KUNSTHAUS AM MUSEUM
CAROLA VAN HAM

VERSTEIGERUNGEN

Alte Kunst	März • Juni • Oktober
Moderne Kunst	April • November
Asiatica • Teppiche	Dezember

G. B. Recco. Stilleben. Zuschlag 170.000 DM

Angebote von Einzelstücken oder
Sammlungen jederzeit erbeten. Kostenlose
Besichtigung und Beurteilung nach
Vereinbarung.

Katalog auf Anfrage und im Abonnement

Drususgasse 1-5 • 50667 Köln
Telefon: 0221/92 58 62-0
Fax: 0221/92 58 62-30

KUNSTHAUS AM MUSEUM

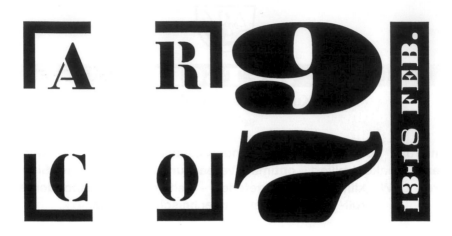

contents:

Modern and Contemporary Art Galleries

Cutting Edge Programmes

Art Edition and Multiples

Photography

Electronic Art

simultaneously:

Latin america at ARCO

I Cibernetica Biennial

IX International Contemporary Art Forum

Major collectors at ARCO

IFEMA
Feria de Madrid

Ministerio de Educación y Cultura
Fundación Coca-Cola España
Iberia
Icex

ARCO
P. O. Box: 67,067
Madrid E-28067 Spain
Tel.: (34-1) 722 50 17
Fax: (34-1) 722 57 98
E-mail: arco@sei.es
Internet: www.arco.sei.es

INTERNATIONAL DIRECTORY OF ARTS

INTERNATIONALES KUNST-ADRESSBUCH

ANNUAIRE INTERNATIONAL DES BEAUX-ARTS

ANNUARIO INTERNAZIONALE DELLE BELLE ARTI

ANUARIO INTERNACIONAL DE LAS ARTES

23. EDITION 1997/98
VOLUME / BAND II

K·G·SAUR   MÜNCHEN   1997

Die Deutsche Bibliothek · CIP-Einheitsaufnahme

International directory of arts = Internationales Kunst-
Adressbuch. München; London; New York; Paris: Saur.
(Edition art address)
Erscheint zweijährlich. – Erscheint in 3 Bd. - Früher im Verl.
Dt. Zentraldruckerei, Berlin, danach im Art-Address-Verl. Müller,
Frankfurt/Main. Aufnahme nach Ed. 21 (1993)
NE: PT

Ed. 21. 1993/94 (1993)
Verl.-Wechsel-Anzeige

Foreign Advertising Representatives:

France:
MG Publicité
22 Rue Drouot
F-75009 Paris
Tel. 01 48 01 86 86
Fax 01 47 70 15 56

Italy:
Marlies Burget
Via Piantarose 12
I-06100 Perugia
Tel. (075) 572 8768
Fax (075) 572 8768

Great Britain and Ireland:
A.R.T. Publicity
281 Cricklewood Lane
NW2 2JJ
London
Tel. (0181) 455 7667
Fax (0181) 455 1772

USA and Canada:
Francesca Zolotov
22 Riverside Dr.
New York, N.Y. 10023
Tel. (212) 877-5385
Fax (212) 877-1729

Printed on acid-free paper

Copyright 1997 by K. G. Saur Verlag & Co. KG, München
Part of Reed Elsevier
Printed in the Federal Republic of Germany

Cover-marmorization: Petra Weinmann, Ansbach
Typesetting: Microcomposition, München
Typesetting of Advertisement: BücherWerkstatt Alexander von Ertzdorff

Printed and bound by Strauss Offsetdruck, Mörlenbach

ISBN 3-598-23075-3

INDEX · INHALT · SOMMAIRE · INDICE

Abbreviations

Museums, Public Galleries

Air	=	Open Air Museum
Arc	=	Archaeological Museum
Art	=	Art Museum
Clas	=	Museum of Classical Antiquities
Chur	=	Church Museum
Dec	=	Museum of Crafts and Decorative Arts
Eth	=	Ethnological Museum
Folk	=	Folklore Museum
Gal	=	Public Gallery
Lib	=	Library with Exhibition
Loc	=	Local or Historical Museum
Mil	=	Military Museum
Nat	=	Natural History Museum
Mus	=	Museum of Musical Instruments
Spec	=	Special Museum
Tech	=	Technical Museum
Uni	=	University Museum

Antiques, Numismatics, Galleries

Ant	=	Antiques
Arch	=	Archaeology, Antiquities
China	=	Porcelain, China, Pottery
Cur	=	Curiosities
Dec	=	Decoration
Draw	=	Drawings
Eth	=	Ethnographica, Primitive Art
Fra	=	Frames
Furn	=	Furniture
Glass	=	Glass
Graph	=	Graphic Art
Ico	=	Icons
Instr	=	Scientific Instruments, Clocks

Jew	=	Jewellery
Lights	=	Lamps, Chandeliers
Mil	=	Armour, Arms, Weapons
Mod	=	Modern Style
Mul	=	Multiples
Music	=	Musical Instruments
Naut	=	Nautical Antiques
Num	=	Numismatics
Orient	=	Oriental and Far Eastern Art
Paint	=	Paintings
Pho	=	Photographs
Rel	=	Religious Art
Repr	=	Reproductions
Sculp	=	Sculptures
Silv	=	Silver
Tex	=	Textiles, Carpets, Tapestries
Tin	=	Tin
Toys	=	Toys, Dolls

Art publishers

ArtBk	=	Art Books
Cal	=	Art Calendars
Card	=	Art Postcards
Graph	=	Graphic Art
Mul	=	Multiples
Per	=	Art Periodicals
Repr	=	Reproductions
Sli	=	Color Slides, Color Transparencies

Antiquarians, Art booksellers

ArtBk	=	Art Books
Autogr	=	Autographs
Engr	=	Engravings
Map	=	Rare Maps
Print	=	Rare Books

Preface

The present 23rd edition 1997/98 of the INTERNATIONAL DIRECTORY OF ARTS contains detailed information of more than 110 000 addresses, names, dates and facts on all spheres of art, the fine art trade and museum organisations. The address material has been revised and updated by a worldwide survey in form of questionnaires. Moreover, numerous national and international associations sent us their newest lists of members, which contained extensive new address material. The 23rd edition contains more than 11 000 new listings and about 25% corrections.

To meet the wishes of numerous customers, the 23rd edition contains for the first time a third volume with an index of institutions and companies and an index of persons (directors, curators, presidents and scientific staff of museums).

Editorial deadline was September 16th, 1996; new listings and corrections, that reached us after this date, could not be included in the 23rd edition any more. In the interest of the users of this book, we therefore ask all persons concerned to return our questionnaires expeditiously in the future and to make clear corrections in legible script.

The INTERNATIONAL DIRECTORY OF ARTS is since 46 years the leading reference book of its kind. Although the greatest possible efforts have been made in compiling this edition, one has to accept errors or missing addresses. We would highly appreciate if our readers would bring such errors or missing addresses to our attention; by doing so they will contribute to the accuracy and reliability of this work. We take the opportunity to point out that we cannot be held responsible for the correctness and completeness of published listing.

The computerized data enables us to make numerous address-collections available to our readers. Please request our extensive address-overview if you happen to be interested.

We express our sincere thanks to all museums, associations, companies and private persons who assisted our endeavours to compile this work as accurately and completely as possible. We hope that this 23rd edition will also become an indispensable source of reference for all users in their daily work.

December 1996   The Publisher

Abkürzungen

Museen, öffentliche Galerien

Air	=	Freilichtmuseum
Arc	=	Archäologisches Museum
Art	=	Kunstmuseum
Clas	=	Antiken- oder Altertums-museum
Chur	=	Kirchenmuseum
Dec	=	Kunstgewerbemuseum
Eth	=	Völkerkundemuseum
Folk	=	Volkskundemuseum
Gal	=	Öffentliche Galerie
Lib	=	Bibliothek mit Ausstellung
Loc	=	Regional oder Geschichts-museum
Mil	=	Militärmuseum
Nat	=	Naturwissenschaftliches Museum
Mus	=	Musikinstrumentenmuseum
Spec	=	Fachmuseum
Tech	=	Technisches Museum
Uni	=	Universitätsmuseum

Antiquitätenhandel, Numismatik, Galerien

Ant	=	Antiquitäten
Arch	=	Archäologie
China	=	Porzellan, Fayencen
Cur	=	Kuriositäten
Dec	=	Einrichter
Draw	=	Zeichnungen
Eth	=	Ethnographica
Fra	=	Rahmen
Furn	=	Möbel
Glass	=	Glas
Graph	=	Graphik
Ico	=	Ikonen
Instr	=	Uhren, wiss. Instrumente

Jew	=	Schmuck
Lights	=	Beleuchtungskörper
Mil	=	Waffen, Militaria
Mod	=	Jugendstil, Art Déco
Mul	=	Multiples
Music	=	Musikinstrumente
Naut	=	Nautische Antiquitäten
Num	=	Numismatik
Orient	=	Ostasiatika, Orientalia
Paint	=	Gemälde
Pho	=	Fotografien
Rel	=	kirchliche Kunst, Devotionalien
Repr	=	Reproduktionen
Sculp	=	Skulpturen
Silv	=	Silber
Tex	=	Textilien, Teppiche, Gobelins
Tin	=	Zinn
Toys	=	Spielzeug, Puppen

Kunstverlage

ArtBk	=	Kunstbücher
Cal	=	Kunstkalender
Card	=	Kunstkarten
Graph	=	Graphik
Mul	=	Auflagenobjekte
Per	=	Kunstzeitschriften
Repr	=	Reproduktionen
Sli	=	Diapositive

Antiquariate, Kunstbuchhandlungen

ArtBk	=	neue Kunstliteratur
Autogr	=	Autographen
Engr	=	alte Graphik
Map	=	alte Landkarten
Print	=	alte Drucke, seltene Bücher

Vorwort

Die vorliegende 23. Ausgabe 1997/98 des INTERNATIONALEN KUNST-ADRESSBUCHS enthält aktuelle und detaillierte Angaben zu mehr als 110 000 Adressen, Namen, Daten und Fakten aus dem weiten Bereich der Kunst, des Kunsthandels und des Museumswesens. Das Anschriftenmaterial wurde im Rahmen einer weltweiten Fragebogenerhebung überprüft und aktualisiert. Darüber hinaus stellten uns zahlreiche nationale und internationale Verbände ihre neuesten Mitgliederlisten zur Verfügung, denen wir umfangreiches neues Anschriftenmaterial entnehmen konnten. Die 23. Ausgabe enthält mehr als 11 000 Neueinträge und ca. 25% Änderungen.

Redaktionsschluß war am 16. September 1996; Neueintragungen und Änderungen, die uns nach diesem Datum erreichten, konnten für die vorliegende 23. Ausgabe leider nicht mehr berücksichtigt werden. Im Interesse aller Benutzer bitten wir nochmals darum, unsere Fragebogen stets umgehend und lesbar ausgefüllt an uns zurückzusenden.

Auf vielfachen Bezieherwunsch enthält die 23. Ausgabe erstmals einen Registerband mit einem Institutionen- und Firmenregister sowie ein Personenregister mit den Namen der Direktoren und leitenden wissenschaftlichen Mitarbeiter aller Museen.

Das INTERNATIONALE KUNST-ADRESSBUCH ist seit 46 Jahren das führende Nachschlagewerk seiner Art. Trotz aller redaktionellen Sorgfalt können Fehler und Lücken nie ganz ausgeschlossen werden. Wir richten daher die herzliche Bitte an unsere Leser, uns auf Fehler bzw. fehlende Institutionen aufmerksam zu machen und so mit dazu beizutragen, die Genauigkeit und Zuverlässigkeit dieses Werkes noch zu erhöhen. Wir weisen an dieser Stelle nochmals darauf hin, daß wir für Richtigkeit und Vollständigkeit der Eintragungen keine Verantwortung übernehmen können.

Die elektronische Speicherung der Daten ermöglicht es uns, Adressenkollektionen anzubieten. Bitte fordern Sie bei Interesse unsere ausführliche Adressenübersicht an.

Unser Dank gilt zahlreichen Museen, Verbänden, Firmen und Privatpersonen für ihre freundliche Unterstützung. Wir hoffen, daß auch die 23. Ausgabe für alle Benutzer zu einem unentbehrlichen Nachschlagewerk für ihre tägliche Arbeit werden möge.

Dezember 1996   Der Verlag

Archaische Figur

Das Register zum *Thieme-Becker, Vollmer* und zum *Allgemeinen Künstlerlexikon* – jetzt inklusive der vollständigen Lexikonartikel aus dem *Allgemeinen Künstlerlexikon!*

Allgemeines Künstlerlexikon – Internationale Künstlerdatenbank

AKL – World Biographical Dictionary of Artists

3. CD-ROM-Ausgabe 1996
DM 2.400,–*
(DM 498,–* für Bezieher der Buchausgabe *Allgemeines Künstlerlexikon*)
(DM 796,–* für Bezieher der *IKD II*)

Die dritte erheblich erweiterte Ausgabe enthält nun neben den Strukturdaten aus den 37 Bänden des *Thieme-Becker* und den 6 Bänden des *Vollmer* die Strukturdaten und die **vollständigen Texteinträge** aus den ersten 12 Bänden des *Allgemeinen Künstlerlexikons.*
Maler, Graphiker, Bildhauer, Architekten – die Vertreter der bildenden Künste aller Kulturräume der Erde von der Antike bis zur Gegenwart können hier nach den verschiedensten Kriterien gesucht und ihre biographischen Daten abgerufen werden.

* unverbindliche Preisempfehlung

Bitte fordern Sie einen ausführlichen Prospekt bei uns an!

K•G•Saur Verlag
Postfach 701620 · D-81316 München · Tel. (089) 7 69 02-0
Fax (089) 7 69 02-150 · E-mail: 100730.1341@compuserve.com

Art and Antique Dealers, Numismatics
Kunst- und Antiquitätenhandel, Numismatik
Commerce d'Antiquités et Numismates
Commercianti d'Antichità i Numismatici
Comercio de Antigüedades y Numismática

Argentina

Buenos Aires

A Troche y Moche, Ortiz de Ocampo 2518, 1425 Buenos Aires. T. (01) 802 49 28. - China / Silv / Glass -   037705
Alberto, R., Peña 1255, 1126 Buenos Aires.
T. (01) 812 45 53.   037706
Alsina Antigüedades, Arenales 1273, Buenos Aires.
- Ant -   037707
Altichiero, Humberto 1449, Buenos Aires.
T. (01) 33 78 96. - Ant / Paint / Sculp -   037708
Alvarez e Hijos, Defensa 973, 1065 Buenos Aires.
T. (01) 362-5755.   037709
Andena, Defensa 1159, 1065 Buenos Aires. T. (01) 361-0678.   037710
Antano, Defensa 1140, Buenos Aires. - Paint / Tex /
Instr -   037711
Antigüedades Esmeralda, Esmeralda 570, 1035 Buenos Aires. T. (01) 393-8319.   037712
Antigüedades PM, Paysandú 2211, 1416 Buenos Aires.
T. (01) 581-9357.   037713
Antique Shop, Avda. del Libertador 15365 Acassuso,
Buenos Aires. T. (01) 743 03 02. - Ant / Paint / Furn /
China / Lights / Instr / Mil -   037714
Antiques, Rue Peña 1711, Buenos Aires.
T. (01) 41 31 20. - Ant / Furn / Dec -   037715
Anzoátegui, Hugo M., Defensa 1122, Buenos Aires.
T. (01) 361 82 48. - Paint / China / Arch -   037716
Apfelbaum, Enrique, Avda. San Juan 3092, 1233 Buenos
Aires. T. (01) 943-0731.   037717
Aries, Rue Peña 1069, 1126 Buenos Aires.
T. (01) 42 99 13. - Ant -   037718
Arte Antica, Defensa 1133, 1065 Buenos Aires.
T. (01) 362-0861.   037719
Arte Colonial, Libertad 1033, Buenos Aires.
T. (01) 44 95 29. - Ant -   037720
Arte Italiana, Libertad 966, Buenos Aires.
T. (01) 393 14 49. - Paint / Furn / China / Instr -   037721
Artemis, Defensa 1124, Buenos Aires. T. (01) 221 14 44.
- Furn / China / Silv / Lights / Instr -   037722
Astrolabio, Beruti 3088 y 3075, Buenos Aires.
T. (01) 82 81 17.   037723
Ballesta, La, Humberto I 417 and Yerbal 341, Buenos Aires. T. (01) 902 341. - Silv / Glass -   037724
Barbazán, Manuel J., Av. Libertad 186, 1012 Buenos Aires. T. (01) 313-8922.   037725
Barral, Angel, Esmeralda 623, 1007 Buenos Aires.
T. (01) 322 88 69.   037726
Barthelmy, Roberto L., Riglos 116, 1424 Buenos Aires.
T. (01) 903 31 87.   037727
Bayard, Arenales 1254, Buenos Aires. T. (01) 42 04 73.
- Ant -   037728
Bebchuck, Julio, Talcahuano 1163, Buenos Aires.
T. (01) 42 51 71. - Furn / Silv -   037729
Belgiorno, Antonio, Avda. Santa Fe 1347, 1059 Buenos
Aires. T. (01) 41 11 17.   037730
Bell, Libertad 966, 1012 Buenos Aires.
T. (01) 393 14 49.   037731
Benedictis, de, Arenales 1739, Buenos Aires.
T. (01) 41 87 43. - Paint / Orient -   037732
Benoit, Raimundo J., Defensa 1152, 1065 Buenos Aires.
T. (01) 361 69 83.   037733
Berlowitz, Enrique, Av. Quintana 229, 1014 Buenos Aires. T. (01) 42 42 72.   037734
Betmalle Germain, Arenales 1140/42, Buenos Aires.
T. (01) 44 53 55. - Ant / Furn / Dec -   037735
Big Ben, Ayacucho 1984, Buenos Aires, 1112.
T. (01) 804-9528. - Ant / Dec -   037736
Bohemia, Libertad 1688, 1016 Buenos Aires.
T. (01) 22 67 75.   037737
Bonifati, Alfredo, Viamonte 895, 1053 Buenos Aires.
T. (01) 322 58 64.   037738
Bouzo, José C., Avda. Bredo 1633, 1407 Buenos Aires.
T. (01) 922 27 99.   037739
Breitmann, Hugo, Av. Pueyrredón 380, Buenos Aires.
T. (01) 89 64 16, 86 19 39. - Ant / Furn / Instr -   037740
Brendans, Arroyo 822, 1007 Buenos Aires.
T. (01) 393 44 47.   037741
Buenos Ayres Anticuarios, Mario Bravo 1108, 1175 Buenos Aires. T. (01) 963 05 02.   037742
Caccia, Julio César e Hijos, Juncal 1316, 1062 Buenos
Aires. T. (01) 41 36 28.   037743

Calderón, Hilda, Avda. San Juan 415, 1147 Buenos Aires. T. (01) 361 01 87.   037744
Capdepont, Av. D. Vélez 5250, Buenos Aires.
T. (01) 982 70 71. - Ant / Furn -   037745
Carballo, Manuel H., Avda. del Trabajo 2565, 1406 Buenos Aires. T. (01) 632 74 95.   037746
Carpet Bazar, Libertad 1056, Buenos Aires.
T. (01) 44 39 41. - Tex -   037747
Casa Capurro, Bulnes 1429, 1176 Buenos Aires.
T. (01) 963 22 14.   037748
Casa Carla, Libertad 120, 1012 Buenos Aires.
T. (01) 37 93 08.   037749
Casa del Balcon, Av. del Libertador 15353, Buenos Aires. T. (01) 743 9111. - Ant / Furn / China / Tex /
Rel -   037750
Casa del Balcon, La, Marcelo T. de Alvear 836, 1058
Buenos Aires. T. (01) 743 9111, 313 0424. - Ant /
Furn / China / Tex / Rel -   037751
Casa José, Av. Corrientes 4535, 1195 Buenos Aires.
T. (01) 862 27 47.   037752
Casa Martes, Corrientes 679, Buenos Aires.
- Num -   037753
Casa Pantin, Av. Callao 2074 Av. del Libertador 1002,
Buenos Aires. T. (01) 42 29 94. - Ant / Dec /
Mil -   037754
Casa Pardo S. A. C., Defensa 1170, Buenos Aires.
T. (01) 30 05 83. - Ant / Furn / Num -   037755
Casa Rodolfo I, Hidalgo 860, 1405 Buenos Aires.
T. (01) 982 94 63. - Ant -   037756
Cereso, Cecilia G. de, Esmeralda 623, 1007 Buenos Aires. T. (01) 394 39 90.   037757
Cores Antigüedades, Charcas 1425, Buenos Aires.
T. (01) 44 48 08. - Furn / China / Lights -   037758
Dart, Arenales 1334, Buenos Aires. T. (01) 22 58 08,
68 16. Doo   037759
Dayan, Lela A. de, Defensa 1016, 1065 Buenos Aires.
T. (01) 362 2285.   037760
Dialogos, Florida 946, shop 2, Buenos Aires.
T. (01) 32 37 24. - Ant / Silv -   037761
Domínguez, Gregoria, Barco del Centenara 1360, 1424
Buenos Aires. T. (01) 923 74 56.   037762
Dover, Guido 1746, Buenos Aires. T. (01) 44 35 03.
- Dec -   037763
Duarte, A., Avda. San Juan 419, 1147 Buenos Aires.
T. (01) 361 5025.   037764
Duffy, Patrick E., Talcahuano 841, 1013 Buenos Aires.
T. (01) 393-9509. - Paint -   037765
Eixarc, Leo, Av. Elcano 3190, 1426 Buenos Aires.
T. (01) 552 79 17.   037766
El Anticuario, 11 de Septiembre 920 Belgrano, Buenos
Aires. T. (01) 772 83 77.   037767
El Balcon de San Telmo, Defensa 1072, 1st floor, Buenos
Aires. - Ant / Silv / Glass -   037768
El Cerro de Potosi, Defensa 1119, Buenos Aires.
T. (01) 221 71 83, 221 49 75. - Ant / Dec / Mil -   037769
El Rastro, Juncal 1180, 1062 Buenos Aires.
T. (01) 42 71 75.   037770
El Rincón, Charcas 3603, 1425 Buenos Aires.
T. (01) 84 96 79.   037771
El Tasador, Avda. Pueyrredón 925, 1032 Buenos Aires.
T. (01) 962 87 70.   037772
El Viejo Bazar, Defensa 941, 1065 Buenos Aires.
T. (01) 362 28 14.   037773
Ezcurra, Ines, Juncal 912, 1062 Buenos Aires.
T. (01) 393 25 37.   037774
Fernandez, Blanco S.R.L., Tucumán 712, Buenos Aires.
T. (01) 392 10 10. - Ant -   037775
Ferrara, Alberto M., México 759, 1097 Buenos Aires.
T. (01) 30 98 20.   037776
Ferrari, Paraguay 1229, Buenos Aires. T. (01) 41 03 24,
41 88 10. - Ant -   037777
Filizzola, Roque, Carlos Calvo 431, 1102 Buenos Aires.
T. (01) 361 54 32.   037778
Finarte-la Defensa, Av. Santa Fe 1660, shops 75/78 and
Defensa 1091, Buenos Aires. T. (01) 44 53 84,
30 24 31. - Ant / Paint / China / Silv -   037779
Fossa, Carlos, Esmeralda 635, 1007 Buenos Aires.
T. (01) 322 76 20.   037780
Franchini, Dante, Arroyo 971, 1007 Buenos Aires.
T. (01) 393 70 83.   037781
Galeria San Martin, Florida 973, Buenos Aires.
T. (01) 31 03 08. - Ant -   037782

Galeria Studio, Libertad 1269-1271, Buenos Aires.
T. (01) 41 16 16, 42 20 46. - Ant -   037783
Goldstein, Andrés G., Avda. Las Heras 3741, 1425 Buenos Aires. T. (01) 801 27 82.   037784
Gran Mercado de Antigüedades, Quintana 360, Buenos
Aires. T. (01) 44 39 40. - Ant / Paint / Furn / Orient / Tex /
Silv -   037785
Grentrajen, Bernardo, Av. San Juan 4017, 1233 Buenos
Aires. T. (01) 361 56 90.   037786
Gualdoni Basualdo, Adrian, Marcelo T. de Alvear 849,
Buenos Aires, 1058. T. (01) 312 35 35. - Ant -   037787
Guerdile, Francisco L., Libertad 1278, 1012 Buenos Aires. T. (01) 42 13 74.   037788
Guido, Avda. Paraguay 1400, 1057 Buenos Aires.
T. (01) 812 96 45.   037789
Haase, Ernesto, Avda. de Mayo 1324, 1085 Buenos Aires. T. (01) 38 95 23.   037790
HC, Montevideo 1785, Buenos Aires. T. (01) 42 07 83.
- Ant -   037791
Hernani, Defensa 1084, 1065 Buenos Aires.
T. (01) 361 43 99/91 46, Fax 361 92 39. - Ant /
Furn -   037792
Iadorola, Hector, Paraná 942, Buenos Aires.
T. (01) 821 3783. - Ant -   037793
Il Sasso, Avda. Juan de Garay 1422, 1153 Buenos Aires.
T. (01) 741 27 86.   037794
Imaginero, Rodriguez Peña 1418, Buenos Aires.
T. (01) 42 59 01. - Furn / Repr / Dec -   037795
Inconagra, Paraguay 1396, 1057 Buenos Aires.
T. (01) 812 96 45.   037796
Innaco, Carlos Calvo 451, Buenos Aires. T. (01) 449 309.
- China -   037797
Jorge, Susana, Esmeralda 758, 1007 Buenos Aires.
T. (01) 322 58 69.   037798
Joyeria Ricciardi, Florida 1001 y Cerrito 360, Buenos Aires. T. (01) 32 30 82. - Ant / Silv -   037799
La Pulga, Arenales 1150, Buenos Aires. T. (01) 44 95 12.
- Ant / Silv -   037800
La Rueda, Av. Rivadavia 7915, 1407 Buenos Aires.
T. (01) 612 24 24.   037801
La Spiga, Cordoba 890-10, Buenos Aires. - Ant / Tex /
Dec -   037802
Las Meninas, Defensa 1070, Buenos Aires.
T. (01) 221 3076. - Orient / Tex -   037803
Lo tenia me abuela, Defensa 995, Buenos Aires.
T. (01) 34 07 52. - Paint / Furn / China / Sculp /
Instr -   037804
Local 2, Esmeralda 623, 1007 Buenos Aires.
T. (01) 322 88 69.   037805
Luines, Quintana 213, Buenos Aires. T. (01) 44 19 33.
- Ant / Dec -   037806
Luz de gas, Defensa 1076, Buenos Aires. - Furn /
Lights / Glass -   037807
Machado, Elena, Florida 537, 1005 Buenos Aires.
T. (01) 393 98 29. - Ant -   037808
Macramé, Defensa 1065, Humberto I 475, Buenos Aires.
T. (01) 33 33 38. - Ant / Cur -   037809
Maison Satuma, Ayacucho 1763, PB, 1112 Buenos Aires. - Ant / Orient / China / Sculp / Draw -   037810
Maple, Suipacha 658, Buenos Aires. - Ant / Furn / China / Tex -   037811
Massini, Ana, De la Feria 1083, Buenos Aires.
T. (01) 362 87 32.   037812
Máster, Talcahuano 841, Buenos Aires.
T. (01) 393 95 09. - Ant / Furn -   037813
Méndez, Marcelo T. de Alvaer 1381, 1058 Buenos Aires.
T. (01) 42 12 83.   037814
Militaria, Azcuénaga 1851, Buenos Aires.
T. (01) 84 72 65. - Mil -   037815
Moctezuma, Fernando G. de, Uruguay 1310, 1016 Buenos Aires. T. (01) 812 76 68. - Ant / Paint / Graph /
Furn / China / Sculp / Tex -   037816
Montecarlo de J. Vazquez, Arenales 1226, 1061 Buenos
Aires. T. (01) 41 78 77.   037817
Montepio, Av. Rivadavia 7701, 1406 Buenos Aires.
T. (01) 612 12 21. - Ant -   037818
Muniz Barreto y Cia., Uruguay 667, Buenos Aires.
T. (01) 46 33 77, 46 71 35. - Ant / Paint / Furn / Tex /
Silv -   037819
Nino de San Telmo, Defensa 1177, 1065 Buenos Aires.
T. (01) 361 49 17.   037820
Nolli, Juan E., Albertí 54, 1082 Buenos Aires.
T. (01) 952 98 32.   037821

Orfaley, Naef George, Arenales 1275 – 60 – 13, Buenos Aires. T. (01) 44 62 13. - Ant / Dec - *037822*

Pallarols-Maugeri, Defensa 1094, Buenos Aires. T. (01) 211 73 60. - Ant / Furn - *037823*

Pantin, Ciprián A., Av. del Libertador 1002 and Callao 2074, Buenos Aires. T. (01) 804 39 70. - Furn / Sculp / Silv / Instr - *037824*

Parist, Carlos A., Austria 1998, Buenos Aires. T. (01) 82 34 73. - Ant - *037825*

Pasini, Juan C.F., Nogoya 3233, 1417 Buenos Aires. T. (01) 53 85 36. *037826*

Peratz Vizourka, Arenales 1388, 1061 Buenos Aires. T. (01) 41 09 67. *037827*

Perla, La, Esmeralda 623, Buenos Aires. T. (01) 392 4963. - Sculp / Jew - *037828*

Pontevecchio, Defensa 1135, 1065 Buenos Aires. T. (01) 362 33 28. *037829*

Portobello, Defensa 1102, Buenos Aires. T. (01) 221 6188. - Furn / Silv - *037830*

Quiven, Marcelo T. de Alvear 472, Buenos Aires. T. (01) 323 722. - Paint / Furn / Sculp / Silv - *037831*

Rawson Decoraciones, Rodríguez Peña 1081 loc. 24, Buenos Aires. T. (01) 41 78 67, 44 49 32. - Ant / Furn - *037832*

Requeteviejo, Vuelta de Obligado 1734, 1426 Buenos Aires. T. (01) 784 96 82. *037833*

Rivero Nina, Av. Caseros 450, 1152 Buenos Aires. T. (01) 23 16 71, Fax 325 6489. *037834*

Rocca, María, Humberto I, 1103 Buenos Aires. T. (01) 362 86 13. *037835*

Rodolfo, Hidalgo 860, 1405 Buenos Aires. T. (01) 981 72 89. *037836*

Saint Loup, Defensa 1092, Buenos Aires. T. (01) 221 2072. - Paint / Furn / China / Instr - *037837*

Salazar, Charcas 790, Buenos Aires. T. (01) 31 02 33. - Dec - *037838*

San Jorge, Defensa 1179, 1065 Buenos Aires. *037839*

São Paulo, Carlos Calvo 449, 1102 Buenos Aires. T. (01) 362 58 50. *037840*

Siglo XIX, Libertad 124, 1012 Buenos Aires. T. (01) 35 19 76. *037841*

Siglos Pasados, Avda. Quintana 229, Buenos Aires. T. (01) 42 42 72. - Ant / China / Tex / Arch / Silv / Glass - *037842*

Siludakis, Horacio, Esmeralda 623, 1035 Buenos Aires. T. (01) 322 63 07. *037843*

Simpson, Libertad 1685, 1016 Buenos Aires. T. (01) 22 47 14. - Furn - *037844*

Sirena, La, Defensa 1088, 1065 Buenos Aires. T. (01) 361 2433. - Ant / Paint / Furn / China / Lights / Glass / Mod - *037845*

Soesthins, Av. Santa Fe 2740, 1425 Buenos Aires. T. (01) 825 67 31. *037846*

Stenta Martha, P.G. de, Gral. J. Perón 1612, Buenos Aires Buenos Aires. T. (01) 35 97 95. *037847*

Sur, Carlos Calvo 407, 1102 Buenos Aires. T. (01) 362 52 89. - Ant / Num - *037848*

Talner, Beatriz & Mauricio, Casilla de Correo 4146, 1000 Buenos Aires. T. (01) 394-0700. - Ant / Paint / Graph / Num / Repr / Glass / Cur / Mod / Ico / Pho / Mul / Draw - *037849*

Ten, Libertad 948, Buenos Aires. T. (01) 41 96 61. - Ant / Dec - *037850*

Thaler Antigüedades, Defensa 1062, Buenos Aires. T. (01) 221 6475. - Furn / Tex / Silv / Glass - *037851*

The Best, Talcahuano 1291, Buenos Aires. T. (01) 42 72 75. - Dec - *037852*

The Clock House, Marcelo T. de Alvear 815-819, Buenos Aires. T. (01) 311 8769. 311 0986. - Instr - *037853*

Tio Antigüedades, Defensa 1075, Buenos Aires. T. (01) 345 364. - Ant / Paint / Tex / Silv - *037854*

Torini, Daniel G., Florida 780, 1005 Buenos Aires. T. (01) 322 21 40. *037855*

Trinidad, Carlos Calvo 409, Buenos Aires. T. (01) 33 04 27. - Paint / Furn / China / Jew / Silv / Rel - *037856*

Tsous, Demetrio, Avda. Boedo 476, 1218 Buenos Aires. T. (01) 97 51 29. *037857*

Vetmas, Libertad 1228, 1272, 1286, Buenos Aires. T. (01) 41 84 60, 44 23 48. - Ant - *037858*

Vilanova, J., Alvear 1427, Buenos Aires. T. (01) 42 41 95. - Ant - *037859*

Vishnu Gallery, Alvear 1910, Buenos Aires. T. (01) 41 89 68. - Ant / Orient - *037860*

Waismel, Samuel, Defensa 1341, 1143 Buenos Aires. T. (01) 361 34 12. *037861*

Wildenstein, Cordoba 618, Buenos Aires. T. (01) 322-0628. - Ant / Paint / Furn / Sculp / Tex / Eth - *037862*

Yapa de San Telmo, La, Carlos Calvo 427, Buenos Aires. T. (01) 337 793. - Silv / Instr - *037863*

Zajac, Lea T., de, Avda. Gaona 2964, 1416 Buenos Aires. T. (01) 582 61 14. *037864*

Zurbaran, Cerrito 1522, 1010 Buenos Aires. T. (01) 22 77 03. - Paint - *037865*

Australia

Adelaide (South Australia)

Elder, J. G., 58 Jerningham St., 5000 Adelaide, 5000. T. (08) 67 28 69. - Ant - *037866*

Megaw and Hogg Pty Ltd., 26 Leigh St., Adelaide, 5000. T. (08) 51 50 14. - Ant / Furn / China / Glass - *037867*

Moghul Antiques, 66 Wyatt St., Adelaide, 5000. T. (08) 223 50 97. - Ant - *037868*

Albury (New South Wales)

Summerfield, T. R., & Co., 553 Smollett St., Albury, 2640. T. (060) 21 38 05. - Ant - *037869*

Armadale (Victoria)

Art Division, 1195 High St., Armadale, 3143. T. 20 1040, 20 2654. *037870*

Geddes, Graham, 877 High St., Armadale, 3143. T. 509 0308. - Furn - *037871*

Grace, 1120 High St., Armadale, 3143. T. 509 86 80. - Paint / Furn / Draw - *037872*

Harper, Lee, 1009 High St., Armadale, Vic. 3143. T. 20 5943. - Furn - *037873*

Monte Cristo, 1199-1201 High St., Armadale, 3143. T. 20 84 13. - Paint / Furn / China - *037874*

Armidale (New South Wales)

Solomons, 121 Beardy St., Armidale, 2350. T. (067) 30 89. - Ant - *037875*

Ballarat (Victoria)

Jones, C. V., 14 Armstrong St., 3350 Ballarat, Vic. 3350. T. (053) 31 1472. - Ant - *037876*

Ballina (New South Wales)

Ballina Antique Shop, Pacific Highway, Ballina. T. (066) 86 27 98. - Furn / Lights / Instr - *037877*

Berrima (New South Wales)

Albury, 2 Jellore St., 2577 Berrima, NSW 2577. T. (048) 77 1525. - Ant - *037878*

Berkelouw, Bendooley, Hume Hwy., 2577 Berrima, 2577. T. (048) 77 13 70. - Ant / Draw - *037879*

Bowral (New South Wales)

Tiptoe et Son, Bong Bong St., 2576 Bowral, 2576, N.S.W. T. (048) 124. *037880*

Brisbane (Queensland)

Cameo Antiques, Cnr Brunswick and Artur St., Fortitude Valley, 4000 Brisbane. T. (07) 358 17 45. - Furn - *037881*

Cordelia Street Antique and Art Centre, 4000 Brisbane POB 28, 4101. T. (07) 844-8514. - Ant / Orient - *037882*

Hardy Bros. Ltd., 118 Queen St., 4000 Brisbane. - Ant / China / Jew / Instr / Glass - *037883*

Morrow's Galleries, 633 Logan Rd. Greenslopes, 4000 Brisbane. T. (07) 97 78 45. - Ant - *037884*

Cairns (Queensland)

St.Clouds, 315c Mulgrave Rd., 4870 Cairns, 4870, Qld. T. (070) 23 32. - Ant - *037885*

Claremont (Western Australia)

Amberley Antiques, 220a Stirling Highway Amberley, Claremont. T. 31 10 05. - China / Jew / Silv / Glass - *037886*

Elwood (Victoria)

Lissauer, H. M., 17 Burns St., 3184 Elwood, 3184. T. 531 23 27. - Ant / Orient / Arch / Eth - *037887*

Faulconbridge

Springwood Antiques, 481 Great Western Highway, 2776 Faulconbridge, 2776. - Ant - *037888*

Gardenvale (Victoria)

Martin Street Antiques, 138 Martin St., 3185 Gardenvale, 3186. T. 596 21 83. - Paint / China / Jew / Silv - *037889*

Geelong (Victoria)

Antiques and Vygones, 175 McKillop St., 3220 Geelong. T. (052) 936 30. - Ant - *037890*

Moorabool Antique Galleries, 200 Moorabool St., 3220 Geelong, 3220. T. (052) 929 70. - Ant - *037891*

Glen Iris (Victoria)

Cook, L.J., & Son, 439-447 Burke Rd., 3146 Glen Iris, Vic. 3156. T. 20 2670. - Ant - *037892*

Goolwa (South Australia)

Havelock House Antiques, Hutchinson St., P.O. Box 96, 5214 Goolwa, 5214. T. (085) 55 21 84. - China - *037893*

Hamilton (Victoria)

Tatlock, Alfred & Sons, 54 Gray St., Hamilton, 3300. T. (055) 225 66. - Ant - *037894*

Hobart (Tasmania)

Battery Point Antiques, 60 Hampden Rd. Battery Point, 7000 Hobart. T. (002) 23 57 95. - Furn / China / Silv - *037895*

Curiosity Shop, 305 Elizabeth St., 7000 Hobart. T. (002) 34 30 69. - Cur - *037896*

Paget, C., 171 Elizabeth St., 7000 Hobart, 7000. *037897*

Hyde Park (Hyde Park)

Antique Galleries, 258 Unley Rd., 5061 Hyde Park, 5061. T. 71 79 87. - Ant - *037898*

Inverell (New South Wales)

Thorley, Beulah, 28 George St., Inverell, 2360. T. (067) 21 51. - China / Silv - *037899*

Jamberoo (New South Wales)

Nerilee, 26 Allowrie St., 2533 Jamberoo, NSW 2533. T. (042) 36 0389. - Ant - *037900*

Kareela (New South Wales)

Australian Art Sales, 11 Tradewinds Pl., Kareela, 2232. T. (02) 528 47 07. - Arch - *037901*

Kiama (New South Wales)

Addison, 33 Collins St., 2533 Kiama, NSW 2533. T. (042) 32 2217. - Ant - *037902*

Launceston (Tasmania)

Rapley, Susan, 12 Lenstan St., 7250 Launceston, 7250. T. (003) 44 28 95. *037903*

Melbourne (Victoria)

Adam, 28 Elizabeth St., Melbourne, Vic. 3000. T. (03) 6545903. - Ant / Paint / Furn / China / Tex / Silv - *037904*

Allen Antiques, 597 Malvern Road Toorak, Melbourne, Vic. 3142. T. (03) 243678. - Furn - *037905*

Bognor, 378 Hawthorn Rd., Caulfield, Melbourne, Vic. 3162. T. (03) 5283831. - Ant - *037906*

Bovill, Miles, 1419 Malvern Rd., Malvern, Melbourne, Vic. 3144. T. (03) 204217. - Ant / Paint / Furn / Dec - *037907*

Brown, Graeme, 591-593 Malvern Rd., Toorak, Melbourne, Vic. 3142. T. (03) 2416303. - Ant - *037908*

Caldwell's Antiques, 542 Glenhuntly Road, Elsternwick, Melbourne, Vic. 3185. T. (03) 5282769. - Ant / Furn / China - *037909*

Connoisseurs' Store, 617 Maluern Rd., Melbourne, Vic.3142. T. (03) 2414185. - Ant - *037910*

Downie, P. J., 242 Swanston Street, Melbourne, Vic. 3000. T. (03) 6634911. - Num - *037911*

Drummond, William, & Co., 384-386 Bourke St., Melbourne, Vic. 3000. T. (03) 678725. - Silv - *037912*

Dunn, John D., 1431 Malvern Rd., Malvern, Melbourne, Vic. 3144. T. (03) 8225637. - Furn / Sculp / Glass - 037913

East and West Art, 665 High St., East Kew, Melbourne, Vic. 3102. T. (03) 8596277. - Ant / Paint / Graph / Furn / Orient / China / Sculp / Arch / Dec / Jew / Rel / Draw -- 037914

Franzi & Filcock, 22 Alma Rd., St. Kilda, Melbourne, Vic. 3182. T. (03) 5341537. - Ant - 037915

Graeme Brown Antiques + Restorations, 591-593 Malvern Rd. Toorak, Melbourne, Vic. 3142. T. (03) 2416303. 037916

Hardy Bros., 338 Collins St., Melbourne, Vic. 3000. - China / Jew / Instr / Glass - 037917

Kehoe, Lesley, 503 Burke Rd., Camberwell South, Melbourne, Vic. 3124. T. (03) 205718. - Orient - 037918

Macedo, G. L., 2 Sydenham Rd., Brookvale, Melbourne, Vic. 2100. T. (03) 933762. - Ant - 037919

McClelland, Joshua, 15 Collins St., Melbourne, Vic. 3000. T. (03) 6545835. - Ant / Paint / Graph / Orient / China - 037920

McPhee, G. D., 200 Chapel St. Prahram, Melbourne, Vic. 3181. T. (03) 512432. - Ant - 037921

Mildenhall Antiques, 423-427 Bay St., Brighton, Melbourne, Vic. 3186. T. (03) 5965633. - Ant / China / Jew / Silv - 037922

Orientique, 531a High St., East Prahran, Melbourne, Vic. 3181. T. (03) 511329. - Orient - 037923

Parkside Antiques, 145 Park St., Melbourne, Vic. 3205. T. (03) 6998114. 037924

Prinny's, 1205-1207 Malvern Rd., Malvern, Melbourne, Vic. 3144. T. (03) 8221676. - Ant - 037925

Prouse PTY, Ltd., Oscar, 347 Burwood Rd. Hawthorn, Melbourne, Vic. 3122. T. (03) 8182892. - Ant - 037926

Rosebud antiques, 1489 Nepean Hwy. Rosebud, Melbourne, Vic. 3939. T. (03) 861223. 037927

Stern, Max, & Co., Flindersstr. 234, Melbourne POB 997.H., Vic. 3001. T. (03) 636751. - Num - 037928

The Jade Gallery, Suite 4, Upper Plaza Southern Cross Centre, Melbourne, Vic. 3000. T. (03) 6548437. - Ant / Furn / Orient / Jew / Silv - 037929

Wiesel, Michael, 256 Toorak Rd. South Yarra, Melbourne, Vic. 3141. T. (03) 2415143. - Jew / Silv / Instr - 037930

Wilson, John, 481-3 Burke Rd., Hawthorn, Melbourne, Vic. 3124. T. (03) 8223344. - Ant / Furn / China / Glass - 037931

Yarrabank Antiques, 588 Chapel St., South Yarra, Melbourne, Vic. 3141. T. (03) 2416987. - Mod - 037932

Moree (New South Wales)

Crowe and Finlay, Linden Arcade, Balo St., 2400 Moree, 2400, NSW. T. (067) 52 13 18. - Silv - 037933

Mount Tamborine (Queensland)

Lurati, W. & P., Eagle Heights, 4272 Mount Tamborine, 4272. T. 45 11 81. - Instr - 037934

Newcastle (New South Wales)

Cottage Gallery, The, 82 Scenic Highway, Merewether, 2300 Newcastle, 2300, NSW. T. (049) 63 22 86. - Paint / China - 037935

Hunter Valley Fine Arts, 145 Beaumont St., Hamilton, 2300 Newcastle, 2303, NSW. T. (049) 61 14 84. - Ant / Paint - 037936

Perth (Western Australia)

R + R Imports, 25 Rokeby Rd., Perth, 6000 Perth, 6008. T. (09) 81 43 50. - Furn / China - 037937

Stirling Galleries, 163 Stirling Hwy., Nedlands, 6000 Perth, 6009. T. (09) 386 51 61. 037938

Young, Marjorie, 836 Hay St., 6000 Perth, 6000. T. (09) 322 5780. - Ant / Paint / Furn / China / Repr / Jew / Silv / Lights / Glass - 037939

Richmond (Victoria)

Mereden, 597-599 Bridge Rd., 3121 Richmond, Vic. 3121. T. 428 3074. - Ant - 037940

Rosebud (Victoria)

Rosebud Antiques, 1489 Nepean Highway, 3939 Rosebud, 3939, Vict. T. (059) 86 12 23. 037941

Seaforth (New South Wales)

Ramornie, 53 Ethel St., 2092 Seaforth, 2092. T. 94 12 86. - Furn / Num / China / Jew / Silv - 037942

Seymour (Victoria)

Smith, T. W., Pty. Ltd., 8 Henry St., 3660 Seymour, 3660. T. (057) 142. - Ant / Furn / Lights - 037943

Sydney (New South Wales)

Abbott, 14 Eastern Rd., Turramurra, Sydney, NSW 2074. T. (02) 498-6561. - Ant / Paint / Furn / China / Jew / Silv / Glass - 037944

Advance Antiques, 306 Railway Pde., Sydney, NSW 2000. T. (02) 587 7797. 037945

Aladdin's Antiques, 241 Sydney Rd., Sydney, NSW 2000. T. (02) 946 737. 037946

Antique Brass Comp., 47 Glebe Point Rd., Sydney, NSW 2000. T. (02) 660 16 08. - Furn / Repr - 037947

Antique International Pty., Ltd., Cnr. Castlereagh, Park Sts., Sydney, NSW 2000. T. (02) 266 814. 037948

Arca Antiques, 115 Stoney Creek Rd., Sydney, NSW 2000. T. (02) 575 023. 037949

Aronson, 317 Pacific Hwy., Crows Nest, Sydney, NSW 2065. T. (02) 922 36 10. 037950

Art of the Pacific, 72-74 Carrington Rd. Waverley, Sydney, NSW 2024. T. (02) 389 74 63. - Eth - 037951

Auchinachie, G. L., 328 Pacific Hwy. Lane Cove, 2000 Sydney, 2000. T. (02) 42 26 47. - Ant / Paint / Furn / Mil - 037952

Avon Print Pty Ltd., 127 Walker St., Sydney, NSW 2000. T. (02) 929 63 37. - Graph - 037953

Balanada, 84 Ingleburn Rd., Sydney. T. (02) 605 1977. 037954

Barefoot Art Gallery, Barefoot Ave., Sydney, NSW 2000. T. (02) 918 6350. 037955

Barton, L, 742 Military Rd., Mosman, Sydney, NSW 2088. T. (02) 960 2271. - Ant - 037956

Barton, L. L., 354 Dowling St. Paddington, Sydney, NSW 2000. T. (02) 31 58 57. - Ant - 037957

Block, Murray, 133 Awaba St. Mosman, Sydney, NSW 2000. T. (02) 969 90 40. - Instr - 037958

Boer, Lloyd, 12-14 Holt St., Double Bay, Sydney, NSW 2028. T. (02) 32 04 49. - Paint - 037959

Boronia, 768 Military Rd., Mosman, Sydney, NSW 2088. T. (02) 969 2100. - Ant - 037960

Bortignons Antiques, Royal Arc., Sydney, NSW 2000. T. (02) 612 100. 037961

Boulken, Ben, Pty. Ltd., 139a Castlereagh St., Sydney, NSW 2000. T. (02) 613 697. 037962

Brackenreg, John, 479 Pacific Hwy., Artarmon, Sydney, NSW 2064. T. (02) 427 03 22. 037963

Bradshaw, W. F., 96 Queen St. Woollahra, Sydney, NSW 2000. T. (02) 32 44 53. - Furn / Instr - 037964

Bulls Hill Pottery, 1273 The Horsley Dr., Sydney, NSW 2000. T. (02) 604 4573. 037965

Burlington Fine Art, 61 Market St., Sydney, NSW 2000. T. (02) 617 911. 037966

Burton, K.G.,&Co., 7 Vincent St., Sydney, NSW 2000. T. (02) 827 1645. - Mil - 037967

Buxton, A., 21 Knox St., Double Bay, Sydney, NSW 2028. T. (02) 327 1489. - Furn / Orient / China / Jew / Silv - 037968

Buxton, A., 21 Knox St., Double Bay, Sydney, NSW 2028. T. (02) 327 1489. - Ant - 037969

Cadry's Oriental Carpets, 158, Pacific Highway, Sydney, NSW North Sydney, 2060. T. (02) 929 8998. - Ant / Tex - 037970

Cadry's Oriental Carpets, 133 New South Head Rd., Edgecliff, Sydney, NSW 2027. T. (02) 328 6059, 328 6144. - Ant / Tex - 037971

Camden Passage, 58 Ourimbah Rd., Mosman, Sydney, NSW 2088. T. (02) 969 4404. - Ant - 037972

Carvendish, 625 Military Rd., Mosman, Sydney, NSW 2088. T. (02) 969 8323. - Ant - 037973

Causeway Bay Antiques, 33a King St., Sydney, NSW 2000. T. (02) 294 047. 037974

Central Dealers, 349 Pitt St., Sydney, NSW 2000. T. (02) 612 790. 037975

Chinese Antique Company, 94 Queen St., Sydney, NSW 2000. T. (02) 325 948. 037976

Chinese Laundry Antiques, 75 George St., Sydney, NSW 2000. T. (02) 277 161. 037977

Coddington Fine Arts, 625 Military Rd., Sydney, NSW 2000. T. (02) 969 8323. 037978

Coniston, 160 Queen St., Woollahra, Sydney, NSW 2025. T. (02) 328 66 01. - Paint - 037979

Copeland & de Soos, 66 Queen St., Woollahra, Sydney, NSW 2025. T. (02) 325 288. - Mod - 037980

Corvell, 557 Willoughby Rd., Sydney, NSW 2000. T. (02) 955 737. 037981

Cresswell, J.D.M., 70 Eastern Rd., Sydney, NSW 2000. T. (02) 482 075. 037982

Crongen, Denis, 67 West St., Sydney, NSW 2000. T. (02) 924 862. 037983

Darling Street Antiques, 409 Darling St., Sydney, NSW 2000. T. (02) 821 927. 037984

Davies, W., 565 Willoughby Rd. Willoughby, Sydney, NSW 2000. T. (02) 95 30 77. - Ant - 037985

Dawson, S., 39 Liverpool St., Sydney, NSW 2021, Paddington. T. (02) 31 40 90. 037986

Doling, G. D., 35 Stanley St. Darlinghurst, Sydney, NSW 2000. T. (02) 31 89 20. - Ant / Furn / China / Silv - 037987

Dorea, 277 Pennant Hills Rd., Sydney, NSW 2000. T. (02) 848 0975. 037988

Eden Antiques, 369 Penshurst St., Sydney, NSW 2000. T. (02) 407 3331. 037989

Elle, 217 Glenmore Rd., Sydney, NSW 2000. T. (02) 338 853. 037990

Excalibur Antiques, Avalon Parade, Sydney, NSW 2000. T. (02) 918 2844. 037991

Flairs Antiques, 133 Pennant Hills Rd., Carlingford, Sydney, 2118, N.S.W. T. (02) 630 31 06. 037992

Ford, Gregory, 264 Oxford St., Paddington, Sydney, NSW 2021. T. (02) 331 5147. - Ant - 037993

Forsyth, Margaret, 1759 Pittwater Rd. Mona Vale, Sydney, NSW 2000. T. (02) 99 64 48. - Ant - 037994

Fraser, 24 Lyndhurst Rd., Glebe, Sydney, NSW 2037. T. (02) 660 30 19. - Furn / China - 037995

Fraser, 152 Mowbray Rd., Sydney, NSW 2000. T. (02) 95 00 93. - Furn / China - 037996

Galleries Primitif, 174 Jersey Rd., Woollahra, Sydney, NSW 2025. T. (02) 32 31 15. - Eth - 037997

Gaslight Antiques of Glebe, 92 Glebe Point Rd., Sydney, NSW 2000. T. (02) 660 2580. 037998

Glenleigh, 73 William St., Sydney, NSW 2000. T. (02) 331 1549. - Ant - 037999

Gliddon, John, 124 Oxford St., Sydney, NSW 2021, Paddington. T. (02) 331 2742. 038000

Grafton, 389 New South Head Rd., Double Bay, Sydney, NSW 2028. T. (02) 327 3567. - Ant / Furn / China / Silv - 038001

Graphics Gallery, 191 Edgecliff Rd., Woollrahra, Sydney, NSW 2025. T. (02) 389 2494. 038002

Hardy Brothers Ltd., 12 Gallery Level Centrepoint, Sydney, NSW 2000. T. (02) 232 2811. - Ant - 038003

Hawk, 370 Pacific Hwy., Crows Nest, Sydney, NSW 2065. T. (02) 436 2350. 038004

Hawkins, J. B., 13 Amhurst St. Cammeray, Sydney, NSW 2000. T. (02) 92 46 92. - Ant - 038005

Hendrikson & Co, 266 George St., Sydney, NSW 2000. T. (02) 773 641. 038006

Hepworth, 415 Old South Head Rd., Sydney, NSW 2000. T. (02) 371 4252. 038007

Ho, David, 39 William St., Paddington, Sydney, NSW 2021. T. (02) 332-8646. - Orient - 038008

Hutson, 147 Castlereagh St., Sydney, NSW 2000. T. (02) 267 61 97. 038009

Hynes Pty Ltd., Bruce C., 121 Military Rd., Sydney, NSW 2089, Neutral Bay. T. (02) 90 50 98. - Mil - 038010

Irwin, Rex, 38 Queen St., Woollrahra, Sydney, NSW 2025. T. (02) 323 212. 038011

Johnson, Clarence, 394-396 Pacific Highway Lane Cove, Sydney, NSW 2000. T. (02) 42 60 10. - Ant - 038012

Jolly, Barry Pty. Ltd., 212 Glenmore Rd., Paddington, Sydney, NSW 2021. T. (02) 357 4494. 038013

Jolyon Warwick James, P.O.Box 142, Woollahra, Sydney, NSW 2025. T. (02) 326 1319, Fax 327 6731. - Silv - 038014

Kansu Gallery, The, 605 Royal Arc., Sydney, NSW 2000. T. (02) 617 211. 038015

Kissing Point Gallery, 2 Kissing Point Rd., Sydney, NSW 2000. T. (02) 449 5600. 038016

Lambert, J.W., 116 Rowe St., Eastwood, Sydney, NSW 2122. T. (02) 858 4601. 038017

Landis, Alan, 140 Castlereagh St., Sydney, NSW 2000.
T. (02) 267-7068. *038018*
Lane, Peter, 14 Martin Pl., Sydney, NSW 2001.
T. (02) 235 01 36. - Ant / Furn / Orient / China / Sculp /
Rel - *038019*
Larkin, Harry, 7 Diments Way, Hurstville, Sydney, NSW
2220. T. (02) 57 15 15. - Ant - *038020*
Lebovic, Josef, 34 Paddington St., Paddington, Sydney,
NSW 2021. T. (02) 332 1840. - Ant / Graph / Pho /
Draw - *038021*
Lipscombe, Stanley, 240 Castlereagh, Sydney, NSW
2000. T. (02) 261 304. *038022*
Loophale Antique, 6 Bellevue Rd., Beverly Hills, Sydney,
NSW 2000. T. (02) 389 8638. *038023*
Maltby, E., 2 Gurner St., Paddington, Sydney, NSW
2021. T. (02) 31 43 17. - Ant - *038024*
Mason's Fine Arts, 165 Castlereagh St., Sydney, NSW
2000. T. (02) 61 26 63. - Ant / Paint / Furn /
China - *038025*
Mayne, B., Corner Palmer and Burton Sts., Sydney, NSW
2000. T. (02) 357 6264. - Rel / Glass - *038026*
McCormick, Tim, 53 Queen St., Woollahra, Sydney, NSW
2025. T. (02) 32 5383. - Paint - *038027*
Metham, Brian Pty Ltd., 17 Princes Hwy., Kog, Sydney,
NSW 2000. T. (02) 587 3035. *038028*
Micawber's Wentworth Hotel, 61-101/15 Phillip St.,
Sydney, NSW 2000. T. (02) 233 2515. - Ant / Paint /
Jew / Silv - *038029*
Moore Michetti Antiques, 110-112 N.S. Head Rd., Dar-
lington Point, Sydney, NSW 2706.
T. (02) 32 61 10. *038030*
Morrison, Robert, 84 Queen St., Woollahra, Sydney,
NSW 2025. T. (02) 32 3273. - Ant - *038031*
Mosman Portobello, 742 Military Rd., Mosman, Sydney,
NSW 2088. T. (02) 960 3427. - Ant - *038032*
Native Art Gallery, 13 Gurner St., Sydney, NSW 2021.
T. (02) 331 48 27. - Eth - *038033*
New Guinea Primitive Arts, 428 George St., Sydney,
NSW 2000. T. (02) 232 47 37. - Orient - *038034*
Newman's Antiques, 212 Castlereagh St., Sydney, NSW
2000. T. (02) 61 34 13. *038035*
Niven, Janet, 118 Queen St., Woollahra, Sydney, NSW
2025. T. (02) 32 2211. - Ant - *038036*
Noblewoods, 318 Oxford St., Woollahra, Sydney, NSW
2025. T. (02) 389 7454. - Ant - *038037*
Nomadic Rug Traders, 125 Harris St., Pyrmont, Sydney,
NSW 2009. T. (02) 660 3753. - Tex - *038038*
Oriental Art Gallery, 545 Royal Hilton Arc., Sydney, NSW
2000. T. (02) 233 28 60. *038039*
Palmer Antiques, 55 Queen St., Woollrahra, Sydney,
NSW 2025. T. (02) 324 478. *038040*
Park Regis, 195a Castlereagh, Sydney, NSW 2000.
T. (02) 617 100. *038041*
Pettigrew,Josiah, 318 Bronte Rd., Sydney, NSW 2000.
T. (02) 389 9339. *038042*
Pines Antiques, Macquarie Rd. Ingleburn, Sydney, NSW
2000. T. (02) 605 12 90. - Ant - *038043*
Polly's Antiques, 307 Military Rd., Sydney, NSW 2000.
T. (02) 908 2506. *038044*
Portobello Shop of Paddington, 94 Hargrave St., Pad-
dington, Sydney, NSW 2021. T. (02) 32 54 62. - Furn /
China / Jew / Lights / Instr - *038045*
Questers, 328 Pacific Hwy., Lane Cove, Sydney, NSW
2066. T. (02) 427 26 47. - Ant - *038046*
Reed, Randall, 83 Moncur St., Woollahra, Sydney, NSW
2025. T. (02) 329 292. *038047*
Schofield, Anne, 36 Queen St., Woollahra, Sydney, NSW
2025. T. (02) 32 1326. - Ant - *038048*
Seaforth Antiques, 51a Ethel St., Sydney, NSW 2000.
T. (02) 947 426. *038049*
Showcase Antiques, 161a Castlereagh St., Sydney, NSW
2000. T. (02) 267 8129. *038050*
Smythe, W., 258 Cumberland Rd., Auburn, Sydney, NSW
2144. *038051*
Spink & Son, 53 Martin Pl., Sydney, NSW 2000.
T. (02) 27 5571. - Num - *038052*
Tavernes Hill Antiques, 125 Bondi Rd., Bondi, Sydney,
NSW 2026. T. (02) 389 7953. *038053*
Tee-Jays, 98 Sydney St., Willoughby, Sydney, NSW
2068. T. (02) 412 31 54. - Ant - *038054*
Tempus, Fugit, 503 Kent St., Sydney, NSW 2000.
T. (02) 617 991. *038055*

Things Antiques, 122 Oxford St., Paddington, Sydney,
NSW 2021. T. (02) 312 740. *038056*
Things Antiques, 6 Glenmore Rd., Paddington, Sydney,
NSW 2021. T. (02) 31 96 71. - Mil - *038057*
Thirty Victoria Street, 30 Victoria St., Potts Point, Syd-
ney, NSW 2011. T. (02) 357 3755. *038058*
Tregaskis, Raymond & Victoria, 43 William St., Padding-
ton, Sydney, NSW 2021. T. (02) 331-2427.
- Orient - *038059*
Trollope, Kerry, 414 Lyons Rd., Five Dock, Sydney, NSW
2046. T. (02) 712 11 02. *038060*
Val, Anthony & Son, 274 Oxford St, Sydney, NSW 2000.
T. (02) 317 625. *038061*
Vande Antiques, 244 b Pitt St., Sydney, 2000.
T. (02) 613 952. *038062*
Victoriana Antiques, 343 Rocky Point Rd., Sans Soucis,
Sydney, NSW 2219. T. (02) 529 6227. *038063*
Walford, Leslie, 282 New South Head Rd., Double Bay,
Sydney, NSW 2028. T. (02) 32 44 46, 32 53 35. - Ant /
Paint / Furn / Silv - *038064*
Waters, R. J., 287 Emmore Rd. Marrickville, Sydney,
NSW 2000. T. (02) 51 74 82. - Ant / Silv - *038065*
Wood, Peter, 35 Majors Bay Rd., Concord, Sydney, NSW
2137. T. (02) 732 145. *038066*
Woollahra Antique Co., 94 Queen St., Woollrahra, Syd-
ney, NSW 2025. T. (02) 325 948. *038067*
Wynyard Gallery, Concourse Arc., Sydney, NSW 2000.
T. (02) 292 184. *038068*
York Antiques, 131 York, Sydney, NSW 2000.
T. (02) 292 009. *038069*
Young, Margaret, 133 Castlereagh, Sydney, NSW 2000.
T. (02) 613 892. *038070*

Toowoomba (Queensland)
Colonial Galleries, 96 Margaret St., 4350 Toowoomba,
4350, Qld. T. (076) 32 71 48. - Furn - *038072*
Toowomba Antiques Centre, 476 Ruthven St., 4350 Toowoomba, Qld. 4350. T. (076) 32 69 78. - Ant - *038073*

Wagga Wagga (New South Wales)
Morrows, Mrs.M., Center Way, 2650 Wagga Wagga,
2650, NSW. T. (069) 42 65. *038074*

Windsor (New South Wales)
Old Wares, 3 Thompson Sq., Windsor, 2756, N.S.W.
T. (045) 77 36 60. - Furn / China / Glass / Cur - *038075*
Whatley, E. L., 128 George St. & 3 Thompson Sq., Wind-
sor, 2756. T. (045) 36 60. - Furn / China /
Glass - *038076*

Wollongong (New South Wales)
Devine's Antique Furniture, Foleys Rd., 2500 Wollon-
gong, 2500, N.S.W. T. (042) 24 053. - Furn - *038077*

Young (New South Wales)
Taggs, 80 Boorowa St., 2594 Young, 2594, N.S.W.
T. (063) 25 94. *038078*

Austria

Allentsteig (Niederösterreich)
Höfinger, Maria, Zwettler Str. 14, 3804
Allentsteig. *038079*

Altaussee (Steiermark)
Kuftner, Renate, Fischerndorf 19, 8992 Altaussee.
T. (06152) 71647. *038080*

Altenmarkt im Pongau (Salzburg)
Hermann, Josef, Haus Nr. 360, 5541 Altenmarkt im
Pongau. *038081*

Amstetten (Niederösterreich)
Hochholzer, Karl, Hauptpl. 27, 3300 Amstetten.
T. (07472) 3212. *038082*
Lechner, Brunhilde, Rathausstr. 11, 3300 Amstetten.
T. (07472) 2366. *038083*
Panico, Friederike, Bahnhofstr. 18, 3300
Amstetten. *038084*
Schimka, G., Postfach 46, 3300 Amstetten. *038085*
Urschitz k5060 Ernst, Hauptplatz 41, 3300 Amstetten.
T. (07472) 22 31. - Mil - *038086*

Andorf (Oberösterreich)
Hofinger, Friedrich, Riedfeldstr. 5, 4770 Andorf.
T. (07766) 2213. *038087*

Anif (Salzburg)
Galerie Anif, 5081 Anif. T. (06246) 3221, 2975.
- Furn - *038088*

Arzl (Tirol)
Kunsthand-Kunsthandel, Kirchgasse 66, 6471 Arzl.
T. (05412) 5231. *038089*

Attnang-Puchheim (Oberösterreich)
Betzwald, Vinzenz, Ahamerstr. 40, 4800 Attnang-
Puchheim. *038090*

Bad Aussee (Steiermark)
Antiquitäten, Ischler Str. 85, 8990 Bad Aussee.
T. (06152) 24 73. *038091*

Bad Hall (Oberösterreich)
Lehner, Hedwig, Kremsmünsterstr.9, 4540 Bad
Hall. *038092*

Bad Hofgastein (Salzburg)
Fritsch, Frank, Kurpromenade 11, 5630 Bad Hofgastein.
T. (06432) 82 08. *038093*
Weidenbacher, Karl, Kirchpl. 7, 5630 Bad Hofgastein.
T. (06432) 6373. *038094*

Bad Ischl (Oberösterreich)
Ressequier, Elinor, Brennerstr. 46, 4820 Bad Ischl.
T. (06132) 405 22. *038095*
Sperlhofer, Gundila Elke, Esplanade 14, 4820 Bad Ischl.
T. (06132) 4424. *038096*
Walter, Wirerstr. 6, 4820 Bad Ischl.
T. (06132) 32 70. *038097*

Bad Leonfelden (Oberösterreich)
Böcksteiner, Peter, Unterlaimbach Nr. 24, 4190 Bad
Leonfelden. T. (07213) 3 10. - Ant - *038098*

Baden bei Wien
Ambrosi, Günther, Heiligenkreuzergasse 3, 2500 Baden
bei Wien. T. (02252) 45380. *038099*
Futschek, Franz, Rohrgasse 63, 2500 Baden bei
Wien. *038100*
Grasl, Gottfried, Wassergasse 1, 2500 Baden bei Wien.
T. (02252) 70 20 10. - Ant / Paint - *038101*
Hruby, Edeltraud, Weilburgstr. 6, 2500 Baden bei
Wien. *038102*
Hutzler, Otto, Melkengasse 9a, 2500 Baden bei Wien.
T. (02252) 883 44. *038103*
Kral, Werner, Annagasse 6, 2500 Baden bei Wien.
T. (02252) 48777. *038104*
Mauthner, Manfred, Beethovengasse 6, 2500 Baden bei
Wien. *038105*
Nicoladoni, Werner, Annagasse 23, 2500 Baden bei
Wien. T. (02252) 44108. *038106*
Schachinger, Rudolf, Pfarrgasse 14, 2500 Baden bei
Wien. *038107*
Schmid, Georg, Heiligenkreuzergasse 5, 2500 Baden bei
Wien. T. (02252) 41225. *038108*
Skarics, Gerhard, Theresiengasse 1, 2500 Baden bei
Wien. T. (02252) 48659. - Ant / Paint / Furn / Jew /
Instr - *038109*
Zweymüller, Hauptpl. 3, 2500 Baden bei Wien.
T. (02252) 484 01. - Ant / Furn - *038110*

Badgastein (Salzburg)
Antiquitäten am Wasserfall, Straubingerpl. 1, 5640 Bad-
gastein. T. (06434) 2766. *038111*
Greyer, Margita, Bismarckstr 14, 5640 Badgastein.
T. (06434) 2652, Fax 2652. - Ant / Paint /
Graph - *038112*
Lang, Franz, Kaiser Franz Josefstr. 17, 5640 Badgastein.
T. (06434) 2652. - Ant / Paint / Orient / China / Sculp /
Jew / Silv / Rel / Glass - *038113*
Urban, Adolf, Straubingerpl. 1, 5640 Badgastein.
T. (06434) 2766. *038114*
Wally's Kunstvitrinen, Kaiserpromenade 350, 5640 Bad-
gastein. T. (06434) 32 54. - Ant - *038115*

Berndorf (Niederösterreich)
Kral, Anton, Kennedy-Pl. 2, 2560 Berndorf.
T. (02672) 22 36, Fax 22 36. *038116*

Bernstein (Burgenland)
Kurz, Wilhelmine, Herrengasse 8, 7434 Bernstein.
T. (03354) 279. *038117*

Birkfeld (Steiermark)
Posch, Franz, Hauptpl. 3, 8190 Birkfeld.
T. (03174) 4477. *038118*
Steiner, Christian, 131, 8190 Birkfeld. *038119*

Bischofshofen (Salzburg)
Ranftl GmbH, Bahnhofstr 30, 5500
Bischofshofen. *038120*

Bleiburg (Kärnten)
Die Bauerntruhe, 9150 Bleiburg. - Ant - *038121*

Blindenmarkt (Niederösterreich)
Schmidradler, Maria, Blindenmarkt 14, 3372
Blindenmarkt. *038122*

Braunau (Oberösterreich)
Schatztruhe, Kirchenpl. 6, 5280 Braunau.
T. (07722) 2270. *038123*

Bregenz (Vorarlberg)
Art House, Ant. Schneiderstr. 20, 6900 Bregenz.
T. (05574) 251 92. *038124*
Dreher, Eduard, Maurachg. 7, 6900 Bregenz.
T. (05574) 2 31 27. - Ant / Paint / Graph / Furn / Num /
China / Sculp / Jew / Instr / Rel / Glass - *038125*
Gasser, Peter, Quellenstr. 30, 6900 Bregenz.
T. (05574) 2 33 29. - Ant - *038126*
Hämmerle, Anton-Schneider-Str 4A/1, 6900 Bregenz.
T. (05574) 47319, Fax 47319. *038127*
Halsegger, Alfred, Viktor-Kleiner-Str. 28, 6900 Bregenz.
T. (05574) 37326. - Num - *038128*
Larisegger, Ferdinand, Neugasse 7, 6900 Bregenz.
T. (05574) 24889. *038129*
Mayer, Helga, Kirchstr. 5, 6900 Bregenz.
T. (05574) 26265. *038130*
Neurater, Hedwig, Anton-Schneider-Str. 30, 6901 Bregenz. - Num - *038131*
Sankt Martin Antiquitäten, Apothekergässele 5, 6900
Bregenz. T. (05574) 26265. - Ant / Paint / Furn /
Sculp - *038132*
Tschanun, Eugen, Deuringstr. 12, 6900 Bregenz.
T. (05574) 26607. *038133*

Brixlegg (Tirol)
Bangheri, Jakob, Neubau, 6230 Brixlegg.
T. (05337) 28 432. *038134*
Schloß Galerie, Schloß Lipperheide, 6230 Brixlegg.
T. (05337) 3318. - Ant / Paint / Graph / China / Sculp /
Tex / Glass / Mod / Ico / Draw - *038135*

Bruck an der Leitha (Niederösterreich)
RAR Realitäten Antiquitäten Raritäten, Kirchengasse 24,
2460 Bruck an der Leitha. T. (02162) 23 27. *038136*

Bruck an der Mur (Steiermark)
Karlon, Anneliese, Koloman-Wallisch-Pl. 2, 8601 Bruck
an der Mur. T. (03862) 518 42. *038137*

Brunn am Gebirge (Niederösterreich)
Vojnicsek, Walter, Arbeitergasse 15, 2345 Brunn am Gebirge. T. (02236) 32331. *038138*

Bürmoos (Salzburg)
Mang, Volker, Lamprechtshausener Str. 8, 5111 Bürmoos. T. (06274) 6456. - Ant - *038139*

Döllach (Kärnten)
Lindsberger, Josef, Schloß Großkirchheim, 9843 Döllach. T. (04825) 23 10 06. *038140*

Dornbirn (Vorarlberg)
Diem, Egbert, Bahnhofstr. 12, 6850 Dornbirn.
T. (05572) 23082, Fax 22667. - Num - *038141*
Feierle, Anna Maria, Littengasse 4a, 6850 Dornbirn.
T. (05572) 64374. *038142*
Gisinger, Charlotte, Altweg 2, 6850 Dornbirn.
T. (05572) 619 34. *038143*
Krebitz, Eleonore, Marktstr. 27, 6850 Dornbirn.
T. (05572) 60444. *038144*
Thurner's, Johannes, Marktstr. 14, 6850 Dornbirn.
T. (05572) 66151-15, Fax 66151-10. *038145*

Ebenthal (Kärnten)
Schawarz, Valentin, Kirchenstr 15, 9065 Ebenthal.
T. (0463) 73111, (0663) 848111. *038146*

Eferding (Oberösterreich)
Falk, Erna, Hörstorf 32, 4070 Eferding. T. (07272) 674.
- Ant / Furn - *038147*
Runge, Brandstätterstr 20, 4070 Eferding.
T. (07272) 2246, Fax 2167. - Ant / Paint / Furn / China /
Sculp / Instr / Rel / Cur / Draw - *038148*

Eisenstadt (Burgenland)
Rötzer, Rudolf Walter, Mattersburger Str. 25, 7000 Eisenstadt. T. (02682) 2494, 3204. *038149*
Wirzel, Gustaf, Pfarrgasse 8, 7000 Eisenstadt. *038150*

Feldbach (Steiermark)
Hasivar, Josef, Hauptpl. 20, 8330 Feldbach.
T. (03152) 2324. *038151*
Kiesslinger, Anna + Gisela, Torplatz 3, 8330
Feldbach. *038152*

Feldkirch (Vorarlberg)
Dürnberger, Sidonia, Altenstadt, Klosterstr.24, 6800
Feldkirch. - Ant - *038153*
Katzenmeyer, Monica & Günther, Raiffeisenpl. 7, 6800
Feldkirch. T. (05522) 23191. *038154*
Villa Mutter, Reichsstr. 170, 6800 Feldkirch.
T. (05522) 719 24. - Ant / Graph / Furn - *038155*

Freistadt (Oberösterreich)
Hofer, B., Salzgasse 26, 4240 Freistadt.
T. (07942) 36 32. *038156*

Friedberg (Steiermark)
Reiss, Maximilian, 8240 Friedberg. - Ant - *038157*

Fügen (Tirol)
Kronthaler, Franz, Hauptstr. 165, 6263 Fügen.
T. (05288) 2265. *038158*

Fulpmes (Tirol)
Shopping-Club, Bahnstr. 19, 6166 Fulpmes.
T. (05225) 26 25. *038159*

Gablitz (Niederösterreich)
Winkler, Josef, Leopold-Schober-Gasse 11, 3003
Gablitz. *038160*

Gars am Kamp (Niederösterreich)
Opitz, Rudolf, Haangasse 23, 3571 Gars am Kamp.
T. (02985) 2 52. - Ant - *038161*

Gaschurn (Vorarlberg)
Rudigier, Otto, 6793 Gaschurn. T. (05558) 8270. - Ant /
Paint / Furn / Sculp / Instr / Rel / Glass - *038162*

Gerlos (Tirol)
Egger, Jakob, Gp. 121/3, 6281 Gerlos.
T. (05284) 5236. *038163*

Gloggnitz (Niederösterreich)
Mempör, Werner, Hauptstr. 35, 2640 Gloggnitz. *038164*

Gmünd (Kärnten)
Maltantik, Fischertratten 9, 9853 Gmünd.
T. (04732) 3183. *038165*
Meissnitzer, Michael, Hauptpl 24, 9853 Gmünd.
T. (04732) 2228, Fax 2228. - Instr - *038166*

Gmunden (Oberösterreich)
Fried, Gunde, Cumberlandpark 85, 4810 Gmunden.
T. (07612) 2261, 4481. *038167*
Fried, Gunde, Franz-Josefpl. 10, 4810 Gmunden.
- Ant - *038168*
Grabner, Ernst, Badgasse 4, 4810 Gmunden.
T. (07612) 4415. *038169*
Harringer, Rudolf, Plentznerstr. 11, 4810 Gmunden.
T. (07612) 48 94. - Ant - *038170*
Loderbauer, Klaus, Traunsteinstr. 41, 4810 Gmunden.
T. (07612) 67513. *038171*
Schober, R., Freygasse 27, 4810 Gmunden.
T. (07612) 4308, 5018, Fax 56 05 31. *038172*
Spiesberger, Karl, Kirchengasse 3, 4810 Gmunden.
T. (07612) 4878. *038173*

Golling (Salzburg)
Kordasch, Erna, Torren 96, 5440 Golling.
T. (06244) 389. *038174*

Graz (Steiermark)
Alt Österreich, Kaiserfeldgasse 24, 8010 Graz.
T. (0316) 70 01 21, 741 85. - Ant - *038175*
Andréewitch, Stephan, Panzenbeckgasse 7, 8010 Graz.
T. (0316) 39 22 09. *038176*
Bobik, Peter Hans, Sackstr. 24, 8010 Graz.
T. (0316) 84 88 54. - Ant / Furn / China / Jew / Silv /
Glass - *038177*
Bobik, Wilhelm, Dr., Schmiedgasse 11, 8010 Graz.
T. (0316) 84 30 78. *038178*
Brodnig, Dr., Sporgasse 23, 8010 Graz.
T. (0316) 849042, Fax 681936. *038179*
Brühl, Kurt, Schmiedgasse 12, 8010 Graz.
T. (0316) 82 16 16. *038180*
Burkert, Helga, Griesgasse 27, 8020 Graz.
T. (0316) 91 11 81. *038181*
Darwisch, Christine, Kastellfeldgasse 10, 8010 Graz.
T. (0316) 83 06 58. *038182*
Eichler, Helmut, Einspinnergasse 2, 8010 Graz.
T. (0316) 71 75 03. *038183*
Erlacher-Bobik, Christa, Stubenberggasse 7, 8010 Graz.
T. (0316) 82 95 53. - Ant / Paint / Furn / Orient / China /
Sculp / Jew / Fra / Silv / Instr / Rel / Glass / Cur / Mod / Ico - *038184*
Fiedler, Gerhard, Am Eisernen Tor 2, 8010 Graz.
T. (0316) 83 05 52. *038185*
Frank, Werner, Weinholdstr. 18, 8010 Graz.
T. (0316) 43 40 35. - Ant / Jew / Instr - *038186*
Galerie zum Glockenspiel, Glockenspielpl. 5, 8010 Graz.
T. (0316) 70 00 28. *038187*
Grabner, Franz, Mariahilferstr 7, 8020 Graz.
T. (0316) 914127, Fax 914127. - Jew / Instr - *038188*
Hadler, Bischofpl. 5, 8010 Graz.
T. (0316) 84 69 10. *038189*
Hermann, Dr., Wastlergasse 2, 8010 Graz.
T. (0316) 33513. - Ant / Furn - *038190*
Holasek, Erich, Sackstr. 34, 8010 Graz.
T. (0316) 84 19 52. - Ant / Furn / China / Sculp / Jew /
Silv / Instr / Mil / Rel / Glass / Cur / Mod / Pho - *038191*
Holasek, Erika, Sackstr. 26, 8010 Graz.
T. (0316) 734 08. *038192*
Kindler, Matthias-Johannes-Andreas, Hofgasse 8, 8010
Graz. T. (0316) 822454, Fax 822454. - Ant / Furn /
Glass - *038193*
Köppel, Orientboutique, Annenstr. 46, 8020
Graz. *038194*
Kunst aus Asien, Reitschulgasse 6, 8010 Graz.
T. (0316) 8 15 85. - Orient / China / Tex / Jew - *038195*
Kunstkabinett Günther Schafschetzy, Färbergasse 2,
8010 Graz. T. (0316) 82 89 82. - Ant / Paint /
Graph - *038196*
Lanz, Hermann, Prof., Hauptpl. 14, 8010 Graz.
T. (0316) 82 93 45. - Num - *038197*
Lendl, Eugen, Gleisdorfergasse 4, 8010 Graz.
T. (0316) 82 55 14. *038198*
Maitz, Theresia, Riesstr. 13, 8010 Graz.
T. (0316) 37625. *038199*
Mölzer, Ortwin, Leonhardstr. 85, 8010 Graz.
T. (0316) 38 13 43. *038200*
Moser, Hans-Sachs-Gasse 14, Passage, I.Stock, 8010
Graz. T. (0316) 82982123, 830110 (Antiquariat),
825696 (Galerie in Antiquitäten), Fax 83011020. - Ant /
Paint / Furn / Repr / Silv / Glass - *038201*
Mostegl, Ernestine, Sackstr. 22, 8010 Graz.
T. (0316) 83 07 85. *038202*
Pichler, Günther, Sporgasse 29b, 8010 Graz.
T. (0316) 76 90 32. - Ant - *038203*
Pretner-Georgi, Christine, Schmiedgasse 38, 8010 Graz.
T. (0316) 84 68 72. *038204*
Regner, Johann, Bischofpl. 5, 8010 Graz.
T. (0316) 82 60 17, Fax 82 60 17. - Rel / Ico - *038205*
Reinisch, Helmut, Hauptpl. 6, 8010 Graz.
T. (0316) 82 11 11. - Tex - *038206*
Schäffer, Thomas, Kollonitschstr. 9a, 8010 Graz.
T. (0316) 35 97 52. *038207*
Scheidel, Harald, Bindergasse 4, 8010 Graz. *038208*
Schullin, Herrengasse 3, 8010 Graz.
T. (0316) 81 30 00. *038209*

Semanek, Rudolf Josef, Glockenspielpl. 5, 8010 Graz.
T. (0316) 83 00 28. 038210
Srna, Manfred, Waldweg 112, 8051 Graz. 038211
Steiner, Gerhard, Sackstr. 24, 8010 Graz.
T. (0316) 731 50. 038212
Steiner, Günther, Glacisstr. 67, 8010 Graz.
T. (0316) 75 304, 73 74 44. - Ant - 038213
Steyerische Kunststube, Engegasse 1, 8010
Graz. 038214
Stiegengalerie, Sporgasse 21, 8010 Graz.
T. (0316) 789 82. 038215
Stoff, Michael, Einspinnergasse 2, 8010 Graz.
T. (0316) 776 67. 038216
Stolberg, Lukas, Grabenstr. 9, 8010 Graz.
T. (0316) 67 13 68. - Instr - 038217
Wittek-Saltzberg, Robert Friedrich, Dr., Maiffredgasse 1,
8010 Graz. T. (0316) 38 15 62. 038218

Grödig (Salzburg)
Galerie Slavi, Kellerstr. 31, 5082 Grödig.
T. (06246) 4448, Fax 4497. 038219

Großgmain (Salzburg)
Haderer, Gertraud, Stauffenstr. 479, 5084 Großgmain.
T. (06247) 473. 038220
Schmidhammer, G., Stauffenstr. 59, 5084 Großgmain.
T. (06247) 8473. - Ant - 038221

Gumpoldskirchen (Niederösterreich)
Oegg, Magret, Wiener Str 26, 2352 Gumpoldskirchen.
T. (02252) 62433, Fax (02252) 63820. 038222

Häselgehr (Tirol)
Immler, Bruno, 6651 Häselgehr.
T. (05634) 6333. 038223

Haidershofen (Niederösterreich)
Alber, Martin, Haidershofen 27, 4431 Haidershofen.
T. 37121. 038224

Hainfeld (Niederösterreich)
Marton, Brigitte, Gölsenstr. 22, 3170 Hainfeld. 038225
Vadlejch, Anton, Sackgasse 6, 3170 Hainfeld.
T. (02764) 364, 611. 038226

Hall (Tirol)
Philipp, Karlmann, Salvatorgasse 6, 6060 Hall.
T. (05223) 3120. 038227
Sattleger, Ferdinand, Sewerstr. 10, 6060 Hall.
T. (05223) 69704. 038228

Hallein (Salzburg)
Dottschadis, J.E., Postgasse 1, 5400 Hallein.
T. (06245) 39382. - Ant / Paint / Graph / Furn / China /
Jew / Silv / Instr / Rel / Glass / Cur / Mod - 038229
Edelmann, Ingo Franz, Molnarpl. 14, 5400 Hallein.
T. (06245) 33 27. 038230
Grundner, Edmund Martin, Bundesstr. Nord 1, 5400
Hallein. 038231
Pliem, Karl, Wiepachstr. 13, 5400 Hallein.
T. (06245) 600 55. 038232

Hard (Vorarlberg)
Hopfgartner, Walburga, Bitzeweg 6, 6971 Hard.
T. (05574) 36703. 038233

Haslach (Oberösterreich)
Wakolbinger, Heinrich, Bahnstr. 10, 4170 Haslach.
T. (07289) 73 94. 038234

Hinterbrühl (Niederösterreich)
Hierzenberger, Lisl, Parkstr.29-31, 2371
Hinterbrühl. 038235

Hirschegg (Vorarlberg)
Stumvoll, Herbert, Walserstr 16, 6992 Hirschegg.
T. (05517) 6428. 038236

Hörbranz (Vorarlberg)
Brauer, Elfriede, Unterhochstegstr. 25, 6912 Hörbranz.
T. (05573) 2404, 2902. 038237

Hörsching (Oberösterreich)
Zdeb, Haidstr. 3, 4063 Hörsching. T. (07221) 722 57.
- Ant - 038238

Hof (Salzburg)
Stangl, H. & I., Haus Nr. 122, 5322 Hof. T. (06229) 23-
29. - Ant - 038239

Hohenems (Vorarlberg)
Linder, Walter, Sägerstr. 1, 6845 Hohenems.
T. (05576) 5595. 038240
Reis, Norbert, Angelika Kaufmann-Str. 1, 6845
Hohenems. 038241
Russegger, Rudolf, Marktstr. 48a, 6845 Hohenems.
T. (05576) 29133. 038242

Hollenstein (Niederösterreich)
Steinhofer, Pauline, Dorf 65, 3343 Hollenstein. 038243

Illmitz (Burgenland)
Klus, Peter, Untere Hauptstr. 14, 7142 Illmitz.
T. (02175) 2933. 038244

Imst (Tirol)
Kienel, Anton, Pfarrgasse 9, 6460 Imst. T. (05412) 3338,
Fax 333 85. - Paint - 038245

Innermanzing (Niederösterreich)
Schuster, G.W., Dr., Barbaraholz, 3052 Innermanzing.
T. 6328. - Orient / Eth - 038246

Innsbruck (Tirol)
Antiquitäten-Galerie Galeothek, Herzog Friedrich Str. 3,
6020 Innsbruck. T. (0512) 58 68 04. - Ant - 038247
Antiquitäten-Galerie Notburga, Maria-Theresien-Str. 55,
6020 Innsbruck. T. (0512) 204 29. - Jew - 038248
Biedermann, Margit, Hilberstr 6, 6080 Innsbruck.
T. (0512) 78548, 846464. 038249
Boschi, Rudolf, Kiebachgasse 8 u. 14, 6020 Innsbruck.
T. (0512) 29224, 21386. - Ant / Paint / Graph / Fra /
Toys - 038250
Cresnjar, Friederike, Pfarrgasse 8, 6020 Innsbruck.
T. (0512) 73 89 44. 038251
Dorighelli, Lorenz, Bachlechnerstr. 24, 6020
Innsbruck. 038252
Engel Bogen, Holiday Inn, Salurner Str. 15, 6020 Inns-
bruck. T. (0512) 58 77 16. - Ant / Instr - 038253
Fischer, Marion, Marktgraben 1, 6020 Innsbruck.
T. (0512) 36 23 23. 038254
Flory, Gertraud, Innrain 21, 6020 Innsbruck.
T. (0512) 56 38 63. 038255
Geußing, Roland, Neurauthgasse 5, 6020 Innsbruck.
T. (0512) 22 55 65. 038256
Graf, Arthur, Wilh.-Greil-Str.15, 6020 Innsbruck.
T. (0512) 23 147. - Tex - 038257
Hallegger, August, Dr., Herzog Friedrich-Str. 22, 6020
Innsbruck. T. (0512) 58 29 53. 038258
Hess, Manfred, Herzog Friedrich-Str. 3, 6020 Innsbruck.
T. (0512) 58 68 04. 038259
Hofinger, Tempelstr. 5, 6010 Innsbruck.
T. (0512) 57 71 82, Fax 57 22 06. - Paint /
Furn - 038260
Hofman, E., Universitätsstr. 10, 6020 Innsbruck.
T. (0512) 24863, 33647. - Num - 038261
Klammer, Alois, Maria Theresien-Str. 20, 6020 Inns-
bruck. T. (0512) 58 93 97. 038262
Konzert, Peter, Erlerstr. 15, 6020 Innsbruck.
T. (0512) 261 39, 243 24. 038263
Mayer, Jutta, Kärntner Str. 64, 6020 Innsbruck.
T. (0512) 44 84 33. 038264
Mayr & Sohn OHG, Margarethe, Leopoldstr. 2, 6020
Innsbruck. T. (0512) 31 21 52. - Ant / Jew / Fra /
Mil - 038265
Oberweger, Innrain 25/5, 6020 Innsbruck.
T. (0512) 579768. 038266
Ostasienhaus, Exlgasse 12, 6026 Innsbruck.
T. (0512) 811 68, 87 823. - Furn / Orient / China / Tex /
Jew - 038267
Reindl, Hubert, Speckbacherstr. 23, 6020 Innsbruck.
T. (0512) 57 61 44, Fax 57 22 28. - Paint /
Furn - 038268
Rhomberg, Templstr. 2, 6010 Innsbruck.
T. (0512) 58 80 80-0, Fax 58 80 80-4. - Ant / Paint /
Graph / Furn / Dec / Lights / Instr / Mod / Draw - 038269
Sailer, Erich, Andreas Hofer-Str. 34, 6020 Innsbruck.
T. (0512) 58 28 57. 038270
Schönpflug, Ingo, Innrain 40, 6020 Innsbruck.
T. (0512) 28037. - Ant - 038271

Sturany, Notburga, Maria Theresien-Str. 55, 6020 Inns-
bruck. T. (0512) 58 04 29. 038272
Trautner, Elfi, Kiebachgasse 12, 6020 Innsbruck.
T. (0512) 58 93 66. - Paint / Paint / Fra - 038273
Trautner, Josef, Pfarrgasse 6, 6020 Innsbruck.
T. (0512) 213 23. 038274
Waritsch, M., Marktgraben 1, 6020 Innsbruck.
T. (0512) 36 23 44. - Ant / Furn - 038275

Kirchberg (Tirol)
Kals, Burkhard, Lindstr. 1, 6365 Kirchberg.
T. (05357) 2247. 038276

Kirchberg am Wechsel (Niederöster-reich)
Leberl, Franz, Kirchberg 63, 2880 Kirchberg am
Wechsel. 038277

Kitzbühel (Tirol)
Erler, Michael, Franz-Erler-Str. 1, 6370 Kitzbühel.
T. (05356) 57413. 038278
Lichtl-Stall, Franz-Reisch-Str. 4, 6370 Kitzbühel.
T. (05356) 26 00, Fax 71345. - Ant / Furn /
Lights - 038279
Reisch, Sigrid, Franz Reischstr.4, 6370 Kitzbühel.
T. (05356) 5252, Fax 52 52 49. 038280
Welwert, Konrad, Josef-Pirchl-Str. 4, Postfach 99, 6370
Kitzbühel. - Ant / Paint / Graph / Furn / China / Sculp /
Rel / Ico / Draw - 038281

Klagenfurt (Kärnten)
Friessnig, Leo, Salmstr. 4, 9020 Klagenfurt.
T. (0463) 80 75 82, 59 75 82. 038282
Habenricht, Wolfgang, Hauptmann-Hermannpl. 4, 9020
Klagenfurt. 038283
Kika, Völkermarkter Str. 165, 9020 Klagenfurt.
T. (0463) 32182. 038284
Prause, Fritz, Neuer Platz, 9020 Klagenfurt.
T. (0463) 55932. - Ant / Paint / Graph / Furn / Sculp /
Jew / Silv - 038285
Prause, Fritz, Pernhartgasse 1, 9010 Klagenfurt.
T. (0463) 55932. - Ant / Paint / Graph / Eth / Jew /
Glass / Cur - 038286
Schilling, Hannemarie, Burggasse 8, 9020 Klagenfurt.
T. (0463) 57925. 038287
Schlambor, Grete, Pernhartgasse 12, 9020
Klagenfurt. 038288
Slama, Hans, Karfreitstr. 1, 9020 Klagenfurt.
T. (0463) 55 63 81. - Paint / Paint - 038289
Treffer, Hans, Burggasse 8, 9020 Klagenfurt. 038290

Klaus (Vorarlberg)
Brugger, Martin Robert, Römerweg 38, 6833
Klaus. 038291

Klosterneuburg (Niederösterreich)
Hampe, Susanna, Weidlinger Str. 3, 3400 Klosterneu-
burg. T. (02243) 69 45. - Ant / Furn / Jew / Cur - 038292
Kolhammer, Alfred, Agnesstr. 50, 3400 Klosterneuburg.
T. (02243) 28 59. - Ant / Paint / China / Sculp / Tex /
Jew / Fra / Silv / Lights / Instr / Mil / Rel / Glass / Cur / M-
od - 038293
Lager, Rudolf, Sachsengasse 6, 3400 Klosterneuburg.
T. (02243) 71 07. - Ant / Jew / Silv / Lights / Instr /
Glass / Mod - 038294

Knittelfeld (Steiermark)
Ebner, Hellmuth, Herrengasse 5, 8720 Knittelfeld.
- Ant - 038295

Kramsach (Tirol)
Zwischenberger, Alfred, Hagau 270b, 6233 Kramsach.
T. (05337) 20 153. 038296

Krems an der Donau (Niederösterreich)
Andrä, Ernst Leopold, Schmidgasse 7, 3500 Krems an
der Donau. 038297
Bauer, Markus, Hohensteinstr. 68, 3500 Krems an der
Donau. 038298
Bröderbauer, Renate, Südtirolerpl., Brauhof, 3500 Krems
an der Donau. 038299
Göschl, Erich, Untere Landstr. 49-51, 3500 Krems an
der Donau. 038300

Heuritsch Antique, Wegscheid 2, 3500 Krems an der Donau. T. (02732) 82133, Fax 827 28 17. - Ant / Paint / Graph / Furn / China / Jew / Silv / Glass - **038301**

Höchtl, Egon, Untere Landstr. 40, 3500 Krems an der Donau. **038302**

Kalteis, Walter, Obere Landstr. 4, 3500 Krems an der Donau. **038303**

Maler, Ernst, Dachsberggasse 8, 3500 Krems an der Donau. **038304**

Müllauer, Thomas, Hoher Markt 5, 3500 Krems an der Donau. T. (02732) 70 42 84. **038305**

Neuhofer, Untere Landstr. 20, 3500 Krems an der Donau. T. (02732) 2347. **038306**

Plöckinger, Walter, Hoher Markt 13, 3500 Krems an der Donau. T. (02732) 37 95. - Ant / Paint / Furn / Sculp / Tex / Arch - **038307**

Saska, Johann, Untere Landstr.15, 3500 Krems an der Donau. **038308**

Schauer, Franz K., Pfarrpl. 13, 3500 Krems an der Donau. T. (02732) 2159. **038309**

Schindler-Aigenbauer, Maria, Hoher Markt 12, 3500 Krems an der Donau. T. (02732) 84207. - Ant - **038310**

Schmid, Karl, Obere Landstr. 5, 3500 Krems an der Donau. T. (02732) 822 43. - Ant - **038311**

Waldbauer, Johann, Hohensteinstr. 12, 3500 Krems an der Donau. **038312**

Walter, Maria, Hafnerpl. 5, 3500 Krems an der Donau. T. (02732) 82756. **038313**

Krieglach (Steiermark)
Gaar, Ernst, Schwöbing 29, 8670 Krieglach. T. (03855) 2731. **038314**

Kufstein (Tirol)
Hochstaffl, Michael, Krankenhausgasse 3, 6330 Kufstein. T. (05372) 64525. - Ant / Furn - **038315**

Pöll, Gerhard, Georg Pirmoser-Str. 5, 6330 Kufstein. T. (05372) 5475. **038316**

Schön, Ingeborg, Kinkstr. 10, 6330 Kufstein. T. (05372) 64535. - Paint / China / Sculp / Jew / Glass - **038317**

Laab im Walde (Niederösterreich)
Kaplan, Helga, Schulgasse 10, 2381 Laab im Walde. **038318**

Lambrechten (Oberösterreich)
Witzmann, Ernestine, Reichergerhagen 21, 4772 Lambrechten. T. (07765) 448. - Ant - **038319**

Landeck (Tirol)
Schrott, Werner, Malserstr. 64, 6500 Landeck. T. (05442) 63801, Fax 63801. - Num - **038320**

Langenlois (Niederösterreich)
Renner, Heinrich, Rudolfstr. 17, 3550 Langenlois. T. (02734) 2600. - Ant / Paint / Furn - **038321**

Laxenburg (Niederösterreich)
Hartl, Friedrich, Hofstr. 1-3, 2361 Laxenburg. **038322**

Leibnitz (Steiermark)
Huallenz, B., Hauptpl.7, 8430 Leibnitz. **038323**
Ranz, Frank, Adalbert-Stifter-Weg 9, 8430 Leibnitz. - Num - **038324**

Leoben (Steiermark)
Berger, Julius, Franz Josef-Str. 23, 8700 Leoben. T. (03842) 45091. **038325**

Ganglberger, Karl, Timmersdorferstr. 5, 8700 Leoben. **038326**

Gruber, Siegfried, Donawitzer Str. 35, 8700 Leoben. T. (03842) 23548. **038327**

Payer, Uschi, Hauptpl 7, 8700 Leoben. T. (03842) 44893. **038328**

Leonding (Linz)
Zauner, Christa, Kauttenstr. 16, 4060 Leonding. T. (0732) 80834. **038329**

Linz (Oberösterreich)
Antiquitäten Nepomuk, Marienstr. 10, 4020 Linz. T. (0732) 27 73 11. - Ant / Furn / China / Sculp / Tex / Jew / Tin - **038330**

Bergsteiger, Anna, Bischofstr. 15, 4020 Linz. T. (0732) 27 91 27. **038331**

Binder, Hans, Mozartgasse 9, 4020 Linz. T. (0732) 27 46 29. - Ant - **038332**

David, Bertha, Schirmerstr. 28, 4020 Linz. T. (0732) 82055. - Furn - **038333**

Eigl, Alois, Dametzstr. 25, 4020 Linz. T. (0732) 77 02 70, Fax 78 56 12. - Graph / Graph - **038334**

Esterbauer, Fritz, Herrenstr. 5, 4020 Linz. T. (0732) 27 28 48. **038335**

Feichtinger, Rolf, Dinghoferstr. 63, 4020 Linz. T. (0732) 661 30 23. **038336**

Gruber, Johann, Ob. Donaulände 119, 4020 Linz. T. (0732) 272 39 13. **038337**

Jahn, Engelbert, Altstadt 17, 4020 Linz. T. (0732) 27 11 58. - Num - **038338**

Jahraus, Gerda, Klammstr. 2, 4020 Linz. T. (0732) 271 98 64. **038339**

Kirchmayr, Richard, Herrenstr. 23, 4020 Linz. T. (0732) 27 46 67. **038340**

Kirchmayr, Richard, Bischofstr. 3a, 4020 Linz. T. (0732) 276 98 43. **038341**

Kriechbaumer, Gudila, Marienstr. 10, 4020 Linz. T. (0732) 27 73 11. **038342**

Kunst aus Asien, Bethlehemstr. 1c, 4020 Linz. T. (0732) 27492. - Furn / Orient / China / Tex / Jew - **038343**

Kunst aus Asien, Stockhofstr. 8, 4020 Linz. T. (0732) 23721. - Furn / Orient / China / Tex / Jew - **038344**

Kunststücke, Spittelwiese 15, 4020 Linz. T. (0732) 794679, Fax 794679. **038345**

Lehner, Hermann, Klammstr. 4, 4020 Linz. T. (0732) 271 98 55. **038346**

Leiner, Rudolf, Anzengruberstr. 18, 4020 Linz. T. (0732) 57461. **038347**

Linzer Kunsthof, F. Muckenhuber, Bischofstr. 11, 4020 Linz. T. (0732) 25 65 38. - Ant / Furn / China / Jew / Fra / Silv / Lights / Rel / Glass - **038348**

Maisgeyer, Angela, Dametzstr. 12, Hauptstr. 43, 4020 Linz. **038349**

Meindl, H. Georg, Steingasse 1, 4020 Linz. T. (0732) 783754, Fax 783754. - Ant / Arch - **038350**

Monetarium, Promenade 11-13, 4041 Linz. T. (0732) 77 48 90, Fax 2391-2801. - Num - **038351**

Neumann, Edith, Rainerstr. 10, 4020 Linz. T. (0732) 58168. **038352**

Pastl, Ute, Dr., Wischerstr. 26, 4040 Linz. T. (0732) 23 73 06. **038353**

Prat, Schmidtorstr. 7, 4020 Linz. T. (0732) 77 16 15, Fax 77 16 15-21. - Paint / Graph / Repr / Fra - **038354**

Puce, L.A., Rainerstr. 10, 4020 Linz. T. (0732) 581 68, Fax 581 68. - Jew / Mod - **038355**

Ratzinger, Johann, Unionstr. 17, 4020 Linz. T. (0732) 66 70 28. **038356**

Roland, Heinrich, Khevenhüllerstr. 25, 4020 Linz. T. (0732) 66 30 03. **038357**

Runge, Herrenstr. 17, 4020 Linz. T. (0732) 78 24 44, Fax 2167. - Ant / Paint / Furn / China / Sculp / Dec / Lights / Glass / Cur - **038358**

Saminger, Erich, Mozartstr. 26, 4040 Linz. T. (0732) 27 16 40. **038359**

Saminger, Ferdinand, Waldeggstr. 20, 4020 Linz. T. (0732) 540 81. - Ant / Furn - **038360**

Schantl, Peter, Landstr. 47, 4020 Linz. T. (0732) 27 98 63. - Tex - **038361**

Schrey, Norbert, Spittelwiese 2, 4020 Linz. T. (0732) 27 63 77. **038362**

Seidler, Wilhelm, Klosterstr. 14, 4020 Linz. T. (0732) 77 00 86, Fax 770 08 64. - Ant / Paint / Jew - **038363**

Silbermayr, Johann, Unionstr. 58, 4020 Linz. **038364**

Skola, Franz, Hauptstr. 7, 4040 Linz. T. (0732) 231 79 82. **038365**

Spreitzer, Maria, In der Auerpeint 9, 4020 Linz. **038366**

Swoboda, Roland, Mozartstr. 9, 4020 Linz. T. (0732) 27 10 54, Fax 28 29 24 (78 29 24). - Num - **038367**

Thalbauer, Hans, Spittelwiese 4, 4020 Linz. T. (0732) 27 53 44, 27 52 27. **038368**

Tober, Theresia, Bethlehemstr. 42, 4020 Linz. T. (0732) 27 75 204. **038369**

Veritas, Harrachstr. 5, 4010 Linz. T. (0732) 276 45 10. **038370**

Zum Taubenschlag, Bischofstr. 3a, 4020 Linz. T. (0732) 27 69 843. - Ant / Paint / Furn / China / Jew / Glass / Mod - **038371**

Lochau (Vorarlberg)
Spöttl, Benedikt, Toni-Russtr. 19, 6911 Lochau. T. (05574) 251 89. **038372**

Marchtrenk (Oberösterreich)
Marchgraber, Erwin, Schafwiesenstr. 39, 4614 Marchtrenk. T. (07243) 523 39, Fax 539 07. - Ant / Paint / Furn / China / Sculp / Instr / Mil / Glass - **038373**

Maria Enzersdorf (Niederösterreich)
Vojnicsek, Wilhelm, Hauptstr. 34, 2344 Maria Enzersdorf. T. (02236) 824 15. **038374**

Maria Saal (Kärnten)
Turrinj, Walter, Arndorferstr. 11, 9063 Maria Saal. T. (04223) 2289. **038375**

Mariapfarr (Salzburg)
Dengg, Erich, Nr. 232, 5571 Mariapfarr. T. (06473) 273. - Jew / Instr - **038376**

Mariazell (Steiermark)
Nitsche, Oswald, Grazer Str. 8, 8630 Mariazell. T. (03882) 2325. **038377**

Martinsberg (Niederösterreich)
Hader, Josef, 3664 Martinsberg. **038378**

Mauterndorf (Salzburg)
Hoogstoel, Reinlinde Berta, Haus Nr. 83, 5570 Mauterndorf. T. (06472) 72 07. - Furn - **038379**

Mauthausen (Oberösterreich)
Lettner, Kurt, Brunngraben 41, 4310 Mauthausen. T. (07238) 21 88. - Ant / Furn - **038380**

Millstatt (Kärnten)
Fundgrube, Haus Nr. 158, 9872 Millstatt. T. (04766) 30 82. **038381**

Mittelberg (Vorarlberg)
Willand, Detlef Eginhart, Hirschegg 240, 6993 Mittelberg. - Ant - **038382**

Mödling (Niederösterreich)
Country House, Brühler Str. 55, 2340 Mödling. T. (02236) 847 56. **038383**

Hanzl, Stefan, Elsa Brandström-Gasse 4, 2340 Mödling. T. (02236) 45569, Fax 45569. **038384**

Kowall, Heinrich, Babenbergergasse 5, 2340 Mödling. T. (02236) 83 92 45, 25290. - Ant / Graph / China / Jew / Silv / Instr / Glass / Mod - **038385**

Roth & Sohn, L., Elisabethstr. 18, 2340 Mödling. T. (02236) 288 95. **038386**

Mondsee (Oberösterreich)
Pichler, Walter, Mondsee 15, 5310 Mondsee. **038387**

Mürzzuschlag (Steiermark)
Empl, Wiener Str. 57, 8680 Mürzzuschlag. T. (03852) 22 34. **038388**

Haindl, Heinrich-Kaiblingergasse 1 b, 8680 Mürzzuschlag. T. (03852) 3481. - Ant / Paint / Graph / Furn / China / Sculp / Jew / Fra / Silv / Lights / Instr / Mil / Glass / Cur - **038389**

Nenzing (Vorarlberg)
Geiger, Rudolf, Heimat 82, 6710 Nenzing. - Ant - **038390**

Neunkirchen (Niederösterreich)
Kornthal, Erwin, Wiesengasse 4, 2620 Neunkirchen. **038391**

Reithmeyer, Rudolf, Hauptpl. 5, 2620 Neunkirchen. T. (02635) 22 84. **038392**

Neusiedl am See (Burgenland)
Mayrberger, Ute, Kirchbergweg 7, 7100 Neusiedl am See. T. (02167) 2351. **038393**

Oberalm (Salzburg)
Haslauer, Matthias, 5411 Oberalm. T. (06245) 2274, 4497. - Ant - **038394**

Obernberg am Inn (Oberösterreich)
Öttl, Margarete, Marktpl. 8, 4982 Obernberg am
Inn. *038395*

Oberndorf (Salzburg)
Flatscher, Anni, Kreuzerleiten 14, 5110 Oberndorf.
T. (06272) 590. *038396*

Obertrum am See (Salzburg)
Zitzler, Rudolf, Obertrum 76, 5162 Obertrum am
See. *038397*

Oberwölz (Steiermark)
Bauer, Leonhard, Wieden 46, 8832 Oberwölz.
T. (03581) 365. *038398*

Ohlsdorf (Oberösterreich)
Knopp, Klaus, Ohlsdorf 56, 4694 Ohlsdorf.
T. (07612) 47611. *038399*

Oslip (Burgenland)
Horvth, Agnes, Hauptstr. 43, 7000 Oslip. *038400*

Ottensheim bei Linz (Oberösterreich)
Lehner, Anna, Linzer Str. 44, 4100 Ottensheim bei Linz.
T. (07234) 22 96. - Ant - *038401*

Perchtoldsdorf (Niederösterreich)
Hitschmann, Irene, Mühlgasse 32-34, 2380 Perchtolds-
dorf. T. (0222) 86 86 53. *038402*
Knapp, Gerhard, Wiener Gasse 46, 2380 Perchtoldsdorf.
T. (0222) 8690467, Fax 8694029. - Mil - *038403*

Perg (Oberösterreich)
Skola, Franz, Dr. Schoberstr.13, 4320 Perg. *038404*

Peuerbach (Oberösterreich)
Sirninger, Josefa, Christoph Zeller-Str. 15, 4722 Peuer-
bach. T. (07276) 2898. *038405*

Pitten (Niederösterreich)
Witzmann, Hannelore, Wiener Neustädter Str. 2, 2823
Pitten. *038406*

Pöllau (Steiermark)
Stalzer, Karl Horst, Herrengasse 14, 8225 Pöllau.
T. (03335) 2451. *038407*

Potzneusiedl (Burgenland)
Collector's Gallery, Schloss Potzneusiedl, 2473 Potzneu-
siedl. T. (02145) 22 49. - Mod - *038408*
Egermann, Gerhard, 2473 Potzneusiedl.
T. (02145) 2249. *038409*

Poysdorf (Niederösterreich)
Fürnwein, Manfred, Römerstr. 4, 2170 Poysdorf.
T. (02552) 2552. *038410*

Purkersdorf (Niederösterreich)
Haider, Harald, Wiener Str. 8, 3002 Purkersdorf.
T. (02231) 4092. *038411*

Rankweil (Vorarlberg)
Häusle, Herbert, St. Peter-Gasse 1, 6830 Rankweil.
T. (0522) 44301. *038412*

Regau (Oberösterreich)
Harringer, Rudolf, Rutzenmoos Pz. Nr. 250, 4844
Regau. *038413*

Reichenau (Niederösterreich)
Eichhorn, Renée, Jägerzeile 2, 2651 Reichenau.
T. (0222) 5230211, (02666) 2061. - Silv - *038414*

Reith (Tirol)
Schmidt, Gottfried, Neudorf 40, 6235 Reith.
T. (05337) 3666. *038415*

Ried (Oberösterreich)
Aigner, Karl, Ornetsmühl 12a, 4910 Ried.
T. (07752) 6700. *038416*
Dietringer, Friedrich, Kränzlstr. 34, 4910 Ried. *038417*
Kössl, P., Roßmarkt 35, 4910 Ried. T. (07752) 4636.
- Furn / Tex - *038418*
Schallmeiner, Karl, Griesgasse 6a, 4910 Ried.
T. (07752) 85600. - Ant / Paint / Furn / Tex / Mod / Jew /
Sculp / Instr - *038419*

Slaby, Dietmar, Mühlbachgasse 5, 4910 Ried.
T. (07752) 7195. *038420*

Riezlern (Vorarlberg)
Zokolowski, Werner, Walserstr. 45, 6991 Riezlern.
T. (05517) 5333. - Ant / Furn / Num / Instr - *038421*

Rust (Burgenland)
Nemeth, Franz, Greinergasse, 7071 Rust.
T. (02685) 568. *038422*

Salzburg
Ahamer, Rüdiger, Itzlinger Hauptstr 45, 5020 Salzburg.
T. (0662) 50264. *038423*
Aichmaier, Johann, Schwarzstr 33, 5020 Salzburg.
T. (0662) 759113. *038424*
Antiquitäten im Franziskanerkloster, Franziskanergasse
5a, 5020 Salzburg. T. (0662) 845210. - Ant / Orient /
China / Dec / Jew / Silv / Rel / Glass / Ico - *038425*
Barta, Manfred, Gorianstr 30, 5020 Salzburg.
T. (0662) 845081. *038426*
Bey Ars, Goldgasse 15, 5020 Salzburg.
T. (0662) 846145, Fax (0662) 848198. - Jew - *038427*
Burges, Peter-Paul, Gstättengasse 23, 5020 Salzburg.
T. (0662) 848115. - Ant / Jew / Glass - *038428*
Dies & Das Antiquitäten, Goldgasse 13, 5020 Salzburg.
T. (0662) 841192. *038429*
Dolejschi, G., Goldgasse 7, 5020 Salzburg.
T. (0662) 842429. *038430*
Dürnberger, Josef, Malerweg 5, 5020 Salzburg.
T. (0662) 877384. *038431*
Eccli, Erika, Gstättengasse 23, 5020 Salzburg.
T. (0662) 843631. *038432*
Englich, Ulf, Franz-Josef-Kai 15, 5020 Salzburg.
T. (0662) 843496. - Ant / Paint / Furn / Jew / Silv /
Glass - *038433*
Englich, Ulf, Getreidegasse 3, 5020 Salzburg.
T. (0662) 843339. - Ant / Paint / Furn / Silv /
Glass - *038434*
Forsthuber, Franz, Bergerbräuhofstr 32, 5020 Salzburg.
- Ant - *038435*
Franklin Mint, Zillnerstr 18, 5020 Salzburg.
T. (0662) 39661. - Num - *038436*
Galerie Linzergasse, Linzergasse, 5020 Salzburg.
T. (0662) 879119, Fax (0662) 879119. - Paint / Graph /
China / Sculp / Glass / Draw - *038437*
Galerie Salis & Vertes, Imbergstr 25, 5010 Salzburg.
T. (0662) 870907, Fax 8708269. - Paint - *038438*
Galerie Weihergut, Linzerg 25, 5020 Salzburg.
T. (0662) 879119, Fax 879119. - Paint / Graph / Sculp /
Glass / Draw - *038439*
Goschler, Herbert v. Karajanpl 3, 5020 Salzburg.
T. (0662) 841695. *038440*
Grims, Wolfgang, Aigner Str 51, 5026 Salzburg.
T. (0662) 629191. - Furn / Mod - *038441*
Grohmann, Volker, Nonntaler Hauptstr 25, 5020 Salz-
burg. T. (0662) 8470792. *038442*
Grünwald, Hans, Makartplatz 4, 5020 Salzburg.
T. (0662) 874491. - Num - *038443*
Gstöttner, Friedrich, Etrichstr 19, 5020
Salzburg. *038444*
Günther, Helmuth, Hans-Sachsgasse 21, 5020 Salzburg.
T. (0662) 32517. *038445*
Guggenberger, Gstättengasse 4-6, 5020 Salzburg.
T. (0662) 843184. *038446*
Halbedel & Saiger, Linzer Gasse 22/IV, 5020 Salzburg.
T. (0662) 79611. - Num - *038447*
Hausleitner, Hans, Moosstr 47, 5020 Salzburg. *038448*
Höllbacher, Erentrud, Paris-Lodron-Str 2, 5020 Salzburg.
T. (0662) 749794. *038449*
Kirchmayer, R. & S., Gstättengasse 3, 5020 Salzburg.
T. (0662) 842219, Fax (0662) 842219-4. - Ant / Furn /
Jew / Silv / Instr - *038450*
Klos, Jana, Maxglaner Hauptstr 12, 5020 Salzburg.
T. (0662) 827838. - Ant / Paint / Graph / Furn / China /
Dec / Lights / Glass / Mod / Draw / Draw - *038451*
Kopfberger, Siegfried, Judengasse 14, 5020
Salzburg. *038452*
Koppenwallner, Paul, Alter Markt 7, 5020 Salzburg.
T. (0662) 842617. *038453*
Kramberger, Antonia, Kleßheimer Allee 29, 5020 Salz-
burg. T. (0662) 33293. *038454*

Lackner, Johann, Baderg 2, 5020 Salzburg.
T. (0662) 842385. *038455*
Lährm, Universitätspl 5, 5020 Salzburg.
T. (0662) 843477, Fax (0662) 840796. *038456*
Lintner, Joachim, Linzer Gasse 31, 5020 Salzburg.
T. (0662) 882525. *038457*
Lochmann, M., Getreidegasse 50, 5020 Salzburg.
T. (0662) 841179. *038458*
Lochmann, V., Basteigasse 3, 5020 Salzburg.
T. (0662) 843668. *038459*
Matern, Peter, Linzer Gasse 5, 5024 Salzburg.
T. (0662) 873795, Fax (0662) 873795. - Paint /
Graph - *038460*
Menzel, Michael, Bürgerspitalpl 5, 5020 Salzburg.
T. (0662) 843393, Fax (0662) 843393. - Paint / Graph /
Furn - *038461*
Moy, Jakob Graf von, Goldgasse 15, 5020 Salzburg.
T. (0662) 840570. *038462*
Müller, Johannes, Hildmannpl 1A, 5020 Salzburg.
T. (0662) 846338, Fax 846338. - Graph - *038463*
Ost Asien Haus, Bristol-Passage, 5020 Salzburg.
T. (0662) 730782. - Furn / Orient / China / Tex /
Jew - *038464*
Pfanzelter, Franz, Judengasse 3, 5020 Salzburg.
T. (0662) 841237. - Dec - *038465*
Pfleger, Elfriede, Franziskanergasse 5a, 5020 Salzburg.
T. (0662) 845210. *038466*
Prinz, Josef, Almgasse 3, 5020 Salzburg.
T. (0662) 841452. - Furn - *038467*
Ranft, Volker, Makartpl 3, 5020 Salzburg.
T. (0662) 876115, Fax 878102. - Ant / Paint / Graph /
Sculp / Jew / Silv / Instr - *038468*
Rautenberg, H. von, Alter Markt 15, 5020 Salzburg.
T. (0662) 843398. - Jew - *038469*
Reitinger, Josef, Straubingerstr 7, 5020 Salzburg.
T. (0662) 827856. - Mil - *038470*
Reuter, Marianne, Gstättengasse 9, 5020 Salzburg.
T. (0662) 842136. - Ant - *038471*
Russmayr, A.M., Rainerstr 24, 5020 Salzburg.
T. (0662) 876216. - Ant - *038472*
Schachtner, Reinhold, Dürlingerstr 4, 5020 Salzburg.
T. (0662) 44405. - Num - *038473*
Schlager, Ingeborg, Bristol Passage, Makartpl 4, 5020
Salzburg. T. (0662) 885696, Fax (0662) 641690. - Ant /
Jew / Silv / Glass / Ico - *038474*
Schlosser, Antoinette, Judengasse 3, 5020 Salzburg.
- Ant - *038475*
Schöppl, Gerhard, Gstättengasse 5, 5020 Salzburg.
T. (0662) 842154. - Ant / Paint / Furn / China / Sculp /
Tex / Instr / Glass / Cur / Tin / Music - *038476*
Schubert, Bürgerspitalgasse 2, 5020 Salzburg.
T. (0662) 843160. - Paint / Furn / China / Sculp / Tex /
Jew / Silv - *038477*
Schwaighofer, G., Giselakai 15, 5020 Salzburg.
T. (0662) 871127, Fax (0662) 871127. - Ant / Num /
Jew / Silv / Instr / Glass / Mod - *038478*
Stubhahn, Manfred, Linzergasse 31, 5020 Salzburg.
T. (0662) 882511, Fax 881022. - Rel - *038479*
Trödelmagazin, Basteig 3, Landhausgasse 3, 5020 Salz-
burg. T. (0662) 843668. *038480*
Voloder, Bernhard, Steingasse 35, 5020 Salzburg.
T. (0662) 871681, Fax (0662) 871681. *038481*
Wagner, Eva, Gemeindeweg 12, 5061 Salzburg.
T. (0662) 23011, 23375. - Ant / Paint / Furn / Fra / Silv /
Glass - *038482*
Wallerstorfer, Marianne, Steingasse 37, 5020 Salzburg.
T. (0662) 876459. - Ant / Furn - *038483*
Wichmann, Horst P., Nonntaler Hauptstr 21, 5020 Salz-
burg. T. (0662) 842393. - Ant / Paint / Furn /
Sculp - *038484*
Winkler, Ina, Willibald-Hauthaler-Str 8, 5020 Salzburg.
T. (0662) 320632. *038485*

Sankt Gilgen (Salzburg)
Kesmarky, Jutta, Pichlerpl 2a, 5340 Sankt Gilgen.
T. (06227) 7368. - Jew - *038486*
Leitner, Egon, Raiffeisenpl. 2, 5340 Sankt Gilgen.
T. (06227) 457. - Ant - *038487*

Sankt Johann (Tirol)
Bendler, Eduard, Paß Thurnstr. 2, 6380 Sankt
Johann. *038488*

Sankt Martin im Innkreis (Oberösterreich)
Slaby, Gerhard, Diesseits 62, 4973 Sankt Martin im Innkreis. T. (07751) 224. *038489*

Sankt Pölten (Niederösterreich)
Bachinger, Alfred, Neugebäudepl. 5, 3100 Sankt Pölten.
T. (02742) 7616. - Ant - *038490*
Figl, Anton, Schreinergasse 4, 3100 Sankt Pölten. *038491*
Jäger, Johann, Dr., Stelzhamerstr. 22, 3100 Sankt Pölten. *038492*
Leiner, Rudolf, Porschestr. 7, 3100 Sankt Pölten. *038493*
Mayer, Eva-Maria, Linzer Str. 13, 3100 Sankt Pölten.
T. (02742) 38193. *038494*
Merz, Reinhard, Franziskanergasse 1a, 3100 Sankt Pölten. T. (02742) 37165. *038495*
Raab & Sauer, Fuhrmanngasse 1, 3100 Sankt Pölten.
T. (02742) 2452. *038496*
Schätz, Heinrich, Rathausgasse 1, 3100 Sankt Pölten. *038497*

Sankt Valentin (Niederösterreich)
Miemelauer, Ludwig, Hauptstr. 14, 4300 Sankt Valentin. *038498*

Sankt Wolfgang (Oberösterreich)
Müller, Ernst Gottfried, Markt 63, 5360 Sankt Wolfgang.
T. (06138) 2 51. - Ant / Num - *038499*

Schärding (Oberösterreich)
Armstark, Burggraben 3, 4780 Schärding.
T. (07712) 3320, Fax 33204. - Ant / Paint / Furn / China / Fra / Lights / Instr / Glass / Cur / Mod - *038500*
Armstark, Unterer Stadtpl 8/Burggraben 3, 4780 Schärding. T. (07712) 3320, Fax 332 04. - Ant / Paint / Furn / China / Fra / Lights / Instr / Glass / Cur / Mod - *038501*
Heindl, Josef, Linzertor 2-3, 4780 Schärding.
T. (07712) 3035, Fax 4708. - Ant / Paint / Graph - *038502*
Palfinger, Otto, Ob. Stadtpl. 21, 4780 Schärding.
T. (07712) 2477. *038503*
Reich, D., Stadtpl. 44, 4780 Schärding. T. (07712) 2173.
- Ant / Jew / Instr - *038504*
Schmierer, Harald, Südtiroler Str. 340, 4780 Schärding.
T. (07712) 4701. *038505*
Strassner, Norbert, Unterer Stadtpl 22, 4780 Schärding.
T. (07712) 2053. - Ant - *038506*

Scharnitz (Tirol)
Steffan, Grenzwechselstube Scharnitz 48, 6108 Scharnitz. *038507*

Scheibbs (Niederösterreich)
BAL-Antiques, Höfingerpromenade 12, 3270 Scheibbs.
T. (07482) 2131. - Ant - *038508*
Ebner, Rudolf, Prof.-Schuh-Gasse 1, 3270 Scheibbs.
T. (07482) 2308. *038509*

Schruns (Vorarlberg)
Feuerstein, Hubert, Dorfstr. 4, 6780 Schruns.
T. (05556) 2129. *038510*
Feuerstein, Josef, Dorfstr. 70, 6780 Schruns.
T. (05556) 2129. - Sculp / Instr - *038511*
Oberwager, Werner, Alte Montjola 22, 6780 Schruns.
T. (05556) 737 92. - Paint / Furn / Sculp / Instr / Mod - *038512*

Schwaz (Tirol)
Chesi, Gerd, Innsbruckerstr.14, 6130 Schwaz. *038513*

Schwertberg (Oberösterreich)
Hinterreiter, Karl Josef, Hafnerstr. 17, 4311 Schwertberg. T. (07262) 61142. *038514*

Seefeld-Grosskadolz (Niederösterreich)
Schuster, Sylvia, Dr, Seefeld 65, 2062 Seefeld-Grosskadolz. T. (02943) 2704. *038515*

Sonnberg (Niederösterreich)
Kepler, Schmiedgasse 56, 2020 Sonnberg. - Furn / Tex / Lights / Mod - *038516*

Spittal an der Drau (Kärnten)
Kukutsch, Leopoldine Elfriede, Neuer Pl. 10, 9800 Spittal an der Drau. T. (04762) 2027, Fax 202 74. - China / Jew / Silv / Glass / Tin - *038517*
Vanzo, Alfred, Brückenstr. 3, 9800 Spittal an der Drau.
T. (04762) 26 98. - Num - *038518*
Weiss, Wilhelm, Ponauer Str. 4, 9800 Spittal an der Drau. T. (04762) 61294. *038519*

Spitz (Niederösterreich)
Mehringer, Ernst, Marktstr. 13, 3620 Spitz.
T. (02713) 2 13. - Ant / Paint / Furn - *038520*

Steyr (Oberösterreich)
Alber, Martin, Rosenegger Str. 5, 4400 Steyr.
T. (07252) 628 00. *038521*
Promberger, H., Pfarrgasse 9, 4400 Steyr. *038522*
Steiners Kunsthandlung, Fischergasse 2, 4400 Steyr.
T. (07252) 62411. - Paint - *038523*

Tamsweg (Salzburg)
Gugg, H. & M., Nr. 62, 5580 Tamsweg. T. (06474) 65 35.
- Ant - *038524*

Tobelbad (Steiermark)
Pro domo, Tobelbader Str. 162, 8144 Tobelbad.
T. (03136) 4355. *038525*

Traun (Oberösterreich)
Dickl, Johann G., Linzer Str. 10, 4050 Traun.
T. (07229) 36 77. *038526*

Traunkirchen (Niederösterreich)
Günter, Anna Rosa, Traunkirchen 21, 4801 Traunkirchen.
T. (07617) 229. *038527*

Tulln (Niederösterreich)
Knollmayer, Othmar, Mühlbachgasse 18, 3430 Tulln. *038528*

Unterpremstätten (Steiermark)
Grom, Hermann, Pz.Nr. 459/6, 8141 Unterpremstätten.
- Ant - *038529*

Vandans (Vorarlberg)
Kaufmann, Alwin, Vandans 797, 6773 Vandans.
T. (05556) 3743. *038530*

Velden (Kärnten)
Schullin & Söhne, Am Korso 21, 9220 Velden.
T. (04274) 3331. - Ant - *038531*
Tsantilas, Konstantin H., Villacher Str. 14, 9220 Velden. *038532*

Villach (Kärnten)
Winding, A., Kirchenpl. 9, 9500 Villach.
T. (04242) 26 224. *038533*

Vöcklabruck (Oberösterreich)
Enzinger, Karl, Industriestr.19, 4840 Vöcklabruck. *038534*

Vöcklamarkt (Oberösterreich)
Böhm, Hedwig, Hatschekstr. 12, 4840 Vöcklamarkt.
T. (07682) 4014. *038535*

Völkermarkt (Kärnten)
Magnet, Wilfried, Hauptpl. 29, 9100 Völkermarkt.
T. (04232) 2444. *038536*
Piskernik, Edgar, Münzgasse 2, 9100 Völkermarkt.
T. (04232) 2361. *038537*

Vormarkt (Oberösterreich)
Mayrhofer, Rosa, Gurten 19, 4982 Vormarkt.
T. (07758) 287. *038538*

Waidhofen (Niederösterreich)
Buschek, Oskar, Bahnhofstr. 28, 3830 Waidhofen.
T. (02842) 25 34, Fax 3434. *038539*
Ecker, Karin, Hamernikgasse 2a, 3830 Waidhofen.
T. (02842) 32004. *038540*
Eder, Viktor Ignaz Johann, Niederleuthnerstr. 2, 3830 Waidhofen. *038541*
Will, Johann, Heidenreichsteinerstr. 18, 3830 Waidhofen. *038542*

Waizenkirchen (Oberösterreich)
Wurnig, Hermann, Kienzlstr. 32, 4730 Waizenkirchen.
T. (07277) 2455. *038543*

Wallern (Oberösterreich)
Perchtold, Norbert, Rosengasse 3, 4702 Wallern.
T. (07249) 8806. *038544*

Wals (Salzburg)
Ronacher, Haus Nr.381, 5071 Wals. T. (0662) 85 03 43.
- Ant - *038545*

Weiz (Steiermark)
Dobida, Karl, Flurgasse 3, 8160 Weiz. T. (03175) 2929.
- Paint / Graph / Draw - *038546*
Tazl, Wolfgang, Birkfelderstr. 9, 8160 Weiz.
T. (03175) 5277. *038547*

Wels (Oberösterreich)
Antik-Möbel-Markt, Mitterweg 1, 4600 Wels.
T. (07242) 67173, Fax 43480. - Ant / Furn - *038548*
Antik-Zentrum, Haiderosenstr. 54, 4600 Wels.
T. (07242) 881 44. *038549*
Bohn, Gertrude, Rainerstr. 4, 4601 Wels. *038550*
Pietsch, Herrengasse 4, 4600 Wels. T. (07242) 44884.
- Tex - *038551*
Preissler, Reinhold, Stadtpl. 58, 4601 Wels.
T. (07242) 67 30. *038552*
Reichel, Christian R., Herrengasse 4, 4600 Wels.
T. (07242) 46964. *038553*
Saminger, Erich, Flugplatzstr. 3, 4601 Wels.
T. (07242) 5458. - Ant / Paint / Graph / Furn / China / Sculp / Jew / Fra / Rel / Glass / Mod - *038554*
Treml, Heinrich, Wallenerstr. 19, 4600 Wels.
T. (07242) 42064. *038555*
Wiesinger, Eleonore, Salzburger Str. 225, 4600 Wels.
T. (07242) 61304, Fax 41854. - Ant - *038556*

Wien
Äolus, Schöffelgasse 25, 1180 Wien.
T. (0222) 47 42 86. *038557*
Aichhorn, August, Taborstr. 24a, 1020 Wien. *038558*
Alt-Wien Kunsthandelsgesellschaft mbH, Bräunerstr. 11, 1010 Wien. T. (0222) 52 91 43. - Ant - *038559*
Alte Kunst bei der Votivkirche, Währinger Str. 16, 1090 Wien. T. (0222) 310 98 80. *038560*
Altes Zeughaus, Burggasse 27, 1070 Wien.
T. (0222) 93 03 43. *038561*
Altkunst Galerie, Spiegelgasse 8-10, 1010 Wien.
T. (0222) 53 41 37. - Paint / China / Silv / Ico - *038562*
Altwaren Galerie, Grosse Sperigasse 24, 1020 Wien.
T. (0222) 33 34 28. *038563*
Altwiener Altwaren, Gymnasiumstr. 3, 1180 Wien.
T. (0222) 31 52 79. - Ant / Paint / Graph / China / Jew / Fra / Silv / Glass / Cur / Mod / Pho / Draw - *038564*
Amend, Walter, Florianigasse 13, 1080 Wien.
T. (0222) 402 95 233. - Num - *038565*
Andréewitch, Stephan, Favoritenstr 10, 1040 Wien.
T. (0222) 5059973, 5050499, Fax 5051438. - Ant / Paint / Furn / China / Silv / Instr / Glass - *038566*
Antikes Dekor, Burggasse 88, 1070 Wien.
T. (0222) 93 16 70. - Ant / China / Dec / Glass - *038567*
Antiquitäten-Keller, Magdalenenstr. 32, 1060 Wien.
T. (0222) 566 95 33. *038568*
ART-Service, Franzensgasse 25, 1050 Wien. *038569*
Art & Decor, Lacknergasse 59, 1170 Wien.
T. (0222) 46 03 62. *038570*
Artaria, Kohlmarkt 9, 1010 Wien. T. (0222) 533 09 36.
- Paint / Graph - *038571*
Asboth, Ute, Spiegelgasse 19, 1010 Wien.
T. (0222) 512 51 37, Fax (0222) 512 13 97. - Ant / Orient / China / Sculp - *038572*
Asenbaum, Herbert, Kärntner Str 28, 1010 Wien.
T. (0222) 5122847, Fax 5350920. - Ant - *038573*
Atlantis-Antique, Schottenfeldgasse 56, 1070 Wien. *038574*
Aurophil, Nußdorfer Str. 72, 1090 Wien.
T. (0222) 3198491. - Num - *038575*
Baier, Robert, Tuchlauben 18/1, 1010 Wien.
T. (0222) 5331265. *038576*
Bakirzoglu, Erika, Schulgasse 65, 1180 Wien.
T. (0222) 4269453. *038577*
BAL-Antiques, Singerstr 27, 1010 Wien.
T. (0222) 5270734. - Paint - *038578*

Banoczay, Invalidenstr. 17, 1030 Wien.
T. (0222) 724 04 84. - Ant -   038579
Basic, Luka, Gaullachergasse 15, 1160 Wien.
T. (0222) 408 39 74, Fax 4088127.   038580
Bauer, Helmut, Favoritenstr. 129, 1100 Wien.
T. (0222) 604 25 27.   038581
Bauernfeind, Antoine, Dorotheergasse 9, 1010 Wien.
T. (0222) 513 10 20.   038582
Bazant, Andreas, Josefstädter Str 52, 1080 Wien.
T. (0222) 4054339.   038583
Bednarczyk, C., Dorotheergasse 12, 1010 Wien.
T. (0222) 5124445, 5127126, Fax (0222) 5124007.
- Ant / Paint / Furn / China / Silv -   038584

```
C. BEDNARCZYK

A-1010 WIEN
DOROTHEERGASSE 12
TELEFON 5 12 44 45-5 12 71 26
FAX 5 12 40 07
```

Behavka, Karl, Gentzgasse 51, 1180 Wien.
T. (0222) 47973952.   038585
bel etage, Mahlerstr 15, 1010 Wien. T. (0222) 5133038,
Fax 5121554. - Ant / Paint / Furn / China / Sculp / Tex /
Jew / Silv / Lights / Glass / Mod -   038586
Bellak's Vitrinchen, Währinger Str. 24, 1090 Wien.
T. (0222) 3198430.   038587
Benda, Wilhelm, Alser Str. 27, 1080 Wien.
T. (0222) 4064519. - Num -   038588
Benedik, Edith, Große Neugasse 6, 1040 Wien.
T. (0222) 563 89 85.   038589
Berger, Devy, Gumpendorfer Str. 99, 1060 Wien.
T. (0222) 5970700, Fax (0222) 5969013.
- Num -   038590
Berger, Devy, Josefstädter Str. 57, 1080 Wien.
T. (0222) 402 83 11. - Num -   038591
Berger, Devy Franz, Grabner Gasse 15, 1060 Wien.
T. (0222) 564 53 72. - Num -   038592
Berger, Hermine, Stephanspl. 4, 1010 Wien.
T. (0222) 5290634.   038593
Besim, Adil, Graben 30, 1010 Wien. T. (0222) 533 09 10.
- Ant / Tex -   038594
Bieler, Herbert, Piaristengasse 62, 1080 Wien.
T. (0222) 4036524, Fax 4026813. - Tex -   038595
Bieler, Herbert, Piaristengasse 62, 1080 Wien.
T. (0222) 403 65 24, Fax 402 68 13. - Tex -   038596
Bienenstein, Franziskaner Pl. 3, 1010 Wien. - Paint /
Graph -   038597
Bienenstein, Weihburggasse 4, 1010 Wien. - Ant /
Paint / Graph / Arch / Eth / Orient -   038598
Bilder & Kunst, Liechtensteinstr. 36, 1090 Wien.
T. (0222) 319 87 91.   038599
Binder, Alfred, Weihburggasse 11, 1010 Wien.
T. (0222) 5135282.   038600
Birchmann, Friedrich, Operngasse 34, 1040 Wien.
T. (0222) 5866193. - Num -   038601
Braunshör, Peter, Bennogasse 6, 1080 Wien.
T. (0222) 4050242. - Ant -   038602
Bühlmayer, C., Michaelerpl. 6, 1010 Wien.
T. (0222) 52 67 59. - Ant / Paint / Fra -   038603
Burger, Wioletka, Kurrentgasse 4, 1010 Wien.
T. (0222) 535 11 51.   038604
Burger, Wioletka, Linke Wienzeile 54, 1050
Wien.   038605
Cejnar, Peter, Lichtenfelsgasse 5, 1010 Wien.
T. (0222) 4063581. - Ant / Fra / Silv / Lights /
Rel -   038606
Cen am Kohlmarkt, Kohlmarkt 7/2, 1010 Wien.
T. (0222) 533 10 57.   038607
Chmel & Söhne, H., Frömmlgasse 40, 1210 Wien.
T. (0222) 38 12 14.   038608
Chudarek, Rudolf, Piaristengasse 46, 1080 Wien.
T. (0222) 4057157. - Ant -   038609
Columbus Münzenhandlung, Columbusgasse 54, 1100
Wien. T. (0222) 64 28 413. - Num -   038610

Czikelj, Maximilian, Döblinger Hauptstr. 69, 1190 Wien.
T. (0222) 36 88 77.   038611
D & S Discogast, Plankengasse 6, 1010 Wien.
T. (0222) 5125885, Fax 512588575. - Instr /
Furn -   038612
Dättel, Rudolf, Zimmermanngasse 8, 1080 Wien.
T. (0222) 402 91 07.   038613
Dan Antiques, Engerthstr 130, 1200 Wien.
T. (0222) 352148. - Ant / Furn / Lights / Instr /
Glass -   038614
Demner, Spiegelgasse 11, 1010 Wien.
T. (0222) 52 07 39.   038615
Demner, M. u. H., Göttweihergasse 1, 1010 Wien.
T. (0222) 512 07 39.   038616
Deutsch, Paul Ernst, Dorotheergasse 13, 1010 Wien.
T. (0222) 5122371. - Ant / Furn / Sculp / Tex /
Lights -   038617
Dirnbacher, Kurt, Westbahnstr. 8, 1070 Wien.   038618
Ditl, Freyung 2, 1010 Wien. T. (0222) 63 84 14.   038619
Donau, Margret, Liechtensteinstr. 117/2, 1090 Wien.
T. (0222) 3195186.   038620
Dorner, Ilse, Plankengasse 6, 1000 Wien.
T. (0222) 52 80 074.   038621
Dorotheer Galerie, Dorotheergasse 6, 1010 Wien.
T. (0222) 512 92 66. - Ant / Paint / Graph / Furn / China /
Sculp / Silv / Mil / Mod / Ico -   038622
Dorotheum, Dorotheergasse 17, 1010 Wien.
T. (0222) 515600, 51560212, Fax (0222) 51560474.
- Ant / Paint / Graph / Furn / Num / Orient / China / Scul-
p / Tex / Eth / Jew / Silv / Mil / Glass / Mod / Toys / Musi-
c -   038623
Dreimäderlhaus, Wiedner Hauptstr. 69, 1010 Wien.
T. (0222) 5054167.   038624
Dürrer, Schönlaterngasse 5, 1010 Wien.
T. (0222) 513 20 53. - Ant -   038625
Duschek & Scheed, Plankengasse 6, 1010 Wien.
T. (0222) 5128585. - Instr / Mod -   038626
Eichhorn, Renee, Kandlgasse 3, 1070 Wien.
T. (0222) 5230211. - Silv -   038627
Einst & Jetzt, Sechskrügelgasse 6, 1030 Wien.
T. (0222) 715 72 52. - Furn / China / Jew / Cur /
Mod -   038628
Eisenberger, Jenö, Rothgasse 2, 1010 Wien.   038629
Eisenberger, Jenö, Formanekgasse 57, 1190
Wien.   038630
Eisenberger, Vera, Getreidemarkt 17, 1050 Wien.
T. (0222) 56 62 40.   038631
Elias, Mathilde, Maxingstr. 2, 1130 Wien.
T. (0222) 829 33 84.   038632
Emberger, Erich, Hernalser Gürtel 43, 1170 Wien.
T. (0222) 43 45 12.   038633
Emlich-Könekampf-Beutel, Ulrike, Franziskanerpl. 1,
1010 Wien. T. (0222) 512 84 28.   038634
English Antiques, Landskrongasse 10, 1010 Wien.
T. (0222) 5357516.   038635
English Antiques, Börsegasse 3, 1010 Wien.
T. (0222) 639855, 637132. - Ant / Furn -   038636
Entzmann & Sohn, Reinhold, Seilerstätte 21, 1010 Wien.
T. (0222) 512 18 90. - Paint / Graph / Fra / Fra /
Draw -   038637
Erdinger, Josef, Handelskai 418/10, 1020 Wien.
T. (0222) 214 51 87. - Ant -   038638
Farron, Guy, Spiegelgasse 8, 1010 Wien.
T. (0222) 512 87 66, Fax 512 87 66. - Ant / Paint / Furn /
Orient / Arch / Dec -   038639
Feldbacher, Peter, Annagasse 6, 1010 Wien.
T. (0222) 5122408, Fax 5122408. - Ant / Paint / Furn /
Dec / Mod -   038640
Feldbacher, Peter, Anton Freunschlagg 59, 1230 Wien.
T. (0222) 6093975, (0663) 809419. - Ant /
Furn -   038641
Figl, Josef, Stallburggasse 2, 1010 Wien.
T. (0222) 513 55 43.   038642
Fischer, Alfred, Sechskrügelgasse 8, 1030 Wien.
T. (0222) 7126207.   038643
Fleihaus, Anton & Günther, Köstlergasse 7, 1060 Wien.
T. (0222) 587 65 89, Fax 587 65 89 76. - Ant / Paint /
Graph / Furn / Fra -   038644
Förster, A., Kohlmarkt 5, 1010 Wien.
T. (0222) 533 20 63.   038645
Formann, Inzersdorfer Str. 63, 1100 Wien.
T. (0222) 621 79 63. - Num -   038646

Forstinger, Taborstr. 36-38, 1020 Wien.
T. (0222) 216 23 730. - Num -   038647
Forstner & Co, Karl, Arndtstr. 53, 1120 Wien.
T. (0222) 85 87 94.   038648
Fosek, Friederike, Prager Str. 61, 1210 Wien.
T. (0222) 38 11 47.   038649
Frank, Heinrich, Teinfaltstr. 3, 1010 Wien.
T. (0222) 533 28 62. - Num -   038650
Frey, Reinhold, Philippovichgasse 1, 1190 Wien.   038651
Gärtner, Michael, Göttweihergasse 1, 1010 Wien.
T. (0222) 52 50 463, 79 17 02. - Ant / Paint / Graph / Chi-
na / Sculp / Jew / Silv / Instr / Glass / Cur / Mod / Ico / Dr-
aw -   038652
Galerie am Kühnplatz, Schleifmühlgasse 17, 1040 Wien.
T. (0222) 587 29 94.   038653
Galerie am Lobkowitzplatz, Lobkowitzpl. 3, 1010 Wien.
T. (0222) 512 13 38. - Ant -   038654
Galerie Ambiente, Lugeck 1, 1010 Wien.
T. (0222) 5131130, Fax 513113014. - Mod -   038655
Galerie bei der Albertina, Lobkowitzpl 1, 1010 Wien.
T. (0222) 5131416, Fax 5137674. - Paint / Graph /
Furn / China / Sculp / Jew / Glass / Mod -   038656
Galerie beim Burgtheater, Teinfaltstr. 3, 1010 Wien.
T. (0222) 535 80 29.   038657
Galerie Comes, Sonnenfelsgasse 15, 1010 Wien.
T. (0222) 5125297. - Cur -   038658
Galerie Corso, Mahlerstr. 4, 1010 Wien.
T. (0222) 513 95 62.   038659
Galerie Gras, Grünangergasse 6, 1010 Wien.
T. (0222) 512 81 06. - Ant / Paint / Graph / Furn / China /
Sculp / Tex / Jew / Lights -   038660
Galerie im Liechtental, Liechtensteinstr. 93, 1090 Wien.
T. (0222) 31 74 92.   038661
Galerie Metropol, Dorotheergasse 12, 1010 Wien.
T. (0222) 5132208, Fax 513 99 63. - Ant / Paint /
Graph / Furn -   038662
Galerie Palais Starhemberg, Dorotheergasse 9, 1010
Wien. T. (0222) 512 01 41. - Ant / Paint / Orient / Mil /
Cur -   038663
Galerie Rauhenstein, Rauhensteingasse 3, 1010 Wien.
T. (0222) 5133009. - Jew -   038664
Galerie Sanct Lucas, Josefspl 5, 1010 Wien.
T. (0222) 5128237, 513320316. - Ant / Paint -   038665
Galerie Sonnenfels, Sonnenfelsg 11, 1010 Wien.
T. (01) 5133919, Fax 5133919.   038666
Galerie Stallburg, Stallburggasse 4, 1010 Wien.
T. (0222) 53 27 38.   038667
Galerie Tropicana, Wattgasse 43, 1160 Wien.
T. (01) 462284. - Tex / Arch / Eth -   038668
Galerie Walfischgasse, Walfischgasse 12, 1010 Wien.
T. (0222) 5123716.   038669
Galerie 1G, Ottakringer Str. 107, 1160 Wien.
T. (0222) 46 34 57.   038670
Geller, Karol, Spiegelgasse 8, 1010 Wien.
T. (0222) 52 41 37.   038671
Das gemütliche alte Heim, Josefstädter-Str. 74, 1080
Wien. T. (0222) 402 65 41.   038672
Genewein, Christian, Stallburggasse 2, 1010 Wien.
T. (0222) 512 38 89.   038673
Giese, Herbert, Dr., Krugerstr 12, 1010 Wien.
T. (0222) 512 38 89.   038674
Giese & Schweiger, Akademiestr 1, 1010 Wien.
T. (0222) 5131843, Fax 5139374.   038675
Gludovacz, Claudia, Josefstädter Str. 70, 1080 Wien.
T. (0222) 4069738. - Ant / Instr -   038676
Grabenhofer-Russy, Viktor, Porzellangasse 54, 1090
Wien. T. (0222) 34 43 12. - Num -   038677
Grabherr, Herbert K., Piaristengasse 54, 1080 Wien.
T. (0222) 408 32 63, Fax 408 32 63. - Paint / Instr / Chi-
na / Silv -   038678
Grass, Roman, Freyung 1, 1014 Wien.
T. (0222) 535 42 76.   038679
Gratelli, Christine, Dr. Ignaz-Seipel-Pl. 1, 1010
Wien.   038680
Gratsos, Constantin, Himmelpfortgasse 19, 1010 Wien.
T. (0222) 513 13 22.   038681
Grzymek, Witold, Habsburgergasse 3, 1010 Wien.
T. (0222) 5335042. - Ant / Paint / Graph / Mod /
Draw -   038682
Gyertyàs, S. u. T., Naglergasse 9, 1010 Wien.   038683
Haberfellner, Gerda, Wimbergergasse 10, 1070 Wien.
T. (0222) 93 42 77.   038684
Häupler, Grazyna, Favoritenstr. 58, 1040 Wien.   038685

Häusler, Martha, Weihburggasse 17, 1010 Wien.
T. (0222) 52 87 87. 038686

Haider, Bianca-Maria, Schlösselgasse 24/2, 1080 Wien.
T. (0222) 43 43 86. 038687

Hammer, Ernst, Spiegelgasse 23, 1010 Wien.
T. (0222) 522 02 32. - Ant / Paint / Furn / China / Sculp /
Silv - 038688

Hampe, Susanna, Weihburgg 9, 1010 Wien.
T. (0222) 5125223. - Jew - 038689

Hardy, Gertrude, Dorotheergasse 14, 1010 Wien.
T. (0222) 512 18 05. - Ant / Furn / Instr / Glass - 038690

Hassfurther, Wolfdietrich, Hohenstaufengasse 7, 1010
Wien. T. (0222) 53509850, Fax (0222) 535098575.
- Ant / Paint / Graph / Glass / Cur / Draw - 038691

Haus der Bilder, Alser Str. 26, 1090 Wien.
T. (0222) 5230550. 038692

Haus der Bilder, Breite Gasse 10, 1070 Wien.
T. (0222) 5230550. 038693

Haus der Bilder, Lerchenfelder Str. 128, 1080
Wien. 038694

Haus der Bilder, Wiedner Hauptstr. 3, 1040
Wien. 038695

Hausmann, Brigitte, Seilerstätte 8, 1010 Wien.
T. (0222) 513 79 44. 038696

Hecht, H., Thaliastr. 49, 1160 Wien.
T. (0222) 92 35 78. 038697

Hegenbarth, Werner, Weihburgg. 20, 1010 Wien.
T. (0222) 520 88 13. - Ant - 038698

Heiler, Burghard, Piaristengasse 56-58, 1080 Wien.
T. (0222) 402 03 18. 038699

Hein, Alfred, Amerlingstr. 13, 1060 Wien.
T. (0222) 56 81 77. 038700

Heintschl, Christine, Kinderspitalgasse 10, 1090 Wien.
T. (0222) 402 94 524. 038701

Heinzel, Josef, Schweglerstr. 21, 1150 Wien.
T. (0222) 924 75 93. - Num - 038702

Heinzl, Helmuth, Neubaugasse 59, 1070 Wien.
T. (0222) 5235432. 038703

Hellmann, Kurt, Schottenfeldgasse 56, 1070 Wien.
T. (0222) 96 11 62. 038704

Helmreich-Hienert, Bauernmarkt 9, 1010 Wien.
T. (0222) 63 72 22, Fax 533 42 75. - Mod / Mul /
Draw - 038705

Hengl, Klaus, Taubstummengasse 8, 1040 Wien.
T. (0222) 5057516, 5055696, Fax 5055696.
- Ant - 038706

Herinek, G., Josefstädter Str. 27, 1082 Wien.
T. (0222) 4064396, Fax (0222) 4064396. - Num / Arch /
Jew - 038707

Hermann, Eva, Stallburggasse 4, 1010 Wien.
T. (0222) 533 90 72. 038708

Hermann, Eva, Weimarerstr. 106a, 1190 Wien.
T. (0222) 36 62 08. 038709

Hieke, Ursula, Dr., Grünangergasse 12, 1010 Wien.
T. (0222) 5133259. - Paint / Graph - 038710

Hirsch, Leonhard, Westbahnstr. 21, 1070 Wien.
T. (0222) 96 78 18. 038711

Hirsch & Kremer, Lerchenfelder Str. 34, 1080 Wien.
T. (0222) 429 46 92. - Num - 038712

Hlopec-Pfaller, Syringgasse 5, 1170 Wien.
T. (0222) 402 21 08. 038713

Hlopec-Pfaller, Hern. Hauptstr. 43, 1170 Wien.
T. (0222) 43 44 30. 038714

Höberter, Walter, Siebensterngasse 17, 1010 Wien.
T. (0222) 963 45 13. 038715

Höhn, Marie, Speisinger Str. 98-100, 1130 Wien.
T. (0222) 8046139. 038716

Hofer, Karl, Schulhof 2, 1010 Wien. T. (0222) 533 45 77,
Fax (0222) 533 45 77. 038717

Hoffmann, F., Gablenzgasse 18, 1160 Wien.
T. (0222) 924 70 15. - Furn - 038718

Hofgalerie, Spiegelg 14, 1010 Wien. T. (0222) 5126350,
Fax 5121406. - Ant / Paint / Furn / Sculp / Tex / Silv /
Mil / Rel / Cur - 038719

Hofstätter, Gabriel Maria, Bäckerstr. 7, 1010 Wien.
T. (0222) 513 11 84. 038720

Hofstätter, Gabriele Maria, Ulrichspl. 2, 1070
Wien. 038721

Hofstätter, Ingrid, Bräunerstr. 7, 1010 Wien.
T. (0222) 512 32 55, Fax 512 16 61. - Paint / Graph /
Jew / Glass - 038722

Hofstätter, Reinhold, Bräunerstr. 12, 1010 Wien.
T. (0222) 533 50 69, 533 50 70, Fax (0222) 5353541.
- Ant / Paint / Furn / Sculp / Tex / Dec / Silv / Lights / Mil /
Rel / Glass / Mod - 038723

Hollander, Anton, Schönbrunner Str. 275, 1120 Wien.
T. (0222) 812 10 65. 038724

Holzer, Werner, Siebensterngasse 32, 1070 Wien.
T. (0222) 52615068, Fax (0222) 5237218. 038725

Horn, Margarita, Habsburgergasse 14, 1010 Wien.
T. (0222) 533 60 93. - Ant - 038726

Hrbek, Brigitte, Raaberbahngasse 19, 1100 Wien.
T. (0222) 604 21 70. 038727

Hübner, Rudolf, Am Graben 28, 1010 Wien.
T. (0222) 5338065, Fax 533806522. - Instr - 038728

Humer, Helga, Währinger Str. 16, 1090 Wien.
T. (0222) 310 98 80. 038729

Hummel, Josef, Premlechnergasse 18, 1120 Wien.
T. (0222) 802 14 62. - Ant / Furn - 038730

Hummel, Julius, Bräuhausgasse 49, 1040 Wien.
T. (0222) 557 23 83. 038731

Imhof Geisslinghof Ohg., Cobenzlgasse 49, 1190 Wien.
T. (0222) 32 67 25. - Paint / Furn - 038732

Internumis, Gumpendorfer Str. 99, 1060 Wien.
T. (0222) 597 07 00. - Num - 038733

Iskra, Johann, Wipplingerstr. 18, 1010 Wien. 038734

Janković, Ratomir, Spiegelgasse 21, 1010 Wien.
T. (0222) 513 87 59. 038735

Janković, Ratomir, Rotenlöwengasse 5-7, 1090 Wien.
T. (0222) 3104762. 038736

Jankowski, Regine, Zedlitzgasse 1, 1010 Wien.
T. (0222) 512 72 12. 038737

Jezek, Johann, Fasangasse 21, 1030 Wien. 038738

Junker, Dorotheerstr 12, 1010 Wien. T. (0222) 5132208,
Fax 5139963. 038739

Kabele, Vinzenz, Penzingerstr. 23, 1140 Wien.
T. (0222) 894 31 89. - Furn - 038740

Der Kachelofen, Sechsschimmelgasse 3, 1090 Wien.
T. (0222) 34 72 94. 038741

Kaesser, Monika, Krugerstr. 17, 1010 Wien.
T. (0222) 512 28 05. - Jew / Lights / Glass /
Mod - 038742

Kaffer, Hannelore, Kühnpl. 5, 1040 Wien. 038743

Kalb, Kurt, Rennweg 2, 1030 Wien.
T. (0222) 7987150. 038744

Kalb, Kurt, Rennweg 2, 1030 Wien. T. (0222) 715 22 50.
- Ant / Paint - 038745

Kalb, Marion, Viktorgasse 20, 1040 Wien. 038746

Kalke, Georg, Lerchenfelderstraße 27, 1070 Wien.
T. (0222) 93 33 06. - Ant / Dec - 038747

Kaplanek, Friedrich, Landgutgasse 27, 1100 Wien.
T. (0222) 604 17 93. 038748

Karoly, Neulerchenfelder Str. 71, 1160 Wien.
T. (0222) 43 30 805. 038749

Kases, A. & M., Dammstr. 3, 1200 Wien.
T. (0222) 337 84 43. 038750

Keil, Helene, Wallnerstr 3, Stg 3, 1010 Wien.
T. (0222) 6340582. 038751

Keil, Robert, Dr., Gloriettegasse 13, 1130 Wien.
T. (0222) 8765574, Fax (0222) 8775034. - Paint /
Draw - 038752

Kerner, Karoline, Nußdorfer Str. 5, 1090 Wien.
T. (0222) 34 70 184. 038753

Kesmarky, Jutta, Invalidenstr 1, 1030 Wien.
T. (0222) 7138833, Fax 7138456. - Jew - 038754

Kettner, Eduard, Seilergasse 12, 1010 Wien.
T. (0222) 513 22 39, 512 98 24. 038755

Kirchengast, Anton, Ungargasse 12, 1030 Wien.
T. (0222) 715 38 803. 038756

Kirsch, Helga, Plankengasse 4, 1010 Wien.
T. (0222) 52 20 865. 038757

Klapetz, Juliana, Plankengasse 7, 1010 Wien.
T. (0222) 513 58 58. - Ant / Orient - 038758

Klein, Johann, Lerchenfeldergürtel 7, 1160 Wien.
T. (0222) 95 47 64. - Paint / Furn / China / Lights /
Glass - 038759

Kleine Galerie, Neubaugasse 59, 1070 Wien.
T. (0222) 93 54 32. 038760

Kleinhagauer, Robert, Arnethgasse 54, 1160 Wien.
T. (0222) 456 21 64. 038761

Kleisinger, Peter, Dr., Suppégasse 7, 1130 Wien.
T. (0222) 829 24 79. 038762

Kloess, Werner, Albertgasse 28, 1080 Wien.
T. (0222) 436 46 84. 038763

Klute, Franziskaner Pl. 6, 1010 Wien. T. (0222) 5135322,
5208674. 038764

Knöll, Friederike, Michaelerplatz 6, 1010 Wien.
T. (0222) 52 92 09. - Ant - 038765

Körbel, Manfred, Bräunerstr. 3, 1010 Wien.
T. (0222) 512 31 67. 038766

Körbel, Maria & Hermann, Domgasse 4, 1010 Wien.
T. (0222) 528 08 73. 038767

Kokorian, Spiegelgasse 19, 1010 Wien.
T. (0222) 5127163. 038768

Kolhammer, Alfred, Dorotheergasse 15, 1010 Wien.
T. (0222) 513 20 63. - Paint / Sculp / Rel - 038769

Konrad, Währinger Str. 155, 1180 Wien.
T. (0222) 47 77 17. - Jew - 038770

Korinek, Hertha, Piaristengasse 39, 1080 Wien.
T. (0222) 436 52 72. - Ant / Furn - 038771

Kotzian, Eva, Lobkowitzpl. 3, 1010 Wien.
T. (0222) 512 13 38. - Ant - 038772

Kotzian, Eva, Dorotheergasse 13, 1010 Wien.
T. (0222) 527389. - Ant - 038773

Kotzian, Friedrich, Lobkowitzpl. 3, 1010 Wien.
T. (0222) 512 13 38. 038774

Kovacek, Michael, Spiegelgasse 12, 1010 Wien.
T. (0222) 5129954, Fax 5132166. - Glass /
Paint - 038775

Kovacs, Patrick, Lobkowitzpl 1, 1010 Wien.
T. (0222) 5879474, Fax (0222) 586084085. - Ant /
Paint / Furn / Sculp - 038776

Kovacs, Patrick, Rechte Wienzeile 31, 1040 Wien.
T. (0222) 5879474, Fax 586084085. - Ant / Paint /
Furn / Sculp - 038777

Kratschmann, Friedrich, Spiegelgasse 15, 1010 Wien.
T. (0222) 512 42 05. - Ant / Paint / Furn / Glass - 038778

Kroupa, Ernst, Spiegelgasse 13, 1010 Wien.
T. (0222) 52 34 72. - Ant / Furn - 038779

Kroupa, Ernst K., Habsburgergasse 14, 1010 Wien.
T. (0222) 535 51 95, Fax (0222) 535 51 95. 038780

Kruschitz, Ludwig, Rennweg 83, 1030 Wien.
T. (0222) 713 06 802. 038781

Kunst- und Stil-Handelsgesellschaft mbH, Kurrentgasse
4, 1010 Wien. T. (0222) 535 11 51. 038782

Kunsthandlung 20th Century, Bauernmarkt 9, 1010
Wien. T. (0222) 63 72 22. - Ant / Paint / Furn / Glass /
Mod - 038783

Kurz, W., Gentzgasse 64-66, 1180 Wien.
T. (0222) 34 65 59, Fax (0222) 4791323. 038784

Lagerhaus Jugendstil Art Deco, Große Neugasse 33,
1040 Wien. T. (0222) 586 69 69, Fax 586 69 69-11.
- Ant / Furn / Dec / Mod - 038785

Lang, Franz, Stammgasse 10, 1030 Wien.
T. (0222) 713 53 54. 038786

Langauer, Elisabeth, Weihburggasse 33, 1010 Wien.
T. (0222) 521 04 75. - Ant / Jew / Glass - 038787

Lechner, Rupert, Taborstr. 53-55/2, 1020 Wien.
T. (0222) 2164863. 038788

Lehner, Ilse, Habsburgergasse 5, 1010 Wien.
T. (0222) 52 73 23. 038789

Leistner, Gustav, Braunschweiggasse 17, 1130 Wien.
T. (0222) 889 19 72. 038790

Leitgeb, Christine, Salesianerg. 17, 1030 Wien.
T. (0222) 715 60 82. 038791

Lindner, Stubenring 20, 1010 Wien. T. (0222) 512 52 99.
- Num - 038792

Lindner (Antikes), J., Lustkandlgasse 41, 1090 Wien.
T. (0222) 3178253, Fax 3174213. - Ant / Paint / Furn /
China / Sculp / Jew / Lights / Instr / Glass / Mod / Tin / T-
oys - 038793

Lipovać, Anton, Dorotheergasse 14, 1010 Wien.
T. (0222) 512 88 46. 038794

**Christian M.
Nebehay, GmbH.**

Annagasse 18, Postfach 303
1015 Wien, Tel. 512 18 01
Fax: 513 50 38

Zeichnungen, Graphik
und wertvolle Bücher

Lorenz, Karl-Horst, Pezlgasse 9, 1170 Wien.
T. (0222) 402 72 27. *038795*
Luft, Erika, Kurrentgasse 12, 1010 Wien. *038796*
Mader, Alfred, Ober Laaer-Str. 104, 1100 Wien.
T. (0222) 685 24 72. *038797*
Mahringer, Rudolf, Aumannpl 2, 1180 Wien.
T. (0222) 4797440, (0664) 3078169. - Paint /
Mod - *038798*
Makoveč, J., Sechskrügelgasse 2, 1030 Wien.
T. (0222) 712 33 88. *038799*
Makovec, J., Hauptstr. 90, 1030 Wien.
T. (0222) 712 32 32. *038800*
Marek, Peter, Gymnasiumstr. 27, 1180 Wien.
T. (0222) 34 32 06. *038801*
Mattes, Antonia, Rainergasse 31, 1040 Wien.
T. (0222) 505 70 592. *038802*
Mautner, Erich M., Herrengasse 2, 1010 Wien.
T. (0222) 63 12 24. - Ant / Ico - *038803*
Mayr, Elisabeth, Grinzinger Str. 117, 1190 Wien.
T. (0222) 37 47 86. *038804*
Mejouscheg, Helga, Plankengasse 4, 1010 Wien.
T. (0222) 512 48 09. *038805*
Meneghel, Susanne, Josefstädter Str. 11, 1080 Wien.
T. (0222) 402 17 852. *038806*
Messina, Josef, Strohgasse 26, 1030 Wien. *038807*
Metlewicz, Thomas, Dr., Seilergasse 14, 1010 Wien.
T. (0222) 5122746. - Paint / Furn / China / Silv /
Glass - *038808*
Metropol, Dorotheergasse 12, 1010 Wien.
T. (0222) 513 22 08, 513 68 38, Fax 513 99 63. - Ant /
Paint / Graph / Furn / Tex / Jew / Silv / Glass / Mod --
038809
Michnowski, Erna, Berggasse 25, 1090 Wien.
T. (0222) 31 12 17. *038810*
Miel, Ingo, Riemergasse 2, 1010 Wien.
T. (0222) 512 48 69. - Instr - *038811*
Mönnig, Friedrich, Schönbrunner Str. 74, 1050 Wien.
T. (0222) 557 87 63. *038812*
Moser, Fritz, Welhburggasse 14, 1010 Wien.
T. (0222) 512 42 10. - Ant / Fra / Lights - *038813*
Moser, Walter E., Nußdorfer Str. 72, 1090 Wien.
T. (0222) 3190870. - Mil - *038814*
Mozelt, Erich, Margartenstr. 50, 1040 Wien.
T. (0222) 5867488, Fax (0222) 5862617.
- Num - *038815*
Mozelt, Erich, Schikanedergasse 13, 1040
Wien. *038816*
Müller, Elisabeth, Dr., Cobenzlgasse 80, 1190 Wien.
T. (0222) 32 21 71. *038817*
Müller, Gerlinde, Mahlerstr. 11, 1010 Wien.
T. (0222) 512 18 97. - Ant - *038818*
Müller, Peter, Kaiserstr. 30, 1070 Wien.
T. (0222) 93 29 453. *038819*
Münzen, Briefmarken, Antiquitäten Ges.mbH, Graben
15, 1010 Wien. T. (0222) 5200632. *038820*
Münzen, Briefmarken, Antiquitäten Ges.mbH, Tuchlau-
ben 6, 1010 Wien. T. (0222) 633312. *038821*
T. (0222) 512 88 44. - Num - *038822*
Münzen und Medaillen, Lambrechtgasse 4, 1040 Wien.
T. (0222) 57 52 46. - Num - *038823*
Münzen-Zentrum, Auerspergstr. 5, 1080 Wien.
T. (0222) 4066805, 4064689, Fax (0222) 4055444.
- Num - *038824*
Münzkistl 1, Neubaugürtel 31, 1150 Wien.
T. (0222) 92 02 99. - Num - *038825*
Murhammer, Rudolf, Heinestr.9, 1020 Wien. *038826*
Nauert, Dierk, Stallburggasse 2, 1010 Wien.
T. (0222) 513 19 27. - Ant / Orient - *038827*

Nauert, Fritz Dierk, Piaristengasse 2-4, 1010 Wien.
T. (0222) 513 19 27. - Num - *038828*
Nebehay, Christian M., Annagasse 18, Postfach 303,
1015 Wien. T. (0222) 5121801, Fax 5135038. - Graph /
Draw - *038829*
Nofredeto, Kurrentgasse 3, 1010 Wien.
T. (0222) 535 31 25. *038830*
Nueber, W., Schönbrunner Str. 182, 1120 Wien.
T. (0222) 8150210. *038831*
Österreichische Werkstätten GmbH, Kärntnerstr.15,
1010 Wien. *038832*
Özelt, Gerhard, Leebgasse 90-92, 1100 Wien.
T. (0222) 627 27 69. *038833*
Orth, Friedrich, Bürgerspitalgasse 8, 1060 Wien.
T. (0222) 57 94 86. - Num - *038834*
Ortner, Ludwig, Siebensterngasse 33, 1070 Wien.
T. (0222) 93 14 60. *038835*
Ostrowsky, Leon, Parkring 12a, 1010 Wien.
T. (0222) 53 37 65. *038836*
Oswald & Kalb, Bäckerstr. 13, 1010 Wien.
T. 5126117. *038837*
Oswald & Kalb, Münzwardeingasse 2, 1060
Wien. *038838*
Otta, Reinhard Johann, Stallburggasse 4, 1010 Wien.
T. (0222) 533 99 21. *038839*
Otto, Seilergasse 1, 1010 Wien. T. (0222) 5125910,
5138039. *038840*
Otto, Mariahilfer Str. 24, 1070 Wien.
T. (0222) 5231066. *038841*
Otto, Lainzer Str. 53, 1131 Wien. T. (0222) 8777500,
Fax (0222) 877750012. - Ant - *038842*
Otto, Währinger Str. 79, 1180 Wien.
T. (0222) 43 13 92. *038843*
Otto, Meidl. Hauptstr. 49, 1120 Wien.
T. (0222) 830152. *038844*
Otto, Hietz. Hauptstr. 22, 1130 Wien.
T. (0222) 8778330. *038845*
Otto, Florisdsf. Hauptstr. 14, 1210 Wien.
T. (0222) 2703737. *038846*
Otto, Heinz, Elßlergasse 4a, 1130 Wien.
T. (0222) 829 16 35. *038847*
Otto, Rudolf, Lainzer Str. 53, 1131 Wien.
T. (0222) 877 75 000, Fax 877 750 012.
- Paint - *038848*
Pabst, Michael, Habsburger Gasse 10, 1010 Wien.
T. (0222) 5337014. *038849*
Padilla-Santander, Angelika, Spiegelgasse 8, 1010
Wien. T. (0222) 513 13 49. *038850*
Pallamar, Friederike, Dorotheergasse 7, 1010 Wien.
T. (0222) 5125228. - Paint - *038851*
Palocz, Ingeborg, Streffleurg. 14, 1200 Wien.
T. (0222) 35 34 474. *038852*
Paltinger, Walter, Wallnerstr. 2, 1010 Wien.
T. (0222) 535 31 93. - Ant - *038853*
La Parete, Tuchlauben 14, 1010 Wien.
T. (0222) 5330133. - Mod - *038854*
Payer Decor, Jasomirgottstr 4, 1010 Wien. *038855*
Pedit, Hermann Gaudentius, Königseggasse 2, 1060
Wien. T. (0222) 587 43 60. *038856*
Peer's Sammlertruhe, Neubaugasse 53, 1070 Wien.
T. (0222) 5261719. - Ant - *038857*
Perco, Mario, Spiegelgasse 11, 1010 Wien.
T. (0222) 513 56 95. *038858*
Peters & Co., Rotenturmstr. 2, 1010 Wien.
T. (0222) 5124962. *038859*
Peters, Axel, Siebensterngasse 24, 1070 Wien.
T. (0222) 5231344. *038860*
Petkowsky, Aleksander, Breitenfurter Str 365, 1230
Wien. T. (0222) 8659340. *038861*
Pfaller, Ingrid, Hernalser Hauptstr. 43, 1170 Wien.
T. (0222) 43 44 30, 42 21 08. *038862*
Pfoser, Wilhelm, Stauraczgasse 5, 1050 Wien.
T. (0222) 553 58 34. *038863*
Pichler, Manfred, Schönbrunner Str. 149, 1050 Wien.
T. (0222) 5451054. - Furn / China / Lights / Glass / Cur /
Mod - *038864*
Pichler & Söhne, Gabriel, Schwarzenbergstr. 1-3, 1010
Wien. T. (0222) 512 14 93. - Ant / Paint / Furn / China /
Sculp / Fra / Silv / Lights / Instr / Glass / Mod - *038865*
Pölzer, Hofburgpassage, 1010 Wien. *038866*
Pointinger, Gertrude, Schönbrunner Str. 105, 1050
Wien. *038867*

Poropatich, Monika, Schüttaustr. 4-10, 1220 Wien.
T. (0222) 23 25 45. *038868*
Portobello, Piaristengasse 24, 1080 Wien.
T. (0222) 408 40 61. *038869*
Prause, Kurt, Spiegelgasse 21, 1010 Wien.
T. (0222) 5124414. *038870*
Prinz, Leopoldine, Dorotheergasse 6-8, 1010 Wien.
T. (0222) 52 47 19. *038871*
Prix, Barbara, Josefstädter Str. 14, 1080 Wien.
T. (0222) 405 74 10, Fax 403 74 40. - Furn / Lights /
Glass / Mod - *038872*
Radetzky, Seilergasse 16, 1010 Wien.
T. (0222) 5131251. *038873*
Radovan, Ivan, Hackenberggasse 29, 1190 Wien.
T. (0222) 32 35 29. *038874*
Rannacher, Gerta, Rotenturmstr. 19/1, 1010 Wien.
T. (0222) 5358066. - Graph / Repr - *038875*
Rauch, Hans Dieter, Graben 15, 1010 Wien.
T. (0222) 533 33 12. - Num - *038876*
Rebhan, Karla, Wurlitzergasse 88, 1170 Wien.
T. (0222) 465 45 42. *038877*
Reichenauer, Ingrid, Pachmüllergasse 6, 1120 Wien.
T. (0222) 813 91 40. *038878*
Reismüller, Erna, Linzer Str. 415, 1140 Wien.
T. (0222) 94 28 142. *038879*
Reti, Stefan, Schönbrunner Str. 274, 1120 Wien.
T. (0222) 934 87 35. *038880*
Rezac, Margit, Gr. Sperlgasse 38, 1020 Wien.
T. (0222) 3562212, Fax (0222) 2165903. - Ant /
Jew - *038881*
Riedl von Seletzky, E. u. W., Spiegelgasse 19, 1010
Wien. T. (0222) 5127930. - Ant - *038882*
Rigler, Wolfgang, Thaliastr. 123, 1100 Wien.
T. (0222) 92 73 964. *038883*
Rogguhn, Günter, Neubaugasse 68, 1070 Wien.
T. (0222) 93 84 19. *038884*
Ruberl, Richard, Himmelpfortg 11, 1010 Wien.
T. (0222) 5131992, Fax 5137709. - Paint /
Graph - *038885*

**RICHARD RUBERL
GALERIE**

Himmelpfortgasse 11
1010 Wien, Tel. 513 19 92, Fax 513 77 09

AQUARELLE U. GEMÄLDE
des 19. und 20. Jahrhunderts

STÄNDIGER ANKAUF

Safari-Shop, Lerchenfelder Str. 104, 1080 Wien.
T. (0222) 402 26 85. *038886*
Salomon, Eugen, Spiegelgasse 19, 1000 Wien.
T. (0222) 52 57 20. - Jew / Silv - *038887*
Salvator Galerie, Salvatorgasse 6, 1000 Wien.
T. (0222) 63 58 01. - Ant / Paint / Furn / China /
Mod - *038888*
Sankt Michael Antiquitäten, Habsburgasse 14, 1010
Wien. T. (0222) 525 01 54. - Ant / Paint / Furn / China /
Tex / Silv / Glass - *038889*
Sauer, Peter, Kärntner Str. 21-23, 1011 Wien.
T. (0222) 512 71 11, Fax 5127888. - Num - *038890*
Schinnerl, Erich, Eslarngasse 26/10, 1030 Wien.
T. (0222) 713 96 645. *038891*
Schmidt, Raimund, Ruthgasse 17, 1190 Wien.
T. (0222) 365 04 75. *038892*
Schneeberger, Hermann, Florianigasse 16, 1080
Wien. *038893*
Schneider, Conrad, Operngasse 10, 1010 Wien.
T. (0222) 575 81 23. - Jew - *038894*
Schöbel, Robert, Dr., Mommsengasse 25, 1040
Wien. *038895*
Schoeller, Renngasse 1-3, 1010 Wien.
T. (0222) 53 47 10, Fax 534 710 433. - Num - *038896*
Schräml, Erwin, Liechtensteinstr. 39, 1090 Wien.
T. (0222) 3170205. - Ant / Paint - *038897*
Schramm, Walter, Himmelpfortgasse 19, 1010 Wien.
T. (0222) 528 07 04. - Ant - *038898*

Schullin, Herbert, Dr., Kohlmarkt 7, 1010 Wien.
T. (0222) 533 90 07, Fax 535 50 60. - Jew /
Silv - 038899
Schuster, Gertrude, Krugerstr. 17, 1010 Wien.
T. (0222) 513 52 34. 038900
Schuster, Susanne, Schwendergasse 20, 1150 Wien.
T. (0222) 83 14 95. 038901
Schweiger, Harald, Akademiestr. 2, 1010 Wien. 038902
Seidenstrasse, Koschatgasse 2-3, 1190 Wien. 038903
Seidl-Finsterer, Elfriede, Stallburggasse 2, 1010 Wien.
T. (0222) 5230152. - Ant / Furn / Sculp / Jew /
Ico - 038904
Shariat, Bagher, Piaristengasse 56-58, 1080 Wien.
T. (0222) 402 46 46. 038905
Siedler, Georg Wilhelm, Kohlmarkt 3, 1010 Wien.
T. (0222) 5339917. - Ant / Paint / Furn / China / Sculp /
Jew / Silv - 038906
Siedler, Wolfgang A., Himmelpfortgasse 13-15, 1010
Wien. T. (0222) 513 29 260, 512 38 95, Fax 513 84 30.
- Ant / Paint / Furn / Sculp / Jew - 038907
Siegl, Peter, Felberstr. 40, 1150 Wien.
T. (0222) 95 21 54. 038908
Siegmeth, A., Lobkowitzplatz 1, 1010 Wien.
T. (0222) 513 37 73, Fax 512 16 59. 038909
Siegmeth GmbH+CO KG, Arta-Julius F., Gr. Sperlgasse
39, 1020 Wien. T. (0222) 336 658, 337 499.
- Instr - 038910
Skalitzki, Elfriede, Längenfeldgasse 8, 1120 Wien.
T. (0222) 83 44 33. 038911
Skvara, Franz, Gr. Schiffgasse 6, 1020 Wien.
T. (0222) 33 52 434. 038912
Smuc, Johann, Barawitzkagasse 12, 1190 Wien.
T. (0222) 36 41 84. 038913
Sommerlatte, Sieglinde, Neustiftgasse 27, 1070
Wien. 038914
Souval, Rudolf, Siebensterngasse 23, 1070 Wien.
T. (0222) 934 95 54. 038915
Spira, Curt, Spiegelgasse 23, 1010 Wien.
T. (0222) 512 68 43. - Ant / Furn / China / Sculp / Instr /
Glass - 038916
Squire, Maria Magdalena, Spiegelgasse 4, 1010 Wien.
T. (0222) 512 13 99. - Ant - 038917
Srna-Modlitby, Martha, Naglergasse 1, 1010 Wien.
T. (0222) 5337445. - Ant - 038918
Steeger, Kurt, Erdbergstr.103, 1030 Wien. 038919
Steffan, Franz, Währinger Str. 75, 1180 Wien.
T. (0222) 43 68 27. - Ant / Jew - 038920
Steffek, Michael, Schönbrunnerstr 71, 1050 Wien.
T. (0222) 5451401, Fax 5451401. - Ant / Furn / Lights /
Instr / Glass / Mod - 038921
Sternat, Reinhold, Dr., Lobkowitzpl 1, 1010 Wien.
T. (0222) 5121871, Fax (0222) 5138517. - Ant / Paint /
Graph / Furn / Mod - 038922
Stöhr, Edith u. Johann, Stallburggasse 2, 1010 Wien.
T. (0222) 512 89 73. - Jew - 038923
Stöhr, Johann, Volkertplatz 14, 1020 Wien.
T. (0222) 214 37 335. - Furn / Instr / Glass - 038924
Stolper, Marianne, Heumühlgasse 13/3, 1040
Wien. 038925
Stranski, Edith, Singerstr 26A, 1010 Wien.
T. (0222) 5126850. - Ant / Furn / Silv - 038926
Strasser, Burggasse 126, 1070 Wien. T. (0222) 93 89 93.
- Num - 038927
Strommer, Alfred, Kurrentgasse 3, 1010 Wien.
T. (0222) 535 31 25. 038928
Stummer, L. H., Mariahilfer Str. 107, 1060 Wien.
T. (0222) 56 43 61. - Num / Instr - 038929
Stumvoll, Elfriede, Troststr. 15, 1100 Wien. 038930
Subal, Anton, Weihburggasse 11, 1010 Wien.
T. (0222) 512 19 81. - Ant / Paint / Furn / Dec / Lights /
Mod - 038931
Suppan, Martin, Habsburgergasse 5, 1010 Wien.
T. (0222) 535 53 520, 535 53 54, Fax 535 53 54 35.
- Paint / Furn - 038932
Szaal, Gerhard, Josefstädter Str. 74, 1080 Wien.
T. (0222) 4066330, Fax (0222) 4028835. 038933
Szaal, Horst, Laudongasse 44, 1080 Wien.
T. (0222) 4066330, Fax (0222) 4028835. 038934
Tellmann, Salomea, Schulerstr. 12/2, 1010 Wien.
- Num - 038935
Tesinsky, Helmut, Augustinerstr. 12, 1010 Wien.
T. (0222) 512 02 58. 038936

GALERIE ZACKE

Alte Kunst aus Asien

Regelmäßig Ausstellungen,
Katalogeversand sowie Editionen

A-1010 WIEN 1   SCHULERSTR. 15
TEL 51 22 23   FAX 513 27 04

Theatergalerie, Josefstädter Str. 32, 1080 Wien.
T. (0222) 408 65 57. - Ant / Fra - 038937
Theuermann, Georg, Dorotheergasse 7, 1010 Wien.
T. (0222) 513 71 32. - Ant - 038938
Theuermann, Valentin, Zollergasse 33, 1070 Wien.
T. (0222) 5237344. 038939
Thiery, Elisabeth-Marie, Wildpretmarkt 1, 1010 Wien.
T. (0222) 5332101, Fax (0222) 5332101. 038940
Thurn-Taxis, Dorothea, Schippergasse 61, 1210 Wien.
T. (0222) 39 14 53. 038941
Tiefenbach, Johann, Plankengasse 4, 1010 Wien.
T. (0222) 522 07 55. - Ant / Orient / China /
Glass - 038942
Titzer, Monika, Singerstr. 5, 1010 Wien. 038943
Toifl, B. u. J., Döblinger Gürtel, Stadtbahnbogen 188,
1190 Wien. T. (0222) 34 23 61. - Ant / Lights - 038944
Topol, Emanuel, Ottakringer Str. 82, 1170 Wien.
T. (0222) 46 42 12. - Num - 038945
Transantik, Rechte Wienzeile 45, 1050 Wien.
T. (0222) 587 92 97. 038946
Tromayer, Erich, Dorotheergasse 7, 1010 Wien.
T. (0222) 513 10 75, Fax 513 81 07. - Paint - 038947
Universum Antiquitäten, Sonnwendgasse 21, 1100
Wien. T. (0222) 78 72 61, 78 72 63. - Ant / Paint / Furn /
China / Fra / Lights / Instr / Rel / Glass / Cur / Mod --
038948
Unterhumer, Alexander, Hauptstr. 63, 1030 Wien.
T. (0222) 712 23 57. - Num - 038949
Valta, H. & J., Rotenlöwengasse 7, 1090 Wien.
T. (0222) 31 64 29. - Ant - 038950
Vanić, Johann, Frauenstiftgasse 1, 1210 Wien.
T. (0222) 39 13 36, 39 55 14. 038951
Vartian & Söhne, Seilergasse 14, 1010 Wien. 038952
Vartian & Söhne, Tuchlauben 8, 1010 Wien.
T. (0222) 533 19 42. - Tex - 038953
Vertiko, Lerchenfelderstr. 30, 1080 Wien.
T. (0222) 402 22 71. - Furn / Lights / Mod - 038954
Vesely, Ilona, Liechtensteinstr. 104, 1090 Wien.
T. (0222) 3109470. 038955
Visconti Art Spectrum, Knöllgasse 16, 1090
Wien. 038956
Vogelhuber, Hans, Vogelweidplatz 2, 1150 Wien.
T. (0222) 9835929. - Ant / Furn - 038957
Vykoukal, Franz, Köllnerhofgasse 2, 1010 Wien.
T. (0222) 513 27 14. 038958
Wallner, Irene, Koppstr. 55, 1160 Wien. 038959
Walter, Erika, Riemergasse 14, 1010 Wien.
T. (0222) 512 94 38, Fax 512 94 38. - Ant / Paint / Furn /
China / Jew / Silv / Glass / Cur / Mod - 038960
Wang, Marcel, Spiegelgasse 25, 1010 Wien.
T. (0222) 5124187. - Ant / Jew - 038961
Wastl, Anna, Porzellangasse 54, 1090 Wien.
T. (0222) 34 24 03. 038962
Weber, Doris, Währinger Str. 147, 1180 Wien.
T. (0222) 479 83 30. - Ant - 038963
Weber, Susanne, Haidgasse 10, 1020 Wien.
T. (0222) 33 93 79. 038964
Weiser, Ingrid, Graf Starhembergg. 5, 1040 Wien.
T. (0222) 5059960. - Ant - 038965
Weithofer, Siebensterngasse 25, 1070 Wien.
T. (0222) 93 58 654. 038966

Welz, Max, Schottenfeldgasse 45, 1070 Wien. 038967
Weninger, Erich, Rennweg 19, 1030 Wien.
T. (0222) 7182821. 038968
Weywoda, Manfred, Köllnerhofg 1, 1010 Wien.
T. (0222) 5120130, Fax 5123377. - Num - 038969
Widder, Margarete, Dr., Singrinergasse 22, 1120
Wien. 038970
Widholm, Bruno, Leitermayergasse 44, 1180 Wien.
T. (0222) 434 05 63, 94 42 30. 038971
Wiener Münzensalon, Schottenring 17, 1010 Wien.
T. (0222) 3197221, Fax 3196486. - Num - 038972
Wiener Waffenkammer, Burggasse 42, 1070 Wien.
T. (0222) 9339725. - Mil - 038973
Wiesner, Leo, Mariahilfer Str. 119, 1060 Wien.
Fax (0222) 5971006. - Num - 038974
Wiesner, Vera, Stumpergasse 41-43, 1060 Wien.
T. (0222) 597 15 11, 597 15 12, Fax 597 15 69.
- Num - 038975
Wilnitsky, Boris, Schulerstr 7, 1010 Wien.
T. (0222) 5134991, Fax 5134991. - Ant - 038976
Wimmer, Naglerg. 8, 1010 Wien. T. (0222) 63 42 39,
63 11 65. - Num - 038977
Wimmer, Kurt, Plankengasse 6, 1010 Wien.
T. (0222) 512 10 47. - Ant / Furn - 038978
Winter, Adalbert, Feldmühlgasse 10, 1120 Wien.
T. (0222) 828 43 26. 038979
Wöhrer, Josef, Stallburggasse 4, 1010 Wien. 038980
Wohnkultur, Mariahilfer Str. 7, 1060 Wien.
T. (0222) 587 87 79. 038981
Wong, Stefan, Penzinger Str. 61, 1140 Wien.
T. (0222) 828 51 15. - Ant / Paint / Furn / China / Jew /
Fra / Silv / Glass / Cur / Mod - 038982
Woratsch, Elisabeth, Wipplingerstr. 20, 1010 Wien.
T. (0222) 5336420. 038983
Würthle & Sohn Nfg, Kaasgraben 108, 1190 Wien.
T. (0222) 3181685, Fax 3181685. - Paint / Graph /
Sculp / Draw - 038984
Zacke, Schulerstr. 15, 1010 Wien. T. (0222) 5122223,
Fax (0222) 5132704. - Orient - 038985
Zapomnel, Erika, Bräunerstr.11, 1000 Wien. 038986
Zendron, Manfred, Kegelgasse 2, 1030 Wien.
T. (0222) 723 81 24. 038987
Zorn, Bräunerstr. 11, 1010 Wien. 038988
Zuba, Karl, Plenergasse 23-25, 1180 Wien.
T. (0222) 47 80 19. 038989

Wiener Neudorf (Niederösterreich)
Vojnniosek, Barbara, Laxenburger Str. 14, 2351 Wiener
Neudorf. T. (02236) 61172. 038990

Wiener Neustadt (Niederösterreich)
Ewanschow, Herta, Böheimgasse 6, 2700 Wiener Neu-
stadt. T. (02622) 23291, Fax 23 29 13. 038991
Payer, Josef, Allerheiligenplatz 3, 2700 Wiener Neu-
stadt. T. (02622) 22 02 72. 038992
Reger, Johannes Maximilian, Brodtischgasse 12, 2700
Wiener Neustadt. 038993
Stirling, Anton, Bahngasse 32, 2700 Wiener Neustadt.
T. (02622) 22 09 15. - Num - 038994

Winzendorf (Niederösterreich)
Schaffler-Glössl, Heide, Winzendorf 172, 2722 Winzendorf. *038995*

Wolfern (Oberösterreich)
Garber, Maximilian, Steyrerstr. 9, 4493 Wolfern.
T. (07253) 272. - Ant / Furn - *038996*

Wolfurt (Vorarlberg)
Moskat, Walter, Lauteracher Str. 32, 6922 Wolfurt.
T. (05574) 347 32. *038997*

Zell am See (Salzburg)
Hölzl, Ferdinand, Färbermühle, 5700 Zell am See.
T. (06542) 23 94. *038998*

Zell am Ziller (Tirol)
Huber, Fritz, Bundesstr. 18a, 6280 Zell am Ziller.
T. (05282) 25 66. *038999*

Zistersdorf (Niederösterreich)
Ludwig Fleckl's, Haupstr. 24, 2225 Zistersdorf. *039000*

Zwettl (Niederösterreich)
Franzus, Christian, Landstr. 61, 3910 Zwettl.
T. (02822) 2453. *039001*

Bahamas

Governor's Harbour (Eleutherd Island)
The Connoisseur, Governor's Harbour. - Ant /
Paint - *039002*

Barbados

Bridgetown
Antiquaria, St. Michael's Row, Bridgetown. T. 426-0635,
Fax 427 6798. *039003*

Saint Michael
Claradon, Pine Rd., Saint Michael. T. (08) 429-
4713. *039004*

Belgium

Aalst (Oost-Vlaanderen)
Alostum, Mathias, Vilainstr 47, 9300 Aalst.
T. (053) 70 13 91. *039005*
Apostelken, 'T, OL Vrouwplein, 9300 Aalst. *039006*
Beeckman, J., D Martensstr 54, 9300 Aalst.
T. (053) 21 02 69. *039007*
Borghmans, Geraardbergsestr 28, 9300 Aalst.
T. (053) 21 04 15. *039008*
Canticleer, Kerkstr 22, 9300 Aalst.
T. (053) 21 42 32. *039009*
Clock-House, Gentsestr 40, 9300 Aalst.
T. (053) 77 97 73. *039010*
Coninck, de, Brusselsesteenweg 80, 9300 Aalst.
T. (053) 70 48 06. *039011*
De Groene Poort, Violettestr 3, 9300 Aalst.
T. (053) 21 28 95. *039012*
Gallery Spaarzaamheidsstraat 65, Spaarzaamheidsstr
65, 9300 Aalst. T. (053) 70 02 17. *039013*
Pintelon, Robert, Pontstr. 19, 9300 Aalst.
T. (053) 287 28. - Ant / Cur - *039014*
Royal Art, Keizerlijkeplaats 28, 9300 Aalst.
T. (053) 21 62 98. *039015*
Soete Huijs, 'T, L de Bethunelaan 45, 9300 Aalst.
T. (053) 21 59 00. *039016*
Steen, van de, Leo de Bethunelaan 10, 9300 Aalst.
T. (053) 70 08 89. *039017*
Verhulst, Keizerlijkepl. 62, 9300 Aalst. T. (053) 21 44 13.
- Ant / Cur - *039018*
Vinck, Eddie, Marcelstr 5a, 9300 Aalst.
T. (053) 78 25 71. *039019*

Aalter (Oost-Vlaanderen)
Recup, Brouwerijstr. 3, 9880 Aalter. T. (051) 746819.
- Furn - *039020*

Taghon, A., Ambachtenln 14, 9880 Aalter.
T. (051) 745166. *039021*

Aarsele (West Vlaanderen)
Pareyn, Jan, Wontergemstr. 16, 8700 Aarsele.
T. (051) 634168, Fax 635922. - Ant / Paint / Graph /
Furn / Orient / China / Sculp / Eth / Silv / Lights / Instr / R-
el / Glass / Cur / Mod / Tin - *039022*

Aartselaar (Antwerpen)
Van Elst, Schelselei 12a, 2630 Aartselaar.
T. (031) 8771010. *039023*
Verantica, De Buerstedelei 9, 2630 Aartselaar.
T. (031) 8870968. - Furn - *039024*

Adinkerke (West-Vlaanderen)
Bart, Jean, Duinkerkekeiweg 5, 8660 Adinkerke.
T. (058) 41256. *039025*
Floorizoone, Urbain, Cabourweg 1, 8660 Adinkerke.
T. (058) 41 21 03. *039026*

Affligem (Vlaams Brabant)
Sompel, Chris van, Brusselbaan 129, 1790 Affligem.
T. 665783. *039027*

Aische-en-Refail (Namur)
Malandre, La, 156 Rue du Château, 5310 Aische-en-Re-
fail. T. (081) 65 65 48. *039028*

Alken (Limburg)
Loix, Jan, Steenweg 306a, 3570 Alken.
T. (011) 312786. *039029*

Alveringem (West-Vlaanderen)
Appel, Den, Appelstr 7, 8690 Alveringem.
T. (058) 28 89 62. *039030*

Ampsin (Liège
Lizein, L., 26 Rue de Jehay, 4540 Ampsin.
T. (085) 318 17. *039031*

Andenne (Namur)
Beaujean, 50 Chaussée d'Anton, 5300 Andenne.
T. (085) 22 22 88. - Ant - *039032*

Antheit (Liège)
Marpaux, A., Chaussèe de Tirlemont, 4520 Antheit.
T. (085) 122 03. *039033*

Antwerpen
A H Antiques, Tabakvest 1, 2000 Antwerpen.
T. (03) 231 61 12. - Ant - *039034*
Adin, Vestingstr 16, 2018 Antwerpen.
T. (03) 233 50 92. *039035*
Adviesbureel voor Antikwiteiten, Lange Leemstr 75,
2000 Antwerpen. T. (03) 232 08 08. *039036*
Agathon Oudheden, Kloosterstr 32, 2000 Antwerpen.
T. (03) 226 18 30. *039037*
Agora 1900-1930, Sint Jansvliet 23, 2000 Antwerpen.
T. (03) 231 13 27. - Ant - *039038*
Akanthos, Kloosterstr 46, 2000 Antwerpen.
T. (03) 248 18 55. *039039*
Alfa Antiques, Platin en Moretuslei 136, 2018 Antwer-
pen. T. (03) 235 30 00. - Ant - *039040*
Amati, Zinkstr 25, 2000 Antwerpen.
T. (03) 232 77 68. *039041*
Amber, Wiegstr. 30, 2000 Antwerpen. T. (03) 231 74 77.
- Ant - *039042*
Anselmo, Anselmostr 32, 2000 Antwerpen.
T. (03) 237 52 72. *039043*
Antiek Brocante, Beeldekenstr 237, 2060 Antwerpen.
T. (03) 235 74 13. *039044*
Antiek Center, Minderbroedersrui 41, 2000 Antwerpen.
T. (03) 226 64 54. *039045*
Antiquiteiten, Lambermontstr 12, 2000 Antwerpen.
T. (03) 248 29 93. *039046*
Antwerpen Antiques Market, Mechelsestw 123, 2018
Antwerpen. T. (03) 218 47 01/14. *039047*
Art Deco, Oever 20, 2000 Antwerpen. T. (03) 225 11 41.
- Ant - *039048*
Avonds, L., Mechelsesteenweg 78, 2018 Antwerpen.
T. (03) 238 51 86. - Ant / Dec - *039049*
Barbarella, Kloosterstr 26, 2000 Antwerpen.
T. (03) 226 45 69. *039050*

Bascourt, M., Mechelsesteenweg 17, 2018 Antwerpen.
T. (03) 233 71 20. - Ant / Paint / Furn / China /
Sculp - *039051*
Bataclan, St Jorispoort 15, 2000 Antwerpen.
T. (03) 226 07 30. *039052*
Blauwe, Mi de, Minderbroedersrui 20, 2000 Antwerpen.
T. (03) 226 30 52. *039053*
Blauwe, Mi de, Minderbroedersrui 20, 2000 Antwerpen.
T. (03) 226 30 52. *039054*
Blondeel, Bernard, Schuttershofstr. 5, 2000 Antwerpen.
T. (03) 2332554, Fax 2324360. - Ant - *039055*

Blue Shop, Steenhouwersvest 15, 2000 Antwerpen.
T. (03) 225 25 54. - Ant - *039056*
Bot, Christiane de, Klosterstr 36, 2000 Antwerpen.
T. (03) 455 09 21, 234 36 62. *039057*
Bourgaux, R., Mechelsesteenweg 31, 2000 Antwerpen.
T. (03) 232 43 52. - Ant - *039058*
Brabo, Melkmarkt 25 a, 2000 Antwerpen.
T. (03) 232 62 33. *039059*
Broll, Wijngaardstr 2, 2000 Antwerpen.
T. (03) 226 15 32. *039060*
Calleja, T., Wijngaardstr. 23, 2000 Antwerpen.
T. (03) 233 28 97. - Mod - *039061*
Campo, Nicole, Leopoldstr. 53, 2000 Antwerpen.
T. (03) 232 62 70, Fax 233 82 80. - Ant / Silv - *039062*
Ceuleneer, R. de, Groendalstr. 16-22, 2000 Antwerpen.
T. (03) 231 63 24. - Ant - *039063*
Chelsea, Oever 28, 2000 Antwerpen.
T. (03) 233 85 77. *039064*
Chelsea, Kloosterstr 10, 2000 Antwerpen.
T. (03) 231 36 43. *039065*
Climats, Leopoldstraat 29, 2000 Antwerpen.
T. (03) 232 88 26. - Ant / Cur - *039066*
D'Avondland, Lange Gasthuisstr 13, 2000 Antwerpen.
T. (03) 232 41 73. *039067*
Daele, Rudi van, Oever 3, 2000 Antwerpen.
T. (03) 225 30 73. - Ant - *039068*
Dajak, Anselmostr. 93, 2018 Antwerpen.
T. (03) 237 51 26. - Eth - *039069*
Decorative Arts, Steenhouwersvest 14, 2000 Antwerpen.
T. (03) 233 19 98. *039070*
Dirven, Jan, Schuttershofstr. 7, 2000 Antwerpen.
T. (03) 233 71 66, Fax 232 43 60. - Ant / Sculp - *039071*
Elchanan, Vestingstr. 16, 2018 Antwerpen.
T. (03) 233 59 92. - Ant - *039072*
Eldeco, Kammenstr. 67, 2000 Antwerpen.
T. (03) 231 75 27. - Ant - *039073*
Eureka Antwerp, Lange Nieuwstr 8, 2000 Antwerpen.
T. (03) 231 77 95. *039074*
Falconantiques, Touwstr 24, 2008 Antwerpen.
T. (03) 271 01 21. *039075*
Fraulahofje, Berchemboslaan 9, 2600 Antwerpen.
T. (03) 230 60 12. *039076*
Gärtner & Co., Steenhouwersvest 18, 2000 Antwerpen.
T. (03) 231 17 61. *039077*
Galeries Versailles, Les, Kammenstr. 36, 2000 Antwer-
pen. T. (03) 233 79 94. - Ant / Paint / Graph / Furn / Chi-
na / Sculp / Jew / Cur - *039078*
Galtraco, Lge Nieuwstr 1, 2000 Antwerpen.
T. (03) 202 02 51. *039079*
Geursts, Valere & Monique, Vleminckstr 5, 2000 Antwer-
pen. T. (03) 232 62 33. *039080*
Geurts, Laurent & Michel, Oever 23, 2000 Antwerpen.
T. (03) 232 45 34. - Ant - *039081*

Gevleugeld Kindje, Drukkerijstr. 7, 2000 Antwerpen.
T. (03) 234 29 32. - Ant -   039082
Goedleven, H., Hardenvoort 9-11, 2060 Antwerpen.
T. (03) 233 66 58, Fax 233 66 53.   039083
Golbert, E., Mechelsesteenweg 85, 2000 Antwerpen.
T. (03) 233 53 34.   039084
Golbert, E., Arenbergstr 16, 2000 Antwerpen.
T. (03) 232 05 67.   039085
Graeve Byzant, de, Aalmoezenierstr. 13, 2000 Antwerpen. T. (03) 232 05 75. - Ant -   039086
Granny, Oever 1, 2000 Antwerpen. T. (03) 232 67 93.
- Ant -   039087
Gray, van, Steenhouwersvest 20, 2000 Antwerpen.
T. (03) 231 61 27. - Ant -   039088
Hansenne-de Vil, J., Breughelstr. 12, 2000 Antwerpen.
T. (03) 239 25 05. - Ant / Paint / Furn / China /
Glass -   039089
Heerenhuis, Paleisstr 28, 2018 Antwerpen.
T. (03) 238 66 03.   039090
Henau, St Jozefstr 10, 2018 Antwerpen.
T. (03) 239 77 58.   039091
Henkes, R., Steenhouwersvest 14, 2000 Antwerpen.
T. (03) 233 19 98.   039092
Herbs & Things, Schrijnwerkersstr 19, 2000 Antwerpen.
T. (03) 234 13 66.   039093
Herck, J. van, Durletstr 37, 2018 Antwerpen.
T. (03) 237 89 35.   039094
Heyman, F., Steenhouwersvest 4, 2000 Antwerpen.
T. (03) 233 07 74.   039095
Hispantics, Coquilhatstr 43-45, 2000 Antwerpen.
T. (03) 237 45 73.   039096
Hofmans, J., Klossterstr 35, 2000 Antwerpen.
T. (03) 233 89 29.   039097
Holman, J., Schuttershofstr 33, 2000 Antwerpen.
T. (03) 226 58 79.   039098
Huize De Roode Catte, Steenhouwersv. 24, 2000 Antwerpen. T. (03) 232 33 38. - Ant -   039099
Ikaros, Steenhouwersvest 45-47, 2000 Antwerpen.
T. (03) 231 54 58.   039100
Ikonencentrum, Geeststr 9, 2000 Antwerpen.
T. (03) 234 17 50.   039101
inerva Harmonie, Harmoniestr. 177a, 2018 Antwerpen.
T. (03) 237 73 97. - Ant -   039102
Jacobs, Charlotte, Kammenstr 67, 2000 Antwerpen.
T. (03) 231 75 27.   039103
Jagersrust, De Keyzerhoeve 16, 2040 Antwerpen.
T. (03) 568 95 18. - Ant -   039104
Jamine, R., Zinkstr. 25, 2000 Antwerpen.
T. (03) 231 80 88. - Ant -   039105
Kailash, Komedieplaats 7-11, 2000 Antwerpen.
T. (03) 231 92 46. - Tex -   039106
Kandelaar, de, Sint-Jorispoortstraat 28, 2000 Antwerpen. T. (03) 231 32 20.   039107
Klavertje, Minderbroedersrui 3, 2000 Antwerpen.
T. (03) 234 25 01. - Ant -   039108
Kumps, L. J., Leopoldstr. 51, 2000 Antwerpen.
T. (03) 233 14 55. - Ant / Paint / Sculp / Tex -   039109
Lady Cant, Welmarkt 25A, 2000 Antwerpen.
T. (03) 232 62 33.   039110
Laet, Francis de, Mechelsesteenweg 81, 2000 Antwerpen. T. (03) 232 77 29. - Jew / Instr -   039111
Leboy, R., Lijnwaadmarkt 20, 2000 Antwerpen.
T. (03) 332 15 90.   039112
Logerij, de, Bleekhofstr 24, 2000 Antwerpen.
T. (03) 233 79 84.   039113
Mabri, Ijzerenwaag 12, 2000 Antwerpen.
T. (03) 231 28 03.   039114
Mahonia, Kasteelpleinstr. 12, 2000 Antwerpen.
T. (03) 216 34 94. - Ant -   039115
Manderley, Lombardenvest 54, 2000 Antwerpen.
T. (03) 233 71 40. - Ant -   039116
Mayfield, Leopoldstr. 47, 2000 Antwerpen.
T. (03) 225 05 52. - Ant -   039117
Meier, B., Grote P. Potstr. 13, 2000 Antwerpen.
T. (03) 232 65 70. - Instr -   039118
Merckx Busselen, Mechelsestw 74, 2018 Antwerpen.
T. (03) 216 97 36.   039119
Mertens, K., Kammenstr. 76, 2000 Antwerpen.
T. (03) 234 21 86. - Ant -   039120
Minerva Harmonie, Harmoniestr 17 a, 2018 Antwerpen.
T. (03) 237 73 97.   039121
Moments, Meir 47, 2000 Antwerpen. T. (03) 233 60 76.
- Ant -   039122

Montebello, Mechelsesteenweg 90, 2018 Antwerpen.
T. (03) 238 50 464. - Ant -   039123
Mot, J. de, Isabellalei 29, 2000 Antwerpen.
T. (03) 230 26 72. - Ant / Furn / Dec / Lights /
Instr -   039124
Mullendorff, Eddy, Leopoldstr. 2-4, 2000 Antwerpen.
T. (03) 231 33 81. - Ant / Furn / Sculp / Tex -   039125
Mullendorff, Eddy, Oude Kerkstr. 28, 2000 Antwerpen.
T. (03) 237 53 81. - Ant / Furn / Mil -   039126
Oude Fortuyne, D', Wolstr 14, 2000 Antwerpen.
T. (03) 233 50 13.   039127
Oude Lamp, de, Schuttershofstr 26, 2000 Antwerpen.
T. (03) 231 97 34.   039128
Pardaf, Gemeentestr 8, 2060 Antwerpen.
T. (03) 232 60 40.   039129
Pascal, Minderbroedersrui 60, 2000 Antwerpen.
T. (03) 231 43 43. - Ant -   039130
Passe Partout, Keizerstr 39, 2000 Antwerpen.
T. (03) 226 17 47.   039131
Past & Present, Schuttershofstr 24, 2000 Antwerpen.
T. (03) 231 26 15.   039132
Phenix 1880-1980, Steenhouwersvest 20, 2000 Antwerpen. T. (03) 231 13 27. - Dec / Jew / Lights / Glass /
Cur / Mod -   039133
Piccolo, Lange Nieuwstr. 4, 2000 Antwerpen.
T. (03) 231 69 21. - Ant -   039134
Poesje, Hoogstr. 58, 2000 Antwerpen. T. (03) 2327363.
- Cur -   039135
Polyedre, Aarschotsestr 26, 2018 Antwerpen.
T. (03) 238 55 01.   039136
Prins van Oranje, Havenmarkt 4, 2040 Antwerpen.
T. (03) 568 66 59.   039137
Proost, C., Melkmarkt 17, 2018 Antwerpen.
T. (03) 232 65 02. - Ant -   039138
Putcuyps, Constant, St. Thomasstraat 31, 2000 Antwerpen. T. (03) 230 82 56. - Ant -   039139
Roode Catte, de, Steenhouwersvest 24, 2000 Antwerpen. T. (03) 232 33 38.   039140
Rueff, Kitty, Mechelsesteenw. 203, 2018 Antwerpen.
T. (03) 230 86 14. - Ant -   039141
Ryckaerts, Erik, Britselei 5, 2000 Antwerpen.
T. (03) 237 13 87. - Ant -   039142
Saritha's Antiques, Mechelsestw 113, 2018 Antwerpen.
T. (03) 281 14 42.   039143
Schuttershofke & Bis, 'T, Schuttershofstr 53, 2000 Antwerpen. T. (03) 235 25 42.   039144
Sels, Dillenstr 21 j, 2018 Antwerpen.
T. (03) 237 44 03.   039145
Shades of the Past, Zirkstr 6, 2000 Antwerpen.
T. (03) 226 23 46.   039146
Show Case, Schuttershofstr. 8, 2000 Antwerpen.
T. (03) 231 25 32. - Ant -   039147
Silberman, Simonstr. 6, 2018 Antwerpen.
T. (03) 232 28 05. - Silv -   039148
Silveren Beer, de, Leeuw v Vlaanderenstr 6, 2000 Antwerpen. T. (03) 226 57 72.   039149
Sluys, S. van, Lange Leemstr. 129, 2018 Antwerpen.
T. (03) 230 65 50. - Ant -   039150
Staf, Kloosterstr. 24, 2000 Antwerpen. T. (03) 231 48 13.
- Ant -   039151
Stevens, de Keyserlei 64, 2000 Antwerpen.
T. (03) 232 18 43. - Num -   039152
Stevens, Vestingstr. 70, 2000 Antwerpen.
T. (03) 232 28 73. - Num -   039153
Stradanus, Belgiëlai 92, 2018 Antwerpen.
T. (03) 218 51 14.   039154
't Woonhuis, Wolstr 43, 2000 Antwerpen.
T. (03) 231 75 35.   039155
Toelen, H., Leopoldstr. 12, 2000 Antwerpen.
T. (03) 232 25 06. - Ant -   039156
Trio, Walter, St Jacobsmarkt 32, 2000 Antwerpen.
T. (03) 232 63 05.   039157
Uniantiek, Drukkerijstr 6, 2000 Antwerpen.
T. (03) 232 64 76.   039158
Van den Broeck-Krämer, Hoogstr. 36, 2000 Antwerpen.
T. (03) 233 55 63. - Ant / Furn / Repr / Fra / Cur - 039159
Verbeeck, P., Wolstr 39, 2000 Antwerpen.
T. (03) 231 36 03.   039160
Verhaegen, L., J van Rijswijckln 25, 2018 Antwerpen.
T. (03) 238 89 37.   039161
Vermeersch, Minderbroedersrui 51, 2000 Antwerpen.
T. (03) 231 48 50.   039162

VG Antiques, Godefriduskaai 50, 2000 Antwerpen.
T. (03) 232 62 33. - Ant -   039163
Viaene, B., Lambermontstr. 12, 2000 Antwerpen.
T. (03) 231 69 21. - Ant / Dec -   039164
Viar, Wolstr 33, 2000 Antwerpen.
T. (03) 231 33 58.   039165
Voiturke, t', Coppenolstr 17, 2000 Antwerpen.
T. (03) 234 17 80.   039166
Voiturke, t', Steenhouwersvest 8, 2000 Antwerpen.
T. (03) 232 38 56.   039167
Waterside Antiques, Sandersstratje 3, 2000 Antwerpen.
T. (03) 226 39 00.   039168
Wijns, Mark, Kloosterstr 72-74, 2000 Antwerpen.
T. (03) 322 35 00.   039169
Zeberg, J., Melkmarkt 37-39, 2000 Antwerpen.
T. (03) 233 82 30. - Ant / Dec / Cur -   039170

Arbre (Hainaut)
Dubois, Léon, rue Mazette 96, 7811 Arbre.
T. (068) 228 40.   039171

Archennes (Brabant Wallon)
Archennes Antiquités, 304 Chaussée de Wavre, 1390
Archennes. T. (010) 840589.   039172
Jacquet, A., 304 Chaussée de Wavre, 1390 Archennes.
T. (010) 840589.   039173

Arendonk (Antwerpen)
Eyckens, Wippelberg 151, 2370 Arendonk.
T. (014) 677600.   039174

Assebroek (West-Vlaanderen)
Fimmers, Baron Rurettelaan 306, 8310 Assebroek.
T. 35 46 22.   039175

Ath (Hainaut)
Baratte, 22 Rue de l'Esplanade, 7800 Ath.
T. (068) 28 35 58/68. - Furn / China / Eth -   039176

Avelgem (West-Vlaanderen)
Grande, R. de, Oudenaardsesteenweg 381, 8580 Avelgem. T. (056) 38 86 89.   039177
Mortier, Yves, Varent 5, 8580 Avelgem.
T. (056) 38 75 91.   039178

Awirs (Liège)
Les Béguines, 34 Rue des Béguines, 4400 Awirs.
T. (041) 75 26 88.   039179

Aye (Luxembourg)
Clinique du Meuble, La, 272 Rue d'Espinthe, 6900 Aye.
T. (084) 31 10 11.   039180
Le Grelle, 272 Rue d'Espinthe, 6900 Aye.
T. (084) 31 10 11.   039181

Aywaille (Liège)
Defosse, J. P., 29a Rue Nicolas-Lambercy, 4920 Aywaille. T. (041) 84 50 52.   039182
La Brocante, av L Libert 18, 4920 Aywaille.
T. (041) 72 42 32.   039183

Baal (Vlaams Brabant)
Van de Velde-Borremans, Langestr 26, 3128 Baal.
T. (015) 23 62 02.   039184

Balegem (Oost Vlaanderen)
Devos, E., Bierman 7, 9860 Balegem.   039185

Balen (Antwerpen)
Ble, D. de, Steegstr 38, 2490 Balen.
T. (014) 81 28 45.   039186
Geuens, F., Vaarstr 162, 2490 Balen.
T. (014) 81 51 00.   039187
Heymans, Wezelln 16, 2490 Balen.
T. (014) 81 40 23.   039188

Basècles (Hainaut)
Serriez, C., rue Grande 45, 7971 Basècles.
T. (069) 7 66 48.   039189

Battice (Liège)
Lejeune, H., 11, rte d'Aubel, 4651 Battice.
T. (087) 6 60 13.   039190

Bavikhove (West-Vlaaderen)
Vanhoutte, Rijksweg 32b, 8531 Bavikhove.
T. (056) 71 04 41.   039191

Bazel (Oost-Vlaanderen)
Brocant Antiquairs, Kruibekestraat 102, 9150 Bazel.
T. (030) 742382.   *039192*
Pien, Dany, Rupelmondestraat 66, 9150 Bazel.   *039193*

Beersel (Vlaams Brabant)
A la Fermette, 313, Ch. d'Uccle, 1650 Beersel.
T. (02) 762355. - Ant / Furn -   *039194*

Beerzel (Antwerpen)
Heikant, Aarschotsebn 1, 2580 Beerzel.
T. (015) 51 60 30.   *039195*

Begijnendijk (Vlaams Brabant)
Old Pine Shop, Liersestr 231, 3130 Begijnendijk.
T. (016) 567767.   *039196*

Bekkevoort (Vlaams Brabant)
Koetshof, 't, Staatsbaan 44, 3460 Bekkevoort.
T. (016) 333635.   *039197*

Bellingen ((Vlaams Brabant)
Herman, Trapstr 19, 1674 Bellingen.
T. (02) 356 50 39.   *039198*

Belsele (Oost-Vlaanderen)
Renaissance, Nieuwebn 108, 9111 Belsele.
T. (031) 772 54 72.   *039199*

Ben-Ahin (Liège)
A la Brocante, 9 Chaussée d'Andenne, 4500 Ben-Ahin.
T. (085) 22 18 75.   *039200*
Bellens, G., 9 Chaussée d'Andenne, 4500 Ben-Ahin.
T. (085) 22 18 75.   *039201*
Lombat, 45 Av de Beaufort, 4500 Ben-Ahin.
T. (085) 21 63 35.   *039202*
Lombat, 95, Ben Lovegnée, 4500 Ben-Ahin.
T. (085) 163 35. - Ant / Dec -   *039203*

Berchem (Antwerpen)
Antique Shop, Elisabethlaan 204, 2600 Berchem.
T. (03) 55 43 58.   *039204*
Ars Antiqua, Lange Markstraat 25, 2600
Berchem.   *039205*
Ceuleneer, Herman de, Pretorjastr 38, 2600 Berchem.
T. (03) 235 98 83.   *039206*
Fraulahofje, T', Berchembosln 9, 2600 Berchem.
T. (03) 230 60 12.   *039207*
Granny's Old Fashion, Diksmuideln 45, 2600 Berchem.
T. (03) 230 35 70.   *039208*
Hellemont, J. van, Elisabethlaan 204, 2600 Berchem.
T. (03) 55 43 58.   *039209*
Lemmens, Jozef, Grote Steenweg 3, 2600 Berchem.
T. (03) 230 67 01   *039210*
Selections-Collections, Fruithoflaan 25, 2600 Berchem.
T. (03) 440 29 54. - Orient -   *039211*

Berlaar, Lier (Antwerpen)
Gysemans, J. & Co., Aarschotsebn 79-81, 2590 Berlaar,
Lier. T. (03) 015/24 14 71.   *039212*

Berlare (Oost-Vlaanderen)
Antiek-Retro, Hertecantln 15 E, 9290 Berlare.
T. (052) 422326.   *039213*
Roels-van de Velde, Lindestr 96, 9290 Berlare.
T. (052) 676471.   *039214*

Berloz (Liège)
Ferronnerie d'Arts, Château de Berlo, 4257 Berloz.
T. (019) 32 23 11.   *039215*

Bertem (Vlaams Brabant)
Eijkenboom, Richard, Tervuursesteenweg 183, 3060
Bertem. T. (016) 48 93 97. - Paint / Furn -   *039216*

Beveren (Oost-Vlaanderen)
Antika, Lange Dreef 2-4, 9120 Beveren.
T. (031) 7757518.   *039217*
Halewijck, A. van, Gravendr 40, 9120 Beveren.
T. (031) 757518.   *039218*
Jet Je Galerij, Spijkerln 104, 8791 Beveren.
T. (056) 704180.   *039219*
van Steenbergen-van de Voorde, Kallobn 57, 9120 Be-
veren. T. (031) 754587.   *039220*
Thijs, André, Irisstraat 19, 9120 Beveren.
T. (031) 756155.   *039221*

Vyver, van de, Bosdamlaan 5, 9120 Beveren.
T. (031) 757059.   *039222*

Bierbeek (Vlaams Brabant)
Beveren, van, Herpendalstr 3, 3360 Bierbeek.
T. (016) 460662.   *039223*
Lucas, Zwartehoekstr 24, 3360 Bierbeek.
T. (016) 463864.   *039224*

Bilzen (Limburg)
Herckenrode, Leten 27, 3740 Bilzen.
T. (011) 41 12 79.   *039225*

Blankenberge (West-Vlaanderen)
Packo, de Meyerstr 60, 8370 Blankenberge.
T. (050) 412259.   *039226*

Boechout (Antwerpen)
Van den Bergh, Provinciestr 556, 2530 Boechout.
T. (031) 4551668.   *039227*

Boekhoute (Oost-Vlaanderen)
Steyaert, Vliet 29, 9961 Boekhoute.
T. (091) 73 70 14.   *039228*

Boezinge (West-Vlaanderen)
Bervoet, G., General Lotzstr 1, 8904 Boezinge.
T. (057) 42 22 51.   *039229*
Oud Luzerne, 'T, General Lotzstr 1, 8904 Boezinge.
T. (057) 42 22 51.   *039230*

Boom (Antwerpen)
Ter Linden, Antwerpsestr 120, 2850 Boom.
T. (03) 844 52 42.   *039231*

Boortmeerbeek (Vlaams Brabant)
Waterschoot, Weerstandsstr 5, 3190 Boortmeerbeek.
T. (015) 512381.   *039232*

Borgerhout (Antwerpen)
Historia, Gitschotellaan 258, 2140 Borgerhout.
T. (031) 36 90 01.   *039233*

Bovesse (Namur)
Le Manoir, R. N. 4, 5081 Bovesse. T. (081) 363 52.
- Ant / Cur -   *039234*
Manoir, Le, Ancienne Rte Bruxelles-Namur, 5081 Bo-
vesse. T. (081) 56 63 52.   *039235*

Braine-l'Alleud (Brabant Wallon)
Antik Shop, 37 Rue Jules Hans, 1420 Braine-l'Alleud.
T. (02) 3846382.   *039236*

Braine-le-Château (Brabant Wallon)
Rzoska, Theresa, Vieux Chemin de Nivelles 120, 1440
Braine-le-Château. T. (02) 3660426.   *039237*

Brasschaat (Antwerpen)
Bouten, Jan, Bredabn 778, 2930 Brasschaat.
T. (031) 663 33 73.   *039238*
Ottow, J. B., Guyotdreef 29, 2930 Brasschaat.
T. (031) 63 15 45.   *039239*

Bree (Limburg)
Javada, Opitterkiezel 45, 3960 Bree.
T. (011) 46 16 24.   *039240*
Witte Engel, Gruitroderkiezel 74, 3960 Bree.
T. (011) 47 38 52.   *039241*

Breendonk (Antwerpen)
Bogaerts, E., Veurtstr 8, 2870 Breendonk.
T. (031) 886 99 78.   *039242*

Broechem (Antwerpen)
Genbrugge, J., Broechemhof, 2520 Broechem.
T. (03) 485 54 71.   *039243*

Brugge (West-Vlaanderen)
Abeele, Pierre van den, Katelijnstr 78, 8000 Brugge.
T. (050) 33 10 25.   *039244*
Angie's Antiques, Grauwwerkersstr 7, 8000 Brugge.
T. (050) 33 72 72.   *039245*
Antiek Apoteek, Ezelstr 68, 8000 Brugge.
T. (050) 34 42 56.   *039246*
Antiekkart, Dudzelesteenweg 64, 8000 Brugge.
T. (050) 33 18 86.   *039247*

Antique & African Art, Ezelstr 139, 8000 Brugge.
T. (050) 34 51 46.   *039248*
Beernaert, St. Salvatorkerkhof 13, 8000 Brugge.
T. (050) 33 56 76. - Ant -   *039249*
Blondeel de Troyer, Gentpoortstr 22, 8000
Brugge.   *039250*
Blondeel., L., Ezelstraat 2, 8000 Brugge. T. (050) 381 04.
- Ant / Cur -   *039251*
Bonte, Werfstr 9, 8000 Brugge.
T. (050) 33 66 00.   *039252*
Broes, Koen, Simon Stevingpl. 12, 8000 Brugge.
T. (050) 33 37 74. - Graph / China / Dec / Jew /
Fra -   *039253*
Brugs Antiekhuis, Hoogstr 27, 8000 Brugge.
T. (050) 33 14 50.   *039254*
Buonarotti, Michelangelo, Predikherenstr 19, 8000
Brugge. T. (050) 33 76 32, Fax 33 68 86.   *039255*
Cantaert, A., Ezelstr 117, 8000 Brugge.
T. (050) 33 72 94.   *039256*
Cantaert, J., Wollestr. 43, 8000 Brugge.
T. (050) 33 59 73. - Ant -   *039257*
Casimirs Collectors Carousel, Markt 7, 8000 Brugge.
T. (050) 34 54 84.   *039258*
Charadan, St.-Anna-Rei 23, 8000 Brugge.
T. (050) 33 66 71. - Paint / Furn / Sculp / Tex /
Instr -   *039259*
Claeys, E., Katelijnestr 48, 8000 Brugge.
T. (050) 33 98 19.   *039260*
Classics, Oude Burg 32-34, 8000 Brugge.
T. (050) 33 90 58. - Ant / Paint / Cur / Ico -   *039261*
Dag & Zonne, Langestr 3, 8000 Brugge.
T. (050) 33 02 93.   *039262*
Depoorter, G., Carmerstr 128, 8000 Brugge.
T. (050) 33 88 83.   *039263*
Despinde, Wijngaardstr 12, 8000 Brugge.
T. (050) 33 25 51.   *039264*
Dewulf, Koning Albertlaan 162, 8000 Brugge.
T. (050) 32 03 28.   *039265*
Fimmers, Anne-Marie, St-Salvator 18-19 Kerkhofstr,
8000 Brugge. T. (050) 34 20 25.   *039266*
Frou-Frou, Wapenmakerstr 9, 8000 Brugge.   *039267*
Galerie Carrousel, Kuiperstr 25, 8000 Brugge.   *039268*
Galerij Ter Gentpoort, Gentspoortstr 6, 8000 Brugge.
T. (050) 33 22 07.   *039269*
Garnier, Korte Zilverstraat 8, 8000 Brugge.
T. (050) 33 01 95. - Ant / Paint / Furn / China /
Ico -   *039270*
Hoorebeke, G. van, Boomgaardstr. 7, 8000 Brugge.
T. (050) 33 35 07. - Graph -   *039271*
Jacquart, Goezeputstr 31, 8000 Brugge.
T. (050) 33 44 12.   *039272*
Kunst en Antiek, Oostendsestw 69, 8000 Brugge.
T. (050) 31 75 34.   *039273*
Lebbe, V., Gistelstw 30, 8200 Brugge.
T. (050) 31 63 01.   *039274*
Lijsterhof, T', Maalsestw 525, 8000 Brugge.
T. (050) 36 22 24.   *039275*
Mahieu, R., Oostendsestw 13, 8000 Brugge.
T. (050) 31 40 66.   *039276*
Mary, St.-Amandstraat 20, 8000 Brugge.
T. (050) 33 96 90. - Ant / Cur -   *039277*
Meire, J.M., St. Salvators Kerkhof 9, 8000 Brugge.
T. (050) 33 68 40, Fax 34 51 07. - Ant -   *039278*
Michot, Marc, Groene Rei 3, 8000 Brugge.
T. (050) 33 97 20. - Orient / China -   *039279*
Moust, J., Mariastr 15, 8000 Brugge.
T. (050) 34 44 35.   *039280*
Mullem, Jan van, Vlamingstr 52, 8000 Brugge.
T. (050) 33 05 94, 33 41 41.   *039281*
Old Fashion, Oostendsestw 20, 8000 Brugge.
T. (050) 31 60 07.   *039282*
Pandje, 'T, St Jacobstr 55, 8000 Brugge.
T. (050) 33 47 92.   *039283*
Papyrus Antiques, Walpln 41, 8000 Brugge.
T. (050) 33 66 87.   *039284*
Prové, W., Hogeweg 8, 8000 Brugge.
T. (050) 31 04 76.   *039285*
Reynaert, Vlamingstr. 26, 8000 Brugge.
T. (050) 33 30 10. - China / Glass -   *039286*
Schelfhout, J.M., St Salvatorskerkhof 16, 8000 Brugge.
T. (050) 33 09 14.   *039287*
Schollin, St Katelijnstr 52, 8000 Brugge.
T. (050) 33 04 72.   *039288*

St.-Georges Antiques, Oostendsestw 36, 8000 Brugge.
T. (050) 31 78 79. 039289
Standaert, André, Witte Leertouwersstr 48, 8000 Brugge. T. (050) 33 27 32. 039290
Traen, J.P., St-Amandstraat 37, 8000 Brugge.
T. (050) 33 49 24. 039291
Tudor Antiques, Oostendesteenweg 45, 8000 Brugge.
T. (050) 31 21 40. - Ant / Furn / China - 039292
Van Meenen, L. & J., Dudzelestw 64, 8000 Brugge.
T. (050) 33 18 86. 039293
Vandenbulcke, Katelijnestr 47, 8000 Brugge.
T. (050) 34 51 53. 039294
Vanderoost, Eddy, Oude Gentweg 60, 8000 Brugge.
T. (050) 33 34 93. - Furn - 039295
Verschave, Birgit, St Annakerkstr 8, 8000 Brugge.
T. (050) 33 06 92. 039296
Vlaminck-Fagneray, St Katelijnstr 98, 8000 Brugge.
T. (050) 33 52 62. 039297
Wiele, M. van de, Jakobünessenstr 5, 8000 Brugge.
T. (050) 33 38 05. 039298
Witte Huis, Gistelsteenweg 30, 8200 Brugge.
T. (050) 32 33 01. 039299

Brustem (Limburg)

Castermans, N., Luikerstr 237, 3800 Brustem.
T. (011) 681408. 039300
Goevaerts, Vliegveldln 2, 3800 Brustem.
T. (011) 689862. 039301

Bruxelles

AA 1900, 13 Rue C Hanssens, 1000 Bruxelles.
T. (02) 502 07 66. 039302
A.B.C. Antiquité, 31 Av E De Molder, 1030 Bruxelles.
T. (02) 241 92 64. 039303
Ahel & Armand, 81 Av du Couronnement, 1200 Bruxelles. T. (02) 733 75 45. 039304
Adauby-Van der Schueren, 14 Rue de la Bourse, 1000 Bruxelles. T. (02) 513 34 00. - Ant - 039305
Adel, A., 54c Rue Dethy, 1060 Bruxelles.
T. (02) 537 62 55. - Ant - 039306
Adelma, 103 Rue P. Baucq, 1040 Bruxelles.
T. (02) 647 49 06. - Ant - 039307
Adriaensens, 127 Av. Rogier, 1030 Bruxelles.
T. (02) 215 10 34. - Ant - 039308
African Art Investment, 19 Rue des Minimes, 1000 Bruxelles. T. (02) 511 16 62. 039309
Al Farahnick, 88 Rue de Namur, 1000 Bruxelles.
T. (02) 511 33 63. - Furn / China / Tex - 039310
Alcazar-Antiques, 393 Ch de Gand, 1080 Bruxelles.
T. (02) 465 91 06. 039311
Alexandre de Leye, 16 Rue Lebeau, 1000 Bruxelles.
T. (02) 514 34 77. 039312
Amandine, 36 Rue J. Stallaert, 1180 Bruxelles.
T. (02) 347 16 59. - Ant - 039313
Amaryllis, 67 Rue Lebeau, 1000 Bruxelles.
T. (02) 512 19 94. - Ant / Cur - 039314
Ambroise, 199 Av du Diamant, 1030 Bruxelles.
T. (02) 735 64 55. - Ant - 039315
Ancart, Philippe, 36 Pl. du Grand Sablon, 1000 Bruxelles. T. (02) 512 20 00. - Ant - 039316
Années 50, 28 Rue de la Régence, 1000 Bruxelles.
T. (02) 512 85 47. - Ant - 039317
Antbrocart, 223 Rue L. Théodor, 1090 Bruxelles.
T. (02) 426 57 95, 731 98 76. - Furn - 039318
Antica, 36 Pl du Grand Sablon, 1000 Bruxelles.
T. (02) 511 34 44. 039319
Antique Elysee, 229-231 Chaussée d'Ixelles, 1050 Bruxelles. T. (02) 647 92 15. - Ant - 039320
Antiques & Design, 6 Pl de la Chapelle, 1000 Bruxelles.
T. (02) 511 86 85. 039321
Antiquidées, 954 Ch de Mons, 1070 Bruxelles.
T. (02) 520 08 89. 039322
Antiquus, 19 Rue Watteeu, 1000 Bruxelles.
T. (02) 514 41 25. - Ant - 039323
Antoine, Michel, 132 Av. de l'Hippodrome, 1050 Bruxelles. T. (02) 649 65 34. - Ant - 039324
Apostrophe, 34 Rue Gén Leman, 1040 Bruxelles.
T. (02) 230 84 82. 039325
Archeologia, 36 Pl. du Grand Sablon, 1000 Bruxelles.
T. (02) 511 15 01. - Paint - 039326
Argus, 45 Pl. du Grand Sablon, 1000 Bruxelles.
T. (02) 511 28 35. - Ant / Cur - 039327

Ars Islamica, 9 Rue Blaes, 1000 Bruxelles.
T. (02) 512 80 60. 039328
Art' Co, Reebokstr 20, 1000 Bruxelles.
T. (02) 512 26 96. 039329
Art Deco, 60-62 Rue Simonis, 1050 Bruxelles.
T. (02) 647 32 71. - Ant - 039330
Art Deco, 49 Rue Lebeau, 1000 Bruxelles.
T. (02) 511 85 23. - Ant - 039331
Art Deco – Art Nouveau, 22 Rue E Allard, 1000 Bruxelles. T. (02) 511 48 94. 039332
Art et Collection, 102 Dr du Duc, 1170 Bruxelles.
T. (02) 660 82 41, 660 83 44. 039333
Art Gallery, 14 Rue Lebeau, 1000 Bruxelles.
T. (02) 513 32 76. - Ant - 039334
Arta-Mangon, 38 Rue Joseph Stevens, 1000 Bruxelles.
T. (02) 511 86 77. - Ant - 039335
Artcade, 81 Av. Lancaster, 1180 Bruxelles.
T. (02) 375 38 41. - Orient - 039336
Artcasting, 247 Av. des Sept. Bonniers, 1190 Bruxelles.
T. (02) 345 37 24. - Ant - 039337
Artimo, 33 Rue Lebeau, 1000 Bruxelles.
T. (02) 512 62 42. - Ant / Mod - 039338
Artisan, 111 Rue du Marché aux Herbes, 1000 Bruxelles. T. (02) 513 46 17. 039339
Arts Anciens, 6 Rue Van Moer, 1000 Bruxelles.
T. (02) 512 14 33. - Ant - 039340
Arts Anciens d'Asie, 88 Rue de Namur, 1000 Bruxelles.
T. (02) 511 33 63. - Ant - 039341
Arts Décoratifs, Les, 49 Rue Lebeau, 1000 Bruxelles.
T. (02) 672 03 32. 039342
Artus S.A. Philippe Denys, 1 Rue des Sablons, 1000 Bruxelles. T. (02) 5123607, Fax (02) 5022567. - Ant / Furn / Sculp / Silv / Mod - 039343
Asie-Afrique, 236 Av Molière, 1050 Bruxelles.
T. (02) 343 24 11. - Orient / Arch / Eth - 039344
Asselman, M., 45 Rue de Rollebeek, 1000 Bruxelles.
T. (02) 511 61 33. 039345
Athena, 11 Rue de la Régence, 1000 Bruxelles.
T. (02) 512 60 33. - Ant - 039346
Atkins, Christopher J. G., 170a Chaussée de Charleroi, 1060 Bruxelles. T. (02) 537 29 28. 039347
Atmosphère, 17 Rue de Rollebeek, 1000 Bruxelles.
T. (02) 513 11 10. 039348
Au Clair de la Lune, 5 Av. d'Oppem, 1150 Bruxelles.
T. (02) 731 33 37. - Ant - 039349
Au petit Rouet, 11 Pl du Petit Sablon, 1000 Bruxelles.
T. (02) 511 49 95. 039350
Autogarden, 20 Rue E. Allard, 1000 Bruxelles.
T. (02) 512 06 58. - Ant - 039351
Bailly, Le, 63 Rue du Bailli, 1050 Bruxelles.
T. (02) 538 70 58. - Ant - 039352
Baldi, L., 112 Tenbosch, 1050 Bruxelles.
T. (02) 344 38 94. 039353
Balloche Brocante, 279 Rue au Bois, 1150 Bruxelles.
T. (02) 762 89 53. - Ant - 039354
Beaufaux, R., 113bis Av de Tervuren, 1040 Bruxelles.
T. (02) 733 34 38. - Ant / Jew / Silv / Mod - 039355
Beaujeu, Anne de, 7 Rue des Sablons, 1000 Bruxelles.
T. (02) 513 56 77. 039356
Becker, Bernard, 482 Ch de Boondael, 1050 Bruxelles.
T. (02) 649 85 93. 039357
Belles Choses, Les, 79 Av. de la Couronne, 1050 Bruxelles. T. (02) 641 91 15. - Furn - 039358
Berbe, M., 39 Rue E. Allard, 1000 Bruxelles.
T. (02) 514 07 43. - Ant - 039359
Berko, 36 Pl du Sablon, 1000 Bruxelles.
T. (02) 511 15 76. 039360
Berkovitch, Marcel, 61 Rue J Lebeau, 1000 Bruxelles.
T. (02) 511 78 95, 358 26 93. 039361
Berkowitsch, S., 7 Rue Lebeau, 1000 Bruxelles.
T. (02) 513 34 87. 039362
Bermann, 82 Rue de l'Arbre Bénit, 1050 Bruxelles.
T. (02) 511 58 88. 039363
Bienaimé, 24 Rue d'Albanie, 1060 Bruxelles.
T. (02) 537 82 04. - Ant - 039364
Blom, S., 38 Rue Ste-Anne, 1000 Bruxelles.
T. (02) 513 75 40. 039365
Bolens, R., 57 Rue Lebeau, 1000 Bruxelles.
T. (02) 511 83 44. - Furn - 039366
Bonheur-du-Jour, Le, 21 Rue des Bollandistes, 1040 Bruxelles. T. (02) 734 23 34. 039367
Borguet, M.-T., 6 Av J-B Depaire, 1020 Bruxelles.
T. (02) 479 77 90. 039368

Boskovitch, 13 Rue Ravenstein, 1000 Bruxelles.
T. (02) 513 01 74. 039369
Braam, 30 Rue A Renard, 1050 Bruxelles.
T. (02) 343 63 77. 039370
Brabant, van, 393 Chaussée de Gand, 1080 Bruxelles.
T. (02) 427 01 77. - Ant / Furn - 039371
Braibant, A., 1a Rue de Livourne, 1060 Bruxelles.
T. (02) 538 08 29. 039372
Brico, Georges, 22 Rue P Hankar, 1180 Bruxelles.
T. (02) 375 81 39. 039373
Brocante & Cie., 5-7 Rue des Coteaux, 1210 Bruxelles.
- Ant - 039374
Brocanteurs Y & B, Les, 13 Rue Verbist, 1210 Bruxelles.
T. (02) 218 08 05. 039375
Bronsin, M., 4 Impasse St Jacques, 1000 Bruxelles.
T. (02) 512 41 34. 039376
Brouwer, W., 35 Rue J Stevens, 1000 Bruxelles.
T. (02) 512 71 86. 039377
Brueker, D. de, 3 Rue du Quesnoy, 1000 Bruxelles.
T. (02) 514 25 41. 039378
Buchanan Antiks, 127a Rue Blaes, 1000 Bruxelles.
T. (02) 513 96 13. 039379
Buchet, 166 Av de la Reine, 1000 Bruxelles.
T. (02) 242 63 05. 039380
Calou, 1333 Chaussée de Waterloo, 1180 Bruxelles.
T. (02) 375 15 44. - Ant - 039381
Camby, M. de Mérode, 1060 Bruxelles.
T. (02) 538 76 40. - Furn - 039382
Canivet, J., 318 Av de Jette, 1090 Bruxelles.
T. (02) 425 05 35. 039383
Cardenas, J., 26-28 Rue Minimes, 1000 Bruxelles.
T. (02) 512 41 92. 039384
Carrez, 18 Rue de Lausanne, 1060 Bruxelles.
T. (02) 538 30 98. 039385
Carton & Taquin, 27 Rue Ducale, 1000 Bruxelles.
T. (02) 513 58 31. 039386
Cassandre, 40 Rue du Châtelain, 1050 Bruxelles.
T. (02) 647 48 80. 039387
Cento, Anni, 31 Pl Grand Sablon, 1000 Bruxelles.
T. (02) 512 53 07, 514 56 33. 039388
Centre du Meuble en Pin, 492 Chaussée de Waterloo, 1050 Bruxelles. T. (02) 538 53 12. 039389
Chamarande, 67 Rue de l'Abbaye, 1050 Bruxelles.
T. (02) 640 42 56/24, Fax 640 42 56. - Jew - 039390
Chandelier, Le, 146 Rue Blaes, 1000 Bruxelles.
T. (02) 512 95 01, 521 05 87. 039391
Changy, M. de, 24 Galerie de la Reine, 1000 Bruxelles.
T. (02) 512 49 93. 039392
Cherche Midi, Au, 16 Rue Ernest-Allard, 1000 Bruxelles.
T. (02) 511 26 08. - Ant / Furn / Lights / Glass / Cur - 039393
Cheverny, 260 Chaussée d'Ixelles, 1050 Bruxelles.
T. (02) 647 67 32. - Ant - 039394
Chez Jean, 21 Ch. de Mons, 1070 Bruxelles.
T. (02) 523 14 06. - Furn - 039395
China Products, 50 Rue des Pierres, 1000 Bruxelles.
T. (02) 513 34 34. - Orient - 039396
Chineur, Yves le, 23 Rue des Minimes, 1000 Bruxelles.
T. (02) 375 03 31. - Ant - 039397
Chintz Shop, 48 Pl du Grand Sablon, 1000 Bruxelles.
T. (02) 513 58 96. 039398
Clarebots, 58 Rue St. Georges, 1050 Bruxelles.
T. (02) 649 58 59. - Ant - 039399
Claude, D., 71 rue Hôtel des Monnaies, 1090 Bruxelles.
T. (02) 537 20 42. - Ant - 039400
Close, Monique, 36 Pl du Grand Sablon, 1000 Bruxelles.
T. (02) 511 16 04. - Furn - 039401
Coffre à Surprises, Le, 548 Rue Vanderkindere, 1180 Bruxelles. T. (02) 344 99 36. 039402
Collem Antique, 26-28 Rue de la Régence, 1000 Bruxelles. T. (02) 511 10 94. - Furn / China / Cur - 039403
Comptoir du Meuble Ancien, 417 Chaussée de Boondael, 1050 Bruxelles. T. (02) 649 16 61.
- Furn - 039404
Contacts, 39 Rue de Rollebeek, 1000 Bruxelles.
T. (02) 511 28 23. - Ant - 039405
Coromandel, 43 Rue de l'Agrafe, 1070 Bruxelles.
T. (02) 521 59 71. 039406
Coster, J. de, 2 Rue Van Moer, 1000 Bruxelles.
T. (02) 512 12 83. - Ant - 039407
Coster, R. de, 525b Chaussée de Waterloo, 1050 Bruxelles. T. (02) 345 68 11. 039408

Costermans, 5 Pl. du Grand Sablon, 1000 Bruxelles.
T. (02) 512 2133. - Ant / Dec - *039409*

Couturier, P., 52 Av VJ Bertraux, 1070 Bruxelles.
T. (02) 524 23 36. *039410*

Crazy Antiques, 152 Rue Blaes, 1000 Bruxelles.
T. (02) 514 27 82. - Ant / Furn - *039411*

Crescendo, 10 Rue Coppens, 1000 Bruxelles.
T. (02) 514 06 96. *039412*

Croës, Gisèle, 54 Blvd. de Waterloo, 1000 Bruxelles.
T. (02) 511 82 16, Fax 514 04 19. - Paint / Orient /
Sculp - *039413*

Crott, H., 40 Rue de Witte, 1050 Bruxelles.
T. (02) 648 69 47. *039414*

Curiosities, 176 Rue Américaine, 1050 Bruxelles.
T. (02) 648 85 88. *039415*

Cuyper, A. de, 13 Rue Lebeau, 1000 Bruxelles.
T. (02) 513 00 89. *039416*

Cyrus, 19 Rue Van Moer, 1000 Bruxelles.
T. (02) 511 29 21. - Ant / Paint / Graph / China /
Sculp - *039417*

Dartevelle, P., 7-8 Impasse Saint-Jacques, 1000 Bruxelles. T. (02) 513 01 75. *039418*

Decharneux, B., 11 Av de Septembre, 1200 Bruxelles.
T. (02) 762 09 43. *039419*

Dehareng, C, 548 Rue Vanderkindere, 1180 Bruxelles.
T. (02) 344 99 36. - Ant - *039420*

Dekens, L., 155 Rue de Linthout, 1200 Bruxelles.
T. (02) 734 59 69. *039421*

Delbosse, 12 Av Nouvelle, 1040 Bruxelles.
T. (02) 640 81 66. *039422*

Delbosse, J.P., 47 Rue Berckmans, 1060 Bruxelles.
T. (02) 539 13 80. *039423*

Deletaille, Emile, 12 Rue Watteeu, 1000 Bruxelles.
T. (02) 512 97 73. - Ant / Orient / Sculp / Arch / Eth /
Cur - *039424*

Delftenco, 11 Rue Lebeau, 1000 Bruxelles.
T. (02) 513 26 49. - Ant - *039425*

Dell'Ale, 84 Chaussée de Wavre, 1050 Bruxelles.
T. (02) 512 23 34. - Ant - *039426*

Delmonte, Albert, 4, Ave. Jette, 1080 Bruxelles.
T. (02) 426 32 35. - Num - *039427*

Demesmaeker, M., 6 Rue du Tabellion, 1150 Bruxelles.
T. (02) 538 69 05. *039428*

Demeter, J., Jaargetijdenln. 14, 1050 Bruxelles.
T. (02) 647 37 67. - Ant - *039429*

Dépozerie, La, 52 Rue du Bailli, 1050 Bruxelles.
T. (02) 648 20 01. *039430*

Descamps, Patrick, 26 Blvd de Waterloo, 1000 Bruxelles. T. (02) 511 94 82. *039431*

Dewindt, 77-79 Rue Lebeau, 1000 Bruxelles.
T. (02) 513 36 12. - Glass / Mod - *039432*

Dieleman, Paule, 11-13 Rue L Lepage, 1000 Bruxelles.
T. (02) 511 91 27. *039433*

Dierickx, 161 Chaussée de Charleroi, 1060 Bruxelles.
T. (02) 5376984. - Paint / Sculp / Eth / Cur - *039434*

Dix-Neuvième, Le, 144 rue Gerard, 1040 Bruxelles.
T. (02) 734 95 82. *039435*

Dubois, M., 61 Av d'Auderghelm, 1040 Bruxelles.
T. (02) 230 40 00. *039436*

Ecuyer, 187-189 Av Louise, 1050 Bruxelles.
T. (02) 6473544. - Ant / Paint / Furn / Sculp /
Cur - *039437*

Eden, P., 177 Av. Pr. Héritier, 1200 Bruxelles.
T. (02) 733 05 93. - Ant - *039438*

Egide, L', 23 Rue du Lombard, 1000 Bruxelles.
T. (02) 502 04 93. *039439*

Elsen, Jean, 65 Av de Tervuren, 1040 Bruxelles.
T. (02) 734 63 56, Fax 735 77 78. - Num - *039440*

En Verre et Contre Tout, 66 Pl du Jeu de Balle, 1000
Bruxelles. T. (02) 502 10 98. *039441*

English Galleries, 166 Chaussée de Charleroi, 1060 Bruxelles. T. (02) 537 29 28. - Ant - *039442*

Epoque Dorée, L', 137 Av de la Couronne, 1050 Bruxelles. T. (02) 647 73 79. *039443*

Escarpolette, L', 28 Rue de Rollebeek, 1000 Bruxelles.
T. (02) 512 77 50. *039444*

Ethnographie des 5 Continents, 28 Rue de Rollebeek,
1000 Bruxelles. T. (02) 513 72 34. *039445*

Eureka, Galerie du Cinquantenaire 6A, 1040 Bruxelles.
T. (02) 736 50 16. *039446*

Everard de Harzir, 133 Tenbosch, 1050 Bruxelles.
T. (02) 538 44 42. *039447*

Eynde, G. van den, 35 Rue J. Stevens, 1000 Bruxelles.
T. (02) 511 97 01. - Ant - *039448*

Fanneau de Lahorie, 48 rue Nothomb, 1040 Bruxelles.
T. (02) 640 94 13. - Ant - *039449*

Ferreira, M., 13 Rue Van Elewyck, 1050 Bruxelles.
T. (02) 646 56 41. *039450*

Fety, Françoise, 32 Rue des Chapeliers, 1000 Bruxelles.
T. (02) 512 18 82. *039451*

Fil du Temps, Au, 7 Rue Lebeau, 1000 Bruxelles.
T. (02) 513 34 87. *039452*

Finck, Alex, 20 rue Ernest Gossart, 1180 Bruxelles.
T. (02) 344 66 22. - Paint - *039453*

Fins de Siècle, 36 R Vieux Marché aux Grains, 1000 Bruxelles. T. (02) 502 11 33. *039454*

Flanders Art Gallery, 36 Rue du Grand Sablon, 1000 Bruxelles. T. (02) 511 00 76. *039455*

Formanoir, Y.L. de, 3 Impasse Saint-Jacques, 1000 Bruxelles. T. (02) 512 08 18. - Ant / Furn - *039456*

Fouineur, 89 Rue du Marché aux Charbons, 1000 Bruxelles. - Ant - *039457*

Franceschi, B., 10, rue Croix de Fer, 1000 Bruxelles.
T. (02) 217 93 95. - Num - *039458*

Fringues & Puces, 98 Rue de Flandre, 1000 Bruxelles.
T. (02) 512 13 58. *039459*

Futur Anterieur, 19 Pl. du Grand Sablon, 1000 Bruxelles.
T. (02) 511 41 72, 512 72 65. - Ant - *039460*

Galerie André, 13 Pl de Londres, 1050 Bruxelles.
T. (02) 513 11 79. *039461*

Galerie Blaes 83, 83-87 Rue Blaes, 1000 Bruxelles.
T. (02) 242 30 75, 513 38 62. - Ant - *039462*

Galerie Brusilia, 33 Rue Herman, 1030 Bruxelles.
T. (02) 215 27 86. *039463*

Galerie Charlemagne, 1166 Chaussée de Waterloo,
1180 Bruxelles. T. (02) 374 7228. - Ant / Paint / Graph /
Furn / China / Jew / Mil - *039464*

Galerie d'Arenberg, 14 Rue aux Laines, 1000 Bruxelles.
T. (02) 512 35 03, Fax 514 53 26. - Sculp - *039465*

Galerie de Poche, 38 Rue E Allard, 1000 Bruxelles.
T. (02) 514 40 05. *039466*

Galerie des Minimes, 23 Rue des Minimes, 1000 Bruxelles. T. (02) 511 28 25. *039467*

Galerie du Pavillon, 60 Rue du Pavillon, 1030 Bruxelles.
T. (02) 241 59 15. *039468*

Galerie du Trône, 168 Rue du Trône, 1050 Bruxelles.
T. (02) 649 49 38. *039469*

Galerie Empire, 8 Pl. du Grand Sablon, 1000 Bruxelles.
T. (02) 512 10 52. - Ant - *039470*

Galerie Jamyro, 59 Rue de Florence, 1060 Bruxelles.
T. (02) 538 42 78. *039471*

Galerie Lampens, 9 Pl de Grand Sablon, 1000 Bruxelles.
T. (02) 512 57 76. *039472*

Galerie Mercure, 426 Av. G. Henrl, 1200 Bruxelles.
T. (02) 736 36 19. - Ant - *039473*

Galerie Nova, 35 Rue du Pépin, 1000 Bruxelles.
T. (02) 512 24 94, 512 32 39, Fax 511 35 35. - Ant /
Paint / Furn / Num / Tex / Silv - *039474*

Galerie Saint-Antoine, 52 Rue Ransfort, 1080 Bruxelles.
T. (02) 410 52 54, Fax 410 53 80. *039475*

Galerie Saint-Eloy, 223 Av. Louise B 28, 1050 Bruxelles.
T. (02) 649 74 35. - Ant - *039476*

Galerie Saint-Louis, 36 Pl du Sablon, 1000 Bruxelles.
T. (02) 522 16 30, 513 82 88. *039477*

Galerie Saint Michel, 22 Rue de l'Escadron, 1040 Bruxelles. T. (02) 735 70 96. - Ant - *039478*

Galerie Saint P., 5 Rue des Minimes, 1000 Bruxelles.
T. (02) 5116427. *039479*

Galerie Temps Perdu, 69 Rue de Namur, 1000 Bruxelles.
T. (02) 513 37 97. - Ant - *039480*

Galeries de Paris, 220 Rue du Trône, 1050 Bruxelles.
T. (02) 648 02 87. *039481*

Galuchat, 182 Av. Louise, 1050 Bruxelles.
T. (02) 647 45 40. - Ant - *039482*

Gdalewitch, J.M., 3 Av. de Jette, 1080 Bruxelles.
T. (02) 426 71 46. - Ant - *039483*

Gérard, 8 Pl J.B. Degrooff, 1200 Bruxelles.
- Ant - *039484*

Ghisoni-Giordano, 148 Blvd. Léopold II, 1080 Bruxelles.
T. (02) 427 40 53. - Ant - *039485*

Goffard, Aline, 8a Rue Bodenbroek, 1000 Bruxelles.
T. (02) 511 27 92. - Ant - *039486*

Grenier d'Amandine, Au, 36 Rue J Stallaert, 1180 Bruxelles. T. (02) 347 16 59. *039487*

Grenier d'Igor, 50 Rue Arenberg, 1000 Bruxelles.
T. (02) 512 70 90. - Ant - *039488*

Grusenmeyer, S., 14 Rue Lebeau, 1000 Bruxelles.
T. (02) 514 03 37, Fax 513 32 76. *039489*

Guillot, L., 20 Rue des Minimes, 1000 Bruxelles.
T. (02) 374 39 67. - Ant - *039490*

Guimiot, Philippe, 138 Av. Louise, 1050 Bruxelles.
T. (02) 640 69 48. - Eth - *039491*

Gulden Snee, 12 Rue Lebeau, 1000 Bruxelles.
T. (02) 512 24 68. *039492*

Haeseleer, Y. d', 36 Rue de la Régence, 1000 Bruxelles.
T. (02) 512 11 50. - Silv - *039493*

Haillez, 127 Rue Voot, 1200 Bruxelles.
T. (02) 770 21 87. *039494*

Harmakhis-Archeologie, 8 Pl. du Grand Sablon, 1000
Bruxelles. T. (02) 380 86 42. - Arch - *039495*

Harzir, Everard de, 149 Tenbosch, 1050 Bruxelles.
T. (02) 538 44 42. *039496*

Hauteville, 132 Av. Louise, 1050 Bruxelles.
T. (02) 648 66 73, 648 62 25. - Ant / Paint / Furn /
Orient / Sculp / Tex / Dec / Silv / Lights / Instr - *039497*

Hemeleers, F., 61 Av des Casernes, 1040 Bruxelles.
T. (02) 640 29 16. *039498*

Henin Planchar, 61a Rue de la Régence, 1000 Bruxelles.
T. (02) 511 81 09. *039499*

Hervy, rue Ernest Allard 10-14, 1000 Bruxelles.
T. (02) 511 1020. - Ant / Silv - *039500*

Heysel, du, 6 Av JB Depaire, 1020 Bruxelles.
T. (02) 479 77 90. *039501*

Hier et Aujourd'hui, 14 Rue des Minimes, 1000 Bruxelles. T. (02) 512 10 71. - Ant / Cur - *039502*

Hoore, D. d', 43 Av du Derby, 1050 Bruxelles.
T. (02) 672 02 98. *039503*

Hornbostel, Diane, 15 Rue des Minimes, 1000 Bruxelles.
T. (02) 511 28 69. *039504*

Horvata, M., 25 Av. Michel-Ange, 1000 Bruxelles.
T. (02) 735 48 10. - Ant - *039505*

Hottat, H., 35 Rue de Rollebeek, 1000 Bruxelles.
T. (02) 511 1384. - Ant / Dec - *039506*

Hove, Mireille van, 125 Rue Keyenveld, 1000 Bruxelles.
T. (02) 514 27 66, 649 25 89. - Ant / Dec / Fra - *039507*

Hove, van, 42 Rue Rollebeek, 1000 Bruxelles.
T. (02) 511 85 10. - Ant - *039508*

Ikodinovic, N., 37 Rue J. Stevens, 1000 Bruxelles.
T. (02) 514 04 77. - Ant / China / Glass - *039509*

Impasse Saint-Jacques, L', 7-8 Impasse Saint-Jacques,
1000 Bruxelles. T. (02) 513 01 75. - Ant / Furn /
Eth - *039510*

Isadora Boutique, 29 Rue Joseph-Stevens, 1000 Bruxelles. T. (02) 513 47 35. *039511*

Ivoire et Chagrin, 49 Rue Lebeau, 1000 Bruxelles.
T. (02) 511 85 23. - Ant - *039512*

Jade, 36 Pl du Grand Sablon, 1000 Bruxelles.
T. (02) 511 66 66. *039513*

Jadoul, 15 Rue de la Régence, 1000 Bruxelles.
T. (02) 512 04 88. - Ant - *039514*

Janson, 18 Av de Laeken, 1090 Bruxelles.
T. (02) 426 80 97. *039515*

Janssens, M., 17 Rue des Sablons, 1000 Bruxelles.
T. (02) 513 46 77. - Ant - *039516*

Jernander, Alain, 19 rue Coppens, 1000 Bruxelles.
T. (02) 514 41 10. - Instr / Mil - *039517*

Jonckheere, Georges de, 55 Blvd de Waterloo, 1000
Bruxelles. T. (02) 5129948, 5121554. - Ant /
Paint - *039518*

Jonge, Willy de, 36 Pl. du Grand Sablon, 1000 Bruxelles.
T. (02) 513 71 92. - Paint - *039519*

Jouets Anciens, 47 Rue de la Madeleine, 1000 Bruxelles. T. (02) 512 92 53. *039520*

Kestemont, 20 Rue des Minimes, 1000 Bruxelles.
T. (02) 513 85 00. *039521*

Keyser, Wilfried de, 440 Ch. de Waterloo, 1050 Bruxelles. T. (02) 534 03 53. - Furn - *039522*

Kinet, Jacques, 23-25 Rue P.E. Janson, 1050 Bruxelles.
T. (02) 538 96 45. - Ant - *039523*

Kinet, Jacques, 8 Rue Bodenbroeck, 1000 Bruxelles.
T. (02) 511 74 49. - Ant - *039524*

Kinet, Jacques, 65 Pl Jourdan, 1040 Bruxelles.
T. (02) 231 08 76. *039525*

Knecht, Raymond, 55 Rue Aux Laines, 1000 Bruxelles.
T. (02) 380 99 68. *039526*

Koenig, Michel, 27 Rue des Minimes, 1000 Bruxelles.
T. (02) 511 75 07. - Ant / Orient / Sculp / Arch / Eth /
Cur - 039527
Kotek, Greta, 157 Av de Tervuren, 1040 Bruxelles.
T. (02) 735 02 37. 039528
Kyoto Gallery, 41 Pl. du Grand Sablon, 1000 Bruxelles.
T. (02) 512 15 78. - Orient - 039529
La Brocantique, 179 et 197 Rue Blaes, 1000 Bruxelles.
T. (02) 514 40 59, 511 89 46. - Furn - 039530
La Feuille d'Armoise, 43 Rue de Rollebeek, 1000 Bruxel-
les. T. (02) 511 86 77. 039531
La Grand Camille, 28 Rue de la Paille, 1000 Bruxelles.
T. (02) 512 60 11. 039532
La Grande Ile, 4 Rue des Pigeons, 1000 Bruxelles.
T. (02) 511 78 08. 039533
Laloux-Dessain, 26 Blvd. de Waterloo, 1000 Bruxelles.
T. (02) 513 56 06. - Ant / Paint / Sculp / Arch - 039534
Laurent, A., 35 Rue des Minimes, 1000 Bruxelles.
T. (02) 512 92 29. 039535
Lavry, J.-P., 4 Rue du Bois de Linthout, 1200 Bruxelles.
T. (02) 734 19 35. 039536
Le Passe Temps, 31 Rue J. Stevens, 1000 Bruxelles.
T. (02) 512 27 47. - Furn - 039537
Le Truandou, 122 Rue Noyer, 1030 Bruxelles.
T. (02) 736 28 12. 039538
Lebizay, Jacqueline, 6 Pl JB Degrooff, 1200 Bruxelles.
T. (02) 734 53 45. 039539
Lefevre, M., 250 Blvd. Lambermont, 1030 Bruxelles.
T. (02) 215 51 75. - Ant - 039540
Legot, A., 55 Rue Simonis, 1050 Bruxelles.
T. (02) 537 31 78. - Ant - 039541
Lemonier, 24 Av des Celtes, 1040 Bruxelles.
T. (02) 735 99 82. 039542
Lenvain, Luc, 25 Rue van den Weyden, 1000 Bruxelles.
T. (02) 502 04 59. 039543
Lepage, Jean-Pierre, 17-19 rue de la Régence, 1000
Bruxelles. T. (02) 512 19 96. - Sculp - 039544
Leys, 56 Pl du Jeu de Balle, 1000 Bruxelles.
T. (02) 502 60 57. 039545
Lhoist, 374 Chaussée d'Alsemberg, 1180 Bruxelles.
T. (02) 344 61 57. - Ant - 039546
Libotte-Prayes, 87 Rue Américaine, 1050 Bruxelles.
T. (02) 538 42 01. - Ant - 039547
Lingot d'Or, Au, 30 Rue au Beurre, 1000 Bruxelles.
T. (02) 511 46 52. 039548
Liverloo, de, 30 Rue Ste-Anne, 1000 Bruxelles.
T. (02) 511 23 61. 039549
Lohest, H., 919 Ch de Waterloo, 1180 Bruxelles.
T. (02) 375 08 12. 039550
London Antiques, 26 Blvd de l'Abattoir, 1000 Bruxelles.
T. (02) 513 22 34. 039551
Lualaba, 15 Rue des Minimes, 1000 Bruxelles.
T. (02) 511 28 69. - Ant - 039552
Ma Campagne, 261 Chaussée de Charleroi, 1060 Bru-
xelles. T. (02) 537 69 09. 039553
Mackers, Robert, 25 Rue de Dublin, 1050 Bruxelles.
T. (02) 511 57 13. - Furn / Instr - 039554
De Maere, Jan, 9 Rue des Minimes, 1000 Bruxelles.
T. (02) 5022400, Fax 5020750. - Paint / Graph - 039555
Magazin Royal, 65A Rue de la Régence, 1000 Bruxelles.
T. (02) 502 09 09. 039556
Magin, 1440 Ch. de Wavre, 1160 Bruxelles.
T. (02) 675 34 42. - Furn - 039557
Mahaux, J., 43 ave. J. Vandersmissen, 1040 Bruxelles.
T. (02) 762 14 26. - Paint / Furn / Silv - 039558
Main d'Or, 12 Rue des Minimes, 1000 Bruxelles.
T. (02) 512 25 99. - Ant / Furn / China - 039559
Maison qui Bouge, 71 Rue du Bailli, 1050 Bruxelles.
T. (02) 538 30 13. - Ant - 039560
Majerus, Pierre, 54-64 Av. de la Chasse, 1040 Bruxelles.
T. (02) 733 87 33. - Glass - 039561
Mansart, Claude, 9 Rue J Stas, 1060 Bruxelles.
T. (02) 537 67 47. 039562
Marc Gallery, 17 Rue des Minimes, 1000 Bruxelles.
T. (02) 514 16 27. 039563
Marie & Luce, 47 Rue des Minimes, 1000 Bruxelles.
T. (02) 502 04 58. 039564
Marine Antique, 27a Rue Berckmans, 1060 Bruxelles.
T. (02) 538 53 13. - Ant - 039565
Marolles, Les, 213 Rue Blaes, 1000 Bruxelles.
T. (02) 512 25 86. 039566
Massot, Thylda, 201 Av Louise, 1050 Bruxelles.
T. (02) 649 76 14. 039567

Mastour, 243 Ch de Waterloo, 1060 Bruxelles.
T. (02) 538 64 32. 039568
Mathieu, R., 40 Rue Sainte-Anne, 1000 Bruxelles.
T. (02) 513 48 21. 039569
Merveilles d'Autrefois, 90a Av. de Tervueren, 1040 Bru-
xelles. T. (02) 736 97 46. - Ant - 039570
Meulemans, Marcel, 64 Rue Marconi, 1190 Bruxelles.
T. (02) 347 11 13. - Ant - 039571
Michel, Alain, 29 Rue des Minimes, 1000 Bruxelles.
T. (02) 512 55 84. 039572
Michiels, J., 14a Rue Simonis, 1060 Bruxelles.
T. (02) 538 81 46. 039573
Michiels, L., 34 Rue de la Régence, 1000 Bruxelles.
T. (02) 511 05 13, 512 49 40. - Ant / China /
Glass - 039574
Michiels, P., 16-18 Av. Adolphe Buyl, 1050 Bruxelles.
T. (02) 648 77 87. - Ant / China / Dec - 039575
Miessens, 18 Rue Lebeau, 1000 Bruxelles.
T. (02) 513 52 54. 039576
Millers English Antiques, 3-7 Rue des Minimes, 1000
Bruxelles. T. (02) 513 42 62. 039577
Minton, 36 Pl. du Grand Sablon, 1000 Bruxelles.
T. (02) 512 75 39. - Ant - 039578
Modern Studio, 11 Rue de la Paille, 1000 Bruxelles.
T. (02) 513 68 02. 039579
Monument Belgium, 178 Av. Van Volxem, 1190 Bruxel-
les. T. (02) 513 51 73. - Num - 039580
Moretti, R., 28 Rue du Beau Site, 1000 Bruxelles.
T. (02) 640 89 70. - Ant - 039581
Nathanaelle, 27 Rue Ducale, 1000 Bruxelles.
T. (02) 512 86 92. 039582
Noelle, Claude, 19-20 Pl. du Grand Sablon, 1000 Bruxel-
les. T. (02) 511 41 72. - Jew - 039583
Objets de Cinq Continents, 23 Galerie du Roi, 1000 Bru-
xelles. T. (02) 513 47 06. 039584
Obsidienne, 24 Rue des Minimes, 1000 Bruxelles.
T. (02) 512 25 99. 039585
Occase, L', 188 Chaussée d'Ixelles, 1050 Bruxelles.
T. (02) 648 19 02. - Ant - 039586
Occasion, L', 41 Rue de la Madeleine, 1000 Bruxelles.
T. (02) 513 16 18. - Ant / Cur - 039587
Oeil, L', 36 Rue Mignot-Delstanche, 1050 Bruxelles.
T. (02) 345 31 28. - Ant / Orient / Eth / Cur - 039588
Olin, S., 50 Rue Dejoncker, 1060 Bruxelles.
T. (02) 537 43 32. 039589
Oosterlinck, 32 Rue des Minimes, 1000 Bruxelles.
T. (02) 513 63 53. 039590
Oriande, 24 Gal de la Reine, 1000 Bruxelles.
T. (02) 512 49 32. 039591
Oultrement, 8, 58 Rue St. Georges, 1050 Bruxelles.
T. (02) 649 58 59. - Ant - 039592
Ouvroir pour Infirmes Rééduques, 78-82a Rue Bodeg-
hem, 1000 Bruxelles. T. (02) 511 04 17. 039593
Overstraeten, J. van, 106 Rue de Laeken, 1000 Bruxel-
les. T. (02) 218 20 91. - Ant - 039594
Palissandre, 17 Rue Lebeau, 1000 Bruxelles.
T. (02) 512 89 23. - Ant - 039595
Palmyre, 83 Rue du Bien Faire, 1170 Bruxelles.
T. (02) 673 51 97. 039596
Palombo, Pierina, 8 Pl du Grand Sablon, 1000 Bruxelles.
T. (02) 511 70 93. 039597
Pandora's Box, 26 Rue Blaes, 1000 Bruxelles.
T. (02) 514 10 10. 039598
Paredes, M.-J., 56 Av E Verhaeren, 1030 Bruxelles.
T. (02) 245 16 16. 039599
Paredis, T., Miniemenstr 25, 1000 Bruxelles.
T. (02) 512 18 38. 039600
Passa Tempo, II, 7 Rue Watteeu, 1000 Bruxelles.
T. (02) 511 59 11. 039601
Passé simple, 103 Galerie Louise, 1050 Bruxelles.
T. (02) 512 27 76. - Ant - 039602
Patrimoine Promotion, 189 Av Albert, 1060 Bruxelles.
T. (02) 346 43 61, Fax 343 09 17. 039603
Paulus Numismates, S.+N., 9 rue Ropsy-Chaudron,
1070 Bruxelles. T. (02) 214 612. - Num - 039604
Peeters, P., 23 Av des Faons, 1180 Bruxelles.
T. (02) 375 43 43. 039605
Penningkabinet, Keizerslaan 4, 1000 Bruxelles.
T. (02) 519 56 08. - Fra - 039606
Petit Magasin, Au, 24 Rue Ernest-Solvay, 1050 Bruxel-
les. T. (02) 511 60 39. 039607
Pic Verre, Le, 18 Rue E Allard, 1000 Bruxelles.
T. (02) 513 70 19. 039608

Pierpont, Olivier de, 409 Av Georges Henri, 1200 Bruxel-
les. T. (02) 734 52 39. 039609
Pin'Art Antiques, 50 Rue Willems, 1210 Bruxelles.
T. (02) 230 80 64. 039610
Pin Blanc et Fantasie, 679 Ch. d'Alsemberg, 1180 Bru-
xelles. T. (02) 347 31 08. - Furn - 039611
Pin et Beurre, 6 Pl. de la Chapelle, 1000 Bruxelles.
T. (02) 511 86 85. - Ant - 039612
Pin et Rotin, Lombardstr. 70-74, 1000 Bruxelles.
T. (02) 511 79 62. - Furn - 039613
Pin & Vin, 78 Av. L. Bertrand, 1030 Bruxelles.
T. (02) 215 46 46. - Ant - 039614
Pinel & Partner, 32 Rue de Rollebeek, 1000 Bruxelles.
T. (02) 514 57 57. 039615
Pipe, 9 Rue E. Allard, 1000 Bruxelles. T. (02) 511 53 24.
- Ant - 039616
Pirouzian, N., 7 Rue Lebeau, 1000 Bruxelles.
T. (02) 502 09 83. 039617
Polo, Ralph Lauren, 52 Blvd de Waterloo, 1000 Bruxel-
les. T. (02) 511 00 04. 039618
Poortere, J.-L. de, 25 Rue de l'Amazone, 1050 Bruxel-
les. T. (02) 538 88 32. 039619
Poussières, 72 Rue Van Oost, 1030 Bruxelles.
T. (02) 216 79 33. - Ant - 039620
Prevost, 43 Rue de Namur, 1000 Bruxelles.
T. (02) 513 49 49. - Ant / Furn - 039621
Rabier, 8-10 Rue des Minimes, 1000 Bruxelles.
T. (02) 512 86 74. - Ant / Furn / Orient / Sculp / Tex /
Arch / Eth / Dec / Jew - 039622
Renard, 27 Rue de la Régence, 1000 Bruxelles.
T. (02) 512 89 01. - Furn / Dec / Jew - 039623
Res Eclectica, 51 Rue du Magistrat, 1050 Bruxelles.
T. (02) 646 57 47. - Furn - 039624
Retromania, 165 Ch de Wavre, 1050 Bruxelles.
T. (02) 512 74 37. 039625
Rigoli, L., 915 Chaussée de Waterloo, 1180 Bruxelles.
T. (02) 375 05 03. - Ant - 039626
Ritter, Grégor, 17 Rue E.-Allard, 1000 Bruxelles.
T. (02) 512 46 79. - Ant / Furn - 039627
Rob, 178 Chaussée de Wavre, 1050 Bruxelles.
T. (02) 511 54 53. - Ant - 039628
Rob, 76 Rue Confédérés, 1000 Bruxelles.
T. (02) 735 88 15. - Ant - 039629
Robert, M.-A., 206 Av de l'Hippodrome, 1050 Bruxelles.
T. (02) 640 88 31. 039630
Romantica, 25 Rue J Stevens, 1000 Bruxelles.
T. (02) 512 37 44. 039631
Ronveaux, J., 227-229 Av. de la Chasse, 1040 Bruxel-
les. T. (02) 736 15 91. - Ant / Paint / Cur - 039632
Roosens, 167 Chaussée de Charleroi, 1060 Bruxelles.
T. (02) 537 58 32. - Ant / Paint / China / Lights /
Instr - 039633
Root, S., 133 Rue Blaes, 1000 Bruxelles.
T. (02) 510 02 71. - Ant - 039634
Root, S., 25 Rue Lebeau, 1000 Bruxelles.
T. (02) 511 17 81. 039635
Ruy du Bourgeois, Le, 50 Chaussée de Charleroi, 1060
Bruxelles. T. (02) 538 02 88. 039636
Salomé, Nils H., 32 Rue de la Paille, 1000 Bruxelles.
T. (02) 513 95 61. 039637
Sand, Gérard, 28b Rue du Lombard, 1000 Bruxelles.
T. (02) 511 70 74. - Orient - 039638
Schelma, 18 Rue de Pervyse, 1040 Bruxelles.
T. (02) 734 97 66. - Ant / Furn - 039639
Schmitz, 49 Rue Lebeau, 1000 Bruxelles.
T. (02) 672 03 32. - Ant - 039640
Schrijver, G. de, 303 Av. de Tervueren, 1150 Bruxelles.
T. (02) 771 48 82. - Ant - 039641
Senny, H., 9 Rue Watteeu, 1000 Bruxelles.
T. (02) 514 03 15. - Ant - 039642
Siècle d'Or, 206 Av. Georges Henri, 1200 Bruxelles.
T. (02) 770 32 27. - Ant - 039643
Simon & Partners, 17 Rue des Sablons, 1000 Bruxelles.
T. (02) 502 18 84. 039644
Smits, Marynen, 171-173 Av. Brugmann, 1190 Bruxel-
les. T. (02) 344 84 55. - Ant / Dec - 039645
Soeteman, Corneille, Zuidstr. 65, 1000 Bruxelles.
T. (02) 513 08 37. - Num - 039646
Solbosch, 2 Av. du Pesage, 1050 Bruxelles.
T. (02) 648 02 55. - Ant - 039647
Speltens, 244 Av. Van Volxem, 1190 Bruxelles.
T. (02) 344 91 22. - Ant - 039648

Stefanovich, 38-39 Galerie Louise, 1050 Bruxelles.
T. (02) 512 94 29, 512 10 21. - Ant / Paint /
Furn – *039649*
Steppe, Karl, 29 Av. de Tervueren, 1040 Bruxelles.
T. (02) 735 58 25. - Ant – *039650*
Steyaert, M., 12 Rue Lebeau, 1000 Bruxelles.
T. (02) 512 24 68. *039651*
Stiernet, 6-8 Rue des Moissonneurs, 1040 Bruxelles.
T. (02) 734 83 31, 734 49 13. *039652*
Struvay, T., 22 Gal du Roi, 1000 Bruxelles.
T. (02) 512 96 88. *039653*
Table Ronde, 438 Chaussée de Waterloo, 1050 Bruxel-
les. T. (02) 538 34 81. - Ant – *039654*
Thirion, Dominique, 72 Blvd. Lambermont, 1030 Bruxel-
les. T. (02) 215 93 96. - Num – *039655*
Timmermans, 36 Rue Declercq, 1150 Bruxelles.
T. (02) 771 80 40. *039656*
Tollemans, Jean, 15 Rue des Sablons, 1000 Bruxelles.
T. (02) 511 34 05. - Ant – *039657*
Topkapi Antiquites, Av. F. Roosevelt 83 Bte. 11, 1050
Bruxelles. T. (02) 640 81 16. - Ant – *039658*
Torrekens, M., 20 Chaussée de Tervueren, 1160 Bruxel-
les. T. (02) 673 52 17. *039659*
Toussaint, J., 27-29 Rue Saint Jean, 1000 Bruxelles.
T. (02) 511 40 36. - Ant – *039660*
Tradart Brussels, 32 Av. Louise, 1050 Bruxelles.
T. (02) 514 58 00, Fax 514 31 35. - Num – *039661*
Treize Quatre Feuilles, 13 Rue du Lombard, 1000 Bru-
xelles. T. (02) 511 61 55. - Ant – *039662*
Tribal Arts, 15 Impasse St-Jacques, 1000 Bruxelles.
T. (02) 511 47 67. - Ant / Eth – *039663*
Trocade du Sablon, 25 Rue des Minimes, 1000 Bruxel-
les. T. (02) 511 79 93. - Ant – *039664*
Trottinette, 4 Rue des Eperonniers, 1000 Bruxelles.
T. (02) 511 00 41. - Ant – *039665*
Trouvaille, La, 7 Rue de Hennin, 1050 Bruxelles.
T. (02) 648 80 84. *039666*
Trouvailles d'Artenice, 1037 Chaussée d'Alsemberg,
1180 Bruxelles. T. (02) 376 81 42. - Ant – *039667*
Turner, Geoffrey, Ave. Louise 90, 1050 Bruxelles.
T. (02) 511 05 77. - Sculp – *039668*
Uguccioni, 145 Drève Pittoresque, 1180 Bruxelles.
T. (02) 374 53 12. *039669*
Un Temps d'Arret, 1a Rue de Livourne, 1060 Bruxelles.
T. (02) 538 08 29. - Ant – *039670*
Val, Marie Luz del, 77 Av Brugmann, 1190 Bruxelles.
T. (02) 343 49 70, Fax 344 67 94. *039671*
Van Petegem, M., 89 Rue M Christine, 1020 Bruxelles.
T. (02) 426 98 53. *039672*
Vandendriessche, M., 125 Rue de Livourne, 1000 Bru-
xelles. T. (02) 649 69 89. *039673*
Vanderborght, Pierre, 9 Rue Ravenstein, 1000 Bruxelles.
T. (02) 512 48 60. - Ant – *039674*
Vanderslyen, 64 Rue de l'Hôtel-des- Monnaies, 1060
Bruxelles. T. (02) 537 80 63. - Ant / Cur – *039675*
Vandersteen, J., 9 Rue de Rollebeek, 1000 Bruxelles.
T. (02) 511 14 84. - Ant / Eth – *039676*
Vannerom, Arcade de la Bonne Reine, 1200 Bruxelles.
T. (02) 762 77 56. - Ant – *039677*
Vanonkelen, L., 36 Rue Rollebeek, 1000 Bruxelles.
T. (02) 511 66 72. - Ant – *039678*
Varosi, C., 32 Chaussée d'Helmet, 1030 Bruxelles.
T. (02) 242 86 21. - Ant – *039679*
Velkens, 157-163 Av. de la Reine, 1030 Bruxelles.
T. (02) 242 63 05. - Ant – *039680*
Vendôme Joaillerie, 49 Rue Au Beurre, 1000 Bruxelles.
T. (02) 512 74 92. - Jew – *039681*
Verackx, L., Vossenpln 27, 1000 Bruxelles.
T. (02) 514 13 69. *039682*
Verbiest, V., 335 Rue de Birmingham, 1070 Bruxelles.
T. (02) 520 00 74. - Ant – *039683*
Verbois, 380 Av Louise, 1050 Bruxelles.
T. (02) 649 73 53. *039684*
Verdeghem, Baudouin van, 69 Rue Lebeau, 1000 Bru-
xelles. T. (02) 511 77 18. - Instr – *039685*
Vieseries, Les, 18 Rue Communale, 1083 Bruxelles.
T. (02) 427 59 81. *039686*
Vieux Bruxelles, Au, 217-219 Rue Blaes, 1000 Bruxel-
les. T. (02) 512 93 01. *039687*
Vieux Charme, Le, 133 Rue du Trône, 1050 Bruxelles.
T. (02) 502 02 27. - Furn – *039688*
Vieux Magasin, Au, 39 Rue Godecharle, 1050 Bruxelles.
T. (02) 648 98 06. *039689*

Villars, 14 Pl. du Grand-Sablon, 1000 Bruxelles.
T. (02) 512 14 17. - Ant / Dec – *039690*
Vokaer, Michel, Chausse'1e de Charleroi 169, 1060 Bru-
xelles. T. (02) 512 13 53. *039691*
Voos Thuiszorg, Vanderlindenstr 46, 1030 Bruxelles.
T. (02) 215 07 15. *039692*
Wachtelaer & Fils, 69 Rue des Mélèzes, 1050 Bruxelles.
T. (02) 343 6043. - Ant / Furn – *039693*
Warche, Robert, 22 Rue Bodenbroek, 1000 Bruxelles.
T. (02) 512 49 35. - Ant / Furn / Jew / Cur – *039694*
Weckmans & Salomé, 32 Rue de la Paille, 1000 Bruxel-
les. T. (02) 513 95 61. *039695*
Wery, L., 111 Rue van Moer, 1000 Bruxelles.
T. (02) 512 75 48. *039696*
Willems, Jean, 5 Rue Ernest Allard, 1000 Bruxelles.
T. (02) 512 03 53, Fax 512 89 50. - Paint /
Draw – *039697*
Williame, Zuidstr. 5, 1000 Bruxelles. T. (02) 511 99 89,
512 76 27. - Num – *039698*
Winster, 304 Av Louise, 1050 Bruxelles.
T. (02) 514 32 08. *039699*
Witmeur, J.-P., 33 Rue de la Madeleine, 1000 Bruxelles.
T. (02) 511 65 86. - Ant – *039700*
Woolf, 225 Av. Louise, 1050 Bruxelles. T. (02) 648 00 20.
- Ant – *039701*
Wouter Brouwer, 35 Rue J. Stevens, 1000 Bruxelles.
T. (02) 5127186. - Furn / China / Glass – *039702*
Wyckaert, 192, rue Royale, 1000 Bruxelles.
T. (02) 217 65 34. - Ant / Cur – *039703*
Yannick, David, 26 Blvd. de Waterloo, 1000 Bruxelles.
T. (02) 513 16 10. - Ant – *039704*
Yetti-Warnotte, 12 Rue R. Chalon, 1050 Bruxelles.
T. (02) 344 10 40. - Ant – *039705*
Zada, 195 Av Louise, 1050 Bruxelles. T. (02) 771 44 46,
647 51 92. *039706*
Zavelberg-Torrekens, M., 20 Ch de Tervuren, 1160 Bru-
xelles. T. (02) 673 52 17. *039707*

ZEN GALLERY
ORIENTAL ART
A. CNUDDE
PARAVENTS JAPONAIS
HAUTE ÉPOQUE CHINOISE
Rue E. Allard, 23 (SABLON)
1000 BRUXELLES
Tél. : 02/511 95 10 Fax 052-37 39 50
Ouv. 14 h – 18 h 30 Fermé dim. et lundi

Zen Gallery, 23 Rue E. Allard, 1000 Bruxelles,
T. (02) 511 95 10, Fax (052) 37 39 50.
- Orient – *039707a*

Casteau (Hainaut)
Vieux Chenêts, Aux, 56 Ch. de Bruxelles, 7061 Casteau.
T. (065) 72 85 57. - Ant / Furn / Dec – *039708*

Charleroi (Hainaut)
Devendt, 48 Rue de la Régence, 6000 Charleroi.
T. (071) 32 81 74. *039709*
Galerie St. Jacques, 19, av. de l'Europe, 6000 Charleroi.
T. (071) 31 28 69. - Ant – *039710*
Hecq, 49-51 Av. de Waterloo, 6000 Charleroi.
T. (071) 33 35 47. - Ant / Paint / Furn – *039711*
Marchal, J. & J.P., 27 Blvd Audent, 6000 Charleroi.
T. (071) 59 14 39. *039712*

Chaudfontaine
Poncin, 31 Voie de Liège, 4050 Chaudfontaine.
T. (041) 65 86 35. *039713*

Chênée (Liège)
Delcour, 31 Rue Alban-Poulet, 4032 Chênée.
T. (041) 65 88 84. *039714*

Cheratte (Liège)
Gerardy-Janssen, 79 Rue Sabaré, 4602 Cheratte.
T. (041) 62 88 72. *039715*

Chimay (Hainaut)
Decroes, M., 2 Rue Rogier, 6460 Chimay.
T. (060) 21 10 40. *039716*
Lagnaux, 26bis Pl Froissard, 6460 Chimay.
T. (060) 21 18 22. *039717*
Macq, M., Les Voûtes, 6460 Chimay.
T. (060) 21 10 40. *039718*

Ciney (Namur)
Demblon, 3 Rue Neufmoulin, 5590 Ciney.
T. (083) 21 10 23. *039719*

Corroy-le-Grand (Brabant Wallon)
Laid Burnia, 6 Rue Laid-Burnia, 1325 Corroy-le-Grand.
T. (010) 68 88 10. *039720*

Couillet (Hainaut)
Antoine, E., 76 Av. de Philippeville, 6010 Couillet.
T. (071) 36 57 68. - Ant / Dec – *039721*
Bosseaux-Meulemen, 405 Chaussée de Philippeville,
6010 Couillet. T. (071) 36 58 49. *039722*

Dadizele (West-Vlaanderen)
Lebon, Ketenstr 2, 8890 Dadizele.
T. (056) 50 90 44. *039723*

Damme (West-Vlaanderen)
Deneve, P., Hoogstr 5, 8340 Damme.
T. (050) 33 81 60. *039724*
Karveel, 'T, Markt 8a, 8340 Damme.
T. (050) 35 57 75. *039725*
Kazemat, Kerkstr 32, 8340 Damme.
T. (050) 35 68 25. *039726*
Wagenhuis, T', Kerkstr 22, 8340 Damme.
T. (050) 35 31 32. *039727*

Daverdisse (Luxembourg)
Duvivier, B., 20 Rue de Porcheresse, 6929 Daverdisse.
T. (084) 388935. *039728*

De Panne (West-Vlaanderen)
Berquin, A., Zeelaan 129, 8660 De Panne.
T. (058) 411 82. - Ant – *039729*
Brocanteur, Zeelaan 39, 8660 De Panne.
T. (058) 41 51 23. *039730*
Godderis, Hugo, Duinhoekstr 13, 8660 De Panne.
T. (058) 41 38 96. *039731*

Deerlijk (West-Vlaanderen)
Galerij Henri, Pontstr 55, 8540 Deerlijk.
T. (056) 71 10 14. *039732*
Priem, E., Diependaele 1, 8540 Deerlijk.
T. (056) 70 21 57. *039733*
Priem, R., Waregemstr 96, 8540 Deerlijk.
T. (056) 71 25 57. *039734*

Deinze (Oost-Vlaanderen)
Centrum voor Oude Effecten, Kouter 126, 9800 Deinze.
T. (091) 869091. *039735*
Danneels, H., G Gezellelaan 56, 9800 Deinze.
T. (091) 86 14 78. *039736*
M. A. S., Emiel Clauslaan 65, 9800 Deinze.
T. (091) 86 11 71. *039737*
Oud Parijs, Dorpstr 20-24, 9800 Deinze.
T. (091) 86 24 19. *039738*
Pine House, Dorpstr 119, 9800 Deinze.
T. (091) 86 58 65. *039739*

Denderleeuw (Oost-Vlaanderen)
'T Oude Meubel, Steenweg 201, 9470 Denderleeuw.
T. (053) 665679. *039740*

Dendermonde (Oost-Vlaanderen)
Buck, P. de, Gentsesteenweg 18, 9200 Dendermonde.
T. (052) 21 30 94. *039741*
Galerij Oud & Nieuw, Dijkstr 11-13, 9200 Dendermonde.
T. (052) 21 94 54. *039742*
Leybaert, Franz Courtensstraat 4, 9200 Dendermonde.
T. (052) 217 52. - Ant / Cur – *039743*
Lucca, Oude Vest 156, 9200 Dendermonde.
T. (052) 22 10 39. *039744*
Segers, R., Brusselsestr 45, 9200 Dendermonde.
T. (052) 21 17 38. *039745*

Dentergem (Oost-Vlaanderen)
Taelman, E., Markegemsestw 146, 8720 Dentergem.
T. (051) 63 52 02. *039746*

Desselgem (Oost-Vlaanderen)
Ostyn, André, Gentseweg 244, 8792 Desselgem.
T. (056) 71 45 40. *039747*

Deurle (Oost-Vlaanderen)
Folknør, G., Park ter Leie 11, 9831 Deurle.
T. (091) 826395. *039748*
Sprang, M., Pontstr. 46, 9831 Deurle. T. (091) 824101.
- Ant - *039749*

Deurne (Antwerpen)
Bakelants, Ivo, Manebruggestr. 247, 2100 Deurne.
T. (03) 321 09 81. - Cur / Glass - *039750*
Beerens, J. F., A Schneiderlaan 97-99, 2100 Deurne.
T. (03) 24 09 30. *039751*
Maru, Boshovestr 56, 2100 Deurne.
T. (03) 324 62 99. *039752*
Wijns, M., Herentalsebn 612, 2100 Deurne.
T. (03) 322 35 00. *039753*

Diepenbeek (Limburg)
Croymans Plaghki, Frank, Wijkstr. 45, 3590 Diepenbeek.
T. (011) 323116. - Furn - *039754*

Dilbeek (Vlaams Brabant)
Artus, L., Kapelstr 145, 1700 Dilbeek.
T. (02) 5228660. *039755*
Charmeraie, La, Molenbergstr 30, 1700 Dilbeek.
T. (02) 5694145. *039756*

Dilsen (Limburg)
Bruyn, S. de, Rijksweg 417, 3650 Dilsen.
T. (011) 75 50 65. *039757*

Dilsen-Stokkem (Limburg)
Daelmans, J., Rijksweg 255, 3650 Dilsen-Stokkem.
T. (011) 75 60 94, Fax 75 69 46. *039758*
Vanstreels, Burg Henryln 127, 3650 Dilsen-Stokkem.
T. (011) 86 44 88. *039759*

Dinant (Namur)
Lurquin, 104 Rue Daoust, 5500 Dinant.
T. (082) 22 26 07. *039760*

Dion-Valmont (Brabant)
Margelle, La, 93 Chaussée de Huy, 1325 Dion-Valmont.
T. (010) 68 81 33. *039761*

Dormaal (Limburg)
Molenhof, Grote Baan 65, 3440 Dormaal.
T. (011) 780967. *039762*

Dottignies (Hainaut)
Union des Ebenistes, 159 Blvd des Alliés, 7711 Dottignies. T. (056) 48 85 14. *039763*

Dour (Hainaut)
Mattelin, P., 169 Rue de Ropaix, 7370 Dour. *039764*

Durbuy (Luxembourg)
Pire, A., 24 Rue de la Haie Himbe, 6940 Durbuy.
T. (086) 21 20 77. *039765*

Ecaussinnes-d'Enghien (Hainaut)
Boite à Sel, 32 Rue Belle Tête, 7190 Ecaussinnes-d'Engh-
hien. T. (067) 44 39 91. *039766*

Eeklo (Oost-Vlaanderen)
Ledeganck, Molenstr 194, 9900 Eeklo.
T. (091) 77 55 22. *039767*
Ramont, A., Leopoldlaan 63, 9900 Eeklo.
T. (091) 77 10 49. *039768*
Verbeelt, Stationstr 8, 9900 Eeklo.
T. (091) 77 72 36. *039769*

Ekeren (Antwerpen)
Markiezenhof, Kloosterstr 127, 2180 Ekeren.
T. (031) 542 27 18. *039770*
Van den Wiel, Bremboslei 44, 2180 Ekeren.
T. (031) 541 92 47. *039771*
Van Laer, F., Prinshoeveweg 42, 2180 Ekeren.
T. (031) 647 18 61. *039772*

Eksel (Limburg)
't Vlaske, Eindhovensebn 61, 3941 Eksel.
T. (011) 734178. *039773*

Elen (Limburg)
Dubois, Rijksweg 942, 3650 Elen.
T. (011) 56 50 47. *039774*

Emblem (Antwerpen)
Alliers, Vruntebn 11, 2520 Emblem.
T. (031) 480 68 61. *039775*
Kammen, de, Oostmallestw. 118, 2520 Emblem.
T. (031) 485 70 35. - Ant / Furn - *039776*

Embourg (Liège)
Poncin, Daniele, 31 Voie de Liège, 4053 Embourg.
T. (041) 65 86 35. *039777*

Epinois (Hainaut)
Lison, J.C., 1-3 Rte. de Charleroi, 7134 Epinois.
T. (064) 33 42 71. - Ant / Dec - *039778*

Erondegem (Oost-Vlaanderen)
Ganzendries, Bloemenstr 28, 9420 Erondegem.
T. (053) 80 73 63. *039779*

Erpe (Oost-Vlaanderen)
Praet, G., Honegemstr 148, 9420 Erpe.
T. (053) 80 52 19. *039780*

Erpent (Namur)
Pompier, E., 578 Chaussée de Marche, 5101 Erpent.
T. (081) 30 15 37. - Ant / Furn / China / Dec / Lights /
Instr / Glass - *039781*

Essene (Vlaams Brabant)
Sompel, J. van, Karlemeersbaan 1, 1790 Essene.
T. (02) 5822641. - Furn - *039782*

Etalle (Luxembourg)
Filipucci, 32 Rue Grande, 6740 Etalle.
T. (063) 45 53 25. *039783*
Hittelet, Rue Gaumiemont, 6740 Etalle.
T. (063) 45 51 92. *039784*
L'Enclos, 82 Rue Lenclos, 6740 Etalle. T. (063) 45 53 26.
- Ant / Furn / Dec - *039785*
Recif, Le, 61 Rue du Moulin, 6740 Etalle.
T. (063) 45 54 46. *039786*

Etikhove (Oost-Vlaanderen)
Kunstgalerij Ladeuze, Ladeuze 3, 9680 Etikhove.
T. (055) 31 10 93. *039787*

Evergem (Oost-Vlaanderen)
Van Verdegem, G., Beekstr 63, 9940 Evergem.
T. (091) 53 26 62. *039788*

Flémalle (Liège)
Trouvaille, La, 74 Chaussée de Chokier, 4400 Flémalle.
T. (041) 754775. *039789*

Fontenoille (Luxembourg)
Watelet, R., La Crolire, 6820 Fontenoille.
T. (061) 31 19 63. *039790*

Fronville (Luxembourg)
Harkey, Château de Denlire, 6990 Fronville.
T. (084) 46 66 16. *039791*

Geel (Antwerpen)
Antiek Boetieka, De Billemontstr 21, 2440 Geel.
T. (014) 58 24 37. *039792*
Jansen, F., Winkelomseheide 34, 2440 Geel.
T. (014) 58 82 88. *039793*
Timmermanns, Pas 119, 2440 Geel.
T. (014) 58 44 05. *039794*

Gelinden (Limburg)
Romantica Antiek, Luikerstw 568, 3800 Gelinden.
T. (011) 485876. *039795*

Genappe (Genepiën) (Brabant Wallon)
Maison Espagnole, La, 8 Rue de France, 1470 Genappe
(Genepiën). T. (067) 771633. *039796*

Genk (Limburg)
Antiek Marleen, Koerlostr 34, 3600 Genk.
T. (011) 35 65 54. *039797*

Classico, St Martinuspl, Shopping III, 3600 Genk.
T. (011) 35 84 92. *039798*
Driessen-Schreurs, Molenstr 47, 3600 Genk.
T. (011) 35 27 06. *039799*
Lorraine, Hoogstr 18, 3600 Genk. T. (011) 35 17 31,
Fax 35 10 33. *039800*
Queen of the South, Hasseltweg 377, 3600 Genk.
T. (011) 35 62 47. *039801*
Roelants, H., Molenstr 21, 3600 Genk.
T. (011) 35 94 22. *039802*

Gent (Oost-Vlaanderen)
Abbaspour, Oude Vest 1, 9000 Gent.
T. (09) 2330808. *039803*
ADG Galerie, Jakobijnenstr 2, 9000 Gent.
T. (09) 2258428. *039804*
Antiek Andre, St Kwintensberg 34, 9000 Gent.
T. (09) 2236293. *039805*
Antiek Brocante Sire Jacob, Herfststr 1, 9000 Gent.
T. (09) 2225695. *039806*
Antiekhoekje, 'T, Zwijnaardsesteenweg 14, 9000 Gent.
T. (09) 2215198. *039807*
Arabesque, Burgstr 21, 5000 Gent.
T. (09) 2330069. *039808*
Ars Antiqua, Kortrijksepoortstr 110, 9000 Gent.
T. (09) 2254292. *039809*
Art & Antiques, St Niklaasstr 44, 9000 Gent.
T. (09) 2233789. *039810*
Arto, Graaf v. Vlaanderenpl. 10-12, 9000 Gent.
T. (09) 2330240. - Furn / Sculp - *039811*
Atelier Steendam, Steendam 42, 9000 Gent.
T. (09) 2236835. *039812*
Baele, Johan, Hoogstr 130, 9000 Gent.
T. (09) 2233837. *039813*
Baete, Roger, Kalandenstraat 12, 9000 Gent.
T. (09) 2250688. - Ant / Paint / Furn / China / Sculp /
Ico - *039814*
Barts Wonderwinkel, Kosteellaan 345, 9000 Gent.
T. (09) 2237220. *039815*
Beir, de, Sint-Baafsplein 4, 9000 Gent. T. (09) 2254680.
- Num - *039816*
Bekoring, de, Steendam 24, 9000 Gent.
T. (09) 2243065. *039817*
Beyst, Ondenbergen 40, 9000 Gent.
T. (09) 2231006. *039818*
Biliet, H., Wijzemansstr 5, 9000 Gent.
T. (09) 2259405. *039819*
Bisscop, Nicole de, Onderbergen 21, 9000 Gent.
T. (09) 3627826. *039820*
Bouckaert, Steendam 110, 9000 Gent.
T. (09) 2242865. *039821*
Bracke, Martelaarsln 436, 9000 Gent.
T. (09) 2257212. *039822*
Braham, Alice, Geldmunt 24, 9000 Gent.
T. (09) 2242614. *039823*
Brocante, Rikelingestr 1, 9000 Gent.
T. (09) 2238087. *039824*
Castle Antiques & Arts, Drabstr 41, 9000 Gent.
T. (09) 2239505, Fax 22240780. *039825*
Coget, Anne, 46 Henegouwestraat, 9000 Gent.
T. (09) 2234450. *039826*
Cooremeters-Huis, Het, Gras Lei 12, 9000 Gent.
T. (09) 2250965. *039827*
Coorevits, A., Koornlei 1, 9000 Gent.
T. (09) 2236143. *039828*
Coppens, P., Kraaln 61, 9000 Gent.
T. (09) 2235399. *039829*
Cosmos, Kortrijksepoortstr 45, 9000 Gent.
T. (09) 2258149. *039830*
Deene, R., Hoogpoort 83, 9000 Gent. T. (09) 2250248.
- Ant - *039831*
Degryse, L., Koestr. 7, 9000 Gent. T. (09) 2255181.
- Ant - *039832*
Demeyer, N., Jan Breydelstr 13, 9000 Gent.
T. (09) 2232054. *039833*
Dhaenens, R., Kraanlei 33, 9000 Gent.
T. (09) 2230587. *039834*
Dragonetti, Ajuinlei 10, 9000 Gent.
T. (09) 2251142. *039835*
Fielding, Blekerijstr 33, 9000 Gent.
T. (09) 3845829. *039836*
Flanders Antiquity, Vaderlandstr 13, 9000 Gent.
T. (09) 2215444, Fax 232 65 18. *039837*

Folklore, Wijzemanstr 5, 9000 Gent.
T. (09) 2259405. *039838*
Galerie Napoleon, Kouterdreef 1, 9000 Gent.
T. (09) 2259865, 2264615. *039839*
Gentse Kunstveilingen St. John, Bij St-Jacobs, 9000
Gent. T. (09) 3573295. *039840*
Gouden Pand, 'T, Onderbergen 72, 9000 Gent.
T. (09) 2258634. *039841*
Hendrycks, Burggravenln 64, 9000 Gent.
T. (09) 2217533. *039842*
Hillaert, M., Salvatorstr. 137, 9000 Gent.
T. (09) 2239243. - Num - *039843*
Hof ter Lieffebrughe, Lievestr. 2, 9000 Gent.
T. (09) 2252492. - Ant - *039844*
Houwen, J., Bij St-Jacobs 17, 9000 Gent.
T. (09) 2237696. *039845*
Ichiban, Ajuinlei 12, 9000 Gent.
T. (09) 2311421. *039846*
Imschoot, van, Burgstr. 6, 9000 Gent. T. (09) 2243867.
- Ant / Cur - *039847*
Intellect, Kalandestr. 1, 9000 Gent. T. (09) 2257351.
- Graph - *039848*
Interieur 13, Kalandenstr 13, 9000 Gent.
T. (09) 2232520. *039849*
Jaeger, F. de, Komijnstr 3, 9000 Gent.
T. (09) 2252310. *039850*
Kartuizerhuys, Kartuizerln 105, 9000 Gent.
T. (09) 2332735. *039851*
Kotek, S., Kortrijksepoortstr 110, 9000 Gent.
T. (09) 2254292. *039852*
Libbrecht, Pensmarkt 1, 9000 Gent.
T. (09) 2231149. *039853*
Magnus, De Kerchoveln 83, 9000 Gent. T. (09) 2238226,
Fax 82 98 36. *039854*
Marin, Guislainstr 48, 9000 Gent.
T. (09) 2279568. *039855*
Michel-Antiquity, Koornlei 2, 9000 Gent.
T. (09) 2251607. *039856*
Monfrans, E., Muinkkaai 13, 9000 Gent.
T. (09) 2252767. *039857*
Mucha, Ottogracht 37, 9000 Gent.
T. (09) 2333164. *039858*
Neckere, Marcel de, Beverhartplein 6, 9000 Gent.
T. (09) 2259856. *039859*
Nieuwenhuyse, H. van, Prinsenhof 55, 9000 Gent.
T. (09) 2232522. *039860*
Numis Artikado, Dampoortstr. 77, 9000 Gent.
T. (09) 2332281. - Num - *039861*
Old Flemish Art, Drongenstationstr. 46, 9000 Gent.
T. (09) 2265325. - Ant / Furn / China / Sculp / Jew / Silv /
Mil / Ico - *039862*
Otantiek, Steendam 12, 9000 Gent.
T. (09) 2252779. *039863*
Oudheden Sorgeloose, Mageleinstr. 19, 9000 Gent.
T. (09) 2236828. - Furn / Jew - *039864*
Pandje, Henegouwenstr 8, 9000 Gent.
T. (09) 2823502. *039865*
Pauw, de, Jakobijnenstr 2, 9000 Gent.
T. (09) 2243635. *039866*
Pearl, Henegouwenstr. 40, 9000 Gent. T. (09) 2243288.
- Glass - *039867*
Pimlico, Onderbergen 23, 9000 Gent.
T. (09) 2221575. *039868*
Poerck, R. de, Zwarte Zustersstr. 12, 9000 Gent.
T. (09) 2253267. - Ant / Furn - *039869*
Rembrandt, Steendamm 58, 9000 Gent.
T. (09) 2236836. *039870*
Renaissance van het Boek, Walpoortstr 7, 9000 Gent.
T. (09) 2254808. *039871*
Rode Koning, De, Kasteellaan 166, 9000 Gent.
T. (09) 2237872. *039872*
Rodon, Brabantdam 56, 9000 Gent.
T. (09) 2257026. *039873*
Rooryck, Michel, Korte Meer 13, 9000 Gent.
T. (09) 2257050. *039874*
Samyn, Voldersstr. 4, 9000 Gent. T. (09) 2252163.
- Ant / Cur - *039875*
Sauvage, A., Ottogracht 5, 9000 Gent.
T. (09) 2300613. *039876*
Sint Baafsgalerij, Limburgstr. 66, 9000 Gent.
T. (09) 2250176. - Ant / Paint / Furn / China / Sculp /
Ico - *039877*

Sire Jacob, Kattenb 109, 9000 Gent.
T. (09) 2225695. *039878*
Sorgeloose, Mageleinstr 19, 9000 Gent.
T. (09) 2236828. *039879*
Steinfeld, E.M., St-Niklaasstr 44, 9000 Gent.
T. (09) 2233789. *039880*
Stijl, Kon Astridln 202, 9000 Gent.
T. (09) 2222182. *039881*
The Fallen Angels, J Breydelstr 29, 9000 Gent.
T. (09) 2239415. *039882*
Thomas, J., Bij St.-Jacobs 12, 9000 Gent.
T. (09) 2241292. - Furn / Mod - *039883*
Uit Steppe en Oase, J Breydelstr 21, 9000 Gent.
T. (09) 2246736. *039884*
Van Durme, O. & F., Sluizekenkaai 1, 9000 Gent.
T. (09) 2242882. *039885*
Vercauteren, Henry, Onderbergen 48, 9000 Gent.
T. (09) 2231128. *039886*
Verhaeghen, Michel, 2 Koornlei, 9000 Gent.
T. (09) 2251607. - Instr - *039887*
Vermeulen, Herman, Kraanlei 3, 9000 Gent.
T. (09) 2243834. - Tex - *039888*
Violet, Laurent Delvauxstr. 1, 9000 Gent.
T. (09) 2252299. - Ant / Paint / Graph / Furn / Sculp /
Rel / Draw - *039889*
Witte, C. de, Bij St-Jacobs 9, 9000 Gent.
T. (09) 2238219. *039890*

Gentbrugge (Oost-Vlaanderen)
Cupido, Tennisstr 108, 9050 Gentbrugge.
T. (091) 30 74 30. *039891*
Dewever, Blockstr 22, 9050 Gentbrugge.
T. (091) 30 28 89. *039892*
Golden Lobster, Brüsselsestw 701, 9050 Gentbrugge.
T. (091) 31 76 99. *039893*
Harlekijn, Blockstr 24e, 9050 Gentbrugge.
T. (091) 30 28 89. *039894*
Parijs, D. van, Kardinal Mercierlaan 85, 9050 Gentbrug-
ge. T. (091) 30 85 68. *039895*

Geraardsbergen (Oost-Vlaanderen)
Barton, Grote Str 79, 9500 Geraardsbergen.
T. (054) 41 12 44. *039896*
Flamant, J., Gentsestr. 191, 9500 Geraardsbergen.
T. (054) 41 28 76. - Furn / Sculp - *039897*
Lorelei, Astridlaan 39, 9500 Geraardsbergen.
T. (054) 41 21 19. *039898*
Schuur, de, Vredestr 44a, 9500 Geraardsbergen.
T. (054) 41 34 53. *039899*
Van der Roost, W., Astridln 184, 9500 Geraardsbergen.
T. (054) 41 39 36. *039900*
Van Quickelberghe, Lessensestr 30, 9500 Geraardsber-
gen. T. (054) 41 27 33. *039901*

Gistel (West-Vlaanderen)
Antiek Hof, Oostendebaan 143, 8470 Gistel.
T. (059) 27 90 61. *039902*

Gosselies (Hainaut)
Les Lions, 6 Rue M Cornil, 6041 Gosselies.
T. (071) 34 08 48. *039903*
Vivart, 32 Rue de la Ferté, 6041 Gosselies.
T. (071) 35 72 18. *039904*

Grand-Rechain (Liège)
Keuninckx, L., 156 Av des Platanes, 4650 Grand-Rech-
ain. T. (087) 33 94 96. *039905*

's Gravenwezel (Antwerpen)
Beddeleem, St Jobsestw 19, 2970 's Gravenwezel.
T. (031) 658 39 93. *039906*
Bellon, V., Kerkstr. 49-51, 2970 's Gravenwezel.
T. (031) 658 21 41. - Ant - *039907*
Extra Muros, St Jobsestw 21b, 2970 's Gravenwezel.
T. (031) 658 63 68. *039908*
Vervoordt, Axel, Kasteel, 2970 's Gravenwezel.
T. (031) 658 14 70. - Furn / Silv - *039909*

Grobbendonk (Antwerpen)
Antico, Herentalsestw 120, 2280 Grobbendonk.
T. (014) 21 03 31. *039910*

Haasdonk (Oost-Vlanderen)
Hof Ter Linden, Melselstr 57a, 9120 Haasdonk.
T. (031) 775 39 09. *039911*

Haine-Saint-Paul (Hainaut)
Pasalli, L., 116 Rue du Queneau, 7100 Haine-Saint-Paul.
T. (064) 22 08 92. *039912*

Halle (Vlaams Brabant)
Art Gallery, 115 Basiliekstraat, 2980 Halle.
T. (031) 3568827. *039913*
Bergensepoort Antiek, Bergensestw. 111, 1500 Halle.
T. (02) 3560710. - Furn - *039914*
Beukenhof, E. & K. Hirsch, Eikenln 18, 2980 Halle.
T. (031) 3841124. *039915*
Brouwer, Paul de, Beestenmarkt 1, 2980 Halle.
T. (031) 3560050. - Furn / Jew - *039916*
Galerie Notre Dame, 17 Quai Williame, 1500 Halle.
T. (02) 3566450. *039917*

Hamme (Oost-Vlaanderen)
Ijsewijn, Willy, Teet 62, 9220 Hamme.
T. (052) 47 73 91. *039918*
Lantaarn, Heirbaan 307, 9220 Hamme.
T. (052) 47 84 42. *039919*
Peelman, J., Zwaarveld 24, 9220 Hamme.
T. (052) 47 83 93. *039920*

Hamont-Achel (Limburg)
Slegers, Henri, Keunenln. 7-11, 3930 Hamont-Achel.
T. (011) 44 61 95. - Ant - *039921*
't Winkelje, Keunenln. 52, 3930 Hamont-Achel.
T. (011) 44 66 72. - Furn - *039922*

Hannut (Liège)
Christiaens, J., 39 Rte de Landen, 4280 Hannut.
T. (019) 51 15 03. *039923*

Harelbeke (West-Vlaanderen)
Debaveye, Nieuwstr. 22, 8530 Harelbeke.
T. (056) 71 15 80. - Furn - *039924*
Dilux, Kortrijksestw 162, 8530 Harelbeke.
T. (056) 71 09 36. *039925*

Hargimont (Luxembourg)
Holtzheimer, J. B., 14 Rue des Capes, 6900 Hargimont.
T. (084) 21 21 39. *039926*

Hasselt (Limburg)
Amfoor Antiek, Genkerstw 187, 3500 Hasselt.
T. (011) 24 31 85. *039927*
Antiek Didden, Graaf de Brigodestr. 16, 3500 Hasselt.
T. (011) 31 37 81. - Furn / Instr - *039928*
Antiek & Design, Demerstr 73, 3500 Hasselt.
T. (011) 22 60 14. *039929*
Fryns-Grutman, 25 Kapelstraat, 3500 Hasselt.
T. (011) 22 73 25, 28 89 71. *039930*
Gathy, Dr Willemstr 4, 3500 Hasselt.
T. (011) 22 38 78. *039931*
Georgien Gallery, Isabellastr. 32-34, 3500 Hasselt.
T. (011) 22 76 41. - Paint / Furn - *039932*
Herckenrode, Dr. Willemsstr. 44, 3500 Hasselt.
T. (011) 22 61 59, 22 56 69. - Paint / Furn /
China - *039933*
Jeurissen, Maagdendries 4, 3500 Hasselt.
T. (011) 22 39 40. *039934*
Kathan, Guldensporenpln 10, 3500 Hasselt.
T. (011) 22 72 48. *039935*
Leboan, Zestienbundersstr 58, 3500 Hasselt.
T. (011) 24 13 35. *039936*
Retro Gallery, Maastrichterstr 113, 3500 Hasselt.
T. (011) 24 30 75. *039937*
Snuffel, F Massystr 13, 3500 Hasselt.
T. (011) 22 26 24. *039938*
't Karrewiel, Kuringerstw 519, 3500 Hasselt.
T. (011) 25 46 02. *039939*

Havré (Hainaut)
Charme du Passé, 1111 Rue de la Chée du Roeulx,
7021 Havré. T. (065) 87 30 92. *039940*
Gossez, A. & J., 1126 Ch. du Roeulx, 7021 Havré.
T. (065) 87 15 89. - Ant / Dec - *039941*

Hechtel (Limburg)
Leukenheide, Lommelsebaan 11, 3940 Hechtel.
T. (011) 73 41 02. *039942*
Van Reet, G., Hasseltsebn 85, 3940 Hechtel.
T. (011) 73 49 64. *039943*

Heinsch (Luxembourg)
Mortier, J. M., 195 Rue de Neufchâteau, 6700 Heinsch.
T. (063) 21 54 04. *039944*

Heist-Op-Den-Berg (Antwerpen)
Brems, Johnny, Bergstr 129, 2220 Heist-Op-Den-Berg.
T. (015) 24 12 99. *039945*
Medussa, Liersestw 199, 2220 Heist-Op-Den-Berg.
T. (015) 24 06 06. *039946*
Oorle, Paul van, Westerlosteenweg 24, 2220 Heist-Op-
Den-Berg. T. (015) 24 67 97. - Paint / Furn / Sculp /
Dec - *039947*
Orley, Barent van, Bergstr. 171, 2220 Heist-Op-Den-
Berg. T. (015) 24 11 10. - Ant - *039948*

Helchteren (Limburg)
Thijs, P., Schutterijstr 12, 3530 Helchteren.
T. (011) 52 19 75. *039949*

Hemiksem (Antwerpen)
Windsor, K de Backerstr 91, 2620 Hemiksem.
T. (031) 877846. *039950*

Herderen (Limburg)
Peters, L., Tongersestr 134, 3770 Herderen.
T. (011) 453216. *039951*

Heule (West-Vlaanderen)
Antika, Kasteelstr 7, 8501 Heule.
T. (056) 21 91 46. *039952*
Desimpel, J., Heulsekasteelstr 15-17, 8501 Heule.
T. (056) 35 32 46. *039953*
Gheysens, Heulse Kasteelstr 15, 8501 Heule. *039954*
Normandie, Kortijksestr 337, 8501 Heule.
T. (056) 35 34 53. *039955*

Heusden (Limburg)
Horenbeeck, F. van, Oude Baan 17, 3550 Heusden.
T. (011) 42 50 78. *039956*
Peuters, E., Dijkstr 181, 3550 Heusden.
T. (011) 43 27 77. *039957*

Heusy (Liège)
Legros, Joseph, Bonaventure, 40 rue Ho Diamont, 4802
Heusy. T. (087) 35 328. *039958*

Hever (Vlaams Brabant)
Spaanse Poort, Leuvensestw 177, 3191 Hever.
T. (015) 51 79 45. *039959*

Heverlee (Vlaams Brabant)
In de Oude Doos, Groenstr 129, 3001 Heverlee.
T. (016) 239442. *039960*

Hoeilaart (Vlaams Brabant)
Wiets, R., 68 Chaussée de Bruxelles, 1560 Hoeilaart.
T. (02) 6579237. *039961*
Wiets, Rene, Brusselsesteenweg 68, 1560 Hoeilaart.
T. (02) 6579237. - Ant / Paint - *039962*

Hornu (Hainaut)
Atelier du Grand Hornu, 80 Rue Sainte-Louise, 7301
Hornu. T. (065) 77 60 88. *039963*
Mattelin, Pierre, 23 Rte de Mons, 7301 Hornu.
T. (065) 77 65 19. *039964*

Hotton (Luxembourg)
Harlez de Deulin, S. de, Château de Deulin, 6990 Hotton.
T. (084) 466616. *039965*

Houdeng-Goegnies (Hainaut)
Belle Brocante, La, 125 Chaussée P-Houtart, 7110 Houdeng-Goegnies. T. (064) 22 34 28. *039966*

Houthalen (Limburg)
Habraken, Raf, Kazerneln. 97, 3530 Houthalen.
T. (011) 521465. - Furn - *039967*

Hove (Antwerpen)
AAC, Mechelsestw 127, 2540 Hove.
T. (031) 454 13 12. *039968*
Lombaert, 42 Av de la Gare, 2540 Hove.
T. (031) 55 56 77. *039969*

Huy (Liège)
Antiquités Marquise, 1 Av Ch et L-Godin, 4500
Huy. *039970*

Pire, 7, rue l'Apleit, 4500 Huy. T. (085) 118 40. - Ant /
Dec - *039971*
Sable, E., 19 Rue de France, 4500 Huy.
T. (085) 21 11 62. *039972*

Ichtegem (West-Vlaanderen)
Engel, Torhoutbaan 5, 8480 Ichtegem.
T. (059) 58 87 64. *039973*

Ieper (West-Vlaanderen)
Galerie Louis XV, Veurnseweg 7, 8900 Ieper.
T. (057) 20 26 02. *039974*
Galerij St. Michiel, 8 Blvd Frenchin, 8900 Ieper.
T. (057) 20 28 55. *039975*
Oud Ieper, Rijselstr 202b, 8900 Ieper.
T. (057) 20 02 86. *039976*

Impe (Oost-Vlaanderen)
Robberechts, Poly, 3 Hofsmeer, 9340 Impe.
T. (053) 219 042. *039977*

Ingelmunster (West-Vlaanderen)
Anim Art & Antiq's AAA, Kortrijkstr 1, 8770 Ingelmunster.
T. (051) 31 53 54. *039978*
West-Antiekhall, Bruggestr 158a, 8770 Ingelmunster.
T. (051) 30 09 53. *039979*

Izegem (West-Vlaanderen)
Desmet & Zoon, Roeselaarsestr 123, 8870 Izegem.
T. (051) 30 62 19. *039980*
Elegast, de, Elegastlaan 2, 8870 Izegem.
T. (051) 31 16 44. *039981*
Vandezante, Zwaluwstr 3, 8870 Izegem.
T. (051) 30 44 59. *039982*
Wyffels, Marktstr, 8870 Izegem.
T. (051) 30 24 80. *039983*

Jambes (Namur)
Marotte, 50 Rue Mottiaux, 5100 Jambes.
T. (081) 30 52 45. *039984*

Jamiolle (Namur)
Antiquités Françaises, 40 Rte de Villers, 5600 Jamiolle.
T. (071) 76 60 67. *039985*
Grenier de Grand-Mère, Le, 24 Rue du Village, 5600 Ja-
miolle. T. (071) 76 69 52. *039986*

Jeuk (Limburg)
Leplat-Ottenburgs, Hundelingenstr. 42, 3890 Jeuk.
T. (011) 485694. - Furn - *039987*

**Jodoigne (Geldenaken) (Brabant
Wallon)**
Byvoet, V., 5 Rue de Pietrain, 1370 Jodoigne (Geldena-
ken). T. (010) 811525. *039988*

Jumet (Hainaut)
Chez Maurice, 2 Rue Fourneaux, 6040 Jumet.
T. (071) 35 02 01. *039989*

Kain (Hainaut)
Bury, A., 40 Rue de la Résistance, 7540 Kain.
T. (069) 22 14 88. - Ant / Furn - *039990*

Kalken (Oost-Vlaanderen)
Van den Bogaert, Nerenweg 1, 9270 Kalken.
T. (091) 67 52 01. *039991*

Kalmthout (Antwerpen)
't Land van Calmthout, Voetboogln 5, 2920 Kalmthout.
T. (031) 666 78 60. *039992*

Kapellen (Antwerpen)
Exclusief Interieur, Antwerpsestw 213, 2950 Kapellen.
T. (03) 664 92 76. *039993*
Groote, de, C Palmansstr 43, 2950 Kapellen.
T. (03) 64 03 33. *039994*
Groote, de, Eikendr 30, 2950 Kapellen.
T. (03) 64 16 71. *039995*
Keyser, W. de, Antwerpsesteenweg 43, 2950 Kapellen.
T. (03) 64 76 79. *039996*
Lindehoeve, Bloemenlei 2, 2950 Kapellen.
T. (03) 64 00 25. *039997*
Midas, Kapelsestr 251, 2950 Kapellen.
T. (03) 665 21 85. *039998*

Oma's Boetiek, Ertbrandstr 228, 2950 Kapellen.
T. (03) 664 62 57. *039999*

Kasterlee (Antwerpen)
Schafer, Turnhoutzebn 31, 2460 Kasterlee.
T. (014) 85 22 18. *040000*

Keerbergen (Vlaams Brabant)
Asian Antiques, Haachtsebn 122, 3140 Keerbergen.
T. (015) 513355. *040001*
Bicoque, Oude Putsebaan 27, 3140 Keerbergen.
T. (015) 512250. *040002*

Kerkhove (West-Vlaanderen)
Mortier, Yves, Varent 5, 8581 Kerkhove. T. (056) 055/
38 75 91. *040003*

Kermt (Limburg)
Antiek Isabelle & Baerts, Molenstr 200, 3510 Kermt.
T. (011) 25 16 61. *040004*
Carmetum, Diesterstw 249, 3510 Kermt.
T. (011) 25 46 55. *040005*
't Spinnewiel, Diesterstw 429, 3510 Kermt.
T. (011) 25 52 26. *040006*

Kessel (Antwerpen)
Dobbelhoef, Terlakenweg 28, 2560 Kessel.
T. (031) 80 58 34. *040007*

Kinrooi (Limburg)
Decor et Antiquo, Breeërstr 121, 3640 Kinrooi.
T. (011) 702178, Fax 702691. *040008*

Kluisbergen (Oost-Vlaanderen)
Cousaert, Stationsstr 160, 9690 Kluisbergen.
T. (055) 387053. *040009*

Knesselare (Oost-Vlaanderen)
Van Loo, Kerkstr 67, 9910 Knesselare.
T. (091) 747884. *040010*

Knokke (West-Vlaanderen)
ABC Antiques & Etnography, Duindistelstr. 16, 8300
Knokke. T. (050) 60 20 54, 61 09 19, Fax 62 14 70.
- Sculp / Cur - *040011*
Allemeersch, S. van, Dorpstr 152, 8300 Knokke.
T. (050) 60 06 72. *040012*
Antiekhoekje, 'T, Zeedijk 608-610, 8300 Knokke.
T. (050) 21 51 98. *040013*
Antique City, T. (050) 60 70 96, 60 55 59. Elizabetlaan 178, 8300
Knokke. T. (050) 60 70 96, 60 55 59. *040014*
Antiques Collection, Leopoldln 17, 8300 Knokke.
T. (050) 60 30 21. *040015*
Antiques Market, 654 Zeedijk, 8300 Knokke.
T. (050) 61 49 05. *040016*
Antwerpen, R. van, Kerkstr. 37, 8300 Knokke.
T. (050) 51 32 22. - Paint / Graph - *040017*
Belleghem, van, Zeedijk 737, 8300 Knokke.
T. (050) 60 70 50. *040018*
Blanckaert, Kustln. 134, 8300 Knokke. T. (050) 60 41 79.
- Arch - *040019*
Boxy, Philippe & L., Dumortierln 105, 8300 Knokke.
T. (050) 61 44 02. *040020*
Castle Antiques & Arts, Lippenslaan 252, 8300 Knokke.
T. (050) 62 18 60, Fax 62 18 61. *040021*
Dajak, Zeedijk 518, 8300 Knokke. T. (050) 61 34 41.
- Eth - *040022*
English Antiques, Kustlaan 243, 8300 Knokke.
T. (050) 60 55 11. *040023*
English Workshop, Dumortierlaan 54, 8300 Knokke.
T. (050) 60 80 09, 61 42 02. *040024*
Gevaert, A. & E., Duivelputlaan 15, 8300 Knokke.
T. (050) 60 18 79. *040025*
Golden Chair Antiques, Zeedijk 654, 8300 Knokke.
T. (050) 61 49 05. *040026*
Grajek, Zeedijk 691, 8300 Knokke. *040027*
Hadley, Dames, Kustln 116 (-Heist), 8300 Knokke.
T. (050) 60 42 52. *040028*
Hallard-Vestringe, Zeedijk 768, 8300 Knokke.
T. (050) 606172. *040029*
Hamilton, Kustlaan 132, 8300 Knokke.
T. (050) 60 95 39. *040030*
Hauteville, Strandstr 7-11, 8300 Knokke.
T. (050) 60 03 34. *040031*

Jonge, Willy de, Zeedijk 708, 8300 Knokke.
T. (050) 61 21 06. - Paint -   040032
Lefèvre, W. & V., Kustlaan 136, Res. St. James, 8300
Knokke. T. (050) 608740. - Paint / Furn / Sculp / Dec /
Silv / Instr -   040033
De Maere, Jan, Kustlaan 136, 8300 Knokke.
T. (050) 603839. - Paint / Draw -   040034
Old Charm Antiques, Zeedijk 764, 8300 Knokke.
T. (050) 60 80 55. - Furn -   040035
Présences, Elisabethlaan 1, 8300 Knokke.
T. (050) 60 74 48.   040036
Thiel, J., Kustlaan 271, 8300 Knokke.
T. (050) 60 15 24.   040037
Thiel, P., Kustlaan 121, 8300 Knokke. T. (050) 60 12 06.
- Ant / Furn / Ico / Mul -   040038
Vervarcke, Dumortierlaan 23, 8300 Knokke.
T. (050) 60 97 05.   040039
Wiele, G. van de, Zoutelaan 16, 8300 Knokke.
T. (050) 60 55 68.   040040

Koekelare (West-Vlaanderen)
Antiek Jean-Marie, Belhutteln 83, 8680 Koekelare.
T. (051) 58 22 91.   040041
Brodeoux, E., Konijnenstr. 4, 8680 Koekelare.
T. (051) 58 89 16. - Ant -   040042

Koksijde (West-Vlaanderen)
Antiekshop, Zeelaan 200, 8670 Koksijde.
T. (058) 51 75 09.   040043
Calcoen & Cie., Veurnestr 24, 8670 Koksijde.
T. (058) 51 12 25.   040044
Dupont, J., Zeelaan 266, 8670 Koksijde.
T. (058) 51 13 30.   040045
Flamen-Desmet, Leopold-III-Ln 16, 8670 Koksijde.
T. (058) 51 66 82.   040046
Ikoon, Zeelaan 180, 8670 Koksijde.
T. (058) 51 75 47.   040047
Pannepot, F., Albert-I-Laan 115, 8670 Koksijde.
T. (058) 51 89 00.   040048
Strandjutter, Westendestr 6-8, 8670 Koksijde.
T. (058) 51 39 75.   040049
Verstraeten, A., Ensorln 9, 8670 Koksijde.
T. (058) 51 41 38.   040050

Kortessem (Limburg)
Kofferke, 'T, Hasseltsesteenweg 61, 3720 Kortessem.
T. (011) 37 66 62.   040051
Ralson, J., Steenweg 53, 3720 Kortessem.
T. (011) 37 66 62.   040052

Kortrijk (West-Vlaanderen)
A Room with a View, Koorniksow 121, 8500 Kortrijk
T. (056) 20 94 64.   040053
Antiek Coudere, Kasteelkai 3, 8500 Kortrijk.
T. (056) 20 28 78.   040054
Antiqua-Corturia, OL Vrouwestr 44, 8500 Kortrijk.
T. (056) 22 38 80.   040055
Beir, de, Lange Steenstr. 7, 8500 Kortrijk.
T. (056) 21 73 05. - Num -   040056
Bouckaert, Jean-Paul, 2 Grijze Zusterstraat, 8500 Kort-
rijk. T. (056) 212 707. - Furn / Sculp / Dec -   040057
Brokantika, Vrouwstraat 44, 8500 Kortrijk.
T. (056) 125 62.   040058
Bruggeman, A., & de Ruyter, Kapittelstr. 1, 8500 Kortrijk.
T. (056) 22 13 59. - Ant / Furn / China / Sculp /
Silv -   040059
Catry, V., Lge Brugstr 35, 8500 Kortrijk.
T. (056) 20 42 40.   040060
Coessens, Torkonjestr. 41-43, 8500 Kortrijk.
T. (056) 22 05 71. - Furn -   040061
Debeyne, A., Begijnhofstr 11, 8500 Kortrijk.
T. (056) 20 11 83.   040062
Grymontprez, Overleiestr 16, 8500 Kortrijk.
T. (056) 35 84 46.   040063
Lefèvre, W. & V., Hendrik Consciencestr 25, 8500 Kort-
rijk. T. (056) 220396. - Paint / Furn / Sculp / Instr / Dec /
Silv -   040064
Marlier, J., Kortrijksestr 406, 8500 Kortrijk.
T. (056) 35 73 03.   040065
Merchie, André, Kasteelstr 15, 8500 Kortrijk.
T. (056) 22 55 37.   040066
Minos, Veldstr 130, 8500 Kortrijk.
T. (056) 21 95 66.   040067

Oud-Cortrycke, Begijnhofstr 2, 8500 Kortrijk.
T. (056) 21 77 15.   040068
Peter Herpels, Begijnhofstr 1, 8500 Kortrijk.
T. (056) 217715, privé: (056) 220363.   040069
Remember, Grote Kring 16, 8500 Kortrijk.
T. (056) 21 74 58. - Jew / Silv -   040070
Sapas, Dolfijnkaai 4, 8500 Kortrijk.
T. (056) 20 40 78.   040071
Scheers, P., H Consciencestr 44, 8500 Kortrijk.
T. (056) 22 61 72.   040072
Speybrouck, O.L. Vrouwestr. 37, 8500 Kortrijk.
T. (056) 20 20 60. - Ant / Paint / Graph / Furn / Orient /
China / Sculp / Tex / Eth / Silv / Lights / Rel / Glass / Cur /
Mod / Draw -   040073
Van Canneyt, J., O-L Vrouwestr 44, 8500 Kortrijk.
T. (056) 22 38 80.   040074

Kraainem (Vlaams Brabant)
Gerard, R., 482 Av Reine Astrid, 1950 Kraainem.
T. (02) 7319613.   040075
Kot, 32 Av d'Oppem, 1950 Kraainem.
T. (02) 7315188.   040076
Pickwick, 97 Rue Van Hove, 1950 Kraainem.   040077

Kuringen (Limburg)
Old Pine Shop, Grote Baan 183, 3511 Kuringen.
T. (011) 254073.   040078

Kuurne (West-Vlaanderen)
Bekaert, Brugsesteenweg 387, 8520 Kuurne.
T. (056) 71 13 89.   040079
Delaere, Frank, Brugsesteenweg 289-397, 8520
Kuurne. T. (056) 71 30 08.   040080
Depypere, Michel, Kruiske Kerkstraat 97, 8520 Kuurne.
T. (056) 713 40.   040081
Galerij Sint-Bernhard, Koning Albertstr 31, 8520 Kuurne.
T. (056) 71 24 17.   040082
Haese, L. d', Leiestr. 115, 8520 Kuurne.
T. (056) 71 93 22. - Ant / Paint / Furn / China / Sculp /
Silv / Cur / Mod -   040083
Saint-Bernard, Kon. Albertstr. 31, 8520 Kuurne.
T. (056) 71 24 17.   040084

La Roche-en-Ardenne (Luxembourg)
Manigart, L., 22 Rue de Harzée, 6980 La Roche-en-Ar-
denne. T. (084) 41 16 83.   040085

Laarne (Oost-Vlaanderen)
Bourgondia, Eeklaan 93, 9270 Laarne.
T. (091) 52 78 07.   040086
Jonge, E. de, Eekhoekstr 82b, 9270 Laarne.
T. (091) 31 63 06.   040087
Standaert, M., Heirweg 140, 9270 Laarne.
T. (091) 69 52 84.   040088

Lacuisine (Luxembourg)
Meubles d'Epoque, Aux, 39 Rte de Neufchâteau, 6821
Lacuisine. T. (061) 31 19 35.   040089

Lantin (Liège)
Michel-Bastien, Y., 11 Rue Freddy-Terwagne, 4450 Lan-
tin. T. (041) 63 37 94.   040090

Lasne-Chapelle-St. Lambert (Brabant Wallon)
Galeries Dolphijn, 7 Rue d'Ottignies, 1380 Lasne-Chapelle-St. Lambert. T. (02) 6531058. - Mul -   040091
Vander Straete, René, Musée Ribauri, 1380 Lasne-Chapelle-St. Lambert. - Eth -   040092

Le Roeulx (Hainaut)
Duquesne, J., 1 Av du Peuple, 7070 Le Roeulx.
T. (064) 66 38 18.   040093

Lebbeke (Oost-Vlaanderen)
Elias, Hendrik, Galerie, Rooienstraat 78, 9280 Lebbeke.
T. (053) 21 44 35. - Ant / Paint / Graph / China / Sculp /
Sculp / Eth / Glass / Cur -   040094
Moonen, P., Baasrodestr 10, 9280 Lebbeke.
T. (053) 21 32 24.   040095

Lede (Oost-Vlaanderen)
Morel-Saey, Hoogstr 34, 9340 Lede.
T. (053) 705437.   040096

Ledeberg (Oost-Vlaanderen)
Boever, A. de, Dr Van Bockxstaelestr 49, 9050 Ledeberg.
T. (091) 25 35 93.   040097
Vervondel, Henk, Kl Kerkstr 50, 9050 Ledeberg.
T. (09) 2317916, Fax 2323393.   040098

VERVONDEL H.

Lic Kunstgeschiedenis Grad Chemie
Inkoop-Verkoop-Expertise
Antiek-Kunst-Curiositeiten-Boeken
Old master pictures

50 Kleine Kerkstraat
9050-Ledeberg-Gent,
Tel. 09 231 7916, Fax 09 232 3393

Leers-et-Fosteau (Hainaut)
Ancien Forestiel, Château de Fosteau, 6530 Leers-et-
Fosteau. T. (071) 59 23 44. - Ant / Furn / Dec /
Lights -   040099

Lendelede (Oost-Vlaanderen)
Raveschot, A., Burg G Dussartln 44, 8860 Lendelede.
T. (056) 35 19 32.   040100

Lennik (Vlaams Brabant)
Roelant, Maurice & Marc, Steenweg op Ninove 34, 1750
Lennik. T. (02) 5822729. - Ant / Cur -   040101

Leopoldsburg (Limburg)
Mertens, Diesterstw 104, 3970 Leopoldsburg.
T. (011) 34 37 32.   040102

Leuven (Vlaams Brabant)
Ars Antiqua, Frederik Lintstr 39, 3000 Leuven.
T. (016) 233449.   040103
Engelen-Casier, Muntstr 10, 3000 Leuven.
T. (016) 233919.   040104
Fine Antiques, Bondgenotenlaan 127, 3000 Leuven.
T. (016) 226472. - Ant / Furn / China / Cur / Cur - 040105
Galerij Uilenspiegel, Tiensestr 127, 3000 Leuven.
T. (016) 238816.   040106
Monica, Schrijnmakersstr 4, 3000 Leuven.
T. (016) 228046.   040107
Oosterlinck, R., Aarschotsestw 34, 3000 Leuven.
T. (016) 463039.   040108
Pauli, L., Bondgenotenln 127, 3000 Leuven.
T. (016) 226472.   040109
Pinus, Diestsestr 176, 3000 Leuven.
T. (016) 238346.   040110
Somers, D., Kapucijnenvoer 79, 3000 Leuven.
T. (016) 228982.   040111
Standard AHZ, Tiensesteenweg 416, 3000 Leuven.
T. (016) 250015.   040112
Szekér, Tiensestw 175, 3000 Leuven.
T. (016) 260491.   040113
Verlinden, J., 46 Tervuursevest, 3000 Leuven.   040114

Lichtaart (Antwerpen)
Wanmolen, de, Leistr 98, 2460 Lichtaart.
T. (014) 55 23 35.   040115

Liège
Ancion & Graulich, 11 Rue Matrognard, 4000
Liège.   040116
Angift, 16 Rue St-Adalbert, 4000 Liège.
T. (04) 2232715.   040117
Astrolabe, L', 2 Rue Laruelle, 4000 Liège.
T. (04) 2232463.   040118
Atelier, L', 19 Rue Louvrex, 4000 Liège.
T. (04) 2237096.   040119
Athanor, L', 2 Rue Sébastien-Laruelle, 4000
Liège.   040120
Au Saint-Thomas', 2, rue St.-Thomas, 4000 Liège.
T. (04) 2231839. - Ant / Dec -   040121
Bare-Delhaise, 20 Rue Saint-Adalbert, 4000 Liège.
T. (04) 2524436.   040122
Bauwens, Joseph, 8 Rue Saint-Thomas, 4000 Liège.
T. (04) 2232246. - Ant -   040123
Borghoms, C., 19 Rue de la Mutualité, 4000
Liège.   040124
Cadran d'Art, Le, 33 Rue St-Paul, 4000 Liège.   040125

Cottiaux, F., 35 Rue de l'Université, 4000 Liège.
T. (04) 2231061. *040126*
Cour Darchis, 5 Rue Darchis, 4000 Liège.
T. (04) 2233233. *040127*
Cremaillere, La, 16-18 Pl des Déportés, 4000 Liège.
T. (04) 2223574. *040128*
Cykorja, J., 62 blvd d'Avroy, 4000 Liège.
I. (04) 2320264. *040129*
Delsemme, 32 Rue Saint-Thomas, 4000 Liège.
T. (04) 2234977. *040130*
Deville, Jacqueline, 16-18 Pl. des Déportés, 4000 Liège.
T. (04) 2223574. - Ant / Paint / Graph / Furn / China /
Sculp / Jew / Silv / Instr / Mil / Glass / Cur / Mod / Tin --
040131
Drisket, 50, bd. Piercot, 4000 Liège. T. (04) 2320875.
- Ant / Dec - *040132*
En St.-Rémy, 6, rue St.-Rémy, 4000 Liège.
T. (04) 2322657. - Ant / Dec - *040133*
Ernes, E., 28 Rue Entre deux Ponts, 4000 Liège.
T. (04) 3436032. *040134*
Fairon, 625 Rue Saint-Léonard, 4000 Liège.
T. (04) 2270382. *040135*
Fourmiliere, la, 6 Quai sur Meuse, 4000 Liège.
T. (04) 2230614. *040136*
Galerie des Antiquaires, La, 23 Rue des Mineurs, 4000
Liège. T. (04) 2323137. *040137*
Galerie Saint-Georges, 10 Pl Saint-Barthélemy, 4000
Liège. T. (04) 2235327. *040138*
Gathy, Armand, 38-40 pass Lemonnier, 4000 Liège.
T. (04) 2235270. *040139*
Gavage-Longrée, 1 Rue Delfosse, 4000 Liège.
T. (04) 2223915. - China - *040140*
Genard, G., 12, rue des Clarisses, 4000 Liège.
T. (04) 2322674. - Ant / Num - *040141*
Gilles, 158, bd. d'Avroy, 4000 Liège. T. (04) 2320491.
- Ant / Cur - *040142*
Gillot, A., 32 Blvd d'Avroy, 4000 Liège.
T. (04) 2224238. *040143*
Gilman, P., 27 Rue de la Casquette, 4000 Liège.
T. (04) 2233934. *040144*
Goossens, Janina, 4 Pl. Sylvain-Dupuis, 4020 Liège.
T. (04) 3420125. - Ant - *040145*
Guffens, H., 29, rue Simonon, 4000 Liège.
T. (04) 2527581. - Ant - *040146*
Ile Saint-Louis, 21, rue du Mouton-Blanc, 4000 Liège.
T. (04) 2231518. - Ant / Dec - *040147*
Koenig, 9 Rue de Campine, 4000 Liège.
T. (04) 2263425. *040148*
Largefeuille, P., 11 Rue Bonne-Fortune, 4000 Liège.
T. (04) 2236605. *040149*
Le Faubourg St.-Gilles, 5 Pl des Déportés, 4000 Liège.
T. (04) 2275174. *040150*
Longrée-Gavage, 1 Rue Delfosse, 4000 Liège.
T. (04) 2223055. *040151*
Louis, J., 13 Rue du Rêve, 4000 Liège.
T. (04) 2237673. *040152*
Mesangère, la, 2 Pl Saint-Barthélemy, 4000 Liège.
T. (04) 2235449. *040153*
Moes, Karl M., 10 Pl. Saint Barthélémy, 4000 Liège.
T. (04) 2235398. - Furn - *040154*
Mooren, Francine, 38, rue Darchis, 4000 Liège.
T. (04) 2235542. - Ant / Dec - *040155*
Mosarm, 4 Blvd. Emile de Laveleye, 4020 Liège.
T. (04) 3440944. - Mil - *040156*
Paulus, André, 5 Rue Saint-Adalbert, 4000 Liège.
T. (04) 2230651. - Ant / Furn - *040157*
Piel, 2 Rue Laruelle, 4000 Liège.
T. (04) 2232098. *040158*
Pin de Campagne, 53 Rue Saint-Gilles, 4000 Liège.
T. (04) 2222137. *040159*
Pirlot, 10 Rue Saint-Thomas, 4000 Liège.
T. (04) 2340596. *040160*
Portes Saint-Thomas, Aux, 3 Rue Saint-Thomas, 4000
Liège. T. (04) 2234377. *040161*
Rapière, la, 26 Rue St.-Thomas, 4000 Liège.
T. (04) 2221127. - Ant / Mil - *040162*
Robin, Eloi, 8-10 Rue Soeurs de Hasque, 4000 Liège.
T. (04) 2233055. *040163*
Schutz, 17, rue St.-Rémy, 4000 Liège. T. (04) 2232303.
- Ant / Dec - *040164*
Somers, A., 5 Rue Saint-Adalbert, 4000 Liège.
T. (04) 2231017. - Ant / Furn / Instr - *040165*

Swinnen, A., 8 Rue Saint-Thomas, 4000 Liège.
T. (04) 2232307. *040166*
Tercaefs, 2, rue St.-Thomas, 4000 Liège. - Ant /
Dec - *040167*
Terwagne-Lamy, 10 Rue Saint-Adalbert, 4000 Liège.
T. (04) 2323490. *040168*
Thiry, 29 Rue de l'Université, 4000 Liège.
T. (04) 2322382. *040169*
Tradition, 29 Rue Simonon, 4000 Liège. T. (04) 2527581.
- Ant / Furn / Repr - *040170*
Trocante, La, 9 Rue Soeurs-de-Hasque, 4000 Liège.
T. (04) 2236495. *040171*
Uhoda, E. & S., 33 Rue Saint-Paul, 4000 Liège.
T. (04) 2320066. *040172*
Vieille Ferme, La, 107, rue du Plan-Incliné, 4000 Liège.
T. (04) 2526920. - Ant / Dec - *040173*
Vieux Saint-Martin, Au, 96 Rue Hors-Château, 4000 Liè-
ge. T. (04) 2230511. *040174*
Voorden, P. van, 146 Rue Feronstrée, 4000 Liège.
T. (04) 2231350. *040175*
Witmeur, J. P. & C., 6 Rue Saint-Adalbert, 4000 Liège.
T. (04) 2222564, 3426431. *040176*
Wynants-Smets, 130 Rue du Paradis, 4000 Liège.
T. (04) 2520447. *040177*
Xhenseval, Fres, 332 Rue St-Gilles, 4000 Liège.
T. (04) 2231254. *040178*

Lier (Antwerpen)
Antiek Boetiek, Timmermanspl 1, 2500 Lier.
T. (03) 489 08 36. *040179*
Antiek Veronique, Hooglachenen 26, 2500 Lier.
T. (03) 80 61 27. *040180*
Antiques White Furniture, P. Krugerstr. 77, 2500 Lier.
T. (03) 489 13 12, 480 01 80. - Furn - *040181*
Timmermans, Werf 10, 2500 Lier.
T. (03) 80 21 49. *040182*
Van der Heyden, H., St. Gummarusstr. 26, 2500 Lier.
T. (03) 80 30 45. - Ant / Cur - *040183*
Willems-Coenen, Mijl 31, 2500 Lier.
T. (03) 489 02 93. *040184*
Zinnia Art Studio, Mechelsestr 83, 2500 Lier.
T. (03) 480 88 88. *040185*

Ligne (Hainaut)
Jonas, C., 332 Chaussée de Tournai, 7812 Ligne.
T. (068) 28 25 25. - Ant - *040186*

Ligny (Namur)
Escaraboucle, L', Château, 5140 Ligny.
T. (071) 81 23 29. *040187*

Limbourg (Liège)
Stroeder, J., 34 Pl d'Andrimont, 4830 Limbourg.
T. (087) 76 22 11. *040188*

Linkebeek (Vlaams Brabant)
Bosch, Jean van den, 96 Rue Hollebeek, 1630
Linkebeek. *040190*
Ringer, M. & E., 85 Rue de la Station, 1630 Linkebeek.
T. (02) 3806717. - Ant - *040191*
Van de Velde, Patrick, 1630 Linkebeek. - Orient / Sculp /
Eth / Rel - *040191a*

Lochristi (Oost-Vlaanderen)
Keppens, G., Ruilare 54, 9080 Lochristi.
T. (091) 559617. *040192*

Lodelinsart (Hainaut)
Tevissen-Anthime, 62 Rue de Bruxelles, 6042 Lodelins-
art. T. (071) 31 28 30. *040193*

Lokeren (Oost-Vlaanderen)
Antiek 'T Anker, C. de Jonghe, Oude Bruglaan 72-74,
9160 Lokeren. T. (091) 48 13 29. *040194*
Muller, Lambert, Gentsesteenweg 288, 9160 Lokeren.
T. (091) 558 178. *040195*
Vuyst, de, Kerkstr. 22-54, 9160 Lokeren.
T. (09) 3485440, Fax 09 3489218. - Ant / Paint / Graph /
Furn / Sculp / Ico / Draw - *040196*

Lommel (Limburg)
Geboers, J., Luikerstw 435, 3920 Lommel.
T. (011) 64 56 53. *040197*

Interior Design Collections, Luikersteenweg 346, 3920
Lommel. T. (011) 64 32 59, 66 23 75, Fax 66 23 76.
- Ant - *040198*
Meulendijks, M., Luikerstw 246, 3920 Lommel.
T. (011) 66 24 91. *040199*
Willem's Antiek, Luikerstw 553, 3920 Lommel.
T. (011) 64 01 06. *040200*

Londerzeel (Vlaams Brabant)
Curiosa Gallery, Berkenlaan 49-51, 1840 Londerzeel.
T. (052) 309838. - Ant / Orient / China / Jew /
Mod - *040201*
Schouwer, K. de, Meerstr 113, 1840 Londerzeel.
T. (052) 309689. *040202*

Loppem (West-Vlaanderen)
Desmet, T., Heidelbergstr 22, 8210 Loppem.
T. (050) 826333. *040203*

Lotenhulle (Oost-Vlaanderen)
Gulden Wijzer, De, Grote Lijkstr 4, 9880 Lotenhulle.
T. (051) 68 89 93. *040204*

Maaseik (Limburg)
Dubois, G., Maastrichtersteenweg 41, 3680 Maaseik.
T. (011) 56 53 14. *040205*
Lemmens, D., Bosstr 7, 3680 Maaseik.
T. (011) 56 43 78. *040206*
Louvre, Rozeboomgaardstr 14, 3680 Maaseik.
T. (011) 56 56 69. *040207*
Prinsenhof, Maastrichterstw 38, 3680 Maaseik.
T. (011) 56 47 30. *040208*
Rietjens, H., Eikerstr 53, 3680 Maaseik.
T. (011) 56 48 08. *040209*

Maasmechelen (Limburg)
Antiek Avenue, Weidestr. 11, 3630 Maasmechelen.
T. (011) 763857. - Furn - *040210*
't Hemelke, Hemelrijkstr 1, 3630 Maasmechelen.
T. (011) 766381. *040211*

Maffe (Namur)
Bertot, J. G., 10 Rue Cherombou, 5374 Maffe.
T. (086) 32 23 88. - Ant / Paint / Furn / Cur - *040212*

Maisières (Hainaut)
Antic-Import, 243 Chaussée de Bruxelles, 7020 Maisiè-
res. T. (065) 72 89 44. *040213*
Château de Garenne, 243 Chaussée de Bruxelles, 7020
Maisières. T. (065) 72 89 44. *040214*

Maldegem (Oost-Vlaanderen)
Albo, Brugsestw 178, 9990 Maldegem.
T. (050) 71 78 08. *040215*
Antiekstock, 2n Butwerwestraat, 9990 Maldegem.
T. (050) 711 939. *040216*
Debbaut, Koning AlbertIn 36, 9990 Maldegem.
T. (050) 71 45 58. *040217*
Nys, W., Aalterbaan 229, 9990 Maldegem.
T. (050) 71 61 76. *040218*
Smitz, J., Noordstr 3, 9990 Maldegem.
T. (050) 71 20 72. *040219*

Malonne (Namur)
Georges, M., 501 Chaussée de Charleroi, 5020 Malonne.
T. (081) 44 49 62. *040220*

Marbais (Brabant Wallon)
Patriarche, J., 1 Rue du Petit-Mont, 1495 Marbais.
T. (071) 878136. *040221*

Marchienne-au-Pont (Hainaut)
Bilboquet, Le, 228 Rue de Beaumont, 6030 Marchienne-
au-Pont. T. (071) 51 58 28. *040222*

Marchin (Liège)
Brocante du Neumoulin, 17 Chem des Gneuses, 4570
Marchin. T. (02) 23 33 53. *040223*

Marcinelle (Hainaut)
Daumerie, 20 Av. Maurée, 6001 Marcinelle.
T. (071) 432 694. - Paint / Furn / China - *040224*

Mariakerke (Oost-Vlaanderen)
Bruinsma, M., De Hemptinnelaan 34, 9030 Mariakerke.
T. (091) 26 33 67. *040225*

Massenhoven (Antwerpen)
Anthonis, J., Bisschoppenbos 76, 2240 Massenhoven.
T. (031) 484 38 41.   040226

Mechelen (Antwerpen)
Antieke Klokken, St Katelijnestr 56, 2800 Mechelen.
T. (015) 211350.   040227
Bon a Bart, Hoveniersstr 14-16, 2800 Mechelen.
T. (015) 41 78 57.   040228
Grandeco, St Janskerkhof 5, 2800 Mechelen.
T. (015) 20 22 17.   040229
Holemans, H.-A., F De Merodestr 7, 2800 Mechelen.
T. (015) 29 07 93.   040230
Lemaire, C., Koningin Astridlaan 142, 2800 Mechelen.
T. (015) 41 60 84. - Ant / Rel -   040231
Mechelse Antiekgalerij, Brusselpoortstr 2, 2800 Meche-
len. T. (015) 42 18 41.   040232
Mechelse Galerij, Overheide 34, 2800 Mechelen.
T. (015) 20 15 32. - Ant / Paint / Graph / Furn / China /
Sculp / Silv / Instr / Cur / Mod / Draw -   040233
Spiegel- en Kristalpalace, F De Marodestr 84, 2800 Me-
chelen. T. (015) 21 77 55.   040234
Storms, Rik, Hallestr 16, 2800 Mechelen.
T. (015) 20 21 65.   040235
't Plantiekje, Leermarkt 6, 2800 Mechelen.
T. (015) 20 25 32.   040236
Van den Camp, Veemarkt 40, 2800 Mechelen.
T. (015) 20 43 05. - Furn -   040237
Verbinnen, Jos, 35 Korenmarkt, 2800 Mechelen.
T. (015) 417 613. - Paint -   040238
Vier Winden, Frederick de Merodestr 51, 2800
Mechelen.   040239
Wolf, I., Augustijnenstr 29, 2800 Mechelen.
T. (015) 20 00 37.   040240

Meerbeke (Oost-Vlaanderen)
Fonteyne Kolbe, van den, Brusselsesteenweg 409, 9402
Meerbeke. T. (054) 33 43 01.   040241

Meeuwen (Limburg)
Gielissen, Leten, Weg naar Helchteren 44, 3670 Meeuwen. T. (011) 791706.   040242

Meix-devant-Virton (Luxembourg)
Roger, J., 5 Rue Eaubruchet, 6769 Meix-devant-Virton.
T. (063) 577539.   040243

Melle (Oost-Vlaanderen)
Ter Schoone, Brüsselsestw 539, 9090 Melle.
T. (091) 52 36 10.   040244
Valmy, Brusselsesteenweg 159, 9090 Melle.
T. (091) 30 26 05.   040245

Menen (West-Vlaanderen)
Meerschaert, Arsenaalstr 46, 8930 Menen.
T. (056) 51 20 16, 017/64 33 40.   040246

Merchtem (Vlaams Brabant)
Zen Galerij, Markt 15, 1785 Merchtem. T. (052) 370843.
- Orient -   040247

Merelbeke (Oost-Vlaanderen)
Haegen, Fernand van der, 188 Gaversesteenweg, 9820
Merelbeke. T. (091) 30 09 10.   040248

Merksem (Antwerpen)
Belgium Antique Exporters, Terlindenhofstr 36, 2170
Merksem. T. (031) 6462911.   040249
Het Wiel, Oude Bareellei 34, 2170 Merksem.
T. (031) 6460074.   040250
Uilenspiegel, Azalealei 78, 2170 Merksem.   040251

Messancy (Luxembourg)
Style-Antiquités, Carrefour, 6780 Messancy.
T. (063) 37 73 22.   040252

Middelkerke (West-Vlaanderen)
Muyle, D., Koninginnelaan 7, 8430 Middelkerke.
T. (059) 30 40 40.   040253

Moelingen (Limburg)
Antik Mouland, 235 Rue de Fouron, 3790 Mouland.
T. (041) 81 06 82.   040274

Moerkerke (West-Vlaanderen)
Ter Polder, Natieln 4, 8340 Moerkerke.
T. (050) 71 22 09.   040254

Mol (Antwerpen)
Bouwkamp, A., Netebeemden 31, 2400 Mol.
T. (014) 31 76 06.   040255
Godfried, Ezaart 335, 2400 Mol.
T. (014) 31 42 33.   040256
Sfinx, Markt 43, 2400 Mol. T. (014) 31 30 84.   040257
Verheyen, Kruisven 63, 2400 Mol.
T. (014) 31 22 67.   040258

Molenstede (Vlaams Brabant)
Antiek Godfried, Ezaart 335, 3294 Molenstede.
T. (013) 31 42 33.   040259

Mons (Hainaut)
Descamps, C., 2 Rue des Chatriers, 7000 Mons.
T. (065) 31 30 61.   040260
Ecu de France, L', 4-8 Av du Belin, 7000 Mons.
T. (065) 31 36 89.   040261
Hennebert, 8 Sq Roosevelt, 7000 Mons.
T. (065) 33 13 53.   040262
Le Charme du Passé, 1111 Ch du Roeulx, 7000 Mons.
T. (065) 87 30 92.   040263
Nivarlet, Fernand, 7bis Rue Samson, 7000 Mons.
T. (065) 333818. - Ant / Furn / Orient / Mil -   040264
Nostalgie, 19 Marché aux Herbes, 7000 Mons.
T. (065) 31 70 48. - Ant / Paint / Graph / Furn -   040265
Passé Simple, 35 Rue de la Coupe, 7000 Mons.
T. (065) 33 76 48. - Ant / Furn -   040266
Roland, 102, rue de Nimy, 7000 Mons. T. (065) 72 86 55.
- Ant -   040267

Moorsele (West-Vlaanderen)
Huyse Grimaldi, Ieperstr 75, 8560 Moorsele.
T. (053) 412828.   040268

Moorslede (West-Vlaanderen)
Deprez, Strobomestr 7, 8890 Moorslede.
T. (056) 501356.   040269
Lepla-Muylle, Jacquesin 10e, 8890 Moorslede.
T. (056) 779570.   040270

Mortsel (Antwerpen)
Apers, W., Krijgsbn 136, 2640 Mortsel.
T. (031) 440 73 34.   040271
Nostalgie, Statielei 13, 2640 Mortsel.
T. (031) 448 05 08.   040272
Pine Antiques, Reypenslei 30, 2640 Mortsel.
T. (031) 440 49 44.   040273

Mouscron (Hainaut)
Antiquart, 121 Rue de la Station, 7700 Mouscron.
T. (056) 34 05 22.   040275
Lambaere, R., 60 Rue du Beau-Site, 7700 Mouscron.
T. (056) 33 51 18.   040276

Muizen (Antwerpen)
Van Meensel, K., Dijleberg 1, 2812 Muizen.
T. (015) 414732.   040277

Namur (Namur)
Art de Namur, 21 Blvd. Baron Huart, 5000 Namur.
T. (081) 22 73 66. - Ant / Paint / Furn / Orient / China /
Ico -   040278
Bolle, 6, Marché St.-Rémy, 5000 Namur.
T. (081) 22 52 88. - Ant / Cur -   040279
Clement, R., 42 Chaussée de Charleroi, 5000 Namur.
T. (081) 71 17 92.   040280
Galerie d'Art de Namur, 21 Blvd. A.-Aquam, 5000 Na-
mur. T. (081) 22 73 66. - Ant / Paint / Furn / Orient / Chi-
na / Ico -   040281
Hendrickx-Gourdin, E., 8 Rue Haute-Marcelle, 5000 Na-
mur. T. (081) 71 26 80.   040282
Lorphevre, A., 29 Rue Haute-Marcelle, 5000 Namur.
T. (081) 71 22 00.   040283
Mailleux, J., 106 Rue Moens-Gelbressée, 5000 Namur.
T. (081) 21 14 19.   040284
Petite Brocante, A la, 36 Rue Haute-Marcelle, 5000
Namur.   040285
Vieux Paris, Au, 6 Marché Saint-Rémy, 5000 Namur.
T. (081) 22 52 88.   040286

Nazareth (Oost-Vlaanderen)
Lombaert-Verzele, 's Gravenstr. 160a, 9810 Nazareth.
T. (091) 85 49 72. - Ant / Paint / Furn / China -   040287

Neerharen (Limburg)
Dubois, N., Staatsbn 85, 3620 Neerharen.
T. (011) 71 36 19.   040288
Zeegers, V., Staatsbn 72, 3620 Neerharen.
T. (011) 76 39 93.   040289

Neufchâteau-Dalhem (Luxembourg)
Klepper, Y., 28 Rue d'Alon, 4608 Neufchâteau-Dalhem.
T. (061) 277218.   040290

Niel-bij-As (Limburg)
Galery Petra, Grotstr. 11, 3668 Niel-bij-As.
T. (011) 658671. - Arch / Furn -   040291

Nil-Saint-Vincent-Saint-Martin (Brabant Wallon)
Gerard, J.B., 49 Rte. de Namur, 1457 Nil-Saint-Vincent-
Saint-Martin. T. (010) 65577. - Ant -   040292

Ninove (Oost-Vlaanderen)
Bremt, A. van den, Brusselstr 102, 9400 Ninove.
T. (054) 33 42 33.   040293
Kolbe, E., Brüsselsestw 409, 9400 Ninove.
T. (054) 33 43 01.   040294
Ville, E. de, Brusselsesteenweg 81-83, 9400 Ninove.
T. (054) 33 19 69.   040295
Walravens, J. M., Lavendelstr 2, 9400 Ninove.
T. (054) 33 40 21.   040296

Nismes (Namur)
Douillez, Jean, 17-19 Rue Vieille-Eglise, 5670 Nismes.
T. (060) 316 25. - Furn -   040297

Nivelles (Brabant Wallon)
Arglane, Georges, 26 Blvd. de la Dodaine, 1400 Nivelles.
T. (067) 213817. - Num -   040298

Noorderwijk (Antwerpen)
Leirs, Morkhovenseweg 79, 2200 Noorderwijk.
T. (014) 21 97 12.   040299

Noville-sur-Mehaigne (Namur)
Haemels-Vertommen, 97, ch. de Louvain, 5310 Noville-
sur-Mehaigne. T. (081) 81 15 64. - Ant / Dec -   040300

Ohain (Brabant Wallon)
Postillon, Le, 13 Rue des Saules, 1380 Ohain.
T. (02) 3540869.   040301
Tri Bizarre, Le, 2 Vallée Gobier, 1380 Ohain.
T. (02) 6333923.   040302
Wood & Silver Antiques, 17 Rue J Philippe, 1380 Ohain.
T. (02) 6532291.   040303

Ohey (Namur)
Godeau, J.-M., 175 Rue du Château, 5350 Ohey.
T. (085) 611780.   040304

Olen (Antwerpen)
Heemhoef, de, Hezewijk 48, 2250 Olen.
T. (014) 22 10 23.   040305
Laenen, G., Stationstr 7, 2250 Olen.
T. (014) 21 17 64.   040306
Naets, V., Statiestr 50, 2250 Olen.
T. (014) 21 47 09.   040307

Olloy-sur-Viroin (Namur)
Douillez, Albert, 9 Grand'Rue, 5670 Olloy-sur-Viroin.
T. (060) 39 92 03. - Furn -   040308

Oordegem (Oost-Vlaanderen)
Sadeleir, Johan de, Grote Steenweg 167, 9340 Oorde-
gem. T. (091) 69 30 66.   040309

Oostduinkerke (West-Vlaanderen)
Bosch, N., Albert-I-Ln 97, 8670 Oostduinkerke.
T. (058) 51 48 24.   040310

Oostende (West-Vlaanderen)
Amfora, Torhoutsestw 15, 8400 Oostende.
T. (059) 80 24 08.   040311
Art Option, A. Hendler, Koningstr 27c, 8400 Oostende.
T. (059) 51 09 10.   040312

Battle Shop, Kapellestr 76, 8400 Oostende.
T. (059) 80 47 40.   *040313*
Beeldens, Vlaanderenstr. 58, 8400 Oostende.
T. (059) 70 03 76. - Furn -   *040314*
David, Langestraat 55, 8400 Oostende.
T. (059) 70 12 90. - Ant / Cur -   *040315*
Decorative Fynaert, Oosthelling, 8400 Oostende.
T. (059) 80 43 45.   *040316*
Ensor & Stephanie, Christinastr 69, 8400 Oostende.
T. (059) 70 22 46, 70 77 55, Fax 80 07 26.   *040317*
Galion, Le, Bucareststr. 12, 8400 Oostende.
T. (059) 70 94 49. - Ant / Cur -   *040318*
Govaert, Serge, 4 Madridstraat, 8400 Oostende. *040319*
Kleine Wapenkamer, Groentenmarkt 10, 8400 Oostende.
T. (059) 50 29 83.   *040320*
La Pipe, 4, rue de Madrid, 8400 Oostende.
T. (059) 70 43 84. - Ant / Paint / Tex -   *040321*
Limbor, Wittenonnenstraat 1, 8400 Oostende.
T. (059) 735 18. - Ant / Cur -   *040322*
Oostende Antiques, Langestr 67, 8400 Oostende.
T. (059) 70 68 94.   *040323*
Ostend Antiques Market, Langestr 67, 8400 Oostende.
T. (059) 50 10 18, 50 75 67.   *040324*
Oude Glorie, Witte Nonnenstr 29, 8400 Oostende.
T. (059) 70 17 82.   *040325*
Rohain, Oosthelling 10, 8400 Oostende.
T. (059) 70 56 47. - Ant / Cur -   *040326*
Sint Jan, Stuiverstr 227, 8400 Oostende.
T. (059) 70 06 62.   *040327*
Uyttenhove, Kerkstr. 10a-12, 8400 Oostende.
T. (059) 50 56 17. - Ant / Paint / Furn / China / Sculp /
Tex / Lights / Rel / Cur / Mod / Draw -   *040328*

Oostkamp (West-Vlaanderen)
Deknock, G., Kortrijksestw 383, 8020 Oostkamp.
T. (050) 278790.   *040329*
Hermi, R., Molenstr 101, 8020 Oostkamp.
T. (050) 826483.   *040330*
Koorstrikerntiek, Bruggestr 107, 8020
Oostkamp.   *040331*

Oostmalle (Antwerpen)
Brauwer, R. de, Lierselei 122, 2390 Oostmalle.
T. (031) 12 31 55.   *040332*

Opwijk (Vlaams Brabant)
Van Hoetegem-Galle, Klei 262-264, 1745 Opwijk.
T. (052) 372618.   *040333*

Ordingen (Limburg)
Beckers, G., Kasteel, 3800 Ordingen.
T. (011) 68 44 22.   *040334*

Oudenaarde (Oost-Vlaanderen)
Old Tower, The, Armenlos 6, 9700 Oudenaarde.
T. (055) 31 48 47.   *040335*
Rogge, M., Achter de Wacht 16-18, 9700 Oudenaarde.
T. (055) 31 55 39.   *040336*
Ruyck, G. de, Burgscheldestr 38, 9700 Oudenaarde.
T. (055) 31 55 86.   *040337*
Tivoli, Tivolistr 171, 9700 Oudenaarde.
T. (055) 31 50 47.   *040338*
Vanderween, Broodstr 16, 9700 Oudenaarde.
T. (055) 31 20 35.   *040339*

Overijse (Vlaams Brabant)
Apolon, Pastorijstr 1, 3090 Overijse.
T. (02) 6877770.   *040340*
Montulet, H., Steenweg op Brussel 587, 3090 Overijse.
T. (02) 6573293.   *040341*

Overpelt (Limburg)
Bartels, Cor., Meerveldstr 5, 3900 Overpelt.
T. (011) 64 15 44.   *040342*
Den Hulst, Napoleonweg 53, 3900 Overpelt.
T. (011) 64 06 53.   *040343*
Mentens, J., Holvenstr 211, 3900 Overpelt.
T. (011) 64 14 51.   *040344*

Paliseul (Luxembourg)
Holtzheimer, J. B., 1 Rue de la Chapelle, 6850 Paliseul.
T. (061) 53 31 79.   *040345*
Holzheimer, J., 22 Rue de Bouillon, 6850 Paliseul.
T. (061) 53 38 64.   *040346*

Pepingen (Vlaams Brabant)
Blok, Steenweg naar Ninove 34, 1670 Pepingen.
T. (02) 3565611.   *040347*

Pepinster (Liège)
Brocantique, 14 Rue Hallet, 4860 Pepinster.
T. (087) 46 93 14,   *040348*

Perk (Vlaams Brabant)
Het Molenhuis, Tervuursesteenweg 78, 1820 Perk.
T. (02) 7518833. - Ant -   *040349*

Pessoux (Namur)
Brocante, 6 Chaussée de Namur-Marche, 5590
Pessoux.   *040350*
Catoul, 7 Rue Jannée, 5590 Pessoux.
T. (083) 68 80 19.   *040351*

Piétrebais (Brabant Wallon)
Carrosse, 10 Chaussée de Namur, 1315 Piétrebais.
T. (010) 840693. - Ant -   *040352*
Duponcheel, C., rue du Village 32, 1315 Piétrebais.
T. (010) 845390. - Ant -   *040353*

Pittem (Oost-Vlaanderen)
Krieke, de, Meulebekestr 107, 8740 Pittem.
T. (051) 46 74 13.   *040354*
Quackelbeen, C., Brugsestw 143, 8740 Pittem.
T. (051) 46 79 72.   *040355*

Plancenoit
Ferme de la Saline, La, 16 Chaussèe de Bruxelles, 1380
Plancenoit. T. (02) 54 49 95. - Ant / Cur -   *040356*

Pondrôme (Namur)
Mengal Jaky, Rte. de Bouillon, 5574 Pondrôme.
T. (082) 71 22 79. - Tex -   *040357*
Vieilleries du Tilleul, Les, 31 Rte de Bouillon, 5574 Pondrôme. T. (082) 71 14 56.   *040358*

Profondeville (Namur)
Autrefois, 112-114 Ch. de Dinant, 5170 Profondeville.
T. (081) 41 23 57. - Ant / Cur -   *040359*
Salentiny, A., 7 Av. Gén. Gracia, 5170 Profondeville.
T. (081) 41 16 55. - Ant / Dec -   *040360*

Proven (West-Vlaanderen)
Alleweireldt, Provenplein 63, 8972 Proven.
T. (057) 30 03 86.   *040361*

Putte (Antwerpen)
Lelie, de, Mechelbaan 571, 2580 Putte.
T. (015) 75 69 99. - Furn / China -   *040362*
Praxel, M., Leuvensebn 142, 2850 Putte.
T. (015) 75 41 62.   *040363*

Ranst (Antwerpen)
Dens Rustique, Schawijkplasweg 14, 2520 Ranst.
T. (03) 3539890.   *040364*

Reet (Antwerpen)
Deweer, Michel, Pierstr. 221, 2840 Reet.
T. (03) 844 02 74. - Furn -   *040365*

Retie (Antwerpen)
Het Antieke Kastenhuis, Provincieln 70, 2470 Retie.
T. (014) 671008.   *040366*
Antiekhoeve, Nonnenstr 25, 2470 Retie.
T. (014) 679078.   *040367*
Kunstgalerij Old Style, St Paulusstr 8, 2470 Retie.
T. (014) 377917.   *040368*
Martens, Postelsebn 10, 2470 Retie.
T. (014) 379225.   *040369*
Veilingen, Rens, Passtr 12, 2470 Retie.
T. (014) 379869.   *040370*

Rhode-Saint-Genèse (Brabant Wallon)
Galerie Saint-Germain, 174 Chaussée de Waterloo,
1640 Rhode-Saint-Genèse. T. (02) 3585134. *040371*
Magasin Pittoresque, Le, 18 Drève Pittoresque, 1640
Rhode-Saint-Genèse.   *040372*
Wauters, Imelda, Bronweg 15, 1640 Rhode-Saint-Genèse. T. (02) 3585775.   *040373*

Riemst (Limburg)
Vanseer, J., Tongertsestw 22, 3770 Riemst.
T. (012) 45 21 07.   *040374*

Rijkevorsel (Antwerpen)
Voeten, Kris, Koekhoven 5, 2310 Rijkevorsel.
T. (031) 3143437. - Ant -   *040375*

Rochefort (Namur)
Brocante, La, 51 Rue Jacquet, 5580 Rochefort.
T. (084) 21 27 87.   *040376*

Rocourt (Liège)
Nissen, 111 Rue Victor-Croisier, 4000 Rocourt.
T. (041) 26 45 54.   *040377*

Roeselare (West-Vlaanderen)
Bolhoed, Bollenstr 21b, 8800 Roeselare.
T. (051) 24 18 39.   *040378*
Loncke, E., Moorseelsestw 2, 8800 Roeselare.
T. (051) 20 63 45.   *040379*
Peter Herpels, Noordstr 68, 8800 Roeselare.
T. (051) 225581.   *040380*
't Oud Spinnewiel, Brugsestw 253, 8800 Roeselare.
T. (051) 21 00 41.   *040381*

Ronquières (Brabant Wallon)
Gehain, M., 152 Rue d'Henripont, 7090 Ronquières.
T. (067) 646371.   *040382*

Ronse (Oost-Vlaanderen)
Aatstraat Brocante, Aatstr 41, 9600 Ronse.
T. (055) 210550.   *040383*
Antiek Ronse, Ninovestr 83, 9600 Ronse.
T. (055) 212261.   *040384*
Brocanteur, St Cornellisstr 44, 9600 Ronse.
T. (055) 212915.   *040385*
Kruissens, Kruisstr 369, 9600 Ronse.
T. (055) 217155.   *040386*
Malander, Nieuwe Brugstr 5, 9600 Ronse.
T. (055) 215692.   *040387*
Princekouter, Opgeeistenstr 126, 9600 Ronse.
T. (055) 215481.   *040388*
Rosnaco, Kruisstr 2, 9600 Ronse.
T. (055) 211659.   *040389*
Sint Hermesgalerij, Aimé Delhayepl 3, 9600 Ronse.
T. (055) 214472.   *040390*

Rosmeer (Limburg)
Briers, D., Kerkstr 49, 3740 Rosmeer.
T. (012) 45 25 80.   *040391*

Rotselaar (Vlaams Brabant)
Den Beuk, Provinciebn 15, 3110 Rotselaar.
T. (016) 446125.   *040392*

Roux (Hainaut)
Bartet, S., 179 Rue de Courcelles, 6044 Roux.
T. (071) 45 02 91.   *040393*

Roux-Miroir (Brabant Wallon)
Choulet, E., 71b Rue de Patruange, 1315 Roux-Miroir.
T. (010) 88 93 12.   *040394*

Rumbeke (West-Vlaanderen)
Loncke, Eric J.G., Château de Rumbeke, 8800 Rumbeke. T. (051) 20 63 45. - Ant -   *040395*
Old Art, Koekuitstr 3, 8800 Rumbeke.
T. (051) 20 57 09.   *040396*

Rummen (Limburg)
Arcada, Grote Str 40, 3454 Rummen.
T. (011) 687077.   *040397*

Schaffen (Vlaams Brabant)
Poelmans, Kerkstr 71, 3290 Schaffen.
T. (013) 31 26 36.   *040398*

Schelle (Antwerpen)
Galerie Tolhuis, Tolhuisstr 70, 2627 Schelle.
T. (031) 87 60 90, 87 61 61.   *040399*

Schepdaal (Vlaams Brabant)
Pede's Hoeve, Lostr 96, 1703 Schepdaal.
T. (02) 5690896.   *040400*

Scherpenheuvel (Vlaams Brabant)
Raeymaekers, G., Vinkenberg 2, 3270 Scherpenheuvel.
T. (013) 334621.   *040401*
Reynders, F., Op 't Hof 68, 3270 Scherpenheuvel.
T. (013) 772651.   *040402*

Schilde (Antwerpen)
Dooren, L. van, Brasschaatsebn 8, 2970 Schilde.
T. (031) 83 40 90.   040403
Van de Velde, Schildedr. 1, 2970 Schilde.
T. (031) 383 63 94, Fax 384 17 38. - Furn -   040404

Schoonaarde (Oost-Vlaanderen)
Terlinden, Oude Brugstr 1, 9200 Schoonaarde.
T. (052) 42 26 36.   040405

Schoten (Antwerpen)
Art-Decor Antiek, Brechtsebaan 262, 2900 Schoten.
T. (031) 51 77 20.   040406
Grote-van Hooydonk, de, Horstebn 107, 2900 Schoten.
T. (031) 58 54 71.   040407
Les Prairies, Alice Nahonlei 19, 2900 Schoten.
T. (031) 658 14 09, Fax 658 20 08. - Paint /
Furn -   040408
Van Hove, Verbertstr 222, 2900 Schoten.
T. (031) 658 96 53.   040409

Serskamp (Oost-Vlaanderen)
Bee, Biesakker 27, 9260 Serskamp.
T. (091) 69 60 35.   040410

Sinaai-Waas (Oost-Vlaanderen)
Amma, Keizerstr 43, 9112 Sinaai-Waas.
T. (031) 772 11 90.   040411
Beirnaert, R., Keizerstr 16, 9112 Sinaai-Waas.
T. (031) 72 37 55.   040412
Smet, E., Stenenmuur 41, 9112 Sinaai-Waas.
T. (031) 72 30 45.   040413

Sint-Denijs-Westrem (Oost-Vlaanderen)
Cleverco, Hoge Heirweg 1a, 9051 Sint-Denijs-Westrem.
T. (091) 22 23 76.   040414
Verstraeten-Declercq, Bevrijdingsstr 12, 9051 Sint-Den-
ijs-Westrem. T. (091) 22 51 90.   040415

Sint-Gillis-Waas (Oost-Vlaanderen)
Drypikkel, Den, Bosstr 10, 9170 Sint-Gillis-Waas.
T. (03) 705048.   040416

Sint-Huibrechts-Lille (Limburg)
Antiek François, Kaulillerweg 69, 3910 Sint-Huibrechts-
Lille. T. (011) 643809. - Furn -   040417

Sint-Kruis (West-Vlaanderen)
Gruyaert, A., Maalse Steenweg 72, 8310 Sint-Kruis.
T. (050) 35 51 78.   040418

Sint-Lamprechts-Herk (Limburg)
Kumpen-Cleeren, Willy en Maggy, St-Truidersteenweg
563, 3500 Sint-Lamprechts-Herk. T. (011) 313197.
- Furn -   040419

Sint-Laureins (Oost-Vlaanderen)
Van Canneyt, E., Beukenhof 47, 9980 Sint-Laureins.
T. (091) 79 94 24.   040420

Sint-Lenaarts (Antwerpen)
Maison, L., Kerkstr 29, 2960 Sint-Lenaarts.
T. (031) 3130570.   040421

Sint-Martens-Latem (Oost-Vlaanderen)
Atelier DMK, Brakelstr. 3, 9830 Sint-Martens-Latem.
T. (091) 82 84 36. - Ant / Furn / Dec / Mod - 040422
Bouckaert, C., Latemstr 19, 9830 Sint-Martens-Latem.
T. (091) 22 91 73.   040423
Kunsthoeve, Dorp 12, 9830 Sint-Martens-Latem.
T. (091) 82 87 92.   040424
Langenhove, Gaetan van, 40 Koperstr, 9830 Sint-Mar-
tens-Latem. T. (091) 823 587.   040425
Naessens & Zonen, Kortrijksesteenweg 209, 9830 Sint-
Martens-Latem. T. (091) 82 39 44.   040426

Sint-Niklaas (Oost-Vlaanderen)
Antika, Kokkelbeekstr 221, 9100 Sint-Niklaas.
T. (03) 76 28 90.   040427
Coppens, Grote Peperstr. 45, 9100 Sint-Niklaas.
T. (03) 776 99 39, Fax 778 13 92. - Eth -   040428
Garsse, van, Stationstr 77, 9100 Sint-Niklaas.
T. (03) 76 11 25.   040429
Halven, F. van, Dalstr 152, 9100 Sint-Niklaas.
T. (03) 76 40 39.   040430

Lutin, F., Dalstr 144, 9100 Sint-Niklaas.
T. (03) 776 72 90.   040431
Muller, de Bondt, Ankerstraat 6, 9100 Sint-Niklaas.
T. (03) 76 66 76. - Ant / Dec -   040432
Paelinck, W., Luccastr 11, 9100 Sint-Niklaas.
T. (03) 776 47 42.   040433
Vanhalven, F., Dalstr 152, 9100 Sint-Niklaas.
T. (03) 76 40 39.   040434

Sint-Truiden (Limburg)
Antikhal, Hasseltsestw 137, 3800 Sint-Truiden.
T. (011) 67 28 79.   040435
Antiqua, Tiensesteenweg 200, 3800 Sint-Truiden.
T. (011) 67 21 90. - Ant / Dec -   040436
Decamp, V., Gootstr 29, 3800 Sint-Truiden.
T. (011) 67 71 43.   040437
Elite, Zoutstr 10, 3800 Sint-Truiden.
T. (011) 67 35 58.   040438
François, Tongersestw 56, 3800 Sint-Truiden.
T. (011) 672391.   040439
Vroonen, L., Beekstr 6, 3800 Sint-Truiden.
T. (011) 68 56 66.   040440

Snellegem (West-Vlaanderen)
Grande, Pol de, Kasteeldreef 5, 8490 Snellegem.
T. (050) 81 36 88, 81 26 86, Fax 81 30 94. - Ant / Furn /
Sculp / Tex -   040441

Soignies (Hainaut)
Capricorne, Le, 10 Rue de Mons, 7060 Soignies.
T. (067) 33 46 81.   040442
Lebon, 294 Chaussée de Mons, 7060 Soignies.
T. (067) 33 48 53.   040443

Spa (Liège)
Gerono-Vivane, J., 2 Rue du Marché, 4900 Spa.
T. (087) 087 772381;087 7724 17. - Ant -   040444

Spouwen (Limburg)
Doomen, Riemsterweg 238, 3744 Spouwen.
T. (011) 414103. - Paint / Furn / Jew -   040445

Stavelot (Liège)
Lemaire, Pierre, 4-6 Rue Neuve, 4970 Stavelot.
T. (080) 88 22 61. - Ant / Furn / Dec -   040446
Temps Jadis, 3 Rue Henri Massange, 4970 Stavelot.
T. (080) 86 31 02.   040447

Sterrebeek (Vlaams Brabant)
Trafalgar, Fazantenlaan 1, 1933 Sterrebeek.   040448

Templeuve (Hainaut)
Bernard, Chez, 63a Rue de Tournai, 7520 Templeuve.
T. (069) 35 29 41.   040449

Temse (Oost-Vlaanderen)
Ganesha, Cauwerburg 47, 9140 Temse.
T. (03) 771 40 88.   040450
Schalienhuis, Cauwerburg 210, 9140 Temse.
T. (03) 71 06 91.   040451
Segers, Stefaan, Scheldestr 2, 9140 Temse.
T. (03) 711 80 43.   040452

Tenneville (Luxembourg)
Teise, 36 Rte de Marche, 6970 Tenneville.
T. (084) 45 52 15.   040453

Ternat (Vlaams Brabant)
Jonge, A. de, Brusselstr 93, 1740 Ternat.
T. (02) 5820871.   040454

Tervuren (Vlaams Brabant)
Antiek-Kot, Leuvensesteenweg 40, 3080 Tervuren.
T. (02) 7675017.   040455
Avaert, D., 40 Rue Saint-Jean, 3080 Tervuren.
T. (02) 7678888.   040456

Terwagne (Liège)
Henkinet, G., 13 Rte de Liège, 4560 Terwagne.
T. (085) 41 19 40.   040457

Theux (Liège)
Belle Epoque, A la, 2, ch. de Spa, 4910 Theux.
T. (087) 54 17 65. - Ant / Cur -   040458
Jacob, L., 701 Chaussée de Spa, 4910 Theux.
T. (087) 22 47 13.   040459

Ramquet, P., 21 Hodbomont, 4910 Theux.
T. (087) 54 23 26.   040460
Vandervelden, La Boverie, face Gendarmerie, 4910
Theux. T. (087) 54 20 83.   040461

Thisnes (Liège)
Distexhe, L., 274 Chaussée de Wavre, 4280 Thisnes.
T. (019) 51 16 37.   040462

Thorembais-les-Béguines (Brabant Wal-
lon)
Velde, R. van de, 6 Rue de Glatigny, 1360 Thorembais-
les-Béguines. T. (081) 655308.   040463

Thuin (Hainaut)
Antiquités, 12 Rue Serstevens, 6530 Thuin.   040464

Tielrode (Oost-Vlaanderen)
Antiekhoeve, Hogenakkerstr 214, 9140 Tielrode.
T. (03) 777 98 43.   040465

Tielt (Vlaams Brabant)
Eterno, Leuvensestw 12, 3390 Tielt.
T. (016) 634595.   040466

Tielt (West-Vlaanderen)
Loontjes, Lucien, Deken Darraslaan 1, 8700
Tielt.   040467
Plettinck, C., Ieperstr 1, 8700 Tielt.
T. (051) 400325.   040468
Verkest, E., Ieperstr 45, 8700 Tielt.
T. (051) 401633.   040469

Tienen (Vlaams Brabant)
Buvens, Rijschoolstr 23, 3300 Tienen.
T. (016) 811147.   040470
Horenbeeck, F. van, Wolmarkt 5, 3300 Tienen.
T. (016) 811773. - Ant / Dec -   040471
Jopan, Peperstr 4, 3300 Tienen.
T. (016) 273756.   040472
Kelderke, 't, Wolmarkt 28, 3300 Tienen.
T. (016) 818445.   040473
Verpoorte, L., Gilainstr 134, 3300 Tienen.
T. (016) 816787.   040474

Tildonk (Vlaams Brabant)
't Groen Kasteel, Lipsestr 154, 3150 Tildonk.
T. (016) 60 20 88.   040475

Tintigny (Luxembourg)
Jacquemin, Georges, 46 Grand'Route, 6730 Tintigny.
T. (063) 441 62. - Furn -   040476
Schwartz, Jacques, 59 Grand'Rue, 6730 Tintigny.
T. (063) 44 40 07. - Ant / Furn / Sculp / Dec /
Rel -   040477

Tohogne (Luxembourg)
Remy, Joseph, 133 Rte de Durbuy, 6941 Tohogne.
T. (086) 21 21 97, Fax 21 31 40.   040478

Tongeren (Limburg)
Antiek Patrick, Luikerstw. 196, 3700 Tongeren.
T. (012) 23 39 73. - Furn -   040479
Castermans, Martin, Leopoldwal 5, 3700 Tongeren.
T. (012) 23 86 00, 23 50 93.   040480
Claes-Gielen, De Schieveldstr 37-39, 3700 Tongeren.
T. (012) 23 19 46.   040481
Claes-Gielen, Luikerstw 96, 3700 Tongeren.
T. (012) 23 63 82.   040482
Conforme, Romeinse Kassei 30, 3700 Tongeren.
T. (012) 23 22 40.   040483
Hansen, B., Waterkuilstr 13, 3700 Tongeren.
T. (012) 23 58 50.   040484
Houbrechts, J., Leopoldswal 8, 3700 Tongeren.
T. (012) 23 06 54.   040485
Jorissen, Luikersteenweg 118, 3700 Tongeren.
T. (012) 23 16 67.   040486
Lycops, T., Jaminstr 37, 3700 Tongeren.
T. (012) 23 78 58.   040487
Nassen-Vanseer, Luikersteenweg 555, 3700 Tongeren.
T. (012) 23 33 70.   040488
Paulussen-Bremaeker, Plein 9, 3700 Tongeren.
T. (012) 334 97. - Ant / Dec -   040489
Peters, J., Maastrichterstw 90, 3700 Tongeren.
T. (012) 23 12 88.   040490

Van den Put, Ton, Veemarkt 9, 3700 Tongeren.
T. (012) 41 34 15. *040491*
Willems, G., Kielenstr 10, 3700 Tongeren.
T. (012) 23 33 27. *040492*
Wolters, W., Stationslaan 24, 3700 Tongeren.
T. (012) 23 14 59. - Ant / Dec - *040493*

Torhout (West-Vlaanderen)
Antiek Brocante, Bruggestr 160, 8820 Torhout.
T. (050) 21 40 78. *040494*
Krommenhaak, Ruddervoordestr 19, 8820 Torhout.
T. (050) 21 16 15. *040495*
Weefhuis, 't, Rijselstr 195, 8820 Torhout.
T. (050) 20 08 47. *040496*

Tournai (Hainaut)
Bury, A., 47 Rue Saint-Brice, 7500 Tournai.
T. (069) 22 70 38. - Ant / Furn - *040497*
Camaieu, Le, 13, rue Saint-Jacques, 7500 Tournai.
T. (069) 22 70 89. - Ant / Dec - *040498*
Jeudy, 54-56 Rue Royale, 7500 Tournai.
T. (069) 22 32 52. *040499*
Maison Verfaille, 26, rue du Bourdon-St.-Jacques, 7500
Tournai. T. (069) 232 31. - Ant / China / Jew - *040500*
Verfaille, 26 Rue du Bourdon St-Jacques, 7500 Tournai.
T. (069) 22 32 31. *040501*
Verfaille, G., 1 Rue du Louvre, 7500 Tournai.
T. (069) 22 32 31. *040502*

Turnhout (Antwerpen)
Avonds, Pierre, de Merodelei 172, 2300 Turnhout.
T. (014) 41 18 65. - Ant / Furn / Sculp / Tex /
Cur - *040503*
Broeckx, Steenweg op Merksplas 2, 2300 Turnhout.
T. (014) 41 32 91. *040504*
Chris, Victoriestr 10, 2300 Turnhout.
T. (014) 41 28 66. *040505*
Chris, Zegepln 2, 2300 Turnhout.
T. (014) 41 88 35. *040506*
Goris, Warandestr 23, 2300 Turnhout.
T. (014) 41 20 40. *040507*
Hiltony's, Grote Markt 67, 2300 Turnhout.
T. (014) 42 32 30. *040508*
Kennis, H., Vianenstr 4, 2300 Turnhout.
T. (014) 41 38 00. *040509*
Tinne Pot, Vianenstr 4, 2300 Turnhout.
T. (014) 41 38 00. *040510*
Van Oprooy, A., Stw op Zevendonk 35, 2300 Turnhout.
T. (014) 41 82 67. *040511*

Uitbergen (Oost-Vlaanderen)
Kirchhoff, Gunter, Moleneindestr 31, 9290 Uitbergen.
T. (091) 67 64 44. *040512*

Vaux-sur-Sûre (Luxembourg)
Candido, E., 176 Rue de Neufchâteau, 6640 Vaux-sur-
Sûre. T. (061) 255449. - Ant - *040513*

Veldegem (West-Vlaanderen)
Goegebeur, Torhoutsteenweg 384, 8210 Veldegem.
T. (050) 27 76 16. *040514*

Veldwezelt (Limburg)
Nelissen, Bernadette, Heserstr 35, 3620 Veldwezelt.
T. (011) 721142. *040515*

Verviers (Liège)
Collette, R., 71 Rue des Saules, 4800 Verviers.
T. (087) 22 66 66. - Paint / Furn - *040516*
Follet, J., 62 Rue des Raines, 4800 Verviers.
T. (087) 33 79 65. *040517*
Legros, J., 55-59 rue du Brou, 4800 Verviers.
T. (087) 33 53 28. - Ant / Cur - *040518*
Polis, Monique, 12 rue du Pont, 4800 Verviers. *040519*
Wilket, 33 Rue du Mont-Moulin, 4800 Verviers.
T. (087) 33 42 77. *040520*

Veurne (West-Vlaanderen)
Ardies, Kasteel St.-Flora, 8630 Veurne.
T. (058) 31 27 02. - Ant / Furn / Orient / China / Sculp /
Cur - *040521*

Viersel (Antwerpen)
Vandenven, A., Liersebn 297, 2240 Viersel.
T. (03) 485 51 19. *040522*

Villers-le-Peuplier (Liège)
Christiaens, M., 8, rue de Huy, 4280 Villers-le-Peuplier.
T. (019) 51 18 55. - Ant / Dec - *040523*

Vlezenbeek (Vlaams Brabant)
Petit Bonheur du Jour, Au, Kamstr 1b, 1602 Vlezenbeek.
T. (02) 532 42 80. *040524*

Vonèche (Namur)
Bruchet, 22 Rte. de Bouillon, 5570 Vonèche.
T. (082) 711 718. - Ant - *040525*

Vorselaar (Antwerpen)
Lyen, A., Heikant 32, 2290 Vorselaar.
T. (014) 514057. *040526*

Vosselaar (Antwerpen)
Amber, Antwerpsestw 238, 2350 Vosselaar.
T. (031) 61 23 33. *040527*
Jaeg, M., 3 Floberg, 2350 Vosselaar. *040528*
Roets, L., Kard Cardijnlaan 43, 2350 Vosselaar.
T. (031) 61 29 51. *040529*

Vreren (Limburg)
Vanseer, L., Luikerstr 406, 3700 Vreren.
T. (012) 234050. *040530*

Vroenhoven (Limburg)
Gielen-Wolters, Maastrichtersteenweg 138, 3770 Vroen-
hoven. T. (012) 452483. *040531*
Wolters-Kusters, Maastrichtersteenweg 179, 3770
Vroenhoven. T. (012) 452252. *040532*

Waardamme (West-Vlaanderen)
La Diligence, Kortrijstr 394, 8020 Waardamme.
T. (050) 27 72 09. *040533*
Ming-k'i Gallery, Bosdreef 25, 8020 Waardamme.
T. (050) 27 82 95. *040534*

Waasmunster (Oost-Vlaanderen)
Hellicon, Neerstr. 135, 9250 Waasmunster.
T. (052) 46 10 83, Fax 46 13 11. - Ant - *040535*

Wakken (West-Vlaanderen)
Desmet, A., J van Severenln, 8720 Wakken.
T. (056) 61 02 57. *040536*

Waltwilder (Limburg)
Moesen, G., Lagestr 57, 3740 Waltwilder.
T. (011) 41 62 72. *040537*

Wandre (Liège)
Schoonbroodt, 66 Rue Rabosée, 4020 Wandre.
T. (041) 62 55 87. *040538*

Wanfercée-Baulet (Hainaut)
Chez Nelly, 16 Rte du Wainage, 6224 Wanfercée-Baulet.
T. (071) 812571. *040539*

Waregem (West-Vlaanderen)
Arttra, Stormestr 118, 8790 Waregem.
T. (056) 60 19 56. *040540*
Uniek Oudheden, DrBohey-VandecWesterlaau 56, 8790
Waregem. T. (056) 60 29 22. *040541*
Volmaakt Verleden, Keukeldamstr 28, 8790 Waregem.
T. (056) 60 89 75. *040542*
Voltaire, Nokerseweg 99, 8790 Waregem.
T. (056) 60 44 86. *040543*

Waremme (Liège)
Alcazar, L', 47 Av H Monjoie, 4370 Waremme.
T. (019) 32 23 51. *040544*
Heymans, 52 Rue Noé-Jacques, 4300 Waremme.
T. (019) 32 40 40. *040545*
Jori, 134 Rue de Hodeige, 4300 Waremme.
T. (019) 32 50 22. *040546*

Waterloo (Brabant Wallon)
Ascot Gallery, 4 Rue M Verbeek, 1410 Waterloo.
T. (02) 3454588. *040547*
Château Cheval, 557 Chaussée de Bruxelles, 1410 Wa-
terloo. T. (02) 3840740, 3580740, 6531254. *040548*
Ferme de l'Ermite, 374 Chaussée de Bruxelles, 1410
Waterloo. T. (02) 3544114. - Ant - *040549*
Feuillet Jauni, Au, 396 Chaussée de Bruxelles, 1410
Waterloo. T. (02) 3547160. *040550*

Joli Pin, 391 Ch. de Bruxelles, 1410 Waterloo.
T. (02) 3540376. - Furn - *040551*
London Antiques, 596 Chaussée de Bruxelles, 1410 Wa-
terloo. T. (02) 3540953. *040552*
Sandy's Antiques, 368 Chaussée de Bruxelles, 1410
Waterloo. T. (02) 3541672. *040553*

Watou (West-Vlaanderen)
Huys-Vercruysse, Abeleplein 8, 8978 Watou.
T. (057) 38 80 14. *040554*

Wavre (Waver) (Brabant Wallon)
Boite à Pin, 266 Chaussée de Louvain, 1300 Wavre (Wa-
ver). T. (010) 225478. - Furn - *040555*
Hautteman, Ferme des Templiers, 1300 Wavre (Waver).
T. (010) 222385, 225348. *040556*
La Halle aux Bois, 122 Rue de Namur, 1300 Wavre (Wa-
ver). T. (010) 224056. *040557*

Westkerke (West-Vlaanderen)
Raaihof, Natieln 287, 8460 Westkerke.
T. (059) 62 13 04. *040558*

Westmalle (Antwerpen)
Europahallen, Delften 23, 2390 Westmalle.
T. (03) 3116152. *040559*
Fimmers, Brechtsestw 31, 2390 Westmalle.
T. (03) 3123718. *040560*

Westmeerbeek (Antwerpen)
Eksternest, Het, Ramselsesteenweg 215, 2235 West-
meerbeek. T. (016) 69 99 55. *040561*

Wetteren (Oost-Vlaanderen)
Baele, Johan, Massemensestw 302, 9230 Wetteren.
T. (091) 69 97 75. *040562*
Baele, N., Markt 2, 9230 Wetteren.
T. (091) 69 07 34. *040563*
Hof ter Wachteke, Schoorstr 47, 9230 Wetteren.
T. (091) 52 23 91. *040564*
Roels, Jabekestr 14, 9230 Wetteren.
T. (091) 69 26 92. *040565*
Van Belleghem, A., Krakeelweg 3, 9230 Wetteren.
T. (091) 69 42 95. *040566*

Wevelgem (West-Vlaanderen)
Antiek Design, Grote Markt 34, 8560 Wevelgem.
T. (056) 41 35 35. *040567*
Stragier, Gullegemstr 119, 8560 Wevelgem.
T. (056) 41 27 40. *040568*

Wijchmaal (Limburg)
Dubrulle, Marien, Stationstr. 48, 3990 Wijchmaal.
T. (011) 632890. - Ant - *040569*

Wijgmaal (Vlaams Brabant)
Collector, Molenstr 20, 3018 Wijgmaal.
T. (016) 448765. *040570*

Willebroek (Antwerpen)
Saerens, Dendermondsesteenweg 220, 2830 Wille-
broek. T. (03) 86 53 61. *040571*

Wilrijk (Antwerpen)
Civitas, Bist 37, 2610 Wilrijk. T. (031) 828 34 92. - Ant /
Paint / Rel - *040572*

Wingene (West-Vlaanderen)
Perquy, Beememsteenweg 52b, 8750 Wingene. *040573*

Wommelgem (Antwerpen)
Philippaerts, Pierre, Herentalsebn 258, 2160 Wommelgem. T. (031) 321 87 84, Fax 322 00 71. *040574*

Wortegem (Oost-Vlaanderen)
Labis, Gilbert, 3 Waregemseweg 9790 Wortegem.
T. (056) 68 82 09. *040575*
Sint-Ignace, Pontstr 24, 9790 Wortegem.
T. (056) 60 61 28. *040576*

Wuustwezel (Antwerpen)
Delvaux, R., Den Bouw 35, 2990 Wuustwezel.
T. (03) 6633155. *040577*

Zandvliet (Antwerpen)
Jagersrust, De Keyzerhoeve 16, 2040 Zandvliet.
T. 5689518. *040578*

Zaventem (Vlaams Brabant)
Paron, H. de, Mechelsesteenweg 401, 1930 Zaventem.
T. (02) 7599323. 040579

Zedelgem (West-Vlaanderen)
Vanderwee, H., Collevijnstr 9, 8210 Zedelgem.
T. (050) 27 61 56. 040580

Zoersel (Antwerpen)
Blank, Max, Bethaniëlei 91, Sint-Antonius, 2980 Zoersel. T. (031) 384 34 49. 040581
Clercq, L. de, Bosin 21, 2980 Zoersel.
T. (031) 383 67 24. 040582
Pine Antiques International, Rodendijk 58, 2980 Zoersel.
T. (031) 312 44 51. 040583

Zolder (Limburg)
Antiek Weekend, Hofeindestr 68, 3550 Zolder.
T. (011) 53 36 68. 040584
Merrenhof, M Scherlersln 111, 3550 Zolder.
T. (011) 53 32 33. 040585

Zomergem (Oost-Vlaanderen)
Antiek Gudrun, Grote Baan 22e, 9930 Zomergem.
T. (091) 72 84 98. 040586

Zonhoven (Limburg)
Awouters, Bremstr 19, 3520 Zonhoven.
T. (011) 81 40 98. 040587

Zottegem (Oost-Vlaanderen)
Antiek Century Brocante, Bruggenhoek 3, 9620 Zottegem. T. (091) 60 25 56. 040588
Breughel, Stw op Aalst 26, 9620 Zottegem.
T. (091) 60 80 63. 040589
Tilia, Gentsesteenweg 291, 9620 Zottegem. 040590

Zulte (West-Vlaanderen)
Patrick, Grote Stw 26, 9870 Zulte.
T. (091) 88 83 61. 040591

Zutendaal (Limburg)
Maenen-Steegmans, Daalstr 96, 3690 Zutendaal.
T. (011) 61 17 91. 040592

Zwijndrecht (Antwerpen)
Wilpa, Verbrandendijk 82, 2070 Zwijndrecht.
T. (03) 52 97 58. 040593

Bermuda

Hamilton
Spencer Drummond, Reid House, Church St., Hamilton POB 1179, 5-24. T. (809) 5-2244. - Paint / Graph / Eth – 040594
Thistle Gallery Antiques, Park Street, Hamilton, GPO 524. T. (809) 2923839. 040595

Southampton
Slope, Eric D., POB 524, Southampton.
T. (809) 238 03 44. - Ant / Num / China / Silv / Glass – 040596

Brazil

Rio de Janeiro (Rio de Janeiro)
Band Joalheiros Antiquarios S. A., Barata Ribeiro 157, 26370 Rio de Janeiro. T. (021) 255 9535, 237 5092. - Ant / Jew / Silv / Cur – 040597
Galeria Bonino, Copacabana Rua Barat Ribeiro, 26370 Rio de Janeiro. T. (021) 235 7831. 040598

São Paulo
Casa e Jardim, Avda. Santo Amaro 34 93, São Paulo.
T. (011) 61 29 15, 34 43 44. - Graph / Repr / Sculp / Dec – 040599
Galeria Império, Rua Dr. Melo Alves 368, São Paulo.
T. (011) 8 84 75. - Ant – 040600
Gouvêa, Renato Magalhães, Rua Pelotas, 475, São Paulo, 04012. T. (011) 549 1700. - Ant / Paint / Graph / Furn / Orient / China / Sculp / Tex / Fra / Silv / Glass / Cur / Mod / Draw – 040601

Vicente, Edmundo, Rua Livreiro Saraiva 236, 01237 São Paulo. - Num – 040602

Canada

Aberfoyle (Ontario)
The Flea Market, Aberfoyle. T. (519) 822 3109.
- Ant – 040603

Amherst (Nova Scotia)
Noburn Antique Shop, Highway 2, Amherst.
T. (902) 667 35 06. 040604
Radones Antiques, 79 Victoria St.W., Amherst.
T. (902) 667 29 49. - Graph / Furn / Instr / Mil / Glass – 040605
Treasure House Ltd., Victoria St., Amherst.
T. (902) 667 24 01. - Ant – 040606

Baddeck (Nova Scotia)
Lynwood Ltd., Baddeck. T. (902) 295 2950. - Ant / Paint / China / Instr / Glass – 040607

Brighton (Ontario)
Dutch Oven, 1 1/2 miles West, Hwy. 2 R. R. 4, Brighton. 040608
Skimble-Skamble Antiques, Cul-de-Sac, R. R. 5, Brighton. 040609

Brockville (Ontario)
Stoneacres, Hwy. 2, Brockville. - Ant / Furn / Tex – 040610

Burgessville (Ontario)
Larmson's Pig'n Plow Antiques, RR1, Burgessville, N0J 1C0. T. (519) 253 84 66. 040611

Burlington (Ontario)
Chandelier Antiques, 2107 Lakeshore Rd., Burlington.
- Ant / Furn / China / Dec / Jew / Silv / Lights / Glass -- 040612

Calgary (Alberta)
Bashford's Corner Ltd., 736 17th Ave. S.W., Calgary, T2S 0B7. T. (403) 269 3560. - Furn / China / Silv – 040613
Birks, H. & Sons Ltd., 314 8th Ave. W., Calgary. - Jew / Silv – 040614
Continental Art Agencies, 921 Riverdale Ave., Calgary.
T. (403) 243 0764. - Ant / Paint / Fra – 040615

Cataraqui (Ontario)
Allie's Antiques, Sydenham Rd., Cataraqui. - Ant / Furn / Jew / Glass – 040616

Charlottetown (Prince Edward Island)
Island Antiques, 80 Highland Ave., Charlottetown.
T. (902) 892 94 37. - Furn / Eth – 040617

Clarkson (Ontario)
Clarkson Market Antiques, 1675 Lake Shore Rd. W., Clarkson. T. (905) 822 0292. - Ant / Furn / China – 040618

Cornwall (Ontario)
Treetops Motel Antique Shop, No. 2 Hwy. W., Cornwall.
- Ant / Furn / China / Silv – 040619

Delhi (Ontario)
Hallmark Shop-REG'D, 3 miles S. on Turkey Point Provincial Park Rd. H.N.10, P. O. Box 248, Delhi, Ont. N4B 2X1. T. (519) 4267059. - Ant / Paint / Furn / China / Tex / Eth / Jew / Silv / Lights / Instr / Glass / Cur – 040620

Fairfield (Prince Edward Islands)
Granary Antiques, The, Rt. 2, Souris, Fairfield.
- Ant – 040621

Gananoque (Ontario)
Beaver Hall Antiques, 21 King St. E, Gananoque.
T. (613) 382 2228. - Furn / China / Eth / Fra / Silv / Glass – 040622

Glen Williams (Ontario)
Beaumont, Marie, 1 mile N. of Georgetown off Hwy. 7, Glen Williams. T. (905) 877 2549. - Ant / Furn / Orient / Lights – 040623

Goderich (Ontario)
Stehs, Dennis, 45 Waterloo St., Goderich. - Ant / Furn / Lights / Mil / Glass – 040624

Guelph (Ontario)
Bedford Antique Shop, 108 Queen St., Guelph. - Ant / Paint – 040625

Halifax (Nova Scotia)
Roberts Ltd., G., 1711 Barrington Rd., Halifax.
T. (902) 422 4516. - Furn / Jew / Silv – 040626
Zwicker's Gallery, 5415 Doyle St., Halifax. 040627

Hamilton (Ontario)
Beaver Coins, Stamps and Antiques, 251 King St. E, Hamilton, Ont. T. (905) 522-3828. - Num / Mil – 040628
Beckett Gallery, 142 James St. S., Hamilton, L8P 3A2.
- Paint / Graph / Sculp / Jew – 040629
Birks, H. & Sons Ltd., 2, King St. E., Hamilton. - Jew / Silv – 040630
Hamilton Antique Market, 2440 Barton St., Hamilton, Ont. - Ant / Furn / Lights / Glass – 040631

Hudson Heights (Québec)
Hudson Antiques of Vaudreuil, P.O.Box 438, Hudson Heights. T. (514) 455 53 53. - Graph / Furn / Eth / Glass – 040632

Jordan (Ontario)
Griffith, Mrs. Audrey E., 25 Main St., Jordan.
- Ant – 040633

Kettleby (Ontario)
Kettlecroft Antiques, Aurora Cloverleaf at Hwy. 400, Kettleby, Ont. T. (905) 727-4184. - Ant – 040634

Kingston (Ontario)
Cottage Antiques, the, 326 University, Kingston.
T. (613) 542 6189. 040635
James, Glen, 4033 Bath Rd., Kingston.
T. (613) 389 1473. 040636
Silveratone Antiques, R R 8, Kingston. T. (613) 544 1364. - Furn – 040637

Lindsay (Ontario)
Burridge Century House, R. R. 6, Lindsay. - Ant – 040638
Harding of Lindsay, 173 Lindsay St. S., Lindsay.
T. (705) 324 2551. - Ant – 040639

Mahone Bay (Nova Scotia)
Pine Shop, the, Main St., Mahone Bay, B0J 2E0.
T. (902) 624 92 20. - Furn – 040640

Markham (Ontario)
The Electric Gallery, 226 Steelcase Road West, Markham, L3R IB3. 040641

Missisauga (Ontario)
Raebinloft Antiques, 1480 Derry Rd. E., Missisauga.
T. (416) 677-3300. - Ant – 040642

Montréal (Québec)
Allice, Harry M., 6370 McLynn Ave, Montreal.
T. (514) 739 0564. - Ant / Paint / Silv – 040643
Artlenders, 318 Victoria Ave., Montreal. 040644
Atelier J. Lukacs, 1504 Sherbrooke St. W, Montreal, Qué. H3G 1L3. T. (514) 933-9877. - Paint / Sculp – 040645
Banko, Walter, Box 97 Westmount PO, Montreal, H3Z 2TI. T. (514) 672 93 64. 040646
Birks, H. & Sons Ltd., 1240 Philips Sq., Montreal.
T. (514) 392 2511. - Ant / China / Jew / Silv – 040647
Bonsecours Antiques, 441 St. Claude St., Montreal.
T. (514) 861 4375. - Ant – 040648
Circa 1880, 2129 Saint Urbain St., Montreal, P.Q.
T. (514) 849 9670. - Ant – 040649
Continental Galleries, 1450 Drummond St., Montreal. 040650
Crescent Antiques, 2137 Crescent St., Montreal, H3G 2C1. T. (514) 849 3061. - Ant / Paint / Graph / Furn / China / Tex / Silv / Lights / Instr / Glass – 040651

Fargeon Bros. Ltd., 5340 Queen Mary Rd., Montreal.
T. (514) 482 9910. - Ant - 040652

Ferroni, 2145 Crescent St., Montreal. T. (514) 849-
1356. - Ant / Graph / Furn / Orient / Dec / Silv / Lights /
Instr / Glass - 040653

Garo, La Maison de l'Art, 305 Ste. Catherine St. E.,
Montreal. T. (514) 844 2924. 040654

Hide Away Antiques, 69 Westminster Ave. North, Montreal. T. (514) 481 90 59. - Furn / China / Silv - 040655

Hoffman's, 1472 Peel St., Montreal. T. (514) 844 2579.
- Ant / Paint / Jew / Silv / Ico - 040656

Johnson, Jan, 2258a Coursol St., Montreal, P.Q. H3J
1C5. T. (514) 935-4721. - Paint - 040657

Klein, Dan, 1494 W Sherbrooke St., Montreal.
T. (514) 937-6161. 040658

Lacasse, Jean, Antiques, 1031 Laurier St. West,
Montreal. 040659

Ohman's Ltd., 1216 Greene Ave., Montreal.
T. (514) 933 4046. - Jew / Silv - 040660

Petit Musée, 1494 Sherbrooke St. W, Montreal, H3G-
1L3. T. (514) 937-6161. - Ant / Paint / Graph / Furn /
Orient / China / Sculp / Tex / Arch / Eth / Dec / Jew / Silv /
Lights / Instr / Mil / Rel / Glass / Cur / Ico - 040661

Plomer, Hubert, 1226 Bishop St., Montreal. T. (514) 866-
0837. - Ant / Furn - 040662

Quebec Antiques, 33 Lakeshore Rd. Pointe Claire, Montreal. T. (514) 697 0643. 040663

Russell, John L., 1504 Sherbrooke St. W., Montreal.
T. (514) 935 2129. - Ant / Paint / Graph / Furn / China /
Repr / Jew / Silv / Lights / Instr / Glass - 040664

Napanee (Ontario)
Graham, 232 W Dundas St., Napanee, K7R 2A8.
T. (613) 354-3454. - Ant - 040665

New Glasgow (Nova Scotia)
Garrett's-By-The-Bridge, 124 Kemp St., New Glasgow.
T. (902) 752 71 61. - Furn / Instr / Glass - 040666

Newmarket (Ontario)
The Penny Farthing, 440 Timothy St., Newmarket.
T. (905) 895 8201. - Ant / Furn / Glass - 040667

Niagara Falls (Ontario)
Olde Country Auction and Antiques, 4604 Evie St., Niagara Falls. T. (905) 356-5523. - Furn - 040668

Niagara-on-the-Lake (Ontario)
Arnold's Antiques, 135 Queen St., Niagara-on-the-Lake.
T. (905) 468-3651. - Ant - 040669

Howe's Antiques, 61 Queen St., Niagara-on-the-Lake.
- Silv / Glass - 040670

Oakville (Ontario)
The Added Touch, 136 Trafalgar Rd., Oakville.
- Ant - 040671

Orangeville (Ontario)
Armstrong Antiques, R. R. 4, Orangeville.
T. (519) 941 4121. - Ant - 040672

Ottawa (Ontario)
Austrian Furniture and Cabinet Making, 3740 Revelstoke
Dr., Ottawa. T. (613) 733- 6474. - Ant / Furn / Jew /
Silv / Lights / Instr / Mil / Glass - 040673

Birks, H., & Sons, 50 Rideau Centre, Ottawa, Ont. K1P
5S5. - Jew / Silv - 040674

Copeland Antiques, 909 Hare Ave., Ottawa, K2A 3J6.
T. (613) 722 9785. - Ant / Furn / Silv / Glass - 040675

Gora's House of Antiques, 484 King Edward Ave., Ottawa. T. (613) 235 4572. - Ant - 040676

Johnson's Furniture Ltd., 111 Murray, Ottawa.
T. (613) 237 1800. - Furn - 040677

Robertson Galleries, 162 Laurier Ave. W.,
Ottawa. 040678

The Snow Goose, 40 Elgin St., Ottawa, K1P 5K5.
T. (613) 232 2213. - Eth - 040679

Wallack, 203 Bank St., Ottawa, K2P 1W7. T. (613) 235-
4339. - Graph / Sculp / Fra / Draw - 040680

Owen Sound (Ontario)
Graham's Antiques, 312 16th St. W., Owen Sound.
- Ant / Furn / China / Lights / Glass - 040681

Perth (Ontario)
Hallett, Maurice W., 27 Leslie St., Perth, K7H 2X5.
T. (613) 267 1182. - China / Silv / Glass - 040682

Philipsburg (Québec)
Lequerme, Frederic „ANtiques", Rte. 133, Philipsburg,
J0J INO. - Ant / Furn - 040683

Picton (Ontario)
House of Falconer, 1 Downs Ave., Picton.
T. (613) CR 6 6546. - Ant / Furn - 040684

Walmsley's Workshop, Elizabeth St., Picton.
T. (613) GR 6 3698. - Ant / Furn / Orient / Glass - 040685

Piedmont (Québec)
Lacasse, Jean, Piedmont, Cte. de Terrebonne.
T. (514) 227 2797. - Furn - 040686

Pike Bay (Ontario)
Lamplighter Antiques, Pike Bay. - Ant - 040687

Plattsville (Ontario)
Dobson, Henry, 66 Albert St. W, Plattsville, Ont. N0J
1S0. T. (519) 684-7434. - Ant / Paint / Furn - 040688

Portland (Ontario)
Greenburnie Antiques, Portland. - Ant / Furn /
Glass - 040689

Old Landing Antiques, Box 12, Portland. T. (613) 5871.
- Ant - 040690

Québec (Québec)
Birks, H. & Sons, Ltd., 16 Fabrique St., Québec. - Jew /
Silv - 040691

Canadian Antique House, 202 Turgeon, Lauzon,
Québec. 040692

Galerie Zanettin, 28 Cote de la Montagne,
Québec. 040693

Galerie 141, 141 St.Paul, Québec. T. (418) 694 97 16.
- Furn / Mod - 040694

L'Héritage Antiquité, 109 Rue St.-Paul, Québec, G1K
3V8. T. (418) 692-1681. - Ant / China / Dec / Glass /
Cur - 040695

Old House Antiques, the, 145 St.Paul, Québec.
T. (418) 694 09 50. - Cur - 040696

Verseau Décor, 137 Rue St.-Paul, Québec, C1K 3V8.
- Ant / Furn / China / Dec / Silv / Lights / Glass / Cur / Mo-
d - 040697

1000 Real Finds, the, 112 St.Paul, Québec.
T. (418) 692 05 81. - Ant - 040698

Regina (Saskatchewan)
Nichol, J., 361 Quebec St., Regina. T. (306) 543 38 53.
- Furn / Silv / Lights / Glass - 040699

Richmond Hill (Ontario)
Beryl Bells Antiques, 11540 Yonge St., Richmond Hill,
L4C 4X7. T. (905) 884-3723. - Furn / China / Silv /
Glass - 040700

Russell (Ontario)
The Castor Shop, Russell. - Ant / Furn / China /
Glass - 040701

Saint Catharines (Ontario)
Haynes Antiques, Adam, 5th St. and Pelham Rd., Saint
Catharines. T. (905) 684-0019. 040702

Town House, 216 King St., Saint Catharines, Ont. L2R
3J9. T. (905) 684 1953. - Ant / China - 040703

Saint Mary's (Ontario)
Irvine, Ruth, 32 St. Andrew's St., Saint Mary's. - Ant /
Orient / Jew / Glass - 040704

Kineman, E. C., Church St., Saint Mary's. - Ant / Lights /
Glass - 040705

O'Hara's Antiques, Queen St. E. Hwy. 7, Saint Mary's.
T. (519) 284 3887. - Ant / Furn / Orient / Lights /
Glass - 040706

Saint Stephen (New Brunswick)
Dover Hill Antiques, 275 Water St., Saint Stephen.
T. (506) 14 66 35 71. - Ant / Glass - 040707

Saskatoon (Saskatchewan)
Birks, H. & Sons, Ltd., 3rd Ave. at 21st St., Saskatoon.
- Jew / Silv - 040708

Simcoe (Ontario)
The Loft, 449 Norfolk St. S, Simcoe. T. (519) 426 6670.
- Ant / Paint / Furn / Silv / Glass - 040709

Smith Falls (Ontario)
Montague House Antiques, RR4, Smith Falls.
T. (613) 283 11 68. 040710

Stanstead (Québec)
Dust + Cobwebs Shop, 66 Zhufferni Rd., Stanstead.
T. (819) 876 22 13. - Furn / Glass - 040711

Stouffville (Ontario)
Jack, Marie, 265 Second St., Stouffville.
T. (905) 640 1311. - Ant - 040712

Stratford (Ontario)
Taylor, Helen, 616 Ontario St., Stratford. - Ant / Furn /
China / Jew - 040713

Streetsville (Ontario)
Manning Hugh, 13 Thomas St., Streetsville.
T. (905) 826 1754. - Ant - 040714

Sudbury (Ontario)
Birks, H. & Sons Ltd., 58 Durham St. S., Sudbury.
- Jew / Silv - 040715

Pit's House of Trasure, 1596 Regent St. S., Sudbury.
- Graph / Furn - 040716

Summerside (Prince Edward Island)
The Cupboard, Summerside, C1N 3J1.
T. (902) 436 94 34. - Furn - 040717

Toronto (Ontario)
A & J, 1130 Yonge St., Toronto. - Ant - 040718

Abacus Antiques, 390 Queen's Quay W, Toronto.
T. (416) 340-9358. - Ant - 040719

Abacus Antiques & Reproduktions, 6 Ripley, Toronto.
T. (416) 760-9358. - Ant - 040720

Accent On Ecletiques, 390 Queen's Quay W, Toronto.
T. (416) 340-2794. - Ant - 040721

Addison, J.S, 1390 Gerrard E, Toronto. T. (416) 466-
1682. - Ant - 040722

Afterglow, 622 Queen W, Toronto. T. (416) 363-9923.
- Ant - 040723

Alf's Antiques, 77 Front E, Toronto. T. (416) 366-0377.
- Ant - 040724

Allery, 322-1/2 Queen W, Toronto. T. (416) 593-0853.
- Ant - 040725

Alpine, 2553 Yonge, Toronto. T. (416) 481-6526.
- Num - 040726

Ann-Teeks, 2670a Danforth Av., Toronto. T. (416) 691-
6002. - Ant - 040727

Antiqua Contents, 482 Roncesvalles, Toronto.
T. (416) 516-9617. - Ant - 040728

Antique Aid, 187a Queen E, Toronto. T. (416) 368-9565.
- Ant - 040729

Antique Art Gallery, 4300 Steeles W, Woodbridge, Toronto. T. (416) 749-2573. - Ant - 040730

Antique Maps at Exploration House, 18 Birch Av., Toronto. T. (416) 922-5193. - Ant - 040731

Antique Quest, 1112 Queen E, Toronto. T. (416) 778-
1668. - Ant - 040732

Antique Warehouse, 39 Richardson, Toronto.
T. (613) 475-3732. - Ant - 040733

Antiquers, 517 Mount Pleasant, Toronto. T. (416) 481-
4474. - Ant - 040734

Antiques by Billy, 390 Queen's Quay W, Toronto.
T. (416) 260-0448. - Ant - 040735

Antiques by Billy, 57 Bloor E, Toronto. T. (416) 922-5534.
- Ant - 040736

Antiques in Time, 111 Jarvis, Toronto. T. (416) 365-
7240. - Ant - 040737

Antiquity K, 1563 Bayview Av., Toronto. T. (416) 489-
4077. - Ant - 040738

Appletree Antiques, 1693 Avenue Rd., Toronto.
T. (416) 781-2054. - Ant - 040739

Architectural Antiques, 43 Britain, Toronto. T. (416) 863-
1590. - Ant - 040740

Art Collector, 786 Saint Clair W, Toronto. T. (416) 656-
2305. - Ant - 040741

Artia, 153 Christie, Toronto. T. (416) 531-7443.
- Ant - 040742

Artifacts Toronto, 360 Davenport, Toronto. T. (416) 963-9605. - Ant -   *040743*

Artistic Two, 1918-A Queen E, Toronto. T. (416) 699-6104. - Ant -   *040744*

Asia Art and Craft, 14 Dundas W, Toronto. T. (416) 977-2502. - Ant -   *040745*

Atelier Fine Arts, 588 Markham, Toronto. T. (416) 532-9244. - Ant -   *040746*

Atop Kuchme, 380 Queen E, Toronto. T. (416) 360-1600. - Ant -   *040747*

Avendale, 1626 Bayview Av., Toronto. T. (416) 487-4279. - Ant -   *040748*

Avenue Antique, 2 Elgin Av., Toronto. T. (416) 972-9936, 960-5913. - Ant -   *040749*

Banyan Tree, 3410 Yonge, Toronto. T. (416) 322-7210. - Ant -   *040750*

Before My Time, 781 Queen E, Toronto. T. (416) 465-4931. - Ant -   *040751*

Beil, Dolly, 986 Eglinton W, Toronto. T. (416) 781-2334. - Ant -   *040752*

Bell, Bert, 3659 Lake Shore, Toronto, B1W. T. (416) 252-9216. - Ant -   *040753*

Bell, Beryl, 11549 Yonge, Toronto. T. (905) 884-3723. - Ant -   *040754*

Benchmark, 1623 Queen W, Toronto. T. (416) 536-8039. - Ant -   *040755*

Benny's Antiques, 272 Church, Toronto. T. (416) 979-5439. - Ant -   *040756*

Bergdon, 180 Davenport Rd., Toronto. T. (416) 924-3865. - Ant / Paint -   *040757*

Bernardi, 707 Mount Pleasant, Toronto. T. (416) 483-6471. - Ant -   *040758*

Bernardi, Sergio, 15040 Yonge, Aurora, Toronto. T. (416) 489-4077. - Ant -   *040759*

Berson, 128 1/2 Cumberland, Toronto. T. (416) 964-1362. - Ant -   *040760*

Beverley Antiques, 83 Front E, Toronto. T. (416) 369-0480. - Ant -   *040761*

Birks, H. & Sons Ltd., 134 Yonge St., Toronto. - Jew / Silv -   *040762*

B.J. Antiques, 64a Queen E, Toronto. T. (416) 366-5537. - Ant -   *040763*

Bloor Yonge Antique Centre, 57 Bloor E, Toronto. T. (416) 967-7676. - Ant -   *040764*

Blue Antiques, 390 Queen's Quay W, Toronto. T. (416) 260-5813. - Ant -   *040765*

Boles, 456 Summerhill Ave, Toronto. T. (416) 922 7653. - Ant / Furn / Lights / Glass -   *040766*

Boston House, Hanna Av., Toronto. T. (416) 538-8789. - Ant -   *040767*

Braem & Minnetti, 1262 Yonge, Toronto. T. (416) 923-7437. - Ant -   *040768*

Braemer Antiques, 2585 Yonge St., Toronto. T. (416) 483 2415. - Ant / Furn -   *040769*

Bremner, 60 Bullock Dr., Toronto. T. (905) 294-1104. - Ant -   *040770*

Camelot Antiques, 529 Queen W, Toronto. T. (416) 366-6036. - Ant -   *040771*

Capricorn Antiques, 600 Markham, Toronto. T. (416) 588-5633. - Ant -   *040772*

Chadwick Shand, 390 Queen's Quay W, Toronto. T. (416) 340-7849. - Ant -   *040773*

Chauvette, C., 311 Rg. 6 Saint Rosaire, Toronto. T. (819) 752-3583. - Ant -   *040774*

Chelsea Shop, 386 Huron St., Toronto. T. (416) 923 7722. - Ant / Graph / Furn / China / Sculp / Dec / Instr / Glass -   *040775*

Chizick & Masters, 744 Queen E, Toronto. T. (416) 461-0609. - Ant -   *040776*

Church Street Gold and Sterling, 155 Church, Toronto. T. (416) 594-1200. - Jew / Silv -   *040777*

Circa Antiques and Interiors, 166 Davenport, Toronto. T. (416) 961-3744. - Ant -   *040778*

Clairman, Alan, 244 Carlton, Toronto. T. (416) 968-6975. - Ant -   *040779*

Clutter, 653 Queen E, Toronto. T. (416) 461-3776. - Ant -   *040780*

Cohen, 1240 Bank, Toronto. T. (613) 738-9243. - Ant -   *040781*

Collins & Chandler, 181 Avenue Rd., Toronto. T. (416) 922-8784. - Ant -   *040782*

Connoisseur Antiques, 390 Queen's Quay W, Toronto. T. (416) 260-0925. - Ant -   *040783*

Contents Connection, 3321 Bathurst, Toronto. T. (416) 256-3566. - Ant -   *040784*

Courage My Love, 14 Kensington, Toronto. T. (416) 979-1992. - Ant -   *040785*

Craig, Granny, 151 Main, Toronto. T. (416) 474-9557. - Ant -   *040786*

Creme de la Creme, 330 Geary Av., Toronto. T. (416) 588-9088. - Ant -   *040787*

Crown Emporium and Auction Services, 3581-B Dundas W, Toronto. T. (416) 761-9008. - Ant -   *040788*

Davenport House Antiques and Interiors, 158 Davenport, Toronto. T. (416) 922-3778. - Ant -   *040789*

Denby, Edward E., 1206 Yonge St., M4Q 1W1. T. (416) 921 2493.   *040790*

Dietemann, D., 747 Broadview, Toronto. T. (416) 462-9013. - Ant -   *040791*

Direct Loom Persian Rugs, 73 Jarvis, Toronto. T. (416) 861-1480. - Tex -   *040792*

Dirocco, Mario, 21 Avenue Rd., Toronto. T. (416) 966-112221. - Ant -   *040793*

Dirstein Robertson, 77 Yorkville Av., Toronto, M5R 1C1. T. (416) 961-6211. - Ant / Furn / Dec -   *040794*

Diva, 566 1/2 Church, Toronto. T. (416) 921-1994. - Ant -   *040795*

Divine Decadence Originals, 7 Charles W, Toronto. T. (416) 922-2105. - Ant -   *040796*

Doc John's Antique Doll Clinic, 194 Carlton, Toronto. T. (416) 323-1864. - Ant -   *040797*

Door Dtore, 43 Britain, Toronto. T. (416) 863-1590. - Ant -   *040798*

Downshire House Clock and Barometers, 178a Davenport, Toronto. T. (416) 927-0279. - Instr -   *040799*

Downstairs Attic, 1645 Bayview Av., Toronto. T. (416) 481-6292. - Ant -   *040800*

English Manor Antiques and Interiors, 518 Mount Pleasant, Toronto. T. (416) 932-1822. - Furn -   *040801*

Estate Antiques and Fine Furniture, 250 Queen W, Toronto. T. (416) 599-5488. - Furn -   *040802*

Evercone, 390 Queen's Quay W, Toronto. T. (416) 260-5337. - Ant -   *040803*

Exploration House, 18 Birch Av., Toronto. T. (416) 922-5153. - Ant -   *040804*

Ferrazzutti, Pam, 390 Queens's Quay W, Toronto. T. (416) 260-0325. - Ant -   *040805*

Fifty-One Antiques, 21 Avenue Rd., Toronto. T. (416) 968-2416. - Ant -   *040806*

Findlay, Cynthia, 390 Queen's Quay W, Toronto, M5V 3A6. T. (416) 340-8281. - Ant -   *040807*

Finishes, 9 Hanna Av., Toronto. T. (416) 588-3850. - Ant -   *040808*

Finlay & Maurin, 259 Kingswood, Toronto. T. (416) 694-4761. - Ant -   *040809*

Florentine Antiques, 198A Davenport, Toronto. T. (416) 944-3018. - Furn -   *040810*

Floyd & Rita's Antiques and Collectables, 390 Queen's Quay W, Toronto. T. (416) 364-1339. - Ant -   *040811*

Fraleigh, 21977 Yonge, Toronto. T. (416) 483-1526. - Jew -   *040812*

French Country Antiques, 160 Pears, Toronto. T. (416) 925-8248. - Ant -   *040813*

Fyte's Antiques and Restorations, 553 Mount Pleasant, Toronto. T. (416) 483-5023. - Ant -   *040814*

Gadsby's, 3433 Yonge, Toronto. T. (416) 322-4895. - Ant -   *040815*

Gallery Kekko, 14 Prince Arthur, Ste. 105, Toronto. T. (416) 960-3905. - Paint / Draw -   *040816*

Gaslight Antiques, 518 Mount Pleasant, Toronto. T. (416) 482-1823. - Ant -   *040817*

Giai Tham, 742 Dundas E, Toronto. T. (416) 866-8498. - Furn -   *040818*

Gilbert & Coles, 160 Pears, Toronto. T. (416) 921-9145. - Ant -   *040819*

Gillespie, Agnes, 5 Brentwood Rd. N, Toronto. T. (416) 233-3895. - Ant -   *040820*

Gillies, David, 66 Avenue Rd., Toronto. T. (416) 969-8464. - Ant -   *040821*

Glass Chimney Art and Antiques, 1661 Eglinton W, Toronto. T. (416) 783-9423. - Ant -   *040822*

Glen Manor Galleries, 102 Avenue Rd., Toronto. T. (416) 961-2286. - Ant -   *040823*

Godard, Mira, 22 Hazelton Av., Toronto, Ont. M5R 2E2. T. (416) 964-8197, Fax 964-5912. - Paint / Graph / Sculp -   *040824*

Gold Shoppe, 25 Bloor St., Toronto, Ont. M4W 1A3. T. (416) 923-5565. - Ant / Jew / Silv -   *040825*

Gold Traders, 390 Queens Quay W, Toronto. T. (416) 599-0083. - Jew -   *040826*

Gray, 203 Queen E, Toronto. T. (416) 363-4860. - Ant -   *040827*

Green, 529 Parliament, Toronto. T. (416) 925-1556. - Ant -   *040828*

Gresham, Sarah, 201 Queen E, Toronto. T. (416) 865-1758. - Ant -   *040829*

Guildhall Antiques Ltd., 111 Jarvis, Toronto. T. (416) 777-0226. - Ant -   *040830*

Harbourfront Antique, 390 Queen's Quay W, Toronto. T. (416) 340-8377. - Ant -   *040831*

Heritage Antique Jewellery and Art, 390 Queen's Quay W, Toronto. T. (416) 260-0398. - Jew -   *040832*

Heritage House Antiques, 390 Queen's Quay W, Toronto. T. (416) 340-2801. - Ant -   *040833*

Hickl-Szabo, 66 Avenue Rd., Toronto. T. (416) T962-4140. - Ant -   *040834*

Hitchin Post, 3823 Bloor w, Toronto. T. (416) 231-8394. - Ant -   *040835*

Homeculture, 3 Southvale Dr., Toronto. T. (416) 421-7573. - Ant -   *040836*

House of Brass and Antiques, 117 Jefferson, Toronto. T. (416) 532-2399. - Ant -   *040837*

Howard, Linda, 581 Mount Pleasant, Toronto. T. (416) 485-2283. - Ant -   *040838*

Hoyt, G., 390 Queen's Quay W, Toronto. T. (416) 340-9366. - Ant -   *040839*

Hummingbird, 1162 Queen E, Toronto. T. (416) 466-4737. - Ant -   *040840*

Hundred and One Antiques, 390 Queen's Quay W, Toronto. T. (416) 340-9862. - Ant -   *040841*

Hundred Antiques, R.R.3, Stirling, Toronto. T. (613) 395-3003. - Ant -   *040842*

In the Attic, 768 Queen E, Toronto. T. (416) 466-7049. - Ant -   *040843*

Inquisitive Antique and Decor Items, 1646 Bayview, Toronto. T. (416) 481-8819. - Ant -   *040844*

Interesting Jewellery Shop, 685 Yonge St., Toronto. T. (416) 923-5744. - Jew / Jew -   *040845*

Jalan, 775 Queen W, Toronto. T. (416) 366-3473. - Ant -   *040846*

Journey's End Antiques, 612 Markham, Toronto. T. (416) 536-2226. - Ant -   *040847*

Karwah, 289 Dundas W, Toronto. T. (416) 598-0043. - Ant -   *040848*

Kershaw, 442 Wilson E, Toronto. T. (905) 648-1991. - Graph -   *040849*

Ket, 6188 Yonge, Toronto. T. (416) 223-5300. - Ant -   *040850*

Lai, C.C., 9 Hazelton, Toronto. T. (416) 928-0662. - Orient -   *040851*

Laing Galleries, 194 Bloor St. W., Toronto.   *040852*

Lake, D. & E., 237 King E, Toronto. T. (416) 863-9930. - Ant -   *040853*

Latimer, Jackie, 390 Queen's Quay W, Toronto. T. (416) 260-5840. - Ant -   *040854*

Lavan, Jose, 179 Queen E, Toronto. T. (416) 369-0508. - Ant -   *040855*

Lavender, 250 Carlton, Toronto. T. (416) 975-9022. - Ant -   *040856*

Les Puces Antiques, 285 Harbord, Toronto. T. (416) 534-0411. - Ant -   *040857*

Lewis, 345 Sorauren, Toronto. T. (416) 588-8104. - Ant -   *040858*

Lillians Fine Collectables, 2594 Danforth Av., Toronto. T. (416) 690-4868. - Ant -   *040859*

Locomotion, 1150 Queen E, Toronto. T. (416) 462-2903. - Ant -   *040860*

Lora's Collectables, 1172 Queen E, Toronto. T. (416) 466-8821. - Ant -   *040861*

Lorenz, 701 Mount Pleasant Rd., Toronto, M4S 2N4. T. (416) 487-2066. - Ant / Furn -   *040862*

M B Furniture and Articles, 1594 Dupont, Toronto. T. (416) 760-7179. - Furn -   *040863*

MacDonald, Harry, 158 Davenport Rd., Toronto. T. (416) 922 3778. - Ant / Furn -   *040864*

Madcap, 112 Sherbourne, Toronto. T. (416) 362-6203. - Ant -   *040865*

Manderley Manor, 515 Mount Pleasant, Toronto. T. (416) 486-3045. - Ant -   *040866*

Markham's Atiques, 559 Mt. Pleasant Rd., Toronto, M4S
2M5. T. (416) 489 6651. - Furn / Lights / Glass - *040867*

Mayhap, 177 Queen E, Toronto. T. (416) 368-5691.
- Ant - *040868*

Mazelow, 3463 Yonge St., Toronto. T. (416) 481-7711,
481-3876. - Paint / Graph / Sculp / Eth / Fra /
Draw - *040869*

McCready Galleries Inc., 192 Davenport Rd., Toronto,
M5R 1J2. *040870*

Mclaine, Mark, Hazelton Lanes, Toronto. T. (416) 927-
7972. - Ant - *040871*

McNichol, 221 Queen S, Toronto. T. (905) 826-1754.
- Ant - *040872*

Michelle Antiques and Collectables, 171-1 King E, Toronto. T. (416) 364-3910. - Ant - *040873*

Military Antiques Trading Post, 1097 O'Connor Dr., Toronto. T. (416) 285-6828. - Mil - *040874*

Mission Craft, 390 Queen's Quay W, Toronto.
T. (416) 482-1325. - Ant - *040875*

Moos Ltd., Gallery, 136 Yorkville Ave., Toronto, M5R
1C2. *040876*

Morris Gallery, Toronto POB 250, Station Q, Ont. M4T
2M1. T. (416) 922-4778. *040877*

Mostly Movables, 785 Queen W, Toronto. T. (416) 865-
9716. - Ant - *040878*

Mount Pleasant Galleries, 563 Mount Pleasant, Toronto.
T. (416) 482-1823. - Ant - *040879*

Movements in Time, Toronto POB 6629, Station A, M5W
1X4. T. (905) 883-1924. *040880*

Narcissus, 1563 Bayview Av., Toronto. T. (416) 489-
4077. - Ant - *040881*

Natara, 1396 Yonge, Toronto. T. (416) 928-7406.
- Ant - *040882*

Nelson, Carole, 2308 Queen E, Toronto. T. (416) 698-
7370. - Ant - *040883*

Nirvana Trading, 1915 Queen E, Toronto. T. (416) 694-
7082. - Ant - *040884*

Nostalgia Nook, 1142 Queen E, Toronto. T. (416) 463-
1695. - Ant - *040885*

Now N Then Collectibles, 390 Queen's Quay W, Toronto.
T. (416) 260-0120. - Ant - *040886*

O'Neil, R. A., 104 Avenue Rd., Toronto, M5R 2H3.
T. (416) 968-2806. - Furn - *040887*

Of Ages Post, 183 Queen E, Toronto. T. (416) 867-8975.
- Ant - *040888*

Old Loves, 2887 Danforth Av., Toronto. T. (416) 693-
4898. - Ant - *040889*

Oldies Antiques, 92 Queen E, Toronto. T. (416) 364-
3798. - Ant - *040890*

Pagnello's Antiques, 1635 Bayview Ave., Toronto.
T. (416) 488 8080. - Ant - *040891*

Paisley, 889 Yonge St., Toronto. T. (416) 923-5830.
- Ant / Furn / Orient / China / Silver / Repr / Sculp / Dec / Silv / Lights / Instr / Glass - *040892*

Pao & Moltke, 21 Avenue Rd., Toronto. T. (416) 925-
6197. - Ant - *040893*

Parkdale Antiques, 1698 Queen W, Toronto. T. (416) 534-
1431. - Ant - *040894*

Perkins, R. G. Ltd., 1198 Yonge St., Toronto, M4T 1WI.
T. (416) 925 0973. - Ant / Paint / Furn / Repr /
Lights - *040895*

Picknick's Choice, 1629 Queen W, Toronto. T. (416) 538-
4419. - Ant - *040896*

Pine Design, 50 Spadina Av., Toronto. T. (416) 340-2532.
- Furn - *040897*

Pinocchio's Collectibles, 1001 Kingston Rd., Toronto.
T. (416) 694-7837. - Ant - *040898*

Plantation, the, 608 Markham St., Toronto, M6G 2L8.
T. (416) 533 6466. - Paint / Furn / Silv - *040899*

Poole Douglas, 116 Sherbourne, Toronto. T. (416) 367-
3255. - Ant - *040900*

Popular Culture, 404 Queen E, Toronto. T. (416) 366-
1761. - Ant - *040901*

Port Dalhousie Trading Company, 104 Avenue Rd., Toronto. T. (416) 920-0323. - Ant - *040902*

Prince of Serendip, 1073 Yonge, Toronto. T. (416) 925-
3760. - Ant - *040903*

Quasi-Modo, 789 Queen W, Toronto. T. (416) 366-8370.
- Ant - *040904*

Queen Street Sales, 635 Queen W, Toronto. T. (416) 363-
4540. - Ant - *040905*

Rasan, 444 Yonge, Toronto. T. (416) 595-0836.
040906

Re Orient, 269 Queen E, Toronto. T. (416) 365-1892.
- Ant - *040907*

Red Indian Art Deco, 507 Queen W, Toronto.
T. (416) 364-2706. - Eth - *040908*

Reeves, Michael, 171 Queen E, Toronto. T. (416) 368-
0257. - Ant - *040909*

Rich and Famous Antique Gallery, 126 Cumberland, To
ronto. T. (416) 929-2357. - Ant - *040910*

Richens, Andrew, 613 Mount Plaesant, Toronto.
T. (416) 487-4437. - Ant - *040911*

Ridpaths, 906 Yonge St., Toronto. *040912*

Ritchie's Appraisals, 24 Bellair, Toronto. T. (416) 923-
7924. - Ant - *040913*

Roberts, 641 Yonge St., Toronto, M4Y 1Z9. T. (416) 924-
8731. *040914*

Robinson, David, Antiques Ltd., 1236 Yonge St., Toronto,
A4T 1W3. T. (416) 921 4858. - Ant - *040915*

Rochelle & Co., 491 Davenport, Toronto. T. (416) 966-
3400. - Ant - *040916*

Rollins Raeburn, 146 Davenport, Toronto. T. (416) 923-
5676. - Ant - *040917*

Rose Antiques, 1586 Dupont, Toronto. T. (416) 588-
1046. - Ant - *040918*

Rotman, M., 44 Sherbourne, Toronto. T. (416) 368-9137.
- Ant - *040919*

Rumi, Richard, & Co., 55 Woodlawn, Toronto.
T. (905) 274-2616. - Ant - *040920*

Ruth's Curiosities, 390 Queen's Quay W, Toronto.
T. (416) 340-9048. - Ant - *040921*

Sabrina & Co., 18 Scarlett, Toronto. T. (416) 762-1215.
- Ant - *040922*

Sam Chandelier Man, 1633 Queen W, Toronto.
T. (416) 537-9707. - Ant - *040923*

Schoolhouse Antiques, 148 Grden Av., Toronto.
T. (416) 530-0000. - Ant - *040924*

Sherman Antiques, 631 Winona Dr., Toronto.
T. (416) 782 5580. - Ant - *040925*

Shiell, Miriam, 16a Hazelton Av., Toronto, Ont. M5R 2E2.
T. (416) 925-2461. - Paint / Graph / Sculp - *040926*

Silverstreak, 1102 Queen E, Toronto. T. (416) 778-5308.
- Ant - *040927*

Smith, Ingrid K., 390 Queen's Quay W, Toronto.
T. (416) 586-0098. - Ant - *040928*

Solway, Carol, 88 Yorkville Av., Toronto, M5R 1B9.
T. (416) 922-0702. - Ant / Furn / China / Glass - *040929*

Somerville, 390 Queen's Quay W, Toronto. T. (416) 586-
0051. - Ant - *040930*

Sugarman, Budd, Antiques and Interior Design, 19 Hazelton Ave., Toronto. T. (416) 925 4471. - Ant /
Furn - *040931*

Susan's Antiques, Mount Pleasant, Toronto.
T. (416) 487-9262. - Ant - *040932*

Swampman's Antiques, R R 3 Guelph Morstn, Toronto.
T. (519) 836-7460. - Ant - *040933*

Tall Ships, 1545 Bayview Av., Toronto. T. (416) 485-
9442. - Ant - *040934*

Taschereau, Michel, 176 Cumberland, Toronto.
T. (416) 923-3020. - Ant - *040935*

Taylor, 1043 Avenue Rd., Toronto. T. (416) 440-0379.
- Num - *040936*

Tea Olive Company, 812 Queen E, Toronto. T. (416) 465-
1244. - Ant - *040937*

The Jared Sable Gallery, 33 Hazelton Ave.,
Toronto. *040938*

Thrift Galleries, 227 Queen St. W., Toronto. T. (416) 598-
3555. - Ant / Paint / Furn / China / Glass / Cur - *040939*

Toronto Antiques House, 1635 Queen W, Toronto.
T. (416) 534-7090. - Ant - *040940*

Town of York Antiques, 184 Davenport, Toronto.
T. (416) 925-4720. - Ant - *040941*

Treasure Chest Antiques, 601 Yonge, Toronto.
T. (905) 722-4411. - Ant - *040942*

Treasure House, 176 Yonge St., Toronto, M5E 1N9.
- Ant - *040943*

Trinkets, 155 Church, Toronto. T. (416) 368-9787.
- Ant - *040944*

Turn of the Century Lighting, 112 Sherbourne, Toronto.
T. (416) 362-6203. - Lights - *040945*

Upper Canada House, 467 Eglinton W, Toronto.
T. (416) 489-9110. - Ant - *040946*

Vaughan, Granny, 140 Woodbridge, Toronto.
- Ant - *040947*

Vernacular, 1130 Yonge, Toronto. T. (416) 961-6490.
- Ant - *040948*

Vicky's Jewellery, 404 Eglinton W, Toronto. T. (416) 488-
1888. - Jew - *040949*

Vintage Radio and Gramaphone, 463 Manor E, Toronto.
T. (416) 481-6708. - Ant - *040950*

Wagman, Stanley, 33 Avenue Rd., Toronto, M5R 1C3.
T. (416) 964-1047. - Furn / Silv - *040951*

Wagner, Odon, 194-196 Davenport Rd., Toronto, M5R
1J2. T. (416) 962-0438. - Paint - *040952*

Walker, 390 Queen's Quay W, Toronto. T. (416) 586-
0103. - Ant / Silv - *040953*

Whim, 517 Mount Pleasant, Toronto. T. (416) 481-4474.
- Ant - *040954*

Whimsy, 597 Mount Pleasant, Toronto. T. (416) 488-
0770. - Ant - *040955*

Windebank, Ronald, 21 Avenue Rd., Toronto.
T. (416) 962-2862. - Ant - *040956*

Wine, Louis, 848A Yonge, Toronto. T. (416) 929-9333.
- Ant - *040957*

Winston, 21 Dundas Sq., Toronto. T. (416) 363-6092.
- Ant - *040958*

Wolfson Antiques, 968 Eglinton Ave., Toronto.
T. (416) 785-4462. - Ant - *040959*

Ye Old Sleigh Antiques, 390 Queen's Quay W, Toronto.
T. (416) 340-7839. - Ant - *040960*

Young Galleries, 2023 Yonge St., Toronto.
T. (416) 483 6304. - Ant - *040961*

Yours Mine & Ours, 390 Queen's Quay W, Toronto.
T. (416) 586-0085. - Ant - *040962*

20th Century, 23 Beverley, Toronto. T. (416) 598-2172.
- Ant - *040963*

507 King Antiques, 507 King E, Toronto. T. (416) 359-
0502. - Ant - *040964*

Trenton (Ontario)

The Attic Shop Antiques, 118 Dundas St. W., Trenton.
T. (613) 392 3424. - Ant / Furn / Orient / Glass - *040965*

Unionville (Ontario)

Roadhouse Antiques, R. R. 1, Unionville.
T. (416) 887 5542. - Ant / Furn / Lights - *040966*

Vancouver (British Columbia)

AA-1 Jim's Used Furniture, 4323 Main, Vancouver.
T. (604) 879-5444. - Furn - *040967*

Abe's Second Hand Store, 4376 Main, Vancouver.
T. (604) 876-4314. - Ant - *040968*

Aileen's Antiques, 422 Richards, Vancouver.
T. (604) 683-1454. - Ant - *040969*

Airmail, 3715 Main, Vancouver. T. (604) 876-6600.
- Ant - *040970*

Alice's Old Furniture and Memorabilia, 4242 Main St.,
Vancouver. T. (604) 876-1838. - Furn - *040971*

Alpine Furniture, 1839 Commercial Dr., Vancouver.
T. (604) 254-1131. - Furn - *040972*

Antiquarius, 341 W Pender, Vancouver. T. (604) 669-
7288. - Ant - *040973*

Antwerp Galleries, 20560 Langley Bypass Lang, Vancouver. T. (604) 534-1247. - Ant - *040974*

Arkay, 3040 Granville St., Vancouver. T. (604) 734-8422.
- Ant - *040975*

Artemis Fine and Decorative Arts, 321 Water, Vancouver.
T. (604) 685-8808. - Ant - *040976*

Artisan Furniture Refinishing, 3396 Dunbar St., Vancouver. T. (604) 736-3828. - Furn - *040977*

Bamboozled Collectibles, 156 W Hastings, Vancouver.
T. (604) 685-1375. - Ant - *040978*

B.C. Jewellers, 11 W Hastings, Vancouver. T. (604) 681-
7012. - Jew - *040979*

Birds of Malden Antiques, 3060 Granville, Vancouver.
T. (604) 733-6812. - Ant - *040980*

Birks, Henry & sons Ltd., 710 Granville St., Vancouver.
- Jew / Silv - *040981*

Blue Heron, 3516 A Main St., Vancouver. T. (604) 874-
8401. - Ant - *040982*

Bohemia Antiques, 2424 Marine W Van, Vancouver.
T. (604) 922-6020. - Ant - *040983*

Burkitt, G., 820 Howe, Vancouver. T. (604) 683-2622.
- Ant - *040984*

California Suite Antiques, 422 Richards, Vancouver.
T. (604) 681-3248. - Ant - *040985*

Canada West Antique Company, 3607 W Broadway, Vancouver. T. (604) 733-3212. - Ant -   040986
Canterbury Curios, 5971 W Boulevard, Vancouver. T. (604) 261-4322. - Ant -   040987
Canterbury Curios Ltd., 5971 W. Boulevard, Vancouver. T. (604) 261 4322. - Ant / Furn / Silv -   040988
Caspian, 3101 Granville St., Vancouver. T. (604) 732-6611. - Tex -   040989
Century House Antiques, 22653 Dewdney Trunk, Maple Ridge, Vancouver. T. (604) 463 3323.   040990
Collectors Shop, 1744 Marine W Van, Vancouver. T. (604) 926-4010. - Ant -   040991
Collectors Shop, 1742 Marine, Vancouver, B.C. T. (604) 926-4010. - Furn / Jew / Silv -   040992
Dodi's Shoppe, 436 Richards, Vancouver. T. (604) 684-5420. - Ant -   040993
Empress Antiques, 422 Richards, Vancouver. T. (604) 684-9822. - Ant -   040994
Equinox Gallery, 1525 W Eighth Av., Vancouver, B.C. V6H 3G3. T. (604) 736-2405.   040995
Finders Keepers, 4785 Kingsway, Vancouver. T. (604) 437-5530. - Ant -   040996
Folkart, 3715 W Tenth, Vancouver. T. (604) 228-1011. - Ant -   040997
Fuller, 466 W Cordova, Vancouver. T. (604) 682-7614. - Ant -   040998
Gastown Antique Emporium, 49 Powell, Vancouver. T. (604) 689-4850. - Ant -   040999
Golden Arts and Curios, 720 Robson, Vancouver. T. (604) 685-3135. - Ant -   041000
Hampshire Antiques, 3149 Granville St., Vancouver. T. (604) 733-1326. - Ant -   041001
Harrison, 2932 Granville St., Vancouver, B.C. V6H 3J7. T. (604) 732-5217, 732-0911. - Ant -   041002
Heirloom Antiques, 6870 King George VI Hwy., Vancouver. T. (604) 597-0133. - Ant -   041003
Jewels and Curios, 474 W Cordovas, Vancouver. T. (604) 681-4102. - Ant / Jew -   041004
Julius, 2310 Granville St., Vancouver. T. (604) 738-9614. - Ant -   041005
Julius, 2310 Granville St., Vancouver, V6H 3G3. T. (604) 738-9614. - Furn / Orient / Silv -   041006
Kelly, 422 Richards, Vancouver. T. (604) 687-8138. - Ant -   041007
Kimono-Ya, 3600 W Fourth, Vancouver. T. (604) 734-0223. - Ant -   041008
La Rouche, Michel, 3958 Main, Vancouver. T. (604) 879-8121. - Ant -   041009
Langmann, 2117 Granville St., Vancouver, B.C. V6H 3E9. T. (604) 736-8825. - Ant / Paint / Furn / Tex -   041010
Langmann Uno, 2117 Granville St., Vancouver. T. (604) 736-8825. - Ant   041011
Legacies Antiques, 438 Richards, Vancouver. T. (604) 681-2033. - Ant -   041012
Lever, 2131 Burrard, Vancouver. T. (604) 736-2711. - Ant -   041013
Lindt, Lothar, 2881 Capilano Rd., Vancouver, B.C. V7R 4H4. T. (604) 980-8910, 986-8712. - Paint -   041014
Mammoth Enterprises, 1286 E 16 St., Vancouver, B.C. V7J 1L3. T. (604) 988-1299, Fax 988-4388.   041015
Marjan, 211 Columbia, Vancouver. T. (604) 687-2001. - Ant -   041016
Marty's Antique and Giftware, 100-3580 Moncton Rmd., Vancouver. T. (604) 271-5637. - Ant -   041017
Memory Lane Antiques and Vintage Lighting, 4386 Main, Vancouver. T. (604) 873-9414. - Ant / Lights -   041018
Metropolitan Home, 353 W Pender, Vancouver. T. (604) 681-2313. - Ant -   041019
Metrotown New and Used Liquidators, 5329 Imperial Bby, Vancouver. T. (604) 438-6629. - Ant -   041020
Moss Brendan, M., 110-332 Water, Vancouver. T. (604) 662-8171. - Ant -   041021
Mount Pleasant Furniture, 4242 Main St., Vancouver. T. (604) 876-5002. - Furn -   041022
Old Country, 3720 W Tenth, Vancouver. T. (604) 224-8664. - Ant -   041023
Old Friends Antiques, 422 Richards, Vancouver. T. (604) 669-7444. - Ant -   041024
Old House and Home, 2507 W Broadway, Vancouver. T. (604) 731-2516. - Ant -   041025
Old Meets New, 84 W Hastings, Vancouver. T. (604) 669-9636. - Ant -   041026

Old Stuff Two, 4510 Main St., Vancouver. T. (604) 872-6939. - Ant -   041027
Oriental Interiors, A-746 SW Marine Dr., Vancouver. T. (604) 321-0171. - Orient -   041028
Panache, 3030 Granville St., Vancouver, V6H 3J8. T. (604) 732-1206. - Ant -   041029
Persian Arts and Crafts, 777 Hornby, Vancouver. T. (604) 681-4639. - Tex -   041030
Portobello Antiques, 3050 Granville St., Vancouver. T. (604) 734-2275. - Ant -   041031
Potter, 1601 W Georgia, Vancouver. T. (604) 685-3919. - Ant -   041032
Rare Find Jewellery, 425-736 Granville, Vancouver. T. (604) 683-4653. - Jew -   041033
Red Barn Antiques, 5553 176 St., Vancouver. T. (604) 576-8737. - Ant -   041034
Robina, B., 4342 Main, Vancouver. T. (604) 877-1500. - Ant -   041035
Robinson, Frankie, 3055 Granville St., Vancouver. T. (604) 734-6568. - Ant -   041036
Scandinavian Antiques, 492 W Hastings, Vancouver. T. (604) 685-7740. - Ant -   041037
Second Time Around Antiques, 4280 Main, Vancouver. T. (604) 879-7016. - Ant -   041038
Sellution Vintage Furniture and More, 2765 W Fourth, Vancouver. T. (604) 736-7355. - Ant / Furn -   041039
Silver Shop, 5628 Dunbar St., Vancouver. T. (604) 263-3113. - Silv -   041040
Source Antiques, 929 Main St., Vancouver, B.C. V6A 2V8. T. (604) 684-9914. - Ant / Furn / Glass -   041041
Stewart, 4391 Main St., Vancouver. T. (604) 872-1155. - Ant -   041042
Sugar Barrel, 4285 Main St., Vancouver. T. (604) 876-5234. - Ant -   041043
Swift, 8211 Granville St., Vancouver. T. (604) 261-1616. - Furn -   041044
T & S Antiques, 422 Richards, Vancouver. T. (604) 687-5334. - Ant -   041045
Tappit Hen Antiques Ltd., 3050 Granville St., Vancouver, V6H 3J8. T. (604) 731 8021. - Ant / Orient -   041046
Tee, R.H.V., & Son, 7963 Granville St., Vancouver. T. (604) 263-2791. - Ant -   041047
Uniques-Collectables with Imagination, 319 W Cordova, Vancouver. T. (604) 684-3711. - Ant -   041048
Uno Langmann, 2117 Granville St., Vancouver. T. (604) 736-8825. - Ant -   041049
Village Antiques and Crafts Mall, 23331 Mavis, Fort Lang, Vancouver. T. (604) 888-3700. - Ant -   041050
Wally's Folly, 3639 W Broadway, Vancouver. T. (604) 736-5848. - Ant -   041051
Winchester Antiques, 422 Richards, Vancouver. T. (604) 682-3573. - Ant -   041052

Victoria (British Columbia)

Antique Shop, 1032 Fort St., Victoria, V8V 3K4. T. (604) 382 4939. - Paint / China / Tex / Jew -   041053
Birks, H. & Sons Ltd., 706 Yates St., Victoria. - Jew / Silv -   041054
Clock Shop, 1037 Fort St., Victoria. - Instr -   041055
Connoisseur's Shop, 1156 Fort St., Victoria. T. (604) 383 0121. - Ant -   041056
Domus Antica Galleries, 1040 Fort St., Victoria. T. (604) 385-5443. - Ant / Furn / Jew / Silv -   041057
Harlequin House, 839 Fort St., Victoria, V8W 1HG. T. (604) 382 2525. - Ant / Graph / Furn / Cur -   041058
Lloyd-El Ceramics & Crafts Ltd. Peter & Dorene Krystalowich, 563 Johnson Street, Victoria, B.Col V8W 1 M2. T. (604) 384 3831. - China -   041059
Newberry's Antiques, 837 Fort St., Victoria, V8W 1H6. T. (604) 383 6541. - Ant / Num / Orient / China -   041060
Pacific Antiques, Ltd., 1025 Fort St., Victoria, V8V 3K5. T. (604) 3885311. - Furn / China / Silv / Glass -   041061
Reynolds, Sydney, 801 Government St., Victoria. T. (604) 383 3931. - Ant -   041062
Rosemary+Wendy Ant., 620 Broughton St., Victoria, V8V 1C7. T. (604) 385 9816. - Ant / Orient / Jew -   041063
The Golden Cameo, 1035 Fort St., Victoria. T. (604) 385 5634. - Orient / Jew -   041064
The Sands of Time, 1033 Fort St., Victoria, V8V 3K5. T. (604) 384-2817. - Furn -   041065
Vanhall Antiques Ltd., 1023 Fort St., Victoria, V8V 3K5. T. (604) 382 7643. - Ant / China / Silv -   041066

Vineland (Ontario)

Barclay Holmes Antiques, P.O.Box 534, Vineland. T. (905) 562 53 16.   041067

Warkworth (Ontario)

Playhouse Antiques, Old Hastings Rd., Warkworth. T. (705) 45. - Ant / Furn / Lights / Instr / Glass -   041068

Westmount (Québec)

Breitman Antiques, S., 1353 Greene Ave., Westmount. T. (514) 937 02 75.   041069
Galerie Art et Style, 4875A Ouest Rue Sherbrooke, Westmount, H3Z 1G9. T. (514) 484-3184.   041070

Windsor (Ontario)

Birks, H. & Sons, Ltd., 375 Quellette Ave., Windsor. - Jew / Silv -   041071
The Gold Shop, 345 Oullette Av., Windsor, N9A 4J1. T. (519) 253-8465. - Jew -   041072

Winnipeg (Manitoba)

Birks, H. & Sons Ltd., 276 Portage Ave., Winnipeg. - Jew / Silv -   041073
Curiosity Shop, 266 Edmonton St., Winnipeg, R3C 1R9. T. (204) 943-2734. - Ant / Graph / Furn / Jew / Mod -   041074
Halls of Art, 134 Douglas Park St., Winnipeg. T. (204) 889-4978. - Furn / Silv / Instr -   041075
Harris, 2571 Portage St., Winnipeg, Man. T. (204) 832-2144. - Ant -   041076
House of Silver Ltd., 743 Wall St., Winnipeg. T. (204) 774 3250. - Silv -   041077
Orient, the, 168 Bannatyne, Winnipeg. T. (204) 956 1703. - Furn / Orient -   041078
Peter's Curios and Antiques, 254-256 Logan Ave., Winnipeg. T. (204) 943-7871. - Ant -   041079
Sugared Mule Antiques and Things Ltd., 600 Broadway, Winnipeg. T. (204) 783 1555. - Paint / Orient / Jew / Silv -   041080
Upstairs Gallery, 266 Edmonton St., Winnipeg, R3C 1R9. T. (204) 943-2734.   041081

Chile

Santiago

Garcia Burr, Alfredo, Arturo Prat 10, Santiago. T. 39 80 77. - Num -   041082
Razeto, Adriano, Pocuro 2826, Santiago. - Paint / Graph / Lights -   041083

China, Republic

Taipei

Bai Win, 5, Lane 728, Chung Shan N Rd., Sec. 6, Taipei. T. (02) 871 4943. - Orient -   041084
Chang, W. C., China Art Export Co., Ltd., P. O. Box 1655, Taipei. T. (02) 293 53; 241 03. - Num -   041085
Chi Hong & Co, l td., Ta Te Bldg., 15 Lane 86, Chungking S. Rd., Sec. 2, Taipei. T. (02) 302-7227/9.   041086
Yih Feng, 40 Hsin Shu Rd., Taipei. T. (02) 281 41 35, 902 67 22. - Orient -   041087

Colombia

Bogotá

Perez, Luis, Calle 81 Nr. 8-72, Bogotá. T. 211 54 03. - Arch -   041088

Ibagué (Tolima)

Taller, Carrera 3 8-80, Ibagué. T. 63 35 02. - Ant -   041089

Croatia

Ljubljana

Antika, Mestrai Trg. 19, 61000 Ljubljana. T. (061) 22285. - Ant -   041090

Czech Republic

Břeclav
Art & Antik, c/o Fosfa, Poštorná, 69141 Břeclav.
T. (0627) 415-159. *041091*

Brno
Patrice, Česka 32, Brno. T. (05) 22534. - Ant - *041092*

České Budějovice
Antiquitäten, Žižkovo nám. 166, České Budějovice.
- Ant - *041093*

Karlovy Vary
Antiquitäten, Dukelskych Hrdinů 2, Karlovy Vary.
- Ant - *041094*
„Tuzex", Tržiště 1, Karlovy Vary. *041095*

Plzeň
Staatlicher Antiquitätenhandel, Nám. Republiky 23,
Plzeň. - Ant - *041096*

Praha
Antiquitäten, Národní tř. 24, Praha. *041097*
Antiquitäten, Vinohradská 45, Praha. *041098*
Antiquitäten, Václavské nám. č. 60, Praha. *041099*
Antiquitäten, Královodvorská 2, Praha. *041100*
ARTIA, Ve Smečkách 30, Praha. T. (02) 24 60 41. *041101*
Direction d'Enterprise des Antiquités, Obránců míru 104,
Praha. *041102*
Klenoty n. p. – Starožitnosti, Mikulandská 7, Praha.
T. (02) 29 86 09. *041103*

Teplice
Antiquitäten, Dlouhá 41, Teplice. *041104*

Denmark

Åbenrå
Petersen, Hans Jørgen, Nørreport 16, 6200 Åbenrå.
T. 74 62 24 79. *041105*

Ålborg
Aalborg Kunst & Antikvitetshandel, Vesterbro 39, 9000
Ålborg. T. 16 06 16. - Ant / Paint / Jew / Instr / Mil /
Glass / Cur / Music - *041106*
Montboden AS, Ostergade 15, 9000 Ålborg. T. 12 70 00.
- Num - *041107*
Pilegaard, G., Algade 65, 9000 Ålborg. T. 98 13 90 00.
- Num - *041108*

Ålsgårde
Scandinavian Antiques, Birkehegnet, 3140 Ålsgårde.
T. 42 10 70 04. - Furn - *041109*

Århus (Jütland)
Aarhus Montgalleri Aps, Ryesgade 23, 8200 Århus.
T. 12 19 24. - Num - *041110*
Antique, Skt. Clemens Str. 7, 8000 Århus C.
- Ant - *041111*
Pedersen, Knud, Vestergade 3, 8000 Århus C.
T. 12 17 99. - Ant / Furn / Instr - *041112*
PR Mønter, Banegaardspl. 9, 8000 Århus C. T. 12 12 95.
- Num - *041113*

Charlottenlund
Kaas, Jaegersborg Allé 39, 2920 Charlottenlund.
T. 31 64 24 76. *041114*
Moes, Karl, Parkvaenget 11, 2920 Charlottenlund.
T. 62 10 89. - Furn / China - *041115*

Espergaerde
Kilde, T., Grøndalsv. 5, 3060 Espergaerde.
T. 42 23 28 97. *041116*

Fanø
„Phillippines Hus", 6720 Fanø. T. 16 23 63. - Ant /
Furn - *041117*

Farum
a2-grafik, Paltholmterr. 46f, 3520 Farum. T. 42 95 50 16.
- Ant - *041118*
Original Graphic Studio, Paltholmterr. 46f, 3520 Farum.
T. 95 50 16. - Graph - *041119*

Fredensborg
Antikgaarden, Endrupvej 45, 3480 Fredensborg.
T. 42 24 82 38. - Ant - *041120*

Gentofte
Donatzsky, Torben, A/S, Anemenovej 62, 2820 Gentofte.
T. 68 22 40. - Ant / Dec - *041121*
Krogh, Brogårdsvej 100, 2820 Gentofte. T. 31 65 84 30.
- Ant - *041122*
Riber, K., Vangedevej 118, 2820 Gentofte. T. 67 00 60.
- Sculp - *041123*

Graested
Esrum Antiuk, Esrum Hovedg. 8, 3230 Graested.
T. 29 05 20. - Ant - *041124*

Gram
Bock, A., 6510 Gram. T. 155. - Ant - *041125*

Hellerup
Hellerup Antik, Strandv 114, 2900 Hellerup.
T. 31 61 02 02. *041126*
Versailles Antiques & Interior Decoration, Strandv. 130
C, 2900 Hellerup. T. 31 61 16 50. - Ant - *041127*

Helsingør
Den Gamle Smedie, Ellenmosevej 1, 3200 Helsingør.
T. 30 64 99. - Furn - *041128*
DK Antique, Strandgade 39, 3000 Helsingør. T. 21 30 72.
- Paint / Draw - *041129*
Guttmann, Max, Stengade 77, 3000 Helsingør.
T. 49 21 65 70. - Ant - *041130*
Sudergaardens Antik, Sudergade 4, 3000 Helsingør.
T. 100 911. *041131*

Herning
Anglo-Dan-Antik, Skolegade 10, 7400 Herning.
T. 122 112. - Cur - *041132*
Cheri, Skolegade 10, 7400 Herning. T. 12 21 12. - Ant /
Furn - *041133*

Hobro
Nordjydsk Kunsthandel, Sallingvej 39, 9500 Hobro.
T. 52 03 36. *041134*

Holte
Artscope, Sollerod Park Blok 15 nr. 13, 2840 Holte.
- Ant - *041135*
Casa Antica, Kongev 29, 2840 Holte.
T. 42 42 15 53. *041136*

Horbelev
Hald, Jens, Brydsbjergvej 2, 4871 Horbelev.
T. 53 84 42 75. *041137*

Horsens
Stovring Antikviteter, Ole, Thonbogade 4, 8700 Horsens.
T. 61 40 10. - Glass - *041138*

Humlebaek
Antikgården i Humlebaek, Ny Strandvej 140 A, 3050
Humlebaek. T. 42 19 17 20. - Ant - *041139*

Hvidovre
Holmegården, Hvidovrevej 94, 2650 Hvidovre.
T. 31 75 23 94. - Ant - *041140*

Karup
Agau Metal, Postboks 56, 7470 Karup. T. 97 10 29 00,
Fax 97 10 29 97. - Num - *041141*

København
A Galerie, Vesterbrog. 171, 1800 København.
T. 31 23 12 65. *041142*
A.A. Antik Lageret, Gl. Kongev. 101, 1850 København V.
T. 31 31 49 59. - Ant - *041143*
A.A.A., Gl. Mønt 2, 1117 København K. T. 33 14 36 17.
- Ant - *041144*
A.A.A. Antik 24, Elmegade 24, 1000 København.
T. 31 37 14 29. - Ant - *041145*
A.B.C. Antik, Ravnsborgg. 15, 1000 København.
T. 31 37 01 58. - Ant - *041146*
Ad Libitum, Strandvejen 185, 2900 København.
T. 31 62 31 32. - Ant - *041147*
Agathe Shop, Nørrebrog. 47, 1000 København.
T. 31 39 74 61. - Ant - *041148*

Almestuen, Jernbane Allé 95, 1000 København.
T. 31 74 40 46. - Ant - *041149*
Alsken, Frederikssundsv. 62B, 1000 København.
T. 31 10 70 15. - Ant - *041150*
Amager Antikstue, Amagerbrog. 156, 1000 København.
T. 31 58 97 62. - Ant - *041151*
Amagerbro Antik, Lyong. 7, 1000 København.
T. 31 58 57 19. - Ant - *041152*
Amanda, Trepkasg. 6, 1000 København. T. 31 37 28 50.
- Ant - *041153*
Amar Antik, Amagerbrog. 16 a, 1000 København.
T. 31 95 50 48. *041154*
Andersen, Bent, Kompagnistraede 7, 1208 København.
T. 33 12 82 84. - Ant / Furn / Glass / Cur - *041155*
Andrejcak, Bent, Gittervej 12, 2100 København.
T. 31 38 66 36/58, Fax 31 26 91 05. - Ant / Paint /
Graph / Furn / China / Sculp / Tex / Fra / Silv / Lights / In-
str / Glass / Cur / Mod - *041156*
Annett Antique, Primulvej 17, 1000 København.
T. 31 10 22 27. - Ant - *041157*
Antik, Jagtvej 23A, 1000 København. T. 82 10 22.
- Ant - *041158*
Antik, Silkegade 11, 1113 København K. T. 33 32 15 91.
- Ant - *041159*
Antik, Gothersg. 153, 1123 København K. T. 33 32 98 37.
- Ant - *041160*
Antik, Bredgade 8, 1260 København K. T. 33 12 60 58.
- Ant - *041161*
Antik, St. Kongensg. 77, 1264 København K.
T. 33 12 31 31. - Ant - *041162*
Antik Expressen, Ryesgade 71, 1000 København.
T. 31 39 90 01. - Ant - *041163*
Antik Huset, N. Fasanvej 114, 1000 København.
T. 31 87 47 47. - Ant - *041164*
Antik-Kate, Vesterbrog. 177, 1800 København V.
T. 22 85 50. - Ant - *041165*
Antik Nordre Frihavn, Nordre Frihavnsg. 49, 2100 Kø-
benhavn Ø. T. 31 42 00 05. - Ant - *041166*
Antik-Shop, Greve Strandv. 27, 1000 København.
T. 42 90 26 15. *041167*
Antik Sofie-Amalie, Rådhusstr. 11, 1466 København K.
T. 33 93 15 75. - Ant - *041168*
Antik & Glasmenageriet, Smallegade 20A, 1000 Køben-
havn. T. 31 86 86 16. - Ant - *041169*
Antik & Kunst, Kompagnistr. 11, 1208 København K.
T. 33 15 23 46. - Ant - *041170*
Antik & Lamper, Gl. Mønt 19, 1117 København K.
T. 33 15 64 63. - Ant - *041171*
Antik Vitrinen, Brolaeggerstr. 6, 1211 København K.
T. 33 15 90 60. - Ant - *041172*
Antik West, Frederiksbergallé 4, 1820 København V.
T. 31 31 64 12. - Ant - *041173*
Antik 141, Gl. Kongevej 141, 1850 København V.
T. 31 22 33 16. - Ant - *041174*
Antik 37, Vodroffsv. 37, 1900 København V.
T. 31 23 22 65. - Ant - *041175*
Antik 50, H.C. Örstedsvej 50B, 1879 København V.
T. 35 71 80. - Ant - *041176*
Antikbutik, Englandsv. 370, 1000 København.
T. 31 51 78 08. - Ant - *041177*
Antikgården, Reerslevv. 23, 1000 København.
T. 46 59 00 26. *041178*
Antikgården, Gl. Jernbanev. 16, 1000 København.
T. 31 46 51 09. - Ant - *041179*
Antikhjønet, Elbag. 35, 1000 København. T. 31 55 12 50,
31 55 20 03. - Ant - *041180*
Antikhjørnet, Bagsvaerd Hovedg. 1, 1000 København.
T. 44 44 23 01. *041181*
Antikkaelderen, Hyskenstraede 16, 1207 København.
T. 33 13 33 01. - Lights - *041182*
Antiknøglen, Rungsted Strandv. 354, 1000 København.
T. 42 24 75 34. *041183*
Antikvitetshuset, St. Kongensg. 44, 1264 København K.
T. 32 72 17. - Ant - *041184*
Antique, Gl. Strand 42, 1202 København K.
T. 33 12 30 04. - Ant - *041185*
Antique Corner, Sølvg. 2, 1307 København K.
T. 33 14 14 65. - Ant - *041186*
Antique Export House, Godthåbsvej 13A, 2000 Køben-
havn. T. 31 19 95 33. - Ant - *041187*
Antique Moderne, Landemaerket 9, 1119 København K.
T. 33 32 63 90. - Ant - *041188*

Antique Traders, Badstuestr. 13, 1209 København K. T. 14 80 79. - Ant - 041189
Antiquete's d'Angleterre, Kongens Nytorv 34, 1050 København. T. 33 93 93 77. 041190
Arms Gallery, Nybrogade 26, 1203 København. T. 33 11 83 38. - Mil - 041191
Art Deco, St. Strandstr. 19, 1255 København K. T. 33 15 52 65. - Ant - 041192
Art Kaj, Helgolandsg. 13, 1653 København V. T. 31 31 32 96. - Ant - 041193
Arts d'Afrique, Pilestraede 29-31, 1112 København K. T. 33 14 26 56. - Orient / Eth - 041194
Bahl, Helge, Blegdamsv. 10, 1000 København. T. 31 37 16 77. - Ant - 041195
Baumann, Lasse, Nabolös 3, 1206 København K. T. 33 11 72 37. - Ant / Paint - 041196
Be-Art, Sankt Pauls Gade 42, 1313 København. T. 33 91 73 13. - Paint / Graph / Draw - 041197
Bechager, Nørre Farimagsg. 72, 1364 København. T. 33 11 01 47. 041198
Bedstemor, Randersgade 41, 1000 København. T. 26 62 46. - Ant - 041199
Bell Epoque Antik, Kompagnistr. 24, 1208 København. T. 33 11 11 86, 33 13 37 13. 041200
Berg, Otto, Toldbodgade 5, 1253 København K. T. 33 13 19 71. - Ant / Paint / Furn / Orient / China / Silv / Glass - 041201
Berndorf, Curt, Fiolstraede 25, 1171 København. T. 33 13 74 76. - Glass - 041202
Bernstorffsvejens Antik, Kildegårdsvej 8, 1000 København. T. 31 61 08 61. - Ant - 041203
Billedantikvariatet, Kompagnistr. 25, 1208 København K. T. 33 12 28 58, 33 12 97 62. - Ant - 041204
Bjaelkerup Antik, Bjaelkerupv. 99, 1000 København. T. 53 70 26 41. 041205
Bohn, Carl, St. Kongensgade 32, 1264 København K. T. 33 13 63 03. 041206
Bolt, Niels, Chr. IX's G. 6, 1111 København. T. 33 13 17 18, 33 12 83 84. 041207
Bondorff, H.J., Hvalsøv. 32, 1000 København. T. 31 80 03 37. - Ant - 041208
Børgesen, Bent, Kompagnistraede 7, 1208 København K. T. 14 83 15. - Ant / Jew / Glass - 041209
Børgesen, Bent, Kompagnistr. 7, 1208 København. T. 33 14 83 15. 041210
Borups Antik, Borupsallé 31, 1000 København. T. 31 19 35 45. - Ant - 041211
Brand, P., Blågrds. 31C, 1000 København. T. 31 39 25 39. - Ant - 041212
Brandt-Jensen, Peter, Bredg. 28, 1260 København. T. 33 32 85 85. 041213
Broberg, P., Hestefolden 1, 1000 København. T. 42 80 16 09. 041214
Brock, J., Gl. Strand 40, 1202 København K. T. 33 15 54 54. - Ant - 041215
Bülow, Gl. Kongevej 37A, 1610 København V. T. 31 77 25. - Ant - 041216
Butik Antik, Store Kongensg. 103, 1264 København K. T. 33 14 21 35. - Ant - 041217
Calli, Løngangstr. 21, 1468 København K. T. 33 12 09 78. - Ant - 041218
Caso, Refshalev. 2, 1432 København K. T. 31 95 30 51. - Ant - 041219
Centrum Antik, Tunnelv. 20, 1000 København. T. 42 96 58 88. 041220
Copenhagen Antique, Hjørringg. 37, 2100 København Ø. T. 31 26 65 65. - Ant - 041221
Dalgaard, Jørgen L., Badstuestraede 16, 1209 København. T. 33 14 09 05. - Ant / Mod - 041222
Danborg, Holbergsg. 17, 1057 København K. T. 33 32 93 94. - Ant - 041223
Danielsen, Eftf., Laederstr. 11, 1201 København K. T. 33 13 02 74. - Ant / China / Silv - 041224
Dansk Antik, Ravnsborgg. 21, 1000 København. T. 37 30 37. - Ant - 041225
Dansk Kunst- & Antikvitetshandler Union, Hestemøllestraede 3, 1464 København K. T. 11 46 36. 041226
Daucke, Børje, Vestebr. 105, 1620 København V. T. 24 74 43. - Ant - 041227
Decorama, Kingosg. 6, 1623 København V. T. 31 24 52 54. - Ant - 041228
Diser 37, Kompagnistr. 37, 1208 København K. T. 33 13 37 75. - Ant - 041229
Dit & Dat, Nordre Frihavnsg. 84, 1000 København. T. 31 38 40 36. 041230
Dragør, Amagerbrog. 28, 1000 København. T. 31 57 94 35. - Ant - 041231
Dukke, Ella, Kompagnistr. 33, 1208 København K. T. 33 15 45 39. - Ant - 041232
Egeskov, Søren, Holbergsg. 13, 1057 København K. T. 33 13 29 29. - Ant - 041233
Eleo, Willy, Arhusg. 37, 1000 København. T. 26 52 41. - Ant - 041234
Elev, Willy, Århusg. 37, 1000 København. T. 31 26 52 41. 041235
English Silver House, Pilestraede 2, 1112 København K. T. 33 14 83 81. - Silv - 041236
Erichsen, J., Guldbergsg. 9, 1000 København. T. 37 62 94. - Ant - 041237
Erud Antik, Birkerød Kongev. 94, 1000 København. T. 42 81 07 91. 041238
Esrum Antik, Hovedg. 8, 1000 København. T. 42 29 05 20. 041239
Falkoner Antik, Falkonerallé 102, 1000 København. T. 31 39 60 93. 041240
Frandsen, Frydendalsvej 3, Frederiksberg, 1809 København. T. 22 50 55. - Ant - 041241
Frederiksberg Antik, Falkonerallé 100, 1000 København F. T. 31 39 60 22. - Ant - 041242
G-B Antik, Ved. Glyptoteket 2, 1575 København V. T. 33 12 73 95. - Ant - 041243
Galerie A, Vesterbrogade 171, Frederiksberg, 1800 København. T. 31 23 12 65. - Ant - 041244
Galerie Antique, Kongens Nytorv. 21, 1000 København. T. 33 11 72 00. - Ant - 041245
Galerie Victoria, St. Strandstr. 20, 1255 København K. T. 15 47 66. - Paint - 041246
Glostrup Antik, Hovedv. 103, 1000 København. T. 42 96 02 15. 041247
Glüsing, Ravnsborgg. 18, 1000 København. T. 31 37 20 24. - Ant - 041248
Godt Køb, Elmegade 2 2001A, 1000 København. T. 31 39 54 77. 041249
Good Old Days, Amagerbrog. 219, 1000 København. T. 31 55 83 10. - Ant - 041250
Good Old Days, Skåneboulevard, 1000 København. T. 42 52 34 36. 041251
Gottschalch, Erik T., Laederstr. 13, 1201 København K. T. 33 12 79 11. - Ant / Glass - 041252
Green Square, Strandlodsvej 11b, 2300 København S. T. 31 57 59 59. - Ant / Furn - 041253
Hansen, Tage Mikkel, Bryggersgade 7, 1460 København K. T. 33 12 53 54. - Ant / Paint / Furn / Mil - 041254
Hartogsohn, Ketti, Palaegade 8, 1261 København K. T. 33 15 53 98. - Ant - 041255
Haslund, Amagertorv. 14, 1160 København K. T. 33 15 88 88. - Ant - 041256
Hede, John, Tingvej 14A, 1000 København. T. 58 010 01. - Ant - 041257
Hendriksen, Lizzi, Jernbane Allé 69, 1000 København. T. 74 47 02. - Ant - 041258
Hendriksen, Lizzi, Jernbaneallé 69, 1000 København. T. 31 74 47 02. 041259
Hindsberg, Egon S., Falkoner Allé 19, 1000 København. T. 31 86 70 76. - Ant - 041260
H.J. Antik, Nordre Dragørv. 53, 1000 København. T. 31 53 51 52. 041261
Hjorth, Emil, & Sønner, Ny Vestergade 1, 1471 København K. T. 33 12 39 89, Fax 33 13 90 30. - Music - 041262
Hold, Kompagnistr. 25, 1208 København K. T. 33 12 73 20. - Ant - 041263
Holmelund, G., Tjørnelunde, 1000 København. T. 53 55 27 01. 041264
Hovedstaden, Fakseg. 19, 1000 København. T. 43 03 84. - Ant - 041265
Igenbo, Alekistev. 92, 1000 København. T. 31 79 07 06. - Ant - 041266
Ind & Ud, Vesterbrog. 120, 1620 København V. T. 31 33 54. - Ant - 041267
Indbo, J.S., Frederiksborgg. 48, 1360 København K. T. 33 11 00 03. - Ant - 041268
Inter Antik, Smalleg. 43, Frederiksberg, 2000 København. T. 31 19 70 35. 041269
Inter Antik Kunst, Smallegade 43, 2000 København V. T. 19 70 35. - Ant - 041270
Ive, Hestemøllestr.3, 1464 København K. T. 33 14 81 71. - Furn / Orient / China / Tex - 041271
Jall, Erik Heide, Nansengade 43. KLD., 1366 København K. T. 33 13 18 67. - Ant / Orient / Arch / Eth - 041272
Jelskov, Poul Thorball, Vestergade 22, 1456 København. T. 33 14 18 95. - Ant - 041273
Jensen, Pilestraede 47, 1112 København. T. 33 11 70 67. - Ant / Furn - 041274
Juncher, Arne, Tårb Strandv. 59, 1000 København. T. 31 63 03 43. - Ant - 041275
Juvélen, Vesterbrog. 50, 1620 København V. T. 31 31 63 73. - Jew - 041276
Jyllinge, Kompagnistr. 9, 1208 København K. T. 33 15 96 50. - Ant - 041277
Kallerup, B., Liselejev. 7 a, 1000 København. T. 42 34 77 90. 041278
Kildesø, Reno, St. Kongensgade 59, 1264 København K. T. 33 15 08 77. - Ant / Furn / China / Eth / Jew / Cur - 041279
Kirsten's Antik, Aegirsg. 4, 1000 København. T. 31 85 26 84. 041280
Kjaer, Flemm., Silkegade 5, 1113 København K. T. 33 15 18 36. - Ant / Furn - 041281
Kofoeds, Georg, St. Kongensg. 59, 1264 København K. T. 33 15 85 44. - Ant - 041282
Krog, Peter, Bredg. 4, 1260 København. T. 33 12 45 55. 041283
Krone, Hulgårdsv. 1, 1000 København. T. 31 86 06 81. - Ant - 041284
Laederstraede Antik, Laederstr. 36, 1201 København. T. 33 11 34 86. 041285
Lange, Jørg, Graekenlandsvej 33, 1000 København. T. 31 58 68 59. - Ant - 041286
Larsen, H.C., Hjortsv. 20, 1000 København. T. 31 46 53 54. - Ant - 041287
Larsen, Jens, Gl. Mønt 27, 1117 København. T. 33 15 62 56. 041288
Larsen, Niels, Borgerg. 91, 1300 København K. T. 33 15 31 70. - Ant - 041289
Leonora Antique, Hyskensstr. 11, 1207 København K. T. 33 14 03 03. - Ant - 041290
Limkilde, T. J., Bredgade 28, 1260 København K. T. 33 13 17 91. - Ant / Furn - 041291
Lundin, Fabricius, Gl. Kongevej 146, 1850 København V. T. 31 24 05 11. - Ant - 041292
Lundin, H.O., Vester Voldg. 21, 1552 København V. T. 33 13 21 11. - Ant - 041293
Lysberg, Hansen & Therp, Bredgade 3, 1260 København K. T. 33 14 47 87. - Ant / Furn / Dec - 041294
Martime Antiques, Toldbodg. 15, 1253 København K. T. 12 12 57. - Ant - 041295
Mathiesen, Ole, Östergade 8, 1100 København. T. 33 14 12 08. - Instr - 041296
Merling, Vesterg. 3, 1456 København K. T. 33 15 78 00. - Ant - 041297
Minell, Lisa, St. Strandstr. 20, 1255 København K. T. 14 99 03. - Ant - 041298
Møbelmessen, Griffenfeldsg. 8, 1000 København. T. 31 39 17 00. - Furn - 041299
Møller, Gl. Kongevej 101, 1850 København V. T. 31 31 49 59. - Ant - 041300
Møller Nielsen, Lis, Kvistgrdsv. 2, 1000 København. T. 42 24 83 42. 041301
Møller, Otto, Gl. Kongevej 135B, 1850 København V. T. 31 24 61 25. - Ant - 041302
Monberg, Morten, Vallerødvaenge 4, 1000 København. T. 42 86 16 66. 041303
Mourier, Vibeke, Frederiksbergallé 42A, 1820 København V. T. 31 22 16 68. - Ant - 041304
Müllertz, Birte, Ordrupv. 123, 1000 København. T. 31 63 60 05. - Ant - 041305
Nelholt, Dennis, Naboløs 1, 1206 København K. T. 33 14 92 15. - Ant - 041306
Nielsen, Otto, Skonbog. 1, 1160 København K. T. 33 11 39 86. - Jew - 041307
Nordun, Olav, Hvidovregade 40, 2650 København. T. 31 75 37 60. - Furn / Instr - 041308
Nørrebros Salgscentral, Nordbaneg. 18, 1000 København. T. 31 81 97 62. - Ant - 041309
Northern Light Gallery, Skt. Bendt's Allé 47, 1000 København. T. 42 99 38 47. 041310
Nyholm, Jytte, Bredgade 78, 1260 København K. T. 33 15 00 12. - Ant - 041311

Österbro Antik, Österbrog. 160, 1000 København.
T. 18 03 87. - Ant -   041312
Opus 57, Ordrupsvej 57, 1000 København. T. 63 41 42.
- Ant -   041313
Ordrup Antikes, Hyldegardsv. 4, 1000 København.
T. 31 63 75 75. - Ant -   041314
Palsager, Allan, Nørre Farimagsg. 72, 13645 København
K. T. 11 01 47. - Ant -   041315
Passer, Nyhavn 18, 1051 København K. T. 33 11 24 66.
- Ant -   041316
Passer, Marchen, Nyhavn. 18, 1051 København K.
T. 33 11 24 66. - Ant -   041317
Pedersen, Tine, Dronningsgårdsv. 2, 1000 København.
T. 42 42 31 81.   041318
PH Antik, Gormsgade 2A, 1000 København. T. 85 29 15.
- Ant -   041319
Phantasie Antik, Ravnsborgg. 20, 1000 København.
T. 37 68 42. - Ant -   041320
Pjot, Nørre, Frederiksborgg. 48, 1360 København.
T. 33 13 34 19.   041321
Qvinten, Karen Olsdatterstr. 15, 1000 København.
T. 42 35 22 87.   041322
Qvistgaard Antique A/S, Laederstraede 32, 1201 Køben-
havn. T. 3314 17 25. - Silv / Glass -   041323
Raabjerg, Folmer, Bredgade 47, 1260 København K.
T. 33130500, Fax 33912331. - Furn / China / Jew /
Silv / Rel / Glass / Mod -   041324
Rasmussen, Bruun, Bredgade 33, 1260 København K.
T. 33136911, Fax 33324920. - Ant -   041325
Rasmussen, Inge, Knabrostr. 14, 1210 København K.
T. 33115892. - Ant -   041326
Regild, V., Gl. Kongevej 33a, 1610 København V.
T. 31 24 63 83. - Ant -   041327
Rekahn, Laederstr. 5, 1000 København.
T. 33 32 92 15.   041328
Resen, Andreas, Kingosg. 1, 1818 København V.
T. 31 89 59. - Ant -   041329
Retro-Antik, Linnésg. 14, 1361 København.
T. 33 13 50 70.   041330
Ristea, Toldbodg. 5 (K), 1253 København. T. 33 13 41 64.
- Ant -   041331
Rosasco, Therese, Ved Stranden 20, 1061 København K.
T. 14 51 37, 33 13 54 10. - Ant -   041332
Roxy Antik, Godthåbsv. 20A, 1000 København.
T. 38 88 02 78. - Ant / Furn / Dec / Glass / Cur -   041333
Royal Copenhagen Antiques, Bredgade 11, 1260 Køben-
havn K. T. (33) 140229. - Ant -   041334
Rundetårn, Købmagersg. 52, 1150 København K.
T. 33 12 81 65. - Ant -   041335
Runge, Erik, Frederiksbergallé 56, 1820 København V.
T. 33 22 67 80. - Ant -   041336
Sankt Jakobs Antique & Art, Sankt Jakobspl. 6, 1000
København. T. 33 26 99 33. - Ant -   041337
Scandinavian House, Vesterbrogade 50, 1620 Køben-
havn. T. 31 22 57 00.   041338
Schmidt, Flemm., V. Voldg. 91, 1000 København.
T. 33 13 65 86. - Ant -   041339
Servanten, Vesterbrog. 127, 1620 København V.
T. 31 22 53 83. - Ant -   041340
Skjalm Petersen, H., Nikolaj Plads 7, 1067 København
K. T. 33 11 82 00. - Ant -   041341
Soelberg, Lars, Kompagnistr. 3, 1208 København K.
T. 33 14 56 60, 33 12 79 77. - Ant / Furn / Instr - 041342
Sølvkaelderen, Kompagnistr. 1, 1208 København K.
T. 33 13 36 34. - Ant -   041343
Sørensen, Birthe, Mønterg. 14, 1116 København K.
T. 33 13 57 66. - Ant -   041344
Sørensen, Elsa, Mønterg. 12, 1116 København K.
T. 33 12 22 27. - Ant -   041345
Steckhahn, Jørg., Kaeragervej 14, 1000 København.
T. 31 74 88 82. - Ant -   041346
Stenstrøm, Edisonsv. 2A, 1856 København V.
T. 31 24 32 34. - Ant -   041347
Store Kongensgade Antik, Store Kongensg. 74, 1264 Kø-
benhavn K. T. 33 15 27 68. - Ant -   041348
Strandvejens Antik, Strandvejen 36, 1000 København.
T. 20 12 58. - Ant -   041349
Strøget, Nygade 7, 1164 København K. T. 33 12 12 65.
- Ant -   041350
Strømann, Marianne, Jaegersb. Allé 7, 1000 København.
T. 31 63 70 95. - Ant -   041351
Strømberg, Gothersg. 7, 1123 København K.
T. 33 32 42 05. - Ant -   041352

Svendsen, H. V., Oehlenschlaegersgade 22-24, 1663
København V. T. 31 22 95 70. - Ant -   041353
Theger, Palle, Gl. Kongevej 39, 1610 København V.
T. 31 24 61 24. - Ant -   041354
Thomsen, Leif, Jagtv. 213, 1000 København.
T. 31 29 05 18. - Ant -   041355
Tisvilde, Tibirkev. 13, 1000 København.
T. 42 30 70 71.   041356
Toftegaard Hansen, Mai-Britt, N. Frihavnsg. 65, 1000
København. T. 31 42 17 75. - Ant -   041357
Tre Falke Antik, Falkoner Allé 10, 1000 København.
T. 22 97 11. - Ant -   041358
Tryde, Niels, Nørrebrog 60, 1000 København.
T. 31 35 31 42. - Ant -   041359
Valby Antik, Toftegardallé 24, 1000 København.
T. 31 17 02 01. - Ant -   041360
Vari-Art, Gothersg. 58, 1123 København.
T. 33 14 19 90.   041361
Veirhanen, Nørrebrog. 60, 2200 København N.
T. 31 35 31 42. - Ant -   041362
Vor Frues Antik, Dyrkøb 3, 1166 København.
T. 33 12 75 41.   041363
Wahl, Kim, Danasv. 38, Frederiskberg, 1910 København.
T. 31 31 27 15.   041364
Wester, Janne, Absalonsg. 7A, 1658 København V.
T. 31 03 22. - Ant -   041365
Wulff, Nordre Frihavnsg. 57, 1000 København.
T. 31 26 08 16. - Ant -   041366
Wulff-Møller, Bredg. 25, 1260 København.
T. 33 91 11 21. - Ant -   041367

Køge

Jacobsen, Arne, Birketoftegaard Køgevej 82, Vallø, 4600
Køge. T. 66 75 84. - Ant -   041368
Køge Antikvitetshandel, Brogade 16, 4600 Køge.
T. 53 66 18 32. - Ant -   041369
Nielsen, Jorgen, N. Juelsgade 1, 4600 Køge.
T. 65 30 40. - Ant -   041370

Kokkedal

Norman Coin + Medals, Egedalsvaenge 20, 2980 Kok-
kedal. T. 24 51 97. - Num -   041371
Strandhuset, Rungsted Strandvej 354, 2980 Kokkedal.
T. 18 02 42. - Ant / Paint / Furn / Orient / China / Dec /
Silv / Lights / Instr / Glass / Cur -   041372

Kolding

Klinge, Laurits, Nørre Bjaert, 6000 Kolding.
T. 75 56 50 32. - Ant -   041373

Krusaa

Krusaa Antikvitets Lager, Madeskovvej 9, 6340 Krusaa.
T. 67 09 99. - Ant -   041374

Lokken

Lighthouse Antiques, Lonstrupvej 46, Rubjerg, 9480
Lokken. T. 99 64 00.   041375

Lyngby (Kopenhagen)

Bartsch, Heine R., Odinsv 5, 2800 Lyngby.
T. 42 87 60 77.   041376

Måløw

Scan Antik, Östergade 22, 2760 Måløw. T. 42 18 10 04.
- Ant -   041377

Maribo

A/S C.-L. Jarvig, 4930 Maribo. T. 203, 690.
- Ant -   041378

Naestved

Fossing, A., Slagelsvej 17, 4700 Naestved. T. 15 51.
- Ant -   041379
Rønne, Palle, Grønneg. 37B, 4700 Naestved.
T. 52 72 08 85. - Ant -   041380

Odense

DPH Trading, Løkkegravene 49, 5270 Odense N.
T. 66 18 95 95. - Ant -   041381
Frøtorp, H., Teisensv. 43, 5000 Odense. - Ant -   041382
Risager, Jørgen, Løkkegravene 49, 5270 Odense.
T. 66 18 95 95.   041383

Præstø

Prästö Antik, Adelgade 79, 4720 Præstø. T. 53791408.
- Furn / Paint / Fra / Ant -   041384

Rödovre

Eskesen Bros. Company, 108-110 Gronlunds Allé, 2610
Rödovre. T. 70 46 55. - Orient -   041385
F.T. Antique, Gunnekaer 26, 2610 Rödovre.
T. 36 72 12 55. - Ant / Orient / China / Repr /
Lights -   041386

Rungsted Kyst

Pennehave Antik, Pennehave 10, 2960 Rungsted Kyst.
T. 42 86 12 32.   041387

Skibby

F.B. Antik, Krabbesholmvej 19, 4050 Skibby.
T. 4232 7530.   041388

Snekkersten

Snekkersten Antique, Strandvejen 210, 3070 Snekkersten. T. 22 13 00. - Ant -   041389

Sønderborg

Wilke & Gehrke, Jernbaneg, 6400 Sønderborg.
T. 225 56. - Ant -   041390

Sørvad

Patina Møbler, Mølletoften 2, 7550 Sørvad.
T. 9743 8400, 9743 8072.   041391

Svendborg

Hansen, Jorgen, Mollergade 63, 5700 Svendborg.
T. 21 79 10.   041392
Rosenthal, J. O., Eghavevej 10D, Troense, 5700 Svend-
borg. - Ant -   041393

Tappernöje

Antiquitäten auf Seeland, Vesterholm, 4733 Tappernöje.
T. 76 44 92. - Ant / Furn / Glass -   041394

Tønder

Hecht's Antik i Tönder, F. K., Nörregade 42, 6270 Tøn-
der. T. 72 17 45. - Ant / Paint / Eth -   041395

Valby

Antique Export House, Trekronerg. 149 C, 2500 Valby.
T. 17 33 88. - Ant -   041396
Kure, Inge, Langg 28, 2500 Valby.
T. 31 30 07 27.   041397
Pepés Antik, Gl Jernbanev 30, 2500 Valby.
T. 31 16 01 34.   041398

Vedbaek

Helle Hovmand, Olesvej 15, 2950 Vedbaek.
T. 89 15 37.   041399

Vejle (Jütland)

Antikstuen i Skovhuset, Skelde, 7100 Vejle.
T. 88 15 01.   041400
Borring, Frank, Grejsdalsvej 326, 7100 Vejle.
T. 85 34 00, 85 33 85. - Ant / Furn / Lights /
Cur -   041401
Rasmussen, Bruun, Pedersholms Allé 42, 7100 Vejle.
T. 75827722, Fax 75724722. - Ant -   041402

Viborg

Viborg Antikvitetshandel, Kompagnistraede 7, 8800 Viborg. - Glass -   041403

Egypt

Cairo

Bajocchi, Pietro, 45 Abdel Khalek Sarwat, Cairo.
T. (2) 391 91 60. - Num -   041404
Boutros, Zaki, Khan Khalili Bazaar Entrance Mousky,
Cairo. T. (2) 90 41 53. - Ant -   041405
Lehnert & Landrock, 44, Sherif Pasha St., Cairo.   041406

Finland

Äänekoski (Keski-Suomen lääni)

Tavallisen Kansan Taidekauppa, Kotakennääntie 13,
44100 Äänekoski. T. (014) 20382.   041407

Espoo (Uudenmaan lääni)
Tarkiainen, Länsituulenkuja 3, 02100 Espoo.
T. (09) 46 16 44. *041408*

Fiskars (Uudenmaan lääni)
Wanha Puoti, 10470 Fiskars. T. (019) 37275. *041409*

Hämeenlinna (Hämeen lääni)
Antiikkiliike Santa Maria, Hallituskatu 7, 13100 Hämeenlinna. T. (03) 27467. *041410*

Hamina (Kymen lääni)
Kehystämö, K., Isoympyräkatu 13, 49400 Hamina.
T. (05) 43677. *041411*
Maarian Antiikki, Maariankatu 10, 49400 Hamina.
T. (05) 44910. *041412*

Hanko/Hangö (Uudenmaan lääni)
Antiqua Vezzi, Bulevardi 3, 10900 Hanko/Hangö.
T. (019) 82293. *041413*

Hattula (Hämeen lääni)
Antiikki Kattila, 13880 Hattula.
T. (017) 71 11 70. *041414*

Heinola (Mikkelin lääni)
Forskullan Taidekartano, 18150 Heinola.
T. (03) 156577. *041415*
Heinolan Keräily ja Antiikki, Siltakatu 1, 18100 Heinola.
T. (03) 154344. *041416*

Helsinki
Aarnio, Liiketie 21, 00730 Helsinki.
T. (09) 36 46 88. *041417*
Ainokainen, Liisankatu 15, 00170 Helsinki.
T. (09) 135 27 65. *041418*
Ajan Antiikki, Tarkk ampujankatu 15, 00120 Helsinki.
T. (09) 63 55 34. *041419*
Ajan Taide, Eurantie 8-10, 00550 Helsinki.
T. (09) 753 55 85. *041420*
Ajanpatria, Museokatu 9, 00100 Helsinki.
T. (09) 49 46 01. *041421*
Albertiina, Mariankatu 24, 00170 Helsinki.
T. (09) 135 28 55. *041422*
Alfa Antiikki, Kapteeninkatu 9, 00140 Helsinki.
T. (09) 66 26 23, 694 80 40. *041423*
Anjan Antiikki, Liisankatu 17, 00170 Helsinki.
T. (09) 135 15 47. *041424*
Antiikki ja Keräily, Liisankatu 12, 00170 Helsinki.
T. (09) 66 41 86. *041425*
Antiikki ja Nykyaika, Viipurinkatu 6, 00510 Helsinki.
T. (09) 146 41 85. *041426*
Antiikki- ja sisustusliike Alfa, Eerikinkatu 31, 00180 Helsinki. T. (09) 694 47 69. *041427*
Antiikki Koru, Eteläranta 20, 00130 Helsinki.
T. (09) 63 68 31. *041428*
Antiikki-, Postimerkki- ja Rahaliike Aarreaitta, Kalevankatu 27, 00100 Helsinki. T. (09) 694 52 48. *041429*
Antiikki Trianon, Eerikinkatu 12, 00100 Helsinki.
T. (09) 64 56 43. *041430*
Antiikkia – Taidetta, N. Magasinsgatan 7, 00100 Helsinki. T. (09) 66 32 74, 66 20 01. - Ant / Furn / Silv /
Mil - *041431*
Antiikkilinja, Viides linja 3, 00530 Helsinki.
T. (09) 753 85 15. *041432*
Antiikkinikkari, Merimiehenkatu 20, 00150 Helsinki.
T. (09) 62 83 06. *041433*
Antik Oskar, Rauhankatu 7, 00170 Helsinki.
T. (09) 135 74 10. *041434*
Antiq. Bulevard, Bulevarden 5, 00100 Helsinki.
T. (09) 64 72 86. - Ant - *041435*
Antique-Castle, Korkeavuorenkatu 15a, 00130 Helsinki.
T. (09) 60 81 99. *041436*
Arin Arkki, Vironkatu 3, 00170 Helsinki.
T. (09) 135 70 81. *041437*
Arin Arkki, Mariankatu 20, 00170 Helsinki.
T. (09) 135 70 81. *041438*
ART-Helsinki, Aleksanterinkatu 26, 00150 Helsinki.
T. (09) 62 70 10. *041439*
Artemis, Mannerheimintie 56, 00260 Helsinki.
T. (09) 49 25 16. *041440*
Artisana, Unioninkatu 28, 00100 Helsinki.
T. (09) 66 52 25. *041441*
Artistica, Kasarmigatan 34, 00100 Helsinki.
T. (09) 66 67 53, 66 41 75. - Tex - *041442*

Berger, Korkeavuorenkatu 13, 00130 Helsinki.
T. (09) 60 83 98. *041443*
Blomqvist, Ritva, Korkeavuorenkatu, 00140 Helsinki.
T. (09) 63 54 91. *041444*
Brocante-Antik, Tehtaankatu 11, 00140 Helsinki.
T. (09) 17 55 15. *041445*
Camelot, Albertinkatu 18, 00120 Helsinki.
T. (09) 63 70 01. *041446*
Church Hill Antiques, Mäntytie 3, 00270 Helsinki.
T. (09) 47 96 25. *041447*
Cul-de-Sac, Sofiankatu 5, 00170 Helsinki.
T. (09) 17 92 99. *041448*
E & L Antiikki, Lönnrotinkatu 16, 00120 Helsinki.
T. (09) 693 24 42. *041449*
Fasaani, Yrjönkatu 25, 00100 Helsinki.
T. (09) 60 25 69. *041450*
Finnantick, Annankatu 13, 00120 Helsinki.
T. (09) 60 54 11. *041451*
Forsström, Hämeentie 28, 00530 Helsinki.
T. (09) 753 15 33. *041452*
Frederik, Karl, Mariankatu 13, 00170 Helsinki.
T. (09) 63 00 14. *041453*
Fyndia, Hietaniemenkatu 6, 00100 Helsinki.
T. (09) 44 41 08. *041454*
Grahn, Patrik, Kalevankatu 16, 00100 Helsinki.
T. (09) 60 50 77, 64 37 82. *041455*
Hamid, Mechelininkatu 26, 00100 Helsinki.
T. (09) 44 64 89. *041456*
Heinänen, Museokatu 23, 00100 Helsinki.
T. (09) 49 58 18. *041457*
Helander, M., Kaarlenkatu 7, 00530 Helsinki.
T. (09) 701 77 49. *041458*
Helsingin Antiikki, Mechelininkatu 51, 00250 Helsinki.
T. (09) 49 95 49. *041459*
Hertza, V., Eteläranta 10, 00130 Helsinki.
T. (09) 62 80 48. *041460*
Hildan ja Huldan Antiikki, Rauhankatu 6b, 00170 Helsinki. T. (09) 17 13 17. *041461*
Hilja, Maria, Rauhankatu 7, 00170 Helsinki.
T. (09) 135 74 49. *041462*
Hirvosen Kehystys- ja Taideliike, Vuorimiehenkatu 33, 00140 Helsinki. T. (09) 63 36 22. *041463*
Hollming, V. & Co., Bulevarden 11, 00100 Helsinki.
T. (09) 66 23 68, 65 97 02. - Ant - *041464*
Holmasto, Snellmaninkatu 15, 00170 Helsinki.
T. (09) 135 7500, Fax 135 5003. - Num - *041465*
Holmasto, Eteläranta 14, 00130 Helsinki.
T. (09) 66 65 00. *041466*
Holmasto Antikshop, Eteläranta 14, 00130 Helsinki.
T. (09) 66 65 00, Fax 135 50 03. - Ant / Num / Silv /
Ico - *041467*
Iso-Äiti Oy, Pääskylänrinne 10, 00100 Helsinki.
T. (09) 76 37 75. - Ant - *041468*
Jokamielenhentori, Järvenpään tori, 00100 Helsinki.
T. (09) 28 80 96. *041469*
Kaarmo, M., Fabianinkatu 17, 00130 Helsinki.
T. (09) 65 46 14. *041470*
Kaivopuiston Antiikki, Kapteeninkatu 9, 00140 Helsinki.
T. (09) 66 37 29. *041471*
Kar Art Nostalgia, Nordenskiöldinkatu 8, 00250 Helsinki.
T. (09) 49 95 40. *041472*
Keräily Galleria, Mechelininkatu 19, 00100 Helsinki.
T. (09) 40 76 56. *041473*
Konstsalongen, Bulevarden 3B, 00100 Helsinki.
T. (09) 64 39 66. - Ant - *041474*
Korvatunturi, Uudenmaankatu 11, 00120 Helsinki.
T. (09) 605 854. - Ant / Furn / China / Silv /
Glass - *041475*
Kotoinen, Kankurinkatu 2, 00150 Helsinki.
T. (09) 65 00 80. *041476*
Kruunuhaan Antiikki, Mariankatu 20, 00170 Helsinki.
T. (09) 135 66 20. *041477*
Kumlin Taide, Bulevardi 15, 00128 Helsinki.
T. (09) 693 25 45. *041478*
Kupari-Taide, Nordenskiöldinkatu 8, 00250 Helsinki.
T. (09) 49 95 40. *041479*
Liinelot, Rauhankatu 7, 00170 Helsinki.
T. (09) 135 77 27. *041480*
Lindberg, B. & M., Töölöntorinkatu 3, 00260 Helsinki.
T. (09) 49 94 16. *041481*
Löytölinja, Viides linja 3, 00530 Helsinki.
T. (09) 76 18 94. *041482*

Malco, Albertinkatu 10, 00150 Helsinki.
T. (09) 65 51 07. *041483*
Mannerheimintien Antiikki, Mannerheimintie 56, 00260 Helsinki. T. (09) 40 78 85. *041484*
Markan Talo, Hämeentie 92, 00550 Helsinki.
T. (09) 71 70 25. *041485*
Maxies Antiikki & Sisustus, Kapteeninkatu 9, 00140 Helsinki. T. (09) 63 82 10. *041486*
Merkki Borg, Keskuskatu 6, Postfach 775, 00100 Helsinki. T. (09) 66 32 23. - Num - *041487*
MMH-Antique, Punavuorenkatu 4, 00120 Helsinki.
T. (09) 66 33 38. *041488*
Muinaisesinekauppa Kagan, Bulevardi 22, 00120 Helsinki. T. (09) 60 12 35. *041489*
Musketti Galleria, Mechelininkatu 19, 00100 Helsinki.
T. (09) 49 59 88. *041490*
Numismaatikko, P.O.Box 895, 00101 Helsinki.
T. (09) 562 49 78. - Num - *041491*
Occasion, Annegatan 15, 00100 Helsinki.
T. (09) 63 49 23. - Ant / Num / China / Jew / Fra / Silv /
Mil - *041492*
Old Art, Georgsgat. 16, 00100 Helsinki. T. (09) 643 818.
- Ant - *041493*
Old Days, Thurmpuistotie 14, 00100 Helsinki.
T. (09) 505 26 81. *041494*
Old Times Antik, Yrjönkatu 25, 00100 Helsinki.
T. (09) 60 40 06. *041495*
Pietari, Töölöntorinkatu 4, 00260 Helsinki.
T. (09) 49 03 61. *041496*
Pop Antik, Iso Roobertinkatu 41, 00120 Helsinki.
T. (09) 66 55 35. *041497*
Pretty Home, Korkeavuorenkatu 17, 00130 Helsinki.
T. (09) 66 00 21. *041498*
Punavuoren Antiikki, Mariankatu 14, 00170 Helsinki.
T. (09) 66 26 82. *041499*
Putinki, Hakaniemen halli, 00530 Helsinki.
T. (09) 73 91 50. *041500*
Rantala A, Solnantie 27, 00330 Helsinki.
T. (09) 48 61 75. *041501*
Ruutu-Ysi, Pursimiehenkatu 1, 00120 Helsinki.
T. (09) 62 68 90. *041502*
Salinpuoli, Mariankatu 10, 00170 Helsinki.
T. (09) 62 64 36. *041503*
Sarvikuono, Kapteeninkatu 9, 00140 Helsinki.
T. (09) 62 84 46. *041504*
Sea Antiques, Tehtaankatu 16, 00140 Helsinki.
T. (09) 66 63 60. *041505*
Senaatin Antiikki, Kirkkokatu 5, 00170 Helsinki.
T. (09) 60 29 40. *041506*
Sepon Penni, Mannerheimintie 92, 00100 Helsinki.
T. (09) 41 88 30. - Num - *041507*
Seriko, Kajaaniksenkatu 10, 00250 Helsinki.
T. (09) 40 88 23. *041508*
Skåne lamppu, Runberginkatu 54, 00260 Helsinki.
T. (09) 49 88 89. *041509*
Taideliike i Hietasalo, Albertinkatu 38, 00180 Helsinki.
T. (09) 60 14 97. *041510*
Taidesalonki, Bulevardi 3, 00120 Helsinki.
T. (09) 64 39 66. *041511*
Taidevälitys, Eerikinkatu 44a, 00180 Helsinki.
T. (09) 694 70 93. *041512*
Tallinvintti, Fabianinkatu 12, 00100 Helsinki.
T. (09) 65 38 78. *041513*
Tanttu, Timo, Liisankatu 21, 00170 Helsinki.
T. (09) 135 55 01. *041514*
Tarkiainen, Mikonkatu 1, 00100 Helsinki.
T. (09) 66 19 16. *041515*
Tonys Art & Antique Magazin, Vironkatu 9, 00170 Helsinki. T. (09) 135 66 30. *041516*
Trianon, Eerikinkatu 12, 00100 Helsinki.
T. (09) 64 56 43. *041517*
Tuomas, Mariankatu 10, 00170 Helsinki.
T. (09) 66 63 60. *041518*
Välitysliike Lux, Uudenmaankatu 7, 00100 Helsinki.
T. (09) 64 23 45. - Ant / Paint / Furn / Num / China / Tex /
Jew / Silv - *041519*
Vanhaa ja Kaunista, Pitkämäentie 24c, 00670 Helsinki.
T. (09) 754 32 64. *041520*
Vanhaisärtä, Igor, Aleksanterinkatu 24, 00100 Helsinki.
T. (09) 66 41 10. - Ant / Paint / Graph / Furn / China /
Sculp / Jew / Silv / Lights / Glass / Cur / Mod - *041521*
Vanhan Tavaran Kauppa Karotti, Dagmarinkatu 8, 00100 Helsinki. T. (09) 44 41 79. *041522*

Vanhat Neidit, Meritullinkatu 6, 00170 Helsinki.
T. (09) 63 64 62.   *041523*
Viiskulman Antiikki, Pursimiehenkatu 1, 00120 Helsinki.
T. (09) 65 71 15.   *041524*
Vinttikamari, Topeliuksenkatu 7, 00250 Helsinki.
T. (09) 49 24 62.   *041525*
Wähäjärvi, Pentti, Makasiininkatu 7, 00130 Helsinki.
T. (09) 66 32 74.   *041526*

Hyrylä (Uudenmaan lääni)
Tuusulan Antiikki, Tuusulantie, 04300 Hyrylä.
T. (09) 25 68 50.   *041527*

Hyvinkää (Uudenmaan lääni)
Vanha Aleksanteri, Suokatu 10, 05800 Hyvinkää.
T. (019) 18440.   *041528*

Imatra (Kymen lääni)
Imatran Taide ja Kehys, Matinkatu 3, 55100 Imatra.
T. (05) 66601.   *041529*
Karjalan Portti, Rauha Asematie 1, 55000 Imatra.
T. (05) 28880.   *041530*
Kekäläinen, Reijo & Tuula, Taimikuja 6, 55000 Imatra.
T. (05) 21004.   *041531*
Liimatainen, Punatulkunkuja 2, 55420 Imatra.
T. (05) 26909.   *041532*
Taide-Aitta, Tapionkuja 3, 55100 Imatra.
T. (05) 64654.   *041533*

Jämsä (Keski-Suomen lääni)
Hirvosen Taide-Aitta, Lukkoilantie 39, 42100 Jämsä.
T. (014) 14151.   *041534*

Järvenpää (Uudenmaan lääni)
Wagon Wheel, 04400 Järvenpää.
T. (09) 271 35 88.   *041535*

Joensuu (Pohjois-Karjalan lääni)
Taide- ja Kehysliike Mesenaatti, Torikatu 19, 80100
Joensuu. T. (013) 25742.   *041536*

Jyväskylä (Keski-Suomen lääni)
Korhonen, Pekka, Gummeruksenkatu 3, 40100 Jyväsky-
lä. T. (014) 21 75 87.   *041537*
Lampetti, Väinönkeskus, 40100 Jyväskylä.
T. (014) 61 28 74.   *041538*
Taide- ja Kehyskeskus, Väinönkatu 38, 40100 Jyväsky-
lä. T. (014) 21 39 19.   *041539*

Kaitjärvi (Kymen lääni)
Samovaari Museotila, Someronnäki, 46550 Kaitjärvi.
T. (05) 74660.   *041540*

Kajaani (Oulun lääni)
Kainuun Kehys ja Taide, Brahenkatu 2, 87100 Kajaani.
T. (08) 12 02 20.   *041541*

Kangasala (Hämeen lääni)
Hämeen Antiikki & Entisöinti, Finnentie 2, 36200 Kanga-
sala. T. (03) 77 02 51.   *041542*
Saarinen, Niilo, 36200 Kangasala.
T. (03) 77 30 78.   *041543*

Kangasniemi (Mikkelin lääni)
Taidepapilla, Salmenkylä, 51200 Kangasniemi.
T. (015) 2549.   *041544*

Karhula (Kymen lääni)
Jokasortti, Karhulantie 34, 48600 Karhula.
T. (05) 62472.   *041545*

Karjaa (Uudenmaan lääni)
Konst- och Pappershandelen, Kauppiaankatu 24, 10300
Karjaa. T. (019) 30752.   *041546*

Kauhava (Vaasan lääni)
Kauhavan Taide ja Kehys, 62200 Kauhava.
T. (06) 34 07 88.   *041547*

Kauniainen (Uudenmaan lääni)
Engl. Antiikkia, Thurmaninpuistotie 14, 02700 Kauniainen. T. (09) 505 26 81.   *041548*

Kemi (Lapin lääni)
Kemin Kehys ja Taide, Keskuspuistokko 10, 94100 Ke-
mi. T. (016) 14970.   *041549*

Kerava (Uudenmaan lääni)
Heikkilä, Esa, Jäspilänkatu 9, 04200 Kerava.
T. (09) 24 91 39.   *041550*

Kivijärvi (Keski-Suomen lääni)
Kotilainen, Pekka, Tiironkylä, 43800 Kivijärvi.
T. (014) 81059.   *041551*

Kokkola (Vaasan lääni)
Antiikkiliike Antique, Länt Kirkkokatu 3, 67100 Kokkola.
T. (06) 12729.   *041552*
Karlström, Rolf, Kirkkokatu 37, 67100 Kokkola.
T. (06) 19261.   *041553*

Kotka (Kymen lääni)
Elfvengren Antiikki, 48100 Kotka. T. (05) 65000.   *041554*
Kehystämö, K., Kirkkokatu 19, 48100 Kotka.
T. (05) 18 63 91.   *041555*
Kotkan Antiikki Narikka, Korkeavuorenkatu 14, 48100
Kotka. T. (05) 17785.   *041556*
Wanha-aika, Kauppakatu 2, 48100 Kotka.
T. (05) 17599.   *041557*

Kouvola (Kymen lääni)
Antiikki Pörssi, Salpausselänkatu 48, 45100 Kouvola.
T. (05) 21001.   *041558*
Kehysmestarit, Valtakatu 21, 45100 Kouvola.
T. (05) 16234.   *041559*
Kouvolan Kehys ja Taide, Kauppamiehenkatu 4, 45100
Kouvola. T. (05) 22441.   *041560*

Kuopio (Kuopion lääni)
Pohjois-Suomen Taide ja Käsityö, Sandelsinkatu 2,
70500 Kuopio. T. (017) 11 87 61.   *041561*
Puljon Talde Ja Antllkkl, Suokatu 41, 70100 Kuopio.
T. (017) 11 55 03.   *041562*
Taidetupa, Puntarhak 10, 70100 Kuopio.
T. (017) 12 51 07.   *041563*

Kuusamo (Oulun lääni)
Taide ja Kehys, Ouluntie 8, 93600 Kuusamo.
T. (08) 11169.   *041564*

Lahti (Hämeen lääni)
Divari, Rautatienkatu 10, 15100 Lahti. T. (03) 82 29 92,
82 37 36.   *041565*
Eskolan Taide- ja Kehysliike, Mariankatu 6, 15110 Lahti.
T. (03) 82 26 62.   *041566*
Feeniks Antique, Vuorikatu 5, 15110 Lahti.
T. (03) 29195.   *041567*
Gabriel, Rautatienkatu 8, 15100 Lahti.
T. (03) 51 34 02.   *041568*
Juhokusti, 15110 Lahti. T. (03) 83 23 25.   *041569*
Jussin, Aleksanterinkatu 29, 15100 Lahti.
T. (03) 20339.   *041570*
Kaarinan Taide ja Antiikki, Vuorikatu 3, 15110 Lahti.
T. (03) 42580.   *041571*
Käyttöantiikki, Vuorikatu 3, 15110 Lahti.
T. (03) 37750.   *041572*
Kultaraami, Aleksanterinkatu 37, 15100 Lahti.
T. (03) 51 31 99.   *041573*
Lahden Kuvastin ja Taidesoppi, Aleksanterinkatu 33,
15100 Lahti. T. (03) 82 66 18.   *041574*
Lahden Taidekauppa, Lahdenkatu 10, 15110 Lahti.
T. (03) 82 42 54.   *041575*
Lyytikäinen, Kolmaskatu 8, 15610 Lahti.
T. (03) 87 81 37.   *041576*
Ristola, P., Vuorikatu 3, 15110 Lahti.
T. (03) 82 70 61.   *041577*
Ritax, Porvoonjoentie 4, 15700 Lahti.
T. (03) 35 31 91.   *041578*
Ritax, Rautatienkatu 16, 15110 Lahti.
T. (03) 35 31 91.   *041579*
Simolan Taide ja Kehys, Hollolankatu 10, 15110 Lahti.
T. (03) 43318.   *041580*
Taide – Kehys, Vesijärvenkatu 2, 15100 Lahti.
T. (03) 37669.   *041581*
Taulun Taika, Vesijärvenkatu 19, 15110 Lahti.
T. (03) 52 03 54.   *041582*

Laitikkala (Hämeen lääni)
Antiikki-Helin, Laitikkala. T. (03) 81230.   *041583*

Laitila (Turun ja Porin lääni)
Ippan Taulu ja Kehys, Välimetsäntie 21, 23800 Laitila.
T. (02) 54170.   *041584*

Lappeenranta (Kymen lääni)
Hirvonen, Kauppakatu 25, 53100 Lappeenranta.
T. (05) 10689.   *041585*
Mai-Art, Brahenkatu 3, 53100 Lappeenranta.
T. (05) 19515.   *041586*

Lapu (Vaasan lääni)
Koivikko, Jouko, Asemakatu 9, 62100 Lapu.
T. (06) 38 83 31.   *041587*
Koti-Taide Malmi, Seinäjoentie, 62100 Lapu.
T. (06) 33 25 14.   *041588*

Lempäälä (Hämeen lääni)
Ruunila, Markku, Nokkatie 4, 37500 Lempäälä.
T. (03) 75 06 32.   *041589*
Saikkonen, Jukka, Myllyvainio, 37500 Lempäälä.
T. (03) 75 00 61.   *041590*

Lemu (Turun ja Porin lääni)
Lemun Wanhaintavarainliike, Niittukartano, 21230 Le-
mu. T. (02) 71 68 31.   *041591*

Littoinen (Turun ja Porin lääni)
Taidepalvelu, Lamellikatu 7, 20660 Littoinen.
T. (02) 44 17 04.   *041592*

Lohja (Uudenmaan lääni)
Le-Olla, Torikatu 3, 08100 Lohja. T. (019) 31107,
48266.   *041593*

Mariehamn (Åland) (Ahvenanmaa)
Bazaren, Torggatan 3, 22100 Mariehamn (Åland).
T. (018) 13540.   *041594*
Ehns, Styrmansgatan 1, 22100 Mariehamn (Åland).
T. (018) 12427.   *041595*
Mariehamns Glas & Ramaffär, Nygatan 14, 22100 Ma-
riehamn (Åland). T. (018) 11891.   *041596*
Mariehamns Konst- & Antikhandel, Storagatan 15,
22100 Mariehamn (Åland). T. (018) 12225.   *041597*

Mikkeli (Mikkelin lääni)
Lyyran, K., Porrassalmenkatu 10, 50100 Mikkeli.
T. (015) 15 17 73.   *041598*
Romantik Antiikki, Mikonkatu 13, 50100 Mikkeli.
T. (015) 15 00 42.   *041599*

Muurla (Turun ja Porin lääni)
Muurlan Taidetalo, 25130 Muurla. T. (02) 80207.   *041600*

Mynämäki (Turun ja Porin lääni)
Entisaika, 23100 Mynämäki. T. (02) 70 61 96.   *041601*

Naantali (Turun ja Porin lääni)
Wanhan Naantalin Antiikki, Luostarinkatu 21, 21100
Naantali. T. (02) 85 05 58.   *041602*

Nastola (Hämeen lääni)
Taidehuone Fundart, Viertotie 11, 15560 Nastola.
T. (03) 62 11 10.   *041603*

Nokia (Hämeen lääni)
Matikka, Pajakatu 7c, 37100 Nokia.
T. (03) 42 34 23.   *041604*
Nokian Osto ja Myynti, Korkeamäenkatu 14, 37100 No-
kia. T. (03) 41 27 03.   *041605*

Noormarkku (Turun ja Porin lääni)
Noormarkun Taide ja Kehystys, 29600 Noormarkku.
T. (03) 55 18 38.   *041606*

Otava (Mikkelin lääni)
Pajatsalo, 50670 Otava. T. (015) 17 02 15,
Fax 17 00 59.   *041607*

Oulainen (Oulun lääni)
Hautala, M., 86300 Oulainen. T. (08) 47 09 60.   *041608*

Oulu (Oulun lääni)
Asemakadun Kehys ja Taulu, Asemakatu 16, 90100 Ou-
lu. T. (08) 22 45 31.   *041609*
Nevalainen, R., Asemakatu 25, 90100 Oulu.
T. (08) 22 82 07.   *041610*

Noble Sisustusliike, Kajaaninkatu 25, 90100 Oulu.
T. (08) 22 28 30, Fax 39 36 94.   041611
Osto- ja Myyntiliike Kellari, Koulukatu 11, 90100 Oulu.
T. (08) 22 44 96.   041612
Oulun Romantiikka, Saaristonkatu 5, 90100 Oulu.
T. (08) 22 50 58.   041613
Oulun Taidetalo, Kirkkokatu 28, 90100 Oulu.
T. (08) 22 26 74.   041614
Pekkala, Asemakatu 12, 90100 Oulu.
T. (08) 22 26 66.   041615

Paimio (Turun ja Porin lääni)
Kankare, Postinkuja 2, 21530 Paimio.
T. (02) 73 28 12.   041616

Palikkala (Turun ja Porin lääni)
Annelin Antiikkia, Ypäjä, 32110 Palikkala.
T. (014) 73709.   041617

Parainen (Turun ja Porin lääni)
Hasse's Antik, Storgårdsgatan, 21600 Parainen.
T. (02) 88 96 29.   041618

Perniö (Turun ja Porin lääni)
Taide ja Kulta, 25500 Perniö. T. (02) 51115.   041619

Pieksämäki (Mikkelin lääni)
Liljalahti, Veikko, Jyväskyläntie 37a, 76150 Pieksämäki.
T. (015) 21998.   041620

Pietarsaari /Jakobstad (Vaasan lääni)
Antik-Boden, Herrholminkatu 12, 68600 Pietarsaari /Ja-
kobstad. T. (06) 15379.   041621
Ståhl, V.W., Kauppiankatu 18, 68600 Pietarsaari /Jakob-
stad. T. (06) 23 05 19.   041622

Pori (Turun ja Porin lääni)
Agentuuri Amfore, Pohjoiskauppatori 3, 28100 Pori.
T. (03) 33 18 78.   041623
An-Ta-Ke, Antinkatu 10, 28100 Pori.
T. (03) 41 10 36.   041624
Antiikki- ja Lahjatavara Eveliina, Isolinnankatu 24,
28100 Pori. T. (03) 33 28 84.   041625
Antiikkiliike Vanha Rouva, Sepänkatu 37, 28130 Pori.
T. (03) 22447.   041626
Jokela, Antinkatu 14, 28100 Pori.
T. (03) 41 11 25.   041627
Porin Taide ja Kehys, Säveltäjänkatu 13, 28100 Pori.
T. (03) 41 29 50.   041628
Taide- ja Posliinikeskus, Isolinnankatu 24, 28100 Pori.
T. (03) 33 25 41.   041629
Valtavainio, Pasi, Itsenäisyydenkatu 68, 28100 Pori.
T. (03) 41 40 36.   041630

Porvoo/Borgå (Uudenmaan lääni)
Aunela, Jorma, Wallgreninkatu 3, 06100 Porvoo/Borgå.
T. (019) 13 15 91, 16 07 03.   041631
Porvoon Antiikki, Jokikatu 14, 06100 Porvoo/Borgå.
T. (019) 172941.   041632

Raahe (Oulun lääni)
Kouvalainen, R., Kauppakatu 40, 92100 Raahe.
T. (08) 235 63 33, Fax 26 37 02.   041633

Raisio (Turun ja Porin lääni)
Aaltonen, Lumilantie 1, 21200 Raisio.
T. (02) 81 03 28.   041634
Raision Huutokauppatoimisto, Torikatu 1, 21200 Raisio.
T. (02) 78 66 88.   041635

Rauma (Turun ja Porin lääni)
Akantus, Kuninkaankatu 29, 26100 Rauma.
T. (02) 22 55 10.   041636

Rauna
Puna-Tupa, Asematie 1, 55300 Rauna.
T. (05) 28880.   041637

Riihimäki (Hämeen lääni)
Ahonen, Siirtola, 11100 Riihimäki.
T. (019) 33140.   041638
Madame Iris Antiquites, Torikatu 3, 11100 Riihimäki.
T. (019) 30066.   041639
Musakka, A., Hämeenkatu 3, 11100 Riihimäki.
T. (019) 33513.   041640

Ruutana (Hämeen lääni)
Virolainen, Pentti, 36110 Ruutana. T. 76 13 78.
- Num -   041641

Salo (Turun ja Porin lääni)
Aarnion Raha ja Antiikki, Asemakatu 2, 24101 Salo.
T. (02) 31 37 43.   041642

Sasi
Antiikkikamari, 39130 Sasi. T. (03) 71 10 88. 041643

Seinäjoki (Vaasan lääni)
Airan Taide ja Kehys, Keskuskatu 17, 60100 Seinäjoki.
T. (06) 14 08 99.   041644
E-P:n Taide ja Kehys, Maamiehenkatu 1, 60100 Seinäjo-
ki. T. (06) 14 18 71.   041645
Taide ja Kehys, Koulukatu 20, 60100 Seinäjoki.
T. (06) 14 18 71.   041646

Taivassalo (Turun ja Porin lääni)
T-Myynti, Inkeranta, 23310 Taivassalo.
T. (02) 85865.   041647

Tammisaari/Ekenäs (Uudenmaan lääni)
Tammisaaren Antiikki ja Taide, Asematie 12, 10600
Tammisaari/Ekenäs. T. (019) 71 15 28.   041648
Werners Konsthandel, Kuninkaankatu 14, 10600 Tammi-
saari/Ekenäs. T. (019) 71 24 81.   041649

Tampere (Hämeen lääni)
Antiikkipörssi, Puutarhakatu 29, 33210 Tampere.
T. (03) 23 47 11.   041650
Art Leonardo, Hämeenkatu 19, 33100 Tampere.
T. (03) 14 00 30.   041651
City-Art, Hämeenkatu 31, 33200 Tampere.
T. (03) 12 28 45.   041652
Divari Tammer-Kanava, Ratinankuja 4, 33100 Tampere.
T. (03) 22 51 27.   041653
Erkkilänsillan Osto-, Myynti- ja Vaihtoliike, Erkkilänkatu
9, 33100 Tampere. T. (03) 12 38 41.   041654
Form & Antik, Hämeenpuisto 35, 33200 Tampere.
T. (03) 14 93 99.   041655
Galleria Annmari's, Aaltosenkatu 31-33, 33500 Tampe-
re. T. (03) 53 20 10.   041656
Husa, Laukontori 6a, 33200 Tampere.
T. (03) 22 89 42.   041657
Kettumäki, Aaro, Hämeenpuisto 16a, 33210 Tampere.
T. (03) 22 88 77.   041658
Köyhän Maalarin Kehys- ja Taidekauppa, Vainiokatu 9,
33500 Tampere. T. (03) 61 13 38.   041659
Laitinen, Pekka L., Koukkutie 5a, 33530 Tampere.
T. (03) 53 14 05.   041660
Lassila, Lauri, Hirvika 23, 33240 Tampere.
T. (03) 22 18 84.   041661
Leskirouva, Verkatehtaankatu 13, 33100 Tampere.
T. (03) 12 88 87.   041662
Miettinen, Arto, Hämeenpuisto 18, 33210 Tampere.
T. (03) 23 85 81.   041663
Old Imperial, Epilänkatu 37, 33270 Tampere.
T. (03) 44 46 37.   041664
Sinisalo, Opiskelijankatu 21a, Tampere.
T. (03) 17 03 68.   041665
Suomen Osto-Myynti ja Antiikki, Pyynikintori 3, 33230
Tampere. T. (03) 22 05 08.   041666
Taide Fox, Hämeenpuisto 16, 33210 Tampere.
T. (03) 13 49 80.   041667
Taidekellari, Mahlankatu 3, 33820 Tampere.
T. (03) 65 18 22.   041668
Taidelainaamo Tampereen Taideyhdistys, Puutarhakatu
35, 33210 Tampere. T. (03) 14 04 67.   041669
Valli, Tuula, Savikukonkatu 35, Tampere.
T. (03) 63 50 41.   041670

Tapiola
Vanha Adam, Menninkäisentie 10b, Tapiola.
T. 46 02 13.   041671

Tre
Suni, Pentti, Rongankatu 2, 33100 Tre. T. 23 45 65.
- Num -   041672

Turku (Turun ja Porin lääni)
Adam Antiques, Puutarhakatu 8, 20100 Turku.
T. (02) 51 08 48.   041673

Ahti & Kni, Eerikinkatu 5, 20110 Turku. T. (02) 32 25 88,
32 96 61.   041674
Åman, Akselintie 14, 20200 Turku.
T. (02) 30 79 80.   041675
Antiikki Piste, Rauhankatu 8, 20100 Turku.
T. (02) 32 53 26.   041676
Antiikki PP, Puutarhakatu 9a, 20100 Turku.
T. (02) 33 39 08.   041677
Antik-Argenta, Humalistonkatu 8, 20100 Turku.
T. (02) 51 08 95.   041678
Art-Galleria, Yliopistonkatu 28, 20100 Turku.
T. (02) 32 95 99.   041679
Artimer, Humalistonkatu 13c, 20100 Turku.
T. (02) 32 71 59.   041680
Huonekalu-Ruola, Aurakatu 8, 20100 Turku.
T. (02) 32 22 28.   041681
Joka Sortti, Kaskenkatu 1, 20000 Turku.
T. (02) 32 88 18. - Num -   041682
Kehys ja Kultaus, Kaskenkatu 2, 20100 Turku.
T. (02) 33 15 51.   041683
Kehysaitta, Hämeentie 20, 20540 Turku.
T. (02) 37 43 08.   041684
Kehyskulma, Aninkaistenkatu 5, 20110 Turku.
T. (02) 51 81 84.   041685
Koti-Puoti, Saarnit 12, 20700 Turku.
T. (02) 31 52 22.   041686
Kuvakehys, Stålarminkatu 1, 20810 Turku.
T. (02) 35 63 82.   041687
Las-Ni, Rauhankatu 10, 20100 Turku. - Ant -   041688
Lehtinen, R., Yliopistonkatu 11a, 20110 Turku.
T. (02) 32 70 40.   041689
LEK Taululiike, Rajakivenkatu 22, 20000 Turku.
T. (02) 42 28 40.   041690
Mäkilän Taidemakasiini, Alakylä Nousiainen, 20000 Tur-
ku. T. (02) 71 56 58.   041691
Muotokuva Taide ja Kehys, Yliopistonkatu 11, 20110
Turku. T. (02) 32 70 40.   041692
Myllykylä, J., Läntinenkatu 15, 20000 Turku.
T. (02) 51 17 54, Fax 31 34 89.   041693
Nurmi, J. A., Kristiinankatu 6, 20100 Turku.
T. (02) 51 16 33.   041694
Old Steamer, Linnankatu 37a, 20100 Turku.
T. (02) 32 22 15.   041695
Palmu, Janne, Vierulanmäki, 20000 Turku.
T. (02) 79 83 50.   041696
Ristolainen, M., Härkämäentie 9, 20100 Turku.
T. (02) 39 77 77.   041697
Taide ja Kehysliike, Stålarminkatu 1, 20810 Turku.
T. (02) 35 63 82.   041698
Taide Santanen, Eerikinkatu 16, 20100 Turku.
T. (02) 31 14 24.   041699
Taidekeidas, Talvitie I I, 20600 Turku.
T. (02) 44 42 00.   041700
Tik Tak Antiikki, Kiinamyllynkatu 2, 20500 Turku.
T. (02) 32 38 15.   041701
Turun Antiikki ja Taide, Läntinen Pitkäkatu 15, 20100
Turku. T. (02) 51 17 54.   041702
Varsinais-Suomen Kehys ja Taide, Hämeenkatu 14,
20500 Turku. T. (02) 33 59 51.   041703
Yli-Tolppa J & K, Kauppiaskatu 15, 20100 Turku.
                                               041704

Uusikaupunki (Turun ja Porin lääni)
Johnsson, Veljet, Ahmatie 18, 23500 Uusikaupunki.
T. (02) 12157.   041705
Kvariaatti & Taulu, Alinenkatu 15, 23500 Uusikaupunki.
T. (02) 23982.   041706

Vaasa/Vasa (Vaasan lääni)
City Taide ja Kehys, Raastuvankatu 18, 65100 Vaasa/Va-
sa. T. (06) 12 94 45.   041707

Vammala (Turun ja Porin lääni)
Vammalan Taide ja Kehys, Onkiniemenkatu 16, 38200
Vammala. T. (02) 13990.   041708

Varkaus (Mikkelin lääni)
Alexin Galleria, Petroskoinkatu 12, 78200 Varkaus.
T. (017) 27135.   041709
Antiikki-Kaluste Galleria, Ahlströminkatu 22, 78250 Var-
kaus. T. (017) 22274.   041710
Lintu & Muusa, Kauppakatu 50, 78200 Varkaus.
T. (017) 27784.   041711

Veikkola (Uudenmaan lääni)
Antiikkitukku, Teollisuustie 6, Halli 6a, 02880 Veikkola.
T. (09) 26 52 13, Fax 26 54 03.   041712
Iso-Äiti Oy, Navalan kartano, 02880 Veikkola.
T. (09) 26 63 53.   041713

Vinkkilä (Turun ja Porin lääni)
Klaara, 23200 Vinkkilä. T. (02) 82 20 10.   041714

France

Abancourt (Nord)
Renaissance, 232 Rue Gén-Leclerc, 59265 Abancourt.
T. 0320757821. - Ant -   041715

Abbeville (Somme)
Cauliers, Jean, 5 Rue Jeanne-d'Arc, 80100 Abbeville.
T. 0322240233. - Ant / Paint / China / Fra -   041716
Courbois, Emile, 6 Av Gare, 80100 Abbeville.
T. 0322244329. - Ant -   041717
Delabie, Gaston, 31 Rue Ledien, 80100 Abbeville.
T. 0322240465. - Ant -   041718
Duval, Daniel, 60 Av Gén-Leclerc, 80100 Abbeville.
T. 0322243284. - Ant -   041719
Pailleux, Daniel, 22 Rue Carmes, 80100 Abbeville.
T. 0322244273. - Ant -   041720
Toutoccas, 12 Rue Jean-Jaurès, 80100 Abbeville.
T. 0322242537. - Ant / Cur -   041721

Abscon (Nord)
Lorthioir, 5 Rue Jean-Jaurès, 59215 Abscon.
T. 0327363499. - Ant -   041722

Acigné (Ille-et-Vilaine)
Leboulanger, Isabelle, 1 Rue Calvaire, 35690 Acigné.
T. 0299625557.   041723

Acquigny (Eure)
Amare, Frédéric, Rue Pacy, 27400 Acquigny.
T. 0232502515.   041724

Dieutre, Christophe, 63 et 65 Rue Aristide-Briand,
27400 Acquigny. T. 0232502750, Fax 0232407610.
- Furn / Dec / Cur -   041725
Lecerf, 27 Rue Louviers, 27400 Acquigny.
T. 0232502103.   041726
Risler, Geneviève, 19 Rue Louviers, 27400 Acquigny.
T. 0232502340, Fax 0232404854.   041727
Tectin, Marcel, 59 Rue Aristide-Briand, 27400 Acquigny.
T. 0232405818.   041728

Agde (Hérault)
Au Petit Brocanteur, 1 Av Gén de Gaulle, 34300 Agde.
T. 0467942776. - Paint / Furn / Dec / Cur -   041729
Félix, France, 4 Rue Esprit-Fabre, 34300 Agde.
T. 0467941185.   041730
Flanquart, C., 63 Rue Alsace-Lorraine, 34300 Agde.
T. 0467948843.   041731
Kolmont, Daniel, 32 Quai Commandant-Réveille, 34300
Agde. T. 0467942799.   041732
Rifa, Joseph, 9 Rue Brescou, 34300 Agde.
T. 0467942526. - Ant -   041733
Robert, Y., 15 Quai Commdt Reveille, 34300 Agde.
T. 0467941306. - Ant -   041734
Ségura, Jacques, 86 Rue de la République, 34300 Agde.
T. 0467210954. - Ant -   041735

Agen (Lot-et-Garonne)
Au Bon Vieux Temps, 12 Rue Cornières, 47000 Agen.
T. 0553669261. - Dec -   041736
Bareyre, Martine & Gérard, 12 Rue Garonne, 47000
Agen. T. 0553669645, Fax 0553967394. - Paint /
Furn / China / Sculp / Tex / Jew / Silv / Lights / Glass / C-
ur -   041737
Chapoulie, 44 Rue Belfort, 47000 Agen. T. 0553668186.
- Furn / Cur -   041738
Charaire, Jean, 31 Rue Jacquard, 47000 Agen.
T. 0553665055.   041739
Cherchari, 53 Rue Richard-Coeur-de-Lion, 47000 Agen.
T. 0553665109.   041740
Galerie d'Art et d'Antiquité, 105 Rue Montesquieu,
47000 Agen. T. 0553667110.   041741

Joorls, Patrice, 5bis Rue Autas, 47000 Agen.
T. 0553876292.   041742
Macé, Jeanne, 78 Rue Bellevue, 47000 Agen.
T. 0553662351.   041743
Mercier, Jean-Marie, 8 Rue Héros-de-la-Résistance,
47000 Agen. T. 0553471801.   041744
Milliard, Colette, 22 Rue Richard-Coeur-de-Lion, 47000
Agen. T. 0553660973.   041745
Mun, André, 19 Rue Centre, 47000 Agen.
T. 0553669995.   041746

Agnac (Lot-et-Garonne)
Cherrier, Francis, Rte Bergerac, La Gare, 47800 Agnac.
T. 0553830380.   041747

Agnetz (Oise)
Gotty, Michèle, 658 RN 31, 60600 Agnetz.
T. 0344781656. - Ant / Furn -   041748

Agon-Coutainville (Manche)
Poinot, Anne, Pl 28-Juillet, 50230 Agon-Coutainville.
T. 0233471000.   041749

Agos-Vidalos (Hautes-Pyrénées)
Meubles du Lavedan, Villages Rte Nationale, 65400
Agos-Vidalos. T. 0562975041. - Furn -   041750

Aignan (Hautes-Pyrénées)
Laethem, Van, Le Paré, 32290 Aignan. T. 0562092043.
- Ant -   041751

Aigues-Mortes (Gard)
Babinot, Francine, 30 Rue Emile-Jamais, 30220 Aigues-
Mortes. T. 0466536936.   041752

Aiguèze (Gard)
Sicard, Christian, Rue Portail-Haut, 30760 Aiguèze.
T. 0466821272.   041753

Ailly-le-Haut-Clocher (Somme)
Boulard, Laurent, 23 Rte nationale, 80690 Ailly-le-Haut-
Clocher. T. 0322280330. - Ant -   041754

Aime (Savoie)
Grange-d'Aime, Av Tarentaise, 73210 Aime.
T. 0479556444. - Ant -   *041755*

Airaines (Somme)
Bourassin-Rancon, Christian, 8 Rue Petits-Prés, 80270
Airaines. T. 0322294014. - Ant -   *041756*

Aire-sur-l'Adour (Landes)
Berdery, Jean-Pierre, Quartier Subéhargues, 40800 Ai-
re-sur-l'Adour. T. 0558717025.   *041757*
Bregeot, Eric de, Pourin, 40800 Aire-sur-l'Adour.
T. 0558719414, Fax 0558719085.   *041758*

Aire-sur-la-Lys (Pas-de-Calais)
Barois, Philippe, 102 Rue Arras, 62120 Aire-sur-la-Lys.
T. 0321390744. - Paint / Furn / Cur -   *041759*
Bouchart, Philippe, 24 Chemin Sablonières-Saint-Mar-
tin, 62120 Aire-sur-la-Lys. T. 0321956862.   *041760*

Airvault (Deux-Sèvres)
Niveleau, Claude, 6 Rue Gendarmerie, 79600 Airvault.
T. 0549647154.   *041761*

Aix-en-Provence (Bouches-du-Rhône)
A Turco, 210 Chemin Gantèse-Puyricard, 13100 Aix-en-
Provence. T. 0442922233.   *041762*
Aix-en-Provence Antiquités, 24 Rue Gaston-de-Saporta,
13100 Aix-en-Provence. T. 0442234253,
Fax 0442216030.   *041763*
Antiquaires de Lignane, 6110 Rte Avignon-Puyricard,
13090 Aix-en-Provence. T. 0442923828.   *041764*
Antiquité Brocante, 18 Rue Lisse-Bellegarde, 13100
Aix-en-Provence. T. 0442966559.   *041765*
Arbaud, 19 Cours Mirabeau, 13100 Aix-en-Provence.
T. 0442266688.   *041766*
Atala, 1 Cours Gambetta, 13100 Aix-en-Provence.
T. 0442969590.   *041767*
Aujoulat, Christian, 6 Rue Pavillon, 13100 Aix-en-Pro-
vence. T. 0442261211.   *041768*
Barletta, Nicole, 2 Rue Jaubert, 13100 Aix-en-Provence.
T. 0442211642.   *041769*
Bercker, Lucien, 10 Rue Matheron, 13100 Aix-en-Pro-
vence. T. 0442214684.   *041770*
Besançon, Philiberte, 19 Rue Cardinale, 13100 Aix-en-
Provence. T. 0442383231.   *041771*
Bianchi, Michel, 3 Rue Granet, 13100 Aix-en-Provence.
T. 0442234998, Fax 0442216023. - Ant -   *041772*
Blanchard, Jacqueline, 5830 Rte Avignon, 13090 Aix-
en-Provence. T. 0442924540.   *041773*
Blanchard, S. & M. Chambert, RN 7 – Puyricard, 13090
Aix-en-Provence. T. 0442924540.   *041774*
Caral dc Montcty Cornut, 4 Rue Jaubert, 13100 Aix-en-
Provence. T. 0442211688. - Jew / Silv -   *041775*
Chiapetta, Claude, 24 Rue Muletiers, 13100 Aix-en-Pro-
vence. T. 0442270469.   *041776*
Forum des Arts, RN 7 – Puyricard, 13090 Aix-en-Pro-
vence. T. 0442925757, Fax 0442925799.   *041777*
Gratte Puces, 15 Rue Boulegon, 13100 Aix-en-Proven-
ce. T. 0442961064.   *041778*
Hermanovits, Jean-François, 36 Rue 4-Septembre,
13100 Aix-en-Provence. Fax 42385894.   *041779*
Hermanovits, Jean-François, 33 Blvd Roy-René, 13100
Aix-en-Provence. T. 0442214599, Fax 0442385894.
- Furn -   *041780*
Import Latino, 42593561, 3797 Rte Galice, 13090 Aix-
en-Provence. T. 0442592943.   *041781*
Jean, Isabelle, 19 Rue Emeric-David, 13100 Aix-en-Pro-
vence. T. 0442385945. - Ant / Furn -   *041782*
Jean, Thierry, 12 Rue Emeric-David, 13100 Aix-en-Pro-
vence. T. 0442381080.   *041783*
Marcelin, Franck, 7 Rue Jaubert, 13100 Aix-en-Proven-
ce. T. 0442231738.   *041784*
Marches du Palais, 1 Rue Chastel, 13100 Aix-en-Pro-
vence. T. 0442380655. - Furn / China / Cur -   *041785*
Matériaux d'Antan, 5580 Rte Avignon-Puyricard, 13090
Aix-en-Provence. T. 0442926212.   *041786*
Mazarin, 8 Rue Frédéric-Mistral, 13100 Aix-en-Proven-
ce. T. 0442271606.   *041787*
Morel, Georges, 6 Rue Jaubert, 13100 Aix-en-Provence.
T. 0442963202, Fax 0442231984.   *041788*
Nostalgia, RN 7 – Puyricard, 13090 Aix-en-Provence.
T. 0442923020.   *041789*

Nostalgia, 7 Av Grassi, 13100 Aix-en-Provence.
T. 0442215175, Fax 0442960993.   *041790*
Paschot, Francis, 9 Rue Thiers, 13100 Aix-en-Provence.
T. 0442385058.   *041791*
Pinet, René Lydie Picard, 1bis Rue Matheron, 13100
Aix-en-Provence. T. 0442219927.   *041792*
Raynaud, Jean-Louis, 3 Pl des Trois Ormeaux, 13100
Aix-en-Provence. T. 0442235232. - Ant / Dec - *041793*
Reboul, Henriette, 25 Rue du 4 Septembre, 13100 Aix-
en-Provence. T. 0442381809. - Ant -   *041794*
Reyre, Robert, 7 Rue Granet, 13100 Aix-en-Provence.
T. 0442233144.   *041795*
Richard, Gérard, 6 Rue Abbé-de-l'Epée, 13100 Aix-en-
Provence. T. 0442202213.   *041796*
Sevat, Hervé, 10 Rue Laurent-Fauchier, 13100 Aix-en-
Provence. T. 0442274104.   *041797*
Toretti, 5 Blvd Carnot, 13100 Aix-en-Provence.
T. 0442214400.   *041798*
Ungaro-Gamard, Yves, 1 Rue Jaubert, 13100 Aix-en-
Provence. T. 0442631033.   *041799*
Veesler, Liliane, 18 Pl de l'Hôtel-de-Ville, 13100 Aix-en-
Provence. T. 0442230322. - Ant / Jew -   *041800*
Vieux Moulin, RN 7, Le Tholonet, 13100 Aix-en-Proven-
ce. T. 0442668976.   *041801*

Aix-les-Bains (Savoie)
Au Passé Simple, 27 Av Grand-Port, 73100 Aix-les-
Bains. T. 0479610675. - Ant -   *041802*
Brocante Aixoise, 6 Rue Alice-Eynard, 73100 Aix-les-
Bains. T. 0479880966. - Furn -   *041803*
Perrin, Josiane, 2 Av Victoria, 73100 Aix-les-Bains.
T. 0479351564. - Ant -   *041804*
Saint-Simond, 48 Rue Saint-Simond, 73100 Aix-les-
Bains. T. 0479888524. - Ant / Paint / Furn -   *041805*
Temple du Diane, 2 Sq Temple-de-Diane, 73100 Aix-
les-Bains. T. 0479350504. - Ant -   *041806*

Aizac (Ardèche)
Nicolas, Michel, les Blanchons, 07530 Aizac.
T. 0475387136. - Ant -   *041807*

Ajaccio (Corse)
A Casa Antica, Résidence Prince-Impérial, 20090 Ajac-
cio. T. 0495231112.   *041808*
A l'Ancien Temps, 17 Rue Forcioli-Conti, 20000 Ajaccio.
T. 0495211865.   *041809*
Arte et Opara, 16 Rue Bonaparte, 20000 Ajaccio.
T. 0495212254. - Paint / Furn / China / Sculp / Tex /
Eth / Instr / Glass -   *041810*
Bartoli, Herminé, 6 Rue Stéphanopoli, 20000 Ajaccio.
T. 0495213302.   *041811*
Bartoli, Saliceti, 8 Rue Emmanuel-Arène, 20000 Ajaccio.
T. 0495510103.   *041812*
Bartoli, Saliceti, 6 Rue Stéphanopoli, 20000 Ajaccio.
T. 0495213302.   *041813*
Boutique Opium, 6 Rue Trois-Marie, 20000 Ajaccio.
T. 0495211217. - Orient / Cur -   *041814*
Ebene, 7 Rue Maréchal-Ornano, 20000 Ajaccio.
T. 0495511022. - Dec -   *041815*
Général Vendémiaire, 4 Rue Zevaco-Maire, 20000 Ajac-
cio. T. 0495214584.   *041816*
Grenier, 19 Cours Napoléon, 20000 Ajaccio.
T. 0495511420.   *041817*
Lantivy, 20 Blvd Pascal-Rossini, 20000 Ajaccio.
T. 0495214190.   *041818*
Mattioli, Jeanne, 37 Rue Cardinal-Fesch, 20000 Ajaccio.
T. 0495215286.   *041819*
Maudrux Miniconi, Marie-France, 23 Rue Bonaparte,
20000 Ajaccio. T. 0495212000.   *041820*
Sicurani, 12 et 14 Cours Grandval, 20000 Ajaccio.
T. 0495213274. - Jew / Cur -   *041821*

Alata (Corse)
Maudrux Miniconi, Marie-France, Village, 20167 Alata.
T. 0495253103.   *041822*

Albertville (Savoie)
Badarelli Antiquités, 1 Rue G.-Perouse-Conflans, 73200
Albertville. T. 0479322011. - Ant / Furn / Eth /
Cur -   *041823*
Il Etait une Fois Demain, 120 Rue Louis-Armand, 73200
Albertville. T. 0479371233. - Ant -   *041824*
Lapierre, Charlette, 55 Rte Provinciale, 73200 Albert-
ville. T. 0479322742. - Ant -   *041825*

Les Trésors de Grand Mère, 2 Rue République, 73200
Albertville. T. 0479371085. - Ant -   *041826*
Persault, Michel, 2 Av de la Tarentaise, 73200 Albert-
ville. T. 0479374091. - Ant / Furn -   *041827*

Albi (Tarn)
Antiquités Saint-Eloi, 11 Pl Sainte-Cécile, 81000 Albi.
T. 0563540573, Fax 0563380660. - Paint / Furn /
Cur -   *041828*
Artaut, Myriam, 18 Rue Peyrolière, 81000 Albi.
T. 0563546158.   *041829*
Au Bonheur du Jour, 13 Rue Peyrolière, 81000 Albi.
T. 0563545713. - Paint / Furn / Cur -   *041830*
Au Dépôt-Vente Albigeois, 5 Av Maréchal-Foch, 81000
Albi. T. 0563547861.   *041831*
Bordes, Gérard, 15 Imp Commandant-Blanché, 81000
Albi. T. 0563542979.   *041832*
Brocante du Lude, 33 Rue Paul-Bodin, 81000 Albi.
T. 0563544991.   *041833*
Brocante Sainte-Cécile, Rue Maîtrise, 81000 Albi.
T. 0563470626.   *041834*
D'Ancien et de Contemporain, 2 Pl Palais, 81000 Albi.
T. 0563479593. - Furn / Dec -   *041835*
Grenier de Clair-Bois, 18 Rue Auguste-Vidal, 81000 Albi.
T. 0563380950.   *041836*
Hahn, Willy, Rte Castres, 81000 Albi.
T. 0563542848.   *041837*
Lescoules, Christian, 5 Rue Roc, 81000 Albi.
T. 0563547119.   *041838*
Malle Anglaise, 5 Rue Oulmet, 81000 Albi.
T. 0563384977.   *041839*
Mazarin, 3 Pl Sainte-Cécile, 81000 Albi.
T. 0563389929.   *041840*
Morgane, 30 Rue Hôtel-de-Ville, 81000 Albi.
T. 0563545808.   *041841*
Penalosa, Jean-Luc, 11 Pl Sainte-Cécile, 81000 Albi.
T. 0563540573, Fax 0563380660.   *041842*
Temps Mêlés, 22 Rue Hôtel-de-Ville, 81000 Albi.
T. 0563384600. - Furn / Tex / Cur -   *041843*

Alençon (Orne)
Dolo-Sallard, Annie, 1 Rue Fresnay, 6100 Alençon.
T. 0233263467. - Ant -   *041844*

Alès (Gard)
Belle Epoque, 33 Av Carnot, 30100 Alès.
T. 0466867389. - Furn -   *041845*
Chez Michel, 32 Rue Faubourg-d'Auvergne, 30100 Alès.
T. 0466789541.   *041846*
Forest, Laurent, 39 Rue Alphonse-Daudet, 30100 Alès.
T. 0466522213.   *041847*
Mon Grenier, 32 Rue Beautéville, 30100 Alès.
T. 0466522011.   *041848*
Regain, Jeune Guy, 40 Rue Faubourg-d'Auvergne,
30100 Alès. T. 0466865524. - Furn / Cur -   *041849*
Tassy, Jean, 20 Rue Brésis, 30100 Alès.
T. 0466524239.   *041850*

Alfortville (Val-de-Marne)
Vonthron, William, 165 Rue Paul-Vaillant-Couturier,
94140 Alfortville. T. 0143756622. - Paint / Furn /
Cur -   *041851*

Allaines (Somme)
Dusart, Jean-Marie, Rue Bertincourt, 80200 Allaines.
T. 0322846231. - Ant / Cur -   *041852*
Picardie Récoup, 4 Rte Arras-Feuillaucourt, 80200 Allai-
nes. T. 0322846479.   *041853*

Allemans-du-Dropt (Lot-et-Garonne)
Cristini, Philippe, Sainte-Anne, 47800 Allemans-du-
Dropt. T. 0553202441.   *041854*

Allériot (Saône-et-Loire)
Joigneault Brocante, Rue du Bois-Verdenet, 71380 Allériot. T. 0385475800. - Ant -   *041855*

Allonzier-la-Caille (Haute-Savoie)
Jacquemin, Gérard, Chez Poraz, 74350 Allonzier-la-
Caille. T. 0450468588.   *041856*

Alvignac (Lot)
Mady, Jouvent, 46500 Alvignac.
T. 0565336640.   *041857*

Ambérieu-en-Bugey (Ain)

Aiglon, 82 Rue Alexandre-Bérard, 01500 Ambérieu-en-Bugey. T. 0474350770. - Ant -   *041858*

Bessière, Georges, Rue Vareilles, 01500 Ambérieu-en-Bugey. T. 0474381239. - Ant -   *041859*

Ambert (Puy-de-Dôme)

Ambert Antiquités, 16 Blvd Henri-IV, 63600 Ambert. T. 0473826084. - Ant -   *041860*

Antique Auvergne, 4 Av Mar-Foch, 63600 Ambert. T. 0473823715. - Paint / Furn -   *041861*

Amboise (Indre-et-Loire)

Alleno, Janine, 96 Rue Nationale, 37400 Amboise. T. 0547574584.   *041862*

Antiquités Victor-Hugo, 93 Rue Victor-Hugo, 37400 Amboise. T. 0547231815.   *041863*

Ecuelle, 12 Rue Nationale, 37400 Amboise. T. 0547570256.   *041864*

Gaillard, Michel, 8 Rue Nationale, 37400 Amboise. T. 0547572291.   *041865*

Guenand, Christian, 38 Quai Charles-Guinot, 37400 Amboise. T. 0547576348.   *041866*

Moreau, Yseult, 8 Pl Général-Leclerc, 37400 Amboise. T. 0547577321.   *041867*

Pépin, Guy, 87 Rte Tours, 37400 Amboise. T. 0547571718.   *041868*

Amiens (Somme)

Ambiani, 47 Blvd Cange, 80000 Amiens. T. 0322923283, Fax 0322923609. - Ant -   *041869*

Atmosphère, 47 Blvd Cange bât B, 80000 Amiens. T. 0322921139. - Ant -   *041870*

Bocquillon, Judith, 47 Blvd Cange, 80000 Amiens. T. 0322929477. - Ant -   *041871*

Bonheur du Jour, 47 Blvd Cange, 80000 Amiens. T. 0322927493. - Ant -   *041872*

Bonocaze, 11 Rue Ducange, 80000 Amiens. - Ant / Cur -   *041873*

Boîte à Clous, 47 Blvd Cange bât C, 80000 Amiens. T. 0322921444. - Ant -   *041874*

Boulot, Jacques, 7 Rue Florimond-Leroux, 80000 Amiens. T. 0322914432. - Ant -   *041875*

Boutique Anglaise, 9 Rue Flatters, 80000 Amiens. T. 0322927492. - Ant -   *041876*

Bray, Pascal, 47 Blvd Cange bât C, 80000 Amiens. T. 0322979153. - Ant -   *041877*

Cabinet d'Expertise Tastet Souchon, 56 Rue République, 80000 Amiens. T. 0322918732. - Ant -   *041878*

Charme du Passé, 45bis Pl René-Goblet, 80000 Amiens. T. 0322918732. - Ant -   *041879*

Coll-Rotger, A., 1 Rue de la Dodane, 80000 Amiens. T. 0322924022. - Ant / Furn -   *041880*

Dartois, Michel, 4 Pl Parmentier, 80000 Amiens. T. 0322927056. - Ant -   *041881*

Desmis, Dominique, 4 Pl Parmentier, 80000 Amiens. T. 0322912645. - Ant -   *041882*

Devillers, Charlie, 47 Blvd Cange, 80000 Amiens. T. 0322809215. - Ant -   *041883*

Devisme, Bruno, 47 Blvd du Cange, 80000 Amiens. T. 0322915225. - Ant -   *041884*

Diable Bouilli, 48 Rue Hocquet, 80000 Amiens. T. 0322917271. - Ant -   *041885*

Duhamel-Hart, Evelyne, 30 Rue Noyon Résid Sainte-Anne, 80000 Amiens. T. 0322924732. - Ant -   *041886*

Fairway, 127 Rue Jules-Barni, 80000 Amiens. T. 0322926410. - Ant -   *041887*

Fanchon, Philippe, 47 Blvd du Cange, 80000 Amiens. T. 0322913439. - Ant / Furn -   *041888*

Fleur Antiquités, 47 Blvd Cange, 80000 Amiens. T. 0322921800. - Ant -   *041889*

Grenier de Saint-Roch, 47 Blvd Cange bât B, 80000 Amiens. T. 0322896971. - Ant -   *041890*

Grodée, Stéphane, 33 Rue Millevoye, 80000 Amiens. T. 0322453234. - Ant / Cur -   *041891*

Heckmann, Gérard, 204 Rue Rouen, 80000 Amiens. T. 0322453234. - Ant / Cur -   *041892*

Lacaze, Nicole de, 47 Blvd Cange, 80000 Amiens. T. 0322920998. - Ant -   *041893*

Le Clerq, Jean-Louis, 46 Rue Saint-Leu, 80000 Amiens. T. 0322912148. - Ant -   *041894*

Lefebvre, Hervé, 57 Croix-Saint-Firmin, 80090 Amiens. T. 0322927615. - Paint -   *041895*

Lescureux, Christian, 69 Rue de Rouen, 80000 Amiens. T. 0322956116. - Paint / Furn -   *041896*

Magnolia, 14 Rue Beauvais, 80000 Amiens. T. 0322918841. - Ant / Furn / Tex -   *041897*

Passé Simple, 46 Rue Saint-Leu, 80000 Amiens. T. 0322912148. - Ant -   *041898*

Potière, 345 Ch Jules-Ferry, 80000 Amiens. T. 0322496400. - Ant -   *041899*

Richard, Marcel, 47 Blvd Cange, 80000 Amiens. T. 0322921597. - Ant -   *041900*

Samara Antiquités, 11 Rue Dusevel, 80000 Amiens. T. 0322924062, Fax 0322925227. - Ant -   *041901*

Sergeant, Hubert, 49 Rue Robert-de-Luzarches, 80000 Amiens. T. 0322925913. - Paint -   *041902*

Tastet, André, 13 Rue Marc-Sangnier, 80000 Amiens. T. 0322916846. - Ant -   *041903*

Ancenis (Loire-Atlantique)

Genneteau, Marie-Thérèse, 94 Rue Général-Leclerc, 44150 Ancenis. T. 40831229.   *041904*

Ancretteville-sur-Mer (Seine-Maritime)

Deneuve, Marie Odile, Ham Ecombarville, 76540 Ancretteville-sur-Mer. T. 0235274675.   *041905*

Andance (Ardèche)

Bebronne, Pierre, les Rioux, 07340 Andance. T. 0475342053. - Ant / Tex -   *041906*

Bebronne, Thierry, Imm-Gilles RN 86, 07340 Andance. T. 0475343596. - Ant -   *041907*

Anduze (Gard)

Pasquier, André & François Fargas, 190 Chemin Serre-de-Lacan, 30140 Anduze. T. 0466618005.   *041908*

Anet (Eure-et-Loir)

Galerie de la Duchesse, 1 Rue Charles-Lechevrel, 28260 Anet. T. 0237414959.   *041909*

Angé (Loir-et-Cher)

Goubert, Gérald, 5 Rte Chaumine, 41400 Angé. T. 0254321175.   *041910*

Angers (Maine-et-Loire)

Acanthe, 47 Rue Mail, 49100 Angers. T. 41875827. - Fra / Glass -   *041911*

Antica, 10 Rue Bodinier, 49100 Angers. T. 41860510.   *041912*

Antiquités du Maine, 1bis Rue Jussieu, 49100 Angers. T. 41605800.   *041913*

Antiquités Toussaint, 27 Rue Toussaint, 49100 Angers. T. 41860756. - Furn / Music -   *041914*

Arts et Antiquités, 17 Pl Sainte-Croix, 49100 Angers. T. 41879966.   *041915*

Atelier, 9 Rue Toussaint, 49100 Angers. T. 41887410. - Paint / Graph / Draw -   *041916*

Au Coin du Feu, 39 Rue Toussaint, 49100 Angers. T. 41883645.   *041917*

Bernard, Béatrice, 66 Rue Fulton, 49000 Angers. T. 41882555.   *041918*

Bernard, Y., 66 Rue Fulton, 49000 Angers. T. 41882555. - Paint / Furn / Cur -   *041919*

Breheret, Michèle, 17 Rue Toussaint, 49100 Angers. T. 41868770.   *041920*

Caprices du Temps, 3 Rue Toussaint, 49100 Angers. T. 41200729. - Furn / Cur / Toys -   *041921*

Centre de Vente entre Particuliers, 137bis Rue Ponts-de-Cé, 49000 Angers. T. 41667931.   *041922*

Chaise de Bois, 48 Blvd Gaston-Ramon, 49100 Angers. T. 41439877. - Furn -   *041923*

Chesneau, Albert, 23 Rue Mare, 49100 Angers. T. 41343356.   *041924*

Colonial Company, 13ter Rue Maillé, 49100 Angers. T. 41873698.   *041925*

Comptoir Anglais, 6 Rue Montault, 49100 Angers. T. 41878349.   *041926*

Duflot, Jacques, 17 Pl Sainte-Croix, 49100 Angers. T. 41873933, Fax 41884917.   *041927*

Ferré, Régis, 13 Rue Haras, 49100 Angers. T. 41873663.   *041928*

Galerie 15, 35 Rue Toussaint, 49100 Angers. T. 41879531. - Paint / Furn / Cur -   *041929*

Girou, Gilles, 19 Rue Toussaint, 49100 Angers. T. 41200344. - Ant -   *041930*

Guéridon, 24 Rue Roë, 49100 Angers. T. 41879782.   *041931*

Ilias, Antonis, 1 Rue Aristide-Justeau, 49100 Angers. T. 41432562. - Furn -   *041932*

Jeanneau, Christian, 34 Rue David-d'Angers, 49100 Angers. T. 41880062.   *041933*

Mouron Rouge, Pl Romain, 49100 Angers. T. 41870013, Fax 41209794.   *041934*

Murcott, Françoise, 67 Rue Beaurepaire, 49100 Angers. T. 41876553.   *041935*

Perrault, Marcel, 62 Rue Baudrière, 49100 Angers. T. 41876241.   *041936*

Silans, Yves de, 2 Chemin Métaboles, 49000 Angers. T. 41483147.   *041937*

Tirault, Rémi, 5 Rue Montault, 49100 Angers. T. 41870424.   *041938*

Trocante, 43 Rue Maître-Ecole, 49000 Angers. T. 41479744.   *041939*

Vacquet-Journiac, Charlette, 57 Rue Saumuroise, 49000 Angers. T. 41666697.   *041940*

Anglès (Tarn)

Ribot, Michel, 81260 Anglès. T. 0563709715.   *041941*

Angles (Vendée)

Duprez, Guy, 10 Rte Tranche-sur-Mer, 85750 Angles. T. 0251975861.   *041942*

Moulin de l'Epinette, 2 Rue Moulins, 85750 Angles. T. 0251975054.   *041943*

Anglet (Pyrénées-Atlantiques)

Amigorena, Jean, Villa Bagheera, Rue Oeillets, 64600 Anglet. T. 0559638840. - Ant -   *041944*

Betbeder, Catherine, 23 Rue Saubadine, 64600 Anglet. T. 0559034076. - Ant -   *041945*

Bordenave, Jean, Haritzaqa Av Brindos, 64600 Anglet. T. 0559038108. - Ant / Furn -   *041946*

Colin, Eric, 21 Rue Chassin, 64600 Anglet. T. 0559032016. - Ant -   *041947*

Peyrecave, Lachiste, Rte Cambo, 64600 Anglet. T. 0559424175. - Ant -   *041948*

Angoulême (Charente)

Antiquités Liselotte, 400 Rue Périgueux, 16000 Angoulême. T. 0545953349. - Furn / Tex / Cur -   *041949*

Choses du Temps, 17 Rue Trois-Notre-Dame, 16000 Angoulême. T. 0545949810.   *041950*

Fragne, Paul, 8 Rue Ludovic-Trarieux, 16000 Angoulême. T. 0545956242.   *041951*

FrouFrou, 55 Rue Genève, 16000 Angoulême. T. 0545380634.   *041952*

Salle des Ventes du Palet, 7 Rue Amiral-Renaudin, 16000 Angoulême. T. 0545952195. - Ant -   *041953*

Slingue, Michel, 10 Rue Raymond-Audour, 16000 Angoulême. T. 0545387974.   *041954*

Tollet, Jean, 73 Rue Abbé-Rousselot, 16000 Angoulême. T. 0545954439.   *041955*

Angresse (Landes)

Volets Bleus, Rte Saint-Vincent-de-Tyrosse, 40150 Angresse. T. 0558435023. - Ant -   *041956*

Anjoutey (Territoire-de-Belfort)

Grenier de Grand'Mère, Rue Etueffont, 90170 Anjoutey. T. 0384546660.   *041957*

Annecy (Haute-Savoie)

Annecy Achat Antiquités, 9 Chemin Croix-Rouge, 74000 Annecy. T. 0450516246.   *041958*

Annecy Antiquités, 4 Av Crêt-du-Maure, 74000 Annecy. T. 0450528732.   *041959*

Antiquités et Puces, 8 Fbg Annonciades, 74000 Annecy. T. 0450514439.   *041960*

Autrefois, 6bis Rue Royale, 74000 Annecy. T. 0450454551.   *041961*

Barbier, Jean-Pierre, 4 Quai Eustache-Chappuis, 74000 Annecy. T. 0450452116.   *041962*

Buttin, Philippe, 6 Rue Jean-Jacques-Rousseau, 74000 Annecy. T. 0450514436.   *041963*

Glazar, 2 Rue Jean-Jaurès, 74000 Annecy. T. 0450452622.   *041964*

Ile au Trésor, 4 Pl Saint-François-de-Sales, 74000 Annecy. T. 0450516736. - Furn / Cur -   *041965*

Leçon des Choses, 1 Quai Cordeliers, 74000 Annecy. T. 0450510085.   *041966*

Malle Poste, 13 Rue Royale, 74000 Annecy.
T. 0450450012. *041967*
Mazot, 9 Rue Collège-Chapuisien, 74000 Annecy.
T. 0450529969. *041968*
Philothée, Passage Evéché, 74000 Annecy.
T. 0450450609. *041969*
Regard Anglais, 5 Rue Perrière, 74000 Annecy.
T. 0450515593. *041970*
Taureilles Antiquités, 2 Rue Jean-Jaurès, 74000 Annecy.
T. 0450514739. *041971*
Trésors de Bornéo, 12 Rue Royale, 74000 Annecy.
T. 0450512018. - Orient - *041972*
Vick de V, 9 Rue Royale, 74000 Annecy.
T. 0450517150. *041973*
Vouillon, François, 4 Rue Jean-Jaurès, 74000 Annecy.
T. 0450455691. *041974*

Annecy-le-Vieux (Haute-Savoie)
Antiquarius, 9 Chemin Abbaye, 74940 Annecy-le-Vieux.
T. 0450232392, Fax 0450099748. *041975*
Forain, Suzanne, 35 Rue Centrale, 74940 Annecy-le-
Vieux. T. 0450233106, Fax 0450098320. *041976*
Pierre et Meuble d'Autrefois, 35 Rue Centrale, 74940
Annecy-le-Vieux. T. 0450236813, Fax 0450098320.
- Furn / Cur - *041977*

Annemasse (Haute-Savoie)
Blanc Occasions, 29 Rte Vallées, 74100 Annemasse.
T. 0450376743. *041978*
Donche, Roland, 9 Chemin Chamarettes, 74100 Anne-
masse. T. 0450920772. - Furn / Cur - *041979*
Doublet, Raphaël, 4 Rue Faucille, 74100 Annemasse.
T. 0450387820. *041980*

Annonay (Ardèche)
A la Montgolfière, 19 Blvd République, 07100 Annonay.
T. 0475334022. - Ant - *041981*
Ateliers du Moulin, 5 Rue César-Filhol, 07100 Annonay.
T. 0475332103. - Ant - *041982*
Bourel, Jean-Paul, Résid. Europe 1, 07100 Annonay.
T. 0475334506. - Ant - *041983*
S.N.E.C., 30 Rue Tournon, 07100 Annonay.
T. 0475333477. - Ant - *041984*

Antibes (Alpes-Maritimes)
Andrin, 13 Imp Aubernon, 06600 Antibes.
T. 0493347878. *041985*
Andrin, Marc, 1 Pl Amiral-Barnaud, 06600 Antibes.
T. 0493344075. *041986*
Antiquités du Vieil Antibes, 10 Rue Docteur-Rostan,
06600 Antibes. T. 0493348901. *041987*
Antiquités Le Patio, 6 Rue Georges-Clemenceau, 06600
Antibes. T. 0493346300. *041988*
Antiquités Le Sire d'Argent, La Brague, R.N. 7, 06600
Antibes. T. 0493 33 49 51. - Ant - *041989*
Aristote, 6 Av Niquet, 06600 Antibes.
T. 0493344220. *041990*
Blum, Charly, 11 Av Philippe-Rochat, 06600 Antibes.
T. 0493741846. *041991*
Brocante du Port, 22 Rue Aubernon, 06600 Antibes.
T. 0493342618. *041992*
Buchart, 110 Blvd Président-Wilson, 06600 Antibes.
T. 0493610457. - Toys / Music - *041993*
Chenevière, Pierre, 16 Av Thiers, 06600 Antibes.
T. 0493340515. *041994*
Geloni, Joseph, 125 Blvd Francis-Meilland, 06600 Anti-
bes. T. 0493617291. *041995*
Gerson, D., 2 Rue Georges Clemenceau, 06600 Antibes.
T. 0493344279. - Ant / Eth - *041996*
Gismondi, Jean, Les Remparts, 06600 Antibes.
T. 0493340667, Fax 0493343584. - Furn - *041997*
Lardin, Victor, 135 Rte Nice, 06600 Antibes.
T. 0493746006. *041998*
Marsala, 3 Rue Tourraque, 06600 Antibes.
T. 0493341515. *041999*
Michelet, 25 Rue Aubernon, 06600 Antibes.
T. 0493340446. *042000*
Passé Présent, 6 Rue Georges-Clemenceau, 06600 Anti-
bes. T. 0493343203. *042001*
Petite Maison, 1 et 4 Blvd Gustave-Chancel, 06600 Anti-
bes. T. 0493347018. - Tex - *042002*
Roy Soleil, 460 Av de Nice, 06600 Antibes.
T. 0493334541. - Ant / Paint / Sculp / Dec / Lights /
Cur - *042003*

Saget, Roger, 15 Av Thiers, 06600 Antibes.
T. 0493348140. *042004*
Sire d'Argens, La Brague, RN 7, 06600 Antibes.
T. 0493334951. - Furn - *042005*
Vert Galant, 24 Rue Thuret, 06600 Antibes.
T. 0493342101. *042006*
Viale, 6 Rue Georges-Clemenceau, 06600 Antibes.
T. 0493345333. *042007*
Vieux Manoir, 6 Av Esterel, 06600 Antibes.
T. 0493678371. *042008*
Yesterday, 16 Rue Aubernon, 06600 Antibes.
T. 0493343255. *042009*

Antoigné (Maine-et-Loire)
Derouard, Michel & Jacqueline, Lernay, 49260 Antoigné.
T. 41509060. - Paint / Furn / Cur - *042010*

Antony (Hauts-de-Seine)
A la Croisée des Temps, 20 Av Division-Leclerc, 92160
Antony. T. 0142374417. - Paint / Furn / Jew /
Silv - *042011*
Antiquités Brocante, 53 Rue Adolphe-Pajeaud, 92160
Antony. T. 0142378711. *042012*
Chonigbaum, 20 Av Division-Leclerc, 92160 Antony.
T. 0142374417. *042013*
Licorne, 104 Rue Marché, 92160 Antony.
T. 0142379244. *042014*
Rousseau, 33 Av Aristide-Briand, 92160 Antony.
T. 0142375405. - Furn / Cur - *042015*

Anzin (Nord)
Nissen, Gérard, 106 Rue Jean-Jaurès, 59410 Anzin.
T. 0327470866. - Ant - *042016*

Aouste (Ardennes)
Dumont, Bruno, Rte Rumigny, 08290 Aouste.
T. 0324544237. - Ant - *042017*

Appenai-sous-Bellême (Orne)
Armenjon, Michel, La Hurlinière, 61130 Appenai-sous-
Bellême. T. 0233731493. - Ant - *042018*

Appoigny (Yonne)
Cordier, Maurice, 3bis Rue Sentier, 89380 Appoigny.
T. 0386530384. - Ant - *042019*
Mainguy, Bernard, 24 Rte Auxerre, 89380 Appoigny.
T. 0386531669. *042020*
Muller, Jean-François, 3bis Rue Pont, 89380 Appoigny.
T. 0386532008. *042021*
Muller, Roger, 5 Rte Joigny, 89380 Appoigny.
T. 0386530132. *042022*
Salah, Jacky, 21 Rte Paris, 89380 Appoigny.
T. 0386531080 *042023*

Apremont (Vendée)
Brocante du Château, Pl Château, 85220 Apremont.
T. 0251552723. *042024*

Apt (Vaucluse)
Chabaud, Jean, Rte Gargas, 84400 Apt. Fax 90744815.
- Ant / Dec - *042025*
Sabatier, Jean-Frédéri, 10 Pl Septier, 84400 Apt.
T. 0490740240. - Ant - *042026*

Arbois (Jura)
Sintot, 34-40 Rue de Courcelles, 39600 Arbois.
T. 0384661368. - Furn - *042027*

Arc-lès-Gray (Haute-Saône)
Hall-Occas, 4 Av Charles-Couyba, 70100 Arc-lès-Gray.
T. 0384651193. *042028*

Arc-sur-Tille (Côte-d'Or)
Heitzmann, Patrick, ZA, 21560 Arc-sur-Tille.
T. 0380370978. - Paint / Furn / Dec / Instr / Cur /
Toys - *042029*

Arcachon (Gironde)
Otternaud, Maurice, 41 Blvd Pierre-Loti, 33120 Arca-
chon. T. 0556330193. *042030*
Oxford-Antiquités, 294 Blvd Plage, 33120 Arcachon.
T. 0556834771, Fax 0556835963. - Furn /
Cur - *042031*
Trouvaille, 20 Cours Tartas, 33120 Arcachon.
T. 0556832988. *042032*

Arcey (Doubs)
Daguet, Christophe, 35 Rue 5ème DB, 25750 Arcey.
T. 0381934144. *042033*

Ardenay-sur-Mérize (Sarthe)
Au Passé Simple, La Butte Fréteau, 72370 Ardenay-sur-
Mérize. T. 0243898866. - Ant - *042034*

Ardin (Deux-Sèvres)
Sécher, Didier, 25bis Rue Jean-de-Saint-Goard, 79160
Ardin. T. 0549043577. *042035*

Argelès-sur-Mer (Pyrénées-Orientales)
Argelès Collection, 55 Rte Collioure, 66700 Argelès-sur-
Mer. T. 0468959898. - Ant - *042036*
Vallés François Antiquités, 79 Rte Collioure, 66700 Ar-
gelès-sur-Mer. T. 0468814348. - Ant / Furn /
Cur - *042037*
Vozelle, Jeanne, 3 Rte Nationale face poste, 66700 Ar-
gelès-sur-Mer. T. 0468810740. - Ant - *042038*

Argent-sur-Sauldre (Cher)
A la Porte de Sologne, 7 Rue Acacias, 18410 Argent-
sur-Sauldre. T. 0248733469,
Fax 0248733469. *042039*
Antiquité La Croix Verte, Av Paris, 18410 Argent-sur-
Sauldre. T. 0248733264. - Ant / China - *042040*

Argentan (Orne)
Arts et Collections d'Antan, 48 Rue du Beigle, 61200 Ar-
gentan. T. 0233359554. - Ant - *042041*
Garcia, Jean-Jacques, 16 Imp Alsace-Lorraine, 61200
Argentan. T. 0233360181. - Ant - *042042*
Souloy, Yanick, 6 Pl Vimal-du-Bouchet, 61200 Argentan.
T. 0233670497. - Ant - *042043*

Argentat (Corrèze)
Peyrou, Eric, 6 Rue Douvisis, 19400 Argentat.
T. 0555281273. *042044*

Argenteuil (Val-d'Oise)
Kobylko, Askold, 32 Rue Raspail, 95100 Argenteuil.
T. 0134102515. *042045*
Michaut, 55 Blvd Jean-Allemane, 95100 Argenteuil.
T. 0130251672. *042046*

Argenton-sur-Creuse (Indre)
Boyer, 2 Rue Paul-Bert, 36200 Argenton-sur-Creuse.
T. 0254240596. *042047*

Argentré-du-Plessis (Ille-et-Vilaine)
Crosnier, Michel, Rue Gennes, 35370 Argentré-du-Ples-
sis. T. 0299966188. *042048*

Argoules (Somme)
Chartiez, Antoine, 2 Grande Rue, 80120 Argoules.
T. 0322299348. - Ant - *042049*

Arles (Bouches-du-Rhône)
Athenoux, Robert, 55 Blvd Emile-Combes, 13200 Arles.
T. 0490930576. *042050*
Cadet Rousselle, 10 Rue Gambetta, 13200 Arles.
T. 0490965660. *042051*
Dervieux, Frédéric, 5 Rue Vernon, 13200 Arles.
T. 0490960239. *042052*
Kachichian, Alain, 38 Pl Balechou, 13200 Arles.
T. 0490935237. *042053*
Maurin, Raymond, 4 Rue de la Grille, 13200 Arles.
T. 0490965157, Fax 0490936900. *042054*
Racon-Dongradi, Irène, 6 Rue Grille, 13200 Arles.
T. 0490967766. *042055*
Rose des Vents, 18 Rue Diderot, 13200 Arles.
T. 0490961585. - Ant / Paint / Furn - *042056*
Roubaud, Joséphine, Chemin Fallet, Résidence La Chau-
mière, 13200 Arles. T. 0490969586. *042057*

Armentières (Nord)
Sainte-Anne, 2 Quai Beauvais, 59280 Armentières.
T. 0320441733. - Ant - *042058*

Armes (Nièvre)
Antiquités, 102 Rte Buissonnière, 58500 Armes.
T. 0386273169. *042059*
Bernier, Simone, 100 Rte Buissonnière, 58500 Armes.
T. 0386271644. *042060*

Arnay-le-Duc (Côte-d'Or)
Marchand d'Oublis, 19 Rue Saint-Jacques, 21230 Ar-
nay-le-Duc. T. 0380900965.   *042061*

Arpajon (Essonne)
Grenier de Pierrot, 12 Pl Marché, 91290 Arpajon.
T. 0164909074.   *042062*
Lefèvre, 47 Grande Rue, 91290 Arpajon.
T. 0164906122.   *042063*
Montagnac, Marion, 6 Rue Gambetta, 91290 Arpajon.
T. 0160839401.   *042064*

Arques (Pas-de-Calais)
Saudemont, Dominique, Garenne, 62510 Arques.
T. 0321989332.   *042065*

Arrancy-sur-Crusne (Meuse)
Blard, Robert, 4 Rue du Château, 55230 Arrancy-sur-
Crusne. T. 0329859278. - Ant -   *042066*

Arras (Pas-de-Calais)
Arvel, 1 Pl Théâtre, 62000 Arras. T. 0321510466.
- Ant -   *042067*
Arvel, Dominique, 1 Pl Théâtre, 62000 Arras.
T. 0321510466.   *042068*
Bremilts, Claude, 3 Rue des Récollets, 62000 Arras.
T. 0321516511. - Paint / Furn / Dec / Cur -   *042069*
Copin, 20 Rue de la Taillerie, 62000 Arras.
T. 0321232808. - Paint / Furn / Cur -   *042070*
Dewasmes, Jean-Charles, 5 Rue 29-Juillet, 62000 Ar-
ras. T. 0321513718.   *042071*
Dworczak, Jacques, 2 Rue Paul-Périn, 62000 Arras.
T. 0321502920.   *042072*
Guisgand, Grégory, 12 Rue Constant-Dutilleux, 62000
Arras. T. 0321241732.   *042073*
Pajic, Milé, 60 Av Fernand-Lobbedez, 62000 Arras.
T. 0321237965.   *042074*
Sellier, Jean-Christian, 13 Rue de Flandre, Résidence
Pierre-Bolle, 62000 Arras. T. 0321595216.
- Mil -   *042075*
Tricard, Maurice, 109 Rue Saint-Aubert, 62000 Arras.
T. 0321713042.   *042076*

Arromanches-les-Bains (Calvados)
Jauzé, Isabelle, 1 Cale Neptune, 14117 Arromanches-
les-Bains. T. 0231213328.   *042077*
Jauzé, Rolande, 6 Rue François-Carpentier, 14117 Arromanches-les-Bains. T. 0231213328.   *042078*

Arry (Somme)
Barjavel, Françoise, lieu-dit Château Blanc, 80120 Arry.
T. 0322299061. - Ant -   *042079*

Ars (Creuse)
Gardner, Timothy-James, Sémenon, 23480 Ars.
T. 0555669876. - Ant -   *042080*

Ars-en-Ré (Charente-Maritime)
Antiquités, Quai Criée, 17590 Ars-en-Ré.
T. 0546295413.   *042081*
Gressler, Patrick, Quai Chabossière, 17590 Ars-en-Ré.
T. 0546292900.   *042082*
Petite Brocante de Caillou, 18 Rue Gambetta, 17590
Ars-en-Ré. T. 0546294773.   *042083*

Artigues-Foulayronnes (Lot-et-Garonne)
Gateau, Annick, RN 121, 40 Av Paris, 47510 Artigues-
Foulayronnes. T. 0553956888.   *042084*

Artigues-près-Bordeaux (Gironde)
Art Antique, 6 Rue Bois-Léger, 33370 Artigues-près-Bor-
deaux. T. 0556400174. - Paint / Furn / China / Sculp /
Cur / Toys -   *042085*

Artix (Pyrénées-Atlantiques)
Abadie, Alain, Av République, 64170 Artix.
T. 0559603734. - Furn -   *042086*

Arzon (Morbihan)
Antique Importers, 7 Quai Volliers, 56640 Arzon.
T. 0297538884. - Ant -   *042087*
Thudot, Georges, 29 Chemin Crouesty, 56640 Arzon.
T. 0297539921, Fax 0297539922. - Ant -   *042088*

Asnières-sur-Seine (Hauts-de-Seine)
Aux Reflets du Passé, 115 Rue Colombes, 92600 Asniè-
res-sur-Seine. T. 0147906659,
Fax 0147901688.   *042089*
Bolton, Martin, 40 Rue Michelet, 92600 Asnières-sur-
Seine. T. 0147337185.   *042090*
Déco Delights, 2 Rue Dentert-Rochereau, 92600 Asniè-
res-sur-Seine. T. 0140860602.   *042091*
Kempf, Jean, 36 Rue Galliéni, 92600 Asnières-sur-Sei-
ne. T. 0147935046.   *042092*
Le Gouil, Dominique, 27 Rue Galliéni, 92600 Asnières-
sur-Seine. T. 0147335500. - Furn / Cur -   *042093*

Athis-Mons (Essonne)
Antiquités des Gobelins, 2 Rue Maréchal-Leclerc, 91200
Athis-Mons. T. 0169381119. - Paint / Furn / Sculp /
Silv / Glass / Toys -   *042094*

Aubagne (Bouches-du-Rhône)
Lys et la Rose, 3 RN 96, 13400 Aubagne.
T. 0442329292, Fax 0442329246.   *042095*
Rome Antique, 28 RN 8, 13400 Aubagne.
T. 0442039143.   *042096*

Aubais (Gard)
Etoile du Midi, Rte Gallargues, 30250 Aubais.
T. 0466807572.   *042097*

Aubenas (Ardèche)
Art Populaire, 44 Rue Quatre-Septembre, 07200 Aube-
nas. T. 0475351488. - Ant -   *042098*
Bacuez, 17 Rue Béranger-de-la-Tour, 07200 Aubenas.
T. 0475350279. - Ant -   *042099*
Dépôt Vente de Tartary, 57 Rue de Tatary, 07200 Aube-
nas. T. 0475933679. - Ant -   *042100*
Jadis & Naguère, 7 Rue Béranger-de-la-Tour, 07200 Au-
benas. T. 0475352666. - Ant / Furn -   *042101*
Nicolas Antiquités, Pl 14-Juillet, 07200 Aubenas.
T. 0475930300. - Ant -   *042102*
Vivarais, Pont d'Aubenas Rte de Privas, 07200 Aubenas.
T. 0475935969. - Ant -   *042103*

Aubencheul-au-Bac (Nord)
Au Vieux Colombier, 29 Rte Nationale, 59265 Auben-
cheul-au-Bac. T. 0327809339. - Ant -   *042104*

Auberchicourt (Nord)
Tondeur, Elina, 71 Rue Doual, 59165 Auberchicourt.
T. 0327926297. - Ant -   *042105*

Aubervilliers (Seine-Saint-Denis)
Au Dépôt des Chineurs, 55 Blvd Félix-Faure, 93300 Au-
bervilliers. T. 0149372011.   *042106*
Boucq, 4 Rue Noyers, 93300 Aubervilliers.
T. 0148345208.   *042107*
Terres Promises, 126bis Rue Cités, 93300 Aubervilliers.
T. 0148119455.   *042108*

Aubeterre-sur-Dronne (Charente)
Antiquités de la Dronne, Rue Saint-Jean, 16390 Aube-
terre-sur-Dronne. T. 0545986028.   *042109*
Galzain, Jean de, Rue Saint-Jean, 16390 Aubeterre-sur-
Dronne. T. 0545986028.   *042110*

Aubiac (Lot-et-Garonne)
Charaire, Jean, Rte Moulins, 47310 Aubiac.
T. 0553678078.   *042111*

Aubigny-au-Bac (Nord)
Au Reflets d'Antan, Rte Nationale, 59265 Aubigny-au-
Bac. T. 0327894555. - Ant -   *042112*

Aubigny-sur-Nère (Cher)
Foucault, Jeanne, 13 Rue Foulons, 18700 Aubigny-sur-
Nère. T. 0248581257.   *042113*
Mercier, Gaëtan, 32 Rue Stuarts, 18700 Aubigny-sur-
Nère. T. 0248580434.   *042114*

Aubusson (Creuse)
Brivet, Gisèle, 57 Rue Vieille, 23200 Aubusson.
T. 0555662797. - Ant -   *042115*
Dessemond, J. – P., 30 Av Jean-Jaurès, 23200 Aubus-
son. T. 0555838745. - Ant / Furn -   *042116*

Auch (Gers)
Bérenguer, Joseph, 7bis Rue Blazy, 32000 Auch.
T. 0562630622. - Furn -   *042117*
Bohard, Marie, 6 Rue Amiral-Péphau, 32000 Auch.
T. 0562054875.   *042118*
Dilhan, Guillaume, 3 Rue Charles-Samaran, 32000
Auch. T. 0562056883.   *042119*
Lespès, Annie, 12 Rue 8-Mai-1945, 32000 Auch.
T. 0562053212, Fax 0562618060. - Furn -   *042120*
Poulain, Philippe, 9 Rue Espagne, 32000 Auch.
T. 0562059521.   *042121*
Vignaux, Claude, 3 Pl 14-Juillet, 32000 Auch.
T. 0562053195.   *042122*
Yverneau, Christophe, 3 Rue Charles-Samaran, 32000
Auch. T. 0562052514, Fax 0562051046.   *042123*

Audincourt (Doubs)
Brisson, Marcelin, 4 Rue Valentigney, 25400 Audincourt.
T. 0381344022. - Furn -   *042124*
Drouin, 30bis Rue Seloncourt, 25400 Audincourt.
T. 0381345880. - Furn -   *042125*
Wettach, Gilles, 36 Rue Champs-Essart, 25400 Audin-
court. T. 0381343356.   *042126*

Augan (Morbihan)
Dépôt Vente de la Roche, 14 Rue Roche, 56800 Augan.
T. 0297934059. - Ant / Furn -   *042127*

Augnax (Gers)
Château, Bernard, 32120 Augnax.
T. 0562651669.   *042128*

Augy (Yonne)
Geoffroy, Michel, 23 Grande Rue, 89290 Augy.
T. 0386538779.   *042129*
Meubles d'Autrefois, 27 Rte Nationale, 89290 Augy.
T. 0386538650.   *042130*

Aulnay-sous-Bois (Seine-Saint-Denis)
Au Bonheur du Jour, 61 Av Dupuis, 93600 Aulnay-sous-
Bois. T. 0148664982.   *042131*
Barraud, Jean-Pierre, 7 Rue Jean-Charcot, 93600 Aul-
nay-sous-Bois. T. 0148792306.   *042132*
Chineur Antiquité, 22 Rue Mâcon, 93600 Aulnay-sous-
Bois. T. 0148699254.   *042133*

Ault (Somme)
Paolozzi, Lionel, 46 Av Gén-Leclerc, 80460 Ault.
T. 0322604302. - Ant -   *042134*

Aumale (Seine-Maritime)
Dumont, Marcel, Rue Saint-Dominique, 76390 Aumale.
T. 0235934021.   *042135*

Auneau (Eure-et-Loir)
Lacombe, Claudine, 52 Grande Rue Equillemont, 28700
Auneau. T. 0237312955.   *042136*

Aups (Var)
Jadis, 3 Pl Marché, 83630 Aups.
T. 0494700469.   *042137*

Auray (Morbihan)
Au Bon Gous'tan, 58 Rue Château, 56400 Auray.
T. 0297566422. - Ant -   *042138*
Basset, Jean-Claude, 43 Rue Château, 56400 Auray.
T. 0297507286. - Ant -   *042139*
Guillou, Alain, 55 Rue Château, 56400 Auray.
T. 0297562752. - Ant -   *042140*
Légende des Siècles, 3 Rue Evêque, 56400 Auray.
T. 0297563263. - Ant / Furn -   *042141*

Aurillac (Cantal)
Astorg, 151 Av Aristide-Briand, 15000 Aurillac.
T. 0471482634.   *042142*
Aurillac Collections, 14 Pl Square, 15000 Aurillac.
T. 0471489363.   *042143*
Aux Nouveautés d'Hier, 13 Blvd Pont-Rouge, 15000 Au-
rillac. T. 0471481138. - Furn / Jew -   *042144*
Berthomieux, Marcelle, 6 Pl Préfecture, 15000 Aurillac.
T. 0471482504.   *042145*
Besson, Jean-Louis, 15 Rue Gare, 15000 Aurillac.
T. 0471482218.   *042146*
Brocante des Fargues, 19 Rue Fargues, 15000 Aurillac.
T. 0471648488.   *042147*

Delclaux, Myriam, 2 Pl Aurinques, 15000 Aurillac.
T. 0471483854. 042148
Fel, Joseph, 8 Rue Noailles, 15000 Aurillac.
T. 0471483383. 042149
Ginioux, Catherine, 8 Pl Hôtel-de-Ville, 15000 Aurillac.
T. 0471482776. 042150
Gonod, Jean-Bernard, 18 Rue Arsène-Vermenouze,
15000 Aurillac. T. 0471643413. 042151
J.B. Antiquité, 7bis Av Aristide-Briand, 15000 Aurillac.
T. 0471488543. 042152
Menez, Marie-Françoise, 14 Rue Victor-Hugo, 15000
Aurillac. T. 0471643740. 042153
Ricros, 9 Rue Guy-de-Veyre, 15000 Aurillac.
T. 0471483888. 042154
Vieux Meubles, 9 Av République, 15000 Aurillac.
T. 0471482574. - Furn - 042155

Ausson (Haute-Garonne)
Lloan, Janine, Chemin Moulin, 31210 Ausson.
T. 0561957198. 042156

Authon-du-Perche (Eure-et-Loir)
Grenier du Perche, 6 Rue Sous-Lieutenant-Germond,
28330 Authon-du-Perche. T. 0237491351. 042157

Autry-le-Châtel (Loiret)
Grange de la Roche, Rte de Bourges, 45500 Autry-le-
Châtel. T. 0238380341. 042158

Autun (Saône-et-Loire)
Au Vieil Autun, 31 Av Charles-de-Gaulle, 71400 Autun.
T. 0385862754. - Ant - 042159
Bouillon, Michel, 3 Rue Cocand, 71400 Autun.
T. 0385520738. - Ant / Furn - 042160
Cavalier, Jean-Pierre, 19 Grande Rue Chauchien, 71400
Autun. T. 0385521320. - Ant - 042161
Héritier, Maurice, La Guinguette, 71400 Autun.
T. 0385524175. - Ant / Furn - 042162
Mancina, Saverio, 31 Av Charles-de-Gaulle, 71400 Au-
tun. T. 0385862754. - Ant - 042163
Marbres, 15 Rue Marbres, 71400 Autun.
T. 0385862834. - Ant / Paint / Furn - 042164
Métra Raoul, 15 Grande-Rue-Chauchien, 71400 Autun.
T. 0385523722. - Furn - 042165
Paillard, F., La Genetoye, 71400 Autun. T. 0385520856.
- Ant - 042166
Transervice 71, 15 Rue Marbres, 71400 Autun.
T. 0385862834. - Ant - 042167

Auvers-Saint-Georges (Essonne)
Busson, Bernard, La Martinière, 39 Rte Morigny, 91580
Auvers-Saint-Georges. T. 0160803445. 042168

Auxerre (Yonne)
A la Dame de Coeur, 38 Rue Egleny, 89000 Auxerre.
T. 0386510719. 042169
Air du Temps, 76 Rue Pont, 89000 Auxerre.
T. 0386516411. - Ant - 042170
Antiquités de la Cathédrale, 9 Pl Saint-Etienne, 89000
Auxerre. T. 0386524512. - Furn / Cur / Toys - 042171
Antiquités Saint-Nicolas, 8 Quai Marine, 89000 Auxerre.
T. 0386526479. 042172
Aux Trois Marchés, 13 Rue Boucheries, 89000 Auxerre.
T. 0386510566. - Ant - 042173
Bérotière, 15 Rue Paul-Bert, 89000 Auxerre.
T. 0386513108. 042174
Broc'Trente, 50 Rue Louis-Richard, 89000 Auxerre.
T. 0386529412. 042175
Doré, 30 Rue Champoulains, 89000 Auxerre.
T. 0386463077. 042176
Duranton, Jean-Louis, 108 Rue Paris, 89000 Auxerre.
T. 0386517550. - Ant - 042177
Eyraud, Emmanuel, 2 Rue Stand, 89000 Auxerre.
T. 0386510365. 042178
Mainguy, Philippe, 16 Rue Engleny, 89000 Auxerre.
T. 0386513859. 042179
Rive Gauche, 81 Rue du Pont, 89000 Auxerre.
T. 0386512710. - Jew / Silv / Mil / Cur - 042180
Romé, 28 Rue Joubert, 89000 Auxerre.
T. 0386512765. 042181
Taxi Mauve, 15 Rue Cochois, 89000 Auxerre.
T. 0386514393, Fax 0386525941. 042182
Taxi Mauve, 7ter Rue Docteur-Labosse, 89000 Auxerre.
T. 0386525645. 042183

Trocante, 7 Rue Maladière, 89000 Auxerre.
T. 0386461954. 042184
Waldteufel, Edouard, 9 Pl Sainte-Etienne, 89000 Auxer-
re. T. 0386524512. - Ant / Furn / Jew / Instr /
Cur - 042185

Auxon (Aube)
Brocante de Saint Leu, 173 Rue Mairie, 10130 Auxon.
T. 0325421547. - Ant / Paint / Dec - 042186
Crédence, 91 Rue Peage, 10130 Auxon. T. 0325420121.
- Ant - 042187

Auxonne (Côte-d'Or)
Trindade, José, 39 Blvd Pasteur, 21130 Auxonne.
T. 0380310218. 042188
Vuillemot-Morel, Jean-Marc, 8 Rue Redoutey, 21130
Auxonne. T. 0380373251, Fax 0380373688. - Ant /
Paint / Sculp / Draw - 042189

Auzances (Creuse)
Joly-Boyer, Bernadette, Le Compas-Prés-d'Auzances,
23700 Auzances. T. 0555671534. - Ant - 042190

Avallon (Yonne)
Billebaude, 9 Rue Mathe, 89200 Avallon.
T. 0386344487. 042191
Bourey Caldarera, Marie-Christine, 67 Rue de Lyon,
89200 Avallon. T. 0386341912. - Ant / Furn - 042192
Portal, Roland, 58 Grande Rue Aristide Briand, 89200
Avallon. T. 0386341028. - Ant - 042193

Avermes (Allier)
Brocantic, l'Epine Rte de Decize, 03000 Avermes.
T. 0470464667. - Ant - 042194
Paquier, Georges, Château de Segange, 03000 Avermes.
T. 0470440663. - Furn / Mil - 042195

Avignon (Vaucluse)
Arjuna, 5 Petite-Saunerie, 84000 Avignon.
T. 0490853910. - Ant / Orient / Jew - 042196
Baume, Hervé, 19 Rue Petite-Fusterie, 84000 Avignon.
T. 0490863766, Fax 0490863766. - Ant / Dec - 042197
Bourret, 5 Rue Limas, 84000 Avignon. T. 0490866502.
- Ant / Paint / Furn / Tex - 042198
Brocante de la Principale, 16 Pl Principale, 84000 Avi-
gnon. T. 0490823751. - Ant - 042199
Brocantes des Carmes, 14 Rue Carreterie, 84000 Avi-
gnon. T. 0490820046. - Ant - 042200
Creange, Colette, 18 Rue Joseph-Vernet, 84000 Avi-
gnon. T. 0490861600. - Ant - 042201
Dame, Christine, 20 Rue Petite-Fuserie, 84000 Avignon.
T. 0490271132. - Ant - 042202
Delhomme, Sylvain, 27bis Rue Thiers, 84000 Avignon.
T. 0490825444. - Ant - 042203
Dervieux, Ferdinand, 11 Rue Félix-Gras, 84000 Avignon.
T. 0490821437. - Ant - 042204
Dumoussaud, Daniel, 9 Rue Limas, 84000 Avignon.
T. 0490860013. - Ant - 042205
En Scène, 8 Rue Carreterie, 84000 Avignon.
T. 0490850611. - Ant / Lights - 042206
Galerie du Limas, 11 Rue Limas, 84000 Avignon.
T. 0490859921. - Ant / Paint / Tin - 042207
Guerre, Gérard, 1 Plan Lunel, 84000 Avignon.
T. 0490864267, Fax 0490856462. - Ant / Paint / Fra /
Glass - 042208
Malbos, Charles, 5 Rue Petite-Calade, 84000 Avignon.
T. 0490866258. - Ant - 042209
Manescau, Raymonde, 2 Rue Mont-de-Piété, 84000 Avi-
gnon. T. 0490822790, Fax 0490149212.
- Ant - 042210
Michel, Eric, 81 Rte Lyon, 84000 Avignon.
T. 0490826283. - Ant - 042211
Pin, Pierre, 11 Rue Limas, 84000 Avignon.
T. 0490859921. - Ant - 042212
Ramadier, Ludovic, 3 Rue Grande-Fusterie, 84000 Avi-
gnon. T. 0490271601. - Ant - 042213
Rebrousse Temps, 20 Rue Petite-Fustierie, 84000 Avi-
gnon. T. 0490271132. - Ant - 042214
Sauco, Claire, 1 Rue Carreterie, 84000 Avignon.
T. 0490854165. - Ant - 042215
Sérignan, 9 Rue Petite-Fuserie, 84000 Avignon.
T. 0490853604. - Ant - 042216

Avon (Seine-et-Marne)
Herode et Bo, 23 Av Général-de-Gaulle, 77210 Avon.
T. 64227777. 042217

Avranches (Manche)
Dodier, Philippe, 6 Rue Brémesnil, 50300 Avranches.
T. 0233580581. 042218
Gervais, Christian, 38 Rue Constitution, 50300 Avran-
ches. T. 0233580254. 042219
Gervais, Gilbert, 1 Rue Collège, 50300 Avranches.
T. 0233582682. 042220
Pinson, Françoise, 2 Pl Angot, 50300 Avranches.
T. 0233584762. 042221
Pouquet, Michel, 80 Rue Constitution, 50300 Avranches.
T. 0233581455. 042222
Vauborel, Maurice de, 176 Rue Liberté, 50300 Avran-
ches. T. 0233580064. 042223

Aydoilles (Vosges)
Toussaint, Denis, 13 Rte Méménil, 88600 Aydoilles.
T. 0329657069. 042224

Baccarat (Meurthe-et-Moselle)
Blot, Laurence, 1 Rue Sainte-Catherine, 54120 Bacca-
rat. T. 0383754614. 042225
Gayer, Paul, 55 Rue Parc, 54120 Baccarat.
T. 0383751232. - Ant - 042226
Hall de l'Occasion, 14 Rue Sainte-Catherine, 54120
Baccarat. T. 0383751366. 042227

Baden (Morbihan)
Kerhervé Antiquités, 56870 Baden. T. 0297571237.
- Ant - 042228
Moulin Pomper, Le Moulin de Pomper, 56870 Baden.
T. 0297571195. - Ant - 042229
Nardon, Jean-François, Kerilio, 56870 Baden.
T. 0297570991. - Ant - 042230
Yesterday, 10 Pl Marhalé, 56870 Baden. T. 0297571460.
- Ant - 042231

Badonviller (Meurthe-et-Moselle)
Keep Cool, 39 Av Jean-Baptiste-Diedler, 54540 Badon-
viller. T. 0383422300. 042232

Bages (Aude)
Galerie Ancien Puits, Rue Ancien-Puits, 11100 Bages.
T. 0468410234. 042233
Vella, William, Ham Prat-de-Cest, 11100 Bages.
T. 0468428017. 042234

Bagnères-de-Luchon (Haute-Garonne)
Azum, Sylvane, 68 All Etigny, 31110 Bagnères-de-Lu-
chon. T. 0561790217. 042235
Oréades, 69 All Etigny, 31110 Bagnères-de-Luchon.
T. 0561790666. - Paint - 042236
Oréades, 4 Pl Mengué, 31110 Bagnères-de-Luchon.
T. 0561793830. - Paint - 042237

Bagneux (Hauts-de-Seine)
Banovsky, Michel, 34 Villa Iris, 92220 Bagneux.
T. 0146658546. 042238
Petit Jacques, 4 Rue Prés, 92220 Bagneux.
T. 0146653717. 042239

Bagnols-sur-Cèze (Gard)
Tarbouriech, Guy & Martine, 25 Av Léon-Blum, 30200
Bagnols-sur-Cèze. T. 0466890779. 042240

Baillargues (Hérault)
Azimont, Jean-Pierre, 41 Rte Nationale, 34670 Baillar-
gues. T. 0467701896. 042241

Bailly (Yvelines)
Antiquités de Bailly, 10 Rue Maule, 78870 Bailly.
T. 0130800330. 042242

Bain-de-Bretagne (Ille-et-Vilaine)
Boulle, Yvon, La Menottière, 35470 Bain-de-Bretagne.
T. 0299439603. 042243
Lemoine, Lande Fleurie, 35470 Bain-de-Bretagne.
T. 0299437081. 042244

Bains-les-Bains (Vosges)
Martin Baudouin, Jeannine, 4 Rue Docteur-André-Leroy,
88240 Bains-les-Bains. T. 0329363176. 042245

Balacet (Ariège)
Cornu, Jean-Pierre, Village, 09800 Balacet.
T. 0561968550.   042246

Balbigny (Loire)
Antiquaire du Fourneau, 34 Rue 11-Novembre, 42510
Balbigny. T. 0477272227, Fax 0477272533.
- Dec -   042247
Félix, Michelle, Rue 11-Novembre, 42510 Balbigny.
T. 0477281053.   042248

Baldersheim (Haut-Rhin)
Ciliento, Franco, 3 Rue Ile-Napoléon, 68390 Balders-
heim. T. 0389561208.   042249

Ballersdorf (Haut-Rhin)
Walter, Irénée, 5 Rue Vergers, 68210 Ballersdorf.
T. 0389251989.   042250

Balma (Haute-Garonne)
Catala d'Oc, 44 Chemin Arènes, 31130 Balma.
T. 0561365139.   042251
Palmada, J., 44 Chemin Arènes, 31130 Balma.
T. 0561243727.   042252

Balsièges (Lozère)
Jeantet, Jean-Jacques, Le Choizal, 48000 Balsièges.
T. 0466470464. - Paint / Furn / Rel -   042253

Balzac (Charente)
Menier, Laurent, 16430 Balzac. T. 0545247380. 042254

Bandol (Var)
Chastagnier, Bernard, Rue Toesca, 83150 Bandol.
T. 0494323569.   042255
Dumaine-Lafare, 22 Rue Docteur-Louis-Marçon, 83150
Bandol. T. 0494294337.   042256

Bar-le-Duc (Meuse)
Au Passé Composé Mangin, 46 Rue Jean-Jacques-
Rousseau, 55000 Bar-le-Duc. T. 0329792640. - Ant /
Lights -   042257
Chodorge, Jean-Louis, 16 Pl Saint-Pierre, 55000 Bar-le-
Duc. T. 0329450799, Fax 0329771672. - Ant - 042258
Galerie Saint-Pierre, 10 Pl Saint-Pierre, 55000 Bar-le-
Duc. T. 0329761458. - Ant -   042259
Hamard, Annette, 2 Rue Moulotte, 55000 Bar-le-Duc.
T. 0329794396. - Ant / Furn -   042260
Troc 55, Rue Bradfer, 55000 Bar-le-Duc.
T. 0329794699. - Ant -   042261

Barbezieux-Saint-Hilaire (Charente)
Merlet, 22 Rue Elie-Vinet, 16300 Barbezieux-Saint-Hi-
laire. T. 0545782956.   042262

Barbizon (Seine-et-Marne)
Brocante de Barbizon, 59 Grande Rue, 77630 Barbizon.
T. 0360662796, Fax 0360664391.   042263
Galerie du Musée, 83 Grande Rue, 77630 Barbizon.
T. 0360662691.   042264
Société La Grange, 8 Rue 23-Août, 77630 Barbizon.
T. 0360664532.   042265
Temps Passé Temps Présent, 44 Grande Rue, 77630
Barbizon. T. 0360664121.   042266

Barcelonette (Alpes-de-Haute-Provence)
Morel, Guy, Rue Commandant-Car, 04400 Barcelonette.
T. 0492810212. - Ant -   042267

Barcelonne-du-Gers (Gers)
Labrouche, Sabine, 13 Rue Pénitents, 32720 Barce-
lonne-du-Gers. T. 0562094056.   042268

Barentin (Seine-Maritime)
Compagnon, Franck, Centre Commercial Mesnil-Roux,
76360 Barentin. T. 0235927610.   042269

Barfleur (Manche)
Boisard, Pierre, 12 Rue Saint-Nicolas, 50760 Barfleur.
T. 0233231214. - Paint / Furn / China / Sculp /
Cur -   042270

Barjac (Gard)
Foire aux Antiquités, Pl Charles-Guynet, 30430 Barjac.
T. 0466245396.   042271

Tassy, Philippe, Mas Jurande, 30430 Barjac.
T. 0466245581.   042272

Barjols (Var)
Quoi de Neuf, 8bis Pl Capit-Vincens, 83670 Barjols.
T. 0494770245.   042273

Barneville-Carteret (Manche)
Antiquités Carteret, 1 Av République, 50270 Barneville-
Carteret. T. 0233529606.   042274
Calèche, 22 Rue Guillaume-le-Conquérant, 50270 Bar-
neville-Carteret. T. 0233533384. - Furn / Cur -   042275

Bartenheim (Haut-Rhin)
Moebel Angèle, 7 Rue Landes, 68870 Bartenheim.
T. 0389683118. - Furn -   042276

Bastelicaccia (Corse)
Arrighi, Mascarone, 20129 Bastelicaccia.
T. 0495200856, Fax 0495238105. - Furn -   042277

Bastia (Corse)
Héritage, Av Libération-Lupino, 20600 Bastia.
T. 0495334651.   042278
Rouif, 47 Blvd Général-Graziani, 20200 Bastia.
T. 0495314352.   042279
Taccola, Claude, 15 Rue Napoléon, 20200 Bastia.
T. 0495315462. - Paint / Furn / Cur -   042280

Bastide-Clairence (Pyrénées-Atlantiques)
Grenier de Labastide Clairence, Rue Notre-Dame, 64240
Bastide-Clairence. T. 0559294770. - Ant / Paint /
Furn -   042281

Battenheim (Haut-Rhin)
Neunlist, André, 12 Rue Prés, 68390 Battenheim.
T. 0389576688. - Furn / Instr / Cur -   042282

Baud (Morbihan)
Mouza, Alain, Parcpin, 56150 Baud. T. 0297391254.
- Ant -   042283
Poulain, Emile, Rte Locminé, 56150 Baud.
T. 0297510133. - Ant / Dec -   042284

Baudrières (Saône-et-Loire)
Guillarme Antiquités, Boulay, 71370 Baudrières.
T. 0385473165. - Ant -   042285

Baugy (Saône-et-Loire)
Cortier, Fernand, Champêtre, 71110 Baugy.
T. 0385251383. - Ant -   042286

Baume-les-Dames (Doubs)
Ferrut, Claudine, 2 Granges-Ravey, 25110 Baume-les-
Dames. T. 0381842599.   042287
Moeglin, Evelyne, 13 Rte Belfort, RN 83, 25110 Baume-
les-Dames. T. 0381840953. - Orient / Dec -   042288
Sthely, Joseph, Rue Myosotis, 25110 Baume-les-Da-
mes. T. 0381840958.   042289

Baume-les-Messieurs (Jura)
Durrenberger, J., Lieu-dit Abbaye, 39570 Baume-les-
Messieurs. T. 0384446180.   042290
Guyon, Albert, Rue Saint-Jean, 39570 Baume-les-Mes-
sieurs. T. 0384446087.   042291
Vuillemey-Broulard, Monique, Pl Mairie, 39570 Baume-
les-Messieurs. T. 0384446433.   042292

Bavilliers (Territoire-de-Belfort)
Bourquard, Claude, 60 Grande Rue, 90800 Bavilliers.
T. 0384218054.   042293

Bayeux (Calvados)
Ellen's, 34 Rue Saint-Jean, 14400 Bayeux.
T. 0231923123.   042294
Lecaudey, Charles, 73 Rue Saint-Malo, 14400 Bayeux.
T. 0231920705.   042295
Leyreloup, Jean, 33 Rue Saint-Laurent, 14400 Bayeux.
T. 0231928097.   042296
Métais, Jeanne, 38 Rue Bouchers, 14400 Bayeux.
T. 0231920473.   042297
Naphtaline, 16 Pl Parvis-Notre-Dame, 14400 Bayeux.
T. 0231215003.   042298
Riboulet, Marie-France, 11 Pl Charles-de-Gaulle, 14400
Bayeux. T. 0231215436.   042299

Vasseur, Michel, 8 Rue Cuisiniers, 14400 Bayeux.
T. 0231225380.   042300

Bayonne (Pyrénées-Atlantiques)
Bayonne Brocante, 4 Rue Sainte-Catherine, 64100
Bayonne. T. 0559551534. - Ant -   042301
Fouineuse, 30 Av Louis-de-Foix, 64100 Bayonne.
T. 0559556063. - Ant -   042302
Grollemund, Michel, 5 Rue Abesque, 64100 Bayonne.
T. 0559591601. - Ant -   042303
Haran, Marc, 24 Rue Faures, 64100 Bayonne.
T. 0559256906. - Ant -   042304
Hourcadette, Pierre, 8 Rue Gramont, 64100 Bayonne.
T. 0559593598. - Ant / Furn / Mil -   042305
International Décoration, 5 Rue Luc, 64100 Bayonne.
T. 0559594946. - Ant -   042306
Jimenez, 11 Av Louis-de-Foix, 64100 Bayonne.
T. 0559554191. - Ant -   042307
Klein, Dominique, 12 Rue Faures, 64100 Bayonne.
T. 0559590076. - Ant -   042308
Lange Antiquités, 5 Pl Monseigneur-Vansteenberghe,
64100 Bayonne. T. 0559254242. - Ant -   042309
Napoléon, 25 Av Capit-Resplandy, 64100 Bayonne.
T. 0559597380. - Ant -   042310
Puzo, Christian, 18 Rue Faures, 64100 Bayonne.
T. 0559590076. - Ant -   042311
Vecchy, Philippe de, 10 Blvd Jean-d'Amou, 64100
Bayonne. T. 0559552964. - Ant -   042312
Yveline Charlett, 38 Blvd Alsace-Lorraine, 64100
Bayonne. T. 0559555562. - Ant -   042313

Bazainville (Yvelines)
Lavoisier, 1 Rte Tacoigneuls, 78550 Bazainville.
T. 0134877432.   042314
Quitard, Pierre, 46 Rte de Paris, 78550 Bazainville.
T. 0134876188, Fax 0134876322. - Ant / Furn / Sculp /
Dec / Cur -   042315

Bazincourt-sur-Epte (Eure)
Jakubowicz, Le Plateau, 27140 Bazincourt-sur-Epte.
T. 0232555476, Fax 0232271012.   042316

Bazoches-sur-Guyonne (Yvelines)
Leca, Rosemania, Houjarray, 78490 Bazoches-sur-
Guyonne. T. 0134860439.   042317

Beaucé (Ille-et-Vilaine)
Angenard, Pierre, La Fumerais, 35133 Beaucé.
T. 0299993563.   042318

Beauchamps (Manche)
Bouillet, Philippe, 2 Rue Bois, 50320 Beauchamps.
T. 0233613979.   042319

Beaucouzé (Maine-et-Loire)
Antic'Eres, Haie du Moulin, 49070 Beaucouzé.
T. 41489898.   042320

Beaufort-en-Vallée (Maine-et-Loire)
Desteve, Paulette, 6 Rue Gare, 49250 Beaufort-en-Val-
lée. T. 41803259.   042321

Beaulieu (Haute-Loire)
Longuet, Bernard, Mariol, 43800 Beaulieu.
T. 0471081291.   042322

Beaulieu-sur-Mer (Alpes-Maritimes)
Androt, Georges, 50 Blvd Général-Leclerc, 06310 Beau-
lieu-sur-Mer. T. 0493010117.   042323
Androt, Pierre, 31 Blvd Gén Leclerc, 06310 Beaulieu-
sur-Mer. T. 0493010356. - Ant -   042324
Conil, Monique, 20 Av Blondelle, 06310 Beaulieu-sur-
Mer. T. 0493016248.   042325
Kat Gilles, 16 Blvd Mar Joffre, 06310 Beaulieu-sur-Mer.
Fax 93010097. - Ant -   042326
Laugier, Jacques, 1 Rue Paul Doumer, 06310 Beaulieu-
sur-Mer. T. 0493011652. - Ant / Paint / Furn - 042327
Masi, Paul, 23 Blvd du Général-Leclerc, 06310 Beau-
lieu-sur-Mer. T. 0493010079. - Ant / Furn / China /
Sculp -   042328
Renard, Adélaïde, 32 Blvd Gén Leclerc, 06310 Beaulieu-
sur-Mer. T. 0493011817. - Ant / Paint / Furn /
China -   042329
Renard, Serge, 2 Rue Paul Doumer, 06310 Beaulieu-
sur-Mer. T. 0493011810. - Furn / Orient / Tex - 042330

Technique et Décor, 50 Blvd Général-Leclerc, 06310 Beaulieu-sur-Mer. T. 0493011094. *042331*

Beaumont (Puy-de-Dôme)
Baptissard, Christiane, Rte Boisséjour, 63110 Beaumont. T. 0473267810. - Ant - *042332*
Coup de Coeur, 43 Rue du-Mont-Doré, 63110 Beaumont. T. 0473269913. *042333*

Beaumont (Vienne)
Au Petit Bonheur, 66 Rte Nationale 10, 86490 Beaumont. T. 0549855313. - Ant - *042334*
Benoît, Jean-Loup, 12 Rue Perrière, 86490 Beaumont. T. 0549855059. - Ant / Sculp / Mil - *042335*

Beaumont-en-Auge (Calvados)
Antiquités de Beaumont, 10 Pl Marché, 14950 Beaumont-en-Auge. T. 0231648645. *042336*

Beaumont-la-Ronce (Indre-et-Loire)
Bachet, Joël, Rue Jacques-Chouinard, 37360 Beaumont-la-Ronce. T. 0547244653. *042337*

Beaumont-le-Roger (Eure)
Varigault, Annie, 93 Rue Saint-Nicolas, 27170 Beaumont-le-Roger. T. 0232446336. *042338*

Beaumont-sur-Sarthe (Sarthe)
Bienvenu Meuble, 1 Pl Dufour, 72170 Beaumont-sur-Sarthe. T. 0243970040, Fax 0243339311.
- Furn - *042339*
Tison, Jacky, Mareschè RN 138, 72170 Beaumont-sur-Sarthe. T. 0243970513. - Ant / Furn - *042340*

Beaune (Côte-d'Or)
Ancienne Guillemin, 24 Pl Carnot, Passage Sainte-Hélène, 21200 Beaune. T. 0380227553.
- Graph - *042341*
Berger, 10 Pl de la Halle, 21200 Beaune. T. 0380220979, Fax 0380240528. - Ant / Furn - *042342*
Billard, Michel, 7 Chemin Barbizottes, 21200 Beaune. T. 0380247885. *042343*
Boutique Antiquités, 18 Rue Maufoux, 21200 Beaune. T. 0380229618. *042344*
Chouet-Darbois, Claude, 8bis Rue Vérottes, 21200 Beaune. T. 0380221804. *042345*
Demouron, Rémy, 30 Rue Cîteaux, 21200 Beaune. T. 0380241850. *042346*
Dumas, François, 91 Rue Fbg-Saint-Nicolas, 21200 Beaune. T. 0380224107. *042347*
Duvillard, André, Gigny, 21200 Beaune. T. 0380223902. *042348*
Duvillard, Guy, 10 Rue Murailles Charrières, 21200 Beaune. T. 0380246933. *042349*
Falce, Philippe, 18 Rte Pommard, 21200 Beaune. T. 0380225428. *042350*
Forey, Jean-Michel, 73 Rte Vignolles, 21200 Beaune. T. 0380225812. - Paint / Furn / Cur / Mod / Music - *042351*
Fourmond, 143 Rte Dijon, 21200 Beaune. T. 0380220052. *042352*
Gaudillat, Michel, Rue Motte-Gigny, 21200 Beaune. T. 0380246121. *042353*
Girard, Jean-Luc, 15 Rue Poterne, 21200 Beaune. T. 0380241754, Fax 0380249177. - Dec - *042354*
Heitzmann, Alain, Rte Challanges, Lot Epinotte-et-Champagne, 21200 Beaune. T. 0380240224. *042355*
Heitzmann Neuville, Daniel, Chemin Barbizottes, 21200 Beaune. T. 0380240249. *042356*
Javouhey, Patrick, 21 Blvd Saint-Jacques, 21200 Beaune. T. 0380227677, Fax 0380222005. *042357*
Krukly, Daniel, 1 Rue Esdouhard, 21200 Beaune. T. 0380227138. *042358*
Lachaux, Jean-Pierre, 37 Rue Vignolles, 21200 Beaune. T. 0380226204. *042359*
Lacote, Andrea-Maria, 6 Pl Fleury, 21200 Beaune. T. 0380226853. *042360*
Marie-Pierre Antiquités, 16 Av République, 21200 Beaune. T. 0380240939. - Paint / Furn / Cur - *042361*
Matériaux d'Autrefois, 88 Rue Fbg-Saint-Nicolas, 21200 Beaune. T. 0380241631. - Furn / Dec / Cur - *042362*
Naudin, Michel, 17 Rue Stand, 21200 Beaune. T. 0380221780. *042363*

Nordera, Bruno, 12 Rue Docteur-Tassin, 21200 Beaune. T. 0380224728. *042364*
Pusset, Jean-Jacques, 88 Rue Fbg-Saint-Nicolas, 21200 Beaune. T. 0380240292. *042365*
Rol, Alain, 166 Rte Dijon, 21200 Beaune. T. 0380223218. *042366*
Roux, Philippe, 3 Chemin Barbizottes, 21200 Beaune. T. 0380220727. *042367*
Ryaux, François, 21 Blvd Saint-Jacques, 21200 Beaune. T. 0380227650. - Paint / Furn / Sculp / Draw - *042368*
Sécula, Eric, 8bis Rte Seurre, 21200 Beaune. T. 0380246201. *042369*
Sécula, François, 17 Rue Murailles-Charrières, 21200 Beaune. T. 0380223339. *042370*
Sécula, Gilles, 36bis Rue Vignolles, 21200 Beaune. T. 0380241464. *042371*
Sécula, Henri, 161 Rte Dijon, 21200 Beaune. T. 0380246945. *042372*
Sécula, Jacky, 41 Rue Docteur-Tassin, 21200 Beaune. T. 0380241758. *042373*
Sécula, Raymond, 22 Chemin La-Champagne, 21200 Beaune. T. 0380247036. *042374*
Sécula, Rodolphe, 41 Rue Docteur-Tassin, 21200 Beaune. T. 07530733. *042375*
Sécula, Yves, 3 Rue Cîteaux, 21200 Beaune. T. 0380247683. *042376*
Sobar, 3 Rue Victor-Millot, 21200 Beaune. T. 0380246627. *042377*
Stéphan, Henri, Rue Vignolles, 21200 Beaune. T. 0380221451. *042378*
Stéphan, Jean-Marc, Rte Verdun, 21200 Beaune. T. 0380222756. *042379*
Tremeaux, Claude, 46 Rte Challanges, 21200 Beaune. T. 0380246975, Fax 0380249048. - Furn / Dec / Cur - *042380*
Tri'Antique, 3 Av République, 21200 Beaune. T. 0380242090, Fax 0380242088. *042381*
Trocaz, Michel, 15 Rue Cîteaux, 21200 Beaune. T. 0380226246. *042382*
Village des Antiquaires, 21 Blvd Saint-Jacques, 21200 Beaune. T. 0380226130. *042383*
Voyemant, Alain, 26 Rue Esdouhard, 21200 Beaune. T. 0380222439. - Furn / Cur - *042384*
Windsor, 5 Rue Cîteaux, 21200 Beaune. T. 0380240925. *042385*

Beaupréau (Maine-et-Loire)
Grimault, Jean-Jacques, Rue Fbg-Gourdon, 49600 Beaupréau. T. 41636770. *042386*

Beaupuy (Lot-et-Garonne)
Pauquet, René, Bourg, 47200 Beaupuy. T. 0553642148. *042387*

Beausoleil (Alpes-Maritimes)
Antiquités, 16 Blvd de la République, 06240 Beausoleil. T. 0493783868. - Ant / Paint / Furn / Cur - *042388*

Beautiran (Gironde)
Atelier du Rostu, Le Couloumey, 14 Rte Landes, 33640 Beautiran. T. 0556675351. - Fra / Glass - *042389*

Beauvais (Oise)
Brocastel, 306 Rte Nationale, 60000 Beauvais. T. 0344842384. - Ant - *042390*
Galerie Mur Antik, 84 Rue Amiens, 60000 Beauvais. T. 0344056555. - Ant / Cur - *042391*
Gorostarzu, Marie-Odile de, 40 Rue de la Madeleine, 60000 Beauvais. T. 0344455383. - Ant - *042392*
Le Roy, Patrick, 2 Rue Guillotin, 60000 Beauvais. T. 0344517543. - Ant - *042393*
Leblond-Magnier, Jacqueline, 55 Rue Saint-Pierre, 60000 Beauvais. T. 0344486981. - Ant - *042394*

Beauvoir-sur-Mer (Vendée)
Régnier, La Maladrie, 85230 Beauvoir-sur-Mer. T. 0251687292. *042395*

Beauzelle (Haute-Garonne)
Lagrange, André, ZI Garossos, 31700 Beauzelle. T. 0561427165. *042396*

Beblenheim (Haut-Rhin)
Klein, Stéfan, 4 Rue Raisins, 68980 Beblenheim. T. 0389490542. *042397*

Bègles (Gironde)
Trocante, 530 Rte Toulouse, 33130 Bègles. T. 0556874181. *042398*

Belabre (Indre)
Chatenet, Jacky, Les Chirons, 36370 Belabre. T. 0254376034. *042399*

Bélesta (Ariège)
Boer, Françoise de, Prince, 09300 Bélesta. T. 0561016040. *042400*

Belfort (Territoire-de-Belfort)
Anthéaume, Fabrice, 17 Rue Hanoï, 90000 Belfort. T. 0384218394. *042401*
Antiquités L'Echoppe, 33 Fbg Ancêtres, 90000 Belfort. T. 0384227246. *042402*
Aux Remparts, 10 Pl Grande-Fontaine, 90000 Belfort. T. 0384218381. *042403*
Cellier, Jean-Pierre, Pl de l'Arsenal, 90000 Belfort. T. 0384281146. *042404*
Grenier au Relais, Pl Grande-Fontaine, 90000 Belfort. T. 0384281756, Fax 0384281756. *042405*
Logistyl, 12 Pl Grande-Fontaine, 90000 Belfort. T. 0384288581. *042406*

Belfort-du-Quercy (Lot)
André Antiquités, Pech Prunel, 46230 Belfort-du-Quercy. T. 0565317079. *042407*

Belgeard (Mayenne)
Pichard Brocante, L'Orerie, 53440 Belgeard. T. 0243044239. - Ant / Furn - *042408*

Belgentier (Var)
Valensi, Gilbert, RN 554, 83210 Belgentier. T. 0494489254. *042409*

Belle-Isle-en-Terre (Côtes-d'Armor)
Crichen, Jean-Yves, 17 Rue Guic, 22810 Belle-Isle-en-Terre. T. 0296433317. *042410*

Bellegarde (Gard)
Dommanget, Jean-Pierre, 22 Rte Beaucaire, 30127 Bellegarde. T. 0466016057, Fax 0466016777. *042411*

Bellegarde-en-Marche (Creuse)
Brocante Service, Rte Aubusson, 23190 Bellegarde-en-Marche. T. 0555676312. - Ant - *042412*

Bellême (Orne)
Baumann, Joël, 1 Rue Paris, 61130 Bellême. T. 0233736850. - Ant - *042413*
Gravures Anciennes, 2 Rue Eglise, 61130 Bellême. T. 0233832104. - Ant - *042414*

Bellevesvre (Saône-et-Loire)
Linsolas-Chaux, Bernard, Rte Torpes, 71270 Bellevesvre. T. 0385723591. - Ant - *042415*

Belleville-sur-Saône (Rhône)
Espalungue d'Arros, Pierre d', 24 Rue Nationale, 69220 Belleville-sur-Saône. T. 0474660734. - Ant - *042416*

Belmesnil (Seine-Maritime)
Desbuissons, Hubert, Rue Mer, 76590 Belmesnil. T. 0235832184. *042417*

Benfeld (Bas-Rhin)
Antic Art Galerie, 4 Av Gare, 67230 Benfeld. T. 0388743178. *042418*
Antiquités de la Tour, 4 Av Gare, 67230 Benfeld. T. 0388741527. *042419*
Arbalète, Village des Antiquaires, 67230 Benfeld. T. 0388747879. *042420*
Charles, Gérard, Village des Antiquaires, 67230 Benfeld. T. 0388742754, Fax 0388740264. *042421*
Chemouni, Sam, Village des Antiquaires, 67230 Benfeld. T. 0388741087. *042422*
Dambron, Arlette, 4 Av Gare, 67230 Benfeld. T. 0388741377. *042423*
Décors, Régine, Village des Antiquaires, 67230 Benfeld. T. 0388316488. - Ant - *042424*
Entz, Ginette, Village des Antiquaires, 67230 Benfeld. T. 0388747272. *042425*
Ghazarian, Alain, 4 Av Gare, 67230 Benfeld. T. 0388744716. *042426*

Quartefeuille, 4 Av Gare, 67230 Benfeld.
T. 0388741307. 042427
Sieso, Laurent, 4 Av Gare, 67230 Benfeld.
T. 0388744972. 042428
Village des Antiquaires, 4 Av Gare, 67230 Benfeld.
T. 0388747856. 042429
Wrublewski, Yann, 4 Av Gare, 67230 Benfeld.
T. 0388742887. 042430

Bennecourt (Yvelines)
Besch, Gérard, 15 Rue La-Roche-Guyon, 78270 Benne-
court. T. 0130930149. 042431

Bénodet (Finistère)
Bothorel, Yves, Moulin du Crann, 29950 Bénodet.
T. 0298570409. - Ant - 042432
Lasserre-du-Rozel, Gérard, 29 Av de l'Odet, 29950 Bé-
nodet. T. 0298570409. - Ant / Paint / Furn - 042433
Meneyer, 52 Av Plage, 29950 Bénodet. T. 0298571197.
- Ant / Paint / Furn / Cur - 042434

Bergerac (Dordogne)
Au Prince du Périgord, 70 Av Paul-Painlevé, 24100 Ber-
gerac. T. 0553588455. 042435
Au Vieux Bergerac, 4 Rue Fontaines, 24100 Bergerac.
T. 0553631639. 042436
Au Vieux Grenier, 8 Rue Professor-Pozzi, 24100 Berge-
rac. T. 0553242861. 042437
Doumenjou-Larroque, Isabelle, 9 Rue Albret, 24100 Ber-
gerac. T. 0553270080. 042438
Dupont, Lucienne, 24 Pl Gambetta, 24100 Bergerac.
T. 0553572126. 042439
Joubert du Cellier, François, Bridet, 24100 Bergerac.
T. 0553272934. 042440
Moreau-Guionneau, Ginette, 22 Rue Saint-James,
24100 Bergerac. T. 0553577838. 042441
Pomme de Pin, 9 Rue Fontaines, 24100 Bergerac.
T. 0553579158. - Furn - 042442

Bergnicourt (Ardennes)
Sabathier-Habrial, Anne-Armelie, 3 Rue Pont-Royal,
08290 Bergnicourt. T. 0324389168. - Ant - 042443

Bernaville (Somme)
Grange, 40 Rte Nationale, 80370 Bernaville.
T. 0322326951. - Ant - 042444

Bernay (Eure)
Broc Shop, 24 Rue Gaston-Folloppe, 27300 Bernay.
T. 0232435180. 042445
Charrette, 15 Rue Gaston-Folloppe, 27300 Bernay.
T. 0232430547. 042446
Chéron, Henry, 34 Rue Charentonne, 27300 Bernay.
T. 0232430894. - Furn / Cur - 042447
Chéron, Henry, 25 Rue Gaston-Folloppe, 27300 Bernay.
T. 0232458434. - Furn / Cur - 042448
Pampille Import, 11 Rue Gaston-Folloppe, 27300 Ber-
nay. T. 0232433271. 042449
Papin, Patrice, 28 Rue Gaston-Folloppe, 27300 Bernay.
T. 0232443764. 042450
Perry-Higgins, Victoria, 5 Rue Gaston-Folloppe, 27300
Bernay. T. 0232440510, Fax 0232440521. 042451

Bernot (Aisne)
Deville, Bernard, 6 Rue Lambert, 02160 Bernot.
T. 0323097817. - Ant / Sculp - 042452

Besançon (Doubs)
Alloccasion, 27 Blvd Léon-Blum, 25000 Besançon.
T. 0381888855. 042453
Au Bonheur du Jour, 7 Rue Gambetta, 25000 Besançon.
T. 0381822759. 042454
Bourgeois, Philippe, 13 Rue République, 25000 Besan-
çon. T. 0381810996. - Paint / Furn / Cur - 042455
Certelli, 98 Rue Dôle, 25000 Besançon. T. 0381515110.
- Paint / Furn / Cur - 042456
Curiosités, 12 Rue Morand, 25000 Besançon.
T. 0381812925. 042457
Debourdeau, Jacqueline, 126 Grande Rue, 25000 Be-
sançon. T. 0381830529. 042458
Galerie Ambre, 4 Pl Pasteur, 25000 Besançon.
T. 0381810373. 042459
Gizard, Antoine, 26 Rue 7ème-Armée-Americaine,
25000 Besançon. T. 0381413333. 042460

Gruillot, Marie-Françoise, 6 Rue Boucheries, 25000 Be-
sançon. T. 0381814587. 042461
Koeller, Jean-Pierre, 184 Rue Dôle, 25000 Besançon.
T. 0381529817. 042462
Koeller, Louis, 3 et 5 Rte Levier, 25720 Beure Besançon.
T. 0381526061. - Paint / Furn / Lights / Instr / Mil /
Glass / Cur / Toys - 042463
Leblond, Gérard, 4 Rue Porteau, 25000 Besançon.
T. 0381810888. 042464
Légende des Siècles, 13 Rue République, 25000 Besan-
çon. T. 0381810996. 042465
Mathieu-Gizard, 1 Rue 7ème-Armée-Americaine, 25000
Besançon. T. 0381811670. 042466
Mathieu, Philippe, 26 Rue 7ème-Armée-Americaine,
25000 Besançon. T. 0381517575. - Paint / Furn / Dec /
Cur - 042467
Merchat, Gérard, 5 Quai Veil-Picard, 25000 Besançon.
T. 0381811640. - Jew - 042468
Meubles d'Autrefois, 83 Rue Granges, 25000 Besançon.
T. 0381833570. - Furn - 042469
Monnier, 31 Rue Préfecture, 25000 Besançon.
T. 0381835187. 042470
Old England, 23 Rue Repos, 25000 Besançon.
T. 0381801078. - Furn - 042471
Village des Antiquaires, 1 Rue 7ème-Armée-Americaine,
25000 Besançon. T. 0381812472. 042472
Villermin, Daniel, 14 Rue Dôle, 25000 Besançon.
T. 0381811207. 042473
Zock, Hazem, 14 Rue Dôle, 25000 Besançon.
T. 0381834193. 042474

Bessan (Hérault)
Fulcrand, R., Domaine de La Valmale, 34550 Bessan.
T. 0467774102/04. 042475

Bessèges (Gard)
Cachemire, 38 Rue République, 30160 Bessèges.
T. 0466252336. 042476

Bessey-lès-Cîteaux (Côte-d'Or)
Charlot, Jack, 13 Rue Amont, 21110 Bessey-lès-
Cîteaux. T. 0380297580. 042477
Schoumer, Pascal, 1 Rue Paquier, 21110 Bessey-lès-
Cîteaux. T. 0380297937. - Ant / Furn - 042478
Stéphan, René, Rte Izeure, 21110 Bessey-lès-Cîteaux.
T. 0380297032. 042479

Bétheny (Marne)
Salle des Ventes de Bétheny, 34 Voie Romaine, 51450
Bétheny. T. 0326022458. - Ant - 042481

Bethoncourt (Doubs)
Sulis, Giancarlo, 8 Rue Léon-Contejean, 25200 Bethon-
court. T. 0381973282. 042482

Béthune (Pas-de-Calais)
Bouretz, 13 Rue Lille, 62400 Béthune. T. 0321572261,
Fax 0321566006. - Furn - 042483
Taranowski, Grégoire, 448 Av Pont-des-Dames, 62400
Béthune. T. 0321573594. 042484

Betton (Ille-et-Vilaine)
Hubert, Christian, 13 Rue Mont-Saint-Michel, 35830
Betton. T. 0299557682. 042485

Beure (Doubs)
Koeller, Frédéric, 11 Rue République, 25720 Beure.
T. 0381410543. 042486

Beuzeville (Eure)
Chiffonnier d'Art, 16 Pl Général-Leclerc, 27210 Beuze-
ville. T. 0232577695. 042487
Eglantine, 124 Pl Général-Leclerc, 27210 Beuzeville.
T. 0232577646. 042488
Hurson-Darduin, Jean-Louis, 12 Rue Louis-Gillain,
27210 Beuzeville. T. 0232425920. 042489
Vaugeois, Gérard, 110 Pl Général-Leclerc, 27210 Beu-
zeville. T. 0232573929. 042490

Beveuge (Haute-Saône)
Ferme du Château, Rte Villers-la-Ville, 70110 Beveuge.
T. 0384205253. 042491

Bévillers (Nord)
Griffart, Jean-Louis, 7 Rue Boussières, 59217 Bévillers.
T. 0327854171. - Ant - 042492

Guidez, Pierre, 7 Rue Boussières, 59217 Bévillers.
T. 0327760227. - Ant - 042493

Bézannes-lès-Reims (Marne)
Pingeon, Christian, 17 Rue Pressoir, 51430 Bézannes-
lès-Reims. T. 0326364242, Fax 0326498377.
- Dec - 042494

Bèze (Côte-d'Or)
Montandon, Jean-Louis, Rue Canes, 21310 Bèze.
T. 0380753206. - Furn - 042495

Béziers (Hérault)
Ascencio, Robert, 5 Av Pierre-de-Coubertin, 34500 Bé-
ziers. T. 0467280604. - Furn - 042496
Au Petit Noyer, 56 Rue Casimir-Péret, 34500 Béziers.
T. 0467490151. 042497
Aux Louis de France, 35 Av Jean-Moulin, 34500 Béziers.
T. 0467491354. 042498
Bonnin, Bernard, 18 Rue Debès, 34500 Béziers.
T. 0467491452. 042499
Bonnin, Christian, 52 Blvd Frédéric Mistral, 34500 Bé-
ziers. T. 0467283350, Fax 0467491010. - Ant / Furn /
China / Repr - 042500
Cadiac, Pradines-Le-Haut, Ancienne Rte Bédarieux,
34500 Béziers. T. 0467307871. 042501
Freitas, 58 Blvd Frédéric-Mistral, 34500 Béziers.
T. 0467281647. 042502
Galerie Mercure, 8 Pl Trois-Six, 34500 Béziers.
T. 0467493787. 042503
Gardes, Alice, 24 Rue Alsace, 34500 Béziers.
T. 0467310416. 042504
Gayraud, Dominique, 63 Av Georges Clémenceau,
34500 Béziers. T. 0467282046. - Ant - 042505
Gayraud, Jacques, 16 Rue Andoque, 34500 Béziers.
T. 0467491354. 042506
Guilhem, Jean-Pierre, 14 Rue du 4 Septembre, 34500
Béziers. T. 0467283405. - Jew - 042507
M.P.B.A., Les Bergeries, Rte Pézenas, 34500 Béziers.
T. 0467314613. 042508
Vigué, Jean-Luc, 48 Blvd Frédéric-Mistral, 34500 Bé-
ziers. T. 0467499931. 042509
Wilson, 17 Rue Giulio-Mattéoti, 34500 Béziers.
T. 0467621640. 042510

Biarritz (Pyrénées-Atlantiques)
Amigorena, Jean, 5 Rue Victor-Hugo, 64200 Biarritz.
T. 0559247390. - Ant - 042511
Athéna Antiquités, Villa Roche Ronde, 15 Av de l'Impéra-
trice, 64200 Biarritz. T. 0559249161. - Ant - 042512
Bakara Antiquités, 23 Rue Mazagran, 64200 Biarritz.
T. 0559220895, Fax 0559245331. - Ant - 042513
Blies, Pierre, 26 Rue Mazagran, 64200 Biarritz.
T. 0559247504. - Ant - 042514
Broc'Adour, 2 Rue Peyroloublih, 64200 Biarritz.
T. 0559247530. - Ant - 042515
Broc Troc, 23 Rue Mazagran, 64200 Biarritz.
T. 0559223463. - Ant - 042516
Cazenave, Edwina, 27 Rue Perpective-Côte-Basque,
64200 Biarritz. T. 0559240572. - Ant - 042517
Damais, Jean, 15 Pl Clemenceau, 64200 Biarritz.
T. 0559240150. - Ant / Paint / Furn / China / Dec / Jew /
Silv / Lights - 042518
Drouet, Fabrice, 8 Av Jaulerry, 64200 Biarritz.
T. 0559246455. - Ant / Paint - 042519
Fontan, 50 Av Maréchal-Foch, 64200 Biarritz.
T. 0559223170. - Ant - 042520
Galerie des Arceaux, 14 Av Edouard VII, 64200 Biarritz.
T. 0559220800. - Ant - 042521
Jeu de l'Oie, 10 Rue Louis-Barthou, 64200 Biarritz.
T. 0559245865. - Ant - 042522
Lasry, 3 Rue Victor-Hugo, 64200 Biarritz.
T. 0559245418, Fax 0559249074. - Ant - 042523
Macé, Maggy, 39 Av Marne, 64200 Biarritz.
T. 0559240715. - Ant - 042524
Majourau, Catherine, 2 Rue Peyroloublih, 64200 Biarritz.
T. 0559247172. - Ant - 042525
Reflets du Temps, 28 Av de Verdun, 64200 Biarritz.
T. 0559246160. - Ant - 042526
Schlaefli, Nine, 13 Rue Luis-Mariano, 64200 Biarritz.
T. 0559231843. - Ant - 042527
Trouvailles Malaterre, 4 Rue Peyroloublih, 64200 Biar-
ritz. T. 0559242672. - Ant / Cur - 042528

Vernière Antiquités, 4 Av de l'Impératrice, 64200 Biarritz. T. 0559246398. - Ant - 042529

Ydais, Annick, Passage du Plaza Av Edouard VII, 64200 Biarritz. T. 0559245228. - Ant - 042530

Bias (Lot-et-Garonne)
Dubois, Nicole, La Landette, 47300 Bias.
T. 0553702898. - Furn - 042531

Bidon (Ardèche)
Mirabel, Monique, Le Village, 07700 Bidon.
T. 0475043806. - Ant - 042532

Biécourt (Vosges)
Petit, Marcel, 564 Grande Rue, 88170 Biécourt.
T. 0329656447. 042533

Biéville-Quétiéville (Calvados)
Ile aux Antiquités, Cours Albert Manuel, Carr St-Jean-le-Lion-d'Or, RN 13, 14270 Biéville-Quétiéville.
T. 0231628320, Fax 0231628320. - Furn /
Cur - 042534

Bignoux (Vienne)
Maitre, Jean-Jacques, 8 Rue Grand-Champ, 86800 Bignoux. T. 0549610167. - Ant - 042535

Biguglia (Corse)
Tragulinu, U., Rte Ortale, 20600 Biguglia.
T. 0495330619. 042536

Billom (Puy-de-Dôme)
Corvinos, Pascal, 9 Rue Antoine-Moillier, 63160 Billom.
T. 0473689810. - Ant - 042537

Demazière, Sylviane, Rte Clermont, 63160 Billom.
T. 0473683903. - Ant / Furn - 042538

Favier, Pierre, 23 Rue Antoine-Moillier, 63160 Billom.
T. 0473689614. - Ant - 042539

Huser, Rose-Marie, 17 Rue Carnot, 63160 Billom.
T. 0473689291. - Ant - 042540

Lassalas, Claude, 2 Av de-la-Gare, 63160 Billom.
T. 0473689028. - Ant - 042541

Binic (Côtes-d'Armor)
Le Bergueleven, La Vallée, 22520 Binic. T. 0296733036,
Fax 0296733001. 042542

Binson-et-Orquigny (Marne)
Despesel, Jean, 4 Rue Blanche, 51700 Binson-et-Orquigny. T. 0326580372. 042543

Biot (Alpes-Maritimes)
Albatros, 1 Chemin Joseph-Durbec, Résidence Albatros, 06410 Biot. T. 0493656315. 042544

Antiquités du Vieux Biot, Chemin Neuf, 06410 Biot.
T. 0493651040. - Furn / Dec / Cur - 042545

Aux Vieilles Voutes, 4 Chemin des Roses, 06410 Biot.
T. 0493650077. - Ant / Furn / China / Cur - 042546

Manni, Jean-Pierre, 614 Rte La-Mer, 06410 Biot.
T. 0493650205, Fax 0493657025. 042547

Savreux, Marine, Chemin Combes, Quartier Saint-Grégoire, 06410 Biot. T. 0493651246. 042548

Biriatou (Pyrénées-Atlantiques)
Geldi Zaizte, Bourg, 64700 Biriatou. T. 0559202776.
- Ant - 042549

Bischoffsheim (Bas-Rhin)
Moor, Alain de, 1 Rue Principale, 67870 Bischoffsheim.
T. 0388502098. 042550

Bizanet (Aude)
Lion, Daniel, Rue Gare, 11200 Bizanet.
T. 0468451606. 042551

Blagnac (Haute-Garonne)
Rail Chimie, 17bis Rue Prosper-Ferradou, 31700 Blagnac. T. 0561714338. 042552

Rivière, Daniel, Chemin Pesayre, 31700 Blagnac.
T. 0561715029. 042553

Servettaz, Christian, 7 Chemin Barrieu, 31700 Blagnac.
T. 0561716441. - Paint / Furn / Cur - 042554

Blainville-sur-l'Eau (Meurthe-et-Moselle)
Remetter, Jean, 38 Rue Saint-Dominique, 54360 Blainville-sur-l'Eau. T. 0383757532. 042555

Blaise-sous-Arzillières (Marne)
Charbonnier, 14 Rue Basse, 51300 Blaise-sous-Arzillières. T. 0326742020. 042556

Blamont (Doubs)
Vacelet, Guy, 7bis Rue Neuve, 25310 Blamont.
T. 0381351665. 042557

Vacelet, Guy, 4 Imp Violettes, 25310 Blamont.
T. 0381351929. 042558

Blanzay (Vienne)
Bealu, Jean-Jacques, La Cotterie, 86400 Blanzay.
T. 0549873652, Fax 0549879283. - Ant - 042559

Blanzy (Saône-et-Loire)
Jacquelin, Pierre, 60 Rte de Macon, 71450 Blanzy.
T. 0385583572. - Ant / Furn - 042560

Jacquelin, Yvette, 60 Rte Mâcon, 71450 Blanzy.
T. 0385583572. - Ant - 042561

Lewandowski, Jean-Pierre, 4 Rte Bizots, 71450 Blanzy.
T. 0385680775. - Ant - 042562

Blaye (Gironde)
Pipat & Morier, 14 Cours Bacalan, 33390 Blaye.
T. 0557423321. 042563

Pipat & Morier, 9 Rue Premayac, 33390 Blaye.
T. 0557428384. 042564

Pipat & Morier, 22 Rue Neuve, 33390 Blaye.
T. 0557420001. - Ant - 042565

Blaymont (Lot-et-Garonne)
Merly Blaymont, Merly, 47470 Blaymont.
T. 0553954062. 042566

Blérancourt (Aisne)
Passé Simple, 3 Rue Sadi-Carnot, 02300 Blérancourt.
T. 0323397215. - Ant / Cur - 042567

Bléré (Indre-et-Loire)
Guillotin Frères, 5 Rue Jules-Boulet, 37150 Bléré.
T. 0547579206. 042568

Blois (Loir-et-Cher)
Antebellum, 12 Rue Saint-Lubin, 41000 Blois.
T. 0254783878. 042569

Antiquité Blésoise, 30 Quai Aristide-Briand, 41000 Blois.
T. 0254743862. - Ant / Furn - 042570

Barbat, 15 Rue Beauvoir, 41000 Blois.
T. 0254781929. 042571

Briau, Jacques, 11 Rue Prêche, 41000 Blois.
T. 0254746780. - Paint / Furn / Sculp / Cur - 042572

Langlois Tapisseries, 1 Rue Voûte-du-Château, 41000 Blois. T. 0254780443. - Tex - 042573

Léal, Eduardo, 14 Rue Bourg-Neuf, 41000 Blois.
T. 0254745376. 042574

Levaye, Patrick, Rue Chemonton, 41000 Blois.
T. 0254784429. - Ant - 042575

Malle aux Lutins, 33 All Pins, Village de l'Arrou, 41000 Blois. T. 0254439364. 042576

Nicko, Nicole, 32 Rue Saint-Lubin, 41000 Blois.
T. 0254781870. 042577

Pastor, Monique, 13 Rue Trois-Marchands, 41000 Blois.
T. 0254748146. 042578

Renaissance du Passé, 45 Rue Saint-Lubin, 41000 Blois. T. 0254742612. 042579

Blonville-sur-Mer (Calvados)
Grenier Antiquité Bar, 157 Av Michel-d'Ornano, 14910 Blonville-sur-Mer. T. 0231879483. 042580

Rohaut Delassus, Françoise, Ferme Lieu Bill, 14910 Blonville-sur-Mer. T. 0231879800. 042581

Blumeray (Haute-Marne)
Barbier, Antoine, Rte Humbercin, 52110 Blumeray.
T. 0325554506. 042582

Bobigny (Seine-Saint-Denis)
Faugère, Olivier, 57 Rue Anjou, 93000 Bobigny.
T. 0148304864. 042583

Bocé (Maine-et-Loire)
Bertho, Bernard, 1 Rue Eglise, 49150 Bocé.
T. 41827316. 042584

Boé (Lot-et-Garonne)
Capot, Franck, Corne, 47550 Boé. T. 0553683628.
- Paint / Furn / China / Toys - 042585

Boeil-Bezing (Pyrénées-Atlantiques)
Irrigaray, Bertrand, RD 937, 64320 Boeil-Bezing.
T. 0559532002. - Ant - 042586

Bogny-sur-Meuse (Ardennes)
Tout Occas, 4 Rue Vallée, 08120 Bogny-sur-Meuse.
T. 0324320920. - Ant - 042587

Weill, Etienne, 20 Rue Jourdes, 08120 Bogny-sur-Meuse. T. 0324321411. - Ant / Furn - 042588

Bois-Colombes (Hauts-de-Seine)
Au Fil des Ans, 5 Rue Victor-Hugo, 92270 Bois-Colombes. T. 0147843537. - Ant - 042589

Grout, Jacqueline, 5 Rue Victor-Hugo, 92270 Bois-Colombes. T. 0142422416. 042590

P'tite Boutique, 1 Pl République, 92270 Bois-Colombes.
T. 0147601767. 042591

Tandart, 7bis Rue Bourguignons, 92270 Bois-Colombes.
T. 0147815795. - Ant / Furn - 042592

Bois-Guillaume (Seine-Maritime)
Au Furet, 3771 Rte Neufchâtel, 76230 Bois-Guillaume.
T. 0235605858. 042593

Phippen, Guy, 3823 Rte Neufchâtel, 76230 Bois-Guillaume. T. 0235617799. 042594

Boisseron (Hérault)
Boisseron Antiquités, Rte Montpellier, 34160 Boisseron.
T. 0467865533. 042595

Grusenmeyer, Philippe, Av Folco-de-Baroncelli, 34160 Boisseron. T. 0467865533. 042596

Paralléles et Méridiens, 260 Av Folco-de-Baroncelli, 34160 Boisseron. T. 0467864120. 042597

Vache, Josian, 32 Av Frédéric-Mistral, 34160 Boisseron.
T. 0467865967. 042598

Bollène (Vaucluse)
Antiquités de la Tour, Rte Suze, 84500 Bollène.
T. 0490305700. - Ant - 042599

Armoire Amoureuse, Rte Pont-Saint-Esprit D 994, 84500 Bollène. T. 0490302393. - Ant - 042600

Vimont, Jacques, Rte Mondragon, 84500 Bollène.
T. 0490301668. - Ant - 042601

Bollwiller (Haut-Rhin)
Ackermann, Gilbert, 4 Rue Staffelfelden, 68540 Bollwiller. T. 0389481910. 042602

Bondues (Nord)
Coup de C'Eôr, 1043 Rte Nationale, 59910 Bondues.
T. 0320032984. - Ant - 042603

Décoration, 1294 Av Gén-de-Gaulle, 59910 Bondues.
T. 0320030854. - Ant - 042604

Flipo, Brigitte, 827 Av Gén-de-Gaulle, 59910 Bondues.
T. 0320467550. - Ant - 042605

Bonnard (Yonne)
Riva, Pascal da, 7 Rte Gare, 89400 Bonnard.
T. 0386732118. 042606

Bonne (Haute-Savoie)
Donche, Roland, 74380 Bonne. T. 0450392342. - Furn /
Cur - 042607

Ducret, Michel, Les Moulins, 74380 Bonne.
T. 0450392168. 042608

Bonneuil-Matours (Vienne)
Bertomeu, Christian, 11 Pl Commerce, 86210 Bonneuil-Matours. T. 0549853060. - Ant - 042609

Debois-Frogé, Solange, 20 Pl Commerce, 86210 Bonneuil-Matours. T. 0549852141. - Ant - 042610

Humarau, Claude, 21 Pl Commerce, 86210 Bonneuil-Matours. T. 0549852495. - Ant / Jew / Silv - 042611

Bonneval (Eure-et-Loir)
Charrier, Fabrice, 8bis Rue Bas-Eglise, 28800 Bonneval.
T. 0237475161. 042612

Bonnières-sur-Seine (Yvelines)
Ancienne Laiterie de Jeufosse, Angle RN 13 – RN 15 et A15, Sortie Bonnières Dir. Vernon, 78270 Bonnières-sur-Seine. T. 0130930772. - Ant - 042613

Bonnieux (Vaucluse)
Delpuech, Ch., 84480 Bonnieux. T. 0490758286. - Ant / Furn / Tex - 042614

Bons-en-Chablais (Haute-Savoie)
Lavy, Bernard, Rue Petit-Paris, Langin, 74890 Bons-en-Chablais. T. 0450361141, Fax 0450394311. 042615

Bonson (Loire)
Royet, Auguste, 34 Av Saint-Marcellin, 42160 Bonson. T. 0477556663. 042616

Bonvillers (Meurthe-et-Moselle)
Collignon, Daniel, 33 Rue Bonvillers, 54111 Bonvillers. T. 0382218766, Fax 0329854071. - Furn - 042617

Boos (Seine-Maritime)
Elie, Jean-François, 184 Rte Paris, 76520 Boos. T. 0235802298. 042618

Bordeaux (Gironde)
Acanthe, 44 Rue Bouffard, 33000 Bordeaux. T. 0556810023. 042619
Afrique-Asie, 23 Cité Lafon, 33300 Bordeaux. T. 0556500414. 042620
Afrique-Asie, 143 Rue Notre-Dame, 33300 Bordeaux. T. 0556444160. 042621
Aghailloff, 13bis Rue Notre-Dame, 33000 Bordeaux. T. 0556516044. 042622
Air du Temps, 87 Rue Notre-Dame, 33000 Bordeaux. T. 0556512991. 042623
Années Folles, 33 Rue Elie-Gintrac, 33800 Bordeaux. T. 0556313891. - Furn / China / Silv / Glass / Jew / Cur / Toys - 042624
Annie & Jacqueline, 94 Cours Maréchal-Juin, 33000 Bordeaux. T. 0556963644. - Furn / China / Silv - 042625
Antica, 16bis Rue A.-Maginot, 33200 Bordeaux. T. 0556172257. - Ant / Furn - 042626
Antiquaire des Chartrons, 77 Rue Notre-Dame, 33000 Bordeaux. T. 0556482044. 042627
Antiquité Notre-Dame, 61 Rue Notre-Dame, 33000 Bordeaux. T. 0556527934. 042628
Antiquités Bouffard, 25 Rue Bouffard, 33000 Bordeaux. T. 0556524296. 042629
Antiquités de l'Alhambra, 14 Rue Lachassaigne, 33000 Bordeaux. T. 0556982746. 042630
Antiquités Salon de Thé, 26 Rue Parlement-Sainte-Catherine, 33000 Bordeaux. T. 0556440634. 042631
Antiquités Sicard, 13 Rue Sicard, 33000 Bordeaux. T. 0556792543. 042632
Antiquités Village Notre-Dame, 61-67 Rue Notre-Dame, 33000 Bordeaux. T. 0556526613, Fax 0556527671. - Ant - 042633
Antiquités 1930-1950, 35bis Pl Pey-Berland, 33000 Bordeaux. T. 0556793547. 042634
Aquitaine Antiquités, 52 Rue Notre-Dame, 33000 Bordeaux. T. 0556814829. 042635
Arar, Florian, 12 Rue Bouffard, 33000 Bordeaux. T. 0556012244, Fax 0556443142. 042636
Armarine, 37 Rue Notre-Dame, 33000 Bordeaux. T. 0556012757. 042637
Art et Style d'Aquitaine, 78 Rue Notre-Dame, 33000 Bordeaux. T. 0556522069. 042638
Arts Primitifs Afrique Océanie, 17 Rue Notre-Dame, 33000 Bordeaux. T. 0556516163. 042639
Assour et Sumer, 58 Rue Bouffard, 33000 Bordeaux. T. 0556441233. 042640
Astruc, Stéphane & François-Xavier, 68 Rue Notre-Dame, 33000 Bordeaux. T. 0556813966. 042641
Atelier du Rostu, 7 Rue Cerf-Volant, 33000 Bordeaux. T. 0556519694. - Fra / Glass - 042642
Au Singe Bleu, 43 Rue Bouffard, 33000 Bordeaux. T. 0556442483, Fax 0556443459. 042643
Auparavant, 95 Rue Notre-Dame, 33000 Bordeaux. T. 0556012752. 042644
Autre Temps, 61 Rue Notre-Dame, 33000 Bordeaux. T. 0556526241. 042645
Bakélite, 35 Rue Faures, 33000 Bordeaux. T. 0556911123. 042646
Barraud, Mannick, 3 Rue Montbazon, 33000 Bordeaux. T. 0556813692. 042647
Belmar, Ange, 282 Av Thiers, 33100 Bordeaux. T. 0556403605. 042648
Bernard, Henri, 78 Rue Loup, 33000 Bordeaux. T. 0556445201. 042649
Besançon, Jacques, 2ter Rue Mably, 33000 Bordeaux. T. 0556816320. 042650
Bethmann, Jean de, 36 Rue Bouffard, 33000 Bordeaux. T. 0556813531. 042651
Bluette, Christian, 17 Rue Cornac, 33000 Bordeaux. T. 0556440266. 042652
Bluette, Christian, 9 Rue Sainte-Elisabeth-Cauderan, 33000 Bordeaux. T. 0556979499. 042653
Bonnaud and Co, 26 Quai Chartrons, 33000 Bordeaux. T. 0556813324. 042654
Bonnet, Marie-Louise, 129 Cours Argonne, 33000 Bordeaux. T. 0556911565. 042655
Boussaroque, Claudine, 69 Rue Croix-Blanche, 33000 Bordeaux. T. 0556481938. 042656
Boutique des Chartrons, 71 Rue Notre-Dame, 33000 Bordeaux. T. 0556816559. 042657
Brocantomanie, 27 Av Thiers, 33100 Bordeaux. T. 0556323560. - Furn / Cur - 042658
Camus, Jean, 5 Imp Sainte-Cadenne, 33000 Bordeaux. T. 0556927721. 042659
Cazaban, 60 Rte Cap-Ferret, Petit-Piquey, 33000 Bordeaux. T. 0556609534. 042660
Cittone, Michel, 48bis Rue Notre-Dame, 33000 Bordeaux. T. 0556790805. 042661
Court, Roger, 33 Rue Bouffard, 33000 Bordeaux. T. 0556813847. - Ant - 042662
Darrouzet, Paule, 60 Rue Remparts, 33000 Bordeaux. T. 0556446344. 042663
Dhelens, Jean-Bernard, 54 Rue Bouffard, 33000 Bordeaux. T. 0556520157. 042664
Drai, Simon, 48 Rue Notre-Dame, 33000 Bordeaux. T. 0556485322. 042665
Dubieilh, Josette, 72 Rue Notre-Dame, 33000 Bordeaux. T. 0556527856. - Furn / Cur - 042666
Dufrèche, Bertrand, 101 Rue Notre-Dame, 33000 Bordeaux. T. 0556449678. 042667
Ecume des Jours, 69 Rue Notre-Dame, 33000 Bordeaux. T. 0556523437. 042668
El Rastro, 21 Rue Bouffard, 33000 Bordeaux. T. 0556522447. 042669
Espace Temps Antiquités, 20 Rue Bouffard, 33000 Bordeaux. T. 0556511730. 042670
Field, Mary, 28 Cours Chapeau-Rouge, 33000 Bordeaux. T. 0556447609. - Furn - 042671
Flash, 96 Rue Amédée-Saint-Germain, 33800 Bordeaux. T. 0556911006. 042672
Galerie d'Art d'Asie, 10 Rue Remparts, 33000 Bordeaux. T. 0556817681. 042673
Galerie L'Horizon Chimérique, 34 Rue Bouffard, 33000 Bordeaux. T. 0556811256. 042674
Galerie La Boétie, 10 Rue La Boétie, 33000 Bordeaux. T. 0556815225. 042675
Galerie Noël, 29 Rue Bouffard, 33000 Bordeaux. T. 0556816182. - Ant / Paint - 042676
Galerie 1900-1930, 32 Rue Bouffard, 33000 Bordeaux. T. 0556792630. 042677
Galerie 73, 73 Rue Remparts, 33000 Bordeaux. T. 0556814528. 042678
Galinie, 29 Rue Cheverus, 33000 Bordeaux. T. 0556442046, Fax 0556810264. - Furn / Dec - 042679
Galinie, 20 Rue des Trois-Conils, 33000 Bordeaux. T. 0556442046, Fax 0556810264. - Furn / Dec - 042680
Garde, 55 Rue Remparts, 33000 Bordeaux. T. 0556440868. - Mil / Toys / Naut - 042681
Gouaux, Jean-Marc, 49 Rue Petit-Parc, 33200 Bordeaux. T. 0556420930. 042682
Guirriec, Pol-Hervé, 42 Rue Notre-Dame, 33000 Bordeaux. T. 0556811312. 042683
Hennichebra, Kader, 56 Rue Notre-Dame, 33000 Bordeaux. T. 0556440063. 042684
Héritage du Bon Vieux Temps, 197ter Rue Georges-Bonnac, 33000 Bordeaux. T. 0556969057. 042685
Hilber, Emmanuel, 10 Terrasse Front-du-Médoc, 33300 Bordeaux. T. 0556241856. 042686
Insolite, 46 Rue Bouffard, 33000 Bordeaux. T. 0556448558. 042687
Jourdain, Mildrède, 11 Rue Sicard, 33000 Bordeaux. T. 0556523146. 042688
Jullion, Christian, 75 Rue Notre-Dame, 33000 Bordeaux. T. 0556482178, Fax 0556513354. 042689
Kronbali, 143 Rue Notre-Dame, 33300 Bordeaux. T. 0556420930. - Orient / Eth - 042690
Labro, Jean-Pierre, 25 Rue Notre-Dame, 33000 Bordeaux. T. 0556793199. 042691
Lafitte, Denise, 26 Quai Chartrons, 33000 Bordeaux. T. 0556519487. 042692
Laügt, Dominique, 36 Rue Desbiey, 33000 Bordeaux. T. 0556514821. 042693
Lefrançois, F.J., 22 Rue Capdeville, 33000 Bordeaux. T. 0556819427. 042694
L.G. Antiquités, 23 Rue Notre-Dame, 33000 Bordeaux. T. 0556523135. 042695
Licorne, 62 Rue Bouffard, 33000 Bordeaux. T. 0556444349. 042696
Lubano, 101 Rue Fondaudège, 33000 Bordeaux. T. 0556441175. 042697
Mazure, Florence, 58 Rue Notre-Dame, 33000 Bordeaux. T. 0556444265. 042698
Meubles Métropole, 61 Rue Notre-Dame, 33000 Bordeaux. T. 0556516148. 042699
Michel, Marie-Claude, 143 Rue Fondaudège, 33000 Bordeaux. T. 0556011113. 042700
Montardy, Marie-Françoise de, 28 Rue Notre-Dame, 33000 Bordeaux. T. 0556790698. 042701
Nansouty, 224 Rue Bègles, 33800 Bordeaux. T. 0556917770. - Paint / Furn / China / Dec / Lights / Mil / Glass / Cur / Toys - 042702
Nom de la Rose, 54 Rue Notre-Dame, 33000 Bordeaux. T. 0556528831, Fax 0556790180. 042703
Or du Temps, 12 Rue Bouffard, 33000 Bordeaux. T. 0556448632. 042704
Passé Antérieur, 115 Rue Notre-Dame, 33000 Bordeaux. T. 0556791130. 042705
Passé au Présent, 3 Av Emile-Counord, 33300 Bordeaux. T. 0556792142. 042706
Passé Simple, 38 Rue Trois-Conils, 33000 Bordeaux. T. 0556480462. 042707
Passicousset, Robert, 35 Rue Bouffard, 33000 Bordeaux. T. 0556813453. - Ant / China - 042708
Patine du Temps, 61 Rue Notre-Dame, 33000 Bordeaux. T. 0556524984. 042709
Péron, François, 76 Rue Notre-Dame, 33000 Bordeaux. T. 0556525325. 042710
Petit Drouot, 39 Rue Remparts, 33000 Bordeaux. T. 0556810022. 042711
Pillot, Emile, 42 Rue Bouffard, 33000 Bordeaux. T. 0556524591. 042712
Pipat & Morier, 64 Rue Notre-Dame, 33000 Bordeaux. T. 0556512809. 042713
Poulard, Guy, 84 Rue Notre-Dame, 33000 Bordeaux. T. 0556525190. 042714
Pruilh, Michel, 23 Rue Bouffard, 33000 Bordeaux. T. 0556482679. 042715
Reflets d'Antan, 260 Cours Somme, 33800 Bordeaux. T. 0556922330. 042716
Roche, Stéphane, 2bis Rue Tourat, 33000 Bordeaux. T. 0556811720. - Paint - 042717
Sabot, Henri, 34 Rue Notre-Dame, 33000 Bordeaux. T. 0556441267. 042718
Salle des Ventes Libres, 29 Rue de Cheverus, 33000 Bordeaux. T. 0556442046. - Ant / Paint / Furn / China / Sculp / Dec / Fra / Lights / Instr / Toys - 042719
Saubot, Roger, 103 Rue Notre-Dame, 33000 Bordeaux. T. 0556517778. 042720
Surabaya, 11 Rue Bouffard, 33000 Bordeaux. T. 0556793164. 042721
Tanguy & Ass, 282 Av Thiers, 33100 Bordeaux. T. 0556329897, Fax 0556320236. 042722
Tanguy, Yves, Mégapole, 282 Av Thiers, 33100 Bordeaux. T. 0556326494, Fax 0556329960. - Furn - 042723
Taxila, 61 Rue Remparts, 33000 Bordeaux. T. 0556446001. - Furn / Orient / Eth - 042724
Thirion, Jean-Luc, 3 Rue Saint-Joseph, 33000 Bordeaux. T. 0556790345. - Furn / Cur / Naut - 042725
Tourny's, 3 Rue Huguerie, 33000 Bordeaux. T. 0556443477. - Naut - 042726
Trouvailles, 37 Cours Victor-Hugo, 33000 Bordeaux. T. 0556521692. 042727
Van Rycke, Evelyne, 25 Cours Martinique, 33000 Bordeaux. T. 0556815655. 042728

Venot, Régine, 3 Rue Notre-Dame, 33000 Bordeaux.
T. 0556529248. *042729*
Villa Vettii, 26 All Tourny, 33000 Bordeaux.
T. 0556790456. *042730*
Vuillier, Cécile, 77 Rue Saint-Joseph, 33000 Bordeaux.
T. 0556482971. - Paint / Fra - *042731*
Zaoui, Salem, 6 Rue Notre-Dame, 33000 Bordeaux.
T. 0556526196. *042732*
99, 99 Rue Notre-Dame, 33000 Bordeaux.
T. 0556011300. *042733*

Bordères-et-Lamensans (Landes)
Harté, Florent, Château de Marras, 40270 Bordères-et-
Lamensans. T. 0558454195. *042734*

Borgo (Corse)
Tudisco, Pascal, Les Chênes-Valrose, 20290 Borgo.
T. 0495307243. - Furn - *042735*

Bormes-les-Mimosas (Var)
Armanet, François, 710 Blvd Soleil, 83230 Bormes-les-
Mimosas. T. 0494711551. *042736*
Guillaume-Petit, Francis, Quartier Ravel, 83230 Bormes-
les-Mimosas. T. 0494711624. *042737*
Panay, Gérard, 22 Rue Jean-Aicard, 83230 Bormes-les-
Mimosas. T. 0494713190. *042738*

Borre (Nord)
Questroy, Danièle, 1561 Rte Nationale, 59190 Borre.
T. 0328407669. - Ant - *042739*
Westelynck, Serge, 1375 Rte Nationale, 59190 Borre.
T. 0328495231. - Ant - *042740*

Bort-les-Orgues (Corrèze)
Antiquités Saint-Thomas, 172 Av Cantal, 19110 Bort-
les-Orgues. T. 0555969050, Fax 0555969070. *042741*

Bosc-Guérard-Saint-Adrien (Seine-Ma-ritime)
Pivain, Claude, Av De-Lattre-de-Tassigny, 76710 Bosc-
Guérard-Saint-Adrien. T. 0235232193. *042742*

Bosmoreau-les-Mines (Creuse)
Clémençon, Martine, Rte du Paris, 23400 Bosmoreau-
les-Mines. T. 0555641143. - Ant / Furn - *042743*

Bouafles (Eure)
Duval, Bernard, 4 Voie-aux-Vaches, 27700 Bouafles.
T. 0232541143. - Furn - *042744*

Bouchain (Nord)
Epoque Meubles d'Antan, 181 Rue Bocquet, 5911 Bou-
chain. T. 0327348282. - Ant - *042745*

Bouchemaine (Maine-et-Loire)
Rangheard, Christiane, 10 Voie Romaine, 49080 Bou-
chemaine. T. 41480303. - Ant / Furn - *042746*

Boudreville (Côte-d'Or)
Echoppe, 21520 Boudreville. T. 0380935216. *042747*

Bougival (Yvelines)
Belle Epoque, 30 Av Jean-Moulin, 78380 Bougival.
T. 0139690411. *042748*
Bougival Antiquités, 14 Quai Rennequin-Sualem, 78380
Bougival. T. 0139180541, Fax 0130822380. *042749*
Pelzer, Alice Hélène, Gérard, 4 Rue du Gén Leclerc,
78380 Bougival. T. 0139690857. - Furn - *042750*
Pelzer, Gérard, 178 Rue Jomard, 78380 Bougival.
T. 0130820243. *042751*

Bouin (Vendée)
Antiquités La Madeleine, 7 Rue Pays-de-Retz, 85230
Bouin. T. 0251490899. *042752*

Boulogne-Billancourt (Hauts-de-Seine)
Aknin, 14 Av Maréchal-de-Lattre-de-Tassigny, 92100
Boulogne-Billancourt. T. 0149090257. *042753*
Antiquité Brocante, 9 Rue Bartholdi, 92100 Boulogne-
Billancourt. T. 0141108521. - Paint / Furn / Cur /
Draw - *042754*
Antiquités Brocante de Boulogne, 88 Av Jean-Baptiste-
Clément, 92100 Boulogne-Billancourt.
T. 0146058206. *042755*
Arestyl, 66 Rue Saussière, 92100 Boulogne-Billancourt.
T. 0146047543. *042756*

Bennazar, Pierre, 14 Rue Galliéni, 92100 Boulogne-Bil-
lancourt. T. 0146091018. *042757*
Derray, Catherine, 98 Blvd Jean-Jaurès, 92100 Boulo-
gne-Billancourt. T. 0146055568. *042758*
Germain, Jacques, 42 Av Général-Leclerc, 92100 Boulo-
gne-Billancourt. T. 0146042844. - Furn / Dec - *042759*
Lelief, Margarette, 12 Rue Mollien, 92100 Boulogne-Bil-
lancourt. T. 0148251281. *042760*
Mayrand-Taieb, Anne, 4 Rue Fessart, 92100 Boulogne-
Billancourt. T. 0146052780. *042761*
Passé Simple, 14 Av Maréchal-de-Lattre-de-Tassigny,
92100 Boulogne-Billancourt. T. 0149090257. *042762*

Boulogne-sur-Mer (Pas-de-Calais)
Broc'Antique, 70 Rue Bréquerecque, 62200 Boulogne-
sur-Mer. T. 0321310403. *042763*
Cap Saint-Louis, 54 Rue Saint-Louis, 62200 Boulogne-
sur-Mer. T. 0321332475. - Paint / Furn / Cur /
Naut - *042764*
Caron, Francis, 24 Rue Porte-Neuve, 62200 Boulogne-
sur-Mer. T. 0321315810. *042765*
Chez nos Anciens, 84 Rue Bréquerecque, 62200 Boulo-
gne-sur-Mer. T. 0321911696. *042766*
Condettan, 9 Parvis Notre-Dame, 62200 Boulogne-sur-
Mer. T. 0321804957. *042767*
Héritage, 32 Rue Victor-Hugo, 62200 Boulogne-sur-Mer.
T. 0321834787. - Furn / Cur - *042768*
Leleu, Gérald, 18 Rue du Doyen (Pl Dalton), 62200 Bou-
logne-sur-Mer. T. 0321872448. - Ant - *042769*
Lentieul, Annie, 89 Blvd Auguste-Mariette, 62200 Bou-
logne-sur-Mer. T. 0321805405. - Furn / Cur /
Toys - *042770*
Marotte de Foucade, 109 Rue Nationale, 62200 Boulo-
gne-sur-Mer. T. 0321833669. - Furn / Cur /
Toys - *042771*
Maupin, Frédéric, 143 Rue Nationale, 62200 Boulogne-
sur-Mer. T. 0321323799. *042772*
Petites Puces, 71 Rue Faidherbe, 62200 Boulogne-sur-
Mer. T. 0321307658. *042773*
Quéhen, Catherine, 54 Rue Saint-Louis, 62200 Boulo-
gne-sur-Mer. T. 0321332475. *042774*
Trouvailles, 67 Rue Félix-Adam, 62200 Boulogne-sur-
Mer. T. 0321872447. *042775*

Bouloire (Sarthe)
Rose Antique, 81 Rue Nationale, 72440 Bouloire.
T. 0243354942. - Ant / Furn - *042776*

Bourbon-Lancy (Puy-de-Dôme)
Antiquités Cimetière, 6 Rue del'Horloge, 71140 Bour-
bon-Lancy. T. 0385891455. - Mil - *042777*

Bourcefranc-le-Chapus (Charente-Marl-time)
Antiquités L'Astelle, 13 Rue Léon-Oriou, 17560 Bourcefranc-le-Chapus. T. 0546853828. *042778*

Bourg-Achard (Eure)
Joly, Jacques, 590 Grande Rue, 27310 Bourg-Achard.
T. 0232562050. - Furn - *042779*

Bourg-de-Péage (Drôme)
Antiquités La Maladière, La Maladière, 26300 Bourg-de-
Péage. T. 0475050650. - Paint / Furn / Cur - *042780*
Passé Présent, 155 Rue Grande, 26300 Bourg-de-Péa-
ge. T. 0475023751. *042781*

Bourg-en-Bresse (Ain)
Corbelin, Raoul, 8 Rue Bourgmayer, 01000 Bourg-en-
Bresse. T. 0474235232. - Ant - *042782*
Foillard, Josette, 160 Blvd Brou, 01000 Bourg-en-
Bresse. T. 0474222586. - Ant - *042783*
Grenier aux Fauteuils, Rte Pont-d'Ain 105 Blvd de Brou,
01000 Bourg-en-Bresse. T. 0474234125.
- Ant - *042784*
Guilliminet, Pierre, 12 Rue de la Prévoyance, 01000
Bourg-en-Bresse. T. 0474212259. - Ant /
Furn - *042785*
M.C.M. Antiquités, 28 Rue Charles-Robin, 01000 Bourg-
en-Bresse. T. 0474239353. - Ant - *042786*

Bourg-lès-Valence (Drôme)
Trocante, 99 Av Lyon, 26500 Bourg-lès-Valence.
T. 0475557788. *042787*

Bourganeuf (Creuse)
Soulie, José, 28 Rue Verdun, 23400 Bourganeuf.
T. 0555641751. - Ant - *042788*

Bourges (Cher)
Agüera-Madrid, Juan, 73 Rue Bourbonnoux, 18000
Bourges. T. 0248242828. *042789*
Belle Epoque, 53 Rue Arènes, 18000 Bourges.
T. 0248240063. - Ant / Furn / Jew / Silv / Mil - *042790*
Charmerie, 77 Rue Bourbonnoux, 18000 Bourges.
T. 0248247571. *042791*
Collectors, 48 Rue Bourbonnoux, 18000 Bourges.
T. 0248249716. - Repr / Cur / Toys - *042792*
Compagnie, Gilles, 2 Rue Samson, 18000 Bourges.
T. 0248656243. *042793*
Coquelet, Sophie, 71 Rue Bourbonnoux, 18000 Bourges.
T. 0248655899. *042794*
Devulder, Jean-Marc, 33 Rue Bourbonnoux, 18000
Bourges. T. 0248651763. - Paint - *042795*
Duchesse de Maillé, 8 Rue Bourbonnoux, 18000 Bour-
ges. T. 0248658687. *042796*
Escuret, Artemon, 14 Rue Porte-Jaune, 18000 Bourges.
T. 0248241407. *042797*
Galerie Samson, 2 Rue Samson, 18000 Bourges.
T. 0248656243. - Furn / Cur - *042798*
Noël, Marcel, 41 Rue Moyenne, 18000 Bourges.
T. 0248700730. - Jew / Silv / Cur - *042799*
Souvenance, 93 Rue Auron, 18000 Bourges.
T. 0248704847. - Furn / Cur - *042800*
Thevenon, Elisabeth, 5 Rue Henri-du-Crot, 18000 Bour-
ges. T. 0248659479. *042801*

Bourgueil (Indre-et-Loire)
Au Charme d'Antan, 3 Rue Commerce, 37140 Bourgueil.
T. 0547979965. *042802*

Bourmont (Haute-Marne)
Arnoud, Liliane, 18 Rue Général-Leclerc, 52150 Bour-
mont. T. 0325011765. *042803*

Bourron-Marlotte (Seine-et-Marne)
Antiquités du Parvis, 30 Rue Général-de-Gaulle, 77780
Bourron-Marlotte. T. 64457900. *042804*
Chailloux, Gisèle, 1 Rue Pasteur, 77780 Bourron-Mar-
lotte. T. 64783095. *042805*
Gaucher, Martine, 1 Rue Egalité, 77780 Bourron-Mar-
lotte. T. 64456910. *042806*
Hassler, Christian, 100 Rue Général-de-Gaulle, 77780
Bourron-Marlotte. T. 64459697. *042807*
Senoble-Roche, Jacqueline, 31 Rue Marceau, 77780
Bourron-Marlotte. T. 64459459. *042808*

Bourseul (Côtes-d'Armor)
Lelandais, Marcel, Le Bourg, 22130 Bourseul.
T. 0296830239. *042809*

Bourth (Eure)
Pasco, Robert, 12 Pl Eglise, 27580 Bourth.
T. 0232326105. *042810*

Boutenac-Touvent (Charente-Maritime)
Berleux, Gilles, Le Bourg, 17120 Boutenac-Touvent.
T. 0546941094. *042811*

Bouville (Seine-Maritime)
Puces, RN 15bis, 76360 Bouville.
T. 0235924100. *042812*

Bouvines (Nord)
Devigne, Danielle, 393 Rue Félix-Dehau, 59830 Bouvi-
nes. T. 0320790409. - Ant - *042813*

Boynes (Loiret)
Hubert Antiquités, 2 Rte de Pithiviers, 45300 Boynes.
T. 0238331007. - Paint / Furn / Cur - *042814*

Bracieux (Loir-et-Cher)
Lagravère, Nicole, 18 Pl Hôtel-de-Ville, 41250 Bracieux.
T. 0254464185. *042815*

Braine (Aisne)
Kapral, Fabrice, 37 Pl Charles-de-Gaulle, 02220 Braine.
T. 0323741082. - Ant - *042816*

Branges (Saône-et-Loire)
Langlois, Michel, Bois-Lichot Dép 978, 71500 Branges.
T. 0385752963. - Ant / Pho -   042817

Bransles (Seine-et-Marne)
Brocante de Bransles, 1 Pl Aristide-Briand, 77620
Bransles. T. 64295115. - Furn -   042818

Brassac (Tarn)
Icher, Claude, 5 Rue Moulin, 81260 Brassac.
T. 0563745704.   042819

Bréal-sous-Montfort (Ille-et-Vilaine)
Lebec, Bel Air, 35310 Bréal-sous-Montfort.
T. 0299853002.   042820

Brécey (Manche)
Bazin, Pascal, 6 Pl Eglise, 50370 Brécey.
T. 0233486039. - Furn / Cur -   042821
Flament, Paul-Michel, 26 Rue Stade, 50370 Brécey.
T. 0233681249.   042822

Brégnier-Cordon (Ain)
Molard Antiquités, Brégnier Village, 01300 Brégnier-Cordon. T. 0479872447. - Ant -   042823

Brens (Ain)
Rosolen, Jean-Pierre, Petit-Brens, 01300 Brens.
T. 0479819509. - Ant -   042824

Brenthonne (Haute-Savoie)
Fauvergue, Arnaud, Puard, 74890 Brenthonne.
T. 0450363460. - Furn / Dec -   042825

Bresles (Oise)
Defrocourt, Cathy, 24 Rue Président Roosevelt, 60510
Bresles. T. 0344079532. - Ant -   042826

Bressuire (Deux-Sèvres)
Baffou, Janine, 19 Pl 5-Mai, 79300 Bressuire.
T. 0549653411.   042827
Bergerie Antiquité, 3 Rue Noiron, 79300 Bressuire.
T. 0549652941.   042828
Maxime Brocante, La Fourchette, 79300 Bressuire.
T. 0549650299.   042829

Brest (Finistère)
Antiquités 29, 29 Rue Voltaire, 29200 Brest.
T. 0298804090. - Ant / Furn -   042830
Belle Epoque, 35 Rue Jean-Macé, 29200 Brest.
T. 0298464477. - Ant / Toys -   042831
Didierjean, Stéphane, 65 Rue Lyon, 29200 Brest.
T. 0298803268. - Ant -   042832
Girard, Eric, 4 Rue Victor-Ségalen, 29200 Brest.
T. 0298444787. - Ant -   042833
Grenier de Recouvrance, 32 Rue Saint-Exupéry, 29200
Brest. T. 0298457666. - Furn -   042834
Grognard, 20 Rue Château, 29200 Brest.
T. 0298802315. - Ant -   042835
Guyader, Jean-Louis, 26 Rue Bohars, 29200 Brest.
T. 0298475228. - Ant -   042836
Jamault, Philippe, 17 Rue Lyon, 29200 Brest.
T. 0298461757. - Ant / Paint / Furn -   042837
Levier, Marie-Jeanne, La Tour-d'Auvergne, 29200
Brest. T. 0298442434. - Ant -   042838
Palette du Boucher, 67bis Rue Victor-Hugo, 29200 Brest.
T. 0298448701. - Ant -   042839
Patris, Françoise, 19 Rue Glasgow, 29200 Brest.
T. 0298800490. - Ant / Furn / Fra -   042840
Remorques, 2 Rue Blaveau, 29200 Brest.
T. 0298436722. - Ant -   042841
Roger, Yves, Rue Jim-Sévellec, 29200 Brest.
T. 0298458434. - Ant -   042842
Salaun, André, 5 Rue Etienne-Dolet, 29200 Brest.
T. 0298445708. - Ant -   042843

Bretenoux (Lot)
Galerie Saint-Martin, Loulié, 46130 Bretenoux.
T. 0565384201.   042844
Ortal, Av Château-de-Castelnau, 46130 Bretenoux.
T. 0565384013.   042845

Breteuil-sur-Iton (Eure)
Audiger, Christian, 314 Rue Théodore-Pierre, 27160
Breteuil-sur-Iton. T. 0232298631.   042846

Brethonne (Haute-Savoie)
Vaisy, Patricia, Chef Lieu, 74890 Brethonne.
T. 0450394475.   042847

Bréville-sur-Mer (Manche)
Vibert, Isabelle, Les Chasses, 50290 Bréville-sur-Mer.
T. 0233503505.   042848

Brévonnes (Aube)
Petit, Francis, 2 Rue Tremblet, 10220 Brévonnes.
T. 0325463877. - Ant / Cur -   042849

Briançon (Hautes-Alpes)
Parisot, René, Chamandrin, 05100 Briançon.
T. 0492211233.   042850
Temps Passé, 11 Rue Temple, 05100 Briançon.
T. 0492203711.   042851

Briare (Loiret)
Boyer, Daniel, 39 Rte Ouzouer, 45250 Briare.
T. 0238312540.   042852
Christoforou, André, Le Bois-Rond, 45250 Briare.
T. 0238314844.   042853
Girault, Pascal, 56 Rue Saint-Firmin, 45250 Briare.
T. 0238312313.   042854
Setti, Stéphane, 23 Rue Port-aux-Pierre, 45250 Briare.
T. 0238313921.   042855

Brie-Comte-Robert (Seine-et-Marne)
Mulsant, Yves, 29 Rue de l'Eglise, 77170 Brie-Comte-
Robert. T. 0164050204. - Paint / Furn / China / Jew /
Silv / Lights / Instr / Mil / Rel / Glass / Mod / Tin -   042856

**Brie-sous-Mortagne (Charente-Mariti-
me)**
Grange aux Vieux Meubles, 49 Av Royan, 17120 Brie-
sous-Mortagne. T. 0546941224.   042857

Brignoles (Var)
Jauneau, Françoise, 14 Rue Lanciers, 83170 Brignoles.
T. 0494591356. - Graph / Pho / Draw -   042858
Styl'Vieil, 23 Av Frédéric-Mistral, 83170 Brignoles.
T. 0494944276.   042859

Brigueuil (Briqueuil)
Airault, Jean-Marc, Les Clidières, 16420 Brigueuil.
T. 0545710530. - Ant -   042861

Briis-sous-Forges (Essonne)
Giraud, Pascal, 3bis Rue Anne-de-Boleyne, 91640 Briis-
sous-Forges. T. 0164907893.   042862

Brin-sur-Seille (Meurthe-et-Moselle)
Lagarde, Hugues, 19 Rue Metz, 54280 Brin-sur-Seille.
T. 0383316866. - Furn -   042863

Brionne (Eure)
Belhache, 37 Rue Maréchal-Foch, 27800 Brionne.
T. 0232454696.   042864
Costentin, Michel, Côte Saint-Sauveur, 27800 Brionne.
T. 0232459125.   042865

Brioude (Haute-Loire)
Sentenat, Michel, 15 Rue 4-Septembre, 43100 Brioude.
T. 0471749142. - Furn -   042866

Brive-la-Gaillarde (Corrèze)
ACCM, 143 Av 8-Mai-1945, 19100 Brive-la-Gaillarde.
T. 0555242455, Fax 0555744755.   042867
Amblard, Albert, 40 Rue Jaubertie, 19100 Brive-la-Gail-
larde. T. 0555231357.   042868
Cherel, Roger, 44 Av Turgot, 19100 Brive-la-Gaillarde.
T. 0555170925.   042869
Coudert, Monique, 9 Rue Récollets, 19100 Brive-la-Gail-
larde. T. 0555741384.   042870
Gaboriaux, Frédéric, Rue Romain-Rolland, 19100 Brive-
la-Gaillarde. T. 0555871024.   042871
Galerie Voltaire, 3 Blvd Voltaire, 19100 Brive-la-Gaillar-
de. T. 0555179726, Fax 0555179727.   042872
Gambarini, Catherine, 7 Rue Sicard, 19100 Brive-la-
Gaillarde. T. 0555231597.   042873
Lapeyre, Françoise, 13 Rue Sicard, 19100 Brive-la-Gail-
larde. T. 0555237541.   042874
Raimondo, Annie, 4 Rue Jaubertie, 19100 Brive-la-Gail-
larde. T. 0555245040.   042875

Valette, Jean-Max, 34 Rue Corrèze, 19100 Brive-la-
Gaillarde. T. 0555242958.   042876

Brives-Charensac (Haute-Loire)
Barrier, Michel, 11bis Av Gare, 43700 Brives-Charensac.
T. 0471091944.   042877

Broglie (Eure)
Selle, Franck, 2bis Rue Bougy, 27270 Broglie.
T. 0232458479.   042878

Brou (Eure-et-Loir)
Karsenti, Josiane, 3 Rue Tête-Noire, 28160 Brou.
T. 0237960150.   042879
Maison de Bois, 23 Pl Halles, 28160 Brou.
T. 0237470288.   042880

Bruguières (Haute-Garonne)
Spettel, Alain, Av Toulouse, 31150 Bruguières.
T. 0561823681. - Ant / Jew -   042881

Brunoy (Essonne)
Au Vieux Meuble, 11 Rue Pasteur, 91800 Brunoy.
T. 0160461282. - Furn -   042882
Gaucher, Maurice, 20 Av Morin, 91800 Brunoy.
T. 0160466328. - Ant -   042883
Lafon, Didier, 18 Rue Dupont-Chaumont, 91800 Brunoy.
T. 0160460607. - Ant -   042884
Picaud, Marcel, 79 Rue Cerçay, 91800 Brunoy.
T. 0160470707, Fax 0160460153.   042885
Vetter, André, 123 Rue Vallées, 91800 Brunoy.
T. 0160468305.   042886

Bruyères-le-Châtel (Essonne)
Brocante du Chatel, 5 Rue Pont-d'Arny, 91680 Bruyères-le-Châtel. T. 0160838673.   042887

Bruz (Ille-et-Vilaine)
Caradec, Gilbert, La Croix-Madame, 35170 Bruz.
T. 0299526484. - Ant / Furn -   042888

Bû (Eure-et-Loir)
Mazenaud, Fabien, 2 Rue Libération, 28410 Bû.
T. 0237821398. - Furn / Cur -   042889

Buchères (Aube)
Guy, Jacques, 38 Rte de Maisons-Blanches, 10800 Buchères. T. 0325419529. - Ant / Cur -   042890

Buhl-Lorraine (Moselle)
Marché aux Puces, 34 Rte Sarrebourg, 57400 Buhl-Lorraine. T. 0387031659.   042891

Bulgnéville (Vosges)
Breton, Benoît, 74 Rue Recollets, 88140 Bulgnéville.
T. 0329092172.   042892

Burlats (Tarn)
Bévilacqua, Raphaël, La Massalarié, 81090 Burlats.
T. 0563355666.   042893
Brochart, Jean-Paul, La Bouloumié, 81090 Burlats.
T. 0563355613.   042894

Busy (Doubs)
Monnier, Frédéric, Lieu-dit Comice, 25320 Busy.
T. 0381572436.   042895

Buzet-sur-Tarn (Haute-Garonne)
Buzantic, Larroque-à-Grès-Basses, 31660 Buzet-sur-
Tarn. T. 0561844579.   042896
Galinier, Marie-Louise, Les Vergnettes, 31660 Buzet-
sur-Tarn. T. 0561840235. - Furn / China / Cur -   042897

Cabanès (Tarn)
Vrins, Jean-Marie, Mas Del-Bosc, 81500 Cabanès.
T. 0563420450.   042898

Cabourg (Calvados)
A la Recherche du Temps Perdu, 3 Av Commandant-
Touchard, 14390 Cabourg. T. 0231915998.   042899
Aigue Marine, Av Bertaux-Levillan, 14390 Cabourg.
T. 0231911187. - Furn / Jew -   042900
Au Grenier de Cabourg, 19bis Av Général-Leclerc,
14390 Cabourg. T. 0231247512.   042901

Cabriès (Bouches-du-Rhône)

Antiquité au Carrosse d'Or, Centre Commercial de Campagne, 13480 Cabriès. T. 0442027002,
Fax 0491925200. - Paint / Furn / Glass / Cur -   *042902*

Cadenet (Vaucluse)

Bergerie, Le Plan, 84160 Cadenet. T. 0490683583.
- Ant -   *042903*
O'Hara, 103 Av Gambetta, 84160 Cadenet.
T. 0490681374. - Ant -   *042904*

Caen (Calvados)

A la Belle Epoque, 68 Rue Saint-Jean, 14300 Caen.
T. 0231856337. - Ant / Jew -   *042905*
Ali Adel, 50 Rue Ecuyère, 14300 Caen. T. 0231853746,
Fax 0231864813. - Paint / Orient / Tex -   *042906*
Art et Décor, 15 Pl Résistance, 14000 Caen.
T. 0231866869.   *042907*
Au Cherche Hier, 19 Rue Teinturiers, 14021 Caen Cédex.
T. 0231856076. - Furn / Lights / Cur -   *042908*
Barbe, Christophe, 40 Rue Ecuyère, 14000 Caen.
T. 0231857293.   *042909*
Basnier, François, 40 Rue Ecuyère, 14000 Caen.
T. 0231853658.   *042910*
Béville, Arnaud, 35 Av Capitaine-Georges-Guynemer,
14000 Caen. T. 0231782734.   *042911*
Briard, Thierry, 24 Rue Demolombe, 14000 Caen.
T. 0231866589.   *042912*
Brillet, Jean-Paul, 38 Rue Ecuyère, 14000 Caen.
T. 0231855775. - Paint / Furn / Sculp / Instr / Glass /
Cur / Music -   *042913*
Brocante Caennaise, 68bis Rue Falaise, 14000 Caen.
T. 0231520063.   *042914*
Brune, Yves, 19 Rue Ecuyère, 14000 Caen.
T. 0231854877.   *042915*
Carrion, Régine, 19 Rue Saint-Sauveur, 14000 Caen.
T. 0231865040.   *042916*
Charton, Marie-Jeanne, 18 Pl Saint-Sauveur, 14000
Caen. T. 0231857727. - Furn / China / Cur -   *042917*
Duffourd, Jean-Claude, 10 Rue Laumonnier, 14000
Caen. T. 0231946441.   *042918*
Echoppe, 21 Rue Demolombe, 14000 Caen.
T. 0231854395.   *042919*
Flambard, Agnès, 7 Rue Clos-Caillet, 14000 Caen.
T. 0231382172.   *042920*
Fontaine, Dominique, 45bis Rue Ecuyère, 14000 Caen.
T. 0231854167.   *042921*
Godey, Georges, 25 Rue Ecuyère, 14000 Caen.
T. 0231864806.   *042922*
Hamminoff, Chris, 50 Rue Ecuyère, 14000 Caen.
T. 0231866273. - Paint / Furn / Sculp / Instr /
Cur -   *042923*
Havas, Frédéric, 13 Rue Ecuyère, 14000 Caen.
T. 0231392890. - Paint / Furn / Sculp / Silv /
Instr -   *042924*
Hubert, Marie, 9 Rue Québec, 14000 Caen.
T. 0231744454. - Furn / Cur -   *042925*
Jean-Louis-Antiquités, 16 Rue Ecuyère, 14000 Caen.
T. 0231856925.   *042926*
Lelong, Pascal, 88 Rue Basse, 14000 Caen.
T. 0231447965.   *042927*
Louaintier, Serge, 25 Rue Falaise, 14000 Caen.
T. 0231838377.   *042928*
Louis, René, 6 Rue Namps, 14000 Caen.
T. 0231501652.   *042929*
Mesnil, Bruno, 46 Passage Grand-Turc, 14000 Caen.
T. 0231772592. - Furn -   *042930*
Morel, Michèle, 32 Rue Ecuyère, 14000 Caen.
T. 0231853459.   *042931*
Quinault, Serge, 3 Rue Belvédère, 14000 Caen.
T. 0231834905.   *042932*
Reine Mathilde, 47 Rue Saint-Jean, 14000 Caen.
T. 0231854552, Fax 0231866493.   *042933*
Roxane's, 2bis Rue aux Fromages, 14000 Caen.
T. 0231866651. - Ant / Furn / Cur -   *042934*
Salaün, Anna, 1 Rue Engannerie, 14000 Caen.
T. 0231853003.   *042935*
Temps Retrouvé, 34 Rue Ecuyère, 14000 Caen.
T. 0231866203. - Paint / Furn / Sculp / Jew / Silv /
Lights / Instr -   *042936*
Toulorge, J., 14 Rue Froide, 14000 Caen.
T. 0231861465.   *042937*

Victoria, 48 Rue Ecuyère, 14000 Caen. T. 0231852454.
- Furn / Silv / Cur -   *042938*

Caestre (Nord)

Goetgheluck, Hubert, 1861 Rte Bailleul, 59190 Caestre.
T. 0328401583. - Ant -   *042939*

Cagnes-sur-Mer (Alpes-Maritimes)

Coquenpot, Michel, 14 Rue du Planastel, 06800 Cagnes-sur-Mer. T. 0493204080. - Ant / Paint / Sculp /
Tex / Cur -   *042940*
Damiano, Lina, 30 Av Auguste-Renoir, 06800 Cagnes-sur-Mer. T. 0493735490.   *042941*
Dolgovo-Sabouroff, Marc, 1 Rue Gardiole, 06800 Cagnes-sur-Mer. T. 0493207216.   *042942*
Remise, 68 Rte Gaude, Résidence Savoies, Bâtiment A,
06800 Cagnes-sur-Mer. T. 0493228826.   *042943*

Cahors (Lot)

Capelle, Nano, 250 Rue Anatole-France, 46000 Cahors.
T. 0565221527.   *042944*
Dubernet de Garros, Agnès, 75 Rue Clément-Marot,
46000 Cahors. T. 0565239310.   *042945*
Fraissinet, Pierre, 99 Rue Château-du-Roi, 46000 Cahors. T. 0565354617, Fax 0565221741. - Paint / Furn /
Tex / Cur -   *042946*
Girard, 64 Chemin Paradis, 46000 Cahors.
T. 0565223803.   *042947*
Lagrèze, Marthe, Regourd, 46000 Cahors.
T. 0565350453.   *042948*
Sagols, Monique-Marthe, 40 Rue Docteur-Bergougnoux,
46000 Cahors. T. 0565350642.   *042949*

Cajarc (Lot)

Beaumel, Gérard, Pl Eglise, 46160 Cajarc.
T. 0565406625.   *042950*

Calais (Pas-de-Calais)

Moulin de Marck, 248 Blvd La-Fayette, 62100 Calais.
T. 0321964140.   *042951*
Passé Simple, 21 Rue Londres, 62100 Calais.
T. 0321977000.   *042952*
Trésors d'Antan, 3 Rue Royale, 62100 Calais.
T. 0321973601.   *042953*

Callian (Var)

Brocante de la Ramade, 11 Rue Ramade, 83440 Callian.
T. 0494765965.   *042954*
Chanay, Catherine, 10 Pl Mairie, 83440 Callian.
T. 0494764063.   *042955*
Morain, Gilbert, Les Cerisiers, Quartier Saint-Pierre,
83440 Callian. T. 0494764891.   *042956*

Calvi (Corse)

Belle Chose, 1 Rue Clemenceau, 20260 Calvi.
T. 0495652043, Fax 0495652043.   *042957*
Broc'Art des Remparts, Rue Alsace-Lorraine, Les Remparts, 20260 Calvi. T. 0495653587. - Ant /
Cur -   *042958*

Calvisson (Gard)

François-Laugier, Maurice, Rue Fontaines, 30420 Calvisson. T. 0466012220.   *042959*
Ortiz, Pierre, Pl Halles, 30420 Calvisson.
T. 0466012497.   *042960*

Cambrai (Nord)

A la Porte Notre Dame, 10 Pl Porte-Notre-Dame, 59400
Cambrai. T. 0327813951. - Ant -   *042961*
Bourgeois, Jacques, 23 Rue Cordiers, 59400 Cambrai.
T. 0327810180. - Ant -   *042962*
Broc Antiquités, 39 Rue Belfort, 59400 Cambrai.
T. 0327817620. - Ant -   *042963*
Godefroy, Olivier, 5 Av Albert 1er, 59400 Cambrai.
T. 0327817620. - Ant -   *042964*
Langlet, Jean-Marie, 39 Rue Belfort, 59400 Cambrai.
T. 0327783210. - Ant -   *042965*
Relais d'Art, 13 Rue Tavelle, 59400 Cambrai.
T. 0327812330. - Ant / Dec -   *042966*
Rifaut, Gilbis, 40 Rue Eswars-Morenchies, 59400 Cambrai. T. 0327780444. - Ant -   *042967*

Camps-en-Amienois (Somme)

Devaux, Alain, Rte Nationale, 80540 Camps-en-Amienois. T. 0322507494. - Ant -   *042968*

Canaples (Somme)

Antiquités Brocantes du Château de Canaples, 93 Rue
Château, 80670 Canaples. T. 0322527958. - Ant /
Cur -   *042969*

Canapville (Calvados)

Lebreton, Alain, Ancien Presbytère, 14800 Canapville.
T. 0231652131.   *042970*

Cancale (Ille-et-Vilaine)

Dumaine, 3 Pl Bricourt, 35260 Cancale.
T. 0299899211.   *042971*

Candé (Maine-et-Loire)

Laurans, Joël, 14 Grande Rue, 49440 Candé.
T. 41927849.   *042972*

Cannes (Alpes-Maritimes)

Antiquaires Associés, 101 Blvd République, 06400 Cannes. T. 0493992230. - Paint / Furn -   *042973*
Antiquité La Tosca, 14 Rue Constantine, 06400 Cannes.
T. 0493385199. - Ant -   *042974*
Antiquités et Argenterie Cannoise, 15 Rue Jean-Macé,
06400 Cannes. T. 0492991143. - Silv / Glass -   *042975*
Antiquités Martine, 167 Blvd République, 06400 Cannes.
T. 0493686030.   *042976*
Antiquités 1900-1950, 121 Blvd République, 06400
Cannes. T. 0493686832.   *042977*
Arts et Philatélie, 14 Rue Bivouac-Napoléon, 06400
Cannes. T. 0493394074. - Paint / Furn / Num -   *042978*
Astori, Françoise, 16 Rue Joseph-Barthélemy, 06400
Cannes. T. 0493909814.   *042979*
Becker, 7 Rue Jean Daumas, 06400 Cannes.
T. 0493383336. - Orient / Arch / Eth / Cur -   *042980*
Bellucci, Nina, 9bis Rue Oran, 06400 Cannes.
T. 0493382371.   *042981*
Bensoussan, Alain, 141 Blvd République, 06400 Cannes.
T. 0492981885.   *042982*
Blanc, Françoise, 12 Pl Marché-Forville, 06400 Cannes.
T. 0493395533.   *042983*
Brocanterie 2, 8 Rue Chabaud, 06400 Cannes.
T. 0493380961.   *042984*
Brunel, 1 Blvd Beausite, 06400 Cannes. T. 0493480916.
- Paint / Cur -   *042985*
Butterfly, Jardin de l'Hôtel Majestic, La Croisette, 06400
Cannes. T. 0493396104. - Furn / Dec / Jew -   *042986*
Canal, Jean-Paul, 14 Rue Constantine, 06400 Cannes.
T. 0493385199.   *042987*
Cannes Brocante, 15 Av Anglais, 06400 Cannes.
T. 0493863060.   *042988*
Casetti, Hélène, 122 Rue Antibes, 06400 Cannes.
T. 0493991159.   *042989*
Comptoir Mondial, 148 Rue Antibes, 06400 Cannes.
T. 0493941447, Fax 0493941202. - Orient -   *042990*
Comtoise, 17 Blvd Montfleury, 06400 Cannes.
T. 0493393992.   *042991*
Cosson, Pierre, 26 Blvd Moulin, 06400 Cannes.
T. 0493391919.   *042992*
Décors Saint-Georges, 33 Rue Suisses, 06400 Cannes.
T. 0493397730.   *042993*
Disy, Jean, 99 Blvd République, 06400 Cannes.
T. 0493384446.   *042994*
Dragonne, 131 Rue d'Antibes, 06400 Cannes.
T. 0493387214. - Mil -   *042995*
Ducoté, Marc-Geoffroy, 99-101 Blvd République, 06400
Cannes. T. 0493383589, Fax 0493994856.
- Paint -   *042996*
Francl, Marc C., 142 Rue Antibes, 06400 Cannes.
T. 0493438643, Fax 0493941133. - Paint / Furn /
Cur -   *042997*
Gagé, Pierre, 89 Blvd République, 06400 Cannes.
T. 0493383671. - Ant -   *042998*
Galerie Albion, 17 Rue Etats-Unis, 06400 Cannes.
T. 0493689348, Fax 0493680355.   *042999*
Galerie Edo, 10 Rue Commandant-Vidal, 06400 Cannes.
T. 0493682574, Fax 0492988289. - Orient -   *043000*
Galerie Marie-France, 7 Rue Maréchal-Fellégara, 06400
Cannes. T. 0493994244.   *043001*
Galeries Saint-Honoré, 12 Rue Notre-Dame, 06400 Cannes. T. 0493392165.   *043002*
Goube, Jean-Pierre, 115 Blvd République, 06400 Cannes. T. 0493991951.   *043003*
Gourier, Paul, 149 Blvd République, 06400 Cannes.
T. 0493382185.   *043004*

Guigue Antiquités, 12 Rue Macé, 06400 Cannes.
T. 0493381566. 043005
Hennocque-Quirin, Jeanne, 27 Blvd de la Croisette,
06400 Cannes. T. 0493391759. - Ant / Furn / China /
Instr / Glass - 043006
Henrik Antiquités, 6 Rue Legoff, 06400 Cannes.
T. 0493390486. 043007
Herpin, Hubert, 20 Rue Macé, 06400 Cannes.
T. 0493395618, Fax 0493395210. - Ant - 043008
Lauretta, Michel, 105 Blvd République, 06400 Cannes.
T. 0493680535. - Paint / Furn / Dec / Silv / Lights /
Cur - 043009
Lavezzari, 175 Av Michel-Jourdan, 06400 Cannes.
T. 0493483970. 043010
Le Forestier, Bernard, 101 Blvd République, 06400 Can-
nes. T. 0493396165. 043011
M.C.M., 20 Av Anglais, 06400 Cannes.
T. 0492986905. 043012
Ming Galerie's, 50 Blvd Croisette, 06400 Cannes.
T. 0493680104, Fax 0493680988. 043013
Moufflet, Pascal, 13 Rue Oran, 06400 Cannes.
T. 0493381364. 043014
Moufflet, Pascal, 30 Blvd Lorraine, 06400 Cannes.
T. 0493381364, Fax 0493689979. - Furn - 043015
Nardini, Pierre, 87 Av Maréchal-Galliéni, 06400 Cannes.
T. 0493680084. 043016
Nissen, Sylvie, 58 Blvd Croisette, 06400 Cannes.
T. 0493387040. - Paint / Sculp / Cur - 043017
Objet d'Art, 132 Blvd République, 06400 Cannes.
T. 0493382433. 043018
Polano, Jacques, 15 Rue Macé, 06400 Cannes.
T. 0492991143. 043019
Ramie, Jean & Huguette, 5 Rue Tony-Allard, 06400 Can-
nes. T. 0493390412. - Arch / Eth - 043020
Raschoffer, Jacques, 53 Blvd République, 06400 Can-
nes. T. 0493384809. 043021
Rebuffel, Michel, 95 Blvd République, 06400 Cannes.
T. 0493994834. 043022
Saramito, Marie-Dominique, 21 Rue Macé, 06400 Can-
nes. T. 0493392025. 043023
Sigal, 21 Rue Jean-de-Riouffe, 06400 Cannes.
T. 0493997420. 043024
Silvy, Jean-François, 5 Rue Pré, 06400 Cannes.
T. 0493391858. 043025
Tambour de Bronze, 28 Rue Hoche, 06400 Cannes.
T. 0493395720. 043026
Trouvaille, 9 Rue Hoche, 06400 Cannes.
T. 0493383609. 043027
Vic, Jacques, 13 Rue Etats-Unis, 06400 Cannes.
T. 0493394057, Fax 0493997943. 043028

Canteleu (Seine-Maritime)
Vétu, Patrice, 17 Rue Gaston Boulet, 76380 Canteleu.
T. 0235363633, Fax 0235363655. 043029

Capbreton (Landes)
Brocante Océane, 4 Av Maréchal-Leclerc, 40130 Capbreton. T. 4 Av Maréchal-Leclerc. 043030

Capdenac (Lot)
Rey, Patrice, Bergounes, 46100 Capdenac.
T. 0565347150. 043031

Capelle-lès-Boulogne (Pas-de-Calais)
Anquez, 116 Rte Nationale, 62360 Capelle-lès-Boulo-
gne. T. 0321911828. - Paint - 043032

Capinghem (Nord)
Belle Epoque, 111bis Rue Poincaré, 59160 Capinghem.
T. 0320935288. - Ant - 043033

Carcassonne (Aude)
Antiquités Le Saint-Georges, 36 Rue Victor-Hugo, 11000
Carcassonne. T. 0468726917. 043034
Argence-Lecaillé, Aurore, 67 Av Franklin-Roosevelt,
11000 Carcassonne. T. 0468723333. 043035
Art de Vivre, 6 Pl Saint-Jean, 11000 Carcassonne.
T. 0468476707, Fax 0468720642. 043036
Bazar, Zl Bouriette, Blvd Joseph-Gay-Lussac, 11000
Carcassonne. T. 0468713177,
Fax 0468718361. 043037
Brocanterie, 97 Rue Aimé-Ramond, 11000 Carcas-
sonne. T. 0468255493. 043038

Brocantique, 54 Rue Verdun, 11000 Carcassonne.
T. 0468256571. - Paint / Furn - 043039
Bruguière de Gorgot, Georges-Henri, 36 Rue Victor-Hu-
go, 11000 Carcassonne. T. 0468475266. - Furn /
Naut - 043040
Deviller-Janda, 37 Rue Jules-Sauzède, 11000 Carcas-
sonne. T. 0468724031. 043041
Escarpolette, 33 Rue Victor-Hugo, 11000 Carcassonne.
T. 0468718997. 043042
Faye, Henriette, 12 Rue Saint-Louis, 11000 Carcas-
sonne. T. 0468470945. 043043
Giacomel, Joseph, 104 Av Général-Leclerc, 11000 Car-
cassonne. T. 0468254669. 043044
Regard Antiquités, 5 Blvd Omer-Sarraut, 11000 Carcas-
sonne. T. 0468724179. 043045
Rouch, Yves, 33 Rue Victor-Hugo, 11000 Carcassonne.
T. 0468718997. 043046
Sarraute Frères, 15 Rue Porte-d'Aude, 11000 Carcas-
sonne. T. 0468724290. 043047

Carcès (Var)
Antiquités Le Lansquenet, 31 Rue Maréchal-Joffre,
83570 Carcès. T. 0494045431. 043048
Seillé, 4 Pl Emile-Zola, 83570 Carcès. T. 0494045027,
Fax 0494043467. 043049

Carentan (Manche)
Harmonie, 5 Rue Château, 50500 Carentan.
T. 0233420024. - Ant / Dec - 043050
Hopking, Eric & Michèle, 53 Rue 101ème-Airborne, RN
13, 50500 Carentan. T. 0233420705. - Furn - 043051
Lecourtois, Jean-Jacques, 9bis Rte Saint-Côme, RN 13,
50500 Carentan. T. 0233423011. 043052

Carnac (Morbihan)
Antiquités de l'Océane, 104 Av Druides, 56340 Carnac.
T. 0297528488. - Ant - 043053
Grenier Saint Pierre, 7 Av Salines, 56340 Carnac.
T. 0297527920. - Ant - 043054
Michaud, Claude, Port-en-Dro, 56340 Carnac.
T. 0297529080. - Ant - 043055
Pilorgé, Jean, 123 Av Druides, 56340 Carnac.
T. 0297520865. - Ant - 043056
Saint Cornély, 11 Rue Saint-Cornély, 56340 Carnac.
T. 0297527401. - Ant - 043057
Soudry-Tharaud, Anne, Ferme Por-en-Dro, 56340 Car-
nac. T. 0297528951, Fax 0297521595. - Ant - 043058

Carnoët (Côtes-d'Armor)
Le Bihan, Gildas, 9 Pl Mairie, 22160 Carnoët.
T. 0296215228. 043059

Carolles (Manche)
Duval, Stéphane, Rte Plage, Villa Suzette, 50740 Carol-
les. T. 0233514280. 043060

Carpentras (Vaucluse)
Augier, Albert, 261 Blvd Alfred-Naquet, 84200 Carpen-
tras. T. 0490632309. - Ant - 043061
Barbotine, 79 Blvd Nord, 84200 Carpentras.
T. 0490600250. - Ant - 043062
Bouscasse, Alain, 37 Rue Porte-de-Mazan, 84200 Car-
pentras. T. 0490601397. - Ant - 043063
Courbet, Francis, 211 Av Mont-Ventoux, 84200 Carpen-
tras. T. 0490672477. - Furn - 043064
Hernandez, René, 89 Rue David-Guillabert, 84200 Car-
pentras. T. 0490632887. - Ant - 043065
Roure, Bruno, 397 Av Jean-Herni-Fabre, 84200 Carpen-
tras. T. 0490605561. - Ant - 043066
Roux, Nelly, 387 Av Victor-Hugo, 84200 Carpentras.
T. 0490671694. - Ant - 043067

Carqueiranne (Var)
Bédier, Claude, 17 Av Jean-Jaurès, 83320 Carquei-
ranne. T. 0494587149. 043068

Carrières-sur-Seine (Yvelines)
Aux Chineurs, 78 Rte Chatou, 78420 Carrières-sur-Sei-
ne. T. 0139143963. - Ant - 043069

Cartigny (Somme)
Bochenek, Edouard, 24 Rue Péronne, 80200 Cartigny.
T. 0322869745. - Ant - 043070

Casamozza (Corse)
Antiquité Saint-Michel, Résidence Saint-Michel, Bât C,
20290 Casamozza. T. 0495383068. - Furn /
Cur - 043071

Cassel (Nord)
Cacool Antiquités, 6 Grand'Place, 59670 Cassel.
T. 0328424590. - Ant - 043072
Grange, Standaert-Strate, 59670 Cassel.
T. 0328424353. - Ant - 043073

Cassis (Bouches-du-Rhône)
Art du Temps, 27 All Mimosas, 13260 Cassis.
T. 0442012197, Fax 0442018855. 043074

Castanet-Tolosan (Haute-Garonne)
Bourdel, Josette, 14 Av Lauragais, 31320 Castanet-To-
losan. T. 0561277412. 043075

Castelculier (Lot-et-Garonne)
Teck en Stock, ZA, 47240 Castelculier. T. 0553965384,
Fax 0553681341. - Furn / Dec - 043076

Casteljaloux (Lot-et-Garonne)
Abadia, 1 Rue Milieu, 47700 Casteljaloux.
T. 0553931510. - Paint / Furn / Cur - 043077
Belle Epoque, Grand'Rue, 47700 Casteljaloux.
T. 0553935307. 043078
Lefranc, Monique-Valérie, 4 Av Lac, 47700 Casteljaloux.
T. 0553201724. 043079

Castellane (Alpes-de-Haute-Provence)
Vaccaretti, Laurent, Quart Colle, 04120 Castellane.
T. 0492836637. - Ant - 043080

Castelmoron-sur-Lot (Lot-et-Garonne)
Dupeyron, Claude, Av Comarque, 47260 Castelmoron-
sur-Lot. T. 0553849746. 043081

Castelnau-de-Médoc (Gironde)
Dartigoeyte, Richard, 15 Rte Saint-Raphaël, 33480 Ca-
stelnau-de-Médoc. T. 0556582342. 043082

Castelnau-le-Lez (Hérault)
Mas du Diable, 34170 Castelnau-le-Lez.
T. 0467720246. - Ant - 043083

Castelnou (Pyrénées-Orientales)
Mannant, Michel, Rue Ourtal, 66300 Castelnou.
T. 0468533546. - Ant - 043084
Pujol, Joan, 7 Rue Avail, 66300 Castelnou.
T. 0468530508. - Ant - 043085

Castelsarrasin (Tarn-et-Garonne)
Destang, 34 Rue Révolution, 82100 Castelsarrasin.
T. 0563951710. - Paint / Furn / Cur - 043086

Castillon-du-Gard (Gard)
Amidon, Pl 8-Mai-1945, 30210 Castillon-du-Gard.
T. 0466371066. 043087
Antiquaires & Brocanteurs du Pont du Gard, Les Croi-
sées, RN 86, 30210 Castillon-du-Gard.
T. 0466371785. 043088
Four Banal, Pl 8-Mai-1945, 30210 Castillon-du-Gard.
T. 0466372600. 043089

Castillon-la-Bataille (Gironde)
Grenier d'Aliénor, 22 Av Maumey, 33350 Castillon-la-
Bataille. T. 0557403916. 043090
Mellier, Jean-Louis, 25 Capitourian, 33350 Castillon-la-
Bataille. T. 0557402532. 043091

Castillon-Massas (Gers)
Mandou, Marie, Pelat, 32360 Castillon-Massas.
T. 0562655579. 043092

Castres (Tarn)
Aldebert, Christian, 3 Av Castres, 81090 Castres.
T. 0563354945. 043093
Aldebert, Comdor, 243 Av Charles-de-Gaulle, 81100
Castres. T. 0563355442. - Paint / Furn / Cur - 043094
Banq, Eric, 181 Av Charles-de-Gaulle, 81100 Castres.
T. 0563352861. 043095
Belle Epoque, 72 Av Albi, 81100 Castres.
T. 0563597656. 043096
Brocante de l'Abinque, 27 Pl Albinque, 81100 Castres.
T. 0563592876. 043097

Caron, Jean-Claude, 8 Rte Naves, 81100 Castres.
T. 0563599654. *043098*
Dondaine, Claude, 11 Blvd Miredames, 81100 Castres.
T. 0563351654. *043099*
Garcia, Marie-Rose, 34 Rue Amiral-Galiber, 81100 Cast-
res. T. 0563725955. - Ant - *043100*
Garcia, Victorio, 221 Av Charles-de-Gaulle, 81100 Cast-
res. T. 0563354135. *043101*
Santos, Jean, 10 Rue Nabrissonne, 81100 Castres.
T. 0563721882. *043102*
Tour du Hobbit, 4 Rue Francisco-Ferrer, 81100 Castres.
T. 0563354034. *043103*

Catenay (Seine-Maritime)
Bertran, Sylvain, 561 Rue Saint-Clair, 76116 Catenay.
T. 0235340564. *043104*

Catus (Lot)
Brocatus, Pl Poste, 46150 Catus.
T. 0565212128. *043105*

Caudebec-en-Caux (Seine-Maritime)
Egels, Damien, 8 Rue Belles-Femmes, 76490 Caude-
bec-en-Caux. T. 0235962574. *043106*

Caudry (Nord)
Prince, Ghislain, 18 Rue République, 59540 Caudry.
T. 0327762390. - Ant - *043107*

Caulnes (Côtes-d'Armor)
Antic Dépôt, 80 Rue Dinan, 22350 Caulnes.
T. 0296838789. - Furn - *043108*

Caumont-sur-Durance (Vaucluse)
Casanova, Danièle, Rte Gadagne, 84510 Caumont-sur-
Durance. T. 0490231107. - Ant - *043109*

Cauneille (Landes)
Carrau, Gilbert, Villa Thiena, RN 117, 40300 Cauneille.
T. 0558730710, Fax 0558731534. - Furn - *043110*

Caurel (Marne)
Mahut-Maillet, G., 3 Rue Witry, 51110 Caurel.
T. 0326971359. - Ant / Paint / Furn / China / Sculp /
Dec / Lights / Instr / Cur / Toys - *043111*

Caussade (Tarn-et-Garonne)
Bergaul, 43 Blvd Léonce-Granie, 82300 Caussade.
T. 0563931628. *043112*
Lancini, Edwige, 38 Pl Notre-Dame, 82300 Caussade.
T. 0563931630. *043113*

Cavaillon (Vaucluse)
Antiquités de la Poste, 14 Av Berthelot, 84300 Cavaillon.
T. 0490719102. - Ant - *043114*
Bey, Patrick, 48 Rue Raphaël-Michel, 84300 Cavaillon.
T. 0490782537. - Ant - *043115*
Serpagli, Daniel, 23 Rte Robion, 84300 Cavaillon.
T. 0490713635. - Ant - *043116*

Cavalaire-sur-Mer (Var)
Levionnais, Marie-Jeannne, Rue Mistral, Croix Sud Be-
linda, 83240 Cavalaire-sur-Mer.
T. 0494643052. *043117*

Cazères (Haute-Garonne)
Canut, Pierre, 7 Blvd Jean-Jaurès, 31220 Cazères.
T. 0561905075. *043118*
Lecussan, Hector, 22 Av Gabriel-Péri, 31220 Cazères.
T. 0561970290. *043119*
Sanchez, Floréal, Chemin Carsalade, 31220 Cazères.
T. 0561970420. *043120*

Cazideroque (Lot-et-Garonne)
Bohl, François, Le Farguiel, 47370 Cazideroque.
T. 0553407848. *043121*

Ceaux-d'Allègre (Haute-Loire)
A la Recherche du Temps Perdu, 43270 Ceaux-d'Allè-
re. T. 0471002050. - Furn / Repr / Cur / Toys - *043122*

Céreste (Alpes-de-Haute-Provence)
Blondel, Jacques, Cours Aristide-Briand, 04110 Céreste.
T. 0492790316. - Ant - *043123*

Céret (Pyrénées-Orientales)
Pont du Diable, 8 Pl Pont, 66400 Céret. T. 0468871363.
- Ant / Paint / Furn - *043124*

Cergy (Val-d'Oise)
Debremaeker, Colette, 14 Av Enclos, 95800 Cergy.
T. 0134200551. *043125*
Delannoy, Patrick, 2 Rue Vauréal, 95000 Cergy.
T. 0130382121. - Ant / Furn - *043126*
Jallier, Alain, 9 Chemin Neuf, 95000 Cergy.
T. 0230325247. *043127*

Cerny (Essonne)
Jadis, 18 Av Carnot, 91590 Cerny.
T. 0164577865. *043128*

Cervières (Hautes-Alpes)
Meyer, Jean-Pierre, Face Mairie de Chef-Lieu, 05100
Cervières. T. 0492201582. - Paint / Furn / Glass /
Cur - *043129*

Cesson-Sévigné (Ille-et-Vilaine)
Antiquités de Vaux, 13 Rue Parc, 35510 Cesson-Sévi-
gné. T. 0299365064. - Paint / Furn / Silv / Cur - *043130*

Chablis (Yonne)
Halle à la Brocante, Rue Serein, 89800 Chablis.
T. 0386428464. - Ant - *043131*
Maunoury Dufour, Jacqueline, 2 Rue Fossés, 89800
Chablis. T. 0386421499, Fax 0386428099.
- Toys - *043132*
Pacault, Philippe, 38 Rue Auxerroise, 89800 Chablis.
T. 0386424496. *043133*

Chabris (Indre)
Tartière, Jean, 11 Rue Pont, 36210 Chabris.
T. 0254400467. - Ant / Furn - *043134*

Chaillé-les-Marais (Vendée)
Mayet, Alain, RN 137, Le Sableau, 85450 Chaillé-les-
Marais. T. 0251567212. *043135*

Chaillon (Meuse)
Barnet, Michel, 55210 Chaillon. T. 0329893356.
- Ant - *043136*

Chailly-en-Bière (Seine-et-Marne)
Susen, Bernard, 25 Rte de Paris, 77960 Chailly-en-Biè-
re. T. 0160664307. - Ant / Furn / China / Lights /
Instr - *043137*
Vieille Grille, 4 Rte Fontainebleau, 77960 Chailly-en-Biè-
re. T. 0360662656. *043138*

Challans (Vendée)
Antiquités du Marais, 182 Rte Saint-Jean-de-Monts,
85300 Challans. T. 0251493783. - Furn / Cur /
Toys - *043139*
Antiquités Les 3 Moulins, 149 Rte Saint-Jean-de-Monts,
85300 Challans. T. 0251931377. - Paint /
Furn - *043140*
Flaire, 16 Rue Nantes, 85300 Challans. T. 0251681081.
- Dec - *043141*

Chalon-sur-Saône (Saône-et-Loire)
Antiquités 2000, 79e Rue François Protheau, 71100
Chalon-sur-Saône. T. 0385430186. - Furn /
Cur - *043142*
Au Bon Vieux Temps, 3 Pl Saint-Vincent, 71100 Chalon-
sur-Saône. T. 0385487385. - Ant / Furn - *043143*
Autrefois, 1 Rue Blé, 71100 Chalon-sur-Saône.
T. 0385480906. - Paint / Furn - *043144*
Couleur Miel, 4 Pl Saint-Vincent, 71100 Chalon-sur-
Saône. T. 0385489625. - Ant - *043145*
Du Cloître, 11 Rue Cloître, 71100 Chalon-sur-Saône.
T. 0385482060. - Ant - *043146*
Duclerc, Marie-Claude, 5 Rue Port-Villers, 71100 Cha-
lon-sur-Saône. T. 0385485663. - Ant - *043147*
Framboisine, 14 Rue Poissonnerie, 71100 Chalon-sur-
Saône. T. 0385486988. - Ant - *043148*
Franck Martial, 13 Rue Carnot, 71100 Chalon-sur-
Saône. T. 0385935188. - Ant / Furn / Jew / Silv /
Mil - *043149*
Galerie des Antiquaires, 9 Rue Blé, 71100 Chalon-sur-
Saône. T. 0385480310. - Ant - *043150*
Girardot, Eugène, 16 Rue Saint-Vincent, 71100 Chalon-
sur-Saône. T. 0385488678. - Ant - *043151*

Gré du Van, 6 Rue Blé, 71100 Chalon-sur-Saône.
T. 0385480958. - Ant / Tex - *043152*
Héry, Georges, 4 Pl Port-Villers, 71100 Chalon-sur-
Saône. T. 0385482491, Fax 0385480130.
- Ant - *043153*
Jacques Antiquités, 9 Rue Poulets, 71100 Chalon-sur-
Saône. T. 0385484311. - Ant - *043154*
Jadis, 23 Rue Fructidor, 71100 Chalon-sur-Saône.
T. 0385485269. - Ant / Furn / Jew - *043155*
Lavirotte, Philippe, 1 Rue Cochons-de-Lait, 71100 Cha-
lon-sur-Saône. T. 0385482668. - Ant - *043156*
Merle, Bernadette, 21 Rue Fructidor, 71100 Chalon-sur-
Saône. T. 0385485269. - Ant - *043157*
Millon-Garnier, Christelle, 6 Rue Poulets, 71100 Chalon-
sur-Saône. T. 0385931542. - Ant - *043158*
Prost, Alain, 5 Rue Poulets, 71100 Chalon-sur-Saône.
T. 0385482516. - Ant / Furn - *043159*
Ravet, Pierre, 79 E Rue François-Protheau, 71100 Cha-
lon-sur-Saône. T. 0385430186. - Ant - *043160*
Richy, Pierre-Maurice, 10 Rue Blé, 71100 Chalon-sur-
Saône. T. 0385486990. - Ant - *043161*
Saint Vincent Antiquités, 11 Pl Saint-Vincent, 71100
Chalon-sur-Saône. T. 0385487751. - Ant - *043162*

Châlons-sur-Marne (Marne)
Archambault, 9 Rue Kellermann, 51000 Châlons-sur-
Marne. T. 0326682470. - Ant / China - *043163*
Dommanget, Daniel, 16 Rue Orfeuil, 51000 Châlons-
sur-Marne. T. 0326211448. *043164*
Orfeuil Antiquités, 12 Rue Orfeuil, 51000 Châlons-sur-
Marne. T. 0326210404. - Furn / Cur - *043165*
Pellot, Germaine, 34 All Paul-Doumer, 51000 Châlons-
sur-Marne. T. 0326683092. *043166*
Pierrejean, Patrick, 4 Rue Gobet-Boisselle, 51000 Châ-
lons-sur-Marne. T. 0326650905. - Ant / Paint / Furn /
Sculp / Dec / Lights / Instr / Cur / Toys - *043167*
Regain Antiquités, 167 Av Paris, 51000 Châlons-sur-
Marne. T. 0326644947. *043168*
Songy, Denise, 16 Rue Juifs, 51000 Châlons-sur-Marne.
T. 0326681889. *043169*

Chambéry (Savoie)
Au Fil des Temps, 12 Rue Porte-Reine, 73000 Cham-
béry. T. 0479600231. - Ant - *043170*
Bellemin, Patrick, 8 Rue Métropole, 73000 Chambéry.
T. 0479750954. - Ant / Paint / Furn - *043171*
Billamoz, Emmanuel, 5 Rue Bonivard, 73000 Chambéry.
T. 0479701932. - Ant / Paint - *043172*
Bonheur du Jour, 68 Rue Dacquin, 73000 Chambéry.
T. 0479852131. - Ant / Furn - *043173*
Chagnon & Massimino, Hubert & Juliette, 8 Pl Porte-
Reine, 73000 Chambéry. T. 0479704701.
- Ant - *043174*
Galerie Saint-Benoit, 4 Rue Guillaume-Fichet, 73000
Chambéry. T. 0479700445. - Ant / Cur - *043175*
Journet, Jean-Claude, 1 Rue Sainte-Barbe, 73000
Chambéry. T. 0479694905. - Ant - *043176*
Pascal, Jean-Pierre, 49 Rue Saint-Réal, 73000 Cham-
béry. T. 0479336259, Fax 0479334260. - Ant - *043177*
Pease, Michèle, 3 Rue Métropole, 73000 Chambéry.
T. 0479701209. - Ant - *043178*
Salle des Ventes des Particuliers, 25 Av Boisse, 73000
Chambéry. T. 0479694480, Fax 0479697666. - Ant /
Furn - *043179*

Chamblanc (Côte-d'Or)
Monot, Robert, Village, 21250 Chamblanc.
T. 0380204617. *043180*

Chambray-lès-Tours (Indre-et-Loire)
S.U.P. Occasions, Rond-Point Hippodrôme, RN 10,
37170 Chambray-lès-Tours. T. 0547282680. *043181*

Chamonix-Mont-Blanc (Haute-Savoie)
Art Populaire, 484 Rue Joseph-Vallot, 74400 Chamonix-
Mont-Blanc. T. 0450536461. *043182*
Au Vieux Chamouny, 53 Gal Alpina, 74400 Chamonix-
Mont-Blanc. T. 0450532054. *043183*
Dépôt Vente du Mont-Blanc, 1869 Rte Pèlerins, 74400
Chamonix-Mont-Blanc. T. 0450535321. *043184*
Dogue Bleu, 168 Av Michel-Croz, 74400 Chamonix-
Mont-Blanc. T. 0450533401. *043185*
Lavaivre, Henriette, 96 Rue Docteur-Paccard, 74400
Chamonix-Mont-Blanc. T. 0450531453. *043186*

Vivie, Gaudérique de, 534 Rue Joseph-Vallot, 74400
Chamonix-Mont-Blanc. T. 0450531476.   *043187*

Chamoux (Yonne)
Boutin, Josiane, Rte Clamecy, 89660 Chamoux.
T. 0386332938.   *043188*

Champagné Ics-Marais (Vendée)
Bouillaud, Alain, 19 Rue Paix, 85450 Champagné-les-
Marais. T. 0251566171.   *043189*

Champagnole (Jura)
Gaiffe, Daniel, 54 Rue Clemenceau, 39300 Champa-
gnole. T. 0384521557.   *043190*
Puces Champagnolaises, 4 Rue Herman Picaud, 39300
Champagnole. T. 0384525271.   *043191*

Champdeuil (Seine-et-Marne)
Betoulières, Michel, 6 Rue Fusées, 77390 Champdeuil.
T. 64388052. - Paint / Furn / Cur -   *043192*

Champenoux (Meurthe-et-Moselle)
Au Grenier, 37 Rue Saint-Barthélémy, 54280 Champe-
noux. T. 0383316675.   *043193*
Galerie Palatine, 25bis Rue Saint-Barthélémy, 54280
Champenoux. T. 0383317346.   *043194*

Champigneulles (Meurthe-et-Moselle)
Baraques Antiquités, Fonds Toul Baraques, RN 4, 54250
Champigneulles. T. 0383966638.   *043195*

Champigny (Yonne)
Denis, Claude, 31 Rue Beaumont-la-Chapelle, 89370
Champigny. T. 0386662425.   *043196*

Champniers (Charente)
Gillard, Colette, Les Rossignols, 16430 Champniers.
T. 0545682269.   *043197*

Champs-sur-Yonne (Yonne)
Grenier de Xavier, 4 Rue La-Poire, 89290 Champs-sur-
Yonne. T. 0386533365.   *043198*

Champtoceaux (Maine-et-Loire)
Pommery, Hervé de, La Bergerie, 49270 Champtoceaux.
T. 41835164.   *043199*

Chanac (Lozère)
Colomb, Alain, La Nojarède, 48230 Chanac.
T. 0466482459.   *043200*

Chancelade (Dordogne)
Pintos, Nicolle & François, 152 Rte Riberac, 24650
Chancelade. T. 0553047553. - Ant -   *043201*

Chandai (Orne)
Antiquaire de Chandai, 46 Rte Paris RN 26, 61300 Chan-
dai. T. 0233342763. - Ant / Furn -   *043202*
Grange des Ongliers, 61300 Chandai. T. 0233244426.
- Ant / Furn / Cur -   *043203*

Changé (Mayenne)
Massot, Régis, Le Louvray Rte Ernée, 53810 Changé.
T. 0243561608. - Ant -   *043204*

Chanos-Curson (Drôme)
Winterstein, Charles, La Motte, 26600 Chanos-Curson.
T. 0475073169.   *043205*

Chantelle (Allier)
Molinari, Jean-Paul, Rue République, 03140 Chantelle.
T. 0470566779. - Ant / Eth / Cur -   *043206*

Chanteloup (Ille-et-Vilaine)
Templon, Jean-Claude, Le Rocher, 35150 Chanteloup.
T. 0299440488, Fax 0299441585.   *043207*

Chantilly (Oise)
Alonso, Boniface, 14 Rue Creil, 60500 Chantilly.
T. 0344571278. - Ant / Furn -   *043208*
Chantebois, 4 Rue Otages, 60500 Chantilly.
T. 0344581725. - Ant -   *043209*
Chantilly Brocante, 12 Rue Gouvieux, 60500 Chantilly.
T. 0344577244. - Ant -   *043210*

Charbuy (Yonne)
Rapin, Philippe, 17 Rue Bac, 89113 Charbuy.
T. 0386471533.   *043211*

Charenton-du-Cher (Cher)
Moreau, Claude, Laugère, 18210 Charenton-du-Cher.
T. 0248607582.   *043212*
Sevret, René, Les Lombards, 18210 Charenton-du-Cher.
T. 0248607576.   *043213*

Charleville-Mézières (Ardennes)
Anthia, 98bis Blvd Gambetta, 08000 Charleville-Mézie-
res. T. 0324334098. - Ant -   *043214*
Fabrizi, Lionel, 20 Cours Aristide-Briand, 08000 Charle-
ville-Mézières. T. 0324590807. - Ant -   *043215*
François, Martine, 15 Quai Henri-Roussel, 08000 Char-
leville-Mézières. T. 0324370763. - Ant -   *043216*
Grenier de Saint-Lié, 20 Pl Mohon, 08000 Charleville-
Mézières. T. 0324377032. - Ant / Paint / Furn /
Glass -   *043217*
Nihotte, Pascal, 26 Rue Moulin, 08000 Charleville-Mé-
zières. T. 0324592014. - Ant -   *043218*
Perrodin, Claude, 17 Rue Saint-Louis, 08000 Charle-
ville-Mézières. T. 0324371305. - Ant -   *043219*

Charlieu (Loire)
Auguste, Philippe, 1 Pl Abbaye, 42190 Charlieu.
T. 0477602253.   *043220*

Charly (Cher)
Trameson, Daniel, 18350 Charly. T. 0248747125.
- Ant -   *043221*

Charly-sur-Marne (Aisne)
Rimbault-Joffard, Robert, 02310 Charly-sur-Marne.
T. 0323820272. - Ant / Furn -   *043222*

Charmes (Vosges)
Lacourt, Maurice, 6 Rue Général-Marion, 88130 Charmes. T. 0329381241.   *043223*

Charmes-sur-l'Herbasse (Drôme)
Pichat, Marcel, Travalers, 26260 Charmes-sur-l'Her-
basse. T. 0475457207.   *043224*

Charmoy (Yonne)
Diligence Maison Atlan, 4 Rte Paris, 89400 Charmoy.
T. 0386912526.   *043225*
Hervieux, Jean-Paul, 17 Rte Paris, 89400 Charmoy.
T. 0386912459.   *043226*
Matériaux Anciens, 14 Rte Paris, 89400 Charmoy.
T. 0386912305.   *043227*
Rivière, Guy, 4 Rte Lyon, 89400 Charmoy.
T. 0386912696.   *043228*

Charolles (Saône-et-Loire)
Dussably, Marie-Thérèse, 6 Pl Champ-de-Foire, 71120
Charolles. T. 0385241909. - Ant / Furn -   *043229*

Chartres (Eure-et-Loir)
Alexandre, Jean-Claude, 6 Rue Porte-Guillaume, 28000
Chartres. T. 0237362303.   *043230*
Baleine, Jean-Emile, 7 Rue Etampes, 28000 Chartres.
T. 0237356790.   *043231*
Chartres Antiquités, 24 Blvd Chasles, 28000 Chartres.
T. 0237362646.   *043232*
Detoeuf, Gérard, 24 E Blvd Chasles, 28000 Chartres.
T. 0237212859.   *043233*
Larvet, Pierre, 5 Rue Volaille, 28000 Chartres.
T. 0237365275.   *043234*
Larvet, Pierre, 24 Blvd Chasles, 28000 Chartres.
T. 0237362878.   *043235*
Lassaussois & Fils, 17 Rue Changes, 28000 Chartres.
T. 0237213774. - Furn / Cur -   *043236*

Chasnais (Vendée)
Engerbeau, Michel, Rte Sables, 85400 Chasnais.
T. 0251977423.   *043237*

Chasseneuil (Indre)
Buthiot, Bernard, Les Tailles, 36800 Chasseneuil.
T. 0254361391.   *043238*

Chasseneuil-sur-Bonnieure (Charente)
Antiquité Charentaise, RN 141, Rte Angoulême, 16260
Chasseneuil-sur-Bonnieure. T. 0545396924.   *043239*

Chassy (Cher)
Devoucoux, Le Chaumois, 18800 Chassy.
T. 0248261651.   *043240*

Château-Chalon (Jura)
Bourdy, Michel, Rte Vallée, 39210 Château-Chalon.
T. 0384852343.   *043241*

Château-Chinon (Nièvre)
Cacciabue-Drac, Delio, 17 Blvd République, 58120 Châ-
teau-Chinon. T. 0386704160.   *043242*

Château-du-Loir (Sarthe)
Simon, Yves, Le Rahart, 72500 Château-du-Loir.
T. 0243794175. - Ant / Furn -   *043243*

Château-Gontier (Mayenne)
Clématires, 6 Rue Glycines, 53200 Château-Gontier.
T. 0243703458. - Ant -   *043244*
Lecomte, Max, Rte Segré, 53200 Château-Gontier.
T. 0243072480. - Ant -   *043245*

Château-Guibert (Vendée)
Chouannerie, 1 Rue Carrières, 85320 Château-Guibert.
T. 0251467697.   *043246*

Château-la-Vallière (Indre-et-Loire)
Antiquités des Années 30, 11 Rue Lezay-Marnésia,
37330 Château-la-Vallière. T. 0547241986.   *043247*
Daluzeau, René, 5 Av Général-de-Gaulle, 37330 Château-la-Vallière. T. 0547241327.   *043248*

Château-Thierry (Aisne)
Au Temps Jadis, 82 Rue Général-de-Gaulle, 02400 Châ-
teau-Thierry. T. 0323835186. - Ant -   *043249*
Chrysalide, 4 Sq Paul-Doumer, 02400 Château-Thierry.
T. 0323833669. - Ant -   *043250*
Delangle-Lafleur, Jean-Pierre, 68 Rue Saint-Martin,
02400 Château-Thierry. T. 0323831389.
- Ant -   *043251*
Epoque, 4 Rue Fère, 02400 Château-Thierry.
T. 0323692044. - Ant / Furn -   *043252*

Châteaubourg (Ille-et-Vilaine)
Morel, Claude, La Beaulière, 35220 Châteaubourg.
T. 0299003177.   *043253*

Châteaudun (Eure-et-Loir)
A la Belle Epoque, 25 Rue Fouleries, 28200 Châteaudun.
T. 0237450193. - Furn -   *043254*
Au Sourire du Passé, 8 Rue Moulin, 28200 Châteaudun.
T. 0237458900. - Furn -   *043255*
Bouhours, William, 31 Blvd Kellermann, 28200 Château-
dun. T. 0237451340.   *043256*
Mahé, Joël, 25 Rue Fouleries, 28200 Châteaudun.
T. 0237450193.   *043257*
Saint-Nicolas, 6 Rue Château, 28200 Châteaudun.
T. 0237450964.   *043258*

Châteaugiron (Ille-et-Vilaine)
Magie du Temps, 10 Rue Madeleine, 35410 Châteaugi-
ron. T. 0299376912.   *043259*

Châteauneuf (Allier)
Dénichoir, Le Bourg, 71740 Châteauneuf.
T. 0385262572. - Ant / Furn -   *043260*

Châteauneuf (Côte-d'Or)
Rouard, Hélène, 21320 Châteauneuf.
T. 0380492171.   *043261*

Châteauneuf (Saône-et-Loire)
Dénichoir, Le Bourg, 71740 Châteauneuf.
T. 0385262572. - Ant / Paint / Furn -   *043262*

Châteauneuf-du-Rhône (Drôme)
Antiquités du Valladas, Pl Poste, 26780 Châteauneuf-
du-Rhône. T. 0475908576.   *043263*

Châteauneuf-en-Thymerais (Eure-et-
Loir)
Iazzourène, Jean-Claude, 49 Rue Dreux, 28170 Châ-
teauneuf-en-Thymerais. T. 0237510822.   *043264*

Châteauneuf-le-Rouge (Bouches-du-
Rhône)
Saurine, Château Galinière, 13790 Châteauneuf-le-Rou-
ge. T. 0442533230, Fax 0442533393.   *043265*

Châteauneuf-sur-Charente (Charente)
Jallet, Christiane, 8 Pl Plaineau, 16120 Châteauneuf-sur-Charente. T. 0545662979. - Furn / Jew /
Toys - *043266*
Salle des Ventes de Châteauneuf, 5 Pl Plaineau, 16120 Châteauneuf-sur-Charente. T. 0545970479. *043267*

Châteauneuf-sur-Loire (Loiret)
Antica, 112 Grande Rue, 45110 Châteauneuf-sur-Loire. T. 0238586685. - Furn / Cur - *043268*
Malle d'Antan, 1 Rue Fontaine-du-Garde, 45110 Châteauneuf-sur-Loire. T. 0238585625. *043269*

Châteauroux (Indre)
Belloy, 9 Rue Lemoine-Lenoir, 36000 Châteauroux. T. 0254340636. - Paint - *043270*

Châteauvillain (Haute-Marne)
Zirotti, Pierre, 24 Rue Penthièvre, 52120 Châteauvillain. T. 0325329575. *043271*

Châtelaillon-Plage (Charente-Maritime)
Arts du Temps, 49 Rue Marché, 17340 Châtelaillon-Plage. T. 0546560403. *043272*
Frances, Lyliane, 35 Av Angoulins, 17340 Châtelaillon-Plage. T. 0546569123. *043273*
Hacault, Alain, 41 Rue Marché, 17340 Châtelaillon-Plage. T. 0546300043. *043274*

Châtellerault (Vienne)
Bagatelle, 39 Rue Louis-Braille, 86100 Châtellerault. T. 0549020287. - Ant - *043275*
Barthélémy, 39 Rue Louis-Braille, 86100 Châtellerault. T. 0549212883. - Ant - *043276*
Cellier, 40 Rue Trois-Pigeons, 86100 Châtellerault. T. 0549859905. - Ant - *043277*
Mabuse Galerie d'Antiquités, 39 Rue Louis-Braille, 86100 Châtellerault. T. 0549930323. - Ant - *043278*
Renault, Claude, 41 Rue Louis-Braille, 86100 Châtellerault. T. 0549234536. - Ant - *043279*
Serrano, 16 Pl de la Croix-Rouge, 86100 Châtellerault. T. 0549931866. - Ant - *043280*

Châtenois (Bas-Rhin)
Antic Brocante des deux Châteaux, 77 Rte Sainte-Marie-aux-Mines, 67730 Châtenois. T. 0388822383. *043281*
Christelle, 25 Rte Sainte-Marie-aux-Mines, 67730 Châtenois. T. 0388827453. *043282*
Herrbach, Pl de la Mairie, 67730 Châtenois. T. 0388820369. - Furn - *043283*
Koch, Liliane, 82 et 101 Rue Maréchal-Foch, 67730 Châtenois. T. 0388821505. - Paint / Furn /
Lights - *043284*
Marianne, 7 Rte Kintzheim, 67730 Châtenois. T. 0388825066. *043285*

Châtenois (Vosges)
Fenouillet, Jean-Claude, Rte Courcelles, 88170 Châtenois. T. 0329946610. *043286*
Hayo, 4 Pl Gare, 88170 Châtenois. T. 0329946922. *043287*
Tourdot, Jean-Claude, 3 Rue Halles, 88170 Châtenois. T. 0329945821, Fax 0329945818. *043288*

Châtillon (Hauts-de-Seine)
Letellier, Dominique, 1 Imp Samson, 92320 Châtillon. T. 0142539683. *043289*
Sauli, 3 All Cadran-Solaire, 92320 Châtillon. T. 0146558388. *043290*

Châtillon-sur-Chalaronne (Ain)
Au Passé Présent, Montplaisir, 01400 Châtillon-sur-Chalaronne. T. 0474550731. - Ant / Furn - *043291*
Bretonnière, Micheline, Pl Eglise, 01400 Châtillon-sur-Chalaronne. T. 0474550602. - Ant - *043292*
Saint-Vincent, Rue Pasteur, 01400 Châtillon-sur-Chalaronne. T. 0474551493. - Ant - *043293*

Châtillon-sur-Loire (Loiret)
Coppin, Jean-Patrick, 7 Rue Hôtel-de-Ville, 45360 Châtillon-sur-Loire. T. 0238314200. *043294*
Dupont, Murielle, 9 Rue Fbg-de-Nancray, 45360 Châtillon-sur-Loire. T. 0238310938. *043295*

Roulin, Jean-Luc, 2 Rue Haute, 45360 Châtillon-sur-Loire. T. 0238314028. *043296*

Châtillon-sur-Marne (Marne)
Grandmaître, Jean-Henri, 3 Rue Raboterie, 51700 Châtillon-sur-Marne. T. 0326581169. *043297*

Châtillon-sur-Seine (Côte-d'Or)
Antiquités Neiges d'Antan, 19 Rue Bourg, Mont, 21400 Châtillon-sur-Seine. T. 0380913869. *043298*
Antiquités Saint-Nicolas, 14 Rue Saint-Nicolas, 21400 Châtillon-sur-Seine. T. 0380911893. *043299*
Burot, Y., 17 Rue Bourg, 21400 Châtillon-sur-Seine. T. 0380910002. *043300*

Châtillon-sur-Thouet (Deux-Sèvres)
Poitou Tout'Occas, 30 Rte Bressuire, 79200 Châtillon-sur-Thouet. T. 0549951926, Fax 0549951090. *043301*
Sinturet, Yves, 24 Av Morinière, 79200 Châtillon-sur-Thouet. T. 0549951985. *043302*

Chatonrupt-Sommermont (Haute-Marne)
Farradèche, Janine, RN 67, 52300 Chatonrupt-Sommermont. T. 0325948166. - Furn / Sculp / Cur - *043303*

Chatou (Yvelines)
Mikaeloff, Yves, 40 Rue Labélonye, 78400 Chatou. T. 0130530691, Fax 0130712420. *043304*

Chaulgnes (Nièvre)
Coudert, Pierre, Pertuiseau, 58400 Chaulgnes. T. 0386378261. *043305*

Chaulnes (Somme)
Lien, 3 Av Jean-Jaurès, 80320 Chaulnes. T. 0322839975. - Ant - *043306*
Maison de Jeager, 12 Rue Framerville, 80320 Chaulnes. T. 0322853621. - Ant - *043307*

Chaumont (Haute-Marne)
Antiquités le Téméraire, 5 Rue Victor-Mariotte, 52000 Chaumont. T. 0325030535. *043308*
Araldi Albin, 41 Rue Bourgogne, 52000 Chaumont. T. 0325032902. *043309*
Broc et Troc, 2 Rue Juvet, 52000 Chaumont. T. 0325036240. *043310*
Decomble, 32 Av Maréchal-Foch, 52000 Chaumont. T. 0325323546. *043311*
Guillaume, Christiane, 15 Av Carnot, 52000 Chaumont. T. 0325030292. *043312*
Raclot, Denis, 28 Rue Félix-Bablon, 52000 Chaumont. T. 0325039419. *043313*
Thieblemont, Gabriel, 2 Rue Tour-Charton, 52000 Chaumont. T. 0325033197. - Ant / Repr - *043314*
Troc Tout, 21 Rue Maréchal-Foch, 52000 Chaumont. T. 0325015431. *043315*
Vançon, Jean-François, 37 Rue Fauvettes, 52000 Chaumont. T. 0325321872. *043316*
Veillerette, Francis, 30 Av Maréchal-Foch, 52000 Chaumont. T. 0325323546. *043317*

Chaumont-sur-Tharonne (Loir-et-Cher)
Brocante Abescat, 9 Pl Mottu, 41600 Chaumont-sur-Tharonne. T. 0254885279. *043318*
Dufour, Edmond, 9 Pl Louis-Blériot, 41600 Chaumont-sur-Tharonne. T. 0254885186. *043319*

Chauny (Aisne)
Baratte, Albert, 3bis Rue Voltaire, 02300 Chauny. T. 0323520782. - Ant - *043320*

Chauray (Deux-Sèvres)
Beaufort, Robert, 39 Rue Château, 79180 Chauray. T. 0549080307. - Furn / Cur - *043321*

Chavanay (Loire)
Linossier, Gérard, Verlieu, Rte Nationale, 42410 Chavanay. T. 0474872358. *043322*

Chécy (Loiret)
Bonnefoy, Richard, 113 Rue Plantes, 45430 Chécy. T. 0238914801. *043323*
En ce Temps là, 2 Pl Jeanne-d'Arc, 45430 Chécy. T. 0238913919. *043324*

Lenoir, Jean-Marc, 98 Av Nationale, 45430 Chécy. T. 0238868809. *043325*
Vaslier, Yves, 114 Av Gien, 45430 Chécy. T. 0238868080. *043326*

Chef-Boutonne (Deux-Sèvres)
Forest, Hervé, Rue Fontaine, 79110 Chef-Boutonne. T. 0549296999. *043327*
Reveillaud, Jacques-Richard, 2 Rue Justice, 79110 Chef-Boutonne. T. 0549296060. *043328*

Chenay (Deux-Sèvres)
Reveillaud, Jacques-Richard, Le Bourg, 79120 Chenay. T. 0549073030. *043329*

Chenonceaux (Indre-et-Loire)
Grange Tourangelle, 5 Rue Docteur-Bretonneau, 37150 Chenonceaux. T. 0547239026. - Furn / China - *043330*
Relais de Chenonceaux, 10 Rue Docteur-Bretonneau, 37150 Chenonceaux. T. 0547238522. *043331*

Cheptainville (Essonne)
Nordin Frères, 5 Rue Francs-Bourgeois, 91630 Cheptainville. T. 0164569544. *043332*

Cherbourg (Manche)
Drieu La Rochelle, Jacques, Rue Blé, 50100 Cherbourg. T. 0233534504. *043333*
Fontaine, Danièle, 16 Rue Tribunaux, 50100 Cherbourg. T. 0233533760. - Furn - *043334*
Fontanet, Hugues, 18 Rue Au-Fourdray, 50100 Cherbourg. T. 0233532569. - Paint / Furn / China / Lights / Glass / Cur - *043335*
Glycines, 181 Av Paris, 50100 Cherbourg. T. 0233441531, Fax 0233221540. - Paint / Furn / Cur - *043336*
Puces de Cherbourg, 3 Rue Port, 50100 Cherbourg. T. 0233010965, Fax 0233431200. *043337*
Puces de Cherbourg, 125 Rue Val-de-Saire, 50100 Cherbourg. T. 0233430448, Fax 0233431200. *043338*

Cherisy (Eure-et-Loir)
Mascré, M., 10 Rue Charles-de-Gaulle, 28500 Cherisy. T. 0237438891. *043339*

Chevagnes (Allier)
Antiquité Brocante, Rte Nationale, 03230 Chevagnes. T. 0470434622. - Ant / Furn - *043340*

Cheval-Blanc (Vaucluse)
Goetz, Franck, 4 Boules-Saint-Gilles, 84460 Cheval-Blanc. T. 0490718506, Fax 0490711208.
- Ant - *043341*

Chevanceaux (Charente-Maritime)
Décorum, Chez Bargeot, 17210 Chevanceaux. T. 0546046604. *043342*

Chevrainvilliers (Seine-et-Marne)
Chappert, Françoise, 15 Rue Milly, 77132 Chevrainvilliers. T. 64287174. *043343*
Morge, Jean-Jacques, 18 Rue Gatinains, 77132 Chevrainvilliers. T. 64287767. *043344*

Chevreuse (Yvelines)
Antiqu'id, 32 Rue Porte-de-Paris, 78460 Chevreuse. T. 0130471635. *043345*
Au Vieux Chevreuse, 16bis Rue Lalande, 78460 Chevreuse. T. 0130520731. - Ant - *043346*
Bourbonnais, Jean-Louis, 12 Rue Renan, 78460 Chevreuse. T. 0130520578. *043347*

Chevry-Cossigny (Seine-et-Marne)
Armes du Chevalier, 2 Rue Jean-Delsol, 77173 Chevry-Cossigny. T. 64054593. *043348*

Chille (Jura)
Atmosphère, 190 Grande Rue, 39570 Chille. T. 0384473298. *043349*

Chilly-Mazarin (Essonne)
Coffret à la Belle Epoque, 18 Rue Passerelle, 91380 Chilly-Mazarin. T. 0169092740. *043350*

Chinon (Indre-et-Loire)
Antiquités La Grange, Saint-Jean, Rte Tours, 37500 Chinon. T. 0547930383. *043351*

Au Vieux Marché, 2 Rte Tours, 37500 Chinon.
T. 0547930410. - Furn / Cur - 043352
Dumartin, Gilles, Château du Plessis, 37500 Chinon.
T. 0547930687. 043353

Chissay-en-Touraine (Loir-et-Cher)
Jaep, Anne-Marie, 27 Rte Tours, 41400 Chissay-en-Tou-
raine. T. 0254321699. 043354

Cholet (Maine-et-Loire)
Antiquités Dudit, 212 Rue Nationale, 49300 Cholet.
T. 41585337. 043355
Braud, Philippe, 4 Rue Roland-Garros, 49300 Cholet.
T. 41584896. 043356
Broc 30, 41 Blvd Hérault, 49300 Cholet.
T. 41710130. 043357
Brosset, Roger, 1 Rue Barjot, 49300 Cholet.
T. 41621177. 043358
Leobon, Frédéric, 22 Rue Sardinerie, 49300 Cholet.
T. 41718505. 043359
Mercier, Jean-Yves, La Petite Simonière, 49300 Cholet.
T. 41652140. 043360
Pruvost, Jacques, 190 Rue Nationale, 49300 Cholet.
T. 41584443. - Furn / Cur - 043361

Chouzé-sur-Loire (Indre-et-Loire)
Boutreux, Patrick, 15 Rue Perruche, 37140 Chouzé-sur-
Loire. T. 0547951674. 043362

Chouzy-sur-Cisse (Loir-et-Cher)
Baronnière Antiquité, 44 Rue Gare, 41150 Chouzy-sur-
Cisse. T. 0254204771. 043363

Ciron (Indre)
Viollet, Evelyne, Scoury, 36300 Ciron.
T. 0254379428. 043364

Clairac (Lot-et-Garonne)
Poitrinet, Jean-Jacques, Marsac, 47320 Clairac.
T. 0553843489. 043365

Clairvaux-les-Lacs (Jura)
Alésina, Eric, 10 Rte Lons-le-Saunier, 39130 Clairvaux-
les-Lacs. T. 0384252144. 043366

Clamart (Hauts-de-Seine)
A l'Espace des Particuliers, 333 Av Général-de-Gaulle,
92140 Clamart. T. 0146323332. 043367
Aber, 183 Av Jean-Jaurès, 92140 Clamart.
T. 0146443259. 043368
Beauclair Klimberg, Françoise, 5 Rue Jeanne Hachette,
92140 Clamart. T. 0146303211. 043369
Gallot, Germain, 7 Rue Montoir, 92140 Clamart.
T. 0140958708. - Ant / Furn - 043370
Gaucher, Maurice, 333 Av Général-de-Gaulle, 92140
Clamart. T. 0146323332. - Ant - 043371
Gaucher, Maurice, 3 Rue Versailles, 92140 Clamart.
T. 0146314080. 043372
JPC, 4 Villa Cour Creuse, 92140 Clamart.
T. 0146382759. 043373
Pascal, 18 Blvd Frères-Vigoureux, 92140 Clamart.
T. 0146447709. 043374
Portman 4, 133 Av Jean-Jaurès, 92140 Clamart.
T. 0146443187. 043375
Tanagra, 15 Rue Hébert, 92140 Clamart.
T. 0146450542. 043376
Weitz, Pascal, 18 Blvd Frères-Vigoureux, 92140 Clam-
art. T. 0140957184. 043377

Clamecy (Nièvre)
Degrémont, Madeleine, 4 Rte Armes, 58500 Clamecy.
T. 0386272323. 043378

Clermont (Oise)
Boudoux, Bernard, Pl Mairie, 60600 Clermont.
T. 0344504140. - Ant - 043379

Clermont-Ferrand (Puy-de-Dôme)
Albareil, Jean-Luc, 6 Rue Paul-Leblanc, 63000 Cler-
mont-Ferrand. T. 0473913965. - Ant - 043380
Ambre, 34 Rue Pascal, 63000 Clermont-Ferrand.
T. 0473928114. - Jew / Silv - 043381
Amélie, 34 Rue Pascal, 63000 Clermont-Ferrand.
T. 0473927940. - Furn / Jew - 043382
Antic'Diffusion, 8 Rue Sainte-Geneviève, 63000 Cler-
mont-Ferrand. T. 0473938384. - Ant - 043383

Antique Annie, 30 Rue Pascal, 63000 Clermont-Ferrand.
T. 0473907765. - Ant - 043384
Antiquités, 78 Rue Lamartique, 63000 Clermont-Fer-
rand. T. 0473935355. - Mod - 043385
Antiquités II, 2 Rue Mont-Mouchet, 63000 Clermont-Fer-
rand. T. 0473938677. - Ant / Paint / Furn /
Jew 043386
Antiquités Lamartine, 78 Rue Lamartine, 63000 Cler-
mont-Ferrand. T. 0473938427. - Ant / Cur - 043387
Antiquités Leroux, 11 Rue Blaise-Pascal, 6300 Cler-
mont-Ferrand. T. 0473901493. - Furn / Music - 043388
Antiquités Saint Eloi, 4 Rue Maurice Busset, 6300 Cler-
mont-Ferrand. T. 0473920204, Fax 0473353871.
- Jew / Silv - 043389
Antix Brocante, 16 Rue Treille, 63000 Clermont-Ferrand.
T. 0473919095. - Cur - 043390
Argus des Monnaies-Curiosités, 30bis Rue Pascal,
63000 Clermont-Ferrand. T. 0473925891. - Ant /
Num / Arch / Mil - 043391
Atara, 5 Pl de-la-Victoire, 63000 Clermont-Ferrand.
T. 0473902280. - Furn - 043392
Aux Sièges d'Autrefois, 30 Rue Petits Gras, 63000 Cler-
mont-Ferrand. T. 0473366379. - Ant - 043393
Bakélite, 12 Rue Massillon, 63000 Clermont-Ferrand.
T. 0473900984. - Ant - 043394
Bauchet & Bitonti, 16 Rue Pascal, 63000 Clermont-Fer-
rand. T. 0473914195. - Ant / Furn / Mul - 043395
Bayssat, Alain, 17 Rue Petit-Gras, 63000 Clermont-Fer-
rand. T. 0473310606. - Graph / Paint - 043396
Bondieu, Roselyne, 15 Pl Terrail, 63000 Clermont-Fer-
rand. T. 0473900504. - Ant - 043397
Buteau, Gérard, 10 Rue Savaron, 63000 Clermont-Fer-
rand. T. 0473914797. - Ant - 043398
Calmels, Marcel, 34 Rue Lauriers, 63000 Clermont-Fer-
rand. T. 0473301093. - Ant / Furn - 043399
Clarysse, Anne-marie, 24 Rue Jacobins, 63000 Cler-
mont-Ferrand. T. 0473901716. - Ant - 043400
Claupier, 10 Rue A.-Moinier, 63000 Clermont-Ferrand.
T. 0473901716. - Furn - 043401
Colas, Jacques, 10 Rue Massillon, 63000 Clermont-Fer-
rand. T. 0473915369. - Ant - 043402
Corvinos, Pascal, 15 Rue Chaussetiers, 63000 Cler-
mont-Ferrand. T. 0473906090. - Ant - 043403
Davioud, Anne, 21 Rue Pascal, 63000 Clermont-Ferrand.
T. 0473910744. - Ant - 043404
Deffarges, Marie-Josephe, 13 Rue Rabanesse, 63000
Clermont-Ferrand. T. 0473938079. - Ant - 043405
Depailler, Chantal, 73 Blvd Lafayette, 63000 Clermont-
Ferrand. T. 0473921567. - Ant - 043406
Desparrain, Christian, 10 Pl Terrail, 63000 Clermont-
Ferrand. T. 0473922150. - Ant - 043407
Foth, Jacqueline, 94 Rue Oradou, 63000 Clermont-Fer-
rand. T. 0473912909. - Ant - 043408
Fournier, Françoise, 16 Pl Terrail, 63000 Clermont-Fer-
rand. T. 0473914174. - Ant / China / Glass /
Cur - 043409
Furlanini, Alexandre, 78 Rue Lamartine, 63000 Cler-
mont-Ferrand. T. 0473938427. - Ant - 043410
H. D. Antiquités, 31 Rue Mouchet, 63000 Clermont-Fer-
rand. T. 0473341070. - Ant - 043411
Jadis Antiquités, 16 Pl Terrail, 63000 Clermont-Ferrand.
T. 0473914174. - Ant / Furn - 043412
Jamet, Geneviève, 2 Rue Mont-Mouchet, 63000 Cler-
mont-Ferrand. T. 0473938677. - Ant - 043413
Jaude Antiquités, 18 Pl Jaude, 63000 Clermont-Ferrand.
T. 0473937249. - Ant - 043414
L'Or des Dômes, 27 Rue Delarbre, 63000 Clermont-Fer-
rand. T. 0473927056. - Paint / Furn / Jew - 043415
Laverroux, Jean-Pierre, 1 Rue Pascal, 63000 Clermont-
Ferrand. T. 0473907239. - Ant / Cur - 043416
Lavest, Georges, 78 Rue Lamartine, 63000 Clermont-
Ferrand. T. 0473935355. - Ant - 043417
Leroux, Marc, 11 Rue Pascal, 63000 Clermont-Ferrand.
T. 0473901493. - Ant - 043418
Mainguet, Nicole, 2 Rue Tranchée-des-Gras, 63000
Clermont-Ferrand. T. 0473912451. - Orient /
Tex - 043419
Mazoyer, Michel, 4 Rue Savaron, 63000 Clermont-Fer-
rand. T. 0473907451. - Ant - 043420
Mercier, Villon, 1 Rue Savaron, 63000 Clermont-Fer-
rand. T. 0473902352. - Ant - 043421
Oprandi, Jean, 35 Rue Chaussetiers, 63000 Clermont-
Ferrand. T. 0473375710. - Ant - 043422

Pautot, Alain, 37 Rue de-la-Treille, 63000 Clermont-Fer-
rand. T. 0473907200, Fax 0473900688. - Furn /
Jew - 043423
Pinard Etellin, Colette, 17 Pl Terrail, 63000 Clermont-
Ferrand. T. 0473906485. - Ant - 043424
Rey, Eric, 11 Rue Pascal, 63000 Clermont-Ferrand.
T. 0473908179. - Ant - 043425
Roux, Eric, 25 Av Margeride, 63000 Clermont-Ferrand.
T. 0473283414. - Ant - 043426
Saint Eloy Antiquités, 4 Rue Maurice-Busset, 63000
Clermont-Ferrand. T. 0473920204. - Ant - 043427
Sakura, 7 Rue Savaron, 63000 Clermont-Ferrand.
T. 0473919371. - Ant - 043428
Speller, Annie, 5 Rue Treille, 63000 Clermont-Ferrand.
T. 0473926997. - Ant - 043429
Sudre, Antoine, 2 Rue Pascal, 63000 Clermont-Ferrand.
T. 0473917646. - Ant - 043430
Thivisol, Yvette, 2 Pl Marché-aux-Poissons, 63000 Cler-
mont-Ferrand. T. 0473915245. - Ant - 043431
Yves Antiquités, 16 Rue Degeorges, 63000 Clermont-
Ferrand. T. 0473920821. - Ant - 043432

Clermont-l'Hérault (Hérault)
Clermont Antiquités, Av Ronzier-Joly, 34800 Clermont-
l'Hérault. T. 0467962397. 043433
Moulin à Huile, Pl Jules-Ballester, 34800 Clermont-
l'Hérault. T. 0467962134. 043434
Thebault, Ginette, Pl République, 34800 Clermont-l'Hérault. T. 0467880620. 043435

Cléry-Saint-André (Loiret)
Baudon, Claude, 141 Rte Orléans, 45370 Cléry-Saint-
André. T. 0238457317. 043436

Clichy (Hauts-de-Seine)
Alexandre, 86 Rue Martre, 92110 Clichy.
T. 0147372732. 043437
Charbonnier, Roger, 3 All Léon-Gambetta, 92110 Clichy.
T. 0142703885. 043438
Cohen, Yvon, 1 Rue Petit, 92110 Clichy.
T. 0142700335. 043439

Clisson (Loire-Atlantique)
Ecrin de Clisson, 8 Rue Docteur-Boutin, 44190 Clisson.
T. 40039326. 043440

Cloyes-sur-le-Loir (Eure-et-Loir)
Guillot-Renou, 34 Rue Docteur-Teyssier, 28220 Cloyes-
sur-le-Loir. T. 0237983165. - Furn - 043441

Cluny (Saône-et-Loire)
Bric à Broc, Pont-de-l'Etang, 71250 Cluny.
T. 0385590621. - Ant - 043442
Capricorne, 7 Rue République, 71250 Cluny.
T. 0385590621. - Ant - 043443
Grenier de Cluny, 8 Rue Municipale, 71250 Cluny.
T. 0385592767. - Ant - 043444
Valentin, Etienne, 6 Rue Filaterie, 71250 Cluny.
T. 0385591149, Fax 0385591254. - Ant / Furn /
China - 043445

Cluses (Haute-Savoie)
Au Petit Grenier, 3 Rue Général-Ferrié, 74300 Cluses.
T. 0450980246. - Furn / China / Mil / Cur - 043446
Verbièse, P., 614 Av Noiret, 74300 Cluses.
T. 0450981835. - Furn - 043447

Coatréven (Côtes-d'Armor)
Stéphan, Yannick, Mézo Moïc, 22450 Coatréven.
T. 0296380187. 043448

Cocquerel (Somme)
Marquette, Frédéric, 20 Rue Abbeville, 80510 Cocquer-
el. T. 0322318277. - Ant - 043449

Cognac (Charente)
Berciaud, Nicole, 5 All Champ-de-Mars, 16100 Cognac.
T. 0545827801. 043450
Hermine d'Orient, 107 Rue Henri-Fichon, 16100 Cognac.
T. 0545324930. - Tex / Jew / Cur - 043451
Lafarge, Jean-Pierre, 171 Av Victor-Hugo, 16100 Co-
gnac. T. 0545353036. 043452
Ricard, 16100 Cognac. T. 0545830080. - Furn / Sculp /
Cur / Toys / Music - 043453

Cogolin (Var)

Foire à la Brocante, ZA, Rte de Saint-Maur, 83310 Cogolin. T. 0494544468, Fax 0494565267. - Ant - 043454

Louis, Françoise, Rte de Saint-Maur, 12 Parc Activité 3, 83310 Cogolin. T. 0494541051. 043455

Coignières (Yvelines)

Debray, M., Rue Pont-des-Landes, 78310 Coignières. T. 0134613081. 043456

Tiphaine, Rue Broderie, 78310 Coignières. T. 0134612425. 043457

Coings (Indre)

Guitter, Claude, La Gaieté, 36130 Coings. T. 0254222679. 043458

Coligny (Ain)

Bastier, Patrick, Les Tilleuls, 01270 Coligny. T. 0474301342. - Furn / Eth / Cur - 043459

Collioure (Pyrénées-Orientales)

Casado, José, 12 Rue Saint-Vincent, 66190 Collioure. T. 0468820085. - Ant - 043460

Collonges (Corrèze)

Antiquités La Boutique, Bourg, 19500 Collonges. T. 0555254505. 043461

Collonges-sous-Salève (Haute-Savoie)

Barreau, Christian, 8 Rte Annecy, 74160 Collonges-sous-Salève. T. 0450437097. 043462

Collorec (Finistère)

Jeanne, Yannig, Penanech, 29126 Collorec. T. 0298739365. - Ant - 043463

Langlais, Marcel, Penanech, 29126 Collorec. T. 0298739365. - Ant - 043464

Colmar (Haut-Rhin)

Antiquités Arcana, 13 Pl Ancienne-Douane, 68000 Colmar. T. 0389415981. - Paint / Furn / Cur - 043465

Antiquités Donato, 14 Rue Tanneurs, 68000 Colmar. T. 0389414006. 043466

Au Vieux Quartier, 1 A Pl Ancienne-Douane, 68000 Colmar. T. 0389241478, Fax 0389410264. 043467

Bally, Gisèle, 3 Rue Mangold, 68000 Colmar. T. 07417726. 043468

Bally, Maurice, 3 Rue Mangold, 68000 Colmar. T. 0389236371. 043469

Biedermann, Jean-Paul, 6 Rue Conseil-Souverain, 68000 Colmar. T. 0389236520. 043470

Brocaphil, 22 Rue Vauban, 68000 Colmar. T. 0389239834. - Ant / Num - 043471

Caffard, Guy, 20 Rue Berthe-Molly, 68000 Colmar. T. 0389237966. - Ant - 043472

Caminade, 10 Rue Porte-Neuve, 68000 Colmar. T. 0389245575. - Graph - 043473

Fontaine, Christophe, 26 Rue Marchands, 68000 Colmar. T. 0389239587. 043474

Franck, Gérard, 34 Rue Marchands, 68000 Colmar. T. 0389245515. 043475

Franck, Judith, 20 Rte Bâle, 68000 Colmar. T. 0389240003. 043476

Franck, Lydia, 34 Rue Marchands, 68000 Colmar. T. 0389245515. 043477

Geismar, Dany, 32 Rue Marchands, 68000 Colmar. T. 0389233041. 043478

Lire et Chiner, 2 Rue Turenne, 68000 Colmar. T. 0389236019. 043479

Pfeiffer, Olivier, 5 C Rue Marchands, 68000 Colmar. T. 0389236208. 043480

Sonrier, Jean-Pierre, 57 Grand-Rue, 68000 Colmar. T. 0389416672. - Furn / China - 043481

Uhlmann, Jean-Pierre, 104 Rte Ingersheim, 68000 Colmar. T. 0389791374. 043482

Colombelles (Calvados)

Camélia Blanc, 12 Pl Hôtel-de-Ville, 14460 Colombelles. T. 0231720575. 043483

Colombes (Hauts-de-Seine)

Aux Reflets du Passé, 97 Rue D'Estienne-d'Orves, 92700 Colombes. T. 0147852303. 043484

Batisse, Michel, 246 Rue D'Estienne-d'Orves, 92700 Colombes. T. 0147808242. 043485

Carrousel des Jouets, 44 Rue Pierre-Brossolette, 92700 Colombes. T. 0147609685. - Toys - 043486

Cigliutti, Carole, 56 Rue Pierre-Géoffroix, 92700 Colombes. T. 0147819125. 043487

Duval, Pl de l'Eglise, 92700 Colombes. T. 0147803817. 043488

Duvauchelle, Frédéric, 57 Rue Jules-Ferry, 92700 Colombes. T. 0147691525. 043489

Fibule, 144bis Henri-Barbusse, 92700 Colombes. T. 0142424440. 043490

Rochas, Sylvain, 36 Rue Gabriel-Péri, 92700 Colombes. T. 0142420302. - Ant - 043491

Combrit (Finistère)

Antiquité du Port de Sainte-Marine, 79 Rue Odet, 29120 Combrit. T. 0298519547. - Ant - 043492

Courtil, Kerlec, 29120 Combrit. T. 0298564664. - Ant - 043493

Courtil, Kerlec, 29120 Combrit. T. 0298564664. - Ant - 043494

Compiègne (Oise)

Bailly, Denise, 34 Rue Bois, 60200 Compiègne. T. 0344414093. - Furn / Rel - 043495

Baudoux-Boitel, 4 Rue Lombards, 60200 Compiègne. T. 0344404772. - Ant / Dec - 043496

Broc 2000, 25 Rue Pierre Sauvage, 60200 Compiègne. T. 0344400692. - Ant - 043497

Challouet, Jacques, 9 Rue Petit Margny, 60200 Compiègne. T. 0344900878. - Ant - 043498

Dénicheur, 387, Av Raymond-Poincaré, 60200 Compiègne. T. 0344833879. - Ant - 043499

Labeye, Gil & Nicole, Pl de l'Eglise, 60200 Compiègne. T. 0344410111. - Ant - 043500

Marie-Tortue, 6 Rue Austerlitz, 60200 Compiègne. T. 0344861280. - Ant - 043501

Nonette Paysanne, 87 Rue Pont-Sainte-Maxence, 60200 Compiègne. T. 0344722276. - Ant / Dec - 043502

Protain, Frédéric, 151 Rue Beauvais, 60200 Compiègne. T. 0344416836. - Ant - 043503

Reflets d'Antan, 21 Rue Pierrefonds, 60200 Compiègne. T. 0344404300. - Ant - 043504

Renardière, 60200 Compiègne. T. 0344760106. - Ant - 043505

Troc 60, 31 Cours Guynemer, 60200 Compiègne. T. 0344865342, Fax 0344866931. - Ant - 043506

Conches-en-Ouche (Eure)

Thoumyre, François, 2 Rue Saint-Etienne, 27190 Conches-en-Ouche. T. 0232300438. - Ant - 043507

Concressault (Cher)

Boin-Schmitt, Rte Vailly, 18260 Concressault. T. 0248737666. 043508

Condé-sur-Vesgre (Yvelines)

Bouquet-Jacoillot, Colette, 4 Rue Vieux-Village, 78113 Condé-sur-Vesgre. T. 0134870464. 043509

Condom (Gers)

Montariol, Jacqueline, 17 Rue Gaichies, 32100 Condom. T. 0562280782. 043510

Salis, Henri, 7 Pl Lucien-Lamarque, 32100 Condom. T. 0562280032. 043511

Confolens (Charente)

Lorthois, Catherine, 14 Rue Pinaguet, 16500 Confolens. T. 0545841090. 043512

Confrançon (Ain)

Au Vieil Artisan Bressan, L'Effondras Rte Nationale 79, 01310 Confrançon. T. 0474302579. - Ant / Furn - 043513

Congerville-Thionville (Essonne)

Zamboni, Pierre, 11 Rue Vignes, 91740 Congerville-Thionville. T. 0164959186. - Furn / Cur - 043514

Conilhac-Corbières (Aude)

Almar Antiquités, RN 113, 11200 Conilhac-Corbières. T. 0468272447. - Ant / Dec / Cur - 043515

Conliège (Jura)

Michel, Narcisse, 14 Rue Neuve, 39570 Conliège. T. 0384241835. 043516

Corbeil-Essonnes (Essonne)

A la Brocante du Cloître, 10 Cloître Saint-Spire, 91100 Corbeil-Essonnes. T. 0164967511. 043517

Brocante Saint-Spire, 63 Rue Saint-Spire, 91100 Corbeil-Essonnes. T. 0160889155. 043518

Didier, 9 Rue Tisseurs, 91100 Corbeil-Essonnes. T. 0160884605, Fax 0160884605. 043519

Mascarin, Jacques, 85 Blvd John-Kennedy, 91100 Corbeil-Essonnes. T. 0164964560. 043520

Corbières (Alpes-de-Haute-Provence)

Bartolomei-Roussel, Yvon, Rue Ferrages, 04200 Corbières. T. 0492783693. - Ant - 043521

Corbigny (Nièvre)

Maroux, Simone, 1 Rue La-Cave, 58800 Corbigny. T. 0386201685. 043522

Cordes (Tarn)

Berthelot, Joël, La Gaudane, 81170 Cordes. T. 0563561080. 043523

Meugnier, Jean-Louis, Rte Albi, 81170 Cordes. T. 0563561318. 043524

Cormainville (Eure-et-Loir)

Legrand, Jean-Luc, 14 Pl Eglise, 28140 Cormainville. T. 0237220047. 043525

Cormatin (Saône-et-Loire)

Poussière du Temps, Bourg, 71460 Cormatin. T. 0385501749, Fax 0385501320. - Ant / Toys / Jew - 043526

Cormeilles (Eure)

Ladevèze, Michel, 15 Rue Pont-Audemer, 27260 Cormeilles. T. 0232578333. 043527

X Taburiaux, 9 Rue Abbaye, 27260 Cormeilles. T. 0232564854. 043528

Cormeilles-en-Vexin (Val-d'Oise)

Caussanel, Gérard, 3 Clos Voirin, 95830 Cormeilles-en-Vexin. T. 0134666782. 043529

Gilles, D., Rue Curie, 95830 Cormeilles-en-Vexin. T. 0134664219. 043530

Strutz, Michel, Rue Curie, 95830 Cormeilles-en-Vexin. T. 0134666691. 043531

Cormeray (Loir-et-Cher)

Arthèmes, Clos Bel-Air, 41120 Cormeray. T. 0254443124. 043532

Corné (Maine-et-Loire)

Brocante du Point du Jour, Rte Point du Jour, 49630 Corné. T. 41450941. - Furn / Cur - 043533

Van Weydevelt, Philippe, ZA Les Magnolias, 49630 Corné. T. 41450788. 043534

Corps-Nuds (Ille-et-Vilaine)

Ado-Ravier, Joëlle, 43 Blvd Gare, 35150 Corps-Nuds. T. 0299440800. 043535

Corseul (Côtes-d'Armor)

Boutique du Meuble Ancien, 8 Rue Temple de Mars, 22130 Corseul. T. 0296279978. 043536

Corte (Corse)

Campana, Félicien, Rte Saint-Pancrace, 20250 Corte. T. 0495610741, Fax 0495460154. 043537

Campana, Félicien, Parc Capuccini, 20250 Corte. T. 0495610949. 043538

Campana, Guérin, Rte Saint-Pancrace, 20250 Corte. T. 0495460219. 043539

Cosne-Cours-sur-Loire (Nièvre)

Alassimone, Maurice, Rte Braults, 58200 Cosne-Cours-sur-Loire. T. 0386261787. 043540

Bertille, 26 Rue Saint-Agnan, 58200 Cosne-Cours-sur-Loire. T. 0386267595. 043541

Borde, Thierry, RN 7, Bois Maillard, 58200 Cosne-Cours-sur-Loire. T. 0386261221. - Furn - 043542

Bric à Brac, Presle, 58200 Cosne-Cours-sur-Loire. T. 0386267843. 043543

Guillemenot, Francis, 1 Rue Lamartine, 58200 Cosne-Cours-sur-Loire. T. 0386283851. 043544

Cosne-d'Allier (Allier)
Bezert, Jean-Pierre, 81 Rue République, 03430 Cosne-d'Allier. T. 0470020112. - Ant -   043545

Cotignac (Var)
Dehennin, Guy, 9 Quartier Basse-Combe, 83570 Cotignac. T. 0494047048.   043546
Schiffino, Antoine, Rte Carcès, 83570 Cotignac.
T. 0494046109.   043547

Cottenchy (Somme)
Richard, M., 4 Rue Louis-Cardon, 80440 Cottenchy.
T. 0322095491. - Ant -   043548

Coublevie (Isère)
Cirieco Antiquités, Rue Lavandes, 38500 Coublevie.
T. 0476057129. - Ant / Furn -   043549

Coubron (Seine-Saint-Denis)
Rambaud, Hervé, 79 Av Jean-Jaurès, 93470 Coubron.
T. 0143305974.   043550

Couches (Saône-et-Loire)
Franck, Patrick, Rue Saint-Nicolas, 71490 Couches.
T. 0385496702. - Ant -   043551

Coudekerque-Branche (Nord)
Piquet Antiquités, 17 Rte Bergues, 59210 Coudekerque-Branche. T. 0328611718. - Ant -   043552

Coufouleux (Tarn)
Tiberto, Alex, La Saudronne, 81800 Coufouleux.
T. 0563419048.   043553

Couhé (Vienne)
Gressler-Vercier, Patric, 2 Rue Mystère, 86700 Couhé.
T. 0549591582. - Ant -   043554
Liévens, Av de Paris, 86700 Couhé. T. 0549432156.
- Furn -   043555
Noëlle & Gérard Antiquaires, 20 Av Bordeaux, 86700 Couhé. T. 0549592592. - Ant -   043556

Coulombs (Eure-et-Loir)
Au Bout de Chandelles, 33 Rue Chandelette-Chandelles, 28210 Coulombs. T. 0237825292. - Furn / Cur -   043557
Tholance, Michèle, 14 Av Abbaye, 28210 Coulombs.
T. 0237513110.   043558

Coulounieix-Chamiers (Dordogne)
Village Périgord, 39 Av Charles-de-Gaulle, 24660 Coulounieix-Chamiers. T. 0553098369, Fax 0553090846.
- Ant -   043559

Couptrain (Mayenne)
Guesne, Pierre, 8 Rue Chevallerie, 53250 Couptrain.
T. 0243038014. - Ant / Furn / Cur -   043560

Cour-Cheverny (Loir-et-Cher)
Cheverny Antiquités, 2 Pl Victor-Hugo, 41700 Cour-Cheverny. T. 0254792266.   043561
Clerc, Alain, 48 Rte Blois, 41700 Cour-Cheverny.
T. 0254799255.   043562
Lenay, Bernard, Les Jacquaudières, 41700 Cour-Cheverny. T. 0254799877.   043563

Courbevoie (Hauts-de-Seine)
Chevalier, Georges, 64 Blvd de la Mission-Marchand, 92400 Courbevoie. T. 0147884141, Fax 0143340899.
- Tex -   043564
Croissy, Bernard, 193 Rue Armand-Silvestre, 92400 Courbevoie. T. 0547884609, Fax 0547886040.
- Mil -   043565
Fourtane-Umbdenstock, Philippe, 2 Blvd Saint-Denis, Bâtiment A, 92400 Courbevoie.
T. 0143338431.   043566
Nouvelles Hybrides, 21 Rue Edith-Cavell, 92400 Courbevoie. T. 0143334016.   043567
Rolland, Emile, 41 Av République, 92400 Courbevoie.
T. 0143333918.   043568
Stoove, Philippe, 77 Blvd Saint-Denis, 92400 Courbevoie. T. 0143333904.   043569
Typhaine, 99 Rue Armand-Silvestre, 92400 Courbevoie.
T. 0147689102.   043570
Wayne, Charlotte, 228 Blvd Saint-Denis, 92400 Courbevoie. T. 0143330174. - Ant / Furn -   043571

Courbouzon (Jura)
Pèle Mèle, 36 Rue Fontaine, 39570 Courbouzon.
T. 0384248782.   043572

Courçay (Indre-et-Loire)
Leclerc, Jean, Moulin de Courçay, 37310 Courçay.
T. 0547941621.   043573
Sterlec, Moulin de Courçay, 37310 Courçay.
T. 0547941621.   043574

Courcelles-lès-Montbéliard (Doubs)
Olman, Jean, 21 Rue Montbéliard, 25420 Courcelles-lès-Montbéliard. T. 0381981878.   043575

Courçon (Charente-Maritime)
Brocante d'Angiré, Moulin de Neuillon, 17170 Courçon.
T. 0546016716.   043576
Chevreau-Drappeau, C., Grande Rue, 17170 Courçon.
T. 0546016293. - Furn -   043577

Courgivaux (Marne)
Leloup-Wallner, Pierrette, 19 Av Europe, 51310 Courgivaux. T. 0326815881, Fax 0326811797.   043578

Courmelles (Aisne)
Riquet Antiquités, 16 Rue Jean-Mermoz, 02200 Courmelles. T. 0323731877. - Ant -   043579

Courpière (Puy-de-Dôme)
Laverroux, Claude, 13 Blvd Gambetta, 63120 Courpière.
T. 0473531440. - Ant -   043580
Maloberti-Miermont, Marie-Claude, 11 Av de-Thiers, 63120 Courpière. T. 0473531724. - Furn / Mul -   043581

Cours (Deux-Sèvres)
Sardet, Claude, Bois Gibert, 79220 Cours.
T. 0549258582.   043582

Coursan (Aude)
Salazan, Antoine, 31 Rue Jean-Jacques-Rousseau, 11110 Coursan. T. 0468339183.   043583

Courtavon (Haut-Rhin)
Humbert, Dominique, 115 Rue Charmes, 68480 Courtavon. T. 0389408072.   043584

Courteilles (Eure)
Hourdé, S., Rte Brézolles, 27130 Courteilles.
T. 0232323494.   043585

Courville-sur-Eure (Eure-et-Loir)
Banquels, 43 Rue Georges-Fessard, 28190 Courville-sur-Eure. T. 0237233305.   043586
Brocante de Courville, 2 Rue Carnot, 28190 Courville-sur-Eure. T. 0237232736.   043587

Coutances (Manche)
Corbet, Auguste, Rte Carentan – Monthuchon, Ecauderie Saint-Nicolas, 50200 Coutances. T. 0233452867.
- Furn / Cur -   043588
Dépôt-Vente des Particuliers, Belle Hostesse, 50200 Coutances. T. 0233074104.   043589
Regnault, Georges, Rte Lessay-Servigny – Lavendelée, 50200 Coutances. T. 0233451801.   043590

Craon (Mayenne)
Longeany Antiquités, 9 Blvd Gustave-Eiffel, 53400 Craon. T. 0243061111. - Ant -   043591

Craponne-sur-Arzon (Haute-Loire)
Barrier, Claude, 36 Fbg Constant, 43500 Craponne-sur-Arzon. T. 0471033946.   043592

Cravent (Yvelines)
Chenuet, 1 Rue Mojard, 78270 Cravent. T. 0134761122, Fax 0134761742.   043593

Crécy-la-Chapelle (Seine-et-Marne)
Broc Antique, 32 Rue Deshuiliers, 77580 Crécy-la-Chapelle. Fax 64636397.   043594
Chapelle Antique, 31 Rue Abbesse, 77580 Crécy-la-Chapelle. T. 64636134. - Furn -   043595
Millord, 4 Pl Marché, 77580 Crécy-la-Chapelle.
T. 64638575, Fax 64636397.   043596

Crépon (Calvados)
Poisson, Anne-Marie, Rte Bazenville, 14480 Crépon.
T. 0231222127.   043597

Cressensac (Lot)
Marie-Agnès, La Paternerie, 46600 Cressensac.
T. 0565377392.   043598

Cresserons (Calvados)
Sevestre, Pascal, 22 Rte Caen, 14440 Cresserons.
T. 0231372196.   043599

Crest (Drôme)
Antiquités des Cordeliers, 5 Rue Cordeliers, 26400 Crest. T. 0475253141.   043600
Gilles, Gilbert, 17 Rue Sadi-Carnot, 26400 Crest.
T. 0475253053. - Paint / Furn / Cur -   043601

Créteil (Val-de-Marne)
Carcanade, Jean-Pierre, 15 Rue Général-Leclerc, 94000 Créteil. T. 0142075895.   043602
Vidal, 8 Av Marie-Amélie, 94000 Créteil. T. (1).   043603

Creuzier-le-Vieux (Allier)
Valentin, Jean-Claude, 38 Rue de l'Industrie, 03000 Creuzier-le-Vieux. T. 0470315513. - Ant / Furn -   043604

Crézancy-en-Sancerre (Cher)
Tanguy, Jean-Pierre, Pl Eglise, 18300 Crézancy-en-Sancerre. T. 0248790822.   043605
Tanguy, Jean-Pierre, Vaudredon, 18300 Crézancy-en-Sancerre. T. 0248790327.   043606

Crissay-sur-Manse (Indre-et-Loire)
Minski, Charles, 1 Rue Château, 37220 Crissay-sur-Manse. T. 0547586102.   043607

Croix (Nord)
Aux Caprices des Temps, 95 Blvd Carnot, 59170 Croix.
T. 0320260654. - Ant -   043608
Menotti, 33 Rue Dupleix, 59170 Croix. T. 0320891827.
- Ant -   043609

Croix-Chapeau (Charente-Maritime)
Antiquités Vieillard, 18 Av Libération, 17220 Croix-Chapeau. T. 0546358127.   043610

Crosne (Essonne)
Antiquaire d'Yerres, 4 All Industrie, 91560 Crosne.
T. 0169482874.   043611

Crozon (Finistère)
Gueguen, Jean-Yves, 1 Rue Louis-Pasteur, 29160 Crozon. T. 0298271202. - Ant -   043612

Cruis (Alpes-de-Haute-Provence)
Morero, Jean-Claude, Pl Eglise, 04230 Cruis.
T. 0492770018. - Ant -   043613

Cublac (Corrèze)
Sowinski, Christiane, Lapoujade, 19520 Cublac.
T. 0555851876.   043614

Cucq (Pas-de-Calais)
Amadeos, 155 Av François-Godin, 62780 Cucq.
T. 0321841197, Fax 0321841226.   043615
Harrewyn, Frédéric, 2 Pl Ancienne-Mairie, 62780 Cucq.
T. 0321948395.   043616
Marotte, 662 Av Maxenge-Van-der-Meersch, Trepied, 62780 Cucq. T. 0321845375. - Furn / Jew / Cur -   043617

Cugnaux (Haute-Garonne)
Bérart, Gérard, 55 Av Toulouse, 31270 Cugnaux.
T. 0561920307.   043618

Cuguen (Ille-et-Vilaine)
Antiquités de la Villate, La Villate, 35270 Cuguen.
T. 0299733334, Fax 0299732979. - Furn / China -   043619

Culan (Cher)
Clément, Rte Montluçon, 18270 Culan. T. 0248566178.
- Furn / Cur -   043620

Curvalle (Tarn)
Moch, Selma, La Claverie, 81250 Curvalle.
T. 0563558815. *043621*

Cussac-sur-Loire (Haute-Loire)
Marcon, Paul, Rte Solignac, 43370 Cussac-sur-Loire.
T. 0471031132. *043622*

Damblain (Vosges)
Brayer, André, 19 Rue Col-Renard, 88320 Damblain.
T. 0329073016. *043623*

Dammarie (Eure-et-Loir)
Ferrand, Michel, 5 Rue Patay, 28360 Dammarie.
T. 0237260110. *043624*

Dampierre-en-Yvelines (Yvelines)
Barre, Laurent-Claude, 3 Pl Eglise, 78720 Dampierre-
en-Yvelines. T. 0130525426. *043625*

Damville (Eure)
Dablanc, Jack, 65 Rue Breteuil, 27240 Damville.
T. 0232345026. *043626*

Daoulas (Finistère)
Longuestre, Franck, 3 Rte Quimper, 29224 Daoulas.
T. 0298259055. - Ant - *043627*

Darois (Côte-d'Or)
Jacquelin, Marie-Thérèse, 22 Rte Troyes, 21121 Darois.
T. 0380356113. *043628*

Davézieux (Ardèche)
Décorama, Rte de Lyon, 07430 Davézieux.
T. 0475676522. - Ant - *043629*
Léorat, Geneviève, 07100 Davézieux. T. 0475332629.
- Ant - *043630*

Dax (Landes)
Clefs de Saint-Pierre, 1 Av Georges-Clemenceau, 40100
Dax. T. 0558741592. *043631*
Ducasse, Patrick, 8 Rue Fusillés, 40100 Dax.
T. 0558741917. *043632*
Duret & Simoneau, 28 Av Saint-Vincent-de-Paul, 40100
Dax. T. 0558740617. - Paint / Furn - *043633*
Etchar, Michel, 2 Rue Eyrose, 40100 Dax.
T. 0558560064. *043634*
Gayan-Sourgen, Henri, 161 Av Saint-Vincent-de-Paul,
40100 Dax. T. 0558740544. *043635*
Gayan-Sourgen, Jean-Louis, 161 Av Saint-Vincent-de-
Paul, 40100 Dax. T. 0558740544. - Furn /
Sculp - *043636*
Petitcol, Xavier & Philippe Ravon, 43 Rue Carmes,
40100 Dax. T. 0558741519, Fax 0558562723. - Furn /
Cur - *043637*

Deauville (Calvados)
Héritage, 8 Rue Albert-Fracasse, 14800 Deauville.
T. 0231984884. *043638*
Lebreton, Alain, 15 Quai Touques, 14800 Deauville.
T. 0231810303. *043639*
Liberty's, 1bis Quai Touques, 14800 Deauville.
T. 0231888554. *043640*
Modestie, 34 Rue Gambetta, 14800 Deauville.
T. 0231981196. *043641*
Tour, Marthe de la, Englesqueville-en-Auge, 14800
Deauville. T. 0231652120. - Paint / Cur - *043642*
Windsor, 5 Pl François-André, 14800 Deauville.
T. 0231882119. - Furn - *043643*

Decize (Nièvre)
Nicard, Philippe, 120 Rte Feuillats, 58300 Decize.
T. 0386252082. *043644*
Thibert, Geneviève, 13 Av Verdun, 58300 Decize.
T. 0386252499. *043645*

Déols (Indre)
Fradet, Jean-Luc, 9 Rue Egalité, 36130 Déols.
T. 0254344951. *043646*

Desvres (Pas-de-Calais)
Faïencerie Masse, 39 Rue Minguet, 62240 Desvres.
T. 0321916399, Fax 0321874938. - China / Repr /
Lights / Dec / Rel - *043647*

Déville-lès-Rouen (Seine-Maritime)
Beurrier, Dominique, 126 Rte Dieppe, 76250 Déville-lès-
Rouen. T. 0235752367. *043648*

Die (Drôme)
Beaumont, Jean, Quart Chamarges, 26150 Die.
T. 0475220083. - Furn / Cur - *043649*

Dieppe (Seine-Maritime)
Antiquités Puits Salé, 188 Grande Rue, 76200 Dieppe.
T. 0232900091. *043650*
Beaufour, Pierre-Louis, 62 Rue De-La-Barre, 76200
Dieppe. T. 0235400355. *043651*
Bric-à-Brac, 8 Rue Oranger, 76200 Dieppe.
T. 0232901201. *043652*
Chineurs, 3 Rue Bains, 76200 Dieppe.
T. 0235842646. *043653*
Gaffé, Daniel, 4 Rue Villate, 76200 Dieppe.
T. 0235841706. *043654*
Milady, 22 Rue De-La-Barre, 76200 Dieppe.
T. 0235844720. - Ant / Jew - *043655*
Saint-Aubin, Roger, 29 Rue Halle-au-Blé, 76200 Dieppe.
T. 0235844594. *043656*

Dierre (Indre-et-Loire)
Potard, Simone, Coquiau, 37150 Dierre.
T. 0547302714. *043657*

Dieulefit (Drôme)
Ami Chemin, 61 Rue Bourg, 26220 Dieulefit.
T. 0475468447. - Furn / Cur - *043658*

Dieupentale (Tarn-et-Garonne)
Dauriac, Jean-Louis, RN 113, 82170 Dieupentale.
T. 0563025094. - Furn - *043659*

Dignac (Charente)
Debord, Claudette, La Clef-d'Or, 16410 Dignac.
T. 0545245177. *043660*
Scamps, François, Rte Angoulême, Chez Nadaud, 16410
Dignac. T. 0545245991. *043661*

Digne (Alpes-de-Haute-Provence)
Gleise, Betty, 93 Blvd Gassendi, 04000 Digne.
T. 0492315533. - Ant / Furn - *043662*

Digoin (Saône-et-Loire)
Jury, Geneviève, 52 Rue Verdier, 71160 Digoin.
T. 0385531008. - Ant - *043663*

Dijon (Côte-d'Or)
Adeline Déco, 23 Rue Condorcet, 21000 Dijon.
T. 0380418871. - Toys - *043664*
Aladdin, 39 Rue Auguste-Comte, 21000 Dijon.
T. 0380701584. *043665*
Atelier de la Tour Saint-Nicolas, 61 Rue Jean-Jacques-
Rousseau, Cour Saint-Nicolas, 21000 Dijon.
T. 0380734169. - Paint / Furn / Cur - *043666*
Atmosphère, 8 Rue Auguste-Comte, 21000 Dijon.
T. 0380732204. *043667*
Au Temps Passé, 54 Rue Jean-Jacques-Rousseau,
21000 Dijon. T. 0380720400. *043668*
Au Vieux Dijon, 8 Rue Verrerie, 21000 Dijon.
T. 0380318908. *043669*
Aux Occasions, 29 Rue Auguste-Comte, 21000 Dijon.
T. 0380735513. - China / Tex / Dec / Lights /
Cur - *043670*
Bouscary, Monique, 53 Rue Jouvence, 21000 Dijon.
T. 0380565364. *043671*
Brocante de Marie-Jeanne, 38 Rue Jeannin, 21000 Di-
jon. T. 0380364977. *043672*
Buisson, Monique, 21 Rue Verrerie, 21000 Dijon.
T. 0380303119. *043673*
Caniou, Fernande, 16 Rue Audra, 21000 Dijon.
T. 0380304998. *043674*
Damidot, Patrick, 56 Rue Forges, 21000 Dijon.
T. 0380300905. - Ant / Furn / China - *043675*
Degiovanni, 38bis Rue Charmette, 21000 Dijon.
T. 0380724780. - Furn / Cur - *043676*
Dubard, 25 B Rue Verrerie, 21000 Dijon.
T. 0380305081, Fax 0380499442. *043677*
Durandot, Denis, 76 Quai Nicolas-Rolin, 21000 Dijon.
T. 0380411492. *043678*
Escabelle, 10bis Rue Auxonne, 21000 Dijon.
T. 0380663157. *043679*

Fouchet, 11 Rue Bons-Enfants, 21000 Dijon.
T. 0380637004. - Paint - *043680*
Galerie Vauban, 3 Rue Vauban, 21000 Dijon.
T. 0380302699. - Paint / Fra - *043681*
Galerie 6, 6 Rue Auguste-Comte, 21000 Dijon.
T. 0380716846. - Paint / Graph / Draw - *043682*
Golmard, 3 Rue Auguste-Comte, 21000 Dijon.
T. 0380671415. - Paint / Furn / Cur - *043683*
Gossot, Renée, 2 Rue Chaudronnerie, 21000 Dijon.
T. 0380671582. *043684*
Graglia, Michel, 45 Rue Verrerie, 21000 Dijon.
T. 0380305497. *043685*
Grande Brocante, 81 Av Drapeau, 21000 Dijon.
T. 0380720419. *043686*
Guillemard, Michel, 22 Rue Verrerie, 21000 Dijon.
T. 0380318911. *043687*
Jacqueson, Jean-Guy, 42 Rue Semur, 21000 Dijon.
T. 0380551672. *043688*
Jadis Antiquités, 15 Rue Am-Roussin, 21000 Dijon.
T. 0380309909. *043689*
Ma Boutique, 11 Rue Verrerie, 21000 Dijon.
T. 0380304365. *043690*
Macassar, 96 Rue Vannerie, 21000 Dijon.
T. 0380672313. - Furn / Cur / Mod - *043691*
M.A.O., 67 Rue Vannerie, 21000 Dijon.
T. 0380671297. *043692*
Mroczek, Geneviève, 34 Rue Chaudronnerie, 21000 Di-
jon. T. 0380676851. *043693*
Mura-Todesco, Béatrice, 12 Pl Ducs-de-Bourgogne,
21000 Dijon. T. 0380301416,
Fax 0380309123. *043694*
Passion des Meubles, 54 Rue Auxonne, 21000 Dijon.
T. 0380667080. - Furn / Cur - *043695*
Perrin, Dominique, 86 Rue Monge, 21000 Dijon.
T. 0380430115. *043696*
Porro, Francis, 37 Rue En-Treppey, 21000 Dijon.
T. 0380671306. - Furn / Cur - *043697*
Positive, 25 Rue Auguste-Comte, 21000 Dijon.
T. 0380748829. *043698*
Pouffier, Elisabeth, 20 Rue Verrerie, 21000 Dijon.
T. 0380318903. *043699*
Ryaux, Evelyne, 7 Rue Verrerie, 21000 Dijon.
T. 0380303306. - Jew / Silv / Cur - *043700*
Turpin, Daniel, 5 Rue Vauban, 21000 Dijon.
T. 0380589364. *043701*

Dinan (Côtes-d'Armor)
Air du Temps, 72 Rue Brest, 22100 Dinan.
T. 0296398411. *043702*
Antiquités des Cordeliers, 13 Pl Cordeliers, 22100 Di-
nan. T. 0296391114. *043703*
Chicawana, 10 Rue Horloge, 22100 Dinan.
T. 0296392956. *043704*
Greniers du Jerzual, 8 Rue Poissonnerie, 22100 Dinan.
T. 0296397404. - Ant / Furn / Jew / Cur - *043705*
Morin, François, 6 Rue Guichet, 22100 Dinan.
T. 0296392520. *043706*
Moulin de la Mer, 14 Rue Ecole, 22100 Dinan.
T. 0296390147. *043707*
Pagner-Guigo, Emilienne, 10 Rue Sainte-Claire, 22100
Dinan. T. 0296395436. *043708*
Pétroff, 31 Rue Horloge, 22100 Dinan. T. 0296390430.
- Paint / Cur - *043709*

Dinard (Ille-et-Vilaine)
Albaret, Claude, 6 Av Harbour, 35800 Dinard.
T. 0299467189. *043710*
Antiquités Anglaises, 25 Rue Maréchal-Leclerc, 35800
Dinard. T. 0299466735. *043711*
Galerie Séraphine, 11 Rue Levavasseur, 35800 Dinard.
T. 0299469488. - Paint / Eth - *043712*
Kervely, Serge, 8 Rue Maréchal-Leclerc, 35800 Dinard.
T. 0299881303. *043713*
Lebourg, Marie-Nicole, 12 Rue Yves-Verney, 35800 Di-
nard. T. 0299881621. *043714*
Lescure, A., 24 Rue Maréchal-Leclerc, 35800 Dinard.
T. 0299469214. *043715*
Motte, Dominique, 21 Av Général-Giraud, 35800 Dinard.
T. 0299461735, Fax 0299465428. *043716*
Reflets d'Antan, 20 Rue Levavasseur, 35800 Dinard.
T. 0299467773. *043717*
Tampé, 22 Blvd Libération, 35800 Dinard.
T. 0299464977. - Furn - *043718*

Tire la Chevillette, 47 Rue Maréchal-Leclerc, 35800 Dinard. T. 0299462488. *043719*

Dinoze (Vosges)
Didier, Yves, 536 Rue Camille-Krantz, 88000 Dinoze.
T. 0329820578. *043720*

Dives-sur-Mer (Calvados)
Antiquités de la Régence 14, 2 Rue Hastings, 14160 Dives-sur-Mer. T. 0231914010. *043721*
Fleury, Benoît, 3 Rue Paul-Canta, 14160 Dives-sur-Mer.
T. 0231913043. *043722*
Mesnil aux Gates, 2 Rue Hastings, 14160 Dives-sur-Mer. T. 0231911909. *043723*

Dol-de-Bretagne (Ille-et-Vilaine)
Laick, Jean, 27 Grande Rue des Stuarts, 35120 Dol-de-Bretagne. T. 0299483346, Fax 0299480767. *043724*
Mandallaz, Michel, Les Rolandières, 35120 Dol-de-Bretagne. T. 0299481980. *043725*

Dole (Jura)
Aladin Line, 43 Rue Arènes, 39100 Dole.
T. 0384823250. - Jew - *043726*
Delaine, Rémi, 34 Rue Julien-Feuvrier-la-Bedugue, 39100 Dole. T. 0384722979, Fax 0384722979.
- Paint / Furn / Dec / Instr / Glass - *043727*
Lemazo, Jean-Claude, 21 Rue Marcel-Aymé, 39100 Dole. T. 0384725317. - Paint / Furn / Instr - *043728*

Dolus-le-Sec (Indre-et-Loire)
Lemoine, Yves, Malicorne, 37310 Dolus-le-Sec.
T. 0547921955. *043729*

Domagné (Ille-et-Vilaine)
Crocq, Guy, La Réusserie, 35113 Domagné.
T. 0299000181. *043730*
Raffenel, Jean-Pierre, Le Haut-Cranne, 35113 Domagné. T. 0299009751. *043731*

Domancy (Haute-Savoie)
Tissot Raymond, Ferme du Pelloux, 74700 Domancy.
T. 0450585391. - Tex - *043732*

Domèvre-en-Haye (Meurthe-et-Moselle)
Art d'Antan, 33 Rue Côte, 54380 Domèvre-en-Haye.
Fax 83231121. *043733*

Dommartin (Rhône)
Girier, Rue Chicotière, RN6, 69380 Dommartin.
T. 0478473708. *043734*

Dommartin-aux-Bois (Vosges)
Jadis, 8 Rue Haut-Bout, Adoncourt, 88390 Dommartin-aux-Bois. T. 0329668299. *043735*

Dommery (Ardennes)
Rolland, Albert, Ferme-Béguines Rte Launois, 08460 Dommery. T. 0324350119. - Ant - *043736*

Dompaire (Vosges)
Aux Armes de Lorraine, 11 Rue Pont-du-Saucy, 88270 Dompaire. T. 0329365555. - Num / Mil - *043737*
Troc de Dompaire, 26 Pl Général-Leclerc, 88270 Dompaire. T. 0329366627. *043738*

Dompierre-sur-Mer (Charente-Maritime)
Pinson, Jean, 1bis Rue Canal-Chagnolet, 17139 Dompierre-sur-Mer. T. 0546446313. *043739*

Domrémy-la-Pucelle (Vosges)
Fruch, Jean-Marie, 1 Rue Eglise, 88630 Domrémy-la-Pucelle. T. 0329069838. *043740*

Doncourt-lès-Conflans (Meurthe-et-Moselle)
Antiquités Auberge Sainte-Marie, 12 Rue Chardebas, 54800 Doncourt-lès-Conflans.
T. 0383330024. *043741*

Donzenac (Corrèze)
Mompart, Michel, 19270 Donzenac.
T. 0555857020. *043742*

Donzy (Nièvre)
Crépin, Serge, 21 Rue Etape, 58220 Donzy.
T. 0386394387. - Paint / Furn / Cur - *043743*

Dordives (Loiret)
Archinard, Mireille, 62 Rte Lyon, 45680 Dordives.
T. 0238928362. *043744*
Barbier, Gérard, 62 Rte Lyon, 45680 Dordives.
T. 0238928534. *043745*
Chartier, Jean-Paul, 62 Rte Lyon, 45680 Dordives.
T 0238928280. *043746*
Valantin, Hugues, 62 Rte de Lyon, 45680 Dordives.
T. 0238928615. - Furn - *043747*

Douai (Nord)
A la Brocante de l'Eglise, 75 Rue Fauqueux, 59500 Douai. T. 0327917477. - Ant - *043748*
A la Mansarde, 72 Pl Marché-aux-Poissons, 59500 Douai. T. 0327879727. - Ant - *043749*
Au Bonheur du Tour, 130 Rue Ferroniers, 59500 Douai. T. 0327879330. - Ant - *043750*
Au Grenier de Gayant, 127 Rue Polygone, 59500 Douai. T. 0327984213. - Ant - *043751*
Maison Sergeur, 6 Rte nationale, 59500 Douai.
T. 0320592298. - Ant - *043752*
Multi'Troc, 42 Rte Cambrai, 59500 Douai.
T. 0327918490. - Ant - *043753*
Poutrain, Pascal, 72 Pl Marché-aux-Poissons, 59500 Douai. T. 0327879727. - Ant - *043754*
Tondeur, Elina, 71 Rue Douai, 59500 Douai.
T. 0327926297. - Ant - *043755*

Douains (Eure)
Aumont, Maryannick, Rte Pacy, 27120 Douains.
T. 0232527348. *043756*

Douarnenez (Finistère)
Goubet, Michel, 23 Rue Pont-Neuf, 29100 Douarnenez. T. 0298743568, Fax 0298743657. - Ant - *043757*

Douchy-les-Mines (Nord)
Cattiaux, Chantal, 250bis Av République, 59282 Douchy-les-Mines. T. 0327444392. - Ant - *043758*
Druon, Sylvie, 159 Av République, 59282 Douchy-les-Mines. T. 0327431147. - Ant - *043759*

Doudeville (Seine-Maritime)
Naze, Michel, Rue Félix-Faure, 76560 Doudeville.
T. 0235965032. *043760*

Doué-la-Fontaine (Maine-et-Loire)
Billy, Dominique, Les Ulmes, 49700 Doué-la-Fontaine.
T. 41670343. - Furn / Cur - *043761*
Moisson, Dominique, 35bis Rue Soulanger, 49700 Doué-la-Fontaine. T. 41590200. - Furn - *043762*
Moisson, Valentin, 35bis Rue Soulanger, 49700 Doué-la-Fontaine. T. 41592139. - Furn - *043763*

Dourdan (Essonne)
Galerie du Grenier, 54 Rue Chartres, 91410 Dourdan.
T. 0164597013. *043764*
Juhan, Liliane, 2 Av Carnot, 91410 Dourdan.
T. 0164596575. *043765*
Tout pour le Plaisir, 29 Av Etampes, 91410 Dourdan.
T. 0164593680. *043766*

Douvres-la-Délivrande (Calvados)
Lair, Joëlle, 3 Av Basilique, 14440 Douvres-la-Délivrande. T. 0231372758. - Furn / Cur - *043767*
Masson, Francis, 31 Rte Caen, 14440 Douvres-la-Délivrande. T. 0231375996. *043768*

Draguignan (Var)
Frèrejacques, 165 Av P-Brossolette, 83300 Draguignan.
T. 0494680578. - Furn / China / Dec - *043769*
Giraud, Patrick, 21 Blvd Jean-Jaurès, 83300 Draguignan. T. 0494687668. *043770*
Mouvement, Rue Blancherie, 83300 Draguignan.
T. 0494471465. *043771*
Raizman, Adolphe, 10 Av Carnot, 83300 Draguignan.
T. 0494680566. - Ant - *043772*
Thème Antique, 573 Av Tuttlingen, 83300 Draguignan.
T. 0494672129. *043773*
Tilbury, Av Général-de-Gaulle, 83300 Draguignan.
T. 0494681385. - Tex - *043774*

Draveil (Essonne)
Bleuse, 6 Blvd Général-de-Gaulle, 91210 Draveil.
T. 0169030517, Fax 0169402068. *043775*

Cornic, 12 All Sports, 91210 Draveil.
T. 0169037247. *043776*

Dreux (Eure-et-Loir)
Rêvantic, 8 Rue Tanneurs, 28100 Dreux.
T. 0237424140. *043777*

Drevant (Cher)
Roussillot, Yves & Marie-Claude, 840 Chemin-Grand-Tertre, 18200 Drevant. T. 0248963018. - Furn / Mil / Cur / Toys - *043778*

Droué (Loir-et-Cher)
Heyraud, Françoise, La Beaudronnière, 41270 Droué.
T. 0254805734. *043779*

Drugeac (Cantal)
Au Siècle Passé, Les Sanioles, 15140 Drugeac.
T. 0471691117. *043780*

Duclair (Seine-Maritime)
Au Bonheur d'Antan, 31 Rue Prés-Sarraut, 76480 Duclair. T. 0235378606. - Furn - *043781*

Dugny-sur-Meuse (Meuse)
Borawiak, Michel, Ecart-de-Billemont, 55100 Dugny-sur-Meuse. T. 0329861969. - Ant / Furn - *043782*

Dun-le-Palestel (Creuse)
Johnson-Feugère, Rue Sabots, 23800 Dun-le-Palestel.
T. 0555891654. - Ant / Furn - *043783*

Dun-sur-Auron (Cher)
Arnoux, Jean-Paul, 66 Rue Hermitage, 18130 Dun-sur-Auron. T. 0248595867. - Furn - *043784*

Dunkerque (Nord)
Bourgogne Antiquités, 54 Rue Bourgogne, 59140 Dunkerque. T. 0328665342. - Ant - *043785*
Claeyssen, Jean-Bernard, 30 Rue Paul-Machy, 59240 Dunkerque. T. 0328663670. - Ant - *043786*
Cuisinier, Ségura, 21 Rue Lion-d'Or, 59140 Dunkerque.
T. 0328668067. - Ant - *043787*
Galerie du Lion d'Or, 21 Rue Lion-d'Or, 59140 Dunkerque. T. 0328630444. - Ant - *043788*
Grenier de Mamy, 16 Rue Soubise, 59140 Dunkerque.
T. 0328631270. - Ant - *043789*
Guichard, Iut Rue Paris, 59140 Dunkerque.
T. 0328606681. - Ant - *043790*
Kiecken Duthoit, 41 Av Kléber, 59240 Dunkerque.
T. 0328206640. - Ant - *043791*
Musardière, 70 Rue Saint-Omer, 59140 Dunkerque.
T. 0328498229. - Furn / China - *043792*

Duras (Lot-et-Garonne)
Ponticq, Michèle, Moulin de Monsieur, 47120 Duras.
T. 0553837402. *043793*

Durtal (Maine-et-Loire)
Antiquités des Chats Bossus, 64bis Av Angers, 49430 Durtal. T. 41760266, Fax 41763337. *043794*
Chalmont, Christophe, 18 Av Angers, 49430 Durtal.
T. 41760452. - Furn / Cur - *043795*

Eaubonne (Val-d'Oise)
Delorme, Michel, 10 Av Liberté, 95600 Eaubonne.
T. 0139598776. *043796*
Grenier du Petit Château, 50 Blvd du Petit-Château, 95600 Eaubonne. T. 0139596454. *043797*
James, Jean, 20 Rue Stéphane-Proust, 95600 Eaubonne. T. 0139595536. *043798*
Jamin, 7 Av Mirabeau, 95600 Eaubonne.
T. 0139590372. - Ant / Paint / Furn / Cur - *043799*
Morateur, Philippe, 5 Rue Louis-Blanc, 95600 Eaubonne.
T. 0139590600. *043800*
Passé Simple, 1 Rue Jeanne-Robillon, 95600 Eaubonne. T. 0139592958, Fax 0139598854. - Furn - *043801*
Trottin, Jean-Claude, 9 Rue Paris, 95600 Eaubonne.
T. 0139592177. *043802*

Eauze (Gers)
Au Grenier Elusate, 34 Blvd d'Artagnan, 32800 Eauze.
T. 0562098967. *043803*

Echalot (Côte-d'Or)
Matériaux d'Autrefois, Rue Lentillet, 21510 Echalot.
T. 0380927075. - Dec - *043804*

Echarcon (Essonne)
Aux Quartiers de France, 9 Rue Paul-Vitalis, 91100 Echarcon. T. 0164571990.   043805

Echenoz-la-Méline (Haute-Saône)
Agrelli, Vincent, Rte Besançon, 70000 Echenoz-la-Mé-line. T. 0384750937.   043806

Echiré (Deux-Sèvres)
Aubisse, G., Logis de Beaulieu, 79410 Echiré. T. 0549257199. - Paint / Furn / Sculp -   043807

Ecole-Valentin (Doubs)
Marotte, 23 Rte Epinal, 25480 Ecole-Valentin. T. 0381800062.   043808

Ecotay-l'Olme (Loire)
Kanel, Gilbert, 1 Chemin Charduron, 42600 Ecotay-l'Olme. T. 0477584104.   043809

Ecouis (Eure)
Lemercier, Michèle, Pl Mairie, 27440 Ecouis. T. 0232694394.   043810
Picard, C., 10 Rte Paris, RN 14, 27440 Ecouis. T. 0232694047. - Paint / Furn / Jew / Silv / Cur -   043811
Tempora Antiquités, 2 Ham Brémules, 27440 Ecouis. T. 0232694531.   043812

Ecrouves (Meurthe-et-Moselle)
Fabing, Catherine, 519 Rue Lieutenant-Ehlé, 54200 Ecrouves. T. 0383644668.   043813

Egletons (Corrèze)
Licorne Saint-Antoine, 79 Av Charles-de-Gaulle, 19300 Egletons. T. 0555933249.   043814

Egreville (Seine-et-Marne)
Grais, Christian, 16 Pl Massenet, 77620 Egreville. T. 64295851.   043815
Rousseau, Maryse, 8 Rue Edmond-Hubert, 77620 Egre-ville. T. 64295645.   043816
Rousseau, Maryse, 48 Rue Saint-Martin, 77620 Egre-ville. T. 64295116.   043817

Eguilles (Bouches-du-Rhône)
Chailloux, Raymonde, 20bis Rue Grand-Logis, 13510 Eguilles. T. 0442925479.   043818

Eguisheim (Haut-Rhin)
Malle aux Lutins, 25 Rue Remparts, 68420 Eguisheim. T. 0389249031. - Furn / Cur -   043819

Eguzon (Indre)
Menant, Paulette, 11 Rue Jean-Jaurès, 36270 Eguzon. T. 0254474429.   043820

Elbeuf (Seine-Maritime)
Kerner, Claude, 86 Rue Martyrs, 76500 Elbeuf. T. 0235782133.   043821
Studio Venise, 15bis Rue Mar-Gallieni, 76500 Elbeuf. T. 0235781966.   043822

Embrun (Hautes-Alpes)
Ligozat, André, 2 Pl Mazelière, 05200 Embrun. T. 0492435289.   043823

Enghien-les-Bains (Val-d'Oise)
Armand, Philippe, 183 Av Division-Leclerc, 95880 Eng-hien-les-Bains. T. 0139641234.   043824
Art Concept, 17 Rue Arrivée, 95880 Enghien-les-Bains. T. 0139642237.   043825
Avrand, 135 Av Division-Leclerc, 95880 Enghien-les-Bains. T. 0139894524, Fax 0139897190.   043826
Cheyrouze, Axel & Claire, 7 Rue Mora, 95880 Enghien-les-Bains. T. 0134128618. - Ant / Paint / Furn / China / Sculp -   043827
Clos, Abel, 1 Pl Foch, 95880 Enghien-les-Bains. T. 0139646643, Fax 0139642762.   043828
Enghien, 10 Pass Dubuisson, 95880 Enghien-les-Bains. T. 0139647443.   043829
Serry, Louis-Marie, 3 Blvd Lac, 95880 Enghien-les-Bains. T. 0134122714. - Ant / Paint / Furn -   043830

Ennordres (Cher)
Laurent, Jean-Claude, Le Grand-Lieu, 18380 Ennordres. T. 0248583202, Fax 0248583242. - Furn -   043831

Epagny (Haute-Savoie)
Trouvailles, 565 Rte de Sillingy, 74330 Epagny. T. 0450220910.   043832

Epernay (Marne)
Bonne Epoque, 106 Av Foch, 51200 Epernay. T. 0326541139. - Furn / Cur -   043833
Brest, Christophe, 24 Av Maréchal-Foch, 51200 Eper-nay. T. 0326540085.   043834
Huzette, Jocelyne, 4 Rue Picardie, 51200 Epernay. T. 0326545852.   043835
Thil, Stéphane, 18 Rue Montarlot, 51200 Epernay. T. 0326553843.   043836

Epinal (Vosges)
Antiquités de la Place, 3 Pl Saint-Goery, 88000 Epinal. T. 0329312800.   043837
Dernier Empire, 23 Rue Bésonfosse-Saint-Laurent, 88000 Epinal. T. 0329354913.   043838
Grenier des Collectionneurs, 2 Rue Jeanmaire, 88000 Epinal. T. 0329822308.   043839
Imagerie Pellerin, 42bis Quai Dognoville, 88000 Epinal. T. 0329822189. - Graph -   043840
Melchior, 13 Pl Edmond-Henry, 88000 Epinal. T. 0329825327.   043841
Spinabroc, 20 Rue Remiremont, 88000 Epinal. T. 0329354786.   043842
Tisserant, Jean-Marie, 16 Rue Louis-Blériot, 88000 Epi-nal. T. 0329343144.   043843
Viant, André, 47 Rue Remiremont, 88000 Epinal. T. 0329353485. - Furn -   043844

Epinay-sur-Odon (Calvados)
Brunet, Jean-Paul, Outreleau, 14310 Epinay-sur-Odon. T. 0231776764.   043845

Epinay-sur-Seine (Seine-Saint-Denis)
Bunel, Marie-Thérèse, 65 Av République, 93800 Epinay-sur-Seine. T. 0148268887.   043846
Wilmes, Maryse, 1 Rue Lille, 93800 Epinay-sur-Seine. T. 0148417655.   043847

Epreville (Seine-Maritime)
Fermette, 76400 Epreville. T. 0235297257.   043848

Ernée (Mayenne)
Lemercier, Roger, 35 Pl Renault-Morlière, 53500 Ernée. T. 0243052055. - Ant -   043849

Erquy (Côtes-d'Armor)
Dodin, Roland, 1 Rue Eglise, 22430 Erquy. T. 0296720894.   043850
Valat, Eric, 2 Rue Eglise, 22430 Erquy. T. 0296720171.   043851

Escornebœuf (Gers)
Hucher, Franck, Rte Mauvezin, 32200 Escornebœuf. T. 0562679168.   043852

Espaly-Saint-Marcel (Haute-Loire)
ID Meubles, 9 Av Paul-Bérard, 43000 Espaly-Saint-Mar-cel. T. 0471059181.   043853

Espelette (Pyrénées-Atlantiques)
Itoiz, Jean-Pierre, Rte Cambo, 64250 Espelette. T. 0559939112. - Ant -   043854

Espinasse-Vozelle (Allier)
Goliard, Paul, Rte Nationale 209, 03110 Espinasse-Vo-zelle. T. 0470565032. - Furn -   043855
Lamarque, Le Breuil, 03110 Espinasse-Vozelle. T. 0470565169. - Ant / Paint / Furn -   043856

Espoey (Pyrénées-Atlantiques)
Rey, Rte de Lourdes, 64420 Espoey. T. 0559046257. - Ant -   043857
Royo, Jésus, 64420 Espoey. T. 0559046809. - Ant -   043858

Espondeilhan (Hérault)
Charme d'Antan, Rue Notre-Dame-des-Pins, 34290 Es-pondeilhan. T. 0467391190. - Furn -   043859

Essert (Territoire-de-Belfort)
Barresi, Joseph, 23 Rue Côteau, 90850 Essert. T. 0384211233.   043860

Essey (Côte-d'Or)
Fougerouge, Village, 21320 Essey. T. 0380841287.   043861

Essey-lès-Nancy (Meurthe-et-Moselle)
Antiquités 89, 123 Av Foch, 54270 Essey-lès-Nancy. T. 0383204952.   043862

Estang (Gers)
Paschal, Nicole, Pl Roger-Bon, 32240 Estang. T. 0562096179.   043863

Etampes (Essonne)
André, Jacques, 11 Av Libération, 91150 Etampes. T. 0164944932.   043864
Castrataro, Giorgio, 6 Av Libération, 91150 Etampes. T. 0169929418.   043865

Etaules (Charente-Maritime)
Galerie Belphégor, 8 Rue Granderie, 17750 Etaules. T. 0546368701, Fax 0546369312.   043866

Eterville (Calvados)
Galerie Ifé, 7 Rue Bois-des-Trentaines, 14930 Eterville. T. 0231266271.   043867

Etival-Clairefontaine (Vosges)
Mathieu, Marie-France, 26 Av Charles-de-Gaulle, 88480 Etival-Clairefontaine. T. 0329418348.   043868

Etouvans (Doubs)
Malesieux, Jean, 29 Rue Dampierre, 25260 Etouvans. T. 0381937228.   043869

Etrépagny (Eure)
Antiquités Les Iris, 38 Rue Georges-Clemenceau, 27150 Etrépagny. T. 0232558878.   043870
Parde, Jean-Pierre, 20 Rue Saint-Maur, 27150 Etrépa-gny. T. 0232558142.   043871

Eu (Seine-Maritime)
Bourjot, Christophe, 15 Rue Normandie, 76260 Eu. T. 0235503757.   043872
Chez Poupy, 66bis Rue République, 76260 Eu. T. 0235863463.   043873
Pignoque, Eric, 44 Rue Paul-Bignon, 76260 Eu. T. 0235864707.   043874

Eugénie-les-Bains (Landes)
D'Hier et d'Aujourd'hui, Résidence Alisiers, 40320 Eugé-nie-les-Bains. T. 0558511191.   043875

Evian-les-Bains (Haute-Savoie)
Duran, Pierre, 35 Quai Paul-Léger, 74500 Evian-les-Bains. T. 0450750248.   043876
Houdebert, Jack, 41 Quai Paul-Léger, 74500 Evian-les-Bains. T. 0450756558. - Furn / Cur -   043877
Lavanchy Brocante Shop, 28 Rue Port, 74500 Evian-les-Bains. T. 0450754815.   043878
Lavanchy, Henri, 5 Av Sources, 74500 Evian-les-Bains. T. 0450751205.   043879
Neyroud, Albert, 1 Pl Port, 74500 Evian-les-Bains. T. 0450752293.   043880
Neyroud, Albert, Rue Genevrilles, 74500 Evian-les-Bains. T. 0450708744.   043881

Evreux (Eure)
Antiquités Saint-Louis, 42 Rue Saint-Louis, 27000 Evreux. T. 0232335427. - Furn / China / Sculp / Lights / Instr / Glass / Cur / Toys -   043882
Au Bonheur du Jour, 20 Rue Horloge, 27000 Evreux. T. 0232385565. - Furn / Cur -   043883
Cabinet d'Expertise en Antiquités, 63 Rue Isambard, 27000 Evreux. T. 0232331903.   043884
Dupont de l'Eure, 3 Pl Dupont-de-l'Eure, 27000 Evreux. T. 0232333599.   043885
Floréal, 41 Rue Harpe, 27000 Evreux. T. 0232332233. - Num / Graph -   043886
Hier et Aujourd'hui, 6 Rue 28e-Régiment-d'Infanterie, 27000 Evreux. T. 0232311685.   043887
Legabilleux, Jean-Paul, 42 Av Aristide-Briand, 27000 Evreux. T. 0232625800. - Paint / Furn / Sculp / Tex / Cur -   043888
Ménard, Christophe, 13 Rue Verdun, 27000 Evreux. T. 0232386780. - Jew -   043889

New Big Antiquités, 1 Rue Cocherel, 27000 Evreux.
T. 0232337231. *043890*

Evron (Mayenne)
Rolland, René, 22 Rue Général-de-Gaulle, 53600 Evron.
T. 0243016007. - Ant / Furn / Jew / Silv - *043891*

Exincourt (Doubs)
Brocanterie, 2 Rue Sochaux, 25400 Exincourt.
T. 0381954221. *043892*

Eyguières (Bouches-du-Rhône)
Lacoste, Sylviane, Rue Treille, 13430 Eyguières.
T. 0490578206. *043893*

Falaise (Calvados)
Bencteux MM, Pl Reine-Mathilde, 14700 Falaise.
T. 0231900641. *043894*
Lair, Christian, 50 Rue Camp-Ferme, 14700 Falaise.
T. 0231900388. *043895*
Ver Eecke, Luc, 21 Av Hastings, 14700 Falaise.
T. 0231401429. *043896*

Faumont (Nord)
Debruille, Pascal, 340 Rue Jean-Jaurès, 59310 Fau-
mont. T. 0320592298. - Ant - *043897*

Faux (Dordogne)
Bacquet, André, La Robertie, 24560 Faux.
T. 0553574781. *043898*

Favars (Corrèze)
Chambon, Claude, Les Loubières, 19330 Favars.
T. 0555293333. *043899*

Faverges (Haute-Savoie)
Mouthon, Sylvain, 41 Rue République, 74210 Faverges.
T. 0450446378. *043900*

Faverolles (Eure-et-Loir)
C'Etait Hier, 12 Rue Eglise, 28210 Faverolles.
T. 0237519879. *043901*
Cour Beaudeval, 4 Rue Fontaines, 28210 Faverolles.
T. 0237514767. *043902*

Fayence (Var)
Allongue, Michel, Le Grand Jardin, Rte Gare, 83440
Fayence. T. 0494761792. *043903*

Fécamp (Seine-Maritime)
Antiquités-Brocante du Grenier à Sel, 34 Blvd Républi-
que, 76400 Fécamp. T. 0235279794. *043904*
Cressent, Bruno, 25 Quai Vicomté, 76400 Fécamp.
T. 0235299646. *043905*
Précieux Sang, 2 Rue Précieux-Sang, 76400 Fécamp.
T. 0235276680. *043906*

Felletin (Creuse)
Boussat, Philippe, rue du Château, 23500 Felletin.
T. 0555664152. - Ant / Paint / Furn / China / Tex / Silv /
Instr / Mod - *043907*

Ferrassières (Drôme)
Nedelec, Bernard, Ferme Lauren, Quart Revaux, 26570
Ferrassières. T. 0475288467. *043908*

Ferrette (Haut-Rhin)
Galerie Mazarin, 3 Carrefour Rte Lucelle, 68480 Ferrette. T. 0389403277. - Furn - *043909*

Ferrières-les-Bois (Doubs)
Brisebard, Dominique, 9 Chemin Vignes, 25410 Ferriè-
res-les-Bois. T. 0381551317. *043910*

Ferrières-Saint-Mary (Cantal)
Boudon, Gilles, Florence, 15170 Ferrières-Saint-Mary.
T. 0471206054. *043911*

Figeac (Lot)
Ducos, M. & B. Henry, 47 Rue Gambetta, 46100 Figeac.
T. 0565346470. *043912*
Molinari, Jacques, 47 Rue Gambetta, 46100 Figeac.
T. 0565346470. *043913*
Serra, Christian, 8bis Rue Clermont, 46100 Figeac.
T. 0565347772. - Furn / Num / Cur - *043914*

Finhan (Tarn-et-Garonne)
Béarzatti, Jean-Pierre, 41 Rue Jean-Lacaze, 82700 Fin-
han. T. 0563655105. *043915*

Fismes (Marne)
Antiquités Vernimont, 2bis Rue Jean-Hubert, 51170 Fis-
mes. T. 0326488784. *043916*

Flassans-sur-Issole (Var)
Babb, Jacques, Domaine Lac, 83340 Flassans-sur-Is-
sole. T. 0494697805. *043917*

Flavigny-sur-Ozerain (Côte-d'Or)
Réty, Michel, Rue Gendarmerie, 21150 Flavigny-sur-
Ozerain. T. 0380962159, Fax 0380962561. *043918*

Flayosc (Var)
Clinique de Poupées, Rte Plans, All Sauges, 83780
Flayosc. T. 0494704592. - Toys - *043919*
Soulard, Jacqueline & Christian, Château du Deffends,
83780 Flayosc. T. 0494704037, Fax 0494703893.
- Ant / Paint / Graph / Furn / China / Sculp / Tex / Jew / Fr-
a / Silv / Lights / Pho / Draw / Toys - *043920*

Flers (Orne)
Lampe à Huile, 53 Rue Messei, 61100 Flers.
T. 0233657527. - Ant - *043921*

Flêtre (Nord)
Westelynck, Serge, Rte nationale, 59270 Flêtre.
T. 0328401320, Fax 0328401842. - Ant - *043922*

Fleurance (Gers)
Antony, Daniel, Rte Auch, Le Roucho, 32500 Fleurance.
T. 0562060977. *043923*
Dépôt 32, 68 Rue Jean-Jaurès, 32500 Fleurance.
T. 0562066436. *043924*
Lepaul, André, 5 All Aristide-Briand, 32500 Fleurance.
T. 0562066863. *043925*

Fleuré (Vienne)
Verdeux, Daniel, 6 Rte Limoges, 86340 Fleuré.
T. 0549420975. - Ant - *043926*

Fleurigné (Ille-et-Vilaine)
Geslin, Patrick, Bellevue, 35133 Fleurigné.
T. 0299952368. - Ant / Sculp - *043927*

Flin (Meurthe-et-Moselle)
Haute Epoque, 24 Rue Vosges-Ménil-Flin, 54120 Flin.
T. 0383715076. *043928*

Flines-lez-Raches (Nord)
Frenoy, Guy, 149bis Blvd Alliés, 59148 Flines-lez-Ra-
ches. T. 0327891584. - Ant - *043929*

Floirac (Lot)
Daubet, Francis, Bourg, 46600 Floirac.
T. 0565325336. *043930*

Florac (Lozère)
Durand, Ida, Rue Baron, 48400 Florac.
T. 0466450118. *043931*

Foix (Ariège)
Benoit, Claude, 4 Pl Parmentier, 09000 Foix.
T. 0561651368. - Furn - *043932*
Cloche d'Or, 12 Rue Lafaurie, 09000 Foix.
T. 0561653955. *043933*
Eventail, 37 Rue Labistour, 09000 Foix.
T. 0561655949. *043934*
Fois, Maurice, 23 Rue Lafaurie, 09000 Foix.
T. 0561650022. *043935*
Toulza, D., Pl Georges-Duthil, 09000 Foix.
T. 0561651834. *043936*

Fondettes (Indre-et-Loire)
Galerie Colombière, Rte Menbrolle, 37230 Fondettes.
T. 0547411305, Fax 0547411402. - Furn /
China - *043937*

Fontaine-le-Dun (Seine-Maritime)
Mythes et Mites, Rue Jules-Lemoine, 76740 Fontaine-
le-Dun. T. 0235973469. *043938*

Fontaine-lès-Dijon (Côte-d'Or)
Antiquités Le Bail, 2 Rue Chambertin-Hauteville, 21121
Fontaine-lès-Dijon. T. 0380564100. - Ant /
Furn - *043939*

Fontainebleau (Seine-et-Marne)
Borg, Bernard, 9 Rue Sablons, 77300 Fontainebleau.
T. 64690883. *043940*
Ducré, 2 Rue des Pins, 77300 Fontainebleau.
T. 64220454. - Paint / Furn / China / Silv / Cur - *043941*
Félix Antiquités, 57 Rue France, 77300 Fontainebleau.
T. 64224235. - Tex / Dec - *043942*
May, Thierry, 213 Rue Saint-Merry, 77300 Fontaine-
bleau. T. 64220546, Fax 60727588. - Furn / Repr /
Cur - *043943*
Mendels, Mme, Marie-Angèle, 29 Rue Grande, 77300
Fontainebleau. T. 0164222020. - Ant - *043944*
Montermini, 28 Rue Cloche, 77300 Fontainebleau.
T. 64227887. *043945*

Fontclaireau (Charente)
Romagne, Raymond, Monpaple, 16230 Fontclaireau.
T. 0545222633. *043946*

Fontenay-aux-Roses (Hauts-de-Seine)
Au Vieux Fontenay, 86 Rue Boucicaut, 92260 Fontenay-
aux-Roses. T. 0147029602. *043947*
Genestal, Claude, 140 Rue Boucicaut, 92260 Fontenay-
aux-Roses. T. 0143502096. *043948*
Vert Antique, 35 Rue Boucicaut, 92260 Fontenay-aux-
Roses. T. 0143508989. *043949*

Fontenay-le-Comte (Vendée)
Achallé, Marc, 36 Av Maréchal Juin, 85200 Fontenay-
le-Comte. T. 0251510220. *043950*
Au Temps Jadis, La Garde, Rte Nantes, 85200 Fonte-
nay-le-Comte. T. 0251692530. - Furn - *043951*
Roussel, Raymond, 94 Rue Loges, 85200 Fontenay-le-
Comte. T. 0251692030. *043952*
Trulla, Joël, 17bis Rte Niort, 85200 Fontenay-le-Comte.
T. 0251694656. *043953*

Fontenay-sous-Bois (Val-de-Marne)
Alain, Bernard, 2 Rue Réunion, 94120 Fontenay-sous-
Bois. T. 0148737340. - Furn - *043954*
Au Temps Jadis, 11 Pl Général-Leclerc, 94120 Fonte-
nay-sous-Bois. T. 0148775123. *043955*

Fontevraud-l'Abbaye (Maine-et-Loire)
Saulnier, Christian, 2 Pl Plantagenets, 49590 Fonte-
vraud-l'Abbaye. T. 41514826. *043956*

Fontiers-Cabardès (Aude)
Ménendez, Claude, 8 Av Le-Bosquet, 11310 Fontiers-
Cabardès. T. 0468265951. *043957*
Ménendez, Pierre, 4 Rte Carcassonne, 11310 Fontiers-
Cabardès. T. 0468265235. *043958*

Fontvieille (Bouches-du-Rhône)
Fouqué, Marcel, 159 Rte Nord, 13990 Fontvieille.
T. 0490547461. - Paint / Furn - *043959*
Pascal, Patrick, 45 Rue La-Tour, 13990 Fontvieille.
T. 0490547032, Fax 0490546126. *043960*

Forbach (Moselle)
Comme Autrefois, 190 Rue Nationale, 57600 Forbach.
T. 0387841299. *043961*

Forcalquier (Alpes-de-Haute-Provence)
Bouscarle, Max, 7 Pl Saint-Michel, 04300 Forcalquier.
T. 0492751926. - Ant / Furn - *043962*
Garrigues, Jean, Le Plan-des-Aires Rte Villeneuve,
04300 Forcalquier. T. 0492753432. - Ant - *043963*
Garrus & Simeray, 5 Pl Saint-Michel, 04300 Forcalquier.
T. 0492751529. - Ant - *043964*
Holvoet, Patrick, 43 Av marcel-André, 04300 Forcal-
quier. T. 0492753200. - Ant - *043965*
Huppert, Bruno, 11 Blvd Latourette, 04300 Forcalquier.
T. 0492752989. - Ant / Furn - *043966*

Forgès (Corrèze)
Brocante, 47 Av Pasteur, 19380 Forgès.
T. 0555286546. *043967*

Forges-les-Eaux (Seine-Maritime)
Grisel, 7 Rue Albert-Bochet, 76440 Forges-les-Eaux.
T. 0235091750. *043968*
Leforestier, Alain, 58 Av Sources, 76440 Forges-les-
Eaux. T. 0235098798. *043969*

Fouesnant (Finistère)
Labous, Jean-Yves, Rte Beg-Meil, 29170 Fouesnant.
T. 0298944965. - Ant - *043970*

Fougères (Ille-et-Vilaine)
Battais, 46 Blvd Rennes, 35300 Fougères.
T. 0299991025. *043971*
Battais, André, 2 Rue Duguay Trouin, 35300 Fougères.
T. 0299990166. - Furn / China / Silv / Lights /
Instr - *043972*
Battais, Francis, 3 Rue Laval, 35300 Fougères.
T. 0299991146. - Furn / China / Silv / Lights / Instr /
Glass / Cur - *043973*
Gledel, Claude, 59 Rue Kléber, 35300 Fougères.
T. 0299990076. *043974*
Gledel, Philippe, 11 Rue Jean-Allain, 35300 Fougères.
T. 0299940844. *043975*
Gledel, Yves, 27 Rue Kléber, 35300 Fougères.
T. 0299994348. *043976*
Marc, 7 Pl Théâtre, 35300 Fougères.
T. 0299943052. *043977*

Fouilloy (Somme)
Poullain, Francis, 2 Rue Aristide-Briand, 80800 Fouilloy.
T. 0322482945. - Ant - *043978*

Fouquebrune (Charente)
Chamouleau, Jean-Claude, La Haute Valade, 16410
Fouquebrune. T. 0545679574. *043979*

Fréjus (Var)
Antic'Fréjus, 12 Rue Grisolle, 83600 Fréjus.
T. 0494537354. *043980*
Brocantomanie, Rue Gustave-Bret, 83600 Fréjus.
T. 0494512338. *043981*
Gauchet, 49 Av Victor-Hugo, 83600 Fréjus.
T. 0494170661. *043982*
Porro, Jean-Bernard, 27 Rue Horace, 83600 Fréjus.
T. 0494531806. *043983*
Tentations, 146 Av Louis-Castillon, 83600 Fréjus.
T. 0494811227, Fax 0494811367. *043984*
Trohay, Jean-Claude, 53 Imp Pinède, Résidence Oasis,
Bâtiment A, 83600 Fréjus. T. 0494442685. *043985*

Fresnes-sur-Escaut (Nord)
Charme d'Antan, 156 Rue Jean-Jaurès, 59970 Fresnes-
sur-Escaut. T. 0327261838. - Ant - *043986*

Frespech (Lot-et-Garonne)
Klinker, Leslie John, La Comberatière, 47140 Frespech.
T. 0553413037. - Ant - *043987*

Fresse (Haute-Saône)
Renaudat, Claudette, Grande Rue, 70270 Fresse.
T. 0384633224. - Toys - *043988*

Fumel (Lot-et-Garonne)
Andrieu-Bourelly, Edmonde, 18 Rue République, 47500
Fumel. T. 0553710122. *043989*
Bulteau, Claude, 58 Av Emile-Zola, 47500 Fumel.
T. 0553713257. *043990*

Fuveau (Bouches-du-Rhône)
Brocante Fuvelaine, RN 96, 13710 Fuveau.
T. 0442680600. - Furn / Cur - *043991*

Gages (Aveyron)
Déco-Rétro, Gages-Le-Pont, 12630 Gages.
T. 0565427493. - Ant / Furn - *043992*

Gagny (Seine-Saint-Denis)
Bréon, 5 et 7 Rue Jules-Vallès, 93220 Gagny.
T. 0143025023. - Paint / Furn / Cur / Music - *043993*

Gaillac (Tarn)
Delherm, Jean-Pierre, 38 Av Jean-Calvet, 81600 Gaillac. T. 0563573603. *043994*

Gaillard (Haute-Savoie)
Fournier, Yves, 8 Rue Emile-Millet, 74240 Gaillard.
T. 0450376663. *043995*

Tassile Lauro, 9 Rue Souville, 74240 Gaillard.
T. 0450398421. - Furn - *043996*

Gaillon-sur-Montcient (Yvelines)
Jourdan, Franck, Moulin de Metz, 78250 Gaillon-sur-
Montcient. T. 0130995501. *043997*

Gallardon (Eure-et-Loir)
Nollet, Jean-Pierre, 2 Rue Templiers, 28320 Gallardon.
T. 0237314015. *043998*
Sabretache, 24 Rue Pierre-Martin, 28320 Gallardon.
T. 0237314397. *043999*

Gambais (Yvelines)
Leda Décors, 27 Rue Goupigny, 78950 Gambais.
T. 0134870232, Fax 0134870653. *044000*

Gambrai (Nord)
Jurande, 22bis Rue Léon-Gambetta, 59400 Gambrai.
T. 0327811436. - Ant - *044001*

Gan (Pyrénées-Atlantiques)
Laur, Norbert, Chemin Vieux-Moulin, 64290 Gan.
T. 0559216263. - Ant - *044002*

Gap (Hautes-Alpes)
Arnoux, Jean, 8 Rue Mazel, 05000 Gap.
T. 0492513347. *044003*
Equipement Culturel Les Pénitents, 21 Rue Imprimerie,
05000 Gap. T. 0492536839. *044004*
Gap Antiquités, Zone Artisanale Eyssagnières, 05000
Gap. T. 0492534014. *044005*
Ligozat, André, 66 Rue Jean-Eymar, 05000 Gap.
T. 0492539948. *044006*
Parruzot, W., 43 Av d'Embrun, 05000 Gap.
T. 0492537619. - Furn - *044007*

Garat (Charente)
Antiquités Le Falcom, Rte Périgueux, Sainte-Catherine,
16410 Garat. T. 0545606140. *044008*

Garches (Hauts-de-Seine)
Charles, Martine, 14 Av Maréchal-Leclerc, 92380 Gar-
ches. T. 0147011227. *044009*
Montabert, Sophie, 149 Grande Rue, 92380 Garches.
T. 0147015111. *044010*

Gardanne (Bouches-du-Rhône)
Car, Jean-Pierre, 25 Av Toulon, 13120 Gardanne.
T. 0442582555. *044011*
Lejeune, Gilles, Quartier La Plaine, 13120 Gardanne.
T. 0442584739. - Paint / Furn / Cur - *044012*

Gassin (Var)
Antic House, Domaine Bourrian, RN 98A, 83990 Gassin.
T. 0494443314, Fax 0494551331. *044013*
Binet, Le Treizain, RN 98, Rte Saint-Tropez, 83990 Gas-
sin. T. 0494977102. *044014*
Poulideto, Rn 98A, Quartier Malheribes, 83990 Gassin.
T. 0494978797. *044015*
Ritzenthaler, RN 98 A, Domaine du Bourrian, 83580 Gas-
sin. T. 0494434314. - Ant / Dec - *044016*
Selli, Daniel, 5 Rue Longue, 83990 Gassin.
T. 0494560480. *044017*

Gavray (Manche)
Grenier d'Annick, Grande Rue, 50450 Gavray.
T. 0233614720. *044018*

Gémenos (Bouches-du-Rhône)
Rouvière, Michel, 1476 Chemin République, 13420 Gémenos. T. 0442320569. - Furn / Repr - *044019*

Gençay (Vienne)
Liaigre, Jacqueline, 13 Rte Civray, 86160 Gençay.
T. 0549593695. - Ant - *044020*
Valade, François, Rue Usson, 86160 Gençay.
T. 0549594549. - Ant - *044021*

Genouillac (Creuse)
Quesnel, Pierre, Chadière, 23350 Genouillac.
T. 0555808155. - Ant - *044022*

Gérardmer (Vosges)
Marion, Josiane, 1 Pl Déportés, 88400 Gérardmer.
T. 0329600657. *044023*

Gerbéviller (Meurthe-et-Moselle)
Aubert, Jacques, 13 Rue Gambetta, 54830 Gerbéviller.
T. 0383428141. *044024*

Gevigney-et-Mercey (Haute-Saône)
François, Roger, Grande Rue, 70500 Gevigney-et-Mer-
cey. T. 0384680100. *044025*

Gevrey-Chambertin (Côte-d'Or)
Follot, Jeannine, Rue La-Croix-des-Champs, 21220 Ge-
vrey-Chambertin. T. 0380343517. *044026*

Ghisonaccia (Corse)
Pieri, Pierrette, Rte Ghisoni, 20240 Ghisonaccia.
T. 0495560121. *044027*

Gibel (Haute-Garonne)
Garrigue, Kate, Village, 31560 Gibel.
T. 0561086238. *044028*
Garrigue, Yves, Rue Eglise, 31560 Gibel.
T. 0561081047. *044029*

Gien (Loiret)
Antiquités La Billebaude, 14 Quai Joffre, 45500 Gien.
T. 0238674174, Fax 0238314543. *044030*
Dupont, 81 Rue Montbricon, 45500 Gien.
T. 0238671730. - Furn / China - *044031*
Salin, Guy, 52 Quai Lenoir, 45500 Gien.
T. 0238671378. *044032*
Setti, 16 Quai Joffre, 45500 Gien.
T. 0238382496. *044033*

Gièvres (Loir-et-Cher)
Vildy, Lydie, Les Arpents, 41130 Gièvres.
T. 0254966265. *044034*

Gif-sur-Yvette (Essonne)
Barbier, Claude, Centre Commercial Chevry II, 91190
Gif-sur-Yvette. T. 0160121934. *044035*
Tarasque, Rue Amodru, 91190 Gif-sur-Yvette.
T. 0169284459. *044036*

Gignac-la-Nerthe (Bouches-du-Rhône)
Aux Reflets d'Antan, RN 568, Av République, Quartier
Mousseline, 13180 Gignac-la-Nerthe. T. 0442884703.
- Glass - *044037*
Pedduzza, Max, Quartier Mousseline, 13180 Gignac-la-
Nerthe. T. 0442881240. *044038*

Gimont (Gers)
Pla, Jérôme, 12 Rue Rhin-et-Danube, 32200 Gimont.
T. 0562677651, Fax 0562677698. - Paint / Furn / Chi-
na / Glass - *044039*

Giromagny (Territoire-de-Belfort)
A la Belle Epoque, 12 Rue Ecoles, 90200 Giromagny.
T. 0384393298. - Ant / Furn - *044040*

Gironde-sur-Dropt (Gironde)
Labonne, Marie-Christine & Nicole Darroquy, 94bis Av
Général-de-Gaulle, Village des Antiquaires, 33190 Gi-
ronde-sur-Dropt. T. 0556711572. *044041*
Schérer, Hélène-Elisabeth, Bourg, 33190 Gironde-sur-
Dropt. T. 0556711029. *044042*

Gironville-sur-Essonne (Essonne)
Air du Temps, 9 Grande Rue, 91720 Gironville-sur-Es-
sonne. T. 0164993073. *044043*

Giroussens (Tarn)
Brunet, Pierre, Saint-Michel, 81500 Giroussens.
T. 0563416319. *044044*

Gisors (Eure)
Au Lion d'Argent, 27 Rue Fbg-Cappeville, 27140 Gisors.
T. 0232273206. - Ant / Furn / Cur - *044045*
Deschamps, Pierre, 7 Rue Raymond-Mordret, 27140 Gi-
sors. T. 0232553949. - Ant / Furn / Cur - *044046*
Lefèvre, Romain, 46 Rue Paris, 27140 Gisors.
T. 0232559424. *044047*

Giverville (Eure)
Martin, Bernard, Bourg, 27560 Giverville.
T. 0232459715. *044048*

Givry (Saône-et-Loire)
Givry Antiquités, 26 Rue République, 71640 Givry.
T. 0385445644. - Ant -   044049

Goderville (Seine-Maritime)
Au Bonheur du Chineur, 1 Rue Guy-de-Maupassant,
76110 Goderville. T. 0235291448.   044050

Gond-Pontouvre (Charente)
Antiquités de Paris, 170 Rte Paris, 16160 Gond-Pon-
touvre. T. 0545690007. - Paint / Furn / Cur -   044051

Gondrecourt-le-Château (Meuse)
Babault, Alain, 36 Rue Patton, 55130 Gondrecourt-le-
Château. T. 0329896058. - Ant -   044052
Lebert, Jean-Claude, 2 Rue Raymond-Poincaré, 55130
Gondrecourt-le-Château. T. 0329896763,
Fax 0329896433. - Ant / Sculp / Dec -   044053

Gondrin (Gers)
Au Passé Antérieur, Rte Nationale, 32330 Gondrin.
T. 0562291579.   044054

Gonfaron (Var)
Oulières, Georges, Quartier Garnaude, 83590 Gonfaron.
T. 0494782622.   044055

Gonfreville-l'Orcher (Seine-Maritime)
Jacqueline, Sylvain & Fils, Manoir de Bevilliers, RN 15,
76700 Gonfreville-l'Orcher. T. 0235454050. - Ant /
Repr -   044056

Gonneville-la-Mallet (Seine-Maritime)
Malle Cauchoise, Rue Gaston-Delahais, 76280 Gonne-
ville-la-Mallet. T. 0235207221.   044057

Gordes (Vaucluse)
Alazarine, Pierre, Les Imberts, 84220 Gordes.
T. 0490769183. - Ant / Paint / China -   044058
Mack, Christian, Les Imberts, 84220 Gordes.
T. 0490769172. - Ant -   044059
Mesureur, Karine, La Beaume, 84220 Gordes.
T. 0490720606. - Ant -   044060

Goudelin (Côtes-d'Armor)
Au Vieux Chaudron, Le Restou, 22290 Goudelin.
T. 0296701866. - Ant / Paint / Furn / Cur -   044061

Gouesnou (Finistère)
Patris, Gilles, 3 Rue brest, 29239 Gouesnou.
T. 0298077115. - Ant -   044062
Roudaut, Robert, Ker-Loïs Rte Brest, 29850 Gouesnou.
T. 0298077645. - Furn -   044063

Gourdon (Lot)
Vignals, J.M. de, 47 Blvd Martyrs, 46300 Gourdon.
T. 0565413765.   044064

Gournay-en-Bray (Seine-Maritime)
Barnet, Bertrand, 23 Rue Notre-Dame, 76220 Gournay-
en-Bray. T. 0235902057.   044065

Grâce-Uzel (Côtes-d'Armor)
Le Verger, Joseph, Tourlanquin, 22460 Grâce-Uzel.
T. 0296262088, Fax 0296288406.   044066

Grâces (Côtes-d'Armor)
Léon, Jean, 23 Rue Château-de-Kéribo, 22200 Grâces.
T. 0296437152.   044067

Gradignan (Gironde)
Cassagrande, Mario, 8 All Rameau, 33170 Gradignan.
T. 0556892876.   044068
Fabre, Nicole, 150 Rte Canéjan, 33170 Gradignan.
T. 0556891024.   044069
Histoire Art, Pl Bernard-Roumegoux, Résidence Bourg,
33170 Gradignan. T. 0556755731. - Toys -   044070

Grande-Rivière (Jura)
Jacquin, Marie-Claude, Ham Bouviers, 39150 Grande-
Rivière. T. 0384601782.   044071

Grandvillars (Territoire-de-Belfort)
Dancelli, Maryse, Rue Général-Leclerc, 90600 Grandvil-
lars. T. 0384235247. - Furn / Cur -   044072

Granville (Manche)
Au Dénicheur, 12 Rue Saintonge, 50400 Granville.
T. 0233515405.   044073
Au Gîte, ZI Maison-Brûlée, 50400 Granville.
T. 0233902600.   044074
Ecume des Jours, 2 Av Libération, 50400 Granville.
T. 0233615722. - Toys -   044075
Granvil'Occasion, 22bis Rue Lecampion, 50400 Gran-
ville. T. 0233504456. - Furn / Cur -   044076
Grizzli, 22 Rue Paul-Poirier, 50400 Granville.
T. 0233614801. - Paint / Furn / Silv / Instr / Cur /
Toys -   044077
Jarneau, Maryvonne, 15 Av Libération, 50400 Granville.
T. 0233515376.   044078
Lerendu, Alain, Pl Albert-Godal, 50400 Granville.
T. 0233512232.   044079
Lerendu, Alain, 7 Rue Hérel, 50400 Granville.
T. 0233907265.   044080
Vaugrante, Jean-Pierre, 62 Av Aristide-Briand, 50400
Granville. T. 0233503741.   044081

Grasse (Alpes-Maritimes)
Antiquités Douce France, 246 Rte Cannes, 06130
Grasse. T. 0493704902.   044082
Boucaud, Philippe, 26 Av F.-de-Croisset, RD 2085,
06130 Grasse. T. 0493362010, Fax 0493401077.
- Ant / Furn / Sculp / Tin -   044083
Dépôt Vente des Casernes, 26 Av Mathias-Duval, 06130
Grasse. T. 0493363118.   044084
Diotallevi, Joseph, 24 Chemin Saint-Marc, 06130
Grasse. T. 0493404656.   044085
Ecritoire et la Plume, 4 Rue Marcel-Journet, 06130
Grasse. T. 0493400578.   044086
Galerie Rosal, 18 Rue Paul-Goby, 06130 Grasse.
T. 0493361132. - Paint / Sculp -   044087
Garcia, 16 Pl aux Aires, 06130 Grasse. T. 0493362390.
- Ant -   044088
Lanterne de Hans, 2 Av Félix-Raybaud, Centre Commer-
cial La Halte, 06130 Grasse. T. 0493708892.   044089
Sanchez del Rio, Joseph, 22 Rue Jean-Ossola, 06130
Grasse. T. 0493362770.   044090
Trois Fontaines, 9 Chemin Cercle, 06130 Grasse.
T. 0493701226.   044091

Graulhet (Tarn)
Dupeyron, Robert, 28 Av Sidobre, 81300 Graulhet.
T. 0563347233.   044092

Grenade-sur-l'Adour (Landes)
Laboudigue, Jacques, 13 Av Mont-de-Marsan, 40270
Grenade-sur-l'Adour. T. 0558459102. - Furn -   044093

Grenoble (Isère)
Aalto, Gandit, 19 Rue Voltaire, 38100 Grenoble.
T. 40623020.   044094
Acanthe Antiquités, 1 Rue Voltaire, 38000 Grenoble.
T. 0476511029. - Ant / Paint / Furn / Music -   044094
Aristoloches, 10 Rue Guétal, 38000 Grenoble.
T. 0476543152. - Ant -   044095
Art d'Antan, 7 Rue Voltaire, 38000 Grenoble.
T. 0476468711. - Ant / Paint / Furn -   044096
Au Chevalier Bayard, 16 Rue Bayard, 38000 Grenoble.
T. 0476441578. - Ant / Paint / Furn -   044097
Berline, 15 Rue Bayard, 38000 Grenoble.
T. 0476426447. - Ant -   044098
Chimène, 3 Rue des Bergers, 38000 Grenoble.
T. 0476584283. - Ant -   044099
Ile aux Trésors, 2 Pl Tilleuls, 38000 Grenoble.
T. 0476431221. - Ant / Furn / Tex -   044100
Mikaëlian, Edouard, 20 Rue Nicolas-Chorier, 38000 Gre-
noble. T. 0476517074. - Ant / Furn / Cur -   044101
Or des Iles, 6 Rue Bayard, 38000 Grenoble.
T. 0476214519. - Ant / Paint / Furn /
Glass -   044102
Prestige Bijoux, 10 Rue Bayard, 38000 Grenoble.
T. 0476427788. - Furn / Orient -   044103
Relais des Epoques, 45 Rue Lesdiguières, 38000 Greno-
ble. T. 0476512777. - Jew -   044104
Rougier, 8 Rue Voltaire, 38000 Grenoble.
T. 0476465115. - Ant -   044105
Soupente Colette Ederlé, 18 Rue Saint-Joseph, 38000
Grenoble. T. 0476442903. - Ant -   044106
                                                        044107
T. 0476434291. - Ant -

Grézet-Cavagnan (Lot-et-Garonne)
Longo, Christine, Roubin, 47250 Grézet-Cavagnan.
T. 0553892160.   044108

Grigny (Essonne)
Antiquités-Brocante-Curiosités, Pl Henri-Barbusse,
91350 Grigny. T. 0169258843,
Fax 0169258905.   044109

Grimaud (Var)
Antiquités de la Queste, Les Roberts, 83310 Grimaud.
T. 0494433065.   044110
Architectural Antiques, RD 61, Rte de Saint-Tropez,
83310 Grimaud. T. 0494432994. - Furn / Dec -   044111
Bardoux, Patrick, La Becassiere, Quartier Caucadis,
83310 Grimaud. T. 0494432994.   044112
Laurin, Françoise, 29 Blvd Aliziers, 83310 Grimaud.
T. 0494432157.   044113

Groisy (Haute-Savoie)
Guillevic, Albert, RN 203, Longchamp, 74570 Groisy.
T. 0450773008.   044114

Gron (Cher)
Nos Ancêtres, 9 Rue Forêt, Saint-Igny, 18800 Gron.
T. 0248685142.   044115

Gron (Yonne)
Grognards, 2bis Rue Bordiot, 89930 Gron.
T. 0386656026. - Furn / Cur -   044116

Groslay (Val-d'Oise)
Antiquités de Groslay, 1bis Rue Anatole-France, 95410
Groslay. T. 0139838480.   044117
Marinesse, Henri, 34 Rue Carrières, 95410 Groslay.
T. 0139838396.   044118
Marinesse, Henri, 38 Rue Général-Leclerc, 95410 Gros-
lay. T. 0139835262.   044119
Rouaud, André, 1bis Rue Anatole-France, 95410 Gros-
lay. T. 0134287315.   044120

Grosley-sur-Risle (Eure)
Leroux, Patrick, Val Gallerand, 27110 Grosley-sur-Risle.
T. 0232453056.   044121

Guebwiller (Haut-Rhin)
Brocante du Florival, 2 Rue Général-de-Gaulle, 68500
Guebwiller. T. 0389761263.   044122
Heberlé, Jean-Jacques, 25 Av Foch, 68500 Guebwiller.
T. 0389768096. - Furn / China -   044123
Mattioli, Gérard, 3 Rue Hôpital, 68500 Guebwiller.
T. 0389766763.   044124

Guérande (Loire-Atlantique)
Aladin, Leniphen, 44350 Guérande.
T. 40623020.   044125
Antiquités Saint-Jean, Rue Hôpital-Saint-Jean, 44350
Guérande. T. 40621051.   044126
Boisguérin, Annick, 24 Rue Saillé, 44350 Guérande.
T. 40248175.   044127
Brocante du Marais, Leniphen, 44350 Guérande.
T. 40150284.   044128
Dépôt-Vente du Particulier, 28 Blvd Emile-Pourieux,
44350 Guérande. T. 40247830. - Paint / Furn -   044129
Henri, Serge, 12bis Fbg-Sainte-Anne, 44350 Guérande.
T. 40248254.   044130
Héral, Quentin, 44350 Guérande.
T. 40247148.   044131
Salle des Ventes Guérandaise, 1 Fbg-Saint-Armel,
44350 Guérande. T. 40620013.   044132

Guéret (Creuse)
Leroy, Henriette, 1 Rue Ascension, 23000 Guéret.
T. 0555520242. - Ant / Paint / Furn / Jew / Silv -   044133

Guermantes (Seine-et-Marne)
Antiquités Les Deux Châteaux, 79 Av Deux-Châteaux,
77600 Guermantes. T. 0360076305.   044134

Guethary (Pyrénées-Atlantiques)
Paturel, Ghislaine, Villa Italiana, 64210 Guethary.
T. 0559265033. - Ant / Jew -   044135

Guignen (Ille-et-Vilaine)
Lemousse, Michel, La Basse-Revachais, 35580 Guig-
nen. T. 0299922614.   044136

Guillestre (Hautes-Alpes)
Chevallier, Stéphane, Av Docteur-Julien-Guillaume,
05600 Guillestre. T. 0492452651.   *044137*

Guilvinec (Finistère)
Quiniou, Patrick, 33 Rte Plomeur, 29115 Guilvinec.
T. 0298581577. - Ant -   *044138*

Guingamp (Côtes-d'Armor)
Bourdon, Louis, 11 Rue Jean-Jacques-Rousseau, 22200
Guingamp. T. 0296439123.   *044139*
Le Jannou, Gildas, 112 Rue Maréchal-Joffre, 22200
Guingamp. T. 0296910233. - Ant / Furn -   *044140*
Vallée, Florence, 8 Rue Pot-d'Argent, 22200 Guingamp.
T. 0296441902.   *044141*

Guipavas (Finistère)
Attic, 17 Rue Pont-Neuf, 29215 Guipavas.
T. 0298424002. - Ant -   *044142*

Guise (Aisne)
Caille, Patrick, 83 Rue Camille-Desmoulins, 01210
Guise. T. 0323612221. - Ant -   *044143*
Rousselle & Vaillant, 137 Rue Général-de-Gaulle, 02120
Guise. T. 0323613137. - Ant / Cur -   *044144*

Haguenau (Bas-Rhin)
Au Fil du Temps, 113 Rte Strasbourg, 67500 Haguenau.
T. 0388932722, Fax 0388061159.   *044145*
Entre-Temps, 14 Rue de la Redoute, 67500 Haguenau.
T. 0388733566. - Furn / Mod -   *044146*
Gasser, M., 61 Grand'Rue, 67500 Haguenau.
T. 0388938163.   *044147*
Henninger, Jean-David, 8 Rue Sainte-Georges, 67500
Haguenau. T. 0388930009.   *044148*
Kibler, Alain, 1 Rue Puits, 67500 Haguenau.
T. 0388733851.   *044149*
Riess, Marguerite, 2 A Rue Tapis, 67500 Haguenau.
T. 0388733566.   *044150*

Hallignicourt (Haute-Marne)
Rousseaux, Jacky, 22 Av Gare, 52100 Hallignicourt.
T. 0325563028.   *044151*

Halloy (Oise)
Aux Vieiseries, 13 Rue Beauvais, 60210 Halloy.
T. 0344466266. - Furn / China -   *044152*

Halluin (Nord)
Meunier, Franck, 26 Rue Bousbecque, 59250 Halluin.
T. 0320466537. - Ant -   *044153*

Ham (Somme)
Delvigne, Hervé, 29 Rue Saint-Quentin, 80400 Ham.
T. 0323365103. - Ant -   *044154*
Vidal, Patricia, 18 Rue du Général-Foy, 80400 Ham.
T. 0322811097. - Ant -   *044155*

Hambye (Manche)
Farradèche, Christian, Rte Granville, 50450 Hambye.
T. 0233904036.   *044156*

Hanches (Eure-et-Loir)
Cailly, Noël, 3 Rue Barre, 28130 Hanches.
T. 0237836389.   *044157*

Hannappes (Aisne)
Broc'Hannapes, 6 Rue Verdun, 012510 Hannappes.
T. 0323606760. - Ant -   *044158*

Hardricourt (Yvelines)
Prigent, Alain, 16 Blvd Carnot, 78250 Hardricourt.
T. 0134745479.   *044159*

Haroué (Meurthe-et-Moselle)
Thouvenot, Robert, 7 Pl Bassompierre, 54740 Haroué.
T. 0383524026.   *044160*

Harquency (Eure)
Deschamps, Sylvie, 10 Rte Pontoise, 27700 Harquency.
T. 0232542745. - Furn / Cur -   *044161*

Hasparren (Pyrénées-Atlantiques)
Navarre-Duplantier, Rue Francis-Jammes, 64240 Ha-
sparren. T. 0559291155. - Ant -   *044162*

Haucourt-Moulaine (Meurthe-et-Mosel-
le)
Scisco, Vincent, 5 Rue George-Sand, 54860 Haucourt-
Moulaine. T. 0383246771. - Furn / China / Cur - *044163*

Haut-de-Gan (Pyrénées-Atlantiques)
Sandona, Mario, 64290 Haut-de-Gan. T. 0559217517.
- Ant -   *044164*

Hautefond (Saône-et-Loire)
Brunel, Didier, Guichard, 71600 Hautefond.
T. 0385814654. - Ant -   *044165*

Hauterives (Drôme)
Chardon, Yves, Village, 26390 Hauterives.
T. 0475688085. - Furn -   *044166*

Hautot-sur-Mer (Seine-Maritime)
Bernar, Ginette, Rue Cabaret, 76550 Hautot-sur-Mer.
T. 0235845952.   *044167*
Hermay, Jacques, Rue Cabaret, 76550 Hautot-sur-Mer.
T. 0235845952.   *044168*

Havelu (Eure-et-Loir)
Biewesch, Roger, Grande Rue, 28410 Havelu.
T. 0237821774.   *044169*

Haybes (Ardennes)
Fagne – Brocante, Rte Nationale 51, 08170 Haybes.
T. 0324412244. - Ant -   *044170*

Hazebrouck (Nord)
Podvin, Roselyne, 110 Rue Aristide-Briand, 59190 Haze-
brouck. T. 0328431744. - Ant -   *044171*
Saint Eloi, 40 Rue Eglise, 59190 Hazebrouck.
T. 0328415098. - Ant -   *044172*

Hendaye (Pyrénées-Atlantiques)
Passe-Temps, 121 Blvd Mer, 64700 Hendaye.
T. 0559480001. - Ant -   *044173*

Hénin-Beaumont (Pas-de-Calais)
Antiquités Brocante, 320 Rue Harnes, 62110 Hénin-
Beaumont. T. 0321755087.   *044174*
Grenier, 10 Rue Denis-Papin, 62110 Hénin-Beaumont.
T. 0321753262. - Furn -   *044175*

Hennebont (Morbihan)
Honeywood, 24 Av République, 56700 Hennebont.
T. 0297361035, Fax 0297365020. - Furn -   *044176*

Henrichemont (Cher)
Au Temps Passé, 1 Rue Bourgogne, 18250 Henriche-
mont. T. 0248267464.   *044177*

Héric (Loire-Atlantique)
Lecomte, Daniel, Rte Rennes, 44810 Héric.
T. 40576383. - Furn -   *044178*

Hérisson (Allier)
M'Bar, Michel, Rue Gambetta, 03190 Hérisson.
T. 0470068929. - Ant -   *044179*

Herm (Landes)
Troc 40, Cluquelardit, Rte Dax-Castets, 40990 Herm.
T. 0558915360. - Furn -   *044180*

Hermanville-sur-Mer (Calvados)
Grillon Antiquités, 497 Rue Prés-de-l'Isle, 14880 Her-
manville-sur-Mer. T. 0231964032.   *044181*
This and That, Rue Tour-de-Ville, 14880 Hermanville-
sur-Mer. T. 0231968810.   *044182*

Héry (Yonne)
Simon, Didier, 2 Rue Sougères, 89550 Héry.
T. 0386477986.   *044183*

Heuchin (Pas-de-Calais)
Vaast, Elisabeth, 2 Grand-Place, 62134 Heuchin.
T. 0321414811.   *044184*

Heugleville-sur-Scie (Seine-Maritime)
Guerrots, François & Chantal des, Le Bosc Michel,
76720 Heugleville-sur-Scie. T. 0235328045.   *044185*

Hiersac (Charente)
Garcia, Y., La Vigerie, 16290 Hiersac. T. 0545969412.
- Ant -   *044186*

Hirsingue (Haut-Rhin)
Grenier de Sundgau, 2 Rue Arc, 68560 Hirsingue.
T. 0389405132.   *044187*

Hirson (Aisne)
Destrés-Lamine, Fabienne, 4 Rue Septembre, 02500
Hirson. T. 0323581408. - Ant / Cur -   *044188*

Hon-Hergies (Nord)
Mirland, 15 Ch du Bois, 59570 Hon-Hergies.
T. 0327669591. - Ant -   *044189*

Honfleur (Calvados)
Agora, 24 Pl Thiers, 14600 Honfleur.
T. 0231894969.   *044190*
Antiquités Allais, Pl Alphonse-Allais, 14600 Honfleur.
T. 0231988849. - Furn / Cur -   *044191*
Antiquités Sainte-Catherine, 10 Pl Sainte-Catherine,
14600 Honfleur. T. 0231890538.   *044192*
Brocanterie, 11 Cours Fossés, 14600 Honfleur.
T. 0231890536. - Paint / Furn / China / Instr /
Cur -   *044193*
Chégaray, Sylvie, 12 Pl Berthelot, 14600 Honfleur.
T. 0231988805.   *044194*
Escale Marine, 7 Rue Homme-de-Bois, 14600 Honfleur.
T. 0231890894. - Paint / Graph / Cur -   *044195*
Rohaut, Françoise, 27 Rue Logettes, 14600 Honfleur.
T. 0231893104.   *044196*

Hossegor (Landes)
Clefs de Saint-Pierre, 651 Av Touring-Club, 40150 Hos-
segor. T. 0558435643.   *044197*
Guilhabert, Françoise, Av Paul-Lahary-Soorts, 40150
Hossegor. T. 0558439743. - Furn / Tex / Silv -   *044198*

Hottot-les-Bagues (Calvados)
Demonchy, Roselyne, Grande Rue, 14250 Hottot-les-Ba-
gues. T. 0231808565.   *044199*

Houdain-lez-Bavay (Nord)
Paindavoine, Marcel, Rte Valenciennes, 59570 Houdain-
lez-Bavay. T. 0327631160. - Ant -   *044200*

Houdemont (Meurthe-et-Moselle)
Uniformologue, 3ter Rue Fonteno, 54180 Houdemont.
T. 0383578202.   *044201*

Houdon (Yvelines)
Ballan, Jean, 34 Rue Epernon, 78550 Houdon.
T. 0130597088.   *044202*
Galerie du Passé, 2 Rue Mont-Rôti, 78550 Houdon.
T. 0130597014.   *044203*

Houilles (Yvelines)
L'Huillier, Thierry, 18 Rue Gabriel-Péri, 78800 Houilles.
T. 0139689450.   *044204*
Truchelut, Daniel, 22 Rue Desaix, 78800 Houilles.
T. 0139682100.   *044205*

Huelgoat (Finistère)
Bothorel, Yves, 24 Pl Aristide-Briand, 29218 Huelgoat.
T. 0298999148. - Ant -   *044206*

Hulsmes (Indre-et-Loire)
Grange aux Moines, La Grande Pièce, 37420 Huismes.
T. 0547954720.   *044207*

Huisseau-en-Beauce (Loir-et-Cher)
Desbordes, Jean-Pierre, 8 Rue 7-Fontaines, 41310
Huisseau-en-Beauce. T. 0254828317.   *044208*

Hyères (Var)
Acxelle Antique, 65 Av Toulon, 83400 Hyères.
T. 0494659720.   *044209*
Art's Gallery, 3 Rue Portalet, 83400 Hyères.
T. 0494659678.   *044210*
Au Vieux Château Saint-Martin, 1000 Chemin Saint-
Martin, 83400 Hyères. T. 0494383207.   *044211*
Boutique La Rosalba, Pl Belvédère, 83400 Hyères.
T. 0494589408.   *044212*
Brault, Denise, 2 Pl Massillon, 83400 Hyères.
T. 0494650999.   *044213*
Caton, 6 Av Paul-Long, 83400 Hyères.
T. 0494658188.   *044214*
Chauveau, Pierre, 3bis Rue Sainte-Catherine, 83400
Hyères. T. 0494652402.   *044215*

Derrive, Nicole, 2509 Rte Almanarre, 83400 Hyères.
T. 0494383682. *044216*

Feuillet, Jean-Claude, 18 Av Paul-Bourget, 83400 Hyères. T. 0494579414. *044217*

Galerie des Ambassadeurs, 1 Rue Pierre-Moulis, 83400
Hyères. T. 0494658260. - Ant - *044218*

Galerie des Iles d'Or, 16 Av des Iles-d'Or, 83400 Hyères.
T. 0494651955. - Furn - *044219*

Garcin, Paul, Le Port, 83400 Hyères.
T. 0494664169. *044220*

Marotte, 3 Rue Portalet, 83400 Hyères.
T. 0494655605. *044221*

Trufaut, Michel, 4 Pl Oustaou Rou, 83400 Hyères.
T. 0494652432. *044222*

Hyèvre-Paroisse (Doubs)
Hyèvre, Village, 25110 Hyèvre-Paroisse.
T. 0381843456. *044223*

Ibos (Hautes-Pyrénées)
Salle des Ventes d'Ibois, Rte Pau, 65420 Ibos.
T. 0562900610. - Ant / Paint / Furn - *044224*

Igoville (Eure)
Hilary, Vincent, Rue Marais, 27460 Igoville.
T. 0232232166. *044225*

Inchy (Nord)
Trifi, Jean-Jacques, 13 Rte Nationale, 59540 Inchy.
T. 0327851777. - Ant - *044226*

Ingrandes-sur-Loire (Maine-et-Loire)
Ferré, Auguste, La Riottière, 49123 Ingrandes-sur-Loire.
T. 41392111. *044227*

Irancy (Yonne)
Cordier, Joël, 9 Chemin Fossés, 89290 Irancy.
T. 0386423106. *044228*

Is-sur-Tille (Côte-d'Or)
Garnier, Serge, 2 et 14 Pl République, 21120 Is-sur-
Tille. T. 0380950098. *044229*

Isles-sur-Suippe (Marne)
Temps Retrouvé, 67 Rte Reims, 51110 Isles-sur-Suippe.
T. 0326033938. *044230*

Isneauville (Seine-Maritime)
Leprévost, Claude, 2807 Rte Neufchâtel, 76230 Isneau-
ville. T. 0235938070. *044231*

Issigeac (Dordogne)
Crédence, Rte Beaumont, 24560 Issigeac.
T. 0553587922. - Paint / Furn / Cur - *044232*

Issoire (Puy-de-Dôme)
Grenier Issoirien, 52 Rte Parentignat, 63500 Issoire.
T. 0473891250. - Ant - *044233*

Guivarch, Janine, Pl République, 63500 Issoire.
T. 0473890568. - Ant - *044234*

Liandier, François, 11 Rue Mas, 63500 Issoire.
T. 0473550088. - Ant - *044235*

Vissi D'Arte, 10 Rue Berbizilae, 63500 Issoire.
T. 0473891165. - Ant - *044236*

Issoudun (Indre)
Aux Arbres à Courges, 1 Rue Minimes, 36100 Issoudun.
T. 0254215632. *044237*

De la Cave au Grenier, Avail, 36100 Issoudun.
T. 0254215442. *044238*

Martin Lehardy, Sylviane, 18 Blvd Roosevelt, 36100 Issoudun. T. 0254218629. *044239*

Moreau, Gérald, 30 Rue Dardault, 36100 Issoudun.
T. 0254030004. *044240*

Saunier, Sylvain, 23bis Rue Manufacture, 36100 Issoudun. T. 0254218320. - Paint / Furn / Cur - *044241*

Issy-les-Moulineaux (Hauts-de-Seine)
Bénalcazar, Robert de, 7 Rue Maximilien-Robespierre,
92130 Issy-les-Moulineaux.
Fax (1) 41080285. *044242*

Coïncidences, 1 Rue Minard, 92130 Issy-les-Moulineaux.
T. 0140934413. *044243*

Daveau, Pascale, 2bis Rue André-Chenier, 92130 Issy-
les-Moulineaux. T. 0146450701. *044244*

Mélancolie, 13ter Rue Auguste-Gervais, 92130 Issy-les-
Moulineaux. T. 0147369543. *044245*

Thomassine, Alice, 37 Rue Henri-Tariel, 92130 Issy-les-
Moulineaux. T. 0146381705. *044246*

Ivry-la-Bataille (Eure)
Antiquités du Moulin, 8 Rue Henri-IV, 27540 Ivry-la-Bataille. T. 0232364171. *044247*

Eaux Vives, 61 Rue Henri-IV, 27540 Ivry-la-Bataille.
T. 0232364172. *044248*

Fouasse, Pierre, 10 Rue René-Dauplay, 27540 Ivry-la-
Bataille. T. 0232367036. *044249*

Ivry-sur-Seine (Val-de-Marne)
Baignoire Délirante, 35 Rue Barbès, 94200 Ivry-sur-Seine. T. 0146720223, Fax 0146712435. *044250*

Caverne des Particuliers, 124 Blvd Stalingrad, 94200
Ivry-sur-Seine. T. 0149599264. *044251*

Iwuy (Nord)
Danjou, Boda, 23 Rue Maréchal-Joffre, 59141 Iwuy.
T. 0327379249. - Furn - *044252*

Gouachi, Serge, 5 Rue Joffre, 59141 Iwuy.
T. 0327796739. - Ant - *044253*

Janvry (Essonne)
Schoettl, Christian, Ham Brosse, 91640 Janvry.
T. 0160120887. *044254*

Janzé (Ille-et-Vilaine)
Boury, Jean-Yves, Zone Artisanale Chauvelière, 35150
Janzé. T. 0299472666. *044255*

Jarnac (Charente)
Jarnac Brocante, 87 Rue Pasteur, 16200 Jarnac.
T. 0545352125. *044256*

Jarny (Meurthe-et-Moselle)
Jacquot, Patrick, 9 Rue Verdun, 54800 Jarny.
T. 0382201332. *044257*

Jasseron (Ain)
Perrin, Noël, 01250 Jasseron. T. 0474300125. - Ant /
Furn – *044258*

Jaulny (Meurthe-et-Moselle)
Barbarot, Claude, 2 Pl Fontaine, 54470 Jaulny.
T. 0383819056. *044259*

Jenlain (Nord)
Belle Epoque, 30 Rte Nationale, 59144 Jenlain.
T. 0327497644. - Ant - *044260*

Joigny (Yonne)
Friess, Jean-Pierre, 13 Av Forêt-d'Othe, 89300 Joigny.
T. 0386622245. - Furn / Cur - *044261*

Friess, Jean-Pierre, Rte Dixmont, 89300 Joigny.
T. 0386623724. - Furn / Cur - *044262*

Pascale, Michèle, 17bis Quai Général-Leclerc, 89300
Joigny. T. 0386620613. *044263*

Joinville-le-Pont (Val-de-Marne)
Antiquités de la Tour, 28 Av Général-Galliéni, 94340
Joinville-le-Pont. T. 0148853183. *044264*

Delhomme, Patrice, 3 Rue Jean-Mermoz, 94340 Joinville-le-Pont. T. 0148862168. *044265*

Maison Philippe, 8 Av Lefèvre, 94340 Joinville-le-Pont.
T. 0148891157, Fax 0148836365. *044266*

Jonquières (Vaucluse)
Maurin, Lydia, 54 Av Libération, 84150 Jonquières.
T. 0490705116. - Ant / Furn - *044267*

Jonzac (Charente-Maritime)
Antiquités du Cloître, 29 Rue Carmes, 17500 Jonzac.
T. 0546482683. - Furn - *044268*

Labrouche, Arnaud, La Maladrerie, 17500 Jonzac.
T. 0546485176, Fax 0546480356. *044269*

Mazurier, Myriam, 5 Pl Champ-de-Foire, 17500 Jonzac.
T. 0546484748. *044270*

Pradeaux, Monique, 3 Rue Tourniquet, 17500 Jonzac.
T. 0546480759. *044271*

Jossigny (Seine-et-Marne)
Ridard, Jean, 2 Rue Tournan, 77600 Jossigny.
T. 64022480. *044272*

Jouars-Pontchartrain (Yvelines)
Arcadie, 15 All André-Le-Nôtre, 78760 Jouars-Pontchartrain. T. 0134899252, Fax 0134899796. *044273*

Février, André, 70 Rte Paris, 78760 Jouars-Pontchartrain. T. 0134898032. - Furn / Cur / Toys - *044274*

Tardif, François, 6 Rte Paris, 78760 Jouars-Pontchartrain. T. 0134890259. - Furn / Cur - *044275*

Joué-lès-Tours (Indre-et-Loire)
Fabry Bonnemazou, Joële, Rte Monts, La Girardère,
37300 Joué-lès-Tours. T. 0547536331. *044276*

Jouet-sur-l'Aubois (Cher)
Antiquités du Pigeonnier, 10 Rue La Chapelle, 18320
Jouet-sur-l'Aubois. T. 0248763110. *044277*

Jouy (Eure-et-Loir)
Bazin, Moulin de la Bussière, 28300 Jouy.
T. 0237222504. *044278*

GLB Création, 5 Rue Berchères, 28300 Jouy.
T. 0237222972. *044279*

Jugon-lès-Lacs (Côtes-d'Armor)
Art Antiquités Artisanat, 24 Rue Penthièvre, 22270 Ju-
gon-lès-Lacs. T. 0296317172. *044280*

Juigné-sur-Loire (Maine-et-Loire)
Trost, André, 107 Grand Rue, 49130 Juigné-sur-Loire.
T. 41546560. *044281*

Juillan (Hautes-Pyrénées)
A la Saisie, 65 Rte Lourdes, 65290 Juillan.
T. 0562329366. - Ant - *044282*

Jurançon (Pyrénées-Atlantiques)
Dargelosse, Noëlle, 4 Av Ossau, 64110 Jurançon.
T. 0559061754, Fax 0559062398. - Ant - *044283*

Vitiello, Christian, 6 Av Charles-Touzet, 64110 Jurançon.
T. 0559063945. - Ant - *044284*

Jussey (Haute-Saône)
Sénille, Laurent, 13 Rue Hospice, 70500 Jussey.
T. 0384680026. *044285*

Juvisy-sur-Orge (Essonne)
Vincent, Bernard, 56 Grande Rue, 91260 Juvisy-sur-Or-
ge. T. 0169455158. - Ant - *044286*

Juzennecourt (Haute-Marne)
Grillet, Jeanne, 52330 Juzennecourt.
T. 0325020110. *044287*

Juziers (Yvelines)
Levecher, Michel, 16 Rue Fontaine, 78820 Juziers.
T. 0134756156. *044288*

Kaltenhouse (Bas-Rhin)
Hager, Gaëlle, 6 Rue Prés, 67240 Kaltenhouse.
T. 0388637855. - Ant / China - *044289*

Kerlaz (Finistère)
Berre, Alain le, Plage du Riz, 29100 Kerlaz.
T. 0298928626. - Ant / Furn - *044290*

Regart, 5 Rue Plomarc'h, 29100 Kerlaz. T. 0298928626.
- Ant - *044291*

Kientzheim (Haut-Rhin)
Riegel, Jacky, 12 Rue Chapelle, 68240 Kientzheim.
T. 0389471270. *044292*

L'Aigle (Orne)
Moulin de Mérouvel, 15 Rue Charles-Mérouvel, 61300
L'Aigle. T. 0233241181. - Ant - *044293*

Vincent, Michel, Pl La Halle, 61300 L'Aigle.
T. 0233246122. - Ant - *044294*

L'Epine (Marne)
Schoentgen, Marie-José, 24 Av Luxembourg, 51460
L'Epine. T. 0326669512. - Ant - *044295*

L'Escarène (Alpes-Maritimes)
Peluet-Altobianchi, César de, Col de Nice, 06440 L'Escarène. T. 0493795048. - Mod - *044296*

L'Etrat (Loire)
Bruyère, Jean, Château-La-Bertrandière, 42580 L'Etrat.
T. 0477747620. *044297*

L'Haÿ-les-Roses (Val-de-Marne)
Rocca, Antoine, 7 Rue Duguesclin, 94240 L'Haÿ-les-Roses. T. 0145474930. *044298*
Terrieres, Claude, 16 All Violettes, 94240 L'Haÿ-les-Roses. T. 0146877608. *044299*

L'Horme (Loire)
Vicente, José, 42 Cours Marin, 42152 L'Horme.
T. 0477314641. *044300*

L'Isle-Adam (Val-d'Oise)
Gueudet-Leroy, 112 Rue Pontoise, 95290 L'Isle-Adam.
T. 0134692550. *044301*
Malais, Rachel, 124 Parc de Cassan, 95290 L'Isle-Adam. T. 0134692899. *044302*
Momon, Marie-France, 327 Parc de Cassan, 95290
L'Isle-Adam. T. 0134692114. *044303*

L'Isle-d'Espagnac (Charente)
Guillebaud, Georges, 159bis Av République, 16340
L'Isle-d'Espagnac. T. 0545682069. *044304*

L'Isle-Jourdain (Gers)
Deu Païs, 30 Av Lombez, 32600 L'Isle-Jourdain.
T. 0562072001. *044305*
Marcazzan, Fabien, Rte Toulouse, ZI, 32600 L'Isle-Jourdain. T. 0562070649, Fax 0562071714.
- Dec - *044306*
Retureau, Philippe, 28 Av Commandant-Parisot, 32600
L'Isle-Jourdain. T. 0562070903. - Paint / Furn / Dec /
Silv / Instr / Glass / Cur - *044307*

L'Isle-sur-la-Sorgue (Vaucluse)
Atelier DL, 4 Av Julien-Guige, 84800 L'Isle-sur-la-Sorgue. T. 0490208608. - Ant - *044308*
Biehn, Michel, 7 Av Quatre-Otages, 84800 L'Isle-sur-la-Sorgue. T. 0490208904, Fax 0490384509.
- Ant - *044309*
Bounias, Christian, 11 Av Libération, 84800 L'Isle-sur-la-Sorgue. T. 0490383802. - Ant - *044310*
Bourgeois, Jean-Jacques, Rte Apt, 84800 L'Isle-sur-la-Sorgue. T. 0490380737. - Ant - *044311*
Boutique de Francine, 1 Av Julien-Guige, 84800 L'Isle-sur-la-Sorgue. T. 0490385581. - Ant - *044312*
Bunel, Patrick, Av Quatre-Otages, 84800 L'Isle-sur-la-Sorgue. T. 0490385176. - Ant - *044313*
Chizky, Jean, 4 Av Julien-Guige, 84800 L'Isle-sur-la-Sorgue. T. 0490207342, Fax 0490385469.
- Ant - *044314*
Collections Passion, 2 Rue Carnot, 84800 L'Isle-sur-la-Sorgue. T. 0490385451. - Ant - *044315*
Cornier, Patrick, 2bis Av Egalité, 84800 L'Isle-sur-la-Sorgue. T. 0490385276. - Ant - *044316*
Djian, Emmanuel, 7 Av Quatre-Otages, 84800 L'Isle-sur-la-Sorgue. T. 0490386358. - Ant - *044317*
Futur Antérieur, 2bis Av Egalité, 84800 L'Isle-sur-la-Sorgue. T. 0490385276. - Ant - *044318*
Gay, André, 7 Av Quatre-Otages, 84800 L'Isle-sur-la-Sorgue. T. 0490382373. - Ant - *044319*
Géva, Rémi, 4 Rue Denfert-Rochereau, 84800 L'Isle-sur-la-Sorgue. T. 0490206371. - Ant - *044320*
Giancatarina, Maria, 4 Av Julien-Guige, 84800 L'Isle-sur-la-Sorgue. T. 0490385802. - Ant - *044321*
Hannotte, Jacques, Rte Caumont, 84800 L'Isle-sur-la-Sorgue. T. 0490208707. - Ant - *044322*
Hermille, Mireille, Av Quatre-Otages, 84800 L'Isle-sur-la-Sorgue. T. 0490385175. - Ant - *044323*
Isle aux Brocantes, 7 Av des Quatre-Otages, 84800
L'Isle-sur-la-Sorgue. T. 0490206993. - Ant - *044324*
Klumpen, Jochem, 4 Av Julien-Guige, 84800 L'Isle-sur-la-Sorgue. T. 0490385766. - Ant - *044325*
Lahmi, Claude, 2bis Av Egalité, 84800 L'Isle-sur-la-Sorgue. T. 0490385176. - Ant - *044326*
Lecomte, Hervé, Av Quatre-otages, 84800 L'Isle-sur-la-Sorgue. T. 0490384217. - Ant - *044327*
Légier, Nathalie, Av Quatre-Otages, 84800 L'Isle-sur-la-Sorgue. T. 0490207517. - Ant - *044328*
Mas de Curebourg, Rte Apt, 84800 L'Isle-sur-la-Sorgue.
T. 0490203006, Fax 0490202342. - Ant - *044329*
Mesureur, Karine, 7bis Av Quatre-Otages, 84800 L'Isle-sur-la-Sorgue. T. 0490384547. - Ant - *044330*
Nicod, Gérard, Le Château de Vellorges, 84800 L'Isle-sur-la-Sorgue. T. 0490382038. - Ant - *044331*

Nicod, Xavier, 9 Av Quatre-Otages, 84800 L'Isle-sur-la-Sorgue. T. 0490380720. - Ant - *044332*
Nossereau-Hauff, Christine, 7 Av Quatre-Otages, 84800
L'Isle-sur-la-Sorgue. T. 0490382586. - Ant - *044333*
Onde, Danielle, 11 Av Quatre-Otages, 84800 L'Isle-sur-la-Sorgue. T. 0490385458. - Ant - *044334*
Peter & Martine, 7 Av Quatre-Otages, 84800 L'Isle-sur-la-Sorgue. T. 0490385178. - Ant - *044335*
Reynaud, Marie-Claire, 4 Av Julien-Guige, 84800 L'Isle-sur-la-Sorgue. T. 0490386027. - Ant - *044336*
Roche, Lysiane, 7 Av Quatre-Otages, 84800 L'Isle-sur-la-Sorgue. T. 0490382579. - Ant - *044337*
Samouraï, 4 Av Julien-Guige, 84800 L'Isle-sur-la-Sorgue. T. 0490208655. - Ant - *044338*
Thomasset, Jean-Pierre, 4 Av Julien-Guige, 84800
L'Isle-sur-la-Sorgue. T. 0490384185. - Ant - *044339*
Thonon, Yannick, 1520 Av Quatre-Otages, 84800 L'Isle-sur-la-Sorgue. T. 0490385620. - Ant - *044340*
Versi, Danièle, L'Orée-de-l'Isle bât B, 84800 L'Isle-sur-la-Sorgue. T. 0490207976. - Ant - *044341*
Vinatier, Richard, 4 Av Julien-Guige, 84800 L'Isle-sur-la-Sorgue. T. 0490380598. - Ant - *044342*
Vincent Mit L'Ane, Rte Apt, 84800 L'Isle-sur-la-Sorgue.
T. 0490206315, Fax 0490208306. - Ant - *044343*

L'Isle-sur-le-Doubs (Doubs)
Antiquités de l'Isle, 4 Rue Ponts, 25250 L'Isle-sur-le-Doubs. T. 0381963952. *044344*

La Barre-de-Semilly (Manche)
Paris Chantal, 1 Rte Saint-Jean, 50810 La Barre-de-Semilly. T. 0233050656. *044345*

La Bassée (Nord)
Grauwin, Nicolas, 9 Rue Lens, 59480 La Bassée.
T. 0320291683. - Ant - *044346*

La Bastide-de-Sérou (Ariège)
Noblet, Michael de, Rue Porte Foix, 09240 La Bastide-de-Sérou. T. 0561645926. - Paint / Cur - *044347*

La Bastide-des-Jourdans (Vaucluse)
Nouchka, Fieraque, 84240 La Bastide-des-Jourdans.
T. 0490778794. - Ant - *044348*

La Baule (Loire-Atlantique)
Anne, 6 Av Pavie, 44500 La Baule.
T. 40603394. *044349*
Antiquités Les Ans Chanteurs, 217 Av Maréchal-de-Lattre-de-Tassigny, 44500 La Baule. T. 40110517,
Fax 40603087. *044350*
Aux Reflets du Passé, 4 Av Marché, 44500 La Baule.
T. 40605145. *044351*
Célette, René, Esplanade François-André, 44500 La
Baule. T. 40242091. - Paint / Furn / Cur - *044352*
Galerie de l'Abbaye, Esplanade François-André, 44500
La Baule. T. 40113161. *044353*
Galerie du Palais, 6 Av Louis Lajarrige, 44500 La Baule.
T. 40245123. *044354*
Garandeau, Maeyvonne, Av Marie-Louise, 44500 La
Baule. T. 40111056. *044355*
Guérin & Fils, Rte Nérac, 44500 La Baule.
T. 40111362. *044356*
Kruydt, Maud, 79 Av Général-de-Gaulle, 44500 La Baule. T. 40603393. - Furn / Jew / Silv - *044357*
Lainé, Marc, Rte Costres, 44500 La Baule.
T. 40012428. *044358*
Lecomte, 4 Blvd Hennecart, 44500 La Baule.
T. 40111174. *044359*
Lecomte, Daniel, Av du Bois d'Amour, 44500 La Baule.
T. 40602697. - Furn - *044360*
London Antiques, 13 Av Général-de-Gaulle, 44500 La
Baule. T. 40600425. *044361*
London Antiquités, 138 Av Général-de-Gaulle, 44500 La
Baule. T. 40240736. *044362*
Nénert, Didier-Jean, 11 Av Pierre-Loti, 44500 La Baule.
T. 40246547. *044363*
Occasions 215, 215 Av Maréchal-de-Lattre-de-Tassigny,
44500 La Baule. T. 40609599. *044364*

La Bazoge (Sarthe)
Giai-Miniet, Daniel, 67 Av Nationale, 72650 La Bazoge.
T. 0243254013. - Ant - *044365*

La Bénisson-Dieu (Loire)
Stubican, Marie-Louise, Parvis Albéric, 42720 La Bénisson-Dieu. T. 0477666396. *044366*

La Boissière-de-Montaigu (Vendée)
Soulard, Claude, Ecole Pont-Légé, 85600 La Boissière-de-Montaigu. T. 0251422415. *044367*

La Bonneville-sur-Iton (Eure)
Chassin, Joëlle, 67 Rue Jean-Maréchal, 27190 La Bonneville-sur-Iton. T. 0232376943. *044368*

La Bouille (Seine-Maritime)
Antiquités Saint-Michel au Vieux Pélican, 3 Pl Saint-Michel, 76530 La Bouille. T. 0235180167. *044369*

La Bresse (Vosges)
Marion, Josiane, 2bis Rue Mougel-Bey, 88250 La
Bresse. T. 0329255983. *044370*

La Cadière-d'Azur (Var)
Wanner, Anne-Marie, Chemin Saint-Côme, 83740 La
Cadière-d'Azur. T. 0494901228. *044371*

La Calmette (Gard)
Atelier de la Regordane, Plan Croix, 30190 La Calmette.
T. 0466810203, Fax 0466810167. *044372*

La Celle-Dunoise (Creuse)
Guilluy, Gérard, 23800 La Celle-Dunoise.
T. 0555890416. - Ant / Furn / Dec - *044373*
Rameix, Christophe, Bourg, 23800 La Celle-Dunoise.
T. 0555892394. - Paint - *044374*

La Celle-Saint-Cloud (Yvelines)
Jackie Antiquités, 42 Av Jonchère, 78170 La Celle-Saint-Cloud. T. 0139183367. *044375*

La Chapelle-aux-Pots (Oise)
Luc, Menant, 15 RN, Les Fontenettes, 60650 La Chapelle-aux-Pots. T. 0344048119. - Ant / Cur - *044376*

La Chapelle-d'Armentières (Nord)
Antique Chapelle, 15 Rue Marle, 59930 La Chapelle-d'Armentières. T. 0320359889. - Ant - *044377*
Jadis, 81 Rue Henri-Matisse, 59930 La Chapelle-d'Armentières. - Ant - *044378*

La Chapelle-des-Fougeretz (Ille-et-Vilaine)
Entrepôt des Antiquités, Zone Artisanale La Brosse,
35520 La Chapelle-des-Fougeretz.
T. 0299664180. *044379*

La Chapelle-la-Reine (Seine-et-Marne)
Chambon, Philippe, 2 Av Fontainebleau, 77760 La Chapelle-la-Reine. T. 64243343. *044380*
Girault, Eliane, 34 Rue Gare, 77760 La Chapelle-la-Reine. T. 64691008. *044381*

La Chapelle-Saint-Luc (Aube)
Drot, Dominique, 1 Rue Lakanal, 10600 La Chapelle-Saint-Luc. T. 0325811485. - Furn - *044382*

La Chapelle-sur-Oudon (Maine-et-Loire)
Journiac, Gilles, 13 Rue Pimodan, 49500 La Chapelle-sur-Oudon. T. 41921221. *044383*

La Charité-sur-Loire (Nièvre)
Bétabois, 19 Cour Château, 58400 La Charité-sur-Loire.
T. 0386696238. *044384*
Brocante Rose, 88 Rue Maréchal-Leclerc, 58400 La
Charité-sur-Loire. T. 0386696641. *044385*
Millet, Jean-Claude, 27 Rue Chapelains, 58400 La Charité-sur-Loire. T. 0386703219. *044386*
Vaissaire-Laurent, Yolande, 19 Cour Château, 58400 La
Charité-sur-Loire. T. 0386700565. *044387*

La Châtre (Indre)
Bellu, Emmanuel, 1 Av Auvergne, 36400 La Châtre.
T. 0254060910. *044388*
Charrier-Villepreux, Brigitte, 83 Rue Nationale, 36400 La
Châtre. T. 0254482076. *044389*

La Chaussée-d'Ivry (Eure-et-Loir)
Antiquaire des Gâtines Rouges, Les Gâtines-Rouges, 28260 La Chaussée-d'Ivry. T. 0237645464.
- Furn -   *044390*

La Chaussée-Saint-Victor (Loir-et-Cher)
Blois Antiquités, 128 Rue Nationale, 41260 La Chaussée-Saint-Victor. T. 0254741455.   *044391*
Coville, Jean, 48bis Rte Nationale, 41260 La Chaussée-Saint-Victor. T. 0254784388.   *044392*

La Ciotat (Bouches-du-Rhône)
Californie Antiquités, Av Guillaume-Dulac, 13600 La Ciotat. T. 0442717875.   *044393*
Contios, Marie-Thérèse, 45 Rue Poilus, 13600 La Ciotat. T. 0442836526.   *044394*

La Clusaz (Haute-Savoie)
Bonzi, Maurice, La Perrière, 74220 La Clusaz. T. 0450024847.   *044395*
Pollet Thiollier, Guy, Les Riffroids, 74220 La Clusaz. Fax 50025129.   *044396*

La Cluse-et-Mijoux (Doubs)
Mesnier, Jacques, 3 Lieu-dit Moulin-Mougain, 25300 La Cluse-et-Mijoux. T. 0381464947.   *044397*

La Colle-sur-Loup (Alpes-Maritimes)
Antiquario, Quartier Plus bas Pilon, 06480 La Colle-sur-Loup. T. 0493325654. - Furn / Dec -   *044398*
Carbonne, Yolande, 2 Blvd Général-Leclerc, 06480 La Colle-sur-Loup. T. 0493328610.   *044399*
Conrad, Michel, 75 Av Maréchal-Foch, 06480 La Colle-sur-Loup. T. 0493326484.   *044400*
Galerie Rive Gauche, 75 Av Maréchal-Foch, 06480 La Colle-sur-Loup. T. 0493327998. - Paint / Furn / Dec / Cur -   *044401*
Maurel, J., 47 Rue Maréchal-Foch, 06480 La Colle-sur-Loup. T. 0493326510.   *044402*
Pastorale, 32 Av Maréchal-Foch, 06480 La Colle-sur-Loup. T. 0493326966.   *044403*
Pigeon, Birgitta, 38 Rue Maréchal-Foch, 06480 La Colle-sur-Loup. T. 0493326515.   *044404*

La Couarde-sur-Mer (Charente-Maritime)
Le Grand, Pol, 46 Grande Rue, 17670 La Couarde-sur-Mer. T. 0546298889.   *044405*

La Coucourde (Drôme)
Au Fil du Temps, Quart Derbières, 26740 La Coucourde. T. 0475900404.   *044406*
Brisou, Joëlle, Quart Derbières, 26740 La Coucourde. T. 0475900586.   *044407*
Brocantine, RN 7, 26740 La Coucourde. T. 0475900883.   *044408*
Gonella, Joseph, Quart Derbières, 26740 La Coucourde. T. 0475900011.   *044409*
Kalao, Quart Derbières, 26740 La Coucourde. T. 0475900123.   *044410*
Maugé, Joëlle, Quart Derbières, 26740 La Coucourde. T. 0475900274.   *044411*
Russo, 26740 La Coucourde. T. 0475900638. - Paint / Furn / Cur -   *044412*

La Couronne (Charente)
Ribardière, Christian, 156 Rte Bordeaux, La Montée, RN 10, 16400 La Couronne. T. 0545671722.   *044413*

La Couture-Boussey (Eure)
Belle Brocante, 4 Rte Ivry, 27750 La Couture-Boussey. T. 0232367846.   *044414*

La Crau (Var)
Arnold, Alice, 22 Av Gare, 83260 La Crau. T. 0494667155.   *044415*
Garcin, Dominique, Quartier Les Martins, 92 Imp Martins, 83260 La Crau. T. 0494667138.   *044416*
Pernin, Rodolphe, 3250 Chemin Long, 83260 La Crau. T. 0494660812.   *044417*
Village Saint-Pierre, 22 Av Gare, 83260 La Crau. T. 0494661194. - Furn -   *044418*

La Crèche (Deux-Sèvres)
Pineau, William, Pied l'Ouaille, 79260 La Crèche. T. 0549756183.   *044419*

La Croix-Saint-Leufroy (Eure)
Marche, Eric, 34 Rue Louviers, 27490 La Croix-Saint-Leufroy. T. 0232677134.   *044420*

La Croix-Valmer (Var)
Fassetti, Henri, 25 Av Tambourinaires, 83420 La Croix-Valmer. T. 0494543859.   *044421*

La Faute-sur-Mer (Vendée)
Favre, Frédéric, Rue Pointe-d'Arçay, 85460 La Faute-sur-Mer. T. 0251564648.   *044422*

La Ferrière (Indre-et-Loire)
Celereau, Fabien, 14 Le Haut-Bourg, 37110 La Ferrière. T. 0547563050.   *044423*

La Ferté-Bernard (Sarthe)
Dépôt Vente de la Porte Saint-Julien, Pl Saint-Julien, 72400 La Ferté-Bernard. T. 0243712515.
- Ant -   *044424*

La Ferté-sous-Jouarre (Seine-et-Marne)
Antiquités des Meulières, 9 Rue Pelletiers, 70260 La Ferté-sous-Jouarre. T. 0360220465.   *044425*
Chapelier, L., 87 Av Franklin-Roosevelt-Sept-Sorts, 77260 La Ferté-sous-Jouarre. T. 0360220853.   *044426*
Leglaive, Jacques, 31 Av Franklin Roosevelt, 77260 La Ferté-sous-Jouarre. T. 0160220242. - Paint / Furn / China / Sculp / Tex / Dec / Instr / Toys / Music -   *044427*
Sénéchal, Georges, 101 Rue Condé, 77260 La Ferté-sous-Jouarre. T. 0360220184. - Ant / Furn -   *044428*
Vasseur, François, 1 Rue Hardy-Guillard, 77260 La Ferté-sous-Jouarre. T. 0360226647.   *044429*

La Ferté-Vidame (Eure-et-Loir)
Cador, Janine, 1 Pl Général-de-Fontanges, 28340 La Ferté-Vidame. T. 0237376017.   *044430*

La Flèche (Sarthe)
Jaffre, Michel, 46 Grande Rue, 72200 La Flèche. T. 0243940636. - Ant / Furn -   *044431*

La Forêt-Fouesnant (Finistère)
Guégaden, Fernande, 43 Rue Baie, 29133 La Forêt-Fouesnant. T. 0298568556. - Ant -   *044432*
Roi Soleil, 25 Rue Charles-de-Gualle, 29133 La Forêt-Fouesnant. T. 0298568211. - Ant -   *044433*

La Fouillouse (Loire)
Porret, Daniel, Le Vernay, 42480 La Fouillouse. T. 0477301666.   *044434*

La Garde (Var)
Antiquaires de la Pauline, RN 98, 83130 La Garde. T. 0494149015, Fax 0494143119.   *044435*
Au Coeur du Temps, 1077 Rue Abel-Gance, 83130 La Garde. T. 0494206955.   *044436*
Colmar, Marcel, Rue Pierre-Loti, Résidence Oliviers, 83130 La Garde. T. 0494232723.   *044437*

La Garde-Freinet (Var)
Ihler, Christian, 1 Rte Nationale 558, 83310 La Garde-Freinet. T. 0494436533.   *044438*

La Grande-Motte (Hérault)
Micheletti Dervieux, Colette, Le Provence, 34280 La Grande-Motte. T. 0467565195.   *044439*
Soulié, Nicole, La Dame-au-Lotus, Av Europe, 34280 La Grande-Motte. T. 0467567344.   *044440*

La Gravelle (Mayenne)
Reine Victoria, Rte nationale 157, 53320 La Gravelle. T. 0243375778. - Ant -   *044441*

La Groise (Nord)
Raout, Roland, Rue Guise, 59360 La Groise. T. 0327776740. - Ant -   *044442*

La Londe-les-Maures (Var)
Calvi, Guy, 11 Rue d'Alger, 83250 La Londe-les-Maures. T. 0494436533.   *044443*

La Loupe (Eure-et-Loir)
Brocante de La Loupe, 25 Rue Chartres, 28240 La Loupe. T. 0237810580.   *044444*

La Madelaine (Nord)
Antiquités Brocante Caractère, 181 Rue Gén-de-Gaulle, 59110 La Madelaine. T. 0320781497. - Ant -   *044445*
Grenier du Chti, 37 Rue Charles-Gounod, 59110 La Madelaine. T. 0320249494. - Ant -   *044446*
Turpin, Pascal, 181 Rue Gén-de-Gaulle, 59110 La Madelaine. T. 0320781497. - Ant -   *011117*

La Mézière (Ille-et-Vilaine)
Matériaux d'Antan, Rte Saint-Malo, 35520 La Mézière. T. 0299665666.   *044448*

La Mothe-Achard (Vendée)
Pruvost, 23 Pl Halles, 85150 La Mothe-Achard. T. 0251386183. - Furn / Cur -   *044449*

La Neuveville-sous-Châtenois (Vosges)
Hubert, Gérard, 18 Rue Village, 88170 La Neuveville-sous-Châtenois. T. 0329944396.   *044450*

La Pacaudière (Loire)
Besson, Roger, Rte Bleue, 42310 La Pacaudière. T. 0477643700.   *044451*
Trois Arcades, RN 7, 42310 La Pacaudière. T. 0477641714.   *044452*

La Queue-en-Brie (Val-de-Marne)
Maison d'Art Oriental, 3 Rue Frères-Lumière, 94510 La Queue-en-Brie. T. 0145933302, Fax 0145933303. - Orient -   *044453*
Royal Antique, 1 Rue Libération, 94510 La Queue-en-Brie. T. 0145769265.   *044454*

La Réole (Gironde)
Au Grenier Grand-Père, RN 113 Lamothe-Landerron, 33190 La Réole. T. 0556617691.   *044455*
Labonne, Albert-Claude, Av Maréchal-de-Lattre-de-Tassigny, 33190 La Réole. T. 0556610409.   *044456*

La Richardais (Ille-et-Vilaine)
Antique Manor, Rue Haut-Chemin, 35780 La Richardais. T. 0299466941.   *044457*
Antiquités Chéron, Zone Artisanale Ermitage, 35780 La Richardais. T. 0299882258. - Furn / Cur -   *044458*
Au Hasard du Temps, Zone Artisanale Ermitage, 35780 La Richardais. T. 0299465540.   *044459*
Lescure, Annick, 7 Rue Gougeonnais, 35780 La Richardais. T. 0299160355. - Ant -   *044460*

La Rivière-Saint-Sauveur (Calvados)
Rico Déco, 8 Chemin Blanc, 14600 La Rivière-Saint-Sauveur. T. 0231895024.   *044461*

La Roche-Bernard (Morbihan)
Philippe Antiquités, 58 Rue Nantes BP 3, 56130 La Roche-Bernard. T. 0299906057. - Ant -   *044462*

La Roche-sur-Foron (Haute-Savoie)
Collectionneur, 26 Rue Perrine, 74800 La Roche-sur-Foron. T. 0450258134.   *044463*
Lavy, Corinne, 47 Rue Plain-Château, 74800 La Roche-sur-Foron. T. 0450031205.   *044464*

La Roche-sur-Yon (Vendée)
AC Vent, 39 Rue Maréchal-Foch, 85000 La Roche-sur-Yon. T. 0251460089. - Furn / Cur -   *044465*
Coffineau, Béatrice, 23 Rue Paul-Doumer, 85000 La Roche-sur-Yon. T. 0251371239.   *044466*
Coffineau, Guy, 23 Rue Paul-Doumer, 85000 La Roche-sur-Yon. T. 0251371239.   *044467*
Engerbeau, Dominique, 39 Rue Maréchal-Foch, 85000 La Roche-sur-Yon. T. 0251052334.   *044468*
Gaillard, Jean-Pierre, 27 Rue Roger-Salengro, 85000 La Roche-sur-Yon. T. 0251360056.   *044469*
Le Déan, 5 Rue Victor-Hugo, 85000 La Roche-sur-Yon. T. 0251361829.   *044470*
Soulas, Didier, 20 Rue Gondoliers, 85000 La Roche-sur-Yon. T. 0251362874.   *044471*

La-Roche-Vineuse (Saône-et-Loire)
Dubief, Régine, Les Prés-Pommiers, 71960 La-Roche-Vineuse. T. 0385377255. - Ant -   *044472*

La Rochefoucauld (Charente)
Montleau, Gérald de, Hôtel Gourville, 16110 La Rochefoucauld. T. 0545630661. - Furn -   *044473*

Reflets du Temps, 35 Rue Halles, 16110 La Rochefoucauld. T. 0545623115.   044474

La Rochelle (Charente-Maritime)
Allo Antiquité, 150 Av Cimetière, 17000 La Rochelle.
T. 0546506228. - Furn / Cur -   044475
Armada, 3bis Rue Fourche, 17000 La Rochelle.
T. 0546417495.   044476
Au Fil des Ans, 50bis Rue Emile-Normandin, 17000 La
Rochelle. T. 0546441829.   044477
Bayeux, Jean-Pierre, 20 Rue Chef-de-Ville, 17000 La
Rochelle. T. 0546417364.   044478
Belle Epoque, 17 Rue Léonce-Vieljeux, 17000 La Ro-
chelle. T. 0546413730.   044479
Caractères, 5 Rue Bazoges, 17000 La Rochelle.
T. 0546411507.   044480
Castaing, Hugues, 17 Rue Cloche, 17000 La Rochelle.
T. 0546413051, Fax 0546505679. - Furn -   044481
Charpentier, Marc, 146 Av Cimetière, 17000 La Rochel-
le. T. 0546270860.   044482
Claudine Antiquités, 18 Rue Saint-Nicolas, 17000 La Ro-
chelle. T. 0546506406. - Furn / Lights / Cur /
Mod -   044483
Dars, André, 19 Quai Valin, 17000 La Rochelle.
T. 0546419047.   044484
Découverte, 10bis Rue Saint-Nicolas, 17000 La Rochel-
le. T. 0546418329. - Graph / Repr -   044485
Denis, Jacques, 24 Rue Templiers, 17000 La Rochelle.
T. 0546414975. - Furn / Cur -   044486
Descateaux, Juany, 28 Rue Saint-Nicolas, 17000 La Ro-
chelle. T. 0546412700.   044487
Grenouillère, 280 Av Jean-Guiton, 17000 La Rochelle.
T. 0546679245.   044488
Guilhabert, Françoise, 112 Av Coligny, 17000 La Rochel-
le. T. 0546345600. - Furn / Tex / Silv -   044489
Michel, Christian, 12 Rue Réaumur, 17000 La Rochelle.
T. 0546506228.   044490
Passion, 14 Rue Ferté, 17000 La Rochelle.
T. 0546505178.   044491
Pin Parasol, 18 Rue Saint-Nicolas, 17000 La Rochelle.
T. 0546411753.   044492
Reix, Chantal, 125 Blvd André-Sautel, 17000 La Rochel-
le. T. 0546341670, Fax 0546003568. - Paint / Furn /
Cur -   044493
Ricard, 17000 La Rochelle. T. 0546341899. - Sculp /
Cur / Toys / Music -   044494
Troc-Antic, 1 Rue Saint-Louis, 17000 La Rochelle.
T. 0546412776.   044495
Verdier, Olivier, 11 Rue Fagots, 17000 La Rochelle.
T. 0546419359.   044496

La Rochette (Charente)
Piqueux, Pierre, Le Bourg, 16110 La Rochette.
T. 0545639193.   044497

La Roquebrussanne (Var)
Aboudaram, Colette, Domaine Menpenti, 83136 La Ro-
quebrussanne. T. 0494869498.   044498
Molières, Ham Molières, 83136 La Roquebrussanne.
T. 0494869395, Fax 0494868281.   044499

La Sentinelle (Nord)
Gardin, Danielle, 53bis Av Jean-Jaurès, 59174 La Senti-
nelle. T. 0327332999. - Ant -   044500

La Seyne-sur-Mer (Var)
Carrera, Guy, 1 Rue Jacques-Laurent, 83500 La Seyne-
sur-Mer. T. 0494872390.   044501
Meublerie, Av Marcel-Paul, 83500 La Seyne-sur-Mer.
T. 0494877374. - Paint / Furn / Cur -   044502
Monjo, Jean-François, 11 Chemin Croix-de-Palun,
83500 La Seyne-sur-Mer. T. 0494942272.   044503
Rouden, André, 282 Rte Janas, 83500 La Seyne-sur-
Mer. T. 0494748494.   044504
Salva, Xavier, 1817 Av Pierre-Auguste-Renoir, 83500 La
Seyne-sur-Mer. T. 0494876214.   044505

La Teste-de-Buch (Gironde)
Mauron, 651 Av Denis-Papin, 33260 La Teste-de-Buch.
T. 0556547038. - Furn / Tex -   044506
Mauron, Pierre, 221 Av Gustave-Eiffel, 33260 La Teste-
de-Buch. T. 0556547260. - Furn / Tex -   044507
Richel, Philippe, 30 Rue Aiguillon, 33260 La Teste-de-
Buch. T. 0556225166.   044508

La Tour-d'Aigues (Vaucluse)
Borin, Edouard, Chemin Cayoux, 84240 La Tour-d'Ai-
gues. T. 0490074892. - Ant -   044509

La Tremblade (Charente-Maritime)
Ecu de France, 43 Blvd Maréchal-Joffre, 17390 La
Tremblade. T. 0546360031, Fax 0546362700.   044510

La Trinité (Alpes-Maritimes)
Troc 06, 6 Blvd Stalingrad, 06340 La Trinité.
T. 0493546097. - Furn / Cur -   044511

La Trinité (Eure)
Antiquités Bigot, Village, 27930 La Trinité.
T. 0232670726.   044512

La Valette-du-Var (Var)
Mondino, Antoine, 420 Av Gabriel-Péri, 83160 La Va-
lette-du-Var. T. 0494610954.   044513
Monnier, Bernard, Av Paul-Valéry, La Coupiane, Bâti-
ment 30, 83160 La Valette-du-Var.
T. 0494202553.   044514
Persico, Didier, 48 Av Moulières, 83160 La Valette-du-
Var. T. 0494612463.   044515

La Varenne-Saint-Hilaire (Val-de-Mar-
ne)
Acanthe, 81bis Av Bac, 94210 La Varenne-Saint-Hilaire.
T. 0148831569.   044517
Au Temps Jadis, 43 Av Bac, 94210 La Varenne-Saint-Hi-
laire. T. 0148891520.   044518
Campion, Noël, 19 Av Raymond-Poincaré, 94210 La Va-
renne. T. 0148832260. - Ant -   044518a
Chenet, 97 Av Bac, 94210 La Varenne-Saint-Hilaire.
T. 0148831602.   044519
Folies Varennoises, 18 Av Mesnil, 94210 La Varenne-
Saint-Hilaire. T. 0148898540.   044520
Guerraz, Pierre, 1 Av Verdun, 94210 La Varenne-Saint-
Hilaire. T. 0148863974.   044521
Kreloufi, Gilbert, 25 Av Bac, 94210 La Varenne-Saint-Hi-
laire. T. 0148835248.   044522
Le Roy, Bianca, 14 Rue Chappelier, 94210 La Varenne-
Saint-Hilaire. T. 0143979343.   044523
Olim, 85 Rue Lafayette, 94210 La Varenne-Saint-Hilaire.
T. 0148836617.   044524

La Vernelle (Indre)
Bruyère, André, Les Mardelles, 36600 La Vernelle.
T. 0254976632.   044525

La Verpillière (Isère)
Brocantine, 44 Rue du Batou, 38290 La Verpillière.
T. 0474944771. - Ant / Furn -   044526

Labarthe (Tarn-et-Garonne)
Casaro, Yvette, Laboulfy-Basse, 82220 Labarthe.
T. 0563676046.   044527

Labarthe-sur-Lèze (Haute-Garonne)
Deldossi, Jacqueline, 285 Chemin Pradets, 31120 La-
barthe-sur-Lèze. T. 0561086704.   044528

Labastide-d'Armagnac (Landes)
Grange Notre Dame, Rue Notre-Dame, 40240 Labastide-d'Armagnac. T. 0558446666. - Paint / Cur -   044529

Labastide-de-Lévis (Tarn)
Tilbury, Saint-Maury, 81150 Labastide-de-Lévis.
T. 0563532832, Fax 0563532393. - Paint / Furn /
Cur -   044530

Labastide-Rouairoux (Tarn)
Grenier Bastidien, 60 Blvd Carnot, 81270 Labastide-
Rouairoux. T. 0563981130.   044531

Labastide-Saint-Pierre (Tarn-et-Garon-
ne)
Cristol, Jean, Rue Victor-Hugo, 82370 Labastide-Saint-
Pierre. T. 0563305148.   044532

Labenne (Landes)
La Branère, La Branère, RN 10, 40530 Labenne.
T. 0559454283. - Paint / Furn / Cur -   044533

Labeuville (Meuse)
Antiquités Brocante Expertises, 16 Grande Rue, 55160
Labeuville. T. 0329875540. - Ant -   044534

Labrihe (Gers)
Laffranque, Jean-Michel, Ligardes, 32120 Labrihe.
T. 0562068957.   044535

Laburgade (Lot)
Combarieu, Charles, Bourg, 46230 Laburgade.
T. 0565316088.   044536

Lachapelle-Auzac (Lot)
Siclet, Martine, Lachapelle Basse, 46200 Lachapelle-
Auzac. T. 0565378277.   044537

Ladoix-Serrigny (Côte-d'Or)
Javouhey, Patrick, Ham Ladoix, 21550 Ladoix-Serrigny.
T. 0380264528.   044538

Lafox (Lot-et-Garonne)
Martini, Terrefort, 47240 Lafox. T. 0553685097,
Fax 0553685388. - Paint / Furn / China / Sculp / Dec /
Glass / Cur / Toys -   044539

Lafrançaise (Tarn-et-Garonne)
Garcia-Montes, Louis, Chemin Brousset, 82130 Lafran-
çaise. T. 0563659279.   044540
Moog, Christophe, 2 Rue Egalité, 82130 Lafrançaise.
T. 0563659600.   044541

Lagnes (Vaucluse)
Degruglier, Hélène, Les Routes-les-Grées, 84800 Lag-
nes. T. 0490203006, Fax 0490202342. - Ant -   044542

Lagorce (Ardèche)
Forissier, Bernard, Fontaine-du-Cade, 07150 Lagorce.
T. 0475377310, Fax 0475377310. - Ant -   044543

Lahoussoye (Somme)
Lenflé, Gaston, 154 Rue Tilleul, 80800 Lahoussoye.
T. 0322405829. - Ant -   044544

Laloubière (Hautes-Pyrénées)
Brocant'oc, 4 Rue Moulin, 65310 Laloubière.
T. 0562452812. - Ant -   044545

Lamastre (Ardèche)
Durrenmath, Jean-Pierre, Rte de Valence, 07270 La-
mastre. T. 0475064716. - Ant / Paint / Furn -   044546

Lamballe (Côtes-d'Armor)
Le Goff, François-Xavier, 14 Rue Guignardais, 22400
Lamballe. T. 0296310882.   044547

Lambersart (Nord)
Balusseau, Arnould, 87 Av Henri-Delecaux, 59130
Lambersart. T. 0320934200. - Ant -   044548
Foulon, Pierre, 87 Av Henri-Delecaux, 59130 Lambers-
art. T. 0320934200. - Ant -   044549
Vert Olive, 63 Rue Bourg, 59130 Lambersart.
T. 0320938098. - Ant -   044550

Lambesc (Bouches-du-Rhône)
Fournier, Yolande, Font d'Arles, RN 7, 13410 Lambesc.
T. 0442927424.   044551
Imbert, J.K., 28 Av Verdun, 13410 Lambesc.
T. 0442928830.   044552

Lamorlaye (Oise)
Antiquités Aras, 13 Av Libération, 60260 Lamorlaye.
T. 0344213199. - Ant -   044553
Antiquités Montaigne, 2 Rue de l'Eglise, 60260 Lamor-
laye. T. 0344213650. - Ant / Paint / Furn -   044554
Kuszelewic, Albert, 17, av Libération, 60260 Lamorlaye.
T. 0344215283. - Ant / Furn -   044555

Lamothe-Fénelon (Lot)
André, Bruno, Emboly, 46350 Lamothe-Fénelon.
T. 0565376116.   044556

Lamotte-Beuvron (Loir-et-Cher)
A Saint-Eterne, 30 Rue Durfort-de-Duras, 41600 La-
motte-Beuvron. T. 0254987536.   044557
Tourelle Antiquités, 39 Av République, 41600 Lamotte-
Beuvron. T. 0254881074, Fax 0254882019.   044558

Lancieux (Côtes-d'Armor)
Sbad, 13 Rue Panorama, 22770 Lancieux.
T. 0296863234.   044559

Landerneau (Finistère)
Billon, Andrée, 23 Rue Brest, 29220 Landerneau. T. 0298850341. - Ant - 044560
Treize Lunes, 4 Pl Saint-Thomas, 29220 Landerneau. T. 0298850834. - Ant - 044561

Landrais (Charente-Maritime)
Niord, 20 Rue Breuil-Saint-Jean, 17290 Landrais. T. 0546277326. 044562

Landudec (Finistère)
Floch, Annie, 7 Rue André-Foy, 29143 Landudec. T. 0298915695. - Ant - 044563

Lanester (Morbihan)
Mouton, Michel, Gal March-Rallye, 56600 Lanester. T. 0297764878. - Ant - 044564

Langeac (Haute-Loire)
Aulanier, Marc, 43300 Langeac. T. 0471771918. - Furn / Cur - 044565
Siozade, Monique, 10 Av Gare, 43300 Langeac. T. 0471772364. 044566

Langoiran (Gironde)
David, Bernadette, 25 Av Général-de-Gaulle, 33550 Langoiran. T. 0556672857. 044567
Foucher, Christian, 11 Av Général-de-Gaulle, 33550 Langoiran. T. 0556670453. - Paint / Furn / China / Sculp / Silv / Lights / Instr / Cur / Toys - 044568

Langon (Gironde)
Cassagne, J.-M. & Joël, 15 Cours Général-Leclerc, 33210 Langon. T. 0556631462. 044569

Langres (Haute-Marne)
Chapusot, Jean-Claude, 7 Rue Diderot, 52200 Langres. T. 0325870901, Fax 0325875811. 044570
Macheret, Michel, 16 Rue Chavannes, 52200 Langres. T. 0325874006. 044571
Relin, Jean-Luc, 15 Chemin Graboue, 52200 Langres. T. 0325875226. 044572

Languet (Ille-et-Vilaine)
Gendrot, Yvon, La Huardais, 35630 Languet. T. 0299698355. 044573

Lannebert (Côtes-d'Armor)
Au Vieux Chaudron, ZA Californie, 22290 Lannebert. T. 0296700429, Fax 0296701866. - Ant / Paint / Furn / Cur - 044574

Lannemezan (Hautes-Pyrénées)
Cazaux, Delphine, 391 Rue Résistants, 65300 Lannemezan. T. 0562980806. - Ant - 044575
Salles des Ventes du Plateau, 64 Rte Toulouse, 65300 Lannemezan. T. 0562980528. - Ant - 044576

Lannilis (Finistère)
Fontaine Rouge, Fontaine-Rouge, 29214 Lannilis. T. 0298041800. - Ant - 044577

Lannion (Côtes-d'Armor)
A à Z Antiquités, ZA Nod-Huel, 22300 Lannion. T. 0296372708. - Furn / Cur - 044578
Antiquités de Viarmes, 6 Quai Viarmes, 22300 Lannion. T. 0296464282. 044579
Atelier, 5 Av Ernest-Renan, 22300 Lannion. T. 0296374283, Fax 0296464125. 044580
Cendrillon, 4 Rue Cie-Roger-Barbé, 22300 Lannion. T. 0296371456. 044581
Dépôt-Vente du Trégor, ZA Nod-Huel, 22300 Lannion. T. 0296371828. 044582
Laurin, Didier, 15 Rue Isidore-Le-Bourdon, 22300 Lannion. T. 0296374207. 044583
Laurin, Jacques, 4 Rue Cie-Roger-Barbé, 22300 Lannion. T. 0296374582. 044584

Lanvallay (Côtes-d'Armor)
Antiquités Tampe, 8 Rue Lion-d'Or, 22100 Lanvallay. T. 0296394406. 044585

Laon (Aisne)
Evrard, Thierry, 81 Rue Arsène-Houssaye, 02000 Laon. T. 0323203173. - Ant - 044586
Grenier, Rue Semilly, 02000 Laon. T. 0323202002. - Ant - 044587

Lapalisse (Allier)
Auscule, Albert, 17 Pl Charles-Bécaud, 03120 Lapalisse. T. 0470990270. - Ant - 044588
Thibur, Robert, 13 Pl Charles-Bécaud, 03120 Lapalisse. T. 0470992770. - Ant - 044589

Lapalme (Aude)
Delacour, Jean-Claude, RN 9, Carrefour Port-La-Nouvelle, 11480 Lapalme. T. 0468481555. 044590

Lapoutroie (Haut-Rhin)
Mantzer, Claudine, 274 Chemin Fossé, 68650 Lapoutroie. T. 0389472387. 044591

Laragne-Montéglin (Hautes-Alpes)
Crédence, 9 Av Provence, 05300 Laragne-Montéglin. T. 0492651290. 044592
Gueyraud Transactions, Les Bellerots, 05300 Laragne-Montéglin. T. 0492650430. 044593
Serres, Fernande, 24 Av Montéglin, 05300 Laragne-Montéglin. T. 0492650849. 044594

Lardy (Essonne)
Acanthe, 69 Grande Rue, 91510 Lardy. T. 0160823747. - Ant - 044595

Larmor-Plage (Morbihan)
Cariatide, 2 Blvd Toulhars, 56260 Larmor-Plage. T. 0297336399. - Ant / Furn - 044596
Occass'affaires, 12 Rue Bretagne, 56260 Larmor-Plage. T. 0297833088. - Ant - 044597

Laroin (Pyrénées-Atlantiques)
Roche-Laclau, Francine, Rue Principale, 64110 Laroin. T. 0559830990. - Ant / Furn - 044598

Laronxe (Meurthe-et-Moselle)
Ledermann, Charles, 54950 Laronxe. T. 0383726017, Fax 0383726662. 044599

Lasalle (Gard)
Arnault, Bruno, 162 Rue Gravière, 30460 Lasalle. T. 0466854392. 044600
Atlan, Figuière, Le Campas-Mouthe, 30460 Lasalle. T. 0466852543. 044601
Quand Pass'.., Le Campas, 30460 Lasalle. T. 0466852543. 044602

Lattes (Hérault)
Rigault, Patrice, La Cereirede, 34970 Lattes. T. 0467582605. 044603

Launois-sur-Vence (Ardennes)
Lenfant, Fernand, la Pereuse, 08430 Launois-sur-Vence. T. 0324350581. - Ant - 044604

Laval (Mayenne)
Antiquités Brocante, 14 Rue Trinité, 53000 Laval. T. 0243530613. - Ant - 044605
Antiquités des 7 Fontaines, 301 Rue Bretagne, 53000 Laval. T. 0243692645. - Ant / Paint - 044606
Aux Puces Lavalloises, 62 Av Mayenne, 53000 Laval. T. 0243490633, Fax 0243538511. - Ant - 044607
Brocante du Pont de Paris, 200 Rue Paris, 53000 Laval. T. 0243560826. - Ant - 044608
Gledel, Gérard, 24 Rue Echelle-Marteau, 53000 Laval. T. 0243534020. - Ant / Furn - 044609
Meyniel, Georges, 29 Rue Saint-Jean, 53000 Laval. T. 0243668238. - Paint / Furn / China / Mul - 044610
Perrier, Jean-Claude, 106 Av de Chanzy, 53000 Laval. T. 0243670558. - Ant / Furn - 044611
Porteboeuf, Franck, 301 Rue Bretagne, 53000 Laval. T. 0243681385. - Ant - 044612
Sauvage, Yannick, 15bis Grande-Rue, 53000 Laval. T. 0243535021. - Ant - 044613

Lavergne (Lot)
Fraux, Patrice, Mirabel, 46500 Lavergne. T. 0565387604. - Ant / Furn - 044614

Lazenay (Cher)
Da Silva, Geneviève, Bourg, 18120 Lazenay. T. 0248517641. 044615

Le Barroux (Vaucluse)
Bourde, Michèle, Le Four-à-Chaux, 84330 Le Barroux. T. 0490624482. - Ant - 044616

Le Beausset (Var)
Guainans, Alain, Quartier Couchoua, RN 8, 83330 Le Beausset. T. 0494986362, Fax 0494905018. - Ant - 044617

Le Bec-Hellouin (Eure)
Antiquités Vad, Pl Mathilde, 27800 Le Bec-Hellouin. T. 0232463680. 044618

Le Bec-Thomas (Eure)
Hamon, Bernard, 2 Rue Eglise, 27370 Le Bec-Thomas. T. 0232353284. 044619

Le Blanc (Indre)
Pailler, Denise, 25 Rue Pierre-Collin-de-Souvigny, 36300 Le Blanc. T. 0254372480. 044620
Vigneux, Rte Trimouille, 36300 Le Blanc. T. 0254371344. - Furn - 044621

Le Bois-Plage-en-Ré (Charente-Maritime)
Castaing, J.J., Le Peu-des-Aumons, 17580 Le Bois-Plage-en-Ré. T. 0546092422. 044622
Puce, 6 Rue Eglise, 17580 Le Bois-Plage-en-Ré. T. 0546091128. 044623

Le Bono (Morbihan)
Atlantiquasie, 37 Rue Pasteur, 56400 Le Bono. T. 0297579384. - Ant - 044624

Le Bourg-Saint-Léonard (Orne)
Gilles, Thomas, 61310 Le Bourg-Saint-Léonard. T. 0233671403. - Ant / Paint / Furn / Silv - 044625
Grenier, Rte de Paris, 61310 Le Bourg-Saint-Léonard. T. 0233671826. - Ant - 044626

Le Breuil (Saône-et-Loire)
Stéphan, Jacky, 11 Rue Montaubry, 71670 Le Breuil. T. 0385553287. - Ant - 044627
Vaillant, Gérard, Rue Pessellière, 71670 Le Breuil. T. 0385553302. - Ant / Furn - 044628

Le Cannet (Alpes-Maritimes)
Ballario, 5 Rue Roses, 06110 Le Cannet. T. 0493382321. 044629
Fouquer, Gérard, 32 Av Mimosas, 06110 Le Cannet. T. 0493695294. - Eth - 044630
Humbert, 102 Av Franklin-Roosevelt, 06110 Le Cannet. T. 0493453634. 044631
Monteil-Durillon, Chemin Garibondy, Hameau du Vieux-Puits, 06110 Le Cannet. T. 0493906067. 044632
Verniers, Martine, 42 Rue Saint-Sauveur, 06110 Le Cannet. T. 0492189380. 044633

Le Castellet (Var)
Dubly, Jacques, 1379 Chemin Fanges, 83330 Le Castellet. T. 0494902333. 044634
Galerie des Remparts, 6 Montée Saint-Eloi, 83330 Le Castellet. T. 0494326698. - Paint / Furn / Sculp - 044635
Guainans, Pl Champ-de-Bataille, 83330 Le Castellet. T. 0494986362. - Ant - 044636

Le Cateau-Cambrésis (Nord)
Denoyelle, Pascal, 19 Rue Mar-Mortier, 59360 Le Cateau-Cambrésis. T. 0327841164, Fax 0327842160. - Ant - 044637

Le Cellier (Loire-Atlantique)
Fourcherot, Josselyn, La Savariais, 44850 Le Cellier. T. 40254014. - Furn / Cur - 044638
Le Poullouin, Emile, La Barre-Peinte, RN 23, 44850 Le Cellier. T. 40254151. - Furn - 044639

Le Chambon-sur-Lignon (Haute-Loire)
Plazanet, Yvonne, 26 Chemin Peyrouet, 43400 Le Chambon-sur-Lignon. T. 0471597266. 044640
Style, 1 Rte Mazet, 43400 Le Chambon-sur-Lignon. T. 0471658892. 044641

Le Chesnay (Yvelines)
Barilleau, Bruno, 13 Rue Docteur-Audigier, 78150 Le Chesnay. T. 0139551312. 044642
Périer, Charles, 2 Rue Pottier, 78150 Le Chesnay. T. 0139544641, Fax 0139542237. 044643

Le Chesne (Eure)
Mouton, Yvan, Les Mares, 27160 Le Chesne.
T. 0232298023. *044644*

Le Cheylard (Ardèche)
Rouzaud, Jean-Marie, 16 Rue des Sabotiers, 07160 Le
Cheylard. - Ant - *044645*

Le Coteau (Loire)
Chaptard, Jean, 35 Rte Commelle, 42120 Le Coteau.
T. 0477681346. *044646*
Fronti, Jean-Claude, 10 Blvd Etines, 42120 Le Coteau.
T. 0477681409. - Furn / Cur - *044647*

Le Crès (Hérault)
Barraud & Bonnet, 102 RN 113, Fbg-Antiquaires, Lot 13,
34920 Le Crès. T. 0467702901. *044648*
Bressoise Transactions, 102 RN 113, Fbg-Antiquaires,
34920 Le Crès. T. 0467871160. *044649*
Bretonneau, Michel, 102 RN 113, Fbg-Antiquaires,
34920 Le Crès. T. 0467872698. *044650*
Cuesta, Antoine, 102 RN 113, Fbg-Antiquaires, 34920
Le Crès. T. 0467871159. *044651*
De Temps en Temps, Lieu dit le Maquet, RN 113, 34920
Le Crès. T. 0467875047. *044652*
Garcia, André, 102 RN 113, Fbg-Antiquaires, 34920 Le
Crès. T. 0467875272. *044653*
Grenier du Pin, 8bis Rue Pointes, 34920 Le Crès.
T. 0467702606. - Furn - *044654*
Otende, Jocelyne, 102 RN 113, Fbg-Antiquaires, 34920
Le Crès. T. 0467871161. *044655*
Pujol, Yvonne, 102 RN 113, Fbg-Antiquaires, 34920 Le
Crès. T. 0467871197. *044656*
Serres, Henry, 102 RN 113, Fbg-Antiquaires, 34920 Le
Crès. T. 0467705904. *044657*
Tarrago, Nicole, 102 RN 113, Fbg-Antiquaires, 34920 Le
Crès. T. 0467871178. *044658*
Thérond, Jean-Pierre, 102 RN 113, Fbg-Antiquaires,
34920 Le Crès. T. 0467871179. *044659*

Le Creusot (Saône-et-Loire)
Liagre, Bernard, 201 Rue Maréchal-Foch, 71200 Le
Creusot. T. 0385563989, Fax 0385787755.
- Ant - *044660*

Le Crotoy (Somme)
Cagnon, Nadine, 42 Rue Porte-du-Pont, 80550 Le Cro-
toy. T. 0322272079. - Ant - *044661*
Sorbier, Germaine, 24 Rue Victor-Petit, 80550 Le Crotoy.
T. 0322278034. - Ant - *044662*

Le Crozet (Loire)
Cizeron, Yves, Le Dauphin, 42310 Le Crozet.
T. 0477643897. *044663*

Le Faou (Finistère)
Arès, Jeannine, 15 Rue Landerneau, 29142 Le Faou.
T. 0298810737. - Ant - *044664*

Le Ferré (Ille-et-Vilaine)
Battais, Bernard, Le Bourg, 35420 Le Ferré.
T. 0299951292. *044665*

Le Fidelaire (Eure)
Antiquité de Sainte-Anne, Ham Sainte-Anne, 27190 Le
Fidelaire. T. 0232307977. - Furn - *044666*

Le Folgoët (Finistère)
Marec, Yves, 24 Rte Brest, 29260 Le Folgoët.
T. 0298831647. - Ant / Furn / Lights - *044667*

Le Garric (Tarn)
Farenc, Michel, 84 RN 88, 81450 Le Garric.
T. 0563367437. - Furn - *044668*

Le Grand-Bornand (Haute-Savoie)
Petitpas, Sur le Villard, 74450 Le Grand-Bornand.
T. 0450023576. - Furn - *044669*

Le Gua (Charente-Maritime)
Roux, Marc, Château Colombier, 17600 Le Gua.
T. 0546947004. *044670*

Le Havre (Seine-Maritime)
Ali Baba, 23 Rue Duguay-Trouin, 76600 Le Havre.
T. 0235263839. *044671*

Antiquités-Brocantic, 136 Rue Maréchal-Joffre, 76600
Le Havre. T. 0235225672. - Furn / China / Dec / Lights /
Instr / Glass / Toys - *044672*
Antiquités de l'Isle, 40 Quai Michel-Féré, 76600 Le Hav-
re. T. 0235424285. *044673*
Antiquités du Mesnil, 77 Rue Président-Wilson, 76600
Le Havre. T. 0235425520. *044674*
Art et Déco, 171 Rue Victor-Hugo, 76600 Le Havre.
T. 0235226221. - Furn / Repr - *044675*
Atelier Saint-Michel, 30 Av Résistance, 76600 Le Havre.
T. 0235434814. - Paint / Instr - *044676*
Au Chat Noir, 14 Rue Victor-Hugo, 76600 Le Havre.
T. 0235430994. *044677*
Au Dé d'Argent, 10 Rue Victor-Hugo, 76600 Le Havre.
T. 0235227079. *044678*
Binet, Carmen, 127 Rue Louis-Brindeau, 76600 Le Hav-
re. T. 0235412896. *044679*
Broc et Puces, 74 Rue Joseph-Morient, 76600 Le Havre.
T. 0235229354. *044680*
Broc'Occasion, 118 Rue Etretat, 76600 Le Havre.
T. 0235420233. *044681*
Colombe, 121 Rue Etretat, 76600 Le Havre.
T. 0235212628. *044682*
Crédence, 20 Rue Béranger, 76600 Le Havre.
T. 0235431191. *044683*
Deux Empires, 51 Rue Louis-Philippe, 76600 Le Havre.
T. 0235211176. *044684*
Ebran, Patrick, 120 Rue Anatole-France, 76600 Le Hav-
re. T. 0235224562. *044685*
Espace Antique, 14 Av Général Archinard, 76600 Le
Havre. T. 0235430153. - Ant - *044686*
Galerie Saint-Philibert, 15 et 17 Pl Halles, 76600 Le
Havre. T. 0235213945. - Paint / Furn - *044687*
Graciano, Joseph, 3 Rue Jean-Bart, 76600 Le Havre.
T. 0235264328. *044688*
Leconte, Thierry, 37 Rue Casimir-Périer, 76600 Le Hav-
re. T. 0235434637. *044689*
Licorne, 50 Rue Maréchal-Joffre, 76600 Le Havre.
T. 0235420892. *044690*
Lombart, 140 Rue Etretat, 76600 Le Havre.
T. 0235433444. - Ant / Furn - *044691*
Malouvier, 77 Rue Louis-Brindeau, 76600 Le Havre.
T. 0235425107, Fax 0235432276. - Paint - *044692*
Rothacker, Christophe, 7 et 9 Rue Casimir-Périer, 76600
Le Havre. T. 0235190857. *044693*
Sainte-Marie, 97 Rue Demidoff, 76600 Le Havre.
T. 0235240767. *044694*

Le Lion-d'Angers (Maine-et-Loire)
Guitton, Bernard, 12 Rue Général-Leclerc, 49220 Le
Lion-d'Angers. T. 41956760. - Paint / Furn / China /
Cur - *044695*

Le Luc (Var)
Calèche, Les Près-D'Audière, RN 7, 83340 Le Luc.
T. 0494734762. *044696*
Kockler, Paul, Quartier Grimaudet, 83340 Le Luc.
T. 0494608550. *044697*

Le Lude (Sarthe)
Albert-Roulhac, Philippe, Rte du Mans, 72800 Le Lude.
T. 0243945483. - Ant / Furn - *044698*

Le Mage (Orne)
Arnaud de Saint-Martin, Le Bourg, 61290 Le Mage.
T. 0233736676, Fax 0233735129. - Ant - *044699*
Fassier, Alain, Le Haut-Chêne, 61290 Le Mage.
T. 0233256688. - Ant - *044700*

Le Mans (Sarthe)
A la Murisserie, 4 Rue Vert-Galant, 72000 Le Mans.
T. 0243876565. - Ant / Furn - *044701*
Allo-Broc, 105 Rue Goncourt, 72000 Le Mans.
T. 0243280909. - Ant / Furn - *044702*
Amaranthe Antiquités, 52 Grande Rue, 72000 Le Mans.
T. 0243877848. - Ant - *044703*
Ancienne Mans, Le Miroir, 72000 Le Mans.
T. 0243860266. - Ant / Furn / Jew - *044704*
Angelus, 84 Rue Montoise, 72000 Le Mans.
T. 0243284299. - Ant - *044705*
Anne Antiquités, 38 Rue Docteur-Leroy, 72000 Le Mans.
T. 0243242383. - Ant - *044706*
Art Antiquités, 165 Rue Mallets, 72000 Le Mans.
T. 0243813450. - Ant - *044707*

Au Rêves d'Antan, 25 Rue Bourg-Belé, 72000 Le Mans.
T. 0243232001. - Ant / Paint / Furn - *044708*
Au Verre à Pied, 48 et 50 Rue de la Mariette, 72000 Le
Mans. T. 0243844000. - Ant - *044709*
Beaucousin, Catherine, 80 Cour Saint-Victor, 72000 Le
Mans. T. 0243771021. - Ant - *044710*
Canivet, Stéphane, 214 Av Jean-Jaurès, 72100 Le
Mans. T. 0243780720. - Ant / Furn - *044711*
Cénomanie Antiquitas, Centre cial République, 72000 Le
Mans. T. 0243243630. - Ant - *044712*
Classiques, 10 Rue Gambetta, 72000 Le Mans.
T. 0243245924. - Ant - *044713*
Cormier, Yves, 59 Blvd Anatole-France, 72000 Le Mans.
T. 0243246099. - Ant - *044714*
Drouet, Sébastien, 48 Rue Nationale, 72000 Le Mans.
T. 0243241682. - Ant - *044715*
Lemercier, Gérard, 57 Cour Saint-Victeur, 72000 Le
Mans. T. 0243241519. - Ant / Furn - *044716*
Longin, Christophe, 165 Rue Maillets, 72000 Le Mans.
T. 0243813450. - Ant - *044717*
Mémin, Gilles, 61 Grande Rue, 72000 Le Mans.
T. 0243242305. - Ant - *044718*
Resserre, 21 Rue Saint-Victeur, 72000 Le Mans.
T. 0243287694. - Ant / Furn - *044719*
Saint-Charles Antiquités, 6 Rue Saint-Charles, 72000 Le
Mans. T. 0243237140. - Ant - *044720*
Serge Roger Vallée, 3 Rue Gougeard, 72000 Le Mans.
T. 0243825946. - Ant - *044721*
Touillet, Philippe, 50 Rue Mariette, 72000 Le Mans.
T. 0243844000. - Ant - *044722*

Le Mas (Alpes-Maritimes)
Berna, Patrick, Les Anthémis, 06910 Le Mas.
T. 0493604018, Fax 0493604018. - Jew /
Silv - *044723*

Le Mêle-sur-Sarthe (Orne)
Ancel, Patricia, 48 Grande Rue, 61170 Le Mêle-sur-Sar-
the. T. 0233271501. - Ant - *044724*

Le Merlerault (Orne)
Saint-Christophe Antiquités, 3 Rue Granville, 61240 Le
Merlerault. T. 0233354375. - Furn - *044725*

Le Mesnil-Esnard (Seine-Maritime)
Comme au Bon Vieux Temps, 73 Rte de Paris, 76240 Le
Mesnil-Esnard. T. 0235800840. *044726*
Dourville, Florent, 2 Rte de Paris, 76240 Le Mesnil-Es-
nard. T. 0235800840. *044727*
Labyrinthe, 2 Rte de Paris, 76240 Le Mesnil-Esnard.
T. 0235800037. *044728*

Le Mesnil-Saint-Denis (Yvelines)
Grauss, Gilles, 4 Av Habert-de-Montmort, 78320 Le
Mesnil-Saint-Denis. T. 0134619724. *044729*
Montjoie, 92 Av Habert-de-Montmort, 78320 Le Mesnil-
Saint-Denis. T. 0134619823. *044730*

Le Muy (Var)
Bourrasset, Daniel, 280 Rte Fréjus, 83490 Le Muy.
T. 0494400759. *044731*
Ferrandi, Paule, RN 7, 83490 Le Muy.
T. 0494451221. *044732*

Le Neubourg (Eure)
Cery, Michel, 11bis Rue Docteur-Couderc, 27110 Le
Neubourg. T. 0232350369. - Furn / Cur - *044733*
Gravigny, Josiane, Village Venon, 27110 Le Neubourg.
T. 0232505155. - China / Glass / Cur - *044734*
Martin & Poot, 17 Rue Général-de-Gaulle, 27110 Le
Neubourg. T. 0232350933. *044735*

Le Pailly (Haute-Marne)
Chez Desserey, Rue Breuil-Saint-Germain, 52600 Le
Pailly. T. 0325874268. *044736*

Le Passage (Lot-et-Garonne)
Habert, Eric & Catherine, 36 Av Pyrénées, 47520 Le
Passage. T. 0553966485. - Paint / Furn / Sculp / Tex /
Cur - *044737*

Le Pecq (Yvelines)
Kerlan, Gwenaëlle de, 34 Rue Président-Wilson, 78230
Le Pecq. T. 0139763630. - Furn - *044738*

Radigois, Isabelle, 33 Blvd Folke-Bernadotte, 78230 Le Pecq. T. 0134800578. *044739*

Le Pellerin (Loire-Atlantique)
Antiquité La Méridienne, 15bis Quai Provost, 44640 Le Pellerin. T. 40056009. *044740*
Foucher, Dominique, 12 Rue Docteur-Sourdille, 44640 Le Pellerin. T. 40046782. *044741*
Guitton, F., 8 Quai Provost, 44640 Le Pellerin. T. 40045531. - Furn / Cur - *044742*

Le Perray-en-Yvelines (Yvelines)
Brocante du Perray, 27 Rue Chartres, 78610 Le Perray-en-Yvelines. T. 0134846682. *044743*
Matagne, Dominique, 28bis Petite-Rue-Verte, 78610 Le Perray-en-Yvelines. T. 0134841876. - Paint / Furn / Cur - *044744*

Le Perreux-sur-Marne (Val-de-Marne)
Albert, Raymond, 26 Rue Jean-d'Estienne-d'Orves, 94170 Le Perreux-sur-Marne. T. 0143243891. - Paint / Furn / Sculp / Jew / Instr - *044745*
Attali, Ange, 22 Av Ledru-Rollin, 94170 Le Perreux-sur-Marne. T. 0148721593. *044746*
Broc'Antique, 89 Rue Victor-Recourat, 94170 Le Perreux-sur-Marne. T. 0148711617. *044747*
Chamak, Raymond Albert, 26 Rue Jean-d'Estienne-d'Orves, 94170 Le Perreux-sur-Marne. T. 0143243891. - Paint / Furn / Sculp / Jew / Instr - *044748*
Deletrain, Maria, 207 Av Général-de-Gaulle, 94170 Le Perreux-sur-Marne. T. 0148729195. - Paint / Furn / Cur - *044749*
Jouandou, Claudine, 25 Rue Station, 94170 Le Perreux-sur-Marne. T. 0143243732. *044750*
Putot, Jacques, 102 Blvd Alsace-Lorraine, 94170 Le Perreux-sur-Marne. T. 0148712802. *044751*

Le Pin-au-Haras (Orne)
Garcia, Gérard, La Gautellerie, 61310 Le Pin-au-Haras. T. 0233674256. - Ant - *044752*
Guérin, Jean, La Frénale, 61310 Le Pin-au-Haras. T. 0233369061. - Ant - *044753*
Tête au Loup, La Frénale, 61310 Le Pin-au-Haras. T. 0233399221. - Ant - *044754*

Le Plessis-Trévise (Val-de-Marne)
Caron, Daniel, 180 Av Maréchale, 94420 Le Plessis-Trévise. T. 0145941979. *044755*
Depresle, Alain, 27 Av Général-de-Gaulle, 94420 Le Plessis-Trévise. T. 0145761100. *044756*

Le Poët (Hautes-Alpes)
Ecuries du Seigneur, Chemin La-Grange-Neuve, 05300 Le Poët. T. 0492657001. *044757*

Le Pont-Chrétien-Chabenet (Indre)
Bauché, Jean-Pierre, 49 Rue Nationale, 36800 Le Pont-Chrétien-Chabenet. T. 0254258043. *044758*

Le Port-Marly (Yvelines)
Florence, Pascale, 6 Rue Jean-Jaurès, 78560 Le Port-Marly. T. 0139581005. *044759*
Mihailescu, Ursula, 6 Rue Jean-Jaurès, 78560 Le Port-Marly. T. 0139160443. - Paint - *044760*

Le Pradet (Var)
Balfet, Christian, Logis du Pin, 83220 Le Pradet. T. 0494756897. *044761*

Le Pré-Saint-Gervais (Seine-Saint-Denis)
Becker, Valérie, 41 Rue Charles-Nodier, 93310 Le Pré-Saint-Gervais. T. 0148402356. *044762*
Berger, Max, 22 Av Belvédère, 93310 Le Pré-Saint-Gervais. T. 0143629899. *044763*
Monnier, Patrick, 12 Rue Béranger, 93310 Le Pré-Saint-Gervais. T. 0149421876. *044764*

Le Puy-en-Velay (Haute-Loire)
A la Recherche du Temps Perdu, 11 Pl Tables, 43000 Le Puy-en-Velay. T. 0471092772. - Furn / Repr / Cur / Toys - *044765*
Bertrandy, Philippe, 27 Rue Raphaël, 43000 Le Puy-en-Velay. T. 0471028523. - Pho - *044766*
Bourgeois, Georges, 30 Rue Raphaël, 43000 Le Puy-en-Velay. T. 0471095597. - Paint / Furn / Cur - *044767*

Centrale de l'Occasion, Rue Latour-Maubourg, 43000 Le Puy-en-Velay. T. 0471096189. *044768*
Le Puy Collection, 7 Rue Portail-d'Avignon, 43000 Le Puy-en-Velay. T. 0471020440. - Jew - *044769*
Marcon, Robert, 19 Rue Saint-Jacques, 43000 Le Puy-en-Velay. T. 0471090334. *044770*
Servoir, 40 Blvd Saint-Louis, 43000 Le Puy-en-Velay. T. 0471093694. - Furn - *044771*
T.E.D., 64 Rue Pannessac, 43000 Le Puy-en-Velay. T. 0471091306, Fax 0471094958. *044772*

Le Raincy (Seine-Saint-Denis)
Bueno, Fabienne, 2bis All Maisons-Russes, 93340 Le Raincy. T. 0143027633. *044773*
Trianon, 5 Rond-Point Montfermeil, 93340 Le Raincy. T. 0143019570. *044774*

Le Rozier (Lozère)
Doussière, Jean-Louis, Bourg, 48150 Le Rozier. T. 0466626548. - Furn - *044775*

Le Sap (Orne)
Lierman, Yves, Rue Raoul-Hergault, 61470 Le Sap. T. 0233362655. - Ant - *044776*

Le Sauze (Alpes-de-Haute-Provence)
Merle, Jean-Claude, Le Super, 04400 Le Sauze. T. 0492811200. - Ant - *044777*

Le Thil-en-Vexin (Eure)
Frège, Jean-Pierre, 25 Grande Rue, 27150 Le Thil-en-Vexin. T. 0232559706. *044778*

Le Thillot (Vosges)
Mougenot, Patricia, 11 Rue Charles-de-Gaulle, 88160 Le Thillot. T. 0329253074. *044779*

Le Tholonet (Bouches-du-Rhône)
Vieux Moulin, Av Paul-Julien, Quartier Bastetti, 13100 Le Tholonet. T. 0442668976. *044780*

Le Thor (Vaucluse)
Altiero, Thierry, Rte Isle-sur-Sorgue, 84250 Le Thor. T. 0490337831. - Ant - *044781*

Le Touquet-Paris-Plage (Pas-de-Calais)
Antikayes, 96 Rue Metz, 62520 Le Touquet-Paris-Plage. T. 0321056396. *044782*
Benel, Eliane, 14 Rue Saint-Louis, 62520 Le Touquet-Paris-Plage. T. 0321053714. - Lights / Cur / Toys - *044783*
Brajou, Gilles, 68 Blvd Daloz, 62520 Le Touquet-Paris-Plage. T. 0321050301. - Furn / Cur - *044784*
Condettan, 81 Rue Saint-Jean, 62520 Le Touquet-Paris-Plage. T. 0321050027. *044785*
Contact, 84 Rue Paris, 62520 Le Touquet-Paris-Plage. T. 0321051296. *044786*
Harrewyn, Frédéric, 42 Av Saint-Jean, 62520 Le Touquet-Paris-Plage. T. 0321051797, Fax 0321054263. *044787*
Lemal, Line, 71 Rue Paris, 62520 Le Touquet-Paris-Plage. T. 0321053595. *044788*
Masson, Jean, 36 Av Saint-Jean, 62520 Le Touquet-Paris-Plage. T. 0321055773, Fax 0321058899. *044789*
Régency, 50 Rue Saint-Jean, 62520 Le Touquet-Paris-Plage. T. 0321051496. *044790*
Régency, 14 Av Saint-Jean, 62520 Le Touquet-Paris-Plage. T. 0321055419. *044791*
Régency, Av Phares, Local Commercial 2, 62520 Le Touquet-Paris-Plage. T. 0321053414. *044792*
Ricard, Jean-Marie, 14 All Quatre-Saisons, 62520 Le Touquet-Paris-Plage. T. 0321051252. *044793*
Wilce, Christine, 86 Rue Paris, 62520 Le Touquet-Paris-Plage. T. 0321053054. *044794*

Le Tréport (Seine-Maritime)
A la Brocante du Musoir, 19 Rue Paris, 76470 Le Tréport. T. 0235503018. *044795*
Temps passe, 1 Rue Hôtel-Ville, 76470 Le Tréport. T. 0235863625. *044796*

Le Tronchet (Ille-et-Vilaine)
Dumaine, Moulin à Vent, 35540 Le Tronchet. T. 0299589165. - Ant / Paint / Furn / Orient / China / Silv / Lights / Instr / Glass / Cur / Mod - *044797*

Le Val-Saint-Germain (Essonne)
Grenier du Val, 76 Rue Village, 91530 Le Val-Saint-Germain. T. 0164590592. *044798*

Le Vaudreuil (Eure)
Dubois, Guy, 46 Rue Bout-des-Jardins, 27100 Le Vaudreuil. T. 0232591614. - Furn / Cur - *044799*

Le Vésinet (Yvelines)
Berthoud, 92bis Rte Montesson, 78110 Le Vésinet. T. 0139765222. *044800*
Dalençon, Annie, 10 Pl Marché, 78110 Le Vésinet. T. 0139760979. *044801*
Marotte, 5 Rue Maréchal-Foch, 78110 Le Vésinet. T. 0139766640. *044802*

Le Vigan (Gard)
Frasse-Sombet, Jacques, Rue 3 Pigeons, 30120 Le Vigan. T. 0467810121. *044803*

Lécousse (Ille-et-Vilaine)
Glédel, Georges, 1 Résidence Hermines, 35133 Lécousse. T. 0299992036. *044804*

Lectoure (Gers)
Cazaux, Evelyne, 3 Rue Dupouy, 32700 Lectoure. T. 0562688153. *044805*
Rêve Antiquité, 10 Rue 14-Juillet, 32700 Lectoure. T. 0562689812, Fax 0562688928. *044806*

Lège-Cap-Ferret (Gironde)
Antiquités de la Presqu'i'5le, 75 Rte Bordeaux, Petit-Piquey, 33950 Lège-Cap-Ferret. T. 0556608837. *044807*
Bordage, Jean-Claude, 9 Rue Trémière, Petit-Piquey, 33950 Lège-Cap-Ferret. Fax 56605278. *044808*

Lembras (Dordogne)
Rigaud, Alexis, Malseinta, 24100 Lembras. T. 0553572861. *044809*

Lens (Pas-de-Calais)
Hamidèche, Dominique, 34 Rue Kléber, 62300 Lens. T. 0321421933. *044810*
Marotte, 130 Rte Lille, 62300 Lens. T. 0321282304. *044811*

Lens-Lestang (Drôme)
Antiquités Le Chatel, 26210 Lens-Lestang. T. 0475319846. - Furn - *044812*

Léon (Landes)
Roulhac, 6 Rue Ecoles, 40550 Léon. T. 0558492219. *044813*

Léré (Cher)
Kadrinoff, 3 Rue Paroisse, 18240 Léré. T. 0248726872. - Paint / Furn / Cur - *044814*

Les Alleuds (Maine-et-Loire)
Horeau Reynaud, Pierrette, Rte Angers, 49320 Les Alleuds. T. 41455917. - Furn / Cur - *044815*
Voloviec, Claude, Rte Notre-Dame Alençon, Prieuré, 49320 Les Alleuds. T. 41455920. - Paint / Furn / Cur - *044816*

Les Andelys (Eure)
Laurent, Odette, 2 Pl Nicolas-Poussin, 27700 Les Andelys. T. 0232544126. - Ant / Furn / Glass / Cur - *044817*
Riquier, Bernard, 47 Côte Feuquerolles, 27700 Les Andelys. T. 0232541406. *044818*

Les Arcs (Var)
Les Arcs Antiquités, 1 Av Jean-Jaurès, 83460 Les Arcs. T. 0494475526. - Ant / Furn - *044819*
Mermod, Andrée, RN 555, 83460 Les Arcs. T. 0494733758. *044820*
Mermod, Patrick, Rte de Draguignan, 83460 Les Arcs. T. 0494733758. *044821*

Les Aubiers (Deux-Sèvres)
Rochard, Yves, 6 Pl Mairie, 79250 Les Aubiers. T. 0549656073. *044822*

Les Authieux (Eure)
Antiquaire des Authieux, Rte Damville, 27220 Les Authieux. T. 0232373132, Fax 0232378107. *044823*

Les Baux-de-Provence (Bouches-du-Rhône)
Mas des Chevaliers, Vallon Fontaine, 13520 Les Baux-de-Provence. T. 0490544448,
Fax 0490544575. *044824*

Les Essards (Vendée)
Au Mobilier Vendéen, 1 Rue Sables, 85140 Les Essards.
T. 0251629264. - Furn - *044825*

Les Essarts-le-Roi (Yvelines)
Caprices de Fleurs, 21 Rue Onze-Novembre, 78690 Les Essarts-le-Roi. T. 0130464117. *044826*

Les Fourgs (Doubs)
Chez Daniel, 25300 Les Fourgs. T. 0381694454. - Furn / Cur - *044827*

Les Islettes (Meuse)
Chandelier, 72 Rue Bancelin, 55120 Les Islettes.
T. 0329882485. - Ant - *044828*
Laforce, Didier, 46 Rue Bancelin, 55120 Les Islettes.
T. 0329882441. - Ant - *044829*
Troc 51, 11 Lot Cardine, 55120 Les Islettes.
T. 0329882078, Fax 0329882132. - Ant - *044830*

Les Issambres (Var)
Marotte, La Marotte, RN 98, 83380 Les Issambres.
T. 0494969261. *044831*
Porro, Jean-Bernard, Pl Ottaviani, Village Provençal, 83380 Les Issambres. T. 0494494423. - Paint / Furn / China / Sculp / Dec / Fra / Instr - *044832*

Les Lucs-sur-Boulogne (Vendée)
Foucault, Fresnel, Les Gâts, 85170 Les Lucs-sur-Boulogne. T. 0251. *044833*

Les Montils (Loir-et-Cher)
Grenier d'Adélaide, ZA Artouillat, 41120 Les Montils.
T. 0254794198. *044834*

Les Mureaux (Yvelines)
Antiquité Foch, 36bis Av Foch, 78130 Les Mureaux.
T. 0130919010. *044835*
Broc'Antiq, 9 Rue Paul-Doumer, 78130 Les Mureaux.
T. 0134749192. *044836*
Forceville, Gérard de, 13 Av Prés, 78130 Les Mureaux.
T. 0134749658. *044837*

Les Ormes-sur-Voulzie (Seine-et-Marne)
Flao, Bernard, 11 Rte Nationale, 77134 Les Ormes-sur-Voulzie. T. 64017599. *044838*
Gidon, Jean-Claude, Le Châtelot, 77134 Les Ormes sur Voulzie. T. 64017542. *044839*

Les Pavillons-sous-Bois (Seine-Saint-Denis)
Boucq, Marcel, 234 Av Aristide-Briand, 93320 Les Pavillons-sous-Bois. T. 0148492563. *044840*
Petite Brocante, 172 Av Aristide Briand, 93320 Les Pavillons-sous-Bois. T. 0148484016. *044841*

Les Pinthières (Eure-et-Loir)
Tholance, Bernard, Rte Prouais, 28210 Les Pinthières.
T. 0237514858. *044842*

Les Ponts-de-Cé (Maine-et-Loire)
Sup'Répart, 10 Rue Maurice-Berne, 49130 Les Ponts-de-Cé. T. 41577443. *044843*

Les Portes-en-Ré (Charente-Maritime)
Antiquités des Fleurs, 5bis Imp Fleurs, 17880 Les Portes-en-Ré. T. 0546296263. *044844*

Les Quatre-Routes (Lot)
Luc, Colette, Rue Armand-Gouygou, 46110 Les Quatre-Routes. T. 0565321169. *044845*
Maison de Louise, Rte Saint-Denis-lès-Martel, 46110 Les Quatre-Routes. T. 0565321442. *044846*

Les Rosiers-sur-Loire (Maine-et-Loire)
Antiquités des Bateliers, 73 Rue Nationale, 49350 Les Rosiers-sur-Loire. T. 41518085. *044847*
Au Bouffon du Roy, 2 Rue Ponts, 49350 Les Rosiers-sur-Loire. T. 41380332. *044848*

Les Rousses (Jura)
Bois de l'Ours, RN 5, 39400 Les Rousses.
T. 0384600669. *044849*

Les Sables-d'Olonne (Vendée)
A.A.B. Atlantique, 20 Av Jean-Jaurès, 85100 Les Sables-d'Olonne. T. 0251238282. - Paint / Furn / Cur - *044850*
Arago Brocante, 25 Blvd Arago, 85100 Les Sables-d'Olonne. T. 0251956445. *044851*
Bonheur du Jour, 16 Rue Eglise, 85100 Les Sables-d'Olonne. T. 0251953457. *044852*
Bourse aux Affaires, 12 Rue Anatole-France, 85100 Les Sables-d'Olonne. T. 0251950613. - Ant / Furn - *044853*
Brocantine, 46bis Rue Palais, 85100 Les Sables-d'Olonne. T. 0251325312. *044854*
Escarpolette, 20 Blvd Castelnau, 85100 Les Sables-d'Olonne. T. 0251951284. *044855*
Estampille, 4 Rue Nicot, 85100 Les Sables-d'Olonne.
T. 0251211228. *044856*

Les Ternes (Cantal)
Antiquités d'Auvergne, 15100 Les Ternes.
T. 0471730040. *044857*

Les Thons (Vosges)
Demange, Pascal, 150 Rue Petits-Thons, 88410 Les Thons. T. 0329079130. *044858*

Les Ulmes (Maine-et-Loire)
Perez, Joseph, 2 Rue Chemin-Vert, 49700 Les Ulmes.
T. 41671899. *044859*

Les Vans (Ardèche)
Leblond Antiquités, Pl du marché, 07140 Les Vans.
T. 0475949019. - Ant - *044860*

Lesneven (Finistère)
Calves Yvon, 27 Pl Château, 29260 Lesneven.
T. 0298211552. - Furn - *044861*

Lesparre-Médoc (Gironde)
Acanthe, 45 Cours Général-de-Gaulle, 33340 Lesparre-Médoc. T. 0556410454. *044862*
Côté Gironde, 24 Cours Georges-Mandel, 33340 Lesparre-Médoc. T. 0556411418. *044863*
Mesuret, Claude, 18 Rte Hourtin, 33340 Lesparre-Médoc. T. 0556412494. *044864*

Lesterps (Charente)
Slade, John, Moulin de Douzy, 16420 Lesterps.
T. 0545715044. *044865*

Levallois-Perret (Hauts-de-Seine)
Antiquités Brocante du Marché, 41 Rue Carnot, 92300 Levallois-Perret. T. 0147584709. *044866*
Brocante du Palais, 1 Pl Henri-Barbusse, 92300 Levallois-Perret. T. 0147576493. *044867*
Peretz, Jean-Claude, 1 Rue Raspail, 92300 Levallois-Perret. T. 0147393287. *044868*
Raphaël, 5 Blvd Bineau, 92300 Levallois-Perret.
T. 0147586707. *044869*
Rider, Michel, 83 Rue Aristide-Briand, 92300 Levallois-Perret. T. 0147392905. *044870*

Levroux (Indre)
Laval, Didier, 7 Av Général-de-Gaulle, 36110 Levroux.
T. 0254356530. - Furn / Cur - *044871*
Nostalgy, 7 Rue 4-Septembre, 36110 Levroux.
T. 0254353443. *044872*

Lézardrieux (Côtes-d'Armor)
Baron, Eric, Kerbourhis, 22740 Lézardrieux.
T. 0296221000. *044873*

Lézat-sur-Lèze (Ariège)
Gaubert, 28 Av Pyrénées, 09210 Lézat-sur-Lèze.
T. 0561691435. - Furn - *044874*
Kirche, Gérard, 5 Blvd Victoire, Villa des Roses, 09210 Lézat-sur-Lèze. T. 0561691707. - Dec - *044875*

Lézignan-Corbières (Aude)
Bac, Margaret, ZI Gaujac, 11200 Lézignan-Corbières.
T. 0468271638. *044876*
Tomatis, Francis, 23 Av Léon-Bourgeois, 11200 Lézignan-Corbières. T. 0468273440. *044877*

Trauque, Betty, Rte Carcassonne, 11200 Lézignan-Corbières. T. 0468270593. *044878*

Libourne (Gironde)
Bouton, Jean-Charles, 6 Rue Jules-Ferry, 33500 Libourne. T. 0557740871. - Ant - *044879*
Brousse, Gilberte, 37 Rue Thiers, 33500 Libourne.
T. 0557511867. *044880*
Dijeau, Pierre, 79 Rue Gambetta, 33500 Libourne.
T. 0557511539. - Furn / Jew / Silv - *044881*
Ile du Temps, 100 Cours Tourny, 33500 Libourne.
T. 0557251540. *044882*
Jean, René, 52 Rue Fonneuve, 33500 Libourne.
T. 0557513185. *044883*

Liehon (Moselle)
Trevy-Ehrmann, Le Clos-du-Buis, 57420 Liehon.
T. 0387762827. *044884*

Ligré (Indre-et-Loire)
Manoir de Beauvais, Rte Champigny-sur-Veude, 37500 Ligré. T. 0547983663, Fax 0547984691. - Ant / Cur - *044885*

Ligueil (Indre-et-Loire)
Joly, Chantal, 59 Rue Aristide-Briand, 37240 Ligueil.
T. 0547920649. *044886*
Joly, Claude, Châteaupin, 37240 Ligueil.
T. 0547599536. *044887*
Taylor, Véra, 4 Pl La-République, 37240 Ligueil.
T. 0547599833. *044888*

Lille (Nord)
A Priori, 10 Façade de l'Esplanade, 59800 Lille.
T. 0320062727. - Ant - *044889*
A.B.B. Antiquités, 35 Rue de-Roubaix, 59800 Lille.
T. 0320552221. - Ant - *044890*
ABC Perrot, 46 Rue Boucher-de-Perthes, 59800 Lille.
T. 0320548547. - Ant - *044891*
Aladin, 26 Ter Rue Basse, 59800 Lille. T. 0320066194.
- Ant - *044892*
Angage, 38 Rue Lepelletier, 59800 Lille. T. 0320511592.
- Ant - *044893*
Antique Shop, 16 Rue Basse, 59800 Lille.
T. 0320515297. - Ant - *044894*
Antiquités du Nouveau Siècle, 106 Rue Hôpital-Militaire, 59000 Lille. T. 0320541317. - Ant - *044895*
Art Antiquités, 18 Rue Basse, 59800 Lille.
T. 0320513732. - Ant - *044896*
Atelier du Bois Passion, 132 Ter Rue Royale, 59800 Lille. T. 0320315669. - Ant - *044897*
A.V.A., 81 Rue Angleterre, 59800 Lille. T. 0320140130.
- Ant - *044898*
Baratte, Rodrigue, 27 Rue Adolphe, 59800 Lille.
T. 0320420639. - Ant - *044899*
Belbezier, 35 Rue Roubaix, 59800 Lille. T. 0320311736.
- Ant - *044900*
Borne, Frédéric, 42 Rue de Cambral, 59000 Lille.
T. 0320521543. - Furn - *044901*
Bouhin, 23 Rue Paris, 59800 Lille. T. 0320065173.
- Ant / Num / Mil - *044902*
Bremilts, Jean-Louis, 61 Rue d'Angleterre, 59800 Lille.
T. 0320515617. - Ant / Paint / Furn / China - *044903*
Brocantic, 20 Rue Henri-Kolb, 59000 Lille.
T. 0320544190. - Ant - *044904*
Cabourdin, Annie, 51 Rue Clef, 59800 Lille.
T. 0320554324. - Ant - *044905*
Chris'Ardy, 114 Rue Jean-Jaurès, 59000 Lille.
T. 0320984365. - Ant - *044906*
Courreur, Christian, 39 Rue Lepelletier, 59800 Lille.
T. 0320748582. - Ant - *044907*
Davioud, André, 8 Rue Baignerie, 59800 Lille.
T. 0320301697. - Ant - *044908*
Delerive, Antoine, 33 Rue Lepelletier, 59800 Lille.
T. 0320513298. - Ant - *044909*
Delobeau, Sandrine, 174 Rue Pierre-Legrand, 59800 Lille. T. 0320044707. - Ant - *044910*
Detrait, Christian, 14 Rue Trois-Mollettes, 59800 Lille.
T. 0320210363. - Lights - *044911*
Dubrulle, Philippe, 10 Rue Bartholomé-Masurel, 59800 Lille. T. 0320553761, Fax 0320210363. - Ant - *044912*
Glibert, Danielle, 24 Rue Basse, 59800 Lille.
T. 0320745829. - Ant - *044913*

Guévenoux, 13 Rue Basse, 59800 Lille. T. 0320510659. - Ant - 044914
Henneghien, Alain, 10 Rue Basse, 59800 Lille. T. 0320550242. - Ant - 044915
Incartade, 17 Rue Halle, 59800 Lille. T. 0320558294. - Ant - 044916
Kita, 5 Rue Royale, 59800 Lille. T. 0320513442. - Orient - 044917
Lamboray, Michel, 21 Rue Roubaix, 59800 Lille. T. 0320064321. - Ant - 044918
Leschevin, Christophe, 22bis Rue Flamen, 59000 Lille. T. 0320228243. - Ant - 044919
Malfaisan, Paul, 77bis Blvd Carnot, 59800 Lille. T. 0320511556. - Ant - 044920
Mevel, Claude le, 12 Rue Basse, 59800 Lille. T. 0320310708. - Ant - 044921
Montupet, Béatrice, 8 Rue Monnaie, 59800 Lille. T. 0320553439. - Ant / Jew / Silv - 044922
Motte, Frédéric, 28 Pl Lion-d'Or, 59800 Lille. T. 0320552543. - Ant - 044923
Old England Shop, 8 Rue Sainte-Anne, 59800 Lille. T. 0320131281. - Ant - 044924
Parenthou, Richard, 4 Rue Saint-Jacques, 59800 Lille. T. 0320066002. - Ant / Graph / Furn / Draw - 044925
Puce a l'Oreille, 10 Pl Louise-de-Bettignies, 59800 Lille. T. 0320741809, Fax 0320150710. - Furn - 044926
Salles des Ventes, 14 Rue Jardins, 59800 Lille. T. 0320061014, Fax 0320510662. - Ant - 044927
Sauvage, Eric, 20 Rue Henri-Kolb, 59000 Lille. T. 0320544190. - Ant - 044928
Sleghem, Jacques, 106 Rue Hôpital-Militaire, 59800 Lille. T. 0320541317. - Ant - 044929
Tibet, 134 Rue Nationale, 59800 Lille. T. 0320545481. - Ant / Orient - 044930
Vanlerberghe, Michel, 35 Rue Saint-J-B-de-la-Salle, 59000 Lille. T. 0320937850. - Ant - 044931
Villers, Monique, 47 Rue Basse, 59800 Lille. T. 0320744951. - Ant - 044932
Wattine, Jacqueline, 10 Pl Lion-d'Or, 59800 Lille. T. 0320558366. - Ant - 044933

Limey-Remenauville (Meurthe-et-Moselle)

David, Philippe, 25 Grande Rue, 54470 Limey-Remenauville. T. 0383843006. 044934

Limoges (Haute-Vienne)

Aubour, Michel, 9 Rue Boucherie, 87000 Limoges. T. 0555344064. - Ant / Paint - 044935
Berthier, Renée, 45 Rue Boucherie, 87000 Limoges. T. 0555333702. - Ant - 044936
Bonnadier, Régis, 27 Rue Elie-Berthet, 87000 Limoges. T. 0555345709. - Furn / Fra - 044937
Cantou, 19 Rue Raspail, 87000 Limoges. T. 0555343647. - Ant - 044938
Chamouleau, Armand, 21 Rue Tanneries, 87000 Limoges. T. 0555326794. - Ant - 044939
Fraignieau-Morin, Virginie, 16 Av Ruchoux, 87000 Limoges. T. 0555775452. - Ant / Furn - 044940
Galerie Corot, 17 Rue Delescluze, 87000 Limoges. T. 0555344911, Fax 0555344911. - Paint / China / Mod - 044941
Galerie 19ème, 16 Blvd Carnot, 87000 Limoges. T. 0555794251. - Ant / Cur - 044942
Lober Valette Thierry, 2 Rue Cruche-d'Or, 87000 Limoges. T. 0555321506. - Furn / Furn - 044943
Lyraud, Jean, 30 Rue Elie-Berthet, 87000 Limoges. T. 0555341107. - Ant - 044944
Marché Brosseau, 8 Rue Brousseau, 87000 Limoges. T. 0555770944. - Ant - 044945
Naudet, Michel, 13 Rue Delescluze, 87000 Limoges. T. 0555326385. - Furn / China - 044946
Nicolier, Josette, 22 Blvd Louis-Blanc, 87000 Limoges. T. 0555336309. - Ant - 044947
Perguet, Gabriel, 285 Rue François-Perrin, 87000 Limoges. T. 0555012772. - Ant - 044948
Presbytére, 29 Rue Elie-Berthet, 87000 Limoges. T. 0555342081. - Ant - 044949
Renardière, 13 Rue Boucherie, 87000 Limoges. T. 0555332004. - Ant / Furn - 044950
Romanet, Céleste, 8 Rue Brousseau, 87000 Limoges. T. 0555798476. - Ant - 044951
Segonds, Jean-Claude, 12 Rue Delescluze, 87000 Limoges. T. 0555333777, Fax 0555035521. - Paint / Furn / China / Mod - 044952
Sigrist, Jacques, 19 Rue Delescluze, 87000 Limoges. T. 0555322027. - Ant / Paint - 044953
Thomain, Andy, 17 Rue Delescure, 87000 Limoges. T. 0555344911, Fax 0555344911. - Ant / Paint / Furn / China - 044954
Vieille Epoque, 285 Rue François-Perrin, 87000 Limoges. T. 0555508684. - Ant / Furn / Tex - 044955
Vigneras, Jacques & Régis, 27 Rue Elie-Berthet, 87000 Limoges. T. 0555331576, Fax 0555329372. - Ant / Furn - 044956

Limours-en-Hurepoix (Essonne)

Martin, Raymonde, 5 Pl Aristide-Briand, 91470 Limours-en-Hurepoix. T. 0164912396. 044957

Limoux (Aude)

Montserrat, Jean-Pierre, 49 Av Fabre d'Eglantine, 11300 Limoux. T. 0468311685. 044958

Linas (Essonne)

Bresan, 12 Rue Lampe, RN 20, 91310 Linas. T. 0169013448. 044959

Linselles (Nord)

Florentin, 80bis Rue Castenau, 59126 Linselles. T. 0320230361. - Ant - 044960
Rousseau, Henri, 161 Av Robert-Descamps, 59126 Linselles. T. 0320463669. - Ant - 044961

Lisieux (Calvados)

Brocante du Rond Point, 16 Rue Docteur-Lesigne, 14100 Lisieux. T. 0231620817. 044962
Brocante Mordant, 47 Rue Théodule-Peulevey, 14100 Lisieux. T. 0231311374. 044963
Verheeke, Roland, 27 Pl République, 14100 Lisieux. T. 0231621559. 044964

Lisle-sur-Tarn (Tarn)

Galerie Raymond Lafage, 2 Rue Raymond-Lafage, 81310 Lisle-sur-Tarn. T. 0563333705. 044965

Liverdun (Meurthe-et-Moselle)

Rouyer, Michel, 7 All Chambéry, 54460 Liverdun. T. 0383245377. 044966
Wolff, Gérard, 14 Rue Aurillac, 54460 Liverdun. T. 0383246071. 044967

Livers-Cazelles (Tarn)

Playe, Aymon, La Ratayre, 81170 Livers-Cazelles. T. 0563560730. 044968

Livron-sur-Drôme (Drôme)

Seauve, Philippe, Rue Docteur-l'Hermier, 26250 Livron-sur-Drôme. T. 0475855112. 044969

Livry (Nièvre)

Werly, Françoise, Haut-Riousse, 58240 Livry. T. 0386374109, Fax 0386372439. 044970

Livry-Gargan (Seine-Saint-Denis)

A.F.A. Brocante, 14 Av Turgot, 93190 Livry-Gargan. T. 0143817021. - Ant / Paint / Furn / Sculp - 044971

Loches (Indre-et-Loire)

Brocante Lochoise, 8 Rue Alfred-de-Vigny, 37600 Loches. T. 0547591683. 044972
Charbonnel, Alain, 9 Rue Balzac, 37600 Loches. T. 0547591760. 044973
Grenier de Capucine, 5 Rue Tours, 37600 Loches. T. 0547593993. 044974
Mauvy, Evrard, 90 Rue Saint-Jacques, 37600 Loches. T. 0547590512. - Furn - 044975
Thuault, Gérard, 9 Pl Blé, 37600 Loches. T. 0547593150. 044976

Locronan (Finistère)

Le-Lay, Philippe, Vieille Rte de Plonévez, 29136 Locronan. T. 0298917622. - Ant - 044977

Loctudy (Finistère)

Larnicol, Danielle, 62 Rue Sébastien-Guiziou, 29125 Loctudy. T. 0298875454. - Ant - 044978
Rolland, Jean-René, 12 Rue Pen-Ar-Veur, 29136 Loctudy. T. 0298875669. - Ant - 044979

Lodève (Hérault)

Calèche Blanche, 58 Av Fumel, 34700 Lodève. T. 0467440652. 044980

Logrian-Florian (Gard)

Chavan, Christian, Le Mas des Elfes, 30610 Logrian-Florian. T. 0466774516. 044981

Lomme (Nord)

Lefebvre, 660 Av Dunkerque, 59160 Lomme. T. 0320926190. - Ant - 044982

Londinières (Seine-Maritime)

Saint-Aubin, Roger, Rue Grainville, 76660 Londinières. T. 0235938070. 044983

Long (Somme)

Bray, Pascal, 5 Rue 8-Mai-1945, 80510 Long. T. 0322318734. - Ant - 044984

Longeville-en-Barrois (Meuse)

Pellerin, Stéphane, 1 Rue Saint-Hilaire, 55000 Longeville-en-Barrois. T. 0329793286. - Furn - 044985

Longeville-lès-Metz (Moselle)

A la Belle Epoque, 28 Blvd Saint-Symphorien, 57050 Longeville-lès-Metz. T. 0387663527. - Furn / Cur - 044986

Longjumeau (Essonne)

Sauvageot, Daniel, 2bis Av Maréchal-Leclerc, 91160 Longjumeau. T. 0164486509. 044987

Longnes (Sarthe)

Adet, Jean-Claude, Rte Laval, 72540 Longnes. T. 0243889258. - Ant - 044988
Adet, Jean-Louis, Le Bourg, 72540 Longnes. T. 0243880123. - Ant - 044989

Longpré-Corps-Saints (Somme)

Ramage, Christiane, 5 Rue Cloîtres, 80510 Longpré-Corps-Saints. T. 0322319120. - Ant / Cur - 044990

Longueville-en-Barrois (Meuse)

Pellerin, Claude, 1 Rue Saint-Hilaire, 55000 Longueville-en-Barrois. T. 0329793286. - Ant - 044991

Longuyon (Meurthe-et-Moselle)

Antiquités de Sainte-Agathe, 13 Rue Sète, 54260 Longuyon. T. 0382265042. 044992

Lons-le-Saunier (Jura)

Berger, Ernest, 60 Rte Besançon, 39000 Lons-le-Saunier. T. 0384474780. 044993
Berger, Victor, 795 Rue Gentianes, 39000 Lons-le-Saunier. T. 0384242334. 044994
Cagne, Edith, 5 Rue Agriculture, 39000 Lons-le-Saunier. T. 0384470877. 044995
Girardet, 205 Rue Regard, 39000 Lons-le-Saunier. T. 0384474824. - Furn - 044996
Martinet, Annie, 75 Rue Saint-Désiré, 39000 Lons-le-Saunier. T. 0384475590. 044997
Salle des Ventes des Particuliers, Chemin Pontot, 39000 Lons-le-Saunier. T. 0384245661. 044998
Temps qui passe, 198 Rue Montaigu, 39000 Lons-le-Saunier. T. 0384245199. - Paint / Furn / Cur - 044999

Lorette (Loire)

Dépôt-Vente Lorettois, Rue Villedieu, 42420 Lorette. T. 0477736626. 045000

Lorient (Morbihan)

Brocante Ouest, 65 Blvd Cosmao-Dumanoir, 56100 Lorient. T. 0297833833. - Ant - 045001
Cariatides, 8 Rue Vauban, 56100 Lorient. T. 0297642222. - Ant - 045002
Carnot Antiquités, 10 Rue Maréchal-Foch, 56100 Lorient. T. 0297215300. - Ant - 045003
D. G. Antiquités, 36 Rue Bayard, 56100 Lorient. T. 0297646316. - Ant - 045004
Débarras Bretons, 9 Av Jean-Jaurès, 56100 Lorient. T. 0297219021. - Ant / Paint / Furn - 045005
Débarras de l'Ouest, 183 Rue Belgique, 56100 Lorient. T. 0297839193. - Ant / Furn - 045006
Décocéan, 29 Rue Liège, 56100 Lorient. T. 0297211177. - Ant - 045007

Estampille, 11 Rue Auguste-Nayel, 56100 Lorient.
T. 0297216372. - Ant - *045008*
Galerie Vauban, 13 Rue Vauban, 56100 Lorient.
T. 0297210102. - Ant - *045009*
Ker Antik, 29 Rue Paul-Guieysse, 56100 Lorient.
T. 0297848547. - Ant - *045010*
Laveyssière, Jean-Pierre, 43 Rue Monistrol, 56100 Lorient. T. 0297377105. - Ant / Jew / Silv - *045011*

Loriol-sur-Drôme (Drôme)
Dubost, Annie, Villa Mado, RN 7, 26270 Loriol-sur-Drôme. T. 0475617774. - Furn / China / Tex / Cur - *045012*

Lormaye (Eure-et-Loir)
Duveau, Philippe, 1 Rue Alexandre-Goislard, 28210 Lormaye. T. 0237519687. *045013*

Louhans (Saône-et-Loire)
Bretin, Béatrice, 80 Grande-Rue, 71500 Louhans.
T. 0385760693. - Ant - *045014*

Loulay (Charente-Maritime)
Logis de Loulay, 6 Rue 8-Mai-1945, 17330 Loulay.
T. 0546339065. - Paint / Furn / Cur - *045015*

Lourdes (Hautes-Pyrénées)
Mouliet, François, Village Jarret, 65100 Lourdes.
T. 0562429654. - Ant - *045016*
Piredi, 5 Av Général Leclerc, 65100 Lourdes.
T. 0562422992. - Ant - *045017*

Louveciennes (Yvelines)
Louve Ancienne, 27 Av Général-Leclerc, 78430 Louveciennes. T. 0139692107. *045018*
Viel, Louis, 8 Rue Général-de-Gaulle, 78430 Louveciennes. T. 0139180828. *045019*

Louviers (Eure)
Au Temps des Cerises, 26 Rue Quai, 27400 Louviers.
T. 0232403689. - Furn / Tex / Cur - *045020*
Beaucousin, Catherine, 17 Rue Remparts, 27400 Louviers. T. 0232505022. *045021*

Louvigné-du-Désert (Ille-et-Vilaine)
Logeais, René, 21 Pl Charles-de-Gaulle, 35420 Louvigné-du-Désert. T. 0299980122. *045022*

Louvroil (Nord)
Belle Epoque, 65 Rte Avesnes, 59720 Louvroil.
T. 0327626544. - Ant - *045023*

Luc-sur-Mer (Calvados)
Fourchon, Serge, 1 Av Lécuyer, 14530 Luc-sur-Mer.
T. 0231971214. *045024*
Maignan, Stéphan, 4 Pl Croix, 14530 Luc-sur-Mer.
T. 0231963996. *045025*

Lucciana (Corse)
Antiquités Barocco, Crucetta, 20290 Lucciana.
T. 0495361121. *045026*
Antiquités Saint-Antoine, RN 193, Lago, 20290 Lucciana. T. 0495383083. *045027*
Jardin du Temps, RN 193, Crocetta, 20290 Lucciana.
T. 0495361979. - Furn / Cur - *045028*

Lucé (Eure-et-Loir)
Centre de l'Antiquité, 17 Rue Malbrosses, 28110 Lucé.
T. 0237358532. *045029*

Luceau (Sarthe)
Bachet, Pierrette, Les Hautes-des-Robiniers, 72500 Luceau. T. 0243440990. - Ant / Ant - *045030*

Luché-sur-Brioux (Deux-Sèvres)
Bassoli, Louis, Grange du Bois, 79170 Luché-sur-Brioux. T. 0549075312. *045031*

Lugny (Saône-et-Loire)
Perrier, Bruno, Saint-Oyen-Montbellet, 71260 Lugny.
T. 0385331716. - Furn / Sculp - *045032*

Luisant (Eure-et-Loir)
Vangeon, Guy, 3 Rue Bienfaisance, 28600 Luisant.
T. 0237351997, Fax 0237309736. *045033*

Lumbres (Pas-de-Calais)
Dubois, Pascal, 35 Av Bernard-Chochoy, 62380 Lumbres. T. 0321930299. *045034*

Lumio (Corse)
Boutet, Lionel, Rte Calvi, Clos des Fleurs, 20260 Lumio.
T. 0495607708. - Paint / Furn / Sculp / Glass - *045035*

Lunel (Hérault)
Bruno-Carles, 235 Av Maréchal-de-Lattre-de-Tassigny,
34400 Lunel. T. 0467713610,
Fax 0467715840. *045036*
Faucher, Christophe, 132 Blvd Diderot, 34400 Lunel.
T. 0467832601. *045037*
Pages, Robert, 310 Av Vidourle, 34400 Lunel.
T. 0467710764. *045038*
Pezon, Fabrice, 14 Blvd Strasbourg, 34400 Lunel.
T. 0467717079. *045039*

Luneray (Seine-Maritime)
Battistella, Aldo, Rue Général-de-Gaulle, 76810 Luneray. T. 0235851989. *045040*
Burel, Y., Rue Général-de-Gaulle, 76810 Luneray.
T. 0235853046. *045041*

Lunéville (Meurthe-et-Moselle)
Antiquités La Puce, 9 Rue Chanzy, 54300 Lunéville.
T. 0383745065. *045042*
Stanislas, 59 Rue République, 54300 Lunéville.
T. 0383738439. *045043*

Lurcy-Levis (Allier)
Cabanne & Maisonneuf, 16 Blvd Gambetta, 03320 Lurcy-Levis. T. 0470678173. - Ant / Furn - *045044*

Lure (Haute-Saône)
Foir'Puces, 90 Av République, 70200 Lure.
T. 0384628100. *045045*

Lusigny-sur-Barse (Aube)
Masse, Vincent, Hameau-de-l'Arivour, 10270 Lusigny-sur-Barse. T. 0325810443. - Ant - *045046*

Luthenay-Uxeloup (Nièvre)
Pignot, Frédéric, Fonderie, 58240 Luthenay-Uxeloup.
T. 0386581078. *045047*

Lutterbach (Haut-Rhin)
Goffinet, Bernard, 23 Rue Aristide-Briand, 68460 Lutterbach. T. 0389524782. *045048*

Luxeuil-les-Bains (Haute-Saône)
Cosson, Robert, 5 Rue Lattre-de-Tassigny, 70300 Luxeuil-les-Bains. T. 0384405090, Fax 0384769652.
- Furn / Cur - *045049*
Girardin, Patrick, 18 Rue Aristide-Briand, 70300 Luxeuil-les-Bains. T. 0384404085. *045050*

Luynes (Indre-et-Loire)
Windsor, Alain, Imp La-Fontaine, 37230 Luynes.
T. 0547555743. *045051*

Luzillé (Indre-et-Loire)
Bellon, 8 Rue Temple, 37150 Luzillé.
T. 0547578810. *045052*

Lyon (Rhône)
Agora, 24 Rue Remparts d'Ainay, 69002 Lyon.
T. 0478382149. - Furn / Cur - *045053*
Alex, 29 Rue Jarente, 69002 Lyon.
T. 0478371635. *045054*
Amarante, 20 Rue Remparts d'Ainay, 69002 Lyon.
T. 0478383329. *045055*
Anne & Thierry, 110 Grande Rue Guillotière, 69007 Lyon.
T. 0478730228. - Furn / Cur - *045056*
Antika 1, 33 Rue Sainte Hélène, 69002 Lyon.
T. 0478372390, Fax 0478422810. - Num - *045057*
Antiquités Baraban, 33 Rue Baraban, 69003 Lyon.
T. 0478548238. - Furn / Cur - *045058*
Antiquités Crinoline, 11 Pl Jules-Guesde, 69007 Lyon.
T. 0478698594. *045059*
Antiquités Gisèle, 50 Rue Sèze, 69006 Lyon.
T. 0472742287. *045060*
Antiquités Marilyn, 55 Rue Auguste-Comte, 69002 Lyon.
T. 0472418812. - Cur / Toys - *045061*

Antiquités 19 20, 50 Rue Auguste-Comte, 69002 Lyon.
T. 0478383825. *045062*
Aquamanile, 50 Rue Sèze, 69006 Lyon.
T. 0472742384. *045063*
Archaïa, 10 Rue Auguste-Comte, 69002 Lyon.
T. 0478929391, Fax 0478372566. *045064*
Art Déco Art Nouveaux, 33 Rue Auguste-Comte, 69002 Lyon. T. 0472418596. - Mod - *045065*
Aryana, 66 Rue Saint-Jean, 69005 Lyon.
T. 0478370181. *045066*
Atelier du Temps, 6 Av Berthelot, 69007 Lyon.
T. 0478721442. - Instr - *045067*
Au Clavier d'Argent, 4 Rue Auguste-Comte, 69002 Lyon.
T. 0478383985. - Jew / Silv - *045068*
Au Fil des Jours, 38 Rue Auguste-Comte, 69002 Lyon.
T. 0472418205. - Tex / Silv - *045069*
Au Jouet d'Autrefois, 105 Rue Pierre-Corneille, 69003 Lyon. T. 0478623645. - Toys - *045070*
Autrefois, 7 Rue Gasparin, 69002 Lyon.
T. 0478378984. *045071*
Autres Choses, 43 Rue Auguste-Comte, 69002 Lyon.
T. 0472419050. *045072*
Balay, Charles, 8 Rue Auguste-Comte, 69002 Lyon.
T. 0478373308, Fax 0472400230. - Ant / Furn - *045073*
Barioz, Christian, 19 Rue Trois-Maries, 69005 Lyon.
T. 0478928174. *045074*
BCMS, 16 Rue Pizay, 69001 Lyon. T. 0478296574,
Fax 0472077578. *045075*
Beltramelli, Angeline, 33 Rue Jarente, 69002 Lyon.
T. 0478378201. *045076*
Bernard, Michel, 1 Pl Antoine Vollon, 69002 Lyon.
T. 0478380214. - Ant - *045077*
Bertouy, Hubert, 33 Rue Franklin, 69002 Lyon.
T. 0478370831. - Ant / Paint / Furn / Sculp / Lights - *045078*
Boisson, Thierry, 113 Grande Rue Guillotière, 69007 Lyon. T. 0472720965. *045079*
Bouvier, Jean, 46 Rue Auguste Comte, 69002 Lyon.
T. 0478371074. - Ant - *045080*
Breda, Chantal de, 27 Pl Bellecour, 69002 Lyon.
T. 0478377705. *045081*
Broc des Docks, 27 Rue Docks, 69009 Lyon.
T. 0478835398. *045082*
Brocante Saint-Antoine, 2 Rue Monnaie, 69002 Lyon.
T. 0478370193. *045083*
Brotteaux Antiquités, 1 Pl Jules-Ferry, 69006 Lyon.
T. 0478242909. *045084*
Brügger, Franck, 36 Rue Cuvier, 69006 Lyon.
T. 0478529121. - Ant - *045085*
Brunet, Patrick, 73 Rue Tronchet, 69006 Lyon.
T. 0472430232. *045086*
Buffet Rouge, 15 Rue Terraille, 69001 Lyon.
T. 0478270669. *045087*
Carnazzi, Jean, 45 Rue Barrier, 69006 Lyon.
T. 0472744727, Fax 0472744727. - China - *045088*
Ceccaldi, Alice, 33 Rue Auguste-Comte, 69002 Lyon.
T. 0478425997, Fax 0478383309. *045089*
Chalvin, Yves, 25 Rue Auguste-Comte, 69002 Lyon.
T. 0478382146, Fax 0478928887. - Paint / Furn / Sculp / Draw - *045090*
Chambrion, Martine, 53 Quai Pierre-Scize, 69005 Lyon.
T. 0478398215. *045091*
Chambrion, Martine, 1 Montée Carmélites, 69001 Lyon.
T. 0478285194. *045092*
Chapeau des Estrets, Guy, 26 Rue Remparts d'Ainay, 69002 Lyon. T. 0478420707. *045093*
Charveriat, Jean, 133 Rue Créqui, 69006 Lyon.
T. 0478526316. *045094*
Choses Antiquités, 52 Rue Auguste-Comte, 69002 Lyon. T. 0478379530. *045095*
Coté, Philippe, 3 Pl Jules-Ferry, 69006 Lyon.
T. 0472742902. *045096*
Creusy, Jean-Philippe, 13 Rue des Remparts-d'Ainay, 69002 Lyon. T. 0478426476, Fax 0472560253.
- Num - *045097*
Creusy, Joël, 14 Rue Vaubecour, 69002 Lyon.
T. 0478376320, Fax 0472410993. - Num - *045098*
Damidot, Daniel, 38 Rue Auguste Comte, 69002 Lyon.
T. 0478378929. - Furn - *045099*
Descours, Michel, 44 Rue Auguste-Comte, 69002 Lyon.
T. 0478373454, Fax 0472419067. - Ant / Paint / Furn / China / Sculp / Tex / Jew / Instr / Cur / Draw - *045100*

Devaux, Hervé, 29 Rue Auguste-Comte, 69002 Lyon.
T. 0478377711. *045101*
Dhikéos, Georges & Michel, 24 Rue Auguste-Comte,
69002 Lyon. T. 0478377556. - Paint - *045102*
Dolls-Toys, 38 Rue Auguste-Comte, 69002 Lyon.
T. 0478429151. - Cur / Toys - *045103*
Dorian, 39 Rue Auguste Comte, 69002 Lyon.
I. 0478374692. - Ant / Furn / Silv - *045104*
Ducoté, Frédéric-Charles, 44 Rue Auguste-Comte,
69002 Lyon. T. 0478373129. - Paint / Furn / Instr / Mil /
Cur / Toys / Naut - *045105*
Ducoté, Vincent, 116 Rue Bugeaud, 69006 Lyon.
T. 0478525455. *045106*
Dulac, Jean, 17 Rue des Remparts-d'Ainay, 69002 Lyon.
T. 0478377860. - Ant / Fra / Glass / Cur / Tin - *045107*
Dumas, Jean-Paul, 8 Rue Auguste Comte, 69002 Lyon.
T. 0478371118. - Ant / Furn / Sculp / Fra - *045108*
Emir, 7 Rue de la République, 69001 Lyon.
T. 0478280522, Fax 0478272211. - Tex - *045109*
England's, 31 Rue Charité, 69002 Lyon.
T. 0478378728. *045110*
Entretemps, 32 Rue Auguste-Comte, 69002 Lyon.
T. 0478400851. *045111*
Espace Vente, 103 Rue Bossuet, 69006 Lyon.
T. 0478249706. - Dec / Cur - *045112*
Favre, Daniel, 39 Cours Vitton, 69006 Lyon.
T. 0478895251. *045113*
Favre, Daniel, 26 Rue Auguste-Comte, 69002 Lyon.
T. 0478420587. *045114*
F.B.D. Croix-Rousse, 18 Rue Pailleron, 69004 Lyon.
T. 0478398855. - Furn / Glass - *045115*
Fournier, Jean-François, 34 Cours Herbouville, 69004
Lyon. T. 0478282137. *045116*
Gaboriaux, Jean-Pierre, 42 Rue Sala, 69002 Lyon.
T. 0478380220, Fax 0472400700. - Ant - *045117*
Galerie Caracalla, 12 Rue du Boeuf, 69005 Lyon.
T. 0478370314. - Graph / Draw - *045118*
Galerie David, 10 Rue Sala, 69002 Lyon.
T. 0478380220, Fax 0472400700. *045119*
Galerie de l'Estampe, 32 Rue Auguste-Comte, 69002
Lyon. T. 0478378826. - Graph - *045120*
Galerie de la Loge, 4 Rue Loge, 69005 Lyon.
T. 0478301508. *045121*
Galerie Désiré, 14 Rue Ferrandière, 69002 Lyon.
T. 0478429850, Fax 0478379703. *045122*
Galerie du Vingtième Siècle, 53 Rue Franklin, 69002
Lyon. T. 0472418036. *045123*
Galerie Fred, 46 Rue Auguste-Comte, 69002 Lyon.
T. 0478381990. - Furn - *045124*
Galerie G, 7 Rue Auguste-Comte, 69002 Lyon.
T. 0472400559. *045125*
Galerie Jacquet, 60 Rue Auguste-Comte, 69002 Lyon.
T. 0472402885. - Paint - *045126*
Galerie L'Eau-Forte, 7 Rue Auguste-Comte, 69002 Lyon.
T. 0478378914. - Graph / Fra - *045127*
Galerie 7, 7 Pl Docteur-Gailleton, 69002 Lyon.
T. 0478422546. - Orient / Tex / Dec - *045128*
Garraud, Philippe, 6 Quai Pêcherie, 69001 Lyon.
T. 0472100028. *045129*
Gérardin, G. & Cie, 6 Rue Auguste-Comte, 69002 Lyon.
T. 0478376149. - Furn / China / Tin / Sculp - *045130*
Gilbert, Annick, 20 Quai Fulchiron, 69005 Lyon.
T. 0478381761. - Lights - *045131*
Grenier de Pauline, 36 Rue Cuvier, 69006 Lyon.
T. 0478529121. - Ant / Furn - *045132*
Guillemin, Pascal, 25 Rue Auguste-Comte, 69002 Lyon.
T. 0478379151. *045133*
Guinand, Michel, 26 Rue Remparts d'Ainay, 69002 Lyon.
T. 0478380367. *045134*
Hauser, Walter, 54 Rue Auguste-Comte, 69002 Lyon.
T. 0478375686. *045135*
Héritier, Micheline, 25 Rue Auguste-Comte, 69002 Lyon.
T. 0472400790. - Paint - *045136*
Hôtel Drouot, 67 Rue Sébastien-Gryphe, 69007 Lyon.
T. 0478610286. *045137*
Houg, Olivier, 14 Rue Ferrandière, 69002 Lyon.
T. 0478429850. - Paint - *045138*
Indifférent, 17 Pl Maréchal-Lyautey, 69006 Lyon.
T. 0478240839. *045139*
Jean-Pierre Antiquités, 142 Blvd Croix-Rousse, 69001
Lyon. T. 0478290914. *045140*
Leleu, Richard, 50 Rue de l'Université, 69007 Lyon.
T. 0478724684. - Ant / Furn / China - *045141*

London Market, 49 Rue Auguste Comte, 69002 Lyon.
T. 0478373073. - Ant / Furn - *045142*
Mansiet, Jacques, 56 Rue Auguste-Comte, 69002 Lyon.
T. 0478379939. - Orient - *045143*
Marcelpoil, Alain, 56 Rue Franklin, 69002 Lyon.
T. 0478374147. *045144*
Martiniani, Roger, 14 Pl Jules-Ferry, 69006 Lyon.
T. 0472742770. *045145*
Masséna Collection, 69 Rue Masséna, 69006 Lyon.
T. 0478520204. - China / Glass - *045146*
Masson, Andrée, 14 Pl Jules-Ferry, 69006 Lyon.
T. 0478525602, Fax 0478522298. *045147*
Miaz, Pierre, 94 Av Frères-Lumière, 69008 Lyon.
T. 0478007738. - Furn - *045148*
Millet, 25 Rue Remparts-d'Ainay, 69002 Lyon.
T. 0472410884, Fax 0478376517. *045149*
Missillier, Philippe, 10 Rue Fleurieu, 69002 Lyon.
T. 0478380811. - Mil - *045150*
Molle, Gilbert, 9 Rue Auguste-Comte, 69002 Lyon.
T. 0478370456, Fax 0478379746. - Paint - *045151*
Monin, 117 Blvd Stalingrad, Cité des Antiquaires, 69100
Lyon. T. 0472442215. *045152*
Monin, Jacques, 34 Rue Auguste-Comte, 69002 Lyon.
T. 0472490050. *045153*
Monnier, Frédéric, 46 Rue Auguste-Comte, 69002 Lyon.
T. 0478381990. *045154*
Morin, Thierry, 6 Rue Auguste Comte, 69002 Lyon.
T. 0478373108. - Paint / Furn / Dec / Lights /
Glass - *045155*
Murgia, Jean-Etienne, 113 Grande Rue Guillotière,
69007 Lyon. T. 0472732434. *045156*
Ogier, Jacques, 3 Rue Auguste-Comte, 69002 Lyon.
T. 0478377983. *045157*
Oxford Antiquités, 54 Cours Vitton, 69006 Lyon.
T. 0478524981, Fax 0472740700. *045158*
Papyvore, 4 Av Général-Brosset, 69006 Lyon.
T. 0478520202. *045159*
Pélissier, Y., 16 Rue Gasparin, 69002 Lyon.
T. 0478428709. *045160*
Perrin, Marie-Jo, 14 Rue Gasparin, 69002 Lyon.
T. 0478373127. - Furn / Cur / Tin - *045161*
Perrin, Marie-Jo, 3 Rue Auguste-Comte, 69002 Lyon.
T. 0478426123. - Furn / Cur - *045162*
Polette, Annie, 14 Pl Jules-Ferry, 69006 Lyon.
T. 0472741974. *045163*
Polette, Jacques, 1 Quai Fulchiron, 69005 Lyon.
T. 0478372710. *045164*
Pour la Galerie, 25 Rue Auguste-Comte, 69002 Lyon.
T. 0472400643. *045165*
Prète, Antoine, 21 Rue Ferrandière, 69002 Lyon.
T. 0478422316. *045166*
Rey, Jean, 23 Rue Auguste Comte, 69002 Lyon.
T. 0478370999. - Paint / Furn / China / Tex /
Instr - *045167*
Richard, Pierre, 41 Rue Auguste-Comte, 69002 Lyon.
T. 0478370119. - Furn / Silv / Instr / Mod - *045168*
Riondet, Bogdan, 124 Rue Sèze, 69006 Lyon.
T. 0478520045. *045169*
Roche, Thierry, 25 Rue Auguste-Comte, 69002 Lyon.
T. 0478371321. - Mod - *045170*
Ropert, Claude, 56 Rue Charité, 69002 Lyon.
T. 0478380678. *045171*
Servan, Andréas, 9 Cours Herbouville, 69004 Lyon.
Fax 78304390. *045172*
Sillage, 21 Rue Remparts-d'Ainay, 69002 Lyon.
Fax 72410641. *045173*
Simon, Simone, 11 Rue Sainte-Hélène, 69002 Lyon.
T. 0478372204. - Ant / Orient / Tex - *045174*
Soulier, Marie-Hélène, 55 Rue Auguste-Comte, 69002
Lyon. T. 0478420320. *045175*
Stylclair, 49 Rue Franklin, 69002 Lyon.
T. 0478428700. *045176*
Temps'Danse, 34 Blvd Brotteaux, 69006 Lyon.
T. 0478521494. *045177*
Thibaudière Brocante Antiquités, 37 Rue Thibaudière,
69007 Lyon. T. 0478589001. *045178*
Thoral, Pierre, 15 Rue Chinard, 69009 Lyon.
T. 0478438163. *045179*
Tic Tac Antiquités, 64 Rue Auguste-Comte, 69002 Lyon.
T. 0478377414. *045180*
Tout l'Art du Meuble, 73 Rue Tronchet, 69006 Lyon.
T. 0472430232. - Furn - *045181*

Trésors de Nathalie, 129 Rue Moncey, 69003 Lyon.
T. 0478710972. *045182*
Trouvailles, 25 Rue Port-du-Temple, 69002 Lyon.
T. 0478373253. - Ant / Furn / Cur - *045183*
Ughetto Turc, 117 Blvd Stalingrad, Cité des Antiquaires,
69100 Lyon. T. 0472430036. *045184*
Valette Antiquités, 40 Rue Camille-Roy, 69007 Lyon.
T. 0478693980. *045185*
Vernay-Chantrel, Bernard, 3 Rue Auguste-Comte, 69002
Lyon. T. 0478428755. - Furn / Cur - *045186*
Verseau, 68 Rue Auguste-Comte, 69002 Lyon.
T. 0478929473. *045187*
Vulliod, François, 30 Rue Maréchal-Foch, 69006 Lyon.
T. 0478932993. *045188*
Wallerand, Béatrice, 17 Pl Maréchal-Lyautey, 69006
Lyon. T. 0478240839. *045189*
Wunschel, Hervé, 14 Pl Jules-Ferry, 69006 Lyon.
T. 0478245217. *045190*

Lyons-la-Forêt (Eure)

Longcamp, Gérard de, Rue Bout-de-Bas, 27480 Lyons-
la-Forêt. T. 0232496143. *045191*
Noblet Martel, Geneviève, Pl Isaac-Benserade, 27480
Lyons-la-Forêt. T. 0232496342. *045192*
Pillet, Jean-François, Pl Isaac-Benserade, 27480 Lyons-
la-Forêt. T. 0232496800. *045193*

Mâcon (Saône-et-Loire)

Besch, Constant, 174 Quais Jean-Jaurès, 71000 Mâcon.
T. 0385381209. - Ant - *045194*
Bourgogne Antiquités, Angle Rue Gambetta et Quais La-
martine, 71000 Mâcon. T. 0385382971.
- Ant - *045195*
Hier et Aujourd'hui, 21 Rue Saint-Niziez Pl Saint-Pierre,
71000 Mâcon. T. 0385390651. - Ant - *045196*
Lopard-Dessolin, Mme, 1054 Quai de Lattre-de-Tassi-
gny, 71000 Mâcon. T. 0385387507, Fax 0385386554.
- Ant - *045197*
Puces Maconnaises, 50 Rue Dufour, 71000 Mâcon.
T. 0385394226. - Ant - *045198*
Rouge, Pierre, 10 Rue Pont, 71000 Mâcon.
T. 0385383440, Fax 0385394109. - Ant / Furn / Tex /
Cur - *045199*

Magenta (Marne)

Au Passé Simple, 21 Av Alfred-Anatole-Thévenet, 51200
Magenta. T. 0326556372. *045200*

Magné (Deux-Sèvres)

Brocante du Marais, 180 Rte Garette, Les Epineaux,
79460 Magné. T. 0549359300. *045201*

Magny-en-Vexin (Val-d'Oise)

Achats Antiquités, 6 Blvd Dailly, 95420 Magny-en-Vexin.
T. 0134672631. *045202*
Avoyne, Claudine, 11 Pl Potiquet, 95420 Magny-en-Ve-
xin. T. 0134670405, Fax 0134673694. *045203*
Jallier, Alain, 9bis Rue Crosne, 95420 Magny-en-Vexin.
T. 0134671126. *045204*
Peghaire, Michel, 6 Blvd Dailly, 95420 Magny-en-Vexin.
T. 0134672631. *045205*
Poisson, Jean-Claude, 53 Rue Paris, 95420 Magny-en-
Vexin. T. 0134670382. *045206*
Ratinaud, Sonia, 6 Rue Crosne, 95420 Magny-en-Vexin.
T. 0134671928. *045207*

Mainneville (Eure)

Dumont, Michel, Pl Marché, 27150 Mainneville.
T. 0232271971. - Ant - *045208*

Maintenon (Eure-et-Loir)

Bézard, Xavier, 6 Av Général-de-Gaulle, 28130 Maintenon. T. 0237230594. *045209*
Plos, Henri, 38 Rue Albert-Gautier-Pierres, 28130 Maintenon. T. 0237271494. *045210*
Schorp, Gérard, Le Clos du Se'1ne'1chal, Eglancourt,
28130 Maintenon. T. 0237825200, Fax 0237787077.
- Ant / Furn / Sculp / Arch / Eth - *045211*

Mairé-Levescault (Deux-Sèvres)

Marchewka, Edmond, Courbanay, 79190 Mairé-Leves-
cault. T. 0549076715. *045212*

Maisons-Alfort (Val-de-Marne)
Genest, Chantal, 138 Av République, 94700 Maisons-Alfort. T. 0143764521. *045213*
Van Houtte, Jean-Louis, 45 Rue Perpignan, 94700 Maisons-Alfort. T. 0143763256. *045214*

Maisons-Laffitte (Yvelines)
Longueville, Daniel, 12 et 21 Rue Vieille-Eglise, 78600 Maisons-Laffitte. T. 0139620996. *045215*
Rivière, Colette, 78 Rue Côtes, 78600 Maisons-Laffitte. T. 0139620239. *045216*

Malakoff (Hauts-de-Seine)
Alter, Hélène, 6 Rue Henri-Martin, 92240 Malakoff. T. 0146577309. *045217*
Chandlée, Véronique, 65 Rue Chauvelot, 92240 Malakoff. T. 0140920939. *045218*
Nunes, 40 Blvd Camelinat, 92240 Malakoff. T. 0146553814. *045219*
Vieux Malakoff, 140 Blvd Gabriel-Péri, 92240 Malakoff. T. 0147357498. *045220*

Malaunay (Seine-Maritime)
Phippen, Hubert, 6bis Rte Montville, 76770 Malaunay. T. 0235760640. *045221*

Mâle (Orne)
Jacpierre Materiaux Anciens, RN 23 Le Chêne-Vert, 61260 Mâle. T. 0237496971. - Ant - *045222*

Malemort-sur-Corrèze (Corrèze)
Delon, Michel, 11 Av 15-Août, 19360 Malemort-sur-Corrèze. T. 0555929659. *045223*
Pendaries, Claude, 50 Av Libération, 19360 Malemort-sur-Corrèze. T. 0555929425. *045224*
Thibault, Jean-Loup, RN 89, Claredent, 19360 Malemort-sur-Corrèze. T. 0555257634. *045225*

Malicorne-sur-Sarthe (Sarthe)
Grenier Malicornais, Rte Parcé, 72270 Malicorne-sur-Sarthe. T. 0243948400. - Ant - *045226*
Plazanet, Nicole, 8 Rue Gambetta, 72270 Malicorne-sur-Sarthe. T. 0243948975. - Ant - *045227*

Mallemort (Bouches-du-Rhône)
Antiquités du Golf, RN 7, 13370 Mallemort. T. 0490591979. *045228*
Antiquités du Mas Chatelan, Mas Chatelan, 13370 Mallemort. T. 0490574565. - Furn / Cur - *045229*

Malves-en-Minervois (Aude)
Autre Jour, Av Château, 11600 Malves-en-Minervois. T. 0468722750. *045230*

Malzéville (Meurthe-et-Moselle)
Morisot, Patrick, 13 Rue Colonel-Driant, 54220 Malzéville. T. 0383332158. *045231*

Mamers (Sarthe)
Pierre, Colette, 13 Rue Charles-Granger, 72600 Mamers. T. 0243979972. - Ant - *045232*

Mandelieu (Alpes-Maritimes)
AB Diffusion, 1145 Auguste-Renoir, 06210 Mandelieu. T. 0492970074, Fax 0493930038. *045233*
Espace Meuble, Av Maréchal-Juin, 06210 Mandelieu. T. 0492976078, Fax 0492971699. - Furn - *045234*
Jean Christophe, 111 Rue Léo-Brun, 06210 Mandelieu. T. 0493493839. *045235*
Joana Village, 809 Av Maréchal-Juin, 06210 Mandelieu. T. 0493493490. *045236*
Puces de la Côte, Chemin Levassor, 06210 Mandelieu. T. 0493477459. *045237*

Mane (Alpes-de-Haute-Provence)
Château de Sauvan, L'Orangerie, 04300 Mane. T. 0492752313. - Ant - *045238*
Lefort, Jean-François, Av Burlière, 04300 Mane. T. 0492751517. - Ant - *045239*
Péroline Antiquités, Rue Haute, 04300 Mane. T. 0492750971. - Ant - *045240*

Manom (Moselle)
Tour de la Brocante et de l'Antiquité, 28 Rue du Luxembourg, 57100 Manom. T. 0382513645. *045241*

Manosque (Alpes-de-Haute-Provence)
Antiquité au Collectionneur, 8 Rue des Tourelles, 04100 Manosque. T. 0492720634. - Ant - *045242*
Barry, Jean-Louis, La Chimère Rte Marseille, 04100 Manosque. T. 0492878587. - Ant / Instr - *045243*
Cheval Volant, 6 Pl Hôtel-de-Ville, 04100 Manosque. T. 0492877342. - Ant - *045244*
Christie's France, 8 Av Luberon, 04100 Manosque. T. 0492724331, Fax 0492725365. - Ant - *045245*
Galerie des Arts et Antiquités, 2 Blvd Martin-Bret, 04100 Manosque. T. 0492873352. - Ant - *045246*
Grelet, Eric, 4 Rue Tanneurs, 04100 Manosque. T. 0492720634. - Ant - *045247*
Ranchu, Michèle, Quart Valveranne, 04100 Manosque. T. 0492876132. - Ant - *045248*

Mantes-la-Jolie (Yvelines)
Levecher, Yvonne, 124 Rue Maurice-Braunstein, 78200 Mantes-la-Jolie. T. 0130942645. *045249*
Renoult, Françoise, 6 Rue Levesque, 78200 Mantes-la-Jolie. T. 0134771345. *045250*
Tiroir aux Secrets, 31 Rue Sangle, 78200 Mantes-la-Jolie. T. 0130927842. *045251*

Marambat (Gers)
Blum, Norbert, 32190 Marambat. T. 0562064678. *045252*

Marans (Charente-Maritime)
Favre, Monique, 27 Rue Aligre, 17230 Marans. T. 0546011473. *045253*
Gaudin, Madeleine, 61 Quai Maréchal-Joffre, 17230 Marans. T. 0546011011. *045254*

Marboué (Eure-et-Loir)
Saison, Gisèle, Lieu-dit Mezelle, 28200 Marboué. T. 0237989357. *045255*

Marcigny (Saône-et-Loire)
Cour des Mirascles en Bourgogne, 6 Rue Chenale, 71110 Marcigny. T. 0385252129, Fax 0385251881. - Ant / Furn - *045256*

Marcillé-Robert (Ille-et-Vilaine)
Barbotin, Auguste, 18 Grande Rue, 35240 Marcillé-Robert. T. 0299436774. *045257*

Marcilly-la-Campagne (Eure)
Deslandes, Alexandre, 9 Pl Eglise, 27320 Marcilly-la-Campagne. T. 0232581001. *045258*
Lehembre, Philippe, 9 Rue Verger, 27320 Marcilly-la-Campagne. T. 0232582943. *045259*

Marcilly-sur-Seine (Marne)
Lebrun, Jean, 48 Rue Tilleuls, 51260 Marcilly-sur-Seine. T. 0326426649. *045260*

Marcoussis (Essonne)
Au Reflets du Passé, 28 Blvd Nélaton, 91460 Marcoussis. T. 0169806656. - Furn / Jew / Cur - *045261*

Marcq-en-Barœul (Nord)
Brocante du Septentrion, Ferme des Marguerites, 59700 Marcq-en-Barœul. T. 0320462742. - Ant - *045262*
Marcq Antiquités, 21 Rue Herrengrie, 59700 Marcq-en-Barœul. T. 0320984558. - Ant - *045263*

Marcy (Nièvre)
Poupée Merveilleuse, Remilly, 58210 Marcy. T. 0386294805. - Toys - *045264*

Marennes (Charente-Maritime)
Favre, Frédéric, 32 Rue Docteur-Roux, 17320 Marennes. T. 0546851921. - Furn - *045265*

Maresché (Sarthe)
Tison, Jacky, La Maison Neuve, 72170 Maresché. T. 0243970513. - Ant - *045266*

Mareuil-le-Port (Marne)
Despesel, 77 Av Paul-Doumer, 51700 Mareuil-le-Port. T. 0326583076. *045267*

Margerie-Chantagret (Loire)
Boczar, Odile, Bourg, 42560 Margerie-Chantagret. T. 0477763234. *045268*

Margon (Eure-et-Loir)
Lafon, Léon, 18 Av Paris, 28400 Margon. T. 0237526204. *045269*

Marignac (Tarn-et-Garonne)
Daventure, Jean-Pierre, Petit Besian, 82500 Marignac. T. 0563652799. *045270*

Marignane (Bouches-du-Rhône)
Deleuil, Huguette, 5 Pl République, 13700 Marignane. T. 0442887885. *045271*

Marin (Haute-Savoie)
A la Poussière d'Or, Rte de Sussinges, 74200 Marin. T. 0450702982. - Paint / Furn / Cur - *045272*

Marly-le-Roi (Yvelines)
A l'Art Antique, 1 Av Saint-Germain, 78160 Marly-le-Roi. T. 0139580096. *045273*
Chabrat, Maurice, 1 Grande Rue, 78160 Marly-le-Roi. T. 0139582388. - Furn / Orient - *045274*
Franc Segent, 1 Rue Alexandre-Dumas, 78160 Marly-le-Roi. T. 0139581292. *045275*

Marmande (Lot-et-Garonne)
Brocante du Pont des Sables, Grande Route Ouest Coussan, 47200 Marmande. T. 0553937195. *045276*
Dubos, Ginette, 11 Rue Toupinerie, 47200 Marmande. T. 0553643045. *045277*
Joret, Patrick, Saint-Aubin, 47200 Marmande. T. 0553895024. *045278*
Vitrat, Francis, RN 113, 47200 Marmande. T. 0553642193. - Furn / China / Cur - *045279*

Marnay-sur-Marne (Haute-Marne)
Grapinet, Alain, 2 RN 19, 52800 Marnay-sur-Marne. T. 0325311109. *045280*

Marnes-la-Coquette (Hauts-de-Seine)
Bordes, Patrick, 2 Pl de la Mairie, 92430 Marnes-la-Coquette. T. 0147410832. - Paint / Furn - *045281*
Dey, J.C.A., 8bis Rue G.-et-X.-Schlumberger, 92430 Marnes-la-Coquette. T. 0147416531. *045282*
Riesen, Didier, 9 Rue Gabriel-Sommer, 92430 Marnes-la-Coquette. T. 0147012461. *045283*
Vitry, Antoine, 8 Pl Mairie, 92430 Marnes-la-Coquette. T. 0147410626. *045284*

Maroilles (Nord)
Vaubourgeix, Serge, Rue Vigniers, 59550 Maroilles. T. 0327847351. - Ant - *045285*

Marolles-en-Hurepoix (Essonne)
Garets, Philippe des, 5 Chemin Poste, 91630 Marolles-en-Hurepoix. T. 0169148549, Fax 0164561901. - Dec - *045286*

Maromme (Seine-Maritime)
Danièle Brocante, 8 Rue Jean-de-Béthencourt, 76150 Maromme. T. 0235740656. *045287*
Puces, 26 Rue Re'1publique, 76150 Maromme. T. 0235754848. *045288*
Trohay, Jean-Claude, 29 Rue Dumont-d'Urville, 76150 Maromme. T. 0235757154. - Furn - *045289*

Marquise (Pas-de-Calais)
LDL, Rue Prés, 62250 Marquise. T. 0321928272. *045290*
Leleu, Gérald, Grande-Place, 62250 Marquise. T. 0321337076. - Ant - *045291*

Marseille (Bouches-du-Rhône)
A la Belle Brocante, 28 Rue Docteur-Escat, 13006 Marseille. T. 0491374609. *045292*
Aegerter, Bernard, 25 Pl aux Huiles, 13001 Marseille. T. 0491547118. *045293*
Aegerter, Bernard, 10 Pl Aux Huiles, 13001 Marseille. T. 0491330612. - Ant / Furn / China - *045294*
Aegeter, 20 Blvd Fifi-Turin, 13010 Marseille. T. 0491255923. *045295*
Aigle Impérial, 20 Blvd Fifi-Turin, 13010 Marseille. T. 0491789111. *045296*
Antiquité au Carrosse d'Or, 2 Blvd Baille, 13005 Marseille. T. 0491794477, Fax 0491925200. - Paint / Furn / Glass / Cur - *045297*

Antiquité au Carrosse d'Or, 254 Chemin Armée-d'Afrique, 13010 Marseille. T. 0491942000, Fax 0491925200. - Paint / Furn / Glass / Cur - *045298*

Antiquité au Carrosse d'Or, 202 Blvd Valbarelle, 13011 Marseille. T. 0491447282, Fax 0491925200. - Paint / Furn / Glass / Cur - *045299*

Antiquités Cérés, 8 Rue Chantier, 13007 Marseille. T. 0491337034. *045300*

Antiquités des Trois Ponts, 55 Cours Julien, 13006 Marseille. T. 0491420400. *045301*

Antiquités Foch, 7 Av Maréchal-Foch, 13004 Marseille. T. 0491349316. *045302*

Antiquités L'Autantique, 174 Av Olives, 13013 Marseille. T. 0491067401. *045303*

Antiquités La Carmagnole, 54 Cours Julien, 13006 Marseille. T. 0491481234. *045304*

Antonioli, Yann, 1 Av Maréchal-de-Lattre-de-Tassigny, 13009 Marseille. T. 0491407334. *045305*

Apkarian, Georges, 71 Cours Julien, 13006 Marseille. T. 0491481207. *045306*

Art 2 Shanghai, 82 Blvd Libération, 13004 Marseille. T. 0491421986. - Furn / Orient - *045307*

Artaud, Jean-Pierre, 19 Rue Augustin Fabre, 13006 Marseille. T. 0491474062. *045308*

Arts et Bronzes, 30 Rue Saint-Jacques, 13006 Marseille. T. 0491813420. *045309*

Au Roi des Puces, 79 Blvd Icard, Nouveau Verdillon, Bâtiment A, 13010 Marseille. T. 0491798831. *045310*

Au Vert Galant, 27 Rue Sylvabelle, 13006 Marseille. T. 0491372208. - Ant / China - *045311*

Au Vieux Bougeoir, 100 Blvd Blancarde, 13004 Marseille. T. 0491860271. *045312*

Au Vieux Marseille, 96 Rue Evêché, 13002 Marseille. T. 0491903114. *045313*

Aux Années Folles, 37 Rue Falque, 13006 Marseille. T. 0491817059. *045314*

Aux Puces, 28 Rue Edmond-Rostand, 13006 Marseille. T. 0491535558. *045315*

Azzopardi, 26 Rue Armand-Bédarrides, 13006 Marseille. T. 0491484610. *045316*

Azzopardi, Joseph, 57 Cours Julien, 13006 Marseille. T. 0491941798. *045317*

Bacciochi, Jean-Jacques, 24 Rue Sylvabelle, 13006 Marseille. T. 0491375631. - Furn - *045318*

Balestra, Christian, 344 Chemin Armée-d'Afrique, 13010 Marseille. T. 0491475500. *045319*

Balestra, Louis, Chemin Madrague-Ville, 13015 Marseille. T. 0491989722. *045320*

Balestra, Louis, 256 Chemin Armée-d'Afrique, 13010 Marseille. T. 0491473145. - Ant - *045321*

Barbaroux, Suzanne, 57 Cours Lieutaud, 13006 Marseille. T. 0491486298. *045322*

Bassan, Michel, 28 Chemin Vallon-de-l'Oriol, 13007 Marseille. T. 0491314997. *045323*

Belleudy, Patrick, 15 Blvd Anjou, 13015 Marseille. T. 0491609533. *045324*

Benichou, Edmond, 69 Rue Breteuil, 13006 Marseille. T. 0491370740, Fax 0491532502. *045325*

Bernard, Lucien, 3 Cours Jean-Ballard, 13001 Marseille. T. 0491542330. *045326*

Bernasconi, Anny-France, 25 Cours Honoré-d'Estienne-d'Orves, 13001 Marseille. T. 0491555972. *045327*

Brès, Martin, 60 Rue Grignan, 13001 Marseille. T. 0491330292, Fax 0491555314. - Paint / Graph - *045328*

Brocante Le Sphinx, 1 Blvd Jean-Eugène-Cabassud, 13010 Marseille. T. 0491426778. *045329*

Brocante 51, 51 Cours Julien, 13006 Marseille. T. 0491471733. *045330*

Brocanterie, 170 Av Mazargues, 13008 Marseille. T. 0491225710. *045331*

Bruno, Alfred, 167 Chemin Four-de-Buze, 13014 Marseille. T. 0491984406. *045332*

Cachou, 10 Rue Crudère, 13006 Marseille. T. 0491426570. *045333*

Caors, Gérard, 93 Rue Paradis, 13006 Marseille. T. 0491814703. - Tex - *045334*

Carmignani, Thierry, 10 Rue Farjon, 13001 Marseille. T. 0491648866. *045335*

Centre Expo du Meuble, 56 Av Camille-Pelletan, 13003 Marseille. T. 0491059700. *045336*

Charbonnier, Michel, 68 Cours Julien, 13006 Marseille. T. 0491940379. *045337*

Chez Patrizia, 10 Rue Bernex, 13001 Marseille. T. 0491646009. *045338*

Chinoiserie, 43 Blvd Baille, 13006 Marseille. T. 0491477490. *045339*

Christophe, 136 Chemin Madrague-Ville, 13015 Marseille. T. 0491630374. *045340*

Ciaparra, Michel, 41 Blvd Gaston-Crémieux, 13008 Marseille. T. 0491532421. *045341*

Cid Antiquités, 3 Rue Aldebert, 13006 Marseille. T. 0491535037. *045342*

Clichés du Passé, 7 Rue Crudère, 13006 Marseille. T. 0491422865, Fax 0491423123. *045343*

Clinique de Poupées, 21 Rue Docteur-Jean-Fiolle, 13006 Marseille. T. 0491376766. *045344*

Colombani, Dominique, 2 Blvd Millière, 13011 Marseille. T. 0491361975. *045345*

Compagnie Anglaise, 113 Rue Paradis, 13006 Marseille. T. 0491530196. *045346*

Davos, 2 Rue Grande-Armée, 13001 Marseille. T. 0491626017. *045347*

Decamp, François, 302 Rue Paradis, 13008 Marseille. T. 0491811800. *045348*

Dell'Aria, Ignace, 138 Blvd Baille, 13005 Marseille. T. 0491798779. - Paint - *045349*

Diaz, Jeanne, 29 Blvd Jean-Labro, 13016 Marseille. T. 0491036558. *045350*

Ecume des Jours, 36 Rue Trois-Rois, 13006 Marseille. T. 0491480709. *045351*

Et le Monde Oublié, 6 Rue Pastoret, 13006 Marseille. T. 0491926005, Fax 0491926004. *045352*

Etienne, Marcel, 22 Cours Joseph-Thierry, 13001 Marseille. T. 0491624843. *045353*

Francine Antiquités, 81 Rue Saint-Ferréol, 13006 Marseille. T. 0491555794. - Jew - *045354*

Galerie d'Art La Poutre, 206 Rue Paradis, 13006 Marseille. T. 0491371093. - Paint / Num / Sculp / Dec / Fra / Mod / Pho - *045355*

Galerie du Multiple, 61 Rue Saint-Savournin, 13005 Marseille. T. 0491920707. *045356*

Galerie du Sud, 32 Rue Saint-Jacques, 13006 Marseille. T. 0491817464. - Paint - *045357*

Galerie Edmond Rostand, 16 Rue Edmond-Rostand, 13006 Marseille. T. 0491819898. - Jew / Silv / Cur - *045358*

Garcia, Jean, 83 Rue Chateaubriand, 13007 Marseille. T. 0491594452. - Furn / China / Lights / Glass / Toys - *045359*

Gay, André, 19 Rue Venture, 13001 Marseille. T. 0491334949. - Furn / Instr / Music / Naut - *045360*

Gershel, 33 Rue Saint-Jacques, 13006 Marseille. T. 0491371680, Fax 0491816683. *045361*

Goyet, 5 Traverse Regny, 13009 Marseille. T. 0491261547. - Paint - *045362*

Grimaud, Thierry, 8 Rue Crudère, 13006 Marseille. T. 0491920860. *045363*

Grivet, Monique, 370 Rue Paradis, 13008 Marseille. T. 0491379165. *045364*

Gulessian, André, 20 Blvd Fifi-Turin, 13010 Marseille. T. 0491790286. *045365*

Gulessian, André, 16 Rue Saint-Savournin, 13001 Marseille. T. 0491471400. *045366*

Hanounou, Moïse, 57 Cours Franklin-Roosevelt, 13004 Marseille. T. 0491482235. *045367*

Jaquenoud, Paula, 2 imp Gardey, 13008 Marseille. T. 0491771269, Fax 0491772833. - Ant / China / Mil - *045368*

Joëlle Perle, 1 Rue Edmond-Rostand, 13006 Marseille. T. 0491375488. *045369*

Kammermann, Georges, 16 Rue Saint-Jacques, 13006 Marseille. T. 0491371143. *045370*

Mandragore, 2 Rue Crudère, 13006 Marseille. T. 0491923088. *045371*

Menard, Henri, 54 Rue Saint-Suffren, 13006 Marseille. T. 0491814826, Fax 0491815263. *045372*

Mercier, Michel, 24 Rue Evêché, 13002 Marseille. T. 0491917249. *045373*

Merdinian, Alain, 8 Rue Fontange, 13006 Marseille. T. 0491491443. *045374*

Moreau, Gérald, 29 Rue Edmond-Rostand, 13006 Marseille. T. 0491570433. *045375*

Mouret, Gilbert, 4 Rue Guy-Fabre, 13001 Marseille. T. 0491507219. - Orient - *045376*

Nadjarian, 137 Rue Paradis, 13006 Marseille. T. 0491370449. - Tex - *045377*

Olibé, William, 166 Blvd Libération, 13004 Marseille. T. 0491429257. *045378*

Pauli, Michel, 28 Rue Docteur-Escat, 13006 Marseille. T. 0491374609. *045379*

Petit Versailles, 4 Rue Versailles, 13003 Marseille. T. 0491500002. - Paint / Furn - *045380*

Phot'Optic, 1 Blvd Dugommier, 13001 Marseille. T. 0491901920. - Instr - *045381*

Plaisir du Bois, 55 Blvd Chave, 13005 Marseille. T. 0491420883. *045382*

Porcher, Fernand, 20 Rue Saint-Saëns, 13001 Marseille. T. 0491337794, Fax 0491334476. - Ant / Paint / Mul / Draw / Tin - *045383*

Poyen, Jane, 6 Rue Edmond Rostand, 13006 Marseille. T. 0491376123. - Ant - *045384*

Présence du Passé, 38 Rue Dragon, 13006 Marseille. T. 0491813111. *045385*

Reflet des Temps, 5 Av André Zénatti, 13008 Marseille. T. 0491252850. *045386*

Ripert de Garam, Mireille, 10 Rue Crudère, 13006 Marseille. T. 0491429804. - Furn / Tex / Jew / Silv / Cur - *045387*

Ripert, Isabelle, 9 Rue Vian, 13006 Marseille. T. 0491481716. *045388*

Roche, Joseph, 31 Rue Edmond-Rostand, 13006 Marseille. T. 0491531454. *045389*

Sablier, 49 Cours Julien, 13006 Marseille. T. 0491427935. *045390*

Salle des Ventes National, 67 Blvd National, 13001 Marseille. T. 0491507867. - Furn / Cur - *045391*

Stammegna, Marc, 74 Rue Breteuil, 13006 Marseille. T. 0491374605, Fax 0491812946. - Paint - *045392*

Sylvia-Jolivet, Jean, 133 Rue Paradis, 13006 Marseille. T. 0491376153. *045393*

Tarrazi, Jean-Pierre, 20 Rue Edmond-Rostand, 13006 Marseille. T. 0491811950. *045394*

Tour d'Oriol, 248 Chemin Vallon-de-l'Oriol, 13007 Marseille. T. 0491522800. - Paint / Cur - *045395*

Vallette-Jaquenoud, 2 Imp Gardey, 13008 Marseille. T. 0491771269, Fax 0491772833. *045396*

Venice, 341 Promenade Corniche-John-Kennedy, 13007 Marseille. T. 0491221575. *045397*

Viala, Maurice, 14 Rue Lafayette, 13001 Marseille. T. 0491083254, Fax 0491626295. *045398*

Vieux Manoir, 57 Cours Julien, 13006 Marseille. T. 0491941798. *045399*

Vigie, Bruno, 66 Rue Grignan, 13001 Marseille. T. 0491555373. *045400*

Vigié, Pierre, 19 Rue Breteuil, 13006 Marseille. T. 0491336829. - Ant / Furn - *045401*

Village Crudère, 10 Rue Crudère, 13006 Marseille. T. 0491484893. *045402*

Vivian, 263 Rue Paradis, 13006 Marseille. T. 0491375282. *045403*

Yvana, 56 Rue Edmond Rostand, 13006 Marseille. T. 0491377554. *045404*

Le 29, 29 Rue Edmond-Rostand, 13006 Marseille. T. 0491571597, Fax 0491374307. *045405*

Marsilly (Charente-Maritime)
Old Shop in Field's, 19 Rue Ecoles, 17137 Marsilly. T. 0546013407. *045406*

Marssac-sur-Tarn (Tarn)
Blanc, Bertrand, 17 Av Albi, 81150 Marssac-sur-Tarn. T. 0563532282. *045407*

Bruyère, Serge, 12 Av Albi, 81150 Marssac-sur-Tarn. T. 0563552437. *045408*

Martainneville (Somme)
Leclerq, Jamy, 5 Rte Nationale, 80140 Martainneville. T. 0322285452. - Ant - *045409*

Martel (Lot)
Abbaye, Rue Barry-de-Brive, 46600 Martel. T. 0565373980, Fax 0565374236. - Furn / Dec / Cur - *045410*

Antiquité Saint-Maur, Rue Droite, 46600 Martel. T. 0565374037. *045411*

Vallée, Yvonne, Pl Léon-Gambetta, 46600 Martel. T. 0565373249. *045412*

Martigues (Bouches-du-Rhône)
Larrieu, André, 35 Rue Langari, 13500 Martigues.
T. 0442073600. *045413*

Marvejols (Lozère)
Comtor, 12 Rue Chanelles, 48100 Marvejols.
T. 0466322214. *045414*
El Ouachni, Ali, 27 Rue Chanelles, 48100 Marvejols.
T. 0466323085. *045415*
El Ouachni, Ali, 45 Rue République, 48100 Marvejols.
T. 0466322877. *045416*

Masny (Nord)
Brocante de l'Eglise, 75 Rue Fauqueux, 59176 Masny.
T. 0327917477. - Ant - *045417*

Massaguel (Tarn)
Mazerand, Joseph, 81110 Massaguel. T. 0563503222.
- Furn / Cur - *045418*

Massangis (Yonne)
Courtois, Georges, Grande Rue, 89440 Massangis.
T. 0386338584. *045419*

Massiac (Cantal)
Miramont, Elie, 70 Av Général-de-Gaulle, 15500 Massiac. T. 0471230389. *045420*

Massy (Essonne)
Au bon Choix, Centre Commercial Moins X, lot 62 et 81, 91300 Massy. T. 0169320475. *045421*

Matha (Charente-Maritime)
Chaton, Philippe, 27 Rue Cognac, 17160 Matha.
T. 0546585511. *045422*

Mathieu (Calvados)
Au Cadran Solaire, 5 Rue Puits, 14920 Mathieu.
T. 0231441237. - Furn / China / Glass / Cur - *045423*

Matignon (Côtes-d'Armor)
Demeulemester, Régis, 8 Pl Gouyon, 22550 Matignon.
T. 0296411181. - Furn / Tex - *045424*
Le Calonnec, Jean-Pierre, L'Hôpital, 22550 Matignon.
T. 0296410835. *045425*

Maubeuge (Nord)
Duval, Luc, 2 Rue Gippus, 59600 Maubeuge.
T. 0327643431. - Ant - *045426*
Marotte, 269 Av Jean-Jaurès, 59600 Maubeuge.
T. 0327646436. - Ant - *045427*
Topkapi, 31 Rue 145ème Rl, 59600 Maubeuge.
T. 0327657812. - Ant - *045428*

Mauriac (Cantal)
Frutière, Valentin, Pl Palais, 15200 Mauriac.
T. 0471681037. *045429*

Maussac (Corrèze)
Antiquités La Coste, La Coste, RN 89, 19250 Maussac.
T. 0555942200. *045430*

Mautes (Creuse)
Château de Boisqueyraux, Boisqueyraux, 23190 Mautes
T. 0555673232, Fax 0555673636. - Ant - *045431*

Mauvezin (Gers)
Matita, Sylvie, 7 Blvd Carnot, 32120 Mauvezin.
T. 0562067733. *045432*

Mayenne (Mayenne)
Art de Vie, 19 Rue Sergent-Louvrier, 53100 Mayenne.
T. 0243042670. - Ant - *045433*
Aubry, Alain, La Ricouillière, 53100 Mayenne.
T. 0243044239. - Ant - *045434*
Lefevre, Jean-Claude, La Courbe Rte d'Alençon, 53100
Mayenne. T. 0243044952. - Ant / Furn - *045435*

Mazamet (Tarn)
Balfet, Olivier, Résid Nore, 81200 Mazamet.
T. 0563615686. *045436*
Brocante des Bausses, 135 Av Maréchal-Foch, 81200
Mazamet. T. 0563989713. *045437*
Brocante 112, RN 112, Face Mammouth, 81200 Mazamet. T. 0563619983. *045438*
Serge, Alain, 5 Rue Arts, 81200 Mazamet.
T. 0563613409. *045439*

Mazan (Vaucluse)
Barbière, Brigitte, 12 Rue Patres, 84380 Mazan.
T. 0490696447. - Ant - *045440*
Beuche, Bernard, 12 Rue Patres, 84380 Mazan.
T. 0490696447. - Ant - *045441*

Mazères (Ariège)
Liberman, Anne-Marie, 33 Rue Gaston-de-Foix, 09270
Mazères. T. 0561694170. - Tex / Dec / Cur - *045442*

Mazerulles (Meurthe-et-Moselle)
Rolin, Gérard, 23 Rue Nancy, 54280 Mazerulles.
T. 0383317116. *045443*

Mazet-Saint-Voy (Haute-Loire)
Brocante Charreyrot, Ferme de Charreyrot, 43520 Mazet-Saint-Voy. T. 0471650166. - Furn - *045444*

Mazières-sur-Béronne (Deux-Sèvres)
Siteau, Michel, Charzay, 79500 Mazières-sur-Béronne.
T. 0549290593. *045445*

Meaux (Seine-et-Marne)
Fabert & Raoult, 7 Av Joffre, 77100 Meaux.
T. 0360254433. *045446*
Vasseur, Jacques, 13 Rue de la Cordonnerie, 77100
Meaux. T. 0164340893. - Ant - *045447*

Médis (Charente-Maritime)
Antiquités Joseph, 60 Rte Saujon, 17600 Médis.
T. 0546067248. *045448*
Chantelauze, Paul, Le Petit Toussauge, 17600 Médis.
T. 0546054940. *045449*

Megève (Haute-Savoie)
Art Actualité, 5 RD, Rochebrune, 74120 Megève.
T. 0450919136. - Sculp / Tex / Dec / Cur - *045450*
Brocantaires, 1866 Rte Nationale, 74120 Megève.
T. 0450214210. - Furn / Cur - *045451*
Fouchault, Jean, 30 Imp Saint-Paul, 74120 Megève.
T. 0450211663. *045452*
Navarro, 2142 Rte Praz-sur-Arly, 74120 Megève.
T. 0450589838. *045453*

Mehun-sur-Yèvre (Cher)
2 RPB, Pl Barmont, 18500 Mehun-sur-Yèvre.
T. 0248570223. *045454*

Melle (Deux-Sèvres)
Tenot-Chome, La Garenne, 79500 Melle.
T. 0549270102. *045455*

Melun (Seine-et-Marne)
Brakha, Yolande, 32 Rue Général-de-Gaulle, 77000 Melun. T. 64523045. *045456*
Domenech, Raynald, 10 Rue Carnot, 77000 Melun.
T. 64378020. - Jew - *045457*
Euménides, 2 Rue Saint-Ambroise, 77000 Melun.
T. 64395494. - Paint / Furn / Cur - *045458*
Gaud & Pirman, 7 Rue Guy-Baudoin, 77000 Melun.
T. 64529045. *045459*

Mende (Lozère)
Bonnal, Av 11-Novembre, 48000 Mende.
T. 0466491355. *045460*
Segala, Georges, Rte Rieucros, 48000 Mende.
T. 0466652530. *045461*

Ménerbes (Vaucluse)
Jongleux, Gérard, Quart Falette, 84560 Ménerbes.
T. 0490723917. - Ant - *045462*
Sacha, Pl Albert-Roure, 84560 Ménerbes.
T. 0490724128, Fax 0490767113. - Ant - *045463*
Saint-Germain Antiquités, Grand'Rue, 84560 Ménerbes.
T. 0490722386, Fax 0490724482. - Ant / Eth /
Cur - *045464*

Ménilles (Eure)
Verdière, René, 17 Rue Honfroy, 27120 Ménilles.
T. 0232361793, Fax 0232362380. *045465*

Mennecy (Essonne)
Jourdain, 2 Rue Chatries, 91540 Mennecy.
T. 0164573432. *045466*

Menton (Alpes-Maritimes)
Bosio, Yves, Pl Herbes, 06500 Menton.
T. 0493354319. *045467*
Falconnet, Pierre, 7 Av Edouard-VII, 06500 Menton.
T. 0493359240. - Paint / Furn / China / Cur - *045468*
Scrudato, Robert, 3 Av Thiers, 06500 Menton.
T. 0493577567. - Paint / Furn / Sculp / Silv /
Glass - *045469*
Tourmondeur, 17 Sq Victoria, 06500 Menton.
T. 0493573303. - Jew / Naut - *045470*

Méounes-lès-Montrieux (Var)
Antiquités aux Tonneaux, Quartier Les Ferrages, Campagne Tonneaux, 83136 Méounes-lès-Montrieux.
T. 0494339075. *045471*
Picard, Henri, Ham Pachoquin, 83136 Méounes-lès-Montrieux. T. 0494489644. *045472*

Mer (Loir-et-Cher)
Cafétérière Emaillée, 1 Rue Nationale, 41500 Mer.
T. 0254813220. *045473*
P'tite Brocante, 44 Av Maunoury, 41500 Mer.
T. 0254810525. *045474*
Sausset, Hubert, 110 Rue Barreau, 41500 Mer.
T. 0254813206. - Paint / Furn / Cur - *045475*

Mercin-et-Vaux (Aisne)
Reflex, 44 Rue de Vaux, 02200 Mercin-et-Vaux.
T. 0323734379. - Paint / Furn - *045476*
Reflex, 44 Rue Vaux, 02200 Mercin-et-Vaux.
T. 0323734379, Fax 0323733613. - Ant - *045477*

Mercurol (Drôme)
Guerdener, Victor, Caravanne Les Odouards, 26600 Mercurol. T. 0475074398. *045478*

Méricourt (Yvelines)
Miroir de Fief, 5 Grande Rue, 78270 Méricourt.
T. 0130420227. *045479*

Mérignac (Charente)
Métayer, Jean-Jacques, Villars, 16200 Mérignac.
T. 0545908047. *045480*

Mérignac (Gironde)
Chaumière d'Antan, 138 Av Saint-Médard, 33700 Mérignac. T. 0556973948, Fax 0556972175. *045481*
Chaumière d'Antan, 138 Av Saint-Médard, 33700 Mérignac. T. 0556973948. - Furn / China / Sculp / Lights /
Instr / Glass / Toys - *045482*
Mérignac Antiquités, 229 Av Marne, 33700 Mérignac.
T. 0556974938. - Ant - *045483*
Otternaud, Maurice, Chemin Pagneau, 33700 Mérignac.
T. 0556363568. *045484*

Mers-les-Bains (Somme)
Broc Antic, 1 Rue Jules-Verne, 80350 Mers-les-Bains.
T. 0235860777. - Ant - *045485*

Mervans (Saône-et-Loire)
Bessy, Jacques, Bois Mercey, 71310 Mervans.
T. 0385761208. - Ant - *045486*

Méry-Corbon (Calvados)
Antiquités du Lion, RN 13, Lion d'Or, 14370 Méry-Corbon. T. 0231235769. *045487*

Meschers-sur-Gironde (Charente-Maritime)
Broux, Jacques, Moulin des Vignes, 17132 Meschers-sur-Gironde. T. 0546025234. *045488*

Mesnil-Clinchamps (Calvados)
Lebouteiller, Joël, La Minotière, 14380 Mesnil-Clinchamps. T. 0231677385. - Furn - *045489*

Mesnil-sur-l'Estrée (Eure)
Brocante Mesniloise, 17 Grande Rue, 27650 Mesnil-sur-l'Estrée. T. 0232829383. *045490*

Messac (Charente-Maritime)
Labrouche, Line, Chez Douteaux, 17130 Messac.
T. 0546706306, Fax 0546706241. *045491*

Metz (Moselle)
A l'Estampille, 116 Av Strasbourg, 57070 Metz.
T. 0387369627. *045492*

A l'Hôtel d'Heu, 21 Rue Fontaine, 57000 Metz.
T. 0387364648. 045493
A La Vieille France, 31 Rue des Jardins, 57000 Metz.
T. 0387366338. - Furn - 045494
Antiquités Modernes, 10 Rue Jardins, 57000 Metz.
T. 0387763364. 045495
Au Bon Vieux, 1bis Rue du Champé, 57000 Metz.
T. 038/740349. - Furn / Cur - 045496
Au Chiabout, 74 Rue des Allemands, 57000 Metz.
T. 0387360934. - Furn - 045497
Au Vieux Chêne, 11 Rue Clercs, 57000 Metz.
T. 0387751217. 045498
Bédébulles, 20 Rue Sainte-Marie, 57000 Metz.
T. 0387369055. - Toys - 045499
Calabria, Gilles, 47 Pl Chambre, 57000 Metz.
T. 0387362405. 045500
Charpentier, Denis, 1bis Rue Champé, 57000 Metz.
T. 0387740349. 045501
Charpentier, Denis, Centre Commercial Saint-Jacques,
57000 Metz. T. 0387741902. 045502
Ecrin, 9 Rue Allemands, 57000 Metz.
T. 0387756985. 045503
Ehrmann, Antoinette, Centre Commercial Saint-Jacques,
57000 Metz. T. 0387757671. 045504
Eventail, 18 Pl Forum, 57000 Metz.
T. 0387752599. 045505
Fort Nicolas, 1 Rue Paris, 57000 Metz.
T. 0387327779. 045506
Girandole, 1bis Rue da la Paix, 57000 Metz.
T. 0387740550. - Paint / Furn / Cur - 045507
Hussard, 13 Rue 20ème-Corps-Américain, 57000 Metz.
T. 0387506502. - Mil - 045508
Il était une Fois, 1 Pl Cormontaigne, 57000 Metz.
T. 0387302626. 045509
Jadis, 36 Rue Pasteur, 57000 Metz.
T. 0387663636. 045510
Jager, Hélène, 10 Rue Petite-Boucherie, 57000 Metz.
T. 0387760797. 045511
Metz Collections, 84 Rue Allemands, 57000 Metz.
T. 0387362574. 045512
Passé Simple, 26 Pl Saint-Simplice, 57000 Metz.
T. 0387368351. 045513
Tour Camoufle, 12 Rue Gambetta, 57000 Metz.
T. 0387663150. 045514
Trevy-Ehrmann, 10 Rue Tête-d'Or, 57000 Metz.
T. 0387577072. 045515
Viola, André, 79 Rte de Plappeville, 57050 Metz.
T. 0387304949. - Paint / Furn / Toys - 045516

Meudon (Hauts-de-Seine)
Au Regard des Anges, 83 Rue Paris, 92190 Meudon.
T. 0145079941. 045517
Fernandez, Josette, 15 Rue Lavoisier, 92190 Meudon.
T. 0145345586. 045518
Henry, 5bis Rue Henri-Barbusse, 92190 Meudon.
T. 0145078136. - Furn / Cur - 045519
Kerdrain, Lionel, 5bis Rue Basse-de-la-Terrasse, 92190
Meudon. T. 0145348960. 045520
Renaudin, 4 Rue Pierre-Wacquant, 92190 Meudon.
T. 0146266282. 045521
Roy, Guillaume, 23 Blvd Nations-Unies, 92190 Meudon.
T. 0146231122. 045522
Setruk, Guy Laurent, 16 Blvd Nations-Unies, 92190
Meudon. T. 0145072030. - Ant / Furn - 045523

Meulan (Yvelines)
Antinéa, 12 Rue Challan, 78250 Meulan.
T. 0130914200. 045524
Antiquités Chrétien, 8 Quai Arquebuse, 78250 Meulan.
T. 0134747872. 045525

Meung-sur-Loire (Loiret)
Garmilla, Jean-Michel, 12 Rue 8-Mai-1945, 45130
Meung-sur-Loire. T. 0238442379. 045526
Jérôme, Jean-Luc, 7 Rue Général-de-Gaulle, 45130
Meung-sur-Loire. T. 0238447903. 045527
Porte d'Amont, 1 Rue Jean-Morin, 45130 Meung-sur-
Loire. T. 0238447971. 045528
Ronssin, Jean-Loup, 43 Rue Général-de-Gaulle, 45130
Meung-sur-Loire. T. 0238444688. 045529

Meursac (Charente-Maritime)
Menier, Michel, Les Epeaux, 17120 Meursac.
T. 0546916683. 045530

Meursault (Côte-d'Or)
Dussort, Maurice, 12 Rue Charles-Giraud, 21190 Meur-
sault. T. 0380216075. 045531

Meylan (Isère)
Michel Antiquités, 23 Chemin Chaumetière, 38240 Meylan. T. 0476410343. - Furn - 045532

Meymac (Corrèze)
Giron, Jeanne, Les Quatre Routes, 19250 Meymac.
T. 0555951212. 045533

Meyriat (Ain)
Pilloud, Eliane, Bohas, 01250 Meyriat. T. 0474518173.
- Ant / Instr / Cur - 045534

Meyrueis (Lozère)
Trésors de la Lozère, Rue Pont-Vieux, 48150 Meyrueis.
T. 0466456060. 045535

Mézy-sur-Seine (Yvelines)
Bouvier, Antoni, Pl des Tilleuls, 78250 Mézy-sur-Seine.
T. 0134740190. - Ant - 045536

Migné (Indre)
Nogrette, Robert, 2 Rte Rosnay-Bonnière, 36800 Migné.
T. 0254378728. 045537

Millau (Aveyron)
Alauzet, Yvon, 22 Av Jean-Jaurès, 12100 Millau.
T. 0565601312. - Ant - 045538
Alauzet, Yvon, 25 Blvd Ayrolle, 12100 Millau.
T. 0565601039. - Ant - 045539
Albanella, 9 Rue Peyrollerie, 12100 Millau.
T. 0565610371. 045540
Bousquel, Alain, 39 Rue Droite, 12100 Millau.
T. 0565608282. 045541
Crouzat, Marie-Rose, 13 Blvd Bonald, 12100 Millau.
T. 0565605075. - Furn / Cur - 045542
Dardenne, Robert, Rue Pont-de-la-Cabre, 12100 Millau.
T. 0565603683. 045543
Dejean, Geneviève, 5 Av République, 12100 Millau.
T. 0565600147. - Furn / Dec / Cur - 045544
Eucher, Micheline, 419 Chemin Viastels, 12100 Millau.
T. 0565601215. 045545
Sahuquet, Philippe, 17 Blvd Saint-Antoine, 12100 Mil-
lau. T. 0565610905. 045546
Storbecher, Daniel, 5 Pl Maréchal-Foch, 12100 Millau.
T. 0565600223. - Ant - 045547

Milly-la-Forêt (Essonne)
Aurélia, 26 Pl Marché, 91490 Milly-la-Forêt.
T. 0164989765. 045548
Aux Epoques, 45 Pl Marché, 91490 Milly-la-Forêt.
T. 0164908444. 045549
Milly, 44 Rue Jean-Cocteau, 91490 Milly-la-Forêt.
T. 0164947410. 045550

Miniac-Morvan (Ille-et-Vilaine)
Lebret, Jean-Louis, Rue Général-de-Gaulle, 35540 Mi-
niac-Morvan. T. 0299585784. 045551

Miramas (Bouches-du-Rhône)
Picard, Monique, 10 Rue Ecoles, 13140 Miramas.
T. 0490500945. - Furn / Tex / Lights / Cur - 045552

Miramont-de-Guyenne (Lot-et-Garonne)
Brunie, Arlette, 6 Rue Jasmin, 47800 Miramont-de-
Guyenne. T. 0553933071. 045553
Cougouille, Serge, 20 Av Paris, 47800 Miramont-de-
Guyenne. T. 0553932211. 045554

Mirande (Gers)
Ténat, René, 9 Rue Gambetta, 32300 Mirande.
T. 0562665398. 045555

Mirepoix (Ariège)
Leduc, Marie, 1 Rue Béal, 09500 Mirepoix.
T. 0561688103. 045556
Tort, Andrée, 5bis Cours Docteur-Chabaud, 09500 Mire-
poix. T. 0561682057. 045557

Miribel (Ain)
Aux Trésors de Grand-Mère, Chemin Belmont-Mas-Ril-
lier, 01700 Miribel. T. 0478553344. - Ant - 045558

Misy-sur-Yonne (Seine-et-Marne)
Millot, Danielle, 26 Rue Grande, 77130 Misy-sur-Yonne.
T. 64312482. 045559

Mitry-Mory (Seine-et-Marne)
Abecassis, Maxime, 56 Av Navarre, 77290 Mitry-Mory.
T. 64678658. 045560

Modane (Savoie)
Favre Antiquité Brocante, 25 Rue République, 73500
Modane. T. 0479050535. - Ant - 045561

Moings (Charente-Maritime)
De la Cave au Grenier, Rte Archiac, 17500 Moings.
T. 0546480919. 045562

Moissac (Tarn-et-Garonne)
Destang, 13 Av Maréchal-de-Lattre-de-Tassigny, 82200
Moissac. T. 0563322249. - Paint / Furn / Cur - 045563
Fournié, Jean-Marc, 1 Rue Daubasse, 82200 Moissac.
T. 0563043102. - Furn - 045564
Sainte-Marie, Jean-Louis, 6 Rue Guilleran, 82200 Mois-
sac. T. 0563040093. 045565

Molompize (Cantal)
Delorme, Bernard, Le Bourg, 15500 Molompize.
T. 0471736305. 045566

Monbalen (Lot-et-Garonne)
Mengès, Gérard, Larricharde-Bas, 47340 Monbalen.
T. 0553417115. 045567

Moncé-en-Belin (Sarthe)
Maison de l'Antiquité, La Belle Etoile RN 23, 72230
Moncé-en-Belin. T. 0243211360. - Ant - 045568

Moncetz-Longevas (Marne)
Lallement, RN 44, 51470 Moncetz-Longevas.
T. 0326675254, Fax 0326675462. - Dec - 045569

Moncontour-de-Bretagne (Côtes-d'Armor)
Papegault, 4 Rue Porte-d'en-Haut, 22510 Moncontour-
de-Bretagne. T. 0296734814. 045570

Mondeville (Calvados)
Harrod's, Rte Paris, ZI, 14120 Mondeville.
T. 0231347200, Fax 0231844080. 045571
Marchand, Pierre, 59 Rte Paris, 14120 Mondeville.
T. 0231781545. 045572

Mondonville (Haute-Garonne)
Roques, Teddy, Chemin de la Cornague, 31700 Mondon-
ville. T. 0561852443. - Paint / Furn / Cur - 045573

Mondoubleau (Loir-et-Cher)
Brocante de la Tour, 6 Pl Marché, 41170 Mondoubleau.
T. 0254807581. 045574
Brocante de la Tour, 3 Rue Edouard-Bezard, 41170
Mondoubleau. T. 0254807581. 045575

Mondreville (Yvelines)
Chalvignac, Pierre, Rte Nationale, 78980 Mondreville.
T. 0130425220. 045576

Monflanquin (Lot-et-Garonne)
Lanteiron, Marie-Agnès, Pl Arcades, 47150 Monflanquin. T. 0553364458. 045577

Monnières (Loire-Atlantique)
Antiquités du Pont, 7 Rue Sèvre, 44690 Monnières.
T. 40546485. 045578

Mons (Charente-Maritime)
Rose des Vents, 12 Rue Poirier-Vert-Tacherie, 17160
Mons. T. 0546250359. 045579

Mons (Gard)
Almeras, Jacky, Rte Alès-Uzès, Le Grand-Chêne, 30340
Mons. T. 0466831487, Fax 0466837334. 045580

Mont-de-Marsan (Landes)
Antiquités, 26 All Brouchet, 40000 Mont-de-Marsan.
T. 0558754145. 045581
Barbier-Cassone, Maryse, 13 Av Sadi-Carnot, 40000
Mont-de-Marsan. T. 0558752752. 045582
Brocante du Sablar, 9 Pl Jean-Jaurès, 40000 Mont-de-
Marsan. T. 0558060740. 045583

Duret & Simoneau, 5 Rue Armand-Dulamon, 40000 Mont-de-Marsan. T. 0558059141. - Paint / Furn - *045584*

Vigier, 1 Rue André-Degoul, 40000 Mont-de-Marsan. T. 0558752264. - Tex - *045585*

Mont-Saint-Aignan (Seine-Maritime)
Antiquités Brocante Filentroc, Pl Colbert, Centre Commercial, 76130 Mont-Saint-Aignan. T. 0235980687. *045586*

Orange Bleue, 31 Rue Edouard-Fortier, 76130 Mont-Saint-Aignan. T. 0235076567. *045587*

Mont-Saint-Martin (Meurthe-et-Moselle)
Au Vieux Fiacre, 25 Rue Pasteur, 54350 Mont-Saint-Martin. T. 0382237915. *045588*

Mont-sous-Vaudrey (Jura)
Godard-Bruand, D., 12 Rue Jules-Grévy, 39380 Mont-sous-Vaudrey. T. 0384717250. *045589*

Montady (Hérault)
Tarrago, Georges, Av Béziers, 34310 Montady. T. 0467905053. *045590*

Tarrago, Nicole & Jean-Louis Berjoan, Av Béziers, 34310 Montady. T. 0467905053. - Ant - *045591*

Montagnieu (Ain)
Varvier, Patrice, Pl de la Mairie, 01470 Montagnieu. T. 0474367755. - Ant - *045592*

Montaigu (Vendée)
Girard, Michel, 56 Av Villebois-Mareuil, 85600 Montaigu. T. 0251940666. *045593*

Picaud, Marc, 45 Av Villebois-Mareuil, 85600 Montaigu. T. 0251488449. *045594*

Montalzat (Tarn-et-Garonne)
Garcia, RN 20, 82270 Montalzat. T. 0563931266. - Furn - *045595*

Montamise (Vienne)
Baudinière, René, D3 Rte Bonneuil-Matours, 86360 Montamise. T. 0549449122. - Ant / Furn - *045596*

Montapas (Nièvre)
Antiq'Art, Saint-Bénin-des-Champs, 58110 Montapas. T. 0386582022. - Furn / Dec / Cur - *045597*

Montargis (Loiret)
Aux Dénicheurs, 19 Rue Loing, 45200 Montargis. T. 0238851632. - Furn / Cur - *045598*

Bernardin, Xavier, 19 Rue Pêcherie, 45200 Montargis. T. 0238856963. *045599*

Dépôt 45 Montargis, 5 Rue Fbg-de-la-Chaussée, 45200 Montargis. T. 0238980934. *045600*

Macon, Jacques, 19 Rue Pêcherie, 45200 Montargis. T. 0238891061. *045601*

Thorez, Liliane, 79 Rue André-Coquillet, 45200 Montargis. T. 0238850039. *045602*

Montauban (Tarn-et-Garonne)
Abbaye Brocante, 7 Rue Carmes, 82000 Montauban. T. 0563630185. - Paint / Furn / Cur - *045603*

Abbaye Brocante, 3 Rue Elie, 82000 Montauban. T. 0563634151. - Paint / Furn / Cur - *045604*

Artous, Paul & Fils, Imp Blancous, 82000 Montauban. T. 0563030936. *045605*

Bonheur du Jour, 1 Rue Princesse, 82000 Montauban. T. 0563667790. *045606*

Bores, Emile, 30 Rue Jules-Ferry, 82000 Montauban. T. 0563633734. *045607*

Chris'Antica, 901 Rue Pater, 82000 Montauban. T. 0563201983. - Paint / Furn / Cur - *045608*

Dufor Quercy, Michel, 8 Pl Franklin-Roosevelt, 82000 Montauban. T. 0563630293. *045609*

Gomez, M., 5 Av 11ème-RI, 82000 Montauban. T. 0563032834. - Furn / Cur - *045610*

Hottin, Sonia, 9 Rue Elie, 82000 Montauban. T. 0563203077. *045611*

Laurens, Paulette, 128 Rte Molières, 82000 Montauban. T. 0563032044. *045612*

Le Bars, 4 Rue Elie, 82000 Montauban. T. 0563200729. *045613*

Le Bars, 16 Rue Princesse, 82000 Montauban. T. 0563634139. *045614*

Rouges, Alain, 97 Grand Rue Sapiac, 82000 Montauban. T. 0563663680. *045615*

Verdier, Pierre, 930 Rue Abbaye, 82000 Montauban. T. 0563633223. *045616*

Montaure (Eure)
Labiche, Nicole, 31 Rue Pasteur, 27400 Montaure. T. 0232259007. *045617*

Montauroux (Var)
Ballade en Jadis, RD 562, 83440 Montauroux. T. 0494857622, Fax 0494857623. *045618*

Joana Village, Grenier Artisanal, Quartier Plan Occidental, 83440 Montauroux. T. 0494857953. *045619*

Terme Saint-Eloi, RD 562, Quartier Plan Oriental, 83440 Montauroux. T. 0494765133. - Ant - *045620*

Montbard (Côte-d'Or)
Bouhin, Jean-Michel, Pl Buffon, 21500 Montbard. T. 0380921079. *045621*

Montbartier (Tarn-et-Garonne)
Lubin, Jocelyne, Combemale, 82700 Montbartier. T. 0563305377. *045622*

Montbéliard (Doubs)
Rerat, Alexis, 19 Av Wilson, 25200 Montbéliard. T. 0381910017. *045623*

Montbonnot-Saint-Martin (Isère)
Objet Direct, 562 Rue Général-de-Gaulle, 38330 Montbonnot-Saint-Martin. T. 0476906694. - Ant - *045624*

Montboyer (Charente)
Torregrossa, Ernest, Jardronne, 16620 Montboyer. T. 0545982987. *045625*

Montbrison (Loire)
Gauchet, Gérard, 10bis Av Libération, 42600 Montbrison. T. 0477580889, Fax 0477588214. - Ant / Furn / Tex / Paint / Glass - *045626*

Harter, Jamil, 9 Blvd Chavassieu, 42600 Montbrison. T. 0477587114. *045627*

Harter, Jean, Rte Nouvelle-Estiallet, 42600 Montbrison. T. 0477581265. *045628*

Montceau-les-Mines (Saône-et-Loire)
Bouchelier Antiquités, 31 Rue Jean-Didier, 71300 Montceau-les-Mines. T. 0385585965. - Ant - *045629*

Durand, Guy, 52 Rue Bruyère, 71300 Montceau-les-Mines. T. 0385570311. - Ant - *045630*

Tanagra, 27 Rue République, 71300 Montceau-les-Mines. T. 0385572655. - Ant - *045631*

Montcel (Puy-de-Dôme)
Godard, Antoine, Lavaure, 63460 Montcel. T. 0473330478. - Ant / Furn - *045632*

Montcenis (Saône-et-Loire)
Boutique d'Antan, 24 Rue Basse, 71710 Montcenis. T. 0385803397. - Ant - *045633*

Monteaux (Loir-et-Cher)
Marand, Claudine, 46 Rte Mesland, Le Portail, 41150 Monteaux. T. 0254702079, Fax 0254702089. *045634*

Montebourg (Manche)
Lefèbvre, Jacques, 38 Rue Général-Leclerc, 50310 Montebourg. T. 0233412485. *045635*

Montélimar (Drôme)
Bernard, Jean-Claude, 60 Rte Saint-Gervais, 26200 Montélimar. T. 0475511574. *045636*

Brocante Saint-Martin, 1 Pl Saint-Martin, 26200 Montélimar. T. 0475537901. *045637*

Deymier, Michel, 120 Av Jean-Jaurès, 26200 Montélimar. T. 0475013624. *045638*

Gillet, Jean-Pierre, 15 Rue Saint-Gaucher, 26200 Montélimar. T. 0475519429. *045639*

Goguel de Toux, Michel, 175 Rte Marseille, 26200 Montélimar. T. 0475014793. *045640*

Grenier du Chapeau Rouge, Pl Léopold-Blanc, 26200 Montélimar. T. 0475015016. *045641*

Lanthelme, Gérard, 25 Rue Saint-Martin, Le Prado, 26200 Montélimar. T. 0475011608. - Paint / Furn / Cur - *045642*

Montereau-Fault-Yonne (Seine-et-Marne)
Jessa, Denise, 15 Rue Docteur-Arthur-Petit, 77130 Montereau-Fault-Yonne. T. 64329132. - China / Cur - *045643*

Montesson (Yvelines)
Parfums du Passé, 6 Av Aristide-Briand, 78360 Montesson. T. 0130714284. *045644*

Renault, Frédéric, 247 Av Gabriel-Péri, 78360 Montesson. T. 0139151368. *045645*

Montfort-en-Chalosse (Landes)
Andrau, Michel, Grand Rue, 40380 Montfort-en-Chalosse. T. 0558986006. *045646*

Montfort-l'Amaury (Yvelines)
Bouquet-Jacoillot, 3 Rue Dion, 78490 Montfort-l'Amaury. T. 0134860297. *045647*

British Gallery, 5 Rue Normande, 78490 Montfort-l'Amaury. T. 0134868575. *045648*

Turiaf, Bernard, 45 Rue Paris, 78490 Montfort-l'Amaury. T. 0134869180. *045649*

Montgeron (Essonne)
Mayer, Michel, 33 Chemin Dessous-du-Luet, 91230 Montgeron. T. 0169403521. *045650*

Montgiscard (Haute-Garonne)
Bensussan, Gérard, RN 113, 31450 Montgiscard. T. 0561811068. *045651*

Sainte-Lauragaise d'Antiquité Bâtiment, 11 Lot Lotge, 31450 Montgiscard. T. 0561279557. *045652*

Montguyon (Charente-Maritime)
Poirrier, Christian, Montguyon, 17270 Montguyon. T. 0546044329. *045653*

Monthou-sur-Bièvre (Loir-et-Cher)
Ehrhardt, Gustave, 35 Rte Montrichard, 41120 Monthou-sur-Bièvre. T. 0254441254. *045654*

Montigny (Seine-Maritime)
Duhamel, Laurence, Rue du Gré, 76380 Montigny. T. 0235360048. *045655*

Montigny-les-Jongleurs (Somme)
Bergerau, Philippe, 18 Rue Principale, 80370 Montigny-les-Jongleurs. T. 0322327001. - Ant - *045656*

Navarro, Françoise, 18 Rue Principale, 80370 Montigny-les-Jongleurs. T. 0322327920. - Ant - *045657*

Montigny-lès-Metz (Moselle)
Bajolet, L.Ch., 93 Rte Pont-à-Mousson, 57158 Montigny-lès-Metz. T. 0387669707. - Furn / Cur - *045658*

Carabinier, 229 Rue Pont-à-Mousson, 57158 Montigny-lès-Metz. T. 0387669532. *045659*

Piccadaci, Lilo, 44 Rue Gibet, 57158 Montigny-lès-Metz. T. 0387550799. - Ant - *045660*

Montigny-sur-Loing (Seine-et-Marne)
Denis, Francisco, 34 Av Gare, 77690 Montigny-sur-Loing. T. 64456684. - Furn - *045661*

Montivilliers (Seine-Maritime)
A la Brocante des Hallettes, 5 Pl Docteur-Chevalier, 76290 Montivilliers. T. 0235550251. *045662*

Blondel, Didier, 8 Pl Docteur-Chevallier, 76290 Montivilliers. T. 0235550251. *045663*

Montlay-en-Auxois (Côte-d'Or)
Au Temps Jadis, Village, 21210 Montlay-en-Auxois. T. 0380644111. *045664*

Montlhéry (Essonne)
Aiguière de Cuivre, 37 Rte Orléans, RN 20, 91310 Montlhéry. T. 0169010103. *045665*

Montlouis-sur-Loire (Indre-et-Loire)
A.M.J.P. Antiquités, 16 Rue Pierre-Maître, 37270 Montlouis-sur-Loire. T. 0547508046. *045666*

Montluçon (Allier)
Arrieta, 19 Pass Barathon, 03100 Montluçon.
T. 0470039905. - Ant -   045667
Baroucheix d'Alembert, 20 Rue d'Alembert, 03100
Montluçon. T. 0470059850. - Ant / Furn -   045668
Bernadines, 6 Rue Joseph-Chantemille, 03100 Montlu-
çon. T. 0470058512. - Ant -   045669
Clément, 1 Rue Pierre-Petit, 03100 Montluçon.
T. 07055630. - Ant / Furn -   045670
Galerie Sainte-Marie, 4 Pl Sainte-Marie, 03100 Montlu-
çon. T. 0470053870. - Ant / Furn -   045671
Lacarin, 5, rue des r-Piliers, 03100 Montluçon.
T. 0470050542. - Ant -   045672
Montjoye, Hugues des, 4 Pl Sainte-Marie, 03100 Mont-
luçon. T. 0470051972. - Ant -   045673
Picaud, Jean, 10 Rue des Cinq-Piliers, 03100 Montlu-
çon. T. 0470290420. - Ant / Furn -   045674
Serveau, Monique, 7 Pl Saint-Pierre, 03100 Montluçon.
T. 0470283049. - Ant -   045675

Montluel (Ain)
Perrier, Raymond, 1350 Rte Nationale La Boisse, 01120
Montluel. T. 0478061663. - Ant -   045676

Montmarault (Allier)
Billon, 1 Rte de Montluçon, 03390 Montmarault.
T. 0470076669. - Furn -   045677
Renaud, Valérie, Les Bégaud, 03390 Montmarault.
T. 0470076884. - Ant -   045678

Montmirail (Sarthe)
Oiseau d'Or, Villemoreau, 72570 Montmirail.
T. 0243719010. - Ant -   045679

Montmorency (Val-d'Oise)
Beauvais, Séverine, 8 Rue du Docteur-Demirleau,
95160 Montmorency. T. 0139642402. - Ant /
Furn -   045680
Gullleray, Christian, 88 Av Division-Leclerc, 95160
Montmorency. T. 0134172109.   045681

Montmorot (Jura)
Salle des Ventes des Particuliers, 38 Av Pasteur, 39570
Montmorot. T. 0384245661. - Ant -   045682
Vichot, Corboz, Le Murger Savagna, 39570 Montmorot.
T. 0384472634.   045683

Montoire-sur-le-Loir (Loir-et-Cher)
Maupas, Catherine, 10 Rue Saint-Jacques, 41800 Mon-
toire-sur-le-Loir. T. 0254852718.   045684
Tabouret, 35 Pl Clemenceau, 41800 Montoire-sur-le-
Loir. T. 0254866653.   045685

Montpellier (Hérault)
Agniel, 30 Rue Chaptal, 34000 Montpellier.
T. 0467584729.   045686
Ailes du Temps, Val de Croze, 72 Rue Sichuan, 34000
Montpellier. T. 0467273277, Fax 0467274043. 045687
Allasio, Claude, 7 Cours Gambetta, 34000 Montpellier.
T. 0467581366.   045688
Anagramme, 5 Rue Gagne-Petit, 34000 Montpellier.
T. 0467527384. - Pho -   045689
Antea, 20 Rue Sainte-Anne, 34000 Montpellier.
T. 0467604210.   045690
Antiquités du Corum, 7 Av Nîmes, RN 113, 34000 Mont-
pellier. T. 0467725070.   045691
Antiquités-Galerie Jean-Jaurès, Pl Jean-Jaurès, 34000
Montpellier. T. 0467663334. - Paint / Sculp / Dec /
Mil -   045692
Antiquités Le Grenier, 17 Cours Gambetta, 34000 Mont-
pellier. T. 0467587865.   045693
Archéologie Monnaie, 18 Rue Palais, 34000 Montpellier.
T. 0467660292, Fax 0467609328. - Paint /
Num -   045694
Bénédictis, Henri de, 14 Rue Gignac, 34080 Montpellier.
T. 0467455420.   045695
Brocantique, 17 Blvd Louis-Blanc, 34000 Montpellier.
T. 0467729928.   045696
Catherine, Jean, 37 Rue de l'Aiguillerie, 34600 Montpel-
lier. T. 0467605210.   045697
Cazes, Jean-Pierre, 2 Rue Jules-Latreilhe, 34000 Mont-
pellier. T. 0467608957.   045698
Clicot, Marie, 15 Blvd Jeu-de-Paume, 34000 Montpel-
lier. T. 0467662903. - Furn -   045699

Fischer, Daniel, 17 Rue Fbg-Nîmes, 34000 Montpellier.
T. 0467720963.   045700
Foucher, Philippe, 11 Rue Palais-des-Guilhem, 34000
Montpellier. T. 0467660036.   045701
Galerie de l'Isle, 1 Rue Vallat, 34000 Montpellier.
T. 0467662124.   045702
Galerie des Guilhems, 6 Rue Plan-Palais, 34000 Mont-
pellier. T. 0467663444.   045703
Galerie du Peyrou, 17 Rue du Palais, 34000 Montpellier.
T. 0467661578. - Ant -   045704
Galerie Saint-Firmin, 10 Rue Saint-Firmin, 34000 Mont-
pellier. T. 0467660918.   045705
Galuchat, 20 Rue Fontaine, 34000 Montpellier.
T. 0467607215.   045706
Garric, Michel, 1 Rue Albisson, 34000 Montpellier.
T. 0467662551.   045707
Glénat, 5 Rue Aiguillerie, 34000 Montpellier.
T. 0467663440. - Graph -   045708
Gresse, Monique, 3 Rue Cambiadours, 34070 Montpel-
lier. T. 0467278760.   045709
Gresse, Monique, 12 Pl Sainte-Anne, 34070 Montpellier.
T. 0467606221.   045710
Guedot, Bernard, 1bis Rue Four-des-Flammes, 34000
Montpellier. T. 0467607744.   045711
Jeanjean, Gisèle, 1 Rue Puits-du-Temple, 34000 Mont-
pellier. T. 0467527256.   045712
Marc, Jean-Pierre, 3 Rue Embouque-d'Or, 34000 Mont-
pellier. T. 0467663790.   045713
Martin, Michel, 14 Rue de Belfort, 34000 Montpellier.
T. 0467 92 56 43. - Ant -   045714
Meubl'Occase, 21 Cours Gambetta, 34000 Montpellier.
T. 0467928764. - Ant -   045715
Molina, Michel, 1 Imp Saint-Côme, 34000 Montpellier.
T. 0467660741.   045716
Randon, Guillaume, 2 Rue Hôtel-de-Ville, 34000 Mont-
pellier. T. 0467663780.   045717
Romieu, Monique, 5 Rue Plan-Palais, 34000 Montpellier.
T. 0467660110.   045718
Rouayroux, Jean-Pierre, 17 Rue Palais, 34000 Montpel-
lier. T. 0467661678. - Paint / Furn / Tex - 045719
Soulier, Marc, 6 Rue Palais-des-Guilhem, 34000 Mont-
pellier. T. 0467604681.   045720
Thérond, Pierre, 38 Blvd Renouvier, 34000 Montpellier.
T. 0467923780.   045721
Varon, Vidal, 16 Rue Thérèse, 34000 Montpellier.
T. 0467723123, Fax 0467022187. - Ant -   045722
Verdier, Bernard, 5 Pl Canourgue, 34000 Montpellier.
T. 0467529059.   045723
Villet, Guilhem, 21 Rue Palais-des-Guilhem, 34000
Montpellier. T. 0467663628.   045724

Montpouillan (Lot-et-Garonne)
Lefranc, Valérie, Lomenie, 47200 Montpouillan.
T. 0553207492.   045725

Montréal-du-Gers (Gers)
Brocante des Cornières, 4 Pl Hôtel-de-Ville, 32250
Montréal-du-Gers. T. 0562294991.   045726

Montréal-la-Cluse (Ain)
Balland, Henri, 54 Rue Savoies, 01460 Montréal-la-
Cluse. T. 0474760320. - Ant -   045727
Coulon, Maurice, 58 Rue Savoies, 01460 Montréal-la-
Cluse. T. 0474761587. - Ant -   045728
Eventail-des-Siècles, 58 Rue des Savoies, 01460 Mont-
réal-la-Cluse. T. 0474761587. - Ant -   045729
Maréchal Antiquité Brocante, 20 Rue du Maquis, 01460
Montréal-la-Cluse. T. 0474760271. - Ant - 045730
Zanol, Alain, 45 Rue Ville, 01460 Montréal-la-Cluse.
T. 0474760174. - Ant -   045731

Montréjeau (Haute-Garonne)
Lloan, Janine, 22 Av Saint-Gaudens, 31210 Montréjeau.
T. 0561956750.   045732
Saulneron, Patrick, 2 Av Tarbes, 31210 Montréjeau.
T. 0561957625.   045733

Montreuil (Seine-Saint-Denis)
Liss, L., 14 Rue Roulettes, 93100 Montreuil.
T. 0142870595.   045734
Vialade, Eric, 2 Rue Lagny, 93100 Montreuil.
T. 0148515104.   045735

Montreuil-aux-Lions (Aisne)
Brocante des Templiers, 27 Av Paris, 02310 Montreuil-
aux-Lions. T. 0323742279. - Ant -   045736

Montreuil-Bellay (Maine-et-Loire)
Albisetti, Sylvie, 42 Pl Marché, 49260 Montreuil-Bellay.
T. 41387163.   045737
Deschamps, Jean-Pierre, 44 Rue Porte-Saint-Jean,
49260 Montreuil-Bellay. T. 41523590.   045738
Galerie des Petits Carreaux, 8 Pl Marché, 49260 Mon-
treuil-Bellay. T. 41387287.   045739

Montreuil-l'Argillé (Eure)
Lapré, Patrick, 34 Rue Grande, 27390 Montreuil-l'Ar-
gillé. T. 0232445155.   045740

Montreuil-sous-Bois (Seine-Saint-Den-is)
Caron, Daniel, 98 Rue Edouard-Vaillant, 93100 Montreu-
il-sous-Bois. T. 0148701300.   045741

Montreuil-sur-Mer (Pas-de-Calais)
A la Cour de France, 81 Rue Pierre-Ledent, 62170 Montreuil-sur-Mer. T. 0321817513.   045742

Montrevault (Maine-et-Loire)
Guinhut, Daniel, 24 Rue Saint-Nicolas, 49110 Montre-
vault. T. 41301030. - Ant -   045743

Montrichard (Loir-et-Cher)
Romanet, Jeannine, 11 Rue Pont, 41400 Montrichard.
T. 0254326538.   045744

Montrond-les-Bains (Loire)
Mallet, Edith, 29 Les Vincents, 42210 Montrond-les-
Bains. T. 0477548946.   045745

Montrouge (Hauts-de-Seine)
Amarante, 22 Rue Gabriel-Péri, 92120 Montrouge.
T. 0146578824.   045746
Artcol, 2 Cité Rondelet, 92120 Montrouge.
T. 0146551761.   045747
Bric à Brac, 31 Rue Racine, 92120 Montrouge.
T. 0142536386.   045748
Burguet, Monique, 128 Rue Maurice-Arnoux, 92120
Montrouge. T. 0146541288.   045749
Delotte, Alain, 46 et 95 Av République, 92120 Montrou-
ge. T. 0142530266.   045750

Montsoreau (Maine-et-Loire)
Borel, Odile, 4 Quai Alexandre-Dumas, 49730 Montso-
reau. T. 41517921. - Furn / Glass / Cur - 045751

Montvendre (Drôme)
Maccari, Patrick, Domaine Villeplat, 26120 Montvendre.
T. 0475592003.   045752

Morancez (Eure-et-Loir)
Foscolo, Patrick, 28 Rue Chartres, 28630 Morancez.
T. 0237352221, Fax 0237910071.   045753

Moret-sur-Loing (Seine-et-Marne)
Brocante du Champs de Mars, 12 Rue Edmond-Dupray,
77250 Moret-sur-Loing. T. 64311322.   045754
Christol, Noélie, 22 Rue Pêcherie, 77250 Moret-sur-
Loing. T. 0360705098.   045755
Grenier Moretain, 30 Rue Peintre-Sislay, 77250 Moret-
sur-Loing. T. 0360704870.   045756
Hassler, Christian, 39 Rue Grande, 77250 Moret-sur-
Loing. T. 0160701495. - Ant -   045757

Morlaix (Finistère)
Belle Epoque, 11 Ven-Archers, 29600 Morlaix.
T. 0298620869. - Ant -   045758
Tréanton, 40 Rue de Paris, 29210 Morlaix.
T. 0298880782. - Ant -   045759

Morre (Doubs)
Galland, Jean-Luc, 2 Rte Lausanne, 25660 Morre.
T. 0381811910.   045760

Morschwiller-le-Bas (Haut-Rhin)
Diaz, Jean-Louis, 21 Rue 1ère-Armée-Française, 68790
Morschwiller-le-Bas. T. 0389430859.   045761

Mortagne-au-Perche (Orne)

Besnard, Michel, 55 Rue Rouen, 61400 Mortagne-au-Perche. T. 0233250141. - Ant - 045762
Bry, François, 31 Rue des Déportés, 61400 Mortagne-au-Perche. T. 0233250399, Fax 0233250399.
- Furn - 045763
Juillard, Marcel, 18 Rue Fbg-Saint-Eloi, 61400 Mortagne-au-Perche. T. 0233251668. - Ant - 045764

Mortcerf (Seine-et-Marne)

Loirat, Christian, 21 Rue de Paris, 77163 Mortcerf.
T. 64043059. 045765

Mougins (Alpes-Maritimes)

Azaïs, Jean, 220 Chemin Fassum, 06250 Mougins.
T. 0493900318. - Mil - 045766
Cremaillère, 463 Av Maréchal-Alphonse-Juin, 06250 Mougins. T. 0493900212. 045767
French Country Living, 2 Rue Muriers, 06250 Mougins.
T. 0493755303, Fax 0493756303. 045768
Heid, Denis, 91 Av Général-de-Gaulle, 06250 Mougins.
T. 0493751662. 045769
Iris, 91 Av Général-de-Gaulle, 06250 Mougins.
T. 0493751875, Fax 0492920473. - Furn - 045770
Mougins Antiquités, 1 Rue Honoré-Henry, 06250 Mougins. T. 0493900508, Fax 0493752157. 045771
Ranc Antiquités, 19 Rue Orfèvres, 06250 Mougins.
T. 0493901388. 045772

Mouilleron-en-Pareds (Vendée)

Allsop, Jonathan, Le Grenouillet, 85390 Mouilleron-en-Pareds. T. 0251003256. - Paint / Furn / Cur - 045773

Mouleydier (Dordogne)

Brac, Jean, Rte Lalinde, 241520 Mouleydier.
T. 0553232306. 045774

Moulins (Allier)

Barale, Paula, 18 Rue Fraternité, 03000 Moulins.
T. 0470449593. - Ant - 045775
Beauger, Jacques, 9 Rue Pont, 03000 Moulins.
T. 0470443337. - Ant - 045776
Bitouzet, Léon, 8 Rue Four, 03000 Moulins.
T. 0470446966. - Ant - 045777
Catala, Pierre-Yves, 28 Pl Vosges, 03000 Moulins.
T. 0470206925. - Ant - 045778
Hall du Particulier, 10 Rue Villars, 03000 Moulins.
T. 0470464792. - Ant - 045779
Jousse, Michel, 6 Pl Vosges, 03000 Moulins.
T. 0470202868. - Ant - 045780
Lemaire, Régis, 50 Rue Fraternité, 03000 Moulins.
T. 0470209561. - Ant - 045781
Millerault, Gilles-Claude, 76 Rue du Pont-Ginguet, 03000 Moulins. T. 0470460334. - Ant - 045782
Paquier, Georges, Château-de-Segange-Avermes, 03000 Moulins. T. 0470440663. - Ant - 045783
Pellegrino, Jean-Claude, 5 Rue Pasteur, 03000 Moulins.
T. 0470443322. - Ant - 045784

Mouriès (Bouches-du-Rhône)

Art du Temps, 44 Rue Roger-Salengro, 13890 Mouriès.
T. 0490475050. 045785

Mouroux (Seine-et-Marne)

Edé, Gérard, La Belle Croix, 1520 Av Paris, 77120 Mouroux. T. 0164030887. - Furn / Mul - 045786

Moutiers-Tarentaise (Savoie)

Boix-Vives, Michel, 83 Rue Sainte-Marie, 73600 Moutiers-Tarentaise. T. 0479240335, Fax 0479240410.
- Ant / Furn - 045787

Muides-sur-Loire (Loir-et-Cher)

Wartelle, Sylvie, 17 Rte Nationale, 41500 Muides-sur-Loire. T. 0254870008. 045788

Mulhouse (Haut-Rhin)

Alsaticarta, 31 Av Clemenceau, 68100 Mulhouse.
T. 0389461357. - Paint - 045789
Altkirch Antiquités, 25 Rue Josué-Hofer, 68200 Mulhouse. T. 0389421225. 045790
Arbalète Antiquités, 10 Rue Loi, 68100 Mulhouse.
T. 0389454979. - Paint / Furn / Cur - 045791
Armand, 4 Rue Couvent, 68100 Mulhouse.
T. 0389463762. - Paint / Furn / Cur - 045792

Aux Charmes d'Antan, 11 Rue Louis-Pasteur, 68100 Mulhouse. T. 0389661475. - Furn / Dec / Silv / Lights / Cur - 045793
Berger, 28 Rue Barrière, 68200 Mulhouse.
T. 0389322667. - Furn / Cur - 045794
Bibelot, 5 Rue Synagogue, 68100 Mulhouse.
T. 0389457745. 045795
Boîte Antique, 3 Pl Concorde, 68100 Mulhouse.
T. 0389460570. - Paint / Furn / Cur - 045796
Frank, Jean, 35 Rue Tanneurs, 68100 Mulhouse.
T. 0389452566. 045797
Ghazarian, 5 Pl Paix, 68100 Mulhouse.
T. 0389562144. 045798
Ghazarian, 3 Rue Raisin, 68100 Mulhouse.
T. 0389661630. 045799
Klein, Bertrand, 17 et 19 Rue Tanneurs, 68100 Mulhouse. T. 0389465141. - Ant / Furn - 045800
Krebs, Robert, 25 Rue Josué-Hofer, 68200 Mulhouse.
T. 0389431323. 045801
Larchèle, 25 Rue Josué-Hofer, 68200 Mulhouse.
T. 0389423570. 045802
Michel, Jean-Louis, 10 Rue Loi, 68100 Mulhouse.
T. 0389454979. 045803
Neff, Charles, 21 Rue Synagogue, 68100 Mulhouse.
T. 0389466138. - Paint / Furn / Num / Arch / Lights / Instr / Mil / Cur / Toys - 045804
Paoletti-Bianelli, Noël, 25 Rue Josué-Hofer, 68200 Mulhouse. T. 0389431667. 045805
Roesch, Fabiola, 25 Rue Josué-Hofer, 68200 Mulhouse.
T. 0389597407. 045806
Trocante, 25 Rue Josué-Hofer, 68200 Mulhouse.
T. 0389435603. 045807
Vieille Garde, 16 Pl Concorde, 68100 Mulhouse.
T. 0389455151. - Paint / Furn / Cur - 045808
Vieille Garde, 25 Rue Josué-Hofer, 68100 Mulhouse.
T. 0389433334. - Paint / Furn / Cur - 045809

Muneville-sur-Mer (Manche)

Dennison, Peter, Bourg, 50290 Muneville-sur-Mer.
T. 0233507713. 045810

Murat (Cantal)

A l'Age de Bronze, 28 Rue Porte-Saint-Esprit, 15300 Murat. T. 0471201482. - Ant - 045811

Muret (Haute-Garonne)

Guedes, Bernard, 97 Rue Saint-Pierre, 31600 Muret.
T. 0562233763. 045812

Mûrs-Erigné (Maine-et-Loire)

Ménager, Benoît, 7 Rte Cholet, 49130 Mûrs-Erigné.
T. 41577449. 045813

Myans (Savoie)

Broc Antique, Lieu-dit-Chacuzard, 73800 Myans.
T. 0479280736. - Ant - 045814

Nançay (Cher)

Auger, Françoise, Pl Eglise, 18330 Nançay.
T. 0248518183. 045815
Besnard, Christian, 9 Rte Salbris, 18330 Nançay.
T. 0248518300. - Furn - 045816
Grenier de Villâtre, 1 Rue Faubourgs, 18330 Nançay.
T. 0248518022, Fax 0248518327. - Paint - 045817

Nancy (Meurthe-et-Moselle)

Antiquités 34, 34 Rue Gustave-Simon, 54000 Nancy.
T. 0383307635. 045818
Aux Vieilles Choses, 15 Blvd Haussonville, 54000 Nancy. T. 0383274633. 045819
Bénichoux, 41 Grande Rue, 54000 Nancy.
T. 0383305547. 045820
Charme du Temps Passé, Centre Commercial Saint-Sébastien, 54000 Nancy. T. 0383327141. 045821
Collignon, Daniel, 81 Grande Rue, 54000 Nancy.
T. 0383328273. 045822
Gargouille, 91 Grande Rue, 54000 Nancy.
T. 0383322187. 045823
Harcos, Ladislas, 33 Rue Stanislas, 54000 Nancy.
T. 0383353545. - Paint / Dec / Mod - 045824
Jantzen, Jean-Claude, 13 Rue Stanislas, 54000 Nancy.
T. 0383352079. 045825
Kayser, Jean-Huber, 9 Rue Général-Clinchant, 54000 Nancy. T. 0383510441. 045826

Lainet Frères, 39 Rue Mon-Désert, 54000 Nancy.
T. 0383901076. 045827
Lepape, Claude, 99 Rue Isabey, 54000 Nancy.
T. 0383986619. 045828
Lhotte, Nicole, 46 Grande Rue, 54000 Nancy.
T. 0383364840. 045829
Lorette, Jean-Paul, 5 Rue Gustave-Simon, 54000 Nancy.
T. 0383356379. 045830
Marotte, 11 Rue Visitation, 54000 Nancy.
T. 0383323809. 045831
Metz-Noblat, Bertrand de, 65 Rue Gabriel-Mouilleron, 54000 Nancy. T. 0383284290. 045832
Pargon, D. & H., 81 Chemin Haut-de-Chèvre, 54000 Nancy. T. 0383983047. 045833
Passé-Présent, 9 Rue Saint-Michel, 54000 Nancy.
T. 0383350278. 045834
Pomme d'Ambre, 135 Grande Rue, 54000 Nancy.
T. 0383303502. 045835
Posalski, Jean-Pierre, 44 Rue République, 54000 Nancy.
T. 0383287506. 045836
Risse, Martine, 3 Rue Stanislas, 54000 Nancy.
T. 0383355225. - Furn / China / Mod - 045837
Sault, Benoît du, 5 Rue Saint-Nicolas, 54000 Nancy.
T. 0383372774. 045838
Schlegel, Pascal, 1 Grande Rue, 54000 Nancy.
T. 0383321538, Fax 0383516616. - Ant / Furn - 045839
Thinus, Emmanuel, 93 Grande Rue, 54000 Nancy.
T. 0383351348. - Paint / Graph / Sculp / Glass / Mod - 045840
Wingerter, I., 87 Grande Rue, 54000 Nancy.
T. 0383350933. - Paint / Graph - 045841

Nangis (Seine-et-Marne)

Neveu, Michel, 9 Rue Noas-Daumesnil, 77370 Nangis.
T. 64082588. 045842

Nannay (Nièvre)

Gillet, Jean-Marie, Nie 151, entre Charité – Clamecy, 58350 Nannay. T. 0386692184. 045843

Nanterre (Hauts-de-Seine)

Alain, 5 Pl Merisiers, 92000 Nanterre.
T. 0147809356. 045844
Chapotot, Claude & Sonia, 32 Rue Philippe-Triaire, 92000 Nanterre. T. 0147244692. 045845
Courtier, 51bis Rue Marcelin-Berthelot, 92000 Nanterre.
T. 0147255091. - Furn / Cur / Mod - 045846
Légende des Siècles, 12 Av Maréchal-Joffre, 92000 Nanterre. T. 0141370223. 045847
Lenoir, Bernard, 17 Av Rueil, 92000 Nanterre.
T. 0147298988. 045848
Naudin, Jeanne, 22 Rue Raymond-Barbet, 92000 Nanterre. T. 0147214473. 045849
Poussier, Charles, 31 Rue Ernest-Renan, 92000 Nanterre. T. 0147215488, Fax 0146950119. 045850
Source aux Trouvailles, 77 Av Georges-Clemenceau, 92000 Nanterre. T. 0147241149. 045851
Zerrouki, Farid, 5 All Henri-Wallon, 92000 Nanterre.
T. 0147247789. 045852

Nantes (Loire-Atlantique)

Air du Temps, 30 Rue Jean-Jaurès, 44000 Nantes.
T. 40895281. - Toys / Naut - 045853
Antiquité Brocante Jean Macé, Pl Jean-Macé-Chantenay, 44100 Nantes. T. 40436969. - Furn / Cur - 045854
Antiquité Le Prieuré Nantais, 13 Rue Marceau, 44000 Nantes. T. 40355173. 045855
Antiquités Brocante des Rochettes, Rue Moulin-Rochettes, 44300 Nantes. T. 40760690. 045856
Antiquités Caroline, 4 Rue Bréa, 44000 Nantes.
T. 0251840442. 045857
Antiquités Clair de Lune, 7 Rue Sarrazin, 44000 Nantes.
T. 0251824707. 045858
Antiquités de France, 18 Rue Paul-Painlevé, 44000 Nantes. T. 40597081. 045859
Antiquités Le Grenier, 23bis Rue Jean-Jaurès, 44000 Nantes. T. 40201697. 045860
Antiquités Saint-Roch, 22 Pl Viarme, 44000 Nantes.
T. 40202799. 045861
Armor, 119 Blvd Doulon, 44300 Nantes. T. 40500492, Fax 40491529. 045862
Au Grand Hussard, 10 Rue Mercoeur, 44000 Nantes.
T. 40484364. - Furn / Mil - 045863

Bachelier Foucauld, 28 Rue Jean-Jaurès, 44000 Nantes. T. 40484364. *045864*
Barbaud, J.Y., 6 Rue de la Gare de Chantenay, 44100 Nantes. T. 40951095. - Furn / Cur - *045865*
Battais, Gilles, 4 Pl E.-Normand, 44000 Nantes. T. 40082629. - Ant - *045866*
Berthelot, Bertrand, 16 Rue Strasbourg, 44000 Nantes. T. 40353595. *045867*
Bohec, Alain, 17 Rue Mathurin-Brissonneau, 44100 Nantes. T. 40695433. *045868*
Bourse aux Affaires, 13 Pl Canclaux, 44100 Nantes. T. 40735050. - Furn / Cur - *045869*
Bourse aux Affaires, 36bis Rue A.-Riom, 44100 Nantes. T. 40739660. - Furn / Cur - *045870*
Brocante, 2 Rue Château, 44000 Nantes. T. 40203160. *045871*
Brocante d'Allonville, 82 Rue Allonville, 44000 Nantes. T. 40744453. *045872*
Buchoul, Jean-Marc, 6 Rue Carmélites, 44000 Nantes. T. 40476063. *045873*
Charline, 11 Rue Jean-de-la-Fontaine, 44000 Nantes. T. 40735082. - Mod - *045874*
Chiché, Bertrand, 21 Rue Mercoeur, 44000 Nantes. T. 40477039. *045875*
Chiron, Marie-Christine, 18 Rue Mercoeur, 44000 Nantes. T. 40485179. - Paint / Furn / China - *045876*
Cibot, 7 Rue Voltaire, 44000 Nantes. T. 40738437. - Paint / Sculp - *045877*
Comptoir aux Occasions, 1bis Blvd De-Launay, 44100 Nantes. T. 40690069. *045878*
Coué, 7 Rue Mercoeur, 44000 Nantes. T. 40082995. *045879*
Coué, Jean-Yves, 108 Rue Hauts-Pavés, 44000 Nantes. T. 40406703. *045880*
Cour des Antiquaires, 7 Rue Industrie, 44100 Nantes. T. 40484849. - Ant - *045881*
Courland, Paul, 27 Rue Jean-Jaurès, 44000 Nantes. T. 40205735. *045882*
Cuny, André, 11 Rue Industrie, 44100 Nantes. T. 40477195. *045883*
Docks Antiques, 5 Blvd Léon-Bureau, 44000 Nantes. T. 0251722709, Fax 0251823943. - Mod - *045884*
Ecritoire, 12 Rue Jean-Jaurès, 44000 Nantes. T. 40477818. *045885*
Ecume des Jours, 12 Rue Brasserie, 44000 Nantes. T. 40692292. *045886*
Etienne, 23 Rue Jean-Jaurès, 44000 Nantes. T. 40892985. - Fra / Silv / Cur - *045887*
Ferré, Yves, 13 Pl Viarme, 44000 Nantes. T. 40203360. *045888*
Fleuret, Jean-Pierre, 39 Rue Jean-Emile-Laboureur, Bâtiment 1, 44000 Nantes. T. 0251819616. *045889*
Galerie du Colombier, 3 Pl Edouard-Normand, 44000 Nantes. T. 40476360. *045890*
Galerie du Palais, 3 Pl Aristide-Briand, 44000 Nantes. T. 40482342. - Furn - *045891*
Garel, 16 Rue Strasbourg, 44000 Nantes. T. 0251820518. *045892*
Genin, Jean-Jacques, 28 Rue Jean-Jaurè, 44000 Nantes. T. 40353412. *045893*
Grenier de la Durantière, 75 Rue de la Durantière, 44000 Nantes. T. 40586868. *045894*
Guidoux, François, 1 Rue Gutenberg, 44100 Nantes. T. 40439847. *045895*
Guillemet, Monique, 19 Rue Mercoeur, 44000 Nantes. T. 40486270. *045896*
Interior's, 9 Rue Général-Leclerc-Hauteclocque, 44000 Nantes. T. 40082563. *045897*
Jadis, 4 Rue Lamoricière, 44100 Nantes. T. 40697485. - Furn / Tex / Dec - *045898*
Lamouret, Patrick, 29 Rue Jean-Jaurès, 44000 Nantes. T. 40890415. *045899*
Le Cam, Françoise & Philippe Belhache, 32 Rte Rennes, 44300 Nantes. T. 40760483. - Paint / Furn / Cur - *045900*
Le Deaut, Jacky, 141 Rue Paul-Bellamy, 44000 Nantes. T. 40140140. *045901*
Ledru, Servane, 11 Rue Kléber, 44000 Nantes. T. 40698171. *045902*
Lew, Didier, 29 Rue Jean-Jaurès, 44000 Nantes. T. 40351283. - Furn - *045903*
Malgioglio, Béatrice, 2ter Rue Harrouys, 44000 Nantes. T. 40890294. *045904*

Malvaux, Bertrand, 2 Rue Franklin, 44000 Nantes. T. 40733600, Fax 40718319. *045905*
Marché d'Erlon, 12ter Rue Erlon, 44000 Nantes. T. 40205878. - Fra / Lights / Glass - *045906*
Marotte, 14 Rue Château, 44000 Nantes. T. 40200065. *045907*
Massias, Jacques, 29 Rue Jean-Jaurès, 44000 Nantes. T. 40896963, Fax 51822640. *045908*
Ouaknine, 26 Rue Adolphe-Moitié, 44000 Nantes. T. 40354365. *045909*
Préard, Yannick, 6 Rue Maisdon-Pajot, 44000 Nantes. T. 40430808. *045910*
Romantic Gallery, 70 Blvd Victor-Hugo, 44200 Nantes. T. 40478411. *045911*
Temps d'Alice, 17 Rue Château, 44000 Nantes. T. 40080299. - Paint / Jew / Silv / Cur - *045912*
Troc 2000, 15 Rte Saint-Sébastien, 44200 Nantes. T. 40032433. - Furn / Cur - *045913*
Trouvailles, 4 Rue Léon-Blum, 44000 Nantes. T. 40200880. *045914*
Turpin, Bernard, 28 Blvd Anglais, 44100 Nantes. T. 40763918. *045915*
Wismes, Michel de, 5 Rue Mercoeur, 44000 Nantes. T. 40484416. - Paint / Furn / Cur - *045916*

Naours (Somme)

Acloque, Thérèse, 25 Rue Arbre, 80260 Naours. T. 0322937701. - Ant - *045917*

Narbonne (Aude)

Antiquités Comtoise Fleurie, 67bis Av Général-Leclerc, 11100 Narbonne. T. 0468414407. *045918*
Antiquités Le Voltaire, 25 Rue Voltaire, 11100 Narbonne. T. 0468411512. *045919*
Bidule, 10 Rue Emile-Zola, 11100 Narbonne. T. 0468324049, Fax 0468325642. *045920*
Borne, Francis, 6bis Av Pyrénées, 11100 Narbonne. T. 0468412322. *045921*
Broc Troc, 4bis Rue Gleizes, 11100 Narbonne. T. 0468501987, Fax 0468655944. - Ant - *045922*
Chanu, Cedric, Rue Ancienne-Porte-de-Béziers, 11100 Narbonne. T. 0468651953. *045923*
Daghlian, Clément, 72 Blvd Frédéric-Mistral, 11100 Narbonne. T. 0468907645. *045924*
Galerie Lutèce, 27 Rue Ancien-Courrier, 11100 Narbonne. T. 0468325568. *045925*
Grenier Narbonnais, Rue Blaise-Pascal, 11100 Narbonne. T. 0468414560. *045926*
Mayaudon, Marie-Thérèse, 46 Av Bordeaux, 11100 Narbonne. T. 0468414374. *045927*
Philippard, 6 Rue Calixte-Camelle, 11100 Narbonne. T. 0468904741. *045928*
Piccadilly, 1 Pl Hôtel-de-Ville, 11100 Narbonne. T. 0468325033. - Jew - *045929*

Neauphle-le-Château (Yvelines)

Grenier de Neauphle, 19 Rue Saint-Martin, 78640 Neauphle-le-Château. T. 0134890915. *045930*

Nemours (Seine-et-Marne)

Hochard, Michel, 15 Pl Jean-Jaurès, 77140 Nemours. T. 64280334. *045931*
Pasquier, Yvonne, 57 Rue Paris, 77140 Nemours. T. 64280166. *045932*

Nérac (Lot-et-Garonne)

Lazartigues, Rue Angle-Droit, 47600 Nérac. T. 0553653810. *045933*
Salis, Michel, 65 Rue Gambetta, 47600 Nérac. T. 0553651662. *045934*
Verdier, Jacques, Rte Condom, 47600 Nérac. T. 0553654811. *045935*

Néris-les-Bains (Allier)

Antiquités de Montassiégé, Château Montassiégé, 03310 Néris-les-Bains. T. 0470649091. - Ant - *045936*
Aubret, Henri, Les Cascades, 03310 Néris-les-Bains. T. 0470301813. - Ant - *045937*
Grenier Bourbonnais, 9bis Blvd Arènes, 03310 Néris-les-Bains. T. 0470032499. - Ant - *045938*
Mancy, Jean-Luc, 12 Blvd Arènes, 03310 Néris-les-Bains. T. 0470031089. - Ant - *045939*

Neufchâteau (Vosges)

Hutinet, Gérard, 3 Av Grande-Fontaine, 88300 Neufchâteau. T. 0329943792. *045940*
Rebourg, Claude, 4 Pl Jeanne-d'Arc, 88300 Neufchâteau. T. 0329940165. *045941*

Neufchâtel-en-Bray (Seine-Maritime)

Ile aux Trésors, 7 Rue Général-de-Gaulle, 76270 Neufchâtel-en-Bray. T. 0235931394. - Furn / China - *045942*

Neufchâtel-Hardelot (Pas-de-Calais)

Boulenger, Daniel, 15 Av Concorde, Hardelot-Plage, 62152 Neufchâtel-Hardelot. T. 0321837510. *045943*
Héritage, 469 Av François-1er, Hardelot-Plage, 62152 Neufchâtel-Hardelot. T. 0321104609. *045944*
Lepoutre, André, Pl La-Fontaine, Hardelot-Plage, 62152 Neufchâtel-Hardelot. T. 0321332240. *045945*

Neuilly-sur-Seine (Hauts-de-Seine)

Aléors, 158 Av Charles-de-Gaulle, 92200 Neuilly-sur-Seine. T. 0147222068, Fax 0146241070. *045946*
Antic Shop, 177 Av Roule, 92200 Neuilly-sur-Seine. T. 0147223535. *045947*
Antiquités 107, 169 Av Achille-Peretti, 92200 Neuilly-sur-Seine. T. 0142627708. - Furn - *045948*
Bacchanales, 28 Rue Orléans, 92200 Neuilly-sur-Seine. T. 0147386615. *045949*
Baroco, 7 Rue Montrosier, 92200 Neuilly-sur-Seine. T. 0147224150. *045950*
Bical, Lydia, 31 Rue Chartres, 92200 Neuilly-sur-Seine. T. 0146241430. *045951*
British Import, 23 Blvd Parc, 92200 Neuilly-sur-Seine. T. 0146372775, Fax 0146372554. *045952*
Chartres, 35 Rue Chartres, 92200 Neuilly-sur-Seine. T. 0147223991. *045953*
Gorvitz, Christian, 18 Rue Hussiers, 92200 Neuilly-sur-Seine. T. 0146244665. *045954*
Groupe Dimension, 7 Rue Montrosier, 92200 Neuilly-sur-Seine. Fax (1) 46246523. *045955*
Pierre, Jean-Claude, 70 Rue Longchamp, 92200 Neuilly-sur-Seine. T. 0146247004. *045956*
Waksberg, Daniel, 72 Blvd Bineau, 92200 Neuilly-sur-Seine. T. 0147574239. *045957*

Neuvéglise (Cantal)

Estival, Bernard, Fressanges, 15260 Neuvéglise. T. 0471238434. *045958*

Neuville-de-Poitou (Vienne)

Aldebert, Alain, 7 Rue Antiquaires, 86170 Neuville-de-Poitou. T. 0549512038. - Ant / Furn - *045959*
Brousseau, Amédée, 39 Rue Vendeuvre, 86170 Neuville-de-Poitou. T. 0549513614. - Ant - *045960*

Neuvy-sur-Loire (Nièvre)

Dépôt-Vente Neuvy, 1 Rue Jean-Jaurès, ZA, 58450 Neuvy-sur-Loire. T. 0386392180. *045961*

Nevers (Nièvre)

A l'Air du Temps, 6 Rue Fer, 58000 Nevers. T. 0386363623. *045962*
Antig'Art, 29 Rue Saint-Etienne, 58000 Nevers. T. 0386367265. - Furn / Dec / Cur - *045963*
Antiquités Parcheminerie, 1 Rue Parcheminerie, 58000 Nevers. T. 0386613069. *045964*
Atelier du 18ème, 23 Rue Jean-Desveaux, 58000 Nevers. T. 0386570949. - Furn - *045965*
Belle Epoque, 7 Rue Barre, 58000 Nevers. T. 0386594804. *045966*
Benoît-Latour, Dominique, 15 Fbg-Lyon, 58000 Nevers. T. 0386377554. *045967*
Brocante Story, 2 Rue Cathédrale, 58000 Nevers. T. 0386612339. *045968*
Collectionneur, 5 Rue Fer, 58000 Nevers. T. 0386367203. - Cur - *045969*
Echauguette, 1 Rue Cathédrale, 58000 Nevers. T. 0386595062. - Paint / Furn / China / Sculp / Silv / Instr / Cur / Toys - *045970*
Ferme, 62 Rue 13ème-de-Ligne, 58000 Nevers. T. 0386366051. *045971*
Forum des Arts, 6 Imp Boullerie, 58000 Nevers. T. 0386369543. *045972*
Galerie du Square, 5 Pl Résistance, 58000 Nevers. T. 0386570504. - Ant / Dec - *045973*

Galerie Saint-Vincent, 9 Rue Ferdinand-Gambon, 58000
Nevers. T. 0386615170. - Paint / Furn / Cur - *045974*
Maraux, Patrick, 15 Rue Cathédrale, 58000 Nevers.
T. 0386591746. *045975*
Passard, Gérard, 28 Rue Midi, 58000 Nevers.
T. 0386574168. *045976*
Puces de Nevers, 7 Rue Récollets, 58000 Nevers.
T. 0386612215. *045977*
Timoléonthos, François, 23 Rue Jean-Desveaux, 58000
Nevers. T. 0386570836. - Furn - *045978*

Neyron (Ain)
Courtois, J. & C., 103 Rte de Genève, 01700 Neyron.
T. 0478551474. - Ant / Furn - *045979*

Nice (Alpes-Maritimes)
Achats Arts Antiquités, 3 A Rue Antoine-Gautier, 06300
Nice. T. 0493555645. *045980*
Amato, Alain d', 34 Rue Catherine-Ségurane, 06300 Ni-
ce. T. 0493551808, Fax 0493899606. - Ant - *045981*
Antic Brocante Californie, 207 Av Californie, 06200 Nice.
T. 0493219087. *045982*
Antic Center Informatique, 8 Rue Antoine-Gautier, 06300
Nice. T. 0493897333. *045983*
Antic Dolls, 22 Rue Lépante, 06000 Nice.
T. 0493804331. - Toys - *045984*
Antiquité Brocante Alberti, 3 Rue Alberti, 06000 Nice.
T. 0493806080. - Paint / Furn / Cur - *045985*
Antiquité et Décoration, Rue Foresta, 06000 Nice.
T. 0493558417, Fax 0493565993. *045986*
Antiquités Art Décoration, 9bis Rue Emmanuel-Philibert,
06300 Nice. T. 0493557702. *045987*
Antiquités Brocante, 18 Corniche André-de-Joly, 06300
Nice. T. 0493555401. - Ant - *045988*
Antiquités Brocante Barbéris, 58 Rue Barbéris, 06300
Nice. T. 0493565080. *045989*
Antiquités Nana, 46 Rue France, 06000 Nice.
T. 0493872238. *045990*
Argenterie Abadie, 1 Rue Antoine-Gautier, 06300 Nice.
T. 0493897399. *045991*
Argenterie Ancienne, 28 Rue Catherine-Ségurane,
06300 Nice. T. 0493264596. *045992*
Armes Anciennes, 10 Rue Cassini, 06300 Nice.
T. 0492041527. *045993*
Art et Conseil, 4 Rue Puget, 06100 Nice.
T. 0492071432, Fax 0492071449. *045994*
Art Music Antic, 4 Rue Am de Grasse, 06000 Nice.
T. 0493887816. *045995*
Artémis, 7 Promenade Anglais, 06000 Nice.
T. 0493889930. *045996*
Arts du XX° Siècle, 2 Rue Antoine-Gautier, 06300 Nice.
T. 0493264242. *045997*
Au Coup de Coeur, 2 Rue Antoine-Gautier, 06000 Nice.
T. 0493269778. *045998*
Au Miroir des Siècles, 37 Rue de la Buffa, 06000 Nice.
T. 0493884861. - Ant / Furn / Silv / Lights - *045999*
Au Petit Grenier, 29 Av Sainte-Marguerite, 06200 Nice.
T. 0493720042. *046000*
Au Roi de Rome, 8 Rue Dalpozzo, 06000 Nice.
T. 0493888446. - Ant / Dec - *046001*
Au Trente et Quarante, 2 Rue Antoine-Gautier, 06300 Ni-
ce. T. 0493567614. *046002*
Au Trente et Quarante, 2 Rue Ségurane, 06300 Nice.
T. 0493567614. - Furn / Cur / Mod - *046003*
Aurore Galerie, 20 Rue Emmanuel-Philibert, 06300 Nice.
T. 0493561633. *046004*
Azaïs, Catherine, 54 Av Ray, 06100 Nice.
T. 0493847133. *046005*
Barailler, Jean-Pierre, 4 Rue Antoine-Gautier, 06300 Ni-
ce. T. 0492042040, Fax 0492041718. - Furn - *046006*
Barailler & Rebuffel, 8 Rue Antoine-Gautier, 06300 Nice.
T. 0493267822. *046007*
Barlian, Georges, Quai Am Infernet, 06300 Nice.
T. 0493553244. *046008*
Bascans, Robert, 5 Rue Antoine-Gautier, 06300 Nice.
T. 0493550079. *046009*
Bastide-Le Petit, Jacqueline, 18 Rue Paris, 06000 Nice.
T. 0493801542. *046010*
Beaulier, Chantal de, 7 Promenade Anglais, 06000 Nice.
T. 0493874500. *046011*
Bémon, Gerald, 3 Rue Antoine-Gautier, 06000 Nice.
T. 0493262674, Fax 0493260485. *046012*

Besch, Léontine, 17 Av Durante, 06000 Nice.
T. 0493884713. *046013*
Biancarelli, François, 28 Rue Catherine-Ségurane,
06000 Nice. T. 0493552724. - Furn / Silv - *046014*
Biglia, Danielle, 2 Rue Antoine-Gautier, 06300 Nice.
T. 0493567449. *046015*
Blanchard, Françoise, 8 Av Verdun, 06000 Nice.
T. 0493871469, Fax 0493884418. - Paint / Furn /
Orient / Cur - *046016*
Bloch, C., 2 Rue Antoine-Gautier, 06300 Nice.
T. 0493558393. *046017*
Bonnafoux, Louis, 21 Rue Paris, 06000 Nice.
T. 0493803328. *046018*
Bottéro, Maryse, 17 Rue Andrioli, 06000 Nice.
T. 0493441900. *046019*
Boucaud, Philippe, 8 Rue Foresta, 06000 Nice.
T. 0493559146. - Furn / Cur - *046020*
Braunstein, Alain, 26 Rue Liberté, 06000 Nice.
T. 0493879628. *046021*
Brocantic, 16 Rue Emmanuel-Philibert, 06300 Nice.
T. 0493567551. *046022*
Butterfly, 4 Rue Catherine-Ségurane, 06300 Nice.
T. 0493892988. - Orient - *046023*
Cabassu, Bernard, 4 Rue Antoine-Gautier, 06300 Nice.
T. 0493267297. *046024*
Canestrier, Jean, 7 Rue Miron, 06000 Nice.
T. 0493802382. *046025*
Caprices du Passé, 2 Rue Antoine-Gautier, 06300 Nice.
T. 0493560161. *046026*
Castres, Jean-Louis, 28 Passage Catherine-Ségurane,
06300 Nice. T. 0493552078. *046027*
Castres, Jean-Louis, 28 Rue Catherine-Ségurane,
06300 Nice. T. 0493552078. - Dec / Cur - *046028*
Cent Garde, 28 Rue Angleterre, 06000 Nice.
T. 0493876445. *046029*
Centa-Damiano, Joseph, 36 Rue Catherine-Ségurane,
06300 Nice. T. 0493896464, Fax 0493261406.
- Ant - *046030*
Chenel, Alain, 7 Prom Anglais, 06000 Nice.
T. 0493871448, Fax 0493858533. - China /
Mod - *046031*
Clémente, 36 Rue Catherine-Ségurane, 06300 Nice.
T. 0493556868. *046032*
Clips Trente, 7 Promenade Anglais, 06000 Nice.
T. 0493883166, Fax 0493876719. *046033*
Collectionnité, 2 Rue Antoine-Gautier, 06300 Nice.
T. 0493269418, Fax 0493267763. - Toys - *046034*
Contraste, 2 Rue Antoine-Gautier, 06300 Nice.
T. 0493894889. *046035*
Corbière, Anne, 33 Rue Droite, 06300 Nice.
T. 0493926534. *046036*
Corpel, Jean-Guy, 7bis Rue Antoine-Gautier, 06300 Ni-
ce. T. 0493564560. *046037*
Dal Farra, Philippe, 7 Promenade Anglais, 06000 Nice.
T. 0493569444. *046038*
Damiano & Macherez, 36 Rue Catherine-Ségurane,
06300 Nice. T. 0493896464,
Fax 0493261406. *046039*
Daulaus, Yves, 344 Blvd Observatoire, 06300 Nice.
T. 0493766101. *046040*
David de Sauzéa, Rambert, 26 Rue Catherine-Ségurane,
06300 Nice. T. 0493558833, Fax 0493565063.
- Ant - *046041*
Dely, 1 Rue Louis-Gassin, 06300 Nice.
T. 0493857845. *046042*
Dervieux, Madeleine, 13 Rue Cassini, 06300 Nice.
T. 0493560011. *046043*
Deville, Michèle, 21 Rue Emmanuel-Philibert, 06300 Ni-
ce. T. 0493561788. *046044*
Diagram, 3 Rue Saint-Vincent, 06000 Nice.
T. 0493620774. *046045*
Diagram, 11 Cours Saleya, 06300 Nice. T. 0493803371,
Fax 0493620739. - Paint / Furn / Dec / Fra / Cur /
Draw - *046046*
Dicken's Antiquités, 13 Rue Emmanuel-Philibert, 06300
Nice. T. 0493556122, Fax 0493556122. *046047*
Dreta, 2 Rue Antoine-Gautier, 06300 Nice.
T. 0493552725. *046048*
Dyka, Corinne, 28 Rue Catherine-Ségurane, 06300 Nice.
T. 0493589746. *046049*
Emery, Jenny, 38 Rue Catherine-Ségurane, 06300 Nice.
T. 0493565020. *046050*

Evrard, André, 23 Rue Lépante, 06000 Nice.
T. 0493852896. *046051*
Farfouillette, 8 Chemin Lauvette, 06300 Nice.
T. 0493543674, Fax 0493270092. *046052*
Fighiéra-Delorme, Michèle, 2 Rue Antoine-Gautier,
06300 Nice. T. 0493563389. *046053*
Fille du Pirate, 21 Rue Emmanuel-Philibert, 06300 Nice.
T. 0492049030. - Paint / Mil / Naut / Instr - *046054*
Fontaine, 15 Blvd du Mont-Boron, 06300 Nice.
T. 0493260674. - Paint / Sculp / Jew / Instr / Glass /
Mod - *046055*
Fontaine Lumineuse, 7 Rue Antoine-Gautier, 06300 Ni-
ce. T. 0493562520, Fax 0493565310. - Ant - *046056*
Galerie Art Lympia, 16 Rue Emmanuel-Philibert, 06300
Nice. T. 0493555119. *046057*
Galerie Art'7, 7 Promenade des Anglais, 06000 Nice.
T. 0493888229. - Paint / Graph / Sculp - *046058*
Galerie des Antiquaires, 7 Promenade Anglais, 06000
Nice. T. 0493870917. *046059*
Galerie L'Albertine, 30 Rue Alberti, 06000 Nice.
T. 0493624973. *046060*
Galerie Miron, 3 Rue Miron, 06000 Nice.
T. 0493621741, Fax 0493626319. *046061*
Galerie Philibert, 18 Rue Emmanuel-Philibert, 06300 Ni-
ce. T. 0493560247. *046062*
Galerie Swan, 9 Rue Emmanuel-Philibert, 06300 Nice.
T. 0493268874. *046063*
Gallon, Jean-Marie, Quai Am Infernet, 06300 Nice.
T. 0493562358. - Tex - *046064*
Garibaldi Antiquités, 4 Rue Catherine-Ségurane, 06300
Nice. T. 0493552659. *046065*
Gautier, Laurence, 28 Rue Catherine-Ségurane, 06300
Nice. T. 0493550685. *046066*
Ginac, Romain, 28 Rue Catherine-Ségurane, 06000 Ni-
ce. T. 0466679815. *046067*
Hangar de la Brocante, 141 Blvd Ariane, 06300 Nice.
T. 0493545484. *046068*
Hassid, Michel, 12 Rue Cassini, 06300 Nice.
T. 0493550200. *046069*
Hermanovits, Jean-François, 4 Rue Antoine-Gautier,
06300 Nice. T. 0492042080. *046070*
Ivanna, 7 B Rue Antoine-Gautier, 06300 Nice.
T. 0493899464. *046071*
Jossaume, Jack, 7 Promenade Anglais, 06000 Nice.
T. 0493880869. - Paint / Furn / Lights / Cur - *046072*
Koson, Bernard, 15 Rue Cassini, 06300 Nice.
T. 0493267737. *046073*
Koson, Sophie, 2 Rue Antoine-Gautier, 06300 Nice.
T. 0492041063. *046074*
Kubera, 7 Promenade Anglais, 06000 Nice.
T. 0493881140. - Orient - *046075*
Lacam, Olivier, 22bis Blvd Jean-Baptiste-Vérany, 06300
Nice. T. 0493261716. *046076*
Lafarge, Muriel, 2 Rue Antoine-Gautier, 06300 Nice.
T. 0493569444. *046077*
Lavoisy, Georges, 11 Rue de la Liberté, 06000 Nice.
T. 0493878873. - Ant - *046078*
Lebra, François, 42 Av Alfred-Borriglione, 06000 Nice.
T. 0493842605. - Ant - *046079*
Légende, 75 Blvd Victor-Hugo, 06000 Nice.
T. 0493880471. *046080*
Lejeune, Gabrielle, 19 Av Notre-Dame, 06000 Nice.
T. 0493851915. *046081*
Leroux, Philippe, 2 Rue Antoine-Gautier, 06300 Nice.
T. 0493552519. *046082*
Lodiana, 3 Blvd Victor-Hugo, 06000 Nice.
T. 0493879309. *046083*
Loft Galerie, 6 Rue Saint-Suaire, 06000 Nice.
T. 0493855120. *046084*
Lord Byron, 8 Av de Verdun, 06000 Nice.
T. 0493871469, Fax 0493884418. - Paint / Furn /
Orient / China / Dec - *046085*
Manuella, 38 Rue Catherine-Ségurane, 06300 Nice.
T. 0493566401. *046086*
Marchands d'Histoires, 21 Rue de Paris, 06000 Nice.
T. 0493272713. - Ant - *046087*
Mathé, Lucile, 7 Promenade Anglais, 06000 Nice.
T. 0493160240. *046088*
Mazières, Serge, 10 Rue Foresta, 06000 Nice.
T. 0493260506. - Paint / Furn - *046089*
M.C.B. de la Tour Saint-François, 35 Rue Pairolière,
06300 Nice. T. 0493807107. *046090*

Mettray, Jean, 4 Rue Catherine-Ségurane, 06300 Nice.
T. 0493561520. *046091*
Molski, Vladimir, 1 Rue Antoine-Gautier, 06300 Nice.
T. 0493564865. *046092*
Moufflet, Pascal, 4 Rue Antoine-Gautier, 06300 Nice.
T. 0493556523, Fax 0493555772. - Furn - *046093*
Moufflet, Raphaële, 6 Rue Foresta, 06000 Nice.
T. 0493555252. *046094*
Müller, Nicolas, 3 Rue Antoine-Gautier, 06300 Nice.
T. 0493552242, Fax 0493558110. *046095*
Nerée, Anne, 15 Av Scudéri, 06100 Nice.
T. 0493530699. *046096*
Numisami, 2 Rue Halevy, 06000 Nice. T. 0493820241.
- Num - *046097*
Objets d'Autrefois, 18 Rue Défly, 06000 Nice.
T. 0493926169. *046098*
Palmieri, Sauveur, 10 et 16 Rue Catherine-Ségurane,
06300 Nice. T. 0493560156. *046099*
Panderis, André, 7 Prom Anglais, 06000 Nice.
T. 0493161766, Fax 0493824406. - Furn - *046100*
Paradis de l'Occasion, 5 Blvd Raimbaldi, 06000 Nice.
T. 0493922998. *046101*
Pedroni, Vasco, 10 Rue Martin-Seytour, 06000 Nice.
T. 0493553678. *046102*
Perrier, Patricia, 2 Rue Antoine-Gautier, 06300 Nice.
T. 0493894475. *046103*
Perrin, Jacqueline, 14 Av Saint-Jean-Baptiste, 06000
Nice. T. 0493925747, Fax 0493925746. - Paint / Furn /
Cur - *046104*
Pope, Philippe, 1 Rue Penchienatti, 06000 Nice.
T. 0493801587. *046105*
Rebuffel, J.-M., 12 Rue Ségurane, 06300 Nice.
T. 0493550890, Fax 0493893637. - Ant - *046106*
Récamier, 50 Rue de France, 06000 Nice.
T. 0493881525. - Paint / Orient - *046107*
Régis, Albert, 34 Rue Catherine-Ségurane, 06300 Nice.
T. 0493267927, Fax 0493891952. *046108*
Ricciotti, Alain, 14 Rue Papon, 06300 Nice.
T. 0493558118. *046109*
Rifaldi, Richard, 4 Rue Sainte-Réparate, 06300 Nice.
T. 0493855697. *046110*
Roboly, Danièle, 32 Rue Catherine-Ségurane, 06300 Ni-
ce. T. 0493897778. *046111*
Roboly, Gérard, 5 Rue Antoine-Gautier, 06300 Nice.
T. 0493266707. *046112*
Rometti, Olivier, 26 Rue Catherine-Ségurane, 06300 Ni-
ce. T. 0493551175, Fax 0493551175. *046113*
Roques Antiquités, 3 Rue Antoine-Gautier, 06300 Nice.
T. 0493896602. *046114*
Rosso, Yolande, 9 Rue Lépante, 06000 Nice.
T. 0493850730. *046115*
Sadaule, Suzanne, 3 Rue Alphonse-Karr, 06000 Nice.
T. 0493878204. - Tex - *046116*
Salager, Eliane, 2 Rue Antoine-Gautier, 06300 Nice.
T. 0493551739. *046117*
Sanson, Jacqueline, 2 Rue Antoine-Gautier, 06300 Nice.
T. 0493553110. *046118*
Scarscelli, Dante, 11 Rue Emmanuel-Philibert, 06300
Nice. T. 0493551826. *046119*
Soisson, Jacqueline, 4 Rue Masséna, 06000 Nice.
T. 0493879094. - Orient - *046120*
Solari, Jean, 16 Blvd Raimbaldi, 06000 Nice.
T. 0493621964. *046121*
Solari, Jean, 17 Rue Melchior-de-Vogüé, 06000 Nice.
T. 0493621964. - Furn - *046122*
Sprugnoli, Marie-Christine, 48 Rue France, 06000 Nice.
T. 0493881503. - Paint / Jew / Silv / Toys - *046123*
Sprugnoli, Michel, 48-50 Rue de France, 06000 Nice.
T. 0493880301. - Paint / Furn / China / Sculp / Jew /
Silv / Lights / Instr / Draw / Toys - *046124*
T.D.M., 21 Rue Emmanuel-Philibert, 06300 Nice.
T. 0493563451, Fax 0493564044. *046125*
Thaïs, 2 Rue Antoine-Gautier, 06300 Nice.
T. 0493550757. *046126*
Transenantic, 12 Rue Emmanuel-Philibert, 06300 Nice.
T. 0493551894. *046127*
Trianon, Marie-Christine, 48 Rue France, 06000 Nice.
T. 0493877593. *046128*
Tudare, Armand, 12 Rue Martin-Seytour, 06000 Nice.
T. 0493268275. *046129*
Vallée, Marc, 28 Rue Catherine-Ségurane, 06300 Nice.
T. 0493267788. *046130*

Vallet, Jeannine, 15 Rue Préfecture, 06300 Nice.
T. 0493850060. *046131*
Variété, 13 Blvd Gambetta, 06000 Nice. T. 0493444243.
- Ant / Lights - *046132*
Webb, Ellis, 6 Rue Lépante, 06000 Nice.
T. 0493923123. *046133*

Nieuil (Charente)
Galerie du Château, Château de Nieuil, 16270 Nieuil.
T. 0545713638. - Paint / Cur / Mod - *046134*

Nieulle-sur-Seudre (Charente-Maritime)
Trémaud, Catherine, 21 Rue Hortensias, 17600 Nieulle-
sur-Seudre. T. 0546850595. *046135*

Niherne (Indre)
Daguenet, Bernard, 29 Rue Saura, 36250 Niherne.
T. 0254298621. - Furn - *046136*

Nîmes (Gard)
Actif Rétro, 14 Rue Auguste, 30000 Nîmes.
T. 0466678088. *046136a*
Antiquités de la Maison Carrée, 9 Rue Racine, 30000
Nîmes. T. 0466219144. *046137*
Antiquité Le Samouraï, 1 Rue Emile-Jamais, 30900
Nîmes. T. 0466760940. *046137a*
Au Logis Provençal, 19 Rue Chapitre, 30000 Nîmes.
T. 0466647704. *046138*
Audibert, Jean-Marie, 42 Av Carnot, 30000 Nîmes.
T. 0466842742. *046139*
Audibert, Jean-Marie, 10 Rue Chapitre, 30000 Nîmes.
T. 0466210585. *046140*
Barbe, Francis, 1 Rue Trois-Maures, 30000 Nîmes.
T. 0466676879. *046141*
Blanchard, 6 Rue Régale, 30000 Nîmes.
T. 0466218446. *046142*
Bonnet, Jean-Pierre, 1 Rue Violette, 30000 Nîmes.
T. 0466217314. *046143*
Chabanel, Jean-Marc, 5 Rue Arènes, 30000 Nîmes.
T. 0466213387. *046144*
Charmoy, Xavier, 9 Rue Guizot, 30000 Nîmes.
T. 0466360747. *046144a*
Chez Delor, 34 Rue Grand-Couvent, 30900 Nîmes.
T. 0466678342. - Ant / Furn - *046145*
Chézeaud, Pierre, 2 Blvd Arènes, 30000 Nîmes.
T. 0466214950. - Furn / China / Tex / Instr - *046145a*
Clos de la Fontaine, 76 Rue République, 30900 Nîmes.
T. 0466847586. *046145b*
Coulloudon, Michel, 2 Pl Grand-Temple, 30000 Nîmes.
T. 0466360774, Fax 0466360787. *046146*
Ecume des Jours, 1 Rue Bachalas, 30000 Nîmes.
T. 0466362568. *046147*
Fages, Jean-Louis, 8 Rue Maison-Carrée, 30000 Nîmes.
T. 0466212103. *046148*
Ginac, Romain, 32 Rue Aspic, 30000 Nîmes.
T. 0466679815. *046148a*
Grenier, 37 Rue Vincent-Faïta, 30000 Nîmes.
T. 0466678041. *046149*
Grenier de Pin, 26 Rue Emile-Jamais, 30900 Nîmes.
T. 0466678743. - Furn - *046150*
Guiot, Georges, 9 Pl Château, 30000 Nîmes.
T. 0466677990. *046151*
Mod Antik, 1 Rue Bachalas, 30000 Nîmes.
T. 0466210405. *046152*
Moline, Florian, 16 Rue Emile-Jamais, 30900 Nîmes.
T. 0466761946. *046153*
Moline, Sélima, 28 Rue Bec-du-Lièvre, 30000 Nîmes.
T. 0466361612. *046154*
Nîm'Or, 28 Rue Nationale, 30000 Nîmes.
T. 0467760081. *046155*
Omphale, 8 Rue Condé, 30000 Nîmes.
T. 0466218844. *046156*
Ortega, Arturo, 41 Rue Grand-Couvent, 30000 Nîmes.
T. 0466215176. *046157*
Pages, Dany, 134 Rte Avignon, 30000 Nîmes.
T. 0466262940. *046158*
Rouflay, Pierrette, 15 Rue Emile-Jamais, 30900 Nîmes.
T. 0466679190. *046159*
Subtil, William, 67ter Av Jean-Jaurès, 30900 Nîmes.
T. 0466291082. *046160*
Vasquez, Patricia, 12 Rue Delon-Soubeyran, 30900
Nîmes. T. 0466762167. *046161*
Vaxelaire, Jean, 61 Rte Sauve, 30900 Nîmes.
T. 0466232450. *046162*

Wagner, Jacques, 15 Rue Meynier-de Salinelles, 30000
Nîmes. Fax 66672058. *046163*

Niort (Deux-Sèvres)
Antiquités du Palais, 7 Rue Thiers, 79000 Niort.
T. 0549281134. - Paint / Furn - *046164*
Austruy, Jean-Claude, 9 Quai Cronstadt, 79000 Niort.
T. 0549246581. *046165*
Laurent, Danièle, 30 Rue Gare, 79000 Niort.
T. 0549284631. - Furn / Silv / Cur - *046166*
Liaigre, Pierre, 38 Rue Gare, 79000 Niort.
T. 0549247791. *046167*
Malle aux Idées, 3 Rue Notre-Dame, 79000 Niort.
T. 0549794110. *046168*
Marquois, Jacky, 172 Av Limoges, 79000 Niort.
T. 0549284178. - Furn - *046169*
Myth et Légend, 5 Av République, 79000 Niort.
T. 0549247722. *046170*
Stouvenel, Marie-Rose, 15 Rue Basse, 79000 Niort.
T. 0549243447. *046171*
Tavard, Freddy, 22 Rue Gare, 79000 Niort.
T. 0549240031. *046172*

Noé (Haute-Garonne)
Mille Ans et Plus, 2 Rte Longages, 31410 Noé.
T. 0561871800. *046179*
Salaignac, Gilbert, Rte Toulouse, 31410 Noé.
T. 0561875377. *046180*

Nogent-en-Bassigny (Haute-Marne)
Magnien, Claude, 7 Rue Emile-Zola, 52800 Nogent-en-
Bassigny. T. 0325318401. - Ant / Dec - *046181*

Nogent-l'Artaud (Aisne)
Chevaliers, Imp Village, 02310 Nogent-l'Artaud.
T. 0323700449. - Ant - *046182*
Maison du 15ème Antiquités, 24 Grande Rue, 02310
Nogent-l'Artaud. T. 0323701035. - Ant - *046183*

Nogent-le-Roi (Eure-et-Loir)
Au Passé Simple, 19 Rue Eglise, 28210 Nogent-le-Roi.
T. 0237513826. - Furn / Cur - *046184*

Nogent-le-Rotrou (Eure-et-Loir)
Hordern, Philip, Lieu-dit La Rédillière, 28400 Nogent-le-
Rotrou. T. 0237528755. *046185*
Sanz, Daniel, RN 23, direction le Mans, 28400 Nogent-
le-Rotrou. T. 0237529143. *046186*

Nogent-sur-Marne (Val-de-Marne)
Bousch, Gilbert, 37 Av Charles-V, 94130 Nogent-sur-
Marne. T. 0148736089. - Furn / Cur - *046187*
Quinsier, Gérard, 171 Grande Rue, 94130 Nogent-sur-
Marne. T. 0148710329. *046188*

Nohant-Vic (Indre)
Rebillot, Jean-Louis, Bourg, 36400 Nohant-Vic.
T. 0254310803. *046189*

Noidans-lès-Vesoul (Haute-Saône)
Toutoccas', ZI Vesoul Ouest, 70000 Noidans-lès-Vesoul.
T. 0384752981. *046190*

Noirétable (Loire)
Véra Ville, Félix, Rte Lyon, 42440 Noirétable.
T. 0477247866. *046191*

Noirmoutier-en-l'Ile (Vendée)
Antic'her, 7 Quai Cassard, 85330 Noirmoutier-en-l'Ile.
T. 0251394189. *046192*
Arnaudeau, Marie-Thérèse, 25 Rue Salle, 85330 Noir-
moutier-en-l'Ile. T. 0251392236. *046193*
Dellus, Jacques, 12 Rue Mardi-Gras, 85330 Noirmou-
tier-en-l'Ile. T. 0251392233. *046194*

Nolay (Côte-d'Or)
Benkert, Daniel, 5 Rue Halles, 21340 Nolay.
T. 0380218443. *046195*
Bernard, Michel, Pl Halles, 21340 Nolay.
T. 0380218555. *046196*
Monnot, Gérard, 18 Rue Sadi-Carnot, 21340 Nolay.
T. 0380217299. *046197*

Nomain (Nord)
Mabille, Roger-Pierre, 23 Rue Coquerie, 59310 Nomain.
T. 0320710523, Fax 0320717582. - Ant - *046198*

Nomdieu (Lot-et-Garonne)
Garnier, Loic, Bourg, 47600 Nomdieu.
T. 0553659679. *046199*

Nonancourt (Eure)
Simon, Gilles, 67 Rue Grande, 27320 Nonancourt.
T. 0232602525. *046200*
Willemin, Jean-Claude, 72 Grande Rue, 27320 Nonancourt. T. 0232582240. *046201*

Nontron (Dordogne)
Lafon, Christian, Rte Thiviers, 24300 Nontron.
T. 0553562251. *046202*

Noron-l'Abbaye (Calvados)
Bertrand, Michel, Rte Deleffard, Manoir du Jageolet,
14700 Noron-l'Abbaye. T. 0231901723. - Ant / Furn /
Cur - *046203*

Notre-Dame-de-Bondeville (Seine-Maritime)
Renault, Daniel, 415 Rue Longs-Vallons, 76960 Notre-Dame-de-Bondeville. T. 0235757440. - Furn - *046204*

Notre-Dame-de-Riez (Vendée)
P'tite Brocante, La Croix-Verte, 85270 Notre-Dame-de-Riez. T. 0251544550. *046205*

Notre-Dame-du-Touchet (Manche)
Lemarié, Jean, Bourg, 50140 Notre-Dame-du-Touchet.
T. 0233590407. - Ant / Cur - *046206*

Nouan-le-Fuzelier (Loir-et-Cher)
Atelier La Patine, 14 Av Paris, 41600 Nouan-le-Fuzelier.
T. 0254968616. *046207*

Novillars (Doubs)
Garnache-Creuillot, Denis, Sq Charles-Nodier, 25220
Novillars. T. 0381556130. *046208*

Noyant (Maine-et-Loire)
Marchand, William, 26 Grande Rue, 49490 Noyant.
T. 41896701. *046209*

Noyelles-sur-Mer (Somme)
Lamy, Philippe, 2 Rue Adéodat-Watripon, 80133 Noyelles-sur-Mer. T. 0322232881. - Ant - *046210*

Noyers (Yonne)
Galerie des Arcades, Pl Hôtel-de-Ville, 89310 Noyers.
T. 0386826005. *046211*

Noyers-sur-Cher (Loir-et-Cher)
Giron Frères, Rte Tours, 41140 Noyers-sur-Cher.
T. 0254754242. - Paint / Furn / Lights / Glass /
Cur - *046212*

Nuits-Saint-Georges (Côte-d'Or)
Carrières de Nuits, Rte Beaune, 21700 Nuits-Saint-Georges. T. 0380611076. - Dec - *046213*
Cuenin, 15 Av Général-de-Gaulle, 21700 Nuits-Saint-Georges. T. 0380612967. *046214*

Nyons (Drôme)
Bourgogne, Francis, 7 Rue 4-Septembre, 26110 Nyons.
T. 0475263510. *046215*
Coquet, Nicole & Jean-Pierre Pourvis, 10 Rue Pasteur,
26110 Nyons. T. 0475264274. *046216*
Fert, Nathalie, 30 Pl Docteur-Bourdongle, 26110 Nyons.
T. 0475261380. - Paint / Furn / Jew - *046217*
Poignant, Rolande, 20 Rue Bas-Bourgs, 26110 Nyons.
T. 0475262014. *046218*

Obernai (Bas-Rhin)
Hartz, Jean-Claude, 173 Rte Ottrott, 67210 Obernai.
T. 0388956258. *046219*
Kleim, 15 Rue Général-Gouraud, 67210 Obernai.
T. 0388951871. *046220*
Klotz, François, 40 Rue Général-Gouraud, 67210 Obernai. T. 0388956492. *046221*

Offranville (Seine-Maritime)
Lahaye, François, 9 Rue Jehan-Veron, 76550 Offranville.
T. 0235049872. *046222*

Olemps (Aveyron)
Ratier Frères, Parc Commercial Les Cassagnettes,
12510 Olemps. T. 0565686600. *046223*

Ollioules (Var)
Antiquaire, 24 Rue Nationale, 83190 Ollioules.
T. 0494632969. *046224*

Olonne-sur-Mer (Vendée)
Bodin-Lemaire, Brigitte, 23 Rue Sables, 85340 Olonne-sur-Mer. T. 0251331130. *046225*
Trois Louis, Rue 8-Mai-1945, 85340 Olonne-sur-Mer.
T. 0251907334. *046226*

Oloron-Sainte-Marie (Pyrénées-Atlantiques)
Laban, Jean-Michel, 13 Rue Auguste-Peyré, 64400 Oloron-Sainte-Marie. T. 0559399445. - Ant - *046227*
Mornet, Colette, 8 Rue Auguste-Peyré, 64400 Oloron-Sainte-Marie. T. 0559390873. - Ant - *046228*

Omméel (Orne)
Lottin, Henriette, Avenelles, 61160 Omméel.
T. 0233368398. - Ant / Cur - *046229*

Omonville-la-Rogue (Manche)
Temps des Secrets, Ferme du Tourps, 50440 Omonville-la-Rogue. T. 0233084184. *046230*

Oncy-sur-Ecole (Essonne)
Antiquaire d'Oncy, 119ter Grande Rue, 91490 Oncy-sur-Ecole. T. 0164987827. *046231*

Onet-le-Château (Aveyron)
Atelier, Rte de Vabre, 12850 Onet-le-Château.
T. 0565780845. - Furn / Repr / Dec - *046232*

Orange (Vaucluse)
Antiquités Brocante de l'Arc, 274 Av Arc-de-Triomphe,
84100 Orange. T. 0490345883. - Ant - *046233*
Jomain, Marie-Claire, 5 Rue Segond-Weber, 84100
Orange. T. 0490347189. - Ant - *046234*
Lagier, Gilbert, Quart Graves Rte Caderousse, 84100
Orange. T. 0490342731. - Ant - *046235*
Pinguet, Bruno, 19 Rue Victor-Hugo, 84100 Orange.
T. 0490346595. - Ant - *046236*

Orchies (Nord)
Grenier du Pévèle, 92 Rue Jules-Ferry, 59310 Orchies.
T. 0320718009. - Ant - *046237*

Orgeval (Yvelines)
A.L.M. Antiquités, 502 Rte Quarante-Sous, 78630 Orgeval. T. 0139759840. *046238*
Compagnie Anglaise, 470 Rte Quarante-Sous, 78630 Orgeval. T. 0139754343. *046239*
Ecurie d'Antan, 2045 RN, 13 Face Habitat, 78630 Orgeval. T. 0139754670. *046240*
Manège du Temps, Centre Commercial Art de Vivre,
78630 Orgeval. T. 0139754275. *046241*
Matthey-Doret, Patrick, 502 Rte Quarante-Sous, 78630
Orgeval. T. 0139754426. *046242*
Passé Simple, 502 Rte Quarante-Sous, 78630 Orgeval.
T. 0139755779. *046243*
Péaron, Monique, Centre Commercial Art de Vivre,
78630 Orgeval. T. 0139754617. *046244*

Orléans (Loiret)
Arche de Noé, 206 Rue Bourgogne, 45000 Orléans.
T. 0238533949. *046245*
Art Ancien, 32 Rue Jeanne-d'Arc, 45000 Orléans.
T. 0238620975. *046246*
Atrema, 18 Rue des Turcies, 45000 Orléans.
T. 0238537610. - Furn - *046247*
Autre Jour, 7 Rue Charles-Sanglier, 45000 Orléans.
T. 0238540517. - Furn / Repr - *046248*
Autre Jour Country, 8 Rue Isaac-Jogues, 45000 Orléans.
T. 0238543062, Fax 0238543074. - Furn /
Repr - *046249*
Barré, Nicolas, 21 Rue Petit-Pont, 45000 Orléans.
T. 0238837243. - Furn - *046250*
Berthelot, 260 Rue Bourgogne, 45000 Orléans.
T. 0238817303. *046251*
Besnard, Alain, 92 Rue Bannier, 45000 Orléans.
T. 0238531802. - Furn / Cur - *046252*

Besnard, Mireille, 92 Rue Bannier, 45000 Orléans.
T. 0238531802. - Furn - *046253*
Bric à Brac, 230 Rue Bourgogne, 45000 Orléans.
T. 0238542737. *046254*
Casciello, Domenico, 30 Rue Jeanne-d'Arc, 45000 Orléans. T. 0238530843, Fax 0238519801. - Paint /
Furn / Sculp / Cur - *046255*
Develon, Paul, 42 Rue Eugène-Vignat, 45000 Orléans.
T. 0238538370. *046256*
Dupeyron, Frank, 9 Rue Vieux-Marché, 45000 Orléans.
T. 0238533208. *046257*
Garmilla, Jean-Michel, 22 Rue Aristide-Maillol, 45000
Orléans. T. 0238639725. *046258*
Grenet, Maryse, 4 Rue Croix-de-Malte, 45000 Orléans.
T. 0238540284. *046259*
Lemray, Ph. & D. Souchard, 22 Quai Augustin, 45100
Orléans. T. 0238513873. - Paint / Furn / Dec / Lights /
Glass - *046260*
Lemray, Ph. & D. Souchard, 1bis Rue Porte Saint-Jean,
45000 Orléans. T. 0238771494. - Paint / Furn / Dec /
Lights / Glass - *046261*
Lidon, Patrick, 192 Rue Bourgogne, 45000 Orléans.
T. 0238538292. - Paint / Furn / Sculp / Cur - *046262*
Liger, Jean-Philippe, 94 Quai Châtelet, 45000 Orléans.
T. 0238536712, Fax 0238817103. - Furn /
Sculp - *046263*
Marie-Andrée, 203 Rue Bourgogne, 45000 Orléans.
T. 0238627637. *046264*
Marit, Pascale, 22 Rue Aristide-Maillol, 45000 Orléans.
T. 0238639725. *046265*
Morcos, Patrice, 64 Rue Bretonnerie, 45000 Orléans.
T. 0238548646. *046266*
Passé Simple, 4 Rue Colombier, 45000 Orléans.
T. 0238420701. - Furn - *046267*
Rouilly, 10 Rue Saint-Etienne, 45000 Orléans.
T. 0238540378. *046268*
Suarez, Pascal, 4 Rue Champ-de-Manoeuvres, 45000
Orléans. T. 0238725409. *046269*
Thomas, Jean-Yves, 8bis Rue de la Bascule, 45100 Orléans. T. 0238564900. - Ant - *046270*
Trompat, Yvette, 13 Rue Vieux-Marché, 45000 Orléans.
T. 0238626118. *046271*

Orsay (Essonne)
Embelle, 12 Rue Archangé, 91400 Orsay.
T. 0169071748. *046272*

Orval (Manche)
Lesigne, Michel, Campagne, 50660 Orval.
T. 0233468248. *046273*

Orvilliers (Yvelines)
Accrall, Marcel, 18 Rue Pré-Saint-Martin, 78910 Orvilliers. T. 0134876187. *046274*

Oullins (Rhône)
Gayet, Jeanne, 10 Rue Ferrer, 69600 Oullins.
T. 0472392049. *046275*
Gayet, Paulette, 10 Rue Ferrer, 69600 Oullins.
T. 0478512456. *046276*
Maurice, Serge, 53 Rue Louis Pasteur, 69600 Oullins.
T. 0478510402. *046277*
Mutel, René, 87 Chemin Buisset, 69600 Oullins.
T. 0478517314. *046278*
Oullins ou l'Autre, 57 Rue République, 69600 Oullins.
T. 0478504641. - Furn / Tex / Cur - *046279*

Oulmes (Vendée)
Czochra, Philippe, 19 Rte Fontenay, 85420 Oulmes.
T. 0251504010. *046280*
Lenestour, 32 Rue Gare, 85420 Oulmes.
T. 0251524818. *046281*

Ousse (Pyrénées-Atlantiques)
Guilhemsans, Jean, 2 Imp Moulin, 64320 Ousse.
T. 0559817619. - Ant / Furn - *046282*

Ozoir-la-Ferrière (Seine-et-Marne)
Garzia, Joël, 74 Av Général-de-Gaulle, 77330 Ozoir-la-Ferrière. T. 0360029607, Fax 0360025080. *046283*

Pacé (Ille-et-Vilaine)
Brié, Alain, 19bis Rue Docteur-Léon, 35740 Pacé.
T. 0299602480. *046284*

Pacy-sur-Eure (Eure)

Atelier B.A., 83 Rue Isambard, 27120 Pacy-sur-Eure.
T. 0232367570. 046285
Atmosphère d'Antan, 115 Rue Isambard, 27120 Pacy-sur-Eure. T. 0232260300. 046286
Aumont, Maryannick, 102 Rue Isambard, 27120 Pacy-sur-Eure. T. 0232261648. 046287
Courtier, 96 Rue Isambard, 27120 Pacy-sur-Eure.
T. 0232360045. - Furn / Cur / Mod - 046288
Leveillé, Eric, 103 Rue Isambard, 27120 Pacy-sur-Eure.
T. 0232360853. - Furn - 046289
Mémoire's, 94bis Rue Isambard, 27120 Pacy-sur-Eure.
T. 0232367393. - Fra / Glass - 046290

Pagny-sur-Moselle (Meurthe-et-Moselle)

Demeure des Prémontrés, 3 Rue Nivoy, 54530 Pagny-sur-Moselle. T. 0383815455. 046291

Paimpol (Côtes-d'Armor)

Coustenoble, Yves, 14 Rue Eglise, 22500 Paimpol.
T. 0296550267. 046292
En ce Temps là, 6 Rue Saint-Vincent, 22500 Paimpol.
T. 0296208035. - Furn / Cur - 046293

Paley (Seine-et-Marne)

Arboré, Jean-François, 18 Rue Vignes, 77710 Paley.
T. 64315340. 046294

Pantin (Seine-Saint-Denis)

Marcus, Ligia, 5 Av 8-Mai-1945, 93500 Pantin.
T. 0148454040. 046295
Occasion Brocante, 166 Av Jean-Lolive, 93500 Pantin.
T. 0148911916. 046296

Paradou (Bouches-du-Rhône)

Antiquité Mas Saint-Roch, Mas Saint-Roch, 13520 Paradou. T. 0490544903. 046297
Antiquités du Braban, Rte Belle-Croix, 13520 Paradou.
T. 0490544293. 046298

Paray-le-Monial (Saône-et-Loire)

Découvertes, 19 Quai Industrie, 71600 Paray-le-Monial.
T. 0385888048. - Ant - 046299

Paray-Vieille-Poste (Essonne)

Gallot, Robert, 174 Av Verdun, 91550 Paray-Vieille-Poste. T. 0169386201. - Ant / Paint / Furn / Silv / Instr / Mil / Toys - 046300
Gallot, Robert, RN 7, 81 Rte de Fontainebleau, 91550 Paray-Vieille-Poste. T. 0169383121. - Ant / Paint / Furn / Silv / Instr / Mil / Toys - 046301

Parigny (Manche)

Leblanc, René, 2 Imp Corral, 50600 Parigny.
T. 0233491302. 046302

Paris

A l'Aigle d'Or, 88 Blvd Magenta, 75010 Paris.
T. 0140378342. - Jew / Silv - 046303
A l'Antique, 74 Rue Charonne, 75011 Paris.
T. 0143559853. 046304
A l'Emeraude, 25 Rue Louis-Legrand, 75002 Paris.
T. 0147424082. - Jew - 046305
A la Bonne Brocante, 47-49 Rue Rendez-Vous, 75012 Paris. T. 0143475145. - Ant / Furn / Tex / Silv / Instr / Cur / Mod / Toys - 046306
A la Bourse d'Or, 102 Rue Dames, 75017 Paris.
T. 0142940953. - Ant - 046307
A la Lorraine, 23 Rue Saints-Pères, 75006 Paris.
T. 0142602784. - Ant - 046308
A la Reine Margot, 7 Quai Conti, 75006 Paris.
T. 0143266250, Fax 0143255982. - Ant - 046309
A la Tour Camouflé, 1 Av Paul-Déroulède, 75015 Paris.
T. 0143063630. - Ant - 046310
A la Vieille Cité, 350 Rue Saint-Honoré, 75001 Paris.
T. 0142606716, Fax 0142606716. - Ant / Jew / Silv / Ico - 046311
Aanor 7ème, 15 Rue Malar, 75007 Paris.
T. 0147058056. 046312
Aaron, 73 Rue Duhesme, 75018 Paris.
T. 0142523131. 046313

DIDIER AARON

118 Fb. St.-Honoré
(75008)
Tél. 01 47 42 47 34
Fax 01 42 66 24 17

Aaron, Didier, 118 Rue Saint-Honoré, 75008 Paris.
T. 0147424734, Fax 0142662417. - Paint / Graph /
Furn / Orient / Dec / Draw - 046314
Aaron, Hervé, 118 Rue Saint-Honoré, 75008 Paris.
T. 0147424734, Fax 0142662417. - Paint /
Furn - 046315
Abacca, 23 Rue Fossés-Saint-Jacques, 75005 Paris.
T. 0140518044. - Orient - 046316
ABC Pascal, 356 Rue Vaugirard, 75015 Paris.
T. 0148283637. - Ant - 046317
Abel, 196 Av Versailles, 75016 Paris. T. 0145258885.
- Ant - 046318
Aboucaya, Georges, 26 Rue Richter, 75009 Paris.
T. 0142468193, Fax 0142467491. - Ant - 046319
Abracadabra, 14 Rue Grenelle, 75006 Paris.
T. 0145487023. - Ant / Cur - 046320
Acanthe, 18 Rue Cortambert, 75016 Paris.
T. 0145031555, Fax 0145032901. - Ant - 046321
Accrosonge, 17 Rue Sainte-Croix-la-Bretonnerie, 75004
Paris. T. 0142774631, Fax 0148870139.
- Eth - 046322
Achkar-Charrière, 232 Blvd Saint-Germain, 75007 Paris.
T. 0145489330, Fax 0142840464. - Ant /
Furn - 046323
Acker, Akko van, 3 Rue Université, 75007 Paris.
T. 0142602203, Fax 0142604687. - Ant - 046324
Acora, Louvre des Antiquaires, 2 Pl Palais-Royal, 75001
Paris. T. 0142615829. 046325
Actéon, 8 Rue Beaune, 75007 Paris. T. 0142612343.
- Naut - 046326
ADL, Louvre des Antiquaires, 2 Pl Palais-Royal, 75001
Paris. T. 0142960527. 046327
ADL, 21 Rue Auguste-Vacquerie, 75016 Paris.
T. 0140700243. 046328
Aernouts, Régis, 78 Av Suffren, 75015 Paris.
T. 0147348510. - Ant - 046329
Agamède, 12 Rue Université, 75007 Paris.
T. 0140159312. - Paint / Graph / Draw - 046330
Ailes du Temps, 9 Rue Alasseur, 75015 Paris.
T. 0147835019. - Ant / Furn - 046331
Ainsi Soient-Ils, 39 Rue Charonne, 75011 Paris.
T. 0148054247. 046332
Air de Chasse, 8 Rue Saints-Pères, 75007 Paris.
T. 0142602598. - Ant / Cur - 046333
Aittouares, 10 Rue Grange-Batelière, 75009 Paris.
T. 0145234113, Fax 0142070390. - Paint / Graph /
Sculp / Draw - 046334
Aittouares, 35 Rue Seine, 75006 Paris. T. 0140518746.
- Paint / Graph / Sculp / Draw - 046335
A.J. Antiquités, 5 Rue Université, 75007 Paris.
T. 0142603394. - Ant - 046336
Aker, Albert, 26 Rue Guynemer, 75006 Paris.
T. 0145444124, Fax 0142840543. - Ant - 046337
Alaux, Jean, 28 Av République, 75011 Paris.
T. 0147005764. - Ant - 046338
Albeck, 11bis Rue Tiphaine, 75015 Paris.
T. 0145777248. - Ant - 046339
Albertine, 9 Rue Maître-Albert, 75005 Paris.
T. 0143293920. - Graph / Draw - 046340
Alcora, 41 Rue Tolbiac, 75013 Paris. T. 0145859321.
- Ant - 046341
Alésia, 233 Rue Alésia, 75014 Paris. T. 0140446200.
- Ant / Paint / Furn / Lights / Instr / Cur / Toys - 046342
Alésia Dépôt-Vente, 123 Rue Alésia, 75014 Paris.
T. 0145455454, Fax 0145395919. - Ant /
Furn - 046343
Allan, David, 13bis Rue Grenelle, 75007 Paris.
T. 0145441705, Fax 0145494889. - Silv - 046344

Allard, 20 Av Suffren, 75015 Paris. T. 0145667743.
- Jew - 046345
Allée, Yannick, Louvre des Antiquaires, 2 Pl Palais-Royal, 75001 Paris. T. 0142615794, Fax 0142615794.
- Ant / Furn - 046346
Almandine, 38 Rue Sèvres, 75007 Paris.
T. 0145492343. - Jew - 046347
Alternative, 3 Rue Rosa-Binheur, 75015 Paris.
T. 0142199372, Fax 0145665100. 046348
Altéro, Nicole, 21 Quai Voltaire, 75007 Paris.
T. 0142611990, Fax 0140200330. - Ant / Furn / Dec /
Glass - 046349
Amateur de Musique, 3 Rue Paul-Strauss, 75020 Paris.
T. 0140302595, Fax 0140302596. 046350
Amélie, 17 Rue Amélie, 75007 Paris. T. 0145559010.
- Ant - 046351
Andréa, 12 Av Théophile-Gautier, 75016 Paris.
T. 0142249077. - Ant - 046352
Andrieux, 5 Rue Beaune, 75007 Paris. T. 0142616835.
- Jew / Cur - 046353
Andrieux & Cie, 15 Rue Sèvres, 75006 Paris.
T. 0145482718. - Jew - 046354
Anka Tomy, 27 Rue Fbg-Montmartre, 75009 Paris.
T. 0147704572, Fax 0147701871. - Paint - 046355
Anne & Pénélopé, 3 Av Champaubert, 75015 Paris.
T. 0147349454. - Ant - 046356
Antan Longtemps, 10 Av Versailles, 75016 Paris.
T. 0145272368. - Ant / Fra - 046357
Antic-Tac, Louvre des Antiquaires, 2 Pl Palais-Royal, 75001 Paris. T. 0142615716, Fax 0142617586.
- Instr - 046358
Antica, 167 Blvd Montparnasse, 75006 Paris.
T. 0143297701. - Ant - 046359
Antikhor, 4 Rue Rambuteau, 75003 Paris.
T. 0142710022. - Jew - 046360
Antipodes, 3 Rue Beaux-Arts, 75006 Paris.
T. 0143294568. - Arch / Eth / Jew - 046361
Antiquaire du Grand Cerf, 8 Passage Grand-Cerf, 75002
Paris. T. 0142336172. 046362
Antiquaires Associés, 10 Rue Eugène-Gibez, 75015 Paris. T. 0145301109. - Ant - 046363
Antiquaréa, 54 Av La-Motte-Picquet, 75015 Paris.
T. 0145676044. 046364
Antique 16, 19 Rue Annonciation, 75016 Paris.
T. 0142886473, Fax 0142309436. - Ant / Paint /
Furn - 046365
Antiquité Bartement, 11 Rue Pierre-Demours, 75017 Paris. T. 0145740936. 046366
Antiquités Chaké, 54 Rue Vasco-de-Gama, 75015 Paris.
T. 0148280415. 046367
Antiquités de Beaune, 14 Rue Beaune, 75007 Paris.
T. 0142612542, Fax 0142612444. 046368
Antiquités du Pont Neuf, 2 Rue Pont-Neuf, 75001 Paris.
T. 0142210326. - Ant / Paint / Furn - 046369
Antiquités du 20ème Siècle, Louvre des Antiquaires, 2
Pl Palais-Royal, 75001 Paris. T. 0149270335. 046370
Antiquités et d'Asie, 4 Av Bugeaud, 75116 Paris.
T. 0145537748, Fax 0147550252. - Orient - 046371
Antiquités Jouffroy, 25 Rue Jouffroy Abbans, 75017 Paris. T. 0140530780. - Ant - 046372
Antiquités Martine, 33 Rue Assomption, 75016 Paris.
T. 0145252498. 046373
Antiquités Rocaille, 25 Rue Sarrette, 75014 Paris.
T. 0145407239. - Ant / Furn - 046374
Antiquités 17, 17 Rue Brochant, 75017 Paris.
T. 0146277204. - Ant - 046375
Antiquités 54, 54 Rue Jacob, 75006 Paris.
T. 0142608361, Fax 0140159313. - Ant - 046376
Antiquités 88, 88 Av Mozart, 75016 Paris.
T. 0142880895. - Ant - 046377
Antoine, 10 Av Opéra, 75001 Paris.
T. 0142960180. 046378
Antoine, André, 31 Rue Beaune, 75007 Paris.
T. 0142612606. - Ant - 046379
Antonovich, François, Louvre des Antiquaires, 2 Pl du
Palais-Royal, 75001 Paris. T. 0142615793,
Fax 0142617116. - Ant / Furn / Sculp / Arch / Rel /
Draw - 046380
Aogai, 36 Rue Verneuil, 75007 Paris. T. 0142611078.
- Graph / Orient / Draw - 046381
Apamée, 3 Rue Maître-Albert, 75005 Paris.
T. 0146340440. - Ant - 046382

L'ARC en Seine
ART DECO / 1930
Christian et Catherine BOUTONNET
Rafaël ORTIZ

27 et 31, rue de Seine
75006 Paris
Tel. : (33) 01 43 29 11 02
Fax : (33) 01 43 29 97 66

Aragon, 21 Rue Jacob, 75006 Paris. T. 0143258769.
- Dec / Cur -   046383

Arc en Seine, 27 Rue de Seine, 75006 Paris.
T. 0143291102, Fax 0143299766. - Paint / Graph /
Furn / Sculp -   046383a

Arcade 127, 33 Rue Valois, 75001 Paris.
T. 0142613291. - Ant -   046384

Arcadiane, Louvre des Antiquaires, 2 Pl Palais Royale,
75001 Paris. T. 0142970500. - Paint / Graph -   046385

Archi-Noire, 19 Rue Victor-Massé, 75009 Paris.
T. 0148780182. - Jew -   046386

Archit-Décor-Conseil, 19 Rue La-Jonquière, 75017 Paris. T. 0142630525. - Ant -   046387

Argana, 33 Rue Jacob, 75006 Paris. T. 0142608923,
Fax 0140200367. - Ant -   046388

Argenterie des Francs-Bourgeois, 17 Rue Francs-Bourgeois, 75004 Paris. T. 0142720400,
Fax 0142720824.   046389

Argiles, 13 Rue Guénégaud, 75006 Paris.
T. 0146334473. - Arch / Eth -   046390

Argonautes, 74 Rue Seine, 75006 Paris. T. 0143267069,
Fax 0143269988. - Graph / Draw -   046391

Arigoni, Catherine, 14 Rue Beaune, 75007 Paris.
T. 0142605099. - Ant -   046392

Ariodante, 17 Rue Lille, 75007 Paris. T. 0142613939.
- Dec -   046393

Aristote, 5 Rue Charlemagne, 75004 Paris.
T. 0142779294.   046394

Arlequin, 8 Rue Dupleix, 75015 Paris. T. 0142731612.
- Ant -   046395

Armengaud, Josette, 19 Rue Bac, 75007 Paris.
T. 0147039907. - Ant / Paint / Furn / Sculp / Tex / Dec /
Cur -   046396

Arnaud, Florence, 10 Rue Saintonge, 75003 Paris.
T. 0142770179. - Graph / Draw -   046397

Art Antiquités Associés, 5 Rue Provence, 75009 Paris.
T. 0145232073. - Ant / Cur -   046398

Art Cadre, 35 Rue Beaune, 75007 Paris. T. 0149279411.
- Fra -   046399

Art de Chine et d'Orient, 88 Rue Chardon-Lagache,
75016 Paris. T. 0145254344. - Orient / China - 046400

Art de la Chine et du Japon, 17 Rue Drouot, 75009 Paris. T. 0147703300, Fax 0140229323.
- Orient -   046401

Art Dépôt, 3 Rue Pont-Louis-Philippe, 75004 Paris.
T. 0142779902. - Lights -   046402

Art Domestique Ancien, 231 Rue Saint-Honoré, 75001
Paris. T. 0140209460. - Eth -   046403

Art Domestique Ancien, 231 Rue Saint-Honoré, 75001
Paris. T. 0140209460. - Eth / Cur -   046404

Art et Curiosités, 10 Rue Saint-Simon, 75007 Paris.
T. 0142229991.   046405

Art Formel, 9 Rue Saint-Paul, 75004 Paris.
T. 0148049333. - Ant -   046406

Art Gallia, 7 Rue Mont-Doré, 75017 Paris.
T. 0143878364. - Ant -   046407

Artel, 25 Rue Bonaparte, 75006 Paris. T. 0143549377.
- Paint / Sculp / Fra / Ico -   046408

Arts Asiatiques, 4 Rue Maître-Albert, 75005 Paris.
T. 0144073131, Fax 0144070318. - Orient -   046409

Arts des Amériques, 42 Rue Seine, 75006 Paris.
T. 0146331831. - Ant / Orient / Sculp / Arch /
Eth -   046410

Arts et Boiseries, 16 Rue Saints-Pères, 75007 Paris.
T. 0142602313. - Ant -   046411

Arts et Marines, 8 Rue Miromesnil, 75008 Paris.
T. 0142652785, Fax 0142653059. - Paint / Instr / Mil /
Cur / Naut -   046412

Asie Antique, 23 Rue Lille, 75007 Paris. T. 0149270443,
Fax 0148346591. - Orient -   046413

Association d'Antiquaires du Village Suisse, 78 Av Suffren, 75015 Paris. T. 0147346904.   046414

Atelier d'Art Damrémont 25, 25 Rue Damrémont, 75018
Paris. T. 0142645220. - Ant -   046415

Atelier du Bois Doré, 80 Av Ternes, 75017 Paris.
T. 0145746758. - Fra -   046416

Ateliers du Matin, 13 Av Théophile-Gautier, 75016 Paris.
T. 0145251711. - Ant -   046417

Atlan, Alain, 56 Rue Caulaincourt, 75018 Paris.
T. 0142552597, Fax 0142526516. - Ant /
Furn -   046418

Atlantis Gallery, 33 Rue Seine, 75006 Paris.
T. 0143268962, Fax 0146336944. - Paint -   046419

Au Cheval de Bronze, 197 Rue Fbg-Saint-Denis, 75010
Paris. T. 0146075785. - Ant -   046420

Au Clair de Lune, 55 Blvd Grenelle, 75015 Paris.
T. 0145757135. - Ant -   046421

Au Collectionneur, 15 Rue Brey, 75016 Paris.
T. 0142276450. - Num / Pho -   046422

Au Complément d'Objet, 112 Rue Sèvres, 75015 Paris.
T. 0145665127. - Ant -   046423

Au Debotté, 2 Rue Charlemagne, 75004 Paris.
T. 0148048520. - Furn / Cur -   046424

Au Directoire, 12 Blvd Raspail, 75007 Paris.
T. 0142226709. - Ant -   046425

Au Fond de la Cour, 49 Rue Seine, 75006 Paris.
T. 0143258189. - Ant -   046426

Au Grand Bazar, 13 Av Théophile-Gautier, 75016 Paris.
T. 0140500513. - Ant -   046427

Au Paradis d'Antan, 36 Rue Bois-le-Vent, 75016 Paris.
T. 0142881015.   046428

Au Passé Retrouvé, 30 Gal Montpensier, 75001 Paris.
T. 0142960945. - Ant -   046429

Au Petit Dunkerque, 67 Rue Saint-Charles, 75015 Paris.
T. 0145781370. - Ant -   046430

Au Petit Hussard, 5 Rue Beaune, 75007 Paris.
T. 0142612986. - Ant / China / Glass -   046431

Au Petit Mayet, 10 Rue Mayet, 75006 Paris.
T. 0145676829. - Ant -   046432

Au Puceron Chineur, 23 Rue Saint-Paul, 75004 Paris.
T. 0142728820. - Jew / Silv -   046433

Au Singe Violet, 46 Rue Assomption, 75016 Paris.
T. 0145273585. - Ant -   046434

Au Vase de Delft, 19 Rue Cambon, 75001 Paris.
T. 0142609429. - Jew / Instr / Ico -   046435

Au Vieux Document, 6bis Rue Châteaudun, 75009 Paris.
T. 0148787784. - Mil / Cur -   046436

Aubinière, Colette, Louvre des Antiquaires, 2 Pl Palais-
Royal, 75001 Paris. T. 0142615759.   046437

Aubry, Eric, 49 Rue Saint-Georges, 75009 Paris.
T. 0142810695.   046438

Auclair, Denise, 178 Av Victor-Hugo, 75016 Paris.
T. 0147276827. - Ant -   046439

Auffret, Marie-Josèphe, 42 Rue Frémicourt, 75015 Paris. T. 0145670959. - Paint / Graph / Draw -   046440

Augeard, Gisèle, 81 Rue Bobillot, 75013 Paris.
T. 0145881750. - Ant / Cur -   046441

Augier, Jeanne, 25 Rue Saint-Paul, 75004 Paris.
T. 0148049031. - Ant -   046442

Aurelio Bis, Louvre des Antiquaires, 2 Pl Palais-Royal,
75001 Paris. T. 0142615798. - Ant -   046443

Autre Jour, 26 Av La-Bourdonnais, 75007 Paris.
T. 0147053660. - Ant -   046444

Autrefois, 10 Rue Ernest-Cresson, 75014 Paris.
T. 0145406163. - Ant -   046445

Autrefois, 156bis Av Daumesnil, 75012 Paris.
T. 0144740224. - Ant -   046446

Aux Armes de France, 4 Rue Babylone, 75007 Paris.
T. 0145480506. - Ant -   046447

Aux Fils du Temps, 33 et 35 Rue Grenelle, 75007 Paris.
T. 0145481468. - Ant -   046448

Aux Reflets du Passé, 36 Rue Delambre, 75014 Paris.
T. 0145385722, Fax 0142798847. - Paint / Furn / Dec /
Instr / Cur / Toys -   046449

Aux Soldats d'Antan, 67 Quai Tournelle, 75005 Paris.
T. 0146334050, Fax 0144073345. - Mil -   046450

Avedis, Louvre des Antiquaires, 2 Pl Palais-Royal,
75001 Paris. T. 0142615689. - Tex -   046451

Aveline, 20 Rue Cirque, 75008 Paris. T. 0142666029,
Fax 0142664591. - Dec -   046452

Aventure, 42 Rue Daguerre, 75014 Paris.
T. 0143200183. - Ant -   046453

Azpitarte, Florence, 41 Rue Acacias, 75017 Paris.
T. 0143800048. - Ant -   046454

Bac, 64 Rue Bac, 75007 Paris. T. 0145480938. - Paint /
Furn / China -   046455

Bac, Georges, 35-37 Rue Bonaparte, 75006 Paris.
T. 0143268267, Fax 0146345158. - Furn / Dec /
Cur -   046456

Bac Street, 1 Rue Bac, 75007 Paris. T. 0142612420,
Fax 0149279085. - Orient / Arch / Jew / Cur -   046457

Badin, 43 Rue Lille, 75007 Paris.
T. 0142868679.   046458

Baillon, Elisabeth, 19 Rue Molière, 75001 Paris.
T. 0140200406. - Paint -   046459

Bailly, Charles & André, 25 Quai Voltaire, 75007 Paris.
T. 0142601647, Fax 0142605492. - Paint -   046460

Bakhtari, Mehdi, 173 Rue Championnet, 75018 Paris.
T. 0142652985. - Ant -   046461

Baladine, 100 Av Daumesnil, 75012 Paris.
T. 0143070519. - China -   046462

Balian, Louvre des Antiquaires, 2 Pl Palais-Royal, 75001
Paris. T. 0142601705, Fax 0142602231. - Dec / Jew /
Cur -   046463

Balmès Richelieu, 21 Pl Vosges, 75003 Paris.
T. 0148872045. - Ant / Furn / Instr / Cur -   046464

Bamyan, 1 Rue Blancs-Manteaux, 75004 Paris.
T. 0144780011.   046465

Barbanel, Claude, 73 Rue Notre-Dame-de-Nazareth,
75003 Paris. T. 0142779379. - Ant / Music -   046466

Barbanel, Roger, 124 Blvd Rochechouart, 75018 Paris.
T. 0142649953. - Ant -   046467

Barbé, Patrice, 16 Rue Grange-Batelière, 75009 Paris.
T. 0147706992, Fax 0147709857. - Ant -   046468

Barbeau, Alain, 1 Rue Moscou, 75008 Paris.
T. 0145222936. - Ant -   046469

Barberousse, Michel, 70 Quai Hôtel-de-Ville, 75004 Paris. T. 0142721644. - Ant -   046470

Barbéry, Jean-Louis, 2 Rue Grands-Degrés, 75005 Paris. T. 0143253376. - Graph / Draw -   046471

Barboza, Pierre, 356 Rue Saint-Honoré, 75001 Paris.
T. 0142606708. - Jew -   046472

Barlor, 125 Rue Rennes, 75006 Paris. T. 0142220963.
- Num -   046473

Baron, Marie-Anne, 6 Rue Lille, 75007 Paris.
T. 0140159760. - Orient / Dec -   046474

Baroni, Jean-François, 12 Rue Louvois, 75002 Paris.
T. 0140200473, Fax 0140200207. - Paint / Graph /
Draw -   046475

Baroques Antiquités, 67 Rue Cherche-Midi, 75006 Paris.
T. 0145493114. - Ant -   046476

Barrère, Jacques, 36 Rue Mazarine, 75006 Paris.
T. 0143265761, Fax 0146340283. - Orient / China /
Sculp / Arch / Eth -   046477

Barrie, Patrick, 186 Blvd Saint-Germain, 75007 Paris.
T. 0145448115. - Ant / Furn / Orient / China / Sculp /
Jew / Silv / Instr / Mod -   046478

Barrié, Philippe, Louvre des Antiquaires, 2 Pl Palais-Royal, 75001 Paris. T. 0142602301. - Ant -   046479

Barry Lindon, 15 Blvd Saint-Germain, 75005 Paris.
T. 0143268885. - Lights / Glass -   046480

Bartleby, 15 Rue Gay-Lussac, 75005 Paris.
T. 0143263659. - Ant -   046481

Bassali, Louvre des Antiquaires, 2 Pl Palais-Royal,
75001 Paris. T. 0142602125. - Ant -   046482

Bastien & Associés, 13 Rue Lille, 75007 Paris.
T. 0142602422. - Furn / Dec -   046483

Bauchet & Bitonti, 84 Rue Folie-Méricourt, 75011 Paris.
T. 0143579400. - Ant -   046484

Baxter, 15 Rue Dragon, 75006 Paris. T. 0145490134.
- Paint / Graph / Draw -   046485

Bayser, Bruno de, 69 Rue Sainte-Anne, 75002 Paris.
T. 0147034987, Fax 0142605932. - Paint / Sculp /
Draw -   046486

Béalu, Christian, 169 Blvd Saint-Germain, 75006 Paris.
T. 0145484653, Fax 0142840980. - Furn / Orient / China / Tex / Fra / Glass / Cur / Draw - *046487*

Béarks, Louvre des Antiquaires, 2 Pl Palais-Royal, 75001 Paris. T. 0142601939. *046488*

Beaujard, Jean-Paul, 25 Rue Varenne, 75007 Paris.
T. 0142229733, Fax 0142229774. *046489*

Beauséjour, 35 Blvd Beauséjour, 75016 Paris.
T. 0145279706. - Paint / Furn / Jew / Silv - *046490*

Beauté Divine, 40 Rue Saint-Sulpice, 75006 Paris.
T. 0143262531. - Glass / Mod - *046491*

Beauvais, Philippe de, 112 Blvd Courcelles, 75017 Paris.
T. 0147632072. - Ant / Paint / Furn / Lights - *046492*

Bechir, Gérard, 59 Rue Condorcet, 75009 Paris.
T. 0142851597. - Ant / Cur - *046493*

Becker, Eugène, 136 Rue Fbg-Saint-Honoré, 75008 Paris. T. 0142894490, Fax 0142894491. - Furn / Sculp - *046494*

Belaych, Christian, 18 Rue Duret, 75116 Paris.
T. 0145004496. - Ant / Paint / Furn - *046495*

Bellanger, Patrice, 198 Blvd Saint-Germain, 75007 Paris. T. 0145441915, Fax 0142840229. - Ant / Sculp - *046496*

Bellier, Jean-Claude, 32 Av Pierre-1er-de-Serbie, 75008 Paris. T. 0147201913, Fax 0147206509.
- Paint - *046497*

Bellou, Guy, 7bis Rue Saints-Pères, 75006 Paris.
T. 0142608133. - Ant / Furn / Instr - *046498*

Benadava, V., 28 Rue La-Boétie, 75008 Paris.
T. 0143591221. - Tex - *046499*

Beneton, Guy, 36 Rue Varenne, 75007 Paris.
T. 0142227802. - Ant / Paint / Orient / China - *046500*

Benli, 17 Rue Saint-Roch, 75001 Paris. T. 0142604976.
- Orient - *046501*

Berès, Huguette, 25 Quai Voltaire, 75007 Paris.
T. 0142612791, Fax 0149279588. - Paint / Graph / Orient - *046502*

Berès-Montanari, Anisabelle, 25 Quai Voltaire, 75007 Paris. T. 0142612791, Fax 0149279588. - Paint / Orient - *046503*

Berger, Alain, 3 Rue Université, 75007 Paris.
T. 0142615501. - Ant - *046504*

Berger, Max, 18 Av Porte-Brunet, 75019 Paris.
T. 0142087481. - Ant - *046505*

Berko, Louvre des Antiquaires, 2 Pl Palais-Royal, 75001 Paris. T. 0142601940, Fax 0142601941.
- Paint - *046506*

Bernard, Pierre-Georges, 1 Rue Anjou, 75008 Paris.
T. 0142652303. - Instr / Cur / Music - *046507*

Bernheim, Denise, 81 Rue Amsterdam, 75008 Paris.
T. 0148740391. - Ant - *046508*

Bernheim, Marcel, 18 Av Matignon, 75008 Paris.
T. 0142652223, Fax 0142652716. - Paint - *046509*

Berthet, Camille, Louvre des Antiquaires, 2 Pl Palais-Royal, 75001 Paris. T. 0142602144. - Jew - *046510*

Berthon, Olivier, 17 Rue Cordelières, 75013 Paris.
Fax (1) 45351651. *046511*

Bertrand, Huguette, 22 Rue Jacob, 75006 Paris.
T. 0143265908. - Ant - *046512*

Besrest, Jean-Jacques, Village Suisse, 10 Av Champaubert, 75015 Paris. T. 0145675961. - Ant - *046513*

Beurdeley & Cie, 200 Blvd Saint-Germain, 75007 Paris. T. 0145489786, Fax 0145449911. - Ant / Furn / Orient / Arch - *046514*

Beyrie, Maria de, 23 Rue Seine, 75006 Paris.
T. 0143257615. - Paint - *046515*

Biaggi, Alexandre, 54 Rue Jacob, 75005 Paris.
T. 0142860840. - Ant - *046516*

Biewesch, Roger, 34 Av Parmentier, 75011 Paris.
T. 0148055530. - Ant - *046517*

Bigot, S., 9 Rue Brémontier, 75017 Paris.
T. 0142278140. - Ant - *046518*

Bijoux du Louvre, Louvre des Antiquaires, 2 Pl Palais-Royal, 75001 Paris. T. 0142601767, Fax 0142605045.
- Jew - *046519*

Birtschansky, Pierre, 156 Blvd Haussmann, 75008 Paris. T. 0145628886, Fax 0142894197. - Paint - *046520*

Bissonnet, André, 6 Rue Pas-de-la-Mule, 75003 Paris.
T. 0148872015. - Music - *046521*

Blanc, Anselme, Louvre des Antiquaires, 2 Pl Palais-Royal, 75001 Paris. T. 0142601843. - Jew - *046522*

Blanc, Cyrille, 9 Rue Provence, 75009 Paris.
T. 0147704270. - Ant - *046523*

Blanchetti, Jean-François de, 2 Rue Saints-Pères, 75007 Paris. T. 0142602243, Fax 0142962347.
- Ant - *046524*

Bleu Passé, 24bis Blvd Courcelles, 75017 Paris.
T. 0142675740. - Ant - *046525*

Blondeel-Deroyan, 11 Rue de Lille, 75007 Paris.
T. 0149279622, Fax 49279618. - Ant / Tex - *046525a*

GALERIE
BLONDEEL-DEROYAN

Antiquities
Medieval art
Tapestries

11, rue de Lille. F-75007 Paris
T. 33/01 49 27 96 22 - F. 33/01 49 27 96 18

Schuttersshofstraat 5 . B-2000 Antwerpen
T. 32.3/232 25 54 - F. 32.3/232 43 60

Boccador, Jacqueline, 1 Quai Voltaire, 75007 Paris.
T. 0142607579, Fax 0142603127. - Furn / Sculp / Tex - *046526*

Bodard, Gilles, Village Suisse, 54 Av La-Motte-Picquet, 75015 Paris. T. 0143064418. - Jew - *046527*

Boix, Christian, 26 Villa Croix-Nivert, 75015 Paris.
T. 0142732281. - Ant - *046528*

Bon Marché, 22 Rue Sèvres, 75007 Paris.
T. 0144398090. - Tex - *046529*

Bon Usage, 21 Rue Saint-Paul, 75004 Paris.
T. 0142788014. - Ant - *046530*

Bonafous-Murat, Arsène, 15 Rue Echaudé, 75006 Paris. T. 0146334231. - Paint / Graph / Draw - *046531*

Boomrang, Louvre des Antiquaires, 2 Pl Palais-Royal, 75001 Paris. Fax (1) 49260581. *046532*

Borowski, Nina, 4 Rue Bac, 75007 Paris.
T. 0145486160, Fax 0145487525. - Ant / Orient / Sculp / Arch / Eth / Jew - *046533*

Boîte à Musique, 96 Rue Bac, 75007 Paris.
T. 0142220130. - Ant - *046534*

Bouche, 41 Rue Richelieu, 75001 Paris.
T. 0142964979. *046535*

Bouché, Charles, 14 Rue Pyramides, 75001 Paris.
T. 0142964979. - Arch / Mil / Cur - *046536*

Bouchoucha, Slim, Louvre des Antiquaires, 2 Pl Palais-Royal, 75001 Paris. T. 0142615725. - Ant / Orient - *046537*

Boucq, 4 Rue Provence, 75009 Paris. T. 0147700095.
- Ant - *046538*

Bourgey, Sabine, 7 Rue Drouot, 75009 Paris.
T. 0147703518, Fax 0142465848. - Num - *046539*

Bourse du Collectionneur, 11 Rue Saint-Marc, 75002 Paris. T. 0145084901. - Num - *046540*

Bousquet, Richard, 38 Rue Sèvres, 75007 Paris.
T. 0145490498. - Ant - *046541*

Bousquet & Cie, 57 Rue Cherche-Midi, 75006 Paris.
T. 0145483350. - Ant / Furn / China - *046542*

Boutersky, Jacques, Louvre des Antiquaires, 2 Pl Palais-Royal, 75001 Paris. T. 0142615796. - Paint / Graph / Draw - *046543*

Boutet, Norbert, 20 Rue Richer, 75009 Paris.
Fax (1) 48000076. - Ant - *046544*

Boutique Anglaise, 11 Rue Daval, 75011 Paris.
T. 0149239405. - Furn - *046545*

Boutique du Marais, 16 Rue Sévigné, 75004 Paris.
T. 0142740365, Fax 0140299828. - Orient / China / Dec - *046546*

Boutique Philippe, Louvre des Antiquaires, 2 Pl Palais-Royal, 75001 Paris. T. 0142615726. - Ant - *046547*

Boutique 34, 34 Rue Saints-Pères, 75007 Paris.
T. 0142222900. - Ant - *046548*

Bouveret, Luc, 8 Rue Furstenberg, 75006 Paris.
T. 0140468281, Fax 0140468283. *046549*

Bouvier, Jacques, 14 Rue Visconti, 75006 Paris.
T. 0143266727. - Ant - *046550*

Bouyer, Michel, 7 Rue Commandant-Guilbaud, 75016 Paris. T. 0146043741. - Ant - *046551*

Boyer, Claude, 14 Rue Lapeyrère, 75018 Paris.
T. 0142573073, Fax 0142571434. - Ant - *046552*

Bozon, Axelle, 78 Av Suffren, 75015 Paris.
T. 0145674444, Fax 0144189544. - Ant / Paint / Graph / Draw - *046553*

Bozon, Michel, 36 Rue Bac, 75007 Paris.
T. 0142612695. - Ant / Paint / Graph / Draw - *046554*

Brakha, 120 Rue Crimée, 75019 Paris.
T. 0142039201. *046555*

Brame & Lorenceau, 68 Blvd Malesherbes, 75008 Paris. T. 0145221689, Fax 0145220167. - Paint - *046556*

Brame & Lorenceau, (B. Lorenceau), 68 Blvd Malesherbes, 75008 Paris. T. 0145221689, Fax 0145220167.
- Paint / Sculp - *046557*

Brame & Lorenceau, (F. Lorenceau), 68 Blvd Malesherbes, 75008 Paris. T. 0145221689, Fax 0145220167.
- Paint - *046558*

Bramy, Louvre des Antiquaires, 2 Pl Palais-Royal, 75001 Paris. T. 0142615748. - Ant - *046559*

Brandicourt, 54 Av Victor-Hugo, 75016 Paris.
T. 0145007616. - Ant - *046560*

Brandsdorfer, Marcel, 21 Rue Moscou, 75008 Paris.
T. 0145229959. - Ant - *046561*

Bresset, 5 Quai Voltaire, 75007 Paris. T. 0142607813, Fax 0142605938. - Ant / Paint / Furn / Sculp - *046562*

BRESSET
MOYEN AGE
RENAISSANCE
17e SIECLE
5, quai Voltaire, 75007 Paris
Tél : (33.1) 42 60 78 13
Fax : (33.1) 42 60 59 38

Bresset, 197 Blvd Saint-Germain, 75007 Paris.
T. 0145481824, Fax 0142605938. - Ant / Paint / Furn / Sculp - *046563*

Brieux, Alain, 48 Rue Jacob, 75006 Paris.
T. 0142602198, Fax 0142605524. - Instr - *046564*

Brisbois, Marie-José, 26 Rue Grands-Augustins, 75006 Paris. T. 0146330963. - Ant - *046565*

British Import, Louvre des Antiquaires, 2 Pl Palais-Royal, 75001 Paris. T. 0142601912. - Furn - *046566*

British Import, Village Suisse, 78 Av Suffren, 75015 Paris. T. 0145678761, Fax 0146372554. - Furn - *046567*

British Import Paris, Louvre des Antiquaires, 2 Pl Palais-Royal, 75001 Paris. T. 0142605400. - Furn - *046568*

Brito, Jeannine de, 12 Rue Université, 75007 Paris.
T. 0142602627. - Ant - *046569*

Broc-Antique, 60 Rue Clichy, 75009 Paris.
T. 0149950077. - Ant - *046570*

Broc'Saint Paul, 9 Rue Saint-Paul, 75004 Paris.
T. 0142744075. - Ant - *046571*

Brocante Atmosphères, 2 Rue Eugène-Varlin, 75010 Paris. T. 0142057003. - Ant - *046572*

Brocante d'Auteuil, 7 Rue Erlanger, 75016 Paris.
T. 0142880212. - Ant - *046573*

Brocanterie, 96 Av Mozart, 75016 Paris. T. 0145204101.
- Ant - *046574*

Brophy, Peter, 26 Rue Charonne, 75011 Paris.
T. 0143557347. - Ant - *046575*

Broutée, William, 44 Rue Dombasle, 75015 Paris.
T. 0148285813. - Ant - *046576*

Brugerolles, Yves, 23 Rue Jean-Jacques-Rousseau, 75001 Paris. T. 0142367571. - Graph / Orient / Mil / Draw - *046577*

Brugier, A., 74 Rue Sèvres, 75007 Paris. T. 0147348327, Fax 0140569140. - Ant - *046578*

Bruneline, 26 Rue Danielle-Casanova, 75002 Paris.
T. 0142869630. - Jew / Silv - *046579*

Bürgi, Camille, 3 Rue Rossini, 75009 Paris.
T. 0148242253, Fax 0147702599. - Ant / Furn / Dec - *046580*

Burawoy, Robert, 12 Rue Le-Regrattier, 75004 Paris.
T. 0143546736, Fax 0140469229. - Ant / Orient - *046581*

Burgan, Claude, 68 Rue Richelieu, 75002 Paris.
T. 0142969557, Fax 0142869243. - Num - *046582*

Buvelot, 9 Quai Voltaire, 75007 Paris. T. 0142618206.
- Ant - *046583*
B.V. Métaux Précieux, 21 Rue Drouot, 75009 Paris.
T. 0148248354. - Jew - *046584*
Byzance, 57 Rue Temple, 75004 Paris. T. 0142724486.
- Jew - *046585*
Cabanel, Victoria, 76 Rue Seine, 75006 Paris.
T. 0143543505. - Ant / Paint - *046586*
Cabinet Versini-Campinchi & Levystone & Ciochetti &
Paviot, 242bis Blvd Saint-Germain, 75007 Paris.
Fax (1) 45448736. - Ant - *046587*
Cabotse, Michel, 75 Rue Notre-Dame-des-Champs,
75006 Paris. T. 0143253483. *046588*
Cabrol, Barbara, 16 Rue Grange-Batelière, 75009 Paris.
T. 0142468183, Fax 0144830854. *046589*
Cacault, Michel, 73 Rue Championnet, 75018 Paris.
T. 0142574152. - Ant - *046590*
Cafler, Michel, Village Suisse, 78 Av Suffren, 75015 Pa-
ris. T. 0144499182. - Furn - *046591*
Cailac, Paule, 13 Rue Seine, 75006 Paris.
T. 0143269888. - Paint / Graph / Draw - *046592*
Caillat & Cie, 24 Rue Fbg-Saint-Antoine, 75012 Paris.
T. 0143439294. - Ant - *046593*
Cailleux, 136 Rue Fbg-Saint-Honoré, 75008 Paris.
T. 0143592524, Fax 0142259511. - Paint / Graph /
Draw - *046594*
Cailleux, Pierre, 13 Rue Monttessuy, 75007 Paris.
T. 0145518000. - Ant - *046595*
Caisse, Jean-François, 5 Rue Beaune, 75007 Paris.
T. 0142612722. - Furn / Fra - *046596*
Calinière, 68 Rue Vieille-du-Temple, 75003 Paris.
T. 0142774046. - Ant - *046597*
Calvet, Gérard, 10 Rue Chauchat, 75009 Paris.
T. 0142461236, Fax 0142461236. - Ant /
Furn - *046598*
Camaieu 13, 13 Rue Saint-Paul, 75004 Paris.
T. 0144598322. - Paint / Graph / Dec / Draw - *046599*
Camoin-Demachy, 9 Quai Voltaire, 75007 Paris.
T. 0142618206, Fax 0142612409. - Ant / Paint / Furn /
Dec - *046600*
Campana, Pierre, 7 Rue Tour, 75016 Paris.
T. 0145203625. - Ant / Cur - *046601*
Campana, Pierre, 148 Av Versailles, 75016 Paris.
T. 0146478081. - Ant - *046602*
Camus, Antoine, 11 Rue Tour, 75016 Paris.
T. 0145200087. - Jew - *046603*
Camus, Roger, 34 Rue Claude-Decaen, 75012 Paris.
T. 0143441402. - Graph - *046604*
Canton, Maria, 3 Rue Provence, 75009 Paris.
T. 0147707566. - Ant - *046605*
Cap Colonies, 84 Rue Cherche-Midi, 75006 Paris.
T. 0145443318, Fax 0142220347. - Rel - *046606*
Capharnaum, 57 Rue Poteau, 75018 Paris.
T. 0142540735. - Ant - *046607*
Capia, Robert, 26 Gal Véro-Dodat, 75001 Paris.
T. 0142362594. - Ant / Furn / China / Eth / Cur / Pho /
Toys - *046608*
Caprices, 53 Rue Legendre, 75017 Paris.
T. 0143802855. - Ant - *046609*
Captier, Bernard, 25 Rue Verneuil, 75007 Paris.
T. 0142610057, Fax 0147490425. - Orient - *046610*
Cariatides, 54 Av La-Motte-Picquet, 75015 Paris.
T. 0147837470. *046611*
Carlier, Philippe, 11 Rue Lille, 75007 Paris.
T. 0142605392, Fax 0142605392. - Ant / Furn /
Sculp - *046612*
Carpentier, Jean, 5 Blvd Voltaire, 75011 Paris.
T. 0148054785. - Ant - *046613*
Carré (Galerie des Orfèvres), 23 Pl Dauphine, 75001 Pa-
ris. T. 0143268130. - Paint / Jew / Graph - *046614*
Carré d'Or, 46 Av George-V, 75008 Paris.
T. 0140701100, Fax 0140709681. - Jew /
Silv - *046615*
Casas, Nadège, 2 Rue Ave-Maria, 75004 Paris.
T. 0148047561. - Ant - *046616*
Casciello, Domenico, Louvre des Antiquaires, 2 Pl Pa-
lais-Royal, 75001 Paris. T. 0142611373. - Paint /
Furn - *046617*
Castaing, Frédéric, 13 Rue Chapon, 75003 Paris.
T. 0142746909, Fax 0142740089. *046618*
Castiglione, Louvre des Antiquaires, 2 Pl Palais-Royal,
75001 Paris. T. 0142601841, Fax 0148780854.
- Jew / Silv - *046619*

Castro, Vincent de, 83 Rue Championnet, 75018 Paris.
T. 0142234929. *046620*
Cathay, 131 Rue Fbg-Saint-Honoré, 75008 Paris.
T. 0142252131. - Ant - *046621*
Cattet, Jean-Pierre, 4 Rue Gén-Camou, 75007 Paris.
T. 0145558616. *046622*
Cazaban, Jean-Louis, 18 Rue Saints-Pères, 75007 Pa-
ris. T. 0142611941. - China - *046623*
Cazals de Fabel, Michel, 97 Rue Courcelles, 75017 Pa-
ris. T. 0147631475. - Ant - *046624*
Cent Un, 101 Rue Charonne, 75011 Paris.
T. 0140091861. - Ant - *046625*
Certain Regard, 71 Rue Dulong, 75017 Paris.
T. 0142120405. - Cur - *046626*
Cézanne, Philippe, Louvre des Antiquaires, 2 Pl Palais-
Royal, 75001 Paris. T. 0142615711, Fax 0142616938.
- Paint / Sculp - *046627*
Chabolle, Edmond, 18 Rue Provence, 75009 Paris.
T. 0142471895. - Ant - *046628*
Chalmont, 150 Rue Saint-Honoré, 75001 Paris.
T. 0142610687. - Ant - *046629*
Chamak, Chantal, 18 Rue Provence, 75009 Paris.
T. 0142466694, Fax 0142463930. - Paint - *046630*
Chamak, Joelle, 6 Rue Batignolles, 75017 Paris.
T. 0143873781, Fax 0144700704. - Ant - *046631*
Chammard, Monique de, 54 Av La-Motte-Picquet,
75015 Paris. T. 0147344738. - Ant / Paint - *046632*
Chamonal, François & Rodolphe, 5 Rue Drouot, 75009
Paris. T. 0147708487, Fax 0142463547.
- Pho - *046633*
Chamouleau, Armand, 5 Rue Université, 75007 Paris.
T. 0142608276. - Ant / Furn - *046634*
Chaplier, Ghyslaine, 8 Av Champaubert, 75015 Paris.
T. 0145673055. - Ant - *046635*
Chapu, Marie-Françoise, 23 Rue Grenelle, 75007 Paris.
T. 0145486327. - Ant / Furn - *046636*
Chastel, Aline, 10 Rue Bonaparte, 75006 Paris.
T. 0140468261, Fax 0143262447. *046637*
Chaudanson, Michel, 14 Rue Bretagne, 75003 Paris.
T. 0142776902. - Ant - *046638*
Chauveau, P.J., 11 Rue Miromesnil, 75008 Paris.
T. 0142654362. - Furn / Orient / Lights - *046639*
Chelly, Anny, 26 Rue Batignolles, 75017 Paris.
T. 0145220789. *046640*
Chemin de Table, 10 Rue Grenelle, 75006 Paris.
T. 0142224021. - Ant - *046641*
Chevalier, 17 Quai Voltaire, 75007 Paris.
T. 0142607268, Fax 0142869906. - Tex - *046642*
Chevalier, 65 Rue Saint-Martin, 75004 Paris.
T. 0142779503, Fax 0142779098. - Jew - *046643*
Chevaux du Vent, 18 Rue Fontaine, 75009 Paris.
I. 0145960532, Fax 0145960546. - Ant /
Orient - *046644*
Chez Will, 55 Rue Damrémont, 75018 Paris.
T. 0142626201, Fax 0142626012. - Ant / Paint / Furn /
Lights - *046645*
Chimère, 5 Rue Grange-Batelière, 75009 Paris.
T. 0142468427. - Ant - *046646*
Chine des Ts'ing, 14 Rue Université, 75007 Paris.
T. 0142606593. - Orient / China - *046647*
Choses et Objets, Village Suisse, 78 Av Suffren, 75015
Paris. T. 0144499534. - Ant - *046648*
Chris, R., 10 Rue Beaux-Arts, 75006 Paris.
T. 0146333402. *046649*
Chrisday Niçaise, Louvre des Antiquaires, 2 Pl Palais-
Royal, 75001 Paris. T. 0142601739. - Jew - *046650*
Christie's France, 6 Rue Paul-Baudry, 75008 Paris.
T. 0140786585, Fax 0142662601. - Ant - *046651*
Ciné-Images, 68 Rue Babylone, 75007 Paris.
T. 0145512750. - Graph / Repr - *046652*
Cinédoc, 45 Passage Jouffroy, 75009 Paris.
T. 0148247136. - Graph / Repr / Cur - *046653*
Cinémagence, 12 Rue Saulnier, 75009 Paris.
T. 0142462121. - Instr - *046654*
Cipière, 26 Blvd Beaumarchais, 75011 Paris.
T. 0147003725. - Instr - *046655*
Circe Aéa, 129 Rue Fbg-Saint-Honoré, 75008 Paris.
T. 0142893913. *046656*
Ciry, Micheline, 35 Rue Charlot, 75003 Paris.
T. 0142726008. - Glass - *046657*
CLAL, 12 Rue Portefoin, 75003 Paris. T. 0144597178,
Fax 0144597173. - Num - *046658*

Claude & Lima, 17 Rue Saint-Paul, 75004 Paris.
T. 0142779802. - Ant / Furn / Orient / Dec - *046659*
Cluzel, Philippe, Av George-V, 75008 Paris.
T. 0147230717. *046660*
Coatalem, Eric, 93 Rue Fbg-Saint-Honoré, 75008 Paris.
T. 0142661717, Fax 0142660350. - Paint /
Draw - *046661*
Cohen, Daniel, 8 Rue Ecoles, 75005 Paris.
T. 0143251408. - Ant - *046662*
Cohen, Gilles, 7 Quai Conti, 75006 Paris.
T. 0143266250, Fax 0143255982. - Sculp / Arch /
Eth - *046663*
Coin de Montcalm, 28 Rue Montcalm, 75018 Paris.
T. 0142586327. - Ant / Paint / Furn - *046664*
Colanne, Louvre des Antiquaires, 2 Pl Palais-Royal,
75001 Paris. T. 0142601672. - Ant - *046665*
Colin-Maillard, 11 Rue Miromesnil, 75008 Paris.
T. 0142654670, Fax 0142654362. - Ant / Paint / Furn /
Orient / Lights - *046666*
Collin, Jean-François, 3 Rue Rossini, 75009 Paris.
T. 0142465792, Fax 0142465792. *046667*
Collin & Delbos, 3 Rue Rossini, 75009 Paris.
T. 0147702857. *046668*
Collin, Yves, Louvre des Antiquaires, 2 Pl Palais-Royal,
75001 Paris. T. 0142615655. - Ant - *046669*
Colombelle, Louvre des Antiquaires, 2 Pl Palais-Royal,
75001 Paris. T. 0142615734. - Toys - *046670*
Comerlati, Didier, 1 Rue Lapeyrère, 75018 Paris.
T. 0142645458. - Ant - *046671*
Comoglio, Georges, 22 Rue Jacob, 75006 Paris.
T. 0143546586, Fax 0140517056. - Ant - *046672*
Compagnie d'Art & Extrême Orient, 3 Rue Mauvais-Gar-
çons, 75004 Paris. T. 0148045834. - Orient - *046673*
Compagnie de la Chine et des Indes, 39 Av Friedland,
75008 Paris. T. 0142890545, Fax 0142891107. - Ant /
Orient / China / Sculp - *046674*
Comptoir d'Achats, 23 Rue Blancs-Manteaux, 75004 Pa-
ris. T. 0140279000, Fax 0140279500. *046675*
Comptoirs du Chineur, 49 Rue Saint-Paul, 75004 Paris.
T. 0142724739. - Ant - *046676*
Conte, Louvre des Antiquaires, 2 Pl Palais-Royal, 75001
Paris. T. 0142601862, Fax 0142601472.
- Dec - *046677*
Conte, Village Suisse, 78 Av Suffren, 75015 Paris.
T. 0147834183. - Dec - *046678*
Corail, Louvre des Antiquaires, 2 Pl Palais-Royal, 75001
Paris. T. 0142615764. - Furn - *046679*
Corbier, Denise, 3 Rue Odéon, 75006 Paris.
T. 0143260320. - Ant / Paint / Furn - *046680*
Cordier, Denis, Louvre des Antiquaires, 2 Pl Palais-Roy-
al, 75001 Paris. T. 0142615653, Fax 0140159545.
- Ant *046681*
Costey, Jean-Paul, 4 Rue Poitou, 75003 Paris.
T. 0142717204, Fax 0142717205. *046682*
Cottage de Deborah, 29bis Rue Pierre-Demours, 75017
Paris. T. 0142275550. - Furn - *046683*
Couderc, Christine, 6 Rue Bûcherie, 75005 Paris.
T. 0143294441. - Paint - *046684*
Coup de Coeur, 3 Rue Charlemagne, 75004 Paris.
T. 0148875031. - China - *046685*
Couque, Philippe, 36 Rue Université, 75007 Paris.
T. 0142964008. - China - *046686*
Cour aux Antiquaires, 54 Rue Fbg-Saint-Honoré, 75008
Paris. Fax (1) 42669663. - Ant - *046687*
Cour aux Antiquaires 3, 54 Rue Fbg-Saint Honoré,
75008 Paris. T. 0142663860. *046688*
Cour Carrée Alcantara, Louvre des Antiquaires, 2 Pl Pa-
lais-Royal, 75001 Paris. T. 0142615819.
- Rel - *046689*
Courteaux-Enault, 41 Rue Saint-André des Arts, 75006
Paris. T. 0143269961. - Ant - *046690*
Courteille, Lydia, 231 Rue Saint-Honoré, 75001 Paris.
T. 0142611171. - Jew - *046691*
Couvin, Marie-Thérèse, 29 Rue Custine, 75018 Paris.
T. 0142572685. - Ant - *046692*
Crédence, 91 Rue Saint-Honoré, 75001 Paris.
T. 0140260544. - Ant - *046693*
Crédit de la Bourse, 2 Rue Quatre-Septembre, 75002
Paris. T. 0142965174, Fax 0142960745.
- Num - *046694*
Cremailleres, 59 Rue Damrémont, 75018 Paris.
T. 0146069933. - Ant - *046695*

Crequier, 70 Rue Saint-Louis-en-l'Ile, 75004 Paris.
T. 0143269366. - Ant - 046696

Croisette, 85 Rue Rosiers, 75004 Paris. T. 0140116532.
- Furn - 046697

Cugnet, Roger, 28 Pl Vosges, 75003 Paris.
T. 0148874110. - Ant - 046698

Cuperty, Roger, 77 Rue Rocher, 75008 Paris.
I. 0145225299. - Ant - 046699

Curiosités, 108 Rue Longchamp, 75016 Paris.
T. 0147271979. - Lights / Cur - 046700

Cygne Vert, 41 Rue Verneuil, 75007 Paris.
T. 0140200841. - Ant - 046701

D B-Vieilleville, Louvre des Antiquaires, 2 Pl Palais-Royal, 75001 Paris. T. 0142615750. - Ant - 046702

Dagommer, Chantal, 52 Rue Doual, 75009 Paris.
T. 0145266902. - Ant - 046703

Dahan, William, 20 Rue Amiraux, 75018 Paris.
T. 0142627708. 046704

Dana, Patrick, 8 Rue Moines, 75017 Paris.
T. 0142260563. - Ant - 046705

Dandois, Ariane, 5bis Passage Charbonniers, 75015 Paris. T. 0145667268. - Ant / Orient / Dec / Ico - 046706

Dandois, Ariane, 1 Rue Staël, 75015 Paris.
T. 0147835133. - Ant / Orient / Dec / Ico - 046707

Dandois, Ariane, 61 Rue Saints-Pères, 75006 Paris.
T. 0142221443, Fax 0145488264. - Ant / Orient / Dec /
Ico - 046708

ARIANE DANDOIS

ARTS D'EXTREME-ORIENT
XIXème SIECLE EUROPEEN
OBJETS D'ART – PEINTURES

61, RUE DES SAINTS-PERES 75006 PARIS
TEL (33.1) 42.22.14.43

Danenberg, Louvre des Antiquaires, 2 Pl Palais-Royal,
75001 Paris. T. 0142615719, Fax 0142617533. - Ant /
Jew - 046709

Danguy, Gérard, 22 Pass Verdeau, 75009 Paris.
T. 0142470679. - Ant - 046710

Daniel, Christiane, Village Suisse, 78 Av Suffren, 75015
Paris. T. 0145675955. - Ant - 046711

Dante France, 6 Rue Valadon, 75007 Paris.
T. 0147537343. - Ant - 046712

Darnault, Véronique, 38 Rue Sèvres, 75007 Paris.
T. 0142221902. 046713

Dary's, 362 Rue Saint-Honoré, 75001 Paris.
T. 0142609523. - Jew / Silv / Instr - 046714

Dauliac Subra, 112 Rue Cherche-Midi, 75006 Paris.
T. 0142221416. - Lights - 046715

Davia de Fer, Louvre des Antiquaires, 2 Pl Palais-Royal,
75001 Paris. T. 0142615755. - Furn - 046716

David, Ghislaine, 1 Quai Voltaire, 75007 Paris.
T. 0142607310, Fax 0142960269. - Furn /
Sculp - 046717

David, Jacques, 2 Rue Juliette-Lamber, 75017 Paris.
T. 0140530143. 046718

David & ses Filles, 27 Rue Bonaparte, 75006 Paris.
T. 0143268140. - Jew / Silv - 046719

De Temps Antan, 16 Rue Lourmel, 75015 Paris.
T. 0145770444. 046720

Debay, Jacqueline, 145 Rue Pompe, 75116 Paris.
T. 0147274233. - Dec / Tin - 046721

Debrunois, 13 Rue Saints-Pères, 75007 Paris.
T. 0142969039. - Ant - 046722

Décalage, 33 Rue Francs-Bourgeois, 75004 Paris.
T. 0142775572. - Ant - 046723

Dechavanne, Muriel, 28 Rue Pierre-Demours, 75017 Paris. T. 0143804313. 046724

Degrave, Jean-Louis, Louvre des Antiquaires, 2 Pl du
Palais-Royal, 75001 Paris. T. 0142615712.
- Ant - 046725

Dehoux, Robert, 29 Rue Buci, 75006 Paris.
T. 0143548201. - Furn / Sculp / Tex / Dec / Lights /
Instr - 046726

Dehoux, Robert, 62 Rue Saints-Pères, 75007 Paris.
T. 0145482847, Fax 0145480692. - Furn / Sculp / Tex /
Dec / Lights / Instr - 046727

Delafoy, Jean-Jacques, 9 Rue Messidor, 75012 Paris.
T. 0143443191. - Ant - 046728

Delalande, Louvre des Antiquaires, 2 Pl Palais-Royal,
75001 Paris. T. 0142605949. - Naut / Instr - 046729

Delalande, Dominique, Louvre des Antiquaires, 2 Pl du
Palais-Royal, 75001 Paris. T. 0142601935. - Ant /
Naut - 046730

Delamare, 108 Rue Cherche-Midi, 75006 Paris.
T. 0142227013. - Dec - 046731

Delarue, 94 Rue Bac, 75007 Paris. T. 0145485674,
Fax 0145480242. - Tex - 046732

Delasalle, F.C., 13 Rue Pierre-Demours, 75017 Paris.
T. 0145721343. - Ant - 046733

Delon, Jeannine, 6 Rue Ouessant, 75015 Paris.
T. 0145670193. - Ant - 046734

Delpierre, Philippe, 3 Rue Bac, 75007 Paris.
T. 0147033225. - Ant / Furn / Lights - 046735

Delvaille, Josette, 15 Rue Beaune, 75007 Paris.
T. 0142612388, Fax 0140159833. - Paint /
Furn - 046736

Demeaux, Maryse, 6 Sq Thimerais, 75017 Paris.
T. 0147640909. - Ant - 046737

Denis, Renée-Luce, 2 Rue Haut-Pavé, 75005 Paris.
T. 0146334363. - Ant / Paint / Furn / Instr - 046738

Dentellière, Village Suisse, 78 Av Suffren, 75015 Paris.
T. 0147344696. - Ant - 046739

Depieds, Jean-Christophe, Louvre des Antiquaires, 2 Pl
Palais-Royal, 75001 Paris. T. 0142611853,
Fax 0142604407. - Furn - 046740

Dépôt-Vente de Paris, 81 Rue Lagny, 75020 Paris.
T. 0143721391. - Furn - 046741

Dépôts & Merveilles, 9 Rue Tour, 75016 Paris.
T. 0142245894. - Ant - 046742

Deroyan, Armand, 13 Rue Drouot, 75009 Paris.
T. 0148000785, Fax 0148000634. - Furn /
Tex - 046743

Derrière la Porte, 76 Rue Pierre-Demours, 75017 Paris.
T. 0144159257. - Ant - 046744

Derrière les Fagots, 8 Rue Abbesses, 75018 Paris.
T. 0142597253. 046745

Dervieux, Denis, 25 Rue Beaune, 75007 Paris.
T. 0140159920. - Ant - 046746

Des Magnolias Comme Autrefois, 72 Av Flandre, 75019
Paris. T. 0140356083. - Ant - 046747

Deschamps, Philippe, 57 Blvd Barbès, 75018 Paris.
T. 0142527887. - Ant - 046748

Deschamps, Stéphane, 19 Rue Guénégaud, 75006 Paris.
T. 0146335800. - Furn / Sculp / Mod - 046749

Descherre, Michel, 131 Rue Fbg-Saint-Honoré, 75008
Paris. T. 0145619847. 046750

Deslandes, Marguerite, 18 Rue Saints-Pères, 75007 Paris. T. 0142602434. - Furn - 046751

Despas, Anne-Marie, 76 Av Suffren, 75015 Paris.
T. 0143065594. - Ant - 046752

Deutsch, Elise, Louvre des Antiquaires, 2 Pl Palais-Royal, 75001 Paris. T. 0142615803. - Ant / Furn - 046753

Deux Orphelines, 21 Pl Vosges, 75004 Paris.
T. 0142726397. - Ant - 046754

Develon, Yves, 11 Rue Charles-V, 75004 Paris.
T. 0142780055, Fax 0148040108. - Eth - 046755

Deville, Bernard, Louvre des Antiquaires, 2 Pl Palais-
Royal, 75001 Paris. T. 0140209537. 046756

Devlay, Ivan, 16 Rue Blomet, 75015 Paris.
T. 0147342213. - Ant - 046757

Diamant Vert, Louvre des Antiquaires, 2 Pl Palais-Royal,
75001 Paris. T. 0142601746. - Jew - 046758

Didier, Gilles, 38 Rue Boileau, 75016 Paris.
T. 0140719809. - Graph / Repr - 046759

Didier, Imbert, 19 Av Matignon, 75008 Paris.
T. 0145621040, Fax 0142258603. - Paint - 046760

Didier Ludot, 19 Gal Montpensier, 75001 Paris.
T. 0142614454. - Ant / Tex - 046761

Dieutegard (Fille du Pirate), Village Suisse N 38, 78 Av
Suffren, 75015 Paris. T. 0147340676. - Naut / Instr /
Mil / Cur - 046762

Dieutegard (Fille du Pirate), Louvre des Antiquaires, 2 Pl
Palais-Royal, 75001 Paris. T. 0142602031. - Naut /
Instr / Mil / Cur - 046763

Dieutegard (Fille du Pirate), Aux Armes de Furstenberg,
1 Rue Furstenberg, 75006 Paris. T. 0143297951.
- Naut / Instr / Mil / Cur - 046764

Dimitrie, Ivana, 36 Gal Montpensier, Jardin du Palais
Royal, 75001 Paris. T. 0142974768. - Eth - 046765

Dion, Isabelle de, 2 Pl Charles-Dullin, 75018 Paris.
T. 0142640316. - Ant - 046766

Dion, Jean-Michel de, 35 Rue Lille, 75007 Paris.
T. 0142601380, Fax 0149270280. 046767

Divine Comédie, 2 Rue Dante, 75005 Paris.
T. 0143544882. - Ant - 046768

Dohm, 41 Rue Turenne, 75003 Paris. T. 0140290607.
- Ant - 046769

Dolce Vita, 25 Rue Charonne, 75011 Paris.
T. 0143382631. - Ant - 046770

Domec, Martine, 40 Rue Mazarine, 75006 Paris.
T. 0143549269. - Ant - 046771

Dorat, Hélène, 78 Rue Michel Ange, 75016 Paris.
T. 0146517706. - Ant - 046772

Doria, 16 Rue Seine, 75006 Paris. T. 0143547349,
Fax 0143256872. 046773

Doria, Florence, 6 Rue Furstenberg, 75006 Paris.
T. 0140460000. - Ant - 046774

Douglas, Charles, 58 Rue Arcade, 75008 Paris.
T. 0145227880. 046775

Dragesco & Cramoisan, 13 Rue Beaune, 75007 Paris.
T. 0142611820, Fax 0142854037. - China /
Glass - 046776

Driguez, Annick, 39 Rue Verneuil, 75007 Paris.
T. 0142860042. - Sculp - 046777

Drouart, 14-16 Rue Grange-Batelière, 75009 Paris.
T. 0147705290, Fax 0148009372. - Paint - 046778

Drouot, 21 Rue Drouot, 75009 Paris. T. 0147702018,
Fax 0147703250. - Ant / Paint / Furn / Tex / Dec / Jew /
Silv / Lights / Instr / Glass / Cur / Mod - 046779

Drouot, 16 Rue Provence, 75009 Paris. T. 0148246000.
- Ant - 046780

Du Côté de chez Viane, 11 Rue Luynes, 75007 Paris.
T. 0145485726. - Ant - 046781

Dubois, Claudine, 50 Rue Caulaincourt, 75018 Paris.
T. 0142550997. - Ant - 046782

Dubois, Eric, 9 Rue Saint-Paul, 75004 Paris.
T. 0142740529. - Eth - 046783

Dubois, Jean-François, 15 Rue Lille, 75007 Paris.
T. 0142604017, Fax 0142960424. 046784

Dubois, Patricia, Louvre des Antiquaires, 2 Pl Palais-
Royal, 75001 Paris. T. 0142601900. - Jew - 046785

Duchange-Garmigny, Louvre des Antiquaires, 2 Pl Palais-Royal, 75001 Paris. T. 0142615838. 046786

Duchange, Roger, 12 Rue Saints-Pères, 75007 Paris.
T. 0142608955, Fax 0149279127. - Ant / Orient /
China - 046787

Ducret, Noël, 21 Quai Malaquais, 75006 Paris.
T. 0142607867. - Ant - 046788

Dugrenot, 18 Rue Montpensier, 75001 Paris.
T. 0142960243. - Ant / Furn / Dec / Lights - 046789

Dumas, Marion, 27 Rue Saint-Paul, 75004 Paris.
T. 0142712145. 046790

Dumonet, Pierre, 82 Rue Maubeuge, 75009 Paris.
T. 0148782882. - Ant - 046791

Dumonteil, Pierre-Michel, 38 Rue Université, 75007 Paris. T. 0142612338, Fax 0142611461. - Ant /
Sculp - 046792

Dumoussaud, Daniel, 13 Rue Grange-Batelière, 75009
Paris. T. 0142466855. - Sculp - 046793

Duo 1900-1930, 15 Rue Lille, 75007 Paris.
T. 0147039263. 046794

Dupard, Henri, 105 Rue Fbg-Saint-Honoré, 75008 Paris.
T. 0142256815. - Orient - 046795

Duperrier, Robert, 14 Rue Beaux-Arts, 75006 Paris.
T. 0143543864. - Eth - 046796

Dupont, René, Louvre des Antiquaires, 2 Pl Palais-Royal,
75001 Paris. T. 0142601719. - Jew - 046797

Dupont, Sophie, 49 Rue Ramey, 75018 Paris.
T. 0142546930. - Ant - 046798

Duprez, Monique, 51 Rue Babylone, 75007 Paris.
T. 0147052857. - Paint / Furn - 046799

Duputel, 20 Rue Beaune, 75007 Paris. T. 0142974792.
- Paint - 046800

Duputel, J. & M., Louvre des Antiquaires, 2 Pl Palais-
Royal, 75001 Paris. T. 0142615751. 046801

Dupuy, Michèle, 108 Rue Tour, 75016 Paris.
T. 0145048527. - Ant - 046802

Dupuy, Michèle, 79 Rue Saint-Charles, 75015 Paris. T. 0145799595. - Ant - 046803
Duseaux, Pierre, 22 Rue Réaumur, 75003 Paris. T. 0142721357, Fax 0142778274. - Num - 046804
Dussordet, Jean-Hervé, 99 Rue Bac, 75007 Paris. T. 0145492239. - Jew - 046805
Dutko, Jean-Jacques, 13 Rue Bonaparte, 75006 Paris. T. 0143269613, Fax 0143292191. - Paint / Mod - 046806
Duval, Anne-Sophie, 5 Quai Malaquais, 75006 Paris. T. 0143545116, Fax 0140469512. - Ant / Mod - 046807
Edrei, Alain, 14 Rue Sablons, 75116 Paris. T. 0147274540. - Furn / Sculp - 046808
Edrei, Jean-Claude, 44 Rue Lille, 75007 Paris. T. 0142612808. - Furn / China / Tex / Cur - 046809
Eleb, Alain, Louvre des Antiquaires, 2 Pl Palais-Royal, 75001 Paris. T. 0142615704. - Num / Pho - 046810
Eléonore, 18 Rue Miromesnil, 75008 Paris. T. 0142651781. - Jew / Silv - 046811
Elisabeth, M., Louvre des Antiquaires, 2 Pl Palais-Royal, 75001 Paris. T. 0142601838. - Ant - 046812
Embden, Antony, 15 Quai Voltaire, 75007 Paris. T. 0142610406, Fax 0142614089. - Ant / China - 046813
Emma, 48 Rue Rochechouart, 75009 Paris. T. 0145260811. - Ant - 046814
English Antiques, 26 Rue Jouffroy-d'Abbans, 75017 Paris. T. 0146226306. - Furn - 046815
Enluminures, Louvre des Antiquaires, 2 Pl Palais-Royal, 75001 Paris. T. 0142601558. 046816
Eolienne, 48 Rue Francs-Bourgeois, 75003 Paris. Fax (1) 42747955. 046817
Epoca, 60 Rue Verneuil, 75007 Paris. T. 0145484866, Fax 0145448582. - Ant / Furn - 046818
Ermenault Mouret, Louvre des Antiquaires, 2 Pl Palais-Royal, 75001 Paris. T. 0142615843. - Ant / Furn - 046819
Escalier d'Argent, 28 Rue Montpensier, 75001 Paris. T. 0140200533. - Furn / Dec / Jew / Silv - 046820
Eskenazi, Djella, 185 Blvd Malesherbes, 75017 Paris. T. 0147638677. - Ant - 046821
Espace Darvill, 54 Rue Fbg-Saint-Honoré, 75008 Paris. T. 0147423891. 046822
Espace Temps, 27 Rue Saint-Paul, 75004 Paris. T. 0142780881. - Paint / Glass - 046823
Estampille, 55 Rue Douai, 75009 Paris. T. 0148741929. 046824
Etats d'Ame, 35 Rue Croix-Nivert, 75015 Paris. T. 0145664176. - Ant / Furn / Paint / Repr / Lights / Tex - 046825
Etudes et Réalisations, 38 Rue Babylone, 75007 Paris. T. 0142224997. - Ant - 046826
Eugénie & Victoria, 1 Rue Lekain, 75016 Paris. T. 0145257910. - Ant / Furn - 046827
Evelyne, 47 Rue La-Fayette, 75009 Paris. T. 0140160860, Fax 0144530858. - Ant - 046828
Exotic Kalagas, 9 All Eiders, 75019 Paris. T. 0140354243. - Ant - 046829
Eymery & Cie, 372 Rue Saint-Honoré, 75001 Paris. T. 0142600525, Fax 0143293407. - Orient / China - 046830
Fabius Frères, 152 Blvd Haussmann, 75008 Paris. T. 0145623918, Fax 0145625307. - Paint / Graph / Furn / Sculp / Jew / Silv / Lights / Instr / Draw - 046831
Fabre, B. & Fils, 19 Rue Balzac, 75008 Paris. T. 0145611752, Fax 0143590397. - Ant / Furn / Sculp / Tex / Instr - 046832
Fabus, 8 Rue Saint-Bernard, 75011 Paris. T. 0144939400. 046833
Faivre-Reuille, Nicole, 13 Rue Saints-Péres, 75006 Paris. T. 0142602874. - Furn / Dec / Cur - 046834
Falaix, Jean-Jacques, 116 Blvd Davout, 75020 Paris. T. 0143611599. - Ant - 046835
Fanette, 1 Rue Alençon, 75015 Paris. T. 0142222173. - Ant - 046836
Farman, P., 122 Rue Bac, 75007 Paris. T. 0145448739. - Ant / Cur - 046837
Farraud, Marc, 24 Rue Surcouf, 75007 Paris. T. 0145555144. - Ant - 046838
Fauchart, Josette, 60 Rue Saint-Louis-en-l'Ile, 75004 Paris. T. 0143540618. - Ant - 046839
Fauteuil pour Deux, 9 Rue Corneille, 75006 Paris. T. 0143297432. 046840
Favand & Ass, 48 Rue Eglise, 75015 Paris. T. 0144260825, Fax 0145580058. 046841
Féau, Joël, 9 Rue Laugier, 75017 Paris. T. 0147636060, Fax 0142675891. - Dec - 046842
Feldman, Marc, 21 Rue Saint-Paul, 75004 Paris. T. 0142729494. - Ant - 046843
Ferre, Jean, Louvre des Antiquaires, 2 Pl Palais-Royal, 75001 Paris. T. 0142615765. - Ant - 046844
Festival du Meuble, 17 Rue Rivoli, 75004 Paris. T. 0142722613, Fax 0142721788. - Ant - 046845
Festor, Pascal, Village Suisse, 78 Av Suffren, 75015 Paris. T. 0147836059. - Jew - 046846
Fey, Marlène, 213 Rue Belleville, 75019 Paris. T. 0142450332. - Ant - 046847
Fibule, 60 Rue Lévis, 75017 Paris. T. 0140538822. - Ant - 046848
Fiesta, 7 Rue Quincampoix, 75004 Paris. T. 0142715334. - Ant - 046849
Finard, Alain, 7 Rue Beaune, 75007 Paris. T. 0142612395, Fax 0140200192. - Ant - 046850
Finaz de Villaine, Manuela, 7 Rue Eugène-Manuel, 75116 Paris. T. 0140727251, Fax 0140507620. - China - 046851
Firch, Jan, 52 Rue Labat, 75018 Paris. T. 0146061236. - Ant - 046852
Fischbacher, 33 Rue Seine, 75006 Paris. T. 0143268487, Fax 0143264884. - Paint / Graph - 046853
Fischer, Dora, 7 Rue Eugène-Sue, 75018 Paris. T. 0142546542. - Jew / Silv - 046854
Fischer-Kiener, 46 Rue de Verneuil, 75007 Paris. T. 0142611782, Fax 0142601337. - Paint / Graph / Sculp / Draw - 046855
Flandrin, Paul-Louis, 158 Rue Grenelle, 75007 Paris. T. 0145512333, Fax 0145518719. 046856
Folavril, 1 Rue Furstenberg, 75006 Paris. T. 0143297951. - Ant - 046857
Fondeur, Marguerite, 24 Rue Beaune, 75007 Paris. T. 0142612578. - Ant - 046858
Fontaine, Francine, 52 Rue Mazarine, 75006 Paris. T. 0146331359. - Ant - 046859
Forceville, France de, 1 Rue Rossini, 75009 Paris. T. 0140220708, Fax 0142469967. - Furn - 046860
Forges, Suzanne, 103 Rue Saint-Dominique, 75007 Paris. T. 0145518159. - Ant - 046861
Forlani, Jacqueline, 7 Rue Saint-Paul, 75004 Paris. T. 0140290197. - Ant - 046862
Fortin, Jean, 28 Rue Henri-Barbusse, 75005 Paris. T. 0140468237. 046863
Four, Robert, 28 Rue Bonaparte, 75006 Paris. T. 0143293060, Fax 0143253395. - Tex - 046864
Fournier, Louvre des Antiquaires, 2 Pl Palais-Royal, 75001 Paris. T. 0147039778. 046865
Fournier-Guérin, Hélène, 25 Rue Saints-Pères, 75006 Paris. T. 0142602181. - Ant / China - 046866
Fragments, Village Saint-Paul, 13 Rue Saint-Paul, 75004 Paris. T. 0142743283. 046867
Fraignoz, Maria, Village Suisse, 78 Av Suffren, 75015 Paris. T. 0145668871. - Ant - 046868
France Asie Trading, 78 Rue Michel-Ange, 75016 Paris. T. 0140716845. - Orient - 046869
Franco, Bernard, 2 Rue Duban, 75016 Paris. T. 0142151544. 046870
François, Denis, 129 Rue Meaux, 75019 Paris. T. 0142061397. - Ant - 046871
Francou, Stanislas, 32 Rue Javelot, 75013 Paris. T. 0145837188. - Ant - 046872
Frank, 14 Rue Pyramides, 75001 Paris. T. 0142606513. - Paint / Graph - 046873
Frémontier, 5 Quai Voltaire, 75007 Paris. T. 0142616490, Fax 0142610496. - Ant / Furn / China / Cur - 046874
Friez, Marie, 2 Rue Provence, 75009 Paris. T. 0142464544. - Paint / Furn - 046875
Froimovici Galai, Pierre, 5 Rue Thouin, 75005 Paris. T. 0143543261, Fax 0143251278. - Ant - 046876
Fryde, Aline, 13 Av Trudaine, 75009 Paris. T. 0144919812. - Ant - 046877
Furuta, Yanusari, Louvre des Antiquaires, 2 Pl Palais-Royal, 75001 Paris. T. 0142615698. 046878
Fustier, Maxime, Village Suisse, 76 & 76bis, 75015 Paris. T. 0147341382. - Ant - 046879
Futur Antérieur, 26 Rue Moines, 75017 Paris. T. 0144859759, Fax 0144853915. - Ant - 046880
Gagnon, Dominique, 76 Av de Suffren, 75015 Paris. T. 0147348439. - Ant / Dec - 046881
Galerie B.J.F., 27 Rue Verneuil, 75007 Paris. T. 0142613646, Fax 0142612200. - Dec - 046882
Galerie d'Almeras, 30 Rue Francs-Bourgeois, 75003 Paris. T. 0142760595. 046884
Galerie d'Auteuil, 13 Av Théophile-Gautier, 75016 Paris. T. 0140506092. - Ant - 046885
Galerie de Beaune, 10 Rue Beaune, 75007 Paris. T. 0142860572, Fax 0140159681. - Furn - 046886
Galerie de la Bourdonnais, 32 Rue Champs-de-Mars, 75007 Paris. T. 0145519531. - Ant / China / Dec / Jew / Silv / Glass / Ico - 046887
Galerie de la Scala, 68 Rue La-Boétie, 75008 Paris. T. 0145632012, Fax 0142894963. - Graph / Sculp / Draw - 046888
Galerie de Monbrison, 2 Rue Beaux-Arts, 75006 Paris. T. 0146340520. - Arch / Eth - 046889
Galerie de Verneuil, 45 Rue Verneuil, 75007 Paris. T. 0140150115. - Furn / Jew / Silv - 046890
Galerie des Laques, 74 Rue Cherche-Midi, 75006 Paris. T. 0145488882, Fax 0145443181. - Furn / Orient - 046891
Galerie des Orfèvres, 66 Quai Orfèvres, 75001 Paris. T. 0143268130. - Paint / Graph - 046892
Galerie du Chevalier et des Collectionneurs, 42 Rue Chevalier-de-la-Barre, 75018 Paris. T. 0142648493, Fax 0142574013. - Paint / Graph - 046893
Galerie du Musée, 58 Rue Bourgogne, 75007 Paris. T. 0145519543. - Ant - 046894
Galerie du Passage, 20 Gal Véro-Dodat, 75001 Paris. T. 0142360113, Fax 0140419886. - Ant - 046895
Galerie du Scorpion, 9 Rue Huchette, 75005 Paris. T. 0143260616. - Orient / Eth - 046896
Galerie H.M., 185 Blvd Saint-Germain, 75007 Paris. T. 0142220114. - Paint - 046897
Galerie Pittoresque, Louvre des Antiquaires, 2 Pl Palais-Royal, 75001 Paris. T. 0142615806. - Eth / Cur - 046898
Galerie 13, 13 Rue Jacob, 75006 Paris. T. 0143269989. - Ant / Furn / Dec - 046899
Galerie 13, 13 Blvd Raspail, 75007 Paris. T. 0145483832. - Ant - 046900
Galerie 34, 34 Passage Jouffroy, 75009 Paris. T. 0147708965, Fax 0148000824. 046901
Galerie 59, 59 Av Kléber, 75016 Paris. T. 0145535825. 046902
Galerie 9, 9 Rue Jacob, 75006 Paris. T. 0143268383, Fax 0143264039. - Paint / Dec / Cur - 046903
Galien et Hippocrate, 13 Rue Monge, 75005 Paris. T. 0143265406. - Ant - 046904
Galilée, 123 Rue Cherche-Midi, 75015 Paris. T. 0145488219. - Ant - 046905
Galion Antiquités, 61 Blvd Batignolles, 75008 Paris. T. 0142933522. 046906
Ganet, Gérard, 10 Pass Verdeau, 75009 Paris. T. 0142463115. - Graph - 046907
Garcia, Maud, Village Suisse, 78 Av Suffren, 75015 Paris. T. 0147839303, Fax 0147832610. - Eth / Jew - 046908
Garland, 13 Rue Paix, 75002 Paris. T. 0142611795, Fax 0142616831. - Jew - 046909
Gary-Roche, 18 Rue Le-Peletier, 75009 Paris. T. 0147703216, Fax 0142868291. - Ant / Paint - 046910
Gastou, Yves, 12 Rue Bonaparte, 75006 Paris. T. 0146347217, Fax 0143296299. - Ant / Furn - 046911
Gattegno, A., 13-15 Rue Grande-Chaumière, 75006 Paris. T. 0143266318. - Fra - 046912
Gaubert, Pierre, 80 Rue Miromesnil, 75008 Paris. T. 0143870988. - Paint / Graph / Sculp / Draw - 046913
Gautier, Marcelle, 184bis Rue Convention, 75015 Paris. T. 0148283957. - Ant - 046914
Gelbard, Maurice, 25 Rue Grands-Augustins, 75006 Paris. T. 0143547474. - Ant - 046915
Gelot, Philippe, 29 Rue Saint-Paul, 75004 Paris. T. 0140270050. - Dec - 046916

Gély, Madeleine, 218 Blvd Saint-Germain, 75007 Paris. T. 0142226335. 046917
Genis, Maurice, 1 Rue Saint-Benoît, 75006 Paris. T. 0142608957. - Ant - 046918
Gérard, Nicole, 28 Rue Jacob, 75006 Paris. T. 0143262643. - Ant / Paint / Furn / Dec - 046919
Ghislaine, David, 1 Quai Voltaire, 75007 Paris. T. 0142607310, Fax 0142960269. 046920
Gillet, Raymond, 19 Rue Arcole, 75004 Paris. T. 0143540083. - Jew - 046921
Giordana, Barbara, 123 Rue Fbg-Poissonnière, 75009 Paris. T. 0142851394. - Ant / Furn / Orient / China - 046922
Girard, Véronique, 7 Rue Saints-Pères, 75006 Paris. T. 0142607400, Fax 0147034154. - Jew / Silv - 046923
Girardi, Guy, 91 Rue Saint-Honoré, 75001 Paris. T. 0142331131. - Ant - 046924
Gismondi, Jean, Louvre des Antiquaires, 2 Pl Palais-Royal, 75001 Paris. T. 0142615671, Fax 0140150390. - Ant / Furn - 046925
Gismondi, Sabrina, 20 Rue Royale, 75008 Paris. T. 0142607389, Fax 0142609894. - Ant - 046926
Gitton, Thierry, 22 Rue Canettes, 75006 Paris. T. 0143293462. - Ant - 046927
Giusti, Iris, 7 Rue Tocqueville, 75017 Paris. T. 0142279081. - Ant - 046928
G.L. Concept, 73 Rue Cherche-Midi, 75006 Paris. T. 0142226726. 046929
Godard-Desmarest, Armand, 1bis Rue Cavalerie, 75015 Paris. T. 0145669746, Fax 0143060332. - Furn / Sculp - 046930
Goldberg, Guy, 13 Av Soeur-Rosalie, 75013 Paris. T. 0147079763. - Ant - 046931
Golditė, Norbert, 32 Rue Turin, 75008 Paris. T. 0142930760. 046932
Golovanoff, 3 Rue Lille, 75007 Paris. T. 0142610375, Fax 0142611299. 046933
Gombert, André, 5 Rue Grange-Batelière, 75009 Paris. T. 0142469497. - Paint - 046934
Gosselin, François, 25 Quai Grands-Augustins, 75006 Paris. T. 0143267619. - Paint / Graph - 046935
Graf, Lise, 58 Av Montaigne, 75008 Paris. T. 0143597789. - Dec - 046936
Grande Roue, 78 Av Suffren, 75015 Paris. T. 0145664238. - Ant - 046937
Grenier d'Alain, 56 Rue Caulaincourt, 75018 Paris. T. 0142552597, Fax 0142526516. - Ant - 046938
Grenier de Grand-Mère, Village Suisse, 78 Av Suffren, 75015 Paris. T. 0147833284. - Furn - 046939
Grivois, Paul, 81 Rue Archives, 75003 Paris. T. 0142721417, Fax 0142726559. - Toys - 046940
Gros, Jean-Pierre, 6bis Rue Saints-Pères, 75007 Paris. T. 0142612815. - Tex / Dec / Lights - 046941
Grunberg, Eric, 40bis Av Bosquet, 75007 Paris. T. 0145510601, Fax 0145512656. - Ant - 046942
Grunspan, Marcel, 6 et 8 Rue Royale, 75008 Paris. T. 0142605757, Fax 0140209550. - Ant / Furn / Mod - 046943
Grunspan, Marcel, 27 Rue Fleurus, 75006 Paris. T. 0145487083. - Ant / Furn / Mod - 046944
Grunspan, Marcel, Louvre des Antiquaires, 2 Pl Palais-Royal, 75001 Paris. T. 0142615839. - Ant / Furn / Mod - 046945
Gudea, 22 Rue Bonaparte, 75006 Paris. T. 0146337862, Fax 0146334230. - Arch - 046946
Guerin, Jean-Claude, 25 Quai Voltaire, 75007 Paris. T. 0142612421, Fax 0149279770. 046947
Guévenoux, 7 Rue Provence, 75009 Paris. T. 0147704697. - Furn - 046948
Guignard, 59 Rue Michel-Ange, 75016 Paris. T. 0146518007, Fax 0146510329. 046949
Guigue, 11 Rue Saint-Gilles, 75003 Paris. T. 0148040495. - Furn - 046950
Guillois, Alain, Louvre des Antiquaires, 2 Pl Palais-Royal, 75001 Paris. T. 0142615655. 046951
Guimiot, Sylvie, 15 Rue Tournelles, 75004 Paris. T. 0140299326. - Furn / Orient - 046952
Guiot, Roberts, 18 Av Matignon, 75008 Paris. T. 0142666584, Fax 0149240793. - Graph / Sculp / Draw - 046953
Guiraud, Raoul, 90 Rue Grenelle, 75007 Paris. T. 0145481182, Fax 0145493790. 046954
Guitline, Georges, 27 Av Matignon, 75008 Paris. T. 0147428234, Fax 0147422416. - Ant - 046955
Guitline, Georges, 41 Rue Vital, 75016 Paris. T. 0142241745. - Ant - 046956
Guyot, Florence, 41 Rue Acacias, 75017 Paris. T. 0143800048. - Ant - 046957
Haboldt & Cie, 137 Rue Fbg-Saint-Honoré, 75008 Paris. T. 0142898463, Fax 0142895881. - Paint / Draw - 046958
Hadjer, Reynold & Fils, 102 Rue Fbg-Saint-Honoré, 75008 Paris. T. 0142666113, Fax 0142666603. - Tex - 046959
Haga, 22 Rue Grenelle, 75007 Paris. T. 0142228240. - Ant - 046960
Hagège, Jean-Joseph, 36 Blvd Batignolles, 75017 Paris. T. 0143871005. 046961
Haggai, Charles, 37 Blvd Pasteur, 75015 Paris. T. 0147349594. - Ant - 046962
Hahn, Joseph, 10 Rue Louvois, 75002 Paris. T. 0147034255, Fax 0147034234. - Paint / Sculp / Draw - 046963
Halfen, Elsa, 14 Rue Jardins-Saint-Paul, 75004 Paris. T. 0148871354. - Eth / Cur - 046964
Harisgain, Charles, 41 Rue Verneuil, 75007 Paris. T. 0142610481. - Ant - 046965
Hassan, Roger, 8 Rue Saint-Bernard, 75011 Paris. T. 0143713624. - Ant / Furn - 046966
Hassan, Roger, Louvre des Antiquaires, 2 Pl Palais-Royal, 75001 Paris. T. 0142616689, Fax 0142616784. - Ant / Furn - 046967
Haut Pas, 15 Rue Feuillantines, 75005 Paris. T. 0146337264. - Ant - 046968
Haute Epoque, 64 Rue Mont-Cenis, 75018 Paris. T. 0142624499. 046969
Hayem, François, 21 Rue Bac, 75007 Paris. T. 0142612560, Fax 0142615902. - Furn - 046970
Hayem, Jean-Patrick, 9 Rue Chaufourniers, 75019 Paris. T. 0142495779. - Ant - 046971
Hayoube, Ahmed, 69 Rue Orteaux, 75020 Paris. T. 0143729571. - Ant - 046972
Heckmann, Pierre, 57 Rue Bonaparte, 75006 Paris. T. 0143547109. - Orient / Cur - 046973
Heimroth, Alain, 11 Rue Auteuil, 75016 Paris. T. 0145207673. - Ant - 046974
Héraclès, 10 Rue Pierre-Demours, 75017 Paris. T. 0145740661. - Ant - 046975
Heran, Jeanne, 171 Blvd Saint-Germain, 75006 Paris. T. 0145489287. - Ant - 046976
Héraud, 24 Av Matignon, 75008 Paris. T. 0142663162. - Paint - 046977
Herbert, 54 Av La-Motte-Picquet, 75015 Paris. T. 0147348361. - Ant - 046978
Héritages, 6 Rue Bréa, 75006 Paris. T. 0143541663, Fax 0143542289. 046979
Herminette, Louvre des Antiquaires, 2 Pl Palais-Royal, 75001 Paris. T. 0142615781. - Eth / Cur - 046980
Heure Bleue, 17 Rue Saint-Roch, 75001 Paris. T. 0142602322. 046981
Higgins, Andrée, 54 Rue Université, 75007 Paris. T. 0145485692, Fax 0145480798. - Furn / Dec - 046982
Histoires de Tables, 14 Rue Jardins-Saint-Paul, 75004 Paris. T. 0140279553. 046983
Hoffer, Jean-Jacques, Village Suisse, 78 Av Suffren, 75015 Paris. T. 0140659617. 046984
Holmsky, Marie de, 80 Rue Bonaparte, 75006 Paris. T. 0143290890, Fax 0145005997. - Paint / Dec - 046985
Homme de Plume, 18 Rue Duret, 75016 Paris. T. 0145019387. - Ant - 046986
Hopkins-Thomas, 2 Rue Miromesnil, 75008 Paris. T. 0142655105, Fax 0142669028. - Paint - 046987
Huard, Germaine, 36 Rue Fondary, 75015 Paris. T. 0145792534. - Ant - 046988
Huguenin, Jean-Michel, 27 Rue Guénégaud, 75006 Paris. T. 0143547856. 046989
Humeurs, 4 Rue Université, 75007 Paris. T. 0142868911, Fax 0142868931. 046990
Il était une fois les Chiffonniers d'art, 12 Rue Rochechouart, 75009 Paris. T. 0148780725. - Ant - 046991
Ilot Trésors, 165 Rue Tolbiac, 75013 Paris. T. 0145880608. 046992
Ilse, B., 56 Rue Université, 75007 Paris. T. 0145489896. - Ant - 046993
Imbert, Didier, 19 Av Matignon, 75008 Paris. T. 0147660131. - Paint - 046994
Imprévu, 21 Rue Guénégaud, 75006 Paris. T. 0143546509. - Ant - 046995
Inard, 179 Blvd Saint Germain, 75007 Paris. T. 0145446688 k703 (1) 40490768. - Tex - 046996
Intemporel, Louvre des Antiquaires, 2 Pl Palais-Royal, 75001 Paris. T. 0142602265. - Graph - 046997
Intemporel, 22 Rue Saint-Martin, 75004 Paris. T. 0142725541. - Graph - 046998
Istria, Michel d', Village Suisse, 78 Av Suffren, 75015 Paris. T. 0143064787, Fax 0144490220. - Ant / Furn - 046999
Izarn, Pascal, 13 Rue Beaune, 75007 Paris. T. 0142609669, Fax 0142602021. - Sculp / Instr - 047000
Jacqueline, Subra, 51 Rue Seine, 75006 Paris. T. 0143545765. - Jew - 047001
Jacquey, Mireille, Louvre des Antiquaires, 2 Pl Palais-Royal, 75001 Paris. T. 0142601856. - Jew - 047002
Jade Antiquités, 52 Rue Verneuil, 75007 Paris. T. 0142860150, Fax 0142860149. - Orient - 047003
Jantzen, Laurence, Louvre des Antiquaires, 2 Pl Palais-Royal, 75001 Paris. T. 0142615805, Fax 0147093555. 047004
Japon Antique, Louvre des Antiquaires, 2 Pl Palais-Royal, 75001 Paris. T. 0142615688. - Orient / Mil - 047005
Jaquenoud, Paula, 54 Rue Fbg-Saint-Honoré, 75008 Paris. T. 0142663860, Fax 0142669663. - Ant / China / Mil - 047006
Jardin du Temps, Palais des Congrès, 2 Pl Porte-Maillot, 75017 Paris. T. 0140682318. - Ant - 047007
Joël Antiquité, Village Suisse, 78 Av Suffren, 75015 Paris. T. 0147832110. 047008
Joerges, Suzanne, 48 Blvd Latour-Maubourg, 75007 Paris. T. 0145517177. - Ant - 047009
Joly, Nicolas, 10 et 14 Rue Royale, 75008 Paris. T. 0142616442, Fax 0149270732. - Paint / Draw - 047010
Jonas, 12 Rue Seine, 75006 Paris. T. 0143265028, Fax 0143296566. - Paint / Graph / Draw - 047011
De Jonckheere, 100 Rue Fbg-Saint-Honoré, 75008 Paris. T. 0142666949, Fax 0142661342. - Paint - 047012
De Jonckheere, Louvre des Antiquaires, 2 Pl Palais-Royal, 75001 Paris. T. 0142602082. - Paint - 047013
Joubert, 38bis Rue Vivienne, 75002 Paris. T. 0142362039. - Num - 047014
Joubert, Jean-Pierre, 18 Av Matignon, 75008 Paris. T. 0142650079, Fax 0147426381. - Paint - 047015
Jours Anciens, 57 Rue Rome, 75008 Paris. T. 0145226886. - Graph / Draw - 047016
Jousseaume, Robert, 91 Rue Martyrs, 75018 Paris. T. 0142545993. - Ant / Cur - 047017
J.P.L.D., 38 Rue Ballu, 75009 Paris. T. 0148744188. - Ant - 047018
Julie Memory's, 38 Rue Bayen, 75017 Paris. T. 0143803688. - Tex - 047019
Julien-Laferrière, Eric, 69 Rue Broca, 75013 Paris. T. 0147074149. - Ant - 047020
Kalfon, Guy, Louvre des Antiquaires, 2 Pl Palais-Royal, 75001 Paris. T. 0140150867, Fax 0140150741. - Ant - 047021
Kaliya, 7 Rue Birague, 75004 Paris. T. 0140279801, Fax 0140279805. 047022
Kalkreuth, Alexis de, 99 Rue Fbg-Saint-Martin, 75010 Paris. T. 0142459458. 047023
Kartir, 11 Rue Bonaparte, 75006 Paris. T. 0143269028. - Tex - 047024
Katia, 7 Rue Bac, 75007 Paris. T. 0142611315. - Ant - 047025
Kellermann, Michel, 55 Rue Varenne, 75007 Paris. T. 0142221124. - Paint / Sculp / Draw - 047026
Képi Rouge, Village Suisse, 78 Av Suffren, 75015 Paris. T. 0145670906. 047027
Kerlir, François, 2 Rue Saints-Pères, 75007 Paris. T. 0142602697. - Furn / Lights / Instr / Mil - 047028
Kevorkian, Carning, 21 Quai Malaquais, 75006 Paris. T. 0142607291, Fax 0142610152. - Ant / Orient / Arch - 047029
Kichelewski, Julien, 55 Blvd Charonne, 75011 Paris. T. 0143700636. - Ant - 047030

Kin Liou, 81 Rue Bac, 75007 Paris. T. 0145488085, Fax 0142843278. - Cur -　*047031*

Kobrine, Danièle, Louvre des Antiquaires, 2 Pl Palais-Royal, 75001 Paris. T. 0142601695. - Jew -　*047032*

Kouki, Village Saint-Paul, 19 Rue Lions-Saint-Paul, 75004 Paris. T. 0148875670, Fax 0148875675. - Furn -　*047033*

Koutoulakis, Emmanuel, 4 Rue Echelle, 75001 Paris. T. 0142606563, Fax 0142602828. - Orient / Sculp / Arch / Eth -　*047034*

Kraemer & Cie, 43 Rue Monceau, 75008 Paris. T. 0145633123, Fax 0145635436. - Furn / Tex / Lights / Instr -　*047035*

Kugel, Jacques, 279 Rue Saint-Honoré, 75008 Paris. T. 0142608623, Fax 0142610672. - Paint / Furn / China / Tex / Jew / Fra / Silv / Instr / Cur -　*047036*

Kugel-Laval, Jeanine, Village Suisse, 78 Av Suffren, 75015 Paris. T. 0147846274. - Ant -　*047037*

Kugiel, Samuel, 5 Rue Tardieu, 75018 Paris. T. 0142645134. - Ant -　*047038*

Kuszelewic, Henri, Village Suisse, 78 Av Suffren, 75015 Paris. T. 0145669124. - Ant / Furn -　*047039*

L'Huillier, Thierry, 42 Rue Verneuil, 75007 Paris. T. 0142602303. - Ant -　*047040*

La Croix, Gérard, 13 Rue Provence, 75009 Paris. T. 0147708888. - Ant -　*047041*

La Fouinerie, 141 Blvd Voltaire, 75011 Paris. T. 0143794506. - Ant -　*047042*

La Palferine, 43 Av Bosquet, 75007 Paris. T. 0145569381. - Ant -　*047043*

La Querrière, Philippe, 27 Rue de Beaune, 75007 Paris. T. 0142610084. - Ant -　*047044*

La Tête d'Or, 54 Rue Verneuil, 75007 Paris. T. 0142603859. - Ant -　*047045*

Lacaze, Bernard, 212 Rue Rivoli, 75001 Paris. T. 0142607727. - Ant -　*047046*

Lachaux, Jean-Christophe, 28 Rue Pierre-Leroux, 75007 Paris. T. 0143066748. - Ant -　*047047*

Ladybird, 91 Rue Saint-Honoré, 75001 Paris. T. 0140139854. - Ant -　*047048*

Lagarde, Jean-Paul, 21 Rue Saints-Pères, 75006 Paris. T. 0142606381. - Ant / Furn -　*047049*

Lagrand, Marc, 25 Rue Bourgogne, 75007 Paris. T. 0145514716, Fax 0144183685. - Furn / Tex / Lights -　*047050*

Lalay, Michel, 2 Rue Saints-Pères, 75007 Paris. T. 0142607162. - Ant -　*047051*

Laloy, Jeanne, 42 Rue Saint-André-des-Arts, 75006 Paris. T. 0143260488. - Ant / Cur -　*047052*

Lambert, Jeanine, 202 Av Maine, 75014 Paris. T. 0145393064.　*047053*

Lampes, 9 Rue Verneuil, 75007 Paris. T. 0140200258, Fax 0140200836. - Lights -　*047054*

Landeau, Alain, 22 Rue Pont-Louis-Philippe, 75004 Paris. T. 0142775211. - Ant / Cur -　*047055*

Landrieux, Pierre, Louvre des Antiquaires, 2 Pl Palais-Royal, 75001 Paris. T. 0142615648. - Jew -　*047056*

Landrot, 5 Rue Jacques-Callot, 75006 Paris. T. 0143267113. - China -　*047057*

Langbain, Martine, 167 Blvd Montparnasse, 75006 Paris. T. 0143297701. - Ant -　*047058*

Langlade, Charles-Edouard de, 5 et 8 Rue Beaune, 75007 Paris. T. 0142610058. - Ant / Furn / Instr -　*047059*

Lantelme, Jean-Claude, Louvre des Antiquaires, 2 Pl Palais-Royal, 75001 Paris. T. 0142615778, Fax 0142615701. - Furn -　*047060*

Lantigner, Benoît, 13 Av Théophile-Gautier, 75016 Paris. T. 0142245040. - Ant -　*047061*

Lapierre, Jean, 58 Rue Vieille-du-Temple, 75003 Paris. T. 0142740770, Fax 0142743760. - Dec -　*047062*

Lapper, Etienne, 14 Rue Hégésippe-Moreau, 75018 Paris. T. 0145227140, Fax 0149270731. - Ant -　*047063*

Laprugne, Jean-Pierre, 52 Rue Mazarine, 75006 Paris. T. 0146338690. - Ant -　*047064*

Laroche, Gabrielle, 12 Rue Beaune, 75007 Paris. T. 0142975918. - Ant / Furn -　*047065*

Laroche, 25 Rue Lille, 75007 Paris. T. 0142603708, Fax 0149270731. - Ant / Furn -　*047066*

De Lattre, 56 Rue Université, 75007 Paris. T. 0145448353. - Graph -　*047067*

Laurendeau, Marie-Noëlle, Louvre des Antiquaires, 2 Pl Palais-Royal, 75001 Paris. T. 0142602030. - Naut -　*047068*

Laurent, Bernard, 44 Rue Galilée, 75008 Paris. T. 0147234409. - Ant -　*047069*

Laurent, François, 45 Rue Lepic, 75018 Paris. T. 0142640280. - Ant -　*047070*

Laurent, Thierry, 65 Rue Verrerie, 75004 Paris. T. 0142722726, Fax 0142725737. - Naut / Instr / Furn -　*047071*

Laurentin-Mercure, 65 Rue Sainte-Anne, 75002 Paris. T. 0142974342. - Ant -　*047072*

Lavergne, Bertrand de, Louvre des Antiquaires, 2 Pl Palais-Royal, 75001 Paris. T. 0142602163, Fax 0139559788. - Orient / China -　*047073*

Lawrence, 54 Rue Miromesnil, 75008 Paris. T. 0142651335.　*047074*

Le Dauphin, Bernard, 87 Av Villiers, 75017 Paris. T. 0140548091, Fax 0142271493. - Ant / Orient / Eth / Mil -　*047075*

Le Poilu, 20 Rue Emile Duclaux, 75015 Paris. T. 0143067732. - Ant -　*047076*

Le Quélançay, 40 Rue Verneuil, 75007 Paris. T. 0142963975. - Ant -　*047077*

Le Vigoureux, Michel, 34 Rue Faisanderie, 75016 Paris. T. 0147278815. - Ant -　*047078*

Léage, François, 178 Rue Fbg-Saint-Honoré, 75008 Paris. T. 0145634346, Fax 0142564630. - Ant / Furn -　*047079*

Lebel, Antoine, 8 Rue Gustave-Doré, 75017 Paris. T. 0147660748. - Ant -　*047080*

Lebrun, 155 Rue Fbg-Saint-Honoré, 75008 Paris. T. 0145610065, Fax 0145619749. - Dec / Fra -　*047081*

Leclercq, J.P.L., Village Suisse, 78 Av Suffren, 75015 Paris. T. 0145679824. - Ant -　*047082*

Lecuyer, 6 Rue Grange-Batelière, 75009 Paris. T. 0142460073, Fax 0142469000.　*047083*

L.E.D.A., 25 Rue Lille, 75007 Paris. T. 0140200179. - Ant / Furn -　*047084*

Leegenhoek, Jacques, 35 Rue Lille, 75007 Paris. T. 0142868551, Fax 0142862552. - Paint -　*047085*

Leegenhoek, Joseph, 23 Quai Voltaire, 75007 Paris. T. 0142963608. - Ant -　*047086*

Lefebure, Bernard, 38 Rue Sèvres, 75007 Paris. T. 0145485791. - Ant -　*047087*

Lefèbvre & Fils, 24 Rue Bac, 75007 Paris. T. 0142611840, Fax 0142869158. - China / Sculp -　*047088*

Lefèvre, Blandine, 8 Rue Grange-Batelière, 75009 Paris. T. 0148000211.　*047089*

Lefort, Pierre, Louvre des Antiquaires, 2 Pl Palais-Royal, 75001 Paris. T. 0142615/65. - Ant -　*047090*

Lefortier, 54 Rue Fbg-Saint-Honoré, 75008 Paris. T. 0142654374. - Tex -　*047091*

Lefran Wuillot, Louvre des Antiquaires, 2 Pl Palais-Royal, 75001 Paris. T. 0142601882. - Jew -　*047092*

Legrand, Jacques, 85 Rue Hauteville, 75010 Paris. T. 0147701316. - Ant -　*047093*

Leloup, Hélène & Philippe, 9 Quai Malaquais, 75006 Paris. T. 0142607591, Fax 0142614594. - Orient / Sculp / Arch / Eth -　*047094*

Lemaire, André, 43 Rue Verneuil, 75007 Paris. T. 0142611255. - Ant / Sculp -　*047095*

Lembessi, Antoinette, 22 Rue Royale, 75008 Paris. T. 0142607358. - Ant / Arch -　*047096*

Lenormand, Xavier, 11 Rue Provence, 75009 Paris. T. 0142468592.　*047097*

Lentz, 3 Rue Général-Roques, 75016 Paris. T. 0146515609.　*047098*

Léonardi, Pierre, 10 Rue Cherche-Midi, 75006 Paris. T. 0145486768. - Ant -　*047099*

Leprince, Christian, 48 Rue Jacob, 75006 Paris. T. 0142600766. - Furn / Sculp / Lights -　*047100*

Leroux, Philippe, 16 Rue Beaune, 75007 Paris. T. 0142611824. - Graph / Furn / Glass / Draw -　*047101*

Les 2 A, 91 Rue Saint-Honoré, 75001 Paris. T. 0145084457. - Ant -　*047102*

Lesieutre, Alain, Louvre des Antiquaires, 2 Pl Palais-Royal, 75001 Paris. T. 0142615713.　*047103*

Lestringant, Philippe, Louvre des Antiquaires, 2 Pl Palais-Royal, 75001 Paris. T. 0142615765. - Ant -　*047104*

Letailleur, Alain, 50 Rue Seine, 75006 Paris. T. 0146332517, Fax 0146330209. - Paint -　*047105*

Levesque, Jeanne, 6 Rue Université, 75007 Paris. T. 0142602240. - Ant / Furn / Lights -　*047106*

Levesque Père & Fils, 3 Rue Saints-Pères, 75006 Paris. T. 0142605657.　*047107*

Lévi, André, 48 Rue Rome, 75008 Paris. T. 0143878806, Fax 0143876437. - Music -　*047108*

Lévy, Etienne, 42 Rue Varenne, 75007 Paris. T. 0145446550, Fax 0145490538. - Ant / Furn / Instr -　*047109*

Lévy, Gérard, 17 Rue Beaune, 75007 Paris. T. 0142612655, Fax 0142960391. - Ant / Orient / Sculp / Pho -　*047110*

Lévy, Jacques, 21 Rue Bourg-Tibourg, 75004 Paris. T. 0142721559. - Ant -　*047111*

Lévy, Jacques, Louvre des Antiquaires, 2 Pl Palais-Royal, 75001 Paris. T. 0142615814. - Ant -　*047112*

Lévy-Leclère, Alice, Village Suisse, 78 Av Suffren, 75015 Paris. T. 0147838564.　*047113*

Lévy, Yvonne, Village Suisse, 78 Av Suffren, 75015 Paris. T. 0147340729. - Ant -　*047114*

Lewin, Henri, 97 Rue Boileau, 75016 Paris. T. 0146476698. - Furn -　*047115*

Leymarie, M., 4 Rue Miromesnil, 75008 Paris. T. 0142659617, Fax 0147424834. - Paint -　*047116*

Liberman, Nadine, 66 Rue Clichy, 75009 Paris. T. 0142829989. - Jew -　*047117*

Licorne, 25 Rue Saint-Paul, 75004 Paris. T. 0142724602. - Ant / Furn -　*047118*

Lièvre, Marylis, 28 Rue Sèvres, 75007 Paris. T. 0145486325. - Ant -　*047119*

Liliane François, 119 Rue Grenelle, 75007 Paris. T. 0145519806.　*047120*

Lille Antiquités, 3 Rue Lille, 75007 Paris. T. 0147033343, Fax 0149279964.　*047121*

Lima, Denise de, 51 Rue Bonaparte, 75006 Paris. T. 0143269006. - Paint / Graph / Draw -　*047122*

Linde, A., 374 Rue Saint-Honoré, 75001 Paris. T. 0142600612, Fax 0142600612. - Jew -　*047123*

Liova, 52 Rue Bac, 75007 Paris. T. 0145485330, Fax 0142840464. - Orient -　*047124*

Litra, 6 Rue Lille, 75007 Paris. T. 0140159501, Fax 0149270984. - Ant -　*047125*

Litybur, 171 Blvd Saint-Germain, 75006 Paris. T. 0145489287.　*047126*

Loft, 17bis Rue Pavée, 75004 Paris. T. 0148874650, Fax 0149849288. - Ant / Furn -　*047127*

London's Market, 38 Rue Fbg-Saint-Antoine, 75012 Paris. T. 0143441716.　*047128*

Longchamp, 81 Rue Longchamp, 75016 Paris. T. 0147045199. - Ant -　*047129*

Loo, C.T. & Cie, 48 Rue de Courcelles, 75008 Paris. T. 0145625315, Fax 0145620702. - Orient / Sculp / Arch / Eth -　*047130*

Lopez, Jean-Michel, 19 Rue Monsigny, 75002 Paris. T. 0140060092.　*047131*

Louis, Henri & les Autres, 15 Rue Saint-Paul, 75004 Paris. T. 0142787939. - Ant -　*047132*

Louis XV, 3 Rue Fbg Saint-Honoré, 75008 Paris. T. 0142663968, Fax 0142662052. - Ant -　*047133*

Loustic, 29 Rue Saints-Pères, 75006 Paris. T. 0142602424. - Jew -　*047134*

Louvre des Antiquaires, 2 Pl Palais-Royal, 75001 Paris. T. 0142972700, Fax 0142970014. - Ant -　*047135*

Louvre-Victoire, 154 Rue Saint-Honoré, 75001 Paris. T. 0140200748. - Ant -　*047136*

Lubicki, Estelle, 50 Rue Général-Brunet, 75019 Paris. Fax (1) 48034216.　*047137*

Lubrano, Michel, 5 Rue Lions, 75004 Paris. T. 0148874188. - Instr / Toys -　*047138*

Luce Brett, 10 Rue Castiglione, 75001 Paris. T. 0142606447. - Ant -　*047139*

Ludion, 175 Av Maine, 75014 Paris. T. 0145395602. - Ant -　*047140*

Lühl, Jan & Hélène, 19 Quai Malaquais, 75006 Paris. T. 0142607697. - Paint / Graph / Orient -　*047141*

Lumière de l'Oeil, 4 Rue Flatters, 75005 Paris. T. 0147076347. - Lights -　*047142*

Lupu, Jean, 43 Rue Fbg-Saint-Honoré, 75008 Paris. T. 0142659319, Fax 0142654916. - Ant / Paint / Furn / Instr -　*047143*

Lupu, Jean, Louvre des Antiquaires, 2 Pl Palais-Royal, 75001 Paris. T. 0140200182. *047144*
Lyons, Olivier des, 9 Rue Beaune, 75007 Paris. T. 0142611681, Fax 0149487001. - Paint - *047145*
Macé, Andrée, 266 Rue Fbg-Saint-Honoré, 75008 Paris. T. 0142274303, Fax 0144400963. - Sculp / Dec - *047146*
Macheret, Michel, Louvre des Antiquaires, 2 Pl Palais-Royal, 75001 Paris. T. 0142615794, Fax 0142615794. - Ant - *047147*
Madel, Pierre, 4 Rue Jacob, 75006 Paris. T. 0143269089, Fax 0140460709. - Ant / Dec - *047148*
Maestracci, Jesuald, 19 Rue Fourcroy, 75017 Paris. T. 0142274317. - Ant - *047149*
Magloire, Philippe & Claude, 13 Pl Vosges, 75004 Paris. T. 0142744067. - Ant / Orient / Sculp / China / Arch / Eth - *047150*
Magnolia, 78 Rue Bac, 75007 Paris. T. 0142223179. - Jew - *047151*
Maison de la Perle, Louvre des Antiquaires, 2 Pl Palais-Royal, 75001 Paris. T. 0142615801. - Jew - *047152*
Maison de Poupée, 40 Rue Vaugirard, 75006 Paris. T. 0146337405. - Toys - *047153*
Maison et Antiquité, 24 Pl Vosges, 75003 Paris. T. 0148878111. - Ant - *047154*
Maison la Vieille Europe, 78 Av Suffren, 75015 Paris. T. 0143066187. - Ant - *047155*
Maison Le Roy, 8 Rue Ecoles, 75005 Paris. T. 0143547303. *047156*
Maison Rouge, 68 Rue Vieille du Temple, 75003 Paris. T. 0148877834. - Ant - *047157*
Maison & Jardin, 120 Rue Fbg-Saint-Honoré, 75008 Paris. T. 0142259350, Fax 0145610551. - Graph / Dec - *047158*
Majestic, 27 Rue Guénégaud, 75006 Paris. T. 0143547856. - Ant / Orient / Eth - *047159*
Majoliques, Village Saint-Paul, 7 Rue Saint-Paul, 75004 Paris. T. 0148874614. - Glass - *047160*
Makassar-France, Louvre des Antiquaires, 2 Pl Palais-Royal, 75001 Paris. T. 0140200425, Fax 0143737812. *047161*
Makassar France, 112 Rue Fbg-Saint-Honoré, 75008 Paris. T. 0142662795. *047162*
Malausséna, Serge, 10 Pl Porte de Champerret, 75017 Paris. T. 0143801729. - Ant - *047163*
Mallarmé Antiquité, 11 Av Stéphane-Mallarmé, 75017 Paris. T. 0148880964. *047164*
Malrait, Marthe, 6 Rue Ouessant, 75015 Paris. T. 0147345938. - Ant - *047165*
Mancel, André, 42 Rue Bac, 75007 Paris. T. 0145480434. - Ant / Furn / China / Sculp / Instr - *047166*
Manevy, Madeleine, 67 Blvd Pasteur, 75015 Paris. T. 0143206668. - Ant - *047167*
Manic, Louvre des Antiquaires, 2 Pl Palais-Royal, 75001 Paris. T. 0142615812, Fax 0142970014. - Ant / Ico / Sculp / Jew - *047168*
Maple & Cie, 5 Rue Boudreau, 75009 Paris. T. 0147425332. - Furn - *047169*
Marc Aurèle, 23 Rue Saint-Sulpice, 75006 Paris. T. 0144072437. *047170*
Marchal, Christiane, 2 Rue Pétel, 75015 Paris. T. 0145334364. *047171*
Marchand d'Oubli, 78 Av Suffren, 75015 Paris. T. 0143068441. - Ant - *047172*
Marchand, Frédéric, 6 Rue Montfaucon, 75006 Paris. T. 0143543282, Fax 0144070482. - Ant / Toys / Glass - *047173*
Marches à suivre, 11 Rue Malebranche, 75005 Paris. T. 0143546025. - Ant - *047174*
Marcilhac, Félix, 8 Rue Bonaparte, 75006 Paris. T. 0143264736, Fax 0143549687. - Paint / Mod - *047175*
Marcus, Claude, 20 Rue Chauchat, 75009 Paris. T. 0147709123, Fax 0145232041. - Paint - *047176*
Marie Maxime, 34 Blvd Batignolles, 75017 Paris. T. 0145224452. - Ant - *047177*
Marine d'Autrefois, 80 Av Ternes, 75017 Paris. T. 0145742397, Fax 0145746170. - Naut - *047178*
Marquiset, Robert, 1 Rue Sophie-Germain, 75014 Paris. T. 0143275127. - Mil - *047179*
Martel-Greiner, 71 Blvd Raspail, 75006 Paris. T. 0145481305. - Glass - *047180*

Martel, Monique, 39 Rue Verneuil, 75007 Paris. T. 0142604797, Fax 0142604709. - Paint / Furn / Draw - *047181*
Martin-Bolton, 48 Rue Archives, 75004 Paris. T. 0142722719. - Furn - *047182*
Martin du Daffoy, Jean-Luc, 334 Rue Saint-Honoré, 75001 Paris. T. 0142604475, Fax 0140150883. - Jew / Silv - *047183*
Martin du Daffoy, Jean-Luc, Louvre des Antiquaires, 2 Pl Palais-Royal, 75001 Paris. T. 0142601992, Fax 0142601996. - Jew / Silv - *047184*
Martin, Florence, 23 Rue Bac, 75007 Paris. T. 0142615288. - Ant - *047185*
Martin, Louis, 19 Rue Odessa, 75014 Paris. Fax (1) 43220926. - Jew - *047186*
Martinez, Fernand, 97 Rue Seine, 75006 Paris. T. 0146330812. - Graph - *047187*
Marx, Jean-Claude, 109 Blvd Malesherbes, 75008 Paris. T. 0145633995. - Ant - *047188*
Mas, Yves, 11bis Rue Chomel, 75007 Paris. T. 0145485606. *047189*
Massenet, Aliette, 169 Av Victor Hugo, 75016 Paris. T. 0147272465, Fax 0147550826. - Ant - *047190*
Mateille, Jean, 10 Av Champaubert, 75015 Paris. T. 0147834708. - Ant - *047191*
Mathonnet, Michel, 10 Rue Bac, 75007 Paris. T. 0142616011. - Ant - *047192*
Maître Billardier, 26 Rue Lappe, 75011 Paris. T. 0143383180, Fax 0140217273. *047193*
Maupin, Constance, 11 Rue Docteur-Goujon, 75012 Paris. T. 0143070128. - Tex - *047194*
Maurin, Paul, 83 Rue Vieille-du-Temple, 75003 Paris. T. 0142781922. - Ant - *047195*
Mauve Boutique, 3 Rue Prêcheurs, 75001 Paris. T. 0142335830. - Ant - *047196*
Maxé, Véronique, 33 Av Matignon, 75008 Paris. T. 0147420252, Fax 0142662834. - Sculp - *047197*
MBA Antiquités, 32 Rue Blomet, 75015 Paris. T. 0145671129. - Ant - *047198*
Méchiche, Jean-Luc, 182 Rue Fbg-Saint-Honoré, 75008 Paris. T. 0145632011, Fax 0142259134. - Paint / Furn / Sculp / Arch / Eth - *047199*
Médicis, Louvre des Antiquaires, 2 Pl Palais-Royal, 75001 Paris. T. 0142610192. *047200*
Meissirel, Christian, 91 Blvd Malesherbes, 75008 Paris. T. 0142259885, Fax 0142259887. - Paint - *047201*
Mercier, Patrice, 58 Rue Pergolèse, 75016 Paris. T. 0145001897. *047202*
Mercier-Ythier, Claude, 20 Rue Verneuil, 75007 Paris. T. 0142602936, Fax 0142613921. - Music - *047203*
Mercure, 52 et 54 Av La-Motte-Picquet, 75015 Paris. T. 0145660811. - Ant / Jew / Silv - *047204*
Mère Grand, 96 Rue Raynouard, 75016 Paris. T. 0145258058. - Ant - *047205*
Mermoz, 6 Rue de Cirque, 75008 Paris. T. 0142258480, Fax 0140750390. - Orient / Sculp / Arch / Eth - *047206*

GALERIE MERMOZ

6 rue de Cirque
75008 Paris
Tél. 01 42 25 84 80
Fax 01 40 75 03 90

**ART
PRECOLOMBIEN**

Méry, Chantal, 75 Av Wagram, 75017 Paris. T. 0147641087. *047207*
Métropolis, Village Saint-Paul, 5bis Rue Saint-Paul, 75004 Paris. T. 0142775871. *047208*
Métrot, André, 34 Rue Faisanderie, 75016 Paris. T. 0147274211. - Ant / Furn - *047209*
Métrot, André, 31 Rue Beaune, 75007 Paris. T. 0142610906. - Ant / Furn - *047210*
Meyer, 17 Rue des Beaux-Arts, 75006 Paris. T. 0143548574. - Eth - *047211*
Meyer, Claude, 56 Rue Four, 75006 Paris. T. 0145487733. - Ant - *047212*

Meyer, Michel, 24 Av Matignon, 75008 Paris. T. 0142666295, Fax 0149240788. - Ant / Furn / Lights / Instr - *047213*
Michael Dan, 176 Rue Fbg Saint-Denis, 75010 Paris. T. 0140372173. - Ant - *047214*
Micheau, Jean-Pierre, 29 Rue Grange-aux-Belles, 75010 Paris. T. 0142381831. Jew - *047215*
Michel, Georges, 26 Rue Richelieu, 75001 Paris. T. 0142613257. - Ant - *047216*
Michel, Philippe, 78 Av Suffren, 75015 Paris. T. 0145679074. - Ant - *047217*
Michel, R.-G., 17 Quai Saint-Michel, 75005 Paris. T. 0143547775. - Graph / Draw - *047218*
Miguet Frères, Louvre des Antiquaires, 2 Pl Palais-Royal, 75001 Paris. T. 0142615825, Fax 0142602379. - Sculp - *047219*
Mikaeloff, Robert, 23 Rue La-Boétie, 75008 Paris. T. 0142652455, Fax 0149240516. - Orient / Tex - *047220*
Mikaeloff, Yves, 10 et 14 Rue Royale, 75008 Paris. T. 0142616442, Fax 0149270732. - Ant / Paint / Furn / China / Sculp / Tex / Draw - *047221*
Milano, D., 11 Av Mozart, 75016 Paris. T. 0142246912. - Orient / Arch / Jew / Cur - *047222*
Miller, 233 Rue Saint-Honoré, 75001 Paris. T. 0142616313. - Jew - *047223*
Mine d'Or, 103 Rue Marcadet, 75018 Paris. T. 0142559089. *047224*
Minot, Guy, 9 Rue Tour, 75016 Paris. T. 0145207127. - Cur - *047225*
Mioche, Sébastien, 42 Rue Bonaparte, 75006 Paris. T. 0143543337. - Ant / Furn / China / Sculp - *047226*
Mireux, Christine, 38 Rue Varenne, 75007 Paris. T. 0140490016. *047227*
Miron, 5 Rue de Provence, 75009 Paris. T. 0147705417, Fax 0148000871. - Ant - *047228*
Moatti, Alain, 77 Rue Saints-Pères, 75006 Paris. T. 0142229104, Fax 0145448617. - Paint / Furn / China / Sculp / Tex / Jew / Silv / Instr / Glass / Cur / Draw -- *047229*
Moatti, Emmanuel, 134 Rue Fbg-Saint-Honoré, 75008 Paris. T. 0142898282, Fax 0142899772. - Paint / Draw - *047230*
Moatti, Emmanuel, 77 Rue Saints-Pères, 75006 Paris. T. 0142229104, Fax 0145448617. - Paint / Draw - *047231*
Monbrison, Alain de, 2 Rue des Beaux-Arts, 75006 Paris. T. 0146340520, Fax 0146346725. - Orient / Sculp / Arch / Eth - *047232*

Monegier du Sorbier, 14 Rue Beaune, 75007 Paris. T. 0142616900. - Ant - *047233*
Monge, Félix, 2 Rue Châtillon, 75014 Paris. T. 0145421752. *047234*
Mongin, Robert, 16 Rue Beaune, 75007 Paris. T. 0142611824. - Ant - *047235*
Monluc, Gérard, 7 Rue de l'Université, 75007 Paris. T. 0142602051. - Ant - *047236*
Monnaie d'Or, 16 Gal Saint-Marc, 75002 Paris. T. 0142331965. *047237*
Monnaies de Lyon, 6 Rue Lyon, 75012 Paris. T. 0143441364, Fax 0143444001. - Num - *047238*

Monnaies de Paris, 11 Quai Conti, 75006 Paris.
T. 0140465666. - Num - *047239*
Montagut, Robert, 20 Rue Verneuil, 75007 Paris.
T. 0142615408, Fax 0142615505. - China /
Instr - *047240*
Monti, Filippo, 56 Rue Verneuil, 75007 Paris.
T. 0145490392, Fax 0142223673. *047241*
Moreau Gobard, Yvonne, 5 Rue Saints-Pères, 75006 Pa-
ris. T. 0142608825. *047242*
Moreau, Jean Luc, 19 Rue Abbé-Grégoire, 75006 Paris.
T. 0145493433. *047243*
Moreau, Jean-Luc, 56 Rue Université, 75007 Paris.
T. 0145499331. - Ant - *047244*
Morlet, 29 Rue Philippe-de-Girard, 75010 Paris.
T. 0146071304, Fax 0146073357. - Graph - *047245*
Mougin-Berthet, Louvre des Antiquaires, 2 Pl Palais-
Royal, 75001 Paris. T. 0142602111. - Jew - *047246*
Mougin, René, 14 Rue Jean-Jacques-Rousseau, 75001
Paris. T. 0140419437. - Ant - *047247*
Mouillefarine, Marie-Anne, 33 Rue Longchamp, 75016
Paris. T. 0147274872. - Ant / Furn / China / Fra / Instr /
Glass - *047248*
Mouseion, Louvre des Antiquaires, 2 Pl Palais-Royal,
75001 Paris. T. 0142615793. - Paint / Arch - *047249*
Mozart, 81 Av Mozart, 75016 Paris. T. 0145272738.
- Ant - *047250*
M.P.A., 9 Rue Verneuil, 75007 Paris. T. 0140200870,
Fax 0140200836. - Ant - *047251*
Muflarz, Eva, 15 Rue Lamartine, 75009 Paris.
T. 0142850578. - Cur / Music - *047252*
Mugler, Nicole, 2 Rue Université, 75007 Paris.
T. 0142963645. - Ant - *047253*
Muller-Dubois, Brigitte, 38 Rue Sèvres, 75006 Paris.
T. 0145485962. - Ant - *047254*
Mundial Coins, 8 Rue Saint-Marc, 75002 Paris.
T. 0145089845. - Num - *047255*
Muné, Carlos, 20 Rue Abbé-Grégoire, 75006 Paris.
T. 0145486829. - Furn / Fra / Glass - *047256*
Muné, Carlos, 59 Rue Cherche-Midi, 75006 Paris.
T. 0145486829. - Furn / Fra / Glass - *047257*
Muné, Jean-Claude, 29 Rue Saints-Pères, 75006 Paris.
T. 0142608295. - Ant / Furn / Fra / Glass - *047258*
Murat, Anne, 7 Rue Benjamin-Franklin, 75016 Paris.
T. 0145206300, Fax 0145515020. - Paint / Furn /
Sculp / Cur - *047259*
Murat-David, Philippe, 3 Rue Beaune, 75006 Paris.
T. 0142616453. - Ant / Furn - *047260*
Mussard, Christian, 54 Av La Motte Picquet, 75015 Pa-
ris. T. 0145660906. - Ant - *047261*
Myers, Myrna, 11 Rue de Beaune, 75007 Paris.
T. 0142611108. - Ant / Orient / China / Tex - *047262*
Mythos et Légendes, 18 Pl Vosges, 75004 Paris.
T. 0142726326, Fax 0142728370. - Ant / Furn / Orient /
Sculp / Arch / Eth - *047263*
Naim, Marie-Amie, 115 Av Villiers, 75017 Paris.
T. 0142676885. - Ant - *047264*
Namaste, 52 Rue Francs-Bourgeois, 75003 Paris.
T. 0142777635. - Jew - *047265*
Narguiz, 13bis Rue Provence, 75009 Paris.
T. 0142465490. - Jew - *047266*
Nataf, Louvre des Antiquaires, 2 Pl Palais-Royal, 75001
Paris. T. 0142602223, Fax 0142602229.
- Paint - *047267*
Navarro, Manuel, 15 Rue Saint-Sulpice, 75006 Paris.
T. 0146336151. - Dec / Fra - *047268*
Nebout, 10bis Passage Clichy, 75018 Paris.
T. 0145224694. - Music - *047269*
Neiges d'Antan, 31 Rue Saint-Paul, 75004 Paris.
T. 0142745304. - Ant - *047270*
Néo Senso, 2 Pl Palais-Royal, 75001 Paris.
T. 0142615741, Fax 0142602464. - Ant - *047271*
Néo Senso, 26 Rue Rondeaux, 75020 Paris.
T. 0144622678, Fax 0144622679. *047272*
Néo Senso, 5 Rue Bonaparte, 75006 Paris.
T. 0143257980, Fax 0143258025. *047273*
News Adam's, Louvre des Antiquaires, 2 Pl Palais-Royal,
75001 Paris. T. 0142606334. *047274*
Nicolas, Jacqueline, 5 Rue Beaune, 75007 Paris.
T. 0142612538, Fax 0142612027. *047275*
Nicolet, Claude, 24 Rue Bourgogne, 75007 Paris.
T. 0145513040. - Ant - *047276*
Nicolier, 7 Quai Voltaire, 75007 Paris. T. 0142607863.
- Furn / Orient / China - *047277*

Niella, 73bis Av Niel, 75017 Paris. T. 0147638210.
- Jew - *047278*
Nissen, Sylvie, 13 Rue Paix, 75002 Paris.
T. 0142616170. - Jew - *047279*
Noé l'Antiquaire du Vin, 12 Rue Malar, 75007 Paris.
T. 0145511467, Fax 0145502987. - Ant - *047280*
Noinville, F. de, 12 Rue Beaune, 75007 Paris.
T. 0143543125. - Orient / Glass / Cur - *047281*
Noir d'Ivoire, 6 Rue Visconti, 75006 Paris.
T. 0143294451. - Eth - *047282*
Noir d'Ivoire, 19 Rue Mazarine, 75006 Paris.
T. 0143549766. - Eth - *047283*
Noir Ebène, 5 Rue Bréa, 75006 Paris. T. 0146347293.
- Ant / Furn / Mod - *047284*
Noisette, Jean-Claude, 117 Rue Damrémont, 75018 Pa-
ris. T. 0142579762. *047285*
Norre, Loraine, 6 Rue Beaune, 75007 Paris.
T. 0142616847, Fax 0149279601. *047286*
Nostalgia, 4 Rue Sorbier, 75020 Paris. T. 0143494883.
- Ant - *047287*
Nostalgie Brocante, 21 Rue Carmes, 75005 Paris.
T. 0146345903. - Ant - *047288*
Notre-Dame, Louvre des Antiquaires, 2 Pl Palais-Royal,
75001 Paris. T. 0142611944. *047289*
Noujaim, Juliette, Louvre des Antiquaires, 2 Pl Palais-
Royal, 75001 Paris. T. 0142601892. - Arch - *047290*
Numismatique et Change de Paris, 3 Rue Bourse, 75002
-Paris. T. 0142974685. - Num - *047291*
Objet, 55 Blvd Batignolles, 75008 Paris. T. 0143872390,
Fax 0142949838. - Ant - *047292*
Objet, 155 Rue de Grenelle, 75007 Paris.
T. 0147054081. - Ant - *047293*
Occasion 240, 240 Rue Vaugirard, 75015 Paris.
T. 0142508452. *047294*
Octernaud, Pierre, 71 Rue Rennes, 75006 Paris.
T. 0142224778. - Jew - *047295*
O.G.N., 64 Rue Richelieu, 75002 Paris. T. 0142974750,
Fax 0142600137. - Num - *047296*
Olim, 92 Rue Grenelle, 75007 Paris. T. 0145494570.
- Paint / Furn - *047297*
Ollier, Jacques, Louvre des Antiquaires, 2 Pl Palais-Roy-
al, 75001 Paris. T. 0142615830, Fax 0142615832.
- Paint / Graph / Furn / Draw - *047298*
Olivary, Paul, 1 Rue Jacob, 75006 Paris.
T. 0146332002. - Ant - *047299*
Onze, 11 Rue Jacob, 75006 Paris.
T. 0143294244. *047300*
Opposite, 8 Rue Tour, 75016 Paris. T. 0145202900.
- Ant - *047301*
Or Antique, 120 Rue Dames, 75017 Paris.
T. 0143876382. - Jew - *047302*
Or du Temps, 2 Rue Donizetti, 75016 Paris.
T. 0145270551. *047303*
Or Verre, 2 Pl Palais-Royal, 75001 Paris.
T. 0142615694. - Ant - *047304*
Orient Antique, 80 Rue Damrémont, 75018 Paris.
T. 0142233497. - Orient - *047305*
Orient-Occident, 5 Rue Saints-Pères, 75006 Paris.
T. 0142607765, Fax 0142600855. - Orient / Sculp /
Arch / Eth - *047306*
Orlando, 68 Rue Rennes, 75006 Paris. T. 0142222866.
- Ant - *047307*
Orphée, 8 Rue Pont-Louis-Philippe, 75004 Paris.
T. 0142726842. *047308*
Ors et Arts, 14 Rue Saints-Pères, 75007 Paris.
T. 0140200503. - Ant - *047309*
Orts, Gérard, 164 Rue Fbg-Saint-Honoré, 75008 Paris.
T. 0142894448, Fax 0145634666. *047310*
Orts, Gérard, 164 Rue Fbg-Saint-Honoré, 75008 Paris.
T. 0142894448, Fax 0145634666. - Paint /
Furn - *047311*
Ottin, Michel, 33 Quai Voltaire, 75007 Paris.
T. 0142611988, Fax 0142613241. - Paint /
Furn - *047312*
Ottocento, Village Saint-Paul, 4 Rue Ave-Maria, 75004
Paris. T. 0142718190. - Furn - *047313*
Ouaiss, Jacques, Louvre des Antiquaires, 2 Pl Palais-
Royal, 75001 Paris. T. 0142615699. - Ant - *047314*
Oxeda, Edmond, 390 Rue Saint-Honoré, 75001 Paris.
T. 0142602757. - Jew / Silv - *047315*
Ozouville, Jean-Claude de, 91 Rue Saint-Honoré, 75001
Paris. T. 0142339639. - Ant - *047316*

Palais du Mandarin, 266 Rue Saint-Honoré, 75001 Paris.
T. 0142606960. - Ant - *047317*
Palais Oriental, 11 Rue Arcole, 75004 Paris.
T. 0143540297. - Ant - *047318*
Palais Oriental, 12 Blvd Montmartre, 75009 Paris.
T. 0147707200. - Ant - *047319*
Palissandre, Louvre des Antiquaires, 2 Pl Palais-Royal,
75001 Paris. T. 0142615739. - Ant - *047320*
Palleau, Jean-Pierre, 54 Av La Motte Picquet, 75015 Pa-
ris. T. 0145660233. - Ant - *047321*
Pallot, Bill, 118 Rue Fbg-Saint-Honoré, 75008 Paris.
T. 0147424734, Fax 0142662417. - Furn - *047322*
Pamyr, 49 Rue Lyon, 75012 Paris.
Fax (1) 49289695. *047323*
Panorama Numismatique, 4 Rue Panoramas, 75002 Pa-
ris. T. 0142333831, Fax 0142369048. - Num - *047324*
Par Hasard, 25 Rue Penthièvre, 75008 Paris.
T. 0153751982. *047325*
Pariente, Xavier, Louvre des Antiquaires, 2 Pl Palais-
Royal, 75001 Paris. T. 0142611853,
Fax 0142604407. *047326*
Paris American Art, 4 Rue Bonaparte, 75006 Paris.
T. 0143267985, Fax 0143543380. - Fra - *047327*
Partouche, Annie, Louvre des Antiquaires, 2 Pl Palais-
Royal, 75001 Paris. T. 0142615839. - Ant - *047328*
Passa Tempo, 54 Rue Lamarck, 75018 Paris.
T. 0142522919. - Ant - *047329*
Passage, 83 Rue Cherche-Midi, 75006 Paris.
T. 0142222646. *047330*
Passé d'Aujourd'hui, 43 Rue Cherche-Midi, 75006 Paris.
T. 0142224121. - Cur - *047331*
Passé Fleuri, 10 Rue Fourcroy, 75017 Paris.
T. 0142271050. - Ant - *047332*
Pastorale, 118 Av Mozart, 75016 Paris. T. 0145257356.
- Ant / Cur - *047333*
Peau d'Ange, 1 Rue Mesnil, 75016 Paris.
T. 0145537811. - Ant - *047334*
Peintre, Christian, 3 Rue Rossini, 75009 Paris.
T. 0147706935. - Ant - *047335*
Pellan, Zoé, 18 Rue Gare de Reuilly, 75012 Paris.
T. 0143442179. - Ant - *047336*
Pellas, Aldo, 15 Rue Payenne, 75003 Paris.
T. 0142781569. - Ant - *047337*
Pellegrin, Jacques, 19 Rue Annonciation, 75016 Paris.
T. 0142886473, Fax 0142309436. - Paint /
Furn - *047338*
Penjab Distribution, 10 Rue Gérando, 75009 Paris.
T. 0142829036. - Ant - *047339*
Pépin, Bruno, Louvre des Antiquaires, 2 Pl Palais-Royal,
75001 Paris. T. 0142602096, Fax 0142605869.
- Jew / Silv - *047340*
Perine, 5 Rue Villebois-Mareuil, 75017 Paris.
T. 0145746503. - Ant - *047341*
Perinet, Michel, 420 Rue Saint-Honoré, 75008 Paris.
T. 0142614916. - Jew - *047342*
Perpitch, Antoine, 240 Blvd Saint-Germain, 75007 Paris.
T. 0145483767, Fax 0142840464. - Ant / Furn / Sculp /
Tex - *047343*
Perreau-Saussine, F., 11 Quai Voltaire, 75007 Paris.
T. 0142611075, Fax 0142615949. - Paint / Sculp /
Draw - *047344*
Perret-Vibert, 170 Blvd Haussmann, 75008 Paris.
T. 0145621585. - Ant / Orient - *047345*
Perrin, Jacques, 3 Quai Voltaire, 75007 Paris.
T. 0142604312, Fax 0142613261. - Paint / Furn /
Lights / Draw - *047346*
Perrin, Jacques, 98 Rue Fbg-Saint-Honoré, 75008 Paris.
T. 0142650138, Fax 0149240408. - Ant /
Furn - *047347*
Perrin, Patrick, 178 Rue Fbg-Saint-Honoré, 75008 Paris.
T. 0140760776, Fax 0140760937. - Paint / Furn /
Draw - *047348*
Perrono, 37 Av Victor-Hugo, 75016 Paris.
T. 0145016788. - Jew - *047349*
Perrono, 4 Rue Chaussée-d'Antin, 75009 Paris.
T. 0147708361. - Jew - *047350*
Petit Palais du Meuble, 13bis Av La Motte Picquet,
75007 Paris. T. 0145516617, Fax 0145516205.
- Ant - *047351*
Petitcollot, Claude, 65 Rue Seine, 75006 Paris.
T. 0143263146. - Ant - *047352*
Pétridès, Gilbert, 63 Rue Fbg-Saint-Honoré, 75008 Pa-
ris. T. 0142664232, Fax 0142652584. - Paint - *047353*

Petrouchka, 18 Rue Beaune, 75007 Paris.
T. 0142616665, Fax 0142610653. - Ant / Ico -   047354
Peyralade, Marie-Thérèse, 54bis Av La Motte Picquet,
75015 Paris. T. 0147346994. - Ant -   047355
Peyre, Jean-Gabriel, 17 Rue Bac, 75007 Paris.
T. 0142611877, Fax 0142611499. - China -   047356
Philippe, Eric, 25 Gal Véro-Dodat, 75001 Paris.
T. 0142332826, Fax 0142211793. - Mod -   047357
Phoenix, 88 Rue Rochechouart, 75009 Paris.
T. 0148780609, Fax 0145235441. - Ant -   047358
Piccolo Téatro, 7 Rue Condé, 75006 Paris.
T. 0140510151. - Ant -   047359
Pierre, Robin, 10 Rue Jacques-Callot, 75006 Paris.
T. 0143263138.   047360
Pietri, Anne & sa Fille, 58 Rue Vieille du Temple, 75003
Paris. T. 0142727042. - Ant -   047361
Pigeron, Xavier, 202 Blvd Saint-Germain, 75007 Paris.
T. 0145488616, Fax 0142228089. - Ant -   047362
Pissarro, Lionel & Sandrine, 6 Rue Beaux-Arts, 75006
Paris. T. 0146337411, Fax 0146330734. - Paint /
Sculp / Draw -   047363
Pistiner, Albert, 20 Rue Yves Toudic, 75010 Paris.
T. 0142034021. - Ant -   047364
Pitel Sabatier, 54 Av La-Bourdonnais, 75007 Paris.
T. 0145555989. - Ant -   047365
Plaisance, Arnaud, 12 Gal Véro-Dodat, 75001 Paris.
T. 0142334590, Fax 0142334595.   047366
Plantard, Jean-Claude, 17 Av République, 75011 Paris.
T. 0143575003. - Ant -   047367
Poindessault, Bernard, 38 Rue Richelieu, 75001 Paris.
T. 0142961012, Fax 0140209466. - Num -   047368
Point de Vue, 91 Rue Saint-Honoré, 75001 Paris.
T. 0142335090, Fax 0145085652.   047369
Poisson, Jacques, 17 Cité-Aubry, 75020 Paris.
T. 0143717309, Fax 0140242620. - Furn /
Instr -   047370
Pollès, Jacqueline, 131 Rue Fbg-Saint-Honoré, 75008
Paris. T. 0142665443. - Graph / China -   047371
Pomme d'Or, 21 Rue Saint-Jacques, 75005 Paris.
T. 0143545713.   047372
Popoff & Cie, 86 Rue Fbg-Saint-Honoré, 75008 Paris.
T. 0142653844, Fax 0140070759.   047373
Porte Etroite, 10 Rue Bonaparte, 75006 Paris.
T. 0143542603, Fax 0140460655. - Print /
ArtBk -   047373a
Portobello, 56 Rue N-D-des-Champs, 75006 Paris.
T. 0143257447. - Tex -   047374
Potignon, Jacques, 54 Rue Fbg-Saint-Honoré, 75008
Paris. T. 0142654374. - Tex -   047375
Pouchin, Max, 67 Rue Convention, 75015 Paris.
T. 0145780342. - Jew -   047376
Pozzoli, Fabio Romano, 157 Rue Fbg-Saint-Honoré,
75008 Paris. T. 0140740858, Fax 0140740870.
- Ant -   047377
Praver, Henri, 32 Rue Solidarité, 75019 Paris.
T. 0142062528. - Ant -   047378
Présents du Passé, 58 Rue de l'Université, 75007 Paris.
T. 0142223407. - Ant / Furn -   047379
Prouté, Paul, 74 Rue de Seine, 75006 Paris.
T. 0143268980, Fax 0143258341. - Graph / Mul /
Draw -   047380
Provost, Michel, 83 Rue Vieille-du-Temple, 75003 Paris.
T. 0142774392. - Ant / Furn / Dec -   047381
Prudou, 2 Rue Rosiers, 75004 Paris. T. 0142741034.
- Ant -   047382
Pythéas, Louvre des Antiquaires, 2 Pl Palais-Royal,
75001 Paris. T. 0140159328. - Arch -   047383
Radé, Michel, 17 Rue Chapelle, 75018 Paris.
T. 0140345225, Fax 0140360340.   047384
Rajon, Gaston, 72 Rue Boursault, 75017 Paris.
T. 0142635812. - Ant -   047385
Rapin, Philippe, 25 Quai Voltaire, 75007 Paris.
T. 0142612421.   047386
Rarissime, 18 Rue Saint-Roch, 75001 Paris.
T. 0142963049. - Paint / Graph / Draw -   047387
Ratton, Charles & Guy Ladrière, 11 Quai Voltaire, 75007
Paris. T. 0142612979, Fax 0142560072. - Paint /
Sculp / Arch / Eth / Cur -   047388
Ratton, Charles & Guy Ladrière, 14 Rue Marignan,
75008 Paris. T. 0143595821, Fax 0142560072.
- Paint / Sculp / Arch / Eth / Cur -   047389
Ratton Hourdé, 10 Rue Beaux-Arts, 75006 Paris.
T. 0146333202.   047390

Raynaud, Bernard, 1 Rue Chaise, 75007 Paris.
T. 0145344769. - Ant -   047391
R.B.A., 7 Rue Bonaparte, 75006 Paris.
T. 0146333193.   047392
RDS Diffusion, 127 Rue Tour, 75016 Paris.
T. 0145046488. - Ant -   047393
Redjala, Mohand, Village Suisse, 4 Av Champaubert,
75015 Paris. T. 0140659580. - Ant -   047394
Reflet d'Antan, Louvre des Antiquaires, 2 Pl Palais-Roy-
al, 75001 Paris. T. 0142615811. - Jew -   047395
Reflets d'Epoques, 17 Blvd Raspail, 75007 Paris.
T. 0145484207. - Ant / Dec -   047396
Regency, 20 Rue Général-Bertrand, 75007 Paris.
T. 0143063025.   047397
Regency, 45 Rue Bac, 75007 Paris. T. 0145483310,
Fax 0145485926. - Furn -   047398
Regis-Saunier, Laurence, 5 Rue Drevet, 75018 Paris.
T. 0142586946. - Ant -   047399
Rein, Jacques, 20 Rue Saint-Romain, 75006 Paris.
T. 0142842096.   047400
Reinold, 233 Rue Fbg-Saint-Honoré, 75008 Paris.
T. 0142273940. - Ant / Furn -   047401
Relais du Passé, 11 Rue Dupont des Loges, 75007 Paris.
T. 0147057570. - Ant -   047402
Renaud, Christophe, 29 Rue Lemercier, 75017 Paris.
T. 0142937719.   047403
Renault, Jacqueline, 19 Rue Victor Massé, 75009 Paris.
T. 0148780182. - Ant -   047404
Renoncourt, Jean, 77 Rue Fbg-Saint-Honoré, 75008 Pa-
ris. T. 0144511160. - Furn / Lights -   047405
Renoncourt, Jean, 1 Rue Saints-Pères, 75006 Paris.
T. 0142607587, Fax 0142601514. - Furn /
Lights -   047406
Renou & Poyet, 164 Rue Fbg-Saint-Honoré, 75008 Paris.
T. 0143593595, Fax 0143389547. - Paint / Sculp /
Draw -   047407
Restoux, Elisabeth, 25 Rue Faidherbe, 75011 Paris.
T. 0143714552. - Ant -   047408
Rétromanie, 81 Rue Vieille du Temple, 75003 Paris.
T. 0148879645. - Ant -   047409
Rétrospective, 45 Rue Pompe, 75016 Paris.
T. 0145042933. - Ant -   047410
Rêveurs Associés, 15 Rue Bouloi, 75001 Paris.
T. 0145085559. - Ant -   047411
Revillon d'Apréval, Marc, 23 Quai Voltaire, 75007 Paris.
T. 0142612736, Fax 0142614370. - Furn / Tex /
Instr -   047412
Rey, Jean & Cie, Louvre des Antiquaires, 2 Pl Palais-
Royal, 75001 Paris. T. 0142615662. - Ant /
Furn -   047413
Ribes, Jean-Charles, 20 Rue Caulaincourt, 75018 Paris.
T. 0142583528. - Ant / Paint / Furn -   047414
Richelieu Numismatique, 48 Rue Richelieu, 75001 Paris.
T. 0142960260. - Num -   047415
Riconti, Bernard, 18 Rue Pétersbourg, 75008 Paris.
T. 0143871871. - Dec -   047416
Rigal, Jean, 12 Av Mac-Mahon, 75017 Paris.
T. 0144090234.   047417
Rimbaud, Jean-Jacques, Louvre des Antiquaires, 2 Pl
Palais-Royal, 75001 Paris. T. 0142615770.
- Jew -   047418
Rimbault-Joffard, Jean-Pierre, 7 Rue Chaptal, 75009
Paris. T. 0145268742. - Ant -   047419
Rimbault-Joffard, Robert, 29 Av Trudaine, 75009 Paris.
T. 0142800700. - Ant -   047420
Rinaldi, Renaud, 8 Rue Rossini, 75009 Paris.
T. 0142463588. - Ant -   047421
Rispal, Antonin, 115 Av La Bourdonnais, 75007 Paris.
T. 0145552731. - Ant -   047422
Rispal, Antonin, 78 Av Suffren, 75015 Paris.
T. 0147837234. - Ant -   047423
Rive Droite, Louvre des Antiquaires, 2 Pl Palais-Royal,
75001 Paris. T. 0140159787, Fax 0142604605.
- Furn / Dec / Cur -   047424
Rivière, Huguette, Louvre des Antiquaires, 2 Pl Palais-
Royal, 75001 Paris. T. 0140200724.   047425
Robin, Pierre, 10 Rue Jacques-Callot, 75006 Paris.
T. 0146346207.   047426
Robyn, J.C., 40 Rue Mazarine, 75006 Paris.
T. 0140472307. - Orient -   047427
Roche de la Celle, Paul, 21 Rue Servandoni, 75006 Pa-
ris. T. 0143252754. - Ant -   047428

Rochefort, Jean-Pierre, 38 Rue Petits Champs, 75002
Paris. T. 0142969228. - Ant -   047429
Rocher, Liliane, Louvre des Antiquaires, 2 Pl Palais-Roy-
al, 75001 Paris. T. 0140200134. - Paint -   047430
Rock, Dominique, 27 Passage Choiseul, 75002 Paris.
T. 0142975212.   047431
Rodriguez, Albert, 16 Rue Provence, 75009 Paris.
T. 0145235339.   047432
Roi Fou, 182 Rue Fbg-Saint-Honoré, 75008 Paris.
T. 0145638259, Fax 0145635891. - Paint / Furn /
Lights / Cur / Mod -   047433
Romaric et les Souvenirs de Gabriel, 17 Rue Saint-Paul,
75004 Paris. T. 0148870835.   047434
Ronsard, 70 Rue Lecourbe, 75015 Paris.
T. 0145666004. - Ant -   047435
Rose des Vents, 25 Rue Beaune, 75007 Paris.
T. 0142601117. - Instr / Naut -   047436
Rossi, Jean-Marie, 20 Rue Cirque, 75008 Paris.   047437
Rossignol, Jacqueline, 73 Av Niel, 75017 Paris.
T. 0140540167. - Ant -   047438
Rouif, Abel, 133 Rue Rome, 75017 Paris.
T. 0142272375. - Paint / Sculp / Glass -   047439
Roumilhac-Bassi, Marie-Jose, 4 Rue Tournon, 75006
Paris. T. 0143259330. - Ant -   047440
Roy, Denis, 8 Rue Saints-Pères, 75007 Paris.
T. 0140200867.   047441
Rullier, Michel, 34 Rue Lille, 75007 Paris.
T. 0142611547. - Ant / Paint / Furn / Sculp / Dec / Instr /
Glass / Cur -   047442
Sabatier, 45 Rue Rome, 75008 Paris. T. 0145221677.
- Music -   047443
Sabban, Louvre des Antiquaires, 2 Pl Palais-Royal,
75001 Paris. T. 0142615762, Fax 0142615763.
- Furn / China / Sculp -   047444
Sabert, René, 133 Rue Mont Cenis, 75018 Paris.
T. 0142520312. - Ant -   047445
Sabot, Henri, 16 Rue Grange Batelière, 75009 Paris.
T. 0147700516. - Ant -   047446
Saboudjian, Lucie, Louvre des Antiquaires, 2 Pl Palais-
Royal, 75001 Paris. T. 0142615785. - Ant -   047447
Saget, Eric, 78 Av Suffren, 75015 Paris. T. 0143060722.
- Ant -   047448
Saget, Roger, Village Suisse, 78 Av Suffren, 75015 Paris.
T. 0143062639.   047449
Sagittaires, 17 Saint-Paul, 75004 Paris. T. 0140290608.
- Ant -   047450
Sagot-Le-Garrec, 10 Rue Buci, 75006 Paris.
T. 0143264338, Fax 0143297747. - Graph /
Draw -   047451
Saint-Honoré, 69 Rue Fbg-Saint-Honoré, 75008 Paris.
T. 0142663663, Fax 0145699265. - Paint -   047452
Saint-Martin, 11 Rue Saints-Pères, 75006 Paris.
T. 0142608365, Fax 0142604419. - Ant -   047453
Saint-Paul 21, 21 Rue Saint-Paul, 75004 Paris.
T. 0148048115.   047454
Saint Petersbourg, 106 Rue Miromesnil, 75008 Paris.
T. 0145639321. - Ant -   047455
Saint-Séverin, 4 Rue Petit-Pont, 75005 Paris.
T. 0146339058. - Ant -   047456
Sakr, Charles, Louvre des Antiquaires, 2 Pl Palais-Royal,
75001 Paris. T. 0142615861. - Ant / Paint /
Furn -   047457
Saling, 14 Rue Fourcy, 75004 Paris.
T. 0140279575.   047458
Salle des Ventes Alésia, 123 Rue Alésia, 75014 Paris.
T. 0145455454, Fax 0145395919. - Ant -   047459
Salloum, Maroun, 6 Rue Lille, 75008 Paris.
T. 0140159501, Fax 0149270984. - Furn -   047460
Salsedo, Antoine, 2 Pl Palais-Royal, 75001 Paris.
T. 0142615802. - Ant -   047461
Sam, 16 Rue Jouffroy d'Abbans, 75017 Paris.
T. 0147549337. - Ant -   047462
Samarcande, 13 Rue Saints-Pères, 75006 Paris.
T. 0142608317. - Orient / Sculp / Arch -   047463
Sandorfi, Maria, 90 Rue Jouffroy d'Abbans, 75017 Paris.
T. 0147639757. - Ant -   047464
Sao, 1 Rue Saint-Benoît, 75006 Paris. T. 0142963260.
- Eth -   047465
Saphir Art, Louvre des Antiquaires, 2 Pl Palais-Royal,
75001 Paris. T. 0142601707. - Jew -   047466
Sarti, G., 137 Rue du Fbg Saint-Honoré, 75008 Paris.
T. 0142893366, Fax 0142893377.   047467

Sartoni-Cerveau, 15 Quai Saint-Michel, 75005 Paris.
T. 0143547573, Fax 0146341288. - Paint /
Graph - *047468*
Saver, 51 Quai Seine, 75019 Paris.
T. 0142057232. *047469*
Scaphandre, Louvre des Antiquaires, 2 Pl Palais-Royal,
75001 Paris. T. 0142601777. - Instr / Naut - *047470*
Scarlett, Louvre des Antiquaires, 2 Pl Palais-Royal,
75001 Paris. T. 0142601726. - Jew - *047471*
S.C.D Antiquités, 106 Blvd Raspail, 75006 Paris.
T. 0145499799. - Ant - *047472*
Scherer & Fils, 19 Rue Valois, 75001 Paris.
T. 0142614624. - Furn / Sculp / Tex - *047473*
Schmit, Manuel, 396 Rue Saint-Honoré, 75001 Paris.
T. 0142603636, Fax 0149279716. - Paint /
Sculp - *047474*
Schmit, Robert, 396 Rue Saint-Honoré, 75001 Paris.
T. 0142603636, Fax 0149279716. - Paint / Sculp /
Draw - *047475*
Schmitt, Michel, 84 Av Breteuil, 75015 Paris.
T. 0143062890. - Ant / Sculp / Draw - *047476*
Schmitz, J. & A., 13 Rue La-Trémoïlle, 75008 Paris.
T. 0147238308. - Ant / Furn / China - *047477*
Schmitz, Jean, 6 Rue Houdon, 75018 Paris.
T. 0142621815. - Ant / Cur - *047478*
Schutz, Edouard, 183 Blvd Saint-Germain, 75007 Paris.
T. 0142221249. - Ant / Furn / Tex - *047479*
S.D.A. Antiquités, Louvre des Antiquaires, 2 Pl Palais-
Royal, 75001 Paris. T. 0149260818,
Fax 0149260819. *047480*
Segoura, Marc, 20 Rue Fbg-Saint-Honoré, 75008 Paris.
T. 0142651103, Fax 0142651608. - Paint /
Draw - *047481*
Segoura, Maurice, 14 Pl François-1er, 75008 Paris.
T. 0142892020. - Paint / Furn / Tex - *047482*
Segoura, Michel, 11 Quai Voltaire, 75007 Paris.
T. 0142611923, Fax 0142600198. - Ant /
Paint - *047483*
Segoura, Pierre, 20 Rue Fbg-Saint-Honoré, 75008 Paris.
T. 0142651103, Fax 0142651608. - Paint /
Draw - *047484*
Seine et Danube, 6 Rue Monsieur-le-Prince, 75006 Pa-
ris. T. 0143250101. - Ant - *047485*
Seine et Danube, 9 Rue Dupuytren, 75006 Paris.
T. 0143250460. *047486*
Sellem, Bernard, 7 Rue Provence, 75009 Paris.
T. 0142463892. - Ant - *047487*
Semarany, 119 Av Emile-Zola, 75015 Paris.
T. 0145770484. - Ant - *047488*
Sender, Mélanie, 18 Rue Grange Batelière, 75009 Paris.
T. 0147701808. - Ant / Furn - *047489*
Senemaud, Monique, Louvre des Antiquaires, 2 Pl Pa-
lais-Royal, 75001 Paris. T. 0142601909.
- Ant - *047490*
Serraire, Patrick, 30 Rue Lille, 75007 Paris.
T. 0147034313. *047491*
Serres, 15 Rue Bonaparte, 75006 Paris. T. 0143257827,
Fax 0146335532. - Arch / Jew - *047492*
Serret-Portier, 17 Rue Drouot, 75009 Paris.
T. 0147708982. - Jew - *047493*
Sevin de Quincy, Edouard de, Louvre des Antiquaires, 2
Pl Palais-Royal, 75001 Paris. T. 0142615799,
Fax 0147033207. - Ant / Jew / Silv - *047494*
Seymour, 9 Rue Dufrenoy, 75016 Paris. T. 0145045465.
- Ant - *047495*
Shangaï's Garden, 30 Rue Saint-Roch, 75001 Paris.
T. 0142614563. - Ant - *047496*
Sidonie, 90 Av Emile-Zola, 75015 Paris.
T. 0140598020. *047497*
Siècle des Lumières, 8 Rue Commaille, 75007 Paris.
T. 0145493554. *047498*
Sigrid, 78 Av Suffren, 75015 Paris. T. 0145674143.
- Ant - *047499*
Silberstein, Claude, 39 Rue Vivienne, 75002 Paris.
T. 0142331955. - Num - *047500*
Simon, Dominique, 147 Blvd Montparnasse, 75006 Pa-
ris. T. 0143267296. - Ant - *047501*
Simon, Emmanuelle, 38 Rue Sèvres, 75006 Paris.
T. 0145449043. - Ant - *047502*
Singe Blanc, 15 Rue Saint-Jacques, 75005 Paris.
T. 0143261470, Fax 0140468536. - Orient - *047503*
Sirène, 22 Rue Echaudé, 75006 Paris. T. 0140517489,
Fax 0143299231. - Graph / Draw - *047504*

Siret, Liliane, 11 Rue Brunel, 75017 Paris.
T. 0145745748. - Jew - *047505*
Sofer, 86 Rue d'Amsterdam, 75009 Paris.
Fax (1) 48745192. - Ant - *047506*
Sonkin, Michel, 10 Rue Beaune, 75007 Paris.
T. 0142612787. - Ant - *047507*
Sophie du Bac, 109 Rue Bac, 75007 Paris.
T. 0145484901. - Toys - *047508*
Sorelle Art Déco, 12 Rue de l'Echaudé, 75006 Paris.
T. 0146335941. - Ant - *047509*
Sotheby's, 3 Rue de Miromesnil, 75008 Paris.
T. 0142664060, Fax 0147422232. - Ant - *047510*
Soubrier, 14 Rue Reuilly, 75012 Paris.
T. 0143729371. *047511*
Souchon, Michel, 14 Rue Grange Batelière, 75009 Paris.
T. 0148000713. - Ant - *047512*
Souillac, Michel, 6 Rue Antoine-Dubois, 75006 Paris.
T. 0143294304. - Ant / Dec / Jew - *047513*
Souris Verte, 23 Rue Saint-Paul, 75004 Paris.
T. 0142747976. - Ant - *047514*
Soustiel, Jean, 146 Blvd Haussmann, 75008 Paris.
T. 0145622776, Fax 0145634463. - Orient / China /
Sculp / Arch / Eth - *047515*
Soyez, Jeannine, 55 Rue Cherche-Midi, 75006 Paris.
T. 0142220420. - Orient / China - *047516*
Spira, Max, 21 Pl Vosges, 75004 Paris. T. 0142771578.
- Ant - *047517*
Spira, Robert, 7 Rue Abbeville, 75010 Paris.
T. 0148744477. - Ant - *047518*
Sportsman, 7bis Rue Henri-Duchêne, 75015 Paris.
T. 0145793893. - Pho - *047519*
Steinitz, Baruch Bernard, 75 Rue Fbg-Saint-Honoré,
75008 Paris. T. 0147423194, Fax 0149249116. - Ant /
Paint / Furn / Sculp / Dec - *047520*
Stolzenberg, Simon, 16 Rue Geoffroy Marie, 75009 Pa-
ris. T. 0147706073. - Ant - *047521*
Storage, 34 Rue Lappe, 75011 Paris.
T. 0143149070. *047522*
Studio Saint-Sulpice, 3 Rue Saint-Sulpice, 75006 Paris.
T. 0140510633. *047523*
Studiolo Antiquités, 2 Rue Yvonne-Le-Tac, 75018 Paris.
T. 0142577438, Fax 0142571172. *047524*
Sudit, Madeleine, 67 Av Suffren, 75007 Paris.
T. 0142730445. - Furn - *047525*
Suffren, 8 Rue Rossini, 75009 Paris.
T. 0148000082. *047526*
Suger, Louvre des Antiquaires, 2 Pl Palais-Royal, 75001
Paris. T. 0142615772. - Jew / Silv - *047527*
Sutton-Grenée, Martine, 78 Av Suffren, 75015 Paris.
T. 0145674629. - Ant - *047528*
Swann, 5 Rue Beaune, 75007 Paris. T. 0142612722.
- Ant - *047529*
Szlos, Lisette, 17 Rue Trétaigne, 75018 Paris.
T. 0142541647. - Ant - *047530*
T Zen, 1 Rue Pierre Lescot, 75001 Paris.
T. 0140399761. - Ant - *047531*
Table en Fête, 71 Pl Docteur-Félix-Lobligeois, 75017 Pa-
ris. T. 0146277549, Fax 0146274919. *047532*
Talabardon, Bertrand, 44 Rue Sainte-Anne, 75002 Paris.
Fax 0147033916, 0147033951. - Ant - *047533*
Tamburini, Roland, 43 Rue Mouffetard, 75005 Paris
T. 0143361575. *047534*
Tanakaya, 4 Rue Saint-Sulpice, 75006 Paris.
T. 0143257291, Fax 0143257291. - Graph /
Orient - *047535*
Tansu, 37 Rue Beaune, 75007 Paris. T. 0142614337.
- Ant - *047536*
Tao, 5 Rue Pont Louis Philippe, 75004 Paris.
T. 0140299545. - Ant - *047537*
Tassel, Jean-Max, 15 Quai Voltaire, 75007 Paris.
T. 0142610201, Fax 0142612563. - Paint - *047538*
Tastet, 15 Rue Grange-Batelière, 75009 Paris.
T. 0147705785. - Ant - *047539*
Tcharny, Lucien, 19 Rue André-del-Sarte, 75018 Paris.
T. 0142642063. - Sculp - *047540*
Teboul, Alain, 30 Rue Claude Decaen, 75012 Paris.
T. 0143442912. - Ant - *047541*
Teboul, Jacqueline, 78 Av Suffren, 75015 Paris.
T. 0143068530, Fax 0140659582. - Ant - *047542*
Templier, 10 Rue Drouot, 75009 Paris. T. 0142470023,
Fax 0142470015. - Jew - *047543*
Temps Retrouvé, 6 Rue Vauvillers, 75001 Paris.
T. 0142336617. - Ant - *047544*

Tentation du Mandarin, 186 Rue Rivoli, 75001 Paris.
T. 0142606589. - Ant - *047545*
Tesson, Robert, 7 Rue Cardinet, 75017 Paris.
T. 0142676004. - Ant - *047546*
Texier, Aliette, 41 Quai Horloge – Pont Neuf, 75001 Pa-
ris. T. 0143542143. - Ant / Furn / Sculp / Eth / Dec /
Cur / Tin - *047547*
Thenadey, Maurice & Cie, 1 Quai Voltaire, 75007 Paris.
T. 0142607733. - Ant / Furn / Tex - *047548*
Théorème, Louvre des Antiquaires, 2 Pl Palais-Royal,
75001 Paris. T. 0140159323. - China - *047549*
Thibaudat, Jacques, 8 Rue Bac, 75007 Paris.
T. 0142612194. - Jew - *047550*
Thibault de la Châtre, 36 Rue Varenne, 75007 Paris.
T. 0145488299, Fax 0145490584. - Ant - *047551*
Thibaut-Pomerantz, Carole, 54 Rue Université, 75007
Paris. T. 0142228341. - Ant / Dec - *047552*
Thiebaut, Bertrand, 4 Av Villiers, 75017 Paris.
T. 0142942571. - Ant / Instr - *047553*
Thomas, 98 Rue Oberkampf, 75011 Paris.
T. 0143553448. - Ant - *047554*
Thomire Roux, Louvre des Antiquaires, 2 Pl Palais-Roy-
al, 75001 Paris. T. 0142615700, Fax 0142615701.
- Paint - *047555*
Tilsam, 21 Rue Odéon, 75006 Paris. T. 0143269407.
- Orient - *047556*
Tomy, Anka, 27 Rue Fbg-Montmartre, 75009 Paris.
T. 0147704572, Fax 0147701871. - Num - *047557*
Tortue Eléctrique, 5 Rue Frédéric-Sauton, 75005 Paris.
T. 0143293708. - Toys - *047558*
Toubalalsar, 5 Rue Muller, 75018 Paris.
T. 0142524227. *047559*
Touchons du Bois, 7 Rue La-Tour-d'Auvergne, 75009
Paris. T. 0142853628. *047560*
Tour Camouflé, Louvre des Antiquaires, 2 Pl Palais-Roy-
al, 75001 Paris. T. 0142602232. - Furn /
Lights - *047561*
Tourbillon, Louvre des Antiquaires, 2 Pl Palais-Royal,
75001 Paris. T. 0142615658. - Ant - *047562*
Touret, Michel, 56 Rue Ruisseau, 75018 Paris.
T. 0142515951, Fax 0142515952. *047563*
Tourneboeuf, Jean-Claude, 38 Rue Sèvres, 75007 Paris.
T. 0145446799. - Ant - *047564*
Toussaint, Daniel, 25 Rue Campo-Formio, 75013 Paris.
T. 0144241529. *047565*
Tovi, Jacques, 31 Rue Raffet, 75016 Paris.
T. 0145279618. - Ant - *047566*
Trévise Antiquités, 43 Rue Trévise, 75009 Paris.
T. 0142471651. *047567*
Triade, 74 Rue Cherche-Midi, 75006 Paris.
T. 0145487419. - Ant - *047568*
Triptyque, 91 Rue Saint-Honoré, 75001 Paris.
T. 0142332374. - Ant / Dec / Jew / Silv / Glass /
Toys - *047569*
Troubadour, 38 Rue Sèvres, 75007 Paris.
T. 0145444989. *047570*
Trouvailles, 17 Rue Henri Monnier, 75009 Paris.
T. 0145266458. - Ant - *047571*
Trouvailles d'Olivier, 13 Av Théophile-Gautier, 75016 Pa-
ris. T. 0145243300. *047572*
Tutino, Dominique, 25 Av George-V, 75008 Paris.
T. 0147205783. *047573*
Ullern, 47 Rue Rome, 75008 Paris. T. 0142935490.
- Music - *047574*
Ulysse, 1 Rue Varenne, 75007 Paris.
T. 0145491985. *047575*
Uraeus, 24 Rue Seine, 75006 Paris. T. 0143269131.
- Sculp / Arch / Eth - *047576*
Urli-Vernenghi, 18 Rue Lille, 75007 Paris.
T. 0142860705, Fax 0142860343. *047577*
Urso, Josiane, 93 Rue Reuilly, 75012 Paris.
T. 0146281243. - Ant - *047578*
Valdi, Claude, 6 Rue Université, 75007 Paris.
T. 0147039490, Fax 0142611467. - Ant - *047579*
Valentin Smith, Michel, 22 Rue Juliette-Lamber, 75017
Paris. T. 0142274636, Fax 0142279280. *047580*
Vallois, 41 Rue Seine, 75006 Paris. T. 0143205084,
Fax 0143299073. - Mod - *047581*
Van Wassenhove, 1 Rue Fontaine, 75009 Paris.
T. 0142814107. *047582*
Vandermeersch, Michel, 27 Quai Voltaire, 75007 Paris.
T. 0142612310, Fax 0149279849. - China - *047583*

Varangue, 25 Rue Bourgogne, 75007 Paris.
T. 0145504241. - Furn / Dec -   *047584*
Vatelot, Etienne, 11bis Rue Portalis, 75008 Paris.
T. 0145221725, Fax 0145220972. - Music -   *047585*
Vautrin & Audouy, 30 Rue Verneuil, 75007 Paris.
T. 0142612462. - China -   *047586*
V.D.A., 8 Rue Vavin, 75006 Paris. T. 0143298482.
- Ant -   *047587*
Vérarose Collection, 3 Rue Pyramides, 75001 Paris.
Fax (1) 40150286.   *047588*
Verdreau Dufresne, 8 Rue N-D des Champs, 75006 Pa-
ris. T. 0145444075. - Ant -   *047589*
Vergnes, Robert, 38 Rue Seine, 75006 Paris.
T. 0143255538. - Ant -   *047590*
Verneuil Bac, 17 Rue du Bac, 75007 Paris.
T. 0142611877, Fax 0142611499. - China -   *047591*

GALERIE
VERNEUIL BAC
Antique pottery.

17, rue du Bac - 75007 Paris
Tél. : 33/01 42 61 18 77
Fax : 33/01 42 61 14 99

Verneuil Saints-Pères, 13 Rue Saints-Pères, 75006 Pa-
ris. T. 0142602830. - Paint -   *047592*
Vernex, Andrée, 90 Rue Bac, 75007 Paris.
T. 0142221261. - Ant -   *047593*
Verreglass, 32 Rue Charonne, 75011 Paris.
T. 0148057843. - Ant -   *047594*
Via Antica, 11 Rue Jacob, 75006 Paris. T. 0140517779.
- Ant -   *047595*
Via Varenne, 38 Rue Varenne, 75007 Paris.
T. 0140490649. - Ant -   *047596*
Vian, 8 Rue Grégoire-de-Tours, 75006 Paris.
T. 0143540269. - Instr / Music -   *047597*
Vichot, Philippe, 37 Rue Lille, 75007 Paris.
T. 0140150081, Fax 0142610752. - Ant / Paint / Tex /
Dec -   *047598*
Vicomte, 15 Rue Saint-Paul, 75004 Paris.
T. 0140279422.   *047599*
Vidal, Eric, 1 Pl Paul-Painlevé, 75005 Paris.
T. 0143294402. - Furn -   *047600*
Vie de Chateau, 17 Rue Valois, 75001 Paris.
T. 0149270982. - Ant / Dec -   *047601*
Vie des Choses, 71bis Rue Tombe Issoire, 75014 Paris.
T. 0143277016. - Ant -   *047602*
Vie en Rose, 73 Pl Docteur-Félix-Lobligeois, 75017 Pa-
ris. T. 0142637071.   *047603*
Vieille Cité, 350 Rue Saint-Honoré, 75001 Paris.
T. 0142606716. - Ico -   *047604*
Vieilleville, Dominique, Louvre des Antiquaires, 2 Pl Pa-
lais-Royal, 75001 Paris. T. 0142615750. - China /
Sculp -   *047605*
Vies Privées, 120 Blvd Raspail, 75006 Paris.
T. 0145491831, Fax 0145480743. - Ant -   *047606*
Vieux Clocheton, 5 Rue Claude Terrasse, 75016 Paris.
T. 0145243652. - Ant -   *047607*
Vieux Manoir, 8 Rue Beaune, 75007 Paris.
T. 0142611750. - China -   *047608*
Vieux Paris, 4 Rue Paix, 75002 Paris. T. 0142610089,
Fax 0142613865. - Jew / Silv / Instr -   *047609*
Vieux Persan, 10 Rue Victor Massé, 75009 Paris.
T. 0145268493. - Ant -   *047610*
Vilaret, Valerie, 81 Rue Saints-Pères, 75006 Paris.
T. 0145447762. - Ant / Furn -   *047611*
Villa Borghese, 5 Rue Philibert-Delorme, 75017 Paris.
T. 0143809758. - Ant -   *047612*
Village de Passy, 19 Rue Annonciation, 75016 Paris.
T. 0145271161. - Ant -   *047613*
Village Suisse, 78 Av Suffren, 75015 Paris.
T. 0147834518. - Ant -   *047614*
Village Suisse, 54 Av La-Motte-Picquet, 75015 Paris.
- Ant -   *047615*
Vincent, Anne, 31 Blvd Raspail, 75007 Paris.
T. 0140490221. - Ant -   *047616*

Vinchon, Annette, 3 Rue Bourse, 75002 Paris.
T. 0142975353, Fax 0142974456. - Num -   *047617*
Vinchon, Jean, 77 Rue Richelieu, 75002 Paris.
T. 0142975000, Fax 0142860603. - Num /
Mil -   *047618*
Virtuoses de la Réclame, 5 Rue Saint-Paul, 75004 Paris.
T. 0142720786. - Repr / Graph -   *047619*
Vivaldi, 39 Rue Rome, 75008 Paris. T. 0143876839.
- Ant -   *047620*
Vivement Jeudi, 52 Rue Mouffetard, 75005 Paris.
T. 0143314452. - Ant -   *047621*
Voeltzel, Thierry, 14 Cité Bergère, 75009 Paris.
T. 0142464267, Fax 0142464269.   *047622*
Voldère, Bernadette de, 78 Av Suffren, 75015 Paris.
T. 0145665453.   *047623*
Voldère, Florence de, Louvre des Antiquaires, 2 Pl Pa-
lais-Royal, 75001 Paris. T. 0140159326.
- Paint -   *047624*
Vos, Jacques de, 34 Rue Seine, 75006 Paris.
T. 0143262926. - Paint / Graph / Sculp / Draw - *047625*
Vos, Jacques de, 7 Rue Bonaparte, 75006 Paris.
T. 0143298894, Fax 0140469545. - Furn / Sculp /
Lights -   *047626*
Vosges Antiquités, 96 Rue Faisanderie, 75016 Paris.
T. 0145004405.   *047627*
Vosges Antiquités, 61 Av Marceau, 75016 Paris.
T. 0147234670. - Ant -   *047628*
Votat, Fernand, 77 Av Kléber, 75116 Paris.
T. 0147279401. - Furn -   *047629*
Votat, Pierre, 133 Rue Michel-Ange, 75016 Paris.
T. 0147430064. - Ant -   *047630*
Waintraub, Henri, 85 Rue Abbé Groult, 75015 Paris.
T. 0145326861. - Ant -   *047631*
Wanooq, Jean, 12 Rue Saints-Pères, 75007 Paris.
T. 0142608364, Fax 0142604148. - Ant / Paint / Furn /
Tex / Dec / Fra / Glass -   *047632*
Watelet, Olivier, 11 Rue Bonaparte, 75006 Paris.
T. 0143260787, Fax 0143259933. - Furn / Dec /
Mod -   *047633*
Weber & Ass, 15 Rue Lille, 75007 Paris. T. 0142602925,
Fax 0142868419. - Paint / Furn / Cur -   *047634*
Widor, 88 Rue Chardon-Lagache, 75016 Paris.
T. 0145204902.   *047635*
Wisen, 102 Rue Fbg-Saint-Honoré, 75008 Paris.
T. 0142666944. - Ant / China -   *047636*
Xavier-Bender, Michèle, 8 Rue Saussaies, 75008 Paris.
T. 0142664245.   *047637*
Yad, 9 Rue Immeubles Industriels, 75011 Paris.
T. 0143706099. - Ant -   *047638*
Yellow Gallery, Louvre des Antiquaires, 2 Pl Palais-Roy-
al, 75001 Paris. T. 0147034945,
Fax 0147034955.   *047639*
Yesterday, 16 Rue Cler, 75007 Paris. T. 0145516560.
- Furn / China -   *047640*
Yveline, 4 Rue Furstenberg, 75006 Paris.
T. 0143265691. - Eth / Cur -   *047641*
Zeitoun, Angel, 10 Rue Véronèse, 75013 Paris.
T. 0145359483. - Ant -   *047642*
Zeitoun, Claude, 42 Rue Maubeuge, 75009 Paris.
T. 0148780606. - Ant -   *047643*
Zins, Michel, 14 Rue Jean Jacques Rousseau, 75001
Paris. T. 0142211311. - Ant -   *047644*
Zola Antiquités, 80 Rue Théâtre, 75015 Paris.
T. 0145799372.   *047645*
Zouari, Mardochée, 22 Rue Frémicourt, 75015 Paris.
T. 0145795223. - Ant -   *047646*
008 Antiquités, 62 Blvd Malesherbes, 75008 Paris.
Fax (1) 45223293. - Ant -   *047647*
1900 Monceau, 62 Blvd Malesherbes, 75008 Paris.
T. 0143879280. - Ant -   *047648*

Parly (Yonne)
Bonnerot, Michel, Chemin de Ronde, 89240 Parly.
T. 0386440552.   *047649*

Parnoy-en-Bassigny (Haute-Marne)
Boudin, Daniel, RN 429, Fresnoy, 52400 Parnoy-en-Bas-
signy. T. 0325908160.   *047650*
Quentin, Rue Château-Fresnoy, 52400 Parnoy-en-Bassi-
gny. T. 0325908137.   *047651*

Paron (Yonne)
Dujeu, Bernard, 39 Rue Saint-Ménard, 89100 Paron.
T. 0386653145.   *047652*

Parthenay (Deux-Sèvres)
Chiparus, 109 Av Aristide-Briand, 79200 Parthenay.
T. 0549942351, Fax 0549641527   *047653*
Chiparus, 1 Rue Henri-Dunant, 79200 Parthenay.
T. 0549942351, Fax 0549641527.   *047654*

Parville (Eure)
Legabilleux, Jean-Paul, RN 13, 27180 Parville.
T. 0232316915. - Paint / Furn / Sculp / Tex /
Cur -   *047655*

Passonfontaine (Doubs)
Vinay, Michel, 19 Grande Rue, 25690 Passonfontaine.
T. 0381432214.   *047656*

Passy-Grigny (Marne)
Gille, Jean-Pierre, 13 Rue Nicolas-Grigny, 51700 Passy-
Grigny. T. 0326529593.   *047657*

Pau (Pyrénées-Atlantiques)
Aéroplane, 6 Av Résistance, 64000 Pau. T. 0559624885.
- Ant -   *047658*
Antiquités du Sud-Ouest, 37 Rue Bayard, 64000 Pau.
T. 0559828887, Fax 0559839142. - Ant -   *047659*
Ascaso Antiquités, 11bis Pl Foirail, 64000 Pau.
T. 0559844426. - Ant -   *047660*
Baute, Daniel, Pl Foirail, 64000 Pau. T. 0559302768.
- Ant -   *047661*
Béarn Antiquités, 12 Rue Henri IV, 64000 Pau.
T. 0559276342. - Ant -   *047662*
Champeau, Georges, Pl Foirail, 64000 Pau.
T. 0559842241. - Ant -   *047663*
Champeau, Georges, 38 Av Edouard VII, 64000 Pau.
T. 0559024003. - Ant / Furn / Sculp / Tex / Silv - *047664*
Colibœuf, Caroline, 1 Rue Gassion, 64000 Pau.
T. 0559274210. - Ant -   *047665*
Country Style, 174 Av Jean-Mermoz, 64000 Pau.
T. 0559627312. - Ant -   *047666*
Delan, 4 Rue Gassion, 64000 Pau. T. 0559274562.
- Ant / Paint / Furn -   *047667*
Durand, Robert, 2 Rue Ségure, 64000 Pau.
T. 0559325387. - Ant -   *047668*
Faget, Jeanne, 34 Rue Emile-Guichenné, 64000 Pau.
T. 0559279355. - Ant -   *047669*
Ferran-Lacome, Pierre, 50 Rue Maréchal-Joffre, 64000
Pau. T. 0559275771. - Ant / Paint / Sculp / Tex - *047670*
Galerie A.J.L, 74 Rue Emile-Garet, 64000 Pau.
T. 0559273639, Fax 0559275442. - Ant -   *047671*
Galerie 64, Pl Foirail, 64000 Pau. T. 0559027280.
- Ant -   *047672*
Galy, Janine, 47 Rue Emile-Guichenné, 64000 Pau.
T. 0559837784. - Ant -   *047673*
Irrigaray, Bertrand, Pl Forail, 64000 Pau. T. 0559848523.
- Ant -   *047674*
Lhoste, Eric, 32 Rue Emile-Garet, 64000 Pau.
T. 0559277550. - Ant / Paint -   *047675*
Maya, 21 Rue Bernadotte, 64000 Pau. T. 0559829538.
- Ant -   *047676*
Orts, Gérard, 30 Rue Henri-IV, 64000 Pau.
T. 0559273130, Fax 0559277780. - Paint /
Furn -   *047677*
Orts, Monique, 52 Rue Maréchal-Joffre, 64000 Pau.
T. 0559273103. - Ant -   *047678*
Pecantet, Guy, 1 Pl Foirail, 64000 Pau. T. 0559800944.
- Ant -   *047679*
Prat Sainte Marie, André, 16 Rue Abbé-Brémond, 64000
Pau. T. 0559023762. - Ant -   *047680*
Rogissart, Jean-Marie, 1 Rue Sully, 64000 Pau.
T. 0559278830. - Ant / Paint / Furn -   *047681*
Rougeaux Bayle, 11 Rue Henri-IV, 64000 Pau.
T. 0559273075. - Ant / Paint / Furn / Dec -   *047682*
Trésarieu, Renée, 7 Rue Henri-IV, 64000 Pau.
T. 0559828092. - Ant -   *047683*

Pavilly (Seine-Maritime)
Antiquité Brocante Mare Blanche, Ham Mare Blanche,
76570 Pavilly. T. 0235916606. - Furn / Cur -   *047684*

Payrin-Augmontel (Tarn)

Veaux, Thierry, RN 112, 81660 Payrin-Augmontel.
T. 0563615285, Fax 0563616798. - Paint / Furn / Dec /
Cur -						*047685*

Penne-d'Agenais (Lot-et-Garonne)

Deconinck, Alain, 7 Av Myre-Mory, 47140 Penne-d'Age-
nais. T. 0553412905.				*047686*

Péreuil (Charente)

Hourdin, Patrice, Graverit, 16250 Péreuil.
T. 0545640452.					*047687*

Périgny (Charente-Maritime)

Débard, André, 113 Rue Grande, 17180 Périgny.
T. 0546441709.					*047688*

Périgueux (Dordogne)

Anaïs, 34 Rue Président-Wilson, 24000 Périgueux.
T. 0553034465.					*047689*
Authier, Thierry, 16 Rue Pierre-Magne, 24000 Périgueux.
T. 0553093233, Fax 0553093233. - Ant -	*047690*
Axpe & Saillard, 73 Rue Combe-Dames, 24000 Péri-
gueux. T. 0553539057. - Ant -			*047691*
Blason, 16 Blvd Georges-Saumande, 24000 Périgueux.
T. 0553087771.					*047692*
Bonnelie, Suzanne, 7 Rue Puy-Limogeanne, 24000 Péri-
gueux. T. 0553097180.				*047693*
Borie, Daniel, 15 All Port, 24000 Périgueux.
T. 0553093400. - Paint / Furn / Cur -		*047694*
Fontaine Saint-Louis, 24 Rue Eguillerie, 24000 Péri-
gueux. T. 0553536003.				*047695*
Galerie du Chineur, 32 Rue Antoine-Gadaud, 24000 Péri-
gueux. T. 0553531115, Fax 0553549746.	*047696*
Jo An, 12 Rue Saint-Front, 24000 Périgueux.
T. 0553533310.					*047697*
Wilde, Yvan de, 3 Rue Limogeanne, 24000 Périgueux.
T. 0553084414, Fax 0553536915.		*047698*

Pernay (Indre-et-Loire)

Daveau, Régis, La Ronde, 37230 Pernay.
T. 0547524804.					*047699*

Pernes-les-Fontaines (Vaucluse)

Brocanterie, 333 Cours Frizet, 84210 Pernes-les-Fontai-
nes. T. 0490664296. - Ant -			*047700*

Péronnas (Ain)

Crapie, 130 Chemin de l'Eglise, 01960 Péronnas.
T. 0474214053. - Ant / Paint / Furn -		*047701*
Crapie Antiquité, Chemin Eglise, 01960 Péronnas.
T. 0474214058. - Ant -				*047702*

Péronne (Somme)

Desmettre, Nadir, 7 Rue Saint-Fursy, 80200 Péronne.
T. 0322841753. - Ant -				*047703*

Pérouges (Ain)

Antiquités Art Ancien, Le Péage, 01800 Pérouges.
T. 0474610711. - Ant -				*047704*
Vénard „La Barbacane", La Porte-d'en-Haut, 01800 Pé-
rouges. T. 0474618427. - Ant -			*047705*

Perpezac-le-Blanc (Corrèze)

Meubles de Jallais, Manoir Bois Noir, 19310 Perpezac-
le-Blanc. T. 0555251964.			*047706*

Perpignan (Pyrénées-Orientales)

Antic Meubles, 19 Av Marcellin-Albert, 66000 Perpig-
nan. T. 0468853173, Fax 0468850052.
- Furn -					*047707*
Antiquaires de Sant-Vincens, Rue Sant-Vincens, 66000
Perpignan. T. 0468508627. - Ant -		*047708*
Berjoan, 13 Av Grande-Bretagne, 66000 Perpignan.
T. 0468353005. - Ant / Furn / Glass / Paint / Lights /
Silv -						*047709*
Boyer, 5 Rue Louis-Béguin, 66000 Perpignan.
T. 0468502072. - Ant -				*047710*
Cadenet, Martine, 32 Blvd Clemenceau, 66000 Perpig-
nan. T. 0468350713. - Ant -			*047711*
Carretero, Thierry, 3 Pl Gambetta, 66000 Perpignan.
T. 0468356128. - Ant -				*047712*
Comteroux, Av Espagne, 66000 Perpignan.
T. 0468546433. - Ant -				*047713*
Curiosités-Décoration 1900-1930, 1 Rue Théâtre,
66000 Perpignan. T. 0468344599. - Ant -	*047714*

Domaine Saint-Roch, 24 Chemin Saint-Roch, 66000
Perpignan. T. 0468674145. - Ant -		*047715*
Fouineuse, 27 Rue Remparts-Villeneuve, 66000 Perpig-
nan. T. 0468350099. - Ant -			*047716*
Gély, Monique, 2 Pl Gambetta, 66000 Perpignan.
T. 0468512312. - Ant -				*047717*
Groupement des Antiquaires et Brocanteurs du Roussil-
lon, 4 Rue André-Bosch, 66000 Perpignan.
T. 0468352782. - Ant -				*047718*
Guiter, Jean-Luc, 18 Rue Doct-Pous, 66000 Perpignan.
T. 0468346861. - Ant -				*047719*
Hansen, G., 3 Rue Romarins, 66000 Perpignan.
T. 0468850302. - Ant / Paint / Furn / Glass /
Tex -						*047720*
Mas Pallaris, 51 Ancien Chemin Bompas, 66000 Perpig-
nan. T. 0468611943. - Ant -			*047721*
Masjo, Rue Sant-Vincens, 66000 Perpignan.
T. 0468670051. - Ant -				*047722*
Maurel, Franck, 1 Pl Révolution-Française, 66000 Per-
pignan. T. 0468341029. - Ant / Furn -		*047723*
Mejean-Gilles, Christine, 7 Rue Grande-des-Fabriques,
66000 Perpignan. T. 0468347145. - Ant /
Paint -						*047724*
Navarro, Antoinette, 2 Rue Stadium, 66000 Perpignan.
T. 0468668095. - Ant -				*047725*
Nérel, Georges, 1 Pl Catalone, 66000 Perpignan.
T. 0468547523. - Ant -				*047726*
Pascot, Guy, 13 Rue Lanterne, 66000 Perpignan.
T. 0468518218. - Ant -				*047727*
Rétro 1900, 17bis Av Lychée, 66000 Perpignan.
T. 0468553718. - Ant / Cur -			*047728*
Rovira, Louis, 21 Av Emile-Roudayre, 66000 Perpignan.
T. 0468613239. - Ant -				*047729*
Saint-Martin, 11 Rue Pierre-Cartelet, 66000 Perpignan.
T. 0468342425. - Furn -				*047730*
Sainte-Anne, Mas Llaro, Rte Canet, 66000 Perpignan.
T. 0468670392. - Ant -				*047731*
Salle de Vente des Tuileries, 28 Rue Tuileries, 66000
Perpignan. T. 0468547523. - Ant -		*047732*
Thomas, Marie-Josée, 5 Rue Cloche-d'Or, 66000 Per-
pignan. T. 0468343485. - Ant -			*047733*
Tout en Images, 70 Rue Mar-Foch, 66000 Perpignan.
T. 0468854614. - Paint / Graph -		*047734*
Trouvailles, 20 Rue Ernest-Renan, 66000 Perpignan.
T. 0468673300. - Ant -				*047735*
Turries, Yves, 35 Rue Courteline, 66000 Perpignan.
T. 0468514443. - Ant -				*047736*

Perriers-sur-Andelle (Eure)

Baveux Le Pennec, Claire, 27 Rue Générale-de-Gaulle,
27910 Perriers-sur-Andelle. T. 0232492067.	*047737*

Perrigny-lès-Dijon (Côte-d'Or)

Gay, Jean-Philippe, 1 Pl Saint-Eloi, 21160 Perrigny-lès-
Dijon. T. 0380512120. - Tex / Lights / Cur -	*047738*

Perros-Guirec (Côtes-d'Armor)

An Ti Coz, 65 Rue Ernest-Renan, 22700 Perros-Guirec.
T. 0296910865.					*047739*
Au Bonheur des Jours, 40 Pl Chapelle, 22700 Perros-
Guirec. T. 0296914739.				*047740*
Sallou, Hervé, Kernivinen, 22700 Perros-Guirec.
T. 0296233453.					*047741*
Stéphan, Yannick, 66 Rue Maréchal-Joffre, 22700 Per-
ros-Guirec. T. 0296233863.			*047742*
Véranda Déco, 25 Blvd Thalassa, 22700 Perros-Guirec.
T. 0296911267.					*047743*

Persac (Vienne)

Raymond, Laurence, La Baudière, 86320 Persac.
T. 0549482276. - Ant -				*047744*
Raymond, Michèle, Pré, 86320 Persac. T. 0549484485.
- Ant -						*047745*

Perthes (Seine-et-Marne)

Lis Gilles, 24 Rue Docteur-Siffre, 77930 Perthes.
T. 0360661357.					*047746*

Pertuis (Vaucluse)

Caula, Jacqueline, 283 Cours République, 84120 Per-
tuis. T. 0490793226. - Ant -			*047747*
Dubois, Adrien, Jas de Beaumont, 84120 Pertuis.
T. 0490792367. - Ant -				*047748*

Fisch, Jeanne, 105 Cours République, 84120 Pertuis.
T. 0490792691. - Ant -				*047749*

Pescadoires (Lot)

Mas Maury, André, Bourg, 46220 Pescadoires.
T. 0565224891.					*047750*

Pesmes (Haute-Saône)

Girardot, Jacques, Rue Tanneurs, 70140 Pesmes.
T. 0384312023.					*047751*

Pessac (Gironde)

Bordan, Michel, 11 Av Pape-Clément, 33600 Pessac.
T. 0556455180. - Furn -				*047752*
Fouillis du Livre, 19 Pl République, 33600 Pessac.
T. 0556453965.					*047753*
Richel, Philippe, Av Pontet, 33600 Pessac.
T. 0556460149.					*047754*
Vert Bleu, 61 Av Général-Leclerc, 33600 Pessac.
T. 0557269996.					*047755*

Peymeinade (Alpes-Maritimes)

Astrolabe, 245 Av Jaïsous, Mas Moghantarah, 06530
Peymeinade. T. 0493660927. - Instr / Cur /
Pho -						*047756*

Peyrieu (Ain)

Carroz Antiquités, Chef-Lieu, 01300 Peyrieu.
T. 0479420116. - Ant -				*047757*

Pézenas (Hérault)

Au Chien Vert, 5 Av Verdun, 34120 Pézenas.
T. 0467983913.					*047758*
Boris Antiquaire, 10 Rue Mercière, 34120 Pézenas.
T. 0467988646.					*047759*
Boularand, Jacques, 4 Pl Etats-du-Languedoc, 34120
Pézenas. T. 0467988538.			*047760*
Cordeliers, 3 Rue de la Grange-des-Prés, 34120 Péze-
nas. T. 0467983992.				*047761*
Cordeliers, 2 Av de Verdun, 34120 Pézenas.
T. 0467981243.					*047762*
Forestier, Pierre, 11 Av Verdun, 34120 Pézenas.
T. 0467980905.					*047763*
Grimaldi, Vital, 12 Rue Potiers, 34120 Pézenas.
T. 0467981199.					*047764*
Paymal, Michel, 21 Av Verdun, 34120 Pézenas.
T. 0467983879. - Ant -				*047765*
Robert, Maurice, 7 Av Verdun, 34120 Pézenas.
T. 0467981730.					*047766*
Robert, Maurice, 12 Av Aristide-Briand, 34120 Pézenas.
T. 0467907236.					*047767*
Vidal, Marie, 17 Fbg-Cordeliers, 34120 Pézenas.
Fax 67989483.					*047768*
Vion, Jean-Paul, 3 Rte Béziers, 34120 Pézenas.
T. 0467980627.					*047769*

Pezou (Loir-et-Cher)

Lahoreau, Patrick, 28 Rue Vendôme, 41100 Pezou.
T. 0254773870.					*047770*
Violeau, Jean-Claude, 5 Av Gare, 41100 Pezou.
T. 0254236026.					*047771*

Phalempin (Nord)

Sainte Rictrude, 32 Rue Gén-Charles-de-Gaulle, 59133
Phalempin. T. 0320327060. - Ant -		*047772*

Piacé (Sarthe)

Tison, Claude, la Détourbe, 72170 Piacé.
T. 0243970397. - Ant -				*047773*

Pierrefitte-sur-Seine (Seine-Saint-Den-is)

Cohen, Raphaël, 45 Rue Delescluze, 93380 Pierrefitte-
sur-Seine. T. 0142358008, Fax 0142359602.	*047774*
Tourneboeuf, Jean-Claude, 65 Blvd Charles-de-Gaulle,
93380 Pierrefitte-sur-Seine. T. 0148262348.	*047775*

Pierrefort (Cantal)

Peyronnet, Gérard, 14 Rue Moulins, 15230 Pierrefort.
T. 0471233744.					*047776*

Pierrelatte (Drôme)

Boîte à Puces, 14 Rue Louis-XI, 26700 Pierrelatte.
T. 0475040847.					*047777*
Calèche, Rue Salins, 26700 Pierrelatte.
T. 0475963499.					*047778*

Pierreville (Manche)
Lemarchand, Jean, Ham ès Haguez, 50340 Pierreville.
T. 0233043371. *047779*

Pignans (Var)
Persico, Didier, La Berlière, Rte Carnoules, 3 Rue Saint-Roche, 83790 Pignans. T. 0494488336. *047780*

Pinel-Hauterive (Lot-et-Garonne)
Peretz, Jean-Claude, Limouzy, 47380 Pinel-Hauterive.
T. 0553011903. *047781*

Pineuilh (Gironde)
Nicouleau, Roland, 24 Av Général-Leclerc, 33220 Pineuilh. T. 0557464295. *047782*

Pinon (Aisne)
Lelièvre, Jean-Luc, 3 Rue Grand-Arrivoir, 02320 Pinon.
T. 0323809125. - Ant - *047783*

Pirey (Doubs)
Ferrey, Laurent, 64 E Rue Collège, 25480 Pirey.
T. 0381599676. *047784*

Placé (Sarthe)
Tison, Claude, Rte Nationale 138, 72170 Placé.
T. 0243970397. - Furn - *047785*

Plainfaing (Vosges)
Aux Puces de Plainfaing, 26 Rue Saint-Dié, 88230 Plainfaing. T. 0329503156. *047786*

Plaisir (Yvelines)
Grenier de Plaisir, 28 Rue Lavoisier, 78370 Plaisir.
T. 0134812836. *047787*

Plancoët (Côtes-d'Armor)
Douvreleur, Paul, 10 Rue Quais, 22130 Plancoët.
T. 0296842160. *047788*
Paul, Marya, 13 Rue Dinard, 22130 Plancoët.
T. 0296842757. *047789*

Planioles (Lot)
Falret, Jérôme, Lestrade, 46100 Planioles.
T. 0565500263. *047790*

Plasne (Jura)
Au Présent du Passé, Rue Château-d'Eau, 39800 Plasne.
T. 0384373667. *047791*

Plassac (Gironde)
Dubreuil, Patrick, 4 La Lande, 33390 Plassac.
T. 0557423941. *047792*
Morier, Bernard, 2 Gazin, 33390 Plassac.
T. 0557423051. *047793*

Plateau-d'Assy (Haute-Savoie)
Jiguet, Philippe, 719 Chemin Cran, 74480 Plateau-d'Assy. T. 0450938723. - Paint / Cur - *047794*

Pleine-Fougères (Ille-et-Vilaine)
Fournier, Michel, Mont Rouault, 35610 Pleine-Fougères.
T. 0299486032. *047795*

Plélan-le-Grand (Ille-et-Vilaine)
Floris, Hubert de, 8 Pl Eglise, 35380 Plélan-le-Grand.
T. 0299068305. *047796*
D'Ogny, La Cour du Gué, 35380 Plélan-le-Grand.
T. 0299069775, Fax 0299069926. *047797*

Pléneuf-Val-André (Côtes-d'Armor)
Antiquités André, 40 Rue Amiral-Charner, 22370 Pléneuf-Val-André. T. 0296722290. *047798*
Dodin, Roland, Quai Terre-Neuvas, 22370 Pléneuf-Val-André. T. 0296729049. *047799*
Le Goff, François-Xavier, 10 Rue Saint-Symphorien, 22370 Pléneuf-Val-André. T. 0296722962. *047800*

Plérin (Côtes-d'Armor)
Catherine & André, 18 Rue Corniche, 22190 Plérin.
T. 0296731460. - China / Cur - *047801*
Galerie des Quais, 16 Quai Chanoine-Guinard, 22190 Plérin. T. 0296521696. - Furn / Cur - *047802*

Plestin-les-Grèves (Côtes-d'Armor)
Antiquités Plestin, 38 Rue Pont-Ménou, 22210 Plestin-les-Grèves. T. 0296356601. *047803*

Pleugueneuc (Ille-et-Vilaine)
Pacserszky, Jean-Yves, Le Tertrais, 35720 Pleugueneuc.
T. 0299694164. *047804*

Pleumeur-Bodou (Côtes-d'Armor)
Suret-Canale, Michèle, 2 Rte Crech-Meur, 22560 Pleumeur-Bodou. T. 0296239201. *047805*

Pleumeur-Gautier (Côtes-d'Armor)
Crémaillère, 6 La Croix-Neuve, 22740 Pleumeur-Gautier.
T. 0296929373. *047806*

Pleurtuit (Ille-et-Vilaine)
Delahaye, Edouard, Le Dick, 35730 Pleurtuit.
T. 0299884214. *047807*
Le Calonnec, Gérard, La Ville-aux-Monniers, 35730 Pleurtuit. T. 0299462557. *047808*
Le Calonnec, Pierre, Les Lions, 35730 Pleurtuit.
T. 0299466079. *047809*

Pleuven (Finistère)
Laurent, Corentin, 37 Moulin-du-Pont, 29170 Pleuven.
T. 0298546328. - Ant - *047810*
Tennier, Emmanuel le, 7 Ty Glas Rte Bénodet, 29170 Pleuven. T. 0298548630. - Ant - *047811*

Pleyber-Christ (Finistère)
Peuchet, Daniel, 73 Rue de la République, 29410 Pleyber-Christ. T. 0298784778. - Ant - *047812*

Plombières-lès-Dijon (Côte-d'Or)
Antiquités Les Classiques, 1 Rue Petites-Roches, 21370 Plombières-lès-Dijon. T. 0380414513. *047813*
Gillard, Joseph, 114bis Rue Velars, 21370 Plombières-lès-Dijon. T. 0380455587. - Ant - *047814*

Plonévez-du-Faou (Finistère)
Nicolas, Patrick, Kervoel, 29530 Plonévez-du-Faou.
T. 0298818226. - Ant / Furn - *047815*

Plouagat (Côtes-d'Armor)
Brocante du Fournello, ZA Fournello, 22170 Plouagat.
T. 0296741641. *047816*

Plouay (Morbihan)
Calèche aux Trésors, 26 Rue Alliés, 56240 Plouay.
T. 0297333581. - Ant - *047817*
Le Stunff, Jean, 26 Rue Alliés, 56240 Plouay.
T. 0297333581. - Ant - *047818*

Ploubezre (Côtes-d'Armor)
Troadec, Pierre, Kerversault, 22300 Ploubezre.
T. 0296059485. *047819*

Ploufragan (Côtes-d'Armor)
Brocantine, 49 Rue Villes-Moisans, 22440 Ploufragan.
T. 0296784462. *047820*

Plougoumelen (Morbihan)
Bardet, Jacques, Château Pont-Sal, 56400 Plougoumelen. T. 0297241107. - Ant / Num - *047821*
Château de Pont-Sal, Château Pont-Sal, 56400 Plougoumelen. T. 0297241107. - Ant / Furn / Num - *047822*
Chaumière Antiquités, Nouvelle-Métairie, 56400 Plougoumelen. T. 0297241055. - Ant - *047823*

Plouguenast (Côtes-d'Armor)
Fichaut, Line, Moulin de la Touche, 22150 Plouguenast.
T. 0296287493. *047824*
Roinet, Jacques, Saint-Théo, 22150 Plouguenast.
T. 0296287568. - Ant / Paint / Furn / Jew / Cur - *047825*

Plouha (Côtes-d'Armor)
Costes, Pierre, Pl Foch, 22580 Plouha.
T. 0296203277. *047826*

Plouharnel (Morbihan)
Le Calvar, Claude, 8 Av Océan, 56720 Plouharnel.
T. 0297523435. - Ant - *047827*
Schitter, Jacqueline, 28 Rue Kerfourchelle, 56720 Plouharnel. T. 0297523435. - Ant - *047828*

Plouigneau (Finistère)
Léon, Philippe, 18 Rte Nationale, 29610 Plouigneau.
T. 0298677146. - Ant / Furn - *047829*

Ploulec'h (Côtes-d'Armor)
Mével, Jacques, Rte Morlaix, 22300 Ploulec'h.
T. 0296465947. - Ant / Furn - *047830*

Plourhan (Côtes-d'Armor)
Tharaud, Annie, Ville Allio, 22410 Plourhan.
T. 0296719060. *047831*

Plurien (Côtes-d'Armor)
Humbert, Allain, 1 Grand'Rue, 22240 Plurien.
T. 0296721127. - Furn / Eth / Cur - *047832*

Pocé-sur-Cisse (Indre-et-Loire)
Fougeron, Max, 42 Rue Cheval-Rouge, 37530 Pocé-sur-Cisse. T. 0547570626. *047833*

Poissy (Yvelines)
Loyer & Fils, 4 Blvd Devaux, 78300 Poissy.
T. 0139650988, Fax 0139651731. - Ant / Furn - *047834*

Poisy (Haute-Savoie)
Fournier, Yves, 3 Chemin Glaves, 74330 Poisy.
T. 0450463377, Fax 0450463537. *047835*

Poitiers (Vienne)
Au Passé Simple, 166 Grand-Rue, 86000 Poitiers.
T. 0549887349. - Ant / Paint / Glass - *047836*
Boutineau, Pierrick, 79 Rte Gençay, 86000 Poitiers.
T. 0549450356. - Ant - *047837*
Bric à Brac, 86 Rue Cathédrale, 86000 Poitiers.
T. 0549602461. - Ant - *047838*
Brocantic, 157 Grand-Rue, 86000 Poitiers.
T. 0549889524. - Ant - *047839*
Corne, Jean-Claude, 2 Rue Arènes-Romaines, 86000 Poitiers. T. 0549888080. - Ant - *047840*
Cotto B, 27 Rue Carnot, 86000 Poitiers. T. 0549887686.
- Ant / China / Mil - *047841*
Dusart, Jean-Luc, 77 Rue Cathédrale, 86000 Poitiers.
T. 0549882278. - Num - *047842*
Forget, Bernard, 30 Pl Charles-de-Gaulle, 86000 Poitiers. T. 0549881623. - Paint - *047843*
G. A. G. Dépôt Ventre, 94 Av Libération, 86000 Poitiers.
T. 0549580861. - Ant - *047844*
Lann, Henri le, 26 Rue Victor-Hugo, 86000 Poitiers.
T. 0549017908, Fax 0549413376. - Ant - *047845*
Mac Crohan Antiquités, 74 Rue Capit-Bés bât A, 86000 Poitiers. T. 0549378427. - Ant - *047846*
P'tit Placard, 62 Grand-Rue, 86000 Poitiers.
T. 0549018061. - Ant - *047847*
Paris Occasion, 8 Pl Alphonse-le-Petit, 86000 Poitiers.
T. 0549889054. - Ant - *047848*
Rullier, Michel, 35 Rue Marché, 86000 Poitiers, BP 236, 86006 Poitiers Cedex. T. 0549882151,
Fax 0549522442. - Sculp / Furn / Dec / Cur - *047849*
Voyer Antiquités, 35 Rue Marché, 86000 Poitiers.
T. 0549889197. - Ant / Paint / Furn - *047850*

Polignac (Haute-Loire)
Marcon, Charles, Rue Donjon, 43000 Polignac.
T. 0471095352. *047851*

Pommerit-le-Vicomte (Côtes-d'Armor)
Le Coz, Gilbert, 15 La Croix-Blanche, 22200 Pommerit-le-Vicomte. T. 0296217874. *047852*

Pommiers-Moulons (Charente-Maritime)
Labrouche, Mathias, Planches, 17130 Pommiers-Moulons. T. 0546706144. - Dec - *047853*

Pompey (Meurthe-et-Moselle)
Villemin, Catherine, 1 Rue Alsace, 54340 Pompey.
T. 0383247125, Fax 0383492614. *047854*

Pompierre (Vosges)
Adam, Philippe, 1 Rue Chevalier-de-la-Barre, 88300 Pompierre. T. 0329065240. *047855*

Pomponne (Seine-et-Marne)
Antic Inter Action, 6 Quai Bizeau, 77400 Pomponne.
T. 64306585. *047856*

Poncé-sur-le-Loir (Sarthe)
Verschoor, Olga, 6 Rue des Coteaux, 72340 Poncé-sur-le-Loir. T. 0243796988. - Ant - *047857*

Pons (Charente-Maritime)

Antiquités Martine, 28 Rue Général-Leclerc, 17800
Pons. T. 0546941126. - Furn / Dec / Cur - *047858*
Brocante Merle, 11 Pl Saint-Vivien, 17800 Pons.
T. 0546961866. *047859*

Pont-à-Mousson (Meurthe-et-Moselle)

Broc'Achat, 13bis Rue Fabvier, 54700 Pont-à-Mousson.
T. 0383820390. *047860*
Dohm, Michèle, 1 Blvd Lattre-de-Tassigny, 54700 Pont-
à-Mousson. T. 0383814085. *047861*
Dolveck, Christian, 386 Rte Norroy, 54700 Pont-à-
Mousson. T. 0383814011. *047862*

Pont-Audemer (Eure)

Perquier, Jacques, 15 Rue Tanneurs, 27500 Pont-Audemer. T. 0232412077. *047863*
Thiétard, A., 3bis Rue Alfred-Canel, 27500 Pont-Audemer. T. 0232421914. *047864*

Pont-Aven (Finistère)

Boutique du Lion d'Or, 1 Rue Auguste-Brizeux, 29930
Pont-Aven. T. 0298091108. - Ant - *047865*
Huguet, Eric, 29 Général-de-Gaulle, 29930 Pont-Aven.
T. 0298061336. - Ant - *047866*
Polychrome Antiquités, 29 Rue Général-de-Gaulle,
29930 Pont-Aven. T. 0298061336. - Ant / Paint /
Furn - *047867*
Rosot, Jean, 17 Rue Général-de-Gaulle, 29930 Pont-
Aven. T. 0298060191. - Ant - *047868*

Pont-d'Ain (Ain)

Carroz, Pascal, 75-77 Rue Saint-Exupéry, 01160 Pont-
d'Ain. T. 0474391190. - Ant - *047869*

Pont-de-Beauvoisin (Isère)

Bertholier, 12 Rue Porte-de-la-Ville, 73330 Pont-de-
Beauvoisin. T. 0476372607. - Ant / Furn - *047870*

Pont-de-Briques-Saint-Etienne (Pas-de-Calais)

Boulogne, 31 Rue Eugène-Huret, 62360 Pont-de-Bri-
ques-Saint-Etienne. T. 0321833645, Fax 0321336530.
- Ant - *047871*
Defachelle, Michel, 29 Rue Eugène-Huret, 62360 Pont-
de-Briques-Saint-Etienne. T. 0321830899. *047872*

Pont-de-l'Arche (Eure)

Galerie de l'Arche, 2 Rue Président-Roosevelt, 27340
Pont-de-l'Arche. T. 0232231527. *047873*
Manoir de Folie Vallée, RN 15, 27340 Pont-de-l'Arche.
T. 0232232193. *047874*
Paviot, Eric, 3 Rue Jean-Prieur, 27340 Pont-de-l'Arche.
T. 0232231996, Fax 0232020268. *047875*
Vieux Hangar, 10 Rue Alphonse-Samain, 27340 Pont-
de-l'Arche. T. 0232021995. *047876*

Pont-de-Vaux (Ain)

Colin, Jean-Pierre, Rte de Saint-Trivier-de-Courtes,
01190 Pont-de-Vaux. T. 0385309306. - Furn - *047878*

Pont-l'Abbé (Finistère)

Aubry, Jacques, 20 Rue Hoche, 29120 Pont-l'Abbé.
T. 0298871610. - Ant / Furn - *047879*
Biger, Yves-Marie, 16 Rue Kérentré, 29120 Pont-l'Abbé.
T. 0298872658. - Ant - *047880*
Binst, Jean, 7 Rue du Lycée, 29120 Pont-l'Abbé.
T. 0298872099. - Furn / Mil - *047881*
Donat-le-Drezen, Simone, 6 Rue Victor-Hugo, 29120
Pont-l'Abbé. T. 0298870662. - Ant - *047882*
Donat, Patrick, 9 Rue Ménez-Bihan, 29120 Pont-l'Abbé.
T. 0298872034. - Ant - *047883*
Euzen, Nicole, 8 Pl Carmes, 29120 Pont-l'Abbé.
T. 0298873500. - Ant / Furn / Tex - *047884*
Martre, Caroline, Rue Pasteur, 29120 Pont-l'Abbé.
T. 0298871681. - Ant / Cur / Pho - *047885*

Pont-l'Evêque (Calvados)

Au Mendigot, Rte Rouen, 14130 Pont-l'Evêque.
T. 0231650267. *047886*

Pont-Noyelles (Somme)

Aguet, Charly, 28 Rue Don, 80115 Pont-Noyelles.
T. 0322401199. - Ant / Cur - *047887*

Pont-Remy (Somme)

Holleville, Jean-Pierre, 17 Rue Jules-Ferry, 80580 Pont-
Remy. T. 0322271643. - Ant / Furn - *047888*

Pont-Saint-Esprit (Gard)

Montagne, Lyonel, 7 Pl Georges-Ville, 30130 Pont-
Saint-Esprit. T. 0466390716. *047889*

Pont-Sainte-Maxence (Oise)

Franzini-Heinen, Arlette, 80 Av Jean-Jaurès, 60700
Pont-Sainte-Maxence. T. 0344722861. - Ant /
Furn - *047890*

Pont-Salomon (Haute-Loire)

Fournier, Nicole, Croix de Trève, 43330 Pont-Salomon.
T. 0471358243. *047891*

Pont-sur-Yonne (Yonne)

Becourt, Thierry, 20 Rue Carnot, 89140 Pont-sur-Yonne.
T. 0386963626. *047892*
Faïences de France, 20 Av Général-Leclerc, 89140
Pont-sur-Yonne. T. 0386963616, Fax 0386672513.
- China - *047893*
Mazaleyrat, Daniel, 15 Av Général-Leclerc, 89140 Pont-
sur-Yonne. T. 0386963458. - Ant - *047894*

Pontaneveaux (Saône-et-Loire)

Coin du Feu, La Lachère RN 6, 71570 Pontaneveaux.
T. 0385338410. - Ant - *047895*

Pontarlier (Doubs)

Boutique d'Art Thomas, 8 Rue République, 25300 Pon-
tarlier. T. 0381395787. *047896*
Cordier, Patrice, 46 Rue République, 25300 Pontarlier.
T. 0381395019. *047897*

Pontaubert (Yonne)

Lafosse, Jean, Rte de Vézelay, 89200 Pontaubert.
T. 0386340213. - Ant / Paint / Furn / Rel - *047898*

Pontigny (Yonne)

Gualbert, Elisabeth, 40 Rte Auxerre, 89230 Pontigny.
T. 0386474088. *047899*

Pontivy (Morbihan)

Jego, Jeanne, 2 Rue Friedland, 56300 Pontivy.
T. 0297252021. - Ant - *047900*

Pontoise (Val-d'Oise)

Taillandier, Jack, 57 Rue Gisors, 95300 Pontoise.
T. 0130381640. - Ant / Furn - *047901*

Pontonx-sur-l'Adour (Landes)

Latour, Jean-Claude, Le Hally, 40465 Pontonx-sur-
l'Adour. T. 0558572177. *047902*

Pontorson (Manche)

Mauxion, 39 Rue Libération, 50170 Pontorson.
T. 0233601277. - Furn - *047903*
Nougues, Henri, 17 Rue Saint-Michel, 50170 Pontorson.
T. 0233601253. - Furn - *047904*

Pontrieux (Côtes-d'Armor)

Collard, 2bis Rue Kérémarch, 22260 Pontrieux.
T. 0296950705. *047905*
Tréméac, Jean-Marie, 2 Rue Galeries, 22260 Pontrieux.
T. 0296951358. *047906*

Pordic (Côtes-d'Armor)

Dentzer, Raymond, Rue Jean-Moulin, 22590 Pordic.
T. 0296790716. *047907*
Le Gallais, Gérard, Imp Lavoisier, 22590 Pordic.
T. 0296793383. *047908*

Portbail (Manche)

Lannaud, T., Village Saint-Siméon, 50580 Portbail.
T. 0233048525. *047909*

Portel-des-Corbières (Aude)

Antiquités Portel, Av Corbières, 11490 Portel-des-Cor-
bières. T. 0468488519. - Furn - *047910*

Portet-sur-Garonne (Haute-Garonne)

Blanc, André, 2 Blvd Europe, 31180 Portet-sur-Garonne.
T. 0561723342. - Mil - *047911*

Porto-Vecchio (Corse)

Grenier d'Adèle, Rte Bastia, Centre Commercial U Centu,
20137 Porto-Vecchio. T. 0495700093. *047912*

Pouancé (Maine-et-Loire)

Expert, Michel, Les Encleuses, 49420 Pouancé.
T. 41924710. *047913*
Expert, Michel, 49 Rue Libération, 49420 Pouancé.
T. 41924122. *047914*
Metzger, Marcel, 84 Rte Chateaubriand, 49420 Pouancé.
T. 41924219, Fax 41924934. *047915*

Pougues-les-Eaux (Nièvre)

Dupard, Yvonne, 70 Av Paris, 58320 Pougues-les-Eaux.
T. 0386685811. *047916*
Jimenez, Christine, 25 Av Paris, 58320 Pougues-les-
Eaux. T. 0386688458. *047917*
Occas 58, RN 7, ZI, 58320 Pougues-les-Eaux.
T. 0386685198, Fax 0386685320. - Ant - *047918*

Pouilly-en-Auxois (Côte-d'Or)

Fougerouge, Av Général-de-Gaulle, 21320 Pouilly-en-
Auxois. T. 0380908611. *047919*

Pouilly-sous-Charlieu (Loire)

Boutique du Sornin, Rte Marcigny, 42720 Pouilly-sous-
Charlieu. T. 0477608216. *047920*
Ducher, François, Rue République, 42720 Pouilly-sous-
Charlieu. T. 0477699580. *047921*

Pouilly-sur-Loire (Nièvre)

Antiquités Saint-Hubert, 87 Rue Waldeck-Rousseau,
58150 Pouilly-sur-Loire. T. 0386390131. *047922*

Poulx (Gard)

Naegel, Christian, 110 Av République, 30320 Poulx.
T. 0466750183. *047923*

Poursac (Charente)

Visseron, Bernadette, Le Bourg, 16700 Poursac.
T. 0545314229. *047924*

Poussay (Vosges)

Occase 88, Rte Mirecourt, 88500 Poussay.
T. 0329374776. *047925*
Rabischung, Lucette, 367 Rue Clos-des-Jards, 88500
Poussay. T. 0329371527. *047926*

Pouxeux (Vosges)

Bataclan, Rue Gare, 88550 Pouxeux.
T. 0329369224. *047927*

Pouzac (Hautes-Pyrénées)

Abadie, Clément, 65 Av La-Mongie, 65200 Pouzac.
T. 0562951243. - Ant - *047928*

Pradelles (Haute-Loire)

Allary, Irène, Pl Foirail, 43420 Pradelles.
T. 0471008463. *047929*

Pré-en-Pail (Mayenne)

Verdière, Gustave, 8bis Rue Aristide-Briand, 53140 Pré-
en-Pail. T. 0243030252. - Ant / Furn - *047930*

Prémery (Nièvre)

Art Ancien, 20 Grand'Rue, 58700 Prémery.
T. 0386681077. *047932*

Presly (Cher)

Jacquemin, Serge, Grande Rue, 18380 Presly.
T. 0248739502. *047933*
Mandra, Rodolphe, 18380 Presly.
T. 0248734094. *047934*

Prey (Vosges)

Cendre, Jean-Luc, 3 Rte Fiménil, 88600 Prey.
T. 0329368537. *047935*

Privas (Ardèche)

Antiquité Brocante, 2bis Av Clément-Faugier, 07000 Pri-
vas. T. 0475658513. - Ant - *047936*
Bribams, Rte Chomérac, 07000 Privas. T. 0475640532.
- Ant - *047937*

Provins (Seine-et-Marne)

Antiquaire, 38 Rue de Changis, 77160 Provins.
T. 64000774. - Furn / Cur - *047938*

Miguaise, Jean-Paul, 12 Rue Friperie, 77160 Provins.
T. 64006255. *047939*
Montchaud, André, 38 Rue Changis, 77160 Provins.
T. 64003991. *047940*

Prunières (Lozère)
Metzger, Jean-Pierre, Tour d'Apcher, 48200 Prunières.
T. 0466312182. *047941*

Pîtres (Eure)
Paviot, Jean-Tony, 4 Rue Féron, 27590 Pîtres.
T. 0232498293. *047942*

Puget-sur-Argens (Var)
Cano, 129 Rue Général-de-Gaulle, 83480 Puget-sur-Ar-
gens. T. 0494815818. *047943*
Géant Occasion, 11 Barestes-Meissugues, 83480 Pu-
get-sur-Argens. T. 0494452905. - Ant / Furn - *047944*
Placier, La Tuilière, RN 7, 83480 Puget-sur-Argens.
T. 0494452592. - Ant - *047945*

Puget-Ville (Var)
Sappey, Huguette, 5 Rte Nationale, 83390 Puget-Ville.
T. 0494483192. *047946*
Sappey, Jacques, 7 Ham Foux, 83390 Puget-Ville.
T. 0494483623. *047947*

Pujols (Lot-et-Garonne)
Dupuy, Daniel, Balassou, 47300 Pujols.
T. 0553709529. *047948*

Pusey (Haute-Saône)
Sainte Foy, Maurice de, 30 Rue Gustave-Courtois,
70000 Pusey. T. 0384764280,
Fax 0384763767. *047949*

Puy-l'Evêque (Lot)
Grenier du Voyageur, Grezels, 46700 Puy-l'Evêque.
T. 0565213879. *047950*

Puycelci (Tarn)
Thuillier, Armand, Le Bourg, 81140 Puycelci.
T. 0563331134. *047951*

Puylaurens (Tarn)
Saunie, Lucien, 11 Rue Cap-de-Castel, 81700 Puylaurens. T. 0563750340. - Furn - *047952*

Puyoô (Pyrénées-Atlantiques)
Antiquité Brocante Puyoô, 117 Rte Nationale, 64270
Puyoô. T. 0559651594. - Ant - *047953*

Puyricard (Bouches-du-Rhône)
Antiquaires de Lignane, RN 7 – Lignane, 13540 Puyri-
card. T. 0442923828. - Ant - *047954*
Turco, Anthony, La Gantèse, 13540 Puyricard.
T. 0442922233, Fax 0442922625. - Furn - *047955*
Varnier, Philippe, 13540 Puyricard. T. 0442578860.
- Paint / Furn / Cur - *047956*

Quers (Haute-Saône)
Sonal, Grande Rue, 70200 Quers.
T. 0384947194. *047957*

Questembert (Morbihan)
Hallier Antiquités, 5 Pl Liberation, 56230 Questembert.
T. 0297266934. - Ant - *047958*

Queyrac (Gironde)
Antiquerie Médoc, Lescapon, 33340 Queyrac.
T. 0556598074. *047959*

Quiberon (Morbihan)
Donatien, Denise, 17 Pl Duchesse-Anne, 56170 Quiber-
on. T. 0297502243. - Ant - *047960*
Le Bayon, Jean-Marie, 12bis Rue Port-Haliguen, 56170
Quiberon. T. 0297304665. - Ant - *047961*
Rettig Antiquités, 42 Rue Point-du-Jour, 56170 Quiber-
on. T. 0297503874. - Ant - *047962*
Rettig, Georges, 14 Rue Phare, 56170 Quiberon.
T. 0297303611. - Ant - *047963*

Quiberville (Seine-Maritime)
Cléon, Alain, Rue Mer, 76860 Quiberville.
T. 0235834622. *047964*

Quillan (Aude)
An Clos, 8 Rue Barbès, 11500 Quillan. T. 0468202616.
- Ant - *047965*
Antiquités Le Cerisiers, 2 Rte Foix, 11500 Quillan.
T. 0468209878. *047966*
Van den Bussche, Dominique, 46 Grand'Rue Vaysse-
Barthélémy, 11500 Quillan. T. 0468202528. *047967*

Quimper (Finistère)
Antiquités des Douves, 19 Rue Douves, 29000 Quimper.
T. 0298951279. - Ant - *047968*
Art de Cornouaille, 12 Pl Saint-Corentin, 29000 Quimper.
T. 0298953924. - Ant - *047969*
Arts et Civilizations, 4 Rue René-Théophile-Laënnec,
29000 Quimper. T. 0298957095. - Ant / Paint - *047970*
Cornet à Dés, 1 Rue Sainte-Thérèse, 29000 Quimper.
T. 0298533751. - Ant / Paint / China - *047971*
Goubet, Michel, 13ter Av de la Liberation, 29000 Quim-
per. T. 0298533504. - Ant - *047972*
Grenier, 60 Rue Près-Sadate, 29000 Quimper.
T. 0298520460. - Ant / Paint / Furn - *047973*
Grenier du Monde, 8 Rue Guéodet, 29000 Quimper.
T. 0298953393. - Ant - *047974*
Guiguen-le-Berre, Annick, 7ter Rue Gentilhommes,
29000 Quimper. T. 0298958967. - Ant / Tex - *047975*
Henry, Ph., 29 Rue Elie-Fréron, 29000 Quimper.
T. 0298954343. - Ant - *047976*
Laurent, Corentin, 31bis Rue Jean-Jaurès, 29000 Quim-
per. T. 0298900903. - Ant / Furn - *047977*
Le Grenier Antiquités, 60 Rue Prés-Sadate, 29000
Quimper. T. 0298520460. - Ant / Paint / Furn - *047978*
Maison de Maud, 5 Rue Laënnec, 29000 Quimper.
T. 0298533889. - Furn - *047979*
Marchadour, Hervé, 23 Rue Penanguer, 29000 Quimper.
T. 0298556378. - Ant - *047980*
Pastorale, 6 Rue Saint-François, 29000 Quimper.
T. 0298958966. - Ant / Paint / Furn - *047981*
Paul, Anne-Marie le, 24 Rue Gentilhommes, 29000
Quimper. T. 0298954722. - Ant - *047982*
Porhiel, René, 18 Rue Elie-Fréron, 29000 Quimper.
T. 0298642660. - Ant - *047983*
Van Hove, 14 Rue Laënnec, 29000 Quimper.
T. 0298958848. - Ant - *047984*

Quinçay (Vienne)
Denis, Betty, Les-Jaudouines, 86190 Quinçay.
T. 0549604278. - Ant - *047985*

Quingey (Doubs)
Monnier-Debroux, Jacqueline, Fbg Sainte-Anne, 25440
Quingey. T. 0381636352. *047986*

Rabastens (Tarn)
Davoy, Stéphane, 33 Rue Cordeliers, 81800 Rabastens.
T. 0563338981. *047987*
Laplane, Aimé, 12 Rue Pont-del-Pa, 81800 Rabastens.
T. 0563406567. *047988*

Ramatuelle (Var)
Develon, Yves, 33 Rue Saint-Esprit, 83350 Ramatuelle.
T. 0494792565. *047989*
Dufour, 45 Rue Sarrazins, 83350 Ramatuelle.
T. 0494792075. - Furn / Orient / Sculp / Arch /
Eth - *047990*
Gilis, 6 Av Pins, Pampelonne, 83350 Ramatuelle.
T. 0494798844. - Paint / Furn / Dec - *047991*
Hervein, Rosemary, Roche des Fées, 83350 Ramatuelle.
T. 0494792503. - Dec / Cur - *047992*
Wagner, Corinne, 13 Av Frédéric-Mistral, Pampelonne,
83350 Ramatuelle. T. 0494798057. - Paint /
Furn - *047993*

Rambervillers (Vosges)
Ferry, Marcel, 10 Pl 30-Septembre, 88700 Rambervillers. T. 0329650832. *047994*

Rambouillet (Yvelines)
Lefèvre, Maurice, 16 Rue Georges-Lenôtre, 78120 Rambouillet. T. 0134856317. *047995*

Rancenay (Doubs)
Moutel, Claude, 25720 Rancenay.
T. 0381523279. *047996*

Randonnai (Orne)
Broc Art Antiquités, 43 Rue Centre, 61190 Randonnai.
T. 0233342406. - Ant / Furn - *047997*

Ranspach (Haut-Rhin)
Vieux Porche, 23 Rue 2-Décembre, 68470 Ranspach.
T. 0389826638. - Furn / China / Cur - *047998*

Raon-aux-Bois (Vosges)
Napo'Broc, 5 Rte Arches, 88220 Raon-aux-Bois.
T. 0329624994. *047999*

Réalmont (Tarn)
Brocante Réalmontaise, 13 Blvd Gambetta, 81120 Réalmont. T. 0563455948. *048000*

Réauville (Drôme)
Kieffer, Jean, RN 541, 26230 Réauville.
T. 0475985053. *048001*

Redon (Ille-et-Vilaine)
A la Vieille Angleterre, 103 Rue Notre-Dame, 35600 Redon. T. 0299721431. *048002*

Regnéville-sur-Mer (Manche)
Amélinerie, Ham Amélinerie, 50590 Regnéville-sur-Mer.
T. 0233454245. *048003*

Régny (Loire)
Meublerie, Rue Roanne, 42630 Régny. T. 0477630342.
- Furn - *048004*

Reignac (Charente)
Forillère, RN 10, 16360 Reignac.
T. 0545782352. *048005*

Reignac-sur-Indre (Indre-et-Loire)
Vandel, Le Château, 37310 Reignac-sur-Indre.
T. 0547941410. *048006*

Reignier (Haute-Savoie)
Pescatore, Jean-Marc, 33 Grande Rue, 74930 Reignier.
T. 0450434824. *048007*

Reims (Marne)
Amarante, 23 Rue Général-Sarrail, 51100 Reims.
T. 0326473147. *048008*
Antiquités Décoration, 6 Rue Capucins, 51100 Reims.
T. 0326400673, Fax 0326977164. *048009*
Artcom Puces de Antiquités, 82 Rue Jacquart, 51100
Reims. T. 0326020406, Fax 0326077340. *048010*
Au Faubourg, 207 Rue Barbâtre, 51100 Reims.
T. 0326827485. *048011*
Aux Meubles Anciens, 45 Blvd Carteret, 51100 Reims.
T. 0326026148. - Furn / Cur - *048012*
Blanckaert, Alain, 51 Rue Neuvillette, 51100 Reims.
T. 0326885252. *048013*
Brasseur, Martine, 4 Rue Tambour, 51100 Reims.
T. 0326404272, Fax 0326476548. *048014*
Caravansérail, 12 Rue Université, 51100 Reims.
T. 0326402446. - Orient - *048015*
Champeaux, 32bis Rue Cernay, 51100 Reims.
T. 0326476217. - Ant / Furn / Cur - *048016*
Churoux, Hervé, 27 Chauss Saint-Martin, 51100 Reims.
T. 0326490557. *048017*
Clef du Passé, 6 Rue Boucheries, 51100 Reims.
T. 0326476420. *048018*
Cocusse, Claudine, 7 Rue Marlot, 51100 Reims.
T. 0326403149. *048019*
Comptoir de l'Antiquité, 47 Cours Jean-Baptiste-Lang-
let, 51100 Reims. T. 0326470417. *048020*
De Keulenaer, Fanny, 23 Rue Colbert, 51100 Reims.
T. 0326474264. *048021*
Gille, Jean-Pierre, 20 Rue Emile-Zola, 51100 Reims.
T. 0326885792, Fax 0326977390. *048022*
Guizzetti, César, 49 Cours Langlet, 51100 Reims.
T. 0326475861. - Ant - *048023*
Leroux, André, 3bis Rue Deville, 51100 Reims.
T. 0326478638. *048024*
Michaud, Henry-François, 2 Rue Carrouge, 51100
Reims. T. 0326490785. *048025*
Mottay, Jean, 56 Rue Buirette, 51100 Reims.
T. 0326477761. *048026*
Mougenot, Michael, 20 Rue François-Dor, 51100 Reims.
T. 0326041889. *048027*

Outters, Christophe, 37 Rue Cérès, 51100 Reims.
T. 0326883377. - Furn / Cur -   *048028*
Passé Joli, 3 Rue Jeanne-d'Arc, 51100 Reims.
T. 0326868761.   *048029*
Perlo, Jean-Louis, 34 Rue Telliers, 51100 Reims.
T. 0326472919.   *048030*
Pierre d'Agate, 11 Cours Jean-Baptiste-Langlet, 51100
Reims. T. 0326474175.   *048031*
Regnier, Jean-Claude, 7 Rue Carrouge, 51100 Reims.
T. 0326881987.   *048032*
Tapis d'Orient Bijoux Anciens, 26 Rue Elus, 51100
Reims. T. 0326883223. - Tex / Jew -   *048033*
Valleise, Paulette, 82 Rue Jacquart, 51100 Reims.
T. 0326020013.   *048034*
Vision d'Asie, 18 Rue Thillois, 51100 Reims.
T. 0326402706.   *048035*
Vivoir, 26 Rue Colbert, 51100 Reims.
T. 0326400735.   *048036*

Relerq-Kerhuon (Finistère)
West Antic, 74 Blvd Léopold-Maissin, 29480 Relerq-Ker-
huon. T. 0298292628. - Ant / Furn -   *048037*

Rémalard (Orne)
Marie, Daniel, 48 Rue Eglise, 61110 Rémalard.
T. 0233737741. - Ant -   *048038*
Théliot, Pierre, 8 Rue Marcel-Louvel, 61110 Rémalard.
T. 0233738320. - Ant -   *048039*

Remiremont (Vosges)
Battou, 20 Rue Général-Leclerc, 88200 Remiremont.
T. 0329231300.   *048040*
Lanterne, 22 Rue La Xavée, 88200 Remiremont.
T. 0329622436.   *048041*

Renescure (Nord)
Musardière, 70 Saint-Omer, 59173 Renescure.
T. 0328498229. - Ant -   *048042*

Rennes (Ille-et-Vilaine)
Air du Temps, 30 Rue Saint-Melaine, 35000 Rennes.
T. 0299635464.   *048043*
Anthéor, 13 Rue Saint-Michel, 35000 Rennes.
T. 0299790997.   *048044*
Antiquités B.G., 5 Rue Edith-Cavell, 35000 Rennes.
T. 0299795066.   *048045*
Arcades, 23 Rue Hypolite-Vatar, 35000 Rennes.
T. 0299389779. - Paint / Furn -   *048046*
Au Temps Jadis, 13 Rue Saint-Michel, 35000 Rennes.
T. 0299795163.   *048047*
Ayesse, Odette, 13 Rue Saint-Michel, 35000 Rennes.
T. 0299790257.   *048048*
Barbay, François, 4 Rue Clisson, 35000 Rennes.
T. 0299782050.   *048049*
Barreau, 3 Rue Victor-Hugo, 35000 Rennes.
T. 0299792888. - Furn / Cur -   *048050*
Battais, Francis, 22 Quai Duguay-Trouin, 35000 Rennes.
T. 0299654597.   *048051*
Beaufils, Serge, 64 Rue Lorient, 35000 Rennes.
T. 0299655931. - Furn / Cur -   *048052*
Bijoux Anciens, 16 Rue Victor-Hugo, 35000 Rennes.
T. 0299639161, Fax 0299631598. - Jew -   *048053*
Bobet, 44 Blvd Jacques-Cartier, 35000 Rennes.
T. 0299654436. - Furn -   *048054*
Chaussavoine, Jules, 27 Blvd de la Liberté, 35000 Ren-
nes. T. 0299795841. - Ant -   *048055*
Chevallier-Clossais, Marie-Thérèse, 11 Rue Victor Hugo,
35000 Rennes. T. 0299388692.   *048056*
Couffon de Trévros, Charles, 15 Rue Hoche, 35000 Ren-
nes. T. 0299387595, Fax 0299314789.   *048057*
Desmeulles, Jacky, 176 Rue Saint-Malo, 35000 Rennes.
T. 0299339064.   *048058*
Divet, 4 Rue Saint-Guillaume, 35000 Rennes.
T. 0299796132.   *048059*
Divet, 45 Rue Motte-Brulon, 35700 Rennes.
T. 0299384429.   *048060*
Girandole, 1 Rue Victor-Hugo, 35000 Rennes.
T. 0299782487.   *048061*
Grenier d'Anaïs, 1 Rue Salomon-de-Brosse, 35000 Ren-
nes. T. 0299795695.   *048062*
Helbert, 15 Rue Victor-Hugo, 35000 Rennes.
T. 0299381133.   *048063*
Jacobert, Philippe, 24 Rue Hoche, 35000 Rennes.
T. 0299367942.   *048064*

Julienne, Patrick, 13 Rue Saint-Michel, 35000 Rennes.
T. 0299783551.   *048065*
Lacour Frères, 354 Rue Nantes, 35200 Rennes.
T. 0299516298.   *048066*
Lices Antiquités, 1 Pl Bas-des-Lices, 35000 Rennes.
T. 0299676194.   *048067*
M.G Communications, 17 Rue Victor-Hugo, 35000 Ren-
nes. T. 0299383974.   *048068*
Palanquin, 19 Rue Chapitre, 35000 Rennes.
T. 0299315710.   *048069*
Petite Boutique d'Antiquités, 10 Rue Derval, 35000 Ren-
nes. T. 0299872780.   *048070*
Priester, Pierre de, 13 Rue Victor-Hugo, 35000 Rennes.
T. 0299633388.   *048071*
Ravier, Daniel, 13 Rue Saint-Michel, 35000 Rennes.
T. 0299782283.   *048072*
Reucheron, Jean-Claude, 3 Rue Guillaume-Lejean,
35000 Rennes. T. 0299367407.   *048073*
Saint-Hélier, 58 Rue Saint-Hélier, 35000 Rennes.
T. 0299302645.   *048074*
Salle des Ventes des Particuliers, 31 Blvd Villebois-Ma-
reuil, 35000 Rennes. T. 0299365151,
Fax 0299631051.   *048075*
Smuggler's, 21 Rue Chapitre, 35000 Rennes.
T. 0299301718.   *048076*
Thiboumery, Jean-Yves, 2 Rue Du-Guesclin, 35000 Ren-
nes. T. 0299782062.   *048077*
Tire la Chevillette, 7 Rue Saint-Georges, 35000 Rennes.
T. 0299388909.   *048078*
Troc-Meubles, 7 Rue Santé, 35000 Rennes.
T. 0299306110. - Furn -   *048079*
Trocante, 37 Blvd Solférino, 35200 Rennes.
T. 0299301512.   *048080*
Trocante, 13 Rue Louis-Guilloux, 35000 Rennes.
T. 0299545064.   *048081*
Trouillard, Marie-Dominique, 17 Rue Monnaie, 35000
Rennes. T. 0299790368.   *048082*

Replonges (Ain)
Au Grenier de Serge, Madeleine-Nord-Ouest, 01750 Re-
plonges. T. 0385311063. - Ant -   *048083*

Restigné (Indre-et-Loire)
Girard, Jacki, 12 Rue Garenne, 37140 Restigné.
T. 0547973573.   *048084*
Puits Chatel, 62 Rue Lossay, 37140 Restigné.
T. 0547973517.   *048085*

Reterre (Creuse)
Garaud, Georges, La CHirade, 23110 Reterre.
T. 0555823620. - Ant -   *048086*

Rethel (Ardennes)
Dufresne, Hubert, 9 Imp Bordeaux, 08480 Rethel.
T. 0324384628. - Ant -   *048087*

Revel (Haute-Garonne)
Gros, Gisèle, Saint-Ferréol, 31250 Revel.
T. 0561835835.   *048088*
Mouton, Gérard, 24 Av Sorèze, 31250 Revel.
T. 0561276514.   *048089*
Souvenirs d'Autrefois, RN 629, 31250 Revel.
T. 0561276162.   *048090*

Revigny (Jura)
Bachellier, Monique, Rue Centre, 39570 Revigny.
T. 0384243814, Fax 0384248732.   *048091*

Ribeauvillé (Haut-Rhin)
Bronner, Philippe, 2 Pl Ancien-Hôpital, 68150 Ribeau-
villé. T. 0389736159.   *048092*

Richelieu (Indre-et-Loire)
Daugé, Claude, 11 Pl Louis-XIII, 37120 Richelieu.
T. 0547581813.   *048093*

Riec-sur-Belon (Finistère)
Coromandel, 7 Rue Alain-Berthou, 29340 Riec-sur-Be-
lon. T. 0298064397, Fax 0298065479. - Ant -   *048094*
Garel, Pierre, 23 Rue Gentilhommes, 29340 Riec-sur-
Belon. T. 0298064921, Fax 0298065346. - Ant /
Orient -   *048095*

Rignac (Lot)
Jouvent, Michel, Bourg, 46500 Rignac.
T. 0565336640.   *048096*

Rilhac-Xaintrie (Corrèze)
Naudet, Jean, Bourg, 19220 Rilhac-Xaintrie.
T. 0555282516.   *048097*

Riom (Puy-de-Dôme)
Cave'Amarthe, 7 Rue Croisier, 63200 Riom.
T. 0473386633. - Furn / Mul -   *048098*
Coté de chez Nane, 137 Blvd Desaix, 63200 Riom.
T. 0473384121. - Ant -   *048099*
Coto, Rosy, 9 Rue Hôtel-de-Ville, 63200 Riom.
T. 0473380881. - Ant -   *048100*
Galerie de l'Horloge, 7 Rue Horloge, 63200 Riom.
T. 0473631783. - Furn / Mul -   *048101*

Riorges (Loire)
Chevreton, Jean, 37 Av Charles-de-Gaulle, 42153 Rior-
ges. T. 0477682253.   *048102*
Debatisse, Jean-Pierre, 59 Imp Chamussy, 42153 Rior-
ges. T. 0477700021.   *048103*

Ris-Orangis (Essonne)
Bric à Brac d'Armelle, 97 Rue Albert-Rémy, 91130 Ris-
Orangis. T. 0169065352.   *048104*
Rousselle, Henrianne, 91 Pl Gare, 91130 Ris-Orangis.
T. 0169435057.   *048105*

Riscle (Gers)
Costa Brocante, Av Adour, 32400 Riscle.
T. 0562698844.   *048106*

Rivarennes (Indre)
Langlet, Geneviève, 7 Pl Valéry-Gilbert-Tournois, 36800
Rivarennes. T. 0254470188.   *048107*

Rive-de-Gier (Loire)
Milliat, Robert, 6 Cours Gambetta, 42800 Rive-de-Gier.
T. 0477755434.   *048108*

Rives (Lot-et-Garonne)
Veysset, Robert, Lascourèges, 47210 Rives.
T. 0553366503. - Furn -   *048109*

Rivière (Pas-de-Calais)
Nicoulaud, 9 Rue Cavée, 62173 Rivière. T. 0321554969.
- Paint / Furn / Toys -   *048110*

Rixheim (Haut-Rhin)
Munch, C., 19 A Rue Wilson, 68170 Rixheim.
T. 0389650161. - Furn -   *048111*

Roanne (Loire)
Bernicat, G., 9 Quai Commandant-Fourcault, 42300
Roanne. T. 0477724112.   *048112*
Bourse du Mobilier, 17 Rue Pierre-Semard, 42300
Roanne. T. 0477711286.   *048113*
CBO Antiquités, 31 Rue Brison, 42300 Roanne.
T. 0477728922.   *048114*
Chatelet Chaume, Didier, 51 Rue Claude-Bochard,
42300 Roanne. T. 0477687506. - Furn / Cur -   *048115*
Collectionneur, 1 Pl Marché, 42300 Roanne.
T. 0477703113.   *048116*
Country House Antique, 10 Pl Marché-de-Lattre-de-Tas-
signy, 42300 Roanne. T. 0477230215.   *048117*
Espace Brocs'Antiks, 38 Rue Nicolas-Cugnot, 42300
Roanne. T. 0477722384.   *048118*
Galerie du Festival, 52 Rue Minimes, 42300 Roanne.
T. 0477700231. - Paint -   *048119*
Kowal, 159 Rue Villemontais, 42300 Roanne.
T. 0477711683.   *048120*
Sartori, Gérard, 52 Rue Minimes, 42300 Roanne.
T. 0477700231.   *048121*

Roche-lez-Beaupré (Doubs)
Bellucci, Marius, 11 Route Nationale, 25220 Roche-lez-
Beaupré. T. 0381570574. - Paint / Furn / Instr -   *048122*

Rochecorbon (Indre-et-Loire)
Trouvailles, 49 Quai Loire, 37210 Rochecorbon.
T. 0547525799.   *048123*

Rochefort (Charente-Maritime)
Aux Meubles Anciens, 22 Av 11-Novembre-1918, 17300
Rochefort. T. 0546995445. - Furn -   *048124*

Ducourtioux, Pierre, 35 Rue Docteur-Paul-Peltier, 17300 Rochefort. T. 0546994267. 048125

Duffour, Pierre, 15 Rue Grimaux, 17300 Rochefort. T. 0546874377. - Furn - 048126

Froger, 41 Rue Docteur-Paul-Peltier, 17300 Rochefort. T. 0546991342. 048127

La Fayette Antiquités, 46 Av Lafayette, 17300 Rochefort. T. 0546873666. 048128

Rochefort-du-Gard (Gard)
Charrin, Christophe, RN 100, La Begude, 30650 Rochefort-du-Gard. T. 0490317774. 048129

Rochefort-en-Terre (Morbihan)
Brion, Jean-Bernard, Pl Puits, 56220 Rochefort-en-Terre. T. 0297433147. - Ant / Paint / Furn / Mil - 048130

Danilo, Denis, Rue Château, 56220 Rochefort-en-Terre. T. 0297433271. - Ant - 048131

Diquero, Yves, Rte Malansac, 56220 Rochefort-en-Terre. T. 0297433273. - Ant / Furn - 048132

Muzerelle, Claude, Pl Puits, 56220 Rochefort-en-Terre. T. 0297433607. - Ant - 048133

Rochegude (Drôme)
Bonillo, Anselme, Village, 26790 Rochegude. T. 0475048572. 048134

Rochemaure (Ardèche)
Fabre, Régis, Mte Château, 07400 Rochemaure. T. 0475490610. - Ant - 048135

Rocheservière (Vendée)
Caillet, Stéphane, 20 Rue Nantes, 85620 Rocheservière. T. 0251949720, Fax 0251949454. 048136

Rocroi (Ardennes)
Bon Vieux Temps, 11 Rue Bourgogne, 08230 Rocroi. T. 0324532488. - Ant - 048137

Rodez (Aveyron)
Lacombe, Jean-Luc, Rue Marc-Robert, 12000 Rodez. T. 0565427754. 048138

Leyrolles, Jean-Marie, 91 Av Paris, 12000 Rodez. T. 0565420605, Fax 0565671297. 048139

Mouysset, Francine & Pierre, 2 Rue Moutiers, 12000 Rodez. T. 0565420086. 048140

Mouysset, Pierre, 9 Rue Grandet, 12000 Rodez. T. 0565420495. 048141

Trésor de Grand-Mère, 37 Rue Liberté, 12000 Rodez. T. 0565674277. - Furn / Jew / Glass / Cur - 048142

Verdeille, Claude, 10 Av Victor-Hugo, 12000 Rodez. T. 0565680975. 048143

Rogues (Gard)
J-B Antiques, Le Cros, 30120 Rogues. T. 0467815303. 048144

Roinville-sur-Auneau (Eure-et-Loir)
Abbaye, 9 Rue Eglise, 28700 Roinville-sur-Auneau. T. 0237318844. - Paint / Furn / China / Sculp / Tex / Silv / Mil / Cur / Toys - 048145

Romans-sur-Isère (Drôme)
Donabedian, Michel, Blvd Gignier, Le Veymont, 26100 Romans-sur-Isère. T. 0475701971. 048146

Eymard, Louis, 10 Quai Dauphin, 26100 Romans-sur-Isère. T. 0475020124. 048147

Pautrot, Yves, 2 Pl Herbes, 26100 Romans-sur-Isère. T. 0475720799. 048148

Rissoan, Alain, 36 Rue Clérieux, 26100 Romans-sur-Isère. T. 0475022258. 048149

Rozand, Christophe, Rue Chossigny, La Presle, 26100 Romans-sur-Isère. T. 0475703754. 048150

Sudre, Gérard, Rue Pierre-Semard, Athéna, 26100 Romans-sur-Isère. T. 0475022534. 048151

Vetter, Michel, 15 Rue Etienne-Dolet, 26100 Romans-sur-Isère. T. 0475701835. 048152

Romenay (Saône-et-Loire)
Ballot, Michel, 71470 Romenay. T. 0385403186. - Ant - 048153

Romilly-sur-Seine (Aube)
Gras, Eric, 64 Rue Marceau, 10100 Romilly-sur-Seine. T. 0325244461. - Ant - 048154

Guillemin, Alain, 37 Rue Milford-Haven, 10100 Romilly-sur-Seine. T. 0325248217. - Ant / Furn / China / Glass - 048155

Romorantin-Lanthenay (Loir-et-Cher)
Camus-Hennebelle, Maurice, 18 Rue Jouannettes, 41200 Romorantin-Lanthenay. T. 0254764855. 048156

Ronchamp (Haute-Saône)
Aux Vieux Meubles, 49 Av République, 70250 Ronchamp. T. 0384635689. - Furn - 048157

Roncq (Nord)
Liebaert, Thierry, 7 cité Mannessier, 59223 Roncq. T. 0320377050. - Ant - 048158

Roppe (Territoire-de-Belfort)
Au Relais, 50 Rte Nationale, 90380 Roppe. T. 0384298082. 048159

Struck, Claude, 52 Rte Nationale, 90380 Roppe. T. 0384298189. 048160

Roquevaire (Bouches-du-Rhône)
Levine-Abile, Jean-Marc, 3 RN 396, 13360 Roquevaire. T. 0442329289. 048161

Lys et la Rose, Quart Valcros, 13360 Roquevaire. T. 0442040211. 048162

Roscoff (Finistère)
Hamon, Claude, 19 Pl Lacaze-Duthiers, 29211 Roscoff. T. 0298697613. - Ant - 048163

Palanquin, 25 Pl Lavaze-Duthiers, 29124 Roscoff. T. 0298697135, Fax 0298697031. - Ant - 048164

Rosières (Haute-Loire)
Prat, Daniel, Grande Rue, 43800 Rosières. T. 0471574519. 048165

Rosières-aux-Salines (Meurthe-et-Moselle)
Aubry, Geneviève, 19 Rue Léon-Bocheron, 54110 Rosières-aux-Salines. T. 0383484413. 048166

Meyer, François, 25 Rue Gambetta, 54110 Rosières-aux-Salines. T. 0383481172. 048167

Roubaix (Nord)
Antoinettes, 22 Rue Marengo, 59100 Roubaix. T. 0320702591. - Ant - 048168

Legrand, Stéphane, 80 Av Alsace, 59100 Roubaix. T. 0320270645. - Ant - 048169

Lenormant, Jacky, 315 Av Nations-Unies, 59100 Roubaix. T. 0320738837. - Ant - 048170

Philippe, 120 Av Jean-Baptiste-Lebas, 59100 Roubaix. T. 0320702402. - Ant - 048171

Thuret, Christian, 24 Rue Bois, 59100 Roubaix. T. 0320708239. - Ant - 048172

Tuileries, 100 Rue Lannoy, 59100 Roubaix. T. 0320738863. - Ant / Furn - 048173

Waxin, Marie-Thérèse, 118 Blvd de-Gaulle, 59100 Roubaix. T. 0320249491. - Ant - 048174

Rouen (Seine-Maritime)
ACR Antiquités, 20 Rue Damiette, 76000 Rouen. Fax 35717510. 048175

Adam T'Elle, 47 Rue Damiette, 76000 Rouen. T. 0235077175. 048176

Antic Saint-Maclou, 178 Rue Martainville, 76000 Rouen. T. 0235895261. - Paint / Jew / Silv - 048177

Antiquité du Vieux Marché, 3 Rue Ancienne-Prison, 76000 Rouen. T. 0235076100. 048178

Antiquités Brocante Le Damiette, 46 Rue Damiette, 76000 Rouen. T. 0235705301. 048179

Antiquités du Donjon, 12 Rue Dupont-Delporte, 76000 Rouen. T. 0235700254. 048180

Antiquités – Numismatique, 21 Rue Damiette, 76000 Rouen. T. 0235884745. - Num - 048181

Arrêt sur Image, 35 Rue Bec, 76000 Rouen. T. 0235076322, Fax 0235890883. 048182

Bayeul, Chantal, 4 Rue Saint-Romain, 76000 Rouen. T. 0235981333. 048183

Bel Gazou, 9 Rue Juifs, 76000 Rouen. T. 0235703919. - Dec / Silv - 048184

Belliard, F., 48 Rue Saint-Romain, 76000 Rouen. T. 0235984629. 048185

Bertran, Etienne, 110 Rue Molière, 76000 Rouen. T. 0235707996. - Paint / Cur - 048186

Bertran, Michel, 108 Rue Molière, 76000 Rouen. T. 0235982406. - Ant / Paint / Furn - 048187

Biville, Laurent, 101 Rue Malpalu, 76000 Rouen. T. 0235888401. 048188

Bloc Acier, 9 Rue Damiette, 76000 Rouen. Fax 35889217. 048189

Boisnard, Jean Luc, 54 Rue République, 76000 Rouen. T. 0235706008, Fax 0235153453. 048190

Brument, Patrick, 14 Rue Ecuyère, 76000 Rouen. T. 0235703739. 048191

Burgaud, Fabrice, 12 Rue Dupont-Delporte, 76000 Rouen. T. 0235706461. 048192

Burgaud, Patrick, 1 All Mozart, 76000 Rouen. T. 0235638144. 048193

Chasset, Patrick, 12 Rue Croix-de-Fer, 76000 Rouen. T. 0235705997. 048194

Cléon, Michel, 33 Rue République, 76000 Rouen. T. 0235886316. 048195

Cléon, Michel, 20 Rue Saint-Romain, 76000 Rouen. T. 0235713506. 048196

Duchemin, Guy, 28 et 50 Rue Damiette, 76000 Rouen. T. 0235719500, Fax 0235703749. - Paint / Furn - 048197

Galerie de l'Archevêché, 64 Rue Saint-Romain, 76000 Rouen. T. 0235893506. 048198

Hart, Catherine, 65 Rue Ganterie, 76000 Rouen. T. 0235887421. - Jew - 048199

Hervieux-Motard, 60 Rue Saint-Romain, 76000 Rouen. T. 0235715966. - Jew / Silv - 048200

Heure Bleue, 3 Rue Percière, 76000 Rouen. T. 0235718435. 048201

Indicible, 37 Rue Saint-Nicolas, 76000 Rouen. T. 0235077012, Fax 0235070723. 048202

Interior's, 59 Rue République, 76000 Rouen. T. 0235896923. 048203

Labiche, Nicole, 10 Rue Damiette, 76000 Rouen. T. 0235899575. 048204

Lalin, Thérèse, 23 Rue Damiette, 76000 Rouen. T. 0235704277. 048205

Langlois, Michel, 17 Rue Harcourt, 76000 Rouen. T. 0235980493. 048206

Loup de Sable, 124 Rue Beauvoisine, 76000 Rouen. T. 0235886640. 048207

Maillon Manquant, 11 Rue Chaine, 76000 Rouen. T. 0235897798. - Toys - 048208

Maine, Leone, 112 Rue Malpalu, 76000 Rouen. T. 0235717575. 048209

Maison de la Poupée, 20 Rue Percière, 76000 Rouen. T. 0235896915. 048210

Manoir de Folie Vallée, 22 Rue Damiette, 76000 Rouen. T. 0235890550. - Ant / Paint / Furn - 048211

Maréchal, Jacques, 239 Rue Eau de Robec, 76000 Rouen. T. 0235880502. 048212

Marie-Hélène, 45 Rue Damiette, 76000 Rouen. T. 0235151415. 048213

Masson, Emmanuelle, 18 Rue Jean-Lecanuet, 76000 Rouen. T. 0235713000, Fax 0235888143. 048214

Mesnil Gaillard, Pierre du, 54 Rue Bons-Enfants, 76000 Rouen. T. 0235710597. 048215

Métais, Henri, 2 Pl Barthélemy, 76000 Rouen. T. 0235709433, Fax 0235711148. - Ant / Paint / Furn / China / Cur - 048216

Or et Bleu, 249 Rue Eau-de-Ropec, 76000 Rouen. T. 0235715052. - Paint / Fra / Glass - 048217

Oubliette, 96 Rue République, 76000 Rouen. T. 0235982025. 048218

Picard, Patrice, 56 Rue Saint-Romain, 76000 Rouen. T. 0235898275. 048219

Pillet, Jean-François, 3 Pl Barthélémy, 76000 Rouen. T. 0235074416. 048220

Pivain, Claude, 54 Rue Damiette, 76000 Rouen. T. 0235702132. 048221

Plachot, Christian, 17 Rue Damiette, 76000 Rouen. T. 0235981525. 048222

Planage, Yves, 41 Rue Damiette, 76000 Rouen. T. 0235070096. 048223

Poulingue & Fils, 4 Pl Barthélémy, 76000 Rouen. T. 0235980956. 048224

Renault, Daniel, 1 Pl Lieutenant-Aubert, 76000 Rouen. T. 0235896171. - Furn - 048225

Rivat, Bertrand, 216 Rue Beauvoisine, 76000 Rouen.
T. 0235159052. *048226*
Robin, Yannick, 54 Rue Damiette, 76000 Rouen.
T. 0235888011. *048227*
Roullet, Dominique, 45 Rue Ganterie, 76000 Rouen.
T. 0235718016. - Jew - *048228*
Scarlett, 4 Rue Ecole, 76000 Rouen. T. 0235071727.
- Jew - *048229*
Schmidt, Gérald, 27 Rue Damiette, 76000 Rouen.
T. 0235076385. *048230*
Tessier, Claude, 103 Rue Malpalu, 76000 Rouen.
T. 0235892691. *048231*
Tételin, Max, 10-14 Rue Saint-Romain, 76000 Rouen.
T. 0235714333. *048232*
Tinti, Olivier, 106 Rue Malpalu, 76000 Rouen.
T. 0235154250. *048233*
Tourraton, Patrick, 13 Rue Damiette, 76000 Rouen.
T. 0235984742. *048234*
Troc en Stock, 44bis Rue Victor-Hugo, 76000 Rouen.
T. 0235702663. *048235*
Vandenhaute, 57 Rue Jeanne-d'Arc, 76000 Rouen.
T. 0235706688. *048236*
Vent d'Est, 68 Rue Fontenelle, 76000 Rouen.
T. 0235888635. *048237*

Royan (Charente-Maritime)
Antiquaire du Port, 15 Rue Jules-Verne, 17200 Royan.
T. 0546385386. - Furn / Cur - *048238*
Antiquités L'Herbaudière, 35 Rue Saules, 17200 Royan.
T. 0546382720. *048239*
Au Bon Vieux Temps, 5 Rue Jules-Verne, 17200 Royan.
T. 0546385939. *048240*
Beaudet, 10 Rue Aunis, 17200 Royan. T. 0546381076.
- Paint / Sculp / Sculp / Dec / Glass / Cur - *048241*
Capet, Patrick, 34 Av Aliénor-d'Aquitaine, 17200 Royan.
T. 0546053014. *048242*
Favre, Christian, 8 Rue Edouard-Branly, 17200 Royan.
T. 0546054377. *048243*
Libre Ebreuil, 48bis Rue Pierre-Dugua, 17200 Royan.
T. 0546387679. - Furn / Tex - *048244*
London Shop, 2 Rue Foncillon, 17200 Royan.
T. 0546239758. - Furn - *048245*
Ontivéros, Jean, 143 Av Rochefort, 17200 Royan.
T. 0546386968. - Ant / Paint / Furn / Sculp /
Cur - *048246*

Roye (Somme)
Art N'Ac Antiquités, 2 Rue du Beffroi, 80700 Roye.
T. 0322870566. - Ant / Cur - *048247*

Ruca (Côtes-d'Armor)
Humbert, Jean-Claude, La Ville Poulet, 22550 Ruca.
T. 0296411947. *048248*

Rueil-Malmaison (Hauts-de-Seine)
Axor, 17 Rue Libération, 92500 Rueil-Malmaison.
T. 0147517085. *048249*
Bosetti, Henri, 33 Rue Lamartine, 92500 Rueil-Malmai-
son. T. 0147080223. *048250*
Cour des Miracles, 20 Rue Docteur-Zamenhof, 92500
Rueil-Malmaison. T. 0147140298. *048251*
Feuille d'Acanthe, 20 Rue Maréchal-Joffre, 92500
Rueil-Malmaison. T. 0147323842. - Ant - *048252*
Galerie Notre-Dame, 7 Rue Gué, 92500 Rueil-Malmai-
son. T. 0147085167, Fax 0147494844. *048253*
Girousse, Claire, 6 Rue Graviers, 92500 Rueil-Malmai-
son. T. 0147518038. *048254*
Pascaline, 2 Rue Réunion, 92500 Rueil-Malmaison.
T. 0147513944. *048255*
Point Rouge, 7 Blvd Maréchal-Joffre, 92500 Rueil-Mal-
maison. T. 0147086506. *048256*
Richelieu, 39 Rue Haute, 92500 Rueil-Malmaison.
T. 0147086756. *048257*

Ruffec (Charente)
Vieille Demeure, 1 Rue Général-Leclerc, 16700 Ruffec.
T. 0545313261. *048258*

Rully (Saône-et-Loire)
Espace Antique, 23 Rue Loppe, 71150 Rully.
T. 0385870949. - Ant - *048259*

Rumilly (Haute-Savoie)
Buttin, Jean-Charles, 11 Rue Terreaux, 74150 Rumilly.
T. 0450010779. *048260*

Rupt-sur-Moselle (Vosges)
Boegly, Serge, 32 Rte Maxonchamp, 88360 Rupt-sur-
Moselle. T. 0329243054. *048261*

Ry (Seine-Maritime)
Aubry, Renaud, Le Bel Event, 76116 Ry.
T. 0235236481. *048262*
Brocante des 3 Vallées, Grande Rue, 76116 Ry.
T. 0235236644. *048263*
Grenier Bovary, Grande Rue, 76116 Ry.
T. 0235232192. *048264*
Lambert, Jean, Grande Rue, 76116 Ry.
T. 0235236644. *048265*

Sablé-sur-Sarthe (Sarthe)
Brière, Michel, 35 Rue Gambetta, 72300 Sablé-sur-Sar-
the. T. 0243953493. - Ant - *048266*
Ronfort-Goeneutte-Lefèvre, Marie-José, 14 Rue Saint-
Nicolas, 72300 Sablé-sur-Sarthe. T. 0243950596.
- Ant - *048267*

Sablonnières (Seine-et-Marne)
Château Morin Antiquités, 9 Rue Montcel, 77510 Sa-
blonnières. T. 64049049. *048268*
Markoff, Youri, 9 Rue Montcel, 77510 Sablonnières.
T. 64049049. *048269*

Saillans (Drôme)
Antiquités du Prieuré, 23 Rue Barnave, 26340 Saillans.
T. 0475215216. *048270*

Saille (Loire-Atlantique)
Aladin, Salorge de Leniphen, 44350 Saille.
T. 40623020. *048271*

Sains-du-Nord (Nord)
Compagnon, Amélia, Rue Sadie-Carnot, 59177 Sains-du-
Nord. T. 0327591823. - Ant - *048272*

Saint-Adrien (Seine-Maritime)
Antiquités Saint-Adrien, 60 Rte de Paris, 76 Saint-Ad-
rien. T. 0235020040, Fax 0235231823. *048273*
Brosolo, Gianpaolo, 11 Rte de Paris, 76 Saint-Adrien.
T. 0235020040. *048274*
Plachot, Christian, 11 Rte de Paris, 76 Saint-Adrien.
T. 0235020040. *048275*

Saint-Aignan (Loir-et-Cher)
Antiquités des Bords du Cher, 13 Quai Jean-Jacques
Delorme, 41110 Saint-Aignan. T. 0254750070.
- Ant - *048276*

Saint-Amand-en-Puisaye (Nièvre)
Féré, Martine, Rte Cosne, 58310 Saint-Amand-en-Puisaye. T. 0386396516. *048277*

Saint-Amand-les-Eaux (Nord)
Au Temps Passée, Rue Marillon, 59230 Saint-Amand-
les-Eaux. T. 0327484443. - Ant - *048278*
Naphtaline, 9 Rue Louise-de-Bettignies, 59230 Saint-
Amand-les-Eaux. T. 0327278313. - Ant - *048279*

Saint-Amand-Montrond (Cher)
Monter, Robert, 19 Rue Nationale, 18200 Saint-Amand-
Montrond. T. 0248966527. *048280*
Pelegrin, 16 Rue Porte-Mutin, 18200 Saint-Amand-Mon-
trond. T. 0248966287. - Furn / Cur - *048281*

Saint-Amans-Soult (Tarn)
Grenier du Maréchal, 69 Rte Nationale, 81240 Saint-
Amans-Soult. T. 0563981486. *048282*

Saint-Amans-Valtoret (Tarn)
Duffourd, Jean-Claude, Roques, 81240 Saint-Amans-
Valtoret. T. 0563983131. *048283*

Saint-André-de-l'Epine (Manche)
Serrant, Pierre, 16 Rue Le-Jardin-Capel, 50680 Saint-
André-de-l'Epine. T. 0233550063. *048284*

Saint-André-de-l'Eure (Eure)
Brocante Normande, 6 Rue Damville, 27220 Saint-An-
dré-de-l'Eure. T. 0232372081. *048285*
Chin'Eure, Rte Damville, 27220 Saint-André-de-l'Eure.
T. 0232374373. *048286*

Saint-André-lez-Lille (Nord)
Acanthe Antiquités Service, 30 Rue Brune, 59350 Saint-
André-lez-Lille. T. 0320517979. - Ant - *048287*

Saint-Angel (Corrèze)
Troq'Tout, Rte Ussel, 19200 Saint-Angel.
T. 0555725110. *048288*

Saint-Antonin-Noble-Val (Tarn-et-Garonne)
Maury, Philippe, Pl Mairie, 82140 Saint-Antonin-Noble-
Val. T. 0563682473. - Furn - *048289*

Saint-Aquilin (Dordogne)
Anne, Jean-François, Château de Bellet, 24110 Saint-
Aquilin. T. 0553049267, Fax 0553549911. - Paint /
Furn - *048290*

Saint-Aquilin-de-Pacy (Eure)
Lamare, Pierre, 32 Rue Charles-Ledoux, 27120 Saint-
Aquilin-de-Pacy. T. 0232360266, Fax 0232261136.
- Furn / Dec - *048291*

Saint-Aubin-Château-Neuf (Yonne)
Carré, Fernand, Rue Chaude, 89110 Saint-Aubin-Châ-
teau-Neuf. T. 0386736413. *048292*

Saint-Aubin-des-Ormeaux (Vendée)
Antiquités du Bocage Vendéen, 4 Rue Gaberneau,
85130 Saint-Aubin-des-Ormeaux.
T. 0251656584. *048293*

Saint-Aubin-Epinay (Seine-Maritime)
Noël, Thierry, 1722 Rte Lyons, 76160 Saint-Aubin-Epi-
nay. T. 0235089873. *048294*

Saint-Aubin-sur-Mer (Calvados)
Baccot, Martine, 13 Av Georges-Pépineaux, 14750
Saint-Aubin-sur-Mer. T. 0231971105. - Paint / Furn /
Cur - *048295*

Saint-Aubin-sur-Scie (Seine-Maritime)
Antiquités-Brocante des Vertus, Les Vertus, 35 Rue Neu-
ve, 76550 Saint-Aubin-sur-Scie.
T. 0235844753. *048296*

Saint-Avertin (Indre-et-Loire)
Haton, Michel, 34 Rue Edouard-Branly, 37550 Saint-
Avertin. T. 0547480110. *048297*

Saint-Benoît-des-Ondes (Ille-et-Vilaine)
Goarnisson-Busson, Emile, La Seigneurie, 35114 Saint-
Benoît-des-Ondes. T. 0299586296. *048298*

Saint-Berthevin (Mayenne)
Aubin, Paul, Rue Croix-des-landes, 53940 Saint-Berthe-
vin. T. 0243691301. - Ant - *048299*
Hermenier Antiquités, 8 Blvd Raphaël-Toutain, 53940
Saint-Berthevin. T. 0243690555. - Furn - *048300*

Saint-Bonnet (Hautes-Alpes)
Zecconi, Auguste, Lot Chanalettes, 05500 Saint-Bonnet.
T. 0492505280. *048301*

Saint-Bonnet-le-Château (Loire)
Galerie Verchère, 2 Pl Commandant-Marey, 42380
Saint-Bonnet-le-Château. T. 0477500044. *048302*

Saint-Brandan (Côtes-d'Armor)
Antiquités du Château de Grénieux, Château de Gré-
nieux, 22800 Saint-Brandan. T. 0296740253,
Fax 0296796099. *048303*
Bannier, Yves, Carboureux, 22800 Saint-Brandan.
T. 0296749148. - Furn - *048304*

Saint-Briac-sur-Mer (Ille-et-Vilaine)
Antiquités Chéron, 1 Blvd du Tertre-Gondan, 35800
Saint-Briac-sur-Mer. T. 0299883254. - Furn /
Cur - *048305*
Galerie Le Vieux Moulin, 2 Rue Vieux-Moulin, 35800
Saint-Briac-sur-Mer. T. 0299880494. - Paint - *048306*

Saint-Brieuc (Côtes-d'Armor)
Albatros de Pitcairn, 24 Rue Jules-Ferry, 22000 Saint-
Brieuc. T. 0296940414. *048307*
André, C., 3 Rue Saint-Gouéno, 22000 Saint-Brieuc.
T. 0296615929. *048308*

Boscher Belleissue, Jacqueline, 2 Rue Baratoux, 22000 Saint-Brieuc. T. 0296338344. *048309*

Grenier Robien, 21 Blvd Carnot, 22000 Saint-Brieuc. T. 0296782367. - Paint / Furn / Cur – *048310*

Héneaux, Emmanuel, 25 Rue Saint-Guillaume, 22000 Saint-Brieuc. T. 0296330790. *048311*

Jubault, Lucienne, 8 Pl Martray, 22000 Saint-Brieuc. T. 0296618563. *048312*

Lutrin, 18 Rue Houvenagle, 22000 Saint-Brieuc. T. 0296335616. *048313*

Méheut, Roland, 63 Rue Théodule-Ribot, 22000 Saint-Brieuc. T. 0296781422. *048314*

Morin, Jacques, 32 Rue Saint-Guillaume, 22000 Saint-Brieuc. T. 0296339056. *048315*

Morin, Jacques, 17 Rue Maréchal-Foch, 22000 Saint-Brieuc. T. 0296618195. *048316*

Trocante, 49 Rue Chaptal, 22000 Saint-Brieuc. T. 0296612861. *048317*

Saint-Bris-le-Vineux (Yonne)
Durot, Gilles, 33 Rue Gouaix, 89530 Saint-Bris-le-Vineux. T. 0386533977. - China – *048318*

Saint-Calais (Sarthe)
Menu, Jean, 1 Rue Sadi-Carnot, 72120 Saint-Calais. T. 0243352625. - Mil – *048319*

Vallée, Suzanne, 8 Rue Sadi-Carnot, 72120 Saint-Calias. T. 0243350069. - Ant – *048320*

Saint-Cannat (Bouches-du-Rhône)
Barse, Gilles, Pl Bascule, 13760 Saint-Cannat. T. 0442506515. *048321*

Mathieu, Jean-Marie, 65 Av Camille-Pelletan, 13760 Saint-Cannat. T. 0442572172. *048322*

Saint-Capraise-de-Lalinde (Dordogne)
Art et Maison, Rte Sarlat, 24150 Saint-Capraise-de-Lalinde. T. 0553249915. - Tex / Fra – *048323*

Saint-Céré (Lot)
Ashley, Brian, 2 Pl Eglise, 46400 Saint-Céré. T. 0565108226. *048324*

Sourzat, Jean-Louis, 4 Av Docteur-Roux, 46400 Saint-Céré. T. 0565381384. - Paint / Furn / Cur – *048325*

Saint-Chéron (Essonne)
Gusthiot, Christian, 13 Cour Mirgaudon, 91530 Saint-Chéron. T. 0164563146. *048326*

Saint-Christophe-sur-Roc (Deux-Sèvres)
Antiquités Saint-Christophe, La Truite, 79220 Saint-Christophe-sur-Roc. T. 0549052054. *048327*

Saint-Cirq-Lapopie (Lot)
Carrin, Christophe, Bourg, 46330 Saint-Cirq-Lapopie. T. 0565312343. *048328*

Saint-Claud (Charente)
Decressat, Signac, 16450 Saint-Claud. T. 0545713105. *048329*

Saint-Claude (Jura)
Petetin, Nicole, 10 Rue Marché, 39200 Saint-Claude. T. 0384456243. *048330*

Saint-Cloud (Hauts-de-Seine)
Au Charme du Passé, 56 Rue Gounod, 92210 Saint-Cloud. T. 0146025091. *048331*

Boulakia, Armand, 14 Rue Gaillons, 92210 Saint-Cloud. T. 0147718960. *048332*

Kaminzer, Nina, 19 Rue Gounod, 92210 Saint-Cloud. T. 0146023389. *048333*

Saint-Congard (Morbihan)
Bougo, Loyc, Le Bourg, 56140 Saint-Congard. T. 0297435008, Fax 0297435383. - Ant – *048334*

Saint-Cristol-lès-Alès (Gard)
Baptiste, Joseph, 544 Av Général-de-Gaulle, 30380 Saint-Cristol-lès-Alès. T. 0466304261. *048335*

Galerie Coup d'Oeil, 544 Av Général-de-Gaulle, 30380 Saint-Cristol-lès-Alès. T. 0466608045. *048336*

Genolhac, Olivier, Château de Montmoirac, 30380 Saint-Cristol-lès-Alès. T. 0466608238. *048337*

Saint-Cyr-les-Colons (Yonne)
Braton, Jean-Pierre, Rue Rollins, 89800 Saint-Cyr-les-Colons. T. 0386414443. *048338*

Guglielmetti, Serge, Porte Cravant, 89800 Saint-Cyr-les-Colons. T. 0386414407. *048339*

Saint-Cyr-sur-Menthon (Ain)
Manigand Mobilier, La Tuillerie, 01380 Saint-Cyr-sur-Menthon. T. 0385363517. - Furn – *048340*

Saint-Cyr-sur-Mer (Var)
Fouqué, Bernard, 1 Av Mer, 83270 Saint-Cyr-sur-Mer. T. 0494263631. *048341*

Saint-Denis (Seine-Saint-Denis)
Export Antic, 20 Rue Catulienne, 93200 Saint-Denis. T. 0142436024. *048342*

Renzi, Clément, 35 Rue Henri-Barbusse, 93200 Saint-Denis. T. 0148290201. - Paint / Furn / Cur – *048343*

Seddiki, Aissa, 1 Rue Boucheries, 93200 Saint-Denis. T. 0148201509. *048344*

Saint-Denis-d'Anjou (Mayenne)
Collet, Henri, 1 Grande-Rue, 53290 Saint-Denis-d'Anjou. T. 0243705209, Fax 0243706686. - Ant – *048345*

Saint-Denis-d'Oleron (Charente-Maritime)
Tournade, François, 5 Rue Tamaris, 17650 Saint-Denis-d'Oleron. T. 0546478623. - Graph / Furn – *048346*

Saint-Denis-des-Monts (Eure)
Windsor, Jean-Pierre, Nouveau-Monde, 27520 Saint-Denis-des-Monts. T. 0232426082. *048347*

Saint-Dié (Vosges)
Galerie Efal, 3 Rue Orient, Pl Marché, 88100 Saint-Dié. T. 0329561456. - Ant / Paint – *048348*

Lemaître, Michèle, 44 Rue Prairie, 88100 Saint-Dié. T. 0329567097. *048349*

Saint-Dizier (Haute-Marne)
Daouzé, André, 264 Av République, 52100 Saint-Dizier. T. 0325561307. *048350*

Saint-Dyé-sur-Loire (Loir-et-Cher)
Cléo Antiquités, 55 Rue Nationale, 41500 Saint-Dyé-sur-Loire. T. 0254816689. - Ant – *048351*

Saint-Emilion (Gironde)
Artaban, 2 Rue Girondins, 33330 Saint-Emilion. T. 0557744714. *048352*

Carrefour des Temps, 8 Rue La-Grande-Fontaine, 33330 Saint-Emilion. T. 0557246090. *048353*

Chartres, Christian, 4 Pl Clocher, 33330 Saint-Emilion. T. 0557246613. *048354*

Métiers du Vin, 10 Rue Petite-Fontaine, 33330 Saint-Emilion. T. 0557246941. *048355*

Saint-Esteben (Pyrénées-Atlantiques)
Haize Hegoa Organisation, Maison Haïtz-Pean Rte Bidegaina, 64640 Saint-Esteben. T. 0559294074, Fax 0559296730. - Ant – *048356*

Saint-Etienne (Loire)
Acrostiche, 34 Rue Badouillère, 42000 Saint-Etienne. T. 0477252439. *048357*

Alisson RP 42, 10 Rue Général-Foy, 42000 Saint-Etienne. T. 0477326507. - Jew – *048358*

Antiquités du Château, Parc du Pilat, Rochetaillée, 42000 Saint-Etienne. T. 0477337177. - Cur – *048359*

Antiquités du Passage, 17 Rue Résistance, 42000 Saint-Etienne. T. 0477416519. *048360*

Arcadius, 14 Rue Notre-Dame, 42000 Saint-Etienne. T. 0477252959, Fax 0477370800. *048361*

Au Temps Passé, 26 Rue Mulatière, 42100 Saint-Etienne. T. 0477371542. *048362*

Blason du Forez, Rue Richelandière, 42100 Saint-Etienne. T. 0477415883. *048363*

Bobèche, Rue Richelandière, 42100 Saint-Etienne. T. 0477340800. *048364*

Bord, Jacques, 2 Rue Richelandière, Parc Giron, 42100 Saint-Etienne. T. 0477210178. *048365*

Caniard, Michel, 2 Rue Marengo, 42000 Saint-Etienne. T. 0477329748. *048366*

Caniard, Stéphane, 19 Rue Dormoy, 42000 Saint-Etienne. T. 0477384148. *048367*

Celant, Geneviève, Rue Richelandière, 42100 Saint-Etienne. T. 0477256538. *048368*

Charpille, Jean-Pierre, 2 Rue Richelandière, 42000 Saint-Etienne. T. 0477338401. *048369*

Clauzier, Bruno, Rue Richelandière, Parc Giron, Case 17, 42100 Saint-Etienne. T. 0477325472. *048370*

Condamin, Jean-Paul, Rue Richelandière, 42100 Saint-Etienne. T. 0477336514. *048371*

Courbon, 5 Rue Parc-Rochetaillée, 42100 Saint-Etienne. T. 0477337177. *048372*

Courbon, 6 Rue Jeu-de-l'Arc, 42000 Saint-Etienne. T. 0477339691. - Paint / Furn / Sculp / Glass / Cur / Toys – *048373*

Delorme, Noëlie-Christiane, Rue Richelandière, Parc Giron, 42100 Saint-Etienne. T. 0477338370. *048374*

Deville, 6 Rue Camille-Collard, 42000 Saint-Etienne. T. 0477323266. *048375*

Deville, Georges, 111bis Cours-Fauriel, 42100 Saint-Etienne. T. 0477253661. *048376*

Draisienne, Rue Combattants-d'AFN, 42000 Saint-Etienne. T. 0477210308. *048377*

Félix, Joël, 1 Rue Résistance, 42000 Saint-Etienne. T. 0477387070. *048378*

Fournel, Gérard, 29 Rue Saint-Jean, 42000 Saint-Etienne. T. 0477326026, Fax 0477337771. *048379*

Fournier, Nicole, Rue Richelandière, 42100 Saint-Etienne. T. 0477325472. *048380*

Gauchet, Gérard, Rue Richelandière, Parc Giron, 42100 Saint-Etienne. T. 0477338541. *048381*

Giraud, Dominique, 21 Rue Antoine-Durafour, 42100 Saint-Etienne. T. 0477253196. *048382*

Godonnier, Henri, 14 Rue Métare, 42100 Saint-Etienne. T. 0477253516. *048383*

Gousset, 30 Rue Paul-Bert, 42000 Saint-Etienne. T. 0477325192. - Instr – *048384*

Gousset, Jean-Pierre, 2 Rue Richelandière, Parc Giron, 42100 Saint-Etienne. T. 0477320060. *048385*

Héliodore, Arcades Hôtel-de-Ville, 42000 Saint-Etienne. T. 0477250848. *048386*

Kanel, Gilbert, Rue Richelandière, Parc Giron, 42100 Saint-Etienne. T. 0477338490. *048387*

Marché des Antiquités, 32 Rue Badouillère, 42000 Saint-Etienne. T. 0477217798. *048388*

Marcou, Marcel, 12 Pl Saint-Roch, 42000 Saint-Etienne. T. 0477211352. *048389*

Maurice Antiquités, 36 Rue Badouillère, 42000 Saint-Etienne. T. 0477386980. *048390*

Rafer, Aline, Rue Richelandière, 42100 Saint-Etienne. T. 0477338396. *048391*

Raveyre, Antoine, 34 Rue Mulatière, 42100 Saint-Etienne. T. 0477251861. *048392*

Retrouvailles, 20 Rue Résistance, 42000 Saint-Etienne. T. 0477321235. *048393*

Reymond, Marcel, 5 Rue Alliés, 42100 Saint-Etienne. T. 0477339546. *048394*

Saint-Antoine, 23 Rue Mulatière, 42100 Saint-Etienne. T. 0477252535. *048395*

Saint-Martin, Alfred, 13 Rue Résistance, 42000 Saint-Etienne. T. 0477341929. *048396*

Therme, Robert, 9 Rue Richelandière, 42100 Saint-Etienne. T. 0477212455. *048397*

Verney-Carron, Patrick, Rue Richelandière, Parc Giron, 42100 Saint-Etienne. T. 0477326549, Fax 0477342404. *048398*

Verzeletti, Serge, 2 Rue Richelandière, 42100 Saint-Etienne. T. 0477883420. *048399*

Saint-Etienne-de-Chigny (Indre-et-Loire)
Martin, Patrice, 52 Quai Loire, 37230 Saint-Etienne-de-Chigny. T. 0547556782. *048400*

Saint-Etienne-de-Cuines (Savoie)
Maurienne Antiquités, Imm Mont-Cuchet, 73130 Saint-Etienne-de-Cuines. T. 0479562836. - Ant – *048401*

Saint-Etienne-de-Fursac (Creuse)
Dourville, Christian, Paulhac, 23290 Saint-Etienne-de-Fursac. T. 0555636711. - Ant – *048402*

Saint-Etienne-du-Vauvray (Eure)
Baude, Magaly, 10 Rue Nationale, 27430 Saint-Etienne-du-Vauvray. T. 0232595868. *048403*

Saint-Etienne-Fontbellon (Ardèche)
Andrieu, Danielle, Rte d'Alès, 07200 Saint-Etienne-Fontbellon. T. 0475352328. - Ant - *048404*

Saint-Fargeau (Yonne)
Pironnet, Gilbert, 4 Rue Eglise, 89170 Saint-Fargeau. T. 0386740719. *048405*

Saint-Fargeau-Ponthierry (Seine-et-Marne)
Maubert, Odette, 14 Rue Gén Patton Tilly, 77310 Saint-Fargeau-Ponthierry. T. 0160657540. - Sculp - *048406*

Penochet, Paul, 33 Rue Caporal-Petit, 77310 Saint-Fargeau-Ponthierry. T. 0164098301. *048407*

Saint-Féliu-d'Amont (Pyrénées-Orientales)
Victoria, 7 Carre la Sardanne, 66170 Saint-Féliu-d'Amont. T. 0468578778. - Furn / Tex - *048408*

Saint-Firmin (Saône-et-Loire)
Bouvet, Roland, Les Caillots, 71670 Saint-Firmin. T. 0385550311. - Ant - *048409*

Saint-Florentin (Yonne)
Quentin, Yannick, 4 Rue Fbg-Saint-Martin, 89600 Saint-Florentin. T. 0386350810. *048410*

Sirieix, Nathalie, 23 Grande Rue, 89600 Saint-Florentin. T. 0386350616. *048411*

Saint-Flour-de-Mercoire (Lozère)
Oziol, Denis, Village, 48300 Saint-Flour-de-Mercoire. T. 0466690909. *048412*

Saint-Floxel (Manche)
Lefèbvre, Jacques, Rue Saint-Clair, 50310 Saint-Floxel. T. 0233213838. *048413*

Saint-Fortunat-sur-Eyrieux (Ardèche)
Antiquités Brocante de la Vallée, Rue Général-Moulin, 07360 Saint-Fortunat-sur-Eyrieux. T. 0475653066. - Ant - *048414*

Temps Retrouvé, Pl Eglise, 07360 Saint-Fortunat-sur-Eyrieux. T. 0475652003. - Ant - *048415*

Saint-Gaudens (Haute-Garonne)
Maison des Ventes, 9 Av Isle, 31800 Saint-Gaudens. T. 0561891923. *048416*

Passé Simple, 3 Av Isle, 31800 Saint-Gaudens. T. 0561890626. *048417*

Vis a Vis, 2 Rue République, 31800 Saint-Gaudens. T. 0561892426. *048418*

Saint-Genest-Malifaux (Loire)
Brocante de Bicêtre, La Digonnerie, 42660 Saint-Genest-Malifaux. T. 0477514379. *048419*

Saint-Genis-de-Saintonge (Charente-Maritime)
Renoux, Yves, RN 137, 17240 Saint-Genis-de-Saintonge. T. 0546498891. - Furn / Cur - *048420*

Saint-Genix-sur-Guiers (Savoie)
Bellen, Robert & Renée, BP 5, 73240 Saint-Genix-sur-Guiers. T. 0476316005. - Ant - *048421*

Merle, Cahrles, Pl Bouverie, 73240 Saint-Genix-sur-Guiers. T. 0476316152. - Ant - *048422*

Saint-Georges-de-Montaigu (Vendée)
Cailliez, Stéphane, La Bonnetière, 85600 Saint-Georges-de-Montaigu. T. 0251420031. *048423*

Saint-Georges-sur-Loire (Maine-et-Loire)
Antiquités du Grand Bras, Le Grand Bras, Rte Chalonnes, 49170 Saint-Georges-sur-Loire. T. 41393031. *048424*

Saint-Germain-de-Longue-Chaume (Deux-Sèvres)
Merceron, Le Patis, 79200 Saint-Germain-de-Longue-Chaume. T. 0549700114. *048425*

Saint-Germain-du-Bel-Air (Lot)
Brocante à la Ferme, Foulquié, 46310 Saint-Germain-du-Bel-Air. T. 0565368567, Fax 0565368373. - Ant / Paint / Furn / Cur - *048426*

Saint-Germain-en-Laye (Yvelines)
Antiquités Dauphine, Pl Dauphine, 78100 Saint-Germain-en-Laye. T. 0134512676. - Ant / Paint - *048427*

Bobby Brocante, 37 Rue Pontel, 78100 Saint-Germain-en-Laye. T. 0139582072. *048428*

Cour de l'Antiquaire, 39 Rue Poissy, 78100 Saint-Germain-en-Laye. T. 0130612489. *048429*

Grenier de Margot, 30 Rue Louviers, 78100 Saint-Germain-en-Laye. T. 0139739150. - Paint / Furn / Jew / Cur - *048430*

Harmonie Décors, 9 Rue Danés-de-Montardat, 78100 Saint-Germain-en-Laye. T. 0134511896. *048431*

Marotte, 20 Rue Danès-de-Montardat, 78100 Saint-Germain-en-Laye. T. 0130611610. - Furn / Cur / Toys - *048432*

Péaron, Monique, 141 Rue Léon-Desoyer, 78100 Saint-Germain-en-Laye. T. 0139739502. *048433*

Reflet d'Antan, 33 Rue Paris, 78100 Saint-Germain-en-Laye. T. 0130870204. *048434*

Saint-Germain Antiquités, 148 Rue Président-Roosevelt, 78100 Saint-Germain-en-Laye. T. 0130610856. *048435*

Saint-Germain-Laval (Loire)
Giroux, Jacques, 51 Rue Huguenots, 42260 Saint-Germain-Laval. T. 0477654042. *048436*

Saint-Germain-sur-Morin (Seine-et-Marne)
Antiquités de Saint-Germain, 19bis Rue Paris, 77740 Saint-Germain-sur-Morin. T. 0360044158. *048437*

Fanchon-Cunhac, 6 Rue Paris, 77740 Saint-Germain-sur-Morin. T. 0360041852. *048438*

Saint-Germain-sur-Sarthe (Orne)
Brocante de la Hutte, Grouas, 72130 Saint-Germain-sur-Sarthe. T. 0243975040. - Ant - *048439*

Saint-Germier (Deux-Sèvres)
Audebault, Dominique, Le Bourg, 79340 Saint-Germier. T. 0549691276. *048440*

Saint-Gilles (Manche)
Serrant, Pierre, 1 Rue Saint-Michel, 50180 Saint-Gilles. T. 0233574113. *048441*

Saint-Gilles-Croix-de-Vie (Vendée)
Atl'Antiquités, 60 Rue Bellevue, 85800 Saint-Gilles-Croix-de-Vie. T. 0251548844, Fax 0251549311. *048442*

Saint-Girons (Ariège)
Antiquités Anglaises, 18 Rue Joseph-Pujol, 09200 Saint-Girons. T. 0561661315. *048443*

Galy, Geneviève, 40 Av Aristide-Bergès, 09200 Saint-Girons. T. 0561660691. *048444*

Sellares, Alain, 84 Av Maréchal-Foch, 09200 Saint-Girons. T. 0561666611. *048445*

Saint-Grégoire (Ille-et-Vilaine)
Julienne, Patrick, 4 Rue Mozart, 35760 Saint-Grégoire. T. 0299687365. *048446*

Saint-Haon-le-Châtel (Loire)
Boutique des Remparts, Bourg, 42370 Saint-Haon-le-Châtel. T. 0477621037. *048447*

Saint-Hilaire-de-Riez (Vendée)
Lucas, Jean, 113 Rue Atlantique, 85270 Saint-Hilaire-de-Riez. T. 0251552006. *048448*

Lucas, Joël, 68bis Rue Georges-Clemenceau, 85270 Saint-Hilaire-de-Riez. T. 0251556728. *048449*

Macker, Gérard, Les Cosses, 85270 Saint-Hilaire-de-Riez. T. 0251543294. - Ant / Furn - *048450*

Migné, Théophile, 283 Rte Perrier-La-Fradinière, 85270 Saint-Hilaire-de-Riez. T. 0251683344. *048451*

Moreau, Annette, 9 Rue Peupliers-Sion, 85270 Saint-Hilaire-de-Riez. T. 0251544501. *048452*

Saint-Hilaire-du-Harcouët (Manche)
Ansel, Alain, 76 Rue République, 50600 Saint-Hilaire-du-Harcouët. T. 0233495741. *048453*

Antiquités Saint-Hilaire, Goberie, 50600 Saint-Hilaire-du-Harcouët. T. 0233495061. - Furn - *048454*

Boudou, Alexandre, Isles, Rte Avranches, 50600 Saint-Hilaire-du-Harcouët. T. 0233491073. *048455*

Saint-Hilaire-Luc (Corrèze)
Soustre, François, Grange de Toine, 19160 Saint-Hilaire-Luc. T. 0555959884. *048456*

Saint-Hilaire-Lusignan (Lot-et-Garonne)
Marrassé, Philippe, RN 113, 47490 Saint-Hilaire-Lusignan. T. 0553676983. *048457*

Saint-Hippolyte-du-Fort (Gard)
Lauriol, Simone, 30170 Saint-Hippolyte-du-Fort. T. 0466772001. *048458*

Saint-James (Manche)
Blivet, Didier, 12 Rue Antoine-Pery, 50240 Saint-James. T. 0233482107. *048459*

Saint-Jean-Bonnefonds (Loire)
Antic-Land, Rue Emile-Zola, 42650 Saint-Jean-Bonnefonds. T. 0477471343. *048460*

Saint-Jean-d'Angély (Charente-Maritime)
Pellissard, Félix, 94 Av Charles-de-Gaulle, 17400 Saint-Jean-d'Angély. T. 0546323001. *048461*

Saint-Jean-d'Aulps (Haute-Savoie)
Antiquités de l'Abbaye, Le Tunnel, 74430 Saint-Jean-d'Aulps. T. 0450796504. - Furn / Cur - *048462*

Saint-Jean-de-Beugne (Vendée)
Leiglat, Francisca, Le Bourg, 85210 Saint-Jean-de-Beugne. T. 0251978076. - Furn / Cur - *048463*

Saint-Jean-de-Gonville (Ain)
Relais-de-l'Antiquité, 01630 Saint-Jean-de-Gonville. T. 0450563963. - Paint / Furn - *048464*

Saint-Jean-de-Luz (Pyrénées-Atlantiques)
Aguer, Hélène, 16 Blvd Thiers, 64500 Saint-Jean-de-Luz. T. 0559510773. - Ant - *048465*

Donibane, 7 Rue Baleine, 64500 Saint-Jean-de-Luz. T. 0559512171. - Ant - *048466*

Frip'ou'net, 21 Rue Loquin, 64500 Saint-Jean-de-Luz. T. 0559269289. - Ant - *048467*

Verrier, Jean, 13 Rue de la République, 64500 Saint-Jean-de-Luz. T. 0559262061. - Ant / Paint - *048468*

Saint-Jean-de-Moirans (Isère)
Chartreuse, Av Gaston-Bonnardel, 38430 Saint-Jean-de-Moirans. T. 0476354963. - Ant - *048469*

Saint-Jean-de-Monts (Vendée)
Antiquités Artémis, 7 Esplanade Mer, Rés Orchidées, 85160 Saint-Jean-de-Monts. T. 0251593504. *048470*

Chaumière Rustique, Le Vieux Cerne, 85160 Saint-Jean-de-Monts. T. 0251582764. *048471*

Galeyrand, Philippe, 200 Rue Sables-Beaulieu, 85160 Saint-Jean-de-Monts. T. 0251586726. - Furn - *048472*

Saint-Jean-de-Thouars (Deux-Sèvres)
Teiller, Joseph, Clos de Vicomte, 79100 Saint-Jean-de-Thouars. T. 0549661773. *048473*

Saint-Jean-du-Gard (Gard)
Jonquière, 132 Grand Rue, 30270 Saint-Jean-du-Gard. T. 0466851714. *048474*

Saint-Jean-Pierre-Fixte (Eure-et-Loir)
Pelletier, Alain, Le Charme, 28400 Saint-Jean-Pierre-Fixte. T. 0237523506. *048475*

Saint-Jean-sur-Vilaine (Ille-et-Vilaine)
Cozette, Maria, La Basse-Bertoisière, 35220 Saint-Jean-sur-Vilaine. T. 0299003964. *048476*

Perrudin, Rémy, Le Pin, 35220 Saint-Jean-sur-Vilaine. T. 0299623744, Fax 0299007854. *048477*

Saint-Jeoire-en-Faucigny (Haute-Savoie)
Perron, Ralph, 1 Rue Melchior, 74490 Saint-Jeoire-en-Faucigny. T. 0450358139. - Furn -   *048478*

Saint-Juery (Tarn)
Farenc, Michel, Rte Ambialet, Les Avalats, 81160 Saint-Juery. T. 0563551209. - Furn -   *048479*

Saint-Julien-de-Peyrolas (Gard)
Maurin, Maria, 30760 Saint-Julien-de-Peyrolas.
T. 0466821865.   *048480*
Sicard, Christian, Colombier, 30760 Saint-Julien-de-Peyrolas. T. 0466821619.   *048481*

Saint-Julien-du-Sault (Yonne)
Hubert, Henry, 15 Rue Fontaine, 89330 Saint-Julien-du-Sault. T. 0386633344. - Furn / Cur -   *048482*

Saint-Julien-en-Genevois (Haute-Savoie)
Jaccaz, 11bis Rte de Lyon, 74160 Saint-Julien-en-Genevois. T. 0450493684. - Furn / Cur -   *048483*
Lacroix, Serge, Norcier, 74160 Saint-Julien-en-Genevois. T. 0450493870.   *048484*

Saint-Julien-les-Villas (Aube)
Hervé, Hugot, 35 Rue Carnot, 10800 Saint-Julien-les-Villas. T. 0325498708. - Ant / Cur -   *048485*

Saint-Julien-Molin-Molette (Loire)
Domaine de Taillis Vert, Taillis Vert, 42220 Saint-Julien-Molin-Molette. T. 0477515392,
Fax 0477515597.   *048486*

Saint-Junien (Haute-Vienne)
Charpentier, Bernard, 9 Blvd Victur-Hugo, 87200 Saint-Junien. T. 0555024156. - Ant -   *048487*
Dussouchaud, Didier, Chemin Goth, 87200 Saint-Junien. T. 0555020761. - Ant -   *048488*

Saint-Just-Saint-Rambert (Loire)
Perret, Paul, Chemin Bechet, 42170 Saint-Just-Saint-Rambert. T. 0477524138.   *048489*

Saint-Lambert-du-Lattay (Maine-et-Loire)
David, Philippe, Paimparé, 49750 Saint-Lambert-du-Lattay. T. 41784021.   *048490*

Saint-Laurent-d'Aigouze (Gard)
Sanier, Marc, Rte Saintes-Maries-de-la-Mer, Mas Saint-Germain, 30220 Saint-Laurent-d'Aigouze.
T. 0466538563.   *048491*

Saint-Laurent-de-Belzagot (Charente)
Fraty, Gilbert, 37 Rue Boulivent, 16190 Saint-Laurent-de-Belzagot. T. 0545603136.   *048492*
Rallion, Jean-Pierre, Logis de Beaulieu, 16190 Saint-Laurent-de-Belzagot. T. 0545602039. - Paint / Furn / Cur / Toys / Music -   *048493*

Saint-Laurent-de-la-Salanque (Pyrénées-Orientales)
Bergeron, Claude, 12bis Rue Alma, 66250 Saint-Laurent-de-la-Salanque. T. 0468281342. - Ant - *048494*
Durant, Eliane, 5 Imp Hector-Berlioz, 66250 Saint-Laurent-de-la-Salanque. T. 0468596332. - Ant - *048495*

Saint-Laurent-des-Vignes (Dordogne)
Vanzo, Rte Bordeaux, 24100 Saint-Laurent-des-Vignes. T. 0553240733.   *048496*

Saint-Laurent-sur-Saône (Ain)
Saône Antiquités, 149 Rue de la Levée, 01750 Saint-Laurent-sur-Saône. T. 0385392147. - Ant - *048497*

Saint-Léger-de-Peyre (Lozère)
Beau-Darmendrail, Serge, Village, Presbytère, 48100 Saint-Léger-de-Peyre. T. 0466320808.   *048498*
Danglehant, Christian, Village, 48100 Saint-Léger-de-Peyre. T. 0466323290.   *048499*

Saint-Léonard (Seine-Maritime)
Manège des Hogues, 76400 Saint-Léonard.
T. 0235273730.   *048500*

Saint-Léonard (Vosges)
Caverne d'Ali Baba, 8 A Rue Lorraine, 88650 Saint-Léonard. T. 0329519085.   *048501*

Saint-Leu-la-Forêt (Val-d'Oise)
Andréas, 111 Rue Evariste-Galois, 95320 Saint-Leu-la-Forêt. T. 0130409964.   *048502*
Antiquaire du Village, 23 Rue Général-Leclerc, 95320 Saint-Leu-la-Forêt. T. 0139605316.   *048503*
Aujourd'hier, 39 Rue Général-Leclerc, 95320 Saint-Leu-la-Forêt. T. 0139957751.   *048504*
Guerrero, Juan, 3 Sentier Gâteau, 95320 Saint-Leu-la-Forêt. T. 0130408429.   *048505*

Saint-Lizier (Ariège)
Rivère, Marie-Louise, Rue Nobles, 09190 Saint-Lizier.
T. 0561561700.   *048506*
Rivière-Pagnon, Nicole, Pl Eglise, 09190 Saint-Lizier.
T. 0561561700. - Ant -   *048507*

Saint-Lô (Manche)
Ancestrale, 79 Rte Villedieu, 50000 Saint-Lô.
T. 0233572413. - Furn / China -   *048508*
Bergmann, Christian, 35 Rue Havin, 50000 Saint-Lô.
T. 0233050668.   *048509*
Galerie des Arts, 61 Rue Neufbourg, 50000 Saint-Lô.
T. 0233572099.   *048510*
Galerie du Ruisseau, 8-10 Rue Marne, 50000 Saint-Lô.
T. 0233561430. - Paint / Furn / Cur -   *048511*

Saint-Lormel (Côtes-d'Armor)
Ancestrale, La Ville Bily, 22130 Saint-Lormel.
T. 0296842357.   *048512*

Saint-Loubès (Gironde)
Pont, Philippe, 86 Av République, 33450 Saint-Loubès.
T. 0556204382.   *048513*
Teynat, Alfred, 1 Rue Saint-Aignan, 33450 Saint-Loubès.
T. 0556789022.   *048514*

Saint-Louis (Haut-Rhin)
Schall, Sonia, 11 Rue Saint-Jean, 68300 Saint-Louis.
T. 0389691597. - Furn / Lights / Cur / Toys -   *048515*

Saint-Lubin-de-la-Haye (Eure-et-Loir)
Mazoyer, Jean-Claude, Manoir de Saint-Lubin, 28580 Saint-Lubin-de-la-Haye. T. 0237820642.   *048516*

Saint-Lubin-des-Joncherets (Eure-et-Loir)
Winter, Richard, La Poterie, 28350 Saint-Lubin-des-Joncherets. T. 0232581535.   *048517*

Saint-Lunaire (Ille-et-Vilaine)
Bihan Antiquités, 107 Blvd Général-de-Gaulle, 35800 Saint-Lunaire. T. 0299463553.   *048518*

Saint-Macaire (Gironde)
Dumeau, Madeleine, Pl Marché-Dieu, 33490 Saint-Macaire. T. 0556622113. - Ant -   *048519*

Saint-Maixent-l'Ecole (Deux-Sèvres)
Bulte, Jean-Marc, 2 Rue Goguet, 79400 Saint-Maixent-l'Ecole. T. 0549765155.   *048520*
Naud, Daniel, 3 Rue Chaigneau, 79400 Saint-Maixent-l'Ecole. T. 0549505294.   *048521*
Pineau, William, 3 Rue Aristide-Briand, 79400 Saint-Maixent-l'Ecole. T. 0549065256,
Fax 0549062948.   *048522*

Saint-Maixme-Hauterive (Eure-et-Loir)
Pouillier, Michel, Brouvilliers, 28170 Saint-Maixme-Hauterive. T. 0237516755.   *048523*

Saint-Malo (Ille-et-Vilaine)
Ancre de Miséricorde, 9 Rue Blatrerie, 35400 Saint-Malo. T. 0299562929.   *048524*
Antiquités Moka, 77 Av Moka, 35400 Saint-Malo.
T. 0299562929. - Jew -   *048525*
Atelier de Solidor, 4 Rue Am Epron, 35400 Saint-Malo.
T. 0299820956.   *048526*
Au Troc Malouin, 36 Rue Georges V, 35400 Saint-Malo.
T. 0299815655.   *048527*
Barré, Gérard, 28 Chaussée Sillon, 35400 Saint-Malo.
T. 0299408958, Fax 0299409646. - Num -   *048528*

Busnel, Jacques-Henry, Manoir de la Perche, 1 Rue Fours-à-Chaux, 35400 Saint-Malo. T. 0299819757.
- Orient / China -   *048529*
Busnel, Jacques-Henry, 12 Rue Dinan, 35400 Saint-Malo. T. 0299409619. - Orient -   *048530*
Busnel, Jean-François, 17 Rue Siam, 35400 Saint-Malo.
T. 0299816054.   *048531*
Chaussavoine, Jules, 31 Rue Dauphine, 35400 Saint-Malo. T. 0299821737.   *048532*
Couet, Yves, 37 Blvd Chateaubriand, 35400 Saint-Malo.
T. 0299560248. - Ant / Paint / Furn / Num / China -   *048533*
Delouche, Olivier, 3 Rue Gouin-de-Beauchêne, 35400 Saint-Malo. T. 0299400102.   *048534*
Douet de la Villefromoy, André, 3 Rue de la Blatrerie, 35400 Saint-Malo. T. 0299408919. - Ant / Furn - *048535*
Le Calvez, Marcel, Rue Général-Patton, 35400 Saint-Malo. T. 0299822326.   *048536*
Le Morvan, Yves-Marie, 3 Rue des Cordiers, 35400 Saint-Malo. T. 0299408656. - Ant -   *048537*
Lereec, Alain, 6 Pl Frères-Lamennais, 35400 Saint-Malo. T. 0299568308.   *048538*
Malle du Corsaire, 21 Pl Canada, 35400 Saint-Malo.
T. 0299405108.   *048539*
Manoir de la Perche, 1 Rue Fours-à-Chaux, 35400 Saint-Malo. T. 0299819757.   *048540*
Néré, Henri, 17 Rue Dauphine, 35400 Saint-Malo.
T. 0299811873.   *048541*
Noël, Hélène, 11 Grand Rue, 35400 Saint-Malo.
T. 0299409882.   *048542*
Petite Brocante, 27 Rue Général-de-Castelnau, 35400 Saint-Malo. T. 0299562323.   *048543*
Sanneville, 1 Pl Gasnier-Duparc, 35400 Saint-Malo.
T. 0299408338, Fax 0299564850.   *048544*
Stephany, Françoise, 5 Rue Puits-aux-Braies, 35400 Saint-Malo. T. 0299563122.   *048545*

Saint-Mammès (Seine-et-Marne)
Delaveau, Jean-Marc, 89 Rue Grande, 77670 Saint-Mammès. T. 64311230.   *048546*

Saint-Marcel-lès-Valence (Drôme)
Aubert, Marcel, 40 Av Provence, 26320 Saint-Marcel-lès-Valence. T. 0475857156.   *048547*

Saint-Marcel-sur-Aude (Aude)
Cadenet, Arlette, Rte Saint-Pons, 11120 Saint-Marcel-sur-Aude. T. 0468935744.   *048548*

Saint-Martin-de-Boscherville (Seine-Maritime)
Marotte, Pl Abbaye, 76840 Saint-Martin-de-Boscherville. T. 0235321001.   *048549*

Saint-Martin-de-Nigelles (Eure-et-Loir)
Schorp, Gérard, 11 Rue Henri-Baillods-Eglancourt, 28130 Saint-Martin-de-Nigelles.
T. 0237825200.   *048550*

Saint-Martin-de-Ré (Charente-Maritime)
Barbotine, 13 Quai Georges-Clemenceau, 17410 Saint-Martin-de-Ré. T. 0546092182, Fax 0546093364.
- Tex / Dec -   *048551*

Saint-Martin-de Ré (Charente-Maritime)
Brandy, Michel, 30 Rue Aristide-Briand, 17410 Saint-Martin-de Ré. T. 0546092770.   *048552*
Couette, Claude, 4 Cours Bailli-des-Ecotais, 17410 Saint-Martin-de Ré. T. 0546093941.   *048553*
Galerie de Thoiras, 9 Av Victor-Bouthillier, 17410 Saint-Martin-de-Ré. T. 0546092989. - Furn -   *048554*
Glineur, Patrick, 4 Cours Bailli-des-Ecotais, 17410 Saint-Martin-de-Ré. T. 0546091090.   *048555*
Puce, 17 Rue Sully, 17410 Saint-Martin-de-Ré.
T. 0546091693.   *048556*
Treille Marine, 4 Pl République, 17410 Saint-Martin-de Ré. T. 0546093622.   *048557*

Saint-Martin-des-Champs (Finistère)
Saint-François, 33 Allée Saint-François, 29600 Saint-Martin-des-Champs. T. 0298638205. - Ant - *048558*

Sherwood Antiques, 39 Allée Saint-François Rte Carantec, 29600 Saint-Martin-des-Champs. T. 0298881795.
- Ant / Furn / Silv -
048559

Saint-Martin-des-Champs (Manche)
Antiquités Saint-Martin, 13 Blvd Luxembourg, 50300 Saint-Martin-des-Champs. T. 0233683516. *048560*
Gervais, Gilbert, 13 Blvd Luxembourg, 50300 Saint-Martin-des-Champs. T. 0233683516. *048561*

Saint-Martin-du-Fouilloux (Maine-et-Loire)
Hexa Décor, RN 23, 49170 Saint-Martin-du-Fouilloux. T. 41397324, Fax 41397677. *048562*

Saint-Martin-du-Fresne (Ain)
Coulon, Maurice, 15 Chemin du Visinal, 01430 Saint-Martin-du-Fresne. T. 0474757356. - Ant - *048563*

Saint-Martin-la-Garenne (Yvelines)
Fallais, Denise, Rue Désirée, 78520 Saint-Martin-la-Garenne. T. 0134779895. *048564*

Saint-Martin-Petit (Lot-et-Garonne)
Au Grenier de Grand-Père, Bourg, 47200 Saint-Martin-Petit. T. 0553948189. *048565*

Saint-Martin-sur-Oust (Morbihan)
Seillon, Jean-Marie, La Croix-Piguel, 56200 Saint-Martin-sur-Oust. T. 0299915575. - Ant - *048566*

Saint-Mathurin-sur-Loire (Maine-et-Loire)
Ferré, Patrick, 38 Quai Roi-René, 49250 Saint-Mathurin-sur-Loire. T. 41570601. *048567*
Ventou-Prentou, 68 Rue Port-la-Vallée, 49250 Saint-Mathurin-sur-Loire. Fax 41570276. - Ant - *048568*

Saint-Maur-des-Fossés (Val-de-Marne)
Abid, Abdelmoumen, 63 Rue Delerue, 94100 Saint-Maur-des-Fossés. T. 0148857778. *048569*
Alma, 3 Av Alma, 94100 Saint-Maur-des-Fossés. T. 0148851836. - Ant - *048570*
Antiquités du Boulevard, 129 Blvd Créteil, 94100 Saint-Maur-des-Fossés. T. 0148836801. - Paint / Graph / Furn / Mil / Cur - *048571*
Antiquités Laurence, 16 Av Docteur-Calmette, 94100 Saint-Maur-des-Fossés. T. 0148831033. *048572*
Au Trésor d'Antan, 6 Blvd Créteil, 94100 Saint-Maur-des-Fossés. T. 0148850897. - Furn / Sculp / Silv / Instr / Mil / Cur / Toys - *048573*
Au Trésor d'Antan, 1 Blvd Général-Giraud, 94100 Saint-Maur-des-Fossés. T. 0148850897. - Furn / Sculp / Silv / Instr / Mil / Cur / Toys - *048574*
Debruille, Luc, 4 Quai Pie, 94100 Saint-Maur-des-Fossés. T. 0148866649. *048575*
Grenier de Saint-Maur, 15 Rue Baratte-Cholet, 94100 Saint-Maur-des-Fossés. T. 0148890016. - Paint / Furn / Cur - *048576*
Lambert, Philippe, 28bis Rue Vassal, 94100 Saint-Maur-des-Fossés. T. 0148895404. *048577*
Lefèvre & Fils, 129 Rue Garibaldi, 94100 Saint-Maur-des-Fossés. T. 0148832760. - Ant - *048578*

Saint-Maurice-l'Exil (Isère)
Bibelot, 24 Rue Sacco-et-Vanzetti, 38550 Saint-Maurice-l'Exil. T. 0474294946. - Ant / Furn - *048579*

Saint-Maurice-la-Clouère (Vienne)
Debarras Express, La Tuillerie, 86160 Saint-Maurice-la-Clouère. T. 0549530213. - Ant - *048580*

Saint-Maurice-sur-Eygues (Drôme)
Coquet, Nicole, Grande Rue, 26110 Saint-Maurice-sur-Eygues. T. 0475276421. *048581*

Saint-Max (Meurthe-et-Moselle)
Artois, 91 Av Carnot, 54130 Saint-Max. T. 0383204390. *048582*
Carte Antique, 33 Rue Louis-Barthou, 54130 Saint-Max. T. 0383297545. *048583*
Oscaria, 85 Av Carnot, 54130 Saint-Max. T. 0383204209. *048584*

Saint-Maximin-la-Sainte-Baume (Var)
Guis, Bruno, 4 Blvd Jean-Jaurès, 83470 Saint-Maximin-la-Sainte-Baume. T. 0494780186. *048585*
Sacha Matériaux, Rte de Barjois, Quartier Régalette, 83470 Saint-Maximin-la-Sainte-Baume. T. 0494593878, Fax 0494593897. *048586*

Saint-Melaine-sur-Aubance (Maine-et-Loire)
Antic Sud Loire, Rte Juigné, ZA Treillebois, 49610 Saint-Melaine-sur-Aubance. T. 41577900. - Furn - *048587*

Saint-Méloir-des-Ondes (Ille-et-Vilaine)
Vannier, Daniel, Les Portes-Rouges, 35350 Saint-Méloir-des-Ondes. T. 0299891345. *048588*

Saint-Memmie (Marne)
Herbelet, Denis, 26 Av Metz, 51470 Saint-Memmie. T. 0326640915. *048589*

Saint-Michel (Aisne)
Frédéric, Francis, 2bis Rue Kinet, 02830 Saint-Michel. T. 0323583037. - Ant / Furn / Cur - *048590*

Saint-Mihiel (Meuse)
Collet, Catherine, 18 Rue Verdun, 55300 Saint-Mihiel. T. 0329891998. - Ant - *048591*
Tonner, Jean-Marie, 12 Rue Docteur-Albert-Thierry, 55300 Saint-Mihiel. T. 0329890220. - Ant - *048592*

Saint-Nabord (Vosges)
Au Réveil du Temps, 24 Rue Centre, 88200 Saint-Nabord. T. 0329233201. *048593*

Saint-Nazaire (Loire-Atlantique)
Antiquité-Brocante de l'Immaculée, 3 Rte Château-de-Beauregard, 44600 Saint-Nazaire. T. 40018379. *048594*
Cloarec, Danielle, 1 All Capucines, 44600 Saint-Nazaire. T. 40537013. *048595*
London Antiques, 10 Rue Louis-Blanquis, 44600 Saint-Nazaire. T. 40221662. *048596*
London Antiquites, 101 Av République, 44600 Saint-Nazaire. T. 40667847. *048597*

Saint-Nicolas-de-Port (Meurthe-et-Moselle)
Antiquités Saint-Nicolas, 36 Av Jolain, 54210 Saint-Nicolas-de-Port. T. 0383467281. *048598*

Saint-Nolff (Morbihan)
Ménézo, Maurice, 6bis Rue Forge, 56250 Saint-Nolff. T. 0297454369. - Ant - *048599*

Saint-Omer (Pas-de-Calais)
Naninck & Lengaigne, 9 Rue François-Ringot, 62500 Saint-Omer. T. 0321382308, Fax 0321383110. *048600*
Quivrin, Olivier, 44 Rue Clouteries, 62500 Saint-Omer. T. 0321984715. *048601*

Saint-Orens-de-Gameville (Haute-Garonne)
Décorantique, 14 Rue Champs-Pinsons, 31650 Saint-Orens-de-Gameville. I. 0561399306. *048602*
Jouanneau, Isabelle, 1 Rue Rivière, 31650 Saint-Orens-de-Gameville. T. 0562248926. *048603*

Saint-Ouen (Seine-Saint-Denis)
Abecassis, Paul, 85 Rue Rosiers, Marché Biron, 93400 Saint-Ouen. T. 0140128238. *048604*
Abel, A., 1 Marché Paul-Bert, 93400 Saint-Ouen. T. 0140102983. *048605*
Abravanelli, Chantal, 142 Rue Rosiers, Marché Malassis, 93400 Saint-Ouen. T. 0140114194. *048606*
Adda, Robert, 142 Rue Rosiers, Marché Malassis, 93400 Saint-Ouen. T. 0140120689. *048607*
Adès, Ginette, 7 Marché Paul-Bert, Stand 410, 93400 Saint-Ouen. T. 0140112819. *048608*
Adjinsoff, Roger, 13 Rue Paul-Bert, 93400 Saint-Ouen. T. 0140112569. *048609*
Agathe, 136 Av Michelet, 93400 Saint-Ouen. T. 0140101819. *048610*
Agora, 142 Rue Rosiers, Marché Malassis, 93400 Saint-Ouen. T. 0140101487. *048611*
Aker, Albert, 85 Rue Rosiers, Marché Biron, 93400 Saint-Ouen. T. 0140102257. *048612*

Aker, Nicole, 142 Rue Rosiers, Marché Malassis, 93400 Saint-Ouen. T. 0140117983. *048613*
Aléors, 99 Rue Rosiers, 93400 Saint-Ouen. T. 0140121262. *048614*
Alpha, 142 Rue Rosiers, Marché Malassis, 93400 Saint-Ouen. T. 0140119933. *048615*
Ambre, 140 Rue Rosiers, Marché Dauphine, 93400 Saint-Ouen. T. 0140118067. *048616*
André, Jeannine, 85 Rue Rosiers, Marché Biron, 93400 Saint-Ouen. T. 0140121150. *048617*
Antiquité du Littoral, 7 Rue Jules-Vallès, Marché Jules-Vallès, 93400 Saint-Ouen. T. 0140123793. *048618*
Antiquité 56, 142 Rue Rosiers, Marché Malassis, 93400 Saint-Ouen. T. 0140118898. *048619*
Antis, 140 Rue Rosiers, Marché Dauphine, 93400 Saint-Ouen. T. 0149450649. *048620*
Apelstein, Katherine, 6 Marché Paul-Bert, Stand 79, 93400 Saint-Ouen. T. 0140114928. *048621*
Arabesque, 142 Rue Rosiers, Marché Malassis, 93400 Saint-Ouen. T. 0140120555. *048622*
Ardalan, Behzad, 5 Marché Paul-Bert, 93400 Saint-Ouen. T. 0140111911. *048623*
Ardif, 136 Av Michelet, 93400 Saint-Ouen. T. 0149450614. *048624*
Arlequin, 136 Av Michelet, 93400 Saint-Ouen. T. 0140111638. *048625*
Art Antic, 142 Rue Rosiers, 93400 Saint-Ouen. T. 0140123251. *048626*
Art Concept, 110 Rue Rosiers, Bâtiment A, Stand 25, 93400 Saint-Ouen. T. 0140111226, Fax 0140118385. *048627*
Art Déco, 110 Rue Rosiers, 93400 Saint-Ouen. T. 0140120283. *048628*
Art Décocom, 142 Rue Rosiers, 93400 Saint-Ouen. T. 0140102014. *048629*
Artcol, 140 Rue Rosiers, 93400 Saint-Ouen. T. 0140128879. *048630*
Artes, 136 Av Michelet, All 8, Stand 173, 93400 Saint-Ouen. T. 0140129899. *048631*
Arts, W., 83 Rue Rosiers, 93400 Saint-Ouen. T. 0140100085. *048632*
Asteix, Christian, 140 Rue Rosiers, Marché Dauphine, Stand 180, 93400 Saint-Ouen. T. 0149450602. *048633*
Au Beau Marché d'Occasions, 1bis Rue Jean-Baptiste-Clément, 93400 Saint-Ouen. T. 0140119351. *048634*
Au Fil des Temps, 85 Rue Rosiers, 93400 Saint-Ouen. T. 0140117777. *048635*
Au Grenier de Lucie, 99 Rue Rosiers, 93400 Saint-Ouen. T. 0140122442. *048636*
Au Petit Mayet, 85 Rue Rosiers, 93400 Saint-Ouen. T. 0140112603. *048637*
Aurélio, 112 Rue Rosiers, 93400 Saint-Ouen. T. 0140122511. *048638*
Autant, Benoît, 85 Rue Rosier, 93400 Saint-Ouen. T. 0140115845. *048639*
Aux Quartiers de France, 8 Rue Lecuyer, 93400 Saint-Ouen. T. 0140122505. *048640*
Aux Trésors Perdus, 99 Rue Rosiers, 93400 Saint-Ouen. T. 0149450732. *048641*
Avner, 85 Rue Rosiers, 93400 Saint-Ouen. T. 0140111923. *048642*
Axana, 134 Rue Rosiers, 93400 Saint-Ouen. T. 0140128777. *048643*
Bachar, Félicita, 85 Rue Rosiers, 93400 Saint-Ouen. T. 0140108357. *048644*
Badaoui, Salima, 110 Rue Rosiers, 93400 Saint-Ouen. T. 0140110632. *048645*
Baillet, Marie-Thérèse, 110 Rue Rosiers, All 5, Stand 24, 93400 Saint-Ouen. T. 0140127743. *048646*
Bakerdjian, 85 Rue Rosiers, 93400 Saint-Ouen. T. 0140112089. *048647*
Balbon, Denise, 136 Av Michelet, 93400 Saint-Ouen. Fax 0140127535. *048648*
Barbanel, Claude, 85 Rue Rosiers, 93400 Saint-Ouen. T. 0140123335. *048649*
Bardot, Stéphane, 142 Rue Rosiers, 93400 Saint-Ouen. T. 0140116178. *048650*
Baroco, 85 Rue Rosiers, 93400 Saint-Ouen. T. 0140120079. *048651*
Barraud, Jean-Pierre, 136 Av Michelet, 93400 Saint-Ouen. T. 0140123809. *048652*

Barre, Dominique, 18 Rue Bons Enfants, 93400 Saint-Ouen. T. 0140115471, Fax 0140101823. *048653*

Barre, Pierre, 103bis Rue Rosiers, 93400 Saint-Ouen. T. 0140102245. *048654*

Barrère, Charles, 136 Av Michelet, All 8, Stand 183, 93400 Saint-Ouen. T. 0140127716. *048655*

Barros, Walfredo de, 136 Av Michelet, 93400 Saint-Ouen. T. 0149450656. *048656*

Bartlett, Michael, 99 Rue Rosiers, 93400 Saint-Ouen. T. 0140108981. *048657*

Bartoli, Louisette, 142 Rue Rosiers, 93400 Saint-Ouen. T. 0140112909, Fax 0140113136. *048658*

Bazin, Patrick, 2 Marché Paul-Bert, Stand 123b, 93400 Saint-Ouen. T. 0140126036. *048659*

Beaucourt, Valérie, 110 Rue Rosiers, 93400 Saint-Ouen. T. 0140120473. *048660*

Belliah, Georges, 1 Marché Paul-Bert, 93400 Saint-Ouen. T. 0140111229. *048661*

Bennazar, Paul, 110 Rue Rosiers, 93400 Saint-Ouen. T. 0140109361. *048662*

Bennazar, Pierre, 110 Rue Rosiers, 93400 Saint-Ouen. T. 0140102936. *048663*

Berdugo, Michel, 136 Av Michelet, 93400 Saint-Ouen. T. 0149450072. *048664*

Besson, Roger, 3 Marché Paul-Bert, 93400 Saint-Ouen. T. 0149450291. *048665*

Beys, Roger, 118 Rue Rosiers, 93400 Saint-Ouen. T. 0140127990, Fax 0140124271. *048666*

Birn, Patricia, 142 Rue Rosiers, 93400 Saint-Ouen. T. 0140129181. *048667*

Biron 75ter, 85 Rue Rosiers, 93400 Saint-Ouen. T. 0140124046. *048668*

Bistrots d'Autrefois, 110 Rue Rosiers, 93400 Saint-Ouen. T. 0140129006. *048669*

Bitoun, Jacques, 85 Rue Rosiers, 93400 Saint-Ouen. T. 0140119654. *048670*

Bodinier, Arlette, 136 Av Michelet, Stand 104bis, 93400 Saint-Ouen. T. 0140108070. *048671*

Boero, Eduardo, 7 Rue Jules-Vallès, Stand 72, 93400 Saint-Ouen. T. 0140121820. *048672*

Bolze, François, 3 Marché Paul-Bert, 93400 Saint-Ouen. T. 0140126075. *048673*

Boîte à Boîtes, 140 Rue Rosiers, 93400 Saint-Ouen. T. 0140127898. *048674*

Bouchet, Guy, 2 Marché Paul-Bert, Stand 40, 93400 Saint-Ouen. T. 0140124024. *048675*

Bouchetard, Catherine, 3 Marché Paul-Bert, Stand 282, 93400 Saint-Ouen. T. 0140115944. *048676*

Bouteloup, Huguette, 85 Rue Rosiers, 93400 Saint-Ouen. T. 0140122408. *048677*

Brick à Barc, 142 Rue Rosiers, 93400 Saint-Ouen. T. 0140113231. *048678*

Bris, Maurice, 85 Rue Rosiers, 93400 Saint-Ouen. T. 0140113230. *048679*

Bruneau, Philippe, 110 Rue Rosiers, All 5, 93400 Saint-Ouen. T. 0140119715. *048680*

Busson, Bernard, 3 Marché Paul-Bert, Stand 165, 93400 Saint-Ouen. T. 0140116791. *048681*

Buzare, Hélène, 140 Rue Rosiers, 93400 Saint-Ouen. T. 0149450363. *048682*

Camus, 5 Rue Eugène-Lumeau, 93400 Saint-Ouen. T. 0140114142, Fax 0140118217. *048683*

Camus, 88 Rue Rosiers, 93400 Saint-Ouen. T. 0140108859, Fax 0140118217. *048684*

Cariatides, 110 Rue Rosiers, 93400 Saint-Ouen. T. 0140101540. *048685*

Carpentier, Jean, 1 Marché Paul-Bert, 93400 Saint-Ouen. T. 0140113330. *048686*

Cassan, Georges-Guillaume, 110 Rue Rosiers, 93400 Saint-Ouen. T. 0140101215. *048687*

Celtill, 142 Rue Rosiers, 93400 Saint-Ouen. T. 0140114270. *048688*

Cervantes, 136 Av Michelet, 93400 Saint-Ouen. T. 0140126989. *048689*

Cervantes, 5 Marché Paul-Bert, Stand 251, 93400 Saint-Ouen. T. 0140113211. *048690*

Chadelaud, Michel, 18 Rue Bons-Enfants, 93400 Saint-Ouen. T. 0149450150, Fax 0140123667. *048691*

Chalbaud, 142 Rue Rosiers, 93400 Saint-Ouen. T. 0140117099. *048692*

Chaumont, Joseph, 85 Rue Rosiers, 93400 Saint-Ouen. T. 0140109375. *048693*

Chauvet, Jean-Paul, 136 Av Michelet, 93400 Saint-Ouen. T. 0140119378. *048694*

Chavanne, Charlotte, 140 Rue Rosiers, 93400 Saint-Ouen. T. 0140113970. *048695*

Chevassus, Lucien, 99 Rue Rosiers, 93400 Saint-Ouen. T. 0140122085. *048696*

Cheyrouse, Axel & Claire, 142 Rue Rosiers, 93400 Saint-Ouen. T. 0140111895. *048697*

Chez Dany, 2 Marché Paul-Bert, Stand 105, 93400 Saint-Ouen. T. 0140111360. *048698*

Chitrit, Marie-Jo, 1 Marché Paul-Bert, 93400 Saint-Ouen. T. 0140129343. *048699*

Chollet, Xavier, 110 Rue Rosiers, 93400 Saint-Ouen. T. 0140122214. *048700*

Choses et Autres Choses, 110 Rue Rosiers, 93400 Saint-Ouen. T. 0140117288. *048701*

Collection's, 142 Rue Rosiers, 93400 Saint-Ouen. T. 0140114767. *048702*

Coridori, Laura, 140 Rue Rosiers, 93400 Saint-Ouen. T. 0149450046. *048703*

Cottreau, Thierry, 140 Rue Rosiers, 93400 Saint-Ouen. T. 0140117271. *048704*

Couderc, Daniel, 140 Rue Rosiers, 93400 Saint-Ouen. T. 0140114290. *048705*

Cougoule-Devergne, Sophie, 111 Rue Docteur-Bauer, 93400 Saint-Ouen. T. 0140120908. *048706*

Cougoule-Devergne, Sophie, 110 Rue Rosiers, 93400 Saint-Ouen. T. 0140124665. *048707*

Couleur du Temps, 136 Av Michelet, All 6, Stand 95, 93400 Saint-Ouen. T. 0140115945. *048708*

Couque, Janine, 142 Rue Rosiers, 93400 Saint-Ouen. T. 0140114898. *048709*

Cuer, Christian, 85 Rue Rosiers, 93400 Saint-Ouen. T. 0140113217. *048710*

Dagommer, Chantal, 1 Marché Paul-Bert, 93400 Saint-Ouen. T. 0140110929. *048711*

Damasse, Charles, 136 Av Michelet, 93400 Saint-Ouen. T. 0140114650. *048712*

Dantan, Maurice, 7 Marché Paul-Bert, Stand 420, 93400 Saint-Ouen. T. 0140112737. *048713*

Darnault, Véronique, 140 Rue Rosiers, Stand 17, 93400 Saint-Ouen. T. 0140127015. *048714*

Daudin, Philippe, 16 Rue Paul-Bert, 93400 Saint-Ouen. T. 0140117722. *048715*

Dauphine International Art 21, 140 Rue Rosiers, 93400 Saint-Ouen. T. 0140119373. *048716*

Déco Bistro, 6 Marché Paul-Bert, Stand 87, 93400 Saint-Ouen. T. 0149450102. *048717*

Delbecque, Roger, Marché Jules-Vallès, 93400 Saint-Ouen. T. 0140108408. *048718*

Delbes, Pierre, 121 Rue Rosiers, 93400 Saint-Ouen. T. 0140115805. *048719*

Delpla, Eric, 3 Marché Paul-Bert, Stand 153, 93400 Saint-Ouen. T. 0149451037. *048720*

Demeter, 6 Marché Paul-Bert, Stand 89, 93400 Saint-Ouen. T. 0149450030. *048721*

Depierre, Rodolphe, 142 Rue Rosiers, 93400 Saint-Ouen. T. 0140126294. *048722*

Deschauwer, Jean-Marie, 140 Rue Rosiers, Stand 37, 93400 Saint-Ouen. T. 0140101619. *048723*

Devot, Céléstin-Henri, 140 Rue Rosiers, 93400 Saint-Ouen. T. 0140114622. *048724*

Disco Puces, 140 Rue Rosiers, 93400 Saint-Ouen. T. 0140119520. *048725*

Drevet, 5 Marché Paul-Bert, Stand 214, 93400 Saint-Ouen. T. 0140119114. *048726*

Dulac, Martine, 26bis Rue Paul-Bert, 93400 Saint-Ouen. T. 0140124330. *048727*

Dupont, 110 Rue Rosiers, 93400 Saint-Ouen. T. 0140108252. *048728*

Dupuy, Martine, 99 Rue Rosiers, 93400 Saint-Ouen. T. 0140120757. *048729*

Eblagon, Jean-Jacques, 17 Rue Pierre-Curie, 93400 Saint-Ouen. T. 0140128550. *048730*

Editions du Père Noël, 140 Rue Rosiers, 93400 Saint-Ouen. T. 0149451134. *048731*

E.D.K., 85 Rue Rosiers, 93400 Saint-Ouen. T. 0140112101. *048732*

El Baz, Patrick, 52 Rue Entrepôts, 93400 Saint-Ouen. T. 0140125642. *048733*

El Sayed Ibrahim, Adel, 26 Rue Voltaire, 93400 Saint-Ouen. T. 0140114977. *048734*

Elcabas, Alain, 115 Rue Rosiers, 93400 Saint-Ouen. T. 0140125522. *048735*

Engler, Fernande, 54 Rue Pasteur, 93400 Saint-Ouen. T. 0140120390. *048736*

Entre Temps, 83 Rue Rosiers, 93400 Saint-Ouen. T. 0140102594. *048737*

Esmeralda, 140 Rue Rosiers, 93400 Saint-Ouen. T. 0140115437. *048738*

Estupina, René, 142 Rue Rosiers, 93400 Saint-Ouen. T. 0140118962. *048739*

Faivre, Marie-Thérèse, 142 Rue Rosiers, 93400 Saint-Ouen. T. 0140119654. *048740*

Favre, Michel, 136 Av Michelet, 93400 Saint-Ouen. T. 0140124265. *048741*

Ferry-Clément, 138 Rue Rosiers, 93400 Saint-Ouen. T. 0140115446. *048742*

Feugère, Isabelle, 140 Rue Rosiers, 93400 Saint-Ouen. T. 0140129350. *048743*

Fidalgo & Frères, 140 Rue Rosiers, 93400 Saint-Ouen. T. 0140100362. *048744*

Finecom, 110 Rue Rosiers, 93400 Saint-Ouen. T. 0140122107. *048745*

Finkel, Michel, 121 Rue Rosiers, 93400 Saint-Ouen. T. 0140117782. *048746*

Fitoussi, Lucien, 20 Rue Bons-Enfants, 93400 Saint-Ouen. T. 0140100570. *048747*

Flajszer, Céline, 142 Rue Rosiers, 93400 Saint-Ouen. T. 0140113649. *048748*

Fortin, Clémence, 110 Rue Rosiers, 93400 Saint-Ouen. T. 0140128740. *048749*

Fortin, Lucien, 110 Rue Rosiers, 93400 Saint-Ouen. T. 0140100243. *048750*

Fourtin, Patrick, 6 Marché Paul-Bert, Stand 81, 93400 Saint-Ouen. T. 0140101787. *048751*

F.P.J.D., 138 Rue Rosiers, 93400 Saint-Ouen. T. 0140127793. *048752*

Franck, 140 Rue Rosiers, 93400 Saint-Ouen. T. 0140127243. *048753*

Franck, 99 Rue Rosiers, 93400 Saint-Ouen. T. 0140118260. *048754*

Gaboriaud, Marc, 110 Rue Rosiers, 93400 Saint-Ouen. T. 0140112692. *048755*

Gaignon, Claude, 85 Rue Rosiers, 93400 Saint-Ouen. T. 0140108681. *048756*

Galai, Pierre, 86 Marché Biron, 93400 Saint-Ouen. T. 0140100658. *048757*

Galerie Christian VIII, 140 Rue Rosiers, 93400 Saint-Ouen. T. 0140122930. *048758*

Galerie Christine, 16 Rue Jules-Vallès, 93400 Saint-Ouen. T. 0140122279. *048759*

Galerie de Beaune, 103 Rue Rosiers, 93400 Saint-Ouen. T. 0140124125. *048760*

Galerie Tourbillon, 136 Av Michelet, 93400 Saint-Ouen. T. 0140129560. *048761*

Galibert, Nicole, 110 Rue Rosiers, All 5, 93400 Saint-Ouen. T. 0149450607. *048762*

Galland, Alain, 110 Rue Rosiers, 93400 Saint-Ouen. T. 0140108563. *048763*

Ganzl, Jacques, 110 Rue Rosiers, 93400 Saint-Ouen. T. 0140109117. *048764*

Garance, 85 Rue Rosiers, 93400 Saint-Ouen. T. 0140117976. *048765*

Garry, 85 Rue Rosiers, 93400 Saint-Ouen. T. 0140100987. *048766*

Gerard, Michel, 99 Rue Rosiers, 93400 Saint-Ouen. T. 0140126733. *048767*

Germand & Fischer, 140 Rue Rosiers, 93400 Saint-Ouen. T. 0140129529. *048768*

Geronimi, Marie, 110 Rue Rosiers, 93400 Saint-Ouen. T. 0140118106. *048769*

Girault, Christiane, 144 Rue Rosiers, 93400 Saint-Ouen. T. 0140114436. *048770*

Gitton, Thierry, 85 Rue Rosiers, 93400 Saint-Ouen. T. 0140115246. *048771*

Glustin, Virginie, 97 Rue Rosiers, 93400 Saint-Ouen. T. 0140122343. *048772*

Goldberg, Henri, 2 Marché Paul-Bert, Stand 115, 93400 Saint-Ouen. T. 0140123892. *048773*

Goldman, Nathalie, 136 Av Michelet, 93400 Saint-Ouen. T. 0140113362. *048774*

Goldmann, Maxime, 138 Rue Rosiers, 93400 Saint-Ouen. T. 0140111538. *048775*

Gomet, Alain, 142 Rue Rosiers, 93400 Saint-Ouen.
T. 0140111675. *048776*
Goulignac, Pascal, 85 Rue Rosiers, 93400 Saint-Ouen.
T. 0140113537. *048777*
Gregorian, 110 Rue Rosiers, 93400 Saint-Ouen.
T. 0140124588. *048778*
Grenier du Louvre, 18 Rue Bons-Enfants, 93400 Saint-Ouen. T. 0140101687. *048779*
Grizot, Cyril, 5 Marché Paul-Bert, 93400 Saint-Ouen.
T. 0140108213. *048780*
Guignard, Gérard, 110 Rue Rosiers, 93400 Saint-Ouen.
T. 0140111785. *048781*
Guignard, Gérard, 140 Rue Rosiers, 93400 Saint-Ouen.
T. 0140126218. *048782*
Guiral de Trenqualie, Elisabeth, 110 Rue Rosiers, 93400 Saint-Ouen. T. 0149450913. *048783*
Guitine, Evelyne, 142 Rue Rosiers, 93400 Saint-Ouen.
T. 0140113734. *048784*
Guy, Claude, 110 Rue Rosiers, 93400 Saint-Ouen.
T. 0140127060. *048785*
Hélène Jordan, 142 Rue Rosiers, 93400 Saint-Ouen.
T. 0140111837. *048786*
Hernandez, Murielle, 136 Av Michelet, 93400 Saint-Ouen. T. 0140109927. *048787*
Hervé, Aline, 136 Av Michelet, 93400 Saint-Ouen.
T. 0140122991. *048788*
Herzog, Christiane, 136 Av Michelet, All 3, Stand 107A, 93400 Saint-Ouen. T. 0140116641. *048789*
Hoffmann, Roland, 85 Rue Rosiers, 93400 Saint-Ouen.
T. 0140128729. *048790*
Homme de Plumme, 142 Rue Rosiers, 93400 Saint-Ouen. T. 0140114933. *048791*
HP, Marché Paul-Bert, All 2, Stand 131, 93400 Saint-Ouen. T. 0140119409. *048792*
Humeurs, 142 Rue Rosiers, 93400 Saint-Ouen.
T. 0140113645. *048793*
Hussard, Jean-Philippe, 110 Rue Rosiers, 93400 Saint-Ouen. T. 0140114255. *048794*
Icône, 138 Rue Rosiers, 93400 Saint-Ouen.
T. 0140113351. *048795*
Ilous, Dominique, 100 Rue Rosiers, 93400 Saint-Ouen.
T. 0140102374. *048796*
Insolite, 136 Av Michelet, 93400 Saint-Ouen.
T. 0140111963. *048797*
International, 59 Rue Rosiers, 93400 Saint-Ouen.
T. 0140108720. *048798*
Iram, 85 Rue Rosiers, 93400 Saint-Ouen.
T. 0140113356, Fax 0140109185. *048799*
Isabelle, 85 Rue Rosiers, 93400 Saint-Ouen.
T. 0140101290. *048800*
J & Jo, 110 Rue Rosiers, 93400 Saint-Ouen.
T. 0140100150. *048801*
Jackie & Jean-Claude, 104 Av Michelet, 93400 Saint-Ouen. T. 0140123666. *048802*
Jackson, 26 Rue Docteur-Bauer, 93400 Saint-Ouen.
T. 0140126033. *048803*
Jacquin, Christiane, 142 Rue Rosiers, 93400 Saint-Ouen. T. 0140113971. *048804*
Jalles, Yves, 136 Av Michelet, 93400 Saint-Ouen.
T. 0140111301. *048805*
James, Dominique, 24 Rue Louis-Dain, 93400 Saint-Ouen. T. 0140115466. *048806*
James, Michel, 136 Av Michelet, 93400 Saint-Ouen.
T. 0140128836. *048807*
Jamin, Laurent, 140 Rue Rosiers, 93400 Saint-Ouen.
T. 0140112406. *048808*
Jonchères, Pierre, 136 Av Michelet, all 7, Stand 65, 93400 Saint-Ouen. T. 0140119459. *048809*
Joscaud, Hugues, 110 Rue Rosiers, 93400 Saint-Ouen.
T. 0140115397. *048810*
Joscaud, Monique, 142 Rue Rosiers, 93400 Saint-Ouen. T. 0140113981. *048811*
Jouen, Daniel, 1 Marché Paul-Bert, 93400 Saint-Ouen.
T. 0140113821. *048812*
Kadrinoff, Alain, Marché Vernaison, 93400 Saint-Ouen.
T. 0140122896. *048813*
Kalfon, Simon, 120 Rue Rosiers, 93400 Saint-Ouen.
T. 0140119311. *048814*
Klein, Michel, 140 Rue Rosiers, 93400 Saint-Ouen.
T. 0140115851. *048815*
Klejman, Edward, 140 Rue Rosiers, 93400 Saint-Ouen.
T. 0140119662. *048816*

Kohn, Francine, 136 Av Michelet, 93400 Saint-Ouen.
T. 0140109336. *048817*
Kolsky, Gisèle, 99 Rue Rosiers, Marché Vernaison, All 1, 93400 Saint-Ouen. T. 0149450755. *048818*
Kuszelevic, Henri, 17 Rue Gambetta, 93400 Saint-Ouen. T. 0140126275. *048819*
Laluque, Claude, 83 Rue Rosiers, 93400 Saint-Ouen.
T. 0140128551. *048820*
Lambrequin, 85 Rue Rosiers, 93400 Saint-Ouen.
T. 0140120771. *048821*
Lapilière, 2 Marché Paul-Bert, Stand26, 93400 Saint-Ouen. T. 0140113204. *048822*
Larousse Trombetta, 85 Rue Rosiers, 93400 Saint-Ouen. T. 0140126851. *048823*
Lasserie, 110 Rue Rosiers, 93400 Saint-Ouen.
T. 0140122019. *048824*
Laurent, B., 140 Rue Rosiers, 93400 Saint-Ouen.
T. 0140128075. *048825*
Laurent, Gisèle, 85 Rue Rosiers, 93400 Saint-Ouen.
T. 0140112599. *048826*
Lavergne, Jean de, 142 Rue Rosiers, 93400 Saint-Ouen. T. 0140113522. *048827*
Lazarovici, Bernard, 140 Rue Rosiers, 93400 Saint-Ouen. T. 0140100046. *048828*
Lazic, Josette, 142 Rue Rosiers, 93400 Saint-Ouen.
T. 0140113804. *048829*
Lazic, Rubens, 136 Av Michelet, 93400 Saint-Ouen.
T. 0140115536. *048830*
Leda, 140 Rue Rosiers, 93400 Saint-Ouen.
T. 0140127488. *048831*
Leday, Yolande, 110 Rue Rosiers, 93400 Saint-Ouen.
T. 0140122651. *048832*
Ledeley, Patrice, 85 Rue Rosiers, 93400 Saint-Ouen.
T. 0140114424. *048833*
Leduc, Sylvia, 99 Rue Rosiers, 93400 Saint-Ouen.
T. 0140101590. *048834*
Lefèvre, Blandine, 85 Rue Rosiers, 93400 Saint-Ouen.
T. 0140122357. *048835*
Lellouche, Abraham, 142 Rue Rosiers, 93400 Saint-Ouen. T. 0140114893. *048836*
Lemay, Yves, 1 Marché Paul-Bert, 93400 Saint-Ouen.
T. 0140126459. *048837*
Lewin, Henri, 3 Marché Paul-Bert, Stand 155, 93400 Saint-Ouen. T. 0140120597. *048838*
Liagre, Bernard, 3 Marché Paul-Bert, 93400 Saint-Ouen. T. 0140101891. *048839*
Luc Antique, 99 Rue Rosiers, All 1, Stand 13, 93400 Saint-Ouen. T. 0140126082. *048840*
Mahé, Gérard, 110 Rue Rosiers, 93400 Saint-Ouen.
T. 0140128122. *048841*
Maison Julien, 136 Av Michelet, 93400 Saint-Ouen.
T. 0140126902. *048842*
Maison Marc, 15 Rue Jules-Vallès, 93400 Saint-Ouen.
T. 0140125228, Fax 0140122647. *048843*
Maison Marc, 18 Rue Bons-Enfants, 93400 Saint-Ouen. T. 0140122776. *048844*
Mape, 85 Rue Rosiers, All 1, Stand 78, 93400 Saint-Ouen. T. 0149451015, Fax 0149451016. *048845*
Maraut, Didier, 11 Rue Docteur-Bauer, 93400 Saint-Ouen. T. 0140109003. *048846*
Marché Biron, 85 Rue Rosiers, 93400 Saint-Ouen.
T. 0140115969, Fax 0140101308. *048847*
Marché des Antiquaires, 46 Rue Jules-Vallès, 93400 Saint-Ouen. T. 0140115966. *048848*
Marché Jules-Vallès, 7 Rue Jules-Vallès, 93400 Saint-Ouen. T. 0140115441. *048849*
Mardfeld, Samuel, 31 Rue Paul-Bert, 93400 Saint-Ouen. T. 0140120332. *048850*
Mardfeld, Samuel, 136 Av Michelet, 93400 Saint-Ouen. T. 0140123371. *048851*
Marnoni, Elisabeth, 80 Rue Rosiers, 93400 Saint-Ouen. T. 0149450203. *048852*
Marugan de Santos, Santi, 83 Rue Rosiers, Marché Biron, Stand 194, 93400 Saint-Ouen.
T. 0140121225. *048853*
Marzet, Claude, 85 Rue Rosiers, 93400 Saint-Ouen.
T. 0140119549. *048854*
Mas Latrie, Jean de, 5 Marché Paul-Bert, 93400 Saint-Ouen. T. 0140102921. *048855*
Masliah, Guy, 85 Rue Rosiers, 93400 Saint-Ouen.
T. 0140126156. *048856*
Mathieu, Alain, 75 Rue Rosiers, 93400 Saint-Ouen.
T. 0140119958. *048857*

Matlis, Bernard, 136 Av Michelet, 93400 Saint-Ouen.
T. 0140119994. *048858*
Mattern, Charles, 7 Marché Paul-Bert, Stand 404, 93400 Saint-Ouen. T. 0140126375. *048859*
Maurielle, 136 Av Michelet, 93400 Saint-Ouen.
T. 0140109137. *048860*
Mazouz, Pascal, 140 Rue Rosiers, 93400 Saint-Ouen.
T. 0140123079. *048861*
M.C. Arts, 140 Rue Rosiers, 93400 Saint-Ouen.
T. 0140128484. *048862*
M.D.M., 6 Marché Paul-Bert, 93400 Saint-Ouen.
T. 0140126190. *048863*
Melis, Antoine, 5 Marché Paul-Bert, 93400 Saint-Ouen.
T. 0149451066. *048864*
Merveilles d'Antan, 40 Rue Jules-Vallès, 93400 Saint-Ouen. T. 0140115364. *048865*
Messager, Michel, 6 Rue Paul-Bert, 93400 Saint-Ouen.
T. 0140121391. *048866*
Meyer, 142 Rue Rosiers, 93400 Saint-Ouen.
T. 0140127074. *048867*
Micoculier, 142 Rue Rosiers, 93400 Saint-Ouen.
T. 0140102858. *048868*
Miechkoup, Léon, 15 Rue Amilcar-Cipriani, 93400 Saint-Ouen. T. 0140121785. *048869*
Milan, Sylvie, 140 Rue Rosiers, Stand 93, 93400 Saint-Ouen. T. 0140129128. *048870*
Minotaure, 140 Rue Rosiers, 93400 Saint-Ouen.
T. 0140102590. *048871*
Montenot, Philippe, 142 Rue Rosiers, 93400 Saint-Ouen. T. 0140114780. *048872*
Morateur, Philippe, 140 Rue Rosiers, 93400 Saint-Ouen. T. 0140120471. *048873*
Mougeot, Julien, 140 Rue Rosiers, 93400 Saint-Ouen.
T. 0140108812. *048874*
Nachtigal, Olivier, 85 Av Michelet, 93400 Saint-Ouen.
T. 0140121891. *048875*
Navon, Gabriel, 99 Rue Rosiers, 93400 Saint-Ouen.
T. 0140125881. *048876*
NPMP Mercure, 2 Marché Paul-Bert, Stand 127, 93400 Saint-Ouen. T. 0140109262. *048877*
O.B.A., 1 Marché Paul-Bert, 93400 Saint-Ouen.
T. 0140127241. *048878*
Ohana, Charles, 140 Rue Rosiers, 93400 Saint-Ouen.
T. 0140128856. *048879*
Olivier-Dythurbide, 110 Rue Rosiers, All 5, Stand 12, 93400 Saint-Ouen. T. 0140128291. *048880*
Opalescences, 136 Av Michelet, 93400 Saint-Ouen.
T. 0140101514. *048881*
Opus 93, 142 Rue Rosiers, 93400 Saint-Ouen.
T. 0140109096. *048882*
Palero, Henri, 83 Rue Rosiers, 93400 Saint-Ouen.
T. 0140128668. *048883*
De la Panneterie, 4 Marché Vernaison, 93400 Saint-Ouen. T. 0140101382. *048884*
Papillon, 4 Marché Paul-Bert, Stand 172, 93400 Saint-Ouen. T. 0140111722. *048885*
Paradis Antique, 142 Rue Rosiers, 93400 Saint-Ouen.
T. 0140124933. *048886*
Parisot, Robert, 30 Rue Lecuyer, 93400 Saint-Ouen.
T. 0140101289. *048887*
Pearon, Michel, 140 Rue Rosiers, 93400 Saint-Ouen.
T. 0140109090. *048888*
Pedezert, Maryse, 4 Marché Paul-Bert, Stand 148, 93400 Saint-Ouen. T. 0140118505. *048889*
Pericoi, Nathalie, 142 Rue Rosiers, 93400 Saint-Ouen.
T. 0140111179. *048890*
Pericoi, Nathalie, 136 Av Michelet, All 8, 93400 Saint-Ouen. T. 0140125151. *048891*
Perruchot, Brigitte, 5 Marché Paul-Bert, Stand 206, 93400 Saint-Ouen. T. 0140100934. *048892*
Peslier, Nicole, 142 Rue Rosiers, 93400 Saint-Ouen.
T. 0140116689. *048893*
Peyre, Jean-Gabriel, 1 Marché Paul-Bert, 93400 Saint-Ouen. T. 0140109200. *048894*
Philippe, Michel, 85 Rue Rosiers, 93400 Saint-Ouen.
T. 0140112777. *048895*
Picot, Jacqueline, 4 Rue Vincent-Palaric, 93400 Saint-Ouen. T. 0140120686. *048896*
Picot, Jacqueline, 140 Rue Rosiers, 93400 Saint-Ouen.
T. 0140125889. *048897*
Pierre, Patrick, 18 Rue Bons-Enfants, 93400 Saint-Ouen. T. 0140108516. *048898*

Piperaud, Pascale, 85 Rue Rosiers, Marché Biron, 93400 Saint-Ouen. T. 0140122692. *048899*

Pistiner, Albert, 85 Rue Rosiers, 93400 Saint-Ouen. T. 0140108432. *048900*

Plaisant, Marie-Thérèse, 142 Rue Rosiers, 93400 Saint-Ouen. T. 0140114882. *048901*

Plantard, Jean-Claude, 1 Marché Paul-Bert, 93400 Saint-Ouen. T. 0140129039. *048902*

Portefaix, Huguette, 85 Rue Rosiers, 93400 Saint-Ouen. T. 0140101340. *048903*

Poustynnikoff, Jacqueline, 142 Rue Rosiers, 93400 Saint-Ouen. T. 0140115098. *048904*

Préférences, 83 Rue Rosiers, 93400 Saint-Ouen. T. 0140116367. *048905*

Preux, Marie-José, 140 Rue Rosiers, 93400 Saint-Ouen. T. 0140114628. *048906*

Prins, Françoise, 59 Rue Rosiers, 93400 Saint-Ouen. Fax (1) 40113183. *048907*

Pytel, Stanislas, 110 Rue Rosiers, 93400 Saint-Ouen. T. 0140101610. *048908*

Quitard, Pierre, Marché Serpette, 110 Rue des Rosiers, Allée 3, Stand 18, 93400 Saint-Ouen. T. 0140100024, Fax 30595205. - Furn / Dec - *048909*

Raspail, Richard, 140 Rue Rosiers, 93400 Saint-Ouen. T. 0140127849. *048910*

Rauzada, Alain, 110 Rue Rosiers, 93400 Saint-Ouen. T. 0140125462. *048911*

Régnier, Jean-Claude, 110 Rue Rosiers, All 2, Stand 4, 93400 Saint-Ouen. T. 0140115606. *048912*

Rémy, Gérald, 138 Rue Rosiers, 93400 Saint-Ouen. T. 0140115561. *048913*

Renaud Inclan, Gisèle, 98 Rue Rosiers, 93400 Saint-Ouen. T. 0140113759. *048914*

Reti, Thomas, 85 Rue Rosiers, 93400 Saint-Ouen. T. 0140124960. *048915*

Reynal, Christophe, 4 Marché Paul-Bert, Stand 227, 93400 Saint-Ouen. T. 0140129077. *048916*

Richard, François, 136 Av Michelet, All 3, Stand 107bis, 93400 Saint-Ouen. T. 0140112913. *048917*

Richard, Renée, 136 Av Michelet, 93400 Saint-Ouen. T. 0140120884. *048918*

Ridder, Thierry, de 85 Rue Rosiers, 93400 Saint-Ouen. T. 0140112838. *048919*

Rizières, 142 Rue Rosiers, 93400 Saint-Ouen. T. 0140128201. *048920*

Roi des Antiquaires, 23 Rue Jules-Vallès, 93400 Saint-Ouen. T. 0140110285. *048921*

Rolland, Roger, 22 Rue Jules-Vallès, 93400 Saint-Ouen. T. 0140114743. *048922*

Rosenthal, Marie-Eve, 110 Rue Rosiers, Stand 11, 93400 Saint-Ouen. T. 0140120485. *048923*

Rudigoz, Céline, 136 Av Michelet, 93400 Saint-Ouen. T. 0140116150. *048924*

Ruiz, Dominique, 3 Rue Paul-Bert, Stand 5, 93400 Saint-Ouen. T. 0140113275. *048925*

Sabatier, Nadine, 85 Rue Rosiers, 93400 Saint-Ouen. T. 0140110724. *048926*

Sabatier, Robert, 87 Rue Rosiers, 93400 Saint-Ouen. T. 0140110524. *048927*

Saguer, Ahmed, 40 Rue Lecuyer, 93400 Saint-Ouen. T. 0140117847. *048928*

Sainsere, Jacqueline, 140 Rue Rosiers, 93400 Saint-Ouen. T. 0140124236. *048929*

Sakr, Charles, 85 Rue Rosiers, All 1, Stand 44, 93400 Saint-Ouen. T. 0140129818. *048930*

Salin, Henri, 136 Av Michelet, All 8, 93400 Saint-Ouen. T. 0140122007. *048931*

Salle des Ventes des Puces, 45 Rue Rosiers, 93400 Saint-Ouen. T. 0140100121. *048932*

Sanchez, Claude, 110 Rue Rosiers, 93400 Saint-Ouen. T. 0140119958. *048933*

Sapet, Christian, 6 Marché Paul-Bert, Stand 81b, 93400 Saint-Ouen. T. 0140122912. *048934*

Sarfati, Odette, 142 Rue Rosiers, Stand 39, 93400 Saint-Ouen. T. 0140112807. *048935*

Sauquet, Jacques, 140 Rue Rosiers, 93400 Saint-Ouen. T. 0140113998. *048936*

Savoir Fer, 110 Rue Rosiers, 93400 Saint-Ouen. T. 0140121358. *048937*

Schneider, Claudie, 142 Rue Rosiers, 93400 Saint-Ouen. T. 0140111309. *048938*

Schwetz, Claude, 85 Rue Rosiers, 93400 Saint-Ouen. T. 0140119874. *048939*

Serres, Christian, 3 Rue Paul-Bert, 93400 Saint-Ouen. T. 0140129765. *048940*

Sicari, Mireille, 85 Rue Rosiers, 93400 Saint-Ouen. T. 0140101429. *048941*

Simonet, Serge, 3 Marché Paul-Bert, Stand 155b, 93400 Saint-Ouen. T. 0140128322. *048942*

Smoker Antiquité, 142 Rue Rosiers, 93400 Saint-Ouen. T. 0140122440. *048943*

Société Gloria, 136 Av Michelet, Marché Vernaison, 93400 Saint-Ouen. T. 0140100262. *048944*

Soret, Philippe, 136 Av Michelet, 93400 Saint-Ouen. T. 0140113525. *048945*

Sourice, Daniel, 18 Rue Bons-Enfants, 93400 Saint-Ouen. T. 0149450776. *048946*

Souyris, Didier, 140 Rue Rosiers, 93400 Saint-Ouen. T. 0140121703. *048947*

Spira, Serge, 7 Marché Vernaison, 93400 Saint-Ouen. T. 0140117431. *048948*

Steinitz, Bernard, 6 Rue Marie-Curie, 93400 Saint-Ouen. T. 0140124761. *048949*

Sterg, A., 85 Rue Rosiers, 93400 Saint-Ouen. T. 0140129327. *048950*

Tempesta Marly, 110 Rue Rosiers, 93400 Saint-Ouen. T. 0140101393. *048951*

Temps et l'Ecrit, 140 Rue Rosiers, 93400 Saint-Ouen. T. 0140128563. *048952*

Tenenbaum, Henri, 99 Rue Rosiers, 93400 Saint-Ouen. T. 0140122355. *048953*

Tétard, Jacques, 136 Av Michelet, 93400 Saint-Ouen. T. 0140112754. *048954*

Themes, Marché Paul-Bert, all 7, Stand 416, 93400 Saint-Ouen. T. 0140113301. *048955*

Thomas, Marie-Thérèse, 142 Rue Rosiers, 93400 Saint-Ouen. T. 0140116694. *048956*

Tourneboeuf, Jean-Claude, 142 Rue Rosiers, 93400 Saint-Ouen. T. 0140114333. *048957*

Tournigand, Yvette, 85 Rue Rosiers, 93400 Saint-Ouen. T. 0140110555. *048958*

Tousaint, Francis, 110 Rue Rosiers, All 3, 93400 Saint-Ouen. T. 0140127945. *048959*

Trouvailles, 7 Rue Jules-Vallès, Marché Jules-Vallès, 93400 Saint-Ouen. T. 0140119070. *048960*

Trouvailles de Théa & Jean-Marc, 136 Av Michelet, 93400 Saint-Ouen. T. 0140118760. *048961*

Turlan, Philippe, 140 Rue Rosiers, 93400 Saint-Ouen. T. 0140122892. *048962*

Turlan, Philippe, 18 Rue Bons-Enfants, 93400 Saint-Ouen. T. 0140101521. *048963*

Valdo, 110 Rue Rosiers, 93400 Saint-Ouen. T. 0140115153. *048964*

Valsyra, 140 Rue Rosiers, 93400 Saint-Ouen. T. 0140117902. *048965*

Van Guygem, Jean-Pierre, 50 Rue Jean-Henri-Fabre, 93400 Saint-Ouen. T. 0140120840. *048966*

Vens, Lucien, 29 Rue Jules-Vallès, 93400 Saint-Ouen. T. 0140108531. *048967*

Verniti, Salvatore, 18ter Rue Lecuyer, 93400 Saint-Ouen. T. 0140123084. *048968*

Verres de nos Grand-Mères, 3 Marché Biron, 93400 Saint-Ouen. T. 0140127219, Fax 0140126513. *048969*

Vidal, Micheline, 110 Rue Rosiers, 93400 Saint-Ouen. T. 0140109370, Fax 0140111213. *048970*

Vieille Epoque, 6 Rue Marceau, 93400 Saint-Ouen. T. 0140117847, Fax 0140111034. *048971*

Vieux Malakoff, 4 Marché Paul-Bert, 93400 Saint-Ouen. T. 0140113755. *048972*

Wayser, Jean, 99 Rue Rosiers, 93400 Saint-Ouen. T. 0140119326. *048973*

Weitz, Dominique, 110 Rue Rosiers, 93400 Saint-Ouen. T. 0140118412. *048974*

Wrobel, Georges, 110 Rue Rosiers, 93400 Saint-Ouen. T. 0149450375. *048975*

Zambakejian, Zohrab, 142 Rue Rosiers, Stand 3r, 93400 Saint-Ouen. T. 0140118608. *048976*

Zelko, Emmanuel, 89 Rue Rosiers, 93400 Saint-Ouen. T. 0140122458. *048977*

Zerline, 142 Rue Rosiers, 93400 Saint-Ouen. T. 0140109251. *048978*

Zoi, Robert, 25 Rue Graviers, 93400 Saint-Ouen. T. 0140119251. *048979*

Saint-Ouen-de-Thouberville (Eure)

Lemaître, La Haizette, 27310 Saint-Ouen-de-Thouberville. T. 0232562237. *048980*

Lemaître d'Estève de Bosch, M.H., La Haizette, 16 Rue Rocques, 27310 Saint-Ouen-de-Thouberville. T. 0232563856, Fax 0232424958. - Furn / China / Fra / Glass - *048981*

Vieille Poste, 118 Rte Nationale, 27310 Saint-Ouen-de-Thouberville. T. 0232565096. - Paint / Graph / Furn / Cur - *048982*

Saint-Ouen-du-Breuil (Seine-Maritime)

Au Dénicheur, La Croix Maltot, 76890 Saint-Ouen-du-Breuil. T. 0235325888. *048983*

Saint-Palais-sur-Mer (Charente-Maritime)

Gouin, Olivier, 93bis Av Ganipote, 17420 Saint-Palais-sur-Mer. T. 0546234511. *048984*

Saint-Parres-aux-Tertres (Aube)

Adonis Antiquités, 28 Rue Gén-de-Gaulle RN 19, 10410 Saint-Parres-aux-Tertres. T. 0325804506. - Ant / Furn - *048985*

Antiquités du Tertre, 67 Av du Général-de-Gaulle, 10410 Saint-Parres-aux-Tertres. T. 0325801417. - Ant / Furn - *048986*

Saint-Paul-en-Jarez (Loire)

Martinez, Hélène, 3 Lot Eglantines, 42320 Saint-Paul-en-Jarez. T. 0477730497. *048987*

Saint-Paul-Trois-Châteaux (Drôme)

Antiquités des Remparts, 6 Rte Garde-Adhémar, 26130 Saint-Paul-Trois-Châteaux. T. 0475967151. *048988*

Saint-Paulet-de-Caisson (Gard)

Lehoucq, Claude, Village, 30130 Saint-Paulet-de-Caisson. T. 0466394503. *048989*

Malbec, 30130 Saint-Paulet-de-Caisson. T. 0466391721. *048990*

Suau, Robert, Quartier Sainte-Agnès, 30130 Saint-Paulet-de-Caisson. T. 0466391712. *048991*

Saint-Paulien (Haute-Loire)

Coudert, Elie, Chemin Lac, 43350 Saint-Paulien. T. 0471004450. *048992*

Marcon, Robert, Pierre Plantée, 43350 Saint-Paulien. T. 0471004352. *048993*

Saint-Péray (Ardèche)

Boucarut, Georges, 31 Rue Ferdinand-Malet, 07130 Saint-Péray. T. 0475403020. - Ant / Cur - *048994*

Charra, Franck, Rd-Pt Pôle 2000, 07130 Saint-Péray. T. 0475405393. - Ant - *048995*

Saint-Pern (Ille-et-Vilaine)

Juette, Christian, Louche, 35190 Saint-Pern. T. 0299667063. *048996*

Saint-Philbert-du-Peuple (Maine-et-Loire)

Antiquités Saint-Vincent, Lande, 49160 Saint-Philbert-du-Peuple. T. 41521002. *048997*

Saint-Pierre-d'Oleron (Charente-Maritime)

Au Grenier Oléronais, RN 734, 17310 Saint-Pierre-d'Oleron. T. 0546473063. *048998*

Buffet du Vieux Temps, Lot Quénole-Bonnemie, 17310 Saint-Pierre-d'Oleron. T. 0546750284. *048999*

Lafon, Josée, Rue Perdriaux-Bonnemie, 17310 Saint-Pierre-d'Oleron. T. 0546470886. *049000*

Saint-Pierre-des-Corps (Indre-et-Loire)

Europ'Occase, Rue Colombier, ZI Yvaudières, 37700 Saint-Pierre-des-Corps. T. 0547443064. *049001*

Saint-Pierre-du-Perray (Essonne)

Douté, Alain, 7 Quai des Platanes, 91280 Saint-Pierre-du-Perray. T. 0160756405. *049002*

Saint-Pierre-Eglise (Manche)

Lutèce Antiquités, 33-37 Rue Calvaire, 50330 Saint-Pierre-Eglise. T. 0233437004. - Furn / Fra / Cur - *049003*

Saint-Pierre-Quiberon (Morbihan)
Beys, Micheline, Rue Clémenceau, 56510 Saint-Pierre-Quiberon. T. 0297308300. - Ant -   *049004*
Francelet-Grosz, Jacqueline, Penthièvre 58 Av Saint-Malo, 56510 Saint-Pierre-Quiberon. T. 0297523273.
- Ant / Graph / Draw -   *049005*

Saint-Pol-de-Léon (Finistère)
Danielou, Léon, Kergompez Rte Clèder, 29250 Saint-Pol-de-Léon. T. 0298690579. - Ant -   *049006*
Stéphan, Monique, 14 Rue Verderel, 29250 Saint-Pol-de-Léon. T. 0298690579. - Ant -   *049007*

Saint-Pourcain-sur-Sioule (Allier)
Malle de Noémie, 23 Blvd Ledru-Rollin, 03500 Saint-Pourcain-sur-Sioule. T. 0470456947. - Ant -   *049008*

Saint-Priest-en-Jarez (Loire)
Boisserenc, Mariane, 24 Rue Voltaire, 42270 Saint-Priest-en-Jarez. T. 0477791338.   *049009*

Saint-Priest-sur-Aixe (Haute-Vienne)
Aurévane, Les Forges, 87700 Saint-Priest-sur-Aixe.
T. 0555702888. - Ant -   *049010*

Saint-Privé (Yonne)
Bougeard, Jean-Paul, Les Creux, 89220 Saint-Privé.
T. 0386749049.   *049011*

Saint-Pryvé-Saint-Mesmin (Loiret)
Casciello, Domenico, 223 Rte Saint-Mesmin, 45750 Saint-Pryvé-Saint-Mesmin. T. 0238519801. - Paint / Furn / Sculp / Cur -   *049012*

Saint-Quay-Portrieux (Côtes-d'Armor)
Mouël Antiquités, 10 Rue Georges-Clemenceau, 22410 Saint-Quay-Portrieux. T. 0296703828.   *049013*
Northcote, Robine, 50 Blvd Général-de-Gaulle, 22410 Saint-Quay-Portrieux. T. 0296705209,
Fax 0296703832.   *049014*

Saint-Quentin (Aisne)
Anthinéa Brocante, 189bis Rue Paris, 02100 Saint-Quentin. T. 0323672471. - Ant -   *049015*
Au Grenier des Michel's, 17 Blvd Cordier, 02100 Saint-Quentin. T. 0323680192. - Ant / Cur -   *049016*
Briatte, Williams, 87 Rue Georges-Pompidou, 02100 Saint-Quentin. T. 0323082431. - Ant -   *049017*
Brocantic, 20 Rue Dachery, 02100 Saint-Quentin.
T. 0323625033. - Ant / Cur -   *049018*
Curios'Art, 23 Rue Sous-Préfecture, 02100 Saint-Quentin. T. 0323670758. - Ant -   *049019*
Fouille Saint-Quentinoise, 70 Chemin Harly, 02100 Saint-Quentin. T. 0323086687. - Ant -   *049020*
Gorlez, Patrice, 14 Rue Gouvernement, 02100 Saint-Quentin. T. 0323621210. - Ant -   *049021*
Grenier de Grand-Mère, 27 Av Faidherbe, 02100 Saint-Quentin. T. 0323626118, Fax 0323626134.
- Ant -   *049022*
Joint, Jacky, 43 Rue Emile-Zola, 02100 Saint-Quentin.
T. 0323647400. - Ant / Cur -   *049023*
Letot, Jean-Paul, 9 Rue Bisson, 02100 Saint-Quentin.
T. 0323642197, Fax 0323648575. - Ant -   *049024*
Lustr Antic, 15 Rue Montmorency, 02100 Saint-Quentin. T. 0323623735. - Lights -   *049025*

Saint-Quentin-Fallavier (Isère)
Bouvier Brocante, Rue Bellevue-le-Furin, 38070 Saint-Quentin-Fallavier. T. 0474945252. - Ant /
Furn -   *049026*

Saint-Quentin-sur-le-Homme (Manche)
Pinson, Joël, Isle-Manière, 50220 Saint-Quentin-sur-le-Homme. T. 0233600454.   *049027*

Saint-Rambert-en-Bugey (Ain)
Ponceblanc, 36 Rue Montferme-Serrière, 01230 Saint-Rambert-en-Bugey. T. 0474363389. - Ant -   *049028*

Saint-Raphaël (Var)
Arstyle, 168 Av Valescure, 83700 Saint-Raphaël.
T. 0494839989.   *049029*
Carlini, Marcel, 175 Quai Albert-1er, 83700 Saint-Raphaël. T. 0494951423.   *049030*
Cassandre, 115 Av Victor-Hugo, 83700 Saint-Raphaël.
T. 0494831171.   *049031*

Piton, J.P., 8 Pl Châteaudun, 83700 Saint-Raphaël.
T. 0494951636. - Ant -   *049032*

Saint-Régis-du-Coin (Loire)
Sauvignet, Hervé, Bourg, 42660 Saint-Régis-du-Coin.
T. 0477518283.   *049033*

Saint-Rémy-lès-Chevreuse (Yvelines)
Bourbonnais, Jean-Louis, 6bis Rue de Port-Royal, 78470 Saint-Rémy-lès-Chevreuse.
T. 0130520578.   *049035*
Riesen, Didier, 7 Rue Victor-Hugo, 78470 Saint-Rémy-lès-Chevreuse. T. 0130529329. - Furn / Cur -   *049036*

Saint-Romain-de-Colbosc (Seine-Maritime)
Bottin, Rte Gommerville, 76430 Saint-Romain-de-Colbosc. T. 0235201838.   *049037*

Saint-Satur (Cher)
Mialane, Raymond, Rue Commerce, 18300 Saint-Satur.
T. 0248541532.   *049038*

Saint-Sauveur (Haute-Saône)
Vivier, Michel, 25 Rue Edouard-Herriot, 70300 Saint-Sauveur. T. 0384401854.   *049039*

Saint-Sauveur-le-Vicomte (Manche)
Lemarchand, Albert, 18 Rue Bottin-Desylles, 50390 Saint-Sauveur-le-Vicomte. T. 0233416644.   *049040*
Lemarchand, Philippe, 2 Rue 8-Mai, 50390 Saint-Sauveur-le-Vicomte. T. 0233951897.   *049041*

Saint-Sébastien-sur-Loire (Loire-Atlantique)
Mignot, 405 Rte Clisson, 44230 Saint-Sébastien-sur-Loire. T. 40031217. - Paint / Furn / Cur -   *049042*

Saint-Senier-sous-Avranches (Manche)
Leprovost, Claude, D 47, 50300 Saint-Senier-sous-Avranches. T. 0233586623.   *049043*

Saint-Sever (Landes)
Loupret, Patrick, Rue du Bellocq, 40500 Saint-Sever.
T. 0558762449. - Paint / Furn / Cur -   *049044*

Saint-Sever-Calvados (Calvados)
Lebouteiller, Joël, Pl Albert-Lebrun, 14380 Saint-Sever-Calvados. T. 0231689451. - Furn -   *049045*

Saint-Siffret (Gard)
Subtil, Williams, Mas Chazel, Chemin Devois, 30700 Saint-Siffret. T. 0466220114.   *049046*

Saint-Simon (Cantal)
Magne, René, 2 Lot Les Sources, Rte Cretes, 15130 Saint-Simon. T. 0471471064.   *049047*

Saint-Simon-de-Bordes (Charente-Maritime)
Labrouche, Arnaud, 40 Rue Arnaudeaux, 17500 Saint-Simon-de-Bordes. T. 0546484624.   *049048*

Saint-Sozy (Lot)
Jauberthie, Alain, Mas Rambert, 46200 Saint-Sozy.
T. 0565322675.   *049049*

Saint-Sulpice (Tarn)
Caussignac, Jean-Claude, 1 Rue Sicard-d'Alaman, 81370 Saint-Sulpice. T. 0563401182.   *049050*
Picart, Jean, 27 Pl Eglise, 81370 Saint-Sulpice.
T. 0563418323.   *049051*

Saint-Sulpice-de-Favières (Essonne)
Causse, Georges, 7 Rue Fèves, 91910 Saint-Sulpice-de-Favières. T. 0164586297.   *049052*

Saint-Sulpice-sur-Risle (Orne)
Ayme, Janine, Le Bois-Aulard, 61300 Saint-Sulpice-sur-Risle. T. 0233241554. - Ant -   *049053*
Ventillard, Michel, 9 Anglures, 61300 Saint-Sulpice-sur-Risle. T. 0233241323. - Ant -   *049054*

Saint-Symphorien (Deux-Sèvres)
Grenier de Bel Air, Ferme de Bel Air, 79270 Saint-Symphorien. T. 0549095103.   *049055*

Saint-Théodorit (Gard)
Roussel, Yves, Lauzette, 30260 Saint-Théodorit.
T. 0466774001.   *049056*

Saint-Trojan-les-Bains (Charente-Maritime)
Elman, Marcelle, Pl Filles de la-Sagesse, 17370 Saint-Trojan-les-Bains. T. 0546761257.   *049057*

Saint-Tropez (Var)
Bagheera, 10 Rue Clocher, 83990 Saint-Tropez.
T. 0494549767, Fax 0494975968. - Ant / Paint /
Mod -   *049058*
Boccador, Jacqueline, 6 Rue Commandant-Guichard, 83990 Saint-Tropez. T. 0494976157. - Furn / Sculp /
Tex -   *049059*
Château Suffren, Pl Mairie, 83990 Saint-Tropez.
T. 0494978515. - Dec -   *049060*
Dumas, Robert, 12 Rue Général-Allard, 83990 Saint-Tropez. T. 0494975893, Fax 0494976895.   *049061*
Fauré, Johane, 18 Rue Citadelle, 83990 Saint-Tropez.
T. 0494977645.   *049062*
Flibusterie, 12 Rue Clocher, 83990 Saint-Tropez.
T. 0494976476. - Paint / Cur / Naut -   *049063*
Francine, 3 Rue F.-Sibilli, Pl de la Garonne, 83990 Saint-Tropez. T. 0494548126. - Jew -   *049064*
Fulcrand, Jacqueline, 5 Rue Sibille, 83990 Saint-Tropez. T. 0494970739. - Paint / Furn -   *049065*
Galerie Suffren, Le Byblo, B4, Av Foch, 83990 Saint-Tropez. T. 0494971980, Fax 0494977598.   *049066*
Garelli, Henri, 8 Rue Clocher, 83990 Saint-Tropez.
T. 0494975510. - Ant / Dec -   *049067*
Girandole, 32 Rue Gambetta, 83990 Saint-Tropez.
T. 0494974561. - Furn / China / Glass -   *049068*
Pigeot, J.M., 8 Rue Etienne-Berny, 83990 Saint-Tropez.
T. 0493387479. - Sculp -   *049069*
Poulideto, 6 Rue Cépoun-Sanmartin, 83990 Saint-Tropez. T. 0494972627, Fax 0494971064. - Ant / Paint /
Cur / Mod -   *049070*
Robichon, François, 8 Rue Commandant-Guichard, 83990 Saint-Tropez. T. 0494970350. - Paint /
Furn -   *049071*
Selli, Daniel, 14 Rue Général-Allard, 83990 Saint-Tropez. T. 0494977327.   *049072*
Style et Décor, 11 Av Foch, 83990 Saint-Tropez.
T. 0494976286, Fax 0494976914. - Furn /
Dec -   *049073*
Suffren, Av Maréchal-Foch, 83990 Saint-Tropez.
T. 0494971980. - Ant / Paint / Furn -   *049074*
Thiénot, Jacqueline, 12 Rue Georges-Clémenceau, 83990 Saint-Tropez. T. 0494970570. - Ant / Furn /
China -   *049075*
Wagner, Corinne, 14 Rue Commandant-Guichard, 83990 Saint-Tropez. T. 0494978583. - Paint / Furn -   *049076*

Saint-Urbain (Vendée)
Antiquités Le Plessis, Le Plessis, 85230 Saint-Urbain.
T. 0251490848.   *049077*

Saint-Uze (Drôme)
Tracol, Roger, Quart Combe-Tourmente, 26240 Saint-Uze. T. 0475032582.   *049078*

Saint-Valery-en-Caux (Seine-Maritime)
Diarra, Françoise, 24 Pl Chapelle, 76460 Saint-Valery-en-Caux. T. 0235573902.   *049079*

Saint-Victor-l'Abbaye (Seine-Maritime)
Beaupuis, Hubert de, RN 29, 76890 Saint-Victor-l'Abbaye. T. 0235326889.   *049080*

Saint-Victor-sur-Rhins (Loire)
Mercade, Richard, Rte Roanne, 42630 Saint-Victor-sur-Rhins. T. 0474640957.   *049081*

Saint-Vincent-de-Tyrosse (Landes)
Minjon, Jeannine, 4 Rue Fontaines, 40230 Saint-Vincent-de-Tyrosse. T. 0558773979.   *049082*

Saint-Vincent-Sterlanges (Vendée)
Fallourd, Claude, 30 Rue Nationale, 85110 Saint-Vincent-Sterlanges. T. 0251402696,
Fax 0251402001.   *049083*

Saint-Vincent-sur-Graon (Vendée)
Allsop, Nicholas, La Grange, Le Champ Hydreau, 85540 Saint-Vincent-sur-Graon. T. 0251314316. *049084*

Saint-Vit (Doubs)
Atelier, 7bis Rue Besançon, 25410 Saint-Vit.
T. 0381877983. *049085*
Aux Charmes d'Antan, 7bis Rue Besançon, 25410 Saint-Vit. T. 0381876230. *049086*
C.K.M., 3 Rue Besançon, 25410 Saint-Vit.
T. 0381876132. *049087*
Escabelle, 6 Rue Besançon, 25410 Saint-Vit.
T. 0381877772. *049088*
Jacquot, Christian, 7bis Rue Besançon, 25410 Saint-Vit.
T. 0381876174. *049089*
Née, Jean-Luc, 7bis Rue Besançon, 25410 Saint-Vit.
T. 0381876198. *049090*
Putod, Jean-Michel, 7ter Rue Besançon, 25410 Saint-Vit. T. 0381875026. *049091*
Raunet, Jean-Louis, 46 Av Dôle, 25410 Saint-Vit.
T. 0381875587. *049092*
Sthely, Joseph, 7bis Rue Besançon, 25410 Saint-Vit.
T. 0381876225. *049093*

Saint-Vrain (Essonne)
Au Passé Rose, 6 Pl Eglise, 91770 Saint-Vrain.
T. 0164560811. - Paint / Furn / Cur - *049094*

Saint-Yrieix-sous-Aixe (Haute-Vienne)
Jouhate, Annette, Le Gué-de-la-Roche, 87420 Saint-Yrieix-sous-Aixe. T. 0555038306. - Ant / Paint /
Furn - *049095*

Saint-Yrieix-sur-Charente (Charente)
Duguet, Claude, Rte Bellevue, 16710 Saint-Yrieix-sur-Charente. T. 0545382840. *049096*

Sainte-Adresse (Seine-Maritime)
Pavillon de la Brocante, 36 Rte Octeville, 76310 Sainte-Adresse. T. 0235460581. *049097*

Sainte-Agathe-la-Bouteresse (Loire)
Madaire, Thierry, La Bouteresse, 42130 Sainte-Agathe-la-Bouteresse. T. 0477241690. *049098*

Sainte-Bazeille (Lot-et-Garonne)
Gajac, Daniel, 38 Av Général-de-Gaulle, 47200 Sainte-Bazeille. T. 0553944992. *049099*
Galerie Saint-Pierre, 20bis Av Général-de-Gaulle, 47200 Sainte-Bazeille. T. 0553943202. *049100*

Sainte-Catherine-lès-Arras (Pas-de-Calais)
A la Croix de Grès, 27 Rte Nationale, 62223 Sainte-Catherine-lès-Arras. T. 0321513833. - Furn /
Cur - *049101*
Campagne, Yves, 12 Résidence Les Genets, 62223 Sainte-Catherine-lès-Arras. T. 0321511411. - Ant /
Furn / Cur - *049102*
Sauriaux, 129 Rte Nationale Lens, 62223 Sainte-Catherine-lès-Arras. T. 0321711287. *049103*
Torris Barrois, Marc-André, 27 Rte Nationale Lens, 62223 Sainte-Catherine-lès-Arras.
T. 0321513833. *049104*

Sainte-Croix-en-Jarez (Loire)
Delorme, Noëlie-Christiane, Bourg, 42800 Sainte-Croix-en-Jarez. T. 0477202181. *049105*

Sainte-Enimie (Lozère)
Causse, Henri, Rue Serre, 48210 Sainte-Enimie.
T. 0466485005. *049106*

Sainte-Foy-la-Grande (Gironde)
Pierson, Pat, 116 Rue République, 33220 Sainte-Foy-la-Grande. T. 0557460354. *049107*

Sainte-Gemme-la-Plaine (Vendée)
Dépôt-Vente de Vendée, Les Quatre Chemins, 85400 Sainte-Gemme-la-Plaine. T. 0251270055. *049108*
P'tite Vendée, RN 137, Les Quatre Chemins, 85400 Sainte-Gemme-la-Plaine. T. 0251270267. *049109*

Sainte-Geneviève-des Bois (Essonne)
Aux Bons Choix, 63 Av Georges-Pitard, 91700 Sainte-Geneviève-des Bois. T. 0160164256. *049110*

Aux Puces de Sainte-Geneviève, 1 Pl Franklin-Roosevelt, 91700 Sainte-Geneviève-des Bois.
T. 0169460054. *049111*
Flash-Mod, 171 Rte Corbeil, 91700 Sainte-Geneviève-des Bois. T. 0160151970. *049112*

Sainte-Hermine (Vendée)
Faucher-Touvron, Brigitte, 26 Rte La Rochelle, 85210 Sainte-Hermine. T. 0251978130. *049113*

Sainte-Marie-du-Mont (Manche)
Martelot, Gisèle, Rte Carentan, 50480 Sainte-Marie-du-Mont. T. 0233715717. *049114*

Sainte-Maxime (Var)
Antiquités de l'Assomption, 1bis Montée du Sémaphore, 83120 Sainte-Maxime. T. 0494962089.
- Furn - *049115*
Au Grenier de Beauvallon, RN 98, Beauvallon, 83120 Sainte-Maxime. T. 0494438892. *049116*
Girardet, Jacqueline, 6 Ancien-Chemin-Guerrevieille, Beauvallon, 83120 Sainte-Maxime. T. 0494961610.
- Paint / Furn - *049117*
Tournebize, Guy, 3 Chemin Cigales, 83120 Sainte-Maxime. T. 0494963101. *049118*

Sainte-Menehould (Marne)
Caniga, Daniel, 16 Rte Verdun, 51800 Sainte-Menehould. T. 0326607425. *049119*
Clergiot, Georges, 65 Rte Nationale, Grange aux Bois, 51800 Sainte-Menehould. T. 0326608687. *049120*
Clergiot, Michel, 67 Rte Nationale, Grange aux Bois, 51800 Sainte-Menehould. T. 0326608563. *049121*

Sainte-Mesme (Yvelines)
Atelier d'Alban, 10 Rue Charles-Legaigneur, 78730 Sainte-Mesme. T. 0130594759. *049122*

Sainte-Montaine (Cher)
Champion, Thierry, Pl Eglise, 18700 Sainte-Montaine.
T. 0248581520. *049123*

Sainte-Pience (Manche)
Morin, Le Parc, 50870 Sainte-Pience.
T. 0233481013. *049124*
Morin, Jean-Yves, Le Parc, 50870 Sainte-Pience.
T. 0233481013. *049125*

Sainte-Savine (Aube)
Agora Patrick Lorne, 130 Av Général-Leclerc, 10300 Sainte-Savine. T. 0325740292, Fax 0325794163.
- Ant / Dec - *049126*
Il Etait Une Fois, 8 Rue Dumont-d'Urville, 10300 Sainte-Savine. T. 0325790413. - Ant / Instr - *049127*
Mariantiquités, 18 Av Général-Leclerc, 10300 Sainte-Savine. T. 0325793279. - Ant / Furn / Jew - *049128*
Pautras Brocante, 148bis Av Galliéni, 10300 Sainte-Savine. T. 0325791928. - Ant / Cur - *049129*

Saintes (Charente-Maritime)
Antiquités La Musardière, 29 Rue Alsace-Lorraine, 17100 Saintes. T. 0546930556. - Paint / Furn / China /
Sculp / Lights / Glass / Cur / Toys / Music - *049130*
Anzemberg, 2 Pl Synode, 17100 Saintes.
T. 0546933138. *049131*
Berthelot, 4 Pl Echevinage, 17100 Saintes.
T. 0546932755. - Ant / Paint / Furn / Cur - *049132*
Brocanteur, 2 Rue Alsace-Lorraine, 17100 Saintes.
T. 0546950555. - Ant / Furn - *049133*
Galerie du Cloître Saint-Pierre, 24 Rue Georges-Clemenceau, 17100 Saintes. T. 0546930819. *049134*
Guillory, Philippe, 4 Rue Georges-Clemenceau, 17100 Saintes. T. 0546931472. *049135*
Noël, Jean-Luc, 1 Rue Comédie, 17100 Saintes.
T. 0546742152. *049136*
Toujouse, Jean-Yves, 25 Rue Saint-Michel, 17100 Saintes. T. 0546933641. - Dec - *049137*

Salbris (Loir-et-Cher)
Hussenot-Desenonges, Bruno, 42 Blvd République, 41300 Salbris. T. 0254970243. *049138*

Salers (Cantal)
Delsol, Jeanine, Rue Beffroi, 15140 Salers.
T. 0471407520. - Paint / Furn / China - *049139*

Salins-les-Bains (Jura)
Depôt Vente Salinois, 14 Rue Orgemont, 39110 Salins-les-Bains. T. 0384379027. *049140*

Sallanches (Haute-Savoie)
A la Belle Epoque, 24 Rte Fayet, 74700 Sallanches.
T. 0450585461. - Paint / Furn / Cur - *049141*
Aux 3 Siècles, 68 Av Genève, 74700 Sallanches.
T. 0450937548, Fax 0450939716. - Graph / Furn / Cur /
Draw - *049142*

Salles-Adour (Hautes-Pyrénées)
Antiquités Brocantine, Imp Iris, 65360 Salles-Adour.
T. 0562453082. - Ant - *049143*

Salon-de-Provence (Bouches-du-Rhône)
Alivon, André, 182 Blvd Capucins, 13300 Salon-de-Provence. T. 0490536598. *049144*
Antique Art, 37 Cours Gimon, 13300 Salon-de-Provence. T. 0490562298. *049145*
Font d'Arles, 3 Rue Horloge, 13300 Salon-de-Provence.
T. 0490565106. *049146*
Troc Salonais, Av Emile-Zola, 13300 Salon-de-Provence. T. 0490566920. *049147*

Saméon (Nord)
Copie d'Ange, 420 Rue du Vieux-Condé, 59310 Saméon.
T. 0320615818. - Ant - *049148*
Restor Bois, 420 Rue Vieux-Condé, 59310 Saméon.
T. 0320615818. - Ant - *049149*

Sampans (Jura)
Damongeot, 9 Rte Dijon, 39100 Sampans.
T. 0384823559. - Furn - *049150*

Sampigny (Meuse)
Broc Line Lainet, Rue Raymond-Poincaré, 55300 Sampigny. T. 0329907515. - Ant / Furn - *049151*

Sanary-sur-Mer (Var)
Bisogno, Denis, 194 Ancien Chemin de Toulon, 83110 Sanary-sur-Mer. T. 0494881037. *049152*
Crouzet, 24 Rue Marcellin-Siat, 83110 Sanary-sur-Mer.
T. 0494883788. - Furn / China - *049153*
Grand Bazar, 194 Ancien Chemin de Toulon, 83110 Sanary-sur-Mer. T. 0494347884, Fax 0494881034.
- Ant - *049154*
Jadis, 2 Rue Laget, 83110 Sanary-sur-Mer.
T. 0494746606. - Jew / Silv - *049155*
Limousin, M., 269 Av Joseph-Lautier, 83110 Sanary-sur-Mer. T. 0494883115. - Ant - *049156*
Relais d'Antan, 8 Imp Prud'Homie, 83110 Sanary-sur-Mer. T. 0494880618. *049157*
Vert Céladon, 20 Rue Barthélémy-de-Don, 83110 Sanary-sur-Mer. T. 0494881901. *049158*

Sannerville (Calvados)
Chereau, Jacques, 3 Rue Maréchal-Leclerc, 14940 Sannerville. T. 0231237730. - Paint / Furn / Cur - *049159*

Santans (Jura)
Sintot, 30 Rue Principale, 39380 Santans.
T. 0384717193. - Furn - *049160*

Saou (Drôme)
Brocante de l'Houme, L'Houme, 26400 Saou.
T. 0475760434. *049161*

Sarlat-la-Canéda (Dordogne)
Barrière, Marie-Luce, Pl Cathédrale, 24200 Sarlat-la-Canéda. T. 0553590484. *049162*
Bennati, Michel, Montfort, Roc Laumier, 24200 Sarlat-la-Canéda. T. 0553591716. - Ant - *049163*
Galerie Fénelon, 1 Rue Fénelon, 24200 Sarlat-la-Canéda. T. 0553592862. *049164*
Gendre, Michel, 4 Rue Fénelon, 24200 Sarlat-la-Canéda. T. 0553298642. *049165*
Hutin, Renaud, 40bis Av Thiers, 24200 Sarlat-la-Canéda. T. 0553312008. *049166*
Perrin, Alain, Les Presses, 24200 Sarlat-la-Canéda.
T. 0553312092. *049167*
Sarlat, 1 Rue Présidial, 24200 Sarlat-la-Canéda.
T. 0553302000. *049168*
Zalacain, Jean-François, Rue Lakanal, 24200 Sarlat-la-Canéda. T. 0553311152. *049169*

Sarrancolin (Hautes-Pyrénées)
Badia, Simone, Quart Ville, 65410 Sarrancolin.
T. 0562987716. - Ant - *049170*

Sarrebourg (Moselle)
Art et Troc, Rte Imling, RN 4, 57400 Sarrebourg.
T. 0387034593. *049171*
Grenier, 7 Rue Marne, 57400 Sarrebourg.
T. 0387033000. *049172*

Sarreguemines (Moselle)
A la Belle Epoque, 8 Rue Bac, 57200 Sarreguemines.
T. 0387957065. *049173*
Jadis, 6 Rue Verdun, 57200 Sarreguemines.
T. 0387986204. *049174*
Tarall, Henri, 74 Rue France, 57200 Sarreguemines.
T. 0387984046. *049175*

Sartrouville (Yvelines)
Bezzina, Marcel, 1 Rue Colonel-Manhes, 78500 Sartrou-
ville. T. 0130574698. *049176*
Debussy, 36 Rue René-Brulay, 78500 Sartrouville.
T. 0139142605. *049177*

Sarzeau (Morbihan)
Antique Importeurs, Tréhiat, 56370 Sarzeau.
Fax 97413914. - Ant - *049178*
Le Boulicaut, Henri, Bourg-Saint-Colombier, 56370 Sar-
zeau. T. 0297264114. - Ant - *049179*
Quinio, Margot, Rte Golfe-le-patis-du-Neret, 56370 Sar-
zeau. T. 0297417889. - Ant / Furn - *049180*
Recherche du Passé, Saint-Colombier, 56370 Sarzeau.
T. 0297264150, Fax 0297264529. - Graph - *049181*

Saujon (Charente-Maritime)
Bacon & Cie, 23 Rue Pierre-de-Campet, 17600 Saujon.
T. 0546028235. *049182*

Saulieu (Côte-d'Or)
Audigier, Georges, 33 Rue Courtepée, 21210 Saulieu.
T. 0380640776. *049183*

Sault (Vaucluse)
Vakanas, Lucien, Av Résistance, 84390 Sault.
T. 0490641166, Fax 0490641182. - Ant - *049184*

Saumur (Maine-et-Loire)
Baury, Raymond, 12 Imp Antoine-Poitou, 49400 Saumur.
T. 41501250. *049185*
Beaumont, Jean, 638 Rue Lamartine, 49400 Saumur.
T. 41672093. *049186*
Bur, Richard, 55 Rue Orléans, 49400 Saumur.
T. 41511959. *049187*
Davy, Michel, 1179 Rue Moulins, 49400 Saumur.
T. 41511254. *049188*
Dépôt-Vente Saumurois, Blvd Benjamin-Delessert,
49400 Saumur. T. 41676646. - Furn / Cur - *049189*
Douillard, Frédéric, 39 Rue Saint-Nicolas, 49400 Sau-
mur. T. 41512168. *049190*
Gautron, Kostia, 87 Rue Orléans, 49400 Saumur.
T. 41513492. *049191*

Saussey (Manche)
Langelier, Jacques, Manoir, 50200 Saussey.
T. 0233451965. *049192*

Sauveterre (Gard)
Monastère de Four, Ham Four, 30150 Sauveterre.
T. 0466826094. *049193*
Vielh-Vernet, Suzette, Av Provence, 30150 Sauveterre.
T. 0466825867. *049194*

Sauveterre-de-Guyenne (Gironde)
Depaire, Alain, 2 Au Closet, 33540 Sauveterre-de-
Guyenne. T. 0556718044. - Instr - *049195*

Sauzet (Drôme)
Maccagnoni, Nadine, Quart Pont-Vert, 26740 Sauzet.
T. 0475461964. *049196*

Savenay (Loire-Atlantique)
Robin, Jean, 10 Blvd Acacias, 44260 Savenay.
T. 40569212. - Pho - *049197*

Saverdun (Ariège)
Peyrègne, Patrick, 18 Rue Croix-Blanche, 09700 Saver-
dun. T. 0561678242. *049198*

Saverne (Bas-Rhin)
Saverne, 27 Rue Saint-Nicolas, 67700 Saverne.
T. 0388916636. *049199*

Savigneux (Loire)
Gauchet, Gérard, Les Jacquins, 42600 Savigneux.
T. 0477586341. *049200*

Savigny-sur-Ardres (Marne)
Passé Composé, 1 Imp Puits-Gras, 51140 Savigny-sur-
Ardres. T. 0326974086. - Ant / Furn / Cur - *049201*

Savigny-sur-Orge (Essonne)
Allo Broc, 16 Rue Victor-Hugo, 91600 Savigny-sur-Orge.
T. 0169243844. - Ant - *049202*
Tétard, Jacques, 22 Rue Coteau, 91600 Savigny-sur-Or-
ge. T. 0169968923. *049203*

Savonnières (Indre-et-Loire)
Prieuré des Granges, 15 Rue Fontaines, 37510 Savon-
nières. T. 0547500967. *049204*

Saxon-Sion (Meurthe-et-Moselle)
Duchatel, Nicolas, 3 Rue Georges-Berger, 54330 Saxon-
Sion. T. 0383251052. *049205*

Sceaux (Hauts-de-Seine)
Dana, Emile, 10 Rue Jean-Giraudoux, 92330 Sceaux.
T. 0147027490. *049206*
Galerie, Florian, 18 Rue Ecoles, 92330 Sceaux.
T. 0146615410. *049207*
Temps Retrouvé, 1 Rue Marguerite-Renaudin, 92330
Sceaux. T. 0147026576. *049208*

Scharrachbergheim (Bas-Rhin)
Antiquité du Bâtiment, 15 Rue Principale, 67310 Schar-
rachbergheim. T. 0388506245,
Fax 0388506333. *049209*

Sciez (Haute-Savoie)
Fauvergue, Arnaud, RN 5, Bonnatrait, 74140 Sciez.
T. 0450725808. - Furn / Dec - *049210*

Sébécourt (Eure)
Boulet, Jean-Claude, La Haisette, 27190 Sébécourt.
T. 0232309551, Fax 0232300870. *049211*

Seclin (Nord)
Wimtetz, Yves, 11 Blvd Hentges, 59113 Seclin.
T. 0320326822. - Ant - *049212*

Sedan (Ardennes)
François Antiquités, 48 Av Stackler, 08200 Sedan.
T. 0324275920. - Ant / Furn - *049213*
Gilardi, Edith, 19 Av du Maréchal-Leclerc, 08200 Sedan.
T. 0324261793. - Ant - *049214*

Sées (Orne)
Graindorge, Jacky, Fontaineriant, 61500 Sées.
T. 0233270678. - Ant - *049215*
Huvé, Philippe, 7 Pl de-Gaulle, 61500 Sées.
T. 0233278121. - Ant - *049216*
Meuble Normands, 18 Rue Aristide-Briand, 61500 Sées.
T. 0233311204. - Ant - *049217*

Segré (Maine-et-Loire)
Delaune, Francis, 45 Rue Lamartine, 49500 Segré.
T. 41611379. *049218*

Seichamps (Meurthe-et-Moselle)
François, Claudine, 3bis Pl Eglise, 54280 Seichamps.
T. 0383290174. *049219*

Seiches-sur-le-Loir (Maine-et-Loire)
Grenier Seichois, 72 Rue Nationale, 49140 Seiches-sur-
le-Loir. T. 41766042. *049220*

Seilhac (Corrèze)
Ronde des Objets, Chez Charrière, 19700 Seilhac.
T. 0555279719. *049221*

Sélestat (Bas-Rhin)
Antiquités-Brocante, 3 Rue Dorlan, 67600 Sélestat.
T. 0388828431. *049222*

Selles-sur-Cher (Loir-et-Cher)
Achat Centrale d'Antiquités, 4 Rue Saint-Roche, 41130
Selles-sur-Cher. T. 0254976378. *049223*

Seloncourt (Doubs)
Autrefois, 120 Rue Général-Leclerc, 25230 Seloncourt.
T. 0381370288. *049224*

Selongey (Côte-d'Or)
Jardin aux Souvenirs, 5 Quai Garnier, 21260 Selongey.
T. 0380755541. *049225*

Séméries (Nord)
Brotonne, Didier, 2 Imp Harcelles, 59291 Séméries.
T. 0327598498. - Ant - *049226*

Semur-en-Auxois (Côte-d'Or)
Diebold, Pascal, 4 Rue Liberté, 21140 Semur-en-Auxois.
T. 0380970862. - Furn - *049227*
Père, 13 Rue Paris, 21140 Semur-en-Auxois.
T. 0380970251. *049228*

Sénas (Bouches-du-Rhône)
Hugues, Gérard, 21bis Av Gabriel-Péri, 13560 Sénas.
T. 0490590243. *049229*

Séné (Morbihan)
Chevalley, 47 Rte Nantes, 56860 Séné. T. 0297475999.
- Furn - *049230*

Senlis (Oise)
Caussin, Mireille, 14 Rue Beauvais, 60300 Senlis.
T. 0344533001. - Ant - *049231*
Gestions d'Intérêts Privés, Rue Petit-Chaâlis, 60300
Senlis. Fax 44536231. - Ant - *049232*
Haustrate, David, 8 Rue République, 60300 Senlis.
T. 0344537971. - Ant - *049233*
Lemoine de Formanoir, Yves, 6 Pl Notre-Dame, 60300
Senlis. T. 0344530674. - Ant - *049234*

Senon (Meuse)
Becq, Pierre, 55230 Senon. T. 0329859817. - Ant /
Mil - *049235*

Sens (Yonne)
A l'Arbre de Jessé, 11 Rue République, 89100 Sens.
T. 0386653876. *049236*
A la Dauphine, 22 Pl de la République, 89100 Sens.
T. 0386650439. - Ant - *049237*
Au Bonheur du Jour, 17 Rue Pépinière, 89100 Sens.
T. 0386644200. *049238*
Condemine, Annie, 12 Blvd Garibaldi, 89100 Sens.
T. 0386954525. *049239*
Darracq, Alain, 62 RN 6, 89100 Sens.
T. 0386979185. *049240*
Mathé, Monique & Jean, 3 Blvd Maréchal-Foch, 89100
Sens. T. 0386656826. - Ant - *049241*
Pigot, Jean-Michel, 6bis Rue Sinson, 89100 Sens.
T. 0386652355. *049242*
Pizon, Brigitte, 13 Rue Binet, 89100 Sens.
T. 0386641811. - Paint / Furn / Sculp / Jew / Silv / Cur /
Toys - *049243*
Poterne Garnier des Prés, 21 Blvd du 14 Juillet, 89100
Sens. T. 0386651138. - Ant / Paint / Furn - *049244*
Saulnier, Régine, 104 Rue Emile Zola, 89100 Sens.
T. 0386651291. - Ant - *049245*
Serrurier, Jean Luc, 48 Blvd 14-Juillet, 89100 Sens
T. 0386640173. *049246*
Serrurier, Jean-Luc, 11 Rue République, 89100 Sens.
T. 0386655848. *049247*
Serrurier, Pierre, 21 Blvd 14-Juillet, 89100 Sens.
T. 0386651138. - Furn - *049248*
Taby, Paul, 8 Rue Trois-Croissants, 89100 Sens.
T. 0386644480. *049249*

Septeuil (Yvelines)
Cheval Blanc, 6 Pl Verdun, 78790 Septeuil.
T. 0134970622. *049250*

Septfonds (Tarn-et-Garonne)
Redon, Daniel, 39 Cours Sadi-Carnot, 82240 Septfonds.
T. 0563312314. *049251*

Sermoise-sur-Loire (Nièvre)
Philippe, Jean, 94 Rte Lyon, 58000 Sermoise-sur-Loire.
T. 0386376077. *049252*

Sermur (Creuse)
Mallet, Robert, La Chaze, 23700 Sermur.
T. 0555670544. - Ant / Furn / Jew - *049253*

Serres (Hautes-Alpes)
Vlahopoulos, Nicolas, Le Moulin, 05700 Serres.
T. 0492670543.   *049254*

Serrière-de-Briord (Ain)
Reginalde, Rue de la Plantaz, 01740 Serrière-de-Briord.
T. 0474367979. - Ant -   *049255*

Serverette (Lozère)
Gauzy-Arnal, Andrée, RN 107, 48700 Serverette.
T. 0466483073.   *049256*

Seurre (Côte-d'Or)
Berbey, Janine, 16 Rue Beauraing, 21250 Seurre.
T. 0380210856.   *049257*

Sevran (Seine-Saint-Denis)
Brette, Robert, 15 All Alençon, 93270 Sevran.
T. 0143832964, Fax 0143859713.   *049258*
Royer, Gilles, 86 Av Livry, 93270 Sevran.
T. 0149369732.   *049259*

Sèvres (Hauts-de-Seine)
Auzanneau, Guy, 52 Grande Rue, 92310 Sèvres.
T. 0146260088.   *049260*
Choquet, Henri, 19 Rue Brongniard, 92310 Sèvres.
T. 0146230048.   *049261*
Le Maire, Jean-Michel, 15 Rue Jules-Ferry, 92310 Sèv-
res. T. 0145349886.   *049262*

Sévrier (Haute-Savoie)
Brocante de Sévrier, Rte Crêt-Morens, 74320 Sévrier.
T. 0450524921.   *049263*
Juillet, Michel, Létraz, 74320 Sévrier.
T. 0450526040.   *049264*
Trimaille, Arlette, 3950 Rte Albertville, 74320 Sévrier.
T. 0450526795.   *049265*

Signes (Var)
Vach, Philippe, 5 Rue Briançon, 83870 Signes.
T. 0494908200.   *049266*

Signy-le-Petit (Ardennes)
Potdevin, Sylvain, 33 Rue Briqueterie, 08380 Signy-le-
Petit. T. 0324535808. - Ant -   *049267*

Sin-le-Noble (Nord)
Kruzina, Antoine, 53 Pl Linerté, 59450 Sin-le-Noble.
T. 0327870927. - Ant -   *049268*

Sisteron (Alpes-de-Haute-Provence)
Chadebec, Michel, 8 Av Jean-Jaurès, 04200 Sisteron.
T. 0492626314. - Ant -   *049269*

Six-Fours-les-Plages (Var)
Félix, 2005 Av Président-John-Kennedy, 83140 Six-
Fours-les-Plages. T. 0494251495. - Ant /
Mod -   *049270*
Ferraris, Jean-Pierre, 403 Av Laënnec, 83140 Six-
Fours-les-Plages. T. 0494257316.   *049271*
Sainte-Hélène, 481 Av Président-John-Kennedy, 83140
Six-Fours-les-Plages. T. 0494254876.   *049272*

Soings-en-Sologne (Loir-et-Cher)
A Saint-Eterne, Corbrande D 765, 41230 Soings-en-So-
logne. T. 0254987536. - Furn / Orient / Sculp / Arch /
Dec / Lights -   *049273*
Chevalier, Bernard, Ferme de Corbrandes, 41230
Soings-en-Sologne. T. 0254987536. - Ant / Furn /
Sculp -   *049274*

Soissons (Aisne)
Fontaine, Martine, 3bis Cité-Gilbert, 02200 Soissons.
T. 0323594666. - Ant -   *049275*
Grenier, Philippe, 21 Rue Paradis, 02200 Soissons.
T. 0323744093. - Ant -   *049276*
Saint-Christophe, 8 Rue Matigny, 02200 Soissons.
T. 0323744510. - Ant / Paint / Furn / Silv -   *049277*
Slastan, Ginette, 8 Rue Matigny, 02200 Soissons.
T. 0323744510. - Ant -   *049278*

Soisy-sur-Ecole (Essonne)
Ricci, Jean, 16 Rue Corbeil, 91840 Soisy-sur-Ecole.
T. 0164980317.   *049279*

Soisy-sur-Seine (Essonne)
Grenier de Soisy, 2bis Rue Meillottes, 91450 Soisy-sur-
Seine. T. 0160753665.   *049280*

Solliès-Pont (Var)
Estagnié, 120 Rue République, 83210 Solliès-Pont.
T. 0494336220.   *049281*

Somme-Vesle (Marne)
Chaspierre, Yvette, 12 Rue Pavillon, 51460 Somme-
Vesle. T. 0326666081.   *049282*

Sommières (Gard)
Horizon Lointain, 1 Pl Jean-Jaurès, 30250 Sommières.
T. 0466804027, Fax 0466804028.   *049283*

Sorel-Moussel (Eure-et-Loir)
Chatelain, Bertrand, 2 Rte Anet, 28520 Sorel-Moussel.
T. 0237418292. - Furn -   *049284*

Sorèze (Tarn)
Blaquière, Geneviève, Rue Puyvert, 81540 Sorèze.
T. 0563741158.   *049285*

Sorgues (Vaucluse)
Jéromine, Quart Sainte-Anne, 84700 Sorgues.
T. 0490322108. - Ant -   *049286*

Sos (Lot-et-Garonne)
Leblanc, Patrick, Rte Gabarret, 47170 Sos.
T. 0553656639.   *049287*

Sotteville-lès-Rouen (Seine-Maritime)
Goude, Lucien, 43 Rue Benjamin-Normand, 76300 Sot-
teville-lès-Rouen. T. 0235721549.   *049288*
Guillard, D., 162 Rue Pierre-Mendès-France, 76300 Sot-
teville-lès-Rouen. T. 0235734244.   *049289*
Paris, Nicole, Rue Henri-Gadeau-de-Kerville, 76300 Sot-
teville-lès-Rouen. T. 0232910899. - Paint / Instr /
Toys -   *049290*

Soual (Tarn)
Galinier Bourdoncle, Josette, 31 Grande Rue, 81580
Soual. T. 0563755233, Fax 0563754126.   *049291*

Soucirac (Lot)
Dalet, Bernard, Bourg, 46300 Soucirac.
T. 0565310321.   *049292*

Souillac (Lot)
André, Bruno, 90 Av Toulouse, 46200 Souillac.
T. 0565327241.   *049293*
Laval, Alain, 18 Rue Louqsor, 46200 Souillac.
T. 0565370939.   *049294*
Marie-Agnès, 3 Pl Doussot, 46200 Souillac.
T. 0565326566.   *049295*

Soulaire-et-Bourg (Maine-et-Loire)
Vieille Forge, 3 Rue Principale, 49460 Soulaire-et-
Bourg. T. 41320591. - Furn -   *049296*

Soulom (Hautes-Pyrénées)
Bimbelotière, 65260 Soulom. T. 0562927958.
- Ant -   *049297*

Souppes-sur-Loing (Seine-et-Marne)
Peyron, Béatrix, 34 Rue Voltaire, 77460 Souppes-sur-
Loing. T. 64297206.   *049298*

Souvigné (Indre-et-Loire)
Quesson, La Joinière, 37330 Souvigné. T. 0547247335.
- Ant / Furn -   *049299*

Soyaux (Charente)
Kulunkian, Stéphane, 14bis Av Général-de-Gaulle,
16800 Soyaux. T. 0545959855.   *049300*
Laporte, Nicole, 104bis Av Général-de-Gaulle, 16800
Soyaux. T. 0545921674.   *049301*
Larapidie, Claude, 15 Rue Marie-Creyssac, 16800
Soyaux. T. 0545387675.   *049302*

Spincourt (Meuse)
George, Paul, 2 Rue Haute, 55230 Spincourt.
T. 0329859315. - Ant -   *049303*

Steinbrunn-le-Haut (Haut-Rhin)
A la Vieille Fontaine, 6 Rue Seigneurs, 68440 Stein-
brunn-le-Haut. T. 0389813600.   *049304*

Strasbourg (Bas-Rhin)
Adler, 7 Rue Bouchers, 67000 Strasbourg.
T. 0388241072, Fax 0388419229. - Mod -   *049305*
Alsace, 21 Rue Molsheim, 67000 Strasbourg.
T. 0388327984.   *049306*
Antiquaires d'Alsace, 18 Rue Ardèche, 67100 Stras-
bourg. T. 0388794494.   *049307*
Antiquités de l'Ill, 23 Quai des Bateliers, 67000 Stras-
bourg. T. 0388369684. - Furn / Cur -   *049308*
Armes Antiques, 10 Rue Bouchers, 67000 Strasbourg.
T. 0388240289. - Mil -   *049309*
Artémis, 15 Rue des Tonneliers, 67000 Strasbourg.
T. 0388324810. - Cur -   *049310*
Au Décor d'Autrefois, 6 Rue Moulins, 67000 Strasbourg.
T. 0388321540.   *049311*
Bastian, Jean, 24 Pl de la Cathédrale, 67000 Stras-
bourg. T. 0388324593. - Ant / Furn / China / Ico / Tin /
Toys -   *049312*
Berauer, 7 A Rue des Frères, 67000 Strasbourg.
T. 0388250646.   *049313*
Blum, 17 Rue Rosheim, 67000 Strasbourg.
T. 0388223840. - Furn / Mod -   *049314*
Bretz-Goustille, Thérèse, 22 Rue Frères, 67000 Stras-
bourg. T. 0388353575. - Furn -   *049315*
Brocanterie, 18 Rue Vieil-Hôpital, 67000 Strasbourg.
T. 0388325279.   *049316*
Brocantique, 125 Rte Schirmeck, 67200 Strasbourg.
T. 0388285878. - Paint / Furn / Cur -   *049317*
Chenkier, Marcel, 10 Rue des Dentelles, 67000 Stras-
bourg. T. 0388328276. - Paint -   *049318*
Chenkier, Marcel, 10 Rue des Dentelles, 67000 Stras-
bourg. T. 0388328276, Fax 0388233164. - Paint /
Furn -   *049319*
Chiara, E. de, 14 Rue du Dôme, 67000 Strasbourg.
T. 0388361281. - Ant -   *049320*
Circé, 24 B Rue Orfèvres, 67000 Strasbourg.
T. 0388224315.   *049321*
Cour Renaissance, 3 Rue Ail, 67000 Strasbourg.
T. 0388520121.   *049322*
Demay, 3 Rue Ail, 67000 Strasbourg.
T. 0388520121.   *049323*
Echelle, 7 Quai Finkwiller, 67000 Strasbourg.
T. 0388371237.   *049324*
Elegia, 28 Rue des Tonneliers, 67000 Strasbourg.
T. 0388223865. - Graph / Fra -   *049325*
Europ'Art, 24 Rue Bouchers, 67000 Strasbourg.
T. 0388356555.   *049326*
Finkwiller, 4 Quai Finkwiller, 67000 Strasbourg.
T. 0388379191.   *049327*
Galerie des Frères, 22 Rue Frères, 67000 Strasbourg.
T. 0388353575.   *049328*
Galerie des Petits Maîtres, 8 Rue Bain-aux-Plantes,
67000 Strasbourg. T. 0388235529.   *049329*
Galerie du Quai, 14 Quai Saint-Nicolas, 67000 Stras-
bourg. T. 0388361329. - Cur -   *049330*
Horn, Claude, 3 Rue Ail, 67000 Strasbourg.
T. 0388320819.   *049331*
Huffschmitt, Marc, 80 A Rue Mélanie, 67000 Stras-
bourg. T. 0388315164, Fax 0388314750.   *049332*
Knoerr, Michel, 13 Cité Spach, 67000 Strasbourg.
T. 0388614433.   *049333*
Labat, Anne, 23 Rue Betschdorf, 67000 Strasbourg.
T. 0388310281. - Cur / Toys -   *049334*
Lacan, 30 Quai Bateliers, 67000 Strasbourg.
T. 0388257852. - Graph -   *049335*
Lamarche, Patrick, 8 Rue Bouchers, 67000 Strasbourg.
T. 0388368236.   *049336*
Le Monnier, Philippe, 10 Rue Vieil-Hôpital, 67000 Stras-
bourg. T. 0388235687.   *049337*
Malbasa, 42 Rue Hallebardes, 67000 Strasbourg.
T. 0388328855.   *049338*
Maudonnet, Philippe, 1 Rue Sainte-Catherine, 67000
Strasbourg. T. 0388251371.   *049339*
Meyer, Mireille, 17 Quai Pêcheurs, 67000 Strasbourg.
Fax 88366700.   *049340*
Mikaeloff, Simon, 7 Rue Orfèvres, 67000 Strasbourg.
T. 0388327445, Fax 0388328061. - Tex -   *049341*
Pfirsch, Bernard, 20 Rue Nuée-Bleue, 67000 Stras-
bourg. T. 0388327279.   *049342*
Sainteff, Denis, 5 Quai Pêcheurs, 67000 Strasbourg.
T. 0388255487. - Toys -   *049343*
Schmidt, 21 Rue Or, 67000 Strasbourg.
T. 0388367369.   *049344*

Schoen, Jean-Pierre, 6 Pl Grande-Boucherie, 67000
Strasbourg. T. 0388326653. *049345*

Tanagra, 19 Pl Marché-Neuf, 67000 Strasbourg.
T. 0388324348. *049346*

Weil, Albert, 8 Rue Bouclier, 67000 Strasbourg.
T. 0388230106. *049347*

Welch, Kathryn, 13 Cité Spach, 67000 Strasbourg.
T. 0388614433. *049348*

Sully-sur-Loire (Loiret)

Antiquités Saint-Germain, 20 Fbg-Saint-Germain, 45600
Sully-sur-Loire. T. 0238364438. *049349*

Brocante du Faubourg, 51 Rue Fbg-Saint-Germain,
45600 Sully-sur-Loire. T. 0238365219. *049350*

Sundhoffen (Haut-Rhin)

Geiger, Pierre, 5 Rue Primevères, 68280 Sundhoffen.
T. 0389714089. *049351*

Suresnes (Hauts-de-Seine)

A la Grange du Val d'Or, 20 Blvd Louis-Loucheur, 92150
Suresnes. T. 0145065088. *049352*

Dubois, Rémi, 22 Rue Moulineaux, 92150 Suresnes.
T. 0145065059. *049353*

Pierres et Vestiges, 26 Rue Henri-Regnault, 92150 Suresnes. T. 0146062694, Fax 0142047278. *049354*

Sévene, 56 Blvd Henri-Sellier, 92150 Suresnes.
T. 0145063413. *049355*

Tain-l'Hermitage (Drôme)

Pélissé, Nicolas, 9 Rue Herbes, 26600 Tain-l'Hermitage.
T. 0475087065. *049356*

Perramond, Alain, 6 Chemin Tortel, 26600 Tain-l'Hermitage. T. 0475085772. *049357*

Talasani (Corse)

Oliver, Jacques, Fiume Olmo, Sud Folelli, RN 198,
20230 Talasani. T. 0495368795. - Ant / Furn /
Fra - *049358*

Tallard (Hautes-Alpes)

Antiquités du Rousine, Pied de la Plaine, 05130 Tallard.
T. 0492540550. *049359*

Talmont-Saint-Hilaire (Vendée)

Belle Epoque, 5bis Rue Nationale, 85440 Talmont-Saint-
Hilaire. T. 0251902222. *049360*

Colaisseau, Jean-Bernard, 301 Rue Querry, 85440 Talmont-Saint-Hilaire. T. 0251222534. *049361*

Grenier d'Ophélie, 15 Rue Centre, 85440 Talmont-Saint-
Hilaire. T. 0251960444. *049362*

Lesourd, Lucien, Rte Bourgenay, L'Aubretière, 85440
Talmont-Saint-Hilaire. T. 0251960111. *049363*

Taponnat-Fleurignac (Charente)

Antiquités Charentaise, Bourdelière, 16110 Taponnat-
Fleurignac. T. 0545620840. *049364*

Tarare (Rhône)

Meunier, Paul, 34 Rue de la République, 69170 Tarare.
- Ant / Furn / China - *049365*

Tarascon (Bouches-du-Rhône)

Bedot, André, Quai du Thor, Rte de Boulbon, 13150 Tarascon. T. 0490913939, Fax 0490914366. *049366*

Château de Panisse, Rte Cellulose, 13150 Tarascon.
T. 0490911530. *049367*

Giraldi-Delmas, Philippe, 15 Rue Hôpital, 13150 Tarascon. T. 0490910580. - Ant - *049368*

Tarascon-sur-Ariège (Ariège)

Laffont, Jacques, Av François-Laguerre, 09400 Tarascon-sur-Ariège. T. 0561051968. - Tex / Cur - *049369*

Tarbes (Hautes-Pyrénées)

Agora, 24 Cours Gambetta, 65000 Tarbes.
T. 0562512504. - Ant / Jew - *049370*

Ariane, 6 Rue Gonnes, 65000 Tarbes. T. 0562346334.
- Ant / Paint / Furn - *049371*

Chabosson, Françoise, 1bis Rue Saint-Vincent-de-Paul,
65000 Tarbes. T. 0562935279. - Ant - *049372*

Garay, 12 Rue Massey, 65000 Tarbes. T. 0562930696.
- Ant / Furn - *049373*

Labat, Claude, 32 Rue Georges-Lassalle, 65000 Tarbes.
T. 0562448222. - Ant - *049374*

Occa Meubles, 13 Av Fould, 65000 Tarbes.
T. 0562512549. - Ant / Furn - *049375*

P'tit Grenier, 61 Rue Brauhauban, 65000 Tarbes.
T. 0562345662. - Ant - *049376*

Salle de Vente Saint-Jean, 20 Av Hoche, 65000 Tarbes.
T. 0562938976. - Ant / Dec / Cur - *049377*

Tavaux (Jura)

Comtoise, 74 Rte Nationale, 39500 Tavaux.
T. 0384811410. - Ant - *049378*

Dejeux, Daniel, 72 Rte Nationale, 39500 Tavaux.
T. 0384811410. *049379*

Pion, Annick, Au Village, 39500 Tavaux.
T. 0384718503. *049380*

Trocaz, André, 44 Rue Châlon, 39500 Tavaux.
T. 0384714405. *049381*

Tavel (Gard)

Mèze, Yoland, Rue La-Condamine, 30126 Tavel.
T. 0466501506. *049382*

Tende (Alpes-Maritimes)

Toesca, Jean, 34 Rue Béatrice-Lascaris, 06430 Tende.
T. 0493046047. - Ant - *049383*

Tendon (Vosges)

Mauchard, François, 61 Rte Cascades, 88460 Tendon.
T. 0329332314. *049384*

Ternuay-Melay-Saint-Hilaire (Haute-Saône)

Spaite, Monique, Rte Servance, Venant de Melay, 70270
Ternuay-Melay-Saint-Hilaire. T. 0384204762. *049385*

Tessé-la-Madeleine (Orne)

Malle d'Andaine, 1 Rue Gilbert-Maître-Jean, 61140
Tessé-la-Madeleine. T. 0233379590. - Ant - *049386*

Oriot, Jean-Marcel, 19 Av Docteur-Joly, 61140 Tessé-
la-Madeleine. T. 0233378135. - Ant - *049387*

Tesson (Charente-Maritime)

Ravon, Philippe & Xavier Petitcol, Maisons Neuves,
17460 Tesson. T. 0546919409, Fax 0546916439.
- Furn / Cur - *049388*

Vieille Saintonge, Moulin Creugnet, 17460 Tesson.
T. 0546916164. - Ant - *049389*

Thairé (Charente-Maritime)

Chaussat, Dominique, 9 Rue Dirac, 17290 Thairé.
T. 0546563645. - Furn - *049390*

Thann (Haut-Rhin)

Dreyer, Marc, 36 Rue Clemenceau, 68800 Thann.
T. 0389374842. *049391*

Themines (Lot)

Rétro Actif, Le Trinquat, 46120 Themines.
T. 0565409219. *049392*

Thénac (Charente-Maritime)

Lervoire, 6 Rte La-Chapelle, 17460 Thénac.
T. 0546916471. *049393*

Thenay (Loir-et-Cher)

Bertrand, Serge, 44 Rue Octave-Gauthier, 41400 The-
nay. T. 0254325360. *049394*

Thiberville (Eure)

Leroux, Régis, RN 13, Les Forgettes, 27230 Thiberville.
T. 0232469793. - Furn - *049395*

Thiers (Puy-de-Dôme)

Bonnemoy, Jean-Luc, 22 Rue Camille-Joubert, 63300
Thiers. T. 0473510812. - Ant - *049396*

Claudet, Anne-marie, 14 Rue Doct-Dumas, 63300
Thiers. T. 0473801360. - Ant - *049397*

Gouttefangeas, Jean-Paul, 3 Rue Camille-Joubert,
63300 Thiers. T. 0473807820. - Ant - *049398*

Herréra-Gutierrez, Jean-Claude, 3bis Rue Camille-Joubert, 63300 Thiers. T. 0473510559. - Ant - *049399*

Thierville-sur-Meuse (Meuse)

Somnard, Claudine, 140bis Av Goubet, 55100 Thierville-
sur-Meuse. T. 0329865465. - Ant - *049400*

Thionville (Moselle)

Brocanthèque, 6 Av Comte-de-Bertier, 57100 Thionville.
T. 0382534350. *049401*

Ehrmann, Fabien, 53 Av Comte-de-Bertier, 57100 Thionville. T. 0382532657. *049402*

Stéphanie, Patrick, 32 Ac Comte-de-Bertier, 57100
Thionville. T. 0382541112. *049403*

Thônes (Haute-Savoie)

Veyret & Fils, Rte Annecy, 74230 Thônes.
T. 0450021556. - Paint / Furn / Sculp - *049404*

Thonon-les-Bains (Haute-Savoie)

Antiquités à la Ferme, Saint-Disdille, Port Ripaille,
74200 Thonon-les-Bains. T. 0450713540. *049405*

Antiquités Bagatelle, 3 Rue Michaud, 74200 Thonon-
les-Bains. T. 0450263344, Fax 0450261220. *049406*

Bric à Brac, 14 Av Dranse, 74200 Thonon-les-Bains.
T. 0450260853. - Furn - *049407*

Grapin, Joël, 26 Chemin Froid-Lieu, 74200 Thonon-les-
Bains. T. 0450710544. - Furn / Cur - *049408*

Lavanchy, 9 Rue Hôtel-de-Ville, 74200 Thonon-les-
Bains. T. 0450716000. - Paint / Furn / Jew - *049409*

Mathusalem, 13 Pl Crête, 74200 Thonon-les-Bains.
T. 0450702320. *049410*

Thorigné-Fouillard (Ille-et-Vilaine)

Antiquités de la Forêt, La Jutauderie, 35235 Thorigné-
Fouillard. T. 0299620034. *049411*

Barreau, RN 12, 35235 Thorigné-Fouillard.
T. 0299620448. - Furn / Cur - *049412*

Beaufils, Serge, 57 Rue Nationale, 35235 Thorigné-
Fouillard. T. 0299624898. *049413*

Thouars (Deux-Sèvres)

Broc Antique, 19 Pl Saint-Médard, 79100 Thouars.
T. 0549680722. *049414*

Grenier Thouarsais, 8 Rue Anatole-France, 79100
Thouars. T. 0549663574. *049415*

Thury-Harcourt (Calvados)

Guée, Jean-Claude, 10 Rue Caen, 14220 Thury-Harcourt. T. 0231797266, Fax 0231790250. *049416*

Troussier, Rémy, 2 Rue Caen, 14220 Thury-Harcourt.
T. 0231390681. *049417*

Tinqueux (Marne)

Salle des Ventes des Particuliers, 25 Rue Gabriel-Péri,
51430 Tinqueux. T. 0326086938. - Ant - *049418*

Tapissier, Michel, 24 Rue Henri-Barbusse, 51430 Tinqueux. T. 0326044173. *049419*

Tonneins (Lot-et-Garonne)

Garrouste, M., Lajaunie, Rte Clairac, 47400 Tonneins.
T. 0553846710. *049420*

Tonnerre (Yonne)

Rouillot, 30 Rue Saint-Pierre, 89700 Tonnerre.
T. 0386553430. *049421*

Torfou (Maine-et-Loire)

Relais de Poste, Colonne, 49660 Torfou.
T. 41465054. *049422*

Torigni-sur-Vire (Manche)

Bergmann, Christian, 23 Rue Notre-Dame, 50160 Torigni-sur-Vire. T. 0233567523. *049423*

Torpes (Doubs)

Flohr, Henri, 31 Rue Vignottes, 25320 Torpes.
T. 0381586547. *049424*

Torvillers (Aube)

Ere du Temps, 20 Grande Rue, 10440 Torvillers.
T. 0325794780. - Ant / Furn - *049425*

Tostes (Eure)

Gribinski, Philippe, 16 Rue Pasteur, 27340 Tostes.
T. 0232404256. *049426*

Tôtes (Seine-Maritime)

Delacroix, Gaston, 13 Rte Havre, 76890 Tôtes.
T. 0235329126. *049427*

Toucy (Yonne)

Carré, Fernand, 30 Rue Pont-Capureau, 89130 Toucy.
T. 0386743210. *049428*

Lescroart Defrance, 18 Rue Paul-Bert, 89130 Toucy.
T. 0386441297. *049429*

Toufflers (Nord)
Lemaire, Dominique, 89 Rue Déportés, 59390 Toufflers.
T. 0320822575. - Ant - *049430*

Touffréville (Calvados)
Cottyn, Lydie, Rue Eglise, 14940 Touffréville.
T. 0231233246. *049431*

Toul (Meurthe-et-Moselle)
Curiosités d'Antan, 18 Rue Michâtel, 54200 Toul.
T. 0383631246. *049432*

Toulon (Var)
Antic JR, Av Fusiliers-Marins, 83000 Toulon.
T. 0494923993. *049433*
Art Peinture, 136 Rue Auffan, 83000 Toulon.
T. 0494423353. - Paint - *049434*
Ascencio, Alain, 15 Av Franklin-Roosevelt, 83000 Toulon. T. 0494411159. *049435*
Blanc, Charles, 71 Av Colonel, Duboin Papillons, 83000 Toulon. T. 0494926545. *049436*
Brunet, Jacques, 6 Rue Molière, 83000 Toulon.
T. 0494922193. *049437*
Cavalière, 257 Blvd Léon Bourgeois, 83100 Toulon.
T. 0494362563. - Ant - *049438*
Chaix, Corine, 4 Pl Noël-Blache, 83000 Toulon.
T. 0494934130. - Ant / Furn / Toys - *049439*
Compagnie Anglaise, 29 Rue Boucheries, 83000 Toulon.
T. 0494917709. *049440*
Cottage, 11 Rue Pomet, 83000 Toulon.
T. 0494920161. *049441*
Crouzet, 219 Av République, 83000 Toulon.
T. 0494899943. *049442*
Descamps, Claire, 9 Rue Vincent-Courdouan, 83000 Toulon. T. 0494930976. *049443*
Dominique, 40 Rue Castillon, 83000 Toulon.
T. 0494424982. *049444*
Estades, Michel, 22 Rue Henri-Seillon, 83000 Toulon.
T. 0494894998. - Paint / Furn / Glass - *049445*
Guenard-d'Abbadie, Andrée & Claude, 40 Rue Lamalgue, 83000 Toulon. T. 0494414659. - Jew / Silv /
Cur - *049446*
Jourdan, Daniel-Louis, 729 Blvd Maréchal-Joffre, 83100 Toulon. T. 0494035282. *049447*
Levina-Swannet, 49-51 Rue Lamalgue, 83000 Toulon.
T. 0494415660. - Paint / Jew / Silv / Mil / Cur - *049448*
Lieutaud, James, Av Entrecasteaux, 83000 Toulon.
T. 0494422632. *049449*
Lou Granieret, 715 Blvd Louis-Picon, 83200 Toulon.
T. 0494929990. *049450*
Louis, 98 Av République, 83000 Toulon.
T. 0494919100. *049451*
Louise, 146 Blvd Maréchal-Joffre, 83100 Toulon.
T. 0494318255. *049452*
Ludopassion, 12 Blvd Lagane, 83000 Toulon.
T. 0494036091. *049453*
Ma Boutique, 54 Av Maréchal-Foch, 83000 Toulon.
T. 0494926625. - Mil - *049454*
Martzloff, Christine, 33 Rue Lamalgue, 83000 Toulon.
T. 0494466632. - Furn / Dec / Jew / Silv - *049455*
Masse, Jean-Sébastien, 88 Blvd Georges-Clémenceau, 83000 Toulon. T. 0494624762. *049456*
Mercure, 12 Pl Vincent-Raspail, 83000 Toulon.
T. 0494926438. *049457*
Mevel, Jean-Pierre, 113 Rue Edouard-Perrichi, 83000 Toulon. T. 0494911202. *049458*
Mikado, Claude, 859 Blvd Jules-Michelet, 83000 Toulon.
T. 0494033760. *049459*
Minerve, 18 Rue Garibaldi, 83000 Toulon.
T. 0494929318. *049460*
Passion Maison, 71 Blvd Sainte-Hélène, 83100 Toulon.
T. 0494031171. - Tex / Dec - *049461*
Philéas Fogg, 3 Rue Henri-Seillon, 83000 Toulon.
T. 0494935450. - Furn / Dec - *049462*
Rivière, Michel, 1397 Vieux Chemin, Sainte-Musse, 83000 Toulon. T. 0494612521. *049463*
Rossi, 18 Rue Revel, 83000 Toulon. T. 0494623020.
- Furn - *049464*
Ruiz, Ramon, 229 Corniche Marius-Escartefigue, 83100 Toulon. T. 0494928113, Fax 0494915207.
- Furn - *049465*

Rumello, Vincent, 4 Rue Dumont-d'Urville, 83000 Toulon. T. 0494920237. *049466*
Serrié, Victor, 60 Rue Lamalgue, 83000 Toulon.
T. 0494416300. *049467*
Succo, V., 10 Rue July, 83000 Toulon.
T. 0494310862. *049468*

Toulon-sur-Arroux (Saône-et-Loire)
Casanova, Pierre, 4 Rue Chalon, 71320 Toulon-sur-Arroux. T. 0385794032. - Ant - *049469*

Toulouse (Haute-Garonne)
Abou, Thérèse & Mireille Benibre, 7 Rue Rempart-Villeneuve, 31000 Toulouse. T. 0561236220. *049470*
Antika du T, 6 Rue Saint-Antoine-du-T, 31000 Toulouse.
T. 0561236261. *049471*
Antiquité Brocante Les Chartreux, 3 Rue Fonderie, 31000 Toulouse. T. 0561534686. - Orient - *049472*
Antiquités, 6 Rue Jean-Suau, 31000 Toulouse.
T. 0561123678. *049473*
Antiquités Colombette, 5 Rue Colombette, 31000 Toulouse. T. 0561993443. *049474*
Antiquités Nazareth, 12 Grande Rue Nazareth, 31000 Toulouse. T. 0561257345. *049475*
Argenterie Ancienne, 10 Pl Carmes, 31000 Toulouse.
T. 0561552305. - Silv - *049476*
Au Bonheur d'Ombeline, 6 Rue Coq-d'Inde, 31000 Toulouse. T. 0561253529. *049477*
Azzola, Max, 3 Rue Perchepinte, 31000 Toulouse.
T. 0561321844. *049478*
Barada, 4 Rue Rempart-Saint-Etienne, 31000 Toulouse.
T. 0561230891. - Furn - *049479*
Barada, 12 Rue Arnaud-Vidal, 31000 Toulouse.
T. 0561626312. - Furn - *049480*
Barbe, Ludovic, 38 Av Hers, 31500 Toulouse.
T. 0561540277. *049481*
Baudet, Laure, 16 Rue Vélane, 31000 Toulouse.
T. 0561250005. *049482*
Besaucèle, Henri, 32 Rue Boulbonne, 31000 Toulouse.
T. 0561210863, Fax 0561219626. - Orient - *049483*
Bonnet, Marie-Claude, 12 Rue Perchepinte, 31000 Toulouse. T. 0561539780. *049484*
Borreau, Pierre, 9 Rue Languedoc, 31000 Toulouse.
T. 0561535551. *049485*
Bourgoin, Suzanne, 2bis Rue Labéda, 31000 Toulouse.
T. 0561233591. *049486*
Brikàbrak, 50 Rte Labège, 31400 Toulouse.
T. 0561342352. *049487*
Brousse, Martine, 94 Rue Riquet, 31000 Toulouse.
T. 0561677073. - Paint / Furn / Cur - *049488*
Cabrol, Pierre, 23 Rue Perchepinte, 31000 Toulouse.
T. 0561524975. *049489*
Calmels, Simone, 2 Pl Montoulieu, 31000 Toulouse.
T. 0561522307. *049490*
Cambus, Isabelle, 61 Rue Pomme, 31000 Toulouse.
T. 0561218556. *049491*
Cardelin, Henri, 11 Rue Fermat, 31000 Toulouse.
T. 0561523110. *049492*
Castella-Ayral, 19 Rue Montoulieu-Velane, 31000 Toulouse. T. 0561256426. *049493*
Chabbert, Patrice, 8 Rue Canard, 31000 Toulouse.
T. 0561555795. *049494*
Costa-Dupuy, Marie-Louise, 7 Rue Croix-Baragnon, 31000 Toulouse. T. 0561527514. *049495*
Cosy Corner, 3 Rue Alexandre-Fourtanier, 31000 Toulouse. T. 0561238754. *049496*
Courtois de Viçose, Germaine, 8 Rue Perchepinte, 31000 Toulouse. T. 0561525155. *049497*
Découverte, 5 Rue Colombette, 31000 Toulouse.
T. 0561637895. *049498*
Delperie, Adrien, 18 Rue Gambetta, 31000 Toulouse.
T. 0561216557. *049499*
Esquerre, Raymond, 34 Pl Mage, 31000 Toulouse.
T. 0561524701. - Paint / Furn / China / Tex / Eth / Jew /
Instr / Glass / Cur / Toys - *049500*
Félix Expertises, 3 Rue Boulbonne, 31000 Toulouse.
T. 0561520153, Fax 0561253939. *049501*
Fenêtres sur Cour, 5 Rue Colombette, 31000 Toulouse.
T. 0561993443. *049502*
Feral, Jacqueline, 8 Rue Fermat, 31000 Toulouse.
T. 0561536334. *049503*
Flahaux, Jacques, 151 Rte Blagnac, 31200 Toulouse.
T. 0561138233. *049504*

Fontanié, Jean, 2 Rue Ninau, 31000 Toulouse.
T. 0561539508. *049505*
Forum des Antiquaires, 388 Av Etats-Unis, 31200 Toulouse. T. 0561708891. *049506*
Fournials, Roger, 12 Blvd Carnot, 31000 Toulouse.
T. 0561625162. - Num / Sculp / Arch / Eth - *049507*
Furgadou, 231 Av Saint-Exupéry, 31400 Toulouse.
T. 0561203059, Fax 0562720006. *049508*
Galerie Athenée, 3 Rue Cantegril, 31000 Toulouse.
T. 0561210881. *049509*
Ganès, Yvette, Rue Trois-Journées, 31000 Toulouse.
T. 0561232113. *049510*
Gérémia, Jean-Louis, 15 Rue Canard, 31000 Toulouse.
T. 0561536270. *049511*
Godéas, Evelyne, 4 Rue Pharaon, 31000 Toulouse.
T. 0561526757. *049512*
Gonzales, Jacqueline, 22 Rue Perchepinte, 31000 Toulouse. T. 0561530912. *049513*
Grenier Colonial, 34 Rue Filatiers, 31000 Toulouse.
T. 0561528559, Fax 0561521962. *049514*
Huc, Marie-Claude, 8 Rue Dupont, 31000 Toulouse.
T. 0561806763. *049515*
Icosium, 32 Rue Marchands, 31000 Toulouse.
T. 0561254475. *049516*
Jaylac, Pierre, 34 Rue Velasquez, 31000 Toulouse.
T. 0561494148. *049517*
Jouanneau, Etienne, 1 Rue Trois-Renards, 31000 Toulouse. T. 0561219104. *049518*
Jouvent, Mady, 13 Pl Dupuy, 31000 Toulouse.
T. 0561996388. *049519*
Juaniquet, Jean, 22 Rue Rempart-Saint-Etienne, 31000 Toulouse. T. 0561218079. - Paint / Furn / China / Silv /
Lights / Instr / Mil / Glass - *049520*
Junqua-Lamarque, Alain, 4 Rue Ninau, 31000 Toulouse.
T. 0561534095. *049521*
Liberman-Langlade, Anne-Marie, 17 Rue Montoulieu-Velane, 31000 Toulouse. T. 0562264222. *049522*
Martin, Patrick, 4 Rue Fermat, 31000 Toulouse.
T. 0561534455. *049523*
Mas, Béatrice, 14 Rue Astorg, 31000 Toulouse.
T. 0561216755. *049524*
Mendès, Martial, 1 Rue Velane, 31000 Toulouse.
T. 0561521497. *049525*
Messerli, Jeanine, 2 Pl Saintes-Scarbes, 31000 Toulouse. T. 0561533309. *049526*
Mussato, Jean-Louis, 9 Rue Tolosane, 31000 Toulouse.
T. 0561523993. *049527*
Naa, M., 13 Rue Rempart-Saint-Etienne, 31000 Toulouse. T. 0561218407. *049528*
Oréades, 39 Rue Pharaon, 31000 Toulouse.
T. 0561539989. - Paint - *049529*
Oushabti, 34 Rue Couteliers, 31000 Toulouse.
T. 0561251928, Fax 0561326855. *049530*
Parade, 47 Grande Rue Nazareth, 31000 Toulouse.
T. 0561522834. *049531*
Payrissat, Annie, 178 Rte Seysses, 31100 Toulouse.
T. 0561402572. - Ant - *049532*
Pecheur, Pierre, 33 Rue Bachelier, 31000 Toulouse.
T. 0561622239. *049533*
Pommerat, Gérard, 388 Av Etats-Unis, Forum des Antiquaires, 31200 Toulouse. T. 0561371360. *049534*
Puces d'Oc, 98bis Rue Fontaines, 31300 Toulouse.
T. 0561593433. - Ant - *049535*
Quercy, 24 Rue Clair-Matin, 31400 Toulouse.
T. 0561808516. - Paint / Cur - *049536*
Rétro Verso, 8bis Rue Bernard-Mule, 31400 Toulouse.
T. 0561808711. *049537*
Riquet'Broc, 94 Rue Riquet, 31000 Toulouse.
T. 0561677073. *049538*
Robardey, Maurice, 324 Rte Espagne, 31100 Toulouse.
T. 0562201545, Fax 0562200580. *049539*
Saint-Paul, Eric, 8 Rue Fermat, 31000 Toulouse.
T. 0561534964. *049540*
Salon des Antiquaires, 31 Rue Rempart-Matabiau, 31000 Toulouse. T. 0561219325. *049541*
Savard, Jean-Christophe, 38 Chemin Moulis, 31200 Toulouse. T. 0561704561. - Furn - *049542*
Savard, Jean-Christophe, 15 Av Minimes, 31200 Toulouse. T. 0561470047. - Furn - *049543*
Schulz Réciproque, 17 Rue Filatiers, 31000 Toulouse.
T. 0561550993. *049544*
Serres, Robert, 10 Rue Languedoc, 31000 Toulouse.
T. 0561526882. *049545*

Sirven, Violette, 5 Rue Réclusane, 31300 Toulouse.
T. 0561426344. *049546*
Sourillan, 20 Av Honoré-Serres, 31000 Toulouse.
T. 0561992200, Fax 0561992300. - Paint /
Cur - *049547*
Subra, Catherine, 1 Pl Sainte-Scarbes, 31000 Toulouse.
T. 0561536282. *049548*
Symonds, Mireille, 5 Rue Lois, 31000 Toulouse.
T. 0561237864. - Furn - *049549*
Syndicat des Antiquaires, 31 Rue Rempart-Matabiau,
31000 Toulouse. T. 0561218126. *049550*
Tayac, Annick, 20 Rue Tolosane, 31000 Toulouse.
T. 0561555525. *049551*
Toulouse Antiquités Brocante, 151 Rte Blagnac, 31200
Toulouse. T. 0561571515. *049552*
Troc du Grand Rond, 7 All Paul-Sabatier, 31000 Tou-
louse. T. 0561637601. *049553*
Troc Toulousain, 390 Av Etats-Unis, 31200 Toulouse.
T. 0561370455. *049554*
Trouvaille, 9 Pl Saintes-Scarbes, 31000 Toulouse.
T. 0561534206. *049555*
Trouvat, Marc, 240 Av Grande-Bretagne, 31300 Tou-
louse. T. 0561150411. *049556*
Vander Elst, Michelle, 5 Rue Colombette, 31000 Tou-
louse. T. 0561634565. *049557*
Vanvincq, Michel, 24 Pl Victor-Hugo, 31000 Toulouse.
T. 0561221393. *049558*
Vidal, Pierrette, 10 Pl Mage, 31000 Toulouse.
T. 0561530874. *049559*
Vieux Noyer, 18 Rue Astorg, 31000 Toulouse.
T. 0561237866. *049560*
Villiers, Frantz-Claude, 22 Rue Sainte-Anne, 31000 Tou-
louse. T. 0561329797. *049561*
Zordan, Pierre, 6 Pl Saintes-Scarbes, 31000 Toulouse.
T. 0561538513. *049562*

Touques (Calvados)
Picard, 25 Av Aristide-Briand, 14800 Touques.
T. 0231984625. *049563*
Sajot, Thérèse, Manoir Croix-Sonnet, 14800 Touques.
T. 0231985270. *049564*

Tour-en-Sologne (Loir-et-Cher)
Brochu, Jean, 124 Rue Petite-Motte, 41250 Tour-en-So-
logne. T. 0254464415, Fax 0254460573. - Furn /
Cur - *049565*

Tourcoing (Nord)
Batteau, Yves, 81 Roubaix Blanc-Seau, 59200 Tour-
coing. T. 0320270878. - Ant - *049566*
Grunwald, Jocelyne, 68 Rue Mouvaux, 59200 Tourcoing.
T. 0320265954. - Ant - *049567*
Lefebvre, Jean-Pierre, 120 Av Gustave-Dron, 59200
Tourcoing. T. 0320251936. - Ant - *049568*
Marchand d'Oublis, 5 Rue Brun-Pain, 59200 Tourcoing.
T. 0320035358. - Ant - *049569*
Nobile, Angelo, 27 Rue Croix-Rouge, 59200 Tourcoing.
T. 0320765585. - Ant - *049570*
Tradition, 40 Blvd Gambetta, 59200 Tourcoing.
T. 0327748729. - Ant - *049571*

Tourdun (Gers)
Dinguidard, Alain, Rte Marciac, 32230 Tourdun.
T. 0562093112. - Tex / Dec / Cur - *049572*

Tournon-d'Agenais (Lot-et-Garonne)
Wang, Maggy, Pl Foirail, 47370 Tournon-d'Agenais.
T. 0553407926. *049573*

Tournon-sur-Rhône (Ardèche)
Ducrocq, Emmanuel, 37 Av Maréchal-Foch, 07300 Tour-
non-sur-Rhône. T. 0475086181. - Ant - *049574*
Millers, Max, 47 Av Maréchal-Foch, 07300 Tournon-sur-
Rhône. T. 0475083429. - Ant / Furn - *049575*

Tournus (Saône-et-Loire)
Bertholon, Nicole, 7 Rue Alexis-Bessard, 71700 Tournus.
T. 0385517208. - Ant / Furn - *049576*
Déco-Bistro, 3 Av Clos-Mouron, 71700 Tournus.
T. 0385511563, Fax 0385517617. - Ant /
Furn - *049577*
Guillemin, Jean-Jacques, 15 Av Gambetta, 71700 Tour-
nus. T. 0385517387. - Ant - *049578*
Perrier, Bruno, 1 Av Clos-Mouron, 71700 Tournus.
T. 0385511359, Fax 0385325457. - Ant - *049579*

Perrier, Catherine, 11 Av Gambetta, 71700 Tournus.
T. 0385513619. - Ant - *049580*
Perrin, Michelle, 6 Rue Gabriel-Jeanton, 71700 Tournus.
T. 0385511114. - Ant / Paint / Furn / Sculp - *049581*

Tourrettes (Var)
Allongue, Michel, Quartier Lac, 83440 Tourrettes.
T. 0494761111, Fax 0494761118. *049582*

Tourriers (Charente)
Seima, Rte Paris, 16560 Tourriers.
T. 0545206024. *049583*

Tours (Indre-et-Loire)
Achtiani, Mehdi, 81 Rue Scellerie, 37000 Tours.
T. 0547644865. *049584*
Antiquités 28, 28 Rue Scellerie, 37000 Tours.
T. 0547611222, Fax 0547611222. - Paint / Furn /
Cur - *049585*
Artica, 45 Rue Scellerie, 37000 Tours. T. 0547201706,
Fax 0547201706. *049586*
Asfeld, Arnaud d', 16 Rue Emile-Zola, Stand 8, 37000
Tours. T. 0547056048. *049587*
Au Vieux Tours, 91 Rue Colbert, 37000 Tours.
T. 0547667394. *049588*
Aury, Mireille, 8 Rue Corneille, 37000 Tours.
T. 0547640545. *049589*
Autrefois, 37 Rue Scellerie, 37000 Tours.
T. 0547054208. - Jew / Silv - *049590*
Balzeau, Liliane, 4 Rue Marcel-Tribut, 37000 Tours.
T. 0547201516. *049591*
Barreau, Patrick, 48 Rue Scellerie, 37000 Tours.
T. 0547209132. *049592*
Bodin, François, 40 Rue Paix, 37000 Tours.
T. 0547643544. *049593*
Bolac, André, 41 Rue Scellerie, 37000 Tours.
T. 0547055564. *049594*
Brillet, Marcel, 39 Pl Gaston-Pailhou, 37000 Tours.
T. 0547611049. - Furn / Dec - *049595*
Brinquin, André, 4 Rue Marcel-Tribut, 37000 Tours.
T. 0547201517. *049596*
Brocante Anglaise, 33 Rue Cygne, 37000 Tours.
T. 0547612026. - Furn / Cur - *049597*
Brocanterie, 81 Rue Scellerie, 37000 Tours.
T. 0547642088. *049598*
Bruneau, Philippe, 62 Rue Scellerie, 37000 Tours.
T. 0547052587, Fax 0547640647. - Paint / Furn / Cur /
Instr - *049599*
Cabotse, Michel, 47 Rue Bernard-Palissy, 37000 Tours.
T. 0547471672, Fax 0547207220. *049600*
Caverne des Particuliers, 184 Rue Pas-Notre-Dame,
37100 Tours. T. 0547417155. *049601*
Chantry, Léon-Noël, 10 Rue Descartes, 37000 Tours.
T. 0547615071. *049602*
Collection Passion, 52 Rue Colbert, 37000 Tours.
T. 0547610556. *049603*
Duchâteau, Bernard, 40 Rue Scellerie, 37000 Tours.
T. 0547665988. *049604*
Espace Scellerie, 45 Rue Scellerie, 37000 Tours.
T. 0547201706. - Furn / Lights / Cur - *049605*
Espinassou, Didier, 6 Rue Lavoisier, 37000 Tours.
T. 0547669020. *049606*
Gabillet, Richard, 18 Rue Cordeliers, 37000 Tours.
T. 0547207226. *049607*
Galerie Méphisto, 45 Rue Scellerie, 37000 Tours.
T. 0547646810. *049608*
Galliot, Philippe, 18 Rue Châteauneuf, 37000 Tours.
T. 0547059050. *049609*
Grizolle, Colette, 16 Pl Résistance, 37000 Tours.
T. 0547616405. *049610*
Hier Pour Demain, 13 Pl Grand-Marché, 37000 Tours.
T. 0547640999. *049611*
Hugon, Paulette, 46 Rue Scellerie, 37000 Tours.
T. 0547201519. *049612*
Jallet, Marie-Christine, 45 Rue Scellerie, 37000 Tours.
T. 0547646270. *049613*
Kalmes, Gérard, 48 Rue Scellerie, 37000 Tours.
T. 0547615800. *049614*
Lalmand, Liliane, 4 Jardin-Andréa-Gabrieli, 37000
Tours. T. 0547058550. *049615*
Lannier, Bernard, 54 Rue Scellerie, 37000 Tours.
T. 0547202074. *049616*

Lannier, Monique, 54 Rue Scellerie, 37000 Tours.
T. 0547202074. - Paint / Furn - *049617*
Leroy-Laveissière, Françoise, 52 Rue Scellerie, 37000
Tours. T. 0547053432. - Orient - *049618*
Magnan, Alain, 25 Rue Colbert, 37000 Tours.
T. 0547666869. *049619*
Manfredi, Dany, 97 Av André-Maginot, 37100 Tours.
T. 0547515758. *049620*
Pageau, Colette, 17 Rue Paul-Louis-Courier, 37000
Tours. T. 0547641703. *049621*
Plat, Jean-Louis, 38 Rue Victoire, 37000 Tours.
T. 0547440242. *049622*
Prot, Didier, 74 Rue Colbert, 37000 Tours.
T. 0547644811. *049623*
Quantin, 27 Rue Emile-Zola, 37000 Tours.
T. 0547057538. *049624*
Renaud, Serge, 2 Pl Victor-Jacquemont, 37200 Tours.
T. 0547274356. *049625*
Robert, Patrice, 4 Rue Marcel-Tribut, 37000 Tours.
T. 0547201524. *049626*
Roma & Cie, 60 Rue Scellerie, 37000 Tours.
T. 0547051743. *049627*
Ronda-Brou, 36 Rue Scellerie, 37000 Tours.
T. 0547203854. *049628*
Ronda, Jean, 71 Rue Scellerie, 37000 Tours.
T. 0547207374. *049629*
Rullon, Jean-Michel, 20 Rue Jules-Favre, 37000 Tours.
T. 0547204276. *049630*
Sabard, P., 33 Rue Scellerie, 37000 Tours.
T. 0547052759. *049631*
Turpault, René, 45 Rue Scellerie, 37000 Tours.
T. 0547057892. *049632*
Vergne, Jean-Claude, 97 Rue Scellerie, 37000 Tours.
T. 0547642319. *049633*
Windsor, Alain, 14 Pl François-Sicard, 37000 Tours.
T. 0547613909. *049634*

Tourtour (Var)
Quercus, Rue Chemin-d'Aups, 83690 Tourtour.
T. 0494705545. *049635*

Tourville-sur-Odon (Calvados)
Toutain, Robert, 38 Rte Bretagne, 14210 Tourville-sur-
Odon. T. 0231806363. *049636*

Tousson (Seine-et-Marne)
Le Floch, Ludovic, 2 Rue Repos, 77123 Tousson.
T. 64247602. *049637*

Touvois (Loire-Atlantique)
Audoire, Roland, 12 Rue Eglise, 44650 Touvois.
T. 40316343. - Instr *049638*

Trangé (Sarthe)
Brocante des Maisons Rouges, RN 157 28 Rue Nationale, 72650 Trangé. T. 0243888137. - Ant - *049639*

Trans-en-Provence (Var)
Belles et Bonnes, 38 Rue Nationale, 83720 Trans-en-
Provence. T. 0495708945. *049640*
Bouxin, Katia, 49 Rue Nationale, 83720 Trans-en-Pro-
vence. T. 0494708672. *049641*

Trébeurden (Côtes-d'Armor)
Mével, Jacques, 14 Rue Sémaphore, 22560 Trébeurden.
T. 0296236931. *049642*
Saint-Jalm, 20 Rue Trozoul, 22560 Trébeurden.
T. 0296474076, Fax 0296474357. *049643*

Trédarzec (Côtes-d'Armor)
Debeir, France-Lise, Traou Meur, 22220 Trédarzec.
T. 0296923028. - Furn / Tex / Cur - *049644*

Trédrez (Côtes-d'Armor)
Antiquités de Locquemeau, Port de Locquemeau, 22300
Trédrez. T. 0296352227. - Furn / Cur - *049645*

Trégastel (Côtes-d'Armor)
Sallou, Hervé, 19 Rue Charles-Le-Goffic, 22730 Tréga-
stel. T. 0296238910. *049646*

Trégon (Côtes-d'Armor)
Le Calonnec, Yann, Le Bourg, 22650 Trégon.
T. 0296272819. *049647*

Tréguier (Côtes-d'Armor)
Atelier du Cuir, 22 Rue Saint-André, 22220 Tréguier.
T. 0296929333. - Furn -   049648
Nicolet, Françoise, 8 Rue Ernest-Renan, 22220 Tréguier.
T. 0296924737.   049649

Trélissac (Dordogne)
Trouvaille, Les Riveaux, 24750 Trélissac.
T. 0553544144. - Paint / China / Sculp / Dec / Jew /
Silv / Glass / Cur -   049650

Trélivan (Côtes-d'Armor)
Pelée, Guy, La Peuvrie, 22100 Trélivan.
T. 0296397526.   049651

Tremblay-les-Villages (Eure-et-Loir)
André, Michel, 11 Rue Prieure-Bilheux, 28170 Trem-
blay-les-Villages. T. 0237653375.   049652

Trementines (Maine-et-Loire)
Humeau, Jean-Claude, La Guilbauderie, 49340 Tremen-
tines. T. 41627553. - Furn -   049653

Tréméreuc (Côtes-d'Armor)
Antique Manor, Ville Aubé, 22490 Tréméreuc.
T. 0296278514.   049654

Tréogat (Finistère)
Huyghe-Cariou, Henri, Pencleuz, 29720 Tréogat.
T. 0298877076. - Ant / Furn -   049655

Triel-sur-Seine (Yvelines)
Brocante de l'Hautil, Chemin des Picardes, 78510 Triel-
sur-Seine. T. 0139707580.   049656
Encaustique, 177 Rue Paul-Doumer, 78510 Triel-sur-
Seine. T. 0139707767. - Furn / Cur -   049657

Trigance (Var)
Remise, Le Village, 83840 Trigance.
T. 0494856808.   049658

Troo (Loir-et-Cher)
Château de la Voûte, Château de la Voûte, 41800 Troo.
T. 0254725252, Fax 0254725252.   049659

Trouville-sur-Mer (Calvados)
Antiquités à Suivre, 80 Rue Bains, 14360 Trouville-sur-
Mer. T. 0231984607.   049660
Antiquités d'Hennequeville, 49 Rte Honfleur, 14360
Trouville-sur-Mer. T. 0231880543.   049661
Biblotine, 120 Blvd Fernand-Moureaux, 14360 Trouville-
sur-Mer. T. 0231814720.   049662
Cettour, 97 Rue Bains, 14360 Trouville-sur-Mer.
T. 0231984449.   049663
Kristofy, Bela, 84 Rue Bains, 14360 Trouville-sur-Mer.
T. 0231984073.   049664
Lutz, Yvan, 81 Rue Bains, 14360 Trouville-sur-Mer.
T. 0231985750. - Jew / Cur -   049665
Mouradian, Georges-Dimitri, Chemin Merles, 14360
Trouville-sur-Mer. T. 0231980532.   049666
Pourquoi Pas, 78 Rue Bains, 14360 Trouville-sur-Mer.
T. 0231881112.   049667

Trouy (Cher)
Musardière, 39 Rue Grand-Chemin, 18570 Trouy.
T. 0248647237.   049668

Troyes (Aube)
Antiquité du Musée, 14 Rue Chrestien de Troyes, 10000
Troyes. T. 0325806091. - Ant -   049669
Antiquités de la Cité, 51 Rue de la Cité, 10000 Troyes.
T. 0325805987. - Ant / Furn -   049670
Dupont, Chantal, 98 Rue Général-de-Gaulle, 10000
Troyes. T. 0325732508. - Ant / Furn / Jew -   049671
Saint Jean, 11bis Rue Champeaux, 10000 Troyes.
T. 0325732938. - Ant / Furn -   049672

Tulle (Corrèze)
Barbazanges, Joëlle, 18 Rue Georges-Thyvent, 19000
Tulle. T. 0555266808.   049673
Boulet, Olivier, 33 Quai Aristide-Briand, 19000 Tulle.
T. 0555203537. - Paint / Furn / Cur -   049674
Catheu, Paul de, 53 Rue Lucien-Sampeix, 19000 Tulle.
T. 0555200667.   049675
Chagot, Francis, 42 Rue Barrière, 19000 Tulle.
T. 0555264858.   049676

Dumaine, Suzanne, 21bis Av Alsace-Lorraine, 19000
Tulle. T. 0555201181.   049677

Ucel (Ardèche)
Baaren, Jasper van, Chemin Vals, 07200 Ucel.
T. 0475935048. - Ant -   049678
Fournier, Jean-Luc, Bréchignac, 07200 Ucel.
T. 0475946522. - Ant -   049679

Ugine (Savoie)
Chenal, Alain, 8 Rue Antoine-Borrel, 73400 Ugine.
T. 0479373167. - Ant -   049680

Urcel (Aisne)
Grenier, 68 Rte Rois, 02000 Urcel. T. 0323211011.
- Ant -   049681
Hutin, Michel, 11 Rte Rois, 02000 Urcel. T. 0323216369,
Fax 0323216107. - Ant -   049682

Urimenil (Vosges)
Petite Ferme, 652 Chapuy-Chantre, 88220 Urimenil.
T. 0329308290. - Paint / Furn / Cur -   049683

Urville-Nacqueville (Manche)
Fontaine, Danièle, Rue Roseaux, 50460 Urville-Nacque-
ville. T. 0233035285. - Furn -   049684

Ury (Seine-et-Marne)
Creat Informatique, 22 Rue Barre, 77116 Ury.
T. 64244260, Fax 64244810.   049685
Léonard, Anne, 20 Rue Nemours, 77116 Ury.
T. 64244717.   049686
Paillard, Arlette, 1 Rue Fontainebleau, 77116 Ury.
T. 64244447.   049687

Ussac (Corrèze)
Mons, François, Saint-Antoine, Les Plantades, 19270
Ussac. T. 0555740916.   049688

Ussel (Corrèze)
Deluermoz, Jean-Marc, 2 Rue Transwal, 19200 Ussel.
T. 0555725272. - Paint / Furn / Cur -   049689
Pont de la Sarsonne, 81 Av Carnot, 19200 Ussel.
T. 0555962654.   049690

Uzerche (Corrèze)
Lafarge, Juliette, Rue Jean-Gentet, 19140 Uzerche.
T. 0555732357.   049691

Uzès (Gard)
Art et Maison, Rue Amiral-Brueys, 30700 Uzès.
T. 0466227845.   049692
Art et Maison, 1 Pl Dampmartin, 30700 Uzès.
T. 0466831487.   049693
Au Bon Vieux Temps, Fouzes, 30700 Uzès.
T. 0466031273.   049694
Favand, Brigitte, 7 Rue Salin, 30700 Uzès.
T. 0466222404.   049695
Simon, Dany, Tourelles Pont-Charrettes, 30700 Uzès.
T. 0466221999, Fax 0466224526.   049696

Vaison-la-Romaine (Vaucluse)
Galant, Catherine, 44 Av Jules-Ferry, 84110 Vaison-la-
Romaine. T. 0490360940. - Ant / Furn -   049697

Val-d'Isère (Savoie)
Pauget, François, Imm Le-Valsnow, 73150 Val-d'Isère.
T. 0479062605. - Ant -   049698

Valaurie (Drôme)
Grenier de Sévigné, Quart Petites-Condamines, 26230
Valaurie. T. 0475986144.   049699

Valence (Drôme)
Arts Décoration Extrême-Orient, 8 Av Romans, 26000
Valence. T. 0475425253. - Orient -   049700
Au Bonheur du Jour, Rte Romans, 26000 Valence.
T. 0475437399.   049701
Au Vieux Rouet, 23 Rue Strasbourg, 26000 Valence.
T. 0475436802.   049702
Centre des Occasions, 471 Av Victor-Hugo, 26000 Va-
lence. T. 0475447006. - Furn / China / Silv /
Cur -   049703
Coulet, Jean-François, 22 Rue d'Athènes, 26000 Valen-
ce. T. 0475435133, Fax 0475557538. - Ant /
Furn -   049704

Dépôt Vente Particuliers, 138 Av Provence, 26000 Va-
lence. T. 0475561617.   049705
Hodot, 8 Rue Théâtre, 26000 Valence.
T. 0475423325.   049706
Knick Knack, 3 Rue Gaston-Rey, 26000 Valence.
T. 0475426270.   049707
Plantier, Pascal, 143 Av Chabeuil, 26000 Valence.
T. 0475556468.   049708

Valenciennes (Nord)
Adélaïde, 120 Pl 8-Mai-1945, 59300 Valenciennes.
T. 0327415040. - Ant -   049709
Argor, 74ter Rue Quesnoy, 59300 Valenciennes.
T. 0327471111. - Ant / Jew -   049710
Decleves, Claude, 87 Rue Saint-Géry, 59300 Valencien-
nes. T. 0327423534. - Ant -   049711
Druon, Jacques, 11 Rue Ferrand, 59300 Valenciennes.
T. 0327461803. - Ant -   049712
Kozak, 90 Famars, 59300 Valenciennes. T. 0327471148.
- Ant -   049713
Tange, 52 Rue Famars, 59300 Valenciennes.
T. 0327294936. - Ant / Paint -   049714
Uribe, Daniel, 42 Rue Famars, 59300 Valenciennes.
T. 0327413642. - Ant -   049715

Valennes (Sarthe)
Varin, Anne-Laurence, 18 Rue Eglise, 72320 Valennes.
T. 0243355051. - Ant -   049716

Vallan (Yonne)
Gaudry, Jacques, 19 Rte Nationale, 89580 Vallan.
T. 0386412538.   049717

Vallauris (Alpes-Maritimes)
Aux 3 Siècles, Rte Vallauris, 06220 Vallauris.
T. 0493632083.   049718
Boisoleil, 52 Av Georges-Clemenceau, 06220 Vallauris.
T. 0493632255.   049719
Brocantissimo, 27 Av Liberté, 06220 Vallauris.
T. 0493631465.   049720
Clef des Choses, 648 Rte Vallauris, 06220 Vallauris.
T. 0493635566.   049721
Loupiote, 47 Av Liberté, 06220 Vallauris.
T. 0493637046.   049722
Marché des Antiquaires, Av du Tapis-Vert, 06220 Vallau-
ris. T. 0493645207. - Ant -   049723
Vallauris Antic, 1 Pl Libération, 06220 Vallauris.
T. 0492951442.   049724

Valleiry (Haute-Savoie)
Gaury, Jean-Pierre, 150 Chemin Biollay, 74520 Valleiry.
T. 0450043421, Fax 0450042480.   049725

Valognes (Manche)
Diguet, 30 Blvd Felix-Buhot, 50700 Valognes.
T. 0233400396. - Furn / Cur -   049726
Duteurtre, Philippe, 40bis Rue Poterie, 50700 Valognes.
T. 0233403416. - Paint / Furn -   049727

Valréas (Vaucluse)
Poignant, Jean-Marc, 9 Chemin Ribeyronne, 84600 Valréas. T. 0490351063. - Ant -   049728

Vandoeuvre-lès-Nancy (Meurthe-et-Mo-selle)
Greniers du Père Sauce, 41 Rue Sainte-Colette, 54500
Vandoeuvre-lès-Nancy. T. 0383567763.   049729
Posalski, Jean-Pierre, 15 All Bruxelles, 54500 Van-
doeuvre-lès-Nancy. T. 0383534242.   049730

Vandrimare (Eure)
Decaux, Marc, 8 Pl Jean-Mary, 27380 Vandrimare.
T. 0232480218.   049731

Vannes (Morbihan)
Acanthe, 13 Rue Saint-Guénhaël, 56000 Vannes.
T. 0297475263. - Ant -   049732
Aristos Broc's, 7 Rue Thomas-de-Closmadeuc, 56000
Vannes. T. 0297543057. - Ant -   049733
Beaupré, 73 Av Edouard-Herriot, 56000 Vannes.
T. 0297543365. - Ant -   049734
Clipper, 16 Rue Saint-Salomon, 56000 Vannes.
T. 0297541724. - Furn -   049735
Cour des Miracles, 13 Rue Porte-Poterne, 56000 Van-
nes. T. 0297541624. - Ant -   049736

Damoutte, Dominique, 14 Rue Saint-Patern, 56000 Vannes. T. 0297471793. - Ant - _049737_

Damoutte, Gérard, 73 Av Edouard-Herriot, 56000 Vannes. T. 0297543365. - ant - _049738_

Estampille, 34 Rue Maréchal-Leclerc, 56000 Vannes. T. 0297424347. - Ant - _049739_

Le Paih, J & B, 17 Pl des Lices, 56000 Vannes. T. 0297427767. - Ant / Furn - _049740_

Maufret-Baugé, Anne-Marie, 3 Rue Porte-Poterne, 56000 Vannes. T. 0297472038. - Ant - _049741_

Moisan, Yves, 49 Rue Quatre-Frères-Créach, 56000 Vannes. T. 0297476362. - Ant - _049742_

Vanves (Hauts-de-Seine)

Domergue, Margaret, 52 Rue Mary-Besseyre, 92170 Vanves. T. 0146449852. _049743_

Guyot, Gérard, 38 Rue Raymond-Marcheron, 92170 Vanves. T. 0140951423. _049744_

Habrekorn, Jean-Pierre, 14 Av Pasteur, 92170 Vanves. T. 0146452008. _049745_

Mivielle, Jean-Pierre, 3 Pl Président-Kennedy, 92170 Vanves. T. 0146454800. _049746_

Varces-Allières et Risset (Isère)

Antiquité Temporel, 36 Gal Saint-Ange, 38760 Varces. T. 0476728980. - Ant / Furn / Lights - _049747_

Chenal, Jacques, Gal Saint-Ange, 38760 Varces-Allières. T. 0476219366. - Ant / Paint / Furn / Glass - _049748_

Dupuis, Gal Saint-Ange, 38760 Varces-Allières-Risset. T. 0476728265. - Ant - _049749_

Varengeville-sur-Mer (Seine-Maritime)

Guiho, Claude, Rte Sainte-Marguerite, 76119 Varengeville-sur-Mer. T. 0235851136. _049750_

Varennes-Vauzelles (Nièvre)

Bellot, Philippe, Les Quatre-Cheminées, 58640 Varennes-Vauzelles. T. 0386380698. _049751_

Stéphan, La Roseraie, 58640 Varennes-Vauzelles. T. 0386594799. - Paint / Furn / Cur / Toys - _049752_

Varetz (Corrèze)

Auger, Patrick, Barrière de Bosredon, 19240 Varetz. T. 0555842285. _049753_

Vieux Fusil, 14 Rue Jean-Baptiste-Bardinal, 19240 Varetz. T. 0555845564. - Furn / Cur - _049754_

Varilhes (Ariège)

Antiquités Ariégeoises, 19 Av Louis-Siret, 09120 Varilhes. T. 0561608400. Furn / Cur - _049755_

Déjean, René, 7 Av 8-Mai-1945, 09120 Varilhes. T. 0561677221. _049756_

Varrains (Maine-et-Loire)

Delaune, Roger, Grande Rue, 49400 Varrains. T. 41529098. _049757_

Vascœuil (Eure)

Cléon, Emmanuel, Village, 27910 Vascœuil. T. 0232322864. _049758_

Vasles (Deux-Sèvres)

Ferme de Firmin, La Coursaudière, 79340 Vasles. T. 0549699255. - Ant / Furn - _049759_

Vasles (Deux-Sèvres)

Ferme de Firmin, 35 km Ouest Poitiers-Coursaudière, 79340 Vasles. T. 0549699255. - Ant / Furn - _049760_

Vatan (Indre)

Belle Epoque, 10 Av Libération, 36150 Vatan. T. 0254499184. - Furn - _049761_

Vattetot-sous-Beaumont (Seine-Maritime)

Odinet, Micheline, La Gentilhommière, Ham Durosay, 76110 Vattetot-sous-Beaumont. T. 0235315676. _049762_

Vaubadon (Calvados)

Bouet, Jean-Loïc, 1 Rte Saint-Lô, 14490 Vaubadon. T. 0231925745. _049763_

Vaujours (Seine-Saint-Denis)

Antiquité Art Ancien, 50 Rue Sevran, 93410 Vaujours. T. 0149631562. _049764_

Dépôt Vente du Grand Cerf, 4 Rue Sevran, 93410 Vaujours. T. 0149630730. _049765_

Vaupillon (Eure-et-Loir)

Bourgeois, Marie, Le Plessis, 28240 Vaupillon. T. 0237810028. _049766_

Vauville (Calvados)

Engler, David, La Cour Notre-Dame, 14800 Vauville. T. 0231879441. _049767_

Vauvillers (Haute-Saône)

Giberton, Marie-Claude, 2 Rue Harpe, 70210 Vauvillers. T. 0384928877. _049768_

Vaux-sous-Aubigny (Haute-Marne)

Guérard, Marc, Couzon-sur-Coulange, 52190 Vaux-sous-Aubigny. T. 0325883416. _049769_

Neuville, Joseph, 23 Rue Bourgogne, 52190 Vaux-sous-Aubigny. T. 0325883062. - Furn / Instr / Cur - _049770_

Vaux-sur-Mer (Charente-Maritime)

Toujouse, Jean-Yves, Rocade Palmyre, ZA, Rte La Tremblade, 17640 Vaux-sur-Mer. T. 0546390869, Fax 0546381862. - Dec - _049771_

Vaux-sur-Seine (Yvelines)

Chrétien, Louis, 170 Rue Général-de-Gaulle, 78740 Vaux-sur-Seine. T. 0134742995. _049772_

Veauche (Loire)

Bonnassieux, Louis, 10 Lot Balmes, 42340 Veauche. T. 0477546922. _049773_

Vélizy-Villacoublay (Yvelines)

Hémon, Jean-Pierre, 5 Rue Racine, 78140 Vélizy-Villacoublay. T. 0139645401. _049774_

Suteau, Jean-François, 7 Av Picardie, 78140 Vélizy-Villacoublay. T. 0139466444. _049775_

Vellefrie (Haute-Saône)

Mairey, Evelyne, Rte Vesoul, 70240 Vellefrie. T. 0384958501. _049776_

Velleron (Vaucluse)

Mas de Laude, 21 Chemin des Arrayies (D938), 84740 Velleron. T. 0490201185. - Ant - _049777_

Venarsal (Corrèze)

Au Vieux Grenier, Les Traverses, 19360 Venarsal. T. 0555257852. _049778_

Vence (Alpes-Maritimes)

Fayolle, Laurence, 9 Av Marcellin-Maurel, 06140 Vence. T. 0493240004. _049779_

Galerie Librairie de la Basse Fontaine, 2 Pl Antony-Mars, 06140 Vence. T. 0493580480. - Repr - _049780_

Martin, Georges, 8 Rue L'Evéché, 06140 Vence. T. 0493581147. - Ant - _049781_

Trouvailles, 30 Pl Antony-Mars, 06140 Vence. T. 0493581227. - Ant - _049782_

Vendôme (Loir-et-Cher)

Bigot, Jean-Claude, 4 Quai Saint-Georges, 41100 Vendôme. T. 0254770545. _049783_

Descotis, Pierre-Marie, 61 Rue Poterie, 41100 Vendôme. T. 0254778407. _049784_

Favrel, Didier, 4 Rue Abbaye, 41100 Vendôme. T. 0254770428. _049785_

Ginis, René, 104 Fbg Chartrain, 41100 Vendôme. T. 0254771498. _049786_

Vendrennes (Vendée)

Robic, Dominique, 6bis La Touche-Bertrand, 85250 Vendrennes. T. 0251661173. _049787_

Vénérand (Charente-Maritime)

Lalonnier, Eddie, La Vieille Verrerie, 17100 Vénérand. T. 0546971417. _049788_

Vénès (Tarn)

Grenier à Meuble, Rte Nationale, 81440 Vénès. T. 0563759370, Fax 0563753336. - Furn - _049789_

Veneux-les-Sablons (Seine-et-Marne)

Brakha, David, 2 Rue Matter, 77250 Veneux-les-Sablons. T. 0360703526. _049790_

Vénissieux (Rhône)

Au Temps Passé, 65 Rue Jules-Ferry, 69200 Vénissieux. T. 0472510263. _049791_

Verberie (Oise)

Vigoureux, Philippe, 9 Rue Juliette-Adam, 60410 Verberie. T. 0344405334. - Ant - _049792_

Verdun (Meuse)

Collections Internationales, 29 Rue Saint-Victor, 55100 Verdun. T. 0329860544. - Ant - _049793_

Potennec, Olivier, Rte Argonne, 55100 Verdun. T. 0329861151. - Ant / Paint / Furn - _049794_

Tassart, Mireille, 3bis Pont-des-Minimes, 55100 Verdun. T. 0329866182. - Ant - _049795_

Verdun-sur-Garonne (Tarn-et-Garonne)

Béarzatti, Jean-Pierre, Clos Roux-Baladels, 82600 Verdun-sur-Garonne. T. 0563028524. _049796_

Verfeil (Haute-Garonne)

Poste aux Chevaux, 12 Grand Faubourg, 31590 Verfeil. T. 0561356690. _049797_

Verjon (Ain)

Gros, Cité-des-Antiquaires, 01270 Verjon. T. 0474515141, Fax 0474515600. - Ant - _049798_

Vermenton (Yonne)

Courtois, Fernand, Château Talent, 89270 Vermenton. T. 0386815060. _049799_

Paret, Michel, 89270 Vermenton. T. 0386815817. _049800_

Vern-sur-Seiche (Ille-et-Vilaine)

Porcher, Dominique, Zone Artisanale Le Bouridel, 35770 Vern-sur-Seiche. T. 0299004527. _049801_

Vernet (Haute-Garonne)

Grosso, Francis, Village, 31810 Vernet. T. 0561085006. _049802_

Verneuil-en-Halatte (Oise)

Binardière, 30 Rue Aristide-Briand, 60550 Verneuil-en-Halatte. T. 0144251001. - Ant - _049803_

Verneuil-sur-Avre (Eure)

Antiquités de la Madeleine, 276 Rue Madeleine, 27130 Verneuil-sur-Avre. T. 0232320704. _049804_

Boulet, Jean-Claude, 163 Rue Docteur-Fabre, 27130 Verneuil-sur-Avre. T. 0232309551. _049805_

Cherruault, Isabelle, 141 Rue Canon, 27130 Verneuil-sur-Avre. T. 0232603810. _049806_

Evènement, 366 Rue Gambetta, 27130 Verneuil-sur-Avre. T. 0232601711. _049807_

Macé, Roland, 539 Rue Madeleine, 27130 Verneuil-sur-Avre. T. 0232323771. _049808_

Miroir du Temps, 561 Rue Madeleine, 27130 Verneuil-sur-Avre. T. 0232602225. _049809_

Nourry-Joannès, Claudine, 105 Rue Thiers, 27130 Verneuil-sur-Avre. T. 0232321985. _049810_

Verneuil-sur-Seine (Yvelines)

Bougerie, Dominique, 8 Rue Rosiers, 78480 Verneuil-sur-Seine. T. 0139711570. _049811_

Brocante de Verneuil, 65 Rue Graviers, 78480 Verneuil-sur-Seine. T. 0139718480. _049812_

Vernon (Eure)

Castreau, Jean, 26 Rue Albuféra, 27200 Vernon. T. 0232510412. _049813_

Simon, Gilles, 31 Rue Potard, 27200 Vernon. T. 0232210601. _049814_

Verrières-le-Buisson (Essonne)

Breton-Proute, Monique, 18 Rue D'Estienne-d'Orves, 91370 Verrières-le-Buisson. T. 0169207498. _049815_

Vers-Pont-du-Gard (Gard)

Brissaud, Jacky, Mas La-Bérangère, Chemin Passeur, 30210 Vers-Pont-du-Gard. T. 0466229088. _049816_

Versailles (Yvelines)
Acanthe, 14bis Rue Baillet-Reviron, 78000 Versailles.
T. 0139530608. 049817
Antic Show, 8 Rue Rameau, 78000 Versailles.
T. 0139537693. 049818
Antiquaires de la Geôle, Passage Geôle, 10 Rue Rameau, 78000 Versailles. T. 0130211513,
- Ant - 049819
Apélian, Monique, 10 Rue Rameau, 78000 Versailles.
T. 0139021727. 049820
Arcane, 17 Rue Anjou, 78000 Versailles.
T. 0139502108. - Furn / Cur - 049821
Au Vieux Souvenir, 33 Av Saint-Cloud, 78000 Versailles.
T. 0139506422. - Furn / Cur - 049822
Au Vieux Versailles, 8 Rue Deux-Portes, 78000 Versailles. T. 0139515918. 049823
Baily, Claire, 20 Rue Royale, 78000 Versailles.
T. 0139504371. - Ant / Paint / Furn / China / Instr / Rel /
Cur - 049824
Barilleau, Ghislaine, 13 Passage Geôle, 78000 Versailles. T. 0139507366. 049825
Bossetti, Michèle, 17 Passage Geôle, 78000 Versailles.
T. 0139021633. 049826
Brocante et Bijoux Saint-Louis, 21 et 25 Rue Général-Leclerc, 78000 Versailles. T. 0130217812. - Paint /
Furn / Sculp / Jew / Silv / Cur - 049827
Brocantique, 25 Rue Etats-Généraux, 78000 Versailles.
T. 0139511192. 049828
Carton, Karin, 16 Passage Geôle, 78000 Versailles.
T. 0139027707. 049829
Daguenet, B., 3 Pl Hoche, 78000 Versailles.
T. 0139506714. - Ant - 049830
Dalençon, 3 Rue Baillage, 78000 Versailles.
T. 0139506438. 049831
Dauphin, 2 Rue Deux-Portes, 78000 Versailles.
T. 0139022844. 049832
Dubois, Rémi, 13 Rue Pourvoierie, 78000 Versailles.
T. 0139495764. 049833
Faucille d'Or, 5 Rue Baillage, 78000 Versailles.
T. 0139513210. 049834
Galerie d'Orphée, 24 Rue Baillet-Reviron, 78000 Versailles. T. 0130218997. - Paint / Furn / Cur - 049835
Galerie du Carré, 25 Passage Geôle, 78000 Versailles.
T. 0139533048. 049836
Galerie Montansier, 13 Rue de la Paroisse, 78000 Versailles. T. 0139502796. - Ant / Furn / Dec - 049837
Galerie Saint-Louis, 11 Rue Orient, 78000 Versailles.
T. 0130215494. - China - 049838
Galerie Seize, 16 Rue Baillet-Reviron, 78000 Versailles.
T. 0139021532. 049839
Grenier d'Hélène, Passage Geôle, 78000 Versailles.
T. 0139021156. 049840
Leclerq, Eric, 4 Rue Baillage, 78000 Versailles.
T. 0139503414. 049841
Lemonnier Frères, 10 Rue Rameau, 78000 Versailles.
T. 0139027961. 049842
Lombard, Jean-Marc, 10 Rue Coste, 78000 Versailles.
T. 0139502780. 049843
Mader, Fanny, Passage Geôle, 78000 Versailles.
T. 0139494356. 049844
Mailly, Chantal, 4 Passage Saladin, 78000 Versailles.
T. 0139506563. - Furn / Cur - 049845
Martin du Buis, 10 Rue Rameau, 78000 Versailles.
T. 0139495464. 049846
Messageot, Charles-Henri, 2 Rue Baillage, 78000 Versailles. T. 0139021460. 049847
Michel, Françoise, 13 Rue Pourvoierie, 78000 Versailles.
T. 0139504521. 049848
Pellat de Villedon, Jean-Yves, 5 Rue Marché-Neuf,
78000 Versailles. T. 0139511672. 049849
Pendule, 5 Rue Baillage, 78000 Versailles.
T. 0139506431. - Instr - 049850
Pouillon, Jacques, 2 Rue Ménard, 78000 Versailles.
T. 0139517860. - Dec - 049851
Ravier, Jeanne, 23 Rue Carnot, 78000 Versailles.
T. 0139501374. 049852
Renaissances, 15 Rue Paroisse, 78000 Versailles.
T. 0139519033. 049853
Séry, Dominique, 13 Rue Pourvoierie, 78000 Versailles.
T. 0139508968. 049854
Simonot-Amigues, 5 Rue Baillage, 78000 Versailles.
T. 0139538572. 049855

Sommerlath, Michèle, 16 Rue Baillet-Reviron, 78000
Versailles. T. 0139511760. 049856
Suissa, Alice, 10 Rue Rameau, 78000 Versailles.
T. 0130211157. 049857
Trésors de Versailles, 9 Rue Saint-Honoré, 78000 Versailles. T. 0139670413. - Paint / Orient / China / Jew /
Silv - 049858
Véronik'Anne, 13 Rue Pourvoierie, 78000 Versailles.
T. 0139517553. 049859

Vert-le-Petit (Essonne)
Acanthe, 11 Rue Amand-Louis, 91710 Vert-le-Petit.
T. 0164934040. 049860

Verteuil-sur-Charente (Charente)
Chat Qui Danse, Rue Halles, 16510 Verteuil-sur-Charente. T. 0545314449. 049861

Vertou (Loire-Atlantique)
Antiquités 44, 446 Rte Clisson, 44120 Vertou.
T. 40334646. - Paint / Furn / Cur - 049862

Vescovato (Corse)
Barone-Stefani, Jean-François, Torra, 20215 Vescovato.
T. 0495366121. 049863

Vesly (Eure)
Lefèvre, Romain, 7 Rue Clos-du-Décret, 27870 Vesly.
T. 0232556033. 049864
Schwob, Pierre, 22 Grande Rue, Clos-des-Saules,
27870 Vesly. T. 0232552528. 049865

Vesoul (Haute-Saône)
Brenner, Michel, 38 Rue Saint-Georges, 70000 Vesoul.
T. 0384757825. 049866
Girard, ZI Regains, 70000 Vesoul. T. 0384761966,
Fax 0384768635. - Dec - 049867
Nova et Vetera, 22 Rue Georges-Genoux, 70000 Vesoul.
T. 0384754280. 049868
Résillot, Michel, 9 Rue Baron-Bouvier, 70000 Vesoul.
T. 0384760819. 049869

Vesseaux (Ardèche)
Court, Bernard, Rte Nationale Les Fargiers, 07200 Vesseaux. T. 0475938759. - Ant - 049870

Vétraz-Monthoux (Haute-Savoie)
Au Temps Jadis, 25 Rte Monthoux, 74100 Vétraz-Monthoux. T. 0450375179. 049871

Veules-les-Roses (Seine-Maritime)
Mythes et Mites, 12 Rue Marché, 76980 Veules-les-Roses. T. 0235979926. 049872

Vézelay (Yonne)
Pacault, André, 1 Pl Eglise, 89450 Vézelay.
T. 0386555473. 049873
Vogade, Philippe, 1 Rue Chapitre, 89450 Vézelay.
T. 0386332313. - Ant / Graph / Furn / China - 049874

Vezins (Maine-et-Loire)
Robic, Albert, 2 Rue Nationale, 49340 Vezins.
T. 41649234, Fax 41649235. 049875

Vic-en-Bigorre (Hautes-Pyrénées)
Bourrut, Lucienne, 2 Av Tarbes, 65500 Vic-en-Bigorre.
T. 0562968090. - Ant - 049876

Vic-Fezensac (Gers)
Fauroux, Philippe, Rte Auch, 32190 Vic-Fezensac.
T. 0562064676. - Furn / Cur - 049877
Marmier, Jean-Maurice, Lagraulas, 32190 Vic-Fezensac. T. 0562063877. 049878

Vic-le-Comte (Puy-de-Dôme)
Galerie Calao, 31 Pl Vieux-Marché, 63270 Vic-le-Comte.
T. 0473690746, Fax 0473690746. - Ant - 049879
Hall, Anita, 50 Pl Vieux-Marché, 63270 Vic-le-Comte.
T. 0473690747. - Ant - 049880
Laurent, François, 27 Pl Liberté, 63270 Vic-le-Comte.
T. 0473692531. - Ant / Eth / Cur - 049881
Laurent & Vimal, Place-de-la-Liberté, 63270 Vic-le-Comte. T. 0473692531. - Ant / Furn - 049882
Rivon, Alexandre, 21 Pl Liberté, 63270 Vic-le-Comte.
T. 0473690284. - Furn - 049883
Vic Antic, 28 Pl Liberté, 63270 Vic-le-Comte.
T. 0473691541. - Ant - 049884

Vimal, Emmanuel, Pl Liberté, 63270 Vic-le-Comte.
T. 0473692193. - Ant - 049885

Vichy (Allier)
Alexandre, Michel, 15 Rue Duchon, 03200 Vichy.
T. 0470977478, Fax 70977499. - Ant - 049886
Au Temps Jadis, 18 Pass Giboin, 03200 Vichy.
T. 0470313713. - Ant - 049887
Crétier, François, Galerie Napoléon, 03200 Vichy.
T. 0470977720, Fax 0470960425. - Ant /
Furn - 049888
Duffar, Nicole, 45 Blvd Gambetta, 03200 Vichy.
T. 0470314210. - Furn - 049889
Fernandez, Noël-Michel, 6 Blvd Russie, 03200 Vichy.
T. 0470975676. - Ant - 049890
Frobert, Suzanne, 7 Pl Allier, 03200 Vichy.
T. 0470321620. - Ant - 049891
Galerie de l'Impératrice, 14 Gal Source-Hôpital, 03200
Vichy. T. 0470315247. - Ant - 049892
Giard, Guy, 5 Av Près-Doumer, 03200 Vichy.
T. 0470983523. - Ant / Cur - 049893
L'Indiscret, 12 Rue Beauparlant, 03200 Vichy.
T. 0470980981. - Ant - 049894
Laurent, Guy, 16 Av de Lyon, 03200 Vichy.
T. 0470590940. - Ant - 049895
Liandier, François, Rue Parc, 03200 Vichy.
T. 0470975592. - Ant / Furn - 049896
Martial Antiquités, 18 Gal Source-Hôpital, 03200 Vichy.
T. 0470974049. - Ant - 049897
Rom'Antiq Antiquités, 24 Rue Montaret, 03200 Vichy.
T. 0470981961. - Ant - 049898
Tournebize, Jean-François, 108 Blvd Nenière, 03200 Vichy. T. 0470985927. - Ant - 049899
Versantic, 26 Rue Montaret, 03200 Vichy.
T. 0470312833. - Ant - 049900

Vidauban (Var)
Au Double Ecot, 1 Lot, ZA, N 7, 83550 Vidauban.
T. 0494736066. 049902
Broc'Brothers, Quartier Plan, 83550 Vidauban.
T. 0494735383. 049903
Moulin, Quartier Moulin, 83550 Vidauban.
T. 0495736608. 049904

Vielle-Saint-Girons (Landes)
Carpe Diem, Rte Lacs-Quartier-Jeantôt, 40560 Vielle-Saint-Girons. T. 0558479491. 049905

Vienne (Isère)
Ronde des Bois, Imp Pilat, 38200 Vienne.
T. 0474849989. - Ant - 049906

Viersat (Creuse)
Baroucheix d'Alembert, 10 Baroucheix, 23170 Viersat.
T. 0555657253. - Ant - 049907

Vierzon (Cher)
Brocantelle, 60 Rue Ponts, 18100 Vierzon.
T. 0248751686. 049908
Hussenot-Desenonges, Bruno, 1 Av Colonel-Frédéric-Manhes, 18100 Vierzon. T. 0248751777. 049909

Vieux-Condé (Nord)
Bazooka, 152 Pl République, 59690 Vieux-Condé.
T. 0327406252. - Ant - 049910

Vieux Moulin
Feuillerale Antiquités, 7 Rue Etanges, 60350 Vieux Moulin. T. 0344859050. - Ant - 049911

Vieux-Thann (Haut-Rhin)
Manoir Antiquités Brocante, 67 Rte Cernay, 68800
Vieux-Thann. T. 0389378451. 049912
Mobiliocase, 35 Rue Charles-de-Gaulle, 68800 Vieux-Thann. T. 0389375314. - Furn - 049913

Vigeois (Corrèze)
Bruneau, Michel & Jean-Pierre Tasserie, Pont de Bleygeat, 19410 Vigeois. T. 0555989265. 049914

Vigneux-sur-Seine (Essonne)
Saguer, 1 All Danton, 91270 Vigneux-sur-Seine.
T. 0169032741. 049915

Vignory (Haute-Marne)

Duplessis, J.V., Rue Général-Leclerc, Le Prieuré, 52320
Vignory. T. 0325318185, Fax 0325312735. - Paint /
Furn / Sculp / Dec / Instr / Cur - *049916*

Vigoulet-Auzil (Haute-Garonne)

Antic Art, Chemin Auzil, 31320 Vigoulet-Auzil.
T. 0561733048. *049917*
Lapointe, Edith, Chemin Causset, 31320 Vigoulet-Auzil.
T. 0561734114. *049918*

Vihiers (Maine-et-Loire)

Jeandrot, Rose-Marie, 38 Rue Nationale, 49310 Vihiers.
T. 41561522. *049919*

Ville-d'Avray (Hauts-de-Seine)

Beaumarie, Jean, 227 Rue Versailles, 92410 Ville-
d'Avray. T. 0147096802. *049920*
Girandole, 56 Rue Saint-Cloud, 92410 Ville-d'Avray.
T. 0147505949. *049921*
Isle d'Avray, 52 Rue Saint-Cloud, 92410 Ville-d'Avray.
T. 0147502485. *049922*
Tempera, 26 Rue Saint-Cloud, 92410 Ville-d'Avray.
T. 0147091298. *049923*

Ville-la-Grand (Haute-Savoie)

Lamouille, Bernard, 6 Rue Commerce, 74100 Ville-la-
Grand. T. 0450373001. *049924*

Villebernier (Maine-et-Loire)

Antiquités Buisson Perron, Le Buisson Perron, 49400
Villebernier. T. 41510052. *049925*
Brocante de la Loire, 29 Rue Nationale, 49400 Villeber-
nier. T. 41677027. - Ant / Furn - *049926*

Villebon-sur-Yvette (Essonne)

Maison Marc & Eva, 6 Av Val-d'Yvette, 91140 Villebon-
sur-Yvette. T. 0160102851. *049927*

Villecroze (Var)

Lions, Jean, Rue Ambroise-Croizat, 83690 Villecroze.
T. 0494706459. - Ant - *049928*

Villedieu-les-Poêles (Manche)

Antiquités Le Grenier, Rte Granville, 50800 Villedieu-les-
Poêles. T. 0233611078. - Furn / Cur - *049929*
Hervy, Eric, 48 Rue Carnot, 50800 Villedieu-les-Poêles.
T. 0233511851. *049930*
Hervy, Eric, 28 Rue Pont-Chignon, 50800 Villedieu-les-
Poêles. T. 0233900089. *049931*
Hervy, Fernand, 28 Rue Pont-Chignon, 50800 Villedieu-
les-Poêles. T. 0233900089. *049932*

Villedieu-sur-Indre (Indre)

Carnet, J.P.H., 50 Rue Général-de-Gaulle, 36320 Ville-
dieu-sur-Indre. T. 0254260716. *049933*

Villefranche-de-Rouergue (Aveyron)

Biard, Michel, 30 Av Ségala, 12200 Villefranche-de-
Rouergue. T. 0565452737. *049934*
Combret, Gabriel, Arcades Consulat, 12200 Villefran-
che-de-Rouergue. T. 0565455966. *049935*
Grésilières, Marie-Hélène, 26 Av Ségala, 12200 Ville-
franche-de-Rouergue. T. 0565811265. *049936*
Paillous, Jacques, La Madeleine, 12200 Villefranche-
de-Rouergue. T. 0565454958. *049937*

Villefranche-sur-Saône (Rhône)

Brocante du Forum, 222 Rue Paix, 69400 Villefranche-
sur-Saône. T. 0474682186. *049938*
Didierjean, Louis, 816 Rue Robert-Schumann, 69400
Villefranche-sur-Saône. T. 0474629417. *049939*
Lautard, Marie-Paule, 78 Rue Nicolas-Rissler, 69400 Vil-
lefranche-sur-Saône. T. 0474091122. *049940*
Nallet, Marie-Thérèse, 191 Rue Belleville, 69400 Ville-
franche-sur-Saône. T. 0474654829. *049941*
Paricot, Franck, 40 Rue Stalingrad, 69400 Villefranche-
sur-Saône. T. 0474091407. *049942*
Temps Passé, 234 Rue Belleville, 69400 Villefranche-
sur-Saône. T. 0474680896. *049943*

Villejuif (Val-de-Marne)

Arthur Laurient's, 14bis Blvd Maxime-Gorki, 94800 Vil-
lejuif. T. 0147264699. *049944*
Au Grenier du Passé, 9 Rue Guynemer, 94800 Villejuif.
T. 0146778703. *049945*

Villemer (Yonne)

Royale Antique, 19 Grande Rue, 89113 Villemer.
T. 0386737021. *049946*

Villemomble (Seine-Saint-Denis)

Delassus, Jean-Louis, 66 Av Raincy, 93250 Villemom-
ble. T. 0148540596. *049947*
Moyer, Christian, 129 Grande Rue, 93250 Villemomble.
T. 0148551737. *049948*

Villemur-sur-Tarn (Haute-Garonne)

Ravez, Joël, 10 Av Franklin-Roosevelt, 31340 Villemur-
sur-Tarn. T. 0561351075. *049949*

Villeneuve (Alpes-de-Haute-Provence)

Trésors du passé, La Ricaude RN 96, 04180 Villeneuve.
T. 0492793124. - Ant - *049950*

Villeneuve-d'Ascq (Nord)

Chris'Ary, 114 Rue Jean-Jaurès, 59650 Villeneuve-
d'Ascq. T. 0320984365. - Ant - *049951*
Motte, Rémy, 202 Rue Jean-Jaurès, 59650 Villeneuve-
d'Ascq. T. 0320898891, Fax 0320459875. - Ant /
Paint / Furn - *049952*
Rousseau, Jean-Noël, 84 Rue Gaston-Baratte, 59650
Villeneuve-d'Ascq. T. 0320790317. - Ant - *049953*

Villeneuve-l'Archevêque (Yonne)

Vieille Forge, 49 Rue République, 89190 Villeneuve-l'Ar-
chevêque. T. 0386868182. *049954*

Villeneuve-la-Garenne (Hauts-de-Seine)

Bonne Aubaine, 20 Rue Bongarde, 92390 Villeneuve-la-
Garenne. T. 0140859881. - Paint / Furn - *049955*

Villeneuve-le-Comte (Seine-et-Marne)

Ozanne, Jean-Pierre, 2 Rue Général-de-Gaulle, 77174
Villeneuve-le-Comte. T. 0360430939. *049956*

Villeneuve-lès-Avignon (Gard)

Quezel Mouchet, Andrée, 10 Blvd Guynemer, 30400 Villeneuve-lès-Avignon. T. 0490250438. *049957*

Villeneuve-Saint-Georges (Val-de-Marne)

Monard, Nicole, 43 Rue Crosne, 94190 Villeneuve-
Saint-Georges. T. 0143890680. *049958*

Villeneuve-sur-Lot (Lot-et-Garonne)

Bellino, Michel, 51 Av Général-Leclerc, 47300 Villeneu-
ve-sur-Lot. T. 0553700291. *049959*
Bertran, Jean-Pierre, Calvétie-Ouest, 47300 Villeneuve-
sur-Lot. T. 0553706075. *049960*
Bordes, Michel, Paga-Ouest, 47300 Villeneuve-sur-Lot.
T. 0553706591. - Furn / Cur - *049961*
Fournier des Corats, Marie-Thérèse, 27 Rue Chasse-
neuil, 47300 Villeneuve-sur-Lot.
T. 0553704191. *049962*
Galerie Edera, 21 Blvd Palissy, 47300 Villeneuve-sur-
Lot. T. 0553704399. - Paint / Furn / Sculp /
Cur - *049963*
Les 3 Tours, Rte Paris-Boutouzet, 47300 Villeneuve-sur-
Lot. T. 0553702798. *049964*
Murari, Max, 8bis Rue Léon-Bonnet, 47300 Villeneuve-
sur-Lot. T. 0553703930. - Paint / Furn / Cur - *049965*
Vecchi, M.C. de, 31 Rue Frères-Clavet, 47300 Villeneu-
ve-sur-Lot. T. 0553015254. - Paint / Furn /
Cur - *049966*

Villeneuve-sur-Yonne (Yonne)

André, Jean-Pierre, 16 Av Général-de-Gaulle, 89500 Vil-
leneuve-sur-Yonne. T. 0386965033. *049967*
Brocante Saint-Nicolas, 1 Blvd Victor-Hugo, 89500 Vil-
leneuve-sur-Yonne. T. 0386965458. *049968*
Hardy, Kléber, 72 Rue Général-de-Gaulle, 89500 Vill-
euve-sur-Yonne. T. 0386871061. *049969*

Villeneuve-Tolosane (Haute-Garonne)

Playe de Boissieu, 21 Rue Saint-Laurent, 31270 Villen-
euve-Tolosane. T. 0561928354. *049970*

Villeperrot (Yonne)

Antony, G., Rue Joignottes, 89140 Villeperrot.
T. 0386671582. *049971*

Villepinte (Aude)

Au Castel, RN 113, Le Castel, 11150 Villepinte.
T. 0468942496. *049972*
Darre, Cosette, 26 Blvd Gambetta, 11150 Villepinte.
T. 0468942496. *049973*

Villeréal (Lot-et-Garonne)

Bouché, Lucette, Rue Saint-Roch, 47210 Villeréal.
T. 0553360093. *049974*

Villers-la-Chèvre (Meurthe-et-Moselle)

Pierson, Marie-Françoise, 9bis Rue Longwy, 54870 Vil-
lers-la-Chèvre. T. 0382449728. *049975*

Villers-lès-Nancy (Meurthe-et-Moselle)

Burté, Bernadette, 38 Av Libération, 54600 Villers-lès-
Nancy. T. 0383287604. - Furn / Cur - *049976*

Villers-Outréaux (Nord)

Poncelet, David, 33 Rue Victor-Hugo, 59142 Villers-Ou-
tréaux. T. 0327820485. - Ant - *049977*

Villers-sur-Mer (Calvados)

Jolly Farm Antiques, Rte Touques, 14640 Villers-sur-
Mer. T. 0231876557. *049978*
Mascarade, 2 Rue Maréchal-Foch, 14640 Villers-sur-
Mer. T. 0231984587, Fax 0231984609. *049979*

Villerville (Calvados)

Duvieu, Jacques, 26 Av Littoral, 14113 Villerville.
T. 0231872318. - Paint / Furn / Sculp / Cur - *049980*
Marie-Watts, Paule, 45 Rue Maréchal-Foch, 14113 Vil-
lerville. T. 0231872025. *049981*

Villette-lès-Arbois (Jura)

Vigoureux, Louise, Rue Résistance, 39600 Villette-lès-
Arbois. T. 0384374014. *049982*

Villeurbanne (Rhône)

Aiglon Galerie des Glaces, 117 Blvd Stalingrad, Cité des
Antiquaires, 69100 Villeurbanne. T. 0478940920.
- Glass - *049983*
Amprino-Félix, Bernard, 117 Blvd Stalingrad, Cité des
Antiquaires, 69100 Villeurbanne.
T. 0478890143. *049984*
Anthoine, Frédéric, 117 Blvd Stalingrad, Cité des Anti-
quaires, 69100 Villeurbanne. T. 0472442025.
- Dec - *049985*
Arbore, Marie-Jeanne, 117 Blvd Stalingrad, Cité des An-
tiquaires, 69100 Villeurbanne. T. 0478932319.
- Paint / Furn - *049986*
Arquebusier, 50 Cours Tolstoï, 69100 Villeurbanne.
T. 0478688783, Fax 0478484763. - Mil - *049987*
Art Campus, 117 Blvd Stalingrad, Cité des Antiquaires,
69100 Villeurbanne. T. 0472820595. *049988*
Au Passé Simple, 117 Blvd Stalingrad, Cité des Antiqui-
res, Stand 184, 69100 Villeurbanne. T. 0478895516.
- Furn / Cur - *049989*
Aux Lucioles, 117 Blvd Stalingrad, Cité des Antiquaires,
69100 Villeurbanne. T. 0478939269. *049990*
Aux Trois Clés, 117 Blvd Stalingrad, Cité des Antiquai-
res, 69100 Villeurbanne. T. 0472442202.
- Cur - *049991*
Baudry, Luc, 117 Blvd Stalingrad, Cité des Antiquaires,
69100 Villeurbanne. T. 0472440970, Fax 0472442616.
- Ant / Paint / Furn / Instr - *049992*
Bayet, Max, 117 Blvd Stalingrad, Cité des Antiquaires,
69100 Villeurbanne. T. 0478897716. *049993*
Because I Love, 117 Blvd Stalingrad, Cité des Antiquai-
res, 69100 Villeurbanne. T. 0472440656. - Dec /
Cur - *049994*
Beronnet, Marcel, 117 Blvd Stalingrad, Cité des Anti-
quaires, 69100 Villeurbanne. T. 0472449523. - Paint /
Furn / Cur - *049995*
Bertholet, Christian, 76 Av Roger-Salengro, 69100 Vil-
leurbanne. T. 0472442258, Fax 0478935896. *049996*
Bouley, Alain, 117 Blvd Stalingrad, Cité des Antiquaires,
69100 Villeurbanne. T. 0478897982. - Ant - *049997*
Bouley, Georges, 117 Blvd Stalingrad, Cité des Antiquai-
res, Stand 119, 69100 Villeurbanne. T. 0478897629.
- Furn - *049998*
Bouley, Jacques, 117 Blvd Stalingrad, Cité des Antiquai-
res, 69100 Villeurbanne. T. 0472443194.
- Furn - *049999*

Bouley, Josiane, 117 Blvd Stalingrad, Cité des Antiquaires, Stand 118, 69100 Villeurbanne.
T. 0478941873. 050000
Bouley, Roger, 117 Blvd Stalingrad, Cité des Antiquaires, 69100 Villeurbanne. T. 0478937024. - Paint / Furn / Cur - 050001
Boutique 155, 117 Blvd Stalingrad, Cité des Antiquaires, 69100 Villeurbanne. 0478898425. 050002
Buhard, Jean-Yves, 117 Blvd Stalingrad, Cité des Antiquaires, 69100 Villeurbanne. T. 0478932748, Fax 0474214103. - Paint / Furn / Cur - 050003
Caverne des Particuliers, 12 Rue Léon-Chomel, 69100 Villeurbanne. T. 0478037587. 050004
Chaintreuil, Marc, 117 Blvd Stalingrad, Cité des Antiquaires, 69100 Villeurbanne. T. 0472430808. - Paint / Furn / Cur - 050005
Chaussinand, Yves, 23 Rue Dedieu, 69100 Villeurbanne. T. 0478523734. - Cur - 050006
Cité des Antiquaires, 117 Blvd Stalingrad, 69100 Villeurbanne. T. 0472449198, Fax 0472442616.
- Ant - 050007
Clerc, Jean-Louis, 117 Blvd Stalingrad, Cité des Antiquaires, 69100 Villeurbanne. T. 0478949842. - Paint / Furn / Cur - 050008
Contre Temps, 117 Blvd Stalingrad, Cité des Antiquaires, 69100 Villeurbanne. T. 0472443148. - Furn / China / Silv / Glass - 050009
Courtois, Jeanine, 117 Blvd Stalingrad, Cité des Antiquaires, 69100 Villeurbanne. T. 0478894509. - Paint / Furn / Cur - 050010
Crapie, 117 Blvd Stalingrad, Cité des Antiquaires, 69100 Villeurbanne. T. 0478932473. - China - 050011
Dauphin, Hervé, 117 Blvd Stalingrad, Cité des Antiquaires, 69100 Villeurbanne. T. 0472440248.
- Mod - 050012
Degioanni, Léopold, 117 Blvd Stalingrad, Cité des Antiquaires, 69100 Villeurbanne. T. 0472449891. - Paint / Sculp / Draw - 050013
Delage, Philippe, 117 Blvd Stalingrad, Cité des Antiquaires, 69100 Villeurbanne. T. 0478897021. 050014
Deville, Michelle, 117 Blvd Stalingrad, Cité des Antiquaires, 69100 Villeurbanne. T. 0478934162.
- Cur - 050015
Dolfus, Paule, 117 Blvd Stalingrad, Cité des Antiquaires, 69100 Villeurbanne. T. 0478937641. - Paint / Furn / Cur - 050016
Druard, Jacques, 117 Blvd Stalingrad, Cité des Antiquaires, 69100 Villeurbanne. T. 0478946636. - Paint / Furn / Cur - 050017
Durand, Gilles, 117 Blvd Stalingrad, Cité des Antiquaires, 69100 Villeurbanne. T. 0472443122. 050018
Favre, Pierre, 117 Blvd Stalingrad, Cité des Antiquaires, 69100 Villeurbanne. T. 0478896121. - Furn - 050019
Fayette, Gilbert, 117 Blvd Stalingrad, Cité des Antiquaires, 69100 Villeurbanne. T. 0472442847.
- Ant - 050020
Félix, Jean-Jacques, 117 Blvd Stalingrad, Cité des Antiquaires, 69100 Villeurbanne. T. 0478896823. - Paint / Furn / Cur - 050021
Franc, Isabelle, 117 Blvd Stalingrad, Cité des Antiquaires, 69100 Villeurbanne. T. 0472449891. - Paint / Furn / Cur - 050022
Fumet, Noëlle, 10 Rue Dedieu, 69100 Villeurbanne. T. 0472742600. 050023
Galerie Hadrien, 117 Blvd Stalingrad, Cité des Antiquaires, 69100 Villeurbanne. T. 0478897801.
- Mod - 050024
Galerie Port-Royal, 117 Blvd Stalingrad, Cité des Antiquaires, 69100 Villeurbanne. T. 0478890671.
- Paint - 050025
Gaudard, Reth, 117 Blvd Stalingrad, Cité des Antiquaires, 69100 Villeurbanne. T. 0478895384. - Paint / Furn / Cur - 050026
Giacone, Daniel, 117 Blvd Stalingrad, Cité des Antiquaires, 69100 Villeurbanne. T. 0478938304.
- Ant - 050027
Grange, Gabriel, 117 Blvd Stalingrad, Cité des Antiquaires, 69100 Villeurbanne. T. 0478932191.
- Furn - 050028
Gros, Robert, 117 Blvd Stalingrad, Cité des Antiquaires, 69100 Villeurbanne. T. 0472442234. 050029
J.C.D., 117 Blvd Stalingrad, Cité des Antiquaires, 69100 Villeurbanne. T. 0472449543. - Jew / Silv - 050030

Jemo, 117 Blvd Stalingrad, Cité des Antiquaires, 69100 Villeurbanne. T. 0478939641. - Jew / Silv - 050031
Lambert, Gérard, 117 Blvd Stalingrad, Cité des Antiquaires, 69100 Villeurbanne. T. 0478949429. 050032
Loison, Jean, Cité des Antiquaires, 117 Blvd Stalingrad, 2.14, 69100 Villeurbanne. - Graph / Repr - 050033
Maire, Jean-Paul, 117 Blvd Stalingrad, Cité des Antiquaires, 69100 Villeurbanne. T. 0478898444.
- Furn - 050034
Marchand, Josephine, 117 Blvd Stalingrad, Cité des Antiquaires, 69100 Villeurbanne. T. 0478894906.
- Mod - 050035
Mariotte-Labe, Pelazzo, 117 Blvd Stalingrad, Cité des Antiquaires, 69100 Villeurbanne. T. 0478949564.
- Dec - 050036
Mas, Jacques, 117 Blvd Stalingrad, Cité des Antiquaires, 69100 Villeurbanne. T. 0472442227. - Ant - 050037
Mathé, Didier, 117 Blvd Stalingrad, Cité des Antiquaires, 69100 Villeurbanne. T. 0478942743. - Paint / Furn / Cur - 050038
Mion, Michèle, 117 Blvd Stalingrad, Cité des Antiquaires, 69100 Villeurbanne. T. 0472443283. 050039
Monier, Lucien, 134 Rue Francis-de-Pressensé, 69100 Villeurbanne. T. 0478031616, Fax 0478682104. 050040
Monin, Jacques, 117 Blvd Stalingrad, Cité des Antiquaires, 69100 Villeurbanne. T. 0478936384. - Paint / Furn / Cur - 050041
Moulin de la Vierge, 117 Blvd Stalingrad, Cité des Antiquaires, 69100 Villeurbanne. T. 0478942554. 050042
Nicole Dentelles, 117 Blvd Stalingrad, Cité des Antiquaires, 69100 Villeurbanne. T. 0478896652.
- Tex - 050043
Oeil de Lynx, 117 Blvd Stalingrad, Cité des Antiquaires, 69100 Villeurbanne. T. 0478939784. - Jew / Silv - 050044
Pandora, 117 Blvd Stalingrad, Cité des Antiquaires, 69100 Villeurbanne. T. 0472440968. - Dec - 050045
Passé du Futur, 117 Blvd Stalingrad, Cité des Antiquaires, 69100 Villeurbanne. T. 0478940475. 050046
Pentecoste, Daniel, 117 Blvd Stalingrad, Cité des Antiquaires, 69100 Villeurbanne. T. 0478898419. - Paint / Sculp / Draw - 050047
Perrier, Anne-Marie, 117 Blvd Stalingrad, 69100 Villeurbanne. T. 0478891291. - Paint / Furn / Dec - 050048
Poulet, Gérard, 44 Rue Alsace, 69100 Villeurbanne. T. 0478847757. 050049
R Antiquités, 117 Blvd Stalingrad, Cité des Antiquaires, 69100 Villeurbanne. T. 0478938898. 050050
Reure, Dominique, 117 Blvd Stalingrad, Cité des Antiquaires, 69100 Villeurbanne. T. 0478891305. - Paint / Furn / Cur - 050051
Robert, Jacqueline, 117 Blvd Stalingrad, Cité des Antiquaires, 69100 Villeurbanne. T. 0478949245.
- Glass - 050052
Rocher, Christophe, 117 Blvd Stalingrad, Cité des Antiquaires, 69100 Villeurbanne. T. 0478934972. - Paint / Furn / Cur - 050053
Sandraz, Didier, 117 Blvd Stalingrad, Cité des Antiquaires, 69100 Villeurbanne. T. 0478940444.
- Furn - 050054
Tradition, 117 Blvd Stalingrad, Cité des Antiquaires, 69100 Villeurbanne. T. 0478941873. - Dec - 050055
Trotignon, Chantal, 117 Blvd Stalingrad, Cité des Antiquaires, 69100 Villeurbanne. T. 0478892578. - Paint / Furn / Cur - 050056
Vairon, Serge, 117 Blvd Stalingrad, Cité des Antiquaires, 69100 Villeurbanne. T. 0478898265. - Paint / Furn / Cur - 050057
Valentin, Patrick, 117 Blvd Stalingrad, Cité des Antiquaires, 69100 Villeurbanne. T. 0478897871. 050058
Vieille Cure, 117 Blvd Stalingrad, Cité des Antiquaires, 69100 Villeurbanne. T. 0478940942. - Paint / Furn / Cur - 050059
Wegiel, Michel, 117 Blvd Stalingrad, Cité des Antiquaires, 69100 Villeurbanne. T. 0478941044.
- Mod - 050060
Wilsor, 42 Rue Anatole-France, 69100 Villeurbanne. T. 0478854097. 050061

Villevallier (Yonne)
Mireau, Jean-Paul, 60 Rue République, 89330 Villevallier. T. 0386911173. 050062

Villey-Saint-Etienne (Meurthe-et-Moselle)
Collard, Yves, 21 Rue Toul, 54200 Villey-Saint-Etienne. T. 0383629753. 050063

Villiers-en-Lieu (Haute-Marne)
Perrot, Jean-Bernard, 4 Grande Rue, 52100 Villiers-en-Lieu. T. 0325056778. 050064

Villiers-sur-Marne (Val-de-Marne)
Au Temps Retrouvé, 15 Rue Louis-Lenoir, 94350 Villiers-sur-Marne. T. 0149300685. - Paint / Furn / China / Tex / Cur - 050065
Blanc, Iris, 7 Rue Marthe-Debaize, 94350 Villiers-sur-Marne. T. 0149305170. - Furn / Cur - 050066
Lelouch, Albertine, 89 Av André-Rouy, 94350 Villiers-sur-Marne. T. 0149300770. 050067

Vincelles (Jura)
Tayeb, Gilbert, Grande Rue, 39190 Vincelles. T. 0384250961. 050068

Vincennes (Val-de-Marne)
Antiquités Dépôt Vente des Laitières, 16 Rue Laitières, 94300 Vincennes. T. 0148084210. 050069
Buche, Pierre, 63 Rue Jarry, 94300 Vincennes. T. 0148085041. - Furn / Cur - 050070
Général Antique Décor, 11 Rue Saulpic, 94300 Vincennes. T. 0143657770. 050071
Grillon, 5 Rue Lejemptel, 94300 Vincennes. T. 0143282630. 050072
Lefèvre, Stéphane, 177 Rue Fontenay, 94300 Vincennes. T. 0143981550. 050073
Vince-Or, 117 Rue Fontenay, 94300 Vincennes. T. 0143741100. 050074

Vindelle (Charente)
Gibus, Le Cluzeau, 16430 Vindelle. T. 0545214827. 050075

Vinneuf (Yonne)
Genetier, Marc, 6 Rue Eugène-Gaudaire, 89140 Vinneuf. T. 0386669183. 050076
Koenig, Serge, 73 Rue Pasteur, 89140 Vinneuf. T. 0386668665. 050077

Vinon-sur-Verdon (Alpes-de-Haute-Provence)
A.J.R., 13 Rue Saint-André, 83560 Vinon-sur-Verdon. T. 0492789797. - Ant / Furn - 050078

Virazeil (Lot-et-Garonne)
Bressan, Daniel, Echars, 47200 Virazeil. T. 0553201899. 050079

Vire (Calvados)
A la Recherche du Passé, 13 Rue Armand-Gasté, 14500 Vire. T. 0231680585. - Ant / Graph / Fra - 050080
Lebouteiller, Jacky, Rue Hippodrôme, 14500 Vire. T. 0231672109. 050081
Vilars, Claude, 7 Rue Emile-Desvaux, 14500 Vire. T. 0231680794. 050082

Viriat (Ain)
Bourdon, Daniel, 470 Chemin But, 01440 Viriat. T. 0474253157. - Ant - 050083
Zagonel, Jacky & Marie, 1117 Rte Paris, 01440 Viriat. T. 0474453795. - Ant - 050084

Viroflay (Yvelines)
Bronidève, 2 Rue Saisons, 78220 Viroflay. T. 0130240851. 050085

Vitré (Ille-et-Vilaine)
Botte Dorée, 20 Rue Embas, 35500 Vitré. T. 0299746827. 050086
Cozette, Martial, 4 Rue Embas, 35500 Vitré. T. 0299747554. 050087
Desmontils, Guy, 36 Rue Beaudrairie, 35500 Vitré. T. 0299752834. 050088
Trottier, Renée, 17 Rue Beaudrairie, 35500 Vitré. T. 0299750401. 050089

Vitry-le-François (Marne)
Delaunay, Fabrice, 14bis Petite Rue Frignicourt, 51300 Vitry-le-François. T. 0326740744. 050090

Noël, Robert, Chemin Marvis, 51300 Vitry-le-François.
T. 0326730928. *050091*

Vitry-sur-Seine (Val-de-Marne)
Sourice, Daniel, 116 B Av André-Maginot, 94400 Vitry-sur-Seine. T. 0146826674. *050092*

Vitteaux (Côte-d'Or)
Bordet, Elisabeth, Rue Edmé-Millot, 21350 Vitteaux.
T. 0380339075. *050093*
Pottier, Jean-Roger, Rue Haute-Saint-Jean, 21350 Vitteaux. T. 0380496724. *050094*

Vittel (Vosges)
Français, Jacky, 27 Pl Général-de-Gaulle, 88800 Vittel.
T. 0329084791. *050095*

Viviers-du-Lac (Savoie)
Aix Antiquités, 970 Rte d'Aix, 73420 Viviers-du-Lac.
T. 0479882917. - Ant / Furn - *050096*
Le Viviers, 980 Rte Aix, 73420 Viviers-du-Lac.
T. 0479882917. - Ant - *050097*

Vix (Vendée)
Fradois, Jean-Philippe, 18 Rue Pont-de-Vix, 85770 Vix.
T. 0251006960. *050098*

Voiron (Isère)
Au Verre Luisant, Rue Tallifardières, 38500 Voiron.
T. 0476661046. - Ant / Glass - *050099*
Foralosso, Michel, 53 Av Paviot, 38500 Voiron.
T. 0476056705. - Furn - *050100*

Voisins-le-Bretonneux (Yvelines)
Messageot, Charles-Henri, 20 Rue Racine, 78960 Voisins-le-Bretonneux. T. 0130435797. *050101*

Volx (Alpes-de-Haute-Provence)
Comptoir du Particulier, 8 ZA Carretière, 04130 Volx.
T. 0492784417. - Ant - *050102*

Vouillé (Vienne)
Irisée, 10 Pl Eglise, 86190 Vouillé. T. 0549514244.
- Ant - *050103*
Lamydécor, Rte Poitiers, 86190 Vouillé. T. 0549514207.
- Ant - *050104*

Voulangis (Seine-et-Marne)
Galerie Brocante de Crécy, 6 Rte Melun, 77580 Voulangis. T. 64638508. *050105*
Mazet, Daniel, 6 Rte Melun, 77580 Voulangis.
T. 64638545. *050106*

Vouvray (Indre-et-Loire)
Orcel, Jean Paul, 10 RN 152, 37210 Vouvray.
T. 0547527718. - Paint - *050107*

Vouzan (Charente)
Martin-Barbier, Colette, Maison-Neuve, 16410 Vouzan.
T. 0545249858. *050108*

Vuillafans (Doubs)
Vuillafans, Antiquité du Moulin, 25840 Vuillafans.
T. 0381609755. *050109*

Wallon-Cappel (Nord)
Bouisson, Jean-Pascal, 14 Rte Nationale, 59190 Wallon-Cappel. T. 0328400174. - Ant - *050110*

Wambrechines (Nord)
Antiquités le Village, 1 Rue Quesnoy, 59118 Wambrechines. T. 0320397178. - Ant - *050111*

Warcq (Ardennes)
Guillaume, Evelyne, 2 Pl Grande-Fontaine, 08000 Warcq. T. 0324331226. - Ant - *050112*

Warmeriville (Marne)
Dépôt-Vente de la Forge, 22 Rue Champs, 51110 Warmeriville. T. 0326038667. *050113*
Salzgeber, Christian, 9 Rue Ragonet, 51110 Warmeriville. T. 0326033961. *050114*

Wasselonne (Bas-Rhin)
Hoff, 7 Rte Strasbourg, 67310 Wasselonne.
T. 0388872559. - Paint / Furn / Sculp / Cur - *050115*
Hoff, Bernard, 1 Pl Tilleuls, 67310 Wasselonne.
T. 0388870887. *050116*

Wattrelos (Nord)
Sinnaeve, Pascal, 44 Rue François-Mériaux, 59150 Wattrelos. T. 0320757543. - Ant - *050117*

Wettolsheim (Haut-Rhin)
Fornasier, Alba, 229 Rte Rouffach, 68000 Wettolsheim.
T. 0389417887. *050118*

Willer-sur-Thur (Haut-Rhin)
Willer Brocante, 39 Rue Grande-Armée, 68760 Willer-sur-Thur. T. 0389823692. *050119*

Wisembach (Vosges)
Sauval-Paradis, Michel, 1 Rue Grotte, 88520 Wisembach. T. 0329517854. *050120*

Wissembourg (Bas-Rhin)
Marie-Galante, 5 Pl Marché-au-Poisson, 67160 Wissembourg. T. 0388941991. *050121*

Witry-lès-Reims (Marne)
Blanc, Philippe, 47 Av Reims, 51420 Witry-lès-Reims.
T. 0326971612. - Furn - *050122*

Woippy (Moselle)
Conrad, René, 11 Rue Ferdinand-Sechehaye, 57140 Woippy. T. 0387308096. - Furn / Dec / Lights / Cur - *050123*

Yébleron (Seine-Maritime)
Hébert, Serge, Rue Forge, 76640 Yébleron.
T. 0235562080. *050124*

Yerres (Essonne)
Antiquaire d'Yerres, Ferme Grange, 91330 Yerres.
T. 0169480181. *050125*
Damasse, Charles, 74 Rue Bellevue, 91330 Yerres.
T. 0169482788. *050126*
Denise, Pierre, 17 Rue Henri-Barbusse, 91330 Yerres.
T. 0169489962. *050127*
Li Wen Ts'ien, 40 Rue Beau-Site, 91330 Yerres.
T. 0169483825. *050128*
Yerres, 7 Rue Michel-Luciani, 91330 Yerres.
T. 0169489505. *050129*

Yssingeaux (Haute-Loire)
Jarnac, Louis, La Besse, 43200 Yssingeaux.
T. 0471590603. *050130*

Yvetot (Seine-Maritime)
Allard, Jean, 18 Av Georges-Clémenceau, 76192 Yvetot.
T. 0235950276. *050131*
His, Simon, 10 Av Foch, 76192 Yvetot.
T. 0235950259. *050132*
Saunier, 9 Rue Guy-de-Maupassant, 76192 Yvetot.
T. 0235955463. - Furn / China - *050133*

Yvoire (Haute-Savoie)
Piccot, André, Rue Eglise, 74140 Yvoire.
T. 0450728113. *050134*

French Guiana

Kourou
Grenier, 17 Impasse Toutouri, 97310 Kourou.
T. (594) 325433. - Ant - *050135*

French Polynesia

Papeete
Galerie Winkler & J. Jacques Laurent, rue Jeanne d'Arc, Papeete. T. 2 81 77. - Ant / Paint / Graph / Orient / Sculp / Eth / Fra / Cur - *050136*
Noanoa, Bard. Pomaré, Papeete. T. 273 47. - Ant / Paint / China / Sculp / Eth - *050137*

Germany

Aachen (Nordrhein-Westfalen)
Aachener Briefmarken- und Münzkontor, Mefferdatisstr. 22, 52062 Aachen. T. (0241) 35039. - Num - *050138*

Anna-Antik, Annastr. 14, 52062 Aachen.
T. (0241) 25230. *050139*
Aykut, E., Annastr. 28, 52062 Aachen.
T. (0241) 25834. *050140*
Bardenheuer, Hof 6-8, 52062 Aachen. T. (0241) 396 77.
- Ant - *050141*
Baum, J., Von-Coels-Str. 195, 52080 Aachen.
T. (0241) 55 59 55. *050142*
Baumhauer, J., Schloßstr. 20, 52066 Aachen.
T. (0241) 50 76 13. *050143*
Bergander, M., Neupforte 12, 52062 Aachen.
T. (0241) 27289. *050144*
Beumers, Manfred, Jakobstr. 37, 52064 Aachen.
T. (0241) 333 95. - Ant / Paint / Graph / Furn / Orient / China / Sculp / Tex / Arch / Jew / Fra / Silv / Lights / Instr / Glass / Cur / Mod / Draw / Tin / Toys - *050145*
Billmann, B., Forellenweg 8, 52074 Aachen.
T. (0241) 17 36 17. *050146*
Bosten, P., Großkölnstr. 56, 52062 Aachen.
T. (0241) 47 47. *050147*
Conrads, Gerhard, Adalbertsteinweg 111, 52070 Aachen. T. (0241) 51 23 85. - Ant / Furn / Instr / Cur - *050148*
Crott, H., Dr. & K. Schmelzer, Pontstr. 21, 52062 Aachen. T. (0241) 36900. *050149*
Dümmer, Kaiserplatz, 52062 Aachen.
T. (0241) 330 89. *050150*
Eick, Alexander, Pontstr. 15-17, 52062 Aachen.
T. (0241) 303 91. - Ant / Paint / Graph / Furn / China / Sculp / Jew / Silv / Instr / Glass - *050151*
Eisen, H., Hochbrück 2, 52070 Aachen.
T. (0241) 15 41 11. *050152*
Geilenkirchen, K., Katschhof 1a, 52062 Aachen.
T. (0241) 275 95. *050153*
Grenzland-Galerie, Theaterstr. 71, 52062 Aachen.
T. (0241) 3 53 16. - Ant / Paint / Tex - *050154*
Greydanus, A., Warmweiherstr. 32, 52066 Aachen.
T. (0241) 54 34 47. *050155*
Grobusch, Münsterpl. 10, 52062 Aachen.
T. (0241) 37665. *050156*
Grobusch, Hannelore, Schopenhauerstr. 19, 52078 Aachen. T. (0241) 52 39 56. *050157*
Hilbert, F.X., Ronheider Berg 221 a, 52076 Aachen.
T. (0241) 79 56 75. *050158*
Hoffmann, K., Steinkaulpl. 7, 52062 Aachen.
T. (0241) 1575. *050159*
I.I.E. Kunst und Antiquitäten, Pontsheide 49, 52076 Aachen. T. (0241) 47 47. *050160*
Kalkoffen, E., Lütticher Str. 597, 52074 Aachen.
T. (0241) 785 53. *050161*
Kuhlow, G., Wirichsbongardstr. 57, 52062 Aachen.
T. (0241) 301 01. - Num - *050162*
Kunsttruhe, Kleinkölnstr. 1, 52062 Aachen. *050163*
Lücker, Angela, Theaterpl. 9-11, 52062 Aachen.
T. (0241) 333 32. - Ant / Furn - *050164*
Lüttgens, Hubert, Münsterpl. 2, 52062 Aachen.
T. (0241) 372 63. - Ant / Paint / Furn - *050165*
Lüttgens, K., Grüner Weg 15, 52070 Aachen.
T. (0241) 15 44 26. *050166*
Lüttgens, K., Münsterpl. 11, 52062 Aachen.
T. (0241) 31152. *050167*
Oelbrecht, Wilhelm, Alte Vaalser Str. 3, 52074 Aachen.
T. (0241) 834 76. - Ant - *050168*
Offermanns, Doris Renate, Annastr. 17, 52062 Aachen.
T. (0241) 363 07. *050169*
Platz, O., Hochstr. 4, 52078 Aachen.
T. (0241) 56 33 97. *050170*
Schumacher, E. & H. C., Wilhelmstr. 59, 52070 Aachen.
T. (0241) 50 43 22. - Ant - *050171*
Schwanen, Peterstr. 77-79, 52062 Aachen.
T. (0241) 278 74. - Ant / Paint / Sculp / Instr / Draw - *050172*
Steinbeck, Hans, Lemierser Berg 137, 52074 Aachen.
T. (0241) 14477. *050173*
Steinle, C., Aureliusstr. 52, 52064 Aachen.
T. (0241) 314 77. - Num - *050174*
Trachterna, Ch., Im Wiesengrund 34, 52078 Aachen.
T. (0241) 02408/1511. *050175*
Wolken, H., Alte Vaalser Str. 127, 52074 Aachen.
T. (0241) 827 05. *050176*

Aalen (Baden-Württemberg)
Kirchner, R.A., Treppacher Str 10, 73434 Aalen.
T. (07361) 6373. - Paint / Graph / Repr / Fra /
Draw -   050177
Kleine Galerie, Mittelbachstr 23, 73430 Aalen.
T. (07361) 68460. - Paint / Graph / Furn / Fra - 050178
Koschwitz, P., Mittelbachstr 17, 73430 Aalen.
T. (07361) 61479.   050179

Abenberg (Bayern)
Baumeister, G., Spalterstr 5, 91183 Abenberg.
T. (09178) 393.   050180

Abtswind (Bayern)
Cotney, J., Pfarrgasse 23, 97355 Abtswind.
T. (09383) 7077.   050181

Achern (Baden-Württemberg)
Birkenfelder, Albert, Sasbacherstr 25, 77855
Achern.   050182

Achim (Niedersachsen)
Dittmar, E., Obernstr. 13, 28832 Achim.   050183
Hiddessen, I., Bremer Str. 1, 28832 Achim.
T. (04202) 29 91.   050184

Adelsdorf (Bayern)
Bibra, Hellmut Freiherr von, Dr., Schloß, 91325 Adelsdorf. T. (09195) 23 41.   050185

Adelsried (Bayern)
Krötz, Franz, Steigfeldstr. 14, 86477 Adelsried.
T. (08294) 1420. - China / Jew -   050186

Ahaus (Nordrhein-Westfalen)
Buddner-Meyer, Am Spieker 2-4, 48683 Ahaus.
T. (02561) 8668.   Ant   050187
ERU Licht & Wohnen, Heisenbergstr. 4, 48683 Ahaus.
T. (02561) 3407.   050188
Steingrube, Bahnhofstr. 7, 48683 Ahaus.
T. (02561) 54 53.   050189

Ahlden (Niedersachsen)
Seidel, Florian, Schloß, 29693 Ahlden. T. (05164) 575.
- Ant -   050190

Ahlen (Nordrhein-Westfalen)
Doder, S., Nordstr 23, 59227 Ahlen.   050191
Gatzemeier, Helga, Hellstr 22, 59227 Ahlen.
T. (02382) 85988. - Furn / China / Silv / Glass - 050192
Görmann, Weststr 89, 59227 Ahlen.
T. (02382) 2047.   050193
Köllermann, I., Markt 6, 59227 Ahlen.
T. (02382) 82050.   050194
Pinas, H., Pferdekamp 17, 59229 Ahlen.
T. (02382) 60654. - Num -   050195
Schneider, Heinz, Nordstr 53, 59227 Ahlen.
T. (02382) 3228.   050196
Westhues, W., Warendorfer Str 19, 59227 Ahlen.
T. (02382) 1202.   050197

Ahrensburg (Schleswig-Holstein)
Antik & Praesent, Große Str. 38, 22926 Ahrensburg.
T. (04102) 56650.   050198
Kollschegg, Uwe, Am Alten Markt 8, 22926 Ahrensburg.
T. (04102) 571 79.   050199
Nostalgie & Phantasie, Manhagener Allee 62, 22926 Ah-
rensburg. T. (04102) 531 35.   050200
Schultz, Swaantje, Reeshoop 14, 22926 Ahrensburg.
T. (04102) 52301.   050201
Steinmetz, J., Bismarckallee 36, 22926 Ahrensburg.
T. (04102) 597 75.   050202

Aichstetten (Baden-Württemberg)
Antikhaus Aichstetten, Hochstr. 75, 88317 Aichstetten.
T. (07565) 1457, Fax (07565) 1057. - Furn / China /
Glass -   050203

Aichtal (Baden-Württemberg)
Harnisch's Münzhandl, Eichendorffstr 29, 72631 Aichtal.
T. (07127) 51313. - Num -   050204

Aken (Sachsen-Anhalt)
Aken-Antik, Dessauer Str. 42, 06385 Aken.
T. (034909) 2651.   050205

Albersdorf (Schleswig-Holstein)
Schönleiter, W., Norderstr. 9, 25767 Albersdorf.
T. (04835) 231.   050206

Albstadt (Baden-Württemberg)
Maier, A.-M., Hechinger Str. 1, 72461 Albstadt.
T. (07431) 126 20.   050207

Aldenhoven (Nordrhein-Westfalen)
Oellers, Josef, Auf der Komm 1, 52457 Aldenhoven.
T. (02464) 10 22.   050208

Aldingen (Baden-Württemberg)
Wilhelm, A., Trossinger Str 35, 78554 Aldingen.
T. (07424) 1286.   050209

Alfeld (Niedersachsen)
Beie, W., Allee 3, 31061 Alfeld.
T. (05181) 25208.   050210
Die Schatulle, Sedanstr 21, 31061 Alfeld.
T. (05181) 81541.   050211

Alfhausen (Niedersachsen)
Klement, Erwin, Ankumer Str. 18, 49594
Alfhausen.   050212
Kreke, Hubert, Hauptstr., 49594 Alfhausen.
T. (05464) 253. - Ant -   050213

Allensbach (Baden-Württemberg)
Hinterskirch, Zur Halde 16, 78476 Allensbach.
T. (07533) 58 10.   050214

Alsfeld (Hessen)
Dravid-Aussenhandels GmbH, Rossmarkt 9, 36304 Alsfeld. T. (06631) 29 86.   050215

Altdort bei Nürnberg (Bayern)
Altdorfer Kunstkammer, Am Marktplatz, 90518 Altdorf
bei Nürnberg. T. (09187) 8600, 5540. - Ant / Furn / China / Tex / Dec / Glass / Cur / Mul -   050216
Späth, B., Am Weingarten 13, 90518 Altdorf bei Nürnberg. T. (09187) 6424. - Num -   050217

Altenberge (Nordrhein-Westfalen)
Zurholt, E., Lindenstr. 8, 48341 Altenberge.
T. (02505) 1236.   050218

**Altenkirchen, Westerwald (Rheinland-
Pfalz)**
Collector Guns, Koblenzer Str 3, 57610 Altenkirchen,
Westerwald. T. (02681) 3688. - Mil -   050219
Troost & R. Micknewitz, J., Kirchstr, 57610 Altenkirchen,
Westerwald. T. (02681) 4266.   050220

Altenkunstadt (Bayern)
Schwarz, W., Kellergasse 5, 96264 Altenkunstadt.
T. (09572) 3088.   050221

Altenmünster (Bayern)
Skogstad, Paul, Joh.-Wisrich-Str. 8, 86450 Altenmünster. T. (08295) 463. - Mil -   050222

Altensteig (Baden-Württemberg)
Neugebauer, F., Welkerstr 107, 72213 Altensteig.
T. (07453) 7749.   050223

Altheim (Baden-Württemberg)
Sauer, K., Hauptstr. 25, 88499 Altheim.
T. (07371) 126 20.   050224

Altötting (Bayern)
Zychlinski, Hildegard von, Gottfr.-Keller-Str. 6, 84503 Altötting. T. (08671) 64 54.   050225

Amberg (Bayern)
Antiquitäten am Marktplatz, 92224 Amberg.
T. (09621) 150 27.   050226
Straubinger, F., Leopoldstr. 10, 92224 Amberg.
T. (09621) 84404.   050227
Stromberg, Axel Baron von, Am Südhang 19, 92224 Am-
berg. T. (09621) 31682, Fax 13961. - Ant / Paint /
Graph / Furn -   050228

Ammerbuch (Baden-Württemberg)
Sauermann-Kern, J., Herrenberger Str. 18, 72119 Ammerbuch. T. (07073) 3821.   050229

Amorbach (Bayern)
Allwarth, R., Schmiedsgasse 8, 63916 Amorbach.
T. (09373) 88 35.   050230
Möller-Stegerwald, M., Abteigasse 1, 63916 Amorbach.
T. (09373) 1047.   050231
Sagasser, Jürgen, Dr., & A., Löhrstr. 48, 63916 Amor-
bach. T. (09373) 2288, Fax 2268. - Graph / Furn / Chi-
na / Tex / Silv -   050232

Andernach (Rheinland-Pfalz)
Baunach, A., Kirchstr. 3, 56626 Andernach.   050233
Belting, Ingrid, Hochstr. 95, 56626 Andernach.
T. (02632) 401 05. - Instr -   050234
Droste zu Vischering, R. von, Steinweg 16, 56626 An-
dernach. T. (02632) 481 98.   050235

Ankum (Niedersachsen)
Kremer, Hugo, Grüner Weg 1, 49577 Ankum.
T. (05462) 331. - Ant -   050236

Anröchte (Nordrhein-Westfalen)
Gerwin, H., Beleckerstr. 55, 59609 Anröchte.
T. (02947) 32 47.   050237
Jablonski, S., Schulburg 2, 59609 Anröchte.
T. (02947) 48 11.   050238

Ansbach (Bayern)
Arneth, Angelika, Würzburgerstr 44, 91522 Ansbach.
T. (0981) 2634.   050239
Eichinger, Max, Neustadt 4, 91522 Ansbach.
T. (0981) 2226. - Ant / Furn / Sculp / Cur -   050240
Hedel, A., Platenstr 4, 91522 Ansbach. T. (0981) 3038.
- Ant -   050241
Meldau, Helmut, Nürnbergerstr 23, 91522 Ansbach.
T. (0981) 3118. - Ant / China / Glass -   050242
Palicka, Vladimir, Liebigstr 4, 91522 Ansbach.
T. (0981) 62014.   050243
Schüßler, A., Urlasstr 8a, 91522 Ansbach.
T. (0981) 17682.   050244
Zucker, Werner, Jahnstr 16b, 91522 Ansbach.
T. (0981) 14087. - Num -   050245

Arnsberg (Nordrhein-Westfalen)
Binhold, A., Lange Wende 6, 59755 Arnsberg.   050246
Gans, Udo, Nordring 22, 59821 Arnsberg.
T. (02931) 129 98. - Num -   050247

Arnstein (Bayern)
Hock, M., Mühlgasse 8, 97450 Arnstein.
T. (09363) 1534.   050248

Arolsen (Hessen)
Greef, G., Bühler Tal 29, 34454 Arolsen.
T. (05691) 12 19.   050249

Arrach (Bayern)
Mangold, P., Ahornstr. 18, 93474 Arrach.
T. (09943) 2753.   050250

Arzberg (Bayern)
Wächter, W., Bauerfeindstr 6, 95659 Arzberg.
T. (09233) 8981.   050251

Aschaffenburg (Bayern)
Breitenbach, Landingstr. 18, 63739 Aschaffenburg.
T. (06021) 147 24.   050252
Brönner, Roßmarkt 35, 63739 Aschaffenburg.
T. (06021) 123 79.   050253
Burger, E., Seebornstr. 9-13, 63743
Aschaffenburg.   050254
Joachimi, M., Wermbachstr. 25, 63739 Aschaffenburg.
T. (06021) 254 97.   050255
Massenkeil, H., Stiftsgasse 10, 63739 Aschaffenburg.
T. (06021) 279 74, Fax (06021) 29813. - China / Draw /
Sculp -   050256
Müller, J., Erthalstr. 16, 63739 Aschaffenburg.
T. (06021) 155 58.   050257
Seeger, C., Treibgasse 5a, 63739 Aschaffenburg.
T. (06021) 23343.   050258
Watzke, Barbara, Badergasse 4, 63739 Aschaffenburg.
T. (06021) 142 47.   050259
Wornast, W., Dalbergstr. 72, 63739 Aschaffenburg.
T. (06021) 24029, Fax (06021) 24039. - Graph /
Fra -   050260

Aschau (Bayern)
Seelig, Klaus, Zellerhornstr. 42, 83229 Aschau. *050261*

Ascheberg (Nordrhein-Westfalen)
Brunnen, Katharinenpl. 4, 59387 Ascheberg.
T. (02593) 7451. *050262*
Sauff, Südstr. 2, 59387 Ascheberg.
T. (02593) 7384. *050263*
Schulte, Fritz Heinrich, Wiedau 32, 59387 Ascheberg.
T. (02593) 12 12. *050264*

Aschheim (Bayern)
Beckert, Wolfgang, Münchner Str. 16, 85609 Aschheim.
T. (089) 9038692, Fax (089) 9030919. - Ant / Paint /
Graph / Ico - *050265*

Asendorf bei Bruchhausen-Vilsen (Niedersachsen)
Clasen, F.A., Heerstr 22, 27330 Asendorf bei Bruchhausen-Vilsen. T. (04253) 1296. *050266*

Aspach (Baden-Württemberg)
Holzwarth, K. & S., Grossaspacher Str. 10, 71546
Aspach. T. (07191) 204 79. *050267*

Asperg (Baden-Württemberg)
Conrad, Traute, Strassenäcker 28, 71679 Asperg. - Ant /
Tex - *050268*

Attendorn (Nordrhein-Westfalen)
Becker, Toni, Ostwall 99, 57439 Attendorn.
T. (02722) 3076. *050269*
Röthling & Springol, Kraghammer Bahnstr 19, 57439 Attendorn. T. (02722) 7771. *050270*

Aub (Bayern)
Lämmermühle, 97239 Aub. T. (09335) 619. *050271*

Augsburg (Bayern)
Anno Domini, Oberer Graben 13, 86152 Augsburg.
T. (0821) 515160. *050272*
Aurel, Marc, Ulrichspl 13, 86150 Augsburg.
T. (0821) 30184. - Ant / Dec - *050273*
Bauch, E., Bauerntanzgäßchen 6, 86150 Augsburg.
T. (0821) 157412. *050274*
Bock, Pfladergasse 5, 86150 Augsburg.
T. (0821) 152367. *050275*
Bolkart, J., Klauckestr 15, 86153 Augsburg.
T. (0821) 30603. *050276*
Brixle, G., Spicherer Str 9, 86157 Augsburg.
T. (0821) 542824. *050277*
Dietzel, I., Klopstockstr 1, 86161 Augsburg.
T. (0821) 151346. *050278*
Dörschug, H., Hillenbrandstr 14, 86156
Augsburg. *050279*
Fiedler, Siegfried, Jahnstr 40, 86179 Augsburg.
T. (0821) 82098/99. - Jew - *050280*
Flohmarkt Antiquitäten, Hermannstr 22, 86150 Augsburg. T. (0821) 39882. - Ant - *050281*
Frank's Antique Shop, Langemarckstr 62, 86156 Augsburg. T. (0821) 406865. - Ant / Glass - *050282*
Ganzenmüller, Philippine-Welser-Str 14, 86150 Augsburg. T. (0821) 519568. - Graph / Repr - *050283*
Gaupties, Eduard, Pferseer Str 20, 86150 Augsburg.
T. (0821) 37930. - Num - *050284*
Grammelsbacher, J., An der Brühlbrücke, 86152
Augsburg. *050285*
Haupt, R., Maximilianstr 48, 86150 Augsburg.
T. (0821) 510544. *050286*
Höhenberger, Karl, Frauentorstr 7, 86152
Augsburg. *050287*
Hrebicek-Hollenburger, Regina, Mittlerer Graben 28,
86152 Augsburg. *050288*
Irbo's Laden, Tannenstr 1, 86179 Augsburg. *050289*
Katzer, W., Jakoberstr 23, 86152 Augsburg.
T. (0821) 38814. *050290*
Knecht, J., Bahnhofstr 29, 86150 Augsburg.
T. (0821) 30555. *050291*
Kühling, Anton, Georgenstr 23, 86152 Augsburg.
T. (0821) 30126. - Ant / Paint / Graph / Furn /
Instr - *050292*
Lang, B., Erstes Quergäßchen 8, 86152 Augsburg.
T. (0821) 152243. *050293*
Loos, K., Heilig-Grab-Gasse 4, 86150 Augsburg.
T. (0821) 518292. *050294*

Matheis, F., Langemarckstr 62, 86156 Augsburg.
T. (0821) 406865, 441113. *050295*
Matschurat, Waltraut, Wilhelm-Hauff-Str 31, 86161
Augsburg. T. (0821) 311982. - Ant / Paint / Furn /
Silv - *050296*
Müller, Günter, Maximilianstr 54, 86150 Augsburg.
T. (0821) 38430. - Ant / Paint / Furn / China / Rel /
Glass - *050297*
Müller, P., Ulmer Str 152, 86156 Augsburg.
T. (0821) 406332. *050298*
Naegele, Hermann, Völkstr 38, 86150 Augsburg.
T. (0821) 33506. - Ant / Num - *050299*
Neichel, U., Mittlerer Graben 6, 86152 Augsburg.
T. (0821) 151825. *050300*
Neider, G., Dominikanergasse 12, 86150 Augsburg.
T. (0821) 35531. *050301*
Reger, Wilhelm, Bürgerm-Aurnhammer-Str 41, 86199
Augsburg. T. (0821) 551001/02. - Ant / Paint / Furn - *050302*
Rehm, Georg, Provinostr 47, 86153 Augsburg.
T. (0821) 551001/02. - Ant / Paint / Furn - *050303*
Scheffler, Römerstädter Str 4, 86199 Augsburg.
T. (0821) 98818, Fax (0821) 95072. - Ant / Paint /
Graph / Orient / Fra - *050304*
Senger, Norbert, Spitalgasse 10, 86150 Augsburg.
T. (0821) 510146. *050305*
Simon, J. & G., Theodor-Sachs-Str 8f, 86199 Augsburg.
T. (0821) 993485. *050306*
Stein, H.-D. von, Vorderer Lech 2, 86150 Augsburg.
T. (0821) 155474. *050307*
Straß, L. & F., Barfüßerstr 8, 86150 Augsburg.
T. (0821) 515868. *050308*
Strauß, Harry, Gratzmüllerstr 8, 86150
Augsburg. *050309*
Wagner, Maria, Kastanienweg 1, 86169 Augsburg.
- Cur - *050310*
Weihreter, Hans, Schertlinstr 11-1/26, 86159 Augsburg.
T. (0821) 572045. - Orient - *050311*
Zwei Mohren Antiquitäten, Katharinengasse 24, 86150
Augsburg. T. (0821) 155745. - Ant / Paint / Graph /
Furn / China / Jew / Silv / Glass - *050312*

Augustdorf (Nordrhein-Westfalen)
Schulz, M., Kohlenweg 1b, 32832 Augustdorf.
T. (05237) 497. *050313*

Auhagen (Niedersachsen)
Kruppa, W., Auf d. Rähden 27, 31553 Auhagen.
T. (05725) 6631. *050314*

Aukrug (Schleswig-Holstein)
Aukrug Antik, Hauptstr. 39, 24613 Aukrug.
T. (04873) 890. *050315*
Kirchenknopf, Heinkenborsteler Str., 02325 Aukrug.
T. (04873) 890. *050316*

Aurich (Niedersachsen)
Alte Schmiede, Domumer Str. 40, 26607 Aurich.
T. (04941) 7915. *050317*
Janssen, Antiquitäten, Grenzstr. 1, 26605 Aurich.
T. (04941) 27 57. *050318*

Aying (Bayern)
Zahn, Johanna, 85653 Aying. T. (08095) 1810. *050319*

Aystetten (Bayern)
Lörcher, Margot, Gartenstr 13, 86482 Aystetten.
T. (0821) 489028, Fax (0821) 485741. - Graph /
Orient - *050320*

Babenhausen (Bayern)
Reiner, Hermann, Silcherweg 3, 87727 Babenhausen.
T. (08333) 1255. *050321*

Bachhagel (Bayern)
Dehner, Georg, jun., 89429 Bachhagel. T. (09077) 521.
- Ant / Num - *050322*

Backnang (Baden-Württemberg)
Griesser, Peter C., Am Rathaus 2, 71522 Backnang.
T. (07191) 15 15. - Paint / Furn - *050323*
Moisel, W., Heutensbacher Str. 27, 71522 Backnang.
T. (07191) 536 57. *050324*

Bad Bentheim (Niedersachsen)
Dubbert, Fr., Wilhelmstr. 10, 48455 Bad Bentheim.
T. (05922) 39 90. *050325*

Bad Berleburg (Nordrhein-Westfalen)
Grau, K.-H., Dorfstr. 40, 57319 Bad Berleburg.
T. (02751) 645. *050326*

Bad Bevensen (Niedersachsen)
Hille, Henning, Medinger Str 18, 29549 Bad Bevensen.
T. (05821) 2474, Fax 42474. - Ant / Tex - *050327*
Sievert, Uta, Medinger Str 10, 29549 Bad Bevensen.
T. (05821) 1894. *050328*

Bad Breisig (Rheinland-Pfalz)
Kunsthandel und Kunstwerkstätte GmbH, Rheintalstr.
40, 53498 Bad Breisig. T. (02633) 951 95. *050329*
Neukirchner, Marianne, Meisenweg 2, 53498 Bad Breisig. T. (02633) 9303, 96850, Fax (02633) 95420.
- Ant / Paint / Furn / China - *050330*
Peters, Bodo, Biergasse 18, 53498 Bad Breisig.
T. (02633) 971 06, 952 14. *050331*
Schmitz-Avila, Thomas, Dr., Koblenzerstr. 42, 53492
Bad Breisig. T. (02633) 979 14, Fax (02633) 7102.
- Ant / Furn - *050332*

Bad Buchau (Baden-Württemberg)
Burger, M., Biberacher Str. 40, 88422 Bad Buchau.
T. (07582) 85 83. *050333*
Prock, C., Wuhrstr. 15, 88422 Bad Buchau.
T. (07582) 2090. *050334*

Bad Camberg (Hessen)
Tunica Galerie, Frankfurter Str. 14, 65520 Bad Camberg.
T. (06434) 32 34. - Ant / Orient / Tex / Arch / Eth /
Jew - *050335*

Bad Dürkheim (Rheinland-Pfalz)
Blüm, Margot, Weinstr. Süd 10, 67098 Bad Dürkheim.
T. (06322) 28 26. - Ant / Paint / Graph / China / Jew /
Silv / Rel / Glass / Mod / Ico - *050336*
Scholz, Sylvia, Weinstr. 24, 67098 Bad Dürkheim.
T. (06322) 5519. *050337*
Ziegler, H., Kurgartenstr. 12, 67098 Bad Dürkheim.
T. (06322) 71 02. *050338*

Bad Ems (Rheinland-Pfalz)
Alexandra, Römerstr. 6, 56130 Bad Ems.
T. (02603) 3827. *050339*
Matthay, Friedrich, Bleichstr. 16, 56130 Bad
Ems. *050340*

Bad Essen (Niedersachsen)
Makoschey, Wimmerstr. 63, 49152 Bad Essen.
T. (05472) 73129. - Furn - *050341*

Bad Füssing (Bayern)
Brückner-Zündorff, J., Kurallee 14, 94072 Bad Füssing.
T. (08531) 229 78. *050342*
Kania, R., Prof.-Böhm-Str. 8, 94072 Bad Füssing.
T. (08531) 221 06. *050343*
Schmid, H., Leonhardistr. 12, 94072 Bad Füssing.
T. (08531)653. *050344*

Bad Harzburg (Niedersachsen)
Hülter, G., Breite Str. 49, 38667 Bad Harzburg.
T. (05322) 805 50. *050345*
Keuck, Herzog-Wilhelm-Str.37, 38667 Bad Harzburg.
T. (05322) 62 05, 44 41. *050346*

Bad Herrenalb (Baden-Württemberg)
Rozic, B., Kurpromenade 27, 76332 Bad Herrenalb.
T. (07083) 1785. *050347*

Bad Hersfeld (Hessen)
Hess, Werner, Ludwig-Braun-Str. 2a, 36251 Bad Hersfeld. T. (06621) 754 34. - Furn - *050348*

Bad Homburg vor der Höhe (Hessen)
Antik am Markt, Louisenstr 13, 61348 Bad Homburg vor
der Höhe. T. (06172) 21619. *050350*
Balzer, Roland A., Herderstr 11, 61350 Bad Homburg vor
der Höhe. T. (06172) 84161. *050351*
Galerie Junge Kunst, Kaiser-Friedrich-Promenade 15,
61348 Bad Homburg vor der Höhe. T. (06172) 21105.
- Paint / Graph / Furn / Orient / Cur / Pho - *050352*

Hill-Kaspar, Mirjam, Louisenstr 13, 61348 Bad Homburg
vor der Höhe. T. (06172) 21619, 21387. *050353*
Indian Arts, A. Bilz & W. Stephan, Kurhaus Ladengalerie,
Louisenstr 56-58, 61348 Bad Homburg vor der Höhe.
T. (06172) 23824. *050354*
Kunst und Antiquitäten, Louisenstr 132, 61348 Bad
Homburg vor der Höhe. T. (06172) 44917,
Fax (06172) 44917. - Paint / Furn / Jew / Mod - *050355*
Rühl, A., Götzenmühlweg 27, 61350 Bad Homburg vor
der Höhe. T. (06172) 34319. *050355a*
Schweizer, Thomasstr 2, 61348 Bad Homburg vor der
Höhe. T. (06172) 23796, Fax (06172) 24558. - Paint /
China / Jew / Silv - *050356*
Waczek, Karl, Elisabethenstr 24, 61348 Bad Homburg
vor der Höhe. *050357*

Bad Honnef (Nordrhein-Westfalen)

Antik- und Kunst-Ecke, Rhöndorfer Str. 32, 53604 Bad
Honnef. T. (02224) 75050, 74701. *050358*
Croce-Brinkmann, Brunnenstr. 5, 53604 Bad Honnef.
T. (02224) 6156. - Paint / Graph / Sculp / Glass - *050359*
Die Galerie Bad Honnef, Hauptstr. 62, 53604 Bad Hon-
nef. T. (02224) 76020, Fax (02224) 7735193. - Graph /
Silv - *050360*
Koschorreck, E., Bahnhofstr. 2b, 53604 Bad Honnef.
T. (02224) 76914. *050361*
Schwan, Paul, Brieberichsweg 12, 53604 Bad
Honnef. *050362*
Treusch, Fritz, Mühlenweg 14c, 53604 Bad Honnef.
T. (02224) 48 65. *050363*

Bad Kissingen (Bayern)

Beck, E., Winkelaerstr. 31, 97688 Bad Kissingen.
T. (0971) 48 95. *050364*
Beck, Otto, Maxstr. 1a, 97688 Bad Kissingen.
T. (0971) 44 91. - Ant / Furn - *050365*
Hassloch, Lindesmühlpromenade 2, 97688 Bad Kissin-
gen. T. (0971) 3257. *050366*
Knabner, H., Martin-Luther-Str. 1, 97688 Bad
Kissingen. *050367*
Paquet, Dietlinde, Lessingstr. 8, 97688 Bad Kissingen.
T. (0971) 64208, Fax (0971) 8023555. - Ant / Paint /
Jew - *050368*
Reichardt, W., Kurhausstr. 1, 97688 Bad Kissingen.
T. (0971) 32 34. *050369*

Bad Königshofen (Bayern)

Zwierlein, Adam-Pfeuffer-Str 3, 97631 Bad Königshofen.
T. (09761) 2654. - Ant - *050370*

Bad Kreuznach (Rheinland-Pfalz)

Becker, Mannheimer Str. 39, 55545 Bad Kreuznach.
T. (0671) 338 25. - Paint / Graph / China / Repr / Fra /
Glass - *050371*
Fuhr, I., Wilhelmstr. 58, 55543 Bad Kreuznach.
T. (0671) 33913. *050372*
Haag & Scott, Kurhausstr. 1, 55543 Bad Kreuznach.
T. (0671) 352 75. *050373*
Lunkenheimer, Römerstr. 18 – 20, 55543 Bad Kreuz-
nach. T. (0671) 46000. *050374*
Müller, P., Industriestr. 21, 55543 Bad Kreuznach.
T. (0671) 645 76. *050375*
Rothenbach, D. & R., Rheinpfalzstr. 15, 55545 Bad
Kreuznach. T. (0671) 67775. *050376*
Zapp, H., Ledderhoser Weg 77, 55543 Bad Kreuznach.
T. (0671) 676 28. *050377*

Bad Krozingen (Baden-Württemberg)

Neumann, R., Basler Str. 12, 79189 Bad Krozingen.
T. (07633) 168 86. *050378*

Bad Lauterberg (Niedersachsen)

Seidel, Hauptstr 89, 37431 Bad Lauterberg.
T. (05524) 3759. *050379*

Bad Liebenzell (Baden-Württemberg)

Huber, M., H.-Sauter-Weg 16, 75378 Bad Liebenzell.
T. (07052) 12 65. *050380*
Stöcklein, U., Maisenbacher Str., 75378 Bad Liebenzell.
T. (07052) 4938. *050381*

Bad Lippspringe (Nordrhein-Westfalen)

Thiele, U., An der Aue 1, 33175 Bad Lippspringe.
T. (05252) 2228. *050382*

Bad Mergentheim (Baden-Württemberg)

Alberth, Marina, Mühlwiesen 1, 97980 Bad Mergent-
heim. T. (07931) 398. - Ant - *050383*
Ali'i Rastani, G.-A., 97980 Bad Mergentheim. *050384*
Götzelmann, Gänsmarkt 9, 97980 Bad Mergentheim.
T. (07931) 82 44. *050385*
Partin & Co., Bahnhofpl 1, 97980 Bad Mergentheim.
T. (07931) 5920, Fax 592445. - Num - *050386*

Bad Münder (Niedersachsen)

Strasser, D., Hamelspringer Str. 91, 31848 Bad Münder.
T. (05042) 17 23. *050387*

Bad Münstereifel (Nordrhein-Westfalen)

Dederichs, Johannes, Euskirchener Str. 26, 53902 Bad
Münstereifel. *050388*
Goossens, H., Kölner Str. 44, 53902 Bad Münstereifel.
T. (02253) 3885. *050389*
Rühle, B., Kölner Str. 92, 53902 Bad Münstereifel.
T. (02253) 2143. *050390*
Tritschkow, J., Euskirchener Str. 25, 53902 Bad Münste-
reifel. T. (02253) 77 00. *050391*

Bad Nauheim (Hessen)

Antiquitäten am Kurpark, Parkstr. 3, 61231 Bad Nau-
heim. T. (06032) 318 61. - Ant - *050392*
Müller, D., Kurstr. 13, 61231 Bad Nauheim.
T. (06032) 2227. *050393*

Bad Nenndorf (Niedersachsen)

Lübke, H., Rodenberger Allee 31/33, 31542 Bad Nenn-
dorf. T. (05723) 28 56. *050394*

Bad Neuenahr-Ahrweiler (Rheinland-Pfalz)

Granow, C., Kreuzstr. 8a, 53474 Bad Neuenahr-Ahrwei-
ler. T. (02641) 29829. *050395*
Müller-Feldmann, Annemarie, Telegrafenstr. 21, 53474
Bad Neuenahr-Ahrweiler. T. (02641) 263 39. - Ant /
Graph / Num / Arch - *050396*
Schwalb, Poststr. 27, 53474 Bad Neuenahr-Ahrweiler.
T. (02641) 250 44. - Orient / Tex - *050397*

Bad Neustadt an der Saale (Bayern)

Breier, Ernst, Theubergstr 13, 97616 Bad Neustadt an
der Saale. T. (09771) 2090. *050398*
Griebel, M. & F., Thenbergstr 15, 97616 Bad Neustadt
an der Saale. T. (09771) 2211. - Ant / Furn / China /
Sculp / Rel / Glass - *050399*

Bad Oeynhausen (Nordrhein-Westfalen)

Clamor, Wilhelm, Am Vorberg 1, 32549 Bad Oeynhau-
sen. T. (05731) 512 38. - Ant / Furn - *050400*
Conrad, Hans, Hahnenkampstr. 15, 32549 Bad Oeyn-
hausen. T. (05731) 55 85, 56 00. - Ant / Furn / China /
Dec / Silv / Lights / Instr / Mil / Glass / Cur - *050401*
Wollesen, Teunis, Falkenweg 1, 32547 Bad Oeynhausen.
T. (05731) 958 88. - Orient / Tex - *050402*

Bad Oldesloe (Schleswig-Holstein)

Corcut, K., Zum Amt 3, 23843 Bad Oldesloe.
T. (04531) 854 61. *050403*
Hansen, O., Dorfstr. 34, 23843 Bad Oldesloe.
T. (04531) 87000. *050404*

Bad Orb (Hessen)

Der Tintenfisch, Wendelinusstr. 7, 63619 Bad Orb.
T. (06052) 25 59. - Ant - *050405*

Bad Pyrmont (Niedersachsen)

Hildebrandt, Hauptallee 3, 31812 Bad Pyrmont.
T. (05281) 60 99 25. - Ant / Paint / Graph / Furn / China /
Dec / Jew / Silv / Lights / Glass / Ico - *050406*
Huneke, Schillerstr. 19, 31812 Bad Pyrmont.
T. (05281) 40 70. *050407*
Schlierkamp, J. & H., Bomberg Allee 4, 31812 Bad Pyr-
mont. T. (05281) 60 65 00. *050408*
Schürk, Arkaden 1, 31812 Bad Pyrmont. *050409*

Bad Rothenfelde (Niedersachsen)

Potthof, Winfried, Hermann-Löns-Weg 2, 49214 Bad Ro-
thenfelde. T. (05424) 718. *050410*

Bad Säckingen (Baden-Württemberg)

Richter, L., Rheinbrückstr. 40, 79713 Bad Säckingen.
T. (07761) 84 70. *050411*

Schön, J.-P., Rheinbrückstr. 25, 79713 Bad Säckingen.
T. (07761) 3451. *050412*

Bad Salzdetfurth (Niedersachsen)

Sommer, K., Amselstieg 1, 31162 Bad Salzdetfurth.
T. (05063) 81 44. *050413*

Bad Salzuflen (Nordrhein-Westfalen)

Antik Lager, Alte Landstr. 5, 32108 Bad Salzuflen.
T. (05222) 222 93. - Furn - *050414*
Antiquitäten am Kurpark, Dammstr. 14, 32105 Bad Salz-
uflen. T. (05222) 35 44. - Furn / Jew / Silv /
Instr - *050415*
Asien Haus, Bismarckstr. 13, 32105 Bad
Salzuflen. *050416*
Böllert, Annastr. 5, 32105 Bad Salzuflen.
T. (05222) 6478. *050417*
Dünne, R., Dammstr. 10c, 32105 Bad Salzuflen.
T. (05222) 59393. *050418*
Junghanns, R., Wenkenstr. 13, 32105 Bad Salzuflen.
T. (05222) 40916. *050419*
Schumann, T., Bleichstr. 6, 32105 Bad Salzuflen.
T. (05222) 586 15. *050420*

Bad Sassendorf (Nordrhein-Westfalen)

Kleines Kunsthaus am Schloß, Bismarckstr. 19, 59505
Bad Sassendorf. - Ant / Furn / China - *050421*
Otto, K., Eichendorffstr. 9, 59505 Bad Sassendorf.
T. (02921) 517 33. *050422*
Wenner, Renate, Kützelbach Str 23, 59505 Bad Sassen-
dorf. - Ant / Furn / China - *050423*

Bad Schönborn (Baden-Württemberg)

Haus der Kunst, Hauptstr. 88, 76669 Bad Schönborn.
T. (07253) 6085, Fax (07253) 6087. *050424*

Bad Schussenried (Baden-Württemberg)

Britsch, Georg, Drümmelbergstr. 9, 88427 Bad Schus-
senried. T. (07583) 24 14. - Ant / Furn / Sculp /
Mil - *050425*

Bad Schwalbach (Hessen)

Schaum, Günter, Adolfstr. 139, 65307 Bad Schwalbach.
T. (06124) 1486. *050426*

Bad Soden (Hessen)

Blumenauer, Hans-Joachim, Am Haag 33, 65812 Bad
Soden. T. (06196) 25081. - Paint - *050427*
Kornmann, Charlotte, Niederhofheimer Str 7a, 65812
Bad Soden. *050428*
Schulz, G., Sperberstr 76a, 65812 Bad Soden.
T. (06196) 24083. - Num - *050429*
Sommer, Harald, Königsteiner Str 20A, 65812 Bad So-
den. T. (06196) 21719. *050430*

Bad Sooden-Allendorf (Hessen)

Kiesow, A., Bahnhofstr. 17, 37242 Bad Sooden-Allen-
dorf. T. (05652) 2766. *050431*

Bad Tölz (Bayern)

Schilling, Marktstr. 31, 83646 Bad Tölz. - Tex - *050432*

Bad Urach (Baden-Württemberg)

Frenzel, E., In den Thermen 2, 72574 Bad Urach.
T. (07125) 70203. *050433*
Rau, Inge, Max-Eyth-Str 11, 72574 Bad Urach. *050434*

Bad Vilbel (Hessen)

Antik-Halle, Frankfurter Str. 24, 61118 Bad Vilbel.
T. (06101) 842 27. - Ant - *050435*
Antiquitäten am Berg, Friedrich-Ebert-Alage 2, 61118
Bad Vilbel. T. (06101) 8211. *050436*
Herget, Alois, Homburger Str. 29, 61118 Bad Vilbel.
T. (06101) 29 52. - Furn - *050437*
Schatztruhe, Frankfurter Str. 58, 61118 Bad Vilbel.
T. (06101) 898 71. - Furn / China / Jew / Silv / Lights /
Glass - *050438*
Umlauf, Osswald, Nidderstr. 19, 61118 Bad Vilbel.
T. (06101) 326 55. - Ant / Furn - *050439*

Bad Waldsee (Baden-Württemberg)

Allgaier, R., Drei Königsgasse 18, 88339 Bad Waldsee.
T. (07524) 6764. *050440*
Fundgrube, 88339 Bad Waldsee.
T. (07524) 56 91. *050441*
Rogg, Philipp, Steinstr. 38, 88339 Bad Waldsee. *050442*

Schmuck, G., Kirrlohstr. 13, 88339 Bad Waldsee. T. (07524) 56 38. 050443
Terwissen, H., & J. Döbele, Schmiedsgasse 18, 88339 Bad Waldsee. T. (07524) 56 91. 050444
Winter, A., Kirrlohstr. 11, 88339 Bad Waldsee. T. (07524) 65 55. 050445
Winter & Schmuck, Schnorrenweg 23, 88339 Bad Waldsee. 050446

Bad Wiessee (Bayern)

Bierstorfer, Richard, Ringbergstr. 10, 83707 Bad Wiessee. T. (08022) 81225. - Ant / Paint / Furn / China / Sculp / Tex / Silv / Rel / Ico - 050447

Bad Wildbad (Baden-Württemberg)

Endres, R., Wilhelmstr 91, 75323 Bad Wildbad. T. (07081) 8663. 050448

Bad Wildungen (Hessen)

Akkoyun, A., Brunnenallee 32, 34537 Bad Wildungen. T. (05621) 72364. 050449
Galerie Bild & Rahmen, Lindenstr. 26, 34537 Bad Wildungen. T. (05621) 723 27. - Paint / Graph / Repr / Fra / Glass - 050450
Mangel, H., Hufelandstr. 11, 34537 Bad Wildungen. 050451

Bad Wimpfen (Baden-Württemberg)

Kuhn, R., Marktrain 1, 74206 Bad Wimpfen. T. (07063) 81 01. 050452
Siber, N., Färberstr. 19, 74206 Bad Wimpfen. T. (07063) 77 40. 050453

Bad Wörishofen (Bayern)

Döring, K., Kneippstr. 9, 86825 Bad Wörishofen. T. (08247) 42 45. 050454
Galerie Alexander, Bgm.-Stöckle-Str. 10, 86825 Bad Wörishofen. T. (08247) 31536. - Paint / Graph / Jew / Glass - 050455

Bad Zwischenahn (Niedersachsen)

Deeken, L., Reihdamm 33, 26160 Bad Zwischenahn. T. (04403) 59158. 050456

Baddeckenstedt (Niedersachsen)

Patzelt, W., An der B6, 38271 Baddeckenstedt. T. (05345) 1220. 050457

Baden-Baden (Baden-Württemberg)

Albrecht, Gebr., Kreuzstr. 3b, 76530 Baden-Baden. - Ant - 050458
Anastasiu, J., Lange Str. 47, 76530 Baden-Baden. T. (07221) 24025. 050459
Apfelbaum-Galerie, Kaiser-Wilhelm Str. 10, 76530 Baden-Baden. T. (07221) 314 82. - Ant - 050460
Bayer, G., Hauptstr. 2, 76534 Baden-Baden. T. (07221) 76 60. 050461
Berlin, W., Geroldsauer Str. 12, 76534 Baden-Baden. T. (07221) 711 09. 050462
Bühler, G., Geroldsauer Str. 137a, 76534 Baden-Baden. T. (07221) 70848. 050463
Christian, O., Kurgarten 21, 76530 Baden-Baden. T. (07221) 23259. 050464
Cresnik, H., Merkurstr. 17, 76530 Baden-Baden. T. (07221) 31495. - Ant / Furn / Arch - 050465
Danner, R., Steinhauerweg 8, 76532 Baden-Baden. T. (07221) 65133. 050466
Furtwengler, U., Gernsbacher Str. 48, 76530 Baden-Baden. T. (07221) 32511. 050467
Holz, Heinrich, Merkurstr. 17, 76530 Baden-Baden. T. (07221) 24975. 050468
Homann, Richard, Gernsbacher Str. 24, 76530 Baden-Baden. T. (07221) 22572. - Ant - 050469
Huster, V., Steinstr. 12, 76530 Baden-Baden. - Num - 050470
Jordan & Matz, Markgraf-Christoph-Str. 9, 76530 Baden-Baden. T. (07221) 315 12. 050471
Kappes, W., Ludwig-Wilhelm-Platz 5, 76530 Baden-Baden. - Num - 050472
Kolb, E., Lichtentaler Str 56, 76530 Baden-Baden. T. (07221) 25575. 050473
Kolb, Erich, Lichtentaler Str. 56, 76530 Baden-Baden. T. (07221) 38972, 25575, Fax (07221) 38982. 050474
Liebmann, Peter, Sophienstr. 13, 76530 Baden-Baden. T. (07221) 31333. 050475
Matz, Dorothea, Markgraf-Christoph-Str. 9, 76530 Baden-Baden. T. (07221) 3112. 050476
Meindl-Pöllmann, A., Werderstr. 1, 76530 Baden-Baden. T. (07221) 31191. - Paint - 050477
Micka, R., Sonnenpl. 2, 76530 Baden-Baden. T. (07221) 384 15. 050478
Niewöhner, A., Werderstr. 18, 76530 Baden-Baden. T. (07221) 31774. 050479
Pavia, A., Lange Str. 64, 76530 Baden-Baden. T. (07221) 31014. 050480
Tatzel, Maximilian, Dr., Balzenbergstr. 63, 76530 Baden-Baden. - Ant / Paint / Furn / China / Sculp / Tex / Jew / Silv / Instr / Glass - 050481
Villa Kunst-Antiquitäten, Gerhard Bayer, Lichtentaler Str. 9 + 16, 76530 Baden-Baden. T. (07221) 23555/54, Fax (07221) 7945. 050482
Weber, Herta, Hermann-Sielcken-Str. 2b, 76530 Baden-Baden. T. (07221) 233 70. - Ant / Furn / China / Silv - 050483
Weber, Peter, Eichstr 12, 76530 Baden-Baden. T. (07221) 25571. - Paint / Graph - 050484
Wirnitzer, Elfriede, Lilienmattstr. 6, Haus Lauschan, 76530 Baden-Baden. T. (07221) 26725. - Graph / Sculp / Draw - 050485

Badenweiler (Baden-Württemberg)

Atzler, Eberhard, Luisenstr. 10, 79410 Badenweiler. T. (07632) 5495. - Paint / China / Silv / Ico - 050486
Felzen, Luisenstr. 9b, 79410 Badenweiler. T. (07632) 54 89. 050487
Schumacher, Kaiserstr. 6, 79410 Badenweiler. T. (07632) 5345. 050488

Baienfurth (Baden-Württemberg)

Ruther, Bergstr. 38, 88255 Baienfurth. 050489

Baiersdorf (Bayern)

Kirchner, Ilse, Bubenreuther Str. 18, 91083 Baiersdorf. T. (09133) 1080. 050490

Balingen (Baden-Württemberg)

Fischer, H., Wilhelmstr. 31, 72336 Balingen. T. (07433) 16162. 050491
Koch, Martha, Tübingerstr. 19, 72336 Balingen. T. (07433) 7173. 050492
Pollermann, Christel, Ebertstr. 3, 72336 Balingen. T. (07433) 7206. 050493
Schönauer, D., Schweizer Str. 40, 72336 Balingen. T. (07433) 5954. 050494

Baltrum (Niedersachsen)

Mindermann, Heinz, 26579 Baltrum. 050495

Bamberg (Bayern)

Antik-Markt der Drogenhilfe Oberfranken, Letzengasse 13a, 96052 Bamberg. T. (0951) 20 30 20. 050496
Arndt, Dr., Karolinenstr. 11, 96049 Bamberg. T. (0951) 56519. - Paint - 050497
Augustyniak, C. &.I., Gertraudenstr. 10, 96050 Bamberg. T. (0951) 24082. 050498
Badum, Dominikanerstr. 1, 96049 Bamberg. T. (0951) 526 96. - Ant / Furn / Glass - 050499
Bamberger Tassenkabinett, Karolinenstr. 22, 96049 Bamberg. T. (0951) 535 42. - China - 050500
Bartl, Memmelsdorfer Str. 7b, 96052 Bamberg. T. (0951) 611 62. 050501
Bauer, Krimhild, Untere Brücke 4, 96049 Bamberg. T. (0951) 55732. 050502
Bauernmöbelmarkt, Letzengasse 13a, 96052 Bamberg. T. (0951) 20 30 20. - Furn - 050503
Blokesch, Karolinenstr. 14, 96049 Bamberg. T. (0951) 554 45. 050504
Essler, V.-Bachstr. 7, 96047 Bamberg. T. (0951) 56376. - Furn - 050505
Franke, C.-F., Karolinenstr. 24, 96049 Bamberg. T. (0951) 28227. 050506
Görtler, Nortbert, Siechenstr. 14, 96052 Bamberg. T. (0951) 67477. - Num - 050507
Härtl, Ulf, Karolinenstr. 9, 96049 Bamberg. T. (0951) 55487, Fax (0951) 55440. - Ant / Paint / Furn / China / Sculp - 050508
Höchstetter, Karolinenstr. 21, 96049 Bamberg. T. (0951) 53577. - Num - 050509
Hottelmann-Schmidt, Irene, Judenstr. 17, 96049 Bamberg. T. (0951) 57106. - Ant / Furn / Jew / Glass / Cur - 050510
Kunsthandlung Christine, Hellerstr. 6, 96047 Bamberg. T. (0951) 260 50. 050511
Liebich, A., Judenstr. 6, 96049 Bamberg. T. (0951) 57784. 050512
Löblein, P., & M. Käßberger, Karolinenstr. 23, 96049 Bamberg. T. (0951) 52400. 050513
Lüffe, Friedrich-Wilhelm, Karolinenstr 24, 96049 Bamberg. T. (0951) 54489, (09544) 7796, Fax 59439. - Graph / Furn / Jew - 050514
Mallkowsky, H., Kaimsgasse 6, 96052 Bamberg. T. (0951) 27346. 050515
Mayer, Michael, Hellerstr. 6, 96047 Bamberg. T. (0951) 26050. - Ant - 050516
Most, Karolinenstr. 1, 96049 Bamberg. T. (0951) 57565, Fax (0951) 57509. - Ant - 050517
Müller, Reinhard, Schranne 6, 96049 Bamberg. T. (0951) 53631. 050518
Murr, Karlheinz, Karolinenstr 4, Untere Brücke 3-5, 96049 Bamberg. T. (0951) 57728, Fax (0951) 56221. - Ant - 050519
Schmutzler, Erika, Herrenstr. 4, 96049 Bamberg. T. (0951) 55270. - Ant - 050520
Senger, Karolinenstr. 8 und 14, 96049 Bamberg. T. (0951) 54030, 23153, Fax (0951) 54420. - Ant - 050521
Triebel, Heinz, Untere Brücke 2, 96049 Bamberg. T. (0951) 26456. 050522
Vogel, G., Karolinenstr. 2, 96049 Bamberg. T. (0951) 53133. 050523
Wenzel, M., Karolinenstr. 16, 96049 Bamberg. T. (0951) 56725. - Ant / Furn / Sculp - 050524
Wohlfahrt, H., Fleischstr. 19, 96047 Bamberg. T. (0951) 23351. 050525

Bargteheide (Schleswig-Holstein)

Janz-Wecke, Marianne, Voßkuhlenweg 62, 22941 Bargteheide. 050526
Roschewitz, B., Langereihe 21, 22941 Bargteheide. T. (04532) 5472. - Ant / Paint / Furn - 050527

Barnstorf (Niedersachsen)

Celmer, Brigitte, Donstorf 8, 49406 Barnstorf. T. (05442) 2712. - Furn - 050528

Barsinghausen (Niedersachsen)

Grabs, Bernhard, Mindener Str. 41, 30890 Barsinghausen. 050529

Bassenheim (Rheinland-Pfalz)

Schmitz, Ilse, Mülheimer Str. 1, 56220 Bassenheim. T. (02625) 4322. - Tin - 050530

Battenberg (Hessen)

Kreis, J., Am Hofenstück 14, 35088 Battenberg. T. (06452) 88 88. 050531

Baunach (Bayern)

Lüffe, Obere Mühle, 96148 Baunach. T. (09544) 7796. - Graph / Furn / Jew - 050532
Wedel, Georg, Haßbergstr. 25, 96148 Baunach. 050533

Bausendorf (Rheinland-Pfalz)

Krohs, M., Am Niederberg 4, 54538 Bausendorf. T. (06532) 3826. 050534

Bawinkel (Niedersachsen)

Gehdke, E., Lingener Str. 11, 49844 Bawinkel. T. (05963) 773. 050535

Bayreuth (Bayern)

Antik-Schneider, Sophienstr. 13, 95444 Bayreuth. T. (0921) 69458. - Ant - 050536
Bayreuther Münzhandlung, Alexanderstr. 15, 95444 Bayreuth. T. (0921) 274 72, 134 84. - Num - 050537
Boutique Rustika, Opernstr. 26, 95444 Bayreuth. T. (0921) 237 72. - Mul - 050538
Fritzsche, Hans-Joachim, Nürnberger Str. 14, 95448 Bayreuth. T. (0921) 22228, 68165. - Ant - 050539
Hemmungen, Friedrichstr. 27, 95444 Bayreuth. T. (0921) 65933. 050540
Kopetz, Hanny, Brandenburger Str. 28 A, 95448 Bayreuth. T. (0921) 22569. 050541

Noworzyn, G., Egerländer Str. 24, 95448 Bayreuth.
T. (0921) 20564. 050542
Rothenbücher, H., Sophienstr. 11, 95444 Bayreuth.
T. (0921) 67447. 050543
Rothenbücher, Peter, Schloßhof Birken, 95447 Bayreuth.
T. (0921) 61878, Fax (0921) 58911. - Ant - 050544
Russ, Christa, Maxstr. 29, 95444 Bayreuth.
T. (0921) 65985. - Ant - 050545
Steingraeber & Söhne, Steingraeber Passage 1, 95444
Bayreuth. T. (0921) 64049, Fax (0921) 58272. - Paint /
Graph / Repr / Sculp / Fra / Lights - 050546
Weder, J., Carl-Schüller-Str. 19a, 95444 Bayreuth.
T. (0921) 23261. 050547
Weithauer, Gert, Ludwigstr. 4, 95444 Bayreuth.
T. (0921) 64656. 050548

Bebra (Hessen)
Brück, Helene, Höhenweg 7, 36179 Bebra.
T. (06622) 2454. - Ant / China / Glass - 050549

Beckeln (Niedersachsen)
Deepe, Werner, Hauptstr. 50, 27243 Beckeln.
T. (04244) 7919. 050550

Bedburg (Nordrhein-Westfalen)
Hirsch, H., Hauptstr 6, 50181 Bedburg.
T. (02272) 2397. 050551

Bedburg-Hau (Nordrhein-Westfalen)
Thyssen, J., Grüner Graben, 47551 Bedburg-Hau.
T. (02823) 48931. 050552

Bendorf (Rheinland-Pfalz)
Hardy, Franz, Bahnhofstr 98, 56170 Bendorf.
T. (02622) 2308. - Paint / Furn - 050553

Bensheim (Hessen)
Edelmann, N., Darmstädter Str. 236, 64625 Bensheim.
T. (06251) 79893. - Ant - 050554
Giesing, Anne-Marie, Friedhofstr. 99, 64625 Bensheim.
T. (06251) 67 03. - Ant / Paint / Graph / Furn /
China - 050555
Meister, W., Gronauerstr. 157, 64625 Bensheim.
T. (06251) 2460. 050556

Berg (Bayern)
Laudenbach, Helmuth, Blaubergstr. 16, 82335 Berg.
- Orient - 050557
Vetter, W., Bachhausen, 82335 Berg.
T. (08151) 5247. 050558

Berg bei Neumarkt (Bayern)
Stützinger, F., Sindbacher Hauptstr. 3, 92348 Berg bei
Neumarkt. T. (09181) 0989/1381. 050559

Berge (Niedersachsen)
Schmidt, W., Börstelerstr. 11, 49626 Berge.
T. (05435) 457. - Furn - 050560

Bergen, Kreis Celle (Niedersachsen)
Lohmann, Michael, Harburgerstr 3, 29303 Bergen, Kreis
Celle. T. (05051) 3113. 050561

Bergheim (Nordrhein-Westfalen)
Hölzer, W., Im Rauland 100, 50127 Bergheim. 050562
Wirf, E., Glescher Str 107, 50126 Bergheim.
T. (02271) 42436. 050563
Wlodarczyk, Margit, Südweststr 5, 50126 Bergheim.
T. (02271) 42505. 050564

Bergisch Gladbach (Nordrhein-Westfalen)
Culmann, Wilhelm-Klein-Str. 16, 51427 Bergisch Glad-
bach. T. (02202) 629 50. 050565
Kürten, Rudolf August, Parkstr. 14, 51427 Bergisch
Gladbach. T. (02202) 61881, 61173. 050566
Löchel, R., Lustheide 26, 51427 Bergisch Gladbach.
T. (02202) 68893. 050567
Menches, V., Brandroster 1, 51427 Bergisch Gladbach.
T. (02202) 61590. 050568
Pisarski, M., Am S-Bahnhof, 51427 Bergisch Gladbach.
T. (02202) 394 50. 050569
Röder, Michael, Ottostr. 22, 51427 Bergisch Gladbach.
T. (02202) 62938. 050570
Schlinkhoff, E., Alter Traßweg 10, 51427 Bergisch Glad-
bach. T. (02202) 62328, 22289. 050571

Schröder, H.M., & U. Dörr, Wingertsheide 59, 51427 Bergisch Gladbach. T. (02202) 64170, Fax 66809. - Paint /
Graph - 050572

Berlin
Achelis, Hans Thomas, Dr., Hüninger Str. 49, 14195 Ber-
lin. T. (030) 832 50 93. 050573
Aconda-Antiquitäten, Malplaquetstr. 36, 13347
Berlin. 050574
Ägyptische Galerie Papyri, Kaiser-Friedrich-Str 4a,
10585 Berlin. T. (030) 3411270. 050575
Afrika Galerie, Etage Urbanhof, Dieffenbachstr. 36,
10115 Berlin. T. (030) 692 59 50. - Eth - 050576
AGO Galerie, Meierottostr 1, 10719 Berlin.
T. (030) 8819024. - Paint / Graph / Furn / Draw - 050577
AGW Münzhandel, Joachimstaler Str. 39-41, 10623 Ber-
lin. T. (030) 882 74 51. - Num - 050578
Akhtary, M., Eisenacher Str. 7, 10777 Berlin.
T. (030) 2131281. - Paint / China / Jew / Silv - 050579
Albrecht, Unter den Eichen 119, 12203 Berlin.
T. (030) 834 47 46. 050580
Alom, van, Meierottostr 1, 10719 Berlin.
T. (030) 8832505. - Paint / Sculp / Eth / Draw - 050581
Alt-Berliner-Truhe, Kaiser-Friedrich-Str. 16, 10585 Ber-
lin. T. (030) 342 22 48. - Ant - 050582
Alterna Kontor für antike Öfen, Pariser Str. 20, 10707
Berlin. T. (030) 2187273. - Graph / Repr - 050583
Amsler & Ruthardt, Nürnberger Str. 53, 10789 Berlin.
T. (030) 2187273. - Graph / Repr - 050584
Annabring, C. Inh. Josip Brajkovic, Nollendorfstr. 28,
10777 Berlin. T. (030) 216 37 26. - Dec - 050585
Antik-Galerie, Goethestr. 81, 10623 Berlin.
T. (030) 31 75 48. 050586
Antik-Kaiser, Viktoria-Luise-Platz 7, 10777 Berlin.
T. (030) 214 27 77. - Ant / Paint / Furn / Dec / Lights /
Mod - 050587
Antik Nr. 1, Maximiliankorso 1, 13465 Berlin.
T. (030) 401 52 93. - Ant - 050588
Antik Royal, Düsseldorfer Str. 10, 10719 Berlin.
T. (030) 883 47 43. - Ant - 050589
Antik Schmuck, Friedbergstr. 37, 14057 Berlin.
T. (030) 321 16 37. - Ant / Repr / Jew / Mod - 050590
Antik-Shop im KaDeWe, Tauentzienstr., 10789 Berlin.
T. (030) 2187482, Fax (030) 8919942. - Ant / Paint /
China / Silv / Ico - 050591
Antik- u. Flohmarkt, Friedrichstr 203, 10117 Berlin.
T. (030) 8834743. 050592
Antik-Waffen, Schlüterstr. 51, 10629 Berlin.
T. (030) 883 86 18. - Mil - 050593
Antik 80, Grunewaldstr. 80, 10823 Berlin.
T. (030) 781 55 75. - Furn / Lights - 050594
Antikhaus-Abou, Bergmannstr. 112, 10961 Berlin.
T. (030) 691 21 28. - Ant - 050595
Antikwerkstatt, Waldemarstr. 24, 10999 Berlin.
T. (030) 651146. - Furn - 050596
Antiquarius, Fasanenstr. 71, 10719 Berlin.
T. (030) 881 36 36. 050597
Antiquitäten-Ankauf, Maxstr 14, 13347 Berlin.
T. (030) 4551394. 050598
Art Deco, Goethestr. 69, 10625 Berlin.
T. (030) 323 17 11. - Mod - 050599
Art Deco- u. Designermöbel, Belziger Str 63, 10823 Ber-
lin. T. (030) 7817384. 050600
Art 1900, Kurfürstendamm 53, 10707 Berlin.
T. (030) 8815627, Fax (030) 8815627. - Paint / Jew /
Mod - 050601
Asien-Center, Europa-Center 81a, 10789 Berlin. 050602
Bader, Alexander, Kalckreuthstr. 14, 10777 Berlin.
T. (030) 2186995. - Ant / Furn - 050603
Bajorat, Horst, Kol. Seebad Elchdamm, II, 7, 10115
Berlin. 050604
Bandoly, Brandenburgische Str 27, 10707 Berlin.
T. (030) 8814910. - Paint / Graph - 050605
Bandtke, Kurt, Hultschiner Damm 33, 12623 Berlin.
T. (030) 527 68 38. - Ant / Paint / Furn / China / Arch /
Eth / Dec - 050606
Barthmann, Martina, Eichborndamm 52, 13403 Berlin.
T. (030) 4138534. 050607
Baues, Irene, Leibnizstr. 60, 10629 Berlin.
T. (030) 324 33 91. 050608
Bellinger-Fuchs, Lisa, Eisenach Str 60, 10823 Berlin.
T. (030) 7848346. 050609

Berbig, Ottomar, Passauer Str. 35, 10789 Berlin.
T. (030) 313 57 27, 313 57 77. - Ant / Cur - 050610
Berendes, P., Bergmannstr. 18, 10961 Berlin.
T. (030) 693 01 43. - Ant - 050611
Bergemann, Drakestr. 43a, 12205 Berlin.
T. (030) 8324889, Fax (030) 8316121. - Ant / Silv /
Mod - 050612
Bergmann, Klaus P., Fasanenstr. 12, 10623 Berlin.
T. (030) 313 74 30. - Ant / Paint / Furn / China /
Glass - 050613
Berliner Fenster, Nürnberger Str. 19, 10777 Berlin.
T. (030) 213 45 24. 050614
Berliner Zinnfiguren, Knesebeckstr. 88, 10623 Berlin.
T. (030) 310802, Fax (030) 316180. - Cur / Tin /
Toys - 050615
Berndt, Dr., Eichenallee 32, 14050 Berlin.
T. (030) 304 25 36. - Ant - 050616
Bethmann-Hollweg, Asta von, Fasanenstr. 68, 10719
Berlin. T. (030) 8821162, Fax (030) 8831761. - Ant /
Paint / Sculp - 050617
Bischoff, Friedrich, Pestalozzistr 54, 10627 Berlin.
T. (030) 3232163. 050618
Bleibtreu-Antik, I. Vieregg-Gülsen, Ludwigkirchstr. 9,
10719 Berlin. T. (030) 883 52 12. - Ant / Cur - 050619
Bleichert, Michael von, Hortensienstr. 9, 12203 Berlin.
T. (030) 831 80 81/82, Fax (030) 831 80 82. - Paint /
Graph / Num - 050620
Blödorn, Klaus, Fechnerstr. 11, 10717 Berlin.
T. (030) 87 52 94. 050621
Bock, Wolfgang, Gardeschützenweg 92, 12203 Berlin.
T. (030) 8332929. 050622
Bodenheim, Bartningallee 7, 10557 Berlin.
T. (030) 853 48 47. - Tex - 050623
Boeck, Roswitha, Beusselstr. 51, 10553 Berlin.
T. (030) 391 72 81. 050624
Böhm, H., Yorckstr 81, 10965 Berlin.
T. (030) 7850078. 050625
Boerner, H., Carmerstr. 19, 10623 Berlin.
T. (030) 313 82 72. 050626
Böttcher, Stephan, Sredzkistr 34, 10435 Berlin.
T. (030) 4422943. 050627
Boldt, Gertrud-Maria, Pestalozzistr. 12, 10625 Berlin.
T. (030) 313 82 01. 050628
Boldt, W.R., Pfalzburger Str. 12, 10719 Berlin.
T. (030) 883 20 09. 050629
Bonasewicz, Barbara, Rheinstr. 32-33, 12161 Berlin.
T. (030) 852 00 80. 050630
Bratz, Jörg P., Pestalozzistr. 88a, 10625 Berlin.
T. (030) 31 72 17. - Ant / Furn / Ico - 050631
Bredow, Hans-Joachim, Kalckreutherstr 13, 10777 Ber-
lin. T. (030) 213 88 77, Fax (030) 301 83 44. - Ant /
Paint / Furn / Mod - 050632
Bredow, Ute, Rankestr. 13, 10789 Berlin.
T. (030) 211 21 09. - Ant / Paint / Furn / Mod - 050633
Brenner, Goltzstr. 42, 10781 Berlin.
T. (030) 216 24 95. 050634
Bresinsky, Hermann, Eisenacher Str. 117, 10777 Berlin.
T. (030) 216 21 67. 050635
Broszat, Goethestr. 69, 10625 Berlin.
T. (030) 3136957. 050636
Bublys, Margot, Wilsnacker Str. 9, 10559 Berlin.
T. (030) 2187007. 050637
Buchen, H.P., Feurigstr 68, 10827 Berlin.
T. (030) 2187007. 050638
Budig-Godolt, R., Leibnizstr. 42, 10629 Berlin.
T. (030) 324 42 13. 050639
Budig, Robert, Schlüterstr. 65, 10625 Berlin.
T. (030) 313 47 58. - Jew / Instr - 050640
Büber, Gisela, Postfach 2946, 10777 Berlin.
T. (030) 8316265. - Ant - 050641
Chalet Antik, Wilmersdorfer Str. 15, 10585 Berlin.
T. (030) 42 14 40. 050642
Charivari, Preußenallee 39, 14052 Berlin.
T. (030) 305 28 39. - Ant - 050643
China-Fritzsche, Rheingaustr. 14, 12161 Berlin.
T. (030) 821 74 10. - Orient - 050644
Christmann, H.G., Görrestr. 30, 12161 Berlin.
T. (030) 851 20 55. 050645
Cibis, Robert, & Christel Conrad, Suarezstr. 63, 14057
Berlin. T. (030) 323 96 63. - Ant / Furn / China /
Silv - 050646
Cohn, E., Paretzer Str. 9, 10713 Berlin.
T. (030) 395 73 33. 050647

Czerny, R., Zillestr. 81, 10585 Berlin.
T. (030) 341 40 04.   050648

Czymoch, Hans, Kaiserin-Augusta-Allee 89, 10589 Berlin. T. (030) 344 13 34. - Num -   050649

Danger, W., Schillerstr. 68, 10625 Berlin.
T. (030) 313 65 43. - Furn -   050650

Deicke, Ullrich, Choriner Str 6, 10119 Berlin.
T. (030) 2316931.   050651

Dekarz, Gerd-Joachim, Leonhardtstr. 4, 14057 Berlin.
T. (030) 323 96 74.   050652

Denk, Peter, Kurfürstendamm 202, 10719 Berlin.
T. (030) 883 62 85.   050653

Dietzel, Goethestr. 6, 10623 Berlin.
T. (030) 31 06 10.   050654

Dobrescu, Luminita, Fasanenstr 29, 10719 Berlin.
T. (030) 8811046. - Ant -   050655

Döbler, R.H., Keithstr. 8, 10787 Berlin.
T. (030) 211 93 44. - Ant / Furn / China / Silv /
Glass -   050656

Döpkens, Hans-J., Alt-Moabit 56, 10555 Berlin.
T. (030) 391 62 29.   050657

Dohnisch, Rudi, Friedrichstr 194, Berlin.
T. (030) 2004372.   050658

Dorau, Gernot, Beusselstr 65, 10553 Berlin.
T. (030) 3911488, Fax (030) 3922984. - Num - 050659

Dralle, Ina-Maria, Schlüterstr. 69, 10625 Berlin.
T. (030) 312 82 93. - Tin -   050660

Drogge, Hans, Heylstr. 1, 10825 Berlin.   050661

Dürlich, M., Keithstr 5, 10787 Berlin. T. (030) 2183660,
Fax (030) 8915529. - Furn / Silv -   050662

Ebel, Wilmersdorfer Str. 78, 10629 Berlin.
T. (030) 323 63 45. - Ant / Jew -   050663

Ebner von Eschenbach, Eisenacher Str 8, 10777 Berlin.
T. (030) 2181117. - Ant / Paint / Graph / Silv /
Glass -   050664

Effenberger, Jan, Friedrichstr 192, 10117 Berlin.
T. (030) 2004391.   050665

Ehrlich, Hans-Jürgen, Carmerstr. 11, 10623 Berlin.
T. (030) 312 33 31.   050666

Elster, Magrit, Rodensteinstr. 7, 13593 Berlin. - Ant /
Paint -   050667

Erdmann, Sonja u. Walter, Bleibtreustr 605, 10623 Berlin. T. (030) 3126464.   050668

Extra-Jochum-1950-heute, Wielandstr. 37, 10625 Berlin. T. (030) 3243302, Fax (030) 3242852. - Furn / Tex /
Jew / Glass -   050669

Farahbaksh, Houshang, Kantstr. 124, 10623 Berlin.
T. (030) 312 22 10. - Num -   050670

Fasanen-Edition, Fasanenstr. 13, 10623 Berlin.
T. (030) 313 97 11. - Ant / Furn -   050671

Feyerabend, Karl, Naumannstr 33, Haus 3, 10829 Berlin. - Ant -   050672

Fournier, G., Mattenbuder Pfad 41, 13503 Berlin.
T. (030) 431 89 19. - Num -   050673

Fries, Ulrich, Bleibtreustr. 53, 10623 Berlin.
T. (030) 313 46 05.   050674

Fritzsche, Ernst, Rheingaustr. 14, 12161 Berlin.
T. (030) 821 74 10. - Orient -   050675

Fuchs, Eisenacher Str 60, 10777 Berlin.
T. (030) 7848346.   050676

Fuhrmann, Jacob, Mommsenstr. 43, 10629 Berlin.
T. (030) 323 57 24. - Ant / Cur -   050677

Gärtner, Rolf, Pestalozzistr 25, 10627 Berlin.
T. (030) 3134566.   050678

Galerie am Südwestkorso, Südwestkorso 65, 12161
Berlin. T. (030) 8218859. - Eth -   050679

Galerie Atige, Leibnizstr. 56, 10629 Berlin.
T. (030) 8821328, Fax (030) 8824736. - Tex - 050680

Galerie Eiszeit, Zeughofstr. 20, 10997 Berlin.
T. (030) 611 60 16.   050681

Gehring, Karl, Gasteiner Str. 9, 10717 Berlin.
T. (030) 872596, Fax (030) 872596. - Ant / Paint /
Orient / China / Jew / Fra / Lights / Glass / Mod - 050682

Gehrt, Karin, Kalckreuthstr. 15, 10777 Berlin.
T. (030) 211 18 10. - Ant / Paint / Graph / Furn / Jew /
Fra / Silv / Lights / Glass / Cur -   050683

Gerber, Elfriede, Bleibtreustr. 48, 10623 Berlin.
T. (030) 881 67 56. - Ant -   050684

Gesell, Horst, Pestalozzistr. 54a, 10627 Berlin.
T. (030) 324 14 63.   050685

Geyer-Manske, Gertrud, Auguste-Viktoria-Str. 63, 13467
Berlin. T. (030) 826 11 07. - Graph -   050686

Glasek, Georgi, Kurfürstendamm 227, 10719 Berlin.
T. (030) 883 11 44.   050687

Gleser, Kurfürstendamm 48, 10707 Berlin.
T. (030) 8617000, 8826050. - Ico -   050688

Globus, Breite Str. 12, 13187 Berlin. T. (030) 482 41 08.
- Num -   050689

Goetz, Gerhard, Grunewaldstr. 80, 10823 Berlin.
T. (030) 781 55 75.   050690

Gojert, Richardstr. 10, 12043 Berlin.
T. (030) 681 20 75.   050691

Gottlieb, P., Emmentaler Str. 87, 13407 Berlin.
T. (030) 496 70 71.   050692

Gozzi & Thymian, Eisenacher Str 117, 10777 Berlin.
T. (030) 2169596.   050693

Grahl, Klaus D., Fasanenstr. 64, 10719 Berlin.
T. (030) 881 59 52. - Ant / Paint / Furn -   050694

Grave, Uhlandstr 83, 10717 Berlin.
T. (030) 874709.   050695

Gronert, Ulrich, Keithstr 10, 10787 Berlin.
T. (030) 2181585. - Paint / China / Silv / Glass /
Mod -   050696

Gropler, Wolfgang, Pestalozzistr. 9a, 10625 Berlin.
T. (030) 312 33 29.   050697

Gropp, Susanne, Fasanenstr. 72, 10719 Berlin.
T. (030) 882 76 16. - Ant -   050698

Grothe, Bernd, Tegeler Str. 35, 13353 Berlin.
T. (030) 453 13 95.   050699

Grzelachowski, Detlef, Tegeler Weg 106, 10589 Berlin.
T. (030) 344 24 66.   050700

Grzimek, Brita, Kurfürstendamm 200, 10719 Berlin.
T. (030) 8814113, Fax (030) 8811459.   050701

Gützlaf, Wolfgang, Friedrichstr 193, 10117 Berlin.
T. (030) 2082555.   050702

Gutschke, Reinhard, Britzer Damm 114, 12347 Berlin.
T. (030) 606 12 12, Fax (030) 6066002.   050703

Haar, Manfred, Richard-Tauber-Damm 5a, 12277 Berlin.
- China / Silv / Instr / Ico -   050704

Haas, Heinz, Seestr. 2, 12589 Berlin. T. (030) 648 08 81.
- Num -   050705

Haas, Wolfgang, Suarezstr. 3, 14057 Berlin.
T. (030) 321 45 70. - Ant / Paint / Graph / Glass /
Mod -   050706

Haase, Dieter, Fritschestr. 65, 10585 Berlin.
T. (030) 342 93 53.   050707

Haersolte, R. van, Mommsenstr. 55, 10629 Berlin.
T. (030) 323 50 54. - Orient / Eth -   050708

Hagbeck, Bodo, Grunewaldstr. 10, 10823 Berlin.
T. (030) 791 67 90.   050709

Hall, G., Pestalozzistr. 25, 10627 Berlin.
T. (030) 312 37 92.   050710

Hansen, Christian, Keithstr 13, 10787 Berlin.
T. (030) 2142899, Fax (030) 2142892. - Tex -   050711

Happel, Erna, Fasanenstr. 14, 10623 Berlin.
T. (030) 881 95 09.   050712

Harmel, Damaschkestr. 24, 10711 Berlin.
T. (030) 324 22 92. - Ant -   050713

Hartwig, Robert, Pestalozzistr. 23, 10625 Berlin.
T. (030) 312 91 24. - Ant -   050714

Harwart, Schlüterstr. 51, 10629 Berlin.
T. (030) 883 86 18. - Mil -   050715

Haß, Matthias, Karl-Marx-Str. 12a, 12043 Berlin.
T. (030) 622 20 91. - Instr -   050716

Heckmann, Manfred, Fasanenstr. 13, 10623 Berlin.
T. (030) 313 97 11.   050717

Heenemann, Jens-Peter, Nassauische Str 47, 10717
Berlin. T. (030) 8618752. - Ant / Paint / Furn / China /
Sculp / Instr / Glass / Mod -   050718

Heides Antiquitäten, Suarezstr. 6, 14057 Berlin.
T. (030) 321 67 91.   050719

Herwick, Egon, Tempelhofer Damm 106, 12099 Berlin.
T. (030) 785 93 17. - Num -   050720

Hett, Ingeborg, Keithstr. 10, 10787 Berlin.
T. (030) 211 31 11. - Eth -   050721

Hildebrandt, Volker, Zossener Str. 50, 10961 Berlin.
T. (030) 693 66 65.   050722

Hiller, R., Osteweg 68, 14167 Berlin.
T. (030) 817 43 62.   050723

Hirschfeld, A. & W., Hauptstr. 72, 10827 Berlin.
T. (030) 8523014. - Instr -   050724

Hirts, Henry E., Sybelstr. 67, 10629 Berlin.
T. (030) 883 53 24. - Ant -   050725

Höche, Kalckreuthstr. 13, 10777 Berlin.
T. (030) 211 60 68. - Ant -   050726

Hofmann, Ruth, Pestalozzistr. 8a, 10625 Berlin.
T. (030) 312 94 12.   050727

Hubert + Jägers, Emser Str. 2, 10719 Berlin.
T. (030) 87 87 30. - Ant / Paint -   050728

Hubert, Klaus, Rheingaustr. 24, 12161 Berlin.
T. (030) 821 55 96.   050729

Hübner, K.-Heinz, Grolmanstr. 46, 10623 Berlin.
T. (030) 883 25 33.   050730

Hurthe, Dieter, Erkstr. 20, 12043 Berlin.
T. (030) 681 93 22. - Ant / Num -   050731

Ilsemann, Bernd, Leonhardtstr 4, 14057 Berlin.
T. (030) 3241460.   050732

Inauen, Margot, Kalckreuthstr. 3, 10777 Berlin.
T. (030) 2187722. - Ant -   050733

International Art Service, Hewaldstr 10, 10825 Berlin.
T. (030) 7844728.   050734

Internationale Sammlerbörse, Nassauische Str. 32,
10717 Berlin. T. (030) 861 34 23. - Mil -   050735

Ital-Park, Kurfürstendamm 121, 10711 Berlin.
T. (030) 891 32 22.   050736

Iwand-Kussin, Mommsenstr. 57, 10629 Berlin.
T. (030) 324 22 27. - Ant -   050737

Jaenichen, Dieter, Weitlingstr. 15, 10317 Berlin.
T. (030) 525 26 56. - Num -   050738

Jörger, Klaus-Peter, Bülowstr 101, 10783 Berlin.
T. (030) 2625500.   050739

Jörger, S., Goethestr. 69, 10623 Berlin.
T. (030) 312 32 28.   050740

Jüptner, Norbert, Pestalozzistr. 13, 10625 Berlin.
T. (030) 313 76 89. - Furn -   050741

Kaganczuk, S., Kurfürstendamm 216, 10719 Berlin.
T. (030) 881 61 62. - Ant / Jew -   050742

Karrer, Jürgen, Eisenacher Str. 7, 10777 Berlin.
T. (030) 2185602. - Ant -   050743

Kaul, Georg, Friedrich-Kayßler-Weg, 12353 Berlin.
T. (030) 6031057.   050744

Kaul GmbH, Knesebeckstr 59, 10719 Berlin.
T. (030) 8838876.   050745

Keller, Werner, Solmsstr. 36, 10961 Berlin.
T. (030) 692 31 42. - China / Glass / Mod -   050746

Kieker, U., Obentrautstr. 68, 10963 Berlin.
T. (030) 892 40 50.   050747

Kitzing, Fritz, Deidesheimer Str. 5, 14197 Berlin.
- Ant -   050748

Klar, Manfred, Motzstr. 32, 10777 Berlin.
T. (030) 213 75 45. - Ant -   050749

Kleber, Horst, Kaiser-Friedrich-Str 16, 10585 Berlin.
T. (030) 3422248.   050750

Kleber, Manfred, Düsseldorfer Str 32, Berlin.
T. (030) 881553.   050751

Klewer, Herbert, Regensburger Str 9, 10777 Berlin.
T. (030) 2114302, Fax (030) 2141878. - Ant / Paint /
Graph / Furn / China / Silv / Lights / Glass / Mod / Draw --   050752

Klingender, Marlies, Goltzstr. 49, 10781 Berlin.
T. (030) 216 37 19.   050753

Klöttschen, H., Reichenberger Str. 102, 10999 Berlin.
T. (030) 618 63 09.   050754

Knuth, Afagh, Goltzstr. 40a, 10781 Berlin.
T. (030) 216 54 92.   050755

Koch, Hans Horst, Kurfürstendamm 216, 10719 Berlin.
T. (030) 8826360, Fax (030) 8824066.
- Graph -   050756

Köhler, Ernst, Kuno-Fischer-Str. 12, 14057 Berlin.
T. (030) 322 10 62/63. - Tex -   050757

Köppen, Uta, Steifensandstr 7, 14057 Berlin.
T. (030) 3211328.   050758

Konny, Suarezstr. 6, 14057 Berlin. T. (030) 3212300,
Fax (030) 3256976. - Ant / Furn -   050759

Kontor für antike Öfen, Pariser Str. 20, 10707 Berlin.
T. (030) 404 40 42. - Ant -   050760

Kopp, Rainer, Kantstr. 29, 10623 Berlin.
T. (030) 3135927, 3123434, Fax (030) 3123434. - Ant /
Paint / Graph / Furn / China / Tex / Jew / Fra / Silv / Lights / Instr / Glass / Mod -   050761

Kosig, Detlev, Pestalozzistr. 9a, 10625 Berlin.
T. (030) 313 78 59. - Ant / Paint / Furn / China / Sculp /
Tex / Jew / Fra / Silv / Lights / Instr / Glass / Cur / Mod /
Draw -   050762

Kowalski, Renate, Markgrafenstr. 85, 10969 Berlin.
T. (030) 251 16 61, Fax (030) 251 75 91. - Ant / Paint /
Graph / Furn / Orient / China / Sculp / Tex / Jew / Silv / Lights / Glass / Mod / Ico -   050763

Kozlowski, Czeslaw, Dr., Kurfürstendamm 59-60, 10707
Berlin. T. (030) 323 70 07. - Ico - 050764
Kramer, Arnold, Kantstr. 49, 10623 Berlin.
T. (030) 313 74 40. - Ant / Furn - 050765
Kramer, Helgard, Ansbacher Str. 11, 10787 Berlin.
- Ant - 050766
Krause, Peter-Jörg, Reichsstr 89, 14052 Berlin.
T. (030) 3044371. 050767
Krawczyk, Johann, Reinhardtstr. 3, 10115 Berlin.
T. (030) 281 33 17. - Num - 050768
Krischke, Dragan u. Babette, Schlüterstr. 49, 10629 Ber-
lin. T. (030) 881 64 87. - Ant / Paint / Jew / Silv /
Mod - 050769
Krüger, Christina, Bergmannstr. 111, 10961 Berlin.
T. (030) 692 54 28. 050770
Krüger, Victoria, Kulmbacher Str. 15, 10777 Berlin.
T. (030) 24 34 00. 050771
Kruppa, Helga, Lorcher Str. 24h, 14197 Berlin.
T. (030) 821 88 16. - Num - 050772
Kuhlmann, Hiltrud, Herbert-Baum-Str. 11, 13088 Berlin.
T. (030) 965 58 11. - Ant / Paint / Furn / China / Tex /
Jew / Fra / Silv / Instr / Glass / Cur / Mod - 050773
Kunst aus Russland, Winterfeldstr. 54, 10781 Berlin.
T. (030) 2153155. - Ant - 050774
Kunst in der Sperlingsgasse, Lietzenburger Str. 82,
10719 Berlin. 050775
Kunst Kontor, Sorauer Str. 14, 10997 Berlin.
T. (030) 618 21 91. 050776
Kunsthandel am Nußbaum, Probststr 1, 10178 Berlin.
T. (030) 8827616. 050777
Kunsthandel GmbH, Friedrichstr 58, 10117 Berlin.
T. (030) 2089194. 050778
Kunstkabinett, Kaiserdamm 32, 14057 Berlin.
T. (030) 301 66 13. - Graph - 050779
Kuo, J.P., Dr., Schlüterstr. 50, 10629 Berlin.
T. (030) 24 35 99. - Orient - 050780
Lärisch, Alfred, Keithstr. 8, 10787 Berlin.
T. (030) 24 65 54. 050781
Lamptique, Grunewaldstr. 16, 10823 Berlin.
T. (030) 2153784, Fax (030) 2151059.
- Lights - 050782
Lau, Christel, Zimmermannstr. 23, 12163 Berlin.
T. (030) 792 34 23. - Ant - 050783
Laurisch, Horst D., Wildenbruchpl. 7, 10115 Berlin.
- Ant / Furn / Tex / Ico - 050784
Lauterbach, Hans, Bötzowstr 31, 10407 Berlin.
T. (030) 4266455. 050785
Lee, Lothar u. Marianne, Kurfürstendamm 32, 10719
Berlin. T. (030) 881 73 33. - Ant - 050786
Lehmann, Rosemarie, Saarower Weg 2, 12589 Berlin.
T. (030) 648 01 96, Fax 6480196. - Ant / Furn /
Rel - 050787
Leibniz-Antiquitäten, Leibnizstr. 28, 10625 Berlin.
T. (030) 31 64 10. 050788
Lemke, M., Schlüterstr. 67-68, 10625 Berlin.
T. (030) 31 66 87. 050789
Lenz & Co, Keithstr. 8, 10787 Berlin.
T. (030) 24 94 05. 050790
Liebchen, Wolfram, Lehrter Str. 25/26, 10557 Berlin.
T. (030) 3943093, Fax (030) 3945985. 050791
Lieckfeldt, Gebr., Alsterweg 34, 14167 Berlin.
T. (030) 817 38 73. 050792
Liesenfeld, Marcus, Willibald-Alexis-Str 20, 10965 Ber-
lin. T. (030) 6929270. 050793
Lietzmann, Rüdiger, Salzbrunner Str 40, 14193 Berlin.
T. (030) 8254944. 050794
Lohmaier, Eva, Keithstr 5, 10787 Berlin.
T. (030) 2136862. - Jew / Silv - 050795
Maaß, Maaß, Rankestr. 24, 10789 Berlin.
T. (030) 211 54 61. 050796
Magnus, Sylvia, Kurfürstendamm 188/89, 10707 Berlin.
T. (030) 8838986. 050797
Mahagonny, Damaschkestr. 23, 10711 Berlin.
T. (030) 324 10 40. 050798
Makosch, A., Pionierstr. 42-61, 13583 Berlin.
T. (030) 372 27 45, 372 45 34. - Ant - 050799
Martin, Holger, Eisenacher Str 118, 10777 Berlin.
T. (030) 2159295, Fax (030) 2159295. - Ant - 050800
Martin, Y., Ehrlichstr. 21, 10318 Berlin.
T. (030) 508 10 00. - Ant - 050801
Martins, Liliana Monica, Königsberger Str 33a, 12207
Berlin. T. (030) 7738216, Fax (030) 7736768. - Paint /
Furn / Cur - 050802

Massow von, Dagmar, Riemeisterstr. 39a, 14169 Berlin.
T. (030) 813 75 78. 050803
Matte, Gina, Schloßstr. 1-2, 12163 Berlin.
T. (030) 792 74 36. - Num - 050804
Maurer, Bernhard, Altensteinstr. 42, 14195 Berlin.
T. (030) 832 79 88. 050805
Mentz, S., Gneisenaustr. 52, 10961 Berlin.
T. (030) 691 20 62. 050806
Menzel, Niels, Beckerstr. 6a, 12157 Berlin.
T. (030) 855 52 96. - Num - 050807
Meyer-Antiquitäten, Pariser Str 21, 10707 Berlin.
T. (030) 8838694. 050808
Meyer, W., Pariser Str. 21-22, 10707 Berlin.
T. (030) 881 57 42, 883 86 94. - Ant / Furn /
China - 050809
Mönnikes & Kirsten Pax, Uwe, Friedrichstr, 10117 Berlin.
T. (030) 2082676. 050810
Morawietz, R., Friedrichstr 191, 10117 Berlin.
T. (030) 2004333. 050811
Müller, Willi, Kantstr 150, 10623 Berlin.
T. (030) 3121031, Fax (030) 3125998. - Ant / Paint /
Tex / Dec - 050812
Münzen am Hansaplatz, Bartningallee 5, 10557 Berlin.
T. (030) 391 44 92. - Num - 050813
Münzengalerie, Uhlandstr. 195/VI, 10623 Berlin.
T. (030) 313 50 43. - Ant / Num / Arch - 050814
Münzfachgeschäft, Frankfurter Allee 106a, 10247 Ber-
lin. T. (030) 89 80 40. - Num - 050815
Münzfachgeschäft Moneta, Friedrichstr. 114, 10115
Berlin. T. (030) 282 67 20. - Num - 050816
Munsky, Helga, Horst-Kohl-Str. 6, 12157 Berlin.
T. (030) 795 99 09. - Instr - 050817
Nell, Thomas, Fuggerstr. 23, 10777 Berlin.
T. (030) 213 37 87. - Cur - 050818
Nesselhut, Helmut, Nithackstr. 24, 10585 Berlin.
T. (030) 341 21 70. 050819
Neue Classic Antiquitäten, Kantstr 31, 10625 Berlin.
T. (030) 3138288, Fax (030) 3137745. 050820
Neumann, Suarezstr. 57, 14057 Berlin.
T. (030) 323 86 77. 050821
Neumann, Lieselotte, Keithstr. 12, 10787 Berlin.
T. (030) 2182590. - Ant / Paint / Furn / China /
Glass - 050822
Neumanns, Suarezstr 57, 10457 Berlin.
T. (030) 3238677. 050823
Nicklaus, Roger, Fröaufstr 7, 12161 Berlin.
T. (030) 8512284. 050824
Niederhäusern, Rudolf von, Krumme Str. 52, 10585 Ber-
lin. T. (030) 312 98 99. 050825
Niermeier, Renate, Belziger Str. 28, 10823 Berlin.
T. (030) 781 31 61. - Num / Jew - 050826
Niklaus, Roger F., Fröaufstr. 7, 12161 Berlin. 050827
Nold, Zobeltitzstr. 68, 13403 Berlin.
T. (030) 413 90 10. 050828
Nostalgie + Kunst, Heesestr 18, 12169 Berlin.
T. (030) 7913866. 050829
Nowak & Beth, Koppenstr. 75, 10243 Berlin.
T. (030) 436 70 72. - Num - 050830
Nowak & Beth, Erich-Lodemann-Str. 117, 12437 Berlin.
T. (030) 632 76 62. - Num - 050831
Olczak, D. Ewa, Bleibtreustr 42, 10623 Berlin.
T. (030) 8834960, Fax 8834828. 050832
Oldenburg, Ulf, Bergstr 13, 12169 Berlin.
T. (030) 7915533. - Ant / Paint / Furn - 050833
Ollrogge, Michael, Körtestr 20, 10967 Berlin.
T. (030) 6936444. 050834
Orangerie, Kalckreutherstr 16, 10777 Berlin.
T. (030) 2177652. - Ant - 050835
Ordens-Sammlung, Wassertorstr. 62, 10969 Berlin.
T. (030) 6143027, Fax (030) 6144559. - Num /
Mil - 050836
Paluschinsky, Heinz-J., Bleibtreustr. 40, 10623 Berlin.
T. (030) 883 37 32. 050837
Peppel-Moore Fine Arts, Kaiserdamm 103-104, 14057
Berlin. T. (030) 321 64 45, Fax (030) 321 36 26. - Repr /
Eth / Pho - 050838
Petsch, Lothar, Stülerstr 4, 10787 Berlin.
T. Fu 01612305029. 050839
Petter, Rainer, Schreinerstr. 64, 10247 Berlin.
T. (030) 588 56 02. - Ant - 050840
Pflanz, Jürgen, Bahnhofstr. 47a, 12159 Berlin. 050841
Pili, Querino, Pestalozzistr. 81, 10627 Berlin.
T. (030) 31 69 69. 050842

Pinus, Koenigsallee 68, 14193 Berlin. 050843
Plickert, R. & B., Residenzstr 139a, 13409 Berlin.
T. (030) 4909288. 050844
Plötz-Peters, Hannelore, Keithstr 8, 10787 Berlin.
T. (030) 2114476. - Paint / China / Jew - 050845
Pluntke, Beate u. Erdmut, Pariser Str 45, 10719 Berlin.
T. (030) 8817166. Ant / Paint / Furn / China / Glass /
Mod - 050846
Politowski, Hannelore, Friedbergstr. 37, 14057 Berlin.
T. (030) 321 16 37. - Ant / Repr / Jew / Mod - 050847
Pregley, Karin, Sarrazinstr. 25, 12159 Berlin. 050848
Prestige Einrichtungen, Kurfürstendamm 206, 10719
Berlin. T. (030) 882 69 07. - Ant / Furn / China / Repr /
Tex / Dec / Silv / Lights - 050849
Prinz-Dunst, Karin, Schlüterstr. 16, 10625 Berlin.
T. (030) 3135965, Fax (030) 3137310. - Ant - 050850
Rathmann, Martina, Eichborndamm 52, 13403 Berlin.
T. (030) 413 85 34. 050851
Reulens, Jörg & Mechthild, Konstanzer Str. 14, 10707
Berlin. T. (030) 870461, Fax (030) 8614116.
- Furn - 050852
Rexhausen, J., Pestalozzistr. 23, 10625 Berlin.
T. (030) 31 61 48, 31 72 44. 050853
Richter, Anne, Kurfürstendamm 203-205, 10719 Berlin.
T. (030) 882 35 30. 050854
Richter, Klaus, Hindenburgdamm 51, 12203 Berlin.
T. (030) 834 49 67. 050855
Riefke, Wolfgang, Gatower Str. 124-126, 13595 Berlin.
T. (030) 361 90 96. 050856
Ritscher, Helga, & Alexander Sandmeier, Prinz-Friedrich-
Leopold-Str. 5, 14129 Berlin. T. (030) 8034598,
Fax (030) 8035152. - Ant / Arch / Jew - 050857
Rohleder, Ilona, Spandauer Str 27, 10178 Berlin.
T. (030) 2415669. 050858
Rohlow, Bernhard, Richtorotr. 12, 12105 Berlin.
T. (030) 706 52 68. 050859
Roho, Sesenheimer Str 19, 10627 Berlin.
T. (030) 3132020. - Ant / Orient - 050860
Sadowski, Peter, Moritzstr 3, 13597 Berlin.
T. (030) 3339752. 050861
Salm, Constanze, Duisburger Str. 4, 10707 Berlin.
T. (030) 881 48 36. 050862
Samawat, Badensche Str. 12, 10715 Berlin.
T. (030) 854 72 60. 050863
Scanform, Joachimstaler Str. 10, 10719 Berlin.
T. (030) 881 98 22. 050864
Schaffarczyk, M., Xantener Str. 10, 10707 Berlin.
T. (030) 882 78 02. - Ant - 050865
Schendel, Winfried G.H., Kamenzer Damm 52, 11249
Berlin. T. (030) 7757002. 050866
Schildhorn-Antiquitäten, Schildhornstr. 87, 12163 Berlin.
T. (030) 791 80 60. - Ant / Paint / Furn / China / Jew /
Lights / Glass / Mod - 050867
Schiller, Eva-Maria, Kantstr. 56, 10623 Berlin.
T. (030) 313 61 60. 050868
Schilling, Teja, Nollendorfstr. 23, 10777 Berlin.
T. (030) 216 60 26. 050869
Schindler, Reimar, Carl-Schurz-Str. 61, 13597 Berlin.
T. (030) 333 79 51. - Num - 050870
Schlebusch, Stefan, Suarezstr. 61, 14057 Berlin.
T. (030) 323 62 56. - Ant - 050871
Schmidt, Michael, Schillerstr. 49, 10625 Berlin.
T. (030) 313 63 81. - Ant - 050872
Schmidt, Ruth, Keithstr 19, 10787 Berlin.
T. (030) 2136049. - Orient / China - 050873
Schmutzler, H., Magdeburger Platz 2, 10785 Berlin.
T. (030) 262 57 28. 050874
Schöne Kunst & Antiquitäten GmbH, Keithstr. 15, 10787
Berlin. T. (030) 213 39 21. - Ant - 050875
Schreiber, Friedhelm, Leonhardtstr. 4, 14057 Berlin.
T. (030) 323 96 74. 050876
Schreyer, Chr., Manfred-von-Richthofen-Str. 19, 12101
Berlin. T. (030) 785 88 84. - Num - 050877
Schröder, Joachim A., Fuggerstr. 4, 10777 Berlin.
T. (030) 2116734, Fax (030) 2115866. - Ant / Furn /
Silv / Glass - 050878
Schröder, R., Yorckstr. 73, 10965 Berlin.
T. (030) 785 65 94. - Ant - 050879
Schüler, Erich, Suarezstr. 59, 14057 Berlin.
T. (030) 324 55 04. - Ant / Paint / Furn / Cur /
Mod - 050880
Schulze, Keithstr. 21, 10787 Berlin.
T. (030) 213 26 32. 050881

Schulze, Martin, Uhlandstr. 130, 10623 Berlin.
T. (030) 861 34 00. 050882
Schulze, Rudolf, Sonnenallee 13, 12047 Berlin.
T. (030) 623 16 28. 050883
Schulze, Thomas, Motzstr. 58, 10777 Berlin.
T. (030) 214 24 87. - Ant - 050884
Schwäneke, Heidi, Savignyplatz 1, 10623 Berlin.
T. (030) 312 10 15. - Ant - 050885
Schwandt, Jörg, Keithstr 10, 10787 Berlin.
T. (030) 2185017. - Silv / Mod - 050886
Schweizer, Erich W., Kurfürstendamm 195, 10707 Berlin. - Tex - 050887
Seidel & Sohn, Fasanenstr 70, 10719 Berlin.
T. (030) 8821621, Fax 8851611. - Ant / Paint / Furn / China / Silv - 050888

Seidel u. Sohn
gegründet 1905
KUNSTHANDEL
Fasanenstr. 70, 10719 Berlin
Tel. (030) 882 16 21
Fax (030) 885 16 11
Filiale:
Eisenacher Straße 113
10777 Berlin
Tel. (030) 216 18 50

Seidel & Sohn, Eisenacher Str 113, 10777 Berlin.
T. (030) 2161850. - Ant / Paint / Furn / China / Silv /
Mil - 050889
Serzisko, Franz, Gieselerstr. 21, 10713 Berlin. 050890
Shimanovich, Bob, Bornstr 8, 12163 Berlin.
T. (030) 8524458. 050891
Sieben, Roland, Hauptstr. 52, 10827 Berlin.
T. (030) 784 32 76. - Ant - 050892
Siemanowitz, Mommsenstr. 21, 10629 Berlin. - Ant /
Paint - 050893
Skiba, Seeburger Str. 9, 13581 Berlin.
T. (030) 331 43 10. - Ant - 050894
Sonnenthal, Karin, Keithstr 19, 10787 Berlin.
T. (030) 2142121. - Ant / Paint / Furn / Fra / Silv /
Cur - 050895
Sorgenicht, Margarete, Suarezstr. 57, 14057 Berlin.
T. (030) 323 70 90. 050896
Sparenberg, Eisenacher Str. 11, 10777 Berlin.
T. (030) 213 92 71. 050897
Sperlich, Lothar, Blissestr 54, 10713 Berlin.
T. (030) 8226180. 050898
Spik, Leo, Kurfürstendamm 66, 10707 Berlin.
T. (030) 8836170, 8836179, Fax (030) 8839734.
- Paint / Furn / Tex - 050899
Staack, Monika, Luisenstr. 19, 12209 Berlin. - Num /
Orient - 050900
Stadnik & Stadnik, Kantstr. 39, 10623 Berlin.
T. (030) 31 04 30. - Furn / Num / China / Glass - 050901
Stahlmach, Adelbert, Eisenacher Str. 19, 10777 Berlin.
T. (030) 2152091, Fax (030) 2152092. - Ant / Furn /
Lights - 050902
Steguweit, Genthiner Str. 36, 10785 Berlin.
T. (030) 261 10 11. - Ant / Furn - 050903
Stolle, Wolf-Rüdiger, Bayreuther Str. 9a, 10789 Berlin.
T. (030) 2181666. - Ant / Graph / Fra - 050904
Strauss, Heidemarie, Waidmannsluster Damm 159,
13469 Berlin. T. (030) 411 20 50. 050905
Strey-Fromm, Lena, Hagelberger Str. 56, 10965 Berlin.
T. (030) 785 40 80. 050906
Strey-Froom, Lena, Hagelberger Str 56, 10965 Berlin.
T. (030) 7854080. 050907
Strube & Dietl, Motzstr. 25, 10777 Berlin.
T. (030) 24 18 60. 050908
studio-galerie-berlin, Frankfurter Allee 36a, 10247 Berlin. T. (030) 2910850. - China / Tex / Glass /
Cur - 050909
Sucksdorff, Jürgen, Meinekestr. 6, 10719 Berlin.
T. (030) 883 88 30. - Furn - 050910
Syrigos, Pestalozzistr. 26, 10627 Berlin.
T. (030) 312 48 81. - Ant - 050911

Tächl, Winfried, Ebertystr. 22, 10249 Berlin.
T. (030) 439 97 08. - Num - 050912
Tchorrek & Partner, Friedrichstr 193, 10117 Berlin.
T. (030) 2082677. 050913
Tempelhofer Münzenhaus, Bacharacher Str. 39, 12099
Berlin. T. (030) 626 33 59, 626 53 13. - Num - 050914
Theis, Neufertstr 6, 14059 Berlin. T. (030) 3212322,
Fax (030) 3224103. - China - 050915
Thiede, Wolfgang, Meierottostr 1, 10719 Berlin.
T. (030) 8819024. 050916
Timberg-Meissen, Kurfürstendamm 214, 10719 Berlin.
T. (030) 881 91 58. - China - 050917
Timberg-Meissen, Keithstr. 10, 10787 Berlin.
T. (030) 24 31 35. - China - 050918
Traube, Erika, Windscheidstr. 23, 10627 Berlin.
T. (030) 324 08 68. 050919
Treppenhauer, F., Mittenwalder Str. 30, 10961 Berlin.
T. (030) 692 11 15. 050920
Trümper, P., Dr., Pfalzburger Str 79, 10719 Berlin.
T. (030) 8817694. - Furn - 050921
Ulrich, Herbert P., Bleibtreustr. 32, 10707 Berlin.
T. (030) 881 26 68. 050922
Utesch, Inge, Breitkopfstr. 82, 13409 Berlin. 050923
Utev, Leibnizstr. 46, 10629 Berlin. T. (030) 323 96 50.
- Paint / China / Glass - 050924
Valentijn, Antonius, Selmapl. 3, 14163 Berlin.
T. (030) 813 72 55. 050925
Valentiner, Max, Kurfürstendamm 59, 10707 Berlin.
T. (030) 323 72 61. 050926
Venzke, G., Fasanenstr. 71, 10719 Berlin.
T. (030) 883 61 17. 050927
Verhoek, Greta, Wielandstr. 31, 10625 Berlin. - Ant /
Furn - 050928
Vicent & Möller, Motzstr 17, 10777 Berlin.
T. (030) 2163786. 050929
Vincent/Möller, Motzstr. 17, 10777 Berlin.
T. (030) 216 37 86. - Ant / Paint / Furn - 050930
Voigt, Hartmut, Uhlandstr. 48, 10719 Berlin.
T. (030) 881 37 10. - Ant / Paint / Furn / China /
Silv - 050931
Vorselaars, Hartmut, Leibnizstr. 28, 10625 Berlin.
T. (030) 313 87 74. 050932
Wagenknecht, Rainer E., Pariser Str. 46, 10719 Berlin.
T. (030) 881 27 33. - Ant / Instr - 050933
Wall, Peter, Eisenacher Str 1, 10777 Berlin.
T. (030) 2184270, Fax (030) 2184270. - Ant /
Furn - 050934
Waroschitz, Lutz, Friedrichstr 195, 10117 Berlin.
T. (030) 8833258. 050935
Wazynski, Detlef, Leibnizstr. 30, 10625 Berlin.
T. (030) 312 44 28. 050936
Wegner, Hans, Leibnizstr. 61, 10629 Berlin. - Ant /
Dec - 050937
Weick, Wilhelm, Eisenacher Str 10, 10777 Berlin.
T. (030) 2187500. - Ant / Paint / Furn - 050938
Weidenbrück, Klaus, Dimitroffstr. 16, 10435 Berlin.
T. (030) 449 20 97. - Num - 050939
Weiß, Josef, Kieler Str 4, 12163 Berlin. 050940
Wende, H.-J., Hoka III, Strasse G Haus 9, 10115
Berlin. 050941
Westphal, Volker, Wundtstr. 52, 14057 Berlin.
T. (030) 321 55 02, 882 11 62, Fax (030) 883 17 61.
- Ant / Paint / Sculp - 050942
Wilson, Joseph P., Hoeppnerstr. 22a, 12101 Berlin.
T. (030) 623 50 32. 050943
Winter, Hildegard, Nürnberger Str. 19, 10777 Berlin.
T. (030) 213 45 24. - Mul - 050944
Wittenborn-Czubaszek, Angelika, Fasanenstr. 61, 10719
Berlin. T. (030) 8831101, Fax (030) 8831101.
- Ant - 050945
Wohlfeil, Helga, Mariendorfer Damm 110, 12109 Berlin.
T. (030) 706 20 51. - Num - 050946
Wollmann, Dieter, Rheinstr 51, 12161 Berlin.
T. (030) 8511722. 050947
Wollmann, Dieter, Rheinstr. 52, 12161 Berlin.
T. (030) 851 17 22. - Ant - 050948
Wolosow, Grigorij, Winterfeldstr. 54, 10115 Berlin.
T. (030) 215 31 55. 050949
Wruck, W., Dr., Niebuhrstr. 78, 10629 Berlin.
T. (030) 881 58 82. - Num - 050950
Wulfes, Karl-Heinz, Kurfürstendamm 207-208, 10719
Berlin. T. (030) 881 41 71. 050951

Zeh, Wolfgang, Fasanenstr. 55, 10719 Berlin.
T. (030) 881 34 97. 050952
Zeidler, M., Leibnizstr. 64, 10629 Berlin.
T. (030) 323 17 11. - Ant - 050953
Zienicke, Karola, Schönwalder Str. 18, 13347
Berlin. 050954
Zille-Hof, Fasanenstr. 12, 10623 Berlin. 050955
Zillemarkt, Bleibtreustr. 48a, 10623 Berlin. 050956

Bernhardswald (Bayern)
Hingerl, E., & E. Walhöfer, Hauptstr. 2, 93170 Bernhardswald. T. (09407) 449. 050957

Bernkastel-Kues (Rheinland-Pfalz)
Masuhr, Erhard, Römerstr. 39, 54470 Bernkastel-Kues.
- Ant / Paint / Graph / Furn / China / Sculp / Tex / Silv / Glass / Mod - 050958

Bernried, Kr. Deggendorf (Bayern)
Hartl, Georg L., Schloß, 94505 Bernried, Kr. Deggendorf.
T. (09905) 13 61. - Orient / China / Sculp / Eth - 050959

Bersenbrück (Niedersachsen)
Dettmer-Schröder, Lindenstr. 10, 49593 Bersenbrück.
T. (05439) 700. 050960

Betzdorf (Rheinland-Pfalz)
Heike, M., Engelsteinstr 86, 57518 Betzdorf.
T. (02741) 24155. 050961
Krug, M., Sandersgarten 16a, 57518 Betzdorf.
T. (02741) 23753. 050962
Wolf, Klaus, Kirchstr 2, 57518 Betzdorf. 050963

Beuren (Baden-Württemberg)
Dix, Inge, Linenhoferstr. 21, 72660 Beuren.
T. (07025) 52 20. 050964

Biberach (Baden-Württemberg)
Antiquitäten Biberach, Birkenweg 1, 88400 Biberach.
- Ant / Paint / Furn / China / Fra - 050965
Helle, G., Ulmer-Tor-Str. 15, 88400 Biberach.
T. (07351) 71366. 050966

Bickendorf (Rheinland-Pfalz)
Kunsthaus Burg Bickendorf, Burgstr. 4, 54636 Bickendorf. T. (06569) 444. - Paint / Furn - 050967

Biedenkopf (Hessen)
Pezus, Knut, An der Warte 5, 35216 Biedenkopf.
T. (06461) 25 10. - Paint - 050968

Bielefeld (Nordrhein-Westfalen)
Anno dazumal Antiquitäten, Altstädter Kirchstr. 2, 33602
Bielefeld. 050969
Antik-Agentur Schröder, Arndtstr. 24, 33615 Bielefeld.
T. (0521) 37 25. 050970
Arendt, Gerhard W., Teutoburger Str. 77, 33607 Bielefeld. T. (0521) 17 33 29. 050971
Brune, Klaus-Peter, Mainzer Str. 1, 33613 Bielefeld.
T. (0521) 88 91 22. 050972
Burckardt, Helga, Niedernstr. 35, 33602 Bielefeld.
T. (0521) 674 82. 050973
Busch, Wilhelm, Gehrenberg 26, 33602 Bielefeld.
T. (0521) 17 11 27, Fax (0521) 17 11 25. 050974
Butz, L., Niederwall 12, 33602 Bielefeld.
T. (0521) 17 19 17. 050975
CDM-Antiquitäten, Kreuzstr. 29, 33602 Bielefeld.
T. (0521) 17 37 61. 050976
Domus Artis, Theresienstr. 1, 33649 Bielefeld.
T. (0521) 45 26 19. 050977
Ewert, Am Brodhagen 119, 33613 Bielefeld.
T. (0521) 89 00 03. 050978
Fee, Altstädter Kirchstr. 10, 33602 Bielefeld.
T. (0521) 65205. - Jew - 050979
Flohmarkt Antik, Neustädter Str. 6, 33602 Bielefeld.
T. (0521) 17 33 38, 29 62 18. 050980
Galerie des 19. Jahrhunderts, Neustädter Str. 16, 33602
Bielefeld. T. (0521) 177924, Fax (0521) 24051. - Furn /
Sculp / Silv - 050981
Garcia, Juan, August-Bebel-Str. 174, 33602 Bielefeld.
T. (0521) 171470, Fax (0521) 138349. - Ant - 050982
Haselhorst, Jakob-Kaiser-Str. 1a, 33615 Bielefeld.
T. (0521) 10 29 72. 050983
Hilker, Bahnhofstr. 47, 33602 Bielefeld.
T. (0521) 17 86 80. - Num - 050984

Höller, H., Schneekoppestr. 13, 33719 Bielefeld.
T. (0521) 33 36 48. - Paint / Graph / Fra / Ico -   050985
Horstmann, Dirk, Obernstr. 42, 33602 Bielefeld.
T. (0521) 665 15.   050986
Keilich & Biasci, Wertherstr. 167, 33615 Bielefeld.
T. (0521) 17 94 67. - Graph / Draw -   050987
Köhler, M., Otto-Brenner-Str. 144, 33604 Biolofold.
T. (0521) 29 79 41.   050988
Kokerbeck, Willy, Hauptstr. 92, 33647 Bielefeld.   050989
Krause, Jochen, Schmale Gasse 2, 33602 Bielefeld.
T. (0521) 611 70, Fax 611 70. - Ant / Furn / China /
Sculp / Dec / Silv / Glass / Tin -   050990
Lehr-Botthof, Rosengarten 8, 33605 Bielefeld.
T. (0521) 232 24.   050991
Mahlmann, J., Kreuzstr. 29, 33602 Bielefeld.
T. (0521) 17 37 61.   050992
Möcking, Ingo, Detmolder Str. 170, 33604 Bielefeld.
T. (0521) 216 78. - Furn -   050993
Nonnenbruch, Splittenbrede 11, 33613 Bielefeld.
T. (0521) 88 79 70. - Graph / Repr / Dec / Fra /
Draw -   050994
Osthoff, Berthold, Humboldtstr. 40, 33615 Bielefeld.
T. (0521) 790 37. - Ant / Paint / Graph -   050995
Pladeck, Friedhelm, Am Brodhagen 97, 33613 Bielefeld.
T. (0521) 82266. - Num -   050996
Rast, Helfried, Rathausstr. 12, 33602 Bielefeld.
T. (0521) 6 55 93. - Num -   050997
Rogge, Felix, Oberntorwall 19a, 33602
Bielefeld.   050998
Stehr, Volker J., Gehrenberg 15, 33611 Bielefeld.
T. (0521) 619 62, 838 70. - Ant / Graph / Furn / Orient /
China / Silv -   050999
Weber, Neustädter Str. 4, 33602 Bielefeld.
T. (0521) 17 00 24.   051000
Winkel, Wolfgang, Hagenkamp 157, 33609 Bielefeld.
T. (0521) 33 27 58, Fax 3369984. - Num -   051001
Zeitwandel, Weststr. 102, 33615 Bielefeld.
T. (0521) 667 88.   051002

Bietigheim (Baden-Württemberg)
Steurer, Arno, Badenstr. 17, 76467 Bietigheim.
T. (07245) 62 14. - Ant -   051003

Bietigheim-Bissingen (Baden-Württemberg)
Thannheimer, M., Geisinger Str. 40, 74321 Bietigheim-
Bissingen. T. (07142) 642 80.   051004

Billerbeck (Nordrhein-Westfalen)
Antik- und Auktionshaus, Holthauser Str 29, 48727 Bil-
lerbeck. T. (02543) 4086, Fax (02543) 4075.
- Ant -   051005
Häder, Alfons, Kolpingstr 1, 48727 Billerbeck.   051006

Bingen (Rheinland-Pfalz)
Altenhofen, G., Römerstr 18, 55411 Bingen.
T. (06721) 43343.   051007
Altenhofen, G., Rathausstr 2, 55411 Bingen.
T. (06721) 15196.   051008
Engelhard-Rotthaus, A., Schmittstr 18, 55411 Bingen.
T. (06721) 15848.   051009
Roos, T. & K., Hasengasse 5, 55411 Bingen.
T. (06721) 12510.   051010

Bippen (Niedersachsen)
Markau, Heinz, Am Feldkamp 18, 49626 Bippen.
T. (05909) 285. - Furn -   051011

Birkenfeld (Baden-Württemberg)
Morlock, B., Kirchweg 51, 75217 Birkenfeld.
T. (07231) 481981.   051012

Birstein (Hessen)
Schmidt, E., Langgasse 2, 63633 Birstein.
T. (06054) 59 30.   051013

Bischberg (Bayern)
Höchstetter, Lerchenweg 12, 96120 Bischberg.   051014
Keller, Jean, Regnitzstr. 7, 96120 Bischberg.
T. (0951) 669 65. - Paint / Furn -   051015
Laschinger, M., & H. Häusler, Hauptstr. 35, 96120 Bisch-
berg. T. (0951) 67854.   051016

Bischofsheim (Hessen)
Hüppauf & Herrmann, Rheinstr 24, 65474
Bischofsheim.   051017

Bispingen (Niedersachsen)
Keuper, K., Tannenwald 1, 29646 Bispingen.
T. (05194) 417.   051018

Bissendorf (Niedersachsen)
Nordmann, L., Mindenerstr. 60, 49143 Bissendorf.
T. (05402) 1843.   051019
Scholtissek, Reinhard, Dürerstr. 1, 49143 Bissendorf.
T. (05402) 72 02, 82 67, Fax 7385.   051020
Szalinski, Peter, Grambergerstr. 7, 49143 Bissendorf.
T. (05402) 88 70. - Ant / Furn -   051021

Bitburg (Rheinland-Pfalz)
Grün, Herbert, Stockstr. 24, 54634 Bitburg.
- Num -   051022
Hein, Gregor, Petersstr. 17, 54634 Bitburg.
T. (06561) 28 12.   051023
Notte, Stockstr. 17/III, 54634 Bitburg. T. (06561) 77 59.
- Num -   051024
Zimmer, Heinrich, Trierer Str. 40, 54634 Bitburg.
T. (06561) 31 92. - Paint / Graph / Repr / Dec / Fra / Ico /
Draw -   051025

Blieskastel (Saarland)
Braun, W., Bliestalstr. 55, 66440 Blieskastel.
T. (06842) 52677.   051026
Krehl, U. & P., Bliesgaustr. 30, 66440 Blieskastel.
T. (06842) 1680.   051027
Numero Uno, Alte Marktstr. 8, 66440 Blieskastel.
T. (06842) 4288.   051028

Blomberg (Nordrhein-Westfalen)
Stachowiak, Wilhelm, Auf dem Bake 5, 32825
Blomberg.   051029

Bobenheim (Rheinland-Pfalz)
Heissler, Willi F. G., Im Wogtal 17, 67273 Bobenheim.
T. (06353) 65 18, 16 66. - Ant -   051030

Bocholt (Nordrhein-Westfalen)
Eichener, Königstr. 23, 46397 Bocholt. - Ant /
Paint -   051031
Hammesfahr, Paul, Osterstr. 43, 46397 Bocholt.   051032
Schulten, F., Wesemannstr. 8, 46397 Bocholt.
T. (02871) 18 34 92.   051033
Tangerding, Julius, Königstr. 32, 46397 Bocholt.
T. (02871) 25 34. - Ant / Furn / Dec -   051034

Bochum (Nordrhein-Westfalen)
Antik am Stadion, Castroper Str. 85, 44791 Bochum.
T. (0234) 50 29 63.   051035
Best-antiques, Herner Str 435, 44807 Bochum.
T. (0234) 538790.   051036
Bochumer Antik Forum, Castroper Str. 100, 44791 Bo-
chum. T. (0234) 51 20 30.   051037
Bochumer Antik-Forum, Castroper Str. 100, 44791 Bo-
chum. T. (0234) 51 11 87. - Ant / Furn / China / Tex /
Jew / Lights / Instr -   051038
Bode, L., Brückstr. 6, 44787 Bochum.
T. (0234) 18138.   051039
Brodowski-Witfeld, Herner Str. 259, 44809 Bochum.
T. (0234) 54 00 96.   051040
Deak Intercoin, Viktoriastr. 43, 44787 Bochum.
T. (0234) 14046, 14057. - Num -   051041
Eiter, B., Wegmannshof 18, 44782 Bochum.
T. (0234) 02327/70968.   051042
England Antik, Hellweg 21, 44787 Bochum.
T. (0234) 67457.   051043
Euromint, Königsallee 178a, 44799 Bochum.
T. (0234) 73016.   051044
Ewert & Knoth, Marthastr. 12, 44791 Bochum.
T. (0234) 58 25 62.   051045
Gudrun's Kämmerchen, Markstr. 315, 44801 Bochum.
T. (0234) 769 75.   051046
Gudrun's Kämmerchen, Castroper Str. 100, 44791 Bo-
chum. T. (0234) 51 11 87.   051047
Haack, Harald, Hattinger Str. 778, 44879 Bochum.
T. (0234) 49 43 15. - Ant / Orient / Arch / Eth -   051048
Hadrys, E., Herner Str 228, 44809 Bochum.
T. (0231) 501964.   051049

Hagermann, L. u. A., Wittener Str. 156, 44803 Bochum.
T. (0234) 35 53 10.   051050
Hellwig, Haferweg 13, 44797 Bochum.
T. (0234) 79 78 39. - Num -   051051
Hülsebus, Hanna, Glockengarten 78, 44803 Bochum.
T. (0234) 35 86 57.   051052
Kintrup, Eberhard & Ingeborg, Gräfin-Imma-Str. 28,
44797 Bochum. T. (0234) 79 11 62. - Jew /
Instr -   051053
Knappmann-Thon, L., Alte Bahnhofstr. 56, 44892 Bo-
chum. T. (0234) 29 35 05.   051054
Kolbus, Große Beckstr. 28, 44787 Bochum.
T. (0234) 68 10 59.   051055
Koop, S., Königsallee 12, 44789 Bochum.
T. (0234) 31 11 51. - Num -   051056
Kroll, Hans-Peter, Am Alten Stadtpark 9, 44791
Bochum.   051057
Krusenbaum, Carl, Westring 5, 44787 Bochum.
T. (0234) 122 50.   051058
Kunst & Antiquitäten, Wittener Str 95, 44803 Bochum.
T. (0234) 331530.   051059
Labedzki, W., Nehringskamp 1, 44879 Bochum.
T. (0234) 49 44 44, 49 20 00.   051060
Makassar, Brüderstr. 4, 44787 Bochum.
T. (0234) 65859. - Ant -   051061
Nieder-Eichholz, D., Hellweg 21, 44787 Bochum.
T. (0234) 67457.   051062
Nottebaum, G., Markstr. 315, 44801 Bochum.
T. (0234) 769 75. - Ant / Furn / China / Tex / Jew /
Lights / Instr -   051063
Portobello, Clemensstr 2, 44789 Bochum.
T. (0234) 330287.   051064
Prior, M., Drückstr. 17, 44787 Bochum. T. (0234) 165 63.
- Mod -   051065
Reich, W., Brunsteinstr. 1, 44789 Bochum.
T. (0234) 30 91 57.   051066
Schwabe & Sterkau, Ückendorfer Str. 109, 44866 Bo-
chum. T. (0234) 34348.   051067
Seidel, Hattinger Str 237, 44795 Bochum.
T. (0234) 450721.   051068
Siewert, Harald, Kemnader Str. 40a, 44795 Bochum.
T. (0234) 478 41. - Num -   051069
Stobbe, Westenfelder Str. 89, 44867 Bochum.
T. (0234) 02327/32 01 32.   051070
Thiele, Wilhelm, Castroper Str. 270, 44791 Bochum.
T. (0234) 676 08.   051071
Tielker, J., Hunscheidtstr. 146, 44789 Bochum.
T. (0234) 33 22 24.   051072
Turner, G., Königsallee 12, 44789 Bochum.
T. (0234) 33 69 99.   051073
Uhlenbruch, H. u. M., Vollmondstr 47, 44894 Bochum.
T. (0234) 286874.   051074
Uhlenbruck & Schoenfeld, Vollmondstr. 47, 44894 Bo-
chum. T. (0234) 28 68 74.   051075
WL-Antik, Nehringskamp 1, 44879 Bochum.
T. (0234) 494444, Fax (0234) 494426. - Ant / Paint /
Graph / Furn / China / Sculp / Dec / Jew / Silv / Instr / Mo-
d / Tin / Toys -   051076
Zur alten Bäckerei, Herner Str. 259, 44809 Bochum.
T. (0234) 54 00 96.   051077

Bodenmais (Bayern)
Ebnet, E., Finkenweg 2, 94249 Bodenmais.
T. (09920) 19 29.   051078
Pongratz, A., Karlhammer, 94249 Bodenmais.
T. (09920) 652.   051079
Seide, W., Marktpl. 5, 94249 Bodenmais.
T. (09920) 71 51.   051080

Bodenwerder (Niedersachsen)
Büngener, Heino, In der Masch 14, 37619 Bodenwerder.
T. (05533) 12 13, 53 27.   051081

Bodman-Ludwigshafen (Baden-Württemberg)
Esslinger, Georg, Möwenstr. 5, 78351 Bodman-Ludwigshafen. T. (07773) 55 49.   051082
Heene, Prinzregentenstr. 29, 78351 Bodman-Ludwigshafen. T. (07773) 52 22 11.   051083

Kikel, Alois, Hauptstr. 15, 78351 Bodman-Ludwigshafen.
T. (07773) 344. - Ant / Furn / Lights / Instr /
Glass - 051084

Böblingen (Baden-Württemberg)
Atelier, Schafgasse 1, 71032 Böblingen.
T. (07031) 229946, Fax 221118. - Graph / Repr / Jew /
Fra / Draw - 051085

Böhl-Iggelheim (Rheinland-Pfalz)
Vogt, M. & E., Am Heidbuckel 2, 67459 Böhl-Iggelheim.
T. (06324) 78851. 051086

Bönningstedt (Schleswig-Holstein)
Dreyer, Hasloher Weg 1, 25474 Bönningstedt.
T. (0411) 5567741. - Ant - 051087

Bohmte (Niedersachsen)
Hollekamp, Wilhelm, Bremer Str. 16, 49163 Bohmte.
T. (05471) 311. - Ant / Furn / Sculp - 051088
Kalde, H., Leverner Str. 41, 49163 Bohmte.
T. (05471) 551. 051089

Bokel (Schleswig-Holstein)
Bokel-Antik, Lindenallee 28, 24802 Bokel.
T. (04330) 1944. - Ant - 051090

Bonn (Nordrhein-Westfalen)
Alefeld, A. W., Bonngasse 44, 53111 Bonn.
T. (0228) 65 51 14. - Paint / Sculp / Jew - 051091
Alefeld, W. F., Sternstr. 5, 53111 Bonn.
T. (0228) 65 66 38. 051092
Ambaum, Kessenicher Str. 61, 53129 Bonn.
T. (0228) 23 67 62. 051093
Antik- und Flohmarkt, Maxstr. 16, 53117 Bonn.
T. (0228) 69 24 22. 051094
Arnim, Hermine von, Nachtigallenstr. 6, 53179
Bonn. 051095
Bartel, Irmgard & Barbara, Oberkasseler Str. 10, 53227
Bonn. T. (0228) 44 07 34/36, Fax 44 44 00. - Ant /
Furn / Tex - 051096
Bödiger, August, Franziskanerstr. 17-19, 53113 Bonn.
T. (0228) 604200, Fax 6042099. - Ant / Paint / Graph /
Furn / Glass / Orient / China / Silv - 051097

Kunstauktionshaus
August Bödiger
GmbH & Co KG
Kunsthandel und Kunstauktionen
Franziskanerstr. 17–19
53113 Bonn
Tel. (02 28) 60 420-0
FAX (02 28) 60 420-99

Bonner Antiquitätenzentrum, Siebenmorgenweg 6,
53229 Bonn. T. (0228) 46 62 00, Fax 46 62 88. 051098
Brand & Rauch, Vivatsgasse 11, 53111 Bonn.
T. (0228) 65 53 36. - Ant - 051099
Cohnen, Hans Karl, Vivatsgasse 12, 53111 Bonn.
T. (0228) 63 66 18, 22 22 17. - Num - 051100
Ehlers, Werner & Peter, Berliner Freiheit 28, 53111
Bonn. T. (0228) 65 72 88. 051101
Fuchs, H.D., Friedrich-Breuer-Str. 52, 53225 Bonn.
T. (0228) 46 24 74. 051102
Galeiski, St., Kessenicher Str. 203, 53129 Bonn.
T. (0228) 23 29 95. 051103
Gantner, Breite Str. 50, 53111 Bonn. T. (0228) 65 71 85.
- Instr - 051104
Goede, S., Ermekeilstr. 42, 53113 Bonn.
T. (0228) 22 94 27. - Ant / Glass / Mod - 051105
Goodmann, R., Bergweg 6, 53225 Bonn.
T. (0228) 46 52 73. 051106
Hagen, Heinrich, Friedrich-Breuer-Str. 52, 53225 Bonn.
T. (0228) 46 24 74. 051107
Hampel, Frithjof, Dr., Königstr. 65, 53115 Bonn.
T. (0228) 21 95 55. - Ant / Furn - 051108
Hansen, Dirk, Sandkaule 13, 53111 Bonn.
T. (0228) 650188. - Paint / Graph / Fra - 051109

Henke, B., Kirschallee 30, 53115 Bonn.
T. (0228) 22 01 38. 051110
HSR-Werkstatt, Richard-Wagner-Str. 20, 53115 Bonn.
T. (0228) 65 86 68, 65 53 84. - Furn - 051111
Kemp, M., Herwarthstr. 10, 53115 Bonn.
T. (0228) 63 61 17. 051112
König & Wolff, Am Neutor 8, 53113 Bonn.
T. (0228) 63 58 06. 051113
Korth, B., Münsterstr. 15, 53111 Bonn.
T. (0228) 65 49 09. 051114
Kunst- und Antiquitäten am Münster, Wesselstr. 14,
53113 Bonn. T. (0228) 65 28 03. 051115
L'Age d'Or-Antiquitäten, Friesdorfer Str. 36, 53173
Bonn. T. (0228) 31 45 56. - Mod - 051116
Leopold, Ludwig, Friedrichstr. 38, 53111 Bonn.
T. (0228) 65 74 22. - Repr / Rel - 051117
Lila Laden, Kaiserpassagen, 53113 Bonn.
T. (0228) 65 07 55. - China / Jew / Fra / Silv / Lights /
Glass / Mod - 051118
Lina & Terry's Antiques, Konstantinstr. 64, 53179 Bonn.
T. (0228) 35 29 09. - Furn - 051119
Möhring & Bode, Meckenheimer Str. 11, 53179 Bonn.
T. (0228) 34 15 96. 051120
Moitz, Elsässer Str. 8, 53175 Bonn. T. (0228) 31 34 69,
31 40 43. - Ant / Paint / Graph / Furn / China /
Lights - 051121
Niemeyer, Lüder H., Simrockallee 34, 53173 Bonn.
T. (0228) 35 12 77. - Paint / Graph / Draw - 051122
Palmer, I. L., Konstantinstr. 64, 53179 Bonn.
T. (0228) 35 53 68. 051123
Pommereit, K., Kölnstr 139-141, 53111 Bonn.
T. (0228) 692722. 051124
Reul, M., Giersbergstr 37, 53229 Bonn.
T. (0228) 481105. 051125
Schierenberg, Philine, Denglerstr. 8, 53173 Bonn.
T. (0228) 31 70 68. - Ant / Glass / Mod - 051126
Schildgen, Gerd, Friesdorfer Str. 68, 53173 Bonn.
T. (0228) 31 54 19. 051127
Schmitt, M., Muffendorfer Hauptstr. 39, 53177 Bonn.
T. (0228) 33 41 72. 051128
Schweitzer's Antiques, Muffendorfer Hauptstr. 37,
53177 Bonn. T. (0228) 36 26 59. - Ant / Paint / Graph /
Furn / China / Tex / Fra / Silv / Lights / Glass - 051129
Schweitzer's Antiques, Löbestr. 1, 53173 Bonn.
T. (0228) 36 26 59. - Ant / Paint / Graph / Furn / China /
Tex / Fra / Silv / Lights / Glass - 051130
Sieger, R., Reuterstr. 38, 53113 Bonn.
T. (0228) 21 63 80. 051131
Stein, Bonner Str. 35, 53173 Bonn.
T. (0228) 31 13 48. 051132
Streck, H.-P., Kölnstr. 127, 53111 Bonn.
T. (0228) 63 33 95. 051133
Stümpel, H., & Sohn, Colmantstr. 22, 53115
Bonn. 051134
Suliak, B., Dürenstr. 3, 53173 Bonn.
T. (0228) 35 76 67. 051135
Theisen, Karl-Helmut, Eltviller Str. 11, 53175 Bonn.
T. (0228) 31 07 03. - Jew - 051136
Wollner, Wilhelm, Vivatsgasse 40, 53115 Bonn.
T. (0228) 22 91 90. - Num - 051137

Bopfingen (Baden-Württemberg)
Eiberle, Elke, Wacholderstr. 5, 73441 Bopfingen.
T. (07362) 44 87. 051138

Boppard (Rheinland-Pfalz)
Nick, Heinrich, Burgstr. 2, 56154 Boppard. 051139

Bordesholm (Schleswig-Holstein)
Brügger, Dorfstr. 2, 24582 Bordesholm.
T. (04322) 15 38. 051140

Borgholzhausen (Nordrhein-Westfalen)
Höke, Herbert, Ravensberger Str. 16, 33829 Borgholz-
hausen. T. (05425) 6554. 051141
Wolframm, S., Kleekamp 54, 33829 Borgholzhausen.
T. (05425) 5551. - Num - 051142

Borken (Nordrhein-Westfalen)
Miethe, H., Ahauser Str. 95, 46325 Borken.
T. (02861) 53 53. 051143
Pöpping, Rudolf, Realschulstr. 22, 46325
Borken. 051144

Rodenberg, Geschw., An Der Grossen Kirche, 46325
Borken. T. (02861) 22 67, Fax 66541. - Ant / Paint /
Graph / Furn / China / Sculp / Rel / Tin - 051145
Sammler-Kabinett, Remigiusstr. 12, 46325 Borken.
T. (02861) 624 35, Fax 66541. - Ant / Paint / Graph /
Furn / China / Sculp / Rel / Tin - 051146

Borkum (Niedersachsen)
Mühe, Curt, Strandstr. 36, 26757 Borkum. 051147

Bornheim (Nordrhein-Westfalen)
Gutowski, Vladimir, Siefenfeldchen 197, 53332 Born-
heim. T. (02227) 614 94, Fax 61013. 051148
Marx, H.-J., Albertusstr. 3, 53332 Bornheim.
T. (02227) 6374. 051149

Borstel (Niedersachsen)
Schoenmakers, A., Nienburger Str. 42, 27246 Borstel.
T. (04276) 344, Fax 344. - Furn - 051150

Bottrop (Nordrhein-Westfalen)
Brammer, Friedrich-Ebert-Str. 136, 46236 Bottrop.
T. (02041) 671 04. 051151
Hüneke, Alfred, Drößlingstr. 14-16, 46244 Bottrop.
T. (02041) 810 56. - Ant - 051152
Ruppert, Ursula, Horster Str. 275, 46238 Bottrop.
T. (02041) 35063. - Num - 051153
Schmitz, M., Hochstr. 41, 46236 Bottrop.
T. (02041) 224 15. 051154
Spirres, Hannelore, Hauptstr. 54, 46244 Bottrop.
T. (02041) 02045/ 821 04. 051155

Boxberg (Baden-Württemberg)
Wrobel, Horst, Uiffinger Str. 53, 97944 Boxberg.
T. (07930) 464. - Furn / China / Instr / Glass - 051156

Brake (Niedersachsen)
Beyer, B., Lange Str 8, 26919 Brake.
T. (04401) 4319. 051157

Brakel (Nordrhein-Westfalen)
Lamers, G., Stegbrede 13, 33034 Brakel.
T. (05272) 8279. 051158

Bramsche (Niedersachsen)
Art Studio, Heinrichstr 6, 49565 Bramsche.
T. (05461) 1362. 051159

Brannenburg (Bayern)
Bauer, Hedwig, Griessenbachstr. 7, 83098 Brannenburg.
- Ant - 051160

Braunfels (Hessen)
Dargies, A., Borngasse 10, 35619 Braunfels.
T. (06442) 4202. 051161

Braunlage (Niedersachsen)
Sprafke, Gerhard, Eichendorffstr. 23, 38700
Braunlage. 051162

Braunschweig (Niedersachsen)

Ambiente, Stephanstr. 1, 38100 Braunschweig.
T. (0531) 76162. 051163
Angela's Antiquitäten, Handelsweg 5, 38100 Braun-
schweig. T. (0531) 405 87. - Ant - 051164
Antik-Keller, Campestr. 23, 38102 Braunschweig.
T. (0531) 74705. 051165
Behrens, R.F., An der Trift 22a, 38124 Braunschweig.
T. (0531) 61 21 42. 051166
Borek, Richard, Theodor-Heuss-Str. 7, 38122 Braun-
schweig. T. (0531) 809 90. - Num - 051167

Caprano, A., Hagenring 18, 38106
Braunschweig. 051168
Frenk, H., Klint 1, 38100 Braunschweig.
T. (0531) 455 19. 051169
Gent, Theodor, Am Alten Petritore 6, 38100 Braun-
schweig. T. (0531) 456 22. - Furn - 051170
Hippler, Angela, Handelsweg 5, 38100 Braunschweig.
I. (0531) 405 87. 051171
Köster, Hubert, Waisenhausdamm 8-11, 38100 Braun-
schweig. T. (0531) 43882, Fax 43848. - Glass - 051172
Kranz, Kristina, Rankestr. 5, 38102 Braunschweig.
T. (0531) 33 57 30. - Ant / Furn - 051173
Krüger, F., Fallersleber Str. 42, 38100 Braunschweig.
T. (0531) 40782. 051174
Langer, G., Am Hasengarten 85, 38126 Braunschweig.
T. (0531) 665 69. 051175
MDM Münzhandelsgesellschaft, Dompl. 4, 38100
Braunschweig. T. (0531) 809 93 41. - Num - 051176
Mühlenberg, Petritorwall 9, 38118 Braunschweig.
T. (0531) 400733, Fax 126303. 051177
Papendieck, Helge, Packhofpassage 3+6, 38100 Braun-
schweig. T. (0531) 650 55. 051178
Schreiber, F., Handelsweg 4, 38100 Braunschweig.
T. (0531) 155 47. 051179
Schublade, Wilhelmstr. 84, 38100 Braunschweig.
T. (0531) 176 59. 051180
Söllner, Gabi, Breite Str. 24, 38100 Braunschweig.
T. (0531) 410 99. 051181
Walkemeyer, R., Raffturm 4, 38116 Braunschweig.
T. (0531) 51 40 93. - Ant / Furn - 051182

Breckerfeld (Nordrhein-Westfalen)
Sommer, H.-G., Epscheiderstr. 39a, 58339 Breckerfeld.
T. (02338) 24 22. 051183

Breisach (Baden-Württemberg)
Hosp, I., Bundesstr. 44, 79206 Breisach.
T. (07667) 07664/3135. 051184
Zimmermann, W. & R., Vogelsang 10, 79206 Breisach.
T. (07667) 3052. 051185

Breitbrunn (Bayern)
Jell-Förg, Marianne, Königstr. 47, 83254 Breitbrunn.
T. (08054) 361. - Ant - 051186

Breitenbrunn (Bayern)
Bednorz, M., Raiffeisenstr. 17, 87739 Breitenbrunn.
T. (08263) 860. 051187

Bremen
Allgemeiner Sammlerdienst, Belgarder Str. 5, 28717
Bremen. T. (0421) 63 20 27. - Num - 051188
Anno Dazumal, Scharnhorststr. 88, 28211 Bremen.
T. (0421) 23 10 24. 051189
Antik, Wulwesstr. 19, 28203 Bremen. T. (0421) 70 45 91.
- Ant - 051190
Antik-Speicher, Bremerhavener Heerstr. 10, 28717 Bre-
men. T. (0421) 63 44 33. - Furn - 051191
Antike Kunst, Fedelhören 79-81, 28203 Bremen.
T. (0421) 32 70 50. - Paint / Mod - 051192
Antikes & Schönes, Morgenlandstr. 14, 28237 Bremen.
T. (0421) 616 55 71. 051193
Ausmeyer & Gerling, Fedelhören 89, 28203
Bremen. 051194
Bahr, F., Schnoor 23, 28195 Bremen.
T. (0421) 32 47 57. 051195
Barbara F., Dobbenweg 4, 28203 Bremen.
T. (0421) 764 88. - Ant - 051196
Barfs, W., Friesenstr. 33, 28203 Bremen.
T. (0421) 721 16. 051197
Beihl, Werner, Vor dem Steintor 34, 28203 Bremen.
T. (0421) 76 6971, Fax 70 54 80. 051198
Bendig, Hanfried, Elsasser Str. 13, 28211 Bremen.
T. (0421) 34 64 70. - Num - 051199
Bertram, W., Contrescarpe 45, 28195 Bremen.
T. (0421) 32 10 93. 051200
Beyer, H., Bismarckstr. 12, 28203 Bremen.
T. (0421) 772 78. 051201
Boie, I., Schnoor 38, 28195 Bremen.
T. (0421) 32 47 34. 051202
Bolland & Marotz, Fedelhören 19, 28203 Bremen.
T. (0421) 32 82 82, Fax 32 85 43. - Ant / China - 051203
Bremer Landesbank, Domshof 26, 28195 Bremen.
T. (0421) 3320. - Num - 051204

Bremer Münzhandlung, Elsasser Str. 13, 28211 Bremen.
T. (0421) 34 64 70. - Num - 051205
Buhse, Karl-Heinz, Prof., Blumenkamp 6, 28759 Bre-
men. T. (0421) 62 55 32. - Num - 051206
Burmester, J., Am Dobben 128, 28203 Bremen.
T. (0421) 744 44. 051207
Drewes, Metzer Str. 11, 28211 Bremen.
T. (0421) 34 91 78. - Ant - 051208
Ehlers, R., Gustavstr. 1c, 28217 Bremen.
T. (0421) 396 29 21. 051209
Faber, Wilfried, Schnoor 25, 28195 Bremen.
T. (0421) 32 33 57. 051210
Fasse, Manfred, Baumwollbörse, Erdgeschoß Zimmer
69, 28195 Bremen. T. (0421) 32 44 04.
- Num - 051211
Feil, Kurt, Am Wall 116, 28195 Bremen.
T. (0421) 125 21. - Paint / Fra - 051212
Feldbusch, K., Landwehrstr. 71, 28217 Bremen.
T. (0421) 39 28 13. 051213
Frers, Karl-Gerhard, Außer der Schleifmühle 14, 28203
Bremen. T. (0421) 32 35 35. - Ant / Dec - 051214
Galerie Afro Asiatica, Marterburg 29, 28195 Bremen.
T. (0421) 32 71 86. - Ant / Eth / Cur - 051215
Galerie im Winter, Richard-Wagner-Str 32, 28209 Bre-
men. T. (0421) 342294. 051216
Galerie Rose, Rockwinkeler Landstr. 59, 28355 Bremen.
T. (0421) 32 77 55, Fax 25 99 80. 051217
Graphik & Buch, St.-Pauli-Str 44, 28203 Bremen.
T. (0421) 74793. - Ant / Paint - 051218
Griesbach, J. & F., Wachmannstr. 47, 28209 Bremen.
T. (0421) 34 54 98. - Ant / Graph / Furn / Orient / China /
Tex / Jew / Silv / Glass / Mod - 051219
Hanseatische Münzenhandlung, Fedelhören 8, 28203
Bremen. T. (0421) 32 10 94. - Num - 051220
Herkules Münzhandel, Oberviolandstr. 17, 28259
Bremen. T. (0421) 50 02 60. - Num - 051221
Hertz, M., Richard-Wagner-Str. 22, 28209 Bremen.
T. (0421) 34 16 70. 051222
Heuer, Peter, Zur Munte 6, 28213 Bremen.
T. (0421) 21 11 26. - Instr - 051223
Heye, T., Dijonstr. 8, 28211 Bremen.
T. (0421) 44 58 93. 051224
Krampitz, H., Am Schwarzen Meer 13, 28205 Bremen.
T. (0421) 1 44 58 88. - Furn - 051225
Krebs, Karin, Schnoor 16, 28195 Bremen.
T. (0421) 32 65 66. - Furn / Jew / Silv - 051226
Lange, F., Kreftingstr. 12, 28203 Bremen.
T. (0421) 785 18. 051227
Manke, W., Fedelhören 79, 28203 Bremen.
T. (0421) 32 64 87. 051228
Mudder, Arnold, Hemelinger Bahnhofstr. 56, 28309 Bre-
men. - Paint / Furn - 051229
Neuse, Contrescarpe 14, 28203 Bremen.
T. (0421) 325642, Fax (0421) 328611. 051230
Plac-art, Humboldtstr. 198, 28203 Bremen.
T. (0421) 768 79. - Graph - 051231
Plöger, Traute, Leher Heerstr. 44, 28359
Bremen. 051232
Popp's Antik, Am Dobben 130, 28203 Bremen.
T. (0421) 32 43 86. 051233
Prieser, Helmut, Gröpelinger Heerstr. 216a, 28237 Bre-
men. T. (0421) 61 72 23. - Num - 051234
Rahmenladen in Steintor, Römerstr. 16, 28203 Bremen.
T. (0421) 74337. 051235
Raup, Günter, Fedelhören 87a, 28203 Bremen.
T. (0421) 32 12 12. - Sculp / Lights / Instr - 051236
Riese, Horst, Kastanienallee 23, 28717 Bremen.
T. (0421) 63 05 66. - Num - 051237
Sankt Jürgen-Antik, St.-Jürgen-Str. 98, 28203 Bremen.
T. (0421) 736 96. 051238
Schmidt, Elisabeth, Hansestr 14, 28217
Bremen. 051239
Schröder & Leisewitz, Carl-Schurz-Str. 39, 28209 Bre-
men. T. (0421) 34 40 83, Fax 345099. - Paint - 051240
Schulz, Gustav G., Tiefer 15, 28195 Bremen.
T. (0421) 32 73 30. - Ant / Num - 051241
Schulz, Johannes, Fedelhören 81, 28203 Bremen.
T. (0421) 32 70 50. - Paint - 051242
Seggern, J. & P. von, Fedelhören 94, 28203 Bremen.
T. (0421) 32 79 18. - Ant / Jew - 051243
Sembach, C., Kornstr. 118, 28201 Bremen.
T. (0421) 55 21 83. 051244

Simon, Brunhild, Feldstr. 52-54, 28203 Bremen.
T. (0421) 785 91. - Jew - 051245
Specht, Alte Hafenstr. 13, 28757 Bremen.
T. (0421) 66 50 16. 051246
Teudloff, Hasso, Am Wall 152, 28195 Bremen. 051247
Thorban, Klaus P., Wachmannstr. 52, 28209
Bremen. 051248
Unbehaun, H., Interlakener Str. 18, 28325 Bremen.
T. (0421) 42 26 31. 051249
Wagner, Hermann, Rolandstr. 40, 28199
Bremen. 051250
Wark, Maria M., Oberneulander Landstr. 183, 28355
Bremen. - Ant / Furn - 051251
William, Evans, Am Schwarzen Meer 9, 28205 Bremen.
T. (0421) 498 81 63. 051252
Wischhusen, Sögestr. 41, 28195 Bremen.
T. (0421) 32 00 68. - Num - 051253
Wolff, Eberhard, Buntentorsteinweg 41, 28201
Bremen. 051254

Bremerhaven (Bremen)
Antik-Werkstatt Alberti, Spichernstr. 8, 27570 Bremer-
haven. T. (0471) 30 13 52. 051255
Art Excusiv, Kanalstr. 3-5, 27520 Bremerhaven.
T. (0471) 864, Fax 864. - Ant - 051256
Boehl & Oppermann, Osterstr. 6, 27568 Bremerhaven.
T. (0471) 46053. 051257
Fuhl, Hartmut, Bürger 55, 27568 Bremerhaven.
T. (0471) 41 32 49. 051258
Hübener, G., An der Mühle 34, 27570 Bremerhaven.
T. (0471) 321 45. 051259
Köter, Heiko, Hafenstr. 18, 27576 Bremerhaven.
T. (0471) 288841. 051260
Rosenberg, A., Lange Str. 18, 27580 Bremerhaven.
T. (0471) 81058. 051261
Schimanietz, W., Zur Siedewurth 3, 27572 Bremerha-
ven. T. (0471) 758 85. 051262
Warrings & Söhne, Rohrstr. 3, 27572 Bremerhaven.
T. (0471) 710 57. 051263

Brensbach (Hessen)
Meinass, F., Kirchstr. 15, 64395 Brensbach.
T. (06161) 1005. 051264

Bretzfeld (Baden-Württemberg)
Maurer, H.-J. & R., Waldbacher Str. 13, 74626 Bretzfeld.
T. (07946) 6213. 051265

Breuberg (Hessen)
Kabel, M., & G. Lang, Wertheimer Str., 64747 Breuberg.
T. (06165) 17 03, 687. 051266

Brilon (Nordrhein-Westfalen)
Kleine Galerie, Spritzengasse 2, 59929 Brilon.
T. (02961) 63 82. - China - 051267
Kracht-Philipp, U., Untere Bahnhofstr. 10, 59929 Brilon.
T. (02961) 02964/741. 051268

Brombachtal (Hessen)
Mück, B., Hauptstr. 24, 64753 Brombachtal.
T. (06063) 3542. - Furn - 051269

Bruchsal (Baden-Württemberg)
Kreischer, A., Spöckweg 37a, 76646 Bruchsal.
T. (07251) 148 05. 051270
Kreischer, E., Werner-von-Siemens-Str. 14, 76646
Bruchsal. T. (07251) 166 43. 051271

Brüggen (Nordrhein-Westfalen)
Heimes, Luise, Burgwall 8a, 41379 Brüggen. 051272
Hoff, Heinrich, Burg-Galerie, Burgwall 1b, 41379 Brüg-
gen. T. (0211) 613755. - Paint / Graph / Jew - 051273

Brühl (Nordrhein-Westfalen)
Kaus, Uhlstr 45, 50321 Brühl. T. (02232) 44817. 051274
Link, M., Uhlstr 41-45, 50321 Brühl.
T. (02232) 44817. 051275
Mattar, Ursula, Eckdorfer Str 22, 50321 Brühl.
T. (02232) 31491. 051276

Brunsbüttel (Schleswig-Holstein)
Müller, M., Koogstr. 32, 25541 Brunsbüttel.
T. (04852) 4040. 051277

Buchholz in der Nordheide (Niedersachsen)

Elstermann, Heidi, Poststr 12, 21244 Buchholz in der Nordheide. T. (04181) 32202. - Ant / Tex / Jew - *051278*

Bückeburg (Niedersachsen)

Waltke, Sablépl. 1, 31675 Bückeburg.
T. (05722) 269 66. *051279*

Büdelsdorf (Schleswig-Holstein)

Johannsen, U. & W., Hollerstr. 123, 24782 Büdelsdorf.
T. (04331) 38846, 31817. *051280*

Bühl (Baden-Württemberg)

Hansmann, C., Hauptstr 50, 77815 Bühl.
T. (07223) 8573. *051281*

Bünde (Nordrhein-Westfalen)

Knollmann, J., Eschstr. 17, 32257 Bünde.
T. (05223) 23 10. *051282*
Niederhommert, Hr., Wielandstr. 20, 32257 Bünde.
T. (05223) 433 38. *051283*
Nienabu, R., Bahnhofstr. 75, 32257 Bünde.
T. (05223) 122 92. - Instr - *051284*

Büren (Nordrhein-Westfalen)

Tomaschewski, G., Lipperhohl 42, 33142 Büren.
T. (02951) 2571. - Ant / Sculp / Arch / Jew / Silv / Mil /
Rel / Ico - *051285*

Bürgstadt (Bayern)

Martin, Günter, Steinerne Gasse 11, 63927 Bürgstadt.
T. (09371) 78 57, Fax 8728. - Ant / Furn - *051286*

Büsingen (Baden-Württemberg)

Hochleitner, Josef, Höhenstr 31, 78266 Büsingen.
T. (07734) 6778. - Ant / Furn / Orient / China / Tex / Dec /
Jew / Silv / Instr / Rel / Glass / Mod - *051287*

Büttelborn (Hessen)

Antiques V.I.P. Gallery, Isarstr. 8, 64572 Büttelborn.
T. (06152) 407 26. *051288*

Bunsloh (Schleswig-Holstein)

Schönleiter, W., Westerau, 25767 Bunsloh.
T. (04835) 583. *051289*

Burgdorf (Niedersachsen)

Görtz, J. & W. von, Peiner Weg 76, 31303 Burgdorf. *051290*
Gude, Wolfgang, Hann. Neustadt 3, 31303 Burgdorf.
T. (05136) 839 45. *051291*

Burgdorf bei Salzgitter (Niedersachsen)

Sapadi, H. & C., Hohenassel, 38272 Burgdorf bei Salzgitter. T. (05347) 1967. *051292*

Burgkunstadt (Bayern)

Häßlein, Bully, Lichtenf. Str. 16, 96224 Burgkunstadt.
T. (09572) 1425. *051293*

Burgwald (Hessen)

Langenfeld, H., Zum Küppel 3, 35099 Burgwald.
T. (06457) 06451/9847. *051294*
Schmidt, H., Tannenstr. 14, 35099 Burgwald.
T. (06457) 06451/9642. *051295*

Burgwedel (Niedersachsen)

Antiquitäten Kabinett, Von-Alten-Str. 23a, 30938 Burgwedel. T. (05139) 3690. *051296*

Burscheid, Rheinland (Nordrhein-Westfalen)

Beckers, Hauptstr 87, 51399 Burscheid, Rheinland.
T. (02174) 63619. *051297*

Buseck (Hessen)

Gansow, G., Großen-Busecker-Str. 40, 35418 Buseck.
T. (064 08) 7939. *051298*
Weppler, H., Am Rinnerborn 45, 35418 Buseck. *051299*

Calw (Baden-Württemberg)

Beutler, Gerhard, Stiegelwiesenweg 8, 75365 Calw.
T. (07051) 63 46. - Num - *051300*

Castrop-Rauxel (Nordrhein-Westfalen)

Galuba, Hans-Dieter, Grutholzstr. 14, 44575 Castrop-Rauxel. *051301*

Celle (Niedersachsen)

Halbach, U., Bergstr. 1b, 29221 Celle.
T. (05141) 28421. *051302*
Krohne, Georg, Mauernstr. 47, 29221 Celle. *051303*
Kuhn, Egbert, Postfach 1245, 29202 Celle.
T. (05141) 238 79. - Num / China - *051304*
Lewitzki, Brandpl. 1, 29221 Celle. T. (05141) 6715,
7888. *051305*
Mariani, Bergstr. 36, 29221 Celle.
T. (05141) 21251. *051306*
Werner, Uwe, Trüllerring 18, 29221 Celle. *051307*
Wolter, Erika, Mauernstr. 35, 29221 Celle.
T. (05141) 293 01. *051308*

Chemnitz (Sachsen)

Ahnert, C., Zöllnerstr. 6, 09111 Chemnitz.
T. (0371) 41 56 28. - Ant - *051309*
Antik, Elisenstr 35, 09111 Chemnitz. T. (0371) 411745.
- Paint / Graph / Furn / China / Repr / Tex / Jew / Silv / Lights / Instr / Mil / Glass / Cur / Mod / Toys - *051310*
Antiquitäten-Galerie Chemnitz, Zöllnerpl. 25, 09111
Chemnitz. T. (0371) 41 13 81. - Ant / Paint / Furn / China / Sculp / Tex / Jew / Silv / Mil / Glass - *051311*
Goy, Renate, Gustav-Adolf-Str. 35, 09116 Chemnitz.
T. (0371) 324 34. - Ant - *051312*
Münzfachgeschäft Pecunia, Brühl 51, 09111 Chemnitz.
T. (0371) 449 62. - Num - *051313*

Clausthal-Zellerfeld (Niedersachsen)

Keller, C., Bergstr. 51, 38678 Clausthal-Zellerfeld.
T. (05323) 781 61. *051314*
Wentzel, J., Osteröderstr. 18, 38678 Clausthal-Zellerfeld. T. (05323) 1637. *051315*

Cloppenburg (Niedersachsen)

Bünger, B., Langestr. 64, 49661 Cloppenburg. *051316*
Studio Antik-Galerie, Löninger Str. 15, 49661 Cloppenburg. T. (04471) 78 00, 844 11. *051317*

Coburg (Bayern)

Galerie 27, Buchbergstr. 16, 96450 Coburg.
T. (09561) 921 62. *051318*
Lüdeke, Mohrenstr. 10, 96450 Coburg.
T. (09561) 396 05, Fax 18464. - Instr - *051319*
Raumschüssel, H., Neugasse 3, 96450 Coburg.
T. (09561) 944 63. *051320*
Schönweiß, Judengasse 34, 96450 Coburg. *051321*
Seifert, E., Webergasse 26, 96450 Coburg.
T. (09561) 951 88. *051322*
Wagner, Klaus, Herrngasse 15, 96450 Coburg.
T. (09561) 940 95. - Num - *051323*

Cochem (Rheinland-Pfalz)

Padovono, U., Burgfrieden 4, 56812 Cochem.
T. (02671) 53 39. *051324*
Steib, Brunhilde, Moselpromenade 22, 56812 Cochem.
T. (02671) 86 27. *051325*

Contwig (Rheinland-Pfalz)

Bumb, I., Landauerstr. 34, 66497 Contwig.
T. (06336) 06336/5142. *051326*

Cottbus (Brandenburg)

Bosse, Sigrid, Finsterwalder Str. 24, 03048 Cottbus.
T. (0355) 42 12 54. - Ant / Paint / Furn / Num / China /
Jew / Glass - *051327*

Crailsheim (Baden-Württemberg)

Sternmann, Math., Lange Str. 60, 74564 Crailsheim.
T. (07951) 75 21. *051328*
Wolf, H., Hüttfeldstr. 14, 74564 Crailsheim.
T. (07951) 8381. *051329*

Cremlingen (Niedersachsen)

Primas, Dagmar, Bäckerstr. 5, 38162 Cremlingen.
T. (05306) 14 08. *051330*

Cuxhaven (Niedersachsen)

Gehlhaar, Manfred, Deichstr. 17, 27472 Cuxhaven.
T. (04721) 379 07. *051331*
Steinhoff, D., Steinmarner Str. 3, 27476 Cuxhaven.
T. (04721) 515 51. *051332*

Veit, A., Nordersteinstr. 10, 27472 Cuxhaven.
T. (04721) 27810. *051333*

Dachau (Bayern)

Jaeppelt, A.E., Schleißheimer Str. 59, 85221 Dachau.
T. (08131) 159 67. *051334*
Nemany, Dorit, Schöttlstr. 2, 85221 Dachau. *051335*
Stadler, E., Konrad-Adenauer-Str. 23, 85221 Dachau.
T. (08131) 829 29. *051336*

Dänischenhagen (Schleswig-Holstein)

Gerhartz, Ulrike, Arp-Schnitger-Weg 28, 02301 Dänischenhagen. T. (04349) 12 74. *051337*

Dagebüll (Schleswig-Holstein)

Alte Stiftung Marienkoog, Westerweg, 25899 Dagebüll.
T. (04667) 202. *051338*

Darmstadt (Hessen)

Antik Galerie, Schulstr. 1a, 64283 Darmstadt.
T. (06151) 256 88, 267 93. - Ant / Paint / Furn / China /
Sculp / Tex / Jew / Silv / Glass / Mod / Draw / Toys -- *051339*
Antikmarkt, Dieburger Str. 10-12, 64287 Darmstadt.
T. (06151) 78 42 16. - Furn - *051340*
Borsdorf-Dagli, Angelika, Brüder-Knauß-Str. 39, 64285
Darmstadt. T. (06151) 61726. *051341*
Darmstädter Galerie, Luisenstr. 24, 64283 Darmstadt.
T. (06151) 208 99. - Ant / Orient / Eth / Jew /
Cur - *051342*
Galerie in der Scheune, Kranichsteiner Str. 108, 64289
Darmstadt. T. (06151) 767 67. - Ant - *051343*
Geilenkeuser, O., Frankensteiner Str. 18, 64297 Darmstadt. T. (06151) 59 47 34. *051344*
Gommermann, R., Luisenstr. 16, 64283 Darmstadt.
T. (06151) 225 68. *051345*
Heymann, Elisabethenstr. 58, 64283 Darmstadt.
T. (06151) 270 32. - Ant - *051346*
Hryciow, Stefan, Dieburger Str. 10-12, 64287 Darmstadt. T. (06151) 78 42 81. - Furn - *051347*
Kabel & Lang, Schulstr. 16, 64283 Darmstadt.
T. (06151) 221 36. - Ant / Paint / China / Jew - *051348*
Lufft, T., Landwehrstr. 3, 64293 Darmstadt.
T. (06151) 207 57. - Graph - *051349*
Otto, Charlotte, & Gerhard Müller, Kittlerstr. 13, 64289
Darmstadt. T. (06151) 201 68. - Ant - *051350*
Sander, Prinz-Christians-Weg 16, 64287 Darmstadt.
T. (06151) 44442. - Paint / Sculp - *051351*
Schmidt, Ellen, Heinrich-Delp-Str. 167, 64297 Darmstadt. T. (06151) 51 44. *051352*
Staschik, G., Landwehrstr. 24 1/2, 64293 Darmstadt.
T. (06151) 274 80. *051353*
Strauß, Daniel, Rheinstr. 16, 64283 Darmstadt.
T. (06151) 256 66. *051354*
Törk, Frankfurter Str. 21, 64293 Darmstadt.
T. (06151) 745 11. - Ant - *051355*
Wentzel, Rolf, Heinheimer Str. 22, 64289 Darmstadt.
T. (06151) 71 64 00. *051356*

Datteln (Nordrhein-Westfalen)

Buskies, Horneburger Str. 50, 45711 Datteln.
T. (02363) 71914. - Paint / Graph / Sculp /
Draw - *051357*
Krahforst, J., Provinzialstr. 32, 45711 Datteln.
T. (02363) 71955. *051358*
Mertins, Jürgen, Provinzialstr. 51, 45711 Datteln.
T. (02363) 0231/668 67, Fax 77 19 26. - Paint / Furn /
China / Tex / Glass - *051359*

Daun (Rheinland-Pfalz)

Mancel, J.-J., Trierer Str. 14, 54550 Daun. *051360*
Vitrine, Borngasse 11, 54550 Daun.
T. (06592) 1030. *051361*

Deggendorf (Bayern)

Eigenschenk, G., Pferdemarkt 5, 94469 Deggendorf.
T. (0991) 75 75. *051362*
Motz, Anton, Bergerstr. 14, 94469 Deggendorf.
T. (0991) 256 59. - Ant / Furn / Tex / Dec - *051363*
Pasquay, J. & H., Berger Str. 42, 94469 Deggendorf.
T. (0991) 239 58. *051364*

Deidesheim (Rheinland-Pfalz)

Hoermann, G., Marktpl. 3, 67146 Deidesheim.
T. (06326) 5756. *051365*

Kämmer, N. & H., Heumarktstr. 17, 6/146 Deidesheim.
T. (06326) 61 10.   051366

Deisenhofen (Bayern)
Puch, Viktor, 82041 Deisenhofen. T. (089) 6132369.
- Ant / Sculp / Ico –   051367

Delmenhorst (Niedersachsen)
Lamping, Rathausplatz, 27749 Delmenhorst.
T. (04221) 183 62.   051368
Staden, van, Lange Str. 3, 27749 Delmenhorst.
T. (04221) 164 56.   051369

Dessau (Sachsen-Anhalt)
Apel, W., Dessauer Str. 68, 06844 Dessau.
T. (0340) 4611.   051370
Edler, B., Königendorfer Str. 12, 06847 Dessau.
T. (0340) 82 36 16.   051371

Detmold (Nordrhein-Westfalen)
Antiqua, Lemgoer Str. 62, 32756 Detmold.
T. (05231) 297 93.   051372
Busche, H., Hornsche Str. 26, 32756 Detmold.
T. (05231) 28896.   051373
Gausmann, S., Schülerstr. 24, 32756 Detmold.
T. (05231) 248 64.   051374
Kopp, Hartwig, Krumme Str. 5, 32756 Detmold.
T. (05231) 226 01.   051375
Laubinger, Albert, Lagesche Str. 166, 32756 Detmold.
T. (05231) 667 22.   051376
Laubinger, Josef, Lagesche Str. 164, 32756 Detmold.
T. (05231) 664 14.   051377
Meyersche Hofbuchhandlung, Krumme Str. 26, 32756
Detmold. T. (05231) 221 31. - Ant / Graph /
Num –   051378
Oebel, Hildegard, Allee 12, 32756 Detmold.
T. (05231) 249 46.   051379
Pilling, Paulinenstr. 5, 32756 Detmold. T. (05231) 21141,
Fax 29827. - Num –   051380
Schnelle, Ernst, Krumme Str. 26, 32756 Detmold.
T. (05231) 221 31. - Num –   051381

Dettenheim (Baden-Württemberg)
Forum-Antik, Leimengrubenweg 4, 76706 Dettenheim.
- Ant –   051382

Dettingen unter Teck (Baden-Württemberg)
Breier, R., Kirchheimer Str. 139, 73265 Dettingen unter
Teck. T. (070 21) 812 15.   051383
Breier, Walter, Bahnhofstr. 2, 73265 Dettingen unter
Teck. T. (070 21) 55122, 52267. - Ant –   051384
Engin & Türkan Yurt, Kirchheimer Str. 154, 73265 Det-
tingen unter Teck. T. (070 21) 464 21.   051385
Fauser, Adolf, Lindenstr. 4, 73265 Dettingen unter Teck.
T. (070 21) 518 06. - Ant –   051386
Yumak, Ahmet, Kirchheimer Str. 158 A/B, 73265 Dettin-
gen unter Teck. T. (070 21) 59748. - Ant –   051387

Deudesfeld (Rheinland-Pfalz)
Koenen, Katharina, Meisenberger Str. 2, 54570 Deudes-
feld. T. (065 99) 861.   051388

Deutsch Evern (Niedersachsen)
Alter, Uwe, Wandelfeld 13, 21407 Deutsch Evern.
T. (04131) 79 10 00, Fax 79 10 07.   051389

Diebach (Bayern)
Weinbeer, K., Insinger Str. 21, 91583 Diebach.
T. (09868) 5444.   051390

Diekhusen-Fahrstedt (Schleswig-Holstein)
Altenau, G. & C., Hauptstr. 12, 25709 Diekhusen-Fahr-
stedt. T. (04851) 1396.   051391

Dielheim (Baden-Württemberg)
A.K.L. Antiques, Markgrafenstr. 6, 69234 Dielheim.
T. (06222) 20 87. - Ant / Furn –   051392

Dießen am Ammersee (Bayern)
Bader, Irene & August, Schornweg 26a, 86911 Dießen
am Ammersee.   051393
Hudler, Josef, Herrenstr. 24, 86911 Dießen am Ammersee. T. (08807) 335. - Ant –   051394

Dietzenbach (Hessen)
Laumann, Günter Rudolf, Am Rebstock 4, 63128 Dietzenbach. T. (06074) 319 06.   051395

Diez (Rheinland-Pfalz)
Amigo Team, Wilhelmstr 37, 65582 Diez.
T. (06432) 2086, Fax 7215. - Orient / Repr /
Arch –   051396

Walbröhl & Co., Felkestr. 48-50, 65582 Diez.
T. (06432) 36 01. - Paint –   051397

Dillenburg (Hessen)
Bertrand, Oranienstr. 8, 35683 Dillenburg.
T. (02771) 211 21.   051398
Bertraud, Helena, Neuhoffstr. 14, 35683
Dillenburg.   051399
Brink, N., Kreuzstr. 4, 35687 Dillenburg.
T. (02771) 7474.   051400

Dillingen (Bayern)
Böhm, Manfred, Frauentalstr. 36, 89407 Dillingen.
T. (09071) 92 46. - Paint / Jew / Instr / Glass –   051401
Schäferling, M., Donauwörther Str. 37 1/2, 89407 Dillin-
gen. T. (09071) 6299.   051402
Waldenmayer, Helmut, Am Mittelfeld 7, 89407 Dillingen.
T. (09071) 26 34. - China / Glass –   051403

Dillingen (Saarland)
Knoll, Hans, Heiligenbergstr. 32 und Jahnstr. 15, 66763
Dillingen. T. (06831) 77307.   051404
Sammler Shop, Friedrich-Ebert-Str. 5, 66763 Dillingen.
T. (06831) 739 91. - Num –   051405

Dingolfing (Bayern)
Goldmann, E., Höfen, 84130 Dingolfing.
T. (08731) 1811.   051406

Dinkelsbühl (Bayern)
Blank, Franz, Brennhof, 91550 Dinkelsbühl.
T. (09851) 622.   051407
DELEIKA, Waldeck, 91550 Dinkelsbühl. T. (09857) 9570,
Fax 93991. - Music –   051408a
Ebert, Herbert & M., Klostergasse 19, 91550 Dinkel-
sbühl. T. (09851) 480. - Ant –   051409
Förster, R., Mückenbrünnlein 16, 91550 Dinkelsbühl.
T. (09851) 25 31.   051410
Fricker, Jürgen H., Hechtzwinger, 91550 Dinkelsbühl.
T. (09851) 36 53. - Ant / Paint / Graph / Furn / China /
Sculp / Silv / Instr / Mil / Glass –   051411

Maier, A., & Chr. Zahradnicek, Siebenbürger Str. 44,
91550 Dinkelsbühl. T. (09851) 33 14.   051412

Dinslaken (Nordrhein-Westfalen)
Elsen, A., Bahnstr. 19, 46535 Dinslaken.   051413
Kasperek, N., Hedwigstr. 30, 46537 Dinslaken.
T. (02064) 539 53.   051414
Oppenberg, B., & R. Goedecke, Wallstr. 1, 46535 Dinsla-
ken. T. (02064) 153 24.   051415
Rieß, Gebr., Sibyllenweg 36, 46537 Dinslaken.
T. (02064) 516 55. - Num –   051416
Veltzke & Woitas, Duisburger Str. 79, 46535 Dinslaken.
T. (02064) 7771.   051417

Dipperz (Hessen)
Weber, Heidelore, Fuldaer Str. 3, 36160 Dipperz.
T. (06657) 72 71. - Ant –   051418

Dissen (Niedersachsen)
Fark & A. Osterheider, F., Große Str 14, 49201 Dissen.
T. (05421) 2146, Fax (05421) 4196. - Ant /
Furn –   051419

Ditzingen (Baden-Württemberg)
Wagner, M., Schillerstr. 3, 71254 Ditzingen.
T. (07156) 7850.   051420

Döhlau (Bayern)
Max, E., Hofer Str. 28, 95182 Döhlau.
T. (09281) 1508.   051421

Dörentrup (Nordrhein-Westfalen)
Alte Form, Hauptstr. 47, 32694 Dörentrup.
T. (05265) 209.   051422

Dörverden (Niedersachsen)
Kubitza, Kurt & Erwin, Langestr. 35, 27313
Dörverden.   051423

Donaueschingen (Baden-Württemberg)
Metzger, R., Zeppelinstr. 4, 78166 Donaueschingen.
T. (0771) 139 99.   051424
Ruby, J., Karlstr. 16, 78166 Donaueschingen.
T. (0771) 13999. - Ant / Furn –   051425

Donzdorf (Baden-Württemberg)
Galerie im Neuen Haus, Dielenstr. 10, 73072 Donzdorf.
T. (07162) 296 13.   051426

Dorfen (Bayern)
Münzenloher, Franz, Furth 1, 84405 Dorfen.
T. (08081) 571, Fax (08081) 1840. - Ant / Furn –   051427

Dormagen (Nordrhein-Westfalen)
Brausen, H., Kölner Str. 114, 41539 Dormagen.
T. (02133) 56 04.   051428
Dormagener Kunsthof, Bismarckstr. 37, 41542 Dorma-
gen. T. (02133) 907 72.   051429

Dornhan (Baden-Württemberg)
Callies, Gerhard, Johannes-Brenz-Weg 17, 72175 Dorn-
han. T. (07455) 22 34.   051430

Dornstetten (Baden-Württemberg)
Theile, S.G., Marktpl. 7, 72280 Dornstetten.
T. (07443) 3369.   051431

Dornumersiel (Niedersachsen)
Antik-Nautic-Schmuck-Kate, Up Börs 3/Kapitänstr. 2,
26553 Dornumersiel. T. (04933) 739. - Ant / Paint /
Furn / Orient / Jew / Silv / Instr –   051432

Dorsten (Nordrhein-Westfalen)
Bendig, Rudi, Schulstr. 4, 46286 Dorsten.
T. (02362) 761 75.   051433

Dortmund (Nordrhein-Westfalen)
Albrecht & Grünert, Balkenstr. 8, 44137 Dortmund.
T. (0231) 52 49 49. - Num –   051434
Anders, R. & B., Martener Str. 280, 44379
Dortmund.   051435
Antiquitäten am Westpark, Lange Str. 67, 44137 Dort-
mund. T. (0231) 14 43 70. - Ant –   051436
Broeldiek, Kaffsackweg 2, 44359 Dortmund.   051437
Eberle, Albrecht, Alter Burgwall 9, 44135 Dortmund.
T. (0231) 52 63 03. - Paint –   051438

Galerie Ambiente, Blickstr 251, 44227 Dortmund. T. (0231) 770234, Fax (0231) 771926. - Paint / Furn / China / Sculp / Tex / Glass - 051439
Heidick, R., Evinger Str. 301, 44339 Dortmund. T. (0231) 85 21 82. - Num - 051440
Henrichsen, Kampstr. 45, 44137 Dortmund. T. (0231) 14 29 70. - Paint / Graph / Fra - 051441
Huste, Liebigstr. 46-48, 44139 Dortmund. T. (0231) 12 26 38, Fax 12 94 95. - Paint / Graph / China / Sculp / Glass / Mod / Pho / Draw - 051442
Ikonen-Galerie Lehmann, Wittener Str. 275, 44149 Dortmund. T. (0231) 17 15 78, Fax 170591. - Ico - 051443
Klemmer, G., Leierweg 29, 44137 Dortmund. T. (0231) 12 27 81. 051444
König, Westfalendamm 275, 44141 Dortmund. T. (0231) 41 54 51. 051445
Kruse, Stockumer Str. 194, 44225 Dortmund. T. (0231) 77 27 29. 051446
Malten, H., Kleppingstr. 28, 44135 Dortmund. T. (0231) 57 19 66. 051447
Markovic, T., Rheinische Str. 134, 44147 Dortmund. T. (0231) 14 68 33. - Ant / Paint / Sculp / Ico / Draw - 051448
Müller, Leopold, Friedrichsruher Str. 3, 44369 Dortmund. 051449
Nöring, Hans, Hohe Str. 16, 44139 Dortmund. T. (0231) 14 15 00. - Num - 051450
Nowak, N., Münsterstr. 170, 44145 Dortmund. T. (0231) 83 52 68. 051451
Schlierkamp, J. & H., Kaiserstr. 46, 44135 Dortmund. T. (0231) 57 20 365. 051452
Schmi-Dau, Am Sprökel 22, 44135 Dortmund. T. (0231) 757 16. 051453
Schmidt, G.H, Hombrucher Str. 60, 44225 Dortmund. T. (0231) 77 99 87. 051454
Schönert, Petra, Sartoristr. 10, 44229 Dortmund. T. (0231) 73 01 87. 051455
Stein, Walter, Blumenstr. 41, 44147 Dortmund. T. (0231) 82 57 03. 051456
Teumer, M., Schwanenwall 4, 44135 Dortmund. T. (0231) 57 15 81. - Ant / Paint / Graph / Furn / Fra / Lights / Mod - 051457
Wilke, H., Kaiserstr. 46, 44135 Dortmund. T. (0231) 52 12 71. 051458
Wortkötter, Paul, Gnadenort 3-5, 44135 Dortmund. T. (0231) 811749. - Ant / Paint / Graph / Furn / China / Repr / Jew / Fra / Silv / Instr / Mil / Cur / Mod / Ico -- 051459

Dossenheim (Hessen)

Bühler, Ute, & Hanno Böttcher, Richard-Wagner-Str. 11, 69221 Dossenheim. T. (062 21) 864271. - Paint / Fra - 051460

Drachselsried (Bayern)

Herrmann, H., Poschingerstr. 12, 94256 Drachselsried. T. (09945) 395, Fax 24 08. 051461

Dreieich (Hessen)

Antikhof Dreieich, Auestr. 8, 63303 Dreieich. T. (06103) 669 03. 051462
Dokter, Ursula, Hainer Trift 25, 63303 Dreieich. T. (06103) 644 88. - Paint / Furn / China / Silv / Instr / Mod - 051463
Galerie R.D., Odenwaldring 112, 63303 Dreieich. T. (06103) 816 95. - Orient - 051464
Garlich, K. B., Albert-Schweitzer-Str. 24a, 63303 Dreieich. T. (06103) 859 70, Fax 83 01 85. - Num - 051465
Leichter, Danica, Röntgenstr. 1, 63303 Dreieich. T. (06103) 82957. - Ant / Paint / Furn / Mod - 051466
Schauer, R. Markus, August-Bebel-Str. 67, 63303 Dreieich. T. (06103) 616 42. 051467

Drensteinfurt (Nordrhein-Westfalen)

Buschmann, H., Ossenbeck 14a, 48317 Drensteinfurt. 051468
Floh- und Antikmarkt Rinkerode, Alte Dorfstr. 1, 48317 Drensteinfurt. T. (02508) 8140. 051469

Dresden (Sachsen)

Am Goldenen Reiter, M. Schuster, Hauptstr. 17-19, 01097 Dresden. T. (0351) 570740. 051470
Antiquitäten, Bautzner Str. 23, 01099 Dresden. T. (0351) 57 02 22. 051471
Arlt, M., Neubühlauerstr 5;Bautzner Landstr 28, 01324;01324 Dresden. T. (0351) 4604760;(0351) 3740708. 051472
Bachmann, E., Böhmische Str 41, 01099 Dresden. T. (0351) 5022830. 051473
Deile, Regina, Hennigsdorfer Str. 31, 01257 Dresden. T. (0351) 2236814, Fax (0351) 2236814. - Ant - 051474
Dresdner Münzhandlung, Dr.-Külz-Ring 11, 01067 Dresden. T. (0351) 4952217. - Num - 051475
Dresdner Münzstube Oesterreich, Leipziger Str 98, 01127 Dresden. T. 01723505021. 051476
Flügel, W., Sebnitzer Str 45, 01099 Dresden. T. (0351) 8011593. 051477
Gebauer, W., Grunaer Str 12, 01069 Dresden. T. (0351) 4940921. 051478
Göldner, L., Blumenstr 73, 01307 Dresden. T. (0351) 4593942. 051479
Gottschalk, A., Troppauerstr 34, 01279 Dresden. T. (0351) 2391527. 051480
Günther, Ernst G., Prellerstr. 25, 01309 Dresden. T. (0351) 309 81. - Paint / Furn - 051481
Hardner, G., Nieritzstr 12, 01097 Dresden. T. (0351) 570758. 051482
Haushalt Gesch. Beräumung, Binger Str 12, 01159 Dresden. T. (0351) 4116803. 051483
Heirler, M., Dr., Königstr 11, 01097 Dresden. T. (0351) 4410553. 051484
Hemmerling Notaphilie, Dr., Konkordienstr 38, 01127 Dresden. T. (0351) 4410082, Fax (0351) 4410082. 051485
Hoche, Herbert W., Gubener Str. 6, 01237 Dresden. T. (0351) 274 32 78. - Num - 051486
Jurk, D., Gubener Str. 6, 01237 Dresden. T. (0351) 2843278. - Num - 051487
Kühl, Johannes, Zittauer Str. 12, 01099 Dresden. T. (0351) 55588. - Orient / Eth - 051488
Künstlerpuppen, Rugestr. 11, 01069 Dresden. T. (0351) 47 01 72. 051489
Kunst der Zeit GmbH, Wilsdrufferstr 7, 01067 Dresden. T. (0351) 4952408. 051490
Kunst und Antiquitäten Am Obergraben, Obergraben 19, 01097 Dresden. T. (0351) 8014331. 051491
Kunst und Antiquitäten Linck, Bautzner Landstr 7, 01324 Dresden. T. (0351) 36616, Fax (0351) 36430. 051492
Lehmann, D., Altseidnitz 15a, 01277 Dresden. T. (0351) 2512320. 051493
Gebr. Lieber, Görlitzer Str 39, 01099 Dresden. T. (0351) 8045658, Fax 8044012. - Ant - 051494
Meyer, Franz, Kaitzer Str. 57, 01187 Dresden. T. (0351) 42729. 051495
Plakity, M., Königsbrücker Str 47, 01099 Dresden. T. (0351) 55078, Fax (0351) 55078. 051496
Radig, T., Veilchenweg 36, 01326 Dresden. T. (0351) 376542. 051497
Rausch, Heinz, Königsbrücker Str. 91, 01099 Dresden. T. (0351) 574986. - Ant / Paint / Furn / China - 051498
Richter, E., Dr., Dachsteinweg 27, 01279 Dresden. T. (0351) 2371008. 051499
Schmidt, H.C., Kamenzer Str 47, 01099 Dresden. T. (0351) 51496. 051500
Schwarzer, Rainer, Dr., Gustav-Adolf-Str. 8, 01219 Dresden. T. (0351) 4710757. - Ant - 051501
Zenker, G., Große Meißner Str 15, 01097 Dresden. T. (0351) 570522. 051502

Duderstadt (Niedersachsen)

Schwedhelm, G., Desingeröderstr., 37115 Duderstadt. T. (05527) 6150. 051503

Dülmen (Nordrhein-Westfalen)

Brock, Coesfelderstr. 103, 48249 Dülmen. T. (02594) 3774. - Furn - 051504
Westphal, H., Dammweg 27, 48249 Dülmen. T. (02594) 3831. 051505

Düren (Nordrhein-Westfalen)

Fornara, P.A., Kölnstr. 74, 52351 Düren. T. (02421) 159 07. - Ant / Silv - 051506
Stemick, Bernhard, Dorfstr. 32, 52353 Düren. T. (02421) 814 82. 051507
Vetter, Oberstr. 10-12, 52349 Düren. T. (02421) 14638, 10461, Fax (02421) 10616. - Paint / Graph / Sculp / Fra / Glass / Ico / Draw - 051508

Düsseldorf (Nordrhein-Westfalen)

Ackens, Carl, Oststr. 162, 40210 Düsseldorf. T. (0211) 36 43 43. - Paint / Tex - 051509
Antik am Bahnhof Bilk, Friedrichstr. 145, 40217 Düsseldorf. T. (0211) 34 27 01. - Ant - 051510
Antik-Markt, Bertastr. 50, 40625 Düsseldorf. T. (0211) 234789 (Altstadt). 051511
Antik-Salon, Worringer Str. 67 und Birkenstr. 40, 40211 Düsseldorf. T. (0211) 35 71 74, 67 44 75. 051512
Antik & Brocante, Niederrheinstr. 220, 40474 Düsseldorf. T. (0211) 43 28 92. 051513
Antiqua Juwelen, Rotthäuser Weg 1A, 40629 Düsseldorf. - Jew - 051514
Antiquitäten am Füstenplatz, Fürstenpl. 1, 40210 Düsseldorf. T. (0211) 37 21 50. - Ant / Furn / China / Dec / Lights / Glass / Mod - 051515
Artis-Galerie in Firma Heinzelmann, Herderstr. 16, 40237 Düsseldorf. T. (0211) 672047. - Tex - 051516
Artis-Galerie in Firma Heinzelmann, Herderstr. 16, 40237 Düsseldorf. T. (0211) 67 20 47. - Tex - 051517
Backes, C., Benderstr. 81, 40625 Düsseldorf. T. (0211) 295509. 051518
Bänder, K., Neubrückstr. 14, 40213 Düsseldorf. T. (0211) 326361. 051519
Baré, Sonja, Grünberger Weg 38, 40627 Düsseldorf. T. (0211) 275265. - Ant - 051520
Bastion Antik, Bastionstr. 23, 40213 Düsseldorf. T. (0211) 32 99 36. 051521
Baumüller, H., Kölner Str. 59, 40211 Düsseldorf. T. (0211) 369238. 051522
Bendgens, Lore, Bilker Str. 31, 40213 Düsseldorf. T. (0211) 132983, Fax (0211) 132986. - Paint / Furn - 051523
Bergemann, Gerrieuspl. 12, 40210 Düsseldorf. T. (0211) 28 39 09. 051524
Bock & A. von Polach, Düsseldorfer Str. 96, 40545 Düsseldorf. T. (0211) 55 43 48, 58 83 63. 051525
Boerner, C.G., Kasernenstr 13, 40213 Düsseldorf. T. (0211) 131805, Fax (0211) 132177. - Graph / Draw - 051526
Bolwerk, B., Berliner Allee 40, 40212 Düsseldorf. T. (0211) 320891. 051527
Borcke, Rüdiger & Gisela von, Blumenstr. 11-15, 40212 Düsseldorf. T. (0211) 32 61 91. 051528
Bosch, Mathias, Oberbilker Allee 101, 40227 Düsseldorf. T. (0211) 784441. - Paint / Furn - 051529
Brandsdörfer, Thomas, Quirinstr. 9, 40545 Düsseldorf. T. (0211) 554401. 051530
Bröhan, Torsten, Graf-Recke-Str 30, 40239 Düsseldorf. T. (0211) 678086, Fax (0211) 672012. 051531
Casati, Pier C., Bastionstr. 13, 40213 Düsseldorf. T. (0211) 326730. 051532
Citadellchen, Citadellstr. 27, 40213 Düsseldorf. T. (0211) 325253. - Ant / Paint - 051533
Cohnen, A., Lorettostr. 14, 40219 Düsseldorf. T. (0211) 307697. - Paint / Repr / Sculp / Fra / Rel - 051534
Conzen, F.G., Schanzenstr 54-56, 40549 Düsseldorf. T. (0211) 577010, Fax 5770141. - Ant / Graph / Furn / China / Fra - 051535
Conzen, F.G., Kö-center, Königsallee, 40212 Düsseldorf. T. (0211) 8668120, Fax 8668129. - Ant / Graph / Furn / China / Fra - 051536
Conzen, F.G., Bilker Str. 5, 40213 Düsseldorf. T. (0211) 8668113, Fax 8668129. - Ant / Graph / Furn / China / Fra - 051537
Conzen, F.G., Trinkaus-Galerie, Königsallee 21-23, 40212 Düsseldorf. T. (0211) 866810, Fax 8668129. - Ant / Graph / Furn / Graph / Repr / Fra - 051538
Daehne, Wilfried, Hermannstr. 22a, 40233 Düsseldorf. T. (0211) 665791. 051539
Deckert, Inge & Bernd, Suitbertusstr. 151, 40223 Düsseldorf. T. (0211) 33 45 45, Fax 33 39 45. - Ant / Instr - 051540
Döhrn, H., Benrodestr. 39, 40597 Düsseldorf. T. (0211) 718 54 96. 051541
Dröge, Rudolf, Brehmstr. 34, 40239 Düsseldorf. T. (0211) 62 21 51. - Tex - 051542

Dué, von, Behrenstr. 62, 40233 Düsseldorf.
T. (0211) 733 88 77. 051543
Dünnebacke, Gisela, Oberbilker Allee 89, 40227 Düssel-
dorf. T. (0211) 36 57 85. 051544
Dünnwald-Rutz, A., Schäferstr. 10, 40479 Düsseldorf.
T. (0211) 4912442. - Ico - 051545
Düsseldorfer Kunstsalon, Tonhallenstr. 16, 40211 Düs-
seldorf. T. (0211) 35 65 97. - Ant / Paint / Furn / China /
Tex - 051546
Egenolf, Herbert, Citadellstr 14, 40213 Düsseldorf.
T. (0211) 320550, Fax 131291. - Orient - 051547
Eichhorst, Günther J., Martin-Luther-Platz 32, 40212
Düsseldorf. T. (0211) 13 22 34. - Ant / Jew - 051548
Eicke, M. & B., Am Schulberg 10, 40625 Düsseldorf.
T. (0211) 36 55 56. 051549
Eisenberg, G., Ackerstr. 77, 40233 Düsseldorf.
T. (0211) 68 68 60. 051550
Esch, Heinz Josef, Schwanenmarkt 12, 40213 Düssel-
dorf. T. (0211) 32 82 80. 051551
Falkenberg, P., Langerstr. 38, 40233 Düsseldorf.
T. (0211) 7331939. 051552
Fischer-Zöller, M., Citadellstr. 25, 40213 Düsseldorf.
T. (0211) 327867, 431441. 051553
Flöck, K., Marienstr. 37, 40210 Düsseldorf.
T. (0211) 463677. 051554
Franz, H., Rosstr. 16, 40210 Düsseldorf.
T. (0211) 463677. 051555
Fritzsche, Karl, Wildenbruchstr. 38, 40545
Düsseldorf. 051556
Fuchs-Greven, Königsallee 38, 40212 Düsseldorf.
- Ant / China - 051557
Gahlen, Marianne van, Ulmenstr. 173, 40468 Düssel-
dorf. T. (0211) 418 09 65. 051558
Galerie am Hofgarten, Arnoldstr. 2, 40479 Düsseldorf.
T. (0211) 491 16 22. - Ant / Paint / Graph / Furn / Orient /
China / Sculp / Tex / Dec / Fra / Silv / Lights / Rel --
051559
Galerie am Stadtgeschichtlichen Museum, Citadellstr.
25, 40213 Düsseldorf. T. (0211) 327867. - Paint /
Furn / China / Silv - 051560
Galerie an der Börse, Klosterstr. 29, 40211 Düsseldorf.
T. (0211) 351575, 351295. - Paint / Tex - 051561
Galerie Arora, Eulerstr. 49, 40477 Düsseldorf.
T. (0211) 44 20 68. 051562
Galerie Ergi, Martin-Luther-Platz 32, 40212 Düsseldorf.
T. (0211) 32 59 65. - Paint / Tex - 051563
Galerie Orientteppiche, Wiga Schuch, Heinrich-Heine-Al-
lee 19, 40213 Düsseldorf. T. (0211) 13 16 71.
- Tex - 051564
Gierhards, E., Bilker Str. 19, 40213 Düsseldorf.
T. (0211) 320464, Fax (0211) 322546. - Ant / Paint /
Furn / China / Silv / Lights / Instr - 051565
Goebel, D., Wilhelm-Kreis-Str. 49, 40595 Düsseldorf.
T. (0211) 7009493. 051566
Guntermann, Lambertusstr. 6, 40213 Düsseldorf.
T. (0211) 32 56 37. - Fra - 051567
Hansen, G., Hauptstr. 10a, 40597 Düsseldorf.
T. (0211) 71 64 61. 051568
Heidkamp, Ludwig, Nordstr. 21, 40477 Düsseldorf.
T. (0211) 491 15 94. - Ant / Fra - 051569
Heintzen & Adams, Hohe Str. 12, 40213 Düsseldorf.
T. (0211) 32 75 52. 051570
Henkel, Tußmannstr. 21, 40477 Düsseldorf.
T. (0211) 48 00 91/92. - Paint / Furn / China /
Tex - 051571
Heubel, Lothar, Bastionstr. 27, 40213 Düsseldorf.
T. (0211) 13 41 03. - Orient - 051572
Heufs, Egon, Talstr. 108, 40217 Düsseldorf.
T. (0211) 34 22 22. - Paint / Tex - 051573
Hoch, Sina, Wallstr. 29, 40213 Düsseldorf.
T. (0211) 13 42 63. - Ant - 051574
Hörle, Hannelore, Mozartstr. 11, 40479 Düsseldorf.
T. (0211) 49 12 56. - Ant / Jew - 051575
Hofmann, Werner, Alt-Niederkassel 47, 40547 Düssel-
dorf. T. (0211) 57 09 24. 051576
Holzwürmchen, Erkrather Str. 286, 40233 Düsseldorf.
T. (0211) 48 29 89. 051577
Huthmann, D.M., Bilker Str. 8, 40213 Düsseldorf.
T. (0211) 13 42 63. 051578
Jockels, Armin, Kaiserswerther Str. 166, 40474
Düsseldorf. 051579
Juric-Beckmann, Simone, Herderstr. 62, 40237 Düssel-
dorf. T. (0211) 66 33 54. - Ant - 051580
Kampf, A., Fürstenwall 216, 40215 Düsseldorf. 051581

Keats, Flachskampstr. 53, 40627 Düsseldorf.
T. (0211) 20 18 36. 051582
Kempkens, S., Am Mönchgraben 6, 40597 Düsseldorf.
T. (0211) 71 40 50. 051583
Kerckerinck zur Borg, Josef Baron, Jägerhofstr. 29,
40479 Düsseldorf. 051584
Knoll, Roßstr. 154, 40476 Düsseldorf.
I. (0211) 45 21 92. 051585
Körs, W., Immermannstr. 2, 40210 Düsseldorf.
T. (0211) 35 15 75. 051586
Kok, G., Hermannstr. 22a, 40233 Düsseldorf.
T. (0211) 66 78 04. 051587
Kraatz, P., Oberkasseler Str. 23, 40545 Düsseldorf.
T. (0211) 57 19 50. 051588
Krauth, Th., Duisburger Str. 19, 40477 Düsseldorf.
T. (0211) 4982961/2, Fax (0211) 4981438. 051589
Kreitlow, R., Am Mühlenturm 6, 40489 Düsseldorf.
T. (0211) 40 77 46. 051590
Kunst-Passage, Worringer Str. 60, 40211 Düsseldorf.
T. (0211) 36 24 73. 051591
Kunze, Lilli E., Kreuzbergstr. 36, 40489 Düsseldorf.
T. (0211) 40 07 82. 051592
Lamers, D., Höherweg 299, 40231 Düsseldorf.
T. (0211) 733 54 08. 051593
Lingenauber, Eckard, Schwerinstr. 38, 40477 Düssel-
dorf. T. (0211) 494202, Fax (0211) 494202. 051594
Lorenz, H.-D., Dahlienweg 1, 40468 Düsseldorf.
T. (0211) 41 05 55. 051595
Maessen, A., & Söhne, Blumenstr. 24, 40212 Düssel-
dorf. T. (0211) 35 34 56. - Tex - 051596
Maga, K., Schanzenstr. 20, 40549 Düsseldorf.
T. (0211) 572120, Fax (0211) 572125. - Paint - 051597
Martinek, Friedrichstr. 145, 40217 Düsseldorf.
T. (0211) 34 27 01. 051598
Mayer, Margit, Malkastenstr. 9, 40211 Düsseldorf.
T. (0211) 32 82 46. - Ant / Furn / Tex / Silv - 051599
Meier-Hahn, Eiskellerberg 1-3, 40213 Düsseldorf.
T. (0211) 323644, 555187, Fax (0211) 134468. 051600
Merkelbach, A. & A.-E. Wuttke, Schillerstr. 7, 40237
Düsseldorf. T. (0211) 68 48 00. 051601
Meschkat, Helga, Tannenstr. 8, 40476 Düsseldorf.
T. (0211) 65 53 85. - Tin - 051602
Model Pool, Rathausufer 23, 40213 Düsseldorf.
T. (0211) 132171, Fax (0211) 132176. 051603
Möbelschmiede, Eintrachtstr. 8, 40227 Düsseldorf.
T. (0211) 72 56 89. - Furn - 051604
Müser, Monika, Schwanenmarkt 12-13, 40213 Düssel-
dorf. T. (0211) 32 73 46. - Ant / Furn - 051605
Nolte, J., Lilienstr. 13, 40474 Düsseldorf.
T. (0211) 432232. 051606
Nothenhof, Bergische Landstr. 509, 40629 Düsseldorf.
T. (0211) 28 97 38. 051607
Nussbaum, Alt-Niederkassel 32, 40547 Düsseldorf.
T. (0211) 57 07 83. 051608
Oberheid, M., Niederrheinstr. 133, 40474 Düsseldorf.
T. (0211) 454 23 80. 051609
Ortenberg, Königsallee 36, 40212 Düsseldorf.
T. (0211) 32 00 93/94. - Jew - 051610
Paashaus, Peter, Uhlandstr. 34, 40237 Düsseldorf.
T. (0211) 682568, 666976. - Ant / Paint / Furn / Silv /
Instr / Glass - 051611
Päpke & Janowitz, Hohe Str. 27, 40213 Düsseldorf.
T. (0211) 131680, Fax (0211) 326948. 051612
Peiffer, Bismarckstr. 61, 40210 Düsseldorf.
T. (0211) 36 52 61. - Paint / Tex - 051613
Peiffer, Wilhelm, Ackerstr. 201, 40235
Düsseldorf. 051614
Peter's Weichholzmöbel, Niederrheinstr. 152, 40474
Düsseldorf. T. (0211) 45 26 72. - Furn - 051615
Plinke, Karin, Tersteegenstr. 63, 40474 Düsseldorf.
- Ant - 051616
Plücker, J., Von-Gahlen-Str. 1, 40625 Düsseldorf.
T. (0211) 297352. 051617
Podhofer, H.-M., Moltkestr. 88, 40479 Düsseldorf.
T. (0211) 48 29 89. 051618
Podszus, E., Naegelestr. 13, 40225 Düsseldorf.
T. (0211) 342237. 051619
Popescu, Victor, Adersstr. 45, 40215 Düsseldorf.
T. (0211) 37 76 60. - Paint / Tex - 051620
Porzellan-Klinik, Nordstr. 26, 40477 Düsseldorf.
T. (0211) 48 54 14. 051621
Puhl, A., Bilker Allee 171 A, 40217 Düsseldorf.
T. (0211) 33 32 24. 051622

Raumann, M., Königsallee 30, 40212 Düsseldorf.
T. (0211) 32 71 66. 051623
Reitzenstein, Christoph von, Ludenberger Str. 30, 40629
Düsseldorf. T. (0211) 66 91 77. - Ant / Furn - 051624
Reusche, H., Kronprinzenstr. 31, 40217 Düsseldorf.
T. (0211) 30 69 51. 051625
Rheinische Münzfreunde, Columbusstr. 36, 40549 Düs-
seldorf. T. (0211) 55 54 34. - Num - 051626
Rincklake van Endert, Schadowpl. 3-5, 40210 Düssel-
dorf. T. (0211) 13 90 60. - Ant / Paint / Graph /
Furn - 051627
Ringel, M., Hoffeldstr. 31, 40235 Düsseldorf.
T. (0211) 67 15 11. 051628
Rive, H., Bastionstr. 10, 40213 Düsseldorf.
T. (0211) 32 46 17. - Ant - 051629
Rix, O., Kronenstr. 66, 40217 Düsseldorf.
T. (0211) 37 38 34. 051630
Ropte, Axel, Ackerstr. 144, 40233 Düsseldorf.
T. (0211) 679 89 43. - Furn - 051631
Rutz, Anita, Schäferstr. 10, 40479 Düsseldorf.
T. (0211) 44 44 42. - Ico - 051632
Rutz, Maria, Königsallee 30, 40212 Düsseldorf.
T. (0211) 133270. - Ant / China / Jew / Silv /
Ico - 051633
Sarx, Willi, Wilhelm-Raabe-Str. 28, 40470 Düsseldorf.
T. (0211) 63 69 48. 051634
Scheelen, Heinz, Akazienstr. 37, 40627 Düsseldorf.
T. (0211) 20 19 29. - Paint / Fra - 051635
Schmäling, Margret, Bilker Str. 31, 40213 Düsseldorf.
T. (0211) 13 25 36. - Mod - 051636
Schmidt, B., Rethelstr 139, 40237 Düsseldorf.
T. (0211) 675967. - Paint / Furn / Silv - 051637
Schmidt, E., Birkenstr. 40 und Worringer Str. 67, 40233
Düsseldorf. T. (0211) 674475, 357174. 051638
Schneider, Friedrich, Louise-Dumont-Str. 1-3, 40211
Düsseldorf. T. (0211) 35 66 39. - Paint / Graph / Repr /
Fra - 051639
Schönauer, Birkenstr. 37, 40233 Düsseldorf.
T. (0211) 66 12 20. 051640
Schröder, H., Im Huferfeld 1, 40468 Düsseldorf.
T. (0211) 42 38 49. 051641
Schürenberg, A., Kasernenstr. 55, 40213 Düsseldorf.
T. (0211) 32 55 49. - Mod - 051642
Schulgen, A.W., Alte Landstr. 77, 40489 Düsseldorf.
T. (0211) 40 12 06. - Graph / Repr / Fra - 051643
Schulte, Eva, Königsallee 56, 40212 Düsseldorf.
T. (0211) 32 82 46. 051644
Schultze, N., Hohenzollernstr. 36, 40211 Düsseldorf.
T. (0211) 35 43 38. 051645
Schwarzer, Klaus, Hüttenstr. 90, 40215 Düsseldorf.
T. (0211) 323658, 374553. 051646
Seidel, Marie-Luise, Rochusstr. 28b, 40479 Düsseldorf.
T. (0211) 46 02 62. 051647
Sieger, P. & M. Rausch, Kaiser-Friedrich-Str. 2a, 40597
Düsseldorf. T. (0211) 71 88 83. 051648
Siemons, Hubert, Mörikestr. 45, 40474 Düsseldorf.
- Ant - 051649
Silber-Börse, Bastionstr. 8, 40213 Düsseldorf.
T. (0211) 32 66 76. - Silv - 051650
Simonis, Poststr. 3, 40213 Düsseldorf. T. (0211) 324873,
Fax (0211) 134792. - Eth - 051651
Soraya, Berliner Allee 22, 40212 Düsseldorf.
T. (0211) 32 77 10. 051652
Staacks, H., Ackerstr. 125, 40233 Düsseldorf.
T. (0211) 66 02 95. 051653
Stecher, W., Graf-Engelbert-Str. 11, 40489 Düsseldorf.
T. (0211) 74 14 82. 051654
Steinbüchel, Hans, Sternstr. 14, 40479 Düsseldorf.
T. (0211) 44 34 22. - Ant / Paint / Tex - 051655
Steinkaul, W., Mindener Str. 13, 40227
Düsseldorf. 051656
Stockermann & Podhofer, Arnoldstr. 2, 40479 Düssel-
dorf. T. (0211) 491 16 22. 051657
Stöhr, B., Steffenstr. 7, 40545 Düsseldorf.
T. (0211) 57 93 22. 051658
Stuckert, Anton, Graf-Adolf-Str. 43, 40210 Düsseldorf.
T. (0211) 38 29 77. - Num - 051659
Stuckert, H., Bismarckstr. 45, 40210 Düsseldorf.
T. (0211) 13 15 54. - Num - 051660
Stuckert, H., Schneider-Wibbel-Gasse 8, 40213 Düssel-
dorf. T. (0211) 32 62 80. - Num - 051661
Studio am Burgplatz, Burgpl. 3, 40210 Düsseldorf.
T. (0211) 13 31 63. - Ant / Furn / Lights - 051662

Stumm, Gert, Lindenstr. 184, 40233 Düsseldorf.
T. (0211) 66 26 23. - Num -   051663
Suchecki, W., Bilker Str. 1, 40213 Düsseldorf.
T. (0211) 327191, Fax (0211) 327191. - Ant /
China -   051664
Taubert, T., Schirmerstr. 4, 40211 Düsseldorf.
T. (0211) 46 28 49.   051665
Tedden, Bilker Str. 6, 40213 Düsseldorf.
T. (0211) 13 35 28. - Ant / Paint -   051666
Tondorf, Paul, Königstr. 5, 40212 Düsseldorf.
T. (0211) 32 96 66.   051667
Ullrich, Angelika, Hohe Str. 4, 40213 Düsseldorf.
T. (0211) 32 81 18. - Ant / Jew / Lights -   051668
Valenta, Hans, Prof., Kaiser-Wilhelm-Ring 34, 40545
Düsseldorf. T. (0211) 57 04 32. - Paint -   051669
Vieler & Bänder, Neubrückstr. 6+14, 40213 Düsseldorf.
T. (0211) 32 63 61.   051670
Vierth, Hans-Heinrich, Kaiserstr 28, 40479 Düsseldorf.
T. (0211) 4912414. - Ant / Furn / China / Instr - 051671
Vierzig, Gabriele, Königsallee 21-23, 40212 Düsseldorf.
T. (0211) 32 49 58. - Ant / Furn / Jew / Fra / Silv /
Lights -   051672
Vinzentz-Kunstberatung, Kaiser-Wilhelm-Ring 19, 40545
Düsseldorf. T. (0211) 57 60 71, Fax (0211) 58 96 58.
- Dec -   051673
Volmer, Königsallee 44, 40212 Düsseldorf.
T. (0211) 32 72 75.   051674
Weber, H.-J., Hohenzollernstr. 23-25, 40211 Düsseldorf.
T. (0211) 35 75 81. - Num -   051675
Wehrens, Horst, Oststr. 13, 40211 Düsseldorf.
T. (0211) 36 34 38. - Paint / Graph -   051676
Wester, H., Aderstr. 30, 40210 Düsseldorf.
T. (0211) 37 29 29.   051677
Wettstein, D., Zaberner Str. 26, 40468 Düsseldorf.
T. (0211) 42 80 67.   051678
Wieczorek, P.-K., Bahnstr. 48, 40210 Düsseldorf.
T. (0211) 32 43 66.   051679
Wiedemann, F., Uhlandstr. 21, 40237 Düsseldorf.
T. (0211) 68 10 06.   051680
Winter, W. A., Kölner Landstr. 298, 40589 Düsseldorf.
T. (0211) 76 32 00.   051681
Wolf, Herbert J., & Verdi, Königsallee 27, 40212 Düssel-
dorf. T. (0211) 802 69. - Ant / Mod -   051682
Zimmermann, A., Haroldstr. 28, 40213 Düsseldorf.
T. (0211) 32 56 92.   051683
Zuny-Gallery, Königsallee 30, 40212 Düsseldorf.
T. (0211) 32 71 66.   051684

Duisburg (Nordrhein-Westfalen)
Ackersgott, A., Grafschafter Str. 25, 47199 Duisburg.
T. (0203) 80 134.   051685
Brauer, M., Heerstr. 2, 47053 Duisburg.
T. (0203) 66 39 77.   051686
Brandes, Düsseldorfer Landstr 305, 47259 Duisburg.
T. (0203) 785843.   051687
Eberlein, D., Schmale Gasse 15, 47051 Duisburg.
T. (0203) 29844.   051688
Gärtner, M., Untermauerstr. 13, 47051 Duisburg.
T. (0203) 266 67. - Ant / Paint / Furn / Lights / Glass /
Mod -   051689
Genner, August, & Co., Sonnenwall 39, 47051 Duisburg.
T. (0203) 257 77.   051690
Haack, J., Düsseldorfer Str. 520, 47055 Duisburg.
T. (0203) 77 61 72.   051691
Kaiser, Manfred, Mülheimer Str. 107-109, 47058 Duis-
burg. T. (0203) 333210, 333636. - Ant -   051692
Kley, E., Bahnhofstr. 157, 47137 Duisburg.
T. (0203) 43 67 53.   051693
Lemaic, N., Lutherstr. 36, 47058 Duisburg.
T. (0203) 35 71 79.   051694
Litzner, P., Bregenzer Str. 43, 47249 Duisburg.
T. (0203) 70 62 64.   051695
Mercatorgalerie, Mercatorstr. 90, 47051 Duisburg.
T. (0203) 264 53. - Ant / Paint -   051696
Nühlen, H., Mühlenstr. 21d, 47137 Duisburg.
T. (0203) 470 27.   051697
Orober, Bismarckpl. 3, 47051 Duisburg. T. (0203) 7165/
67. - Paint / Graph / Repr / Sculp / Draw -   051698
Rauch, N., Kreuzstr. 10, 47198 Duisburg.
T. (0203) 444 97.   051699
Reitzenstein, C. von, Düsseldorfer Landstr. 303, 47259
Duisburg. T. (0203) 78 08 52.   051700

Rempe, Weseler Str. 103a, 47169 Duisburg.
T. (0203) 40 34 34. - Num / Jew / Silv -   051701
Rey, B., Raiffeisenstr. 147, 47259 Duisburg.
T. (0203) 78 68 69.   051702
Scheib, G. & H., Angermunder Str. 198, 47269 Duisburg.
T. (0203) 76 69 76. - Ant / Dec -   051703
Schuischel, H., Mercatorstr. 90, 47051 Duisburg.
T. (0203) 264 53.   051704
Schulte-Bahrenberg, Ralf, Erftstr. 9, 47051 Duisburg.
T. (0203) 33 65 63.   051705
Schwertner, K., Düsseldorfer Landstr. 314, 47259 Duis-
burg. T. (0203) 78 94 58.   051706
Sprünken, A., Dellpl. 1, 47051 Duisburg.
T. (0203) 230 84.   051707
Weyer, D., Kaiser-Wilhelm-Str. 297, 47169 Duisburg.
T. (0203) 40 17 41.   051708

Durmersheim (Baden-Württemberg)
Dollenbacher, E. & S., Benzstr. 4, 76448 Durmersheim.
T. (07245) 7779.   051709

Eberbach (Baden-Württemberg)
Polygraphicum, Backgasse 1, 69412 Eberbach.
T. (06271) 1387. - Paint / Graph / Fra / Draw -   051710

Ebergötzen (Niedersachsen)
Conrad, U., Holzerode, 37136 Ebergötzen.
T. (05507) 1418.   051711

Ebern (Bayern)
Pawlas, Karl R., Am Kirschrangen 9, 96106 Ebern.
T. (09531) 15 50. - Num -   051712

Ebersbach-Musbach (Baden-Württem-
berg)
Zern, Hans, Am Rathaus, 88371 Ebersbach-Musbach.
T. (07584) 18 39. - Paint / Graph -   051713

Ebersberg (Bayern)
Fischer-Böhler, Hohenlindener Str 4-6, 85560 Ebers-
berg. T. (08092) 22534, 22274. - Furn / China /
Silv -   051714
Veit, Erhard, Wasserburger Str 8, 85560 Ebersberg.
T. (08092) 8477. - Ant -   051715

Ebersburg (Hessen)
Nass, F.-D., Goerg-August-Zinn-Str. 15, 36157 Eber-
sburg. T. (06656) 5106, 5585. - Num -   051716

Eckernförde (Schleswig-Holstein)
Peters, St. Nicolai-Str. 7, 24340 Eckernförde.
T. (04351) 2891.   051717

Edemissen (Niedersachsen)
Böddecker & Wagner, Wiesengrund 9, 31234 Edemis-
sen. T. (05176) 10 13. - Mil -   051718

Edesheim (Rheinland-Pfalz)
Hintz, H.-D., Staatsstr. 32, 67483 Edesheim.
T. (06323) 3823.   051719

Edling (Bayern)
Braune, Irmgard, Hart 2, 83533 Edling. - Ant -   051720
Braune, J., Schloss Hart, 83533 Edling.   051721

Eggenfelden (Bayern)
Binder, W., Öttingerstr. 2, 84307 Eggenfelden.
T. (08721) 39 96.   051722
Hiermeier, Centa, Ludwig-Thoma-Str. 39, 84307 Eggen-
felden. T. (08721) 17 71. - Ant -   051723

Eggstätt (Bayern)
Diener von Schönberg-Pfaffroda, Hubertus & Helene,
Kirchpl. 2, 83125 Eggstätt. T. (08056) 500. - Ant /
Furn -   051724

Eglfing (Bayern)
Mack, Renate, Hauptstr. 12, 82436 Eglfing.
T. (08847) 315, Fax (08847) 254. - Ant / Paint / Furn /
Sculp -   051725

Egling (Bayern)
Bleymaier, E. A., Schallkofen, 82544 Egling.
T. (08176) 7403. - Ant / Paint / Graph / China / Fra /
Glass / Ico -   051726
Zum Sande, Stefan, Dettenhausen 10 A, 82544 Egling.
T. (08176) 313.   051727

Egloffstein (Bayern)
Preis, Norbert, Markgrafenstr. 100, 91349 Egloffstein.
T. (09197) 1266. - Ant / Paint / Graph / Furn /
Glass -   051728

Ehrenkirchen (Baden-Württemberg)
Fehrenbach, K., Belzgasse 17, 79238 Ehrenkirchen.
T. (07633) 146 37.   051729

Eichstetten (Baden-Württemberg)
Wolf, Nimburgerstr. 13, 79356 Eichstetten.   051730

Einbeck (Niedersachsen)
Leske, W., Maschenstr. 9, 37574 Einbeck.
T. (05561) 738 59. - Paint / Graph / Repr / Sculp / Jew /
Fra / Glass -   051731
Omas Trödelladen, Möncheplatz 8, 37574 Einbeck.
T. (05561) 14 68.   051732

Eitorf (Nordrhein-Westfalen)
Pschribülla, Claus, Huckenbröl 12, 53783 Eitorf. 051733

Ellwangen (Baden-Württemberg)
Eckart, Karl-Heinz, Höhenweg 2, 73479 Ellwangen.
T. (07961) 90450, Fax 904545. - Ant / Paint / Graph /
Furn / China / Jew / Silv / Glass -   051734
Maier, A., Spitalstr 11, 73479 Ellwangen.   051735
Raible, Aloys, Marktplatz 12, 73479 Ellwangen.
T. (07961) 2281.   051736
Schindler, R., Marienstr 8, 73479 Ellwangen.
T. (07961) 4755. - Num -   051737

Elmshorn (Schleswig-Holstein)
Schaefer, R., Ramskamp 60, 25337 Elmshorn.
T. (04121) 736 65.   051738
Weise, U., Reichenstr. 23, 25336 Elmshorn.
T. (04121) 6911.   051739

Eltville (Hessen)
Heimes, I., Kiedricher Str 41, 65343 Eltville.
T. (06123) 5153.   051740
Ruppert, E., Hauptstr 23+42, 65343 Eltville.
T. (06123) 3825.   051741
Weißenrieder, W., Neumühle, 65343 Eltville.
T. (06123) 2478.   051742

Elze (Niedersachsen)
Antik-Hof, Calenberger Str 3, 31008 Elze.
T. (05124) 8333. - Ant -   051743
Arendt, B., Gudinger Gasse 6, 31008 Elze.
T. (05124) 1637.   051744

Emden (Niedersachsen)
Lüttje, Koophus, Faldernstr. 31, 26725 Emden.
T. (04921) 23766.   051745
Mietz, W., Mühlenstr. 39, 26725 Emden.
T. (04921) 25446, Fax (04921) 26725. - Cur -   051746

Emmelshausen (Rheinland-Pfalz)
Francke, Marlis, Rhein-Mosel-Str. 50, 56281 Emmels-
hausen. T. (06747) 6569, 8306. - Paint -   051747

Emmendingen (Baden-Württemberg)
Senftleben-Gudrich, M., Hochburgerstr. 25, 79312 Em-
mendingen. T. (07641) 53111.   051748

Emmerich (Nordrhein-Westfalen)
Convent, Eltenerstr. 1, 46446 Emmerich.
T. (02822) 70453.   051749

Emsdetten (Nordrhein-Westfalen)
Lohmann, Alfons, Austum 3, 48282 Emsdetten.
T. (02572) 7707.   051750

Emstek (Niedersachsen)
Rüwe-Wulfers, Clemens-August-Str. 6, 49685 Emstek.
T. (04473) 370. - Ant / Furn / China / Silv -   051751

Endorf (Bayern)
Ziegler, Eva, Hemhof 16, 83093 Endorf. T. (08053) 2270.
- Ant / Tex -   051752

Engelskirchen (Nordrhein-Westfalen)
Donner, E., Hauptstr. 12, 51766 Engelskirchen.
T. (02263) 64 20.   051753
Odendahl & Kretschmer, Im Auel 38, 51766 Engelskir-
chen. T. (02263) 21 62, Fax 801024. - Furn -   051754

Schenk, M. W., Am Bleiberg 2, 51766 Engelskirchen.
T. (02263) 7774, 5096. *051755*

Ennepetal (Nordrhein-Westfalen)
Azteca, Milsperstr. 165, 58256 Ennepetal.
T. (02333) 4011. *051756*
Beste, Hans, Buchenstr. 42, 58256 Ennepetal.
T. (02333) 705 43. - Num - *051757*
Seiermann, Azteca, Loherstr. 8, 58256
Ennepetal. *051758*

Ennigerloh (Nordrhein-Westfalen)
Niewöhner, Eta, Am Kreuzkämpken 16, 59320
Ennigerloh. *051759*

Epfenbach (Baden-Württemberg)
Kettering, Rolf, Bethelweg 6, 74925 Epfenbach.
T. (07263) 3436. *051760*

Eppelborn (Saarland)
Recktenwald, L., Erlenweg 1, 66571 Eppelborn.
T. (06827) 82219, Fax (06827) 84497. - Ant - *051761*

Eppingen (Baden-Württemberg)
Kreischer, A. & F., Rohrbacherstr. 9, 75031 Eppingen.
T. (07262) 072 60/4 74. - Furn - *051762*

Eppstein (Hessen)
Vandeberg, M.-T., Zum Kohlwaldfeld 9a, 65817 Eppstein. T. (06198) 7352. *051763*

Erbach (Hessen)
Glenz, Rainer, Jahnstr. 10, 64711 Erbach.
T. (06062) 4744. - Ant / Furn / Glass - *051764*
Kolletzky, Friedrich, Werner-von-Siemens-Str. 14, 64711 Erbach. T. (06062) 3061, 1808,
Fax (06062) 61454. - Sculp / Rel - *051765*

Erfde (Schleswig-Holstein)
Beier, R. & Mückenheim, Landstr. 18, 24803 Erfde.
T. (04333) 324. *051766*

Erftstadt (Nordrhein-Westfalen)
Bach, M., Bonnerstr. 9-11, 50374 Erftstadt.
T. (02235) 75103, 77726. - Num - *051767*
Bungarten, Günther, Kerpener Str. 1, 50374 Erftstadt.
- Ant - *051768*
Erftstädter Münzkabinett, Bonner Str. 9-11, 50374 Erftstadt. T. (022 35) 2916, 75103. - Num - *051769*

Erfurt (Thüringen)
Antiquitäten-Galerie Krämerbrücke, Krämerbrücke 6, 99084 Erfurt. T. (0361) 26372. - Ant / Paint / Graph / Furn / China / Repr / Sculp / Tex / Jew / Silv / Glass / Mod- *051770*
Pappeler, T., Krämerbrücke 8, 99084 Erfurt.
T. (0361) 6422873. - Num / Mil - *051771*

Erkelenz (Nordrhein-Westfalen)
Staab, I., Lauerstr. 47, 41812 Erkelenz.
T. (02431) 68 98. *051772*
Toepfer, Lothar H.-J., Gormannsstr. 4, 41812 Erkelenz.
T. (02431) 3138. *051773*

Erkner (Brandenburg)
Kroll, I., Holzfällerstr. 11, Woltersdorf, 15537 Erkner.
T. (03362) 5462. *051774*

Erkrath (Nordrhein-Westfalen)
Rath, K.H., Fasanenstr. 21, 40699 Erkrath.
T. (0211) 24 32 19. *051775*
Reif, L., Neanderstr. 71, 40699 Erkrath.
T. (0211) 24 44 08. *051776*

Erlangen (Bayern)
Beck, H., Schiffstr. 4, 91054 Erlangen.
T. (09131) 23505. *051777*
Csonth, Istvan, Paulistr. 4, 91054 Erlangen.
T. (09131) 211 14. - Ant / Paint / Furn / China / Silv / Glass / Ico - *051778*
Dürr, C., Werner-von-Siemens-Str 13, 91052 Erlangen.
T. (09131) 25353. *051779*
Dürr, C., Luitpoldstr 5, 91054 Erlangen.
T. (09131) 25733. *051780*
Gradl & Hinterland, Bohlenplatz 1, 91054 Erlangen.
T. (09131) 20 92 92. - Num - *051781*

Hahn, G., Pfarrstr. 18, 91054 Erlangen.
T. (09131) 20 70 61. *051782*
Kippert, B., Obere Karlstr. 7, 91054 Erlangen.
T. (09131) 274 03. *051783*
Pilz, Bernhard, Schallershofer Str. 17, 91056 Erlangen.
T. (09131) 411 25. *051784*
Prahse, G., Hauptstr. 114, 91054 Erlangen.
T. (09131) 20 87 40. *051785*
Scheuermann, Ludwig, Walburgastr. 3, 91056 Erlangen.
T. (09131) 431 50. *051786*
Scholl, Carl, Hauptstr. 13, 91054 Erlangen.
T. (09131) 219 28. - China / Repr / Jew / Fra / Glass - *051787*
Schröter, Barbara, Heuwaagstr., 91054 Erlangen.
T. (09131) 27740. *051788*
Sitzmann, Lannersberg 7, 91058 Erlangen.
T. (09131) 600 11/12. *051789*
Walter, Gerhard, Goethestr. 17, 91054 Erlangen.
T. (09131) 275 73. *051790*
Wannemacher, H., Franzosenweg 2, 91058 Erlangen.
T. (09131) 60 34 43. - Furn - *051791*

Erlensee (Hessen)
Pagel, Valerie, Raiffeisenstr. 25, 63526 Erlensee.
T. (06183) 46 54. - Ant - *051792*

Erwitte (Nordrhein-Westfalen)
Köhler, J., Merklinghauserstr. 146, 59597 Erwitte.
T. (02943) 24 56. *051793*

Eschborn (Hessen)
Kunst & Antik, Rödelheimer Str 44, 65760 Eschborn.
T. (06196) 45245. - Ant / Graph / China / Fra / Silv / Glass - *051794*

Eschenlohe (Bayern)
Hebeisen, Peter, Loisachstr. 35, 82438 Eschenlohe.
- Ant / Paint / Furn / China / Sculp - *051795*

Eschershausen (Niedersachsen)
Die Galerie, Wickensen 25a, 37632 Eschershausen.
T. (05534) 2062, Fax (05534) 3898. - Paint / Graph / Fra / Ico - *051796*

Eschweiler (Nordrhein-Westfalen)
Conzen, A.M., Grabenstr 13, 52249 Eschweiler.
T. (02403) 33936. *051797*
Jantzen, Hanni, Dreiers Gärten 3, 52249 Eschweiler.
T. (02403) 21014. - Ant - *051798*
Kenkmann, W., Grabenstr 13, 52249
Eschweiler. *051799*
Neffgen, Peter, Grabenstr 79, 52249 Eschweiler. *051800*

Esens (Niedersachsen)
Textil-Werkstätte, Westerstr. 13, 26427 Esens. *051801*

Espelkamp (Nordrhein-Westfalen)
Schiermeier, Udo, Grüner Weg 14, 32339 Espelkamp.
T. (05772) 8772. *051802*
Thiel, Otto, Wacholderweg 8, 32339 Espelkamp. *051803*

Espenau (Hessen)
Möller, Heideweg 2, 34314 Espenau. T. (056 73) 21 79.
- Num - *051804*

Essen (Nordrhein-Westfalen)
Angelbeck, Günter, Ostpreußenstr. 15, 45259 Essen.
T. (0201) 46 01 65, 46 51 49. *051805*
Becker, Anna-Greta, Seibertzstr. 17, 45144 Essen.
T. (0201) 74 81 51. *051806*
Beltz, Tina, Markuspfad 3, 45133 Essen.
T. (0201) 41 14 18, Fax (0201) 42 30 53. - Ant / Paint / Furn / China / Jew / Silv / Lights / Instr - *051807*
Bock, H., Im Löwental 48, 45239 Essen.
T. (0201) 49 10 10. *051808*
Borgwardt, Almut, Rüttenscheider Str. 288, 45131 Essen. T. (0201) 42 36 96. *051809*
Busch, U., Am Langensiepen 24, 45259 Essen.
T. (0201) 46 55 46. *051810*
Coenen, Heide, Rüttenscheider Str. 218, 45131 Essen.
T. (0201) 42 41 41. - Jew / Silv / Glass / Furn / Instr - *051811*
Deres, U., Kahrstr. 5, 45128 Essen. T. (0201) 77 35 91.
- Furn - *051812*

Döring, J., Girardetstr. 46, 45131 Essen.
T. (0201) 77 56 54. *051813*
Freienstein, Am Gerichtshaus 97, 45257 Essen.
T. (0201) 48 11 53. - Furn / Jew - *051814*
Friedrich, E., Alfredstr. 340, 45133 Essen.
T. (0201) 42 34 61. *051815*
Glass, H., Hans-Luther-Allee 21, 45131 Essen.
T. (0201) 782810. - Ant / Furn / Tex - *051816*
Die Gravüre, Rüttenscheider Str 56, 45130 Essen.
T. (0201) 793182, Fax (0201) 794949. *051817*
Grunewald, P., Gemarkenstr. 130, 45147 Essen.
T. (0201) 70 68 28. *051818*
Hermann, W., Heckstr. 3, 45239 Essen.
T. (0201) 49 63 87. *051819*
Herz, W., Veronikastr 69, 45131 Essen.
T. (0201) 79 26 85, Fax 792685. - Ant - *051820*
Höller, Hannelore, Akazienallee 12, 45127 Essen.
T. (0201) 22 66 81. - Ant / Paint / Fra / Ico / Mul - *051821*
Hörr, E., Ahornstr. 5, 45134 Essen.
T. (0201) 47 05 52. *051822*
Holberndt, Günter, Alfredstr. 6, 45130 Essen.
T. (0201) 78 29 91, 78 17 04. - Ant - *051823*
Hümmling, L., Rüttenscheider Str. 164a, 45131 Essen.
T. (0201) 42 45 69. *051824*
Im Himmel, Grafenstr. 49, 45239 Essen.
T. (0201) 49 11 38. - Ant - *051825*
Klaus, Helmut, Hans-Horl-Str. 7, 45357 Essen.
T. (0201) 66 59 11. - Ant / Num / Mil - *051826*
Knappe, H. Ch., Kastanienallee 90, 45127 Essen.
T. (0201) 23 99 65. - Num - *051827*
Kramm, Huyssenallee 58, 45128 Essen.
T. (0201) 23 37 77. - Tex - *051828*
Krüper, A., Kennedyplatz 5, 45127 Essen.
T. (0201) 230490, Fax (0201) 235949. *051829*
Krüper, J., Moltkepl. 5, 45138 Essen.
T. (0201) 263742. *051830*
Kullik-Collande, E.-W., Kopstadtplatz 12, 45127 Essen.
T. (0201) 22 43 67. *051831*
Kunst, R., Bochumer Str. 216, 45276 Essen.
T. (0201) 53 59 06. *051832*
Kunzi, Edgar, Eduard-Lucas-Str. 25, 45131 Essen.
T. (0201) 41 06 16. - Paint / Graph / Sculp / Fra - *051833*
L & B Antiquitäten, Klarastr. 44, 45130 Essen.
T. (0201) 79 84 39. *051834*
L & B Antiquitäten, Elfriedenstr. 8, 45130 Essen.
T. (0201) 79 03 79. *051835*
Lackmann, S., Rüttenscheider Str. 118, 45131 Essen.
T. (0201) 78 28 22. *051836*
Lindner, Ramon, Rüttenscheider Str. 242, 45131 Essen.
T. (0201) 42 16 78. *051837*
Lücker, F., Laurastr. 10, 45289 Essen.
T. (0201) 57 83 54. *051838*
Menke, A., Ruhrtalstr. 435, 45219 Essen.
T. (0201) 3486. *051839*
Nettesheim, Karlheinz, Kupferdreher Str. 350, 45257 Essen. T. (0201) 48 20 12. - Ant / Furn - *051840*
Nikolic, Z., Werneraue 1, 45279 Essen.
T. (0201) 53 25 98. *051841*
Oepen, K. von, Rüttenscheider Str. 200, 45131 Essen.
T. (0201) 41 15 59. *051842*
Offermann, G., Sabinastr. 1, 45136 Essen.
T. (0201) 25 38 35. *051843*
Pendule-Antiquitäten, Gemarkenstr. 130, 45147 Essen.
T. (0201) 70 68 28. *051844*
Roth, M., Wildbannstr. 7a, 45329 Essen.
T. (0201) 344748, 341311, 368413. *051845*
Rumpelstilzchen, Klarastr. 45, 45130 Essen.
T. (0201) 77 82 09. *051846*
Ruttloff, R., Stoppenberger Platz 1, 45141 Essen.
T. (0201) 29 38 24. *051847*
Schenk-Behrens, Karla W., Moltkepl. 9, 45127 Essen.
T. (0201) 26 23 90. - Num - *051848*
Schichtel, M., Meisenburgstr. 153, 45133 Essen.
T. (0201) 71 16 97. *051849*
Schilling, Marion, Dohmanns Kamp 7, 45130 Essen.
T. (0201) 78 32 39. *051850*
Schlabach-Stil, Huyssenallee 89-93, 45128 Essen.
T. (0201) 22 81 69. *051851*
Schniedermeier, Klarastr. 21, 45130 Essen.
T. (0201) 77 22 15. - Furn / China / Silv - *051852*
Stubing, Margret, Münzenstudio, Viehofer Str. 60, 45127 Essen. T. (0201) 23 95 16. - Num - *051853*

Wagner, K., Berliner Str. 178, 45144 Essen.
T. (0201) 74 31 55.   051854
Wegener, Karin, III Hagen 31, 45127 Essen.
T. (0201) 22 77 92. - Ant / Paint / Furn / China / Silv /
Lights / Instr / Glass -   051855
Weidig-Bödeker, I., Rübezahlstr. 33, 45134 Essen.
T. (0201) 47 12 86.   051856
Westmeyer, A., Rüttenscheider Str. 172, 45131 Essen.
T. (0201) 42 09 07.   051857
Wirtz, I., Krayer Str. 12, 45276 Essen.
T. (0201) 50 47 45.   051858
Zippel, K., I.-Weber-Str. 11, 45127 Essen.
T. (0201) 22 65 13.   051859

Essingen (Rheinland-Pfalz)
Odenwälder, G. W., Kirchstr. 42, 76879
Essingen.   051860

Esslingen (Baden-Württemberg)
Asia-Antik, Am Postmichelbrunnen, 73728 Esslingen.
T. (0711) 357193. - Ant / Orient / Mil -   051861
Bilder-Fingerle, Unterer Metzgerbach 2, 73728 Esslin-
gen. T. (0711) 356651. - Paint / Repr / Jew /
Fra -   051862
B.T.T., Im Heppächer 3, 73728 Esslingen.
T. (0711) 356412, Fax (0711) 356412. - Ant / Paint /
Graph / Furn / Sculp / Fra / Glass / Draw -   051863
Carmi, D., Roßmarkt 13, 73728 Esslingen.
T. (0711) 350062.   051864
Dengler, Erik, Im Heppächer 29, 73728
Esslingen.   051865
Domizil, Roßmarkt 15, 73728 Esslingen.
T. (0711) 352077.   051866
Ermel, G., Obere Beutau 77, 73728 Esslingen.
T. (0711) 375504.   051867
Fingerle, H., Unterer Metzgerbach 2, 73728 Esslingen.
T. (0711) 356651.   051868
Hetzinger, R., Webergasse 3, 73728 Esslingen.
T. (0711) 312881, 352129. - Instr -   051869
Kübler & Ganz-Kübler, Oberhofweg 1, 73730 Esslingen.
T. (0711) 3160019.   051870
Limpert, H.-W., Alte Talstr 23, 73732 Esslingen.
T. (0711) 375285.   051871
Schmid, H., Fischbrunnenstr 8, 73728 Esslingen.
T. (0711) 357193.   051872
Trittner, Ernst, Katharinenstr 8, 73728 Esslingen.
T. (0711) 3160187.   051873

Ettenheim (Baden-Württemberg)
Breiden, Karin hr, Postfach 8, 77949 Ettenheim.
- Mod -   051874
Münzen und Medaillen, Blumenberg 16, 77955 Etten-
heim. T. (07822) 5927, Fax (07822) 8133.
- Num -   051875

Etterzhausen (Bayern)
Balters, Willy, Sonnenstr. 1, 93152 Etterzhausen.
T. (09404) 214. - Ant -   051876

Ettlingen (Baden-Württemberg)
Battaglia-Merkle, M., Seminarstr. 14, 76275 Ettlingen.
T. (07243) 16647.   051877
Fuchs, G., Markstr. 16, 76275 Ettlingen.
T. (07243) 793 33.   051878
Jonderko, R., Bulacherstr. 32, 76275 Ettlingen.
T. (07243) 319 04. - Furn / Lights / Mod -   051879

Euskirchen (Nordrhein-Westfalen)
Hausen, Luisa, Wilhelmstr. 67, 53879 Euskirchen.
T. (02251) 2969.   051880
Smet, de, Jakobsgasse 16, 53879 Euskirchen.
T. (02251) 527 27.   051881

Eutin (Schleswig-Holstein)
Krafczyk, S., Riemannstr. 34, 23701 Eutin.
T. (04521) 73380.   051882
Layard, V., Königstr. 1, 23701 Eutin.
T. (04521) 3544.   051883
Riessen, Petra, Riemannstr. 18, 23701 Eutin.
T. (04521) 722 22.   051884

Feldafing (Bayern)
Ferk, Michaele, Bahnhofstr. 21, 82340 Feldafing.
T. (08157) 663.   051885

Feldkirchen (Bayern)
Holey, G., 94351 Feldkirchen, Niederbayern.
T. (09420) 251, 336.   051886

Fellbach (Baden-Württemberg)
Bergler, H.-P. & H., H.-P. & H., Wernerstr. 7, 70736 Fel-
lbach. T. (0711) 580535.   051887
Seeger, B., Bahnhofstr 139, 70736 Fellbach.
T. (0711) 574424.   051888
Steger, H., Bruckwiesenweg 2, 70734 Fellbach.
T. (0711) 579803, 579905.   051889
Uhlig, Johannes, Maicklerstr 31, 70736 Fellbach.
T. (0711) 582790. - Ant -   051890

Fernwald (Hessen)
Wahle, Hella, Hellenweg 26, 35463 Fernwald. - China /
Cur -   051891

Fichtenau (Baden-Württemberg)
Mugele, Werner, Kapellenstr. 26, 74579 Fichtenau.
T. (07962) 551. - Furn / Cur -   051892

Filderstadt (Baden-Württemberg)
Antik-Häusle, Hohenheimer Str. 25, 70794 Filderstadt.
T. (0711) 77 46 34. - Ant / Furn / China / Fra /
Cur -   051893
Heck, Otto, Hohenzollernweg 3, 70794 Filderstadt.
T. (0711) 77 31 22. - Ant / Mil -   051894
Schulz, U.D., Moltkestr. 4, 70794 Filderstadt.
T. (0711) 77 43 25.   051895
Zimmermann, F., Pulsstr. 33, 70794 Filderstadt.
T. (0711) 70 11 86.   051896

Fischach (Bayern)
Schäbel, G., Schlössleweg 7a, 86850 Fischach.
T. (08236) 207.   051897
Schäbel, R., Marktplatz 5, 86850 Fischach.
T. (08236) 1693.   051898

Fischbachau (Bayern)
Roth, F.-R., Am Sägfeld 21, 83730 Fischbachau. 051899

Flein (Baden-Württemberg)
Unger, Michael, Bildstr. 78, 74223 Flein.
T. (07131) 255466, Fax (07131) 578692. - Ant / Paint /
Graph / Furn / China / Tex -   051900

Flensburg (Schleswig-Holstein)
Antiquitäten Nordfriesland, Norderstr. 35, 24939 Flens-
burg. T. (0461) 23044.   051901
Bootsmann, Heinz, Mozartstr. 12, 24943
Flensburg.   051902
Cornwall, Frank, Norderstr. 4, 24939 Flensburg.
T. (0461) 364 39. - Ant / Paint / Furn / Orient / Jew /
Silv / Ico -   051903
Dohm, Gabriele, Fuchskuhle 4, 24941
Flensburg.   051904
Ellenberg, D., Rote Str. 14, 24937 Flensburg.
T. (0461) 25643.   051905
Fick, L., Vor der Koppe 12, 24937 Flensburg.
T. (0461) 76 01.   051906
Gampert & Hansen, Große Str. 48, 24937 Flensburg.
T. (0461) 12444. - Ant -   051907
Gründker, Horst, Thomas-Mann-Str. 26, 24937 Flens-
burg. T. (0461) 524 05.   051908
Jensen, J., Norderstr. 11, 24939 Flensburg.
T. (0461) 25111.   051909
Kunst und Antiquitäten Rote Straße, Rote Str. 10, 24937
Flensburg. T. (0461) 291 61.   051910
Rojahn, Rote Str. 14, 24937 Flensburg. T. (0461) 25 643.
- Ant / Paint / Graph / Furn / China / Silv / Lights / Glass --
                                                           051911
Schwiewager, E., Rote Str. 16, 24937 Flensburg.
T. (0461) 13142.   051912
Werner, E., Zur Bleiche 46, 24941 Flensburg.
T. (0461) 98080.   051913
Wolfram, Heinz, Apenrader Str. 76, 24939 Flensburg.
- Num -   051914

Flieden (Hessen)
Spahn, Reinhold, Franz-Winter-Str. 1, 36103
Flieden.   051915

Flintbek (Schleswig-Holstein)
Horstmann, Dieter, Schurkamp 12, 24220 Flintbek.
- Num -   051916

Florstadt (Hessen)
Jakobi, Lindenstr. 18, 61197 Florstadt. T. (06041) 69 77.
- Ant / Furn -   051917

Fockbek (Schleswig-Holstein)
Stender, K.-H., Elsdorfer Str. 20, 24787 Fockbek.
T. (04331) 614 32.   051918

Föhren (Rheinland-Pfalz)
Clasen, H., Am Reichelbach 6, 54343 Föhren.
T. (06502) 5854.   051919

Forchheim, Oberfranken (Bayern)
Deckmann, W., von-Brun-Str 4, 91301 Forchheim, Oberfranken. T. (09191) 80395.   051920
Greim, G., Dr., John-F.-Kennedy-Ring 60, 91301 Forchheim, Oberfranken. T. (09191) 80155. - China - 051921

Forst (Baden-Württemberg)
Velhage, Josef, Kronauer Allee 11, 76694 Forst. 051922

Forst (Brandenburg)
Gärtner, W., Berliner Str. 76, 03149 Forst.
T. (03562) 8542.   051923

Frankenberg, Eder (Hessen)
Ante, D., Hauptstr 3, 35066 Frankenberg, Eder.
T. (06451) 21287.   051924
Denaro, G., Auf der Heide 11, 35066 Frankenberg, Eder.
T. (06451) 22537.   051925

Frankenthal, Pfalz (Rheinland-Pfalz)
Schlitt, J., Westliche Ringstr 32, 67227 Frankenthal,
Pfalz. T. (06233) 9729.   051926

Frankfurt am Main (Hessen)
Ambiente, Egonolffstr 38, 60316 Frankfurt am Main.
T. (069) 495419.   051927
Antik-Altkönig, Mittelweg 27, 60318 Frankfurt am Main.
T. (069) 556185, Fax (069) 556185. - Paint / Furn /
Silv / Jew -   051928
Antik-Art-Galerie, Kurfürstenstr 8a, 60486 Frankfurt am
Main. T. (069) 771799.   051929
Antik-Eck, Rotlinstr 39, 60316 Frankfurt am Main.
T. (069) 491936, 4950544.   051930
Antik Office, Weckmarkt 5, 60311 Frankfurt am Main.
T. (069) 283021, Fax (069) 734771. - China / Sculp /
Glass / Mod -   051931
Antik-Warenhaus, Friedberger Landstr 325, 60389
Frankfurt am Main. T. (069) 5963766, 513086.
- Furn -   051932
Antiken-Kabinett, Ganghoferstr 24, 60320 Frankfurt am
Main. T. (069) 519015, Fax (069) 519026.
- Arch -   051933
Asia Gallery, Gutleutstr 294, 60327 Frankfurt am Main.
T. (069) 233311.   051934
Barras, Cornelia C., Neue Mainzer Str 22, 60311 Frank-
furt am Main. T. (069) 251455. - Ant / Jew /
Silv -   051935
Bauer-Schatztruhe, Oeder Weg 56, 60318 Frankfurt am
Main. T. (069) 555998. - Ant / Paint / Furn / Num / Chi-
na / Jew / Silv -   051936
Beacon Hill Antiques, Jahnstr 60, 60318 Frankfurt am
Main. T. (069) 5971561. - Mod -   051937
Bechler, Max, Wendelsweg 118, 60599 Frankfurt am
Main. T. (069) 682930.   051938
Bienert, Erich, Dompl 10, 60311 Frankfurt am Main.
T. (069) 288980. - Ant -   051939
Blechschmidt, Gotthard, Wallstr 5, 60594 Frankfurt am
Main. T. (069) 612818. - Ant / Paint / Graph / Furn /
Num / Fra / Cur / Mod / Draw / Ant -   051940
Bodenheimer, Max, Rosenbergstr 6, 60313 Frankfurt am
Main. T. (069) 287795, Fax (069) 288359.
- Pho -   051941
British Corner, Große Bockenheimer Str 35, 60313
Frankfurt am Main. T. (069) 287765. - Ant / Jew /
Silv -   051942
Brumme, Siegfried, Braubachstr 34, 60311 Frankfurt
am Main. T. (069) 287263, Fax (069) 296682.
- Graph -   051943

Büttgen, Wolfgang, Brückenstr 37, 60594 Frankfurt am Main. T. (069) 628788. - Instr -   *051944*
Buren, J, Oeder Weg 66, 60318 Frankfurt am Main. T. (069) 559423.   *051945*
Buttlar, von, Eppsteiner Str 24, 60323 Frankfurt am Main. T. (069) 721880, Fax (069) 172393.   *051946*
Cachet, Schweizer Str 16, 60594 Frankfurt am Main. T. (069) 622995. - Mod -   *051947*
Czakainski, A., Oberer Kalbacher Weg 3, 60437 Frankfurt am Main. T. (069) 5071709.   *051948*
Dameru, I., Rotlintstr 39, 60316 Frankfurt am Main. T. (069) 491936.   *051949*
Deutsche Numismatik, Mainzer Landstr 131, 60327 Frankfurt am Main. T. (069) 235034/35.
- Num -   *051950*
Döbritz, Wilhelm M., Braubachstr 10-12, 60311 Frankfurt am Main. T. (069) 721118, 287733. - Ant - *051951*

Wilhelm M. Döbritz
Kunst- u. Auktionshaus

Antiquitäten
Braubachstr. 10–12
60311 Frankfurt
Tel. (069) 28 77 33 + 72 11 18

Essel, W., Friedberger Landstr 98, 60316 Frankfurt am Main. T. (069) 434179.   *051952*
Fassler, Marianne, Kettenhofweg 123, 60325 Frankfurt am Main. - Tin -   *051953*
Fichter, H.W., Arndtstr 49, 60325 Frankfurt am Main. T. (069) 746741, Fax (069) 747946. - Paint /
Draw -   *051954*
Fine Antiques, Fahrgasse 25, 60311 Frankfurt am Main. T. (069) 288239. - Ant / Furn / Instr -   *051955*
frankfurter kunstgalerie, Justinianstr 22, 60322 Frankfurt am Main. T. (069) 558582.   *051956*
Frankfurter Numismatik, Corneliusstr 13, 60325 Frankfurt am Main. T. (069) 748666. - Num -   *051957*
Gärtner, Heinz, Kaiserhofstr 13, 60313 Frankfurt am Main. T. (069) 624614.   *051958*
Galerie am Goethe Haus, Berliner Str 66, 60311 Frankfurt am Main. T. (069) 565416, 285695. - Ant / Graph /
China / Sculp / Glass / Mod -   *051959*
Gellman, Leo, Fahrgasse 22, 60311 Frankfurt am Main. T. (069) 281422, Fax 281422. - Furn -   *051960*

ANTIQUITÄTEN
L. GELLMAN

Große Auswahl von Möbeln
des Biedermeier bis Barock

Fahrgasse 22, 60311 Frankfurt
Tel. 0 69 / 28 14 22
Fax 0 69 / 28 14 22

Geppert-Rahm, Marth, Reinhardstr 6, 60433 Frankfurt am Main. T. (069) 511323. - Furn / China -   *051961*
Giegerich, Karl, Schwalbacher Str 25, 60326 Frankfurt am Main. T. (069) 737805.   *051962*
Graf, Eckenheimer Landstr 126, 60318 Frankfurt am Main. T. (069) 557261.   *051963*
Gressler, R., Dillenburgerstr 15, 60439 Frankfurt am Main. T. (069) 586497.   *051964*
Hanke, H., Töngesgasse 48, 60311 Frankfurt am Main. T. (069) 281515.   *051965*
Harder, J., Auf der Kuhr 40, 60435 Frankfurt am Main. T. (069) 544782. - Paint / Graph -   *051966*
Hauck-Jäcklin, Anne, Oeder Weg 51, 60318 Frankfurt am Main. T. (069) 558047.   *051967*
Heijnigen, G. van, Fahrgasse 20, 60311 Frankfurt am Main. T. (069) 284690.   *051968*

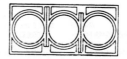

Heilig, Andreas B., Königslacher Str 4, 60528 Frankfurt am Main. T. (069) 673856, Fax (069) 6771171. - Paint /
Draw -   *051969*
Hermann-Simsch, M., Römerberg 8, 60311 Frankfurt am Main. T. (069) 292818.   *051970*
Herrlein, Klaus, Schulstr 1a, 60594 Frankfurt am Main. T. (069) 613933, 624928. - Furn -   *051971*
Heubel, Lothar, Braubachstr 9, 60311 Frankfurt am Main. T. (069) 283190.   *051972*
Hilpert, Annemarie, Liliencronstr 17, 60320 Frankfurt am Main. T. (069) 563868, Fax (069) 563868. - Ant /
Furn / China / Tex / Toys -   *051973*
Hirsch, Höhenstr 49, 60385 Frankfurt am Main. T. (069) 442368. - Furn / China / Silv / Glass -   *051974*
Historisches Portfolio, Kaiserstr 24, 60311 Frankfurt am Main. T. (069) 231010. - Ant -   *051975*
Hoedt, Wolf, Mittlerer Hasenpfad 1, 60598 Frankfurt am Main. T. (069) 626122. - Ant / Paint / Furn / Fra / Instr /
Cur -   *051976*
Houston, William P., Böcklinstr 2, 60596 Frankfurt am Main. T. (069) 637742. - Furn -   *051977*
Iser, Gerda, Neumannstr 92, 60433 Frankfurt am Main. T. (069) 522478. - Ant -   *051978*
Ivacic, I., Ferdinand-Dirichs-Weg 1, 60529 Frankfurt am Main. T. (069) 355330.   *051979*
Jammer, D., Niemandsfeld 18, 60435 Frankfurt am Main. T. (069) 546688. - Furn -   *051980*
Janus Antik, Glauburgstr 83a, 60318 Frankfurt am Main. T. (069) 591799. - Ant -   *051981*
Japan Art Galerie, Braubachstr 9, 60311 Frankfurt am Main. T. (069) 282839. - Furn -   *051982*
Jasper, Rolf, Kl. Hochstr 16-18, 60313 Frankfurt am Main. T. (069) 282268.   *051983*
Kaiser, Rüdiger, Mittelweg 54, 60318 Frankfurt am Main. T. (069) 5971109. - Num -   *051984*
Karlsson, Germaniastr 46, 60389 Frankfurt am Main. T. (069) 458646, Fax (069) 458646. - Paint / Graph /
Repr / Sculp -   *051985*
Kastl, Albanusstr 16, 65929 Frankfurt am Main.   *051986*
Kegelmann, P. Michael, Saalgasse 3, 60311 Frankfurt am Main. T. (069) 288461, Fax 288462. - Ant /
Instr -   *051987*
K.G. Kunsthandels-GmbH, Auf der Körnerwiese 19-21, 60322 Frankfurt am Main. T. (069) 550939, 557022,
Fax (069) 5971755. - Ant / Furn / Sculp / Jew / Silv /
Lights / Glass / Mod -   *051988*
Klein, W., Mörfelder Landstr 10, 60598 Frankfurt am Main. T. (069) 616485. - Furn -   *051989*
Klementz, Henrika, Westendstr 95, 60325 Frankfurt am Main. T. (069) 752666.   *051990*

Kopp, H., Talstr 106a, 60437 Frankfurt am Main. T. (069) 503203.   *051991*
Krause, Helmut, Postfach 160454, 60067 Frankfurt am Main. T. (06105) 74306, Fax 74190. - Ant /
Paint -   *051992*
Kreitz, J., Thorwaldsenplatz 1, 60596 Frankfurt am Main. T. (069) 635634.   *051993*
Kress, Matthias, Eschersheimer Landstr 554b, 60433 Frankfurt am Main. T. (069) 526434.   *051994*
Kuehn, Georg, Weißfrauenstr 2-8, 60311 Frankfurt am Main. T. (069) 288230. - Mod -   *051995*
Kümmel, R., Wallstr 12, 60594 Frankfurt am Main. T. (069) 628609, Fax (069) 628609. - Graph / Tex / Eth /
Jew -   *051996*
Kunst und Antiquitäten, Oeder Weg 51, 60318 Frankfurt am Main. T. (069) 558047. - Paint / Furn / Jew /
Mod -   *051997*
Kunsthandlung am Frankfurter Hof, Bethmannstr 50-54, 60311 Frankfurt am Main. T. (069) 289742,
Fax (069) 292346. - Paint -   *051998*
Kupfermann, J., Rohrbachstr 8, 60389 Frankfurt am Main. T. (069) 467321.   *051999*
Lappé, Kornmarkt 5, 60311 Frankfurt am Main. T. (069) 284377. - Furn -   *052000*
Laterna Magica, Textorstr 58, 60594 Frankfurt am Main. T. (069) 628744, Fax (069) 628744. - Ant -   *052001*
Leichter, Danica, Fahrgasse 27, 60311 Frankfurt am Main. T. (069) 292385. - Ant / Paint / Furn /
Mod -   *052002*
Loewinstein, A., Rothschildallee 11a, 60389 Frankfurt am Main. T. (069) 439567. - Lights / Mod -   *052003*
Lugner, Gärtnerweg 1, 60322 Frankfurt am Main. T. (069) 553809, Fax (069) 5962332. - Jew -   *052004*
Magus, Weißadlergasse 8, 60311 Frankfurt am Main. T. (069) 282835, Fax (069) 287619.   *052005*
Maier, Heinz, Höhenstr 22, 60385 Frankfurt am Main. T. (069) 446239. - Furn / Instr -   *052006*
Mandala Antikschmuck, Adalbertstr 7b, 60486 Frankfurt am Main. T. (069) 776238. - Jew -   *052007*
Masic, Große Bockenheimer Str 46, 60313 Frankfurt am Main. T. (069) 285289.   *052008*
Merry Old England, Opernplatz 2, 60313 Frankfurt am Main. T. (069) 288262. - Ant -   *052009*
Miclescu, Radu A., Fahrgasse 29, 60311 Frankfurt am Main. T. (069) 293763. - Ant / Furn -   *052010*
Mitzlaff, Otto von, Römerberg 34, 60311 Frankfurt am Main. T. (069) 284401.   *052011*
Morbe, Thomas, De-Neufville-Str 7, 60599 Frankfurt am Main. T. (069) 656201.   *052012*
Morneweg, Norbert, Rüsterstr 4d, 60325 Frankfurt am Main. T. (069) 727855.   *052013*

Müller, Frank M., Schweizer Str 16, 60594 Frankfurt am
Main. T. (069) 616342. *052014*
Münzkontor Frankfurt, Reifenberger Str 57, 60489
Frankfurt am Main. T. (069) 784133,
Fax (069) 7896813. - Num - *052015*
Neunert, Peter A., Schultheißenweg 105b, 60489 Frank-
furt am Main. T. (069) 788488. - Num - *052016*
Niederlintner, Fahrgasse 17, 60311 Frankfurt am Main.
T. (069) 288239. *052017*
Nietzsch, Rudolf, Ackermannstr 74, 60326 Frankfurt am
Main. - Ant - *052018*
Nitsche, E., Berger Str 286, 60385 Frankfurt am Main.
T. (069) 466285. *052019*
Nitsche, Hans Helmut, Genfer Str 2, 60437 Frankfurt am
Main. T. (069) 5071011, Fax (069) 5072612. - Ant /
Graph / Furn / Repr / Dec / Instr / Cur - *052020*
Numberger, J., Weckmarkt 4, 60311 Frankfurt am Main.
T. (069) 285687. *052021*
Nuovo 2 Design 1950-1970, Fahrgasse 1, 60311 Frank-
furt am Main. T. (069) 283918. *052022*
Oberhack, D., Berger Str 200, 60385 Frankfurt am Main.
T. (069) 463336. *052023*
Olli Antik, Sandgasse 2, 60311 Frankfurt am Main.
T. (069) 291199. *052024*
Ostasien-Galerie, Gotenstr 9, 65929 Frankfurt am Main.
T. (069) 302552. - Ant / Paint / Furn / Orient / China /
Sculp / Tex / Arch / Eth - *052025*
Pellengahr, Ingo, Fahrgasse 29, 60311 Frankfurt am
Main. T. (069) 2978837. *052026*
Petri, K., Wallstr 9, 60594 Frankfurt am Main.
T. (069) 616506. *052027*
Peus, Busso, Dr., Bornwiesenweg 34, 60322 Frankfurt
am Main. T. (069) 9596620, Fax 555995.
- Num - *052028*
Pieroth, Heinz, Fahrgasse 23, 60311 Frankfurt am Main.
T. (069) 284282, Fax (069) 284282. - Ant / Furn /
Sculp - *052029*
Poller, Thomas, Neue Mainzer Str 60, 60311 Frankfurt
am Main. T. (069) 285269, Fax (069) 288869. - Ant /
Furn - *052030*
Reichard, Bernusstr 18, 60487 Frankfurt am Main.
T. (069) 706860, Fax (069) 708771. *052031*
Reichert, A., Neue Mainzer Str, 60311 Frankfurt am
Main. T. (069) 293493. *052032*
Reimer, H., Bolongarostr 131, 65929 Frankfurt am Main.
T. (069) 316982. *052033*
Reimsbach-Kounatze, Egenolffstr 19, 60316 Frankfurt
am Main. T. (069) 4930508. *052034*
Reinhard, Helmut, Fahrgasse 9, 60311 Frankfurt am
Main. T. (069) 283220. - Num - *052035*
Richert, Dieter P., Im Trutz Frankfurt 13, 60313 Frankfurt
am Main. T. (069) 283381. - Paint / Tex / Fra /
Mul - *052036*
Roccioletti, W., Berger Str 4, 60316 Frankfurt am Main.
T. (069) 441073. *052037*
Roos, M. & D., Fahrgasse 89, 60311 Frankfurt am Main.
T. (069) 287223. - China - *052038*
Rumbler, Helmut H., Börsenstr 7-11, 60313 Frankfurt
am Main. T. (069) 291142, Fax (069) 289975.
- Ant - *052039*
Ruttmann, Fr., Fahrgasse 19, 60311 Frankfurt am Main.
T. (069) 285019. - Ant - *052040*
Schneider, Carl, Eschersheimer Landstr 74, 60322
Frankfurt am Main. T. (069) 556726. - Ant / Paint /
Furn / China / Sculp / Silv / Instr / Glass - *052041*
Scholz, M.S., Mühlgasse 3, 60486 Frankfurt am Main.
T. (069) 703899. *052042*
Schreiter, N., Glauburgstr 83a, 60318 Frankfurt am
Main. T. (069) 591799. *052043*
Seemann, Helmut, Pferdskopfweg 9, 65931 Frankfurt
am Main. - Num - *052044*
Sekulić, Friedrich, Berliner Str 39, 60311 Frankfurt am
Main. T. (069) 291800. - Silv / Jew - *052045*
Shahidi, Seilerstr 9, 60313 Frankfurt am Main.
T. (069) 285619. *052046*
Siebert, Fritz, Berliner Str 68, 60311 Frankfurt am Main.
T. (069) 284685, Fax (069) 541523. - Paint / Graph /
Lights - *052047*
Silbernagel-Löffler, Andrea, Lersnerstr 36, 60322 Frank-
furt am Main. - Ant - *052048*
Sommer, B., Fahrgasse 97, 60311 Frankfurt am Main.
T. (069) 282775. - Num - *052049*

Soosten, Karsko von, Klingerstr 8, 60313 Frankfurt am
Main. T. (069) 287456. *052050*
Spreitzer, H., Reifenberger Str 57, 60489 Frankfurt am
Main. T. (069) 784133. - Num - *052051*
Starl, Edith, Oeder Weg 25, 60318 Frankfurt am Main.
T. (069) 556661. - Ant - *052052*
Stelzner, Irmgard, Butzbacher Str 48, 60389 Frankfurt
am Main. T. (069) 455599. - Ant - *052053*
Stief, Friedrich-Kahl-Str 8, 60489 Frankfurt am Main.
T. (069) 787777. *052054*
Stingl, R., Fahrgasse 27, 60311 Frankfurt am Main.
T. (069) 1310659. *052055*
Stör, Hans & Else, Fahrgasse 7-9, 60311 Frankfurt am
Main. T. (069) 295858. - Ant / Mil - *052056*
Stolzenberg, Kurt G., Große Seestr 63, 60486 Frankfurt
am Main. T. (069) 701379. - Paint / Graph / Repr /
Arch / Eth - *052057*
Studio Art Deco, Römerberg 8-10, 60311 Frankfurt am
Main. T. (069) 292818. - Mod - *052058*
Szönyi, Katalin, Steinweg 2, 60313 Frankfurt am Main.
T. (069) 287905. - Num - *052059*
Techno Antik, Bolongarostr 141, 65929 Frankfurt am
Main. T. (069) 316085. - Ant - *052060*
Teutschbein, Weckmarkt 7, 60311 Frankfurt am Main.
T. (069) 288516. - Paint / Furn / Draw - *052061*
Traut, C., Leipziger Str 77, 60487 Frankfurt am Main.
- Ant - *052062*
Tresor am Römer, Braubachstr 15, 60311 Frankfurt am
Main. T. (069) 281248, Fax (069) 282160.
- Graph - *052063*
Urlass, Rüdiger, Fahrgasse 19, 60311 Frankfurt am
Main. T. (069) 295727, 284932, Fax (069) 284932.
- Mod - *052064*
Urlass, Sabine, Ziegelgasse 3, 60311 Frankfurt am
Main. T. (069) 291026. - Mod - *052065*
Vonderbank, Goethestr 11, 60313 Frankfurt am Main.
T. (069) 282490, Fax (069) 296148. *052066*
Wagner, W., Hainer Weg 24, 60599 Frankfurt am Main.
T. (069) 683511. *052067*
Weinheber, J. & B., Börsenplatz 1, 60311 Frankfurt am
Main. T. (069) 288079. - Ant / Paint / Jew - *052068*
Weißmantel, Helmut, Mechtildstr 31, 60320 Frankfurt
am Main. T. (069) 554192. - Ant - *052069*
Weka-Numismatik, An der Walkmühle 21, 60437 Frank-
furt am Main. T. (069) 501539. - Num - *052070*
Wendel, G.E.F., Langweidenstr 38, 60488 Frankfurt am
Main. T. (069) 786431, 7893999. - Num - *052071*
Westenburger, Lore, Oskar-Schindler-Str 21, 60437
Frankfurt am Main. T. (069) 507213. - Ant - *052072*
Wilson, J., Weißadlergasse 8, 60311 Frankfurt am Main.
T. (069) 282835. *052073*
Wittwer, H., Ulmerstr 10, 60325 Frankfurt am Main.
T. (069) 724580. *052074*
Yeganeh, Mohammed, Bundenweg 7, 60320 Frankfurt
am Main. T. (069) 562241. - Arch - *052075*
Zeller, H., Berger Str 140, 60385 Frankfurt am Main.
T. (069) 4960259. *052076*
Zidarics, Norbert, Gutzkowstr 1, 60594 Frankfurt am
Main. T. (069) 618328; 621191. Ant / Furn - *052077*
Zimmermann, Helmut, Bethmannstr 50-54, 60311
Frankfurt am Main. T. (069) 280820, Fax (069) 287273.
- Ant / Paint / Graph / Furn / Num / China / Sculp / Tex / A-
rch / Jew / Fra / Silv / Lights / Rel / Glass / Mod / Ico / Dr-
aw - *052078*

Frauenau (Bayern)

Lemberger, W., Hauptstr. 21, 94258 Frauenau.
T. (09926) 243. *052079*

Frechen (Nordrhein-Westfalen)

Cottin, I., Hauptstr. 141, 50226 Frechen.
T. (02234) 559 69. *052080*
Gil-Antiques, Augustinusstr. 7-11, 50226
Frechen. *052081*
Malta, Starenweg 68, 50226 Frechen.
T. (02234) 53 43 93. - Mil - *052082*
Rick, R., Mauritiusstr. 48, 50226 Frechen.
T. (02234) 541 97. *052083*

Freiburg (Baden-Württemberg)

Acker, R., Konviktstr. 9, 79098 Freiburg.
T. (0761) 35498. *052084*

Antik-Einrichtungsgesellschaft, Oberlinden 10, 79098
Freiburg. T. (0761) 33407. - Furn - *052085*
Birkenfelder, O., Badenweilerstr. 16, 79115 Freiburg.
T. (0761) 44 35 22. *052086*
Bric a Brac, Gerberau 11, 79098 Freiburg.
T. (0761) 38 27 55. *052087*
Casana, Salzstr. 26, 79098 Freiburg. T. (0761) 329 55.
- Ant / Paint - *052088*
Dick, R. & K., Hildastr. 17, 79102 Freiburg.
T. (0761) 753 13. *052089*
Dingler, Günterstalstr. 53, 79102 Freiburg.
T. (0761) 70 22 68. *052090*
Dold, Tony, Gerberau 2, 79098 Freiburg.
T. (0761) 241 17. *052091*
Ebner, Karlstr. 5, 79104 Freiburg. T. (0761) 24455,
Fax (0761) 286888. - Num - *052092*
Elsenhans, Veith, Rempartstr. 5, 79098 Freiburg.
T. (0761) 261 26. - Glass - *052093*
Förnbacher, K., Schloßbergstr. 10, 79098 Freiburg.
T. (0761) 266 65. *052094*
Geiger, Hans, Dr., Schwarzwaldstr. 169, 79102 Freiburg.
T. (0761) 232 32. - Paint / Graph / Sculp /
Draw - *052095*
Haering, Jürgen, Gerberau 38, 79098 Freiburg.
T. (0761) 25330, Fax (0761) 25330. - Num /
Arch - *052096*
Heyden, von H., Fischerau 10, 79098 Freiburg.
T. (0761) 265 71. *052097*
Historia Verlag, In den Weihermatten 13, 79108 Frei-
burg. T. (0761) 54821, Fax 57994. - Repr /
Glass - *052098*
Jacob, Friedrichring 24, 79098 Freiburg.
T. (0761) 353 14. *052099*
Jahrendt, Herbert, Kartäuserstr. 8, 79102 Freiburg.
T. (0761) 223 76. - Ant / Num / Lights / Glass /
Mod - *052100*
Janz, Max, Sundgaualllee 35, 79114 Freiburg.
T. (0761) 811 80. *052101*
Kaiser, V., Gerberau 10, 79098 Freiburg.
T. (0761) 246 53. - Ant / China / Lights / Glass - *052102*
Kanstinger, Klaus, Rehhagweg 9, 79100 Freiburg.
T. (0761) 294 10. *052103*
Kircher, T., Klarastr. 31, 79106 Freiburg.
T. (0761) 27 31 32. *052104*
Konvikt-Antik, Konviktstr. 16, 79098 Freiburg.
T. (0761) 32720. - Ant / Furn / Jew / Instr /
Mod - *052105*
Kopf, Peter, Am Kreuzsteinacker 18, 79117 Freiburg.
- Ant / Graph / Instr - *052106*
Kraus, M., Klarastr. 55, 79106 Freiburg.
T. (0761) 28 18 98. - Ant / Jew / Silv / Instr - *052107*
Kricheldorf, H.H., Günterstalstr. 16, 79100 Freiburg.
T. (0761) 739 13. - Num / Arch / Rel - *052108*
Kricheldorf, I., Merzhauser Str. 157d, 79100 Freiburg.
T. (0761) 40 34 33. - Num - *052109*
Lahde, J., & C. Hartenstein-Lahde, Untere Entengasse 4,
79112 Freiburg. T. (0761) 1713. *052110*
Langenbach, H.J., Habsburgerstr. 57, 79104 Freiburg.
T. (0761) 55 31 58. *052111*
Lankoff, Peter, Lorettostr 40, 79100 Freiburg.
T. (0761) 402140. - Ant / Paint / Graph / Furn / Num /
Orient / China / Sculp / Tex / Arch / Eth / Jew / Silv / Ligh-
ts / Mil / Glass / Cur / Mod - *052112*
Lesch, I., Stadtstr. 46, 79104 Freiburg.
T. (0761) 301 57. *052113*
Maier, Linnestr. 23, 79110 Freiburg. T. (0761) 845 38.
- Instr - *052114*
Oma's Möbel, Schwarzwaldstr. 88, 79102 Freiburg.
T. (0761) 70 90 93. - Furn - *052115*
Passmann, W., Leinhaldenweg 17, 79104 Freiburg.
T. (0761) 539 62. - Paint / Sculp / Glass - *052116*
Puhze, Günter, Stadtstr. 28, 79104 Freiburg.
T. (0761) 25476, Fax (0761) 26459. - Arch - *052117*
Reichenbach, Jürgen, Gerberau 8, 79098 Freiburg.
T. (0761) 250 60. - Ant / Furn - *052118*
Reichert, A., Gerberau 7a, 79098 Freiburg.
T. (0761) 390 19. *052119*
Reinhardt, R., Auggener Weg 5, 79114 Freiburg.
T. (0761) 44 50 34. *052120*
Ruf, Rosemarie, Ziegelhofstr. 12, 79110 Freiburg.
- Num - *052121*
Scherb, W., Kartäuserstr. 32, 79102 Freiburg.
T. (0761) 22267. *052122*

Schumann, U., Talstr. 35, 79102 Freiburg.
T. (0761) 74173. *052123*
Schwer, D., Schwarzwaldstr. 88, 79102 Freiburg.
T. (0761) 70 90 93. *052124*
Simmermacher, René, Talstr 5, 79102 Freiburg.
T. (0761) 73676. - Ant / China / Sculp - *052125*
Spiegelhalter, J., Konviktstr. 51, 79098 Freiburg.
T. (0761) 243 84. *052126*
Vennemann, B., Günterstalstr. 68, 79100
Freiburg. *052127*
Volle, S., Talstr. 45, 79102 Freiburg. T. (0761) 733 03.
- Num - *052128*
Wehmer, Bernd, Reiterstr. 4, 79100 Freiburg.
T. (0761) 40 28 35. - Furn / China / Glass /
Mod - *052129*
Wehrle, Alexander, Gartenstr. 10, 79098 Freiburg.
- Ant - *052130*
Wolff, Ulrike, Glümerstr. 35, 79102 Freiburg.
T. (0761) 725 66. - Ant / Arch / Eth - *052131*

Freigericht (Hessen)
Bendt, H. & M., Am Trieb 12, 63579 Freigericht.
T. (06055) 4561. *052132*

Freisen (Saarland)
Lauer, H.-D., Mühlenweg 7, 66629 Freisen.
T. (06855) 1656. *052133*

Freising (Bayern)
Antik-Palette, Ziegelgasse 17, 85354 Freising.
T. (08161) 13410, Fax (08161) 50000. - Ant / Paint /
Graph / Silv / Mil / Rel / Glass / Cur - *052134*

Freital (Sachsen)
Antiquitätenmarkt Martin, Dresdner Str. 55, 01705 Frei-
tal. T. 64 18 65. - Ant / Paint / Furn / China / Sculp / Tex /
Jew / Silv / Glass / Mod - *052135*
Martin, A., Dresdner Str. 55, 01705 Freital.
T. (0351) 641865. *052136*

Freudenstadt (Baden-Württemberg)
Groth, Uwe, Karl-von-Hahn-Str. 125/33, 72250 Freuden-
stadt. T. (07441) 811 68. - Orient - *052137*
Michel, Walter, Münzversand, Johann-Sebastian-Bach-
Weg 9, 72250 Freudenstadt. T. (07441) 47 02.
- Num - *052138*

Frickenhausen (Baden-Württemberg)
Landenberger, Hauptstr. 58, 72636 Frickenhausen.
T. (07022) 49350. *052139*

Fridolfing (Bayern)
Hummel, Ina, Lieseich, 83413 Fridolfing.
T. (08684) 410. *052140*

Friedberg (Bayern)
Külmer, Renate von, Thomas-Mann-Str. 23, 86316
Friedberg. T. (0821) 635 40. - Ant - *052141*
Rahn, Rüdiger, Bauernbräustr. 2, 86316 Friedberg.
T. (0821) 60 11 32. - Num - *052142*

Friedberg (Hessen)
Severin, G. & P., Görbelheimer Mühle 1a, 61169 Friedberg. T. (06031) 34 18. - Ant / Furn / Lights - *052143*

Friedelsheim (Rheinland-Pfalz)
Babilon, A., Hauptstr. 77, 67159 Friedelsheim.
T. (06322) 672 04. *052144*

Friedrichsdorf, Taunus (Hessen)
Anlauf, M. & G., M. & G., Junkernfeldstr 5, 61381 Fried-
richsdorf. T. (06175) 79726. *052145*
Antik-Haus, Hugenottenstr 111, 61381 Friedrichsdorf,
Taunus. T. (06175) 5504. *052146*
Grützner, P., Wilhelmstr 7, 61381 Friedrichsdorf, Taunus.
T. (06175) 79417. *052147*
Hahn, K.-P., Hugenottenstr 111, 61381 Friedrichsdorf,
Taunus. T. (06175) 5518. *052148*
Hofer, Alt Seulberg 43, 61381 Friedrichsdorf, Taunus.
T. (06175) 79797. *052149*

Friedrichshafen (Baden-Württemberg)
Albano, K., Karlstr. 49, 88045 Friedrichshafen.
T. (07541) 25300. - Num - *052150*

Alt Buchhorn, Seestr. 1, Heiseloch 5, 88045 Friedrichs-
hafen. T. (07541) 23377, 54941, Fax (07541) 54947.
- Ant / Furn / Mul - *052151*
Brugger, Hedy, Dornierstr. 99, 88048 Friedrichshafen.
- Num - *052152*
Tunc, Neset, Friedrichstr. 47, 88045 Friedrichshafen.
T (07541) 242 83. *052153*

Friedrichsthal (Saarland)
Fundgrube, Saarbrückerstr. 113, 66299 Friedrichsthal.
T. (06897) 84 05 10. *052154*

Friesenheim (Baden-Württemberg)
Reichmann, Bruno, Adlerstr. 8, 77948
Friesenheim. *052155*

Fröndenberg (Nordrhein-Westfalen)
Temme-Becker, T., & M. Becker, Graf-Adolf-Str. 109,
58730 Fröndenberg. T. (02378) 02373/76463. *052156*

Fronhausen (Hessen)
Schenk zu Schweinsberg, Ekkehard, Giessener Str.4,
35112 Fronhausen. T. (06426) 63 43. - Paint / Graph /
Instr / Cur / Draw - *052157*

Fürstenau bei Bramsche, Hase (Nieder-
sachsen)
Koenig, K.-H., Robert-Bosch-Ring 14, 49584 Fürstenau
bei Bramsche, Hase. T. (05901) 726. *052158*
Vogt, Ernst, Hauptstr 18, 49584 Fürstenau bei Bramsche, Hase. T. (05901) 845. *052159*

Fürstenfeldbruck (Bayern)
Adelhoch, Paul, Fürstenfeld 3, 82256 Fürstenfeldbruck.
T. (08141) 4514, 43718, Fax 42670. - Ant / Paint /
Paint / Furn / Sculp / Tex / Dec / Fra - *052160*
Böttcher, G., Geisinger Steig 13, 82256 Fürstenfeld-
bruck. T. (08141) 105 65. *052161*
Fine Antiques, Kloster Fürstenfeld1, 82256 Fürstenfeld-
bruck. T. (08141) 6820, Fax (08141) 42104.
- Furn - *052162*
Herzhoff, Pucherstr. 7, 82256 Fürstenfeldbruck.
T. (08141) 210 18. *052163*
Reinegger, P., Landsberger Str. 11, 82256 Fürstenfeld-
bruck. T. (08141) 10417, Fax (08141) 18971. - Paint /
Graph / Repr / Fra / Draw - *052164*
Schönberger, G., Adolf-Kolping-Str. 2, 82256 Fürsten-
feldbruck. T. (08141) 910 65. *052165*
Vonderbank, Ledererstr. 2, 82256 Fürstenfeldbruck.
T. (08141) 170 07. *052166*

Fürth (Bayern)
Antik-Boutique, Vacher Str. 10, 90766 Fürth.
T. (0911) 75 77 41. *052167*
Antikmagazin, Johannisstr. 7, 90763 Fürth.
T. (0911) 74 69 99. - Ant - *052168*
Banknoten-Münz-Börse, Königstr. 77, 90762 Fürth.
T. (0911) 77 40 42. - Num - *052169*
Biersack, Sperlinggstr. 14, 90768 Fürth.
T. (0911) 75 11 14, 75 24 81. - Furn - *052170*
Döhler, I., Würzburger Str. 44, 90766 Fürth.
T. (0911) 73 14 81. *052171*
Galerie am Theater, Königstr. 107, 90762 Fürth.
T. (0911) 77 07 27. - Ant - *052172*
Gitta's Antikboutique, Waagstr. 3, 90762 Fürth.
T. (0911) 77 40 10. *052173*
Haag, J., Waldstr. 25, 90763 Fürth. T. (0911) 70 54 64.
- Ant - *052174*
Hamper, Else, Amalienstr. 27, 90763 Fürth.
T. (0911) 77 26 10. *052175*
Kropf, Otmar, Wiesenstr. 8, 90765 Fürth.
T. (0911) 79 88 11. - Mil - *052176*
Münz-Börse, Königstr. 77, 90762 Fürth.
T. (087 04) 77 40 42. - Num - *052177*
Ostermayer, W., Cadolzburger Str. 12, 90766 Fürth.
T. (0911) 73 62 72. *052178*
Palicka, Jakobinenstr. 18, 90762 Fürth.
T. (0911) 709559, Fax (0911) 709559. - Jew - *052179*
Reuther, Sandbergstr. 18, 90768 Fürth.
T. (0911) 76 75 65. - Ant / Furn - *052180*
Schrepf, Rudolf, Nürnberger Str. 31, 90762 Fürth.
T. (0911) 790 72 10. - Ant / Graph / China / Glass /
Mod - *052181*

Striegel, W., Johannisstr. 7, 90763 Fürth.
T. (0911) 74 69 99. *052182*
Thomas, Nürnberger Str. 12, 90762 Fürth.
T. (0911) 77 11 92. *052183*
Weichardt, Rudolf-Breitscheid-Str. 17, 90762 Fürth.
T. (0911) 77 40 87, Fax (0911) 77 53 61.
- Num - *052184*

Fürth (Hessen)
Ruhr, Klaus, Dr., Schlierbacher Str. 50, 64658 Fürth.
T. (06253) 4437, Fax (06253) 1638. - Ant /
Furn - *052185*

Füssen (Bayern)
Frübing, Ruth & Horst, Magnuspl. 4, 87629 Füssen.
T. (08362) 66 71. - Ant - *052186*
Kubath, Bernhard, Geometerweg 20, 87629 Füssen.
T. (08362) 3125. *052187*
Spicker, P., Reichenstr. 37, 87629 Füssen.
T. (08362) 66 30. *052188*
Wille, Irmgard, Lechhalde 1, 87629 Füssen.
T. (08362) 7874, Fax (08362) 7874. - Ant / Paint /
Graph / Furn / China / Sculp / Jew / Silv / Glass / Draw /
Tin - *052189*

Fulda (Hessen)
Deisenroth, A., Petersberger Str. 33, 36037 Fulda.
T. (0661) 776 59. *052190*
Galerie Bohemica, Franz-Schubert-Str. 1, 36043 Fulda.
T. (0661) 37377. - Graph / China / Sculp / Tex / Jew /
Glass - *052191*
Galerie Meistergasse 10, Meistergasse 10, 36037 Fulda.
T. (0661) 719 08. *052192*
Kleinod, Karlstr. 37, 36037 Fulda. T. (0661) 736 20.
- Jew / Instr - *052193*
Leipold, Günther, Löherstr. 26, 36037 Fulda.
T. (0661) 777 75. *052194*
Maierhof, Eckhard, Heinrichstr. 38, 36037 Fulda.
T. (0661) 77528. *052195*
Nüdling, Charlotte K., Luckenberg 11, 36037 Fulda.
T. (0661) 223 03. - Ant / Paint / Furn / China / Jew / Silv /
Glass - *052196*
Raab, Helene, Mittelstr. 29, 36037 Fulda.
T. (0661) 714 71. *052197*
Schmidt, J. & E., Abtstor 41, 36037 Fulda.
T. (0661) 723 43. - Ant / Paint / Repr / Sculp / Jew / Fra /
Silv / Lights - *052198*
Seuring, Mathilde, Severiberg 2, 36037 Fulda.
T. (0661) 752 82. *052199*
Sorg, Josef, Mainzer Str. 6, 36039 Fulda.
T. (0661) 513 30, 787 92. - Jew / Instr - *052200*

Fuldatal (Hessen)
Stark, S. & H., Veckerhagener Str. 48a, 34233 Fuldatal.
T. (05607) 81 77 32. *052201*

Furth im Wald (Bayern)
Gaschler, G., Pfarrstr. 8, 93437 Furth im Wald.
T. (09973) 1285. *052202*

Gaggenau (Baden-Württemberg)
Häffner, P., Badstr. 2, 76571 Gaggenau.
T. (07225) 71113. *052203*
Scherer-Metzler, M., Badstr. 2, 76571 Gaggenau.
T. (07225) 76614. *052204*

Galmsbüll (Schleswig-Holstein)
Alte Stiftung, Marienkoog, Westerweg, 25899 Galms-
büll. T. (04661) 202. *052205*
Feddersen, B., Kleiserkoog, 25899 Galmsbüll.
T. (04661) 8365. *052206*
Kirchner, Stephan, Nordersterweg, 25899 Galmsbüll.
T. (04661) 53 17. - Ant / Furn - *052207*

Gangelt (Nordrhein-Westfalen)
Mieden, W.J., Hanxlerstr. 15, 52538 Gangelt.
T. (02454) 26 93. *052208*
Wichert, G. & U., Frankenstr. 34, 52538 Gangelt.
T. (02454) 15 81. - Ant - *052209*

Gangkofen (Bayern)
Suschinski, Edmund, Frontenhausener Str. 3, 84140
Gangkofen. T. (08722) 8409. *052210*

Garbsen (Niedersachsen)

Meyer, B., Burgstr. 8, 30826 Garbsen.
T. (05131) 75722. *052211*

Garding (Schleswig-Holstein)

Schinske, G., Tatingerstr. 3, 25836 Garding. *052212*

Garmisch-Partenkirchen (Bayern)

Heissenberger, A., Ludwigstr. 68, 82467 Garmisch-Par-
tenkirchen. T. (08821) 58886. *052213*
Jaud, Georg, Bahnhofstr. 24, 82467 Garmisch-Partenkir-
chen. T. (08821) 50008, Fax (08821) 79208. - Ant /
Paint / Furn / Tex / Fra - *052214*
Kleines Antiquarium, Königstandstr. 7, 82467 Garmisch-
Partenkirchen. - Ant / Paint / Furn / China / Silv / Instr /
Rel / Glass / Cur / Mod - *052215*
Loreck-Zimmermann, Ludwigstr. 27, 82467 Garmisch-
Partenkirchen. T. (08821) 558 03. *052216*
Merry Old England, Bahnhofstr. 4, 82467 Garmisch-Par-
tenkirchen. T. (08821) 599 09. - Ant / Paint / Furn /
Num / China / Jew / Silv / Instr / Mil / Mil - *052217*
Neuner, Georg, Ludwigstr. 11, 82467 Garmisch-Parten-
kirchen. T. (08821) 26 52. - Ant / Furn - *052218*
Pritschow im Kainzenfranz, Am Kurpark 16, 82467 Gar-
misch-Partenkirchen. T. (08821) 22 17. - Paint / Furn /
Tex - *052219*
Simon, A., Ludwigstr. 59, 82467 Garmisch-Partenkir-
chen. T. (08821) 35 22. *052220*
Wünsch, G., Ludwigstr. 96, 82467 Garmisch-Partenkir-
chen. T. (08821) 554 94. *052221*
Zeiler, Jutta, Triftstr. 28b, 82467 Garmisch-
Partenkirchen. *052222*

Gauting (Bayern)

Pfirrmann, Arno, Buchendorfer Str. 2, 82131 Gauting.
T. (089) 850 07 57. - Furn - *052223*

Gefrees (Bayern)

Heller, Th., Hauptstr. 45, 95482 Gefrees. T. (09254) 262.
- Furn - *052224*

Geilenkirchen (Nordrhein-Westfalen)

Gutschi, D., Konrad-Adenauer-Str. 189, 52511 Geilenkirchen. T. (02451) 3097. *052225*

Geisenheim (Hessen)

Presser, I., Römerberg 2, 65366 Geisenheim.
T. (06722) 50726. *052226*

Geislingen an der Steige (Baden-Würt-temberg)

Fritsch, P., Rorgensteig 6, 73312 Geislingen an der Stei-
ge. T. (07331) 45122. *052227*
Steck, Wolfgang, Stuttgarter Str 50, 73312 Geislingen
an der Steige. T. (07331) 63538. - Graph /
Furn - *052228*
Unterlöhner, E., Lange Gasse 5, 73312 Geislingen an der
Steige. T. (07331) 44717. *052229*

Geldern (Nordrhein-Westfalen)

Brückner, Harttor 2, 47608 Geldern. T. (02831) 86674.
- Furn - *052230*
Orphey, N., Martinistr. 50g, 47608 Geldern.
T. (02831) 4004. *052231*

Gelnhausen (Hessen)

Porsch, M., & M. de Vries, Langgasse 17, 63571 Gelnhausen. T. (06051) 179 53. *052232*

Gelsenkirchen (Nordrhein-Westfalen)

Achtelik, P.-M., Maximilianstr. 12, 45894 Gelsenkirchen.
T. (0209) 390012, Fax (0209) 390012. - Paint / Graph /
Furn / Silv / Instr - *052233*
Antik 2000, Hobackestr. 67, 45899 Gelsenkirchen.
T. (0209) 58 46 43. - Ant - *052234*
Berkenbusch, Blindestr. 1, 45894 Gelsenkirchen.
T. (0209) 37 54 41. - Paint / Graph / Repr / Sculp / Jew /
Fra / Rel / Glass - *052235*
Decker, D., Maximilianstr. 11, 45894 Gelsenkirchen.
T. (0209) 30335. *052236*
Grüterich, Ingrid, Allmendenweg 2, 45894 Gelsenkir-
chen. T. (0209) 59 36 82. - Orient / China - *052237*
Jürgensen, Elly, Möckernhof 15, 45886
Gelsenkirchen. *052238*

Kurth, U., Auf dem Schollbruch 44, 45899 Gelsenkir-
chen. T. (0209) 552 45. *052239*
Löwe, Ernst, Kirchstr. 7, 45879 Gelsenkirchen. *052240*
Misch, U., Hagenstr. 41, 45894 Gelsenkirchen.
T. (0209) 37 06 71. *052241*
Roth, H., Weberstr. 17, 45879 Gelsenkirchen.
T. (0209) 27 02 23. *052242*
Sehnert-Schucht, I., Blindestr. 1, 45894 Gelsenkirchen.
T. (0209) 37 54 41. *052243*
Seidler, C., Rheinelbestr. 42, 45886
Gelsenkirchen. *052244*
Volz, Grillostr. 47, 45881 Gelsenkirchen.
T. (0209) 861 60. - Num - *052245*
Voss, Helmut, Mühlenstr. 45, 45894
Gelsenkirchen. *052246*
Wiemann, A., Am Fettingkotten 39, 45891 Gelsenkir-
chen. T. (0209) 72288. *052247*

Gemünden (Hessen)

Zoll, S., Zur Burg 1, 35285 Gemünden.
T. (06453) 555. *052248*

Gengenbach (Baden-Württemberg)

Ruck, Melitta, Brückenhäuserstr. 2, 77723 Gengenbach.
T. (07803) 57 17. - Ant / Furn / Instr - *052249*

Georgensgmünd (Bayern)

Schwarz, L., Marktpl. 11, 91166 Georgensgmünd.
T. (09172) 8633. *052250*

Georgsmarienhütte (Niedersachsen)

Schatztruhe, Oeseerstr. 91, 49124 Georgsmarienhütte.
T. (05401) 40443. - Ant / Furn - *052251*

Gera (Thüringen)

Saskia – Kleinantiquitäten, Zschochernstr. 36, 07545
Gera. T. (0365) 26932. *052252*
Thüringer Antiquitäten und Einrichtungshaus, Von-Os-
sietzky-Str. 32, 07552 Gera. T. (0365) 29317. *052253*

Gerabronn (Baden-Württemberg)

Arnim, Christoph Graf von, Villa Kuperhof, 74582 Gera-
bronn. T. (07952) 67014. *052254*
Hoffmann, E., Rechenhausenstr 2, 74582 Gerabronn.
T. (07952) 5238. *052255*

Geretsried (Bayern)

Hassel, Gert von, Breslauer Weg 44, 82538 Geretsried.
T. (08171) 8566. - Arch - *052256*

Gerlingen (Baden-Württemberg)

Arp, A., Kirschstr 3, 70839 Gerlingen.
T. (07156) 217268. *052257*

Germersheim (Rheinland-Pfalz)

Haaff, August-Keiler-Str. 19, 76726 Germersheim.
T. (07274) 2444. - Ant / Paint / Graph / Furn - *052258*

Gernsbach (Baden-Württemberg)

Balser, Helmuth, Igelbachstr. 16, 76593 Gernsbach.
T. (07224) 70 10, 16 67. - Ant / Paint / Furn / China /
Tex / Eth / Fra / Silv - *052259*

Gerolzhofen (Bayern)

Taupp, Angy, Lülsfelder Weg 1, 97447 Gerolzhofen.
T. (09382) 5774. - Lights - *052260*

Gescher (Nordrhein-Westfalen)

Hessing, H., Borkener Damm 51, 48712 Gescher.
T. (02542) 6343. *052261*
Kreiter, R., Stadtlohnerstr. 46, 48712 Gescher.
T. (02542) 6101. *052262*

Gettorf (Schleswig-Holstein)

Broocks, C. & M., Herrenstr. 29, 24214 Gettorf.
T. (04346) 7435. *052263*

Gevelsberg (Nordrhein-Westfalen)

Grafen, F., Mittelstr. 71, 58285 Gevelsberg.
T. (02332) 140 36. *052264*

Giengen (Baden-Württemberg)

Göttler, Franz, Tannenstr 17, 89537 Giengen.
T. (07322) 3882. - Mil - *052265*

Gießen (Hessen)

Farben-Schmidt, Neuenweg 7, 35390 Gießen. - Paint /
Graph / Repr / Fra / Draw - *052266*
Galerie Krauch & Fincke, Schulstr. 11, 35390 Gießen.
T. (0641) 357 48. *052267*
Niederlintner, Grünberger Str. 13, 35390 Gießen.
T. (0641) 35263, Fax (0641) 78173. - Ant / Furn /
Instr - *052268*
Rätzel, Georg, Grünberger Str. 11, 35390 Gießen.
T. (0641) 32440, Fax (0641) 33454. - Paint / Graph /
Repr / Sculp / Fra / Lights - *052269*
Reuß, B., Seltersweg 46, 35390 Gießen.
T. (0641) 74417. - Num - *052270*
Roden, R., Zu den Mühlen 19, 35390 Gießen.
T. (0641) 775 14. *052271*
Sammlerzentrale, Frankfurter Str. 11, 35390 Gießen.
T. (0641) 745 45. - Ant - *052272*

Gifhorn (Niedersachsen)

Winkelmann, R., Braunschweiger Str. 3, 38518 Gifhorn.
T. (05371) 164 70. *052273*

Gilching (Bayern)

MNA, Postfach 1408, 82199 Gilching. - Num - *052274*

Gladbeck (Nordrhein-Westfalen)

Reuer, Rentforter Str 52-62, 45964 Gladbeck.
T. (02143) 21819. - Furn - *052275*
Werner, I., Hochstr 51, 45964 Gladbeck.
T. (02143) 63390. *052276*

Gladenbach (Hessen)

Burk, D., Kreuzstr. 35, 35075 Gladenbach.
T. (06462) 23 52. *052277*

Gleisweiler (Rheinland-Pfalz)

Groß, F., Kirchstr. 13, 76835 Gleisweiler.
T. (06345) 3178. *052278*

Glienicke (Brandenburg)

Brandenburgischer Antiquitätenhandel, Ernst-Thäl-
mannstr. 11-13, 16548 Glienicke. *052279*

Glinde

Siemen, A., Otto-Hahn-Str 3, 21509 Glinde.
T. (040) 7279342. *052280*

Glonn (Bayern)

Kotzinger, H., Am Kupferbach 2, 85625 Glonn.
T. (08093) 691. - Ant / Paint - *052281*

Gmund (Bayern)

Duensing, Tölzer Str. 2, 83703 Gmund.
T. (08022) 754 23, 745 80. - Paint - *052282*
Hölzermann, Ulrich, Muhlthalstr. 16, 83703 Gmund.
T. (08022) 74350, Fax (08022) 74340. - Ant / Paint /
Graph / Orient / Mod - *052283*
Maurer, W., An der Mangfall 1, 83703 Gmund.
T. (08022) 1653. - Paint / Sculp / Arch / Mul - *052284*
Sievert, H. J., Tölzer Str. 129, 83703 Gmund.
T. (08022) 74877. - Ant - *052285*

Goch (Nordrhein-Westfalen)

Hühn, G., An der Waterkuhl 4, 47574 Goch.
T. (02823) 33 08. *052286*
Lübeck, Benzstr. 2, 47574 Goch. T. (02823) 5483.
- Paint - *052287*

Göllheim (Rheinland-Pfalz)

Schraven, J., Gundheimerhof 2, 67307 Göllheim.
T. (06351) 8286. *052288*

Göppingen (Baden-Württemberg)

Becke, L., Hauptstr. 36, 73033 Göppingen.
T. (07161) 68 33 00. *052289*
Becke, M., Kirchstr. 8, 73033 Göppingen.
T. (07161) 71959. *052290*
Dundalek, Peter-Moritz, Poststr. 33, 73035 Göppingen.
T. (07161) 682 24. - Ant - *052291*
Fauser, Adolf, Boller Str. 37, 73035 Göppingen.
T. (07161) 490 67. - Ant / Paint / Furn / China / Instr /
Glass - *052292*
Frenzel, E., Schulstr. 6, 73033 Göppingen.
T. (07161) 721 75. *052293*
Garmisch, W. & J. Helmer, Lange Str. 6, 73033 Göppin-
gen. T. (07161) 741 57. *052294*

Haenle, Schulstr. 12, 73033 Göppingen.
T. (07161) 699 96. *052295*
Haisch, Elisabeth, Schottstr. 19, 73033 Göppingen.
T. (07161) 758 88. - Ant - *052296*
Herrmann, Rathausstr. 2, 73035 Göppingen.
T. (07161) 12864. *052297*
Immig, A., Kaiserbergsteige 15, 73037 Göppingen.
T. (07161) 570. *052298*
Lietzmann, Vordere Karlstr. 45, 73033
Göppingen. *052299*
Pfrommer, W., Jebenhäuser Str. 90, 73035 Göppingen.
T. (07161) 723 28. - Ant / Furn / Dec - *052300*
Reik, Karl, Schillerstr. 77, 73033 Göppingen.
- Num - *052301*
Scheck, W., Schloßstr. 2, 73033 Göppingen.
T. (07161) 73808. *052302*
Seeger, B., Querstr. 14, 73033 Göppingen.
T. (07161) 76229. *052303*
Seeger, D., Spitalstr. 17, 73033 Göppingen.
T. (07161) 762 29. *052304*
Winkler, Wühlestr. 32, 73033 Göppingen.
T. (07161) 716 61. - Num - *052305*
Zoller, E., Pflegstr. 1, 73033 Göppingen.
T. (07161) 752 37. *052306*

Göttingen (Niedersachsen)
Antiklager Ascherberg, Ascherberg 1, 37081 Göttingen.
T. (0551) 70 31 29. *052307*
Artemjew, Nikolai, Friedländer Weg 46, 37085 Göttin-
gen. T. (0551) 592 82. - Ant - *052308*
Bockum-Dolffs, von, Bühlstr. 19, 37073 Göttingen.
- Ant / Furn - *052309*
Bohm, S., Barfüßerstr. 12, 37073 Göttingen.
T. (0551) 57086, Fax (0551) 67832. Ant / Paint / Furn /
Mul - *052310*
Bricoles, Papendiek 2, 37073 Göttingen.
T. (0551) 55016. - Mod - *052311*
Brust, Hanns, Jüdenstr. 22, 37073 Göttingen.
T. (0551) 424 75. *052312*
Eberwein, Roswitha, Bismarckstr. 4, 37085 Göttingen.
T. (0551) 47083, Fax (0551) 41543. - Ant / Orient / Tex /
Arch - *052313*
English Antiques, Rote Str. 16, 37073 Göttingen.
T. (0551) 577 75. - Ant / Furn / China / Tex / Fra / Silv /
Lights / Instr / Glass - *052314*
Krickmeyer, E., Rote Str. 30, 37073 Göttingen.
T. (0551) 577 38. - Num - *052315*
Maas, Sylvia, Rote Str. 15, 37073 Göttingen.
T. (0551) 578 43. - Furn - *052316*
Mayer, Joachim, Lange Geismarstr. 55, 37073 Göttin-
gen. T. (0551) 41761, Fax (0551) 58694. - Ant / Paint /
Furn / Jew / Silv / Glass / Mod - *052317*
Mayer, Ursula, Kurze Str. 7, 37073 Göttingen.
T. (0551) 477 22. - Ant - *052318*
Müller, Klaus, Am Weißen Steine 11, 37085 Göttingen.
T. (0551) 465 74. *052319*
Sparenberg, F., Lange Geismarstr. 69, 37073 Göttingen.
T. (0551) 451 63. *052320*
Stratemann, Kurt-R., Burgstr. 19, 37073 Göttingen.
T. (0551) 41981. *052321*
Uta's Vitrinchen, Lange Geismar 16, 37073 Göttingen.
T. (0551) 434 87. - Toys - *052322*
Wolf, Jüdenstr. 31, 37073 Göttingen. T. (0551) 433 77.
- Ant / Paint / Graph / Num / Jew / Silv / Mil / Cur --
052323
Yesterday, Ewaldstr. 79, 37075 Göttingen.
T. (0551) 55402, 47246. - Mod - *052324*
Zöllner, H. & C. Hexel, Lange Geismarstr. 49, 37073
Göttingen. *052325*

Gollhofen (Bayern)
Ofenhäusle, 97258 Gollhofen. T. (09339) 10 06. *052326*

Goslar (Niedersachsen)
Antikhof Goslar, Hoher Weg 5, 38640 Goslar.
T. (05321) 269 45. - Ant / Furn / Mil / Ico - *052327*
Deierling, Hermann, Kaiserbleek 1, 38640 Goslar.
T. (05321) 265 60. *052328*
Flügge, Hans R., Wittenstr. 7, 38640 Goslar.
T. (05321) 220 17. - Ant - *052329*
Horizont Laden, Petersilienstr. 29, 38640 Goslar.
T. (05321) 296 86. *052330*

Krebs & Tippach GmbH, Petersilienstr. 3, 38640 Goslar.
T. (05321) 226 76. - Ant - *052331*
Mittendorf, Karl-Heinz, Hoher Weg 15, 38640 Goslar.
T. (05321) 261 22. - Ant / China / Silv / Mil /
Glass - *052332*
Richter, K., Auf dem Berge 26, 38644 Goslar.
T. (05321) 843 18. *052333*
Richter, Karsten, Clausthaler Str. 52, 38640 Goslar.
T. (05321) 4711. *052334*
Schwartz, Moritz, Bäckerstr. 2, 38640 Goslar.
T. (05321) 46 11. *052335*

Gottmadingen (Baden-Württemberg)
Ritter, M., Hauptstr. 22, 78244 Gottmadingen.
T. (07731) 73481. *052336*

Gräfelfing (Bayern)
Langer, Karl J., Rottenbucherstr. 33a, 82166 Gräfelfing.
T. (089) 8543590, Fax (089) 8544293. - Instr - *052337*
Puttfarken, Bahnhofstr. 103, 82166 Gräfelfing.
T. (089) 85 25 61. *052338*
Stadelmayr, Susanne, Scharnitzer Str. 39, 82166 Gräfel-
fing. T. (089) 85 24 65. - Ant - *052339*

Gräfenberg (Bayern)
Frank, G., Am Sportpl. 12, 91322 Gräfenberg.
T. (09192) 8590. - Num - *052340*

Grafenau (Baden-Württemberg)
Klöter, Peter, Schloß Dätzingen, 71117 Grafenau.
T. (07033) 43484, Fax 44619. - Instr - *052341*
Schlichtenmaier, Schloß Dätzingen, 71117 Grafenau.
T. (07033) 41394, Fax (07033) 44923. - Paint / Graph /
Sculp / Draw - *052342*

Grafenau (Bayern)
Driendl, H. & C., Voitschlag, 94481 Grafenau.
T. (08552) 39 19. *052343*
Wolf, G., Kröllstr. 5, 94481 Grafenau.
T. (08552) 3320. *052344*

Grafenhausen (Baden-Württemberg)
Mangeon, G., Rehgasse, 79865 Grafenhausen. *052345*

Grafschaft (Rheinland-Pfalz)
Kohlhass, K., Heppinger Str. 62, 53501 Grafschaft.
T. (02641) 24553. *052346*

Grasberg (Niedersachsen)
Grewe, R., Neu-Rautendorfer Str. 86, 28879
Grasberg. *052347*
Stelten, H., Otterstein 48, 28879 Grasberg.
T. (0408) 39 28. *052348*

Grasbrunn (Bayern)
Funk, Werner, Beethovenring 7, 85630 Grasbrunn.
T. (089) 46 64 33, Fax (089) 460 69 42. - Ant / Num /
Arch - *052349*

Grassau (Bayern)
Blüml, J. & A., Achentalstr. 11, 83224 Grassau.
T. (08641) 14 57. *052350*

Grebenhain (Hessen)
Stöhr, Hand, Frankfurter Str. 10, 36355 Grebenhain.
T. (06644) 12 86. *052351*

Grebin (Schleswig-Holstein)
Zorndt, E., Rantzau, 24329 Grebin.
T. (04383) 604. *052352*

Greding (Bayern)
Franz, Christof & Manfred Ehrl, Schloss, Nürnberger Str.
1, 91171 Greding. T. (08463) 1459, 9545. - Paint /
Eth / Mil - *052353*

Greifenstein (Hessen)
Klein, N., Hauptstr. 31, 35753 Greifenstein.
T. (02779) 1288. *052354*

Greussenheim (Bayern)
Demling, M. & Silvia, Bergstr. 14, 97259 Greussenheim.
T. (09369) 1515. *052355*

Greven, Westfalen (Nordrhein-Westfalen)
Höning, Erwin, Kirchstr 3, 48268 Greven, Westfalen.
- Instr - *052356*
Lindenbaum, Lindenstr 32, 48268 Greven, Westfalen.
T. (02571) 2012. *052357*
Mader, Martinistr 49, 48268 Greven, Westfalen.
T. (02571) 2137, Fax (02571) 52469. - Num - *052358*
Putzer, K., Guntrunperbg. 3, 48268 Greven, Westfalen.
T. (02571) 51382. *052359*

Grevenbroich (Nordrhein-Westfalen)
Engels, E. & H., Gruissem 31a, 41516 Grevenbroich.
T. (02181) 28 07. *052360*
Geller, Arndtstr. 3, 41515 Grevenbroich.
T. (02181) 22 88. - Ant / Paint / Furn / China /
Mil - *052361*
Kellerweßel, K., Lindenstr. 32, 41515 Grevenbroich.
T. (02181) 93 92. *052362*
Krapohl, Jakob, Schloß Hülchrath, 41516 Grevenbroich.
T. (02181) 7104, Fax 69149. - Ant / Furn - *052363*

Griesbach (Bayern)
Diezmann, R., Karpfham-Schneider-Str 2, 94086 Griesbach. T. (08532) 1262. *052364*

Griesheim (Hessen)
Golden Pendulum, Postfach 1166, 64343 Griesheim.
T. (06155) 2231, Fax (06155) 2433. - Jew / Cur /
Instr - *052365*
Swetec, Franz, Friedrich-Ebert-Str. 48, 64347 Gries-
heim. T. (06155) 783 91. - Paint - *052366*
Zum Fleißigen Biber, Postfach 1166, 64343 Griesheim.
T. (06155) 2231, Fax (06155) 6155. *052367*

Gröbenzell (Bayern)
Kreutz, I., Kreiubreitlstr. 10, 82194 Gröbenzell. *052368*

Gronau (Nordrhein-Westfalen)
Almsick, Georg van, Merschstr. 21, 48599 Gronau.
T. (02562) 10 61/63. *052369*
Antike-Fundgrube, Gildehauser Str. 68, 48599 Gronau.
T. (02562) 5180, Fax (02562) 1615. - Furn - *052370*
Gremegro, An der Eßseite 219, 48599 Gronau.
T. (02562) 52 52. - Ant - *052371*
Subgang, Alfons, Enscheder Str. 352, 48599 Gronau.
T. (02562) 6542. *052372*

Groß Nordende
Maus, Philipp, Altendeichsweg 25, 25436 Groß Norden-
de. T. (04125) 635. - Ant - *052373*

Groß Rönnau (Schleswig-Holstein)
Tabernakel, Segeberger Str. 29, 23795 Groß Rönnau.
T. (04551) 833 62. *052374*

Groß-Umstadt (Hessen)
Brunner, Andrea, Rodensteinerstr. 4, 64823 Groß-Um-
stadt. T. (06078) 56 80, 715 66. *052375*
Buchal, P., Heinrich-Ritzel-Str. 3, 64823 Groß-Umstadt.
T. (06078) 72361. *052376*
Die Schatulle, An der Wehrkirche 5, 64823 Groß-
Umstadt. *052377*
Galerie im Hof, Friedr.-Ebert-Str. 5, 64823 Groß-Um-
stadt. T. (06078) 4973. - Furn - *052378*
Schuh, G., Marktplatz, 64823 Groß-Umstadt.
T. (06078) 3550. *052379*
Ziesler, G., Schlierbacherstr. 4, 64823 Groß-Umstadt.
T. (06078) 65 67. *052380*

Grossefehn (Niedersachsen)
Antik an der Mühle in Westgroßfehn, Timmel, 26629
Grossefehn. T. (04945) 454. - Ant - *052381*

Grosserlach (Baden-Württemberg)
Schmidt, R., Neufürstenhütte, 71577 Grosserlach.
T. (07903) 3206. - Ant / Furn / Tex - *052382*

Großkarolinenfeld (Bayern)
Thaler, Georg, 83109 Großkarolinenfeld. *052383*

Großniedesheim (Rheinland-Pfalz)
Bruckert, A. & C., Beindersheimer Str. 4, 67259 Großnie-
desheim. T. (06239) 3354. *052384*

Grünstadt (Rheinland-Pfalz)
Schilling, H., Mozartstr. 32, 67269 Grünstadt.
T. (06359) 23 10, 29 88. - Ant -   *052385*

Grünwald (Bayern)
Bierstorfer, Josef, Ricarda-Huch-Str 1, 82031 Grünwald.
T. (089) 6411779.   *052386*
Griebert, Peter, Ricarda-Huch-Str 4, 82031 Grünwald.
T. (089) 6413054. - Ant -   *052387*
Leuchtenberger, Regina, Gabriel-von-Seidl-Str 30a,
82031 Grünwald.   *052388*
Matzke, Helga, Wörnbrunner Str 11, 82031 Grünwald.
T. (089) 641067. - Ant -   *052389*
Nordström, Ninna, Rathauspl 1, 82031 Grünwald.
T. (089) 6411830. - Ant / Paint / Furn / Repr / Tex / Dec /
Lights -   *052390*

Günzburg (Bayern)
Gawlik, C., Bahnhofstr. 5, 89312 Günzburg.
T. (08221) 8122.   *052391*
Neumann, Ernst, Wättepl. 6, 89312 Günzburg.
T. (08221) 321 87. - Num -   *052392*

Gütersloh (Nordrhein-Westfalen)
Büteröwe, Waltraud, Auf der Benkert 23a, 33330
Gütersloh.   *052393*
Grabenheinrich, H., Kökerstr. 5a, 33330 Gütersloh.
T. (05241) 294 50.   *052394*
Grosse-Hainbrock, Hohenzollernstr. 2, 33330 Güters-
loh. T. (05241) 15956.   *052395*
Hanna's Kommodenboden, Nordring 23, 33330 Güters-
loh. T. (05241) 14769.   *052396*
Jentsch, Detlef, Kahlertstr 2, 33330 Gütersloh.
T. (05241) 13168, Fax 13168. - Ant -   *052397*
Meyreiß, Pavenstädter Weg 5, 33334 Gütersloh.
T. (05241) 28171.   *052398*
Oelker, Engelbert, Berliner Str. 39, 33330
Gütersloh.   *052399*
Ohlbrock, Christoph, Reckenberger Str. 22, 33332 Gü-
tersloh. T. (05241) 514 86.   *052400*
Strothotte, B., Andreasweg 8, 33335 Gütersloh.
T. (05241) 784 83. - Num -   *052401*
Weber-Haus, Münsterstr. 9, 33330 Gütersloh.
T. (05241) 283 06. - Ant / Graph / Furn / China / Dec /
Jew / Silv / Instr / Glass / Cur -   *052402*

Gummersbach (Nordrhein-Westfalen)
Lindner, Hunstiger Str. 37, 51645 Gummersbach.
T. (02261) 766 35.   *052403*
Pannhuis, H., Lingestenstr. 8, 51645 Gummersbach.
T. (02261) 53954.   *052404*
Sarcander, Arthur, Frömmersbacher Str. 9, 51647 Gum-
mersbach. T. (02261) 267 65. - Paint -   *052405*
Schmitt, Otto, Glockenweg 2, 51647 Gummersbach.
T. (02261) 02266/3502. - Ant -   *052406*

Gunzenhausen (Bayern)
Sprengel, K.D., Wagstr, 91710 Gunzenhausen.
T. (09831) 8484. - Ant / Paint / Graph / Fra /
Glass -   *052407*

Gutenzell-Hürbel (Baden-Württemberg)
Meier, Hans, Schlüsselbergstr. 11, 88484 Gutenzell-Hür-
bel. T. (073 52) 07352/ 88 65. - Ant -   *052408*

Haan (Nordrhein-Westfalen)
Albrecht, Norbert, Alter Kirchpl 23, 42781 Haan.
T. (02129) 4850.   *052409*
Bockhacker, M., Eschenweg 7, 42781 Haan.
T. (02104) 61113.   *052410*
Burton, J., Am Quell 12, 42781 Haan.
T. (02104) 61413.   *052411*
Scholzen, Werner, Jahnstr 12, 42760 Haan.
T. (02129) 52783, Fax (02129) 53982. - Ant / Paint /
Furn / Orient / China / Sculp -   *052412*
Schwaneberg, H., Wilhelmstr 30, 42781 Haan.
T. (02129) 8855. - Ant -   *052413*

Hänichen (Sachsen)
Friedrich, U., Hauptstr 9, 01728 Hänichen.
T. (0351) 4030616.   *052414*

Hagen (Niedersachsen)
Gäng, A., Im Lorenkamp 32, 49170 Hagen.
T. (054 01) 71 11.   *052415*

Hagen (Nordrhein-Westfalen)
Cercle d'Art Orthodoxe du Sud-Est, Bolohstr. 39, 58093
Hagen. T. (02331) 520 60.   *052416*
Freter, H., Dahlenkampstr. 2, 58095 Hagen.
T. (02331) 256 66. - Paint / Graph / Repr / Fra -   *052417*
Kaiser, Hans, Am Höing 7, 58097 Hagen.
T. (02331) 87 02 66.   *052418*
Klaproth, Bernd, Bergstr. 110, 58095 Hagen.
T. (02331) 159 85.   *052419*
Lange, W., Helfer Str. 2, 58099 Hagen.
T. (02331) 606 56.   *052420*
Nordmeier, Walter, Buschstr. 79, 58099 Hagen. - Ant /
Mil -   *052421*
Paffrath, Marie, Spinngasse 4, 58095 Hagen.
T. (02331) 235 05.   *052422*
Schürmann, H., Altenhagener Str. 42, 58097 Hagen.
T. (02331) 889 55.   *052423*
Syplacz, A., Lenneuferstr. 15, 58119 Hagen.
T. (02331) 02334 / 40630.   *052424*
Vogel, J., Rembergstr. 58, 58095 Hagen.
T. (02331) 281 26.   *052425*

Halle (Nordrhein-Westfalen)
Ambiente, Rosenstr. 10, 33790 Halle.   *052426*
Antiklager, Bismarckstr. 5, 33790 Halle.
T. (05201) 9785.   *052427*
Haller Nostalgie Stübchen, Rosenstr. 3, 33790 Halle.
T. (05201) 4789.   *052428*
Ravensberger Kunstspeicher, Ascheloher Weg 5, 33790
Halle. T. (05201) 7963, Fax (05201) 7664. - Ant / Furn /
Sculp -   *052429*

Halle (Sachsen-Anhalt)
Jacobshagen, K., Geiststr. 45, 06108 Halle.
T. (0345) 33398.   *052430*

Hallstadt (Bayern)
Motschenbacher, A., Am Ziedergraben 19, 96103 Hall-
stadt. T. (0951) 755 88.   *052431*

Halstenbek (Schleswig-Holstein)
Galerie Eisberg, 25469 Halstenbek. T. (04101) 310 71.
- Jew -   *052432*

Haltern (Nordrhein-Westfalen)
Seppmann, Werner A., Dr., Arenbergstr 31, 45721 Hal-
tern. T. (02364) 3224799. - Ant -   *052433*

Halver (Nordrhein-Westfalen)
Lange, U., Volmestr. 45, 58553 Halver.
T. (02353) 02351/71904.   *052434*
Sieper, Wolfgang & Waltraud Schaub, Höhenweg 31,
58553 Halver. T. (02353) 27 78.   *052435*

Hamburg
Abrahams, Heegbarg 31, 22391 Hamburg.
T. (040) 602 48 33.   *052436*
Abrahams Ankauf, Berliner Allee 42, 22850 Hamburg.
T. (040) 5233243.   *052437*
Abrahams, Käte, Einkaufszentrum Alstertal, 20095 Ham-
burg. T. (040) 602 48 33.   *052438*
Acoustic Art, Borselstr 16c, 22765 Hamburg.
T. (040) 39863350.   *052439*
Aderholz, L., Ruhrstr. 11, 22761 Hamburg.
T. (040) 850 81 22.   *052440*
Afghan-Haus, Lehmweg 41, 20251 Hamburg.
T. (040) 48 10 21. - Ant -   *052441*
African Arts Gallery, Hegestr 2, 20251 Hamburg.
T. (040) 4804600.   *052442*
African Arts Gallery, Hegestr. 2, 20251 Hamburg.
T. (040) 4804600.   *052443*
Aktien Galerie, Rathausstr. 12, 20095 Hamburg.
T. (040) 323948. - Num -   *052444*
Aktiv Art & Print, Lokstedter Weg 86, 20251 Hamburg.
T. (040) 464355.   *052445*
Alpers, Blankeneser Bahnhofstr. 9, 22587 Hamburg.
T. (040) 86 96 75. - Ant -   *052446*
Alter, Anneliese, Elbchaussee 10, 22765 Hamburg.
T. (040) 397182. - Ant -   *052447*
Ande, Hermann, Colonnaden 70, 20354 Hamburg.
T. (040) 35 21 65. - Jew / Mul / Instr -   *052448*
Ankauf Bildat, Gr. Burstah 40, 22457 Hamburg.
T. (040) 363950.   *052449*

Anno dazumal, Schlüterstr. 77, 20146 Hamburg.
T. (040) 455467.   *052450*
Anthony, Dorette, Blankeneser Landstr. 39, 22587 Ham-
burg. T. (040) 86 05 55. - Furn / Lights -   *052451*
Antic-Kaufhaus Falkenried, Falkenried 85, 20251 Ham-
burg. T. (040) 47 93 73.   *052452*
Antik Bau Stawe, Dockenhudener Str 7, 22587 Ham-
burg. T. (040) 864566.   *052453*
Antik-Kontor, Goldbekpl 2, 21303 Hamburg.
T. (040) 2806482.   *052454*
Antik-Laden, Wilstorfer Str 114a, 21073 Hamburg.
T. (040) 776467.   *052455*
Antik Speicher, Eifflerstr. 1, 22769 Hamburg.
T. (040) 43 30 40, Fax (040) 4304445. - Furn -   *052456*
Antik & Kunst, Eichenstr. 29, 20259 Hamburg.
T. (040) 49 89 81.   *052457*
Antikbau, Dockenhudener Str. 7, 22587 Hamburg.
T. (040) 86 45 66.   *052458*
Antike Schmuckwaren, Poststr. 22, 20354 Hamburg.
T. (040) 35 28 63.   *052459*
Antikes & Dekoratives, Flughafenstr. 85, 22415 Ham-
burg. T. (040) 531 53 91.   *052460*
Antikfundgrube-Krenz, Wendemuthstr 57, 22041 Ham-
burg. T. (040) 681627.   *052461*
Antikmarkt, Volksdorfer Weg 226, 22393 Hamburg.
T. (040).   *052462*
Antique Jewellery, Eppendorfer Baum 38, 20249 Ham-
burg. T. (040) 48 10 74, Fax 04778/7252.
- Jew -   *052463*
Antiquitäten am Hofweg, Hofweg 65, 22085 Hamburg.
T. (040) 2205584, Fax (040) 224863.   *052464*
Antiquitäten am Michel, Martin-Luther-Str. 6, 20459
Hamburg. - Ant -   *052465*
Antiquitäten am Park, Flemingstr. 16, 22299 Hamburg.
T. (040) 48 53 88. - Ant / Paint / Furn / Jew / Silv /
Lights -   *052466*
Antiquitäten bei der Uni, Hoheluftchaussee 21, 20253
Hamburg. T. (040) 420 05 54.   *052467*
Antiquitäten-bric-a-brac, Martinistr 6, 20251 Hamburg.
T. (040) 484855.   *052468*
Antiquitäten Colonnade 70, Colonnaden 70, 20354
Hamburg. T. (040) 353154. - Furn / Sculp / Silv /
Glass -   *052469*
Antiquitäten im Alstertal, Wellingsbüttler Weg 188,
22391 Hamburg. T. (040) 536 58 26.   *052470*
Antiquitäten No. 6, Herderstr. 6, 22085 Hamburg.
T. (040) 220 96 20.   *052471*
Antiquitäten-Scheune, Osdorfer Landstr. 233, 22549
Hamburg. - Paint / Furn / Tex / Silv / Ico -   *052472*
Arkady, Alter Steinweg 11, 20459 Hamburg.
T. (040) 346047. - Orient -   *052473*
Arndt, Klosterwall 9-21, 20095 Hamburg.
T. (040) 32 62 85. - Ant / Mod -   *052474*
Art Connection, Johnsallee 65, 20146 Hamburg.
T. (040) 4107715.   *052475*
Art Galerie von Sturm, Gr. Flottbeker Str 30, 22607
Hamburg. T. (040) 893971.   *052476*
Art & Book GmbH, Grindelallee 132, 20146 Hamburg.
T. (040) 447936.   *052477*
Art & Trading oHG, Auedich 22, 21129 Hamburg.
T. (040) 7426826.   *052478*
Aschmutat, R., Feldnerstr. 2, 21075 Hamburg.
T. (040) 765 03 60.   *052479*
Asian Art, Mittelweg 21, 20148 Hamburg.
T. (040) 410 40 03. - Orient -   *052480*
Ateliers für die Kunst, Klosterwall 15, 20095 Hamburg.
T. (040) 335731.   *052481*
Bachner, R., Max-Brauer-Allee 196, 22765 Hamburg.
T. (040) 439 89 52.   *052482*
Bakschis, J., Eppendorfer Landstr. 130, 20251 Ham-
burg. T. (040) 480 79 12.   *052483*
Bambus Art & Design GmbH, Duvenstedter Triftweg 95,
22397 Hamburg. T. (040) 6074238.   *052484*
Bauernstuben, Grindelhof 69, 20146 Hamburg.
T. (040) 45 13 678.   *052485*
Beckmanns, Tarpenbekstr. 65, 20251 Hamburg.
T. (040) 48 95 58. - Ant -   *052486*
Begemann, E., Beimoorstr. 33, 22081 Hamburg.
T. (040) 29 28 06.   *052487*
Bergmann, H., Klosterwall 7, 20095 Hamburg.
T. (040) 33 66 55.   *052488*
Binikowski, J. Buddelschiffladen, Lokstedter Weg 68,
20251 Hamburg. T. (040) 46 28 52.   *052489*

Birgfeld, Hummelbütteler Weg 28, 22339 Hamburg.
T. (040). 052490
Blass, Ernst, Hohe Bleichen 26, 20354 Hamburg.
T. (040) 34 60 50. - Mil - 052491
Blochwitz, J., & H. Bergmann, Klosterwall 9, 20095
Hamburg. T. (040) 33 53 83. 052492
Blume, B., ABC-Str. 51, 20354 Hamburg.
T. (040) 34 45 35. 052493
Blume, Doris, Elbchaussee 10, 22765 Hamburg.
T. (040) 390 45 03. 052494
Bobsien, W., ABC-Str 50, 20354 Hamburg.
T. (040) 344406. 052495
Bobsien, Winfried, ABC-Str 50, 20354 Hamburg.
T. (040) 344406. - Ant / Furn / China / Silv / Glass /
Draw - 052496
Brammer, Krista, Wellingsbüttler Weg 32, 22391 Ham-
burg. T. (040) 5362898. 052497
Brekenfeld, Kathrin, Frauenthal 13, 20149
Hamburg. 052498
Bric-a-Brac, Martinistr. 6, 20251 Hamburg.
T. (040) 48 48 55. 052499
Brinkama, Edda, Rondeel 39, 22301 Hamburg.
T. (040) 271 30 39. - Ant / Paint / Furn / China / Tex /
Silv / Lights / Glass - 052500
Bristol Antiques, Bleichenbrücke 9, Passage Bleichen-
hof, 20354 Hamburg. T. (040) 34 28 00. - Ant / Paint /
Furn / Jew / Silv / Lights / Cur - 052501
Brocantique Mildner, Papenhuder Str 30, 22087 Ham-
burg. T. (040) 2200993, Fax (040) 2209566. - Ant /
Furn / Lights - 052502
Brose, O., Jagersredder 25, 22397 Hamburg.
T. (040) 605 42 64. 052503
Bruns, Thomas, Neuer Wall 46, 20354 Hamburg.
T. (040) 364419, Fax (040) 374649. - Paint / Furn /
Mul - 052504
Büker, Eberhard, Donauweg 1, 22393 Hamburg.
T. (040) 6401031, Fax (040) 6402026. - Mil - 052505
Bugatti, Osdorfer Landstr. 233, 22549 Hamburg.
T. (040) 800 82 56. - Ant - 052506
Buhr, Carl, Hamburger Str 23, 22083 Hamburg.
T. (040) 221180. 052507
Bunzendahl, Karl, Stralsunder Str. 4, 20099
Hamburg. 052508
Busse, Holger, Lange Reihe 71, 20099 Hamburg.
T. (040) 249771. 052509
Busse, M., Hofweg 65, 22085 Hamburg.
T. (040) 220 55 84. 052510
Butt Verlag, Robert, Mundsburger Damm 54, 22087
Hamburg. (040) 2203365. 052511
Cabinett der Geschichte, Esplanade 17, 20354 Ham-
burg. T. (040) 34 56 21. - Num - 052512
Cheikh, D. T., & Cie., Rethelstr. 52, 22607 Hamburg.
- Tex - 052513
Claire, T. le, Elbchaussee 156, 22605 Hamburg.
T. (040) 8810646. 052514
Clausen, C., Papenhuderstr 31, 22087 Hamburg.
T. (040) 225138. 052515
Consequence Artwork & Concept, Mittelweg 49, 20149
Hamburg. T. (040) 444014. 052516
Credé, H.-D. & Marieluise, M., Seestr. 16, 22607 Ham-
burg. T. (040) 829014. 052517
Czerwonatis, G., Emilienstr. 74a, 20259 Hamburg.
T. (040) 49 50 11. 052518
Dehn & Bathke, Tibarg 56, 22459 Hamburg.
T. (040) 586507. 052519
Dehn & Bathke, Tibarg 56, 22459 Hamburg.
T. (040) 586057. 052520
Denneberg, J., Bahrenfelder Str. 1, 22765 Hamburg.
T. (040) 390 40 08. 052521
Detjens, Hans, Hermann-Behn-Weg 8, 20146 Hamburg.
T. (040) 45 33 56. - Paint / Tex / Silv - 052522
Dickel, Martin, Sillemstr 60, 20257 Hamburg.
T. (040) 495885, Fax 4916531. - Fra - 052523
Digital art of Music, Bekkampsweg 6, 22045 Hamburg.
T. (040) 65493457. 052524
Dreipunkt GmbH, Osterbekstr 90a, 22083 Hamburg.
T. (040) 2789705. 052525
Dürfeldt, Albrecht, Sierichstr. 158, 22299 Hamburg.
T. (040) 480 23 94. 052526
Dürkop, P., Hochallee 6, 20149 Hamburg.
T. (040) 4101513. 052527
Dzubba, Stefan A., Milchstr. 23, 20148 Hamburg.
T. (040) 44 99 36. - Ant / Furn / Dec - 052528

Eismann, Günter, Mörkenstr. 8, 22767 Hamburg.
T. (040) 380 02 92. - Ant / Furn / China / Instr - 052529
Elbe-Antik-Hof, Osdorfer Landstr. 233, 22549 Hamburg.
T. (040) 800 49 53. 052530
Elise, Lüdemannstr. 2, 22607 Hamburg.
T. (040) 899 22 67. 052531
Emporium Hamburg, Sorbenstr 47, 20537 Hamburg
T. (040) 257990, Fax (040) 25799100. - Num - 052532
Emporium Hamburg, Ernst-Scherling-Weg 5b, 22119
Hamburg. T. (040) 6519052. 052533
Engel Sammlerhaus, Methfesselstr 60, 20257 Hamburg.
T. (040) 4911071. 052534
EPOCA, Isestr 16, 20144 Hamburg.
T. (040) 4207115. 052535
Farbraum Digital Art + Litho GmbH, Borselstr 16b,
22765 Hamburg. T. (040) 3984660. 052536
Fehrenz, Gustav, Dorfwinkel 15, 22359 Hamburg.
T. (040) 6036019. 052537
Final Artwork GmbH, Tesdorpfstr 11, 20148 Hamburg.
T. (040) 45025200. 052538
Finck, Claus, Erlenkamp 18, 22087 Hamburg.
T. (040) 229 02 36. 052539
Finckenstein, Charlotte Gräfin Finck von, Elbchaussee
31, 22765 Hamburg. T. (040) 3903011,
Fax 3903011. - China / Glass - 052540
Firmin, A., Klosterwall 9, 20095 Hamburg.
T. (040) 330890. 052541
Fischer, K., Peiffersweg 8, 22307 Hamburg.
T. (040) 6918779. 052542
Fowler & CO, Große Bleiche 36, 20354 Hamburg.
T. (040) 343392. 052543
Freese-Seiler, Karolinenstr. 25, 20357 Hamburg.
T. (040) 43 39 36. 052544
Galerie Aldona, Mittelweg 19, 20148 Hamburg.
T. (040) 4100519. 052545
Galerie an der Staatsoper, Große Theaterstr. 32, 20354
Hamburg. T. (040) 34 25 16. 052546
Galerie Condor, Volksdorfer Damm 33, 22359 Hamburg.
T. (040) 6039816, Fax (040) 6036158. 052547
Galerie d'histoire, Dammtorstr. 12, 20354 Hamburg.
T. (040) 34 31 31. - Ant - 052548
Galerie in Eppendorf, Lehmweg 46, 20251 Hamburg.
T. (040) 47 01 57. - Graph / Sculp / Fra / Draw - 052549
Galerie in Flottbek, Alexander-Zinn-Str. 25, 22607 Ham-
burg. T. (040) 82 64 74. - Paint / Graph / Sculp /
Mod - 052550
Galerie Lehmann, Harburger Ring 17, 21073 Hamburg.
T. (040) 7664567. 052551
Galerie Maritim, Martin-Luther-Str. 21, 20459 Hamburg.
T. (040) 364312, Fax (040) 363367. - Naut - 052552
Galerie Menssen, Ulzburger Str 308, 22846 Hamburg.
T. (040) 5228822. 052553
Galerie Mewes, Lehmweg 51, 20251 Hamburg.
T. (040) 481126. 052554
Galerie Morganti, Wandsbeker Chaussee 3, 22089 Ham-
burg. T. (040) 2513003. 052555
Galinski, U., Ditmar Koel Str 19, 20459 Hamburg.
T. (040) 312016. 052556
Galinski & Hein, Marktstr. 36, 20357 Hamburg.
T. (040) 430 06 81. 052557
Garg, Dr., Bergstedter Chaussee 64, 22395 Hamburg.
T. (040) 6048663, 665540. 052558
Gemälde Zeiner, Voßstraat 75, 22399 Hamburg.
T. (040) 6021534. 052559
Gerdts, C., Klosterwall 9, 20095 Hamburg.
T. (040) 32 69 10. 052560
Gerlach, A., Mittelweg 30, 20148 Hamburg.
T. (040) 447958. 052561
Glanz & Gloria Sammler Ecke, Hohe Bleichen 26, 20354
Hamburg. T. (040) 34 39 73. 052562
Gohar Pour, M., Am Rathenaupark 13, 22763 Hamburg.
T. (040) 8813769. 052563
Golshan, An der Alster 81, 20099 Hamburg.
T. (040) 24 58 09. - Tex - 052564
Goritzka, R., Martinistr. 20, 20251 Hamburg.
T. (040) 483884. 052565
Grau, G., Tangstedter Landstr. 182, 22415 Hamburg.
T. (040) 520 03 44. 052566
Greiff, Konstantin, Poststr. 29, 20354 Hamburg.
T. (040) 34 65 04. - Ant - 052567
Griep, R., Hartungstr. 18, 20146 Hamburg.
T. (040) 44 76 48. - Ant - 052568

Grimm, Karl W., Hütten 65, 20355 Hamburg.
T. (040) 31 28 94. - Fra - 052569
Guckel, Henriette E., Eifflerstr. 1, 22769 Hamburg.
T. (040) 43 30 40. - Furn - 052570
Günnemann, Karl, Ehrenbergstr 57, 22767 Hamburg.
T. (040) 387264. 052571
Günnemann, Karl, Ehrenbergstr. 57, 22767 Hamburg.
T. (040) 387264, Fax (040) 384089. - Ant / Paint / Furn /
China / Sculp / Arch / Silv / Glass - 052572
Günther, H., Deichstr. 30, 20459 Hamburg.
T. (040) 37 11 30. 052573
Guhr, Andreas, Jungfernstieg 8, 20354
Hamburg. 052574
Hacker, R., Klosterallee 104, 20144 Hamburg.
T. (040) 48 12 09. 052575
Hamburger Flohmarkt, Weidenstieg 20, 20259 Ham-
burg. T. (040) 49 36 72. - Ant - 052576
Harcken, Moorweidenstr. 7, 20148 Hamburg.
T. (040) 449777, Fax (040) 44809804. - China - 052577
Hargens, H., Giffeyweg 1, 22175 Hamburg.
T. (040) 6431256. 052578
Harries, Hofweg 12, 22085 Hamburg. T. (040) 229 00 77.
- Num - 052579
Hartwig, Marianne, Poelchaukamp 20, 22301 Hamburg.
T. (040) 27 70 92. 052580
Hartwig, Monika, Schlüterstr. 75, 20146 Hamburg.
T. (040) 45 54 67. 052581
Hauswedell & Nolte, Pöseldorfer Weg 1, 20148 Ham-
burg. T. (040) 4132100, Fax 41321010. - Paint /
Graph / Sculp / Draw - 052582
Hazeborg, Bernhard ter, Milchstr. 11, 20148 Hamburg.
T. (040) 410 10 16/17, Fax 410 10 16. - Ant / Paint /
Furn / Silv - 052583
Heinrich, P., Mittelweg 138, 20148 Hamburg.
T. (040) 45 78 05. Ant 052584
Helling, Otto, Nagelsweg 10, 20097 Hamburg.
T. (040) 24 50 66. - Num - 052585
Hellkamp, I., Bergwinkel 14, 21075 Hamburg.
T. (040) 7907637. 052586
Henk, Anne, Klosterwall 9, 20095 Hamburg.
T. (040) 32 61 57. 052587
Hennig, K., Wexstr 35, 20355 Hamburg.
T. (040) 352585. 052588
Henning, Karl, Dr., Wexstr. 35, 20355 Hamburg.
T. (040) 32 25 85. 052589
Hentschel, D., Clemens-Schultz-Str. 94, 20359 Ham-
burg. T. (040) 313650. 052590
Hermsen, Jean, Hofweg 8, 22085 Hamburg.
T. (040) 345171, Fax (040) 2201284. - China /
Silv - 052591
Herold, R., Loogeplatz 1, 20249 Hamburg.
T. (040) 478060. 052592
Heuser, Dr., & Grete, Hohe Bleichen 14-16, 20354 Ham-
burg. T. (040) 24 51 26. 052593
Heuts, H., Dr., Milchstr. 4, 20148 Hamburg.
T. (040) 442423. - Ant - 052594
Hillmann, Gertrud, Lehmweg 6, 20251 Hamburg.
T. (040) 420 53 00. 052595
HKV GmbH, Ruhrstr 90, 22761 Hamburg.
T. (040) 8514970. 052596
Hochhuth, Walter D., Poststr 11, 20354 Hamburg.
T. (040) 342211, Fax 352020. - Ant / Glass / Jew / Silv /
Toys - 052597
Holz, J., Wellingsbüttler Weg 188, 22391 Hamburg.
T. (040) 536 58 26. - Ant - 052598
Homberger, Bahrenfelder Str. 15, 22765 Hamburg.
T. (040) 39 41 27. 052599
Horstmann, Rainer, Dr., Hofweg 69, 22085 Hamburg.
T. (040) 270 04 28. 052600
House of Bewlay, Bleichenbrücke 10, 20354 Hamburg.
T. (040) 35 34 33. - Ant - 052601
Hühne, Wolfgang, Mittelweg 21, 20148 Hamburg.
T. (040) 410 40 03. 052602
Huelsmann, F.K.A., Hohe Bleichen 15, 20354 Hamburg.
T. (040) 342017, Fax 354534. - Ant / Paint / Graph /
Fra / Rel / Draw - 052603
Huelsmann, F.K.A., Hohe Bleichen 15, 20354 Hamburg.
T. (040) 342017. 052604
Hy-editions, Glashüttenstr 3, 20357 Hamburg.
T. (040) 4304189. 052605
Iglinski, G., Eichenstr. 29, 20259 Hamburg.
T. (040) 49 89 81. 052606

Ilgenstein, C., Gärtnerstr. 16, 20253 Hamburg. T. (040) 480 84 61. *052607*
Isman-Fänder, Anat, Neue ABC-Str. 3, 20354 Hamburg. T. (040) 353113. - Jew - *052608*
Jackson, D., Osdorfer Landstr. 233, 22549 Hamburg. T. (040) 800 49 53. *052609*
Jacobs, Erika, Johnsweg 2, 21077 Hamburg. T. (040) 760 20 38. - Furn - *052610*
Jacobsen, Kai, Hartungstr 18, 20146 Hamburg. T. (040) 447648, Fax (040) 447648. - Ant - *052611*
Jiujiu Galerie, St. Georgstr. 6, 20099 Hamburg. T. (040) 24 55 55. - Orient - *052612*
Jora, B., Lokstedter Weg 112, 20251 Hamburg. T. (040) 480 2266. *052613*
Kadach, E., Dorotheenstr 54, 22301 Hamburg. T. (040) 2790877. *052614*
Kadel, W., Rothenbaumchaussee 27, 20148 Hamburg. T. (040) 45 11 86. *052615*
Kandemir, E., Rappstr. 15, 20146 Hamburg. T. (040) 44 95 32. *052616*
Kegel & Konietzko, Breckwoldtstr 8, 22587 Hamburg. T. (040) 860920, Fax 862415. - Eth - *052618*

KEGEL und KONIETZKO
Exotische Kunst
Afrika – Oceanien
Expertisen-Schätzungen
22587 Hamburg (Blankenese)
Breckwoldtstraße 8
Telefon: (0 40) 86 09 20
Telefax: (0 40) 86 24 15

Kessler, Ralph, Eichendorffstr. 21, 22587 Hamburg. T. (040) 86 96 62. - Ant / Paint / Graph / Furn / China / Sculp / Tex / Dec / Glass / Draw - *052619*
Kiefernrausch, Tarpenbekstr. 51, 20251 Hamburg. T. (040) 480 14 97. *052620*
Kittel, Werner, Corneliusstr. 5, 22607 Hamburg. T. (040) 36 59 33. - Ant / Paint / Furn / China / Sculp / Tex / Jew / Silv / Glass / Mod - *052621*
Klement, Ina, Eppendorfer Weg 2, 20259 Hamburg. T. (040) 439 89 57. - Furn - *052622*
Klose, Gustav, Steinstr. 13, 20095 Hamburg. Fax (040) 327196. *052623*
Klose, Gustav, Holsteinischer Kamp 17, 22081 Hamburg. T. (040) 29 46 63. *052624*
Klosterfelde, H., Caprivistr. 14, 22587 Hamburg. T. (040) 866 33 96. *052625*
Knudsen, J., Esplanade 17, 20354 Hamburg. T. (040) 345621. *052626*
Koglin, M., Große Elbstr 262, 22767 Hamburg. T. (040) 384781. *052627*
Konietzko, Julius, Gerhofstr. 2, 20354 Hamburg. T. (040) 345289, Fax (040) 362709. - Num / Arch / Eth - *052628*
Korte, K., Poststr. 51, 20354 Hamburg. T. (040) 34 26 44. *052629*
Kovacs, B., Bramfelder Chaussee 423, 22175 Hamburg. T. (040) 6010797. *052630*
Kramm, Günter, Hegestr. 17, 20251 Hamburg. T. (040) 48 30 16. - Ant / Fra / Glass / Mod - *052631*
Kratz, Edmund J., & Co., Dockenhudener Str. 25, 22587 Hamburg. T. (040) 86 14 45, Fax 86 14 30. - Ant / Paint / Furn / China / Sculp / Tex / Silv - *052632*
Krause, Hermann, Strandweg 87, 22587 Hamburg. T. (040) 860215. *052633*
Krenz, H., Wendemuthstr 57, 22041 Hamburg. T. (040) 681627. *052634*
Kroyer, H., Gerhart-Hauptmann-Platz 46, 20095 Hamburg. T. (040) 335303. *052635*
Kroyer, Helmut, Münzcontor, Gerhart-Hauptmann-Platz 46, 20095 Hamburg. T. (040) 33 53 03. - Num - *052636*
Krüger, Lokstedter Weg 11, 20251 Hamburg. T. (040) 46 29 71. *052637*
Krystof, Großer Burstah 40, 20457 Hamburg. T. (040) 36 39 50. - Num - *052638*
Kuball, Ralf-Matthias, Hohe Bleichen 22, 20354 Hamburg. T. (040) 35 27 35. - Paint / China - *052639*
Kuchel, Johannes, Osdorfer Landstr. 233, 22549 Hamburg. T. (040) 82 51 21, 800 49 42. - Furn / China - *052640*
Kunst- und Uhrhandelsgesellschaft mbH, Große Bleichen 21, 20354 Hamburg. T. (040) 35719623. *052641*
Kunsthaus City, Gerhofstr 2, 20354 Hamburg. T. (040) 343291. - Ant / Furn - *052642*
Kurz, Arthur, Fischers Allee 56-58, 22763 Hamburg. - Ant / Lights - *052643*
Kuschel, K., Klosterwall 9, 20095 Hamburg. T. (040) 33 64 24. *052644*
Lange, G., Hallerpl. 14, 20095 Hamburg. T. (040) 44 51 11. *052645*
Langhagen & Harnisch, Jungfernstieg 44, 20354 Hamburg. T. (040) 344097, Fax (040) 344353. *052646*
Laurence Art Products, Hofweg 22, 22085 Hamburg. T. (040) 2202859. *052647*
Le Claire, Thomas, Elbchaussee 156, 22605 Hamburg. T. (040) 8810646, Fax (040) 8804612. - Draw - *052648*
Lehmann, Monika, Ballindamm 25, 20095 Hamburg. T. (040) 326367. *052649*
Liedigk, T., Rothenbaumchaussee 207, 20149 Hamburg. T. (040) 456139. *052650*
Limburg, Th., Hofweg 15, 22085 Hamburg. T. (040) 2291001, Fax (040) 2273379. *052651*
Limpopo, Margaretenstr 31, 20357 Hamburg. T. (040) 4302121. *052652*
Link, C., Schulterblatt 55, 20357 Hamburg. T. (040) 435162. *052653*
Lührs, Joachim, Michaelisbrücke 3, 20459 Hamburg. T. (040) 371194, Fax (040) 371103. - Graph / Draw - *052654*
Macoun, Dietrich, Gärtnerstr 28, 20253 Hamburg. T. (040) 4227422. *052655*
Magic Art, Behringstr 42, 22763 Hamburg. T. (040) 3908175. *052656*
Mannshardt, H., Neustädter Neuer Weg 18, 20459 Hamburg. T. (040) 724 76 15. *052657*
Masmeier, B., Lange Reihe 76, 20099 Hamburg. T. (040) 24 47 11. *052658*
Maus, P., Möhlmannweg 6, 22587 Hamburg. T. (040) 86 97 34. *052659*
Medusa, Gärtnerstr. 50-52, 20253 Hamburg. T. (040) 4911101, Fax (040) 4905193. - Ant / Furn / Lights - *052660*
Meendsen, G., Parkallee 18, 20144 Hamburg. T. (040) 44 83 90. *052661*
Meißner-Edition, Heegbarg 14, 22391 Hamburg. T. (040) 6026010. *052662*
Meißner Edition, Heebarg 31, 22391 Hamburg. T. (040) 6026010. *052663*
Menez, D., Max-Brauer-Allee 194, 22765 Hamburg. T. (040) 4394538. *052664*
Menzel, Hermann, Mohnhof 10, 21029 Hamburg. T. (040) 721 21 31. *052665*
Merkator Münzhandelsgesellschaft, Sorbenstr. 45, 20537 Hamburg. T. (040) 25 70 91. - Num - *052666*
Methmann & Co., An der Alster 83, 20099 Hamburg. T. (040) 280 11 45. - Num - *052667*
Mewes, Axel, Lehmweg 51, 20251 Hamburg. T. (040) 48 11 26. - Paint / Graph / Sculp / Jew / Glass / Draw - *052668*
Meyburg, K.-J., Pool 36, 23555 Hamburg. T. (040) 345397. *052669*
Meyer, F., Lehmweg 36, 20251 Hamburg. T. (040) 481957. *052670*
Meyer, H., Elbchaussee 11, 22765 Hamburg. T. (040) 396469. *052671*
Meyer, Harry, Haydnstr. 21, 22761 Hamburg. T. (040) 899 13 31. *052672*
Meyerdiercks, Kurt, Wagnerstr. 14, 22081 Hamburg. T. (040) 29 47 26. *052673*
Michèle, Beselerplatz 11, 22607 Hamburg. T. (040) 89 87 63. - Furn - *052674*
Minden, M. von, Bergedorfer Schloßstr 5a, 21029 Hamburg. T. (040) 7247730. *052675*
Missal, F., Grindelhof 77, 20146 Hamburg. T. (040) 410 63 92. *052676*
Missal, R., Maria Louisenstr 63, 22301 Hamburg. T. (040) 484814. *052677*
Modschiedler, K., Neue ABC-Str. 10, 20354 Hamburg. T. (040) 34 20 60. *052678*
Möhl, B., Oberstr. 18b, 20144 Hamburg. T. (040) 420 40 13. *052679*
Moeller, Martin, Klosterallee 78, 20144 Hamburg. T. (040) 420 63 88, Fax (040) 420 10 49. - Draw - *052680*
Montag, John, Ballindamm 25, 20095 Hamburg. T. (040) 33 85 60. - Ant / China - *052681*
Müller, C., Eppendorfer Landstr. 85-87, 20249 Hamburg. T. (040) 48 66 75. - Ant - *052682*
Multiple Art, Heegbarg 31, 22391 Hamburg. T. (040) 6026077. *052683*
Musik Antik am Weidenstieg, Weidenstieg 14, 20259 Hamburg. T. (040) 400272. - Music - *052684*
Nagel, K., Holländische Reihe 6, 22765 Hamburg. T. (040) 390 55 35. - Ant - *052685*
Navigator-Schiffsantiquitäten, Sorbenstr. 39, 20537 Hamburg. T. (040) 25 70 01, Fax (040) 250 55 66. - Ant / Instr - *052686*
Neubarth, Michael, Lehmweg 40, 20251 Hamburg. T. (040) 480 16 52, Fax (040) 490 46 89. - Ant / Furn / Dec / Cur - *052687*
Niederoest, Urs S., & Co., Hohe Bleichen 22, 20354 Hamburg. T. (040) 34 42 11. - Ant / Furn / China / Sculp / Tex / Silv - *052688*
Niemann, Große Bäckerstr. 4, 20095 Hamburg. T. (040) 37 81 71, Fax (040) 37 81 72. - Mil - *052689*
Niemann, R., Eppendorfer Weg 177, 20253 Hamburg. T. (040) 4226366. *052690*
Nitschke, A., Wexstr. 33, 20355 Hamburg. T. (040) 34 69 91. *052691*
Nossitex, Am Sandtorkai 33, 20457 Hamburg. - Tex - *052692*
Nowack, Am Sooren 89b, 22149 Hamburg. T. (040) 6733134. *052693*
Nowlahka, S., Bramfelder Str 95c, 22305 Hamburg. T. (040) 6918072. *052694*
O Sopha, Hoheluftchaussee 2, 20253 Hamburg. T. (040) 4204444, Fax (040) 4204447. *052695*
O & M Orden & Militaria, Stresemannstr 149, 22769 Hamburg. T. (040) 4306200. *052696*
Oberwemmer, Günter, Bussestr. 37, 22299 Hamburg. T. (040) 511 74 42. *052697*
Opus Art, Landwehr 25, 22087 Hamburg. T. (040) 2513885. *052698*
Osarek, Hauersweg 14, 22303 Hamburg. T. (040) 2807696. *052699*
Otteni, Elbchaussee 264, 22605 Hamburg. T. (040) 82 92 19, Fax (040) 82 62 23. - Ant / Furn / China / Tex / Silv - *052700*
Padberg & Viehbrock GmbH, Hammerbrookstr 5, 20097 Hamburg. T. (040) 2800970. *052701*
Pamminger, Reinhilde, Martin-Luther-Str. 6, 20459 Hamburg. T. (040) 364201, Fax (040) 364201. - Ant / Furn / Glass - *052702*
PATIO-Antiques, Hohe Bleichen 11, 20354 Hamburg. T. (040) 343525. *052703*
Patrick, Adenauerallee 32, 20097 Hamburg. T. (040) 280 31 34. - Ant - *052704*
Paulsen, Ulrike, Alsterdorfer Str. 383, 22297 Hamburg. T. (040) 51 25 05. - Furn / Fra - *052705*
Peetz, P., Koppel 104, 20099 Hamburg. T. (040) 24 72 56. - Furn - *052706*
Pendulum, Maria-Louisen-Str. 5, 22301 Hamburg. T. (040) 48 62 14. *052707*
Peters, G., Köhnestr 8, 20539 Hamburg. T. (040) 787181. *052708*
Peyk-Wiegel, H., Koldingstr. 6, 22769 Hamburg. T. (040) 850 65 99. *052709*
Pohl, C. & M., Eberhofweg 64, 22415 Hamburg. T. (040) 531 72 58, 48 92 26. - Ant - *052710*
Pohl, Max, Sierichstr 116, 22299 Hamburg. T. (040) 489226. *052711*
Pommer Esche, R., Hofweg 8, 22085 Hamburg. T. (040) 2273330. *052712*
Prager & Prinz, Neue ABC-Str 8, 20354 Hamburg. T. (040) 344882. *052713*
Prott Art & Präzision, W., Große Brunnenstr 120, 22763 Hamburg. T. (040) 3906800. *052714*
Quittenbaum, Sülldorfer Kirchenweg 51, 22587 Hamburg. T. (040) 868491, Fax (040) 865484. - Furn / China / Glass - *052715*
Quittenbaum, Askan, Sülldorfer Kirchenweg 51, 22587 Hamburg. T. (040) 8663906. *052716*

Radloff, E., Mundsburger Damm 46, 22087 Hamburg. T. (040) 227 94 39. - Ant - 052717
Rathmann, H.-W., Herderstr. 6, 22085 Hamburg. T. (040) 2209620. 052718
Raum & Kunst GmbH, Große Bleichen 35, 20354 Hamburg. T. (040) 3589632. 052719
Raza Afghan-Haus, Lehmweg 41, 20251 Hamburg. T. (040) 48 10 21. - Ant / Furn / Draw / Tex / Arch / Jew / Mil / Glass - 052720
Reitz, K. & M., ABC-Str. 50, 20354 Hamburg. T. (040) 35 33 82. - Ant / Instr - 052721
Rey, Erich-Wilhelm, Alte Rabenstr. 19, 20148 Hamburg. T. (040) 44 54 76. - Ant - 052722
Richter, M., Grindelhof 69, 20146 Hamburg. T. (040) 45 13 67. 052723
Riegamer, D., Gotenstr. 14, 20097 Hamburg. T. (040) 23 24 32. 052724
Rieken, Jochen, Rothenbaumchaussee 49, 20148 Hamburg. T. (040) 44 57 41. - Ant / Furn / Orient - 052725
Ritscher, Karsten, 902314, 21075 Hamburg. T. (040) 7905402, Fax (040) 7903230. 052726
Ritter, Marion, Lehmweg 5, 20251 Hamburg. T. (040) 422 07 50. - Ant - 052727
Röhrdanz, Herta, ABC-Str. 19, 20354 Hamburg. T. (040) 342592. 052728
Rohse, Christina, Oberstr. 133, 20149 Hamburg. T. (040) 44 22 32. - Ant - 052729
Roos, Uwe, Rodigallee 232, 22043 Hamburg. T. (040) 654 70 46. 052730
Rose, L., Papenhuder Str. 42, 22087 Hamburg. T. (040) 2202425. 052731
Rosenthal, Werner, Naumannplatz 21, 22049 Hamburg. 052732
Roubeni, A., & Co, Borsteler Chaussee 85, 22453 Hamburg. - Tex - 052733
Rowlett, R., Bleichenbrücke 9, 20354 Hamburg. T. (040) 342800. 052734
Rühmkorf, Bei St. Johannis 5, 20148 Hamburg. T. (040) 44 54 76. 052735
Rüsch, A., Fabriciusstr 121, 22177 Hamburg. T. (040) 6427264. 052736
Rüsch, M., Ringstr 51, 22145 Hamburg. T. (040) 6781193. 052737
Rusch, Amtsstr. 22, 22143 Hamburg. T. (040) 677 51 01. 052738
Ryan's Antiques, Eppendorfer Weg 231, 20251 Hamburg. T. (040) 460 23 23, Fax (040) 480 20 27. - Ant - 052739
Sakakini, Klosterwall 9, 20095 Hamburg. T. (040) 33 70 10. 052740
Salewski, E., Jessenstr. 20, 22767 Hamburg. T. (040) 38 69 50. 052741
Sankt Georg Antiquitäten, Koppel 40, 20099 Hamburg. T. (040) 24 65 00. 052742
Schaede, Peter A., Alter Fischmarkt, 20457 Hamburg. T. (040) 33 73 12. - Paint - 052743
Schäfer, A.-C., Alte Holstenstr. 22, 21031 Hamburg. T. (040) 721 91 05. - Ant - 052744
Schäfer, M., Klosterallee 104, 20144 Hamburg. T. (040) 47 96 49. 052745
Schapp, Ahrensburger Str 121, 22045 Hamburg. T. (040) 6684660. 052746
Schimpl, C., Flemingstr. 16, 22299 Hamburg. T. (040) 48 53 88. - Ant - 052747
Schletzer, Dieter, Neuer Wall 63, 20354 Hamburg. T. (040) 362327, Fax (040) 3743395. - Orient / Tex / Eth - 052748
Schliemann, Schleusenbrücke 1, 20355 Hamburg. T. (040) 36 28 89, Fax (040) 37 11 32. - Furn / China / Silv - 052749
Schlondes, Frohmestr. 11, 22457 Hamburg. T. (040) 5594774. - Furn - 052750
Schlondes, Große Bleiche 31, 22457 Hamburg. T. (040) 345588. 052751
Schlüter, Carl F., Alsterufer 12, 20354 Hamburg. T. (040) 410 10 49/40. 052752
Schmidt Artwork + Service, Heiko, Winterhuder Weg 40, 22085 Hamburg. T. (040) 2274620. 052753
Schmoller, Bernd, Dr., Poststr. 36, 20354 Hamburg. T. (040) 34 47 35. - Instr - 052754
Schrader, G., Süderstr 159a, 20537 Hamburg. T. (040) 2512412. 052755
Schrape, R., Frahmredder 10, 22393 Hamburg. T. (040) 601 49 43. 052756
Schüler, Karen, Eppendorfer Baum 20, 20249 Hamburg. T. (040) 47 47 59. - Ant / Jew - 052757
Schultz, Holger, Breite Str. 159, 22767 Hamburg. 052758
Schultz & Dahms, Lehmweg 28, 20251 Hamburg. T. (040) 5361416. 052759
Schulz, Bahrenfelder Chaussee 55, 22761 Hamburg. T. (040) 890 31 59. 052760
Schulz, Martina, Poppenbütteler Chaussee 110, 22397 Hamburg. T. (040) 607 26 41. 052761
Schulz, U., Eilbeker Weg 40, 22089 Hamburg. T. (040) 200 50 15. 052762
Schulz, Wolfgang & Ingrid, Lehmweg 30, 20251 Hamburg. T. (040) 420 46 50. - Mod - 052763
Seifarth, M., Klosterwall 7, 20095 Hamburg. T. (040) 33 61 82. - Ant - 052764
Select Novo, Holländische Reihe 6, 22765 Hamburg. T. (040) 390 55 35. - Mod - 052765
Shipsantiques, Sorbenstr. 39, 20537 Hamburg. T. (040) 25 70 01. - Naut - 052766
Siemer, Peter, Beim Andreasbrunnen 5, 20249 Hamburg. T. (040) 47 00 04. - Num - 052767
Silver Art, Alte Holstenstr 49, 21031 Hamburg. T. (040) 7245976. 052768
Simonian, N. u Dr S., Oberstr 119, 20149 Hamburg. T. (040) 455060. 052769
Somschor, Eppendorfer Weg 77, 20259 Hamburg. T. (040) 490 43 89. - Ant - 052770
Sonntag, D., & E. Vermeulen-Sonntag, Alte Rabenstr. 20, 20148 Hamburg. T. (040) 44 35 66. 052771
Spanka, W., Hegestr. 28a, 20251 Hamburg. T. (040) 460 22 47. 052772
Specht, K., Maria-Louisen-Str. 2, 22301 Hamburg. T. (040) 47 27 03. - Ant - 052773
Spieß, K., Osdorfer Landstr. 233, 22549 Hamburg. T. (040) 800 49 28. 052774
Spitzer, B., Einkaufszentrum Alstertal, 20095 Hamburg. T. (040) 602 54 25. - Num - 052775
Spott, Weddinger Weg 1, 22143 Hamburg. T. (040) 6770970, Fax (040) 6779340. - Ant - 052776
Stahl, Hans, Hohe Bleichen 28, 20354 Hamburg. T. (040) 342325, Fax 3480432. - Ant / Paint / China - 052777
Stamm, A., Eilbeker Weg 20, 22089 Hamburg. T. (040) 200 29 85. 052778
State of Art, Willhoop 7, 22453 Hamburg. T. (040) 5894213. 052779
Steen, K., Bundesstr. 60, 20144 Hamburg. T. (040) 44 75 67. 052780
Steen, Klaus, Hohe Bleichen 22, 20354 Hamburg. T. (040) 34 50 20. 052781
Steinnetz, A., Uhlenhorster Weg 14, 22085 Hamburg. T. (040) 229 60 59. - Ant - 052782
Stentzel, G., Koboldweg 46, 21077 Hamburg. T. (040) 760 68 43. 052783
Stewen, Holger, Hohe Bleichen 21, 20354 Hamburg. T. (040) 35 16 09. - Furn / Dec - 052784
Stobbe, Jörg, Mundsburger Damm 60, 22087 Hamburg. T. (040) 2207002. 052785
Stordel, P., Milchstr. 26,, 20148 Hamburg. T. (040) 44 97 85. 052786
Sweet Home, Klosterallee 67, 20144 Hamburg. T. (040) 420 26 91. - Ant - 052787
Swietlik, G., Kirchenweg 2, 20099 Hamburg. T. (040) 280 38 56. - Ant - 052788
Sytnyk, Klosterwall 9, 20095 Hamburg. T. (040) 33 88 06. 052789
Tarp, R., Schottmüllerstr. 35, 20251 Hamburg. T. (040) 47 44 80. 052790
Teetzmann, P., Hoheluftchaussee 21, 20253 Hamburg. T. (040) 420 05 54. 052791
Thiesen, Wandsbeker Königstr. 64, 22041 Hamburg. T. (040) 652 33 25. - Ant - 052792
Thora-Antiquitäten, Milchstr. 3, 20148 Hamburg. T. (040) 45 31 91. 052793
Tietjen & Co., Spitalerstr 30, 20095 Hamburg. T. (040) 330368, Fax 323035. - Num - 052794
Tilitz, N., Herbert-Weichmann-Str 47, 22085 Hamburg. T. (040) 2299010. 052795
Troge, Birgit, Hochallee 127-128, 20149 Hamburg. T. (040) 48 32 55. - Ant / Paint / Furn / Lights - 052796
Trosiner, R., Grasweg 5, 22299 Hamburg. T. (040) 48 10 33. 052797
Trzebiatowski, Eimsbütteler Ch 43, 20259 Hamburg. T. (040) 4304209, Fax (040) 4307841. 052798
Urban, M., Klosterwall 21, 20095 Hamburg. T. (040) 337836. 052799
Volcen, von, Eppendorfer Landstr. 24, 20249 Hamburg. T. (040) 47 09 25. 052800
Villa Lupi, Heußweg 40, 20255 Hamburg. T. (040) 4904372. 052801
Voss, Claudia, Neue ABC-Str. 8, 20354 Hamburg. T. (040) 34 05 31. 052802
Wäsche-Stübchen, Bahrenfelder Str. 3, 22765 Hamburg. T. (040) 390 41 05. - Tex - 052803
WAH, Hermann-Behn-Str. 17, 20095 Hamburg. T. (040) 45 47 49. 052804
Wandsbeker Kunsthandlung, Wandsbeker Allee 62, 22041 Hamburg. T. (040) 682016. 052804a
Wandsbeker Puppenhaus, Wandsbeker Marktstr. 144, 22041 Hamburg. T. (040) 68 23 70. 052805
Warburg, Maria Luisa, Rothenbaumchaussee 60, 20148 Hamburg. T. (040) 45 52 11. 052806
Wasiluk, W., Kirchenweg 2, 20099 Hamburg. T. (040) 280 24 81. 052807
Watson, Isestr. 14, 20144 Hamburg. T. (040) 420 14 71. 052808
Weber, Eva-Vera, Mittelweg 156, 20148 Hamburg. T. (040) 410 12 04. 052809
Weber, Helga Maria, Eppendorfer Baum 23, 20249 Hamburg. T. (040) 478593. - Fra - 052810
Weber, J., Eppendorfer Weg 67, 20259 Hamburg. T. (040) 4911187. 052811
Wege, Kai, Röbbek Str 15a, 22607 Hamburg. T. (040) 8226692. 052812
Wehling, G., Steinstr. 13a, 20095 Hamburg. T. (040) 32 43 09. - Num - 052813
Weidle, Ingrid, Isestr. 76, 20149 Hamburg. T. (040) 460 49 41. - Ant / Glass - 052814
Weiss, H., Kampchaussee 41, 21033 Hamburg. T. (040) 7244981. 052815
Weitze, Helmut, Neuer Wall 18, 20354 Hamburg. T. (040) 35 27 61. - Instr - 052816
Wellmann, Poppenbüttler Landstr 1, 22391 Hamburg. T. (040) 6062801. 052817
Wense, Gebhard, Ferdinandstr. 35, 20095 Hamburg. T. (040) 33 71 38. 052818
Werner, Fruchtallee 110, 20259 Hamburg. T. (040) 4900377. 052819
Westend Antiquitäten, Waitzstr. 5, 22607 Hamburg. T. (040) 890 32 90. - Ant / Furn / China / Jew / Silv / Glass - 052820
Wettig, C., Hegestr 33, 20249 Hamburg. T. (040) 4602115. 052821
Wiechmann, Kai, Bogenstr. 52, 20144 Hamburg. T. (040) 4204921. 052822
Wiemann, R., Eppendorfer Weg 79, 20259 Hamburg. T. (040) 406131. - Furn - 052823
Wieseler, Julius, Ohlsdorfer Str. 5, 22299 Hamburg. T. (040) 473183. 052824
Wildt, Helen, Klosterallee 104, 20144 Hamburg. T. (040) 48 95 09. 052825
Wingert, T., Geschwister-Scholl-Str. 114a, 20251 Hamburg. T. (040) 47 94 48. 052826
Winkler, R., Klosterwall 9, 20095 Hamburg. T. (040) 33 75 34. - Ant - 052827
Witt, I., Luruper Hauptstr. 50, 22547 Hamburg. T. (040) 831 74 38. 052828
Wolter, ABC-Str 12, 20354 Hamburg. T. (040) 3589423, 3589494. 052829
Wulf, Renate, Gertigstr. 27, 22303 Hamburg. T. (040) 279 83 08. - Furn / China / Silv - 052830
Wulff, Jürgen, Blankeneser Landstr. 3, 22587 Hamburg. 052831
Zeiner, F., Voßstraat 75, 22399 Hamburg. T. (040) 6021534. 052832
Zen Galerie, Wexstr. 35, 20355 Hamburg. T. (040) 352585, Fax (040) 8663550. - Paint / Graph / Orient - 052833
Zeugner, A., Methfesselstr. 78, 20257 Hamburg. T. (040) 491 98 07. 052834

Hameln (Niedersachsen)

Beckmann, Uwe E.R., Kaiserstr. 57, 31785 Hameln.
T. (05151) 165 94. - Mil -   *052836*
Beier, Hartmut, Bäckerstr. 49, 31785 Hameln.
T. (05151) 3297, Fax (05151) 3297. - Ant / Furn / Num /
Mil / Cur -   *052837*
Bilitzka-Franken, U., Wendenstr. 6, 31785 Hameln.
T. (05151) 44388.   *052838*
Büngener, Alte Marktstr. 15, 31785 Hameln.
T. (05151) 24762.   *052839*
Eichenberg, I., Neue Marktstr. 23, 31785 Hameln.
T. (05151) 42220.   *052840*
Fargel, Bäckerstr. 55, 31785 Hameln.
T. (05151) 24901.   *052841*
Fargel, C., Bäckerstr. 55, 31785 Hameln.
T. (05151) 2 49 01.   *052842*
Höllings, A., Kopmanshof 75, 31785 Hameln.
T. (05151) 279 00.   *052843*
Jung, Albert, Lohstr. 7, 31785 Hameln.
T. (05151) 36 13.   *052844*
Kuhlmann, Antje D., Wendenstr. 8, 31785 Hameln.
T. (05151) 274 28.   *052845*
Schwarz, U., Platzstr. 5, 31785 Hameln.
T. (05151) 434 59. - Furn -   *052846*
Stammer, H., Reuteranger, 31789 Hameln.
T. (05151) 124 03.   *052847*

Hamm (Nordrhein-Westfalen)

Antikmarkt auf dem Bauernhof, Werler Str 327, 59069
Hamm. T. (02381) 598296. - Ant / Furn / Instr -   *052848*
Bähner, M. & W., Dolberger Str 242, 59073 Hamm.
T. (02381) 38602.   *052849*
Kallerhoff, Franz, Oststr 46, 59065 Hamm.   *052850*
Kohl, A., Werler Str 20, 59065 Hamm.
T. (02381) 29163.   *052851*
Kuhlmann, V., Nordstr 8, 59065 Hamm.
T. (02381) 21324.   *052852*
Siegfried, Doris, Von-Galen-Str 98, 59063
Hamm.   *052853*

Hammelburg (Bayern)

Neder, Cornelia, Berliner Str. 38, 97762 Hammelburg.
T. (09732) 25 10.   *052854*

Hamminkeln (Nordrhein-Westfalen)

Bratke, B., Schlößstr. 8, 46499 Hamminkeln.
T. (02852) 4161.   *052855*
Fischer, J., Telgerhuck 6, 46499 Hamminkeln.
T. (02852) 1622.   *052856*

Hanau (Hessen)

Becker, Friedrich, Hanauer Vorstadt 13, 63450 Hanau.
T. (06181) 22733. - Num -   *052857*
Brüggemann, Moselstr. 40, 63452 Hanau.
T. (06181) 169 68.   *052858*
Hesters, Alter Rückinger Weg 2, 63452 Hanau.
T. (06181) 833 38.   *052859*
Patzelt, L., Ludwigstr. 11, 63456 Hanau.
T. (06181) 65 94 94.   *052860*

Handewitt (Schleswig-Holstein)

Derouet, Wolfgang, Unaften 5, 24983 Handewitt.
T. (04608) 61 89.   *052861*
Fischer, K.H., Meynautal 2, 24983 Handewitt.
T. (04608) 1374.   *052862*

Hann. Münden (Niedersachsen)

Antique Angelique, Lange Str. 10, 34346 Hann. Münden.
T. (05541) 43 92.   *052863*
Kaltenstadler, Rosenstr. 18, 34346 Hann. Münden.
T. (05541) 712 83.   *052864*
Seute, G., Waschbergweg 4, 34346 Hann. Münden.
T. (05541) 31124.   *052865*

Hannover (Niedersachsen)

Adamiec, Wolf-D., Rotermundstr. 13c, 30165 Hannover.
T. (0511) 350 20 35.   *052866*
Anticus, Anderter Str. 62, 30629 Hannover.
T. (0511) 59 22 94.   *052867*
Antik & Art, Königstr. 47, 30175 Hannover.
T. (0511) 348 68 00.   *052868*
Antik und Trödel, Passerelle, Raschpl. 3q, 30159 Hanno-
ver. T. (0511) 34 52 15.   *052869*
Antikladen Kirchrode, Großer Hillen 8, 30559 Hannover.
T. (0511) 52 02 48.   *052870*

Antiquitäten am Thielenplatz, Thielenplatz 3, 30159
Hannover. T. (0511) 32 34 54.   *052871*
Antiquitäten in Herrenhausen, Alleestr. 15, 30167 Han-
nover. T. (0511) 71 77 74.   *052872*
Ars Mundi Collection, Bödekerstr. 13, 30161 Hannover.
T. (0511) 348 43 43. - Ant -   *052873*
A&S, Bessemerstr. 17, 30177 Hannover.   *052874*
Bartholomaei, Pawils von, Am Marstall 21, 30159 Han-
nover. T. (0511) 66 93 48, Fax (0511) 62 12 85. - Paint /
Graph -   *052876*
Baumert, Gisela, Walderseerstr. 24, 30177 Hannover.
Beckmann, Erich, Georgstr. 48, 30159 Hannover.
T. (0511) 323074, Fax (0511) 329922. - Paint / Furn /
Orient / China / Sculp / Jew / Ico -   *052877*
Blancon, Gilles, Goethepl. 11, 30159 Hannover.
T. (0511) 170 18. - Num -   *052878*
Brenske, Helmut, Machandelweg 11, 30419 Hannover.
T. (0511) 633667, Fax 633667. - Ico -   *052879*
Bühnemann, Lothar, Heymesstr. 26, 30539 Hannover.
T. (0511) 526127, Fax (0511) 323744. - Num /
Mil -   *052880*
Degener, Lilo, Hindenburgstr. 33, 30175 Hannover.
T. (0511) 81 20 68. - Ant / China / Sculp / Silv - *052881*
Deppe, Mary, Galerie Luise, Theaterstr., 30159 Hanno-
ver. T. (0511) 32 95 65.   *052882*
Effective Accessoires, Friesenstr. 13, 30161 Hannover.
T. (0511) 31 40 84 / 85. - Furn / Dec / Lights / Instr /
Cur / Mul / Tin -   *052883*
Eickriede, H. & A., Engelbosteler Damm 81, 30167
Hannover.   *052884*
Eiden, Knochenhauerstr. 9, 30159 Hannover.
T. (0511) 32 98 89, 549 09 71. - Furn -   *052885*
El Gendi, Osterstr. 59, 30159 Hannover.
T. (0511) 363 16 36, Fax (0511) 363 27 01.   *052886*
Ellinger, C., Böckerstr. 14, 30659 Hannover.
T. (0511) 647 73 78.   *052887*
Ersmann, Ernst-Wilhelm, Koppelweg 36A, 30655 Hanno-
ver. T. (0511) 64 57 24.   *052888*
Fischer, H., Schlägerstr. 46, 30171 Hannover.
T. (0511) 88 16 04.   *052889*
Garbs, Walter, Deisterstr. 15, 30449 Hannover.
T. (0511) 44 01 67.   *052890*
Gebhardt, H.-J., Königsworther Str. 37, 30167 Hannover.
T. (0511) 320618, 1316286.   *052891*
Glashoff, Nordfeldstr. 29, 30459 Hannover.
T. (0511) 41 66 67, 42 31 93. - Mod -   *052892*
Greiser, I. B., Georgstr. 46, 30159 Hannover.
T. (0511) 32 50 37. - Num -   *052893*
Grüttner, A., Chemnitzer Str. 1, 30179 Hannover.
- Num -   *052894*
Hallenflohmarkt, Passerelle Raschpl. 5, 30159 Hanno-
ver. T. (0511) 31 81 71.   *052895*
Haller, Wilfried W., Spinozastr. 14, 30625 Hannover.
T. (0511) 55 31 00.   *052896*
Herbart, Wolfgang, Rotermundstr. 13d, 30165 Hannover.
T. (0511) 350 23 70.   *052897*
Heydenreich, R., Meersmannufer 17, 30655 Hannover.
T. (0511) 64 17 45.   *052898*
Holz, Marianne, Seelhorststr 50, 30175 Hannover.
T. (0511) 819918.   *052899*
Honscha, Siegward, Kurt-Schumacher-Str. 15, 30159
Hannover. T. (0511) 32 29 31. - Num -   *052900*
Huth, Lutz, Rathenaustr. 13-14, 30159 Hannover.
T. (0511) 32 73 04.   *052901*
Kämper, Königstr. 30, 30175 Hannover.
T. (0511) 34 21 51.   *052902*
Kambeck, Björn Uwe, Roßkampstr. 69b, 30519 Hanno-
ver. T. (0511) 83 57 24. - Instr -   *052903*
Kempin, Hermann, Marienstr. 62, 30171 Hannover.
T. (0511) 81 72 89, Fax (0511) 819392.   *052904*
Klöver, H., Podbielskistr. 282, 30655 Hannover.
T. (0511) 69 77 13.   *052905*
Koch, Jürgen, Königstr. 50, 30175 Hannover.
T. (0511) 34 20 06, Fax (0511) 388 03 60.   *052906*
Koch, W., Volgersweg 19, 30175 Hannover.
T. (0511) 34 50 48. - Paint / Graph / Sculp /
Draw -   *052907*
Krätzer, Hermann, Rampenstr. 15, 30449 Hannover.
T. (0511) 44 11 51. - Ant / Furn / Repr / Dec - *052908*
Kruppa, Walter, Calenberger Str. 35, 30169 Hannover.
T. (0511) 141 18. - Ant / Paint -   *052909*

Kühle, Gustav, Wegenerstr. 18, 30175
Hannover.   *052910*
Kurz, Peter O., Bödekerstr. 57, 30161 Hannover. *052911*
Laubinger, Adolf, Kansteinweg 2, 30419 Hannover.
T. (0511) 79 18 73.   *052912*
Menges & Söhne, Aloys, Königstr 51, 30175 Hannover.
T. (0511) 343522, Fax 3885652. - Ant / Paint / Furn /
China / Silv / Glass -   *052913*

Meyer, Ernst, Henleinweg 20, 30519 Hannover. - Paint /
Graph / Repr / Fra / Draw -   *052914*
Mielenz, Greitheweg 5, 30559 Hannover.
T. (0511) 52 66 33. - Ant / Mil -   *052915*
Mooshage, Hermann, Kramerstr. 23, 30159 Hannover.
T. (0511) 320173. - Ant / Paint / Furn / Silv / Instr /
Glass -   *052916*
Mühlnikel, S., Marienstr. 85, 30171 Hannover.
T. (0511) 85 19 71.   *052917*
Münzen- und Medaillengalerie Susanne Wimmelmann,
Hausmannstr. 1, 30159 Hannover. T. (0511) 1 43 83.
- Num -   *052918*
Pawelzik, Lister Meile 52, 30161 Hannover.
T. (0511) 34 58 87. - Num -   *052919*
Ramin, Jürgen, Lindener Marktpl. 7, 30159
Hannover.   *052920*
Saal, Harald, Theodor-Lessing-Pl. 1b, 30159 Hannover.
T. (0511) 32 87 70. - Ant / Furn / China / Silv /
Glass -   *052921*
Sammler-Markt, Knochenhauerstr. 8, 30159 Hannover.
T. (0511) 30 65 40.   *052922*
Sandvoss, Kantstr. 2, 30625 Hannover.
T. (0511) 554411, Fax (0511) 554400.
- Orient -   *052923*
Schöpke & Lange, Rathenaustr. 13, 30159 Hannover.
T. (0511) 32 67 34. - Num -   *052924*
Schumm, B., Hildesheimer Str. 59, 30169 Hannover.
T. (0511) 88 42 42.   *052925*
Schwiete, J., Alleestr. 15, 30167 Hannover.
T. (0511) 71 77 74.   *052926*
Seemeyer, Adolf, Podbielskistr. 5, 30163 Hannover.
T. (0511) 66 14 57.   *052927*
Senden, von, Yorckstr. 1, 30161 Hannover.
T. (0511) 33 21 24. - Ant -   *052928*
Steinmeyer, Klaus, Voßstr. 57-58, 30163 Hannover.
T. (0511) 66 07 28.   *052929*
Teppichhaus Germania, Karmarschstr. 31, 30159 Han-
nover. T. (0511) 32 79 21. - Tex -   *052930*
Trödelhalle Lister Platz, Lister Platz 3, 30163 Hannover.
T. (0511) 39 35 46. - Ant -   *052931*
Voigt, Gerhard, Limmerstr. 44, 30451 Hannover.
T. (0511) 45 66 40.   *052932*
Waldmann, Susanne, Tiergartenstr. 104, 30559 Hanno-
ver. T. (0511) 52 78 66, 52 15 10.   *052933*
Wedekind, Lutz, Feuntstr. 30, 30161 Hannover.
T. (0511) 32 36 32.   *052934*
Weigelt, Jörg, Oskar-Winter-Str. 3, 30161 Hannover.
T. (0511) 628375, 628376, Fax (0511) 628377. *052935*
Wentzel, Willmerstr. 20, 30519 Hannover.
T. (0511) 83 54 90.   *052936*
Wickel, D., Mittelstr. 9, 30169 Hannover.
T. (0511) 18186.   *052937*

Wiedenroth, Alfred, Gellertstr. 50, 30175 Hannover.
T. (0511) 85 88 33. *052938*
Wintering, Auf dem Hollen 15, 30165 Hannover.
T. (0511) 66 37 56. - Ant - *052939*
Wroblewski, Knochenhauerstr. 1, 30159 Hannover.
T. (0511) 32 48 31. *052940*
Zemlin, I., Brehmstr. 49, 30173 Hannover.
T. (0511) 81 09 77. - China / Glass - *052941*
Zörnig & Mock, Marienstr. 18, 30171 Hannover.
T. (0511) 819495, Fax 2834459. *052942*

Hanstedt (Niedersachsen)
Tillybs, Heinz, Achterdieck, 21271 Hanstedt.
T. (04184) 7441, Fax (04184) 7441. - Ant / Paint /
Furn - *052943*

Hardegsen (Niedersachsen)
Ellermeier, Friedrich, Dr., 2. Burgmannshof, 37181 Hardegsen. T. (05505) 5413. - Music - *052944*

Harsewinkel (Nordrhein-Westfalen)
Gausling, G. M., Klosterhof 7, 33428 Harsewinkel.
T. (05247) 89 38. *052945*

Hasbergen (Niedersachsen)
Böggemeyer, Walter, Hansastr. 15, 49205 Hasbergen.
T. (05405) 34 13. *052946*

Hasloh (Schleswig-Holstein)
Giesecke, Horst, Kieler Str. 45, 25474 Hasloh. *052947*

Haßfurt (Bayern)
Bopp & Hußlein, Truchseßpassage, 97437 Haßfurt.
T. (09521) 2586. *052948*

Haßloch (Rheinland-Pfalz)
Ireland, A., Bahnhofstr. 67454 Haßloch.
T. (06324) 59237. *052949*
Kastenholz, G., Kirchgasse 27, 67454 Haßloch.
T. (06324) 59681. *052950*

Hatten (Niedersachsen)
Sylvester, Günter, Am Tempelberg 4, 26209 Hatten.
T. (04482) 8612. *052951*

Hattingen (Nordrhein-Westfalen)
Alt, Robert, Krämersdorf 8, 45525 Hattingen. *052952*
Hendriks, H., Kohlenstr 401, 45529 Hattingen.
T. (02324) 40737. *052953*
Klöden, E., Emschestr 54, 45525 Hattingen.
T. (02324) 202745. *052954*

Hattstedt (Schleswig-Holstein)
Gebauer, U., Bundesstr. 48, 25856 Hattstedt.
T. (04846) 1036. *052955*
Schwermer, H., Ostermarsch 16, 25856 Hattstedt.
T. (04846) 325. *052956*

Hatzfeld (Hessen)
Schmolling, W., Edertalstr. 4, 35116 Hatzfeld.
T. (06467) 8235. *052957*

Hausach (Baden-Württemberg)
Boscia, S., Waldstr 8, 77756 Hausach. *052958*

Hausham (Bayern)
Stampfl, Walter, Geißstr. 5, 83734 Hausham. *052959*

Heessen (Niedersachsen)
Theiß, Norbert, Im Siek 21, 31707 Heessen.
T. (05722) 85580. - Fra - *052960*

Heide (Schleswig-Holstein)
Reimers, B., Markt 67, 25746 Heide.
T. (0481) 87964. *052961*
Rogalla, F. & K., Husumer Str 87, 25746 Heide.
T. (0481) 72956. *052962*
Werner, C., Sylterstr 1, 25746 Heide.
T. (0481) 87044. *052963*

Heidelberg (Baden-Württemberg)
Antiquitäten & Weine, Rahmengasse 12, 69120 Heidelberg. T. (06221) 41 28 83, Fax (06221) 40 25 26. - Ant /
Furn / Fra / Lights / Glass / Cur / Mod / Mul - *052964*
Arabeske, Ladenburger Str. 51, 69120 Heidelberg.
T. (06221) 462 74. - Ant - *052965*

B & B Antiques, Sofienstr. 27, 69115 Heidelberg.
T. (06221) 230 03. - Ant - *052966*
Berg, E., Handschuhsheimer Landstr. 6, 69120 Heidelberg. T. (06221) 47 45 95. - Ant - *052967*
Bernards, Friedrich-Ebert-Platz 20, 69117 Heidelberg.
- Ant / Furn - *052968*
Bromor, R., Haspelgasse 14, 69117 Heidelberg.
T. (06221) 16 23 00. *052969*
Brook's English Antiques, St.-Anna-Gasse 1, 69117 Heidelberg. T. (06221) 250 52. *052970*
Castle, Im Sand 3a, 69115 Heidelberg.
T. (06221) 105 62. - Ant - *052971*
Corniello, Domenico, Hauptstr. 122, 69117 Heidelberg.
T. (06221) 283 12. - Num - *052972*
Doss, A., Fröbelstr. 2, 69123 Heidelberg.
T. (06221) 82343. *052973*
Eichendorff, Amalienstr. 2a, 69126 Heidelberg.
T. (06221) 31 49 99, Fax (06221) 37 24 34. - Furn /
Dec / Silv / Ant - *052974*
Eid, G., & V. Sengle, Bergheimer Str. 101a, 69115 Heidelberg. T. (06221) 205 16. - Paint /
Fein, Heinz Gerhard, Schloß Wolfsbrunnenweg 21a,
69118 Heidelberg. T. (06221) 205 16. - Paint /
Draw - *052976*
Ginilewicz, Dossenheimer Landstr. 83, 69121 Heidelberg. T. (06221) 41 34 37. *052977*
Greiser, Olaf, Schröderstr. 14, 69120 Heidelberg.
T. (06221) 40 15 87. - Paint / Graph / Draw - *052978*
Hörrle, Oskar, Kaiserstr. 70, 69115 Heidelberg.
T. (06221) 209 14. *052979*
Hofmann, Karlsruher Str. 52, 69126 Heidelberg.
T. (06221) 37 44 88. - Ant / Furn / Num / China / Jew /
Silv / Glass - *052980*
Holub, Arnold, Hirtenaue 25, 69118 Heidelberg.
Furn - *052981*
Humboldt, D. Freifrau von, Rohrbacher Str. 18, 69115
Heidelberg. T. (06221) 16 19 99. *052982*
Kammerer, U., Neugasse 5, 69117 Heidelberg.
T. (06221) 213 96. - Paint / Tex - *052983*
Kerle, Kurfürsten Anlage 8, 69115 Heidelberg.
T. (06221) 131 13. *052984*
Kratzert, R., Mittelbadgasse 7, 69117 Heidelberg.
T. (06221) 18 42 62. - Ant / Instr - *052985*
Leitz, Berthold, Nadlerstr. 3, 69117 Heidelberg.
T. (06221) 135 32. *052986*
Lux, Michael, Akademiestr 1, 69117 Heidelberg.
T. (06221) 23851. - Num / Ant / China / Jew /
Silv - *052987*
Mein Lädchen, Brückenstr. 34, 69120 Heidelberg.
T. (06221) 47 13 98. *052988*
Melnikow, M., Theaterstr. 11, 69117 Heidelberg.
T. (06221) 18 36 26. *052989*
Metz, Gisela, Mittelbadgasse 10, 69117 Heidelberg.
T. (06221) 235 71. *052990*
Neanders, Ingrimstr. 8, 69117 Heidelberg.
T. (06221) 244 35. - Orient / Sculp / Tex / Arch / Eth /
Jew - *052991*
Nuzinger, C., St.-Anna-Gasse 11, 69117 Heidelberg.
T. (06221) 161670, Fax (06221) 181204.
- Paint - *052992*
Piccobello, Klingentorstr. 6, 69117 Heidelberg.
T. (06221) 16 41 00. - Ant - *052993*
Renner, W., Rathausstr. 62, 69126 Heidelberg.
T. (06221) 323 41. - Ant / Dec - *052994*
Röcker, W., Brückenkopfstr. 6b, 69120 Heidelberg.
T. (06221) 437 22. *052995*
Rudolf, G., Kurfürsten Anlage 1-3, 69115 Heidelberg.
T. (06221) 13733. *052996*
Saghy, Andreas von, Friedrich-Ebert-Anlage 19, 69117
Heidelberg. T. (06221) 231 04. - Ant / Tex / Mil - *052997*
Schatztruhe, Kaiserstr. 62, 69115 Heidelberg.
T. (06221) 251 50. - Ant - *052998*
Schmidt, A., Brückenkopfstr. 6a, 69120 Heidelberg.
T. (06221) 47 31 13. - Ant - *052999*
Schultz, G., Ziegelgasse 26, 69117 Heidelberg.
T. (06221) 16 69 90. - Ant / Paint / Jew / Mod - *053000*
Siber, Margarete, Bergheimer Str. 45, 69115 Heidelberg.
T. (06221) 241 69. - Ant / Paint / Graph / China / Sculp /
Jew / Silv / Glass / Cur - *053001*
Souterrain, Handschuhsheimer Landstr. 6, 69120 Heidelberg. T. (06221) 47 45 96. - Ant - *053002*
Spiess & Walther, Friedrich-Ebert-Anlage 23a, 69117
Heidelberg. T. (06221) 222 33. *053003*

Strobel, C.B., Plöck 62, 69117 Heidelberg.
T. (06221) 203 08. *053004*
Stühmer & Heincke, Schillerstr. 29, 69115 Heidelberg.
T. (06221) 76 74 30. - Ant - *053005*
Stümpges, Hertzstr. 1, 69126 Heidelberg.
T. (06221) 30 06 71. *053006*
Treusch, Sofienstr 29, 69115 Heidelberg.
T. (06221) 23974. - Jew - *053007*
Tschantaridis, A., Haspelgasse 16, 69117 Heidelberg.
T. (06221) 16 18 17. *053008*
Welker, W., Hauptstr. 106, 69117 Heidelberg.
T. (06221) 226 12. *053009*
Winnikes, Heinrich, & Sohn, Steingasse 14, 69117 Heidelberg. T. (06221) 216 84. - Ant / Furn - *053010*
Winnikes, Helmut & Annemarie, Hauptstr. 138, 69117
Heidelberg. T. (06221) 216 43. - Furn / China / Silv - *053011*
Winterstein, R., Bluntschlistr. 17, 69115 Heidelberg.
T. (06221) 147 61. *053012*

Heidenheim an der Brenz (Baden-Württemberg)
Florian's Schatztruhe, Clichystr 2-6, 89518 Heidenheim an der Brenz. T. (07321) 46677. *053013*
Geiselhart, W., Hintere Gasse 12, 89522 Heidenheim an der Brenz. T. (07321) 22412. *053014*
Kleines Kunsthaus, Clichystr 49, 89518 Heidenheim an der Brenz. T. (07321) 46101. *053014a*
Maier, Hans, Hans-Holbein-Str 53, 89520 Heidenheim an der Brenz. T. (07321) 62346. *053015*
Nehring, Clara, Clichystr 69, 89518 Heidenheim an der Brenz. T. (07321) 44450. - Ant / Paint / Graph / Furn /
China / Sculp / Fra / Lights / Instr / Mil / Glass / Mod / Tin / Toys - *053016*
Neils, Elfriede / Tatjana, Leonhardstr 39, 89518 Heidenheim an der Brenz. T. (07321) 44614. - Ant / Paint /
Furn / Jew / Instr - *053017*
Schulz, E., Am Radkeller 3, 89518 Heidenheim an der Brenz. T. (07321) 44450. *053018*

Heidesheim (Rheinland-Pfalz)
Elsner, K.J., Berndesallee 12, 55262 Heidesheim.
T. (06132) 57896. *053020*

Heilbronn (Baden-Württemberg)
Blech, Wolfgang, Allee 12, 74072 Heilbronn.
T. (07131) 84151. *053021*
Conny's Lädle, Klingenberger Str 12, 74080 Heilbronn.
T. (07131) 31275. - Ant - *053022*
Fischer, Jürgen, Trappensee, 74074 Heilbronn.
T. (07131) 73064/65, Fax (07131) 77428. - Ant /
Glass - *053023*
Freyer, Conny, Klingenberger Str 12, 74080 Heilbronn.
T. (07131) 31275, 163919. *053024*
Hartmann, A., Hauptstr 34, 74081 Heilbronn.
T. (07131) 55245. *053025*
Krämer, P., Postpassage, 74072 Heilbronn.
T. (07131) 83308. - Num - *053026*
Porzellan-Klassiker, Blücherstr 46, 74074 Heilbronn.
T. (07131) 570273. - China - *053027*
Vock, Eduard, Kilianspl 3, 74072 Heilbronn.
T. (07131) 84314. *053028*

Heiligenhafen (Schleswig-Holstein)
Schlünsen, Ferienpark, 23774 Heiligenhafen.
T. (04362) 2471. *053029*

Heiligenhaus (Nordrhein-Westfalen)
Müller, H.-J., Gohrstr 10, 42579 Heiligenhaus.
T. (02126) 23466/67. *053030*

Heiligkreuzsteinach (Baden-Württemberg)
Münch, Hüttengasse 40, 69253 Heiligkreuzsteinach. *053031*

Heilsbronn (Bayern)
Lowig, Max-Gerd & Gisela, Abteigasse 3, 91560 Heilsbronn. T. (09872) 396. - Ant - *053032*

Heinersreuth (Bayern)
Redel, A., Bayreutherstr. 21, 95500 Heinersreuth.
T. (0921) 46564. *053033*

Heinsberg (Nordrhein-Westfalen)
Linzen, H.J., Werlo 47, 52525 Heinsberg.
T. (02452) 8273.   053034

Heitersheim (Baden-Württemberg)
Kanzler, Walter H., Eschbacher Str. 1, 79423 Heitersheim. T. (07633) 61 87. - Mil -   053035

Hemer (Nordrhein-Westfalen)
Limbrock, G., Nieringser Weg 26a, 58675 Hemer.
T. (02372) 615 91.   053036

Hemhofen (Bayern)
Härtl, Ulf, Ringstr. 33, 91334 Hemhofen.
T. (09195) 7186, Fax (09195) 55440. - Ant / Paint /
Furn / China / Sculp -   053037
Kraus, M., Am Vogelherd 10, 91334 Hemhofen.
T. (09195) 2258.   053038

Henstedt-Ulzburg (Schleswig-Holstein)
Küchel, Angelika, Rhener Kehre 13a, 24558 Henstedt-
Ulzburg. T. (041 93) 796 46.   053039
Molles, Ruth, Virchowring 42, 24558 Henstedt-Ulzburg.
T. (041 93) 3429.   053040

Heppenheim (Hessen)
Antiquitäten An- und Verkauf, Darmstädter Str 25,
64646 Heppenheim. T. (06252) 76939.   053041
Meinberg, E., Wormser Tor 4, 64646 Heppenheim.
T. (06252) 2553.   053042

Herborn (Hessen)
Dietrich, G., Turmstr 23, 35745 Herborn.
T. (02772) 41336.   053043
Haase, Helga, Kallenbach's Wäldchen 27, 35745 Her-
born. T. (02772) 3818. - Furn -   053044
Paproth, E., Am Reuterberg 15, 35745 Herborn.
T. (02772) 54435. - Num -   053045
Schneider, R., Kleine Gasse 3, 35745 Herborn.
T. (02777) 6393.   053046

Herford (Nordrhein-Westfalen)
Bloemers, Günter, Hermannstr. 47, 32052
Herford.   053047
Lülf-Steffen, Hämelinger Str. 6, 32052 Herford.
T. (05221) 53730, 55662.   053048
Tobisch-Wimmer, H., Berliner Str. 24, 32052
Herford.   053049

Hermannsburg (Niedersachsen)
Ermgassen, H., P.-Schütze-Weg 10, 29320 Hermanns-
burg. T. (05052) 2430.   053050
Müller, S., Am Lutterbach 1, 29320 Hermannsburg.
T. (05062) 28 84.   053051

Hermsdorf (Sachsen)
Löwe, Claus Dieter, Neue Str 10, 01458 Hermsdorf.
- Paint / Graph / Furn / China / Tex / Jew / Fra / Silv / Gla-
ss / Cur / Mod / Toys -   053052

Herne (Nordrhein-Westfalen)
Gabert, Gerold, Bahnhofstr. 8b, 44623 Herne.
T. (02323) 507 33. - Paint / Graph -   053053
Henrichs, R., Martinistr. 28, 44652 Herne.
T. (02323) 02325/61479.   053054
Klecks-Herne, Neustr. 25, 44623 Herne.
T. (02323) 57262, Fax (02323) 53278.   053055
Oelmann, Heinz, Mozartstr. 5, 44649 Herne.
T. (02323) 704 73. - Ant -   053056
Tapper, Erwin, Heinrich-Schütz-Str. 3, 44627
Herne.   053057
Wurm-Schleimer, H., Hauptstr. 153, 44652 Herne.
T. (02323) 712 97.   053058
Zur alten Bäckerei, Mühlhauser Str. 19, 44627 Herne.
T. (02323) 634 89.   053059

Heroldstatt (Baden-Württemberg)
Frenzel, Lange Str. 6, 72535 Heroldstatt.
T. (07389) 12 88/89.   053060

Herrenberg (Baden-Württemberg)
Böhmländer, Christine, Tübinger Str. 28, 71083 Herren-
berg. T. (07032) 44 70.   053061
Györfi, G. & S., Schuhgasse 2, 71083 Herrenberg.
T. (07032) 5730.   053062

Herrmann, Klemens, Marktpl. 1, 71083 Herrenberg.
T. (07032) 265 85.   053063

Herrsching (Bayern)
Ramer, A., Schloß, 82211 Herrsching.
T. (08152) 5214.   053064

Herrstein (Rheinland-Pfalz)
Gerhard, R., Hauptstr. 41, 55756 Herrstein.
T. (06785) 1440.   053065
Knospe, B., Schloßweg 18, 55756 Herrstein.
T. (06785) 7534.   053066

Herscheid (Nordrhein-Westfalen)
Bergmann, Unterdorfstr 4, 58849 Herscheid.
T. (02357) 4161. - Furn -   053067

Herten (Nordrhein-Westfalen)
Irmer, W.E., Hermannstr 15, 45699 Herten.
T. (02366) 35132. - Num -   053068
Westenweller, Lore, Schreberstr 20, 45701 Herten.
T. (02366) 43226. - Num -   053069

Herxheim bei Landau (Rheinland-Pfalz)
Verstegen, R. & W., Untere Hauptstr. 111, 76863 Her-
xheim bei Landau. T. (07276) 6681.   053070

Herzberg (Brandenburg)
Röhner, Werner, Torgauer Str. 20, 04916 Herzberg.
T. (03535) 3919, Fax (03535) 3919.   053071

Herzogenaurach (Bayern)
Herrmann, Heidi, Kurstr. 8, 91074 Herzogenaurach.
T. (09132) 42 63.   053072

Herzogenrath (Nordrhein-Westfalen)
Bücken, H., Südstr. 182, 52134 Herzogenrath.
T. (02406) 22 49.   053073
Pieters Antiquitäten, Rolandstr. 42, 52134 Herzogenrath.
T. (02406) 02407/2450.   053074

Hessisch Lichtenau (Hessen)
Kiehlmann, E. & H., Kirchstr. 7, 37235 Hessisch Lichtenau. T. (05602) 3117.   053075

Heubach (Baden-Württemberg)
Ising, Dr., Gmünder Str 28, 73540 Heubach.
T. (07173) 8913. - Num -   053076
Stephan, J., Im Bürglesbühl 28, 73540 Heubach.
T. (07173) 8740.   053077

Heusenstamm (Hessen)
Kronat, Rudolf W., Hubertusanlage 90, 63150 Heusenstamm. T. (06104) 56 14.   053078

Heusweiler (Saarland)
Bauernstube, Kirchstr 21, 66265 Heusweiler.
T. (06806) 79065.   053079
Kirchschlager, Walter, Akazienweg 2, 66265 Heusweiler.
- Num -   053080

Hiddenhausen (Nordrhein-Westfalen)
Niemjetz, Karl, Bünderstr. 375, 32120 Hiddenhausen.
- Ant -   053081
Onken, Peter, Ziegelstr. 177, 32120 Hiddenhausen.
T. (05221) 32069.   053082

Hilden (Nordrhein-Westfalen)
de Fries, E., Hagelkreuzstr. 5, 40721 Hilden.
T. (02103) 85 20.   053083
Galerie 51, Schulstr. 25, 40721 Hilden.
T. (02103) 534 00.   053084
Kloeters, Gisela, Kurt-Kappel-Str. 1, 40721 Hilden.
T. (02103) 522 29.   053085
Köster, H., Schulstr. 25, 40721 Hilden.
T. (02103) 53400.   053086
Maskaric, N., Benrather Str. 16, 40721 Hilden.
T. (02103) 51454.   053087
Naiv Art Center Nedo's Stuben, Benrather Str. 16, 40721
Hilden.   053088
Okroy, P., & A. Zenker, Beckersheide 24, 40724 Hilden.
T. (02103) 881 57.   053089
Safa, A., Walder Str. 1, 40724 Hilden.
T. (02103) 626 21.   053090
Weiss, K., Benrather Str. 34, 40721 Hilden.
T. (02103) 546 86.   053091

Hildesheim (Niedersachsen)
Gauen, Rudolf, Marktstr. 18, 31134 Hildesheim.
- Rel -   053092
Kohlenberg, Horst, Dammstr. 14, 31134 Hildesheim.
T. (05121) 386 18. - Num -   053093
Krüger, Ch., Marktstr. 2-3, 31134 Hildesheim.
T. (05121) 314 91.   053094
Langstein, Roland, 31134 Hildesheim. - Num -   053095
Scholz, Reinhard G., Osterstr. 12, 31134 Hildesheim.
T. (05121) 361 07.   053096

Hilpoltstein (Bayern)
Haußner, Freystädterstr 38, 91161 Hilpoltstein.
T. (09174) 1240. - Furn -   053097
Hossner, Magda, Industriestr 21, 91161 Hilpoltstein.
T. (09174) 9551, 2334.   053098
Karl, R., Kolpingstr 3, 91161 Hilpoltstein.
T. (09174) 9604.   053099
Willmitzer, H., Bahnhofstr 12, 91161 Hilpoltstein.
T. (09174) 3436.   053100

Hilter (Niedersachsen)
Marquart, Osnabrücker Str. 19, 49176 Hilter.
T. (05409) 38201.   053101

Hochdonn (Schleswig-Holstein)
Schmidt, J., Dreeßenweg 7, 25712 Hochdonn.
T. (04825) 2343.   053102

Hochheim (Hessen)
Kissel & Strüver, Weiherstr 25, 65239 Hochheim.
T. (06146) 4117.   053103
Riese, E., Frankfurter Str 24, 65239 Hochheim.
T. (06146) 9565.   053104
Weißmantel, H., Hintergasse 42, 65239 Hochheim.
T. (06146) 7442.   053105

Höchberg (Bayern)
Busch, Peter M., Karwinkel 12, 97204 Höchberg.
T. (0931) 484 69. - Mil -   053106
Römer Antiquariat, Am Hessental 12, 97204
Höchberg.   053107

Höchstädt, Oberfranken (Bayern)
Rohrer, K., Schloßpl. 19, 95186 Höchstädt, Oberfranken.
T. (09205) 1464.   053108

Hörden (Niedersachsen)
Victoria Antique, Hauptstr. 6, 37412 Hörden.
T. (05521) 65 61. - Ant -   053109

Hördt (Rheinland-Pfalz)
Manenti, J., Wörthstr. 65, 76771 Hördt.
T. (07272) 2895.   053110

Hörstel (Nordrhein-Westfalen)
Göcke, Josef, Kanalstr. 116, 48477 Hörstel.   053111

Hof (Bayern)
Lankes, Heinz-Dieter, Klosterstr 22, 95028 Hof.
T. (09281) 18200.   053112
Pfadenhauer, A., Kreuzsteinstr 13, 95028 Hof.
T. (09281) 3341.   053113
Rudorf, Horst, Schützenweg 22, 95028 Hof.
T. (09281) 16909.   053114
Weidmann, W., Luitpoldstr 15, 95028 Hof.
T. (09281) 85939.   053115
Wolf, Alfred und Karin, Karolinenstr 26, 95028 Hof.
T. (09281) 85578.   053116

Hofgeismar (Hessen)
Jakisch, L. & E., Zwischen den Brücken 9, 34369 Hof-
geismar. T. (05671) 45 40.   053117
Seifert, E., Steinweg 1, 34369 Hofgeismar.
T. (05671) 2424. - Num -   053118

Hofheim (Bayern)
Meindl, P., Eichelsdorf 28, 97461 Hofheim.
T. (09523) 432. - Ant / Furn -   053119

Hofheim (Hessen)
English Antiques, Wiesbadener Str 7a, 65719 Hofheim.
T. (06192) 8770, 6584.   053120
Ernst, Rolf August, Im Klingen 5a, 65719 Hofheim.
T. (06192) 22138. - Orient -   053121

Haslbeck, Karl, Nordring 13, 65719 Hofheim.
T. (06192) 21071. - Ant -   053122
Kahl, G.A., Nachtigallenweg 7, 65719 Hofheim.
T. (06192) 1418.   053123
Kaiser, D., Wiesbadener Str 7a, 65719 Hofheim.
T. (06122) 8770.   053124
Koppe, Taunusstr 1a, 65719 Hofheim. T. (06192) 15461
- Ant / Furn -   053125
Werthern, J. von, Kurhausstr 2, 65719 Hofheim.
T. (06192) 25906.   053126
Witte, U., Mainzerstr 44, 65719 Hofheim.
T. (06192) 37573.   053127

Hohenhameln (Niedersachsen)
Welge, Hans-Jürgen, Alte Molkerei, 31249 Hohenha-
meln. T. (05128) 54 07.   053128

Holm (Schleswig-Holstein)
Dietz, U., Hauptstr. 21, 25488 Holm.
T. (04103) 138 94.   053129

Holzgerlingen (Baden-Württemberg)
Schwedler, Schwalbenweg 4, 71088 Holzgerlingen.
T. (07031) 41278.   053130

Holzhausen (Rheinland-Pfalz)
Neuhäusel, P., Nikolaus-August-Otto-Str. 7, 56357 Holz-
hausen. T. (06772) 81 60.   053131

Holzkirchen, Oberbayern (Bayern)
Wimmer, Anton, Tölzer Str 3, 83607 Holzkirchen, Oberbayern. T. (08024) 2425. - Ant / Furn -   053132

Holzminden (Niedersachsen)
Ludwig, F., Kirchstr. 3, 37603 Holzminden.
T. (05531) 7298.   053133
Maximilian Antiquitäten, Mittlere Str. 8, 37603 Holzmin-
den. T. (05531) 37 38.   053134

Homberg (Hessen)
Antikhaus Homberg, Holzhäuser Str. 20, 34576 Hom-
berg. T. (05681) 4030.   053135
Hartmann, E., Breslauerstr. 24, 34576 Homberg.
T. (05681) 2772.   053136

Homburg (Saarland)
Beck, M., Am Schwedenhof 4, 66424 Homburg.
T. (06848) 554, 6654.   053137
Jeromin, J., Saarbrücker Str 104, 66424 Homburg.
T. (06841) 67733, 5767.   053138
Lauer, Bertold, Talstr 55, 66424 Homburg.
T. (06841) 60400. - Ant -   053139
Miles, E., Talstr 36, 66424 Homburg.
T. (06841) 62728.   053140

Horb (Baden-Württemberg)
Hehl, W., Mühlgässle 19, 72160 Horb.
T. (07451) 8533.   053141
Potrebny, H., Johanniterstr 53, 72160 Horb.
T. (07451) 3079.   053142
Stölzel, J., Seestr 20, 72160 Horb.
T. (07486) 7524.   053143

Horn-Bad Meinberg (Nordrhein-Westfalen)
Bruckmann, Hans, Mauerstr 9, 32805 Horn-Bad Meinberg. T. (05234) 2893. - Ant -   053144

Horst (Schleswig-Holstein)
Klaushenke, Joachim, Horstmühle, 25358 Horst.
T. (04126) 480, 04129/1313, Fax (04126) 1099.
- Furn / Repr / Eth -   053145
Rothmar, H.V., Schulstr. 2, 25358 Horst.
T. (04126) 10 10.   053146

Horstmar (Nordrhein-Westfalen)
Dober, I., Schöppinger Str. 18, 48612 Horstmar.
T. (02558) 7152.   053147

Hude (Niedersachsen)
Eilers, M., Friedrichstr 27, 27798 Hude.
T. (04408) 348.   053148

Hünxe (Nordrhein-Westfalen)
Koch, J., Dinslakener Str. 142, 46569 Hünxe.
T. (02856) 31691.   053149

Kühne, D., Schmerbecker Landstr. 25, 46569 Hünxe.
T. (02856) 7633.   053150

Hürth (Nordrhein-Westfalen)
Antiquitäten-Centrum, Bonnstr 409, 50354 Hürth.
T. (02233) 45299. - Ant -   053151

Hütterscheid (Rheinland-Pfalz)
Klinkert, O., Hauptstr. 27, 54636 Hütterscheid.
T. (06527) 710.   053152

Husum (Schleswig-Holstein)
Alt-Friesischer Kunsthandel, Süderstr 13, 25813 Husum.
T. (04841) 3030/31.   053153
List-Petersen, P.-C., Hörn 8 und Wilhelmstr 29, 25813
Husum. T. (04841) 62657, Fax (04841) 63847. - Ant /
Paint / China / Repr / Fra / Lights / Instr -   053154
Tobien, J., Neustadt 10, 25813 Husum.
T. (04841) 64800.   053155

Ibbenbüren (Nordrhein-Westfalen)
Landhaus-Antik, Stettiner Str. 24a, 49479 Ibbenbüren.
T. (05451) 05455/1058.   053156
Leonhardt, Jochen, Münsterstr. 50, 49477 Ibbenbüren.
T. (05451) 15550, Fax (05451) 49550. - Ant /
Sculp -   053157

Idar-Oberstein (Rheinland-Pfalz)
Afghan Basar Gems, Mainzerstr. 34, 55743 Idar-Ober-
stein. T. (06781) 47508.   053158

Immenstadt (Bayern)
Kennerknecht, Julius-Kunert-Str 13, 87509 Immenstadt.
T. (08323) 1861.   053159

Imsbach (Rheinland-Pfalz)
Maurer, R. & E., Röderhof, 67817 Imsbach.
T. (06302) 389.   053160

Ingelheim (Rheinland-Pfalz)
Leimer, Hochstr 44, 55218 Ingelheim. T. (06132) 8094,
Fax (06132) 86563. - Furn -   053161
Rhein-Main-Antik Widmer, Steingasse 2, 55218 Ingel-
heim. T. (06132) 76091. - Ant / Furn -   053162
Westphal, Martin, Belzerstr 10, 55218 Ingelheim.
T. (06132) 4608. - Ant / Paint / Furn / China / Jew /
Glass / Mod -   053163

Ingersheim (Baden-Württemberg)
Grünwald, Sabine, Heckenstr. 18, 74379 Ingersheim.
- Mil -   053164

Ingolstadt (Bayern)
Anlauf, R., Goldknopfgasse 5, 85049 Ingolstadt.
T. (0841) 33374.   053165
Antik und Deco, Milchstr 12, 85049 Ingolstadt.
T. (0841) 34152, 87990, Fax (0841) 51961. - Ant /
Furn / Repr / Dec -   053166
Gaiser, E., Hagauer Str 78, 85051 Ingolstadt.
T. (0841) 34192.   053167
Gauß, H., Griesmühlstr 2, 85049 Ingolstadt.
T. (0841) 34192.   053168
Nemec, V., Neubaustr 2, 85049 Ingolstadt.
T. (0841) 33696, Fax (0841) 17113.   053169
Scheiner, Große Zellgasse 63, 85049 Ingolstadt.
T. (0841) 32398, 56533, Fax (0841) 17498.
- Num -   053170
Schwarz, Moritzstr 11, 85049 Ingolstadt.
T. (0841) 34527. - Paint / China / Repr / Fra /
Glass -   053171
Tollkühn, H., Taschenturmstr 2, 85049 Ingolstadt.
T. (0841) 34031.   053172
Zech, Schmalzingergasse 3, 85049 Ingolstadt.
T. (0841) 34844. - Paint / Graph / Silv -   053173

Inning (Bayern)
Galerie Désirée, Marktpl. 3, 82266 Inning.
T. (08143) 14 86, 16 93. - Ant / Furn / China /
Instr -   053174

Insul (Rheinland-Pfalz)
Hövel, Gustav, 53520 Insul.   053175

Iphofen (Bayern)
Grötsch, H.-H., Ringsbühlweg 2, 97346 Iphofen.
T. (09323) 1079.   053176

Schmidt, E., Breite Gasse 9, 97346 Iphofen.
T. (09323) 51 93. - Paint / Jew / Mil -   053177

Ipsheim (Bayern)
Pfeiffer, H., Altheim, 91472 Ipsheim.
T. (09846) 272.   053178

Iserlohn (Nordrhein-Westfalen)
Jacobi, Paul, Alter Rathausplatz 11, 58636 Iserlohn.
T. (02371) 239 93. - Mil -   053179
Sanchez, Hochstr. 30, 58638 Iserlohn.
T. (02371) 20358.   053180
Sittler, M., Baarstr. 146, 58636 Iserlohn.
T. (02371) 42647.   053181

Isernhagen (Niedersachsen)
Antik-Deele, Burgwedeler Str. 19a, 30916 Isernhagen.
T. (0511) 72 37 86.   053182
Honscha, Siegward, Isernhagener Str. 49, 30916 Isern-
hagen. T. (0511) 61 23 54. - Num -   053183
Kuhrmeier, M., Gleiwitzer Str. 16, 30916
Isernhagen.   053184
Rombourg, Franck, Am Ostfelde 118, 30916 Isernhagen.
T. (0511) 73 78 79.   053185
Voss, D., Moorstr. 6, 03001 Isernhagen.
T. (0511) 39 31.   053186

Ismaning (Bayern)
Hesse, Gisela, Mayerbacherstr. 28, 85737
Ismaning.   053187
Senn, Renate A., Konradstr. 14, 85737 Ismaning.
- Orient -   053188

Isny (Baden-Württemberg)
Hommanner, I., Friedhag 2, 88316 Isny.
T. (07562) 3905.   053189
Roller, R., Eberzstr 3, 88316 Isny.
T. (07562) 8751.   053190

Ispringen (Rheinland-Pfalz)
Tusch, Karlheinz, Karlstr 1, 75228 Ispringen.
T. (07231) 82646, Fax (07231) 86215.   053191

Issum (Nordrhein-Westfalen)
Knoor, Klotenstr. 9, 47661 Issum.
T. (02835) 41069.   053192
Vaupel, P. & R., Floorsweg 10, 47661 Issum.
T. (02835) 5278.   053193

Jena (Thüringen)
Beyreuther, Jürgen, Fürstengraben 18, 07743 Jena.
T. (03641) 54452. - Ant -   053194

Jersbek (Schleswig-Holstein)
Roschewitz, B., Langereihe 21, 22941 Jersbek.
T. (04532) 5472, Fax (04532) 7672. - Ant / Paint / Furn /
Repr -   053195

Jesteburg (Niedersachsen)
Jesteburger Mühle, Hauptstr. 76, 21266 Jesteburg.
T. (041 83) 41 70.   053196
Sammans Hus-Antik, Hauptstr. 26, 21266 Jesteburg.
T. (041 83) 37 39.   053197

Jettingen (Baden-Württemberg)
Hoyer, Anne, Nagolder Str. 15, 71131 Jettingen.
T. (07452) 755 72. - Ant / Paint / Eth -   053198

Jettingen-Scheppach (Bayern)
Stuttfeld, G., Burgauer Weg 1, 89343 Jettingen-Schep-
pach. T. (08225) 615.   053199

Jevenstedt (Schleswig-Holstein)
Galerie Jevenstedt, Itzehoer Chaussee 24, 24808 Jevenstedt. T. (04337) 757.   053200

Jever (Niedersachsen)
Habersetzer, Gartensweg 8, 26441 Jever.
T. (04461) 5204.   053201
Sassmannshausen, Jägerkamp 20, 26441
Jever.   053202

Jüchen (Nordrhein-Westfalen)
Eder, K.B., Niersstr. 24, 41363 Jüchen. T. (02165) 2030,
Fax (02165) 7632. - Paint / Graph / Repr / Sculp /
Fra -   053203

Lorenz, Hans, Kirchstr. 3, 41363 Jüchen.
T. (02165) 12 71. - Ant -   053204

Jülich (Nordrhein-Westfalen)
Schlefers, Magdalene, Kapuzinerstr. 3, 52428 Jülich.
T. (02461) 39 64, 18 97.   053205

Kaarst (Nordrhein-Westfalen)
Gross, Maubisstr. 31, 41564 Kaarst.
T. (021 01) 693 27.   053206
Lennartz, S., August-Thyssen-Str. 3, 41564 Kaarst.
T. (021 01) 62033.   053207
Rieckhof, P.M., August-Thyssen-Str. 4, 41564 Kaarst.
T. (021 01) 60 37 63.   053208
Ringes, Heinz, Mittelstr. 4, 41564 Kaarst.   053209
Tschöpe, Reinhild, Bruchweg 8, 41564 Kaarst.
T. (021 01) 60 27 56.   053210
Wessendorf, G., Neusserstr. 101e, 41564 Kaarst.
T. (021 01) 632 38. - Paint / Graph / Sculp / Fra / Pho /
Mul / Draw -   053211

Kahl (Bayern)
Wenzel, Anne, An den Franzosenäckern 4, 63796 Kahl.
- Ant -   053212

Kaisersesch (Rheinland-Pfalz)
Portobello, Koblenzer Str. 51, 56759 Kaisersesch.
T. (02653) 82 08.   053213

Kaiserslautern (Rheinland-Pfalz)
Behr, A.A., Mannheimer Str. 37, 67655 Kaiserslautern.
- Paint / Repr / Fra -   053214
Boschert, Hermann, Eisenbahnstr. 20, 67655 Kaisers-
lautern. T. (0631) 932 98.   053215
Galerie Exquisit, Distelstr. 12, 67657 Kaiserslautern.
T. (0631) 401 88.   053216
Gleiche, Rudolf, Dr., Rudolf-Breitscheid-Str. 5, 67655
Kaiserslautern. T. (0631) 164 29.   053217
Heinrichs, L., Mannheimer Str. 117, 67657 Kaiserslau-
tern. T. (0631) 421 40.   053218
Hoffmann, A. & J., Distelstr. 12, 67657 Kaiserslautern.
T. (0631) 401 88.   053219
Nebling, Monika, Theodor-Heuss-Str. 7, 67663 Kaisers-
lautern. T. (0631) 686 70. - Ant / Paint / Graph -   053220
Ohk, M., Fruchthallstr., 67655 Kaiserslautern.
T. (0631) 643 02.   053221
Prass, U., Schillerstr. 5, 67655 Kaiserslautern.
T. (0631) 637 51.   053222
Roos, M., Benzinoring 39, 67657 Kaiserslautern.
T. (0631) 932 88.   053223

Kalkar (Nordrhein-Westfalen)
Aldenhoff, H. & H., Markt 16, 47546 Kalkar.
T. (02824) 5082.   053224
Antiquitäten im Mühlenhof, Düffelsmühle 34, 47546 Kal-
kar. T. (02824) 20 14/15. - Ant -   053225
Wilmsen, Johannes, Föckenhof 3, 47546 Kalkar.
T. (02824) 2014/15. - Ant -   053226

Kalletal (Nordrhein-Westfalen)
Strohmeier, H.-C., Echternhagen 9, 32689 Kalletal.
T. (05264) 93 91.   053227

Kamp-Lintfort (Nordrhein-Westfalen)
Holzhauer, J., Rundstr. 31a, 47475 Kamp-Lintfort.
T. (02842) 87 17.   053228

Kampen (Schleswig-Holstein)
Flachsmann, H., Kurhausstr., 25999 Kampen.
T. (04651) 43166.   053229
Kampener Galerie, Wattweg 19, 25999 Kampen.
T. (04651) 42924, Fax (04651) 46596. - Paint /
Graph -   053230
May, H., Kurhausstr., 25999 Kampen.
T. (04651) 45322.   053231
Schäfer, W., Kupferkanne, 25999 Kampen.   053232

Kandern (Baden-Württemberg)
Graf, Basler Str. 16, 79400 Kandern. T. (07626) 74 04.
- Furn -   053233

Kappeln (Schleswig-Holstein)
Birkenheuer, Franz, Querstr 2a, 24376 Kappeln.
T. (04642) 2112.   053234

Karben (Hessen)
Spreen, C., Am Schloß 18, 61184 Karben.
T. (06039) 72 60.   053235
Volkskunst, Burg-Grafenröder Str. 2, 61184 Karben.
T. (06039) 17 07.   053236

Karlsruhe (Baden-Württemberg)
Abel, E., Herrenstr. 33, 76133 Karlsruhe.
T. (0721) 23427.   053237
Bettini, A. & F., Markgrafenstr. 38, 76133 Karlsruhe.
T. (0721) 69 52 02.   053238
Boss, Jürgen, Daxlander Str. 68, 76185 Karlsruhe.
T. (0721) 59 01 79.   053239
Boss, Jürgen, Kaiserstr. 169, 76133 Karlsruhe.
T. (0721) 230 66.   053240
Boss, Jürgen, Am Berg 28, 76228 Karlsruhe.
T. (0721) 45 08 12.   053241
Büchle, E., Kreuzstr. 19, 76133 Karlsruhe.
T. (0721) 69 93 87, 75 16 27.   053242
Burhenne, H., Scheffelstr. 68, 76135 Karlsruhe.
T. (0721) 84 26 81.   053243
Chalet, Waldstr. 95, 76133 Karlsruhe. - Ant -   053244
Champangne, Joel, Klauprechtstr. 1, 76137 Karlsruhe.
- Ant -   053245
Demmer, Gerwigstr. 34, 76131 Karlsruhe.
T. (0721) 62 17 56. - Ant -   053246
Dorer, J., Erbprinzenstr. 19, 76133 Karlsruhe.
T. (0721) 257 57.   053247
Drechsel, Gerlinde, Herrenstr. 42, 76133 Karlsruhe.
T. (0721) 216 07. - Ant / Paint / China / Sculp -   053248
Ferstl, Robert, Enzstr. 2, 76199 Karlsruhe.
T. (0721) 887368, Fax (0721) 885000. - Instr -   053249
Fischer, S., Karlstr. 91, 76137 Karlsruhe.
T. (0721) 28018.   053250
Furrer, Karin, Amalienstr. 14a, 76133 Karlsruhe.
T. (0721) 25748.   053251
Glaser, T., Jägerstr. 10, 76227 Karlsruhe.
T. (0721) 40 77 08, 40 61 37. - Ant -   053252
Gromer, Herta, Tulpenstr. 39, 76199 Karlsruhe.
T. (0721) 302 42. - Paint / Furn -   053253
Hansen, M., Herrenstr. 44, 76133 Karlsruhe.
T. (0721) 232 47.   053254
Heil, A., Weinbrennerstr. 15, 76135 Karlsruhe.
T. (0721) 85 42 40.   053255
Hess, Dietrich, Kaiserstr. 36, 76133 Karlsruhe.
T. (0721) 69 81 24.   053256
Hild, Claus, Dr., Rintheimer Str. 2, 76131 Karlsruhe.
T. (0721) 698476, Fax (0721) 691619. - Num -   053257
Jägel-Bettini, Markgrafenstr. 38, 76133
Karlsruhe.   053258
Kirrmann, J., Herrenstr. 38-40, 76133 Karlsruhe.
T. (0721) 247 04. - Furn / Dec -   053259
Kreitz, B., Lessingstr. 78, 76135 Karlsruhe.
T. (0721) 85 55 61.   053260
Kroker, L., & D. Walsch, Amalienstr. 89, 76133 Karlsru-
he. T. (0721) 297 44. - Num -   053261
Kunz, E., Hardtstr. 47, 76185 Karlsruhe.
T. (0721) 59 18 16.   053262
Kutzner, Thomas, Hirschstr. 35a, 76133 Karlsruhe.
T. (0721) 253 53.   053263
Leis, Karl, Herrenstr. 52, 76133 Karlsruhe.
T. (0721) 294 71. - Ant -   053264
Leonardy, Peter, Jean-Ritzert-Str. 1, 76227 Karlsruhe.
T. (0721) 447 77. - Ant / Furn / Instr -   053265
Löffel, M., Wilhelmstr. 28, 76137 Karlsruhe.
T. (0721) 66 11 68.   053266
Mehl, N., Werderstr. 53, 76137 Karlsruhe.
T. (0721) 37 57 86.   053267
Paramount Internationale Münzgesellschaft, Rheinstr.
117a, 76185 Karlsruhe. T. (0721) 55 59 22.
- Num -   053268
Raab, N., Nelkenstr. 33, 76135 Karlsruhe.
T. (0721) 84 21 19.   053269
Schach, Horst, Herrenstr. 50a, 76133 Karlsruhe.
T. (0721) 262 22.   053270
Schade, B., Kaiserstr. 67, 76131 Karlsruhe.
T. (0721) 37 41 92.   053271
Schäfer, Kaiserstr. 86, 76133 Karlsruhe.
T. (0721) 278 60. - Jew -   053272

Schmittger, V., Friedrichstr. 6, 76229 Karlsruhe.
T. (0721) 48 41 45.   053273
Schork, G., Karlsruher Str. 41, 76139 Karlsruhe.
T. (0721) 68 11 89.   053274
Tandem, Hirschstr. 54, 76133 Karlsruhe.
T. (0721) 264 65.   053275
Ubu, Karlstr. 6, 76133 Karlsruhe.
T. (0721) 230 39.   053276
Usine, Rheinstr. 65, 76185 Karlsruhe.
T. (0721) 59 27 94.   053277
Wackernah, G., Amalienstr. 42, 76133 Karlsruhe.
T. (0721) 294 26.   053278
Wolf, Günter, Am Pfinztor 20, 76227 Karlsruhe.
T. (0721) 401414, Fax (0721) 42613. - Num -   053279
Zimmermann, W., Erbprinzenstr. 28, 76133 Karlsruhe.
T. (0721) 241 60.   053280

Karlstadt (Bayern)
Gömling, M., Arnsteinerstr 40, 97753 Karlstadt.
T. (09353) 2272.   053281

Kassel (Hessen)
Asiatica, Obere Königsstr. 1, 34117 Kassel.
T. (0561) 748 31. - Orient -   053282
Baus, Werner, Ihringshäuser Str. 77, 34125
Kassel.   053283
Bollerhey, Dörnbergstr. 7, 34119 Kassel.
T. (0561) 28 15 07.   053284
Bornmann, M., Untere Königsstr. 50, 34117 Kassel.
T. (0561) 18474. - Num -   053285
Drube, P., Goethestr. 55, 34119 Kassel.
T. (0561) 77 71 94.   053286
Eichholz, J., Wilhelmshöher Allee 286, 34131 Kassel.
T. (0561) 31 15 06.   053287
Galerie Eule, Wolfsschlucht 8a, 34117 Kassel.
T. (0561) 127 40.   053288
Gross, Günther, Wilhelmshöher Allee 9, 34117 Kassel.
T. (0561) 161 49. - Graph -   053289
Hoppe, Goethestr. 67, 34119 Kassel.
T. (0561) 77 33 25.   053290
Krantz, F.-M., Rudolf-Schwander-Str. 23, 34117 Kassel.
T. (0561) 10 28 48.   053291
Kunsthandlung Wolfsanger, Wolfsangerstr. 92, 34125
Kassel. T. (0561) 87 57 45.   053292
Leck, Irmgard, Friedrich-Ebert-Str. 124, 34119 Kassel.
T. (0561) 77 22 35, 174 03.   053293
Loida, E., Friedrich-Ebert-Str. 95, 34119 Kassel.
T. (0561) 777777.   053294
Mißler, Pestalozzistr. 12, 34119 Kassel.
T. (0561) 77 65 25.   053295
Moosburger, Roland, Friedrich Ebert Str. 96, 34119 Kas-
sel. T. (0561) 77 27 58.   053296
Pflüger, Fernando, Holländische Str. 95, 34127 Kassel.
- Num -   053297
Prior, W., Friedrich-Ebert-Str. 91, 34119 Kassel.
T. (0561) 77 35 88. - Ant / Paint / Furn / China / Jew /
Fra / Silv / Lights / Glass -   053298
Rogowski, C., Elfenbuchenstr. 12, 34119 Kassel.
T. (0561) 13171.   053299
Rudolf, J., Friedrich-Ebert-Str. 115, 34119 Kassel.
T. (0561) 72042, 81 22 52. - Num -   053300
Rühl, Otto Horst, Wilhelmshöher Allee 40-42, 34125 Kassel.
T. (0561) 873012, Fax (0561) 873012. - Ant / Paint /
Graph / Furn / Tex / Dec / Silv / Lights / Instr / Glass / Cu-
r / Mod -   053301
Schatzinsel, Untere Königsstr. 50, 34117 Kassel.
T. (0561) 184 74. - Ant -   053302
Schmidt, Renate, Saarlandstr. 5, 34131 Kassel.
T. (0561) 337 86. - China -   053303
Schulte, J., Friedrich-Ebert-Str. 93, 34119 Kassel.
T. (0561) 166 49.   053304
Schumann, Reinhold, & Co., Sachsenstr. 1, 34131 Kas-
sel. T. (0561) 169 23. - Ant -   053305
Schumann, Reinhold, & Co., Wilhelmshöher Allee 82,
34119 Kassel. T. (0561) 169 23. - Ant / Furn -   053306
Simon, J., Weserstr. 42, 34125 Kassel.
T. (0561) 87 35 14. - Num -   053307

Kastl (Bayern)
Haisch, J., Klosterbergstr. 8, 92280 Kastl.
T. (09625) 743. - Arch -   053308

Kaufbeuren (Bayern)
Effenberger, Kurt, Hüttenstr. 103, 87600 Kaufbeuren.
T. (08341) 64346. - Furn -   053309
Schlegel, Walter, Pfarrgasse 13, 87600 Kaufbeuren.
T. (08341) 150 59. - Paint / China / Jew / Instr /
Glass -   053310
Schmid, H., Ledergasse 17, 87600 Kaufbeuren.
T. (08341) 129 87.   053311

Kaufungen (Hessen)
Weber, W., Siedlerweg 9, 34260 Kaufungen.
T. (05605) 40 98.   053312

Kayhude (Schleswig-Holstein)
Brose, O., Segeberger Str. 121, 23863 Kayhude.
T. (04535) 6424.   053313
Schümann, P., Segeberger Str. 121, 23863 Kayhude.
T. (04535) 1364.   053314

Kehl (Baden-Württemberg)
Jacquier, Paul-Francis, Honsellstr. 8, 77694 Kehl.
T. (07851) 1217. - Num -   053315
Schwebius, H., Marktstr. 2, 77694 Kehl.
T. (07851) 722 48.   053316
Walter, S., Blumenstr. 8, 77694 Kehl.
T. (07851) 4672.   053317

Kelberg (Rheinland-Pfalz)
Schäfer, G., Bergstr. 14, 53539 Kelberg.
T. (02692) 553.   053318

Kelkheim (Hessen)
Antikes & Kreatives im Holunderhof, Frankfurter Str 21,
65779 Kelkheim. T. (06195) 2000. - Furn -   053319
Mayrl, J., Hornauerstr 95, 65779 Kelkheim.
T. (06195) 63353.   053320
Merry Old England, Frankfurter Str 107, 65779 Kelk-
heim. T. (06195) 2222. - Ant / Furn / China / Silv /
Instr -   053321

Kell (Rheinland-Pfalz)
Frank & Henrich, Trierer Str. 25, 54427 Kell.
T. (06589) 1559.   053322

Kelsterbach (Hessen)
Hilda's Antik, Waldstr. 69, 65451 Kelsterbach.   053323

Kempen (Nordrhein-Westfalen)
Bienefeld, M., Ellenstr 2, 47906 Kempen.
T. (02152) 53726. - Ant / Furn / China / Tex -   053324
Leendert, A. Eulen 7, 47906 Kempen.
T. (02152) 6061.   053325

Kempten (Bayern)
Botzenhardt, Rudolf, Ludwigstr 103, 87437
Kempten.   053326
Botzenhardt, Walburga, Bei der Rose 9, 87435 Kempten.
T. (0831) 24587.   053327
Brianza, Bruno, Schützenstr 6, 87435 Kempten.
T. (0831) 14859.   053328
Gorlik, J., Zwingerstr 15, 87435 Kempten.
T. (0831) 12483.   053329
Heyer, P., Salzstr 32, 87435 Kempten.
T. (0831) 27446.   053330
Knaup, Heinz, Lessingstr 46, 87435 Kempten.
- Ant -   053331
Matzner, Dieter, Rathauspl 2, 87435 Kempten.
T. (0831) 15996, Fax (0831) 202629. - Graph / Repr /
Fra -   053332
Nuber, M., Gerberstr 24, 87435 Kempten.
T. (0831) 13100.   053333
Reutter, S., Kaufbeurer Str 29, 87437 Kempten.
T. (0831) 78200.   053334
Roeben, R. & M., Bahnhofstr 1, 87435 Kempten.
T. (0831) 22562.   053335
Seith, H., Memminger Str 21, 87439 Kempten.
T. (0831) 14381.   053336

Kenzingen (Baden-Württemberg)
Flemming, L., Oberes Schloß, 79341 Kenzingen.
T. (07644) 74 45.   053337

Kerken (Nordrhein-Westfalen)
Altertumsfundgrube, 47647 Kerken.   053338
Geisler, Paul, Hubertusstr. 1, 47647 Kerken.   053339

Grüne, J., Aldekerker Landstr. 57, 47647 Kerken.
T. (02833) 7727, 4325.   053340

Kernen (Baden-Württemberg)
Antiquitäten am Rathaus, Stettener Str. 9, 71394 Kern-
en. T. (07151) 41387. - Ant / Paint / Graph / China /
Arch / Eth / Silv / Rel / Glass / Cur / Toys -   053341

Kerpen (Nordrhein-Westfalen)
Rieke, Barbara Maria, Am Schloßpark 27, 50169 Ker-
pen. T. (02237) 18800. - Instr -   053342
Scharff, A., Hauptstr 329, 50169 Kerpen.
T. (02273) 2531.   053343
Will, H.-D., Heerstr 401, 50169 Kerpen.
T. (02237) 8168.   053344

Kevelaer (Nordrhein-Westfalen)
Bauer, Busmannstr. 1, 47623 Kevelaer.
T. (02832) 53 61.   053345
Gesthüsen, T., Gelderner Str. 127, 47623 Kevelaer.
T. (02832) 1720.   053346
Görtzen, F.J., & Marie T. Helgers, Busmannstr. 1, 47623
Kevelaer. T. (02832) 5361.   053347
Hanßen, Hermann, Grenzweg 4, 47624
Kevelaer.   053348
Janssen, H., Busmannstr. 2, 47623 Kevelaer.
T. (02832) 6966, Fax (02832) 3902. - Paint / Graph /
Sculp / Fra / Rel -   053349
Janssen, H., Hoogeweg 16, 47623 Kevelaer.
T. (02832) 2281, Fax (02832) 3902. - Paint / Graph /
Sculp / Fra / Rel -   053350
Kocken, Hauptstr. 23, 47623 Kevelaer. T. (02832) 78136,
Fax (02832) 70007. - Paint / Graph / China / Sculp /
Jew / Fra / Lights / Rel / Glass / Draw -   053351
Niessen, A. & M., Busmannstr. 26, 47623 Kevelaer.
T. (02832) 702 70.   053352
Schröer, Heinrich, Basilikastr. 3, 47623 Kevelaer.
T. (02832) 20 48. - Ant -   053353
Timmermann, Maria, Hauptstr. 20, 47623 Kevelaer.
T. (02832) 26 30. - Ant -   053354

Kiel (Schleswig-Holstein)
Antik-Möbel-Markt, Ziegelteich, 24103 Kiel.
T. (0431) 932 47.   053355
Antiques, Küterstr. 8-12, 24103 Kiel.
T. (0431) 94436.   053356
Galerie Hinterhaus, Wilhelminenstr. 19, 24103 Kiel.
T. (0431) 55 40 11. - Paint / Graph / Pho /
Draw -   053357
Grensing, Knooper Weg 78, 24103 Kiel. T. (0431) 81360,
Fax (0431) 554033. - Ant / Paint / Furn / China / Dec /
Fra / Lights / Glass -   053358
Hass, J.-R., Brunsrade 3, 24114 Kiel.
T. (0431) 67 63 71.   053359
Haus der Kunst, Dänische Str. 15, 24103 Kiel.
T. (0431) 970077, Fax (0431) 970079. - Ant -   053360
Heibel, Bärbel, Rathausstr. 15, 24103 Kiel.
T. (0431) 921 72. - Ant / Paint / Furn / China /
Sculp -   053361
Hense, T., Damperhofstr. 14, 24103 Kiel.
T. (0431) 938 10.   053362
Kapitzke, Siegfried, Langenfelde 165, 24159 Kiel.
- Num -   053363
Kasper & Richter, Hanssenstr. 6, 24106 Kiel.
T. (0431) 33 70 09. - Ant / Furn -   053364
Krug, K.-H., Möllingstr. 3, 24103 Kiel.
T. (0431) 917 72.   053365
Kühl, D., Hamburger Chaussee 30, 24113 Kiel.
T. (0431) 68 52 78.   053366
Lehmkuhl, A., Holtenauer Str. 84, 24105 Kiel.
T. (0431) 56 37 81.   053367
Manthey, G., Holtenauer Str. 105, 24105 Kiel.
T. (0431) 81473.   053368
Melson, R., Ziegelteich 16, 24103 Kiel.
T. (0431) 93247.   053369
Möbius, Manfred, Esmarchstr. 58, 24105 Kiel.
T. (0431) 81893. - Ant / Paint / Graph / Furn / China /
Silv / Glass -   053370
Müller, Walter, Andreas-Gayk-Str. 19, 24103 Kiel.
T. (0431) 953 05.   053371

Negelein, Feldstr. 70, 24105 Kiel. T. (0431) 802140,
Fax (0431) 82144. - Paint / Furn / China / Sculp / Silv /
Lights / Glass / Mod / Tin -   053372
Neubauer, U., Eggerstedtstr. 5, 24103 Kiel.
T. (0431) 917 01.   053373
Oldenburg, Holstenstr. 22, 24103 Kiel. T. (0431) 94676,
Fax (0431) 96656. - Num -   053374
Raritäten-Stübchen, Andreas-Gayk-Str. 19, 24103 Kiel.
T. (0431) 953 05.   053375
Richter, Fred, Dänische Str. 18, 24103 Kiel.
T. (0431) 953 17. - Ant / Furn / Jew -   053376
Richter, J., Hanssenstr. 6, 24106 Kiel.
T. (0431) 33 70 09.   053377
Wischhausen, Rolf, Bergstr. 5, 24103 Kiel.
T. (0431) 55 49 59. - Num -   053378

Kindsbach (Rheinland-Pfalz)
Mertel, W., Kaiserstr. 65, 66862 Kindsbach.
T. (06371) 16885.   053379
Mueller, A., Hörnchenstr.16, 66862 Kindsbach.
T. (06371) 62585.   053380
Wagner, T.E., Kaiserstr. 35, 66862 Kindsbach.
T. (06371) 151 44.   053381

Kinheim (Rheinland-Pfalz)
Lücker, R., Burgstr. 73, 54538 Kinheim.
T. (06532) 1049.   053382

Kirchbrak (Niedersachsen)
Brunnarius, Karl, Westerbraker Str. 4, 37619 Kirchbrak.
T. (05533) 4220.   053383

Kirchhain (Hessen)
Frank, G., Stettiner Str. 33, 35274 Kirchhain.   053384

Kirchheim (Baden-Württemberg)
Durst, H., Max-Eyth-Str. 42, 73230 Kirchheim.
T. (07021) 29 02.   053385
Hauff, Fritz, Marktstr. 1-3, 73230 Kirchheim.
T. (07021) 26 24. - Graph / Furn -   053386
Maslewski, Klaus & R., Hindenburgstr. 18, 73230 Kirch-
heim. T. (07021) 34 22.   053387
Reinhardt, A., Lindorfer Weg 15, 73230 Kirchheim.
T. (07021) 60 71.   053388
Saam, Ludwig, Dettinger Str. 48, 73230 Kirchheim.
T. (07021) 71222. - Num -   053389
Zigan & Niecke, Alleenstr. 8, 73230 Kirchheim.
T. (07021) 6023.   053390

Kirchlengern (Nordrhein-Westfalen)
Guszahn, Peter, Weststr. 74, 32278 Kirchlengern.
T. (05223) 74549. - Num -   053391

Kirchlinteln (Niedersachsen)
Schrader, Lange Str. 5, 27308 Kirchlinteln.
T. (04237) 04237/846.   053392

Kirchzarten (Baden-Württemberg)
Baum, I., Hauptstr 9a, 79199 Kirchzarten.
T. (07661) 3035.   053393
Seifarth, M., Bahnhofstr 1, 79199 Kirchzarten.
T. (07661) 7382.   053394

Kirrweiler (Rheinland-Pfalz)
Masanek, H.-P. & G. Wessa, Am Bahnhof 12, 67489 Kirr-
weiler. T. (06321) 58192.   053395

Kissenbrück (Niedersachsen)
Säbel, Gerhard, Hinter dem Dorfe 34, 38324 Kissen-
brück. T. (05337) 843. - Mil -   053396

Kitzingen (Bayern)
Kamler, E., Klosterbauhof 2, 97318 Kitzingen.
T. (09321) 63 20. - Ant -   053397
Singer, J., Südtiroler Str. 6, 97318 Kitzingen.
T. (09321) 347 33.   053398
Steinruck, Paul J., Luitpoldstr. 3, 97318
Kitzingen.   053399

Klein Berssen (Niedersachsen)
Novel, U., Sögeler Str. 80, 49777 Klein Berssen.
T. (05965) 627.   053400

Holler

Bauernmöbel
Eckart Holler
Volkskunst · Spielzeug
bäuerlicher Hausrat und Werkzeuge
Weststraße 22
09128 Kleinolbersdorf (Chemnitz)
☎(0371) 77 21 67
tel. Anmeldung erbeten
Ausstellung im
Wasserschloß Klaffenbach

Kleinolbersdorf (Sachsen)
Holler, Eckart, Weststr 22, 09128 Kleinolbersdorf.
T. (0371) 772167. - Furn -　　　　　　053401

Kleinostheim (Bayern)
Bauer, E., Grabenstr. 10, 63801 Kleinostheim.
T. (06027) 6330.　　　　　　　　　053402
Koberstein, E., Hanauer Str. 35, 63801 Kleinostheim.
T. (06027) 8436.　　　　　　　　　053403

Kleve (Nordrhein-Westfalen)
van Ackeren, Kavarinerstr 31, 47533 Kleve.
T. (02821) 20794.　　　　　　　　053404
Elbers, Grosse Str 20, 47533 Kleve. T. (02821) 23118.
- Ant / Paint / Graph / China / Repr / Jew / Fra / Glass --
　　　　　　　　　　　　　　　053405
Hövelmann, J., Hölderlinstr 19, 47533 Kleve.
T. (02821) 40700.　　　　　　　　053406
Kacier, G., Lambertusstr 12, 47533 Kleve.
T. (02821) 27509.　　　　　　　　053407
Sanders, J.G., Wasserstr 4, 47533 Kleve.
T. (02821) 20477.　　　　　　　　053408
Schroer, M., Lindenallee 46, 47533 Kleve.
T. (02821) 17105.　　　　　　　　053409
Sevens, U., Werftstr 1, 47533 Kleve. T. (02821) 25540.
- Ant -　　　　　　　　　　　　053410
Weber-Kiffe, F., Nieler Str 51, 47533 Kleve.
T. (02821) 30881, Fax (02821) 31316. - Ant / Furn /
Sculp -　　　　　　　　　　　　053411

Koblenz (Rheinland-Pfalz)
Ameln, E., Hofstr. 270, 56077 Koblenz.
T. (0261) 70 25 66. - Ant -　　　　　053412
Antica Antiquitäten, Firmungstr. 44, 56068
Koblenz.　　　　　　　　　　　053413
Eckels, Max, Firmungstr. 36, Görresstr. 10, 56068 Ko-
blenz. T. (0261) 345 73, 365 60. - Ant / Paint / Graph /
Furn / China / Sculp / Tex / Silv / Glass / Mod / Draw --
　　　　　　　　　　　　　　　053414
Forneck, Gerd Martin, Hohenzollernstr. 149, 56068 Ko-
blenz. T. (0261) 16382, Fax (0261) 34741.
- Num -　　　　　　　　　　　053415
Hardy, Bernd, Lüderitzstr. 7, 56076 Koblenz.
T. (0261) 754 53.　　　　　　　　053416
Hoffmann, R., Kornpfortstr. 25, 56068 Koblenz.
T. (0261) 372 72.　　　　　　　　053417
Huther, B., Firmungstr. 40, 56068 Koblenz.
T. (0261) 344 23.　　　　　　　　053418
Knödgen, Hugo, Florinsmarkt 14, 56068 Koblenz.
T. (0261) 323 91. - Ant / Paint / Furn / China -　053419
Lein, P., Grabenstr. 19, 56072 Koblenz.
T. (0261) 258 50.　　　　　　　　053420
Mau, S., Emser Str. 50a, 56076 Koblenz.
T. (0261) 747 92.　　　　　　　　053421
Meister, Gebrüder, Firmungstr. 13, 56068 Koblenz.
T. (0261) 333 57. - Ant / Paint / Furn / Repr /
Fra -　　　　　　　　　　　　053422
Meurer, Lieselotte, Firmungstr. 17, 56068 Koblenz.
- Paint -　　　　　　　　　　　053423
Schild, Jürgen, Münztr. 10, 56068 Koblenz.　053424
Schmitt, Rudolf, Görresstr. 2, 56068 Koblenz.　053425
Seelhoff, E., Schloßstr. 34a, 56068 Koblenz.
T. (0261) 314 84. - China / Repr / Sculp / Rel /
Ico -　　　　　　　　　　　　053426
Tent, E., Florinspfaffengasse 5, 56068 Koblenz.
T. (0261) 167 27. - Paint -　　　　　053427

Köfering (Bayern)
Köferinger Antik und Bauernmöbel, Kirchstr. 14, 93096
Köfering. T. (09406) 2425. - Furn -　　053428

Köln (Nordrhein-Westfalen)
A + B Art und Bijou, Severinstr. 133, 50678 Köln.
T. (0221) 31 51 38. - Jew -　　　　053429
Albrecht & Hoffmann, Rubensstr. 42, 50676 Köln.
T. (0221) 230848, Fax (0221) 231837. - Num - 053430
Alte Kunst, Thürmchenswall 15, 50668 Köln.
T. (0221) 135477.　　　　　　　053431
Altertümchen-Weichholzmöbel, Am Duffesbach 41,
50677 Köln. T. (0221) 31 31 52. - Ant -　053432
Alträucher, Wahlenstr 10, 50823 Köln.
T. (0221) 512246.　　　　　　　053433
Ankiewicz, U., Berrenrather Str. 176, 50937 Köln.
T. (0221) 44 49 72. - Ant -　　　　053434
Antik am Severinstor, Severinstr. 23, 50678 Köln.
T. (0221) 32 61 23.　　　　　　　053435
Antik Depot, Kartäuserhof 29, 50678 Köln.
T. (0221) 31 21 32.　　　　　　　053436
Antik 25, Gertrudenstr. 25, 50667 Köln.
T. (0221) 21 17 34.　　　　　　　053437
Antiqua-nova, Buttermarkt 31, 50667 Köln.
T. (0221) 2583010, Fax (0221) 2401834 (2587886).
- Dec -　　　　　　　　　　　053438
Antiquitäten am Stadtwald, Dürener Str 254, 50931
Köln. T. (0221) 4303927.　　　　　053439
Antiquitäten Kupfergasse, Kupfergasse 14-16, 50667
Köln. T. (0221) 2577330. - Ant / Repr / Silv / Glass /
Cur / Mod / Draw / Tin -　　　　　053440
Art Air Klein, Wahlenstr 37, 50823 Köln.
T. (0221) 513971.　　　　　　　053441
Balkhausen, I., Salierring, 50677 Köln.
T. (0221) 248077.　　　　　　　053442
Balkhausen, J., Lindenstr. 15, 50674 Köln.
T. (0221) 23 89 17.　　　　　　　053443
Balkhausen, J. u I., Aachener Str 27, 50674 Köln.
T. (0221) 251834.　　　　　　　053444
Bauer, Inka, Neuenhöfer Allee 10, 50937 Köln.
T. (0221) 46 32 55. - Arch -　　　053445
Baum Antiquitäten, Kupfergasse 14-16, 50667 Köln.
T. (0221) 2577330.　　　　　　　053446
Bazzanella, Roonstr. 37a, 50674 Köln.
T. (0221) 24 77 51. - Ant -　　　　053447
Becher, Lübecker Str. 17, 50858 Köln.
T. (0221) 430 12 00. - Ant / Furn / China / Silv / Lights /
Instr / Glass -　　　　　　　　　053448
Beltracchi, Berg. Gladbacher Str. 1000a, 51069 Köln.
T. (0221) 68 37 22. - Ant -　　　　053449
Bibelots, Neumarkt-Passage, 50667 Köln.
T. (0221) 25 33 89. - Jew / Mod / Mul -　053450
Bibra, V., Friesenwall 31, 50672 Köln.
T. (0221) 251364.　　　　　　　053451
Biergans, Walter, Frankfurter Str. 215, 51147 Köln.
T. (0221) 632 50. - Ant / Furn / Eth -　053452
Binhold, Hohe Str. 96, 50667 Köln. T. (0221) 214222,
2578971, Fax (0221) 254401. - Ant / Paint /
Tex -　　　　　　　　　　　　053453
Birkenfeld, A., Lindenstr 18, 50674 Köln.
T. (0221) 237140.　　　　　　　053454
Bischoff, J., Berrenrather Str. 194, 50937 Köln.
T. (0221) 41 23 47. - Furn -　　　053455
Blaue Galerie, Auf dem Berlich 13, 50667 Köln.
T. (0221) 231679, 2578010.　　　　053456
Bogumil, G., Bayenstr. 28, 50678 Köln.
T. (0221) 31 72 53. - Ant -　　　053457
Bohn & H. Schmidt, W., Marsilstein 6, 50676 Köln.
T. (0221) 21 66 96. - Ant / Furn / China / Silv / Lights /
Instr -　　　　　　　　　　　053458
Braszczok, Am Heidstamm 9, 50859 Köln.
T. (0221) 70218.　　　　　　　053459
Brockmann-Lemke, Neven-du-Mont-Str. 17-19, 50667
Köln. T. (0221) 257 42 33. - Ant / Furn / Dec - 053460
Burleson, R., Marsilstein 25, 50676 Köln.
T. (0221) 21 10 61. - Ant -　　　053461
Christoffels, E., Gladbacher Str 29, 50672 Köln.
T. (0221) 519809.　　　　　　　053462
Coeln-Antik, Brüsseler Str 63, 50672 Köln.
T. (0221) 522662.　　　　　　　053463
Cottin, J., Alpenroder Weg 30, 50767 Köln.
T. (0221) 790 17 48.　　　　　　053464
Cremer, Helmut, Taubengasse 19, 50676 Köln.
T. (0221) 245465.　　　　　　　053465
Damani, Ubierring 41, 50678 Köln.
T. (0221) 325396.　　　　　　　053466

Dautzenberg, Bruno, St.-Apern-Str. 56, 50667 Köln.
T. (0221) 257 70 60. - Ant / Furn -　053467
Delitz, R.-E., Gertrudenstr 31, 50667 Köln.
T. (0221) 2576091.　　　　　　　053468
Deuerling-Wegener, D., Berrenrather Str. 274, 50937
Köln. T. (0221) 42 67 15.　　　　053469
Devroede-Archeologie, Zeughausstr. 10, 50667 Köln.
T. (0221) 131417. - Arch -　　　053470
Devroede-Missinne, Zeughausstr 14-22, 50667 Köln.
T. (0221) 131417, 134702. - Ant / Arch / Furn - 053471
Die Vitrine, Komödienstr. 13, 50667 Köln.
T. (0221) 21 27 65.　　　　　　　053472
Dietze, A., Riehler Pl 3, 50668 Köln.
T. (0221) 728813.　　　　　　　053473
Drinhausen, A., Buttermarkt 22, 50667 Köln.
T. (0221) 258 12 96. - Ant -　　　053474
Edel, Neumarkt 1c, 50667 Köln. T. 21 67 12 (257 54 35).
- Ant / Paint / Silv -　　　　　　053475
Effelsberg, K., Bergisch Gladbacher Str 616, 51067
Köln. T. (0221) 639130.　　　　053476
Evers, J., Innere Kanalstr. 13, 50931 Köln.
T. (0221) 51 11 77. - Ant -　　　053477
Fahrbach, Georg, Pfeilstr. 28-30, 50672 Köln.
T. (0221) 2575425, Fax (0221) 2575429. - Ant /
Lights -　　　　　　　　　　　053478
Fard, A. E., Kirchstr. 11, 50996 Köln.
T. (0221) 39 50 30.　　　　　　　053479
Faust, Aloys, Am Hof 34-36, 50667 Köln.
T. 21 81 90 (258 20 38). - Ant / Furn -　053480
Feyen, R., Frechener Weg 57, 50859 Köln.
T. (0221) 75131.　　　　　　　053481
Feyen, Roderich, St.-Apern-Str. 48-50, 50667 Köln.
T. (0221) 257 70 42. - Ant / Paint / Furn / Sculp /
Rel -　　　　　　　　　　　　053482
Fidow-Fiddickow, A., Herzogstr. 32, 50667 Köln.
T. (0221) 244783, 2575648.　　　053483
Friedrich, Walter, Deutzer Freiheit 103, 50679 Köln.
T. (0221) 81 34 94, Fax 81 39 79. - Paint /
Furn -　　　　　　　　　　　053484
Gün, I., Ludwigstr. 15, 50667 Köln. T. (0221) 257 65 97,
257 66 55.　　　　　　　　　053485
Günter's, Palmstr 28, 50672 Köln.
T. (0221) 253357.　　　　　　　053486
Ha-Ge Raritäten, Zechenstr 11, 51103 Köln.
T. (0221) 8701800.　　　　　　　053487
Halm, E.P., Postfach 101708, 50455 Köln.
T. (0221) 258 20 34. - Ant / Paint / Graph / Num / Jew /
Silv / Ico / Draw -　　　　　　　053488
Hampel, F., Dr., Neumarkt 18a, 50667 Köln.
T. (0221) 25 57 25, 25 64 73. - Ant -　053489
Hanner, A., Birkenstr. 9, 50996 Köln.
T. (0221) 35 26 86.　　　　　　　053490
Hart, Otto, Zeughausstr. 26, 50667 Köln.
T. (0221) 13 53 76. - Ant / Paint / Furn / Orient / China /
Glass / Mod -　　　　　　　　　053491
Hasenkamp, Mittelstr. 1, 50672 Köln. T. (0221) 23 60 80,
25 60 90. - Graph / Ico -　　　　053492
Heckelei, N., Gottesweg 169, 50939 Köln.
T. (0221) 446363.　　　　　　　053493
Hennig, von & Haymasy, Auf dem Berlich 11, 50667
Köln. T. 21 16 30 (257 80 31).　　053494
Herr, W.G., Friesenwall 35, 50672 Köln.
T. (0221) 254548, Fax 254548. - Ant -　053495
Heubel, L., Odenthaler Str. 371, 51069 Köln.
T. (0221) 60 46 87, 60 18 25.　　　053496
Heubel, Lothar, Breite Str. 118, 50667 Köln.
T. (0221) 216004. - Ant / Mil / Ico -　053497
Heuts, M., St.-Apern-Str. 42, 50667 Köln.
T. 21 48 63 (257 51 23).　　　　053498
Hoffmann, R., Brüsseler Str 87, 50672 Köln.
T. (0221) 517698.　　　　　　　053499
Holborn, J., Greesbergstr. 2, 50668 Köln.
T. (0221) 12 43 40.　　　　　　　053500
Hünerbein, Bernhard von, Lintgasse 22-26, 50667 Köln.
T. (0221) 21 07 10.　　　　　　　053501
Huhn, E., Olpener Str. 524, 51109 Köln.
T. (0221) 89 71 12. - Ant -　　　053502
Hundt, H., Dellbrücker Hauptstr. 49, 51069 Köln.
T. (0221) 68 27 20. - Ant -　　　053503
Inhoffen, U., Sülzburgstr. 205, 50937 Köln.
T. (0221) 425006.　　　　　　　053504
Jahns, Wolfgang, Trierer Str. 19, 50676 Köln.
T. (0221) 32 89 78.　　　　　　　053505

Juchem, M., Rösrather Str. 612 m, 51107 Köln. *053506*
K plus K, Unter Goldschmied 5, 50667 Köln.
T. (0221) 253733. *053507*
Kameke Antik, Kamekestr 3, 50672 Köln.
T. (0221) 513110. *053508*
Katebi, G., Neven-du-Mont-Str. 5, 50667 Köln.
T. 23 82 81 (257 63 33). *053509*
Kirchhoff, Genovevastr. 26-32, 51065 Köln. *053510*
Klefisch, Ubierring 35, 50678 Köln. T. (0221) 32 17 40,
Fax (0221) 32 52 17. - Orient - *053511*
Klein, H.G., St. Apern-Str 2, 50667 Köln.
T. (0221) 2576133, Fax (0221) 2583264. - Ant / Paint /
Silv - *053512*
Knopek, Hans Jürgen, Alter Markt 55, 50667 Köln.
T. (0221) 253600. - Num - *053513*
Kölner Münz-Antiquariat, Alter Markt 36-42, 50667
Köln. T. (0221) 2582223. - Num - *053514*
Kölner Münzkabinett, Neven-du-Mont-Str. 15, 50667
Köln. T. (0221) 2574238, 211438, Fax (0221) 254175.
- Num - *053515*
Köntges, Werner, Virchowstr. 12, 50935 Köln. - Ant /
Orient / Arch / Eth / Mil - *053516*
Korth, Benedikt, St.-Apern-Str. 7, 50667 Köln.
T. (0221) 2574838, Fax (0221) 23 18 24.
- Paint - *053517*
Krings, Antonio, Richmodstr 27, 50667 Köln.
T. (0221) 2577286/2577264, Fax (0221) 252956.
- Ant / China / Jew - *053518*
Kroha, Tyll, Neven-DuMont-Str 15, 50667 Köln.
T. (0221) 2574238, Fax (0221) 254175. *053519*
Küppers, Pfarriusstr. 13, 50935 Köln. T. (0221) 21 58 95.
- Ant - *053520*
Kunsthandlung Küppers, Teutoburger Str 12, 50678
Köln. T. (0221) 343973. *053521*
Kunsthaus am Museum, Drususgasse 1-5, 50667 Köln.
T. (0221) 252057, Fax (0221) 236077, 2578558. - Ant /
Paint - *053522*
Lackner, M., Pfeilstr. 46, 50672 Köln.
T. (0221) 2573251. *053523*
Lackner, Martin, Palmstr 14, 50672 Köln.
T. (0221) 254427. *053524*
Lädchen, Appellhofplatz 17-19, 50667 Köln.
T. (0221) 21 72 60. - Ant / China / Jew / Silv - *053525*
Lang, A., Bergisch Gladbacher Str. 1000A, 51069 Köln.
T. (0221) 68 37 22. - Ant / Lights / Glass / Cur /
Mod - *053526*
Leichenich, Hans, Dünnwalder Mauspfad 280, 51069
Köln. T. (0221) 602235. *053527*
Lempertz, Neumarkt 3, 50667 Köln. T. (0221) 9257290,
Fax 9257296. - Ant / Paint / Graph / Furn / Orient / Chi-
na / Sculp / Tex / Arch / Eth / Jew / Silv / Instr / Mil / Glas-
s / Mod / Ico / Pho / Draw - *053528*
Lewandowski, Hans, Stefan-Lochner-Str 11, 50999
Köln. T. (0221) 393404. - Furn / Dec / Jew /
Silv - *053529*
Lilienthal, von, Buttermarkt 9, 50667 Köln.
T. (0221) 257 06 43. - Ant / Instr - *053530*
Linnartz, Hans, Alter Markt 36-42, 50667 Köln.
T. (0221) 24 65 79. - Num - *053531*
Löffler, Karin, Kartäuserhof 3, 50678 Köln.
T. (0221) 318702, 319614. *053532*
Löhmer-Müller, U., Berrenrather Str 176, 50937 Köln.
T. (0221) 444972. *053533*
London Antiques, Pferdmengesstr. 3, 50968 Köln.
T. (0221) 37 21 62. - Ant / Furn / Silv - *053534*
Lützow-Antik, Lützowstr 1, 50674 Köln.
T. (0221) 243544. *053535*
Luhr, K.-H., Kartäuserhof 29, 50678 Köln.
T. (0221) 31 21 32. *053536*
Lyck, B., Balthasarstr. 61, 50670 Köln.
T. (0221) 72 23 61. *053537*
Makel, R. & G., Höxterstr. 16, 51109 Köln.
T. (0221) 84 28 92. *053538*
Malchow, Wittgensteinstr. 18, 50931 Köln.
T. (0221) 40 42 82. - Graph - *053539*
Massenbach, Fabian von, Bremer Str. 5, 50670 Köln.
T. (0221) 12 15 50. - Orient - *053540*
May, Zeughausstr. 9, 50667 Köln. T. (0221) 23 46 14.
- Paint / Furn / Orient - *053541*
Melhorn, H., Bahnhofstr 1, 50667 Köln.
T. (0221) 66590. *053542*
Meller, I., Thürmchenswall 72, 50668 Köln.
T. (0221) 125809. *053543*

KUNSTHAUS AM
MUSEUM
CAROLA VAN HAM

Drususgasse 1-5 • 50667 Köln
Telefon: 0221/92 58 62-0
Fax: 0221/92 58 62-30

GEMÄLDE
ANTIQUITÄTEN
MOBILIAR
ORIENTTEPPICHE
SKULPTUREN
GRAPHIK
KUNST DES 20. JH.

Meul, Theodor, Paulstr. 10, 50676 Köln.
T. (0221) 31 72 41. - Ant - *053544*
M.G. Modern Grafic Kunsthandel, Maarweg 143, 50825
Köln. T. (0221) 495000. *053545*
Mischell, Hans H., Von-Werth-Str. 33, 50670 Köln.
T. (0221) 134104. - Ant / Furn / China / Silv - *053546*

HANS H. MISCHELL
ANTIQUITÄTEN

50670 KÖLN
VON-WERTH-STR. 33
TEL. (02 21) 13 41 04

Mohrholz, Helmut P., St.-Apern-Str. 13, 50667 Köln.
T. (0221) 24 25 71. - Ant / Furn - *053547*
Molsberger, Elmar, Komödienstr. 13, 50667 Köln.
T. (0221) 257 75 55. *053548*
Moog, Eike, Albertusstr. 9-11, 50667 Köln.
T. (0221) 2574916, 2574839. - Paint / Graph /
Orient - *053549*
Moos, Brüsseler Str 2, 50674 Köln.
T. (0221) 238144. *053550*
Morgenland, Zülpicher Str. 4, 50674 Köln.
T. (0221) 21 07 80. *053551*
Müller, Alfred Otto, Sternengasse 1, 50676 Köln.
T. (0221) 231513. - Fra - *053552*
Münz Zentrum, Rubenstr 42, 50676 Köln.
T. (0221) 230848, Fax (0221) 231837. *053553*
Münzlädchen, Clodwigpl. 17, 50667 Köln.
T. (0221) 32 47 49. - Num - *053554*
Naescher, Gertrudenstr. 25, 50667 Köln.
T. (0221) 21 17 34. *053555*
Nagel, Ch., Friedrichstr 63, 50676 Köln.
T. (0221) 36 50. - Ant - *053556*
Nijmeijer, Günter, Kemperbachstr. 53, 51069 Köln.
T. (0221) 68 67 74. - Furn - *053557*
Nolden, Alfred, Wendelinusstr. 48, 50933 Köln.
T. (0221) 49 16 26. *053558*
Nowaczysnki, A., Höninger Weg 145, 50969 Köln.
T. (0221) 3603911. *053559*
Nowak, K.W., Flandrische Str. 10, 50674 Köln.
T. (0221) 25 14 53. - Ant - *053560*
Olefanten, Aachener Str. 32, 50674 Köln.
T. (0221) 51 53 69. - Ant - *053561*
Osper, Knut, Pfeilstr. 29, 50672 Köln. T. (0221) 9257100,
Fax (0221) 92571010. - Paint / Graph / Sculp / Fra /
Mod / Ico / Draw - *053562*
Pan, M. Lackner, Pfeilstr. 46, 50672 Köln.
T. (0221) 240 18 65 (257 32 51). - Lights /
Mod - *053563*
Panahmand, M., Händelstr. 26, 50674 Köln.
T. (0221) 24 82 76. *053564*
Parmentier, H., Palmstr. 21, 50672 Köln.
T. (0221) 253790. *053565*
Pasek, P., Gottesweg 135, 50939 Köln.
T. (0221) 44 62 84. - Ant - *053566*

Pasque, J., Bonner Str. 242, 50677 Köln.
T. (0221) 38 86 51. *053567*
Patina, Lindenstr. 73, 50674 Köln. T. (0221) 21 92 99.
- Ant - *053568*
Pelster, M., Kleine Budengasse 13, 50667 Köln.
T. (0221) 258 20 40. - Ant - *053569*
Pesch-Galerie-Atrium, Kaiser-Wilhelm-Ring 22, 50672
Köln. T. (0221) 161 30. - Ant / Furn - *053570*
Petri, E., Olpener Str 234, 51103 Köln.
T. (0221) 874068. *053571*
Pirotte, S., Chlodwigpl 17, 50678 Köln.
T. (0221) 324749. *053572*
Pohl, Karl H., Lintgasse 5, 50667 Köln.
T. (0221) 2577605, Fax (0221) 253350. - Instr - *053573*
Prangenberg, Th., Alteburger Str 22, 50678 Köln.
T. (0221) 323214. *053574*
Pütz, Peter, St.-Apern-Str. 17-21, 50667 Köln.
T. (0221) 2574995, Fax (0221) 2574995.
- Jew - *053575*
Puppenstube, Hospeltstr. 1, 50825 Köln.
T. (0221) 54 47 39. - Toys - *053576*
Pydde, B., Aachener Str. 549, 50933 Köln.
T. (0221) 49 13 69. - Ant - *053577*
Ralle, An Groß St. Martin 7-8, 50667 Köln.
T. (0221) 258 05 09. - Ant - *053578*
Ramacher, M., & R. Boesmans, Virchowstr. 21, 50935
Köln. T. (0221) 43 47 75. - Ant - *053579*
Rath, Christian, Hohenstaufenring 5, 50674 Köln.
T. (0221) 23 24 55. - Num - *053580*
Redetzky, Lothar, Wahlenstr. 10, 50823 Köln.
T. (0221) 51 22 46. *053581*
Rehborn, Ernst, Lülsdorfer Str. 158, 51143 Köln.
T. (0221) 819 91. - Ant - *053582*
Reinelt & Temp, Am Weizenacker 23, 51105 Köln.
T. (0221) 83 45 96. *053583*
Rhenania, Bayenstr 28, 50678 Köln.
T. (0221) 312812. *053584*
Rieder, W., Alteburger Str. 37, 50678 Köln.
T. (0221) 31 36 17. - Ant - *053585*
Rieger, Theodor, Homburger Str. 14, 50969 Köln.
T. (0221) 36 28 39. - Num - *053586*
Ries, K., Kalker Hauptstr. 168, 51103 Köln.
T. (0221) 870 30 60. *053587*
Roeder, M., Neusser Str. 46, 50670 Köln.
T. (0221) 72 08 26. - Ant - *053588*
Rötel, Carl von, Großer Griechenmarkt 113, 50676 Köln.
- Ant - *053589*
Röther, J., Benesisstr. 52, 50672 Köln. T. (0221) 239387,
2573689. *053590*
Romeleit, M. L., Pfeilstr. 31, 50672 Köln.
T. (0221) 2573087, Fax (0221) 2570899. - Graph /
Furn / Orient / Fra / Silv / Lights / Mod - *053591*
Rotmann, E., St.-Apern-Str. 11, 50672 Köln.
T. (0221) 2574827, 2574874, Fax (0221) 2574874.
- Jew / Silv / Ico - *053592*
Ruland, R., Werheider Str. 8, 51069 Köln.
T. (0221) 68 44 41. - Ant / Eth - *053593*
Rust, Iris, Zeughausstr. 10, 50674 Köln.
T. (0221) 13 55 11, 76 13 66. - Ant - *053594*
Safiriou, Georg, St.-Apern-Str 14-18, 50667 Köln.
T. (0221) 2576030, Fax 2573497. *053595*
Saubert, W., Salzgasse 15, 50667 Köln.
T. (0221) 25 41 82. - Ant - *053596*
Schäselong, Brüsseler Str. 63, 50672 Köln.
T. (0221) 52 26 62. - Furn - *053597*
Scharifeh-Center, Piusstr. 26, 50823 Köln.
T. (02219 523135. *053598*

Scheller, F.H., Braugasse 6, 50859 Köln.
T. (0221) 497752. 053599
Schichel, W., Kolumbastr. 1, 50667 Köln. 053600
Schindler, M., Robert-Heuser-Str. 20, 50968 Köln.
T. (0221) 34 14 36. - Ant - 053601
Schirow, G., Abshofstr 7, 51109 Köln.
T. (0221) 692733. 053602
Schloesser, R., Hospeltstr. 1, 50825 Köln.
T. (0221) 545156. - Ant - 053603
Schmitt, Lahnstr, 50996 Köln.
T. (0221) 8304799. 053604
Schoder, S., Am Duffesbach 41, 50677 Köln.
T. (0221) 31 31 52. 053605
Schrader, Joseph, Melatengürtel 103, 50825
Köln. 053606
Schuhmacher, L., Wickrather Str 5, 50670 Köln.
T. (0221) 7392703. 053607
Schumacher, G., Mozartstr. 22, 50674 Köln.
T. (0221) 23 67 53. 053608
Schwarzenhofer, J., Palmstr 26, 50672 Köln.
T. (0221) 255353. 053609
Schwarzer Elefant, Quatermarkt 5, 50667 Köln.
T. (0221) 24 29 97. - Orient - 053610
Schwingelen, Barbara, Wendelinusstr. 48, 50933 Köln.
T. (0221) 49 16 26. - Furn - 053611
Seegert, Hochwaldstr. 12, 50935 Köln.
T. (0221) 43 03 198. - Ant / Paint / Jew - 053612
Seifert, Hans-Ulrich, Unter Taschenmacher 10, 50667
Köln. T. (0221) 2580645. - Num - 053613
Siegel, B., Lindenallee 28, 50968 Köln. 053614
Simon, h., Brauweilerstr 58, 50859 Köln.
T. (0221) 79256. 053615
Sistig, M., Berliner Str. 955, 51069 Köln.
T. (0221) 60 14 22. - Ant - 053616
Sponholz, E., Pfeilstr. 23, 50672 Köln.
T. 21 87 77 (257 30 09). 053617
Spreen, E., Pfeilstr 23, 50672 Köln.
T. (0221) 2570766. 053618
Stähli, P., Neusser Str. 46, 50670 Köln.
T. (0221) 73 20 19. - Ant - 053619
Steinsträsser, Salierring 26a, 50677 Köln.
T. (0221) 23 74 79. - Instr - 053620
Stemmler, Christophstr 20-22, 50670 Köln.
T. (0221) 136470. 053621
Sterzenbach, J.P., Lintgasse 5, 50667 Köln.
T. (0221) 21 84 35. 053622
Stockhausen, F. von, Moltkestr. 91, 50674 Köln.
T. (0221) 52 71 74. 053623
Streminski, K., Friesenstr. 35, 50670 Köln.
T. (0221) 25 46 77. - Ant - 053624
Strick, Agnes, Venloer Str. 552, 50825 Köln.
T. (0221) 550 20 47. 053625
Sültrup, K., Ehrenfeldgürtel 110, 50823 Köln.
T. (0221) 55 50 60. - Ant - 053626
Tarzan, Benesisstr 52, 50672 Köln.
T. (0221) 2573689. 053627
Theves, Herbert, Bechergasse 5, 50667 Köln.
T. (0221) 2580742. 053628
Thieler, Hartmut, Aachener Str. 60-62, 50674 Köln.
T. (0221) 52 61 22. 053629
Thomas, G., Friesenwall 66, 50672 Köln.
T. (0221) 253578. 053630
Tober, Hans D., Marienweg 42, 50858 Köln. 053631
Trompka, G., Aachener Str. 514, 50933 Köln.
T. (0221) 49 50 86. - Ant - 053632
Uedelhoven, h., Hahnenstr. 18, 50667 Köln.
T. (0221) 25 60 71. - Ant / Furn / Cur - 053633
Vierhaus, K., St.-Apern-Str. 64, 50667 Köln.
T. (0221) 2577073. 053634
Vigelius, Egon, Pfeilstr. 45, 50672 Köln.
T. (0221) 2573352. - Ant - 053635
Weber, Axel G., Gertrudenstr. 29, 50667 Köln.
T. (0221) 2576087, Fax (0221) 255156. - Num /
Arch - 053636
Weber, Gerlinde, Kirchweg 82, 50858 Köln.
T. (0221) 48 23 31. - Ant - 053637
Weick, W., St. Apernstr. 56, 50667 Köln.
T. (0221) 25 33 22. - Ant - 053638
Weinberg, D., Theodor-Heuss-Ring 14, 50668 Köln.
T. (0221) 12 25 05. 053639
Weiss, Hans-Heinrich, Breite Str. 159, 50667 Köln.
T. (0221) 2576069. - Ant / Furn / Instr / Mod - 053640

Wendt, H., Riehler Str. 51, 50668 Köln.
T. (0221) 72 19 90. 053641
Weßling, W. 6000 Erfurter Str 44, 51103 Köln.
T. (0221) 8703602. 053642
West Antik, Aachener Str. 514, 50674 Köln.
T. (0221) 49 50 86. 053643
Wiedenfeld, M. 6000 Aachener Str 21, 50674 Köln.
T. (0221) 252439. 053644
Winterscheid, A., Merheimer Str 85, 50733 Köln.
T. (0221) 738313. 053645
Wünsch, W., Houdainer Str 2, 51143 Köln.
T. (0221) 85115. 053646
Wurlitzer, B., Lindenstr 20, 50765 Köln.
T. (0221) 231830. 053647
Zenz, C., Venloer Str 27, 50672 Köln.
T. (0221) 518549. 053648
Zerhusen, Klaus, Sankt-Apern-Str 40, 50667 Köln.
T. (0221) 2575129. - Ant / Paint / Graph / Furn / Silv /
Instr - 053649
Zientek, W., Friesenwall 102, 50672 Köln.
T. (0221) 254343. 053650
Zöllner, Pipinstr 3, 50667 Köln.
T. (0221) 256271. 053651
Zühlsdorf, Karl Heinz, Auf den Rothenberg 13, 50667
Köln. T. (0221) 257 79 76. - Num / Sculp / Arch /
Jew - 053652

Köngen (Baden-Württemberg)
Inceisa, M., Lilienweg 18, 73257 Köngen.
T. (07024) 830 92. 053653
Inceisa, M., Untere Neue Str. 8a, 73257 Köngen.
T. (07024) 842 09. 053654

Königheim (Baden-Württemberg)
König & Reinelt, Neue Heimat 28, 97953 Königheim.
T. (09341) 093 41/75 77. 053655

Königsberg (Bayern)
Sommer-Fuchs, C., Pfarrgasse 44, 97486 Königsberg.
T. (09525) 260. 053656

Königsbrunn (Bayern)
Volkskunststube, Hunnstetterstr 81, 86343 Königsbrunn.
T. (08231) 1574. 053657

Königslutter (Niedersachsen)
Bittner, John, Haus Nr 161, 38154 Königslutter. 053658
Hippler, A., Kleine Steimke, 38154 Königslutter.
T. (05365) 2886. 053659

Königstein (Hessen)
Antik-Haus, Am Ellerhang 3, 61462 Königstein.
T. (06174) 25126. 053660
Herzer, Hildegard, Schwalbenweg 5, 61462 Königstein.
T. (06174) 23281. - Ant / Paint / Graph - 053661
Richter, Rita, Kuckucksweg 16, 61462 Königstein.
T. (06174) 3530. 053662
Toepfer, Eva, Dr., Friedrich-Bender-Str 15, 61462 Kö-
nigstein. T. (06174) 4115, Fax (06174) 7605.
- Silv - 053663
Vogel, H.-D., Wiesbadener Str 35, 61462 Königstein.
T. (06174) 4254. - Num - 053664

Königswinter (Nordrhein-Westfalen)
Holz, Dagmar, Dr., Im Rothsiefen 17, 53639 Königswin-
ter. T. (02244) 1212, Fax (02244) 5776. - Ant - 053665
Köhne, H., Klotzstr. 12, 53639 Königswinter.
T. (02223) 267 39. - Ant - 053666

Köthen (Sachsen-Anhalt)
Haase, Schalaunische Str. 10-11, 06366 Köthen.
T. (03496) 3704. 053667

Kötzting (Bayern)
Klepsch Kunst, Schattenaustr. 23, 93444
Kötzting. 053668

Kolbermoor (Bayern)
Kugler, Anton & Ilse, Sepp-Straßberger-Str. 3, 83059
Kolbermoor. T. (08031) 915 86. - Ant / Furn - 053669

Konstanz (Baden-Württemberg)
Blatz, A., Zollernstr. 15, 78462 Konstanz.
T. (07531) 263 41. 053670
Buch & Kunst, Münzgasse 16, 78462 Konstanz.
T. (07531) 241 71. - Ant / Graph / Repr - 053671

Endele, Elmar, Turnierstr. 21, 78462 Konstanz.
T. (07531) 22225. - Furn - 053672
Epp, F., St.-Stephans-Platz 47, 78462 Konstanz.
T. (07531) 264 64. 053673
Hörenberg, I., Hussenstr. 64, 78462 Konstanz.
T. (07531) 230 00. 053674
Mehrpahl, Karl, Hofhalde 12, 78462 Konstanz.
T. (07531) 231 83. - Ant - 053675
Messmer, W., Schiffstr. 27, 78464 Konstanz.
T. (07531) 311 38. - Orient / Mil - 053676
Ottinger, M., Hans-Lobisser-Str. 9, 78465 Konstanz.
T. (07531) 07533/61 91. 053677
Schweizer, K., Kreuzlinger Str. 13, 78462 Konstanz.
T. (07531) 16160. 053678
Schwenkglenks, R., Zollernstr. 25, 78462 Konstanz.
T. (07531) 26130. 053679
Wesner, Bodanstr. 15, 78462 Konstanz. 053680

Kornwestheim (Baden-Württemberg)
Oettling, Peter, Ulrichstr. 31, 70806 Kornwestheim.
T. (07154) 2230 08. - China / Instr - 053681

Korschenbroich (Nordrhein-Westfalen)
Beier, H., Hauptstr. 101, 41352 Korschenbroich.
T. (02161) 02182/5589, 59168. 053682
Jozefowski, M., Raitz-von-Frentz-Str. 6, 41352 Kor-
schenbroich. T. (02161) 67 22 55. 053683
Köhnen, G., Konrad-Adenauer-Str. 33, 41352 Korschen-
broich. T. (02161) 67 09 30. 053684
Rive, Gilleshütte 99, 41352 Korschenbroich.
T. (02161) 646 41, Fax 641341. - Ant - 053685
Waude, I., Scherfhausen 10, 41352 Korschenbroich.
T. (02161) 02182/59257. 053686

Krailling (Bayern)
Heigl, M.M., Meisenweg 16, 82152 Krailling.
T. (089) 857 43 84. - Ant / Graph / Orient - 053687

Kranenburg (Nordrhein-Westfalen)
Weber, Heidi, Galileistr. 6, 47559 Kranenburg. 053688

Krefeld (Nordrhein-Westfalen)
Addisow, R., Neusser Str. 49, 47798 Krefeld.
T. (02151) 39 94 71. 053689
ars domus, Mennonitin-Kirch-Str. 50, 47798 Krefeld.
T. (02151) 223 28. - Ant - 053690
Bildt, K., Kölner Str. 605, 47807 Krefeld.
T. (02151) 30 11 45. 053691
Brückmann, Monika, Kölner Str. 202, 47805 Krefeld.
T. (02151) 31 26 88. 053692
Burger, Hartmut, Moerser Str. 106, 47803 Krefeld.
T. (02151) 692 08. - Mil - 053693
Golubarsch, K., Im Heggelsfeld 49, 47802 Krefeld.
T. (02151) 56 02 55. 053694
Großjung, S., Philadelphiastr. 138, 47799 Krefeld.
T. (02151) 282 16. 053695
Grünen, T., St.-Anton-Str. 57, 47798 Krefeld.
T. (02151) 80 08 53. 053696
Heeseler, G., Prinz-Ferdinand-Str. 115, 47798 Krefeld.
T. (02151) 77 17 05. 053697
Hock, W., Dr., Südwall 80, 47798 Krefeld.
T. (02151) 77 45 04. 053698
Jansen, Wolfgang, Krefelder Str. 222, 47839 Krefeld.
T. (02151) 73 34 52. 053699
Keyserlingk, Barbara Gräfin, Uerdinger Str. 295, 47800
Krefeld. T. (02151) 50 10 70. - Furn - 053700
Krüzner, M., Liesentorweg 17, 47802 Krefeld.
T. (02151) 56 06 74. 053701
Leibenguth, R., Höppnerstr. 38, 47809 Krefeld.
T. (02151) 54 02 95. 053702
Lennertz, E., Evertsstr. 18, 47798 Krefeld.
T. (02151) 697 53. 053703
Lichtenberg, Busenpfad 48, 47802 Krefeld.
T. (02151) 56 00 17. 053704
Mainz, Maria, Borsigstr. 24, 47809 Krefeld.
T. (02151) 259 23. - Graph / Draw - 053705
Neumann, K., Breite Str. 58, 47798 Krefeld.
T. (02151) 286 86. 053706
Oellers, R., Moerser Str. 390, 47803 Krefeld.
T. (02151) 59 30 00. 053707
Olbrich, Renate, Westwall 188, 47798 Krefeld.
T. (02151) 77 36 53. 053708
Papeler, H., Hülser Str. 102, 47803 Krefeld.
T. (02151) 75 51 26. 053709

Relners, H., Schnelderstr. 56, 47798 Krefeld.
T. (02151) 63 10 31. *053710*
Rose, Ekkehard, Rheinbabenstr. 50, 47809 Krefeld.
T. (02151) 57 31 07. - Furn - *053711*
Rudolph/Seidengalerie, Ostwall 64-66, 47798 Krefeld.
T. (02151) 297 09. *053712*
Schleiffenbaum, Gebr., Vinzenzstr. 16, 47799 Krefeld.
T. (02151) 225 69. - Ant - *053713*
Stevens, I., Industriestr. 33, 47803 Krefeld.
T. (02151) 75 89 81. *053714*
Stevens, W., Seidenstr. 70, 47799 Krefeld.
T. (02151) 80 02 96. *053715*
Vogt, H.-G., Prinz-Ferdinand-Str. 115, 47798 Krefeld.
T. (02151) 77 79 55. *053716*
Weber, M., Evertsstr. 45, 47798 Krefeld.
T. (02151) 699 72. *053717*

Kronberg (Hessen)

Brook's English Antiques, Frankfurter Str 13, 61476
Kronberg. T. (06173) 2931. - Ant / Paint / Furn / China /
Jew / Silv / Instr / Glass / Cur - *053718*
Croop, M., Frankfurter Str 13, 61476 Kronberg.
T. (06173) 5531. - Furn - *053719*
Flachsmann, Hildegard, Kellergrundweg 22, 61476
Kronberg. T. (06173) 79333. - Ant / Orient - *053720*
Opper, Uwe, Tanzhausstr 1, 61476 Kronberg.
T. (06173) 640518, Fax 940194. - Paint - *053721*
Schiffmann, Herbert, Jaministr 2b, 61476 Kronberg.
T. (06173) 2542. - Ant / China / Glass - *053722*
Spektakel-Antik, Tanzhausstr 17, 61476 Kronberg.
T. (06173) 1031. - Ant - *053723*
Stumpf-Behrens, Karin, Friedrich-Ebert-Str 31, 61476
Kronberg. T. (06173) 1371. - Ant - *053724*
Winzer, Axel, Dr., Tannenweg 18, 61476 Kronberg.
I. (06173) 63568. - Ant / Num / Orient - *053725*

Kronshagen (Schleswig-Holstein)

Weltzien, Sigrid, Hasselkamp 116, 24119
Kronshagen. *053726*

Krumbach (Bayern)

Albrecht, H., Lichtensteinstr, 86381 Krumbach.
T. (08282) 5573. *053727*

Krummhörn (Niedersachsen)

Koch, R.G., Katrepel 7, 26736 Krummhörn.
T. (04926) 5 40. *053728*
Korth, Adolf, Mühlenstr., 26736 Krummhörn.
T. (04926) 744. *053729*

Künzell (Hessen)

Semler, Rudolf, An der Röthe 6, 36093 Künzell.
T. (0661) 66556/222. - Ant - *053730*

Künzelsau (Baden-Württemberg)

Ehrhardt, H., Keltergasse 15, 74653 Künzelsau.
T. (07940) 35 92. *053731*
Pekers, H., Langenburgerstr. 7, 74653
Künzelsau. *053732*

Kulmbach (Bayern)

Kathrin's Geschenkstadel, Langgasse 9, 95326 Kulm-
bach. T. (09221) 4557. *053733*
Wagner, M., Spitalgasse 14, 95326 Kulmbach.
T. (09221) 2353. - Num - *053734*

Laatzen (Niedersachsen)

Afro-asiatisches Kunsthandwerk, Oesseler Str. 38,
30880 Laatzen. - Orient - *053735*

Lachendorf (Niedersachsen)

Roth, H., Garßener Str 19, 29331 Lachendorf.
T. (05145) 6010. *053736*

Ladbergen (Nordrhein-Westfalen)

Schulte-Freckling, Heinrich, Dorfstr. 11, 49549
Ladbergen. *053737*

Ladenburg (Baden-Württemberg)

Anders, F., Kirchenstr. 37, 68526 Ladenburg.
T. (06203) 152 22. *053738*
Gerstenberger, B., Kirchenstr. 3, 68526
Ladenburg. *053739*
Menrad, W., Hauptstr. 29, 68526 Ladenburg.
T. (06203) 141 32. *053740*

Schmidt, G., Am Bahndamm 8, 68526 Ladenburg.
T. (06203) 25 08. *053741*

Lage, Lippe (Nordrhein-Westfalen)

Antiquitäten vom Biedermeier bis Jugendstil, Schillerstr
14, 32791 Lage, Lippe. T. (05232) 66439. *053742*

Lahnstein (Rheinland-Pfalz)

Blaser, R., Hochstr. 19, 56112 Lahnstein.
T. (02621) 55 05. *053743*
Jost, R., Braubacherstr. 52, 56112 Lahnstein.
T. (02621) 46 23. *053744*

Lahr (Baden-Württemberg)

Breithaupt, W., Kaiserstr 38, 77933 Lahr. *053745*
Röger, S., Bertholdstr 56, 77933 Lahr.
T. (07821) 23738. *053746*
Timing Center, Schlehenweg 49, 77933 Lahr.
T. (07821) 25069. - Num - *053747*
Trapp, E., Heerstr 21, 77933 Lahr.
T. (07821) 43524. *053748*
Warthmann, T., Alstadtquartier 14, 77933 Lahr.
T. (07821) 26443. *053749*
Wild, Rathauspl 6, 77933 Lahr. T. (07821) 23847,
Fax (07821) 271631. *053750*

Lampertheim (Hessen)

Hamm, Sedanstr 15, 68623 Lampertheim.
T. (06206) 3768. *053751*

Landau (Bayern)

Tixier, F., Gansmühle 10, 94405 Landau.
T. (09951) 1080. *053752*

Landau (Rheinland-Pfalz)

Auerswald, Martin-Luther-Str 8, 76829 Landau.
T. (06341) 82525. *053753*
Baumann, T., Jostweg 10, 76829 Landau.
T. (06341) 85225. *053754*
Berger, M., Geiselgasse 1, 76829 Landau.
T. (06341) 62756. *053755*
Boos, Meerweibchenstr 7, 76829 Landau.
T. (06341) 20742. - Ant / Furn / Repr / Lights - *053756*
Boschert, Eberhard, Martin-Luther-Str 10, 76829 Land-
au. T. (06341) 82011. *053757*
Götz, G., Trappengasse 9, 76829 Landau.
T. (06341) 82679. *053758*
Klotz, Ferdinand, Hainbachstr 88, 76829 Landau.
T. (06341) 60071. *053759*
Robertz, K.-Heinz, Röntgenstr 47, 76829 Landau.
T. (06341) 30702. *053760*
Schöneberg, Kleiner Pl 11, 76829 Landau.
T. (06341) 85917. *053761*
Zinnkann, Martin-Luther-Str 4, 76829 Landau.
T. (06341) 86972. - Ant / Paint / Graph / Lights /
Mod - *053762*

Landsberg (Bayern)

Bechter, Jutta, Vordere Mühlgasse 187, 86899 Lands-
berg. T. (08191) 4346, Fax (08191) 4346.
- Furn - *053763*

Landshut (Bayern)

Albecker, A., Weidenweg 23, 84032 Landshut.
T. (0871) 33639. *053764*
Antiquitäten an der Heiliggeistkirche, Heilig-Geist-Gasse
398, 84028 Landshut. T. (0871) 21376, 26358. - Ant /
Paint / Furn / China / Sculp / Tex / Jew / Instr / Glass -- *053765*
Böhmische Antiquitäten, Altstadt 26, 84028 Landshut.
T. (0871) 26339, 68107. *053766*
Bogner, I., Neustadt 472, 84028 Landshut.
T. (0871) 23503. *053767*
English Antiques, Altstadt 72, 84028 Landshut.
T. (0871) 25458. *053768*
Forstner, H., Neustadt 461, 84028 Landshut.
T. (0871) 89878. *053769*
Hudorovac, R., Querstr 23, 84034 Landshut.
T. (0871) 65738. *053770*
Mandel, Ludwig, Ludwig-Thoma-Str 49, 84036 Lands-
hut. T. (0871) 44341. *053771*
Meindl, A., Röntgenstr 10a, 84030 Landshut.
T. (0871) 74564. *053772*
Pfaffinger, K., Eugenbacher Str 24, 84028 Landshut.
T. (0871) 72941. *053773*

Richter, B., Altstadt 69, 84028 Landshut.
T. (0871) 28101. *053774*
Richter, Gabi, Ländgasse 37, 84028 Landshut. *053775*
Rödig, Gertrud, Altstadt 369, 84028 Landshut.
T. (0871) 28141. - Ant - *053776*
Romberger, S., Schirmgasse 276, 84028 Landshut.
T. (0871) 28198. *053777*
Sax, Liesl, Jodoksgasse 585, 84028 Landshut.
T. (0871) 22231. *053778*
Schuh, B., Grasgasse 332, 84028 Landshut.
T. (0871) 26747. *053779*
Seidl, Josef, Altstadt 17, 84028 Landshut.
T. (0871) 26626. - Ant - *053780*
Seyed-Ghaemi, S., Schirmgasse 272, 84028 Landshut.
T. (0871) 89318. *053781*
Stein, W., Fliederstr 38, 84032 Landshut.
T. (0871) 76703. *053782*
Wegrzyniak, Schönfeldstr 2, 84036 Landshut.
T. (0871) 51142. *053783*
Weiss, E. & K., Obere Ländgasse 49a, 84028 Landshut.
T. (0871) 22614. - Ant / Furn / China / Dec / Jew / Silv /
Lights / Instr / Rel / Glass / Mod / Toys - *053784*

Landstuhl (Rheinland-Pfalz)

Feuerabend, M., Schubertstr. 9, 66849 Landstuhl.
T. (06371) 64 13. *053785*
L'Antiquaire, Ludwigstr. 32, 66849 Landstuhl.
T. (06371) 26 37. - Ant / Furn / Jew / Silv / Instr / Ico /
Mod - *053786*
Lieser, H., Ludwigstr. 32, 66849 Landstuhl.
T. (06371) 2637. *053787*
Zoller, U., Weiherstr. 2, 66849 Landstuhl.
T. (06371) 158 54. *053788*

Langen (Hessen)

Wannemacher, W., Frankfurter Str 11, 63225 Langen.
T. (06103) 29419. - Ant - *053789*
Winskowsky, Horst, Feldbergstr 27, 63225 Langen.
T. (06103) 25363. - Num - *053790*

Langenargen (Baden-Württemberg)

Hanser, H. & S., Gräbenen 50, 88085 Langenargen.
T. (07543) 1458. *053791*
Probst, G., Krokusweg 3, 88085 Langenargen.
T. (07543) 39 78. *053792*

Langenau (Baden-Württemberg)

Riedel, O., Hindenburgstr 14, 89129 Langenau.
T. (07345) 3455. *053793*

Langenfeld (Nordrhein-Westfalen)

Holtum, Manfred von, Ursulaweg 53, 40764 Langenfeld.
- Ant / Paint / Graph - *053794*
Holtum, Roswitha von, Ursulaweg 53, 40764 Langen-
feld. T. (02173) 19509. - Graph - *053795*

Langenhagen (Niedersachsen)

Antiquitäten Nr. 1, Hindenburgstr 1, 30851 Langenha-
gen. T. (0511) 772504. - Ant - *053796*
Ehlers, R., Twenger Weg 4, 30855 Langenhagen.
T. (0511) 775006. *053797*
Kassler, W., Hermansburger Str 10, 30855 Langenha-
gen. T. (0511) 743640. *053798*

Langenlonsheim (Rheinland-Pfalz)

Remmet, Angelika, Naheweinstr. 141, 55450 Langen-
lonsheim. T. (06704) 1895. *053799*
Remmet, K.-H., Guldenbachstr. 11, 55450 Langenlons-
heim. T. (06704) 2339. *053800*

Langquaid (Bayern)

Trützschler, Johannes, Schloß, 84085 Langquaid.
T. (09452) 666. - Furn / China / Silv / Glass - *053801*

Lastrup (Niedersachsen)

Carstensen, Ernst, Timmerlage 10, 49688 Lastrup.
- Instr - *053802*

Laubach (Hessen)

Graulich, H., Untere Langgasse 7, 35321 Laubach.
T. (06405) 1792. *053803*

Lauchhammer (Brandenburg)

Christ, Elsterwerdaer Str. 22, 01979 Lauchhammer.
T. (03574) 7217. *053804*

Lauda-Königshofen (Baden-Württemberg)
Berl, U., Kapellenstr.13, 97922 Lauda-Königshofen.
T. (09343) 3592. 053805

Laudenbach (Bayern)
Breitenbach, C., Dorfstr. 24, 63925 Laudenbach.
T. (09372) 2362. 053806

Lauf (Bayern)
Bäuerliche Antiquitäten, Schloßstr 3, 91207 Lauf.
T. (09123) 7165. - Furn - 053807
Gerstacker, H. & R., Hopfenstr 10, 91207 Lauf.
T. (09123) 75807. 053808
Kellner, Brigitte, Kolerschloß, 91207 Lauf.
T. (09123) 7165. 053809
Steckenpferd-Antik, Siebenkeesstr 7, 91207 Lauf.
T. (09123) 4447. 053810

Lauingen (Bayern)
Reichert, W., Donaustr. 3a, 89415 Lauingen.
T. (09072) 44 52. 053811

Laupheim (Baden-Württemberg)
Brohl, Volker, Bahnhofstr. 1, 88471 Laupheim.
T. (07392) 89 76. 053812

Lauter (Bayern)
Müller, R., Birkenstr. 5, 96169 Lauter.
T. (09544) 305. 053813

Lauterstein (Baden-Württemberg)
Gelmar, S., Hauptstr. 263, 73111 Lauterstein.
T. (07332) 55 65. 053814
Haenle, Hauptstr. 257, 73111 Lauterstein.
T. (07332) 50 54. 053815

Lautertal (Hessen)
Greb, Norbert, Storndorfer Str. 38, 36369 Lautertal.
T. (06630) 573. 053816

Lautrach (Bayern)
Mulzer, Georg, Deybachstr. 12, 87763 Lautrach.
- Ant - 053817

Leer (Niedersachsen)
Arians, Rathausstr 7, 26789 Leer.
T. (0491) 3868. 053818
Dopmann, Dietrich, Breslauer Str 6, 26789 Leer. 053819
Pache, Johannes, Neuestr 42, 26789 Leer.
T. (0491) 3291. - Ant / Instr / Cur - 053820

Legden (Nordrhein-Westfalen)
Im Kreuzgang, Stiftsstr. 6, 48739 Legden.
T. (02566) 12 31. 053821

Lehre (Niedersachsen)
Vitrine, Berliner Str. 67, 38165 Lehre.
T. (05308) 1500. 053822

Lehrte (Niedersachsen)
Sander, Henning, Katt'sche Str. 7, 31275 Lehrte.
T. (05132) 05175/7242. 053823

Leinfelden-Echterdingen (Baden-Württemberg)
Brill, M., Echterdinger Str. 30, 70771 Leinfelden-Echterdingen. T. (0711) 75 03 50. 053824
Hoch, P., Taxiswald 6, 70771 Leinfelden-Echterdingen.
T. (0711) 754 56 46. 053825

Leipzig (Sachsen)
Antiquitäten an der Oper, Ritterstr. 16, 04109 Leipzig.
T. (0341) 281651. - Ant / Orient / China / Sculp / Tex /
Jew / Fra / Silv / Instr / Rel / Glass / Cur / Mod / Ico --
053826
Antiquitäten- und Münzengalerie, Schulstr. 3, 04109
Leipzig. T. (0341) 27 18 76. - Ant / Num - 053827
Antiquitätencafe Kleinod, Käthe-Kollwitz-Str. 71, 04109
Leipzig. T. (0341) 471555,4011267. - Ant / Paint /
Graph / Furn / Num / Orient / China / Sculp / Tex / Jew /
Silv / Lights / Instr / Mil / Glass / Cur / Mod / Ico / Pho --
053828
Beier, H., Nikolaistr. 55, 04109 Leipzig.
T. (0341)980 02 50. 053828a

Brauer, Eberhard, Braustr. 29, 04107 Leipzig.
T. (0341) 2130651. - Ant / Paint / Furn / China / Jew /
Fra / Silv / Glass / Cur - 053829
Brinkmann, Thomaskirchhof 11, 04109 Leipzig.
T. (0341) 9603006. - Paint / Graph / China / Jew / Silv /
Instr / Mil / Glass / Cur / Tin / Toys / Naut - 053830
Frank, M., Nikolaistr. 55, 04109 Leipzig.
T. (0341) 29 20 07. 053831
Freyer, R., Grimmaische Str. 1-7, 04109 Leipzig.
T. (0341) 20 96 94. - Ant - 053832
Galerie Kleinod, Käthe-Kollwitz-Str. 71, 04109 Leipzig.
T. (0341) 47 15 55, 401 12 67. - Ant / Paint / Graph /
Furn / China / Jew / Instr / Glass - 053833
Görg, W., Waldstr. 44, 04105 Leipzig. T. (0341) 28 71 38.
- Ant - 053834
Höhn, Heidrun, Brühl 52, 04109 Leipzig.
T. (0341) 9602386, 9613464, Fax 2117245. 053835
Leipziger Münzhandlung und Auktion, Katharinenstr. 11,
04109 Leipzig. T. (0341) 29 11 30, Fax 211 72 45.
- Num - 053836

Lemförde (Niedersachsen)
Möbel Deele, Im Dorf 23, 49448 Lemförde.
T. (05443) 81 32. - Furn - 053837

Lemgo (Nordrhein-Westfalen)
Antik-Eck, Breite Str. 20, 32657 Lemgo.
T. (05261) 16072. - Ant - 053838
Förster & Ludwig, Bhf. Horstmann, 32657 Lemgo.
T. (05261) 726 26. 053839
Kiek in beim Turm, Ostertor 1, 32657 Lemgo.
T. (05261) 124 11. 053840
Klein, Robert, Kluskampstr. 46, 32657 Lemgo.
T. (05261) 175 98. 053841
Kramp, Werkstr. 3, 32657 Lemgo.
T. (05261) 64 64. 053842
Maatz, Eckhard, Voßheiderstr. 98, 32657 Lemgo.
T. (05261) 881 64. 053843
Reinecke & Heinrich, Osterf. 23, 32657 Lemgo.
T. (05261) 6186. 053844
Rosteck, Stift St. Marien 22-27, 32657 Lemgo.
T. (05261) 4077, 13105. - Ant / Paint / Furn / China /
Fra - 053845

Lengerich (Nordrhein-Westfalen)
Antik-Diele, Wechterstr 42, 49525 Lengerich.
T. (05482) 1603. 053846
Knirsch, Rainhard, In der Hiärken 7, 49525 Lengerich.
T. (05481) 1210. 053847
Marx, M., Mühlenweg 13, 49525 Lengerich.
T. (05481) 82355. 053848

Lennestadt (Nordrhein-Westfalen)
Hufnagel, Am Schützenpl. 3, 57368 Lennestadt.
T. (02721) 828 10. - Graph - 053849

Lensahn (Schleswig-Holstein)
Boie, Heinz, Brunskrug, 23738 Lensahn.
T. (04363) 3457. 053850

Leonberg (Baden-Württemberg)
Felstead, J., Theodor-Heuss-Str 1, 71229 Leonberg.
T. (07152) 22212. 053851
Krauß & Kühnel, Schloßstr 8, 71229 Leonberg.
T. (07152) 23609. 053852
Markt 28, Marktpl 28, 71229 Leonberg.
T. (07152) 21396. - Ant - 053853
Müller, H.-J., Marktpl 13, 71229 Leonberg.
T. (07152) 6178. 053854
Neumann, Schloßstr 15, 71229 Leonberg.
T. (07152) 22595. 053855
Pfisterer, Helmut, Brandenburgerstr 7, 71229 Leonberg.
T. (07152) 25459. 053856
Walter, Hans-Willi, Postfach 1804, 71208 Leonberg.
T. (07152) 24800, Fax (07152) 24698. - Ant - 053857

Leuchtenberg (Bayern)
Schösser, F., Döllnitz, 92705 Leuchtenberg.
T. (09659) 898. 053858

Leupoldsgrün (Bayern)
Oertel + Co., Am Löwenberg 5, 95191 Leupoldsgrün.
T. (09292) 60-0, Fax 1640. - Orient / Tex / Ico - 053859

Leverkusen (Nordrhein-Westfalen)
Becker, Alice, Im Kalkfeld 24, 51379 Leverkusen.
T. (0214) 02171/467 11. - Ant / Jew - 053860
Dollmann, Matthias, Berliner Str. 163, 51377 Leverkusen. T. (0214) 911 89. 053861
Gutmann, H.-J., Stixchesstr. 201, 51377 Leverkusen.
T. (0214) 75304. 053862
Lindner, J., Kölner Str. 1, 51379 Leverkusen.
T. (0214) 02171/2447. 053863
Lütke, Wilhelm & Manfred, Kölner Str. 19, 51379 Leverkusen. T. (0214) 02171/18 84. - Paint / Furn / Orient /
Tex / Jew / Fra - 053864
Schulten, E., Altstadtstr. 114, 51379 Leverkusen.
T. (0214) 02171/43803. 053865

Lich (Hessen)
Licher Kunstmöbel-Werkstätten, Bahnhofstr. 46, 35423
Lich. T. (06404) 61652. - Furn - 053866
Seharsch, P., Lessingstr. 3, 35423 Lich.
T. (06404) 18 03. 053867

Lichtenau (Nordrhein-Westfalen)
Möller, H., Grundsteinheim, 33165 Lichtenau.
T. (05295) 1465. 053868

Lichtenfels, Bayern (Bayern)
Feulner, R., Sonnenweg 3, 96215 Lichtenfels, Bayern.
T. (09571) 4206. 053869
Heck, & R. Feulner, W., Abteistr. 20, 96215 Lichtenfels,
Bayern. T. (09571) 308. - Furn / China / Sculp - 053870

Lilienthal (Niedersachsen)
Antik und Trödel, Mittelbauer 13, 28865 Lilienthal.
T. (04298) 04292/568. 053871
Gerken-Hermut, Kathrin, Falkenberger Landstr. 79, 28865 Lilienthal. T. (04298) 31396. 053872
Meenen, Heinz, Goebelstr 23, 28865 Lilienthal.
T. (04298) 3277. 053873

Limburg an der Lahn (Hessen)
Antiquitäten am Salzmarkt, Salzgasse 17-19, 65549
Limburg an der Lahn. T. (06431) 25637, Fax 5712.
- Ant / Furn / Repr / Tex / Dec - 053874
Antiquitäten im Türmchen, Frankfurter Str 40-42, 65549
Limburg an der Lahn. T. (06431) 44754.
- Furn - 053875
Bachmann, Rübsanger Str 52, 65551 Limburg an der
Lahn. T. (06431) 72320. 053876
Fischer, D., Koblenzer Str 73, 65556 Limburg an der
Lahn. T. (06431) 3774. 053877
Jordan, Udo, Frankfurter Str 40, 65549 Limburg an der
Lahn. T. (06431) 44754. 053878
Küster, Käthe, Fleischgasse 22, 65549 Limburg an der
Lahn. 053879
Stoltenburg, Ernst, Hospitalstr 1, 65549 Limburg an der
Lahn. T. (06431) 6756. 053880
Topp, Hans-Jürgen, Grabenstr 31, 65549 Limburg an
der Lahn. T. (06431) 6490, Fax 24172. - Paint /
Graph - 053881
Weiland, K., Lindenstr 3, 65549 Limburg an der
Lahn. 053882
Weiland, Klaus, Rütsche 10, 65549 Limburg an der
Lahn. T. (06431) 6609. - Ant - 053883

Lindau, Bodensee (Bayern)
Christl, Willi, Vordere Metzgergasse 4, 88131 Lindau,
Bodensee. T. (08382) 6419. 053884
Kürn, H.U., Salzgasse 6, 88131 Lindau, Bodensee.
T. (08382) 5133. - Tex - 053885
Schönfelder, Ludwigstr 14, 88131 Lindau, Bodensee.
T. (08382) 4384, 5823. - Ant / Paint / China /
Sculp - 053886
Schrade, Ewald und Dorothea, Krummgasse 3, 88131
Lindau, Bodensee. T. (08382) 28459,
Fax (08382) 28459. 053887
Spielberg, B., Salzgasse 5, 88131 Lindau, Bodensee.
T. (08382) 28225. 053888
Walter, P.J., Maximilianstr 2a, 88131 Lindau, Bodensee.
T. (08382) 22736. 053889
Zeller, Michael, Bindergasse 7, 88131 Lindau, Bodensee. T. (08382) 93020, Fax 26535. - Jew / Ant / Paint /
Glass / Graph / Mod / Orient / China / Silv / Mil / Instr --
053890

Linden (Hessen)
Mulitze, Traute, Tannenweg 39, 35440 Linden. T. (06403) 619 61. - Ant - 053891

Lindenberg, Pfalz (Rheinland-Pfalz)
Matthaei, A., Lambrechterstr, 67473 Lindenberg, Pfalz 053892

Lindenthal (Sachsen)
Lindenthal, Bahnhofstr 47, 04466 Lindenthal. T. (0341) 4614666, Fax (0341) 4612660. - Paint / Mil / Furn / Silv - 053893

Lindlar (Nordrhein-Westfalen)
Winterberg, H., Habbacherstr 8, 51789 Lindlar. T. (02266) 2017. 053894

Lingen (Niedersachsen)
Antiquitäten und Kunst, Burgstr 31, 49808 Lingen. T. (0591) 2441. 053895
Birkle, W. & A., Langschmidtsweg 68, 49808 Lingen. T. (0591) 51022. - Num - 053896
Ilsemann, V., Mühlentorstr 5, 49808 Lingen. T. (0591) 49421. 053897
Suiver, M.-L., Große Str 7, 49808 Lingen. T. (0591) 2406. - Num - 053898

Lippstadt (Nordrhein-Westfalen)
Flohmarkt, Cappelstr. 49, 59555 Lippstadt. T. (02941) 49 48. - Ant - 053899
Rahmacher, Cappelstr. 74, 59555 Lippstadt. T. (02941) 46 03. 053900
Schneider, Claus, Geiststr. 9, 59555 Lippstadt. T. (02941) 43 07. 053901

Löningen (Niedersachsen)
Knappert, Willy, Bunner Str., 49624 Löningen. T. (05432) 2911. 053902

Lörrach (Baden-Württemberg)
Milohnic, Marino, Hermann-Albrecht-Str. 32, 79540 Lörrach. - Num - 053903
Pempelfort, S., Basler Str. 159, 79539 Lörrach. T. (07621) 434 48. 053904
Risch, Katharina, Basler Str. 154, 79539 Lörrach. T. (07621) 464 03. 053905
Treiling, T., Feerstr. 1, 79541 Lörrach. T. (07621) 545 45. 053906
Wechlin, Karl, Basler Str. 172, 79539 Lörrach. T. (07621) 462 23. - Ant / Fra - 053907
Wolter, P., Brombacher Str. 3, 79539 Lörrach. 053908
Zernke, W., Grabenstr. 2a, 79539 Lörrach. T. (07621) 828 92. 053909

Lohfelden (Hessen)
Göbel, E., Berliner Str. 71, 34253 Lohfelden. 053910

Lohmar (Nordrhein-Westfalen)
Blum, G., Altenratherstr. 1, 53797 Lohmar. T. (02246) 5900. 053911
Bornkast, M., Meigermühle, 53797 Lohmar. T. (02246) 2886. - Furn - 053912

Lohne, Oldenburg (Niedersachsen)
Krogmann, Hermann, Wickeler Flur 4, 49393 Lohne, Oldenburg. T. (04442) 1789. - Furn - 053913

Lohra (Hessen)
Wolter, Martin, Scheunengalerie, Kauzenhof, 35102 Lohra. T. (06462) 1234. - Paint - 053914

Lorch (Baden-Württemberg)
Kerler, G., Reissergasse 6, 73547 Lorch. T. (07172) 48 87. 053915
Sieger, H.E., Am Venusberg 32-34, 73547 Lorch. T. (06726) 4031. - Num - 053916

Loßburg (Baden-Württemberg)
Hoenig, W., & G. Rodt, Schröderstr. 10, 72290 Loßburg. T. (07446) 2809. 053917

Ludwigsburg (Baden-Württemberg)
Boss, J., Myliusstr. 8, 71638 Ludwigsburg. T. (07141) 250 46. 053918
Feigl, Günter, Gartenstr. 3, 71638 Ludwigsburg. 053919
Fischer, G., Lindenstr. 27, 71634 Ludwigsburg. 053920
Krust, F., Alte Gasse 1, 71634 Ludwigsburg. T. (07141) 238 68. 053921
Meister, Michael, Moltkestr. 6, 71634 Ludwigsburg. - Num - 053922
Pohl, E.-M., Marktplatz 13, 71634 Ludwigsburg. 053923
Reimann & Monatsberger, Palais Graevenitz, Marstallstr. 5, 71634 Ludwigsburg. T. (07141) 90955, Fax (07141) 901071. - Ant / Paint / Graph / Furn / Orient / China / Sculp / Tex / Jew / Silv / Instr / Mil / Rel / Glass / Cur / Mod / Draw - 053924

Ludwigshafen am Rhein (Rheinland-Pfalz)
Dropmann, B., Prinzregentenstr 47, 67063 Ludwigshafen am Rhein. T. (0621) 525240. 053925
Hoffmann, V., Amtsstr 8, 67059 Ludwigshafen am Rhein. T. (0621) 523838. - Ant - 053926
Lauth, Robert, Mundenheimer Str 252, 67061 Ludwigshafen am Rhein. T. (0621) 563840. 053927
Zintl, Maria, Heinigstr 55, 67059 Ludwigshafen am Rhein. T. (0621) 522887. - Ant / Furn / Repr - 053928

Lübbecke (Nordrhein-Westfalen)
Tantius, Hans-Gerd, Andreasstr 6, 32312 Lübbecke. T. (05741) 31877, Fax 318799. - Paint / Graph / Repr / Sculp / Fra / Glass / Mul / Draw - 053929
Wiegmann, Kaiserstr 1a, 32312 Lübbecke. T. (05741) 8855. 053930
Wiegmann, K. & D., Am Markt 1, 32312 Lübbecke. T. (05741) 5527. 053931

Lübeck (Schleswig-Holstein)
Alte und Neue Kunst, Trelleborgallee 2, 23570 Lübeck. T. (0451) 74949, Fax (0451) 74949. - Ant / Paint / Furn / Repr / Fra / Silv / Lights / Glass / Mod / Naut - 053932
Antik-Engelsgrube, Engelsgrube 6-8, 23552 Lübeck. T. (0451) 771 60. - Ant / Paint / Furn / China / Jew / Mod - 053933
Antik-Möbelhof, Große Burgstr. 27, 23552 Lübeck. T. (0451) 728 68. - Ant / Furn - 053934
Antikhalle Travemünde, Vogteistr. 13, 23570 Lübeck. T. (0451) 2217. 053935
Bannow, Günther, Fleischhauerstr. 87, 23552 Lübeck. T. (0451) 773 38. 053936
Beetz, K., Hüxstr. 101, 23552 Lübeck. T. (0451) 74284. 053937
Bollmeyer, J., Engelsgrube 68, 23552 Lübeck. T. (0451) 787 65. 053938
Captain's Corner, Strandpromenade 1b, 23570 Lübeck. T. (0451) 738 03. 053939
Hantsch, Helena, Kohlenhof 5, 23570 Lübeck. T. (0451) 3833. 053940
Herzog, H., Kohlenhof 5, 23570 Lübeck. T. (0451) 3833. 053941
Hill, Horst, Kurgartenstr. 111, 23570 Lübeck. T. (0451) 35 02. - Ant - 053942
Hingst, Rüdiger, Sandstr. 6, 23552 Lübeck. T. (0451) 7 33 68. - Num - 053943
KIB-Kunstbild Vertriebsgesellschaft, Moislinger Allee 191, 23558 Lübeck. T. (0451) 89 32 70, Fax (0451) 89 25 90. - Repr - 053944
Krumpeter, C., Große Burgstr. 27, 23552 Lübeck. T. (0451) 72868. 053945
Mewes, Carl, Mühlenstr. 33, 23552 Lübeck. 053946
Neumann, Andrea, Breite Str. 17, 23552 Lübeck. T. (0451) 739 93. - Ant / Furn / Dec / Jew / Silv - 053947
Nonkovic, D., Beckergrube 64, 23552 Lübeck. T. (0451) 70 42 95. 053948
Oloff, Hans-Erwin, Marlesgrube 40, 23552 Lübeck. T. (0451) 70 52 53. 053949
Richter, Engelsgrube 40, 23552 Lübeck. T. (0451) 723 38. 053950
Stanke, P. & H., Königstr. 124, 23552 Lübeck. T. (0451) 760 49. 053951
Stoffer, H., Beckergrube 97, 23552 Lübeck. T. (0451) 711 91. 053952
Ungethüm, Karin, Maritim Passage, 23552 Lübeck. T. (0451) 73803. 053953
Weigt, P., Große Burgstr. 22, 23552 Lübeck. T. (0451) 766 38. 053954
Winzösch, Lothar, Ahrensböker Str. 5, 23554 Lübeck. T. (0451) 779 60. 053955
Zitzewitz, Jutta von, Hüxstr. 66, 23552 Lübeck. T. (0451) 752 53. 053956

Lüchow, Wendland (Niedersachsen)
Paas, Kurt, Hegelstr 1, 29439 Lüchow, Wendland. - Num - 053957

Lüdenscheid (Nordrhein-Westfalen)
Branscheid, U., Luisenstr. 2, 58511 Lüdenscheid. T. (02351) 290 51. 053958
Hoffmeister, Liebigstr. 9, 58511 Lüdenscheid. T. (02351) 23372, Fax (02351) 26739. - Paint / Sculp / Pho / Mul / Draw - 053959
Kessler, Gisbert, Hochst. 44, 58507 Lüdenscheid. T. (02351) 274 03. - Num - 053960
Petrikat, P., Weststr. 41, 58509 Lüdenscheid. T. (02351) 293 47. 053961

Lüdinghausen (Nordrhein-Westfalen)
Brüggemann & Co., H.-Böckler-Str., 59348 Lüdinghausen. T. (02591) 30 57. 053962
Wittkamp, F. & A., Lindostr. 9, 59348 Lüdinghausen. T. (02591) 4422. 053963

Lülsfeld (Bayern)
Volk, B., Frankenwinheimerstr. 10, 97511 Lülsfeld. T. (09382) 8473. 053964

Lüneburg (Niedersachsen)
Beckhaus, H., Am Markt 6, 21335 Lüneburg. T. (04131) 311 61. 053965
Bottke, Sylvia, Wilhelm-Reinecke-Str. 76, 21302 Lüneburg. T. (04131) 42724. - Ant / Paint / Silv - 053966
König, Antonie, Am Berge 37, 21335 Lüneburg. T. (04131) 624 75. 053967
Nikolai, Lüner Str. 2+3, 21335 Lüneburg. T. (04131) 326 22. - Ant / Paint / Furn / China / Jew / Fra / Silv / Instr / Glass / Mod - 053968

Lünen (Nordrhein-Westfalen)
Baak, Rudolf, Dr., Marienstr. 19, 44534 Lünen. T. (02306) 546 82. - Paint / Furn - 053969
Heseler, Walter, Lange Str. 65, 44532 Lünen. T. (02306) 121 50. 053970
Niggeling, D., Dortmunder Str. 93., 44536 Lünen. T. (02306) 126 12. 053971

Lunden (Schleswig-Holstein)
Malta, Traute, Lehe, 25774 Lunden. T. (04882) 322. 053972

Magdeburg (Sachsen-Anhalt)
Haller, M., Weberstr. 18, 39112 Magdeburg. T. (0391) 61 39 55. 053973
Mauritius, Max-Josef-Metzger-Str. 2, 39104 Magdeburg. T. (0391) 34 43 39. 053974
Rahn, R., Breiter Weg 255, 39104 Magdeburg. T. (0391) 32918. 053975

Maikammer (Rheinland-Pfalz)
Maikammer, Hartmannstr. 9, 67487 Maikammer. T. (06321) 59130. - Ant / Paint / Furn / China - 053976
Masanek, H.P., Marktstr. 5, 67487 Maikammer. T. (06321) 5374. - Ant / Furn - 053977

Mainaschaff (Bayern)
Horlebein, U., Goethestr. 28, 63814 Mainaschaff. - Ant / Furn / China / Instr / Glass / Cur - 053978

Mainburg (Bayern)
Fuchs, A., & Renate Puttenhausen, Kirchstr. 1, 84048 Mainburg. T. (08751) 2660. 053979

Mainhardt (Baden-Württemberg)
Gutjahr, R., Mönchstr. 18, 74535 Mainhardt. T. (07903) 26 95. 053980

Mainhausen (Hessen)
Antik-Haus Mainhausen, Sudetensiedlung 4, 63533 Mainhausen. T. (06182) 261 02. - Furn / Instr - 053981

Mainz (Rheinland-Pfalz)
Alexander & Möschler, Kartäuserstr. 6, 55116 Mainz. T. (06131) 201 54. - Ant - 053982
Arnold & Mayer, Hauptstr. 16g, 55252 Mainz. T. (06134) 25272. 053983

Berg, Christa, Fuststr. 17, 55116 Mainz.
T. (06131) 230053. — 053984
Beuerbach, W. M., Pfitznerstr. 8, 55118 Mainz.
T. (06131) 67 43 90. — 053985
Brumme, Siegfried, Kirschgarten 11, 55116 Mainz.
T. (06131) 228074, Fax (06131) 230717.
- Graph - — 053986
Buse, Heidelbergerfaßgasse 8, 55005 Mainz.
T. (06131) 234015, Fax 236594. - Instr - — 053987
Cene, H., Klarastr. 21, 55116 Mainz.
T. (06131) 22 19 85. — 053988
Düx, Heinrich, Schönbornstr. 9, 55116 Mainz. — 053989
Jasmin, Binger Str. 1, 55116 Mainz.
T. (06131) 22 19 84. — 053990
Krabler, J. & M., Hintere Bleiche 7, 55116 Mainz.
T. (06131) 22 74 37. — 053991
Kumpmann, Udo, Rheinstr. 33, 55116 Mainz.
T. (06131) 23 30 08, Fax (06131) 22 75 66. - Ant /
Paint / Furn / Tex / Dec - — 053992
Lehr, D., & J.A., Kirschgarten 21, 55116 Mainz.
T. (06131) 22 87 55. — 053993
Lehr, Sigrid, Van-Gogh-Str. 25, 55127 Mainz.
T. (06131) 713 60. - China - — 053994
Lunkenheimer, Inselstr. 4, 55116 Mainz.
T. (06131) 22 30 63. — 053995
Maria's Antik Boutique, Nackstr. 8, 55118 Mainz.
T. (06131) 67 38 58. — 053996
Metzner, Eberhard, Rheinstr. 40, 55116 Mainz.
T. (06131) 231180. - Furn - — 053997
Metzner, Wolfgang Jakob, Liebfrauenstr. 1, 55116
Mainz. T. (06131) 22 82 54. - Ant / Paint / Furn /
Glass - — 053998
Möschler, A., Kartäuserstr. 6, 55116 Mainz.
T. (06131) 201 54. — 053999
Müller, E. und R., Rheinstr. 101, 55116 Mainz.
T. (06131) 22 38 73. — 054000
Müller, W., Kaiserstr. 41, 55116 Mainz.
T. (06131) 61 44 86. — 054001
Namokel, Ute-Elisabeth, Rheinstr. 39, 55116 Mainz.
T. (06131) 286 35. — 054002
Neuhäuser, Roland G., Budenheimer Str. 25, 55124
Mainz. T. (06131) 413 46. — 054003
Nicollier, Augustinerstr. 73, 55116 Mainz.
T. (06131) 222557, Fax (06131) 224144. - Jew /
Silv - — 054004
Rehberg, Dagmar, Uferstr. 17, 55116 Mainz.
T. (06131) 22 46 05. — 054005
Roesgen, I. von, Uferstr. 43, 55116 Mainz. — 054006
Roland's Antiquitäten, Budenheimer Str. 25, 55124
Mainz. — 054007
Rousin, K., Zanggasse 1, 55116 Mainz.
T. (06131) 22 28 99. — 054008
Schorr, Jürgen, Stolze-Schrey-Str. 24, 55124 Mainz.
- Orient / Tex / Rel / Glass / Ico - — 054009
Schott, M., Kirschgarten 3, 55116 Mainz.
T. (06131) 22 02 11. — 054010
Schublade, Die, Kirschgarten 1, 55116 Mainz.
T. (06131) 22 00 04. — 054011
Steckenpferd, Bleichgarten 11, 55120 Mainz.
T. (06131) 68 61 68, 68 68 11. — 054012
Tusar, H., Binger Str. 3, 55116 Mainz.
T. (06131) 22 88 22. — 054013
Wenz, R., Am Rathaus 8, 55116 Mainz.
T. (06131) 22 77 94, Fax (06131) 22 89 08. - Ant /
Repr / Silv / Glass - — 054014

Malente (Schleswig-Holstein)
Lück, Lindenweg 16, 23714 Malente.
T. (04523) 3020. — 054015

Malsch (Baden-Württemberg)
Göckel, Hauptstr. 30, 69254 Malsch.
T. (07253) 221 40. — 054016

Mannheim (Baden-Württemberg)
Bauer, Rheinhäuser Str. 110, 68165 Mannheim.
T. (0621) 44 27 90. — 054017
Bausback, Franz, N 3, 9, 68161 Mannheim.
T. (0621) 25808, Fax (0621) 105957. - Ant /
Tex - — 054018
Brinkmann, Volker, Augusta-Anlage 18, 68159 Mann-
heim. T. (0621) 44 85 14, 41 33 28. - China - — 054019

Engelhardt, 0 6,3, 68159 Mannheim. T. (0621) 15 10 51.
- Tex - — 054020
Erlich, N 7, 7, 68161 Mannheim. T. (0621) 288 26.
- Tex - — 054021
Fifty-Fifty, Seckenheimer Str. 75, 68165 Mannheim.
T. (0621) 40 28 21. — 054022
Freund, Q 3, 9, 68161 Mannheim.
T. (0621) 10 55 31. — 054023
Gentile, C., Gaswerkstr. 1, 68307 Mannheim.
T. (0621) 77 39 32. — 054024
Gloria-Schmuck und Antiquitäten, R 3, 1, 68161 Mann-
heim. T. (0621) 15 54 31. - Ant / China / Jew / Silv /
Glass / Mod - — 054025
Gremm, T., R 3, 12, 68161 Mannheim.
T. (0621) 15 14 41. - Ant / Paint / Furn - — 054026
Gruber, P 6, 24, 68161 Mannheim.
T. (0621) 25087. — 054027
Harms, Molly, Hortenpassage, Friedrichspl. 5, 68159
Mannheim. T. (0621) 25132. — 054028
Hauck, M., Q 2, 5, 68161 Mannheim.
T. (0621) 29 18 45. — 054029
Huss, M., Mühldorfer Str. 4, 68165 Mannheim.
T. (0621) 44 12 31. - Ant - — 054030
Kaeflein, Walter, M 2, 10, 68161 Mannheim.
T. (0621) 15 14 54. - Graph - — 054031
Kazinik, Postfach 1224, 68001 Mannheim.
- Tex - — 054032
Kroker & Walsch GmbH, Quadrat Qu 3, 10, 68159 Mann-
heim. T. (0621) 2 05 14. - Num - — 054033
Kurpfälzische Münzhandlung, Augusta-Anlage 52,
68159 Mannheim. T. (0621) 44 95 66, 44 88 99,
Fax (0621) 40 37 52. - Num - — 054034
Lehnert, Hubertus, M 4, 5, 68161 Mannheim.
T. (0621) 10 24 72, Fax (0621) 57 75 59. - Ant /
Instr - — 054035
Merkel, H. K., Moselstr. 7, 68167 Mannheim.
T. (0621) 33 14 87. — 054036
Metz, W. & W., Friedrich-Engelhorn-Str. 7, 68167
Mannheim. — 054037
Nagel, Felicitas, Augusta-Anlage 15, 68159 Mannheim.
T. (0621) 442 77. - Ant / Paint / China / Silv - — 054038
Neskudla, R., T 3, 9, 68161 Mannheim.
T. (0621) 15 53 92. — 054039
Pontow, Harry, Hirschhorner Str. 20, 68259 Mannheim.
T. (0621) 79 44 84. - Paint - — 054040
Reffert, G., S 6, 26, 68161 Mannheim.
T. (0621) 272 48. — 054041
Rheinstädtler, M, M 3, 9, 68161 Mannheim.
T. (0621) 210 22. — 054042
Roth, L., B 4, 13, 68159 Mannheim. T. (0621) 15 36 21.
- Ant - — 054043
Rudolf, Hans-Jürgen, Seckenheimer Str. 25, 68165
Mannheim. T. (0621) 44 38 98. - Ant / Paint /
Furn - — 054044
Schreiber, Elke & Werner, Augusta-Anlage 30, 68165
Mannheim. T. (0621) 44 43 30. - Ant / China - — 054045
Schubert, W., Friedrichsring 40, 68161 Mannheim.
T. (0621) 14756. — 054046
Schulz, Karl-Friedrich, Friedrichspl. 15, 68159 Mann-
heim. T. (0621) 40 69 46. - Ant / China / Jew / Silv /
Glass / Cur / Mod - — 054047
Seider, Herbert, Augustaanlage 5, 68165 Mannheim.
T. (0621) 41 44 50. — 054048
Spenn, R., P 5, 11, 68161 Mannheim.
T. (0621) 202 46. — 054049
Stahl, Karl-Theodor, P 7, 16-17, 68161 Mannheim.
T. (0621) 220 22. - Paint / Graph - — 054050
Welsch, Karin, Eichendorffstr. 19, 68167 Mannheim.
T. (0621) 33 18 78. — 054051
Zürn, Maria, F 2, 6, 68159 Mannheim. — 054052

Marburg (Hessen)
Käfer, Winfried, Hofstatt 2, 35037 Marburg.
T. (06421) 27884. — 054053
Kirchhain, Daniel, Lingelgasse 5a, 35037
Marburg. — 054054
Mangner, Josef, Schwanallee 20, 35037 Marburg.
T. (06421) 292102. - Ant - — 054055
Ring, A., Bei St Jost 24, 35039 Marburg.
T. (06421) 27561. — 054056
Schneider, Hans, Damaschkeweg 5, 35039 Marburg.
T. (06421) 41492. — 054057
Schulz, Otto, Untergasse 5, 35037 Marburg. — 054058

Weber-Sobotzki, Heidelore, Ketzerbach 17 und 19 1/2,
35037 Marburg. T. (06421) 66746. - Ant / Paint / Furn /
China - — 054059
Wolff, Michael, Steinweg 4, 35037 Marburg.
T. (06421) 67552. - Ant / Paint / Graph / Furn /
China - — 054060

March (Baden-Württemberg)
Schwörer, M., Waldstr. 7a, 79232 March.
T. (07665) 25 61. — 054061

Marienhafe (Niedersachsen)
Graf, K., Bogenstr. 18, 26529 Marienhafe.
T. (04934) 1420. — 054062

Mariental (Niedersachsen)
Bugenhagen, Horst, Berliner Platz 1, 38368
Mariental. — 054063

Markdorf (Baden-Württemberg)
Thum, Ittendorf, 88677 Markdorf.
T. (07544) 3201. — 054064

Markt Rettenbach (Bayern)
Freistädter, O., Buchenbrunn 26, 87733 Markt Retten-
bach. T. (08392) 529. - Num - — 054065

Marktbreit (Bayern)
Hueth, A. van, Ochsenfurtherstr. 23, 97340 Marktbreit.
T. (09332) 35 12. — 054066

Marktheidenfeld (Bayern)
Schmelz & Marshel, Georg-Mayr-Str. 1, 97828 Marktheidenfeld. T. (09391) 5678. — 054067

Marktleugast (Bayern)
Ott, A., Helmbrechtserstr. 4b, 95352 Marktleugast.
T. (09255) 684. — 054068

Marktoberdorf (Bayern)
Schröder, Alexander, Salzstr. 5, 87616 Marktoberdorf.
T. (08342) 5272, 6375. — 054069

Marktredwitz (Bayern)
Antik-Schneider, Markt 48, 95615 Marktredwitz.
T. (09231) 3684. - Ant - — 054070
Fraß, R., Dammstr. 20, 95615 Marktredwitz.
T. (09231) 63684. — 054071
Glass, Astrid von, Dammstr. 18, 95615 Marktredwitz.
T. (09231) 2609. — 054072

Marquartstein (Bayern)
Bachmann, Nora, 83250 Marquartstein. - Ant - — 054073
Wimmer, Nina & Sohn, Pettendorfer Str. 51, 83250
Marquartstein. T. (08641) 25 22. - Furn - — 054074

Marxzell (Baden-Württemberg)
Latzko, Albtalstr. 4, 76359 Marxzell.
T. (07248) 8281. — 054075
Reißner, A., Gertrudenhof, 76359 Marxzell.
T. (07248) 55 07, Fax (07248) 13 97. - Ant - — 054076

Mastershausen (Rheinland-Pfalz)
Christ, Leo, Mautzbach 7, 56869 Mastershausen.
- Ant - — 054077

Mauer (Baden-Württemberg)
Jautz, Ferenc, Schneeberg 12, 69256 Mauer. — 054078

Maulbronn (Baden-Württemberg)
Asperger, W., Klosterhof 21, 75433 Maulbronn. - Paint /
Graph / China / Jew / Pho / Draw - — 054079
Galerie im Hof, Im Klosterhof 34, 75433 Maulbronn.
T. (07043) 69 90. — 054080
Ziegelbauer, Dieter, Schafhof 8, 75433 Maulbronn.
T. (07043) 28 64. — 054081

Mayen (Rheinland-Pfalz)
Mohr, Helmut, Nettetal 9, 56727 Mayen.
T. (02651) 26 44. - Mil - — 054082
Müller-Johnston, Habsburgring 22, 56727 Mayen.
T. (02651) 29 76. — 054083

Mechernich (Nordrhein-Westfalen)
Beissel von Gymnich, Graf F.J., Burg Satzvey, 53894
Mechernich. T. (02443) 1834. - Ant / Graph / Furn /
Sculp / Dec - — 054084

Meckenbeuren (Baden-Württemberg)

Fricker, A., Hauptstr. 71, 88074 Meckenbeuren.
T. (07542) 48 54. *054085*

Meckenheim (Nordrhein-Westfalen)

Ruland, K., Hauptstr 1, 53340 Meckenheim.
T. (02225) 14325. *054086*

Meckesheim (Baden-Württemberg)

Haaf, Franz-Josef, Hauptstr 50, 74909 Meckesheim.
T. (06226) 8174. *054087*

Meerbusch (Nordrhein-Westfalen)

Bredelin, H.R. & B., Nachtigallenweg 2, 40668 Meer-
busch. T. (02132) 18 73. *054088*
Emminghaus, H., Krefelder Str. 13, 40670 Meerbusch.
T. (02132) 56 76. *054089*
English Interiors, Moerser Str. 16, 40667 Meerbusch.
T. (02132) 762 88. - Furn - *054090*
Heinen, R., Meerbuscher Str. 48, 40670 Meerbusch.
T. (02132) 1828. *054091*
Kramer, K., Düsseldorfer Str. 31a, 40667 Meerbusch.
T. (02132) 2620. - Ant / Furn / Lights - *054092*
Leendert, F. van, Düsseldorfer Str. 49, 40667 Meer-
busch. T. (02132) 21 04. *054093*
Lethgau, R., Poststr. 58, 40667 Meerbusch.
T. (02132) 103 81. *054094*
Meerbuscher Kunstauktionshaus, Kanzlei 3, 40667
Meerbusch. T. (02132) 5711, Fax 5337. *054095*
Rosthal, H., Kanzlei 3, 40667 Meerbusch.
T. (02132) 57 11. *054096*
Schneider, E. D., Düsseldorfer Str. 79, 40667 Meer-
busch. T. (02132) 712 39. *054097*
Steinmann Kursmünzenversand, Schulstr. 29, 40668
Meerbusch. T. (02132) 3680. - Num - *054098*
Tigges, Ika, Wanheimer Str. 7, 40667
Meerbusch. *054099*

Meersburg (Baden-Württemberg)

Geiger, B., Stettener Str 1, 88709 Meersburg.
T. (07532) 7446. *054100*
Geiger, M., Gehauweg 22, 88709 Meersburg.
T. (07532) 5650. *054101*
Reinen, H., Kronenstr 17, 88709 Meersburg.
T. (07532) 9116. *054102*
Schneider, W., Unterstadtstr 15, 88709 Meersburg.
T. (07532) 5646. *054103*
Thum, Bismarkpl 1, 88709 Meersburg. T. (07532) 6533.
- Ant - *054104*
Thum, Unterstadtstr 4, 88709 Meersburg.
T. (07532) 6533. - Ant / Furn / China / Repr / Fra /
Lights / Instr / Glass / Cur - *054105*
Ulmer, M., Schlossplatz 3, 88709 Meersburg.
T. (07532) 5788. *054106*

Meine (Niedersachsen)

Wendt, Günter, Abbesbütteler Str. 14, 38527 Meine.
T. (05304) 3535. *054107*

Meinerzhagen (Nordrhein-Westfalen)

Röthling, M., Lortzingstr. 3, 58540 Meinerzhagen.
T. (02354) 6465. *054108*

Meldorf (Schleswig-Holstein)

Bohr, Christel, Zollstr. 10, 25704 Meldorf.
T. (04832) 31 04. *054109*
Kaluza, F., Roggenstr. 3, 25704 Meldorf.
T. (04832) 26 21. *054110*
Voit, Harro, Weidenbaum 1, 25704 Meldorf. *054111*

Melle (Niedersachsen)

Antik-Möbel, Am Denkmal 8, 49324 Melle.
T. (05422) 7250. - Furn - *054112*
Hörstemeier, I., Mühlenstr 11, 49324 Melle.
T. (05422) 44017. *054113*
Oberdiek, H., Ligusterstr. 6, 49328 Melle.
T. (05422) 734. *054114*
Raude, A., Schützenstr 35, 49326 Melle.
T. (05422) 1640. *054115*

Memmelsdorf (Bayern)

Braun, Rebenstr. 2, 96117 Memmelsdorf.
T. (0951) 30165. *054116*

Memmingen (Bayern)

Ghanipour, M.-M., Herrenstr. 14, 87700 Memmingen.
T. (08331) 805 00. *054117*
Harzenetter, L., Theaterplatz 11, 87700 Memmingen.
T. (08331) 59 50. *054118*

Menden (Nordrhein-Westfalen)

Siebert, Peter, Bahnhofstr 12, 58700 Menden.
T. (02373) 2307. - Num - *054119*

Merzen (Niedersachsen)

Mertens, J., Osteroden. Weg 13, 49586 Merzen.
T. (05466) 385. *054120*
Voss, Paul, Hauptstr. 1a, 49586 Merzen.
T. (05466) 1412. *054121*

Merzig (Saarland)

Lansch, J., Schankstr. 24, 66663 Merzig.
T. (06861) 75398. *054122*
Weber, D., Wendelinusstr. 74, 66663 Merzig.
T. (06861) 88196. *054123*

Meschede (Nordrhein-Westfalen)

Kirschstein, H., Berge, 59872 Meschede.
T. (0291) 72 42. *054124*
Peters, Doris, Im schwarzen Bruch 7, 59872 Meschede.
T. (0291) 19 00. - Furn - *054125*

Mettmann (Nordrhein-Westfalen)

Biesenbruch, W., Bahnstr. 37, 40822 Mettmann.
T. (02104) 22857. *054126*
English Antiques, Mittelstr. 20, 40822 Mettmann.
T. (02104) 224 90. - Ant / Furn / Jew / Silv / Instr /
Glass / Cur - *054127*
Zanders, R., Breitestr. 10, 40822 Mettmann.
T. (02104) 225 26. *054128*

Metzingen (Baden-Württemberg)

Kienzlen, Adelheid, Kastanienweg 17, 72555 Metzingen.
T. (07123) 41796. - Toys - *054129*

Meudt (Rheinland-Pfalz)

Edition Tietze, Nachtigallenweg 10, 56414 Meudt.
T. (06435) 88 22. *054130*

Michelau (Bayern)

Würstlein, K.H., Am Nonnenbach 20, 96247 Michelau.
T. (09571) 243. *054131*

Michelstadt (Hessen)

Antiquitäten am Diebsturm, Häfnergasse 7, 64720 Mi-
chelstadt. T. (06061) 712 84. *054132*
Pfaff, G., Neutorstr. 1, 64720 Michelstadt.
T. (06061) 30 60. *054133*

Miesbach (Bayern)

Burger, Ilona, Tölzer Str. 28, 83714 Miesbach.
T. (08025) 15 89. - Jew / Silv - *054134*
Moser, Eberhard, Stadtpl. 10, 83714 Miesbach.
T. (08025) 3967, Fax 5468. - Ant / Furn / Dec /
Paint - *054135*
Schwab, Eckhard, Waldecker Höhe 6, 83714 Miesbach.
T. (08025) 3967, Fax 5468. - Ant / Furn / Dec /
Paint - *054136*

Mindelheim (Bayern)

Bednorz, M., Memmingerstr. 6, 87719 Mindelheim.
T. (08261) 95 59. *054137*
Kleele, M., Traminerstr. 1, 87719 Mindelheim. *054138*

Minden, Westfalen (Nordrhein-Westfalen)

Diesenberg, Wilfried, Königstr 26, 32423 Minden, West-
falen. T. (0571) 20514. *054139*
Jettmann, Carl, Obermarktstr 17, 32423 Minden, West-
falen. T. (0571) 26379. *054140*
Klaffki, J., Königstr 40a, 32423 Minden,
Westfalen. *054141*
Lübking, Dorothea, Königstr 247, 32427 Minden, West-
falen. T. (0571) 28826. *054142*
Möller-von Stiften, Vinckestr 5, 32423 Minden, Westfa-
len. T. (0571) 22150. - Ant - *054143*
Schönbeck, Todtenhauser Str 77, 32425 Minden, West-
falen. T. (0571) 47310. *054144*
Schulz, R., Ziethenstr. 6, 32425 Minden, Westfalen.
T. (0571) 45569. - Furn / China / Instr / Glass - *054145*
Theiß, H., Schwerinstr 7, 32425 Minden, Westfalen.
T. (0571) 48360. *054146*

Mittelbiberach (Baden-Württemberg)

Moser, Paul, Waldhoferstr. 17, 88441 Mittelbiberach.
T. (07351) 716 73. - Num - *054147*

Mittelneufnach (Bayern)

Güttner, B., 86868 Mittelneufnach.
T. (08262) 15 37. *054148*

Mitterteich (Bayern)

Leibold, M., Vorstadt 36, 95666 Mitterteich.
T. (09633) 22 20. *054149*

Möglingen (Baden-Württemberg)

Frank, Kurt, Neuffenstr. 12, 71696 Möglingen.
- Num - *054150*

Möhnesee (Nordrhein-Westfalen)

Bartke, H., Günnerstr., 59519 Möhnesee.
T. (02924) 387. *054151*

Mölln (Schleswig-Holstein)

Petersen, Am Markt 1, 23879 Mölln. T. (04542) 1470,
Fax (04542) 7126. - Ant - *054152*

Mönchengladbach (Nordrhein-Westfalen)

Busch, Rainer, Bismarckstr. 108, 41061 Mönchenglad-
bach. T. (02161) 12105, Fax (02161) 12746. - Ant /
Paint / Furn / Dec / Silv - *054153*
Carat, Kleiststr. 10, 41061 Mönchengladbach.
T. (02161) 18 15 35. - Ant / Paint / Graph / Furn / China /
Sculp / Fra / Silv / Glass / Mod / Mul / Draw - *054154*
Cohnen, Carl, Hindenburgstr. 160, 41061 Mönchenglad-
bach. T. (02161) 156 55. - Ant / Paint / Furn /
Sculp - *054155*
Deußen, Heinrich, Gasstr. 17, 41236 Mönchengladbach.
T. (02161) 421 37. *054156*
Dreyer, H., Oberheydener Str. 76, 41061 Mönchenglad-
bach. T. (02161) 41945. *054157*
Evans, D., Düsseldorfer Str. 52, 41238 Mönchenglad-
bach. T. (02161) 155 00. *054158*
Grandt, E. & R. Rieger, Wallstr. 19, 41061 Mönchenglad-
bach. T. (02161) 23703. *054159*
Heil, Karl, Kaiserstr. 3, 41061 Mönchengladbach.
T. (02161) 234 94. - Ant / Paint / Graph - *054160*
Krichel, Josef, Bettrather Str. 76, 41061 Mönchenglad-
bach. T. (02161) 227 75. - Paint / Graph / Repr / Sculp /
Fra / Rel / Glass - *054161*
Küppers, J.M., Friedrichstr. 4, 41061 Mönchengladbach.
T. (02161) 151 40. - Ant / Paint / Furn / China / Sculp /
Jew / Rel / Glass / Mod / Ico / Tin / Toys - *054162*
Kunstkammer, Albertusstr. 4, 41061 Mönchengladbach.
T. (02161) 124 30. - Ant / Paint / Graph / China /
Glass - *054163*
Leuchten, E., Eickener Str. 81, 41061 Mönchenglad-
bach. T. (02161) 152 18. - Paint / Graph / Fra - *054164*
Lodes, N., Friedrich-Ebert-Str. 251, 41236 Mönchen-
gladbach. T. (02161) 218 08. *054165*
Maaßen, W., Neusser Str. 13, 41065 Mönchengladbach.
T. (02161) 60 55 97. *054166*
Pilgrim, Gustav, Markt 6, 41236
Mönchengladbach. *054167*
Rüttgers, M., Gasstr. 114, 41236 Mönchengladbach.
T. (02161) 40811. *054168*
Sanders, J., Alsstr. 18, 41063 Mönchengladbach.
T. (02161) 146 09. *054169*
Sönnert, Günther, Wetschewell 77, 41199 Mönchen-
gladbach. - Ant - *054170*
Thönnessen, Marinus, Hindenburgstr. 35, 41061 Mön-
chengladbach. T. (02161) 211 14. - Ant - *054171*
Tietz, Agnes, Regentenstr. 84, 41061 Mönchengladbach.
T. (02161) 129 97. *054172*
Vischer, Erwin, Bismarckstr. 59, 41061
Mönchengladbach. *054173*
Wagner, U., Hohenzollernstr. 58, 41061 Mönchenglad-
bach. T. (02161) 20 03 80. *054174*
Waude, Lockhütter Str. 177, 41066 Mönchengladbach.
T. (02161) 66 29 29. *054175*
Wolf, Marlene, Volksbadstr. 85, 41065 Mönchengladbach.
T. (02161) 39 14 33. *054176*

Mönsheim (Baden-Württemberg)

mobilart, Leonberger Str 21, 71297 Mönsheim.
T. (07044) 5760. - Ant - *054177*

Mörfelden-Walldorf (Hessen)

Hornivius, Sabina, Jousdanallee 16, 64546 Mörfelden-
Walldorf. *054178*

Mörnsheim (Bayern)

Huber, Rudger, Plattenberg 11, 91804 Mörnsheim.
T. (09145) 63 00. *054179*

Moers (Nordrhein-Westfalen)

Breitung, G., Friedrichstr. 1, 47441 Moers.
T. (02841) 26102. *054180*
Burk, R., Haagstr. 61, 47441 Moers.
T. (02841) 27725. *054181*
Hennen, B., Weygoldstr. 4, 47441 Moers.
T. (02841) 235 28. *054182*
IC Antiquitäten, Steinstr. 19, 47441 Moers.
T. (02841) 234 40. *054183*
Kramps-Klenke, Neustr. 10, 47441 Moers.
T. (02841) 21854. *054184*
Meyer, M., Dorfstr. 39, 47447 Moers.
T. (02841) 30377. *054185*
Schmitz, L., Neustr. 34, 47441 Moers.
T. (02841) 236 27. *054186*

Mössingen (Baden-Württemberg)

Ebner, Werner, Pappelstr. 37, 72116 Mössingen. *054187*

Mözen (Schleswig-Holstein)

Köhler, Margrit, Wiesengrund 22, 23795 Mözen.
T. (04551) 34 46. - Ant / Furn - *054188*

Molbergen (Niedersachsen)

Thomas, L., Ginsterstr. 8, 49696 Molbergen.
T. (04475) 13 44. *054189*

Monschau (Nordrhein-Westfalen)

Bongartz, D., Laufenstr. 58, 52156 Monschau.
T. (02472) 34 07. *054190*
Schumacher, Hermann, Laufenstr. 30-32, 52156 Mon-
schau. T. (02472) 23 19. - Ant / Furn / Lights - *054191*

Moormerland (Niedersachsen)

Gräfe, Westerwieke 128, 26802 Moormerland.
T. (04954) 4321. - Furn - *054192*

Morsum (Niedersachsen)

Proll, K., Beppener Str. 27, 27321 Morsum.
T. (04204) 1245. *054193*

Mosbach, Baden (Baden-Württemberg)

Trub, Paul, Kesslergasse 9, 74821 Mosbach,
Baden. *054194*

Much (Nordrhein-Westfalen)

Habernickel & Mahlberg, Oberdreisbach 6, 53804 Much.
T. (02245) 3818. - Ant - *054195*

Mühldorf (Bayern)

Fluhrer, Ernst P., Stadtpl. 77, 84453 Mühldorf.
T. (08631) 80 10. - Ant / Num - *054196*

Mülheim an der Ruhr (Nordrhein-West-falen)

Brechlin, Karsten, Kölner Str 387, 45481 Mülheim an
der Ruhr. T. (0208) 480451. *054197*
Dalwig-Nolda, Ulrike von, Kohlenkamp 2, 45468 Mül-
heim an der Ruhr. T. (0208) 36463. *054198*
Hartmann, Rudolf, Kettwiger Str 16, 45468 Mülheim an
der Ruhr. T. (0208) 36799. *054199*
Kunst-Kabinett, Bleichstr 16, 45468 Mülheim an der
Ruhr. T. (0208) 31806. - Paint / Graph / Orient / Sculp /
Eth - *054200*
Maar, Fr., Mendener Str 61, 45470 Mülheim an der Ruhr.
T. (0208) 34101. *054201*
Mensing, J., Rhein-Ruhr-Zentrum, 45468 Mülheim an
der Ruhr. T. (0208) 497797. *054202*
Pape, Marlene, Friedrichstr 26, 45468 Mülheim an der
Ruhr. T. (0208) 383933. - Furn - *054203*
Peichert, Uwe, Ruhrorter Str 6, 45478 Mülheim an der
Ruhr. T. (0208) 55212. - Glass / Mod - *054204*
Rotermund, C., Delle 45, 45468 Mülheim an der Ruhr.
T. (0208) 381616. *054205*
Schmellekamp, R., Wöllenbeck 11, 45470 Mülheim an
der Ruhr. T. (0208) 372363. *054206*
Schwutke, A., Duisburger Str 105, 45479 Mülheim an
der Ruhr. T. (0208) 427092, 54851. *054207*

Sluma, B., Düsseldorfer Str 144, 45481 Mülheim an der
Ruhr. T. (0208) 483837. - Furn / China / Repr / Jew /
Silv / Lights / Glass / Mod - *054208*
Steinen, M., Mausegattstr 69, 45472 Mülheim an der
Ruhr. T. (0208) 57785. *054209*
Stirnberg, G., Langenfeldstr 69, 45481 Mülheim an der
Ruhr. T. (0208) 489627. *054210*
Sund, M., Hingbergstr 130, 45470 Mülheim an der Ruhr.
T. (0208) 33061. *054211*
Terjung, H., Kesselbruchweg 93, 45478 Mülheim an der
Ruhr. T. (0208) 51707. *054212*
Vehreschild, Friedrich, Hochfelder Str 46, 45478 Mül-
heim an der Ruhr. T. (0208) 590502. *054213*

Müllheim (Baden-Württemberg)

Erhardt, H., Badstr. 6, 79379 Müllheim.
T. (07631) 57 44. *054214*
Steck, Helene, Hebelstr. 11, 79379 Müllheim. *054215*

Münchberg (Bayern)

Schloßbauer, V. & R., Burgstr. 62, 95213 Münchberg.
T. (09251) 803 20. *054216*

München (Bayern)

AHM Antiquitäten & Kunsthandel, Wörthstr. 3, 81667
München. T. (089) 448 36 68. *054219*
Ahrend & Wagner A.-M., E. Helga, Prannerstr. 4, 80333
München. T. (089) 22859681. - Ant / Jew - *054220*
Aigner, Kurt F., Türkenstr. 96, 80799 München.
T. (089) 28 33 50. - Paint / Furn / Jew / Silv - *054221*
Akanthus, Bismarckstr 6, 80803 München.
T. (089) 331431, Fax (089) 342095. *054222*
Alte Bäuerliche Kunst, Amalienstr. 21, 80333 München.
T. (089) 28 45 37. - Ant / Furn - *054223*
Amabile Kunst & Mode, Forstenrieder Allee 63, 81476
München. T. (089) 759 39 69. - China / Tex / Silv /
Glass - *054224*
Andrews, L., Isabellastr. 13, 80798 München.
T. (089) 271 48 57. *054225*
Andriot, B., Milchstr. 10, 81667 München.
T. (089) 448 77 38. *054226*
Anter, Theresienstr. 63, 80333 München.
T. (089) 52 98 56. *054227*
Antic-Puppen, Nymphenburger Str. 78, 80636 München.
T. (089) 18 27 93. - Ant / Cur - *054228*
Antiqua Merlin, Viktoriastr. 7, 80803 München.
T. (089) 339043. - Ant - *054229*
Antiquitäten Alte und Neue Kunst, Hochbrückenstr. 14,
80331 München. T. (089) 22 23 94. - Ant / Paint / Chi-
na / Glass - *054230*
Antiquitäten am Kosttor, Falkenturmstr. 14, 80331 Mün-
chen. T. (089) 22 41 31. - Ant / Furn / Sculp / Tex /
Silv *054231*
Antiquitäten am Wiener Platz, Wiener Platz 2, 81667
München. T. (089) 48 81 88. - Ant / Paint / Graph /
Furn / China / Jew / Silv / Glass / Cur / Mod - *054232*
Antiquitäten 66, Theresienstr. 66, 80333 München.
T. (089) 280 07 75. - Ant / Furn - *054233*
Apel, Günter, Karlstr. 42a, 80333 München.
T. (089) 55 49 56. - Paint / Draw - *054234*
Arco-Zinneberg, Maximilian Graf, Brienner Str 10,
80333 München. T. (089) 284080. *054235*
Arens, L., Amalienstr 33, 80799 München.
T. (089) 2802176. *054236*
Arpos, Paganinistr. 47, 81247 München.
T. (089) 811 90 13. - Ant - *054237*
Ars-Antik, Hohenzollernstr. 95, 80796 München.
T. (089) 271 61 36. - Ant - *054238*
ars mundi collection, Maximiliansplatz 12b, 80331 Mün-
chen. T. (089) 226440. - Orient / China / Repr / Sculp /
Jew / Silv / Instr / Ico - *054239*
Art, Lucile-Grahn-Str. 36a, 81675 München.
T. (089) 470 60 06. - Ant - *054240*
Art Appeal, Kurfürstenstr. 4, 80799 München.
T. (089) 33 35 73. - Lights / Mod - *054241*
Art Deco, Georgenstr. 68, 80799 München.
T. (089) 271 26 13, 271 74 41. - Furn / China / Lights /
Glass / Mod - *054242*
Artaria, Schellingstr. 33, 80799 München.
T. (089) 280 94 52. *054243*
Arte Andino, Promenadeplatz 12, 80333 München.
T. (089) 225089, Fax (089) 225089. - Repr / Tex / Eth /
Jew - *054244*

Artemis, Maximianspl 15, 80331 München.
T. (089) 295581. *054245*
Atelier Janine, Elisabethstr. 28, 80796 München.
T. (089) 271 82 00. *054246*
Athena Galerie, Ottostr 5, 80333 München.
T. (089) 591147, Fax 598220. - Num / Arch - *054247*
Aufhäuser, H., Löwengrube 12, 80333 München.
T. (089) 23932711, Fax (089) 23932879.
- Num - *054248*
Bachmaier, P., Frauenhoferstr. 9, 80331 München.
T. (089) 26 45 91. *054249*
Baier, T., Ainmillerstr 22, 80801 München.
T. (089) 390462. *054250*
Baindl, Altostr 10, 81245 München.
T. (089) 8633231. *054251*
Ballack, F.H.H., Bismarckstr 6, 80803 München.
T. (089) 335138, Fax 342095. - Ant / Furn / Tex /
Dec - *054252*
Balzer, Hermann, Kapuzinerpl. 1, 80331 München.
T. (089) 77 67 72. - Ant - *054253*
Bary, Evret von, Königinstr. 37, 80539 München.
T. (089) 28 53 01. - Ant - *054254*
Bauer-Magg, Postfach 340142, 80098 München.
T. (089) 28 13 89. - Furn / China / Tex / Jew / Silv / Instr /
Glass - *054255*
Baur, C.M., Prannerstr 5, 80333 München.
T. (089) 223251. *054256*
Bear Gallery, The, Gabelsbergerstr. 7, 80333 München.
T. (089) 280 03 33, Fax (089) 641 31 18. - Ant / Furn /
Fra / Silv - *054257*
Bednarek, S., Arcisstr. 61, 80801 München.
T. (089) 271 38 29. *054258*
Beer, Franz X., Schraudolphstr. 26, 80799 München.
T. (089) 278 00 89. - Furn - *054259*
Bellinger, Katrin, Rauchstr. 2, 81679 München.
T. (089) 98 34 65, Fax (089) 981 02 53. - Draw - *054260*

**Katrin Bellinger
Kunsthandel**

Meisterzeichnungen
Master Drawings
1500–1900

Rauchstraße 2
D-81679 München
Tel.: 0 89 / 98 34 65
Fax: 0 89 / 9 81 02 53

Besuch nach Vereinbarung
By appointment only

Berendes, Lüder, Innere Wiener Str 24, 81667 München.
T. (089) 482512. *054261*
Berghammer, Peter, Alb.-Roßhaupter-Str. 11, 81369
München. T. (089) 78 23 37, 769 14 82. - Ant - *054262*
Bernheimer, Promenadepl 13, 80333 München.
T. (089) 226672, Fax 226037. - Ant / Paint / Furn /
Orient / China / Tex / Dec / Lights - *054263*
Betz, D., Clemensstr. 9, 80803 München.
T. (089) 340 11 28. *054264*
Beyer, Harry, Salvatorstr. 8, 80333 München.
T. (089) 29 36 64. - Ant / Paint / Jew - *054265*
Biedermeierhaus, Preysingstr 4, 81667 München.
T. (089) 4470523. *054266*
Biehler, M., Georgenstr. 28, 80799 München.
T. (089) 33 72 62. *054267*
Bierhaus, H., Gabelsbergerstr 52, 80333 München.
T. (089) 528734. *054268*
Biermann, K.H., Karlstr. 60, 80333 München.
T. (089) 59 48 98. *054269*
Bierstorfer, R., Residenzstr. 25, 80333 München.
T. (089) 22 95 18. - Ant - *054270*
Bissinger, George C., Klenzestr. 12, 80469 München.
T. (089) 22 35 67. - Instr - *054271*
Blechschmidt, Richard, Amalienstr. 24, 80333 München.
T. (089) 28 47 57. - Ant - *054272*

Blumenfeld, E., Neuhauser Str. 24, 80331 München.
T. (089) 260 36 49.   054273
Bodendiek, K., Herzogstr. 89, 80796 München.
T. (089) 301501.   054274
Böhler, Julius, Briennerstr 10, 80333 München.
T. (089) 281165, Fax (089) 280636. - Ant / Paint /
Sculp / Draw -   054275
Bohm, H.J., Grillparzerstr. 35, 81675 München.
T. (089) 47 64 96, Fax (089) 4705347. - Ant -   054276
Bohm, S., Prannerstr 5, 80333 München.
T. (089) 220735.   054277
Bohnhoff & Pluntke, Adalbertstr. 54, 80799 München.
T. (089) 271 75 62.   054278
Bordihn, G., Burgstr. 8, 80331 München.
T. (089) 298340. - Num -   054279
Born, Herbert, Gabelsbergerstr. 32, 80333 München.
T. (089) 52 98 94. - Ant / Furn / Dec / Lights -   054280
Borsoe, K., Herzog-Heinrich-Str. 15, 80336 München.
T. (089) 53 72 22.   054281
Boysen, Ileana, Frauenstr 12, 80469 München.
T. (089) 292798. - Glass / Mod -   054282
Bracciali, Carlo, Landsberger Str 61, 80339 München.
T. (089) 50 90 26.   054283
Breede, Residenzstr. 11, 80333 München.
T. (089) 228 56 38, Fax (089) 228 56 39.
- Jew -   054284
Brigantine 1900, Türkenstr. 40, 80799 München.
T. (089) 28 48 16. - Ant / Furn / Mod -   054285
Brill, E., Herzogstr. 12, 80803 München.
T. (089) 34 64 32.   054286
Brum, Türkenstr. 96, 80799 München.
T. (089) 280 00 05.   054287
Brunsch, J., Theresienstr. 19, 80333 München.
T. (089) 28 28 29. - Ant / China / Mil / Glass -   054288
Burgemeister, K., Senftlstr. 1, 81541 München.   054289
Busch, J., Cosimastr. 123, 81925 München.
T. (089) 95 62 91.   054290
Butschal, Leo, Schützenstr. 1, 80335 München.
T. (089) 597492, Fax (089) 5501751. - Jew -   054291
Buttermilch & Kaspar, Metzstr. 28, 81667 München.
T. (089) 448 83 77.   054292
Cada, Maximilianstr 13, 80539 München.
T. (089) 296014. - Ant / China / Jew / Silv -   054293
Captain's Saloon, Westenriederstr. 20, 80331 München.
T. (089) 22 10 15. - Instr -   054294
Caspari, S., Lindwurmstr. 207, 80337 München.
T. (089) 77 76 74.   054295
Century Box, Steinstr. 73, 81667 München.
T. (089) 48 16 62, Fax (089) 50 40 85. - Dec / Cur /
Mod -   054296
China-Laden, Reichenbachstr. 15, 80469 München.
T. (089) 26 82 34. - Orient / China / Jew -   054297
City-Mint, Bahnhofspl 2, 80335 München.
T. (089) 593731, Fax (089) 594262. - Num -   054298
Color, Westenriederstr. 20, 80331 München.
T. (089) 228 38 22. - Mil -   054299
Czarny, V., Perhamerstr. 9, 80687 München.
T. (089) 580 64 00.   054300
Daxer & Marschall, Wittelsbacher Pl 6, 80333 München.
T. (089) 280640, Fax 281757. - Ant / Paint / Furn /
Sculp / Instr / Draw -   054301

DAXER & MARSCHALL

Möbel, Gemälde, Zeichnungen und Skulpturen
des 18. und frühen 19. Jahrhunderts

Wittelsbacher Pl. 6
Eingang Briennerstraße
D-80333 München
Telefon (0 89) 28 06 40 und
Fax (0 89) 28 17 57

Degens, Jan, Hermann-Schmidt-Str. 4, 80331 München.
- Ant -   054302
Deschler, Maximilian, Wirtstr 9, 81539 München.
T. (089) 6923675. - Paint / Graph -   054303
Deubl & Söhne, Türkenstr. 29, 80799 München.
T. (089) 28 72 18. - Fra / Glass -   054304
Diller, Johannes, Ohlstadter Str 21, 81373 München.
T. (089) 7603550.   054305

Bernheimer
seit 1864

München – London
Altmeistergemälde
Chinesische Porzellane
Möbel 18. Jahrhundert

Promenadeplatz 13
80333 München
Tel: 089-22 66 72
Fax: 089-22 60 37

By appointment only
1 Mount Street, London W1Y 5AA
Tel: 0044-171-495 7028
Fax: 0044-171-495 7027

DOSAS, Thomas-Dehler-Str. 12, 81737 München.
T. (089) 670 79 71.   054306
Drindl, H., Corneliusstr. 12, 80469 München.
T. (089) 26 64 79. - Ant / Furn -   054307
Eder, Prannerstr. 4, 80333 München. T. (089) 22 03 05,
Fax (089) 22 63 41. - Instr -   054308
Eder, H. A., Elfenstr. 17, 81739 München.
T. (089) 60 22 92.   054309
Ehmer, Erich, Südliche Auffahrtsallee 77, 80639 Mün-
chen. T. (089) 178 11 30. - Fra -   054310
Ehrhardt, Konrad, Kreittmayrstr. 32, 80335 München.
T. (089) 129 64 15. - Ant / Paint / Sculp / Rel -   054311
Einrichtung, Die, Brienner Str. 12, 80333 München.
T. (089) 230 90.   054312
Emery, R., Preysingstr. 52, 81667 München.
T. (089) 448 67 71.   054313
Engel, Adolf von, Ottostr. 6, 80333 München.
T. (089) 59 66 06.   054314
Engelbrecht, A., Kaulbachstr. 77, 80802 München.
T. (089) 397576, 348800, Fax (089) 332707. - Ant /
Paint / Furn -   054315
England Antiques, Hochbrückenstr. 10, 80331 München.
T. (089) 227867, Fax (089) 2289374. - Ant / Furn /
Repr / Dec / Silv / Cur / Mod -   054316
English Arts & Antiques, Ungererstr. 80, 80805 Mün-
chen. T. (089) 361 65 23. - Furn -   054317
Enthammer, Sollner Str. 29, 81479 München.
T. (089) 791 31 26. - Furn -   054318
Erdmann, K., Theresienstr. 77, 80333 München.
T. (089) 52 40 99.   054319
Ertürk, E., Steinsdorfstr. 21, 80538 München.
T. (089) 29 52 59. - Tex -   054320
Ettl, German, Thierschstr. 1, 80538 München.
T. (089) 22 32 49. - Num -   054321
Fassnacht, Emeran, Josephspitalstr. 15, 80331 Mün-
chen. T. (089) 592336, 605708. - Ant / Paint /
Fra -   054322
Feine, Willimar A., Stockmannstr. 47, 81477 München.
- China -   054323
Fenk, P., Am Kosttor 2, 80331 München.
T. (089) 29 98 67.   054324
Fink, Peter, Gabelsbergerstr 7, 80333 München.
T. (089) 285122.   054325
Finke, R. & F., Herterichstr. 51, 81479 München.
T. (089) 791 88 73.   054326
Fischer, Wilhelm Thomas, Maximilianstr 31, 80539
München. T. (089) 222787. - Ant / Sculp / Silv /
Rel -   054327
Fleischmann, Elisabethstr. 23, 80796 München.
T. (089) 2717100, Fax (089) 2800144. - Paint / Graph /
Draw -   054328
Foraum Bereiteranger, Bereiteranger 15, 81541 Mün-
chen. T. (089) 655413, Fax (089) 656997.   054329
Forchhammer, Lenbachplatz 7, 80333 München.
T. (089) 29 39 44. - Paint / Furn -   054330
Frank, R., Schellingstr. 130, 80797 München.
T. (089) 1292393.   054331
Frank, Zangl & Co., Türkenstr. 48, 80799 München.
T. (089) 283267, Fax (089) 288207. - Ant / Paint / Furn /
China / Sculp / Fra / Lights / Glass / Cur / Mod -   054332

Frantz, W. & R., Erhardtstr. 5, 80469 München.
T. (089) 201 03 17.   054333
Fresen, Dr., Ottostr. 13, 80333 München.
T. (089) 592170.   054334
Frisch, D., Landsberger Str. 8, 80339 München.
T. (089) 50 66 81.   054335
Frisch, Gertrud, Westenriederstr. 19, 80331 München.
T. (089) 22 91 54. - Ant / Furn / China / Instr / Glass /
Ico -   054336
Frowein, Dagmar, Scheinerstr. 7, 81679 München.
T. (089) 98 35 56. - Paint / Silv -   054337
Fuchs, Willy, Westenriederstr. 17, 80331 München.
T. (089) 22 08 39. - Ant -   054338
Füchter, S., Harthauser Str. 17, 81545 München.
T. (089) 692 65 16.   054339
Führer, W.T., Falkenturmstr. 8, 80331 München.
T. (089) 220056, Fax (089) 297864. - Ant /
Dec -   054340
Galerie Acade, Prannerstr. 5, 80333 München.
T. (089) 22 41 26. - Ant -   054341
Galerie am Haus der Kunst, Franz-Josef-Strauß-Ring 4,
80539 München. T. (089) 222315, Fax (089) 2800044.
- Orient -   054342
Galerie Arcis, Flemingstr. 47, 81925 München.
T. (089) 98 44 33, Fax (089) 98 06 00. - Paint / Glass /
Mod -   054343
Galerie Glas + Handwerk, Türkenstr. 29, 80799 Mün-
chen. T. (089) 28 79 34.   054344
Galerie in der Fürstenstrasse, Theresienstr. 19, 80333
München. T. (089) 2809797, Fax (089) 2809797.
- Mod -   054345
Galerie Johanna, Planeggerstr. 33, 81241 München.
T. (089) 834 61 72. - Ant / Paint / Furn / Orient / China /
Tex / Jew / Lights / Instr / Glass -   054346
Gemini, Herrnstr. 13, 80539 München. T. (089) 22 40 46,
Fax (089) 28 37 17. - Orient -   054347
Gensmantel-Keck, Margot, Westenriederstr. 8, 80331
München. T. (089) 29 22 93. - Furn -   054348
Giessener Münzhandlung, Maximilianspl 20, 80333
München. T. (089) 226876, Fax 2285513.
- Num -   054349

ANKAUF
VERKAUF
BERATUNG
SCHÄTZUNG
AUKTIONEN

GIESSENER
MÜNZHANDLUNG
Dieter Gorny GmbH
80333 München
Maximiliansplatz 20

Tel.: 0 89 – 22 68 76
Fax: 0 89 – 2 28 55 13

Gitbud, Leo, Dr., Residenzstr. 11, 80333 München.
T. (089) 22 41 85. - Num -   054350
Glogger, B., Beltweg 20, 80805 München.
T. (089) 361 25 74.   054351
Göbl, A., Augustenstr. 14, 80333 München.
T. (089) 59 49 95.   054352

Goering Institut e.V., Giselastr 7, 80802 München.
T. (089) 3839500, Fax 396781. *054353*

Götzenbrugger-Zwigart, Wörthstr. 13, 81667 München.
T. (089) 140 72 98, 448 83 97. *054354*

Gold + Silver Market, Türkenstr. 63, 80799 München.
T. (089) 28 88 07. *054355*

Gräf, Friedrich, Chamissostr 12, 81925 München.
T. (089) 982009. - Ant - *054356*

Graf, R., Reichenbachstr. 16, 80469 München.
T. (089) 26 63 40. *054357*

Grassani, P., Friedenheimer Str. 33, 80686 München.
T. (089) 57 81 35. - Num - *054358*

Griffel, M., Oefelestr. 9, 81543 München.
T. (089) 66 48 08. *054359*

Gripekoven & Söhne, Residenzstr. 27,, 80333 München.
T. (089) 29 50 92, 291 32 45, Fax (089) 228 30 18.
- Tex / Dec - *054360*

Grolitsch, G., Hippmannstr. 5, 80639 München.
T. (089) 178 41 79. *054361*

Gromotka, P., Theresienstr. 19, 80333 München.
T. (089) 280 97 97. - Ant - *054362*

Gronert, Schäfflerstr. 18, 80333 München.
T. (089) 22 61 70. - Ant - *054363*

Grünwald, Michael D., Dr., Römerstr. 26, 80803 München. T. (089) 34 75 62, Fax (089) 34 83 91. - Paint /
Sculp / Draw - *054364*

Grundner, Heinz, Habermannstr 12, 80638 München.
T. (089) 176368. - Furn / Instr - *054365*

Haas, P., Hans-Sachs-Str. 3, 80469 München.
T. (089) 260 99 39. *054366*

Haberzettl, Anna-Maria, Augustenstr. 16, 80333 München. T. (089) 59 10 27, 271 61 40. *054367*

Härtel, M., Wasserburger Landstr. 186, 81827 München.
T. (089) 4303117. *054368*

Häusler-Halrid, Inge, Hohenlohestr. 27, 80637 München.
T. (089) 15 57 20. *054369*

Haller-Nemelka, D., Prinzregentenstr. 108, 81677 München. T. (089) 470 48 90. *054370*

Hammer, Klaus, Augustenstr. 2, 80333 München.
T. (089) 59 81 34. - Num - *054371*

Hartl, Georg L., Ludwigstr. 11, 80539 München.
T. (089) 28 38 54. - Orient / China / Sculp / Eth - *054372*

Hartwig, H., Blutenburgstr. 112, 80636 München.
T. (089) 129 41 73. *054373*

Haunschild, Franz, Müllerstr. 22, 80469 München.
T. (089) 24 06 90. - Ant / Furn - *054374*

Hawari, Dreimühlenstr. 16, 80469 München.
T. (089) 76 46 69. - Furn - *054375*

Hecht, Herzogspitalstr. 7, 80331 München.
T. (089) 260 82 20. *054376*

Hedler, Dall Armistr 57, 80638 München.
T. (089) 170417. *054377*

Heigermoser, D., Friedenspromenade 27, 81827 München. T. (089) 42 17 13. *054378*

Heinrich, Theresienstr. 58, 80333 München.
T. (089) 28 23 06. - Ant - *054379*

Heise, T., Türkenstr. 82, 80799 München.
T. (089) 284877. *054380*

Heiss, Günther, Balanstr. 12, 81669 München.
T. (089) 48 59 14. *054381*

Heitmann, R., Dr., Schraudolphstr. 14a, 80799 München. T. (089) 272 23 22. - Ant - *054382*

Hemmerle, Gebr., Maximilianstr 14, 80539 München.
T. (089) 220189. - Jew - *054383*

Henkenjohann, Frauenstr 12, 80469 München.
T. (089) 222727. *054384*

Henrich, R., Theresienstr. 58, 80333 München.
T. (089) 28 23 06. - Ant / Paint / Furn / China / Tex / Dec /
Silv / Glass / Cur / Mod - *054385*

Henseler, Galeriestr. 2a, 80539 München.
T. (089) 22 11 76. - Eth - *054386*

Hermann, Sandstr 33, 80335 München.
T. (089) 5237296, Fax (089) 5237103. - Mil - *054387*

Hermann, A., Dachauer Str. 48, 80335 München.
T. (089) 59 50 84. *054388*

Hernitz, Lilo, Peter-Kreuder-Str. 1, 81245 München.
T. (089) 88 07 80. - Jew / Silv / Glass - *054389*

Herrmansdörfer, Benno, Kapuzinerpl. 2, 80331 München. T. (089) 76 63 29. - Ant / Paint / Furn /
Sculp - *054390*

Herzer, Heinz, Maximilianstr 43, 80538 München.
T. (089) 297729, Fax (089) 297730. - Arch - *054391*

Heubel, L., Westenriederstr. 8, 80331 München.
T. (089) 221876. *054392*

Hiebl, Hans, Am Glockenbach 11, 80469 München.
T. (089) 26 59 82. *054393*

Hirsch, Gerhard, Promenadepl 10, 80333 München.
T. (089) 292150, Fax 2283675. - Num - *054394*

MÜNZENHANDLUNG
Gerhard Hirsch
Nachfolger
PROMENADEPLATZ 10
83333 MÜNCHEN
TELEFON (0 89) 29 21 50
TELEFAX (0 89) 2 28 36 75
Jährlich mehrere Auktionen
MÜNZEN - MEDAILLEN -
NUMISMATISCHE LITERATUR -
ANTIKE KLEINKUNST
ANKAUF - VERKAUF -
KUNDENBETREUUNG
Kataloge durch den Auktionator

Hirsch, Krischan, Ismaninger Str. 91, 81675 München.
T. (089) 98 30 42. - China / Silv / Glass - *054395*

Hoch, A., Schwanthalerstr 86, 80336 München.
T. (089) 532533. *054396*

Höllersberger, M., Graubündener Str. 39, 81475 München. T. (089) 759 36 75. - Num - *054397*

Hofer, Josef, Ottostr. 6, 80333 München.
T. (089) 55 56 36. - China - *054398*

Hoffmann, Maximilian, Kurzhuberstr. 2, 81825 München.
T. (089) 42 93 59. *054399*

Hofmann, Kurzhuberstr 2, 81825 München.
T. (089) 429359. *054400*

Holfert, C., Angertorstr 1b, 80469 München.
T. (089) 263115. *054401*

Holzwurm-Galerie, Pestalozzistr. 34, 80469 München.
T. (089) 26 51 21. - Furn / Jew - *054402*

Hovis, Subal & Co., Neuturmstr. 1, 80331 München.
T. (089) 228 95 11, Fax 22 25 39. - Ant / Paint / Graph /
Furn / China / Sculp / Dec / Silv / Lights / Glass / Mod -- *054403*

Huber, Andreas, Residenzstr. 11, 80333 München.
T. (089) 29 82 78. - Ant / Instr - *054404*

Huber, I., Ottostr 13, 80333 München.
T. (089) 597541. *054405*

Huber-Oberholzner, Prannerstr. 4, 80333 München.
T. (089) 29 97 17. - Furn - *054406*

Hürland, R., Kreuzstr. 15, 80331 München.
T. (089) 26 72 01. - Ant / Jew / Lights / Mul - *054407*

Ikonengalerie, Theresienstr. 9, 80333 München.
T. (089) 28 46 47. - Ico - *054408*

Iliu, Julia F., Barerstr 46, 80799 München.
T. (089) 2800688. - Graph - *054409*

IMM Münz-Institut, Rindermarkt 7, 80331 München.
T. (089) 23110405. - Num - *054410*

Injuka, Martina Str. 15a, 80804 München.
T. (089) 36 43 25. *054411*

Irrgang, I., Stahlgruberring 13, 81829 München.
T. (089) 420 22 97. - Ant - *054412*

Jagemann, Carl, Residenzstr. 3, 80333 München.
T. (089) 22 54 93. - Jew / Instr - *054413*

Jaschinski, Detlef, Westenriederstr. 27, 80331 München. T. (089) 29 97 32. *054414*

Jordan, Stefan, Amalienstr. 14-16, 80333 München.
T. (089) 28 38 66. - Ant / Furn / Silv / Cur - *054415*

Jorde, Ursula, Theresienstr. 9, 80333 München.
T. (089) 28 15 95. - Ant / China / Jew / Silv / Glass /
Cur - *054416*

Joseph, Monika, Händelstr. 7, 81675 München.
T. (089) 98 77 85. - Ant / Furn / Dec / Lights / Glass /
Cur - *054417*

Jung, Ferdinand-Miller-Pl 12, 80335 München.
T. (089) 187669. *054418*

Kabinett Lerchenfeld, Herzog-Rudolf-Str 9, 80539 München. T. (089) 2283950. *054419*

Kagerer, U., Nymphenburger Str. 192, 80634 München.
T. (089) 123 40 00. *054420*

Kaiser, Antonie, Rindermarkt 1, 80331 München.
T. (089) 24 15 93. - Sculp / Rel - *054421*

Kaiser, Kurt, Nymphenburger Str. 115, 80636 München.
T. (089) 129 29 66, 129 74 75. - Ant - *054422*

Kamm, H., & B. Lindermayr, Sonnenstr. 9, 80331 München. T. (089) 555596. *054423*

Kammerl, A., Neusser Str 21, 80636 München.
T. (089) 36101028. *054424*

Kellnberger, Otto, Heiligegeiststr 8, 80331 München.
T. (089) 226479. - Ant - *054425*

Kempe, Frank, Galeriestr. 6a, 80539 München.
T. (089) 298626, Fax (089) 225879. - Paint / Graph /
Draw - *054426*

Ketterer, Wolfgang, Brienner Str 25, 80333 München.
T. (089) 552440, Fax (089) 55244166. *054427*

Khoshbakht, C., Viktoriastr 7, 80803 München.
T. (089) 339044. *054428*

Kiehl, Günter, Hörwarthstr. 51, 80804 München.
T. (089) 36 39 19. - Ant / Paint / Furn / China / Dec /
Lights - *054429*

KIFO, Kulturheimstr. 13, 80939 München.
T. (089) 325389, Fax 325389. - Orient - *054430*

King Kong, Baumstr 4e, 80469 München.
T. (089) 2021696. *054431*

Kirsch, H., Talstr. 59, 80331 München.
T. (089) 292907. *054432*

Kirschner, Ludwig, Leopoldstr. 76, 80802 München.
T. (089) 34 85 55. - Instr - *054433*

Kleindienst, A., Buttermelcherstr. 14, 80469 München.
T. (089) 201 65 24. *054434*

Kleinert, I., Westenriederstr. 20, 80331 München.
T. (089) 29 37 40. *054435*

Klingmann, Hermine A., Prößlstr. 8, 81545 München. *054436*

Kloiber, U., Pacellistr 5, 80333 München.
T. (089) 299255. *054437*

Klose, W., Pfarrstr. 16, 80538 München.
T. (089) 22 11 02. *054438*

Knobloch, Hans, Preysingstr 22, 81667 München.
T. (089) 488643. *054439*

Knotty-Lane, Winterstr. 4, 81543 München.
T. (089) 651 6791. - Ant / Furn - *054440*

Köck, Beichstr 5, 80802 München. T. (089) 337538,
Fax 337538. *054441*

Koeppen, Karin, Isabellastr. 12, 80798 München.
T. (089) 37 48 42. - Sculp / Jew / Silv / Glass /
Mod - *054442*

Kohut, Westendstr. 31, 80339 München.
T. (089) 50 56 28. *054443*

Kohut, Nymphenburger Str 115, 80636 München.
T. (089) 1292966. *054444*

Kolb, Am Haag 7, 80937 München. T. (089) 3164499.
- Ant - *054445*

Koller, H.C., Westenriederstr. 19, 80331 München.
T. (089) 29 68 62. *054446*

Konrad, A. & I., Gneisenaustr. 16, 80992 München.
T. (089) 149 66 44. *054447*

Kortländer, Karin, Kurfürstenstr. 7, 80799 München.
T. (089) 272 13 51. - Ant / Furn - *054448*

Krätzler, W.M., Isabellastr. 49, 80796 München.
T. (089) 271 27 38. *054449*

Krattenmacher, Theresienstr. 124, 80333 München.
T. (089) 52 29 82. - Ant - *054450*

Kraus, I., Sebastiansplatz 7, 80331 München.
T. (089) 26 31 54. *054451*

Kreß, E., Agnes-Bernauer-Str. 92, 80687 München.
T. (089) 58 28 69. *054452*

Krüger, W.A., Georgenstr. 123, 80797 München.
T. (089) 129 99 69. *054453*

Kube, Jan K., Thomas-Wimmer-Ring 17, 80539 München. T. (089) 29 66 59. *054454*

Kühnel, Am Eulenhorst 61, 81827 München.
T. (089) 4391919. *054455*

Kugler-Eder, A., Prinzregentenpl. 17, 80331 München.
T. (089) 474911. *054456*

Kujümzian, Dikran, Rosental 16, 80331 München.
T. (089) 24 06 58. - Ant / Paint / Num / Orient / Tex /
Jew / Mil - *054457*

Kunst im Tal, Talstr. 32, 80331 München.
T. (089) 292907. *054458*

Kunst-Oase, Hohenzollernstr. 58, 80801 München.
T. (089) 39 68 75. 054459
Kunst- und Antiquitätenhandelsgesellschaft, Amalienstr.
16, 80333 München. T. (089) 28 38 66. - Ant - 054460
Kunstring München, Briennerstr. 4, 80333 München.
T. (089) 28 15 32, 28 24 85. - China - 054461
Kunstsammlung Tumulka GmbH, Grillparzerstr 46,
81675 München. T. (089) 45555522. 054462
Kunstzentrum Moosach, Pelkovenstr. 46, 80992 Mün-
chen. T. (089) 1494302, Fax 1412729. - Paint / Graph /
Sculp / Fra - 054463
Kurfner, Klenzestr 16, 80469 München.
T. (089) 267333. 054464
La Belle Epoque, Augustenstr. 41, 80333 München.
T. (089) 52 73 77. - Ant / Mod - 054465
Labiner, Oscar, Ferdinand-Miller-Platz 3, 80335 Mün-
chen. T. (089) 129 55 72. - China / Jew / Silv - 054466
Laimer Schlößl, Agnes-Bernauer-Str. 112, 80687 Mün-
chen. T. (089) 56 26 77. 054467
Landhausmöbel, Nymphenburger Str. 21-23, 80335
München. T. (089) 55 42 68. 054468
Langemann, M., Nusselstr. 49, 81245 München.
T. (089) 83 86 43. 054469
Lanz, Hubert, Dr., Maximiliansplatz 10, 80331 München.
T. (089) 2913086, Fax (089) 2913086. - Num - 054470
Laszlo, A., Gabelsbergerstr. 56, 80333 München.
T. (089) 52 87 52. 054471
Laue, J. G., Theresienstr. 33, 80333 München.
T. (089) 280 09 72. - Furn / Mil - 054472
Lechner, E., Ambacher Str. 8, 81476 München.
T. (089) 75 33 59. - China - 054473
Lechner, E., Ottostr. 13/V, 80333 München.
T. (089) 59 63 44. - China - 054474
Ledebur, Briennerstr. 5, 80333 München.
T. (089) 22 48 69. 054475
Loikoim, Androoo Rainor, Adolhoidotr. 18, 80798 Mün
chen. T. (089) 272 18 60. 054476
Lerch, Max, Ottostr. 1b, 80333 München.
T. (089) 59 37 67. 054477
Lettenbauer, Antonie, Voßstr. 1, 81543 München.
T. (089) 65 90 44. - Ant - 054478
Leuthenmayr, Albert, Hartmannstr. 2, 80333 München.
T. (089) 22 67 64. - Ant / Paint - 054479
Leuthenmayr, Karl, Agnes-Bernauer-Str. 112, 80687
München. T. (089) 56 49 81. - Ant - 054480
Lienhard, M., Lautensackstr. 13, 80687 München.
T. (089) 57 14 52. 054481
Limbacher, Konradstr 10, 80801 München.
T. (089) 3455350, Fax (089) 396732. 054482
Linckersdorff, C.E., Galeriestr. 2a., 80539 München.
T. (089) 22 20 56. - Ant / Jew / Instr - 054483
Lindner, Ulla, Elektrastr. 11, 81925 München.
T. (089) 91 16 59. - Arch - 054484
Linsmaier, Paul, Augustenstr. 56, Hinterhaus, 80333
München. T. (089) 52 27 37. - Ant - 054485
Lipah, Herbert, Nördliche Auffahrtsallee 63, 80638 Mün-
chen. T. (089) 17 75 23. 054486
Lips, Doris, Wiener Platz 8, 81667 München.
T. (089) 480 17 82. - Furn - 054487
Littomericzky, E., Vollmannstr. 57, 81925 München.
T. (089) 91 12 31. 054488
Ljubicic, R., Hohenwaldeckstr. 18, 81541 München.
T. (089) 692 95 92, Fax 692 38 65. - Furn - 054489
Löcherer, E., Rosenheimer Str. 94, 81669 München.
T. (089) 48 76 65. 054490
Löwe, Edmund, Amalienstr. 24, 80333 München.
T. (089) 28 17 09. - Ant - 054491
Lohner, Ursula, Hochbrückenstr. 3, 80331 München.
T. (089) 22 09 15. - Jew - 054492
Lomnasan, J., Hedwigstr. 12, 80636 München.
T. (089) 18 44 66. 054493
London House, Rotbuchenstr. 6, 81547 München.
T. (089) 690 93 93. - Furn - 054494
Lun, Münchener Freiheit 4, 80802 München.
T. (089) 344420. 054495
Lustinger, H., Schellingstr. 40, 80799 München.
T. (089) 272 09 87. 054496
Mages, Otto, Schüleinpl 10, 81673 München.
T. (089) 438802. 054496a
Mahler & Partner, Maximilianstr 21, 80539 München.
T. (089) 299595. - Paint - 054497
Maier, Reichenbachstr. 15, 80469 München.
T. (089) 260 53 72. - Ant - 054498

Mander, Lissy, Georgenstr. 22, 80799 München.
T. (089) 39 72 75. - Ant / Paint - 054499
Marouchian, Postfach 860408, 81631 München.
T. (089) 9577619, Fax 9295272. 054500
Marwitz, Eduard, Sindoldstr. 2, 80639 München.
- Jew - 054501
Maurer, W., Kurfürstenstr 17, 80801 München.
T. (089) 2711345. 054501a
Mayer, Franz, Seidlstr. 25, 80335 München.
T. (089) 59 54 84. - Rel / Glass - 054502
Mayer, Gunar, Karlstr. 45, 80333 München.
T. (089) 59 51 05. - Jew / Instr - 054503
Mayr, Rudolf, Max-Weber-Platz 2, 81675 München.
T. (089) 448 57 33. 054504
Mayr, W., Reichenbachstr. 26, 80469 München.
T. (089) 201 45 63. 054505
Mehl, O., & Co., Augustenstr. 45, 80333 München.
T. (089) 52 93 92. - Ant - 054506
Mehringer, S., Merzstr 12, 81679 München.
T. (089) 987431, Fax (089) 9827543. - Sculp - 054507
Meier, Gisela, Prannerstr 4, 80333 München.
T. (089) 226340, Fax 2289481. - Paint - 054508
Meißner, K.H., Pütrichstr. 4, 81667 München.
T. (089) 485997. 054509
Meletta, Eric, Wittelsbacherpl 1, 80333 München.
T. (089) 283239. - Ant - 054510
Menzel, Radlsteg 2, 80331 München.
T. (089) 29 14 64. 054511
Merkl, F., Franz-Josef-Str. 46, 80331 München.
T. (089) 34 91 50. 054512
Merkl, L., & Co., Dienerstr. 19, 80331 München. 054513
Merry Old England, Reichenbachstr. 16, 80469 Mün-
chen. T. (089) 59 44 43. 054514
Meusburger, Marlis, Georgenstr. 50, 80799 München.
T. (089) 271 09 69, Fax 54274. - Lights - 054515
MGM Antikschmuck, Stiglmaierpl. 2, 80333 München.
T. (089) 5233660, Fax 525393. 054516
Michael Peter, Leopoldstr 48, 80802 München.
T. (089) 3816270. 054517
Mikorey, Theresienstr. 51, 80333 München.
T. (089) 52 53 22. 054518
Mittenzwei, J., Dr., Fliegenstr. 12, 80337 München.
T. (089) 26 30 27. - Ant - 054519
Morvan, Alain, Salvatorstr. 2, 80333 München.
T. (089) 29 94 20. - Ant / Furn / China / Jew / Silv /
Glass / Cur - 054520
Mory, Ludwig, Marienpl. 8, 80331 München.
T. (089) 22 45 42. - Ant - 054521
Motschmann, Hans, Sollner Str. 30, 81479 München.
T. (089) 79 72 51. 054522
Mühlbauer, Florian, Türkenstr. 92, 80799 München.
T. (089) 280 96 94. 054523
Münchener Gobelin Manufaktur, Notburgastr. 5, 80639
München. T. (089) 17 03 61. - Tex - 054524
Münchner Antiquitätenmarkt, Fürstenstr. 8, 80333 Mün-
chen. T. (089) 28 14 47. 054525
Münzen und Antiken an der Oper, Residenzstr. 18,
80333 München. T. (089) 22 41 85. - Num /
Arch - 054526
Muggenthaler, M., Fraunhoferstr. 9, 80469 München.
T. (089) 26 45 91. 054527

Nägel-Jaspers, Michael, Josephspl. 5, 80331 München.
T. (089) 271 83 93, Fax 273 08 34. - Paint - 054528
Nehmann, Wilhelm, Rosenheimer Str. 46, 81669 Mün-
chen. T. (089) 486994. - Paint / Graph / Fra - 054529
Neidhardt, Brienner Str 11, 80333 München.
T. (089) 223510, 220619, Fax (089) 2913702. - Ant /
Paint / Furn / China / Sculp / Tex / Silv / Instr - 054530
Nein, G., Rosenheimer Str. 105, 81667 München.
T. (089) 4807472. 054531
Neuhausener Kleine Kunsthalle, Blutenburgstr. 45,
80636 München. T. (089) 123 10 42. - Ant - 054532
Neupert, Herold, Westenriederstr. 8, 80331 München.
T. (089) 29 60 87. 054533
Niederecker, Ursula, Kufotoinor Platz 5, 81670 Münohon.
T. (089) 98 18 00. - Furn - 054534
Niemann, H., Isabellastr. 6, 80798 München.
T. (089) 272 13 09. 054535
Nierhaus, Thessa, Arthur-Kutscher-Pl. 2, 80802 Mün-
chen. T. (089) 34 16 81, Fax 34 16 81. - Jew - 054536
Nietsch, S., Innere Wiener Str. 58, 81667 München.
T. (089) 480 21 42. - Ant - 054537
Nikolaus, H., Preysingstr. 15, 81667 München.
T. (089) 448 52 86. 054538
Nowak, Schillerstr. 7, 80336 München.
T. (089) 591660. 054539
Obermüller, A., Schloßstr. 5, 81675 München.
T. (089) 476384. 054540
Odesser, Roman, Westenrieder Str 16, 80331 München.
T. (089) 226388. 054541
Oeffner, H., Passauerstr. 35, 81369 München.
T. (089) 769 35 62. 054542
Oexmann, Knuth H., Franz-Josef-Strauß-Ring 4, 80539
München. T. (089) 22 19 67. - Furn - 054543
Offeney, B., Montgelasstr 6, 80639 München.
T. (089) 983687. 054544
Ohlendorff, I. von, Virchowstr. 18, 80805 München.
T. (089) 36 27 72. - Num - 054545
Oppenheimer, C., Humboldtstr. 13, 81543 München.
T. (089) 65 26 19. 054546
Orcutt, James, Schulstr. 34, 80634 München.
T. (089) 16 44 66. 054547
Orny, L. & H., Herzog-Heinrich-Str. 15, 80336 München.
T. (089) 532015. 054548
Ostasiatika, Fürstenstr. 10, 80333 München.
T. (089) 280 90 91, Fax 28 44 38. - Ant / Furn / Orient /
Sculp / Tex - 054549
Ostler, Thomas-Wimmer-Ring 3, 80539 München.
T. (089) 2289264, Fax 220377. - Paint / Sculp /
Tex - 054550
Otto, Sendlinger Str 45, 80331 München.
T. (089) 2608485. 054551
Otto-Galerie, Augustenstr 45, 80333 München.
T. (089) 529392, Fax (089) 1784033/34. - Paint / Furn /
Sculp / Silv - 054552
Otto, Rudolf, Schrammerstr 3, 80333 München.
T. (089) 223818. 054553
Pachinger, Grillparzerstr. 37, 81675 München.
T. (089) 470 24 29. - Ant - 054554
Penkert, Fürstenstr. 6, 80333 München.
T. (089) 28 12 71. - Ant / Furn - 054555

NORBERT POKUTTA

GEMÄLDE ALTER MEISTER

Chamissostraße 11 · 81925 München · Telefon 98 40 55 · Fax 9 82 73 14

· Besuche nach Vereinbarung ·

Persau, R., Anglerstr. 3, 80339 München.
T. (089) 502 60 73. 054556
Pescoller, Karlspl 5, 80335 München. T. (089) 553091.
- China - 054557
Peters, M., Neuturmstr 5, 80331 München.
T. (089) 2285860. 054558
Pfadenhauer, Karl, Hackenstr. 4, 80331 München.
T. (089) 26 36 19. - Paint / Graph / Eth / Mod - 054559
Pfefferle, Karl, Gewürzmühlstr 5, 80538 München.
T. (089) 295292. - Fra - 054560
Pichl & Hrdlicka J., L., Theresienstr 27, 80333 München.
T. (089) 288244. 054561
Pilati, Amiraplatz 3, 80333 München.
T. (089) 22 90 71. 054562
Pluntke & Bohnhoff, Adalbertstr. 54, 80799 München.
T. (089) 37 75 62. - Ant / Paint / Furn / China / Jew /
Silv / Lights / Glass - 054563
Pokutta, Norbert, Chamissostr 11, 81925 München.
T. (089) 984055, Fax 9827314. - Paint - 054564
Pollmer, Alexander, Landsberger Str 3, 80339 München.
T. (089) 505546, Fax (089) 374729. - Orient - 054565
Potamianos, Frundsbergstr. 9, 80634 München.
T. (089) 16 25 77. - Ant - 054566
Prasch, Elisabeth, Möwestr. 43a, 81827 München.
T. (089) 430 51 23. - Graph - 054567
Praske, D., Ohmstr. 12, 80802 München.
T. (089) 34 82 86. 054568
Preller, M.C., Christophstr. 4, 80538 München.
T. (089) 29 79 83. 054569
Püchler, P., Ganghoferstr. 2, 80339 München.
T. (089) 50 95 92. 054570
Queen Mum, Ohlmüllerstr 6, 81541 München.
T. (089) 668807, Fax (089) 527636. - Furn - 054571
Raab, J., Fraunhoferstr. 22, 80469 München.
T. (089) 201 39 53. 054572
Ramer, Andreas, Fürstenstr. 8, 80333 München.
T. (089) 28 41 71. - Furn / Silv / Cur - 054573
Raritäten-Kabinett, Fürstenstr. 8, 80333 München.
T. (089) 28 41 71. 054574
Reichert, Heinz, Prannerstr 7, 80333 München.
T. (089) 220846, Fax (089) 299877. - China - 054575
Reile, M., Wörthstr 7, 81667 München.
T. (089) 4470881, Fax (089) 9827378. 054576
Reinmund, D., Nymphenburger Str. 78, 80636 München.
T. (089) 18 27 93. 054577
Ressmann u Stieglmeier, Georgenstr 45a, 80799 München. T. (089) 2713433. 054578
Reuther, Christel, Seestr. 4, 80802 München.
T. (089) 39 17 11, Fax 395789. - Ant / Fra - 054579
Riggauer, Konrad, Lilienstr. 11-13, 81669 München.
T. (089) 48 15 85, Fax 481587. - Ant / Fra - 054580
Ritter, Herbert M., Fürstenstr. 6, 80333 München.
T. (089) 283639, Fax 2800936. - Ant / Paint / Furn /
Silv - 054581

Ritthaler, Albert, Bismarckstr 2, 80803 München.
T. (089) 399959, Fax (089) 391113. - Paint / Graph /
Glass / Mod - 054582
Riverside Antiques, Eversbuschstr. 14, 80999 München.
T. (089) 812 06 94. - Ant - 054583
Röbbig, Gerhard, Prannerstr. 5, 80333 München.
T. (089) 299758. - Ant / Furn / China - 054584
Rößler, Albrecht, Postfach 101228, 80086 München.
T. (089) 931388, Fax (089) 932904. - Num - 054585
Rößler, Gisela, Kurfürstenstr 15, 80799 München.
T. (089) 2710127. - Ant / Paint / Furn / China / Sculp /
Fra / Glass - 054586
Romann, Henri, Blumenstr. 25, 80331 München.
T. (089) 26 40 29. - Ant / Instr - 054587
Rosch, Heidi, St.-Anna-Str. 16, 80538 München.
T. (089) 29 40 61. 054588
Roßner, Werner, Thelottstr. 14, 80933 München.
T. (089) 314 4423. - Num - 054589
Roth, Hermann, Ottostr. 11, 80333 München.
T. (089) 55 78 10. - Ant / Furn - 054590
Rudigier, Gertrud, Arcostr. 1, 80333 München.
T. (089) 595432. - Ant / China - 054591
Ruef, Gabriele, Ottostr. 13, 80333 München.
T. (089) 55 74 20. - Ant - 054592
Ruef, Rosemarie, Stiftsbogen 16, 81375
München. 054593
Ruetz, G. & U. Ruetz-Seidel, Richildenstr. 10, 80639
München. T. (089) 17 38 69, Fax 17 49 43.
- Orient - 054594
Rummel, S. von, Prinzregentenstr. 112, 81677 München. T. (089) 470 71 83, Fax 470 17 85.
- Mod - 054595
Rung, D., Reitmorstr 18, 80538 München.
T. (089) 2904357. 054596
Rutzky, M., Augustenstr. 39, 80333 München.
T. (089) 523 42 55. 054597
Sammlerquelle GmbH, Frauenhoferstr.20, 80331 München. T. (089) 260 35 87. - Ant / Num - 054598
Sanct Romedius, Maximilianstr 31, 80539 München.
T. (089) 222776, 222787. - Paint - 054599
Sarkander, H., Pachemstr. 2, 81673 München.
T. (089) 43 45 87. 054600

Schäffner, H., Sparkassenstr 11, 80331 München.
T. (089) 294993. 054601
Scharnowski, Günter, Lechelstr 58, 80997 München.
T. (089) 8114006. - Paint - 054602
Scheidwimmer, Xaver, Barerstr 3, 80333 München.
T. (089) 594979, Fax 557187. - Ant / Paint /
Sculp - 054603
Scheppmann, I., Nymphenburger Str. 86, 80636 München. T. (089) 190 28 83. 054604
Schierl, L., Friedenheimer Str. 119, 80686 München.
T. (089) 57 63 23. 054605
Schilling, C. Freifrau von, Franz-Joseph-Str. 14, 80801
München. T. (089) 33 32 69. 054606
Schimmel, J., Frauenstr. 15, 80469 München.
T. (089) 22 39 75. - Ant - 054607
Schlapka, Gabelsbergerstr. 9, 80333 München.
T. (089) 28 86 17. - Furn - 054608
Schley, Kardinal-Faulhaber-Str. 14a, 80333 München.
T. (089) 226188, Fax (089) 2913959. - Instr - 054609
Schmalzl, Bernhard J., Bräuhausstr. 10, 80331 München. T. (089) 29 93 51. - Jew / Silv - 054610
Schmidt, Auenstr 104, 80469 München.
T. (089) 7460653. 054611
Schmitt, Vorherstr. 10a, 80997 München.
T. (089) 812 41 86. - Num - 054612
Schmitz-Petri, W., Besselstr. 4, 81679 München.
T. (089) 98 82 55. 054613
Schneider, Kardinal-Döpfner-Str 4, 80333 München.
T. (089) 283600. 054614
Schneider, Herbert, Innere Wiener Str. 26, 81667 München. T. (089) 4807378. - Ant - 054615
Schneider, Ulrich, Postfach 401 712, 80717 München.
T. (089) 29 32 20. - Ant / China / Mil / Mod / Tin - 054616
Schnick-Schnack Kunsthandelsgesellschaft, Prannerstr.
11, 80333 München. T. (089) 29 37 17. 054617
Schönberger, Heiglhof, 81377 München.
T. (089) 7143471. 054618
Schöninger, H., Karlspl. 25, 80331 München.
T. (089) 592148. - Paint / Graph / Sculp / Fra - 054619
Schöninger & Co., Sonnenstr. 21, 80331 München.
T. (089) 59 68 72, Fax 52 64 16. - Ant / Paint /
Graph - 054620
Schoettle-Ostasiatica/Joachim Baader, Ehrenfelsstr. 2,
81375 München. T. (089) 714 15 15. - Furn - 054621
Schott, Alexander, St.-Anna-Str 29, 80538 München.
T. (089) 297436. - Graph - 054622
Schütz, I., Artilleriestr. 7, 80636 München.
T. (089) 129 45 84. 054623
Schütze, Bavariaring 41, 80336 München.
T. (089) 763470. 054624
Schuler, Ottostr. 13, 80333 München.
T. (089) 595356. 054625
Schultheiss, G. B., Georgenstr. 35, 80799 München.
T. (089) 34 10 50. - Ant / Furn / Repr / Jew / Silv /
Lights / Glass / Mod - 054626
Schulz, Günter, Prannerstr. 5, 80333 München.
T. (089) 29 87 89. - Instr - 054627
Schulze, Manfred, Glückstr. 2, 80333 München.
T. (089) 28 41 38, Fax (089) 281683. - Num - 054628
Schuster, Franz, Schwanthalerstr. 7, 80336 München.
T. (089) 59 80 11. - Num - 054629
Schwabinger Münzstube, Hohenzollernstr. 67, 80796
München. T. (089) 271 00 80, 278 00 21.
- Num - 054630
Schwarz, H. & I., Schellingstr. 10, 80799 München.
T. (089) 280 95 56. - Jew / Fra / Silv / Glass - 054631
Schweizer, Babette, Schellingstr. 81, 80799 München.
T. (089) 272 26 66. 054632
Seidl, J., Gräfelfinger Str. 136, 81375 München.
T. (089) 70 24 34. 054633

Seidl, Josef, Siegesstr. 21, 80802 München.
T. (089) 34 95 68, Fax 396597. - Ant -   *054634*

Seiler, D.E., Georgenstr. 51, 80799 München.
T. (089) 2718010, 6804648. - Paint / Sculp -   *054635*

Seitz, Günther, Hochbrückenstr. 4, 80331 München.
T. (089) 228 32 23. - Instr -   *054636*

Seling, H. W., Dr., Oskar-von-Miller-Ring 31, 80333
München. T. (089) 28 48 65. Ant / Silv   *054637*

Serapis, Residenzstr. 18, 80333 München.
T. (089) 22 41 85.   *054638*

Setzer, O., Ostpreußenstr. 43, 81927 München.
T. (089) 930 28 30, Fax 9294018.   *054639*

Silber-Keller, Stievestr. 9, 80638 München.
T. (089) 1781956, Fax (089) 173290. - Silv -   *054640*

Silla-Steiner, Therese, Frauenstr. 13, 80469 München.
T. (089) 29 95 37. - Paint / Furn / China / Jew / Instr /
Glass / Cur / Mod -   *054641*

Simon, Zittauer Str. 26, 80997 München.
T. (089) 223453.   *054642*

Singer, A. & M., Widenmayerstr. 42, 80538 München.
T. (089) 223453.   *054643*

Skarecky, E., Schellingstr. 63, 80799 München.
T. (089) 28 23 97.   *054644*

Skiri, Angela, Ursulastr. 9, 80802 München.
T. (089) 34 45 44. - Ant / Furn / Instr / Glass /
Mod -   *054645*

Soheili, D., Ungererstr. 80, 80805 München.
T. (089) 361 65 23.   *054646*

Soin, Leopoldstr. 116, 80802 München. T. (089) 334040,
7603585, Fax 346000. - Orient -   *054647*

Sonnleitner, W., Sulenstr. 10, 81477 München.
T. (089) 79 60 84.   *054648*

Spaeth, von, Theresienstr 19, 80333 München.
T. (089) 2809132, Fax (089) 2809132. - Ant / Glass /
Mod -   *054649*

Spindler, Klaus, Baaderstr. 45, 80469 München.
T. (089) 201 61 68, Fax 2016168. Furn /
Instr -   *054650*

Sprink, Hans U., Dachauer Str 14, 80335 München.
T. (089) 598908.   *054651*

Steinbach, Michael, Demollstr 1, 80638 München.
T. (089) 1571691, Fax (089) 1577096. - Ant -   *054652*

Steiner, A., Frauenstr. 13, 80469 München.
T. (089) 29 95 37.   *054653*

Stölzle, Prannerstr. 5, 80333 München.
T. (089) 297366.   *054654*

Störmer, C., Theresienstr. 66, 80333 München.
T. (089) 280 07 75.   *054655*

Storr, Karl, Kaufingerstr. 25, 80331 München.
T. (089) 229514. - Ant / Sculp / Rel -   *054656*

Stummer, Ludwig-Richter-Str. 21a, 80687
München.   *054657*

Sturm, R.-M., Großhesseloher Str. 4, 81479 München.
T. (089) 79 46 75.   *054658*

Style Francais, Le, Westenriederstr. 27, 80331 München. T. (089) 29 97 32.   *054659*

Suschko, Wassily, Westenriederstr. 20, 80331 München.
T. (089) 29 31 31. - Ant / Paint / Furn / Orient / China /
Sculp / Jew / Silv / Glass / Mod / Ico -   *054660*

Tachjian, C., Stachus, Untergeschoss, 80331 München.
T. (089) 59 50 74.   *054661*

Telkamp, Karoline, Maximilianstr 6, 80539 München.
T. (089) 226283. - Jew / Silv / Glass / Mod -   *054662*

Terminus Theatiner-Kunsthandel, Salvatorstr. 2, 80333
München. T. (089) 22 52 48.   *054663*

Thomas, Wolfgang, Belgradstr.9, 80796 München.
T. (089) 304648. - Ant / Num -   *054664*

Tidjina, Zlatko, Gabelsbergerstr. 69, 80333 München.
T. (089) 52 21 26;52 59 77. - Num -   *054665*

Timberg, Helmut, Maximilianstr 15, 80539 München.
T. (089) 295235. - China -   *054666*

Tivoli, Montgelasstr. 6, 81679 München.
T. (089) 98 36 87, Fax 98 36 87. - Ant / Paint / Furn / China / Jew / Silv / Lights -   *054667*

Tomic, Z.F., Maximilianstr 56, 80538 München.
T. (089) 225035. - Ant -   *054668*

Trost, Ottostr 11, 80333 München. T. (089) 592333.
- Furn -   *054669*

Troynikow, T., Kanalstr. 11, 80538 München.
T. (089) 22 77 01. - Ant -   *054670*

Tudjina, Z., Gabelsberger Str 69, 80333 München.
T. (089) 522126.   *054671*

Unger, Briennerstr. 7, 80333 München. T. (089) 22 75 15.
- Ant -   *054672*

Urban & Pierigal, Prannerstr. 5, 80333 München.
T. (089) 29 35 84. - Ant -   *054673*

Velde, H. van der, Wiener Platz 2, 81667 München.
T. (089) 48 81 88.   *054674*

Vogdt, Stefan A., Kurfürstenstr. 5, 80799 München.
T. (089) 2716857, Fax (089) 272 12 68. - Paint / Num /
Dec / Jew / Silv / Cur / Draw -   *054675*

Vogt, Gerhard F., Fürstenstr. 10, 80333 München.
T. (089) 28 31 64 + 280 99 77. - Ant / Furn /
Dec -   *054676*

Vogt, P., Nederlinger Str. 42, 80638 München.
T. (089) 157 16 68.   *054677*

Vogt, Peter, Marienpl. 8, 80331 München.
T. (089) 29 41 32, Fax 22 71 53. - China -   *054678*

Voigtmann & Co., Seitzstr. 17, 80538 München.
T. (089) 29 77 44. - Tex -   *054679*

Wager, Anna-Maria, Prannerstr. 4, 80333 München.
T. (089) 29602128.   *054680*

Wahrmann-Kleber, Dr, Barerstr 72, 80799 München.
T. (089) 2723354.   *054681*

Waldherr, Hubert, Tal 69, 80331 München.
T. (089) 29 89 86. - Furn -   *054682*

Wallach, Residenzstr. 3, 80333 München.
T. (089) 22 08 71, Fax 29160954. - Ant -   *054683*

Weichinger & Ostertag, Brucknerstr. 27, 81677 München. T. (089) 470 21 47.   *054684*

Weiner, J., Reichenbachstr. 11, 80469 München.
T. (089) 260 30 31. - Ant / Tex / Jew / Silv / Instr / Glass /
Mod / Draw / Tin -   *054685*

Weller, Egon, Martiusstr. 6, 80802 München.
T. (089) 34 72 86. - Ant / Furn / Tex -   *054686*

Wenzel, G., Wiener Platz 7, 81667 München.
T. (089) 448 60 49.   *054687*

Wenzel, P., Blutenburgstr. 29, 80636 München.
T. (089) 129 77 33.   *054688*

Wiechmann, K., Sollner Str 59, 81479 München.
T. (089) 7914959.   *054689*

Wieser, B. & H., Fürstenrieder Str. 70, 80686 München.
T. (089) 56 13 35.   *054690*

Wieser, M., Leonrodstr. 6, 80634 München.
T. (089) 16 20 40. - Ant -   *054691*

Wilhelm, C., Pestalozzistr. 5, 80469 München.
T. (089) 268671.   *054692*

Wilmerdinger, R., Wendl-Dietrich-Str. 32, 80634 München. T. (089) 16 92 87.   *054693*

Winkelmann, E.M., Preysingstr. 45, 81667 München.
T. (089) 447 05 23.   *054694*

Winkler, S., Baaderstr. 64, 80469 München.
T. (089) 201 53 18. - Ant -   *054695*

Winning, W., Bräuhausstr. 10, 80331 München.
T. (089) 29 93 51. - Num -   *054696*

Witt, Hermann Harry, Maximiliansplatz 12, 80333 München. T. (089) 221101. - Ant / Furn / China / Dec /
Silv -   *054697*

Wörndl, M. & M., Falkenturmstr. 14, 80331 München.
T. (089) 28 36 26.   *054698*

Wohlert, Werner H., Lindwurmstr. 46, 80337 München.
T. (089) 77 36 17. - Ant / Paint / Furn / China / Jew /
Silv / Instr / Glass / Cur -   *054699*

Wohlgemuth, J., Walter-Otto-Str. 2b, 80997 München.
T. (089) 812 52 99.   *054700*

Wohlschlager, Otto, Burgstr 7, 80331 München.
T. (089) 220789. - Num -   *054701*

Wulfs, Habsburgerstr. 1, 80801 München.
T. (089) 39 23 36.   *054702*

Wunderlich, W., Liebigstr. 12 a, 80538 München.
T. (089) 22 34 22.   *054703*

Zambelli, Josef, Herterichstr. 57a, 81479 München.
T. (089) 79 69 63. - Ant / Furn / Silv -   *054704*

Zannoth, Wilhelm, Westenriederstr. 24, 80331 München.
T. (089) 294246. - Ant / Paint / Graph / China / Silv /
Instr / Glass / Mod -   *054705*

Zausch, R., Wendl-Dietrich-Str. 21a, 80634 München.
T. (089) 167 54 78. - Ant -   *054706*

Zeitwende, Barerstr. 86a, 80799 München.
T. (089) 271 60 03. - Furn -   *054707*

Ziegler, Winfried, Herzogstr 77, 80796 München.
T. (089) 582221.   *054708*

Zinn-Mory, Marienpl., 80331 München.
T. (089) 22 45 42.   *054709*

Zolghadar, Maximilianstr 33, 80539 München.
T. (089) 294398, 294107. - Tex -   *054710*

Zorn, Askolf W., Fallmerayerstr 9a, 80796 München.
T. (089) 3081023. - Ico -   *054711*

Zscheyge, T., Hochbrückenstr. 14, 80331 München.
T. (089) 22 23 94.   *054712*

Zuber, W., Siegfriedstr. 16, 80803 München.
T. (089) 33 30 08. - Ant -   *054713*

Münster (Nordrhein-Westfalen)

Aegidii-Galerie, Aegidiimarkt, 48143 Münster.
T. (0251) 5 80 95.   *054714*

Antik Alte Möbel, Aldruper Str. 132, 48159 Münster.
T. (0251) 21 68 50.   *054715*

Antik und Neu, Gartenstr. 57, 48147 Münster.
T. (0251) 27 45 86.   *054716*

Antiquitäten am Stadtmuseum, Salzstr. 30, 48143 Münster. T. (0251) 42021.   *054717*

Antiquitäten-Center, Auf der Laer 21, 48157 Münster.
T. (0251) 31 43 61. - Furn -   *054718*

Antiquitätenhaus Alte Pleistermühle, Pleistermühlenweg,
48155 Münster. T. (0251) 31 67 18.   *054719*

Aulock, Andrea von, Grenkuhlenweg 2, 48167 Münster.
T. (0251) 02506/21 19. - Furn / China / Silv -   *054720*

Ballestrem, Gräfin, Weseler Str. 311, 48151 Münster.
T. (0251) 75291. - Furn / Silv -   *054721*

Becker, Rita, Palestrinastr. 6, 48147 Münster.
T. (0251) 23 36 13, Fax 236190. - Ant / Paint / Furn /
Fra / Lights / Instr / Glass / Mod -   *054722*

Belle Epoque, Rosenpl. 10, 48143 Münster.
T. (0251) 51 13 07.   *054723*

Bröker, Joh., Georgskommende 9, 48143 Münster.
T. (0251) 4 53 83. - Ant / Furn -   *054724*

Bruens, U., Bohlweg 19a, 48147 Münster.
T. (0251) 54209. - Jew -   *054725*

CM Uhren- und Schmuckgalerie, Bahnhofstr. 12, 48143
Münster. T. (0251) 540 11. - Jew / Instr -   *054726*

Dötsch, H. U. & A., Ludgeritstr. 85, 48143 Munster.
T. (0251) 473 28. - Jew / Silv / Mod -   *054727*

Falger, W.A., Salzstr. 37, 48143 Münster.
T. (0251) 79 44 92. - Ant -   *054728*

Flasse, Rüdiger, Friedrich-Ebert-Str. 69, 48153 Münster.
T. (0251) 75913.   *054729*

Frye & Sohn, Hörsterstr. 47-48, 48143 Münster.
T. (0251) 466 62. - Paint / Graph -   *054730*

Galerie Scheherazade, Windthorststr. 45, 48143 Münster. T. (0251) 556 40. - Ant / Paint / Graph / Orient /
Eth / Jew / Cur -   *054731*

Götting, Heinrich, Alter Fischmarkt 7, 48143 Münster.
T. (0251) 544 00. - Ant / Paint / Graph / Repr /
Fra -   *054732*

Gripekoven & Söhne, Spiekerhof 6-11, 48143 Münster.
T. (0251) 43262, 42724, Fax 42724. - Tex -   *054733*

Hachmeister, Klosterstr. 12, 48143 Münster.
T. (0251) 51210, Fax (0251) 57217. - Paint / Graph /
Eth -   *054734*

Heemann, Annette, Warendorfer Str. 75, 48145 Münster.
T. (0251) 368 78.   *054735*

Hessing, M., Horstmarer Landweg 263, 48149 Münster.
T. (0251) 827 43.   *054736*

Heuer, U., Ostmarkstr. 65, 48145 Münster.
T. (0251) 39 37 89.   *054737*

Holthaus, Wolfgang, Dahlweg 68a, 48153
Münster.   *054738*

Husmann, Am Burloh 43, 48159 Münster.
T. (0251) 21 13 31. - Ant -   *054739*

Kiene, Rolf, Pleistermühlenweg 194, 48157 Münster.
T. (0251) 31 67 18.   *054740*

Klosterbusch und Wilsmann, Klosterbusch 12, 48167
Münster. T. (0251) 61 56 83.   *054741*

Klümke, Charlotte, Warendorfer Str. 78a, 48145 Münster. T. (0251) 35222. - Furn / Mod -   *054742*

Knirim, Ingrid, Kanalstr. 113, 48147 Münster.
T. (0251) 22682. - Graph / Draw -   *054743*

Koch, Richard, Bahnhofstr. 12, 48143 Münster.
T. (0251) 44649. - Num -   *054744*

Kösters, Wilhelm, Prinzipalmarkt 45/46, 48143 Münster.
T. (0251) 448 95/96.   *054745*

Kuhlmann, Heinrich, Salzstr. 11, 48143 Münster.
T. (0251) 434 37.   *054746*

Kunst im Speicher, An der Kleimannbrücke 36, 48157
Münster. T. (0251) 32 41 73.   *054747*

Laumann, F., Pröbstingstr. 6, 48157 Münster.
T. (0251) 32 90 32.   *054748*

Ludgerigalerie, Windthorststr. 65, 48143 Münster.
T. (0251) 56613. - Ant / Tex / Eth -   054749
Mikus, Lothar, Engelstr. 68, 48143 Münster.
T. (0251) 530 50, Fax 530 51 95.   054750
Münstersches Kunst- und Auktionshaus, Buddenstr. 3-6,
48143 Münster. T. (0251) 513 56, Fax 51 90 36.
- Ant -   054751
Nolte, Michael, Bogenstr. 11-12, 48143 Münster.
T. (0251) 448 09, Fax 51 13 60. - Ant / Furn / Dec /
Lights -   054752
Peter, B., Ostmarkstr. 67, 48145 Münster.
T. (0251) 37 58 81.   054753
Rincklake van Endert, Rothenburg 14-17, 48143 Mün-
ster. T. (0251) 405 31. - Paint / Furn / Tex /
Instr -   054754
Roxel-Antik, A-v-Droste-Hülsh.-Str 13, 48161 Münster.
T. (0251) 76 06. - Furn / China / Silv / Glass - 054755
Schepers, Ralf, Bohlweg 19b, 48147 Münster.
T. (0251) 51 14 99, Fax 54765. - Silv -   054756
Schiras, Warendorfer Str. 48, 48145 Münster.
T. (0251) 37 56 78.   054757
Schlummer, Ringoldsgasse, 48143 Münster.
T. (0251) 472 31.   054758
Skandia, Ludgeripl. 4-6, 48143 Münster.
T. (0251) 53 24 63.   054759
Steins, Hansjürgen, Bahnhofstr. 14, 48143 Münster.
T. (0251) 5 84 41. - Paint -   054760
Stenderhoff, Theresia, Alter Fischmarkt 21, 48143 Mün-
ster. T. (0251) 44749, Fax (0251) 51526.   054761
Wawerzonnek, Armin, Tischlerweg 13, 48161 Münster.
T. (0251) 02534/27 17. - Ant / Furn / Tex / Dec / Jew /
Silv / Instr -   054762
Weber, Til, Königsstr. 15, 48143 Münster.
T. (0251) 56042.   054763
Wehse, P. & R., Nordstr. 2, 48149 Münster.
T. (0251) 27 31 75.   054764
Wilmsen, D., Schadowstr. 5, 48163 Münster.
T. (0251) 02501/58088.   054765

Münstertal (Baden-Württemberg)
Dukić, R., Neuhäuser Str. 22, 79244 Münstertal.
T. (07636) 519.   054766

Murnau (Bayern)
Beurer, Elli, Johannisgasse 18, 82418 Murnau.
T. (08841) 1810. - Ant / Graph / Furn -   054767
Bredow-König, von, Postgasse 1, 82418 Murnau.
T. (08841) 1695.   054768

Murrhardt (Baden-Württemberg)
Monier, H., Nägelestr. 2, 71540 Murrhardt.
T. (07192) 45 40.   054769

Nagold (Baden-Württemberg)
Galerie Lotos, In der Heide 16/2, 72202 Nagold.
T. (074 59) 440. - Ant / Orient / China / Arch /
Eth -   054770
Gerster, W., Steinbergstr. 2, 72202 Nagold.
T. (07452) 45 77. - Num -   054771

Naila (Bayern)
Pfeifer, S. & E., Bergstr. 2, 95119 Naila.
T. (09282) 8539.   054772

Neckargemünd (Baden-Württemberg)
Adam, Pfluggasse 22, 69151 Neckargemünd.
T. (06223) 8718.   054773
Palette, Bahnhofstr. 9, 69151 Neckargemünd.
T. (06223) 66 29.   054774

Neckarsteinach (Hessen)
Pedersen, Gerd, Kirchenstr. 5, 69239 Neckarsteinach.
T. (06229) 10 30.   054775

Neckarsulm (Baden-Württemberg)
Lorenz, T., Friedenstr. 9, 74172 Neckarsulm.
T. (07132) 374 33.   054776
Lorenz, T., Rathausstr. 32, 74172 Neckarsulm.
T. (07132) 374 11.   054777

Neresheim (Baden-Württemberg)
Maier, Beurener Weg 1, 73450 Neresheim.
T. (07326) 2610. - Ant / Paint -   054778

Nettetal (Nordrhein-Westfalen)
Erkens, August, Niedieckstr. 25, 41334 Nettetal.
T. (02153) 2605.   054779
Esch, Heinz Josef, Hochstr. 16, 41334 Nettetal.
T. (02153) 81 46. - Paint / Furn / Orient / China / Sculp /
Silv -   054780
Goertz, Johannes, Josefstr. 43, 41334 Nettetal.
T. (02153) 701 35.   054781
Notz-Erkens, Niedieckstr. 25, 41334 Nettetal.
T. (02153) 2659. - Ant / Paint / Furn / Jew -   054782

Neu-Isenburg (Hessen)
Antik im Hof, Frankfurter Str. 143, 63263 Neu-Isenburg.
T. (06102) 230 43. - Furn -   054783
Bader, A., Frankfurter Str. 9, 63263 Neu-Isenburg.
T. (06102) 40 38. - Ant -   054784
Durak-von Freyberg, A., Frankfurter Str. 143, 63263
Neu-Isenburg. T. (06102) 230 43. - Furn -   054785
Klüppel, M., Bahnhofstr. 96, 63263 Neu-Isenburg.
T. (06102) 6445.   054786
Liebhart & Heuberger, Isenburg-Zentrum, 1. Etage,
63263 Neu-Isenburg.   054787
Michael's Antiques, Frankfurter Str. 16-18, 63263 Neu-
Isenburg. T. (06102) 391 07. - Ant / Paint / Furn / Chi-
na / Silv -   054788
Wipfler, Hans-Peter, Schönbornring 24, 63263 Neu-Isen-
burg. T. (06102) 51555. - Ant / Paint / China / Silv /
Glass / Mod -   054789

Neu-Ulm (Bayern)
Erhardt, H., Turmstr. 43, 89231 Neu-Ulm.
T. (0731) 785 09.   054790
IPA Galerie, Brühlweg 9-11, 89233 Neu-Ulm.
T. (0731) 67 91. - Paint -   054791

Neu Wulmstorf (Schleswig-Holstein)
Spitzer, H., Elchpfad 18, 21629 Neu Wulmstorf.
T. (040) 7008117.   054793

Neubeuern (Bayern)
Alex Antiques-Galerie, Winkl Haus Nr. 25, 83115 Neubeuern. T. (08035) 491. - Paint / Paint / Graph / Furn /
Orient / China / Jew / Fra / Silv / Lights / Instr / Mil / Glas-
s / Cur -   054794

Neuburg (Bayern)
Maier, J., Ingolstädter Str. 7, 86633 Neuburg.
T. (08431) 440 84. - Ant -   054795
Schwarz, K.H. & J. Ziemba, Beim Jägerhaus 21, 86633
Neuburg. T. (08431) 83 26.   054796

Neuenhaus (Niedersachsen)
Reinink, Gerhard, Danziger Str. 5, 49828
Neuenhaus.   054797

Neuenkirchen, Lüneburger Heide (Nie-
dersachsen)
Plum, H., Delmsen, 29643 Neuenkirchen, Lüneburger
Heide. T. (05195) 339.   054798
Zander, B. von, Hauptstr. 15, 29643 Neuenkirchen, Lü-
neburger Heide. T. (05195) 2111.   054799

Neuenstadt (Baden-Württemberg)
Birchall, John, Eberstädterstr. 4, 74196 Neuenstadt.
T. (07139) 79 63. - Ant -   054800
Kappes, Kurmainzstr. 5, 74196 Neuenstadt.
T. (07139) 73 29.   054801
Lawes, U., Turmhahnstr. 3, 74196 Neuenstadt.
T. (07139) 88 87.   054802

Neuenstein, Hessen (Hessen)
Antikhof Neuenstein, Domäne, 36286 Neuenstein, Hes-
sen. T. (06677) 472, Fax 633. - Ant / Paint / Graph /
Furn -   054803

Neuenstein, Württemberg (Baden-Würt-
temberg)
Momo, Bahnhofstr 48, 74632 Neuenstein, Württemberg.
T. (07942) 3550.   054804

Neuffen (Baden-Württemberg)
Scheithauer, U., Hauptstr. 20, 72639 Neuffen.
T. (07025) 5348.   054805
Scheithauer, U., Oberer Graben 2, 72639 Neuffen.
T. (07025) 2875.   054806

Neumarkt (Bayern)
Hailer, H., Kirchengassen 4, 92318 Neumarkt.
T. (09181) 7602.   054807
Hanel, Josef, Löwenthalstr 12, 92318 Neumarkt.
T. (09181) 8210. - Ant -   054808
Maschauer, S., Rosengasse 1a, 92318 Neumarkt.
T. (09181) 21446.   054809
Schwarz, Sieglinde, Sandstr 40, 92318 Neumarkt.
T. (09181) 8210.   054810
Trescher, H., Weichselsteiner Weg 1a, 92318 Neumarkt.
T. (09181) 21285. - Furn -   054811

Neumünster (Schleswig-Holstein)
Die kleine Galerie, Fürsthof 4, 24534 Neumünster.
T. (04321) 16 32. - Glass -   054812

Neunburg (Bayern)
Wachter, R., Ritter-von-Pflug-Str 15, 92431 Neunburg.
T. (09672) 705.   054813

Neunkirchen, Saar (Saarland)
Maeckel, Heinrich, Langenstrichstr 4, 66538 Neunkir-
chen, Saar. - Ant -   054814
Schubert, Ludwig, Stummstr 15, 66538 Neunkirchen,
Saar. T. (06821) 2208. - Ant -   054815

Neunkirchen-Seelscheid (Nordrhein-
Westfalen)
Rust, G., Gutmühlenweg 6, 53819 Neunkirchen-Seel-
scheid. T. (02247) 7337. - Ant / Furn / Instr -   054816

Neuötting (Bayern)
Blachian, Franz Eligius, Frauenhoferstr. 7, 84524 Neuöt-
ting. T. (08671) 200 03. - Ant -   054817

Neuss (Nordrhein-Westfalen)
Antik-Haus, Krefelder Str. 43, 41460 Neuss.
T. (02131) 27 72 68.   054818
Ex-Clou, Klarissenstr. 2, 41460 Neuss.
T. (02131) 27 34 34. - Ant / Paint / Furn / China / Dec /
Jew / Lights / Glass -   054819
Mariacher, I., Erprather Str. 38, 41466 Neuss.
T. (02131) 46 56 89.   054820
Müller, H., Quirinusstr. 2, 41460 Neuss.
T. (02131) 27 55 66. - Num -   054821
Oehmen-Krieger, A., Krefelder Str. 43, 41460 Neuss.
T. (02131) 27 72 68.   054822
Offelder, W., Michaelstr. 70, 41460 Neuss.
T. (02131) 241 90.   054823
Postall, Josef, Niederstr. 47, 41460 Neuss.
T. (02131) 83 26.   054824
Rieder, E., Hamtorstr. 2, 41460 Neuss.
T. (02131) 232 69.   054825
Roßlenbroich, K., Koblenzer Str. 63, 41468 Neuss.
T. (02131) 397 77.   054826
Schubert, M., Münsterplatz 2, 41460 Neuss.
T. (02131) 212 57.   054827

Neustadt am Rübenberge (Niedersach-
sen)
Röpke, Gudrun, Ahnser Weg 5, 31535 Neustadt am Rübenberge. T. (05032) 2474. - Ant / Furn / Tex /
Dec -   054828

Neustadt an der Aisch (Bayern)
Pabst, P., Riedfelder Ortsstr 32a, 91413 Neustadt an der
Aisch. T. (09161) 7755.   054829
Remshard, F., Nürnberger Str 7, 91413 Neustadt an der
Aisch. T. (09161) 4445. - Num -   054830

Neustadt an der Weinstraße (Rheinland-
Pfalz)
Abresch, H., Bergstr 1, 67434 Neustadt an der Weinstra-
ße. T. (06321) 38 24.   054831
Brune, Haardter Schloß, 67433 Neustadt an der Wein-
straße. T. (06321) 32625, Fax 82240. - Furn / Repr /
Instr -   054832
Denzinger, Herbert, Hauptstr 63, 67433 Neustadt an der
Weinstraße.   054833
Eidel, P., Kunigundenstr 12, 67433 Neustadt an der
Weinstraße. T. (06321) 83074. - Furn -   054834
Emde, R., Hohenzollernstr 28, 67433 Neustadt an der
Weinstraße. T. (06321) 88570.   054835
Glaser, G., Chemnitzer Str 13 B, 67433 Neustadt an der
Weinstraße. T. (06321) 31376.   054836

Kurpfälzische Kupferstichhandlung, Dochnahlstr 14, 67434 Neustadt an der Weinstraße. T. (06321) 31619. - Graph - *054837*

Masanek, H.-P., Branchweilerhofstr 88b, 67433 Neustadt an der Weinstraße. T. (06321) 5374. *054838*

Meta's Pfälzer Kunsthandlung, Friedrichstr 18, 67433 Neustadt an der Weinstraße. T. (06321) 2061. *054839*

Raab, I., Kunigundenstr 8, 67433 Neustadt an der Weinstraße. T. (06321) 32890. - Ant / Furn - *054840*

Raule, Rolf, Hirschhornring 41a, 67435 Neustadt an der Weinstraße. T. (06321) 69079. - Ant / Furn - *054841*

Rübel, H., Marktpl 9, 67433 Neustadt an der Weinstraße. T. (06321) 31619. - Graph - *054842*

Schanzenbächer, G., Fröbelstr 10, 67433 Neustadt an der Weinstraße. T. (06321) 30210. *054843*

Szopinski, Bauerndoktor-Gros-Str 36, 67435 Neustadt an der Weinstraße. T. (06321) 4640. *054844*

Wessa, K., Amalienstr 31, 67434 Neustadt an der Weinstraße. T. (06321) 7628. *054845*

Neustadt, Hessen (Hessen)

Ruhl, H., Am Schalkert 9, 35279 Neustadt, Hessen. T. (06692) 8522. *054846*

Neustadt in Holstein (Schleswig-Holstein)

Boller, A., Kreienredder 62, 23730 Neustadt in Holstein. T. (04561) 8146. *054847*

Held, U., Waschgrabenstr 5, 23730 Neustadt in Holstein. T. (04561) 9348. *054848*

Neutraubling (Bayern)

Zimmermann, Horst, Waldenburger Str. 3, 93073 Neutraubling. T. (09401) 8706, 7771. - Ant / Paint / Graph / Furn / Num / China / Jew / Instr / Mil / Glass - *054849*

Neuwied (Rheinland-Pfalz)

Faber, Schloßstr. 40, 56564 Neuwied. T. (02631) 231 38. *054850*

Failer, Marktstr. 52, 56564 Neuwied. T. (02631) 25750. - Paint / Graph / Fra - *054851*

Hentrich, L., Marktstr. 91, 56564 Neuwied. T. (02631) 484 48. *054852*

Nidderau (Hessen)

Gruber, Ingrid, Kleine Gasse 7, 61130 Nidderau. - Furn - *054853*

Rohde, W., Hüttenweg 13, 61130 Nidderau. T. (06187) 23983, Fax 264435. - Ant / Paint / Furn / Silv / Lights / Mod - *054854*

Nieblum (Schleswig-Holstein)

Hübner, A. & C., 25938 Nieblum. T. (04681) 8280. *054855*

Köhler, M., 25938 Nieblum. T. (04681) 2662. *054856*

Niebüll (Schleswig-Holstein)

Andersen, H., Hauptstr. 6, 25899 Niebüll. T. (04661) 8179. *054857*

Derouet, W., Koogsreihe 5, 25899 Niebüll. T. (04661) 35 10. *054858*

Feddersen, B. H., Hauptstr. 41a, 25899 Niebüll. - Paint / Graph / Draw - *054859*

Niederzier (Nordrhein-Westfalen)

Hertel, Niederfeld 2, 52382 Niederzier. T. (02428) 02428/34 54. - Ant / Paint / Furn - *054860*

Nienburg, Weser (Niedersachsen)

Mauersberg, R., Bisquitstr 2, 31582 Nienburg, Weser. *054861*

Menge, Karl, Lange Str 43, 31582 Nienburg, Weser. *054862*

Nienstädt (Niedersachsen)

Bollmohr, Bahnhofstr. 277, 31688 Nienstädt. T. (05721) 6207. *054863*

Waldeck, Hüttenstr. 84, 31688 Nienstädt. T. (05721) 34 72. - Furn - *054864*

Nördlingen (Bayern)

Hamich-Rafensteiner, I., Marktpl. 15, 86720 Nördlingen. T. (09081) 22626. *054865*

Nonnenhorn (Bayern)

Schempp, Dieter, Seehalde 13, 88149 Nonnenhorn. T. (08382) 84 46. - Mil - *054866*

Norden (Niedersachsen)

Eden, J., Westerstr. 11, 26506 Norden. T. (04931) 2557. *054867*

Norderney (Niedersachsen)

Eggen, Georg, Winterstr. 14b, 26548 Norderney. *054868*

Huber, Heike, Poststr. 10, 26548 Norderney. T. (04932) 829 66. - Ant / Paint / Graph / Furn / China / Sculp / Arch / Dec - *054869*

Huber, Peter, Langestr. 2, Postfach 1257, 26534 Norderney. T. (04932) 826 00, Fax 2754. - Ant / Paint / Graph / Furn / China / Jew / Silv / Lights / Instr / Glass / Cur -- *054870*

Lührs, Johann, Strandstr. 4, 26548 Norderney. *054871*

Mindermann, Uwe, Jann-Berghaus-Str. 81, 26548 Norderney. *054872*

Rossbach, Hannes, Jann-Berghaus-Str. 17, 26548 Norderney. T. (04932) 82802. - Ant / Furn / Jew / Fra / Silv / Lights / Mod - *054873*

Rozmer, G., Strandstr. 12, 26548 Norderney. T. (04932) 17 30. *054874*

Norderstedt (Schleswig-Holstein)

Abrahams, Herold Center, 22844 Norderstedt. T. (040) 5233243, Fax 5231623. - Ant - *054876*

Bochers & Sven Droigk, Sven, Ohechaussee 13, 22848 Norderstedt. T. (040) 5479750. *054877*

Bohlens & Zopp, Rathausallee 19c, 22846 Norderstedt. T. (040) 5217825. *054878*

Bolz, F., Segeberger Chaussee 362, 22851 Norderstedt. T. (040) 529 20 04. *054879*

Fowler & Co., Am Gehölz 16-18, 22844 Norderstedt. T. (040) 522 19 15. *054880*

Holste, K., Rosa-Luxemburg-Weg 4, 22846 Norderstedt. T. (040) 5228818. *054881*

Leifeld, U., Ohechaussee 8, 22848 Norderstedt. T. (040) 5296838. *054882*

Prinz & Möller, Ochsenzoller Str. 187-189, 22848 Norderstedt. T. (040) 523 99 15. - Furn - *054883*

Schüssler, Franz, Waldstr. 7, 22846 Norderstedt. T. (040) 522 25 75. *054884*

Ulmer, Detlef, Glashütter Damm 266, 22851 Norderstedt. T. (040) 5292371. *054884a*

Nordhackstedt (Schleswig-Holstein)

Magnussen, E. G., 24980 Nordhackstedt. T. (04639) 413. - Ant - *054885*

Nordhastedt (Schleswig-Holstein)

Ott, R., Fiel Nr. 1, 25785 Nordhastedt. T. (04804) 1279. *054886*

Nordhorn (Niedersachsen)

Giorgi, M. de, Neuenhauser Str. 4, 48529 Nordhorn. T. (05921) 36806. - Num - *054887*

Kupschus, Stadtring 41, 48527 Nordhorn. T. (05921) 64 35. - Furn / China / Jew / Instr - *054888*

Moeken, Bernhardstr. 22, 48529 Nordhorn. T. (05921) 755 83. *054889*

Reinink, Geert, Nordhorner Weg 55, 48527 Nordhorn. T. (05921) 67 02. - Furn - *054890*

Scholten & Sohn, H., Hakenstr. 14, 48527 Nordhorn. *054891*

Wiggers, Johann, Südstr. 9, 48531 Nordhorn. - Ant - *054892*

Nottuln (Nordrhein-Westfalen)

Bross, B., Am Hagenbach 30, 48301 Nottuln. T. (02502) 10 98. *054893*

Gausepohl, Bernhard, Liebigstr. 20, 48301 Nottuln. - Furn - *054894*

Notzingen (Baden-Württemberg)

Auch, A., Kirchheimer Str 9, 73274 Notzingen. T. (07021) 46421. *054895*

Nümbrecht (Nordrhein-Westfalen)

Drinhausen, A., Heddinghausen 108, 51588 Nümbrecht. T. (02293) 66 49. - Ant / Paint / Graph / Furn / China / Eth / Fra / Lights / Instr / Glass / Cur / Mod / Pho / Tin / Toys / Music - *054896*

Werner, Karl-Heinz, Grunewald 11, 51588 Nümbrecht. T. (02293) 6150, Fax 4446. - Furn - *054897*

Nürnberg (Bayern)

Albrecht, C.P., Hauptmarkt 29, 90403 Nürnberg. T. (0911) 221955. - Ant / Num - *054898*

Artificial Design & Objekte, Bucher Str. 19, 90419 Nürnberg. T. (0911) 33 55 75, Fax 33 82 51. - Furn / Dec - *054899*

AT home, Eibacher Hauptstr. 91, 90451 Nürnberg. T. (0911) 64 60 09, Fax 64 64 04. - Ant - *054900*

Bach, Guido & Peter, Peter-Henlein-Str. 71, 90459 Nürnberg. T. (0911) 45 89 09. - Furn - *054901*

Barthelmeß, Eugen, Kaiserstr. 32, 90403 Nürnberg. T. (0911) 22 72 42. *054902*

Baumeister, Wiesenstr. 84, 90459 Nürnberg. T. (0911) 45 59 11. *054903*

Beck, R.M., Wilhelm-Max-Str. 68, 90402 Nürnberg. T. (0911) 33 55 21. *054904*

Behringer, E. & W., Krelingstr. 47, 90408 Nürnberg. T. (0911) 35 49 79. *054905*

Bergmann, Rudolf W., Äussere Großweidenmühlstr. 19, 90419 Nürnberg. T. (0911) 332096, Fax 332084. - Ant / Silv - *054906*

Bingold, Hans, Färberstr. 21, 90402 Nürnberg. T. (0911) 22 51 14. *054907*

Bretschneider, Ernst, Winklerstr. 24, 90403 Nürnberg. T. (0911) 22 68 66. - Ant - *054908*

Bretschneider, Max, Neutorgraben 11, 90419 Nürnberg. *054909*

China-Laden, Kaiserstr. 8, 90403 Nürnberg. T. (0911) 207 61. *054910*

Egon, Fritz, Leiblstr. 11, 90431 Nürnberg. T. (0911) 32 93 88. - Furn - *054911*

Erlinger, Günter, Obere Wörthstr. 5, 90403 Nürnberg. T. (0911) 22 48 09. *054912*

Feller, R., Sulzbacher Str. 76, 90489 Nürnberg. T. (0911) 53 51 59. *054913*

Frank, Günther, Pillenreuther Str. 59, 90459 Nürnberg. T. (0911) 44 43 52. - Num - *054914*

Galerie Auch Weinhandel, Weißgerbergasse 22, 90403 Nürnberg. T. (0911) 221670. *054915*

Galerie Sorko, Hessestr 8, 90443 Nürnberg. T. (0911) 267496. - Paint / Graph / Orient / Draw - *054916*

Gebert, U., Breite Gasse 13, 90402 Nürnberg. T. (0911) 24 30 67. - Num - *054917*

Ginko Bilobo, Bergstr. 12, 90403 Nürnberg. T. (0911) 22 22 09. *054918*

Gradl & Hinterland, Theatergasse 13, 90402 Nürnberg. T. (0911) 20 83 39. - Num - *054919*

Grieb, M., Lahmannstr. 21, 90419 Nürnberg. T. (0911) 34 49 17. *054920*

Gugel, Schwabacher Str. 100, 90439 Nürnberg. T. (0911) 61 40 88. - Num - *054921*

Haisch, J., Bergstr. 10, 90403 Nürnberg. T. (0911) 23 28 59. - Ant / Eth - *054922*

Hanauer, Rudolf, Allersberger Str. 33, 90461 Nürnberg. T. (0911) 45 50 28. - Num - *054923*

Hartmann, Artur, Weinmarkt 1, 90403 Nürnberg. T. (0911) 22 45 69. - Ant / Paint / Furn / Instr - *054924*

Herzog, R., Leonhardstr. 1, 90443 Nürnberg. T. (0911) 26 15 31. - Ant / Paint / Graph / Furn / China / Sculp / Jew / Silv / Instr / Mod / Toys - *054925*

Höfler, Johannisstr. 109, 90419 Nürnberg. T. (0911) 33 38 43. *054926*

Horlbeck, Pillenreuther Str. 44, 90459 Nürnberg. T. (0911) 44 77 66. *054927*

Kachelriess, Gisela, Weinmarkt 10, 90403 Nürnberg. T. (0911) 20 83 11. *054928*

Klarner, Helmut, Freyjastr 12, 90461 Nürnberg. T. (0911) 472908. - Furn - *054929*

Klinger, K., Bucher Str. 17, 90419 Nürnberg. T. (0911) 33 06 90. *054930*

König, Bucher Str 17, 90419 Nürnberg. T. (0911) 338182, Fax (0911) 337960. - Ant / Paint / Graph / Furn / China / Repr / Sculp / Tex / Jew / Silv / Lights / Instr / Mil / Rel / Glass / Cur / Mod / Ico / Pho / Draw - *054931*

Krausser, Marie, Sylter Str. 20, 90425 Nürnberg. T. (0911) 34 32 38. *054932*

Kreitlein, M., Karl-Grillenberger-Str. 20, 90402 Nürnberg. T. (0911) 20 40 30. *054933*

Maly, V. von, Einsteinring 20, 90453 Nürnberg.
T. (0911) 64 04 53. - Num -   *054934*
Mögeldorfer Lädle, Laufamholzstr. 35, 90482 Nürnberg.
T. (0911) 54 78 22.   *054935*
Müller, M., Untere Kreuzgasse 2, 90403 Nürnberg.
T. (0911) 22 26 49.   *054936*
Nürnberger Gobelin-Manufaktur, Bingstr. 40, 90480
Nürnberg. T. (0911) 40 75 66. - Tex -   *054937*
Nürnberger Rahmenkunst, Haus der Gemälde, Kaiserstr.
38, 90403 Nürnberg. T. (0911) 22 52 38. - Orient /
Repr / Fra -   *054938*
Oettner, G., Weißgerbergasse 8, 90403 Nürnberg.
T. (0911) 22 57 13.   *054939*
Plasberger, Ralf-D., Regensburger Str. 35, 90478 Nürn-
berg. T. (0911) 47 23 86.   *054940*
Raimond, J., Muggenhofer Str. 39, 90429 Nürnberg.
T. (0911) 32 83 56.   *054941*
Reichel, Robert, Bessemerstr. 52, 90411 Nürnberg.
T. (0911) 51 25 56. - Ant / Furn / Repr -   *054942*
Reis, R., Peter-Henlein-Str. 22, 90443 Nürnberg.
T. (0911) 44 82 77. - Ant -   *054943*
Roth, U., Hauptmarkt 1, 90403 Nürnberg.
T. (0911) 22 59 15.   *054944*
Russo, Anton, An den Weihern 29, 90455 Nürnberg.
T. (0911) 88 21 92.   *054945*
Saffer, H.G., Untere Turnstr. 14a, 90429 Nürnberg.
T. (0911) 26 21 43, 26 85 84.   *054946*
Sammel Surium, Heroldstr. 11, 90408 Nürnberg.
T. (0911) 34 30 43. - Ant -   *054947*
Sander, Georg, Zirndorfer Str. 94, 90449 Nürnberg.
- Ant / Paint / Sculp -   *054948*
Schlosser, Joseph, Albrecht-Dürer-Str. 1, 90403 Nürn-
berg. T. (0911) 20 92 65. - Furn / Glass -   *054949*
Schrag, Heinrich, Königstr. 15, 90402 Nürnberg.
T. (0911) 20 46 08. - Graph / Repr / Fra -   *054950*
Schubladen, Der, Brettergartenstr. 97b, 90427 Nürnberg.
T. (0911) 326 27 47. - Furn -   *054951*
Seckendorff, Christoph von, Füll 8, 90403 Nürnberg.
T. 22 63 06, (09844) 225. - Ant / Paint / Furn / Orient /
China / Silv / Glass -   *054952*
Seiffert, A., Bergstr. 12, 90403 Nürnberg.
T. (0911) 22 22 09.   *054953*
Spielzeug-Galerie, Weißgerbergasse 35, 90403 Nürn-
berg. T. (0911) 22 21 01.   *054954*
Spielzeug von Damals, Siegfriedstr. 2, 90461 Nürnberg.
T. (0911) 47 67 56, 45 25 64. - Toys -   *054955*
Steinbach, A., Johannisstr. 100, 90419 Nürnberg.
T. (0911) 33 16 28.   *054956*
Südstadt Antiquitäten, Wilhelm-Spaeth-Str. 10, 90461
Nürnberg. T. (0911) 46 62 50.   *054957*
Träg, A., Obere Wörthstr. 16, 90403 Nürnberg.
T. (0911) 22 23 31. - Cur -   *054958*
Träg, E., Obere Wörthstr. 18, 90403 Nürnberg.
T. (0911) 20 92 99.   *054959*
Venzlaff, Peter-Vischer-Str. 21, 90403 Nürnberg.
T. (0911) 241 85 55.   *054960*
Voigt, Obere Wörthstr. 1, 90403 Nürnberg.
T. (0911) 22 65 86.   *054961*
Wegener, V., Obere Schmiedgasse 24, 90403 Nürnberg.
T. (0911) 22 29 75.   *054962*
Wehner, Edith, Handwerkerhof Alt Nürnberg, 90402
Nürnberg.   *054963*
Weidler, Herbert, Morgensternstr. 1, 90451 Nürnberg.
T. (0911) 64 66 64.   *054964*
Weller, Bauerngasse 32, 90443 Nürnberg.
T. (0911) 28 91 60.   *054965*
Wiedl, G., Rosental 23, 90403 Nürnberg.
T. (0911) 22 26 99.   *054966*
Ziegler, Helmut, Pirckheimerstr. 134, 90409 Nürnberg.
T. (0911) 53 48 60. - China / Tin -   *054967*
Zintl, Herbert, Obere Mentergasse 1, 90443 Nürnberg.
T. (0911) 41 33 42.   *054968*
Zwissler, B., Weinmarkt 12a, 90403 Nürnberg.
T. (0911) 24 12 58.   *054969*

Nürtingen (Baden-Württemberg)

Hamisch, J., Brunnsteige 3, 72622 Nürtingen.
T. (07022) 314 24.   *054970*
Mehlhorn, W., Schloßgartenstr. 12, 72622 Nürtingen.
T. (07022) 323 05.   *054971*
Winkler, Michael, Marktstr. 9, 72622 Nürtingen.
T. (07022) 86 30. - Ant / Paint / Furn / Dec -   *054972*

Nußloch (Baden-Württemberg)

Bach, Ingeborg, Dreikönigstr. 11, 69226 Nußloch.
T. (06224) 107 22. - China / Jew / Silv -   *054973*
Ohrnberger, N., Gartenstr. 3, 69226 Nußloch.
T. (06224) 101 79.   *054974*

Oberasbach (Bayern)

Dallner, H., Bruckwiesenstr. 89, 90522 Oberasbach.
T. (0911) 69 89 19. - Ant -   *054975*
Ludwig, R., Rosenstr. 11, 90522 Oberasbach.
T. (0911) 69 54 89. - Ant -   *054976*
Müller, M., Wilhelmstr. 12, 90522 Oberasbach.
T. (0911) 69 23 32. - Ant -   *054977*

Oberbiberg (Bayern)

Kunst & Gemälde Marsie, Walstr. 2, 82041 Oberbiberg.
T. (089) 613 41 93. - Paint -   *054978*

Oberderdingen (Baden-Württemberg)

Kuhn, Ernst, Obere Gasse 11, 75038 Oberderdingen.
T. (07045) 80 10.   *054979*

Obergünzburg (Bayern)

Ullwer, Werner, Gartenweg 3, 87634 Obergünzburg.
T. (08372) 13 79.   *054980*

Oberhausen, Rheinland (Rheinland-Pfalz)

Cremer, Clemens, Poststr 5a, 46045 Oberhausen,
Rheinland. T. (0208) 227 10. - Ant / Furn / China /
Instr -   *054981*
Falk, Horst, Wielandstr 8, 46045 Oberhausen, Rhein-
land. T. (0208) 285 79.   *054982*
Kulbrock, H. Jürgen, Willi-Brandt-Pl 1, 46045 Oberhau-
sen, Rheinland. T. (0208) 808282. - Ant -   *054983*
Rüter, F.-J., Gustavstr 104, 46049 Oberhausen, Rhein-
land. T. (0208) 855803.   *054984*
Westhoff, Alfons, Beethovenstr 34, 46145 Oberhausen,
Rheinland.   *054985*

Oberkirch (Baden-Württemberg)

Müller, E., Löwengasse 6, 77704 Oberkirch.
T. (07802) 21 55.   *054986*

Oberlahr (Rheinland-Pfalz)

Buschulte, Alter Bahnhof, 57641 Oberlahr.
T. (02685) 12 86. - Furn -   *054987*

Obernburg (Bayern)

Muschik, N., Römerstr 55, 63785 Obernburg.
T. (06022) 5778.   *054988*

Obernkirchen (Niedersachsen)

Hentschel, Heinz, Rintelner Str 104, 31683 Obernkir-
chen. T. (05724) 2375.   *054989*

Obernzell (Bayern)

Munzinger, Susanne, Gasthof zur Post, 94130 Obernzell.
T. (08591) 1030.   *054990*

Obernzenn (Bayern)

Winterstein, B., Urphertshofen 9, 91619
Obernzenn.   *054991*

Oberstaufen (Bayern)

Antiquitäten-Cabinet, Schloßstr. 7, 87534 Oberstaufen.
T. (08386) 7564.   *054992*
Antiquitäten und Wein, Schloßstr. 1, 87534 Oberstaufen.
T. (08386) 72 28, Fax 4758. - Ant / Furn / Sculp / Dec /
Lights / Instr / Rel / Glass -   *054993*
Schulze, G., Hinterreute, 87534 Oberstaufen.
T. (08386) 27 43.   *054994*

Oberstdorf (Bayern)

Schädler, Oststr. 7, 87561 Oberstdorf.
T. (08322) 22 18.   *054995*

Oberteuringen (Baden-Württemberg)

Fitzko, K., Rosenstr. 15, 88094 Oberteuringen.
T. (07546) 56 95, 54 52.   *054996*

Oberursel (Hessen)

Antik Scheune, Vorstadt 6, 61440 Oberursel.   *054997*
Antiquitäten Krebsmühle, Krebsmühle, 61440 Oberursel.
T. (06171) 79572.   *054998*

Ochsenfurt (Bayern)

Giolda, Manfred, Theatergasse 5, 97199 Ochsenfurt.
T. (09331) 14 82. - Paint / Furn / Silv / Instr -   *054999*

Ochsenhausen (Baden-Württemberg)

Biechele, Margret, Schloßstr. 67, 88416 Ochsenhausen.
T. (07352) 82 37. - Ant / Furn / Sculp / Rel -   *055000*
Oberschwäbische Barockgalerie, Schloßstr 67, 88416
Ochsenhausen. T. (07352) 8237, Fax (07352) 4623.
- Paint / Furn / Sculp -   *055001*

Ockenheim (Rheinland-Pfalz)

Geib, Renate, Am St. Jakobsberg 33, 55437 Ockenheim.
T. (06725) 17 04, Fax 3749. - Graph -   *055002*

Odenthal (Nordrhein-Westfalen)

Blau, H.G., Höffer Weg 9, 51519 Odenthal.
T. (02202) 72 77.   *055003*

Öhringen (Baden-Württemberg)

Häuser, S., Poststr. 69, 74613 Öhringen.
T. (07941) 627 83.   *055004*
Rosenhagen, J., Am Bahndamm 17, 74613 Öhringen.
T. (07941) 25 08.   *055005*

Oelde (Nordrhein-Westfalen)

Antik An- und Verkauf, Stromberger Tor 2, 59302 Oelde.
T. (02522) 632 64. - Ant -   *055006*
Antik-Markt, Westrikweg 4, 59302 Oelde.
T. (02522) 6850.   *055007*
Dahms, P., Bahnhofstr. 7, 59302 Oelde.
T. (02522) 21 59.   *055008*
Diewald, Alfried, Schultenfeld, 59302 Oelde.
- Ant -   *055009*
Jakobi, K., Ahornweg 10, 59302 Oelde.
T. (02522) 18 44.   *055010*
Klosterbusch und Wilsmann, Zur dicken Linde 40,
59302 Oelde. T. (02522) 1386.   *055011*
Rusche, Egon, Enningerloher Str. 16, 59302 Oelde.
T. (02522) 82620, Fax 82629. - Ant / Paint -   *055012*

Oestrich-Winkel (Hessen)

Heich, D., Schnitterstr. 39, 65375 Oestrich-Winkel.
T. (06723) 55 29. - Mil -   *055013*
Sokel, H., Goethestr. 10, 65375 Oestrich-Winkel.
T. (06723) 45 57.   *055014*
Spreitzer, Bernhard, Hauptstr. 121, 65375 Oestrich-Win-
kel. T. (06723) 35 65. - Ant -   *055015*

Östringen (Baden-Württemberg)

Schmidt, H., Heinrich-Mann-Str. 6, 76684 Östringen.
T. (07253) 233 63.   *055016*

Oettingen (Bayern)

Klingel, E., Zeilstr. 6, 86732 Oettingen.   *055017*

Offenbach (Hessen)

Cosigo, Löwenstr. 24, 63067 Offenbach.
T. (069) 88 08 67. - Num -   *055018*
Häggele, K., Frankfurter Str. 80, 63067 Offenbach.
T. (069) 88 23 11.   *055019*
Herold, Manfred, Ludwigstr. 151, 63067 Offenbach.
T. (069) 81 35 29.   *055020*
Kindel, Kaiserstr. 61, 63065 Offenbach.
T. (069) 88 68 75. - Tin -   *055021*
Kitzinger, Annemarie, Mühlheimer Str. 386, 63075 Of-
fenbach. T. (069) 86 27 96.   *055022*
Klein, Wolfgang, Bieberer Str. 64, 63065 Offenbach.
T. (069) 88 69 12.   *055023*
Kohlpoth, Waldstr. 324, 63071 Offenbach.
T. (069) 85 18 88.   *055024*
Leidecker, M., Bieberer Str. 266, 63071 Offenbach.
T. (069) 85 50 03.   *055025*
Offenbacher Kunstkabinett, Mittelseestr. 52, 63065 Of-
fenbach. T. (069) 81 13 33, Fax 81 16 15. - Paint /
Graph / Repr / Tex / Dec / Fra / Glass / Draw -   *055026*

Offenburg (Baden-Württemberg)

Erdrich, W., Hauptstr. 119, 77652 Offenburg.
T. (0781) 244 33.   *055027*
Hofmann, R., Kesselstr. 8, 77652 Offenburg.
T. (0781) 232 29.   *055028*
Karrle, Katharina, Resedenweg 8, 77656 Offenburg.
T. (0781) 543 19.   *055029*

Leberer, U., Badstr. 2, 77652 Offenburg. T. (0781) 741 67. 055030
Schulz, Erwin, Tullastr. 41, 77652 Offenburg. T. (0781) 68 70. - Num - 055031
Schulz, Erwin, Tullastr. 41, 77652 Offenburg. T. (0781) 268 70. - Num / Mil - 055032

Offingen (Bayern)
Arndt, Martin, Steigstr. 29, 89362 Offingen. T. (08224) 72 80. - Ant - 055033

Ofterdingen (Baden-Württemberg)
Winter, Roman, Hechinger Str. 21, 72131 Ofterdingen. T. (07473) 41 77. 055034

Oggelshausen (Baden-Württemberg)
Burger, Max, 88422 Oggelshausen. - Ant - 055035

Ohrum (Niedersachsen)
Rautmann, P., Brückenstr. 13, 38312 Ohrum. - Mil - 055036

Olching (Bayern)
Huss, G., Hauptstr. 73, 82140 Olching. T. (08142) 185 72. - Furn - 055037

Oldenburg (Schleswig-Holstein)
Frenzel, Günter, Gr.-Schmütz-Str. 206, 23758 Oldenburg. T. (04361) 28 00. - Num - 055038

Oldenburg (Niedersachsen)
Anno Domini, Schloßpl. 19, 26121 Oldenburg, Oldenburg. T. (0441) 26070. - Ant - 055039
Antik- und Trödelkeller, Ammerländer Heerstr. 60, 26129 Oldenburg, Oldenburg. T. (0441) 77 65 18. 055040
Böhm, Donnerschweer Str. 60, 26123 Oldenburg, Oldenburg. T. (0441) 87532. 055041
Friedrich, O., Herrenweg 55a, 26135 Oldenburg, Oldenburg. T. (0441) 20 30 63. 055042
Kaluza, P., Alexanderstr. 13, 26121 Oldenburg, Oldenburg. T. (0441) 82870, 86500, Fax 86500. - Furn - 055043
Kunst & Antiquitäten, Peterstr. 46, 26121 Oldenburg, Oldenburg. T. (0441) 27170. 055044
Leo, M., Dr., Von-Müller-Str. 14, 26123 Oldenburg, Oldenburg. T. (0441) 817 29. 055045
Lühr, E., Haarenstr. 43, 26122 Oldenburg, Oldenburg. T. (0441) 164 09. 055046
Menges, A., Kurwickstr. 28, 26122 Oldenburg, Oldenburg. T. (0441) 15353. 055047
Rudolf, A., Ziegelhofstr. 6, 26121 Oldenburg, Oldenburg. T. (0441) 88 20 26. 055048
Smid, Klaus J., Burgstr. 30, 26122 Oldenburg, Oldenburg. T. (0441) 1 37 77. - Ant / Furn / China / Silv / Glass - 055049
Völker, Ernst, Lange Str. 45, 26122 Oldenburg, Oldenburg. T. (0441) 264 06. - Paint / Graph / Furn / Repr - 055050
Witt, H., Helmsweg 16, 26135 Oldenburg, Oldenburg. T. (0441) 20 28 22. 055051
Witt, L., Osterkampsweg, 26131 Oldenburg, Oldenburg. T. (0441) 575 21. 055052
Zeiner, Ludwig, Donnerschweer Str. 60, 26123 Oldenburg, Oldenburg. T. (0441) 875 32. - Ant / Silv / Lights / Rel / Cur / Ico - 055053

Olpe (Nordrhein-Westfalen)
Antik am Hexenturm, Frankfurter Str 16, 57462 Olpe. T. (02761) 3267. - Ant / Furn - 055054

Olsberg (Nordrhein-Westfalen)
Hees, H., Steinstr. 4, 59939 Olsberg. T. (02962) 24 57. 055055
Rath, I., & R. Meiswinkel, Bahnhofstr. 2, 59939 Olsberg. T. (02962) 2917. 055056

Opfenbach (Bayern)
Steinbauer, Franz, Allgäustr. 2-4, 88145 Opfenbach. T. (08385) 544. - Ant / Furn - 055057

Ortenberg (Baden-Württemberg)
Danner, P., Farrengasse 5, 77799 Ortenberg. T. (0781) 336 11. 055058

Osnabrück (Niedersachsen)
Anno dazumal, Lotter Str. 27, 49078 Osnabrück. T. (0541) 48002. - Ant - 055059
Atsch, A., Fritz-Reuter-Str. 17a, 49080 Osnabrück. T. (0541) 43 08 76. 055060
Bartel, A., Jeggener Weg 116, 49084 Osnabrück. T. (0541) 768 89. - Num - 055061
Blechkiste-Blechspielzeugversand, Stüvestr. 11, 49076 Osnabrück. T. (0541) 676 06, Fax 67606. - Toys - 055062
Böggemeyer, Walter, Lönsweg 20, 49076 Osnabrück. T. (0541) 43 33 78. 055063
Bosse, P., Große Gildewart 20, 49074 Osnabrück. T. (0541) 296 34. 055064
Boutique Antik, Lotter Str. 111, 49078 Osnabrück. T. (0541) 439 73. - Ant / Furn - 055065
Breitenkamp, W., Heger Str., 49074 Osnabrück. T. (0541) 480 01. - Ant / Paint / Graph / Furn / China / Dec / Jew / Silv / Lights / Glass - 055066
British-Möbel, Bramscher Str. 251, 49090 Osnabrück. T. (0541) 58 89 40. - Furn - 055067
Buddemeier, E., Dr., Marienstr. 17, 49074 Osnabrück. T. (0541) 257 44. - Ant - 055068
Delden, Dr. van, & Cie., Marienstr. 17, 49074 Osnabrück. T. (0541) 257 44, Fax 46261. - Ant / Paint / Furn / China / Jew / Silv / Glass - 055069
Dühme, Wilhelm, Markt 12, 49074 Osnabrück. 055070
Esch, Domhof 2, 49074 Osnabrück. T. (0541) 23556. 055071
Foth, Lothar, Heger Str. 24, 49074 Osnabrück. T. (0541) 22834. 055072
Fritz, P., Bierstr. 17, 49074 Osnabrück. T. (0541) 221 88. 055073
Hülsmeier, Dorothea, Heger Str. 7, 49074 Osnabrück. T. (0541) 224 16. 055074
Kersling, Ulf, Liebigstr. 31, 49074 Osnabrück. T. (0541) 290 36. 055075
Kreienbrink, Ansgar, Kleine Schulstr. 26, 49078 Osnabrück. T. (0541) 44 15 29. - Furn - 055076
Kremer, H., Heger Str. 10, 49074 Osnabrück. T. (0541) 2 23 24. - Ant - 055077
Künker, Fritz-Rudolf, Gutenbergstr. 23, 49076 Osnabrück. T. (0541) 680 51. - Num - 055078
Laubinger, Max, Piesberger Str. 56, 49090 Osnabrück. 055079
Laubinger, Rudolf, Piesberger Str. 58, 49090 Osnabrück. T. 616 50 (12 39 50). 055080
Liebmann, Lortzingstr. 1, 49074 Osnabrück. T. (0541) 261 76. 055081
Marquardt, Hannoversche Str. 19, 49084 Osnabrück. T. (0541) 57 33 35. 055082
Montana, Meller Str. 49, 49084 Osnabrück. T. (0541) 58 89 89. 055083
Moser, M., Heger Str. 26, 49074 Osnabrück. T. (0541) 294 56. 055084
Perrey, Dr., Krahnstr. 42, 49074 Osnabrück. T. (0541) 22522. 055085
Steinbrink, H., Hasemauer 7, 49074 Osnabrück. T. (0541) 244 25. - Num - 055086

Osterburken (Baden-Württemberg)
Reinhard, Bahnhofstr. 2, 74706 Osterburken. T. (06291) 8046, Fax 8662. - Orient / Tex - 055087

Ostercappeln (Niedersachsen)
Möller, Bremer Str. 40, 49179 Ostercappeln. T. (05473) 21 11. 055088

Osterhofen (Bayern)
Haber, Günther, Passauer Str. 27, 94486 Osterhofen. T. (09932) 20 06. - Furn - 055089

Osterode am Harz (Niedersachsen)
Elchlepp, A., Schillerstr 14a, 37520 Osterode am Harz. T. (05522) 4660. 055090

Ostfildern (Baden-Württemberg)
Petto, C., Kaiserstr. 12, 73760 Ostfildern. T. (0711) 34 31 94. 055091
Vitrine, Hauptstr. 14, 73760 Ostfildern. T. (0711) 456 02 22. 055092

Osthofen (Rheinland-Pfalz)
Fischer, Heinz, Carlo-Mierendorff-Str. 36, 67574 Osthofen. T. (06242) 76 68. 055093

Ostrach (Baden-Württemberg)
Wallrer, Ernst, Mörikestr. 16, 88356 Ostrach. 055094

Otterbach (Rheinland-Pfalz)
Lacmann, A., Kirchenstr 15, 67731 Otterbach. T. (06301) 1291. 055095

Otterberg (Rheinland-Pfalz)
Schäfer, K., Lutherstr. 5, 67697 Otterberg. T. (06301) 9903, Fax 9903. 055096

Ottersberg (Niedersachsen)
Blanken, H., Zum Dieker Ort 18, 28870 Ottersberg. T. (04205) 04293/262. 055097
Conreder, H., Wilhelmshauerstr. 4, 28870 Ottersberg. T. (04205) 7087. 055098

Otterstadt (Rheinland-Pfalz)
Jeschke, W., Frankenstr. 14, 67166 Otterstadt. T. (06232) 4534. - Tex - 055099
Miro, Mannheimer Str. 46, 67166 Otterstadt. T. (06232) 41089. 055100

Ottobrunn (Bayern)
Gaßner, Hermann, Unterhachinger Str. 1, 85521 Ottobrunn. T. (089) 6098986. 055101
Klaeber, Rolf, Spitzwegstr. 41a, 85521 Ottobrunn. - Ant - 055102

Ottweiler (Saarland)
Bost, M., Am Felsenkeller 4, 66564 Ottweiler. 055103

Otzberg (Hessen)
Studio für Kunst, Rodensteiner Weg 5, 64853 Otzberg. T. (06162) 22 07. 055104

Overath (Nordrhein-Westfalen)
Heppekausen, J., Kölnerstr. 43, 51491 Overath. T. (02206) 80403. - Ant - 055105
Kraus, E., Auf dem Lohkuppen 14, 51491 Overath. T. (02206) 717 44, 731 25. 055106
Schirow, Gerd H.R., Zoellnerstr. 27, 51491 Overath. T. (02206) 7710. - Furn / Silv - 055107

Paderborn (Nordrhein-Westfalen)
Altmeyer, R., Alte Torgasse 9, 33098 Paderborn. T. (05251) 259 38. 055108
Fuest, E., Rathenaustr. 80, 33102 Paderborn. T. (05251) 35945. 055109
Hagedorn, R., Theodorstr. 19, 33102 Paderborn. T. (05251) 28 14 15. 055110
Harlinghausen, Fritz, Giersstr 29, 33098 Paderborn. T. (05251) 23437. - Graph / Num - 055111
Hoffmann-Frigge, G., Hathumarstr. 5, 33098 Paderborn. T. (05251) 28 12 20. 055112
Janssen, Grube 9, 33098 Paderborn. T. (05251) 254 44. - Paint / Graph - 055113
Kabella, Wolfgang, Mühlenstr. 20, 33098 Paderborn. T. (05251) 28 15 55. 055114
Kafsack, Margareta, Michaelstr. 2-6, 33098 Paderborn. T. (05251) 25598, Fax 7273. - Ant / Paint / Furn / Silv / Draw - 055115
Krehota, Karl, Detmolder Str. 41, 33100 Paderborn. T. (05251) 567 72. 055116
Kunst- und Heimathaus, Mühlengrund 27, 33106 Paderborn. T. (05251) 61 81. 055117
Lammersen, August, Kamp 14, 33098 Paderborn. T. (05251) 236 69. - Ant - 055118
Poppinga, R., Ükern, 33098 Paderborn. T. (05251) 223 11. 055119
Rodehutscord, H., Stettiner Str. 1, 33106 Paderborn. T. (05251) 75712. 055120
Rossi, G., Michaelstr. 7, 33098 Paderborn. T. (05251) 262 70. 055121
Schlingmann, Renate, Krumme Grube 2, 33098 Paderborn. T. (05251) 288 77. 055122
Stecker, Karl-Heinz, Am Ikenberg 1, 33098 Paderborn. 055123
Tüshaus K. & I., Mühlenstr. 42, 33098 Paderborn. 055124

Witte, Königstr. 2, 33098 Paderborn. T. (05251) 234 22.
- Num - *055125*

Passau (Bayern)
Böhmisch, H.L., Rindermarkt 1, 94032 Passau.
T. (0851) 31516. *055126*
Böhmisch, H.L., Rindermarkt 1, 94032 Passau.
T. (0851) 31516. - Ant / Instr / Glass - *055127*
Haidinger, E., Ort 8, 94032 Passau.
T. (0851) 2802. *055128*
Maier, J., Neuburger Str. 41, 94032 Passau.
T. (0851) 65 93. *055129*
Michalski, Görlitzer Str. 34, 94036 Passau.
T. (0851) 542 09. *055130*
Thurnreiter, P. & G., Grabengasse 28, 94032 Passau.
T. (0851) 352 01. - Ant - *055131*
Zanella, F., Residenzplatz 3, 94032 Passau.
T. (0851) 2983. *055132*

Pattensen (Niedersachsen)
Kretzberg, Göttingerstr 40, 30982 Pattensen.
T. (05101) 12456. *055133*
Schulz, H., Dammstr 23, 30982 Pattensen.
T. (05101) 15398. *055134*

Pegnitz (Bayern)
Blechschmidt, H., Ostpreussenstr. 5, 91257 Pegnitz.
T. (09241) 58 39. *055135*

Pennigsehl (Niedersachsen)
Gossée, Jens-Helmut, Eichenhof, 31621
Pennigsehl. *055136*

Petersaurach (Bayern)
Hartmann, D., Kirschenstr. 13, 91580
Petersaurach. *055137*

Pfaffenhofen an der Ilm (Bayern)
Hitzler, Auenstr 13, 85276 Pfaffenhofen an der Ilm.
T. (08441) 71818. - Ant - *055138*

Pfaffing (Bayern)
Finster, Herbert, Berg 17, 83539 Pfaffing.
T. (08076) 1083. - Ant / Paint / Graph - *055139*

Pforzen (Bayern)
Leistner & Viebrock, Kaufbeurer Str. 6, 87666
Pforzen. *055140*

Pforzheim (Baden-Württemberg)
Bencik, Östliche Karl-Friedrich-Str. 7, 75175 Pforzheim.
T. (07231) 10 12 07. *055141*
Bode, Michael, Wilhelmshöhe 2, 75173 Pforzheim.
T. (07231) 243 47. - Ant / Paint / Graph / Furn / China /
Jew / Fra / Silv / Glass - *055142*
Breitsprecher, Bodo, Östl Karl-Friedr-Str. 11, 75175
Pforzheim. - Ant / Jew - *055143*
Dittus, M., Lotthammerstr. 9, 75172 Pforzheim.
T. (07231) 445 38. *055144*
Henninger-Tavcar, K., Hachellalee 7, 75179 Pforzheim.
T. (07231) 3 11 89. - China / Sculp - *055145*
Jäck, Lilo, Dillsteiner Str. 30, 75173 Pforzheim.
T. (07231) 219 27. *055146*
Krings, J.P., Albert-Schweitzer-Str 9, 75181 Pforzheim.
T. (07231) 79191. - Ant / Paint / Jew / Instr - *055147*
Müller, Klaus Emanuel, Würmtalstr. 11b, 75181 Pforz-
heim. T. (07231) 69343, 680485, Fax 67166.
- Ant - *055148*
Pforzheimer Münzhandelsgesellschaft, Bertholdstr. 15,
75177 Pforzheim. T. (07231) 325 71. - Num - *055149*
Ratz, Bernd, Oranierstr. 5, 75175 Pforzheim.
T. (07231) 3 21 16. - Ant - *055150*
Schmidt, T., Am Nagoldhang 9, 75173 Pforzheim.
T. (07231) 24740. *055151*
Starck, Rüdiger, Lammstr. 20, 75172 Pforzheim.
T. (07231) 14743. *055152*
Weber, Felix, Durlacher Str. 23, 75172 Pforzheim.
T. (07231) 329 41. - Ant - *055153*

Pfullingen (Baden-Württemberg)
Henderson, Römerstr 96, 72793 Pfullingen.
T. (07121) 790633, Fax 790688. - Eth / Orient - *055154*

Pfungstadt (Hessen)
Gansel, Rheinstr. 116, 64319 Pfungstadt.
T. (06157) 7758. *055155*

Schilke, Am Hintergraben 6, 64319 Pfungstadt.
T. (06157) 37 72, 846 96. - Ant - *055156*

Pinneberg (Schleswig-Holstein)
Hilffert, Franz, Kiefernweg 39, 25421 Pinneberg.
T. (04101) 625 43. - Instr - *055158*
Stahl, H., Prisdorf, 25421 Pinneberg.
T. (04101) 718 42. *055159*
Wendland, Mühlenstr 21a, 25421 Pinneberg.
T. (040) 24709, Fax (040) 200844. *055159a*

Pirmasens (Rheinland-Pfalz)
Numiversal, Schachenstr. 21, 66954 Pirmasens.
T. (06331) 640 51/53. - Num - *055160*
Reppa, Georg, Schachenstr. 61, 66954 Pirmasens.
T. (06331) 630 61. - Num - *055161*
Schmölz, Helmut, Mozartstr. 4, 66954 Pirmasens.
T. (06331) 980 67. - Ant / Paint / Graph / Num - *055162*
Schwalier, R., Jakob-Schunk-Str. 51, 66953
Pirmasens. *055163*

Pirna (Sachsen)
Großmann, Schmiedestr. 1, 01796 Pirna.
T. (03501) 3571, Fax 3571. - Paint / Graph / Repr /
Fra - *055164*

Plettenberg (Nordrhein-Westfalen)
Flesch, W., Christian-Rohlfs-Weg 2, 58840
Plettenberg. *055165*

Pöcking (Bayern)
Lorenz-Haramus, Eichenstr 21, 82343 Pöcking.
T. (08157) 8518. - Ant - *055166*

Poing (Bayern)
Gallon, Malcolm, Welfenstr. 29c, 85586 Poing.
T. (08121) 816 04. - Jew / Silv / Instr / Glass - *055167*

Pommelsbrunn (Bayern)
Stadler, M., Hübmersberg, 91224 Pommelsbrunn.
T. (09154) 85 29. - Ant - *055168*

Porta Westfalica (Nordrhein-Westfalen)
Das alte Fachwerkhaus, Portastr. 50, 32457 Porta West-
falica. T. (05706) 53666, 58676. *055169*
Möllenhoff, Irmgard, Portastr. 51, 32457 Porta Westfali-
ca. T. (05706) 552 84. - Ant / Jew / Silv / Glass /
Mod - *055170*
Theiß, R., Eisbergerstr. 15, 32457 Porta
Westfalica. *055171*

Potsdam (Brandenburg)
Antiquitäten-Galerie Potsdam, Kleine Gasse 3, 14467
Potsdam. T. (0331) 21320. - Ant / Paint / Furn / Orient /
China / Sculp / Tex / Jew / Silv / Glass / Mod - *055172*

Preetz, Holstein (Schleswig-Holstein)
Kunstboutique, Langebrückstr 6, 24211 Preetz,
Holstein. *055173*
Sütel, Hans-Richard, Klosterstr 18, 24211 Preetz,
Holstein. *055174*

Pressath (Bayern)
Weiterer, K., Riggau 14b, 92690 Pressath.
T. (09644) 657. *055175*

Preußisch Oldendorf (Nordrhein-Westfa-len)
Möller, H., Am Kamp 12, 32361 Preußisch Oldendorf.
T. (05742) 22 82. *055176*
Spreen, Hauptstr. 18, 32361 Preußisch Oldendorf.
T. (05742) 20 75. - Ant - *055177*

Prien (Bayern)
Antiquitäten und Wohnkultur, Bernauer Str 79, 83209
Prien. T. (08051) 3234, 4543. - Ant / Paint / Graph /
Furn / Arch / Dec / Jew / Fra / Silv / Lights / Instr / Glass /
Mod / Ico - *055178*
Kronast, Benedikt, Marktplatz 7, 83209 Prien.
T. (08051) 2123. - Ant / Sculp / Glass - *055179*

Prittriching (Bayern)
Okon-Chan, Kirchbergstr. 4D, 86931 Prittriching.
T. (08206) 6482. - Orient - *055180*

Pronstorf (Schleswig-Holstein)
Westphal & Niehusen, Lindenstr. 5, 23820 Pronstorf.
T. (04353) 04553/572, Fax 04506/1092. - Ant / Graph /
Furn / Lights / Instr - *055181*

Prüm (Rheinland-Pfalz)
Wangen, K., St.-Vither-Str. 23, 54595 Prüm.
T. (06551) 2276. *055182*

Püttlingen (Saarland)
Weber, C., Marktstr. 5, 66346 Püttlingen.
T. (06898) 63090. *055183*

Pulheim (Nordrhein-Westfalen)
Weber & Barth, Apfelweg 6, 50259 Pulheim.
T. (02238) 3329. *055184*

Pullach (Bayern)
Brenske, Wettersteinstr 25, 82049 Pullach.
T. (089) 795969, Fax (089) 795953. - Ico - *055185*

Quakenbrück (Niedersachsen)
Justus, Gerd, Lange Str. 12, 49610 Quakenbrück.
T. (05431) 29 57. *055186*
Wehlburg, Bahnhofstr. 36, 49610 Quakenbrück.
T. (05431) 6716. - Ant / Furn - *055187*

Quedlinburg (Sachsen-Anhalt)
Antiquitäten – Münzen, Pölkenstr. 50, 06484 Quedlinburg. T. (03946) 3256. *055188*

Radebeul (Sachsen)
Dähn, M., Bahnhofstr 16a, 01445 Radebeul.
T. (0351) 74965. *055189*
Vogel, M., Pestalozzistr 2, 01445 Radebeul.
T. (0351) 2811061. *055190*

Radevormwald (Nordrhein-Westfalen)
Hardt, Sieplenbusch 1, 42477 Radevormwald.
T. (02195) 80 58. - Orient - *055191*

Radolfzell (Baden-Württemberg)
Bodin, N., Singenerstr. 20, 78315 Radolfzell.
T. (07732) 534 93. *055192*

Raesfeld (Nordrhein-Westfalen)
Pelzer, Freiheit 10, 46348 Raesfeld.
T. (02865) 6504. *055193*
Wolter, Schlossallee 2, 46348 Raesfeld.
T. (02865) 7070. *055194*

Ramstein-Miesenbach (Rheinland-Pfalz)
Galerie K, Landstuhler Str. 69, 66877 Ramstein-Miesen-
bach. T. (06371) 707 37. *055195*
Hemm, T., Am Hocht 12, 66877 Ramstein-Miesenbach.
T. (06371) 524 07. *055196*

Randersacker (Bayern)
Demling, Ochsenfurterstr. 7, 97236 Randersacker.
T. (0931) 70 98 97. *055197*

Ransbach-Baumbach (Rheinland-Pfalz)
Letschert, Peter, Bergstr. 20, 56235 Ransbach-Baum-
bach. T. (02623) 2271, Fax 4768. - Ant / Furn /
Lights - *055198*
Schenkelberg, J., Masselbach 9, 56235 Ransbach-
Baumbach. T. (02623) 21 21. - China - *055199*
Sollbach, E., In der Bornwiese, 56235 Ransbach-Baum-
bach. T. (02623) 24 78. *055200*

Rastatt (Baden-Württemberg)
Bader, K.-F., Hauptstr. 47, 76437 Rastatt.
T. (07222) 522 41. - Ant - *055201*
Bollian, C., Lochfeldstr. 23, 76437 Rastatt.
T. (07222) 516 55. - Ant - *055202*
Clausnitzer, C., Finkenstr. 8, 76437 Rastatt.
T. (07222) 81041. - Ant / Paint / Graph / Fra /
Draw - *055203*
Ehrlich, Richard A., Kehlerstr. 13, 76437 Rastatt.
T. (07222) 2 39 39. - Ant / Num - *055204*
Ruf, Wolfgang, Brahmsweg 3, 76437 Rastatt.
T. (07222) 283 53, Fax 29034. - Tex - *055205*

Rastede (Niedersachsen)
Kieler, Dieter, Am Nordkreuz 6, 26180 Rastede.
T. (04402) 814 43. - Furn - *055206*

Studio Galerie, Bahnhofstr. 2, 26180 Rastede.
T. (04402) 82666. - Paint - 055207

Ratingen (Nordrhein-Westfalen)

Antikscheune, Heiligenhauser Str. 23, 40883 Ratingen.
T. (08669) 66138. 055208
Blees, E., Kirchfeldstr. 44, 40882 Ratingen.
T. (02102) 518 70. 055209
Schmitz, B., Düsseldorfer Str. 69, 40878 Ratingen.
T. (02102) 25847. 055210
Schützdeller, P., Lintorfer Str. 11, 40878 Ratingen.
T. (02102) 23825. 055211
Tanculski, Siegfried, Am Södrath 63, 40885 Ratingen.
T. (02102) 02054/4060, Fax 02054/7640. 055212
Thelen, R., Am Ostbahnhof 3, 40878 Ratingen.
T. (02102) 22114. 055213

Ratzeburg (Schleswig-Holstein)

Hartenberger, K., Herrenstr. 22, 23909 Ratzeburg.
T. (04541) 3792. - Ant - 055214

Ratzenhofen (Bayern)

Junkelmann, Erich, Dr., Schloß, 84094 Ratzenhofen.
- Ant / Arch / Eth - 055215

Rauschenberg (Hessen)

Kilian, H., Ellerweg 1, 35282 Rauschenberg.
T. (06425) 06427/8805. 055216

Ravensburg (Baden-Württemberg)

Dalfino, Wilhelmstr. 1, 88212 Ravensburg.
T. (0751) 165 85. 055217
Endraß, Werner, Tettnanger Str. 29, 88214 Ravensburg. 055218
Kamberger, M., Mühlbruckstr. 11, 88212 Ravensburg.
T. (0751) 332 38. 055219
Rieser, Rudolf, Eichelstr. 8, 88212 Ravensburg.
T. (0751) 22761. - Ant / Tex - 055220

Recklinghausen (Nordrhein-Westfalen)

Böcker, W., Feldstr. 46, 45661 Recklinghausen.
T. (02361) 65 27 58. 055221
Bomheuer, Hermann, Bochumer Str. 145, 45661 Recklinghausen. 055222
Brokbais, Wilhelm, Tiroler Str. 36a, 45659 Recklinghausen. T. (02361) 317 59. 055223
Dick, Augustinessenstr. 2a, 45657 Recklinghausen.
T. (02361) 18 42 26. - Paint / Furn / China / Jew / Glass - 055224
Gesterkamp, M.D., Herzogswall 10, 45657 Recklinghausen. T. (02361) 23891. 055225
Giesel, G. & M., Bochumer Str. 193, 45661 Recklinghausen. T. (02361) 65 34 91. 055226
Kaupel, J., Bochumer Str. 258, 45661 Recklinghausen.
T. (02361) 65 49 88. 055227
Knick, Martinistr. 12, 45657 Recklinghausen.
T. (02361) 229 30. - Paint / Graph / Repr / Fra / Glass - 055228
Lutat, Turmstr. 2, 45657 Recklinghausen.
T. (02361) 57851. 055229
Meyer, Kaiserwall 24, 45657 Recklinghausen.
T. (02361) 57673. - Num - 055230
Pfeil, W.P. Graf von, Beisinger Weg 2a, 45657 Recklinghausen. T. (02361) 234 74. - Paint / Paint / Graph / Furn / Dec - 055231
Schröder, Martinistr. 5, 45657 Recklinghausen. 055232
Spitmann, Wickingstr. 6, 45657 Recklinghausen.
T. (02361) 263 61. 055233

Rees (Nordrhein-Westfalen)

Brüderle, U., Schloß Sonsfled, 46459 Rees.
T. (02851) 02850/268. 055234
Peters, T., Sebastianstr. 7, 46459 Rees.
T. (02851) 1268. 055235

Regen (Bayern)

Wießner, H., Moizerlitzpl. 4, 94209 Regen.
T. (09921) 2520. 055236

Regensburg (Bayern)

Antik-Laden, Thundorferstr. 2, 93047 Regensburg.
T. (0941) 536 49, Fax 53649. - Ant / Paint / China / Sculp / Jew / Fra / Silv / Instr / Rel / Glass - 055237
Asia, Weiße-Hahnen-Gasse 2, 93047 Regensburg.
T. (0941) 590 39. 055238
Balters, E., & R. Löffler, Wahlenstr. 6, 93047 Regensburg. T. (0941) 56 04 14. 055239
Baumann, Eduard, Kramgasse 6, 93047 Regensburg.
T. (0941) 533 22, Fax 562198. - Ant / Paint / Graph / Furn - 055240
Berg, R., Wahlenstr. 3, 93047 Regensburg.
T. (0941) 522 29. 055241
Der Kleine Kunstladen, Rathausplatz 4, 93047 Regensburg. T. (0941) 56 01 44. 055242
Dietzel, H., Engelburgergasse 9, 93047 Regensburg.
T. (0941) 51300. 055243
Feiner, Franz, Brauergasse 8, 93059 Regensburg.
T. (0941) 86840. 055244
Fisch, P., Weißgerbergraben 6, 93047 Regensburg.
T. (0941) 56 01 75. 055245
Hackel-Bleibtreu, Christine, Wöhrdstr 7, 93059 Regensburg. T. (0941) 560674, Fax (0941) 57199. - Graph / Orient / Fra / Draw - 055246
Hahn, C., Hinter der Grieb 3, 93047 Regensburg.
T. (0941) 52425. 055247
Inhofer, C., Andreasstr. 26, 93059 Regensburg.
T. (0941) 842 57. 055248
Insam, Tändlergasse 11, 93047 Regensburg.
T. (0941) 510 74. - Ant / Paint / Furn / Dec / Jew / Silv / Lights / Instr - 055249
Mehrbrey, M., Rathausplatz, 93047 Regensburg.
T. (0941) 57167. 055250
Molière, M. M., Engelburgergasse 6, 93047 Regensburg.
T. (0941) 542 16. 055251
Otto, R., Thundorferstr. 2, 93047 Regensburg.
T. (0941) 53649, Fax 53649. - Ant - 055252
Pospieszczyk, R., Seifensiedergasse 14, 93059 Regensburg. T. (0941) 867 39. 055253
Radny, Günther V., Schwerdner Mühle, 93047 Regensburg. T. (0941) 828 77 055254
Rampfel, H., Untere Bachgasse 11, 93047 Regensburg.
T. (0941) 519 25. 055255
Schilling, Fritz, Steckgasse 4, 93047 Regensburg. 055256
Schindler, L., Ardennenstr. 23, 93057 Regensburg.
T. (0941) 612 39. 055257
Sichert, Hans, Adolf-Schmetzer-Str. 18, 93055 Regensburg. T. (0941) 5 32 23. - Ant / Paint - 055258
Watzlawik, S., Pfarrergasse 9, 93047 Regensburg.
T. (0941) 56 07 05. 055259
Wingerter, Rennweg 19, 93049 Regensburg.
T. (0941) 340 35. 055260

Rehau (Bayern)

Antiquitäten- und Bauernmöbel-Markt, Maxpl 15, 95111 Rehau. T. (09283) 1508. 055261
Stanka, H., Schildstr 4, 95111 Rehau.
T. (09283) 2871. 055262

Rehburg-Loccum (Niedersachsen)

Frantz, J., Heidtorstr. 8, 31547 Rehburg-Loccum.
T. (05037) 1415. 055263
Wagner, H., Münchehägerstr. 2, 31547 Rehburg-Loccum. T. (05037) 05766/1537. 055264

Rehlingen-Siersburg (Saarland)

Schon, E., Niedstr 107, 66780 Rehlingen-Siersburg.
T. (06833) 67143. 055265

Reichshof (Nordrhein-Westfalen)

Feustel, Karl, Auf der Bre 5, 51580 Reichshof. 055266

Reinbek (Schleswig-Holstein)

Antik Haus, Schmiedesberg 16, 21465 Reinbek.
T. (040) 7228800. 055267
Becker, J., Schönningstedter Str 57, 21456 Reinbek.
T. (040) 7227028. 055268
Jantzen, Margret, Schmiedesberg 16, 21465 Reinbek.
T. (040) 722 88 00. 055269
Kukla, Irmgard, Schulstr. 6, 21465 Reinbek. - Ant / Tex - 055270

Remagen (Rheinland-Pfalz)

Kessel, D., Im Gretenhof 5, 53424 Remagen.
T. (02642) 75 25, Fax 0228/31 02 22. - Sculp / Fra - 055271
Unikat, Mainzer Str. 87, 53424 Remagen.
T. (02642) 02288/8061. - Paint / Graph / Sculp / Fra / Mul / Draw - 055272

Remscheid (Nordrhein-Westfalen)

Hämmerling, Leana, Burger Str. 63a, 42859 Remscheid.
T. (02191) 38393, 38326, Fax 38390. 055273
Kranjc, F., Bergisch Born 124, 42897 Remscheid.
T. (02191) 66 71 48. 055274
Krielke, H., Krimstr. 7, 42855 Remscheid.
T. (02191) 77005. 055275
Müller, G., Alleestr. 71, 42853 Remscheid.
T. (02191) 259 10. 055276
Pauler, G., Königstr. 111, 42853 Remscheid.
T. (02191) 72147. 055277
Sauer, K.-J., Freiheitstr. 103, 42853 Remscheid.
T. (02191) 29 30 20. 055278

Remseck (Baden-Württemberg)

Döser, Fr. Paul, Blumenstr. 11, 71686 Remseck.
T. (07146) 77 00. 055279
Knyphausen, Graf, Schloß, 71686 Remseck.
T. (07146) 6321. 055280

Remshalden (Baden-Württemberg)

A und B, Antiquitäten und Bücher, Haus der Kunst, 73630 Remshalden. T. (07181) 749 71. - Ant - 055281
Haus der Kunst, Kanalstr. 10, 73630 Remshalden.
T. (07181) 73505, Fax 74933. - Ant - 055282

Rendsburg (Schleswig-Holstein)

Johannsen, U. & W., Hollerstr. 123b, 24768 Rendsburg.
T. (04331) 388 46, 318 17. 055283

Retterath (Rheinland-Pfalz)

Harrer, R. & W., Hauptstr. 1a, 56769 Retterath.
T. (02657) 1625. 055284

Reutlingen (Baden-Württemberg)

Galerie unter den Linden, Bahnhofstr. 30, 72764 Reutlingen. T. (07121) 408 76. 055285
Heck, Thomas, Kaiserstr. 64, 72764 Reutlingen.
T. (07121) 37 09 11, Fax 874 08. - Ant / Paint / Graph / Furn / China / Arch / Jew / Silv / Cur / Mul / Draw -- 055286
Horwarth, Metzgerstr. 9, 72764 Reutlingen.
T. (07121) 366 02. 055287
Kouril, Leo, Gaylerstr. 30, 72766 Reutlingen. 055288
Lang, R., Krämerstr. 10, 72764 Reutlingen.
T. (07121) 371 76. 055289
Rauscher, Norbert, Nürtingerhofstr. 1, 72764 Reutlingen.
T. (07121) 30 26 46. - Mil - 055290
Reutlinger Kunstkabinett, Nürtingerhofstr. 7, 72764 Reutlingen. T. (07121) 30 02 88. - Ant / Paint / Graph / Jew / Instr - 055291
Schröder, M., Riedstr. 23, 72766 Reutlingen.
T. (07121) 412 00. 055292
Tireli, Halil, Hofstattstr. 15, 72764 Reutlingen. 055293
Uhren-Sommer, Wilhelmstr. 111, 72764 Reutlingen.
T. (07121) 3 46 80. - Mod - 055294
Waimer, S., Albstr. 9, 72764 Reutlingen.
T. (07121) 378 01. 055295

Rheda-Wiedenbrück (Nordrhein-Westfalen)

Anno-Aktuell, Kirchstr 2, 33378 Rheda-Wiedenbrück.
T. (05242) 2698. 055296
Dreier, I.H., Lange Str 33, 33378 Rheda-Wiedenbrück.
T. (05242) 8452. - Furn - 055297
Galerie im Kertenhof, Moorweg 77, 33378 Rheda-Wiedenbrück. T. (05242) 42842, Fax 49774. - Paint / Graph / Sculp - 055298
Praske, Berliner Str 63, 33378 Rheda-Wiedenbrück.
T. (05242) 49227. 055299

Rheinbach (Nordrhein-Westfalen)

Haimann, Roswitha, 53359 Rheinbach. T. (02226) 69 40.
- Num - 055300
Kahmen, Dr. Hartmut, Todenfelderstr. 1, 53359 Rheinbach. T. (02226) 54 91. 055301

Rheinberg (Nordrhein-Westfalen)

Vorderstrase, R., Binsheimerstr. 11, 47495 Rheinberg.
T. (02843) 02844/792. 055302

Rheine (Nordrhein-Westfalen)

Büchter, E., Peterstr 30, 48429 Rheine.
T. (05971) 85552. 055303

Schulte, Pappelstr 22, 48431 Rheine.
T. (05971) 54189. 055304
Soisch, Herrenschreiberstr 17, 48431 Rheine.
T. (05971) 15292. 055305
Stegemann-Nienkemper, Markt 1, 48429 Rheine.
T. (05971) 12270. 055306
Stiegemann-Schöpper, Markt 15, 48429 Rheine.
T. (05971) 56566. 055307

Riedenburg (Bayern)
Richter, K., Schambacherweg 13a, 93339 Riedenburg.
T. (09442) 1342. 055308

Riedlingen (Baden-Württemberg)
Johannsen, W. & C., Schloßberg 12, 88499 Riedlingen.
T. (07371) 5700. 055309

Riedstadt (Hessen)
Bilinski, E., Hollagasse 1, 64560 Riedstadt.
T. (06158) 725 09. 055310

Riegelsberg (Saarland)
Hoppstädter, I., Wolfskaulstr. 59, 66292 Riegelsberg.
T. (06806) 47994. 055311

Rimbach, Oberpfalz (Bayern)
Döll, Anne, Fasanenweg 4, 93485 Rimbach, Oberpfalz.
T. (09977) 46 95. - Paint / Graph - 055312

Rimsting (Bayern)
Kietzmann, Edgar, Hochrießstr. 9, 83253 Rimsting.
T. (08051) 13 93. - Tex - 055313

Rinnthal (Rheinland-Pfalz)
Braun, H., Sportpl. 29, 76857 Rinnthal.
T. (06346) 8617. 055314

Rinteln (Niedersachsen)
Ritter, Extertalstr. 4, 31737 Rinteln. T. (05751) 43543,
42135. 055315

Rodenbach, Kr. Kaiserslautern (Rheinland-Pfalz)
Kunst-Studio, Fuchsstr. 41, 67688 Rodenbach, Kr.
Kaiserslautern. 055316

Rodgau (Hessen)
Wolff, M., Seestr 85, 63110 Rodgau. T. (06106) 72019.
- Num - 055317

Rödermark (Hessen)
Schöning, Rudolf, Jägerstr. 19, 63322 Rödermark.
T. (06074) 98289. 055318

Rödinghausen (Nordrhein-Westfalen)
Obrock, Helmut, Bahnhofstr. 6, 32289 Rödinghausen.
T. (05746) 81 04. - Ant / Furn - 055319

Römerberg (Rheinland-Pfalz)
Böh, E. & M., Am Friedhof, 67354 Römerberg.
T. (06232) 841 25. 055320

Rösrath (Nordrhein-Westfalen)
Herkoe, Holunderweg 2, 51503 Rösrath.
T. (02205) 820 44. 055321
Schlösser, Scharrenbroicher Str. 64, 51503 Rösrath.
T. (02205) 24 37. 055322
Wilden, Th., Kölnerstr. 62, 51503 Rösrath.
T. (02205) 26 43. 055323

Roetgen (Nordrhein-Westfalen)
Wynands, J., Bundesstr. 77, 52159 Roetgen.
T. (02471) 3594. 055324

Röthenbach, Allgäu (Bayern)
Immler, G., Tobelbachstr. 13, 88167 Röthenbach, Allgäu.
T. (08384) 268. 055325

Rohrdorf (Bayern)
Meyer van den Bergh, Zwillingshof, 83101 Rohrdorf.
T. (08032) 12 77. - Ant - 055326

Ronnenberg (Niedersachsen)
Nistahl, Holger, Empelder Str. 5, 30952 Ronnenberg.
T. (05109) 90 79. - Ant - 055327

Rosche (Niedersachsen)
Werner, R., Neumühle, 29571 Rosche.
T. (05803) 594. 055328

Rosenheim (Bayern)
Burger, Christine, Salinstr. 1, 83022 Rosenheim.
T. (08031) 159 29. - Paint / Furn / Jew / Mod /
Ico - 055329
Heibl, G., Neubeuerer Str. 1, 83026 Rosenheim.
T. (08031) 133 06. 055330
Paulinger, G., Ahornweg 17, 83022 Rosenheim. 055331
Urscher, Ludwigsplatz 32, 83022 Rosenheim.
T. (08031) 156 15. 055332
Weiß, Hildegard, Brünnsteinstr. 1, 83026 Rosenheim.
T. (08031) 45513. - Ant / Paint - 055333

Roßdorf bei Darmstadt (Hessen)
Otto, Ulrich, Buchwiesenweg 2, 64380 Roßdorf bei
Darmstadt. T. (06154) 9549. - Ant - 055334

Rostock (Mecklenburg-Vorpommern)
Mau, August, Am Brink 1, 18057 Rostock. T. (0381) 081/
22919. 055335

Roth, Mittelfranken (Bayern)
Schäfer, H., Leonhardsmühle, 91154 Roth, Mittelfranken. T. (09171) 63883. 055336
Sponsel, K., Kohlengasse 19, 91154 Roth, Mittelfranken. T. (09171) 3900. 055337

Rothenburg ob der Tauber (Bayern)
Eisenmann, Ludwig, Kirchplatz 2, 91541 Rothenburg ob
der Tauber. 055338
Hornn, Hermann, Kirchplatz 4, 91541 Rothenburg ob der
Tauber. 055339
Kenzen, G., Rödergasse 23, 91541 Rothenburg ob der
Tauber. T. (09861) 8136. 055340
Lindner, Georg, Herrngasse 6, 91541 Rothenburg ob der
Tauber. T. (09861) 3139. 055341
Mörmann, E. & Uschi, E. & Uschi, Uhlandstr 10, 91541
Rothenburg ob der Tauber. T. (09861) 7756. 055342
Schweitzer, Theodor, Herrngasse 11, 91541 Rothenburg
ob der Tauber. T. (09861) 3480. 055343
Sebald, G., Herrngasse 6, 91541 Rothenburg ob der
Tauber. T. (09861) 3139. 055344
Weiß, Fritz, Untere Schmiedgasse 5, 91541 Rothenburg
ob der Tauber. T. (09861) 2343. - Ant - 055345
Weiß, Peter, Herrngasse 23, 91541 Rothenburg ob der
Tauber. T. (09861) 3459. - Ant - 055346
Wohlfahrt, Käthe, Herrngasse 2, 91541 Rothenburg ob
der Tauber. T. (09861) 4090. - China / Cur - 055347

Rottach-Egern (Bayern)
Böck, Ernst & Betty, Seestr. 11, 83700 Rottach-Egern.
T. (08022) 51 34. - Ant / Paint / Furn / China / Sculp /
Silv / Rel / Ico - 055348
Böck, Thomas, Seestr. 3, 83700 Rottach-Egern.
T. (08022) 62 60. - Ant - 055349
Galerie am See, Ganghoferstr. 15, 83700 Rottach-Egern.
T. (08022) 672 13. - Ant / Furn / Sculp - 055350
Huber-Oberholzner, Nördliche Hauptstr. 7, 83700 Rottach-Egern. T. (08022) 265 40. - Furn - 055351
Lange, Günther, Hagerweg 12, 83700 Rottach-Egern.
T. (08022) 22 57. 055352
Marx, Werner, Seestr. 24, 83700 Rottach-Egern.
T. (08022) 21 72. - Paint - 055353
Prechtl, Peter, Seestr. 51, 83700 Rottach-Egern.
T. (08022) 248 28. - Ant / Paint / Graph / Furn / Sculp /
Dec / Jew / Fra / Instr / Rel / Glass / Cur - 055354
Richter, G.A., Pitscherweg 2, 83700 Rottach-Egern.
T. (08022) 52 22, Fax 26591. - Paint / Graph /
Draw - 055355
Rischer, Rolf, Nördliche Hauptstr. 13, 83700 Rottach-
Egern. T. (08022) 266 92, Fax 26069. - Ant /
Tex - 055356

Ruderting (Bayern)
Straub, L., Fischerhaus, 94161 Ruderting.
T. (08509) 579. 055357

Rüsselsheim (Hessen)
Friedrichs, Heinz A., Danziger Str. 24, 65428 Rüsselsheim. T. (06142) 422 85. - Num - 055358
Hück, K., Brunnenstr. 3, 65428 Rüsselsheim.
T. (06142) 72240. 055359

Ruhpolding (Bayern)
Dorrer, Rupert, Biberlöd 4, 83324 Ruhpolding.
T. (08663) 1873. 055360

Runkel (Hessen)
Quaschinski, B. & W., Burgstr. 31, 65594 Runkel.
T. (06482) 771, Fax 5712. - Ant / Furn / Repr / Tex /
Dec - 055361

Saarbrücken (Saarland)
Ball, Eisenbahnstr. 70, 66117 Saarbrücken.
T. (0681) 54942. 055362
Dawo, Udo, Kaiserstr. 133, 66111 Saarbrücken.
T. (0681) 81 23 21. - Furn - 055363
Der Saar Spezialist, Sulzbachstr. 3, 66111 Saarbrücken.
T. (0681) 35190. - Num - 055364
Ebrahimzadeh, L., Talstr. 48-50, 66119 Saarbrücken.
T. (0681) 584 71 90, 58 37 81. 055365
Ernst, Albert J., Im Flürchen 59, 66133 Saarbrücken.
T. (0681) 815767, 06805/7172, Fax 06805/21571.
- Paint / Sculp - 055366
Euler & Lösch, Mainzer Str. 58, 66121 Saarbrücken.
T. (0681) 63063. 055367
Herburger, Heinz, Dudweilerstr. 13, 66111 Saarbrücken.
T. (0681) 2 16 31. - Paint / Graph / Fra / Draw - 055368
Hofer, Jürgen, Bahnhofstr. 93, 66111 Saarbrücken.
T. (0681) 362 66. - Jew - 055369
Hoffmann, Günter, Sulzbachstr. 3, 66111 Saarbrücken.
T. (0681) 351 90. - Num - 055370
Hoffmann, H.-J., Wilhelm-Heinrich-Str. 22, 66117 Saarbrücken. T. (0681) 56791. - Num - 055371
Hupprich, E., Talstr. 64, 66119 Saarbrücken.
T. (0681) 516 47. 055372
Kohl, C., Am Sandberg 34, 66125 Saarbrücken.
T. (06897) 765153, 762230. - Num - 055373
Kohlbacher, P., Kaiserstr. 22, Schafbrücke, 66111 Saarbrücken. T. (0681) 89 22 20. 055374
Kohlert, Franz, Ormesheimer Str., 66131 Saarbrücken.
T. (0681) 06893/ 36 05. 055375
Konkel, Marian, Saargemünder Str. 154a, 66119 Saarbrücken. T. (0681) 87 12 78. 055376
Kopp, Obertorstr. 8, 66111 Saarbrücken.
T. (0681) 365 79. 055377
Kuriosa & Antik, Talstr. 48-50, 66119 Saarbrücken.
T. (0681) 584 71 90, 58 37 81, 558 33. 055378
Laborenz-Huber, D., Keltermannpassage, 66111 Saarbrücken. T. (0681) 320 79. 055379
Langer, Martin, Neumagener Weg 3, 66113 Saarbrücken. T. (0681) 7 16 03. - Ant / Paint / Tex - 055380
Lauer, K., Nauwieser Str. 44, 66111 Saarbrücken.
T. (0681) 35305. 055381
Möhringer, R., Feldmannstr. 28, 66119 Saarbrücken.
T. (0681) 584 63 44. 055382
Müller, K., St. Johanner Markt 18, 66111 Saarbrücken.
T. (0681) 358 24. 055383
Neuheisel, Gernot, Johannisstr. 3, 66111 Saarbrücken.
T. (0681) 390 44 60. 055384
Peretz, Dudweilerstr. 9, 66111 Saarbrücken.
T. (0681) 356 97. - Ant - 055385
Preisegger, Kaiserstr. 2, 66111 Saarbrücken.
T. (0681) 3 34 19. - Ant - 055386
Rase & Fromm, Im Rosengarten 7, 66130 Saarbrücken.
T. (0681) 87 41 18. 055387
Schmitt, Karlheinz, Dudweilerstr. 3, 66111 Saarbrücken.
T. (0681) 39 85 63. - Ant / Paint / Tex - 055388
Strauß, Kaiserstr. 170, 66111 Saarbrücken.
T. (0681) 81 45 73. 055389
Weber, Frank, Kaiserstr. 69A, 66111 Saarbrücken.
T. (0681) 81 37 76. 055390

Saarlouis (Saarland)
Bickelmann, G. H., Gymnasiumstr. 1, 66740 Saarlouis.
T. (06831) 14 31. - Num - 055391
Schirra, Überherrner Str. 1, 66740 Saarlouis.
T. (06831) 42173, Fax 41524. - Furn / Silv /
Mod - 055392
Volp, R., Alte Poststr. 28, 66740 Saarlouis.
T. (06831) 814 66. 055393
Walzinger, A. & A., Pavillonstr. 8, 66740 Saarlouis.
T. (06831) 495 41. 055394
Wilhelm, P., VII. Gartenreihe 7, 66740 Saarlouis.
T. (06831) 43324. 055395

Salem (Baden-Württemberg)
Credé, Eduard, Alte Neufracher Str. 149, 88682 Salem.
T. (07553) 75 78. - Ant / Orient / Arch / Eth / Cur / Mod /
Ico - *055396*

Salzgitter (Niedersachsen)
Magazin, Denzstr. 8, 38259 Salzgitter.
T. (05341) 39 37 57. *055397*

Salzhemmendorf (Niedersachsen)
Wenzel, R., Kummerstr., 31020 Salzhemmendorf.
T. (05153) 7743. *055398*

Salzkotten (Nordrhein-Westfalen)
Smajgl, Andreas, Wewelsburger Str. 13, 33154 Salzkotten. T. (05258) 76 83. - Ant / Paint / Graph / Furn / Num /
China / Sculp / Tex / Dec / Jew / Fra / Silv / Instr / Rel / Glass / Mod / Ico - *055399*

Salzwedel (Sachsen-Anhalt)
Müller, Burgstr. 37, 29410 Salzwedel. T. (03901) 23510.
- Paint - *055400*

Sandberg (Bayern)
Ertl, Harald, Langenleiten, 97657 Sandberg.
T. (09701) 373. *055401*

Sande (Niedersachsen)
Wolff, Wilfried, Sanderahmer Str. 33a, 26452 Sande.
T. (04422) 4000, Fax 4000. - Ant / Paint / Graph / Furn /
Orient / China / Sculp / Tex / Arch / Jew / Fra / Rel / Glas-
s / Draw / Tin / Naut - *055402*

Sandhausen (Baden-Württemberg)
Galerie für englische Keramik, Allmendstr. 31, 69207
Sandhausen. T. (06224) 3317. - Furn / Silv - *055403*

Sankt Augustin (Nordrhein-Westfalen)
Fandreyer, An der Hongsburg 13, 53757 Sankt Augustin.
T. (02241) 33 87 88. - Tex - *055404*
Lassche, H., Waldstr. 3, 53757 Sankt Augustin. *055405*
Schacher, R., Im Rosengarten 44, 53757 Sankt
Augustin. *055406*

Sankt Goarshausen (Rheinland-Pfalz)
Heuser, S., Bahnhofstr 4, 56346 Sankt Goarshausen.
T. (06771) 2195. *055407*

Sankt Ingbert (Saarland)
Thielen, H., Im Alten Tal 32, 66386 Sankt Ingbert.
T. (06894) 52210. *055408*

Sassnitz (Mecklenburg-Vorpommern)
Hartwich, Hauptstr. 30, 18546 Sassnitz.
T. (038392) 22390. - Paint / Graph / Furn / China /
Sculp / Mul / Draw - *055409*

Saterland (Niedersachsen)
Haendel, Julia, In der Lee 20, 26683 Saterland.
T. (04498) 12 26. - Furn / Silv / Instr - *055410*

Sauensiek (Niedersachsen)
Grunau, P., Wiegersen, 21644 Sauensiek.
T. (04169) 292. *055411*

Saulgau (Baden-Württemberg)
Friedmann, K., Lindenstr. 12, 88348 Saulgau.
T. (07581) 40 55. *055412*
Jörg, Werner H., Kasper-Kohler-Weg 12, 88348 Saulgau.
T. (07581) 85 32. - Num - *055413*

Schafflund (Schleswig-Holstein)
Neumann, M., Kätnerweg 8, 24980 Schafflund.
T. (04639) 234. *055414*

Schellerten (Niedersachsen)
Langstein, R., Steinkamp 9, 31174 Schellerten.
T. (05123) 12170. - Num - *055415*

Schesslitz (Bayern)
Liska, Hans, Oberend 15, 96110 Schesslitz.
T. (09542) 568. - Ant - *055416*

Schillingsfürst (Bayern)
Weinbeer, K., Insingerstr. 21, 91583 Schillingsfürst.
T. (09868) 5444. *055417*

Schlangen (Nordrhein-Westfalen)
Mania, Hornsche Str. 30, 33189 Schlangen.
T. (05252) 81632. *055418*

Schlangenbad (Hessen)
Balzer, Schloßpark Hohenbuchau, 65388 Schlangenbad.
T. (06129) 2319. - Paint - *055419*
Gärtner, Rheingauerstr 31, 65388 Schlangenbad.
T. (06129) 8930. *055420*
Kunstgalerie Hohenbuchau, Weiherallee 1-3, 65388
Schlangenbad. T. (06129) 2319. - Paint - *055421*
Weissenrieder's Neumühle, Schlangenbaderstr 167A,
65388 Schlangenbad. T. (06129) 2478. - Ant / Furn /
China / Dec - *055422*

Schleiden (Nordrhein-Westfalen)
Thiel, L., Klosterpl 3, 53937 Schleiden.
T. (02444) 1918. *055423*

Schleswig (Schleswig-Holstein)
Jänner, J., Michaelistr. 56a, 24837 Schleswig.
T. (04621) 237 04. *055424*
Schrape, Lollifuß 15, 24837 Schleswig.
T. (04621) 29258. *055425*
Steinhusen, E., Friedrichstr. 77, 24837 Schleswig.
T. (04621) 332 25. *055426*
Thomsen, E., Faulstr. 14, 24837 Schleswig.
T. (04621) 27264. *055427*

Schliersee (Bayern)
Greinwald, A. & M., Seestr. 13a und 16, 83727 Schlier-
see. T. (08026) 42 27. - Ant / Paint / Furn / Sculp /
Rel - *055428*

Schloß Holte-Stukenbrock (Nordrhein-Westfalen)
Gorecki, Georg, Buchenweg 17, 33758 Schloß Holte-
Stukenbrock. *055429*

Schmallenberg (Nordrhein-Westfalen)
Tröster, H., Burgweg 1, 57392 Schmallenberg.
T. (02972) 1460. *055430*

Schmelz (Saarland)
Freis, H. & E., Talstr. 40, 66839 Schmelz.
T. (06887) 3800. *055431*

Schneverdingen (Niedersachsen)
Schmidt, L., Oststr. 6, 29640 Schneverdingen.
T. (05193) 1885. *055432*

Schöllkrippen (Bayern)
Antiquitäten am Geisberg, Geisbergstr. 7, 63825 Schöll-
krippen. T. (06024) 9488, Fax 5603. - Paint / Furn / Chi-
na / Dec / Jew / Silv / Lights / Glass - *055433*
Borst, M., Aschaffenburgerstr.36, 63825 Schöllkrippen.
T. (06024) 9937. *055434*

Schönaich (Baden-Württemberg)
Krug, R., Wettgasse 12, 71101 Schönaich. *055435*

Schönecken (Rheinland-Pfalz)
Propson, R., Unter de Pfordt 50, 54614 Schönecken.
T. (06553) 2435. *055436*

Schonungen (Bayern)
Götz, Winfried, Schwarzland 2, 97453 Schonungen.
T. (09721) 09727/1475. *055437*

Schopfheim (Baden-Württemberg)
Matt, J., Hauptstr. 235, 79650 Schopfheim.
T. (07622) 61298. *055438*
Münzen-Neef, Hauptstr. 111, 79650 Schopfheim.
T. (07622) 2788, Fax 2788. - Num - *055439*

Schorndorf (Baden-Württemberg)
Hochleitner, C., Remsstr. 27, 73614 Schorndorf.
T. (07181) 697 68. *055440*
Hochleitner, C., Welzheimer Str. 17, 73614 Schorndorf.
T. (07181) 77254. *055441*
Ilzhöfer, P., Welzheimer Str. 27, 73614 Schorndorf.
T. (07181) 752 93. *055442*
Kreeb, E., Gottlieb-Daimler-Str. 51, 73614 Schorndorf.
T. (07181) 649 56. *055443*

Pilz, E., Westergasse 6, 73614 Schorndorf.
T. (07181) 748 28. *055444*
Smital, Adolf, Wieslauftalstr. 59, 73614 Schorndorf.
T. (07181) 637 32. *055445*

Schramberg (Baden-Württemberg)
Grimm, Rolf, Oberndorfer Str. 147, 78713
Schramberg. *055446*
Rapp, Eugen, Jorgenmichelshof 2, 78713
Schramberg. *055447*

Schriesheim (Baden-Württemberg)
Mohr, I., Ruhweg 3, 69198 Schriesheim.
T. (06203) 654 10. *055448*

Schutterwald (Baden-Württemberg)
Kunst und Leben, Schutterstr. 12, 77746 Schutterwald.
T. (0781) 510 84. *055449*

Schwabach (Bayern)
König, M., Am Rothbock 6a, 91126 Schwabach.
T. (09122) 824 40. *055450*
Ramsenthaler, K., Königspl. 21, 91126 Schwabach.
T. (09122) 2555. *055451*

Schwäbisch Gmünd (Baden-Württemberg)
Fischer, R., Kappelgasse 3, 73525 Schwäbisch Gmünd.
T. (07171) 304 69. *055452*
Gelmar, Josef, Rinderbacher Gasse 28, 73525 Schwä-
bisch Gmünd. T. (07171) 631 49. *055453*
Hoffmann, U. & M., Rinderbacher Gasse 21, 73525
Schwäbisch Gmünd. T. (07171) 679 93. *055454*
Ma-celo's, Ackergasse 2, 73525 Schwäbisch Gmünd.
T. (07171) 39814. *055455*
Merz, D., Akazienweg 25, 73527 Schwäbisch Gmünd.
T. (07171) 66696. *055456*
Schmidt, Wolfgang, Wilhelmstr. 38, 73525 Schwäbisch
Gmünd. T. (07171) 64528. - Graph / Repr / Pho /
Draw - *055457*
Ulrich, T., Aalener Str. 54, 73529 Schwäbisch Gmünd.
T. (07171) 635 43. *055458*

Schwäbisch Hall (Baden-Württemberg)
Baumann, J., Bahnhofstr. 2, 74523 Schwäbisch Hall.
T. (0791) 88 05. *055459*
Pfeiffer, K. H., Obere Herrengasse 6, 74523 Schwäbisch
Hall. T. (0791) 63 31. *055460*

Schwalmstadt (Hessen)
Pfau, Rolf, Am grossen Wallgraben 31, 34613 Schwalm-
stadt. T. (06691) 48 92. - Ant / Furn - *055461*
Rode, Chinapark 1, 34613 Schwalmstadt.
T. (06691) 43 87. - Orient - *055462*
Wollmann, Industriestr. 1a, 34613 Schwalmstadt.
T. (06691) 2988, Fax 24224. - Paint / Graph /
Sculp - *055463*

Schwalmtal, Niederrhein (Nordrhein-Westfalen)
Heimes, L., Burgwall 1, 41366 Schwalmtal, Niederrhein.
T. (02163) 5595. *055464*

Schwandorf (Bayern)
Schwarz, P., Garrstr, 92421 Schwandorf.
T. (09431) 42906. *055465*

Schwanewede (Niedersachsen)
Lawrence, Horst, Dorfstr. 59, 28790 Schwanewede.
T. (04209) 0421/ 68 23 03. - Ant - *055466*

Schwangau (Bayern)
Antikhaus-Sammlerstube, Unterdorf 1, 87645 Schwangau. T. (08362) 88110, Fax 88130. - Ant - *055467*

Schwarzenbruck (Bayern)
Rötzer, F. & E., Fröschauerstr. 3, 90592 Schwarzenbruck. T. (09128) 32 09. *055468*

Schwegenheim (Rheinland-Pfalz)
Prosotowitz, Hans, Bahnhofstr. 86, 67365 Schwegenheim. T. (06344) 37 78. - Silv / Instr - *055469*

Schweich (Rheinland-Pfalz)
Hoflädchen, Oberstiftstr 50, 54338 Schweich.
T. (06502) 2335. *055470*

Schweinfurt (Bayern)

Brembs, B., Zehntstr. 3, 97421 Schweinfurt.
T. (09721) 24772.   055471
Marotte, Bauerngasse 16, 97421 Schweinfurt.
T. (09721) 285 99. - Ant -   055472
Reusch, C., Zehntstr. 1, 97421 Schweinfurt.
T. (09721) 23505.   055473
Vorndran, Obere Str. 9, 97421 Schweinfurt.
T. (09721) 18 53 79.   055474
Wansch, Ludwig, Obere Str. 28, 97421
Schweinfurt.   055475
Wolff, Klaus, Schultesstr. 18, 97421 Schweinfurt.
T. (09721) 223 73.   055476
Wolz, Fridolin, Schönerstr. 3, 97422 Schweinfurt.
- Num -   055477

Schwelm (Nordrhein-Westfalen)

Mahl, M., Hauptstr. 6a-10a, 58332 Schwelm.
T. (02336) 75 06, Fax 7506. - Ant / Furn -   055478

Schwendi (Baden-Württemberg)

Irg, Franz, Biberacher Str. 16, 88477 Schwendi.
T. (07353) 20 10. - Ant / Furn / Sculp / Dec / Lights /
Instr / Rel / Glass / Cur -   055479

Schwerin (Mecklenburg-Vorpommern)

Antiquitäten-Galerie Schwerin, Am Markt 10, 19055
Schwerin. T. (0385) 812485. - Ant / Paint / Furn /
Orient / Sculp / Tex / Jew / Glass / Mod / Ico -   055480

Schwerte (Nordrhein-Westfalen)

Vasarhelyi, Günter, Meinerweg 5, 58239 Schwerte.
T. (02304) 67034. - Mil -   055481

Schwetzingen (Baden-Württemberg)

Rapp, K.-H., Lunevillerstr. 18, 68723 Schwetzingen.
T. (06202) 32 90.   055482

Schwissel (Schleswig-Holstein)

Brunke, M. & B., Lüttredder 6, 23795 Schwissel.
T. (04551) 2285.   055483

Seefeld (Bayern)

Ramer, Andreas, Schloss, 82229 Seefeld.
T. (08152) 788 77. - Furn -   055484
Schloßscheune, 82229 Seefeld.
T. (08152) 784 13.   055485

Seeheim-Jugenheim (Hessen)

Poorhosaini, Hauptstr 48, 64342 Seeheim-Jugenheim.
T. (06257) 7809. - Ant -   055486
Siegmayer, H., Außerhalb 31, 64342 Seeheim-Jugen-
heim. T. (06257) 81905.   055487

Seeon (Bayern)

Schott-Goller, Grete, Schulstr. 5, 83370 Seeon.   055488

Seevetal (Niedersachsen)

Fey, Thomas, Jesteburger Str. 5, 21218 Seevetal.
T. (04105) 524 95, Fax 54935. - Ant / Paint /
Furn -   055489
Hansen, Nikolaus, Liedholz 3, 21217 Seevetal.   055490

Selb (Bayern)

Aldewereld, Cornelis, Hammergut, 95100 Selb.
T. (09287) 788 33.   055491

Selfkant (Nordrhein-Westfalen)

Hensgens, Anita, Hauptstr. 38, 52538 Selfkant.
T. (02456) 12 92.   055492
Schenkelberg, B., Landstr. 31, 52538 Selfkant.
T. (02456) 18 02.   055493

Seligenstadt (Hessen)

Alban, E., Kaiser-Karl-Str. 31, 63500 Seligenstadt.
T. (06182) 21320.   055494

Selters, Taunus (Hessen)

Hochhaus, P., Grabenstr. 23, 65618 Selters, Taunus.
T. (06483) 6682.   055495

Senden (Bayern)

Siemann, Ursula, Fuggerstr. 8, 89250 Senden.   055496

Senden, Westfalen (Nordrhein-Westfalen)

Vorspohl, Klara, Dorfstr. 5, 48308 Senden, Westfalen.
T. (02597) 15 61.   055497

Siegburg (Nordrhein-Westfalen)

Grunschel, K., Siegfeldstr.15, 53721 Siegburg.
T. (02241) 652 15.   055498
Micus, Herbert, Augustastr. 25, 53721 Siegburg.
T. (02241) 512 27.   055499
Schmidt, J., Luisenstr. 42, 53721 Siegburg.
T. (02241) 698 32.   055500

Siegen (Nordrhein-Westfalen)

Intarsia, Hermannstr 16, 57072 Siegen.   055501
Isermann, I., Löhrstr 13, 57072 Siegen.
T. (0271) 52573.   055502
Kiss, J., Breite Str 11, 57076 Siegen.
T. (0271) 45400.   055503
Nohl, Ruth, Kölner Str 44, 57072 Siegen.
T. (0271) 55108. - Ant -   055504
Pothmann, W., Juliusstr 16, 57072 Siegen.
T. (0271) 53339.   055505
Richter, U., Hinterstr 73, 57072 Siegen. T. (0271) 52360,
Fax 50257. - Ant / Paint / China / Sculp / Jew / Silv /
Lights / Cur -   055506
Schütz, H.-W., Gießenreistr 12, 57072 Siegen.
T. (0271) 46546.   055507
Spyra-Hanssen, Edelgard, Tillmann-Stolz-Str 35, 57074
Siegen.   055508

Sigmaringen (Baden-Württemberg)

Riempp, Julius, Apothekergasse, 72488 Sigmaringen.
T. (07571) 123 76.   055509

Simmerath (Nordrhein-Westfalen)

Menzerath, H., Paustenbacherstr. 51, 52152 Simmerath.
T. (02473) 81 43.   055510

Sindelfingen (Baden-Württemberg)

Höhn, M., Ziegelstr. 5, 71063 Sindelfingen.
T. (07031) 842 61.   055511
Leibfried, Fr., Böblinger Str. 3, 71065 Sindelfingen.
T. (07031) 845 49.   055512
Strehler, Brigitte, Hermelinweg 7, 71063 Sindelfingen.
T. (07031) 801043, Fax (07031) 806906.   055513

Singen (Baden-Württemberg)

Förg, Alfons, Hauptstr 40, 78224 Singen.
T. (07731) 63577.   055514
Frauendienst, A., Schaffhauser Str 51, 78224 Singen.
T. (07731) 65575.   055515
Lenz, Heinrich, Thurgauer Str 1, 78224 Singen.
- Num -   055516
Rädler, H.-P., Heganstr 4, 78224 Singen.
T. (07731) 68555.   055517

Sinn (Hessen)

Lampasiak, Josef, Ballersbacher Weg 21, 35764 Sinn.
T. (02772) 523 29.   055518

Sinsheim (Baden-Württemberg)

Antikcenter, Louis-Goos-Str 6, 74889 Sinsheim.
T. (07261) 12036.   055519
Büchner, H., Am Hohen Stein 1, 74889 Sinsheim.
T. (07261) 4895.   055520
Deberle, J., Burghäldeweg 13, 74889 Sinsheim.
T. (07261) 2783.   055521
Schwald, G., Waibstadterstr 19, 74889 Sinsheim.
T. (07261) 4292.   055522
Stoll, R., Dörntelsberg 3, 74889 Sinsheim.
T. (07261) 61027.   055523
Zimnoch, Luis-Goos-Str 6, 74889 Sinsheim.
T. (07261) 12036.   055524

Sinzheim (Baden-Württemberg)

Müller, A., Landstr. 60, 76547 Sinzheim.
T. (07221) 825 60.   055525

Sinzig (Rheinland-Pfalz)

Meis, Bachovenstr 5, 53489 Sinzig. T. (02642) 42933.
- Paint -   055526

Söhlde (Niedersachsen)

Wanfahrt, K., An der Bundesstr. 8, 31185 Söhlde.
T. (05129) 1666. - Ant / Paint / Graph / Furn / Orient /
Sculp -   055527

Soest (Nordrhein-Westfalen)

Antik-Galerie Soest, Märkische Str B1, 59494 Soest.
T. (02921) 61603. - Furn -   055528
Kiko, W., Märkische Str 22a, 59494 Soest.
T. (02921) 61603.   055529
Knop, H.-D., Paradieser Holzweg 23, 59494 Soest.
T. (02921) 60703.   055530
Reimann-Wehr, C., An der Lanner 2, 59494 Soest.
T. (02921) 02928/1005.   055531
Soester Münzcabinett, Markt 3-5, 59494 Soest.
T. (02921) 2211. - Num -   055532
Die Werkstatt, Auf der Borg 38-40, 59494 Soest.
T. (02921) 3976.   055533

Solingen (Nordrhein-Westfalen)

Antikhaus am Weyer, Weyerstr. 265, 42719 Solingen.
T. (0212) 31 62 63.   055534
Bärz, Elisabeth, Schloßbergstr. 7, 42659
Solingen.   055535
Burger Kunststuben, Schloß Burg, 42651 Solingen.
T. (0212) 403 03. - Paint / Graph / China / Jew -   055536
Demessieur, Thomas, Pfaffenberger Weg 87, 42659 So-
lingen. T. (0212) 447748, Fax 20 27 01. - Ant / Paint /
Furn -   055537
Fischer, F.-P., Nibelungenstr. 25, 42653 Solingen.
T. (0212) 53 08 33.   055538
Grimm, Helmut, Merscheider Str. 16, 42699
Solingen.   055539
Grusser, G., Friedrich-Ebert-Str. 243, 42719 Solingen.
T. (0212) 31 37 99.   055540
Kamm, G., Kuller Str. 57, 42651 Solingen.
T. (0212) 54 94 98.   055541
Lommel, M., Eiland 14, 42651 Solingen.
T. (0212) 20 39 52. - Num -   055542
Müllenmeister, K.J., Börsenstr 69, 42657 Solingen.
T. (0212) 809004, Fax 809617. - Paint -   055543
Müller, Heinz-W., Wermelskirchener Str. 46, 42659 So-
lingen. T. (0212) 420 24, Fax 46691. - Num -   055544
Schaaff, C.D., Mummstr. 31, 42651 Solingen.
T. (0212) 106 61.   055545
Schröder, Detlef, Merscheider Str. 316, 42699 Solingen.
T. (0212) 33 11 24.   055546
Wick, E., Hübben 25, 42655 Solingen.
T. (0212) 20 79 90.   055547

Soltau (Niedersachsen)

Bauer, F. & R., Grenzwall 6, 29614 Soltau.
T. (05191) 5808.   055548
Stephan, Siegmund, Walsroder Str. 41, 29614 Soltau.
T. (05191) 162 85, Fax 17823. - Num / China / Tex /
Jew / Silv / Mil -   055549

Sonthofen (Bayern)

Hohenegg, G., Mühlenweg 7, 87527 Sonthofen.
T. (08321) 810 57.   055550
Metzeler, A., Hochstr. 20, 87527 Sonthofen.
T. (08321) 9253.   055551
Schaake, Gustentr. 27, 87527 Sonthofen.
T. (08321) 42 00. - Mil -   055552

Spahnharrenstätte (Niedersachsen)

Bley, Hermann, Hauptstr. 81, 49751 Spahnharrenstätte.
T. (05951) 05952/6 62.   055553

Spalt (Bayern)

Bussinger, R., Lange Gasse 36, 91174 Spalt.
T. (09175) 464.   055554

Spangdahlem (Rheinland-Pfalz)

Kremer, J.W., Tannenweg 6a, 54529 Spangdahlem.
T. (06565) 4681.   055555

Spenge (Nordrhein-Westfalen)

Sarpe, R., Am Schürhof 196, 32139 Spenge.   055556

Speyer (Rheinland-Pfalz)

Drawe, G., Gilgenstr. 15, 67346 Speyer.
T. (06232) 791 66, 784 33. - Ant -   055557
Dusch, Peter, Gutenbergstr. 19, 67346 Speyer.
T. (06232) 745 72. - Ant / Furn / Fra -   055558

Göbel, Hannelore, Johannesstr. 20, 67346 Speyer. T. (06232) 240 68. - Ant - 055559

Kopp, D., Mühlturmstr. 7, 67346 Speyer. T. (06232) 76151. 055560

Memmel, F., Wormser Str. 47, 67346 Speyer. T. (06232) 72337. 055561

Weingärtner, H., Korngasse 34, 67346 Speyer. T. (06232) 751 36. 055562

Wilde, Werner, Breslauer Str. 8, 67346 Speyer. 055563

Sprockhövel (Nordrhein-Westfalen)

Dr. Klusmann Fine Art, Schulstr 23, 45549 Sprockhövel. T. (02324) 77190. - Paint - 055564

Nasenberg, B., Mittelstr 97, 45549 Sprockhövel. T. (02324) 02339/4357. 055565

Stade (Niedersachsen)

Anton, E., Steiermarkstr. 32, 21680 Stade. T. (04141) 668 54. 055567

Stadtallendorf (Hessen)

Budrus, R., Litau 18, 35260 Stadtallendorf. T. (06429) 1495. 055568

Zon, R. van, Ohäusermühle, 35260 Stadtallendorf. T. (06429) 75 18. 055569

Stadthagen (Niedersachsen)

Bolte, Niedernstr. 31, 31655 Stadthagen. T. (05721) 6313. 055570

Oberschür, Detlev, Oberntorstr. 2, 31655 Stadthagen. T. (05721) 48 97. - Ant / Graph / Furn / China / Repr / Tex / Dec / Jew / Silv / Lights / Glass / Jew - 055571

Stadtlohn (Nordrhein-Westfalen)

Hintemann, Felix, Estern 53, 48703 Stadtlohn. T. (02563) 242. - Furn - 055572

Leuker, Bernhard, Büren 1, 48703 Stadtlohn. T. (02563) 025 66/43 55. 055573

Temme, A., Richters Kp. 18, 48703 Stadtlohn. T. (02563) 78 39. 055574

Staffelstein (Bayern)

Schwendner, Franz, 96231 Staffelstein. 055575

Starnberg (Bayern)

Rischkopf, Günter, Jägersbrunn 5, 82319 Starnberg. T. (08151) 163 47, Fax (08151) 3387. - Ant - 055576

Scholler, Lotte von, Bahnhofspl. 4, 82319 Starnberg. 055577

Schwarzmann, Maximilianstr. 14, 82319 Starnberg. T. (08151) 167 59, Fax 89753. - Ant / Paint / Furn / Jew - 055578

Steinbach, Taunus (Hessen)

Cenkovcan, I., Niederhöchstädter Str 20, 61449 Steinbach, Taunus. T. (06171) 78077. 055579

Schmitt, L., Berlinerstr 31, 61449 Steinbach, Taunus. T. (06171) 71823. 055580

Steinbergkirche (Schleswig-Holstein)

Wendrich, U., Schöne Aussicht 14, 24972 Steinbergkirche. T. (04632) 75 33. 055581

Steinenbronn (Baden-Württemberg)

Meier, K.-D., & S. Staudenraus, Plieningerstr. 10, 71144 Steinenbronn. T. (07157) 725 14. - Ant - 055582

Steinfurt (Nordrhein-Westfalen)

Antiquitäten und Geschenke, Markt 5, 48565 Steinfurt. T. (02551) 82836. - Ant / Paint / Furn / China / Jew / Silv / Silv - 055583

Steinhagen (Nordrhein-Westfalen)

Bock, Melitta, Bielefelder Str. 90, 33803 Steinhagen. T. (05204) 8621. 055584

Butz, L., Azaleestr. 44, 33803 Steinhagen. T. (05204) 4145. 055585

Rother, E., Alte Kirchstr. 12, 33803 Steinhagen. T. (05204) 8644. 055586

Steinwenden (Rheinland-Pfalz)

Gensinger, E., Reichswaldring 43, 66879 Steinwenden. T. (06371) 51353. 055587

Stephanskirchen, Simssee (Bayern)

Bachmayr, Walter, Grillparzerstr. 9, 83071 Stephanskirchen, Simssee. T. (08036) 71533. - Ant - 055588

Zahn, Hans, 83071 Stephanskirchen, Simssee. - Ant - 055589

Stockach (Baden-Württemberg)

Emwid, Industriestr. 19, 78333 Stockach. T. (07771) 2804. - Num - 055590

Fundgrube, Dillstr. 8a und Goethestr. 25, 78333 Stockach. T. (07771) 1708. 055591

Stolberg (Nordrhein-Westfalen)

Gorissen, H., Vennstr 99, 52224 Stolberg. T. (02402) 8177. 055592

Kaussen, Ingrid, Vennstr 99-101, 52224 Stolberg. T. (02402) 02408/58377. - Ant - 055593

Neuerburg, Ch., Langerweher Str 47, 52224 Stolberg. T. (02402) 02409/247. 055594

Strasslach (Bayern)

Altbayrische Antiquitäten, Kleindingharting 5, 82064 Strasslach. T. (08170) 72 42, Fax 7242. - Ant / Furn / China / Lights / Glass / Tin - 055595

Scheibal, Hans B., Dinghartingerstr. 4, 82064 Strasslach. T. (08170) 687, 089/201 54 18. - Paint / Graph / Draw - 055596

Straubing (Bayern)

Liberté, Stadtturm, 94315 Straubing. T. (09421) 10136. 055597

Meier, M., Theresienplatz 6, 94315 Straubing. T. (09421) 13 50. 055598

Schneeberger, R., Schenkendorfstr. 5, 94315 Straubing. T. (09421) 306 53. 055599

Wimmer, F., Fraunhoferstr. 8, 94315 Straubing. T. (09421) 126 13. 055600

Winkelmeier, J., Fraunhoferstr. 14, 94315 Straubing. T. (09421) 128 90. 055601

Strehla (Sachsen)

Hebecker, Annelies, Am Markt 112, 01616 Strehla. T. (035264) 593. 055602

Stuhr (Niedersachsen)

Glasfuchs, Der, Elzstr. 2, 28816 Stuhr. T. (0421) 56 15 00. 055603

Koenig, Hermann, Bahnhofstr. 6, 28816 Stuhr. T. (0421) 89 04 81. - Furn - 055604

Stuttgart (Baden-Württemberg)

Aichele, Frieder, Calwer Str. 38, 70173 Stuttgart. T. (0711) 364613, Fax 400608. - Ant / Orient / China / Tin - 055605

Albion Antiquitäten, Birkenwaldstr. 213b, 70191 Stuttgart. T. (0711) 29 57 58. - Ant / Furn / China / Jew / Silv / Lights / Instr / Glass / Cur / Mod - 055606

Antik-Markt, Stöckachstr. 17a, 70190 Stuttgart. T. (0711) 26 05 49, 28 13 24. - Furn - 055607

Antiquitäten Kabinett, Königstr. 20, 70173 Stuttgart. T. (0711) 29 89 23. - Ant / Paint / Furn / China / Jew - 055608

Atelier Glas und Kunst, Gutbrodstr. 8, 70197 Stuttgart. T. (0711) 63 29 64. - Glass - 055609

Bader, R., Fritz-Elsas-Str. 34, 70174 Stuttgart. T. (0711) 29 77 47. 055610

Bärchen, Heidi, Königstr. 20, 70173 Stuttgart. T. (0711) 29 89 23. 055611

Baetzner, Herilt, Falbenhennenstr. 15, 70180 Stuttgart. T. (0711) 640 75 22. - Ant - 055612

Bäurle, Peter, Dr., Relenbergstr. 70, 70174 Stuttgart. T. (0711) 22 17 90, 22 17 99. 055613

Baisch, D.K., Eberhardstr. 35, 70173 Stuttgart. T. (0711) 24 16 24. 055614

Barth, Lisa, Konradstr. 10, 70327 Stuttgart. T. (0711) 33 11 97. - Paint / Graph - 055615

Belger, K.-R., Mozartstr. 55, 70180 Stuttgart. T. (0711) 64 44 49. 055616

Bischoff, Barbara, Industriestr. 24, 70565 Stuttgart. T. (0711) 73 24 78. - Paint / Furn / Lights / Instr - 055617

Bock, Wolfgang, Kächeleweg 3, 70619 Stuttgart. 055618

Botnanger Kunsthaus, Beethovenstr. 7, 70195 Stuttgart. T. (0711) 69 45 57. 055619

Brem, Brigitte M., Katharinenstr. 16, 70182 Stuttgart. T. (0711) 236 98 79. - Ant / Furn / China / Jew / Instr - 055620

Brenner, Dieter, Großglocknerstr. 16, 70327 Stuttgart. T. (0711) 33 07 23. - Ant - 055621

Breunig, Eugen, Katharinenstr. 17, 70182 Stuttgart. T. (0711) 23 44 35. 055622

Bühler, Wagenburgstr 4, 70184 Stuttgart. T. (0711) 240507, Fax (0711) 2361153. - Paint / Graph / Sculp - 055623

Chou, Alwine, Hauptmannsreute 107, 70193 Stuttgart. 055624

CWS Antiques, Bludenzer Str. 24, 70469 Stuttgart. T. (0711) 85 37 18. - Ant - 055625

Dahesch, Dr. N., Königstr. 22, 70173 Stuttgart. T. (0711) 29 10 15. - Tex - 055626

Dargel, Joh.-Joachim, Schwabstr. 36b, 70197 Stuttgart. T. (0711) 617475. - Ant / Furn - 055627

Dassler, Gomaringer Str. 32, 70597 Stuttgart. T. (0711) 76 41 50. - Ant / Furn / China / Mil / Glass / Tin / Toys - 055628

Dayss, Barbara, Calwer Str. 38a, 70173 Stuttgart. T. (0711) 29 51 75. - Ant - 055629

Durst, B., Rosenstr. 31, 70182 Stuttgart. T. (0711) 24 14 38. 055630

Edeltrödel, Leonhardstr. 13, 70182 Stuttgart. T. (0711) 23 33 85. - Ant / Jew / Cur / Mod - 055631

Feister, Karola, Im Asemwald 26/19, 70599 Stuttgart. T. (0711) 61 22 45. 055632

Felstead, J. P., Olgastr. 53, 70182 Stuttgart. T. (0711) 24 78 89. - Ant / Furn - 055633

Fischle, Erwin, Rosenstr. 34, 70182 Stuttgart. T. (0711) 24 29 87. 055634

Galerie Alt-Amerika, Schwabstr 82, 70193 Stuttgart. T. (0711) 6363184, Fax (0711) 634913. - Arch / Eth - 055635

Galerie Riedenberg, Helga Stoll, Brunnenwiesen 42 D, 70619 Stuttgart. T. (0711) 47 07 08. 055636

Ginter, M., Alosenweg 32, 70329 Stuttgart. T. (0711) 42 12 14. 055637

Glauner, E., & M. Marazzi, Rienzistr. 17, 70597 Stuttgart. T. (0711) 765 51 41. - Ant / Arch / Jew - 055638

Gulumjan, W., Abstatter Str. 3, 70437 Stuttgart. T. (0711) 61 12 91. 055639

Hamma, Im Schießgärtle 16, 70567 Stuttgart. 055640

Ikonen-Galerie, Lenzhalde 20, 70192 Stuttgart. T. (0711) 257 82 28. - Ant / Paint / Sculp / Ico - 055641

Jongleur, Urbanstr. 68, 70182 Stuttgart. T. (0711) 22 57 61. 055642

Joniskeit, Rainer D., Lazarettstr. 14, 70182 Stuttgart. T. (0711) 24 06 24, Fax 649 49 01. - Paint - 055643

Katz, A., Liststr. 25, 70180 Stuttgart. T. (0711) 60 94 33. 055644

Kem, Raija, Gustav-Siegle-Str. 72, 70193 Stuttgart. T. (0711) 65 90 90. - Ant / Jew - 055645

Korea, Wiener Str. 91a, 70469 Stuttgart. T. (0711) 85 07 57. 055646

Kroker + Walsch GmbH, Charlottenstr. 42, 70182 Stuttgart. T. (0711) 24 46 34. - Num - 055647

Kunstraum, Filderstr. 34, 70180 Stuttgart. T. (0711) 6491001, Fax 6409708. - Graph - 055648

Landesgirokasse-Numism. Abt., Königstr. 3-5, 70173 Stuttgart. T. (0711) 2061 24 74. - Num - 055649

Lang, M. R., Bebelstr. 60, 70193 Stuttgart. T. (0711) 63 53 05. 055650

Lauster, Horst, Krokodilweg 27, 70499 Stuttgart. T. (0711) 86 15 00. - Num - 055651

Maas, Werner, Dorotheenstr. 2, 70173 Stuttgart. T. (0711) 24 64 86. - Jew / Silv - 055652

Matti, W.K., Reinsburgstr. 70, 70178 Stuttgart. T. (0711) 61 23 01. 055653

Mauler, Gerhard, Überkinger Str. 4, 70372 Stuttgart. T. (0711) 51 45 74. 055654

Mayer, H., Katharinenstr. 35, 70182 Stuttgart. T. (0711) 24 36 76. 055655

Metropolis, Augustenstr 117, 70197 Stuttgart. T. (0711) 610099, Fax (0711) 610099. - Mod - 055656

Mokry, K.M., Heusteigstr. 106, 70180 Stuttgart. T. (0711) 60 40 10. 055657

Münzen- und Medaillenhandlung Stuttgart, Charlottenstr. 4, 70182 Stuttgart. T. (0711) 24 44 57, Fax 23 39 36. - Num - 055658

Münzenetage, Marktpl. 14, 70173 Stuttgart. T. (0711) 24 46 79, Fax 2360192. - Num - 055659

Münzpallette West, Schwabstr. 100, 70193 Stuttgart. T. (0711) 61 76 75. - Num - 055660

Nagel, Ursula, Mörikestr. 17-19, 70178 Stuttgart.
T. (0711) 649 15 12, Fax 60 86 52. - Ant / Paint / Graph /
Furn / Orient / China / Sculp / Tex / Jew / Silv / Instr / Mi-
l / Glass / Cur / Mod -   055661
Neubauer, Günter, Böckinger Str 20a, 70437 Stuttgart.
T. (0711) 841632.   055662
Opferkuch, Rolf, Wernlinstr. 1, 70193 Stuttgart.
T. (0711) 29 55 27.   055663
Paul, Christoph, Blautopfstr. 12, 70329
Stuttgart.   055664
Privileg-Club, Charlottenstr. 44, 70182 Stuttgart.
T. (0711) 24 75 32.   055665
Raible, Hauptstr. 64, 70563 Stuttgart. T. (0711) 73 24 66.
- Paint / Graph -   055666
Rieber, Bernd, Reinbeckstr. 29E, 70565 Stuttgart.
T. (0711) 74 89 69. - Ant / Paint / Furn / China / Sculp /
Jew / Silv -   055667
Römmelt, Alois, Schloßstr. 80, 70176 Stuttgart.
T. (0711) 62 44 80. - Num -   055668
Röth, L.G., Pfarrstr 21, 70182 Stuttgart.
T. (0711) 241852/241873, Fax (0711) 2360310.
- Graph -   055669
Roos, Werner, Wallmerstr. 36, 70327 Stuttgart.
T. (0711) 33 37 49. - Paint / China / Jew /
Glass -   055670
Rothenbacher, M., Elisabethenstr. 26, 70176 Stuttgart.
T. (0711) 63 64 34.   055671
Ruff, Oskar, Salzmannweg 17, 70192 Stuttgart.
T. (0711) 295096, Fax (0711) 297614.   055672
Ruzek, F., Torstr. 17, 70173 Stuttgart. T. (0711) 24 56 11,
60 02 95. - Ant / Paint / Furn / China / Silv /
Glass -   055673
Sabet, M. & Sons, Maybachstr. 16, 70469 Stuttgart.
T. (0711) 89 99-0. - Tex -   055674
Sammler Eck, Gablenberger Hauptstr. 55, 70186 Stutt-
gart. T. (0711) 46 38 73. - Ant -   055675
Schäfer, Albert, Libanonstr. 90, 70186 Stuttgart.
T. (0711) 46 73 73. - Tin -   055676
Schaible, Hilde, Eberhardstr. 53, 70173 Stuttgart.
T. (0711) 23 47 30.   055677
Schaller, Marienstr. 3, 70178 Stuttgart.
T. (0711) 162650, Fax (0711) 2261677. - Paint /
Graph / Repr / Sculp / Fra -   055678
Schatzinsel, Königstr. 1, 70173 Stuttgart.
T. (0711) 29 64 82. - Orient -   055679
Schüppel, I., Thingstr. 68, 70565 Stuttgart.
T. (0711) 74 83 63. - Tin -   055680
Stieglitz, Otto, Kreuznacher Str. 15, 70372
Stuttgart.   055681
T. (0711) 62 09 18. - Ant -   055682
Szepanski, P., Immenhofer Str. 13, 70180 Stuttgart.
T. (0711) 64 50 77.   055683
Tausendschön, Lautenschlagerstr. 17, 70173 Stuttgart.
T. (0711) 29 40 32, Fax 295112. - China / Jew / Glass /
Cur -   055684
Teppichgalerie, Eberhardstr. 65, 70173 Stuttgart.
T. (0711) 23 27 23, 23 47 61. - Tex -   055685
Titze, M., Sigmaringer Str. 242, 70597 Stuttgart.
T. (0711) 72 19 79.   055686
Walter, Maja, Hauptmannsreute 91, 70193 Stuttgart.
T. (0711) 22 02 46, Fax 29 24 74. - Paint -   055687
Weber, Calwer Str. 52, 70173 Stuttgart.
T. (0711) 22 85 27.   055688
Weidemann, I., Herdweg 94e, 70193 Stuttgart.
T. (0711) 29 57 58. - Ant / Furn / Jew / Silv / Instr /
Glass / Cur / Mod -   055689
Weissenburger, Ruth, Marienstr. 24, 70178 Stuttgart.
T. (0711) 62 19 96. - Ant -   055690
Winkler, P., Hauptstr. 58, 70563 Stuttgart.
T. (0711) 73 64 71.   055691
Wonderful, Pfarrstr. 5, 70182 Stuttgart.
T. (0711) 24 37 05. - Ant / Furn / Lights / Mod -   055692
Zimmermann, Fritz, Echterdinger Str. 4, 70599
Stuttgart.   055693

Sülfeld (Schleswig-Holstein)
Bolz, S., Am Dorfpl 3, 23867 Sülfeld.
T. (04537) 7211.   055694

Süßen (Baden-Württemberg)
Hörsch, J., Kernerstr. 1, 73079 Süßen.
T. (07162) 41084.   055695

Schömig, R., Vordere Stelle 2, 73079 Süßen.
T. (07162) 41133.   055696

Sugenheim (Bayern)
Kube, Jan K., Altes Schloss, 91484 Sugenheim.
T. (09165) 13 86, Fax 1292. - Mil -   055697

Sulingen (Niedersachsen)
Schwecke, L., Bassumer Str. 25, 27232 Sulingen.
T. (04271) 4537.   055698

Sulzbach (Saarland)
Krüger, P.U., Sulzbachtalstr 111, 66280 Sulzbach.
T. (06897) 54213.   055699
Mertes, Horst Heinz, Goldene-Au-Str 25, 66280 Sulz-
bach. T. (06897) 4597. - Num -   055700
Spang, Edmund, Marktstr 8, 66280 Sulzbach.   055701

Sulzfeld (Bayern)
Rung, Detlev, Kirchpl. 1, 97320 Sulzfeld.
T. (09321) 66 29. - Ant / Jew -   055702

Sulzheim (Bayern)
Pöter, P.H., Wilhelm-Behr-Str. 34, 97529 Sulzheim.
T. (09382) 8628.   055703

Sundern (Nordrhein-Westfalen)
Plaesier, Sibylle, Markt 2, 59846 Sundern.
T. (02933) 1738. - China / Sculp -   055704

Sylt-Ost (Schleswig-Holstein)
Haus Damaskus, Boysenstr. 6, 25980 Sylt-Ost.
T. (04651) 228 15. - Ant / Tex -   055705
Kirchner, Stephan, Gaat, 25980 Sylt-Ost.
T. (04651) 32260.   055706
Mylin, J., C.P.-Hansen-Allee 10, 25980 Sylt-Ost.
T. (04651) 317 07.   055707
Nordfriesische Kunstwerkstätten, Kampende 17, 25980
Sylt-Ost. T. (04651) 60 88. - Ant -   055708

Tacherting (Bayern)
Ziegler, Erika, Alter Pfarrhof 2a, 83342 Tacherting.
T. (08622) 08622/1272. - Ant / Furn -   055709

Tamm (Baden-Württemberg)
Windsor Gallery, Bahnhofstr. 28, 71732 Tamm.
T. (07141) 60 38 45.   055710

Tangermünde (Sachsen-Anhalt)
Guth, K., Schloßfreiheit 3, 39590 Tangermünde.
T. (039322) 2025. - Paint / China / Eth / Cur -   055711

Tangstedt (Schleswig-Holstein)
Burkhardt, Wolfgang, Beekmoorweg 4, 22889 Tang-
stedt. T. (04109) 60 03.   055712

Taufkirchen (Bayern)
Huber, Rudolf, Kögelweg 2, 82024 Taufkirchen.
T. (089) 6122547. - Ant -   055713

Taunusstein (Hessen)
Käsdorf, A., Rolandstr. 11, 65232 Taunusstein.
T. (06128) 719 11.   055714
Matuschek, B., Aarstr. 94, 65232 Taunusstein.
T. (06128) 425 79.   055715

Tecklenburg (Nordrhein-Westfalen)
Alte Kunst, Ledder Dorfstr. 104, 49545 Tecklenburg.
T. (05482) 18 57.   055716
Steinigeweg, W., Ibbenbürener Str. 1, 49545 Tecklen-
burg. T. (05482) 13 10.   055717

Tegernsee (Bayern)
Die Palette, Hauptstr. 32, 83684 Tegernsee.
T. (08022) 30 07. - Ant / Paint -   055718

Telgte (Nordrhein-Westfalen)
Dondrup, Eduard, Dorf 32a, 48291 Telgte.
T. (02504) 74 73. - Ant -   055719
Wessels, Ruth, Münstertor 18, 48291 Telgte.
T. (02504) 31 30. - Ant / Sculp -   055720
Willach, Gabriele, Grevener Str. 10,, 48291 Telgte.
T. (02504) 88184. - Ant / Paint -   055721

Tengen (Baden-Württemberg)
Müller, M., Zollstr. 11, 78250 Tengen.
T. (07736) 12 33.   055722

Tettenweis (Bayern)
Schwetz, Erna, Unterschwärzenbach, 94167 Tettenweis.
T. (08534) 71 66.   055723

Thalmassing (Bayern)
Schuberth, Franz, St.-Wolfgang-Str 1, 93107 Thalmas-
sing. T. (09173) 8370. - Ant / Paint / Furn /
China -   055724

Tholey (Saarland)
Münzen der Antike, Theltalstr 10a, 66636 Tholey.
T. (06853) 7170, Fax 7784. - Num -   055725

Thurnau (Bayern)
Grießhammer, G., Hopfenleithe 1, 95349 Thurnau.
T. (09228) 5588.   055726

**Timmendorfer Strand (Schleswig-Hol-
stein)**
Kunsthaus Timmendorf, Strandallee 62, 23669 Timmendorfer Strand. T. (04503) 21 00.   055727

Tirschenreuth (Bayern)
Antikhöle, Falkenberger Str. 40, 95643 Tirschenreuth.
T. (09631) 2525, 4747, 4568.   055728
Berr, K., Marktpl. 5, 95643 Tirschenreuth.
T. (09631) 1581.   055729
Molwitz, Angerweg 15, 95643 Tirschenreuth.
T. (09631) 22 77.   055730

Titisee-Neustadt (Baden-Württemberg)
Colucci, M., Parkstr. 2, 79822 Titisee-Neustadt.
T. (07651) 880 24.   055731

Tittmoning (Bayern)
Zellhuber, M., Blumenstr. 15, 84529 Tittmoning.   055732

Titz (Nordrhein-Westfalen)
Rasenberger, G., Lommertzheimstr. 10, 52445 Titz.
- Ant -   055733
Velmerig, Linnicher Str. 85, 52443 Titz. T. (02463) 10 62,
Fax 3641. - Glass -   055734
Zur Gilde, Landwehr 1, 52445 Titz. T. (02463) 89 76.
- Ant / Furn / China / Lights -   055735

Töging (Bayern)
Meyer, Georg, Königsberger Str. 10a, 08261
Töging.   055736

Traunstein (Bayern)
Danes, Loni, Schaumburger Str 25, 83278
Traunstein.   055737
Schneeberger, Carl, Taubenmarkt 7, 83278 Traunstein.
T. (0861) 4500. - Paint / Furn / China / Sculp /
Cur -   055738

Trier (Rheinland-Pfalz)
Gaber, Heinrich, Maarstr. 42, 54292 Trier.
T. (0651) 288 83.   055739
Grotowski, Paulinstr. 5, 54292 Trier. T. (0651) 22500,
22533. - Tex -   055740
Habernicht, M., Genovevastr. 4, 54293 Trier.
T. (0651) 62995.   055741
Haubrich, Bernd, Palaststr. 15, 54290 Trier.
T. (0651) 4 84 48. - Ant -   055742
Hermersdorf, K., An der Meerkatz 2, 54290 Trier.
T. (0651) 741 84.   055743
Kaschenbach, Peter, Fleischstr. 50, 54290 Trier.
T. (0651) 73487, Fax (0651) 42397. - Paint / Graph /
Repr / Fra / Ico -   055744
Kaurisch, E., Paulinstr. 32, 54292 Trier.
T. (0651) 445 53.   055745
Kläs, W., Engelstr. 3, 54292 Trier.
T. (0651) 780 28.   055746
Kottmeier, H.-J., Bitburger Str. 2, 54294 Trier.
T. (0651) 833 00, Fax 84622. - Ant / Furn -   055747
Kreuz, Nikolaus, Irscher Berg 17, 54296 Trier.
- Ant -   055748
Kuntz, L., Saarstr. 61, 54290 Trier.
T. (0651) 452 71.   055749
Lamberti, Hans, Im Schankenbungert 15, 54294 Trier.
- Num -   055750
Minault, R., Markusstr. 36, 54294 Trier.
T. (0651) 83983.   055751
Stoffels, Joh., Fleischstr. 66, 54290 Trier.
T. (0651) 486 30.   055752

Weber, P., Maarstr. 6, 54292 Trier.
T. (0651) 752 01. *055753*

Troisdorf (Nordrhein-Westfalen)
Friede, R., Lindlaustr. 27, 53842 Troisdorf.
T. (02241) 470 13. *055754*
Kajan, W., Im Kreuzfeld 7, 53842 Troisdorf.
I. (02241) 445 10. *055755*
Schröder, S., Kölner Str. 5, 53840 Troisdorf.
T. (02241) 779 00. *055756*
Theisen, Siegi, Kölner Str. 103, 53840 Troisdorf.
T. (02241) 734 35. - Ant - *055757*

Tuchenbach (Bayern)
Läumer, E. & Gabriele, Elsternstr. 3, 90587 Tuchenbach.
T. (0911) 75 46 76. *055758*

Tübingen (Baden-Württemberg)
Antiquitäten-Salon, Pfleghofstr., 72070 Tübingen.
T. (07071) 21 21 88 und 653 33. *055759*
Conrad, A., Westbahnhofstr. 60, 72070 Tübingen.
T. (07071) 411 55. *055760*
Conrad, D.& B. Cecillon, Haaggasse 25, 72070 Tübingen. T. (07071) 228 08. *055761*
Doster, Thomas, Haaggasse 30, 72070 Tübingen.
T. (07071) 265 39. - Ant / Graph / Furn / Jew / Fra / Silv /
Glass / Mod - *055762*
Galerie Tabula, Mühlstr. 18, 72074 Tübingen.
T. (07071) 248 50, Fax 23015. - Ant / Paint / Graph /
Num / Orient / China / Repr / Sculp / Tex / Arch / Eth / Je-
w / Fra / Silv / Glass / Cur / Pho / Draw - *055763*
Greiner-Plath, B., Ammergasse 23, 72070 Tübingen.
T. (07071) 57 63. *055764*
Haus für alte Kunst, Denzenberghalde 6, 72074 Tübingen. T. (07071) 21 13 47. - Ant / Paint / Furn / Sculp /
Tex *055765*
Heck, Thomas, Hafengasse 10, 72070 Tübingen.
T. (07071) 263 06, Fax 874 08. - Ant / Paint / Graph /
Furn / China / Arch / Jew / Silv / Cur / Mul / Draw --
055766
Kaiser, R., Kronenstr. 5, 72070 Tübingen.
T. (07071) 512 12. *055767*
Marr, Ferdinando, Haaggasse 5, 72070 Tübingen.
T. (07071) 27056. *055768*
Merx, Hans-Ulrich, Burgsteige 2, 72070 Tübingen.
T. (07071) 221 20. *055769*
Metzen, T., Haaggasse 17, 72070 Tübingen.
T. (07071) 21523. *055770*
Patterson, N., Haaggasse 23, 72070 Tübingen.
T. (07071) 217 08. *055771*
Rui, T. & F. Marro, Haaggasse 5, 72070 Tübingen.
T. (07071) 270 56. *055772*
Schindler, Obere Haldenstr. 11, 72074 Tübingen.
T. (07071) 833 04. - Ant / Furn - *055773*
Schwarz, K.-H., Münzgasse 5, 72070 Tübingen.
T. (07071) 231 00. - Num - *055774*
Wahl, D. R., Neustadtgasse 3, 72070 Tübingen.
T. (07071) 217 65. *055775*

Tuttlingen (Baden-Württemberg)
Güthinger, R., Heubergweg 8, 78532 Tuttlingen.
T. (07461) 5382. - Paint / Graph - *055776*
Wilhelm, Bruno, Heinrich-Rieker-Str. 6, 78532 Tuttlingen. - China / Glass - *055777*

Tutzing (Bayern)
Schneider, Hans, Dr., Mozartstr 6, 82327 Tutzing.
T. (08158) 3050, Fax (08158) 7636. - Ant - *055778*

Überlingen (Baden-Württemberg)
Arenz, B., An der Bleiche 5, 88662 Überlingen.
T. (07551) 64598. *055779*
Kunsthaus zur Löwenzunft, Hofstatt 7, 88662 Überlingen. T. (07551) 836. - Orient / China - *055780*
Mathias, Gotthold B., Münsterstr 10, 88662 Überlingen.
T. (07551) 63413. - Ant / Graph - *055781*

Uelzen (Niedersachsen)
Arlt, Harry, Holdenstedter Str. 40, 29525 Uelzen.
T. (0581) 74066. *055782*
Barduhn, J., Lindenstr. 20a, 29525 Uelzen.
T. (0581) 6247. *055783*
Brinckmann, Gerhard, Kagenbergstr. 22, 29525 Uelzen.
T. (0581) 73831. *055784*

Stolte, Friedhelm, Bischof-Bruno-Str. 12, 29525 Uelzen.
T. (0581) 128 07. *055785*

Uettingen (Bayern)
Brehm, W., Hauptstr. 3, 97292 Uettingen.
T. (09369) 2284. *055786*
Heß, D., Altes Pfarrhaus, 97292 Uettingen.
T. (09369) 1516. *055787*

Uhingen (Baden-Württemberg)
Banzhaf, I., Fichtenstr. 4, 73066 Uhingen.
T. (07161) 31284. *055788*

Uhldingen-Mühlhofen (Baden-Württemberg)
Roeder, Roland, Tüfingerstr. 6a, 88690 Uhldingen-
Mühlhofen. T. (07556) 8554. - Ant / Paint /
Furn - *055789*

Ulm (Baden-Württemberg)
Braun, Hanne, Fünf-Bäume-Weg 48, 89081
Ulm. *055790*
Düsterer, F., Fischergasse 8, 89073 Ulm.
T. (0731) 69184, 610944. *055791*
Dunkel, B., Kornhausgasse 4, 89073 Ulm.
T. (0731) 63689. *055792*
Fischerplatz – Galerie, Fischergasse 21, 89073 Ulm.
T. (0731) 63349, Fax (0731) 619159. - Ant / Paint /
Graph / Furn / Sculp / Silv / Draw - *055793*
Frenzel, E., Neue Str 103, 89073 Ulm.
T. (0731) 63622. *055794*
Frey, E. & M., Schwörhausgasse 9, 89073 Ulm.
T. (0731) 63526. *055795*
Heise, Albrecht, Keplerstr 24, 89073 Ulm.
T. (0731) 62825. *055796*
Hoche, I., Judenhof 10, 89073 Ulm.
T. (0731) 69493. *055797*
Jakober, Siegfried, Hafengasse 15, 89073 Ulm.
T. (0731) 64880. - Ant / Orient - *055798*
Kölle, Rolf, Herdbrucker Str 8, 89073 Ulm.
T. (0731) 68937. - Instr - *055799*
Mewes, Werner, Ensingerstr 50, 89073 Ulm.
T. (0731) 63577. - Orient / Mil - *055800*
Ölgemälde im Bilderhaus, Olgastr 14, 89073
Ulm. *055801*
Steinberger, L., Lehrer-Tal-Weg 201, 89081 Ulm.
T. (0731) 54363. *055802*
Wickert, R., Kohlgasse 13, 89073 Ulm. T. (0731) 68335.
- Num - *055803*

Ulmen (Rheinland-Pfalz)
Meurer, E., Mühlenweg 8, 56766 Ulmen.
T. (02676) 6 89. *055804*

Umkirch (Baden-Württemberg)
Hercher, Hans W., In der Breite 6, 79224 Umkirch.
T. (07665) 70 55. - Num - *055805*

Unna (Nordrhein-Westfalen)
Wassmann, Erich, Waalwijker Str. 39, 59425
Unna. *055806*
Weise, Christian, Massener Str. 74, 59423
Unna. *055807*

Unsleben (Bayern)
Watermann, U. & B., Enggasse 12, 97618
Unsleben. *055808*

Untergruppenbach (Baden-Württemberg)
Schaupp, R., Abstatterstr. 30, 74199 Untergruppenbach.
T. (07131) 07130/6776. *055809*

Uplengen (Niedersachsen)
Arians, Horst, Ostertorstr. 144, 26670 Uplengen.
T. (04956) 739. *055810*

Usingen (Hessen)
Ruths, Walter, Am Sportplatz, 61250 Usingen.
T. (06081) 33 93. - Ant / Paint / Furn / Sculp /
Silv - *055811*
Tröger, H. G., Scheunengasse 4, 61250 Usingen.
T. (06081) 24 67. *055812*

Vaihingen (Baden-Württemberg)
Ramge, B., An der Reichsstr 4, 71665 Vaihingen.
T. (07042) 14791. *055813*

Valley (Bayern)
Antiquitäten in der Aumühle, Aumühler Weg 2, 83626
Valley. T. (08024) 2713. - Ant / Furn - *055814*

Varel (Niedersachsen)
Baumann Nachf., H., Lange Str. 8, 26316 Varel.
T. (04451) 5841. - Ant / Paint / Graph / Furn / China /
Sculp / Glass - *055815*
Friedrichs, Rolf G., Lange Str 12, 26316 Varel.
T. (04451) 6858, 2373. - Ant / Paint / Furn / China /
Silv / Instr / Glass - *055816*
Hartmann, Werner, Flachsweg 41 b, 26316 Varel.
T. (04451) 2403. - Furn - *055817*

Vechta (Niedersachsen)
Korth, Werner, Große Str. 95, 49377 Vechta.
T. (04441) 29 28. *055818*
Weuffen, P., Bakumer Str. 3, 49377 Vechta.
T. (04441) 3261. *055819*

Veitshöchheim (Bayern)
Oppmann, Marianne, Wolfstalstr. 6, 97209 Veitshöchheim. T. (0931) 926 44. - Furn / Instr - *055820*

Velbert (Nordrhein-Westfalen)
Bruckmann, G., Hauptstr 51, 42555 Velbert.
T. (02124) 1637. *055821*
Kessels, Botho, Hölterhoffstr. 14, 42549 Velbert.
T. (02124) 6 48 56. - Ant / Orient / Mil - *055822*
Obach, Dieter, Friedrichstr. 120, 42551 Velbert.
T. (02124) 538 62. *055823*
Schubert, Richard, Friedrichstr. 89, 42551 Velbert.
T. (02124) 50919. - Ant - *055824*

Velburg (Bayern)
Sprenger, G., Kapellenweg 11, 92355 Velburg.
T. (09182) 12 55. *055825*

Verden (Niedersachsen)
Heyden, Hubertus von, Obere Strasse 44, 27283 Verden.
T. (04231) 84566. *055826*
Sabatier, Bergstr 2, 27283 Verden. T. (04231) 3055.
- Ant - *055827*

Vetschau (Brandenburg)
Patzschke, C., M.-Kerk-Str. 38, 03226 Vetschau.
T. (035433) 2982. *055828*

Viechtach (Bayern)
Heinzl, L., Stadtpl. 1, 94234 Viechtach.
T. (09942) 24 41. *055829*
Kunsthaus Ostbayern, Stadtpl. 1, 94234 Viechtach.
T. (09942) 5055. - Paint / Graph - *055830*

Vienenburg (Niedersachsen)
HP-Sammler-Service, Wasserburg Wiedelah, 38690 Vi-
enenburg. T. (05324) 4088. - Mil / Naut - *055831*
Mittendorf, K., Bergenroderstr. 2, 38690 Vienenburg.
T. (05324) 63 50. - Ant / China / Silv / Mil /
Glass - *055832*

Vierhöfen (Niedersachsen)
Ther, Ann-Gabriele, 21444 Vierhöfen.
T. (04172) 6113. *055833*

Viernheim (Hessen)
Baureis, H., Kettelerstr. 46, 68519 Viernheim.
T. (06204) 3453. *055834*
Leinweber, Irene, Kirschenstr. 75a, 68519
Viernheim. *055835*

Viersen (Nordrhein-Westfalen)
Alarta, Greefsallee 51, 41747 Viersen.
T. (02162) 13515. *055836*
Antikstube, Große Bruchstr. 7, 41747 Viersen. - Ant /
Furn / Num / China / Jew / Silv / Instr - *055837*
Art-Galerie-Antiquitäten, Gladbacher Str. 32, 41747
Viersen. T. (02162) 31818, 30733. *055838*
Benden, K., Ratsallee 5, 41749 Viersen. *055839*
Berger, H., Hauptstr. 21, 41747 Viersen.
T. (02162) 345 32. *055840*

Meulengraf, A. van de, Peterstr. 7a, 41747 Viersen.
T. (02162) 24171.   055841
Pauly, A., Hauptstr. 70, 41747 Viersen.
T. (02162) 124 64. - Ant / Paint / Graph / Furn / Repr /
Jew / Lights / Glass -   055842
Roth, Franz, Blumenstr. 48, 41749 Viersen.   055843
Schmidt, S., Dechant-Stroux-Str. 38, 41748 Viersen.
T. (02162) 156 23. - Num -   055844
Sixel, Herbert, Tönisvorster Str. 53, 41749 Viersen.
T. (02162) 72 23.   055845
Stein, K.-J., Gladbacher Str. 65, 41747 Viersen.
T. (02162) 291 00.   055846
Winzen, H., Große Bruchstr. 7a, 41747 Viersen.
T. (02162) 234 74.   055847

Villingen-Schwenningen (Baden-Württemberg)
Bennett, G., Carl-Haag-Str. 2, 78054 Villingen-Schwen-
ningen. T. (07721) 07720/21180.   055848
Hald, Volker, Alte Herdstr. 19, 78054 Villingen-
Schwenningen.   055849
Heinzmann, G., Rietstr. 2, 78050 Villingen-Schwennin-
gen. T. (07721) 551 35. - Paint / Graph / Repr /
Ico -   055850

Villmar (Hessen)
Müller, Karlheinz, Lahnstr. 14, 65606 Villmar.
T. (06474) 80 38/39, Fax 13 37. - Ant / Paint / Furn / Chi-
na / Silv / Mil / Glass -   055851

Völklingen (Saarland)
Lange, H. & M., Hunsrückstr. 26, 66333 Völklingen.
T. (06898) 425 08.   055852

Voerde (Nordrhein-Westfalen)
Schulz, U., Bahnhofstr 157 A, 46562 Voerde.
T. (02855) 5755.   055853

Vreden (Nordrhein-Westfalen)
Noldes, Heinrich, Burgstr. 7, 48691 Vreden.
T. (02564) 10 63.   055854

Wabern (Hessen)
Danz, H. & H.-J., Cappelerstr. 5, 34590 Wabern.
T. (05683) 363.   055855

Wacken (Schleswig-Holstein)
Knoop, F., Kohlenbek 1, 25596 Wacken.   055856

Wadern (Saarland)
Barbian, H., Im Hufengarten 14, Morscholz, 66687 Wa-
dern. T. (06871) 7295.   055857

Wadgassen (Saarland)
Antik-Möbel, Abteistr. 1-5, 66787 Wadgassen.
T. (06834) 41540. - Furn -   055858
Interieur Antique, Schelmeneich 35, 66787 Wadgassen.
T. (06834) 431 84.   055859
Maurer, Francine, Ludweilerstr. 135, 66787 Wadgassen.
T. (06834) 6239, Fax 61680. - Arch / Eth -   055860

Wächtersbach (Hessen)
Jäger, R., Pfarrgasse 20, 63607 Wächtersbach.
T. (06053) 10 22.   055861
Mitzlaff, Otto von, Schloß, Prinzessenhaus, 63607
Wächtersbach. T. (06053) 39 27. - Furn -   055862

Wahlstedt (Schleswig-Holstein)
Gerling, J., 23812 Wahlstedt. T. (04554) 64 22.
- Num -   055863

Waibstadt (Baden-Württemberg)
Ries, Kurt, Lammstr 4, 74915 Waibstadt.
T. (07263) 5819. - Ant -   055864

Waidhaus (Bayern)
Dierl, Xaver, Am Wiesenbergl 3, 92726 Waidhaus.
T. (09652) 302. - Ant -   055865

Waldbröl (Nordrhein-Westfalen)
Rose, M.-S., Westerwaldstr. 11, 51545 Waldbröl.
T. (02291) 5865.   055866
Schneider, Gregor, Nümbrechterstr. 4, 51545 Waldbröl.
T. (02291) 35 90.   055867
Sohnius, Otto, Vennstr. 25, 51545 Waldbröl.   055868

Waldbronn (Baden-Württemberg)
Neuhoff, G., Esternaystr. 48, 76337 Waldbronn.
T. (07243) 691 75.   055869

Waldeck (Hessen)
Bialowitz, N., Korbacher Str. 19, 34513 Waldeck.
T. (05634) 1570.   055870

Waldenbuch (Baden-Württemberg)
Mayer, Hannelore, Beethovenstr. 3, 71111 Waldenbuch.
T. (07157) 33 34.   055871

Waldkirch (Baden-Württemberg)
Krupinski, B., Hödlerstr. 2, 79183 Waldkirch.
T. (07681) 23774.   055872

Waldkirchen (Bayern)
Armstark, Alfred, Kellerweg 7, 94065 Waldkirchen.
T. (08581) 3152.   055873

Waldmohr (Rheinland-Pfalz)
Jacob, G., Rathausstr. 42, 66914 Waldmohr.
T. (06373) 31 75.   055874
Schmidt, H. W., Lessingstr. 34, 66914 Waldmohr.
T. (06373) 1240, 4664.   055875

Waldshut-Tiengen (Baden-Württemberg)
Daniels, R., Weihergasse 12, 79761 Waldshut-Tiengen.
T. (07741) 622 20.   055876
Langenfeld, G., Eschbacher Str. 24, 79761 Waldshut-
Tiengen. T. (07751) 2741.   055877
Neumann, Heinz, Kaitlestr. 1, 79761 Waldshut-Tiengen.
T. (07741) 53 37.   055878

Walldorf (Baden-Württemberg)
Albrecht, Rudolf, Rudolf-Diesel-Str. 42, 69190 Walldorf.
T. (06227) 94 48. - Rel -   055879
Görlach, B, Hauptstr. 47, 69190 Walldorf.
T. (06227) 99 00.   055880

Walldürn (Baden-Württemberg)
Berberich, R., Waldstr. 41, 74731 Walldürn.
T. (06282) 398.   055881
Englert, Oskar, jr., Hornbacherstr. 29, 74731 Walldürn.
T. (06282) 7441, Fax 7641. - Ant / Paint / Furn /
Silv -   055882

Wallenhorst (Niedersachsen)
Kolker, Richard, Boerskamp 61, 49134
Wallenhorst.   055883
Kremer, Karl, Am Bockholt 3, 49134 Wallenhorst.
T. (05407) 16 14.   055884

Wallersdorf (Bayern)
Hochleitner, Josef F., Haidlfinger Str. 27, 94522 Wallers-
dorf. T. (09933) 621.   055885

Wallertheim (Rheinland-Pfalz)
Bielitz, Orden, Obergasse 24, 55578 Wallertheim.
T. (06732) 81 44.   055886

Wallhausen (Baden-Württemberg)
Nesplak, K., Hauptstr. 125, 74599 Wallhausen.
T. (07533) 25 71.   055887

Walluf (Hessen)
Veit, H., Kapellenstr. 8a, 65396 Walluf.
T. (06123) 733 01.   055888

Walsdorf (Bayern)
Horn, W., Neiglersdorfer Str. 5, 96194 Walsdorf.
T. (09549) 8069.   055889

Walsdorf (Rheinland-Pfalz)
Stanisby, G.R., Hauptstr. 8, 54578 Walsdorf.
T. (06593) 1535.   055890

Walsrode (Niedersachsen)
Ahlden, M. sen., Am Bahnhof 93a, 29664 Walsrode.
T. (05161) 72906. - Num -   055891
Best, W., Stellichte, 29664 Walsrode. T. (05161) 05168/
413.   055892
Kalender, C., Lange Str. 25, 29664 Walsrode.
T. (05161) 53 27.   055893
Zargari, G., Moorstr. 26, 29664 Walsrode.
T. (05161) 6434.   055894

Waltrop (Nordrhein-Westfalen)
B. und B. Antiquitäten, Isbruchstr. 2, 45731 Waltrop.
T. (02309) 75577.   055895

Wangels (Schleswig-Holstein)
Jipp, Karl, Dorfstr. 16, 23758 Wangels.
T. (04382) 1330.   055896

Wangen (Baden-Württemberg)
Birk, Renate, 88239 Wangen. T. (07522) 2628.
- Num -   055897
Gunzert, E., Am Waltersbühl 16, 88239
Wangen.   055898
Weiner, Günter, Humpisstr 18, 88239 Wangen.
T. (07522) 2870. - Num -   055899

Waren an der Müritz (Mecklenburg-Vor-pommern)
Bischoff, Beethovenstr. 2, 17192 Waren an der Müritz.
T. (0391) 3120. - Paint / Graph / Furn -   055900

Warendorf (Nordrhein-Westfalen)
Budde, Ernst, Brünebede 34, 48231 Warendorf.
T. (02581) 3453.   055901
Friedrichs, Maria, Oststr. 47, 48231 Warendorf.   055902
Recker, Burkhard, Lilienstr. 1, 48231 Warendorf.
T. (02581) 63 24 94.   055903
Röttger, F., Beckumer Str. 21, 48231 Warendorf.
T. (02581) 60238. - Ant / Furn -   055904
Vöcking, L., Königstr. 1, 48231 Warendorf.
T. (02581) 1375.   055905
Weiler, Aenne, Marktstr. 1, 48231 Warendorf.   055906

Warstein (Nordrhein-Westfalen)
Berger, Andreas S., Sebastianshof, 59581 Warstein.
T. (02902) 22 11.   055907
Göbel, H., Kreisstr. 34, 59581 Warstein.
T. (02902) 2700.   055908

Wassenberg (Nordrhein-Westfalen)
Staas, A., Kreusstr. 32, 41849 Wassenberg.
T. (02432) 209 91.   055909

Wasserburg (Bayern)
Göttler, Josef, Schmidzeile 10, 83512 Wasserburg.
T. (08071) 360. - Ant / Furn / Dec -   055910
Göttler, Josef, Marienpl. 7, 83512 Wasserburg.
T. (08071) 28 52. - Ant / Paint / Furn -   055911
Göttler, Werner, Frauengasse 4, 83512 Wasserburg.
T. (08071) 6991. - Ant / Furn -   055912

Wattenheim (Rheinland-Pfalz)
Breyther, D., Hauptstr. 27, 67319 Wattenheim.
T. (06356) 1451.   055913

Weddingstedt (Schleswig-Holstein)
Norddeutsche-Antiquitäten, Dorfstr. 2, 25795 Wedding-
stedt. T. (0481) 873 88. - Ant -   055914
Ratke, Günter, Alter Landweg 85, 25795 Weddingstedt.
T. (0481) 879 23. - Num -   055915

Wedel (Schleswig-Holstein)
Eitzenberger, Hans, Rosengarten 6a, 22880 Wedel.
T. (04103) 896 89, Fax 97734. - Tex -   055916

Wedemark (Niedersachsen)
Kunst-Antiquitäten-Café, Werner-v.-Negenborn-Str. 9,
30900 Wedemark. T. (05130) 2016.   055917
Wassmann, Waltraud, Am Kuckuckshof 7, 30900 Wede-
mark. T. (05130) 52 03, Fax 39057. - Num -   055918
Wichert, P., Scherenb. 15, 30900 Wedemark.
T. (05130) 6869.   055919

Weener (Niedersachsen)
Meertens, T., Kirchstr. 33a, 26826 Weener.
T. (04951) 38 11.   055920

Wegberg (Nordrhein-Westfalen)
Wegberger-Antik-Stube, Bahnhofstr. 52, 41844 Weg-
berg. T. (02434) 1867.   055921

Wehrheim (Hessen)
Rupar, R., Wintersteinstr. 15, 61273 Wehrheim.
T. (06081) 14919.   055922

Weiden (Bayern)
Hand in Hand, Rathauspassage, 92637 Weiden.
T. (0961) 43350. *055923*
Turbanisch, In der Weiding 10, 92637 Weiden. *055924*
Weiss, H. & B., In der Weiding 10, 92637 Weiden.
T. (0961) 22894. *055925*

Weil am Rhein (Baden-Württemberg)
Braitsch, E., Alte Str. 61, 79576 Weil am Rhein.
T. (07621) 754 96. *055926*
Stahlberger, Pfädlistr 4, 79576 Weil am Rhein.
T. (07621) 74650. *055927*

Weilburg (Hessen)
Hahn, Bahnhofstr.5, 35781 Weilburg.
T. (06471) 30343. *055928*
Heumann, M., Kleisterstr. 4, 35781 Weilburg. *055929*
Scherbaum, R., Salbenhäuser Weg 2, 35781 Weilburg.
T. (06471) 2685. *055930*

Weilersbach (Bayern)
Stegmeyer, Jürgen, Schloßpl 8, 91365 Weilersbach.
T. (09191) 65794. - Instr - *055931*

Weilerswist (Nordrhein-Westfalen)
Strohmenger, A., Kölnerstr. 150, 53919 Weilerswist.
T. (02254) 51 65. - Ant / Paint / Furn / China / Arch /
Jew / Fra / Silv / Lights / Instr / Glass / Mod / Tin / Toys --
055932

Weilheim an der Teck (Baden-Württemberg)
Pasqualini, B., Obere Mühlstr. 36, 73235 Weilheim an
der Teck. T. (07023) 83 24. *055934*
Schmidt, Luise, Brunnenstr. 25, 73235
Weilheim. *055934a*

Weimar (Thüringen)
Eckard, Dr., Neugasse 1, 99423 Weimar.
T. (03643) 61573. *055936*
Kunst und Antiquitäten am Eckermannhaus, Bauhaus-
gasse 15, 99423 Weimar. T. (03643) 59458.
- Ant - *055937*
Monti, Kaufstr. 22, 99423 Weimar. Fax 06218/22138.
- Orient - *055937a*

Weingarten (Baden-Württemberg)
Böser, D., Bahnhofstr. 1, 76356 Weingarten.
T. (07244) 2890. *055939*
Uhrig & Kufahl, Bahnhofstr. 24, 76356 Weingarten.
T. (07244) 32 85. - Ant - *055940*

Weingarten, Württemberg (Baden-Württemberg)
Eggler, Erika, Hölderlinstr 18, 88250 Weingarten, Württemberg. T. (0751) 0751/411 52. - Num - *055941*
Wettstein, Karl-Viktor, Haldenweg 33, 88250 Weingarten, Württemberg. *055942*

Weinheim (Baden-Württemberg)
Deinhardt, R., Karlstr 2, 69469 Weinheim.
T. (06201) 66202. *055943*
Klüber, Marktplatz 5, 69469 Weinheim.
T. (06201) 16790. - Paint / Graph / Fra - *055944*
Langeloh, Elfriede, Am Michelsgrund 14, 69469 Wein-
heim. T. (06201) 67335, 67354, Fax (06201) 182862.
- China - *055945*

Loßmann, Hans-Jürgen, Rote-Turm-Str 28, 69469 Wein-
heim. - Ant - *055946*
Weise, H.-D., Sommergasse 137, 69469 Weinheim.
T. (06201) 58773. - Ant - *055947*

Weinsberg (Baden-Württemberg)
Guttenberger, Rolf, Stadtseestr. 32, 74189 Weinsberg.
- Ant - *055948*

Weisendorf (Bayern)
Vollath, Am Windflügel 7, 91085 Weisendorf.
T. (09135) 8305. - Paint - *055949*

Weiskirchen (Saarland)
Scheune, Dorfstr. 42, 66709 Weiskirchen.
T. (06876) 06874/1593. *055950*

Weißenhorn (Bayern)
Letzner, G., Herzog-Georg-Str. 12, 89264 Weißenhorn.
T. (07309) 7772. *055951*

Weiterstadt (Hessen)
Antiklädchen, Hauptstr. 12, 64331 Weiterstadt.
T. (06150) 536 49. *055952*
Pfister, M., Niedergartenweg 5, 64331 Weiterstadt.
T. (06150) 513 60. *055953*

Welmbüttel (Schleswig-Holstein)
Siercks, I., An der Bundesstr. 15, 25782 Welmbüttel.
T. (04838) 7331. *055954*

Welzheim (Baden-Württemberg)
Bubeck, Bernd, Kastellstr. 39, 73642 Welzheim.
- Num - *055955*

Wenden (Nordrhein-Westfalen)
Bulbach, W., Johann-von-Bever-Str. 3, 57482 Wenden.
T. (02762) 73 88. *055956*

Wendlingen (Baden-Württemberg)
Lörz, B. & H., Behrstr 76, 73240 Wendlingen.
T. (07024) 3866. *055957*

Wenningstedt (Schleswig-Holstein)
Missal, Gisela, Hauptstr. 21, 25996 Wenningstedt.
T. (04651) 434 68. *055958*

Werl (Nordrhein-Westfalen)
Bandulet-Höpping, B., Steinergraben 34, 59457 Werl.
T. (02922) 843 21, 843 40. *055959*
Gossling, A., Spitalgasse 6, 59457 Werl.
T. (02922) 02922/4553. *055960*
Hill-Antik, Schloß Lohe, 59457 Werl.
T. (02922) 7400. *055961*
Knabe, Kurt, An der Steinerbrücke 23, 59457 Werl.
T. (02922) 20 46. *055962*
Kunst und Antik Börse, Bundesstr. 29, 59457 Werl.
T. (02922) 61 60. *055963*
Reimann-Wehr, Cornelia, Klosterstr. 5, 59457 Werl.
T. (02922) 64 94. *055964*
Rensmann, E., Büdericher Bundesstr. 29, 59457 Werl.
T. (02922) 22 83, 61 60. - Paint / Furn / Instr - *055965*

Werlaburgdorf (Niedersachsen)
Schoenawa, Hartmut, Ostlandstr. 12, 38315 Werlaburg-
dorf. T. (05335) 400, Fax 415. - Num - *055966*

Wermelskirchen (Nordrhein-Westfalen)
Frembgen, D., Thomas-Mann-Str. 2, 42929 Wermelskir-
chen. T. (02196) 833 33. *055967*
Siebel, Th., Kreuzstr. 1, 42929 Wermelskirchen.
T. (02196) 82613. *055968*
Stoßberg, R., Eipringhausen 5, 42929 Wermelskirchen.
T. (02196) 916 65. *055969*

Wernau (Baden-Württemberg)
Boiger, Roswitha, Röntgenstr 28, 73249 Wernau. - Ant /
Ico - *055970*

Werne (Nordrhein-Westfalen)
Fred's, Tigge 18a, 59368 Werne.
T. (02389) 533772. *055971*
Sauff, H., Penningrode 41, 59368 Werne.
T. (02389) 45636. *055972*

Wertheim (Baden-Württemberg)
Gimple, W., Nebenmaingasse 3, 97877 Wertheim.
T. (09342) 38537. *055973*

Wesel (Nordrhein-Westfalen)
Raadts & Goedeck, Heuberg 6, 46483 Wesel.
T. (0281) 216 77. *055974*
Schlüsener, Hermann, Schermbecker Landstr. 231,
46485 Wesel. T. (0281) 502 10. *055975*
Scholten, D., In der Dell 6, 46483 Wesel.
T. (0281) 618 65. *055976*
Scholten, J., Esplanade 2, 46483 Wesel.
T. (0281) 237 42. *055977*
Siegersma, W., Schwanenhofstr. 56, 46487 Wesel.
T. (0281) 02803/4415. *055978*

Wesselburen (Schleswig-Holstein)
Mohr, J.-P., Lollfuss 6a, 25764 Wesselburen.
T. (04833) 25 23. *055979*

Wesseling (Nordrhein-Westfalen)
Bürger, Gerhard, Hubertusstr 82, 50389 Wesseling.
T. (02236) 40989. *055980*

Westensee (Schleswig-Holstein)
Westensee Antik, Dorfstr. 23, 24259 Westensee.
T. (04305) 681. *055981*

Westerland (Schleswig-Holstein)
Abeling, K., Käpt'n Christiansenstr. 13, 25980 Wester-
land. T. (04651) 23265. *055982*
Antiquitäten zur alten Dorfschmiede, Keitumer Chaussee
11, 25980 Westerland. T. (04651) 22136. *055983*
China-Bohlken, Friedrichstr. 38, 25980 Westerland.
T. (04651) 230 80. - Orient - *055984*
Grillfeldt, Ole, Keitumer Chaussee 11, 25980 Wester-
land. T. (04651) 22136. - Furn - *055985*
Moussali, M., Boysenstr. 6, 25980 Westerland.
T. (04651) 28 15. *055986*
Petersen-Suckau, K., Dr., Nicolasstr. 2, 25980 Wester-
land. T. (04651) 6113. *055987*
Radzuweit, H. & M., Kjeirstr. 2, 25980 Westerland.
T. (04651) 73 31. - Ant - *055988*
Trödler Rantum, Rantum, 25980 Westerland.
T. (04651) 212 77. *055989*
Zellermann, Ursula, Friedrichstr. 38, 25980 Westerland.
T. (04651) 3080. *055990*
Zur alten Dorfschmiede, Keitumer Chaussee 11, 25980
Westerland. T. (04651) 221 36. *055991*

Westerstede (Niedersachsen)
Siebrecht, A., Hüllstede, 26655 Westerstede.
T. (04488) 1605. *055992*

Wettenberg (Hessen)
Shafie-Zadeh, R., Magdeburger Str. 26, 35435
Wettenberg. *055993*

Wetzlar (Hessen)
Antik am Dom, Schwarzadlergasse 1a, 35578 Wetzlar.
T. (06441) 451 46. *055994*
Hensoldt, Rainer M., Wertherstr. 29, 35578 Wetzlar.
T. (06441) 42720. - Ant - *055995*
Moser, Hans, Lahninsel 1, 35578 Wetzlar.
T. (06441) 459 46. *055996*
Siebert, U., Weißadlergasse 4, 35578 Wetzlar.
T. (06441) 47433. *055997*

Weyhe (Niedersachsen)
Kirchwyher Antiquitätenstube, Richtweg 15, 28844
Weyhe. T. (04203) 95 80. *055998*

Wiefelstede (Niedersachsen)
Krawczyk, S., Parkstr. 10, 26215 Wiefelstede. *055999*
Zimmermann, H., Hauptstr. 27, 26215 Wiefelstede.
T. (0441) 04402/6677. *056000*

Wiesbaden (Hessen)
Antik, Jahnstr. 10, 65185 Wiesbaden. T. (0611) 30 53 93.
- Ant / Furn - *056001*
Antik am Kochbrunnen, Saalgasse 36, 65183 Wiesba-
den. T. (0611) 51483. *056002*
Antik & Design, Taunusstr. 34, 65183 Wiesbaden.
T. (0611) 59 92 10. - Paint / Graph / Furn / Sculp / Dec /
Jew / Fra / Silv / Lights - *056003*

Beisac, Hermien de, Taunusstr. 38, 65183 Wiesbaden. T. (0611) 52 21 41. - Ant / Furn / China / Glass / Cur / Mod - 056004
Beisac, Philipp de, Taunusstr. 38, 65183 Wiesbaden. T. (0611) 37 11 71. - Ant - 056005
Besier, R., Taunusstr. 25, 65183 Wiesbaden. T. (0611) 52 17 75. - Ant / Furn / Num / China / Jew / Silv / Instr / Glass - 056006
Bolognesi, Gianni, Bismarckring 6, 65185 Wiesbaden. T. (0611) 44 22 97. - Ant - 056007
Classic-Münzen, Moritzstr. 50, 65185 Wiesbaden. T. (0611) 37 34 78. - Num - 056008
Czenkusch, E., Beethovenstr. 14, 65189 Wiesbaden. T. (0611) 30 09 94. 056009
Dagi's Flohmarkt, Wielandstr. 12, 65187 Wiesbaden. T. (0611) 30 15 90. 056010
Danker, Anton, Friedrichstr. 14, 65185 Wiesbaden. T. (0611) 30 00 25. - Tex / Dec - 056011
Dorr, Rheinstr. 101, 65185 Wiesbaden. T. (0611) 37 14 72. 056012
Engel, P., Kurt-Schumacher-Ring 47, 65197 Wiesbaden. T. (0611) 40 58 76. 056013
Franz, M., Grabenstr. 9, 65183 Wiesbaden. T. (0611) 37 04 73. 056014
Fuhr, W., Marcobrunnerstr. 18, 65197 Wiesbaden. T. (0611) 44 40 02. 056015
Gill, Bärenstr. 2, 65183 Wiesbaden. T. (0611) 30 02 86, Fax 30 02 86. - Jew / Fra / Silv / Mod - 056016
Goebel, U., Blücherstr. 32, 65195 Wiesbaden. T. (0611) 47602. 056017
Golden Oldies, Alte Dorfstr. 35, 65207 Wiesbaden. T. (0611) 06122/12369. 056018
Grübel, E., Dambachtal 10, 65193 Wiesbaden. T. (0611) 52 79 11. 056019
Handwerk & Kunst, Wilhelmstr. 56, 65183 Wiesbaden. 056020
Harkort, U., Taunusstr. 31, 65183 Wiesbaden. T. (0611) 59 04 42. - Ant / Paint / Mod - 056021
Heimann, R., Am Lindenborn 14, 65207 Wiesbaden. 056022
Heinemann, Taunusstr. 39, 65183 Wiesbaden. T. (0611) 52 29 56. - Ant / Paint / Furn / Sculp - 056023
Heller, S., Mauergasse 15, 65183 Wiesbaden. T. (0611) 30 25 95. 056024
Hinterhaus, Karlstr. 15, 65185 Wiesbaden. T. (0611) 30 99 91. 056025
Hubatschek, B., Nerostr. 32, 65183 Wiesbaden. T. (0611) 52 28 91. 056026
Janson, Ludwig, Siegfriedring 4b, 65189 Wiesbaden. T. (0611) 73966. - Silv - 056027
Jonker, Hans, & Hans-Joachim Roloff, Taunusstr. 32, 65183 Wiesbaden. T. (0611) 52 92 02, Fax 05103. - Ant / Paint / Furn / China / Silv - 056028
Keul & Sohn, Taunusstr. 33-35, 65183 Wiesbaden. T. (0611) 52 26 61, Fax 522661. - Paint / Furn - 056029
Knab, Alfred, Taunusstr. 47, 65183 Wiesbaden. T. (0611) 52 23 01. - Ant / Paint / Furn / Tex / Sculp / Dec / Jew / Silv - 056030
Kranepfuhl, Gerhart, Trommlerweg 1, 65195 Wiesbaden. 056031
Kumpf, Daniela, Parkstr. 33, 65189 Wiesbaden. T. (0611) 52 83 57, Fax 333365. - Ant / China - 056032
Kumpf, Dieter, Taunusstr. 30, 65183 Wiesbaden. T. (0611) 59 72 97. - Ant / China - 056033
Kunz, Taunusstr. 24, 65183 Wiesbaden. T. (0611) 518 09. - Ant - 056034
Marschalleck-Babelsberg, Carl H., Stettiner Str. 8a, 65203 Wiesbaden. T. (0611) 6 18 42. - Paint / Repr - 056035
Mersmann, P. & E., Wagemannstr. 25, 65183 Wiesbaden. T. (0611) 37 83 37. 056036
Mohr, Heinz, Kleine Weinbergstr. 1, 65193 Wiesbaden. T. (0611) 52 12 12. - Graph - 056037
Molzberger, K., Luisenstr. 27, 65185 Wiesbaden. 056038
Müller & Kühn, Zietenring 5, 65195 Wiesbaden. T. (0611) 40 75 06. 056039
Neess, Ferdinand Wolfgang, Bingertstr. 10, 65191 Wiesbaden. T. (0611) 56 14 39. - Ant / Furn / Glass - 056040
Nied, Pavillon am Bahnhofsvorpl., 65183 Wiesbaden. T. (0611) 71 91 03, 70 10 03. - Paint / Graph / Repr / Sculp / Jew / Fra - 056041

Oberacker, Rolf, Taunusstr. 28, 65183 Wiesbaden. T. (0611) 517 73. - Ant / China - 056042
Oldenburg, W., Lahnstr. 87, 65195 Wiesbaden. T. (0611) 46 86 97. 056043
Paulig, Frank, Wörthstr. 17, 65185 Wiesbaden. T. (0611) 37 63 23. - Ant / Paint - 056044
Reinsbacher, B., Herrmmühlgasse 9, 65183 Wiesbaden. T. (0611) 30 19 18. 056045
Rendelsmann, Heijo, Taunusstr. 34, 65183 Wiesbaden. T. (0611) 59 84 85, Fax 591 45. - Ant / Paint / Graph / Furn / Jew / Silv / Instr - 056046
Rinnelt, C., Taunusstr. 36, 65183 Wiesbaden. T. (0611) 523307, Fax (0611) 9590951. - Ant / Paint / Arch / Pho - 056047
Schmidt, M., Yorckstr. 13, 65195 Wiesbaden. T. (0611) 40 65 92. 056048
Schmiech, B., Albrechtstr. 46, 65185 Wiesbaden. T. (0611) 37 88 38. - Ant - 056049
Schröter, Hans, Waldstr. 72, 65187 Wiesbaden. T. (0611) 8 42 99. - Ant - 056050
Simon's, Taunusstr. 28, 65183 Wiesbaden. T. (0611) 52 28 41. - Ant / Paint / Furn / Silv - 056051
Stahlstich-Galerie, H.-J. Hörner, Saalgasse 1, 65183 Wiesbaden. T. (0611) 37 05 33. 056052
Strebel, Wilhelmstr. 56, 65183 Wiesbaden. T. (0611) 30 40 21, Fax 37 36 76. - Orient - 056053
Tremus, Karl & Elke, Nerostr. 22, 65183 Wiesbaden. T. (0611) 517 69, 518 02. - Ant / Furn / China / Dec - 056054
Vicevic, S., Hasenspitz 19, 65199 Wiesbaden. T. (0611) 46 71 09. 056055
Wemmers, Dirk, Steubenstr. 22, 65189 Wiesbaden. T. (0611) 30 18 21. - Ant - 056056
Witkowski's, Taunusstr. 24, 65183 Wiesbaden. T. (0611) 59 04 65. - Mod - 056057
Ziffzer, Elke, Grabenstr. 26, 65183 Wiesbaden. T. (0611) 06127/6362. 056058
Zimmermann, U., Bremthaler Str. 23, 65207 Wiesbaden. T. (0611) 373341. 056059
Zinnlade, Wilhelmstr. 56, 65183 Wiesbaden. T. (0611) 373341. 056060

Wiesloch (Baden-Württemberg)
Engelhorn, H., Hauptstr. 132, 69168 Wiesloch. T. (06222) 1436. 056061
Haeveker, H., Marktstr. 10, 69168 Wiesloch. T. (06222) 59394. - Num - 056062

Wietze (Niedersachsen)
Antiquitäten-Café, Steinförderstr. 126, 29323 Wietze. T. (05146) 14 44. 056063

Wildberg, Württemberg (Baden-Württemberg)
Esser-Zilleßen, G., Weingartenweg 1, 72218 Wildberg, Württemberg. T. (07054) 7191. 056064

Wilhelmshaven (Niedersachsen)
Picker, Heinrich, Gökerstr. 83, 26384 Wilhelmshaven. 056065
Popken, Gebr., Gökerstr. 24-26, 26384 Wilhelmshaven. T. (04421) 420 51. 056066

Willich (Nordrhein-Westfalen)
Bildt, K., Enger Weg 7, 47877 Willich. T. (02154) 02156/2885. 056067
Blum, K., Fischelner Str. 3, 47877 Willich. T. (02154) 2684. - Ant / Furn - 056068
Dau, I., Herzogweg 10, 47877 Willich. T. (02154) 2163. 056069
Kock, I., Moltkestr. 9, 47877 Willich. T. (02154) 1500. 056070
Kunst im Handwerk, Martin-Rieffert-Str. 11, 47877 Willich. T. (02154) 21 64. - Ant / Furn / Repr - 056071
Weimann-Modexa, Daimlerstr. 13, 47877 Willich. T. (02154) 4658. 056072

Windeck (Nordrhein-Westfalen)
Brecht, Regina, In Übersehen 16, 51570 Windeck. T. (02292) 02243/805 27. - Paint / China / Tex / Jew / Glass - 056073

Windelsbach (Bayern)
Koch, H., Schloßstr. 1, 91635 Windelsbach. T. (09867) 373. 056074

Winden (Rheinland-Pfalz)
Walz, Hauptstr. 36, 76872 Winden. T. (06349) 7545. 056075

Wingst (Niedersachsen)
Lukas, Klaus, Alt Kehdingen 41, 21789 Wingst. T. (04778) 04777/691. 056076

Winnenden (Baden-Württemberg)
Grafer, W.-D., Im Hummerholz 29, 71364 Winnenden. T. (07195) 62291. 056077

Wipperfürth (Nordrhein-Westfalen)
Berger, M. & H., Kleppersfeld 7, 51688 Wipperfürth. T. (02281) 4752. 056078

Wissen (Rheinland-Pfalz)
Tomandl, Vera, Im Kreuztal 78 und 104, 57537 Wissen. T. (02742) 1014. 056079

Wittdün (Schleswig-Holstein)
Behrendt, N., Hauptstr. 23, 25946 Wittdün. T. (04682) 1221. 056080

Witten (Nordrhein-Westfalen)
Grabski, H., Winsheimstr. 17, 58454 Witten. T. (02302) 69 04 39. 056081
Grabski, H., Ardeystr. 61, 58452 Witten. T. (02302) 82542. 056082
Wiedenbrüg, Karin, Gerichtsstr. 6, 58452 Witten. T. (02302) 578 14. 056083
Wulff, Hansjoachim, Auf den Stücken 15, 58455 Witten. T. (02302) 539 49. - Tex / Ico - 056084

Wittlich (Rheinland-Pfalz)
Wollscheid, K.-H., Rudolf-Diesel-Str. 17, 54516 Wittlich. T. (06571) 39 57. 056085

Wittmund (Niedersachsen)
Carol-Antiques, An der Kirche, 26409 Wittmund. T. (04462) 04464/8288. 056086
Onken, Dorfstr. 11, 26409 Wittmund. T. (04462) 6901. 056087
Pemöller, Karin, Wittmunder Str. 6, 26409 Wittmund. T. (04462) 1260. 056088
Reichert, Lothar, Kirchstr. 2, 26409 Wittmund. T. (04462) 386. 056089

Witzenhausen (Hessen)
Sammelsurium, Steinstr. 2, 37213 Witzenhausen. T. (05542) 44 77, 66 55. - Ant / Furn / China / Cur - 056090

Wörth (Bayern)
Wallrabenstein, I., Landstr. 14, 63939 Wörth. I. (09372) 71460. 056091

Wörth (Rheinland-Pfalz)
Lang, M., Pfarrstr. 5, 76744 Wörth. T. (07271) 70 67. 056092
Peitl, F., Marienstr. 31, 76744 Wörth. T. (07271) 417 49. 056093

Wörthsee (Bayern)
Antique Shop, Münchener Str. 3, 82237 Wörthsee. T. (08153) 77 66. - Ant - 056094
Downstairs Antiques, Alte Hauptstr. 18, 82237 Wörthsee. T. (08153) 82 39. - Ant / Furn - 056095
Gut Schluifeld, 82237 Wörthsee. T. (08153) 10 51. 056096

Wolfenbüttel (Niedersachsen)
Antik, Wallstr. 23, 38300 Wolfenbüttel. T. (05331) 1000. - Ant - 056098
Freunde Historischer Wertpapiere, Am Hogrevenkamp 4, 38302 Wolfenbüttel. T. (05331) 72890, Fax 31575. 056098a
Fricke, S., Harzstr. 16, 38300 Wolfenbüttel. T. (05331) 2505. 056099
Koch Kunsthaus, Lange Herzogstr. 9, 38300 Wolfenbüttel. 056100
Krause, Großer Zimmerhof 16, 38300 Wolfenbüttel. T. (05331) 24 27. 056101

Wolframs-Eschenbach (Bayern)
Storck, C., Hauptstr. 13, 91639 Wolframs-Eschenbach. T. (09875) 438, 256. - Ant - 056102

Storck, E., Hartmann-von-der-Aue-Str. 18, 91639 Wolframs-Eschenbach. T. (09875) 256.　　056103

Wolfratshausen (Bayern)
Graf-Pauli, A., Obermarkt 46, 82515 Wolfratshausen.
T. (08171) 17788.　　056104
Leder, Jutta, Aurikelstr. 2, 82515 Wolfratshausen.
T. (08171) 7386.　　056105

Wolfschlugen (Baden-Württemberg)
Zellmeier, Erich, Goethestr. 28, 72649 Wolfschlugen.
- Num -　　056106

Wolsfeld (Rheinland-Pfalz)
Pauls, J., Europastr. 5, 54636 Wolsfeld.
T. (06568) 7479.　　056107

Worms (Rheinland-Pfalz)
Carlé, Heinz, Altmühlstr. 3, 67547 Worms.　　056108
Kraft, Karin, Valckenbergstr. 12, 67547 Worms.
T. (06241) 221 59, 546 99. - Ant / Paint / Furn -　　056109
Lohmann, E., Brunnerstr. 17, 67549 Worms.
T. (06241) 750 09.　　056110
Moser, Liesel, Martinsgasse 31, 67547 Worms.
T. (06241) 259 19. - China / Glass -　　056111
Steuer, Helmut, Kämmererstr 41, 67547 Worms.
T. (06241) 238.　　056112

Worpswede (Niedersachsen)
Behrend, L., Osterwederstr. 21, 27726 Worpswede.
T. (04792) 25 65.　　056113
Geertz, C., Lindenallee 3, 27726 Worpswede.
T. (04792) 13 02.　　056114
Gerdes, Hembergstr. 25, 27726 Worpswede.
T. (04792) 14 05.　　056115
Hofmeister, Ane, Marcushof, 27726
Worpswede.　　056116
Kornadt, I., Findorffstr. 17, 27726 Worpswede.
T. (04792) 18 27.　　056117
Stelten, Hembergstr. 3, 27726 Worpswede.
T. (04792) 76 44, 39 58.　　056118
Stelten de Wiljes, A., Bergstr. 32, 27726 Worpswede.
T. (04792) 71 84.　　056119
Stengel, M., Bergstr. 23, 27726 Worpswede.
T. (04792) 22 92.　　056120
Tietjen, H., Alte Molkereistr. 21, 27726 Worpswede.
T. (04792) 2928.　　056121
Viebahn, Wörpedahlerstr. 12, 27726 Worpswede.
T. (04792) 3030, Fax (04792) 4086. - Ant / Paint / Furn /
China / Sculp / Tex / Dec / Lights / Instr -　　056122
Weingart, W., Sophie-Bötjer-Weg 7, 27726 Worpswede.
T. (04792) 2607. - Glass -　　056123
Worpsweder Gemälde Galerie Cohrs-Zirus, Bergstr. 5,
27726 Worpswede. T. (04792) 17 48. - Paint -　　056124

Wrohm (Schleswig-Holstein)
Schönleiter, W., Raiffeisenstr., 25799 Wrohm.
T. (04802) 416.　　056125

Wülfrath (Nordrhein-Westfalen)
Christ, Kochof 12, 42489 Wülfrath.
T. (02128) 73155.　　056126

Würselen (Nordrhein-Westfalen)
Das Lädchen, Kaiserstr. 35, 52146 Würselen.
T. (02405) 4958.　　056127

Würzburg (Bayern)
Amelung, Wolf-D., Karmelitenstr. 15, 97070 Würzburg.
T. (0931) 584 48, Fax 59648. - Ant / Furn / China /
Glass -　　056128
Antiquitäten am Rathaus, Wolfhartsgasse 5, 97070
Würzburg. T. (0931) 520 02.　　056129
Baum, Joachim, Rottendorfer Str. 22, 97074 Würzburg.
T. (0931) 765 61. - Ant / Furn / Sculp / Rel -　　056130
Baum, Wolfgang, Karmelitenstr. 23, 97070 Würzburg.
T. (0931) 592 53. - Ant / Furn / Sculp / Glass -　　056131
Brände, W., Büttnererstr. 25, 97070 Würzburg.
T. (0931) 15942.　　056132
Büchner, Gebr., Hofstr. 10, 97070 Würzburg.
T. (0931) 54529. - Ant -　　056133
Carstensen, Dominikanerpl. 4, 97070 Würzburg.
T. (0931) 50151. - Jew / Silv -　　056134
Detzer, Evelyn, Semmelstr. 25, 97070 Würzburg.
T. (0931) 591 64.　　056135

Drexler, Christl, Luitpoldstr. 8, 97082 Würzburg. - Ant /
Furn / China / Instr / Mil / Glass -　　056136
Ebinger, Michael, Karmelitenstr. 19, 97070 Würzburg.
T. (0931) 594 49. - Ant -　　056137
Ewald, Gustav, Bronnbachergasse 33, Eingang: Graben-
gasse, 97070 Würzburg. T. (0931) 16237. - Ant /
Lights -　　056138
Fischer, Burkarderstr. 32, 97082 Würzburg.
T. (0931) 41 66 50. - Num -　　056139
Gild, Wolfhartsgasse 6, 97070 Würzburg.
T. (0931) 54118. - Orient -　　056140
Giolda, Manfred, Kardinal-Faulhaber-Platz 4, 97070
Würzburg. T. (0931) 557 04, Fax 55779. - Paint / Furn /
Silv / Instr -　　056141
Hetzler, Gerhard, Franziskanergasse 1, 97070 Würzburg.
T. (0931) 5 80 94. - Ant / Furn / China / Silv -　　056142
Hillenbrand, A., Pommergasse 2, 97070 Würzburg.
T. (0931) 519 44.　　056143
Hübner, Heide, Domstr. 2, 97070 Würzburg.
T. (0931) 15151, Fax 50236. - Paint -　　056144
Kelim, Büttnerstr. 25, 97070 Würzburg.
T. (0931) 159 42.　　056145
Knabenbauer, Edgar, Rotkreuzstr. 5, 97080 Würzburg.
T. (0931) 55878. - Ant -　　056146
Küfner, H., Dr., Textorstr. 14, 97070 Würzburg.
T. (0931) 125 54.　　056147
Leonhardt, K., Wolfhartsgasse 5, 97070 Würzburg.
T. (0931) 520 02.　　056148
Lockner, Hermann P., Heinestr. 7, 97070 Würzburg.
T. (0931) 567 24. - Ant / China / Sculp / Silv /
Glass -　　056149
Mainfränkische Münzenhandlung, Textorstr. 16/18,
97070 Würzburg. T. (0931) 54519, Fax 59716.
- Num -　　056150
Mantei, Willi, Semmelstr. 60, 97070 Würzburg.
T. (0931) 543 49 und 729 44.　　056151
Meixner, A., Spessartstr. 27a, 97082 Würzburg.
T. (0931) 422 49.　　056152
Michalke, W., Sanderglacisstr. 4, 97072 Würzburg.
T. (0931) 754 92.　　056153
Michel, Gerd, Semmelstr. 42, 97070 Würzburg.
T. (0931) 139 08. - Graph -　　056154
Müller, Franz Xaver, Kardinal-Faulhaber-Platz 2, 97070
Würzburg. T. (0931) 526 24.　　056155
Neuhaus, Albrecht, Heinestr. 9, 97070 Würzburg.
T. (0931) 568 49, Fax 54286. - Ant / Paint / Furn /
Sculp / Jew / Silv -　　056156
Oberle, Steinbachtal-Rossberg, 97070 Würzburg.
T. (0931) 88 75 01, Fax 97082. - Ant / Paint / Furn / Chi-
na / Sculp / Tex / Dec / Cur -　　056157
Pfrang, W., Sieboldstr. 6, 97072 Würzburg.
T. (0931) 88 11 19.　　056158
Rummel, Barbara, Textorstr. 13-15, 97070 Würzburg.
T. (0931) 129 39, Fax 880176. - Ant / Paint / Graph /
Furn / Jew -　　056159
Schaller, E., Buchengraben 14, 97080 Würzburg.
T. (0931) 923 14.　　056160
Schlaud, J., Eichhornstr. 23, 97070 Würzburg.
T. (0931) 525 23. - Ant -　　056161
Schubert, Werner, Karmelitenstr. 19, 97070 Würzburg.
T. (0931) 594 49. - Ant / Paint / Furn / Jew /
Instr -　　056162
Sommer, Pleicherkirchpl. 13, 97070 Würzburg.
T. (0931) 582 58.　　056163
Stieber, Anni, Bronnbachergasse 37, 97070 Würzburg.
T. (0931) 513 55.　　056164
Villinger, Radegundis, Kaiserstr. 13, 97070 Würzburg.
T. (0931) 588 86, 938 26, Fax 93826. - Ant / Paint /
Graph / Sculp / Jew / Instr / Ico / Draw -　　056165
Volk, Konrad, Domstr. 41, 97070 Würzburg.
T. (0931) 588 54.　　056166
Wildmeister, Karmelitenstr., 97070 Würzburg.
T. (0931) 529 42. - Paint / Graph / Fra -　　056167
Winterstein, E., Vierter Siedlungsweg 4, 97082 Würz-
burg. T. (0931) 41 27 82.　　056168
Zemanek-Münster, Peterpl. 2, 97070 Würzburg.
T. (0931) 158 43. - Ant / Furn / China / Tex / Jew /
Glass / Mod -　　056169

Wunstorf (Niedersachsen)
Antikes u. d. Storchennest, Seeweg 8, 31515 Wunstorf.
T. (05031) 711 66.　　056170

Antiquitäten und Moden, Alter Winkel 16, 31515 Wun-
storf. T. (05031) 05033/1791.　　056171
Kirst, Siegfried, Alter Winkel 18, 31515 Wunstorf.
T. (05031) 050 33/81 36.　　056172

Wuppertal (Nordrhein-Westfalen)
Ackermann, W., Jaegerstr. 8, 42117 Wuppertal.
T. (0202) 74 35 82. - Paint / China / Jew / Silv -　　058173
Antik-Markt, Färberstr. 4-6,, 42275 Wuppertal.
T. (0202) 64 65 81. - Furn -　　056174
Becker, H., Sonnborner Str. 93, 42327 Wuppertal.
T. (0202) 74 53 76.　　056175
Brusten, A., Wormser Str. 53, 42119 Wuppertal.
T. (0202) 42 45 66.　　056176
Büttner, W., & D. Müller, Oppdorferstr. 50, 42103 Wup-
pertal. T. (0202) 394 60 33.　　056177
Delorette, H., Grönhoffstr. 8, 42285 Wuppertal.
T. (0202) 81109.　　056178
E & B Antik-Möbel-Import, Hatzfelder Str. 135, 42281
Wuppertal. T. (0202) 70 22 54. - Furn -　　056179
Fischer, G., Viehhofstr. 115, 42117 Wuppertal.
T. (0202) 43 60 70.　　056180
Fischer, P., Am Friedenshain 93, 42349 Wuppertal.
T. (0202) 40 26 43.　　056181
Galerie Palette, Sedanstr. 68-68a, 42281 Wuppertal.
T. (0202) 50 67 69. - Ant -　　056182
Gottschalk, Ursula, Friedrich-Ebert-Str. 79, 42103 Wup-
pertal. T. (0202) 30 17 16, 30 15 25. - Furn / China /
Silv -　　056183
Höller, Alfred N., Färberstr. 4, 42275 Wuppertal.
T. (0202) 64 65 81.　　056184
Hohage, J., Gräfrather Str. 16, 42329 Wuppertal.
T. (0202) 73 54 22.　　056185
Jindra, G., & P. Palluk, Schmitteborn 19, 42389 Wupper-
tal. T. (0202) 60 60 00.　　056186
Krause, G., Concordienstr. 9, 42275 Wuppertal.
T. (0202) 59 33 49.　　056187
Mühlenbeck, H., Sadowastr. 12, 42115 Wuppertal.
T. (0202) 31 38 44, Fax 31 60 00. - Ant / Mod -　　056188
Mumbeck, Bernd, Luisenstr. 104, 42103 Wuppertal.
T. (0202) 31 16 26.　　056189
Offermann & Schmitz, Wittelsbacherstr 31, 42287 Wup-
pertal. T. (0202) 555873, Fax (0202) 572267. - Orient /
Eth -　　056190
Runte, Carl, Wikingerstr. 1, 42275 Wuppertal.
T. (0202) 66 42 42. - Ant / Paint / Graph / Furn / China /
Silv / Instr / Glass -　　056191
Saxenhammer, K., Luisenstr. 69, 42103 Wuppertal.
T. (0202) 30 45 79.　　056192
Schott, J., Hippenhaus 31b, 42329 Wuppertal.
T. (0202) 73 62 27.　　056193
Schwarzkopf, E., Bredde 99, 42275 Wuppertal.
T. (0202) 59 33 49.　　056194
Speer, F., Alemannenstr. 35, 42105 Wuppertal.
T. (0202) 30 95 70.　　056195
Stöhr, H & W., Jägerhofstr. 43, 42119 Wuppertal.
T. (0202) 42 33 23.　　056196
Stosberg, H.-U., Westkotter Str. 158, 42277 Wuppertal.
T. (0202) 50 16 66.　　056197
Tichmann, A., Luisenstr. 81, 42103 Wuppertal.
T. (0202) 31 37 04. - Ant -　　056198
Zylka, Franz J., Erbschlöer Str. 22, 42369 Wuppertal.
T. (0202) 46 55 77. - Num -　　056199

Wyk (Schleswig-Holstein)
Lüden, Catharina, Waldstr. 11, 25938 Wyk.
T. (04681) 639. - Ant / Graph / China -　　056200
Richter-Levsen, Martha, Mittelstr. 10, 25938
Wyk.　　056201
Winkels, Renate & D., Strandstr. 75, 25938
Wyk.　　056202

Xanten (Nordrhein-Westfalen)
Adam, Viktorstr. 3, 46509 Xanten.
T. (02801) 5350.　　056203
Görtzen u. Sohn, Josef, Marsstr. 30, 46509 Xanten.
T. (02801) 14 76. - Furn -　　056204
Helgers, N., Siegfriedstr. 2, 46509 Xanten.
- Furn -　　056205

Zellingen (Bayern)
Felgenhauer, J., Mäderweg 32, 97225 Zellingen.
T. (09364) 9876.　　056206
Jung, Klaus, Hans Böcklerstr. 13, 97225
Zellingen.　　056207

Zeven (Niedersachsen)

Franz, Gerhard, Hoftohorn 15, 27404 Zeven.
T. (04281) 12 56. 056208
Liebig, Friedrich, Kattrepel 3, 27404 Zeven.
T. (04281) 5618. 056209
Michaelis, G., Beethovenweg 7, 27404 Zeven.
T. (04281) 25 19, 76 22, Fax 8475. - Num - 056210

Zirndorf (Bayern)

Classic-Kunst und Handwerk, Marktplatz 1, 90513 Zirndorf. T. (0911) 607487. 056211
Schultheiss, H., Weiherhofer Hauptstr 15, 90513 Zirndorf. T. (0911) 605312. 056212
Zickler, Egon, Wielandstr 16, 90513 Zirndorf. 056213

Zweibrücken (Rheinland-Pfalz)

Czerny, W., Ritterstr. 4, 66482 Zweibrücken.
T. (06332) 171 36. 056214
Nickel, Heinz, Oselbachstr 72, 66482 Zweibrücken.
T. (06332) 16384. - Mil - 056215

Zwickau (Sachsen)

Briefmarken- und Münzfachgeschäft, Marienpl. 1,
08056 Zwickau. T. (0375) 25965. - Num - 056216

Zwiesel (Bayern)

Pongratz, A., Oberzwieselauerstr. 1, 94227 Zwiesel.
T. (09922) 22 59. 056217
Schmitt, H., Langdorferstr. 30, 94227 Zwiesel.
T. (09922) 9463. 056218

Zwingenberg, Bergstr. (Hessen)

Backs, Bahnhofstr. 3, 64673 Zwingenberg, Bergstr.
T. (06251) 75503. 056219

Greece

Athinai

Adams, Bassilios, Kraterou 19 Ilissia, 136 71 Athinai.
T. (01) 770 1290. 056220
Antiqua, 4 Blvd. Amalias, 105 57 Athinai.
T. (01) 323 22 20, Fax 324 17 00. - Paint / Furn / Orient /
Tex / Jew / Silv / Instr / Mil / Rel / Glass / Cur / Ico --
056221
Antiques & Things, 24 Ifestou St., 105 55 Athinai.
T. (01) 321 96 85. - Silv / Lights / Instr / Mil - 056222
Apostolakis, Chr. Markos, Arionos 6, 105 54 Athinai.
T. (01) 324 2094. 056223
Art Chinois, 41 Od. Skoufa, 106 73 Athinai.
T. (01) 363 73 64. - Orient / China - 056224
Assimakis, Dimitrios, 2 Pindarou St., 106 71 Athinai.
T. (01) 611244. - Paint / Furn 056225
Astor Gallery, 16, kar Servias Str, Athinai. 056226
Bassilis, Platia Avissinias 16, 105 55 Athinai.
T. (01) 32 42 582. 056227
Bikos, V. Panagiotis, Ermou 101, 105 55 Athinai.
T. (01) 32 46 575. 056228
Bostanzoglou, Mentis, 21 Omirou St, 106 72 Athinai.
T. (01) 9214783. 056229
Chatsopoulos, Ioannis, Iphaestou 20, 105 55 Athinai.
T. (01) 32 51 156. 056230
Collectors, c/o Athens Hilton Hotel, 46 Leof Vass Sophi-
as, 106 76 Athinai. 056231
Dascalopoulos, Athanassios, 69 Pandrossou St., 105 55
Athinai. T. (01) 3213096. - Arch - 056232
Delezos, K. Panagiotis, Artemissiou 8, 104 35 Athinai.
T. (01) 89 40 856. 056233
Digran, Serapian, 31 Efaistou St, 105 55 Athinai.
T. (01) 3212579. 056234
Dimitressis, Constantin, 61 Pandrossou St., 105 55 Athi-
nai. T. (01) 3213124. - Arch - 056235
Eliadis, Efthifron, 20 Panepistimou St., 106 72 Athinai.
T. (01) 612719. - Paint / Arch - 056236
Emirzas, Dimitrios, 1 Antimou Gazi St., Athinai.
T. (01) 322. - Paint / Furn - 056237
Filaretos, 26 Ephaestou St., 105 55 Athinai.
T. (01) 324 0287. - Ant / Num / Arch / Jew / Lights / Mil /
Cur / Ico - 056238
Fortunas, Steve, 27 Voucourestiou St., 106 71 Athinai.
T. (01) 611221. - Orient / Jew - 056239
Galbinos, Konstantinos, Kimolou 8, 113 62 Athinai.
T. (01) 48 16 872. - Ant - 056240

Galerie Antiqua, 2 Rue Messoghion, 115 27 Athinai.
T. (01) 770 58 81. - Ant / Paint / Furn / Orient / China /
Tex / Silv / Instr / Mil / Rel / Glass / Cur / Ico - 056241
Genisarlis, Eleftherios, 2 Pindarou St., 106 71 Athinai.
T. (01) 36 11 244. - Paint / Furn - 056242
Giannacopoulos, John, 16 Kydatheneon St., 105 58
Athinai. T. (01) 3233728. - Paint / Mil - 056243
Gikas, Alexander, 7 Pindarou St., 106 71 Athinai.
T. (01) 635909. - Paint / Furn - 056244
Goutas, Vassilios, 42 Solonos St., 106 72 Athinai.
T. (01) 624648. - Ant / Paint - 056245
Goutis, Odos Pandrosou 4 + 40, 105 55 Athinai.
T. (01) 32 13 212, 32 13 044. - Jew / Rel - 056246
Hatopoulos, Theodosis, 71 Pandrossou St., 105 55 Athi-
nai. T. (01) 3213148. - Arch / Ico - 056247
Hatzimeletiadis, George, 7 Pindarou St., 106 71 Athinai.
T. (01) 611239. - China - 056248
Kagalos, Fotios, Platia Avissinias, 105 55 Athinai.
T. (01) 32 10 071. - Ant - 056249
Kapsoulaki, Martha, 63 Pandrossou St., 105 55 Athinai.
T. (01) 321 31 18. - Ant / Arch / Ico - 056250
Karamichalis, Anthony, 5 Havriou St., 105 62 Athinai.
T. (01) 3233574. - Num / Arch - 056251
Katisiaris, John, 31 Kydathineon St., 105 58 Athinai.
T. (01) 3228955. - Ant - 056252
Kazantsidis, Th. Bassilios, Astingos 19, 105 55 Athinai.
T. (01) 32 41 462. - Ant - 056253
Kazantzoglou, Xenofon, 17 Valaoritou St., 106 71 Athi-
nai. T. (01) 635656. - Ant / Furn / Jew - 056254
Kioussis, Michael, 3 Iraklitou St., 106 73 Athinai.
T. (01) 627097. - Ant / Paint - 056255
Kougheas, I. Bassilios, Aghisilaou 106, 104 35 Athinai.
T. (01) 34 20 504. - Ant - 056256
Koughianos, Spyr. & Sons, PLatia Avissinias 6 Monasti-
raki, 105 55 Athinai. T. (01) 32 12 473. - Ant /
Furn - 056257
Kourt, John, 17 Ifaistou St., 105 55 Athinai.
T. (01) 3210029. - Ant / Ico - 056258
Kourtidis, John, 6 Canaris St., 106 71 Athinai.
T. (01) 610524. - Paint / Furn - 056259
Kromidas, Constantin, 43 Solonos St., 106 72 Athinai.
T. (01) 603294. - Paint / Num - 056260
Liakopoulou, Mary, 4 Glyconos St., 106 75 Athinai.
T. (01) 713938. - Paint - 056261
Liapakis, Achilleas, 20 Efaistou St., 105 55 Athinai.
T. (01) 3245827. - Arch / Ico - 056262
Lihnostatis, 14, Odos Patr Ioakim, 106 75
Athinai. 056263
Maleas, Fotinos, 33 Solonos St., 106 71 Athinai.
T. (01) 362 99 06, 644 83 61. - Paint / Furn - 056264
Malteos, Anargyros, Orpheos 31, 105 64 Athinai.
T. (01) 94 23 074. - Ant - 056265
Manessis, George, 34 P. Ioakim St., 106 75 Athinai.
T. (01) 726531. - Ant / Paint / Furn - 056266
Martinos, John, 50 Pandrossou, 105 55 Athinai.
T. (01) 321 3110. - Ant - 056267
Mavromatis, Alkis, 3 Marasli St., 106 76 Athinai.
T. (01) 738341. - Paint / Furn - 056268
Michalakonas, Michael, 32 Solonos St., 106 73 Athinai.
T. (01) 626182. - Paint / Furn - 056269
Mikiditsian, O. Stella, Iphaestou 48, 105 55 Athinai.
T. (01) 32 42 726. - Ant - 056270
Miraraki, K. Despina, Leof. Kifissias 116, 115 24 Athinai.
T. (01) 69 29 709. - Ant / Furn - 056271
Motakis, Bassilios, Platia Avissinias 3, 105 55 Athinai.
T. (01) 32 14 993. - Ant - 056272
Moukanis, G. Nikolaos, Thermopylon 19, 104 35 Athinai.
T. (01) 24 66 010. - Ant - 056273
Othonaiou, Helen, 1 Charitos St., 106 75 Athinai.
T. (01) 741456. - Paint - 056274
Palaiologos, Pasiouras, 12 Solonos St., 106 73 Athinai.
T. (01) 637405. - Ant / Furn - 056275
Papadakis, Anthony, 23 Praxitelous St., 105 62 Athinai.
T. (01) 3226617. - Paint / Fra - 056276
Papaghergiou, Aspasia, Satobriandou 46 Omonia, 104
32 Athinai. T. (01) 52 41 247. - Ant - 056277
Patrikiadis, George N., 58-62 Pandrossou St., 105 55
Athinai. T. (01) 321 99 28. - Ant / Num / Repr / Sculp /
Arch / Jew / Silv / Ico - 056278
Petropoulos, S. Evthimios, Platia Avissinias 8, 105 55
Athinai. T. (01) 32 42 850. - Ant - 056279
Politis, G. Dion., Assomatou 5, 105 53 Athinai.
T. (01) 32 52 415. 056280

Rogotis, Paul, 8 Kinetou St., 105 55 Athinai.
T. (01) 3212604. - Ant / Furn - 056281
Roussos, Nikolaos, Od. Stadiou 3, 105 62 Athinai.
T. (01) 322 2815. - Ant / Num / Orient / China / Sculp /
Dec / Jew / Fra / Lights / Instr / Mil / Glass / Cur / Ico --
056282
Sepheriades, E., Havriou 5, 105 62 Athinai.
T. (01) 323 35 74. - Num - 056283
Sepheriades, Euripides, 9 Praxitelous, 105 62 Athlnal.
T. (01) 335 74. - Num - 056284
Sirapian, Iphaestou 6, 105 55 Athinai.
T. (01) 32 10 169. 056285
Sokaras, Takis, 2 Nissou St., 105 55 Athinai.
T. (01) 321758. - Ant - 056286
Souleles, Ioannis, Platia Avissinias 14, 105 55 Athinai.
T. (01) 32 18 771. 056287
Spanopoulos, Constantin, 26-28 Anagnostopoulou St.,
106 73 Athinai. T. (01) 625693. - Paint / Furn - 056288
Stratis, Frangiskos, Aghia Marinis 37 Aegaleo, 122 44
Athinai. T. (01) 56 13 684. 056289
Tatalias, Charalambos, 1 Agathoupoleos St., 112 57
Athinai. T. (01) 87 63 67. - Ant / Furn - 056290
Tiffany Gallery, Od. Solonos 28, 10 673 Athinai.
T. (01) 363 62 12. - Ant / Paint / Furn / Num / Tex / Jew /
Fra / Silv / Lights / Instr / Draw - 056291
Tsanetatos, A. Konstantinos, Kladou 9, 105 55 Athinai.
T. (01) 32 19 636. 056292
Tsannis, Ioannis, Aghiou Philippou 11, 105 55 Athinai.
T. (01) 32 19 706. 056293
Tsantilis, 31, Mitropoleos Str, 105 57 Athinai. 056294
Tsilalis, Kifissias 297 Kifissia, 145 63 Athinai.
T. (01) 80 82 488. 056295
Tsipitsis, Constantin, 265 Kifissias Ave., 145 64 Athinai.
T. (01) 8012403. - Furn / China - 056296
Vangeli, Platia Avissinias 3, 105 55 Athinai.
T. (01) 32 12 604. 056297
Vassiliadis, 22 Solonos Str, 106 73 Athinai.
T. (01) 363 05 73. 056298
Vitalis, Peter, 75 Pandrossou St., 105 55 Athinai.
T. (01) 3213123. - Arch / Ico - 056299
Voyatzis Bros., 10 Monastiraki Sq, 105 55 Athinai, 116.
T. (01) 325 08 84, 325 08 87. 056300
Zoumboulakis, Kolonaki Sq. 20, 106 73 Athinai.
T. (01) 360 82 78, 324 80 39. - Ant / Paint / Paint /
Graph / Sculp - 056301
Zoumboulakis Brothers, 1 Kriezotou, 106 71 Athinai.
T. (01) 61 34 33. - Ant - 056302

Irakleion (Kriti)

Pouranis, John, 48 25th August Ave., 712 02 Irakleion.
T. (081) 28 06 79. - Ant / Furn - 056303

Piraeus

Chatsiakos, Ioannis, Omir Skilitsi 19, 185 33 Piraeus.
T. (01) 41 79 337. 056304
Flamouris, Georghios, Omir. Skilitsi 9, 185 32 Piraeus.
T. (01) 41 74 648. - Ant - 056305
Georgas, George, 1 Plataiou St., 185 40 Piraeus.
T. (01) 426243. - Ant / Furn - 056306
Karalis, Sotirios, L. Bas. Georghiou A3, 185 31 Piraeus.
I. (01) 41 34 165, 41 78 265. - Num - 056307
Kritikos, Evang., Platia Ippodamias 12, 185 31 Piraeus.
T. (01) 41 76 925. 056308
Moudakis, Michael, 1 Filonos St, 185 31 Piraeus.
T. (01) 4171538. 056309
Pantasi, A., Filonos 6, 185 31 Piraeus. T. (01) 41 22 602.
- Ant / Furn - 056310
Theodorakakos, Nikolaos, Alipedou 36, 185 31 Piraeus.
T. (01) 41 25 846. - Ant / Furn - 056311
Touliatos, Panaghiotis, Om. Skilitsi 3, 185 32 Piraeus.
T. (01) 41 79 285. - Ant / Lights - 056312

Skiathos

Archipelagos, 370 02 Skiathos. T. (0424) 0427/22163.
- Ant / Paint / Furn / Num / China / Tex / Dec / Jew / Silv /
Lights / Glass / Ico / Mul - 056313

Syros

Threpsiadis, Demetrios, 19 Protopapadaki St., Syros.
- Paint / Furn - 056314

Thessaloniki

Alexander, 25 Tsimiski Str, 546 24 Thessaloniki. 056315

Antiques Co., 8, Vogatsikou, 546 22
Thessaloniki. 056316
Athanassiadis, 16 Tsimiski Str, 546 24
Thessaloniki. 056317
Bruno, 54 Tsimiski Str, 546 23 Thessaloniki. 056318
El Greco, 93 Tsimiski Str, 546 22 Thessaloniki. 056319
Knossos, 16, Komninon Str, 546 24
Thessaloniki. 056320
Reïsis, Dimitrios, pros Oraeokastro, 570 13 Thessaloni-
ki. T. (031) 65 68 09. 056321
Scaperda & Sons, 3, Fil Eterias St, 546 21
Thessaloniki. 056322
Siogas, Angelos, 70 km Odou Lagada, Thessaloniki.
T. (031) 65 43 89. 056323

Guadeloupe

Le Gosier
Christiane, 5 Montauban, 97190 Le Gosier.
T. (590) 845251. 056325

Pointe-à-Pitre
A la Recherche du Passé, Centre Commercial La Marina,
97110 Pointe-à-Pitre. T. (590) 908415,
Fax (590) 909739. - Graph / Dec - 056326
Brocante des Isles, 3 Rue Brissac, 97110 Pointe-à-Pitre.
T. (590) 915281. 056327
Mas, Christian, 33bis Rue Henri-IV, 97110 Pointe-à-Pi-
tre. T. (590) 915269, Fax (590) 832728.
- Graph - 056328
Pérès-Sol, Michèle, 14 Pl Victoire, 97110 Pointe-à-Pitre.
T. (590) 914702. 056329
Tim-Tim, 15 Rue Jean-Jaurès, 97110 Pointe-à-Pitre.
T. (590) 834071. Graph / Furn / Tex / Jew /
Cur - 056330

Saint-Claude
Pinard, Laurence, Rte Choisy, 97120 Saint-Claude.
T. (590) 803577. 056331

Hong Kong

Hong Kong
Altfield, 38 Hollywood Rd., Central, Hong Kong.
- Orient - 056332
Art Treasures Gallery, 42 Hollywood Rd., Hong Kong.
T. 5-430430. - Orient - 056333
Arts House, 36 Chungking Arcade, Nathan Rd., Kowloon,
Hong Kong. T. 3-682 665. 056334
Arts of China, Hong Kong Hotel, Shop 325, Kowloon,
Hong Kong. T. 3-7225073, 3-699525.
- Orient - 056335
Asian African Arts Co., J. Hotung House, 49 Peking Rd.,
Kowloon, Hong Kong. T. 3-669977. 056336
Benny Chow, A5 Mandarin Hotel Arcade, Hong Kong.
T. 5-228521. 056337
Casabella, 18-GIF Hilton Hotel, Hong Kong. 056338
Cat Street Galleries, 38 Lok Ku Rd., Sheung Wan, Hong
Kong. T. 5-431609. - Orient - 056339
Cathay, 10A Carnarvon Rd., Kowloon, Hong Kong. T. 3-
7391172, 3-7391284. - Orient - 056340
Chang Chinese Arts & Crafts, 127 Tai Shan Gallery,
Ocean Terminal, Kowloon, Hong Kong. T. 3-
665883. 056341
Chang, Robert, 124 Waglan Gallery, Deck 1, Ocean Ter-
minal, Kowloon, Hong Kong. T. 3-672397.
- Orient - 056342
China Art-Craft Co., 73 bis 75 Nathan Rd. Kowloon,
Hong Kong. T. 6 66 84 18. - Ant / Furn - 056343
China Arts Co., 7a Humphreys Ave., Kowloon, Hong
Kong. T. 3-669689. 056344
China Arts & Gift Centre, 25a Lock Rd., Kowloon, Hong
Kong. T. 3-665 909. 056345
China Curio Centre, 12 Upper Lascar Row, Hong Kong.
T. H-43 10 06. - Ant / Cur - 056346
Chinese Arts and Crafts, 30 Canton Rd., Tsimshatsui,
Kowloon, Hong Kong. T. 731 13 33. - Orient - 056347
Ching, C.P., 21 Hollywood Rd., Central, Hong Kong. T. 5-
438638. - Orient - 056348

Chow's Jewelery, 34 Hankow Rd., Kowloon, Hong Kong.
T. 3-664 651, 3-663 834. - Orient / Jew - 056349
Chu, Royal Garden Hotel, Shop 106, Kowloon, Hong
Kong. T. 3-7220110. - Orient - 056350
Chung Fat Ivory Factory, 15 Cameron Rd., Kowloon,
Hong Kong. T. 3-669833. 056351
Coleman, Teresa, 37 Wyndham St., Ground Fl., Hong
Kong. T. 526-2450, Fax 845-0793. - Ant / Paint / Furn /
Tex / Jew - 056352
Comaisseur Antique Decoration, 307 Lane Crawford
House, Hong Kong. T. 5-244407. 056353
David Arts Co., 5a Ice House St., G/F, Hong Kong. T. 5-
248875. 056354
Dunt King, 6 Lyndhurst Terrace Central District, Hong
Kong. T. 5-450703. 056355
Dynasty Arts & Crafts Co., 174-5 Sheraton Hotel, 1/F
Kowloon, Hong Kong. T. 3-691568. 056356
Everlasting Chinese Arts Studio, 1 Harbour Village, Star
House, 4/F, Kowloon, Hong Kong. T. 3-
662574. 056357
Flieger, Cynthia, 122 Ocean Terminal Kowloon, Hong
Kong. T. 3-668047. 056358
Foo Cheong Co., 78 Chung King Arcade Kowloon, Hong
Kong. T. 3-665534. 056359
Foochow Art Co., 16 E Carnarvon Rd., Kowloon, Hong
Kong. T. 3-671495. - Ant - 056360
Foochow Art Co., 16F Carnarvon Rd., Kowloon, Hong
Kong. T. 3-671495. 056361
Fordley Arts, 43 Peking Rd., Kowloon, Hong Kong. T. 3-
669011. 056362
Frederick Arts Ltd., 101b Ocean Terminal, Kowloon,
Hong Kong. T. 3-662912. 056363
Fung, Martin, 38 Lok Ku Rd., Central, Hong Kong. T. 5-
459330. - Orient - 056364
Gala Enterprises, 350 Hong Kong Hotel Arkade, Kow-
loon, Hong Kong. T. 3-682474. 056365
Good Brothers & Co., D7 Sheraton Hotel, St/Fl., Kow-
loon, Hong Kong. T. 3-664215. 056366
Grand Arts Co., B5 Hyatt Hotel Arcade, Kowloon, Hong
Kong. T. 3-688381. 056367
Grand Dragon Co., 206 Lin Tin Gallery, Ocean Terminal,
Kowloon, Hong Kong. T. 3-672222. 056368
Han Dynasty Art & Craft, 35 Hilton Hotel, Hong Kong.
T. 5-235728. 056369
Han Fung, 50 Mirador Mansion, Kowloon, Hong Kong.
T. 3-660094. 056370
Hing Co., Lee, 15 Ambassador Hotel, G/F Nathan Rd.,
Kowloon, Hong Kong. T. 3-662403. 056371
Honeychurch, 29 Hollywood Rd., Hong Kong. T. 5-
432433. - Orient - 056372
Hong Kong Artisans, 311 Shopping Arcade, Excelsior
Hotel, Hong Kong. T. 5-765857. 056373
Horstmann, Charlotte, & Gerald Godfrey, Ocean Termi-
nal, Kowloon, Hong Kong. T. 735 7167.
- Orient - 056374
Jade House, 1-D Mody Rd., Kowloon, Hong Kong. T. 3-
680491. - Orient - 056375
Jeiwah, 2-10 Lyndhurst Terrace, Suite 1001-2, Central,
Hong Kong. T. 5-417236. - Orient - 056376
Jun Alday, 77 Wyndham St., Central, Hong Kong. T. 5-
261285. - Orient - 056377
Kee, D. Y., G35 Hyatt Hotel Arcade, Nathan Rd., Kow-
loon, Hong Kong. T. 3-674220. 056378
Ken Shing Hing Chong, 180 Ocean Terminal, Kowloon,
Hong Kong. T. 3-677285. 056379
Kershaw, Eileen, M-20 Peninsula Hotel Arcade, Kow-
loon, Hong Kong. T. 3-664083. 056380
King Feng, 335 Hong Kong Hotel Shopping Arcade, Kow-
loon, Hong Kong. T. 3-679370. - Orient - 056381
King & Sons, Y. C., 7 Carnarvon Road, G/F, Kowloon,
Hong Kong. T. 3-684 222. 056382
Konn & Fine Arts, 39 Hilton Hotel Arcade, Hong Kong.
T. 5-230902. 056383
Kung, Y. M., 142 Prince's Building, Hong Kong. T. 5-
240 326. 056384
Lam Luen Kee Co., 52 Lyndhurst Terrace, Hong Kong.
T. 5-437226. 056385
Lee, Sammy Y., & Wangs, 29-31 Chatham Rd. Kowloon,
Hong Kong. T. 3 663935, 3 7235661. - Ant - 056386
Limb, P. K., 36 Queen's Road Central Room 106 Hing
Wai Bldg., Hong Kong. T. H-23 57 44. 056387
Lohan, Shop 39, Hilton Hotel, Central, Hong Kong. T. 5-
262 202. 056388

Lu, P.C., & Sons, Peninsula, West Arcade, G/F Shop W-
10, Hong Kong. T. 3-672589. - Orient - 056389
Lu, P.C., & Sons, Peninsula, Mezzanine Shop ML-7,
Hong Kong. T. 3-688436. - Orient - 056390
Lu, P.C., & Sons, Mandarin Hotel, Mezzanine Shop M-9-
11, Hong Kong. T. 5-243395. - Orient - 056391
Luen Chai Curios Store, 22 and 23 Upper Lascar Row,
Hong Kong. T. H-44 11 38, H-44 59 17. - Ant /
Cur - 056392
Ma, C.L., 24 Hollywood Rd., Hong Kong. T. 5-254369, 5-
8451524. - Orient - 056393
Mandarin Gem & Jade, 10 Harbour Village, Kowloon,
Hong Kong. T. 67 72 64. - Ant / Paint / Orient / China /
Sculp / Dec - 056394
Ming Dynasty, 104 Prince's Building, Hong Kong. T. 5-
241286. 056395
Nathan, 81 Peking Rd., Kowloon, Hong Kong. T. 3-
688914,3-688940. - Orient - 056396
Nelson Chan Art & Co., 23 Far East Mansion G/F, Kow-
loon, Hong Kong. T. 3-67 63 65. 056397
Ngan Hing Shun Co., 112/116a Ap Lei Chau Gallery,
Ocean Terminal, Hong Kong. T. 3-661210. 056398
Noble Arts Ltd., 3 Excelsior Hotel, 1/F, Hong Kong. T. 5-
762614. 056399
Oriental Arts House, 28 Hankow Rd., Kowloon, Hong
Kong. T. 3-672863. 056400
Oriental Arts & Crafts, 131 Tai Shan Gallery, Ocean Ter-
minal, Kowloon, Hong Kong. T. 3-666947. 056401
Oriental Arts & Handicraft, Shop 21, Star House, 106
Prince's Bldg., Kowloon, Hong Kong. T. 3-677652, 5-
241868. - Orient - 056402
Oriental Ivory & Arts Ltd., 316 Hong Kong Hotel Arcade,
Kowloon, Hong Kong. T. 3-672791. 056403
Peking House of Art, 33 Hilton Hotel Arcade G/F. 2,
Queen's Rd. C., Hong Kong. T. 5-252611. 056404
Plum Blossoms, 306-307 Exchange Sq. One, Hong
Kong. T. 5-212189. - Orient - 056405
Pok Art House, 18 Granville Rd., Kowloon, Hong Kong.
T. 3-664796. 056406
Pui Kee, 56 Mirador Mansion, Kowloon, Hong Kong. T. 3-
670335. 056407
Royal Arts, 19 Carnarvon Rd., Kowloon, Hong Kong. T. 3-
660 375. 056408
Shanghai Jade Carving Factory, 58-64 Nathan Rd., Kow-
loon, Hong Kong. T. 3-682757. - Orient - 056409
Sovereign Company, 18-24 Salisbury Rd., Kowloon,
Hong Kong. T. 3-695666,3-698081. - Orient - 056410
Tai Sing, 22, Wyndham St., Hong Kong. T. 5-
259 365. 056411
Tai Sing, 122 Hollywood Rd., Hong Kong. T. 5-491289,
5-491295. - Ant / Furn - 056412
Tai Yip, 30A Stanley St., Hong Kong. T. 5-250496.
- Orient - 056413
The Bangkok Capital Antique Co Ltd., 5 Carnarvon Rd.,
Kowloon, Hong Kong. T. 3-665 479. 056414
The China-Art-Craft Co., 73 Nathan Road, Kowloon,
Hong Kong. T. 3-668418. 056415
The Collections Shop, 120 Hong Kong Hotel, Arcade,
Kowloon, Hong Kong. T. 3-682 372. 056416
The Oriental Arts Co., D2 Sheraton Hotel 2/F, Nathan
Road, Kowloon, Hong Kong. T. 3-690 820. 056417
The Paul Young, Shop-11, Lower Basement Connaught
Centre, Hong Kong. T. 5-259 828. 056418
The Treasure Co., 278 Ocean Terminal, Kowloon, Hong
Kong. T. 3-673 686. 056419
The Union Arts Co., 6a Cameron Road, Kowloon, Hong
Kong. T. 3-666 676. 056420
Tih, C. C., Prince's Bldg., Hong Kong. T. H-22 89 13.
- Ant / China - 056421
Treasures of China, Shop 312, Ocean Galleries Harbour
City, Kowloon, Hong Kong. T. 3-681387.
- Orient - 056422
Tse, C.Y, Hilton Hotel, Shop 39, Hong Kong. T. 5-256557.
- Ant / Orient / Jew - 056423
Universal Artists Co., Shop 26 Star House, G/F, Kowloon,
Hong Kong. T. 3-666 359. 056424
Vintage China, Princes Bldg., Shop 252, Central, Hong
Kong. T. 5-253866. - Orient - 056425
Wing Fung Arts Co., 19 Star House, G/F Kowloon, Hong
Kong. T. 3-679-762. 056426
Wing Fung Arts Co., 104 Hong Kong Hotel Arcade, Kow-
loon, Hong Kong. T. 3-690 679. 056427

Wing Hing, 18 Salisbury Rd., Kowloon, Hong Kong. T. 3-664923. - Orient - 056428

Wo Kee Arts, Shop 18, Mirador Mansions Arcade, Kowloon, Hong Kong. T. 3-688 920. 056429

Wong's Arts Co., D6 Sheraton Hotel, 2/F, Kowloon, Hong Kong. T. 3-672 976. 056430

Woo's Curios, 101 Hong Kong Hotel, 1/F, Kowloon, Hong Kong. T. 3-692 471. 056431

Yang & Co., Y. F., 163c Ocean Terminal, Kowloon, Hong Kong. T. 3-679 474. 056432

Young, Paul Co., 5 bis 6 Middle Rd. Kowloon, P.O. Box 6355, Hong Kong. T. K-66 37 48. - Ant - 056433

Yuan Feng & Co., 18 Ashley Rd. Kowloon, Hong Kong. T. 3-664 663. - Ant / Orient - 056434

Yue Po Chai, 132-136 Hollywood Rd., Hong Kong. T. 5-404374-5. - Ant / Jew - 056435

Yuen Cheong & Co., 248 Lamma Gallery Ocean Terminal, Kowloon, Hong Kong. T. 3-674 765. 056436

Yung Kee Curios, 11 Lyndhurst Terrace, Hong Kong. T. H-44 02 32. - Ant / Cur - 056437

Hungary

Budapest

Artex, Münnich F. u. 31, Budapest. T. (01) 31 33 30.
- Paint / Graph / Sculp / Tex - 056438

Artunion, Szep u. 5, 1053 Budapest. T. (01) 17 17 28.
- Ant / Paint / Graph / China / Tex / Dec / Jew / Lights / Glass / Pho / Draw - 056439

Galéria, Galerie des Verbandes Ungarischer Radierkünstler, Petöfi S. u. 18, 1052 Budapest. - Paint / Graph / Repr / Sculp - 056440

Képcsarnok Közületi, Dózsa György Str. 38, 1076 Budapest. - Graph / Num / Sculp - 056441

Konsumturist, Hess András tér 3, Budapest.
T. (01) 75 03 92. - Ant / Furn / Num / China / Sculp - 056442

Iceland

Reykjavik

Benediktsson, Sigurdur, Hafnarstraeti 11, Reykjavik.
- Ant / Paint / Graph - 056443

Kristjonsson, Bragi, Vatnsstigur 4, Box 775, 121 Reykjavik. T. (91) 351-129 720. 056444

Listidjan, Njalsg 94, 105 Reykjavik. T. (91) 91/124 04. 056445

India

Agra

Munshi, 9 Mahatma Gandhi Rd., 282 001 Agra.
T. 7 42 39. - Ant / Paint / Jew - 056446

Raj Emporium, 71 Taj Rd., Agra, 282001. T. 7 39 74.
- Ant / Paint / Orient / Tex / Dec / Jew / Silv / Lights / Draw - 056447

Bangalore (Mysore)

Natesan's Antiqarts, 64 Mahatma Gandhi Rd., Bangalore, 560001. T. 58 74 27, 58 83 44, Fax 58 61 05.
- Eth - 056448

Bombay (Maharashtra)

Dialdas, M. & Son, 190 Shamaldas Gandhi Marg, POB 2356, Bombay, 400002. T. (022) 311124.
- Ant - 056449

Essajee, A.K., Suleman Chambers Appollo Pier Rd, Bombay, 400039. T. (022) 231071. 056450

Hassamal, 538 Kalbadevi Rd, POB 2236 (2), Bombay.
T. (022) 312001/2. - Ant / Tex / Silv - 056451

Nanavatty, Suresh, 16 Apollo St, Bombay. - Paint / Graph / Furn / Sculp / Tex / Jew / Lights - 056452

Calcutta (West Bengal)

Gem Company, Great Fastern Hotel, Calcutta.
T. 23 41 23. - Ant / Paint / Jew - 056453

Delhi (Delhi)

Art Museum, 1726 Burn Bastion Rd., Delhi.
- Ant - 056454

Kumar, Virendra, 11 Sundar Nagar Market, Delhi, 110003. T. 61 88 75, 61 11 13. - Ant / Paint / Orient / Tex / Arch / Eth - 056455

Kumar, Virendra, Ashok Hotel, Delhi, 110021.
T. 37 01 01/ 21 60. - Ant / Paint / Orient / Tex / Arch / Eth - 056456

Hoshiarpur (Punjab)

Kanhaya Lal Brij Lal, Dabbi Bazaar, Hoshiarpur.
- Ant - 056457

Karm Chand Payara Lal, B., Dabbi Bazaar, Hoshiarpur.
T. 446. - Ant / Eth - 056458

Hyderabad (Andhra Pradesh)

Mittal, Kamla, 1-2-214 Gagan Mahal Rd., Hyderabad.
- Ant / Arch - 056459

New Delhi

Bharany's Curio House, 14 Sunder Nagar Market, New Delhi, 110003. T. (011) 618528. - Ant / Arch / Cur - 056460

Boutique, 20 Sunder Nagar Market, New Delhi, 110003.
T. (011) 619066. - Ant / Sculp / Jew / Mil - 056461

Nath, 50 Hanuman Rd, New Delhi. T. (011) 40688.
- Ant / Lights / Mil - 056462

Srinagar (Kashmir)

ShaHab-Ud-Din, M., & Sons, POB 348, Srinagar.
- Ant - 056463

Udaipur (Rajasthan)

Curious House, Chetak Circle, Udaipur. T. 3206. - Ant / Paint / China / Silv / Mil / Cur / Music - 056464

Varanasi (Uttar Pradesh)

Banaras Art Stores, Thatheri Bazar, Varanasi. T. 29 91.
- Ant / Orient / Arch / Eth - 056465

Curio Cottage, S.19/3 Nai Bazar, Burna Bridge, Varanasi.
T. 32 29. - Ant / Orient / Arch / Eth - 056466

Indonesia

Bandung

„Chiam Brothers", Pasar Baroe 21 B, Bandung. - Ant / Paint / Num / Sculp / Arch / Eth / Jew / Silv - 056467

Iran

Isfahan

Persepolis, Nagush Jahan Square 50, Isfahan.
T. 2 69 20. 056468

Ziba, Honarhayeh, Ave. Chaharbagh 304, Isfahan.
T. 54 17 6. 056469

Teheran

Aziz, 82 Ave. Ferdowsi, Teheran. - Ant - 056470

Caravan, 212 Ave. Takhte Jamshid, Teheran.
T. (021) 825 999. - Ant - 056471

Djavaherian Handicrafts, Bazar Bozorg, Passage Favardine, Teheran. T. (021) 203 554. - Ant - 056472

Easatis, Ave. Pahlavi, Bazar Safavieh, Teheran.
T. (021) 890 710. - Ant - 056473

Honor Esfahan, Ave. Estambol, Plasco Building, Teheran.
T. (021) 302 230. - Ant - 056474

Iran Hedieh, Ave. Estambol, Plasco Passage, Teheran.
T. (021) 318 852. - Ant - 056475

Kennedy, 212 Ave. Takhte Jamshid, Teheran.
T. (021) 822 532. 056476

Louvre, 132 Ferdowsi, Teheran.
T. (021) 319 684. 056477

Moses Saidian, Av. Manutchehri 218, Teheran.
T. (021) 31 31 16. 056478

Opaline Rose, Ave. Pahlavi, Bazar Safayieh 6-7, Teheran. T. (021) 820 710. - Ant - 056479

Panjeh Talai, Ave. Villa 151, Teheran.
T. (021) 66 07 78. 056480

Rafael, 279 Ave. Manoutchehri, Teheran.
T. (021) 310 348. - Ant - 056481

Riahi Antiques, Ferdowsi Ave., Teheran. - Ant - 056482

Saman, Ave. Ferdowsi 48, Teheran.
T. (021) 39 39 02. 056483

Serai, Zivar, Ave. Schah Abbas 74, Teheran.
T. (021) 82 17 47. 056484

Soleiman & Haroun, 170 Ave. Ferdowsi, Teheran.
T. (021) 318 689. - Ant - 056485

Sulivan Gallery, 136 Fakhrerazy Ave. Shahreza Ave, Teheran. T. (021) 649 751. - Paint / Graph / Furn / Repr / Sculp / Dec / Fra / Mod - 056486

Teheran Gallery, Av. Abbasse Abad, Carrefour Ghasre 9, Teheran. - Ant / Paint / Graph / Repr / Sculp / Tex / Eth / Dec / Silv / Glass / Mod / Pho / Mul / Draw - 056487

Iraq

Baghdad

Hasso, N. A. & Co., Hasso Building, Baghdad. 056488

Ireland

Adare (Co. Limerick)

Adare Antiques, Adare. - Ant / China / Glass - 056489

Stacpoole, George, Adare. T. (061) 396409, Fax 396733.
- Ant / Paint / Furn / China / Tex / Dec / Jew / Silv / Glass / Draw - 056490

Ashford (Co. Wicklow)

Clonattin Antiques, Mount Usher, Wicklow, Ashford.
T. (0404) 4116. - Ant / Paint / China / Jew / Silv / Glass - 056491

Ballina (Co. Mayo)

Maguire, Martin, Tone St., Ballina. T. (096) 22598.
- Ant - 056492

Mount Falcon Estates, Mount Falcon Castle, Ballina.
T. (096) 146. - Ant / China / Silv / Glass - 056493

Ballyduff (Co. Waterford)

Lodge, Flower Hill, Ballyduff. T. (058) 6, 29. - Furn / China / Silv / Glass - 056494

Blackrock (Co. Dublin)

Hazley Godsil, 4 Main St., Blackrock. T. (01) 88 50 11.
- Ant - 056495

Miskelly, 19a Main St., Blackrock. T. (01) 83 36 55.
- Ant - 056496

Roberts & Little, 49 Main St., Blackrock.
T. (01) 88 99 61. - Ant - 056497

Bray (Co. Wicklow)

Bray Antiques, 37 Main St., Bray. T. (01) 86 25 25.
- Ant - 056498

Clancy Chandeliers, Ballywaltrim, Bray. T. (01) 86 34 60.
- Ant - 056499

Buttevant (Co. Cork)

Arts Antiques, St. Joseph's Stores, Buttevant.
T. (022) 2 31 78. - Ant - 056500

Cahir (Co. Tipperary)

Burke, John F., & Sons, Cahir. T. (052) 255. - Ant / China / Silv - 056501

Cork (Co. Cork)

Antique Shop Ltd., 6, Cook St., Cork. T. (021) 2 29 50.
- Furn / Silv - 056502

Feehan & Co. Ltd., 2 Bridge St., Cork. T. (021) 2 60 79.
- Furn / China / Silv / Instr - 056503

O'Connel, C., Ltd., 5 & 6 Lavitt's Quay, Cork.
T. (021) 2 03 46. - Ant - 056504

The Curio Shop, 2 Sheares St., Cork. T. (021) 4 35 99.
- Ant / Paint / Num / Cur - 056505

Dalkey (Co. Dublin)

Crawford, 1 Convent Rd., Dalkey. T. (01) 85 02 85.
- Ant - 056506

Donegal (Co. Donegal)

Antique Shop, The Diamond, Donegal. T. (073) 144.
- China / Jew / Silv / Glass - 056507

Drogheda (Co. Louth)
Greene, The Mall, Drogheda. T. (041) 62 12. - Furn /
Silv -   056508

Dublin
Acanthus Woodcarvers, U4 Liffey Trust Centre, North
Wall, Dublin 1. T. (01) 36 57 63. - Sculp -   056509
Alexander, Malcolm, 46 Dawson St., Dublin 2.
T. (01) 679 1548, Fax 679 6667. - Ant -   056510
Allen, David W., 46a Capel St., Dublin 1. T. (01) 73 05 92.
- Ant -   056511
Allen & Townsend, 10 Saint Stephen's Garden, Dublin 1.
T. (01) 71 00 33. - Paint -   056512
Anthony, 7-9 Molesworth St., Dublin 2. T. (01) 77 72 22.
- Ant -   056513
Antiqcurios, 33 Clarendon St., Dublin. T. (01) 71 49 32.
- Ant -   056514
Antique Fireplace Centre, 79 Francis St. (8), Dublin.
T. (01) 54 22 59. - Ant -   056515
Antique Prints and Paintings, 16 Anne St. South, Dublin
2. T. (01) 71 96 23. - Paint / Graph -   056516
Antique Shop, 2 Bedford Row, Dublin 2. T. (01) 77 28 76.
- Ant -   056517
Bird, Christy, 32 Richmond St. South, Dublin 2.
T. (01) 75 40 49. - Furn -   056518
Bits and Pieces Antiques, 78 Francis St., Dublin 8.
T. (01) 54 11 78. - Lights / Instr -   056519
Browsing, 59 South William St., Dublin 2.
T. (01) 679 3820. - Ant -   056520
Butler, Edward, 14 Bachelor's Walk, Dublin 1.
T. (01) 73 02 96. - Ant / Paint / Furn / Instr /
Glass -   056521
C & M Upholstery, 9 Upper Basin St., Dublin 8.
T. (01) 53 75 50. - Furn -   056522
Circa Antiques, 58 Upper Stevens St., Dublin 8.
T. (01) 78 49 59. - Ant -   056523
City Brass Shop, 74 Francis St., Dublin 8.
T. (01) 54 26 96. - Ant -   056524
Clifford, 5 Parnell St., Dublin 1. T. (01) 72 60 62.
- Furn -   056525
Clontarf Antiques, 47a Clontarf Rd., Dublin 3.
T. (01) 33 15 92. - Ant -   056526
Collectors Corner, 323 Saint Michael's Mall, Dublin.
T. (01) 80 15 43. - Ant -   056527
Conlon, 21-22 Lower Clanbrassil St., Dublin 8.
T. (01) 53 73 23. - Paint / Furn -   056528
Conlon, G., 3 Fumbally Ln., Dublin 8. T. (01) 53 22 06.
- Ant -   056529
Coombe Antiques, 117 The Coombe, Dublin 8.
T. (01) 53 74 93. - Ant -   056530
Courtville, 59 South William St., Dublin 2.
T. (01) 679 4042. - Paint / Jew -   056531
Danker, H., 10 South Anne St., Dublin 2. T. (01) 77 40 09.
- Ant / Jew / Silv -   056532
Domain, 4-6 Bridgefoot St., Dublin 8. T. (01) 77 55 05.
- Ant -   056533
Elizabeth Antiques, 59 South William St., Dublin 2.
T. (01) 679 1983. - Ant -   056534
Finders Antiques, 37 Francis St., Dublin 8.
T. (01) 54 20 07. - Ant -   056535
Fine Pine Rere, 3 Williams Park, Dublin 6.
T. (01) 97 10 52. - Furn -   056536
Fitzsimon, 59 South William St., Dublin 2.
T. (01) 679 6576. - Ant -   056537
Gibson O'Neill, 64 Patrick St., Dublin 2. T. (01) 53 91 85.
- Ant -   056538
Gift Exchange, 17 Ormond Quay, Dublin 2.
T. (01) 77 87 68. - Ant -   056539
Ha' Penny Bridge Galleries, 15 Bachelors Walk, Dublin
1. T. (01) 72 39 50. - Ant -   056540
Kenyon, Gerald, 10 Great Strand St., Dublin 1.
T. (01) 73 06 25. - Paint / Furn -   056541
Kenyon, Gerald, 10 Ormond Quay, Dublin 1.
T. (01) 73 04 88. - Paint / Furn -   056542
Kildare Antiques, 19 Kildare St., Dublin 2.
T. (01) 76 35 76. - Paint / Furn -   056543
Lace Lady, 129 Upper Luson St., Dublin 4.
T. (01) 60 45 37. - Tex -   056544
Lantern Antiques, 57 Francis St., Dublin 8.
T. (01) 53 45 93. - Ant -   056545
Lawler Briscoe & Co., 35 Lower Ormond Quay, Dublin 1.
T. (01) 77 30 60. - Ant -   056546

Liberties Antiques, 34 Francis St., Dublin 8.
T. (01) 54 24 80. - Ant -   056547
Liffey Lore, 24 Lower Liffey St., Dublin 1.
T. (01) 72 78 37. - Ant -   056548
Lucius, 25 Wellington Quay, Dublin 2. T. (01) 679 3642.
- Ant -   056549
Molesworth Antiques Gallery, 28 Molesworth St., Dublin
2. T. (01) 61 49 86. - Ant -   056550
Moorhead, Roxane, 77 Francis St., Dublin 8.
T. (01) 53 39 62. - Furn / China / Glass -   056551
Natural Pine Antiques, 101 Francis St., Dublin 8.
T. (01) 54 18 12. - Furn -   056552
Neptune Gallery, 41 South William St., Dublin 2.
T. (01) 71 50 21. - Paint / Graph / Fra / Draw - 056553
Nickol, Gordon, 59 Patrick St., Dublin 8. T. (01) 54 33 22.
- Ant -   056554
O'Connell, Joe, 46 Clanbrassil St., Dublin 8.
T. (01) 54 18 00. - Ant -   056555
O'Keeffe, 104 Lower Clanbrassil St., Dublin 8.
T. (01) 53 71 88. - Ant -   056556
Old Curiosity Shop, 30 South Market Arcade, Great Ge-
orges St., Dublin 2. T. (01) 71 15 40. - Ant -   056557
Oman's Antiques, 114 Capel St., Dublin 1.
T. (01) 72 44 77. - Ant -   056558
Orken Bros., 24 Dufferin Av., Dublin 8. T. (01) 54 28 27.
- Ant -   056559
Ormond Antiques, 32 Lower Ormond Quay, Dublin 1.
T. (01) 72 72 57. - Furn / China / Lights / Instr /
Glass -   056560
Pembroke, 114 Baggot Ln., Dublin 4. T. (01) 60 39 55.
- Ant -   056561
Phoenix Gallery, 59 South William St., Dublin 2.
T. (01) 679 49 08. - Ant -   056562
Rembrandt Antiques, 24 South Anne St., Dublin 2.
T. (01) 77 93 74. - Ant / China / Silv / Glass - 056563
Riverside Antiques, 29 Lower Ormond Quay, Dublin 1.
T. (01) 73 01 01. - Ant -   056564
Saskia Antiques, 24 Fitzwilliam Sq., Dublin.
T. (01) 61 04 40. - Ant -   056565
Seventy Seven Antiques, 77 Francis St., Dublin 8.
T. (01) 53 18 69. - Ant -   056566
Silver Shop, 59 South William St., Dublin 2.
T. (01) 679 4147. - Silv -   056567
South William Street Antiques, 6 South William St., Dub-
lin 2. T. (01) 77 74 64. - Ant -   056568
Sugan, 97 Francis St., Dublin 8. T. (01) 53 19 48.
- Ant -   056569
Vander, Jenny, 20 South City Markets, Dublin 2.
T. (01) 77 04 06. - Ant -   056570
Weldon, J.W., 55 Clarendon St., Dublin 2.
T. (01) 77 16 38. - Ant / Jew / Silv -   056571
Weldon, J.W., 18 South Anne St., Dublin 2.
T. (01) 77 27 42. - Ant -   056572
Williams, 153 Capel St., Dublin 1. T. (01) 73 25 88.
- Ant -   056573

Dun Laoghaire (Co. Dublin)
Anglesea Antiques, 1a Corrig Av., Dun Laoghaire.
T. (01) 84 33 52. - Ant / Furn -   056574
Sylvan Nook, 61 Upper George's St., Dun Laoghaire.
T. (01) 80 60 21. - Ant -   056575
Thro the Looking Glass, 2 Salthill Pl., Dun Laoghaire.
T. (01) 80 65 77. - Ant -   056576
Tudor Galleries, Sandycove, Dun Laoghaire.
T. (01) 80 34 27. - Furn / Instr -   056577

Enniskerry (Co. Wicklow)
Primrose Antiques, The Hill, Enniskerry. T. (01) 86 82 04.
- Ant -   056578

Ferbane (Co. Offaly)
Antique Shop, Upper Main St., Ferbane. - Furn / China /
Silv / Glass -   056579

Fermoy (Co. Cork)
The Grange Antique Shop, The Grange, Fermoy.
T. (025) 23. - Furn / China / Silv -   056580

Freshford (Co. Kilkenny)
Upper Court Manor Antiques, Upper Court Manor, Freshford. T. (056) 321 74. - Ant -   056581

Gort (Co. Galway)
Lough Cutra Castle Antiques, Gort. T. (091) 19.
- Furn -   056582

Kanturk (Co. Cork)
The Cottage, Kanturk. T. (029) 7. - Furn -   056583

Killorglin (Co. Kerry)
Unique Antiques, Killorglin. T. (066) 6. - Ant / China /
Silv / Glass / Cur -   056584

Kilmallock (Co. Limerick)
Ash Hill Towers, Kilmallock. T. (065) 35. - Ant / Furn /
China -   056585

Loughrea (Co. Galway)
Century Pine, Raheen, Loughrea. T. (091) 414 04.
- Furn -   056586

Malahide (Co. Dublin)
Malahide Antique Shop, 14 New St., Malahide.
T. (01) 45 29 00. - Ant -   056587

Newtownmountkennedy (Co. Wicklow)
Old Corner Shop, Newtownmountkennedy. T. (01) 90.
- Ant -   056588

Oughterard (Co. Galway)
Bridge Antiques, Bridge Cottage, Oughterard.
T. (091) 107. - Furn / China / Silv / Glass -   056589
Oughterard Antiques, Main St.), Oughterard. T. (091) 45.
- Furn / China / Instr -   056590

Roscrea (Co. Tipperary)
Antique Shop, Rosemary St., Roscrea. T. (0505) 313.
- China / Silv / Lights / Instr / Mil -   056591

Tipperary (Co. Tipperary)
Courtville Antiques, The Corner House, St. Michael's St.,
Tipperary. T. (062) 512 49. - Furn / China / Jew / Silv /
Glass -   056592

Tramore (Co. Waterford)
Antique Shop, Main St., Tramore. - Furn / China / Jew /
Glass -   056593

Westport (Co. Mayo)
Westport Antiques and Art Centre, Lodge Rd., Westport.
T. (098) 261 32. - Ant -   056594

Israel

Bat Yam
C.O.I.N.S., 59100 Bat Yam POB 3311. T. (03) 58 36 30.
- Num -   056595

Bethlehem
Barakat, Rachel's Tomb Rd., Bethlehem.
T. (02) 74 37 37. - Arch -   056596

Haifa
M.F.G., 31040 Haifa POB 44502. T. (04) 66 19 23,
Fax 972-4-671525. - Paint / Graph / Num / Repr /
Sculp / Cur / Ico / Draw -   056597
Zohar, Supersol Building Central Carmel, Haifa.
T. (04) 86 726.   056598

Jerusalem
Barakat, Jerusalem Plaza Hotel, 47 King George St.,
91000 Jerusalem. T. (02) 28 42 56. - Arch -   056599
Collector, Jerusalem Hilton Hotel, PO Box 4075, 91000
Jerusalem, 91040. T. (02) 53 38 90. - Ant / Paint /
Graph / Sculp / Arch / Jew / Silv / Rel -   056600
Doron Arts & Crafts, 31 Yaffo Road, 91000 Jerusalem.
T. (02) 22 50 86.   056601
Doron, Esther, 9, Shlomzion Hamalka St., 91000
Jerusalem.   056602
Yossi S. Masters Workshop, 28 King David St., 91000
Jerusalem, 94101. T. (02) 22 33 29, 22 17 86. - Jew /
Rel -   056603

Tel Aviv
Au Charme du Passé, Kikar Kedumim 6, 68037 Tel Aviv.
T. (03) 829336. - Ant / Paint / Jew / Jew / Ico - 056604

Dolphin Shop, Hilton Hotel, Tel Aviv.
  T. (03) 5245712. *056605*
Jacobi, 10 Ben Yehuda St, Tel Aviv. *056606*
Kaufman, 81 Ben Yehuda St, 63435 Tel Aviv.
  T. (03) 234113. - Graph / Furn / Sculp - *056607*
Stieglitz, Joseph, 71 Allenby Rd, Tel Aviv. T. (03) 291389.
  - Ant / Paint / Num / Arch / Eth - *056608*

Italy

Abano-Terme (Padova)

La Scaletta, Piazza Sacro Cuore 33, 35031 Abano-Ter-
  me. T. (049) 66 89 06. *056609*
Piccola Londra, Largo Marconi, 35031 Abano-Terme.
  T. (049) 63 75 28, 66 84 15. *056610*

Acireale e Città del Fanciullo (Catania)

Castogiovanni, Orazio, Via Galatea 83, 95024 Acireale e
  Città del Fanciullo. T. (095) 60 81 63. *056611*
Vecchia Epoca, Via Vittorio Emanuele 132, 95024 Acireale e Città del Fanciullo. T. (095) 60 65 94,
  60 61 73. *056612*

Acqui Terme e Bagni (Alessandria)

Il Tarlo, Via Monteverde 30, 15011 Acqui Terme e Bagni.
  T. (0144) 545 07. *056613*

Adro (Brescia)

La Boutique della Ceramica Antica, Via Cairoli 39,
  25030 Adro. T. (030) 735 91 84. *056614*
Zanardi, Luigi, Via Bettoni 1, 25030 Adro.
  T. (030) 735 61 84. *056615*

Agnone (Isernia)

Celli, Via Vittorio Emanuele 90, 86081 Agnone.
  T. (0865) 772 95. *056616*

Agrate Brianza (Milano)

Fraternali, Giuseppe, Via Lecco 159, 20041 Agrate
  Brianza. T. (039) 65 01 79. *056617*

Alassio (Savona)

Bl.BA Antiques, Viale Hambury 59, 17021 Alassio.
  T. (0182) 40 78 84, 46 91 04. *056618*
Bottega d'Arte, Via Leonardo da Vinci 86, 17021 Alassio.
  T. (0182) 40294. - Furn - *056619*
Chiapuzzi, Giovanni, Via XX Settembre 187, 17021 Alas-
  sio. T. (0182) 46 00 65. *056620*
Gibb, Viale Gibb 2, 17021 Alassio.
  T. (0182) 409 42. *056621*
Leonardiana, Via Leonardo da Vinci 72, 17021 Alassio.
  T. (0182) 444 88. - Ant / Paint / Furn / China /
  Tex - *056622*
Michelangelo, Via Vittorio Veneto 142, 17021 Alassio.
  T. (0182) 432 45, 47 03 74. *056623*
Orient Express, Via XX Settembre 85, 17021 Alassio.
  T. (0182) 424 82. *056624*
Pittigliani, Piazza Ferrero 76, 17021 Alassio.
  T. (0182) 441 67. - Ant / Paint / Furn / China / Repr /
  Jew / Silv / Glass - *056625*
Sani, Via Mazzini 52, 17021 Alassio.
  T. (0182) 428 52. *056626*
Stalla, Biagio, Corso Marconi 53, 17021 Alassio.
  T. (0182) 407 84. *056627*

Alba (Cuneo)

della Piana, Flavio, Via Paruzza 10, 12051 Alba.
  T. (0173) 41 02. *056628*
Sandri, Ivan, Via Vivaro 7, 12051 Alba.
  T. (0173) 44 18 70, 28 05 04, 28 10 67. *056629*

Albano Laziale (Roma)

Casa Antica, Via Appia 38, 00042 Albano Laziale.
  T. (06) 93 20 210. *056630*

Albenga (Savona)

Valeriano, Santino, Via Medaglie d'Oro 84, 17031 Albenga. T. (0182) 508 11. *056631*

Albignasego (Padova)

Broggiato, Giancarlo, Strada Battaglia 67, 35020 Albignasego. T. (049) 69 01 11. *056632*
Franceson Jole, Maria, Strada Battaglia 93, 35020 Albignasego. T. (049) 68 04 54, 68 40 55. *056633*

Selezione di Vecchi Mobili, Strada Battaglia 165, 35020
  Albignasego. T. (049) 68 59 17. *056634*

Albinea (Reggio Emilia)

Poli, Renato, Piazza Cavicchioni 5-6, 42020 Albinea.
  T. (0522) 644 11. *056635*

Albino

L & W Trade Import Antiquarie Mobili e Oggetti Inglesi,
  Via G. Marconi 7G, 10125 Albino. T. (035) 774014,
  Fax (035) 774050. *056636*

Alessandria

Bongiorni, Via S Pio V 11, 15100 Alessandria.
  T. (0131) 430 75. *056637*
Bric a Brac, Via Legnano 6-8, 15100 Alessandria.
  T. (0131) 541 84. - Ant / Paint / Graph / Furn - *056638*
Cairo, Francesco, Via Mazzini 98, 15100 Alessandria.
  T. (0131) 540 09. - Ant - *056639*
Ghalibaf, Via Cavour 19, 15100 Alessandria.
  T. (0131) 556 88. *056640*

Almè (Bergamo)

Dani, Viale Italia 85, 24011 Almè.
  T. (035) 54 14 15. *056641*
Rota, Luigi, Via Milano 12, 24011 Almè.
  T. (035) 54 10 45. *056642*

Altamura (Bari)

Loizzo, L., Via Gravina 19, 70022 Altamura.
  T. (080) 870 11 51. *056643*

Ancona

Belluzzi, Gianni, Corso Amendola 49, 60100 Ancona.
  T. (071) 226 17. *056644*
Bric á Brac, Via Maratta 32, 60100 Ancona.
  T. (071) 343 87. *056645*
Bugari, Austillo, Strada Statale 16, 60100 Ancona.
  T. (071) 80 46 355, 20 16 10. *056646*
Delle Muse, Via Gramsci 1, 60100 Ancona.
  T. (071) 517 04. *056647*
La Bottegadi Mary, Piazza Kennedy 12, 60100 Ancona.
  T. (071) 264 67. *056648*
Mazzanti, Sandro, Via Matas 37, 60100 Ancona.
  T. (071) 530 94, 331 32. *056649*
Vecchia Inghilterra, Via Trieste 9, 60100
  Ancona. *056650*

Andria (Bari)

Antiqua 81, Via d'Azeglio 110, 70031 Andria.
  T. (0883) 23007. *056651*
Guglielmi, Michele, Via Bologna 9-11, 70031 Andria.
  T. (0883) 23833. *056652*
Regano, A, Estr Trentino 72, 70031 Andria.
  T. (0883) 82413. *056653*

Anghiari (Arezzo)

Bianchi, Gino, Via Lidia 67, 53031 Anghiari.
  T. (0575) 781 71. *056654*
Calli, Loris, Piazza IV Novembre, 53031 Anghiari.
  T. (0575) 782 39. *056655*
Calli, Piero, Piazzetta della Croce 14, 53031 Anghiari.
  T. (0575) 784 91, 783 81. *056656*
Poggini, Milton, Piazzo Baldaccio 5, 53031 Anghiari.
  T. (0575) 780 24. - Ant - *056657*
Villa Miravalle, Via Circonvallazione 2, 53031 Anghiari.
  T. (0575) 781 31. *056658*

Aosta

Leslin, Jacques, Via Sant'Anselmo 12, 11100 Aosta.
  T. (0165) 318 67. *056659*
Michelangelo Due, Via Porta Praetoria 19, 11100 Aosta.
  T. (0165) 405 68. *056660*

Aprilia (Latina)

Tonon, Via Torre Bruna 19, 04011 Aprilia.
  T. (06) 925 60 02. *056661*

Aramengo (Asti)

Nicola Anna Rosa, Via Mazzini 12, 14020 Aramengo.
  T. (0141) 48 92 81. *056662*

Arco (Trento)

Jannello, Antonio, Strada Statale, 38062 Arco.
  T. (0464) 52 06 63. *056663*

Arezzo

AIG, Piazza Risorgimento 4, 52100 Arezzo.
  T. (0575) 222 57. *056664*
Aliciati, Gianni, Via Roma 3, 52100 Arezzo.
  T. (0575) 288 45, 30 00 76. *056665*
Amar, Logge Vasari 6, 52100 Arezzo.
  T. (0575) 266 40. *056666*
Art Gallery, Corso Italia, 52100 Arezzo.
  T. (0575) 35 44 22. *056667*
Art Gallery, Piazza S Jacopo, 52100 Arezzo.
  T. (0575) 28 82 90. *056668*
Art Gallery, Piazza San Jacopo 288, 52100 Arezzo.
  T. (0575) 35 66 45. *056669*
Badiali, Claudio, Piazza Vasari 2, 52100 Arezzo.
  T. (0575) 35 47 20. *056670*
Bardi, Alma, Corso Italia 97, 52100 Arezzo.
  T. (0575) 216 35. *056671*
Bindi, Paolo, Corso Italia 58, 52100 Arezzo.
  T. (0575) 350782. - Tex - *056672*
Bottega Antiquaria, Via Cavour 28, 52100
  Arezzo. *056673*
Bracciali, Via Seteria 14, 52100 Arezzo.
  T. (0575) 30 21 08. *056674*
Bruschi, I, Piazza San Francesco 1, 52100 Arezzo.
  T. (0575) 218 69. *056675*
Burzi, Corso Italia 22, 52100 Arezzo.
  T. (0575) 30 22 84. *056676*
Casa Vendite Antiquarie, piazza San Francesco 1, 52100
  Arezzo. T. (0575) 218 69. - Ant / Furn / China / Arch /
  Mil - *056677*
Ceccatelli, Corso Italia 10, 52100 Arezzo.
  T. (0575) 53 59 37. *056678*
Chiostro, Il, Piazza Grande 6-8, 52100 Arezzo.
  T. (0575) 276 76. *056679*
Dall' Ara, Franco, Corso Italia 52, 52100 Arezzo.
  T. (0575) 35 30 11. - Graph / Glass - *056680*
Dall'Ara, Franco, Corso Italia 52, 52100 Arezzo.
  T. (0575) 35 30 11. - Graph / Glass / Mod - *056681*
Dei Bardi, Tina, Piazza Grande 7, 52100 Arezzo.
  T. (0575) 268 86, 272 12. *056682*
Del Porto, Donato, Piazza Grande 8, 52100 Arezzo.
  T. (0575) 276 76. *056683*
Don Chisciotte, Via Leon Battista Alberti 7, 52100 Are-
  zzo. T. (0575) 276 36. *056684*
Etruria, Corso Italia 12, 52100 Arezzo.
  T. (0575) 35 07 73. *056685*
Faltoni, Galleria G. Monaco 2/5, 52100 Arezzo.
  T. (0575) 35 46 11. - Num - *056686*
Grace Gallery, Via Cavour 30, 52100 Arezzo.
  T. (0575) 35 49 63. *056687*
Gral, Via Seteria 8, 52100 Arezzo.
  T. (0575) 36 15 18. *056688*
Il Negozietto, via di Seteria 30, 52100 Arezzo.
  T. (0575) 35 30 08. *056689*
Il Raffaello, Corso Italia 34, 52100 Arezzo.
  T. (0575) 236 05. *056690*
Kalòs, Corso Italia 83, 52100 Arezzo. T. (0575) 34634.
  - Silv - *056691*
La Piaggia, Piaggia San Martino 6, 52100 Arezzo.
  T. (0575) 266 19. *056692*
La Pleve, Seterla 14, 52100 Arezzo. *056693*
La Pieve, Via Garibaldi 43, 52100 Arezzo.
  T. (0575) 35 91 08. *056694*
La Piroga, Corso Italia 38, 52100 Arezzo.
  T. (0575) 210 03. *056695*
La Vetrinetta, Corso Italia 60, 52100 Arezzo.
  T. (0575) 35 66 45. *056696*
Lebole, Nicoletta, Corso Italia, 52100 Arezzo.
  T. (0575) 35 66 45. *056697*
Mattesini, Via Seteria 8, 52100 Arezzo.
  T. (0575) 36 15 18. *056698*
Mercationo, Via Sette Panti 145, 52100 Arezzo.
  T. (0575) 38 10 10. *056699*
Michelangelo, Corso Italia 10, 52100 Arezzo.
  T. (0575) 35 59 37. *056700*
Numifil, Via Morconi 1b, 52100 Arezzo.
  T. (0575) 35 54 00. - Num - *056701*
Nuovo Chimera, Via San Francesco 15, 52100 Arezzo.
  T. (0575) 35 01 55. *056702*
Passerotti, Marisa, Corso Italia, 52100 Arezzo.
  T. (0575) 228 79. *056703*
Pozzo, Piazza Grande 40, 52100 Arezzo.
  T. (0575) 35 27 04. *056704*

Puglisi, M. P., Via Cavour 35, 52100 Arezzo.
T. (0575) 30 22 39. *056705*
Rossi, Flora, Piazza Grande 34, 52100 Arezzo.
T. (0575) 29678. *056706*
San Giorgio, Via di Seteria 22, 52100 Arezzo.
T. (0575) 35 77 23. *056707*
Schirazi, Corso Italia 55-57, 52100 Arezzo.
T. (0575) 233 92. *056708*
Vanneschi Bracciali, Via della Minerva 5, 52100 Arezzo.
T. (0575) 35 68 40. *056709*

Argenta (Ferrara)
Il Mulino, Via Garibaldi 4, 44011 Argenta.
T. (0532) 85 44 98. *056710*

Asagio (Vicenza)
Guya, Via Monte Valbella 23, 36012 Asagio.
T. (0424) 639 52. *056711*

Ascoli Piceno (Pisa)
Tomassini, Luigi, Via Dino Angelini 65, 63100 Ascoli
Piceno. *056712*

Asolo (Treviso)
Asolana, Via Dante 22, 31011 Asolo. *056713*

Asparetto (Verona)
Merlin's Organisation, 37050 Asparetto.
T. (0442) 830 02. *056714*
Taccini, Luigi, Via Isolabella 229, 37050 Asparetto.
T. (0442) 831 56. *056715*

Assisi (Perugia)
Antichità 3 Esse, Loc San Pietro Campagna, 06081 Assi-
si. T. (075) 81 63 63. *056716*
Canqi, A., Via G Mazzini 6, 06081 Assisi.
T. (075) 81 60 67. *056717*
Carloni, A., Via Los Angeles 7, 06081 Assisi.
T. (075) 804 14 04. *056718*
Il Duomo, Orietta Fiorelli, Via Porta Perlici 13, 06081 As-
sisi. T. (075) 81 65 06, 81 62 19. *056719*
Piccolo Mondo Antico, Via San Paolo 7, 06081 Assisi.
T. (075) 81 62 22. *056720*
Ponti, P., Via San F d'Assisi 3, 06081 Assisi.
T. (075) 81 64 29. *056721*
Ranocchia, M., Corso Mazzini 27A, 06081 Assisi.
T. (075) 81 67 70. *056722*
Riccardi, Ennio & Piero, Piazza Santa Chiara 3, 06081
Assisi. T. (075) 81 28 77. - Ant / Graph - *056723*
Trionfetti, Luciana, Via Porta 16A, 06081 Assisi.
T. (075) 81 61 41. *056724*

Asti
Bottega d'Arte, Corso Dante 20, 14100 Asti.
T. (0141) 546 85. - Ant - *056725*
Cussotto, Pietro Paolo, Via Ariosto 10, 14100 Asti.
T. (0141) 21 41 75. *056726*
Il Quadrifoglio, Corso Alfieri 116, 14100 Asti.
T. (0141) 302 84. *056727*
Jug, Corso Torino 60, 14100 Asti. T. (0141) 321 03,
21 56 39. *056728*
Novarese, Piergiorgio, Via Roero 26, 14100 Asti.
T. (0141) 500 36. *056729*
Valente, Corso Dante 69, 14100 Asti.
T. (0141) 21 17 68. *056730*
Valente, Corso Dante 69, 14100 Asti. T. (0141) 21 1768,
507 23. *056731*

Avellino
Numismatica Becker, Parco Cappuccini 877 C.P. 111,
83100 Avellino. T. (0825) 388 01. - Num - *056732*

Badia al Pino (Arezzo)
Fura, Mirella, Autostrada del Sole, 52041 Badia al Pino.
T. (0575) 492 49. *056733*

Bagnone (Massa Carrara)
Cacciamani, Gino, Piazza G Marconi 3, 54021 Bagnone.
T. (0187) 49 61 05. *056734*

Barberino Val d'Elsa (Firenze)
Cose del Passato, Via Cassia 25, 50021 Barberino Val
d'Elsa. T. (055) 80 75 098. *056735*

Barcelona
Daedvus, Consejo de Ciento 286, 08011 Barcelona.
T. (93) 317 47 90. *056736*
Sala Nonell, Juan Sebastián Bach 16, 08021 Barcelona.
T. (93) 201 69 11. - Ant - *056737*

Bardello (Varese)
Pellegrini, Alberto, Via Piave 55, 21020 Bardello.
T. (0332) 74 30 17. *056738*

Bardonecchia (Torino)
Piazzetta, La, Via Medail 57, 10052 Bardonecchia.
T. (0122) 97 09. - Ant / Paint / Furn / China / Tex / Dec /
Jew / Silv / Instr / Cur / Ico - *056739*

Bareggio (Milano)
Baiardo, Via Madonna Pellegrina 179, 20010
Bareggio. *056740*

Bari
Andriani, Via Putignani 144, 70122 Bari.
T. (080) 521 24 11. *056741*
Apulia, Via Cognetti 37, 70121 Bari.
T. (080) 54 03 63. *056742*
Barberini, Michele, Via Lombardi 26, 70122 Bari.
T. (080) 21 41 10. *056743*
Carnevale, Francesco, Via Cairoli 71, 70122 Bari.
T. (080) 521 25 56. *056744*
Coluccia, Piero, Via Dante Alighieri 330, 70122 Bari.
T. (080) 521 28 02. - Paint / Furn - *056745*
Conte, Fratelli, Via Oreste 4, 70123 Bari.
T. (080) 34 42 76. *056746*
D'Eliso, Via Principe Amedeo 145, 70122 Bari.
T. (080) 524 17 30. *056747*
Drouot, Corso Vitt Emanuele II 76, 70122 Bari.
T. (080) 521 14 00. *056748*
Galleria d'Arte e Moderna, Via De Nicolò 52, 70121 Bari.
T. (080) 521 63 48. *056749*
Galleria San Ferdinando, Via Calefati 76, 70121 Bari.
T. (080) 521 86 05. - Furn - *056750*
Galleria San Ferdinando, Via Carlo Guarnieri 16A, 70126
Bari. T. (080) 558 34 31. - Furn - *056751*
Gibbons Arredamenti, Via Putignani 29A, 70122 Bari.
T. (080) 521 35 19. *056752*
Il Canterano, Via Nicolai 85, 70122 Bari.
T. (080) 521 35 49, 521 04 49. *056753*
Il Federico, Via Putignani 122, 70122 Bari.
T. (080) 521 60 35. - Paint / Furn / Fra - *056754*
L'Ottocento, Via Piccinni 189, 70122 Bari.
T. (080) 521 62 96. *056755*
Lo Zodiaco, Via Dalmazia 12, 70121 Bari.
T. (080) 558 86 37. *056756*
Misia Arte, Via Putignani 97, 70122 Bari.
T. (080) 521 28 26. - Furn - *056757*
Ragtime, Via Ottavio Serena 43, 70126 Bari.
T. (080) 33 73 86. *056758*
Snob, Via del Rossi 30A, 70122 Bari.
T. (080) 521 51 73. *056759*
Toto, Domenico, Via Andrea da Bari 96, 70121 Bari.
T. (080) 521 45 06. *056760*

Barletta (Bari)
Centro Mercato Antiquariato, Via Foggia 49, 70051 Bar-
letta. T. (0883) 52 60 56. *056761*
Parente, Via Gabbiani 1, 70051 Barletta.
T. (0883) 30 26 71. *056762*
Samarelli, A., Via Municipio 19, 70051 Barletta.
T. (0883) 51 45 89. *056763*

Bassano del Grappa (Vicenza)
Azizian, Piazza Giardino 13, 36061 Bassano del Grappa.
T. (0424) 272 06. *056764*
Bernardi, Mario e C., Via Capitelvecchio 9, 36061 Bas-
sano del Grappa. T. (0424) 27 19 77. *056765*
Bussandri, Villa Marchesane 116, 36061 Bassano del
Grappa. T. (0424) 275 45. - Ant / Dec - *056766*
Guidolin, Egidio, Via Gamba 41-43, 36061 Bassano del
Grappa. T. (0424) 27539. - Furn - *056767*
Mauro, Bonato, Via Marcello 6-8, 36061 Bassano del
Grappa. T. (0424) 29723. - Furn / Silv - *056768*
Ottocento, Via Parolini 1, 36061 Bassano del Grappa.
T. (0424) 224 52. - Ant / Paint / Furn / Dec / Silv /
Glass - *056769*

Sartori, Antichita, Via Vittorelli 50, 36061 Bassano del
Grappa. T. (0424) 225 85. *056770*
Scalabrin, Ginalberto, Via Menarola 24, 36061 Bassano
del Grappa. T. (0424) 272 50. *056771*

Bastia Umbra (Perugia)
Di Clementi, Cristina & C., Ospedalicchio, 06083 Bastia
Umbra. T. (075) 80 I 01 38. *056772*
Fraia, B., Via Garibaldi 10, 06083 Bastia Umbra.
T. (075) 801 05 81. *056773*
Fraia, B. Simona, SS di Assisi 147, 06083 Bastia Umbra.
T. (075) 800 48 37. *056774*

Bedizzole (Brescia)
Allemandi, G., Via Sonvigo 11, 25081 Bedizzole.
T. (030) 67 60 53. *056775*

Beinette (Cuneo)
Aram, Regione Colombero 34, 12081 Beinette.
T. (0171) 40 16 33. *056776*

Belluno
Canzan, Via Mezzaterra 71, 32100 Belluno.
T. (0437) 200 59. *056777*
Chierzi, via Meotti, 32100 Belluno. - Ant - *056778*
Scremin, Luigi, Via Pellegrini 14-18, 32100 Belluno.
T. (0437) 231 17. - Ant - *056779*

Bergamo
Ardrizzo, Andrea, Via Mazzini 8c-d, 24100 Bergamo.
T. (035) 22 31 94. *056780*
Ars Antiqua, Via Borfuro 14, 24100 Bergamo.
T. (035) 23 25 05. - Ant - *056781*
Balzaretti, Daniela, Via XX Settembre 70, 24100 Berg-
amo. T. (035) 21 40 68. *056782*
Day, Clelia, Piazza Vecchia, 24100 Bergamo.
T. (035) 21 93 19. *056783*
Bergamo, Via Vittorio Emanuele 18, 24100 Bergamo.
T. (035) 22 48 31. *056784*
Boselli Vannini, Fiorenza, Via Monte S. Michele 1b,
24100 Bergamo. T. (035) 23 76 39. - Ant - *056785*
Bottarlini, Via San Benedetto 3, 24100 Bergamo.
T. (035) 23 28 53. *056786*
Bottega del Gombito, Via Gombito 13, 24100 Bergamo.
T. (035) 22 11 87. *056787*
Crespi, Via Garibaldi 3m, 24100 Bergamo.
T. (035) 21 22 11. - Furn / Sculp - *056788*
Galleria Permanente d'Arte, Piazza Dante 1, 24100
Bergamo. T. (035) 24 85 34. - Ant / Paint /
Furn - *056789*
Invernnici Fratelli, Via Locatelli 3, 24100 Bergamo.
T. (035) 24 31 79. - Num - *056790*
La Torre, Piazza Vittorio Veneto 6, 24100 Bergamo.
T. (035) 22 22 34. *056791*
Lorenzelli, Via S. Michele 1, 24100 Bergamo.
T. (035) 24 86 67. - Ant - *056792*
Michelangelo, Via Locatelli 7, 24100 Bergamo.
T. (035) 22 13 00. *056793*
Nurchis, Elvio, Via Broseta 21-23, 24100 Bergamo.
T. (035) 21 32 37. *056794*
Pasini, Via Broseta 43, 24100 Bergamo.
T. (035) 24 83 32. *056795*
Previtali, Gianmaria, Via Tasso 21, 24100 Bergamo.
T. (035) 24 83 93. - Ant / Paint / Furn - *056796*
Quarenghi, Piazza Vecchia 1, 24100 Bergamo.
T. (035) 22 00 17. *056797*
Radaelli, Carlo, Via Sant'Alessandro 32, 24100 Berg-
amo. T. (035) 21 32 48. *056798*
Riva, Ferdinando, Via Paglia 7, 24100 Bergamo.
T. (035) 24 90 71. *056799*
Rossi, Gianmaria, Via Colleoni 15, 24100 Bergamo.
T. (035) 22 06 75. - Furn - *056800*
Scaccabarozzi, Giorgio, Viale Vittorio Emanuele 52b,
24100 Bergamo. T. (035) 21 73 73. - Paint / Furn /
Sculp - *056801*
Serra, Patrick, Via Sant'Orsola 37, 24100 Bergamo.
T. (035) 21 71 45. *056802*
Tironi, Simona, Via Broseta 13, 24100 Bergamo.
T. (035) 21 41 09, 24 42 83. - Paint - *056803*
Tuman, Via Locateli 24, 24100 Bergamo.
T. (035) 22 31 85. *056804*

Besana Brianza
Unique Antiques, Via G. Puccini 50, Besana Brianza.
T. (0362) 995118, Fax (0362) 995397. *056805*

Besana Brianza (Milano)
Unique Antiques, Via Puccini 50, 20045 Besana Brianza.
T. (0362) 99 51 18. - Furn - *056806*
Uniques Antiques, Via G Puccini 50, 20045 Besana
Brianza. T. (0362) 941 40. *056807*

Bibbiena (Arezzo)
Dei, Via Nazionale 86, 52011 Bibbiena.
T. (0575) 59 39 57. *056808*
Ferroni, Giuseppe, Via Garibaldi 1, 52011 Bibbiena.
T. (0575) 59 39 68. *056809*

Bibbona (Livorno)
Novecento, Stazione di Bolgheri, 57020 Bibbona.
T. (0586) 60 01 76. *056810*

Biella (Vercelli)
Arredamenti d'Arte, Via Milano 129, 13051 Biella.
T. (015) 269 21. *056811*
Ciocchetti Bertola, Rosa, Piazza S Giacomo 3, 13051
Biella. T. (015) 217 37. *056812*
Grossi, de, Via Repubblica 30, 13051 Biella.
T. (015) 35 25 40, 212 29. *056813*
Ternengo Tre, Piazza San Giacomo 3, 13051 Biella.
T. (015) 209 28. *056814*

Bientina (Pisa)
Antichita', Neri Carlo, Via Jacopo del Polta 24, Via della
Vecchia Stazione 14/16, 56031 Bientina.
T. (0587) 756076, Fax (0587) 756076. *056815*
Cose Vecchie, Piazza Vittorio Emanuele 150, 56031
Bientina. T. (0587) 75 55 67. *056816*
Lambertucci, Vasco, Via Sarzanese 189, 56031 Bientina.
T. (0587) 75 57 00. *056817*
Menicucci, Daniele, Piazza Vittorio Emanuele, 56031
Bientina. T. (0587) 553 46. *056818*
Neri, Carlo, Via San Pietro 1, 56031 Bientina.
T. (0587) 75 60 76, 75 59 05. *056819*
Serretti, Luigi, Via Sarzanese Valdera 94, 56031 Bienti-
na. T. (0587) 75 56 91. *056820*

Bisceglie (Bari)
Ferrante, Via Bovio 75, 70052 Bisceglie.
T. (080) 96 19 80. *056821*

Boario Terme (Brescia)
Galleria dell'Antiquariato, Corso Italia 44, 25041 Boario
Terme. T. 53 55 44, 55109. *056822*

Bologna
A.B.C. Antiche Belle Cose, Via Guerrazzi 9c, 40125 Bolo-
gna. T. (051) 22 99 80. - Paint / Furn / China - *056823*
A.E.A., Via C Battisti 21, 40123 Bologna. *056824*
Aesse, Via Castiglione 30, 40124 Bologna.
T. (051) 27 77 79. *056825*
Aia-Bordoli, S., Piazza Galvani, 40124 Bologna.
T. (051) 22 26 03. *056826*
Al Collegio, Via Collegio di Spagna 7, 40123 Bologna.
T. (051) 27 98 61. *056827*
Al Grillo, Via Marchesana 6, 40124 Bologna.
T. (051) 23 74 62. *056828*
All'Oratorio, Via Val d'Aposa 4, 40123 Bologna.
T. (051) 27 38 58. *056829*
Antichità Galliera, Via Galliera 19, 40121 Bologna.
T. (051) 23 08 33. *056830*
Antichità G.B., Via Farini 32, 40124 Bologna.
T. (051) 23 36 98. *056831*
Antichità G.B., Via Castiglione 62, 40124
Bologna. *056832*
Antichità Porta di Castello, Via Porta di Castello 5,
40121 Bologna. T. (051) 26 32 13. *056833*
Antichità San Vitale, Via San Vitale 3, 40125 Bologna.
T. (051) 23 79 97. *056834*
Antiquari Riuniti, Via N Sauro 14, 40121 Bologna.
T. (051) 23 91 06, 23 96 64, 26 06 19. *056835*
Antiques, Via dei Mille 16, 40121 Bologna.
T. (051) 26 47 75. *056836*
Approdo, L', Via Altabella 3, 40126 Bologna.
T. (051) 22 57 04. *056837*
Archivio, Via Guerrazzi 10, 40125 Bologna.
T. (051) 22 57 68. *056838*

Ariete, L', Via Marsili 7, 40124 Bologna.
T. (051) 33 12 02. *056839*
Art Gallery, Via Fossalta 3, 40125 Bologna. *056840*
Arte Antica, Via Altabella 15, 40126 Bologna.
T. (051) 22 24 54, 26 36 96. *056841*
Arte Antica, Altabella 15, 40126 Bologna.
T. (051) 22 24 54. - Ant / Paint / Furn / China - *056842*
Arti Decorative, Via Santo Stefano 12, 40125 Bologna.
T. (051) 22 27 58. *056843*
Bagnolati, Via Castiglione 50, 40136 Bologna.
T. (051) 27 09 62. *056844*
Balaustra, La, Via dei Giudei 3, 40126 Bologna.
T. (051) 27 56 31. *056845*
Barberia Antichità, Via Barberia 8, 40123 Bologna.
T. (051) 33 24 72. - Paint / Furn - *056846*
Bastardini, de, Via M. d'Azeglio 41c-45b, 40123 Bolo-
gna. T. (051) 33 11 58. - Furn - *056847*
Bellei, M., Via IV Novembre 14, 40123 Bologna.
T. (051) 22 75 41. *056848*
Borgo Antichità, Via del Borgo S Pietro 101a/b, 40126
Bologna. T. (051) 25 10 36. *056849*
Bottega del Luzzo, Via del Luzzo 6, 40125 Bologna.
T. (051) 23 91 80. *056850*
Bottega dell'Antiquario, Via Marchesana 12, 40124 Bo-
logna. T. (051) 23 85 45. - Ant - *056851*
Brighenti, Duilio & C., Via M d'Azeglio 15, 40123 Bolo-
gna. T. (051) 22 07 43. *056852*
Brini, Costantino, Strada Maggiore 54, 40125 Bologna.
T. (051) 22 47 72. *056853*
Brunori, Gabriele, Via Belle Arti 25, 40126 Bologna.
T. (051) 23 38 99. *056854*
Ca' d'Oro, Via Amendola 10, 40121 Bologna.
T. (051) 55 42 05. *056855*
Cacciari Salvati, Via Drapperie 8, 40 124 Bologna.
T. (051) 27 45 03. *056856*
Cagliostro 15, Via Cesare Battisti, 40123 Bologna.
T. (051) 22 49 48. *056857*
Canonica, Via Canonica 3, 40126 Bologna.
T. (051) 26 62 16. *056858*
Caselli Morsisi, R., Via Galliera 19, 40121 Bologna.
T. (051) 23 08 33. *056859*
Cicognani, Strada Maggiore 19, 40125 Bologna. *056860*
Colores, Patricia, Via dei Poeti, 40124 Bologna. *056861*
Cortinovis, Via Castiglioni 12, 40124 Bologna.
T. (051) 22 97 11. - Paint / Furn / China / Dec - *056862*
Cose di Altri Tempi, Via Galliera 12, 40121 Bologna.
T. (051) 23 72 82. *056863*
Cose di Ieri, Via Musei 4, 40124 Bologna.
T. (051) 23 96 12. - Ant - *056864*
Costa, Silvia Maria, Via Mazzini 36, 40138
Bologna. *056865*
Cristiani & Foschini, Porta di Castello, Via S. Stefano
36d, 40125 Bologna. T. (051) 22 64 55. - Paint /
Furn - *056866*
Curiosità d'Altri Tempi, Via Lame 32, 40122 Bologna.
T. (051) 54 76 10. *056867*
Cuscini-Lancellotti, Strada Maggiore 56c, 40125 Bolo-
gna. T. (051) 23 79 48. - Furn - *056868*
D'Epoca, Via de'Toschi 2i, 40124 Bologna.
T. (051) 27 52 74. - Furn - *056869*
Diamants, Les, Piazza Cavour 5, 40124 Bologna.
T. (051) 26 92 14. *056870*
Droghetti, Ugo, Vicolo Malgrado 2, 40125 Bologna.
T. (051) 39 27 69. *056871*
Due Torri, Strada Maggiore 17, 40125 Bologna.
T. (051) 23 64 48. *056872*
Emporio dell'Antico, Via Guerrazzi 9, 40125
Bologna. *056873*
Fazzini, Via Galleria Cavour 91, 40124 Bologna.
T. (051) 52 02 81. *056874*
Ferrini, Altabella 15, 40126 Bologna.
T. (051) 22 24 54. *056875*
Fiumicelli, Via Griffoni 1e, 40123 Bologna.
T. (051) 23 57 63. *056876*
Franzoni, Dino & Gastone, Via Rialto 28, 40124 Bologna.
T. (051) 23 21 64. *056877*
Galleria Antichità, Via Galleria Cavour 19, 40124 Bolo-
gna. T. (051) 23 08 33. *056878*
Galleria Caldarese, Via Caldarese 1, 40125 Bologna.
T. (051) 23 97 71. *056879*
Galleria d'Arte del Caminetto, Via Marescalchi 2, 40123
Bologna. T. (051) 23 33 13. *056880*

Galleria d'Arte 56, Via Murri 56, 40137 Bologna.
T. (051) 39 68 22. *056881*
Galleria d'Azeglio, Via d'Azeglio 14, 40123 Bologna.
T. (051) 26 66 90. *056882*
Galleria Maggiore, Via M. de Azeglio 15/2, 40123 Bolo-
gna. T. (051) 23 58 43, Fax 22 27 16. - Paint / Furn /
Tex - *056883*
Galleria Saragozza, Via Saragozza 115, 40135 Bologna.
T. (051) 41 39 34. *056884*
Galli, Lorenzo, Via Castiglione 42, 40124 Bologna.
T. (051) 23 50 53. *056885*
Garisenda, Strada Maggiore 14, 40125 Bologna.
T. (051) 23 18 93. *056886*
Gaudenzi, Luciano, Via S. Vitale 2, 40125 Bologna.
T. (051) 23 79 31. - Num - *056887*
Geneve, Via Farini 9, 40124 Bologna.
T. (051) 22 44 40. *056888*
Giannantoni, Renato, Via Farini 31, 40124 Bologna.
T. (051) 23 21 74. - Num - *056889*
Giordani, Giancarlo, Prof., Strada Maggiore 21, 40125
Bologna. T. (051) 22 44 40. - Num - *056890*
G.N. Antichità, Via San Gervasio 5f, 40121 Bologna.
T. (051) 23 83 63. - Paint - *056891*
Govoni, Via Galliera 12, 40121 Bologna.
T. (051) 23 72 82. *056892*
Haas, Via Castiglione 1, 40124 Bologna.
T. (051) 23 24 18. *056893*
Il Tarlo, Via Collegio di Spagna 7, 40123 Bologna.
T. (051) 22 75 03. *056894*
Il Tarlo, Via Collegio di Spagna 7, 40123 Bologna.
T. (051) 22 75 03. *056895*
Iran Bazar, Via Guerrazzi 30, 40125 Bologna.
T. (051) 26 48 89. *056896*
La Musa, Via L. C. Farini 35/b, 40124 Bologna.
T. (051) 22 76 38. - Ant / Fra - *056897*
Maglia, Giampiero, Piazza San Francesco 1/b, 40122
Bologna. T. (051) 26 26 92. *056898*
Mancini, Libero, Via degli Orti 15, 40137 Bologna.
T. (051) 44 07 88. *056899*
Marchesi, Viale Pietro Pietramellara 35, 40121 Bologna.
T. (051) 55 52 64. - Num - *056900*
Marchesi, Maurizio, Via S Stefano 16, 40125 Bologna.
T. (051) 27 20 83. *056901*
Maricampo, Via Massimo d'Azeglio 3, 40123 Bologna.
T. (051) 22 46 85. *056902*
Maricampo, Via Massimo d'Azeglio 3, 40123 Bologna.
T. (051) 22 46 85. *056903*
Mariella, Via S Felice 33, 40122 Bologna.
T. (051) 26 82 54. *056904*
Mazzoni, Gianni, Via S Mamolo 58, 40136 Bologna.
T. (051) 58 01 30. *056905*
Melotti, Vittorio, Via S Vitale 27, 40125 Bologna.
T. (051) 22 02 41. *056906*
Modernista, Via Solferino 14, 40124 Bologna. *056907*
Mondini, Graziano, Via Indipendenza 3/c, 40121 Bolo-
gna. T. (051) 26 32 76. *056908*
Moneti & Tartarini, Piazza di Porta S Mamolo 4, 40136
Bologna. T. (051) 58 04 33. *056909*
Montegrappa Maison d'Art, Viale Monte Grappa 12/a,
40121 Bologna. T. (051) 22 85 64. - Paint / Jew / Silv /
Instr - *056910*
Mordakhai, Via de' Foscherari 15, 40124 Bologna.
T. (051) 27 50 52. *056911*
Naldi, Via Testori 3, 40123 Bologna.
T. (051) 23 47 99. *056912*
Nevola, Via Santo Stefano 12, 40125 Bologna.
T. (051) 22 27 58. *056913*
Occipinti, Via Santo Stefano 47, 40125 Bologna.
T. (051) 22 48 08. *056914*
Old Gallery, Via Clavature 20/a, 40124 Bologna.
T. (051) 23 36 69. - Paint / Furn / Tex - *056915*
Ornamenti d'Epoca, Via del Luzzo 6/a, 40125 Bologna.
T. (051) 26 54 17. - Jew / Silv - *056916*
Pepoli, Via de Toschi 2, 40124 Bologna.
T. (051) 27 52 74. *056917*
Peri, Cesare, Via Begatto 1, 40125 Bologna.
T. (051) 27 27 25. *056918*
Persia, Via Clavature 17/a, 40124 Bologna.
T. (051) 26 76 85. - Silv - *056919*
Petrucci, Via Petroni 23, 40126 Bologna.
T. (051) 27 08 25. *056920*
Poli, Flora, Via G Petroni 32, 40126 Bologna.
T. (051) 26 75 01. *056921*

Porta di Castello, Via Porta di Castello, 40121 Bologna. T. (051) 26 32 13. 056922
Portafoglio Storico, Via Malvasia 1, 40131 Bologna. T. (051) 52 09 92. - Ant / Num - 056923
Portobello, Via M d'Azeglio 67, 40123 Bologna. T. (051) 58 33 11. 056924
R 2 Enrico Righi, Via Clavature 22 c/d, 40124 Bologna. T. (051) 22 48 37. - Num - 056925
Reale, Maria, Via de'Pignattari 1, 40124 Bologna. T. (051) 27 55 47. 056926
Rimondi, Luigi, Via Nasadella 19, 40123 Bologna. T. (051) 33 06 54. 056927
Riva Reno, Via Galleria 23, 40124 Bologna. T. (051) 27 08 93, 23 74 80. - Num - 056928
Ronchi, Giovanni, Via Farini 31, 40124 Bologna. T. (051) 23 25 49. - Ant / Furn / China - 056929
Rosa Carpets, Via C Battisti 20, 40123 Bologna. T. (051) 22 14 18. 056930
San Petronio, Via San Vitale 7, 40125 Bologna. 056931
San Vitale Antichita, Via San Vitale 3, 40125 Bologna. T. (051) 23 79 97. 056932
Santo Stefano, Via Santo Stefano 15, 40125 Bologna. T. (051) 27 12 57. - Furn - 056933
Santoro, P., Via Zamboni 26, 40125 Bologna. T. (051) 26 09 19. 056934
Savini, Francesco, Via Portanova 18, 40123 Bologna. T. (051) 27 79 12. 056935
S.E.A.B., Via Marsala 25, 40126 Bologna. T. (051) 23 21 73. 056936
Serrazanetti, Via Orefici 5, 40124 Bologna. T. (051) 22 46 54. - Ant / Furn / Tex - 056937
Sette Chiese, Le, Via de' Pepoli 2, 40125 Bologna. T. (051) 26 60 17. 056938
Simoni e Berdini, Via de Pepoli 2/b, 40125 Bologna. T. (051) 26 60 17. - Furn - 056939
Studio Nave 1888, Via Santo Stefano 14, 40125 Bologna. T. (051) 23 13 32, 26 08 39. 056940
Studio 900, Via del Carro 6b, 40126 Bologna. T. (051) 26 30 99. - Paint / Graph / Furn / Sculp / Glass / Mod - 056941
Teheran Carpets, Via V Bassi 12, 40137 Bologna. T. (051) 22 49 06. 056942
Terziani, Via Castiglione 5, 40124 Bologna. T. (051) 26 40 10. - Num - 056943
Testoni, Piazza de' Celestini 1, 40123 Bologna. T. (051) 23 24 04. - Num - 056944
Tubertini, Via Rizzoli 9, 40125 Bologna. T. (051) 22 26 60. - Jew - 056945
Vaccari, Via Fondazza 14, 40125 Bologna. T. (051) 43 68 81. 056946
Vascello, Il, Via Altabella 7, 40126 Bologna. T. (051) 27 38 42. 056947
Vecchi, Raffaellla, Via Cartoleria 26, 40124 Bologna. 056948
Veronesi, Ferdinando, & Figli, Piazza Maggiore 4, 40124 Bologna. T. (051) 22 48 35. 056949
Vianini, R., Via Santo Stefano 15, 40125 Bologna. T. (051) 27 12 57. 056950
Vigarani, Via Ferruccio Magnani 6, 40134 Bologna. T. (051) 41 48 05. - Ant / Paint - 056951
Zacchini, Franco, Via G Bertini 14, 40127 Bologna. T. (051) 51 24 40. 056952
Zanetti & Selleri, Via G Petroni 1, 40126 Bologna. T. (051) 23 06 37. 056953
Zironi, Vittorio, Via Saragozza 23, 40123 Bologna. T. (051) 33 11 54. 056954
Zucchelli, Galleria Cavour 2, 40124 Bologna. T. (051) 22 37 22. 056955
2 di Quadri, Il, Via Cartoleria 4, 40124 Bologna. T. (051) 23 44 02. 056956

Bolzano

Furlan, Via Cappuccini 7, 39100 Bolzano. T. (0471) 239 21. 056957
Horus, Corso Liberta 22, 39100 Bolzano. T. (0471) 375 45. 056958
Milan, Corso Liberta 37, 39100 Bolzano. T. (0471) 303 21. 056959
Morandell, Arnold, Via Museo 16, 39100 Bolzano. T. (0471) 393 59. 056960
Numismatica-Sixt, Piazza Erbe 15, 39100 Bolzano. T. (0471) 236 26. - Num - 056961
Persian Gallery, Via Leonardo da Vinci 1, 39100 Bolzano. T. (0471) 232 88. 056962
Vivena Gioielleria, Galleria Sernesi 25, 39100 Bolzano. T. (0471) 246 66. 056963

Bordighera e Alta (Imperia)

Antichita del Settecento, Via Romana 83, 18012 Bordighera e Alta. T. (0184) 26 17 56. 056964
Bregliano, Ampelio, Via Vittorio Emanuele 102, 18012 Bordighera e Alta. T. (0184) 26 29 80. 056965

Borgo

Antichita' D'Artibale Dario, Antiquariato del Borgo, Via di Porta Montopoli 3, 02030 Borgo. T. (0765) 27023. 056966

Borgo San Lorenzo (Firenze)

Il Tarlo, Ficini Margheri, Via S Francesco 12, 50032 Borgo San Lorenzo. T. (055) 845 88 81. 056967
Porta Fiorentina, Piazza del Mercato 2, 50032 Borgo San Lorenzo. T. (055) 84 57 259. 056968

Borgosatollo (Brescia)

Berta, B., Via Marconi 55, 25010 Borgosatollo. T. (030) 270 10 80. 056969

Borgosesia (Vercelli)

Ghisleri, Via Montrigone 105, 13011 Borgosesia. T. (0163) 215 79. 056970
Pasqualin, Angelo, Corso Vercelli 144, 13011 Borgosesia. T. (0163) 230 61. 056971

Boves (Cuneo)

Boves l'Antiquario, Corso Bisalta 45, 12012 Boves. T. (0171) 88 05 03. 056972

Bovolone (Verona)

Al Cancello, Via San Francesco 1, 37051 Bovolone. T. (045) 714 50 49, 714 52 18. 056973
Bottega Florentina, Via Madonna 7, 37051 Bovolone. T. (045) 71 00 813. 056974
Il Tarocco, Via Madonna 359, 37051 Bovolone. T. (045) 71 00 099. 056975
Mirandola, Via Madonna 144-46, 37051 Bovolone. T. (045) 710 01 34. 056976

Bra (Cuneo)

Chiesa, Michele, Strada Statale Bra/Alba 4, 12042 Bra. T. (0172) 42 50 27. 056977
Mollo, Andrea e Figlio, Via Vittorio Emanuele 142, 12042 Bra. T. (0172) 41 53 75, 447 83. 056978
Mollo, Giuseppe, Via Vittorio Emanuele 305, 12042 Bra. T. (0172) 42 16 78. 056979
Mollo, Lino, Via Vitt. Emanuele 164-152, 12042 Bra. T. (0172) 41 22 63, 4 40 97. - Ant / Paint / Graph / Num / Jew / Instr / Mod - 056980

Breno (Brescia)

Balada, B., Via Mazzini 19, 25043 Breno. T. (0364) 22621. 056981
Ongaro, A., Via Prudenzini 16, 25043 Breno. T. (0364) 22861. 056982
Pezzotti, E., Piazza Vittoria 13, 25043 Breno. T. (0364) 32 00 10. 056983

Brescia

Adam's Antiquariato, Corso Martiri Libertà 10c, 25122 Brescia. T. (030) 377 07 71. - Furn / Jew / Silv - 056984
Al Cantarane, Daniela Garioni, Via Trieste 57A, 25121 Brescia. T. (030) 43280. 056985
Albrici, Antonio, Via Fratelli Baniera 5, 25100 Brescia. T. (030) 510 66. - Ant / Furn / Repr - 056986
Allemandi & Beltrametti, Via Trieste 54/a, 25100 Brescia. T. (030) 45509. - Paint / Furn / Silv - 056987
Altro-Avanguardia nel' 900, Via Fratelli Ugoni 4, 25100 Brescia. T. (030) 56525. - Furn / China - 056988
Antichità, Via Milano 51C, 25126 Brescia. T. (030) 31 80 58. 056989
Antichità San Giovanni, Via Capriolo 22, 25100 Brescia. T. (030) 406 10. 056990
Antichità Santa Giulia, Via Musei 50, 25100 Brescia. T. (030) 495 76. 056991
Antiquas Santa Caterina, Dott. Beatrice Albrici, Via Trieste 16D, Piazza Duomo, 25121 Brescia. T. (030) 240 05 84. 056992
Antiquitas, Corso Mameli 24, 25100 Brescia. T. (030) 28 02 92. 056993
Arca, Via Mazzini 26, 25122 Brescia. T. (030) 29 57 40. 056994
Armondi, Corso Palestro 37/B, 25121 Brescia. T. (030) 295550. 056995
Ars Studio, Giuseppe Duse, Via Mazzini 14B, 25121 Brescia. T. (030) 510 91. 056996
Azizian, Bahman, Viale Venezia 42, 25100 Brescia. T. (030) 29 14 83. 056997
Baldo, Via X Giornate 1, 25100 Brescia. T. (030) 454 01. 056998
Baresi, Giulio Bruno, Via Valcamonica 49A, 25132 Brescia. T. (030) 241 13 66. 056999
Beltrametti, Mauro, Via Trieste 51, 25100 Brescia. T. (030) 543 20. 057000
Bettini, Via Trieste 23, 25100 Brescia. T. (030) 480 20. 057001
Bettoni, F., Via Crispi 33A, 25121 Brescia. T. (030) 29 35 42. 057002
Bianchetti, Carlo & Mario, Vicolo dell'Aria 7, 25121 Brescia. T. (030) 53443. 057003
Bottega Antiquaria, Via Vittorio Emanuele 12, 25100 Brescia. T. (030) 531 28. 057004
Botteghina, La, Via Solferino 17, 25100 Brescia. T. (030) 571 50. 057005
Bussi, Angelo Rodolfo, Via Capriolo 3, 25100 Brescia. T. (030) 562 98. 057006
Camnasio, Albrici, Via Fratelli Bronzetti 14A, 25122 Brescia. T. (030) 41135. 057007
Capponi, Ettore, Via S Faustino 54, 25100 Brescia. T. (030) 29 04 14. 057008
Castellini, Ernesto, Via Trieste 64, 25100 Brescia. T. (030) 524 51. 057009
Centro Italiano del Lampadario e del Mobile d'Epoca, Viale S Eufemia 39, 25100 Brescia. T. (030) 36 11 74. 057010
Chiminelli, Paolo, Via Trieste 56, 25100 Brescia. T. (030) 571 60. - Ant - 057011
Coen, Virginia Peroni, Via Trieste 56, 25100 Brescia. T. (030) 411 10. 057012
Colantonio, Luciano, Via Orientale 18, 25121 Brescia. T. (030) 40012. 057013
Curti, P., Via Solferino 26, 25121 Brescia. T. (030) 41174. 057014
D'Ambrosio, M., Rua Sovera 37, 25122 Brescia. T. (030) 45273. 057015
Ellero, M., Via XXIV Maggio 2, 25122 Brescia. T. (030) 47301. 057016
Ersego, O., Via E Capriolo 16, 25100 Brescia. T. (030) 29 57 32. 057017
Ferrante, Giovanni, Via Trieste 60, 25100 Brescia. T. (030) 403 66. 057018
Fontanella, Roberto, Via Mazzini 24A, 25121 Brescia. T. (030) 29 57 40. 057019
Galleria Antiquaria Bresciana, Via Trieste 43D, 25121 Brescia. T. (030) 46453. 057020
Galleria Bistro, Piazza della Loggia 11, 25100 Brescia. T. (030) 29 61 28. 057021
Galvani, L., Via Turati 68, 25123 Brescia. T. (030) 39 24 34. 057022
Garzoni, Contrada delle Bassiche 2, 25100 Brescia. T. (030) 29 03 81. 057023
Il Balconico, Via Cattaneo 32, 25121 Brescia. T. (030) 50502. 057024
Il Grifone, Vicolo dell' Arciprete 9, 25100 Brescia. T. (030) 28 05 36. - Paint / Furn - 057025
Il Segno di Fuoco, Lisa Lucchetti, Via Moretto 61E, 25121 Brescia. T. (030) 29 59 73. 057026
Inselvini, Via Capriolo 18, 25100 Brescia. T. (030) 406 10. 057027
International House, Via Vittorio Emanuele 46, 25100 Brescia. T. (030) 585 32. 057028
L'Alta Epoca, Vincenzo Vinella, Piazza Brusato, 25121 Brescia. T. (030) 29 31 52. 057029
L'Eredita, Maria Bottarel, Via delle Antiche Mura 14, 25100 Brescia. T. (030) 515 25. 057030
Loggia, La, Via Beccaria 3, 25100 Brescia. T. (030) 470 04. 057031
Maghini, Corso Mameli 49, 25100 Brescia. T. (030) 59453, 377 24 66. 057032
Majorana, G., Tresanda del Territorio 8, 25122 Brescia. T. (030) 377 00 29. 057033

Malatesta, Via Musei 50 B, 25121 Brescia.
T. (030) 50393. - Graph -   057034
Mangeri, Via Trieste 62C, 25121 Brescia.
T. (030) 59250.   057035
Maria Teresa, Via XXIV Maggio 14, 25100 Brescia.
T. (030) 473 01.   057036
Mazzucchelli, Angela, Contrada Santa Chiara 1, 25100
Brescia. T. (030) 98 82 64.   057037
Morini, Lucio, Via Trieste 54, 25100 Brescia.
T. (030) 482 68.   057038
Navoni, Franco, Via Milano 20, 25100 Brescia.
T. (030) 540 23.   057039
Nember, Angelo, Via C Beccaria 16, 25100 Brescia.
T. (030) 29 47 93.   057040
Numismatica, La, Via Ferramola 1, 25100 Brescia.
T. (030) 562 11. - Num -   057041
La Numismatica – Rivista, Via Ferramoia 1A, 25121
Brescia. T. (030) 56211, 3756211.   057042
Parolari, Osvaldo, Via Turati 18, 25100 Brescia.
T. (030) 522 35.   057043
Piccolo Mondo Antico, Via Tosio 27, 25121 Brescia.
T. (030) 56077.   057044
Rovetta, Angelo, Corso Cavour 2, 25100 Brescia.
T. (030) 562 89.   057045
Rusconi, Via Independenza 89, 25100 Brescia.
T. (030) 36 27 10.   057046
Scarampella, G.G., Viale Venezia 86, 25123 Brescia.
T. (030) 56334.   057047
Schreiber, Manlio, Corso Magenta 26, 25100 Brescia.
T. (030) 461 53.   057048
Schreiber, Manlio, Corso Zanardelli 17, 25100 Brescia.
T. (030) 534 87.   057049
Spagnoli, F., Via Trieste 68B, 25121 Brescia.
T. (030) 29 57 46.   057050
Stoppini, Pierluigi, Corso Palestro 28, 25100 Brescia.
T. (030) 48100.   057051
Studio Linea, Piazza Martiri di Belfiore 3, 25100 Brescia.
T. (030) 55279. - Paint / Furn -   057052
Torri, A., Via Gadola 51, 25136 Brescia.
T. (030) 200 53 71.   057053
Tre Archi, Contrada S Chiara 13, 25100 Brescia.
T. (030) 493 69.   057054
Triboldi, Aldo, Corso Palestro 48, 25100 Brescia.
T. (030) 533 20, 404 97.   057055
Uggeri, Giorgio, Corso Matteotti 38, 25100 Brescia.
T. (030) 424 07.   057056
Vannini, Via A Mario 49, 25121 Brescia.
T. (030) 29 41 36.   057057
Vezzoli, S., Via Casazza 25, 25136 Brescia.
T. (030) 200 07 08.   057058
Zani, Aldo, Corso Martiri Libertà 24, 25100 Brescia.
T. (030) 423 16. - Num -   057059
Zanoletti, Giulia, Via Trieste 58, 25100 Brescia.
T. (030) 425 71.   057060

Brindisi
Morelli, Antonia, Via XX Settembre 65, 72100 Brindisi.
T. (0831) 212 72.   057061

Brisighella (Ravenna)
Bric à Brac, Via Baccarini 23, 48013 Brisighella.
T. (0546) 273 00.   057062

Busto Arsizio (Varese)
Arte Bella, Via Cavallotti 2, 21052 Busto Arsizio.
T. (0331) 63 94 06.   057063
Dei Salvi, Luisa, Via Matteotti 6, 21052 Busto Arsizio.
T. (0331) 67 92 73. - Furn -   057064
Il Tarlo, Piazza Santa Maria 1, 21052 Busto Arsizio.
T. (0331) 62 70 47.   057065
Nedalini, Anna & C., Via Ugo Foscolo 13, 21052 Busto
Arsizio. T. (0331) 32 00 70. - Furn / Jew / Silv /
Instr -   057066
Nedalini, Maurizio, Via F. Guerrazzi 5, 21052 Busto Arsi-
zio. T. (0331) 62 90 63. - Instr -   057067
Turba, Narciso, Via XX Settembre 11, 21052 Busto Arsi-
zio. T. (0331) 63 32 05.   057068

Cagliari
Antiren, Via Puccini 49, 09100 Cagliari.
T. (070) 49 34 62. - Paint / Graph / Furn -   057069
Apollo, Via Mameli 120, 09100 Cagliari.
T. (070) 66 38 26.   057070

Arte Antica e Moderna, Via Sassari 122, 09100 Cagliari.
T. (070) 66 81 82.   057071
Bellezza Antiquity, Largo Carlo Felice 19, 09100 Cagliari.
T. (070) 66 42 04.   057072
Bellezza Antiquity, Via Roma 129, 09100
Cagliari.   057073
Cose Antichità, Via Dante 59, 09100 Cagliari.
T. (070) 48 82 87.   057074
Epicureo, Giulio, Viale Trento 5, 09100 Cagliari.
T. (070) 66 64 87.   057075
Falorni, Luigi, Via Farina 49-51, 09100 Cagliari.
T. (070) 65 22 81. - Furn -   057076
Fior di Ioto, Corso Vittorio Emanuele 215, 09100 Caglia-
ri. T. (070) 66 37 38. - Furn / Jew -   057077
Il Guscio di M.S.M., Portico di Sant'Antonio 5, 09100 Ca-
gliari. T. (070) 65 88 57.   057078
Invito al Collezionismo, Via Giotto 26, 09100 Cagliari.
T. (070) 54 20 29. - Num -   057079
Nucita, Antonio, Via Mameli 103, 09100 Cagliari.
T. (070) 65 83 40.   057080
Porta d'Oro, La, Via Garibaldi 191, 09100 Cagliari.
T. (070) 65 07 34. - Paint -   057081
Portobello Antiquity, Via Costituzione 14, 09100 Cagliari.
T. (070) 65 77 04.   057082

Calamandrana (Asti)
Moraglio, Angelo, Via Roma 123, 14042 Calamandrana.
T. (0141) 752 59.   057083

Calcara di Crespellano
British Antiques, Via Allende 1, 40010 Calcara di Crespellano. T. (051) 962603.   057084

Calliano (Asti)
Zanetti, Giuseppina, Via Asti 136, 14031 Calliano.
T. (0141) 92 83 76.   057085

Caltanissetta
L'Antiquariato, Viale Libertà 98, 93100 Caltanissetta.
T. (0934) 328 92.   057086

Camogli (Genova)
Marcacci, Piazza Amendola 10, 16032 Camogli.
T. (0185) 77 06 76.   057087

Campogalliano (Modena)
Apparuti, Giorgio, C.P. 42, 41011 Campogalliano.
T. (059) 52 53 95. - Num -   057088

Camucia (Arezzo)
Marri, Franco, Via Italo Scotoni 2, 52042 Camucia.
T. (0575) 60 35 70. - Jew -   057089

Canale (Cuneo)
Cauda, Mario, Via San Martino 25, 12043 Canale.
T. (0713) 95 327, 97 83 27.   057090

Canazei di Fassa (Trento)
Arte Design, Via Roma, 38032 Canazei di Fassa.
T. (0462) 621 37.   057091

Cannobio (Novara)
Alberigo, Piazza Indipendenza 27, 28052 Cannobio.
T. (0323) 702 50, 703 65.   057092

Cantù (Como)
Motta, Carlo, Via Virgilio 28, 22063 Cantù.
T. (031) 70 32 97.   057093

Capezzano Pianore (Lucca)
Baldi, Via Bocchette 11, 55040 Capezzano Pianore.
T. (0584) 94 03 393.   057094
Lotio e Mazzera, Via Ghivizzani, 55040 Capezzano Pia-
nore. T. (0584) 94 02 16.   057095

Capri (Napoli)
Bowinkel, Uberto, Via Camerelle 49, 80073 Capri.
T. (081) 837 06 81. - Graph / Repr / Fra / Cur /
Pho -   057096

Capriolo (Brescia)
La Capriolese Immobiliare, Via Bremola 2, 25031 Ca-
priolo. T. (030) 73 61 77.   057097
Ricci, Curbastro Evelina, Via Adro 37, 25031 Capriolo.
T. (030) 746 02 75.   057098
Zanni, D., Via Roma, 25031 Capriolo.
T. (030) 73 61 28.   057099

Zanni, R., Via Parini 4, 25031 Capriolo.
T. (030) 736 40 24.   057100

Cardito (Napoli)
Di Napoli, Raffaele, Via Nazionale 43, 80024 Cardito.
T. (081) 831 35 20.   057101

Carmagnola (Torino)
Tosadori, Nicla, Via Torino 81, 10022 Carmagnola.
T. (011) 977 07 62.   057102

Carrara (Massa Carrara)
Lattanzi, Corrado, Via Cavour 6, 54033 Carrara.
T. (0585) 703 15. - Ant -   057103
Lazzarini, Gualtiero, Via Don Minzoni 4, 54033 Carrara.
T. (0585) 718 69.   057104

Casagiove (Caserta)
Amico, Via Nazionale Appia 36, 81022 Casagiove.
T. (0823) 46 64 59.   057105

Casale di Scodosia (Padova)
Casumaro, Oscar, Via Marconi, 35040 Casale di Scodo-
sia. T. (049) 871 42.   057106
Crema, Vittorio, Via Grande 23, 35040 Casale di Scodo-
sia. T. (049) 871 65.   057107
La Zia, Francesco, Via de Luca, 35040 Casale di Scodo-
sia. T. (049) 871 20.   057108
Missaglia, Adremas, Via Giovanni XXIII, 35040 Casale di
Scodosia. T. (049) 870 39.   057109
Missaglia, Leandro, Via Giovanni XXIII, 35040 Casale di
Scodosia. T. (049) 870 97.   057110
Modenese, Sergio, Via Giovanni XXIII, 35040 Casale di
Scodosia. T. (049) 870 98.   057111
Mostra Mercato Antiquariale, Piazza Moro, 35040 Ca-
sale di Scodosia. T. (049) 870 41, 870 44.   057112
Patti, Giuseppe, Via Marconi 15, 35040 Casale di Scodo-
sia. T. (049) 871 64.   057113

Casale Monferrato (Alessandria)
Aleramo, Via Alessandria 16, 15033 Casale Monferrato.
T. (0142) 702 03, 790 80.   057114
Bacchio, Giuliano, Piazza Rattazzi 5, 15033 Casale Mon-
ferrato. T. (0142) 27 72.   057115
Negri, Dino, Via G. Mameli 57, 15033 Casale Monferra-
to. T. (0142) 760 33. - Furn -   057116
Pampuro, Mauro, Corso Lanza 136, 15033 Casale Mon-
ferrato. T. (0142) 230 05, 80 63 40.   057117
Pietro, Gino, Piazza Brigata Casale 18, 15033 Casale
Monferrato. T. (0142) 34 39.   057118

Casaleone (Verona)
Pasotto, Luigi, Via Venera 23, 37052 Casaleone.
T. (0442) 305 26.   057119

Casalgrande (Reggio Emilia)
Bottega dell'Antichità, La, Via Statale 37, 42013 Casal-
grande. T. (0522) 84 61 69, 84 03 60.   057120

Casarano (Lecce)
Epoque, Via San Giuseppe 40, 73042 Casarano.   057121
Epoque 2, Via San Giuseppe 15, 73042
Casarano.   057122

Cascia (Perugia)
Luca, Carmela de, Loc Molinella, 06043 Cascia.
T. (0743) 76908.   057123

Cascina (Pisa)
Il Tarlo, Via Giuseppe Cei 3, 56021 Cascina.   057124

Caserta
Il Tornese, Via C Battisti 75, 81100 Caserta.
T. (0823) 32 95 98.   057125

Casorezzo (Milano)
Mereghetti, Carlo, Via Europa 5, 20010 Casorezzo.
T. (02) 90 10 037. - Paint / Fra -   057126

Cassacco (Udine)
Rsolo, Bruno, Via Pontebbana 30, 33010 Cassacco.
T. (0432) 85 16 05.   057127

Cassino (Frosinone)
Santulli, Via d'Annunzio 65, 03043 Cassino.   057128
Santulli, Via Virgilio 45-47, 03043 Cassino.
T. (0776) 21 248, 24 260. - Ant -   057129

Castelfranco Emilia (Modena)
Antiquarien, L', Via Emilia est 15, 41013 Castelfranco
Emilia. T. (059) 92 49 80.   057130

Castelfranco Veneto (Treviso)
Il Melograno, Corso XXIV Aprile 46, 31033 Castelfranco
Veneto. T. (0423) 49 33 01.   057131

Castelguelfo (Parma)
Corradini, Enrico, Via Emilia 103, 43010 Castelguelfo.
T. (0521) 616 27.   057132

Castell'Arquato (Piacenza)
Romano's, Via Rigolli 4, 29014 Castell'Arquato.
T. (0523) 80 36 47.   057133

Castellammare di Stabia (Napoli)
Filippo, R. de, Corso Garibaldi 44, 80053 Castellammare
di Stabia. T. (081) 87 13 042, 87 12 110.   057134

Castellazzo Bormida (Alessandria)
Molinari, Mario, Via Roma 17, 15073 Castellazzo Bormi-
da. T. (0131) 722 81.   057135

Castelleone (Cremona)
Cappellini, Giuseppe, Via Roma, 26012 Castelleone.
T. (0374) 563 89, 52 63.   057136

Castello di Annone
CRI Il segno di essere Mobili antichi – Tappeti Tessuti
per l'arredamento, Via Roma 56, 14034 Castello di An-
none. T. (0141) 401766.   057137

Castelnaso (Bologna)
Menegatti, Via Ca' dell'Orbo 44, 40055 Castelnaso.
T. (051) 78 12 57.   057138

Castelnuovo Don Bosco (Asti)
Montabone, Carlo, Piazza Dante 18, 14022 Castelnuovo
Don Bosco. T. (011) 98 76 664.   057139

Castelnuovo Magra (La Spezia)
Polini, Mario, Via Aurelia 28, 19030 Castelnuovo Magra.
T. (0817) 67 32 71.   057140

Castelnuovo Rangone (Modena)
Bottega del Portico, La, Portici Via Roma 2, 41051 Castelnuovo Rangone. T. (059) 53 55 72.   057141

Castelvetro Piacentino (Piacenza)
Bonetti, Mirocleto, Strada Statale, Località Mezzano Chi-
tantolo, 29010 Castelvetro Piacentino.
T. (0523) 82 34 34.   057142

Castiglione del Lago (Perugia)
Arte e Decorazioni, Via del Forte, 06061 Castiglione del
Lago. T. (075) 95 18 59.   057143

Castiglione della Pescaia (Grosseto)
Piccola Galleria d'Arte e Antichita, Via Marconi 66,
58043 Castiglione della Pescaia.
T. (0564) 93 31 89.   057144

Castione Andevenno (Sondrio)
Fontana, Olimpio, Via Andevenno 1, 23012 Castione Andevenno. T. (0342) 35 81 06.   057145

Castrezzato (Brescia)
Manenti, Marchesi, Via Piave 73-75, 25030 Castrezzato.
T. (030) 71 40 86.   057146

Catania (Sicilia)
Cannella, Via Teramo 8, 95100 Catania.
T. (095) 37 45 88. - Furn -   057147
Cirinio Capra Antonio, Via Fiamingo 8/g, 95100 Catania.
T. (095) 32 74 42. - Num -   057148
Fecarotta Fratelli, Via Etnea 170, 95100 Catania.
T. (095) 31 79 27.   057149
G. Antichità, P., Via Firenze 102, 95100 Catania.   057150
Il Tarlo, Via Oberdan 116, 95129 Catania.
T. (095) 32 60 09.   057151
Medusa, Via M. Ventimiglia 245, 95100 Catania.
T. (095) 31 78 75. - China -   057152
Nuova Studio, Via XX Settembre 33, 95100 Catania.
T. (095) 44 83 33.   057153
Porta, Michele La, Viale Ionio 10, 95129 Catania.
T. (095) 38 72 02.   057154

Portobello, Via V Giuffrida 234, 95128 Catania.
T. (095) 437565.   057155
Scaglione, Via Messina 250, 95100 Catania.
T. (095) 38 27 23.   057156
Scionti, Oreste, Via Rosso di San Secondo 16, 95100
Catania.   057157
Stampe Antiche, Viale Ionio 83, 95100 Catania.
T. (095) 38 35 32.   057158
Toluian, Viale XX. Settembre 29 e 64, 95129 Catania.
T. (095) 44 75 90, 31 69 72. - Tex -   057159

Catanzaro
La Porta d'Oro, Via Acri 26, 88100 Catanzaro.
T. (0961) 204 34.   057160

Cattolica (Forli)
Ghelfi, Roberto, Via G Bovio 20, 47033 Cattolica.
T. (0541) 96 23 09.   057161

Cavriago (Reggio Emilia)
Antiques Corner, Via Gramsci, 42025 Cavriago.
T. (0522) 573 28, 57 55 58.   057162

Cecina e Marina (Livorno)
Antiquariato, Via Risorgimento 44, 57023 Cecina e Mari-
na. T. (0586) 64 30 27.   057163
My Silvers, Via Buozzi 3, 57023 Cecina e Marina.
T. (0586) 64 01 34.   057164

Cellatica (Brescia)
La Tarsia, Via Montebello 64, 25060 Cellatica.
T. (030) 252 10 02.   057165

Cento (Ferrara)
La Balaustra, Corso Guercino 24, 44042 Cento.
T. (051) 90 47 91.   057166

Ceparana (La Spezia)
City of London, Via Genova 3, 19020 Ceparana.
T. (0187) 93 31 65.   057167

Cerea (Verona)
Marani, Giorgio & C., Via XXV Aprile 31, 37053 Cerea.
T. (0442) 802 63.   057168
Taccini, Luigi, Via Isolella 29, 37053 Cerea.
T. (0442) 831 56.   057169
Ziviani, Via Roma 13, 37053 Cerea.
T. (0442) 802 13.   057170

Cervasca (Cuneo)
Ristorto, Via Borgo San Dalmazzo 84, 12010 Cervasca.
T. (0171) 854 74.   057171

Cervia (Ravenna)
Purbion, E., Viale Oriani 2, 48015 Cervia.
T. (0544) 99 26 92.   057172
Venturi, Patrizia, Via Brenta 4, 48015 Cervia.
T. (0544) 92 74 06.   057173

Cervo (Imperia)
Ca'da Nin, Via Vicoletto 1, 18010 Cervo.
T. (0183) 40 81 00.   057174

Cesena (Forli)
Belletti, Mirko, Via Strinati 12, 47023 Cesena.
T. (0547) 299 83.   057175
Belletti, Pierluigi, Via Marinelli 5, 47023 Cesena.
T. (0547) 258 34.   057176
Casadei, Gabriella, Via Chiaramonti 59, 47023 Cesena.
T. (0547) 268 78.   057177
Guerra, Antonella, Via Baschi 17, 47023 Cesena.
T. (0547) 242 18.   057178
Leri e Oggi, Via Bovio 453, 47023 Cesena.
T. (0547) 273 48.   057179
Porta e Trova, Via Cesare Finiali 86, 47023
Cesena.   057180
Porta e Trova, Via Strinati 11, 47023 Cesena.
T. (0547) 299 35, 257 27.   057181
Raggi R, Via Scevola 4, 47023 Cesena.
T. (0547) 258 39.   057182
Stagni, Loris, Via Rovella 50, 47023 Cesena.   057183

Cesenatico (Forli)
Trianon, Le, Viale Roma 1-3, 47042 Cesenatico.
T. (0547) 833 06.   057184

Ceva (Cuneo)
Eredi Minetti, Via Doria 9, 12073 Ceva.
T. (0174) 711 00.   057185

Cherasco (Cuneo)
Passone, Felice e Figlio, Via Ferraretto 7, 12062 Cheras-
co. T. (0172) 480 07.   057186
San Pietro, Via San Pietro 9, 12062 Cherasco.
T. (0172) 481 45.   057187

Chianciano Terme (Siena)
Montresor, Rosanna, Piazza Italia 1, 53042 Chianciano
Terme. T. (0578) 643 41.   057188

Chiari (Brescia)
Grassini, Roberto, Via B Varisco 1, 25032 Chiari.
T. (030) 71 15 63.   057189
Royal Antiques, Rosy Pasini, Via San Martino della Bat-
taglia 44, 25032 Chiari. T. (030) 700 06 56.   057190

Chiavari (Genova)
Carlini, Piazza Sanfront 13, 16043 Chiavari.
T. (0185) 30 76 77.   057191
La Poubelle, Piazza Milano 13, 16043 Chiavari.
T. (0185) 30 67 18.   057192
Oneto, Via Magenta 29, 16043 Chiavari.
T. (0185) 36 03 67. - Furn -   057193
Studio di Antiquariato, Via Mongiardini 22, 16043 Chia-
vari. T. (0185) 31 18 24.   057194

Chieti
Antiqua, Via F Salomone 162, 66100 Chieti.
T. (0871) 646 81.   057195
Co.Gia.RA., Via Benedetto Croce 40, 66100 Chieti.
T. (0871) 512 78.   057196

Chiomonte (Torino)
Cose di ieri, Via Levis 38 bis, 10050 Chiomonte.
T. (0122) 542 64.   057197

Chiusi Città (Siena)
Mencarelli, Enrico, Localita Querce al Pino 53, 53043
Chiusi Città. T. (0578) 270 18.   057198

Ciano d'Enza (Reggio Emilia)
Art Canossa, Via Carbonizzo 94, 42026 Ciano d'Enza.
T. (0522) 87 84 41.   057199
Manelli, Via Val d'Enza Nord 98, 42026 Ciano d'Enza.
T. (0522) 87 83 44.   057200

Cigliano (Vercelli)
Gavinelli, Teresa, Via Garibaldi 80, 13043 Cigliano.
T. (0161) 447 17.   057201

Ciliverghe (Brescia)
Albini, Battista, Via Panda Superiore 22, 25080 Ciliverg-
he. T. 262 01 68.   057202

Cinisello Balsamo (Milano)
Ali Babà, Viale Fulvio Testi 176, 20092 Cinisello Balsamo. T. (02) 24 02 128, 24 06 357.   057203

Cirie
Antichita' Blotto, Via Canavere 6, 10073 Cirie.
T. (011) 9207415, (0336) 510333.   057204

Ciserano (Bergamo)
Gambirasio, Via Piave 1, 24040 Ciserano.
T. (035) 88 32 00.   057205

Città di Castello (Perugia)
Caselli, Antonio, Zona Industriale Regnano, 06012 Città
di Castello. T. (075) 85 03 186.   057206
Luciano, Nardi, Nucleo San Stefano del Piano, 06012
Città di Castello. T. (075) 851 05 49.   057207
Migliorati, Mario, Via del Gatto 18, 06012 Città di Ca-
stello. T. (075) 855 79 54.   057208

Cittadella (Padova)
Scalco, Sebastiano, Borgo Treviso 23, 35013 Cittadella.
T. (049) 59 10 21.   057209

Cividate Camuno (Brescia)
Morandini, A., Via Borgo Olcese, 25040 Cividate Camu-
no. T. (0364) 45219.   057210

Civitanova Marche (Macerata)
Ahmadi Galleria Persiana, Corso Umberto I 183, 62012 Civitanova Marche. T. (0733) 733 96. *057211*

Centro d'Arte Marche, Via Monfalcone 15, 62012 Civitanova Marche. T. (0733) 77 09 36. *057212*

Marazzi, Via De Amicis 34, 62012 Civitanova Marche. T. (0733) 728 27, 791 29. *057213*

Cocquio (Varese)
Del Monaco, Wanda, Via Milano 104, 21034 Cocquio. T. (0332) 70 02 78. *057214*

Mele, Felice, Via Milano 11, 21034 Cocquio. T. (0332) 70 06 84. *057215*

Colloredo di Mont'Albano (Udine)
Taboga Plinio, Via Ermes 5, 33010 Colloredo di Mont'Albano. T. (0432) 85 90 34. *057216*

Cologno al Serio (Bergamo)
Carrara, Omobono, Via Mazzini 8, 24055 Cologno al Serio. T. (035) 89 61 02. *057217*

Ranica, Angelo, Via B Croce 9, 24055 Cologno al Serio. T. (035) 89 63 62. *057218*

Colorno (Parma)
Gelati, Maurizio, Via Lavacher 25, 43052 Colorno. T. (0521) 81 53 19. *057219*

San Rocco, Via San Rocco 60, 43052 Colorno. T. (0521) 81 64 42. - Paint / Furn - *057220*

Comelico Superiore (Belluno)
Sacco Sonador, Giovannino, Via Roma 5, 32040 Comelico Superiore. T. (0435) 688 52. *057221*

Comerio (Varese)
La Corte, Via Garibaldi 50, 21025 Comerio. T. (0332) 74 61 04. *057222*

Como
Andermarck, Carlo, Via Milano 97, 22100 Como. T. (031) 24 09 25. *057223*

Antique Runner, Via Rezzonico 27A, 22100 Como. T. (031) 30 37 88, Fax 30 21 24. *057224*

Galleria Volta, Via Volta 52, 22100 Como. T. (031) 27 70 78. - Paint / Furn / China - *057225*

Lietti, Giorgio, Via Milano 94, 22100 Como. T. (031) 46 21 16. *057226*

Manoukian Noseda, Giacomo, Via Indipendenza 55, 22100 Como. T. (031) 26 35 64. *057227*

Molteni, Giampiero, Via Rezzonico 27/a, 22100 Como. T. (031) 24 04 41. - Furn - *057228*

Pecco, Mario, Via Diaz 47, 22100 Como. T. (031) 27 23 91. *057229*

Spinelli, Silvna, Via Borgonovo 125, 22100 Como. T. (031) 55 99 66. *057230*

The Antique Runner, Via Rezzonico 27A, 22100 Como. T. (031) 303788, Fax (031) 302124. *057231*

The Antique Runner, Via Rezzonico 27A, 22100 Como. T. (031) 303788, Fax 8031) 302124. *057232*

Conegliano (Treviso)
Studio Europa, Via Isonzo 30/5, 3115 Conegliano. T. (0438) 327 26. *057233*

Conversano (Bari)
Cipriani Felicia, Cafagna, Largo Cattedrale 1, 70014 Conversano. T. (080) 995 23 24. *057234*

Iudice, M., Via Beethoven 1, 70014 Conversano. T. (080) 995 70 65. *057235*

Corato (Bari)
Fiore, Gino & Anna Maino, Viale Vittorio Veneto 174, 70033 Corato. T. (080) 872 44 86. *057236*

Cortina d'Ampezzo (Belluno)
Auriga, L', Via Roma 2, 32043 Cortina d'Ampezzo. T. (0436) 600 60. *057237*

Cacciari Salvati, Corso Italia 138, 32043 Cortina d'Ampezzo. T. (0436) 33 31. *057238*

Di Rosa-Bonaventura, Corso Italia 12, 32043 Cortina d'Ampezzo. T. (0436) 56 81. *057239*

Galleria del Tarlo, Via Battisti 20, 32043 Cortina d'Ampezzo. T. (0436) 603 29. *057240*

La Ruota, Galleria Croce Bianca 100, 32043 Cortina d'Ampezzo. T. (0436) 663 33. *057241*

Marco Polo, Corso Italia 111, 32043 Cortina d'Ampezzo. *057242*

Red, Ernest, & Figli, Corso Italia 220, 32043 Cortina d'Ampezzo. T. (0436) 37 62. - Ant - *057243*

Cortona (Arezzo)
Billi, Giorgio, Piazza Signorelli 25 e 26, 52044 Cortona. T. (0575) 629 88. *057244*

Castellani, Lorenzo, Piazza Signorelli 4, 52004 Cortona. T. (0575) 60 37 82. *057245*

Poccetti, Paolo, Piazza Signorelli 28, 52044 Cortona. T. (0575) 60 31 08. *057246*

Stanganini, Giulio, Piazza Signorelli 29, 52044 Cortona. T. (0575) 60 32 58. *057247*

Cosenza
Giuliani Attilio, Via Duca degli Abruzzi 7, 87100 Cosenza. T. (0984) 250 24. *057248*

Il Piccolo Mondo Antico, Via Serra 51, 87100 Cosenza. T. (0984) 358 21. *057249*

Cossato (Vercelli)
Villa Katiuscia, Strada per Vallemosso 571, 13014 Cossato. T. (015) 98 15 26. *057250*

Costigliole d'Asti (Asti)
Gerbi, Via Asti-Nizza 100, 14055 Costigliole d'Asti. T. (0141) 96 60 46. *057251*

Cotignola (Ravenna)
Parra, Balilla, Via Fratelli Kennedy 14, 48010 Cotignola. T. (0545) 403 94. *057252*

Courmayeur (Aosta)
Bich, Celestino, Via Monte Bianco 26, 11013 Courmayeur. T. (0165) 84 29 23. - Ant - *057253*

Dell'Antico, Viale Monte Bianco 33, 11013 Courmayeur. T. (0165) 84 10 12. *057254*

Guichardaz, Ettore, Via Roma 51, 11013 Courmayeur. T. (0165) 84 30 44. *057255*

Cremona
Bernuzzi, Luigi, Corso Matteotti 23, 26100 Cremona. T. (0372) 277 79. *057256*

Cremona Fedelissima, Via Manzoni 20/a & 45/a, 26100 Cremona. T. (0372) 24439. - Graph / Jew / Silv - *057257*

Crespellano (Bologna)
Fid Art Antichita', Via Papa Giovanni XXIII 6, 40056 Crespellano. T. (051) 969022, 969384. *057258*

Fiumicelli, Via Giovanni XXIII 6, 40056 Crespellano. T. (051) 96 90 22. *057259*

Cuggione (Milano)
Cooperativa Antiquari d'Italia, Via Beolchi 11, 20012 Cuggione. T. (02) 97 46 253. *057260*

Cuneo
Aram, Via Roma 38, 12100 Cuneo. T. (0171) 549 62. *057261*

Cavaglion Fratelli, Via Statuto 4, 12100 Cuneo. T. (0171) 20 07. *057262*

Fulcheri, G., & Figli, Corso Francia 48, 12110 Cuneo. T. (0171) 49 12 35. - Ant / Paint / Paint / Furn / China / Tex / Dec / Lights / Instr - *057263*

Giordano, Michelangelo, Via San Giacomo 2, 12100 Cuneo. T. (0171) 694 16. *057264*

Harmony l'Antiquario, Via Saluzzo 28, 12100 Cuneo. T. (0171) 678 44. *057265*

Il Cartiglio, Borgo San Giuseppe, 12100 Cuneo. T. (0171) 40 12 54. *057266*

Il Cartiglio, Via Savona 39, 12100 Cuneo. *057267*

Peano, Roberto, Corso Nizza 96, 12100 Cuneo. T. (0171) 69 32 42. - Ant / Furn / Tex / Dec - *057268*

Toselli, Fraz Madonna dell'Olmo, Villa Tornaforte, 12100 Cuneo. T. (0171) 671 38. *057269*

Darfo (Brescia)
Gregorini, L., Corso Italia 42, 25047 Darfo. T. (0364) 53 55 44. *057270*

Lombardo, Giovanni, Via Marconi 72, 25047 Darfo. T. (0364) 53 13 23. - Furn - *057271*

Daverio (Varese)
Morotti l'Antico, Piazza Monte Grappa 9, 21020 Daverio. T. (0332) 94 71 23. *057272*

Silbernagl, Via Fiume 14, 21020 Daverio. T. (0332) 94 71 66. *057273*

Desenzano del Garda (Brescia)
Antiquario del Garda, Via dal Molin 4, 25015 Desenzano del Garda. T. (030) 914 25 82. *057274*

Cajola, D., Via Roma 67, 25015 Desenzano del Garda. T. (030) 991 17 07. *057275*

Cinquetti, A., Via Porto Vecchio 7, 25015 Desenzano del Garda. T. (030) 914 16 53. *057276*

Gnutti, S., Via Bardolino 14, 25015 Desenzano del Garda. T. (030) 91 42 406. *057277*

Lido, Via dal Molin 45, 25015 Desenzano del Garda. T. (030) 914 12 15. - Furn / Jew / Instr - *057278*

Mucchetti, A., Via Milano 22, 20515 Desenzano del Garda. T. (030) 914 33 17. *057279*

Viola, P., Via SA Merici, 25015 Desenzano del Garda. T. (030) 914 35 38. *057280*

Zerlotti Nerjs, Via Stretta Castello 33, 25015 Desenzano del Garda. T. (030) 914 04 66. *057281*

Desio (Milano)
Aliprandi, Gianantonio, Via Garilbaldi 193, 2033 Desio. T. (0362) 63 00 15. - Furn / Jew - *057282*

Dogliani (Cuneo)
Galleria Grafica Antica, Piazza Carlo Alberto 10, 12063 Dogliani. T. (0173) 704 05, 701 58. *057283*

Il Mobilio, Via Vittorio Emanuele 41, 12063 Dogliani. T. (0173) 702 01. *057284*

Domodossola (Novara)
Borgnis, Giovanni, Via Rosmini 8, 28037 Domodossola. T. (0324) 2795. *057285*

Jussi, Sergio, Piazza Convenzione 2, 28037 Domodossola. *057286*

Proarte Antichitá, Via Gramsci 38, 28037 Domodossola. T. (0324) 42835. - Ant / Paint / Graph / Furn - *057287*

Empoli (Firenze)
Santa Chiara, Via Chiara 71, 50053 Empoli. T. (0571) 766 27. *057288*

Enna
Toluian, Via Roma 271, 94100 Enna. T. (0935) 255 55. *057289*

Erba (Como)
L'Antiquario di via Dante, Via Dante 26, 22036 Erba. T. (031) 64 31 08, 64 06 75. *057290*

Mary Lory, Via Volta 15, 22036 Erba. T. (031) 64 21 51. *057291*

Faenza (Ravenna)
Baraccani, Anco, Via Zanzi 8, 48018 Faenza. *057292*

Casadio, Franco, Via Croce 33, 48018 Faenza. T. (0546) 230 04, 304 99. *057293*

Castellari, Fausto, Via Oberdan 22, 48018 Faenza. T. (0546) 226 73. *057294*

Castellari, Valeria, Via San Martino 7, 48018 Faenza. T. (0546) 325 22. *057295*

Lama, Giovanni, Via Naviglio 37, 48018 Faenza. T. (0546) 267 64. *057296*

Mazzotti, Antoinetta, Via Firenze 52, 48018 Faenza. T. (0546) 431 99, 431 56. *057297*

Palazzo Pasi, Via Mazzini 52, 48018 Faenza. T. (0546) 66 31 88. - Paint / Furn / China - *057298*

Pini, Ivo, Corso Mazzini 139, 48018 Faenza. T. (0546) 250 81. *057299*

Piovaccari, Erminio, Via Vittorio Veneto 37, 48018 Faenza. T. (0546) 62 03 59. *057300*

Righini, Tiziano, Via Santa Maria d'Angelo 13, 48018 Faenza. T. (0546) 204 78. *057301*

Sartoni, Sergio, Via Mezzarisa 5, 48018 Faenza. T. (0546) 292 75. *057302*

Sire-Mil-Mar, Via N Sauro 12, 48018 Faenza. T. (0546) 296 02. *057303*

Zoli, Giuseppe, Via Forlivese 53, 48018 Faenza. T. (0546) 304 11. *057304*

Fano (Pesaro e Urbino)

Antichità, Viale Buozzi 20, 61032 Fano. T. (0721) 825 53, 825 33. *057305*

Antonacci, Piazza XX Settembre 40, 61032 Fano.
T. (0721) 839 78. *057306*

La Stanzina, Corso Matteotti 55, 61032 Fano.
T. (0721) 87 98 44, 87 63 81. *057307*

La Torchiera, Via Galantara, 61032 Fano.
T. (0721) 87 47 40, 87 73 85. *057308*

Ottalevi, Via Cavallotti 10, 61032 Fano.
T. (0721) 87 77 09. *057309*

Fauglia (Pisa)

Epoca, Via Colline 10bis, 56043 Fauglia.
T. (050) 64 32 70. - Paint / Furn - *057310*

Felino (Parma)

Bola, Ermes, Via Caumon Caimi 6, 43035 Felino.
T. (0521) 80 21 41. *057311*

Feltre (Belluno)

Conzada, Carlo, Via Mezzaterra 19, 32032 Feltre.
T. (0439) 834 88. *057312*

Conzada Nascimbene, Franca, Piazza Isola 1, 32032
Feltre. T. (0439) 836 33. - Jew - *057313*

Conzada Nicola, Rina, Via Gaggia 7, 32032 Feltre.
T. (0439) 836 34. *057314*

Vecchia Bottega, Via Vecellio 5, 32032 Feltre.
T. (0439) 836 77. *057315*

Ferrara

Antica Epoque, Corso Giovecca 112, 44100 Ferrara.
T. (0532) 26690. - Paint / Furn - *057316*

Antichità Viale Po, Viale Po 7, 44100 Ferrara.
T. (0532) 520 90. *057317*

Bric a Brac, Via dei Romei 44, 44100 Ferrara.
T. (0532) 390 22. *057318*

Calabria, Giordano, Via Garibaldi 90, 44100 Ferrara.
T. (0532) 343 27. - Ant / Furn - *057319*

Campanella, Giancarlo, Via Alfonso I d'Este 30, 44100
Ferrara. T. (0532) 349 98. *057320*

Cavacoli, Giulio, Via Aldighieri 43, 44100 Ferrara.
T. (0532) 391 93. *057321*

Cavalcoli, Giulio, Via Zandonai 88, 44100 Ferrara.
T. (0532) 922 92. *057322*

Cinti, Nazzareno, Via Cairoli 40, 44100 Ferrara.
T. (0532) 216 66. *057323*

Giulietta, Via Giovecca 75, 44100 Ferrara.
T. (0532) 351 07. *057324*

Il Tarlo, Via Bersaglieri del Po 25, 44100 Ferrara.
T. (0532) 366 54. *057325*

Italcoins s.r.l., Via Bologna 68/4, 44100 Ferrara.
- Num - *057326*

La Bottega, Via Saraceno 43, 44100 Ferrara.
T. (0532) 925 00. *057327*

La Cisterna, Via Bersaglieri del Po 27, 44100 Ferrara.
T. (0532) 392 60. *057328*

La Pulca, Via Degli Adelardi 5, 44100 Ferrara.
T. (0532) 480 10. *057329*

Landi, Maria, Via Ariosto 98, 44100 Ferrara.
T. (0532) 478 33. *057330*

Lodi, Andrea, Corso Giovecca 92, 44100 Ferrara.
T. (0532) 470 30, 381 88. *057331*

Pari, Ivano, Via L Borsari 91, 44100 Ferrara.
T. (0532) 289 47. *057332*

Torelli Raffaele, Via Vignatagliata 29, 44100 Ferrara.
T. (0532) 217 19. *057333*

Fiano (Tonno)

Aries, Via Borla 1, 10070 Fiano.
T. (011) 92 21 93. *057334*

Fidenza (Parma)

Chiusa, Mino, Via Ponteghiera 47, 43036 Fidenza.
T. (0524) 502 83. *057335*

Finale Ligure (Savona)

Ventura, Gisella, Via Molinetti 16, 17024 Finale Ligure.
T. (019) 60 16 71. *057336*

Fino Mornasco (Como)

Lotti, Via Scalabrini 1, 22073 Fino Mornasco.
T. (031) 92 71 35. *057337*

Firenze

Agliozzo Manilo Antiquariato, Sdrucciolo dei Pitti 27R,
50125 Firenze. T. (055) 2396805. *057338*

Aguzzoli F., 2 Via Buonvichni, 50132 Firenze.
T. (055) 575206. *057339*

Albertosi, Giorgio, Piazza Frescobaldi 1r, 50125 Firenze.
T. (055) 21 36 36. - Paint / Furn - *057340*

Almaviva, Piazza S. Felice 14r, 50125 Firenze.
T. (055) 28 07 34. *057341*

Altri Tempi, Via della Spada 38r, 50123 Firenze.
T. (055) 21 51 91. *057342*

Alunno, Carlo, 9r Via Ninna, 50122 Firenze.
T. (055) 217611. *057343*

Anti-Quariato, Via Palazzuolo 58r, 50123 Firenze.
T. (055) 29 34 31. *057344*

Antichita' mobili d'Arte, Cassettoni, credenze, scrittoi e
vetrine '800, oggettistica, stampe – Restauri, Via Toti
25, 51037 Firenze. T. (055) 952203. *057345*

Antichita' San Pancrazio, 33R Via Spada, 50123 Firenze.
T. (055) 215473. *057346*

Antichità Santo Spirito, Via S. Spirito 58, 50125 Firenze.
T. (055) 28 42 84. *057347*

Antigua, Via Federighi 3r, 50123 Firenze.
T. (055) 29 21 25. *057348*

Archimede & Lazzerini, Via Fossi 13r, 50123 Firenze.
T. (055) 1 230 22 91. *057349*

Arredamenti D.A.M.A., Via L. Ghiberti 18, Firenze.
T. (055) 8071335, Fax (055) 8071335. *057350*

Arrighetti G., 3r Piazza Cimatori, 50122 Firenze.
T. (055) 212653. *057351*

Ars Antiquaria, 3 Lgarno Soderini, 50124 Firenze.
T. (055) 294626. *057352*

Arte 4, Borgo Ognissanti 23r, 50123 Firenze.
T. (055) 28 95 84. *057353*

Artedue Mobili di Travelli E. & C., 21 Via Nullo, 50137
Firenze. T. (055) 613979. *057354*

Artstudio Cappuzo, Via Maggio 41r, 50125 Firenze.
T. (055) 28 29 87. - Ant / Paint / Graph / Furn /
Orient - *057355*

Astronomi, Giorgio, Via Maggio 19/21 r, 50125 Firenze.
T. (055) 295148. *057356*

Azzolini, D., Via S. Monaca 13r, 50124 Firenze.
T. (055) 21 43 56. *057357*

Bacarelli B., 33R Via Fossi, 50123 Firenze.
T. (055) 215457. *057358*

Baccei D., 30R Via Masaccio, 50136 Firenze.
T. (055) 579920. *057359*

Il BA.CO., 33b/r Via S. Zanobi, 50129 Firenze.
T. (055) 480068. *057360*

Bagatto di Lupi M. e di Grazia, 80 Via Orcagna, 50121
Firenze. T. (055) 670424. *057361*

Baggi Angela Collections immob., Via Mugnana, Firenze.
T. (055) 8544628. *057362*

Balsimelli F., 33r Borgo S. Lorenzo, 50123 Firenze.
T. (055) 292322. *057363*

Banchi, Davide, Via Condotta 11r, 50122 Firenze.
T. (055) 28 27 65. *057364*

Banco 22, Via del Sole 8r, 50123 Firenze.
T. (055) 28 02 39. *057365*

Baracchi, P., Piazza Ciompi, Stand 23, 50122 Firenze.
T. (055) 24 39 41. *057366*

Baroni, G. C. et Fils, Borgo Ognissanti 50-52r, 50123 Firenze. T. (055) 28 29 77. - Ant - *057367*

Bartoli, R., Via della Fonderia 4r, 50142 Firenze.
T. (055) 22 22 71. *057368*

Bartolozzi, Guido, Via Maggio 18r/11, 50125 Firenze.
T. (055) 21 56 02, Fax (055) 292296. - Ant - *057369*

Bassi R., 3R Via Serragil, 50124 Firenze.
T. (055) 215776. *057370*

Bassi, R., Borgo S. Fredino 91, 50124 Firenze.
T. (055) 21 31 44. *057371*

Battaglini, Luca, Borgo S. Jacopo 76r, 50125 Firenze.
T. (055) 238 22 06. *057372*

Bazzanti, Pietro, Borgo S. Jacopo 80r, 50123 Firenze.
T. (055) 292164. *057373*

Bellini, Luigi, Lungarno Soderini 5, 50124 Firenze.
T. (055) 214031, (0337) 686268. - Paint / Furn / Sculp /
Tex – *057374*

Benvenuti A., 69R Via Maggio, 50125 Firenze.
T. (055) 280991. *057375*

Berti, A., Via del Moro 28r, 50123 Firenze.
T. (055) 28 22 81. *057376*

Berti, Berto, B., Via dei Fossi 29r, 50123 Firenze.
T. (055) 29 45 49. *057377*

Berti G., 26 Via Pontignale, 50142 Firenze.
T. (055) 7310520. *057378*

Berti L., 76r Via Romana, 50125 Firenze.
T. (055) 221690. *057379*

Berti, Mauro, Via de Fossi 15r, 50123 Firenze.
T. (055) 28 36 05. *057380*

Biagiotti, Roberta, Via Maggio 49r, 50125 Firenze.
T. (055) 29 21 17. *057381*

B.M., 47R Via Agnolo, 51022 Firenze.
T. (055) 242812. *057382*

Bonanni, Giancarla, Via del Parione 47, 50123 Firenze.
T. (055) 21 38 90. *057383*

Bondi Antichita', 71R Borgo Albizi, 50122 Firenze.
T. (055) 2340698. *057384*

Boralevi Antiquanato, Via Maggio 84r, 50122 Firenze.
T. (055) 28 17 56. - Tex - *057385*

Botega S. Felice, Via Maggio 39r, 50125 Firenze.
T. (055) 21 54 79. *057386*

Bottega delle Stampe, Borgo S. Jacopo 56r, 50125 Firenze. T. (055) 295396. *057387*

Botticelli, Via Maggio 38r, 50125 Firenze.
T. (055) 29 42 29. - Sculp - *057388*

Bracci, Giulino, Lungarno Guicciardi 15r, 50125 Firenze.
T. (055) 21 24 70. *057389*

Brown, Cristina, Piazza Ciompi (Stand 29), 50122 Firenze. T. (055) 2346560. *057390*

Bruno, S., Via Maggio 38, 50125 Firenze.
T. (055) 289795. - Paint / Sculp - *057391*

Bruschi, Piazza Rucellai 1, 50123 Firenze.
T. (055) 29 47 59, 230 26 71. *057392*

Bruschi, Alberto, Via S. Spirito 40r, 50125 Firenze.
T. (055) 217033. - Paint / Furn / Sculp - *057393*

Bruschi Casa d'arte, Via dei Fossi 42r, 50123 Firenze.
T. (055) 21 01 41. *057394*

Bruzzichelli, Giovanni, Borgognissanti 31r, 50123 Firenze. T. (055) 29 23 07. - Ant / Furn / Cur - *057395*

C'era una Volta, Via Madonna della Tosse 32/34r, 50129
Firenze. T. (055) 57 43 10. *057396*

Cafulli, L., Borgo San Frediano 53, 50124 Firenze.
T. (055) 21 90 21. *057397*

Cagliostro, Piazza S. Giovanni 5r, 50124 Firenze.
T. (055) 28 38 62. *057398*

Camiciotti, U., Via S. Spirito 9r, 50125 Firenze.
T. (055) 29 48 37, 239 80 72. - Ant - *057399*

Campolmi, Alessandro, Via Maggio 5, 50125 Firenze.
T. (055) 29 53 67. - Paint / Furn - *057400*

Cappuzzo, G., Via Maggio 41r, 50125 Firenze.
T. (055) 28 29 87. *057401*

Carati, Via de Barbadori 17-19r, 50125 Firenze.
T. (055) 21 75 33. *057402*

Carnevali, Carlo, Borgo S. Jacopo 64r, 50125 Firenze.
T. (055) 295064. - Ant / Paint / Furn / Sculp / Tex /
Rel - *057403*

Carocci, A., Via Romana 40r, 50125 Firenze.
T. (055) 22 45 92. *057404*

Il Cartiglio, 78r Via Maggio, 50125 Firenze.
T. (055) 287961. *057405*

Casa d'Arte Bruschi, Via dei Fossi 42, 50125 Firenze.
T. (055) 210141. - Num - *057406*

Casa D'Arte G. Paoletti, Via B. Gozzoli 20/22R, Borgo S.
Jacopo 53R, 50124 Firenze. T. (055) 2336038,
294942, Fax (055) 2336039. *057407*

Casa Schlatter, 14 Viale Mille, 50131 Firenze.
T. (055) 570588. *057408*

Casa Wolf, Via di Parione 58r, 50123 Firenze.
T. (055) 28 80 85. *057409*

Caselli, L., Via Maggio 17r, 50125 Firenze.
T. (055) 239 64 22. *057410*
Cassi, M., Via di S. Nicolò 72r, 50125 Firenze.
T. (055) 234 24 01. *057411*
Castelnuovo Tedesco G., 22 Via Calo', 50141 Firenze.
T. (055) 411974. *057412*
Castelnuovo Tedesco, G., Via Bezzecca 11, 50139 Firenze. T. (055) 47 05 95. *057413*
Castelnuovo Tedesco, G., Via Grocco 14, 50139 Firenze.
T. (055) 436 04 60. *057414*
Cavet, Borgo S. Frediano 14r, 50124 Firenze.
T. (055) 21 60 00. *057415*
Cei, Leone, Via dei Fossi 17, 50123 Firenze.
T. (055) 2396039. - Ant / Furn / Num / Repr / Sculp /
Fra - *057416*
Censi, S., Via Mazzetta 15r, 50125 Firenze.
T. (055) 29 49 35. *057417*
Centonze, C., Via Maggio 72r, 50125 Firenze.
T. (055) 21 28 09. *057418*
Ceri, M., Via dei Serragli 30r, 50124 Firenze.
T. (055) 21 79 78, 28 84 57. *057419*
Chelini, A. & C., Via Maggio 28, 50125 Firenze.
T. (055) 21 34 71. - Ant / Furn / China - *057420*
Chelini Chelini Produzione mobili e accessori per arredamento, Via don Lorenzo Perosi 15, Firenze.
T. (055) 756031, Fax (055) 756476. *057421*
Chelsea Antichità, M. Cosci, Via Ginori 21r, 50123 Firenze. T. (055) 21 46 55. *057422*
Chesne Dauphine' B., 31R Via S. Agostino, 510143 Firenze. T. (055) 2302261. *057423*
Chesne Dauphiné, Mario, Via Palazzuolo 66r, 50123 Firenze. T. (055) 287002. *057424*
Chiarantini, Giacomo, Piazza Pitti 8, 50125 Firenze.
T. (055) 284410. *057425*
Chiavacci Fratelli, Via della Spada 41r/60r, 50123 Firenze. T. (055) 2398696/213865. *057426*
Colao, Via S. Spirito 11r, 50125 Firenze.
T. (055) 239 67 12. *057427*
Colao Antichita', 10R Via Isola Stinche, 50122 Firenze.
T. (055) 264033. *057428*
Conti, Giovanni, Lungarno Guicciardini 11, 50125 Firenze. T. (055) 28 23 53. - Ant / Furn - *057429*
Coppini, M. A., Via Palazzuolo 33r, 50123 Firenze.
T. (055) 29 42 70. *057430*
Cose del Passato, Via dei Fossi 3r, 50123 Firenze.
T. (055) 29 46 89. - Ant - *057431*
CS 1, Piazzale Donatello 28, 50132 Firenze.
T. (055) 571349. *057432*
Davico, Umberto, Via Parioncino 5r, 50123 Firenze.
T. (055) 28 32 06. - Paint - *057433*
De Benedictis, G., Porta dei Ciompi, 50122 Firenze.
T. (055) 234 61 05. *057434*
De Benetti, Paola, 65R Via Maggio, 50125 Firenze.
T. (055) 294267. *057435*
De Carlo Pavan, Via Maggio 1r, 50125 Firenze.
T. (055) 26 32 02, 28 93 02. *057436*
De Caro, F., Via Barbadori 27r, 50125 Firenze.
T. (055) 21 38 92. *057437*
Del Guerra, Umbertina, Via di Parione 53/55r, 50123 Firenze. T. (055) 28 36 30. - Ant / China - *057438*
Di Clemente, R., Via Maggio 64r, 50125 Firenze.
T. (055) 239 66 49. *057439*
Dinolevi, Via Maggio 53r, 50125 Firenze.
T. (055) 21 28 15, Fax (055) 212700. - Tex - *057440*
Duncan's, 101 Via Ghibelina, 50122 Firenze.
T. (055) 2381039. *057441*
Elyasy, Mehdy, Via Por Santa Maria 41, 50122 Firenze.
T. (055) 29 86 05. - Tex - *057442*
Eurocambio Numismatica, Via Verdi 6r, 50122 Firenze.
T. (055) 24 47 77. - Num - *057443*
F. Cicco, Borgo Allegri 17r, 50122 Firenze.
T. (055) 24 56 17. *057444*
Faini Fratelli, Via dei Benci 18r, 50122 Firenze.
T. (055) 24 12 40. *057445*
Falchini S., 75R Via Moro, 51023 Firenze.
T. (055) 292315. *057446*
Falegnameria Lo Stile – Rocchini e Allegranti, 13r Via
Casine, 51022 Firenze. T. (055) 2480759. *057447*
Fallani Best, 15R Borgo Ognissanti, 51023 Firenze.
T. (055) 2381419. *057448*
Fallani Best, Borgo Ognissanti 15r, 50123 Firenze.
T. (055) 21 49 86. *057449*

Falteri, Via dei Benci 20r, 50122 Firenze.
T. (055) 243704. *057450*
Fattorini, Gisella, Via Federighi 1r, 50123 Firenze.
T. (055) 239 80 47. *057451*
Fattorini, Massimo, Via S. Nicolo' 71r, 50125 Firenze.
T. (055) 234 27 60. *057452*
Fattorini P., 17R Via Fossi, 51023 Firenze.
T. (055) 2381097. *057453*
Fattorini, Stefano, Via S. Nicoló 61r, 50125 Firenze.
T. (055) 234 26 74. *057454*
Fedi M., 47r Via Chiesa, 50125 Firenze.
T. (055) 229581. *057455*
Ferrari, Ennio, Via dei Serragli 22, 50124 Firenze.
T. (055) 239 66 59. - Ant - *057456*
Fiaschi, F., Via Guicciardini 2, 50125 Firenze.
T. (055) 239 64 94, 21 37 58. *057457*
Filistrucchi, A., Via Mazzetta 14r, 50125 Firenze.
T. (055) 239 88 81. *057458*
Finck, Michele e Catherine, Via della Vigna Nuova 15r,
50123 Firenze. T. (055) 21 32 43. *057459*
Fioretto, Borgo Ornissanti 43r, 50123 Firenze.
T. (055) 21 49 27. - Ant / Paint / Furn / China / Sculp /
Tex / Fra / Silv / Glass / Draw - *057460*
Five o'clock, Via S. Guiseppe 14r, 50122 Firenze.
T. (055) 24 43 75. *057461*
Fontanini, M., Via S. Spirito 20r, 50125 Firenze.
T. (055) 21 12 47. *057462*
Fortebraccio, 12R Borgo Croce, 50121 Firenze.
T. (055) 2343882. *057463*
Franco Semenzato, 11 Via Maggio, 50125 Firenze.
T. (055) 282905, 293000, 2302823. *057464*
Frascione, Enrico, Via dei Fossi 61r, 50123 Firenze.
T. (055) 29 40 87. *057465*
Frascione, Giulio, Via S. Spirito 19r, 50125 Firenze.
T. (055) 28 37 84. - Ant - *057466*
Freisleben, Meacci, Borgo S. Jacopo 45r, 50125 Firenze.
T. (055) 28 34 91. *057467*
Freschi, Roberto, Via dei Fossi 49r, 50123 Firenze.
T. (055) 28 70 51. *057468*
Frivo' di Fontani F. e Bernard I., 26R Ciompi, 50122 Firenze. T. (055) 2347023. *057469*
Frullini, Vera, Strucciolo de' Pitti, 50125 Firenze.
T. (055) 296805. *057470*
Funghini, Luciano, Via dei Fossi 32r, 50123 Firenze.
T. (055) 29 42 16. - Ant / Furn - *057471*
G. Fundoni Antichità, Via dei Fossi 34/36r, 50123 Firenze. T. (055) 28 71 36. *057472*
Gabellieri, Mirna, Borgo S. Japoco 80r, 50125 Firenze.
T. (055) 292164. - Jew / Fra - *057473*
Gabellini, A. M., Borgo Tegolaio 48r, 50125 Firenze.
T. (055) 29 42 33. *057474*
Galleria Antiquaria, Borgo Ognissanti 6r, 50123 Firenze.
T. (055) 28 41 75. *057475*
Galleria Guelfa, Via Guelfa 4, 50129 Firenze.
T. (055) 28 49 85. *057476*
Galleria Guicciardini, Via S. Spirito 26r, 50125 Firenze.
T. (055) 28 31 77. *057477*
Galleria Pasti Bencini, Via Maggio 26r, 50125 Firenze.
T. (055) 28 23 84. *057478*
Galleria San Giovanni, 10R Via Sprone, 51025 Firenze.
T. (055) 2302102. *057479*
Gallori Turchi, N., Via Maggio 14r, 50125 Firenze.
T. (055) 28 22 79. - Ant / Paint / Furn / China / Sculp /
Mil - *057480*
Gensini, Adriano, Piazza Nazario Sauro 11r, 50125 Firenze. T. (055) 29 87 75. *057481*
Gentilini, Carlo, Via S. Spirito 5, 50123 Firenze.
T. (055) 214289. - Ant / Furn / Dec - *057482*
Giaconi, Sergio & Patrizio, Via Maggio 43r, 50125 Firenze. T. (055) 21 33 97, Fax (055) 213397. - Ant - *057483*
Gioe, S., Via Maggio 76r, 50125 Firenze.
T. (055) 230 22 28. *057484*
Giorgi, Via della Vigna Nuova 51, 50123 Firenze.
T. (055) 21 16 31. - Ant - *057485*
Gobbi, A., Via Macci 101r, 50122 Firenze.
T. (055) 24 11 02. *057486*
Gonnelli, A. & F., Via del Moro 32/34r, 50123 Firenze.
T. (055) 239 68 43. - Ant - *057487*
Gonnelli, Luigi & Figli, Via Ricasoli 14r, 50122 Firenze.
T. (055) 21 68 35. *057488*
Gozzini – Palmieri, Via dei Fossi 41r, 50123 Firenze.
T. (055) 21 35 08. *057489*

Granchi, Giovanni, Via dei Fossi 43r, 50123 Firenze.
T. (055) 282915/213795. - Ant - *057490*
Griffo, M., Via Palazzuolo 37r, 50123 Firenze.
T. (055) 28 75 17. *057491*
Guidi, Marcello, Via del Porcellana 3, 50123 Firenze.
T. (055) 28 70 10. - Ant / Paint / China / Sculp /
Fra - *057492*
Hermes, Via dei Fossi 23r, 50123 Firenze.
T. (055) 21 81 19. *057493*
Il Cartiglio, Via Romana 39r, 50125 Firenze.
T. (055) 229 81 51. *057494*
Il Fiorino, Via Porta Rossa 81r, 50123 Firenze.
T. (055) 21 83 15. *057495*
Il Maggiolino, Via Maggio 80r, 50125 Firenze.
T. (055) 21 66 60. *057496*
Il Veliero, Via Maggio 44r, 50125 Firenze.
T. (055) 239 88 65. *057497*
Ilinja, Via Pandolfini 20r, 50122 Firenze.
T. (055) 489527. *057498*
Innocenti, Roberto & C., Borgo Pinti 11r, 50121 Firenze.
T. (055) 247 86 68. *057499*
Intercambio di Balsimelli Fabio, 8 Borgo Santi Apostoli,
50123 Firenze. T. (055) 264448. *057500*
Investimenti Finanziari, 53r Via Cavour, Firenze.
T. (055) 215764. *057501*
Italiana Antiquariato, 1r Via Fossi, 50123 Firenze.
T. (055) 2381487. *057502*
Iwanejko, A., Via Maggio 74r, 50125 Firenze.
T. (055) 28 80 63. *057503*
L'Auriga, Sdrucciolo dei Pitti 20r, 50125 Firenze.
T. (055) 29 49 28. - Ant / Paint / Graph / Furn / Orient /
China / Sculp / Tex / Arch / Eth / Dec / Fra / Silv / Lights /
Instr / Mil / Rel / Glass / Draw / Tin - *057504*
L. Lupi e C., 9 Via Maggio, 50125 Firenze.
T. (055) 288266. *057505*
L. Lupi e C., 5 Via Tornabuoni, 50125 Firenze.
T. (055) 212068. *057506*
La Loggetta, Via dello Sprone 1, 50125 Firenze.
T. (055) 28 44 31. *057507*
La Moneta, Via Porta Rossa 27r, 50123 Firenze.
T. (055) 28 75 72. *057508*
Lapiccirella, Leonardo, Via Maggio 4/6r, 50123 Firenze.
T. (055) 216598/284902. - Ant / Graph - *057509*
Lazzeri, Alberto, Piazza Ghiberti 43r, 50122 Firenze.
T. (055) 2480772. *057510*
Le Colonne, Via del Moro 38r, 50123 Firenze.
T. (055) 28 36 90. - Furn - *057511*
Le Gemme – Il Veliero, Via Maggio 44r, 50125 Firenze.
T. (055) 2398865. - Jew / Silv - *057512*
Leone & Figli, Via dei Fossi 47r, 50123 Firenze.
T. (055) 29 60 39. *057513*
Levi D., 53r Maggio, 50125 Firenze.
T. (055) 210054. *057514*
Limongiello, M. G., Via Faenza 24r, 50123 Firenze.
T. (055) 21 03 38. *057515*
Lo Spillo, Borgo S. Jacopo 72r, 50125 Firenze.
T. (055) 29 31 26. *057516*
Lo Stripo, 24r Via Maggio, 50125 Firenze.
T. (055) 292398. *057517*
Lorena, Via Maggio 10r, 50125 Firenze.
T. (055) 21 17 26. - Ant / Furn / Lights - *057518*
Lupi, G., Borgo Croce 21r, 50121 Firenze.
T. (055) 234 27 55. *057519*
Lupi, M., Via V. Gioberti 100r, 50121 Firenze.
T. (055) 67 97 80. *057520*
Luzzetti, Gianfranco, Borgo S. Jacopo 28A, 50125 Firenze. T. (055) 211232. *057521*
Magazzini del Borgo, Borog la Croce 21r, 50121 Firenze.
T. (055) 234 27 55. *057522*
Manetti, J., Borgo Tegolaio 46r, 50125 Firenze.
T. (055) 21 52 85. *057523*
Manzini A., 10r Via Bolognese, 50139 Firenze.
T. (055) 489469. *057524*
Marcelli & Fancelli, Porta Rossa 6r, 50123 Firenze.
T. (055) 230 26 18. *057525*
Margua, Via Magliabechi 1, 50122 Firenze.
T. (055) 24 46 64. - Ant / Furn / Tex - *057526*
Marianelli, Enzo, Via Maggio 9, 50125 Firenze.
T. (055) 21 37 30. *057527*
Marino, Via S. Spirito 8r, 50125 Firenze.
T. (055) 21 31 84. *057528*
Mariotti, 9 Via S. Spirito, 50125 Firenze.
T. (055) 283300. *057529*

Masini S., 21r Sdrucciolo Pitti, 50125 Firenze.
T. (055) 293093. 057530
Mazzoni, Andrea, Via Maggio 15r, 50125 Firenze.
T. (055) 239 86 30. 057531
Mei Brenti, Daisy, Via Guicciardini 16, 50125 Firenze.
T. (055) 21 06 53. 057532
Melli, Gustavo, Ponte Vecchio 44/48r, 50125 Firenze.
T. (055) 21 14 13. - Ant / Jew / Silv - 057533
Meoni, P., Via della Spada 45r, 50123 Firenze.
T. (055) 28 40 62. 057534
Michail Gallery, Lungarno Guicciardi 21r, 50125 Firenze.
T. (055) 29 20 00. 057535
Moncini, Giuliano, Via S. Paolino 6, 50123 Firenze.
T. (055) 28 30 82. 057536
Morelli, Sandro, Via Maggio 51r, 50125 Firenze.
T. (055) 28 27 89. 057537
Neri, Anna Maria, Via dei Fossi 57r, 50123 Firenze.
T. (055) 29 21 36. 057538
Nobili F., 25r Borgo Pinti, 50121 Firenze.
T. (055) 2347443. 057539
Nocentini P., 41r Piazza Ghilberti, 50122 Firenze.
T. (055) 2343885. 057540
Noel Dutilieul G., 46r Via Moro, 50123 Firenze.
T. (055) 295173. 057541
Pacci, Ponte Vecchio 41, 50125 Firenze.
T. (055) 29 42 69. 057542
Palloni, A., Borgo Ognissanti 19r, 50123 Firenze.
T. (055) 239 87 09. - Paint / Furn / Sculp - 057543
Palloni, M., Piazza dei Ciompi 5, 50122 Firenze.
T. (055) 248 09 44. 057544
Palloni Picchi, L., Via del Porcellana 8r, 50123 Firenze.
T. (055) 230 28 70. 057545
Palmieri V., 41r Via Fossi, 50123 Firenze.
T. (055) 213508. 057546
Panconi, M., Via Maggio 35, 50125 Firenze.
T. (055) 28 93 15. 057547
Paoletti, Paolo, Via Maggio 30r, 50125 Firenze.
T. (055) 21 47 28. 057548
Parronchi, Via dei Fossi 18r, 50123 Firenze.
T. (055) 21 51 09, Fax (055) 294097. 057549
Li Pera, Maria Renata, 2r Piazza S. Spirito, 50125 Firen-
ze. T. (055) 268328. 057550
Petrini, A., Via S. Spirito 4, 50125 Firenze.
T. (055) 28 96 73. 057551
Picciani, Jacopo, Borgo Croce 17r, 50121 Firenze.
T. (055) 234 57 12. 057552
Piccolo Mondo Antico, Borgo la Croce 24r, 50121 Firen-
ze. T. (055) 2343152. 057553
Pierini, Borgo Ognissanti 22r, 50123 Firenze.
T. (055) 239 81 38. - Ant / Dec - 057554
Pillori, I. M., Via del Moro 54r, 50123 Firenze.
T. (055) 283358. 057555
Pintucci, A., Via S. Spirito 14, 50125 Firenze.
T. (055) 21 48 51. 057556
Pippi, Via Antonio Pacinotti 1r, 50135 Firenze.
T. (055) 57 95 82. 057557
Piselli, Balzano, Via Maggio 23r, 50125 Firenze.
T. (055) 239 80 29. 057558
Pitti, Via Maggio 15, 50125 Firenze.
T. (055) 287138. 057559
Pratesi A., 7r Via Fossi, 50123 Firenze.
T. (055) 287683. 057560
Pratesi, Givoanni, Via Maggio 13, 50125 Firenze.
T. (055) 239 65 68. 057561
Pratesi P., 100 Via Campofiore, 50136 Firenze.
T. (055) 678921. 057562
Rafanelli, P., Borgo Ognissanti 32r, 50123 Firenze.
T. (055) 21 57 14. 057563
Rangoni, Viale G. Mazzini 53, 50132 Firenze.
T. (055) 234 63 71. 057564
Rizzi G., 22r Via Mazzetta, 50125 Firenze.
T. (055) 213965. 057565
Romanelli, Raffaello, Lungarno Acciaioli 72-78r, 50123
Firenze. T. (055) 239 66 62, Fax (055) 2396047. - Ant /
Repr / Sculp / Dec / Mod - 057566
Romano, A., Borgo Ognissanti 54r, 50123 Firenze.
T. (055) 21 16 07. - Ant / Paint / Sculp - 057567
Romano, P., Borgo Ognissanti 20, 50123 Firenze.
T. (055) 293294. 057568
Romano, S., Borgo Ognissanti 36, 50123 Firenze.
T. (055) 239 60 06. 057569
Sani A., 58r Via S. Spirito, 50125 Firenze.
T. (055) 284284. 057570

Santoro, J. L., Via Mazzetta 8r, 50125 Firenze.
T. (055) 21 31 16. 057571
S.A.V.I.A., Via degli Alfani 50/r, 50121 Firenze.
T. (055) 247 63 75. 057572
Scarselli, A., Borgo S. Jacopo 33r, 50125 Firenze.
T. (055) 28 40 02. - Ant - 057573
Senatori S., 20r Via Presto di S. Martino, 50125 Firenze.
T. (055) 282935. 057574
Senatori, Saverio, Via S. Spirito 4r, 50125 Firenze.
T. (055) 21 03 63. 057575
Il Sigillo Antichita', 7r Via Ripoli, 50126 Firenze.
T. (055) 6580166. 057576
Soldi mobili e oggetti di antiquariato, Via delle Oche
15R, 50122 Firenze. T. (055) 2302153. 057577
Sommazzi-Wettstein, Piazza Tommaseo 10r, 50135 Fi-
renze. T. (055) 697612, 697747. 057578
Sotheby, Via Gino Capponi 26, 50121 Firenze.
T. (055) 57 14 10. 057579
Spennato, A. G., Via della Spada 32/34r, 50123 Firenze.
T. (055) 28 37 45. 057580
Spini, Ernesto & Figlio, Via di Casellina 61, 50018 Firen-
ze. T. (055) 751304, 750342,
Fax (055) 754306. 057581
Straniquario di Talenti, Carlo, 1r Via Giusti, 50143 Firen-
ze. T. (055) 2347208. 057582
Il Tarlo di Fincini Margheri Antichita – Restauri, Via G. M.
Brocchi 122, Borgo S. Lorenzo, Firenze.
T. (055) 8458881. 057583
Tedesco, E., Via Macci 89r, 50122 Firenze.
T. (055) 234 02 34. 057584
Teglia, Marco & Luca, Via dei Bardi 27, 50125 Firenze.
T. (055) 234 27 21. 057584a
Tozzi, Pier Giacomo, Ponte Vecchio 19r, 50125 Firenze.
T. (055) 28 35 07. - Jew / Silv / Ico - 057585
Traslucido, Via Maggio 95, 50125 Firenze.
T. (055) 21 27 50. - Paint / Furn / China / Sculp - 057586
Trimarchi, R., Via Pandolfini 4, 50122 Firenze.
T. (055) 248 09 16. 057587
Vanefti, Luciano, Piazza dei Ciompi, Stand 22, 50122
Firenze. 057588
Varando S., 18r Via Romana, 50125 Firenze.
T. (055) 2336977. 057589
Vecchio Lotto, 13 Via Studio, 50122 Firenze.
T. (055) 289115. 057590
Vedovato, Rodolfo, Borgo S. Frediano 3r, 50124 Firenze.
T. (055) 21 74 67. 057591
Velona, Via dei Fossi 31r, 50123 Firenze.
T. (055) 28 70 69. - Furn / Silv - 057592
Veneziano G., 53r Via Fossi, 50123 Firenze.
T. (055) 287925. 057593
Veneziano, Guiseppe, Via dei Fossi 56r, 50123 Firenze.
T. (055) 2396497. - Ant - 057594
Ventura, Borgo Ognissanti 16/18r, 50123 Firenze.
T. (055) 21 09 14. - Ant - 057595
Vespucci, Giordano, Borgo Albizi 72r, 50123 Firenze.
T. (055) 234 47 19. 057596
Vetus, Via Verdi 29r, 50122 Firenze.
T. (055) 234 48 78. 057597
Vitali, Gianfranco, Via dei Moro 68r, 50123 Firenze.
T. (055) 238 26 38. 057598
Volterra, Ponte Vecchio 55r, 50125 Firenze.
T. (055) 21 26 62. 057599
Zalum, A., Via Terme 2r, 50123 Firenze.
T. (055) 239 60 36. 057600
Zecchi, Via Maggio 34r, 50125 Firenze.
T. (055) 29 33 68. - Ant / Furn - 057601

Fiuggi (Frosinone)
Bruscino, Via dei Villini, 03014 Fiuggi.
T. (0775) 550 25. 057603

Foligno (Perugia)
Fabbri, F., Via Nazionale, Scopoli, 06034 Foligno.
T. (0742) 63 21 10. 057604
Il Monile, Via Cesare Agostini 30, 06034 Foligno.
T. (0742) 59471. 057605
Infraportas, Piazza San Domenico 5, 06034 Foligno.
T. (0742) 500 77, 520 08. 057606
Moretti, R., Piazza Santa Domenica 5, 06034 Foligno.
T. (0742) 34 06 77. 057607
Romagnoli, Corso Cavour 133, 06034 Foligno.
T. (0742) 34 01 85. 057608

Fondi
Rigamonti Lionello & Figli, Via Appia, 04022 Fondi.
T. (0771) 512424, Fax (0771) 512425. 057609

Fontanellato (Parma)
Zinelli, Ermes & Alessandro, Via IV Novembre, 43012
Fontanellato. T. (0521) 87 72 69. 057610
Zinelli, Ermes & Alessandro, Via Veneto, 43012 Fonta-
nellato. T. (0521) 87 76 12. 057611

Fonte (Treviso)
Gazzola, Gianfranco, Via Monte Grappa, 31010 Fonte.
T. (0423) 580 68. - Ant / Furn / Repr / Dec / Fra - 057612

Forli
Biondi, Ivan, Via Orsini 30, 47100 Forli.
T. (0543) 251 08. 057613
Camporesi, Briccolani, Piazza Guido da Montefeltro,
47100 Forli. T. (0543) 282 87, 601 77. 057614
Casadei, Corrado, Via Marcolini 27, 47100 Forli.
T. (0543) 681 87. 057615
Collini, Azelio, Via Morattini 6, 47100 Forli.
T. (0543) 260 76. 057616
Filgros, Corso Garibaldi 132, 47100 Forli.
T. (0543) 345 64. 057617
L'Acquario, Corso Mazzini 8, 47100 Forli.
T. (0543) 340 27. 057618
L'Arte della Cornice, Corso A Diaz 68, 47100 Forli.
T. (0543) 293 04. 057619
Martoni, Mauro, Via Bella 22, 47100 Forli.
T. (0543) 256 79. 057620
Minelli, Gabriele, Via P Merlonia 26, 47100 Forli.
T. (0543) 265 24. 057621
Partisani, Mirella, Viale della Liberta 39, 47100 Forli.
T. (0543) 301 27. 057622
Polvere, Corso Diaz 42, 47100 Forli.
T. (0543) 201 75. 057623
Pretolani, William, Piazza D Alighieri 17, 47100 Forli.
T. (0543) 342 05. 057624
Sirtori, Laura, Corso Diaz 30, 47100 Forli.
T. (0543) 261 74. 057625
Zampiga, Guglielmo, Via Flli Zanetti 24, 47100
Forli. 057626

Formigine (Modena)
Bellei, Raoul, Via Marconi 7, 41043 Formigine.
T. (059) 55 88 15. 057627
Ceci & Spagnoli, Via Giardini 322, 41043 Formigine.
T. (059) 55 86 14, 55 61 19. 057628
Giusti, Domenico, Via Giardini Sud 34, 41043 Formigine.
T. (059) 55 70 79. 057629
Medici, Cesare, Via del Bondone 10, 41043 Formigine.
T. (059) 55 80 32. 057630

Forte dei Marmi (Lucca)
Antichità il Forte, Via Carducci 16, 55042 Forte dei Mar-
mi. T. (0584) 86238. - Ant - 057631
La Bottega dell'Ancona, Viale Morin 58, 55042 Forte dei
Marmi. T. (0584) 833 66. 057632
Veneri, Via IV Novembre 15, 55042 Forte dei Marmi.
T. (0584) 801 24. 057633

Fossato di Vico (Perugia)
Amico del Tarlo, L', V Eugubina, Osteria del Gatto,
06022 Fossato di Vico. T. (075) 91 91 59. 057634
Marinelli, V., Via Flaminia 53, Osteria del Gatto, 06022
Fossato di Vico. T. (075) 91 98 98. 057635

Francavilla (Brindisi)
Apulia, Viale Lilla 49, 72021 Francavilla.
T. (0831) 94 30 51. 057636

Frosinone
Bragaglia Eredi, Corso Repubblica 149, 03100 Frosi-
none. T. (0775) 85 17 25. 057637
Laretti, Via del Plebiscito 45, 03100 Frosinone.
T. (0775) 85 03 74. 057638

Gallarate (Varese)
L'Antico, Via Trombini 8, 21013 Gallarate.
T. (0331) 79 63 43. 057639
Old England, Via Posporta 2, 21013 Gallarate.
T. (0331) 78 42 08. 057640
Old England, Via Giovanni Bosco 10/18, 21013 Gallara-
te. T. (0331) 78 63 25. 057641

Gardone Val Trompia (Brescia)
Cotelli, L., Via Matteotti 219, 25063 Gardone Val Trompia. T. (030) 83 12 97. 057642

Gargnano (Brescia)
Cani, R., Via XXIV Maggio, 25084 Gargnano.
T. (0365) 71983. 057643
Contato, C., Via Villavetro 23, Bogliaco, 25084 Gargnano. T. (0365) 72194. 057644

Gazzola (Piacenza)
Vasaia, La, Castello di Zinardi Landi, Frazione Rivalta, 29010 Gazzola. T. (0523) 376 75. 057645

Genola (Cuneo)
Faccanoni, Giampietro, Via Marconi 1, 12040 Genola.
T. (0172) 682 65. 057646

Genova
Anticarte, Via Cairoli 1, 16124 Genova. T. (010) 20 05 10.
- Ant / Paint / Furn / China / Sculp - 057647
Bacobru, Via Santa Zita 22, 16129 Genova.
T. (010) 58 97 62. 057648
Beringheli, Via Caffaro 39/r, 16129 Genova.
T. (010) 29 84 07. - Furn - 057649
Bo Massimo, Via Garibaldi 11-13/r, 16124 Genova.
T. (010) 28 26 71. - Furn - 057650
Bric a Brac, Via Borgo Incrociati 90, 16137 Genova.
T. (010) 87 38 82. 057651
Brutto, Roberto, Via Sant' Ilario 102/b, 16167 Genova.
T. (010) 32 13 08. - Num - 057652
Cabib, Manlio, Via Roma 8, 16121 Genova.
T. (010) 58 15 31. - Tex - 057653
Capozzi, Adolfo e Figlio, Via Cairoli 38, 16124 Genova.
T. (010) 20 46 42. 057654
Capozzi, Marco Dr., Via Cairoli 38, 16124 Genova.
T. (010) 20 46 42. - Ant - 057655
Cardona, Via Garibaldi 12, 16124 Genova.
T. (010) 20 85 88. 057656
Casarino, Teresa, Via Cairoli 19/r, 16124 Genova.
T. (010) 20 45 97. - Ant / Furn / Graph / China /
Tex - 057657
Cattarinich, Silvio, Dr., Via Luccoli 26, 16123 Genova.
T. (010) 20 74 26. 057658
Chiostro, II, Via Cairoli 17, 16124 Genova.
T. (010) 20 17 56. - Ant / Paint - 057659
Clemente, Fulgenzio, Via Rimassa 146, 16129 Genova.
T. (010) 58 16 00. 057660
Di Cristina, Alessandro, Via Caffaro Arcate Ponte, 16125
Genova. T. (010) 29 06 03. - Furn / Sculp - 057661
Durbiano, Via Garibaldi 14, 16124 Genova.
T. (010) 28 05 85. - Ant - 057662
Errepi, Borgo Incrociati 49, 16137 Genova.
T. (010) 87 58 24. 057663
Fulgenzio, C, Via Allessandro Rimassa 146, 16129 Genova. T. (010) 58 16 00. 057664
Ghiglione, Piazza San Matteo 6/a/r, 16123 Genova.
T. (010) 20 87 07, 20 78 87. - Num - 057665
Gori, Via Roma 55, 16121 Genova.
T. (010) 58 05 06. 057666
Il Convegno, Galleria Mazzini 3, 16121 Genova.
T. (010) 56 18 37. 057667
La Cupola d'Oro, Vicolo Chiesa Vigne 22, 16124 Genova.
T. (010) 20 46 59. 057668
La Cupola d'Oro, Via Chiossone 20, 16124 Genova.
T. (010) 29 81 58. 057669
„La Vela", via Caprettari 16-18 R, 16123 Genova.
T. (010) 292 577. - Num - 057670
Lassa-Scalese, Salita S Caterina 3, 16123 Genova.
T. (010) 58 18 30. 057671
Loleo, M., Via Pegli 34, 16155 Genova.
T. (010) 68 73 28. 057672
Marra, Via dei Giustiniani 44, 16123 Genova.
T. (010) 20 49 37. 057673
Massone, Via di Canneto il Lungo 111, 16123 Genova.
T. (010) 29 78 45. 057674
Meschoulam, Via Domenico Fiasellla 20, 16121 Genova.
T. (010) 59 54 89. 057675
Meschoulam, Fabrizio Sem, Via Garibaldi 3, 16124 Genova. T. (010) 29 08 33. 057676
Mesciulam, Plinio, Via Tullio Molteni 4-16 sc A, 16151
Genova. T. (010) 46 32 51. 057677
Montagnani, M., Piazza Paolo da Novi 36, 16129 Genova. T. (010) 58 58 44. 057678

Montanari, Vico delle Compere 2, 16123 Genova.
T. (010) 29 59 37. 057679
Naphtaline, Via Gugliemo Oberdan 19-21, 16167
Genova. 057680
Oddone, Attilio & Marco, Via Garibaldi 7, 16124 Genova.
T. (010) 31 20 48. - Ant - 057681
Oddone, Attilio & Marco, Via Lurago, 16124 Genova.
T. (010) 31 20 48, 20 14 39. 057682
Old and Beautiful, Coro della Maddalena 23, 16124 Genova. T. (010) 20 17 43. 057683
Old Times, Via Cesarea 58, 16121 Genova.
T. (010) 58 58 21. 057684
Oliva, Guido, Galleria Mazzini 24/r, 16121 Genova.
T. (010) 58 79 90. - Num - 057685
Panzano, Giancarlo, Via Cairoli 13, 16124 Genova.
T. (010) 20 65 55. - Ant / Num - 057686
Panzano, Giancarlo, Via Cairoli 13, 16124 Genova.
T. (010) 20 65 55. 057687
Panzano, Guido, Via Cairoli 14, 16124 Genova.
T. (010) 29 27 24. - Ant / Paint / Furn / China / Dec /
Silv / Instr - 057688
Panzano, Mario, Via Garibaldi 5, 16124 Genova.
T. (010) 20 05 68. 057689
Panzano, Mario, Via Garibaldi 5, 16124 Genova.
T. (010) 20 05 68. 057690
Picasso, di Cardona Mario, Via Garibaldi 12, 16124 Genova. T. (010) 20 85 88. 057691
Portobello, Vico del Fieno 9, 16123 Genova.
T. (010) 20 84 61. 057692
Preziophil, Via Carducci 17, 16123 Genova.
T. (010) 56 11 84. 057693
Quaglia, Giorgio, Vico del Fieno 8/r, 16123 Genova.
T. (010) 28 10 60. 057694
Riccio, Via Aurelia 34, 16167 Genova.
T. (010) 32 29 59. 057695
Rubinacci, Via Garibaldi 8, 16124 Genova.
T. (010) 29 87 58. 057696
Rubinacci, Via Garibaldi 8, 16124 Genova.
T. (010) 29 87 58. 057697
San Sebastian, Via San Sebastian 57, 16123 Genova.
T. (010) 59 36 85. 057698
Savalli, Pietro, Via Canneto il Lungo 63, 16123 Genova.
T. (010) 20 05 35. 057699
Savalli, Pietro, Via Canneto il Lungo 63, 16123 Genova.
T. (010) 20 05 35. 057700
Savarese, Via XX Settembre 139/b/r, 16121 Genova.
T. (010) 54 30 02. - Num - 057701
Savarese, Oliva Bruno, Via XX Settembre 139/b/r, 16121
Genova. T. (010) 54 30 02. - Num - 057702
Squarcina, Fratelli, Via Chiossone 20, 16123 Genova.
T. (010) 29 81 58. 057703
Studio, Via Cairoli 19, 16124 Genova.
T. (010) 20 45 97. 057704
Terzaghi, Alfredo, Vle Ponte dell'Ammiraglio 30, 16148
Genova. T. (010) 33 23 50. 057705
Tola, A., Via Borgo degli Incrociati 66, 16137 Genova.
T. (010) 88 77 00. 057706
Vigliero, Giorgio, Via Cairoli 3, 16124 Genova.
T. (010) 29 58 49. - Ant - 057707
Vivioli, Via Devoto 15, 16131 Genova. T. (010) 39 94 252, 30 88 56. 057708
Wannenes, Aldo, Piazza Meridiana 2, 16124 Genova.
T. (010) 20 14 55. - Ant / Lights - 057709

Germignaga (Varese)
Germignaga, Via Stheli 110, 21010 Germignaga.
T. (0332) 53 05 42. 057710

Ghedi (Brescia)
Gaydum Antikà, Piazza Roma 42, 25016 Ghedi.
T. (030) 90 12 26, 903 20 57. - Paint / Jew /
Silv - 057711

Ghiffa (Novara)
Mori, Via Nazionale 45, 28055 Ghiffa.
T. (0323) 591 72. 057712

Giulianova (Teramo)
Magazzeni, Via Amendola, 64021 Giulianova.
T. (085) 86 25 32. 057713

Giussano
Monterosa Arredi, Via Milano 69/71, 20034 Giussano.
T. (0362) 850764, Fax (0362) 850764. 057714

Gorizia
Adamo, Via Cascino 10, 34170 Gorizia.
T. (0481) 835 44. 057715
Orientappeti di Farias, Via Mazzini 9, 34170 Gorizia.
T. (0481) 334 60, 322 70. 057716

Gorle (Bergamo)
I Tre Tarli, Via Celadina 5, 24020 Gorle.
T. (035) 29 61 64. 057717

Gradisca d'Isonzo (Gonzia)
Bottega d'Arte, Via C Battisti 55, 34072 Gradisca d'Isonzo. T. (0481) 922 61. 057718

Grado (Gonzia)
Bottega d'Arte, Viale Dante Alighieri 35, 34073 Grado.
T. (0431) 807 60, 806 29. 057719
Boutique dell'Antiquariato, Via Marina 42, 34073 Grado.
T. (0431) 72 63 41. 057720
Helios, Viale Europa Unit 11, 34073 Grado.
T. (0431) 0463/80806, 38041. 057721

Gressoney Saint-Jean (Aosta)
Casaliscoz, Piazza Umberto 1, 11025 Gressoney Saint-Jean. T. (0125) 35 55 93. 057722

Greve in Chianti (Firenze)
Baggi, Angela, Piazza Matteotti 21, 50022 Greve in
Chianti. T. (055) 854 46 28. 057723

Groppello di Gavirate
Ntichità Brocanter, Via Rovera 39, 20126 Groppello di
Gavirate. T. (0332) 745270. 057724

Grosseto
Barbini, Gastone, Via dell'Unione 40-42, 58100 Grosseto. T. (0564) 238 42. 057725
La Ragnatela, Via Battisti 23, 58100 Grosseto.
T. (0564) 41 24 68. 057726
Vecchia Marina International, Corso Carducci 21, 58100
Grosseto. T. (0564) 41 52 69. 057727

Gubbio (Perugia)
Cecchini, S., Via Baldassani 62, 06024 Gubbio.
T. (075) 927 20 76. 057728
Marcelli, A., Via Baldassani 44, 06024 Gubbio.
T. (075) 927 33 70. 057729
Marcelli, A.M., Via del Popolo 23, 06024 Gubbio.
T. (075) 927 36 87. 057730
Vantaggi, G., Loc Torre Calzolari, 06024 Gubbio.
T. (075) 925 63 98. 057731

Gussago (Brescia)
Mobil Restauro, Via Mandolussa 191, 25064 Gussago.
T. (030) 32 02 16. 057732

Imola (Bologna)
Cose d'Altri Tempi, Via Appia 35, 40026 Imola.
T. (0542) 359 07. 057733
Grillini, Tomaso, Via Quaini 33-35, 40026 Imola.
T. (0542) 296 42. 057734
Pilatimirri, Rosanna, Via Emilia 150, 40026 Imola.
T. (0542) 302 44. 057735

Imperia
VIB, Via Aurelio Saffi 19, 18100 Imperia.
T. (0183) 618 51. 057736

Ischia (Napoli)
Rustica Domus, Corso Vittorio Colonna 167, 80070
Ischia. T. (081) 992 10. 057737

Iseo (Brescia)
Fava, Franco, Piazza Statuto 2, 25049 Iseo.
T. (030) 98 02 58. 057738
Turro, Via per Rovato 2, 25049 Iseo. T. (030) 982 17 75.
- Ant - 057739

Isola Vicentina (Vicenza)
Carobin, Luigi, Via Chiodo 1, 36033 Isola Vicentina.
T. (0444) 55 83 69. 057740

Ivrea (Torino)
Cecconello, Ettore, Via Aosta 33, 10015 Ivrea.
T. (0125) 49716. 057741
La Madia, Corso Nigra 19, 10015 Ivrea.
T. (0125) 468 50. 057742

Lazzari, Via Arduino 66, 10015 Ivrea. T. (0125) 449 28. 057743
Piccolo Mondo Antico, Corso Palestro 15, 10015 Ivrea. T. (0125) 481 44. 057744

Jesi (Ancona)

Bottega della Nonnina, Via Setificio 28, 60035 Jesi. T. (0731) 561 20. 057745
Dante, Piazza Spontini 7, 60035 Jesi. T. (0731) 570 63, 211 76. 057746
Pacenti, Via Mura Occidentali 19, 60035 Jesi. T. (0731) 520 18, 48 87. 057747

L'Aquila

Di Brisco, Luigi, Viale Nizza 6, 67100 L'Aquila. T. (0862) 260 81. 057748
Piccirilli, Romano, Piazza Palazzo 1, 67100 L'Aquila. T. (0862) 295 06, 264 32. 057749

La Spezia

Arte e Antichita, Via Vittorio Veneto 82, 19100 La Spezia. T. (0187) 274 68. 057750
Battolla e Carabelli, Via San Bartolomeo 659, 19100 La Spezia. T. (0187) 50 03 06. 057751
Botto, Viale San Bartolomeo 89, 19100 La Spezia. T. (0187) 50 63 46, 50 67 63. 057752
Il Quadrifoglio, Via XXIV Maggio 263, 19100 La Spezia. T. (0187) 50 09 94. 057753
Il Relitto, Via San Bartolomeo 128, 19100 La Spezia. T. (0187) 50 52 58. 057754
Il Relitto, Viale San Bartolomeo 21, 19100 La Spezia. T. (0187) 201 17. 057755
Marcacci, G., Via XXIV Maggio 13, 19100 La Spezia. T. (0187) 251 54. 057756
Marcacci, G., Via Gioberti 13, 19100 La Spezia. T. (0187) 290 56. 057757
Michi, Edoardo e C., Via Biassa 53, 19100 La Spezia. T. (0187) 222 97. 057758
Michi, Edoardo e C., Piazza Beverini 14, 19100 La Spezia. T. (0187) 362 09. 057759
Romagnani, Giancarlo, Via Cavallotti 39, 19100 La Spezia. T. (0187) 303 13. 057760

Lacchiarella (Milano)

Old Imports, Il Girasole Pad 6 Negozio 5, 20084 Lacchiarella. T. (02) 90 09 15 26. - Ant - 057761

Lacco Ameno (Napoli)

Il Tarlo, Corso Angelo Rizzoli 61, 80076 Lacco Ameno. T. (081) 98 60 08. 057762
Prado, El, Piazza Santa Restituta, 80076 Lacco Ameno. T. (081) 98 61 97. 057763

Lanciano (Chieti)

Ragnatela, La, Via De Titta 3-5, 66034 Lanciano. T. (0872) 393 19. 057764

Langhirano (Parma)

Puntobi, Via Tanara 6, 43013 Langhirano. T. (0521) 85 26 55. 057765

Latisana (Udine)

Fiorindo, Piazza Indipendenza 67, 33053 Latisana. T. (0431) 51 00 33. 057766

Lavagna (Genova)

Lanata, Angelo e Figli, Piazza Vittorio Veneto 27, 16033 Lavagna. T. (0185) 30 31 48. 057767
Porta d'Oro, La, Piazza Marini 18, 16033 Lavagna. T. (0185) 30 23 96. - Ant / Furn / Jew / Silv / Instr / Cur - 057768

Laveno Mombello (Varese)

Longobardi, Walter, Via Cittiglio 12 e Via Ceretti 23+25, 21014 Laveno Mombello. T. (0332) 66 87 00. - Tex - 057769

Lazise (Verona)

Bottega d'Arte, Piazza Vittorio Emanuele, 37017 Lazise. T. (045) 64 30 09. 057770

Lecce

Anastasia, Giovanni, Statale 274 Taviano-Racale, 73100 Lecce. T. (0832) 98 24 26. 057771
Arkè, Via L. Prato 28, 73100 Lecce. T. (0832) 402 64. - Graph / Furn / Tex - 057772
Epoque, Via Braccio Martello 41, 73100 Lecce. 057773
L.E.C., Via Libertini 69, 73100 Lecce. T. (0832) 28803. 057774
Vecchie Cose, Vico Dei Sotterrani 23, 73100 Lecce. T. (0832) 229 11, 255 47. 057775

Legnano (Milano)

Fabbrica Arredamenti Negozi, Via per Castellanza 33, 20025 Legnano. T. (0331) 540946. 057776
Mandelli, Corrado, Via Giulini / Via Palestro, 20025 Legnano. T. (0331) 54 00 44. - Furn - 057777
Marlacchi, Via Cavallotti 19, 20025 Legnano. T. (0331) 54 12 50. - Tex - 057778

Lerici (La Spezia)

Il Ventaglio, Largo Marconi 3 e 4, 19032 Lerici. T. (0187) 96 85 33. 057779

Lesa (Novara)

Bordogna, Giorgio, Lungo Lago, 28040 Lesa. - Ant - 057780
Giobbi, Evandro, Via Portici 32 Capo Maggiore, 28040 Lesa. T. (0322) 779 24. 057781

Levane (Arezzo)

Resti, Marino, Via 2 Giugno 83, 52023 Levane. T. (055) 97 80 62. 057782

Lido di Camaiore (Lucca)

Fabbiani, Via Italica 60, 55043 Lido di Camaiore. T. 679 96, 676 11. 057783
Il Tarlo della Vigna, Via Aurelia 140, 55043 Lido di Camaiore. T. 90 51 65. 057784
Lotito, Riccardo, Via dei Chivazzani, 55043 Lido di Camaiore. T. 678 06. 057785
Rossi, Giovanna, Viale Colombo 300, 55043 Lido di Camaiore. T. 660 67. 057786
Rossi, Luigi, Via Italica, 55043 Lido di Camaiore. T. 90 057. 057787
Vornoli, Romano, Via Aurelia 39, 55043 Lido di Camaiore. 057788

Lignano Sabbiadoro (Udine)

L'Arco, Via Arco del Grecale 1, 33054 Lignano Sabbiadoro. 057789
Oriental Haus, Via Arco della Paranza 1, 33054 Lignano Sabbiadoro. T. (0431) 727 58, 36 33 64. 057790
Pancotto Ceschelli, Piazza del Sole 48, 33054 Lignano Sabbiadoro. T. (0431) 42 21 35. 057791

Limone Piemonte (Cuneo)

Archivolto Ambiente, Largo Roma 7, 12015 Limone Piemonte. T. (0171) 92 70 70. 057792
Costa, Giuliano, Via Roma 44, 12015 Limone Piemonte. T. (0171) 92 76 36. 057793
Il Negozietto, Via Roma 23, 12015 Limone Piemonte. T. (0171) 926 50. 057794
Il Tarlo, Via Roma 71, 12015 Limone Piemonte. T. (0171) 92 61 15, 92 77 91. 057795

Livorno

Ambrosini e Marinari, Via del Fante 22, 57100 Livorno. T. (0586) 230 20. 057796
Ayres, Via Borra 21, 57100 Livorno. T. (0586) 271 12. 057797
Bernini, Via Marrachi 156, 57100 Livorno. T. (0586) 80 83 20. 057798
Bock, Corso Amedeo 50, 57100 Livorno. T. (0586) 344 90. 057799
Conti, Via Verdi 19, 57100 Livorno. T. (0586) 304 65. 057800
Cose del Passato, Via de Larderel 34, 57100 Livorno. T. (0586) 225 69. 057801
Dinozzi, Via Fanciulli 24, 57100 Livorno. T. (0586) 89 96 70. - Furn / Jew / Silv - 057802
Funaro, Via Fanciulli 24, 57100 Livorno. T. (0586) 34 670. 057803
Gemme, Le, Via Ricasoli 66, 57100 Livorno. T. (0586) 23222. - Ant / Jew - 057804
Il Veliero, Via Ricasoli 68, 57100 Livorno. T. (0586) 305 47. 057805
Liburnia, Corso Amedeo 118, 57100 Livorno. T. (0586) 322 30. 057806
Piccola Parigi, Via Maggi 63, 57100 Livorno. T. (0586) 262 03. 057807
Scarabeo, Lo, Via Fiume 47-49, 57100 Livorno. T. (0586) 89 12 49. - Ant / Furn / Fra - 057808
Silver Fox, Via Magenta 28, 57100 Livorno. T. (0586) 262 29. 057809
Volpi, Via Magenta 24, 57100 Livorno. T. (0586) 283 31. - Silv / Instr - 057810

Loano (Savona)

Piazzico d'Arte, Via Stella 14, 17025 Loano. T. (019) 66 74 24. 057811

Lodi (Milano)

Bottega d'Arte Antichità, Via Garibaldi 36, 20075 Lodi. T. (0371) 637 32. 057812
San Bassan, Via Cingia 17, 20075 Lodi. T. (0371) 636 55. 057813

Lonato (Brescia)

Gitti, Itala, Via San Giuseppe 6, 25017 Lonato. T. (030) 91 30 120. 057814

Loreggia (Padova)

Pataviumart, Villa Wollemberg, 35010 Loreggia. T. (049) 57 09 03. 057815

Lucca

Angelini, B., v. del Battistero 25, 55100 Lucca. - Ant - 057816
Arca, L', Via del Battistero 13, 55100 Lucca. T. (0583) 437 55. - Ant - 057817
Bocconi, Maria, Via del Battistero 52, 55100 Lucca. T. (0583) 476 21. 057818
Carli, Costantino, Via del Battistero 54, 55100 Lucca. T. (0583) 477 41. 057819
Carli, Pietro, Via Fillungo 93, 55100 Lucca. T. (0583) 411 19. 057820
Carlino, Piazza del Suffragio 21, 55100 Lucca. T. (0583) 470 06. 057821
Casa Antiquaria, Via Arcivesovado 37-35, 55100 Lucca. T. (0583) 41412. - Furn - 057822
Del Debbio, Via dei Borghi 106, 55100 Lucca. T. (0583) 498 27. 057823
Fistemaire, Carlo, Via del Battistero 8, 55100 Lucca. T. (0583) 449 06. - Ant / Furn / Dec - 057824
Frediani, R., Via del Battistero 14, 55100 Lucca. T. (0583) 426 23. 057825
Ieri e l'Altro Ieri, Via Calderia 13, 55100 Lucca. T. (0583) 41 95. 057826
Ilaria, Via Battistero 28, 55100 Lucca. T. (0583) 489 41. 057827
Kostner, Liliana, Via Battistero 21, 55100 Lucca. T. (0583) 437 12. 057828
Kraag, Via del Battistero 15, 55100 Lucca. T. (0583) 460 74. 057829
Mandoli, Piazzetta del Battistero 50, 55100 Lucca. 057830
Marchini, Leonardo, Via del Battistero 24, 55100 Lucca. T. (0583) 465 17. 057831
Martini, Corso Garibaldi, 55100 Lucca. T. (0583) 421 20. 057832
Nieri, P., Via dell'Arancio 3-5, 55100 Lucca. T. (0583) 432 50. 057833
San Giovanni, Piazza San Giovanni 12, 55100 Lucca. T. (0583) 498 45. 057834
Santa Croce, Via Santa Croce 57, 55100 Lucca. T. (0583) 422 09. 057835
Santucci, Andrea, Via Arcivescovado 35, 55100 Lucca. T. (0583) 414 12. - Ant - 057836
Tessiture Artistiche Lucchesi, Via del Duomo 12, 55100 Lucca. T. (0583) 498 45. 057837
Vangelisti, Bruno, Galleria d'Arte, v. S. Donnino 4, 55100 Lucca. T. (0583) 451 35. - Ant - 057838
Vecci, R., Via del Gallo 20, 55100 Lucca. T. (0583) 499 30. 057839

Lugo di Ravenna (Ravenna)

Bottega del Restauro, Via Cirondario Ponente 72, 48022 Lugo di Ravenna. T. (0545) 275 43. 057840
Cortesi, Antonio, Via C Donati 11, 48022 Lugo di Ravenna. T. (0545) 232 71. 057841
Emiliani, Oriano, Via Manfredi 44, 48022 Lugo di Ravenna. T. (0545) 222 28. 057842
Lo Stemma, Via Risorgimento 19, 48022 Lugo di Ravenna. T. (0545) 228 21. 057843

Neri, Giuseppe, Via Amendola 20, 48022 Lugo di Raven-
na. T. (0545) 252 00. *057844*
Pronim, Piazza Baracca 12, 48022 Lugo di Ravenna.
T. (0545) 212 55. *057845*
Stoppa, Antonio, Via Circondario Ponente 72, 48022 Lu-
go di Ravenna. T. (0545) 275 43. *057846*
Visani, Paolo, Via Sant'Andrea 16, 48022 Lugo di Raven-
na. T. (0545) 268 93. *057847*

Luzzara (Reggio Emilia)
Conetrali, Arturo, Via Tagliavini 60, 42045 Luzzara.
T. (0522) 83 51 66. *057848*

Macerata
Ahmadi Galleria Persiana, Via Ancona 15, 62100 Mace-
rata. T. (0733) 473 33. *057849*
Immagini, Via Mozzi 84, 62100 Macerata.
T. (0733) 334 16. *057850*
Zuccari, Nello, Via Crescimbeni 13, 62100 Macerata.
T. (0733) 458 28. *057851*

Madesimo (Sondrio)
Vanossi, Arnaldo, Via alle Fonti 7, 23024 Madesimo.
T. (0343) 530 76. *057852*

Madonna di Campiglio (Trento)
La Bifora, Piazza Righi 27, 38084 Madonna di Campi-
glio. T. (0465) 427 42. *057853*

Malè (Trento)
La Bifora, Via Brescia 18, 38027 Malè.
T. (0463) 914 15. *057854*

Manta (Cuneo)
Antichiga' Carignano G., Restauri – Compra vendita Mo-
bili antichi, S.S. Saluzzo-Cuneo, 12030 Manta.
T. (0175) 85924. *057855*
Carignano, G., S.S. Saluzzo-Cuneo, 12030 Manta.
T. (0175) 85924. - Ant / Furn - *057856*

Mantova
Ballerini, Via Cavour 59, 46100 Mantova.
T. (0376) 36 18 10. - Furn / China / Silv - *057857*
Il Prisma, Via Corrado 42, 46100 Mantova.
T. (0376) 36 90 92, 32 36 04. *057858*
Mazzucchini, Sergio, Via S Anselmo 12, 46100 Mantova.
T. (0376) 32 47 91. *057859*
Morgan, Via Chiassi 57, 46100 Mantova.
T. (0376) 36 90 56. *057860*
Mossini, Via Cavour 100, 46100 Mantova.
T. (0376) 36 89 10. *057861*

Marciana Marina (Livorno)
Bigi, Walter, Via Mentana 5, 57033 Marciana Marina.
T. (0565) 994 03. *057862*

Margherita di Savoia (Foggia)
Il Tarlo, Corso Ricco 29, 71044 Margherita di Savoia.
T. (0883) 65 21 51. *057863*

Marina di Pietrasanta (Lucca)
Orvieto, Paolo, Via Versilia 49, 55044 Marina di Pietrasanta. T. (0584) 229 08. *057864*

Marsala (Trapani)
Coppola, Via San Michele 38, 91025 Marsala.
T. (0923) 95 88 41, 95 78 12. *057865*
Toluian, Via Fazio 54, 91025 Marsala.
T. (0923) 95 11 75. *057866*

Martina Franca (Taranto)
Abat Jour, Via Vitt Emanuele 15, 74015 Martina Franca.
T. (080) 70 14 32. *057867*
Capodiferro, D., Via Pergolesi 34, 74015 Martina Franca.
T. (080) 883 18 72. *057868*

Massa
De Arte, Piazza Puccini 8, 54100 Massa.
T. (0585) 48 84 61. *057869*
Jacques, dott. Enrico, v. Zoppi 16, 54100 Massa.
- Num - *057870*
Ornacasa, Piazza De Gasperi 4, 54100 Massa.
T. (0585) 433 66. *057871*
Paoletti, Leonardo, Via Matteotti 23, 54100 Massa.
T. (0585) 439 40. *057872*

Massa Finalese (Modena)
Dal Conte, Via Per Modena 276, 41035 Massa Finalese.
T. (059) 990 74. *057873*

Massa Lombarda (Ravenna)
Marabini, Franco e Patrizia, Via Veneto 14, 48024 Massa
Lombarda. *057874*

Massarosa (Lucca)
Antico Truciolo, Vla Portovecchio 1, 55054 Massarosa.
T. (0584) 934 82. *057875*

Matelica (Macerata)
Mori, Nando e Dino, Via G Veneziani 42, 62024 Matelica.
T. (0737) 804 01. *057876*
Mori, Nando e Dino, Arco Campamante 13, 62024 Mate-
lica. T. (0737) 801 75. *057877*
Mori, Nando e Dino, Via G Veneziani 60, 62024 Matelica.
T. (0737) 824 83. *057878*
Mori, Nando e Dino, Corso Vittorio Emanuele 50, 62024
Matelica. T. (0737) 804 22. *057879*

Mazzin-Pera di Fassa (Trento)
Mogno, Giovanni, Via Dolomiti 18, 38030 Mazzin-Pera di
Fassa. T. (0462) 671 12. *057880*

Meda (Milano)
Art-Decor di Galimberti, Via Indipendenza 167, 20036
Meda. T. (0362) 70194. *057881*
Galimberti, Via Indipendenza 167, 20036 Meda.
T. (0362) 70194. *057882*

Megliadino San Fidenzio (Padova)
Guariso, Ludovico, Strada Statale 10, 35040 Megliadino
San Fidenzio. T. (0429) 892 20. *057883*

Merano
Gava e Fortuna, Via Cavour 75-77, 39012 Merano.
T. (0473) 240 98. *057884*
Lizzi, Enrico, Via Roma 28, 39012 Merano.
T. (0473) 367 64. *057885*

Messina
Bottegone del Mobile d'Arte, Via Garibaldi 130, 98100
Messina. T. (090) 551 98. *057886*
Sciarrone, Viale Boccetta 20, 98100 Messina.
T. (090) 439 46. *057887*
Toluian, Viale S Martino 92, 98100 Messina.
T. (090) 71 09 15. *057888*

Milano
Abafil Produzione e Vendita Accessori e Pubblicazioni,
Via S. Maria Fulcorina 17, 20123 Milano.
T. (02) 866636. *057889*
Acquistamo Antichita' Pagamento Contanti, Via Euripide
7 – Zona Fiera, 20145 Milano. T. (02) 4818269,
4812517. *057890*
Acquisti e Stime di Collezioni di Qualsiasi Importanza
Italphil, Via G. Morone 8, 20121 Milano.
T. (02) 76023396, Fax (02) 76020517. *057891*
Acquisto Antichita' C'era Ulna Volta, Certifichiamo l'au-
tenticita' dei nostri oggetti, Via T. Prisco 1, 20122 Mi-
lano. T. (02) 4818813, (0337) 348515. *057892*
Acquisto Antichita' Maffezzoni Massimiliano, Corso Co-
mo 9, 20154 Milano. T. (02) 6599066. *057893*
African – Art, Viale Caterina da Forli 28, 20146 Milano.
T. (02) 40091571. *057894*
Al Piccolo Naviglio, 34 Alz. Nav. Grande, 20144 Milano.
T. (02) 8376028. *057895*
A.LA. Antichi Lavori D'Argento, 5 Via Havez, 20129 Mila-
no. T. (02) 29403300. *057896*
Ale.B. di Alesia Brunelli & C., 21 Via Olmetto, 20123 Mi-
lano. T. (02) 8052408. *057897*
Alessandri, M.V., 42 Via Sarpi, 20154 Milano.
T. (02) 33605875. *057898*
Aliprandi, Gianantonio, Via Madonnina 9, 20121 Milano.
T. (02) 869 39 48. *057899*
Alkame, Corso Magenta 22, 20123 Milano.
T. (02) 805 71 56. *057900*
Alle Antiche Armi, Via Bigli 24, 20121 Milano.
T. (02) 76022318. *057901*
Alliata, 2 Via Castelbarco, 20136 Milano.
T. (02) 89402647. *057902*

Allusystem Cornici Antiche im Marmo e Pietra per Cami-
netti, Via Settala 59, 20124 Milano.
T. (02) 29523070. *057903*
American Oak Furniture di Antoniazzi, Maria Teresa, 36
Via Lamamora, 20122 Milano.
T. (02) 5400721. *057904*
Amiras, S., Corso Venezia 25, 20121 Milano.
T. (02) 79 33 97. *057905*
Ammiraglio Benbow, Via Col di Lana 8, 20136 Milano.
T. (02) 58 10 06 28. - Furn - *057906*
Ammiraglio Benbow Mobili d'epoca, Alzaia Naviglio
Grande 48, 20144 Milano. T. (02) 58106279. *057907*
Anni Cento, Viale Piave 17, 20129 Milano.
T. (02) 78 40 75. - Jew - *057908*
Anti's Antichita' di A. Tomba & C., 10 Corso Concordia,
20129 Milano. T. (02) 76002431. *057909*
Anticherie Acquisto e Vendo, Via Piazza della Francesca,
Milano. T. (02) 347767. *057910*
Antichi Ricordi di Vitella, Rosanna, 3 Viale Col di Lana,
20136 Milano. T. (02) 89409460. *057911*
Antichita' Acquisto in Contanti, Via Pisacane 53, 20129
Milano. T. (02) 29403146. *057912*
Antichita' alle Grazie, 2 Via Caradosso, 20123 Milano.
T. (02) 4818505. *057913*
Antichità Baiardo Acquista in Contanti, Milano.
T. (02) 93569979. *057914*
Antichita dell'Ottocento, Via Caminadella 5, 20123 Mila-
no. T. (02) 86452324. *057915*
Antichità della Moscova, Via della Moscova 47A, 20121
Milano. T. (02) 29 00 07 63. *057916*
Antichita' di Giancarlo Ricco e, 2 Via Senato, 20121 Mi-
lano. T. (02) 76003953. *057917*
Antichità Dover, Viale Premuda 27, 20129 Milano.
T. (02) 79 57 27. *057918*
Antichita' Drake di Ceppi, Elisabetta, 8 Viale Glan Ga-
leazzo, 20136 Milano. T. (02) 89404308. *057919*
Antichita' e Arte, 11 Via S. Maurilio, 20123 Milano.
T. (02) 20123. *057920*
Antichità e Stile, Viale Monte Nero 44, 20135 Milano.
T. (02) 55 18 00 54. *057921*
Antichita' Fabio Trivoli, 21 Via Cellini, 20129 Milano.
T. (02) 76009993. *057922*
Antichita' G. – N., Guagenti – Nobile, Via Maddalena 2
(Piazza Missori), Via S. Stefano 23B, 20122 Milano.
T. (02) 8052039, Fax (02) 8052039. *057923*
Antichita' Leo, 1 Ig. Usuelli, 20133 Milano.
T. (02) 76002416. *057924*
Antichita' Maestro Zitti, Serravalle Scrivia Villa Ginestra,
20144 Milano. T. (0143) 633454. *057925*
Antichita' Marciana, 18 Via Lanzone, 20123 Milano.
T. (02) 86451727. *057926*
Antichita' Neri, Carlo, Via Jacopo del Polta 24, Via della
Vecchia Stazione 14/16, 56031 Milano.
T. (0587) 756076, Fax (0587) 756076. *057927*
Antichita' Perfetto di Perfetto, Lucia Sabrina, 4 Via Raso-
ri, 20145 Milano. T. (02) 4817451. *057928*
Antichita' Petruni, Via Washington 80, Via Garian, 20146
Milano. T. (02) 48006911. *057929*
Antichita' San Marco, Acquisto Antiquariato, Via S. Mar-
co 26, 20121 Milano. T. (02) 6555388,
(0337) 299993. *057930*
Antichita Venezia, Corso Venezia 6, 20121 Milano.
T. (02) 78 01 12. *057931*
Antiquariato Selezionato, 2 Via Formentini, 20121 Mila-
no. T. (02) 86460529. *057932*
Antiquariato Selezionato, Via Formentini 2, 20121 Mila-
no. T. (02) 8058316. *057933*
Antiquinvest, 23 Via Quarenghi, 20151 Milano.
T. (02) 33400626. *057934*
Antonini M.M., 1 Piazza Lega Lomb., 20154 Milano.
T. (02) 314477. *057935*
Antonucci, Cosima, Corso Indipendenza 5, 20129 Mila-
no. T. (02) 7388543. *057936*
Arcadia Antichità, Ripa di Porta Ticinese 61, 20143 Mi-
lano. T. (02) 8375787. *057937*
Archeo Galleria, Via Olona 7, 20123 Milano.
T. (02) 837 20 65. - Arch - *057938*
Archita de Vittori, Via Pantano 19, 20122 Milano.
T. (02) 58304392. *057939*
Argenti Antichi Icone Russe Antichità, Via Turati 6,
20121 Milano. T. (02) 6599305,
Fax (02) 6599384. *057940*

Arienti, Via Volta 5, 20121 Milano.
T. (02) 6555003. 057941
Ariosto, Carlo, Via Monte Napoleone 22, 20121 Milano.
T. (02) 79 87 98, 76 00 20 02,
Fax (02) 76004231. 057942
Arly, Via Ragutta 3, 20121 Milano.
T. (02) 76002002. 057943
Arredamenti Duomo, 47 Via A. Sforza, 20136 Milano.
T. (02) 8356365. 057944
Arredamenti Solferino, 46 Via Solferino, 20121 Milano.
T. (02) 6599029. 057945
Arredare, 24 Corso Indipendenza, 20129 Milano.
T. (02) 712514, 7490293. 057946
Arrivabene G., 9 Via Corsico, 20144 Milano.
T. (02) 58101729. 057947
Ars Minor, Via Boscovich 30, 20124 Milano.
T. (02) 669 22 93. 057948
Arsitalia, Via S. Vittore 8, 20123 Milano. T. (02) 87 81 45,
805 27 37. 057949
Arsorient's, Via Scarpa 9, 20145 Milano.
T. (02) 43 32 47. - China / Tex - 057950
Art & Idea' 900 di Emilio de Tullio, 50 Via Dezza, 20144
Milano. T. (02) 48013217. 057951
Arte Antica, Via S. Andrea 11, 20121 Milano.
T. (02) 798675/76021776. 057952
Artero, Corso Magenta 27, 20123 Milano.
T. (02) 80 57 394. 057953
Arts Decoratifs, 10 Via Guicciardini, 20129 Milano.
T. (02) 794685. 057954
Au Temps Passe, Via Brera 30, 20121 Milano.
T. (02) 877538. 057955
Bagatti, Arturo, Piazza Risorgimento 3, 20129 Milano.
T. (02) 76 00 63 53. - Furn / Fra / Mil - 057956
Raleni R., 31 Corso Piazzetta Vigentina, 20122 Milano.
T. (02) 58314469. 057957
Ballerini, Umberto, Via Palermo 20, 20121 Milano.
T. (02) 657 15 57. 057958
Balzani & Pedriali, Via Borgospesso 8, 20121 Milano.
T. (02) 76003596. 057959
Balzaretti, Daniela, Via Solferino 19, 20121 Milano.
T. (02) 29 00 37 72, 657 55 17. 057960
Bandello Antichità, Via Matteo Bandello 18, 20123 Mila-
no. T. (02) 469 45 21. 057961
Barillet M.J., 24 Via Lamarmora, 20122 Milano.
T. (02) 55195047. 057962
Bellini e Pesapane, Via S. Maurilio 24, 20123 Milano.
T. (02) 866 26 15. 057963
Bellini, Tino, Via Madonnina 12, 20124 Milano.
T. (02) 86462086. - Ant / Furn / Sculp / Tex - 057964
Bellini, Tino, Via S. Carpoforo 4, 20121 Milano.
T. (02) 89 01 09 49. 057965
BE.MA., 61 Ripa Piazzetta Ticinese, 20143 Milano.
T. (02) 8375787. 057966
Benbassa Porta C., Via Bramante da Urbino 1, 20154
Milano. T. (02) 33 60 83 79. 057967
Benedetti, Adriano & C., Adriano & C., Via Lazzaro Palaz-
zi 7, 20124 Milano. T. (02) 29 51 04 24. 057968
Bensi, Antonella, Via Santo Spirito 15, 20121 Milano.
T. (02) 76023007. 057969
Bensi Santini A., 15 Via S. Spirito, 20121 Milano.
T. (02) 76022914. 057970
Bernardi C., 1 Piazza Cavour, 20121 Milano.
T. (02) 29005389. 057971
Bernardini, Via Caradosso 2, 20123 Milano.
T. (02) 4818697. 057972
Bersia Antiquariato, 45 Corso Magenta, 20123 Milano.
T. (02) 48011450. 057973
Bianchin L., 7 Via Olona, 20123 Milano.
T. (02) 8372065. 057974
Bianco, P., Via Spallanzani 6, 20129 Milano.
T. (02) 2049038. 057975
Bigli 21, Via Bigli 21, 20121 Milano.
T. (02) 76 00 22 53. 057976
Biglidieci Antichità', 10 Via Bigli, 20121 Milano.
T. (02) 76003446. 057977
Bini, Teodolinda, Via Faravelli 18, 20149 Milano.
T. (02) 33 61 05 74. 057978
Il Biscione, 15/17 Via Santa Marta, 20123 Milano.
T. (02) 86452726. 057979
BI.TI.E., 6 Vicolo Lavandai, 20144 Milano.
T. (02) 8372860. 057980
Blanchaert, Via Nirone 19, 20123 Milano.
T. (02) 86451700. 057981

Blasco, Francesco, Corso Porta Romana 111, 20122 Mi-
lano. T. (02) 551 01 78. 057982
Bo E., 15 Ripa Piazzetta Ticinese, 20143 Milano.
T. (02) 8372992. 057983
Boggiali, Gaetano, Via Torino 34, 20123 Milano.
T. (02) 80 14 91. 057984
Bogonovo Morena Maria, Via Ponte Vetero 21, 20121
Milano. T. (02) 86464839. 057985
Bonarrigo A., 15 Corso S. Gottardo, 20136 Milano.
T. (02) 8323092. 057986
Bonatelli, Franco, Franco, Via Niccolini 25A, 20154 Mila-
no. T. (02) 331 19 57. - Paint / Graph - 057987
Bonatti, G., Via Abamonti 2, 20129 Milano.
T. (02) 29 40 50 91. 057988
Boni, Lucio, Via S. Giovanni sul Muro 3, 20121 Milano.
T. (02) 86460415. 057989
Borgonuovo 4, Via Borgonuovo 4, 20121 Milano.
T. (02) 655 17 01, 659 60 19. 057990
Bortolotti, Via Aurelio Saffi 33, 20123 Milano.
T. (02) 463628. 057991
La Bottega del Lando' di Ascione, Ernesto, 25 Via Leo-
pardi, 20123 Milano. T. (02) 4816430. 057992
Bottega del Mago, Via Bigli 7, 20121 Milano.
T. (02) 76021528. 057993
Bottega dell'Antiquario, Corso XXII Marzo 20 e Viale
Monte Nero 50, 20135 Milano. T. (02) 5511507,
5517986, 5512155. 057994
Bottega Della Nonna, Via Maddalena 5, 21022 Milano.
T. (02) 805 36 50. 057995
Bottini, Franco, Via Agnello 19, 20121 Milano.
T. (02) 87 80 96. 057996
Botton, J., Via Brighenti 40, 20155 Milano.
T. (02) 39210208. 057997
Brucoli, M., Via Spiga 46, 20121 Milano.
T. (02) 76020361/76023767. 057998
Brucoli, Mauro, Via della Spiga 46, 20121 Milano.
T. (02) 76023767. 057999
Brunella, M., Via Boccaccio 26, 20123 Milano.
T. (02) 805 30 17, 498 56 21. 058000
Il Bulino Antiche Stampe di Tamburini, Giovanna, 50
Corso Magenta, 20123 Milano.
T. (02) 48011448. 058001
Bungalow Country, 128 Via Gadames, 20151 Milano.
T. (02) 38008886, 38008934. 058002
C'Era Una Volta, Piazza Argentina, 20124 Milano.
T. (02) 29524779. 058003
Caiati, Corso Porta Vigenta 6, 20122 Milano.
T. (02) 58 31 44 20, 58 31 49 03. 058004
Camelini, Maria Gracia & C., Corso Magenta 52, 20123
Milano. T. (02) 48 01 14 00. 058005
Camisasca, A., Via San Carpoforo 6, 20121 Milano.
T. (02) 89 01 05 54. 058006
Campi, A., Via V. Monti 27, 20123 Milano.
T. (02) 439 03 68. 058007
Campogiani, Marco, Via Modena 22, 20129 Milano.
T. (02) 738 69 78. 058008
Candeliere Fratelli, 4 Via Ala, 20159 Milano.
T. (02) 6883037. 058009
Canelli, Paolo, Via S. Spirito 14, 20121 Milano.
T. (02) 76 00 21 24. - Ant / Paint / Furn - 058010
Capasso, Paola, Via Madonnina 3, 20121 Milano.
T. (02) 86 46 04 12. 058011
Capitani S., 22 Via Comelico, 20135 Milano.
T. (02) 5517263. 058012
Carducci M., 20 Via C. da Sesto, 20148 Milano.
T. (02) 58114717. 058013
Care Vecchie Cose di, Panbianco Alberto, 38 Alz. Nav.
Grande, 20144 Milano. T. (02) 89407560. 058014
Carozzi, Maria Felicia, Via Moscova 7, 20121 Milano.
T. (02) 65 97 695. 058015
Carravieri, Via Madonnina 3, 20121 Milano.
T. (02) 86 46 05 16. 058016
Il Carrobiolo galleria di antiquariato oggetti d'arte, Via
Carlo Alberto 31, 20052 Milano.
T. (039) 321863. 058017
Cattaneo C., 18 Via Caminadella, 20123 Milano.
T. (02) 72022304. 058018
Cattaneo, Guido, Via Soresina 16, 20144 Milano.
T. (02) 48 00 05 51. 058019
Caviglia E., 6 Via turati, 20121 Milano.
T. (02) 29005740. 058020
Cazzaniga, Bino, Via Lanzone 1, 20123 Milano.
T. (02) 863067. 058021

Ceralacca, 5 Via Rovello, 20121 Milano.
T. (02) 876618. 058022
Ceralacca, Angela, Via Rovello 18, 20121 Milano.
T. (02) 86465075. 058023
Ceresa, A., Via Washington 3, 20146 Milano.
T. (02) 43 71 00. 058024
Cervi V., 99 Ripa Piazetta Ticinese, 20143 Milano.
T. (02) 8392093. 058025
Cesatl, Alessandro, Via S.G. sul Muro 3, 20129 Milano.
T. (02) 86460928. 058026
Cesati, Alessandro, Via Baldissera 9, 20129 Milano.
T. (02) 29 52 13 61. - Ant - 058027
Chimera, Via Cerva 8, 20122 Milano.
T. (02) 76 00 69 58. 058028
Choccio Antichità', Via Sansovino 28, 20133 Milano.
T. 802) 26680465. 058029
Ciardi, V., Via Fiori Chairi 16, 20121 Milano.
T. (02) 87 89 06. 058030
Ciottoli Solazzo G.L., 33 Ripa Piazzetta Ticinese, 20143
Milano. T. (02) 58111711. 058031
Cislaghi, C., Alzaia Naviglio Grande 56, 20144 Milano.
T. (02) 836 10 15. 058032
Citterio, Aldo, Via Orefici 18, 20123 Milano.
T. (02) 876214. 058033
Cittone, Elio, Via Bigli 2, 20121 Milano.
T. (02) 76001745, Fax (02) 76013345. 058034
Clang, 12 Via Borgospesoo, 20121 Milano.
T. (02) 796411. 058035
Clem Antiquariato, 10 Via Vico, 20123 Milano.
T. (02) 48006852. 058036
Cocepa Centro Numismatico Internazionale, 6 Via Tem-
peranza, 20127 Milano. T. (02) 2892451. 058037
Cogliolo, Luisa, Corso Porta Ticinese 30, 20143 Milano.
T. (02) 837 90 14. 058038
Collezioni, Via Piazza Sottocorno 27, 20129 Milano.
T. (02) 7387057. 058039
Colombi, Elda, Corso Monforte 21, 20122 Milano.
T. (02) 76 00 21 46. 058040
Comacchi, G., Via Turati 6, 20121 Milano.
T. (02) 654536. 058041
Comensoli, M., Viale Corsica 1, 20133 Milano.
T. (02) 73 03 96. 058042
Compagnia D'Architettura di Garini Angelo & C., 57 Via
de Amicis, 20123 Milano. T. (02) 58112205. 058043
Compro Antichita', Milano. T. (02) 4818733,
(0337) 312925. 058044
Consulenza D'Arte, Via Passione 7, 20122 Milano.
T. (02) 76000774. 058045
Container, 3 Corso Garibaldi, 20121 Milano.
T. (02) 876194. 058046
Conzada C., 23 Corso Piazzetta Romana, 20122 Milano.
T. (02) 58315868. 058047
Copello & Rizzo, Via de Castillia Gaetano 21, 20124 Mi-
lano. T. (02) 688 20 61. 058048
Cortona, E., Corso Monforte 38, 20122 Milano.
T. (02) 78 46 17. - Paint / Graph / Sculp / Draw - 058049
Cose d'Epoca, Via Melzo 22, 20129 Milano.
T. (02) 29 51 80 24. 058050
Cose del Passato, Via Vittorio Colonna 25, 20149 Mila-
no. T. (02) 46 21 34. 058051
Le Cose di, Alessandra, 4 Via Novati, 20123 Milano.
T. (02) 8055447. 058052
Cose Vecchie, Via Vincenzo Foppa 5, 20144 Milano.
T. (02) 46 38 21. 058053
Cosima, Corso Independenza 5, 20129 Milano.
T. (02) 738 85 43. 058054
C.R.A.C., 34 Sismondi, 20133 Milano.
T. (02) 70101584. 058055
Crazymport, 4 Via Custodi, 20136 Milano.
T. (02) 8361266. 058056
Crippa, Carlo, Via degli Omenoni 2, 20121 Milano.
T. (02) 87 86 80, Fax (02) 878680. - Num - 058057
Criptonit di Chammaa E. C., Eveline, 30 Corso Magenta,
20123 Milano. T. (02) 862323. 058058
Cris, 6 Via Piacenza, 20135 Milano.
T. (02) 55180214. 058059
Cristallo, Paola, Corso Garibaldi 46, 20121 Milano.
T. (02) 72 02 27 47. 058060
Croffi, C., Via Vigevano 3, 20144 Milano.
T. (02) 837 64 70. 058061
Cuoccio, Antonio, Via Lanzone 27, 20123 Milano.
T. (02) 72022355, 72011055. 058062

Cuoccio Fratelli, Via Plinio 40, 20129 Milano. T. (02) 29 40 16 54. 058063
Curti, R. & A. Fabbroni, Via Solferino 31, 20121 Milano. T. (02) 659 96 70. 058064
D'Aloja, Andrea, Via Manzoni 19 e Piazza del Carmine 6, 20121 Milano. T. (02) 86463269/879866, Fax (02) 86461101. 058065
Dabbene, Largo Treves 2, 20121 Milano. T. (02) 6554406. 058066
Dalzini R., 67 Via Ornato, 20162 Milano. T. (02) 6425202. 058067
Daolio M., 49 Via Verro, 20141 Milano. T. (02) 8467304. 058068
Dast, Via Alessandro Manzoni 12, 20121 Milano. T. (02) 76006807. 058069
De Giovanni, Viale Jenner 69/3, 20159 Milano. T. (02) 6886462. - Silv - 058070
De Giulio, J., Via Lomazzo 8, 20154 Milano. T. (02) 349 10 23. 058071
Decomania, Via Formentini 7, 20121 Milano. T. (02) 86 46 34 13. 058072
Dedalo, Viale Premuda 23, 20129 Milano. T. (02) 79 85 36. 058073
Del Ventisette, Renzo, Viale Premuda 7, 20129 Milano. T. (02) 5401373. 058074
Dell'Occhino, G., Via Molino delle Armi 19-21, 20123 Milano. T. (02) 58 31 02 91. 058075
Derbylius, Via Piatti 6, 20123 Milano. T. (02) 870289. 058076
Di Bari, Antonio, 102 Viale Monza, 20127 Milano. T. (02) 26111190. 058077
Di Loreto A., 12 Via Meravigli, 20123 Milano. T. (02) 8056493, 8693875. 058078
Di Vittori Archita, Luigia, 19 Via Pantano, 20122 Milano. T. (02) 58304392. 058079
Dimorae, 69 Corso Magenta, 20123 Milano. T. (02) 48011803. 058080
Distintivi e Medaglie Numismatica Investments, Via Mazzini 12, 20123 Milano. T. (02) 8052161, 879893, 875507, 72023501, Fax (02) 879384. 058081
Due Civette Sul Como' di Caputo e Dal Magro, 68 Corso Piazetta Ticinese, 20143 Milano. T. (02) 8392558. 058082
Duse & C., Corso Magenta 85, 20123 Milano. T. (02) 48 00 02 36. 058083
Eikon, 14 Via Palermo, 20121 Milano. T. (02) 6554999. 058084
El Botteghin, Piazza Lima, 20124 Milano. T. (02) 29 40 96 89. 058085
El Rebelott, Via Lazzaretto 7, 20124 Milano. T. (02) 29 00 04 74. 058086
Enea di Bracciali Enea Magazzino, Via Romilli 7, 20139 Milano. T. (02) 5396211, 57403904, Fax (02) 57302059. 058087
Enrico, Maria, 48 Alz. Nav. Grande, 20144 Milano. T. (02) 58106279. 058088
Enrico, Maria, Viale Col di Lana 8, 20136 Milano. T. (02) 58 10 06 28. 058089
Epifani, M., Via Madonnina 5, 20121 Milano. T. (02) 86 05 89. 058090
Epipla, Via Mascheroni 22, 20145 Milano. T. (02) 48 01 16 95. 058091
Esagono Antichità, Via S. Giovanni sul Muro 21, 20121 Milano. T. (02) 86455041. 058092
Eskenazi, Via Monte Napoleone 15, 20121 Milano. T. (02) 76000022, Fax 78 25 57. - Orient / China / Tex - 058093
Etro, Roberto, Via Pontaccio 17, 20121 Milano. T. (02) 72003720. 058094
Euronummus, 10 Viale Marino, 20129 Milano. T. (02) 781919, 76003287. 058095
Fabroni, A., Via Copernico 18, 20125 Milano. T. (02) 607 03 38. 058096
Falcieri, Armando, Via Verdi 2, 20121 Milano. T. (02) 876550. 058097
Farina, G., Via Saffi 7, 20123 Milano. T. (02) 481 88 33. 058098
Farsciran, Via Rovello 1, 20121 Milano. T. (02) 87 29 47. 058099
Fasanella, M., Via Caminadella 5, 20123 Milano. T. (02) 86 45 23 24. 058100
Fedetto, A., Via Vincenzo Monti 28, 20123 Milano. T. (02) 481 53 91. 058101
Ferro, Paola, Via Oltrocchi 8, 20137 Milano. T. (02) 55 18 84 65. 058102
Filatelia Metro', Via Cordusio, 20123 Milano. T. (02) 878113. 058103
Filatelia Metro', 15 Corso Vitt. Eman. II, 20122 Milano. T. (02) 76004256. 058104
Finarte, Piazetta Maurilio Bossi 4, 20121 Milano. T. (02) 87 70 41, Fax 86 73 18. 058105
Foroni, F., Via Sottocorno 27, 20129 Milano. T. (02) 738 70 57. 058106
Franzin, Dino, Corso Matteotti 7, 20121 Milano. T. (02) 76021034. 058107
Fratelli Sala, Viale Coni Zugna 54, 20144 Milano. T. (02) 8376809. 058108
Il Fratino di Marcenaro, Rosanita, 27 Via Fabbri, 20123 Milano. T. (02) 8375235. 058109
Freschi, R., Via Lanzone 19, 20123 Milano. T. (02) 86 67 36. 058110
Frigerio, E., E., Piazzale Baracca 10, 20123 Milano. T. (02) 43 72 15. 058111
Fusaro & Lovazzano, Largo Europa 9/129, 15057 Milano. T. (0131) 811528, 814975. 058112
Galetti, Gianfranco, Via Vallarsa 10, 20139 Milano. T. (02) 53 47 04, 57 40 03 20. 058113
Galignani A., 17 Fiamma, 20129 Milano. T. (02) 70107822. 058114
Galleria D'Orlane, 13 Via S. Maurilio, 20123 Milano. T. (02) 72000779. 058115
Galleria di Porta Ticinese di Pellegrini, Giancarla & C., 87 Corso Piazetta Ticinese, 20143 Milano. T. (02) 8394374. 058116
Galleria Gierre, Via del Fusaro 2, 20146 Milano. T. (02) 4691812/(0336) 339019. - Furn / Tex / Fra - 058117
Galleria Hermitage, Via Vincenzo Monti 56, 20123 Milano. T. (02) 498 59 07, 48 01 95 59, Fax (02) 48019559. 058118
Galleria Il Cannocchiale, Via Brera 4, 20121 Milano. T. (02) 86 75 18. 058119
Galleria Mandala, Via Lanzone da Corte, 20123 Milano. T. (02) 86 67 36. - Ant / Furn - 058120
Galleria Rizzardi, Via Solferino 56, 20121 Milano. T. (02) 657 05 63, Fax (02) 6570563. 058121
Galleria Salamon, Via San Damiano 2, 20122 Milano. T. (02) 76 01 31 42, 76 02 39 49, 76 02 22 30, Fax 76 00 49 38. - Paint / Graph / Num - 058122
Gallo, M., Alzaia Naviglio Grande 158, 20144 Milano. T. (02) 42 70 34. 058123
Gavioli, Vico, 9 Via Fatebenefratelli, 20121 Milano. T. (02) 29005586, 29005596. 058124
Gemelli F., 16 Via Pacini, 20131 Milano. T. (02) 70638599. 058125
Ghelli, Andrea & Monica, Via Osti 6, 20122 Milano. T. (02) 805 48 45. - Silv - 058126
Ghio, Dario, Corso Magenta 30, 20123 Milano. T. (02) 86 23 24. 058127
Gianetti, Maria Antonia, Via Gesu 23, 20121 Milano. T. (02) 76 00 83 62. - Ant / Paint / Sculp / Eth - 058128
Il Giardino dei Ricordi, Como – Piazza San Fedele 5, 22028 Milano. T. (031) 271034. 058129
Giglio Pasquale e C., 53 Via Pisacane, 20129 Milano. T. (02) 29403146. 058130
Gilardelli G., 38 Via G. Carcano, 20141 Milano. T. (02) 89511583. 058131
Gilli, R., Via Gesú 17, 20121 Milano. T. (02) 79 40 87. 058132
Giusti & Podesta, Via S. Maria alla Porta 11, 20123 Milano. T. (02) 80 48 21. 058133
Gloria E., 1 Piazza Plo XI, 20123 Milano. T. (02) 804106. 058134
Gracis P.G., 6 Via S. Simplicano, 20121 Milano. T. (02) 877807. 058135
Granocchia, Marcello, Viale Piave 28, 20129 Milano. T. (02) 29521392. 058136
Grichina N., 76 Viale M.te Nero, 20135 Milano. T. (02) 55182032. 058137
Guindani A., 98 Corso Piazetta Ticinese, 20135 Milano. T. (02) 8372313. 058138
Halevim, Davide, Via S. Spirito 13, 20121 Milano. T. (02) 76002292, Fax 78 43 28. 058139
Hazan, Vittorio, Via Pietro, 20122 Milano. T. (02) 76005240. 058140
Horologium, Via Cerva 16, 20122 Milano. T. (02) 709326. 058141
Horologium, 16 Via Cerva, 20122 Milano. T. (02) 76005473. 058142
Idea Books, Via Vigevano 41, 20144 Milano. T. (02) 8373949, 8360395, 8390284, Fax (02) 8357776. - Pho - 058143
Idea Studio, Oggetti antichi e moderni, Via Mascheroni 14, 20145 Milano. T. (02) 48001016. 058144
Ideal Mobili – Lux Casa, 16 Viale Abruzzi, 20131 Milano. T. (02) 29406730. 058145
Ieri e Oggi, 51 Corso S. Gottardo, 20136 Milano. T. (02) 58101780. 058146
Il Biscione, Via S. Marta 15, 20123 Milano. T. (02) 86 45 27 26. 058147
Il Campiello, Via Santa Radegonda 16, 20121 Milano. T. (02) 86462407. 058148
Il Cancelletto, Viale Piave 41, 20129 Milano. T. (02) 201016. 058149
Il Cirmolo, Via Lanzone 16, 20123 Milano. T. (02) 86 71 73. 058150
Il Giardino del Re, Via Solferino 41, 20121 Milano. T. (02) 655 48 80. 058151
Il Paiolo, Via Morone 3, 20121 Milano. T. (02) 80 94 45. 058152
Il Palanchino, Via Zuara 22, 20146 Milano. T. (02) 422 61 36. 058153
Il Pontaccio, Via Pontaccio 19, 20121 Milano. T. (02) 86 75 19. 058154
Il Ponte, Via Pontaccio 12, 20121 Milano. T. (02) 72 00 37 49, Fax (02) 72022083. 058155
Il Posto delle Bricóle, Via Lambrate 18, 20131 Milano. T. (02) 284 29 33. 058156
Il Quindici, Via Moscova 25, 20121 Milano. T. (02) 655 44 92. 058157
Il Terrazzino, Via Bagutta 1, 20121 Milano. T. (02) 78 14 47. 058158
Illulian, M., Via Anfossi 19, 20135 Milano. T. (02) 546 01 61. 058159
In.Arte, 5 Via Rossari, 20121 Milano. T. (02) 76001837. 058160
Incontri Gacaru' di Somaglia, Clara Maria, 37 Via Spartaco, 20135 Milano. T. (02) 55192604. 058161
Ingoglia Acquisto Antichita', Giuseppe, Via Volta 20, Via Astesani 2, 20121 Milano. T. (02) 66200861. 058162
Ingoglia, Giuseppe, Via Volta 20, 20121 Milano. T. (02) 29 00 30 97. 058163
Intercoins, Via Carducci 9, 20123 Milano. T. (02) 8900404, Fax (02) 8056065. 058164
Intercoins, Via Carducci 9, 20123 Milano. T. (02) 8900404, Fax (02) 870189. 058165
Intercoins, Via Carducci 9, 20123 Milano. T. (02) 8900404, Fax (02) 870189. 058166
Intercoins Monete, Via Carducci 9, 20123 Milano. T. (02) 8900404, Fax (02) 8056065. 058167
International Business Brokers, 18 Via Aselli, 20133 Milano. T. (02) 70105555. 058168
Investments, 12 Via Mazzini, 20123 Milano. T. (02) 862247, 864427, 8052537, 8690469. 058169
Ippogrifo, Via S. Maurilio 18, 20123 Milano. T. (02) 72 02 20 10. 058170
Ital Centro Numimatico, Corso Vittorio Emanuele II 37b, 20122 Milano. T. (02) 798080, Fax (02) 795873. 058171
Iuric, Emilia, Corso Italia 35, 20122 Milano. T. (02) 58 31 32 51. 058172
Izzillo, M., Via Vetere 10, 20123 Milano. T. (02) 89 40 15 53. 058173
Jammal, M., Via Washington 105, 20146 Milano. T. (02) 422 50 22. 058174
Kalos, Via Carlo Farini 6, 20154 Milano. T. (02) 657 21 65. 058175
L'Albero del Tempo, Via Molino Armi 25, 20123 Milano. T. (02) 839 43 25. 058176
L'Antenato di Groppo Alberto, Via Canonica 9, 20154 Milano. T. (02) 349 00 77. - Paint / Furn - 058177
L'Antenato Raccoglitore Antichita', Via Canonica 9, 20154 Milano. T. (02) 3490077. 058178
L'Eccelso By, Max, 37 Ripa Piazetta Ticinese, 20143 Milano. T. (02) 89406031. 058179
L'Emporium, 23 Corso Monforte, 20122 Milano. T. (02) 76000452. 058180

L'Eredità, Via Solferino 11, 20121 Milano.
T. (02) 86462530. 058181
L'Eroica, Via S. Simpliciano 5, 20121 Milano.
T. (02) 86 46 01 41, Fax 869 05 98. 058182
L'Iris, Via Bertani 2, 20154 Milano.
T. (02) 33 60 89 02. 058183
L'Officina Casa D'Aste Antiquariato Arte Moderna, 29
Corso Vercelli, 20144 Milano. T. (02) 48008882,
48011906. 058184
L'Oro dei Farlocchi, Via Madonnina 5, 20121 Milano.
T. (02) 86 05 89. 058185
L'Unicorno, Via S. Giovanni sul Muro 17, 20121 Milano.
T. (02) 86451512/8900955. 058186
L'800, Via Aselli 22, 20133 Milano.
T. (02) 738 54 00. 058187
La Biscaglina, Via Caminadella 22, 20123 Milano.
T. (02) 8057272. 058188
La Bottega Solferino, Via Marsala 4, 20121 Milano.
T. (02) 659 75 57. 058189
La Canonica, Corso Porta Vigentina 12, 20122 Milano.
T. (02) 58314784. 058190
La Grange, Viale Monte Nero 63, 20135 Milano.
T. (02) 545 86 56. 058191
La Porta Antica, Via Meravigli 18, 20123 Milano.
T. (02) 86 01 25. 058192
La Portantina, Via Vigna 6, 20123 Milano.
T. (02) 80 53 315. - Graph / Mul - 058193
La Roccia, Via Annunciata 2, 20121 Milano.
T. (02) 65 36 08. 058194
La Tenda Gialla, Via Castelfidardo 2, 20121 Milano.
T. (02) 29 00 09 81. 058195
La Trouvaille, Via S. Giovanni sul Muro 10, 20121 Mila-
no. T. (02) 86 36 90. - Furn / Silv - 058196
La Zaffera, Corso Porta Romana 54, 20122 Milano.
T. (02) 58 30 33 01. 058197
Lanzone 16, Via Lanzone 16, 20123 Milano.
T. (02) 86 45 21 86. 058198
Le Antiquarie, Via Fiori Chiari 14, 20121 Milano.
T. (02) 86 4617 30. 058199
Le Gioie di Funaro, Via Pontaccio 17, 20121 Milano.
T. (02) 86 53 54. 058200
Le Muse, Via Maroncelli 2, 20154 Milano.
T. (02) 29 00 25 68. 058201
Le Pleiadi, Via Broletto/Via Bossi, 20121 Milano.
T. (02) 7202 27 34. 058202
Le Quinte di Vita Dell'Orso, Via dell'Orso 14, 20121 Mila-
no. T. (02) 805 58 56. 058203
Lega U., 19 Via Lamarmora, 20122 Milano.
T. (02) 59901861. 058204
Ligorio Antichità, Via Kramer 23, 20129 Milano.
T. (02) 76 01 34 44. - Ant / Furn / China / Fra - 058205
Lo Scarabattolo, Via Solferino 14, 20121 Milano.
T. (02) 659 02 53. 058206
Lobasso, G., Via Orti 35, 20122 Milano.
T. (02) 546 24 68. 058207
Longari, Nella, Via Bigli 15, 20121 Milano.
T. (02) 78 03 22, 79 42 87. 058208
Longo M.LE., 36 Via V. Monti, 20123 Milano.
T. (02) 4801393. 058209
Longo, V., Via Carducci 9, 20123 Milano.
T. (02) 72 01 01 50, 86 45 36 31. 058210
Lorenzelli, Via S. Andrea 19, 20121 Milano.
T. (02) 78 30 35, Fax (02) 76005692. 058211
Louvre Tchen Arte Antica E. Moderna Plinio Expertise,
10 Via Pinio, 20129 Milano. T. (02) 29400347. 058212
Lozommasi, Rosa, Via Gustavo Fara 4, 20124 Milano.
T. (02) 66980395. 058213
Lucon M., 21 Via Tito Livio, 20137 Milano.
T. (02) 5465259. 058214
Maccaferri, Luigi, Via Caminadella 17, 20123 Milano.
T. (02) 72 00 01 18. 058215
Machine Age di Ciocca, Giuseppe e C., 27 Via Solferino,
20121 Milano. T. (02) 29006332. 058216
Magda, Via Domenico Cimarosa 5, 20154 Milano.
T. (02) 498 59 58. 058217
Magnetti, Via Manzoni 45, 20121 Milano.
T. (02) 33608826. 058218
Magnetti, Dr. Luigi, Via Principe Eugenio 6, 20155 Mila-
no. T. (02) 33608826. 058219
Mainetti, Ugo, Galleria Unione 3, 20122 Milano.
T. (02) 86 27 97. 058220
Mainieri, Via Bagutta 24, 20121 Milano.
T. (02) 78 39 74. 058221

Malang, Viale Bligny 13, 20136 Milano.
T. (02) 58 30 04 79. 058222
Malastrana Antica, Corso Garibaldi 104, 20121 Milano.
T. (02) 65 41 73. 058223
Maltinti, Bruno, Via Fratelli Brozetti 26, 20129 Milano.
T. (02) 74 92 580. 058224
Manusardi, Anna & Marina, Via Caminadella 13, 20123
Milano. T. (02) 87 88 36. 058225
Manzoni Architettura D'Interni, 20 Via Uberti, 20129 Mi-
lano. T. (02) 29510687. 058226
Marcopolo, Via Borromeo 10, 20123 Milano.
T. (02) 87 41 18. 058227
Mardkha, Abdorrahim, Via Capuccio 19, 20123 Milano.
T. (02) 86 45 31 69. 058228
Marelli, R., Via Venini 34, 20127 Milano.
T. (02) 26 14 50 85. 058229
Margiotta Liberfilo, Via Agnello 1, 20121 Milano.
T. (02) 8053197. 058230
Maria, Cristina, 14 Via Palermo, 20121 Milano.
T. (02) 29006216. 058231
Marino Affaitati, Giovanni, Via Ariberto 19, 20123 Mila-
no. T. (02) 832 11 92. - China - 058232
Mastromatteo F., 1 Via Pordenone, 20132 Milano.
T. (02) 2152405. 058233
Mazzi Milano, 1 Via Piazza Cossa, 20122 Milano.
T. (02) 76015377, 76015379. 058234
Mazzoleni Arte, 6 Via Morone, 20121 Milano.
T. (02) 76002650. 058235
Mazzoleni, Gianfranco, Via Monte Napoleone 22, 20121
Milano. T. (02) 78 03 48, 76 00 85 24,
Fax 76008524. - Jew / Eth / Silv - 058236
Mecozzi, Carlo, Via Roma 81, 20081 Milano.
T. (02) 9420131, Fax (02) 9420131. 058237
Medda G., 17 Via Madonnina, 20121 Milano.
T. (02) 862900, 86463718. 058238
Medio Arte, Via Albani 9, 20149 Milano.
T. (02) 48 00 49 45. 058239
Mediolanum, Via Montebello 240, 20121 Milano.
T. (02) 65 36 37. 058240
Meravigli Antiquariato, Via Meravigli, 20123 Milano.
T. (02) 8693875, Fax (02) 8056493. 058241
Meridiana, Via V. G. Orsini 8, 20147 Milano.
T. (02) 404 66 23. 058242
La Meta' del Cielo, Corso Piazetta Ticinese 83, 20143
Milano. T. (02) 8361325. 058243
Michail di David Sorgato & C., 18 Via Caminadella,
20123 Milano. T. (02) 86453592. 058244
Michail, Louise, Via S. Spirito 19, 20121 Milano.
T. (02) 76001064. 058245
Michel, Leo, Via Solferino 35, 20121 Milano.
T. (02) 659 83 33. 058246
Milano 15, 22 Via M.te Napoleone, 20123 Milano.
T. (02) 798798. 058247
Milanoro, 7 Piazza Sant Agostino, 20123 Milano.
T. (02) 89406047, 89406432, 8379115,
8321359. 058248
Mithos di Napoli Carmine, 13 Ripa Piazetta Ticinese,
20143 Milano. T. (02) 89400543. 058249
Modernariato Paganoni, G., Corso Vittorio Emanuele/ Via
S. Paolo 1, 20122 Milano. T. (02) 8690948,
Fax (02) 875972. 058250
Modo Antiquo di Fedrizzi, Cristina e Cinzia, 31 Via Cado-
re, 20135 Milano. T. (02) 55194776. 058251
Mondini, Carla, Via Fiori Chiari 8, 20121 Milano.
T. (02) 805 39 07, Fax (02) 8053907. - Ant - 058252
Monete D'Oro, Via del Bollo 7, 20123 Milano.
T. (02) 86455047, 86455048. 058253
La Moneteria di Pandolfi C. & C., Via Bassano Porrone 4,
20121 Milano. T. (02) 877889, 870633, 878505,
(0337) 330813, Fax (02) 870633, 878505. 058254
Montesi, M. G., Via Marsala 13, 20121 Milano.
T. (02) 29 00 20 57. 058255
Monteverde, L., Via S. Sofia 18, 20122 Milano.
T. (02) 58312906. 058256
Monti F., 24 Viale S. Michele del Carso, 20144 Milano.
T. (02) 48015100. 058257
Morli, Silvano, Via Cimarosa 5, 20144 Milano.
T. (02) 498456. 058258
Mornata N., 3 Corso Piazetta Ticinese, 20143 Milano.
T. (02) 8376473. 058259
Moroni S., 5 Via Bollo, 20123 Milano.
T. (02) 8051813. 058260

Moscatelli G., 20 Via G.B. Martini, 20131 Milano.
T. (02) 2892441. 058261
Motta, Luigi, Via S. Giovanni sul Muro 3, 20121 Milano.
T. (02) 87 86 51. 058262
Mottola, Via S. Marta 21, 20123 Milano.
T. (02) 8692922. 058263
Mozzoni, Carlo, Corso Monforte 15, 20122 Milano.
T. (02) 76023270. 058264
Musa, Via Pisacane 40, 20129 Milano. T. (02) 204 67 32,
Fax (02) 29524183. - Furn - 058265
N.A.K., 24 Via Bagutta, 20121 Milano. T. (02) 76002609,
76005948. 058266
Nava, Graziella, Via Rovello 18, 20121 Milano.
T. (02) 86 46 20 26. 058267
Nazarri, Laura, Via S. Calocero 31, 20123 Milano.
T. (02) 837 90 57. 058268
Nettori, A., Via Corsico 9, 20144 Milano.
T. (02) 832 38 93. 058269
New Light di Caltagirone e Agrusa, Via Fogazzaro 11,
20135 Milano. T. (02) 55015920. - Ant / Furn /
Dec – 058270
Nicholls, Via Alessandro Manzoni 41, 20121 Milano.
T. (02) 6575874. 058271
Nicotra D., 23 Via Caminadella, 20123 Milano.
T. (02) 72002624. 058272
Novecento, Via Donizetti 8, 20122 Milano.
T. (02) 55187767. 058273
Numismatica Investments, Via Mazzini, 20123 Milano.
T. (02) 8052161, 879893, 72023501, 875507,
Fax (02) 879384, 801149. 058274
Numismatica Milanese, Via Fontana 6, 20122 Milano.
T. (02) 55195418, Fax (02) 55195418. 058275
Numismatica Speronari, Via Speronari 7, 20123 Milano.
T. (02) 86463417. 058276
Numismatica Vigentina, Via Ripamonti 18, 20136 Mila-
no. T. (02) 5455730. 058277
La Nuova Compagnia delle Indie, Via Tiepolo 67, 20129
Milano. T. (049) 8071292, Fax (049) 8073600. 058278
Occhiuto, A., Ripa Porta Ticinese 13, 20143 Milano.
T. (02) 89401210. 058279
Oggetti Smarriti, 2 Via del Don, 20132 Milano.
T. (02) 58317263. 058280
Old Britannia, Piazzale Biancamano 2, 20129 Milano.
T. (02) 6552667. 058281
Old English Furniture, Via S. Simpliciano 6, 20121 Mila-
no. T. (02) 87 78 07. - Furn - 058282
Old London, Via Melzi d'Eril 3, 20154 Milano.
T. (02) 31 50 26. 058283
Old Russian di Castella, Antonio, Via Scarlatti 19, 20124
Milano. T. (02) 29 40 65 05, 29 40 83 53. 058284
Old Silver, Via Gesù 3, 20121 Milano.
T. (02) 794808. 058285
Old Store di Morzulli e Passeroni, 7 Via Petrarca, 20123
Milano. T. (02) 4815367. 058286
Old World, Via S. Giovanni sul Muro 6, 20121 Milano.
T. (02) 87 82 61. 058287
Orientart, Via Bazzini 23, 20131 Milano.
T. (02) 23 03 45. 058288
Orsi, Alessandro, Via Bagutta 14, 20121 Milano.
T. (02) 76002214. 058289
Orsolini, Via Lanzone 27, 20123 Milano.
T. (02) 72 01 07 35. 058290
Orvieto, Paolo, Piazzale Baracca 8, 20123 Milano.
T. (02) 498 99 46. 058291
Osservatorio Libri, 36 Via Palmieri, 20141 Milano.
T. (02) 89516015. 058292
Overseas Store, 3 Via Morone, 20121 Milano.
T. (02) 86464571. 058293
Palanzona, Paola Giorgia, Via Lupetta 2, 20123 Milano.
T. (02) 89 01 08 13. 058294
Palazzi Litta, Via Solari 23, 20144 Milano.
T. (02) 832 35 34. 058295
De Palo Studio D'Arte 56, Michele, Viale Monza 56,
20127 Milano. T. (02) 26823463, 26823457. 058296
Papa' del Lumi Rinnova – Crea – Sostituisce, Via V.
Monti 8, 20123 Milano. T. (02) 48013259. 058297
Papazian, Corso Garibaldi 117, 20121 Milano.
T. (02) 65 41 40. 058298
Pars, Corso Monforte 28, 20122 Milano.
T. (02) 700409. 058299
Patrassi, A., Via Solferino 27, 20121 Milano.
T. (02) 659 94 86. 058300

Pavesi, Arnaldo, Via G. d'Arezzo 17, 20123 Milano.
T. (02) 439 04 19. *058301*

Paviato, Gastone Franco, Via Borgospesso 22, 20121 Milano. T. (02) 76 00 58 25. *058302*

Pegaso Antichità, Via San Marco 18, 20121 Milano.
T. (02) 29 00 20 81. *058303*

Pelgoron, 22 Corso Matteotti, 20121 Milano.
T. (02) 76001591, 76002074. *058304*

Pennisi, Giovanni, Via Manzoni 29, 20121 Milano.
T. (02) 86 22 32. *058305*

Perotto, Via Gesù 17, 20121 Milano. T. (02) 76008338/ 76020527. *058306*

Persico, R., Via Cherubini 8, 20145 Milano.
T. (02) 481 83 98. *058307*

Persico R., 6 Via Cherubini, 20145 Milano.
T. (02) 4816228. *058308*

Pesapane, Giovanna, Via S. Maurillo 20, 20123 Milano.
T. (02) 80 46 90. *058309*

Phidias, Corso Venezia 18, 20121 Milano.
T. (02) 76014157/76020991. *058310*

Piantoni Antichita', 7 Via S. Tomaso, 20121 Milano.
T. (02) 879365. *058311*

Piatti, Nene, Via Francesco Sforza 14, 20122 Milano.
T. (02) 76 00 52 84. *058312*

Piccolo Mondo Antico, Via Bronzetti 6, 20129 Milano.
T. (02) 71 58 20. *058313*

Piccolo Mondo Antico di Signori Angelo, Villa Eugenia – Piazza di Legino 7, Milano. T. (019) 860947. *058314*

Pippa, Luigi, Via Durini 26, 20122 Milano.
T. (02) 79 42 97. - Instr - *058315*

Piva, Domenico, Via S. Andrea 1, 20121 Milano.
T. (02) 76 02 04 19, 76 00 06 78, Fax (02) 783440. *058316*

Piva, Francesco, Via S. Damiano 5, 20122 Milano.
T. (02) 76 00 02 36. *058317*

Plinio il Giovane, Via Borgonuovo 27, 20121 Milano.
T. (02) 869 09 04. *058318*

Podesta' P., 6 Via Turati, 20121 Milano.
T. (02) 6575995. *058319*

Pojaga, L., Via Scaldasole 1, 20123 Milano.
T. (02) 58 10 36 59. *058320*

Polenghi, Dario & Patrizia Maffeo, Via S. Marta 23, 20123 Milano. T. (02) 875032, Fax 72 02 23 58. - Ant / Paint - *058321*

Poliart, Via S. Marta 15, 20123 Milano.
T. (02) 86 45 09 92. *058322*

Il Ponte Casa D'Aste, Via Pontaccio 12, 20121 Milano.
T. (02) 72003749, Fax (02) 72022083. *058323*

Pontremoli, Via Montenapoleone 22, 20121 Milano.
T. (02) 76001394, 798456, 76001120, Fax 76014147.
- Furn / Orient / Tex / Dec / Rel - *058324*

Pontremoli s.r.l.

Via Montenapoleone 22
Via Borgospesso 17
20121 Milano – Italy

Tel. (02) 76001394 – 798456
76001120
Fax 76014147

Milan's Largest Antique Dealer

La Porta Giusta Antichita', Via S. Pellico 21, 20019 Milano. T. (02) 3281500. *058325*

Portobello, Corso Magenta 11, 20123 Milano.
T. (02) 87 02 54. *058326*

Pozzi, Giovanni, Via F. Sforza 49, 20122 Milano.
T. (02) 54 60 610. *058327*

Pozzi, Guido, Via Raffaello Sanzio 30, 20149 Milano.
T. (02) 498 69 89. *058328*

Pozzi, Ugo & Giorgio Fontana, Via Orso 14, 20121 Milano. T. (02) 58 58 56. *058329*

Premoli-Lorandi, Via C. Stazio 18, 20131 Milano.
T. (02) 26 14 59 28. *058330*

Preti, B., Via S. Marco 26, 20121 Milano.
T. (02) 6555388. *058331*

Provvisier di Trovarelli, Maria e C., 43 Corso XXII Marzo, 20129 Milano. T. (02) 7381134. *058332*

Provvisier di Trovarelli, Maria & C., 43 Corso XXII Marzo, 20129 Milano. T. (02) 70126640. *058333*

Psaculia, V., Via Scaldasole 3, 20123 Milano.
T. (02) 832 31 30. *058334*

Pulpito, Antonio, Via Felice Casati 2, 20124 Milano.
T. (02) 204 77 18. *058335*

Pulvirenti, C., Via Corridoni 4, 20122 Milano.
T. (02) 546 22 85. *058336*

Rachtian, Parviz, Via Bianca di Savoia 14, 20122 Milano.
T. (02) 583301021. *058337*

Radice A., 55 Via de Amicis, 20123 Milano.
T. (02) 58113277. *058338*

Radici Antiquari, Dr. Luigi & C. Ragici, Via S. Marta 19, 20123 Milano. T. (02) 86 45 09 48. *058339*

Raimondi, Corso Venezia, 6, 20121 Milano.
T. (02) 76002412, 76021422, Fax 76014489. *058340*

DITTA RAIMONDI

Casa fondata nel 1776

Stampe
Antiche e Moderne

CORSO VENEZIA, 6-MILANO
TEL.: 76002412 – 76021422
FAX 76014489

Raiti, G., Ripa Porta Ticinese 49, 20143 Milano.
T. (02) 837 92 70. *058341*

Raspa, G., Via Montegani 1, 20141 Milano.
T. (02) 89 50 05 63. *058342*

Ratto, Mario, Via Alessandro Manzoni 14, 20121 Milano.
T. (02) 799380. *058343*

Rebughini, R., Corso Porta Ticinese 83, 20123 Milano.
T. (02) 836 13 25. *058344*

Reggiani, Via Foppa 7, 20144 Milano.
T. (02) 46 38 21. *058345*

Renzo del Ventisette, Viale Premuda 7, 20129 Milano.
T. (02) 5401372, 5401062, Fax (02) 5470623. *058346*

Resi, G., Via Giulini 5, 20123 Milano.
T. (02) 80 44 08. *058347*

Ricco, Via S. Maria alla Porta 11, 20121 Milano.
T. (02) 87 59 56. *058348*

Ricco, E. & C., Via Senato 2, 20121 Milano.
T. (02) 76 00 39 53. *058349*

Ricetti, Augusta, Corso Genova 11, 20123 Milano.
T. (02) 837 99 60. *058350*

Rinaldi A., 13 Via Ceriani, 20153 Milano.
T. (02) 48916102. *058351*

Rinaudo, Nicola, Via G. G. Mora 9, 20123 Milano.
T. (02) 837 23 07. *058352*

Ripa Antica, Ripa di Porta Ticinese 27, 20143 Milano.
T. (02) 89 40 41 67. - Furn - *058353*

Rivière, James, Via Fiori Chiari 7, 20121 Milano.
T. (02) 80 62 86. *058354*

Roberta e Basta, Via Fiori Chairi 2, 20121 Milano.
T. (02) 861593, Fax (02) 86464519. *058355*

Roberto Martinoli, Acquisto Antichità, Via Calabiana 3, Milano. T. (02) 5692475, (0337) 344399. *058356*

Rodolfo IV, Via Pontaccio 17, 20121 Milano.
T. (02) 800363. - Jew / Cur / Mod - *058357*

Roncato M.C., 6 Via Piatti, 20123 Milano.
T. (02) 870289, 8055155. *058358*

Rossi, L., Corso Porta Vigentina 34, 20122 Milano.
T. (02) 58314046. *058359*

Rossini, Aldo, Corso Venezia 33, 20121 Milano.
T. (02) 76000194. *058360*

Rusconi Antichità, Via Fiori Chiari 26, 20121 Milano.
T. (02) 86 34 67. *058361*

Russkaja Gallereja, Via Ripa Ticinese 33, 20143 Milano.
T. (02) 89 40 16 40. - China / Tex / Silv / Ico - *058362*

Russo, Gianni, Via Cerva 16, 20122 Milano.
T. (02) 76 02 09 47. - Ant / Furn - *058363*

Russo, Toto, Corso Venezia 12, 20121 Milano.
T. (02) 79 67 32, 76 02 26 95. *058364*

Rustiquario, Via Terraggio 21, 20148 Milano.
T. (02) 86 45 21 77, Fax 86 50 87. *058365*

S. Maurilio Antichita' di Donatella Dottorini e C., 18 Via S. Maurilio, 20123 Milano. T. (02) 86462396. *058366*

Sabetelli, Franco, Via Fiori Chiari 5, 20121 Milano.
T. (02) 8052688. *058367*

Sacerdoti, Edmondo, Via S. Andrea 17, 20121 Milano.
T. (02) 79 51 51. *058368*

Saitz, F., Corso di Porta Romana 25, 20122 Milano.
T. (02) 58 30 75 24. *058369*

La Saletta di Evy Tomassini, 1 Via Bezzecca, Milano.
T. (02) 55185449. *058370*

Sammy, Via Dogana 3, 20123 Milano.
T. (02) 86 46 10 00. *058371*

Sampieri P., 71 Via M.te Ceneri, 20155 Milano.
T. (02) 39214374. *058372*

San, 10 Via Cenisio, 20154 Milano.
T. (02) 33609328. *058373*

San Maurilio, Via S. Maurilio 18, 20123 Milano.
T. (02) 86 46 23 96. *058374*

Sanesi, M., Via S. Fermodella Battaglia, 20121 Milano.
T. (02) 659 27 10. *058375*

Sani, J., Alzaia Naviglio Pavese 12, 20143 Milano.
T. (02) 835 77 75. *058376*

Sani, O., Ripa di Porta Ticinese 37, 20143 Milano.
T. (02) 836 06 45. *058377*

Santa Marta, Via S. Marta 23, 20123 Milano.
T. (02) 72 02 23 58. *058378*

Santa Sofia 18, Via S. Sofia 18, 20122 Milano.
T. (02) 87 79 80. - Furn - *058379*

Santabrogio, A., Corso C. Colombo 11, 20144 Milano.
T. (02) 89 40 06 73. *058380*

Santolin, Giustiniano, Via dei Bossi 8, 20121 Milano.
T. (02) 86 46 00 30. *058381*

Santoro, L., Via Serlio 11, 20139 Milano.
T. (02) 569 62 23. *058382*

Sapori P., 12 Via Manzoni, 20121 Milano.
T. (02) 76024101. *058383*

Sassone, F., Viale Monte Nero 29, 20135 Milano.
T. (02) 55 19 04 91. *058384*

Scarfone, M., Via Nino Bixio 37, 20129 Milano.
T. (02) 29514633/29513061. *058385*

Scarlatella, Via Codara, 20135 Milano.
T. (02) 58111278. *058386*

Schieppati, Corso G. Garibaldi 22, 20121 Milano.
T. (02) 86 46 16 67. *058387*

Il Segno del Tempo di Carboni, Piero Luigi & C., 6 Via Cagnola, 20154 Milano. T. (02) 316035. *058388*

Seniora Antichita' e Restauri, 20 Via S. Vincenzo, 20123 Milano. T. (02) 58104562. *058389*

Sevi, Daniele, Via Fiori Chiari 6, 20121 Milano.
T. (02) 876169. - Tex - *058390*

Signorini, A., Via Maiocchi 11, 20129 Milano.
T. (02) 29 40 19 08. *058391*

Silva, Gabriella, Via Sant'Andrea 8, 20121 Milano.
T. (02) 7950 64. *058392*

Silvestri C., 34a Via Pisacane, 20129 Milano.
T. (02) 29520145. *058393*

Silvestri, Carla, Via Borgospesso 5, 20121 Milano.
T. (02) 76 02 06 31. *058394*

Silvestri, Claudio, Via Borgonuovo 26, 20121 Milano.
T. (02) 659 29 09. *058395*

Societa' Numismatica Italiana, 3 Via Orti, 20122 Milano.
T. (02) 55194970. *058396*

Solzi, Franco, Via Giulio Romano 1, 20135 Milano.
T. (02) 58309017. *058397*

Sorgato, via Cerva 18, 20122 Milano.
T. (02) 78 43 23. *058398*

Spairani, S., Via Pantano 15, 20122 Milano.
T. (02) 58 30 40 94. *058399*

Speronari, 7 Via Speronari, 20123 Milano.
T. (02) 863607. *058400*

Spinella, Andrea, Via F Sforza 3, 20122 Milano.
T. (02) 551 29 94. *058401*

Spreafico, M. E., Via dal Re Marcantonio 2, 20156 Milano. T. (02) 33 00 17 60. *058402*

Stanza del Borgo, Via G. Puccini 5, 20121 Milano.
T. (02) 87 05 44, 86 53 92. *058403*

Storti G., 2 Piazza Cordusio, 20123 Milano.
T. (02) 86463785. *058404*

Studio D., 8 Via Stampa, 20123 Milano.
T. (02) 72022189. *058405*
Studio d'Arte Veronesi, Via de Amicis 47, 20123 Milano.
T. (02) 89 40 04 24. *058406*
Subert, Alberto, Viadella Spiga 22, 20121 Milano.
T. (02) 799594. *058407*
Subert, G., Via San Pietro all'Orto 26, 20121 Milano.
T. (02) 76 02 32 20. *058408*
Supino, G., Alzaira Naviglio Pavese 52, 20143 Milano.
T. (02) 835 83 59. *058409*
Swop Il Baratto, Via Alberti 12, 20149 Milano.
T. (02) 34 15 72. *058410*
Taccani, Florence, Via Turati 6, 20121 Milano.
T. (02) 655 40 25. *058411*
Tanzini, Luigi, Piazza Risorgimento 6, 20129 Milano.
T. (02) 79 45 93. *058412*
Tardo, Carlo, Via Turati 6, 20121 Milano.
T. (02) 659 93 05. - Ant / Silv / Mul - *058413*
Teardo, Carlo, Via Maggiolini 2, 20122 Milano.
T. (02) 76 02 13 56. *058414*
Tedeschi, G., Piazza Duomo 17, 20121 Milano.
T. (02) 86461809. *058415*
Tedeschi Numismatica, Piazza Duomo 17, 20121 Mila-
no. T. (02) 86461809. *058416*
Tema e Varianzioni, 13 Ripa Piazetta Ticinese, 20143
Milano. T. (02) 58100209. *058417*
Il Terrazzino di C. Olivares & C., 1 Via Bagutta, 20121
Milano. T. (02) 782420. *058418*
I Tesori di Brera, 6 Via S. Carpoforo, 20121 Milano.
T. (02) 72004740. *058419*
The Old America, Via Bagutta 9, 20121 Milano.
T. (02) 76006019/794691. *058420*
Titbits di F. Donagemma, 7 Via F.ili Gabba, 20121 Mila-
no. T. (02) 72022471. *058421*
Toffoletto, Laura, Via Guido d'Arezzo 1, 20145 Milano.
T. (02) 481 35 27. - Paint / Furn - *058422*
Tosi, A., Viale Monte Nero 73, 20135 Milano.
T. (02) 545 75 37. *058423*
Trani, S., Viale Monte Nero 63, 20135 Milano.
T. (02) 545 86 56. *058424*
Trinity Fine Art, 17 Via Olmetto, 20123 Milano.
T. (02) 72011805. *058425*
Turchet, Umberto, Via Andegari 18, 20121 Milano.
T. (02) 867112/86461374. *058426*
Tursellino, Dr. Ignazio, Via S. Maurillo 20, 20123 Milano.
T. (02) 890 00 47. *058427*
Vaduz Antichità, Ripa Porta Ticinese 21, 20143 Milano.
T. (02) 837 39 37. *058428*
Valcarenghi, Dario, Via Corridoni 6, 20122 Milano.
T. (02) 59901811. - Tex - *058429*
Valeria Bella Stampe, Via S. Cecilia 2, 20122 Milano.
T. (02) 76 00 44 13. - Graph - *058430*
Vantellini, Via Manzoni 30, 20151 Milano.
T. (02) 79 41 83. *058431*
Vantellini, Leonardo e Carlo, 44 Corso Venezia, 20121
Milano. T. (02) 76001695. *058432*
Vasoli, C. & F. Mascheretti, Via Eustachi 22, 20129 Mila-
no. T. (02) 29510297/29510299. *058433*
Venturini, C., Via Marghera 18, 20149 Milano.
T. (02) 48 00 46 21. *058434*
Vertemati A., 60 Via Venini, 20127 Milano.
T. (02) 2846037. *058435*
Vezzani, Giuseppina, Via Morone 6, 20121 Milano.
T. (02) 79 47 74. - Ant / Paint / Furn / Sculp - *058436*
Victory, Piazza Mentana 3, 20123 Milano.
T. (02) 86 45 25 82. *058437*
Vignati S., 16 Via Meravigli, 20123 Milano.
T. (02) 860158. *058438*
VIP Arkstudio, 13 Via S. Vincenzo, 20123 Milano.
T. (02) 8357278. *058439*
Vip 7, Ripa Porta Ticinese 7, 20143 Milano.
T. (02) 58101429/58106600. *058440*
Viscontea, 1 Piazza Santa M. Beltrade, 20123 Milano.
T. (02) 8900893. *058441*
Visconteum, Via Manzoni 12, 20121 Milano.
T. (02) 76 02 08 29. - Ant - *058442*
Wannenes, Giacomo, Via Bigli 21, 20121 Milano.
T. (02) 76 02 24 00. *058443*
Yes i do Arte ed Antiquariato di Giraldi Dr. Giancarlo, 2
Viale Gran Sasso, 20131 Milano.
T. (02) 29400748. *058444*
Zambon, Violetta, Ripa di Porta Ticinese 23-27, 20143
Milano. T. (02) 835 62 33. *058445*

Zannoni A., 5 Viale Cassiodoro, 20145 Milano.
T. (02) 4693908. *058446*
Zecchini, Napoleone, Via della Spiga 9, 20121 Milano.
T. (02) 76 00 40 49. *058447*
Zonco, C., Via Fiori Chiari 14, 20121 Milano.
T. (02) 805 26 26. *058448*

Mira Porte (Venezia)
Da Tos, Renzo, Villa Franceschi, 30030 Mira Porte.
T. (041) 42 02 80, 285 65. *058449*

Mirandola (Modena)
Il Vascello, Via C Battisti, 41037 Mirandola.
T. (0535) 205 27. *058450*
Malaguti, Silvano, Via Amendola 5, 41037 Mirandola.
T. (0535) 223 63. *058451*

Modena
Benzi, Vittorio, Via dello Zono 8, 41100 Modena.
T. (059) 21 66 73. *058452*
Bertacchi, Orfeo, Rua Frati 8, 41100 Modena.
T. (059) 21 76 00. *058453*
Bertarini, Aldo, Rua Muro 89, 41100 Modena.
T. (059) 21 78 78, 36 71 54. *058454*
Cantore, Corso Adriano 15/e, Rua Pioppa 37, 41100 Mo-
dena. T. (059) 24 32 09. - Furn - *058455*
Cattinari, Via Coltellini 16, 41100 Modena.
T. (059) 21 88 42. *058456*
Darsena, La, Piazza S Domenico 2, 41100 Modena.
T. (059) 21 99 42. *058457*
Della Casa, Pietro, Via Roccociolo 36, 41100 Modena.
T. (059) 35 11 84. *058458*
Diegoli, Franco, Via del Correggi 12, 41100 Modena.
T. (059) 68 60 15. *058459*
Fabbi, Miranda, Via Battisti 60/a, 41100 Modena.
T. (059) 21 73 62. - China - *058460*
Ferraresi, Via Stella 30, 41100 Modena.
T. (059) 21 66 19. *058461*
Franceschini, Luise Maria, Rua Frati Minori 28, 41100
Modena. T. (059) 24 31 22. *058462*
Franco, Bruno, Via Emilia Ovest 737, 41100 Modena.
T. (059) 33 81 74. *058463*
Gennaro, Domenico, Via Lanfranco 18, 41100 Modena.
T. (059) 23 53 46. *058464*
Magni, Savino, Via J Barozzi 130, 41100 Modena.
T. (059) 24 38 67. *058465*
Marchesi, Maria Luisa, Via Torre 51, 41100 Modena.
T. (059) 23 62 32. - Furn / China - *058466*
Maria Grazia, Corso Canal Grande 65, 41100 Modena.
T. (059) 22 53 51. *058467*
Martinelli, Graziella, Via Scarpa 8, 41100
Modena. *058468*
Muratori, Largo Garibaldi 38, 41100 Modena.
T. (059) 22 38 06. - Jew / Silv / Instr - *058469*
Piccinini, Franco, Via Gallucci 40, 41100 Modena.
T. (059) 23 90 53. *058470*
Pollastri, Bruno, Via Modonella 9, 41100 Modena.
T. (059) 23 72 69. *058471*
Portici, I, Via Buon Pastore 234, 41100 Modena.
T. (059) 39 12 16. - Paint / Furn - *058472*
Posta Vecchia, Via C Battisti 44, 41100 Modena.
T. (059) 22 52 45. *058473*
Riva, Maria Pia, Via Taglio 22, 41100 Modena.
T. (059) 21 45 30. *058474*
San Giorgio, Corso Canal Grande 86, 41100 Modena.
T. (059) 23 36 11. *058475*
Sereni, Luigi, Corso Adriano 54, 41100 Modena.
- Num - *058476*
Sinionazzi, Piazza della Torre 8, 41100 Modena.
T. (059) 58 51 50. *058477*
Sogliani, Guido, Via Giardini 704, 41100 Modena.
T. (059) 35 85 54, 35 11 50. *058478*
Surprise, Via Ganaceto 28, 41100 Modena.
T. (059) 23 74 53. *058479*

Moena (Trento)
Arte Design, Piazza Italia, 38035 Moena. *058480*

Mogliano Veneto (Treviso)
Toniolo, Narciso, Via De Gasperi 15, 31021 Mogliano Veneto. T. (041) 45 07 80. *058481*

Molfetta (Bari)
Calo, D., Via Aligheri 54A, 70056 Molfetta.
T. (080) 91 54 26. *058482*
Foglie, Michele delle, Piazza Vitt Emanuele 5, 70056
Molfetta. T. (080) 914014. *058483*

Molinella (Bologna)
Cose Vecchie e Antiche, Via Calzolari 40, 40062 Molinella. T. (051) 88 05 53. *058484*

Moncalieri (Torino)
Marotta, Strada Carpice 22, 10024 Moncalieri.
T. (011) 64 60 31, 64 61 65, 646 73 21,
Fax 646 71 93. *058485*
Migliore, Piazza Martiri d Libertà 14, 10024 Moncalieri.
T. (011) 64 45 04. *058486*
Vecchio Piemonte, Via Galileo Galilei 8, 10024 Monca-
lieri. T. (011) 64 46 17. *058487*

Mondovi (Cuneo)
Avico, Via Carassone 22, 12084 Mondovi.
T. (0174) 448 48. *058488*
Cigliero, Francesco, Via Annunziata 3, 12084 Mondovi.
T. (0174) 40771. *058489*
Comino, Via Sant'Agostino 19, 12084 Mondovi.
T. (0174) 423 35. *058490*

Monopoli (Bari)
Intini, Franco, Via Conchia 2, 70043 Monopoli.
T. (080) 77 70 52. *058491*

Monselice (Padova)
Canazza, Angelo, Via Colombo 20, 35043 Monselice.
T. (0429) 725 78. *058492*

Montagnana (Padova)
Cose del Passato, Borgo Eniano 25, 35044 Montagnana.
T. (0429) 822 55. *058493*
Il Torrione, Porta Vicenza, 35044 Montagnana.
T. (0429) 892 20. *058494*

Montalcino (Siena)
da Michelangelo, Via Matteotti 1, 53024 Montalcino.
T. (0577) 84 87 43. *058495*

Monte San Savino (Arezzo)
Fabiani, Via della Stazione 27, 52048 Monte San Savino.
T. (0575) 84 42 78. *058496*

Montebelluna (Treviso)
Minato, Danilo, Via Piave 57, 31044
Montebelluna. *058497*
Vignola, Carlo ALberto, Via Piave 57, 31044 Montebellu-
na. T. (0423) 211 91, 237 20. *058498*

Montecatini Terme e Tettuccio (Pistoia)
Bottega d'Arte Livorno, Piazza D'Azeglio 12, 51016
Montecatini Terme e Tettuccio.
T. (0572) 795 52. *058499*
Cose d'Altri Tempi, Corso Roma 17, 51016 Montecatini
Terme e Tettuccio. T. (0572) 717 89, 734 57. *058500*
Di Rosa-Bonaventura, Via San Martino 13, 51016 Mon-
tecatini Terme e Tettuccio. T. (0572) 720 87. *058501*
Il Quadrifoglio, Via Mazzini 11, 51016 Montecatini Terme
e Tettuccio. T. (0572) 783 77. *058502*
La Cupola, Piazza del Popolo 9, 51016 Montecatini Ter-
me e Tettuccio. T. (0572) 782 20. *058503*
Mazzoncini, Pietro, Via Ballerini 2, 51016 Montecatini
Terme e Tettuccio. T. (0572) 728 14. *058504*
Old England, Corso Roma 53, 51016 Montecatini Terme
e Tettuccio. T. (0572) 746 42. *058505*
Pitti, Corso Matteotti 57, 51016 Montecatini Terme e
Tettuccio. T. (0572) 76 68 93. - Furn / Tex - *058506*

Montecchio Emilia (Reggio Emilia)
Bezzi, Eligio, Via Reverberi 15, 42027 Montecchio Emi-
lia. T. (0522) 86 61 04. *058507*
Bolognesi, Rino, Strada S Polo 15, 42027 Montecchio
Emilia. T. (0522) 86 46 12. *058508*
Boni, Lucio, Via Franchini 92, 42027 Montecchio Emilia.
T. (0522) 86 43 53. *058509*
Cantarelli, Peppino, Via Franchini 1, 42027 Montecchio
Emilia. T. (0522) 86 45 25. *058510*
Medici, de, Piazza Cavour 3, 42027 Montecchio Emilia.
T. (0522) 86 45 70. *058511*

Poli, Galdino, Via Prampolini 20, 42027 Montecchio Emilia. T. (0522) 86 45 75. *058512*

Scalabrini, Marco, Via dei Mille 5, 42027 Montecchio Emilia. T. (0522) 86 44 88. *058513*

Scalabrini, Umberto, Via dei Mille 24, 42027 Montecchio Emilia. T. (0522) 86 44 88. *058514*

Montefiascone (Viterbo)
Venanzini, Carlo, Via Cassia 3, 01027 Montefiascone. T. (0761) 863 31. *058515*

Montepulciano (Siena)
Barccuci, Eros, Località San Pietro 17, 53045 Montepulciano. T. (0578) 77167. *058516*

Barcucci, Eros, Località S Pietro 17, 53045 Montepulciano. T. (0578) 771 67. *058517*

Galluzzi Azerbi, Via Roma 58, 53045 Montepulciano. T. (0578) 770 64. - Ant / Paint / Furn / Sculp / Arch - *058518*

Le Stanze del Poliziano, Palazzo del Poliziano 2, 53045 Montepulciano. T. (0578) 772 85. *058519*

Rossi, Franco, Via delle Terme 36, 53045 Montepulciano. T. (0578) 790 13. *058520*

Monterotondo (Roma)
Natangelo, Via Marsala 34, 00015 Monterotondo. T. (06) 900 19 06. *058521*

Montespertoli (Firenze)
Antichità Stilmobil, Via Taddeini 295, 50025 Montespertoli. T. (0571) 60 80 95, 60 84 06. *058522*

Montevarchi (Arezzo)
Farolfi, Tosca, Via Diaz 97, 52025 Montevarchi. T. (055) 98 06 14. *058523*

Montevideo
Bergamaschi, Maria Teresa, Via Passerini 9, 20052 Montevideo. T. (02) 231 42. *058524*

Montichiari (Brescia)
L'Arcolaio, Viale Europa 2, 25018 Montichiari. T. (030) 96 17 58. *058525*

La Fonte, Via Mantova 189, 25018 Montichiari. T. (030) 96 20 93. *058526*

Mose, Via T Speri 30, 25018 Montichiari. T. (030) 96 10 57. *058527*

Montone (Perugia)
Galleria Antiquaria L'Angelo, Corso Garibaldi 17, 06014 Montone. T. (075) 93 06 205, 93 06 200. *058528*

Montone (Teramo)
Antiques, Via Fonte Alessio 9, 64020 Montone. T. 864 81 71. *058529*

Montorio Veronese (Treviso)
Il Tridente, Via Olivè 40, 37033 Montorio Veronese. T. (045) 55 72 64. *058530*

Monza (Milano)
Bergamaschi, Maria Teresa, Via Passerini 8, 20052 Monza. T. (039) 32 31 42. - Furn / Jew / Silv - *058532*

Bergomi, Eugenio, Via Carlo Alberto 34, 20052 Monza. T. (039) 32 23 80. - Ant - *058533*

Il Carrobiolo, Via Carlo Alberto 31, 20052 Monza. T. (039) 32 18 63. *058534*

La Fila, Via Manzoni 1, 20052 Monza. T. (039) 36 52 03. *058535*

Fiordi Biondi, Viale Lombardia 127, 20052 Monza. T. (039) 745114. *058535a*

Lanesi, Arnaldo, Via dei Mille 4, 20052 Monza. T. (039) 213 29. *058536*

Le Pleiadi, Via Vittorio Emanuele 20, 20052 Monza. T. (039) 263 62, 757 39. *058537*

Montrasio Arte, Via Cortelonga, 20052 Monza. T. (039) 217 70. *058538*

Portobello Cose Vecchie, Via S Paolo 4, 20052 Monza. T. (039) 235 80, 46 52 64. *058539*

Muggia (Trieste)
La Soffitta, Calle Verdi 3, 34015 Muggia. T. (040) 27 30 98. *058540*

Muggiò (Milano)
Naboni Amadio, Guiseppina, Via Abba 5, 20053 Muggiò. T. (039) 79 16 32. *058541*

Napoli
A.B.F., Viale Kennedy 333, 80125 Napoli. T. (081) 760 81 94. *058542*

Affaitati, Antonio, Via S. Maria di Constant. 18, 80138 Napoli. T. (081) 34 96 22. - Ant - *058543*

Affaitati, Cesare, Via Michele Morelli 45, 80121 Napoli. T. (081) 40 75 29. *058544*

Angeli, de, Via D Morelli 26, 80121 Napoli. T. (081) 40 68 84. *058545*

Arca, L', Via Chiatamone 53, 80121 Napoli. T. (081) 42 23 01. - Ant - *058546*

Arte e Cose Antice, Piazza dei Martiri 28, 80121 Napoli. T. (081) 40 05 46. *058547*

Ascierto, Rubens & I. Ferdinando, Via D, Morelli 6, 80121 Napoli. T. (081) 40 53 72. *058548*

Ascione, Nicola, Via E Toti 10, 80134 Napoli. T. (081) 32 34 14. *058549*

Avant'Art, Via S Maria a Cappella 10, 80121 Napoli. T. (081) 41 20 34. *058550*

Bianchi d'Espinosa, Via dei Mille 16, 80121 Napoli. T. (081) 41 45 01. - Paint - *058551*

Bottega della Nonna, La, Via Foria 240, 80139 Napoli. T. (081) 29 77 72. *058552*

Bowinkel, Uberto, Via S. Lucia 25, 80132 Napoli. T. (081) 41 77 39. - Graph / Repr / Fra / Cur / Pho - *058553*

Brandi, Gennaro, Via Domenico Morelli 9-11, 80121 Napoli. T. (081) 42 15 81. - Ant - *058554*

British Trade, Via Domenico Morelli 39, 80121 Napoli. T. (081) 40 00 11. - Ant / Graph / Furn / Dec / Silv / Lights / Glass / Cur / Mod - *058555*

Bugli, Francesco, Via S. Maria di Constant. 34, 80138 Napoli. T. (081) 34 83 26. - Ant - *058556*

Caiafa, Via G Arcoleo 57 e Via del Poggio 50-54, 80121 Napoli. T. (081) 743 59 94. *058557*

Capace, Renato, Via C Poerio 41, 80121 Napoli. T. (081) 42 20 80. *058558*

Capuano, Emanuele, Via SMaria di Costant52, 80138 Napoli. T. (081) 45 98 41. *058559*

Carbone, Via Domenico Morelli 33, 80121 Napoli. T. (081) 40 79 77. - Ant - *058560*

Carignani, Mario, Via Carducci 2, 80121 Napoli. T. (081) 41 56 71. *058561*

Casella, Via Carlo Poerio 92, 80121 Napoli. T. (081) 764 26 27. - Ant / Graph - *058562*

Caso, P.zza S. Domenico Maggiore 16, 80134 Napoli. T. (081) 551 67 33, Fax 522 01 08. - Furn / Jew - *058563*

Cocchia, Eugenio, Largo Sant'Orsola a Ch3, 80121 Napoli. T. (081) 41 12 66, 68 20 70. *058564*

Compra Tutto, Via Salvator Rosa 54, 80135 Napoli. T. (081) 21 32 22. *058565*

Corcione, G., Piazza Bernini 117, 80129 Napoli. T. (081) 36 43 34. *058566*

Corte, Ileana della, Via Santa Lucia 65, 80132 Napoli. T. (081) 42 11 93. - Jew - *058567*

Cucchiarone, Pasquale, Via S Maria di Const46, 80138 Napoli. T. (081) 45 25 83. *058568*

D'Amodio, Antimo, Via SMaria a CappVe14, 80121 Napoli. T. (081) 41 55 79. *058569*

D'Amodio, Antimo, Via Domenico Morelli 20, 80121 Napoli. T. (081) 764 34 74. *058570*

D'Angelo, Mario, Via Bisignano 11, 80121 Napoli. T. (081) 42 64 14. *058571*

Decina Giovanni Giulio, Vico Ischitella 1, 80121 Napoli. T. (081) 764 22 42. *058572*

Dello Ioio, Carmine, Via Domenico Morelli 8, 80121 Napoli. T. (081) 41 60 46. *058573*

Dello Ioio, dott. Guiseppe, Riviera di Chiaia 213/14, 80121 Napoli. T. (081) 41 85 02. - Paint / Furn - *058574*

Domus, Via dei Mille 1, 80121 Napoli. T. (081) 40 48 09. - Ant / Furn / Tex - *058575*

Falanga, Giuseppe, Via D Morelli 6, 80121 Napoli. T. (081) 41 81 57. *058576*

Falco, Giuseppe de, Corso Umberto I 24, 80138 Napoli. T. (081) 20 62 66. - Num - *058577*

Fasano, Attilio, Via D Morelli 73, 80121 Napoli. T. (081) 41 85 44. *058578*

Fiorillo, Elio, Via C. Battisti 9, 80134 Napoli. T. (081) 32 49 87. - Furn - *058579*

Galleria Florida, Via Domenico Morelli 13, 80121 Napoli. T. (081) 41 64 00. - Ant - *058580*

Gallotta, Via Chiaia 139, 80121 Napoli. T. (081) 42 11 64. - Jew - *058581*

Giglio, Giuseppe, & Figli, Via Carlo Poerio 46, 80121 Napoli. T. (081) 40 09 43. - China - *058582*

Giuffrida, Italo, Via Chiaia 41, 80121 Napoli. T. (081) 41 79 84. - Num - *058583*

Iavarone, Tommaso, Via G Arcoleo 8-10, 80121 Napoli. T. (081) 40 58 62. *058584*

Iermano, Salvatore, Via S Maria a Cap Vecch 44, 80121 Napoli. T. (081) 40 31 22. *058585*

Il Noce di Silvana Casolaro, Via S Rosa 326, 80147 Napoli. T. (081) 21 17 12. *058586*

Improta, Via C. Poerio 24, 80121 Napoli. T. (081) 42 75 75. - Furn - *058587*

L'Ottocento, Via D. Morelli 28, 80121 Napoli. T. (081) 41 63 16. - Paint / Furn - *058588*

Maison d'Art, Pzza dei Martiri a Cappella Vecchia 18, 80121 Napoli. T. (081) 40 27 44. *058589*

Manfredonia, Via S Maria a Capp Vecc 18, 80121 Napoli. T. (081) 40 27 44. *058590*

Mantovano, Piazza dei Martiri 58, 80121 Napoli. T. (081) 41 80 03, Fax 41 68 16. - Jew - *058591*

Martucci, Raffaele, Riviera di Chiaia 119, 80121 Napoli. T. (081) 68 54 09. - Furn - *058592*

Morelli, Via Domenico Morelli 43, 80121 Napoli. T. (081) 764 44 81. *058593*

Napoli Nobilissima, Piazza Vittoria 6, 80121 Napoli. T. (081) 41 19 76. *058594*

Natale, Luigi, Via Cappella Vecchia 31, 80121 Napoli. T. (081) 42 58 22. *058595*

Navarra, Piazza dei Martiri 23, 80121 Napoli. T. (081) 41 70 03. - Ant - *058596*

Pagliuca, Stefano, Via Chiatamone 56, 80121 Napoli. T. (081) 42 61 41. *058597*

Palmieri, Alfeo, Vico Ischitella 7, 80121 Napoli. T. (081) 764 17 16. *058598*

Paragona, Massimo, Vico Ischitella 2, 80121 Napoli. T. (081) 41 26 26. *058599*

Pecorella, Luigi, P.zza San Pasquale 17-19, 80121 Napoli. T. (081) 42 69 10. - Furn - *058600*

Persepolis, Piazza dei Martiri 23/d, 80121 Napoli. T. (081) 764 38 24. - Tex - *058601*

Portico, Il, Via Domenico Morreli 39, 80121 Napoli. T. (081) 40 00 11. - Furn - *058602*

Rapuano, Salvatore, Via Sapienza 12, 80138 Napoli. T. (081) 46 38 20. *058603*

Ravel, E.J., Via Toledo 205, 80134 Napoli. T. (081) 40 37 21. *058604*

Razzano, Via V Gaetani 8, 80121 Napoli. T. (081) 42 15 14. *058605*

Regency House, Via D Morelli 36, 80121 Napoli. T. (081) 41 70 25. *058606*

Regency House, Via Michelangelo 11 e Via Monteoliveto 36, 80129 Napoli. T. (081) 36 65 04, 32 42 46. - Furn / Silv - *058607*

Rigattiere, Le, Via C Poerio 109, 80121 Napoli. T. (081) 764 24 88. *058608*

Rojo, Francesco, Supportico Fondo di Separazione 3, 80121 Napoli. T. (081) 351 40 04. *058609*

Rojo, Renato, Via S Maria di Const 20, 80138 Napoli. T. (081) 34 32 47. *058610*

Ruocco, Gabriele, Via G. Arcoleo 35, 80121 Napoli. T. (081) 42 65 71, 764 40 17. - Paint / Furn / China / Fra - *058611*

Scippa, Raffaele, Via V. Gaetani 20/21, 80121 Napoli. T. (081) 40 05 43. - Furn - *058612*

Scrigno, Lo, Via Cilea 132, 80127 Napoli. T. (081) 64 99 54. - Jew - *058613*

Sebastiano 36, Via Sant Anna dei Lombardi 58-59, 80134 Napoli. T. (081) 32 72 81. - Furn - *058614*

Serrao, Andrea, Via San Gennaro ad Antignano 108, 80128 Napoli. T. (081) 37 33 50. *058615*

Sessantasei, Via Bisignano 58, 80121 Napoli. T. (081) 41 13 90. *058616*

Siniscalco, Maurizio, Via C Poerio 116, 80121 Napoli. T. (081) 40 09 83. *058617*

Studio d'Arte Antica, Vico Ischitella 1, 80121 Napoli. T. (081) 40 33 65. *058618*

Surcontre, Corso V Emanuele 46 e Via Posillipo 317, 80121 Napoli. T. (081) 66 09 21, 575 04 04.　058619
Trade Antiques, Via Martucci 35/a, 80147 Napoli.
T. (081) 66 94 15.　058620

Narni (Terni)
Petracchini, Via Roma 17, 05035 Narni.
T. (0744) 72 60 84.　058621

Nerviano (Milano)
Bernasconi Romigioli, Corso Sempione 29, 20014 Nerviano. T. (0331) 58 76 06.　058622

Nizza Monferrato (Asti)
Onesti, Carlo, Via Lanero 21, 14049 Nizza Monferrato.
T. (0141) 72 61 46.　058623

Noceta (Parma)
Angilella, Via Emilia Ovest 5, 43015 Noceta.
T. (0521) 613 81.　058624
Le Due Torri, Via Centolance, 43015 Noceta.
T. (0521) 621 81.　058625
Tomasi, Giovanna, Via Matteotti 60, 43015 Noceta.
T. (0521) 621 81.　058626

Nogara (Verona)
Berardo, Adriano, Via G di Vittorio 7, 37054 Nogara.
T. (0442) 887 30.　058627

None (Torino)
Portobello, Strada Statale 23, 10060 None.
T. (011) 98 65 584.　058628

Norcia (Perugia)
Regoli, A., Corso Sertorio 23, 06046 Norcia.
T. (0743) 81 66 75, 81 64 40.　058629

Novara
Baldini, Renzo, Via Porta 16, 28100 Novara.
T. (0321) 21715. - Paint -　058630
Cancello, Corso Cavour 11, 28100 Novara.
T. (0321) 313 08.　058631
Conte Annelise, Via XX Settembre 12, 28100 Novara.
T. (0321) 39 10 98.　058632
Cose Vecchie Della Nonna, Corso della Vittoria 67, 28100 Novara. T. (0321) 47 28 00.　058633
Folk-Art, Via Omar 18, 28100 Novara.
T. (0321) 39 23 64.　058634
Galli, Michele, via dei Caccia 5, 28100 Novara.
T. (0321) 23 026. - Ant -　058635
Pozzi, Via C Perazzi 2, 28100 Novara.
T. (0321) 223 85.　058636
Urbano Quinto e Figlio, Via D Bello 9/A, 28100 Novara.
T. (0321) 233 13.　058637

Novi Ligure (Alessandria)
Antiquaria, Via Roma 90, 15067 Novi Ligure.
T. (0143) 25 79.　058638
Bagnasco, Giulio, Strada Serravalle 42, 15067 Novi Ligure. T. (0143) 74 17 82.　058639

Numana e Lido (Ancona)
La Muffa, Via Roma 8, 60026 Numana e Lido.
T. (071) 93 60 59.　058640

Oggiono (Como)
Milani, Mario, Via Lazzaretto 58, 22048 Oggiono.
T. (0341) 57 72 51.　058641

Olgiate Comasco (Como)
Amarcord, Via San Gerardo 40, 22077 Olgiate Comasco.
T. (031) 94 66 33, 98 65 589.　058642

Orbetello (Grosseto)
Vascello, Il, Via Mazzini 12, 58015 Orbetello.
T. (0564) 86 79 84.　058643

Oria (Brindisi)
Timurian, Via Asmara 3, 72024 Oria. T. (0831) 94 72 95, 94 51 97.　058644

Orio Litta (Milano)
Littantiqua, Palazzo Litta, 20080 Orio Litta.
T. (0377) 867 77. - Furn -　058645

Orvieto (Terni)
Antichità Soliana, Via Soliana 10, 05018 Orvieto.
T. (0763) 322 75.　058646
Botteguccia, La, Piazza Duomo 4, 05018 Orvieto.
T. (0763) 332 91.　058647
Cannucciari, Strada Amerina 65, 05018 Orvieto.
T. (0763) 780 25.　058648
Cavour, Corso Cavour 19, 05018 Orvieto.
T. (0763) 321 06.　058649
Mencarelli, Marcello, Corso Cavour 127, 05018 Orvieto.
T. (0763) 351 69.　058650
Riccardi, Via Duomo 33, 05018 Orvieto.
T. (0763) 330 74.　058651
Tomaccini, P.zza Duomo 4, 05018 Orvieto.
T. (0763) 42171. - Jew -　058652

Ospedaletti (Imperia)
A.R.S. Ars Arte Antica, corso Marconi 10, 18014 Ospedaletti. T. (0184) 896 40.　058653
Il Tarlo, Corso Regina Margherita 176, 18014 Ospedaletti. T. (0184) 589 62.　058654
Zora, Via Cavour 40, 18014 Ospedaletti.
T. (0184) 589 32, 602 6.　058655

Ostiglia (Mantova)
Gavioli, Nadia, Via Brennero 71, 46035 Ostiglia.
T. (0386) 24 13.　058656

Ostuni (Brindisi)
Bagnulo, Santo Felice, Via Cattedrale 41, 72017 Ostuni.
T. (0831) 97 36 32.　058657

Oulx (Torino)
Pozzallo, Flavio, Via Monginevro 73, 10056 Oulx.
T. (0122) 83 13 14.　058658

Ozzano Taro (Parma)
Berziga, Anna Maria, Via Nazionale 66, 43046 Ozzano Taro. T. (0521) 80 91 87.　058659

Paderno Dugnano (Milano)
Borhi, Pietro, Via G Casati 65, 20037 Paderno Dugnano.
T. (02) 91 87 595.　058660

Padova (Belluno)
Antiquarlo Gemmologo, Via Davila 6, 35137 Padova.
T. (049) 66 41 95. - Jew / Fra / Silv / Mod / Ico -　058661
Baggio, Franco, Rivera Mugnai 8, 35100 Padova.
T. (049) 65 85 03.　058662
Berto, Alessandro, Via Soncin 21, 35100 Padova.
T. (049) 62 01 47.　058663
Bianca Maria, via Roma 39A, 35100 Padova.
T. (049) 251 00. - Ant / Furn / Num / Tex -　058664
Bordin, corso Umberto I. 10, 35100 Padova.
T. (049) 361 30. - Ant / Paint / Paint / Furn / China / Sculp -　058665
Bric a Brac, Via Sant'Andrea 13, 35100 Padova.
T. (049) 248 73.　058666
Broggiato, Giancarlo, Strada Battaglia 87 -Albignasego, 35 100 Padova. T. (049) 69 0 11.　058667
Bucceri, Piazza dei Signori 5, 35100 Padova.
T. (049) 875 06 41. - Furn / Silv / Ico -　058668
Buzzanca, Giampaolo, via S. Andrea 5, 35100 Padova.
T. (049) 65 18 31. - Repr -　058669
Cesaro, Giorgio, Corso Vittorio Emanuele 106, 35100 Padova. T. (049) 68 11 68.　058670
Cesaro, Romano, Riviera Paleocapa 2/a, 35100 Padova.
T. (049) 30175.　058671
Copercini, Giuseppin, Via San Francesco 34, 35100 Padova. T. (049) 66 02 19.　058672
Croce d'Oro, Via C Battisti 97, 35100 Padova.
T. (049) 353 39.　058673
Da Rin, Maria Luisa, Via Cesare Battisti 34, 35100 Padova. T. (049) 361 73.　058674
Galleria dell'Antico, Via San Francesco 65, 35100 Padova. T. (049) 202 93.　058675
Gallimberti Carosio, Via Roma 103, 35100 Padova.
T. (049) 34716. - Furn -　058676
Gorenc, Corso del Popolo 16, 35100 Padova.
T. (049) 380 41. - Ant / Paint / Furn / China / Sculp / Fra / Glass / Draw -　058677
Govetosa Boranga, Via Altinate 76, 35100 Padova.
T. (049) 657948.　058678
Il Cavallino, Via Cesare Battisti 114, 35100 Padova.
T. (049) 66 20 09, 262 51.　058679

Lucio, Via Umberto I 53, 35100 Padova.
T. (049) 329 49.　058680
Marzi, de, Galleria Duomo 8, 35100 Padova.
T. (049) 446 38.　058681
Matteis Cappuzzo, Via Altinate 77, 35100 Padova.
T. (049) 39474. - Orient -　058682
Nogarotto, Via Galileo Galilei 5, 35100 Padova.
T. (049) 457 64.　058683
Ragazzi, Pietro, Via della Valle 2, 35100 Padova.
T. (049) 39825. - Furn -　058684
Schiavinato, Pier Paolo, Via S Francesco 192, 35100 Padova. T. (049) 66 14 20.　058685
Schiavinato, Pierpaolo, Via San Francesco 192, 35100 Padova. T. (049) 66 14 20, 51 00 73.　058686
Silva, Tullio, Via dei Fabbri 36, 35122 Padova.
T. (049) 39826.　058687
Teheran Carpets, Via Roma 33, 35100 Padova.
T. (049) 65 59 29.　058688
Vanotti, Gino, Piazza delle Erbe 12, 35100 Padova.
T. (049) 228 17.　058689

Paina (Milano)
Brenna, Ambrogio, Via Maddalena 2, 20030 Paina.
T. (0362) 23 81 56.　058690

Palermo (Sicilia)
Abanti'Cu, Via P Paternostro 86, 90141 Palermo.
T. (091) 58 60 32.　058691
Al Bastione, Corso Alberto Amedeo 116, 90138 Palermo.
T. (091) 32 87 75, 32 21 92.　058692
Al Firriato di Villafranca, Via Principe di Villafranca 42, 90141 Palermo. T. (091) 33 20 33, 54 93 03.　058693
Al Sansovino, Via Liberta 129, 90143 Palermo.
T. (091) 29 69 38.　058694
Altamura, Via Liberta 102/A, 90145 Palermo.
T. (091) 625 16 90. - Paint / Furn / China -　058695
Antichita e Liberty, Viy XII Gennaio 1, 90139 Palermo.
T. (091) 32 25 03.　058696
Antiqua Domus, Via Wagner 11/b, 90139 Palermo.
T. (091) 611 07 77. - Furn / China -　058697
Antiquity, Via XX Settembre 17, 90139 Palermo.
T. (091) 33 26 06.　058698
Armonia della Casa, Via Parisio 46, 90145 Palermo.
T. (091) 56 11 65.　058699
Astrel, Via Piersanti Mattarella 22, 90145 Palermo.
T. (091) 29 12 18.　058700
Athena, Corso Alberto Amedeo 184, 90138 Palermo.
T. (091) 58 97 86.　058701
Bartorelli, Egidio, Via R. Wagner 11/r, 90139 Palermo.
T. (091) 32 38 23. - Paint / Furn -　058702
Boscia, Corso Alberto Amedeo 122, 90138 Palermo.
T. (091) 33 28 37.　058703
Burgio, Emanuele, Via Villareale 21, 90138 Palermo.
T. (091) 32 53 95.　058704
Burgio, Giuseppe, Corso Alberto Amedeo 212, 90138 Palermo. T. (091) 58 33 07. - Ant -　058705
Casa delle Aste e delle Esposizioni, Via Mariano Stabile 172, 90139 Palermo. T. (091) 58 22 48, 32 95 82.　058706
Conti, Via Roma 420, 90139 Palermo. T. (091) 32 35 60. - Num -　058707
Corimbo, Via Pr. di Belmonte 96-98-100, 90139 Palermo. T. (091) 58 94 26. - Paint / Furn / China -　058708
Daneu, Corso Vittorio Emanuele 452, 90134 Palermo.
T. (091) 23 05 29. - Ant / Eth -　058709
Fecarotta, Via Principe di Belmonte 103, 90139 Palermo. T. (091) 33 15 18. - Ant / Paint / Furn / Jew / Silv / Rel -　058710
Fieravecchia, Via N. Garzilli 73, 90141 Palermo.
- Furn -　058711
Gl.Bl., Corso Alberto Amedeo 54, 90138 Palermo.
T. (091) 32 98 58, 33 12 32.　058712
Governale, Antonello, Corso Alberto Amedeo 60, 90138 Palermo. T. (091) 321977. - Ant / Paint / Furn / China -　058713
Governale, Patella Donatello, Via E. Parisi 36, 90141 Palermo. T. (091) 58 49 98. - Paint / Silv -　058714
Hera, Via Liberta 3, 90139 Palermo. T. (091) 58 48 76, 32 98 81.　058715
Il Caminetto, Via Pipitone Federico 97, 90144 Palermo.
T. (091) 26 65 64.　058716
Il Perseo, Via Principe di Paterno 4, 90144 Palermo.
T. (091) 29 85 84.　058717

L'Oro dei Farlocchi, Via Florestano Pepe 12, 90139 Palermo. T. (091) 32 54 57. - Furn - 058718
La Medusa, Piazza Unita d'Italia 3, 90144 Palermo.
T. (091) 26 03 61. 058719
La Portantina, Via Liberta 42, 90141 Palermo.
T. (091) 29 80 93, 32 85 24. 058720
Le Blason, Via Petraca 19, 90144 Palermo.
T. (091) 25 13 12. 058721
Loga, Via Abela 7, 90141 Palermo.
T. (091) 32 89 92. 058722
Mercante, Il, Via N Garzilli 77, 90141 Palermo.
T. (091) 30 01 89. 058723
Migliore, Pzza G Amendola 6, 90141 Palermo.
T. (091) 33 41 94. 058724
Migliore, Via Paolo Paternostro 39, 90141 Palermo.
T. (091) 58 42 64. 058725
Migliore, Piazza G. Amendola 6, 90141 Palermo.
T. (091) 33 41 94. - Num - 058726
Oggi, Spazio, Via Torrearsa 11, 90139 Palermo.
T. (091) 58 54 03. 058727
Old England, Via Arimondi 2, 90143 Palermo.
T. (091) 25 13 54, 25 36 30. 058728
Paladino Barone, Anna, Via Mariano Stabile 141, 90139 Palermo. T. (091) 58 43 83, 20 23 69. - Ant / China / Silv - 058729
Patella, Corso Vitt. Emanuele 474, 90134 Palermo.
T. (091) 28 36 60. - Paint / Furn / China - 058730
Perfetto, Randisi, Corso Alberto Amedeo 112, 90138 Palermo. T. (091) 32 18 74, 33 44 25. 058731
Sacco, Francesco, Via Pepe 15, 90139 Palermo.
T. (091) 33 37 70. 058732
Toluian, Via della Liberta 31, 90139 Palermo.
T. (091) 32 33 13, 58 66 29. 058733
Torta, Giulio, Via I. Carini 34, 90138 Palermo.
T. (091) 32 34 61. - Paint / Jew / Silv - 058734
Trionfante, Via Altofonte 80, 90129 Palermo.
T. (091) 59 98 37, 42 32 58, Fax 59 68 35. 058735
Zucchetto, Via Cavour 65, 90100 Palermo.
T. (091) 243062. - Num - 058736

Panicale (Perugia)

Il Vecchia Convento, Loc Poggio di Braccio, 06064 Panicale. T. (075) 83 62 20. 058737

Parma

A Galleria, Vicolo Assistenza 6, 43100 Parma.
T. (0521) 399 13. 058738
Adorni, Via XX Settembre 47, 43100 Parma.
T. (0521) 982 31. 058739
Alexanian, Via Emilia Est 140, 43100 Parma.
T. (0521) 423 70. 058740
Amadei, Ezio, Borgo del Correggio 34, 43100 Parma.
T. (0521) 365 60. 058741
Angelo d'Oro, B. Onorato 4, 43100 Parma.
T. (0521) 3 37 45. - Ant / Paint / Graph / China / Arch / Mod - 058742
Antiquaria Arte, Borgo Riccio da Parma 43, 43100 Parma. T. (0521) 28 60 30. - Paint / Furn / China / Sculp - 058743
Au Temps Jadis, Via San Silvestro 20, 43100 Parma.
T. (0521) 30160. 058744
Ballotta, Alcide, Via A Braga 23, 43100 Parma.
T. (0521) 569 20. 058745
Baroni, Donatella, Borgo Antini 7, 43100 Parma.
T. (0521) 340 94. 058746
Baroni, Luigi, Via Emilia Ovest 139, 43100 Parma.
T. (0521) 99 81 20. 058747
Bertogalli, Borgo A Mazza 2, 43100 Parma.
T. (0521) 293 92. 058748
Bocchia, Ettore, Viale Campanini 2, 43100 Parma.
T. (0521) 943 78. 058749
Borgobello, Borgo Montasuù 3, 43100 Parma.
T. (0521) 367 38. 058750
Brigenti, Giuseppe, Via La Spezia 179, 43100 Parma.
T. (0521) 96076. - Paint / Furn - 058751
Canasi, Ugo, Borgo Parmigianino 29, 43100 Parma.
T. (0521) 349 88. 058752
Cantoni, Angela, Via A. Mazza 2/d, 43100 Parma.
T. (0521) 28 29 21. - Furn / Jew - 058753
Chippendale, Piazzale Cervi 7, 43100 Parma.
T. (0521) 358 50. 058754

Consigli, Borgo Longhi 4, 43100 Parma.
T. (0521) 333 10. - Ant / Paint / China / Sculp / Instr / Cur / Mod / Draw - 058755
Consigli, Bruno, Borgo Antini 3, 43100 Parma.
T. (0521) 336 60. 058756
Esposito, Mauro, Via Emilia Est 142, 43100 Parma.
T. (0521) 49 42 98. 058757
Esposito, Mauro, Via Bodoni 1, 43100 Parma.
T. (0521) 398 35. 058758
Faldistorio, Il, Via XXII Luglio 27, 43100 Parma.
T. (0521) 35784. - Jew / Silv - 058759
Felisi, Sergio, Borgo Regale 1, 43100 Parma. 058760
Ferraglia, Fabio, Via XXII Luglio 19, 43100 Parma.
T. (0521) 388 02. 058761
Galleria arti visive, Via Bruno Longhi 6, 43100 Parma.
T. (0521) 28 26 87. 058762
Gazebo, Borgo G Tommasini 3, 43100 Parma.
T. (0521) 315 63. 058763
Gazzabuglio, Via XX Marzo 13, 43100 Parma.
T. (0521) 233 79. 058764
La Bottega del Mobile, Via Garibaldi 32, 43100 Parma.
T. (0521) 386 42, 49 41 41. 058765
La Rosa d'Irlanda, Borgo Riccio da Parma 24, 43100 Parma. T. (0521) 405 83. 058766
Le Arti Decorative, Via XX Marzo 11, 43100 Parma.
T. (0521) 343 53. 058767
Levrieri, Gianfranco, Via Paganini 7, 43100 Parma. 058768
Lo Scrigno, Via Repubblica 104, 43100 Parma.
T. (0521) 357 30, 432 12. 058769
Maria Luigia, Borgo Regale 24, 43100 Parma.
T. (0521) 20 88 16. 058770
Michelotti, Claudio, Borgo della Posta 8, 43100 Parma.
T. (0521) 303 88. - Furn / Sculp - 058771
Mistrali, Emilio, Via Pastrengo 2, 43100 Parma.
T. (0521) 59 21 81, 59 21 81. 058772
Nautilus, Via Pisacane 12, 43100 Parma.
T. (0521) 20 88 74. 058773
Oliva, Via al Duomo 1, 43100 Parma.
T. (0521) 33920. 058774
Passato prossimo, Borgo del Canale 2/c, 43100 Parma.
T. (0521) 20 63 45. - Silv - 058775
Pellegrini, Lidia, Via Lepido 30, 43100 Parma.
T. (0521) 49 28 78. 058776
Picchi Arizzi Picchi, Via N Sauro 24, 43100 Parma.
T. (0521) 369 47. 058777
Ramenzoni, Via XX Marzo 3, 43100 Parma.
T. (0521) 220 82. 058778
Regency, Pzza della Macina, 43100 Parma.
T. (0521) 35495. 058779
Revival, Via XXII Luglio 30, 43100 Parma.
T. (0521) 578 11. 058780
Riccardi Benati, Anna Maria, Via N Sauro 18, 43100 Parma. T. (0521) 229 62. 058781
Rossetti, Maurizio, Via Scutellari 2, 43100 Parma.
T. (0521) 236 80. 058782
Sfinge, La, Borgo Maroldo 21, 43100 Parma.
T. (0521) 53223. 058783
Sir Donald, Borgo Riccio 43, 43100 Parma.
T. (0521) 385 26. 058784
Vescovi, Piazzale San Vitale 11, 43100 Parma.
T. (0521) 23 13 59. 058785
Zerbini, Via Zaccagni 3, 43100 Parma. T. (0521) 273 50. - Furn / Mod - 058786

Pasturo (Como)

Ticozzi, Ernesto, Via Provinciale 1, 22040 Pasturo.
T. (0341) 95 502. 058787

Pavia

Antichità le Due Colonne, Via dei Mille 121, 27100 Pavia. T. (0382) 29056. 058788
Galleria Antiquaria, Strada Nuova 8, 27100 Pavia.
T. (0382) 373 63. 058789
Il Trovarobe, Via San Giovannino 9, 27100 Pavia.
T. (0382) 46 03 54. 058790
Kronos California Classics, Viale A. Brambilla 52, 27100 Pavia. T. (0382) 42 30 10. - Furn - 058791
Lualdi, Luca, Via dei Mille 88, 27100 Pavia.
T. (0382) 230 33. - Paint / Furn / Silv - 058792
Paviarte, Via Bossolaro 16, 27100 Pavia.
T. (0382) 338 08. - Graph / Sculp - 058793

Zanoletti, Via Teodorico 4, 27100 Pavia.
T. (0382) 30 26 86, 48 21 45. 058794
Zetti, Piero, Strada Nuova 32, 27100 Pavia.
T. (0382) 200 34. 058795

Pedavena (Belluno)

Righes, Luigi, Villa Pasole, 32034 Pedavena.
T. (0439) 836 77. 058796

Perugia

Antichità Piantarose, Via Piantarose 9, 06122 Perugia.
T. (075) 573 11 25. 058797
Arte Antiquaria, Piazza Piccinino 9, 06122 Perugia.
T. (075) 666 06. 058798
Bottega del Sagittario, La, Via Ulisse Rocchi 8, 06122 Perugia. T. (075) 261 54. 058799
Bruschelli, Via dei Priori 84, 06123 Perugia.
T. (075) 66020. 058800
Cecchini, Corso Vannucci 66, 06121 Perugia.
T. (075) 258 53. 058801
D'Alfonso M.F., Via Settevalli 995, Pilla, 06139 Perugia.
T. (075) 514 00 03. 058802
Galleria Gul, Via Baglioni 38, 06121 Perugia.
T. (075) 65313. 058803
Il Vecchio Convento, Via Boncambi 21, 06123 Perugia.
T. (075) 66025. - Ant / Paint / Furn - 058804
L'Amuleto, Via del Coppetta 36, 06124 Perugia.
T. (075) 65897. 058805
Luna, Piazza Giordano Bruno 5, 06121 Perugia.
T. (075) 66901. 058806
Mancini, Via Baldeschi 10, 06123 Perugia.
T. (075) 61631. 058807
Mearini, F., Via Boncampi 21, 06123 Perugia.
T. (075) 66025. 058808
Perugia Arte e Antiquariato, Piazza Piccinino 9, 06122 Perugia. T. (075) 66606. 058809
Piantarose, Forasiepi-Raggi, Via Piantarose 9, 06100 Perugia. T. (075) 573 11 25. - Ant / Furn / Sculp / Jew / Fra / Silv / Lights / Instr / Glass / Draw - 058810
Piccola Londra, Via Campo di Marte 8M, 06124 Perugia.
T. (075) 75 11 97. 058811
Rufini, Piazza IV Novembre 31, 06122 Perugia.
T. (075) 61007. - Furn - 058812
San Andrea, Via Manzoni 396, Ponte San Giovanni, 06154 Perugia. T. (075) 39 53 46. 058813
Shanti, Giovanni Discenza, Via Mazzini 4, 06121 Perugia. T. (075) 20783. 058814

Pesaro

Astarta, Via Picciola 8, 61100 Pesaro.
T. (0721) 679 27. 058815
H e W Fayaz, Piazzale 1 Maggio 13, 61100 Pesaro.
T. (0721) 659 48. 058816
Mari R. e Pedini M., Via Varese 16, 61100 Pesaro.
T. (0721) 682 50. 058817
Oliveriana Antichita, Via Mazza 54, 61100 Pesaro.
T. (0721) 682 50. 058818
Paolucci, Via Petrucci 32, 61100 Pesaro.
T. (0721) 668 01. 058819

Pescara

Castaldi, Via Venezia 12, 65100 Pescara.
T. (085) 273 98. 058820
Coen & Pieroni, Corso Vittorio Emanuele 94, 65100 Pescara. T. (085) 225 50, 226 52. 058821
DE.MI.CE, Corso Manthone 49, 65100 Pescara.
T. (085) 662 50, 83 99 40. 058822
L'Antiquariato Piga, Corso Vittorio Emanuele 32, 65100 Pescara. T. (085) 29 71 57. 058823
Recherche, Corso G Manthone 65, 65100 Pescara.
T. (085) 242 23, 223 32. 058824

Pescia (Pistoia)

Cose Vecchie, Via Oberdan 10, 51017 Pescia.
T. (0572) 47 98 71. 058825
Giuntini, Giuntino, Via Oberdan 38, 51017 Pescia.
T. (0572) 471 35. 058826

Pescocostanzo (L'Aquila)

Cattoli, Piazza Municipio 3, 67033 Pescocostanzo. 058827

Piacenza

Alternariato, Via Citadella 27, 29100 Piacenza.
T. (0523) 21729. - Furn / China - 058828

Arca, Via Verdi 19, 29100 Piacenza.
T. (0523) 304 37.   058829
Arcadia, Via Pace 30, 29100 Piacenza.
T. (0523) 273 36.   058830
Art & Craft, Via Mandelli 4, 29100 Piacenza.
T. (0523) 370 52.   058831
Art & Craft, Via Mandelli 4, 29100 Piacenza.
T. (0523) 370 52.   058832
Arte Nova, Via San Giovanni 22, 29100 Piacenza.
T. (0523) 24720. - Furn -   058833
Arte 6, Via Cittadella 2, 29100 Piacenza.
T. (0523) 289 48.   058834
Buttala, Via Sant'Antonino 31, 29100 Piacenza.   058835
Cerati, Renzo, Via G Landi 9, 29100 Piacenza.
T. (0523) 255 25.   058836
Farina, Fulvio, Via San Giuseppe 1 int., 29100 Piacenza.
T. (0523) 75 51 94. - Furn -   058837
Gioia, Ludovico, Via Verdi 9, 29100 Piacenza.
T. (0523) 269 43.   058838
Kalamian, Ehsan, Via Genova 2, 29100 Piacenza.
T. (0523) 381 60.   058839
Leoni, Luigi, Strada Bobbiese 45, 29100 Piacenza.
T. (0523) 703 47.   058840
Losi, Jose, Galleria Borsa 26, 29100 Piacenza.
T. (0523) 24642. - Num -   058841
Madia, La, Via Chiapponi 39, 29100 Piacenza.
T. (0523) 28639. - Furn -   058842
Malair, Via Borghetto 33, 29100 Piacenza.
T. (0523) 352 03.   058843
Oxford Antiques, Via Conciliazione 55, 29100 Piacenza.
T. (0523) 591919, Fax (0523) 591919.   058844
Singarella, Conte, Via Garibaldi 62, 29100 Piacenza.
T. (0523) 20252. - Paint / Furn -   058845
Viani, Via Mandelli 2, 29100 Piacenza.
T. (0523) 226 09.   058846

Pianella Val Tidone (Piacenza)
Nemi, Largo Dal Verme, 29010 Pianella Val Tidone.
T. (0523) 995 26.   058847

Pietra Ligure (Savona)
Schiaroli-Peluzi, Egle, Via XXV Aprile 38, 17027 Pietra
Ligure. T. (019) 62 54 43. - Ant / Furn / China / Sculp /
Rel / Cur -   058848

Pieve Ligure (Genova)
Il Cucciolo, Via XXV Aprile 247, 16030 Pieve Ligure.
T. (010) 346 03 90.   058849

Piggio Berni (Forli)
Zoffoli, Via Santo Marino 30, 47030 Piggio Berni.
T. (0541) 62 95 66. - Repr -   058850

Pinerolo (Torino)
Bordunale, Giovanni, Via Orbassano 39, 10064 Pinerolo.
T. (0121) 225 30.   058851
Bresso, Angelo, Corso Torino 6, 10064 Pinerolo.
T. (0121) 225 68.   058852

Piombino (Livorno)
Ceccarelli e Calastri, Via Lombroso 66, 57025
Piombino.   058853
Gasperi, Ubaldo, Corso Italia 41, 57025 Piombino.
T. (0565) 334 41.   058854

Pisa
C'era Una Volta, Via San Martino 74, 56100 Pisa.
T. (050) 494 30.   058855
Costa, Pierluigi, Vie Pietro Gori 33, 56100 Pisa. 058856
Costa, Pierluigi, Via Turati 31, 56100 Pisa.
T. (050) 227 51.   058857
Ferretti, Giovanni, Via Cottolengo 19, 56100 Pisa.
T. (050) 50 02 68.   058858
Gallani, M. G., Via Santa Maria 113, 56100 Pisa.
T. (050) 233 30. - Paint / Graph / Furn / Tex /
Dec -   058859
Kinzika, Via San Martino 86, 56100 Pisa.
T. (050) 248 80.   058860
La Bottega dell'Architetto, Via San Bernardo 55, 56100
Pisa. T. (050) 403 78.   058861
Melograno, Il, Via Santa Cecilia 25, 56100 Pisa.
T. (050) 470 27.   058862
Melograno, Il, Via Santa Cecilia 25, 56100 Pisa.
T. (050) 470 27.   058863

Torre, La, Via Crispi 75, 56100 Pisa.
T. (050) 272 51.   058864

Pistoia
Andreini, Marco, Viale Patrocchi 116, 51100 Pistoia.
T. (0573) 32993. - Paint / Furn / China / Sculp - 058865
Art Shop, Via Curtatone e Montanara 56, 51100 Pistoia.
T. (0573) 348 01.   058866
Della Custodia, Via del Canbianco 16, 51100 Pistoia.
T. (0573) 318 34.   058867
La Casa del Collezionista, Corso Amendola 38, 51100
Pistoia. T. (0573) 33860. - Graph / Num -   058868
La Cornice, Via Palestro 5, 51100 Pistoia.
T. (0573) 36 72 96.   058869

Pollenza (Macerata)
Cantarini, Via Menichelli 23, 62010 Pollenza.
T. (0733) 42 84 87.   058870
Gattucci, Via Raffaello Sanzio 9, 62010 Pollenza.
T. (0733) 51 91 36, 51 92 18.   058871
Marinozzi, Caterina, Via Monsignor Marinozzi 61, 62010
Pollenza. T. (0733) 51 91 74.   058872
Marinozzi, Caterina, Via Leopardi 98, 62010 Pollenza.
T. (0733) 51 93 79.   058873
Marinozzi, Giuliana, Via Giacomo Leopardi 96, 62010
Pollenza. T. (0733) 51 92 59, 51 94 01.   058874

Ponsacco (Pisa)
L'Antico, Via Valdera P59, 56038 Ponsacco.
T. (0587) 73 04 95.   058875

Pont Cavanese (Torino)
Cresto, Ernestina Luciana, Via Soana 24, 10085 Pont
Cavanese. T. (0124) 846 14.   058876

Ponte della Priula (Treviso)
Gaborin, Emilio, Via IV Novembre 67, 31010 Ponte della
Priula. T. 27242.   058877
Sari, Vittorio, Via Ortigara 3, 31010 Ponte della Priula.
T. 271 68.   058878

Ponte di Piave (Treviso)
Dalle Crode Casagrande, Adriana, Via Jesolo 1, 31047
Ponte di Piave. T. (0422) 75 98 36.   058879

Ponte San Giovanni (Perugia)
Sant'Andrea, Via Manzoni 398, 06087 Ponte San Giovanni. T. (075) 39 53 46, 385 26.   058880

Ponte Tarlo (Parma)
Bandini, Carla, Via Emilia 9, 43010 Ponte Tarlo.
T. (0521) 611 07.   058881
Corradini, Enrico, Via Emilia 103, 43010 Ponte Tarlo.
T. (0521) 616 27.   058882
Nasciuti, Giovanni, Via Emilia 43, 43010 Ponte Tarlo.
T. (0521) 611 12.   058883
Quadretti, Ettore, Via Raffaello 2, 43010 Ponte Tarlo.
T. (0521) 612 01.   058884

Pontedera (Pisa)
Il Tarlo, Viale Repubblica 3, 56025 Pontedera.
T. (0587) 520 37.   058885

Pordenone
Etching, Viale S Martelli 25, 33170 Pordenone.
T. (0434) 277 85, 0337/53 48 36, Fax 53 48 36.   058886
La Gioconda, Viale Marconi 20, 33170 Pordenone.
T. (0434) 25 58 45, 62 05 05.   058887

Porto Mantovano (Mantova)
Bonfogo, Via delle Artigianato 13-14, 46047 Porto Mantovano. T. (0376) 39 89 89. - Furn -   058888

Porto San Giorgio (Ascoli Piceno)
Il Rigattiere, Via Mazzini 133, 63017 Porto San Giorgio.
T. (0734) 493 59, 202 80.   058889

Porto Valtravaglia (Varese)
L'Antenato, Piazza Imbarcadero, 21010 Porto
Valtravaglia.   058890

Portofino (Genova)
Artarmi, Calata Marcconi 3, 16034 Portofino.
T. (0185) 694 94, 694 91.   058891
Pisani, Massimo, Via Roma 20, 16034 Portofino.
T. (0185) 692 80.   058892

Positano (Salerno)
Le Myricae, Piazza Mulini 71, 84017 Positano.
T. (089) 87 58 82. - Ant / Furn -   058893

Possagno (Treviso)
Marchet, Via Masiere 2, 31054 Possagno.
T. (0423) 542 28.   058894

Potenza
Memoli, Luigi, Via Cavour 20, 85100 Potenza.
T. (0971) 345 77.   058895

Prato (Firenze)
Fioravanti, Via Gobetti 46, 50047 Prato.
T. (0574) 266 77.   058896
Iannettone, Via dell'Accademia 27, 50047 Prato.
T. (0574) 31654.   058897
Moretti, Alfredo, Via Pomeria 29, 50047 Prato.
T. (0574) 422 50.   058898

Preganziol (Treviso)
Alle Grazie, Via F Baracca 1, 31022 Preganziol.
T. (0422) 44663.   058899

Premosello Chiovenda (Novara)
Poppi, Ermanno, Via Nazionale 27, 28020 Premosello
Chiovenda. T. (0324) 801 37.   058900

Primaluna (Como)
Monticelli, Michele, Via Provinciale 89, 22040 Primaluna. T. (0341) 98 02 55.   058901

Punta Ala (Grosseto)
Samarkanda, Piazza del Porto, 58040 Punta
Ala.   058902
Servizi Galleria, Il Gualdo, 58040 Punta Ala.
T. (0564) 92 22 96.   058903

Punta Marina (Ravenna)
Cangini, Maria, Via della Lampara 20, 48020 Punta Marina. T. (0544) 43 80 84.   058904

Putignano (Bari)
Antiquariato Sud, Via Ten Sbiroli 7-11, 70017 Putignano.
T. (080) 73 33 77, 895 43 60.   058905

Quart (Aosta)
Il Tarlo, Regione America, 11020 Quart.
T. (0165) 621 23.   058906

Quattro Castella (Reggio Emilia)
Croci, Via Volta 4, 42020 Quattro Castella.
T. (522) 88 72 28.   058907
Davoli, Via Prampolini 17, 42020 Quattro Castella.
T. (522) 88 72 06.   058908

Ragusa
Il Tappeto, Via Risorgimento 85, 97100 Ragusa.
T. (0932) 486 22.   058909
Marco, di, Via Orfanotrofio 91, 97100 Ragusa.
T. (0932) 20781. - Ant -   058910

Rapallo (Genova)
Covre, Emila, Via Vico Della Pista 7, 16035 Rapallo.
T. (0185) 639 14.   058911
Cristallo, Galleria Cristallo 9, 16036 Rapallo.
T. (0185) 27 06 10.   058912
Fedele Covre, Emilia, Corso Italia 36, 16035 Rapallo.
T. (0185) 639 14.   058913
Patanè, Via Rossetti 10, 16035 Rapallo.
T. (0185) 548 77.   058914
San Camillo, Galleria Raggio 14, 16035 Rapallo.
T. (0185) 536 82.   058915
Tigullio, Corso Matteotti 5, 16035 Rapallo.
T. (0185) 536 02.   058916

Ravenna
A.B. Antiquariato Brocchi, Via Cairoli 6, 48100 Ravenna.
T. (0544) 22252. - Paint / Furn / Sculp -   058917
Alessi, Carlo, Via Calatafimi 47, 48100 Ravenna.
T. (0544) 46 49 70.   058918
Bartolotti, Giorgio, Via di Roma 84, 48100 Ravenna.
T. (0544) 343 2.   058919
Bratti, Adriano, Via Luca Longhi 21, 48100 Ravenna.
T. (0544) 351 98.   058920
Casemurate, Piazza San Francesco 3, 48100 Ravenna.
T. (0544) 323 93.   058921

Cenacolo, II, Via Mura San Vitale 4, 48100 Ravenna.
T. (0544) 382 28. 058922

Cimatti, Gianpaolo, Via Canale Molinette 3, 48100 Ravenna. T. (0544) 625 99. 058923

Coccio, II, Via Andrea Agnello 6, 48100 Ravenna.
T. (0544) 342 69. - Paint - 058924

Dragoni & Ranieri, Piazza del Popolo 12, 48100 Ravenna. T. (0544) 224 35. - Num - 058925

Fietta, Donata, Via Argentario 1, 48100 Ravenna.
T. (0544) 237 28. - Ant - 058926

Marani, Antonio, Piazza Duomo 8, 48100 Ravenna.
T. (0544) 354 76. 058927

Ponte, II, Via di Roma 82, 48100 Ravenna.
T. (0544) 357 68. 058928

P.Z.B., Via Ricci 23, 48100 Ravenna.
T. (0544) 334 38. 058929

Raffa, Antonio, P.zza del Popolo 12, 48100 Ravenna.
T. (0544) 22435, 27619. - Num - 058930

Romini, Francesco, Via Mariani 22, 48100 Ravenna.
T. (0544) 30150. - Num - 058931

San Giorgio, Via S Vitale 34, 48100 Ravenna.
T. (0544) 396 34. 058932

Savoia, Adride, Via IX Febbraio, 48100 Ravenna. 058933

Senni, Romano, Via Luca Longhi 22, 48100 Ravenna.
T. (0544) 361 39. 058934

Recanati (Macerata)
Tempi Passati, Antichita, Viale C Battista, 62019 Recanati. T. (071) 9786822. 058935

Reggio Calabria
Abenavoli, Via Campanella 53, 89100 Reggio Calabria.
T. (0965) 208 6. 058936

La Diligenza, Via Vittorio Veneto 76, 89100 Reggio Calabria. T. (0965) 294 23. 058937

Old House, V Annunziata Argine Destro 23, 89100 Reggio Calabria. T. (0965) 905 66. 058938

Parigi, Lavinio, Corso Vittorio Emanuele 39, 89100 Reggio Calabria. T. (0965) 904 15. 058939

Pecoraro, Lucia, Via Tripepi 123, 89100 Reggio Calabria.
T. (0965) 940 23. 058940

Reggio Emilia
Al Voltone, Via Don Minzoni 10, 42100 Reggio Emilia.
T. (0522) 85 82 34, 342 66. 058941

Berti, Franco, Via S. Bernardino 2a, 42100 Reggio Emilia. T. (0522) 29 47 01. - Furn / Dec - 058942

Borciani, Via del Cristo 2, 42100 Reggio Emilia.
T. (0522) 383 56, 30728. 058943

Bric á Brac, Via Roma 22, 42100 Reggio Emilia.
T. (0522) 368 75. 058944

Cocchi, Roberto, Via Tassoni 217, 42100 Reggio Emilia.
T. (0522) 58 21 88. 058945

Edda, Via Secchi 16, 42100 Reggio Emilia.
T. (0522) 424 10. 058946

Emporio Novecento, Via Ariosto 4/a, 42100 Reggio Emilia. T. (0522) 41603. 058947

Erriques, Vincenzo, Via Secchi 6, 42100 Reggio Emilia.
T. (0522) 318 65. - Num - 058948

Esposito Alfonso, Via Roma 22/a, 42100 Reggio Emilia.
T. (0522) 36875. - Furn - 058949

Fiumicelli, Italo, Via Edison 8, 42100 Reggio Emilia.
T. (0522) 918 35. - Ant / Paint - 058950

Fontanesi, Piazza Montanesi 8, 42100 Reggio Emilia.
T. (0522) 43350. 058951

Fornaciari, Via del Mercato 1, 42100 Reggio Emilia.
T. (0522) 225 16. 058952

Gualdi F.lli, Via Ponte Besolario 3, 42100 Reggio Emilia.
T. (0522) 403 17. 058953

Il Gioiello, Via Crispi 1, 42100 Reggio Emilia.
T. (0522) 449 89. 058954

Il Tarlo, Piazza Fontanesi 1, 42100 Reggio Emilia.
T. (0522) 48 51 83, 389 97. 058955

Jotti, Aldo, & Figli, Via Amendola 57, 42100 Reggio Emilia. T. (0522) 927 21. 058956

La Madia, Via Filippo Re 10, 42100 Reggio Emilia.
T. (0522) 352 89, 373 59. 058957

Leon d'Oro, Via dei Due Gobbi 1, 42100 Reggio Emilia.
T. (0522) 427 82. 058958

Lodesani, Via G da Castello 7, 42100 Reggio Emilia.
T. (0522) 382 86, 202 62. 058959

Magnaini Croci, Claudia, Via S Girolamo 1, 42100 Reggio Emilia. T. (0522) 396 75. 058960

Menozzi Nay, Via Navona 1, 42100 Reggio Emilia.
T. (0522) 397 56. 058961

Morani, Alfredo, Via L Ariosto 4, 42100 Reggio Emilia.
T. (0522) 416 03. 058962

Nocco, Silvestro, Via G da Castello 27, 42100 Reggio Emilia. T. (0522) 443 11. 058963

Numismatica Emiliana, Via Secchi 6/a, 42100 Reggio Emilia. T. (0522) 31865. - Num - 058964

Old Wood, Bosco di Scandiano, 42100 Reggio Emilia.
T. (0522) 85 59 58. 058965

Persian Gallery, Via Emilia S Stefano 9/M, 42100 Reggio Emilia. T. (0522) 44239. 058966

Phidias, Via Roma 22/a, 42100 Reggio Emilia.
T. (0522) 43 68 75. - Sculp - 058967

Piolanti, Dante, Via L Fornaciari 12, 42100 Reggio Emilia. T. (0522) 455 11. 058968

Sassi, Atos, Via del Cristo 6, 42100 Reggio Emilia.
T. (0522) 448 50. 058969

Tedeschi, Anna, Vicolo Corbelli 2/d, 42100 Reggio Emilia. T. (0522) 41846. - Jew - 058970

Vescovado, Via Vescovado 3, 42100 Reggio Emilia.
T. (0522) 348 51. 058971

Zamboni, Massimo, Via Palestro 3, 42100 Reggio Emilia.
T. (0522) 367 76. 058972

Reggiolo (Reggio Emilia)
Pavarini, Via Guastalla 114, 42046 Reggiolo.
T. (0522) 82 91 43. 058973

Riccione (Forli)
San Martino, Via Nievo 11, 47036 Riccione.
T. (0541) 40719. 058974

Volpe, Celio, Via Dante 255, 47036 Riccione.
T. (0541) 409 47. 058975

Rieti
La Soffitta della Nonna, Via Loreto Mattei 29, 02100 Rieti. T. (0746) 407 80. 058976

Rio Antiquariato, Via Salaria 58, 02100 Rieti.
T. (0746) 607117, Fax (0746) 607143. 058977

Rio Antiquariato, Via Cintia 57, 02100 Rieti.
T. (0746) 202793. 058978

Rimini (Forli)
Antiquariato Ariminensis, Via Soardi 16, 47037 Rimini.
T. (0541) 545 19, 231 75. - Ant - 058979

Ariminensis, Piazza 3 Martiri 30, 47037 Rimini.
T. (0541) 545 76. 058980

Cose Vecchie, Corso d'Augusto 211, 47037 Rimini.
T. (0541) 541 92. 058981

Domeniconi, Vezia, Corso Giovanni XXIII, 47037 Rimini.
T. (0541) 542 39 058982

I Monili di Dama Elche, Viale Ceccherini, 47037 Rimini. 058983

L'Ottocento, Via Ravegnani 26, 47037 Rimini.
T. (0541) 535 92. 058984

Leonardi, Via Tempo Malatestiano 12, 47037 Rimini.
T. (0541) 287 59. 058985

Milvia, Via Roma 6, 47037 Rimini.
T. (0541) 485 85. 058986

Pagliarani Rossi, Albertina, Piazza Cavour 11, 47037 Rimini. T. (0541) 275 64. 058987

Pironi, Corso Giovanni XXIII, 47037 Rimini.
T. (0541) 286 16. 058988

Sigismondo, Via Sigismondo 77, 47037 Rimini.
T. (0541) 78 11 81. - Num - 058989

Via Soardi 16, 47037 Rimini. T. (0541) 545 19.
- Ant - 058990

Riva del Garda (Trento)
Facincani, Viale Prati 20, 38066 Riva del Garda.
T. (0464) 51 37 39. 058991

Jannello, Via Ricamboni 5, 38066 Riva del Garda.
T. (0464) 51 22 14. 058992

Riva Trigoso (Genova)
Montaldi Verdino, Paolo e Anna Rita, Via Bartolomeo Brin 86, 16037 Riva Trigoso. T. (0185) 425 10. 058993

Rivanazzano (Pavia)
Bazar, Via Marconi 36, 27055 Rivanazzano.
T. (0383) 917 28. 058994

Rivoli (Torino)
Damiano, Fratelli, Via Flli Piol 43 Torino, 10098 Rivoli.
T. (011) 958 92 62. 058995

Fiorio Fratelli, Piazza Martiri d Libertà 4, 10098 Rivoli.
T. (011) 958 03 60, 958 93 77. 058996

Robecco sul Naviglio (Milano)
Garavaglia, Pierino, Via Matteotti 32, 20087 Robecco sul Naviglio. T. (02) 947 06 25. - Furn - 058997

Rocca Malatina (Modena)
Vecchi, V.C., 41050 Rocca Malatina. T. (059) 79 58 39.
- Ant / Num - 058998

Roccaraso (L'Aquila)
Il Tesoretto, Via Roma 45, 67037 Roccaraso. 058999

Roma
A 6 B, 34 Viale Milizie, 00192 Roma.
T. (06) 3213929. 059000

Acajou di Roberto Cavalieri, 177 Via Valsolda, 00141 Roma. T. (06) 00141. 059001

Achilli G., 32 Via Mascherino, 00193 Roma.
T. (06) 68307286. 059002

Acquista Soprammobili, Via P. Micheli 36, 00198 Roma.
T. (06) 3610773. 059003

Acquista Soprammobili, Viale Regina Margherita 82, 00198 Roma. T. (06) 8552451, 8547728. 059004

Acquisti e Stime di Collezioni di Qualsiasi Importanza Italphil, Piazza Mignanelli 3, 00187 Roma.
T. (06) 6787617, 6840468, Fax (06) 6794045. 059005

Adriani, S., Via A. Loria 3, 00191 Roma.
T. (06) 36309443. 059006

Agostinelli Antichita', Via Donato Bartolomeo 44, 00126 Roma. T. (06) 5219058. 059007

Agostini, Piazza Borghese 1, 00186 Roma.
T. (06) 6784074. - Paint / Furn / Orient / Tex - 059008

Agostino M., 182 Via Flavio Stilicone, 00175 Roma.
T. (06) 76900151. 059009

Akka, Via Pié di Marmo 13-14, 00186 Roma.
T. (06) 679 20 66. 059010

A.L., Via Vittoria 28, 00187 Roma.
T. (06) 679 46 71. 059011

Albertosi L., 20 Via S. Croce Gerusalemme, 00185 Roma. T. (06) 7028006. 059012

Alvaro, N., Via Coronari 126, 00186 Roma.
T. (06) 68802457. 059013

Ambrogi, Via Aurelia 101/107, 00165 Roma.
T. (06) 63 42 93. 059014

Ambrosi M., 47 Via Banchi Vecchi, 00186 Roma.
T. (06) 6879685. 059015

Ambrosi, Tomasi, Via D. Fontana 44, 00185 Roma.
T. (06) 70495889. 059016

Angel's Station Arte e Antiquariato, Via Panisperna 244, 00184 Roma. T. (06) 4820675, 58202437. 059017

Angelo Di Castro, 20 Via Alibert, 00187 Roma.
T. (06) 69941757. 059018

Angolo del collezionista, Via S. Marino, 2 (Adiacente C.so Trieste), 00198 Roma. T. (06) 8543796, (0337) 794594. 059019

Angolo Delle Cose Belle, 26 Via Velletri, 00198 Roma.
T. (06) 8548714. 059020

Antica Roma di Alberti Angelo e C., 6b/bc Via Accumoli, 00135 Roma. T. (06) 30814041. 059021

Anticaja, Via dei Filippini 3, 00186 Roma.
T. (06) 687 56 58. 059022

Antiche Art Decorative, Via Marcello Prestinari 21, 00195 Roma. T. (06) 2619753. 059023

Antichita', Alibert, 27 Via Alibert, 00187 Roma.
T. (06) 3207726. 059024

Antichita' Brighton Restauro Mobili (Nuovo Salario), Via Antonio Silvani 58/60, 00139 Roma.
T. (06) 8103204. 059025

Antichita' e Curiosita' di Antonio Gallo & C.S.N.C., 74 Via Vigne Nuove, 00139 Roma. T. (06) 8188740. 059026

Antichita' e Dintorni di Scribano, Claudia Maria Piera & Orietta, 96 Via F. Nocolai, 00136 Roma.
T. (06) 343400. 059027

Antichita Giorgini, Via Chiana, 55/a (Parioli), 00198 Roma. T. (06) 8848694. 059028

Antichita Grossista degli Antiquari, Via Nomentana 1141, 00162 Roma. T. (06) 86802237, 8273737. 059029

Antichita' La Botteghina di Annoscia, Maria Pia, 49 Via Cipro, 00136 Roma. T. (06) 39387766. 059030
Antichita', Margutta, 67 Via Margutta, 00187 Roma. T. (06) 3207649. 059031
Antichità Margutta, Via Margutta 68-69, 00187 Roma. T. (06) 6790349. 059032
Antichità Monserrato 30 di Carozzi & Vecci, 30 Via Monserrato, 00186 Roma. T. (06) 6868242. 059033
Antichità Roma, Via in Arcione 104, 00187 Roma. T. (06) 679 23 83. 059034
Antichita' & Curiosita' di Antonio Gallo & C.SNC, Via Vigne Nuove, 00139 Roma. T. (06) 87182170. 059035
Antico e.. Carlo Marx 36, Viale Marx 3645, 00137 Roma. T. (06) 86 89 72 09. 059036
Anticuus, 408 Via Gregorio VII, 00165 Roma. T. (06) 6628147. 059037
Anticuus di Nicolucci & Gentili, Ricci & Flavio, Via Gregorio VII 400, 00165 Roma. T. (06) 663 72 52. 059038
Antiqua Domus, 6 Via Giraud, 00186 Roma. T. (06) 6869542. 059039
Antiqua Domus, Via dei Coronari 39/43, 00186 Roma. T. (06) 6875384, 6861186, Fax (06) 6861530. 059040
Antiqua Domus, Via Paola 25/27, 00186 Roma. T. (06) 686 15 30. 059041
Antiqua Res, Via dei Coronari 44a, 00186 Roma. T. (06) 686 79 23. 059042
Antiquari Acquisto, Via G. Cerbara 84, 00147 Roma. T. (06) 51600935. 059043
Antiquariato – Mobili Porcelanne – Import d'arte, Viale Marconi 578, 00146 Roma. T. (06) 5582214. 059044
Antiquariato 3000, Via Giulia 58, 00186 Roma. T. (06) 689 23 29. 059045
Le Antiquarie di Botto, Maria, 19 Via Consolato, 00186 Roma. T. (06) 6896898. 059046
Antiques Studio, Via Pio Foà 74, 00100 Roma. T. (06) 531 01 52. 059047
Antonacci Efrati, Via del Babuino 146, 00187 Roma. T. (06) 6781595/6789087. - Ant / Furn - 059048
Apolloni, M. P., Via Avignonesi 29A, 00187 Roma. T. (06) 482 82 21. 059049
Apolloni, W., Via del Babuino 133-134, 00187 Roma. T. (06) 36002216. - Paint / Furn / Draw - 059050

W. APOLLONI

Objets d'Art - Orfèvrerie
Tableaux Anciens et Modernes
Meubles du 18ème Siècle

Via del Babuino 132-133-134
T. 36 00 22 16

Arcadia, Via del Babuino 70a, 00187 Roma. T. (06) 679 10 23. 059051
Archè Antichità, Via Etruria 71, 00183 Roma. T. (06) 700 17 24. 059052
Archeos Studio, 36a Viale Med D'Oro, 00136 Roma. T. (06) 39735889. 059053
Arcobaleno, Di Alessandro Basile, 65 Via Panico, 00186 Roma. T. (06) 6893223. 059054
Arinvest, 117 Via Ripetta, 00186 Roma. T. (06) 6874146, 6876458. 059055
Arnaboldi, Fratelli, Via Gregorio VII 110, 00165 Roma. T. (06) 39376876, Fax (06) 39376878. 059056
Arredamenti Capitani di Capitani Adrio e C., 157 Via Pietralata, 00158 Roma. T. (06) 4500904. 059057
Arredamenti Marconi, 44/45/46 Piazza Monteleone Spoleto, 00191 Roma. T. (06) 3338162. 059058
Arredamenti Marconi, 139 Via Camposampiero, 00191 Roma. T. (06) 3330743. 059059
Arrivabene M., 70 Via S. Simone, 00186 Roma. T. (06) 68300568. 059060
Art Déco Gallery, Via dei Coronari 14, 00186 Roma. T. (06) 686 53 30. - Ant / Furn / Sculp - 059061
Arte Antica, 79 Via Coronari, 00186 Roma. T. (06) 6865046. 059062
Arte Antica, 75/d Via Trionfale, 00192 Roma. T. (06) 39738279. 059063

Arte Antica, Via Coronari 147, 00186 Roma. T. (06) 686 75 93. 059064
AR.TE.S. Arredamenti Telerie Stile, 23 Via F. Caracciolo, 00197 Roma. T. (06) 3252002. 059065
Artestile, 87 Via Fratina, 00197 Roma. T. (06) 6791082. 059066
ArtImport, Piazza Borghese 2/2A, 00186 Roma. T. (06) 6873633/6873634, Fax (06) 69941402. - Ant / China / Silv / Cur - 059067
Artinvest, Via Ripetta 117, 00186 Roma. T. (06) 6876138. 059068
Arvim, Via Pietra 70 e 41, 00186 Roma. T. (06) 678 33 44, 679 69 31. 059069
Astrologo, E., Via dei Banchi Nuovi 29, 00186 Roma. T. (06) 6861606. 059070
Bacchi, Dr. Antonio, Via Salaria 121B, 00198 Roma. T. (06) 884 22 50. - Ant / Furn - 059071
Baglioni, Via di Ripetta 139, 00186 Roma. T. (06) 6877121. 059072
Baldascini, M., Via Prati dei Papa 51F, 00146 Roma. T. (06) 559 42 32. 059073
Il Balon 2 di Fornasieri, 51 Piazza Navona, 00186 Roma. T. (06) 6879639. 059074
Bandinelli, R., Via Polacchi 2A, 00186 Roma. T. (06) 6788805/6793119. 059075
Baranowsky, Via del Corso 184, 00187 Roma. T. (06) 679 15 02. - Num - 059076
Barbarisi E., Via Palombella, 00186 Roma. T. (06) 68807048. 059077
Basini P., 31 Via Venticinque, 00136 Roma. T. (06) 37513540. 059078
Belardi, Giarcarlo, Rampa Mignanelli 11, 00187 Roma. T. (06) 678 31 90. 059079
Belle Epoque Antichità, 2/a Via Silvestro II, 00167 Roma. T. (06) 6630375. 059080
Benedetti, C., Via Panisperna 105, 00184 Roma. T. (06) 482 66 14. 059081
Benedetti, C., Via Coronari 37, 00186 Roma. T. (06) 68801326. 059082
Benedetti R., 7 Via Verolengo, 00167 Roma. T. (06) 66414423. 059083
Benetti, A., Via Banchi Nuovi 48, 00186 Roma. T. (06) 689 33 93. 059084
Benucci, Ida, Babuino 153, 153A, 153B, 00123 Roma. T. (06) 6786251, 6786858. 059085
Benucci, Ida, Via Babuino 33, 00123 Roma. T. (0337) 741461, Fax (06) 6797573. 059086
Benucci, J., Via Giulia 174, 00186 Roma. T. (06) 687 52 20. 059087
Berardi, G., Corso Rinascimento 9, 00186 Roma. T. (06) 687 71 09. 059088
Berardo, Silvia, Via Biella 13, 00182 Roma. T. (06) 7027042. 059089
Bernabei, M. C., Via Chini 59/61, 00147 Roma. T. (06) 513 90 43. 059090
Berni, Luigi, Via S. Vincenzo 11, 00152 Roma. T. (06) 678 59 61. 059091
Bertugno, Bruno, Via P. De Cristofaro 86/88, 00136 Roma. T. (06) 39721149. 059092
Bettini A. – Il Fiorino, Compravendita monete oro, argento Medaglie, collezioni, Via Veneto 4A, 00187 Roma. T. (06) 4741063, 4871458. 059093
Biagiarelli, 97 Piazza Capranica, 00186 Roma. T. (06) 69940728. 059094
Biagiarelli, G. M., Piazza Caparnica 97, 00187 Roma. T. (06) 678 49 87. 059095
Bianchini, Via Giulia 23, 00186 Roma. T. (06) 687 53 09. 059096
Big Ben Antiques, Via del Pellegrino 111, 00186 Roma. T. (06) 687 57 94. - Furn - 059097
Big Ben Antiques, 21 Via Agnello, 00184 Roma. T. (06) 6791367. 059098
Bigetti M., 31 Via Laurina, 00187 Roma. T. (06) 3203783, 3611044. 059099
Bigetti, Mario, Via M. de Fiori 67, 00187 Roma. T. (06) 679 00 48. 059100
Bilenchi, D., Via Spagnoli 41, 00186 Roma. T. (06) 686 74 27. 059101
Bilenchi '900, Via della Stelletta 17, 00186 Roma. T. (06) 6875222. 059102
Boncompagni Sturni, Via Babuino 115, 00187 Roma. T. (06) 6783847/6797907. - Jew - 059103

Bongarzoni, E., Via Leonina 68, 00184 Roma. T. (06) 481 76 73. 059104
Bono, G., Via Coronari 190, 00186 Roma. T. (06) 687 71 45. 059105
Borrazzi, L., Via del Babuino 65, 00187 Roma. T. (06) 678 05 67. 059106
Bottega d'Arte, Via Appia Nuova 712A, 00181 Roma. T. (06) 785 63 25. 059107
Bottega dell'Antiquariato Edilizio, Piazza Cancelleria 74-75, 00186 Roma. T. (06) 689 23 53. 059108
La Bottega, Margutta, 58 Via Margutta, 00187 Roma. T. (06) 3207981. 059109
Il Bottegone Dell'Antiquariato, 32 Via Margutta, 00187 Roma. T. (06) 3614140. 059110
Il Bottegone Dell'Antiquariato, 40 Viale Colli Portuensi, 00151 Roma. T. (06) 58237055. 059111
Il Bottegone Dell'Antiquariato, 5 Via Falda, 00152 Roma. T. (06) 5800824. 059112
Il Bottegone Dell'Antiquariato di Parenza Gianfranco & C., 10 Via F. Vettori, 00164 Roma. T. (06) 6663511. 059113
Il Bottegone Dell'Antiquariato, 2000 Mq di Esposizione Import Diretto – Vendita a Commercianti, Via Margutta, Roma. T. (06) 3614140. 059114
Il Bottegone Dell'Antiquariato, 2000 Mq di Esposione Import Diretto – Vendita a Commercianti, Via F. Vettori 10, Roma. T. (06) 6663511. 059115
Il Bottegone Dell'Antiquariato, 2000 Mq di Esposizione Import Diretto – Vendita a Commercianti, Viale dei Colli Portuensi 40/48, Roma. T. (06) 5826162, 58237238, Fax (06) 58237055. 059116
Bracci, A., Via Andrea Doria 34B, 00192 Roma. T. (06) 39737425. 059117
Bracci, C., Via Funari 18A, 00186 Roma. T. (06) 68308212. 059118
Brancaccio, S., Via Città delle Pieve 34, 00191 Roma. T. (06) 333 61 44. 059119
Brancatelli, Calogero, Via Pereira 99, 00136 Roma. T. (06) 345 21 05. 059120
Bric A' Brac, 20 Via Macchia Saponara, 00125 Roma. T. (06) 52310146. 059121
Bric à Brac ai Coronari, Via Coronari 163, 00186 Roma. T. (06) 68806393. 059122
Briganti, M., Via Panisperna 247, 00184 Roma. T. (06) 482 50 12. 059123
Il Brillocco di Aurora Piras, 28 Via Mocenigo, 00192 Roma. T. (06) 3700275. 059124
British Trade, Via Scrofa 39, 00186 Roma. T. (06) 687 95 64. 059125
Brogi, Giovanna, Via Catullo 22, 00193 Roma. T. (06) 687 46 69. - Furn - 059126
Bruni, A., Via Giulia 101, 00186 Roma. T. (06) 68805323. 059127
Buceti, D., Via Banchi Vecchi 60, 00186 Roma. T. (06) 68802907. 059128
Buceti, U., Piazza Montevecchio 16, 00186 Roma. T. (06) 68308604. 059129
Bulgari, Via dei Condotti 10, 00187 Roma. T. (06) 679 38 76. - Ant / Jew / Silv - 059130
Calabretta, P. L., Via Mastro Giorgio 62, 00153 Roma. T. (06) 575 85 06. 059131
Calabrò e Colasanti, Via del Babuino 51, 00187 Roma. T. (06) 6791804. 059132
Calabro' M., 11 Via Stoppani, 00197 Roma. T. (06) 8070500. 059133
Calo' F., 159 Via Coronari, 00186 Roma. T. (06) 6865053. 059134
Calò, Fabrizio, Via dei Coronari 85, 00186 Roma. T. (06) 68806512. 059135
Calò, Giuseppe, Via Basento 73/75, 00198 Roma. T. (06) 844 16 63. 059136
Cambio Rosati Acquisto e vendita monete, Via Nazianale, 00184 Roma. T. (06) 4885498. 059137
Cammisa T., 20 Piazza Teatro Pompec, 00186 Roma. T. (06) 6876769. 059138
Camponi, E., Via Stelletta 32, 00186 Roma. T. (06) 686 52 49. 059139
Canto, U., Via S. Aurea 132, 00186 Roma. T. (06) 68 30 86 72. 059140
Capitolium, Via Fedele 56, 00179 Roma. T. (06) 78346516. 059141
Carlucci, F., Via Salaria 224C, 00198 Roma. T. (06) 841 62 14. 059142

Carnovale, Aurelio, Via del Governo Vecchio 71, 00186 Roma. T. 806) 6864850. *059143*

Caroselli M., 49 Cironv. Trionfale, 00195 Roma. T. (06) 39736227. *059144*

Carpi P., 50 Via Conte Verde, 00185 Roma. T. (06) 4464769. *059145*

Carpi P., 14 Via Rimini, 00182 Roma. T. (06) 70476477. *059146*

Casa del Turista, 97 Via Giolitti, 00185 Roma. T. (06) 4467251. *059147*

Castellano F., 26 Via Panico, 00186 Roma. T. (06) 6873818. *059148*

Catena Annibale, Antichita' – Importazione diretta, Via S. Gherardi 80, 00146 Roma. T. (06) 5587906. *059149*

Cattaneo, Via al Mezzocammino 195A, 00128 Roma. T. (06) 508 49 17. *059150*

Cavaglia' E., 20/f Via Paul di Calboli, 00195 Roma. T. (06) 37517911. *059151*

Ceccarelli G., 110 Via Coronari, 00186 Roma. T. (06) 6875358. *059152*

Ceccherini V., 109 Via Jenner, 00151 Roma. T. (06) 5373887. *059153*

Cecilia Antiquariato, Via dei Filippini 10, 00186 Roma. T. (06) 68801593. *059154*

Cegna A., 52 Via Banchi Nuovi, 00186 Roma. T. (06) 68804915. *059155*

Cenacolo, Via dei Coronari 190, 00186 Roma. T. (06) 6877145. *059156*

Centro Antiquariato Lubrano, Via Migiurtinia 14-16, 00199 Roma. T. (06) 838 09 05. *059157*

Centro Serena, 1601 Via Prenestina, 00132 Roma. T. (06) 2080144. *059158*

Centro Serena, 1061 Via Prenestina, 00132 Roma. T. (06) 2080042, 2080275, 2080335. *059159*

Centrro Serena, 1601 Via Prenestina, 00132 Roma. T. (06) 2080050. *059160*

Cerboni T., 48 Via S. Carmignano, 00151 Roma. T. (06) 58232429. *059161*

Chelsea, 88 Via Pricilla, 00199 Roma. T. (06) 86213692. *059162*

Chelsea di Cesare Saccani, 86 Via Pricilla, 00199 Roma. T. (06) 86211572. *059163*

Chiericoni G., 901/f Via Cassia, 00189 Roma. T. (06) 3762591. *059164*

La Chimera di Paola Cipriani, 128/129 Via Giulia, 00186 Roma. T. (06) 6874869. *059165*

Christie's, Piazza Navona 114, 00186 Roma. T. (06) 6872787. *059166*

Ciccalotti M., 167a Via Merulana, 00185 Roma. T. (06) 7003493. *059167*

Ciciani A., 79 Via Arcaia, 00183 Roma. T. (06) 77209942. *059168*

Cicolani, Marani S., 28 Via G. Serafino, 00136 Roma. T. (06) 39737388. *059169*

Cigna A., 34 Via Bregno, 00196 Roma. T. (06) 3244969. *059170*

Cirincione M., 59 Viale Vignola, 00196 Roma. T. (06) 3224946. *059171*

Civile A., 29 Via Sannazzaro, 00196 Roma. T. (06) 82000931. *059172*

Club dell' Antiquariato Internazionale, Via Bernardino Ramazzini 91, 00151 Roma. T. (06) 534 69 30, 537 30 87.
- Ant / Paint / Furn / Tex / Silv - *059173*

C.M. International, 44 Via Giuliana, 00195 Roma. T. (06) 3700253, 3722479. *059174*

C.M.I., 12 Vicolo Campanella, 00186 Roma. T. (06) 6874874. *059175*

Cocozza, Antonio, Via Luigi Rizzo 40, 00136 Roma. T. (06) 39720391/39720590. *059176*

Cocozza, Osvaldo, Via Margutta 41, 00187 Roma. T. (06) 3614056. *059177*

Coen, Luciano, Via Margutta 65, 00187 Roma. T. (06) 3207604. - Orient - *059178*

Cofimes, 7 Via Calabria, 00187 Roma. T. (06) 4820002. *059179*

Cohen, Via del Babuino 59, 00187 Roma. T. (06) 678 43 11. *059180*

Colca, 17 Via S. Giacomo, 00187 Roma. T. (06) 6782851, 6783846, 6791156, 6798089. *059181*

Collalti A., 11 Via Val Chienti, 00141 Roma. T. (06) 8102925. *059182*

Collalti, Sergio, Viale Somalia 151, 00199 Roma. T. (06) 86201044. - Furn - *059183*

Collati, A., Via Teulada 5/7, 00195 Roma. T. (06) 37515914. *059184*

Il Collezionista, 51 Via Cossa, 00193 Roma. T. (06) 3213892. *059185*

Colonia Artistica, 3 Via Sesini, 00124 Roma. T. (06) 50914118. *059186*

Colonna, F., Via Vittoria 50, 00187 Roma. T. (06) 6794481. *059187*

La Conchiglia Dell'Ottocento, 145 Via Stampa, 00137 Roma. T. (06) 86801616. *059188*

Condotti Fine Arts, 56 Via Condotti, 00187 Roma. T. (06) 6791973. *059189*

Constantini, Giuseppe, Piazza Navona 104, 00186 Roma. T. (06) 68806643. *059190*

COR.DA, 22 Via Collazia, 00183 Roma. T. (06) 70454827. *059191*

Corrado M., 58 Via G.G. Belli, 00193 Roma. T. (06) 3226823. *059192*

Corsetti S., 49 Via Banco di S. Spirito, 00186 Roma. T. (06) 6832768. *059193*

Cose D'Altri Tempi, 170 Viale Tor Quinto, 00191 Roma. T. (06) 3340475. *059194*

Cose D'Altri Tempi, 170 Viale Tor Quinto, 00191 Roma. T. (06) 3340476. *059195*

Cose di Ieri, 26 Via Vittoria, 00187 Roma. T. (06) 6990648. *059196*

Cossiau C., 102 Via Governo Vecchio, 00186 Roma. T. (06) 68308910. *059197*

Costa, Nito, Via Panisperna 238, 00184 Roma. T. (06) 4819379. *059198*

Costantino A.M., 10 Via Ripetta, 00186 Roma. T. (06) 3610269. *059199*

Covatti A., 91/a Via Margutta, 00187 Roma. T. (06) 6792798. *059200*

Cramersteter N., 18 Via Sciacca, 00182 Roma. T. (06) 7001717. *059201*

Crisafi – La Regina, Mobili antichi e d'occasione, Via Casse Basse 222, 00126 Roma. T. (06) 5250231. *059202*

Cutri S., 26 Via Banchi Nuovi, 00186 Roma. T. (06) 6861453. *059203*

Cynthia Antichita' – Vendita, Mobili e dipinti 800 Francia Inghilterra – Importazone diretta Acquisto da privati, Via Genzano 67/B – 67/C, 00179 Roma. T. (06) 7802225. *059204*

D'Amora F., Via Ombrellari, 00193 Roma. T. (06) 6879816. *059205*

D'Antoni, Luciana, Via del Pellegrino 88, 00186 Roma. T. (06) 6875156. *059206*

D'Arpino, Rosa Bianca, Via Salaria 276, 00198 Roma. T. (06) 8419986. *059207*

Dalpiaz R., Vicolo Sugarelli, 00186 Roma. T. (06) 68801083. *059208*

Das C., 43/a Via Monserrato, 00186 Roma. T. (06) 6892356. *059209*

Davoli A., 168 Via Giulia, 00186 Roma. T. (06) 6896097. *059210*

De Angelis A., 325 Via Casetta Mattei, 00148 Roma. T. (06) 66161412. *059211*

De Angelis A., 325 Via Casetta Mattei, 00148 Roma. T. (06) 66154046, 66154246. *059212*

De Angelis A., 315 Via Casetta Mattei, 00148 Roma. T. (06) 66161410. *059213*

De Angelis C., 8 Via Pacinotti, 00146 Roma. T. (06) 5561654. *059214*

De Marchi, Mario E Walter, Via dei Tre Archi, 00186 Roma. T. (06) 6864486. *059215*

De Matteis D., 28 Via Palumbo, 00195 Roma. T. (06) 39730682. *059216*

De Sanctis S., 219 Via Coronari, 00186 Roma. T. (06) 68801254. *059217*

De Simone M., 2 Via Belsiana, 00186 Roma. T. (06) 6780185. *059218*

De Sisinno, Via dei Banchi Nuovi 17, 00186 Roma. T. (06) 68804012. *059219*

De Stefani Arte e Antichita, 6 Via Boschetto, 00184 Roma. T. (06) 485897. *059220*

Del Borgo G., 114 Via Giulia, 00186 Roma. T. (06) 68806243. *059221*

Del Borgo, Guido, Via Giulia 8, 00186 Roma. T. (06) 687 98 17. - Ant / Paint / Draw - *059222*

Di Castro Adolfo di Servio e Lea di Castro, Via del Babuino 80/81, 00187 Roma. T. (06) 3207684. *059223*

Di Castro, Alberto, Piazza di Spagna 5, 00187 Roma. T. (06) 679 22 69. *059224*

di Castro, Aldo, Via del Babuino 71, 00187 Roma. T. (06) 6794900/69940267. *059225*

Di Castro, Amedeo, Via del Babuino 77/78, 00187 Roma. T. (06) 3207650. *059226*

Di Castro Angelo di Angelo e Lucilla, Via Alibert 20/21/ 22, 00187 Roma. T. (06) 69941757. *059227*

Di Castro, L., 78/a Via Croce, Roma. T. (06) 6790972. *059228*

Di Castro, Nicola, Via del Babuino 92, 00187 Roma. T. (06) 679 02 10. *059229*

Di Castro R., 49 Via Margutta, 00187 Roma. T. (06) 3614054. *059230*

Di Fabio T., 60 Vicolo Governo Vecchio, 00186 Roma. T. (06) 68803725. *059231*

Di Giorgio C., 42 Via Monserrato, 00186 Roma. T. (06) 68801707. *059232*

Di Giorgio, D., Via del Babuino, 00187 Roma. T. (06) 3218624. *059233*

Di Iacovo R., 52 Borgo Pio, 00193 Roma. T. (06) 68801967. *059234*

Di Matteo, G., Via Chiana 17/19, 00198 Roma. T. (06) 854 93 82. *059235*

Di Nepi, S. e P., Via del Babuino 87/88, 00187 Roma. T. (06) 3207654. *059236*

Di Paolo L., 44/a Via Lungara, 00165 Roma. T. (06) 6893662. *059237*

Di Sora E., 29 Via Molajoni, 00159 Roma. T. (06) 4390601. *059238*

Di Virgilio di, Stefanoni Rosa Felice, 33 Via Serpenti, 00184 Roma. T. (06) 485744. *059239*

Diana G., 13 Passeg. Ripetta, 00186 Roma. T. (06) 3612053, 3219073. *059240*

Dilor, 188 Via Giulia, 00186 Roma. T. (06) 6864291. *059241*

Dini S., 51/a Via Fontelana, 00152 Roma. T. (06) 5815218. *059242*

Doninelli P.I., 337 Via Corso, 00186 Roma. T. (06) 6791893. *059243*

Dragonfly, Arte moderna – Orologi – Perizie Si acquista da privati contanti, Via Tacito 38, 00193 Roma. T. (06) 3244411. *059244*

Due C, 15 Via Giuliana, 00195 Roma. T. (06) 3721320. *059245*

Durante, G., Piazza di Spagna 9, 00187 Roma. T. (06) 679 59 54. *059246*

El Euteri F., 39/a Via M. de' Fiori, 00172 Roma. T. (06) 6794806. *059247*

El Greco, Via Pontina, 00128 Roma. T. (06) 5070380, 5070616. *059248*

Emporio Floreale, Via delle Carrozze 46, 00187 Roma. T. (06) 678 02 07. - Paint / Mod - *059249*

Ercolani, 25 Borgo Vittorio, 00193 Roma. T. (06) 68801083. *059250*

Eredi Tanca, 10/11/12 S. Crescenzi, 00186 Roma. T. (06) 68803328. *059251*

Esercizio 2000, 2 Via Bellotti Bon, 00197 Roma. T. (06) 8587153. *059252*

Eur Antiquariato, 105 Viale Aeronautica, 00144 Roma. T. (06) 5915428. *059253*

Euro Antichita' Giulia, 140/a Via Giulia, 00186 Roma. T. (06) 68308048. *059254*

Eurocambio, 92 Via Crispi, 00187 Roma. T. (06) 4819834. *059255*

Fabbri F., 107 Via Urbana, 00184 Roma. T. (06) 4885608. *059256*

Fabbrini C., 46 Viale Adriatico, 00141 Roma. T. (06) 898391, 8173659. *059257*

Fabbrini C., Via U. Balzani, 00162 Roma. T. (06) 8604495. *059258*

Fallani, Via del Babuino 58A, 00187 Roma. T. (06) 3207982. - Ant / Num / Sculp / Arch - *059259*

Farenza Il Bottegone dell' Antiquariato, Viale dei Colli Portuensi 48, 00153 Roma. T. (06) 58237238. *059260*

Farnese Arte, 106 Via Monserrato, 00186 Roma. T. (06) 6876280. *059261*

F.A.R.O., Via Casalmonferrato 7A e Via Spadola 27, 00182 Roma. T. (06) 7029390/7234975. - Furn - *059262*

Fasoli, C., Via Giuseppe Zanardelli 1, 00186 Roma.
T. (06) 654 18 27. 059263
Fauro, Via di Monserrato 120, 00186 Roma.
T. (06) 6867747. 059264
Fauro, 16 Via Archimede, 00197 Roma.
T. (06) 8082534. 059265
Favà, Via del Babuino 180, 00187 Roma.
T. (06) 361 08 07. - Ant / Paint / Furn / Sculp /
Silv - 059266
Fazio M.C., 37/39 Via Rendano, 00199 Roma.
T. (06) 86212472. 059267
Febbi G., 98 Via Clementino, 00186 Roma.
T. (06) 6873777. 059268
Febo, Via delle Carrozze 48, 00187 Roma.
T. (06) 6785430. - Paint / Furn - 059269
Felici V., 135 Via Casale Lumbroso, 00166 Roma.
T. (06) 66180596. 059270
La Fenice, 297 Via Prati Fiscali, 00141 Roma.
T. (06) 8104654. 059271
Ferrante, Arturo, Via del Babuino 42/43, 00187 Roma.
T. (06) 678 36 13. 059272
Ferrareis A., 49 Via Prisciano, 00136 Roma.
T. (06) 3498121. 059273
Ferrari G., 9 Via Valle Vescovo, 00189 Roma.
T. (06) 3336479. 059274
Ferrazza R., 24 Via C. Paoletti, 00198 Roma.
T. (06) 00198. 059275
Ferretti E Guerrini Antichita', 22 Via Banchi Nuovi,
00186 Roma. T. (06) 68307448. 059276
Ferri, Via Sistina 10, 00187 Roma. T. (06) 4827893.
- Num - 059277
Fiano, Via Giulia 150, 00186 Roma.
T. (06) 6879712. 059278
Ficarra F., 21 Via Monserrato, 00186 Roma.
T. (06) 6893211. 059279
Filateria Don Bosco, 12 Viale Salesiani, 00175 Roma.
T. (06) 71510220. 059280
Finarte, Via Margutta 54, 00187 Roma.
T. (06) 3207721. 059281
Fine Art, 12 Via Laurina, 00187 Roma.
T. (00187. 059282
Fiore C., 15 Via Reggio E., 00198 Roma.
T. (06) 8541496. 059283
Fiore, Giuseppe, 6 Piazza Aruleno Celio Sabino, 00174
Roma. T. (06) 715102/2. 059284
Fiore, Maria Giuseppina, Via Giulia 173, 00186 Roma.
T. (06) 68308903. - Paint / Furn - 059285
Fiorentini, Enrico, Via Margutta 53B, 00187 Roma.
T. (06) 3207660. 059286
Flavoni, Ugo, Via del Governo Vecchio 97, 00186 Roma.
T. (06) 6861534. 059287
Fontana M., 82 Viale reg. Margherita, 00198 Roma.
T. (06) 8552451. 059288
Fontana M., 36 Via P.A. Micheli, 00197 Roma.
T. (06) 3610773. 059289
La Fontanella Fotografico, Antiquariato, Via S. Giovanni
in Laterano 166, Roma. T. (06) 7008126,
Fax (06) 5740175. 059290
Forin G., Via Giulia, 00186 Roma.
T. (06) 6861651. 059291
Formichi F., 41 Via Parione, 00186 Roma.
T. (06) 6880186. 059292
Fortuna, Alberto, Via dei Coronari 198, 00186 Roma.
T. (06) 6867948. 059293
FRA.BO.NO, 2/b Via Sciamanna, 00168 Roma.
T. (06) 3381905. 059294
Funghini, Via di Ripetta 149, 00186 Roma.
T. (06) 8307128. - Furn / Sculp - 059295
G. Ruiz & C., 109 Via Margutta, 00187 Roma.
T. (06) 69941800. 059296
G.A.D., 77/78 Via Babuino, 00187 Roma.
T. (06) 3207650. 059297
Gaggia, Anna, Via dei Coronari 112, 00186 Roma.
T. (06) 68804997. 059298
Gagnolato G., 63 Via Boccardo, 00191 Roma.
T. (06) 3338971. 059299
Galardi Carlandrea Antiquario, Via Franco Sacchetti 2/A,
00137 Roma. T. (06) 87137616. 059300
Galleria Akka, 14 Via Pie' di Marmo, 00186 Roma.
T. (06) 6792066. 059301
Galleria Antiquaria dell'Arco, Via Giulia 178, 00186 Ro-
ma. T. (06) 68801520. 059302

Galleria Antiquariato Europeo, Via Margutta 76, 00165
Roma. T. (06) 3207729. 059303
Galleria Antiquariato Europeo, Via Gregorio VII 272,
00165 Roma. T. (06) 630233, 39376627,
Fax (06) 39387189. 059304
Galleria Coronari di Laura Dall'Aglio, Collezionismo d'Ar-
te, 00186 Roma. T. (06) 6869917. 059305
Galleria D'Arte Cattaneo, 195/a Via Mezzocammino,
00128 Roma. T. (06) 5084917. 059306
Galleria dei Cosmati, Via Cavallini 8, 00193 Roma.
T. (06) 361 11 41. 059307
Galleria del Francobollo, 204 Via Nazioanle, 00184 Ro-
ma. T. (06) 4818247. 059308
Galleria Dell'Antiquariato Europeo, 272 Gregori VII,
00165 Roma. T. (06) 630233, 39387189. 059309
Galleria Dell'Antiquariato Europeo, 272 Via Gregori VII,
00165 Roma. T. (06) 39376627. 059310
Galleria Fauro, 120 Via Monserrato, 00168 Roma.
T. (06) 6832586. 059311
Galleria Mario dei Fiori, Via Mario dè Fiori 24 C, 00187
Roma. T. (06) 678 08 33. 059312
Galleria Pinciana, Via Pinciana 61-65, 00198 Roma.
T. (06) 8414889. 059313
Galleria Romana Antichita', 81/a Via Giulia, 00186 Ro-
ma. T. (06) 68801447. 059314
Galleria Romana Dell'Ottocento, 14 Via Sardegna,
00187 Roma. T. (06) 4821862. 059315
Galleria S. Emiliano, Via Canada 3, 00181 Roma.
T. (0734) 997359. 059316
Galleria S. Emiliano, Via Tuscolana 226 c/d, Via Assisi
148, 00181 Roma. T. (06) 7802722, 7811789,
Fax (06) 7858178. 059317
Galleria, Verde, 40 Via Monserrato, 00186 Roma.
T. (06) 68307695. 059318
Gallo R., 103 Via Val Maira, 00141 Roma.
T. (06) 88640174. 059319
Galpada – Import – Export, 380 Via Ojetti, 00137 Roma.
T. (06) 8273706, 86802500. 059320
Gamberini, Via di Monserrato 121A, 00186 Roma.
T. (06) 8802629. 059321
Gandini L., 13 Via 7 Metri, 00137 Roma.
T. (06) 79844453. 059322
Gargiulo M., 37 Via Vittoria, 00187 Roma.
T. (06) 6789465. 059323
Gasparini, C., Via della Fontanella di Borghese 46,
00186 Roma. T. (06) 6876658. - Ant / Paint /
Furn - 059324
Gasparrini C., 48 Via Fontan di Borghese, 00186 Roma.
T. (06) 6790620. 059325
Gasparrini C., 46 Via Fontan di Borghese, 00186 Roma.
T. (06) 6785820. 059326
Gauzzi P., 199 Via Pellegrino, 00186 Roma.
T. (06) 6832728. 059327
Gentile L., 104 Via Monserrato, 00186 Roma.
T. (06) 6879014. 059328
Gentile, Roberto, Piazza di Tor Sanguigna 1, 00186 Ro-
ma. T. (06) 6868623. 059329
Gerardini, Viale Regina Margherita 147, 00198 Roma.
T. (06) 85 06 94. 059330
Gherardi C., 33/33a Via Prefett, 00186 Roma.
T. (06) 6873730. 059331
Gherardi, Claudio, Via Pallacorda 1, 00186 Roma.
T. (06) 68801412. 059332
Giancaterini, Luigi, 25 Via Licia, 00183 Roma.
T. (06) 7001540. 059333
Gierre Antichita' di, Roberto Gallo, 103 Via Val Maira,
00141 Roma. T. (06) 88328005. 059334
Giorgi, Giuliano, Via dei Coronari 25, 00186 Roma.
T. (06) 6875968. 059335
Giorgio Ferrari, 9 Via Valle Vescovo, 00189 Roma.
T. (06) 3336496. 059336
Giovannetti A., Via Aurella, 00165 Roma.
T. (06) 6697141. 059337
Giuffrida M., 20/21 Via Coronari, 00186 Roma.
T. (06) 6877358. 059338
Giusti, L., Via Giulia 117, 00186 Roma.
T. (06) 68801991. 059339
Goffi – Carboni, G., Piazza Augusto Imperatore 7, 00186
Roma. T. (06) 3227184. 059340
Gold & Silver Exchange Bank, Oro, argento. kingotti, ge-
ttoni d'oro, Via D'Azeglio 3A, 3B, 00184 Roma.
T. (06) 4885047, 4743116. 059341

Gombacci S., 11 Via Giulia, 00186 Roma.
T. (06) 6875225. 059342
Grieco R., 29/30 Via Banchi Vecchi, 00186 Roma.
T. (06) 68801689. 059343
Guerra C., 124b Via XX Settembre, 00187 Roma.
T. (06) 4827569. 059344
Guerrieri, G.L., 199a Via Alessandria, 00198 Roma.
T. (08) 8845502. 059345
Gussio, Lucia, Via Laurina 27A, 00187 Roma.
T. (06) 3614156. 059346
Hastings Enterprises, 57 Via Fauro, 00197 Roma.
T. (06) 8587259. 059347
Hastings Enterprises, 61 Via Fauro, 00197 Roma.
T. (06) 8070898. 059348
Hastings Enterprises, 399 Via Gregorio VII, 00165 Roma.
T. (06) 633604. 059349
Hastings G., 3 Via Piccinini, 00135 Roma.
T. (06) 3767673. 059350
Hastings G.J., 13840 Via Trionfale, 00136 Roma.
T. (06) 3763076. 059351
Hendy, J., Piazza di Pietra 42, 00186 Roma.
T. (06) 678 58 04. 059352
Hobbies, 2e Via A. Farnese, 00192 Roma.
T. (06) 3210447. 059353
Home Antiquariato, 138/140 Via Conta D'Org, 00141 Ro-
ma. T. (06) 8109773. 059354
Home Antiquariato, 72a/b Viale Tirreno, 00141 Roma.
T. (06) 87190273. 059355
Idone N., 5/5a/5b Via Giuochi Istmici, 00194 Roma.
T. (06) 36304611. 059356
IG.OR.Societa' in Nome Collettivo di Ricci Beatrice & C.,
2 Via Banchi Nuovi, 00186 Roma.
T. (06) 6893243. 059357
Il Collezionista, Via Panico 65, 00186 Roma.
T. (06) 6893223, Fax (06) 6893223. - China - 059358
Il Globo, Via Gregorio VII 354, 00165 Roma.
T. (06) 663 60 88. 059359
Il Gonfalone, Via Giulia 88, 00186 Roma.
T. (06) 63308882. 059360
Il Leoncino, Via del Leoncino 25, 00186 Roma.
T. (06) 6876503. 059361
Il Leone Azzurro, Via Angelo Brunetti 35/39, 00186 Ro-
ma. T. (06) 68802585. 059362
Il Postiglione, Via Mario de' Fiori 4/5, 00187 Roma.
T. (06) 69940659. 059363
Il Pozzo, Via dei Coronari 180, 00186 Roma.
T. (06) 656 59 38. 059364
Il Sagittario, Via Caio Mario 6A, 00192 Roma.
T. (06) 324 16 77. 059365
Il Sagittario, Piazza Unità 14, 00192 Roma.
T. (06) 321 24 48. 059366
Il Silenus, Via Margutta 91, 00187 Roma.
T. (06) 6792798. 059367
Il Trittico, Via dei Coronari 81, 00186 Roma.
T. (06) 6877431. 059368
International Art Center di, De Leo Marcello, 37 Via Pa-
lombella, 00186 Roma. T. (06) 68802920. 059369
Internazionale, 57 Piazza Cinquecento, 00185 Roma.
T. (06) 4885005. 059370
Interni di Pieroni, Maria Luisa, 64a Via Orso, 00186 Ro-
ma. T. (06) 68801519. 059371
Invito A Casa, 27 Circonv. Clodia, 00195 Roma.
T. (06) 39735298. 059372
Istituto Europeo di Design, 212 Via Salaria, 00198 Ro-
ma. T. (06) 8842186. 059373
Izzo A., 902 Via Appia Nuova, 00178 Roma.
T. (06) 7184136, 7186419. 059374
Izzo A., 51a Via Margutta, 00187 Roma.
T. (06) 3210135. 059375
Jandolo, A., Via Margutta 51A, 00187 Roma.
T. (06) 3207659. 059376
Kown Y.O., 11 Via Chiavari, 00186 Roma.
T. (06) 68801118. 059377
L'Angolo – Antiquariato, Dipinti – Mobili – Marmi, Via
degli Orsini 36, 00186 Roma. T. (06) 6896003. 059378
L'Antico di Principali F., Viaggio intorno ad un oggetto,
Via Catanzaro 41, 00161 Roma.
T. (06) 44233724. 059379
L'Antiquus, 15 Via Giuliana, 00195 Roma.
T. (06) 37513550. 059380
L'Antiqvario, Via A. Sogliano 49, 00164 Roma.
T. (06) 66141565. 059381

L'Arca, 9 Via Campo Marzio, 00186 Roma.
T. (06) 6789395. *059382*
L'Arcidiagus, 33 Via Delfini, 00186 Roma.
T. (06) 6990619, 6990634. *059383*
L' Art Nouveau, Via dei Coronari 221, 00100 Roma.
T. (06) 6545230. *059384*
La Chicciola, Via dei Coronari 185/186, 00186 Roma.
T. (06) 68801954. *059385*
La Chimera, Via Giulia 122-124, 00186 Roma.
T. (06) 68308344. *059386*
La Colonna, Via dei Coronari 14, 00186 Roma.
T. (06) 6865330. *059387*
La Coroncina, Via dei Coronari 21, 00186 Roma.
T. (06) 6896704. *059388*
La Fantasia, Via Barberini 69, 00187 Roma.
T. (06) 474 54 29. *059389*
La Mansarde, Via dei Coronari 203, 00186 Roma.
T. (06) 6879266. - Ant - *059390*
La Piazzetta, Via dei Coronari 125, 00186 Roma.
T. (06) 68802242. *059391*
La Ragnatela, Via del Castel di Leva 392, 00134 Roma.
T. (06) 71 35 31 27, 71 35 30 67,
Fax (06) 71353252. *059392*
La Spelonca, Via S. Constanza 18, 00198 Roma.
T. (06) 8558900/8292664. *059393*
Lacoste, Romano, Via Giulia 18, 00186 Roma.
T. (06) 6869590. - Ant - *059394*
Lampronti, Cesare, Via del Babuino 67, 00187 Roma.
T. (06) 679 58 00. - Furn / China / Tex / Draw - *059395*
Lampronti, Dr. Carlo, Via del Babuino 69/152, 00187 Roma. T. (06) 6782947/6790306. *059396*
Laneri L., 10 Via Bodoni, 00153 Roma.
T. (06) 5757886. *059397*
Lanni, M., Via degli Orsini 26, 00186 Roma.
T. (06) 68308195. *059398*
Lapedota, Via Margutta 14, 00187 Roma.
T. (06) 3614002. *059399*
Le Muse, Piazza dell'Orologio 14, 00186 Roma.
T. (06) 6861764. *059400*
Le Myricae, Via F. Palucci de Calboli Fulcieri 55, 00195 Roma. T. (06) 37516209. - Furn - *059401*
Le Pleiadi, Via del Pellegrino 110, 00186 Roma.
T. (06) 687 31 80. - Ant / Furn / Silv - *059402*
Le Troc, Via dei Greci 38, 00187 Roma.
T. (06) 679 60 91. *059403*
Lebran, S., Piazza del Parlamento 9, 00186 Roma.
T. (06) 6871358. *059404*
Leone Azzurro, 102 Via Clementino, 00186 Roma.
T. (06) 68802585. *059405*
Leone V., Via Boezio, 00192 Roma.
T. (06) 6878756. *059406*
Leoni L., 86 Via Belsiana, 00187 Roma. T. (06) 6783210,
6790514. *059407*
Littera G., 194/196 Viale Somalia, 00186 Roma.
T. (06) 8601796. *059408*
Lo Scrittoio, Via dei Coronari 102/103, 00186 Roma.
T. (06) 6875536. *059409*
Lombardelli A., 78b Via Macchia Saponara, 00124 Roma. T. (06) 5216154. *059410*
Lombardi A., 29 Via Coronari, 00186 Roma.
T. (06) 68307823. *059411*
London Bridge, Via G. Gioacchino Belli 58, 00193 Roma.
T. (06) 360 68 23. *059412*
Lorenzale, Elio, Via dei Coronari 2/3, 00186 Roma.
T. (06) 6864616. - Num / China - *059413*
LO.RO.DI Collatti, Claudio & C., 40 Via Colonna Antonina,
00186 Roma. T. (06) 69940855. *059414*
Lubrano, G., Piazza Elio Callistio 1, 00199 Roma.
T. (06) 86208757. *059415*
Lucchetti Soldi, Paola, 172 Via Salaria, 00198 Roma.
T. (06) 8541284. *059416*
Lucchini A., 12 Via Acacie, 00171 Roma.
T. (06) 2414131, 2427327. *059417*
Luciani L., 10 Via S. Casciano Bagni, 00146 Roma.
T. (06) 55268897. *059418*
Lukacs – Donath, Via Vittorio Veneto 183, 00187 Roma.
T. (06) 482 18 24, Fax (06) 4821824. - Ant / Paint / China / Silv - *059419*
Lullo, Gsare, Via del Babuino 127, 00187 Roma.
T. (06) 6791561. *059420*
M S. 80, 30 Via Nizza, 00198 Roma.
T. (06) 8412648. *059421*

MA.BI. Art, Via Nuvolari, 00142 Roma.
T. (06) 51956014. *059422*
Mada, Via Savonarola 31/33, 00195 Roma.
T. (06) 39737752. *059423*
Maffettone P., 110/111 Via Banchi Vecchi, 00186 Roma.
T. (06) 68804127. *059424*
Magistri R., 44 Via Pellegrino, 00186 Roma.
T. (06) 6879272. *059425*
Maino M.P., 46 Via Carrozze, 00187 Roma.
T. (06) 6780207. *059426*
La Maison Antiquariato, Arredamento d'epoca Sheffield
– Orologi antichi, Viale Amelia 42/42A, 00181 Roma.
T. (06) 7827639. *059427*
Malliani F., 18 lg. Febo, 00186 Roma.
T. (06) 68802873. *059428*
MA.MO di Massaroni, Rosina, 46 Via Governo Vecchio,
00186 Roma. T. (06) 6874957. *059429*
MA.MO. di Massaroni, Rosina, 3 Via Orto Napoli, 00187
Roma. T. (06) 6785772. *059430*
Manasse, Via di Campo Marzio 44, 00186 Roma.
T. (06) 6871007. *059431*
Mancini & Pianosi, Via Giolitti 63A, 00185 Roma.
T. (06) 4881509. - Num - *059432*
Mangiavacchi G., 56 Via Nievo, 00153 Roma.
T. (06) 5811093. *059433*
Manno G.I., 143 Via Banchi Vecchi, 00186 Roma.
T. (06) 68802814. *059434*
Mapad, 157 Via Pietralata, 00158 Roma.
T. (06) 4182060. *059435*
Marcrellino V., 5/9 Via Boccanegra, 00162 Roma.
T. (06) 44290831. *059436*
Mariani F., 8 Via M.te Cristallo, 00141 Roma.
T. (06) 87182833. *059437*
Marmoidea, 35 Via Monserrato, 00186 Roma.
T. (06) 68308441, 68308442. *059438*
Marra, Dr. Giorgio, Via O. Gasparri 4, 00152 Roma.
T. (06) 58209715. - Furn - *059439*
Martinoja A., 107a Via Babuino, 00187 Roma.
T. (06) 6798263. *059440*
Marzocco, Via Giulia 11, 00186 Roma.
T. (06) 68 75 225. *059441*
Megna, Fabio, Via del Babuino 148A, 00187 Roma.
T. (06) 679 51 50. *059442*
Menat, 16 Via Carrozze, 00187 Roma.
T. (06) 6786986. *059443*
Mensura, 38 Via Baullari, 00186 Roma.
T. (06) 6879972. *059444*
Micioni M., 13840 Via Trionfale, 00136 Roma.
T. (06) 3762855. *059445*
Mieli, Via dei Coronari 163, 00186 Roma.
T. (06) 654 03 93. *059446*
Molayem, Albert, Via Bocca di Leone 30, 00187 Roma.
T. (06) 0790841/0790841. - Arch / Jew - *059447*
Mondo Antico, Via dei Coronari 32, 00186 Roma.
T. (06) 6868298. *059448*
Monetti, Via Giulia 169, 00186 Roma.
T. (06) 6547436. *059449*
Monserrato Arte, 14 Via Monserrato, 00186 Roma.
T. (06) 6875776. *059450*
Moratti P., 34 Via Scrofa, 00186 Roma.
T. (06) 6873825. *059451*
Moretti A., 95 Via Coronari, 00186 Roma.
T. (06) 6873963. *059452*
Moretti Antiquariato – Marmi, C. & A., Via dei Coronari
233A, Roma. T. (06) 68801369. *059453*
Moretti, Claudio, 00186 Roma.
T. (06) 68801369. *059454*
Morgantini G., 8 Piazza Orologia, 00186 Roma.
T. (06) 6877549. *059455*
Morgantini, G., Via Stelletta 10, 00186 Roma.
T. (06) 6865481. *059456*
Moroni R., 82/83 Via Governo Vecchio, 00186 Roma.
T. (06) 6875284. *059457*
Moroni U., 43 Via Bocca Leone, 00187 Roma.
T. (06) 6786073. *059458*
Moroni U., 22 Via Cardello, 00184 Roma.
T. (06) 6790793. *059459*
Morosi, Luciano, Via dei Coronari 13, 00186 Roma.
T. (06) 68307313. *059460*
Morosini, 37 Viale Liegi, 00198 Roma.
T. (06) 8848195. *059461*
Morvzzi Nvmismatica, Via Dei Salesiani 12a, 00175 Roma. T. (06) 71510220, 71545937. *059462*

Moscati G., 192 Via Coronari, 00186 Roma.
T. (06) 68805924. *059463*
Moschitti, Guido, Via degli Spagnoli 30, 00186 Roma.
T. (06) 6869937. *059464*
Munzi G., 90 Via Giulia, 00186 Roma.
T. (06) 68805420. *059465*
Muzzioli M., 35 Via Pavone, 00186 Roma.
T. (06) 6869711. *059466*
My Fair Lady, 24 Via G. Antonelli, 00197 Roma.
T. (06) 8088450. *059467*
Navona Antiquariato, Oggettistica – Mobili – Dipinti,
Piazza Navona 52, 00186 Roma.
T. (06) 6879639. *059468*
Neri, A., Via di S. Giovanni in Laterano 264, 00184 Roma. T. (06) 70450679. *059469*
Nicoletta Lebole, 38 Via Babuino, 00187 Roma.
T. (06) 6783902. *059470*
Nicoletti R., 23/27 Via Albenga, 00183 Roma.
T. (06) 7027442. *059471*
Noce S., 20 Via Scrofa, 00186 Roma.
T. (06) 6861837. *059472*
Nostalgia Dell'Antico, 4 Via Maccarese, 00057 Roma.
T. (06) 6678101. *059473*
Nuccia Sbardella di Sbardella e Trita & C., 47 Via Babuino, 00187 Roma. T. (06) 3235493. *059474*
Numismatica Merulana Monete – Cartamonete – Medaglie, Via Merulana 167A, 00185 Roma.
T. (06) 7003493. *059475*
Oasi, Mario Attilio, Via del Babuino 83, 00187 Roma.
T. (06) 3207585. *059476*
Old Design Piccola bottega antiquaria 800 e 900 inglese, Via Bellinzona 25, 00198 Roma.
T. (06) 8547258. *059477*
Old England, Via di Panico 55-59, 00186 Roma.
T. (06) 6868606. *059478*
Old Home, 26 Via Amatrice, 00199 Roma.
T. (06) 8608972. *059479*
Old Home, 36 Via Amatrice, 00199 Roma.
T. (06) 86203516. *059480*
Old Scotland, Via Ce Carolis 84d, 00136 Roma.
T. (06) 349 78 96. - Furn - *059481*
Old Times, Via dei Pastini 112, 00186 Roma.
T. (06) 678 01 95. *059482*
Olivi, Giovanni, Via del Babuino 136, 00187 Roma.
T. (06) 679 86 82. - Ant / Dec - *059483*
Orsini A., 8 Via Quintili, 00175 Roma.
T. (06) 76961430. *059484*
Orts Berenguer M.E., 60 Via Mad. Monti, 00184 Roma.
T. (06) 4740804. *059485*
Ottaviani, Via dei Banchi Vecchi 27, 00186 Roma.
T. (06) 6877465. *059486*
Over the Stars di Zizzo Volga, 244 Via Panisperna,
00184 Roma. T. (06) 4820675. *059487*
Pacchera, Dario, Via dei Greci 7, 00187 Roma.
T. (06) 679 50 81. - Ant / Furn - *059488*
Pace Anna Mobili Antichi, Vicolo Sforza Cesarini 51,
00186 Roma. T. (06) 6865556. *059489*
Pam Elettroforniture, 7/13 Via Fucini, 00137 Roma.
T. (06) 87137107. *059490*
Papadato, Via del Babuino 147, 00187 Roma.
T. (06) 678 38 80. - Ant / Silv - *059491*
Papaleo V., 19 Via Leutari, 00186 Roma.
T. (06) 6874014. *059492*
Passeri M., 199 Via Cavour, 00184 Roma.
T. (06) 4745112. *059493*
Pea A., 42 Piazza Teatro Pompeo, 00186 Roma.
T. (06) 68801293. *059494*
Pea C., 13 Via S. Maria Anima, 00186 Roma.
T. (06) 68802623. *059495*
Pea L., 31a/31b Via Orazio, 00193 Roma.
T. (06) 6876764. *059496*
Pea U., 39 Piazza Teatro Pompeo, 00186 Roma.
T. (06) 6869217. *059497*
Pedoni, Roberto, Via Vespasiano 7, S. Pietro/Metro Ottaviano, 00192 Roma. T. (06) 39733744. *059498*
Peretti, Arnaldo, Via del Governo Vecchio 120, 00186
Roma. T. (06) 68802563. - Paint - *059499*
Pesciaioli L., 12 Via Pallacorda, 00186 Roma.
T. (06) 6873710. *059500*
Pesciaioli, L., Via della Fontarella di Borghese 59, 00186
Roma. T. (06) 6876646. *059501*
Petochi, G., Piazza di Spagna 23, 00187 Roma.
T. (06) 679 06 35. *059502*

Piazza G., 2 Via F. di Savola, 00198 Roma. T. (06) 3610916. 059503
Picciati, Via di Priscilla 39/41/43, 00199 Roma. T. (06) 86206273. - Mil - 059504
Piccirilli, Via Giulia 103, 00186 Roma. T. (06) 6864088. - Furn / Sculp / Jew - 059505
Piccirilli, Francesco, Via di Torre Argentina 82/83, 00186 Roma. T. (06) 6540804. 059506
Piccirilli W., 103 Via Giulia, 00186 Roma. T. (06) 68802374. 059507
Piccolo Antiquariato, 45 Via E.Q. Visconti, 00193 Roma. T. (06) 3216297. 059508
Pierantognetti G., 280 Via Appla Nuova, 00183 Roma. T. (06) 7027611. 059509
PI.GA., 65/66 Via Coronari, 00183 Roma. T. (06) 6869623. 059510
Pinci Fratelli, 92/94 Via Galfia, 00183 Roma. T. (06) 7009532. 059511
Piperno A., 31 Piazza Pio XI, 00165 Roma. T. (06) 39377074. 059512
Pirri A., 74 Via Pettinari, 00186 Roma. T. (06) 68803856. 059513
Pivetta S., 22 Viale, 00153 Roma. T. (06) 5800447. 059514
Poggi, S, 16 Via Parione, 00186 Roma. T. (06) 68308881. 059515
Portavia A., 142 Via Germanico, 00192 Roma. T. (06) 39737325. 059516
Posani E., 18 Via S. Maria Anima, 00186 Roma. T. (06) 6864202. 059517
Prestigio Interni, 38 Via Governo Vecchio, 00186 Roma. T. (06) 68805134. 059518
Prili Cav. Luciano, Via Banchi Nuovi 27, 00186 Roma. T. (06) 68805660. 059519
Prili Cav. Luciano, Via degli Orsini 35, 00186 Roma. T. (06) 6832589. 059520
Prili F., 110 Via Monserrato, 00186 Roma. T. (06) 6865349. 059521
Prili M., 249 Corso Vitt. Eman II, 00186 Roma. T. (06) 6868311. 059522
Prili, Mario, Via dei Banchi Nuovi 42, 00186 Roma. T. (06) 6868816, 6868311. 059523
Prili, Mario, Via dei Banchi Nuovi 42, 00186 Roma. T. (06) 6868816. - Furn - 059524
Principali F., 8 Via Padova, 00161 Roma. T. (06) 44291620. 059525
Profili G., 16a Via Bisagno, 00199 Roma. T. (06) 8605903. 059526
Quaranta S., 213 Via Coronari, 00186 Roma. T. (06) 6896704. 059527
Quasar Corsi Antiquariato, Via le Reg Margherita 192, 00198 Roma. T. (06) 8440144, 8557078, Fax (06) 8547311. 059528
Quattrini A., 185 Via Coronari, 00186 Roma. T. (06) 68801954. 059529
R. & B., 11 Via rampa Mignanelli, 00187 Roma. T. (06) 6783190. 059530
Ramoni, Roberto, Via del Governo Vecchio 76, 00186 Roma. T. (06) 68802003. 059531
Rancini S., 77a Via Boschetto, 00184 Roma. T. (06) 4814212. 059532
Randazzo R., 31 Via Casale Ghella, 00189 Roma. T. (06) 3761596. 059533
Raoli M., 19 Via Rieti, 00198 Roma. T. (06) 8555635. 059534
Raoli M., 52 Via Velletri, 00198 Roma. T. (06) 8442901, 85301401. 059535
Raucci O., 17 Via Faa' di Bruno, 00195 Roma. T. (06) 3728483. 059536
Ravasi M., 78 Via Risaro, 00127 Roma. T. (06) 52372794. 059537
Recanati A., 104 Via Margutta, 00187 Roma. T. (06) 69942150. 059538
Renn Rain F., 123 Via Babuino, 00187 Roma. T. (06) 6783384. 059539
Res Allestimenti e C., 33/34 Via Banchi Vecchi, 00186 Roma. T. (06) 6875747. 059540
Riccardi, Angelo, Via di Parione 11, 00186 Roma. T. (06) 6877248. 059541
Ricci A, 41a Via Rotonda, 00186 Roma. T. (06) 6864877. 059542
Ricci B., 67 Viale Ippocrate, 00161 Roma. T. (06) 44237696. 059543
Ricci M.T., 39 Via Tirso, 00198 Roma. T. (06) 8417411. 059544
Riganti Fausto, 41 Via M. de' Fiori, 00172 Roma. T. (06) 6790680. 059545
Rinaldi R., 27 Via d'Ascanio, 00186 Roma. T. (06) 6861028. 059546
Rinascimento 87, 13 Corso Rinascimento, 00186 Roma. T. (06) 6869823. 059547
Ritorto I., 39 Via T. Campanella, 00186 Roma. T. (06) 39732546. 059548
Robe D'Arte, 14 Via Tuscolana, 00182 Roma. T. (06) 7023626. 059549
Robe D'Arte, 49 Piazza Re di Roma, 00183 Roma. T. (06) 77204022. 059550
Roberto Della VIle Disgn, 85 Via Margutta, 00187 Roma. T. (06) 3207693. 059551
Roberto Pedoni Numismatica e Arte, 7 Via Vespasiano, 00192 Roma. T. (06) 39733744. 059552
Roccantica, 12 Via Roccantica, 00199 Roma. T. (06) 8601652. 059553
Romano Antichita', Via Villa Chigi 80, 00199 Roma. T. (06) 86212449. 059554
Romano F., 24 Via Palombella, 00186 Roma. T. (06) 6865718. 059555
Romano, Licia, Via del Babuino 141a 142, 00187 Roma. T. (06) 679 11 98. - Ant / Paint / Sculp - 059556
Rosatelli, F., Viale Somalia 23, 00183 Roma. T. (06) 86200271. 059557
Rosati, R., Via Giulia 114, 00186 Roma. T. (06) 654 02 43. 059558
Rose M., 14 Via S. Teodoro, 00186 Roma. T. (06) 6796513. 059559
Rosenfelder W., 53 Via Babuino, 00187 Roma. T. (06) 6790964. 059560
Rossi, F., Via della Stelletta 31, 00186 Roma. T. (06) 6868978. 059561
Rovelli L., 41a Viale Parioli, 00197 Roma. T. (06) 8075575. 059562
Ruschiak, Via E.Q. Visconti 8B, 00193 Roma. T. (06) 321 31 52. - Paint / Furn / China / Tex - 059563
Russo D., 119 Via Babuino, 00187 Roma. T. (06) 6790161. 059564
Sabeni C., 222 Via Case Basse, 00126 Roma. T. (06) 5250231. 059565
Saccetti G., 4 Via Monserrato, 00186 Roma. T. (06) 68801797. 059566
Salbitani, Gabriella, Via di Ripetta 141 B, 00186 Roma. T. (06) 6875130. 059567
Salvati S., 22 Via Giulia, 00186 Roma. T. (06) 68805233. 059568
Santamaria, Pio & Pietro, Piazza di Spagna 35, 00187 Roma. T. (06) 679 04 16. - Num - 059569
Sartori A.M., 61 Via Badoero, 00154 Roma. T. (06) 5137025. 059570
Sassi A., 11 Via Moro, 00153 Roma. T. (06) 5816470. 059571
Scalzotto C., 89 Borgo Vittorio, 00153 Roma. T. (06) 6869150. 059572
Scarabellin A., 103 Via Monserato, 00186 Roma. T. (06) 68804393. 059573
Scarchilli R., 138 Via Coronari, 00186 Roma. T. (06) 6869704. 059574
Schettino U., 25 Via Panico, 00186 Roma. T. (06) 6896246. 059575
Schiaparelli, Giampaolo, Viale Parioli 168, 00197 Roma. T. (06) 8084697. 059576
Schiavello A., 21 Via Prestinari, 00195 Roma. T. (06) 3219753. 059577
Sciarra R., 2 Via San Marino, 00198 Roma. T. (06) 8543796. 059578
La Seggiola, 89 Via Panisperna, 00184 Roma. T. (06) 4826602. 059579
Sellarione D., 58 Via Ant. Silvani, 00139 Roma. T. (06) 8103204. 059580
Selvi C., 26 Via Rivaldi, 00151 Roma. T. (06) 58232594. 059581
Sensi F., 86 Via Margutta, 00187 Roma. T. (06) 3207643. 059582
Sèra del Bechetin, Largo Toniolo 7/8, 00186 Roma. T. (06) 68803722. 059583
Sestieri Antichita' Di Andrea e Lorenzo Sestieri, 18/29 Via Alibert, 00187 Roma. T. (06) 6793915. 059584
Sestieri Antichita' Di Andrea e Lorenzo Sestieri, 9 Via Gesu' e Maria, 00187 Roma. T. (06) 6780073. 059585
Sestrieri, D., Via Margutta 57, 00187 Roma. T. (06) 3207590. 059586
Sette Arredamenti, 53 Via della Giovanna, 60166 Roma. T. (06) 66180404. 059587
Severa, G., Via Margutta 59 A, 00187 Roma. T. (06) 3207711. 059588
Sganga G., 74 Via Marche, 00187 Roma. T. (06) 4821954. 059589
Sheraton Antichita', Vendita All'Ingrosso, Via Verolengo 7 (Zona Boccea), 00167 Roma. T. (06) 66414423. 059590
Silme, 1 Via Tor Sanguigna, 00186 Roma. T. (06) 6865139. 059591
Silvestri M.T., 91/a Via Margutta, 00187 Roma. T. (06) 6790655. 059592
Simotti-Rocchi, M., Largo della Fontanella di Borghese 76, 00186 Roma. T. (06) 6876656. 059593
Sineo, Via dei Coronari 57, 00186 Roma. T. (06) 68806866. 059594
Sineo L., 38 Via Coronari, 00186 Roma. T. (06) 6880209. 059595
La Sinopia, 21c Via Banchi Nuovi, 00186 Roma. T. (06) 6872869. 059596
Sirio, 36 Via Bevagna, 00191 Roma. T. (06) 3337097. 059597
Societa' Il Timone, 27 Via Alibert, 00187 Roma. T. (06) 3207605. 059598
Societa' MA.MO, 215 Via coronari, 00186 Roma. T. (06) 6864717. 059599
La Soffitta, 27a Via Farnesia, 00165 Roma. T. (06) 3333774. 059600
Sola G., 230 Via Meruiana, 00185 Roma. T. (06) 4872709. 059601
Solarte, 6 Via Brunetti, 00186 Roma. T. (06) 3200407. 059602
Soligo, Aldo, Via del Babuino 161, 00187 Roma. T. (06) 361 41 58. 059603
Il Soppalco, 10 Via Menotti, 00191 Roma. T. (06) 3217389. 059604
Spagnoletto, P., Vialle delle Medaglie d'Oro 6B, 00136 Roma. T. (06) 39731544. 059605
Sterling Gallery di Tidia Innocenti, 94b Viale Parioli, 00197 Roma. T. (06) 8075135. 059606
Stoduto M.T., 239 Via Sicilia, 00187 Roma. T. (06) 4885492. 059607
Studio Antiquaria Lampade, 107 Via Giulia, 00186 Roma. T. (06) 6892814. 059608
Studio Antiquario, Via Giulia 103 A, 00186 Roma. T. (06) 68803840. 059609
Lo Studio di Restauro di Ricotta Sergio, 45 Via M.te Giordano, 00186 Roma. T. (06) 6877472. 059610
Studio Ripetaa di Nardo e C., 134 Via Ripetta, 00186 Roma. T. (06) 6873575. 059611
Studio 9, Vicolo della Moretta 9, 00186 Roma. T. (06) 654 08 94. 059612
Studio 99 di Manzollino Massimo & D'Alessio, 98 Via Cappellari, 00186 Roma. T. (06) 6896340. 059613
Sturni, Via di Campo Marzio 81, 00186 Roma. T. (06) 69940781. 059614
Sturni A., 13 Via Stelletta, 00186 Roma. T. (06) 68802194. 059615
Sturni, Dr. Vito, Via Campo Marzio 81, 00186 Roma. T. (06) 6784240. 059616
Sturniolo, Giovanni, Piazza S Eustachio 49, 00186 Roma. T. (06) 68802116. 059617
Taiuti, Anna e Andrea, Via Bettolo 31/33, 00195 Roma. T. (06) 3701183. - Paint / Furn / China - 059618
Taloni, Piero, Via del Curato 10/11, 00186 Roma. T. (06) 6875450/6892373. 059619
Tanca, Giuseppe, Salita dei Crescenzi 12, 00186 Roma. T. (06) 687 52 72, Fax (06) 68803328. - Ant / Paint / Furn / China / Silv / Lights / Instr - 059620
Tanca, Milena, Via dei Coronari 230, 00186 Roma. T. (06) 68806052. 059621
Le Tartarughe, 14 Piazza Mattei, 00186 Roma. T. (06) 68801645. 059622
Tempi Moderni, Via del Governo Vecchio 108, 00186 Roma. T. (06) 6877007. 059623
Il Tempo E L'Arte, 2 Via Cassini, 00197 Roma. T. (06) 8070754. 059624

Tempo Retrovato, Via dei Bianchi Nuovi 28A, 00186 Roma. T. (06) 654 87 07. *059625*

Terenzi, L., Via dei Coronari 108, 00186 Roma.
T. (06) 6865626. *059626*

Tiraforti L., 82 Via Volsci, 00185 Roma.
T. (06) 4451613. *059627*

Tomada A., 53 Via Germanico, 00192 Roma.
T. (06) 39723505. *059628*

Tomassetti, Antonietta, Via Margutta 11/12, 00187 Roma. T. (06) 3614007. - Ant - *059629*

Tornato V., 29 Via M. Clementi, 00193 Roma.
T. (06) 3215958. *059630*

Traco O., 4 Piazza Citta' Leonina, 00193 Roma.
T. (06) 68801252. *059631*

Tradardi, Oliviero, Via Margutta 99, 00187 Roma.
T. (06) 679 28 85. - Paint - *059632*

Tuena B., F., Via Margutta 53, 00187 Roma.
T. (06) 3207987. *059633*

Tuena F.M., 53 Via Margutta, 00187 Roma.
T. (06) 3207641. *059634*

Valadier Antichità', 53 Via Valadier, 00135 Roma.
T. (06) 3244411. *059635*

Valgimigli M., 67 Via Litta Modignani, 00144 Roma.
T. (06) 5201053. *059636*

Valligiano, Via Giulia 193, 00186 Roma.
T. (06) 686 95 05. *059637*

Vangelli, Laolo, Via del Babuino 25, 00187 Roma.
T. (06) 678 09 90. - Ant - *059638*

Vangelli, Raoul, Via Margutta 52, 00187 Roma.
T. (06) 3207666. *059639*

Vantaggio Uno, 5 Via Vantaggio, 00186 Roma.
T. (06) 3219178. *059640*

Vattani, Gino, Via dei Coronari 6, 00186 Roma.
T. (06) 6861827. - Furn - *059641*

Vattani, Marcello, Via dei Coronari 150, 00186 Roma.
T. (06) 6864535. *059642*

Vattani Mobili Antichi, Marcello, Italiani e Inglesi, 00186 Roma. T. (06) 6864535. *059643*

Vecchi Sogni, 161b Cironv. Clodia, 00195 Roma.
T. (06) 3252145. *059644*

Vecchia Rimessa, Via dei Coronari 41, 00186 Roma.
T. (06) 6861186. - Ant / Furn - *059645*

Venanzini, Franco, Via dei Coronari 15, 00186 Roma.
T. (06) 68801190. *059646*

Veneziano M., 54a Via Margutta, 00187 Roma.
T. (06) 3207617. *059647*

Venti M., 33 Via O. da Gubbio, 00181 Roma.
T. (06) 5585017. *059648*

Venturi, Simona kVia A. Ripa 12, Via A Ripa 12, 00198 Roma. T. (06) 841 26 58. *059649*

Venturi Spada, 14 Via Giulia, 00186 Roma.
T. (06) 6865448. *059650*

Verdini C., 22 Via Zanardelli, 00186 Roma.
T. (06) 6861268. *059651*

Virgilio, C., Via della Lupa 10, 00186 Roma.
T. (06) 6871093. *059652*

Visconti, 15 Via Scrofa, 00186 Roma.
T. (06) 6868052. *059653*

Vitale, Lidia, Via dei Coronari 160, 00186 Roma.
T. (06) 6865347. *059654*

Vitali, Vicola del Bottino 8A, 00187 Roma.
T. (06) 679 42 36. *059655*

Vittoria Antichita', 25 Via Vittoria, 00187 Roma.
T. (06) 6796758, 69941951. *059656*

Vivanti, Via del Babuino 73, 00187 Roma.
T. (06) 678 97 06. *059657*

Vivanti, G., Via del Babuino 138, 00187 Roma.
T. (06) 679 80 69. *059658*

Volterra Settimio, 100 Via Monserrato, 00186 Roma.
T. (06) 6872164. *059659*

Zampetti I., 63 Via Crescenzio, 00193 Roma.
T. (06) 6868523. *059660*

Zanardelli Antichita', 22 Via Zanardelli, 00186 Roma.
T. (06) 6861850. *059661*

Zanna A., 18 Via Ischia d Castro, 00189 Roma.
T. (06) 33251543. *059662*

Zecca Privata di Roma, 3 Via Leoncavallo, 00199 Roma.
T. (06) 86202495. *059663*

Zenobi 10, Via d'Ascanio, 10086 Roma.
T. (06) 6869693. *059664*

Zoffoli, Renato, Via del Babuino 137, 00186 Roma.
T. (06) 679 06 28. *059665*

Zumbe' R., 18 Via Leccosa, 00186 Roma.
T. (06) 68308772. *059666*

1900 di Marina Gargiulo, Art nouveau e art deco', Via Vittoria 37, Roma. T. (06) 6789465. *059667*

2 P Antiquariato, Piazza R. Ardigo 36/37, 00142 Roma.
T. (06) 5409716, 5192599. *059668*

Romano d'Ezzelino (Vicenza)
Guidolin, Via Spin, 36060 Romano d'Ezzelino.
T. (0424) 309 68. *059669*

Romano di Lombardia (Milano)
Roncalli, Lino, Via Alighieri 31, 24058 Romano di Lombardia. T. (0363) 980 51. *059670*

Rosà (Vicenza)
Fiorese, Giusto, Via Piave, Cusinati, 36027 Rosà.
T. (0424) 842 92. *059671*

Rosignano Marittimo (Livorno)
Le Scuderie, Via Antonio Gramsci 115, 57016 Rosignano Marittimo. T. (0586) 79 93 39, 79 92 02. *059672*

Rovereto (Trento)
Ferrario, Corso Verona 3, 38068 Rovereto.
T. (0464) 369 24. *059673*

Rovigo
Cose d'Altri Tempi, Via Oberdan 5, 45100 Rovigo.
T. (0425) 233 53. *059674*

Rubiera (Reggio Emilia)
Fiumicelli, Italo, Piazza XXIV Maggio 1, 42048 Rubiera.
T. (0522) 918 35. *059675*

Fiumicelli, Italo, Via Marsala, 42048 Rubiera.
T. (0522) 62 06 62, 62 07 60. *059676*

Russi (Ravenna)
Mazzotti, Bruna, Via Michelangelo 3, 48026 Russi.
T. (0544) 58 08 04. *059677*

Ruta (Genova)
Pallotta, Via Aurelia 257-58 Genova, 16030 Ruta.
T. (0185) 77 14 93. *059678*

Sinatra, Via Aurelia 203, 16030 Ruta. T. (0185) 77 11 12, Fax 77 11 12. *059679*

Rutigliano (Bari)
Poli, Giangrazio, Via Pietro De Bellis 5, 70018 Rutigliano.
T. (080) 66 27 17. *059680*

S. Stefano Belbo
Eldoardo Bussi antichità, Via XX Settembre, Via Martiri Belfiore, Via Porta Sottana 12, 12058 S. Stefano Belbo. T. (0141) 840389. *059681*

Eldoardo Bussi antichità, Via XX Settembre, Via Martiri Belfiore, Via Porta Sottana 12, 12058 S. Stefano Belbo. T. (0141) 840389. *059682*

Sabaudia (Latina)
Taloni, Via Mediana km 8700, 04016 Sabaudia.
T. (0773) 500 56. *059683*

Sabbio Chiese (Brescia)
Meridiana, La, Via Belvedere 1, 25070 Sabbio Chiese.
T. (0365) 851 27. *059684*

Saint-Pierre (Aosta)
Biondi, Marcella, Via PS Bernardo 4, 11010 Saint-Pierre.
T. (0165) 950 82, 78 52 90. *059685*

Salerno
Schiavone, Matteo, Piazza Altano 5, 84100 Salerno.
T. (089) 22 61 55. *059686*

Tafuri & La Scala, Via Mercanti 108, 84100 Salerno.
T. (089) 22 77 47. - Jew - *059687*

Salò (Brescia)
Chiocciola, La, Lungolago Zanardelli 9, 25087 Salò.
T. (0365) 201 86. *059688*

Salsomaggiore Terme (Parma)
Alfieri, G., & Figlio, Via Romagnosi 5, 43039 Salsomaggiore Terme. T. (0524) 772 19, 742 03. - Paint - *059689*

Il Trovarobe, Via Copelli 4, 43039 Salsomaggiore Terme.
T. (0524) 773 26. *059690*

Saluzzo (Cuneo)
Ansaldi F.lli, Corso Italia 100, 12037 Saluzzo.
T. (0175) 434 27. *059691*

Bellino, Gianfranco, Via Marucchi 2, 12037 Saluzzo.
T. (0175) 446 19. *059692*

Bertoni, Amleto, Via Griselda 22, 12037 Saluzzo.
T. (0175) 455 41. *059693*

Brancaccio, Franco, Piazza Mondagli 9, 12037 Saluzzo.
T. (0175) 451 59. *059694*

Capellotti, Michele, Corso Piemonte 38, 12037 Saluzzo.
T. (0175) 43362. *059695*

Chiriaco, Manlio, Via Torino 100, 12037 Saluzzo.
T. (0175) 41232. *059696*

Collovati, Bruno, Strada Salita al Castello 6, 12037 Saluzzo. T. (0175) 450 49. *059697*

Costa, Giuliano, Salita al Castello 8, 12037 Saluzzo.
T. (0175) 428 67. *059698*

Dutto, Sergio, Via Spielberg 57, 12037 Saluzzo.
T. (0175) 41876. *059699*

Galliano, Edoardo, Salita al Castello 2, Via Spielberg 39, 12037 Saluzzo. T. (0175) 436 35, 429 65. *059700*

Seia, Giampiero, Piazza Castello 32, 12037 Saluzzo.
T. (0175) 41273. *059701*

San Arcangelo di Romagna (Bologna)
Beato, Simone, Via Saffi 29, 47038 San Arcangelo di Romagna. T. (0541) 62 65 51. *059702*

San Bartolomeo al Mare (Imperia)
La Rovere, Via Aurelia 118, 18016 San Bartolomeo al Mare. T. (0183) 40 08 58. *059703*

San Benedetto del Tronto (Ascoli Piceno)
Ahmadi, Galleria Persiana, Via Gramsci 9, 63039 San Benedetto del Tronto. T. (0735) 682 00. *059704*

Anticaglie, Via Manara 12, 63030 San Benedetto del Tronto. T. (0735) 28 93. *059705*

Antiquarius, Via Roma 63, 63039 San Benedetto del Tronto. *059706*

Antiquarius, Via Volta 106, 63030 San Benedetto del Tronto. T. (0735) 817 56. *059707*

Scipi, Corso Mazzini 8, 63030 San Benedetto del Tronto.
T. (0735) 35 55. *059708*

Vecchie Cose, Via CL Gabrielli 28, 63039 San Benedetto del Tronto. T. (0735) 843 91, 630 39. *059709*

San Casciano Val di Pesa (Firenze)
Migliori, Dino, Borgo Sarchiani 30, 50026 San Casciano Val di Pesa. T. (055) 82 01 77. *059710*

San Colombano Belmonte (Torino)
Belmonte, Via Boasca 12, 10080 San Colombano Belmonte. T. (0124) 66 66 03. *059711*

San Dona di Piave (Venezia)
Old Imports, Via 13 Martiri 63, 30027 San Dona di Piave.
T. (0421) 518 24. *059712*

San Donato Milanese (Milano)
Domus Artis, Via Libertà 16, 20097 San Donato Milanese. T. (02) 52 72 017. *059713*

San Gimignano (Siena)
Focarile, Il, Via S Matteo 8, 53037 San Gimignano.
T. (0577) 94 06 94. *059714*

L'Eringio, Via del Castello 13, 53037 San Gimignano.
T. (0577) 94 15 44. *059715*

Migliorini Curini, Via S Matteo 81, 53037 San Gimignano. T. (0577) 94 06 65. *059716*

San Giorgio Canavese (Torino)
Graglia, Mario, Via della Repubblica 31, 10090 San Giorgio Canavese. T. (0124) 324 49. *059717*

San Giustino (Perugia)
Cancellieri, Maria, Piazza Municipio, 06016 San Giustino. T. (075) 85 61 89. *059718*

Cerboni, Francesco, Via Garibaldi, Via Umbra 18, 06016 San Giustino. T. (075) 85 61 43, 787 54. *059719*

Polverini, Piazza Municipio 8, 06016 San Giustino.
T. (075) 85 61 89. *059720*

San Pellegrino Terme (Bergamo)
Walri San Pellegrino, Via Mazzoni 1, 24016 San Pellegrino Terme. T. (0345) 216 48. *059721*

San Polo d'Enza (Reggio Emilia)
Lodi Prati, Maria, Viale Risorgimento, 42020 San Polo d'Enza. T. (0522) 87 81 17. 059722

San Prospero Parmense (Parma)
Levrieri, Gianfranco, Via E Lepido 287, 43027 San Prospero Parmense. T. (0521) 49 93 05. 059723

San Romano (Pisa)
Il Tempo, Via Tosco Romagnola 226, 56020 San Romano. T. (0571) 458 70. 059724

Sanguinetto (Verona)
Francioli, Andriano, Via Capitello Conca Marise, 37058 Sanguinetto. T. (0442) 812 96. 059725

Sanremo (Imperia)
Ammirati, Augusta, Via Garibaldi 113, 18038 Sanremo. T. (0184) 757 82. - China - 059726
Arte Antic e Moderna, Corso Imperatrice 104, 18038 Sanremo. T. (0184) 718 93. 059727
Cavour 2, Corso Matteotti, 18038 Sanremo. T. (0184) 84375. - Furn / Sculp / Silv - 059728
L'Angolo del Tarlo, Corso Cavallotti 168, 18038 Sanremo. T. (0184) 724 36. 059729
La Conchiglia, Piazza Borea d'Olmo 9, Sede: Via Cavour 2, 18038 Sanremo. T. (0184) 843 75, 53 09 55. - Ant / Paint / Furn / Sculp / Silv / Instr / Ico - 059730
Studio d'Arte, Via Padre Semeria 170, 18038 Sanremo. T. (0184) 801 82. 059731
Zoccai, Corso Imperatrice 12, 18038 Sanremo. T. (0184) 858 07. - Ant / Jew / Silv - 059732

Sansepolcro (Arezzo)
Tarducci, Angelo, Via XX Settembre 123, 52037 Sansepolcro. T. (0575) 752 71. 059733

Sant'Angelo Lodigiano (Milano)
Esmeralda, Piazza Libertà 15, 20079 Sant'Angelo Lodigiano. T. (0371) 924 53. 059734
Mattioli, Franco, Via Cavour 79, 20079 Sant'Angelo Lodigiano. T. (0371) 928 96. 059735

Sant'Eufemia (Brescia)
Rusconi, Rudiano, Via Indipendenza 89, 25080 Sant'Eufemia. T. (030) 36 27 10. 059736

Santa Margherita Ligure (Genova)
Bernardi, de, Via Partigiani d'Italia 15, 16038 Santa Margherita Ligure. T. (0185) 870 68. 059737
Boero, Aldo, Via Algeria 1, 16038 Santa Margherita Ligure. T. (0185) 871 74. 059738
Casanova, Carlo, Via Gramsci 21, 16038 Santa Margherita Ligure. T. (0185) 28 70 11. - Paint - 059739
Gli Archi, Via Roma 22, 16038 Santa Margherita Ligure. T. (0185) 2871 52. - Ant - 059740
Grosso, Michele, Via Bottaro 30, 16038 Santa Margherita Ligure. T. (0185) 871 81. - Ant / Furn / China - 059741
Il Cantuccio, Corso Marconi 5, 16038 Santa Margherita Ligure. T. (0185) 875 46. 059742
Portobello, Via Gramsci 99, 16038 Santa Margherita Ligure. T. (0185) 288 170. - Ant / Paint / Furn / Orient / China / Tex / Dec / Jew / Silv - 059743
Quaquaro, Emanuele, & Figli, Via Gramsci 69, 16038 Santa Margherita Ligure. T. (0185) 865 78. 059744
Quaquaro, L. B., Via Pescino 1, 16038 Santa Margherita Ligure. T. (0185) 871 16. 059745
Sacchetti, Mario, Via Roccatagliata 69, 16038 Santa Margherita Ligure. T. (0185) 882 04. 059746
Terzaghi, Alfredo, Via della Vittoria 10, 16038 Santa Margherita Ligure. T. (0185) 870 81. 059747

Santa Maria Capua Vetere (Caserta)
Galleria dell'Arco, P. Saccone, Via Aldo Moro 331, 81055 Santa Maria Capua Vetere. T. (0823) 84 55 76. 059748
Munno, Francesco, Via Aldo Moro 22, 81055 Santa Maria Capua Vetere. T. (0823) 84 29 12. 059749

Santa Maria degli Angeli (Perugia)
Carloni, Antonio, Via Los Angeles 38, 06088 Santa Maria degli Angeli. T. (075) 81 93 15. 059750
Carloni, Antonio, Via Los Angeles 7, 06088 Santa Maria degli Angeli. T. (075) 81 99 04. 059751
Elite, Via Porta d'Italia, 06080 Santa Maria degli Angeli. T. (075) 804 08 06, Fax 804 08 06. - Paint / Furn / Tex / Jew / Silv - 059752
Il Tarlo, Strada Statale 75, 06088 Santa Maria degli Angeli. T. (075) 81 98 59, 81 95 76. 059753

Santo Stefano Belbo (Cuneo)
Bussi, Edoardo, Via XX Settembre- Via Martiri Belfiore, 12058 Santo Stefano Belbo. T. (0141) 84 03 89. - Ant - 059754
Bussi, Piera, Via Stazione 22, 12058 Santo Stefano Belbo. T. (0141) 848 82. 059755

Saronno (Varese)
L'Antica Bottega, Via Verdi 23, 21047 Saronno. T. (02) 96 09 208. 059756
La Tortuga, Via L. Caronnl 8, 21047 Saronno. T. (02) 962 37 87. - Furn / Dec / Silv - 059757
Passerini, F.lli, Corso Italia 30, 21047 Saronno. T. (02) 960 26 22. - Tex - 059758

Sarzana (La Spezia)
Albertosi, Giorgio, Via Mascardi 56, 19038 Sarzana. T. (0187) 62 43 79. 059759
Battistini, Franco, Via Mascardi 33, 19038 Sarzana. T. (0187) 62 19 72. 059760
Bellotto, Oscar, Variante Aurelia, 19038 Sarzana. T. (0187) 62 20 95. 059761
Bellotto, Oscar, Via Mascardi 22, 19038 Sarzana. T. (0187) 62 04 13. 059762
Buongiovanni, Alfonso, Via Mascardi 52, 19038 Sarzana. T. (0187) 62 08 03. 059763
Carozzi, Marco, Via Fiasella 41, 19038 Sarzana. T. (0187) 62 62 49. 059764
Carozzi Mattioli, Donnina, Via Fiasella 27, 19038 Sarzana. T. (0187) 62 41 56. 059765
Carozzi Mattioli, Donnina, Via Mascardi 12, 19038 Sarzana. 059766
Di Sarcina, Guido, Via Fiasella 55, 19038 Sarzana. T. (0187) 62 14 50. 059767
Ferasso, Via Pecorina 1, 19038 Sarzana. T. (0187) 62 19 98. 059768
Il Tarlo, Via Bertolini 23, 19038 Sarzana. T. (0187) 62 15 66. - Paint / Jew - 059769
Il Ventuno, Via Mascardi 21, 19038 Sarzana. T. (0187) 62 11 51. 059770
Isoppo e Parma, Via Pecorina 2, 19038 Sarzana. T. (0187) 62 11 44. 059771
Paganini, Mario, Via Mascardi 55, 19038 Sarzana. T. (0187) 62 11 95. 059772

Sassari
Carrabs, Via Roma 83, 07100 Sassari. T. (079) 273135. 059773
Michelangelo Due, Via Mazzini 37, 07100 Sassari. T. (079) 23 12 20. 059774
Michelangelo Due, Viale Umberto 90, 07100 Sassari. T. (079) 27 20 50. 059775
Michelangelo Due, Via Cavour 57, 07100 Sassari. T. (079) 27 20 50. 059776
Rubattu, Viale Umberto 85, 07100 Sassari. T. (079) 35501. 059777

Sassuolo (Modena)
Frisieri, Giuseppe, Piazza Martiri Antifascisti 50, 41049 Sassuolo. T. (0536) 88 14 43. 059778
Il Bugigattolo, Via Fenuzzi 4, 41049 Sassuolo. T. (0536) 88 4125. 059779
Pennoni, Via F Cavallotti 94, 41049 Sassuolo. T. (0536) 88 50 58. 059780

Savignano sul Panaro (Modena)
Migliori, Diana, Via Claudia 4351, 41056 Savignano sul Panaro. T. (059) 73 01 35. 059781

Savignano sul Rubicone (Forli)
Belli, Paolo, Via Matteotti 69, 47039 Savignano sul Rubicone. T. (0541) 94 44 55. 059782

Savona
Averla, Vittorio, Via Spinola 10, 17100 Savona. T. (019) 353 54. 059783
Bottega d'Arte Antica, Via Mistrangelo 55, 17100 Savona. T. (019) 266 18. - Ant / Paint / Furn / China / Eth / Dec / Jew / Silv - 059784
Cabib, Corso Italia 14 e 172, 17100 Savona. T. (019) 206 58, 356 09. 059785
Dedalo, Piazza del Vescovato, 17100 Savona. T. (019) 34327. 059786
Delfino, Via Luigi Corsi 7, 17100 Savona. T. (019) 217 98. 059787
Delfino, Via Paleocapa 73, 17100 Savona. T. (019) 256 73. 059788
Gigliotti, Francesco, Corso Mazzini 8, 17100 Savona. T. (019) 226 19. 059789
Gigliotti, Gianni, Piazetta dei Consoli 7, Sant Andrea, 17100 Savona. T. (019) 35688. 059790
Hobby Invest, Piazz Sisto IV 13, 17100 Savona. T. (019) 253 83. 059791
La Fonte, Via Nizza 155, 17100 Savona. T. (019) 88 15 78. 059792
La Navicella, Via Vacciuoli 1, 17100 Savona. T. (019) 38 77 72. - Paint / China - 059793

Scandiano (Reggio Emilia)
La Cassapanca, Via Garibaldi 33, 42019 Scandiano. T. (0522) 85 67 33. 059794
Old Wood, Strada Statale 467, 42019 Scandiano. T. (0522) 855 95. 059795

Scandicci (Firenze)
Corazzi, Via Pisana 412, 50010 Scandicci. T. (055) 72 12 63. 059796
Pieri, Alessandro, Via Pisana 530, 50018 Scandicci. T. (055) 79 03 76. 059797

Scheggino (Perugia)
Amadio, Gregorio, Via di Borgo 2, 06040 Scheggino. T. (0743) 61109. 059798

Senago (Milano)
Arzuffi, Angelo, Via Montale 26, 20030 Senago. T. (02) 998 75 00. - Sculp / Fra / Silv - 059800

Senigallia (Ancona)
La Fiera di Sinigaglia, Via Fratelli Bandiera 49, 60019 Senigallia. T. (071) 65 90 18. 059801
Olmo Bello, Via Armellini 51, 60019 Senigallia. T. (071) 607 14. 059802

Seregno (Milano)
Cantù di cantù, Piazza Italia 6, 20038 Seregno. T. (0362) 22 14 71. 059803

Serravalle Sesia (Vercelli)
Piasio, Dino, Frazione Naula 23, 13037 Serravalle Sesia. T. (0163) 45 01 10. 059804

Sestri Levante (Genova)
Luxardo, Piazza Bò 11, 16039 Sestri Levante. T. (0185) 424 40. 059805
Rinaldi del Cogliano, Via XXV Aprile 32, 16039 Sestri Levante. T. (0185) 416 91. 059806
Sole, Al, Via XXV Aprile 143, 16039 Sestri Levante. T. (0185) 417 10. 059807
Traversaro, Via XXV Aprile 32, 16039 Sestri Levante. T. (0185) 446 18. 059808

Sestriere (Torino)
Costa, Giuliano, Piazza Giovanni Agnelli 2, 10058 Sestriere. T. (0122) 764 56. 059809

Settimo Milanese (Milano)
La Porta Giusta, Via Pellico 21, 20019 Settimo Milanese. T. (02) 32 81 500. 059810

Sforzacosta (Macerata)
Zecchini, Frezotti, Franca, Via Nazionale 29, 62010 Sforzacosta. T. (0733) 458 01. 059811

Siena
Andrei, Piazza Indipendenza 3, 53100 Siena. T. (0577) 28 44 80. 059812
Bottega dell'Antiquariato, Via del Capitano 13, 53100 Siena. T. (0577) 28 80 68. 059813
CMC Antichità, Piazza Indipendenza 3-4, 53100 Siena. T. (0577) 28 44 80. - Furn - 059814
Giuliani, Via di Citta 77, 53100 Siena. 059815
La Balzana, Via della Sapienza 26, 53100 Siena. T. (0577) 420 03. 059816

La Pia, Via Cecco Angiolieri 31, 53100 Siena.
T. (0577) 28 83 33. *059817*
Mazzoni, Piazza San Giovanni 8, 53100 Siena.
T. (0577) 28 20 91. *059818*
Monna, Agnese, Via di Città 45, 53100 Siena.
T. (0577) 28 22 88. - Jew / Silv - *059819*
Red Baron's Liberty & Déco, Via Salicotto 11, 53100
Siena. T. (0577) 28 33 96. *059820*
Saena Vetus, Via di Città 53, 53100 Siena.
T. (0577) 423 95. - Paint / Furn - *059821*
San Giovanni, Piazza S. Giovanni e Via dei Fusari 3,
53100 Siena. T. (0577) 28 92 08. - Furn - *059822*
Taddeucci, D., Via di Città 136, 53100 Siena.
T. (0577) 28 91 60. - Paint / Furn - *059823*
Vizia, Enzo, Via di Citta 99, 53100 Siena.
T. (0577) 28 22 41, 39 42 55. *059824*

Siracusa
Il Tappeto, Corso Matteotti 65, 96100 Siracusa.
T. (0931) 613 36. *059825*

Sirmione (Brescia)
Da Luigi, Via Emilia 21, 25019 Sirmione.
T. (030) 91 93 89. *059826*
Le Due Fontane, Via Emilia 54, 25019 Sirmione.
T. (030) 91 93 19. *059827*
Minozzo, Renzo, Via I Maggio, 25019 Sirmione.
T. (030) 91 90 23. *059828*
Mosè, Via Statale 38, 25019 Sirmione.
T. (030) 91 91 79. *059829*

Solesino (Padova)
Gallo, G., Via XXVIII Aprile, 79/bis, 35047 Solesino.
T. (0429) 70173. *059830*
Gallo, Gianni, Via XXVIII Aprile 120, 35047 Solesino.
T. (0429) 701 73, 701 48. *059831*
Polato, Luciano, Via Lombardia 1, 35047 Solesino.
T. (0429) 70193. *059832*
Rocchetto, Ivano, Via Gramsci 4, 35047 Solesino.
T. (0429) 70162. *059833*
Scarparo, Via Nazionale 23, 35047 Solesino.
T. (0429) 701 32. *059834*
Seno, Via Galilei Galileo 3, 35047 Solesino.
T. (0429) 70157. *059835*

Somma Lombardo (Varese)
Old England, Via Milano 122, 21019 Somma Lombardo.
T. (0331) 25 42 33. *059836*

Sondrio
Bavieri, Duilio, Via Stelvio 13, 23100 Sondrio.
T. (0342) 21 60 83. *059837*
Belintende, Oscar, Via Valeriana 6, 23100 Sondrio.
T. (0342) 21 42 18. *059838*

Soragna (Parma)
Mussi, Via Garibaldi 17, 43019 Soragna.
T. (0524) 693 48. *059839*

Sorrento (Napoli)
Minerva, Corso Italia 219, 80067 Sorrento.
T. (081) 878 51 54. - Ant - *059840*
Vecchio Cose, Corso Italia 261, 80067 Sorrento.
T. (081) 878 36 48. *059841*

Spinetoli (Ascoli Piceno)
Forlini, Luigi e Marino, Via Salaria 103, 63030 Spinetoli.
T. (0736) 895 41. *059842*

Spino d'Adda (Cremona)
Petroni, Severino, Strada Paullese 26, 26016 Spino
d'Adda. T. (0373) 96 60 70. *059843*

Spoleto (Perugia)
Ciarletti, Alfredo, Via Arco di Druso 19, 06049 Spoleto.
T. (0743) 211 02. *059844*
Fiori, P., Via Norvegia 8, San Giacomo, 06049 Spoleto.
T. (0743) 52 02 17. *059845*
Galleria del Mobile Antico, Via Arco di Druso 15, 06049
Spoleto. T. (0743) 43586. *059846*
Graffiti, Via Palazzo Duchi 17, 06049 Spoleto.
T. (0743) 47300. *059847*
La Fontana, Via del Mercato 19, 06049 Spoleto.
T. (0743) 391 28. *059848*

Lucentini, Armando e Alessandro, via del Palazzo dei
Duchi 18, 06049 Spoleto. T. (0743) 22 32 58. *059849*
Marucci, G., Fr Monte Martano 31, 06049 Spoleto.
T. (0743) 64036. *059850*
Milanese, Eugenio, Via Nuova 2, 06049 Spoleto.
T. (0743) 22 35 49. *059851*
Palatium, Via Aurelio Saffi 11, 06049 Spoleto.
T. (0743) 477 59. *059852*
Sapori, Paolo, Piazza Fontana 1, 06049 Spoleto.
T. (0743) 45641. *059853*
Umbria Sud, Via Strada Romana 8, 06049 Spoleto.
T. (0743) 361 07. *059854*

Stanghella (Padova)
Contiero, Q., Via Nazionale 109, 35048 Stanghella.
T. (0425) 95241. *059855*

Stefano Belbo (Cuneo)
Bussi, Edoardo, Via Porta Sottana 12, 12058 Stefano
Belbo. T. (0141) 84 03 89. - Ant / Furn - *059856*

Stia (Arezzo)
Casa del Vecchio Mobile, Piazza Tanucci 23, 52017 Stia.
T. (0575) 589 89. *059857*

Stupinigi
Galleria D'Arte Juvarra Antiquariato Palazzina, Piazza
Principe Amedeo, Stupinigi. T. (011) 3580990,
Fax (0121) 352310. *059858*

Susegana (Treviso)
Dionisi, Via Conegliano 39, 31058 Susegana.
T. (0438) 735 47. *059859*

Tabiano (Parma)
Antichita di Tabiano Bagni, Via Salsomaggiore, 43030
Tabiano. T. (0524) 502 83. *059860*

Taormina (Messina)
Arte Antica, Corso Umberta 110, 98039 Taormina.
T. (0942) 239 10, 237 27. *059861*
Chez le Francais, Via San Domenico 6, 98039 Taormina.
T. (0942) 232 89. *059862*
Forin, Marina, Corso Umberto 148, 98039 Taormina.
T. (0942) 230 60, 230 20. *059863*
Gallodoro, Salvatore, Piazza San Domenico 2, 98039
Taormina. T. (0942) 246 97. *059864*
Novelli, Corso Umberto 92, 98039 Taormina.
T. (0942) 243 49. *059865*
Panarello, Carlo, Corso Umberto 122, 98039 Taormina.
T. (0942) 239 51. *059866*
Pandora, Salite Dente 2, 98039 Taormina. - Ant / Sculp /
Rel / Glass / Cur - *059867*
Saro, Corso Umberto 210, 98039 Taormina.
T. (0942) 251 84. *059868*

Taranto
Margherita, Corso Umberto 79a, 74100 Taranto.
T. (099) 920 78. *059869*

Tarvisio (Udine)
Arte e Dimora, Via Roma 24, 33018 Tarvisio.
T. (0429) 29 77. *059870*

Tavagnacco (Udine)
Luca, Aldo de, Viale Trieste 15, 33010 Tavagnacco.
T. (0432) 66 02 87. *059871*

Tavernelle (Massa Carrara)
Polaris, Via Roma 169, 54010 Tavernelle.
T. (055) 807 78 30. *059872*

Terni
Cangioli Bartolozzi, Via Barberini 15, 05100 Terni.
T. (0744) 553 80, 591 19. *059873*
Galleria Barbarasa, Via Barbarasa 6, 05100 Terni.
T. (0744) 599 05. *059874*
Galleria Barberini, Via Barberini 9, 05100 Terni.
T. (0744) 584 57. - Ant / Furn - *059875*
Leonardo, Via Barberini 1, 05100 Terni.
T. (0744) 479 68. *059876*

Terranuova Bracciolini (Arezzo)
Wendland, Marcel von, Piansalipano Penna 135, 52028
Terranuova Bracciolini. - Paint - *059877*

Todi (Perugia)
Alexandris, A. de, Via Ciuffelli 1, 06059 Todi.
T. (075) 894 29 84. *059878*
Alexandris, Giordano Bruno de, Via Ciuffelli 19, 06059
Todi. T. (075) 894 25 05. *059879*
Biagi, M., Via A Ciuffelli 6, 06059 Todi.
T. (075) 894 31 97. *059880*
Caiello Galletti, Via del Seminario 4, 06059 Todi.
T. (075) 88 23 93. *059881*
Cionco, Bruno, Via Augusto Ciuffelli 7, 06059 Todi.
T. (075) 894 33 08. *059882*
Il Vicolo, Via del Seminario 21, 06059 Todi. *059883*
Il Vicolo, via Ciuffelli 33, 06059 Todi.
T. (075) 88 27 15. *059884*
Sargeni, Cesare, Piazza Umberto I 18, 06059 Todi.
T. (075) 894 33 00. *059885*
Studio d'Arte, Via Mazzini 10, 06059 Todi. *059886*

Tolentino (Macerata)
Antiquary, Zona Industriale Le Grazie, 62029 Tolentino.
T. (0733) 97 19 95, 996 75. *059887*

Tolmezzo (Udine)
Mecchia, Via Grialba 30, 33028 Tolmezzo.
T. (0433) 28 01, 21 17. *059888*

Torino
Abrate Antichità, Via Pietro Micca 6B, 10122 Torino.
T. (011) 5623495. *059889*
Acquista Anceh Antichita' Cristiani, Via della Rocca 6,
10123 Torino. T. (011) 8178391; (0337) 220476,
4369600. *059890*
Acquisto per Contanti da Privati, Via S. Martino 25,
10122 Torino. T. (0173) 978327, 979355. *059891*
Aimone Riccardo Antichità – Perizie Acquisto – Vendita,
Via Gradisca 50 Bis/C, 10136 Torino.
T. (011) 356476. *059892*
Ajassa, Corso Moncalieri 234, 10133 Torino.
T. (011) 6615252/6615020, Fax (011) 6615252. - Ant /
Orient / Silv - *059893*
Alberto, Carlo, Via Carlo Alberto 7, 10123 Torino.
T. (011) 8173420. *059894*
Albina Forestier Antichia', 98b Corso Vitt. Eman. II,
10121 Torino. T. (011) 539832, 542035. *059895*
Alfa – Castellano Rag., Claudio, Corso U. Sovietica 381,
10135 Torino. T. (011) 615276. *059896*
All'Angolo dell'Antichità, Via Bava 2, 10124 Torino.
T. (011) 87 35 54. - Ant - *059897*
All'Angolo Dell'Antichita', 2 Via Bava, 10124 Torino.
T. (011) 8173554. *059898*
Alternariato, 16b Piazza Via Veneto, 10123 Torino.
T. (011) 882384. *059899*
Amarilli, Via M. Vittoria 8b, 10121 Torino.
T. (011) 54 15 30. - Ant / Graph / Furn / Orient / China /
Sculp / Dec / Silv / Cur - *059900*
Amigoni, Annarosa, Via delle Rosine 8, 10121 Torino.
T. (011) 88 56 06. - Ant - *059901*
Angotti, Giuseppe, Via della Rocca 20, 10123 Torino.
T. (011) 83 12 87. - Ant - *059902*
Antichita' Acquisto in Contanti, Via F. lli Calandra 21,
10123 Torino. T. (011) 8126596. *059903*
Antichita' – Baghai 6000 Via Bogino 10E, 10123 Torino.
T. (011) 8178204, (0337) 228099. *059904*
Antichita' Cavour, 3 Piazza Cavour, 10123 Torino.
T. (011) 8179316. *059905*
Antichità Cavour, Galleria Principe Eugenio, Via Cavour
17, 10123 Torino. T. (011) 5625650. *059906*
Antichita' Griffa Vendo – Acquisto, Via Maria Vittoria
22C, 10123 Torino. T. (011) 8127073. *059907*
Antichita' Zecchino, Via Porta Palatina 3, 10122 Torino.
T. (011) 4363397, 3187184. *059908*
Antinori G.L., 17 Via Covour, 10123 Torino.
T. (011) 5626295. *059909*
Antique di Ferrero, Enrico & C., 10 Via Borgo Dora,
10152 Torino. T. (011) 4362106. *059910*
Antix di Matteo, Bruno e C., 5 Via Rattazzi, 10123 Torino.
T. (011) 5625264. *059911*
Aries, Galleria Principe Eugenio, Via Cavour 17, 10123
Torino. T. (011) 5628266. - Furn - *059912*
Arredamenti, Emy, 127 Corso Racconigi, 10141 Torino.
T. (011) 3850854. *059913*
Arsenal Armi, Corso Turati 11, 10123 Torino.
T. (011) 50 29 68. *059914*

Art Maruska Collezionismo – Regalerie Bambole e mobili d'epoca Porcellane, ventagli e vertri, Via Vassalli Eandi 38, 10138 Torino. T. (011) 4344473, Fax (011) 4344473. *059915*

Arte Antica, Via Accademia Albertina 1, 10123 Torino. T. (011) 812 28 47. *059916*

Arte Antica Compra-vendita tappeti, restauro mobili antichi, Oggetti d'arte Vetri Vecchia Murano – Porcellane, Via Chiesa della Salute 88, 10147 Torino. T. (011) 2166059, (0337) 228843. *059917*

Artemobili, 99/7 Via Orbetello, 10148 Torino. T. (011) 251679. *059918*

Arts T Crafts Studio, 32 Via M. Vittoria, 10123 Torino. T. (011) 836217. *059919*

Attilio Riva in Frossasco Antichita' – Dipinti, Via Pinerolo 11, 10152 Torino. T. (0121) 352310, 353888, Fax (0121) 352310. *059920*

Baghai Sain S., 10h Via Bogino, 10123 Torino. T. (011) 8178204. *059921*

Baldin, Giulia, Via Po 11, 10124 Torino. T. (011) 8121227/8396881. *059922*

Basso, F., Via Giolitti Giovanni 11, 10123 Torino. T. (011) 54 97 20. *059923*

Battilossi, Via Giolitti 45f, 10123 Torino. T. (011) 839 59 68, Fax 812 38 90. *059924*

Behrouz Carpets, Via Mazzini 52, 10123 Torino. T. (011) 88 24 67. - Tex - *059925*

Bellomonte, Via Maria Vittoria 10, 10123 Torino. T. (011) 53 83 62. - Furn / China - *059926*

Beltramino, Luigi, Via Maria Vittoria 15, 10123 Torino. T. (011) 889703. *059927*

Benappi, Mario, Galleria Principe Eugenio, Via Cavour 17, 10123 Torino. T. (011) 5627794. *059928*

Benappi, R., Via Valprato 68, 10155 Torino. T. (011) 248 38 77. *059929*

Benappi, V., Via Gioberti 8, 10128 Torino. T. (011) 53 11 68. *059930*

Benatti M., 17 Via Valperga Caluso, 10125 Torino. T. (011) 6693464. *059931*

Berman, Via Arcivescavado 9-18, 10121 Torino. T. (011) 53 74 30. *059932*

Bernardis, Corso Inghilterra 27, 10138 Torino. T. (011) 434 32 57. - Ant / Paint / Graph / Num - *059933*

Berto9la, L., Via S. Pellico 29E, 10125 Torino. T. (011) 6689712. *059934*

Biazzi, Tina, Via Maria Vittoria 29B, 10123 Torino. T. (011) 8170421. *059935*

Bottega Antiquaria il Caduceo, 3 Via Cernaia, 10121 Torino. T. (011) 530202. *059936*

Bottega d'Arte, Via Monte di Pietà 13L, 10121 Torino. T. (011) 547822. *059937*

La Bottega die San Luca, 20 Via Cavour, 10123 Torino. T. (011) 8127358. *059938*

Brancaccio, C., Strada Basse Stura 63, 10154 Torino. T. (011) 20 40 14. *059939*

Bravin T., 5 Via Somis, 10138 Torino. T. (011) 4345309. *059940*

Breuza & Larizza, Via Monginevro 8, 10138 Torino. T. (011) 4331243. *059941*

Briotti S., 21 Corso Cadore, 10153 Torino. T. (011)8990888. *059942*

Brusasca Spalazzo, G., Via della Rocca 1, 10123 Torino. T. (011) 83 52 09. *059943*

Brusasca U., 15 Piazza Corso Emanuele II, 10123 Torino. T. (011) 8171185. *059944*

Burzio, Vincenzo, Via S. Dalmazzo 9, 10122 Torino. T. (011) 54 53 31. *059945*

Candellero M., 115 Corso Un. Sovietica, 10134 Torino. T. (011) 3190927. *059946*

Capone Silvia, 23 Via M. Vittoria, 10123 Torino. T. (011) 884031. *059947*

Capuani, Giovanni, Corso Siracusa 177-1, 10137 Torino. T. (011) 35 54 21. *059948*

Caramagna Luciano – Cambio, Sterline – Monte d'oro correnti, Via Cernaia 40, 10122 Torino. T. (011) 539014. *059949*

Carbone, Vicenzo & Figli, Galleria Principe Eugenio, Via Cavour 17, 10123 Torino. T. (011) 516268. *059950*

Caretto, Via Maria Vittoria 10, 10123 Torino. T. (011) 53 72 74. - Paint - *059951*

Carpet's Gallery, Galleria Subalpina 9-13, 10123 Torino. T. (011) 54 48 96. *059952*

Casa D'Aste della Rocca, 33 Via Rocca, 10123 Torino. T. (011) 836244, 8123070. *059953*

Casale E., 35 Corso de Gasperi, 10129 Torino. T. (011) 599555. *059954*

Casartelli, Via Maria Vittoria 25A, 10123 Torino. T. (011) 88 31 81, Fax (011) 883181. - Furn / Silv - *059955*

Cascino, N., Via Monte di Pietà 23, 10122 Torino. T. (011) 54 02 90. *059956*

Cassino, Gianni, Via della Rocca 1, 10123 Torino. T. (011) 83 62 98. *059957*

Cassino, Loredana, Via della Rocca 1, 10123 Torino. T. (011) 8397832. *059958*

Catalano, G., Via Stampini 14, 10148 Torino. T. (011) 2267261. *059959*

Cavallo, Carlo, Via Berthollet 30, 10125 Torino. T. (011) 6699958, 4364965. - Ant / Furn - *059960*

Chimenti C., 14 Via Andreis, 1052 Torino. T. (011) 4365004. *059961*

Chimenti R., 36h Via Arsenale, 10121 Torino. T. (011) 882475. *059962*

Chiriotti, L., Galleria Principe Eugenio, Via Cavour 17, 10123 Torino. T. (011) 5625816. *059963*

Cicogna Casanova di Cicogna Casanova R. & C., 19 Corso Moncalieri, 10131 Torino. T. (011) 6604757. *059964*

Cicogna Casanova R., 12 Via Villa Regina, 10131 Torino. T. (011) 8193350. *059965*

Cigales et Lavandes, 51a Via M. Vittoria, 10123 Torino. T. (011) 8193233. *059966*

Ciraulo A., 23 Via Borgo Dora, 10152 Torino. T. (011) 5211317. *059967*

Circolo Numismatico Torinese, 9 Via Ozanam, 10123 Torino. T. (011) 8173822. *059968*

La Clessidra di Tazzetti V. & C., 29 Via Rocca, 10123 Torino. T. (011) 837038. *059969*

Coccimiglio, U., Via dell'Accademia Albertina 21C, 10123 Torino. T. (011) 83 65 79. *059970*

Cohen, Giuseppe, Galleria San Federico 41, 10123 Torino. T. (011) 5628769. - Orient / Tex - *059971*

Colombari, Giorgio & C., Piazza Carignano 2, 10123 Torino. T. (011) 51 05 55, 53 28 21. *059972*

Colombari, Giorigio & C., 17 Via Cavour, 10123 Torino. T. (011) 5620555. *059973*

Combi, Gianni & C., Via Teofilo Rossi di Montelera 3, 10123 Torino. T. (011) 561 35 82. *059974*

Corvino, M., Via Chiesa Salute 88, 10147 Torino. T. (011) 216 60 59. *059975*

Cose Antiche Vendita mobili autentici – Quadri Camini d'epoca, Specchiere e cornici, Via Provinciale 334/338, 10141 Torino. T. (011) 9700400. *059976*

Cristiani, C., 13 Via Piazza Palat, Torino. T. (011) 4360715. *059977*

Cristiani, Giancarlo, Via della Rocca 6, 10123 Torino. T. (011) 8178391. - Ant / Paint / Furn / China - *059978*

Curreli R., 16 Via Monferrato, 10131 Torino. T. (011) 8191421. *059979*

Cutica, Via Maria Vittoria 1, 10123 Torino. T. (011) 54 27 36. - Num - *059980*

Damiano Fratelli & C., Galleria Principe Eugenio, Via Cavour 17, 10123 Torino. T. (011) 5624868. - Paint / Furn / China / Silv - *059981*

De Luca L., 20 Via Napione, 10124 Torino. T. (011) 8171113. *059982*

Dellacha, Vaj, M. L., Via della Rocca 2, 10123 Torino. T. (011) 812 53 42. *059983*

Dutto, Via S. Francesco da Paola 14M, 10123 Torino. T. (011) 8178663. *059984*

E Libreria Numismatica di Nirino Osvaldo e C., 15 Via Micca, 10121 Torino. T. (011) 539835. *059985*

Eco di Forme, 10f Via Bogino, 10123 Torino. T. (011) 8123083. *059986*

Eco di Forme, 19 Via M. Vittoria, 10123 Torino. T. (011) 8395177. *059987*

Extempora di Capone Silvia Antiquariato – Oggestistica Tessuti d'arredamento, Via M. Vittoria 23A, 10123 Torino. T. (011) 884031. *059988*

Fascino del Passato, Via Pellico 2, 10125 Torino. T. (011) 650 36 52. *059989*

Fassino M., 55d Corso de Gasperi, 10129 Torino. T. (011) 505276. *059990*

Feira, M., Via Pescatore 11B, 10124 Torino. T. (011) 812 45 60. *059991*

Filatelica, 14 Via Golto, 10125 Torino. T. (011) 6503063. *059992*

Filtor, Via Amerigo Vespucci 32, 10129 Torino. T. (011) 50 23 07. - Num - *059993*

Fina, Gianfranco, Gallerie Principe Eugenio, Via Cavour 17, 10123 Torino. T. (011) 5621173/597778. - Furn / Silv - *059994*

Fiore C., 12 Via Borgo Dora, 10152 Torino. T. (011) 5213216. *059995*

Fiore C., 17/14 Via Cavour, 10123 Torino. T. (011) 5623833. *059996*

Fiorio, Pietro, Via V. Porri 6A, 10153 Torino. T. (011) 8981585. - Ant - *059997*

Fiorio S., 11 Via Giolitti, 10123 Torino. T. (011) 10123. *059998*

Fitzcarraldo, 24 Via S. Franc. d'Assisi, 10121 Torino. T. (011) 538982. *059999*

Follies, Via Barbaroux 9, 10122 Torino. T. (011) 53 55 36. *060000*

Fulcheri, Giuseppe & Figli, Gallerie Principe Eugenio, Via Cavour 17, 10123 Torino. T. (011) 5624688. *060001*

Galleria d'Arte Torre di Mare, Via Maria Vittoria 26, 10123 Torino. T. (011) 8125940. - Furn - *060002*

Galleria del Ponte, Corso Moncalieri 3, 10131 Torino. T. (011) 8193233. *060003*

La Galleria di Floriana Maturi & C., 2b Via Lanino, 10152 Torino. T. (011) 5213137. *060004*

Gallerie Principe Eugenio Arte e Antiquariato, 24 Antiquari in un Palazzo, Via Cavour 17, 10123 Torino. T. (011) 5624209. *060005*

Gallino, Cecilia & Carlotta, Via Andrea Doria 19, 10123 Torino. T. (011) 8128013. - Paint / Fra - *060006*

Gallo Antichità, Galleria Principe Eugenio, Via Cavour 17, 10123 Torino. T. (011) 5625659. *060007*

Ganesh, Via Bogino 19D, 10123 Torino. T. (011) 8170074. *060008*

Gentile & Scarfò, Via Bava 9B, 10124 Torino. T. (011) 8123403. *060009*

Geronzi, Italo, Via Cibrario 43, 10144 Torino. T. (011) 4376189. *060010*

GFC Radio Hobby Acquisto – Vendita Scambio – Noleggio Riparazioni – Ricambi, Via Fontanesi 25, 10153 Torino. T. (011) 888263, 8173694. *060011*

Ghalibaf, Corso Vittorio Emanuele II 40, 10123 Torino. T. (011) 878093. *060012*

Ghigo, Daniele, Corso S. Maurizio 52, 10124 Torino. T. (011) 8174555. - Ant / Furn / Orient / Tex - *060013*

G.I.M., 38 Via Vassalli Eandi, 10138 Torino. T. (011) 4344473. *060014*

Gioielleria Mangia, Via amendola 14, 10121 Torino. T. (011) 518587. *060015*

Giordanino G., 46 Via Vespucci, 10129 Torino. T. (011) 10129. *060016*

Giraudo di Alberto Giraudo & C., 8 Via Rubiana, 10139 Torino. T. (011) 745073. *060017*

Giraudo di Alberto Giraudo & C., 7 Via Palazza Citta, 10122 Torino. T. (011) 4361336. *060018*

Giubergia, F., Corso Giulio Cesare 261, 10155 Torino. T. (011) 2464533. *060019*

Grasso, Teresio, Via Cavour 13, 10123 Torino. T. (011) 5621279. - Ant - *060020*

Guaraldo D., 12 Via Borgo Dora, 10152 Torino. T. (011) 4362543. *060021*

I Segni di Bob Ben, 20c Via S. Teresa, 10121 Torino. T. (011) 5176552. *060022*

I Segni di bob Ben, 20 Via S. Teresa, 10121 Torino. T. (011) 539280. *060023*

I Segni di Bob Ben, Via S. Teresa 20C, 10121 Torino. T. (011) 5628947. *060024*

Il Capitello, Via Mazzini 13, 10123 Torino. T. (011) 8170477. *060025*

Il Cassetto della Nonna, Corso Regina Margherita 148, 10152 Torino. T. (011) 5213127. - Ant / Paint / Furn / Jew / Silv - *060026*

Il Conte Anselmo, Via Po 32, 10123 Torino. T. (011) 812 66 76. *060027*

Il Saggio e La Luna, Via Nizza 107, 10126 Torino. T. (011) 669 93 18. *060028*

Il Tarlo Bottega Antiquaria, Galleria Principe Eugenio, Via Cavour 17, 10123 Torino. T. (011) 5623332. - Furn / China - *060029*

Italia, Louis Robert, 109 Corso Vitt. Eman. II, 10128 Torino. T. (011) 541150. *060030*

L'Angolo, Via Bonafous 8, 10123 Torino.
T. (011) 8174104. *060031*
L'Arte Antica, Via A. Volta 9, 10121 Torino.
T. (011) 562 58 34, 54 90 41, Fax 534 154. - Graph /
Orient - *060032*
L'Omnibus di Serre, Via Borgo Dora 22, 10152 Torino.
T. (011) 521 22 31. - Ant / Furn - *060033*
La Lanterna Magica, Alberta Bossi, Via S. Francesco
d'Assisi 26G, 10123 Torino. T. (011) 543753/5171268.
- Ant / Furn / Cur - *060034*
La Pellegrina, Corso Francia 15, 10138 Torino.
T. (011) 434 22 81. *060035*
La Pulce, Via G. Botero 19C, 10122 Torino.
T. (011) 546444. - Paint / Furn / Jew - *060036*
L.A.R.T. di Pischetola Compravendita mobili, soprammo-
bili, oggettistica Restauri – Perizie, Via Governolo 14,
10128 Torino. T. (011) 500742. *060037*
Lazzarini, Galleria Principe Eugenio, Via Cavour 17,
10123 Torino. T. (011) 5625970. - Paint / Furn /
Instr - *060038*
Les Fleurs Animées Antiquariato insolito, Via Plana 1/I,
10123 Torino. T. (011) 884912. *060039*
Les Voleurs, Via Villa della Regina 9, 10131 Torino.
T. (011) 8194267. *060040*
Liistro S., 48 Corso S. Maurizio, 10124 Torino.
T. (011) 882287. *060041*
La Lira di Lombardo A. Monete cartomoneta francobolli,
Via Alloni 10D, 10122 Torino.
T. (011) 4369644. *060042*
Lo Zodiaco, Via dei Mercanti 13, 10123 Torino.
T. (011) 54 26 17. *060043*
Lombardo A, 10 Via Allioni, 10122 Torino.
T. (011) 4369644. *060044*
Loqui D., 200 Corso Francia, 10145 Torino.
T. (011) 745985. *060045*
La Madia di Falco D. e Galleano G., 40 Via Mad. Cristina,
10125 Torino. T. (011) 6689889. *060046*
Maimome, E., Corso Stati Uniti 9, 10128 Torino.
T. (011) 53 75 11. *060047*
Malloggia, A., Via delle Rosine 1, 10123 Torino.
T. (011) 88 58 68. *060048*
Marchisio Arredamenti, 86 Via Frelius, 10139 Torino.
T. (011) 3859713. *060049*
Marotta Importazione Mobili Antichi, Francia – Inghilter-
ra – oriente Tappeti Antichi e Vecchi Porcellane Cinesi
e Sculture, Moncalieri S. Maria, Strada Carpice, 22,
10124 Torino. T. (011) 6467427,
Fax (011) 6467193. *060050*
Martano O., 113c Via Tripoli, 10137 Torino.
T. (011) 3141775. *060051*
Massone, Giuseppe, Via della Rocca 2G, 10123 Torino.
T. (011) 88 53 36. *060052*
Mazzone, E., Via S. Francesco da Paolo 11E, 10123 Tori-
no. T. (011) 8173701. *060053*
Mogliasso, Michele, Via Maria Vittoria 44, 10123 Torino.
T. (011) 884455. *060054*
Monete oro – argento – rame antiche e moderne Carta-
moneta, francobolli, Piazza Paleocapa 3, Via Lagrange
15, 10121 Torino. T. (011) 544535, 532573. *060055*
Montenegro Numismatica, Corso Vittorio Emanuelle II,
65, 10128 Torino. T. (011) 546365,
Fax (011) 544856. *060056*
Montenegro Numismatica, Corso Vittorio Emanuele II
65, 10128 Torino. T. (011) 546365,
Fax (011) 544856. *060057*
Morgana di Righetti Baraldo & C., 14 Via Piazza Citta',
10122 Torino. T. (011) 4361423. *060058*
M.S. di Milano Pierra e C., 2 Piazza Carignano, 10123
Torino. T. (011) 545472. *060059*
Mussato S., 51 Via Giolitti, 10123 Torino.
T. (011) 884522. *060060*
Neirotti, Via Gradisca 52, 10136 Torino.
T. (011) 36 55 89. - Furn - *060061*
Nigra, M., Via Borgo Dora 35, 10123 Torino.
T. (011) 740584/5213913. *060062*
Nikzad Opere D'Arte, 91 Via Osasco, 10141 Torino.
T. (011) 3821411. *060063*
Nirino – Numismatica e liberia numismatica, Via P. Mic-
ca 15, 10121 Torino. T. (011) 539835. *060064*
Nizza, Giulio, Via Mazzini 40, 10123 Torino.
T. (011) 835244/8127844. *060065*
Novarese, D., Via Maria Vittoria 20, 10123 Torino.
T. (011) 8125289. *060066*

Novarese, M., Via Maria Vittoria 6, 10123 Torino.
T. (011) 54 57 39. *060067*
Novecento, Via Po 5, 10123 Torino. T. (011) 543697.
- Ant / Furn / China / Jew / Cur - *060068*
Numart, 9 Piazza G. dalle Bande Nere, 10132 Torino.
T. (011) 8994947. *060069*
Numismatica Eupremio Montenegro, Corso Vittorio Ema-
nuele II 65, Via Gioberti 2, 10128 Torino.
T. (011) 546365, 5621930, Fax (011) 544856. *060070*
Obligato, F., Via Maria Vittoria 13, 10123 Torino.
T. (011) 8395190. *060071*
Old England Gallery, Via S. Massimo 42, 10123 Torino.
T. (011) 812 20 21. *060072*
Old Turin, Via Valprato 68, 10155 Torino.
T. (011) 248 50 51, Fax (011) 2485315. - Ant - *060073*
Ornamenta, 18 Via M. Vittoria, 10123 Torino.
T. (011) 837170. *060074*
Otini Galleria di Ottini G. e C., 27b Via M. Vittoria, 10123
Torino. T. (011) 884430. *060075*
Paglia e Fieno, Corso Fiume 5, 10123 Torino.
T. (011) 65 88 42. - Furn / China / Fra - *060076*
Palbert Antichità, Corso Vittorio Emanuele II 28, 10123
Torino. T. (011) 8127431. *060077*
Papa S., 10 Via Lanino, 10152 Torino.
T. (011) 4365018. *060078*
Parigi, A., Via Borgo Dora 14, 10152 Torino.
T. (011) 521 13 90. *060079*
Parigi, D., Via Monferrato 10 e 20, 10131 Torino.
T. (011) 8196722. *060080*
Parigi Pido, Daniela, Via Monferrato 10 e 20, 10131 To-
rino. T. (011) 8196722. *060081*
Pascale T., 8g Via Mazzini, 10123 Torino.
T. (011) 8122146. *060082*
Peirani S., 216a Via Tripoli, 10137 Torino.
T. (011) 365514. *060083*
Pellegrino, Bartelomeo, Via Maria Vittoria 27, 10125 To-
rino. T. (011) 889262. *060084*
Pellegrino, Bartolomeo, Galleria Principe Eugenio, Via
Cavour 17, 10123 Torino. T. (011) 5623376. *060085*
Perito Numismatico Presso Gamera die Commercio, Tri-
bunale, Dogana, Via Sacchi 44, Viale Vittoria 1, 10128
Torino. T. (011) 595966, 9674186. *060086*
Perotti G., 12 Via Andreis, 10152 Torino.
T. (011) 5211692. *060087*
Peyrani, Sergio, Via Tripoli 216, 10137 Torino.
T. (011) 36 55 14, 309 59 30. *060088*
Polo, Marco, Via Po 59, 10124 Torino. T. (011) 8177782,
Fax (011) 8177782. *060089*
Pozzallo, Flavio, Galleria Principe Eugenio, Via Cavour
17, 10123 Torino. T. (011) 5625025. *060090*
Pregliasco – Libri Antichi, Stampe – Disegni – Manos-
critti, Via Acc. Albertina 3/Bis, 10123 Torino.
T. (011) 8177114. *060091*
Pron, Lino, Via Plana 19E, 10135 Torino.
T. (011) 83 79 75. *060092*
Quaglia, L., Via Borgo Dora 31, 10152 Torino.
T. (011) 521 15 59. *060093*
Il Quattrino, 15 Via Lagrange, 10123 Torino.
T. (011) 532573. *060094*
Il Quattrino, 3 Piazza Paleocapa, 10121 Torino.
T. (011) 544535. *060095*
Questa, Enrico, Via Camerana 10, 10123 Torino.
T. (011) 5622422. - Furn / Orient / China / Sculp / Silv /
Instr / Glass / Cur – *060096*
Remagnino A., 25c Via Piazza Amedeo, 10123 Torino.
T. (011) 8171635. *060097*
Riccardino Arredamenti, 53 Via Borgaro, 10149 Torino.
T. (011) 2163730. *060098*
Rollero Perito – Monete da collezione, Via Arsenale 35/
Bis, 10121 Torino. T. (011) 5621450. *060099*
Romanelli, R., Via Maria Vittoria 46D, 10123 Torino.
T. (011) 8171300. *060100*
Salomone, S., Corso Trapani 34, 10139 Torino.
T. (011) 74 02 79. - Ant / Furn - *060101*
Samuele B., 1 Via Mazzini, 10123 Torino.
T. (011) 549735. *060102*
San Federico, Galleria S. Federico 30, 10121 Torino.
T. (011) 541455. *060103*
San Francesco Antichita', 12 Via S. Franc. da Paola,
10123 Torino. T. (011) 8122273. *060104*
Santini, Norico, Corso Einaudi 45, 10123 Torino.
T. (011) 50 31 95. *060105*

Scarfo' R., 9 Via Bava, 10124 Torino.
T. (011) 8123403. *060106*
Schreiber, 27 Corso S. Maurizio, 10124 Torino.
T. (011) 8171731, 835621. *060107*
Sciolla, Piero, Via Principe Amedeo 11, 10123 Torino.
T. (011) 8170514. - Furn - *060108*
Secol-Art, Via S. Francesco da Paola 14A, 10123 Torino.
T. (011) 8174063. - Ant / Paint / Furn / Mod - *060109*
Securizzo sekur, Via Refrancore 28/14, 10151 Torino.
T. (011) 7392397, Fax (011) 7399522. *060110*
Serin, Galleria Subalpina 18, 10127 Torino.
T. (011) 557 01 48. *060111*
Sibona P.L., 18 Via Corso Alberto, 10123 Torino.
T. (011) 5176007. *060112*
Signetti, Angela, Via Maria Vittoria 41, 10123 Torino.
T. (011) 88 59 68. *060113*
Sikander, Via Valprato 68, 10155 Torino.
T. (011) 85 96 61, 85 98 29. *060114*
Stella, S., Via Viterbo 123, 10149 Torino.
T. (011) 25 29 61. *060115*
Targa, Andrea, 28 Via pr. Amedeo, 10123 Torino.
T. (011) 8170642. *060116*
Tina, Via Maria Vittoria 29B, 10123 Torino.
T. (011) 839 71 94. - Mod - *060117*
Tonso, A., Via Carlo Capelli 39, 10146 Torino.
T. (011) 79 70 27. *060118*
Totem e Tabu', 31f Via Catania, 10153 Torino.
T. (011) 284095, 859230, 2488619. *060119*
Totem e Tabù, Via Catania 31F, 10153 Torino.
T. (011) 284095, Fax 8011) 2488619. *060120*
Turbiglio E., 10 Via Rocca, 10123 Torino.
T. (011) 835032. *060121*
Vaccarino M., 38 Via S. Massimo, 10123 Torino.
T. (011) 8127338. *060122*
Valabrega, Via della Rocca 29, 10123 Torino.
T. (011) 812 10 42. *060123*
Valabrega, Vittorio, e Via della Rocca 29, 10123 Torino.
T. (011) 515606/8121042. *060124*
Varallo Gian Domenico Monete d'oro correnti, Corso Via
Emanuele II 27, 10125 Torino.
T. (011) 6692994. *060125*
Vecchia Europa, Via Bertola 26, 10123 Torino.
T. (011) 541680. *060126*
Veneto, B., Via Bava 8, 10124 Torino.
T. (011) 88 59 60. *060127*
Vercelli, Leonarda, Galleria Principe Eugenio, Via Cavour
17, 10123 Torino. T. (011) 5628265. *060128*
Verniti S., 12 Via Porri, 10153 Torino.
T. (011) 8981345. *060129*
Vitrotto, C., Via Carlo Alberto 6, 10123 Torino.
T. (011) 54 27 49. *060130*
Vitrotto, Clotilde e C., 52 Via Giolitti, 10123 Turino.
T. (011) 8171742. *060131*
Voena, Via dei Mille 36, 10123 Torino. T. (011) 88 98 84,
Fax 956 13 93. *060132*
Yesterday, Via Francesco Petrarca 11C, 10126 Torino.
T. (011) 650 33 19. - Furn / Silv - *060133*
Zabert, Gilberto, Piazza Cavour 10, 10123 Torino.
T. (011) 8178627/8175516, Fax (011) 8178627. - Ant /
Paint / Furn / Sculp / Dec - *060134*
Zaza, A. G., Via dei Mercanti 3G, 10154 Torino.
T. (011) 541523. *060135*
Zengiaro A., 23 Piazza Via Veneto, 10124 Torino.
T. (011) 8174420. *060136*
Zengiaro, Angelo, Piazza Carlo Emanuele II 19, 10123
Torino. T. (011) 8170725. - Furn / Paint - *060137*
Zucco, E., Corso Casale 180F, 10132 Torino.
T. (011) 8980392. *060138*
Zurfletti, Via Roma 351, 10123 Torino. T. (011) 530073.
- Instr - *060139*

Torre Annunziata (Napoli)
Maria, Domenico de, Corso Umberto I 259, 80058 Torre
Annunziata. T. (081) 861 46 54. *060140*

Torre Canavese (Torino)
Datrino, Castello di Torre Canavese, 10010 Torre Cana-
vese. T. (0124) 50 10 71, 50 11 14,
Fax 50 11 17. *060141*

Torre del Greco (Napoli)
Luna, Luigi, Via Nazionale 191, 80059 Torre del
Greco. *060142*

Torre San Giorgio (Cuneo)
Bertero, Lucio, Prov Giovanni Giolitti, 12030 Torre San Giorgio. T. (0172) 960 76. 060143

Torrechiara (Parma)
La Bottega del Gallo, Vicolo del Borgo 13, 43010 Torrechiara. T. (0521) 77 11 33. 060144

Tortona (Alessandria)
Guagnini, Via Emilia 79, 15057 Tortona. T. (0131) 86 14 77. 060145
Taroppio, Mario, Via Massa Saluzzo, 15057 Tortona. 060146

Toscolano (Brescia)
Felina, Via Donizetti 35, 25088 Toscolano. T. (0365) 64 27 30. - Furn - 060147

Trani (Bari)
Liserre e C., Corso Italia 27, 70059 Trani. T. (0883) 440 15, 423 88. 060148
Todisco, Giuseppe, Via Ognissanti 2, 70059 Trani. T. (0883) 433 96. 060149

Tremezzo (Como)
Peschiera, Ugo, Via Portici San Pietro 8, 22019 Tremezzo. T. (0344) 406 42. 060150

Trento
Cappelletti, Via Alfieri 13, 38100 Trento. T. (0461) 254 52. - Ant - 060151
Gasperetti, Bruno, Via Torre Verde 52, 38100 Trento. T. (0461) 246 71. - Ant - 060152
S.C.F., Via Mantova 30, 38100 Trento. T. (0461) 251 57. 060153

Trestina (Perugia)
Pettenella, P., Viale Parini 64, 06018 Trestina. T. 85 45 29. 060154

Trevi (Perugia)
La Piccolo Galleria, Via Roma 18, 06039 Trevi. T. (0742) 78 08 47. 060155

Treviglio (Bergamo)
Banfi, Innocente, Via M d'Azeglio 33, 24047 Treviglio. T. (0363) 482 17. 060156

Treviso
Allegrini, Viale C. Batisti 20, 31100 Treviso. T. (0422) 45 608. - Ant / Paint / Furn / China / Tex / Silv / Glass - 060157
Amadio, Oscar, Viale Bixio 23, 31100 Treviso. T. (0422) 609 97. 060158
Barasciutti, Via Carlo Alberto 25, 31100 Treviso. T. (0422) 40623. 060159
Brunello, Enrico, Via Castelmenardo 49, 31100 Treviso. T. (0422) 54795. 060160
Bruneria, Piazza Vittorio 24, 31100 Treviso. T. (0422) 466 54. 060161
Chinellato, Gianni, Via Manzoni 24, 31100 Treviso. T. (0422) 48788. 060162
Galleria Soraya, Via C. Battisti 2, 31100 Treviso. T. (0422) 54 08 12. - Tex - 060163
Mora, Felicita, Piazza Pola 16, 31100 Treviso. T. (0422) 513 57. 060164
Piccolo, Alba & Palo del, Via A. Diaz 26, 31100 Treviso. T. (0422) 55885. - Jew - 060165
Plataroli, Pino, Via Siora Andriana del Vescovo 50, 31100 Treviso. T. (0422) 658 87. 060166
Plataroli, Pino, Via Terraglio 72, 31100 Treviso. 060167
Postiglione, Via Diaz 34, 31100 Treviso. 060168
Sancin, L., Via Paris Bordone 18, 31100 Treviso. T. (0422) 43730. 060169
Stefani, Ida de, Via Paris Bordone 38, 31100 Treviso. T. (0422) 518 93. 060170
Tiziano, Borgata Cavour 53, 31100 Treviso. T. (0422) 41884. 060171
Trevisana, Via Orioli 8, 31100 Treviso. T. (0422) 51661. - Num - 060172
Zanon, Adriano, Via Feltrina 39, 31100 Treviso. 060173
Zanon, Adriano, Via Dotti 42, 31100 Treviso. T. (0422) 539 82. 060174

Trezzano (Milano)
Antiquario di Bregorio, Giuseppe, Via Tintoretto 2, 20090 Trezzano. T. (02) 48400796, 4883197. 060175
Gregorio, Guiseppe, Via Pirandello 8, Cascina Mezzetta, 20090 Trezzano. T. (02) 48 40 07 96, 488 31 97. - Furn - 060175a
Manelli Antichita', Via San Cristofora 75, 20090 Trezzano. T. (02) 48401339. 060176

Trieste
Antiquitas, Via dei Rettori 1, 34121 Trieste. T. (040) 659 44, 681 13. 060178
Bellon e C., Via Ciamician 7, 34131 Trieste. T. (040) 77 14 10. 060179
Bernardi, Giulio, Via Roma 3, 34121 Trieste. T. (040) 690 86. - Num - 060180
Bottega Vecia, Via del Trionfo 1, 34121 Trieste. T. (040) 649 58. 060181
Boutique dell'Antiquariato, Via dell'Annunziata 6, 34124 Trieste. T. (040) 72 63 41, 72 39 31. 060182
Bravin, Mario, Piazza Vecchia 5, 34121 Trieste. T. (040) 686 48, 695 89. - Furn / Dec / Mod - 060183
Casa d'Arte, Via dell'Orologio 6, 34121 Trieste. T. (040) 76 08 61. - Ant / Paint / Furn / Dec - 060184
Casa d'Arte Orientale, Via Pier Luigi da Palestrina 8, 34133 Trieste. T. (040) 76 80 07, 63 02 89. 060185
Corso, Al, Galleria Rossoni, 34122 Trieste. T. (040) 615 39. 060186
Cose Vecchie, Via Timeus 9, 34125 Trieste. T. (040) 76 18 01, 74 47 16. 060187
El Trovarobe, Via San Michele 6, 34124 Trieste. T. (040) 682 23, 63 10 52. 060188
Filatelia Nazionale, Capo di Piazza 2, 34121 Trieste. T. (040) 63 17 08. - Num - 060189
Gaber, Frida, Via della Beccherie 15, 34139 Trieste. T. (040) 694 10. 060190
Galleria Tappeti Orientali, Viale XX Settembre 39, 34125 Trieste. T. (040) 954 23. 060191
Gioielleria Liberty, Via Malcanton 14, 34121 Trieste. T. (040) 63 16 41, 77 15 83. 060192
Giubilo, Giuseppe, Via del Teatro 1, 34121 Trieste. T. (040) 62180. - Tex - 060193
Iesu, Gianfranco, Via Cadorna 13, 34124 Trieste. T. (040) 76 07 19. 060194
Il Giardino, Via Mazzini 12, 34121 Trieste. T. (040) 682 42. 060195
La Miniera, Via del Ponte 4, 34124 Trieste. T. (040) 659 10, 76 62 44. 060196
Pozza, Claudio, Via Torrebianca 29, 34132 Trieste. T. (040) 681 73. 060197
Saxida, Paolo, Piazza Barbacan 2, 34143 Trieste. T. (040) 648 22. 060198
Saxida, Paolo, Via Negrelli 12, 34143 Trieste. T. (040) 73 44 04. 060199
Sfiligoi, Vittoria, Via Einaudi 3, 34121 Trieste. T. (040) 64431. - Num - 060200
Taccari, Clodio, Via Giustiniano 6, 34133 Trieste. T. (040) 693 42. 060201
Tagliante, Donato e Vincenzo, Via delle Beccherie 1, 34121 Trieste. T. (040) 79 56 68, 57 62 31. 060202
Tagliente, Giuseppe, Via delle Beccherie 6, 34121 Trieste. T. (040) 63 16 21. 060203
Veci Ricordi, Via Rossetti 20, 34125 Trieste. T. (040) 72 86 08. 060204
Zucco, de, Riva Nazario Sauro 6/A e B, 34121 Trieste. T. (040) 30 82 99, Fax 30 83 99. - Paint / Furn / China / Silv - 060205

Triggiano (Bari)
Bucci, C., Corso Vittorio Emanuele 56, 70019 Triggiano. T. (080) 878 12 36, 68 30 28. 060206

Trino (Vercelli)
Savio, Via Picco 7, 13039 Trino. T. (0161) 820 83. 060207

Tuoro sul Trasimeno (Perugia)
Renzoni, O., Via del Lavoro 15, 06069 Tuoro sul Trasimeno. T. (075) 82 61 83. 060208

Udine
Antiquità, Via Paolo Sarpi 20, 33100 Udine. T. (0432) 29 06 82. 060209
Marchetti & C., Via B. Stringher 25/3, 33100 Udine. T. (0432) 29 91 29. - Ant / Paint / Graph / Furn / Orient / China / Sculp / Tex / Silv / Glass / Cur / Ico / Draw -- 060210
Muschietti, Galleria Astra, 33100 Udine. T. (0432) 50 57 54. - Num - 060211
Samarcanda, Vicolo Pulesi7, 33100 Udine. T. (0432) 29 12 72. 060212

Umbertide (Perugia)
Vecchio Cose, Rosa Ferranti, Via Stella 12, 06019 Umbertide. T. (075) 941 54 91. 060213

Urbino (Pesaro e Urbino)
Bernardini, Via Piano Santa Lucia 10, 61029 Urbino. T. (0722) 31 97. 060214
Bernardini, Via Vittorio Veneto 52, 61029 Urbino. T. (0722) 26 22. 060215
Fotomero, Via Puccinotti 27, 61029 Urbino. T. (0722) 27 96, 27 00. 060216

Vado (Bologna)
Piretti, Via Val di Setta 24, 40040 Vado. T. (051) 93 90 76, 93 91 34. 060217

Vago (Verona)
Scarpolini, Via A Volta 15, 37050 Vago. T. (045) 98 22 32. 060218

Valenza (Alessandria)
Pasetti, Maria Rosa, Viale Dante 14, 15048 Valenza. T. (0131) 97 46 91. - Jew / Instr - 060219

Valfabbrica (Perugia)
Gatti, A., Via Monte Serra Casacastalda 12, 06029 Valfabbrica. T. (075) 90 91 37. 060220
Spiti, R., Via Roma 17, Casacastalda, 06029 Valfabbrica. T. (075) 90 91 71. 060221

Valperga (Torino)
Colombatto, Via Battisti 15 bis, 10087 Valperga. T. (0124) 61 73 19, 61 71 16. 060222

Varese
Sogliani, Via Fratelli della Rovere 12, 21100 Varese. T. (0332) 22 89 98. 060223
Studio R, Via Leopardi 13, 21100 Varese. T. (0332) 23 03 66, 22 99 92. 060224
Wolf, Viglio, Piazza Podestà 2, 21100 Varese. T. (0332) 28 01 13. 060225
Yanni, Via Bagaini 14, 21100 Varese. T. (0332) 23 50 80, 31 05 62. 060226
Zebert, Piazza del Podestà 2, 21100 Varese. T. (0332) 24 06 67. 060227

Varzo (Novara)
Cunioni, Amilcare, Via Nazionale del Sempione, 28039 Varzo. T. (0324) 71 31. 060228

Venaria
Antichita' Burzio Luca, Via A. Mensa 13B, 10078 Venaria. T. (011) 495046. 060229

Venezia
Arredi d'Arte, S. Marco 2438, 30124 Venezia. T. (041) 318 58. - Ant - 060230
Barozzi, San Marco 2052, Calle delle Veste, 30124 Venezia. T. (041) 896 15. - Ant - 060231
Biban, F., San Marco 2437, 30124 Venezia. T. (041) 22082. 060232
Bonato, Patrizia, Castello 6490, 30122 Venezia. T. (041) 522 77 34. 060233
Casellati, Pippo, San Marco 2404, 30124 Venezia. T. (041) 309 66. 060234
Cesana, San Marco 4392, 30124 Venezia. T. (041) 23 90 5. 060235
Di Rizzoli, Herriz & C., Via XXII Marzo 2381, 30124 Venezia. T. (041) 520 42 76, 522 93 33. - Jew / Silv - 060236
Dominici, Giuseppe, San Marco, Spadaria 549/64, 30124 Venezia. T. (041) 522 38 92. 060237
Emmer, Piccoli Nicoletta, Isola di Torcello 24, 30121 Venezia. T. (041) 522 84 73. 060238
L'IXa, San Marco 2958/a & 3357/a, 30124 Venezia. T. (041) 522 96 56, 522 15 80. - Furn - 060239
Laura, San Marco 3724, 30124 Venezia. T. (041) 522 80 93. - Furn - 060240

Martin, Bruno, San Giovanni Crisostomo 5781, 30121 Venezia. T. (041) 25540. - Num - 060241

Micossi, Gianni & C., Dorsoduro 3212, 30123 Venezia. T. (041) 522 83 25. - Tex - 060242

Mirate, Francesco S., S. Marco 1904, 30124 Venezia. T. (041) 276 00. - Paint / Furn / China / Sculp / Tex / Dec / Fra / Silv / Instr / Rel / Glass / Draw - 060243

Nummisfil, San Marco 4862, 30124 Venezia. T. (041) 523 20 95. - Num - 060244

Orfino, via Verdi 88 Mestre, 30171 Venezia. T. (041) 95 74 24. - Num - 060245

Patitucci, Beppe, San Marco 2511, 30124 Venezia. T. (041) 363 93. - Sculp - 060246

Rahaim, Rascid & C., Via XXII Marzo 2380, San Marco, 30124 Venezia. T. (041) 522 47 36. 060247

Rizzo, Orlando, San Marco 706, 30124 Venezia. T. (041) 29380. 060248

San Giorgio, Calle Fiubera San Marco, 30124 Venezia. T. (041) 522 66 10. - Furn - 060249

Sant Angelo, San Marco 3537, 30124 Venezia. T. (041) 522 68 40. 060250

Santomaco della Toffola, Antonietta, San Marco 1504-Frezzaria, 30124 Venezia. T. (041) 523 66 43. - Graph / Furn / Silv - 060251

Scarpa, Pietro, Via XXII Marzo 2089, 30124 Venezia. T. (041) 522 71 99. - Graph / Sculp / Tex / Draw - 060252

Tolotti, Paolo, San Marco 2520, 30124 Venezia. T. (041) 85262. 060253

Trevisan, Via Einaudi 29, 30174 Venezia. T. (041) 95 21 65. - Paint / Furn / Instr - 060254

Trois, Vittorio, San Marco 2666, 30124 Venezia. T. (041) 522 29 05. - Ant / Paint / Furn / China / Tex - 060255

Xantippe, San Barnaba 2774, 30123 Venezia. - Paint / Furn / Draw - 060256

Zancopè, Paolo, Campo S Maurizio 2677, 30124 Venezia. 060257

Zanutto, Enzo, San Marco 2360, 30124 Venezia. T. (041) 353 59. 060258

Venezia Mestre

Barovier, Marina/Franco de Boni, Via Palazzao, 30174 Venezia Mestre. T. (041) 95 79 60. - Ant / China - 060259

Berto, Marzia, Via Ciardi 50, 30174 Venezia Mestre. T. (041) 98 06 65. - Tex - 060260

Marameo, Via Caneve 85, 30173 Venezia Mestre. T. (041) 98 37 25. 060261

Pozzo, Al, Via Olivi 68, 30171 Venezia Mestre. T. (041) 94 09 55. 060262

Rezen, Viale Garibaldi 2, 30173 Venezia Mestre. T. (041) 98 58 41. - Tex - 060263

Torre, La, Torre Belfreddo 56, 30174 Venezia Mestre. T. (041) 98 44 27. - Ant / Paint / Furn / Orient / China / Sculp / Lights / Instr / Rel / Glass / Cur / Mod / Draw -- 060264

Vianello, Vinicio, Via del Rio Storto 3, 30174 Venezia Mestre. T. (041) 91 46 16. 060265

Verano Brianza (Milano)

Colciago, Renato, Via A Grandi 74, 20050 Verano Brianza. T. (0362) 90 47 20. 060266

Interni Arte, Via Brandi 73, 20050 Verano Brianza. T. (0362) 90 26 41. - Jew - 060267

Verbania Fondotoce (Novara)

Muzzi, Walter, Via Quarantadue Martiri 122, 28040 Verbania Fondotoce. T. (0323) 49 61 36. 060268

Verbania Pallanza (Novara)

Antichita, Via Vittorio Veneto 122, 28048 Verbania Pallanza. T. (0323) 427 19. 060269

Zago, Rita, Via 42 Martiri 18, 28048 Verbania Pallanza. T. (0323) 49 60 65, 50 34 82. 060270

Vercelli

Artearredo, Via Fratelli Ponit 24, 13100 Vercelli. T. (0161) 544 15. 060271

Bellaguardia, Luigi, Corso Libertà 295, 13100 Vercelli. T. (0161) 570 70, 632 78. 060272

Cassetta, Romeo, Via Tigrai 11, 13100 Vercelli. T. (0161) 64252. - Furn - 060273

Dazza, Arturo, Piazza Paietta 9, 13100 Vercelli. T. (0161) 524 88. - Ant / Paint / Furn - 060274

Donati, Via Paggi 84, 13100 Vercelli. T. (0161) 2326. - Paint / Furn - 060275

Gaggi, Enrico & Dada, Viale Garibaldi 39, 13100 Vercelli. T. (0161) 624 89. - Ant / Furn / Tex - 060276

Il Tarlo, Via Crispo 6, 13100 Vercelli. T. (0161) 640 09. 060277

Isola, Anna, Via Failla 14, 13100 Vercelli. T. (0161) 67890. - Furn / Sculp - 060278

Ottobrini, Corso Libertà 290, 13100 Vercelli. T. (0161) 60035. 060279

Ressia, Via Pastrengo 9, 13100 Vercelli. T. (0161) 65154. 060280

Santa Chiara, Corso Libertà 327, 13100 Vercelli. T. (0161) 571 46, 664 57, 684 98. 060281

Vergato (Bologna)

Bruni, Graziano, Strada Porrettana 50, 40038 Vergato. T. (051) 91 10 02. 060282

Verolengo

Mattarte il Fascino Dell'Antico, Via Torino, 10038 Verolengo. T. (011) 9148141. 060283

Verolengo (Torino)

Mattarte, Strada Torino 12, 10038 Verolengo. T. (011) 914 91 77, Fax 914 81 41. 060284

Verona

Antichità Sottoriva, Via Sottoriva 34, 37121 Verona. T. (045) 596634. - Ant / Furn - 060285

Antiquaria Veronese, Piazza Santa Anastasia 9, 37121 Verona. T. (045) 285 89. - Ant / Paint / Furn / Orient / China / Tex / Arch - 060286

Bia, Marta, Via Catullo, 37121 Verona. T. (045) 800 91 91. - China / Sculp / Jew - 060287

Cancello, Al, Piazza Cittadella 7, 37122 Verona. T. (045) 59 22 74. 060288

Dalla Persia, Alberto, P.zza Erbe, Palazzo Maffei, 37121 Verona. T. (045) 800 69 89. - China - 060289

Graffiti, Corso Sant'Anastasia 36, 37121 Verona. T. (045) 327 79. 060290

Il Tarlo, Via Sottoriva 24, 37121 Verona. T. (045) 211 46. 060291

Lonardelli, Franco, Corso Sant'Anastasia 29-31, 37121 Verona. T. (045) 226 53. - Ant / Paint / Furn / Tex / Dec / Lights - 060292

Lugo Poiesi, Via Portici 7, 37121 Verona. T. (045) 266 99. - Ant - 060293

Malavasi, Fernando, Corso Sant'Anastasia 18, 37121 Verona. T. (045) 336 24. 060294

Mercante d'Oriente, Il, Corso Santa Anastasia 34, 37121 Verona. T. (045) 59 41 52. 060295

Negrini, A., C. S. Anastasia 18, 37121 Verona. T. (045) 303 98. - Sculp / Silv / Glass - 060296

Negrini, Maurizio, Corso Sant'Anastasia 34, 37121 Verona. T. (045) 326 50. 060297

Rinaldi, Oscar, & Figlio, Via Capello 23, 37121 Verona. T. (045) 380 32. - Num / Arch - 060298

Sansone & Alloro, Via Unità d'Italia 105, 37132 Verona. T. (045) 52 01 47. 060299

Teheran Carpets, Via Roma 1, 37121 Verona. T. (045) 323 95. 060300

Valbusa, Corso Sant'Anastasia 38, 37121 Verona. T. (045) 260 30. 060301

Veronese-Baldo, Corso Cavour 9, 37121 Verona. T. (045) 59 69 79. - Ant - 060302

Verzuolo (Cuneo)

Bessone, Osvaldo, Via Villanovetta 1, 12039 Verzuolo. T. (0175) 85 840. 060303

Viadana (Mantova)

Berni, Via Marconi 15, 46019 Viadana. T. (0375) 83 31 37. - Paint / Furn / Tex / Jew - 060304

Bottoli Antiques, Viale Kennedy 2, 46019 Viadana. T. (0375) 816 74. 060305

Old England, Via Verdi 17, 46019 Viadana. T. (0375) 823 78. 060306

Viareggio (Lucca)

Brocchini, Vincenzo, Via Aurelia sud 360, 55049 Viareggio. T. (0584) 39 07 36. 060307

Cercietti Pasquini, Via Marconi 107, 55049 Viareggio. T. (0584) 517 24. 060308

Parodi, Via IV Novembre 6, 55049 Viareggio. T. (0584) 470 33. 060309

Rafaelli, Giovanni, Via Coppino 193, 55049 Viareggio. T. (0584) 39 39 88. 060310

Vicenza

Antichità S. Barbara, Contrà S Barbara 25, 36100 Vicenza. T. (0444) 233 90. 060311

Bicciato, Corso Fogazzano 119, 36100 Vicenza. T. (0444) 23 49 28. 060312

Boschetti, Gianfranco, Piazza delle Erbe 3, 36100 Vicenza. T. (0444) 310 07. 060313

Bottega Fiorini, Via Ponte Pietra 15 a, 36100 Vicenza. T. (0444) 800 71 55. - Ant - 060314

Cepellini Ruggero, Corso Palladio 138 b, 36100 Vicenza. T. (0444) 54 37 06. - Paint / Jew / Silv - 060315

Demunari, Via Vescovado 119, 36100 Vicenza. T. (0444) 54 26 63. - Ant - 060316

Galleria Santa Barbara 14, Santa Barbara 14, 36100 Vicenza. T. (0444) 23 63 32. - Paint / Tex - 060317

Il Tritone, Corso Fogazzaro 119, 36100 Vicenza. T. (0444) 23 38 63. 060318

La Cassaforte, Via S Gaetano da Thiene 2 a, 36100 Vicenza. T. (0444) 50 71 75. 060319

Menato, Corso Fogazzaro 35, 36100 Vicenza. T. (0444) 285 99. 060320

Milan, Viale Roma 14, 36100 Vicenza. T. (0444) 274 31. 060321

Pasamoglu, Hasan, Via Molon 8, 36100 Vicenza. T. (0444) 54 57 83. - Tex - 060322

Pascià, Corso Palladio 186, 36100 Vicenza. T. (0444) 54 57 83. - Tex - 060323

Tomasi, Luigi de, Contrà Sant Apostoli 14, 36100 Vicenza. T. (0444) 23 24 15. 060324

Tommaso, Franco, Via San Domenico 2, 36100 Vicenza. T. (0444) 344 66. 060325

Vico Equense (Napoli)

Lincar, Charles, corso Filangieri 44, 80069 Vico Equense. T. (081) 879 88 16. - Num - 060326

Vicoforte (Cuneo)

Regis, Luciano, Strada Statale 28 sud, 12080 Vicoforte. T. (0174) 637 40. 060327

Vigevano (Pavia)

Agli Archi Rosa, Piazza Sant Ambrogio 5, 27029 Vigevano. T. (0381) 822 74. 060328

Al Portone, Via XX Settembre 37, 27029 Vigevano. T. (0381) 856 74. 060329

Cose Antiche, Via Cadutti d Liberatzione 33, 27029 Vigevano. T. (0381) 751 10. 060330

Galleria dell'Antiquariato, Via Simone del Pozzo 12, 27029 Vigevano. T. (0381) 755 75. 060331

Il Nome, Via del Popolo 20, 27029 Vigevano. T. (0381) 835 07. 060332

Zambon, Carlo, Via Dante 23, 27029 Vigevano. T. (0381) 715 46. 060333

Zambon, Carlo, Via Del Carrobbio 8, 27029 Vigevano. T. (0381) 751 87. 060334

Vignola (Modena)

Maculan, Loredana, Via Ponte Muratori 2, 41058 Vignola. T. (059) 77 33 66. 060335

Maculan, Loredana, Via Ponte Muratori 2, 41058 Vignola. T. (059) 77 33 66, 77 52 44. 060336

Villa Adriana (Tivoli-Roma)

Laboratorio Falegnameria – Restauro – Tappezzeria, Via Tiburtina 153/155, 00010 Villa Adriana (Tivoli-Roma). T. (0774) 533362, 535191. 060337

Villa Carcina (Brescia)

Bosio, Giuseppe, Via Garibaldi 56, 25069 Villa Carcina. T. (030) 88 10 29. 060338

Villa Vicentina (Udine)

Il Mercato dell'Arte, Via Gorizia 38, 33059 Villa Vicentina. T. (0431) 966 78. 060339

Villanova (Cuneo)

Neve, Sergio, Via Mondovì 59, 12089 Villanova. T. (0174) 69 93 10. 060340

Villanova D'Asti
Antichita' Lentini, Strada per Asti 81, 14019 Villanova
D'Asti. T. (0141) 946112. 060341
Lentini Compra vendita, Strad per Asti 81, 14019 Villanova D'Asti. T. (0141) 946112. 060342

Villaricca (Napoli)
Andretta, Erminio, Circumvallazione Esterna Napoli,
80010 Villaricca. T. (081) 894 15 15. 060343

Villastanza (Milano)
Morlacchi, Via Gorizia 5, 20010 Villastanza.
T. (0331) 55 31 12, 55 42 36. - Tex - 060344

Viterbo
Bentivegna Fiorillo, Maria, Via San Pellegrino 88, 01100
Viterbo. T. (0761) 348 63. 060345
Cose del Passato, Via S Pellegrino 3, 01100 Viterbo.
T. (0761) 348 03. 060346
Fiorillo, Franco, QuartMedievale SPellegrino88, 01100
Viterbo. T. (0761) 348 63. 060347
Foglietta, Antonio, Via Cardinale La Fontaine 10, 01100
Viterbo. 060348
Marchi, de, Via Macel Maggiore 12, 01100 Viterbo.
T. (0761) 22 37 73. 060349
Regni, Enio, Via Cardinale La Fontaine 1, 01100 Viterbo.
T. (0761) 22 16 22. 060350

Vittorio Veneto (Treviso)
Bottega d'Antiquariato, Via Martiri della Liberta 7,
31029 Vittorio Veneto. T. (0438) 534 39. 060351
Nardi, Fratelli de, Via Rizzera 282, 31029 Vittorio Veneto. T. (0438) 592 55. 060352

Voghera (Pavia)
Barisonzi, Fausto, Via XX Settembre 11, 27058 Voghera.
T. (0383) 443 76. 060353
Limosini, Ugo, Via Piacenza 39, 27058 Voghera.
T. (0383) 40147. - Furn - 060354

Zepponami (Viterbo)
Venanzini, Carlo, Via Cassia 5, 01020 Zepponami.
T. (0761) 863 31. 060355

Zibello (Parma)
Allegri, Raffaella, Via Roma 24, 43010 Zibello.
T. (0524) 991 02. 060356

Zola Predosa (Bologna)
Surprise, Via Risorgimento 242, 40069 Zola Predosa.
T. (051) 75 17 53. 060357

Japan

Hiroshima (Hiroshima-ken)
Japanese Gallery, 1-5-1 Fukushima-cho, Hiroshima.
T. (082) 231-6066. 060358

Kanazawa (Ishikawa-ken)
Tanisho Co. Ltd., 44 Jukken-machi, Kanazawa.
T. (0762) 21 7000. - China - 060359

Kobe (Hyogo-ken)
Hanshin, 3-45 Motamachi, Ikutaku, Kobe.
T. (078) 33 2516. - Orient - 060360
Uedakincokudo, 5-54 Motomachidori, Ikutaku, Kobe.
T. (078) 34 5108. - Orient - 060361

Kyoto
Akai, Mituru, 231-1 Yamatooji- Higashi-irum Shinmonzen St., Higashiyama-ku, Kyoto. T. (075) 541-6547.
- Ant / Furn / China / Sculp - 060362
Antique Kumura, Higashi-ooji Nishi-iru, Shinmonzen-dori, Kyoto. T. (075) 561-8871. 060363
Curtis, Robert E., Ltd., 2-16 Sanjobo-cho, Awataguchi
Higashiyama-ku, Kyoto. T. (075) 561-2560. - Ant /
Orient - 060364
G. Nakajima Antiques & Carlos Shop, 238 Shinmonzendori, Higashiyama-ku, Kyoto. T. (075) 561-
7771. 060365
Gashoken, 251 Umemotocho, Shinmonmaedori Higashiyamaku, Kyoto. T. (075) 561 1586. - Orient - 060366
Gwasendo Co. Ltd., Kawaramachi-Gojo Agaru, Shimogyo-ku, Kyoto 600. T. (075) 075 341-3288. 060367

Hayashitok, 83 Nakanocho Ogawa-Marutamachi, Makagyo-ku, Kyoto. T. (075) 222 0231, 231 2222.
- Sculp - 060368
Heian Art, Sanjo-sagaru, Jingu-michi, Higashiyama-ku,
Kyoto. T. (075) 771-6340. 060369
Heian Art, 373-38 Horrike-cho, Sanjo- agaru-, Jingumichi-agaru, Kyoto 605. T. (075) 751-0277.
- Ant - 060370
Holland Gwabo, Nishijin PO Box 65, Kyoto 602.
T. (075) 414-1076, Fax 431-8958. 060371
Ikegami, T., Shinmonzen Higashiyama-ku, Kyoto.
T. (075) 541-4563. - Ant / Furn / Orient / China /
Tex - 060372
Inaba Cloisonne Co., Ltd., Sanjo Shirakawabashi Nishi
Higashiyama-ku, Kyoto 605. T. (075) 761-1161/3.
- Orient - 060373
Izumi & Co., Higashioji-mishiiru Shinmonzen-dori, Kyoto.
T. (075) 531-4033. 060374
Kaji's Antique, Shinmonzen St., Higashi-ohji Higashiyama-ku, Kyoto 605. T. (075) 561-4114, Fax 531-1250.
- Ant / Orient / China - 060375
Kakumoto, C., 245 Nakano-cho, Shinmonzen St. Higashiyama-ku, Kyoto. T. (075) 56-3164. - Ant / Orient /
Sculp / Dec - 060376
Kashu & Co., Shinmonzen-dori, Higashi-ohji Nishi-iru,
Higashiyama-ku, Kyoto 605. T. (075) 561-
7568. 060377
Kato Co., Ltd., Shinmonzen St. Higashiyama-ku, Kyoto
605. T. (075) 561-1580, Fax 561-5297. - Ant / Orient /
Repr / Sculp / Dec - 060378
Kazuo Kotera, 245 Shinmonzen St. Higashiyama-ku,
Kyoto. T. (075) 525-2100. - Ant / Orient - 060379
Kidd, David, 17 Ebisudani Hi-No-Oka Yamashina, Kyoto.
T. (075) 751 8552. - Ant / Paint / Furn / Orient /
Sculp - 060380
Kita, R., 256, Shinmonzen-dori, Higashi- ohji, Nishi-iru
Higashiyama-ku, Kyoto. T. (075) 561-
6023. 060381
Kondo, 278 Kitagawa, Shijodori – Gionmachi, Higachiyamaku, Kyoto. T. (075) 561 4367. - Orient - 060382
Kozuyoshije, 85 Oichicho, Omaedori-Nishiiru Ichijodori,
Kamagyoku, Kyoto. T. (075) 461 8814.
- Orient - 060383
Kyoto Washington, Teianno-cho, Teramadi-Higashi- iru,
Shijo-dori, Shimokyo-ku, Kyoto. T. (075) 221-
0807. 060384
Mikumo Wood-Block Hand Print Co., Ltd., Shijo Kakashinmichi Nishi-Iro, Kyoto. - Ant - 060385
Murray's Co., Sanjyo st. Higashiyama-ku, Kyoto.
T. (075) 771-6233. 060386
Murrys Co., Sanjo Keage Awata-Jing Kado Higashiyama-ku, Kyoto 605. T. (075) 771-1984, Fax 771-
7233. 060387
Nakajima, G., 238 Shinmonzen St., Higashiyama-ku,
Kyoto. T. (075) 561-7771. - Ant / Tex / Eth – 060388
Nakamura, T., 372 Nawate-dori Sanjo Minami- iru, Higashiyama-ku, Kyoto 605. T. (075) 3561-
4726. 060389
Nakashiu Co., Umemoto-cho, Shinmonzen- dori, Higashi-ohji Nishi-iru, Kyoto 605. T. (075) 561-
2906. 060390
Okudarenhode, 244 Kitagawa, Shijodori- Gionmachi,Higachiyamaku, Kyoto. T. (075) 561 3655.
- Orient - 060391
Okumura, S., Shinmonzen St., Kyoto. T. (075) 561-2385.
- Ant - 060392
Rakuyo Shoten, Shinmonzen St., Higashiyama-ku, Kyoto. T. (075) 541-4825. - Ant / Lights - 060393
Ren Ko Do, Shinmonzen, Nawate, Higashi Higashiyama-ku, Kyoto. T. (075) 525-2121. - Ant / Paint / Orient / China - 060394
Robert E. Curtis Ltd., 2-16 Sanjobo-cho, Awataguchi, Higashiyama-ku, Kyoto. T. (075) 561-2560. 060395
Sakaikuzuqki, 113 Higashikataicho, Omaedori Ichijo-Agaru, Kitano, Kamig., Kyoto.
T. (075) 462 2723. 060396
Shibunkaku, Matubara-Kudaru Nishiteracho, Shimogyo-ku, Kyoto. T. (075) 801 2375. - Orient - 060397
Shibunkaku, Furumonzen-dori, Yamato-oji, Higashi-iru,
Higashiyama-ku, Kyoto 605. T. (075) 531 0001,
Fax 561 4386. 060398

Taniguchi, H., 247 Nakano-cho Shinmonzen Higashiyama-ku, Kyoto. T. (075) 561-1371. - Ant / Paint /
Cur - 060399
Tenpyo-do Co., Umemoto-cho, Shinmonzen-dori Higashiyama-ku, Kyoto 605. T. (075) 561-5688. 060400
The Red Lantern Shop, 236 Shimmonsen St., Nakanocho Higashiyama-ku, Kyoto 605. T. (075) 561-6314.
- Graph - 060401
Tikuan, Motocho, Yamatooji-Higashiiru Komonmaedori,
Higashiyamaku, Kyoto. T. (075) 531 0684.
- Orient - 060402
Tsuruki, Y., & Co., Shinmonzen St. Higashiyama-ku,
Kyoto. T. (075) 561-1886. - Ant / Paint / Graph / Furn /
Orient / China / Repr / Sculp / Arch / Dec - 060403
Uchida Art Co., Kumanojinja-Higashi Sakyo-Ku, Kyoto
606. T. (075) 761-0345, Fax 761-0349. 060404
Ushio Gallery, Shinmonzen St., Higashiyama- nishi-iru
Higashi, yama-ku, Kyoto. 060405
Yagi Art Shop, 200 Shinmonzen St., Hanamikoji Nishi-iru, Higashiyama-ku, Kyoto 605. T. (075) 541-1671.
- Ant / Orient / China - 060406
Yamada Art Gallery, 253 Umemoto-cho, Shinmonzendori, Higashiyama-ku, Kyoto 605. T. (075) 561-
5382. 060407
Yamanaka & Co., 14 Awataguchi Sanjobo-cho, Higashiyama-ku, Kyoto. T. (075) 5610931, Fax 531-0490.
- Ant - 060408
Yokoyama, Nawate-dori Shinbashi-agaru, Higashiyama-ku, Kyoto 605. T. (075) 541-1321, Fax 541-
1325. 060409
Yoshidashoundo, Karasuma-Higashiiru Anekoji, Nakagyoku, Kyoto. T. (075) 221 7328. - Orient - 060410
Zenta Shoundo Co., Ltd., Higashi Karasumaru, Anekoji
Nakagyo-ku, Kyoto. T. (075) 22-7328. - Ant / Paint /
Orient / China / Silv / Glass - 060411

Nagoya (Aichi-ken)
Gayudo, 2-17 Shuzaicho, Higashiku, Nagoya.
T. (052) 941 3937. - Orient - 060412
Itoubijututen, 3-16-25 Nishiki, Nakaku, Nagoya.
T. (052) 971 3190. - Orient - 060413
Japanese Art Gallery, 401 Takara Dai-ichi Bldg., 2-5-1
Sakae, Naka-ku, Nagoya 460. T. (052) 231-0855.
- Orient - 060414
Minoi, 2-11-4 Nishiki, Nakaku, Nagoya.
T. (052) 231 3353. - Orient - 060415
Ohgiya Oriental Antiques, 5-11 Chikusa Dori Chikusa-Ku, Nagoya 464. T. (052) 732-3639. - Ant / Furn / China / Instr - 060416
Yonaman, 1-16 Sakashitacho, Tikusaku, Nagoya.
T. (052) 751 2044. - Orient - 060417
Yonekin, 3-12 Nagaregawacho Nakaku, Nagoya.
T. (052) 241 3937. - Orient - 060418

Nara (Nara-ken)
Gakugndo, 16 Higashimukainakacho, Nara.
T. (0742) 22 2147. - Orient - 060419
Nanmeido, 58 Noboriojicho, Nara. T. (0742) 22 3764.
- Orient - 060420
Seitaro, Kimura, 42 Shimo Sanjomachi, Nara.
- Ant - 060421
Shokodo, Kadofuricho, Sanjodori, Nara.
T. (0742) 22 2147. - Orient - 060422
Tamabayashi, Z., Sanjo-dori, Nara. T. (0742) 2-2147.
- Ant - 060423

Okayama (Okayama-ken)
Sanyo-do Antiques, 13-20 Chuo 2-chome, Kurashiki,
Okayama 710. T. (0862) 25-4577. 060424

Osaka
Chohoan, 36 Tatamiyacho, Midmiku, Osaka.
T. (06) 211 3628. - Orient - 060425
Gallery Kawachi, 43, Shinsaibashi-suxi, 1-chome, Minami-ku, Osaka 542. T. (06) 252-5800. 060426
Hachimando, 3-56 Nishinakajimacho Higashiyodogawa-Ku, Osaka. T. (06) 301 5007. - Orient - 060427
Hayashitok Co Ltd., Chiyodo-kita Bld. 17 Naniwacho, Kita-ku, Osaka. T. (06) 3733021. - Ant / Sculp - 060428
Henkotin, 2-1476 Kawaramachi, Naniwaku, Osaka.
T. (06) 541 0795. 060429
Hiranikotoken, 3-8 Oimatsucho, Kitaku, Osaka.
T. (06) 363 5869. - Ant / Orient - 060430

Hiranosaikodo, Hahkyu Dep. Store, Sumidacho, Kitaku, Osaka. T. (06) 361 1381. - Orient - 060431

Inoueryukodo, 2-39 Koraibashi, Higashi-Ku, Osaka. T. (06) 231 2488. - Orient - 060432

Kawanabe Corporation, 3,6-chome Uehonmachi Tennoji-ku, Osaka. T. (06) 7612543. - China / Sculp - 060433

Kitabynji, 9 Hatimancho Minamiku, Osaka. T. (06) 211 8245. - Ant - 060434

Komodo, Hankyu Dep. Store 41 Sumidacho, Kita-Ku, Osaka. T. (06) 361 1381. - Orient - 060435

Onkodo, Yambumoto, 6th floor, Hankyu Dep. Store, Osaka. T. (06) 361 1381. - Paint - 060436

Onoshigeo Shoten, Hankyu Dep. Store 41 Sumidacho, Kita-Ku, Osaka. T. (06) 361 1381. - Orient - 060437

Riseido, Taiyuji-cho, Kita-ku, Osaka 530. T. (06) 311 7487. - Orient - 060438

Sakumaharuzoshoten, 2-36 Shinsaibashisuji Minamiku, Osaka. T. (06) 211 4596. - Ant - 060439

Sekai Bijutsu Co Ltd., Henkochin, 1476 2-chome Kawaracho, Naniwaku, Osaka. T. (06) 641 0795. - Ant / Orient - 060440

Shosendo, 4-3 Awakimachi,Higashi-Ku, Osaka. T. (06) 231 8797. - Orient - 060441

Shugado, 4-25 Kitahama, Higashi-Ku, Osaka. T. (06) 231 0860. - Orient - 060442

Taigado, 2-6-18 Inari, Naniwa-ku, Osaka 556. T. (06) 568-7691. 060443

Takigawahoseido, 45 Kitatamayacho, Minami-Ku, Osaka. T. (06) 211 2126. - Orient - 060444

Tenyu Co., 13-5 Nishi Tenma 4-chome, Kita-ku, Osaka 530. T. (06) 364-5519. 060445

Todamasa Shoten, Hankyu Dep. Store 41 Sumidacho, Kita-Ku, Osaka. T. (06) 361 1381. - Orient - 060446

Todashoten, 4-31 Fushimicho, Higashi-Ku, Osaka. T. (06) 321 5272. - Orient - 060447

Toyo Handicrafts, Rm. 201 Junes Andoji Bldg., 5-13 Andoji-machi, Chuo-ku, Osaka 542. T. (06) 761-8599, Fax 761-8499. 060448

Umeda, 2-3-9 Sonezaki, Kita-ku, Osaka. T. (06) 364-3212. 060449

Yokoyama, Inc., Nawate Shinbashi Agara Higashiyama-ku, Osaka 605. T. (06) 541-1321. 060450

Yokoyama Kogei Ltd., Osaka Intl. Airport Bldg. 2F, 555 Hotarugaike-Nishimadu, Osaka. T. (06) 56-7456. 060451

Yonada Shoten, 37 Hachimancho, Miniami-Ku, Osaka. T. (06) 211 1467. - Orient - 060452

Tokyo

Art Plaza Magatani, 10-13 Toranomon 5-chome, Minato-ku, Tokyo 105. T. (03) 3433-6321, Fax 3431-6325. 060453

Asahi Art Center, Hibiya Park Bldg., 1-8-1 Yuraku-cho, Chiyoda-ku, Tokyo 100. T. (03) 3271-6260. 060454

Asahi Art Co., Ltd., 3-10, Jingumae 4-chome Shibuya-ku, Tokyo 150. T. (03) 3408-4624, Fax 3408-5651. - Ant - 060455

Azuma Co., Ltd., 9-3, Ginza 5-chome, Chuo-ku, Tokyo. - Ant / Paint / Orient / China / Sculp / Eth / Dec / Silv / Lights / Mil / Glass - 060456

Daijindo, 5-7 Minami Aoyama 6-chome, Minatu-ku, Tokyo 107. T. (03) 3400-0504, Fax 3400-0666. - Orient - 060457

Friendship Trading, Maruishi Bldg., 10-4 Kaji-cho 1-chome, Chiyoda-ku, Tokyo 101. T. (03) 3258-0331, Fax 3258-0334. 060458

Fugendo, 3-1 Nipponbashi-Douri, Chuo-Ku, Tokyo. T. (03) 3271 6671. - Orient - 060459

Fuji Fine Arts, Azabudai Houei Bldg., 2-3-20 Azabudai, Minato-ku, Tokyo 106. T. (03) 3582-1870, Fax 3582-1870. 060460

Gallery, 11-6, Akasaka 1-chome, Minato-ku, Tokyo 107. T. (03) 3585-4816, 3585-5019. - Orient - 060461

Geishinda, 3rd Fl., Sanyo Bldg., 1-8-10, Kyobashi, Chuo-ku, Tokyo 104. T. (03) 3564-0123, Fax 3564-3116. 060462

Godoy, George & Sandra, 3-27-7 Nozawa, Setagaya-ku, Tokyo. T. (03) 3414-6601. - Orient - 060463

Hanabishi, 6-19 Ginza 6-chome, Chuo-ku, Tokyo 104. T. (03) 3572-0873. 060464

Harumi, 9-6-14, Akasaka, Minata-ku, Tokyo 107. T. (03) 3403-1043. - Orient - 060465

Heisando Co., Ltd., 2-4, 1 Chôme Shiba Park Minato-ku, Tokyo 105. T. (03) 3434-0588, 3443-0589. - Ant / Paint / Orient / China / Sculp / Arch / Eth / Dec / Instr / Mi-l - 060466

Hioki Tenroku, 4-36 Roppongi 3-chome, Minato-ku, Tokyo 106. T. (03) 3584-3880. 060467

Honma, S., 4-8 Azabudai 3-chome, Minato-ku, Tokyo 106. T. (03) 3583-2950. 060468

Ishikatsu Garden Co., 3-4-7, Minami Aoyama, Minato-ku, Tokyo. T. (03) 3401-1677. - Orient - 060469

Japan Traditional Craft Center, 2nd. Fl., Plaza 246 Bldg., 3-1-1 Minami Aoyama, Minato-ku, Tokyo 107. T. (03) 3403-2460, Fax 3403-1587. 060470

Kanae Art Salon, 32-17 Kakinokizaka 1-chome, Meguro-ku, Tokyo 152. T. (03) 3723-5040. 060471

Keinan, 2-4, Yuraku-cho, Chiyoda-ku, Tokyo. T. (03) 3501-4015. 060472

Kite Museum, Taimeiken Bldg., 12-10, 1-chome, Nihonbashi, Chuo-ku, Tokyo 103. T. (03) 3271-2465. - Ant / Paint / Sculp - 060473

Kochukyo, 3-8-5, Nihonbashi, Chuo-ku, Tokyo. T. (03) 3271-1835. - Ant / Orient / China / Arch / Eth - 060474

Kurofune, 7-7-4 Roppongi, Minato-ku, Tokyo. T. (03) 3479-1552. - Orient - 060475

Matsunaga Art Shop, Sukiyabashi, 1 Ginza 5-chome Chuo-ku 104, Tokyo. T. (03) 3571-7818. 060476

Mayuyama & Co., 5-9 Kyobashi 2-chome, Chuo-ku 104, Tokyo. T. (03) 3561-5146, Fax 3561-6716. 060477

Mikazuki Gallery, Crescent Hse, 8-20 Shiba Koen 1-chome, Minato-ku, Tokyo 105. T. (03) 3436-3216, Fax 3436-5608. 060478

Mildred Warder, Ltd., 10-4 Toranomon 2-chome, Minato-ku 105, Tokyo. T. (03) 3585-8274. 060479

Mitochu, 3-1 Nipponbashi-Douri, Chuo-Ku, Tokyo. T. (03) 3271 9574. - Orient - 060480

Mitokoshokai, 3-4-25 Roppongi, Minato-Ku, Tokyo. T. (03) 3583 4378. - Orient - 060481

Mukashiya K.K., 1-14-32-210 Jingumae, Shibuya-ku, Tokyo 150. T. (03) 3404-1170, Fax 3401 2821. 060482

Murakami Hojido, 4-36 Roppongi 3-chome, Minato-ku, Tokyo 106. T. (03) 3583-0662. 060483

Nakazawa Co., M., 1-2-15, Yuraku-cho Chiyoda-ku, Tokyo 100. T. (03) 3591-1553/2553. 060484

Nanbando, 3-8, Roppongi 2-chome Minato-ku, Tokyo 106. T. (03) 358345582203. - Ant / Orient - 060485

Nippon Gallery, 3-1-4, Nihonbashi, Chuo-ku, Tokyo. T. (03) 3272-0011-13. 060486

Nishida, Yuzo, 15-18, 3-chome, Roppongi Minato-ku 106, Tokyo. - Cur - 060487

Nurihiko Gallery, 1 Nurihiko Bldg., 2-9-2 Kyobashi, Chuo ku, Tokyo 104. T. (03) 3561-5807, Fax 3561-6329. 060488

Odawara, Imperial Hotel Arcade, 1, 1-chome, Uchisaiwaicho, Chiyoda-ku, Tokyo. T. (03) 3591-0052. - Paint / Orient - 060489

Ohno, 31-23, 2chome Yushima Bunkyo-ku, Tokyo. T. (03) 3811 43 65. - Orient / China - 060490

Olympic Coin Gallery, Hoki Building, 31-8 Taito 4 Chome Taito-ku, Tokyo 110. T. (03) 3835 3093. - Num - 060491

Omiya, Y., Imperial Hotel Arcade, 1-1-1 Uchisaiwai-cho, Chiyoda-ku, Tokyo 100. T. (03) 3591-3667. 060492

Oriental Bazaar, 9-13 Jingumae 5-chome, Shibuya-ku, Tokyo 150. T. (03) 3400-3933, Fax 3499-6910. 060493

Oriental House, 12-1, Minami Aoyama 6-chome, Minato-ku, Tokyo. T. (03) 3400-0504. - Ant - 060494

Sagamiya, 6-13-9 Minami-Aoyama Minato-ku, Tokyo. T. (03) 3571 1222. - Paint - 060495

Sagemonoya, Yotsuya 4-28-20-703 Shinjuku-ku, Tokyo 160. T. (03) 33526286, Fax 33566581. - Orient - 060496

Saikodo, 2-7-18, Ginza Chuo-ku, Tokyo 104. T. (03) 3564-0711. 060497

Sankeido, 4-1 Nipponbashi-Muromati Chuo-Ku, Tokyo. T. (03) 3241 0935. - Orient - 060498

Sante, 4th Fl., Shinjuku Kokuto Bldg., 6-11-3 Nishi Shinjuku, Tokyo 160. T. (03) 3343-0310, Fax 3343-0307. 060499

Seigandobijuto, 6-11-3 Minami-Aoyama Minato-ku, Tokyo. T. (03) 3400 6270. - Orient - 060500

Sekaido Co., 1-29 Shinjuku 3-chome, Shinjuku-ku 160, Tokyo. T. (03) 3351-2961. 060501

Setsu Gatodo Co, 7-9, 3-chome, Nihombashi, Chuo-ku, Tokyo 103. T. (03) 3271-9630. - Ant / Paint / Orient / Arch - 060502

Sumisho Art Gallery, UN Bldg., 3F, 2-15 Yurakucho, 1-chome, Chiyoda-ku, Tokyo 100. T. (03) 3593-0777, Fax (03) 3593-0848. - Paint - 060503

Taisei Stamps & Coins Co., 19-8, Kyobashi 1-chome, Chuo-ku, Tokyo 104. T. (03) 3562-0711. - Num - 060504

Tajima, 8-19 Gainza 1-chome, Chuo-ku, Tokyo 104. T. (03) 3567-7576, Fax 3567-7576. 060505

Takaoka Shokai, 5 Kanda Jinbo-cho 1-chome, Chiyoda-ku, Tokyo 101. T. (03) 3291-5868. 060506

Terada Craft Studio, 8-15 Akasaka 3-chome, Minato-ku, Tokyo 107. T. (03) 3583-0558, Fax 3583-0527. 060507

Tokyo Art Salon, Hotel New Otani Arc. 4, Koi-cho, Chiyoda-ku, Tokyo. T. (03) 3265-0785, Fax 03 3265-0785. 060508

Tokyo Bijutsu Club (The Art Dealers Association), 6-19-15 Shimbashi Minato-ku, Tokyo 105. 060509

Tokyo Central Kaigakan, Ginza Boeki Bldg. 8th Floor 7-18, 2-chome Ginza, Chuo-ku, Tokyo 104. T. (03) 3564-0711. - Ant / Paint / Graph / Orient / China / Sculp / Tex / Lights / Draw - 060510

Toraya Co., 13-1 Minami Aoyama 5-chome, Minato-ku, Tokyo 107. T. (03) 3400-8121. 060511

Uchida Art Co., Sukiyabashi Shopping Ctr., Tokyo. T. (03) 3571-8077. 060512

Uchida Woodblock Printing Co., Ltd., 2nd Floor, Sukiyabashi Shopping Center, Ginza-Nishi, Tokyo. T. (03) 3571-8077. 060513

Watanabe + Co., 11 Akefune-cho, Shiba Minato-Ku, 11 Mori Blg., Tokyo. T. (03) 35914527. - China / Sculp - 060514

Watanabe, K., Co., 14, 1-chome, Yurako-cho, Tokyo. - Ant / Orient / China - 060515

Yabumoto, 3-2, Ginza 6-chome, Chuo-ku, Tokyo 104. T. (03) 3572-2748. - Ant - 060516

Yanagawa Art Store, 5-4-27 Minami-Aoyama, Minato-ku, Tokyo 107. T. (03) 3407 2244, Fax 3407 7943. - Orient - 060517

Yokoyama, Inc., Sukiya-bashi Shopping Center Ginza-Nishi, Chuo-ku, 2nd Fl., Tokyo. T. (03) 3572-5066/7. - Ant - 060518

Yokoyama, Tokyo Hilton Arcade, 10-3, 2-chome, Nagatacho, Chiyoda-ku, Tokyo 100. T. (03) 3580-9017. - Ant - 060519

Kenya

Mombasa

African Arts, Digo Rd., Mombasa. T. 25 507. 060520

Afro Crafts, Kihudini Rd., Mombasa. T. 23081. 060521

Articraft, Kihudini Rd., Mombasa. T. 26232. 060522

Nairobi

Antique Gallery, Kaunda St, POB 47616, Nairobi. T. (02) 227759. - Ant / Furn / Eth / Jew / Silv - 060523

Antiquity Shop, Nairobi Hilton, Mama Ngina St, POB 32182, Nairobi. T. (02) 331705. - Eth / Jew / Instr / Cur / Ico - 060524

Jewels and Antiques, Kimathi St, Nairobi. T. (02) 332002. 060525

Korea, Republic

Seoul

Gold House, II Insa Dong, Chongro-Ku, Seoul. T. (02) 73-42 44. - Furn / China / Jew - 060526

Period Antiques & Clocks, 74-62 Itaewon-Dong, Yongsan-Ku, Seoul. T. (02) 44-4423. - Furn - 060527

Tong-in, 16 Kwanhun-dong, Chongro-ku, Seoul, 100. T. (02) 74-4827, 74-4867, 75-9094. - Ant / Paint / Furn / Orient / China / Repr / Sculp / Jew / Silv - 060528

Lebanon

Beirut

Abousleiman, Farid, Rue de Damas, Immeuble Roxy, Beirut. T. (961) 22 52 85. 060529

Galerie „L'Amateur", rue Hamra, Capucins, Beirut POB 11982. T. (961) 342 930, 345 384. - Paint / Orient / China / Jew / Silv - 060530

Maison Habis, avenue Français, P.O. Box 116116, Beirut. T. (961) 22 61 03. - Tex / Jew / Silv - 060531

Liechtenstein

Balzers

Attikadellarte, Heeraweg 629, 9496 Balzers. T. (075) 41541. 060532

Nigg, Franz, Unterm Stein 598, 9496 Balzers. T. (075) 42408. 060533

Scherini, L., Kohlbruckweg 314, 9496 Balzers. 060534

Eschen

Antiquitätenhandelsanstalt, 9492 Eschen. 060535

Batliner, Elmar, 9492 Eschen. T. (075) 266 95. 060536

Steffling, Brigitte, 9492 Eschen. 060537

Mauren

Antique Export Establishment, P.O. Box 146, 9493 Mauren. T. (075) 3731252, Fax (075) 3731239.
- Furn - 060538

Nendeln

Militär-Stüble, Churerstr. 73, 9485 Nendeln. T. (075) 373 30 24. - Ant / Mil - 060539

Ruggell

Dome, Spiegelstr., 9491 Ruggell. T. (075) 33376. 060540

Schaan

Batliner, E., Landstr. 94, 9494 Schaan. 060541

Haas, Heinrich, Zollstr. 74a, 9494 Schaan. T. (075) 251 32. 060542

Jacky Antiquitäten, Landstr. 43, 9494 Schaan. T. (075) 235 10. 060543

Karst, Jean, Landstr 65, 9494 Schaan. T. (075) 2322935, Fax (075) 2323103. - Ant / Paint / Furn / China / Fra / Instr / Glass / Cur / Mod - 060544

Karst, Jean, Landstr 65, 9494 Schaan. T. (075) 2322935. 060545

Kübelbeck, Sylvia, Bildgass 70, 9494 Schaan. T. (075) 26052. 060546

Vaduz

Demarchi, Helene, Städtle 36, 9490 Vaduz. 060547

Ikonengalerie, Schaanerstr. 32, 9490 Vaduz. T. (075) 221 69. 060548

Leon Apeiron, Herrengasse 35, 9490 Vaduz. T. (075) 26122. 060549

Marlborough International Fine Art Est., Bartlegroschstr. 34, 9490 Vaduz. T. (075) 232 43 27. - Paint / Graph / Sculp / Draw - 060550

Schlegel + Schneider, Herrengasse 13, 9490 Vaduz. T. (075) 24 64 72. - Ant / China / Instr - 060551

Schneider, Lothar, Herrengasse 13, 9490 Vaduz. T. (075) 24647. 060552

Studer, Alfred Carl, St.-Markus-Gasse 23, 9490 Vaduz. T. (075) 265 40. 060553

Lithuania

Vilnius

Senamiesčio Antikvariatas, Universiteto 10, 2001 Vilnius. T. (02) 629146, Fax 628138. - Ant / Paint / Graph / Furn / China / Sculp / Lights / Glass / Mod / Ico / Tin - 060554

Luxembourg

Luxembourg

Adam, 16 Rue des Capucins, 1313 Luxembourg. T. (0352) 47 41 01. - Ant / Furn / China - 060555

Galerie Marie-Thérèse, 24 Av Marie-Therese, 2132 Luxembourg. T. (0352) 41509, 23712. 060556

Malaysia

Kelantan

Kelantan Malay Arts and Crafts, Jalan Sultanah Zainab, Kota Bharu, Kelantan. 060557

Kuala Lumpur (Selangor)

Asia Arts and Crafts Syndikat, Hilton Hotel, Kuala Lumpur. 060558

China Arts, Jalan T. Abdul Rahman, Kuala Lumpur. 060559

Dame de Malacca, La, 11 Jalan Pinang, Kuala Lumpur. T. (03) 48 47 09. 060560

Dame de Malacca, La, 367-1 Ampang, Rd., 8th Mile, Kuala Lumpur. 060561

Kashmir Arts Pro Sharmans, 174 Jalan T. Abd. Rahman, Kuala Lumpur. 060562

Kotabukiya Syndikat, 16 Jalan T. Abd. Rahman, Kuala Lumpur. 060563

Peiping Store Syndikat, 17 A Suleiman Ct., Kuala Lumpur. 060564

Malacca (Malaya)

Chin Nang Store, 44 Jalan Munshi Abdullah, Malacca. 060565

Syarikat, Abdul, 26 Jalan Hang Jebat, Malacca. T. 223 633. 060566

Penang

China Handicraft Company, 3D Jalan Penang, Penang. 060567

Eastern Curious Company, 35 Lbh Bishop, Penang. 060568

Leong Thin Lien, 175 Lbh Campbell, Penang. 060569

Oriental Arts Company, 35 F. Jalan Penang, Penang. 060570

Sharikat Kamsis Commercial Enterprise, 3-G Penang Rd., Penang. T. 60054. 060571

Malta

Valletta

Azzopardi & Sons, 18 Zachary St., Valletta. T. 282 15, 247 75. - Jew / Silv - 060572

Martinique

Fort-de-France

Au Petit Pavois, 96 Rte Phare, 97200 Fort-de-France. T. (596) 610214. - Graph / Furn / Dec / Silv - 060573

Baldaquin, 28 Rte Clairière, 97200 Fort-de-France. T. (596) 700080. - Furn - 060574

Gold Dolphin, 7 Blvd Chevalier-Sainte-Marthe, 97200 Fort-de-France. T. (596) 631742. - Dec - 060575

Rivière-Salée

Hier et Aujourd'hui, Petit Bourg, 97215 Rivière-Salée. T. (596) 778098, Fax (596) 778099. 060576

Schoelcher

Air du Temps, Batelière, 97233 Schoelcher. T. (596) 618612. 060577

Big Ben, Patio de Cluny, 97233 Schoelcher. T. (596) 609363. - Furn / Cur - 060578

Mexico

Cuernavaca (Morelos)

Galeria „Trini", Ruiz de Alarcon 7, Cuernavaca. 060579

„Tianguis" Arte Popular, Jardin del Palacio de Cortés, Cuernavaca. 060580

Guadalajara (Jalisco)

„El Diamante", Calle Juarez 351, Apartado 213, Guadalajara. - Jew / Instr - 060581

Mérida (Yucatán)

„El Paso", Calle 59 no. 501, Mérida. 060582

Puerto, Guy, Hotel Mérida, Mérida. T. 1-61-99, 1-74-72. - Ant - 060583

México (D.F.)

Antigüedades Impero, Hamburgo 149 103, México. 060584

Coloniart, Calle Estocolmo 37, Colonia Juarez, México. T. 525 89 28, 514 47 99. - Ant / Paint / Furn / Sculp / Fra - 060585

Cosio de Ortiz, Emma, Callejon de San Antonio 44, San Angel, México. - Arch / Eth - 060586

Echaniz, Mar Arafura 8, México. T. 527 29 51. - Arch - 060587

Fernandez, Guillermo, Av. Insurgentes Sur 76 A, México. 060588

Galeria Eugenio, Allende 84, México. T. 29 28 49. - Ant - 060589

Galerias Kant, Hamburgo 157, México. - Orient - 060590

Kamffer, Raul, Orizaba 62 Plaza Rio de Janeiro, México. - Ant - 060591

Lanai, Hamburgo 151, México, 06600, D.F. T. 511 33 32. - Paint / Graph / Sculp / Dec / Mod / Draw - 060592

Lazarin, Eduardo, Palma Norte 414-C, México. 060593

Mina, Mercedes de, Durango 103, México. - Instr - 060594

Mondragon, Lydia M. Vda. de, Allende 62-G, México. 060595

Perez e Hijos, S. A., Bolivar 13, México. 060596

Monterrey (Nuevo León)

Carapan, Hidalgo 305 Ote., Monterrey. - Ant / Eth - 060597

Galerias Elena, Hidalgo 2724 Pte., Monterrey. - Ant / Eth - 060598

Madero, Rodolfo Garza, Padre Mier 429 Pte., Monterrey. 060599

Puebla (Puebla)

Bazar de los Sapos, S. A., 7 riente No. 401, Casa de la Cupula, Puebla. T. 244 97, 110 82. - Ant - 060600

San Miguel de Allende (Guanajuato)

Casas Coloniales, Canal 5, San Miguel de Allende. - Ant - 060601

Veracruz (Veracruz)

Galerias Imperial, Lerdo 165, Hotel Imperial, Veracruz. T. 209 36, 219 82. - Ant - 060602

Monaco

Monaco Ville

Quernheim/Hohenlohe, 4 Ave de la Madone, 98000 Monaco Ville. T. 93 15 00 11. 060603

Monte Carlo

Antiquité, 1, av. Henry-Dunant, 98000 Monte Carlo. T. 93 50 58 22. - Ant - 060604

Athenaeum, 5 Av Princesse Alice, 98000 Monte Carlo. T. 93 50 77 72, Fax 93 16 03 94. 060605

Blaise, Emile, 21, bd. du Jardin Exotique, 98000 Monte Carlo. T. 93 30 56 96. - Ant / Paint / Furn - 060606

Fersen, Sporting d'Hiver, Pl. du Casino, 98000 Monte Carlo. T. 93 50 91 77. - Ant / Paint - 060607

Gadoury, Victor, 38 Blvd. des Moulins, 98000 Monte Carlo. T. 93 25 12 96. - Num - 060608

Galerie d'Art Ancien et Moderne, 21, Bd. Princesse-Charlotte, 98000 Monte Carlo. T. 93 30 76 22. - Ant / Paint / Furn / China - 060609

Galerie du Palais de la Scala, rue Henri Dunant, 98000 Monte Carlo. T. 93 30 58 22. - Ant - *060610*

Galerie Park Palace, 46 R Grimaldi, 98000 Monte Carlo. T. 93 50 68 44. - Ant - *060611*

Ghilardi, 6 Rue Saint-Michel, 98000 Monte Carlo. T. 93 30 94 88. - Paint / Furn - *060612*

L'Intemporal, 21 Blvd Princesse Charlotte, 98000 Monte Carlo. T. 93 50 60 16. *060613*

Laura, Luigi Anton, Impasse de la Fontaine, 98000 Monte Carlo. T. 93 25 09 15, Fax 93 25 77 80. *060614*

Lorenzi, Madeleine, 26, bd des Moulins, 98000 Monte Carlo. T. 93 30 62 33. - Jew / Silv - *060615*

Mint State, Pl. du Casino, 98000 Monte Carlo. T. 93 50 82 74. - Num - *060616*

Monte-Carlo Antiquités, 27 Blvd. des Moulins, 98000 Monte Carlo. T. 93 30 82 61. - Ant - *060617*

Park-Palace, 46 rue Grimaldi, 98000 Monte Carlo. T. 93 50 68 44. *060618*

Ribolzi, Adriano, 6 Av. des Beaux-Arts, 98000 Monte Carlo. T. 93 30 06 25. - Ant / Furn / Sculp / Tex - *060619*

SAPJO, 16, bd des Moulins, 98000 Monte Carlo. T. 93 50 54 34. - Ant / China / Jew / Silv - *060620*

Stauffer, 1 blvd. du Jardin-Exotique, 98000 Monte Carlo. T. 93 50 97 72. - Paint / Furn - *060621*

Trianon, 6 Blvd. des Moulins, 98000 Monte Carlo. T. 93 25 11 22. - Ant / Eth - *060622*

Walpole, 15 Blvd. du Jardin Exotique, 98000 Monte Carlo. T. 93 30 70 14. - Ant / Eth / Dec - *060623*

Myanmar

Yangon

Choo Seng & Co., 54 22nd St., Yangon. *060624*

Nepal

Kathmandu

Bhakta Bahadur Sreshtha, 20/239 Gyaneswor, Sano Gaucharan, Naksal, P.O. Box 699, Kathmandu. T. 4-14665. - Ant / Paint / Orient / Arch / Jew / Fra - *060625*

Handicrafts Impex Enterprises, Kathmandu GPOB 1069. - Ant / Paint / Orient / Cur - *060626*

Nepal Crystal Works & Curio House, 6/31 Juddha Sadak, Kathmandu. - Ant - *060627*

Silk Road Textiles, Kathmandu POB 3391. T. 411-391. - Orient / Tex - *060628*

Lalitpur (Patan)

Nepal Curio Works Shop, Mangal Bazar, Bhimsensthan, Lalitpur. - Ant - *060629*

Netherlands

Aardenburg (Zeeland)

Haneghem, les, Weststraat 68, 4527 BV Aardenburg. T. (0117) 491271. - Furn / Silv / Instr - *060630*

Aerdenhout (Noord-Holland)

Schreuder, René, Teding van Berkhout laan 57, 2111 ZB Aerdenhout. T. (023) 5323987, Fax 5420550. - Paint - *060631*

Alkmaar (Noord-Holland)

Dickhout, J. G., Kennemerstr 30w, 1815 LB Alkmaar. *060632*

Doofpot, Fnidsen 68, 1811 NH Alkmaar. T. (072) 5111120. - Ant - *060633*

Drie Kronen, Luttik Oudorp 114, 1811 MZ Alkmaar. T. (072) 5116311. *060634*

Duijneveld, G., Oudegracht 39, 1811 CA Alkmaar. *060635*

Henke, Ben, Koningstr 8, 1811 LV Alkmaar. *060636*

Henke, P., Gedempte Nieuwesloot 20-22, 1811 KT Alkmaar. T. (072) 5117041. *060637*

Het Huis met de Kogel, Appelsteeg 2, 1811 NA Alkmaar. *060638*

Schaddenhorst, C., Spoorstr. 31, 1815 BG Alkmaar. T. (072) 5116492. - Ant / Paint / Furn / China / Sculp / Jew / Silv - *060639*

Almelo (Overijssel)

Alberts, Henk, Grotestr. 117-123, 7607 CH Almelo. - Ant / Paint / Graph / Repr / Sculp / Dec / Jew / Fra / Rel / Draw - *060640*

Hagedorn, J. H., Nijreesdwarsweg 6a, 7609 PD Almelo. *060641*

Klooster-Esch, de, Westerstr 9, 7607 GL Almelo. *060642*

Koridon, W. G., Bornerbroeksestr 112, 7601 BH Almelo. *060643*

Alphen a/d Rijn (Zuid-Holland)

Doofpot, De, Ruysdaelstr 100, 2406 TH Alphen a/d Rijn. T. (0172) 474596. *060644*

Lee, J. P. van der, Vondelstr 8, 2406 XH Alphen a/d Rijn. T. (0172) 475652. *060645*

Amersfoort (Utrecht)

Eykelboom, I., Kamp 7, 3811 AM Amersfoort. T. (033) 4721870. *060646*

Homann, U. M. E. C., Hof 38, 3811 CK Amersfoort. T. (033) 415906. *060647*

Ramselaar, van, Havick 47, 3811 EX Amersfoort. T. (033) 4613494. - Ant / Dec - *060648*

Amstelveen (Noord-Holland)

AMNU, Berkenrodelaan 14, 1181 AJ Amstelveen. T. (020) 643 29 33. - Ant / Num - *060649*

Blokhoff, Tineke, Marg van Borsselenlaan 65, 1181 CZ Amstelveen. T. (020) 643 38 25. *060650*

Burijn Prenten, De, Amstelzijde 44, 1184 VA Amstelveen. T. (020) 963 18 68. - Ant - *060651*

Klinkhamer, J. A., Gr Willemlaan 33, 1181 EE Amstelveen. T. (020) 643 28 16. *060652*

Niele, Ed van, Oude Karselaan 4, 1182 CR Amstelveen. T. (020) 643 77 57. - Ant - *060653*

Vingerhoed, De, Bos en Vaartlaan 34, 1181 AB Amstelveen. T. (020) 643 19 54, 641 55 01. - Ant - *060654*

Westerbos & V. Schaik, Dorpsstr. 33, 1182 JA Amstelveen. T. (020) 641 46 17. - Ant - *060655*

Amsterdam

Aalderink, Spiegelgracht 15, 1017 JP Amsterdam. T. (020) 623 02 11, Fax 639 05 33. - Ant / Eth - *060656*

Aartuin, A. di, Valeriusstr 208, 1075 GK Amsterdam. T. (020) 679 59 32. *060657*

Acon, Nieuwe Spiegelstr. 46 sout, 1017 DG Amsterdam. T. (020) 624 92 88. - Ant - *060658*

Agora, Corn. Schuytstr. 9, 1071 JC Amsterdam. T. (020) 679 92 34. - Tex / Glass / Mod - *060659*

Amstel Antiques, Amstel 110, 1017 AD Amsterdam. T. (020) 638 44 45. - Ant - *060660*

Amsterdam Antiques Gallery, Nieuwe Spiegelstr 34, 1017 DG Amsterdam. T. (020) 625 33 71. *060661*

Ank-Tiek, Planciusstr. 18, 1013 MH Amsterdam. T. (020) 622 03 45. - Ant - *060662*

Antiek & Curiosa, Hogeweg 46A, 1098 CD Amsterdam. T. (020) 693 09 45. - Ant - *060663*

Antiekbeurs 700, van Slingelandstr 24, 1051 CH Amsterdam. T. (020) 686 43 72. *060664*

Antiekmarkt De Looier, Elandsgracht 109, 1016 TM Amsterdam. T. (020) 624 90 38. - Ant / Paint / Graph / Furn / Orient / China / Repr / Sculp / Dec / Jew / Silv / Lights / Instr / Rel / Glass / Mod / Pho / Mul / Tin - *060665*

Antique Arcade, Kerkstr. 176, 1017 GT Amsterdam. T. (020) 624 75 19. - Graph / Furn / China / Instr - *060666*

Antique Shop Hilton, Apollolaan 138, 1077 BG Amsterdam. T. (020) 673 57 37. *060667*

Antiques Gallery, Kerkstr. 142, 1017 GR Amsterdam. T. (020) 625 26 25. - Furn / China - *060668*

Appenzeller, Hans, Grimburgwal 1-5, 1012 GA Amsterdam. T. (020) 626 82 18. - Jew - *060669*

Ariadne, Leo en Martin Gerritzen, Rosmarijnsteeg 2, 1012 RP Amsterdam. T. (020) 624 59 66. - Num - *060670*

Ariëns Kappers, E.H., Nieuwe Spiegelstr. 32, 1017 DG Amsterdam. T. (020) 623 53 56, Fax 638 43 71. - Graph - *060671*

Aronson, Nieuwe Spiegelstr. 39, 1017 DC Amsterdam. T. (020) 6233103, Fax (020) 6383066. - Furn / China / Silv / Instr - *060672*

Art and Antiques Fair-Delft, Keizersgracht 207, 1016 DS Amsterdam. T. (020) 623 89 04. *060673*

Art Deco, Molsteeg 5-7, 1012 SM Amsterdam. T. (020) 623 21 89. - Furn / China / Dec / Lights / Glass / Cur - *060674*

Art Promotion Amsterdam, Diepenbrockstr 28, 1077 VZ Amsterdam. T. (020) 676 26 16. *060675*

Astamangala, Kerkstr 165, 1017 GH Amsterdam. T. (020) 623 44 02. *060676*

Atelier voor Antiek Textiel, Brouwersgracht 195/639, 1015 GJ Amsterdam. T. (020) 627 60 45. - Ant - *060677*

Ates, E. A., 1e Helmersstr. 167, 1054 DS Amsterdam. T. (020) 612 62 13. - Ant / Jew - *060678*

Aussen, R., Oudezijds Voorburgwal 189, 1012 EW Amsterdam. *060679*

Avanti, Haarlemstr. 59, 1013 EK Amsterdam. T. (020) 620 83 92. - Ant - *060680*

Aziatica, Weteringstr 20, 1017 SN Amsterdam. T. (020) 623 53 58. *060681*

Baken van Koekshaven, Lindengracht 5, 1015 KB Amsterdam. T. (020) 623 94 96. *060682*

Bakker, Bartje, Nieuwe Spiegelstr 50, 1017 DG Amsterdam. T. (020) 626 54 88. *060683*

Bartlema De Sloot, Velserweg 32, 1014 AH Amsterdam. T. (020) 686 15 66. - Ant - *060684*

Bartlema De Sloot, Spaarndammerdk. 715, 1014 AE Amsterdam. T. (020) 686 15 66. - Ant - *060685*

Becker, Jan, Willemsparkweg 117, 1071 GW Amsterdam. T. (020) 662 98 65. - Ant / Furn / China / Sculp / Tex / Lights - *060686*

Beeke & van Bree, Keizersgracht 82, 1015 CT Amsterdam. T. (020) 622 47 27. *060687*

Beeling, J.P., Stadionplein 23-III, 1076 CG Amsterdam. T. (020) 6763501, Fax (020) 6790622. - China - *060688*

Berg, H. van den, Rynstr. 192, 1079 HS Amsterdam. T. (020) 642 29 82. - Ant - *060689*

Berlijn, Ger, Prinsengracht 534-40, 1017KJ Amsterdam. T. (020) 625 91 97. *060690*

Beveren, van, Borgerstr 224, 1053 RE Amsterdam. T. (020) 683 42 24. *060691*

Bijleveld, Benjamin, Nieuwe Spiegelstr. 45, 1017 DC Amsterdam. T. (020) 627 77 74, Fax 27 27 47. - Ant / Instr / Mil / Naut - *060692*

Bill, H.F., Singel 443, 1012 WP Amsterdam. T. (020) 623 87 26. - Ant - *060693*

Blitz Antiek en Kunsthandel, Nieuwe Spiegelstr. 37a, 1017 DC Amsterdam. T. (020) 6232663, Fax (020) 6277839. - Orient - *060694*

Boeijen, J. H. van, Rozengracht 212, 1016 NL Amsterdam. T. (020) 625 14 82. *060695*

Boer, P. de, Herengracht 512, 1017 CC Amsterdam. T. (020) 6236849, Fax (020) 6231285. - Paint - *060696*

Boerenmeubelen, Rozengracht 145, 1016 LW Amsterdam. T. (020) 626 00 53. - Furn - *060697*

Boltjes, P., Zeeburgerpad. t/o 76, 1019 AD Amsterdam. T. (020) 693 40 64. - Num - *060698*

Bont, W. van, Huidenstr 9, 1016 ER Amsterdam. T. (020) 623 35 62. *060699*

Borkulo, J.C. van, Admiraal de Ruyterweg 95, 1056 ET Amsterdam. T. (020) 685 41 20. *060700*

Borkulo, Loes van, Van Woustr. 220, 1073 NB Amsterdam. T. (020) 662 48 97, 664 64 30. - Num - *060701*

Borsje, C., Utrechtsestr. 108, 1017 VS Amsterdam. T. (020) 623 82 47. - Ant / Dec - *060702*

Boudoir, Het, Buiten Dommerstr. 14, 1013 HW Amsterdam. T. (020) 625 74 89. - Ant - *060703*

Bouvy & Joosten, Keizersgracht 318, 1016 EZ Amsterdam. T. (020) 625 70 04. - Ant - *060704*

Braal, A. de, Amstelveensew 23, 1054 MB Amsterdam. T. (020) 616 18 18. *060705*

Brinkman, A.P., Keizersgracht 584-586, 1017 EN Amsterdam. T. (020) 627 44 66. - Ant / Paint / Furn / Orient / China / Tex - *060706*

Brocante, Kerkstr. 383 A, 1017 HX Amsterdam. T. (020) 627 43 75. - China / Cur - *060707*

Brownie's Old Shop, Eerste van der Helststr 74, 1072 NZ Amsterdam. T. (020) 693 96 29. *060708*

Budil, S., Haarlemmerstr 113, 1013 EM Amsterdam. T. (020) 626 77 86. *060709*

Bussel, Loed van, Jan Luykenstraat 25, 1071 CK Amsterdam. T. (020) 671 34 33. - Eth - 060710

Cassirer, Paul, Keizersgracht 109, 1015 CJ Amsterdam. T. (020) 6248337. - Paint - 060711

Celsius, Singel 389, 1012 WN Amsterdam. T. (020) 626 51 17. 060712

Chop, Hendel & Mendel, Transvaalkade 3a, 1092 JH Amsterdam. I. (020) 694 46 30. 060713

Chronos, 1e Constantijn Huyensstr. 74, 1054 BW Amsterdam. T. (020) 612 90 83. - Instr - 060714

Citroen, Karel A., Kalverstr. 1, 1001 EH Amsterdam. T. (020) 626 55 34. - Jew / Silv / Mod - 060715

Cornwall, Theo, Rozengracht 162, 1016 NK Amsterdam. T. (020) 624 55 42. 060716

Couperus, Heisteeg 4, 1012 WC Amsterdam. - Ant / Dec - 060717

Cserno, Spiegelgracht 28, 1017 JS Amsterdam. T. (020) 626 36 97. - Orient / China / Sculp - 060718

Cuyp, Albert, A. Cuyperstr. 156, 1073 BK Amsterdam. T. (020) 671 01 37. - Ant - 060719

D'Aghtsteen, Oude Doelenstr 16, 1012 ED Amsterdam. 060720

Damme, Th. van, Van der Pekplein 5, 1031 GZ Amsterdam. 060721

Degenaar, E.R., Nieuwe Spiegelstr. 60, 1017 DH Amsterdam. T. (020) 638 10 10. - Instr - 060722

Dekker, H., Spiegelgracht 9, 1017 JP Amsterdam. T. (020) 623 89 92. - Jew / Instr - 060723

Demandt & Dullaert, Keizersgracht 570, 1017 EM Amsterdam. T. (020) 620 30 47. - Ico - 060724

Denijs, J., Nieuwe Spiegelstr. 29, 1017 DB Amsterdam. T. (020) 624 32 58, 623 47 49. - Ant / Furn / China / Jew / Silv - 060725

Diemer auf dem Kampe, A. Durerstr. 31, 1077 LV Amsterdam. T. (020) 673 25 23. - Ant - 060726

Dolfijn, Spiegelgracht 7, 1017 JP Amsterdam. T. (020) 6222810. - Paint / Draw - 060727

Douma, A.R., Singel 352, 1016 AG Amsterdam. T. (020) 624 75 94. 060728

Douma, Mark, Lange Leidsedwarsstr. 224, 1017 NR Amsterdam. T. (020) 623 15 23. - Graph / Instr - 060729

Douw, G., 1e vd. Helststr. 15, 1073 AB Amsterdam. T. (020) 662 24 88. - Ant - 060730

Douwes, Stadhouderskade 40, Amsterdam, 1071 ZD. T. (020) 6643262, Fax 6640154. - Paint / Graph / China / Lights - 060731

Drayer, A., Pr Hendrikkade 139, 1011 AS Amsterdam. T. (020) 623 75 17. 060732

Dreven & Toebosch, Nieuwe Spiegelstr. 68, 1017 DH Amsterdam. T. (020) 625 27 32. - Instr - 060733

Duifjes, Oosterparkstr. 2e-322, 1092 BV Amsterdam. T. (020) 665 20 77. - Ant / Dec - 060734

Dullaert, Keizersgracht 570, 1017 EM Amsterdam. T. (020) 620 30 47. - Ant - 060735

Dusarduyn, R., Molsteeg 5-7, 1012 SM Amsterdam. T. (020) 624 85 99. - Ant - 060736

Duyvendijk, Pieke van, Nieuwe Spiegelstr. 46, 1017 DG Amsterdam. T. (020) 624 85 99. - Ant - 060737

Egelantier, Egelantiersgracht 93, 1015 RE Amsterdam. T. (020) 626 20 61. - Ant / Instr / Draw - 060738

English Antiques, Utrechtsedwstr 65, 1017 WC Amsterdam. T. (020) 625 72 92. 060739

Eurasia Antiques, Nieuwe Spiegelstr. 40, 1017 DG Amsterdam. T. (020) 626 15 94. - Ant / Furn / Orient / China - 060740

Ex-Coenders, Keizersgracht 150, 1015 CX Amsterdam. T. (020) 625 51 80. - Tex - 060741

Fabery de Jonge, Keizersgracht 574, 1017 EM Amsterdam. T. (020) 6387195, Fax (020) 6387657. - Jew - 060742

Fifties-Sixties, Huidenstr. 13, 1016 ER Amsterdam. T. (020) 623 26 53. - Cur - 060743

Fijnaut, Jacques, Nieuwe Spiegelstr. 31, 1017 DC Amsterdam. T. (020) 625 63 74. - Furn - 060744

Galerie Binnenkant, Binnenkant 48, 1011 BR Amsterdam. T. (020) 622 22 91. - Ant / Paint - 060745

Gallerie Oppo, Spiegelgracht 30, 1017 DG Amsterdam. T. (020) 624 11 92. - Ant - 060746

Gasseling, Christiaan, Nieuwe Spiegelstr. 66, 1017 DH Amsterdam. T. (020) 623 10 02. - Ant - 060747

Gem'Gold, Hogehilweg 14, 1101 CD Amsterdam. T. (020) 691 90 61, Fax 91 59 01. - Jew - 060748

Geurs Aziatisch Antiek, Tolstr. 120, 1074 VK Amsterdam. T. (020) 662 90 91. - Eth / Mil - 060749

Glassinico, 2e Egelantdwarstr. 18, 1015 SC Amsterdam. T. (020) 638 57 09. - Ant - 060750

Glazen, R. & R., Rusland 27, 1012 CK Amsterdam. T. (020) 626 81 07. - Ant - 060751

Goltzius, Nieuwe Spiegelstr. 37-I, 1017 DC Amsterdam. T. (020) 6380094. - Ant / Graph - 060752

Gomex, Prins Hendrikkade 135, 1011 AR Amsterdam. T. (020) 626 18 29, 626 37 97. - Num - 060753

Graal, J. P., Weteringstraat 45, 1017 SM Amsterdam. - Ant / Dec - 060754

Groen, Barend, Spiegelgracht 13, 1017 JP Amsterdam. T. (020) 623 02 57. - Ant / Furn / Dec - 060755

Grosbard, S.H., Molstg 9, 1012 SM Amsterdam. T. (020) 624 77 65. 060756

Gude & Meijer, Overtoom 152, 1054 HP Amsterdam. T. (020) 6129742, Fax (020) 6850112. - Instr - 060757

Haaksman, Diane, Elandsgracht 55, 1016 TN Amsterdam. - Furn / Lights / Cur - 060758

Haas, De, Kerkstr. 155, 1017 GG Amsterdam. T. (020) 626 59 52. - Ant - 060759

Handkar, De, Rozengracht 60, 1016 ND Amsterdam. T. (020) 622 09 73. 060760

Hart, Mathieu, Rokin 122, 1012 LC Amsterdam. T. (020) 6231658, Fax (020) 6248688. - Ant / Graph / Furn / Lights / Instr / Toys - 060761

Heek, G.H. van, Nieuwe Spiegelgstr 47, 1017 DD Amsterdam. T. (020) 625 00 50. 060762

Hekma & De Mol, Oude Braak 21, 1012 PS Amsterdam. T. (020) 625 58 97. 060763

Hendriks, Elisabeth, Nieuwe Spiegelstr. 61, 1017 DD Amsterdam. T. (020) 623 00 85. - Orient - 060764

Hennenquin, C.F., NZ Voorburgwal 383, 1012 RM Amsterdam. T. (020) 623 41 90. 060765

Het Kabinet J.F.H.H. Beekhuizen, Nieuwe Spiegelstr. 49, 1017 DD Amsterdam. T. (020) 6263912, Fax (020) 6275905. - Ant / Furn / China / Sculp / Toys - 060766

Het Prentenhuys, Reguliersdwarsstr 39, 1017 BK Amsterdam. T. (020) 625 07 57. 060767

Hoogkamp, B.L., Nieuwe Spiegelstr. 27, 1017 DB Amsterdam. T. (020) 625 88 52. - Ant - 060768

Hoogkamp, B.L., Singel 496, 1017 AX Amsterdam. T. (020) 625 55 78. - Ant - 060769

Horn, C., Weteringstraat 39, 1017 SM Amsterdam. T. (020) 624 19 45. - Ant / Dec - 060770

Horst, S.M., van der, Spiegelgracht 20, 1968 LL Amsterdam. T. (020) 623 26 80. - Ant / Dec - 060771

Houthakker, Bernard, Rokin 98, 1012 KZ Amsterdam. T. (020) 623 39 39, Fax 27 35 48. - Paint / Draw - 060772

Houwink, R., Nieuwe Spiegelstr. 57, 1017 DD Amsterdam. T. (020) 623 66 42. - Ant - 060773

Huisman, Th., Majofskistraat 9, 1065 SN Amsterdam. T. (020) 615 34 79. - Ant - 060774

Icon Antiekmarkt, Frederiksplein 16, 1017 XM Amsterdam. T. (020) 624 92 88. - Paint / China / Cur - 060775

In the Oldfashioned Way, Keizersgracht 1, 1015 CC Amsterdam. T. (020) 624 90 11. 060776

Israel, Nico, Keizersgracht 489-491, 1017 DM Amsterdam. T. (020) 622 25 55. - Ant / Furn - 060777

Italiaander Galleries, Prinsengracht 526, 1017 KJ Amsterdam. - Arch / Eth - 060778

Ivo, Emil, Brouwersgracht 807, 1015 GK Amsterdam. T. (020) 627 79 60. - Ant - 060779

Jelske Wagenaar-Terpstra, N. Spiegelstraat 52, 1017 DG Amsterdam. T. (020) 625 44 31. - China - 060780

Jenner, H. W., Kloveniersburgwal 46, 1012 CW Amsterdam. T. (020) 624 31 60. 060781

Jong, M. D. de, Jacob v Lennepkade 336, 1053 NJ Amsterdam. T. (020) 612 96 33. 060782

Jong, Rea, Weteringstraat 22, 1017 SN Amsterdam. - China - 060783

Kaan, Rens J., Lijnbaansgracht 292, 1017 RM Amsterdam. T. (020) 624 85 00, 626 84 66. - Furn / Instr - 060784

Kajuit, De, Prinsengracht 809, 1017 KA Amsterdam. T. (020) 625 44 31. - Ant - 060785

Kalpa Art, Wijde Heisteeg 9, 1016 AS Amsterdam. T. (020) 622 19 89. - Orient / Eth - 060786

Karlsson, L., Overtoom 182, 1054 HR Amsterdam. T. (020) 616 83 32. - Ant - 060787

Kattenburg, Rob, De Lairessestr. 96, 1071 PJ Amsterdam. T. (020) 662 23 37. - Paint / Draw - 060788

Kengen & De Siegte, Nieuwe Spiegelstr. 37, 1017 DC Amsterdam. T. (020) 624 03 22. - Ant - 060789

Kersten, L., Koninginneweg 69, 1075 CH Amsterdam. T. (020) 671 36 51. - Ant / Dec - 060790

Kinébanian, D. W., Heiligeweg 35, 1012 XN Amsterdam. T. (020) 6287019. 060791

Klavertje Vier, Oude Looiersstr 55, 1016 VG Amsterdam. T. (020) 623 00 84. 060792

Klein, Duimpje, Grimburgwal 4, 1012 GA Amsterdam. T. (020) 624 63 15. 060793

Klein, J., Potgieterstr 22, 1053 XX Amsterdam. T. (020) 616 31 56. 060794

Klein, T., Binnen Oranjestr 24, 1013 JA Amsterdam. T. (020) 624 55 33. 060795

Klift, Hans van der, Warmoesstraat 56, 1012 JG Amsterdam. - Ant / Paint / Furn - 060796

Knijpfles, de, Kerkstr. 153, 1017 GG Amsterdam. T. (020) 623 21 18. - China / Glass - 060797

Kooiman, Karen, Weteringstr. 29, 1017 SM Amsterdam. T. (020) 625 53 46. - Mod - 060798

Korenaer, T., NZ Kolk 4, 1012 PV Amsterdam. T. (020) 622 60 30. 060799

Korf de Gidts, Peter, Nieuwe Spiegelstr. 28, 1017 DG Amsterdam. T. (020) 625 26 25, Fax 625 26 25. - China / Glass - 060800

Koster, Vijzelstr 85, 1017 HG Amsterdam. T. (020) 623 90 85. 060801

Koster, Vaartstr 50, 1075 RR Amsterdam. T. (020) 673 82 10. 060802

Koster, A. G., Keizersgracht 145, 1015 CK Amsterdam. T. (020) 624 13 74. 060803

Kramer, E., Nieuwe Spiegelstr. 64, 1017 DH Amsterdam. T. (020) 623 08 32. - China / Eth - 060804

Kreymborg, E., N. Z. Voorburgwal 350, 1012 RX Amsterdam. T. (020) 626 52 03. - Ant - 060805

Krijnen, J., Schoolstr 3, 1054 KC Amsterdam. T. (020) 616 96 81. 060806

Kroon, Koninginneweg 77, 1075 CJ Amsterdam. T. (020) 673 04 25. - Ant / Dec - 060807

La Finestra, Plant Kerkin 24, 1018 TB Amsterdam. T. (020) 626 94 43. - Ant - 060808

Laan, C., Nieuwe Spiegelstraat 61, 1017 DD Amsterdam. T. (020) 623 27 89. - Orient / China - 060809

Lameris, Frides, Nieuwe Spiegelstr 55, 1017 DD Amsterdam. T. (020) 6264066, Fax 6265893. - China / Glass - 060810

Laseur, Weteringschans 199, 1017 XG Amsterdam. 060811

Lassen, A., Nwe Spiegelstr.59, 1017 DD Amsterdam. T. (020) 624 41 02. - Jew / Mil - 060812

Lebbing, Prinsengracht 805-807, 1017 KA Amsterdam. T. (020) 624 12 53. - Furn - 060813

Leeuwe, E. de, 1e Boerhaavestr. 5, 1091 RZ Amsterdam. - Ant / Dec - 060814

Leidelmeijer, Frans, Nieuwe Spiegelstr. 58, 1017 DH Amsterdam. T. (020) 6254627, Fax (020) 6205672. - Mod - 060815

Lemaire, Reguliersgracht 80, 1017 LV Amsterdam. T. (020) 6237027. - Orient / Eth - 060816

Levitus, Singel 361, 1012 WL Amsterdam. T. (020) 625 89 48. - Ant / Furn / China / Repr / Tex / Jew / Silv / Lights / Instr / Glass / Cur / Mod - 060817

Limburg, Nieuwe Spiegelstr. 33-35, 1017 DC Amsterdam. T. (020) 623 57 63, Fax 623 64 09. - Furn / China / Glass - 060818

Lust, B., Singel 64, 1015 AC Amsterdam. T. (020) 623 10 60. - Ant - 060819
Lyppens, Langebrugsteeg 8, 1012 GB Amsterdam. T. (020) 627 09 01. - Ant / Dec - 060820
Marcus, Johannes, N.Z. Voorburgwal 284, 1012 RT Amsterdam. T. (020) 6236920. - Paint / Graph / Draw - 060821
Mary en William, Runstr 10, 1016 GK Amsterdam. T. (020) 625 66 48. 060822
Matthijs, Elandsgracht 67, 1016 TP Amsterdam. T. (020) 626 66 07. 060823
May, H.K., Nieuwe Spiegelstr. 25, 1017 DB Amsterdam. T. (020) 624 91 29. - Ant - 060824
May, J.E., Heisteeg 4, 1012 WC Amsterdam. T. (020) 626 54 62. 060825
Meek, G. H. van, Prinsengracht 586, 1017 KR Amsterdam. - Ant - 060826
Meer, A. van der, Keizersgracht 503, 1017 DN Amsterdam. T. (020) 662 19 36. - Paint - 060827
Meeuwen, van, PC Hooftstr 101, 1071 BR Amsterdam. T. (020) 662 11 09, 671 95 81. 060828
Meubeltje, 't, Herenstr. 23, 1015 BZ Amsterdam. T. (020) 625 31 21. - Furn - 060829
Meurs, W. J. G. van, Keizersgracht 578, 1017 EN Amsterdam. T. (020) 623 77 32. - Orient / China - 060830
Mevius, Rob, Hendrik Jacobszstr. 7, 1075 PA Amsterdam. T. (020) 676 64 44. - Ant - 060831
Miko, J van Galenstr 166, 1056 CJ Amsterdam. T. (020) 616 25 78. 060832
Möller, Max, Willemsparkweg 15, 1071 GN Amsterdam. T. (020) 6625425. 060833
Morpurgo, Joseph M., Rokin 108, 1012 LA Amsterdam. T. (020) 6235883, Fax (020) 6209812. - Ant / Furn / Orient / China / Arch / Silv / Glass - 060834
Morsink, Jan, Keizersgracht 562, 1017 EM Amsterdam. T. (020) 6200411, Fax (020) 6201939. - Ico - 060835
Mustert, W.J.H., Tweede van der Helststr42, 1072 PE Amsterdam. T. (020) 671 69 70. 060836
Nederlandsche Muntenveiling, Rokin 60, 1012 KV Amsterdam. T. (020) 623 02 61. - Num - 060837
Nijs, A. de, Singel 110, 1015 AE Amsterdam. T. (020) 623 34 46. 060838
Olifant Antiekzaak, De, Alb Cuypstr 192-194, 1073 BL Amsterdam. T. (020) 671 94 21. 060839
Oorschot, Nico van, Bosboom Toussaintstr. 20, 1054 AR Amsterdam. T. (020) 612 59 61. - Furn - 060840
Oostermeijer, Frits & Jan, Elandsgracht 91, 1016 TS Amsterdam. T. (020) 622 10 39. - Ant - 060841
Patriasz, G., Weteringstr. 48, 1017 SP Amsterdam. T. (020) 626 62 22. - Ant - 060842
Petit Marchand, Kerkstr 155, 1017 GG Amsterdam. T. (020) 626 59 52. 060843
Pijl, T. C. van der, Tweede Jan Steenstr 4, 1073 VN Amsterdam. T. (020) 672 26 89. 060844
Plenge, H. H., Nieuwe Spiegelstr. 38, 1017 DG Amsterdam. T. (020) 625 69 27. - Ant / China / Sculp / Rel - 060845
Poel, van de, Valeriusstr. 238A, 1075 GL Amsterdam. T. (020) 676 64 44. - Ant - 060846
Polak, J., Spiegelgracht 3, 1017 JP Amsterdam. T. (020) 6279009, Fax (020) 6222379. - Ant / Furn / Orient / Sculp / Eth / Glass - 060847
Portaal, 'T, Vijzelstraat 101, 1017 HH Amsterdam. T. (020) 666147. - Ant / Paint / Furn / Instr - 060848
Pot Grenen, Prinsengracht 276, 1016 HJ Amsterdam. T. (020) 625 32 10. - Furn - 060849
Pothuys, 'T, Gasthuismolensteeg 18-20, 1016 AN Amsterdam. T. (020) 671 67 44. - Ant / Dec - 060850
Premsela & Hamburger, Rokin 120, 1012 LC Amsterdam. T. (020) 6249688, 6275454. - China / Jew / Silv / Instr - 060851
Prestige Art Gallery, Regliersbreestr. 42, 1017 LS Amsterdam. T. (020) 624 01 04. - Ant - 060852
Rarekiek, Runstraat 31, 1016 GJ Amsterdam. T. (020) 623 35 91. - Eth - 060853
Reeker, P.C. Hooftstr. 75, 1071 BP Amsterdam. T. (020) 671 28 59. - Ant - 060854
Roelofs, Jan, Spiegelgracht 5, 1017 JP Amsterdam. T. (020) 6259114, Fax (020) 6383039. - Furn / Instr - 060855
Roelofsz, Charles, Leidsegracht 42, 1016 CM Amsterdam. T. (020) 6255568, Fax (020) 6268951. - Paint - 060856
Rolf, Kerkstr 93, 1017 GD Amsterdam. T. (020) 624 83 50. 060857
Rommelmarkt Looiersgracht, Looiersgracht 38, 1016 VS Amsterdam. T. (020) 627 47 62. - Ant / China / Repr / Jew / Silv / Instr / Glass / Cur / Mod - 060858
Rueb, Banstraat 4, 1071 ZP Amsterdam. T. (020) 6767566, Fax (020) 6755700. - Paint - 060859
Rummertje, 'T, Runstraat 32, 1016 GK Amsterdam. T. (020) 624 37 35. 060860
Russum, Th. N. R. van, Adriaan van Oordthof 8, 1064 RW Amsterdam. T. (020) 611 35 12. - Furn - 060861
Rutten, Paul, Keizersgracht 568, 1017 EM Amsterdam. T. (020) 6277057. - Orient / Eth - 060862
Salomon, S., Rokin 70, 1012 KW Amsterdam. T. (020) 623 16 92. - Ant - 060863
Saundarya Lahari, Nwe. Looiersstr. 23, 1017 VA Amsterdam. T. (020) 627 87 37. - Ant / Ant / Orient / Sculp - 060864
Schavot, 'T, NZ Voorburgwal 146, 1012 SJ Amsterdam. T. (020) 625 45 20. 060865
Scheepens, Matthieu, Nassankade 128, 1052 ED Amsterdam. T. (020) 684 38 36. - Furn - 060866
Schilling, F. W., Nwe. Spiegelstraat 23, 1017 DB Amsterdam. T. (020) 62 39 66, 623 53 56. - Jew / Silv - 060867
Schlichte Bergen, Velazquezstr 8, 1077 NH Amsterdam. T. (020) 6769344, 6751701, Fax (020) 6734786. - Paint / Draw - 060868
Schlichte Bergen, P.C. Hooftstr. 53, 1071 BN Amsterdam. T. (020) 6751701, 6769344, Fax (020) 6734786. - Paint / Draw - 060869
Schnitzler, W., Nwe Spiegelstr.59, 1017 DD Amsterdam. T. (020) 625 86 39. - Graph / Silv / Glass - 060870
Schreuders, J., Spiegelgracht 7, 1017DB Amsterdam. T. (020) 623 97 92. - Ant - 060871
Silverplate, Nes 89, 1012 KD Amsterdam. T. (020) 624 83 39. - Ant - 060872
Simon, C., C. P. Hooftstraat 82, 1071 CB Amsterdam. T. (020) 673 68 04. - Ant / Dec - 060873
Simons, Kalverstr. 98, 1012 PJ Amsterdam. T. (020) 6239833, Fax (020) 6240956. - Jew / Silv - 060874
Smit, Wilbert & Coster, Rudolph, Nieuwe Spiegelstraat 67, 1017 DD Amsterdam. T. (020) 6273975, Fax (020) 6265592. - Furn / Paint / China / Sculp - 060875
Smits, C. A., Nieuwe Spiegelstr. 53, 1017 DD Amsterdam. T. (020) 673 16 52. - Ant / Furn - 060876
Smokiana, Prinsengracht 488, 1017 KH Amsterdam. T. (020) 4211779. - Ant / Cur / Eth - 060877
Spaans Galjoen, 23 Weteringdwarsstr. 33b, 1017 SR Amsterdam. T. (020) 625 94 62. - Ant - 060878
Spaans, S., Nassaukade 128, 1052 ED Amsterdam. T. (020) 684 38 36. 060879
Spanish Galleon, The, 2e Weteringdwarsstr. 33, 1017 SR Amsterdam. T. (020) 625 94 62. - Furn / Instr / Glass - 060880
Speeldoos, De, Middenw 161, 1098 AL Amsterdam. T. (020) 692 26 98. 060881
Spiegeltje, Nieuwe Spiegelstr. 63, 1017 DD Amsterdam. T. (020) 624 87 03. - Jew - 060882
Spiegeltje-Spiegeltje, Huidenstr 26, 1016 ET Amsterdam. T. (020) 625 74 07. 060883
Stalpaert't, Weteringschans 173, 1017 XD Amsterdam. T. (020) 624 54 34. - Ant - 060884
Stein, Benjamin J., Nieuwe Spiegelstr. 70, 1017 DH Amsterdam. T. (020) 623 27 89. - Orient - 060885
Stender, Stadionweg 190-I, 1077 TC Amsterdam. T. (020) 6751909. - Instr - 060886
Stilnovo, Haarlemmerstr 20, 1014 BE Amsterdam. T. (020) 627 45 95. 060887
Stodel, Spiegelgracht 23, 1017JP Amsterdam. T. (020) 627 18 66. - Ant - 060888
Stodel, Bernhard, Rokin 70, 1012 KW Amsterdam. T. (020) 623 16 92. - Ant / Furn / China / Silv - 060889
Stodel, Inez, Nieuwe Spiegelstr. 65, 1017 DD Amsterdam. T. (020) 6232942, Fax (020) 6248982. - Ant / Dec / Jew / Cur - 060890
Stodel, Inez, Kerkstr. 195, 1017 GJ Amsterdam. T. (020) 623 29 42. - Ant / Dec / Jew / Cur - 060891
Stolk, Frits, Koninginnenweg 77, 1075 CJ Amsterdam. T. (020) 673 15 62. 060892
Streumer, J.N., Lynbaansgracht 279, 1017 RM Amsterdam. T. (020) 627 88 08. - Ant - 060893
Süss, René, Nieuwe Spiegelstr. 46, 1017 DG Amsterdam. T. (020) 624 85 99. - Ant / Furn / Sculp - 060894
Swaen, de, Langebrugsteeg 2, 1012 GB Amsterdam. T. (020) 624 22 99. 060895
Terra, Reestr. 21, 1016 DM Amsterdam. T. (020) 638 59 13. - Ant - 060896
Tets, van, Keizersgracht 528, 1017 EK Amsterdam. T. (020) 625 37 66. 060897
The Silver Box, M. van Pol-Henquet, Nieuwe Spiegelstr. 53, 1017 DD Amsterdam. T. (020) 622 22 40. - Jew / Silv - 060898
Tichel, De, Tichelstr 5, 1015 KR Amsterdam. T. (020) 626 27 06. 060899
Tiller, J., Eerste J. van Campenstr. 1, 1072 BB Amsterdam. T. (020) 672 27 25. - Ant / Dec - 060900
Traanberg, K.F., Sarphatipark 52, 1073 CZ Amsterdam. T. (020) 671 67 44. 060901
Uitje voor Leuke Dingen, Binnen Oranjestr 24, 1013 JA Amsterdam. T. (020) 624 55 33. 060902
Van Os, Yu, Herengracht 298, 1016 BX Amsterdam. T. (020) 625 73 50. 060903
Van Os, Yu, Nieuwe Spiegelstr. 68, 1017 DH Amsterdam. T. (020) 622 07 40. - Furn / Instr - 060904
Van Rossum & Co., Herengracht 518, 1017 CC Amsterdam. T. (020) 6221010, Fax (020) 6242541. - China / Sculp / Furn / Silv / Glass - 060905

Vecht, A., Rokin 30, 1012 KT Amsterdam. T. (020) 623 47 48. - Ant / China / Sculp - 060906
Veenendaal de la Haye, Celntuurbaan 207, 1074 CV Amsterdam. T. (020) 679 15 08. 060907
Veilinggebouw De Zwann, Keizersgracht 474, 1017 EG Amsterdam. T. (020) 622 04 47. 060908
Veltman, P.S.M., Eerste Looiersdwarsstr 23, 1016 VL Amsterdam. T. (020) 627 69 68. 060909
Vier Luijkjes, De, Sint Nicolaasstr 45, 1012 NJ Amsterdam. T. (020) 622 33 50. 060910
Visser, Jan, Nieuwe Spiegelstr. 58, 1017 DH Amsterdam. T. (020) 624 56 25. - Eth - 060911
Vliet, H. C. van, Nieuwe Spiegelstr. 74, 1017 DH Amsterdam. T. (020) 6227782. - China / Glass - 060912
Voorvelt, J.H., Oude Doelenstr 16, 1012 ED Amsterdam. T. (020) 626 54 61. 060913
Vredespijp, Eerste vd. Heiststr. 5-11, 1073 AA Amsterdam. T. (020) 676 48 55. - Furn - 060914
Vredevoogd, Willem, PCHooftstr 82, 1071 CB Amsterdam. T. (020) 673 68 04. 060915
Vries, Bruno de, Elandsgracht 67, 1016 TP Amsterdam. - Furn / Lights / Cur - 060916
Vries, P. de, Spiegelgracht 36, 1017 JS Amsterdam. T. (020) 625 16 09. - Ant / Cur - 060917
Wagenaar-Terpstra, T., Prinsengracht 811, 1017 KA Amsterdam. T. (020) 625 44 31. 060918
Wassenaar, Eduard, Hobbemastr. 10a, 1071 ZB Amsterdam. T. (020) 679 51 38. - Mil - 060919
Waterman, K. & V., Rokin 116, 1012 LB Amsterdam. T. (020) 6232958, Fax (020) 6206149. - Paint - 060920
Weller, M.A., Planciusstr 18, 1013 MH Amsterdam. T. (020) 622 03 45. 060921

Wieg, A., Murillostraat 10-II, 1077 NE Amsterdam. T. (020) 6762094, Fax (020) 6762094. - Paint / Draw - 060922
Wijttenbach, Wijttenbachstr 23, 1093 HS Amsterdam. T. (020) 665 59 98. 060923
Wildbret, Cas O., Het Laagt 81, 1025 GD Amsterdam. T. (020) 637 03 20. 060924
Wilhelmina, van Spoijkstr 112, 1057 HH Amsterdam. T. (020) 683 51 57. 060925
Will, C.J., Nieuwe Spiegelstr 67, 1017 DD Amsterdam. T. (020) 624 88 26. 060926
Winkeltje, 'T, Weteringstraat 22, 1017 SN Amsterdam. - Glass - 060927
Wolf, Bettina & Carola, Nes 89, 1012 KD Amsterdam. T. (020) 624 83 39. 060928
Woltering, M.L., Nieuwe Spiegelstr 53, 1017 DD Amsterdam. T. (020) 622 22 40. 060929
Wouter Sterk, Valeriusstr. 112 hs, 1075 GD Amsterdam. T. (020) 664 36 34. - Furn - 060930
Yesterday, Weteringstraat 46, 1017 SP Amsterdam. T. (020) 623 95 01. - China / Lights / Glass / Mod - 060931
Zadick, Nieuwe Spiegelstr 37, 1017 DD Amsterdam. T. (020) 623 01 05. 060932
Zedde, van der, De Clercqstr. 85, 1053 AG Amsterdam. T. (020) 616 50 06. - Ant - 060933
Zilverberg, M., Rokin 30, 1012 KT Amsterdam. T. (020) 6259518, Fax (020) 62595180008. - Arch / Num - 060934
Zoomers, Prinsengracht 489, 1016 HP Amsterdam. T. (020) 620 30 57. - Ant - 060935
Zotos, Christos, Nieuwe Spiegelstr. 51, 1017 DD Amsterdam. T. (020) 622 88 05. - Furn - 060936

Apeldoorn (Gelderland)

Graaf, J.J. de, Mariannelaan 6, 7316 DT Apeldoorn. 060938
Hamas, 'T, Korenstr 21, 7311 LL Apeldoorn. 060939
Keuning, J., Bartelsweg 63, 7311 DJ Apeldoorn. 060940
Kunst- en Antiekgalerie "Het Loo", Loolaan 83, 7314 AH Apeldoorn. T. (055) 5217832, Fax 5789265. - China / Furn / Paint - 060940a

Arnhem (Gelderland)

Aalberg, F. W. H., Bakkerstr. 67a-68, 6811 EK Arnhem. - Ant / Furn - 060941
Aalbers, F.W.H., Kluizeweg 218, 6815 EH Arnhem. T. (026) 4435337. - Ant / Furn - 060942
Con & Verdonck, Gele Rijdersplein 41, 6811 AR Arnhem. T. (026) 4420495. - Tex - 060943
Dijken, B., Adolf van Nieuwenaarlaan 2, 6824 AN Arnhem. T. (026) 4420939. - Ant / Paint / Furn / Sculp - 060944
Driessen, Gebr., Sonsbeeksingel 32, 6814 AB Arnhem. T. (026) 4455314. 060945
Driessen, J. K., Bakkerstr. 16, 6811 EG Arnhem. T. (026) 4451098. - Ant / Paint / Furn / Orient / China / Tex / Silv / Glass - 060946
Gemert, van, & Peters, Kruizemuntstr 6, 6833 GB Arnhem. T. (026) 4421427. 060947
Gildehuys, Bakkerstr 67, 6811 EK Arnhem. T. (026) 4436585, 4420604. 060948
Hartlief & Baars, Rijnstr 71, 6811 EZ Arnhem. T. (026) 4456318. 060949
Leijser, Margot, Bakkerstr 11b, 6811 EG Arnhem. T. (026) 4454415. 060950
Museum of Modern Art, Utrechtseweg 87, 6812 AA Arnhem. T. (026) 3512431, Fax 4435148. 060951
Rijnders, B.A.H., & Zn., Pastoorstr 4, 6811 ED Arnhem. T. (026) 4456756. 060952
Van Os, P.P., Bakkerstr. 67 A, 6811 EK Arnhem. T. (026) 4422009, Fax 4436418. - Ant / Paint / Graph / Furn / Orient / China - 060953

Assen (Drenthe)

Coins Group Select, Cederlaan 1, 9401 RC Assen. T. (0592) 314384. - Num - 060954
Dijkstra, W., Vaart Zuidzijde 87, 9401 GJ Assen. T. (0592) 317509. 060955

Baarn (Utrecht)

Calis, W., Veldheimweg 20, 3741 SG Baarn. 060956
Hoogendijk, M.H.P., Eemnesserweg 91, 3743 AG Baarn. T. (035) 5420459, Fax 5422237. - Ant / Paint / Furn / China / Dec / Instr - 060957
Porto-Bello, Laanstr 25, 3743 BA Baarn. 060958
Rubingh, H., Laanstr 16, 3743 BE Baarn. 060959
Vermaten, A., Vondellaan 3, 3743 HW Baarn. 060960

Baexem (Limburg)

Meer, A. A. B. van der, Rijksweg 10, 6095 NB Baexem. 060961

Beek (Limburg)

Antiek Frica, Kleingenhouterstr 44, 6191 PP Beek. 060962
Oreeland, M. M., Prins Mauritslaan 109, 6191 EE Beek. - Num - 060963

Beekbergen (Gelderland)

Konstkabinet, Het, Arnhemseweg 625, 7361 TR Beekbergen. T. (055) 5061539. - Ant / Paint / Orient / Sculp - 060964

Bemmel (Gelderland)

Wegh, Henk, Ressensestr. 2, 6681 DX Bemmel. T. (0481) 462534. - Ant / Furn / Instr - 060965

Bergen (Noord-Holland)

Boerenhuys, 'T, Ruinelaan 14, 1861 LL Bergen. - Ant / Dec - 060966
galerie de sfinx, Tuindorpweg 11, 1862 VG Bergen. - Ant / Orient / Sculp / Arch / Eth - 060967
Pluym, van de, Kruisweg 19, 1861 LA Bergen. - Ant / Dec - 060968
Sfinx Gallery, Tuindorpweg 11, 1862 VG Bergen. T. (072) 5895617. - Arch - 060969

Bergen op Zoom (Noord-Brabant)

Gans, De, Grote Markt 28, 4611 NT Bergen op Zoom. T. (0164) 236473. - Ant - 060970
Oude Lantaarn, D', Engelsestraat 36, 4611 RR Bergen op Zoom. - Ant / Furn / China / Silv - 060971
Sanden, A. J. van de, Borgvlietsedreef 30, 4615 ED Bergen op Zoom. T. (0164) 234561. 060972

Best (Noord-Brabant)

Isphording, Bosseweg 33, 5682 BA Best. 060973

Beverwijk (Noord-Brabant)

Gugnum, M. van, Baanstr 16-18, 1942 CJ Beverwijk. T. (0251) 224643. 060974

Bilthoven (Utrecht)

IKAVO, 1. Brandenburgerweg 24, 3721 MJ Bilthoven. T. (030) 2211754. - Ant - 060975
Koperen Lantaarn, De, Julianalaan 30, 3722 GR Bilthoven. 060976

Blaricum (Noord-Holland)

Albers, B., Tweede Molenweg 18, 1261 HC Blaricum. T. (035) 5314730. 060977
Atelier, Het, Eemnesserweg 29b, 1261 HH Blaricum. T. (035) 5383856. 060978
Raven, A.H.J., Fransepad 17, 1261 JD Blaricum. T. (035) 5314329. 060979
Rebel, C., Tweede Molenweg 15, 1261 HA Blaricum. T. (035) 5315324. 060980

Bloemendaal (Noord-Holland)

Zonnehoek, De, Verbindingsweg 4, 2061 EK Bloemendaal. T. (023) 5251479. 060981

Bolsward (Friesland)

Toonstra, A., Kleine Dylakker 4, 8701 HV Bolsward. T. (0515) 572750. 060982

Borculo (Gelderland)

Wentink, G., Tourton-Bruynsstr 3, 7271 VL Borculo. 060983

Borger (Drenthe)

Old Borger, Hunebedstr 14, 9531 JV Borger. T. (0599) 235802. 060984

Borne (Overijssel)

Riet, P.J. ter, Bekenhorst 6, 7622 CK Borne. 060985

Breda (Noord-Brabant)

Van Aalst, L.P.M., Nieuwe Ginnekenstraat 34, 481 NS Breda. T. (076) 5142664, Fax 5225422. - Furn / China / Sculp / Glass - 060986
Akkermans, M., Kerkhofweg 65, 4835 GA Breda. T. (076) 5650630. 060987
Antiekhuis, 'T, Nieuwe Huizen 25, 4811 TK Breda. - Ant - 060988
Brandtijser Antiek, Grote Markt 39, 4811 XP Breda. - Ant - 060989
Couvreur, Havermarkt 21, 4811 WG Breda. T. (076) 5219231. 060990
Crijns & Stender, Ginnekenweg 328, 4835 NL Breda. T. (076) 5100102, Fax 5100410. - Instr - 060991
Dieckmann, T. J., Nw. Boschstr. 41, 4811 CV Breda. - Ant - 060992
Galerie des Arts, Raadhuisstr. 28, 4835 JB Breda. T. (076) 5652291. - Ant / Paint / Furn / Sculp / Tex / Jew / Silv / Mil / Rel - 060993
Grootswagers, H. & R. Postma, St. Janstr. 21, 4811 ZK Breda. T. (076) 5142917. - Furn / Silv - 060994
Hofkens, A., Haagdijk 16, 4011 TT Breda. T. (076) 5145259. 060995
Jansen, A., Catharinastr. 34, 4811 XJ Breda. - Ant / Furn / Lights - 060996
Joris, E.E., Nonnenveld 25, 4811 HN Breda. T. (076) 5139338. 060997
Kandelaar, De, Barionielaan 2, 4818 RA Breda. T. (076) 5130049. 060998
Karoly, J. M., Torenstraat 23, 4811 XV Breda. T. (076) 5142726. - Cur - 060999
Kuijper, J. G., & Zn., Haagdijk 64-66, 4811 TV Breda. T. (076) 5217281. - Ant / Furn / China / Glass - 061000
Pels, Theo, Ulvenhoutselaan 147, 4834 ME Breda. T. (076) 5651765. - Ant - 061001
Poes, de, Nwe Boschstr 37, 4811 CV Breda. T. (076) 5145113. 061002
Pomp, De, Ginnekenmarkt 3, 4835 JC Breda. T. (076) 5652802. 061003
Schreurs, M. H., Catharinastr. 40-42, 4811 XJ Breda. T. (076) 5219024. - Instr - 061004
Spinnewiel, Het, Kerkhofweg 65, 4835 GA Breda. T. (076) 5650630. 061005
Twee Bogen, De, Wilhelminastr. 42, 4818 SH Breda. T. (076) 5131154. - Paint / Furn / China / Silv - 061006
Vegten, N. van, Ginnekenmarkt 3, 4835 JC Breda. - Ant - 061007
Zegers, Kloosterplein 4, 4811 GN Breda. T. (076) 5144439. 061008

Breukelen (Utrecht)

Kattenburg, Rob, Oudaen, Zandpad 80, 3621 NG Breukelen. T. (0346) 265098, Fax 266437. 061009

Brielle (Zuid-Holland)

Romein, J. S., G. J. v. d. Boogerdw. 21, 3232 EB Brielle. T. (0181) 412208. - Ant / Paint / Furn / Mul / Instr / Cur / Draw - 061010
Stoep, van de, Voorstraat 25, 3231 BE Brielle. - Ant / Dec - 061011

Bussum (Noord-Holland)

Goede Oude Tijd, Die, Vlietlaan 70, 1404 CE Bussum. T. (035) 6912388. 061012
Gouwswaard, Kruislaan 3, 1401 TX Bussum. T. (035) 6932303. 061013
Haspers, Raadhuisstr 38, 1404 CX Bussum. T. (035) 6918035. 061014
Kulsen, Wichmanlaan 43, 1405 GZ Bussum. T. (035) 6943354. 061015
Schulman, Laurens, Brinklaan 84 A, 1404 GM Bussum. T. (035) 6916632, Fax 6910878. - Num - 061016

Buurmalsen (Gelderland)

Eck, C. van, Rijksstraatweg 2, 4197 BE Buurmalsen. 061017

Buurse (Overijssel)

Woudenberg, Alsteedseweg 12, 7481 RV Buurse. 061018

Delft (Zuid-Holland)

Arkesteijn, P.J.M., Vrouwenrecht 2, 2611 KK Delft. T. (015) 2136313. 061019

Balk, J.J., Broerhuisstr 4, 2611 GD Delft. *061020*
Bestman, Vrouw Juttenland 24-26, 2611 LC Delft.
T. (015) 2124351. *061021*
Bokhoven, W. van, Oude Delft 226, 2611 CG Delft.
- Ant / Furn - *061022*
Bosch, W.v.d., Vrouwenrecht 8, 2611 KK Delft.
T. (015) 2142384. - Ant - *061023*
Brouwerhuys, 'T, Voldersgracht 29, 2611 EV Delft.
T. (015) 2140716. *061024*
Felius, Markt 71, 2611 GS Delft. - Eth - *061025*
Galerie De Fetisch, Markt 73, 2611 GS Delft.
T. (015) 2130445, 2565534. - Eth - *061026*
Geenen, C.V., Oosteinde 171, 2611 VD Delft.
T. (015) 2143869. *061027*
Henry Deux, Nieuwe Langendijk 68, 2611 VL Delft.
T. (015) 2124582. *061028*
Hof van Eden, Beestenmarkt 14, 2611 GB Delft.
T. (015) 2124118. - Ant / Paint / Graph / Furn / China /
Tex / Instr - *061029*
Huize Oud Delft, Vrouwenrecht 10, 2611 KK Delft.
- Ant - *061030*
Iperen, M. I. F. van, Oude Delft 160a, 2611 HG Delft.
- Ant / Paint / Furn / Eth - *061031*
J.F. Graphics, Markt 1, 2611 GP Delft. T. (015) 2142578.
- Paint - *061032*
Kaerskorff, de, Markt 2, 2611 GT Delft.
T. (015) 2141479. - China - *061033*
Kassies Import, Choorstr. 36, 2611 JH Delft.
T. (015) 2132518. - Furn - *061034*
Keramos, Billitonstr 33, 2612 AT Delft.
T. (015) 2140016. *061035*
Koch, Gebr., Voorstr 19, 2611 JJ Delft.
T. (015) 2135637. *061036*
Leeuwen & Hoogeveen, Oosteinde 171, 2611 VD Delft.
T. (015) 2146370. *061037*
Loenen, Van, Markt 63, 2611 GS Delft.
T. (015) 2123735. *061038*
Lüpker, T., Simonsstr 49, 2628 TE Delft.
T. (015) 2568062. *061039*
Lupker-Ruiterman, J.P., Oosteinde 175, 2611 VD Delft.
T. (015) 2131425. *061040*
Orangerie, Markt 71, 2611 GS Delft.
T. (015) 2136723. *061041*
Ruyter, Pieter de, Donkerstr 3, 2611 TE Delft.
T. (015) 2122017. *061042*
Schaften, Van, Vrouwenrecht 10, 2611 KK Delft. - Ant /
Dec - *061043*
Snuffelhal, De, Breestr. 17, 2611 RE Delft.
T. (015) 2126243. *061044*
Waagschaal, De, Gasthuissteeg 13A, 2611 RH Delft.
T. (015) 2143825. *061045*
Zoetmulder, Ingrid, Voorstr. 63, 2611 JI Delft.
T. (015) 2142097. - Mul - *061046*

Denekamp (Overijssel)
Blokius & Zn, Oldenzaalsestr 30, 7591 GM
Denekamp. *061047*

Deventer (Overijssel)
Antic Huis, Walstr. 79, 7411 GK Deventer.
T. (0570) 618871. - Ant / Dec - *061048*
Arsenaal, Het, Grote Kerkhof, 7411 KT Deventer.
T. (0570) 615538. - Ant - *061049*
Bugter, Martin, Stromarkt 6, 7411 PJ Deventer.
T. (0570) 613684, Fax 613684. *061050*
Dieckman, Hooykaas, Roggestr 22, 7411 EP Deventer.
T. (0570) 617341. *061051*
Dokter, Spijkerboorsteeg 6, 7411 JG Deventer.
T. (0570) 614107. *061052*
Meubelhoek, In de, Grote Kerkhof 29, 7411 KV Deventer.
T. (0570) 614426. *061053*
Meursing, Rijkmanstr. 48, 7411 GC Deventer.
T. (0570) 619071. - Ant / Paint - *061054*
Pypenlade, Grote Kerkhof 36, 7411 KV Deventer.
T. (0570) 614426. *061055*

Diepenveen (Overijssel)
Refuge, Kieftenweg 1, 7431 PT Diepenveen.
T. (0570) 591751. *061056*

Dieren (Gelderland)
Lackroy, Zutphensestraatweg 10a, 6953 CK
Dieren. *061057*

Dinxperlo (Gelderland)
Slaghekke-van't Erve, Aaltenseweg 36, 7091 AG Dinx-
perlo. T. (0315) 651509. *061058*

Doesburg (Gelderland)
Dam, van, Prunusstr. 21, 6982 CG Doesburg. - Ant /
Dec - *061059*
Geereking, Gasthuisstr. 3-5, 6981 CP Doesburg.
T. (0313) 473330. - Furn - *061060*
Roelofsen, W., Gastelaarsstr. 15, 6981 BH Doesburg.
T. (0313) 473196. - Ant / Paint / Jew / Silv - *061061*

Doetinchem (Gelderland)
La Capitana, Oude Terborgseweg 254, 7004 KA Doetin-
chem. T. (0314) 345889, Fax 345889. - Paint /
Jew - *061062*
Jansen, Terborgseweg 381, 7004 GE Doetinchem.
T. (0314) 324085. - Paint / Furn - *061063*
Sars, J. W. M., Missetstr 5, 7005 AA Doetinchem.
T. (0314) 332834. *061064*
Voorhuis, Rob., Waterstr. 30, 7009 CK Doetinchem.
T. (0314) 333649, 344137. - Instr - *061065*

Doezum (Groningen)
Huizinga, J., Doezemertocht 1, 9863 TE
Doezum. *061066*

Domburg (Zeeland)
Vreeke, C. J., Singel 35, 4357 BV Domburg.
T. (0118) 581725. *061067*

Dordrecht (Zuid-Holland)
Dolphyn, De, Voorstr 8, 3311 ER Dordrecht. *061068*
Genderen, J. C. van, Grote Kerkbuurt 2, 3311 CB Dord-
recht. T. (078) 6139123. *061069*
Hond, Jan d', Stadhuisplein 3-4, 3311 CR Dordrecht.
T. (078) 6136803. *061070*
Jongeneel, D., Stadhuisplein 4, 3311 CR Dordrecht.
- Ant - *061071*
Oud-Dordrecht Antiquariaat, Wijnstr 37, 3311 BT
Dordrecht. *061072*
Rijsdijk, J., Voorstr 136, 3311 EN Dordrecht.
T. (078) 6131108. *061073*
Rijsdijk, P. H., Voorstr 128, 3311 ER Dordrecht. *061074*
Rode Deur, Voorstr. 128, 3311 ER Dordrecht.
T. (078) 6139902. - Paint / Graph / Mod - *061075*
Sengers, Voorstr 179, 3311 EN Dordrecht. *061076*
Sigtermans, E., Spuiweg 26, 3311 GV Dordrecht.
- Ant - *061077*
Smits, A., Voorstr. 475, 3311 CV Dordrecht. - Ant /
Dec - *061078*
Stoop, Bert, Grote Keerksbuurt 2, 3400 Dordrecht.
- Ant - *061079*
Valen, J. van, Visstr. 25, 3311 KX Dordrecht. - Ant /
Paint / Graph / Furn / China / Sculp / Silv / Glass / Draw -
061080
Vermeulen, G., & Zn., Wijnbrug 3, 3311 EV Dordrecht.
- Ant / Paint / Furn - *061081*
Verwoerdt, A., Voorstr. 420, 3311 CX Dordrecht.
- Ant - *061082*

Dreumel (Gelderland)
Webo, Rooijsestr 41, 6621 AH Dreumel.
T. (0487) 571571. *061083*

Driebergen (Utrecht)
Antiekhuis Driebergen, Traay 140, 3971 GT Driebergen.
- Furn / Instr - *061084*
Beem, van, Koningine Wilhelminalaan 22, 3972 EX Drie-
bergen. - Ant / Dec - *061085*

Echt (Limburg)
Tanis, Hans, St-Jorisstr 3, 6101 CA Echt.
T. (0475) 485026. *061086*
Verjeijen, M., Kerkveldweg 45, 6101 HR
Echt. *061087*

Edam (Noord-Holland)
Klaassens, Lingerzijde 42, 1135 AR Edam. *061088*
Wagenmakers, W.A., & W.R. den Haan, Jan van Nieu-
wenhuizenplein 8', 1135 WV Edam.
T. (0299) 372973. *061089*

Ede (Gelderland)
Simonis & Buunk, Notaris Fischerstr. 30-32, 6711 BD
Ede. T. (0318) 614825. - Paint - *061090*
Spits, N. Stationsstr. 4, 6711 AG Ede. T. (0318) 619697.
- Ant / Dec - *061091*
Villa Antica, Hessenweg 34, 6718 TD Ede.
T. (0318) 613156. - Furn - *061092*

Eefde (Gelderland)
Enkzicht, Zutphenseweg 57-59, 7211 EB Eefde.
T. (0575) 540322. - Furn - *061093*

Eemnes (Utrecht)
Impression Art Gallery, Hasselaarlaan 8, 3755 AW Eem-
nes. T. (035) 5316174. - Paint - *061094*
Lip, van der, Wakkerendijk 236, 3755 DK Eemnes.
T. (035) 5383290. *061095*

Eersel (Noord-Brabant)
Mollen, Schadewijkstr. 1, 5521 HD Eersel. - Ant / Furn /
Instr - *061096*
Ruimte, de, Nieuwstr. 63, 5521 CB Eersel.
T. (0497) 514001. - Ant - *061097*

Eindhoven (Noord-Brabant)
Bies, A.H., Boschdijk 221a, 5612 HC Eindhoven.
T. (040) 2431377. - Paint - *061098*
Boeren, Tongelresestr 375a, 5642 NC Eindhoven.
T. (040) 2816998. *061099*
Bonus Intro, Leenderweg 191, 5643 AG Eindhoven.
T. (040) 211479. - Ant / Dec - *061100*
Con & Verdonck, Piazzagalerie 51, 5611 AE Eindhoven.
T. (040) 2441522. - Tex - *061101*
Doofpot, De, Smalle Haven 6, 5611 EJ Eindhoven.
T. (040) 2444737. - Ant / Furn - *061102*
Ducker, J.M., Manusstr 9, 5612 RA Eindhoven. *061103*
Ganzenwinkel, G. van, Mirachstr 27, 5632 CD Eindho-
ven. T. (040) 2441331. *061104*
Hurk, A. A. C. van der, Hoenderberglaan 18, 5628 EC
Eindhoven. T. (040) 2415522. *061105*
Meerhoff, Stratumsedijk 51, 5611 NC Eindhoven.
T. (040) 2117129. - Ant / Paint / Furn - *061106*
Megchelen, Cock van, Floraplein 11, 5643 JH Eindho-
ven. T. (040) 2120645. - Fum / Sculp - *061107*
Mont Martre, Fransebaan 54, 5627 JE Eindhoven.
T. (040) 2481531. - Ant - *061108*
Rimmermans-de Wit, R., Hoogstr 151, 5615 PC Eindho-
ven. T. (040) 2520452. *061109*
Sommen, van der, Brugmanstr. 20, 5621 BX Eindhoven.
T. (040) 2447348. - Ant - *061110*
Van Leeuwen, D. van, Gestelsestr. 81, 5615 LC Eindho-
ven. T. (040) 229410. - Ant / Furn / Glass - *061111*

Enschede (Overijssel)
Achterberg, M., Begoniastr 4, 7514 ZX Enschede.
T. (053) 428902. *061112*
Boogaard, T. C., Redemtoristenpark 37, 7532 AB
Enschede. *061113*
Brejaart, R., Sogtoenlanden 15, 7542 CP Enschede.
T. (053) 4762207. - Arch - *061114*
Combes, Berns, Schouwingstr 32, 7531 AH
Enschede. *061115*
Gelink, G. W., J Obrechtstr 6, 7512 DG Enschede.
T. (053) 428850. *061116*
Horst, G. H. ter, Oldenzaalsestr 296, 7523 AH Enschede.
T. (053) 418172. *061117*
Koelink, G. B. V., Haverstraatpassage 30-38, 7511 EX
Enschede. T. (053) 4324433. - Ant - *061118*
Meinema, A., Janninksweg 60, 7513 DL Enschede.
T. (053) 426688. *061119*
Staarman-Kleine, J. L., Sterkerstr 49, 7545 TG Ensche-
de. T. (053) 425417. *061120*

Enter (Overijssel)
Mennegart, C. J., Zwiksweg 6, 7468 BR Enter. *061121*

Epse-Gorssel (Gelderland)
Hermitage, De, Lochemseweg 1, 7214 RA Epse-Gorssel.
T. (0575) 492443. - Ant / Furn / China / Silv / Lights /
Rel - *061122*
Jonge, Fabery de, Weerdsweg 3, 7214 DM Epse-Gors-
sel. T. (0575) 494234, Fax 494288. *061123*
Van Kranendonk Duffels, Weerdsweg 3, 7214 DM Epse-
Gorssel. T. (0575) 491875. - China / Silv - *061124*

Esch (Noord-Brabant)
Vucht, H. van, Groenweg 3, 5296 LZ Esch.
T. (0411) 601620. *061125*

Etten (Noord-Brabant)
Klep-van Unen, Bisschopsmolenstr. 79, 4876 AJ Etten.
T. (076) 5012227. - Furn - *061126*
Piersma, L Brugstr 56, 4876 AP Etten.
T. (076) 5034435. *061127*
Stolker, M., Sander 24, 4871 NA Etten.
T. (076) 5012169. *061128*

Franeker (Friesland)
Meulen, van der, Dijkstr 34, 8801 LW Franeker. *061129*

Gasteren (Drenthe)
Jobing & Zonen, Brink 6, 9466 PE Gasteren.
T. (0592) 231363. - Ant / Furn / Dec / Cur / Mod /
Ico - *061130*

Geffen (Noord-Brabant)
Essing Antiquairs, Kerkstraat 12, 5386 AC Geffen.
T. (073) 5322457, Fax 5325678. - China /
Furn - *061131*
Gielis, P. G. H., Bergstr 27, 5386 KJ Geffen. *061132*

Geldrop (Noord-Brabant)
Anita & Andre, Dwarsstr 118, 5666 BG Geldrop.
T. (040) 2863401. *061133*
Berg, van den, Hulst 2, 5662 TH Geldrop.
T. (040) 2855803. - Ant / Furn / Sculp / Tex / Silv / Instr /
Rel - *061134*
Keulen, R., Berkenhof 25, 5664 VC Geldrop.
T. (040) 2863385. *061135*

Geleen (Limburg)
Houten, R., Groenseykerstr 41a, 6161 SE
Geleen. *061136*
Muntgalerie Limburg, Mauritslaan 61, 6161 HR Geleen.
- Num - *061137*

Gendringen (Gelderland)
Brunsveld, hoek Grotestr. – Ulftseweg, 7081 CE Gendringen. T. (0315) 681423. - Ant / Furn / Instr - *061138*

Giessenburg (Zuid-Holland)
Overduin, Pieter, Dorpsstraat 28, 3381 AG Giessenburg.
T. (0184) 652652, Fax 651056. - Paint - *061139*

Goes (Zeeland)
Schraaf, van der, Korte Kerkstr. 5, 4461 JE Goes. - Ant /
Dec - *061140*

Gorinchem (Zuid-Holland)
Bergman, F., Westwagenstr 41, 4201 HE Gorinchem.
T. (0183) 623761. *061141*
Ship's Antiques, Hoofdwal 43, 4207 EB Gorinchem.
T. (0183) 631766. *061142*

Gorssel (Gelderland)
Bonnema, Wiltinkhof 7, 7213 CJ Gorssel.
T. (0575) 491656. *061143*

Gouda (Zuid-Holland)
Disseldorp, N., Westhaven 70, 2801 PN Gouda.
T. (0182) 517049. *061144*
Lameris, Pieter, Lage Gouwe 48, 2801 LG Gouda.
T. (0182) 512077. - Ant / Furn / Sculp / Eth - *061145*
Roemer, de, Westhaven 26, 2801 PJ Gouda.
T. (0182) 516825. *061146*

Grijpskerk (Groningen)
Koetshuis, 't, Groningerstr 64, 9843 AC
Grijpskerk. *061147*
Schippenhuis, 't, Stationstr 4, 9843 AD
Grijpskerk. *061148*

Groede (Zeeland)
Verhage, A., Pr Marijkeplein 8, 4503 AG Groede. *061149*
Verhage, J. P., Dijckmeesterstr 3, 4503 AR
Groede. *061150*
Verhage, P., Blekestr 13, 4503 BE Groede. *061151*

Groningen
Groningana, Oude Kijk in 't Jatstraat 60, 9712 EL Groningen. T. (050) 3135858. - Num - *061152*

Koolma, P.F., Gedempte Zuiderdiep 81, 9711 HC Gronin-
gen. T. (050) 3134230. *061153*
Lameris, Zuiderdiep 86, 9744 AP Groningen.
T. (050) 532467. - Ant / Dec - *061154*
Ninck Blok, D.H.J., Noorderhaven 40, 9712 LD Gronin-
gen. T. (050) 3127232. - Furn - *061155*
Rozema, J. K., Zuiderdiep 87, 9745 AC Groningen.
T (050) 3132708. *061156*
Wiersema, Zuiderdiep 114a, 9744 AP Groningen.
T. (050) 3181358. *061157*

Den Haag (Zuid-Holland)
A & A, Hoefkade 649, 2525 LD Den Haag.
T. (070) 380 40 92. - Ant - *061160*
Aa-Bee Antiekhandel, Denneweg 114c, 2514 CK Den
Haag. T. (070) 364 35 56. *061161*
AAP, Mies Noot, Goudenregenstr. 113, 2565 EP Den
Haag. T. (070) 360 84 54, 368 22 74. - Lights /
Cur - *061162*
Aardewerk, A., Jan van Nassaustr. 76, 2596 BV Den
Haag. T. (070) 3240987, Fax (070) 3242051. - Furn /
China / Silv / Instr / Glass - *061163*
Abbacus, Heemskerckstr. 9, 2518 EH Den Haag.
T. (070) 345 73 70. - Ant - *061164*
ABC der Boeken, Het, Obrechtstr 94, 2517 VX Den Haag.
T. (070) 360 60 44. *061165*
Acart, W. Pymontkade 881, 2518 JT Den Haag.
T. (070) 345 64 42. - Fra - *061166*
Akkolades, Waldeck Pyrmontkade 882, 2518 JT Den
Haag. T. (070) 345 55 79. - Ant - *061167*
Aldenbeuring, Prinsestr. 53, 2513 CB Den Haag.
T. (070) 364 83 18. - Ant / Cur - *061168*
Amazone, Zoutmanstr. 94, 2518 GT Den Haag.
T. (070) 346 03 49. - Furn / Lights / Glass - *061169*
Andelos, Dr. Lelykade 54, 2583 CM Den Haag.
T. (070) 358 56 08. - Ant - *061170*
Angelique, Panamaplein 48, 2000 Den Haag.
T. (070) 325 16 88. *061171*
Anna, Christa, Deltaplein 528, Kijkduin, 2554 GH Den
Haag. T. (070) 368 20 22. - Ant / Cur - *061172*
Antartica, Noordeinde 45-45a, 2514 GC Den Haag.
T. (070) 364 93 35. - Ant - *061173*
Antes, Frederikstr. 46, 2514 LL Den Haag.
T. (070) 360 76 22. - Ant - *061174*
Antiekpalais, Het, Frederikstr 56, 2514 LL Den Haag.
T. (070) 346 27 92. *061175*
Any, Geestr. 40-42, 2513 VB Den Haag.
T. (070) 364 01 44. - Ant - *061176*
Aram, Denneweg 134, 2514 CL Den Haag.
T. (070) 365 74 54. - Ant - *061177*
Archipel Antiek, Denneweg 37, 2514 CC Den Haag.
T. (070) 346 77 84, 363 10 57. - Ant - *061178*
Art Agencies International, Noordeinde 111, 2514 GE
Den Haag. T. (070) 364 51 83. - Ant - *061179*
Artemis, Molenstr. 51, 2513 BJ Den Haag.
T. (070) 361 69 55. - Ant - *061180*
Bakker, Prins Hendrikstr. 97, 2518 HM Den Haag.
T. (070) 346 59 53. - Ant - *061181*
Bal, J.A., Bylandstr 119, 2562 GB Den Haag.
T. (070) 360 12 85. *061182*
Beaux Arts, Les, Noordeinde 113a, 2514 GE Den Haag.
T. (070) 360 58 91. - Ant - *061183*
Beelen, Paul, Noordeinde 96, 2514 GM Den Haag.
T. (070) 365 68 58. - Orient / Eth - *061184*
Ben Bor, Vreeswykstr. 1, 2546 AA Den Haag.
T. (070) 364 00 91. - Furn - *061185*
Bennies Fifties, G. Deynootweg 990, 2586 BZ Den Haag.
T. (070) 351 40 62. - Ant - *061186*
Bodes & Bode, Denneweg 50, 2514 CH Den Haag.
T. (070) 364 99 50. - Ant / Eth / Jew / Silv - *061187*
Boheemen, Burg Hooftstr. 27, 2552 TM Den Haag.
T. (070) 397 49 05. - Fra - *061188*
Boom, H. ten, Noordeinde 132, 2514 GN Den Haag.
T. (070) 360 57 54. - Instr - *061189*
Bouwman, Ivo, Jan van Nassaustraat 80, 2596 BW Den
Haag. T. (070) 3283660, Fax (070) 3283881.
- Paint - *061190*
Brocante Antiek, Fred Hendriklaan 255, 2582 CD Den
Haag. T. (070) 350 10 23. - Ant - *061191*
Bronzen Paard, Het, Ln. v. Meerdervoort 308, 2563 AL
Den Haag. T. (070) 360 44 05. - Ant - *061192*
Burg, Jac. A. van der, & Co., Denneweg 3a, 2514 CB
Den Haag. T. (070) 346 07 85. - Furn / Sculp - *061193*

Bussel, Loed van, Thomsonlaan 123, 2565 JA Den
Haag. T. (070) 338 85 70. - Orient / Eth - *061194*
Buys, P., Denneweg 114, 2514 CK Den Haag.
T. (070) 364 35 56. - Ant / Paint / Repr - *061195*
Cachot, Maliestr. 18, 2514 CA Den Haag.
T. (070) 365 99 79. - Ant - *061196*
Centrum 't Veilinghuis, Nassau Dillenburgstr. 3, 2596 AB
Den Haag. T. (070) 3244271. - Ant - *061197*
Corenger, Javastr. 90, 2585 AT Den Haag.
T. (070) 31 07 69 99. - Dec - *061198*
Cramer, G., Javastr. 38, 2585 AP Den Haag.
T. (070) 3630758, Fax (070) 3630759. - Paint - *061199*
Damen, J.H.S., Noordeinde 95, 2514 GD Den Haag.
T. (070) 360 58 95. - Ant / Paint / Furn / China / Silv /
Glass - *061200*
Darco, Vlamingstr. 17, 2511 AZ Den Haag.
T. (070) 346 17 17. - Ant - *061201*
Dat Antiek, Breitnerlaan 285, 2596 HA Den Haag.
T. (070) 324 22 22. - Furn - *061202*
Declemij, Noordeinde 157a, 2514 GG Den Haag.
T. (070) 360 03 25. *061203*
Denijs, P.A., Denneweg 57, 2514 CD Den Haag.
T. (070) 345 03 13. - Paint - *061204*
Dreese B.V., Korte Poten 32, 2511 EE Den Haag.
T. (070) 363 04 10. *061205*
E. & R., Noordeinde 86-88, 2514 GL Den Haag.
T. (070) 346 58 92. - Ant - *061206*
Ellemaat, de, Rijswijkseweg 422, 2516 HP Den Haag.
T. (070) 399 58 53. *061207*
Elshout, J.A.P. van der, A. Paulownastr. 27, 2518 BA Den
Haag. T. (070) 363 71 92. - Ant - *061208*
Ende, M. van den, Hooikade 29-31, 2514 BJ Den Haag.
T. (070) 346 06 51. - Ant - *061209*
Eybergen, Denneweg 3a, 2514 CB Den Haag.
T. (070) 363 47 48. - Ant - *061210*
Floor, Denneweg 33, 2514 CC Den Haag.
T. (070) 364 23 26. - Ant - *061211*
Franken, P. H., Noordeinde 182, 2514 GR Den Haag.
T. (070) 3605744. - Jew - *061212*
Frantzen, P., Kazernestr. 34a, 2514 CT Den Haag.
T. (070) 363 72 57. - Ant - *061213*
Gaag, J.A., Thompsonplein 3, 2565 KS Den Haag.
T. (070) 360 17 64. - Ant - *061214*
Gaemers, A., Noordeinde 155, 2514 GG Den Haag.
T. (070) 346 38 68. - Ant / Instr - *061215*
Gaemers, P., Javastr. 273-273a, 2585 AL Den Haag.
T. (070) 365 77 77. - Ant / Instr - *061216*
Galerie A1, Roggeveenstr. 144, 2518 TT Den Haag.
T. (070) 345 55 09. - Ant - *061217*
Galerie Dali, Noordeinde 184, 2514 GR Den Haag.
T. (070) 364 01 80. - Ant - *061218*
Galerie des Arts, Noordeinde 128, 2514 GN Den Haag.
T. (070) 365 77 91. - Ant / Paint - *061219*
Galerie Edison, Javastr. 16, 2585 AN Den Haag.
T. (070) 363 50 00. - Paint / Graph / China / Sculp / Tex /
Pho / Mul / Draw - *061220*
Galerie Passage, Passage 33, 2511 AB Den Haag.
T. (070) 346 02 59. - Ant - *061221*
Geradts, Spakenburgsestraat 61, 2574 JS Den Haag.
T. (070) 339 42 40. - Ant / Dec - *061222*
Gesloten Huis, Het, Weteringkade 96, 2515 AS Den
Haag. T. (070) 385 91 95. *061223*
Geus, de, Laan van Meerdervoort 515, 2563 AT Den
Haag. T. (070) 363 15 92. - Ant - *061224*
Graaf, J. van den, Noordeinde 192, 2514 GS Den Haag.
T. (070) 365 73 70. - Glass - *061225*
Grenen Stal, De, Grote Markstr. 14, 2511 BJ Den Haag.
T. (070) 364 65 32. - Furn - *061226*
Grijspaardt, Zuiderparklaan 216, 2574 HV Den Haag.
T. (070) 364 96 03. - Ant - *061227*
Hagedoorn, Denneweg 182, 2514 CM Den Haag.
T. (070) 360 68 86. - Ant - *061228*
Hart, E., Noordeinde 152a, 2514 GR Den Haag.
T. (070) 360 58 81, 360 74 21. - Furn / China /
Lights - *061229*
Heeneman, M., Prinsestr. 47, 2513 CA Den Haag.
T. (070) 364 47 48. - Ant - *061230*
Heytveldt, H. F., Balistraat 26, 2585 XT Den Haag.
T. (070) 363 87 88. - Ant / Dec - *061231*
Hollandische Huijsje, Het, Denneweg 114a, 2514 CK
Den Haag. T. (070) 360 01 39. - Ant - *061232*

Hoogsteder, Lange Vijverberg 15, 2513 AC Den Haag.
T. (070) 3615575, Fax (070) 3617074. - Ant / Paint /
Furn - 　　　　　　　　　　　　　　　　　　　　　*061233*
Hooijmans, J.L., Frederikstr. 80, 2514 LM Den Haag.
T. (070) 346 66 39. - Ant - 　　　　　　　　　　　　*061234*
Hooykaas Fine Arts, (The Hague Fine Arts), Lange Voorh-
out 27, 2514 EB Den Haag. T. (070) 3609083,
Fax (070) 3609314. - China / Glass / Furn / Sculp / Silv /
Orient / Paint - 　　　　　　　　　　　　　　　　　*061234a*
Horst, Ronald van der, Toussaintkade 18 + 39, 2513 CJ
Den Haag. T. (070) 345 16 50. - Ant - 　　　　　*061235*
Hut, De, Oranjelaan 4, 2515 RH Den Haag.
T. (070) 380 91 00. - Ant - 　　　　　　　　　　　*061236*
Huyser, Jan A., Heinsiusstr 23, 2582 VR Den Haag.
T. (070) 355 03 04. 　　　　　　　　　　　　　　　*061237*
In de Drie Molen, Molenstraat 9a-11, 2513 BH Den
Haag. T. (070) 360 51 86. - Ant / Dec - 　　　　*061238*
In de Vergulde Tuitlamp, Denneweg 110a, 2514 CK Den
Haag. T. (070) 364 31 43. - Ant - 　　　　　　　*061239*
In 't Duifje, Frederikstr. 3, 2514 LA Den Haag.
- Ant - 　　　　　　　　　　　　　　　　　　　　　*061240*
Inter Antiques, Noordeinde 115a, 2514 GE Den Haag.
T. (070) 364 37 36. - Ant - 　　　　　　　　　　　*061241*
John's Antique, Vaillantlaan 141, 2526 HD Den Haag.
T. (070) 363 30 94. 　　　　　　　　　　　　　　　*061242*
Kam, W.A., Molenstr 30a, 2513 BL Den Haag.
T. (070) 346 09 20. 　　　　　　　　　　　　　　　*061243*
Karma, Prinsestr. 18, 2513 CD Den Haag.
T. (070) 365 78 88. - Ant - 　　　　　　　　　　　*061244*
Kettenis Sandor, Javastr. 116, 2585 AW Den Haag.
T. (070) 365 47 98. - China - 　　　　　　　　　　*061245*
Kleef, van, & Hart, Noordeinde 152a, 2514 GR Den
Haag. T. (070) 360 58 81, 332 14 24. - Ant / Paint /
Furn / China - 　　　　　　　　　　　　　　　　　*061246*
Koch, Gebr., Hoogstraat 7, 2513 AN Den Haag.
T. (070) 346 33 05. - Ant / Furn / Repr / Sculp / Silv /
Lights / Mil - 　　　　　　　　　　　　　　　　　　*061247*
Konstkabinet, Noordeinde 159, 2514 GG Den Haag.
T. (070) 346 28 86. - Ant / Paint / Orient /
Sculp - 　　　　　　　　　　　　　　　　　　　　　*061248*
Kouw, C.J.J., Surinamestr. 32, 2585 GK Den Haag.
T. (070) 346 17 86. - Ant - 　　　　　　　　　　　*061249*
Van Kranendonk Duffels, Van Alkemadelaan 253, 2597
AH Den Haag. - Jew / Silv - 　　　　　　　　　　*061249a*
Kreuk, Wil de, Kastanjestr. 7, 2565 HJ Den Haag.
T. (070) 360 14 54. - Num - 　　　　　　　　　　*061250*
Kroeze, J.T., Noordeinde 20, 2514 GJ Den Haag.
T. (070) 362 00 74. - Ant - 　　　　　　　　　　　*061251*
Krol, Kazernestr. 142, 2514 CW Den Haag.
T. (070) 362 12 16. - Ant - 　　　　　　　　　　　*061252*
Kunstcentrum, Het, Molenstr. 16, 2513 BK Den Haag.
T. (070) 346 36 97. - Ant - 　　　　　　　　　　　*061253*
L'Agenterie Antique, Korte Poten 61, 2511 EC Den Haag.
T. (070) 346 21 24. - Ant - 　　　　　　　　　　　*061254*
Lantaarn, De, Thomsonlaan 91 en 122, 2565 HZ Den
Haag. T. (070) 363 24 27. - Furn - 　　　　　　　*061255*
Le Bonheur, Stevinstr. 192, 2587 ET Den Haag.
T. (070) 354 08 55. - Ant - 　　　　　　　　　　　*061256*
Leeuwen, B.V., Denneweg 114a, 2514 CK Den Haag.
T. (070) 360 01 39. - Ant - 　　　　　　　　　　　*061257*
Lelle, De, Dr. Lelykade 40, 2583 CM Den Haag.
T. (070) 354 99 33. - Ant - 　　　　　　　　　　　*061258*
Liesker, A.J., Molenstr. 5, 2513 BH Den Haag.
T. (070) 365 84 61. - Ant - 　　　　　　　　　　　*061259*
Lucas, Groenewegje 113, 2515 LP Den Haag.
T. (070) 346 16 49. 　　　　　　　　　　　　　　　*061260*
Luden, Frederikstr. 50-52a, 2514 LL Den Haag.
T. (070) 361 66 07. - Ant / Dec - 　　　　　　　*061261*
Maranta, Elandstr. 81, 2513 GM Den Haag.
T. (070) 356 30 03. - Ant - 　　　　　　　　　　　*061262*
Marktje, A. vd. Goesstr. 2, 2582 AK Den Haag.
T. (070) 355 40 86. - Ant - 　　　　　　　　　　　*061263*
Marral, Fuchsiastr. 42, 2565 PS Den Haag.
T. (070) 323 82 16. - Ant - 　　　　　　　　　　　*061264*
Mocenni, Mario, Denneweg 75, 2514 CE Den Haag.
T. (070) 346 81 06. - Ant / Furn - 　　　　　　　*061265*
Mont-Blanc, Korte Poten 38, 2511 EE Den Haag.
T. (070) 364 98 71. - Ant - 　　　　　　　　　　　*061266*
Montmartre Doorduin, Vos in Tuinstr. 3, 2514 BX Den
Haag. T. (070) 360 01 16. - Ant - 　　　　　　　*061267*
Muiselaar, C.C., Denneweg 29, 2514 CC Den Haag.
T. (070) 318 04 31. - Ant / Furn / China - 　　　*061268*

Muiselaar, Emile, Koningsplein 30a, 2518 JG Den Haag.
T. (070) 360 60 43. - Ant / Dec - 　　　　　　　　*061269*
Nederveen, S.J., Frederikstr 4, 2514 LK Den Haag.
T. (070) 346 26 85. 　　　　　　　　　　　　　　　*061270*
Neeltje, Denneweg 10, 2514 CG Den Haag.
T. (070) 346 77 68. - Ant - 　　　　　　　　　　　*061271*
Nieuwkoop, J. van, & Zoon, Stevinstr 143, 2587 ED Den
Haag. T. (070) 355 70 78. 　　　　　　　　　　　*061272*
Ninua, Hooftskade 97, 2526 KB Den Haag.
T. (070) 363 88 35. 　　　　　　　　　　　　　　　*061273*
Nova Spectra, Ln. v. Meerdervoort 41, 2517 AD Den
Haag. T. (070) 365 52 33. - Ant - 　　　　　　　*061274*
Numint, v. Alkemadeln 201, 2597 AG Den Haag.
T. (070) 324 13 89. - Num - 　　　　　　　　　　　*061275*
Nystad, S., Ruychrocklaan 442, 2597 EJ Den Haag.
T. (070) 324 50 24. - Paint - 　　　　　　　　　　*061276*
Omega, Noordeinde 117, 2514 GE Den Haag.
T. (070) 365 57 51. - Ant - 　　　　　　　　　　　*061277*
Ottevanger, Mauritskade 61, 2514 HG Den Haag.
T. (070) 362 09 47. - Ant - 　　　　　　　　　　　*061278*
Oude Centrum, Stille Veerkade 34, 2512 BG Den Haag.
T. (070) 363 83 44. - Ant / Cur - 　　　　　　　　*061279*
Oude Denne, D', Denneweg 37, 2514 CC Den Haag.
T. (070) 311 68 87. - Ant / Dec - 　　　　　　　*061280*
Oude Hof, Het, Javastraat 72, 2585 AS Den Haag.
T. (070) 360 60 12. - Ant / Paint / Furn / China / Silv /
Cur - 　　　　　　　　　　　　　　　　　　　　　　*061281*
Oude Stijl, J. Bildersstr. 71, 2596 EG Den Haag.
T. (070) 324 97 35. - China / Silv / Lights - 　　*061282*
Paix, La, Anna Paulownastr. 111, 2518 BD Den Haag.
T. (070) 363 33 22. - Ant / Paint / Jew / Silv - 　*061283*
Paljas Pineshop, Frederikstr. 38, 2514 LL Den Haag.
T. (070) 360 75 68. - Ant - 　　　　　　　　　　　*061284*
Persepolis, Denneweg 43a-45, 2514 CD Den Haag.
T. (070) 311 78 85. - Ant - 　　　　　　　　　　　*061285*
Peterson, Paul, Jul. v. Stolberglaan 349, 2595 CJ Den
Haag. T. (070) 383 65 56. - Fra - 　　　　　　　*061286*
Petite Merle, La, Beeklaan 498, 2562 BD Den Haag.
T. (070) 360 25 84. - Ant - 　　　　　　　　　　　*061287*
Poel, J., Denneweg 63, 2514 CD Den Haag.
- Ant - 　　　　　　　　　　　　　　　　　　　　　*061288*
Polak, R., Jan van Nassaustr 17, 2596 BL Den Haag.
T. (070) 3280020, Fax (070) 3241663. 　　　　　*061289*
Ponsen, A.E., Fisherstr 374, 2572 RL Den Haag.
T. (070) 365 81 76. 　　　　　　　　　　　　　　　*061290*
Prix d'Amis, Ln. v. Meerdervoort 3, 2517 AA Den Haag.
T. (070) 365 13 46. - Ant - 　　　　　　　　　　　*061291*
Pukkie, Badhuisstr. 49, 2584 HE Den Haag.
T. (070) 350 72 69, 355 15 24. - Ant - 　　　　*061292*
Quik, L., Suezkade 138, 2517 CC Den Haag.
T. (070) 360 74 74. 　　　　　　　　　　　　　　　*061293*
Résidence, La, Laan van Meerdervoort 306, 2563 AL
Den Haag. T. (070) 346 69 83. 　　　　　　　　　*061294*
Rich, Stevinstr. 150, 2587 ES Den Haag.
T. (070) 352 35 55. - Ant - 　　　　　　　　　　　*061295*
Rietdijk Veilingen, Noordeinde 41, 2514 GC Den Haag.
T. (070) 364 78 31, 364 79 57. - Num - 　　　　*061296*
Rive-Gauche, Denneweg 21 A, 2514 CC Den Haag.
T. (070) 346 40 44. 　　　　　　　　　　　　　　　*061297*
Roger, Spekstr. 3, 2514 BL Den Haag.
T. (070) 365 35 22, Fax 365 35 22. - Ant /
Paint - 　　　　　　　　　　　　　　　　　　　　　*061298*
Roos, Keizerstr. 36a, 2584 BJ Den Haag.
T. (070) 352 37 97. - Ant - 　　　　　　　　　　　*061299*
Rutten, F., All Piersonlaan 179, 2522 MK Den Haag.
T. (070) 390 53 54. - Ant - 　　　　　　　　　　　*061300*
Sanders, Nico, Noordeinde 188, 2514 GR Den Haag.
T. (070) 365 73 75. - Ant / Paint / Graph / Dec - 　*061301*
Schatkamer, De, Denneweg 68, 2514 CJ Den Haag.
T. (070) 346 01 49. - Ant / Furn / China / Cur - 　*061302*
Schoonens, A., Zoutmanstr. 71, 2518 GN Den Haag.
T. (070) 345 19 59. - Furn - 　　　　　　　　　　*061303*
Schooners, Zuidwal 101a, 2512 XV Den Haag.
T. (070) 360 08 33. - Ant / Dec - 　　　　　　　*061304*
Simons, Plein 9a, 2511 CR Den Haag. T. (070) 3658800,
Fax (070) 3560001. - Jew / Silv - 　　　　　　　*061305*
Smelik & Stokking, Noordeinde 156, 2514 GR Den Haag.
T. (070) 364 99 94. - Ant / Paint / Furn / China / Sculp /
Tex / Silv / Lights - 　　　　　　　　　　　　　　*061306*
Smidje van der Wiel, Laan van Meerdervoort 315a, 2563
AN Den Haag. T. (070) 339 50 46. 　　　　　　　*061307*
Spinnewiel, Het, Molenstr 37, 2513 BJ Den Haag.
T. (070) 360 51 71. 　　　　　　　　　　　　　　　*061308*

Spoor, Fred, Denneweg 68-68a, 2514 CJ Den Haag.
T. (070) 346 01 49. - Furn - 　　　　　　　　　　*061309*
Stil, J.W., Obrechtstr. 387, 2517 VB Den Haag.
T. (070) 346 01 24. - Furn - 　　　　　　　　　　*061310*
Straaten, M.F. van, Barentszstr. 39, 2518 XD Den Haag.
T. (070) 345 48 14. - Orient - 　　　　　　　　　*061311*
Tijdspiegel, De, Noordeinde 202, 2514 GS Den Haag.
T. (070) 360 70 55, 347 86 35. - Ant / Jew /
Instr - 　　　　　　　　　　　　　　　　　　　　　*061312*
Tiron Ned, G. Deynootweg 980, 2586 BZ Den Haag.
T. (070) 358 52 55. - Ant - 　　　　　　　　　　　*061313*
Toko Dik, Hobbemastr 232, 2526 JV Den Haag.
T. (070) 363 22 03. 　　　　　　　　　　　　　　　*061314*
Toussaint, Toussaintkade 8-18, 2513 CJ Den Haag.
T. (070) 339 86 63. - Ant / Furn / Instr - 　　　*061315*
Triep, J. M., Grote Hertoginnenlaan 145, 2517 EP Den
Haag. T. (070) 346 64 37. 　　　　　　　　　　　*061316*
Twee Wapens, De, Frederikstr. 4, 2514 LK Den Haag.
T. (070) 346 26 85. - Ant - 　　　　　　　　　　　*061317*
Twee Wijzers, De, Molenstr 35, 2513 BJ Den Haag.
T. (070) 360 96 78. 　　　　　　　　　　　　　　　*061318*
Van Leeuwen-Bersee, R., Lijsterbestr 16, 2563 KW Den
Haag. T. (070) 360 61 68. 　　　　　　　　　　　*061319*
Van Leeuwen, S., Noordeinde 164-164a, 2514 GR Den
Haag. T. (070) 3653907. - Ant / Furn / China /
Instr - 　　　　　　　　　　　　　　　　　　　　　*061320*
Verbove, A. J., Denneweg 108-108a, 2514 CK Den
Haag. T. (070) 311 29 93. - Ant - 　　　　　　　*061321*
Victoria Pine Shop, Weissenbruchstr. 123, 2596 GD Den
Haag. T. (070) 324 75 79. - Ant - 　　　　　　　*061322*
Victorine, Badhuisweg 247, 2597 JR Den Haag.
T. (070) 355 66 75. - Ant - 　　　　　　　　　　　*061323*
Vlam, Michiel De, Sumatrastr. 200, 2585 CV Den Haag.
T. (070) 358 56 33. - Ant - 　　　　　　　　　　　*061324*
Voorst, van & P.B. van Beest, A. Paulownastr. 107, 2518
BD Den Haag. T. (070) 364 43 34. - Ant - 　　　*061325*
Vuurduiveltje, Fuchsiastr. 2, 2565 PR Den Haag.
T. (070) 323 53 10. - China - 　　　　　　　　　　*061326*
Weegenaar, C. J. J., Frederikstr. 12-12b, 2514 LK Den
Haag. T. (070) 346 28 74. - Ant / Furn / China /
Instr - 　　　　　　　　　　　　　　　　　　　　　*061327*
Weissenbruch, Weissenbruchstr. 126, 2596 GL Den
Haag. T. (070) 324 93 65. - Ant - 　　　　　　　*061328*
Wensveen, J. H. B. van, Haagsestr 1, 2587 TE Den
Haag. T. (070) 355 07 22. 　　　　　　　　　　　*061329*
Wilart, Noordeinde 105, 2514 GE Den Haag.
T. (070) 365 78 88. - Orient / Eth - 　　　　　　*061330*
Wittenberg, P., Korte Poten 38, 2511 EE Den Haag.
T. (070) 364 98 71. - Paint - 　　　　　　　　　　*061331*
Zetz, P.M., Lutherse Burgwal 26, 2512 CB Den Haag.
T. (070) 364 37 36. 　　　　　　　　　　　　　　　*061332*
Zuurveen, T.H., Denneweg 134, 2514 CL Den Haag.
T. (070) 346 23 58. - Ant / Cur - 　　　　　　　*061333*

Haaren (Noord-Brabant)

Hüsstege, Driehoeven 12, 5076 BB Haaren.
T. (0411) 621264. - Ant / Paint / Graph / Furn / Sculp /
Dec / Ico - 　　　　　　　　　　　　　　　　　　　*061334*

Haarlem (Noord-Holland)

Au Tricolore, Ridderstr. 6, 2011 RS Haarlem.
T. (023) 5320455. - Ant / Dec - 　　　　　　　　*061335*
Becker, H., Gierstr. 50, 2011 GE Haarlem.
T. (023) 5312839. - Ant / Graph - 　　　　　　　*061336*
Boerenantiek t'Halster, Kleine Houtstr. 88, 2011 DR
Haarlem. T. (023) 5320455. - China / Lights / Mil / Cur /
Mod - 　　　　　　　　　　　　　　　　　　　　　*061337*
Bonte, de, Schagchelstr 6, 2011 HX Haarlem.
T. (023) 5327118. 　　　　　　　　　　　　　　　*061338*
Boomsma, Warmoesstr. 20, 2011 HP Haarlem.
T. (023) 5323834. - Ant / Furn / Dec / Jew / Glass /
Cur - 　　　　　　　　　　　　　　　　　　　　　　*061339*
Cassée, A., Ged. O. Gracht 93, 2011 GN Haarlem.
T. (023) 5321289. - Ant / Dec - 　　　　　　　　*061340*
Eck-Gieben, A. J. van, Oude Groenmarkt 14-16, 2011
HL Haarlem. T. (023) 5323462. 　　　　　　　　*061341*
Friesche Schathuis, Jansstr. 8, 2011 RX Haarlem.
T. (023) 5310054. - Ant - 　　　　　　　　　　　*061342*
Gulik, Anton K. J. van der, Frankestr. 37, 2011 HT Haar-
lem. T. (023) 5329244. - Ant / Furn / Orient / China /
Glass - 　　　　　　　　　　　　　　　　　　　　*061343*

Heerkens Thijssen, Wagenweg 6, 2012 ND Haarlem.
T. (023) 5312725. - Ant / Paint / Graph / Furn / China /
Sculp / Dec / Silv / Instr / Glass / Cur / Draw -   *061344*
Hof, J. van t', Gedempte Oude Gracht 113, 2011 GP
Haarlem. T. (023) 5326141.   *061345*
Marel, C. M. van de, Radboudstr 6, 2025 BK Haarlem
T. (023) 5379179.   *061346*
Mariteam, Korte Margarethastr 4, 2011 PK Haarlem.
T. (023) 531689.   *061347*
Neut, R. A. G. van der, Klein Heiligland 43, 2011 EC
Haarlem. T. (023) 5317272. - Furn / China -   *061348*
Oprecht Veiling, De, Bilderdijkstr 1a, 2013 EG Haarlem.
T. (023) 5316486.   *061349*
Oude Ambracht, 't, Breestr 14, 2011 ZZ Haarlem.
T. (023) 5316781.   *061350*
Plas, A. van der, Spekstr 14, 2011 HM Haarlem.
T. (023) 5325744.   *061351*
Pothuys, 't, Laurierstr 25, 2023 NA Haarlem.
T. (023) 5250491.   *061352*
Reijgersberg, Patrick, Damstr. 27, 2011 HA Haarlem.
T. (023) 5316118. - Ant -   *061353*
Seynhuis, 't, Duvenvoordestr 36, 2013 AG Haarlem.
T. (023) 5314692.   *061354*
Smith & Wieringa, Zijlweg 52, 2013 DJ Haarlem.
T. (023) 5311252, 5257824.   *061355*
Tak, John. J. Ph. van der, Oude Groenmarkt 12, 2011 HL
Haarlem. T. (023) 5322008. - Furn / Lights /
Instr -   *061356*
Van Leeuwen, J., Korte Begijnestr 1, 2011 HC Haarlem.
T. (023) 5321563.   *061357*
Van Ravenstein, Spekstr. 10, 2011 HM Haarlem.
T. (023) 5320274. - China / Silv -   *061358*
Van't Hof, A., Grote Markt 23, 2011 RC Haarlem.
T. (023) 5310704. - Ant / Furn / Instr -   *061359*
Venus Antiek, Gierstr 37, 2011 GA Haarlem.
T. (023) 5312993.   *061360*
Visser, Paul, Damstr 25, 2011 HA Haarlem.
T. (023) 5323957.   *061361*
Waaygat, 't, Nassaustr 11, 2011 PH Haarlem.
T. (023) 5320833   *061362*
Zadelhoff, W. G. F. van, Lorentzplein 26, 2012 HH Haar-
lem. T. (023) 5317673.   *061363*

Heemskerk (Noord-Holland)
Horst, P. J. van der, Rijksstraatweg 112, 1968 LL
Heemskerk. T. (0251) 236997.   *061364*

Heemstede (Noord-Holland)
Beukenkamp-Keur, A. E., Zandvoortselaan 93, 2106 CL
Heemstede. T. (023) 5288085.   *061365*
Brokke, H., Zandvoortselaan 93, 2106 CL
Heemstede.   *061366*
Dare, Herenweg 149, 2106 MH Heemstede.
T. (023) 5283182. - Ant / Instr -   *061367*
Tinkamer, De, Herenweg 142, 2101 MT Heemstede.
T. (023) 5283127.   *061368*

Heerlen (Limburg)
Alberts, G., Geleenstr. 5, 6411 HP Heerlen.
T. (045) 5713609. - Ant / Dec -   *061369*
Driessens, F., Honigmanstr 45, 6411 LJ Heerlen.
T. (045) 5712590.   *061370*
Vaessen, S., Bongerd 11, 6411 LD Heerlen.
T. (045) 5712240. - Jew / Silv / Instr / Rel -   *061371*

Heeze (Noord-Brabant)
Saes, A., Jan Deckersstr 7, 5591 HN Heeze.   *061372*

Heinenoord (Zuid-Holland)
Linden, B. van der, Reedijk 27, 3274 KE Heinenoord.
T. (0186) 601620.   *061373*

Helden (Limburg)
Haffmans, F. J., Pastoor Knippenberghstr 55, 5988 CT
Helden.   *061374*

Helvoirt (Noord-Brabant)
Berkelmans, H. W. M., Rijksweg 1, 5268 KJ Helvoirt.
T. (0411) 641828.   *061375*
Koldewey, J., Antwerpsebaan 2, 5268 KB Helvoirt.
T. (0411) 641306. - Ant / Furn / China / Sculp / Dec /
Rel -   *061376*

Hem (Noord-Holland)
Antiek Boerderij Houtlust, de Hout 26, 1607 HC Hem.
- Furn -   *061377*

Hengelo (Overijssel)
Jonge, G. de, Woltersweg 105, 7552 DC
Hengelo.   *061378*
Lubbers, H. C., Bothastr 24, 7551 GH Hengelo.
T. (074) 2422289.   *061379*
Morsink, Jan, Wolter ter Catestr. 56, 7551 HZ Hengelo.
T. (074) 2421977, Fax 2424141. - Ico -   *061380*
Weustink, H., Castorweg 304, 7557 KS
Hengelo.   *061381*

's-Hertogenbosch (Noord-Brabant)
Borzo, Verwersstr. 21, 5211 HT 's-Hertogenbosch.
T. (073) 6135012, 6133706. - Paint / Graph -   *061382*
Gelder, van, Oude Dieze 15, 5211 KT 's-Hertogenbosch.
T. (073) 6146254. - Jew -   *061383*
Kranendonk Duffels, J. van, Oude Dieze 15, 5211 KT 's-
Hertogenbosch. T. (073) 61462154. - Fra -   *061384*
Laat, H. de, Vughterstr 162, 5211 GN 's-Hertogenbosch.
T. (073) 6133536.   *061385*
Linden, N. B. W. van der, Andriessenstr 1, 5224 JE 's-
Hertogenbosch. T. (073) 6137501.   *061386*
Mes, F. F., Postelstr. 42, 5211 EB 's-Hertogenbosch.
T. (073) 6144854. - Ant / Furn / China / Sculp / Lights /
Rel -   *061387*
Ouden Huls, den, St. Jorisstr. 24, 5211 HB 's-Hertogen-
bosch. T. (073) 6142200. - Ant / Dec -   *061388*
Spoor, J., Verwersstr. 59, 5211 HV 's-Hertogenbosch.
T. (073) 6130158. - Ant / Furn -   *061389*
Vanderven & Vanderven, Peperstr. 6, 5211 KM 's-Herto-
genbosch. T. (073) 0140251. - Ant / Furn / China /
Silv -   *061390*

Heusden (Noord-Brabant)
Tegenbosch, Lambert, Putterstr. 48, 5256 ZG Heusden.
T. (0416) 622772, Fax 623340. - Paint -   *061391*

Hillegom (Zuid-Holland)
Wiegel, Riet, Vincent van Goghsingel 38, 2182 LP Hille-
gom. T. (0252) 519368. - Mod -   *061392*

Hilvarenbeek (Noord-Brabant)
Vijver-Mommersteeg, van der, Groot Westerwijksestr. 2,
5081 NE Hilvarenbeek. T. (013) 5051445. - Ant /
Furn -   *061393*

Hilversum (Noord-Holland)
Antiek Boutique, Soestdijkerstr 39, 1213 VR Hilversum.
T. (035) 648621.   *061394*
Fieret, M., Wolvenlaan 259, 1216 EV Hilversum.
T. (035) 615134.   *061395*
Hertog, de, de Genestetlaan 32, 1215 EB Hilversum.
T. (035) 611125. - Ant / Dec -   *061396*
Kok, A., Nieuwlandseweg 37, 1215 AW Hilversum.
T. (035) 612136.   *061397*
Luifel, De, Havenstr 89, 1211 KJ Hilversum.
T. (035) 616831.   *061398*
Schaaf, Vaartweg 1-3, 1211 JD Hilversum.   *061399*
Smit & van Asselt, s'Gravelandseweg 3, 1211 BN Hilver-
sum. T. (035) 6214998. - Jew / Silv -   *061400*
Snel, C., Herenstr 34, 1211 CC Hilversum.
T. (035) 610598.   *061401*
Taalvriend, De, Langestr 22, 1211 GZ Hilversum.
T. (035) 647030.   *061402*
Waag, De, Bodemanstr 2, 1216 AK Hilversum.
T. (035) 612687.   *061403*
Warnars, E.G.M.J., Snelliuslaan 43, 1222 TC Hilversum.
T. (035) 6852651.   *061404*
Wigman, W., De Genestetlaan 32, 1215 EB Hilversum.
T. (035) 611125.   *061405*

Hindeloopen (Friesland)
Bootsma, Nieuwstad 28, 8713 JL Hindeloopen.   *061406*

Hoensbroek (Limburg)
Evers, Th., De Koumen 58, 6433 KJ Hoensbroek.
T. (045) 5223333.   *061407*
Verstegen, Kouvenderstr 220, 6431 HJ
Hoensbroek.   *061408*

Hoevelaken (Gelderland)
Slijkerman & Slijkerman, Oosterdorpsstr. 97, 3871 AC
Hoevelaken. T. (033) 2535167. - Glass -   *061409*

Hoorn (Noord-Holland)
Molenaar, K., Grote Noord 116, 1621 KL Hoorn.
T. (0229) 215972   *061410*
Rijn, van, Breestr 11, 1621 CG Hoorn.   *061411*

Huizen (Noord-Holland)
Snel, C., Nieuwe Bussumerweg 99, 1272 CE
Huizen.   *061412*

Katwoude (Noord-Holland)
Grenen, Lagedijk 3, 1145 PL Katwoude.
T. (0299) 651257.   *061413*

Kloosterburen (Groningen)
Top, T., Leensterweg 55, 9977 PB Kloosterburen. - Ant /
Dec -   *061414*

Laag-Keppel (Gelderland)
Venema, Rijksweg 92, 6998 AK Laag-Keppel.
T. (0314) 381917. - Instr -   *061415*

Laren (Noord-Holland)
Calis, T., Tuintje 17, 1251 RZ Laren.
T. (035) 5387957.   *061416*
Enneking, F.A., Hoog Hoefloo 35, 1251 EC Laren.
T. (035) 5387639.   *061417*
Karrewiel, 't, St Jansstr 24a, 1251 LB Laren.
T. (035) 5382947.   *061418*
Kikkertje, 't, C Bakkerlaan 19, 1251 BP Laren.
T. (035) 5382817.   *061419*
Nieuwenhuyzen, Klaaskampen 4c, 1251 KP Laren.
- Ant / Dec -   *061420*
Vischschoonmaker, Abbie, Galleries International, 2 Ze-
venend, 1251 RN Laren. T. (035) 5383806.
- Ant -   *061421*

Leeuwarden (Friesland)
Beeling, A. C., & Zn., Nieuwestad 91, 8911 CL Leeuwar-
den. T. (058) 2136325. - Ant / Furn / China /
Silv -   *061422*
Beuneker, Nieuwestad 53, 8911 CJ Leeuwarden.
T. (058) 2125452.   *061423*
Esveld-Riemersma, J. L. van, Bagijnestr 58a, 8911 DS
Leeuwarden. T. (058) 225869.   *061424*
Gerbenzon & Zoon, Weerd 15-17, 8911 HL Leeuwarden.
T. (058) 2125553. - Furn / China / Tex / Silv -   *061425*
Hielkema, A., Nieuweburen 134, 8911 GB Leeuwarden.
T. (058) 225799. - Num -   *061426*
Mercuur, M., Louisastr 9, 8933 AN Leeuwarden.
T. (058) 220464.   *061427*
Smit, P., Willem Frisostr 22b, 8933 BP Leeuwarden.
T. (058) 234372.   *061428*
Veen, S. van der, J Evenhuisstr 41, 8923 EE Leeuwar-
den. T. (058) 220686.   *061429*
Vries-Mebius, F. de, 8901 EA Leeuwarden Postbus
4025. T. (058) 262803.   *061430*

Leiden (Zuid-Holland)
Blansjaar, Hogewoerd 48, 2311 HN Leiden.
T. (071) 530919. - Ant / Paint / Dec -   *061431*
Cruysen, R. Jacques van, Rapenburg 20, 2311 EW Lei-
den. T. (071) 5120072. - Paint / Furn / China -   *061432*
„De Rijn", Nieuwe Rijn 60, 2312 JH Leiden.
T. (071) 522150. - Ant / Dec -   *061433*
Gysen et Schoonderwoerd, Breestr 13, 2311 CG Leiden.
T. (071) 525110.   *061434*
Pierement, 't, Rapenburg 54, 2311 EX Leiden.
T. (071) 5134534. - Ant / Dec / Glass / Mod -   *061435*
Ruiten, J. C. van, & Zn., Kort Rapenburg 12, 2311 GC
Leiden. T. (071) 5126290. - Ant / Num / China / Jew /
Silv / Cur -   *061436*
Sint Lucas Society, Rapenburg 83, 2311 GK Leiden.
T. (071) 525514. - Ant / Dec -   *061437*

Leidschendam (Zuid-Holland)
Bos, T., Voorburgseweg 34a, 2264 AG Leidschendam.
T. (070) 3588.   *061438*

Lekkerkerk (Zuid-Holland)
Ridder, de, & Zoon, Schwacht 346, 2941 EM Lekker-
kerk. T. (0180) 6622290.   *061439*

Lochem (Gelderland)

Dyck-den Hartog, Zutphenseweg 114, 7241 SG
Lochem. *061440*

Fontein, S.J., Laan Ampsen 7, 7241 NG Lochem.
T. (0573) 256842. - Draw - *061441*

Lunteren (Gelderland)

Scharrenburg, Van, Edeseweg 11a, 6741 CP Lunteren.
T. (0318) 482355. - Ant / Dec - *061442*

Spies, G.J., Dorpsstr 130, 6741 AP Lunteren.
T. (0318) 483129. *061443*

Maarssen (Utrecht)

Paroxis International, Bisonspoor 5006, 3605 LW Maarssen. T. (0346) 573998. *061444*

Maastricht (Limburg)

Antiekgro-Exclusief, Akersteenweg 144, 6227 AC Maastricht. T. (043) 3616926, 3648018. - Ant / Paint /
Graph / Sculp / Tex / Silv / Lights - *061445*

Bärwaldt, K.H., Tongersestr. 11, 6211 LL Maastricht.
T. (043) 3216823. - Ant / China / Dec - *061446*

Bakker, R., Stokstraat 22, 6211 GD Maastricht.
T. (043) 3216277. - Instr - *061447*

Blauwe Olifant, St. Servaasklooster 38, 6211 TE Maastricht. T. (043) 3254383, Fax 3259103.
- Orient - *061448*

Claessens, Roger, Brusselsestr 22, 6211 PE Maastricht.
T. (043) 314789. *061449*

Eyck, A. J. van, & Zn., Boschstr 72, 6211 AX Maastricht.
T. (043) 314382. *061450*

Gabriels, E., & Zn., Bourgognestr 28, 6221 BZ Maastricht. T. (043) 315457. *061451*

Gielen-Wolters, Hertogsingel 104, 6214 AG Maastricht.
T. (043) 318079. *061452*

Heritage, Stokstr. 13, 6211 GB Maastricht.
T. (043) 3216711. - Ant / China / Sculp / Arch - *061453*

Jurrissen, M., Kleine Gracht 4, 6211 CB Maastricht.
T. (043) 318994. - Ant / Paint / Furn / China /
Instr - *061454*

Leuken, M. van, Pieterstr 15, 6211 JM Maastricht.
T. (043) 311708. *061455*

Lommen, M. J., St. Bernardusstr. 33-35, 6211 HK
Maastricht. T. (043) 3219113. - Ant / Sculp / Arch /
Eth - *061456*

Molenaar, V.A.C., Pergamijndonk 134, 6218 GX Maastricht. T. (043) 319979. - Instr - *061457*

Noortman, Vrijthof 49, 6211 LE Maastricht.
T. (043) 3216745, Fax 3213899. *061458*

Peeter-Antiek, St Pieterstr 30, 6211 JN Maastricht.
T. (043) 319140. *061459*

Vaessen, S., M. Smendenstr. 11, 6211 GK Maastricht.
T. (043) 3211428. - Jew / Silv / Instr - *061460*

Verspeek, J., St Pieterskade 11, 6212 AC Maastricht.
T. (043) 315186. *061461*

Wolters, J., Cannerweg 111, 6213 BH Maastricht.
T. (043) 319776. *061462*

Middelburg (Zeeland)

Flipse, J., Segeerstr. 56-70, 4331 JP Middelburg.
- Ant - *061463*

Hooge, A. J. de, Kinderdijk 24, 4331 HG Middelburg.
T. (0118) 627988. - Ant / Furn - *061464*

Vlier, G. L. C. van, Hoogstr 17, 4331 KR Middelburg.
T. (0118) 616536. *061465*

Middelharnis (Zuid-Holland)

Gerbrand, A., Voorstr 6, 3241 EG Middelharnis. *061466*

Krijnsman, A. S., Eendrachtstr 30, 3241 CD
Middelharnis. *061467*

Middelie (Noord-Holland)

Stolp, De, Middelie 33, 1472 GP Middelie. *061468*

Mierlo (Noord-Brabant)

Huybregts, J. H., Pastoor de Winterstr. 16, 5731 EJ
Mierlo. - Ant / Dec - *061469*

Welvaars, A. B., Broekstr 47, 5731 RA Mierlo. *061470*

Montfoort (Utrecht)

Argent International B.V., Heeswijk 84, 3417 GP Montfo-
ort. - Num - *061471*

Moordrecht (Zuid-Holland)

Scheve Hoeve, De, Westeinde 227, 2841 BT Moord-
recht. T. (0182) 373097. - Ant / Dec - *061472*

Muiden (Noord-Holland)

Floris, Weesperstr 10, 1398 XX Muiden. *061473*

Hartje van Muiden, Het, Amsterdamsestr 7, 1398 BK
Muiden. *061474*

Naarden (Noord-Holland)

Buys, F., Marktstr. 38, 1411 EA Naarden.
T. (035) 6941351. - Ant / Furn / China / Repr / Glass /
Instr / Cur - *061475*

Van Wisselingh, E.J., Valkeveenselaan 46, 1411 GT
Naarden. T. (035) 6943708, Fax 6949358.
- Paint - *061476*

Nieuwerkerk a.d. Ijssel (Zuid-Holland)

Looze, Alice de, 's Gravenweg 62, 2911 CG Nieuwerkerk
a.d. Ijssel. T. (0180) 314662. - Ant / Furn - *061477*

Nijmegen (Gelderland)

Antiek- en Kunsthandel, In de Betouwstr 40, 6511 GD
Nijmegen. T. (024) 3220848. *061478*

Beekhuizen, Mr Franckenstr 17, 6522 AB Nijmegen.
T. (024) 3221955. *061479*

Darantanas, A., & Co., Timorstr 12, 6524 KB Nijmegen.
T. (024) 3220841. *061480*

Eijndhoven, van, Weurtseweg 52, 6541 AX Nijmegen.
T. (024) 3774487. *061481*

Gerritsen, H. G., Van Welderenstr 88, 6511 MR Nijmegen. T. (024) 3224387. *061482*

Giovanni, W., Populierstr 16, 6522 JH Nijmegen.
T. (024) 3222217. *061483*

Groen, H., Lange Hezelstr 58, 6511 CL Nijmegen.
T. (024) 3550082. *061484*

Janssen, G.W., Mr Franckenstr 5, 6522 AA Nijmegen.
T. (024) 3231835. *061485*

Osinga & Co., Tooropstr 185, 6521 NM Nijmegen.
T. (024) 3231373. *061486*

Smulders, Van Welderenstr. 30, 6511 ML Nijmegen.
T. (024) 3200029. - Ant / Furn / Dec / Instr /
Cur - *061487*

Teunissen, H. A. J., Kannenmarkt 16, 6511 KC Nijmegen. T. (024) 3232129. *061488*

Wilhelm, A. M., Frans Halsstr 60, 6523 CM Nijmegen.
T. (024) 3232401. *061489*

Noordwijk aan Zee (Zuid-Holland)

Enneking, F.A., Marevista 22, 2202 BX Noordwijk.
T. (071) 3647645, Fax 3647645. - Paint *061490*

Zoetmulder, Arnold, Strandwijck 20, 2202 BV Noordwijk
aan Zee. T. (071) 3616417. - Ant / Paint / Furn / Mil /
Ico - *061491*

Nuenen (Noord-Brabant)

Sesam Gallery, Berg 41, 5671 CB Nuenen.
T. (040) 2831668. - Furn / Sculp - *061492*

Ochten (Gelderland)

Zuu, L.J.M., Perengaard 1, 4050 EC Ochten.
T. (0344) 641601. - Furn - *061493*

Oegstgeest (Zuid-Holland)

Almondehoeve, Almondew 2, 2343 AA Oegstgeest.
T. (071) 5172757. *061494*

Plessen, F., Geversstr 47, 2341 GA Oegstgeest.
T. (071) 552151. *061495*

Wurfbain, M.L., Dorpsstr. 67, 2343 AX Oegstgeest.
T. (071) 5173387, Fax 5155731. - Paint - *061496*

Oirschot (Noord-Brabant)

Kollenburg, F.V., van Rijkeshuisstr. 19, 5688 EC Oirschot.
- Instr - *061497*

Oostburg (Zeeland)

Dierkx, J., Burg Erasmusstr 12, 4501 BK
Oostburg. *061498*

Oosterland (Zeeland)

Limburg, Kantoor J. Stuy, Koninginneplein 1-3, 4307 BA
Oosterland. T. (0111) 641232, Fax (0111) 641232.
- Glass / Furn / China - *061499*

Ospel (Limburg)

Arphi, Alain & Odette, Meijelsedijk 67, 6035 RJ Ospel.
T. (0495) 641455. *061500*

Oss (Noord-Brabant)

Bastings & van Tuijl, Walstr. 64, 5341 CK Oss.
T. (0412) 623843. - Ant / Paint / Furn / China - *061501*

Leyten-Ebbeling, Houtstr 2, 5341 GG Oss. *061502*

't Poezenest, Kortfoortstraat 85, 5342 AC Oss.
T. (0412) 625108. - Ant / Dec - *061503*

Ottoland (Zuid-Holland)

Binnenweg, B., Lange Zijde A 29, 2975 BB Ottoland.
T. (0184) 642147, Fax 641503. - Ant / Furn / Instr /
Cur - *061504*

Ouderkerk a.d. Amstel (Noord-Holland)

Pennink-Clous, M. D., Amstelzijde 33, 1191 LK Ouder-
kerk a.d. Amstel. T. (020) 4963198. - Ant /
Cur - *061505*

Poederooijen (Gelderland)

Oude Veerhuis, 't, Maasdijk 90, 5307 TD
Poederooijen. *061506*

Poortugaal (Zuid-Holland)

Romantiek, Breebartlaan 3, 3171 CC Poortugaal.
T. (010) 502585. *061507*

Purmerend (Noord-Holland)

Antiek Centrum Purmerend, Gedempte Singelgracht 17-
19, 1441 AN Purmerend. T. (0299) 426485. *061508*

Het Spitshuis de Grenen Neus, Ged Singelgracht 17,
1441 AN Purmerend. *061509*

Rijswijk (Zuid-Holland)

Bogaerde, Paulus, Passage C 26-27, 2280
Rijswijk. *061510*

Roermond (Limburg)

Berden, J. F., Veldstr 16, 6041 GS Roermond.
T. (0475) 314273. *061511*

Romunt, Roerzicht 1, 6041 XV Roermond.
T. (0475) 316010, 316910. - Num - *061512*

Walschot, Bakkerstr. 26, 6041 JR Roermond.
T. (0475) 317001. - Ant / Dec - *061513*

Wolters, J., Neerstr 11, 6041 KA Roermond.
T. (0475) 314038. *061514*

Roosendaal (Noord-Brabant)

Berting, A. J. M., Marconistr 3, 4702 SE Roosendaal.
T. (0165) 543517. *061515*

Meakk, Brugstr 1a, 4701 LA Roosendaal.
T. (0165) 542036. *061516*

Vier Wilgen, De, Biezenstr 1, 4703 SM Roosendaal.
T. (0165) 541453. *061517*

Witte Raaf, De, St Josephstr 55, 4702 CV Roosendaal.
T. (0165) 534470. *061518*

Rosmalen (Noord-Brabant)

Raad, Matthé de, Hintham 16, 5246 AG Rosmalen.
- Furn / China / Sculp / Glass - *061519*

Rotterdam (Zuid-Holland)

Abstract Raadsveld, Nieuwe Binnenweg 112, 3015 BE
Rotterdam. T. (010) 436 42 31. - Ant - *061520*

Ambiente, Straatweg 63, 3051 BD Rotterdam.
T. (010) 461 22 81. - Ant - *061521*

Anamorfosen, Oudedijk 62a, 3062 AE Rotterdam.
T. (010) 412 40 62. - Ant - *061522*

Antieke Schuit, De, Putsebocht 111, 3073 HE Rotterdam. T. (010) 484 74 69. *061523*

Antiekhal Kralingen, Goudesingel 44a-48a, 311 KC Rotterdam. T. (010) 433 07 17. - Ant - *061524*

Antiekstal, De, 's Gravenweg 639, 3065 SC Rotterdam.
T. (010) 412 11 91. *061525*

Antiquiteiten en Oude Kunst, Hoflaan 96, 3062 JK Rotterdam. T. (010) 411 06 63. - Ant / Instr / Cur - *061526*

Arabesque, Spoorsingel 55a, 3033 GH Rotterdam.
T. (010) 466 90 53. - Ant - *061527*

Ars Antiqua, Meent 73a, 3011 JE Rotterdam.
T. (010) 412 77 77. - Ant - *061528*

Arti, Adm. de Ruyterweg 30, 3031 AC Rotterdam.
T. (010) 412 97 94. - Ant - *061529*

Assumburgh, Nobelstr. 11B, 3039 SC Rotterdam.
T. (010) 467 92 18. - Ant - *061530*

Barendse, H., Nieuwe Binneweg 126a, 3015 BE Rotterdam. T. (010) 423 82 78. *061531*

Barometer, De, Bergweg 201-207, 3037 EJ Rotterdam. T. (010) 434 05 06, 467 76 58. - Ant / Furn - *061532*

Bon-Art, Zwart Janstr. 86, 3035 AW Rotterdam. T. (010) 467 02 27. - Ant - *061533*

Boogert van der Reyken, Wolle Foppenweg 89, 3069 LX Rotterdam. T. (010) 456 07 13. - Ant - *061534*

Boshart-de Leeuwe, E., Zaagmolendrift 6b, 3035 JA Rotterdam. T. (010) 465 62 80. *061535*

Bouclier, Le, Kleiweg 201B, 3051 SL Rotterdam. T. (010) 418 61 63. - Ant - *061536*

Brouwer, C.A., Koedoodstr. 66, 3089 ST Rotterdam. T. (010) 429 33 51. - Ant - *061537*

Butterfly, The, Zenostr. 184, 3076 AZ Rotterdam. T. (010) 419 46 11. - Ant - *061538*

Castendijk, C. P. A. & G. R., Mecklenburglaan 51, 3061 BD Rotterdam. T. (010) 413 89 37. - Paint / China - *061539*

Coolsingel, De, Coolsingel 87 c, 3012 AE Rotterdam. T. (010) 414 62 18. - Ant - *061540*

Czerwinski's Lijstenwinkel, Rodenrijselaan 19B, 3037 XB Rotterdam. T. (010) 466 73 06. - Ant - *061541*

Dam, W. van, Kellogpl 217, 3068 JH Rotterdam. T. (010) 420 65 82. *061542*

Degens, Beijerlandselaan 144, 3074 EP Rotterdam. T. (010) 419 30 21. - Ant - *061543*

Donderbus, De, Oostzeedk. Beneden 231A, 3061 VW Rotterdam. T. (010) 414 02 67. - Ant - *061544*

Dubbele Deur Antiek, De, Dreef 74, 3075 HC Rotterdam. T. (010) 432 20 74. *061545*

Eerden, Leo van der, Mauritsweg 55, 3012 JX Rotterdam. T. (010) 413 57 47. - Paint - *061546*

Erf't, Noordsingel 58, 3032 BG Rotterdam. T. (010) 467 27 00. - Ant - *061547*

Europoort, Bergweg 148A, 3036 BJ Rotterdam. T. (010) 466 02 44. - Num - *061548*

Extravaganza, Rodenryselaan 17B, 3037 XB Rotterdam. T. (010) 466 73 45. - Ant - *061549*

Flartvof, Nieuwe Binneweg 196, 3021 GK Rotterdam. T. (010) 477 97 23. - Ant - *061550*

Fritsch, J. S., Dordtselaan 144a, 3073 GM Rotterdam. T. (010) 484 85 59. *061551*

Galerie 2000, Westersingel 30, 3014 GR Rotterdam. T. (010) 436 30 18. - China / Sculp / Eth / Jew / Glass - *061552*

Gildehuis, 't, Zwart Janstr 108, 3035 AX Rotterdam. T. (010) 424 93 32. *061553*

Goosen, K., Hordijk 63, 3079 DE Rotterdam. T. (010) 419 05 53. *061554*

Graaf, J.A. van der, Zaagmolenstr. 116A, 3035 HH Rotterdam. T. (010) 466 32 85. - Ant - *061555*

Grenen Huis, Het, Bergweg 299-301, 3037 EN Rotterdam. T. (010) 467 81 82. - Ant - *061556*

Groenewoud, Adriaan, Aelbrechtskolk 3b, 3025 HA Rotterdam. T. (010) 425 80 11. - Furn - *061557*

Hillegersbergse Antiekhal, Straatweg 35, 3051 BC Rotterdam. T. (010) 418 48 25. *061558*

Hooga, Oudedijk 146A, 3061 AP Rotterdam. T. (010) 413 82 22. - Ant - *061559*

Kaleidoskoop, De, Beyerlandselaan 173, 3074 EH Rotterdam. T. (010) 486 60 75. - Ant - *061560*

Kandelaar, De, Van Cittersstr 72, 3022 LM Rotterdam. T. (010) 423 75 46. *061561*

Kats, F., Voorhaven 4, 3024 RM Rotterdam. T. (010) 4764475, Fax (010) 4772226. - Instr / Cur - *061562*

Keulsche Pot, In de, Overschiese Dorpsstr. 37, 3043 CN Rotterdam. T. (010) 415 89 63. - Ant - *061563*

Klarenbeek, M., Oude Binnenweg 102, 3012 JG Rotterdam. T. (010) 412 35 70. - Ant - *061564*

Klerk, D. de, Voorschoterlaan 139, 3062 KM Rotterdam. T. (010) 413 31 90. - Ant - *061565*

Koch, Gebr., Lynbaan 78, 3012 ER Rotterdam. T. (010) 413 59 92. - Ant / Sculp / Fra / Lights / Mil - *061566*

Kolé, K., Hoogstr. 26, 3011 PP Rotterdam. T. (010) 413 09 75. - Ant - *061567*

Koopman, B.B., Zweedsestr. 141, 3028 TS Rotterdam. T. (010) 425 80 11. *061568*

Kooy, Henk van, Aelbrechtskolk 10, 3024 RE Rotterdam. T. (010) 476 97 24. - Glass - *061569*

Kreft, Hans, Mathenesserlaan 195, 3014 HB Rotterdam. T. (010) 436 15 29. - Instr - *061570*

Kuijpers, Dirck, Havenstr 11, 3024 SE Rotterdam. T. (010) 476 46 26. *061571*

Kunstkabinett, Havenstr. 11, 3024 SE Rotterdam. T. (010) 476 46 26. - Ant - *061572*

Langstraat, W. P., Maurltsweg 54a, 3012 JX Rotterdam. T. (010) 412 88 14. *061573*

Liberty, Meent 58, 3011 JM Rotterdam. T. (010) 411 06 76. - Ant - *061574*

Lorijn, J.M.A., Putselaan 146, 3074 JH Rotterdam. T. (010) 485 54 12. - Num - *061575*

Martin, Hoogstr 72, 3011 PT Rotterdam. T. (010) 413 00 44. *061576*

Mastrigt, J. van, Botersloot 18-20, 3011 HG Rotterdam. T. (010) 414 35 80. - Num - *061577*

Nieuwe Giessen, Av. Concordia 136, 3062 LP Rotterdam. T. (010) 413 80 75. - Ant - *061578*

Nieuwkoop, C. L. van, Mauritsweg 54a, 3012 JX Rotterdam. T. (010) 412 88 14. - Ant - *061579*

Nostalgia, F. Rujsstr. 22D, 3061 ME Rotterdam. T. (010) 452 04 78. - Ant - *061580*

Old Curiosity Shop, Bergse Dorpsstr. 42 A, 3054 GE Rotterdam. T. (010) 418 60 44. - Ant - *061581*

Oudedijk, D', Oudedijk 194, 3061 AS Rotterdam. T. (010) 414 20 00. - Ant - *061582*

Overschie Kunsthandel, Overschiese Dorpsstr. 34, 3043 CS Rotterdam. T. (010) 462 48 72. - Ant - *061583*

Peeters, Groene Hilledijk 167 A, 3073 AB Rotterdam. T. (010) 484 77 76. - Ant - *061584*

Quay Gallery, Schiedamseweg 119-121, 3026 AG Rotterdam. T. (010) 476 76 80. *061585*

Relakado, Groene Hilledijk 253 A, 3073 AJ Rotterdam. T. (010) 486 58 56. - Ant - *061586*

Rodenburg, K., Mauritsweg 54, 3012 JX Rotterdam. T. (010) 412 12 68. - Ant - *061587*

Rotterdamse Antikhallen, De, Bergweg 196, 3035 BM Rotterdam. T. (010) 466 69 30. - Ant - *061588*

Schouw, De, Statenlaan 45, 3051 HL Rotterdam. T. (010) 422 22 00. - Ant - *061589*

Select, Overschiese Dorpsstr. 54, 3043 CS Rotterdam. T. (010) 462 70 33. - Ant - *061590*

Siepman, Putsebocht 45-47-49, 3073 HD Rotterdam. T. (010) 485 54 63. - Ant - *061591*

Sierantuur, Proveniersstr. 70B, 3033 CN Rotterdam. T. (010) 465 54 11. - Ant - *061592*

Smit, J.T., Crooswijkseboocht 75, 3034 NC Rotterdam. T. (010) 412 58 25. - Ant - *061593*

Snuifdoos, De, Bergweg 128, 3036 BH Rotterdam. T. (010) 467 25 98. - Ant - *061594*

Stalco, Geyssendorfferweg 5-15, 3088 GJ Rotterdam. T. (010) 429 00 71. *061595*

't Prentenkabinet, Oostzeedijk 350, 3063 CD Rotterdam. T. (010) 411 11 93, 420 77 27. - Graph - *061596*

Tiffany Works, Witte de Withstr 41b, 3012 BM Rotterdam. *061597*

Twietwintig, Botersloot 42A, 3011 HH Rotterdam. T. (010) 413 21 94. - Ant - *061598*

Veiling, Mira, Stationsplein 45 Postbus 29040, 3001 GA Rotterdam Postbus 29040. T. (010) 433 02 38. - Num - *061599*

Vellinga, G.J., Bergse Dorpsstr. 132, 3054 GH Rotterdam. T. (010) 418 13 25. - Ant - *061600*

Ven, G.W.H. van de, Dorpsweg 72A, 3083 LD Rotterdam. T. (010) 480 01 78. - Ant - *061601*

Waag, A. H. van der, Overschiese Dorpsstr 39b, 3043 CN Rotterdam. T. (010) 415 30 45. *061602*

Waag, De, Spoorsingel 67a, 3033 GJ Rotterdam. T. (010) 428 68 23. - Ant / Dec - *061603*

Waning, Jan J. van, Westersingel 35, 3014 GS Rotterdam. T. (010) 436 01 98. - Ant - *061604*

Wapen van Delfshaven, Het, Albrechtskolk 55, 3025 HB Rotterdam. T. (010) 476 05 55. *061605*

Wemmers, Dirk, Lange Welle 66, 3075 XW Rotterdam. T. (010) 432 46 94. - Glass / China - *061606*

Wendingen, Bajonetstr. 49, 3014 ZC Rotterdam. T. (010) 436 65 26. - Ant - *061607*

Wolf, K.M. van der, Cl de Vrieselaan 12, 3021 JN Rotterdam. T. (010) 425 86 26. *061608*

Ruurlo (Gelderland)

Meulenbroek-Hoolsema, J., Barchemseweg 51, 7261 DB Ruurlo. T. (0573) 451567. *061609*

Santpoort (Noord-Holland)

Kastanjeloot, Wstelaan 32, 2071 KR Santpoort. T. (023) 5378135. *061610*

Petite Fleur, Hoofdstr 202, 2071 EN Santpoort. T. (023) 5375097. *061611*

Santpoort, Overbiltweg 35, 2071 XM Santpoort. T. (023) 56282. *061612*

Sassenheim (Zeeland)

Kengen, Charles, Rijksstraatweg 75, 2171 AK Sassenheim. T. (0252) 214682. - Furn - *061613*

Schiedam (Zuid-Holland)

Bijl, Simon, A., Boterstr 2, 3111 NC Schiedam. T. (010) 426 22 42. *061614*

Hoeven, van der, Lorentzplein 12a, 3112 KS Schiedam. *061615*

Plantage, De, Lange Nieuwestr 171, 3111 AJ Schiedam. *061616*

Verhal, E. H., De Wildestr 5, 3119 PK Schiedam. *061617*

Schipluiden (Zuid-Holland)

Konstkabinet, Vlaardingsekade 57, 2636 BD Schipluiden. T. (015) 3808311. - Ant - *061618*

Schoonhoven (Zuid-Holland)

Antiquax Holland, Voorhaven 2-4, 2871 CJ Schoonhoven. T. (0182) 33840, 34035. *061619*

Schoonhovense Antiekhandel, Voorhaven 19, 2871 CH Schoonhoven. T. (0182) 32534. *061620*

Sint Michielsgestel (Noord-Brabant)

Pijnenburg-Vink, A. C., De Ruwenbergstr 12-14, 5271 AG Sint Michielsgestel. *061621*

Witte Boerderij, De, Hezelaar 2, 5271 SK Sint Michielsgestel. T. (073) 5512778. *061622*

Sneek (Friesland)

Dijkstra, Nauwe, Nauwe Noorderhorn 21, 8601 CX Sneek. *061623*

Roosjen, R., Gabbemastr 34, 8602 VD Sneek. *061624*

Westerhof, J.B., Hoogend 18, 8601 AE Sneek. T. (0515) 417198. - Num - *061625*

Soest (Utrecht)

Doofpot, De, Koninginnelaan 99, 3762 DC Soest. *061626*

Leuveren, van, Koninginnelaan 152, 3762 DK Soest. *061627*

Meurer, P. K., Talmalaan 33, 3761 AL Soest. *061628*

Staphorst (Overijssel)

Talen, G., Gemeenteweg 220, 7951 CV Staphorst. *061629*

Weerd, H. de, Gemeenteweg 90, 7951 CP Staphorst. *061630*

Swalmen (Limburg)

Pot, Nicolaas A. M., Rijksweg Zuid 32, 6071 HW Swalmen. T. (0475) 501965. - Ant / Furn / China / Jew / Silv / Instr - *061631*

Teteringen (Noord-Brabant)

Crijns & Stender, Tilburgsebaan 1, 4847 NM Teteringen. T. (076) 5875700, Fax 5877776. - Instr - *061632*

Tilburg (Noord-Brabant)

Galerie Aquarius, Postbus 10415, 5000 JK Tilburg. T. (013) 5421792. - Ant / Furn / China / Sculp - *061633*

Lampke, 't, Stevenzandsestr 23, 5021 HA Tilburg. T. (013) 5430510. *061634*

Spijkers, Berdijksestr 61, 5025 VD Tilburg. T. (013) 5422197. *061635*

Ulestraten (Limburg)

Rococo, Groot-Bergheim 61, 6235 BK Ulestraten, Post Meerssen. T. (043) 3643325. *061636*

Utrecht

Achter de Dom, Achter de Dom 6, 3512 JP Utrecht. T. (030) 2334773. - Ant - *061637*

Antique Centre de Ossekop, Voorstr. 19, 3512 AH Utrecht. T. (030) 2315756. - Ant - *061638*

Blauwe Kater, De, Klintgenshaven 1, 3512 GX Utrecht. T. (030) 2319013. - Furn / Cur - *061639*

Bunnik, Hoogravenseweg 24, 3523 TL Utrecht.
T. (030) 2892356. - Ant - 061640
Bylsma, Henk, Merwedekade 132bis, 3522 JA
Utrecht. 061641
Couwenbergh, Nachtegaalstr. 48, 3581 AK Utrecht.
T. (030) 2310283. - Ant - 061642
Daalhuizen, J. M., Julianaweg 60, 3525 VH Utrecht.
T. (030) 2883154. 061643
Daatselaar & Godhelp, Korte Jansstr. 17-19, 3512 GM
Utrecht. T. (030) 2318266, Fax 2316474.
- Ant - 061644
Doesburg, J., Bem. Weerd Osstzijde 55-56, 3514 ASD
Utrecht. T. (030) 2711821. - Furn - 061645
Eisendoorn, E., Lepelaarstr. 25, 3582 SL Utrecht.
T. (030) 2319612. 061646
Forger, J. H. C., Voorstr 34, 3512 AP Utrecht.
T. (030) 231186. 061647
Gieling, Marcel, Weerdsingel Oostzijde 37, 3514 AC Ut-
recht. T. (030) 2734661. - Ant - 061648
Groot, A.W.J. de, Lichte Gaard 6, 3511 KT Utrecht.
T. (030) 2319252. - Ant - 061649
Haasnoot, N., Teelingstr. 10, 3512 GV Utrecht.
T. (030) 2313505. - Ant - 061650
Haffmans, F. J., Hoogravenseweg 22-24, 3523 TL Ut-
recht. T. (030) 2892356. - Furn / Num / Instr - 061651
Harder, P., Voorstr. 30, 3512 AN Utrecht.
T. (030) 2314259. - nat - 061652
Hofpoort Grenen, Voorstr. 21, 3512 AH Utrecht.
T. (030) 2319482. - Furn / Lights - 061653
HS Goud Zilver, Springweg 18, 3511 VP Utrecht.
T. (030) 2341631. - Num - 061654
Interior Consultants, Oudegracht 295, 3511 PA Utrecht.
T. (030) 2312001. - Furn / Orient / Tex - 061655
Jurcka, Smeestr 3, 1251 RN Utrecht.
T. (030) 2315454. 061656
Kleijn, Ludy, Boterstr. 15, 3511 LZ Utrecht.
T. (030) 2317127. - Ant - 061657
Kleinjan, W., Vismarkt 17, 3511 KS Utrecht.
T. (030) 2310069. - Ant - 061658
Kleinjan, W., Herenstr. 21, 3512 KA Utrecht.
T. (030) 2317235. - Ant - 061659
Kleyn, F., Oudkerkhof 38, 3512 GL Utrecht.
T. (030) 2310856. - Ant / Paint / Sculp - 061660
Krijnen, J. W. H., Nobelstr 20, 3512 EP Utrecht.
T. (030) 2316019. 061661
Lisman, G. A., Vismarkt 10, 3511 KR Utrecht.
T. (030) 2312835. - Ant / Furn / China / Glass - 061662
Marinus, L. Nieuwstr. 75, 3512 PE Utrecht.
T. (030) 2317347. - Furn / Lights - 061663
Meeuwen, van, Oudkerkhof 7, 3512 GH Utrecht.
T. (030) 2316119. 061664
Meissie, L. Smeestr. 7, 3511 PS Utrecht.
T. (030) 2367720. - Ant - 061665
Mennink, L. J., Schoutenstr 4, 3512 GB Utrecht.
T. (030) 2315371. 061666
Neos, Hartingstr. 16a, 3511 HV Utrecht.
T. (030) 2317338. - Ant - 061667
Nouveau Art, Zadelstr. 37, 3511 LS Utrecht.
T. (030) 2328878. - Mod - 061668
Old-Pine-Store, Oudegracht 288, 3511 NW Utrecht.
T. (030) 2340066. - Ant - 061669
Olthoff, P.A., Prinsenstr. 22, 3581 JS Utrecht.
T. (030) 2517569. - Ant - 061670
Oog Kunst & Antiekhandel, Het, Voorstr. 43, 3512 AJ Ut-
recht. T. (030) 2318609. - Ant - 061671
Oort Logerij, Van, Vlampijpstr. 55, 3534 AR Utrecht.
T. (030) 2441671. - Ant - 061672
Oud Holland, Vismarkt 8, 3511 KR Utrecht.
T. (030) 2313179. - Ant - 061673
Oude Dingenhuis, Het, Oudegracht 405, 3511 PH Ut-
recht. T. (030) 2319252. 061674
Oude Pijpenlade, De, Oude Gracht 199, 3511 NG Ut-
recht. T. (030) 2311464. - Ant / Furn / Dec / Cur /
Ico - 061675
Overbeek, Oudegracht 90, 3511 AV Utrecht.
T. (030) 2322108. - Paint - 061676
Palet, Mariastr. 36, 3511 LP Utrecht. T. (030) 2317333.
- Paint - 061677
Petilion, Lichte Gaard 5, 3511 KT Utrecht.
T. (030) 2310843. - Ant - 061678
Petit Boyeau, Le, Korte Smeestr. 10, 3512 NX Utrecht.
T. (030) 2310759. 061679

Rijks Munt, Leidseweg 90, 3531 BG Utrecht.
T. (030) 2910342. - Num - 061680
Rijn, Van, Oudegracht 90, 3511 AV Utrecht.
T. (030) 2312080. - Ant - 061681
Royal Art, Livingstonelaan 104, 3526 HP Utrecht.
T. (030) 2889111. - Ant - 061682
Schoonheim, Vinkenburgstr. 3, 3512 AA Utrecht.
T. (030) 2312136. - Ant - 061683
Seelig, Ternatestr. 5, 3531 RW Utrecht.
T. (030) 2948660. 061684
Sint Maarten, Oud Kerkhof 33, 3512 GJ Utrecht.
T. (030) 2318975. - Ant - 061685
Soeten, F. de, Lichte Gaard 5, 3511 KT Utrecht.
T. (030) 2313626. 061686
Studio 73, Bermuurde Weerd Oostzijde 73, 3514 AT Ut-
recht. T. (030) 2719777. - Ant - 061687
Swatow, H. Graaflandstr. 167, 3525 VS Utrecht.
T. (030) 2870090. - nat - 061688
Trajectum, Croeselaan 249, 3521 BR Utrecht.
T. (030) 2949709. - Num - 061689
Walsemann, Carel, Ganzenmarkt 30, 3512 GE Utrecht.
T. (030) 2311253. - Ant / Furn - 061690
Wezel, van, Biltstr. 20, 3572 BB Utrecht.
T. (030) 2717113. - Ant - 061691
Zalm, S. A. van der, Ooftstr. 25, 3572 HR Utrecht.
T. (030) 2712842. 061692

Valkenswaard (Noord-Brabant)
Bekelaar, M., Ooistr. 1, 5555 KB Valkenswaard.
T. (040) 2042499. 061693
Brangers, Beelmanstr. 5, 5554 CJ Valkenswaard.
T. (040) 2043390. 061694

Veldhoven (Noord-Brabant)
Dücker, J., Dorpsstr. 120, 5504 HL Veldhoven.
T. (040) 2534290. - Furn - 061695

Velp (Gelderland)
Becker, H.P.C., Hoofdstr. 22, 6881 TJ Velp.
T. (026) 3613987. - Ant / Dec - 061696

Venlo (Limburg)
Knippenberg, L. van, Straelseweg 566-568, 5916 AD
Venlo. T. (077) 315936. - Ant / Dec - 061697
Linssen, Roermondsestr. 25, 5912 AH Venlo.
T. (077) 3540707. - Ant / Dec - 061698
Linssen, P.H.A., Parade 15, 5911 CA Venlo.
T. (077) 3544032. - Ant - 061699

Vinkeveen (Utrecht)
Buying, Hillegonda, Donkereind 11, 3645 TC
Vinkeveen. 061700

Vlaardingen (Zuid-Holland)
Antiekzolder, 't, Westhavenkade 58, 3131 AG Vlaardin-
gen. - Ant / Furn / Glass / Cur - 061701
Boer, J. W., Van Hogendorpplein 214, 3135 CM
Vlaardingen. 061702
Bolderheij, J. J., Hoogstr. 99, 3131 BM Vlaardingen.
T. (010) 434 99 90. 061703
Bot, G. P, Smalle Havenstr. 21, 3131 BS
Vlaardingen. 061704
Groen, J. W., Smalle Havenstr. 13, 3131 BS
Vlaardingen. 061705
Thomas & de Wee, Hoogstr. 37, 3131 BL Vlaardingen.
T. (010) 5916518. 061706
Vogel, Westhavenplaats 8, 3131 BT
Vlaardingen. 061707
Wapen van Holland, Westhavenkade 69, 3131 AG
Vlaardingen. 061708

Vlissingen (Zeeland)
Dalen, van, Palingstr. 18, 4381 AG Vlissingen. 061709

Voorburg (Zuid-Holland)
Melse-Vahrenkamp, Pompe-van-Meerdervoortstr. 4,
2274 PR Voorburg. - Ant / Dec - 061710

Voorschoten (Zuid-Holland)
Laurentius, Th., Orangerie Duivenvoorde, 2252 AK Voor-
schoten. - Paint / Graph - 061711

Waalre (Noord-Brabant)
Schäfer, Eindhovenseweg 44, 5582 HT Waalre. - Ant /
Instr - 061712

Wageningen (Gelderland)
Bohmer, A., Lawickse Allee 112, 6707 AN Wageningen.
T. (0317) 411218. 061713
Nije, Ohe, Hoogstr. 42, 6701 BW Wageningen.
T. (0317) 415529. 061714

Warmenhuizen (Noord-Holland)
Soest, Arthur van, De Baan 1, 1749 VR Warmenhuizen.
T. (0226) 393900. - Graph - 061715

Warnsveld (Gelderland)
Helm, P. van der, Rijksstraatweg 162, 7231 AL Warn-
sveld. T. (0575) 512661. - Ant - 061716

Wassenaar (Zuid-Holland)
Fischer, F. J. T., & Zn., Luifelbaan 48, 2242 KV Wasse-
naar. T. (070) 5112648. - Ant / Furn / Cur - 061717
Metz, Loekie, Zijdeweg 33, 2244 BD Wassenaar.
T. (070) 5177732. - Num - 061718
Smith, Leslie, Hertelaan 15, 2243 EK Wassenaar.
T. (070) 5179079. - Paint - 061719
't Oude Kabinet, Langstr. 93, 2242 KP Wassenaar.
T. (070) 5115932. 061720

Weert (Limburg)
Werz, Eloy, Oelemarkt 12, 6001 ES Weert.
T. (0495) 532218. - Ant / Dec - 061721

Westerbork (Drenthe)
Klomp, L., Hoofdstr. 42-44, 9431 AE
Westerbork. 061722

Wijchen (Gelderland)
Uilenhof, De, Valendrieseweg 82, 6603 AD
Wijchen. 061723

Willemsoord (Overijssel)
Kok, B., Steenwijkerweg 214, 8338
Willemsoord. 061724

Winschoten (Groningen)
Waslander, J., Venne 137, 9671 ER Winschoten. 061725

Woerden (Zuid-Holland)
Buysert, J.C., Haven 13, 3441 AS Woerden. 061726
Romantica, Voorstr. 1, 3441 CA Woerden. 061727
Speerstra, Sierkersstr. 5, 3442 GR Woerden. 061728

Wormerveer (Noord-Holland)
H.P.V. Antieke Verlichtings Groothandel, Wandelweg 44-
46, 1521 AH Wormerveer. T. (075) 66216373. 061729

Zaandam (Noord-Holland)
Het Spitshuis de Grenen Neus, Westzijde 136, 1506 EK
Zaandam. T. (075) 6163545. 061730
Jagershuis, Zeilenmakerspad 2, 1509 BZ Zaandam.
T. (075) 6168886. 061731
Kliffen, R.J., Stationsstr. 91, 1506 DE Zaandam.
T. (075) 6162685. 061732
Spits, Albert, Westzijde 125b, 1506 GB Zaandam.
T. (075) 6175287. 061733
Takkenberg, M., Botenmakersstr. 115, 1506 TC Zaan-
dam. T. (075) 6163078. 061734

Zandvoort (Noord-Holland)
Kion, H. J. Bob, Haltestr. 75-77, 2042 LL Zandvoort.
- Ant / Paint / Furn / China / Tex / Silv / Mil / Cur - 061735
Koremans, Hermine, Cort v.d. Lindenstr. 26, 2042 CB
Zandvoort. 061736
Oude Tijd, De, Oranjestraat 2a, 2042 GS Zandvoort.
T. (023) 57242472. - Ant / Dec - 061737

Zeist (Utrecht)
Becker, Gebr., Oude Arnhemseweg 16, 3702 BE Zeist.
T. (030) 6917425. - Furn / China / Glass - 061738
Becker, Gebr., Eerste Hogeweg 22, 3701 HL Zeist.
T. (030) 6913620. - Furn / China / Glass - 061739
Becker, J. H. Hendr. Zn., Tweede Hogeweg 119, 3701
AX Zeist. T. (030) 6912776. - Ant - 061740
Hoevelaak & Zn., van, Erste Dorpsstr. 10, 3701 HB Zeist.
T. (030) 6913230. 061741
Ikonen-Galerie, Slotlaan 128, 3701 GR Zeist.
T. (030) 6923285. - Ico - 061742

Zierikzee (Zeeland)
Burgerweeshuis, Poststr. 45, 4301 AB Zierikzee.
T. (0111) 412683. - Ant / Paint / China / Sculp / Jew /
Cur - *061743*

Zundert (Noord-Brabant)
Galerij Ria, Molenstr. 45, 4881 CP Zundert.
T. (076) 5971849. *061744*

Zutphen (Gelderland)
Het Oude Geveltje, Nieuwstad 36, 7201 NR Zutphen.
T. (0575) 516601. *061745*
Hof van Flodorf, Halterstr. 22, 7201 MX Zutphen.
T. (0575) 514021. *061746*
Ott, J.B.A.M., Zaadmarkt 76, 7201 KM Zutphen.
T. (0575) 518100, Fax 543897. - Furn / Orient / China /
Glass - *061747*
Turfje, Turfstraat 10, 7201 KG Zutphen.
T. (0575) 515807. - Ant / Paint / Sculp / Sculp /
Eth - *061748*
Veterman, B., Warnsveldseweg 56, 7204 BE Zutphen.
T. (0575) 513054. *061749*

Zwijndrecht (Zuid-Holland)
Antiekkooi, Ringdijk 386, 3331 LK Zwijndrecht.
T. (078) 6126815. - Ant / Furn / Tex / Silv / Instr / Tin /
Toys - *061750*

Zwolle (Overijssel)
Kate, E. ten, Gombertstr. 112, 8031 MC Zwolle.
T. (038) 415759. *061751*
Ruitenberg, J., Spoorstr. 1-3, 8012 AV Zwolle.
T. (038) 4213687. - Furn / China / Glass - *061752*
Stibbe, D., Luttekstr. 19, 8011 LN Zwolle.
T. (038) 411412. - Ant / Furn / China / Jew /
Silv - *061753*

New Zealand

Auckland
New Zealand Antique Dealers Association, 99 Shortland
St., Auckland. T. (09) 734 3251. *061756*

Auckland (Auckland)
Cooke, David, 99 Shortland St., Auckland.
T. (09) 73 43 25. - Ant / Paint / Furn / China / Tex /
Silv - *061757*
Dixon, John, 488 Remuera Rd., Auckland.
T. (09) 50 26 03. - Ant - *061758*

Wellington
Willeston, Level 2, AA Centre Lambton Quay, Wellington,
GPOB 736. T. (04) 730 664. - Paint / Graph / Repr /
Fra - *061759*

Westmere (Auckland)
Antiquities Consultants, 32 Rawene Av., Westmere.
T. (0649) 360 21 45. *061760*

Nicaragua

Managua
Exclusivas Europeas, Apartado 1626, Managua. - Ant /
Paint / Furn / Sculp - *061761*

Norway

Bergen
Bryggen Brukthandel, Bredsgarden 2, Bryggen, 5000
Bergen. *061762*
Kunst, Torvalm. 9, 5000 Bergen. - Ant - *061763*
Prydkunst, Torgalm. 8, 5000 Bergen. - Ant - *061764*
Skjensvold, Veiten 4, 5000 Bergen. - Ant - *061765*

Fevik
Brukthandek-Antik, E. W. Tollefsen, 4870 Fevik.
T. 37047555. *061766*
Tollefsen, E. W., 4870 Fevik. T. 37147555. *061767*

Fredrikstad
Galerie Antique, Villa Glommen, 1600 Fredrikstad.
- Ant / Furn / Silv - *061768*

Halden
Dahle, Villa Antique, Svinesund, 1750 Halden.
T. 94395190. - Ant / Cur - *061769*
Kuriosa, Storgt. 18, 1750 Halden. I. 94385050. *061770*

Oslo
Anno 87-Brukt-Antik, Wm. Thranes G. 65b, 0173 Oslo.
T. 22 38 40 09. - Ant - *061771*
Antik-Brukt Markedet, Trondheimsv. 13, 0560 Oslo.
T. 22 67 61 02. - Ant - *061772*
Antik U-12, Uranienborgv. 12, 0258 Oslo. T. 22 43 08 60.
- Ant - *061773*
Antik 7, Majorstuv. 35, 0367 Oslo.
T. 22 69 88 75. *061774*
Antikboden, Fredensborgv. 17, 0177 Oslo.
T. 22 42 64 78. - Ant - *061775*
Antikfunn, Wilhelmsg. 2, 0168 Oslo. T. 22 60 38 41.
- Ant - *061776*
Antikkhuset, Grefsenv. 6, Box 4433 Torshov, 0403 Oslo.
T. 22 15 39 80, Fax 22 22 51 14. *061777*
Antiqua, Wilhelmsg. 4, 0168 Oslo. T. 22 46 10 04.
- Ant - *061778*
Antique, Mandalls G. 4, 0190 Oslo. T. 22 68 28 21.
- Ant - *061779*
Antique Plus, Hovseterv. 86a, 0768 Oslo. T. 22 14 94 82.
- Ant - *061780*
BA 47 Antikviteter, Bygdøy Allé 47, 0265 Oslo.
T. 22 44 25 09. - Ant - *061781*
Beka Antik, Grønlandsleiret 5, 0190 Oslo. T. 22 68 82 38.
- Ant - *061782*
Berntsen, Kaare, Universitetsgt. 12, 0164 Oslo.
T. 22 20 34 29, Fax 22 11 01 08. - Ant / Furn - *061783*
Bestefars Ly & Løsøre, Huitfeldts G. 36, 0253 Oslo.
T. 22 83 05 21. - Ant - *061784*
Blomqvist, Tordenskioldsgt. 5, 0160 Oslo.
T. 22 41 26 31. - Ant / Paint / Tex - *061785*
Bolin, Kari M., Cam Colletts V. 5, 0258 Oslo.
T. 22 43 42 36. - Ant - *061786*
Captain's Cabin, Hier Heyerdahlsg. 1, Oslo.
T. 22 41 88 71. - Ant - *061787*
Centrum Fornikling, Storg. 51, 0182 Oslo.
T. 22 20 48 41. - Ant - *061788*
City Auksjon, Kont. Maserud Allé 23, 0268 Oslo.
T. 22 44 99 91. - Ant - *061789*
Damm, Tollbug 25, 0157 Oslo. T. 22 41 04 02,
22 33 66 15. - Ant - *061790*
Enhjørningen, Skovvn. 12, 0257 Oslo. T. 22 44 00 45.
- Ant - *061791*
Eventyrhuset, Banksjet Frølichs G. 2c, 0454 Oslo.
T. 22 60 75 28. - Ant - *061792*
Fryd & Pryd, Trondheimsv. 13, 0560 Oslo.
T. 22 68 55 46. *061793*
Galleri Nordstrand, Nordstrandv. 36, 1163 Oslo.
T. 22 28 79 27. - Ant - *061794*
Gamlesmia, Maridalsv. 293b, Oslo. T. 22 23 10 77.
- Ant - *061795*
Gamlestua, Frognerv. 4, 0257 Oslo. T. 22 44 05 09.
- Ant - *061796*
Gammel & Rart, Colbjørnsens G. 14, 0256 Oslo.
T. 22 44 40 62. - Ant - *061797*
Gard, Schønings G. 7, 0356 Oslo. T. 22 69 44 83.
- Ant - *061798*
Gyldenløve, Niels Juels G. 5, 0272 Oslo. T. 22 43 44 22.
- Ant - *061799*
Hammerlunds Kunsthandel, Tordenskioldsgt. 3, 0160
Oslo. T. 22 42 36 26, 22 41 27 44. - Ant / Paint / Paint /
Graph / Furn / Sculp / Silv / Glass - *061800*
Hesteskoen, Grønlandsleiret 55, 0190 Oslo.
T. 22 67 44 30. - Ant - *061801*
Lille Antik, Åse Sørli Skovv. 7, 0257 Oslo. T. 22 44 36 92.
- Ant - *061802*
Loftet, President Harbitz G. 25, 0259 Oslo.
T. 22 44 45 66. - Ant - *061803*
London Bridge Trading, Skovv. 13, 0257 Oslo.
T. 22 44 67 34. - Ant - *061804*
Markveien Brukthandel, Markv. 58, 0550 Oslo.
T. 22 39 02 90, 22 71 51 43. *061805*
Mathisen, Bjørn, Maridalsv. 31, 0175 Oslo.
T. 22 36 24 27. - Ant - *061806*

Norges Kunst & Antikvitethandleres Forening, Universi-
tetsgaten 12, Oslo. T. 20 34 29. *061807*
Nostalgi, Prof. Dahls G. 39, 0353 Oslo. T. 22 55 15 72.
- Ant - *061808*
Ny York, Markv. 56c, 0550 Oslo. T. 22 37 38 33.
- Ant - *061809*
Oslo Marsjandise, Basarhallene, Dronningengs G. 27,
0154 Oslo. T. 22 42 41 08. - Ant - *061810*
Oslo Mynthandel, Kongensgate 31, 0101 Oslo.
T. 22 41 60 78, Fax 22 33 32 36. - Num - *061811*
Roggema, Chriss J., Neubergg. 6f, 0367 Oslo.
T. 22 43 02 87. - Ant - *061812*
Rønning, N.K., Oberst Rodes V. 42, 1152 Oslo.
T. 22 29 49 76. - Ant - *061813*
Samleren, Hegdehangsv. 14a, 0167 Oslo. T. 22 56 84 56.
- Ant - *061814*
Sirikit, Uranienborgv. 4, 0258 Oslo. T. 22 44 58 49.
- Ant - *061815*
Skattekisten Basarhallene, Dronningens G. 27, 0154 Os-
lo. T. 22 42 57 79. - Ant - *061816*
Skrapoteket, Bogstadv. 25, 0355 Oslo. T. 22 46 16 76.
- Ant - *061817*
Smith, Bjørn, Trondheimsv. 13, 0560 Oslo.
T. 22 67 61 02. *061818*
Solberg, Esaias, Dronningens G. 27, 0154 Oslo.
T. 22 41 63 49. - Ant - *061819*
Studio Hansteen, Drammensv. 4, 0010 Oslo.
T. 22 41 41 13, 22 42 70 63. - Ant - *061820*
Victoria & Albert, Kirkev. 77, 0364 Oslo. T. 22 46 89 57.
- Ant - *061821*
Vika Antikk, Løkkev. 11, 0253 Oslo. T. 22 44 12 48,
22 44 60 21. - Ant - *061822*
West Sølv. og Mynt, Niels Juels G. 27, 0257 Oslo.
T. 22 55 75 83. - Ant - *061823*

Skien (Telemark)
Eek, Marth., Lundegt. 2, 3700 Skien. T. 35523831.
- Ant - *061824*

Tønsberg
Ulving, Tore, Ö. Langgt. 18, 3100 Tønsberg.
T. 33313283. - Ant - *061825*

Tromsø
Maehle, Brødrene, & Ramme, Skippergt. 12, 9000 Trom-
sø. T. 77683562. *061826*
Tollefsen, Harald, Bispegt. 4, 9000 Tromsø.
T. 77683532. - Ant / Furn - *061827*

Peru

Lima
Art Center Shop, Alameda Ricardo Palma 246 Miraflo-
res, Lima. T. 25 60 97, 45 94 11. - Ant / Paint / Tex /
Eth - *061828*

Philippines

Makati
Cappricci Jewelers and Goldsmith, Ayala Center, Makati.
T. (02) 8186031. *061829*
Katutubo, Ayala Center, Makati. T. (02) 8186031. *061830*
Luz Gallery, Makati Av. L.V. Locsin Bldg., Makati.
T. (02) 8156906. *061831*
Osmundo Antique Gallery, Ayala Center, Makati.
T. (02) 8174891. *061832*

Manila
Banzon Antiques, 1219 A.Mabani St, Manila.
T. 591691. *061833*
Decorall-Antique and Thrift Shop, Mercedes Benz Lane,
Virra Mall Shopping Center, Manila.
T. (02) 963012. *061834*
Emperor Arts and Antiques, Harrison Plaza, Vito Cruz St,
Ermita, Manila. T. (02) 5217481. - Ant - *061835*
Kabul Antique Center, Harrison Plaza, Vito Cruz St, Ermi-
ta, Manila. T. (02) 572960. *061836*
Likha Antiques and Crafts Inc., 1415 A. Mabini Street,
Ermita, Manila. T. (02) 588125. *061837*

Nice Twice Thrift Shop, Tindalo Lane 2/F, Virra Mal-
lShopping Center, Manila. T. (02) 795230.   061838
Recuerdos de Bacolod Arts and Antiques, 55 Padre Fau-
ra Mall, 472 P. Faura St, Manila.
T. (02) 57206175.   061839
Terry's Antiques, 1401 A.Mabini St, Manila.
T. (02) 588020.   061840
Via Antica, 1411 A.Mabani St, Manila.
T. (02) 591234.   061841

Pasay
Galerias Bravo, NAIA Departure Area, Pasay.
T. (02) 8317974.   061842
Galleon Shop, Phillipine Plaza, CCP Complex, Pasay.
T. (02) 8320701.   061843

Quezon City
Arts and Antiques Phils, 7812 St, Quezon City.
T. (02) 702175.   061844
Bravo, 192-194 Tomas B. Morato Av, Quezon City.
T. (02) 985441.   061845
Josephine's, Ali Mall, Cubao, Quezon City.
T. (02) 9215187.   061846

Poland

Bydgoszcz
Salon Sztuki DESA, P. Zjednoczenia 2, 85-006 Bydgoszcz. - Ant -   061847

Częstochowa
Antykwariat i Salon Sztuki Współczesnej, ul. Szymanow-
skiego 1, 42-200 Częstochowa.   061848

Gdańsk
Antykwariat, ul Długa 2, 80-827 Gdańsk.
T. 31 59 68.   061849

Gdynia (Gdańsk)
Salon Sztuki Współczesnej, ul 22 Lipca 25, 81-395
Gdynia.   061850

Katowice
Antykwariat, ul Dworcowa 7, 40-012 Katowice.
- Ant -   061851
Salon Sztuki Współczesnej, ul Wieczorka 8, 40-013 Ka-
towice. - Ant -   061852

Kraków
Antykwariat, Rynek Glówny 43, 31-013 Kraków.   061853
Ars Christiana, Mały Rynek, 31-041 Kraków.   061854
Salon Sztuki DESA, Hynek Gł. 43, 31-013 Kraków.
- Ant / China / Tex / Jew / Silv / Lights / Instr -   061855
Salon Sztuki Współczesnej, ul. Św. Jana 3, 31-017 Kra-
ków. - Ant / Paint / Furn / Sculp -   061856

Łódź
Antykwariat i Salon Sztuki Współczesnej, ul. Piotrkowska 117, 90-430 Łódź. - Ant -   061857

Opole
Antykwariat i Salon Sztuki Współczesnej, ul 1 Maja 1,
45-068 Opole.   061858

Poznań
Antykwariat, ul Ratajczaka 35, 61-816 Poznań.
- Ant -   061859
Kruk, W., ul Pułaskiego 11, 60-607 Poznań.
T. (061) 5 08 10. - Num / Jew / Silv -   061860
Salon Sztuki DESA, Stary Rynek 48, 61-772 Poznań.
- Ant -   061861
Salon Sztuki Współczesnej, ul Czerwonej Armii 63, 61-
806 Poznań. - Ant -   061862

Szczecin
Antykwariat i Salon Plastyki Współczesnej, Pl Żołnierza
Polskiego, 70-551 Szczecin.   061863

Warszawa
Antykwariat DESA, ul Nowy Świat 51, 00-042 Warsza-
wa. T. (022) 27 47 60. - Paint / Furn / China /
Sculp -   061864
Antykwariat DESA, ul Nowy Świat 48, 00-363 Warsza-
wa. T. (022) 26 44 66. - Jew -   061865

Antykwariat DESA, ul Marszałkowska 34/50, 00-554
Warszawa. T. (022) 28 77 05. - Paint / Furn / China /
Tex / Silv -   061866
Antykwariat „Veritas", Pl. Trzech Krzyzy 18, 00-499
Warszawa. - Ant -   061867

Wrocław
Antykwariat i Salon Plastyki Wspolszesnej, Pl Kościuszki
16, 106 Wrocław.   061868

Portugal

Albergaria-a-Velha
Osseloa Antiguidades, 3850 Albergaria-a-Velha.
T. 521 52. - Ant -   061869

Alcobaca (Estremadura)
Casa Alcobaça, Praça D. Alfonso Henriques 6 e 7, 2460
Alcobaca. T. 424 08. - Ant / Paint / China / Sculp /
Mil -   061870
Casa Cisterciense, Frei Antonio Brandao 1, Alcobaca.
T. 421 61.   061871
Casa Cistericense, Rua Frei Antomio Brandao 1 3 5,
2460 Alcobaca. T. 421 61. - Ant / Furn / China / Instr /
Glass -   061872
Casa Trindade, Praça Dr. Oliveira Salazar 60, 2460 Alco-
baca. T. 422 43. - Ant / Paint / China / Instr /
Mil -   061873
Trindade, Antonio Pereira da, Rua da Trindade 15, 2460
Alcobaca. T. 32 46 60. - Ant / Instr / Rel -   061874
Trindade, Joao, Praca 25 Abril 59-60, 2460 Alcobaca.
T. 42534. - Furn / China / Instr / Glass -   061875

Alverca (Ribatejo)
Sociedade Luso-Oriental de Tapetes, Lda., Estrada da
Estaçao 56, 2615 Alverca. T. 25 88 42. - Ant /
Tex -   061876

Caldas da Rainha (Estremadura)
Soares de Oliveira, Jose, Rua Dr. Miguel Bombarda 21,
2500 Caldas da Rainha. T. 223 47. - Ant -   061877

Carcavelos
Cavaco, Av. Jorge V. 40, Carcavelos. T. (01) 247 04 23.
- Ant -   061878

Cascais (Estremadura)
Antico-Artes, Rua Afonso Sanches 36, 2750 Cascais.
T. (01) 28 09 34. - Ant -   061879
Antiguidades Rainer, Rua Federico Arouca 33A, 2750
Cascais. T. (01) 28 28 14. - Ant -   061880
Duarte, M. H., Rua Alexandre Herculano 19, 2750 Cas-
cais. T. (01) 284 16 88. - Furn -   061881
Ferro-Velho de Cascais, Av. José Frederico Arouca 33A,
2750 Cascais. T. (01) 28 28 14. - Ant -   061882
Lotos-Chinese Art Shop, Hotel Estoril Sol, Loja 9, 2750
Cascais. T. (01) 28 33 58. - Orient -   061883

Coimbra
Celso Franco, Jose, Rue Freitoria dos Linhos 46, 3000
Coimbra.   061884

Elvas (Alto Alentejo)
Cas Velha, Av. S. Domingos 614, 7350 Elvas.
- Ant -   061885

Entre-os-Rios
Casa Bodo, Lugar das Casas Novas, 4575 Entre-os-Rios.
T. (055) 60401. - Ant / Paint / Graph / Furn / China /
Sculp / Tex / Dec / Jew / Silv -   061886

Estoril
Antique Bernardo de Lencastre, Av. de Nice 8, 2765
Estoril. T. (01) 26 18 90. - Ant / Furn / Silv -   061887
Galeria Gauvin, Av. Saboia 25, 2765 Estoril.
T. (01) 26 01 06. - Ant -   061888
Gauvin, Av. Saboia 25, Estoril. T. (01) 26 01 06.   061889
Noelke, Raymund D., Rua Santa Rita 11, 2765 Estoril.
T. (01) 26 11 73. - Paint / China / Sculp -   061890

Evora (Alto Alentejo)
Proença, Gertrudes, Rua do Raimundo 77, 7000 Evora.
T. 222 75. - Ant -   061891

Funchal (Madeira)
Arte Antiga, Rua Escola Politécnica 22/24, 1200 Fun-
chal. - Paint / Furn / China / Dec -   061892
Caires, João Silvéro, Rue Fernão de Ornelas 56 A/B
Apartado 102, 9002 Funchal. T. 249 54. - Paint / Furn /
China -   061893
Chagas, Rua dos Ferreiros 113, 9000 Funchal.
T. 212 00.   061894
Franca, Julio Albuquerque, Rua Ivens 4, 9000 Funchal.
T. 204 00.   061895
Galerias Madeira, Rua Betencouth, 9000 Funchal.
T. 217 75. - Ant -   061896
Tapecarias da Madeira, Lda., Rua da Carreira 194, 9000
Funchal. T. 220 73. - Tex -   061897

Lagos (Algarve)
Casa do Papagaio, Rua Dr. Oliveira Salazar 27, 8600
Lagos.   061898

Lisboa
Adorno, Rua S. Bernardo 16, 1200 Lisboa.
T. (01) 66 69 55.   061899
Afra, Jaime, Rua Don Pedro V 49, 1200 Lisboa.
T. (01) 32 84 41. - Ant / Paint / Furn / Orient / China /
Sculp / Silv / Mil / Rel -   061900
Albuquerque & Sousa, Rua D. Pedro V 68-70, 1200 Lis-
boa. T. (01) 36 55 22. - Ant / Furn / China / Sculp /
Lights / Rel / Toys -   061901
Almeida e Sousa, Lda., Rua do Alecrim 54, 1200 Lisboa.
T. (01) 32 67 11. - Ant / Furn -   061902
Alvaro Matos Vide, Manuel, Rua das Praças 13A, 1200
Lisboa. T. (01) 84 26 14. - Ant -   061903
Alves Gama, Jose, Rua da Rosa 235 – 237, 1200 Lis-
boa. T. (01) 36 81 13. - Ant -   061904
Anacleto, Joaquim, Heliodoro Salgado 53 B, 1100 Lis-
boa. T. (01) 830614.   061905
Andrade Heredeira, Jeronimo de, Rua de S. Bento 52,
1200 Lisboa. T. (01) 67 15 89. - Ant -   061906
Antiqualia, Praça Luis de Camoes 37, 1200 Lisboa.
T. (01) 32 32 60.   061907
Antiqualia de Portugal Lda., Rua de D. Pedro V. 69 71,
1200 Lisboa. T. (01) 32 81 78. - Ant -   061908
Antiqualia Lda., Praça de L. Camoes 37 39, 1200 Lis-
boa. - China -   061909
Antiquario de S. Bento, Rua de S. Bento 79, 1200 Lis-
boa. T. (01) 67 64 28. - Furn / China / Cur -   061910
Antiquario do Principe Real, Rua D. Pedro V. 107, 1200
Lisboa. T. (01) 37 09 10. - Furn / Sculp -   061911
Antiquario do Ritz, Rua Rodrigo da Fonseca Hotel Ritz,
1200 Lisboa. T. (01) 65 23 91. - Ant -   061912
Antunes, Praça Dr. Nuno P. Torres 9, 1200 Lisboa.
T. (01) 70 60 41.   061913
Araujo, Maria de Lourdes, Rua Filipe Folque 36, 1000
Lisboa. T. (01) 41590.   061914
Atelier Teixeira Lopes, Rua Infantaria 16, 95, 1200 Lis-
boa. T. (01) 68 83 00. - Ant -   061915
Atrio, Rua das Chagas 17C, 1200 Lisboa.
T. (01) 36 87 08. - Ant / Paint / Furn / China / Repr / Dec /
Lights / Rel / Glass / Cur / Mod / Mul -   061916
Azevedo, Tv. St. Idefonso 4a, 1200 Lisboa.
I. (01) 66 72 87.   061917
Baptista, A.M. Salgueiro, Rua do Alecrim 85-89, 1200
Lisboa. T. (01) 362069. - Furn / China -   061918
Bazar de S. José, Rua de S. José 162, 1100 Lisboa.
T. (01) 334 16. - Ant / Paint / Graph / Furn /
China -   061919
Bazar Duque, Calçada do Duque 43A, 1200 Lisboa.
T. (01) 36 76 60. - Ant / Furn / China -   061920
Bazar Nobre Lda., Rua S. Bento 224 225, 1200 Lisboa.
T. (01) 66 11 27. - Ant -   061921
Belchior, Rua de Escola Politecnica 241, 1200 Lisboa.
T. (01) 68 58 88. - Ant -   061922
Biblarte Lda., R. Sao Pedro Alcântara 71, 1200 Lisboa.
T. (01) 36 37 02. - Ant / Paint / China -   061923
Bilbao e Adorno, Jesus, Rua da Horta Seca 1, 1200 Lis-
boa. T. (01) 32 01 60. - Ant / China -   061924
Borges, Jose, Rua Ponta Delgada 58, 1000 Lisboa.
T. (01) 517 00. - Ant -   061925
Bricabrauqe Mobrel Lda., Rua S. Bento 386/388, 1200
Lisboa. T. (01) 66 18 91. - Ant -   061926
Cabral Moncada, Isabel, Rua Dom Pedro V 34, 1200 Lis-
boa. T. (01) 36 82 95.   061927

Caires, João Silvério de, Av. Oscar Monteiro Torres 50/B, 1000 Lisboa. T. (01) 32 89 88. - Paint / Furn / China / Tex - *061928*

Candeias de Jesus, Victor, Rue D. Pedro V 44, 1200 Lisboa. T. (01) 37 30 72. *061929*

Canova, Rua do Alecrim 117-121, 1200 Lisboa. T. (01) 32 83 43. - Ant / Furn / China / Sculp - *061930*

Cardoso, Jose Maria, Rua S. Bento 257/259, 1200 Lisboa. T. (01) 66 75 16. - Ant / Furn - *061931*

Carvalho e Gil, Lda., Rua da Escola Politecnica 31 33, 1200 Lisboa. T. (01) 36 94 17. - Ant - *061932*

Carvalho e Raimundo, Lda., Rua de S. Bento 19, 1200 Lisboa. T. (01) 66 39 55. *061933*

Casa dos Bordados Central de Macau, Rua Ferreira Borges 96A, 1300 Lisboa. T. (01) 68 42 62. - Orient - *061934*

Casa dos Dourados, Tv. do Ferragial 12, 1200 Lisboa. T. (01) 32 86 69. - Ant - *061935*

Casa dos Tapetes de Arraiolos, Rua da Imprensa Nacional 116-E, 1200 Lisboa. T. (01) 66 82 46. - Tex - *061936*

Casa Jesus, Rua St. José 181, 1200 Lisboa. T. (01) 32 27 44. *061937*

Casa Quintão, Rua Ivens 30/34, 1200 Lisboa. T. (01) 358 37 bis 8. - Furn / Tex - *061938*

Casa Quioto, Rua de S. José 99/105, 1100 Lisboa. T. (01) 32 06 25. - Ant / Furn - *061939*

Casa Terenas, Rua de Prata 158, 1100 Lisboa. T. (01) 32 21 49. - Orient - *061940*

Casa Velha, Rua das Chagas 33, 1200 Lisboa. T. (01) 32 04 63. *061941*

Cavaco, Francisco N., Rua do Alecrim 107-109, 1200 Lisboa. T. (01) 34234 65, Fax (01) 346 39 07. - Ant / Furn / China / Jew - *061942*

Centro Antiquario do Alecrim Lda., Rua do Alecrim 48 50, 1200 Lisboa. T. (01) 36 68 92. - Furn / China - *061943*

Chung LDA., Rua dos Douradores 133, 1100 Lisboa. T. (01) 36 96 55. - Orient - *061944*

Costa, Antonio, Rua do Alecrim 76/78, 1200 Lisboa. T. (01) 32 58 89. - Ant / Paint / China / Furn - *061945*

Cousas de Antanho-Objectos de Arte Lda., Rua Dom Pedro V 24, 1200 Lisboa. T. (01) 324725. *061946*

Cruz, Arnaldo, Rua do Embaixador 37, 1300 Lisboa. T. (01) 63 84 46. - Ant - *061947*

Cruz Pereia-Antiquidades, Rua D. Pedro V 65, 1200 Lisboa. T. (01) 320645. - Paint / China - *061948*

Curado, Ribeiro, Av. Alm Gago Continho 101B, 1700 Lisboa. T. (01) 89 08 66. - Ant / Furn - *061949*

Da Silva, Praça Luis de Camoès 40-41, 1200 Lisboa. T. (01) 32 27 28, 32 63 69. *061950*

Dinastia-Antiquarios, Rua da Ecola Politecnica 183, Lisboa. T. (01) 66 89 73, 66 83 44. - Ant - *061951*

Dom Pedro V, Rua Dom Pedro V, 1200 Lisboa. T. (01) 321105. - Ant / Furn - *061952*

Dourarte, Av. Joao 21 51A, Lisboa. T. (01) 76 25 91. - Ant - *061953*

Duff, George Robert, M.A., Rua Artilharia 34 r/C, Lisboa. T. (01) 68 43 40. - Paint / Orient / China - *061954*

Esteves Rodrigues, Jose, Rua do Meio a Lapa 37 c/v, 1200 Lisboa. T. (01) 67 35 82. - Ant - *061955*

Fernandes Gomes, Armando, Rua Nova do Loureiro 4, Lisboa. T. (01) 32 74 07. - Ant - *061956*

Ferreira, A.J., Rua de S. José 161 167, 1100 Lisboa. T. (01) 32 37 65. - Ant / Paint / Furn / China / Dec - *061957*

Ferreira, Carlos Simoes, Rua de S. Bento 79, 1200 Lisboa. T. (01) 676428. - Ant - *061958*

Ferreira Santos, Antonio, Rua Alexandre Herculano 19A, Lisboa. T. (01) 430 61. *061959*

Ferreira Ventura, Henrique, Rua de S. Bento 170, 1200 Lisboa. T. (01) 67 95 59. - Ant - *061960*

Ferrolho, rua Nova de S. Mamede 6, 1100 Lisboa. T. (01) 669221. - Paint / Furn / China / Tex / Silv - *061961*

Galeria da Arcade, Rua D. Pedro V 56, Porta A, 1200 Lisboa. T. (01) 36 85 18. - Ant - *061962*

Galeria da Sé, Rua Augusto Rosa 46-48, 1100 Lisboa. T. (01) 86 42 41. - Furn / Sculp / Rel / Mul - *061963*

Galeria de Antiguidades, Rua do Alecrim 62, 1200 Lisboa. T. (01) 32 79 60. - Ant / Paint - *061964*

Galeria Goyarte, Rua D. Estefania 84C, 1000 Lisboa. T. (01) 53 64 11. - Ant - *061965*

Galeria 111, Compo Grande 113, 1700 Lisboa. T. (01) 77 74 18. *061966*

Galerias Star, Av. Sidonio Pais, 1000 Lisboa. T. (01) 495 00. - Jew - *061967*

Gaspurgo – Empresa Esterilizadora Lda., Rua de Marvila 88 90, 1900 Lisboa. T. (01) 38 39 15. - Ant - *061968*

Goyarte, Rua D. Estefania 84, 1200 Lisboa. T. (01) 53 64 11. *061969*

Hapetian, J.Z., Rua D. Pedro V 56-F, 1200 Lisboa. T. (01) 335 42, 77 34 91. - Tex - *061970*

Henriques de Carvalho, Manuel, Rua da Escola Politecnica 88-99, 1200 Lisboa. T. (01) 66 28 16. - Ant - *061971*

Holterman, Rua da Misericordia 137-141, 1200 Lisboa. T. (01) 32 72 72. *061972*

Hortega, Elena Adorno, Rua de S. Bernardo 16, 1200 Lisboa. T. (01) 66 33 76, 66 69 55. - Ant / Paint / Furn / China / Jew - *061973*

Ideal Mercantil, Rua Marques de Fronteira 68A, 1000 Lisboa. T. (01) 68 36 60. - Ant - *061974*

Jalco – Moveis e Decoraçoes, SARL, Rua Ivens 44, 1200 Lisboa. T. (01) 32 80 95. - Ant / Furn - *061975*

Jesus, Antonio de, Rua de S. Jose 181, 1100 Lisboa. T. (01) 322 744. - Ant - *061976*

Leal, Luis L., Lda., Rua D. Pedro V. 59 61, 1200 Lisboa. T. (01) 32 45 46. - Ant / Furn - *061977*

Leiloes-Afralilhos, Av. Duqué de Loulé 1, 1200 Lisboa. T. (01) 514 78. *061978*

Leiria e Nascimento Lda., Rua da Emenda 30 10, Lisboa. T. (01) 36 94 98. - Ant - *061979*

Levy, Sam, Rua Castilho 57, Lisboa. T. (01) 572698. - Tex / Arch - *061980*

Livraria Portugal, Rua do Carmo 70, 1200 Lisboa. T. (01) 36 05 82, 36 05 83, 32 82 20. - Num - *061981*

Lourdes Araujo, Jaria de, Rua Filipe Folque 36, 1000 Lisboa. T. (01) 415 90. - Ant - *061982*

Machado + Pedrosa Lda., S. José 182, 1100 Lisboa. T. (01) 40338. *061983*

Marques, R., Misericordia 92, 1200 Lisboa. T. (01) 349 77. *061984*

Martins, Abel, Rua S. Bento 63, 1200 Lisboa. T. (01) 67 95 13. - Ant - *061985*

Martins, Joaquim, Rua José Estevao 2-C, 1100 Lisboa. T. (01) 4 70 72. - Ant / Furn / China / Glass - *061986*

Mayer, José, Rua do Loreto 18, 1200 Lisboa. T. (01) 32 28 81. - Paint / China / Silv - *061987*

Melo, Otilia Sampaio, Rua do Alecrim 62, 1200 Lisboa. T. (01) 327960. *061988*

Mendes e Silva Lda., Alberto, Rua Rodrigues Sampaio 96 c/v E, Lisboa. T. (01) 547 20. - Ant - *061989*

Mitnitzky, Joachim, Lda., Calçada de S. Francisco 1, 1200 Lisboa. T. (01) 32 68 63, 36 82 33. - Ant / Paint / Furn / China / Sculp - *061990*

Mobrel, Rua de S. Bento 386, 1200 Lisboa. T. (01) 66 18 91. *061991*

Molder, A., Rua 1.0 de Dezembro 101, 3.0, Lisboa. T. (01) 32 15 14. - Ant - *061992*

Moncada, Isabel Cabral, Rua Dom Pedro V 34, 1200 Lisboa. T. (01) 368295. *061993*

Noelke, Rua Antonio Maria Cardoso 15, 1200 Lisboa. T. (01) 32 17 91. *061994*

Noelke, Raymond D., Rua Vitor Cordon 1, 1200 Lisboa. T. (01) 36 70 70. - Ant / Paint / Orient / China / Sculp - *061995*

Nunes de Oliveira, Manuel, Lda., C. de Santana 160, 1100 Lisboa. T. (01) 443 87. - Ant - *061996*

O'Donnell + Roldao Madeira, 67 Escola Politecnica, 1200 Lisboa. T. (01) 369419. - Furn / China - *061997*

Oom Veiga, Palmira, Rua do Alecrim 44, 1200 Lisboa. T. (01) 36 98 76. - Ant - *061998*

Ourivesaria de Santo Eloi, Lda., Augusta 181 183, 1100 Lisboa. T. (01) 36 17 87. - Jew / Silv - *061999*

Ourivesaria Sanata Filomena, Largo Manuel E. Silva 9, 1500 Lisboa. T. (01) 783092. *062000*

Ouro Velho, Av. Elias Garcia 54 B, 1000 Lisboa. T. (01) 779381. - Mod - *062001*

Panoplia, Largo Andaluz 26, 1000 Lisboa. T. (01) 42336. *062002*

Parente, J., Rua Quirino da Fonseca 39b, 1000 Lisboa. T. (01) 52 39 33. - Furn / China - *062003*

Pecardi Decoraçoes Lda., Rua Nova da Trinidade 1C, 1200 Lisboa. T. (01) 328 10. - Ant - *062004*

Pereira, A. Paes, Rua Dom Pedro V 145, 1200 Lisboa. T. (01) 326121. - China - *062005*

Pereira, Fernando Mauricio, Rua do Triângulo Vermelho 27, 3.0, 1100 Lisboa. T. (01) 83 74 30. - Ant - *062006*

Pimenta, M.C., Lda., Rua Augusta 253/255, 1100 Lisboa. T. (01) 32 45 64. - Num / Jew / Silv / Instr - *062007*

Pintassilgo + Almeido, Rua Nova de S. Mamede 6, 1200 Lisboa. T. (01) 669221. - Paint / Furn / China / Tex / Silv - *062008*

Pintassilgo e Fernandes Lda., Rua da Escola Politecnica 183, 1200 Lisboa. T. (01) 66 89 73. - Ant / China - *062009*

Pinto, Rua de Alecrim 81, 1200 Lisboa. T. (01) 36 65 18. *062010*

Pinto, Alfredo, Rua do Alecrim 81, 1200 Lisboa. T. (01) 366518. - Ant - *062011*

Pinto Machado Lda., J., 25-27 Praca S. Bento, 1200 Lisboa. T. (01) 671433. *062012*

Pires, Largo da Trinade 11, 1200 Lisboa. T. (01) 36 99 51. *062013*

Pires Vieito, Daniel, Calç. da Estrela 21, Porta 6, 1200 Lisboa. T. (01) 67 94 52. - Ant - *062014*

Poliartis Lda., Rua da Alegria 94, c/v, 1200 Lisboa. T. (01) 32 08 39. - Furn / Sculp / Dec - *062015*

Portico, Rua Misericordia 31, 1200 Lisboa. T. (01) 36 79 93. - Ant - *062016*

Pra Antigo, Rua S. Jose 126/128, 1100 Lisboa. T. (01) 36 63 29. - Paint / Furn / China - *062017*

Quito, Rua de S. José 99, 1200 Lisboa. T. (01) 32 06 25. *062018*

Ramos Pestana, Alfredo, Rua D. Pedro V. 8 e 10, 1200 Lisboa. T. (01) 36 93 44. - Ant - *062019*

Restauradora da Queimada Lda., Tv. da Queimada 32, Lisboa. T. (01) 32 75 87. - Ant - *062020*

Rirade Antiguidades, Rua de S. Marta 26, 1200 Lisboa. *062021*

Rodrigues, Luis, Rua D. Pedro V 84 86, 1200 Lisboa. T. (01) 36 88 36. - Ant - *062022*

Rodriguez, Jaime, Rua da Assunção 88, 1100 Lisboa. T. (01) 36 77 27. - Paint / China / Jew / Silv / Dec - *062023*

Rombauer, Eleonora, R. Remedios à Lapa 60, 1200 Lisboa. T. (01) 66 15 38. - Ant / Furn - *062024*

Rosa, Jose, Rua José Estevao 2A e B, 1100 Lisboa. T. (01) 53 18 43. - Ant - *062025*

Salao de Antiguidades Lda., Rua D. Pedro V. 31/37, 1200 Lisboa. T. (01) 32 52 80. - Ant / Furn / China - *062026*

Salgado, Jose Jesus, Rua de S. Bento 246, 1200 Lisboa. T. (01) 66 23 40. - Furn - *062027*

Salgueiro Baptista, A.M., Rua do Alecrim 85/89, 1200 Lisboa. T. (01) 36 20 69. - Furn / China - *062028*

Salvador, Joao, Rua Eng. Vieira da Silva 14, 1300 Lisboa. T. (01) 537642. *062029*

San Carlos Lda., Largo de São Carlos 15, 1200 Lisboa. T. (01) 36 83 23. - Ant / China - *062030*

Silva, Trav. de Queimada 28, 1200 Lisboa. T. (01) 36 85 89. *062031*

Silva, Antonio P. da, Lda., Praça Luis de Camoes 40/41, 1200 Lisboa. T. (01) 32 27 28. - Ant / Jew / Silv - *062032*

Silva, Domingos da, Rua de Santa Marta 49, Lisboa. T. (01) 500 56. - Ant - *062033*

Silva, Joao Duarte, Rua Dom Pedro V 56, P.A., 1200 Lisboa. T. (01) 862924. *062034*

Simoes, Carlos D. & Irmãos, Rua de Santa Marinha 3, 1100 Lisboa. T. (01) 862527. - Paint / Furn / China / Glass - *062035*

Simoes e Irmaos, Carlos Domingues, Lda., Rua Santa Marinha 3, 1100 Lisboa. T. (01) 86 25 27. - Ant / Furn / China - *062036*

Soares e Mendonça, Rua Luz Soriano 53, 1200 Lisboa. T. (01) 32 13 12. - Ant - *062037*

Sociedade Inglesa de Decoraçoes e Antiguidades Lda., Rua da Emenda 26, 1.0, 1200 Lisboa. T. (01) 32 46 06. - Ant - *062038*

Sopal, Rua Ivens 58, 1200 Lisboa. T. (01) 37 01 66. - Dec - *062039*

Sousa Braga, Rua do Alecrim 69, 1200 Lisboa. T. (01) 345 62. *062040*

Tavares de Carvalho, Av. da Republica 46, 1200 Lisboa. T. (01) 77 03 77. *062041*

Teixeira Bastos Lda., Rua Aurea 214, Lisboa.
T. (01) 32 65 15. - Ant - 062042
Tralha, Calçada do Graca 6, 1200 Lisboa.
T. (01) 86 66 71. 062043
Trindade, Antonio, Rua do Alecrim 81, 1200 Lisboa.
T. (01) 32 46 60. - Ant / Orient / China / Eth / Instr /
Rel - 062044
Vasco, J., Rua Alexandre Herculano 21A, Lisboa.
T. (01) 512 60. 062045
Vaz + Melo, Rua da Imprensa Nac. 116-E 2, 1200 Lisboa. T. (01) 66 82 46. 062046
Veiga, Palmira Oom, Rua do Alecrim 44, 1200 Lisboa.
T. (01) 369876. 062047
Velha do Camoes, Rua das Chagas 33, 1200 Lisboa.
T. (01) 32 04 63. - Ant - 062048
Ventura, Rua S. Bento 176, 1200 Lisboa.
T. (01) 66 15 39. - Ant - 062049
Vide, Eugenio, Rua da Bombarda 72, 8.0E, 1100 Lisboa.
T. (01) 82 26 14. - Ant - 062050
Vitrine, Rua D. Pedro V.9 e 11, 1200 Lisboa.
T. (01) 36 88 36. - Ant - 062051
V.S. Antiguidades + Valharias, Rua Eduardo Coelho 37,
1200 Lisboa. T. (01) 35249. - Furn / Glass - 062052
Vultos e Duarte, J., Lda., Rua de Santa Marta 41A e B,
Lisboa. T. (01) 431 67. - Ant / Furn / Mil - 062053
Xairel Antiguidades, Rua D. Pedro 111, 1200 Lisboa.
T. (01) 302 66. - Ant - 062054

Porto

A Leiloeira Lda., Dr. Barbosa Castro 55, 4000 Porto.
T. (02) 365 67. - Ant - 062055
Alves, Alfredo de Sa Aires, Rua de Santo Antonio 197,
4100 Porto. T. (02) 250 10. - Ant / China / Jew - 062056
„Arca Velha", Rua Jose Falcao 230, 4000 Porto.
- Ant - 062057
Baganha, Dom Hugo 13, 4000 Porto.
T. (02) 348 83. 062058
Baptista e Pinto, Lda., Rua Alberto Aires Gouveia 55 7,
4000 Porto. T. (02) 345 67. - Ant - 062059
Baptista-Joalheiro, Rua Passos Manuel 2, 4000 Porto.
T. (02) 228 31, 278 88. - Ant / Dec / Silv - 062060
Baptista, Pedro A., Rua das Flores 231, 4000 Porto.
T. (02) 251 42. - Ant / Jew - 062061
Baptista, Pedro A., Rua das Florès 235, 4000 Porto.
T. (02) 251 42. 062062
Barros, Sara, Rua das Oliveiras 67, 4000 Porto.
T. (02) 233 70. - Ant - 062063
„Bons Tempos", Rua de Conceiçao 27 29, 4000 Porto.
T. (02) 224 99. - Ant - 062064
Brito, Viuva de Antonio Jose de, Rua da Lapa 17, 4000
Porto. T. (02) 255 35. - Ant - 062065
Casa Azul, Praça Carlos Alberto 84 85, 4000 Porto.
T. (02) 234 50. - Ant - 062066
Casa Caruncho, Av. Boavista 1059, 4000 Porto. - Ant /
Furn - 062067
Casa de Moveis Tanger, Rue Marechal Saldanha 129,
4100 Porto. T. (02) 68 00 40. - Ant - 062068
Casa do Campo, Praça da Republica 186, Porto.
T. (02) 315 30. - Ant - 062069
Correia de Sousa, J. Baptista, Rua de Costa Cabral 750,
4200 Porto. T. (02) 49 23 41. - Ant / Paint / Cur - 062070
Correira, Domingos da Silva, Rua Martires de Libertade
119, 4000 Porto. - Ant - 062071
Costa, A.S., Av. Camilo 227, 4300 Porto.
T. (02) 57 38 33. - Ant / Furn - 062072
Da Silva, Rua Martires de Libertade 119, 4000
Porto. 062073
„Elmo", Alberto Aires Gouveia 9, 4000 Porto.
T. (02) 334 09. - Ant - 062074
Ferreira, Luiz & Filhos, 9, Rua Trindade Coelho, 4000
Porto. T. (02) 31 61 46. - Jew - 062075
Lencastre, Av. da Bravista 1059, 4000 Porto.
T. (02) 609 63. 062076
Lopes e C. Armando, Rua Marechal Saldanha 121, 4100
Porto. T. (02) 68 32 74. - Ant - 062077
Martins, Abigail, Rua de Nossa, Senhora de Fatima 125,
4000 Porto. - Ant - 062078
Mendoca, Rua Formosa 112, 4000 Porto.
T. (02) 339 09. 062079
Mota, Antonio Pereira, Rua Cedofeita 80, 4000 Porto.
T. (02) 224 72. - Ant - 062080
Pereira, Francisco, Rua Oliveiras 14-16, 4000 Porto.
T. (02) 263 92. - Ant - 062081

Portocarrero Baganha, Dom Hugo 13, Porto.
T. (02) 348 83. - Ant / Furn / Rel - 062082
Silva, Mario, Lda., Rua D. Manuel II 20, 4000 Porto.
T. (02) 263 67. - Ant - 062083
Simoes, Praça Carlos Alberto 85, 4000 Porto.
T. (02) 234 50. 062084
Souto, Rui, Av. da Boavista 868, 4100 Porto.
T. (02) 609 14 55, 606 49 55, Fax 606 49 55. 062085
Uniao de Bancos Portugueses, Dept. Numismatica, Rua
de Sa da Bandeira 53, 4000 Porto. T. (02) 201 33.
- Num - 062086
Vilarinha, Rua de Cedofeita 210-216, 4000 Porto.
- Ant - 062087

Sesimbra

Bazar Lota d'Arcada, Av. Salazar 25A, 2970 Sesimbra.
T. 229 12 27. - Ant - 062088

Sintra (Estremadura)

„Antiguidades", Antiquario de San Pedro de Sintra, Av.
Conde de Sucena 23, 2710 Sintra. T. 98 13 73. - Furn /
Tex - 062089
Antiquiario, Av. Conde de Sucena 23, 2710 Sintra.
T. 98 13 73. 062090
Ferreira, Christiano Conceiçao, San Pedro de Sintra, Rua
Marqués Viana 3, 2710 Sintra. T. 981538.
- Ant - 062091
Galeria Real de San Pedro, San Pedro de Sintra, 2710
Sintra. T. 31 49 68. - Ant / Sculp / Lights / Instr /
Mil - 062092
Mayer, Galeria-Real, Lojas 10-12, S. Ped. de Sintra,
2710 Sintra. - Paint / Furn / China - 062093
Pedro de Sintra, S., Ave. Conde de Sucena 23, 2710
Sintra. T. 981373. - Ant / Furn - 062094
Real de Sintra, Galeria, S. Pedro de Sintra Eestrada Na-
cional, 2710 Sintra. T. 981663. - Ant - 062095
Relicario de San Pedro, San Pedro de Sintra, Rua Trude
Sousa 3 7, 2710 Sintra. - Ant - 062096

Vila Viçosa (Alentejo)

Silva Jardim, Francisco, Av. Duarte Pacheco 41, 7160
Vila Viçosa. T. (068) 158. 062097

Viseu (Beira Alta)

Madeira, Antonio, Ruo do Goncalinho 55, 3500 Viseu.
T. 22430. - Ant - 062098
Pereira, Serafim Rodrigues, Rua de Picadeiro 244, 3500
Viseu. T. 229 98. - Ant - 062099

Réunion

Saint-Denis

Chineuse, La Montagne, 97400 Saint-Denis.
T. (262) 238090. - Ant - 062100
Samarkand, 16 Rue Sainte-Anne, 97400 Saint-Denis.
T. (262) 413580. - Ant - 062101

Saint-Paul

Compagnie Orientale, Rte Cambale, 97460 Saint-Paul.
T. (262) 455049, Fax (262) 455669. - Ant - 062102

Saint-Pierre

Grenier, 69 Rue François-de-Mahy, 97410 Saint-Pierre.
T. (262) 251840. - Ant - 062103
Malle d'Anton, RN3, 127 Rue Archambaud-les-Caser-
nes, 97410 Saint-Pierre. T. (262) 354365.
- Ant - 062104

Sainte-Clotilde

Antiquaire, 51 Rue Eudoxie-Nonge, 97490 Sainte-Clotil-
de. T. (262) 283309. - Ant - 062105

Russia

Moskva

Aktsiya, Bryusov per 6, 103009 Moskva.
T. (095) 2291975. 062106
Aktsiya, ul Arbat 43 stroenie 3, 121002 Moskva.
T. (095) 2413191. 062107
Antik, ul Arbat 6, 121002 Moskva.
T. (095) 2917041. 062108

Antikvar, Bryusov per 2-14, 103006 Moskva.
T. (095) 2290610. - Furn - 062109
Antikvar, ul Myasnitskaya 13, 101000 Moskva.
T. (095) 9257608, Fax 9286757. 062110
Antikvar, 2-oi Truzhennikov per 4, 119121 Moskva.
T. (095) 2466728. - Furn - 062111
Antikvariat, ul Bolshaya Yakimanka 54-56, 117049 Mos-
kva. T. (095) 2389545. 062112
Antikvarny salon, Karmanitski per 5, 121002 Moskva.
T. (095) 2414985. 062113
Arbatskaya nakhodka, ul Arbat 11, 121002 Moskva.
T. (095) 2917038. 062114
Art-Akademiya, Krymski val 10-14 komnata A-20,
117049 Moskva. 062115
Art-Kollektor, ul Arbat 12, 121002 Moskva.
T. (095) 2022738. 062116
Atribut, ul Preobrazhenski val 17, 107061 Moskva.
T. (095) 9643113. 062117
Chastnaya kollektsiya, ul Novoslobotskaya 17, 103030
Moskva. T. (095) 9788675. 062118
Diana, ul Berkhnyaya Radishchevskaya 9-a, 109004
Moskva. T. (095) 9150551. 062119
Forte-Bank, ul Kuusinena 25, 125252 Moskva.
T. (095) 1959877. 062120
Galeeya na Smolenskoi naberezhnoi, Smolenskaya na-
berezhnaya 5-13, 121002 Moskva.
T. (095) 2442381. 062121
Galereya Shon, Nikitski bulvar 12-a, 121019 Moskva.
T. (095) 2914579. 062122
Galereya v Atriume gostinitsy Balchug, ul Balchug 1,
Moskva. T. (095) 2306500. 062123
Globus-Galereya, Kamergerski per 3, 103009 Moskva.
T. (095) 2926336. 062124
Kartiny-Baget-Antikvariat salon, Arbatski per 2, 121019
Moskva. T. (095) 2915995. 062125
Kupina, ul Arbat 6-2 stroenie 1-2, 121019 Moskva.
T. (095) 2020571. 062126
Kupina, ul Arbat 18-1 stroenie 1, 121002 Moskva.
T. (095) 2024462. 062127
Mezhnumizmatika, ul Bolshaya Dmitrovka 9, 103009
Moskva. T. (095) 292431. 062128
Mir iskusstva, ul Pyatnitskaya 16, Moskva.
T. (095) 2313302. 062129
Muzyka-Antikvar, ul Pushechnaya 1-8, 103031 Moskva.
T. (095) 9257356. - Music - 062130
Numizmat, Goncharny proezd 8-40, 109172 Moskva.
T. (095) 9156563. 062131
Raritet, ul Arbat 31, 121002 Moskva.
T. (095) 2412381. 062132
Starina, ul Petrovka 24, 103051 Moskva.
T. (095) 2093215. 002133
Universum, Maly Nikitski per 16, 121069 Moskva.
T. (095) 2904082. 062134
Yuniset-Art, Bolshoi Nikolopeskovski per 17, 121002
Moskva. T. (095) 2447766. 062135
Zvezda, ul Arbat 11, Moskva. T. (095) 2917143. 062136

Sankt-Peterburg

Antikvar, ul Nalichnaya 21, Sankt-Peterburg.
T. (812) 2171010. - China / Ico - 062137
Antikvariat, ul Michurinskaya 14/3, Sankt-Peterburg.
T. (812) 2323355. 062138
Antikvariat, ul Pochtamskaya 5, Sankt-Peterburg.
T. (812) 3112643. 062139
Antikvariat Russkaya starina, ul Nekrasova 6, Sankt-Pe-
terburg. T. (812) 2732859. - Jew / Ico - 062140
Bronza, ul Sadovaya 26, Sankt-Peterburg.
T. (812) 3109578. 062141
Gelos, Nevski prosp ekst 151, Sankt-Peterburg.
T. (812) 2770503. 062142
Greviti, Sytninskaya pl 3, 197101 Sankt-Peterburg.
T. (812) 2333744. - Jew - 062143
Karneya-Diamond, ul Kolomenskaya 3, 191119 Sankt-
Peterburg. T. (812) 124841. - Jew - 062144
Kollektsioner, Ligovski prosp 61, Sankt-Peterburg.
T. (812) 1648226. - Num - 062145
Lavka antikvara, Mosskovskoe shosse 16 kv1, 196158
Sankt-Peterburg. T. (812) 2937300. 062146
Lavka antikvara, ul Kazanskaya 39, Sankt-Peterburg.
T. (812) 3127253. 062147
Na Liteinom, Liteiny prosp 61, Sankt-Peterburg.
T. (812) 2753873, 2753874. - China - 062148

Nasledie, Nevski prosp ekt 116, Sankt-Peterburg. T. (812) 2795067. - Graph / Jew - 062149
Natasha, Rizhski prosp 19, Sankt-Peterburg. T. (812) 2514863. - Paint / Graph / Ico / Draw - 062150
Numizmatika, Maly proezd 10, Sankt-Peterburg. T. (812) 2137395. - Num 062151
Panteleimonovski, ul Pestelya 13/15, 191028 Sankt-Peterburg. T. (812) 2797235. - Jew - 062152
Peterburg, ul Furshtatskaya 42, Sankt-Peterburg. T. (812) 2730341. 062153
Rapsodiya, ul Bolshaja Konyushennaya 13, Sankt-Peterburg. T. (812) 3144801. - Paint / China / Jew / Furn - 062154
Rus, Kamennoostrovski prosp 17, Sankt-Peterburg. - Graph / China / Jew / Ico - 062155
Sankt-Peterburg, Nevski prosp 54, Sankt-Peterburg. T. (812) 3114020. - Paint / Graph / Furn / China - 062156
Sekunda, Litejny prosp 61, Sankt-Peterburg. T. (812) 2757524. 062157
Starinnye chasy, ul Bolshay Konyushennaya 19, Sankt-Peterburg. T. (812) 3141559. - China / Instr - 062158
Starye gody, ul Bolshaya monetnaya 23, Sankt-Peterburg. T. (812) 2338701. 062159
Sudarushka, Apraskin dvor korpus 1, Sankt-Peterburg. T. (812) 3102859. 062160
Terciya, ul Italyanskaya 5, Sankt-Peterburg. T. (812) 1105568, Fax (812) 3118048. 062161

Singapore

Singapore

Aipotu Art Commercial, 204 Blk. 178 Toa Payoh Central, Singapore. T. 2550388. 062162
Aizia Discovers, 33-A/35-A Cuppage Rd., Singapore. T. 2357866. 062163
Art and Woodcraft Company, G-75 Lucky Plaza, Singapore. T. 2354929. 062164
Arts and Crafts Trading, 304 Far East Shopping Centre, Singapore. T. 2355680. 062165
Arts Centre, G-15 Tangein Shopping Centre, Singapore. T. 7377577. 062166
Arts Centre, M32 Far East Shopping Centre, Singapore. T. 2352449. 062167
Asia Arts, 17-B International Bldg, Singapore. T. 7373631, 7371169. 062168
Bareo, 19 Tanglin Rd., Singapore, 1024. T. 737 3211. - Orient / Eth - 062169
Borobudur Arts + Crafts, 545 Orchard Rd., Singapore, 0923. 062170
Chalamay Co., BLK 129, Bedok North St. 2, Nr. 01-36, Singapore, 1648. T. 782 0752, 545 2412, Fax 545 3379. 062171
Chan Gallery, 167-E Singapore Handicraft Centre, Singapore. T. 2355374. 062172
Chan Ngee, 85 Bek 18 Outram Pk, Singapore. T. 2201127. 062173
Chan Pui Kee, 86 Neil Rd., Singapore, 0208. T. 223 48 06. 062174
Changi Junk Store, 442 Changi Rd., Singapore. T. 4484914. 062175
Chanrai's Art and Crafts, Cold Storage (9), Singapore. T. 2355189. 062176
Chen Yee Shen, G 12 and B 27 Orchard Towers, Singapore. T. 7371174. 062177
Cheong Kee & Co., G-15 Far East Shopping Centre, Singapore. T. 7370227. 062178
China Crafts, 3 Coleman St., Peninsula Shopping Centre, Singapore, 0617. T. 336 1970, 336 6243. 062179
China Trading Company, Raffles Hotel, Singapore. T. 328298. 062180
Chinese Heritage, 304 Orchard Rd., 02-55 Lucky Plaza, Singapore, 0923. T. 235 9714. - Ant / Orient / China / Draw - 062181
Chong Hwa, M 54 Lucky Plaza, Singapore. T. 7373707. 062182
Crystal Art Commpany, 32 Ripley Cres, Singapore. T. 2844734. 062183
Delingent Trading Company, 3 Larut Rd., Singapore. T. 2945750. 062184
Doviehallen Butikk, 16-A Enggor St, Singapore. T. 2201678. 062185
Dragon House, 132/133 Lucky Plaza, Singapore. T. 2359439. 062186
Dynasty Crafts, 28 Up Weld Rd., Singapore. T. 2949507. 062187
Eastern Art Company, 63 Stamford Rd., Singapore. T. 322394. 062188
Fine Arts of Asia, 227-B Holland Ave, Singapore. T. 669443. 062189
Hongkong Craft, G-08 Peninsula Shopping Complex, Singapore. T. 33 35 45. 062190
Hsu Bros, 04-06 Funan Centre, Singapore, 0617. T. 337 32 70. 062191
Island Arts and Crafts, Hotel Royal Ramada 11, Singapore. T. 2553309. 062192
Ismail, 4723 Appt. Blk. 1, Beach Rd., Singapore, 0719. T. 258 22 08. 062193
Ju-I Antiques, 1-15 Tanglin Shopping Centre, Singapore. T. 37 78 97. 062194
Kingsley Art Centre, 68 Orchard Rd. 03-14, 0923 Singapore. T. 337 04 68. 062195
Kong Onn, 67 Victoria St, Singapore. T. 362264. 062196
Kumra & Co., 1 Colombo Court, No.08-16, Singapore, 0617. T. 337 2130, 338 1745, Fax 337 3129. 062197
Kwok, 545 Orchard Rd., 03-01 Far East Shopping Centre, Singapore, 0923. T. 235 2516, 235 4042. - Orient - 062198
Leng Siang Hin, 184 Golden Mill Food Centre, Singapore. T. 2933623. 062199
Little Paris, 293-A/295-A Outram Pk, Singapore. T. 2201705. 062200
Mandarin Galleries, Mandarin Hotel Arcade, Orchard Rd., Singapore. T. 375970. - Ant / Paint - 062201
Maywood, 227 Shaw Centre, Singapore. T. 7379074. 062202
Ming Blue, 1 Scotts Rd. 04-26 / 04-27 Shaw Centre, Singapore, 0922. T. 734 6541. 062203
Ming Shop, G4 Orchard Towers, Singapore. T. 7372 656. 062204
Moon Gate, 19 Tanglin Rd., Singapore, 1024. T. 737 67 71. - Ant / Paint / Furn / Orient / China / Sculp / Arch / Jew / Rel / Cur / Draw - 062205
Ngian Hln, 1270-B People's Pk., Singapore. T. 982588. 062206
Novelty Departmental Store, 66-A Blk. 28 Chai Chee Ave, Singapore. T. 417864. 062207
Paul Art Gallery, G 14-A Supreme House, Singapore. T. 31217. 062208
Peking Lace, 66 North Bridge Rd., Singapore. T. 333380. 062209
Philippine Arts + Crafts, F25 S'pore Hilton Shop. Arc., Singapore. T. 7371 585. 062210
Seah Galleries, Shangri-La Hotel, Singapore. - Ant / Paint / Orient / China / Sculp - 062211
Seng Huat Chop, 287 Victoria St, Singapore. T. 2943185. 062212
Shanghai Art House, 210 Shaw Centre, Singapore. T. 2352305. 062213
Shantung, 01-28 Orchard Towers, Singapore, 0923. T. 737 25 91. 062214
Sing Kwong + Co., 465 North Bridge Rd, Singapore. T. 2940421. 062215
Soon Hong, 428 Joo Chiat Rd, Singapore. T. 499753. 062216
Straits Commercial Art Co., 65 Stamford Road, Singapore, 0617. T. 338 1710. 062217
Supreme Arts House, G4/G5 Lucky Plaza, Singapore. T. 2356303. 062218
Supreme Souvenirs Corner, Supreme House, Singapore. T. 30701. 062219
Taisei Stamps & Coins, River Valley Rd., 01-33 Liang Court, 0617 Singapore. T. 336 9222, 336 8585, Fax 339 7769. 062220
Tang Heng Lee, 149 Hill St., Singapore. T. 333304. 062221
Tang Horse, 1-10 Tanglin Shopping Centre, Singapore. T. 7374941. 062222
Tanti, 188 Bt Timah Rd, Singapore. T. 2351116. 062223
Thai Handicraft, 1005 BB Up Thomson Rd., Singapore. T. 4524400. 062224
Thye Nam & Co., 13 Temple St, Singapore. T. 2230341. 062225
Tiong Guan Craft Store, 136-31 Sembawang Rd., Singapore. T. 2571843. 062226
Toh Foong, 5 Temple St., Singapore. T. 2231343. 062227
Tzen Gallery, M 19 Far East Shopping Centre, Singapore. T. 2353156. 062228
Wei Lin Jewellery, F4, Mandarin Hotel, Shopping Arcade, Orchard Rd., Singapore, 0923. T. 73 75 970. 062229
Wing On Cheun Arts, 133-A South Bridge Rd., Singapore. T. 981474. 062230
Ying Kee Hong, 25-H Lor 12 Geylang, Singapore, 1439. T. 744 69 11. 062231
Yue Chu Tang Art Gallery, Block 22, Outram Park, Nr 02-287, Singapore 0316. T. 2275123, Fax 2275389. - Ant / Paint / Orient / China / Repr - 062232

Slovakia

Bratislava

Antiquitäten, Nalepkova 17, Bratislava. 062233
Antiquitäten, Leningradska 7 „Tuzex", Gorkeho 12, Bratislava. 062234

South Africa

Cape Town (Cape Province)

Adler, Julian, 2 Corwen St., Claremont, Cape Town. T. (021) 64 24 40. - China / Instr - 062235
Anne's Antiques, 95 Regent Rd., Sea Point, Cape Town, 8000. T. (021) 44 49 10. - Ant / Silv - 062236
Bonzakein Persian Carpets Ltd., 50 Shortmarket St., Cape Town, 8000. T. (021) 2 40 67. - Tex - 062237
Brevan Art Gallery, Corner of Church and Burg St., Cape Town. 062238
Castle Galleries, 5 Wolfe St. Old Wynberg, Cape Town, 8000. T. (021) 71 04 70. - Ant / Furn - 062239
Isfahan Ltd., Heerengracht Centre Foreshore, Cape Town, 8000. - Tex - 062240
Peters, C.M., 52 Albert Rd., Landsowne, Cape Town. 062241
Thorp, P. A. Lee, 12 Fountain Centre, Rondebosch, Cape Town, 8001. T. (021) 66 31 59. - Ant / Paint / Graph / Repr / Fra / Glass / Pho / Mul / Draw - 062242
Visser, Peter, 117 Long St., Cape Town. T. (021) 237870. - Paint / Graph / Furn / China - 062243

Durban (Natal)

Antiques & Bygones, The Old Church, 50 Aliwal St., Durban, 4001. T. (031) 368-1414, Fax 32 15 23. - Paint / Furn / China / Jew / Silv / Instr / Glass - 062244
Zell's Curios, 78 bis 80 West St., Durban. - Ant / Cur - 062245

Germiston (Transvaal)

Kaplan, Alec & Son, P.O.Box 132, Germiston, 1400. T. 22 12 18. - Num / Eth / Mil - 062246
Verteegh, T.J.C., Art Gallery, 1 Market St., Germiston. 062247

Johannesburg (Tvl.)

Adams, 97A Harrison St. Braamfontein, Johannesburg, 2001. T. (011) 403 1453. - Ant / Furn / Silv - 062248
Cottage, The, Corner of Eighth Ave. and Main Rd., Melville, Johannesburg. T. (011) 726 7506. - Furn - 062249
Cowen, Sidney Ltd., The Vestibule Shop, Medical Centre 209 Jeppe St., Johannesburg. T. (011) 22 49 60. - China / Jew / Silv - 062250
Culverwell, Peter, 12 Keyes Av., Rosebank, 2196 Johannesburg. T. (011) 788-3029. 062251
Eastern House for Art + Craft, 60 Plein St., Johannesburg. T. (011) 234684. 062252
Editions Graphiques, 99 Market St., Johannesburg, 2001. T. (011) 440 24 77. - Graph / Sculp - 062253
Guenther, Egon Gallery, 4 Krans St. Linksfield, Johannesburg. - Eth - 062254
Heirlooms, Hurlingham Court Chaplin Rd., Illovo, Johannesburg. T. (011) 42 18 40. - Furn / Silv - 062255
Kaplan, Alec & Son Ltd., 87 Delvers St., Johannesburg. T. (011) 22 12 18. - Num / China / Eth - 062256

Ming, 73a Kruis St., 2001 Johannesburg. T. (011) 337-
5482. - Ant - *062257*
Norwood Cottage Antiques, 50 Grant Ave., Norwood, Jo-
hannesburg. - Ant - *062258*
Old Dutch Antique Shop, Northlands, P.O.Box 55020, Jo-
hannesburg. - Ant / Paint / Furn / Tex - *062259*
Read's, 4 Knightsbridge, Rosebank, Johannesburg,
2196. T. (011) 47 26 07. - Ant / Furn / Orient / China /
Silv - *062260*
Westgate, Eloff St., Johannesburg POB 9854, 2000.
T. (011) 331 2117. - Paint / Draw - *062261*
Whippman's Gallery, 107B Eloff St., Johannesburg.
T. (011) 23 76 88, 22 38 35. *062262*

Kalk Bay (Cope Province)
Gallery Medici, 22 Main Rd., Dalebrook, Kalk Bay.
T. 8 10 64. - Orient / China / Silv / Glass - *062263*
Sylvester, H.W. + Sons, 66 Main Rd., Kalk Bay. T. 84780.
- Furn - *062264*

Paarl (K.P.)
Klein Vredenburg Gallery, 155 Main St., Paarl. *062265*
Paarl Antiques, 154 Main St., Paarl. - Ant - *062266*

Plettenberg Bay (Cape Province)
Old and New, 23 Main St., Plettenberg Bay POB 282.
T. 323 15. - Ant / Silv / Lights / Glass - *062267*

Pretoria (Tvl.)
Schweickerdt, E., 89 Queen St., Pretoria, 0002.
T. (012) 21 65 57. - Paint / Repr / Fra - *062268*

Sandton (Transvaal)
Goodman Gallery, The, 3B Hyde Sq.,m Hyde Park,
Sandton. *062269*
Sherry's Antiques, 27 Benmore Gardens Sandown,
Sandton. T. 33 83 75. - Furn / Silv / Instr -
Glass - *062270*
Templar's Antiques Ltd., 11 Benmore Gardens, Sand-
own, 2096 Sandton. T. 783-1163. - Furn /
Silv - *062271*

Stellenbosch (K.P.)
Art Centre, Bloem St., Die Braak, Stellenbosch. *062272*
Gun O'Clock, 152 Dorp St., 7600 Stellenbosch.
T. (02231) 768 89. - Instr - *062273*

Tulbagh
Silberberg, Helmut K., Dr., Monbijou, Tulbagh, 6820.
T. (02362) 100. - Ant / Furn / Orient / Tex / Arch / Eth /
Silv / Cur - *062274*
Tulbagh Antiques, Dorpstraat, Tulbagh. - Furn - *062275*

Wynberg
Chelsea Gallery, 51 Waterloo Rd., 7800 Wynberg, 7800.
T. 761 6805. - Paint / Graph / Sculp / Tex /
Draw - *062276*

Spain

Alcoy (Alicante)
Decoradora, Mayor 18, 03002 Alcoy. T. (965) 21 30 27,
21 38 94, 20 14 24. - China - *062277*

Alicante (Alicante)
Correspondence-Club, Avda. Costa Blanca 28, Alicante.
T. (96) 65 12 54. - Ant / Paint / Furn / China / Sculp /
Fra / Silv / Glass / Mod / Pho - *062278*

Almeria (Almeria)
Dominguez Cazorla, Miguel, Segura, 3, 04003 Almeria.
T. (951) 21 42 78. *062279*

Badajoz
Almoneda, Vasco Nunez, 2, 06001 Badajoz.
T. (924) 2 06 16. - Ant / Paint / Furn / China - *062280*

Barcelona
Alonso Navarro, A., Aribau 22, 08011 Barcelona.
T. (93) 209 09 41. *062281*
„Ambrosio", Sacristans, 3, Barcelona. T. (93) 221 79 83.
- Ant / Furn - *062282*
Amoros Carrera, A., Arragón 526, 08026 Barcelona.
T. (93) 225 53 13. *062283*

Ancien Bijou, Paeso de Gracia 55, 08007 Barcelona.
T. (93) 2158519. *062284*
Anglada, Pedralbes 3, 08033 Barcelona.
T. (93) 247 30 21. *062285*
Antiguedades L'Art, Calle Baños Nuevos 20, 08002 Bar-
celona. T. (93) 302 06 87. *062286*
Antiguedades Pedro, Independencia 238, 08026 Barce-
lona. T. (93) 225 23 58. *062287*
Antiquary Market, Pl. Francesc Marcia 8, 08029 Barce-
lona. T. (93) 322 10 52. *062288*
Aragonés Corominas, Veguer, 13, 08002 Barcelona.
T. (93) 221 42 04. - Furn / China / Dec / Instr - *062289*
Arteuropa, Paeso de Gracia 41, 08007 Barcelona.
T. (93) 15 73 68. *062290*
Aureo, Beethoven, 13, 08021 Barcelona.
T. (03) 2018733, Fax 2023306. - Ant / Num - *062291*

Austerlitz, Paja 3, 08002 Barcelona.
T. (93) 318 03 88. *062292*
Bacardi, D., Paja 4, 08002 Barcelona.
T. (93) 301 56 87. *062293*
Balari-Galobart, J. J., Mallorca 419, 08013 Barcelona.
T. (93) 215 14 67. *062294*
Balari, Juan J., Bruc 144, 08037 Barcelona.
T. (93) 207 45 56. - Ant / Paint / Furn - *062295*
BalcLi's, Calle Rosellón,. 227, 08008 Barcelona.
- Ant - *062296*
Barcino Antiguedades, Aragón 526, 08013 Barcelona.
T. (93) 225 25 13. *062297*
Baron Cornal, Calle Baños Nuevos 18, 08002 Barcelona.
T. (93) 318 39 86. *062298*
Baròn-Hermanos, Banys Nous 18, 08002 Barcelona.
T. (93) 318 39 86. - Ant - *062299*
Bayt, Muntaner 499, 08022 Barcelona.
T. (93) 212 58 87. *062300*
Bellido Aguilar, Aragón 528, 08026 Barcelona.
T. (93) 225 55 91. *062301*
Benthem Gross, Federico, Diputacion 304, 08009 Barce-
lona. T. (93) 318 47 23. - Orient / Sculp / Eth - *062302*
Berenguer-Jimenez, n., Espronceda 305, 80818 Barce-
lona. T. (93) 308 03 82. *062303*
Binomi, Sant Lluís 63, 08024 Barcelona.
T. (93) 210 81 01. - Graph - *062304*
Blanco Monsell, G., Via Augusta 106, 08006 Barcelona.
T. (93) 200 89 42. *062305*
Boada Saquero, Agustin, Pl. de San José Oriol 6, 08002
Barcelona. T. (93) 302 33 31. - Ant - *062306*
Bofil Pellicer, Boters 15, 08002 Barcelona.
T. (93) 318 79 43. *062307*
Bolet Farré, J. F., Milans, 4, 08002 Barcelona.
T. (93) 232 23 53. - Ant - *062308*
Brocante, Mallorca 279, 08037 Barcelona.
T. (93) 215 46 72. - Ant / Paint / Furn / China / Sculp /
Fra / Lights / Instr / Cur - *062309*
Cali Antiguedades, Aragón 534, 08026 Barcelona.
T. (93) 226 55 47. *062310*
Calico, X. & F., Pl. del Angel 2, 08002 Barcelona.
T. (93) 310 55 12/16, Fax 310 27 56. - Num - *062311*
Campanera Mata, J., Paja, 10, 08002 Barcelona.
T. (93) 222 90 43. - Ant - *062312*
Carlota, Paja 4, 08002 Barcelona.
T. (93) 301 56 87. *062313*

Cartago, Aragón 515, 08013 Barcelona.
T. (93) 246 25 81. *062314*
Casa Estrada, San Severo 3, 08002 Barcelona.
T. (93) 301 08 29. *062315*
Casa Maria Esclasans, Piedad 10, 08002 Barcelona.
T. (93) 315 02 58. - Ant - *062316*
Casa Yelmo, Travesera de Gracia, 123, 08012 Barcelo-
na. T. (93) 217 47 96. - Ant - *062317*
Casals, Calle Baños Nuevos 12, 08002 Barcelona.
T. (93) 317 93 96. *062318*
Chester Antiques, Sátalo 105-113, 08021 Barcelona.
T. (93) 200 97 60. *062319*
Chincho, Juan, Paja, 19, 08002 Barcelona.
T. (93) 222 90 43. - Ant - *062320*
Climent-Benaiges, V., Paris 205, 08008
Barcelona. *062321*
Coll Ros, V., Rossellón 224, 08008 Barcelona.
T. (93) 215 71 68. *062322*
Collection R, Calle Montcada 19, 08003 Barcelona.
T. (93) 3 310 33 11. - Orient - *062323*
Comart, Passaje Cataluña 100, 08026 Barcelona.
T. (93) 215 77 78. *062324*
Cordoba Garabain, Granados 147, 08017 Barcelona.
T. (93) 200 73 73. *062325*
Crisce, Muntaner 233, 08021 Barcelona.
T. (93) 200 43 28. - Ant / Graph / Furn / Repr / Dec /
Lights / Glass / Cur / Mod - *062326*
Cugat, Calle Baños Nuevos 20, 08002 Barcelona.
T. (93) 302 06 87. *062327*
Demel Pogorny, L., Aribau 129, 08036 Barcelona.
T. (93) 322 12 25. *062328*
Diabolo Cajuelo, Juan Sebastián Bach 22, 08021 Barce-
lona. T. (93) 239 52 88. *062329*
El Candil, Urgel, 280, Barcelona. T. (93) 230 84 12.
- Ant - *062330*
Eladio, Corchón Fernandez, Petrixol 1, 08002 Barcelona.
T. (93) 2 22 39 19. - Furn / Sculp - *062331*
Esclasans, Maria, Piedad 10, 08002 Barcelona.
T. (93) 315 02 58. - Ant / Paint / Furn / Cur - *062332*
Estrada-Fernandez, E., San Severo 3, 08002 Barcelona.
T. (93) 301 08 29. *062333*
Falgueras Carreras-Almato, B., Pza. San José Oriol, 4,
08001 Barcelona. T. (93) 301 71 91. - Paint / Furn /
Mil / Glass - *062334*
Forcada Rovira, R., Puerta del Angel, 3 y 5, 08002 Bar-
celona. T. (93) 231 05 74. - Ant - *062335*
Galan Cortes, A., Valencia 281, 08009 Barcelona.
T. (93) 215 39 96. *062336*
Galeria Oriol, Provenza 264, 08008 Barcelona.
T. (93) 215 21 13. *062337*
Galerias Linares, Plaza de Cristo Rey, 2bis, 08002 Bar-
celona. T. (93) 210 15 41. - Ant / Paint / Furn /
Eth - *062338*
Galerias Sant Jordi, Pl. del Rey, 9, 08002 Barcelona.
T. (93) 221 13 76. - Ant / Dec - *062339*
Galve, E., Paris 177, 08036 Barcelona.
T. (93) 245 45 42. *062340*
Gonzalez Sintes, Isidro, San Severo, 1, 08002 Barcelo-
na. T. (93) 229 01 00. - Ant - *062341*
Gothsland, Consell de Cent, 331, 08007 Barcelona.
T. (93) 302 49 91. *062342*
Grasas, Calle Baños Nuevos 14, 08002 Barcelona.
T. (93) 318 08 53. *062343*
Grasas Codina, Alberto, Baños Nuevos, 14, 08002 Bar-
celona. T. (93) 318 08 53, 317 88 38. - Paint / Furn /
China / Sculp - *062344*
Greca, Baños Nuevos 14, 08002 Barcelona.
T. (93) 302 57 39. - Ant / Paint / Furn / Sculp /
Silv - *062345*
Greca, Ganduxer 45, 08021 Barcelona.
T. (93) 201 04 70. *062346*
Grifé y Escoda, Avda. Glmd. Franco, 484, Barcelona.
T. (93) 228 78 61. - Paint / Furn / China / Sculp / Sculp /
Tex / Dec / Lights / Glass - *062347*
Herman's, Gran Via Carlos 59, 08028 Barcelona.
T. (93) 241 62 23. *062348*
Jacas, M., Valencia 544, 08026 Barcelona.
T. (93) 245 10 55. *062349*
Kensington, Paris 177, 08036 Barcelona.
T. (93) 200 45 42. *062350*
Las Lanzas, Aribau 116, 08036 Barcelona.
T. (93) 253 28 06. *062351*

Las Meninas, Paris, 205, 08008 Barcelona. T. (93) 230 63 18. - Ant / China - 062352
Leonora, Beethoven 13, 08021 Barcelona. T. (93) 239 04 16. 062353
Linares-Reyes, Pl. de la Catedral 2, 08002 Barcelona. T. (93) 310 15 41. 062354
Lottier, Pierre, Pérez Galdos, 4, 08012 Barcelona. T. (93) 217 35 37. 062355
Maassot, Emilio, Valencia, 170, 60, 08002 Barcelona. T. (93) 253 81 66. - Paint / Orient - 062356
Maragall, Calle Petrixol 5, 08002 Barcelona. T. (93) 318 70 20. 062357
Maragall, Pasaje Catalûna 116, 08026 Barcelona. T. (93) 218 29 60. 062358
Marti-Lluma, S., Provenza 243, 08008 Barcelona. T. (93) 215 93 82. 062359
Marti, Santiago, Provenza 243, 08008 Barcelona. T. (93) 215 93 82, Fax 215 9474. - Ant / Paint / Furn / China / Sculp / Tex - 062360
Martin Torrents, J. L., Ganduxer 45, 08021 Barcelona. T. (93) 201 04 70. 062361
Masip Pascual, José, Paja, 33, 08002 Barcelona. T. (93) 231 85 22. 062362
Milicua Inza, Florencio, Casanova, 97, 08010 Barcelona. T. (93) 253 63 19. 062363
Miro, Ramon, Floridablanca 110-112, 08015 Barcelona. T. (93) 223 41 40. - Ant / Furn - 062364
Nilo, Mallorca, 252, 08008 Barcelona. T. (93) 215 15 19. 062365
Ninfas, Paseo de Gracia 55-57, 08007 Barcelona. T. (93) 215 68 76. 062366
Noirjean, Alfredo, San Severo, 9, 08002 Barcelona. T. (93) 231 20 61. - Ant / Furn / Sculp / Dec - 062367
Novell, Calle Baños Nuevos 12, 08002 Barcelona. T. (93) 221 74 67. 062368
Ocasion, Dos de Mayo 211, 08013 Barcelona. T. (93) 226 31 51. 062369
Pardo, Enamorados 77, 08013 Barcelona. T. (93) 246 57 58. 062370
Pasaje, Mallorca 237, 08008 Barcelona. T. (93) 215 13 58. 062371
Pascual-Miro, Calle Baños Nuevos 14, 08002 Barcelona. 062372
Perez Hitacugat, Valliriana 79, 08006 Barcelona. T. (93) 212 50 44. 062373
Pérez Pagés, E., Paja, 8, 08002 Barcelona. T. (93) 231 83 50. - Ant - 062374
Pickwick, Rosellon 224, 08008 Barcelona. T. (93) 215 41 48, 215 74 68. 062375
Pinos-Sanchez, F., Consejo di Ciento 331, 08007 Barcelona. T. (93) 302 49 91. 062376
Pintó, Ramon, Passeig Sant Joan 176, 08037 Barcelona. T. (93) 258 38 16. - Graph - 062377
Pio-Cabello, C., Calle Paja 37, 08002 Barcelona. T. (93) 317 84 90. 062378
Pio-Cabello, J. M., San Honorato 9, 08002 Barcelona. T. (93) 317 10 79. 062379
Pironti, Mangos, Ernesto, Calle de la Paja, 3, 08002 Barcelona. T. (93) 221 44 72. - Ant / Cur - 062380
Pla de la Fuente, Aragón 517-519, 08013 Barcelona. T. (93) 231 15 08. 062381
Povo, Fernando, Baños Nuevos, 5, 08002 Barcelona. T. (93) 222 30 22. - Furn - 062382
Povo Sanchez, Codols 16, 08002 Barcelona. T. (93) 302 54 34. 062383
Puces Antiguedades, Vallmajor 31, 08021 Barcelona. T. (93) 211 79 96. 062384
Puig, Calle Banôs Nuevos 17, 08002 Barcelona. T. (93) 301 78 80. 062385
Quintana, San Severo 7, 08002 Barcelona. T. (93) 317 92 42. 062386
Ramon, Arturo, Paja 25, 08002 Barcelona. T. (93) 302 59 70, 302 59 74. - Ant / Paint / Furn / Sculp - 062387
Ramon Roman, Enriqueta, Paja, 5, 08002 Barcelona. T. (93) 231 21 01. - Furn / Sculp - 062388
Rampoines, Enrique-Granados 147, 08008 Barcelona. T. (93) 200 73 73. 062389
Roig-Hermanos, Aragón 526, 08013 Barcelona. T. (93) 226 00 31. 062390
Roure, Calle Paja 21, 08002 Barcelona. T. (93) 231 07 82. 062391
Rovira, Rambla Cataluña 62, 08002 Barcelona. T. (93) 215 20 92. 062392
Royo-Ruilopez, San Severo 5, 08002 Barcelona. T. (93) 317 82 81. 062393
Ruilopez Alonso, Pedro, San Severo, 8, 08002 Barcelona. T. (93) 221 56 73. - Furn / Sculp - 062394
Sabartés Massagué, Carmen, Paja, 21, 08002 Barcelona. T. (93) 231 07 82. - Ant - 062395
Sala-Brok, Via Layetana 180, 08010 Barcelona. 062396
Sala Gaspar, Consejo de Ciento 323, 08007 Barcelona. T. (93) 318 87 40. - Paint - 062397
Sanchez Cascales, Josefa, Bânos Nuevos, 20, 08002 Barcelona. T. (93) 222 85 28. - Ant - 062398
Sanchez, Hijos de A., Baños Nuevos 20, 08002 Barcelona. T. (93) 301 42 43. 062399
Sanchez Rovira, Juan José, Baños Nuevos, 17E, 08002 Barcelona. T. (93) 317 6230. - Ant - 062400
Santa Clara, Bajada Santa Clara, 2, 08002 Barcelona. T. (93) 221 93 02. - Ant - 062401
Santa's, Paeso de Gracia 55-57, 08007 Barcelona. T. (93) 216 04 41. 062402
Santos Palacios, Pilar, Ciudad de Balaguer, 54, 08002 Barcelona. T. (93) 247 42 72. - Ant - 062403
Sanz Blanco, German, Paja, 10, C, 2a, 08002 Barcelona. T. (93) 231 21 69. - Ant / Cur - 062404
Selvaggio-Montserrat, F., Freneria 12, 08002 Barcelona. T. (93) 315 15 56. 062405
Sir John, Rambla Cataluña 99, 08002 Barcelona. T. (93) 215 14 67. - Ant / Paint / Furn - 062406
Sitjas-Rosello, J., Aragón 530, 08026 Barcelona. T. (93) 225 55 21. 062407
Subastas, Provenza 257, 08008 Barcelona. 062408
Subex, Mallorca 253, 08008 Barcelona. T. (93) 204 05 45. 062409
Temps d'Ahir, Durán y Bas, 08002 Barcelona. T. (93) 317 62 27. 062410
Tirvia, Via Augusta 168, 08021 Barcelona. T. (93) 209 37 27. 062411
Tobajas-Purroy, A., Dos de Mayo 225, 08013 Barcelona. T. (93) 245 10 55. 062412
Toledo, Paja, 13-15, 08002 Barcelona. T. (93) 222 33 55. - Furn / Sculp - 062413
Torrente, Calle Baños Nuevos 14, 08002 Barcelona. T. (93) 231 07 67. 062414
Torres, José Antonio, Balmes 470, 08022 Barcelona. T. (93) 247 06 49. - Ant / Paint / Furn / Orient - 062415
Trallero, Aragón 530, 08013 Barcelona. T. (93) 232 91 60. 062416
Trallero-Sancho, M., Aragón 530-532, 08013 Barcelona. T. (93) 225 55 21. 062417
Truis-Esclanas, Piedad 10, 08002 Barcelona. T. (93) 315 02 58. 062418
Ubach, M., Paeso de Gracia 55, 08007 Barcelona. T. (93) 216 05 94. 062419
Urgell Llorens, Lorenzo, Piedad, 8, 08002 Barcelona. T. (93) 221 75 95. - Furn / China / Sculp / Silv - 062420
Valenti S. A., Provenza, 308, 08037 Barcelona. T. (93) 215 45 25. - Ant / Furn / Silv - 062421
Valro, Provenza 308, 08037 Barcelona. T. (93) 215 45 25. 062422
Vayreda, Rambla Cataluña 116, 08002 Barcelona. T. (93) 218 29 60. 062423
Verd-House, Mallorca 243, 08008 Barcelona. T. (93) 215 17 39. 062424
Vila, Xavier, Pasaje Mercader 10, 08008 Barcelona. T. (93) 215 92 05. - Paint / Furn - 062425
Vilaseca-Serratosa, Aribau 106, 08036 Barcelona. T. (93) 253 28 06. - Paint / Furn - 062426
Virallonga-Llunch, Consejo de Ciento 106, 08015 Barcelona. 062427
William's, Calle Provenza 215, 08036 Barcelona. T. (93) 21550 29. 062428
Xarrie-Rovira, J., Aribau 129, 08036 Barcelona. T. (93) 322 12 25. 062429
Xicranda, Consejo de Ciento 592, 08013 Barcelona. T. (93) 225 22 35. 062430

Benidorm (Alicante)

Linares Muonoz, Abelardo, Gambo, 3, 03500 Benidorm. T. (965) 36 15 62. - Ant - 062431

Bilbao (Vizcaya)

Eguia Lopez, Ma. Belén, Bolosticalle, 1, 48000 Bilbao. 062432
Herederos de Luis Loureiro, Marqués del Puerto, 9, 48008 Bilbao. T. (94) 21 44 09. - Ant - 062433
Rica Basagoiti, Marques del Puerto, 1, 48009 Bilbao. T. (94) 423 02 44. - Ant / Furn / Tex / Cur - 062434

Burgos

Arte Antigüedades, Paloma, 12, 09003 Burgos. T. (947) 20 03 01. - Ant / Furn / Sculp / Lights / Instr / Mil - 062435
Mediavilla, Avda. Reyes Catolicos, 21, 09005 Burgos. 062436

Bustillo de Cea (León)

Gonzalez Bello, Edesio, 24172 Bustillo de Cea. - Ant - 062437

Cádiz

Casa Rodriguez, Enrique de las Marinas, 1, 11003 Cádiz. T. (956) 21 31 04. - Paint / Furn / Sculp - 062438
El Jerazano, Sacramento, 18, 11001 Cádiz. T. (956) 21 48 45. - Furn - 062439
Gonzalez Ramos, Rafael, Vea Murguia, 8, 11003 Cádiz. T. (956) 21 37 31. - Ant / Furn - 062440

Callosa de Ensarriá (Alicante)

Galeria Arrabal, Arrabal 13, 03510 Callosa de Ensarriá. T. (965) 88 07 68. - Ant - 062441

Castellón de la Plana

Forcadell, Cristobal, Zaragoza, 24, 12001 Castellón de la Plana. - Ant - 062442

Córdoba

Aguilera Canete, Juan, Encarnacion, 7, 14013 Córdoba. T. (957) 22 32 19. - Ant / Arch - 062443
Casa Adarve Gonzalez, Magistral Gonzales Francés 11, 14013 Córdoba. T. (957) 22 64 91. - Paint / Furn / China / Mil - 062444

Corella (Navarra)

Agudo Sanchez, Joaquin, La Cruz, 6 Ü, 31591 Corella. T. (948) 780 298, 780 195. - Paint / Furn / Sculp / Mil - 062445
Siete Villas, Pérez Onate, 37, 31591 Corella. T. (948) 194. - Ant / Furn - 062446

El Ferrol del Caudillo (La Coruna)

La Ocasion, Canalejas, 116, 15400 El Ferrol del Caudillo. T. (981) 35 50 56. - Ant - 062447

Estella (Navarra)

Peral Vda. de Serapio Peral, Julio Ruiz de Alda, 1, 31200 Estella. T. (948) 15. - Ant - 062448

Figueres (Girona)

Quintana, Joan, Alvarez de Castro 29, 17600 Figueres. T. (972) 50 46 06. - Ant / Paint / Furn / China / Sculp / Fra / Instr / Mil / Cur - 062449
Quintana, Joan, Pep. Ventura 24-27, 17600 Figueres. T. (972) 50 46 06, 50 29 39. - Ant / Paint / Furn / China / Sculp / Fra / Instr / Mil / Cur - 062450

Fuenterrabia (Guipuzcoa)

Bidasoa, Plaza de Armas, 1, 20280 Fuenterrabia. T. (943) 643 096. 062451

Gijon (Asturias)

Miranda Fernandez, Alfredo, Covadonga, 3, 33201 Gijon. T. (985) 34 11 56. - Furn / Dec / Mil - 062452

Ginzo de Limia (Orense)

Lamas Lamas, Juan A., Gral. Franco, 104 Chalet Villa Antonia, Ginzo de Limia. - Ant - 062453

Girona

Pera Planells, Agustin, Subida Barrufa 15, 17007 Girona. T. (972) 20 63 56. - Ant - 062454
Valenti Clua, Fernando, Força, 19, 17004 Girona. T. (972) 20 18 67. - Ant / Furn / Silv - 062455

Granada

Guillermina Contreras del Pino, Ganivet, 7, Granada. T. (958) 22 76 29. - Paint / Furn / China / Mil - 062456

Linares Reyes, Josefa, Hotel Alhambra, Palacios, 18009 Granada. T. (958) 22 14 68. - Paint / Furn / Jew / Mil - *062457*

Lopez Benarte, Alcaiceria, s/n, 18001 Granada. - Ant - *062458*

Ruiz Linares, Alhambra 64, Puerta del Vino 2, 18009 Granada. T. (958) 22 19 71, 22 29 85. - Paint / Furn / China / Sculp / Glass - *062459*

Ibero (Navarra)

Echenique, Agapito Tina, 31173 Ibero. T. (948) 4. - Ant - *062460*

Jaén

Antaño, Virgen de la Capilla 7, 23001 Jaén. T. (953) 25 37 35. - Ant / Paint / China / Arch - *062461*

Jerez de la Frontera (Cádiz)

Isabelita, Clavel, 11, 11402 Jerez de la Frontera. T. (956) 25 28 52. - Paint / Furn - *062462*

La Coruña

Galerias Casimiro, Marcial del Adalid, 19, 15005 La Coruña. T. (981) 23 20 90. - Ant / Furn - *062463*

Vencia, Orzan, 40, 15003 La Coruña. T. (981) 22 60 94. - Paint / Furn / China / Instr / Mil - *062464*

La Junquera (Gerona)

Galerias Pirineos, Carretera de Francia, s/n, 17851 La Junquera. T. (972) 143. - Ant - *062465*

Las Arenas (Vizcaya)

Puente, M. a. Luisa, Calvo Sotelo, 18, 48930 Las Arenas. - Ant / Dec - *062466*

Las Palmas de Gran Canaria

Estoril, Triana 35, 35002 Las Palmas de Gran Canaria. T. (928) 37 31 36, 36 79 50, 36 40 85. - Ant / Paint / Paint / Num / Orient / China / Repr / Sculp / Instr / Cur -- *062467*

Logroño (La Rioja)

Martin Domingo, Francisco, Queipo de Llano, 35, 1, 26005 Logroño. T. (941) 24 78 34. - Furn / Repr - *062468*

Ochoa Rioja, José, Once de Junio, 3, e.0, 26001 Logroño. T. (941) 22 09 17. - Num / Sculp - *062469*

Lorca (Murcia)

Manzanera, Mariano, Fajardo el Bravo, s/n, 30800 Lorca. *062470*

Madrid

Abelardo-Linares, Pl. Cortes 11, 28014 Madrid. T. (91) 429 55 51. *062471*

Abolengo, Gal. Piquer, teinda, 4 Ribera de Curtidores, 29, 28005 Madrid. - Ant - *062472*

Acueducto, Ribera de Curtidores 29, 28005 Madrid. T. (91) 230 99 09. *062473*

Alcaraz Gonzalez, Francisco, Prim, 17, 5.0, 28004 Madrid. T. (91) 222 16 97. *062474*

Alcocer-Anticuarios, Pelayo, 68, 28004 Madrid. - Paint / Furn / China - *062475*

Alcocer Garcia, Jesus, Hortaleza, 104, 28004 Madrid. T. (91) 231 43 57. - Cur - *062476*

Alecon, Narcisos 60, Prado 29, 28016 Madrid. T. (91) 2 32 14 94, 23 13 029. - Ant / Paint / Furn / China / Instr - *062477*

Alenson, Villanueva 21, 28001 Madrid. T. (91) 225 98 63. *062478*

Alfonso, Ribera de Curtidores, 12 Nueves Galerias, 28005 Madrid. T. (91) 227 20 57. - Ant / Furn / Mil - *062479*

Almoneda, Recoletos, 4, 28001 Madrid. T. (91) 225 98 23. - Furn / Cur - *062480*

Almoneda, Carnero 17, 28005 Madrid. T. (91) 265 83 85. - Ant - *062481*

Almoneda, General Mola, 28, 28001 Madrid. T. (91) 225 67 25. - Ant / Paint - *062482*

Almoneda, Nuñez de Balboa, 85, 28006 Madrid. T. (91) 275 94 51. - Ant - *062483*

Almoneda, Plaza Gral. Vara del Rey, 5, 28045 Madrid. T. (91) 265 18 26. - Ant - *062484*

Almoneda, Illescas 22, 28024 Madrid. T. (91) 218 43 14. - Ant - *062485*

Almoneda, Ribera de Curtidores 29, 28005 Madrid. T. (91) 467 42 24. *062486*

Almoneda Doldan, Gal. Piquer, tda. 60 Ribera de Curtidores, 29, 28005 Madrid. T. (91) 227 06 68. - Ant - *062487*

Almoneda El Acueducto, Gal. Piquer, tienda 41 Ribera de Curtidores, 29, 28005 Madrid. T. (91) 228 00 29. - Furn - *062488*

Almoneda Palacios, Mira el Rio Baja, 21, 28005 Madrid. T. (91) 267 30 32. - Furn / China - *062489*

Almoya Bento, M. C., Hermosilla 37, 28001 Madrid. T. (91) T. 267 04 40. *062490*

Alonso, de Vda., Jorge Juan, 56, 28001 Madrid. T. (91) 435 95 74. - Ant / China / Fra / Silv / Instr / Cur - *062491*

Alonso Ojeda, Antonio, Ribera de Curtidores, 12, 28005 Madrid. T. (91) 222 90 13. - Ant - *062492*

Alvarez Gordon, Mercedes, Ribera de Curtidores, 29 Gal. Piquer, 28005 Madrid. T. (91) 239 49 66. - Ant - *062493*

Amieva Alonso, R., Huerta 17, 28004 Madrid. T. (91) 429 58 12. *062494*

Andrée y Hipola, Serrano, 16 y 28, 28001 Madrid. T. (91) 226 52 23. - Ant / Paint / Paint / Dec - *062495*

Andrés del Barrio, Antonia, Gal. Piquer Ribera de Curtidores, 29, 28005 Madrid. *062496*

Angel-Lucas, Jorge Juan 11, 28001 Madrid. T. (91) 276 17 40. *062497*

Angel Martinez, J., Barco 18, 28004 Madrid. T. (91) 221 08 30. *062498*

Antigüedadas Atelier, Ribera de Curtidores 15, 28005 Madrid. T. (91) 468 34 33. - Ant - *062499*

Arienza, Bravo, Carnero 17, 28005 Madrid. T. (91) 265 90 56. - Ant / Furn - *062500*

Arte, Gal. Piquer, tda. 69 Ribera de Curtidores, 29, 28005 Madrid. T. (91) 239 91 89. - Ant / Furn - *062501*

Arte de Reloxes, Plaza Santa Ana 10, 28012 Madrid. T. (91) 429 64 63. *062502*

Arte y Hogar, Gal. Piquer, tda. 29 Ribera de Curtidores, 29, 28005 Madrid. T. (91) 227 61 15. - Ant - *062503*

Aryan, Av. Alberto Alcocer 47, 28016 Madrid. T. (91) 250 84 40. - Ant - *062504*

Ateneo de Madrid, Prado 21, 28014 Madrid. T. (91) 429 74 42, 429 17 50. - Graph / Eth - *062505*

Auba Soro, Maria Teresa, Ribera de Curtidores 29 Gal. Piquer, tdas. 2 y 3, 28005 Madrid. T. (91) 239 84 60. - Ant / Paint / Furn / China / Tex / Cur - *062506*

Aurello, Serrano, 48, 28001 Madrid. T. (91) 225 91 12. - Ant / Dec - *062507*

Ayala Rodriguez, Pl. General Vara del Rey 15, 28045 Madrid. T. (91) 467 38 06. *062508*

Azipilicueta Aguilar, Zurbarán 20, 28010 Madrid. T. (91) 410 10 37. *062509*

Balboa, Nuñez de Balboa 13, 28001 Madrid. T. (91) 275 04 18. *062510*

Barragan Ramos, Almirante 10, 28004 Madrid. T. (91) 231 70 62. *062511*

Barranco, José, Gal. Ribera, tda. 10 Ribera de Curtidores, 15, 28005 Madrid. - Paint / China - *062512*

Begoña Zunzunegui, Lope de Vega, 31, 28014 Madrid. *062513*

Benavente Sanz, Francisca, Ribera de Curtidores, 14, 28005 Madrid. T. (91) 227 47 40. - Ant - *062514*

Benezit, Castillo Pineiro 8, 28039 Madrid. T. (91) 234 83 48. *062515*

Benito Blasco, Pedro, Ribera de Curtidores, 9, 28005 Madrid. - Ant - *062516*

Beralia, Barquillo 20, 28004 Madrid. T. (91) 221 08 73. - Paint - *062517*

Berenguer Lamdea, Antonia, Gal. Piquer, tda. 54 Ribera de Curtidores, 29, 28005 Madrid. T. (91) 227 06 68, 251 87 76. - Ant / Furn / Sculp - *062518*

Berkowitsch-Isgur, J., Velázquez 4, 28001 Madrid. T. (91) 411 21 73. *062519*

Bermejo del Moral, Marta, Nuevas Galerias Ribera de Curtidores, 12, 28005 Madrid. - Ant - *062520*

Bernatets Lesbat, Andrea, Serrano, 16, 28001 Madrid. - Ant - *062521*

Blanco Monsell, Principe de Vargara 25, 28001 Madrid. T. (91) 275 18 20. *062522*

Bolano-Rodriguez, L., Carnero 27, 28005 Madrid. T. (91) 265 88 49. *062523*

Botticelli, Juan Bravo, 33, 28006 Madrid. T. (91) 411 14 78. *062524*

Bravo-Arienza, Carnero 17, 28005 Madrid. T. (91) 265 90 56. *062525*

Brunswick, Prado 12, 28014 Madrid. T. (91) 429 51 69. - Ant / Paint / Graph / Furn - *062526*

Caballero-Calvo 29, Ribera de Curtidores 29, 28005 Madrid. *062527*

Caballero Chozas, Justo, Donoso Cortés, 18, 28015 Madrid. T. (91) 223 16 20. *062528*

Cacheiro, Puebla, 15, 28004 Madrid. T. (91) 221 24 44. - Ant - *062529*

Canada-Cordero, A., Ribera de Curtidores 29, 28005 Madrid. *062530*

Canas Sans, J., Ribera de Curtidores 15, 28005 Madrid. T. (91) 468 65 26. *062531*

Càrabe, Nuevas Galerias Ribera de Curtidores 12, 28005 Madrid. T. (91) 2 27 20 57, 2 30 65 21. - Ant - *062532*

Carabe-Palacio, L., Ribera de Curtidores 29, 28005 Madrid. T. (91) 230 58 46. *062533*

Cardani Art Search, Prof Waksman, 12, 28036 Madrid. T. (91) 4588279, Fax 4588974. - Paint / Sculp - *062534*

Cardani, Daniel, Prof Waksman, 12, 28036 Madrid. T. (91) 4588279, Fax 4588974. - Paint / Sculp - *062535*

Carmela, Gal. Piquer Ribera de Curtidores, 29, 28005 Madrid. T. (91) 239 99 67. - Ant - *062536*

Carretero Duran, Rosalia, Carnero, 1, 28005 Madrid. - Cur - *062537*

Casa Apolinar Sanchez-Villalba, Santa Calatina, 5, 28014 Madrid. T. (91) 222 38 85. - Ant - *062538*

Casa y Jardin, S. A., Padilla, 21 y 32, 28006 Madrid. T. (91) 225 39 52. - Furn / Dec / Cur - *062539*

Castan, Carlos, Colmenares 9, 28004 Madrid. T. (91) 232 58 37. - Num - *062540*

Castillejos Tejero, Rafaela, Ribera de Curtidores, 29, 28005 Madrid. T. (91) 230 96 90. - Ant - *062541*

Cayard-Reig, M. C., Claudio Coello 93, 28006 Madrid. T. (91) 225 76 98. *062542*

Caylus, Lagasca 28, 28001 Madrid. T. (91) 578 30 98, Fax 577 77 79. *062543*

Cayon, A. Figueroa 4, 28004 Madrid. T. (91) 222 62 67, 222 63 32. *062544*

Cayon, Juan R., Fuencarral 41, 28004 Madrid. T. (91) 211 08 32, 221 43 72. - Num - *062545*

Cayon, Juan R., Mayor 27, 28013 Madrid. T. (91) 266 50 33, 266 39 96. - Num / Arch / Eth / Cur - *062546*

Centro de Anticuarios Lagasca, Lagasca 36, 28001 Madrid. *062547*

Colecciones Particulares, Victor Pradera 32, Madrid. T. (91) 2 47 48 58. - Paint - *062548*

Concha Barrios, Claudio Coello 17, 28001 Madrid. T. (91) 275 14 39. *062549*

Cortés Oliver, Nicolas, Plaza de la Cebada, 7, 28005 Madrid. T. (91) 265 36 95. - Ant - *062550*

Crimea, Ribera de Curtidores 12, 28005 Madrid. T. (91) 230 80 29. *062551*

Curiosidades, Gal. Piquer, tda. 14 Ribera de Curtidores, 29, 28005 Madrid. T. (91) 227 73 89. - Ant - *062552*

Davenport, Ribera de Curtidores 29, 28005 Madrid. T. (91) 230 57 16. *062553*

Decoracion 25, Autopista de Valencia 25 km, Madrid. T. (91) 231 82 80. - Paint - *062554*

Del Carmen Perez, Pl. General Vara del Rey 5, 28005 Madrid. T. (91) 266 28 36. *062555*

Del Rey Canana, Jose Maria, Ribera de Curtidores 12, 28005 Madrid. T. (91) 227 61 46. *062556*

Delgado Baquerizo, J., San Agustin 7, 28014 Madrid. T. (91) 429 94 03. *062557*

Desvan de Madrid, Alcalá 211, 28028 Madrid. T. (91) 255 60 16. *062558*

Diaz, A., Hortaleza 110, 28004 Madrid. T. (91) 419 04 88. *062559*

Diaz Nieto, Esther, Castelló 3, 28001 Madrid. - Furn / Cur - *062560*

Diaz Recuero, F., Atocha 111, 28012 Madrid. T. (91) 429 10 65. *062561*

Diez Colomo, Pedro, Feijoo, 3, 28010 Madrid. T. (91) 224 72 76. - Ant - *062562*

Diez Monsalve, Prado 28, 28014 Madrid. T. (91) 429 33 35. *062563*

Doldan, Ribera de Curtidores 29, 28005 Madrid.
T. (91) 468 33 36. 062564
Dominguez Borrajo, Victor, Lucio del Valle, 12, 28003
Madrid. T. (91) 254 04 82. 062565
Don Braulio, C., Coello 38, 28001 Madrid.
T. (91) 435 01 27. 062566
Dona Urraca, S. A., Velazquez 86, 28006 Madrid.
T. (91) 225 50 62. - Ant / Furn / Dec - 062567
Donvito Ontiveros, Gurtubay 4, 28001 Madrid.
T. (91) 275 54 97. 062568
Duran, Pedro, S. A., Serrano, 12 y 30, 28001 Madrid.
T. (91) 276 30 00, 226 54 17. 062569
El Arca de Noé, Gal. Piquer, tda. 50 Ribera de Curtidores,
29, 28005 Madrid. T. (91) 230 96 90. - Paint / Furn /
Sculp - 062570
El Monasterio, Gal. Piquer, tda. 47 Ribera de Curtidores,
29, 28005 Madrid. T. (91) 230 99 09. - Ant /
Furn - 062571
Encarnacion, Claudio Coello 88, 28001 Madrid.
T. (91) 226 50 02. 062572
Escudero Bayo, José, General Mola, 28, 28001 Madrid.
T. (91) 225 67 25. - Ant - 062573
Espinosa Ruiz, M., Nuñez de Balboa 42, 28001 Madrid.
T. (91) 276 17 31. 062574
Establecimientos Maragall, S. A., Po Eduardo Dato 17,
28010 Madrid. T. (91) 223 80 53. - Ant / Paint /
Paint - 062575
Esteban Rodriguez, Avda. Betanzos 28, 28029 Madrid.
T. (91) 201 11 33. 062576
Esther, Castello, 3, 28001 Madrid. - Furn / Cur - 062577
Eutiquiano Garcia, S. A., Plaza Santa Ana, 7, 28012 Ma-
drid. T. (91) 221 47 72. - Ant / Paint / Furn / China /
Sculp / Tex / Jew - 062578
Fernandez Arriola, Ribera de Curtidores 12, 28005 Ma-
drid. T. (91) 239 72 50. 062579
Fernandez Jaldon Vindel, J. M., Hermosilla 59, 28001
Madrid. T. (91) 275 99 50. 062580
Ferrari, Tienda 28 Ribera de Curtidores 29, 28005 Ma-
drid. T. (91) 2 28 13 27. - Ant - 062581
Fortuny Antiguedades, Fortuny 13, 28010 Madrid.
T. (91) 410 10 37. 062582
Frame, General Pardiñas 69, 28006 Madrid.
T. (91) 411 33 62. 062583
Fresno Ruiz, Angel, Gal. Piquer, tda. 26 Ribera de Curti-
dores, 29, 28005 Madrid. T. (91) 230 64 97. - Paint /
China / Sculp - 062584
Fresno Ruiz, Manuel, Gal. Piquer, tda. 40 Ribera de Cur-
tidores, 29, 28005 Madrid. T. (91) 228 00 29. - Ant /
Furn - 062585
Galeria Kreisler, Serrano, 19, 28001 Madrid.
T. (91) 226 05 43. - Ant - 062586
Galeria Velazquez, Velazquez, 40, 28001 Madrid.
T. (91) 276 26 20, 276 45 04. - Ant / Paint / Paint / Chi-
na / Tex / Instr - 062587
Galerias San Agustin, San Agustin 3, 28014 Madrid.
T. (91) 221 98 13. - Paint / Dec - 062588
Gambara, Jose Ortega y Gasset 33, 28006 Madrid.
T. (91) 276 90 55. 062589
Gamero, Francisco Silvela, 45, 28028 Madrid.
T. (91) 226 04 23, 230 40 60, 275 66 89. - Ant / Furn /
Sculp / Tex / Lights - 062590
Garcia + Fresno, Goya 28, 28001 Madrid.
T. (91) 2 25 12 25. - Ant - 062591
Garcia Albuquerque, A. Jesus, Ribera de Curtidores, 19,
28005 Madrid. T. (91) 227 32 20. 062592
Garcia de Arriba, Manuel, Plaza Santa Ana, 12, 28012
Madrid. - Ant - 062593
Garcia Saro, Jesus, Serrano, 48, 28001 Madrid.
T. (91) 226 81 62. - Cur - 062594
Gavar, Almagro 32, 28010 Madrid.
T. (91) 410 45 77. 062595
Gil Albarran, J., Pl. General Vara del Rey 13, 28005 Ma-
drid. T. (91) 227 07 12. 062596
Gil, F., Mira el Rio Alta 4, 28005 Madrid.
T. (91) 265 90 96. 062597
Giner Jurado, Fernando, José Abascal 26, 28003 Ma-
drid. T. (91) 448 58 56. 062598
Gomez Coronel, Embajadores 30, 28012 Madrid.
T. (91) 468 75 01. 062599
Gomez Ramos, Amparo, Ribera de Curtidores, 14,
28005 Madrid. - Cur - 062600
Gonzales-Gonzales, J., Jorge Juan 51, 28001
Madrid. 062601

Gonzales-Salina, E., Ribera de Curtidores 12, 28005
Madrid. 062602
Gorzan Fridman, Moreria 2, 28005 Madrid.
T. (91) 226 14 75. 062603
Guardia Martin, M. L., Ribera de Curtidores 29, 28005
Madrid. T. (91) 230 64 99. 062604
Guillamon Leon, José, Nuevas Galerias, tda. 33 Ribera
de Curtidores, 12, 28005 Madrid. T. (91) 227 00 44.
- Ant - 062605
Guinea, José, Gal. Piquer, tda. 6 Ribera de Curtidores,
29, 28005 Madrid. T. (91) 227 95 45. - Ant - 062606
Gurich, Mq. de Viana 40, 28025 Madrid.
T. (91) 442 96 36. - Ant / Furn / China - 062607
Gurtubay, Gurtubay 4, 28001 Madrid.
T. (91) 275 54 97. 062608
Gutiérrez Barbero, Emeterio, Nuevas Galerias, tda. 19
Ribera de Curtidores, 12, 28005 Madrid.
T. (91) 239 00 11. - Ant - 062609
Hernandez Martinez, J., Santa Ana 23, 28005 Madrid.
T. (91) 265 03 09. 062610
Hernandez Rodriguez, Agustin, Mira el Sol, 13, 28005
Madrid. T. (91) 228 55 42. - Ant - 062611
Herranz Garcia, Eugenio, Casado del Alisal 6, 28014
Madrid. T. (91) 227 15 07. - Ant / Furn / Sculp - 062612
Hidalgo Malaguilla, Jesus, Gal. Piquer, tdas. 23 y 25 Ri-
bera de Curtidores, 29, 28005 Madrid.
T. (91) 230 56 53. - Paint / Furn / Num - 062613
Hinojosa Garcia, F., Prado 9, 28014 Madrid.
T. (91) 231 18 36. 062614
Hipola, Galeria Serrano 16, 28001 Madrid.
T. (91) 431 25 56, 431 67 37. - Paint / Furn / China /
Sculp / Silv / Glass - 062615
Humanes Lopez Dechaves. M., Velasquez 46, 28001
Madrid. T. (91) 275 36 56. 062616
Ibero Americana de Numismatico, S.A., Galeria, Plaza
Salamanca 9, 28006 Madrid. T. (91) 226 44 65.
- Num - 062617
Iglesia, Gal. Piquer, tda. 32 Ribera de Curtidores, 29,
28005 Madrid. - Ant - 062618
Iglesia Caro, J., Lopez Silva 3, 28005 Madrid.
T. (91) 265 62 80. 062619
Iglesias Cubria, J., Lopez de Hayos 5, 28006 Madrid.
T. (91) 261 62 17. 062620
Ilarri Ortiz, Nuevas Galerias, Ribera de Curtidores, 12,
28005 Madrid. - Ant - 062621
Illary Oritz, Ribera de Curtidores 12, 28005
Madrid. 062622
Ispahan, Serrano 6, 28001 Madrid.
T. (91) 431 41 20. 062623
Italica, Velazquez 54, 28001 Madrid. T. (91) 275 29 15.
- Ant / Paint / Graph / Furn / Orient / China / Sculp / Tex /
Dec / Lights / Instr / Rel / Cur / Mod / Ico / Draw - 062624
Jabato-Jimenez, L., Ribera de Curtidores 29, 28005 Ma-
drid. T. (91) 239 91 89. 062625
Jaraba Mesas, J., Carnero 17, 28005 Madrid.
T. (91) 265 88 49. 062626
Jeronimo, Carnero 6, 28005 Madrid.
T. (91) 239 98 76. 062627
Jimenez Fernandez, J., Rodas 4, 28005 Madrid.
T. (91) 227 69 77. 062628
Juan Silva, Gal. Piquer Ribera de Curtidores, 29, 28005
Madrid. - Ant - 062629
Julfe, Nuevas Galerias Ribera de Curtidores, 12, 28005
Madrid. T. (91) 239 00 11. - Ant - 062630
Kilim, Velazquez 75, 28001 Madrid. T. (91) 276 95 86.
- Ant - 062631
La Llave, Nuevas Galerias, tda. 35 Ribera de Curtidores,
12, 28005 Madrid. T. (91) 239 72 60. - Furn /
Dec - 062632
Lage, Nuevas Galerias Ribera de Curtidores, 12, 28005
Madrid. T. (91) 239 93 41. - Ant - 062633
Leon Marin, P., Santa Catalina 7, 28014 Madrid.
T. (91) 247 45 50, 429 79 63. 062634
Linares, Abelardo, S. A., Carrera San Jeronimo, 48,
28014 Madrid. T. (91) 221 46 27, 221 14 99.
- Ant - 062635
Linares Rodriguez de Velasco, C., San Agustin 3, 28014
Madrid. T. (91) 221 98 13. 062636
Linson S.A., Calle del Prado 29, 28014 Madrid. - Furn /
China / Sculp / Tex - 062637
Lopez Alonso, Maria, Nuevas Galerias, Ribera de Curti-
dores, 12, 28005 Madrid. - Ant - 062638

Lopez Bouza, E., Goya 44, 28001 Madrid.
T. (91) 275 28 42. 062639
Lopez de Aragon, Felix, Serrano, 87, 28006 Madrid.
T. (91) 276 85 92. 062640
Lopez Montero, Pedro, Péz, 15, 28004 Madrid.
T. (91) 221 74 87. 062641
Lopez Palomar, Pedro, Prado, 3, 28014 Madrid.
T. (91) 222 42 57. - Silv - 062642
Lopez Reiz, Gal. Piquer, tda. 59 Ribera de Curtidores,
29, 28005 Madrid. T. (91) 239 50 80. - Ant - 062643
Los Andes, Ribera de Curtidores 29, 28005 Madrid.
T. (91) 468 09 52. - Ant - 062644
Los Toledanos, Gal. Piquer, tda. 20 Ribera de Curtidores,
29, 28005 Madrid. T. (91) 228 52 49. - Ant - 062645
Los Tres Luises, Prado 16, 28014 Madrid.
T. (91) 221 06 21. - Ant / Paint / Arch - 062646
Lotus Imports, Azulinas 7, 28036 Madrid.
T. (91) 457 65 66. 062647
Lozano Delgado, I., Ribera de Curtidores 12, 28005 Ma-
drid. T. (91) 468 29 73. 062648
Lozano Delgado, S., Ribera de Curtidores 29, 28005 Ma-
drid. T. (91) 228 41 65. 062649
Lucas Villar, Angel, Gal. Piquer, tda. 16 Ribera de Curti-
dores, 29, 28005 Madrid. T. (91) 227 51 12.
- Ant - 062650
Lugo Hernandez, C., Rodas 26, 28005 Madrid.
T. (91) 467 04 31. 062651
Luis Carabe, Ribera de Curtidores, 12 Nuevas Galerias,
28005 Madrid. T. (91) 227 20 57, 230 65 21. - Paint /
Furn / Silv / Mil - 062652
Mahogany, S. L., Bravo 41, 28005 Madrid.
T. (91) 402 92 95. 062653
Maquiscut, C., Claudio Coello 141, 28006 Madrid.
T. (91) 262 87 61. 062654
Marco Polo, Paseo de la Habana 56, 28036 Madrid.
T. (91) 2 50 26 09. - Graph / Repr - 062655
Marfé, Gal. Piquer, tda. 28 Ribera de Curtidores, 29,
28005 Madrid. - Ant - 062656
Martin-Davila, C., Carnero 2, 28005 Madrid.
T. (91) 467 33 32. 062657
Martin Franco, Manuel, Santa Catalina, 4, 28014 Ma-
drid. T. (91) 232 25 78. - Ant - 062658
Martin Nieto, I., Nuñez de Balboa 85, 28001 Madrid.
T. (91) 411 32 38. 062659
Martinez de Luis, F., Jardines 12, 28013 Madrid.
T. (91) 231 16 95. 062660
Martinez Hernandez, Patricio, Plaza Gral. Vara de Rey,
15, 28045 Madrid. T. (91) 468 34 33. 062661
Martinez, Ricardo Martin de Diego, Carnero 4, 28005
Madrid. T. (91) 539 31 00. - Ant / Furn / China / Dec /
Lights / Instr - 062662
Martinez Ruiz, A., Ribera de Curtidores, 29 Gal. Piquer,
tda. 30, 28005 Madrid. T. (91) 228 69 75.
- Ant - 062663
Martinez-Santamaria, B., León 3, 28014 Madrid.
T. (91) 429 51 97. 062664
Mateos-Garcia, Nuñez de Balboa 27, 28001 Madrid.
T. (91) 276 36 21. 062665
McGregor, Graham Kennth, Ribera de Curtidores 45,
28005 Madrid. T. (91) 468 34 33. 062666
Mendoza Solano, M. R., José Ortega y Gasset 33, 28006
Madrid. T. (91) 276 90 55. 062667
Merino Gil, C., Pl. de Santa Barbara 3, 28004 Madrid.
T. (91) 447 75 42. 062668
Merodio Ibanez, Recoletos 4, 28001 Madrid.
T. (91) 225 98 23. 062669
Mexico Antiguedades, Huertas 17, 28012 Madrid.
T. (91) 429 58 12. 062670
Mi Casa del Rastro, Ribera de Curtidores, 31, 28005
Madrid. T. (91) 227 77 03, 239 71 76. - Ant /
Furn - 062671
Miro Coll, E., Pl. General Vara del Rey 15, 28005 Madrid.
T. (91) 468 01 22. 062672
Momplet, Antonio, Velazquez, 27, 28001 Madrid.
T. (91) 275 24 55. - Ant / Furn - 062673
Morales Garcia, Lagasca, 37, 28001 Madrid.
T. (91) 221 77 23. - Ant - 062674
Morcillo Lopez, E., Ribera de Curtidores 29, 28005 Ma-
drid. T. (91) 228 13 00. 062675
Morueco Rodriguez, L., Praqdo 16, 28014 Madrid.
T. (91) 221 02 81. 062676
Morueco Rodriguez, L., Prado 15, 28014 Madrid.
T. (91) 429 36 59. 062677

Moya Castro, Gerardo, Pelayo 5, 28004 Madrid.
T.(91) 221 37 37. - Ant -   062678
Muebles Aurelio, Serrano 48, 28006 Madrid.
T. (91) 431 81 62.   062679
Munoz Garcia Martin, Almagro, 30, 28010 Madrid.
T. (91) 257 12 57. - Paint / Num -   062680
Nogues Huguet, J., Orense 37, 28020 Madrid.
T. (91) 455 05 26.   062681
Novart, Monte Esquinza 46, 28010 Madrid.
T. (91) 419 79 86.   062682
Ontalva Rodriguez, J., Pl. Santa Ana 10, 28012 Madrid.
T. (91) 429 64 63.   062683
Ordaz y Norris, S. L., Jorge Juan 9, 28001 Madrid.
T. (91) 431 36 02.   062684
Orno, Covarrubias 20, 28010 Madrid. T. (91) 447 71 95.
- Ant / Furn -   062685
Palacios de Paz, Manuela, Plaza Gral. Vara del Rey, 15,
28045 Madrid. T. (91) 227 31 70.   062686
Pascual Bermejo, M., Ribera de Curtidores 12, 28005
Madrid. T. (91) 227 16 01.   062687
Paternina, Alvaro, Velazquez, 38, 28001 Madrid.
T. (91) 575 3820, 431 2778. - Ant / Paint / Furn / Orient /
Tex / Dec / Silv / Instr -   062688
Pelta Martin, E., Ribera de Curtidores 29, 28005
Madrid.   062689
Pena, Prado 5, 28014 Madrid. T. (91) 429 61 34.   062690
Pérez Llinador, Marcial, Gal. Piquer, tda. 58 Ribera de
Curtidores, 29, 28005 Madrid. T. (91) 230 96 59.
- Ant -   062691
Perez-Munos, J., Hilarión Eslava 13, 28015 Madrid.
T. (91) 244 02 51.   062692
Pérez Pérez, Roman, Ribera de Curtidores, 12, 28005
Madrid.   062693
Perez Silva, M., Ribera de Curtidores 12, 28005 Madrid.
T. (91) 228 40 36.   062694
Pergamino, Juan Bravo 22, 28006 Madrid.
T. (91) 275 94 51.   062695
Pessan Louche, N., Ribera de Curtidores 29, 28005 Ma-
drid. T. (91) 467 23 94.   062696
Pidal Alvarez, J. J., Joaquin Costa 59, 28002 Madrid.
T. (91) 261 16 67.   062697
Pinto-Coelho, Don Pedro 8, 28005 Madrid.
T. (91) 265 86 59.   062698
Pinto Torrijos, Laureano, Ribera de Curtidores, 29 Galeri-
as Piquer, tda. 65, 28005 Madrid. T. (91) 467 35 43.
- Ant / Mil -   062699
Pinto Torrijos, V., Ribera de Curtidores 29, 28005 Ma-
drid. T. (91) 475 65 32.   062700
Quintanilla Gutiérrez, Angel, Carnero, 6, 28005 Madrid.
T. (91) 239 32 09. - Ant -   062701
Quintanilla Serrano, Jeromino, Carlos Arniches, 7,
28005 Madrid. T. (91) 227 94 04. - Ant -   062702
Rafael, Plaza Gral. Vara del Rey, 12, 28045 Madrid.
T. (91) 265 88 19. - Ant / Graph / Furn / Dec -   062703
Rena Perales, Enrique, Prado, 11, 28014 Madrid.
T. (91) 231 88 46. - Ant -   062704
Retiro, Alfonso XII 10, 28014 Madrid.
T. (91) 232 67 71.   062705
Rey Camara, José Maria del, Ribera de Curtidores, 12
Nuevas Galerias, 28005 Madrid. T. (91) 227 61 46.
- Ant / Furn -   062706
Rey Fernandez-Latorre, E. C., Claudio Coello 35, 28001
Madrid. T. (91) 275 30 11.   062707
Reyna Perales, E., Prado 11, 28014 Madrid.
T. (91) 2 31 88 46. - Ant -   062708
Rios Garcia, Carlos, Nuevas Galerias, tda. 25 Ribera der
Curtidores, 12, 28005 Madrid. T. (91) 230 78 83.
- Ant / Paint / Furn / Sculp -   062709
Robles Pérez, Federico, Nuevas Galerias Ribera de Curti-
dores, 12, 28005 Madrid. - Ant -   062710
Rodriguez Encarnacion, Antonio, Claudio Coello, 88,
28001 Madrid. T. (91) 226 50 02. - Ant / Paint /
Sculp -   062711
Rodriguez y Jiménez S. L., Calle del Prado, 15, 28014
Madrid. T. (91) 222 33 32. - Paint / Furn /
Sculp -   062712
Romero Fernandez, Rafael, Calle del Prado, 23, 28014
Madrid. T. (91) 231 14 46. - Ant / Paint / Furn / Sculp /
Arch -   062713
Romero, L., Plaza General Vara de Rey 14, 28045 Ma-
drid. T. (91) 467 35 42. - Ant / Paint / Furn -   062714

Rosales Padin, Rosario, Nuevas Galerias Ribera de Curti-
dores, 12, 28005 Madrid. T. (91) 239 98 71. - Furn /
China -   062715
Sala-Franca, Carr. San Jeronimo 46, 28014 Madrid.
T. (91) 222 04 99. - Ant -   062716
Salinas Gonzalvez, Elena, Nuevas Galerias Ribera de
Curtidores, 12, 28005 Madrid. - Ant -   062717
San-Say, Nuevas Galerias Ribera de Curtidores, 12,
28005 Madrid. T. (91) 227 05 81. - Paint / Furn /
Sculp -   062718
Sanchez Sanchez, Pedro, Ribera de Curtidores, 6,
28005 Madrid. T. (91) 227 05 10. - Paint / Furn /
Mil -   062719
Sanchiz Pérez, Pilar, Gal. Piquer, tda. 5 Ribera de Curti-
dores, 29, 28005 Madrid. T. (91) 227 28 96.
- Ant -   062720
Santiso, Nuevas Galerias Ribera de Curtidores, 12,
28005 Madrid. T. (91) 239 75 70. - Ant -   062721
Selobo, Goya 44, 28001 Madrid. T. (91) 275 28 42.
- Ant -   062722
Serrano Pombo, J. C., Claudio Coello 43, 28001 Madrid.
T. (91) 431 40 56.   062723
Setien Alvarez, Juan, Carnero, 6, 28005 Madrid.
- Ant -   062724
Silva, Fruto de Juan, Ribera de Curtidores 29, 28005
Madrid. T. (91) 4 67 23 94.   062725
Silva Maese, Magdalena, Ribera de Curtidores, 12,
28005 Madrid. T. (91) 228 40 36. - Ant -   062726
Silva Pita, Ofelia, Ribera de Curtidores, 33, 28005 Ma-
drid. - Ant -   062727
Sobrina de Martinez, Nuevas Galerias Ribera de Curtido-
res, 12, 28005 Madrid. T. (91) 239 00 11. - Ant / Paint /
Sculp -   062728
Somacarrera Carbonell, Manuel, Gal. Piquer, tda. 17 Ri-
bera de Curtidores, 29, 28005 Madrid.
T. (91) 228 65 34. - Ant / Furn -   062729
Sontillana, Velazquez 47, 28001 Madrid.
T. (91) 276 35 98, 276 28 44. - Furn / Dec -   062730
Suarte, calle del Prado no. 8, 28014 Madrid.
T. (91) 222 56 82. - Ant / Tex -   062731
Sugesa, Domingo Fernández 5, 28036 Madrid.
T. (91) 457 66 33/99 60, Fax 457 86 29. - Ant / Paint /
Furn / China -   062732
Teodora, Ribera de Curtidores, 29, 28005 Madrid.
- Ant -   062733
Tomas, Gal. Piquer, tda. 56 Ribera de Curtidores, 29,
28005 Madrid. T. (91) 228 02 17. - Paint /
Furn -   062734
Torre, de la, Almirante 23, 28004 Madrid.
T. (91) 231 98 96.   062735
Turrero Lucia, Manuel, Ribera de Curtidores, 12, 28005
Madrid. T. (91) 239 86 63. - Mil -   062736
Usallan Pérez, Eloy, Gal. Piquer, tda. 27 Ribera de Curti-
dores, 29, 28005 Madrid. T. (91) 227 61 84. - Furn /
China / Sculp / Mil -   062737
Valenti S. A., Juan Bravo 9, 28006 Madrid.
T. (91) 276 89 57, 276 89 58. - Ant -   062738
Vázquez, Antonio, Nuevas Galerias, Ribera de Curtidores
12, 28005 Madrid. T. (91) 2 39 93 41. - Ant -   062739
Venavente Sanz, Francisca, Ribera de Curtidores 14,
28005 Madrid. - Ant -   062740
Vindel Cuesta, José Pedro, Prado, 7, 28014 Madrid.
T. (91) 222 08 80. - Ant / Graph -   062741
Viudas Munoz, Antonio, Cruz, 6, 28012 Madrid.
T. (91) 221 02 75. - Ant -   062742
Zazo Jiménez, Gonzalo, Gal. Piquer, tda. 15 Ribera de
Curtidores, 29, 28005 Madrid. T. (91) 227 06 56.
- Paint / Furn / China -   062743
Zurdo, M. J., Ribera de Curtidores 15, 28005
Madrid.   062744

Málaga (Malaga)

Blasco Alarcon, Salvador, Molina Larios, 4, 29015 Mála-
ga. T. (952) 21 20 02. - Ant -   062745
Delgado de Mayorga, Isidora, Carreteria, 125, 29008
Málaga. T. (952) 22 24 31. - Paint / Furn /
China -   062746
Lozano Delgado, Sebastian, Alamos, 10, 29012 Málaga.
T. (952) 21 09 22, 25 08 30. - Ant -   062747
Paquita, Ollerias, 4, 29002 Málaga. T. (952) 21 97 17.
- Ant -   062748

Marbella (Málaga)

Crevisa, Muelle Ribera, Casa N, 29600 Marbella.
T. (952) 81 56 53. - Ant / Paint / Furn / Repr /
Draw -   062749
La Caracola, Oritz de Molinillo, 10, 29600 Marbella.
T. (952) 82 30 59. - Num / China -   062750
Moufflet, Louis, Carretera de Cadiz, El Rosario, 29600
Marbella. T. (952) 77 48 41.   062751

Mataro (Barcelona)

Soler Gonzalez José, San Benito, 34, 08302 Mataro.
- Cur -   062752

Murcia

Chys, Traperia, 11, 30001 Murcia. - Ant / Cur -   062753
Numismatica Llorente, San José, 34, 30003 Murcia.
T. (968) 21 64 34. - Num -   062754

Navarra

El Rastro, Descalzos, 11, 31001 Navarra.
T. (948) 21 47 01. - Ant / Furn -   062755

Orense

Angel, Lamas Carvajal, 8, Orense. T. (988) 11 94.
- Ant -   062756
Casa Ros, Marinamansa, 11, Orense. T. (988) 21 36 34,
21 44 68. - Furn / Sculp -   062757
Lopez, Abel, Avda. de Portugal 96, 32002
Orense.   062758
Pérez Ferreiro, Urbano, Avda. de Portugal, 96, 32002
Orense. T. (988) 217427. - Ant -   062759

Orihuela (Alicante)

Fenoll Martinez, Antonio, San Agustin, 27, 03300
Orihuela.   062760

Oviedo (Asturias)

Esperanza, Mon, 20, 33003 Oviedo. T. (985) 21 29 28.
- Ant / Furn -   062761

Palafrugell (Gerona)

Antigüedades Marti, Palamos, 16, 17200 Palafrugell.
T. (972) 30 01 18. - China -   062762

Palamós (Gerona)

Antigüedades Altamira, Paseo 18 de Julio, 27, 17230
Palamós. - Ant -   062763

Palma de Mallorca (Baleares)

Casa Buades, Pla. de Cort, 32, 07001 Palma de Mallorca. T. (971) 21 21 40.   062764
Casa Delmonte, via Roma, 16, 07012 Palma de Mallor-
ca. T. (971) 21 50 47. - Furn / Cur -   062765
Juan, Juan de, Arabi 5, 07003 Palma de Mallorca.
T. (971) 71 58 86. - Ant -   062766
Linares, Plaza de la Almoina 4, 07001 Palma de Mallorca. T. (971) 71 72 19, 71 38 34. - Ant / Paint / Furn / China / Sculp / Arch / Jew / Silv -   062767

Pamplona (Navarra)

Cenoz, M., Errotaza, 9, 31014 Pamplona.
T. (948) 21 69 94. - Ant / Cur -   062768
Gonzalez Martinez, Miguel, Dormitaleria, 36, 31001
Pamplona. T. (948) 21 52 17. - Paint / Furn -   062769
Migueleiz, Florencia, Avda. de Roncesvalles, 11, 31002
Pamplona. T. (948) 21 32 90. - Cur -   062770

Polop (Alicante)

Sotano Medieval, 18 de Julio 8, 03520 Polop. - Paint /
China / Sculp -   062771

Pontevedra

Altamira, Charino 14, 36002 Pontevedra.
T. (986) 859 910. - Ant / Furn / Orient / Sculp / Jew /
Silv / Rel / Cur / Mul -   062772
Cofré, Baron, 12, 36002 Pontevedra. T. (986) 85 21 13.
- Ant -   062773

Puerto de la Cruz (Tenerife)

Arcon, Blanco 8, 38400 Puerto de la Cruz.
T. (922) 37 12 11.   062774

Puerto de Santa Maria (Cádiz)

Gonzalez Suarez, Antonio, San Sebastián, 5, 11500 Puerto de Santa Maria. - Ant -   062775

Rincón del Soto (Logroño)
Jiménez, Alfredo, Carrera, 28, 26550 Rincón del Soto.
- Ant - 062776

Sabadell (Barcelona)
Cau d'Art Sabadell, Sant Cugat 9, Sabadell.
T. (93) 728 07 35. - Paint / Sculp - 062777
Centellas, Virgén de Montserrat, 68, 08201 Sabadell.
- Cur - 062778
Numismatica Sabadell, San Jaime 4, 08201 Sabadell.
T. (93) 725 85 16. - Num - 062779

Sahagún (Leon)
Gil, Pedro, 24320 Sahagún. - Ant - 062780

Salamanca
Antigüedades Alonso, Eloy Bullon, 15, Salamanca.
T. (923) 21 29 26. - Ant - 062781
Martin Sanchez, Sebastian, Eloy Bullon, 36, Salamanca.
T. (923) 21 28 88, 22 21 18. - Ant - 062782
Nieto, Cuesta de la Raqueta, 8, 37001 Salamanca.
T. (923) 24 32 06. - Ant - 062783
Zafiro, Meléndez, 21, 37008 Salamanca.
T. (923) 21 27 44. - Ant - 062784

San Sebastián (Guipuzcoa)
Echevarria, Arturo, Puerto, 14 30, 4a, 20003 San Sebastián. T. (943) 188 72. - Ant / Paint / Cur - 062785
Ibero Antigüedades, Serrano de Anguita, 4, 20008 San Sebastián. T. (943) 215 908. - Ant / Cur - 062786
Munos Roiz, Manuel Rafael, Aldamar, 28, 20003 San Sebastián. T. (943) 1 04 57. - Fra / Silv - 062787
Valenti Clua, Fernando, Plaza Zaragoza, 2, 20007 San Sebastián. T. (943) 1 1 18 25. - Ant / Furn / Silv - 062788

Sanchonuño (Segovia)
Antigüedades y Talleres de Forja Artisticas, Carretera de Valladolid 31, 40297 Sanchonuño. T. (911) 16 00 09.
- Ant / Cur - 062789

Santa Elena (Jaen)
Arte Tipico, Caudillo Franco, 78, 23213 Santa Elena.
- Num / Arch - 062790

Santander (Cantabria)
Atenas, Somorrostro, 3, 39002 Santander.
T. (942) 22 95 32. - Ant - 062791
Dintel, Santa Clara, 8, 39001 Santander.
T. (942) 227 876. 062792
Simancas, Cadiz 18, 39002 Santander. T. (942) 220 308.
- Ant - 062793

Santiago de Compostela (La Coruña)
Casa Hortensia, Bautizados, 8 y Azabacheria, 7, 15702 Santiago de Compostela. T. (981) 31 11. - Ant / China / Instr - 062794
Tenda, Gelmirez, 2, 15702 Santiago de Compostela.
T. (981) 58 25 20. 062795

Segovia
Escribano Velasco, Pedro, Conde Cheste, 6, 40001 Segovia. T. (911) 45 16. - Cur - 062796
La Fuencisla, Isabel la Catolica, 12, 40001 Segovia.
- Furn / Cur - 062797
Viloria, Simon, Plaza de los Huertos, 2, 40001 Segovia.
T. (911) 34 23. - Mil - 062798
Zuloaga, Juan, S. Juan de los Caballeros,s/n, 40001 Segovia. - Cur - 062799

Sevilla
Casa Saavedra, Hernando Colon, 34 y 36, 41004 Sevilla.
T. (954) 21 37 94. - Paint / Cur - 062800
Galerias Adarve Linares, Santo Tomas, 1, 41004 Sevilla.
T. (954) 22 52 16. - Ant - 062801
Linares Munoz, Abelardo, Mateos Gago 4, 41004 Sevilla. T. (954) 22 05 90. - Ant - 062802
Linares Munoz, Antonio, Rodrigo Caro 11, 41004 Sevilla. T. (954) 21 34 63. - Ant / Paint / China / Repr / Sculp / Silv / Instr / Mil / Mul - 062803
Linares Reyes, Alberto, Mateos Gago, 5, 41004 Sevilla.
T. (954) 22 21 45. - Ant - 062804
Moreno, Deogracias, Vida, 11, 41004 Sevilla.
- Cur - 062805
Moro Gonzales, Placentines, 18, 41004 Sevilla.
T. (954) 22 46 33. - Paint / Furn / China / Sculp - 062806

Ortega, Av. de la Constitución 5, 41004 Sevilla.
T. (954) 22 33 45. - Ant - 062807
Pinanes de Tena, Manuel, Alemanes, 13, 41004 Sevilla.
T. (954) 22 32 00. - Ant - 062808

Sitges (Barcelona)
Museo del Cau Ferrat, Calle Fonollar s.n., 08870 Sitges.
T. (93) 8940364, Fax (93) 8948529. 062809
Museo Maricel, Calle Fenollar s.n., 08870 Sitges.
T. (93) 8940364, Fax (93) 8948529. 062810

Tarragona
Antigüedades Javier, Portella, 2, 43003 Tarragona.
T. (977) 20 54 75. - Num / Dec / Mil - 062811
Castellanau, Fernando de, Caballeros, 11, 43003 Tarragona. T. (977) 23 97 30. - Ant / Furn / China / Sculp / Arch / Dec / Tin - 062812
Javier, Portella, 2, 43003 Tarragona. T. (977) 20 54 75.
- Num - 062813
Rigau Mestre, Miguel, Bajada Misericordia 14, 43003 Tarragona. T. (977) 23 76 28. - Ant / Instr - 062814

Toledo
Arte Español, Reyes Catolicos 10, 45002 Toledo.
T. (925) 22 22 14. - Ant / Paint / Furn / China / Sculp / Jew / Silv / Mil - 062815
Casa Balaguer, Pasadizo Ayuntamiento, 12, 45002 Toledo. T. (925) 27 17. - China - 062816
Diaz Moya, José Miguel, San Miguel, 3, 45001 Toledo.
T. (925) 21 23 39. - Furn / Num / Mil - 062817

Tossa de Mar (Gerona)
Collado, San Miguel, s/n., 17320 Tossa de Mar.
T. (972) 34 03 07. - Furn / Dec - 062818

Trespaderme (Burgos)
Saiz Gallo, Pedro, Ntra. Sra. de Begona letra F, 09540 Trespaderme. T. (947) 57. - Ant / Furn - 062819

Valencia
Artesania Puerto, Tejedores, 5, 46001 Valencia. 062820
Barriocanal Morquillas, Cecilia, Mar, 1, 46003 Valencia.
T. (96) 22 23 46. - Ant - 062821
Casa Victoria, Jorge Juan, 34, 41004 Valencia.
T. (96) 21 80 06. - Furn / China / Mil - 062822
Cot Casanova, Pedro, Correjeria, 29, 46001 Valencia.
T. (96) 22 22 50. - Furn / China - 062823
Jacob's, Caballeros, 41, 46001 Valencia. - Ant / Dec - 062824
Niu D'art, Gran Via Germania, 7, 46006 Valencia.
T. (96) 334 97 25. 062825
Solaz Rufino, Alfredo, Pintor Fillol, 9, 46003 Valencia.
T. (96) 31 15 02. - Furn / China - 062826
Terol de Solis, José F., Poeta Querol 1, 46002 Valencia.
T. (96) 3 22 25 58. - Furn / China - 062827

Valencia de Don Juan (León)
Tabares, Inés, 24200 Valencia de Don Juan.
- Ant - 062828

Valladolid
Galeria de Arte Castilla, Pza. Universidad, 2, 47002 Valladolid. T. (983) 227 360. - Paint / Furn / China / Mil - 062829

Veguellina de Orbigo (León)
Junquera, Deogracias, 24350 Veguellina de Orbigo.
- Ant - 062830

Vic (Barcelona)
Antigüedades Dorca, Montserrat, 15, 08500 Vic.
T. (93) 289 14 32. - Ant - 062831
Font Sellabona, José, Plaza de la Catedral, s/n. Apdo. 77, 08500 Vic. - Ant - 062832
Portet, José, Plaza de la Catedral, s/n., 08500 Vic.
- Ant - 062833

Vigo (Pontevedra)
Angel, Marqués de Valladares, 7, 36201 Vigo.
- Ant - 062834
Arte, Pl. de la Constitucion, 6, 36202 Vigo.
T. (986) 21 27 09. - Ant - 062835
Sevres, Carral 8, 36202 Vigo. T. (986) 21 89 83. - Ant / Mil - 062836

Villagarcia de Arosa (Pontevedra)
El Hogar, José Antonio, 16, 36600 Villagarcia de Arosa.
T. (986) 219. - Furn / China - 062837

Vitoria (Alava)
Arco Iris Antigüedades, Correria, 57, 01001 Vitoria.
T. (945) 72 68, 52 68. - Ant / Paint / Furn / Sculp / Mil - 062838
Casa el Rey, Portal del Rey, 18, 01001 Vitoria.
T. (945) 21 37 70. - Furn / Sculp / Mil - 062839
Flor de Lis, Correria, 5, 01004 Vitoria. T. (945) 21 34 00.
- Furn / Sculp / Tex / Silv - 062840
Galerias Apellaniz, General Alava, 8, 01005 Vitoria.
T. (945) 23 30 78. - Ant / Paint / Furn / Num / Sculp / Mil - 062841
Larruy Bandellou, RamSon, Zapateria 86, 01001 Vitoria.
- Paint / Num / China / Sculp / Instr - 062842
Objetos de Arte, Correria 6, 55 y 71, 01001 Vitoria.
T. (945) 25 72 68. - Ant - 062843
Rabasco Campo, José Luis, Correria, 6, 01001 Vitoria.
T. (945) 21 26 88. - Ant - 062844
Txitxillu, Correria 33, 01001 Vitoria. T. (945) 25 16 49.
- Ant / Paint / Furn / Num / China / Sculp / Eth / Mil / Rel - 062845
Urbina, Gomez, Correria, 26, 01001 Vitoria.
T. (945) 54 27. - Ant - 062846

Zaragoza
Hesperia, Plaza de José Antonio 10, 50010 Zaragoza.
T. (976) 23 53 67. - Ant - 062847

Sri Lanka

Colombo
Arts and Crafts, 6 Mackinnon Bldg., Colombo. - Ant / Arch / Eth - 062848
Hemachandra Bros., 4 York St., Colombo. T. 219 21, 251 47. - Ant / Eth / Jew / Silv - 062849

Kandy
Asian Crafts, 14 Dalada Veediya, Kandy. T. 294. - Ant / Jew / Rel - 062850
Asian Crafts, 14 Dalada Veediya, Kandy.
T. 232 83. 062851

Sweden

Eldsberga
Oppenheimer, Jonny, Tönnersjö, 310 31 Eldsberga.
T. (035) 430 82. - Ant / Orient / Jew / Glass - 062852

Falkenberg
Lennart Castelius, Färegaresträret 3, 31131 Falkenberg.
T. (0346) 15284, 84393. 062853

Falsterbo
Seklar, Sju, 230 11 Falsterbo. - Ant - 062854

Frufällan
Persson, Thomas, Box 27, 50014 Frufällan.
T. (033) 24 70 66, 010/33 37 30. 062855

Gävle
Göran Gudmundsson Byggnadsvård & Bohag, Kyrkogatan 23, 803 11 Gävle. T. (026) 11 79 48. - Ant - 062856

Göteborg
Adonbolagen, Olsson, Vegagatan 22B, 41135 Göteborg.
T. (031) 24 24 75. - Tex - 062857
Antik Björn, Västra Hamngatan, 41117 Göteborg.
T. (031) 13 97 98. - Ant / Furn / Cur - 062858
Antik West, Södra vägen 41, 412 54 Göteborg.
T. (031) 18 51 60, 20 90 50, Fax 186930. - Orient / China / Tex / Silv / Cur / Ico - 062859
Antikamiralen, Västra Hamngatan 6, 41117 Göteborg.
- Ant / Graph / China - 062860
Antikhallarna, Västra Hamngatan 6, 41117 Göteborg.
- Num - 062861
Antikhörnan Johansson & Co, Västra Hamngatan 6, 41117 Göteborg. T. (031) 13 58 55. - Ant / Furn - 062862

Antikt Porslin, Västra Hamngatan 6, 41117 Göteborg.
T. (031) 13 77 99. - Ant / Orient -   *062863*
Ateljé Varia, Västra Hamngatan 6, 41117 Göteborg.
T. (031) 11 78 55. - China -   *062864*
Beso Ur & Antik, Västra Hamngatan 6, 411 17 Göteborg.
T. (031) 13 94 84, Fax 13 20 86. - Num / Jew /
Instr -   *062865*
Bohème Konst & Antikvitetshandel, Övre Husargatan
25a, 413 14 Göteborg. T. (031) 11 83 01. - Ant / Paint /
Furn / China / Silv / Glass -   *062866*
Collectors Corner AB, Västra Hamngatan 6, 41117 Göte-
borg. T. (031) 13 61 35. - Ant / Paint / Furn / Orient / Chi-
na / Arch / Silv / Mil / Glass -   *062867*
Fortuna Antik, Kristinelundsgatan 7, 41137 Göteborg.
T. (031) 16 16 36. - Ant / Dec -   *062868*
Galerie Tizian, Västra Hamngatan 6, 41117 Göteborg.
T. (031) 13 70 57. - Ant / Paint / China -   *062869*
Galleri Elvan, Västra Hamngatan 6, 41117
Göteborg.   *062870*
Gamle Bengt, Förengsg. 34, 41127 Göteborg.
T. (031) 11 31 12. - Ant / Orient / Dec / Mil /
Cur -   *062871*
Gåvan, Västra Hamngatan 6, 41117 Göteborg.
T. (031) 11 56 95. - Ant / Furn / Orient / China /
Dec -   *062872*
Göteborgs Mynthandel, Västra Hamngatan 6, 41117 Gö-
teborg. T. (031) 11 01 44. - Num -   *062873*
Juvelbörsen, W.P.F. Juveler och ädelstenar, Västra
Hamngatan 6, 41117 Göteborg.
T. (031) 13 98 04.   *062874*
Klockmakare John Innes, Västra Hamngatan 6, 41117
Göteborg. T. (031) 13 28 71. - Instr -   *062875*
Konst & Antikviteter, Sten Sturesg. 6, 41139 Göteborg.
- Ant -   *062876*
Koppa-Boden, Västra Hamngatan 6, 41117 Göteborg.
- Paint -   *062877*
Lansenfeldts Antikviteter, Västra Hamngatan 6, 41127
Göteborg. T. (031) 11 13 24. - Ant / Paint / Dec -   *062878*
Martins Antik, Magasinsgatan 3, 411 18 Göteborg.
T. (031) 11 36 91.   *062879*
Mölndals Auktionsbyra AB, Th. Prohaska, Fridkullagatan
15, 41262 Göteborg. T. (031) 18 46 64. - Ant / Instr /
Mil -   *062880*
Moneta Mynthandel, Västra Hamngatan 6, 41117 Göte-
borg. T. (031) 13 92 23. - Num -   *062881*
Myntaffaeren Numis, Vallgatan 1, 40315 Göteborg
P.O.B. 2332. T. (031) 13 33 45. - Num -   *062882*
No. 14, Västra Hamngatan 6, 41117 Göteborg.
T. (031) 13 94 52. - Instr / Cur / Mod -   *062883*
Nordiska Konstgalleriet, Västra Hamngatan 6, 41117
Göteborg. T. (031) 11 78 86. - Ant / Paint -   *062884*
Persepolis AB, Västra Hamngatan 6, 41117 Göteborg.
T. (031) 11 10 50. - Tex -   *062885*
Samlarshopen, Västra Hamngatan 6, 41117 Göteborg.
T. (031) 11 06 06.   *062886*
Skepparn, Vasagatan 23, 411 24 Göteborg.
T. (031) 13 60 82. - Ant / Paint -   *062887*
Tobison, Hallegatan 15, 417 02 Göteborg.
T. (031) 23 49 68. - Ant / Furn / China / Glass -   *062888*
Trägardh, Gunnar, Kungsportsavenyn 34, 41136 Göte-
borg. T. (031) 16 68 48. - Ant / Graph / Furn / Repr / Tex /
Dec / Instr -   *062889*
Yngves Mynt & Antik, Västra Hamngatan 6, 41117 Göte-
borg. T. (031) 13 57 82. - Ant / Num -   *062890*

Halmstad

Larsson, Hasse, Magnus Stenbocksv. 57, 30233 Halmstad. T. (035) 15 63 40, 010/94 11 48.   *062891*

Helsingborg

Jabi Antik, Järnvägsgatan 13, 252 24 Helsingborg.
T. (042) 18 16 14.   *062892*

Hillerstorp

Petersson, Kenneth, Storgatan 12, 33033 Hillerstorp.
T. 22380.   *062893*

Höör

Scandia Armco Inc., Parkgatan 13, 24300 Höör.
T. (0413) 205 16. - Num / Mil -   *062894*

Jönköping

Svenska Antikbyran, Veragatan 3, 55268 Jönköping.
T. (036) 16 30 80. - Ant -   *062895*

Kävlinge

Essen, Alexander Baron von, Box 149, 244 00 Kävlinge.
T. (046) 70 95 30. - Paint -   *062896*

Kalmar

Florins Eftr., Södra Langgatan 24, 38100 Kalmar.
- Ant -   *062897*
Ugglas, Kungsgatan 19, 39246 Kalmar.
T. (04 80) 194 07, 671 76. - Ant -   *062898*

Karlstad

Larsson, Stefan, Kungsgatan 4, 65224 Karlstad.
T. (054) 15 20 25, Fax 18 59 04.   *062899*

Kungälv

Gammelboden Ragnhild Bergling, Västragatan 55,
44200 Kungälv. T. (0303) 123 69. - Ant -   *062900*

Kungsbacka

Ardins, Knut, S. Torggatan 6, 43400 Kungsbacka.
T. (0300) 124 97. - Ant -   *062901*

Leksand

Jonsson, Stig, Yttermo 3192, 79300 Leksand.
T. (0247) 14177, 52 54 33.   *062902*

Ljungsbro

Backes Antik, Gullhem, 59060 Ljungsbro.
T. (013) 65807.   *062903*

Löddeköping

Albumet, Malmövägen 8, 240 21 Löddeköping.
T. 70 50 01. - Ant / Paint / Furn -   *062904*

Löderup

Gula Huset, Semaforgatan 4, 27020 Löderup.
T. (0411) 24536.   *062905*

Malmö

Artium, Kalendegatan 7, 20090 Malmö. T. (040) 22580.
- Furn / China / Instr / Glass -   *062906*
Falkkloos, Hamng. 2, 211 22 Malmö. T. (040) 11 86 95.
- Ant -   *062907*

Marieholm

Collectors Corner, Folke Abrahamsson, Reslövs Kvarn,
24030 Marieholm. T. (0413) 70055.   *062908*

Mellerud

Stens Antik, Sten Torstensson, Landsvägsgatan 61,
46400 Mellerud. T. (0530) 12225.   *062909*

Nässjö

Konstsalongen, Gunvor Johnson, Storgatan 39, 57122
Nässjö. T. (0380) 11884, Fax 75754.   *062910*

Örebro

Prima Galleri, Fredsgatan 13, 703 61 Örebro.
T. (019) 13 53 34. - Furn / China -   *062911*

Rättvik

Lennerthson, Torsten, Altsarbyn, 795 00 Rättvik.
T. (0248) 300 36. - Furn -   *062912*

Skanör

Artium, Box 79, 23010 Skanör. T. 122580. - Ant / Graph /
Furn / China / Sculp / Silv / Instr / Glass -   *062913*

Stockholm

A & A Artesan Antik, Sibylleg. 69, 114 43 Stockholm.
T. (08) 660 24 86. - Ant -   *062914*
Afrodite Antik, Odeng. 92, 113 22 Stockholm.
T. (08) 31 75 00. - Ant -   *062915*
Afrodite Möbler, Odeng. 94, 113 22 Stockholm.
T. (08) 31 51 51. - Ant -   *062916*
Ahlström, B., Kungsgatan 28-30, 111 35 Stockholm.
T. (08) 14 02 20. - Num -   *062917*
Albatross Antikviteter, Scheeleg. 6, 112 23 Stockholm.
T. (08) 50 04 47. - Ant -   *062918*
Albert & Herbert, Hornsg. 29A, 116 49 Stockholm.
T. (08) 42 34 10. - Ant -   *062919*
Alfort, J.M., Köpmangatan 14, 111 31 Stockholm.
T. (08) 20 64 05.   *062920*
All Uppköpet, Vanadisv. 30, 113 46 Stockholm.
T. (08) 33 05 25. - Ant -   *062921*

Amell, Regeringsgatan 52, 111 56 Stockholm.
T. (08) 11 41 91, 11 09 87. - Ant / Furn / China /
Silv -   *062922*
Åmell, Verner, Danderydsgatan 17, 11426 Stockholm.
T. (08) 611 41 93, Fax 611 80 05.   *062923*
Ancient Art & Antiques, Sture Larsson, Riddargatan 12,
114 35 Stockholm. T. (08) 21 22 30. - Ant / Orient / Chi-
na / Tex / Jew -   *062924*
Anno Domini Antikhandel, Hagbyv. 3, 171 40 Stockholm.
T. (08) 27 06 65. - Ant -   *062925*
Anno 1900, Södermannag. 40, 116 40 Stockholm.
T. (08) 42 93 36. - Ant -   *062926*
Antik-Kronan, Storkyrkobr. 3, 100 90 Stockholm.
T. (08) 21 96 96.   *062927*
Antik 66, Östgötag. 66, 102 73 Stockholm.
T. (08) 40 22 43. - Ant -   *062928*
Antika Leksaksmagasinet, Karlbergsv. 75, 113 35
Stockholm. T. (08) 31 61 60. - Ant -   *062929*
Antika o. Begagnade Möbler, S:t Eriksg. 79, 113 32
Stockholm. T. (08) 34 28 50. - Ant -   *062930*
Antikaffären, Grevg. 69, 114 59 Stockholm.
T. (08) 662 05 44. - Ant -   *062931*
Antikaffären, Storkyrkobr. 10, 111 28 Stockholm.
T. (08) 10 50 47. - Ant -   *062932*
Antiken, Scheeleg. 24, 112 28 Stockholm.
T. (08) 53 58 63. - Ant -   *062933*
Antiklagret, Kungsholmsg. 13, 100 90 Stockholm.
T. (08) 53 13 31.   *062934*
Antikmagasinet- Lampverkstad, Riddarg. 11, 114 51
Stockholm. T. (08) 661 61 60. - Ant -   *062935*
Antikman, Hornsg. 28, 117 20 Stockholm.
T. (08) 40 10 10, 40 40 40. - Ant -   *062936*
Antikt, Hantverkarg. 34, 112 21 Stockholm.
T. (08) 53 56 12. - Ant -   *062937*
Antiquea, V. Trädgårdsg. 11A, 111 53 Stockholm.
T. (08) 24 17 71. - Ant -   *062938*
Antiquea, Hamngatan Dept. Store, 3rd Floor, 111 47
Stockholm. T. (08) 762 8820.   *062939*
Antiquitas, Rörstrandsg. 18, 113 40 Stockholm.
T. (08) 30 85 23. - Ant -   *062940*
Antonsson, Skåneg. 78, 116 37 Stockholm.
T. (08) 41 10 10. - Ant -   *062941*
Apelkrona, Köpmang. 10, 111 31 Stockholm.
T. (08) 11 78 28. - Ant -   *062942*
Apollo Antik & Konsthandel, Tegnergatan 5, 111 40
Stockholm. T. (08) 21 90 98, 11 04 92. - Ant / Furn / Chi-
na / Silv -   *062943*
Arca'dia Form, Kindstug. 12, 111 29 Stockholm.
T. (08) 10 27 51, 10 86 59. - Ant -   *062944*
Ariadne, Köpm. Gatan 22, 11131 Stockholm.
T. (08) 11 85 35.   *062945*
Artema, Kornhamnstorg., 111 27 Stockholm.
T. (08) 20 95 95, 21 56 30. - Ant -   *062946*
Artemis Antik, Droteringholmsv. 1, 112 42 Stockholm.
T. (08) 54 64 44. - Ant -   *062947*
Artilleri-Brahe, Braheg. 7A, 114 37 Stockholm.
T. (08) 662 03 79, 667 60 92. - Ant -   *062948*
Ateljé Nygammalt, Grevg. 17, 114 59 Stockholm.
T. (08) 667 27 92. - Ant -   *062949*
Auktionshuset National, Stureg. 4, 114 35 Stockholm.
T. (08) 98 88 70. - Ant -   *062950*
Award Antik, Kralav. 15A, 114 49 Stockholm.
T. (08) 10 27 07, 660 41 21. - Ant -   *062951*
Bakos, Stefan, Stureg. 44B, 114 36 Stockholm.
T. (08) 662 03 05. - Ant -   *062952*
Bissinger, Köpmang. 16, 111 31 Stockholm.
T. (08) 20 03 79. - Ant -   *062953*
Björklund, Tomas, Skomakarg. 32, 111 29 Stockholm.
T. (08) 21 60 44. - Ant -   *062954*
Blå Stolen, L. Dracke Sveav. 108, 113 50 Stockholm.
T. (08) 32 09 16. - Ant -   *062955*
Blasius, Helene Gerschman, Arsenalsg. 1, 111 47
Stockholm. T. (08) 11 01 71. - Ant -   *062956*
Bocca Tigris, Kungsholmsg. 4A, 112 27 Stockholm.
T. (08) 53 50 90. - Orient / Tex / Eth -   *062957*
Broberg, Lars, Grev Tureg. 56, 114 38 Stockholm.
T. (08) 660 40 26. - Ant -   *062958*
Bröderna Hagelin, Tjärhovsg. 16, 116 21 Stockholm.
T. (08) 44 52 26. - Ant -   *062959*
Bröderna Hagelin, Odeng. 44, 113 51 Stockholm.
T. (08) 34 29 40. - Ant -   *062960*

Bukowski, Arsenalsgt. 8, 111 47 Stockholm. T. (08) 10 25 95, Fax 11 46 74. - Ant / Paint / Graph / Furn / Orient / China / Sculp / Tex / Silv / Lights / Instr / Glass / Mod / Ico / Draw - 062961
Carlin, Upplandsg. 40, 113 28 Stockholm. T. (08) 31 34 01. - Ant - 062962
Comet Invest, Box 1136, 171 22 Stockholm. T. (08) 83 66 03. - Ant - 062963
Copelia, Köpmantorget. 2, 111 31 Stockholm. T. (08) 11 59 69. - Ant - 062964
Corona Antik, Odeng. 80, 113 22 Stockholm. T. (08) 30 55 05. - Ant - 062965
Decker, Kurt, Biblioteksgatan 12, 10090 Stockholm. T. (08) 20 00 29, 11 69 85. - Jew / Silv - 062966
Domino Antik, Drottningg. 81A, 111 60 Stockholm. T. (08) 11 37 09. - Ant - 062967
Draken, Köpmantorget 2, 111 31 Stockholm. T. (08) 20 26 38, 717 30 29. - Ant - 062968
Druvan Antik, Sibylleg. 43- 45, 10090 Stockholm. T. (08) 661 96 66. - Ant - 062969
Dybecks Antikhandel, Köpmangatan 16, 10090 Stockholm. T. (08) 11 57 83. - China / Silv / Glass - 062970
Ebra, Askrikeg. 13, 115 29 Stockholm. T. (08) 667 33 06. - Ant - 062971
Edelstam, Karlav. 59, 114 49 Stockholm. T. (08) 660 49 80. - Ant - 062972
Eklunds, Rune, Hornsg. 61, 116 49 Stockholm. T. (08) 669 44 45. - Ant - 062973
Eko Antik, Hornsg. 149, 117 28 Stockholm. T. (08) 84 40 75. - Ant - 062974
Engströmer, Nalle, Kommendörsg. 25, 100 90 Stockholm. T. (08) 660 26 46. 062975
Eriksdal, Ringstr. 89, 116 60 Stockholm. T. (08) 43 66 43. - Ant - 062976
Ernsjöö, Elof, Sibyllegatan 31, 114 42 Stockholm. T. (08) 662 82 77, Fax 661 14 73. - Ant - 062977
Fartygsmagasinet i Stockholm, Österlångg. 19, 111 31 Stockholm. T. (08) 20 93 98. - Ant - 062978
Fataburen Antik, Fatbursg. 18A, 116 52 Stockholm. T. (08) 41 83 64. - Ant - 062979
Fifty-Fifty, Rörstransg. 11, 113 40 Stockholm. T. (08) 31 03 34. - Ant - 062980
Findia Trading, Florag. 17, 114 31 Stockholm. T. (08) 21 38 24. - Ant - 062981
Fiskarn, Timmermansg. 37, 116 49 Stockholm. T. (08) 40 10 93. - Ant - 062982
Flexi-Form, Lillåv. 71, 121 59 Stockholm. T. (08) 48 38 80. - Ant - 062983
Förri Tiden, Sibylleg. 36, 114 43 Stockholm. T. (08) 660 80 98. - Ant - 062984
Forsell, Sibylleg. 59, 114 43 Stockholm. T. (08) 661 20 43. - Ant - 062985
Fyndmarknaden Varnhuset, Sergels Torg 12, 111 57 Stockholm. T. (08) 21 81 45. - Ant - 062986
Galerie Morgan, Morgan Cazorec, Köpmangatan12, 11131 Stockholm. T. (08) 20 07 19, 20 90 62, Fax 791 22 73. 062987
Gamla Hem, Folkungag. 93, 116 30 Stockholm. T. (08) 44 45 63. - Ant - 062988
Gamla Minnen Antik, Hantverkarg. 74, 112 38 Stockholm. T. (08) 51 05 03. - Ant - 062989
Gamla Stadens Möbel, Nygatan 20, 100 90 Stockholm. T. (08) 20 51 67. 062990
Gesällen, Storg. 10, 114 51 Stockholm. T. (08) 661 35 40. 062991
Glencarse, Odeng. 86, 113 22 Stockholm. T. (08) 30 35 40. - Ant - 062992
Grefvens Renoveringsateljé, Grevg. 46, 114 58 Stockholm. T. (08) 660 63 06. - Ant - 062993
Gustavianska Konsthandeln, Arsenalsg. 1, 111 47 Stockholm. T. (08) 611 63 63. - Ant - 062994
Haage, Kommendörsg. 24, 114 48 Stockholm. T. (08) 660 10 40. - Ant - 062995
Hälsingemöbler, Hälsingeg. 2, 113 23 Stockholm. T. (08) 34 10 36. - Ant - 062996
Håkans Auktionsgods, Upplandsg. 76, 113 44 Stockholm. T. (08) 33 83 40. - Ant - 062997
Hantverk & Tradition, Rånöv. 5, 161 51 Stockholm. T. (08) 80 15 40. - Ant - 062998
Harrison, Steven, Karlav. 74, 114 59 Stockholm. T. (08) 661 87 12. - Ant - 062999
Hedvig Antik, Artillerig. 14, 114 51 Stockholm. T. (08) 660 68 40. - Ant - 063000
Heinbrandt Addie, Norrlandsgatan 21, 11143 Stockholm. T. (08) 20 75 72. 063001
Högvalten, Herkulesg. 9, 111 52 Stockholm. T. (08) 10 50 15. - Ant - 063002
Höijer, Upplandsg. 11, 111 23 Stockholm. T. (08) 20 95 05, 20 87 30. - Ant - 063003
Hopareboden, Österlanggatan 31, 11131 Stockholm. T. (08) 10 75 30. - Ant - 063004
Hud-Juhlin, Järntorgsg. 6, 111 29 Stockholm. T. (08) 10 15 53. - Ant - 063005
Järntorgsboden, Hantverkarg., 122 43 Stockholm. T. (08) 53 45 45, 53 49 70. - Ant - 063006
Johansson, Lars & Smycken, Kommendörsg. 20B, 102 48 Stockholm. T. (08) 783 03 83. - Ant - 063007
Jojjes Fyndhörna Enskede Antik, Nynäsv. 322, 122 34 Stockholm. T. (08) 48 80 70. - Ant - 063008
Kajsas Prylgömma, Upplandsg. 43, 113 28 Stockholm. T. (08) 31 10 27. - Ant - 063009
Keruben, Kungsg. 57, 111 22 Stockholm. T. (08) 21 82 55. - Ant - 063010
Kleo, Nybrog. 36, 114 40 Stockholm. T. (08) 661 72 42. - Ant - 063011
Klostervalvet Cupiditas Antik, Svartmang. 27, 111 29 Stockholm. T. (08) 11 11 29, Fax 54 64 46. - Ant - 063012
Knutssons, Kommendörsg. 9, 11448 Stockholm. T. (08) 66 08 17. 063013
Kokoro Asian Art, Österlångg. 12, 111 31 Stockholm. T. (08) 11 68 87, Fax 758 46 49. - Orient - 063014
Kreuter, Björn, Köpmanng. 18, 111 31 Stockholm. T. (08) 20 88 99, 21 03 33. - Furn / Num / Silv / Instr - 063015
Kronberg Esbjörn, Karlav. 46, 114 49 Stockholm. T. (08) 660 60 07. - Ant - 063016
Kulan, Skomakarg. 24B, 10090 Stockholm, 111 29. T. (08) 10 25 23. - Ant - 063017
Latona, Sturegatan 20, 114 36 Stockholm. T. (08) 662 90 45, Fax 662 90 45. - Ant - 063018
Leksaker, Västerlångg. 11, 111 29 Stockholm. T. (08) 10 41 58. - Ant - 063019
Lilla Klenoden, Roslagsg. 22, 113 55 Stockholm. T. (08) 15 20 65. - Ant - 063020
Lindkvist och Sjöberg, Grevgatan 6, 114 53 Stockholm. T. (08) 660 64 54, Fax 660 5819. - Ant - 063021
Ljunggren, Bertil H., Nybrogatan 42, 11440 Stockholm. T. (08) 660 97 19. - Ant / Instr - 063022
Lovisa, Ulrika, Köpmang. 9, 111 31 Stockholm. T. (08) 20 37 03. - Ant - 063023
Lundgren, Kommendörsgatan 20 A, 114 48 Stockholm. T. (08) 662 25 82, Fax 662 05 10. - Ant - 063024
Lundin, L., Stureg. 38, 114 36 Stockholm. T. (08) 667 54 82, 667 32 76. - Ant - 063025
M-B Antik, Norrtullsg. 21, 113 27 Stockholm. T. (08) 32 69 29. - Ant - 063026
Magaliff, Bernhard, Gustav Adolfs Torg 16, 111 52 Stockholm. T. (08) 20 00 74. - Ant / Paint / Furn / China / Jew - 063027
Malm Konsthandel, Torstenssonsg. 7, 114 56 Stockholm. T. (08) 661 74 51. - Ant - 063028
Maria Antik, Torkel Knutssonsg. 31, 116 51 Stockholm. T. (08) 84 71 20. - Ant - 063029
Melander, Birger Jarlsg. 1, 111 45 Stockholm. T. (08) 20 71 69. - Ant - 063030
Min Skattkammare, Upplandsg. 47, 113 28 Stockholm. T. (08) 31 07 06. - Ant - 063031
Molander, Odeng. 100, 113 22 Stockholm. T. (08) 34 85 00. - Ant - 063032
Molvidson, M., Nybrogatan 21, 114 39 Stockholm. T. (08) 661 86 84, Fax 661 86 60. - Ant - 063033
Monias Antikaffär, Kungstensg. 69, 113 29 Stockholm. T. (08) 33 20 69. - Ant - 063034
Mormors Spegel, Odeng. 84, 113 22 Stockholm. T. (08) 31 21 53. - Ant - 063035
Munkeborg, Pierre, Grev Tureg. 13A, 114 46 Stockholm. T. (08) 660 90 38. - Ant - 063036
Naga, Österlångg. 10, 111 31 Stockholm. T. (08) 20 41 07. - Ant - 063037
Neuman, Torsten, Samuelsg. 6, 112 20 Stockholm. T. (08) 611 42 59. - Ant - 063038
Noaks Ark Old Animals, Runebergsg. 3, 114 29 Stockholm. T. (08) 20 98 15, 21 25 89. - Ant - 063039
Nordiska Antikhandeln, Riddarg. 11 a, 100 90 Stockholm. T. (08) 660 97 02. 063040
Nordlinds Mynthandel A.B., Ulf, Nybrogatan 36, Box 5132, 10243 Stockholm. T. (08) 626261, 616213. - Num - 063041
Nordlings Antikbod, Skånegatan 86, 10090 Stockholm. T. (08) 43 01 16. 063042
Norrmalm, Roslagsg. 19, 113 55 Stockholm. T. (08) 15 70 24, 15 60 50. - Ant - 063043
Novara Guld Silver Antik, Karlav. 59, 114 49 Stockholm. T. (08) 661 67 00. - Ant - 063044
Oden, Uppl. g. 41, 113 28 Stockholm. T. (08) 34 65 22. - Ant - 063045
Ögren, Erik Dahlbergsg. 21, 115 35 Stockholm. T. (08) 664 44 10. - Ant - 063046
Östermalmsövre Fyndmarknad, Karlav. 89, 115 22 Stockholm. T. (08) 662 74 38. - Ant - 063047
Östermalmstorgs Konst & Antik, Grev Magnig. 13, 114 55 Stockholm. T. (08) 660 83 62. - Ant - 063048
Old Arthur, Odeng. 90, 113 22 Stockholm. T. (08) 34 81 70, 34 81 85. - Ant - 063049
Oles Konstantik, Erik Segersälls Väg 7, 126 50 Stockholm. T. (08) 19 41 86. - Ant - 063050
Olsson, Roslagsg. 17, 113 55 Stockholm. T. (08) 15 64 97. - Ant - 063051
Olsson, Lars, Köpmangatan 7, 111 31 Stockholm. T. (08) 10 25 00, 317 080. - Ant / Draw - 063052
Orima, Nybrogatan 25, 114 39 Stockholm. T. (08) 667 11 50, 661 36 10. - Tex - 063053
Oxelberg, Hornsg. 52, 100 90 Stockholm. T. (08) 41 41 71. 063054
Pabo, Folke Hammenström, Birg. Jarlsg. 103B, 114 20 Stockholm. T. (08) 15 69 10. - Ant - 063055
Peensalu, Grev Tureg 23, 114 38 Stockholm. T. (08) 660 87 60. - Ant - 063056
Peo Mynt & Frimärken AB, Drottinggatan 29, Box 16 245, 10385 Stockholm. T. (08) 211 210. - Num - 063057
Polar Antik, Bondeg. 57, 100 90 Stockholm. T. (08) 43 76 17. 063058
Polstjernan, Arsenalsg. 5, 111 47 Stockholm. T. (08) 611 39 73/75, Fax 611 39 72. - Ant / Furn / China / Tex / Dec / Silv / Lights - 063059
Ramsden, S:t Eriksg. 52, 112 34 Stockholm. T. (08) 52 82 45. - Ant - 063060
Rehns Antikhandel, Kommendörsgatan 20B, 11448 Stockholm. T. (08) 663 34 51, Fax 663 31 51. 063061
Ribbhagen, Kurt, Birger Jarlsgatan 13, 111 45 Stockholm. T. (08) 679 82 36, Fax 611 10 88. - Ant / Jew / Silv / Ico - 063062
Rocaille, Stureg. 38, 114 36 Stockholm. T. (08) 667 32 76, 667 54 82. - Ant - 063063
Roslagsfyndet i Stockholm, Roslagsg. 7, 113 55 Stockholm. T. (08) 32 29 90. - Ant - 063064
Rostiek, Skåneg. 71, 116 37 Stockholm. T. (08) 44 43 97. - Ant - 063065
Runhällen Antik Lager, Kungsholmsg. 13, 112 27 Stockholm. T. (08) 53 13 34. - Ant - 063066
Sahlström, Frejg. 17, 113 49 Stockholm. T. (08) 15 63 76. - Ant - 063067
Saker Man Minns, Linnég. 28, 114 47 Stockholm. T. (08) 662 10 60. - Ant - 063068
Samir, Linnég. 26, 114 47 Stockholm. T. (08) 662 76 11. - Ant - 063069
Samlarboden, Nytorgsg. 36A, 114 40 Stockholm. T. (08) 41 48 08. - Ant - 063070
Sankt Eriks Antik, Sankt Erikplan 2, 100 90 Stockholm. T. (08) 34 89 00. 063071
Sankt Görans Konst + Antikhandel, Ingrid Nordlund, Köpmanbrinken 6, 11131 Stockholm. T. (08) 20 14 20. 063072
Sjöström, Hans Göran, Nybrogatan 6, 10243 Stockholm. T. (08) 660 42 00. 063073
Skaj, Curt, Master Lästmakargatan 6, 111 44 Stockholm. T. (08) 611 76 80. - Ant - 063074
Snäckan Antik, Ann Norelid, Sibyllegatan 45, 11442 Stockholm. T. (08) 661 01 01. 063075
SPAK A/B Epokernas Varuhus, Klarabergsgatan 37, 11121 Stockholm. T. (08) 23 12 80. - Ant / Paint / Furn / China / Sculp / Tex / Silv / Lights / Instr / Glass - 063076
Stopalo, Jean & Casrten, Tegnérgatan 12, 11358 Stockholm. T. (08) 673 44 40, 35 72 27. - Ant - 063077
Strandbergs Mynthandel, Arsenalsgatan 8, 10391 Stockholm. T. (08) 208 120. - Num - 063078

Svea-Mynt- & Frimaerkshandel AB, Stureplan 4, Box
5358, 10246 Stockholm. T. (08) 144 640.
- Num -   *063079*
Thunér, Lars, Karlavägen 12, 11431 Stockholm.
T. (08) 21 40 04, 010/38 20 06.   *063080*
Trangsunds Boden, Trangsund 10, 11129 Stockholm.
T. (08) 20 05 18. - Ant -   *063081*
Tropius Antik, B.& L. Wahlström, Nybrogatan 42, 11440
Stockholm. T. (08) 662 33 37, 010/76 00 28,
Fax 661 10 61.   *063082*
Viktoria Antik, Norrtullsg. 1, 113 29 Stockholm.
T. (08) 32 17 00. - Ant -   *063083*
Vita Valvet, Odeng. 90, 113 22 Stockholm.
T. (08) 32 82 05, 32 82 70. - Ant -   *063084*
Wärnling, Ake, Sibylleg. 26, 114 42 Stockholm.
T. (08) 660 58 29. - Ant -   *063085*
Wasa Antik- & Auktionsgodaffär, Uppl.-gatan 66, 10090
Stockholm. T. (08) 33 00 80.   *063086*
Westerberg, Kindstug. 6, 111 31 Stockholm.
T. (08) 20 75 14. - Ant -   *063087*
Willborg, J.P., Sibylleg. 41, 114 42 Stockholm.
T. (08) 783 02 65, 783 03 65. - Ant -   *063088*
Wirén, B.E., Köpmangatan 3, 11131 Stockholm.
T. (08) 21 64 62, 11 26 24.   *063089*
Zedell, Ragnar, Köpmangatan 3, 111 31 Stockholm.
T. (08) 21 02 39.   *063090*

Sundsvall
Dahlin, Bengt, Mosjön, 85590 Sundsvall. - Paint /
Arch -   *063091*

Svärdsjö
Antikkonsult-Åke Eriksson, Borgärdetsvägen 7, 79023
Svärdsjö. T. (0246) 11275, 10386, 010/
52 71 41.   *063092*

Svedala
Excelsior Antik, Lena af Ekenstam, Kyrkogatan 23,
23300 Svedala. T. (040) 40 30 40,
Fax 40 01 30.   *063093*

Teckomatorp
Tumlaren Antikaffär, Kurt Nilsson, Norrvidinge 1248,
26020 Teckomatorp. T. (0418) 60152, 010/
42 42 11.   *063094*

Uppsala
Kavaletten, Svartbg. 30, 755 90 Uppsala. - Ant -   *063095*
Mattssous Mynt, Kungssängsgatan 21/B, 75322 Uppsa-
la. - Num -   *063096*

Vänersborg
Knutssons, Kungsgatan 3, 462 33 Vänersborg.
T. (0521) 66077, 010/87 03 50, Fax 12635.   *063097*

Västerås
Persson, Georg, Sturegatan 16, 72213 Västerås.
T. (021) 311 58. - Ant / Jew / Silv -   *063098*

Växjö
Galleri Wärend, Ulriksbergspr. 2, 35236 Växjö.
T. (0470) 24422, 010/45 45 70.   *063099*
Växjö Antikaffär, Dalbovägen 10, 35238 Växjö.
T. (0470) 133 11. - Ant -   *063100*

Switzerland

Aarau (Aargau)
Dika-Antik, Entfelderstr. 51, 5000 Aarau.
T. (064) 22 86 32.   *063101*
Diriwächter, Hans, & Paul Kasper, Entfelderstr. 51, 5000
Aarau. T. (064) 22 86 32. - Ant -   *063102*
Galerie zur Zinne, Rathausgasse 9, 5000 Aarau.
T. (064) 24 76 26. - Paint / Graph / China -   *063103*
Lissil, Kirchgasse 13, 5000 Aarau.
T. (064) 22 51 52.   *063104*
Schärz, Roland & Hulda, Obere Vorstadt 34, 5001 Aarau.
T. (064) 8221360.   *063105*

Aarburg (Aargau)
Eichenberger, Roland, Oltnerstr. 104, 4663 Aarburg.
T. (062) 41 11 68.   *063106*

Spiess-Hillmer, Michel, Bahnhofstr 3, 4663 Aarburg.
T. (062) 7914166.   *063107*

Aathal-Seegräben (Zürich)
Böckli, J., Lehnhof, 8607 Aathal-Seegräben.
T. (01) 932 17 24.   *063108*

Abtwil (Sankt Gallen)
Antiquitäten-Galerie, Sonnenbergstr. 10, 9030 Abtwil.
T. (071) 3113831.   *063109*

Aeschi (Solothurn)
Jäggi, Hansulrich & Regina, Gallishofst. 84, 4556 Ae-
schi. T. (062) 9615829. - Ant -   *063110*

Agiez (Vaud)
Aquet, Ernest, Le Pressoir, 1352 Agiez.
T. (024) 4413787.   *063111*

Allaman (Vaud)
Allegri, Claude, Château d'Allaman, 1165 Allaman.
T. (021) 807 32 06.   *063112*
Au Lieutenant Baillival, Château d'Allaman, 1165 Alla-
man. T. (021) 807 37 56.   *063113*
Au Vieux Logis, Château d'Allaman, 1165 Allaman.
T. (021) 807 40 41.   *063114*
Boteh, Château d'Allaman, 1165 Allaman.
T. (021) 807 33 63.   *063115*
Château des Antiquaires, Château d'Allaman, 1165 Alla-
man. T. (021) 807 38 05. - Ant / Paint / Furn / Tex / Jew /
Silv / Instr / Mod -   *063116*
Grand Argentier, Château, 1165 Allaman.
T. (021) 807 37 09, 36 54 62. - Jew / Silv -   *063117*
Kruet, Paul, Château d'Allaman, 1165 Allaman.
T. (021) 807 39 42.   *063118*
Mermier, Hean, Château d'Allaman, 1165 Allaman.
T. (021) 8074131.   *063119*
Rigaldo & Fils, Chateau des Antiquaires, 1165 Allaman.
T. (021) 3235021, 8073518.   *063120*
Stucky, Nini, Château d'Allaman, 1165 Allaman.
T. (021) 807 38 46.   *063121*

Allschwil (Basel-Land)
Cattelani, Vincenzo, Hegenheimermattweg 119a, 4123
Allschwil. T. (061) 481 69 15.   *063122*
Gürtler, Lina, Baslerstr. 14, 4123 Allschwil.
T. (061) 481 62 62.   *063123*
Trouvaille Cattelani, Hegenheimer Str. 119 a, 4123 All-
schwil. T. (061) 481 69 15.   *063124*

Altendorf (Schwyz)
Stählin, Betli, Zürcher Str.7, 8852 Altendorf.
T. (052) 4422574.   *063125*

Altstätten (Sankt Gallen)
Frewi, Churer Str. 2, 9450 Altstätten.
T. (071) 7552433.   *063126*

Amriswil (Thurgau)
Pfister, Erna, Arboner Str. 35, 8580 Amriswil.
T. (071) 4114515.   *063127*

Andermatt (Uri)
Ackermann, R. & Th., Turmmaststr. 11, 6490 Andermatt.
T. (041) 8877320. - Ant -   *063128*
Galerie im Verkehrsbüro, Gotthardstr. 2, 6490 Ander-
matt. T. (041) 8877454, Fax 681 85. - Paint / Furn / Chi-
na / Sculp / Tex / Jew / Cur / Pho / Draw -   *063129*

Anières (Genève)
Linder, Armand, 297a Rte. d'Hermance, 1247 Anières.
T. (022) 751 11 08. - Ant / Sculp -   *063130*
Pittet, Eric, 50 Chemin des Avallons, 1247
Anières.   *063131*

Appenzell (Appenzell Innerrhoden)
Dörig & Caviezel, Hirschgasse 10, 9050
Appenzell.   *063132*
Fässler, Hermann & Söhne, Weissbadstr 22 u. 33, 9050
Appenzell. T. (071) 7871284. - Ant / Furn -   *063133*
Fischli, Markus, Gaiser Str. 4a, 9050 Appenzell.
T. (071) 7871006.   *063134*
Leimbacher, Karl, Weissbadstr. 45, 9050 Appenzell.
T. (071) 7871263.   *063135*
Rechsteiner, Arnold, Hirschberg 11, 9050 Appenzell.
T. (071) 7872245.   *063136*

Rechsteiner, T., Mettlenstr. 1, 9050 Appenzell.
T. (071) 7871630.   *063137*

Ardon (Valais)
Au Temps Jadis, Rue du Vieux-Village, 1957 Ardon.
T. (027) 3062058.   *063138*
Delaloye, Romain, Rue du Vieux-Village, 1957 Ardon.
T. (027) 3062058.   *063139*

Arlesheim (Basel-Land)
Vier Jahreszeiten Antiquitäten, Eremitagestr. 13, 4144
Arlesheim. T. (061) 701 73 52. - Ant -   *063140*

Arosa (Graubünden)
Bottega Antica, Castellino, 7050 Arosa.
T. (081) 3773446.   *063141*

Arth (Schwyz)
Pfister, Hans & Rudolf, Bernerhöhe, 6415 Arth.
T. (041) 855 17 95.   *063142*

Ascona (Ticino)
Antichità Mona Lisa, Via Collegio 6, 6612 Ascona.
T. (091) 7914552. - Ant / Paint / Graph / Orient / China /
Sculp / Jew / Silv / Instr / Glass / Cur / Mod -   *063143*
Arte e Scienza, Passagio San Pietro 8, 6612 Ascona.
T. (091) 7914666, Fax 7922187. - Orient -   *063144*
Bottega d'Arte, Via Locarno 23, 6612 Ascona.
T. (091) 7911713. - Ant / China -   *063145*
La Corona, Via Rondonico 3, 6612 Ascona.
T. (091) 7913559.   *063146*
Flori, Willy, Via Muraccio 7, 6612 Ascona.
T. (091) 7917937.   *063147*
Galleria Serodine, Vic. S. Pietro 9, 6612 Ascona.
T. (091) 7911861, Fax 7912820. - Ant / Sculp / Arch /
Ico -   *063148*
Galleria Turri, Contrada Maggiore 26, 6612 Ascona.
T. (091) 7913615. - Ant / Paint / Furn / Sculp / Instr /
Rel / Ico -   *063149*
Kohler, Via Orelli 4, 6612 Ascona.
T. (091) 7911357.   *063150*
Masini, Daniela e Mauro, Via Rondonico 3, 6612 Ascona.
T. (091) 7915979.   *063151*
Fratelli Scaglia, Via Muraccio 63, 6612 Ascona.
T. (091) 7912693.   *063152*
Studio d'Arte, Via Collegio 38, 6612 Ascona.
T. (091) 7916662.   *063153*
Tobler, Walter A., Via Buonamano 69, 6612 Ascona.
T. (091) 7913512.   *063154*
Turri, 26 Via Contrada Maggiore, 6612 Ascona.
T. (091) 7913615.   *063155*

Au (Sankt Gallen)
Rutz, Angelo, Hauptstr. 107, 9434 Au.
T. (071) 7226808.   *063156*
Spirig, Othmar, Hauptstr. 40, 9434 Au.
T. (071) 7446685.   *063157*

Au (Zürich)
Schneider, Roger, Moosacherstr. 3, 8804 Au.
T. (01) 781 23 80. - Ant / Furn / China / Tex / Cur /
Mod -   *063158*

L'Auberson (Vaud)
Burgoz, Michel, 23 Grand-Rue, 1454 L'Auberson.
T. (024) 4543388, Fax 4544166.   *063159*
Crausaz, Pierre, 63 Grand-Rue, 1454 L'Auberson.
T. (024) 4544251.   *063160*

Aubonne (Vaud)
Chez l'Antiquaire, 8 Château-Verd, 1170 Aubonne.
T. (021) 808 70 50.   *063161*
Galerie de l'Amiral Duquesne, 6 Rue Amiral-Duquesne,
1170 Aubonne. T. (021) 808 57 00, Fax 808 68 73.
- Ant / Furn / China -   *063162*

Aurigeno (Ticino)
Bovien, Ursula, Castello Ciappui 9, 6671 Aurigeno.
T. (091) 7531831.   *063163*

Auvernier (Neuchâtel)
Richard, Jean-Francis, 7 Rte. du Lac, 2012 Auvernier.
T. (032) 7319579.   *063164*

Avenches (Vaud)
Andralys, 1 Rte. de Berne, 1580 Avenches.
T. (026) 6751124.   063165
Brog, Albert, 71 Rue Centrale, 1580 Avenches.
T. (026) 6751320.   063166
Guillard, Alain, 14 Rue Centrale, 1580 Avenches.
T. (026) 6751640.   063167

Baar (Zug)
Baumann, Hansjörg, Neugasse 24a, 6340 Baar.
T. (041) 761 46 36.   063168
Jenni, Josef, Büelstr. 10a, 6340 Baar.
T. (041) 761 07 86.   063169

Bachenbülach (Zürich)
Ginsig, Markus, Kasernenstr. 4, 8184 Bachenbülach.
T. (01) 860 90 76.   063170
Zum Holzwurm, Kapp-Haus, Kasernenstr. 4, 8184 Bachenbülach. T. (01) 860 90 76.   063171

Bad Ragaz (Sankt Gallen)
Balsiger, Walter, Bahnhofstr 14, 7310 Bad Ragaz.
T. (085) 3023830.   063172

Baden (Aargau)
Antiquitäten & Gegenwartskunst, Zürcherstr 7, 5400 Baden. T. (056) 2220285, Fax 2228986. - Ant / Paint /
Graph / Orient / China / Sculp / Arch / Jew / Fra / Silv / Lights / Instr / Mil / Rel / Glass / Cur / Mod / Ico / Draw --   063173
SAMPL, Restaurationswerkstatt für Antiquitäten und Kunst aller Art, Zürcherstr 7, 5400 Baden.
T. (056) 2220285, Fax 2228996.   063174
Wagner, Claus, Stadtturmstr. 11, 5400 Baden.
T. (056) 222 95 00.   063175

Baldegg (Luzern)
Adolpho Antiquitäten, Ferrenweg 4, 6283 Baldegg.
T. (041) 910 34 30.   063176

Balerna (Ticino)
Bernadis, Leonardo, Casa Vescovile, 6828 Balerna.
T. (091) 6836671.   063177
Il Tario, Casa Vescoville, 6828 Balerna.
T. (091) 6836671.   063178

Balgach (Sankt Gallen)
Nüesch, Ernst, Mühlsteinstr. 15, 9436 Balgach.
T. (071) 7221612.   063179

Basadingen (Thurgau)
Elliott, Chris, Hauptstr., 8254 Basadingen.
T. (052) 6571379.   063180

Basel (Basel-Stadt)
Aeschbacher, Kurt, Totenpl. 3, 4051 Basel.
T. (061) 261 90 62.   063181
Altes en vogue, Güterstr. 245, 4053 Basel.
T. (061) 331 14 38.   063182
Antik Lädeli 108, Sankt Johanns-Ring 108, 4056 Basel.
T. (061) 321 60 87. - Ant -   063183
Antiques am Heuberg, Heuberg 34, 4051 Basel.
T. (061) 261 30 97.   063184
Antiquitäten Sankt Johannstor, Sankt Johannsvorstadt 106, 4056 Basel. T. (061) 322 42 40. - Ant / China /
Jew / Lights / Glass / Mod -   063185
Antiquitäten zum Rosshof, Petersgraben 49, 4051 Basel.
T. (061) 261 38 39.   063186
Antiquités du 1900-1930, Schützenmattstr. 8, 4051 Basel. T. (061) 261 31 10.   063187
Art Antica, Schliengerweg 12, 4057 Basel.
T. (061) 691 98 68. - Ant -   063188
Arte & Licht, Spalenvorstadt 31, 4051 Basel.
T. (061) 261 08 72. - Lights -   063189
Artinba, Sankt Jakobs Str 25, 4052 Basel.
T. (061) 2775429, Fax (061) 2775588. - Ant / Paint /
Graph / Furn / Sculp / Jew / Silv -   063190
Asiatica, Rümelinspl. 14, 4001 Basel.
T. (061) 261 52 95.   063191
Audion, Wasgenring 45, 4055 Basel.
T. (061) 321 43 72.   063192
Baggenstos-Annen, A., Ochsengasse 14, 4058 Basel.
T. (061) 261 22 80. - Ant / Furn / Sculp / Instr /
Rel -   063193

Basels 1. Kuriositätengeschäft, Spalenberg 12, 4051
Basel. T. (061) 261 93 23. - Ant / Cur -   063194
Basilea Münzhandel, Gerbergässlein 26, 4001 Basel.
T. (061) 261 95 66. - Num -   063195
Bieder, Hans, Barfüsserpl 21, 4051 Basel.
T. (061) 261 08 69, Fax (061) 921 12 35. - Ant / Paint /
Furn / China / Dec / Instr / Glass -   063196
Billeter, Madeleine, Leimenstr. 16, 4051 Basel.
T. (061) 272 16 65.   063197
Blöchle, Peter, Spalenvorstadt 31, 4051 Basel.
T. (061) 2610872.   063198
Bohnenblust, Max, Clarastr. 34, 4058 Basel.
T. (061) 691 26 81.   063199
Braitmaier, Werner, Petersgraben 73, 4051 Basel.
T. (061) 261 53 21.   063200
Cachet, Münsterberg 13, 4051 Basel.
T. (061) 2723594.   063201
Christen-Shamoon Objets, Elisabethenstr. 42, 4051 Basel. T. (061) 272 61 68.   063202
Cimicchi, Sandro, Angensteinerstr. 15, 4052 Basel.
T. (061) 312 85 46.   063203
Damioli, Sandro, Schützenmattstr. 8, 4051 Basel.
T. (061) 261 18 08.   063204
Eberwein, Felix, Spalenberg 30, 4051 Basel.
T. (061) 261 03 48. - Num -   063205
Egli, René, Blotzheimerstr. 19, 4055 Basel.
T. (061) 321 68 67.   063206
Eichenberger, Jean, Rheingasse 32, 4058 Basel.
T. (061) 261 30 68. - Ant -   063207
Erlanger & Althaus, Klybeckstr. 29, 4057 Basel.
T. (061) 692 32 18. - Ant -   063208
Erni, Dolores, Rümelinsplatz 14, 4051 Basel.
T. (061) 261 52 95. - Ant / Orient -   063209
Galerie Demenga, Henric-Petri-Str. 19, 4051 Basel.
T. (061) 272 45 62, Fax (061) 272 44 00. - Paint /
Graph / Sculp / Fra / Glass / Mul / Draw -   063210
Galerie Ethno-Art, Schnabelgasse 1, 4051 Basel.
T. (061) 2622250. - Ant / Eth / Orient / Jew -   063211
Galerie Sevogel, Sevogelstr. 76, 4052 Basel.
T. (061) 312 26 59.   063212
Galerie Varia, Rümelinspl. 6, 4051 Basel.
T. (061) 261 45 51, Fax (061) 261 35 57. - Orient /
Eth -   063213
Gasser, Philippe, Spalentorweg 48, 4051 Basel.
T. (061) 271 60 48.   063214
Gerber, Waldemar, Schneidergasse 18, 4001 Basel.
T. (061) 2611773, Fax 2614150. - Paint /
Graph -   063215
Glasstettler, Fritz, Petersgraben 19, 4051 Basel.
T. (061) 261 30 24. - Ant -   063216
Goepfert, Roger, Sissacherstr. 11, 4052 Basel.
T. (061) 312 62 35.   063217
Graf-Marti, Paul, Breisacherstr 6-8, 4057 Basel.
T. (061) 6910488.   063218
Graf, Rudolf J., Rheingasse 31, 4005 Basel.
T. (061) 6810066.   063219
Hablützel, Frank, Falknerstr. 32, 4051 Basel.
T. (061) 261 88 22, Fax (061) 261 33 52. - Dec - 063220
H.A.C. Kunst der Antike, Malzgasse 23, 4052 Basel.
T. (061) 271 67 55, Fax (061) 271 57 33. - Ant /
Arch -   063221
Handschin, Rudolf, Neuhausstr. 3, 4057 Basel.
T. (061) 631 58 80.   063222
Henrich, Anna, Lenzg 6, 4025 Basel. T. (061) 3228733.
- Ant / Paint / Graph -   063223
Herzog, Peter, Holbeinstr. 79 a, 4051 Basel.
T. (061) 272 79 23.   063224
Horlogerie de Collection A. & A. Ciprian, Binningerstr.
15, 4051 Basel. T. (061) 271 57 90.   063225
Hutter, Jolanda, Riehentorstr. 14, 4058 Basel.
T. (061) 681 45 01. - Ant -   063226
Katz, David, Dufourstr. 5, 4052 Basel. T. (061) 272 73 51,
Fax (061) 272 73 51. - Paint -   063227
Knöll, Niklaus, Herbergsg. 4, 4003 Basel.
T. (061) 261 60 06.   063228
Knöll, Thomas, Utengasse 52, 4058 Basel.
T. (061) 6922988, Fax 6922942.   063229
Krieg, Hans-Peter, Allschwilerstr. 24, 4055 Basel.
T. (061) 302 78 24.   063230
Kübli, Josua, Kornhausgasse 8, 4051 Basel.
T. (061) 261 51 67. - Ant -   063231

Kübli, Martin, Leonhardsberg 14, 4051 Basel.
T. (061) 261 03 15, Fax (061) 261 03 57. - Ant / Paint /
Furn / Sculp -   063232
Labyrinth, Nadelberg 17, 4001 Basel.
T. (061) 261 57 67.   063233
Leingruber, Rolf, Oberwilerstr 159, 4054 Basel.
T. (061) 421 44 33, Fax 4214433.   063234
Leinweber, Ilona, Postfach, 4001 Basel.
T. (061) 261 18 01.   063235
Libelle, Hegenheimerstr. 90, 4055 Basel.
T. (061) 381 35 56.   063236
Lüdin, Paul, Riehenstr. 6, 4058 Basel.
T. (061) 681 73 75.   063237
Lutz, Werner, St. Alban Rheinweg 42, 4052
Basel.   063238
Martins da Costa, J.B., Amberbachstr. 87, 4057
Basel.   063239
Micheluzzi, Silvia, Lothringerstr. 31, 4056 Basel.
T. (061) 382 96 06.   063240
Mohler, Karl, Rheinsprung 7, 4051 Basel.
T. (061) 2619882, Fax (061) 2619881.
- Graph -   063241
Mohler, Trudy, Drahtzugstr 57, 4001 Basel.
T. (061) 6818289.   063242
Münzer, Adolf, Hammerstr. 92, 4057 Basel.
T. (061) 6914681. - Furn / Mod -   063243
NS Antiquitäten, Blumenrain 3, 4051 Basel.
T. (061) 382 34 13.   063244
Oldiana, Auf der Lyss 24, 4003 Basel.
T. (061) 261 77 00.   063245
Palladion, Rennweg 51, 4052 Basel. T. (061) 3123400,
3120344. - Ant / Sculp -   063246
Pawelzik, Martin, Isteiner Str 86, 4058 Basel.
T. (061) 6929613.   063247
Peter, Margrit, Aeschenvorstadt 24, 4051 Basel.
T. (061) 2720270. - Ant / Furn / Silv / Glass -   063248
Petitjean, Roland A., Steinentorstr 35, 4051 Basel.
T. (061) 2819900. - Ant / Graph / Furn / Orient /
Mil -   063249
Pfau, Tamara, Güterstr. 147 p, 4053 Basel.
T. (061) 281 01 30. - Ant -   063250
Pfister, Annemarie, Petersgraben 18, 4051 Basel.
T. (061) 261 75 02.   063251
Richers, Margrit, Altrheinweg 54, 4057 Basel.
T. (061) 631 51 74.   063252
Rossi, André, Bruderholzweg 46, 4053 Basel.
T. (061) 361 47 54. - Ant / Paint / Graph -   063253
Russo, Rosario, Oetlingerstr. 189, 4057 Basel.
T. (061) 692 09 33. - Num -   063254
Sankt Johannstor, St. Johanns-Vorstadt 106, 4056 Basel. T. (061) 322 42 40. - Ant -   063255
Scheidegger, Fritz, Zürcherstr. 91, 4052 Basel.
T. (061) 311 37 30.   063256
Schiess, Patricia, Güterstr. 122, 4053 Basel.
T. (061) 361 14 19.   063257
Schmidt, Ernesto, Gerbergasse 53, 4001 Basel.
T. (061) 261 10 08.   063258
Schneider, Eduard, Claragraben 160, 4057 Basel.
T. (061) 691 42 88.   063259
Schnell-Markes, H. & T., Klosterberg 19, 4051 Basel.
T. (061) 272 57 62.   063260
Schwabe, Andreas, Spalenberg 28, 4003 Basel.
T. (061) 2613663.   063261
Ségal, M. & G., Aeschengraben 14-16, 4051 Basel.
T. (061) 272 39 08, Fax (061) 272 29 84. - Ant / Paint /
Furn / China / Sculp / Silv / Instr / Glass -   063262
Senn, Rudolf, Klosterberg 7, 4051 Basel.
T. (061) 2726262.   063263
Siegrist, Willy, Steinenvorstadt 79, 4051 Basel.
T. (061) 271 49 39.   063264
Simmermacher, René, Augustinergasse 7, 4001 Basel.
T. (061) 2611458. - Ant / Paint / Graph / Num / China /
Silv / Glass / Toys -   063265
Steiner, Nordfrid, Blumenrain 3, 4051 Basel.
T. (061) 2616837. - Num -   063266
Stöcklin, Daniel, Spalenberg 61, 4051 Basel.
T. (061) 261 76 26. - Num -   063267
Thorens, Daniel Blaise, Aeschenvorstadt 15, 4051 Basel. T. (061) 271 72 11, Fax (061) 271 72 06.
- Paint -   063268
Timeless Antiques, Hammerstr 3, 4058 Basel.
T. (061) 6928020, Fax 6928675. - Instr -   063269

Trouvaille, Petersgraben 3, 4051 Basel.
T. (061) 261 38 78. - Ant / Furn - *063270*
Varia, Rüemlinspl. 6, 4001 Basel. T. (061) 261 45 51.
- Ant - *063271*
Vögtli, Heinz, Nadelberg 45, 4051 Basel.
T. (061) 261 49 40. *063272*
Volkskunst St. Clara, Clarastr. 7, 4058 Basel.
T. (061) 681 62 22. - Eth - *063273*
W & W Antiqua, Freie Str. 95, 4051 Basel.
T. (061) 272 81 00, Fax (061) 261 81 52. - Ant / China /
Jew / Silv / Instr - *063274*
Wanner, J., Spalenberg 14, 4051 Basel.
T. (061) 261 48 26. *063275*
Zabiello, Irena, Heuberg 34, 4051 Basel.
T. (061) 261 30 97. *063276*
Zum Basilisk, Elisabethenstr. 15, 4051 Basel.
T. (061) 272 18 23. *063277*
Zum Glungenen Stübli, Wettsteinallee 47, 4058 Basel.
T. (061) 6811712. - Toys - *063278*
Zur Krähe, Spalenvorstadt 13, 4051 Basel.
T. (061) 261 22 65. *063279*

Bassecourt (Jura)
Chariatte, Marc, 91 Longchamp, 2854 Bassecourt.
T. (032) 4267967. *063280*

Beckenried (Nidwalden)
Achermann, Franz, Kirchweg 23, 6375 Beckenried.
T. (041) 620 12 17. *063281*

Beinwil am See (Aargau)
Eichenberger, Walter, Dr., Aarauerstr 12, 5712 Beinwil
am See. T. (062) 7714421, Fax 7714421. *063282*

Bellach (Solothurn)
Siegrist, Gertrud, Hangenmoosstr. 4, 4512 Bellach.
T. (032) 6183041. *063283*

Bellevue (Genève)
Janner, Rue 53 Rte. de Collex, 1293 Bellevue.
T. (022) 774 15 48. - Ant - *063284*

Bellinzona (Ticino)
Castel Arte, P. Collegiata 1, 6501 Bellinzona.
T. (091) 8256710. *063285*
Jemora, Jean-Daniel, Via Teatro 9, 6500 Bellinzona.
T. (091) 8262957. *063286*
Il Tario, Via Teatro 9, 6500 Bellinzona.
T. (091) 8262957. *063287*

Belmont-sur-Lausanne (Vaud)
Lutz, Robert, Rte. du Signal, 1092 Belmont-sur-Lausanne. T. (021) 7287616. *063288*

Belp (Bern)
Qualig, Robert, Hühnerhubelstr. 3, 3123 Belp.
T. (031) 819 07 29. *063289*

Benken (Sankt Gallen)
Harder, Jakob, Haldenstr. 24, 8717 Benken.
T. (052) 2832991. *063290*
Helbling, Max, Unterhaldenstr., 8717 Benken.
T. (052) 2831818. *063291*

Bern
Amacker, Regula, Münstergasse 42, 3011 Bern.
T. (031) 311 04 03. *063292*
Andreani, Luciano, Postgasse 6, 3011 Bern.
T. (031) 3114280. *063293*
Antiquitätengalerie zum Bärengraben, Nydegg. 17, 3011
Bern. T. (031) 311 44 44. - Ant - *063294*
Antix, Rathausgasse 23, 3011 Bern.
T. (031) 311 31 05. *063295*
Art Deco, Rathausgasse 55, 3011 Bern.
T. (031) 311 58 59. *063296*
Art moderne et ancien, Gerechtigkeitsgasse 33, 3011
Bern. T. (031) 311 24 72. - Ant / Furn - *063297*
Artex – Expertenbüro für Bildende Kunst, Dr. Franz Josef
Sladeczek, Dufourstr 21, 3005 Bern. T. (031) 3527278,
Fax 3527804. - Ant / Paint / Graph / Sculp - *063298*
Bagnoud, Agathe, Postgasse 50, 3011 Bern.
T. (031) 311 64 98. - Ant - *063299*
Barth, Kurt, Wabernstr. 54, 3007 Bern.
T. (031) 371 03 03. *063300*

Baumann, Marcel, Aarbergergasse 16-18, 3011 Bern.
T. (031) 3116866, 3121747. *063301*
Baumann, René, Aarbergergasse 16-18, 3011 Bern.
T. (031) 3116866. *063302*
Berger-Kohler, Louise, Burgunderstr. 72, 3018 Bern.
T. (031) 992 13 06. - Ant / Paint / China - *063303*
Berti, Luciano, Gerechtigkeitsgasse 64, 3011 Bern.
T. (031) 311 04 13. *063304*
Bloch-Diener, Elsa, Kramgasse 60, 3011 Bern.
T. (031) 3110406. - Ant / Arch / Ico - *063305*
Bloch-Diener, Elsa, Obstbergweg 7, 3006 Bern.
T. (031) 3526765. - Ant / Arch / Ico - *063306*
Bolsoni Antik AG, Postfach 5575, 3001 Bern.
T. (031) 3027778, Fax 3027774. *063307*
Brändlin, Susanne, Kramgasse 84, 3011 Bern.
T. (031) 311 55 84. *063308*
Brand, Joachim, Herzogstr. 23, 3014 Bern.
T. (031) 331 70 60. *063309*
Bühler, Jäcky, Stauffacherstr. 16, 3014 Bern.
T. (031) 331 31 01. - Ant - *063310*
Burgfeld, Breiteweg 28, 3006 Bern.
T. (031) 932 11 44. *063311*
Comor Watch, Theaterpl. 8, 3007 Bern.
T. (031) 311 23 61. *063312*
Dietrich, M., Rathausgasse 62, 3011 Bern.
T. (031) 311 50 82. - Num - *063313*
Dinbau, Holenackerstr. 5, 3027 Bern.
T. (031) 991 98 73. *063314*
Duinmeyer, Eddy, Nydeggstalden 32, 3011 Bern.
T. (031) 311 90 91. *063315*
Ethnographica Marcopolo, Münstergasse 47, 3011 Bern.
T. (031) 311 88 44. *063316*
Feller, G., Schifflaube 48, 3011 Bern. T. (031) 311 56 06.
- Ant - *063317*
Fidanza, Alberto, Könizstr. 53a, 3008 Bern.
T. (031) 371 88 45. *063318*
Fine Arts, Rathausgasse 39, 3011 Bern.
T. (031) 311 11 77. *063319*
Fries, Liesbeth, Nydeggstalden 32, 3011 Bern.
T. (031) 311 57 75. - Ant - *063320*
Galerie de Berne, Aarbergerg. 16-18, 3011 Bern.
T. (031) 311 68 66. - Ant / Furn - *063321*
Geelhaar, W., Thunstr. 7, 3005 Bern. T. (031) 351 11 44.
- Ant - *063322*
Gilgen, Marianne, Rathausgasse 14, 3011 Bern.
T. (031) 311 15 80. *063323*
Guatelli, Edgar, Gerechtigkeitsgasse 72, 3011 Bern.
T. (031) 311 04 04. *063324*
Halter, Martin, Klösterlistutz 10, 3013 Bern.
T. (031) 331 42 66. - Glass - *063325*
Hermann, Ernst, Egghölzlistr. 41, 3006 Bern.
I. (031) 351 50 49. *063326*
Himmelreich, Beat, Reichenbachstr 3, 3004 Bern.
T. (031) 3011331. *063327*
Holenacker Antiquitäten, Holenackerstr. 1, 3027 Bern.
T. (031) 992 12 19. *063328*
Max Howald's Erben, Gerechtigkeitsgasse 54, 3011
Bern. T. (031) 3111410, Fax 3118315. - Ant / Jew /
Silv - *063329*

MAX HOWALD'S ERBEN AG.

Bijoux anciens – Argenterie
Ständige Schmuck + Silber Ausstellung
18., 19. Jh., Jugendstil, Art Déco

Gerechtigkeitsgasse 54 – 3011 Bern
Tel. 031 / 311 14 10

Innocenti, Angelo, Oberweg 3, 3013 Bern.
T. (031) 332 27 73. *063330*
Irmak, Abdulkadir, Kramgasse 47, 3011 Bern.
T. (031) 3120604. - Tex - *063331*
Jakob, Teo, Gerechtigkeitsgasse 23-36, 3011 Bern.
T. (031) 311 53 51, Fax (031) 311 91 18.
- Furn - *063332*
Käbat, Michel, Eigerpl. 5, 3007 Bern.
T. (031) 371 56 92. *063333*

Kaynak, Kramgasse 35, 3011 Bern.
T. (031) 311 01 11. *063334*
Knecht, Hawa, Viktoriarain 12, 3013 Bern.
T. (031) 331 72 86. *063335*
Kogal, Burkhard, Kramgasse 53, 3011 Bern.
T. (031) 311 89 19. - Paint / Graph / Num - *063336*
Kornfeld, Laupenstr 41, 3008 Bern. T. (031) 3814673,
Fax 3821891. - Graph / Draw - *063337*
Kräter, Ida & Isolde, Kramgasse 55, 3011 Bern.
T. (031) 311 61 09. - Ant / Dec - *063338*
Kunst und Antiquitäten am Breiteweg, Breiteweg 28,
3006 Bern. T. (031) 931 54 88. - Ant / Paint / Graph /
Furn / Dec / Fra / Lights / Instr / Glass / Cur / Mod / Toys /
Music - *063339*
Kunstklause, Seftigenstr 65, 3007 Bern.
T. (031) 3716259. - Ant / Paint / Fra / Graph - *063340*
Kunstsalon, Wabernstr. 54, 3007 Bern.
T. (031) 371 07 44. *063341*
Läderach, Germaine, Münstergasse 24, 3011 Bern.
T. (031) 311 80 04. *063342*
Liz Antiquitäten, Rathausgasse 39, 3011 Bern.
T. (031) 311 11 77. *063343*
Lowositz, W., Rathausgasse 62, 3011 Bern.
T. (031) 311 50 82. - Num - *063344*
Lüthy, Charles, Seftigenstr. 45, 3007 Bern.
T. (031) 371 31 16. *063345*
Mäder, Max, Kramgasse 54, 3011 Bern.
T. (031) 311 62 35, Fax (031) 311 76 32. - Ant / Paint /
Graph / Furn / Orient / China / Sculp / Tex / Dec / Fra / Sil-
v / Lights / Instr / Mil / Ico / Toys / Music - *063346*
Meyer, Hans, Kramgasse 35, 3011 Bern.
T. (031) 312 00 00. *063347*
Meyer-Mueller SA, Monbijoustr. 10, 3001 Bern.
T. (031) 381 41 31. *063348*
Moeri, Fritz, Monbijoustr. 89, 3007 Bern.
T. (031) 371 71 35. - Ant - *063349*
Müller, Johannes, Neuengasse 38, 3001 Bern.
T. (031) 311 70 24. *063350*
Alfred Müllers Söhne, Aebistr. 10, 3012 Bern.
T. (031) 301 12 72. *063351*
Muff, A., Cedernstr. 4, 3018 Bern. T. (031) 992 00 58.
- Ant / Cur - *063352*
Negro, Giuseppe Dal', Gerberngasse 22, 3011 Bern.
T. (031) 311 31 58. *063353*
Nyffeler, Rathauspl. 6, 3008 Bern.
T. (031) 311 07 71. *063354*
Poyet, Kramgasse 59, 3011 Bern. T. (031) 311 65 15.
- Mil - *063355*
Pulitzer & Knöll, Kramgasse 62, 3011 Bern.
T. (031) 311 56 91, 22 93 33. - Paint / Graph /
Fra - *063356*
Rentsch, Paul, Rathausgasse 8, 3011 Bern.
T. (031) 312 09 10. *063357*
Rieder, J.P., Gerechtigkeitsgasse 79, 3011 Bern.
T. (031) 3126646. - Ant / Furn - *063358*
Ritschard, Matthias, Kramgasse 5, 3011 Bern.
T. (031) 311 86 60. *063359*
Rolli, Bernard, Breiteweg 28, 3006 Bern.
T. (031) 9315488. - Furn / Fra / Mod - *063360*
Rolli, Jean, Schwabstr. 80, 3018 Bern.
T. (031) 992 74 77. *063361*
Romagosa, Jaime, Hirschengraben 6, 3011 Bern.
T. (031) 3815943. *063362*
Rüfenacht, Rudolf, Brunngasse 46, 3011 Bern.
T. (031) 311 29 22. *063363*
Schatzchäschtli, Gerechtigkeitsgasse 13, 3011 Bern.
T. (031) 312 03 19. *063364*
Scherer & Sohn, Otto, Kramgasse 26, 3011 Bern.
T. (031) 311 73 69. - Instr - *063365*
Schmidt, Daniel, Scheibenstr. 38, 3014 Bern.
T. (031) 332 08 07. *063366*
Schwab, Kurt, Spitalackerstr 26, 3013 Bern.
T. (031) 332 96 16. *063367*
Sonne, Iljos, Münstergasse 46, 3011 Bern.
T. (031) 311 90 11. *063368*
Stähli, Roland, Mattenhofstr. 34, 3007 Bern.
T. (031) 381 48 10. *063369*
Stettler, Amthausgasse 1, 3000 Bern. T. (031) 312 03 33,
Fax 3112329. - Tex - *063370*
Strauss, Jean, Morgenstr. 123, 3018 Bern.
T. (031) 991 42 42. *063371*
Streit, Ursula, Brunngasse 25, 3011 Bern.
T. (031) 3116906. *063372*

Stucker, Hermann, Güterstr. 9, 3008 Bern.
T. (031) 381 22 06.   063373
Stucki, Suzanne, Lorbeerstr. 1, 3018 Bern.
T. (031) 992 10 54. - Ant -   063374
Thedy's Lamps Shop, Rathausgasse 51-53, 3011 Bern.
T. (031) 311 62 35, 52 62 52, Fax (031) 311 76 32.
- Ant / Lights -   063375
Tout Style Antiquités, Gerechtigkeitsgasse 30, 3011
Bern. T. (031) 311 11 04. - Ant -   063376
Vitrine, Gerechtigkeitsg 73, 3000 Bern 8.
T. (031) 3118570, Fax 3118269. - Ant / Furn / Tex /
Dec / Instr / Glass / Lights / Mod -   063377
Wälti, Thérèse H., Monbijoustr. 17, 3011 Bern.
T. (031) 381 72 02. - Ant -   063378
Werro, Jean, Zeitglockenlaube 2, 3011 Bern.
T. (031) 311 27 96.   063379
Wild, Alexander, Rathausgasse 30, 3011 Bern.
T. (031) 311 44 80, Fax (031) 311 44 70.
- Num -   063380
Wirz, Peter, Kramgasse 10, 3011 Bern.
T. (031) 311 20 03.   063381
Zeller, Michèle, Kramgasse 20, 3000 Bern 13.
T. (031) 3119388, Fax 3123242. - Ant / Jew / Fra /
Draw -   063382
Zemp, Rudolf, Rathausgasse 45, 3011 Bern.
T. (031) 311 72 61.   063383
Zinngrube Bern, Gerechtigkeitsgasse 9, 3011 Bern.
T. (031) 311 64 49.   063384
Zobrist, Charles, Reichenbachstr. 77, 3004 Bern.
T. (031) 301 50 89.   063385

Bettlach (Solothurn)
Bischof, Cesar, Bischmattstr 7, 2544 Bettlach.
T. (032) 6452574.   063386

Bex (Vaud)
Brocante du Glarey, 15 Rte. de Gryon, 1880 Bex.
T. (024) 4632010.   063387

Biberist (Solothurn)
Kurmann, Schachenstr. 23, 4562 Biberist.
T. (032) 6724250. - Ant / Furn / Num / China / Sculp /
Fra / Silv / Lights / Mil / Glass / Cur / Mod -   063388

Biberstein (Aargau)
Pfenninger, W., Gislifluhweg 50, 5023
Biberstein.   063389

Biel (Bern)
Antikschreinerei, Bßzingenstr. 191, 2504 Biel.
T. (032) 3425848. - Furn -   063390
Burkhardt, Paul, Obergässli 13, 2502 Biel.
T. (032) 3234160. - Ant / Furn -   063391
Columbus Intérieur, Nidaugasse 14, 2502 Biel.
T. (032) 3233011.   063392
Donno, Rocco de, 191 Rue de Boujean, 2504 Biel.
T. (032) 3425848.   063393
Engeli, Dora, Brüggstr. 6, 2503 Biel.
T. (032) 3653439.   063394
Flury, Max, Zentralstr. 12, 2501 Biel. T. (032) 3224505,
Fax 3226865.   063395
Flury, Max, Zentralstr. 12, 2502 Biel.
T. (032) 3224505.   063396
Houriet, Armand, 47 Rue du Midi, 2504 Biel.
T. (032) 3410438. - Ant -   063397
Jegge, Martin, Obergasse 4, 2502 Biel.
T. (032) 3234958.   063398
Loetscher, Marc-André, R. Basse 46, 2502 Biel.
T. (032) 3226386. - Ant / Paint / Graph / Instr -   063399
Marti, Théo, Zentralstr. 14, 2502 Biel.
T. (032) 3235940.   063400
Mathys, Heinz, Neumarktstr. 24, 2502 Biel.
T. (032) 3222565.   063401
Meyer, Claude, 5 Rue B. Rechberger, 2502 Biel.
T. (032) 3232607. - Ant -   063402
Meyer, Francis, 76 Quai du Bas, 2502 Biel.
T. (032) 3223077. - Ant -   063403
Muri, Charles-Louis, 48 Rue Basse, 2500 Biel.
T. (032) 3232341.   063404
Pandolfino, Ignazio, Madretschstr. 56, 2503 Biel.
T. (032) 3653608.   063405
Pro Antica, 11 Rue de Flore, 2502 Biel.
T. (032) 3222383.   063406

Schöni, Denis, 47 Rue Basse, 2502 Biel.
T. (032) 3220134.   063407
Schweizer, Max, Zentralstr. 23, 2502 Biel.
T. (032) 3224679.   063408
Stalder, Anton, Ländtestr. 35, 2503 Biel.
T. (032) 3231312.   063409
Tièche, Roland, Mattenstr. 11, 2503 Biel.
T. (032) 3226475. - Ant / Furn / China / Sculp -   063410
Top Style, Obergasse 29, 2502 Biel.
T. (032) 3228049.   063411
Vifan & Co., S., Ischeneyweg 7, 2504 Biel.
T. (032) 3222062. - Ant -   063412

Bière (Vaud)
Corthesy, Karine, Le Soleil, 1145 Bière.
T. (021) 809 51 70.   063413

Binningen (Basel-Land)
Bieli, Josef, Oberwiler Str. 61, 4102 Binningen.
T. (061) 421 49 72. - Ant / Furn / China / Sculp -   063414

Binz (Zürich)
Antik-Fundgrube, Witikonstr. 14, 8122 Binz.
T. (01) 825 12 28.   063415

Birmensdorf (Zürich)
Meier, Jacques, Lärchenstr. 20, 8903 Birmensdorf.
T. (01) 737 27 24.   063416

Birrwil (Aargau)
Zum blauen Pfauen, In den Ländern 79, 5708 Birrwil.
T. (064) 74 12 67. - Ant / Furn / Paint / Draw -   063417

Birsfelden (Basel-Land)
Noblesse Antiquités, Hauptstr. 3, 4127 Birsfelden.
T. (061) 312 48 97. - Ant -   063418
Zumsteg, Ernst, Schillerstr. 7, 4127 Birsfelden.
T. (061) 312 21 45.   063419

Bischofszell (Thurgau)
Zur Antikecke, Schottengasse 16, 9220 Bischofszell.
T. (071) 4221140.   063420

Bissone (Ticino)
Ferrario, Giuseppe, Via Collina 21, 6816 Bissone.
T. (091) 6499768.   063421
Galeazzi, Giuseppe, 6816 Bissone.
T. (091) 6499282.   063422

Blonay (Vaud)
Kellenberger, Eric, 22 Ch. Planaz, 1807 Blonay.
T. (021) 943 44 44, Fax 9437777. - Graph / Mod /
Mul -   063423
Papon, Jean, 8 Ch. Champsavaux, 1807 Blonay.
T. (021) 943 15 76.   063424

Bottmingen (Basel-Land)
Hirsig, Willi, Gustackerstr. 10, 4103 Bottmingen.
T. (061) 421 51 34.   063425

Boussens (Vaud)
Gentilhommiere, 1034 Boussens. T. (021) 91 18 15.
- Ant -   063426

Bouveret (Valais)
Ostertag, Robert, Villa Domino, Ch. Brison, 1897 Bouveret. T. (024) 4811344.   063427

Bowil (Bern)
Thierstein, Samuel, 3533 Bowil. T. (031) 711 15 95.
- Ant -   063428

Bremgarten (Aargau)
Mühlemann & Co, Am Bogen 6, 5620 Bremgarten.
T. (056) 6334953. - Jew / Instr -   063429

Bremgarten (Bern)
Sollberger, Walter, Seftaurain 9, 3047 Bremgarten.
T. (031) 301 43 32.   063430

Les Brenets (Neuchâtel)
Galerie du Bourg, Bourg-Dessous 55, 2416 Les Brenets.
T. (032) 9321886.   063431

Isole di Brissago (Ticino)
Constantini, Marco, 6614 Isole di Brissago.
T. (091) 7931813.   063432

Ponti, Enea, Piodina, 6614 Isole di Brissago.
T. (091) 7931639.   063433

Brügg bei Biel (Bern)
Bissat, Théo, Pfeideck 4, 2555 Brügg bei Biel.
T. (032) 3734868. - Ant -   063434

Brüttisellen (Zürich)
Dobi, Herbert, Riedmühlestr. 12, 8306 Brüttisellen.
T. (01) 833 13 10.   063435

Brugg (Aargau)
Roth, Rolf, Baslerstr. 2, 5200 Brugg.
T. (056) 441 40 84.   063436

Brunnen (Schwyz)
Frefel, Felix, Sportplatzweg 8, 6440 Brunnen.
T. (041) 820 14 54.   063437

Buchenegg (Zürich)
Lutz, H.P., Alte Sennhütte, 8143 Buchenegg.
T. (01) 710 55 88. - Ant -   063438

Buchillon (Vaud)
Eméry, Jean-Claude, Rte Cantonale Etoy, 1164 Buchillon. - Ant -   063439

Buchs (Aargau)
Brockoli, Mitteldorfstr. 82, 5033 Buchs.
T. (064) 22 72 92.   063440
Kleiner, Lochmattweg 37, 5033 Buchs. T. (064) 22 33 20,
Fax 24 36 83. - Ant / Paint / China / Sculp / Silv / Glass /
Draw -   063441

Bülach (Zürich)
Rakita, Alex, Winterthurer Str. 5, 8180 Bülach.
T. (01) 860 23 88.   063442

Büren (Solothurn)
Moser, Stefan, Gempenstr. 20, 4413 Büren.
T. (061) 911 01 94.   063443

Büren an der Aare (Bern)
Maurer, Erica & Paul, Kreuzgasse 20, 3294 Büren an der
Aare. T. (032) 3513168.   063444

Bulle (Fribourg)
Barras, David, 8 Rue Victor Tissot, 1630 Bulle.
T. (026) 9121377.   063445
Dupasquier, Pierre-Alain, 26 Rue Pierre Sciobéret, 1630
Bulle. T. (026) 9121454.   063446
Nater, Albert, 34 Rue de Gruyères, 1630 Bulle.
T. (026) 9127994.   063447
Remy, Bernard, 24 Ch. d'Ogoz, 1630 Bulle.
T. (026) 9127463.   063448

Burgdorf (Bern)
Fink, Eduard, Metzgergasse 18, 3400 Burgdorf.
T. (034) 4226044, 4224711. - Graph -   063449
Willener, Brigitte, Schmiedengasse, 3402
Burgdorf.   063450
Willener, Brigitte, Hohengasse 17, 3400 Burgdorf.
T. (034) 4228104.   063451

Bussigny-près-Lausanne (Vaud)
Jaton, Christine, 12 Rue du Château, 1030 Bussigny-
près-Lausanne. T. (021) 701 38 71.   063452
Steiner, René, 5 Rte. de la Chaux, 1030 Bussigny-près-
Lausanne. T. (021) 701 04 61.   063453

Busswil bei Büren (Bern)
Rickli, Edith Lydia, Hinterfeldweg 7, 3292 Busswil bei
Büren. T. (032) 3848078. - Ant -   063454

Cagiallo (Ticino)
Fluri, Hans, 6955 Cagiallo. T. (091) 9434171.   063455

Campione d'Italia (Ticino)
Belcaro, Giacinto, Via Bonino 10, 6911 Campione d'Italia. T. (091) 6498640.   063456

Canobbio (Ticino)
Ferrari, Franco, Via Viganelli 2, Al Maglio, 6952 Canobbio. T. (091) 9410520.   063457

Carona (Ticino)
Sommerhalder, Otto, 6914 Carona.
T. (091) 6496052.   063458

Carouge (Genève)

Aellen, Charly, 26 Rue Ancienne, 1227 Carouge.
T. (022) 342 16 56. - Ant / Furn - *063459*
Ange du Bizarre, 10 Rue Ancienne, 1227 Carouge.
T. (022) 343 50 56. *063460*
Atelier 5, 5 Rue Saint-Victor, 1227 Carouge.
T. (022) 343 08 82. - Ant - *063461*
Bosson, Huguette, 4 Rue Joseph-Girard, 1227 Carouge.
T. (022) 342 21 11. - Ant - *063462*
Brand, Marianne, 20 Rue Ancienne, 1227 Carouge.
T. (022) 343 35 65. *063463*
Challandes-Calame, P., 10 Rue Ancienne, 1227 Carouge. T. (022) 342 54 81. - Ant - *063464*
Chauve, Jacques, 4 Pl. de l'Octroi, 1227 Carouge.
T. (022) 343 00 72. - Ant - *063465*
De Tout un Peu, 21 Rue Saint-Victor, 1227 Carouge.
T. (022) 342 34 96. - Ant - *063466*
Does, Dorle van der, 20 Rue St.-Victor, 1227 Carouge.
T. (022) 3421100. *063467*
Dürr, 22 Rue Jacques-Dalphin, 1227 Carouge.
T. (022) 343 85 90/342 62 25, Fax 343 85 90.
- Num - *063468*
Gallinari, Jacques, 21 Rue St.-Victor, 1227 Carouge.
T. (022) 342 34 96. - Ant / Paint / Sculp /
Lights - *063469*
Graff, Guy, 4 Rte. de Drize, 1227 Carouge.
T. (022) 3430930. *063470*
Kilcher, Bernard, r. Caroline 44, 1227 Carouge.
T. (022) 3432547. - Ant - *063471*
Objets d'Asie, 3 Rue Saint-Victor, 1227 Carouge.
T. (022) 343 83 23. - Orient - *063472*
Passé Composé, 42 Rue Jacques-Dalphin, 1227 Carouge. T. (022) 342 68 27. - Furn - *063473*
Reymond, Jacques, 8 Rue Ancienne, 1227 Carouge.
T. (022) 3420821. *063474*

Caslano (Ticino)

Frunz, Eduard, Via Torrazza, 6987 Caslano.
T. (091) 6062340. *063475*

Cernier (Neuchâtel)

Masmejan, Gérard, 1 Rue Guillaume-Farel, 2053 Cernier. T. (032) 8533544. *063476*

Le Châble (Valais)

Gailloud, Yvan, Villette, 1934 Le Châble.
T. (027) 7761358. *063477*

Cham (Zug)

Wyss, Fritz, Sinserstr. 41, 6330 Cham.
T. (041) 780 19 38. *063478*
Zollinger, Karl, Parkweg 2, 6330 Cham.
T. (041) 780 27 88. *063479*

Chambésy (Genève)

Moret, 17 Ch. de Valérie, 1292 Chambésy.
T. (022) 758 17 59. *063480*

Champagne (Vaud)

Hofmann, Edouard, 1424 Champagne.
T. (024) 4361354. *063481*

Champéry (Valais)

Perrin, Etienne, Chalet Perrin, 1874 Champéry.
T. (024) 4791286. *063482*

Charmey (Fribourg)

Antiqua, Planpraz, 1637 Charmey. T. (026) 9271257.
- Ant - *063483*

Château-d'Oex (Vaud)

Rosat, Alois, La Petite Maison, Les Moulins, 1837 Château-d'Oex. T. (026) 9246633. *063484*
Sadeleer, Stanislas de, Le Bercail, 1837 Château-d'Oex.
T. (026) 9247833. *063485*

La Chaux-de-Fonds (Neuchâtel)

Antica, Av. L. Robert 39, 2300 La Chaux-de-Fonds.
T. (032) 9135488. - Ant / Paint / Furn - *063486*
Antiquités Brocante, 2 Rue Numa-Droz, 2300 La Chaux-de-Fonds. T. (032) 9685959. - Ant - *063487*
Artesania, 4 Prom. des Six-Pompes, 2300 La Chaux-de-Fonds. T. (032) 9687651. *063488*
Aux Antiquites d'Horlogerie, 27 Rue Jaquet-Droz, 2300 La Chaux-de-Fonds. T. (032) 9130969. *063489*

Brocante de la Ronde, 3 Rue de la Ronde, 2300 La Chaux-de-Fonds. T. (032) 9681622. - Ant - *063490*
Diglio, Elio, 43 Rue D.-Jeanrichard, 2300 La Chaux-de-Fonds. T. (032) 9130383. *063491*
Dubois, Claude, 8 Rue de la Concorde, 2300 La Chaux-de-Fonds. T. (032) 9686624. *063492*
Galerie d'Horlogerie Ancienne, Rue des Musées 26, 2300 La Chaux-de-Fonds. T. (032) 9138526. *063493*
Genis, José, 11 Rue de la Ronde, 2300 La Chaux-de-Fonds. T. (032) 9683094. *063494*
Guinand, Jean-Paul, 20 Ruelle de l'Aurore, 2300 La Chaux-de-Fonds. T. (032) 9134183. *063495*
L'Ile au Trésor, Jardinière 11, 2300 La Chaux-de-Fonds.
T. (032) 9134934. *063496*
Macchi, Serge, 2 Rue Numa Droz, 2303 La Chaux-de-Fonds. T. (032) 9685959. *063497*
Parel, Charles, 12 Rue du Grenier, 2300 La Chaux-de-Fonds. T. (032) 9132673. - Ant - *063498*
Schenk, Claudine, 3 Rue de la Ronde, 2300 La Chaux-de-Fonds. T. (032) 9681622. *063499*
Schnegg, Christian, 19 Rue du Collège, 2300 La Chaux-de-Fonds. T. (032) 9682228. *063500*
Wasem, Willy, 31 Rue de la Serre, 2300 La Chaux-de-Fonds. T. (032) 9138831. *063501*

Chavannes-près-Renens (Vaud)

Binz, M., 18 Rte. Maladière, 1022 Chavannes-près-Renens. *063502*

Chêne-Bourg (Genève)

Patthey, Jean-Claude, 5 Rue Gotthard, 1225 Chêne-Bourg. T. (022) 348 71 03. - Ant - *063503*
Philnova, 6 Ch. Chalets, 1225 Chêne-Bourg.
T. (022) 349 33 00. - Ant - *063504*
Schlesser, Jean-Pierre, 12 Rue Gotthard, 1225 Chêne-Bourg. T. (022) 349 53 49. - Ant - *063505*
Shopping Puces, Rue Peillonnex 79, 1225 Chêne-Bourg. *063506*

Chermignon-d'en-Bas (Valais)

Galerie des Neiges Chaux & von Siggenthal, Crans pl. de l' anc. Poste, 3971 Chermignon-d'en-Bas.
T. (027) 4816839. *063507*

Cheseaux-sur-Lausanne (Vaud)

Armes Anciennes, 2 Ruelle du Temple, 1033 Cheseaux-sur-Lausanne. T. (021) 731 43 13. *063508*
Esponton, 2 Ruelle de Temple, 1033 Cheseaux-sur-Lausanne. T. (021) 731 43 13. *063509*

Cheyres (Fribourg)

Schenk, Jacques, Le Château, 1468 Cheyres.
T. (026) 6632872. - Ant - *063510*

Chézard (Neuchâtel)

Jacot-Descombes, Pierre, 2 Ch. du Forvy, 2054 Chézard.
T. (032) 8534916. *063511*

Chiasso (Ticino)

Finarte, Via Pasteur 1, 6830 Chiasso.
Fax (091) 430012. *063512*
Heltrophy, Via Soldini 23, 6830 Chiasso.
T. (091) 6837117. - Num - *063513*
Monnaies Or Argent, Via E. Bossi 1, 6830 Chiasso.
T. (091) 6823767. - Num - *063514*

Chur (Graubünden)

Barandun, David, Brändligasse 36, 7000 Chur.
T. (081) 2841144. *063515*
Graf, Albert, Sandstr. 59, 7000 Chur.
T. (081) 2529031. *063516*
Mari, Giovanni, Obere Gasse 39, 7000 Chur.
T. (081) 2520383. *063517*
Padrutt, Marlies, Vazerolgasse 16, 7002 Chur.
T. (081) 2524515. *063518*
Schmid, Mia & Hans, Obere Gasse 38, 7000 Chur.
T. (081) 2521058. - Ant / Paint / Furn / Sculp / Silv / Mil / Glass / Ico - *063519*
Wassenberg, Maria Helena, Rheinstr. 43, 7000 Chur.
T. (081) 2847176. *063520*

Clarens (Vaud)

Galitch, Paul, 9 Rue Artisans, 1815 Clarens.
T. (021) 964 40 34. *063521*

Claro (Ticino)

Mercato, Roberto, Via Cantonale, 6702 Claro.
T. (091) 8632444. *063522*

Colombier (Neuchâtel)

Dessarzin, Jean-Daniel, 8 Ch.-Notre-Dame, 2013 Colombier. T. (032) 8411000. *063523*

Conches (Genève)

Briner, Janet F., Av Paul-Chaix 2, 1231 Conches.
T. (022) 7893458. *063524*

Corcelles-près-Concise (Vaud)

Payot, Eric, 1426 Corcelles-près-Concise.
T. (024) 4341663. *063525*

Corgémont (Bern)

Waelchli, Christian, 10 Quart-Dessus, 2606 Corgémont.
T. (032) 4891076. *063526*

Corminboeuf (Fribourg)

Piller, Yves, 1 Impasse de la Colline, 1720 Corminboeuf.
T. (026) 4752177. *063527*

Cornol (Jura)

Antiquités, Rte. St.-Gilles, 2952 Cornol.
T. (032) 4622774. *063528*

Cortaillod (Neuchâtel)

Au Fil du Temps, 1 Goutte d'Or, 2016 Cortaillod.
T. (032) 8423878. *063529*

Cossonay-Vill (Vaud)

Brunner, F. & C.O., Rue du Temple, 1304 Cossonay-Vill.
T. (021) 861 09 86. *063530*

Courgenay (Bern)

Snoriguzzi, Michel, 663 Rue du Général Comman, 2892 Courgenay. T. (032) 4712345. *063531*
Tallone, Marlyse, 110 Mont-Lave, 2892 Courgenay.
T. (032) 4712113. *063532*

Courroux (Jura)

Chariatte, Guy, 355 Rue Général-Guisan, 2822 Courroux.
T. (032) 4222516. *063533*

Courtepin (Fribourg)

Scheidegger, Claude, 40 Rte. Marais, 1784 Courtepin.
T. (026) 6842678. *063534*

Crans-sur-Sierre (Valais)

Les Ateliers Georges Banoud, 3963 Crans-sur-Sierre.
T. (027) 4812067. *063535*
Mayfair Antiques, 3963 Crans-sur-Sierre.
T. (027) 4815289. *063536*

Crémines (Bern)

Spart, Michel, Zatte 4, 2746 Crémines.
T. (032) 4999548. - Ant / Furn / Dec - *063537*

Cressier (Fribourg)

Tschanz, Fritz, 1785 Cressier. T. (026) 6741959. *063538*

Cuarnens (Vaud)

Virgilio, Jean-François, La Combe, 1309 Cuarnens.
T. (021) 864 54 51. *063539*

Cugy (Fribourg)

Rossier, Jean-Blaise, Au Village, 1482 Cugy.
T. (026) 6606474. *063540*

Cully (Vaud)

Mounoud, René-Marcel, Pl. du Major Davel, 1096 Cully.
T. (021) 799 18 95. *063541*

Deitingen (Solothurn)

Kofmel, Walter, Baschistr 231, 4707 Deitingen.
T. (032) 6141686. *063542*

Delémont (Jura)

Bloch, Francis, 5 Rue du Marché, 2800 Delémont.
T. (032) 4223715. - Ant / Furn / China / Dec - *063543*

Develier (Jura)

Sugnaux, Irma, 77 Rte. Principale, 2802 Develier.
T. (032) 4227778. *063544*

Disentis/Mustér (Graubünden)

Kunstgalerie Art-Deco, 7180 Disentis/Mustér. *063545*

Domat/Ems (Graubünden)
Martinis, G.-M. de, Rieven 17, 7013 Domat/Ems.
T. (081) 6323808.   063546

Dongio (Ticino)
Wüthrich, Max, Cà del Pacifico, 6715 Dongio.
T. (091) 8712561.   063547

Dornach (Solothurn)
Peter, Margrit, Steinmattweg 14, 4143 Dornach.
T. (061) 701 71 16. - Ant / Furn / Silv / Glass -   063548

Dübendorf (Zürich)
Stall-Lädeli, Wallisellenstr. 28, 8600 Dübendorf.
T. (01) 8217473, Fax 8217473.   063549
Suremann, Walter, Täschenstr. 5, 8600 Dübendorf.
T. (01) 821 37 34.   063550
Wyss, Jaime, Zürichstr 98, 8600 Dübendorf.
T. (01) 8213366, Fax 8213354. - Lights / Instr /
Pho -   063551

Dürnten (Zürich)
Michelsen, Christian, Manssarde 31, 8635 Dürnten.
T. (052) 2464344.   063552

Ebikon (Luzern)
Bachmann, Hermann, Zentralstr. 14 a, 6030 Ebikon.
T. (041) 440 19 22.   063554
Hlinavsky, Jaroslav, Riedmattstr. 10, 6030 Ebikon.
T. (041) 440 26 53. - Ant -   063555
Portmann, Alfred, Luzerner Str 53, 6030 Ebikon.
T. (041) 4207080.   063555a
Stadelmann, Josef, Schachenweidstr. 41, 6030 Ebikon.
T. (041) 420 00 30.   063556
Weibel, Karl, Gerbering 2, 6030 Ebikon.
T. (041) 440 66 76.   063557

Ebmatingen (Zürich)
Baehler, Steinmueri 24a, 8123 Ebmatingen.
T. (01) 980 19 53, Fax 980 38 49. - Repr / Dec / Jew /
Silv / Instr -   063558

Echallens (Vaud)
Amstutz, Jean-Claude, Rte. Lausanne, 1040 Echallens.
T. (021) 881 25 14.   063559
Dagon, Françoise, Rue des Terrasses, 1040 Echallens.
T. (021) 881 15 96.   063560

Ecublens (Vaud)
Dépraz, Josette, Rte. de la Pierre, 1024 Ecublens.
T. (021) 691 64 80. - Ant / Instr -   063561
Dufour, W.B., 12 Rue de Bassenges, 1024 Ecublens.
T. (021) 691 36 35.   063562

Egg bei Zürich
Gura AG, Bachtelweg 13, 8132 Egg bei Zürich.
T. (01) 984 14 00.   063563
Lüthy, Barbla, Dorfstr. 1, 8132 Egg bei Zürich.
T. (01) 984 08 83.   063564

Eglisau (Zürich)
Riedi, Ursula, Obergass 31, 8193 Eglisau.
T. (01) 8673259, 2623510.   063565
Zanoni, Peter, Rheinsfelderstr 24, 8193 Eglisau.
T. (01) 8673429.   063566
Zum Buurehus, Rheinsfelderstr. 24, 8193 Eglisau.
T. (01) 867 34 29.   063567

Egnach (Thurgau)
Damasco, Gino, Wiedenhorn 481, 9322 Egnach.
T. (071) 4772459.   063568

Eich (Luzern)
Wenger, Paul, Brand, 6205 Eich.   063569

Einigen (Bern)
Fuhrer, Hansruedi, Gheiweg 53, 3646 Einigen.
T. (033) 545363.   063570

Einsiedeln (Schwyz)
Birchler, Josef, Hauptstr. 47, 8840 Einsiedeln.
T. (052) 4123142. - Ant -   063571
Schatt, Josef, Züricher Str. 66, 8840 Einsiedeln.
T. (052) 4121251. - Ant / Furn -   063572

Elgg (Zürich)
Gisler, Armin, Vorderg. 11, 8353 Elgg. T. (052) 3854388.
- Ant -   063573

Embrach (Zürich)
Brunner, Fritz, Dorfstr 64, 8424 Embrach.
T. (01) 8652570.   063574

Emmetten (Nidwalden)
Müller, Kurt, Gumprechtstr. 39, 6376 Emmetten.
T. (041) 620 10 62. - Graph -   063575

Engelburg (Sankt Gallen)
Kuster, Hugo, Höhenstr. 8, 9032 Engelburg.
T. (071) 2782604.   063576

Epagny (Fribourg)
Sigg, Jacques, La Vertchire, 1664 Epagny.
T. (026) 9212486.   063577

Erlenbach (Zürich)
Engelmann, Lotte, Freihofstr. 1, 8703 Erlenbach.
T. (01) 910 58 60.   063578
Savardi & Rossi, Bahnhofstr. 33, 8703 Erlenbach.
T. (01) 910 80 88.   063579

Ersigen (Bern)
Isenring, Walter, Dorfstr. 44, 3423 Ersigen.
T. (034) 4452112.   063580

Eschenbach (Luzern)
Barmet, Eduard, Luzernstr. 12, 6274 Eschenbach.
T. (041) 448 35 25.   063581

Eschenz (Thurgau)
Weber-Züllig, F., Hauptstr. 166, 8264 Eschenz.
T. (052) 89173. - Ant / Furn / Instr / Glass / Cur /
Mod -   063582

Eschert (Bern)
Le Grand Toit, 5a Sous la Rive, 2743 Eschert.
T. (032) 4934014.   063583

Etoy (Vaud)
Emery, Jean-Claude, Rte. Suisse, 1163 Etoy.
T. (021) 807 32 13.   063584

Fällanden (Zürich)
Graf, Peter, Zürichstr. 5, 8117 Fällanden.
T. (01) 825 35 11.   063585
Ruffini & Sohn, R., Schwerzenbachstr. 3, 8117 Fällan-
den. T. (01) 825 46 35. - Ant / Furn / China / Dec / Instr /
Lights / Glass -   063586

Farvagny-le-Grand (Fribourg)
Martin, Francine, 1726 Farvagny-le-Grand.   063587

Feldbrunnen (Solothurn)
Hert, Emil, Rehhubelstr. 1, 4532 Feldbrunnen.
T. (032) 6220853.   063588

Feldmeilen (Zürich)
Bosch, Rudolf, Seestr 11, 8706 Feldmeilen.
T. (01) 9237477.   063589

Ferreyres (Vaud)
Pascalin, Georges, Rte. de Moiry, 1313 Ferreyres.
T. (021) 87 76 43. - Ant / Paint / Graph / Furn / China /
Arch / Silv / Glass / Cur / Draw / Toys -   063590

Flaach (Zürich)
Rösli Antiquitäten, Hauptstr. 1, 8416 Flaach.
T. (052) 3181620.   063591
Zimmermann-Kretz, Kurt & Silvia, Oberdorfstr 9, 8416
Flaach. T. (052) 3181147, Fax 3181969.
- Furn -   063592

Flawil (Sankt Gallen)
Huser, Robert, Wiler Str. 204, 9230 Flawil.
T. (071) 3934161.   063593

Flendruz (Vaud)
Allegri, Claude, 1839 Flendruz. T. (026) 9258276,
Fax 9259327. - Ant / Paint / Furn / Cur -   063594

Founex (Vaud)
Ferrari, Lucien, Grand-Rue, 1297 Founex.
T. (022) 776 18 84.   063595

Frauenfeld (Thurgau)
Baur, Rolf, Zürcherstr 124, 8500 Frauenfeld.
T. (052) 7201018.   063596
Hartmann, H.G., Zürcherstr. 195, 8500 Frauenfeld.
T. (052) 7212267.   063597
Sasso, Eleonore, Zürcherstr. 132, 8500 Frauenfeld.
T. (052) 7215670. - Ant -   063598

Frenkendorf (Basel-Land)
Aebischer, Erwin, Talstr 11, 4402 Frenkendorf.
T. (061) 9017020.   063599

Fribourg
Ansermet, Adèle, Rue de Lausanne 56, 1700 Fribourg.
T. (026) 3223833. - Ant / Furn / Mil -   063600
Antiquaire, Rue de Zaehringen 94, 1700 Fribourg.
T. (026) 3222174. - Ant / Paint / China -   063601
Artcurial Suisse, Villars-les-Joncs, 1700 Fribourg.
T. (026) 4814877.   063602
Beaux Arts, 46 Grand-Rue, 1700 Fribourg.
T. (026) 3245919. - Ant -   063603
Dumont, Michel, Pl. du Petit-St.-Jean 3, 1700 Fribourg.
T. (026) 3221848. - Silv -   063604
Egger, André, 8 Rue de l'Industrie, 1700 Fribourg.
T. (026) 3249874.   063605
Ettlin, Michel, 110 Rte. Morat, 1700 Fribourg.
T. (026) 3226070.   063606
Macherel, Blanche, 54 Rue Zaehringen, 1700 Fribourg.
T. (026) 3222174. - Ant -   063607
Margelle, 6 Rue Epouses, 1700 Fribourg.
T. (026) 3224483. - Ant -   063608
Monferini, G. & M.-P., 2 a Rue Hans-Geiler, 1700 Fri-
bourg. T. (026) 3227001.   063609
Neuhaus, Beat, 7 Imp. Forêt, 1700 Fribourg.
T. (026) 4812142.   063610
Numisma Gold, C.P. 286, 1700 Fribourg.
T. (026) 4753437. - Num -   063611
Rieder, Nicole, 1 Rue des Bouchers, 1700 Fribourg.
T. (026) 3224178.   063612
Stauffacher, Max, Av. Jean-Marie Musy 22, 1700 Fri-
bourg. T. (026) 4814360.   063613
Trouvailles, 37 Rue des Alpes, 1700 Fribourg.
T. (026) 3224769.   063614

Frutigen (Bern)
Germann, Christian, Paradiesli Ried, 3714 Frutigen.
T. (033) 6712844.   063615
Reichen, Hans, Flugplatz, Wisoeystr., 3714 Frutigen.
T. (033) 6711925. - Ant -   063616
Schmid, Jürg, Parallelstr., 3714 Frutigen.
T. (033) 6715118.   063617

Fuyens (Fribourg)
Paudex, Gilbert, 1690 Fuyens. T. (026) 6531704. - Furn /
Num / Sculp -   063618

Gais (Aargau)
Herzenauer, H., Weierweid 1231, 9056 Gais.   063619

Galmiz (Fribourg)
Spack, Robert, Bahnhofstr. 74, 3285 Galmiz.
T. (026) 6704131.   063620

Genève
ACB Art Créations et Bibliophilie, 35 Ch. Grange-Canal,
1208 Genève. T. (022) 735 29 00.   063621
Altamira, 5-7 Rue Céard, 1204 Genève.
T. (022) 328 84 24. - Ant -   063622
Amateurs, 15 Grand-Rue, 1204 Genève.
T. (022) 321 33 13. - Ant -   063623
Andata Ritorno, 37 Rue Stand, 1204 Genève.
T. (022) 329 60 69. - Ant -   063624
Antiquités et Decoration, 2 Rue de la Fontaine, 1204 Ge-
nève. T. (022) 321 37 85.   063625
Antiquités Scientifiques, Rue du Perron 19, 1211 Genè-
ve. T. (022) 3287731.   063626
Antiquorum, 2 Rue du Mont-Blanc, 1201 Genève.
T. (022) 9092850, Fax 9092860. - Ant / Instr -   063627
Arcade Chausse-Coqs, 16 Rue Chausse-Coqs, 1204 Ge-
nève. T. (022) 320 06 30. - Ant -   063628
Ars Antiqua, 3 Rue Albert-Gos, 1206 Genève.
T. (022) 347 02 18. - Num / Arch -   063629
Ars Nova, 6 Rue Calvin, 1204 Genève.
T. (022) 321 86 60. - Ant / Mod -   063630

Art-Monnaies, 10 Rue Berne, 1201 Genève.
T. (022) 731 67 48. - Num -   *063631*
Asprey, 40 Rue du Rhône, 1204 Genève.
T. (022) 310 72 77. - Instr -   *063632*
Athina, 21 Rue Mont-Blanc, 1201 Genève.
T. (022) 738 71 55. - ant -   *063633*
Au Bonheur du Jour, 27 Pl. Bourg-de-Four, 1204 Genè-
ve. T. (022) 329 82 43.   *063634*
Au Picpus, 19 Blvd. du Pont-d'Arve, 1205 Genève.
T. (022) 329 00 75.   *063635*
Au Temps Perdu, Rue Georges-Leschot 6, 1205 Genève.
T. (022) 329 29 50.   *063636*
Au Vieux Canon, 40 Grand-Rue, 1204 Genève.
T. (022) 328 57 58. - Ant / Furn -   *063637*
Au Vieux Paris, 1 Rue de la Servette, 1201 Genève.
T. (022) 734 25 76, Fax 7347709. - Toys -   *063638*
Au Vieux St.-Gervais, 10 Rue des Corps-Saints, 1201
Genève. T. (022) 731 75 75.   *063639*
Bach, G., 8 Av. Pictet-de-Rochemont, 1207 Genève.
T. (022) 736 90 00.   *063640*
Bachmann, Christian, 25 Rue Alfred-Vincent, 1201 Ge-
nève. T. (022) 731 83 11.   *063641*
Bachofner, M., 30 Rue Montbrillant, 1201 Genève.
T. (022) 733 25 00. - Ant -   *063642*
Baird, Maria, 14 Rue Perron, 1204 Genève.
T. (022) 328 88 20. - Ant -   *063643*
Battolo, Luigi, 20 Av. Pictet-de-Rochemont, 1207 Genè-
ve. T. (022) 735 02 54.   *063644*
Baumann, Jacques-Claude, 12 Grand-Rue, 1204 Genè-
ve. T. (022) 321 90 38. - Ant -   *063645*
Benador, Jacques, 7 Rue Hôtel-de-Ville, 1204 Genève.
T. (022) 3116136, Fax 3113205. - Paint /
Sculp -   *063646*
Berndt, Pierre, 34-36 Grand-Rue, 1204 Genève.
T. (022) 311 74 85.   *063647*
Bolle, Pierre-Alain, 17 Rue de Montchoisy, 1207 Genève.
T. (022) 735 01 96. - Ant -   *063648*
Bordier, Jean-Claude, 59 Blvd. Saint-Georges, 1205 Ge-
nève. T. (022) 328 21 80.   *063649*
Bounica, 8 Rue Terrassière, 1207 Genève.
T. (022) 736 54 57. - Ant -   *063650*
Burgener, Jean-Pierre, 11 Rue Hôtel-de-Ville, 1204 Ge-
nève. T. (022) 310 42 70.   *063651*
Byron Galerie, 9 Rue Sismondi, 1201 Genève.
T. (022) 731 62 74.   *063652*
Cabinet de Curiosités, 34 Pl. Bourg-de-Four, 1204 Genè-
ve. T. (022) 329 99 30. - Ant -   *063653*
Camagna, 14 Cours de Rive, 1204 Genève.
T. (022) 736 74 78. - Ant / Paint / Furn / Tex /
Dec -   *063654*
Cangialosi, Vittorio, 28 Rue des Grottes, 1201 Genève.
T. (022) 734 92 77.   *063655*
Catala, Marie-Christine, 19 Blvd. Georges Favon, 1204
Genève. T. (022) 321 88 16.   *063656*
Charbonnier, Georges L., 19 Rue de la Cite, 1204 Genè-
ve. T. (022) 328 28 10. - Paint / Furn / Ico -   *063657*
De Charrière, 57, route de Frontenex, 1207 Genève.
T. (022) 7367050, Fax 7367050.   *063658*
Cheneviere, Bertrand, 22 Prom. Saint-Antoine, 1204 Ge-
nève. T. (022) 321 30 07. - Ant -   *063659*
Cigarini, Romano, 1 Rue Rôtisserie, 1204 Genève.
T. (022) 329 29 33. - Ant -   *063660*
Colucci, Marco, 48 Rue de Lyon, 1203 Genève.
T. (022) 344 17 62.   *063661*
Comte, Roland, 25 Rue Montchoisy, 1207 Genève.
T. (022) 736 05 89.   *063662*
Conchon, Ginette-Marie, 14 Rue du Perron, 1204 Genè-
ve. T. (022) 3285260.   *063663*
Dammron, Claude, 4 Rue du Mont-Blanc, 1201 Genève.
T. (022) 732 30 86.   *063664*
Decolony, 16bis Blvd. Helvétique, 1207 Genève.
T. (022) 736 34 04. - Ant -   *063665*
Desbiolles, Yvon, 7 Blvd. du Théâtre, 1204 Genève.
T. (022) 321 72 05.   *063666*
Desforges, Sylvia, 24 Pl. Bourg-de-Four, 1204 Genève.
T. (022) 311 25 20.   *063667*
Desmeules, J.P., 83 Rue des Eaux-Vives, 1207 Genève.
T. (022) 735 93 20.   *063668*
Devanthéry, Yves, 44 Blvd. Carl-Vogt, 1205 Genève.
T. (022) 781 25 18. - Ant -   *063669*
Diamantart, 19 Rue du Rhône, 1207 Genève.
T. (022) 321 40 05.   *063670*

Dike, Catherine, 4 Rue de Hesse, 1204 Genève.
T. (022) 7218888. - Ant / China / Jew / Silv / Instr / Mil /
Glass / Cur / Mod / Pho / Music -   *063671*
Domus Balexert, 27 Av. Louis-Casaï, 1209 Genève.
T. (022) 321 22 92.   *063672*
Ducor, Pierre, 8 Pl. Bourg de Four, 1204 Genève.
T. (022) 320 47 32. - Ant -   *063673*
Farina, Lydie, 1 Rue Emile Yung, 1205 Genève.
T. (022) 346 46 81. - Ant -   *063674*
Ferrero, Roger, 9 Rue Hôtel de Ville, 1204 Genève.
T. (022) 3286091.   *063675*
Filippini, Jean, 29d Ch. Grange-Canal, 1208 Genève.
T. (022) 735 02 86. - Ant -   *063676*
Foëx, Raymonde, Rue Terrassière 8, 1207 Genève.
T. (022) 7365457.   *063677*
Galerie de la Haute-Ville, 13 Grand-Rue, 1204 Genève.
T. (022) 321 51 54. - Ant -   *063678*
Galerie de Loës, 9 Rue Beauregard, 1204 Genève.
T. (022) 3116001, 3206001, Fax (022) 3124704.
- Graph -   *063679*
Galerie de Saint-Jean, 92 Rue de Saint-Jean, 1201 Ge-
nève. T. (022) 732 32 52.   *063680*
Galerie des Templiers, Ruelle des Templiers 5, 1207 Ge-
nève. T. (022) 7359188, 3445397, Fax 7000785.
- Ant / Arch / Eth / Tex -   *063681*
Galerie Dutta, 15 Rue des Etuves, 1201 Genève.
T. (022) 7386422, Fax (022) 7385731. - Ant / Orient /
Mil -   *063682*
Galerie Grand-Rue, 25 Grand-Rue, 1204 Genève.
T. (022) 3117685.   *063683*
Galerie Persane, 16 Rue de la Corraterie, 1204 Genève.
T. (022) 311 99 74.   *063684*
Galerie Un Deux Trois, 5 Rue Gérard-Muzy, 1207 Genè-
ve. T. (022) 7861611, Fax (022) 7868833. - Graph /
Dec / Mod / Mul -   *063685*
Galerie 5, 5 Place du Bourg-de-Four, 1204 Genève.
T. (022) 320 78 24. - Furn -   *063686*
Gamberini, Elio, 7 Rue du Lac, 1207 Genève.
T. (022) 735 58 48. - Ant -   *063687*
Garcia, Maria-Angèle, 48 bis Rue Terrassière, 1207 Ge-
nève. T. (022) 735 25 87.   *063688*
Giacometti, Pierre, 12 Rue Vallin, 1201 Genève.
T. (022) 320 57 35.   *063689*
Girardin, Gilbert, 7 Blvd. Théâtre, 1204 Genève.
T. (022) 3293960, 3113383. - Ant -   *063690*
Givaudon, Claude, 8a Ch. des Clochettes, 1206 Genève.
T. (022) 347 10 10.   *063691*
Glass-Story, 6 Rue Sismondi, 1201 Genève.
T. (022) 738 71 60.   *063692*
Gonzalez, Antonio, 10 Rue de Berne, 1201 Genève.
T. (022) 731 67 48. - Num -   *063693*
Gottret, Maurice, 12 Rue Jules-Gottret, 1255 Genève.
T. (022) 784 20 48.   *063694*
Grand-Rue, 25 Grand-Rue, 1204 Genève.
T. (022) 3117685. - Paint / Graph / Draw -   *063695*
Grillet, Bernard & Patricia, 81 Rue des Eaux-Vives, 1207
Genève. T. (022) 786 22 21.   *063696*
Héritage, 3 Rue Pierre Fatio, 1204 Genève.
T. (022) 786 96 30.   *063697*
Hirsch, Claude, 24 Rue St Léger, 1204 Genève.
T. (022) 3111377.   *063698*
Horngacher, François, 34 Pl. du Bourg-de-Four, 1204
Genève. T. (022) 3113186, 299930.   *063699*
Huchette, 4 Rue Tour-Maîtresse, 1204 Genève.
T. (022) 321 37 02. - Ant -   *063700*
Huguenin, Monique, 39 Grand-Rue, 1204 Genève.
T. (022) 321 67 19. - Ant -   *063701*
Hunziker, Berthe, 10 Rue Emile-Yung, 1205 Genève.
T. (022) 347 32 08. - Ant -   *063702*
Illi, Raymond, 20 Rue de l'Arquebuse, 1204 Genève.
T. (022) 321 43 47. - Ant / Paint / Graph / Furn / China /
Sculp -   *063703*
Jadis Montres et Bijoux, 21 Grand-Rue, 1204 Genève.
T. (022) 781 24 02.   *063704*
Max N. Knöll, 4 bis Route des Jeunes, 1211 Genève 26.
T. (022) 8111111, Fax 8111118. - Ant / China / Sculp /
Silv / Rel / Glass / Cur -   *063704a*
Koller, 2 Rue de l'Athénée, 1205 Genève.
T. (022) 3210385, Fax (022) 3287872. - Ant -   *063705*
Kurz, 1 Rue Hôtel-de-Ville, 1204 Genève.
T. (022) 321 36 70. - Ant -   *063706*
Latham, Lionel, 5 Rue Sismondi, 1201 Genève.
T. (022) 7313761, Fax 7313761. - Mod -   *063707*

Lavanchy, André, 17 Rue Montchoisy, 1207 Genève.
T. (022) 7731429. - Furn -   *063708*
Lechner & Penet, 1 Rue Hôtel-de-Ville, 1204 Genève.
T. (022) 321 36 70.   *063709*
Letu, Bernard, Rue Calvin 2, 1204 Genève.
T. (022) 3104757, Fax 3108492. - Ant -   *063710*
Maggy Antiquités, 16 Cours-de-Rive, 1204 Genève.
T. (022) 736 74 11.   *063711*
Masis Metna, 12 Gal. J. Malbuisson, 1204 Genève.
T. (022) 311 22 20.   *063712*
Mieville, Claude, 4 Rue Henri-Fazy, 1204 Genève.
T. (022) 321 37 76.   *063713*
Miguel-Fajardo, Ramon de, 36 Rue Rousseau, 1201 Ge-
nève. T. (022) 731 05 65.   *063714*
Miroir aux Alouettes, 15 Rue 31. Décembre, 1207 Genè-
ve. T. (022) 786 63 66.   *063715*
Monnaies et Timbres, 36 Rue Rousseau, 1201 Genève.
T. (022) 731 05 65. - Num -   *063716*
Montparnasse, 39 Grand-Rue, 1204 Genève.
T. (022) 321 67 19.   *063717*
Morand, Chantal, 9 Blvd. des Philosophes, 1205 Genève.
T. (022) 321 68 92.   *063718*
Nespolo, Carlo, 33 Rue du Stand, 1204 Genève.
T. (022) 3296306.   *063719*
New York – New York, 5 Rue Sismondi, 1201 Genève.
T. (022) 731 87 65.   *063720*
Niederer, Boris, 32 Grand-Rue, 1204 Genève.
T. (022) 321 95 65. - Ant -   *063721*
Nostalgie Art, 18 Rue des Etuves, 1201 Genève.
T. (022) 738 31 30. - Ant -   *063722*
Novel, Jean, 1 Rue de la Muse, 1205 Genève.
T. (022) 328 15 57.   *063723*
Numisart, 4 Rue Barques, 1207 Genève.
T. (022) 736 75 93. - Num -   *063724*
Numismatica Genevensis, 1 Rond-Point de Plainpalais,
1205 Genève. T. (022) 3204640, Fax 3292152.
- Num -   *063725*
Obermann, Pierre, 12 Rue du Perron, 1204 Genève.
T. (022) 3213654, 3113654.   *063726*
Oceanide, Port Franc de Genève, 1211 Genève.
T. (022) 342 48 52. - Ant -   *063727*
Perrin, Anne-Marie, 27 Pl. Bourg-de-Four, 1204 Genève.
T. (022) 329 82 43. - Ant -   *063728*
Persia, 2 Pl. Neuve, 1204 Genève.
T. (022) 3247310.   *063729*
Peyrolliers Antiquités, 14 Rue des Chaudronniers, 1204
Genève. T. (022) 320 00 56. - Ant / Furn / Sculp / Glass /
Ico -   *063730*
Ponce, Marlène, 32 Rue Rothschild, 1202 Genève.
T. (022) 3311537. - Ant -   *063731*
Rajic-Cretegny, Hélène, 4 Rue Leschot, 1205 Genève.
T. (022) 329 07 97. - Ant -   *063732*
Rasty, Amir, 4 Rue de Hesse, 1205 Genève.
T. (022) 3213477.   *063733*
Reich, Rosemarie, 4 Rue du Vieux-Billard, 1205 Genève.
T. (022) 321 14 37.   *063734*
Richard, Gérard, 4 Rue Fribourg, 1201 Genève.
T. (022) 732 76 62. - Ant -   *063735*
Rigotti, Pascal, 63 Rte. de Chêne, 1208 Genève.
T. (022) 7358981   *063736*
Rios, Avelino, 7 Rue des Pâquis, 1201 Genève.
T. (022) 731 25 93.   *063737*
Royal-Art Antiquités, R. du Rhône 82, 1204 Genève.
T. (022) 3214041. - Ant -   *063738*
Saccon, Florent, 3 Rue Sismondi, 1201 Genève.
T. (022) 732 98 13.   *063739*
Salon d'Antiquités, 32 Rue Rothschild, 1202 Genève.
T. (022) 731 15 37.   *063740*
Schmitt & Cie., Ernest, Rue de l'Hôtel-de-Ville 3, 1204
Genève. T. (022) 3283540.   *063741*
Shaman Gallery, 25 Rue de la Cité, 1204 Genève.
T. (022) 781 41 18.   *063742*
Shanghai Arts & Crafts, 1 Pl. des Florentins, 1204 Genè-
ve. T. (022) 321 02 53.   *063743*
Sonsino, Edwin, 2 Parc Château-Banquet, 1202 Genève.
T. (022) 732 60 04. - Ant -   *063744*
Sonsino, Ralph, 6 Parc Château-Banquet, 1202 Genève.
T. (022) 732 75 24. - Ant -   *063745*
Sormani, 4 Rue Saint-Victor, 1206 Genève.
T. (022) 346 46 77.   *063746*
Stefanelli, Luigi, 20 Rue Prévost-Martin, 1205 Genève.
T. (022) 329 06 21.   *063747*

Témoin, 27 Grand-Rue, 1204 Genève.
T. (022) 3216538.   *063748*
Tonon, Paolo, rue du Village-Suisse 1, bd. St.-Georges
52, 1205 Genève. T. (022) 3280938, 3288221. - Ant /
Furn -   *063749*
Tradart Genève, 29 Quai des Bergues, 1201 Genève.
T. (022) 7313831, Fax (022) 7314590. - Num -   *063750*
Vonctoulis, 54 Rte. de Florissant, 1206 Genève.
T. (022) 346 05 66.   *063751*
Vuilleumir, Francis, 32 Rue Prieuré, 1202 Genève.
T. (022) 732 09 81. - Ant -   *063752*
Wagner, B., Ruelle des Templiers 5, 1207 Genève.
T. (022) 7359188, Fax 7000785. - Arch / Eth -   *063753*
Weiss, René & Yvonne, 5 Av. Calas, 1206 Genève.
T. (022) 346 32 29. - Ant -   *063754*
Zimmermann, D., 9 Rue Hôtel-de-Ville, 1204 Genève.
T. (022) 310 62 52.   *063755*
Zinnanti, Calogero, 7 Pl. Fusterie, 1204 Genève.
T. (022) 328 91 97. - Ant -   *063756*

Genolier (Vaud)
Au Temps qui Passe, 1 Rte. de Coinsins, 1261 Genolier.
T. (022) 366 25 15, Fax 366 37 02. - Ant / Furn / Lights /
Mul -   *063758*

Gipf-Oberfrick (Aargau)
Staub, Ernst, Kornberghof 185, 5073 Gipf-Oberfrick.
T. (062) 8713649.   *063759*

Giubiasco (Ticino)
Fasciani, Leonardo, 2 Strada delle Gaggiole, 6512 Giu-
biasco. T. (091) 8576480, Fax 8577850.   *063760*
Moro, Franca Diana, Via Borghetto 1, 6512 Giubiasco.
T. (01) 27 61 19.   *063761*

Givrins (Vaud)
Klein, Ursula, Ch. de Savy, 1261 Givrins.
T. (022) 3691550.   *063762*

Gland (Vaud)
Bondi, Delmo, Ch. Vermy, 1196 Gland.
T. (022) 364 23 71.   *063763*
Mangone, Antonio, Pont-Farbel, 1196 Gland.
T. (022) 3642042.   *063764*

Glarus (Glarus)
Gähler, Walter, Abläschstr. 10, 8750 Glarus.
T. (055) 6406233.   *063765*
Gisler, Migli, Bahnhofstr. 23, 8750 Glarus.
T. (055) 6405254.   *063766*
Lötscher, Peter, Spielhof 16, 8750 Glarus.
T. (055) 6404526.   *063767*
Zweifel, Hannelore, Burgstr. 26, 8750 Glarus.
T. (055) 6401294. - Ant -   *063768*

Glattbrugg (Zürich)
Schatt, Erich, Rohrstr. 31, 8152 Glattbrugg.
T. (01) 810 01 33.   *063769*

Glattfelden (Zürich)
Grossbacher, Frank, Gottfried-Keller-Str. 14, 8192 Glattfelden. T. (01) 867 06 66.   *063770*

Goldau (Schwyz)
Pfister, Walter, Bernerhöhe, 6410 Goldau.
T. (041) 855 19 97.   *063771*

Gonten (Appenzell)
Ziffero AG, Unterberg, 9108 Gonten. T. (071) 7941243.
- Ant -   *063772*

Gordola (Ticino)
Baumgartner, Gerhard, Via Tratto di Cima 10, 6596 Gor-
dola. T. (093) 676575.   *063773*

Gorgier (Neuchâtel)
Nembrini, Aldo, Cerisiers 7, 2023 Gorgier.
T. (032) 8551704.   *063774*

Gossau (Sankt Gallen)
Kuster, Rolf, Büelwiesstr. 1 c, 9202 Gossau.
T. (071) 3858316.   *063775*
Tschudin, Esther, Sonnenstr. 6 + 7, 9202 Gossau.
T. (071) 3856393.   *063776*
Wüst, Arno, St. Gallerstr. 51, 9202 Gossau.
T. (071) 3852528. - Ant -   *063777*

Grand-Lancy (Genève)
Champod, Michel, 85 Rte. Grand-Lancy, 1212 Grand-
Lancy. T. (022) 794 41 35.   *063778*
Novel, Jean-Pierre, 31 Ch. des Palettes, 1212 Grand-
Lancy. T. (022) 794 27 44. - Ant -   *063779*

Grandvaux (Vaud)
Jeanneret, Yves-Rollin, Le Tronchet, 1603 Grandvaux.
T. (021) 799 12 14. - Ant -   *063780*
Parolini, Jean Jaques, Cret Mouton, 1603 Grandvaux.
T. (021) 7991957.   *063781*
Parolini, Marietta, Cret Mouton, 1603 Grandvaux.
T. (021) 7991957, 3234885.   *063782*

Grandvillard (Fribourg)
Echenard, Michel, Villars-sous-Mont, 1666 Grandvillard.
T. (026) 9281049.   *063783*
Zenoni, Roland, 1666 Grandvillard.
T. (026) 9281741.   *063784*

Greifensee (Zürich)
Schnurrenberger, Susan, Müllermies 11, 8606 Greifen-
see. T. (01) 940 65 53.   *063785*

Grenchen (Solothurn)
Billaud, Gilbert, Kapellstr. 7, Brockenhaus, 2540 Gren-
chen. T. (032) 6525449. - Ant -   *063786*

Grosswangen (Luzern)
Marti, Hans, Feldstr., 6022 Grosswangen.
T. (041) 980 21 31. - Ant / China / Instr / Toys - *063787*

Grüt (Zürich)
Antiquar zum Leopard, 8624 Grüt. T. (051) 932 25 86.
- Ant / Furn -   *063788*
Bachman, Josef, Grüningerstr., 8624 Grüt.
T. (051) 932 25 86.   *063789*

Gryon (Vaud)
Vieux Gryon Antiquités, 1882 Gryon.
T. (024) 4981409.   *063790*

Gstaad (Bern)
Romang, Werner, Hauptstr., 3780 Gstaad.
T. (033) 7443848.   *063791*

Gsteig b. Gstaad (Bern)
Romang, Werner, Feuters. Zelg, 3785 Gsteig b. Gstaad.
T. (033) 7551003.   *063792*

Gümligen (Bern)
Rösti, Fritz, Worbstr 219, 3073 Gümligen.
T. (031) 9527262.   *063792a*
Walch Antiquités, Walchstr. 9, 3073 Gümligen.
T. (031) 951 62 52. - Ant -   *063793*

Guntershausen (Thurgau)
Baur, Rolf, Resigartenstr. 6, 8357 Guntershausen.
T. (052) 3651463.   *063795*
Zur Alte Pressi, Hauptstr. 4, 8357 Guntershausen.
T. (052) 3852071.   *063796*

Hägendorf (Solothurn)
Kubierske, Helmuth, Solothurner Str. 535, 4614 Hägen-
dorf. T. (062) 46 41 49.   *063797*

Hägglingen (Aargau)
Schmid, Rita, Mitteldorfstr. 22, 5607 Hägglingen.
T. (056) 6241208.   *063798*

Hagenbuch (Zürich)
Studer, Elisabeth, Hagenstal, 8523 Hagenbuch.
T. (052) 3641088.   *063799*

Hagenstal (Zürich)
Studer, Elisabeth, Antiquitäten im Hagenstal/Elgg, 8523
Hagenstal. T. (052) 3641088.   *063800*

Hallau (Schaffhausen)
Pfund, Erwin, Horbelstr. 79, 8215 Hallau.
T. (052) 6813623.   *063801*

Hausen am Albis (Zürich)
Hegglin, Hans, Oberdorfstr. 4, 8915 Hausen am Albis.
T. (01) 764 08 50.   *063802*
Ulker, August & Traudel, Müseggweg 1, 8915 Hausen
am Albis. T. (01) 764 04 53.   *063803*

Hedingen (Zürich)
Kühne, Franz, Zürcherstr. 9, 8908 Hedingen.
T. (01) 761 05 34.   *063804*

Heiden (Aargau)
Hochreutener, Emil, Oberegger Str. 24, 9410 Heiden.
T. (071) 8912880. - Ant / Furn / Instr -   *063805*

Hergiswil (Nidwalden)
Lussi-Langensand, Mattli 5, 6052 Hergiswil.
T. (041) 630 31 77. - Ant -   *063806*

Herisau (Aargau)
Bellaggio, B., Ob. Sonnenbergstr. 3, 9100 Herisau.
T. (071) 3513241. - Ant -   *063807*
Galerie Windegg, Windegg 4, 9100 Herisau.
T. (071) 3521868. - Sculp / Tex / Jew / Glass / Cur /
Draw / Tin / Toys -   *063808*

Herrliberg (Zürich)
Antiquitäten Herrliberg, Seestr. 180, 8704 Herrliberg.
T. (01) 915 27 38.   *063809*

Herzogenbuchsee (Bern)
Flückiger, René, Thörigenstr. 37, 3360 Herzogenbuch-
see. T. (062) 9613605.   *063810*
Schaffer, A., Unterholzstr. 10, 3360
Herzogenbuchsee.   *063811*
Winistörfer, René, Zürichstr. 55, 3360 Herzogenbuchsee.
T. (062) 9614626.   *063812*

Hinterkappelen (Bern)
Witschi, Rudolf, Eymattstr. 123, 3032 Hinterkappelen.
T. (031) 381 02 66.   *063813*

Hinwil (Zürich)
Antiquarische Gesellschaft, Langenrainstr. 7, 8340 Hin-
wil. T. (01) 937 20 20.   *063814*
Rüthemann, Roland, Schloss Girenbad 109, 8340 Hinwil.
T. (01) 937 36 42.   *063815*

Hirzel (Zürich)
Antik-Galerie Melusine, Zugerstr. 41, 8816 Hirzel.
T. (01) 729 99 66.   *063816*

Hochdorf (Luzern)
Barmet, Edy, Luzernstr. 35, 6280 Hochdorf.
T. (041) 910 48 20.   *063817*

Hochwald (Solothurn)
Vögtli, Benno, Baselweg 10, 4146 Hochwald.
T. (061) 7513317.   *063818*

Hofstetten bei Elgg (Zürich)
Haegi, Pierre, Dickbuch, 8354 Hofstetten bei Elgg.
T. (052) 3631943.   *063819*

Hombrechtikon (Zürich)
Dolder, Hans-Rudolf, Wydum, 8634 Hombrechtikon.
T. (052) 2442042.   *063820*
Gigengack, G., Widmenstr. 656, 8634 Hombrechtikon.
- Furn / Instr -   *063821*

Horgen (Zürich)
Murbach, Gottfried, Seestr. 295, 8810 Horgen.
T. (01) 725 0701. - Ant / Furn -   *063822*
Rössler & Stampfli, Seestr. 126, 8810 Horgen.
T. (01) 725 09 77.   *063823*
Sieber, Hans, Neugasse 8, 8810 Horgen.
T. (01) 7257311.   *063824*

Horw (Luzern)
Antik e Nuovo, Bahnhofstr. 20, 6048 Horw.
T. (041) 340 29 29.   *063825*
Borstel, J. von, Kantonsstr. 56, 6048 Horw.
T. (041) 310 03 44.   *063826*
Gjotas, Charalambos, Bahnhofstr. 20, 6048 Horw.
T. (041) 340 19 50.   *063827*
Gravura, Spierstr. 5, 6048 Horw. T. (041) 340 31 32.
- Graph -   *063828*

Hünenberg (Zug)
D'Vitrine, Dorfgässli 1, 6331 Hünenberg.
T. (041) 780 33 03.   *063829*

Hunzenschwil (Aargau)
Meyer, E., Gränicherweg 17, 5502 Hunzenschwil.
T. (064) 8971739. *063830*
Sitte-Jost, Gisela, Sonnenrain 13, 5502 Hunzenschwil.
T. (062) 8973050. *063831*

Igis (Graubünden)
Marmet, Untergasse 48, 7206 Igis.
T. (081) 3225013. *063832*

Ins (Bern)
La Torre, Annemarie, Müntschemiergasse 34, 3232 Ins.
T. (032) 3131910. *063833*

Interlaken (Bern)
Löwe-Egge, Marktgasse 6, 3800 Interlaken.
T. (033) 8222900. *063834*

Ittigen (Bern)
Antiquitäten Lilly, Niesenweg 16, 3063 Ittigen.
T. (031) 921 00 44. *063835*
Baumann, Geraldine, Badhausstr. 5, 3063 Ittigen.
T. (031) 921 68 39. *063836*

Jegenstorf (Bern)
Duinmeyer, Eddy, Oberdorfstr. 23a, 3303 Jegenstorf.
T. (031) 761 00 68. - Ant / Furn / Sculp - *063837*

La Joux (Fribourg)
Ferronnerie d'Art, 1697 La Joux.
T. (026) 6551249. *063838*

Jouxtens-Mézery (Vaud)
Marguet, M., Ch. de la Batiaz, 1008 Jouxtens-
Mézery. *063839*

Kaiserstuhl (Aargau)
Ruth, Ernst, Bleicherweg 114, 8434 Kaiserstuhl.
T. (01) 858 15 14. - Ant - *063840*

Kaltbrunn (Sankt Gallen)
Harder, Jakob, Schulhausstr. 15, 8722 Kaltbrunn.
T. (052) 2831130. *063841*
Romer, L., Rickenstr. 13, 8722 Kaltbrunn.
T. (052) 2831691. *063842*

Kandergrund (Bern)
Perreten, Walter, Fürten, 3716 Kandergrund.
T. (033) 6712136. *063843*

Kehrsatz (Bern)
Diesslin, Hansruedi, Talstr. 8, 3122 Kehrsatz.
T. (031) 961 51 89. *063844*
Wiesendanger, Samuel, Sandbühlstr. 33, 3122 Kehrsatz.
T. (031) 961 30 96. - Ant - *063845*

Kerns (Obwalden)
Weisser, Hans, 6064 Kerns. T. (041) 660 18 24.
- Ant - *063846*

Kilchberg (Zürich)
Trotte, Seestr. 152, 8802 Kilchberg.
T. (01) 715 33 30. *063847*
Wittwer, Samuel, Neuweidstr. 19, 8802 Kilchberg.
T. (01) 715 40 59. *063848*

Kirchberg (Bern)
Foto Antic, Hauptstr. 9, 3422 Kirchberg.
T. (034) 4455400. *063849*
Maurer, E., Bernstr. 3, Rüdtligen-Alchenflüh, 3422
Kirchberg. *063850*

Kirchberg (Sankt Gallen)
Klaus, Rolf, Rätenbergstr. 19, 9533 Kirchberg.
T. (071) 9313946. *063851*

Kirchdorf (Aargau)
Vouga, Elizabeth, Hirschengasse 3, 5416 Kirchdorf.
T. (056) 2825292. - Ant / Silv - *063852*

Kirchlindach (Bern)
Lörtscher, Theo, Lindenrain 9, 3038 Kirchlindach.
T. (031) 829 34 06. *063853*

Klosters (Graubünden)
Kessely, Hans & Nina, Im Tolli, 7250 Klosters.
T. (081) 4222066. *063854*

Kloten (Zürich)
Stähli, H.P., Dietlikerstr. 36, 8302 Kloten.
T. (01) 814 30 41. *063855*
Wanner, Gerda, Kanzlerweg 3, 8302 Kloten.
T. (01) 813 21 36, 311 97 04. *063856*
Werder, Beatrice, Zipfelstr. 38, 8302 Kloten.
T. (01) 813 36 66. *063857*
Wullschleger, John R., Gerbegasse 6, 8302 Kloten.
T. (01) 813 38 55. *063858*

Krattigen (Bern)
Bergauer, Peter, Krattigstr. 134, 3704 Krattigen.
T. (033) 6548081. *063859*

Kreuzlingen (Thurgau)
Art Apollo Galerie, Hauptstr. 26, 8280 Kreuzlingen.
T. (071) 67272928, 054. *063860*
Hugle, M., Grenzbachstr. 5, 8280 Kreuzlingen.
T. (071) 6727535. - Num - *063861*
Lauer, Kurt, Finkenstr. 24, 8280 Kreuzlingen.
T. (071) 6726154. *063862*
Rutishauser, Hans E., Hauptstr 100-104, 8280 Kreuzlin-
gen. T. (071) 6721972, Fax 6721948. - Ant / Graph /
Furn / Tex / Dec / Fra / Instr - *063863*
Signer, Werner, Haus Avantgarde, 8280 Kreuzlingen.
T. (071) 6724383. - Ant / Paint / Graph / Furn / Repr /
Sculp / Tex / Dec / Silv / Mil / Draw - *063864*
Zbornik, Fritz, Seestr. 50, 8280 Kreuzlingen.
T. (071) 6725571. *063865*

Kriens (Luzern)
Kammermann, Werner, Luzernerstr. 71, 6010 Kriens.
T. (041) 311 17 28. - Ant / Furn - *063866*
Meyers, Albert, Luzernerstr. 51a, 6010 Kriens.
T. (041) 311 20 00. - Num - *063867*

Küsnacht (Zürich)
Dolder, Hans-Rudolf, Bahnhofstr. 8, 8700 Küsnacht.
T. (01) 910 85 15. *063868*
Oriental Art Gallery, Silbergrundstr. 10, 8700 Küsnacht.
T. (01) 910 55 65. *063869*

Küssnacht am Rigi (Schwyz)
Beetschen, Eduard, Luzerner Str. 66, 6403 Küssnacht
am Rigi. T. (041) 850 20 58. *063870*
Pauli, Dagmar, Ländihöhi 17, 6403 Küssnacht am Rigi.
T. (041) 8503182. *063871*
Räber, Alois, Luzerner Str 30, 6403 Küssnacht am Rigi.
T. (041) 8501005. *063872*
Reichlin, Ernst, Grepperstr 8, 6403 Küssnacht am Rigi.
T. (041) 8501650. *063873*
Reichlin, Urs, Grepperstr 8, 6403 Küssnacht am Rigi.
T. (041) 8501650. *063874*

Lamone (Ticino)
Birth, Ernesto & Alice, Strada Cantonale, 6814 Lamone.
T. (091) 9664656. *063875*

Le Landeron (Neuchâtel)
Chez le Banneret, 5 Ville, 2525 Le Landeron.
T. (032) 7513931. *063876*
Marcozzi, Jimmy, 19 Ville, 2525 Le Landeron.
T. (032) 7514682. *063877*
Muttner, Marcel, 7 Ville, 2525 Le Landeron.
T. (032) 7511447. *063878*
Wermeille, Marie-José, 30 Ville, 2525 Le Landeron.
T. (032) 7512033. *063879*

Langendorf (Solothurn)
Odermatt, Markus, Industriestr 8, 4513 Langendorf.
T. (032) 6183646. *063880*

Langenthal (Bern)
Bartolo, Gaetano di, Farbgasse 21a, 4900 Langenthal.
T. (062) 9227726. *063881*
Nyffeler & Co., Max, Jurastr 16, 4901 Langenthal.
T. (062) 9231818. - Ant / Furn - *063882*
Schüpbach, Mathias, Lotzwilstr. 3, 4900 Langenthal.
T. (062) 9222570. *063883*

Langnau am Albis (Zürich)
Lachat, Irma, Weidstr. 4, 8135 Langnau am Albis.
T. (01) 713 37 96. - Num - *063884*

Lantsch (Graubünden)
Rustica Tgeasa, Hauptstr., 7083 Lantsch.
T. (081) 6812122. *063885*

Lausanne (Vaud)
Antiquaille, 15 Blvd. de Grancy, 1006 Lausanne.
T. (021) 616 22 01. *063886*
Antiquité Vieux-Bourg, Rue Cheneau-de-Bourg 7, 1003
Lausanne. T. (021) 323 22 12. *063887*
Art Ancien, 126 Av. d'Echallens, 1004 Lausanne.
T. (021) 625 20 05. *063888*
L'As de Coeur, 5 a Pl. de la Cathèdrale, 1005 Lausanne.
T. (021) 312 05 41. *063889*
Au Bon Vieux Temps, 21 Rue Grand-St.Jean, 1003 Lau-
sanne. T. (021) 312 43 06. - Ant - *063890*
Au Bonheur du Jour, Bd. Grancy 28, 1006 Lausanne.
T. (021) 616 25 65. - Ant / Furn - *063891*
Au Foyer d'Autrefois, 3 Rue de la Mercerie, 1003 Lau-
sanne. T. (021) 323 44 27. - Ant / Paint / China / Dec /
Silv - *063892*
Au Grand Argentier, 3 Av. Davel, 1004 Lausanne.
T. (021) 646 54 62. *063893*
Au Numismate, 24 Rue du Simplon, 1006 Lausanne.
T. (021) 616 92 62. *063894*
Au Reliquaires, 4 rue de la Paix, 1003 Lausanne.
T. (021) 323 22 27. *063895*
Au Vieux Logis, 15 Rue Beau-Séjour, 1003 Lausanne.
T. (021) 323 43 61. *063896*
Aubaine, Rue du Tunnel 11, 1005 Lausanne.
T. (021) 3223033. *063897*
Aux Présents du Passé, 19 Av. de Béthusy, 1005 Lau-
sanne. T. (021) 3227276. *063898*
Benois, Patrick, 17 Bd. de Grancy, 1006 Lausanne.
T. (021) 616 22 01. *063899*
Black, Petrita, 27 Av. d'Ouchy, 1006 Lausanne.
T. (021) 616 01 70. - Paint - *063900*
Bogdanovitch, Caroline, 16 Rue du Midi, 1003 Lau-
sanne. T. (021) 312 79 47. *063901*
Boppart, Daniel, 48 Rte. Aloys-Fauquez, 1018 Lausanne.
T. (021) 646 83 06. *063902*
Brocantica, 33 Av. de Morges, 1004 Lausanne. *063903*
Burette, René, 12 Côtes de Montbenon, 1003 Lausanne.
T. (021) 624 04 94. *063904*
La Calèche, 29 Rue de Bourg, 1003 Lausanne. *063905*
Cardas Boyer & Pingard, 10 Rue de Bourg, 1003
Lausanne. *063906*
Caruso, Antonio, Av de la Harpe 12, 1007 Lausanne.
T. (021) 6163612. *063907*
Castellucci, Guerrino, 24 Rue de Simplon, 1006 Lau-
sanne. - Num - *063908*
Castle Antiques, 5 Rue Cheneau-de-Bourg, 1003 Lau-
sanne. T. (021) 323 71 00. - Furn / China / Silv /
Glass *063909*
Cazzaniga & Marguet, Rue de la Paix 4, 1003 Lausanne.
T. (021) 323 22 27. - Ant / Furn - *063910*
Chatelain, Daniel, Rue du Pont 10, 1003 Lausanne.
T. (021) 323 58 54. *063911*
Chez Angela, 12 Av. de France, 1004 Lausanne.
T. (021) 624 15 77. *063912*
Cottet, Jean-Claude, Pl Pépinet 3, 1003 Lausanne.
T. (021) 3233635. *063913*
Dalimier, Guy, 13 Rue Pré-du-Marché, 1004 Lausanne.
T. (021) 3220482. *063914*
Danese-Milano, Rue Centrale 31, 1003 Lausanne.
T. (021) 323 01 14. *063915*
Deillon, Louis, Rue Beau-Séjour 9-11, 1003 Lausanne.
T. (021) 3231460. *063916*
Denoyel, Claude, 15 Av. du Temple, 1012 Lausanne.
T. (021) 617 95 33. *063917*
Dick, Jacques, 1 Rue de la Paix, 1003 Lausanne.
T. (021) 312 78 19. - Ant / Jew / Silv - *063918*
L'Ecrin, 1 Pl. Benjamin-Constant, 1003 Lausanne.
T. (021) 323 66 53. *063919*
La Ferme des 3 Chasseures, Rte. d'Oron, 1000 Lau-
sanne. T. (021) 784 33 40, Fax (021) 784 33 10. *063920*
Filambule, Rue des Terreaux 18 bis, 1003 Lausanne.
T. (021) 323 12 23. - Tex - *063921*
Fontannaz, Serge, Rue St.-Laurent 8, 1003 Lausanne.
T. (021) 3126482. *063922*
Frey, Otto, Chemin de Lucinge 2, 1006 Lausanne.
T. (021) 323 26 55. *063923*
Füllemann, Hans, 19 Av de Chailly, 1012 Lausanne.
T. (021) 6532282. *063924*

Galerie du Château, 2, Palace du Tunnel, 1004 Lausanne. T. (021) 3126959. *063925*

Gismondi, 1 Ch. Beau-Rivage, 1006 Lausanne. T. (021) 616 24 14. *063926*

Goumaz, Jean-Pierre, 29-31 Rue Centrale, 1003 Lausanne. T. (021) 323 01 14. *063927*

GPL Antiquités SA, Rue du Simplon 45, 1006 Lausanne. T. (021) 616 63 15. - Ant - *063928*

Guillod, Frédéric, 10 Blvd. de Grancy, 1004 Lausanne. T. (021) 616 95 93. *063929*

Hämmerli, Armand, Av. Mousquines 14, 1005 Lausanne. T. (021) 323 64 81. - Ant - *063930*

Horloger, 38bis Av. de Béthusy, 1005 Lausanne. T. (021) 3229297. *063931*

Images Antiquités, Rue Cheneau-de-Bourg 17, 1003 Lausanne. T. (021) 323 97 35. - Ant / Paint / Graph / Furn / China / Silv - *063932*

Imoberdorf, Av. de Chailly 49, 1012 Lausanne. T. (021) 728 26 20. - Num - *063933*

Jadis Antiquités, Rue Beau-Séjour 9-11, 1003 Lausanne. T. (021) 323 14 60. - Ant / Paint / Furn / Orient / China / Sculp / Tex / Silv / Lights / Instr / Glass / Cur / Mod - *063934*

Jouet Ancien, 8 Av de Rumine, 1005 Lausanne. T. (021) 3125869. *063935*

Keller, Bernard, 126 Av. d'Echallens, 1004 Lausanne. T. (021) 624 02 71. *063936*

Koenig & Cie., CP, 1000 Lausanne. T. (021) 625 55 41. *063937*

König, Tapis, 4 Rue Haldimand, 1000 Lausanne. T. (021) 320 89 41. *063938*

Lena, Mario, Rue César-Roux 7, 1005 Lausanne. T. (021) 320 07 41. *063939*

Marino, Pierre, Avenue Béthusy 19, 1005 Lausanne. T. (021) 3127276, 233380. *063940*

Martin, Jean L., 13 Ch des Pyramides, 1007 Lausanne. T. (021) 6259836. *063941*

May, Michel, Chêneau-de-Bourg 7, 1003 Lausanne. T. (021) 323 22 12. - Ant - *063942*

Mermond, Françoise, 7 Rue Mercerie, 1003 Lausanne. T. (021) 323 18 58. *063943*

Michaud, Christine, 22 Rue des Terreaux, 1003 Lausanne. T. (021) 323 85 07. *063944*

Naharro, J.L., 77 Av. du Léman, 1005 Lausanne. T. (021) 728 18 05. *063945*

Neuffer, Gaston, 28 Av. de la Harpe, 1007 Lausanne. T. (021) 617 40 50. *063946*

Neuffer, Simone, Blvd de Grancy 34, 1006 Lausanne. T. (021) 6162624. *063947*

Niederhauser, Catherine, 8 Grand-Chêne, 1003 Lausanne. T. (021) 312 98 18/19, Fax (021) 323 51 38. - Ant / Paint / Furn / Sculp / Jew / Silv - *063948*

Nightingale, Cheneau-de-Bourg 10, 1003 Lausanne. T. (021) 323 32 57. - Orient - *063949*

L'Occa Broc, 42 Av. d'Echallens, 1004 Lausanne. T. (021) 625 60 40. *063950*

Oesch, Madeleine, 9 Rue Cheneau-de-Bourg, 1003 Lausanne. T. (021) 323 47 87. *063951*

Orangerie-Reinz, Rue Mercerie 7, 1003 Lausanne. T. (021) 323 18 58. *063952*

Parolini, Jean-Jacques, Rue Dr. César-Roux 5, 1005 Lausanne. T. (021) 323 48 85. *063953*

Passé Présent, 2 Av. Tribunal-Fédéral, 1005 Lausanne. T. (021) 312 22 54. *063954*

Péquignet, J.P., 17 Av. de la Gare, 1003 Lausanne. T. (021) 323 62 49. *063955*

Picconi, Jean-Maxime, 17 Rue Cheneau-de-Bourg, 1003 Lausanne. T. (021) 323 20 21. *063956*

Porchet, Carmen, Av de Cour 29, 1007 Lausanne. T. (021) 8074131, 6173242. *063957*

Potterat, Robert, 8 Av. du Théâtre, 1005 Lausanne. T. (021) 3224453. *063958*

Rauch, 3 Ch. de Chandolin, 1005 Lausanne. T. (021) 323 02 92. *063959*

Régné, André, 29 Rue de Bourg, 1003 Lausanne. T. (021) 320 73 55. *063960*

Relier, 22 Rue des Terreaux, 1003 Lausanne. T. (021) 323 85 07. *063961*

Rigaldo, Michel, Escaliers du Marché 9, 1003 Lausanne. T. (021) 3235021, 8073518. *063962*

Rime, Marcel, 34 Rue Pré-du-Marché, 1004 Lausanne. T. (021) 323 50 94. - Num - *063963*

Rivas, Ramon, 25 Rue St.-Martin, 1003 Lausanne. T. (021) 323 41 43. - Ant - *063964*

Rosa, Giovanni di, 4 Rte. Aloys-Fauquez, 1018 Lausanne. T. (021) 647 73 84. *063965*

Rouhani, Ahmad, 11 Av. Juste-Olivier, 1006 Lausanne. T. (021) 323 82 53. *063966*

Salon des Antiquaires, Av Agassiz 2, 1001 Lausanne. T. (021) 319/111, Fax 3197910. *063967*

Ségalat, Roger J., 4 Rue Pontaise, 1018 Lausanne. T. (021) 6483601, Fax 6482585. *063968*

Solana, Janine, 22 Av. Parc-Rouvraie, 1018 Lausanne. T. (021) 647 89 32. *063969*

Somenzi, Roméo, 15 Av. d'Echallens, 1003 Lausanne. T. (021) 624 49 39. *063970*

Steiner, René, 17 Av. de la Gare, 1003 Lausanne. *063971*

La Tabatière, 10 Av. William Fraisse, 1006 Lausanne. T. (021) 616 70 04. *063972*

Trautmann, Stéphanie-C., 43 Rue de la Borde, 1018 Lausanne. T. (021) 647 29 86. *063973*

Trois Chasseurs, 33 Av. de Morges, 1004 Lausanne. T. (021) 624 02 02. *063974*

Les Trouvailles, 13 Rue du Pré-du-Marché, 1004 Lausanne. T. (021) 312 04 82. *063975*

Vallotton, Paul, 2 Av J.-J.-Mercier, Postfach, 1002 Lausanne. T. (021) 3129166, Fax (021) 3208463. - Paint / Draw - *063976*

Verdan & Fils, 2 Blvd. de Grancy, 1006 Lausanne. T. (021) 616 56 60. - Furn - *063977*

Vieille Fontaine, 9-13 Rue Cheneau-de-Bourg, 1003 Lausanne. T. (021) 3234787, Fax 3112823. - Ant / Orient / Cur - *063978*

Vieux Bourg, 7 Cheneau-de-Bourg, 1003 Lausanne. T. (021) 323 22 12. *063979*

Wartensleben, Elisabeth, 4 Av. Jurigoz, 1006 Lausanne. T. (021) 616 13 26. - Paint - *063980*

Zosso, Roger, Rue du Pont 10, 1003 Lausanne. T. (021) 3222109. - Instr - *063981*

Lenzburg (Aargau)

Collection Bärenburg, Schlößchen Bärenburg, 5600 Lenzburg. T. (064) 51 21 73. - Ant / Orient - *063982*

Roth, H. Fritz, Oberer Haldenweg 38, 5600 Lenzburg. T. (064) 51 21 73. *063983*

Zur Laterne, Rathausgasse 17, 5600 Lenzburg. T. (064) 51 47 66. *063984*

Les Ponts-de-Martel (Neuchâtel)

Benoit & Gentil, 5 Rue de la Prairie, 2316 Les Ponts-de-Martel. T. (032) 9371458. *063985*

Leukerbad (Valais)

Ferrari, Bruno, Haus Végé, 3854 Leukerbad. T. (027) 4701235. *063986*

Leuzigen (Bern)

Big-Horn, Bürenstr. 45, 3297 Leuzigen. T. (032) 6793922. *063987*

Big-Horn, Unterdorf 137, 3297 Leuzigen. T. (032) 6793922. - Ant - *063988*

Lichtensteig (Sankt Gallen)

Künzle, Fredy, Haus Frohburg, 9620 Lichtensteig. T. (071) 9887663. - Lights - *063989*

Liestal (Basel-Land)

Bieder, Hans, Schleifewuhrweg 2, 4410 Liestal. T. (061) 921 12 41, Fax (061) 921 12 35. - Ant / Paint / Furn / China / Dec / Instr / Glass / Cur - *063990*

Bugmann, M. & E., Rheinstr. 2, 4410 Liestal. T. (061) 921 37 77. *063991*

Ile au Trésor, Amtshausgasse 3, 4410 Liestal. T. (061) 921 41 11. - Ant - *063992*

Locarno (Ticino)

Bellerio, Timothy & Atsuko, Via Sant'Antonio 11, 6600 Locarno. T. (091) 7515794, Fax 7515774. - Ant / Furn / Sculp / Jew / Silv / Lights / Instr - *063993*

Bretscher, Alfred, Via F. Rusca 6, 6600 Locarno. T. (091) 7515847. *063994*

Cassovia, Szirmay, Via Borghese 2, 6600 Locarno. T. (091) 7511527. - Ant / Paint / Graph / China / Sculp / Silv / Cur - *063995*

Gatto, Vincenzo, Via S. Jorio 21, 6600 Locarno. T. (091) 7514259. *063996*

Pedrazzi, Renato, Via Torretta 5, 6600 Locarno. T. (091) 7517418. *063997*

Rüsch, Valdemaro, 9 Via S. Antonio, 6600 Locarno. T. (091) 7514688. *063998*

Longirod (Vaud)

La Fermette, Le Pessey-d'En-Haut, 1261 Longirod. T. (022) 368 11 57. *063999*

Losone (Ticino)

Centro Intercasa, Via Locarno 43, 6616 Losone. T. (091) 7911621. *064000*

Fiori, Willy, Via Madonna d. Fontana, 6616 Losone. T. (091) 7915304. *064001*

Ponti, Enea, Via Locarno 90, 6616 Losone. T. (091) 7911733. - Ant / Furn - *064002*

Tobler, Walter, Contrada Maggiore 2, 6616 Losone. T. (091) 7913512. *064003*

Lucens (Vaud)

Koller, Château de Lucens, 1522 Lucens. *064004*

Lüchingen (Sankt Gallen)

Grabherr-Ritter, Walter, Rorschacher Str.112-116, 9438 Lüchingen. T. (071) 7552036. - Ant / Paint / Furn / China / Sculp / Tex / Dec / Fra / Silv / Lights / Instr / Rel / Glass / Cur - *064005*

Lugano (Ticino)

Antichità J.D.M., Via Peri 21a, 6900 Lugano. T. (091) 9213051, Fax 212501. *064006*

Bader-Koller, Edith, Via C. Cantù 3, 6900 Lugano. T. (091) 9239360, Fax 9239350. - Arch / Draw - *064007*

Bernasconi, Mario, Via P. Peri 7, 6900 Lugano. T. (091) 9237860. *064008*

Bottega dell'Antiquario, Via P. Peri 7, 6900 Lugano. T. (091) 9237860. *064009*

Bottega delle stampe e delle cornici, P. Indipendenza 1, 6900 Lugano. T. (091) 9226821. *064010*

Calvi, Sergio & Gaby, Via Ferri 5, 6900 Lugano. T. (091) 9724229. *064011*

Casoli, Rolando, Via Nassa 68, 6900 Lugano. T. (091) 9228355. *064012*

Caviglia, Enrico, Viale Cattaneo 1, Postfach 2345, 6901 Lugano. T. (091) 9234015. - China / Glass - *064013*

Giorgio Dannecker & Paola Garbini, Via Marconi 3a, 6900 Lugano. T. (091) 9228341, 9231880. *064014*

Donati, Pino, Nassa 17, 6900 Lugano. T. (091) 9233854. - Ant - *064015*

Evan, Via Pessina 9, 6900 Lugano. T. (091) 9234224. *064016*

Filarco, Via Cattedrale 4, 6900 Lugano. T. (091) 9228618. *064017*

Galitzky, M., Via Nassa 17, 6900 Lugano. T. (091) 9231687. - Ant / China / Jew - *064018*

Galleria Anfitrite, Via Pessina 22-23, 6900 Lugano. T. (091) 9220967. - Furn / China / Jew / Silv / Instr - *064019*

Galleria d'Arte, Via Ginevra 4, 6900 Lugano. T. (091) 9227589. *064020*

Galleria dell'Angelo, Piazza Cioccaro 11, 6900 Lugano. T. (091) 9229858. - Ant / Furn / Orient / Sculp / Tex - *064021*

Garbini, Paolo, Via Marconi 3a, 6900 Lugano. T. (091) 9228341. *064022*

Gatti, Luciano, Via Moncucco 3, 6900 Lugano. T. (091) 961896. *064023*

Gattopardo, Via Pessina 20, 6900 Lugano. T. (091) 9227589. *064024*

Ghin, Angelo, Via Campo Marzio 13, 6900 Lugano. T. (091) 9228843. *064025*

Giambelli, Franco, Via G. Marconi 2, 6900 Lugano. T. (091) 9220744. *064026*

Merlo, Marcello, Via Zurigo 38, 6900 Lugano. T. (091) 9239201. *064027*

Miler, Sonja, Piazza Manzoni 8, 6900 Lugano. T. (091) 9227302. *064028*

Moosmann, Franco, Via Cattedrale 11, 6900 Lugano. T. (091) 9234538. *064029*

Pagivo, Via Nassa 29, 6900 Lugano. T. (091) 9231888. *064030*

Papiri, Adriana, Via Ginevra 4, 6900 Lugano. T. (091) 9227589. *064031*

Pierini & Rossini, Via Lavizzari 10, 6900 Lugano.
T. (091) 9237569. *064032*
Rommel, Tony, Via Bagutti 33, 6904 Lugano.
T. (091) 9727731. *064033*
Scardeoni, Bruno, Via Nassa 54, 6900 Lugano.
T. (091) 9229236, Fax 22 92 91. *064034*
Spirig 5A, Kurt, Via Nassa 4, 6900 Lugano.
T. (091) 9234560, Fax 9237332. *064035*
Tonella, Danielle, Via Stauffacher 2, 6900 Lugano.
T. (091) 9226484. *064036*
Walter, Alfredo, Via Moncucco 3, 6900 Lugano.
T. (091) 9660894. *064037*

Lungern (Obwalden)
Ming, Josef, Eistr., 6078 Lungern.
T. (041) 678 16 03. *064038*

Lussy-sur-Morges (Vaud)
Gonet, Marylène, 1133 Lussy-sur-Morges.
T. (021) 801 44 52. *064039*
Zanone, Pierre, En St.-Martin, 1133 Lussy-sur-Morges.
T. (021) 801 58 55. - Ant / Paint / Graph / Furn - *064040*

Lutry (Vaud)
Au Semainier Antiquité, 76 Grand-Rue, 1095 Lutry.
T. (021) 7914687. *064041*
Dentan, Silvie, 3 Rue Verdaine, 1095 Lutry.
T. (021) 7915064. *064042*
Desarzens, M.-G., Résidence des Vignes, 31 Ch. Bur-
quenet, 1095 Lutry. T. (021) 7912375. *064043*
Five o'Clock, 6 Rue de l'Horloge, 1095 Lutry.
T. (021) 7913844. *064044*
Galerie Pomone, 15 Rue Friporte, 1095 Lutry.
T. (021) 7912884. *064045*
Giaguinto, Ottaviano, 4 Pl. du Temple, 1095 Lutry.
T. (021) 7914607. *064046*
Piaget, Eva, & Jean Marc, 2 Rue de l'Horloge, 1095 Lu-
try. T. (021) 791 43 59. *064047*
Revel Mergegne, Rue de l'Horlogerie 1, 1095 Lutry.
T. (021) 7915543. *064048*
Vieux Lutry, 1 Rue de l'Horloge, 1095 Lutry.
T. (021) 7915543. *064049*

Luzern
Amrein, Werner J., Hirschmattstr. 56, 6003 Luzern.
T. (041) 210 60 25. *064050*
Antik-Eggli, Unter der Egg 8 a, 6004 Luzern.
T. (041) 410 15 21. *064051*
Art-Galerie, Maihofstr. 52, 6004 Luzern.
T. (041) 420 33 18. - Ant - *064052*
Bachmann, Irène, Weinmarkt 17, 6004 Luzern.
T. (041) 410 23 83. *064053*
Bachmann, Lisbeth, Hofstr 14, 6006 Luzern.
T. (041) 410 19 16. *064054*
Bader, Haldenstr 2, 6006 Luzern. T. (01) 4106210,
Fax 4106310. - Ant / Paint / Furn / Sculp / Tex / Arch /
Rel - *064055*

BADER

KUNST DER ANTIKE, DES MITTELALTERS UND DER RENAISSANCE

CH-6006 LUZERN
HALDENSTRASSE 7

TEL. 041 - 410 62 10
FAX 041 - 410 63 10

Bärenbold, Maria, Moosstr. 15, 6003 Luzern.
T. (041) 210 83 34. - Ant - *064056*

Bammert, Urs, Kauffmannweg 12, 6003 Luzern.
T. (041) 210 29 96. *064057*

Bendetti, Armando, Kauffmannweg 5, 6003 Luzern.
T. (041) 240 22 82. *064058*
Borstel, Mario von, Unterlachenstr. 9, 6005 Luzern.
T. (041) 360 98 66. *064059*
Boss, Jean-Pierre, Kramgasse 1, 6004 Luzern.
T. (041) 410 47 82. - Jew - *064060*
Büel, Otto, Hertensteinerstr. 12, 6003 Luzern.
T. (041) 410 55 23. - Ant / Paint / Furn / China / Sculp /
Jew / Silv - *064061*
Diriwächter, Kurt, Bireggstr. 1, 6003 Luzern.
T. (041) 360 58 48. *064062*
Emmenegger, Franz, Neustadtstr. 8, 6003 Luzern.
T. (041) 210 62 86. - Ant - *064063*
Franke, Jürgen W., Hirschmattstr. 24, 6003 Luzern.
T. (041) 210 71 71. *064064*
Galerie du Quai, Schweizerhofquai 4, 6004 Luzern.
T. (041) 410 66 77. - Furn - *064065*
Galerie Meile, Rosenberghöhe 4a, 6004 Luzern.
T. (041) 4203318, Fax 4202169. *064066*
George, Franziskanerpl. 16, 6003 Luzern.
T. (041) 210 24 00. *064067*
Gilda, Furrengasse 15, 6004 Luzern.
T. (041) 410 28 21. *064068*
Gilhofer & Ranschburg, Trullhofstr. 20 a, 6004 Luzern.
T. (041) 240 10 15. *064069*
Gilhofer & Ranschburg, Trüllhofstr 20a, 6004 Luzern.
T. (041) 2401015, Fax 2405001. *064070*
Hirsiger, W., Hertensteinstr. 37, 6000 Luzern.
T. (041) 410 39 33. - Num - *064071*
Kaeslin, Otto, Haldenstr. 5, 6006 Luzern.
T. (041) 410 63 44. *064072*
Keller, Dieter, Pfistergasse 25, 6003 Luzern.
T. (041) 240 23 82. *064073*
Kleiner, Postfach, 6000 Luzern 15. T. (041) 3721074,
Fax 3721073. - Ant / Paint - *064074*
Kunstsalon, Habsburgerstr. 35, 6003 Luzern.
T. (041) 210 17 33. - Ant / Paint / Graph - *064075*
Kupferstich Boutique, Weinmarkt 17, 6004 Luzern.
T. (041) 410 23 83. *064076*
Led Line Art & Wear Mazziotta, Maihofstr. 29, 6004 Lu-
zern. T. (041) 420 30 92. *064077*
Linsi, Zentralstr. 2, 6003 Luzern.
T. (041) 210 31 73. *064078*
Meier, Arno, Wesemlinstr. 40, 6006 Luzern.
T. (041) 420 69 21. *064079*
Meile, Peter, Bramberghöhe 9, 6004 Luzern.
T. (041) 4106706. - Paint / Graph / Sculp / Draw /
Draw - *064080*
Montrésor Antiquités, Kauffmannweg 12, 6003 Luzern.
T. (041) 210 29 96. *064081*
Perot, René, Gartenheimstr. 36, 6006 Luzern.
I. (041) 420 28 23. *061082*
R & S Kunsthandel, Waldstätterstr. 18, 6003 Luzern.
T. (041) 27 51 21. *064083*
Schloss Oberlöchli, Adligenswilerstr. 90, 6006 Luzern.
T. (041) 420 03 64. *064084*
Schmidt, Helmut, Schweizerhofquai 4, 6004 Luzern.
T. (041) 410 19 76. - Jew / Instr - *064085*
Schwingruber, Markus, Maihofstr. 20, 6006 Luzern.
T. (041) 420 95 68. *064086*
Sieber, Bruno, Hans-Holbein-Gasse 4, 6004 Luzern.
T. (041) 4106040. *064087*
Sury, Marc von, Tannegg 11, St. Niklausen, 6005 Lu-
zern. T. (041) 340 12 45. - Furn / Instr - *064088*
Ulmann, Bernhard, Fruttstr. 17, 6005 Luzern.
T. (041) 360 88 47. *064089*
Vögeli, R. & J., Alpenstr. 7, 6004 Luzern.
T. (041) 410 55 10. *064090*
Vonlaufen, Hugo, Vonmattstr. 20, 6003 Luzern.
T. (041) 240 87 43. *064091*
Wey & Co., Haldenstr. 11, 6006 Luzern.
T. (041) 410 55 07, Fax (041) 410 19 49. - Ant / Paint /
China / Sculp / Jew / Rel / Glass / Ico - *064092*
Willimann, Joseph, Theaterstr. 3, 6003 Luzern.
T. (041) 210 86 48. - Ant / Paint / Furn / China / Sculp /
Tex / Silv - *064093*

Lyss (Bern)
Bürgi, Robert, Ob. Aareweg 24, 3250 Lyss.
T. (032) 3842052. *064094*
Messerli, Paul, Herrengasse 25, 3250 Lyss.
T. (032) 3846473. *064095*

Madulain (Graubünden)
Helvetische Münzenzeitung HMZ, Gemeindehaus, 7523
Madulain. T. (081) 8540055, Fax 8540054. *064096*

Magliaso (Ticino)
Arts & Decor, Via Cantonale, 6983 Magliaso.
T. (091) 6064717. *064097*
Galleria Arte Primitiva, Via Fiume, Casa Calao, 6983 Ma-
gliaso. T. (091) 6061962, Fax 6062057. - Sculp /
Eth - *064098*
Meiermazzega, Anna, Via Cantonale, 6983 Magliaso.
T. (091) 6064717. *064099*
Morigi, Paolo, Via Fiume 21, 6983 Magliaso.
T. (091) 6061962, Fax 6062057. *064100*

Malleray (Bern)
Devaud, Roland, 1 Rue du Frête, 2735 Malleray.
T. (032) 4922253. *064101*

Margrethen (Sankt Gallen)
Emberger, Paul, Bahnhofstr. 12a, 9430 Margrethen.
T. (071) 7444480. - Ant - *064102*

Martigny (Valais)
Bussien, Carlo, 22 Rue Marc Morand, 1920 Martigny.
T. (027) 7222965. *064103*
Hiob International, 35 Rue du Léman, 1920 Martigny.
T. (027) 7223883. *064104*

Matten bei Interlaken (Bern)
Kämpf, Willy, Hauptstr. 57, 3800 Matten bei Interlaken.
T. (033) 8226305. *064105*

Meggen (Luzern)
La Puerta del Sol, Lerchenhalde 9, 6045 Meggen.
T. (041) 377 14 24. - Ant - *064106*

Meilen (Zürich)
Beck, H., Seestr 615, 8706 Meilen. T. (01) 9234774,
Fax 9234774. - Instr - *064107*
Galerie La Charpenna, Grübstr., 8706 Meilen.
T. (01) 9152147, 9233202. *064108*
Grob, Hans, Dollikerstr. 4/31, 8706 Meilen.
T. (01) 923 16 07. - Furn - *064109*
Komatzki, Dorfstr. 140, 8706 Meilen. T. (01) 9234512,
Fax (01) 9236158. *064110*

Meinier (Genève)
Château de Corsinge, Rte. de la Pallanterie 2, 1252
Meinier. *064111*

Meisterschwanden (Aargau)
Roggwiler, Barbara, Hauptstr. 46, 5616 Meisterschwanden. T. (056) 6273229. *064112*

Mellingen (Aargau)
Kleinert, Udo, Salzmattstr. 11, 5507 Mellingen.
T. (056) 491 26 80. *064113*

Mendrisio (Ticino)
Ferrari, Gian-Mario, 2 Rue Bello, 6850 Mendrisio.
T. (091) 6468586. *064114*
Monetti, Raoul, Via Motta 11, 6850 Mendrisio.
T. (091) 6461026. *064115*
Sanguin, Adriano, Via Industria 1, 6850 Mendrisio.
T. (091) 6465314. *064116*

Mergoscia (Ticino)
Pedroni, Casimiro, Rivapiana, 6647 Mergoscia.
T. (091) 7453491. *064117*

Mesocco (Graubünden)
Steiner, Bernadetta, San Bern Centro Lumbreida, 6563
Mesocco. T. (092) 941514. *064118*

Mézières (Vaud)
Wilmart, Sacha, Face au Théâtre, 1083 Mézières.
T. (021) 903 24 81. - Ant / Furn - *064119*

Minusio (Ticino)
Mediatore, Via Simen 9, 6648 Minusio.
T. (091) 7431854. *064120*

Möhlin (Aargau)
Au Charme Ancien, Sonnenweg 4, 4313 Möhlin.
T. (061) 851 19 89. *064121*
Riedel, Melana, Bahnhofstr. 79, 4313 Möhlin. *064122*

Mörel (Valais)
Stucky, Bruno, 3983 Mörel. T. (027) 9271832.   *064123*

Möriken (Aargau)
Spreuer, Gerhard, Unteräschstr. 11, 5115 Möriken.
T. (064) 53 33 41.   *064124*

Mörschwil (Sankt Gallen)
Aschi's Raritätenkeller, Rorschacher Str. 377, 9402 Mörschwil. T. (071) 8661955.   *064125*
Winiger, Ernst Alois, Fahrnstr. 39, 9402 Mörschwil.
T. (071) 8661955.   *064126*

Moiry (Vaud)
Schopfer, Maurice, 1314 Moiry.
T. (021) 866 73 68.   *064127*

Mollis (Glarus)
Gubser, Willi, Wiesstr. 9, 8753 Mollis.
T. (055) 6122443.   *064128*
Kamm, Hans-Rudolf, Hinterdorfstr. 14, 8753 Mollis.
T. (055) 6124063.   *064129*

Mont-la-Ville (Vaud)
Jaggi, Pierre-André, La Pièce, 1328 Mont-la-Ville.
T. (021) 864 54 25.   *064130*

Le Mont-sur-Lausanne (Vaud)
Laffely, Jules, 19 Rte. de Cugy, 1052 Le Mont-sur-Lausanne. T. (021) 652 93 28.   *064131*

Mont-sur-Rolle (Vaud)
Regazzoni, Serge, Les Pelluettes, 1185 Mont-sur-Rolle.
T. (021) 825 22 87.   *064132*

Montagny-la-Ville (Fribourg)
Zeller, Walter, Château de Gottreau, 1776 Montagny-la-Ville. T. (026) 6606461.   *064133*

Montana-Vermala (Valais)
Bagnoud, Georges, 3962 Montana-Vermala.
T. (027) 4812067.   *064134*
La Brocante, Av. de la Gare, 3962 Montana-Vermala.
T. (027) 4815968.   *064135*

Monthey (Valais)
Caveau de l'Antiquité, 2 Pl. Eglise, 1870 Monthey.
T. (024) 4719196.   *064136*
Jentsch, Claudine, 2 Av. du Crochetan, 1870 Monthey.
T. (024) 4716656.   *064137*

Montreux (Vaud)
Au Vieux Mazot, 42 Av. des Alpes, 1820 Montreux.
T. (021) 963 31 63.   *064138*
Blatter, Bernard, 11 Av. du Casino, 1820 Montreux.
T. (021) 963 36 42.   *064139*
Brocante des Planches, 26 Rue du Pont, 1820 Montreux.
T. (021) 963 74 72.   *064140*
L'Exotique, 16 Grand-Rue, 1820 Montreux.
T. (021) 963 43 10.   *064141*
Galerie 58, 58 Av. Alpes, 1820 Montreux.
T. (021) 963 46 24.   *064142*
Galitch, Paul, 9 Rue des Artisans, 1820 Montreux.
T. (021) 964 40 34.   *064143*
Haldy, Jacques, Rue Industrielle 10, 1820 Montreux.
T. (021) 63 57 15. - Ant / Furn -   *064144*
Les Planches, 1 Ruelle Chauderon, 1820 Montreux.
T. (021) 963 78 91.   *064145*

Morcote (Ticino)
Al Portico, 6922 Morcote. T. (091) 9961370.   *064146*
Hegar, Peter, Via Piana, 6922 Morcote.
T. (091) 9961996.   *064147*

Morges (Vaud)
Aubry, Roger, 86 Rue Louis de Savoie, 1110 Morges.
T. (021) 801 62 27. - Ant / Graph / Fra / Draw -   *064148*
Bezzola, Georges, 40 Rue Louis-de-Savoie, 1110 Morges. T. (021) 801 31 88. - Ant / Paint / Graph / Furn /
Dec -   *064149*
Boutique Louis-de-Savoie, 67 Rue L.-de-Savoie, 1110
Morges. T. (021) 801 84 11.   *064150*
Bovi, Alain, 84 Rue L.-de-Savoie, 1110 Morges.
T. (021) 801 90 10.   *064151*
Centre Rives-de-Morges, 47 c Rte. de Lausanne, 1110
Morges. T. (021) 802 29 47.   *064152*

Challet, Danielle, 47c Rue Lausanne, 1110 Morges.
T. (021) 802 29 47.   *064153*
Dufaux, Jacques, 3 Rue Couvaloup, 1110 Morges.
T. (021) 801 04 49.   *064154*
Grenier de la Côte, 47 g Rte. de Lausanne, 1110
Morges.   *064155*
Koch, Geneviève, 67 Rue Louis-de-Savoie, 1110 Morges. T. (021) 801 84 11. - Ant -   *064156*
Moyard, 83-87 Grand-Rue, 1110 Morges.
T. (021) 801 62 41. - Ant / Furn / Tex / Dec /
Lights -   *064157*

Morgins (Valais)
Lange, Gérald, Chalet Primevère, 1875 Morgins.
T. (024) 4771442.   *064158*

Moudon (Vaud)
La Bohème, 14.-Avril 4, 1510 Moudon.
T. (021) 905 14 95.   *064159*
Grosjean, Gilbert, 12 Vieux-Bourg, 1510 Moudon.
T. (021) 905 21 68.   *064160*
Ricca, Michel, 1 Rue des Terreaux, 1510 Moudon.
T. (021) 905 15 36.   *064161*

Moutier (Bern)
Au Grenier du Viaduc, 29 Viaduc, 2740 Moutier.
T. (032) 4931727.   *064162*

Mühledorf (Solothurn)
Alte Seilerei, Murfistr. 97, 4583 Mühledorf.
T. (032) 6451176.   *064163*

Münchenbuchsee (Bern)
Grosjean, Lilian, Hofwilstr. 136, 3053 Münchenbuchsee.
T. (031) 869 00 81.   *064164*

Münchenstein (Basel-Land)
Neuschwander, Otto, Lindenstr. 39, 4142 Münchenstein.
T. (061) 411 05 23.   *064165*
Oppliger, B., Wasserhausweg 18, 4142 Münchenstein.
T. (061) 411 36 91.   *064166*

Münchwilen (Thurgau)
Leutenegger, Hansfred, Badstr. 5, 9542 Münchwilen.
T. (071) 9662221.   *064167*

Münsingen (Bern)
Rentsch, Bernstr. 3, 3110 Münsingen.
T. (031) 312 09 10. - Ant -   *064168*

Müswangen (Luzern)
Klaus, Ernst, Linden, 6289 Müswangen.
T. (041) 917 15 28.   *064169*

Muntelier (Fribourg)
Schwarz, Hauptstr. 221, 3286 Muntelier.
T. (026) 6705530. - Furn -   *064170*

Muralto (Ticino)
Cavargna, Maria Luisa, Viale Verbano 33, 6600 Muralto.
T. (091) 7438161.   *064171*
La Fonte, Viale Verbano 33, 6600 Muralto.
T. (091) 7438161.   *064172*
Pedroni, Carlo, Postgebäude, 6600 Muralto.
T. (091) 7431247. - Paint / Graph / Furn / Orient / China /
Sculp / Arch / Eth / Jew / Fra / Silv / Rel / Glass / Mod --
  064173

Muri (Aargau)
Feiss-Koella, Reinhard, Aettenbergstr 13, 5630 Muri.
T. (056) 6441589.   *064174*

Muri bei Bern (Bern)
Bugmann & Engel, Thunstr 86, 3074 Muri bei Bern.
T. (031) 9514030.   *064175*
Kampf, Heinz Hubertus, Ob. Wehrliweg 2, 3074 Muri bei
Bern. T. (031) 9515580.   *064176*

Murten (Fribourg)
Baho Quilt Gallery, Hauptgasse 38, 3280 Murten.
T. (026) 6702070. - Tex -   *064177*
Bruni, Anton, Schlossgasse 14, 3280 Murten.
T. (026) 6702809. - Ant -   *064178*
Hegar, Peter, Ryf 34, 3280 Murten. T. (026) 6701805.
- Ant -   *064179*
Schluep, Hans, Schlossgasse 12, 3280 Murten.
T. (026) 6702347.   *064180*

Schwarz, Beat, Bernstr. 23, 3280 Murten.
T. (026) 6701656. - Paint / Furn / Repr / Dec / Lights /
Instr / Cur / Ico / Tin -   *064181*
Ugrinovits, Gerlinde, Deutsche Kirchgasse 9, 3280 Murten. T. (026) 6702321.   *064182*

Muttenz (Basel-Land)
Bernard, Peter, Hauptstr. 2, 4132 Muttenz.
T. (061) 461 02 33. - Ant / Instr -   *064183*
Gerber, J. & K., Bahnhofstr. 39, 4132 Muttenz.
T. (061) 461 62 97.   *064184*
Hausamann, Claudine, Hauptstr. 43, 4132 Muttenz.
T. (061) 461 95 61.   *064185*
Schröder, Ruth, St. Jakobs-Str. 55, 4132 Muttenz.
T. (061) 461 33 51. - Ant / Furn -   *064186*
Spreng, Katrin, Hauptstr. 65, 4132 Muttenz.
T. (061) 461 48 22. - Ant -   *064187*

Näfels (Glarus)
Fischli, Hans, Freulerweg 4, 8752 Näfels.
T. (055) 6122125.   *064188*
Hauser, Theo & Hedwig, Bahnhofstr. 4, 8752 Näfels.
T. (055) 6121108.   *064189*

Nänikon (Zürich)
Au Vieux Cadran, Stationsstr. 11, 8606 Nänikon.
T. (01) 941 30 33.   *064190*

Naters (Valais)
Fasciani, Renato, Landstr. 60, 3904 Naters.
T. (027) 9232943.   *064191*

Nax (Valais)
Jacquod, Jean-Bernard, Cordamou, 1961 Nax.
T. (027) 2031953.   *064192*

Neuchâtel
Alder, Charles, 24 Av. de Bellevaux, 2000 Neuchâtel.
T. (032) 7251560.   *064193*
Au Bonheur du Jour, 24 Rue du Seyon, 2000 Neuchâtel.
T. (032) 7254533.   *064194*
Fahrny, Jean, 10 Rue du Coq d'Inde, 2000 Neuchâtel.
T. (032) 7246484.   *064195*
Galitch, Pierre, 21 Rue des Moulins, 2000 Neuchâtel.
T. (032) 7250266.   *064196*
Gennari, Romano, 78 Ch. de la Caille, 2006 Neuchâtel.
T. (032) 7305467.   *064197*
Gretillat, Jean-Claude, 90 Rue des Draizes, 2006 Neuchâtel. T. (032) 7311962.   *064198*
Guyot, Jacques, 6 Rue F.-C. de Marval, 2000 Neuchâtel.
T. (032) 7259590.   *064199*
Loup, Alphonse, 15 Rue des Saars, 2000 Neuchâtel.
T. (032) 7253062.   *064200*
Meylan, Jacques-E., Pl. des Halles 2, 2000 Neuchâtel.
T. (032) 7252806.   *064201*
Ray, Jacques, 10 Rue des Parcs, 2001 Neuchâtel.
T. (032) 7244824.   *064202*
Richard, Jean-Francis, 31 Rue des Poudrières, 2006
Neuchâtel. T. (032) 7244453. - Ant -   *064203*
Rossato, Silvio, 24 Rue de Maillefer, 2000 Neuchâtel.
T. (032) 7243931.   *064204*
Rothplatz, Michèle, 31 Rue des Parcs, 2000 Neuchâtel.
T. (032) 7254480.   *064205*
Schneider, Claude, 9 Rue de l'Evole, 2000 Neuchâtel.
T. (032) 7252289.   *064206*
Vuille, Claudine, 46 Av. Portes-Rouges, 2000 Neuchâtel.
T. (032) 7252081.   *064207*

Neuenegg (Bern)
Ugrinovits, Gerlinde, Riedh, 3176 Neuenegg.
T. (031) 741 14 18.   *064208*

Neuenkirch (Luzern)
Bühlmann, Friedrich, Sonnmattstr. 15, 6206 Neuenkirch.
T. (041) 467 21 83.   *064209*
Steinemann, Tino, Rippertschwand, 6206 Neuenkirch.
T. (041) 467 12 97, Fax 4671117. - Graph / China / Tex /
Dec / Glass -   *064210*

Neuhausen am Rheinfall (Schaffhausen)
Liebefels, Rosenbergstr. 17, 8212 Neuhausen am Rheinfall. T. (052) 6727736. - Ant -   *064211*

Neunkirch (Schaffhausen)
Chelsea Gallery, Vordergasse 44, 8213 Neunkirch.
T. (052) 6813411. - Ant / Paint / Furn -   *064212*

La Neuveville (Bern)
Hirt, Patrice, Rue du Port, 2520 La Neuveville.
T. (032) 7513440, 7513010. - Ant / Furn -   *064213*

Nidau (Bern)
Patzer, Paul & Lilian, Lyssstr. 21, 2560 Nidau.
T. (032) 3656748.   *064214*

Niederbuchsiten (Solothurn)
Zeltner, Georg, Bodenmatt 136, 4626 Niederbuchsiten.
T. (062) 63 15 35.   *064215*

Niedererlinsbach (Solothurn/Aargau)
Antiques Peter von der Mühl, Tulpenweg 6, 5015 Niedererlinsbach. T. (064) 34 18 95.   *064216*

Niederhasli (Zürich)
Antigua, Haldenstr. 1, 8155 Niederhasli.
T. (01) 850 50 15.   *064217*

Niederneunforn (Thurgau)
Fischer, G. & R., Zum Schwanen, 8525 Niederneunforn.
T. (052) 7451629.   *064218*

Niederönz (Bern)
Antiquitäten-Galerie zum Waldhus, Juraweg 1, 3362 Niederönz. T. (062) 9612085.   *064219*

Niederrohrdorf (Aargau)
Sprenger, Margot, Fohrhölzlistr. 7, 5443 Niederrohrdorf.
T. (056) 496 31 05.   *064220*

Niederteufen (Aargau)
Küng, Freddie, Steinwichslenstr. 2, 9052 Niederteufen.
T. (071) 3331626, Fax 3331626. - Instr -   *064221*

Niederurnen (Glarus)
Bisig, Peter, Hauptstr. 27, 8867 Niederurnen.
T. (055) 6101617.   *064222*

Novaggio (Ticino)
Atelier Amadeo, Casa Catarina, 6986 Novaggio.
T. (091) 6062345.   *064223*

Nürensdorf (Zürich)
Lüssi, Hans, Spitalackerstr. 3, 8309 Nürensdorf.
T. (01) 836 75 62.   *064224*

Nyon (Vaud)
Courroisier, Olga, 58 Rue de Rive, 1260 Nyon.
T. (022) 361 34 84.   *064225*
Delley-Paltani, F. & M., 68 Rue de Rive, 1260 Nyon.
T. (022) 361 86 32.   *064226*
Detruche, Anne, 11 Ruelle des Moulins, 1260 Nyon.
T. (022) 3622195.   *064227*
La Fenestre, 55 Rue de Rive, 1260 Nyon.
T. (022) 361 07 84.   *064228*
Guignet, Bernard, 27 Ch. Plantaz, 1260 Nyon.
T. (022) 3614844.   *064229*
La Marotte, 55 Rue de Rive, 1260 Nyon.
T. (022) 3623077.   *064230*
Mégevet, Marguerite, Ch. de l'Argilliere 2, 1260 Nyon.   *064231*
Paltani, rue de Rive 57, 1260 Nyon. T. (022) 3614070.
- Ant / Furn / China -   *064232*
Pelichet, Edgar, 6 Château Mafroi, 1260 Nyon.
T. (022) 361 18 19.   *064233*
Ratcliff, 64 Rue de Rive, 1260 Nyon.
T. (022) 361 14 41.   *064234*
Rivereine Antiquités, 57 Rue Rive, 1260 Nyon.
T. (022) 361 40 70.   *064235*
Zanchiello, Cosimo, 9 Rue de la Colombière, 1260 Nyon.
T. (022) 361 63 18. - Ant -   *064236*

Oberdorf (Solothurn)
Etter, Louis, Dorfplatz 100, 4515 Oberdorf.
T. (032) 6223283. - Instr -   *064237*

Oberembrach (Zürich)
Klerk, Jan de, Oberwagenburg 217, 8425 Oberembrach.
T. (01) 865 05 20.   *064238*

Oberentfelden (Aargau)
Kyburg, Hanspeter, Jubiläumsweg 10, 5036 Oberentfelden. T. (064) 43 35 59.   *064239*

Obergerlafingen (Solothurn)
Rüeggsegger, Werner, Schulhausstr. 48, 4564 Obergerlafingen. T. (032) 6756189.   *064240*

Oberkirch (Luzern)
Origoni, Gregor, Luzernstr. 66, 6208 Oberkirch.
T. (041) 921 31 36.   *064241*

Oberönz (Bern)
Antiquitäten-Galerie im Moos, Bernstr. 27, 3363 Oberönz. T. (062) 9611794.   *064242*

Oberriet (Sankt Gallen)
Wüst, Martin, Steigstr., 9463 Oberriet.
T. (071) 7611958.   *064243*

Oftringen (Aargau)
Meier, Erwin, Zürichstr. 77, 4665 Oftringen.
T. (062) 97 17 87.   *064244*
Meyer, Am Tych 14a, 4665 Oftringen.
T. (062) 97 01 11.   *064245*

Ollon (Vaud)
Fernandez, Ivy, Villars-Soleil, 1867 Ollon.
T. (024) 4951619.   *064247*
Marie-Noëlle, Marclay, Pallueyres, 1867 Ollon.
T. (025) 372388.   *064247a*

Olten (Solothurn)
Antiquitäten am Zielemp, Hauptgasse 10, 4600 Olten.
T. (062) 32 31 10.   *064248*
Bösch, Peter, Hardfeldstr. 7, 4600 Olten.
T. (062) 26 13 26.   *064249*
Borner, Markus, Hauptgasse 10, 4600 Olten.
T. (062) 2123110, 2162360.   *064250*
Hersperger, Urs, Ringstr. 2a, 4600 Olten.
T. (062) 22 32 14. - Ant -   *064251*
IH Ikonen Handel, Konradstr 31, 4600 Olten.
T. (062) 325918. - Ico -   *064252*

Onnens (Vaud)
Schenk, Sabine, 1425 Onnens.
T. (024) 4361749.   *064253*

Orbe (Vaud)
Lale-Demoz, Roger, 28 Rue Abbaye, 1350 Orbe.
T. (024) 4411414.   *064254*

Orpund (Bern)
Jobin, Eduard, Jurastr. 8, 2552 Orpund.
T. (032) 3552282.   *064255*
Zeller, Madeleine, Hauptstr. 226, 2552 Orpund.
T. (032) 3551282. - Ant -   *064256*

Ossingen (Zürich)
Galerie Usserdorf 68, Steinerstr. 60, 8475 Ossingen.
T. (052) 3171907.   *064257*
Klimbim, Andelfingerstr. 278, 8475 Ossingen.
T. (052) 3172576.   *064258*

Ottenbach (Zürich)
Ghinolfi, Albert, Tobelhof, 8913 Ottenbach.
T. (01) 761 22 55. - Ant / Paint / Furn / China / Sculp / Tex / Glass / Cur -   *064259*

Oulens-sous-Echallens (Vaud)
Oberson, Michel, 1041 Oulens-sous-Echallens.
T. (021) 881 34 47. - Furn -   *064260*

Paradiso (Ticino)
Casoli, Roberto, Via Corona 15, 6900 Paradiso.
T. (091) 9941141.   *064261*
Hagner, Louis, Via Boggia 4, Postfach 557, 6902 Paradiso. T. (091) 994578. - Ant / Fra -   *064262*

Payerne (Vaud)
Caillet, Gérard, 5 Rue Boverie, 1530 Payerne.
T. (026) 6601572.   *064263*
Plumettaz, Fernand, Rue des Granges 28, 1530 Payerne.
T. (026) 6604633.   *064264*

Penthaz (Vaud)
Chapuis, Charles-Henri, Rue du Bornalet, 1303 Penthaz.
T. (021) 861 24 34.   *064265*

Peseux (Neuchâtel)
Sauser, Pierre, 7 Rue de Neuchâtel, 2034 Peseux.
T. (032) 7315171.   *064266*
Steiner, David, 7 Rue du Stand, 2034 Peseux.
T. (032) 7313977.   *064267*

Pfäffikon (Schwyz)
Blattmann, Josef, Rosenhof 5, 8808 Pfäffikon.
T. (052) 4104802. - Ant / Paint / Graph / Tex -   *064268*

Pfäffikon (Zürich)
Zürcher, Kurt, Obermattstr. 72, 8330 Pfäffikon.
T. (01) 950 31 97.   *064269*

Pfeffingen (Basel-Land)
Maurer, Lotty, Hauptstr. 37, 4148 Pfeffingen.
T. (061) 7512148.   *064270*

Pieterlen (Bern)
Fritz-Shaar, Robert, Hauptstr. 26, 2542 Pieterlen.
T. (032) 3771382. - Ant / Paint / Graph -   *064271*

Plan-les-Ouates (Genève)
Yersin, Charles, 23 Ch. Plein-Vent, 1228 Plan-les-Ouates. T. (022) 7711129.   *064272*

Ponte Tresa (Ticino)
Portobello-antiquario, Via Lugano, 6988 Ponte Tresa.   *064273*

Porrentruy (Jura)
Moine, Paul, 15 Rue Vaucher, 2900 Porrentruy.
T. (032) 4666825. - Ant -   *064274*
Müller, Philippe, 22 Rue de l'Eglise, 2900 Porrentruy.
T. (032) 4664928.   *064275*
Paratte, Maurice, 13 Rue des Annonciades, 2900 Porrentruy. T. (032) 4662247.   *064276*

Porsel (Fribourg)
Ponzo, Josiane, En Corbès, 1699 Porsel.
T. (021) 907 70 20.   *064277*

Poschiavo (Graubünden)
Jensen, Leticia, Via Maestra, 7742 Poschiavo.
T. (081) 8440012.   *064278*

Pully (Vaud)
Atica, S., 23 Rue du Port, 1009 Pully.
T. (021) 7296029.   *064279*
Grosjean, Jean-Jacques, Ch. des Roches 7, 1009 Pully.
T. (021) 7299378. - Ant -   *064280*

Puplinge (Genève)
Mayor, José, Rte. de Presinge, 1241 Puplinge.   *064281*

Radelfingen bei Aarberg (Bern)
Hersberger & Westerhof, 17e Au, 3271 Radelfingen bei Aarberg. T. (032) 3923904.   *064282*

Rapperswil (Sankt Gallen)
Brenner, Annette, Herengasse 4, 8640 Rapperswil.
T. (052) 2108158.   *064283*
Dür, Irma, Kluggasse 10, 8640 Rapperswil.
T. (052) 2109870.   *064284*
Galerie zum Schloss, Hauptpl. 10, 8640 Rapperswil.
T. (052) 2107453. - Ant / Paint / Graph / Instr -   *064285*
Hungerbühler, Urs, Marktgasse 18, 8640 Rapperswil.
T. (055) 2104720.   *064286*
Massimo, Feliciani, Alte Jonastr. 104, 8640 Rapperswil.
T. (052) 2102000.   *064287*
Verena R. Antiquitäten, Marktgasse 10, 8640 Rapperswil. T. (052) 2105902.   *064288*

Regensdorf (Zürich)
Grosjean, A., Ostring 36, 8105 Regensdorf.
T. (01) 840 28 59.   *064289*

Reinach (Aargau)
Lienhard, Viehmarktstr. 7, 5734 Reinach.
T. (064) 71 63 48.   *064290*

Reinach (Basel-Land)

Bernard, Robert, Baselstr 108, 4153 Reinach.
T. (061) 711 01 76, Fax 7110565. - Instr - 064291

Bütschi, Adrian, Kirchg. 7, 4153 Reinach.
T. (061) 711 56 57. - Ant / Furn - 064292

Roth, Aldo, Kägenhofweg 8, 4153 Reinach.
T. (061) 711 86 16. 064293

Stierli, Paul Graham, Bellstr. I, 4153 Reinach. 064294

Vasatko, Jan, Im Stockacker 39, 4153 Reinach.
T. (061) 711 58 97. 064295

Rheineck (Sankt Gallen)

Spirig, Lydia, Gruebstr 89, 9424 Rheineck.
T. (071) 8885292. 064296

Riaz (Fribourg)

Blanc, Fernand, 1632 Riaz. T. (026) 9128228. 064297

Rickenbach (Solothurn)

Borner, Andreas, Kirchweg 29, 4613 Rickenbach.
T. (062) 2162360, 2123110. 064298

Riehen (Basel-Stadt)

Antikstube Riehen, Baselstr. 45, 4125 Riehen.
T. (061) 641 33 30. 064299

Luchsinger, Hans, Äussere Baselstr. 255, 4215 Riehen.
T. (061) 601 88 18. - Ant / Furn - 064300

Muster, Rösly, Baselstr. 45, 4125 Riehen.
T. (061) 641 33 30. 064301

Phila Service, Burgstr. 10, 4125 Riehen.
T. (061) 641 35 87. - Num - 064302

Schibli, Robert, Bettingerstr.1, 4125 Riehen.
T. (061) 641 66 51. - Ant - 064303

Seckinger, Hansueli, Burgstr. 7, 4125 Riehen.
T. (061) 641 15 72. - Ant - 064304

Zum Buurekäschtli, Baselstr. 67, 4125 Riehen.
T. (061) 641 42 64. - Ant / Furn - 064305

Rodersdorf (Solothurn)

Huber, Roland, Biederthalstr. 46, 4118 Rodersdorf.
T. (061) 731 13 43. 064306

Rohrbach bei Huttwil (Bern)

Antiquitäte-Schopf, Längacher, 4938 Rohrbach bei Huttwil. T. (062) 9652384. 064307

Rolle (Vaud)

Aebi, Louis, 18 Grand-Rue, 1180 Rolle.
T. (021) 825 21 08. 064308

Brossy, Robert, 12 Rte. de Genève, 1180 Rolle.
T. (021) 825 26 07. 064309

Chez l'Artisan, 96 Grand-Rue, 1180 Rolle.
T. (021) 825 37 78. 064310

Gasparetto, Antoine, 48 Grand-Rue, 1180 Rolle.
T. (021) 825 31 30. 064311

Micello, Luigi, 8 Ch. J. Berney, 1180 Rolle.
T. (021) 825 31 81. 064312

Romainmôtier (Vaud)

Surer, Th. D., Au Lieutenant Baillival, 1323 Romainmôtier. T. (024) 4531458, Fax 4531830. - Ant / Paint /
Furn / China / Jew / Silv - 064313

Romanel-sur-Lausanne (Vaud)

Au Temps Retrouvé, 13 Rte. d'Echallens, 1032 Roma-
nel-sur-Lausanne. T. (021) 371437, 6471437. 064314

Romanshorn (Thurgau)

Antiquitäten Galerie, Hafenstr. 10, 8590 Romanshorn.
T. (071) 4632747. - Furn - 064315

Burgstaller, Kurt, Arbonerstr. 64, 8590 Romanshorn.
T. (071) 4635255. - Ant - 064316

Stampfer, Rudolf, Bahnhofstr. 3, 8590 Romanshorn.
T. (071) 4635655. - Paint / Graph / Repr / Fra - 064317

Rona (Graubünden)

Poltera, Louis Alpo, 7454 Rona.
T. (081) 6845226. 064318

Ronco sopra Ascona (Ticino)

Galleria Decorama, Via Ciseri, 6622 Ronco sopra Ascona. T. (091) 7916841. - Paint / China / Sculp / Jew /
Glass - 064319

Ropraz (Vaud)

Fondation L'Estrée, Espace Culturel, 1088 Ropraz.
T. (021) 9031173, Fax 9031173. 064320

Rorschach (Sankt Gallen)

Bayard, Armin, Kirchstr. 15, 9400 Rorschach.
T. (071) 8418044. 064321

Engensperger, Hauptstr. 42-44, 9400 Rorschach.
T. (071) 8416212/14, Fax 8416002. - Ant / Furn / China / Sculp / Dec / Lights - 064322

Huber-Signer, Ulrich, Trischlistr. 12, 9400 Rorschach.
T. (071) 8412993. 064323

Martha, Karl, Dr., Mariabergst. 11, 9400 Rorschach.
T. (071) 8413421. - Ant - 064324

Romano, Venerando, Hauptstr. 20, 9400 Rorschach.
T. (071) 8412163. 064325

Rosé (Fribourg)

Guex, Gilbert, 7 Rte. Côte, 1754 Rosé. T. (026) 4701622.
- Ant - 064326

Rothenburg (Luzern)

Koller, Magda, Bertiswilstr. 86, 6023
Rothenburg. 064327

Rothrist (Aargau)

Thut, Hanspeter, Gländstr. 19, 4852 Rothrist.
T. (062) 44 22 73. 064328

Rotkreuz (Zug)

Galerie zur uralten Uhr, Luzernerstr. 8, 6343 Rotkreuz.
T. (041) 790 13 04. - Instr - 064329

Hainbuchner, Josef, Buonaserstr. 9, 6343 Rotkreuz.
T. (041) 790 14 69. 064330

Rougemont (Vaud)

Rochat, Claude, La Vieille Cure, 1838 Rougemont.
T. (026) 9258288. 064331

Rossier-Barrier, David, Le Pont-de-Pierre, 1838 Rougemont. T. (026) 9258280. - Ant / Orient - 064332

Rüdlingen (Schaffhausen)

Hürsch, Paul, Schneehalde 68, 8455 Rüdlingen.
T. (01) 867 30 27. 064333

Rueyres-les-Prés (Fribourg)

Brülhart, Gisèle, 1542 Rueyres-les-Prés.
T. (026) 6671572. 064334

Rupperswil (Aargau)

Weber, Hilda, Rotholzweg 2, 5102 Rupperswil.
T. (064) 47 27 94. 064335

Russin (Genève)

La Lampisterie, 6 Rte. des Molards, 1281 Russin.
T. (022) 754 12 32. 064336

Ruswil (Luzern)

Albisser, Ruth, Neuenkirchstr. 43, 6017 Ruswil.
T. (041) 495 18 25. - Ant - 064337

Saanen (Bern)

Au Foyer, Hauptstr., 3792 Saanen.
T. (033) 7442607. 064338

Kohli, Christine, Oberdorf, 3792 Saanen.
T. (033) 7443440. 064339

Sachseln (Obwalden)

Ah, Theo von, Bahnhofstr. 12, 6072 Sachseln.
T. (041) 660 14 44. - Ant / Furn - 064340

Ars Antiqua Antiquitäten, Brünigstr. 49, 6072 Sachseln.
T. (041) 660 61 55. 064341

Saint Antoni (Fribourg)

Binz, Erich, Menzishaus, 1713 Saint Antoni.
T. (026) 4951791. 064342

Saint-Blaise (Neuchâtel)

Le Brocantique, 1 Rue de Vigner, 2072 Saint-Blaise.
T. (032) 7531476. 064343

Franc, Ginette, 6 Grand-Rue, 2072 Saint-Blaise.
T. (032) 7534732. 064344

Schneider, Paul, 6 Ch. des Plaines, 2072 Saint-Blaise.
T. (032) 7532392. 064345

Saint-Léonard (Valais)

Hager, Nelly, 3958 Saint-Léonard.
T. (027) 2032193. 064346

Saint-Prex (Vaud)

Cuendet, Jean-Pierre, 2 Rue de la Gare, 1162 Saint-
Prex. T. (021) 806 14 64. 064347

Emery, Raymond, En Senaugin, 1162 Saint-Prex.
T. (021) 806 12 46. 064348

Saint-Sulpice (Vaud)

Weigle, Walter, 23 Ch. du Russel, 1025 Saint-Sulpice.
T. (021) 691 49 88. 064349

Sainte-Croix (Vaud)

Hediguer, Paul, 26 Rue Centrale, 1450 Sainte-Croix.
T. (024) 4543971. 064350

Salavaux (Vaud)

Antiquus, 1581 Salavaux. T. (026) 6752737. 064351

Sâles (Fribourg)

Ferraglia, Aldo, Le Clos, 1625 Sâles.
T. (026) 9178369. 064352

Salmsach (Thurgau)

Hunziker, R.K., Kehlhofstr. 18, 8599 Salmsach.
T. (071) 4633828. - Num - 064353

Samedan (Graubünden)

Galerie riss, Haus Nr. 6, POB 202, 7503 Samedan.
T. (081) 8525556. 064354

Sutter, Chasper, Bahnhofstr. 47, 7503 Samedan.
T. (081) 8525414. 064355

Sankt Gallen

Ackermann, T., Wasserg 12, 9000 Sankt Gallen.
T. (071) 2223679. - Ant / Furn / China / Glass /
Toys - 064356

African Arts, Schmiedgasse 18, 9000 Sankt Gallen.
T. (071) 2225555. - Eth - 064357

Anno Domini, Metzgergasse 13, 9000 Sankt Gallen.
T. (071) 2226346. - Ant / Fra / Lights / Glass / Cur /
Toys - 064358

Antiquitäten Heiligkreuz, Hinterlauben 13, 9000 Sankt
Gallen. T. (071) 236663. - Ant / Paint / Graph / Furn /
China / Sculp / Jew / Lights / Instr / Rel - 064359

Art-Kabinet, Goethestr. 61, 9008 Sankt Gallen.
T. (071) 2454565. 064360

Atelier-Galerie, Greithstr. 6a, 9008 Sankt Gallen.
T. (071) 2456261. - Ant / Paint / Graph / Furn / China /
Eth / Instr / Glass / Mod / Mul / Draw - 064361

Bruderer, Robert, Schmiedgasse 18, 9000 Sankt Gallen.
T. (071) 2225555. - Ant - 064362

Bucher, Edwin, Müller-Friedberg-Str. 1, 9000 Sankt Gallen. T. (071) 2227540. - Ant - 064363

Comba, Markus, Magnihalden 3, 9000 Sankt Gallen.
T. (071) 2226074. - Ant - 064364

Eichholzer, Werner, Goliathgasse 33, 9006 Sankt Gallen.
T. (071) 2440641, Fax 2440641. - Instr - 064365

Erker-Galerie, Gallusstr. 30-32, 9000 Sankt Gallen.
T. (071) 2227979, Fax 22 79 19. - Ant / Paint - 064366

Falch, Hermann, Buchentalstr. 13 a, 9000 Sankt Gallen.
T. (071) 2458654. 064367

Feldmann, Jürgen, Demutstr. 3, 9000 Sankt Gallen.
T. (071) 2223589. 064368

Fenner, Silvia, Hinterlauben 13, 9000 Sankt Gallen.
T. (071) 2236663, 2452179. 064369

Fröhlich, Emil Konrad, Goliathgasse 23, 9004 Sankt Gallen. T. (071) 2220963. - Ant - 064370

Fröhlich, Hansueli, Marktgasse 26, 9000 Sankt Gallen.
T. (071) 2233212, Fax 2233241. - Ant / Furn / China /
Sculp / Lights / Instr / Rel / Glass - 064371

Galerie am Park, Notkerstr 14, 9000 Sankt Gallen.
T. (071) 2459555. 064372

Graphica Antiqua, Oberer Graben 46, 9001 Sankt Gallen.
T. (071) 2235016. - Graph - 064373

Hartmann, Roland, Dr, Zwinglistr 3, Postfach 213, 9004
Sankt Gallen. T. (071) 2221870. 064374

Hediger, Thomas, Gallusstr 3, 9000 Sankt Gallen.
T. (071) 2226767, Fax 2226788. - Ant / Num - 064375

Heinzmann, M. & E., Sankt Jakobstr. 60, 9000 Sankt
Gallen. T. (071) 2448621. - Ant / Paint / Orient / China /
Sculp / Silv / Cur - 064376

Hinterberger, J., Langgasse 107a, 9008 Sankt Gallen.
T. (071) 2452762. - Furn -   064377
Hinterhoflade, Hintere Davidstr. 14, 9000 Sankt Gallen.
T. (071) 2220828.   064378
Hirzel, Fritz, Felsenstr. 34, 9000 Sankt Gallen.
T. (071) 2230401. - Ant -   064379
Hobi, Anna & Andreas, Hintere Davidstr. 14, 9000 Sankt
Gallen. T. (071) 2220828. - Ant -   064380
Howarth, Kräzernstr. 66, 9015 Sankt Gallen.   064381
Keller, Alfons J., Greithstr. 6a, 9000 Sankt Gallen.
T. (071) 2456261.   064382
Klopfer, Herbert, Kirchgasse 14, 9000 Sankt Gallen.
T. (071) 2225366.   064383
Kühne, Kurt, Sankt-Josefen-Str. 25, 9001 Sankt Gallen.
T. (071) 2776011. - Graph -   064384
Kunst-Antik zum Adlerberg, Sankt Jakob Str. 60, 9000
Sankt Gallen. T. (071) 2448627.   064385
Langenegger, Sonja, Rosenbergstr. 44, 9000 Sankt Gal-
len. T. (071) 2234888. - Ant -   064386
Nenning, Alfred, Metzgergasse 25, 9000 Sankt Gallen.
T. (071) 2231210. - Ant -   064387
Nostalgie-Keller, Gallusstr. 35, 9000 Sankt Gallen.
T. (071) 2236166.   064388
im Obersteg-Bucher, Markus, Dr., Müller-Friedberg-Str
1, 9000 Sankt Gallen. T. (071) 2227540, Fax 2227540.
- Jew / Silv / Furn -   064389
Opus Zwei, Kirchgasse 3, 9000 Sankt Gallen.
T. (071) 2233888.   064390
Osvald, Niklaus von, Dr., Sankt Jakobstr. 61, 9000 Sankt
Gallen. T. (071) 2455011.   064391
Osvald, Oliver, Oberer Graben 46, 9001 Sankt Gallen.
T. (071) 2235016.   064392
Pethö, Maria, Rorschacher Str. 159, 9006 Sankt Gallen.
T. (071) 2453319.   064393
Raubach, Neugasse 39-41, 9000 Sankt Gallen.
T. (071) 2222766, Fax 2226842. - Furn / Paint - 064394
Senn, Martin, Langgasse 20, 9008 Sankt Gallen.
T. (071) 2446533. - Graph / Fra -   064395
Sennhauser & Partner, Altenwegenstr. 71, 9015 Sankt
Gallen. T. (071) 3113579. - Furn -   064396
Speck, Alfred, Kesselhaldenstr. 6, 9004 Sankt Gallen.
T. (071) 2233473. - Ant -   064397
Stäheli, Arthur, Sonderstr. 45, 9011 Sankt Gallen.
T. (071) 2225888. - Ant -   064398
Staub, Erich, Moosstr. 21a, 9000 Sankt Gallen.
T. (071) 2779196. - Ant -   064399
Widmer, Hans, Löwengasse 3, 9004 Sankt Gallen.
T. (071) 2233581, Fax 2234280. - Ant / Paint / Graph /
Sculp -   064400
Zum Fundgrübli, Wassergasse 5 a, 9000 Sankt Gallen.
T. (071) 2223356.   064401
Zum Goldige Herzli, Metzgergasse 10, 9000 Sankt Gal
len. T. (071) 2235277.   064402

Sankt Moritz (Graubünden)
Birth, E. & A., Via Somplaz 13, 7500 Sankt Moritz.
T. (081) 8337564.   064404
Katz, David, Via Serlaz 27-29, 7500 Sankt Moritz.
T. (081) 8333090, Fax 8333090. - Paint -   064405
Krattiger, Willy, Via Sela 2, 7500 Sankt Moritz.
T. (081) 8335333.   064406
Zervudachi, Peter, Palace-Arcade, 7500 Sankt Moritz.
T. (081) 8333531. - Ant / Paint / Furn / Tex / Jew / Silv /
Ico -   064406a

Sarnen (Obwalden)
Galerie Silverlady, Engellohstr. 11, 6060 Sarnen.
T. (041) 660 33 87.   064407

Satigny (Genève)
Constantin, P., 116 Rte. du Mandement, 1242
Satigny.   064408

Savièse (Valais)
roten, Thérèse, Saint Germain, 1965 Savièse.
T. (027) 3951689.   064409

Schaffhausen
Abt, Eugen & Susi, Abendstr. 27, 8200 Schaffhausen.
T. (052) 6241617. - Ant -   064410
Antik und Kunst Emilian, Neustadt 49, 8200 Schaffhau-
sen. T. (052) 6259080.   064411
Bartl, Johanna, Unterstadt 25, 8200 Schaffhausen.
T. (052) 6256065.   064412

Galerie zum Schlüssel, Neustadt 49, 8200 Schaffhau-
sen. T. (052) 6259080. - Ant / Paint / Graph / Furn /
Orient / Fra / Lights -   064413
Henry's Antik-Shop, Repfergasse 8, 8200 Schaffhausen.
T. (052) 6259839. - Ant -   064414
Maurer, Walter, Hornbergstr. 33, 8200 Schaffhausen.
T. (052) 6248619. - Ant -   064415
Rutishauser, Max, Schloss Herblingen, 8207 Schaffhau-
sen. T. (052) 6432720. - Ant / Paint / Furn / China /
Sculp / Tex / Jew / Silv -   064416
Schmid, Bernhard, Neustadt 69, 8200 Schaffhausen.
T. (052) 6248284.   064417
Seelhofer, Jacqueline, Eschenweg 12, 8200 Schaffhau-
sen. T. (052) 6257016.   064418

Scheuren (Bern)
Zaugg, Victor, Hauptstr. 50, 2556 Scheuren.
T. (032) 3732419.   064419

Schindellegi (Schwyz)
Kyburz, Rudolf, Dorfstr. 7 a, 8834 Schindellegi.
T. (01) 784 69 38.   064420

Schlatt bei Winterthur (Zürich)
Vogel, Fritz, In der Säge, 8418 Schlatt bei Winterthur.
T. (052) 3631060. - Instr -   064421

Schleitheim (Schaffhausen)
Kradolfer, Samuel, Zur oberen Mühle, 8226 Schleitheim.
T. (052) 6801147.   064422
Ullmann-Meier, Hölderli 7, 8226 Schleitheim.
T. (053) 649 00.   064423
Wanner, Hermann, Adlerstr. 19, 8226 Schleitheim.
T. (052) 6801396.   064424

Schmerikon (Sankt Gallen)
Gebert, Paul, Hauptstr. 83, 8716 Schmerikon.
T. (052) 2822305.   064425
Müller, Franz, St. Galler-Str 26, 8716 Schmerikon.
T. (052) 2821552. - Ant -   064426

Schmitten (Fribourg)
Schafer, Hugo, Müllerstr. 16, 3185 Schmitten.
T. (026) 4961225.   064427

Schöftland (Aargau)
Buchser, Markus, Aarauerstr. 22, 5040 Schöftland.
T. (064) 81 19 59.   064428

Schönenwerd (Solothurn)
Amsler, H., Gartenstr. 40, 5012 Schönenwerd.
T. (064) 41 32 07. - Num -   064429

Schwarzenburg (Bern)
Galerie Schmiedgasse, Schmiedgasse 10, 3150
Schwarzenburg. T. (031) 7311030. - Ant -   064430
Hauser, Heinz, Dorfpl 8, 3150 Schwarzenburg.
T. (031) 7310173.   064431

Schwerzenbach (Zürich)
Gut & Collectors Corner, Gfennstr. 47, Gut Werner, 8603
Schwerzenbach. T. (01) 825 47 82.   064432

Schwyz (Schwyz)
Beeler, Peter, Kollegiumstr. 4, 6430 Schwyz.
T. (041) 811 53 10.   064433
Felchlin, Xaver, Gotthardstr. 47, 6430 Schwyz.
T. (041) 811 24 41.   064434
Gasser, Heinz, Maihof, Hauptplatz, 6430 Schwyz.
T. (041) 8112020, 8116626.   064435
Maihof, Schlagstr., 6430 Schwyz. T. (041) 811 56 26.
- Ant -   064436
Reichmuth, Anton, Ibach Gottardstr., 6430 Schwyz.
T. (041) 811 52 52. - Ant -   064437
Trutsch, Annemarie, Saint-Martinsstr. 1, 6430 Schwyz.
T. (041) 811 33 32.   064438

Seegräben
Böckli, August, Lehenhof, 8607 Seegräben.
T. (01) 9321724.   064439

Seon (Aargau)
Bock, Dieter, Reussgasse 25, 5703 Seon.
T. (064) 55 29 36.   064440

Sierre (Valais)
Antille, Fernand, 3 Rue du Bourg, 3960 Sierre.
T. (027) 4551257.   064441
Steyaert, Paul, Planzette 26, 3960 Sierre.
T. (027) 4552385.   064442

Signau (Bern)
Rupp, Rosalie, Gässli 1, 3534 Signau.
T. (034) 4971237.   064443

Sils/Segl-Maria (Graubünden)
Fümm, Elsy, Segl Maria, 7514 Sils/Segl-Maria.
T. (081) 8265268.   064444

Sion (Valais)
Au Troc Retro, 4 Rue des Châteaux, 1950 Sion.
T. (027) 3224146.   064445
Baumann, Alfred, 9 Rue de Conthey, 1950 Sion.
T. (027) 3224594.   064446
Bonvin, René, 19 Rue du Rhône, 1950 Sion.
T. (027) 3222110.   064447
Grosjean, André, 24 Rue de Savièse, 1950 Sion.
T. (027) 3229635.   064448
Juillerat, Michel, 8 Rue Grand-Pont, 1950 Sion.
T. (027) 3234232.   064449
Martin, Edgar, 25 Rue de Loèche, 1950 Sion.
T. (027) 3222349.   064450
Nodari, Silvia, 26 Av. de Tourbillon, 1950 Sion.
T. (027) 3220060.   064451
Sauthier, Michel, Rue des Tanneries 1, 1950 Sion.
T. (027) 3222526. - Ant -   064452
Surroca, François, 53 Rue des Creusets, 1950 Sion.
T. (027) 3228378.   064453
Tour d'Argent, Rue de Savièse 10, 1950 Sion.
T. (027) 3227007.   064454
Vergeres, Jean, 19 Rue de la Lombardie, 1950 Sion.
T. (027) 3220879.   064455

Siselen (Bern)
Galerie 25, Juchen 25, 2577 Siselen. T. (032) 3962071,
Fax 3962071.   064456

Solothurn
Eberhard, Weissensteinstr. 63, 4500 Solothurn.
T. (032) 6222046. - Ant -   064457
Flury, Arthur, Weissensteinstr. 9, 4500 Solothurn.
T. (032) 6234423.   064458
Kräuchi, Werner, Römerstr. 22, 4500 Solothurn.
T. (032) 6232957.   064459
Nussbaum, Ruedi, Barfüssergasse 6, 4500 Solothurn.
T. (032) 6227958.   064460
Tablo, Niklaus-Konrad-Str. 26, 4500 Solothurn.
T. (032) 6220747.   064461
Tranzer, Erika, Barfüssergasse 12, 4500 Solothurn.
T. (032) 6225955.   064462

Speicher (Aarau)
Waldburger, S., Einfang 725, 9042 Speicher.   064463

Spiez (Bern)
Atelier Trunz, Asylstr. 56, 3700 Spiez.
T. (033) 6541163.   064464

Spreitenbach (Aargau)
Antiquitäten Galerie am Dörfliplatz, Tivoli, 8957 Sprei-
tenbach. T. (056) 4014455.   064465

Staad (Sankt Gallen)
Blum, Egon, Schlössliweg 8, 9422 Staad.
T. (071) 8554747.   064466
Sigi's Antiquitäten, Schlössliweg 6, 9422 Staad.
T. (071) 8551888. - Ant / Furn -   064467

Stadel (Winterthur) (Zürich)
Steiner, E., Haldenrainstr. 51, 8543 Stadel (Winterthur).
T. (052) 3371588. - Furn -   064468

Stadel b. Niederglatt (Zürich)
Müller, Ernst, Stäglistr. 16, 8174 Stadel b. Niederglatt.
T. (01) 858 12 22.   064469

Stäfa (Zürich)
Hediger, Max, Glärnischstr 48b, 8712 Stäfa.
T. (01) 9263696.   064470
Kehlhof-Galerie, Seestr. 185, 8712 Stäfa.
T. (01) 926 60 79.   064471

Kunz, Maria, Grundstr. 90, 8712 Stäfa.
T. (01) 926 24 56. *064472*
Neff, Beat, Bergstr. 9, 8712 Stäfa.
T. (01) 926 54 80. *064473*
Rodriguez, Manuel, Bergstr. 38, 8712 Stäfa.
T. (01) 926 17 27. *064474*
Schibli, Helga, Bergstr. 14, 8712 Stäfa.
T. (01) 926 28 20. *064475*

Stallikon (Zürich)
Lutz, Hanspeter, Hinterbuchenegg 572, 8143 Stallikon.
T. (01) 710 55 88. *064476*

Stans (Nidwalden)
Lehmann & Sohn, W., Schmiedgasse 35, 6370 Stans.
T. (041) 610 21 86. *064477*

Steckborn (Thurgau)
A-Z Kunstservice, Seestr. 117, 8266 Steckborn.
T. (052) 7613435. - Ant - *064478*

Steffisburg (Bern)
Brechbühl, Leni, Hombergstr. 56, 3612 Steffisburg.
T. (033) 4378000. *064479*
Santschi, Christian, Weidenweg 11, 3612 Steffisburg.
T. (033) 4372502. *064480*

Stein am Rhein (Schaffhausen)
Galerie am Undertor, Understadt 24, 8260 Stein am
Rhein. T. (052) 7414176, Fax 3762280. - Ant / Graph /
Fra - *064481*
Oriental Gallery zum Rosenberg, Oberstadt 12, 8260
Stein am Rhein. T. (052) 7414319. *064482*

Steinhausen (Zug)
Bolli, Elfi, Grabenackerstr. 46, 6312 Steinhausen.
T. (041) 741 19 55. *064483*
Orlandi, Tonino, Grabenackerstr. 50, 6312 Steinhausen.
T. (041) 741 18 21. *064484*

Süderen (Bern)
Müller, Fritz, Beim Schulhaus, 3618 Süderen.
T. (033) 4531172. *064485*

Suhr (Aargau)
Binder, Willi, Neue Aarauerstr. 6, 5034 Suhr.
T. (064) 31 53 92. *064486*

Surpierre (Fribourg)
Château de Surpierre, 1528 Surpierre.
T. (026) 6681558. *064487*

Sursee (Luzern)
Fundgrube zur Laterne, Unterstadt 14, 6210 Sursee.
T. (041) 921 78 77. *064488*
Stadelmann, Arnold, Mühlepl. 1, 6210 Sursee.
T. (041) 921 27 35. *064489*

Susten (Valais)
Sewer, Ernest, 3952 Susten. T. (027) 4731058. *064490*

Tägerig (Aargau)
Erni, Paul, Grütweg 4, 5522 Tägerig. T. (056) 491 27 49.
- Num - *064491*

Tafers (Fribourg)
Tinguely, Peter, Freiburgstr. 217, 1712 Tafers.
T. (026) 4942474. *064492*

Tagelswangen (Zürich)
Struchen, Rietstr 3, 8317 Tagelswangen.
T. (052) 3435331, Fax 3434930. - Ant / Paint / Furn /
Pho - *064493*

Tavannes (Bern)
Francescoli, Rosemary, 14 Grand-Rue, 2710 Tavannes.
T. (032) 4812214. - Ant - *064494*
Schöni, Wilfred, 20 Pierre-Pertuis, 2710 Tavannes.
T. (032) 4811278. *064495*

Teufenthal (Aargau)
Schweigerlehner, Erich, Linzenthalbodenweg 489, 5723
Teufenthal. T. (064) 46 14 14. *064496*

Thal (Sankt Gallen)
Suhm, Walter, Wolfsgrube, 9425 Thal.
T. (071) 8881717. *064497*

Zürcher, E., Buriet 446, 9425 Thal. *064498*

Thalwil (Zürich)
Brunner, Katrin, Oberdorfstr. 29, 8800 Thalwil.
T. (01) 720 33 70. *064499*
Widmeier, Kurt, Schorenstr. 37, 8802 Thalwil.
T. (01) 715 47 76. *064500*

Thörishaus (Bern)
Ecker, Helmut, Sensemattstr. 20a, 3174 Thörishaus.
T. (031) 889 06 06. *064501*

Thun (Bern)
Bergauer, P., Feuerwerkerstr. 46 f, 3603 Thun.
T. (031) 839 33 30. - Ant / Furn / Tex - *064503*
Krebser, Bälliz 64, 3601 Thun. T. (033) 2221922. *064504*
OCC-Antik, Feuerwerkerstr. 46F, 3603 Thun.
T. (033) 2225330. - Furn / Tex - *064504a*
Zeller & Zumkehr, Ob. Hauptgasse 48, 3600 Thun.
T. (033) 2224931. *064505*

Toffen (Bern)
Old-Timer Garage, Gürbestr. 3a, 3125 Toffen.
T. (031) 819 38 38, 819 00 00,
Fax (031) 819 51 91. *064506*

La Tour-de-Peilz (Vaud)
Domingo, Louis, 20 Rue du Château, 1814 La Tour-de-
Peilz. T. (021) 944 60 31. *064507*
Graf, Patrice, 12 Pl. Anciens-Fossés, 1814 La Tour-de-
Peilz. T. (021) 944 51 72. *064508*
Loubet, Pierre, 6 Rue du Temple, 1814 La Tour-de-Peilz.
T. (021) 944 12 54. *064509*
Ostertag, Pierre, 19 Av. des Baumes, 1814 La Tour-de-
Peilz. T. (021) 944 10 34. *064510*
Savioz, Christian, 209 Rte. de Chailly, 1814 La Tour-de-
Peilz. T. (021) 944 22 22. *064511*
Stettler, Marcel, 128 Ch. Béranges, 1814 La Tour-de-
Peilz. T. (021) 944 22 79. *064512*
Wieland, Nicolas, 80 Av. Bel-Air, 1814 La Tour-de-Peilz.
T. (021) 944 28 31. *064513*

La Tour-de-Trême (Fribourg)
Christin, René, 84 Rue Ancien-Comté, 1635 La Tour-de-
Trême. T. (026) 9122029. *064514*
Vigna, Joseph, Rue Ancien Comt, 1635 La Tour-de-
Trême. T. (026) 9123456. - Ant - *064515*

Tramelan (Bern)
Calderoli, Gilbert, 181 Grand-Rue, 2720 Tramelan.
T. (032) 4874805. *064516*
Votano, Guiseppe, 69 Grand-Rue, 2720 Tramelan.
T. (032) 312 76 46. *064517*

Triengen (Luzern)
Gut, Werner, Kantonsstr 61, 6234 Triengen.
T. (041) 9332727, Fax 9332727. - Ant / Paint / Graph /
Furn / China / Sculp / Instr / Rel / Cur / Mod - *064518*
Muccillo, Antonio, Buchenweg, 6234 Triengen.
T. (041) 933 13 52. - Ant - *064519*

Trimstein (Bern)
Zeller, Anreas, Bühl 12, 3083 Trimstein.
T. (031) 839 36 35. *064520*

Trogen (Aargau)
Bucher, Edwin O., Blatten, 9043 Trogen.
T. (071) 3443210. *064521*

Tüscherz (Bern)
Tschantré, Thomas H., Dorfweg 15, 2512 Tüscherz.
T. (032) 3236527. *064522*

Turbenthal (Zürich)
Stephani, Jürg, Im Bühl, 8488 Turbenthal.
T. (052) 3852386. *064523*

Ueken (Aargau)
Bellin, Angela, Hauptstr. 20, 5028 Ueken.
T. (064) 61 46 15. *064524*

Uerikon (Zürich)
Schatztrückli Hütten, Schwarzbachstr. 87, 8713 Uerikon.
T. (01) 926 26 17. *064525*

Uetikon am See (Zürich)
Blum, Michael, Auf der Rüti, 8707 Uetikon am See.
T. (01) 9204979. *064526*
Magener, Jörg, Auf der Rüti, 8707 Uetikon am See.
T. (01) 9204979. *064527*

Uhwiesen (Zürich)
Dietrich, Erwin, Dorfstr 29, 8248 Uhwiesen.
T. (052) 6591343. - Num - *064528*

Uitikon-Waldegg (Zürich)
Curiger, Carl-Rudolf, Birmensdorferstr. 24, 8142 Uitikon-
Waldegg. T. (01) 493 16 66. *064529*

Unterlangenegg (Bern)
Gunten, Werner von, Russachen, 3614 Unterlangenegg.
T. (033) 4532121. - Ant / Furn - *064530*

Unterseen (Bern)
Galerie Weissenau, Weissenaustr. 6, 3800 Unterseen.
T. (033) 8221041. *064531*

Uster (Zürich)
Antique Dolls, Sonnenbergstr. 61, 8610 Uster.
T. (01) 940 91 72. *064532*
Lüthy, Edgar, Sandstr. 1, 8610 Uster.
T. (01) 940 92 35. *064533*

Uttwil (Thurgau)
Hügli, Jörg, Romanshornerstr 14, 8592 Uttwil.
T. (071) 4631053. *064534*
Zur Alten Tenne, Romanshorner Str. 14, 8592 Uttwil.
T. (071) 4634772. *064535*

Uznach (Sankt Gallen)
Arnold, Karl, Ernetschwilerstr. 6, 8730 Uznach.
T. (052) 2802828. *064536*
Hipp, Max, Remigihofstr. 14, 8730 Uznach.
T. (052) 2803574. *064537*

Vacallo (Ticino)
Bernardis, Leonardo, Via Bellinzona, 6833 Vacallo.
T. (091) 6838562. *064538*

Valangin (Neuchâtel)
Wittwer, Jacques, Le Bourg, 2042 Valangin.
T. (032) 8572406. *064539*

Vallorbe (Vaud)
Au Vieux Soufflet, 24 Grand-Rue, 1337 Vallorbe.
T. (021) 843 11 39. *064540*

Vandoeuvres (Genève)
Antonini, Maurice E., 110 Rte. de Meinier, 1253 Vandoeuvres. T. (022) 750 21 04. *064541*

Vaulion (Vaud)
Tripet, Raoul, Bas-du-Village, 1325 Vaulion.
T. (021) 843 31 10. *064542*

Vaz/Obervaz (Graubünden)
Moser, Paulina, Via Nora Lain, 7082 Vaz/Obervaz.
T. (081) 3843833. *064543*

Vernayaz (Valais)
Centre de Brocante, 1904 Vernayaz.
T. (027) 7641376. *064544*

Versoix (Genève)
Uhlmann, Jean, Ch. Molard 27-29, 1290 Versoix.
T. (022) 755 26 20. - Ant - *064545*

Vésenaz (Genève)
Alivertti, René, 52 Rte. de Thonon, 1222 Vésenaz.
T. (022) 752 47 07. - Ant / Dec - *064546*
Mermier, Jean-Eric, Rte de Thonon 72, 1222 Vésenaz.
T. (022) 7521177, Fax 7523515. *064547*

Vevey (Vaud)
Amstein, Gilbert, 22 b Quai Perdonnet, 1800 Vevey.
T. (021) 922 81 11. *064548*
Anderson, 6-8 Rue du Torrent, 1800 Vevey.
T. (021) 921 30 72. *064549*
L'Art de Vivre, 4 Pl. de l'Ancien-Port, 1800 Vevey.
T. (021) 922 84 27. *064550*
Bernasconi, Giovanni, 10 Pl. de l'Ancien-Port, 1800 Ve-
vey. T. (021) 922 64 44. *064551*

Celotti, Louis, 5 Rue de l'Hôtel-de-Ville, 1800 Vevey.
T. (021) 921 33 85.   *064552*
Collet, Serge-A., 30 Rue du Simplon, 1800 Vevey.
T. (021) 923 51 23.   *064553*
Duvanel, Gérard, 10 Rue d'Italie, 1800 Vevey.
T. (021) 921 25 56. - Ant -   *064554*
Guignard, Ad., 32 Rue du Lac, 1800 Vevey.
T. (021) 921 36 24. - Ant -   *064555*
Hennessy, Clive, 1 Rue du Château, 1800 Vevey.
T. (021) 921 93 45.   *064556*
Longo, Luigi, 3 Rue Simplon, 1800 Vevey.
T. (021) 921 30 87.   *064557*
Papon, Jean, 3 Rue Hôtel-de-Ville, 1800 Vevey.
T. (021) 921 62 50.   *064558*
Rivollet, Madeleine, 8 Ruelle du Lac, 1800 Vevey.
T. (021) 921 95 77. - Ant / China / Draw -   *064559*
Vauthey, Roger, 14 Rue d'Italie, 1800 Vevey.
T. (021) 921 00 91.   *064560*
Zervudachi Antiquités, 5-7 Rue du Lac, 1800 Vevey.
T. (021) 9210958, Fax 9219537. - Ant / Paint / Furn /
Tex / Jew / Silv / Ico -   *064561*

Peter Zervudachi

Antiquités

5–7 rue du Lac, 1800 **VEVEY**
Tél. (021) 9 21 09 58

et

Palace-Arcade, 7500 **St. Moritz**
Tél. (0 81) 833 3531

Veyrier (Genève)
Lugrin, 6 Ch. J.-E. Gottret, 1255 Veyrier.   *064562*

Veytaux (Vaud)
Au Caprices des Temps, 4 Rue Ancien-Collège, 1820
Veytaux. T. (021) 963 61 79.   *064563*
Clerc, René, 37 Av. de Chillon, 1820 Veytaux.
T. (021) 963 23 90.   *064564*
Gaillard, Olivier, 4 Rue de l'Ancien Collège, 1820
Veytaux.   *064565*

Vezia (Ticino)
Righini, Nicola, Via Morbio 13, 6943 Vezia.
T. (091) 9663942.   *064566*
Rigilio, Giovanni, Via San Gottardo 10, 6943 Vezia.
T. (091) 9663260.   *064567*

Viganello (Ticino)
Burani, Umberto, Ai Gelsi 7, 6962 Viganello.
T. (091) 9722739.   *064568*
Leemann, Siglinde, Via Capelli 2, 6962 Viganello.
T. (091) 9727605.   *064569*
Monza, Emilio, Via La Santa 17, 6962 Viganello.
T. (091) 9416263. - Ant / Paint / Furn / China / Sculp /
Arch / Jew / Silv / Instr / Instr / Mil / Rel / Glass -   *064570*

Vilars (Neuchâtel)
Picci & Fils, 2063 Vilars. T. (032) 8535366,
Fax 8535522. - Ant / Furn -   *064571*

Villaraboud (Fribourg)
Dougoud, Jean-Louis, Ferme, 1679 Villaraboud.
T. (026) 6551464.   *064572*

Villarlod (Fribourg)
Karst, André, 1695 Villarlod. T. (026) 4112175. *064573*

Villars-sur-Ollon (Vaud)
Artisane, Rue Centrale, 1884 Villars-sur-Ollon.
T. (024) 4953490.   *064574*
Fernandez, Ivy, Villars-Soleil, 1884 Villars-sur-Ollon.
T. (024) 4951619.   *064575*

Villaz-Saint-Pierre (Fribourg)
Paudex, Gilbert, 1758 Villaz-Saint-Pierre.
T. (026) 6531704.   *064576*

Villeneuve (Vaud)
Au Vieux Villeneuve, 27 Grand-Rue, 1844 Villeneuve.
T. (021) 960 23 61.   *064577*

Deillon, Robert, 8 Rue du Nord, 1844 Villeneuve.
T. (021) 960 15 25. - Ant -   *064578*

Villeret (Bern)
Gerber, Bertile, 14 Rue Principale, 2613 Villeret.
T. (032) 9412658.   *064579*

Vordemwald (Aargau)
Bähler, Hermann, Langenthalerstr. 8, 4803 Vordemwald.
T. (062) 51 61 15.   *064580*

Vouvry (Valais)
Gillioz, Maurice, Av. de Savoie 57, 1896 Vouvry.
T. (024) 4811907.   *064581*

Vullierens (Vaud)
Gasset, Edvige, 1115 Vullierens.
T. (021) 869 91 26.   *064582*

Wabern (Bern)
Bigler, Margrite, Nesslerenweg 72, 3084 Wabern.
T. (031) 961 13 66.   *064583*

Wädenswil (Zürich)
Schneider, R. & S., Au Moosackerstr. 3, 8820 Wädenswil. T. (01) 780 70 80.   *064584*

Wäldi (Thurgau)
Zimmermann, Hans, Bildäckerli 110, 8564 Wäldi.
T. (071) 6571701.   *064585*

Wald (Zürich)
Michelsen, Christian, Wasserschloß Jonathal, 8636
Wald. T. (052) 2464344.   *064586*

Wallenwil (Thurgau)
Jezler, Peter, Waldbachstr 14, 8360 Wallenwil.
T. (071) 9711083.   *064587*

Wallisellen (Zürich)
Müller, Robert, In den Weissenäckern 3, 8304 Wallisellen. T. (01) 8300227, 8301777.   *064588*
Schneider, Helen, Glattmärt, 8304 Wallisellen.
T. (01) 830 21 41.   *064589*

Walzenhausen (Aargau)
Graf, Walter, Höhe 821, 9428 Walzenhausen.
T. (071) 8884565.   *064590*

Wangen a/Aare (Bern)
Wittmer, Ursula, Städtli 17, 4705 Wangen a/Aare.
T. (065) 712323, (032) 6312323.   *064591*

Wangen bei Dübendorf (Zürich)
Appenzeller, Werner, Im Oberdorf 11, 8602 Wangen bei
Dübendorf. T. (01) 833 10 64.   *064592*
Galerie am Dorfplatz, Dorfplatz, 8602 Wangen bei Dübendorf. T. (01) 833 34 06.   *064593*

Weesen (Sankt Gallen)
Flütsch, Claudio, Marktgasse, 8872 Weesen.
T. (055) 6161677.   *064594*
Kieni, Peter, Flistr., 8872 Weesen.
T. (055) 6161672.   *064595*

Weggis (Luzern)
Ulrich, Josef, Lützelau, 6353 Weggis.
T. (041) 390 24 80.   *064596*

Weissenburg (Bern)
Matter, Willy, Dorf, 3764 Weissenburg.
T. (033) 7831384.   *064597*

Weisslingen (Zürich)
Denzler, Max, Lendikonerstr. 15, 8484 Weisslingen.
T. (052) 3841260.   *064598*
Mülli-Galerie, Dorfstr. 65, 8484 Weisslingen.
T. (052) 3841514.   *064599*

Wetzikon (Zürich)
Antik-Shop, Zentralstr. 7, 8623 Wetzikon.
T. (01) 930 11 50.   *064600*

Widen (Aargau)
Stocker, H., In der Rüti 2, 8967 Widen.   *064601*
Strebel, Hans, Imbissmattstr. 15, 8967 Widen.
T. (056) 6337619.   *064602*

Wiedlisbach (Bern)
Chällerlädeli, Städtli 16, 4537 Wiedlisbach.
T. (032) 6362633, Fax 6361287. - Paint /
China -   *064603*
Frauchiger, S., Städtli 23, 4537 Wiedlisbach.
T. (032) 6363516. - Mil -   *064604*
Günther, Hans, Bielstr. 2, 4537 Wiedlisbach.
T. (032) 6362389.   *064605*

Wikon (Luzern)
Felten, Helmut, Oberdorfstr. 3, 4806 Wikon.
T. (062) 51 99 73.   *064606*

Wila (Zürich)
Vescoli's Antik-Schöpfli, Aegertswil, 8492 Wila.
T. (052) 3852390. - Ant -   *064607*

Wilderswil (Bern)
Giovanni, Heidy A. di, Lehngasse 79 b, 3812 Wilderswil.
T. (033) 8221814.   *064608*

Winkel bei Bülach (Zürich)
Zum Holzwurm, Lufingerstr. 19, 8185 Winkel bei Bülach.
T. (01) 861 06 88.   *064609*

Winterthur (Zürich)
The Clock Shop, Steinberggasse 4, 8400
Winterthur.   *064610*
Galerie Wülfinger, Wülfingerstr. 235, 8408 Winterthur.
T. (052) 2215361.   *064611*

Wohlen (Aargau)
Geissmann, Beatrice, Bremgartenstr. 7, 5610 Wohlen.
T. (056) 622 24 74.   *064612*
Roetheli, Romana, Bifangstr. 5, 5610 Wohlen.
T. (056) 622 59 04. - Ant / Cur -   *064613*

Wolfhausen (Zürich)
Bühler, Edy, Hauptstr. 1, 8633 Wolfhausen.
Fax 552431455.   *064614*

Wollerau (Schwyz)
Blattmann, Martha, Verenastr. 29, 8832 Wollerau.
T. (01) 784 05 89.   *064615*

Würenlos (Aargau)
Güntli & Stocker, Shopping Brücke 1, 8116 Würenlos.
T. (056) 4242985.   *064616*
Markwalder, Beatrice, Mühle 21, 5436 Würenlos.
T. (056) 4242757. - Ant -   *064617*

Yverdon-les-Bains (Vaud)
Bouquinerie Brocante, 11 Rue des Pêcheurs, 1400 Yverdon-les-Bains. T. (024) 4256343.   *064618*
Brocante du Castrum, 54 Rue du Valentin, 1400 Yverdon-les-Bains. T. (024) 4254719.   *064619*
Chaumière, 78 Rue de la Plaine, 1400 Yverdon-les-Bains. T. (024) 4252762.   *064620*
Croset, Jean-François, 3 Rue du Four, 1400 Yverdon-les-Bains. T. (024) 4258645.   *064621*
Gatabien, Jacqueline, 5 Rue Sablonnaire, 1400 Yverdon-les-Bains. T. (024) 4254162.   *064622*
Poncet, Daniel, 8 Rue Prés-du-Lac, 1400 Yverdon-les-Bains. T. (024) 4451475.   *064623*
Rive de la Thiele, 16 Quai des Ateliers, 1400 Yverdon-les-Bains. T. (024) 4250908 001007341-733-X.   *064624*
Techni Puces, 13 Rue du Collège, 1400 Yverdon-les-Bains. T. (024) 4261920.   *064625*
Vuille, Louis, Maison-Rouge 5, 1400 Yverdon-les-Bains.
T. (024) 210626, Fax 212544. - Graph / Fra - *064626*
Zwygart, Werner, 7 Av. des Bains, 1400 Yverdon-les-Bains. T. (024) 4256343.   *064627*

Yvonand (Vaud)
Altmann, René, Maison du Pont, 1462 Yvonand.
T. (024) 4301475.   *064628*

Zofingen (Aargau)
Baudenbacher, Alice, Nussweg 3, 4800 Zofingen.
T. (062) 51 23 71.   *064629*
Meier, Erwin, Pappelweg 5, 4800 Zofingen.
T. (062) 51 64 50.   *064630*
Peyer & Aeschlimann, Bärengasse 11, 4800 Zofingen.
T. (062) 51 70 21. - Ant / Paint / Graph / Furn / Fra / Silv /
Lights / Instr / Mil / Glass -   *064631*

Schenk, Evamaria, Bottenwilerstr 25, 4800 Zofingen. T. (062) 7513687. - Ant - 064632

Zollikofen (Bern)

Perla, Pasquale, Schloss Reichenbach, 3052 Zollikofen. T. (031) 911 18 06. 064633
Ramseyer, K., Schulhausstr. 18, 3052 Zollikofen. T. (031) 911 12 57. 064634

Zollikon (Zürich)

Zemp, Nick, Zollikerstr. 106, 8702 Zollikon. T. (01) 391 48 70. 064635

Zürich

A-B Einrahmungen, Badenerstr 254, 8004 Zürich. T. (01) 242 28 96, Fax 2422896. 064636
ABC Antiquariat, Zähringerstr 31, 8001 Zürich. T. (01) 2527145, Fax 2526132. 064637
Aladin Antik, Seefeldstr 226, 8008 Zürich. T. (01) 3815380, Fax 3822913. - Ant / Lights / Glass / Mod - 064638
Alte Galerie Enge, Seestr. 11, 8002 Zürich. T. (01) 202 44 45. 064639
Alte Uhren, Rotbuchstr. 54, 8000 Zürich. T. (01) 363 23 53. 064640
American Folk Art Gallery, Spiegelgasse 7, 8001 Zürich. T. (01) 261 58 88. - Ant / Sculp / Tex - 064641
Amman, Thomas, Restelbergstr 97, 8044 Zürich. T. (01) 2529052, Fax 2528254. 064642
Amodio, Pasquale, Meinrad Lienert-Str. 23, 8003 Zürich. T. (01) 462 20 52. 064643
Andreoni, Domenico, Lindenstr. 32, 8008 Zürich. T. (01) 252 46 45. - Ant - 064644
Annapurna, Scheitergasse 10, 8001 Zürich. T. (01) 262 07 80. 064645
Antica Rustica, Friesenbergstr. 205, 8055 Zürich. T. (01) 462 60 65. - Ant / Furn / Mil - 064646
Antik-Fundgrueb, Krugg. 7, 8001 Zürich. T. (01) 261 00 01. - Ant - 064647
Antik-Galerie Irchel, Winterthurerstr 66, 8006 Zürich. T. (01) 3626474, Fax 3626474. 064648
Antik-Markt, Stüssihof 10, 8001 Zürich. T. (01) 252 63 52. 064649
Antiquarius, Zeltweg 12, 8032 Zürich. T. (01) 261 13 30. 064650
Antique Collector, General Wille-Str. 8, 8002 Zürich. T. (01) 202 67 40. 064651
Antiquitäten & Fundus, Mommsenstr. 2, 8044 Zürich. T. (01) 252 38 33. 064652
Arts & Decors, Kirchgasse 33, 8001 Zürich. T. (01) 261 32 21. 064653
Aschbacher, L., Fraumünsterstr. 9, 8001 Zürich. T. (01) 211 86 20. - Ant / Paint / Furn / China / Tex / Lights / Instr - 064654
Atelier d'Art, Neumarkt 1, 8001 Zürich. T. (01) 252 66 70. - Graph / Fra - 064655
Atelier d'Art, Mühlebachstr. 126a, 8008 Zürich. T. (01) 383 36 60. 064656
Atelier im Bärenhof, Talacker 16, 8001 Zürich. T. (01) 211 45 41. - Ant - 064657
Atelier 3, Froschaugasse 3, 8001 Zürich. T. (01) 261 34 67. 064658
Au Meuble Ancien, Seestr. 92, 8002 Zürich. T. (01) 202 24 08. 064659
Aux Barbus, Klosbachstr. 13, 8032 Zürich. T. (01) 251 91 12. - Furn - 064660
Baumann, Susanne, Schipfe 49, 8001 Zürich. T. (01) 261 81 53. 064661
Baumgartner, Willy, Schaffhauserstr. 440, 8050 Zürich. T. (01) 301 37 12. 064662
Baviera, Peter, Segantinistr. 129, 8049 Zürich. T. (01) 341 42 51. 064663
Berweger, Willi, Zähringerstr. 27, 8001 Zürich. T. (01) 383 15 12. 064664
Best English Antiques, Kreuzbühlstr. 8, 8008 Zürich. T. (01) 261 02 42. 064665
Biondi, Massimo, Trittligasse 36, 8001 Zürich. T. (01) 221 02 03. 064666
Blum, Ellen, Kirchgasse 33, 8001 Zürich. T. (01) 251 31 20. - Ant / Furn / China / Dec / Silv - 064667
Bodmer, Stadelhoferstr 34, 8001 Zürich. T. (01) 251 93 54, Fax 2512905. 064668
Boni, Louise de, Rolandstr. 25, 8004 Zürich. T. (01) 241 75 05. 064669
Braumandl, Eugen, Zähringerstr. 20, 8001 Zürich. T. (01) 252 71 89. 064670
Britschgi, Melchior, Rämistr. 33, 8001 Zürich. T. (01) 261 56 32. 064671
Brun, Jeanette G., Dufourstr 119, 8008 Zürich. T. (01) 3836300. - Sculp / Arch - 064672
Bucher, Frieda, Schlüsselgasse 12, 8001 Zürich. T. (01) 221 12 37. 064673
Büttiker, Katharina, Wühre 9, 8001 Zürich. T. (01) 2116758, Fax 2121168. 064674
Camerin, Giuseppe, Birchstr. 72, 8057 Zürich. T. (01) 363 45 34. 064675
Camonica, Mario, Egertenstr. 56, 8003 Zürich. T. (01) 463 79 51. 064676
Carrara, Austr. 22, 8045 Zürich. T. (01) 462 36 31. 064677
Colombo, Angelo, Limmatquai 40, 8001 Zürich. T. (01) 2622191, Fax 2622205. - Instr - 064678
Coray, Jürg, Pflugstr. 16, 8006 Zürich. T. (01) 362 22 07. 064679
Cottage Antiques, St. Peterhofstatt 12, 8001 Zürich. T. (01) 2210239. - Ant / Furn / China / Lights / Glass / Instr / Tin - 064680
Deak & Co., Freigutstr. 27, 8002 Zürich. T. (01) 281 16 81. - Num - 064681
Deurzen, Laura von, Grossalbis 10, 8045 Zürich. T. (01) 463 62 40. 064682
Dietrich, Erwin, Werdmühlepl. 4, 8001 Zürich. T. (01) 211 01 67. - Num - 064683
Dolezal, Peter, Dr., Wehntalerstr. 492, 8046 Zürich. T. (01) 371 96 11. - Ant / Paint / Graph / Furn / China / Jew / Silv / Mil / Glass / Ico / Draw - 064684
Dorigo, Richard, Tobelhofstr. 320, 8044 Zürich. T. (01) 251 98 34. - Ant / Furn / China / Sculp / Dec - 064685
Ehrbar, Othmar, Universitätsstr. 17, 8006 Zürich. T. (01) 252 88 78. 064686
English Antiques, Strehlgasse 9, 8001 Zürich. T. (01) 211 01 31. 064687
English-Center-Antiques, Erismannstr. 55, 8004 Zürich. T. (01) 241 19 04, Fax 241 11 66. 064688
English Workshop Antiques Gallery, Oberdorfstr. 25, 8001 Zürich. T. (01) 383 34 80. - Ant / Paint / Furn / Jew / Silv - 064689
Färber & Sohn, J.J., Dufourstr. 104, 8008 Zürich. T. (01) 383 66 49. 064690
Falk + Falk, Kirchgasse 28, 8001 Zürich. T. (01) 2625657, Fax 2616202. - Graph / Draw - 064691
Fehr, Jean, Postfach 145, 8043 Zürich. T. (01) 492 52 33, Fax 401 07 37. - Tex - 064692
Feilchenfeldt, Walter, Freie Str 116, 8032 Zürich. T. (01) 3837960, Fax 3839948. - Paint / Draw - 064693
Fine Art, Restelbergstr. 97, 8044 Zürich. T. (01) 252 90 52. 064694
Frangos, Efstratios, Winterthurerstr. 142a, 8057 Zürich. T. (01) 363 47 15. 064695
Frangos, Stratjs, Sternenstr. 30, 8002 Zürich. T. (01) 201 04 96. 064696
Frey, Charles, Kreuzpl 9, 8032 Zürich. T. (01) 2516868. - Ant - 064697
Galerie Antike Ecke, Klosbachstr. 1, 8032 Zürich. T. (01) 252 10 72. 064698
Galerie Ars Antiqua, Brandschenkestr. 5, 8039 Zürich. T. (01) 201 09 33, Fax 201 09 33. - Jew / China - 064699
Galerie für Glasmalerei, Sternenstr. 24, 8002 Zürich. T. (01) 202 19 51. - Ant - 064700
Galerie Meister, Kirchgasse 28, 8001 Zürich. T. (01) 262 56 57/252 67 73, Fax 261 62 02. - Ant / Furn / China / Dec / Silv / Glass - 064701
Galerie Nefer, Postfach 6636, 8023 Zürich. T. (01) 211 48 05, Fax 211 59 47. - Sculp / Arch - 064702
Galerie Ypsilon, Augustinergasse 6, 8001 Zürich. T. 2116501. 064703
Gertsch, Hansruedi, Zollstr. 120, 8005 Zürich. T. (01) 271 42 45. 064704
Ghinolfi, André, Bederstr. 91, 8002 Zürich. T. (01) 201 12 92. 064705
Glaser, W., Kasernenstr. 75, 8004 Zürich. T. (01) 242 43 43. 064706
Grafica Antica, Fortunagasse 20, 8001 Zürich. T. (01) 221 04 17. 064707
Guggenheim, René, St. Peterhofstatt 12, 8001 Zürich. T. (01) 2210239. 064708
Guyer, Annemarie, Auf der Mauer 1, 8001 Zürich. T. (01) 261 33 43. 064709
Haas, Walter, Trittlig 24, 8001 Zürich. T. (01) 2623288, Fax 2616729. - Ant / Furn / Mod - 064710
Häberling, M., Freudenbergstr. 101, 8044 Zürich. T. (01) 362 62 47. - Num - 064711
Hafter, Robert, St. Peterstr 10, 8001 Zürich. T. (01) 2114400, Fax 2118773. - Ant / Paint / Graph / Furn / Orient / Dec / Silv / Lights / Glass / Cur - 064712
Haftmann, Roswitha, Rütistr 28, 8030 Zürich. T. (01) 2512435, Fax 2514519. 064713
Hannibal, St. Jakobstr. 39, 8004 Zürich. T. (01) 242 60 44. 064714
Harper's Shop, Stadelhoferstr. 42, 8001 Zürich. T. (01) 252 89 87. 064715
Hassler-Anderegg, Elisabeth, Kirchgasse 26, 8001 Zürich. T. (01) 2616858. - Ant / Furn / Glass / Cur - 064716
Heinimann, Kirchgasse 17, 8001 Zürich. T. (01) 251 13 68. 064717
Hellman, Monica, Strehlgasse 9, 8001 Zürich. T. (01) 2110131. 064718
Hipp, Wilhelm, Scheideggerstr. 120, 8038 Zürich. T. (01) 482 65 75. 064719
Hofmann & Co., Harry, Bahnhofstr. 87, 8001 Zürich. T. (01) 221 33 93. 064720
Hofmann & Reinhard, Stauffacherquai 56, 8004 Zürich. T. (01) 241 16 32, 241 55 40. - Mil - 064721
Hohl, Marcel, Schaffhauserstr. 248, 8057 Zürich. T. (01) 311 36 00. 064722
Hollinger, Walter, St. Jakobstr. 54, 8004 Zürich. T. (01) 241 02 48. - Ant / Graph / Furn - 064723
Hüsler, Peter, Greblerweg 16, 8047 Zürich. T. (01) 491 09 70. 064724
Hutter, F., Erlachstr. 36, 8003 Zürich. T. (01) 35 84 22. 064725
Ikonen Galerie Sophia, Weggengasse 3, 8001 Zürich. T. (01) 211 25 44, Fax 212 12 90. - Ico - 064726
Ikonengalerie Peter & Paul, Zähringerstr. 28, 8001 Zürich. T. (01) 261 61 28. 064727
Imhof, Postfach 697, 8025 Zürich. T. (01) 462 06 36. - Num - 064728
Immonag, Hohlstr. 415, 8048 Zürich. T. (01) 492 42 52. 064729
Inauen, André, Rotbuchstr. 16, 8006 Zürich. T. (01) 363 14 61. 064730
Insinna, Louis, Bertastr. 4, 8036 Zürich. T. (01) 242 52 69. - Instr - 064731
Iseli-Mooser, M., Kirchgasse 33, 8001 Zürich. T. (01) 261 18 60. 064732
The Jade Dragon, Segantinistr. 35, 8049 Zürich. T. (01) 341 09 53. 064733
Jecklin & Co., Rämistr. 30, 8001 Zürich. T. (01) 261 35 20. 064734
Jent, H.R., Spiegelgasse 26, 8001 Zürich. T. (01) 2610573. - Ant / Cur - 064735
Jezler, Peter W., Kirchgasse 30, 8001 Zürich. T. (077) 973083, Fax (01) 2519181. - Mil - 064736
Kahane, L., Hechtpl. 12, 8001 Zürich. T. (01) 251 67 30. 064737
Kalberer, Paula, Schwamendingerstr. 12, 8051 Zürich. T. (01) 322 03 53. 064738
Karpf, Roland, Kreuzbühlstr. 8, 8008 Zürich. T. (01) 261 76 42. 064739
Keller & Söhne, Eugen, Im Maas 6, 8049 Zürich. T. (01) 341 77 80. 064740
Kempf, Stephan J., Strehlgasse 19, 8001 Zürich. T. (01) 2213830. - Paint / Graph - 064741
Kiener, Martin, Neumarkt 23, 8001 Zürich. T. (01) 2624221 (Antiquitäten), 2624235 (Antiquariat), Fax 2624275. - Ant / Furn / Silv / Lights - 064742
Kluge, Eduard von, Seefeldstr 173, 8008 Zürich. T. (01) 4226389, Fax 4221545. - Ant / Cur - 064743
Kluge, Eduard, Seefeldstr 173, 8008 Zürich. T. (01) 4226389. 064744
Knecht, Karl, Hagenbuchrain 8, 8047 Zürich. T. (01) 492 01 09. 064745

Bedeutendes antikes Silber
des 16. - 18. Jahrhunderts

F. PAYER
Kunsthandel

Pelikanstraße 6, «Felsenhof»
8001 Zürich, Telefon 01/2 21 13 82
Fax 01/2 12 25 13

Knöbel, Albert, Sennhauserweg 9, 8032 Zürich.
T. (01) 251 24 49. *064746*

Knuchel & Kahl, Rämistr. 17, 8024 Zürich.
T. (01) 252 53 53. *064747*

Koenig, Peter, Kreuzpl 5, 8032 Zürich.
T. (01) 2513261. *064748*

Koller, Hardturmstr 102, 8031 Zürich. T. (01) 2730101,
Fax 2731966. - Paint / Orient / Jew - *064749*

Kunchel & Kahl, Rämistr. 17, 8024 Zürich.
T. (01) 252 53 53. *064750*

Kunst Shop Has, Weinbergstr. 15, 8001 Zürich.
T. (01) 252 69 24. *064751*

Kupferstich-Boutique Zum Augustiner, Augustinergasse
52, 8001 Zürich. T. (01) 211 34 20. *064752*

Langer, Wolfgang, Predigerpl 26, 8001 Zürich.
T. (01) 2526950. *064753*

Laube, Dr, Trittligasse 19, 8001 Zürich. T. (01) 2518550,
Fax 2527527. - Graph / Draw - *064754*

Lazertis, Universitätsstr. 21, 8006 Zürich.
T. (01) 261 14 13. *064755*

Leu Numismatik, In Gassen 20, 8001 Zürich.
T. (01) 2114772, Fax 2114686. - Num - *064756*

Limmat, Rämistr. 45, 8001 Zürich.
T. (01) 252 84 33. *064757*

Lotos, K. Egloff, Mühlebachstr 28, 8008 Zürich.
T. (077) 691659. - Orient - *064758*

Lutz, Edmond, Kirchgasse 21, 8001 Zürich.
T. (01) 252 43 36. - Furn - *064759*

Madliger-Schwab, Wohllobgasse 8, 8001 7ürich.
T. (01) 221 06 86. - Ant / Paint - *064760*

Manor House Collection, Kirchgasse 25, 8001 Zürich.
T. (01) 252 05 04. *064761*

Marti, Sonja F., Nelkenstr. 15, 8006 Zürich.
T. (01) 362 86 83. *064762*

von Matt, Hansjakob, Dr, Weinbergstr 20, 8001 Zürich.
T. (01) 2525277. - Sculp / Rel - *064763*

Maurer, Ruth, Münsterstr 14+18, 8001 Zürich.
T. (01) 261 85 00. *064764*

Meissner, Bruno, Bahnhofstr 14, 8001 Zürich.
T. (01) 2103355, Fax 2103357. - Paint - *064765*

Meissner, Kurt, Florastr 1, 8008 Zürich. T. (01) 3835110,
Fax 3836066. - Paint / Draw - *064766*

Merk, Oberdorfstr. 21, 8024 Zürich.
T. (01) 261 11 41. *064767*

Merten-Münzel, Charlotte, Lavaterstr. 46, 8002 Zürich.
T. (01) 202 32 88. - Ant - *064768*

Meyer-Muller, Stampfenbachstr. 6, 8023 Zürich.
T. (01) 251 90 50. *064769*

Monetarium, Bahnhofstr. 89, 8001 Zürich.
T. (01) 333 25 26. *064770*

Müller, Reinhold, Uetlibergstr. 109, 8045 Zürich.
T. (01) 35 12 88. *064771*

Münger, Heinrich, Rindermarkt 11, 8001 Zürich.
T. (01) 252 20 52. *064772*

Muhrer, Angela, Dufourstr. 134, 8008 Zürich.
T. (01) 383 76 66. *064773*

Muralto Wohnungseinrichtungen, Nüschelerstr. 24, Postfach, 8021 Zürich. T. (01) 211 06 70,
Fax 2112611. *064774*

NAAG; Numismatics & Ancient Art Gallery, Glärnischstr
36, 8002 Zürich. T. (01) 202 72 52, Fax 2027258.
- Num / Arch - *064775*

Nido, Attilio, Regensbergstr. 150, 8050 Zürich.
T. (01) 312 06 14. - Instr / Glass - *064776*

Nonvaleurs, Edisonstr. 10, 8050 Zürich.
T. (01) 312 30 97. *064777*

Oehry, Benedicte, Widdergasse 10, 8001 Zürich.
T. (01) 2121290. *064778*

Oettinger, René, Dorfstr. 71, 8126 Zürich.
T. (01) 918 01 21. *064779*

Pantasis, Peter, Tobelhofstr. 355, 8044 Zürich.
T. (01) 821 16 60. *064780*

Payer, Fritz, Pelikanstr 6, Felsenhof, 8001 Zürich.
T. (01) 2211382, Fax 2122513. - Silv - *064781*

Pedrabissi, Anita, Schaffhauserstr. 76, 8057 Zürich.
T. (01) 362 06 82. *064782*

Peyer, Enrico G., Rämistr 45, 8001 Zürich.
T. (01) 2528433. *064783*

Pinkus-Genoss. Antiquariat, Froschaugasse 7, 8001 Zürich. T. (01) 251 26 47. *064784*

Redding, Richard, Strehlgasse 9, 8001 Zürich.
T. (01) 2120014. *064785*

Rhéa Gallery, Zürichbergstr. 26, 8032 Zürich.
T. (01) 252 06 20, Fax 252 06 26. - Ant / Paint / Furn /
China / Arch / Jew / Ico - *064786*

Riedi, Ursula, Torgasse 5, 8001 Zürich. T. (01) 262 35 10.
- China - *064787*

Rigamonti's English Antiques, Birmensdorferstr. 172,
8003 Zürich. T. (01) 462 46 10. *064788*

Ritter, Paul, Seestr. 92, 8002 Zürich.
T. (01) 202 24 08. *064789*

Riz à Porta Domenic, Zeltweg 14, 8032 Zürich.
T. (01) 252 36 02. - Ant - *064790*

Römer, Rämistr 23, 8001 Zürich. T. (01) 2616087,
Fax 2610736. - Paint / Sculp - *064791*

Roth, Willy, Seefeldstr. 18, 8008 Zürich.
T. (01) 252 38 04. *064792*

Rouiller, Maurice, Affolternstr. 180, 8050 Zürich.
T. (01) 311 96 66. *064793*

RR English Antiques, Strehlg. 9, 8001 Zürich.
T. (01) 211 01 31. *064794*

Rüegg, Ernst, Am Wasser 161, 8049 Zürich.
T. (01) 341 65 65. *064795*

Rufini, Hermina, Schipfe 25, 8001 Zürich.
T. (01) 221 06 45. *064796*

Saint James' Gallery, Rämistr. 5, 8001 Zürich.
T. (01) 252 24 25. - Ant / Paint / Graph / Furn / Jew /
Silv / Instr / Glass - *064797*

Saint James' Workshop, Hardpl 21, 8004 Zürich.
T. (01) 4015365, Fax 4015365. - Ant / Paint / Furn /
Repr / Jew / Fra / Silv / Lights / Instr / Glass / Cur / Mul --
064798

S.A.L.D.I., Stadelhoferstr 10, 8001 Zürich.
T. (01) 2626656, Fax 2627033. - Orient / Eth /
Jew - *064799*

Sammelsurium, Rötelstr. 69, 8037 Zürich.
T. (01) 362 65 15. *064800*

Santschi, Alfred, Alfred-Strebel-Weg 15, 8047 Zürich.
T. (01) 492 21 81. *064801*

Schade, Harald, Waaggasse 5, 8001 Zürich.
T. (01) 221 10 42. - Ant / Paint / Furn / Tex / Jew /
Instr - *064802*

Schaerli, Pia-Maria, Spiegelgasse 29, 8001 Zürich.
T. (01) 252 76 43. *064803*

Schaufelberger, Max, Bäckerstr. 35, 8004 Zürich.
T. (01) 242 65 88, Fax 291 17 85. - Mil - *064804*

Schuster & Co., Bahnhofstr. 18, 8022 Zürich.
T. (01) 211 66 03, Fax 212 13 28. - Dec - *064805*

Schweizer, Christophe, Bertastr. 19, 8003 Zürich.
T. (01) 4510051, (01) 3641278. *064806*

Simmermacher, René, Kirchgasse 25, 8024 Zürich.
T. (01) 2525512. - Ant / Paint / Graph / Num / China /
Silv / Glass / Toys - *064807*

Stäbler, Erwin, Mutschellenstr. 46, 8002 Zürich.
T. (01) 201 01 61. *064808*

Stand der Jungen Sammler, Postfach 757, 8037 Zürich.
T. (01) 362 23 00. *064809*

Steiner, Max, Predigergasse 12, 8001 Zürich.
T. (01) 2523949. *064810*

Stendler, Ruth, Nussbaumstr. 12, 8003 Zürich.
T. (01) 461 70 87. *064811*

Sternberg, Frank, Schanzengasse 10, 8001 Zürich.
T. (01) 2523088, Fax 2524067. - Num / Arch - *064812*

Steudler, Ruth, Nussbaumstr. 12, 8003 Zürich.
T. (01) 461 70 87. *064813*

Stiefel, Harry, Neustadtgasse 9, 8001 Zürich.
T. (01) 383 20 39. *064814*

Strassberg, Max, Sonneggstr. 49, 8006 Zürich.
T. (01) 262 03 43. *064815*

Sturzenegger, Alice, Überlandstr 387, 8051 Zürich.
T. (01) 3211914. - Furn - *064816*

Tanner, Robert, Forchstr 19, 8032 Zürich.
T. (01) 3837072. - Instr - *064817*

Tanner, Wilhelmine, Sihlstr. 24, 8001 Zürich.
T. (01) 211 77 64. - Paint - *064818*

Tschümperlin, Josef, Rothstr. 14, 8057 Zürich.
T. (01) 363 87 24. *064819*

Vidal, Bahnhofstr. 31, 8001 Zürich. T. (01) 221 25 73.
- Tex - *064820*

Villa Ulmberg, Thujastr. 14, 8038 Zürich.
T. (01) 481 88 33. *064821*

Vock, Carl, Schipfe 10-16, 8001 Zürich.
T. (01) 2113434. *064822*

Vollmoeller, Heidi, Kurhausstr 17, 8032 Zürich.
T. (01) 2513103, Fax (01) 2514249. - Ant / Orient /
Eth - *064823*

VSAR Sekretariat, Ursula Riedi, Torgasse 5, 8001 Zürich.
T. (01) 2623510. *064824*

Waehry, Toni, Münzpl. 1, 8000 Zürich.
T. (01) 211 56 30. *064825*

Weilemann & Co., Oberdorfstr. 25, 8001 Zürich.
T. (01) 383 34 80. - Ant / Paint / Furn / Silv - *064826*

Weilenmann, André, Wibichstr. 21, 8037 Zürich.
T. (01) 363 47 23. *064827*

Weinberg & Co., Bahnhofstr. 10, 8022 Zürich.
T. (01) 221 36 61. *064828*

Wohngalerie W. Zwahlen, Weinbergstr 145, Postfach,
8006 Zürich. T. (01) 3635515,
Fax (01) 3634383. *064829*

Wolpe, A. & L., Bederstr. 28, 8002 Zürich.
T. (01) 202 91 46. *064830*

Zell, Werner, Zeltweg 12, 8032 Zürich. T. (01) 261 13 30.
- Ant / Paint - *064831*

Ziegler-Ardessi, Loredana, Bahnhofstr 27, 8001 Zürich.
T. (01) 2120606. *064832*

Ziegler, Renée, Rämistr 34, 8001 Zürich.
T. (01) 2512322, Fax 2512546. *064833*

Zoé, Florastr. 32, 8008 Zürich. T. (01) 383 29 88. *064834*

Zug

Antik Galerie, Gotthardstr. 20, 6300 Zug.
T. (041) 711 72 17. - Ant / Graph / Furn / China / Tex /
Jew / Fra / Silv / Lights / Instr / Rel / Glass / Cur / Mod / I-
co - *064835*

Walter Barth Erben, Grabenstr 1a, 6300 Zug.
T. (041) 7114815, Fax 7113324. - Graph - *064836*

Bild & Schmuck, Untere Altstadt 6, 6300 Zug.
T. (041) 710 39 32. *064837*

Brugger, Matthias, Hasenbühlweg 40, Postfach 2279,
6300 Zug. T. (041) 711 46 52. - Num - *064838*

Franklin, Mint, Baarerstr. 12, 6300 Zug.
T. (041) 711 11 06. - Num - *064839*

Koller, Hermann, Baarerstr. 47, 6300 Zug.
T. (041) 711 56 18. *064840*

Trojanowski, Albisstr 7, 6300 Zug. T. (041) 7114818,
Fax 7116392. - Furn - *064841*

Willi, H.J. Erich, Baarerstr. 43, 6300 Zug.
T. (041) 711 53 77. *064842*

Zumikon (Zürich)

Timo-Kunsthandel, Schöntalstr. 3, 8126 Zumikon.
T. (01) 918 04 77. *064843*

Zurzach (Aargau)

Burghalde Antiquitäten, Burghaldenweg 5, 8437 Zurzach. T. (056) 249 20 55. - Ant / Furn - *064844*

Burghalde-Antiquitäten, Burghaldenweg 5, 5330 Zurzach. T. (056) 2492055. *064845*

Zuzwil (Sankt Gallen)

Euw, Norbert von, Stockerstr. 1, 9524 Zuzwil.
T. (071) 9443127, Fax 9442332. - Num - *064846*

Spiess, Herbergstrasse, 9524 Zuzwil.
T. (071) 9441833. *064847*

Zweisimmen (Bern)
Dreyfuss, Lenkstrasse, 3770 Zweisimmen.
T. (033) 7221053. *064848*
Nacht, Ernst, Postfach 366, 3770 Zweisimmen.
T. (033) 7221567. *064849*

Thailand

Bangkok
Angsana, 32/1 Sukhumvit 81 Phra Khanong, Bangkok POB 11-167. *064850*
Art and Antique Centre, River City Shopping Complex, Bangkok. T. 235-2966. - Orient - *064851*
Asia Arts, Yatikon, 1159 New Rd., Bangkok.
T. 233 4184. *064852*
Asian Antiques, 16 19 Siam Square, Bangkok POB 414. *064853*
Chai Ma, 799-801 Silom Rd., Wat Khaek, Bangkok.
T. 236-4390. - Ant / Paint / China - *064854*
Chieng Huat Antique Ltd., Henry Dunant Rd., Bangkok.
T. 252-5265. - Ant / Graph / Mod - *064855*
GoLden Tortoise, Y. Pintaud, 249/l Sukhumvit Soi 49, Bangkok, 10110. T. 391-4983, Fax 216-6527. - Paint / Furn / Orient / Sculp / Dec - *064856*
Hoon, Royal Orchid Sheraton Hotel, Suite 321, Yota Rd., Bangkok, 10100. T. 235-2966. - Orient - *064857*
House of Siam Ltd., 8 Sathorn Nua Rd. 5, Bangkok.
T. 233-2797, 233-4516. - Ant - *064858*
Lotus, 155-157 Rajdamri Rd., Bangkok, 10500.
- Orient - *064859*
Pure Design, 3062 Ruam Rudee Road, Bangkok.
T. 2522338, 2526393. *064860*
Rama Antiques, 981 Silom Road, Bangkok.
T. 2357991. *064861*
Sukhotai Antiques, 975/3 Rajaprasong Rd., Bangkok.
T. 587 00. - Ant - *064862*
Vichitchai Antiques Co. Ltd., 124/33 4 Soi Nakornkasem New Rd., Bangkok. T. 22 55 76. - Ant - *064863*

Chiengmai
Boriscothi Antiques, 406/1 Tapae Road, Chiengmai. *064864*

Tunisia

Tunis
Evangelisti, 48, rue Djemâa-Ez Zitouna, Tunis.
T. 24 31 27. - Num - *064865*

Turkey

Istanbul
Akmucat, Asmalimescit 41, Istanbul.
T. 44 53 05. *064866*
Aseo, Carsil Kebir Sahaflar Sok, 97, Istanbul.
T. 22 73 40. - Ant - *064867*
Aykac Ziya, Kapaliçarsi Takkelicer 66-72, Istanbul.
T. 27 60 82. *064868*
Bardakci, Kapaliçarsi Iç Bedestan 5-7, Serif Aga, Istanbul. T. 527 04 38. *064869*
Bicen, Asmalimescit 42, Tepebasi, Istanbul. T. 49 38 87, 49 88 39. - Ant - *064870*
Karakus Yusuf ve Üzülmez Farac, Sandal Bedesteni sok.
19 Kapalicarsi, Istanbul. T. 27 09 36. - Ant - *064871*
Kazgan, Ali, Kapalicarsi ic Bedesten 26 35, Istanbul.
T. 27 52 56. - Ant / China / Tex / Jew / Silv / Mil - *064872*
Kent, Zincirli 8, Istanbul. T. 27 33 97. *064873*
Kent, Abdullah Ist.-Kapalicarsi, Zincirli Han 7 9, Istanbul.
T. 27 33 97. *064874*
Orient, Bankalar Cad. Bankalar Han Kat 5 No. 37, P.O.Box 176 Sisli, Istanbul. - Ant / Num / Orient / Tex / Arch / Mil - *064875*
Sevsevil, Lüfti, Kapali Carsi Zincirli Han 6, 34440 Istanbul. T. 522 09 77, 527 02 79, 512 75 46. - Ant / Furn / Orient / China / Dec / Lights / Glass - *064876*
Takmaz Yahya, Mucevheratbedestin, Istanbul.
T. 27 63 33. *064877*

Uganda

Kampala
National Handicrafts, 81, Kampala Rd., P.O.Box 7136, Kampala. *064878*

United Kingdom

Abbots Bromley (Staffordshire)
Birchwood Antiques, Bromleys, Bagot St., Abbots Bromley Staffs. T. (01283) 840288. - Ant / Tex - *064879*
Ivy House Antiques, Ivy House, High St., Abbots Bromley Staffs. T. (01283) 840259. - Ant / Furn / China / Glass - *064880*

Aberaeron (Dyfed)
Colectomania, Corner Shop, Albert St., Aberaeron Dyfed.
T. (01545) 597. - Ant / Furn / China - *064881*

Aberdare (Mid Glamorgan)
Market Antiques, Aberdare Market, Aberdare Glam.
T. (01685) 870242. - Ant - *064882*

Aberdeen (Aberdeenshire)
Atholl Antiques, 322 Great Western Rd., Aberdeen AB1 6PL. T. (01224) 593547. - Paint / Furn - *064883*
Benzie, James, 651 George St., Aberdeen AB2 3XQ.
- Ant / Furn / Fra / Jew / Mil - *064884*
Gallery, 41 Justice St., Aberdeen Aberdeens.
T. (01224) 625909. - Paint / Graph / Jew - *064885*
McCalls, 90 King St, Aberdeen Aberdeens.
T. (01224) 641916. - Ant - *064886*
McCalls, 11 Bridge St., Aberdeen Aberdeens.
T. (01224) 584577. - Jew - *064887*
Rendezvous Gallery, 100 Forest Av., Aberdeen Aberdeens. T. (01224) 323247. - Ant / Paint / China / Jew - *064888*
Reynolds, 162-164 Skene St., Aberdeen Aberdeens.
- Ant - *064889*
Thistle Antiques, 28 Esslemont Av., Aberdeen Aberdeens. T. (01224) 643692. - Ant - *064890*
Watt, Elizabeth, 69 Thistle St., Aberdeen Aberdeens.
T. (01224) 647232. - Ant - *064891*
Waverley Gallery, 18 Victoria St., Aberdeen Aberdeens.
T. (01224) 640633. - Paint / Graph - *064892*
Wood, Colin, 25 Rose St., Aberdeen Aberdeens.
T. (01224) 643019. - Paint / Furn / Silv - *064893*
Young Antiques & Fine Art, William, 1 Gaelic Lane, Aberdeen AB1 1JR. T. (01224) 644757. - Ant / Furn - *064894*

Aberfeldy (Perthshire)
Young Antiques, Denis, Glenlyon, Aberfeldy Perts.
T. (01887) 877232. - Paint / China - *064895*

Aberford (Yorkshire)
Aberford Antiques, Hicklam House, Aberford Yorks.
T. (01532) 813209, Fax (01532) 813121. - Ant / Graph / Furn - *064896*

Abergavenny (Gwent)
Close, Henry H., 36 Cross St., Abergavenny Gwent.
T. (01873) 853583. - Furn / China / Glass - *064898*
Lockyer, H.K., 22 Monk St, Abergavenny Gwent.
T. (01873) 855825. - China / Silv - *064898a*

Abersoch (Gwynedd)
Annteaks, Main St., Abersoch Gwynedd.
T. (0175881) 2353. - Furn / China / Silv / Glass - *064899*
Bridge Antiques, Tymawr, Abersoch Gwynedd.
T. (0175881) 2484. - Ant - *064900*

Aberystwyth (Dyfed)
Furniture Cave, 33 Cambrian St., Aberystwyth Dyfed.
T. (01970) 611234. - Furn - *064901*
Howards of Aberystwyth, 10 Alexandra Rd., Aberystwyth SY23 1LE. T. (01970) 624973. - Graph / Furn / China / Silv / Glass - *064902*
Mann Antiques, Chris, Westminster Yard, High St., Aberystwyth Dyfed. - Ant / Instr - *064903*

Abinger Hammer (Surrey)
Abinger Bazaar, Guildford Rd., Abinger Hammer Surrey.
T. (01306) 730756. - China / Silv / Glass - *064904*
Stirling Antiques, Aberdeen House, Abinger Hammer.
T. (01306) 730706. - Furn / China / Jew / Silv / Glass - *064905*

Abridge (Essex)
Abridge Antique Centre, Market Pl., Abridge Essex.
T. (0137881) 311512. - Ant - *064906*

Accrington (Lancashire)
Coin and Jewellery Shop, 129a Blackburn Rd., Accrington Lancs. T. (01254) 384757. - Num / Jew - *064907*

Acle (Norfolk)
Ivy House Antiques, Ivy House, The Street, Acle Norfolk.
T. (01493) 750682. - Paint / Furn / China / Glass - *064908*
Lion Antiques, Old Sale Ring, Cattle Market, Acle Norfolk. T. (01493) 751836. - Furn - *064909*

Acrise (Kent)
Kirby, R., Caroline Cottage, Ridge Row, Acrise Kent.
T. (0130389) 3230. - Furn - *064910*

Addingham (Yorkshire)
Addingham Antiques, 70-72 Main St., Addingham LS29 0PL. T. (01943) 830788. - Paint / Furn / China / Instr - *064911*
Manor Barn, Burnside Mill, Main St., Addingham.
T. (01943) 830176. - Furn - *064912*

Adversane (Sussex)
Antique Centre and Collectors Market, Old House, Adversane Sussex. T. (01403) 783594. - Ant - *064913*

Albrighton (Shropshire)
Doveridge House of Neachley, Long Lane, Albrighton TF11 8PJ. T. (01902) 373131/2. - Furn / Instr - *064914*

Alcester (Warwickshire)
High Street Antiques, 11a High St., Alcester Warks.
T. (01789) 764009. - China / Silv / Glass - *064915*
Malthouse Antiques Centre, Market Pl., Alcester Warks.
T. (01789) 764032. - Paint / Graph / Furn - *064916*

Aldeburgh (Suffolk)
Aldeburgh Galleries, 132 High St., Aldeburgh Suffolk.
T. (01728) 453963. - Ant - *064917*
Guillemot, 134-136 High St., Aldeburgh Suffolk.
T. (01728) 453933. - Furn - *064918*
Mole Hall Antiques, 102-104 High St., Aldeburgh Suffolk. T. (01728) 452361. - Furn - *064919*
Thompson's Gallery, 175 High St., Aldeburgh Suffolk.
T. (01728) 453743. - Paint / Furn - *064920*

Alderley Edge (Cheshire)
Alderley Antiques, 17 London Rd., Alderley Edge SK9 7JT. T. (01625) 584819. - Ant / Paint / Furn / China / Jew - *064921*
Baker Antiques, Anthony, 14 London Rd., Alderley Edge Cheshire. T. (01625) 582674. - Furn / China / Instr / Glass - *064922*
Brook Lane Antiques, 93 Brook Lane, Alderley Edge Cheshire. T. (01625) 582717. - Furn - *064923*
Massey and Son, D.J., 51a London Rd., Alderley Edge Cheshire. T. (01625) 583565. - Jew / Silv - *064924*

Alderney (Alderney)
Victoria Antiques, St. Catherine's, Victoria St., Alderney Channel Islands. T. (0148182) 3260. - Furn / China / Silv / Glass - *064925*

Alford (Aberdeenshire)
Gordon, R.S., Main St., Alford Aberdeens.
T. (019755) 62404. - Ant / Furn / Jew / Instr - *064926*

Alfriston (Sussex)
Alfriston Antiques, The Square, Alfriston Sussex.
T. (01323) 870498. - Paint / Jew / Silv / Instr - *064927*
Radford Antiques, Twytton House, High St., Alfriston Sussex. T. (01323) 870440. - Graph / China / Jew / Mil / Glass - *064928*

Allonby (Cumbria)

Cottage Curios, Main St., Allonby Cumbria.
- Ant -   064929

Alnwick (Northumberland)

Country Pine Antiques, 22 Bailiffgate, Alnwick Northumbs. T. (01665) 603616. - Furn -   064930
Pottergate Antiques, 24 Narrowgate, Alnwick Northumbs. T. (01665) 510034. - Ant -   064931
Robertson, Ian A., Castle Corner, Narrowgate, Alnwick Northumbs. T. (01665) 602725. - Ant / Furn / China / Jew -   064932
Tamblyn, 12 Bondgate Without, Alnwick Northumbs. T. (01665) 603024. - Paint / Furn / China / Glass -   064933

Alresford (Hampshire)

Artemesia, 16 West St., Alresford Hants. T. (01962) 732277. - Furn / China -   064934
Close Antiques, 32 East St., Alresford Hants. T. (01962) 732189. - Furn / Orient / Sculp -   064935
Evans & Evans, 40 West St., Alresford Hants. T. (01962) 732170. - Instr -   064936

Alrewas (Staffordshire)

Poley Antiques, 5 Main St., Alrewas Staffs. T. (01283) 791151. - Ant / Furn / China / Glass - 064937

Alsager (Cheshire)

Trash'n' Treasure, 48 Sandbach Rd., Alsager Cheshire. T. (01270) 872972. - Paint / Furn / China -   064938

Althorne (Essex)

Bailey, John, 5 Austral Way, Althorne Essex. T. (01621) 740279. - Furn / Instr -   064939

Altrincham (Cheshire)

Baron Antiques, 64-66 Manchester Rd, Altrincham Cheshire. T. (0161) 9282943. - Ant -   064940
Halo, 97 Hale Rd., Altrincham Cheshire. T. (0161) 9411800, Fax (0161) 9299565. - Furn -   064941
Halo, 2a Beech Rd., Altrincham Cheshire. - Furn -   064942
New Street Antiques, 48 New St., Altrincham Cheshire. T. (0161) 9284827. - Ant / Furn / China / Silv - 064943
Squires Antiques, 25 Regent Rd, Altrincham Cheshire. T. (0161) 9280749. - Furn / Silv -   064944

Amersham (Buckinghamshire)

Amersham Antiques and Collectors Centre, 20-22 Whielden St., Amersham Bucks. T. (01494) 431282. - Ant -   064945
Cupboard Antiques, 80 High St., Amersham Bucks. T. (01494) 722882. - Furn -   064946
Mon Galerie, Old Forge, Broadway, Amersham Bucks. T. (01494) 661884. - Paint / Graph -   064947
Partridges, 67 High St., Amersham HP7 0DT. T. (01494) 728452. - Ant -   064948
Quilter, Michael, 38 High St., Amersham. T. (01494) 433723. - Furn -   064949
Sundial Antiques, 19 Whielden St., Amersham Bucks. T. (01494) 727955. - Ant / Furn / Orient / Mil - 064950

Ammanford (Dyfed)

Amman Antiques, 29 Station Rd., Ammanford Wales. T. (01269) 592730. - Ant -   064951

Ampthill (Bedfordshire)

Ampthill Antiques, Market Sq., Ampthill Beds. T. (01525) 403344. - Furn / Paint / Jew -   064952
Ampthill Emporium, 6 Bedford St., Ampthill Beds. T. (01525) 402131. - Furn -   064953
Bently Antiques, Pat, 7 Kings Arms Yard, Ampthill Beds. T. (01525) 404939. - Furn -   064954
Harman Antiques, Robert, 11 Church St., Ampthill Beds. T. (01525) 402322. - Furn -   064955
Pine Parlour, 82a Dunstable St., Ampthill Beds. T. (01525) 403030. - Furn -   064956
Roberts Antiques, Ann, 1 Kings Arms Yard, Ampthill Beds. T. (01525) 403394. - Furn / Instr - 064957
Timms Antiques, S. & S., 1618 and 20 Dunstable St, Ampthill Beds. T. (01525) 403067. - Ant / Furn -   064958

Angarrack (Cornwall)

Jennings Antiques, Paul, Millbrook House, Angarrack Cornwall. T. (01736) 754065. - Furn / Instr - 064959

Angmering (West Sussex)

Bygones, The Square, Angmering Sussex West. T. (01903) 786152. - Furn -   064960

Annahilt (Co. Down)

Period Architectural Features and Antiques, 263 Ballynahich Rd, Annahilt N. Ireland. T. (01846) 638091. - Ant -   064961

Antrim (Co. Antrim)

Country Antiques, 219b Lisnevenagh Rd., Antrim N. Ireland. T. (018494) 29498. - Furn / China / Jew - 064962

Ardersier (Highland)

Ardersier Antiques, Ardersier Cottage, Ardersier Scotland. T. (01667) 462237. - Paint -   064963

Ardingly (West Sussex)

Ardingley Antiques, 64 High St., Ardingly. T. (01444) 892680. - Furn / China / Silv / Glass - 064964

Armagh (Co. Armagh)

Hole-in-the-Wall, Market St., Armagh. - Ant -   064965

Arundel (West Sussex)

Armstrong-Davis Gallery, The Square, Arundel Sussex West. T. (01903) 882752. - Sculp -   064966
Baynton-Williams, 37 A High St, Arundel Sussex West. T. (01903) 883588. - Ant -   064967
Country Life by Bursig, 1 Tarrant Sq., Arundel Sussex West. T. (01903) 883456. - Paint / Furn / China -   064968
Davidson, Richard, Romsey House, Arundel Sussex West. T. (01903) 883141, Fax (01903) 883141. - Paint / Furn -   064969
Golding, Pat, 6 Castle Mews, Tarrant St., Arundel Sussex West. - China / Glass -   064970
Lasseters, 8a High St., Arundel Sussex West. T. (01903) 882651. - Jew / Silv -   064971
Mamie's Antiques Centre, 5 River Rd., Arundel Sussex West. T. (01903) 882012. - Ant -   064972
Riverside Gallery and Tearooms, River Rd., Arundel Sussex West. T. (01903) 882921. - Paint / China / Silv / Glass -   064973
Serendipity Antiques, 27 Tarrant St., Arundel Sussex West. T. (01903) 882047. - Paint / Graph - 064974
Sussex Fine Art, 7 Castle Mews, Tarrant St., Arundel Sussex West. T. (01903) 884055. - Paint - 064975
Swaffer, Spencer, 30 High St., Arundel Sussex West. T. (01903) 882132, Fax (01903) 884564. - Furn / Cur -   064976
Tarrant Street Antique Centre, Nineveh House, Tarrant St., Arundel Sussex West. T. (01903) 884307. - Ant -   064977
Treasure House Antiques and Collectors Market, 31b High St., Arundel Sussex West. T. (01903) 507446. - Furn / China / Jew / Silv -   064978
Upstairs Downstairs Antique Centre, 29 Tarrant St., Arundel Sussex West. T. (01903) 883749. - Ant -   064979
Whitehouse Antique Interiors, 4 Tarrant Sq., Arundel Sussex West. T. (01903) 882443. - Furn / China -   064980

Ascott-under-Wychwood (Oxfordshire)

Wychwood Antiques, Four Centuries, London Ln., Ascott-under-Wychwood Oxon. T. (01993) 831571. - Furn -   064981

Ash Priors (Somerset)

Granary Galleries, Court House, Ash Priors Somerset. T. (01823) 432402. - Ant / Furn -   064982
Hall's Antiques, Court House, Ash Priors Somerset. T. (01823) 432402. - Paint / Furn -   064983

Ash Vale (Surrey)

House of Christian Antiques, 5-7 Vale Rd., Ash Vale Surrey. T. (01252) 314478. - Furn -   064984

Ashbourne (Derbyshire)

Adams Antiques, Yvonne, 47 Church St., Ashbourne Derbys. T. (01335) 346466. - Furn -   064985

Ashbourne Fine Art, Agnes Meadow Farm, Offcote, Ashbourne Derbys. T. (01335) 344072. - Paint - 064986
Elsom Antiques, Pamela, 5 Church St., Ashbourne Derbys. T. (01335) 343468. - Ant / Furn / China / Glass -   064987
Manion Antiques, 23 Church St., Ashbourne Derbys. T. (01335) 343207. - Furn / China / Jew / Silv - 064988
Out of Time Antiques, 21 Church St., Ashbourne Derbys. T. (01335) 342096. - Furn / Tex -   064989
Rose Antiques, 37 Church St., Ashbourne Derbys. T. (01335) 343822. - Furn / China / Jew / Silv - 064990
Spurrier-Smith Antiques, 28, 29 and 41 Church St, Ashbourne Derbys. T. (01335) 343669. - Ant / Paint / Furn / China -   064991
Upchurch, Kenneth, 30B Church St, Ashbourne Derbys. T. (01332) 754499. - Furn -   064992

Ashburton (Devon)

Ashburton Marbles, Great Hall, North Street, Ashburton Devon. T. (01364) 53189. - Ant -   064993

Ashby-de-la-Zouch (Leicestershire)

Ivanhoe Antiques, 53 Market St., Ashby-de-la-Zouch Leics. T. (01530) 415424. - Ant / Furn -   064994

Ashtead (Surrey)

Bumbles, 90 The Street, Ashtead Surrey. T. (01372) 276219. - Furn -   064995
Memory Lane Antiques, 102 The Street, Ashtead Surrey. T. (01372) 273436. - Ant -   064996
Temptations, 88 The Street, Ashtead Surrey. T. (01372) 277713. - Jew / Silv -   064997

Ashton-under-Lyne (Lancashire)

Kenworthys, 226 Stamford St., Ashton-under-Lyne OI6 7LW. T. (0161) 330 30 43. - Jew / Silv - 064998

Askham (Nottinghamshire)

Mitchell Fine Arts, Sally, Thornlea, Askham NG22 0RN. T. (0177) 783234. - Paint / Graph -   064999

Aslockton (Nottinghamshire)

Neville Gallery, Jane, Elm House, Abbey Lane, Aslockton Notts. T. (01949) 50220. - Paint -   065000

Astwood Bank (Hereford and Worcester)

Bracebridge Gallery, 49 The Ridgeway, Astwood Bank Herefs & Worcs. T. (01527) 893557. - Paint - 065001

Atcham (Shropshire)

Mytton Antiques, Norton Cross Rd., Atcham Shrops. T. (01952) 86229. - Ant / Instr -   065002

Atherton (Greater Manchester)

Victoria's, 144/146 Bolton Rd, Atherton Lancs. T. (01942) 882311. - Ant / Furn -   065003

Attleborough (Norfolk)

Bush & Partners, A. E., Vineyards Antiques Gallery, Leys Lane, Attleborough Norfolk. T. (01953) 454239. - Furn -   065004

Atworth (Wiltshire)

Campbell, Peter, 59 Bath Rd, Atworth Wilts. T. (01225) 709742. - Ant -   065005

Auchterarder (Tayside)

Hayes Gallery, Paul, 71 High St., Auchterarder Scotland. T. (01764) 662320. - Paint -   065006
Stanley & Son, K., Regal Bldg Townhead, Auchterarder Scotland. - Ant / Furn / China / Tex -   065007
Times Past Antiques, Broadfold Farm, Auchterarder Scotland. T. (01764) 663166. - Furn -   065008
Whitelaw & Sons, John, 120 High St., Auchterarder. T. (01764) 662482. - Ant / Furn -   065009

Auldearn (Highland)

Auldearn Antiques, Dalmore Manse, Lethen Rd., Auldearn Scotland. T. (01667) 53087. - Furn / China / Tex -   065010

Avening (Gloucestershire)

Upton Lodge Galleries, Avening House, Avening Glos. T. (0145) 383. - Paint -   065011

Axbridge (Somerset)
Old Post House, Weare, Bridgewater Rd., Axbridge Somerset. T. (01934) 732372. - Ant / Furn -　　065012

Axminster (Devon)
Potter & Son, W. G., West St., Axminster Devon.
T. (01297) 32063. - Furn / Instr -　　065013

Aylesbury (Buckinghamshire)
Harvey Antiques, Morton, 21 Wendover Rd., Aylesbury Bucks. T. (01296) 84307. - Ant / Paint / Furn -　　065014

Aylsham (Norfolk)
Pearse Lukies, Bayfield House, White Hart St., Aylsham Norfolk. T. (01263) 734137. - Furn -　　065015

Ayr (Strathclyde)
Antiques, 39 New Rd., Ayr Scotland. T. (01292) 265346.
- Ant -　　065016
Old Curiosity Shop, 27 Crown St., Ayr Scotland.
T. (01292) 280222. - Paint / Furn -　　065017

Bagillt (CLwyd)
Mayfair Antiques, Green Park House, Green Park, High St., Bagillt Wales. T. (01352) 711891. - Ant -　　065018

Bakewell (Derbyshire)
Beedham Antiques, Holme Hall, Bakewell Derbys.
T. (01629) 813285. - Furn -　　065019
Chappell Antiques and Fine Art, K., King St., Bakewell DE4 1DZ. T. (01629) 812496, Fax (01629) 814531.
- Ant / Furn / China -　　065020
Goldstone, Michael, Avenel Court, Bakewell Derbys.
T. (01629) 812487. - Furn -　　065021
Harper, Martin & Dorothy, King St., Bakewell Derbys.
T. (01629) 814757. - Furn / Glass -　　065022
Water Lane Antiques, Water Lane, Bakewell Derbys.
T. (01629) 814161. - Furn -　　065023

Balcombe (West Sussex)
Pine and Design, Haywards Heath Rd., Balcombe Sussex West. T. (01444) 811700. - Furn / Eth -　　065024
Woodall & Emery, Haywards Heath Rd., Balcombe Sussex West. T. (01444) 811608. - Ant -　　065025

Baldock (Hertfordshire)
Attic, 20 Whitehorse St., Baldock Herts.
T. (01462) 893880. - Furn -　　065026
Butt Antiques, Anthony, 7/9 Church St, Baldock Herts.
T. (01462) 895272. - Furn -　　065027
Howards, 33 Whitehorse St., Baldock Herts.
T. (01462) 892385. - Instr -　　065028
Moss, Ralph & Bruce, 26 Whitehorse St., Baldock SG7 6QB. T. (01462) 892751. - Ant / Furn -　　065029
Porter, Arthur, 31 Whitehorse St., Baldock Herts.
T. (01462) 895351. - Furn -　　065030
Wheelwright, 1 Mansfield Rd., Baldock Herts.
T. (01462) 893876. - Furn / China / Jew -　　065031

Balfron (Central)
Amphora Galleries, 16-20 Buchanan St., Balfron G63 0TT. T. (01360) 40329. - Ant / Furn -　　065032

Ballater (Grampian)
McEwan Gallery, Bridge of Gairn, Ballater Scotland.
T. (013397) 55429, Fax 55995. - Paint / Graph -　065033

Ballyclare (Co. Antrim)
Antique Shop, 64a Main St., Ballyclare N. Ireland.
T. (019603) 52550. - Furn / China / Instr / Glass -　　065034

Bampton (Devon)
Bampton Antiques, 9 Castle St., Bampton Devon.
T. (01398) 331658. - Furn / China / Glass -　　065035
Byles, Robert, 7 Castle St., Bampton Devon.
T. (01398) 331515. - Ant / Furn -　　065036

Bampton (Oxfordshire)
John Antiques, Angela, Market Sq, Bampton Oxon.
T. (01993) 772448. - Furn / China / Glass -　　065037

Banbridge (Co. Down)
Cameo Antiques, 41 Bridge St., Banbridge N. Ireland.
T. (018206) 23241. - Ant -　　065038

Banbury (Oxfordshire)
Vedmore Furniture and Antiques, Judy, 42 Parson's St., Banbury Oxon. T. (01295) 269626. - Furn -　　065039

Banchory (Grampian)
Bell of Aberdeen, John, 26 High St., Banchory Scotland.
T. (013302) 5676. - Furn -　　065040
Bygones, 6 Dee St., Banchory Scotland.
T. (013302) 3095. - Ant / Furn -　　065041

Bangor (Gwynedd)
Wellfield Antique Centre, Wellfield Court, Bangor Wales.
T. (01248) 361360. - Ant -　　065042
Windsor Gallery, David, 201 High St., Bangor Wales.
T. (01248) 364639. - Paint / Graph -　　065043

Bankfoot (Tayside)
Antiques and Bygones, Tighvallich, Dunkeld Rd., Bankfoot Scotland. T. (01738) 87452. - Lights -　　065044

Barkham (Berkshire)
Barkham Antique and Craft Centre, Barkham St., Barkham Berks. T. (01734) 761355. - Furn -　　065045
David, John E., Edneys Hill Farm, Edneys Hill, Barkham Berks. T. (01734) 783181. - Ant -　　065046

Barmouth (Gwynedd)
Aspley Antiques and Reproductions, Llanaber Rd, Barmouth Wales. T. (01341) 281057. - Furn -　　065047

Barnard Castle (Durham)
Collector, Douglas House, The Bank, Barnard Castle Durham. T. (01833) 37783. - Paint / Furn / Silv -　　065048
Town House Antiques, 7 Newgate, Barnard Castle Durham. T. (01833) 37021. - Furn -　　065049

Barnet (Greater London)
Bellinger, Carl, 91 Wood St., Barnet Herts.
T. (0181) 449 3467. - Ant / Furn -　　065050

Barnoldswick (Lancashire)
Bunn, Roy W., 34/36 Church St, Barnoldswick BB8 5UT.
T. (01282) 813703. - China -　　065051

Barnsley (Gloucestershire)
Denzil Verey, Barnsley House, Barnsley GL7 5EE.
T. (01285) 740402. - Furn -　　065052

Barnsley (South Yorkshire)
Charisma Antiques Trade Warehouse, Market St, Hoyland, Barnsley Yorks South. T. (01226) 747599. - Ant / Paint / Furn -　　065053
Simmons, Christine, Saint Pauls former Methodist Chapel, Market St., Hoyland, Barnsley Yorks South.
T. (01226) 747599. - Paint -　　065054

Barnstaple (Devon)
Artavia Gallery, 80 Boutport St., Barnstaple Devon.
T. (01271) 71025. - Paint / Graph / Pho -　　065055
Nostalgia, 48B Bear St, Barnstaple Devon.
T. (01271) 73751. - Furn / China / Tex / Glass -　065056
Parkhouse Antiques and Jewellery, Mark, 106 High St., Barnstaple Devon. T. (01271) 74504. - Paint / Furn / China / Instr / Glass -　　065057

Barnt Green (Hereford and Worcester)
Barnt Green Antiques, 93 Hewell Rd., Barnt Green B45 8NE. T. (0121) 445 4942. - Furn -　　065058

Barrhead (Strathclyde)
C.P.R. Antiques and Services, 96 Main St., Barrhead Scotland. T. (0141) 881 5379. - Ant / Furn -　　065059

Barrington (Somerset)
Stuart Interiors, Barrington Court, Barrington TA19 0NQ.
T. (01460) 40349. - Furn -　　065060

Barrow-in-Furness (Cumbria)
Antiques, 237 Rawlinson St, Barrow-in-Furness Cumbria. T. (01229) 823432. - Paint / Furn / Jew / Silv / Instr -　　065061

Barry (Tayside)
Hwkins Bros. Antiques, 5 Romily Bldgs Roodham Rd, Barry Wales. T. (01446) 746561. - Ant -　　065062
Irena Art and Antiques, 111 Broad St., Barry Wales.
T. (01446) 747626. - Ant / Furn / China / Glass -　065063

Barton (Cheshire)
Rayment Antiques, Derek, Orchard House, Barton Rd., Barton Cheshire. T. (01829) 270429. - Instr　　065064

Barton-upon-Humber (Humberside)
Streetwalker Antiques, Brigg Rd., Barton-upon-Humber Humberside South. T. (01652) 660050. - Ant / Furn -　　065065
Streetwalker Antiques, 35 High St., Barton-upon-Humber Humberside South. T. (01652) 33960.
- Ant -　　065066

Basingstoke (Hampshire)
Squirrel Collectors Centre, 9 New St., Basingstoke Hants. T. (01256) 464885. - Jew / Silv -　　065067

Baslow (Derbyshire)
Westfield Antiques, Rigel, Church View Dr., Baslow Derbys. T. (01246) 582386. - Orient / China -　　065068

Bath (Avon)
Abbey Galleries, 9 Abbey Churchyard, Bath Avon.
T. (01225) 460565. - Jew / Silv -　　065069
Adam Gallery, 13 John St., Bath Avon.
T. (01225) 480406. - Paint -　　065070
Alderson, 23 Brock St., Bath BA1 2LW.
T. (01225) 421652. - Furn / Silv / Glass -　　065071
Antique Linens and Lace, 11 Pulteney Bridge, Bath Avon. T. (01225) 465782. - Tex -　　065072
Arkea Antiques, 10 Monmouth Pl, Bath Avon.
T. (01225) 429413. - China / Silv / Instr -　　065073
Baines of Bath, G. and J., 14-15 John St., Bath Avon.
T. (01225) 332566. - Furn -　　065074
Bartlett Street Antique Centre, 5-10 Bartlett St, Bath Avon. T. (01225) 310457. - Ant -　　065075
Bath Antiques Market, Guinea Lane off Lansdow Rd, Bath Avon. T. (01225) 337638, Fax (01225) 422510.
- Ant -　　065076
Bath Galleries, 33 Broad Street, Bath Avon.
T. (01225) 462946. - Paint / Furn / Jew / Silv -　065077
Bath Saturday Antiques Market, Walcot St., Bath Avon.
T. (01225) 317 837. - Ant -　　065078
Bath Stamp and Coin Shop, Pulteney Bridge, Bath Avon.
- Num -　　065079
Beau Nash House Antiques, Beau Nash House, Union Passage, Bath Avon. T. (01225) 447806. - Paint / Furn -　　065080
Bladud House Antiques, 8 Bladud Bldgs., Bath Avon.
T. (01225) 462929. - Jew -　　065081
Blyth Antiques, 28 Sydney Bldgs., Bath Avon.
T. (01225) 469766. - Furn -　　065082
Brass & Sons, Lawrence, 93-95 Walcot St., Bath Avon.
T. (01225) 464057. - Furn -　　065083
Breeze & Behan, 6 George St., Bath Avon.
T. (01225) 466499. - Furn -　　065084
Bryers Antiques, 12a Manvers Street, Bath Avon.
T. (01225) 460535. - Furn / China / Dec / Glass -　　065085
Casemate, 12 Bartlett St., Bath Avon.
T. (01225) 465142. - Ant -　　065086
Cooper, Sheila, 7-10 Bartlett St., Bath Avon.
T. (01225) 442730. - Ant -　　065087
Craik, Brian and Caroline, 8 Margret's Bldgs., Bath Avon.
T. (01225) 33 7161. - Ant / Paint / Dec -　　065088
Croft, John, 3 George St., Bath BA1 2EH.
T. (01225) 466211. - Paint / Furn / Instr -　　065089
Dando, Andrew, 4 Wood St., Bath BA1 2JQ.
T. (01225) 422702. - Ant / Furn / China -　　065090
Dickinson, D. and B., 22 New Bond St., Bath BA1 1BA.
T. (01225) 466502. - Jew / Silv -　　065091
Dodge Interiors, Martin, 15-16 Broad St., Bath Avon.
T. (01225) 462202. - Paint / Furn -　　065092
Dollin & Daines, 2 Church St., Bath Avon.
T. (01225) 462752. - Music -　　065093
Dryden, Peter, 2 Prince's Buildings, George St, Bath Avon. T. (01225) 423038. - Furn -　　065094
Dux Antiques, Frank, 33 Belvedere, Lansdown Rd., Bath Avon. T. (01225) 312367. - Furn / Glass / Dec -　065095
Emm, Anthony, York St., Bath BA1 1NH.
T. (01225) 447992. - Furn / Orient -　　065096
Galleon, 33 Monmouth St., Bath BA1 2AN.
T. (01225) 312330. - Furn / Jew / Silv -　　065097
Gibson, David, 4 Wood St, Queen Sq, Bath BA1 6QB.
T. (01225) 446646. - Instr -　　065098

Graylow & Co., George St., Bath Avon.
T. (01225) 469859, Fax (01272) 215405.
- Furn - *065099*
Great Western Antique Centre, Bartlett St., Bath BA1
2QZ. T. (01225) 424243. - Ant / Paint / Furn / Orient /
China / Tex / Eth / Jew / Silv / Lights / Instr / Mil / Glass /
Cur - *065100*
Gregory, George, Manvers St, Bath BA1 1JW.
T. (01225) 466055. *065101*
Haliden Oriental Rug Shop, 98 Walcot St., Bath Avon.
T. (01225) 469240. - Tex / Paint / China - *065102*
Hood & Co, Helma, 3 Margarets Bldgs., Brock St., Bath
BA1 2LP. T. (01225) 424438. - Paint / Graph / Furn /
China - *065103*
Jadis, 17 Walcot Bldgs., London Rd., Bath Avon.
T. (01225) 338797, Fax (01225) 338797.
- Furn - *065104*
Jones, Orlando, 10b Monmouth Pl., Bath Avon.
T. (01225) 422750. - Ant - *065105*
King, Ann, 38 Belvedere, Lansdown Rd., Bath Avon.
T. (01225) 336245. - Tex - *065106*
Kingsley Gallery, 16 Margarets Bldgs., Brock St., Bath
Avon. T. (01225) 448432. - Ant - *065107*
Lansdown Antiques, 23 Belvedere, Lansdown Rd., Bath
Avon. T. (01225) 313417. - Furn - *065108*
Linford, Carr, 10-11 Walcot Bldgs., London Rd., Bath
Avon. T. (01225) 317516. - Furn - *065109*
Mallory & Sons, E. P., 1-4 Bridge St and 5 Old Bond St,
Bath BA2 4AP. T. (01225) 465885. - Jew / Silv - *065110*
No. 12 Queen Street, 12 Queen St., Bath Avon.
T. (01225) 462363. - Furn / Tex - *065111*
Paragon Antiques and Collectors Market, 3 Bladud
Bldgs., Paragon, Bath Avon. T. (01225) 463715.
- Ant - *065112*
Pennard House Antiques, 3-4 Piccadilly, London Rd.,
Bath Avon. T. (01225) 313791, Fax (01225) 448196.
- Furn - *065113*
Quiet Street Antiques, 3 Quiet St., Bath Avon.
T. (01225) 315727. - Ant / Furn / China - *065114*
Rainsford, P. R., 23a Manvers St., Bath Avon.
T. (01225) 445107. - Ant - *065115*
Robinson, T. E., 3-4 Bartlett St., Bath BA1 2OZ.
T. (01225) 463982. - Ant / Furn / Glass - *065116*
Sainsbury, M., 35 Gay St., Bath BA1 2NT.
T. (01225) 424808. - Ant / Paint / Silv - *065117*
Saville Row Gallery, 1 Saville Row, Bath Avon.
T. (01225) 334595. - Paint / Sculp - *065118*
Scott Antiques, 11 London St., Bath Avon.
T. (01225) 462423. - Ant - *065119*
Susannah, 142/144 Walcot St, Bath Avon.
T. (01225) 445069. - Ant / Tex - *065120*
Town and Country Antiques, 11 Queen St., Bath Avon.
T. (01225) 463176. - Furn - *065121*
Trimbridge Galleries, 2 Trimbridge, Bath Avon.
T. (01225) 466390. - Paint / Graph - *065122*
Walcot Reclamation, 108 Walcot St., Bath Avon.
T. (01225) 444404. - Ant - *065123*
Wallis and Mosdell, Glenda and Gerry, 6 Chapel Row,
Queen Sq, Bath Avon. T. (01225) 424677.
- Ant - *065124*
Widcombe Antiques and Pine, 9 Claverton Bldgs. Wid-
combe, Bath Avon. T. (01225) 428767. - Furn - *065125*

Battle (East Sussex)
Magpie Antiques, 38 Mount St., Battle Sussex East.
T. (01424) 772194. - Ant - *065126*

Battlesbridge (Essex)
Battlesbridge Antique Centre, A130 mid-way between
Chelmsford and Southend, Battlesbridge Essex.
- Ant - *065127*
Cromwell House Antique Centre, Cromwell House, Batt-
lesbridge Essex. T. (01268) 734005. - Ant - *065128*
Haybarn and Bridgebarn Antique Centres, Battlesbridge
Essex. T. (01268) 763500, 735884. - Ant - *065129*
Muggeridge Farm Warehouse, Battlesbridge Essex.
T. (01268) 769392. - Ant - *065130*
Old Granary Antique and Craft Centre, Battlesbridge Es-
sex. T. (01268) 763344. - Ant - *065131*

Bawdeswell (Norfolk)
Norfolk Polyphon Centre, Wood Farm, Bawdeswell Norfolk. T. (0136) 288230. - Instr / Music - *065132*

Bawtry (South Yorkshire)
Swan Antiques, 4 Swan St., Bawtry Yorks South.
T. (01302) 710301. - Furn / China / Silv / Glass - *065133*
Treasure House Antiques Centre, 4-10 Swan St., Bawtry
Yorks South. T. (01302) 710621. - Ant / Furn / China /
Silv - *065134*
Wilson, Timothy D., Grove House, Wharf St., Bawtry
Yorks South. T. (01302) 710040. - Ant / Furn - *065135*

Beaconsfield (Buckinghamshire)
Cole (Fine Paintings), Christopher, 1 London End, Be-
aconsfield Bucks. T. (01494) 671274. - Paint - *065136*
Elsworth – Beaconsfield, June, 16 London End, Be-
aconsfield Bucks. T. (01494) 675611, Fax 671273.
- Furn / Silv - *065137*
Grosvenor House Interiors, 51 Wycombe End, Beacons-
field HP9 1LX. T. (01494) 677498. - Furn - *065138*
Norton Antiques, 56 London End, Beaconsfield HP9 2JH.
T. (01494) 673674. - Ant / Paint / Furn - *065139*
Old Curiosity Shop, 47-49 Wycombe End, Beaconsfield
Bucks. T. (01494) 674473. - Ant / Furn - *065140*
Period Furniture Showrooms, 49 London End, Beacons-
field Bucks. T. (01494) 674112. - Furn - *065141*
Spinning Wheel, 86 London End, Beaconsfield.
T. (01494) 673055. - Ant / Furn / China / Glass - *065142*

Beaminster (Dorset)
Beaminster Antiques, 4 Church St., Beaminster Dorset.
T. (01308) 862591. - Paint / Furn / China / Jew - *065143*
Cottage Antiques, 17 The Square, Beaminster Dorset.
T. (01308) 862136. - Paint / Graph / Furn /
Instr - *065144*
Good Hope Antiques, 2 Hogshill St., Beaminster Dorset.
T. (01308) 862119. - Furn / Instr - *065145*
Hennessy, Daniels House, Hogshill St., Beaminster Dor-
set. T. (01308) 862635. - Furn - *065146*

Beaulieu (Hampshire)
Beaulieu Fine Arts, Malt House, High St., Beaulieu
Hants. T. (01590) 612089. - Paint / Graph /
Draw - *065147*

Beauly (Highland)
Marr Antiques, Iain, 3 Mid St., Beauly IV4 7DP.
T. (01463) 782372. - Paint / Furn / China / Silv /
Instr - *065148*

Beaumaris (Gwynedd)
Castle Antiques, 13 Church St., Beaumaris Wales.
T. (01248) 810474. - Ant / Graph / Furn - *065149*
Museum of Childhood, 1 Castle St, Beaumaris Wales.
T. (01248) 712498. - Ant / Toys - *065150*

Beccles (Suffolk)
Saltgate Antiques, 11 Saltgate, Beccles Suffolk.
T. (01502) 712776. - Furn / Instr - *065151*
Waveney Antiques Centre, Peddars Lane, Beccles Suf-
folk. T. (01502) 716147. - Ant / Furn / Jew /
Silv - *065152*

Beckenham (Greater London)
Beckenham Antique Market, Old Council Hall, Bromley
Rd., Beckenham Kent. T. (0181) 7776300.
- Ant - *065153*
Horton's, 428 Croydon Rd., Beckenham Kent.
T. (0181) 6586418. - Paint / Furn / Jew / Silv - *065154*
Pepys Antiques, 9 Kelsey Park Rd, Beckenham Kent.
T. (0181) 650 0994. - Ant / Paint / Furn / China /
Silv - *065155*
Scallywag, 22 High St., Beckenham BR3 1AY.
T. (0181) 658 6633. - Ant - *065156*
Witham, Norman, 2 High St., Beckenham Kent.
T. (0181) 650 4651. - Ant / Furn / China / Glass - *065157*

Bedale (North Yorkshire)
Thornton Gallery, Snape, Bedale Yorks North.
T. (01677) 70318. - Paint - *065158*

Bedford (Bedfordshire)
Stapleton's Antiques, 51 Ford End Rd., Bedford Beds.
T. (01234) 211087. - Ant / Furn / Instr - *065159*

Bedingfield (Suffolk)
Olde Red Lion, The Street, Bedingfield Suffolk.
T. (0172876) 491. - Ant / Furn - *065160*

Beeston (Nottinghamshire)
Bailey, Elizabeth, 33 Chilwell Rd., Beeston Notts.
T. (01602) 255685. - Ant / Furn - *065161*

Belfast (Co. Antrim)
Bell Gallery, 13 Adelaide Park, Belfast.
T. (01232) 662998. - Paint - *065162*
Kearney & Sons, T. H., 123 University St., Belfast.
T. (01232) 231055. - Ant - *065163*
Lambe, Charlotte and John, 41 Shore Rd., Belfast.
T. (01232) 370761. - Paint / Graph / Furn - *065164*
Sinclair's Antique Gallery, 19 Arthur St., Belfast.
T. (01232) 322335. - Num / Jew / Glass - *065165*

Belper (Derbyshire)
Sweetings (Antiques 'n' Things), 1-1a The Butts, Belper
Derbys. T. (01773) 825930. - Furn - *065166*
Wayne "Le Razov Man", Neil, 72 Bridge St., Belper Der-
bys. T. (01773) 827910, Fax 825662. - Instr - *065167*

Bembridge (Isle of Wight)
Solent Antiques, 1 Dennett Rd., Bembridge i. of Wight.
T. (01983) 872107. - Furn / Instr - *065168*
Windmill Antiques, 1 Foreland Rd., Bembridge i. of
Wight. T. (01983) 873666. - Furn / China / Jew /
Silv - *065169*

Bentley Heath (West Midlands)
Widdas Fine Paintings, Roger, 7 Bullivents Close, Be-
ntley Heath West Mids. T. (01564) 773217. - Paint /
Draw - *065170*

Berkeley (Gloucestershire)
Antique Shop, 11 High St., Berkeley Glos.
T. (01453) 811085. - Paint / Furn / China /
Glass - *065171*
Berkeley Market, Berkeley Glos. T. (01453) 511032.
- Ant - *065172*

Berkhamsted (Hertfordshire)
Park Street Antiques, 350 High St., Berkhamsted HP4
1HT. T. (01442) 864790, Fax 864790. - Ant / Furn /
Instr - *065173*

Berry Hill (Gloucestershire)
Forest Antiques, Dean, Corner House, Berry Hill Glos.
T. (01594) 833211. - Paint / Furn / China - *065174*

Berwick-on-Tweed (Northumberland)
Castlegate Antiques, 83 Castlegate, Berwick-on-Tweed
Northumbs. T. (01289) 306009. - Ant / Furn /
Instr - *065175*
Treasure Chest, 43 Bridge St., Berwick-on-Tweed Nor-
thumbs. T. (01289) 307738. - Furn / China / Silv /
Glass - *065176*

Betley (Staffordshire)
Betley Court Gallery, Main Rd., Betley Staffs.
T. (01270) 820652. - Paint / Graph / Furn - *065177*

Beverley (Humberside)
Hawley Antiques, 5 North Bar Within, Beverley HU17
8AP. T. (01482) 868193. - Ant / Paint / Furn / China /
Silv - *065178*
Ladygate Antiques, 8 Ladygate, Beverley Humberside
North. T. (01482) 881494. - Ant / Furn / Instr - *065179*
Starkey Galleries, James H., 49 Highgate, Beverley
HU17 9QN. T. (01482) 881179, Fax 861644. - Paint /
Graph / Draw - *065180*
Well Lane Antiques, 10 Well Lane, Beverley Humberside
North. T. (01482) 882868. - Ant - *065181*

Bewdley (Hereford and Worcester)
Ma's Antiques, 89 Welch Gate, Bewdley Merefs &
Worcs. T. (01299) 403845. - Instr - *065182*

Bexhill-on-Sea (East Sussex)
Barclay Antiques, 7 Village Mews, Little Common, Be-
xhill-on-Sea Sussex East. T. (01797) 222734. - Paint /
Furn / China / Glass - *065183*
Bexhill Antique Exporters, 56 Turkey Rd, and Quakers
Mill, Bexhill-on-Sea Sussex East. T. (01424) 210182.
- Furn - *065184*
Old Mint House, 45 Turkey Rd., Bexhill-on-Sea Sussex
East. T. (01323) 762337, Fax (01323) 762337. - Furn /
Naut - *065185*

Springfield Antiques, 127 Ninfield Rd., Bexhill-on-Sea Sussex East. T. (01424) 211225. - Paint / Furn / China / Silv - 065186

Stewart Gallery, 48 Devonshire Rd., Bexhill-on-Sea Sussex East. T. (01424) 223410. - Paint / China / Glass - 065187

Village Antiques, 17 Village Mews, Little Common, Bexhill-on-Sea Sussex East. T. (01424) 772035. - Furn - 065188

Bexley (Greater London)

Argentum Antiques, 18-20 High St., Bexley Kent. T. (01322) 527915. - Paint / Furn / China / Jew / Silv / Instr - 065189

Bicester (Oxfordshire)

Barn, Crumps Butts, off Bell Lane, Bicester Oxon. T. (01869) 252958. - Furn - 065190

Lissetter of Bicester, 3 Kings End, Bicester OX6 7DR. T. (01869) 252402. - Ant / Furn - 065191

Bickerstaffe (Lancashire)

Webster, E. W., Wash Farm, Rainford Rd., Bickerstaffe Lancs. T. (01695) 24326. - Furn - 065192

Biddenden (Kent)

Two Maids Antiques, 6 High St., Biddenden Kent. T. (01580) 291807. - Paint / Furn - 065193

Bideford (Devon)

Acorn Antiques, 11 Rope Walk, Bideford Devon. T. (01237) 470177. - Furn - 065194

Collins & Son, J., 63 High St and 28 High St, Bideford EX39 2AN. T. (01237) 473103, Fax 475658. - Paint / Furn - 065195

Medina Gallery, 20 Mill St., Bideford Devon. T. (01237) 476483. - Paint / Graph / Pho - 065196

Petticombe Manor Antiques, Petticombe Manor, Monkleigh, Bideford Devon. T. (01237) 475605. - Paint / Graph / Furn / China / Glass - 065197

Red House Antiques, 25-26 Bridgeland St., Bideford Devon. T. (01237) 470686. - Furn - 065198

Riverside Antiques, Market Pl., Bideford Devon. T. (01237) 471043. - Ant / China - 065199

Scudders, Emporium, Bridge St., Bideford Devon. T. (01237) 479567. - Ant - 065200

Bidford-on-Avon (Warwickshire)

Antiques Centre, High St., Bidford-on-Avon Warks. T. (01789) 773680. - Ant / Furn / Jew - 065201

Crown Antiques, 14 High St., Bidford-on-Avon Warks. T. (01789) 772939. - Ant / Furn - 065202

Biggleswade (Bedfordshire)

Shortmead Antiques, 46 Shortmead St., Biggleswade Beds. T. (01767) 601780. - Ant / Furn / China - 065203

Billingham (Cleveland)

Bedi Antiques, Margaret, 5 Station Rd., Billingham Cleveland. T. (01642) 782346. - Paint / Furn - 065204

Bingham (Nottinghamshire)

Cheshire, E. M., Manor House, Market Pl., Bingham Notts. T. (01949) 838861. - Furn - 065205

Bingley (West Yorkshire)

Bingley Antiques Centre, Keighley Rd., Bingley York West. T. (01274) 567316. - Furn / China - 065206

Carrol, E., 5 Ryshworth Hall, Keighley Rd. Crossflatts, Bingley Yorks West. T. (01274) 568800. - Paint - 065207

Curio Cottage, 3 Millgate, Bingley Yorks West. T. (01274) 612975. - Furn - 065208

Victorian House Shop, 88 Main St., Bingley Yorks West. T. (01274) 569278. - Ant - 065209

Birchington (Kent)

Chawner, John, 36 Station Approach, Birchington Kent. T. (01843) 43309. - Instr - 065210

Birdbrook (Essex)

Westrope, I., The Elms, Birdbrook Essex. T. (0144085) 365. - Ant / Furn / China - 065211

Birkenhead (Merseyside)

Bodhouse Antiques, 379 New Chester Rd., Birkenhead Merseyside. T. (0151) 644 9494. - Paint / Graph / Furn / China / Silv - 065212

Courtney, William, Tunnel Entrance, Cross St, Birkenhead Merseyside. T. (0151) 647 8693. - Ant - 065213

Rose Mount, 2 Rose Mount, Birkenhead Merseyside. T. (0151) 653 9060. - Ant - 065214

Birmingham (West Midlands)

Always Antiques, 285 Vicarage Rd., Kings Heath, Birmingham West Mids. T. (0121) 444 8701. - Furn / Tex / Toys - 065215

Architectural Antiques of Moseley, 23 A Saint Mary's Row, Moseley, Birmingham West Mids. T. (0121) 442 4546. - Ant - 065216

Archives, 496 Bristol Rd., Selly Oak, Birmingham West Mids. T. (0121) 472 4026. - Furn / Instr - 065217

Asbury Antiques, Peter, 162 Vicarage Rd., Langley, Birmingham West Mids. T. (0121) 552 1702. - Ant - 065218

Ashleigh House Antiques, 5 Westbourne Rd., Birmingham West Mids. T. (0121) 454 6283. - Paint / Furn / Instr - 065219

Cameo, 4 Lonsdale Rd., Harborne, Birmingham West Mids. T. (0121) 426 6900. - Ant / China - 065220

Carleton Gallery, 91 Vivian Rd., Harborne, Birmingham West Mids. T. (0121) 427 2487. - Graph - 065221

Chesterfield Antiques, 181 Gravelly Lane, Birmingham West Mids. T. (0121) 373 3876. - Ant - 065222

City of Birmingham Antique Market, Saint Martins Market, Edgbaston St., Birmingham B5 5BD. T. (0171) 6244848. - Ant - 065223

Clark Antiques, Peter, 36 Saint Mary's Row, Moseley, Birmingham West Mids. T. (0121) 449 8245. - Furn / Silv - 065224

Collectors Shop, 63 Station St., Birmingham West Mids. T. (0121) 631 2072. - Num / Jew / Silv / Mil - 065225

Collyer, R., 185 New Rd., Rubery, Birmingham West Mids. T. (0121) 453 2332. - Jew / Instr - 065226

Eden Coins, Birmingham West Mids. T. (0121) 422 5357. - Num - 065227

Edgbaston Gallery, 42 Islington Row, Five Ways, Edgbaston, Birmingham West Mids. T. (0121) 454 4244. - Paint / Furn / Instr - 065228

Fellows, Maurice, 21 Vyse St., Hockley, Birmingham West Mids. T. (0121) 554 0211, Fax 507 0807. - Jew - 065229

Fine Pine, 75 Mason Rd., Erdington, Birmingham West Mids. T. (0121) 373 6321. - Ant / Furn - 065230

Format of Birmingham, 18 Bennetts Hill, Birmingham West Mids. - Num - 065231

Garratt Antiques, 35 Stephenson St., Birmingham West Mids. T. (0121) 6439507. - Jew / Silv / Toys - 065232

Graves Gallery, 3 Augusta St, Birmingham West Mids. T. (0121) 212 1635. - Ant / Paint - 065233

Harris, Bob, 2071 Coventry Rd., Sheldon, Birmingham B26 3DY. T. (0121) 743 2259. - Ant / Furn - 065234

Hubbard Antiques, John, 224-226 Court Oak Rd.,Harborne, Birmingham West Mids. T. (0121) 426 1694. - Paint / Furn / Dec - 065235

James Antiques-Canalside, Gas St., Basin, Birmingham West Mids. T. (0121) 643 3131. - Ant / Furn - 065236

James Antiques, Tim, 47 Dogpool Ln., Stirchley, Birmingham. T. (0121) 414 0051. - Ant / Furn - 065237

Johnson & Sons, Rex, 28 Lower Temple St., Birmingham West Mids. T. (0121) 643 9674. - China / Jew / Silv / Glass - 065238

Johnson & Sons, Rex, 23 Union St., Birmingham West Mids. T. (0121) 643 7503. - China / Jew / Silv / Glass - 065239

Kestrel House Antiques and Auction Salerooms, 72 Gravelly Hill North, Erdington, Birmingham B23. T. (0121) 3732375. - Paint - 065240

March Medals, 113 Gravelly Hill North, Erdington, Birmingham West Mids. T. (0121) 384 4901. - Dec / Mil - 065241

Moseley Antiques, Unit 5, Woodbridge Rd., Moseley, Birmingham West Mids. T. (0121) 449 6186. - Furn / Instr - 065242

Moseley Pianos, Unit L, 68 Wyrley Rd., Witton, Birmingham B6 7BN. T. (0121) 449 6869. - Music - 065243

Nathan & Co., 31 Corporation St., Birmingham B2 4LS. T. (0121) 643 5225. - Jew / Silv - 065244

Piccadilly Jewellers, Piccadilly Arcade, New St., Birmingham West Mids. T. (0121) 643 5791. - Jew / Silv - 065245

Smithsonia, 14-16 Piccadilly Arcade, Birmingham West Mids. T. (0121) 643 8405. - Furn / Jew - 065246

Tatters of Tyselery, 590 Warwick Rd., Tyseley, Birmingham West Mids. T. (0121) 707 4351. - Ant - 065247

Treasure Chest, 1407 Pershore Rd., Stirchley, Birmingham West Mids. T. (0121) 458 3705. - Ant - 065248

Victoriana Antiques, 287 Bearwood Rd., Bearwood, Warley, Birmingham West Mids. T. (0121) 429 8661. - Furn / Tex / Jew / Silv - 065249

Windmill Gallery, 6 Ernest St., Holloway Head, Birmingham West Mids. T. (0121) 6223986, Fax 666 6630. - Paint / Draw - 065250

Yesterdays Antiques, 125 Pottery Rd., Oldbury, Birmingham West Mids. T. (0121) 420 3980. - Ant / Furn / Instr / China - 065251

Birstwith (North Yorkshire)

Pearson Antique Clock Restauration, John, Church Cottage, Birstwith Yorks North. T. (01423) 770828. - Instr - 065252

Bishop's Cleeve (Gloucestershire)

Cleeve Picture Framing, Church Rd., Bishop's Cleeve Glos. T. (01242) 672785. - Paint / Graph - 065253

Priory Gallery, Priory, Station Rd., Bishop's Cleeve Glos. T. (01242) 673226. - Paint - 065254

Bishops Stortford (Hertfordshire)

Northgate Antiques, 21 Northgate End, Bishops Stortford Herts. T. (01279) 656957. - Ant - 065255

Windhill Antiquary, 4 High St., Bishops Stortford Herts. T. (01279) 651587. - Ant / Furn - 065256

Bishops Waltham (Hampshire)

Pinecrafts, 4 Brook St., Bishops Waltham Hants. T. (01489) 892878. - Furn - 065257

Blackburn (Lancashire)

Ancient and Modern, 56 Bank Top, Blackburn Lancs. T. (01254) 263256. - Jew - 065258

Edwards Group, Charles, 4-8 Lynwood Rd., Blackburn Lancs. T. (01254) 691748. - Jew - 065259

Mitchell's, 76 Bolton Rd., Blackburn Lancs. T. (01254) 664663. - Ant / Jew / Silv - 065260

Walmsley, Anthony, 93 Montague St., Blackburn Lancs. T. (01254) 698755. - Ant / Furn / Instr - 065261

Blackmore (Essex)

Hay Green Antiques, Haygreen Farmhouse, Blackmore Essex. T. (01277) 821275. - Furn - 065262

Blackpool (Lancashire)

Antique Dolls, 29a Caunce St., Blackpool Lancs. T. (01253) 20701. - Toys - 065263

Arundel Coins, 521 Lytham Rd., Blackpool Lancs. T. (01253) 43081. - Paint / Num / Jew / Silv - 065264

Blackpool Antiques Centre, 105-107 Hornby Rd., Blackpool Lancs. T. (01253) 752514. - Furn - 065265

Christian, Peter & Ann, 400/402 Waterloo Rd, Blackpool Lancs. T. (01253) 763268. - Furn - 065266

Ireland, Peter, 31 Clifton St., Blackpool Lancs. T. (01253) 21588. - Num / Jew / Mil - 065267

Latham Antiques, R. H., 45 Whitegate Dr., Blackpool Lancs. T. (01253) 393950. - Furn / China - 065268

Nostalgia, 95 Coronation St., Blackpool Lancs. T. (01253) 293251. - China - 065269

Past and Present, 126 Harrowside, Blackpool Lancs. T. (01253) 42729. - Ant - 065270

Pine Dresser, 1 Ball St., South Shore, Blackpool Lancs. T. (01253) 403862. - Furn - 065271

R. & L. Coins, Fyldex House, 521-523 Lytham Rd., Blackpool FY4 1RJ. T. (01253) 43081. - Num - 065272

Bladon (Oxfordshire)

Carter Antiques, Mark, 25 Park St., Bladon OX7 1RW. T. (01993) 811841. - Furn - 065273

Park House Antiques, 26 Park St., Bladon Oxon. T. (01993) 812817. - Furn - 065274

Blaenau Ffestiniog (Gwynedd)
Antique Shop, 74 A Manod Rd, Blaenau Ffestiniog
Wales. T. (01766) 830629. - Ant / Instr -   *065275*

Blairgowrie (Tayside)
Sim, Roy, Granary Warehouses, Lower Mill St., Blairgowrie Scotland. T. (01250) 873860. - Furn / Silv /
Instr -   *065276*

Blakedown (Worcestershire)
Hay Antiques, 20 Birmingham Rd., Blakedown Herefs. &
Worcs. T. (01562) 700791. - Furn -   *065277*

Blandford (Dorset)
A & D Antiques, 21 East St., Blandford DT11 7DU.
T. (01258) 455643. - Glass -   *065278*
Havelin Antiques, 42 Salisbury St., Blandford Dorset.
T. (01258) 452431, Fax 450664. - Furn / China /
Tex -   *065279*
Stour Gallery, 28 East St., Blandford Dorset.
T. (01258) 456293. - Paint -   *065280*
Strowger of Blanford, 13 East St., Blandford Dorset.
T. (01258) 454374. - Furn -   *065281*

Blaydon (Tyne and Wear)
Blaydon Antique Centre, Bridge House, Bridge St., Blaydon Tyne & Wear. T. (0191) 414 3535. - Paint / Furn /
China / Music -   *065282*

Bletchingley (Surrey)
Cider House Galleries, 80 High St., Bletchingley RH1
4PA. T. (01883) 742198, Fax (01883) 744014.
- Paint -   *065283*
John Anthony Antiques, 71 High St., Bletchingley Surry.
T. (01883) 743197, Fax 742108. - Furn -   *065284*
Marsh, Simon, Old Butchers Shop, High St., Bletchingley
Surrey. T. (01883) 743350. - Furn / Instr -   *065285*
Post House Antiques, 32 High St., Bletchingley Surrey.
T. (01883) 743317. - Ant -   *065286*
Quill Antiques, 86 High St., Bletchingley Surrey.
T. (01883) 743755. - Ant / China / Tex -   *065287*

Blewbury (Oxfordshire)
Blewbury Antiques, London Rd., Blewbury OX11 9NX.
T. (01235) 850366. - Ant / Instr -   *065288*

Bloxham (Oxfordshire)
Dickins, H. C., High St., Bloxham Oxon.
T. (01295) 721949. - Paint / Graph / Draw -   *065289*

Bognor Regis (Sussex)
Gough Bros. Art Shop and Gallery, 71 High St., Bognor
Regis Sussex West. T. (01243) 823773.
- Paint -   *065290*

Bolton (Lancashire)
Bolton Antique Centre, Central St., Bolton Lancs.
T. (01204) 362694. - Ant -   *065291*
Corner Cupboard, 2 Hawarden St., Bolton Lancs.
T. (01204) 58948. - Ant -   *065292*
Curiosity Shop, 832 Bury Rd., Breightmet, Bolton Lancs.
T. (01204) 21290. - Naut -   *065293*
Drop Dial Antiques, Last Drop Village, Hospital Rd.,
Bromley Cross, Bolton Lancs. T. (01204) 307186.
- Ant / Paint / Silv / Instr -   *065294*
Last Drop Antique and Collectors Fair, Last Drop Hotel,
Bromley Cross, Bolton Lancs. - Ant -   *065295*
Memory Lane Antique Centre, Gilnow Lane off Deane
Rd., Bolton Lancs. T. (01204) 380383. - Ant -   *065296*
Oakes & Son, G., 160-162 Blackburn Rd., Bolton Lancs.
T. (01204) 26587. - Furn -   *065297*
Park Galleries Antiques, Fine Art and Decor, 167 Mayor
St., Bolton Lancs. T. (01204) 29827. - Ant / Furn / China / Silv / Glass -   *065298*

Bolton-by-Bowland (Lancashire)
Farmhouse Antiques, 23 Main St., Bolton-by-Bowland
Lancs. T. (012007) 294. - China / Tex / Jew -   *065299*
Harrop Fold Clocks, Harrop Fold, Lane Ends, Bolton-by-
Bowland Lancs. T. (012007) 665. - Instr -   *065300*

Boreham Street (East Sussex)
Camelot Antiques, Boreham Street Sussex East.
T. (01323) 833460. - Furn / China / Silv / Glass - *065301*

Boroughbridge (North Yorkshire)
Bates Antiques, Jeffrey, Aberure, Bridge St., Boroughbridge Yorks North. T. (01423) 324258. - Paint / Furn /
Silv -   *065302*
Eyles Antiques, Joan, The Stone Yard, 12 Fishergate,
Boroughbridge YO5 9AL. T. (01423) 323357. - Ant /
Paint / Furn / China / Instr -   *065303*
Galloway Antiques, High St., Boroughbridge Yorks North.
T. (01423) 324602. - Paint / Furn -   *065304*
Graham Antiques, Anthony, Aberure, Bridge St., Boroughbridge Yorks North. T. (01423) 324258. - Ant /
Paint / Furn -   *065305*
Saint James House Antiques, Saint James Sq., Boroughbridge Yorks North. T. (01423) 322508. - Furn /
China -   *065306*
Wilson & Sons, R. S., Hall Sq., Boroughbridge Yorks
North. T. (01423) 322417. - Furn -   *065307*

Bosham (West Sussex)
Bosham Antiques, Bosham Sussex West.
T. (01243) 572005. - Ant / Furn -   *065308*

Boston (Lincolnshire)
Boston Antiques Centre, 12 West St., Boston Lincs.
T. (01205) 361510. - Jew / Silv -   *065309*
Holland, Mary, 7A Red Lion St, Boston Lincs.
T. (01205) 363791. - Ant -   *065310*
Pen Street Antiques, 9A Pen St, Boston Lincs.
T. (01205) 364118. - China / Silv / Glass -   *065311*
Portobello Row Antiques Centre, 93-95 High St., Boston
Lincs. T. (01205) 369456. - Furn / Naut / Instr - *065312*
That Little Shop, 7 Red Lion St, Boston Lincs.
T. (01790) 53060. - Ant / Jew -   *065313*

Boston Spa (West Yorkshire)
London House Oriental Rugs and Carpets, London House, High St., Boston Spa Yorks West.
T. (01937) 845123. - Tex -   *065314*

Botley (Hampshire)
Burnham-Slipper Antiques, Jane, 8 Winchester St., Botley Hants. T. (01489) 782354. - Ant / Furn / China /
Silv -   *065315*

Bottesford (Leicestershire)
Keen, Thomas, 51 High St., Bottesford Leics.
T. (01949) 42177. - Paint / Furn / Dec -   *065316*

Bottisham (Cambridgeshire)
Cambridge Pine, Hall Farm, Lode Rd., Bottisham Cambs.
T. (01223) 811208. - Furn -   *065317*

Boughton (Kent)
Clock Antiques, 187 The Street, Boughton Kent.
T. (01227) 751258. - Instr -   *065318*
Collyer Antiques, Jean, 194 The Street, Boughton Kent.
T. (01227) 751454. - Ant / Furn / China / Glass - *065319*

Bournemouth (Dorset)
Andrews Antiques, Michael, 916 Christchurch Rd., Bournemouth Dorset. T. (01202) 427615. - Ant / Furn /
Naut -   *065320*
Antique Centre, 837/839 Christchurch Rd, East Boscombe, Bournemouth Dorset. T. (01202) 421052. - Furn /
China / Silv / Mod -   *065321*
Antique Shop, 646 Wimborne Rd., Winton, Bournemouth
Dorset. T. (01202) 527205. - Ant -   *065322*
Antiques and Furnishings, 339 Charminster Rd., Bournemouth Dorset. T. (01202) 527976. - Furn / China / Tex /
Dec -   *065323*
Artist Gallery, 1086 Christchurch Rd, Boscombe, Bournemouth Dorset. T. (01202) 417066. - Graph -   *065324*
Blade and Bayonet, 884 Christchurch Rd., Boscombe,
Bournemouth Dorset. T. (01202) 429891.
- Mil -   *065325*
Boscombe Antiques, 731 Christchurch Rd., Boscombe,
Bournemouth Dorset. T. (01202) 398202.
- China -   *065326*
Boscombe Militaria, 86 Palmerston Rd., Boscombe,
Bournemouth Dorset. T. (01202) 304250.
- Mil -   *065327*
Collectors Corner, 63 Seabourne Rd., Southbourne,
Bournemouth Dorset. T. (01202) 420945. - Ant /
Furn -   *065328*

Denver Antiques, Peter, 36 Calvin Rd., Winton, Bournemouth Dorset. T. (01202) 532536. - Paint / Furn / China / Glass -   *065329*
Dunton Antiques, Richard, 920 Christchurch Rd., Boscombe, Bournemouth Dorset. T. (01202) 425963,
Fax 418456. - Furn / China / Glass -   *065330*
Geneen, Lionel, 781 Christchurch Rd., Boscombe, Bournemouth Dorset. T. (01202) 422961. - Furn /
China -   *065331*
Georgian House Antiques, 110-112 Commercial Rd.,
Bournemouth Dorset. T. (01202) 554175. - Ant / Num /
Jew / Silv -   *065332*
Green Room, 796 Christchurch Rd., Boscombe, Bournemouth Dorset. T. (01202) 392634. - Furn / Dec /
Lights -   *065333*
Hampshire Gallery, 18 Lansdowne Rd., Bournemouth
Dorset. T. (01202) 551211. - Paint -   *065334*
Hardy's Market, 862 Christchurch Rd., Boscombe, Bournemouth Dorset. T. (01202) 422407. - Ant -   *065335*
H.L.B. Antiques, 139 Barrack Rd., Bournemouth Dorset.
T. (01202) 429252. - Ant -   *065336*
Moordown Antiques, 885 Wimborne Rd., Bournemouth
Dorset. T. (01202) 513732. - Ant -   *065337*
Mussenden & Son Antiques, Jewellery and Silver, G. B.,
24 Seamoor Rd., Westbourne, Bournemouth Dorset.
T. (01202) 764462. - Ant / Jew / Silv -   *065338*
Payne & Son, Geo. A., 742 Christchurch Rd., Boscombe,
Bournemouth Dorset. T. (01202) 394954. - Jew /
Silv -   *065339*
Porter, R.E., 2-6 Post Office Rd, Bournemouth BH1 1BA.
T. (01202) 554289. - Jew / Silv / Instr -   *065340*
Portique, 15-17 Criterion Arcade, Bournemouth BH1
1BU. T. (01202) 552979. - Orient / China / Jew / Silv /
Glass -   *065341*
Russell Cotes Art Gallery and Museum, East Cliff, Bournemouth BH1 3AA. T. (01202) 451800.   *065342*
Sainsbury, Jonathan L. F., 21-22 The Arcade, Bournemouth Dorset. T. (01202) 557633. - Ant / Paint /
Furn -   *065343*
Sainsburys of Bournemouth, 23-25 Abbott Rd., Bournemouth BH9 IEU. T. (01202) 529271,
Fax (01202) 510028. - Furn -   *065344*
Saint Andrew's Market, 4b Wolverton Rd, Boscombe,
Bournemouth Dorset. T. (01202) 394470. - Furn /
Dec -   *065345*
Sandy's Antiques, 790 Christchurch Rd., Boscombe,
Bournemouth Dorset. T. (01202) 301190. - Ant /
Orient / Naut -   *065346*
Shickell Antiques, 869 Christchurch Rd., Boscombe,
Bournemouth Dorset. T. (01202) 432331. - Ant / Furn /
Jew -   *065347*
Shippey's of Boscombe, 15-16 Royal Arcade, Boscombe, Bournemouth Dorset. T. (01202) 396548. - China /
Jew / Silv / Glass -   *065348*
Stebbing, Peter, 7 Post Office Rd., Bournemouth BH1
1BB. T. (01202) 552587. - Furn / China / Jew / Silv /
Glass -   *065349*
Sterling Coins and Medals, 2 Somerset Rd., Boscombe,
Bournemouth Dorset. T. (01202) 423881. - Num /
Mil -   *065350*
Stuart, D. C., 34-40 Poole Hill, Bournemouth Dorset.
T. (01202) 555544. - Ant / Furn -   *065351*
Swift & Sons, R. A., 4b Wolverton Rd Boscombe, Bournemouth Dorset. T. (01202) 394470. - Paint / Furn /
China / Silv -   *065352*
Victorian Chairman, 883 Christchurch Rd., Boscombe,
Bournemouth Dorset. T. (01202) 420996.
- Furn -   *065353*
Victorian Parlour, 874 Christchurch Rd., Boscombe,
Bournemouth Dorset. T. (01202) 433928.
- Furn -   *065354*
Yesterday Tackle and Books, 42 Clingan Rd., Boscombe
East, Bournemouth Dorset. T. (01202) 476586.
- Ant -   *065355*
York House Gallery, Queens Park, Bournemouth Dorset.
T. (01202) 394275. - Paint -   *065356*

Bovey Tracey (Devon)
Thomas & James Antiques, 6A Station Rd, Bovey Tracey
Devon. T. (01626) 835350. - Furn / China /
Dec -   *065357*

Bow Street (Dyfed)
Garn House Antiques, Garn House, Bow Street Wales.
T. (01970) 828562. - Ant / Furn / China / Jew /
Glass - 065358

Bowdon (Greater Manchester)
Eureka Antiques and Interiors, 7a Church Brow, Bowdon
Cheshire. T. (0161) 926 9722. - Furn / China /
Jew - 065359

Bowness-on-Windermere (Cumbria)
Thornton Antiques Supermarket, J. W., North Terrace,
Bowness-on-Windermere Cumbria. T. (015394) 42930.
- Ant / Paint / Furn - 065360
Utopia Antiques, Lake Rd., Bowness-on-Windermere
Cumbria. T. (015394) 88464. - Furn - 065361
White Elephant Antiques, 66 Quarry Rigg, Lake Rd.,
Bowness-on-Windermere Cumbria. T. (015394) 46962.
- Ant / Furn / Tex - 065362

Boxford (Suffolk)
Corner Cupboard, The Old Bakery, Boxford Suffolk.
T. (01787) 210123. - Furn - 065363

Brackley (Northamptonshire)
Brackley Antiques, 69 High St., Brackley Northants.
T. (01280) 703362. - Furn / China - 065364
Jackson Antiques, Peter, 3 Market Pl., Brackley Nor-
thants. T. (01280) 703259. - Paint / Furn / China / Silv /
Glass - 065365
Juno's Antiques, 4 Bridge St., Brackley Northants.
T. (01280) 700639. - Ant - 065366
Right Angle, 24 Manor Rd., Brackley Northants.
T. (01280) 702462. - Paint / Graph - 065367

Bradfield Saint George (Suffolk)
Denzil Grant Antiques, Hubbards Corner, Bradfield Saint
George Suffolk. T. (01449) 736576. - Furn - 065368

Bradford (West Yorkshire)
Collectors' Corner, 5-7 Frizinghall Rd., Bradford Yorks
West. T. (01274) 487098. - Ant - 065369
Corner Shop, 89 Oak Lane, Bradford Yorks West.
- Furn / China / Instr - 065370
Langley's (Jewellers), 59 Godwin St., Bradford Yorks
West. T. (01274) 722280. - Jew - 065371
Low Moor Antiques, 233-234 Huddersfield Rd., Low
Moor, Bradford Yorks West. T. (01274) 671047. - Ant /
Furn / Naut - 065372

Bradford-on-Avon (Wiltshire)
Avon Antiques, 25, 26-27 Market St, Bradford-on-Avon
BA15 1LL. T. (01225) 862052. - Furn / Instr - 065373
Harp Antiques, 17 Woolley St., Bradford-on-Avon BA15
1AD. T. (01225) 865770. - Furn / China / Silv - 065374
Humble Antiques, 7-9 Wooley St., Bradford-on-
Avon Wilts. T. (012216) 6329. - Ant / Furn - 065375
Moxham Antiques, 17, 23 and 24 Silvr St, Bradford-on-
Avon BA15 1JZ. T. (01225) 862789,
Fax (01225) 867844. - Furn / China - 065376

Bramhall (Greater Manchester)
Dickinson, David H., Bramhall POB 29.
T. (0161) 440 0688. - Furn - 065377

Bramley (Surrey)
Drummonds of Bramley, Birtley Farm, Bramley Surrey.
T. (01483) 898766, Fax 894393. - Ant - 065378
Memories, High St., Bramley Surreys.
T. (01483) 892205. - Furn / China / Silv / Glass - 065379

Brampton (Cambridgeshire)
Brampton Mill Antiques, 87 High St., Brampton Cambs.
T. (01480) 411402. - Ant - 065380

Brampton (Cumbria)
Fell Antiques, Mary, 32-34 Main St., Brampton Cumbria.
T. (01228) 22224. - Paint / Furn / China / Jew - 065381

Brancaster Staithe (Norfolk)
Brancaster Staithe Antiques, Coast Rd., Brancaster Staithe Norfolk. T. (01485) 210600. - Furn - 065382

Brandsby (North Yorkshire)
Ward & Son, L. L., Bar House, Brandsby.
T. (013475) 651. - Furn - 065383

Branksome (Dorset)
Allen's, 447/449 Poole Rd, Branksome Dorset.
T. (01202) 763724, Fax 763724. - Furn - 065384
Branksome Antiques, 370 Poole Rd., Branksome Dorset.
T. (01202) 763324. - Ant / Furn / Instr - 065385
Mack Antiques, David, 434-437 Poole Rd, and 43 a
Langley Rd, Branksome Dorset. T. (01202) 760005.
- Furn / Naut - 065386

Brantham (Suffolk)
Brantham Mill Antiques, Brantham Suffolk.
- Furn - 065387

Brassington (Derbyshire)
Knights Antiques, Old Barn, Middle Lane, Brassington.
T. (0162) 985317. - Paint / Furn - 065388

Brasted (Kent)
Barrington, David, High St., Brasted Kent.
T. (01959) 562537. - Furn - 065389
Brasted Antiques and Interiors, High St., Brasted Kent.
T. (01959) 564863. - Paint / Furn - 065390
Brooker Antiques at the Village Gallery, Elizabeth, High
St., Brasted Kent. T. (01959) 562503. - Furn /
Instr - 065391
Courtyard Antiques, High St., Brasted Kent.
T. (01959) 564483. - Ant / Furn / Jew / Silv - 065392
Ivy House Antiques, High St., Brasted Kent.
T. (01959) 564581. - Paint / Furn / China - 065393
Keymer, Son & Co., The Green, Swaylands Pl., Brasted
Kent. T. (01959) 564203. - Furn / Instr - 065394
Massingham Antiques, Roy, Coach House, Brasted Kent.
T. (01959) 562408. - Furn / Dec - 065395
Old Manor House Antiques, The Green, High St., Brasted
Kent. T. (01959) 562536. - Ant / Instr - 065396
Rashleigh, High St., Brasted Kent. T. (01959) 563938.
- Ant - 065397
Southdown House Antique Galleries, Southdown House,
High St., Brasted TN16 1JE. T. (01959) 563522.
- Paint / Furn / China / Tex / Glass - 065398
Stoodley, Dinah, High St., Brasted Kent.
T. (01959) 563616. - Furn / China - 065399
Tilings Antiques, High St., Brasted TN16 1JA.
T. (01959) 564735. - Furn / China - 065400
Warner, W. W., The Green, Brasted Kent.
T. (01959) 563698. - Furn / China - 065401
Weald Gallery, High St., Brasted Kent.
T. (01959) 562672. - Paint - 065402

Braunton (Devon)
Cooper Antiques, Eileen, Challoners Rd., Braunton EX33
2ES. T. (01271) 813320. - Ant / Paint / China / Jew /
Silv - 065403
Coward Fine Silver, Timothy, Marisco, Saunton, Braun-
ton Devon. T. (01271) 890466. - Silv - 065404

Brecon (Powys)
Hazel of Brecon, 2 Dukes Arcade, Brecon Wales.
T. (01874) 625274. - Jew - 065405
Ship Street Galleries, 14 Ship St., Brecon LD3 9AD.
T. (01874) 623926. - Furn / Glass - 065406
Silver Time, 2 Dukes Arcade, Brecon Wales.
T. (01874) 625274. - Silv / Instr - 065407

Brentwood (Essex)
Brandler Galleries, 1 Coptfold Rd., Brentwood Essex.
T. (01277) 222269. - Paint - 065408

Brereton (Staffordshire)
Rugeley Antique Centre, 161-163 Main Rd., Brereton
Staffs. T. (01889) 577166. - Paint / Furn / China / Tex /
Glass - 065409

Bressingham (Norfolk)
Bateson Antiques, David, Lodge Farm, Bressingham.
T. (0137) 988629. - Furn - 065410

Bridge-of-Earn (Tayside)
Imrie Antiques, Back St, Bridge-of-Earn Scotland.
T. (01738) 812784. - Naut - 065411

Bridgnorth (Shropshire)
English Heritage, 2 Whitburn St., Bridgnorth Shrops.
T. (01746) 762097. - Ant / Jew / Mil - 065412

Micawber Antiques, 64 Saint Mary's St., Bridgnorth
Shrops. T. (01746) 763254. - Furn / China - 065413
Norton Galleries, Pauline, Bank St., Bridgnorth Shrops.
T. (01746) 764889. - Paint - 065414
Parmenter Antiques, 5 Central Court, High St., Bridg-
north Shrops. T. (01746) 765599. - Paint / Silv - 065415

Bridgwater (Somerset)
Bridgwater Antiques Market, Marycourt Shopping Mall,
Bridgwater. T. (01823) 451433. - Ant - 065416

Bridlington (Humberside)
Antique Militaria, 2 Princess Terrace, Bridlington Hum-
berside North. T. (01262) 676846. - Mil - 065417
Dixon, C.J. and A.J., 23 Prospect St., Bridlington Hum-
berside North. T. (01262) 676877, Fax 606600.
- Num - 065418
Priory Antiques, 47-49 High St., Bridlington Humberside
North. T. (01262) 601365. - Furn - 065419
Sedman Antiques, Carnaby Court, Bridlington Humbersi-
de North. T. (01262) 674039. - Ant / Furn /
China - 065420
Sweet's Antiques, 24 West St., Bridlington Humberside
North. T. (01262) 677396. - Ant / China /
Glass - 065421

Bridport (Dorset)
Batten's Jewellers, 26 South St., Bridport Dorset.
T. (01308) 56910. - Jew / Silv - 065422
Bridport Antiques Centre, 5 West Allington, Bridport Dor-
set. T. (01308) 25885. - Ant / Furn / China /
Jew - 065423
Cox's Corner, 40 Saint Michael's Lane, Bridport Dorset.
T. (01300) 23451. - Paint / Furn - 065424
Hobby Horse Antiques, 29 West Allington, Bridport Dor-
set. T. (01308) 22801. - China / Jew / Silv /
Toys - 065425
Tudor House Antiques, 88 East St., Bridport DT6 3LL.
T. (01308) 427200. - Ant - 065426
Westdale Antiques, 4a Saint Michael's Trading Estate,
Bridport Dorset. T. (01308) 27271. - Furn /
Tex - 065427

Brierfield (Lancashire)
Blakey & Sons, J. H., Church St., Brierfield BB9 5AD.
T. (01282) 691655. - Ant / Furn / Instr - 065428

Brightling (East Sussex)
Hunt Galleries, John, Willingford Lane, Brightling Sussex
East. T. (0142) 482239. - Paint / Sculp - 065429

Brighton (East Sussex)
Alexandria Antiques, 3 Hanover Pl., Brighton Sussex
East. T. (01273) 688793. - Paint / Furn / China - 065430
Antiques and Bedsteads, 105 Gloucester Rd., Brighton
Sussex East. T. (01273) 621434. - Ant / Furn /
Tex - 065431
Art Deco Etc., 73 Upper Gloucester Rd., Brighton Sussex
East. T. (01273) 329268. - Paint / Furn / China /
Mod - 065432
Ashton's Antiques, 1-3 Clyde Rd., Preston Circus, Brigh-
ton Sussex East. T. (01273) 605253. - Furn /
Naut - 065433
Attic Antiques, 23 Ship St., Brighton Sussex East.
T. (01273) 326378. - Ant / Paint / Furn / China /
Instr - 065434
Balchin & Son, H., 18-19 Castle St., Brighton Sussex
East. - Ant - 065435
Bears and Friends, 32 Meeting House Ln., Brighton Sus-
sex East. T. (01273) 208940, Fax (01273) 202736.
- Toys - 065436
Brighton Antique Wholesalers, 39 Upper Gardner St.,
Brighton Sussex East. T. (01273) 695457.
- Furn - 065437
Brighton Architectural Salvage, 33-34 Gloucester Rd.,
Brighton Sussex East. T. (01273) 681656. - Ant /
Furn - 065438
Brown, Mary, 42 Surrey St., Brighton Sussex East.
T. (01273) 721160. - Tex / Jew - 065439
Carmichael, P., 33 Upper North St., Brighton Sussex
East. T. (01273) 328072, Fax (01273) 328072.
- Furn - 065440

C.A.R.S., 4-4a Chapel Terrace Mews, Brighton Sussex
East. T. (01273) 601960, Fax (01273) 623846.
- Toys - 065441

Cashin Gallery, Sheila, 40 Upper North St., Brighton Sussex East. T. (01273) 326619. - Paint / Furn - 065442

Circus Antiques, 2B Clyde Rd, Brighton Sussex East.
T. (01273) 696553. - Paint / Furn / China /
Glass - 065443

Connoisseur Antique Gallery, 113 Church Rd., Hove,
Brighton Sussex East. T. (01273) 777398.
- Ant - 065444

Cowen Antiques, Christopher G., 60 Middle St., Brighton
BN1 1AL. T. (01273) 205757. - Ant / Furn - 065445

Deane Antiques, Graham, 39 Upper North St., Brighton
Sussex East. T. (01273) 207207. - Ant / Furn /
China - 065446

Deane, Graham, 18-19 Marlborough St., Brighton Sussex East. T. (01273) 207207. - Ant / Furn /
China - 065447

Diamond, Harry, 9 Union St., Brighton Sussex East.
T. (01273) 29696. - Jew / Silv / Instr - 065448

Doyle Antiques, James, 10 Union St., Brighton BN1 1HA.
T. (01273) 323694, Fax (01273) 324330. - Jew /
Silv - 065449

Edmonds, D. H., 27-28 Meeting House Ln., Brighton
Sussex East. T. (01273) 327713, 328871. - Jew / Silv /
Instr - 065450

Fitchett Antiques, Alan, 5-5A Upper Gardner St, Brighton
Sussex East. T. (01273) 600894. - Furn / Silv - 065451

Goble, 44 Meeting House Ln., Brighton BN1 1HB.
T. (01273) 202801, Fax (01273) 202736. - Jew / Silv /
Instr - 065452

Gold and Silversmiths of Hove, 3 Planet House, 1 The
Drive, Brighton Sussex East. T. (01273) 738489.
- Jew / Silv - 065453

Hall, Douglas, 23 Meeting House Ln., Brighton Sussex
East. T. (01273) 325323. - Jew / Silv - 065454

Hallmarks, 4 Union St., Brighton Sussex East.
T. (01273) 725477. - Jew / Silv / Instr - 065455

Hatchwell Antiques, Simon, 94 Gloucester Rd., Brighton
BN1 4AP. T. (01273) 691164. - Ant / Paint /
Instr - 065456

Hawkins, Mark and David, 27 Meeting House Lane,
Brighton Sussex East. T. (01273) 321357. - Ant /
Mil - 065457

House of Antiques, 17 Prince Albert St., Brighton Sussex
East. T. (01273) 327680. - Jew / Silv - 065458

Hume, Dudley, 46 Upper North St., Brighton Sussex East.
T. (01273) 323461. - Furn - 065459

Hyndford Antiques, 143 Edward St., Brighton Sussex
East. T. (01273) 602220. - Ant / China - 065460

Kingsbury Antiques, 4 Union St., Brighton Sussex East.
T. (01273) 725477. - Jew / Silv / Instr / Glass - 065461

Leoframes, 70 North Rd., Brighton Sussex East.
T. (01273) 695862. - Graph - 065462

Leopard, 35 Kensington Gardens, Brighton Sussex East.
T. (01273) 695427. - Tex - 065463

Mason, Harry, 21A Prince Albert St, Brighton Sussex
East. T. (01273) 29540. - Jew / Silv - 065464

Miller Antiques, H., 22a Ship St., Brighton Sussex East.
T. (01273) 326255. - Jew / Silv - 065465

Moorhead Antiques, Patrick, 22 Ship St., Brighton.
T. (01273) 326062. - Ant / Paint / Furn / China - 065466

Norman Antiques, Michael, 15 Ship St., Brighton BN1
1AD. T. (01273) 326712, Fax (01273) 206556.
- Furn - 065467

Oasis Antiques, 39 Kensington Gardens, Brighton Sussex East. T. (01273) 683885. - Furn / Tex / Glass /
Mod - 065468

Page Antiques, Brian, 8 Foundry St., Brighton Sussex
East. T. (01273) 609310, Fax (01273) 620055. - Furn /
Orient / Instr - 065469

Palmer Antiques, Devmot & Jill, 7-8 Union St., Brighton
Sussex East. T. (01273) 328669, Fax (01273) 777641.
- Paint / Furn / Tex - 065470

Pearson, Sue, 13 1/2 Prince Albert St., Brighton Sussex
East. T. (01273) 329247. - Toys - 065471

Ponting Antiques, Ben, 53 Upper North St., Brighton
Sussex East. T. (01273) 329409. - Furn - 065472

Prinny's Gallery, 3 Meeting House Ln., Brighton Sussex
East. T. (01273) 204554. - Ant / China / Jew - 065473

Pyramid, 9a Kensington Gardens, Brighton Sussex East.
T. (01273) 607791. - Paint / Furn / China /
Lights - 065474

Recollections, 1a Sydney St., Brighton Sussex East.
T. (01273) 681517. - Furn / Lights - 065475

Resners', 1 Meeting House Lane, Brighton Sussex East.
T. (01273) 329127. - Jew / Silv - 065476

Rodney Classics, Arthur, Rear of 64-78 Davigdor Rd.,
Hove, Brighton Sussex East. T. (01273) 326550.
- Furn / Naut - 065477

Rogers Oriental Rugs, Clive, 22 Brunswick Rd., Hove,
Brighton Sussex East. T. (01273) 738257,
Fax (01273) 738687. - Orient / Tex - 065478

Rutland Antiques, 48 Upper North St., Brighton Sussex
East. T. (01273) 329991. - Ant / Furn / China /
Tex - 065479

Shelton Arts, 4 Islingword Rd., Brighton Sussex East.
T. (01273) 698345. - Paint / Graph - 065480

Shop of the Yellow Frog, 10-11 The Lanes, Brighton
Sussex East. T. (01273) 325497. - China / Jew /
Silv - 065481

Simmons, S. L., 9 Meeting House Lane, The Lanes,
Brighton sussex East. T. (01273) 327949. - Jew /
Silv - 065482

Sussex Commemorative Ware Centre, 88 Western Rd.,
Hove, Brighton Sussex East. T. (01273) 773911.
- Ant - 065483

Tapsell Antiques, 59-59a Middle St., Brighton BN1 1AL.
T. (01273) 328341. - Ant / Paint / Furn / Orient /
Instr - 065484

Tidey, Michael, 87 Saint Georges Rd., Kemptown, Brighton Sussex East. T. (01273) 602389. - Furn - 065485

Webb, Graham, 59 Ship St., Brighton Sussex East.
T. (01273) 321803, Fax (01273) 321803.
- Music - 065486

Welbourne, Stephen & Sonia, 43 Denmark Villas, Hove,
Brighton Sussex East. T. (01273) 722518.
- Paint - 065487

White, E. & B., 43-47 Upper North St., Brighton Sussex
East. T. (01273) 328706. - Furn - 065488

Wigdor, David, 30 Trafalgar St., Brighton Sussex East.
T. (01273) 677272. - Ant - 065489

Witch Ball, 48 Meeting House Lane, Brighton Sussex
East. T. (01273) 326618. - Graph - 065490

Woolman Antiques, L., 29 Gloucester Rd., Brighton Sussex East. T. (01273) 609645. - Paint / Furn / China /
Instr - 065491

Yellow Lantern Antiques, 34 Holland Rd., Brighton BN3
1JL. T. (01273) 771572. - Furn / China / Instr - 065492

Zebrak at Barnes Jewellers, 24 Meeting House Ln.,
Brighton Sussex East. T. (01273) 202929,
Fax (01273) 321021. - Jew / Silv / Instr - 065493

Bristol (Avon)

Alexander Gallery, 122 Whiteladies Rd., Bristol Avon.
T. (0117) 9734692, Fax (0117) 466991. - Paint /
Graph - 065494

Antique Beds, 3 Litfield Pl., Bristol BS8 3LT.
T. (0117) 9735134. - Furn - 065495

Barometer Shop, 2 Lower Park Row, Bristol Avon
T. (0117) 9272565. - Furn / Instr - 065496

Bizarre Antiques, 210 Gloucester Rd., Bishopston, Bristol Avon. T. (0117) 9427888. - Ant - 065497

Bristol Antique Market, Corn St, Bristol Avon.
T. (0117) 9224014. - Ant - 065498

Bristol Guild of Applied Art, 68/70 Park St, Bristol.
T. (0117) 9265548. - Furn - 065499

Bristol Trade Antiques, 192 Cheltenham Rd., Bristol
Avon. T. (0117) 9422790. - Ant - 065500

Butler, Robin, 20 Clifton Rd., Bristol BS8 1AQ.
T. (0117) 9733017. - Furn / Silv / Glass - 065501

Carnival Antiques, 607 Sixth Av, Bristol Avon.
T. (0117) 892166, Fax (0117) 891333. - Furn / China /
Glass - 065502

Cleeve Antiques, 282 Lodge Causeway, Bristol Avon.
T. (0117) 9658366. - Furn - 065503

Clifton Antiques Market, 26/28 The Mall, Clifton, Bristol.
T. (0117) 734531. - Ant - 065504

Cotham Galleries, 22 Cotham Hill, Cotham, Bristol Avon.
T. (0117) 9730626. - Furn / Glass - 065505

Cross, David, 7 Boyces Av., Clifton, Bristol Avon.
T. (0117) 9732614. - Paint / Graph / Draw - 065506

Frocks and Tails, 39A Cotham Hill, Cotham, Bristol Avon.
T. (0117) 9737461. - Tex - 065507

Grey-Harris & Co., 12 Princess Victoria St., Bristol Avon.
T. (0117) 9737365. - Jew / Silv - 065508

Grimes Militaria, Chris, 13 Lower Park Row, Bristol
Avon. T. (0117) 9298205. - Instr / Mil / Naut - 065509

Kemps, 9 Carlton Court, Westbury-on-Trym, Bristol
Avon. T. (0117) 9505090. - Jew - 065510

Mall Gallery, 16 The Mall, Bristol Avon.
T. (0117) 9736263. - Paint - 065511

Mall Jewellers, 4 The Mall, Clifton, Bristol Avon.
T. (0117) 9733178. - Jew / Silv - 065512

Michael's Antiques, 150 Wells Rd., Bristol Avon.
T. (0117) 9713943. - Ant - 065513

Mills Architectural Antiques, Unit 3, Satellite Business
Park, Blackswarth Rd., Bristol BS5 8AX.
T. (0117) 9556542, Fax (0117) 558146. - Ant - 065514

Oldwoods, 1 Colston Yard, Bristol Avon.
T. (0117) 9299023. - Furn - 065515

Oriental Carpet Centre, 3 Queen's Rd., Clifton, Bristol
Avon. T. (0117) 9290165. - Tex - 065516

Potter's Antiques and Coins, 60 Colston St., Bristol BS1
5AZ. T. (0117) 9262551. - Ant / Furn / Num /
Glass - 065517

Relics – Pine Furniture, 109 Saint George's Rd, Bristol
Avon. T. (0117) 9268453. - Furn - 065518

Saunders, R. A., 162 Raleigh Rd., Bristol Avon.
T. (0117) 9662637. - Furn - 065519

Vintage Wireless Company, Tudor House, Cossam St.,
Bristol BS17 3EN. T. (0117) 9565472,
Fax (0117) 575442. - Instr - 065520

Brixham (Devon)

Prestige Antiques, John, 1-2 Greenwood Court, Greenwood Rd., Brixham Devon. T. (01803) 856141,
Fax (01803) 851649. - Furn / Naut - 065521

Brixworth (Northamptonshire)

Gunnett, B. R., 128 Northampton Rd., Brixworth Northants. T. (01604) 880057. - Furn - 065522

Broadstairs (Kent)

Broadstairs Antiques and Collectables, 49 Belvedere
Rd., Broadstairs Kent. T. (01843) 861965. - Ant / Furn /
China - 065523

Broadstone (Dorset)

Galerie Antiques, 4-4a Station Approach, Broadstone
Dorset. T. (01202) 695428. - China / Jew / Silv /
Mod - 065524

Broadway (Hereford and Worcester)

Court Antiques, Unit 5, Cotswold Court, The Green,
Broadway Herefs & Worcs. T. (01386) 853472. - Ant /
China - 065525

Ewart, Garina, 58 High St, Broadway WR12 7DT.
T. (01386) 853371, Fax (01386) 858948. - Paint / Furn /
China / Silv - 065526

Fenwick & Fisher, 88-90 High St., Broadway Herefs &
Worcs. T. (01386) 853227. - Furn - 065527

Gormley Antiques, J. and S., Leamington Rd, Broadway
Herefs & Worcs. T. (01386) 853035. - Furn - 065528

Hagen, Richard, Yew Tree House, Broadway Herefs &
Worcs. T. (01386) 853624, 858561,
Fax (01386) 852172. - Paint - 065529

Hay Loft Gallery, Berry Wormington, Broadway Herefs &
Worcs. T. (01242) 621202. - Paint - 065530

Haynes Fine Art, 69 High St., Broadway Herefs & Worcs.
T. (01386) 852649, Fax (01386) 858187.
- Paint - 065531

High Park Antiques, 62 High St., Broadway Herefs &
Worcs. T. (01386) 853130. - Paint / Furn / China /
Silv - 065532

Howards of Broadway, 27a High St., Broadway Herefs &
Worcs. T. (01386) 858924. - Silv - 065533

Keil, H. W., Tudor House, Broad Close, Broadway WR12
7DP. T. (01386) 852408. - Furn - 065534

Noott Fine Paintings, John, 14 Cotswold Court, The
Green, Broadway Herefs & Worcs. T. (01386) 852787,
Fax (01386) 858348. - Paint - 065535

Olive Branch Antiques, 80 High St., Broadway Herefs &
Worcs. T. (01386) 853831. - Furn / China /
Instr - 065536

Picton House Antiques, High St., Broadway Herefs & Worcs. T. (01386) 853807. - Furn - 065537

Brobury (Hereford and Worcester)
Brobury House Gallery, Brobury. T. (019817) 229. - Paint / Graph - 065538

Brockdish (Norfolk)
Brockdish Antiques, Commerce House, Brockdish Norfolk. T. (0137) 975498. - Furn - 065539

Brodick (Strathclyde)
Village Studio, Kames Cottage, Shore Rd., Brodick Scotland. T. (01770) 302213. - Ant / Jew / Silv - 065540

Bromley (Greater London)
Antica, 35-41 High St., Bromley Kent. T. (0181) 464 7661. - Ant - 065541
Bromley Antique Market, Widmore Rd., Bromley Kent. - Ant / Num / Jew - 065542
Paraphernalia Antiques and Collectors' Centre, 171 Widmore Rd., Bromley Kent. T. (0181) 318 2997. - Ant - 065543

Bromsgrove (Hereford and Worcester)
Strand Antiques, 22 The Strand, Bromsgrove Herefs & Worcs. T. (01527) 72686. - Ant - 065544

Bromyard (Hereford and Worcester)
Lennox Antiques, 3 Broad St., Bromyard Herefs & Worcs. T. (01885) 483432. - Furn / China - 065545

Broseley (Shropshire)
Gallery 6, 6 Church St., Broseley Shrops. T. (01952) 882860. - Paint - 065546

Broughton (Lancashire)
Cowell Architectural Antiques, W. J., Church Hill Lodge, d'Urton Ln, Broughton Lancs. T. (01772) 864551. - Ant - 065547
Village Antiques, 488 Garstang Rd., Broughton Lancs. T. (01772) 862648. - Ant / Jew / Toys - 065548

Broughton Astley (Leicestershire)
Old Bakehouse Antiques and Gallery, 10 Green Rd., Broughton Astley Leics. T. (01455) 282276. - Furn - 065549

Bruton (Somerset)
Gallery 16, 16 High St., Bruton Somerset. T. (01749) 812269. - Paint - 065550
Lewis Gallery, Michael, 17 High St., Bruton Somerset. T. (01749) 813557. - Graph - 065551
M.G.R. Exports, Unit 1, Bruton Ind. Estate, Bruton Somerset. T. (01749) 812460, Fax 812882. - Furn / Naut - 065552

Buchlyvie (Central)
Amphora Galleries, Main St., Buchlyvie Scotland. T. (01360) 85203. - Furn - 065553

Buckingham (Buckinghamshire)
Flappers, 2 High St., Buckingham Bucks. T. (01280) 813115. - Furn / Tex - 065554

Budleigh Salterton (Devon)
New Gallery, 9 Fore St., Budleigh Salterton EX9 6NG. T. (01395) 443768. - Paint / Graph / Draw - 065555
Old Antique Shop, 15 Fore St., Budleigh Salterton Devon. T. (01395) 271451. - Furn / China - 065556
Quinney's, High St., Budleigh Salterton Devon. T. (01395) 442793. - Furn / China / Silv / Glass - 065557
Thorn, David J., 2 High St., Budleigh Salterton EX9 6LQ. T. (01395) 442448. - Ant / Paint / Furn / China / Silv - 065558

Bulkington (Warwickshire)
Sport and Country Gallery, Northwood House, Bulkington Warks. T. (01203) 314335. - Paint - 065559

Bungay (Suffolk)
Black Dog Antiques, 51 Earsham St., Bungay Suffolk. T. (01986) 895554. - Ant - 065560
Cork Brick Antiques, 6 Earsham St., Bungay Suffolk. T. (01986) 894873. - Ant / Furn - 065561
Country House Antiques, 30 Earsham St., Bungay Suffolk. T. (01986) 892875. - Furn / China - 065562

Burford (Oxfordshire)
Burford Gallery, Classica House, High St., Burford Oxon. T. (01993) 822305. - Paint - 065563
Denver House Antiques and Collectables, Denver House, Witney St., Burford Oxon. T. (01993) 822040, Fax (01993) 822769. - Num - 065564
Fyson Antiques, Jonathan, 50 High St, Burford Oxon. T. (01993) 823204. - Furn / China / Jew - 065565
Horseshoe Antiques and Gallery, 97 High St., Burford Oxon. T. (01993) 823244. - Paint / Furn / Instr - 065566
Howards of Burford, 51 High St., Burford Oxon. T. (01993) 823172. - Jew / Silv - 065567
Nielsen Antiques, Anthony, 80 High St, Burford Oxon. T. (01993) 822014. - Furn - 065568
Pickup, David k6150 oxon, 115 High St., Burford. T. (01993) 822555. - Ant / Furn - 065569
Purdon, Richard, 158 High st., Burford Oxon. T. (01993) 823777, Fax (01993) 823719. - Tex - 065570
Schotten Antiques, Manfred, 109 High St., Burford OX18 4RH. T. (01993) 822302, Fax 80993) 822055. - Furn - 065571
Shield Antiques, Robin, 134 High St., Burford OX8 4QU. T. (01993) 822462. - Paint / Furn - 065572
Sinfield Gallery, Brian, 128 High St., Burford Oxon. T. (01993) 822603. - Paint - 065573
Swan Gallery, High St., Burford Oxon. T. (01993) 822244. - Paint / Furn / China / Sculp - 065574
Walker, Zene, Bull House, High St., Burford Oxon. T. (01993) 823284. - Ant / Furn / China - 065575
Williams, Frank, Old Post Office, High St., Burford Oxon. T. (01993) 822128. - Ant / Furn - 065576
Wren Gallery, 4 Bear Court, High St., Burford Oxon. T. (01993) 823495. - Paint / Draw - 065577

Burgess Hill (West Sussex)
British Antique Exporters, Queen Elizabeth Av, Burgess Hill RH15 9RX. T. (01444) 245577. - Ant - 065578
British Antique Replicas, Queen Elizabeth Av, Burgess Hill Sussex West. T. (01444) 245577. - Furn - 065579

Burghfield Common (Berkshire)
Graham Gallery, Highwoods, Burghfield Common Berks. T. (01734) 832320. - Graph - 065580

Burley (Leicestershire)
Burley Workshops, Home Farm, Burley-on-the-Hill, Burley Leics. T. (01572) 757333. - Furn - 065581

Burneston (North Yorkshire)
Greenwood, W., Oak Dene, Church Wynd, Burneston Yorks North. T. (01677) 424830. - Paint / Fra - 065582

Burnham Market (Norfolk)
Cringle, M. and A., Old Black Horse, Burnham Market Norfolk. T. (01328) 738456. - Furn / China / Glass - 065583
Hamilton Antiques, Anne, North St., Burnham Market Norfolk. T. (01328) 738187. - Furn / China - 065584
Market House Antiques, Burnham Market PE31 8HF. T. (01328) 738475. - Ant / Furn - 065585

Burnham-on-Crouch (Essex)
Quay Antiques, 28 High St., Burnham-on-Crouch CM0 8AA. T. (01621) 782468. - Paint / China / Jew - 065586

Burnham-on-Sea (Somerset)
Adam Antiques, 30 Adam St., Burnham-on-Sea Somerset. T. (01278) 783193. - Furn / China / Instr - 065587
Heap's Antiques, 39 Victoria St., Burnham-on-Sea Somerset. T. (01278) 782131. - Furn / China / Glass - 065588

Burnley (Lancashire)
Brun Lea Antiques, Dane House Mill, Dane House Rd., Burnley Lancs. T. (01282) 413513. - Furn - 065589

Burscough (Lancashire)
West Lancashire Antiques, Victoria Mill, Victoria St., Burscough Lancs. T. (01704) 894634. - Naut - 065590

Burton-on-Trent (Staffordshire)
Broadway Studios, 127 New St., Burton-on-Trent Staffs. T. (01283) 41802. - Paint / Graph - 065591

Burton Antiques, 1-2 Horninglow Rd., Burton-on-Trent Staffs. T. (01283) 42331. - Furn - 065592
Pinewood, Justin, The Maltings, Wharf Rd., Burton-on-Trent Staffs. T. (01283) 510860. - Furn - 065593
Scattergood, C. & P., 132 Branston Rd., Burton-on-Trent Staffs. T. (01283) 46695. - Ant / China - 065594

Burwash (East Sussex)
Chateaubriand Antiques Centre, High St., Burwash Sussex East. T. (01435) 882535. - Ant / Furn / Tex - 065595
Chaunt House, High St., Burwash Sussex East. T. (01435) 882221. - Instr - 065596

Burwell (Cambridgeshire)
Norman Antiques and Restoration, Peter, 57 North St., Burwell Cams. T. (01638) 742197. - Furn / Instr / Mil - 065597

Bury (Lancashire)
Newtons, 151 The Rock, Bury Lancs. T. (0161) 7641863. - Ant - 065598

Bury Saint Edmunds (Suffolk)
Corner Shop Antiques, 1 Guildhall St., Bury Saint Edmunds Suffolk. T. (01284) 701007. - China / Jew / Silv - 065599
Guildhall Gallery, 1-1a Churchgate St., Bury Saint Edmunds Suffolk. T. (01284) 762366. - Paint / Graph - 065600
Guildhall Street Antiques, 27 Guildhall St., Bury Saint Edmunds Suffolk. T. (01284) 703060. - Ant - 065601
Mac, Winston, 65 Saint John's St., Bury Saint Edmunds Suffolk. T. (01284) 767910. - Silv - 065602
Pepper, 23 Churchgate St., Bury Saint Edmunds IP33 1RG. T. (01284) 768786. - Ant / Furn / China - 065603

Bushey (Hertfordshire)
Circa Antiques, 43 High St., Bushey Village, Bushey Herts. T. (0181) 950 9233. - Ant / Furn / China - 065604
Country Life Antiques, 33a High St., Bushey Herts. T. (0181) 950 8575. - Paint / Furn / China - 065605
Thwaites & Co., 33 Chalk Hill, Oxney, Bushey Herts. T. (01923) 232412. - Music - 065606

Bushmills (Co. Antrim)
Dunluce Antiques, 33 Ballytober Rd., Bushmills N. Ireland. T. (012657) 31140. - Paint / China / Silv - 065607

Buxton (Derbyshire)
Antiques Warehouse, 25 Lightwood Rd., Buxton Derbys. T. (01298) 72967. - Furn / Furn - 065608
G. and J. Antiques, George St., Buxton Derbys. T. (01298) 72198. - Furn / Instr - 065609
Lewis Antiques, 64 Fairfield Rd., Buxton Derbys. T. (01298) 78648. - Ant / Furn / Tex - 065610
Penny Post Antiques, 9 Cavendish Circus, Buxton Derbys. T. (01298) 25965. - Ant / Furn / China - 065611
West End Galleries, 8 Cavendish Circus, Buxton SK17 6AT. T. (01298) 24546. - Paint / Furn / Silv - 065612
What Now Antiques, Cavendish Arcade, The Crescent, Buxton Derbys. T. (01298) 27178. - Ant / China / Toys - 065613

Cadeby (Leicestershire)
Stanworth, P., The Grange, Cadeby Leics. T. (01455) 291023. - Paint - 065614

Cadnam (Hampshire)
Buckingham, C. W., Twin Firs, Southampton Rd., Cadnam Hants. T. (01703) 812122. - Furn - 065615
Hingstons, Minstead Cottage, Romsey Rd., Cadnam Hants. T. (01703) 812301. - Ant / Furn - 065616

Caerphilly (Mid Glamorgan)
Gittings & Son, G. J., 10 Clive St., Caerphilly. T. (01222) 868835. - Ant / Jew / Naut - 065617

Calne (Wiltshire)
Calne Antiques, 2a London Rd., Calne Wilts. T. (01249) 816311. - Furn / Naut - 065618

Camberley (Surrey)
Pedlar, 231 London Rd., Camberley Surrey. T. (01276) 64750. - Ant / Furn / China - 065619
235 Antiques, 235 London Rd., Camberley Surrey. T. (01276) 32123. - Furn / Silv / Instr - 065620

Camborne (Cornwall)

Grate Expectations, West Charles St., Camborne Cornwall. T. (01209) 719898. - Ant - 065621
Victoria Gallery, 28 Cross St., Camborne Cornwall. T. (01209) 719268. - Ant / Furn / Jew - 065622

Cambridge (Cambridgeshire)

Applin, 8 Lensfield Rd., Cambridge Cambs. T. (01223) 315168. - Furn - 065623
Beazor & Sons, John, 78-80 Regent St., Cambridge CB2 1DP. T. (01223) 355178. - Furn / Instr - 065624
Benet Gallery, 19 Kings Parade, Cambridge CB2 1SP. T. (01223) 353783. - Graph - 065625
Buckies, 31 Trinity St., Cambridge CB2 1TB. T. (01223) 357910. - Jew / Silv - 065626
Cambridge Fine Art, 33 Church St, Cambridge CB2 5HG. T. (01223) 842866, 843537. - Paint - 065627
Collectors Centre, Hope St, Cambridge Cambs. T. (01223) 211632. - Ant / Furn - 065628
Collectors' Market, Dales Brewery, Gwydir St., Cambridge Cambs. T. (01223) 311047. - Ant / Graph / Furn - 065629
Collins & Clark, 14-17 Regent Terrace, Cambridge CB2 1AW. T. (01223) 353801. - Furn / Orient / China - 065630
Cossa Antiques, Grabov, 34 Trumpington St., Cambridge CB2 1QY. T. (01223) 356049. - China / Jew / Glass - 065631
Cottage Antiques, 16-18 Lensfield Rd., Cambridge Cambs. T. (01223) 316698. - Ant / Furn / China - 065632
Crabbe, Peter Ian, 3 Pembroke St., Cambridge Cambs. T. (01223) 357117. - Furn / China - 065633
Gwydir Street Antiques, Gwydir St., Cambridge Cambs. T. (01223) 460548. - Ant / Furn / China - 065634
Hyde Park Corner Antiques, 12 Lensfield Rd., Cambridge Cambs. T. (01223) 353654. - Furn / China / Jew - 065635
Pearson Paintings, Prints and Works of Art, Sebastian, 3 Free School Lane, Cambridge CB2 3QA. T. (01223) 323999. - Paint / Graph - 065636
Rose Cottage Antiques, Brewery Rd., Pampisford, Cambridge Cambs. T. (01223) 834631. - Furn / Lights - 065637
Strover, Barry, 55 Sturton St., Cambridge Cambs. T. (01223) 66302. - Furn - 065638
Webster-Speakman, S. J., 79 Regent St., Cambridge Cambs. T. (01223) 315048. - Ant / Furn / China - 065639

Canterbury (Kent)

Antique and Design, The Old Oast, Mollow Ln, Canterbury. T. (01227) 762871. - Furn - 065640
Baker, R.J., 16 Palace St., Canterbury Kent. T. (01227) 463224. - Jew / Silv - 065641
Burgate Antique Centre, 10 Burgate, Canterbury Kent. T. (01227) 456500. - Furn / China / Mil - 065642
Canterbury Weekly Antique Market, Saint Peter's St, Canterbury Kent. - Ant - 065643
Coach House Antiques, Duck Lane, Saint Radigund's, Canterbury Kent. T. (01227) 463117. - Ant / Furn / China - 065644
Conquest House Antiques, 17 Palace St., Canterbury Kent. T. (01227) 464587, Fax 451375. - Furn - 065645
Greenfield Gunmakers & Son, H. S., 4-5 Upper Bridge St., Canterbury Kent. T. (01227) 456959. - Mil - 065646
Harvey Centre, 22/24 Stour St, Canterbury Kent. T. (01227) 452677. - Ant / Furn - 065647
Henley Antiques, R. and J. L., 37a Broad St., Canterbury Kent. T. (01227) 769055. - Ant / Furn - 065648
Leadenhall Gallery, 12 Palace St., Canterbury Kent. T. (01227) 457339. - Graph - 065649
Leith's Brocanterbury, Nan, 68 Stour St., Canterbury CT1 2NZ. T. (01227) 454519. - Jew / Glass - 065650
Parker Williams Antiques, 22 Palace St., Canterbury Kent. T. (01227) 768341. - Furn / China / Silv - 065651
Pearson Antiques, Michael, 2 The Borough, Northgate, Canterbury Kent. T. (01227) 459939. - Furn / Instr - 065652
Pine and Things, Oast Interiors, Wincheap Rd., Canterbury Kent. T. (01227) 470283. - Furn - 065653

Rastro Antiques, 44a High St., Canterbury Kent. T. (01227) 463537. - Ant / Furn - 065654
Saracen's Lantern, 8-9 The Borough, Canterbury CT1 2DR. T. (01227) 451968. - Ant / Furn / Instr - 065655
Stablegate Antiques, 19 The Borough, Palace St., Canterbury Kent. T. (01227) 764086. - Ant / Furn / China - 065656
Town and Country Furniture, 141 Wincheap Rd., Canterbury Kent. T. (01227) 762340. - Furn - 065657
Victorian Fireplace, 92 Broad St., Canterbury Kent. T. (01227) 767723. - Furn - 065658

Cardiff (South Glamorgan)

Alexander Antiques, 312 Whitchurch Rd., Cardiff Wales. T. (01222) 621824. - Furn / Jew / Instr - 065659
Back to the World, West Canal Wharf, Cardiff Wales. T. (01222) 390939. - Furn - 065660
Burge Antiques, A., 54 Crwys Rd., Cardiff Wales. T. (01222) 383268. - Ant / Instr - 065661
Charlotte's Wholesale Antiques, 129 Woodville Rd., Cardiff Wales. T. (01222) 759809. - Ant / Furn / Naut - 065662
Cronin Antiques, 12 Mackintosh Pl., Roath, Cardiff Wales. T. (01222) 498929. - Ant / Jew / Silv - 065663
Douglas, W. H., 161 Cowbridge Rd., Cardiff Wales. T. (01222) 224861. - Ant / Naut - 065664
Grandma's Goodies, 31 Mortimer Rd., Pontcanna, Cardiff Wales. T. (01222) 383142. - Furn / China / Tex - 065665
Heritage Antiques and Stripped Pine, 83 Pontcanna St., Cardiff Wales. T. (01222) 390097. - Ant / Furn - 065666
Jacobs Antique Centre, West Canal Wharf, Cardiff Wales. T. (01222) 390939. - Ant / Furn - 065667
King Fireplaces, Antiques and Interiors, 163 Cowbridge Rd. East, Canton, Cardiff Wales. T. (01222) 225014. - Furn - 065668
King Fireplaces & Architectural Antiques, All Saints Church, Adamstown Sq., Splott, Cardiff Wales. T. (01222) 492439. - Ant / Furn - 065669
Llanishen Antiques, 26 Crwys Rd., Cathays, Cardiff Wales. T. (01222) 397244. - Furn / China / Silv - 065670
Manor House Fine Arts, 73 Pontcanna St., Cardiff CF1 9HS. T. (01222) 227787. - Ant / Paint - 065671
Past and Present, 242 Whitchurch Rd., Heath, Cardiff Wales. T. (01222) 621443. - Furn / China / Instr - 065672
San Domenico Stringed Instruments, 175 Kings Rd., Canton, Cardiff Wales. T. (01222) 235881, Fax (01222) 344510. - Music - 065673

Carlisle (Cumbria)

Carlisle Antique and Craft Centre, Cecil Hall, Cecil St., Carlisle Cumbria. T. (01228) 21970. - Ant - 065674
Charm Antiques, Lonsdale St., Carlisle Cumbria. T. (01228) 23035. - Furn / China / Glass - 065675
Clements, James W., 19 Fisher St., Carlisle CA3 8RF. T. (01228) 25565. - Ant / Furn / China - 065676
Layne, A. C., 48 Cecil St., Carlisle Cumbria. T. (01228) 45019. - Instr - 065677
Saint Nicholas Galleries, 28 London Rd., Carlisle Cumbria. T. (01228) 34425. - Ant - 065678
Saint Nicholas Galleries, 39 Bank St., Carlisle Cumbria. T. (01228) 44459. - China / Jew / Instr - 065679
Second Sight, 4A Mary St, Carlisle Cumbria. T. (01228) 591525. - Paint / Furn / China - 065680
Souvenir Antiques, Treasury Court, Fisher St., Carlisle Cumbria. T. (01228) 401281. - Graph / Furn / China - 065681

Carmarthen (Dyfed)

Cwmgwili Mill, Bonwydd Arms, Carmarthen Wales. T. (01267) 231500. - Furn - 065682
Merlins Antiques, Albion Arcade, Blue St., Carmarthen Wales. T. (01267) 237728. - China - 065683

Carshalton (Greater London)

Antiques, 314 Carshalton Rd., Carshalton Surrey. T. (0181) 6422108. - Ant / Lights - 065684
Cambridge Parade Antiques, 229-231 Carshalton Rd., Carshalton Surrey. T. (0181) 643 0014. - Ant - 065685
Carshalton Antique Galleries, 5 High St, Carshalton SM5 3AP. T. (0181) 647 5664. - Ant / Furn / Instr - 065686

Cherub Antiques, 312 Carshalton Rd., Carshalton Surrey. T. (0181) 643 0028. - Ant / Furn - 065687

Cartmel (Cumbria)

Anthemion-The Antique Shop, Cartmel Cumbria. T. (0153) 9536295. - Furn - 065688
Bacchus Antiques, Longlands, Cartmel Cumbria. T. (0153) 953675. - Ant - 065689

Castle Ashby (Northamptonshire)

Castle Ashby Gallery, Old Farmyard, Castle Ashby Northants. T. (01604) 696787, Fax (01604) 696787. - Paint - 065690

Castle Cary (Somerset)

Cary Antiques, 2 High St., Castle Cary Somerset. T. (01963) 50437. - Furn / China / Glass - 065691
Martin Antiques, John, High St., Castle Cary Somerset. T. (01963) 50733. - Jew / Lights / Instr - 065692

Castle Combe (Wiltshire)

Combe Cottage Antiques, Castle Combe SN14 7HU. T. (01249) 782250. - Furn / China - 065693

Castle Douglas (Dumfries and Galloway)

Bendall, 221-223 King St., Castle Douglas Scotland. T. (01556) 2113. - Ant - 065694

Castle Hedingham (Essex)

Orbell House Gallery, Orbell House, Castle Hedingham Essex. T. (01787) 60298. - Tex - 065695

Castletown (Isle of Man)

Bell Antiques, J. and H., 22 Arbory St., Castletown I. of Man. T. (01624) 823132. - China / Jew / Silv - 065696

Ceres (Fife)

Ceres Antiques, 19 Main St., Ceres Scotland. T. (0133) 482384. - Ant / China - 065697

Cerne Abbas (Dorset)

Cerne Antiques, Cerne Abbas Dorset. T. (01300) 341490. - Furn / China / Silv - 065698

Chagford (Devon)

Meredith, John, 41 New St., Chagford Devon. T. (01647) 433474. - Furn / Mil - 065699
Payton Antiques, Mary, Old Market House, Chagford Devon. T. (01647) 432428. - Graph / China / Glass - 065700
Whiddons Antiques and Tearooms, 6 High St., Chagford Devon. T. (01647) 433406. - Paint / Graph / Furn - 065701

Chalfont Saint Giles (Buckinghamshire)

Gallery 23 Antiques, High St., Chalfont Saint Giles Bucks. T. (01494) 871512. - Furn / China / Silv - 065702
Images in Watercolour, 8 The Lagger, Chalfont Saint Giles Bucks. T. (01494) 875592. - Paint / Draw - 065703
Smith, T., Furniture Village, London Rd., Chalfont Saint Giles Bucks. T. (01494) 873031. - Ant - 065704

Chapel-en-le-Frith (Derbyshire)

Clock House, 48 Manchester Rd., Chapel-en-le-Frith Derbys. T. (01298) 815174, Fax (01298) 816192. - Ant / Jew / Instr - 065705

Chard (Somerset)

Guildhall Antique Market, Guildhall, Chard Somerset. - Ant - 065706

Charing (Kent)

Peckwater Antiques and Interiors, 13 and 17 High St, Charing Kent. T. (01233) 712592. - Ant - 065707

Cheadle Hulme (Greater Manchester)

Allan's Antiques and Reproductions, 10 Ravenoak Rd., Cheadle Hulme Cheshire. T. (0161) 4853132. - Furn / Silv - 065709

Cheam (Greater London)

Franzer Antiques, Malcolm, 19 Brooklyn Crescent, Cheadle Cheshire. T. (0161) 4283781. - Instr / Naut - 065709a

Rogers Antiques, 22 Ewell Rd., Cheam Surrey. T. (0181) 643 8466. - Furn - 065710

Cheddleton (Staffordshire)

Jewel Antiques, 63 Basford Bridge Ln., Cheddleton Staffs. T. (01538) 360744. - Paint / Jew / Instr - 065711

Cheltenham (Gloucestershire)

Antiques, 22 Montpellier, Cheltenham Gloi. T. (01242) 522939. - Ant / Furn / China - 065712

Bailey's Quality Antique, 16 Suffolk Rd., Cheltenham Glos. T. (01242) 255897. - Ant / Lights - 065713

Bed of Roses, 12 Prestbury Rd., Cheltenham Glos. T. (01242) 231918. - Furn - 065714

Beer, John, 23 Priory St., Cheltenham Glos. T. (01242) 576080. - Furn - 065715

Bottles and Bygones, 96 Horsefair St., Charlton Kings, Cheltenham Glos. T. (01242) 236393. - Ant / Furn / Jew - 065716

Bradbury, Edward, 32 High St., Cheltenham Glos. T. (01242) 221486. - Furn - 065717

Butler & Co., 111 Promenade, Cheltenham Glos. T. (01242) 522272. - Num - 065718

Cameo Antiques, 31 Suffolk Parade, Cheltenham Glos. T. (01242) 236467. - Ant / Paint / Furn - 065719

Charlton Kings Antique Centre, 199 London Rd., Charlton Kings, Cheltenham Glos. T. (01242) 510672. - Ant - 065720

Cheltenham Antique Market, 54 Suffolk Rd., Cheltenham Glos. T. (01242) 529812. - Ant - 065721

Cocoa, 7 Queens Circus, Cheltenham Glos. T. (01242) 233588. - Tex - 065722

Country Life Antiques, Montpellier St, Cheltenham Glos. T. (01242) 226919. - Furn / Instr - 065723

Greens of Montpellier, 15 Montpellier Walk, Cheltenham GL50 1SD. T. (01242) 512088. - China / Jew / Silv - 065724

Heydens Antiques and Militania, 420 High St., Cheltenham Glos. T. (01242) 582466. - Ant / Mil - 065725

Howard, David, 42 Moorend Crescent, Cheltenham Glos. T. (01242) 243379. - Paint / Draw - 065726

Kyoto House Antiques, 14 Suffolk Rd., Cheltenham Glos. T. (01242) 519566. - Orient - 065727

Latchford Antiques, 215 London Rd., Charlton Kings, Cheltenham Glos. T. (01242) 226263. - Paint / Furn / China - 065728

Leckhampton, 215 Bath Rd., Cheltenham Glos. T. (01242) 570230. - Ant - 065729

Manor House Antiques, 42 Suffolk Rd., Cheltenham Glos. T. (01242) 232780. - Ant / Furn / Naut - 065730

Martin & Co., 19 The Promenade, Cheltenham GL50 1LP. T. (01242) 522821. - Jew / Silv - 065731

Montpellier Clocks, Montpellier St, Cheltenham Glos. T. (01242) 242178. - Instr - 065732

Niner Antiques, Elizabeth, 53 Great Norwood St., Cheltenham Glos. T. (01242) 516497. - Graph / Furn - 065733

Oliver, Patrick, 4 Tivoli St., Cheltenham Glos. T. (01242) 513392. - Furn / Naut - 065734

Pirde Oriental Rugs, Eric, 44 Suffolk Rd., Cheltenham Glos. T. (01242) 580822. - Tex - 065735

Scott-Cooper, 52 The Promenade, Cheltenham Glos. T. (01242) 522580. - Jew / Silv / Instr - 065736

Tapestry, 33 Suffolk Parade, Cheltenham Glos. T. (01242) 512191. - Furn - 065737

Townsend, John P., Ullenwood Park Farm, Cheltenham Glos. T. (01242) 870223. - Furn - 065738

Triton Gallery, 27 Suffolk Parade, Cheltenham Glos. T. (01242) 510477. - Furn - 065739

Turner Antiques, Joy, 100 Leckhampton Rd., Cheltenham Glos. T. (01242) 522939. - Ant - 065740

Turtle Fine Art, 30 Suffolk Parade, Cheltenham Glos. T. (01242) 241646. - Paint / Graph - 065741

Chepstow (Gwent)

Davies Antiquex Centre, 12 Saint Marys St., Chepstow Wales. T. (01291) 625957. - Ant / Furn / Naut - 065742

Glance Gallery, 17a Upper Church St., Chepstow Wales. - Graph - 065743

Plough House Interiors, Upper Church St, Chepstow Wales. T. (01291) 625200. - Furn / Naut - 065744

Cherhill (Wiltshire)

Oxley Antique Clocks and Barometers, P. A., Old Rectory, Main Rd., Cherhill Wilts. T. (01249) 816227, Fax (01249) 821285. - Instr - 065745

Chertsey (Surrey)

Chertsey Antiques, 8 Windsor St., Chertsey Surrey. T. (01932) 563565. - Ant - 065746

Mister Sun Antiques, 96 Guildford St., Chertsey Surrey. T. (01932) 566323. - Ant - 065747

Surrey Antiques Centre, 10 Windsor St., Chertsey Surrey. T. (01932) 563313. - Ant / Furn / China - 065748

Chesham (Buckinghamshire)

Bartram, Albert, 177 Hivings Hill, Chesham HP5 2PN. T. (01494) 783271. - Ant / Furn / China - 065749

Chess Antiques, 85 Broad St., Chesham Bucks. T. (01494) 783043. - Furn / Instr - 065750

For Pine, 340 Berkhampstead Rd., Chesham Bucks. T. (01494) 776119. - Furn - 065751

Omniphil, Germains Lodge, Fullers Hill, Chesham Bucks. T. (01494) 771851. - Graph - 065752

Queen Anne House, 57 Church St., Chesham Bucks. T. (01494) 783811. - Furn / China / Glass - 065753

Tooley, M. V., 85 Broad St., Chesham Bucks. T. (01494) 783043. - Instr - 065754

Chester (Cheshire)

Adams Antiques, 65 Watergate Row, Chester CH1 2LE. T. (01244) 319421. - Furn / Instr / Mod - 065755

Antique Exporters of Chester, Rossett Mill, Rossett, Chester Cheshire. T. (01829) 41001. - Furn - 065756

Avalon Postcard and Stamp Shop, 1 City Walls, Northgate St, Chester Cheshire. T. (01244) 318406. 065757

Baron Fine Art, 68 Watergate St., Chester Cheshire. T. (01244) 342520. - Paint / Graph - 065758

Boddle & Dunthorne, 52 Eastgate St., Chester CH1 1LE. T. (01244) 326666. - Jew / Silv / Instr - 065759

Boustead Antiques, Olwyn, 61 Watergate Row, Chester Cheshire. T. (01244) 342300. - Ant / Furn / Instr - 065760

Chester Furniture Cave, 97a Christleton Rd., Boughton, Chester Cheshire. T. (01244) 314798. - Furn - 065761

Farmhouse Antiques, 21-23 Christleton Rd., Boughton, Chester CH3 5UF. T. (01244) 322478. - Ant / Furn / Instr - 065762

Grosvenor Antiques of Chester, 22 Watergate St., Chester Cheshire. T. (01244) 315201. - Ant - 065763

Guildhall Fair, Watergate St., Chester Cheshire. - Ant - 065764

Harper, Erica and Hugo, 27 Watergate Row, Chester CH1 2LE. T. (01244) 323004. - Furn / China / Glass - 065765

Jamandic, 22 Bridge St. Row, Chester Cheshire. T. (01244) 312822. - Graph / Furn / China - 065766

Kayes of Chester, 9 Saint Michaels Row, Chester Cheshire. T. (01244) 327149. - Paint / Jew / Silv - 065767

Lowe & Sons, 11 Bridge St. Row, Chester CH1 1PD. T. (01244) 325850. - Jew / Silv - 065768

Made of Honour, 11 City Walls, Chester CH1 1LD. T. (01244) 314208. - Ant / China / Tex - 065769

Melody's Antique Galleries, 32 City Rd., Chester Cheshire. T. (01244) 328968. - Furn / Silv / Lights - 065770

Nicholson, Richard A., 25 Watergate St., Chester CH1 2LB. T. (01244) 326818, Fax (01244) 336138. - Graph / Draw - 065771

Richmond Galleries, Watergate Bldg., New Crane St., Chester Cheshire. T. (01244) 317602. - Furn - 065772

Saint Peters Art Gallery, Saint Peters Churchyard, Northgate St., Chester Cheshire. T. (01244) 345500. - Paint - 065773

Titchner & Sons, John, 67 Watergate Row, Chester Cheshire. T. (01244) 326535. - Furn - 065774

Walsh, Bernard, 11 Saint Michaels Row, Chester CH1 1EF. T. (01244) 326032. - Ant / Jew / Silv - 065775

Watergate Antiques, 56 Watergate St., Chester CH1 2LD. T. (01244) 344516, Fax (01244) 320350. - Ant / China / Silv - 065776

Whitehead, Joyce and Rod, 11 City Walls, Chester Cheshire. T. (01244) 314208. - Ant / Tex - 065777

Chesterfield (Derbyshire)

Coleman Antiques, Polly, 424 Chatsworth Rd., Brampton, Chesterfield Derbys. T. (01246) 278146. - Paint / Graph / Furn - 065778

Goodlad, Anthony D., 26 Fairfield Rd., Brampton, Chesterfield Derbys. T. (01246) 204004. - Mil - 065779

Hackney House Antiques, Hackney Lane, Barlow, Chesterfield Derbys. T. (01742) 890248. - Paint / Furn / Silv - 065780

Morris, Ian, 479 Chatsworth Rd., Brampton, Chesterfield Derbys. T. (01246) 235120. - Paint / Furn - 065781

Times Past, 13 Chatsworth Rd, Chesterfield Derbys. T. (01246) 557077. - Graph / Furn / China - 065782

Yates Antiques, Brian, 420 Chatsworth Rd., Brampton, Chesterfield Derbys. T. (01246) 220395. - Furn / China - 065783

Chichester (West Sussex)

Almshouses Arcade, 19 The Hornet, Chichester Sussex West. - Ant - 065784

Antique Shop, Frensham House, Hunston, Chichester Sussex West. T. (01243) 782660. - Furn - 065785

Canon Gallery, Lane End, Appledram Ln., Chichester Sussex West. T. (01243) 786063. - Paint - 065786

Gems Antiques, 39 West St., Chichester Sussex West. T. (01243) 786173. - Paint / Furn / China - 065787

Green & Stone of Chichester, 1 North House, North St., Chichester Sussex West. T. (01243) 533953. - Paint / Graph - 065788

Hancock Antiques, Peter, 40-41 West St., Chichester PO19 1RP. T. (01243) 786173. - Ant - 065789

Heritage Antiques, 77, 83 and 84 Saint Pancras, Chichester Sussex West. T. (01243) 783470. - Furn - 065790

Saint Pancras Antiques, 150 Saint Pancras, Chichester Sussex West. T. (01243) 787645. - Furn / China / Mil - 065791

Chiddingfold (Surrey)

Manor House Interiors, 1 Petworth Rd., Chiddingfold Surrey. T. (01428) 682727. - Paint / Silv / Lights - 065792

Chiddingstone (Kent)

Lane Antiques, Barbara, Tudor Cottage, Chiddingstone Kent. T. (01892) 870577. - Ant / Furn / China - 065793

Chilham (Kent)

Peacock Antiques, The Square, Chilham Kent. T. (01227) 730219. - Furn / Silv / Glass - 065794

Chingford (Greater London)

Slater Antiques, Nicholas, 8 Station Approach, Station Rd., Chingford Essex. T. (0181) 529 2938. - Furn / China / Tex - 065795

Chipping Campden (Gloucestershire)

Antique Heritage, High St., Chipping Campden Glos. T. (01386) 840727. - China - 065796

Pedlars, Lower High St., Chipping Campden Glos. T. (01386) 840680. - Ant - 065797

Saxton House Gallery, High St., Chipping Campden Glos. T. (01386) 840278. - Paint / Furn / Instr - 065798

School House Antiques, School House, High St., Chipping Campden Glos. T. (01386) 841474, Fax (01386) 841367. - Furn / Instr - 065799

Stuart House Antiques, High St., Chipping Campden Glos. T. (01386) 840995. - Ant / China - 065800

Swan Antiques, High St., Chipping Campden GL55 6HB. T. (01386) 840759. - China / Jew / Silv - 065801

Chipping Norton (Oxfordshire)

Bugle Antiques, 9 Horsefair, Chipping Norton Oxon. T. (01608) 643322. - Ant / Furn - 065802

Chipping Norton Antique Centre, 1 Middle Row, Chipping Norton Oxon. T. (01608) 644212. - Ant / Furn - 065803

Emporium, 26 High St., Chipping Norton Oxon. T. (01608) 643103. - Graph / China - 065804

Georgian House Antiques, 21 West St., Chipping Norton Oxon. T. (01608) 641369. - Paint / Furn - 065805

Howard, Jonathan, 21 Market Pl., Chipping Norton Oxon. T. (01608) 643065. - Instr - 065806

Key Antiques, 11 Horse Fair, Chipping Norton Oxon. T. (01608) 643777. - Ant / Furn - 065807

Stroud Antiques, Peter, 35 New St., Chipping Norton OX7 5LL. T. (01608) 642571. - Ant / Furn - 065808

Wiggins, Peter, Raffles Farm, Southcombe, Chipping Norton Oxon. T. (01608) 642652. - Instr - 065809

Chipping Sodbury (Avon)
Sodbury Antiques, 70 Broad St., Chipping Sodbury Avon.
T. (01454) 273369. - Furn / China / Jew -   065810

Chirk (Clwyd)
Seventh Heaven, Chirk Mill, Chirk Wales.
T. (01691) 777622, Fax (01691) 777313.
- Furn -   065811

Chislehurst (Greater London)
Chislehurst Antiques, 7 Royal Parade, Chislehurst Kent.
T. (0181) 467 1530. - Furn / China -   065812
Sim, Michael, 1 Royal Parade, Chislehurst BR7 5PG.
T. (0181) 467 7040, Fax (0181) 4674352. - Paint /
Furn / Instr -   065813

Chobham (Surrey)
Greengrass Antiques, Hookstone Farm, Hookstone Ln.,
Chobham Surrey. T. (01276) 857582. - Furn /
Naut -   065814
Tarrystone, 40-42 High St., Chobham Surrey.
T. (01276) 857494. - Furn / China -   065815

Chorley (Lancashire)
Charisma Curios and Antiques, 91 Wigan Rd., Euxton,
Chorley Lancs. T. (0125) 7276845. - Ant /
Furn -   065816

Christchurch (Dorset)
Arditti, J. L., 88 Bargates, Christchurch Dorset.
T. (01202) 485414. - Tex -   065817
Christchurch Carpets, 55/57 Bargates, Christchurch Dor-
set. T. (01202) 482712. - Tex -   065818
Hamptons, 12 Purewell, Christchurch Dorset.
T. (01202) 484000. - Ant / Furn / Instr -   065819
Lankshear Antiques, M. & R., 149 Barrack Rd., Christ-
church Dorset. T. (01202) 473091. - Ant -   065820
Old Stores, West Rd., Brandgore, Christchurch Dorset.
T. (01425) 72616. - Ant -   065821

Christian Malford (Wiltshire)
Harley Antiques, The Comedy, Christian Malford Wilts.
T. (01249) 720112. - Furn -   065822

Church Stretton (Shropshire)
Antiques on the Square, 2 Sandford Court, Sandford Av.,
Church Stretton Shrops. T. (01694) 724111. - Furn /
China / Glass -   065823
Old Barn Antiques, High St., Church Stretton Shrops.
T. (01694) 723742. - Ant / Furn / China -   065824
Stretton Antiques, 9 High St, Church Stretton Shrops.
T. (01694) 781330. - Ant -   065825
Stretton Antiques Market, 36 Sandford Av., Church
Stretton Shrops. T. (01694) 723718. - Ant -   065826

Cirencester (Gloucestershire)
Beech Antique Clocks, Jonathan, Nurses Cottage, Ciren-
cester Glos. T. (01285) 851495. - Instr -   065827
Cirencester Antique Market, Market Pl., Cirencester
Glos. T. (0171) 2335786. - Ant -   065828
Cirencester Antiques Centre, The Waterloo, Cirencester
Glos. T. (01285) 644040. - Furn / Jew / Silv -   065829
Corner Cupboard Curios, 2 Church St., Cirencester Glos.
T. (01285) 655476. - Ant -   065830
Forum Antiques, 20 West Way, Cirencester Glos.
T. (01285) 658406. - Furn -   065831
Gray Antiques, Jay, 1 Cheltenham Rd., Cirencester GL7
2HS. T. (01285) 652755. - Ant / Furn / China -   065832
Hares, 17-19 Gosditch St., Cirencester Glos.
T. (01285) 640077. - Furn -   065833
Hudson, Thomas and Pamela, 19 Park St., Cirencester
Glos. T. (01285) 652972. - Ant / Glass -   065834
Legg & Son, E. C., Tetbury Rd, Cirencester Glos.
T. (01285) 650695. - Furn -   065835
Ponsford Antiques, A. J., 51-53 Dollar St., Cirencester
GL7 2AS. T. (01285) 652355. - Furn / Fra -   065836
Stokes, William H., 6/8 Dollar St, Cirencester GL7 2AJ.
T. (01285) 653907, Fax (01285) 653907.
- Furn -   065837
Taylor Antiques, Rankie, 34 Dollar St., Cirencester Glos.
T. (01285) 652529. - Furn / Silv / Glass -   065838
Ward Fine Paintings, P. J., 11 Gosditch St., Cirencester
Glos. T. (01285) 658499. - Paint -   065839
Weaver Antiques, Bernard, 28 Gloucester St., Cirence-
ster GL7 2DH. T. (01285) 652055. - Furn -   065840

Clacton-on-Sea (Essex)
Sharman, L. R., 80B Rosemary Rd, Clacton-on-Sea Essex. T. (01255) 424620. - Furn / Instr / Mil -   065841

Clare (Suffolk)
Agnus, 41A Nethergate St, Clare Suffolk.
T. (01787) 278547. - Furn / Jew -   065842
Clare Antique Warehouse, The Mill, Malting Lane, Clare
Suffolk. T. (01787) 278449. - Ant -   065843
Clare Collector, 1 Nethergate St., Clare Suffolk.
T. (01787) 277909. - Paint / Furn / China -   065844
Clare Hall Company, The Barns, Clare Hall, Cavendish
Rd., Clare CO10 8PJ. T. (01787) 277510.
- Furn -   065845
Granny's Attic, 22 High St., Clare Suffolk.
T. (01787) 277740. - Tex -   065846
Salter Antiques, F. D., 1-2 Church St., Clare Suffolk.
T. (01787) 277693. - Furn / China -   065847

Clayton-le-Moors (Lancashire)
Phillips, Edward V., 238 Whalley Rd., Clayton-le-Moors
Lancs. T. (01254) 396739. - Furn / Naut -   065848
Sparth House Antiques, Sparth House, Whalley Rd.,
Clayton-le-Moors Lancs. T. (01254) 872263.
- Ant -   065849

Cleobury Mortimer (Shropshire)
Cleobury Mortimer Antique Centre, Childe Rd., Cleobury
Mortimer Shrops. T. (01299) 270513. - Ant /
Furn -   065850

Clevedon (Avon)
Beach Antiques, 13 The Beach, Clevedon Avon.
T. (01272) 876881. - China / Jew / Glass -   065851
Clevedon Fine Arts, 14 Woodside Rd., Clevedon Avon.
T. (01272) 872304. - Graph -   065852

Clitheroe (Lancashire)
Castle Antiques, 15 Moor Lane, Clitheroe Lancs.
T. (01200) 26568. - Furn / Naut -   065853
Ethos Gallery, 4 York St., Clitheroe Lancs.
T. (01200) 27878. - Paint -   065854
Lee's Antiques, 59 Whalley Rd., Clitheroe Lancs.
T. (01200) 24921. - Ant -   065855
Rebecca Antiques, 22 Moor Lane, Clitheroe Lancs.
T. (01200) 29461. - Paint / Furn -   065856

Clutton (Avon)
McCarthy, Ian & Diane, 112 Station Rd., Clutton Avon.
T. (01761) 53188. - Lights -   065857

Coalville (Leicestershire)
Keystone, 9 Ashby Rd., Coalville Leics.
T. (01530) 835966. - Paint / Furn / Jew -   065858
Massey's Antiques, 26 Hotel St., Coalville Leics.
T. (01530) 832374. - Ant / Furn -   065859

Coatbridge (Strathclyde)
Stewart Antiques, Michael, Hornock Cottages, Gartsher-
ry Rd., Coatbridge Scotland. T. (01236) 422532.
- Furn -   065860

Cobham (Surrey)
Antics, 44 Portsmouth Rd., Cobham Surrey.
T. (01932) 865505. - Ant / Furn / Naut -   065861
Cobham Galleries, 65 Portsmouth Rd., Cobham KT11
1JQ. T. (01932) 867909. - Paint / Furn / Instr -   065862

Cockermouth (Cumbria)
Cockermouth Antiques, 5 Station St., Cockermouth
Cumbria. T. (01900) 826746. - Ant / Paint /
Furn -   065863
Cockermouth Antiques Market, Courthouse, Main St.,
Cockermouth Cumbria. T. (01900) 824346.
- Ant -   065864
Holmes Antiques, 1 Market Pl., Cockermouth Cumbria.
T. (01900) 826114. - Paint / Graph / Furn -   065865

Codford (Wiltshire)
Tina's Antiques, 75 High St., Codford Wilts.
T. (01985) 50828. - Ant -   065866

Codicote (Hertfordshire)
Kimbell, Richard, Country Gardens, High St., Codicote
Herts. T. (01438) 821616. - Furn -   065867

Codsall (Staffordshire)
Dam Mill Antiques, Birches Rd., Codsall Staffs.
T. (01902) 843780. - Ant / Furn / China -   065868

Coggeshall (Essex)
Antique Metals, 9A East St, Coggeshall Essex.
T. (01376) 562252. - Ant -   065869
Antique Pine, 63/65 West St, Coggeshall Essex.
T. (01376) 561972. - Furn -   065870
Chairs, 11 Market Hill, Coggeshall Essex.
T. (01376) 562766. - Furn -   065871
Coggeshall Antiques, Doubleday Corner, Coggeshall Es-
sex. T. (01376) 562646. - Paint / Furn -   065872
Jobson's, Joan, 5A Church St, Coggeshall Essex.
T. (01376) 561717. - Ant / Furn / Naut -   065873
Marchant, Mark, 3 Market Sq., Coggeshall CO6 1TS.
T. (01376) 561188. - Furn / Dec / Instr -   065874

Colchester (Essex)
Badger, The Street, Elmstead Market, Colchester Essex.
T. (01206) 822044. - Furn / Tex / Instr -   065875
Barntiques, Lampitts Farm, Turkeycock Lane, Colchester
Essex. T. (01206) 210486. - Ant / Furn -   065876
Bond & Son, S., 14 North Hill, Colchester Essex.
T. (01206) 572925. - Paint / Furn -   065877
Cannon Antiques, Elizabeth, 85 Crouch St., Colchester
Essex. T. (01206) 575817. - Furn / Jew / Silv -   065878
Davana Original Interiors, 88 Hythe Hill, Colchester Es-
sex. T. (01206) 797853. - Furn / Tex / Lights -   065879
Dean Antiques, Margery, Hill Farm, Harwich Rd, Colche-
ster Essex. T. (01206) 250485, Fax (01206) 252040.
- Furn -   065880
Essex Antiques Centre, Priory St., Colchester Essex.
T. (01206) 871150. - Ant -   065881
Grahams of Colctester, 19 Short Wyre St., Colchester
Essex. T. (01206) 576808. - Jew / Silv -   065882
Iles Gallery, Richard, 10a, 10 and 12 Northgate St, Col-
chester Essex. T. (01206) 577877. - Paint -   065883
Partner & Puxon, 7 North Hill, Colchester CO1.
T. (01206) 573317. - Ant / Furn / China -   065884
Stock Exchange Antiques, 40 Osborne St., Colchester
Essex. T. (01206) 561997. - Ant -   065885
Trinity Antiques Centre, 7 Trinity St., Colchester CO1
1JN. T. (01206) 577775. - Ant / Furn -   065886
Wilkinson Antiques, Rita M., Heath Farm House Station
Rd, Colchester Essex. T. (01206) 822805.
- Furn -   065887

Coldstream (Borders)
Coldstream Antiques, 44 High St., Coldstream Scotland.
T. (01890) 2552. - Furn / Silv / Instr -   065888

Coleraine (Co. Londonderry)
Forge Antiques, 24 Long Commons, Coleraine N. Ireland.
T. (01265) 51339. - Ant / Silv / Instr -   065889

Colne (Lancashire)
Enloc Antiques, Birchenlee Mill, Lenches Rd., Colne
Lancs. T. (01282) 867101. - Furn -   065890

Colsterworth (Lincolnshire)
Underwood Antiques, Clive, 46 High St., Colsterworth
Lincs. T. (01476) 860689. - Paint / Furn /
China -   065891

Coltishall (Norfolk)
Allport-Lomax, Liz, Church St., Coltishall Norfolk.
T. (01603) 737631. - Paint / Furn / China -   065892
Bates & Sons, Eric, High St., Coltishall NR12 7AA.
T. (01603) 738716. - Ant / Furn -   065893
Bradbury Antiques, Roger, Church St., Coltishall Norfolk.
T. (01603) 737444. - Furn -   065894
Coltishall Antiques Centre, High St., Coltishall Norfolk.
T. (01603) 738306. - Ant -   065895
Golder, Gwendoline, Point House, High St., Coltishall
Norfolk. T. (01603) 738099. - Furn -   065896
Neal Cabinet Antiques, Isabel, Bank House, High St.,
Coltishall Norfolk. T. (01603) 737379. - Ant / Furn /
China -   065897

Colwyn Bay (Clwyd)
North Wales Antiques, 56-58 Abergele Rd., Colwyn Bay
Wales. T. (01492) 530521. - Ant / Furn -   065898

Colyton (Devon)
Brookfield Gallery, Market Pl., Colyton Devon.
T. (01297) 553541. - Graph / Furn / Instr -　065899
Colyton Antique Centre, Dolphin St., Colyton Devon.
T. (01297) 552339. - Ant -　065900

Combe Martin (Devon)
Retrospect Antiques, Sunnymede, King St., Combe Martin EX34 0AD. T. (01271) 882346. - Ant -　065901

Comberton (Cambridgeshire)
Comberton Antiques, 5a West St., Comberton Cambs.
T. (01223) 262674. - Ant / Furn / Naut -　065902

Compton (Surrey)
Old Post Office Antiques, The Street, Compton Surrey.
T. (01483) 810303. - Paint / Furn / China -　065903

Comrie (Tayside)
Coach House, Dundas St., Comrie Scotland.
T. (01764) 670765. - China -　065904

Congleton (Cheshire)
Buckley Antiques Exports, W., 35 Chelford Rd., Congleton Cheshire. T. (01260) 275299. - Furn / Naut -　065905
Congleton Antiques, 2 Cross St., Congleton Cheshire.
T. (01260) 298909. - Ant / Furn -　065906
Pine Too, 8/10 Road Hill, Congleton Cheshire.
T. (01260) 279228. - Furn -　065907

Coniston (Cumbria)
Old Man Antiques, Yewdale Rd., Coniston Cumbria.
T. (0153) 9441389. - Ant / Instr -　065908

Conwy (Gwynedd)
Black Lion Antiques, 11 Castle St., Conwy Wales.
T. (01492) 592470. - Furn / China -　065909
Char Bazaar, 25 Castle St., Conwy Wales.
T. (01492) 593429. - China -　065910
Conway Antiques, 17 Bangor Rd., Conwy Wales.
T. (01492) 592461. - Ant -　065911
Gibbs Antiques and Decorative Arts, Paul, 25 Castle St., Conwy Wales. T. (01492) 593429. - China / Mod -　065912

Cookham (Berkshire)
Phillips & Son, Dower House, Cookham SL6 9SN.
T. (016285) 529337. - Paint -　065913

Cookstown (Co. Tyrone)
Cookstown Antiques, 16 Oldtown St, Cookstown N. Ireland. T. (016487) 65279. - Ant / Paint / Mil -　065914
Saddle Room Antiques, 4 Coagh St., Cookstown N. Ireland. T. (0164) 8762033. - Furn / China / Silv -　065915

Corby Hill (Cumbria)
Langley, The Forge, Corby Hill Cumbria.
T. (01228) 560899. - Furn -　065916

Corringham (Essex)
Bush House, Church Rd., Corringham Essex.
T. (01375) 673463. - China -　065917

Corsham (Wiltshire)
Eden, Matthew, Pickwick End, Corsham SN13 0JB.
T. (01249) 713335, Fax (01249) 713644.
- Furn -　065918

Corwen (Clwyd)
Caxton House Antiques, Bridge St., Corwen Wales.
T. (01490) 413276. - Furn / China / Lights -　065919

Costessey (Norfolk)
Coach House, Townhouse Rd., Costessey Norfolk.
T. (01603) 742977. - Paint / Graph / Draw -　065920

Coulsdon (Greater London)
Decodream, 233 Chipstead Valley Rd, Coulsdon Surrey.
T. (0181) 6685534. - China -　065921
Potashnik Antiques, David, 7 The Parade, Stoats Nest Rd., Coulsdon Surrey. T. (0181) 660 8403. - Ant / Furn -　065922

Coupar Angus (Tayside)
Henderson Antiques, 35 Lintrose, Coupar Angus Scotland. T. (01828) 27450. - Furn -　065923

Coventry (West Midlands)
Antique Shop, 107 Spon End, Coventry West Mids.
T. (01203) 525915. - Ant -　065924
Memories Antiques, 400A Stoney Stanton Rd, Coventry West Mids. T. (01203) 687994. - Ant / Paint / Furn -　065925
Milton Antiques, 93 Dane Rd., Coventry West Mids.
T. (01203) 456285. - Furn / Naut -　065926
Spon End Antiques, 115-116 Spon End, Coventry West Mids. T. (01203) 228379. - Furn / Jew / Toys -　065927

Cowbridge (South Glamorgan)
Bulmer's, 42 Eastgate, Cowbridge Wales.
T. (01446) 775744. - Furn / China -　065928
Cowbridge Antiques, 55 Eastgate, Cowbridge Wales.
T. (01446) 774774. - Furn -　065929
Eastgate Antiques, 3 The Limes, Cowbridge Wales.
T. (01446) 775111. - Paint / Furn / Jew -　065930
Havard & Havard, 59 Eastgate, Cowbridge Wales.
T. (01446) 775021. - Furn -　065931
Owen Gallery, John, 55 Eastgate, Cowbridge Wales.
T. (014463) 774774. - Paint -　065932
Renaissance Antiques, 49 High St., Cowbridge Wales.
T. (01446) 773893. - Ant / Furn / China -　065933
Watercolour Gallery, Old Wool Barn, Verity's Court, Cowbridge Wales. T. (01446) 773324. - Paint -　065934

Cowes (Isle of Wight)
Galerias Segui, 75 High St., Cowes I. of Wight.
T. (01983) 292148. - Paint / Graph / Furn -　065935
Marine Gallery, 1 Bath Rd., Cowes I. of Wight.
T. (01983) 200124, Fax (01983) 297282. - Paint / Graph -　065936

Cowfold (West Sussex)
Cowfold Clocks, Old House, The Street, Cowfold Sussex West. T. (01403) 864505. - Ant / Furn / Instr -　065937
Squires Pantry Antiques, Station Rd., Cowfold Sussex West. T. (01403) 864869. - Furn -　065938

Cranborne (Dorset)
Tower Antiques, The Square, Cranborne Dorset.
T. (0172) 54552. - Furn -　065939

Cranbrook (Kent)
Cranbrook Antique Centre, 15 High St., Cranbrook Kent.
T. (01580) 712173. - Ant -　065940
Cranbrook Gallery, 21B Stone St, Cranbrook Kent.
T. (01580) 713021. - Paint / Graph -　065941
Old Bakery Antiques, Old Bakery, St. David's Bridge, Cranbrook TN17 3HN. T. (01580) 713103.
- Furn -　065942
Swan Antiques, Stone St., Cranbrook Kent.
T. (01580) 712720. - Ant / Furn / China -　065943
Wooden Chair Antiques, Waterloo Rd., Cranbrook Kent.
T. (01580) 713671. - Ant / Furn -　065944

Cranham (Gloucestershire)
Newman Gallery, Heather, Cranham GL6 6TX.
T. (01452) 812230. - Paint / Draw -　065945

Cranleigh (Surrey)
Rubenstein Fine Art, Barbara, Smithwood House, Smithwood Common, Cranleigh Surrey. T. (01483) 267969, Fax (01483) 267535. - Paint -　065946

Craven Arms (Shropshire)
I and S Antiques, Stokesay, Ludlow Rd., Craven Arms Shrops. T. (01588) 672263. - Furn -　065947

Crawley (West Sussex)
Hardman Antiques, Jennie, Spikemead Farm, Poles Ln., Lowfield Heath, Crawley Sussex West.
T. (01293) 560294, Fax (01293) 539826.
- Furn -　065948

Crayford (Greater London)
Watling Antiques, 139 Crayford Rd., Crayford Kent.
T. (01322) 523620. - Ant / Naut -　065949

Cremyll (Cornwall)
Cremyll Antiques, The Cottage, Cremyll Beach, Cremyll Cornwall. T. (01752) 822934. - Jew / Naut -　065950

Crewkerne (Somerset)
Antique and Country Pine, 14 East St., Crewkerne Somerset. T. (01460) 75623. - Furn -　065951
Crewkerne Furniture Emporium, Viney Bridge, South St., Crewkerne Somerset. T. (01460) 75319. - Furn / Naut -　065952
Oscars – Antique Market, 13-15 Market Sq., Crewkerne TA18 7LE. T. (01460) 72718. - Ant / Furn -　065953

Cricklade (Wiltshire)
Gwilliam, Edred A. F., Candletree House, Bath Rd., Cricklade Wilts. T. (01793) 750241. - Mil -　065954

Crieff (Tayside)
Antiques and Fine Art, 11 Comrie St., Crieff PH7 4AX.
T. (01764) 654496. - Ant / Paint / Furn -　065955
Crieff Antiques, Comrie Rd., Crieff Scotland.
T. (01764) 653322. - Furn / China / Lights -　065956
Strathearn Antiques, 2 Comrie St., Crieff Scotland.
T. (01764) 654344. - Ant / Num / Jew -　065957

Cromer (Norfolk)
Bond Street Antiques, 6 Bond St, and 38 Church St, Cromer Norfolk. T. (01263) 513134. - Furn / China / Jew -　065958
Rust Antiques, Benjamin, 3 Saint Margaret's Rd., Cromer Norfolk. T. (01263) 511452. - Instr / Glass -　065959
Seago, A. E., 15 Church St., Cromer Norfolk.
T. (01263) 512733. - Furn -　065960

Crosby Ravensworth (Cumbria)
Jennywell Hall Antiques, Crosby Ravensworth Cumbria.
T. (01931) 715288. - Paint / Furn -　065961

Croughton (Northamptonshire)
Croughton Antiques, 29 High St., Croughton Northants.
T. (01869) 810203. - Ant / Naut -　065962

Crowmarsh Gifford (Oxfordshire)
Pennyfarthing, 49 The Street, Crowmarsh Gifford Oxon.
T. (01491) 837470. - Furn / China / Silv -　065963

Croydon (Greater London)
Collectors Corner Antiques, 43 Brighton Rd., Croydon Surrey. T. (0181) 6807511. - Furn / Toys -　065964
Griffin G. E., 43a Brighton Rd., Croydon Surrey.
T. (0181) 6883130. - Ant -　065965
Trengove, 46 South End, Croydon CRO 1DP.
T. (0181) 6882155. - Ant / Paint -　065966
Whitgift Galleries, 77 South End, Croydon Surrey.
T. (0181) 6880990. - Paint -　065967

Cuckfield (West Sussex)
Foord-Brown Antiques, David, High St., Cuckfield Sussex West. T. (01444) 414418. - Furn / China -　065968
Hopkins, John, 1 The Courtyard, Ockenden Manor, Cuckfield Sussex West. T. (01444) 454323. - Paint / Furn -　065969
Usher Antiques, Richard, 23 South St., Cuckfield Sussex West. T. (01444) 451699. - Furn -　065970

Culham (Oxfordshire)
Dixon Fine Engravings, Rob, Warren Farmhouse, Thame Ln., Culham Oxon. T. (01235) 524676. - Graph / Fra -　065971

Cullompton (Devon)
Cobweb Antiques, Old Tannery, Exeter Rd., Cullompton Devon. T. (01884) 38207. - Furn -　065972
Cullompton Old Tannery Antiques, Exeter Rd, Cullompton Devon. T. (01884) 38476. - Furn / China -　065973
Mills Antiques, Old Tannery, Exeter Rd., Cullompton Devon. T. (01884) 32462. - Furn -　065974
Sunset Country Antiques, Old Tannery, Exeter Rd., Cullompton Devon. T. (01884) 32890. - Furn -　065975

Dalbeattie (Dumfries and Galloway)
Wildman's Antiques, 3 Maxwell St., Dalbeattie Scotland.
T. (01556) 610260. - Furn / Jew / Silv -　065976

Darlington (Durham)
Brown & Sons, S., 26 Hollyhurst Rd., Darlington Durham.
T. (01325) 354769. - Ant -　065977
Bygones, 3/5 McMullen Rd, Darlington Durham.
T. (01325) 461399. - Furn -　065978

Finnegan, Robin, 83 Skinnergate, Darlington Durham.
T. (01325) 489820. - Ant / Num / Jew -   065979
Nichol & Hill, 20 Grange Rd., Darlington Durham.
T. (01325) 357431. - Furn -   065980
Ramsey Antiques, Alan, Unit 10, Dudley Rd, Darlington
Durham. T. (01325) 361679. - Furn -   065981

Dartford (Kent)
Dartford Antiques, 27 East Hill, Dartford Kent.
T. (01322) 291350. - Furn -   065982

Darwen (Lancashire)
Cottage Antiques, 135 Blackburn Rd., Darwen Lancs.
T. (01254) 775891. - Furn / China -   065983
Darwen Antique Centre, Provident Hall, The Green, Darwen Lancs. T. (01254) 760565. - Paint / Furn /
China -   065984
K.C. Antiques, 538 Bolton Rd., Darwen Lancs.
T. (01254) 772252. - Furn -   065985

Datchet (Berkshire)
Alway Fine Art, Marian and John, Riverside Corner,
Windsor Rd., Datchet Berks. T. (01753) 541163,
Fax (01753) 541163. - Paint -   065986

Davenham (Cheshire)
Davenham Antique Centre, 461 London Rd., Davenham
Cheshire. T. (01606) 44350. - Ant / Graph /
Furn -   065987
Magpie Antiques, 4 Church St., Davenham Cheshire.
T. (01829) 260360. - Paint / Furn -   065988

Deal (Kent)
Decors, 67 Beach St., Deal Kent. T. (01304) 368030.
- Ant -   065989
Morales Antiques, José, 138 High St., Deal Kent.
T. (01304) 361461. - Graph / Furn -   065990
Print Room Gallery, 95a Beach St., Deal Kent.
T. (01304) 368904. - Graph -   065991
Quill Antiques, 12 Alfred Sq., Deal Kent.
T. (01304) 375958. - Ant / China -   065992
Serendipity, 168/170 High St, Deal Kent.
T. (01304) 369165. - Paint / Furn / China -   065993

Debenham (Suffolk)
Debenham Antiques Centre, Foresters Hall, High St., Debenham IP14 6QW. T. (01728) 860777. - Furn / China /
Glass -   065994
Lanchester, N., 21 High St., Debenham Suffolk.
T. (01728) 860756. - Ant / Naut -   065995

Deddington (Oxfordshire)
Castle Antiques, Manor Farm, Clifton, Deddington OX5
4PA. I. (01869) 38888. - Furn / China / Silv   065996
Deddington Antique Centre, Laurel House Market Sq,
Deddington Oxon. T. (01869) 38968. - Ant -   065997
Tuckers Country Store and Art Gallery, Market Pl., Deddington Oxon. T. (01869) 38215. - Paint / Furn /
Instr -   065998

Derby (Derbyshire)
Abbey House, 115 Woods Ln., Derby Derbys.
T. (01332) 31426. - Ant / Toys -   065999
Derby Antique Centre, 11 Friargate, Derby Derbys.
T. (01332) 385002. - Furn / China / Instr -   066000
Friargate Pine and Antiques Centre, Pump House, Stafford St, Derby Derbys. T. (01332) 41215. - Ant /
Furn -   066001
Tanglewood, 142 Ashbourne Rd., Derby Derbys.
T. (01332) 46005. - Furn -   066002
Ward, Charles H., 12 Friar Gate, Derby Derbys.
T. (01332) 42893. - Paint -   066003

Devizes (Wiltshire)
Cross Keys Jewellers, The Ginnel, Market Pl., Devizes
Wilts. T. (01380) 726293. - Jew / Silv -   066004

Dingwall (Highland)
Dingwall Antiques, 6 Church St., Dingwall Scotland.
T. (01349) 65593. - Graph / China / Glass -   066005

Disley (Cheshire)
Crescent Antiques, 7 Buxton Rd., Disley Cheshire.
T. (01663) 765677. - Ant / Furn / China -   066006
Mill Farm Antiques, 50 Market St., Disley SK12 2DT.
T. (01663) 764045. - Ant / Furn / Instr -   066007

Diss (Norfolk)
Diss Antiques, 2 Market Pl., Diss Norfolk.
T. (01379) 642213. - Furn / China / Instr -   066008
Gostling, 13 Market Hill, Diss Norfolk.
T. (01379) 650360. - Ant -   066009

Ditchling (East Sussex)
Dycheling, 34 High St., Ditchling Sussex East.
T. (01273) 842929. - Furn -   066010
Shaw Antiques, Nona, 4 and 8 West St, Ditchling Sussex
East. T. (01273) 843290. - Furn / China / Silv -   066011

Doddington (Cambridgeshire)
Doddington House Antiques, 2 Benwick Rd., Doddington
PE15 0TG. T. (01354) 740755. - Paint / Furn /
Instr -   066012

Donaghadee (Co. Down)
Furney, 3-4 Shore St., Donaghadee N. Ireland.
T. (01247) 883517, Fax (01247) 888729.
- Furn -   066013

Doncaster (South Yorkshire)
Doncaster Sales and Exchange, 20 Copley Rd., Doncaster Yorks South. T. (01302) 344857. - Ant -   066014

Dorchester (Dorset)
Colliton Antique and Craft Centre, Colliton St., North
Square, Dorchester Dorset. T. (01305) 269398. - Furn /
Jew -   066015
Dorchester Antiques Market, Hardy Hall, Dorchester Dorset. T. (01963) 62478. - Ant -   066016
Legg Antiques, Michael, 15 High East St., Dorchester
Dorset. T. (01305) 264596. - Paint / Furn /
China -   066017
Walker Antiques, John, 52 High West St., Dorchester
Dorset. T. (01305) 260324. - Furn / Tex -   066018

Dorchester-on-Thames (Oxfordshire)
Dorchester Galleries, Rotten Row, Dorchester-on-Thames OX9 8LJ. T. (01865) 341116. - Paint / Graph /
China -   066019
Giffengate Antiques, 16 High St., Dorchester-on-Thames
Oxon. T. (01865) 340028. - Paint / Furn /
China -   066020
Hallidays Antiques, Old College, High St., Dorchester-on-Thames OX9 8HL. T. (01865) 340028. - Ant / Paint /
Furn -   066021
Shambles Antiques, 3 High St., Dorchester-on-Thames
Oxon. T. (01865) 341373. - Furn -   066022

Dorking (Surrey)
Antiquaries Antique Centre, 56 West St., Dorking Surrey.
T. (01306) 743398. - Ant / Furn / Silv -   066023
Colins, Noel, 15 West St., Dorking Surrey.
- Jew -   066024
Collins, T. M., 70 High St., Dorking Surrey.
T. (01306) 880790. - Jew -   066025
Coombes, J. and M., 44 West St., Dorking Surrey.
T. (01306) 885479. - Ant -   066026
Dorking Antique Centre, 17-18 West St., Dorking Surrey.
T. (01306) 740915. - Ant -   066027
Dorking Desk Shop, 41 West St., Dorking RH4 1BU.
T. (01306) 883327, Fax (01306) 875363.
- Furn -   066028
Dorking Emporium Antiques Centre, 1A West St, Dorking
Surrey. T. (01306) 876646. - Furn -   066029
Hampshires of Dorking, 50-52 West St, Dorking Surrey.
T. (01306) 887076. - Furn -   066030
Hebeco, 47 West St., Dorking Surrey. T. (01306) 875396.
- China / Silv -   066031
Hollander, E., Dutch House, Horsham Rd., Dorking RH5
4NF. T. (01306) 888921. - Silv / Instr -   066032
Holmwood Antiques, Norfolk Rd., South Holmwood, Dorking Surrey. T. (01306) 888174. - Furn -   066033
King's Court Galleries, 54 West St., Dorking Surrey.
T. (01306) 881757, Fax (01306) 875305.
- Graph -   066034
Lang Antiques, John, Old King's Head Court, High St.,
Dorking Surrey. T. (01306) 882203. - Ant /
Furn -   066035
Norfolk House Galleries Antique Centre, 48 West St, Dorking Surrey. T. (01306) 881028. - Furn -   066036
Nostalgia, 1 West St., Dorking Surrey.
T. (01306) 880022. - Tex -   066037

Ockley Antiques, 43 West St., Dorking Surrey.
T. (01306) 712266. - Furn -   066038
Oriental Carpets and Decorative Arts, 37 West St., Dorking Surrey. T. (01306) 876370. - Tex -   066039
Owl House, 4 Lyons Court, Dorking Surrey.
T. (01306) 740239. - Furn -   066040
Quilt Room, 20 West St., Dorking Surrey.
T. (01306) 740739. - Tex -   066041
Saunderson Antiques, Elaine, 18-18a Church St., Dorking Surrey. T. (01306) 881231. - Furn -   066042
Thorpe & Foster, 49-52 West St, Dorking Surrey.
T. (01306) 881029. - Furn -   066043
Victoria and Edward Antiques Centre, 61 West St., Dorking Surrey. T. (01306) 889645. - Ant -   066044
Watson, Pauline, Old King's Head Court, High St., Dorking Surrey. T. (01306) 885452. - Jew / Silv -   066045
West Street Antiques, 63 West St., Dorking Surrey.
T. (01306) 883487. - Furn / China / Mil -   066046
Worth Antiques, Patrick, 11 West Street, Dorking Surrey.
T. (01306) 884484. - Furn -   066047

Dorney (Berkshire)
Old School Antiques, Old School, Village Rd., Dorney
SL4 6QW. T. (01628) 603247. - Ant / Furn /
China -   066048

Douglas (Isle of Man)
Corrin Antiques, John, 73 Circular Rd., Douglas I. of
Man. T. (01624) 629655. - Furn / Instr -   066049

Dover (Kent)
Bonnies, 18 Bartholomew St., Dover Kent.
T. (01304) 204206. - Ant -   066050
Morill, W. J., 437 Folkestone Rd., Dover Kent.
T. (01304) 201989. - Paint -   066051
Saunders, J. and L., 196-197 London Rd., Dover Kent.
T. (01304) 214003. - Ant -   066052
Stuff, 87 London Rd., Dover Kent. T. (01304) 215405.
- Ant -   066053

Droitwich (Hereford and Worcester)
Grant Fine Art, 9A Victroia Sq, Droitwich Herefs & Worcs.
T. (01905) 778155, Fax (01905) 794507. - Paint /
Graph -   066054
Wolt Antiques, H. and B., 128 Worcester Rd., Droitwich
WR9 8AN. T. (01905) 772320. - Ant / China /
Glass -   066055

Dronfield (Derbyshire)
Bardwell Antiques, 51 Chesterfield Rd., Dronfield Derbys. T. (01246) 412183. - Ant -   066056

Drumnadrochit (Highland)
Frere Antiques, Joan, Drumbule House, Drumnadrochit
Scotland. T. (0145) 62210. - Furn -   066057

Duffield (Derbyshire)
Wayside Antiques, 62 Town St., Duffield Derbys.
T. (01332) 840346. - Paint / China / Silv -   066058

Dulford (Devon)
Mounter, G., Bakers Farm, Dulford Derbys.
T. (018846) 358. - Furn -   066059

Dulverton (Somerset)
Acorn Antiques, 39 High St., Dulverton Somerset.
T. (01398) 23286. - Furn / China / Tex -   066060
Faded Elegance, 39 High St., Dulverton Somerst.
T. (01398) 23286. - Tex -   066061

Dumfries (Dumfries and Galloway)
Antiquarian, 71 Queensberry St., Dumfries Scotland.
T. (01387) 59970. - Furn / China / Silv -   066062
Cairnyard Antiques, Cairnyard, Beeswing, Dumfries
Scotland. T. (01387) 73218. - Ant / Furn / Instr -   066063
Dix, 100 English St., Dumfries Scotland.
T. (01387) 64234. - Ant -   066064

Dunchurch (Warwickshire)
Dunchurch Antique Centre, 16-16a Daventry Rd., Dunchurch Warks. T. (01788) 817147. - Ant -   066065

Dundee (Tayside)
Angus Antiques, 4 Saint Andrews St, Dundee Scotland.
T. (01382) 22128. - Jew / Mil -   066066

Livingstone, Neil, Unit South Grove Works, Brewery Ln.,
Dundee Scotland. T. (01382) 21618. - Furn -   066067
Westport Gallery, 3 Old Hawkhill, Dundee DD1 5EU.
T. (01382) 21751. - Ant / Paint -   066068

Dunkeld (Tayside)

Dunkeld Antiques, Tay Terrace, Dunkeld Scotland.
T. (01350) 720032. - Ant -   066069
Dunkeld Interiors, 14 Bridge St., Dunkeld Scotland.
T. (01350) 727582. - Furn -   066070
Stanley, K., High St., Dunkeld Scotland. - Ant -   066071

Dunmow (Essex)

Bennett, Julia, Flemings Hill Farm, Great Easton, Dunmow Essex. T. (01279) 850279. - Furn -   066072
Hilton, Simon, Flemings Hill Farm, Great Easton, Dunmow Essex. T. (01279) 850107. - Paint / Graph /
Sculp -   066073

Dunstable (Bedfordshire)

Castle Coins and Chiltern International Antiques, 47a
High St. South, Dunstable Beds. T. (01582) 606751.
- Ant / Num / Jew -   066074

Duxford (Cambridgeshire)

Mooney, Riro D., 4 Moorfield Rd., Duxford Cambs.
T. (01223) 832252. - Ant -   066075

Eaglescliffe (Cleveland)

Jordan, T. B. and R., Aslak, Aislaby, Eaglescliffe Cleveland. T. (01642) 782599. - Paint -   066076

Eaglesham (Southclyde)

Eaglesham Antiques, 73 Montgomery St., Eaglesham
Scotland. T. (0135) 532814. - Ant / China /
Silv -   066077

Easingwold (North Yorkshire)

Bow Antiques, 94 Long St., Easingwold Yorks North.
T. (01347) 822596. - Furn / China / Glass -   066078
Chapman Medd & Sons, Market Pl., Easingwold Yorks
North. T. (01347) 821370. - Furn -   066079
Mrs Reynolds, B.A.S., 42 Long St., Easingwold Yorks
North. T. (01347) 821078. - Ant -   066080
White House Farm Antiques, Thirsk Rd., Easingwold
Yorks North. T. (01347) 821479. - Ant -   066081

East Budleigh (Devon)

Antiques at Budleigh House, Budleigh House, East Budleigh EX9 7ED. T. (01395) 445368. - Ant / Furn /
China -   066082

East Grinstead (West Sussex)

Antique Atlas, 31A High St, East Grinstead Sussex West.
T. (01342) 315813. - Graph -   066083
Antique Print Shop, 11 Middle Row, East Grinstead RH19
3AX. T. (01342) 410501, Fax (01342) 322149. - Paint /
Graph / Draw -   066084
Atkinson Antiques, Keith, Moorhawes Farm, East Grin-
stead Sussex West. T. (01342) 870765,
Fax (01342) 870767. - Furn -   066085

East Horsley (Surrey)

Gould & Sons, A., Old Rectory Cottage Ockham Rd.
South, East Horsley KT24 6QJ. T. (0148) 653747.
- Furn / Instr -   066086

East Molesey (Surrey)

Abbott Antiques, 75 Bridge Rd., East Molesey Surrey.
T. (0181) 941 6398. - Instr -   066087
Antiques Arcade, 77 Bridge Rd., East Molesey Surrey.
T. (0181) 979 7954. - Ant -   066088
B.S. Antiques, 39 Bridge Rd., East Molesey Surrey.
T. (0181) 941 1812. - Graph / Furn / Instr -   066089
Court Gallery, 16 Bridge Rd., East Molesey Surrey.
T. (0181) 941 2212. - Paint / China -   066090
Gooday Shop and Studio, 48-50 Bridge Rd., East Mole-
sey Surrey. T. (0181) 979 9971. - Ant -   066091
Hampton Court Antiques, 75 Bridge Rd., East Molesey
Surrey. T. (0181) 941 6398. - Ant / Furn / Instr - 066092
Hope Phonographs and Gramophones, Howard, 21 Brid-
ge Rd., East Molesey Surrey. T. (0181) 941 2472.
- Instr / Music -   066093
Nicholas Antiques, 31 Bridge Rd., East Molesey Surrey.
T. (0181) 979 0354. - Ant / Furn / Dec -   066094

Sovereign Antique Centre, 53 Bridge Rd., East Molesey
Surrey. T. (0181) 783 0595. - Paint / Furn -   066095
Speed, Martin, 5 Bridge Rd., East Molesey Surrey.
T. (0181) 979 6690. - Ant / Furn -   066096

East Peckham (Kent)

North, Desmond and Amanda, The Orchard, Hale St ,
East Peckham Kent. T. (01622) 871353. - Tex - 066097

Eastbourne (East Sussex)

Barsley Antiques, Douglas, 44 Cornfield Rd., Eastbourne
Sussex East. T. (01323) 733666. - Furn / China /
Silv -   066098
Bell Antiques, 47 South St., Eastbourne Sussex East.
T. (01323) 641339. - Paint / Furn -   066099
Bruford & Son, Wm., 11/13 Cornfield Rd, Eastbourne
BN21 3NA. T. (01323) 725452. - Jew / Silv /   066100
Bygones, 24 Willingdon Rd., Eastbourne Sussex East.
T. (01323) 737537. - Tex -   066101
Cowderoy Antiques, John, 42 South St., Eastbourne
BN21 4XB. T. (01323) 720058. - Ant -   066102
Crest Antiques, 52 Grove Rd., Eastbourne Sussex East.
T. (01323) 721185. - Ant -   066103
Day of Eastbourne Fine Art, John, 9 Meads St., East-
bourne Sussex East. T. (01323) 725634.
- Paint -   066104
Eastbourne Antiques Market, 80 Seaside, Eastbourne
BN22 8QP. T. (01323) 720128. - Ant -   066105
Elliott & Scholz Antiques, 12 Willingdon Rd., Eastbourne
Sussex East. T. (01323) 732200. - Furn / Instr - 066106
Ludby Antiques, James, 34 Church St., Eastbourne Sus-
sex East. T. (01323) 732073. - Furn / China /
Glass -   066107
Old Town Hall Antique Centre, 52 Ocklynge Rd., East-
bourne Sussex East. T. (01323) 416016. - Furn / Chi-
na / Jew -   066108
Partridge Antiques, Timothy, 46 Ocklynge Rd., East-
bourne Sussex East. T. (01323) 638731.
- Furn -   066109
Pharoahs Antiques Centre, 28 South St., Eastbourne
Sussex East. T. (01323) 738655. - Ant -   066110
Pickering, Ernest, 44 South St., Eastbourne Sussex East.
T. (01323) 730483. - Furn / China / Instr -   066111
Premier Gallery, 24-26 South St., Eastbourne Sussex
East. T. (01323) 736023. - Paint -   066112
Stacy-Marks, E., 24 Cornfield Rd., Eastbourne Sussex
East. T. (01323) 720429, Fax (01323) 733897.
- Paint -   066113
Stewart Gallery, 25 Grove Rd., Eastbourne Sussex East.
T. (01323) 729588, Fax (01323) 729588. - Paint / Chi-
na / Glass -   066114
Weller Restoration Centre, W. H., 12 North St., East-
bourne BN21 1AA. T. (01323) 410972. - Ant /
Silv -   066115

Eastleigh (Hampshire)

Tappers Antiques, 186 Southampton Row, Eastleigh
Hants. T. (01703) 643105. - Ant -   066116

Eccleston (Lancashire)

Bygone Times, Times House, Grove Mill, The Green, Eccleston Lancs. T. (01257) 453780. - Ant -   066117
3 L's Antiques, Unit 4, The Arches, Grove Development
Centre, Eccleston Lancs. T. (01257) 450290. - Furn /
China -   066118

Edenbridge (Kent)

Chevertons, 67-71 High St, Edenbridge Kent.
T. (01732) 863196, Fax (01732) 864298. - Ant /
Furn -   066119

Edenfield (Lancashire)

Antique Shop, 17 Market St., Edenfield Lancs.
T. (0170) 6823107. - Ant / Naut -   066120

Edgware (Greater London)

Edgware Antiques, 19 Whitchurch Lane, Edgware HA8
6JZ. T. (0181) 952 1608. - Graph / Furn /
China -   066121

Edinburgh (Lothian)

Another World, 25 Candlemaker Row., Edinburgh EH1
2QG. T. (0131) 225 1988. - Orient -   066122

Antiques, 48 Thistle St., Edinburgh Scotland.
T. (0131) 226 3625. - Paint / China / Glass -   066123
Behar Carpets, 12a Howe St., Edinburgh Scotland.
T. (0131) 225 1069. - Tex -   066124
Black, Laurance, 45 Cumberland St., Edinburgh Scot-
land. T. (0131) 557 4545. - Paint / Furn /
China -   066125
Bonnar Jewellers, Josph, 72 Thistle St., Edinburgh Scot-
land. T. (0131) 226 2811. - Jew -   066126
Bourne Fine Art, 4 Dundas St., Edinburgh Scotland.
T. (0131) 557 4050. - Paint -   066127
Calton Gallery, 10 Royal Terrace, Edinburgh Scotland.
T. (0131) 556 1010, Fax (0131) 5581150. - Paint /
Graph / Sculp -   066128
Cinders, 3 East Trinity Rd, Edinburgh Scotland.
T. (0131) 5520491. - Furn -   066129
Clark Gallery, Carson, 173 Canongate, Royal Mile, Edin-
burgh Scotland. T. (0131) 556 4710. - Graph - 066130
Collectors Shop, 49 Cockburn St., Edinburgh Scotland.
T. (0131) 226 3391. - Num / Silv / Mil -   066131
Court Curio Shop, 519 Lawnmarket, Edinburgh Scotland.
T. (0131) 225 3972. - Ant -   066132
Davidson & Begg Antiques, 183-189 Causewayside,
Edinburgh EH1 2JV. T. (0131) 6624221. - Ant / Paint /
Furn -   066133
Day Antiques, Alan, 13c Dundas St., Edinburgh Scotland.
T. (0131) 557 5220. - Ant / Furn -   066134
Drysdale, A. F., 20 and 35 Noth West Circus Pl, Edin-
burgh EH3 6TW. T. (0131) 225 4686,
Fax (0131) 2257100. - Ant / Lights -   066135
Duff Antiques, George, 254 Leith Walk, Edinburgh Scot-
land. T. (0131) 554 8164. - Naut -   066136
Dunedin Antiques, 4 North West Circus Pl., Edinburgh
Scotland. T. (0131) 220 1574. - Furn -   066137
Edinburgh Coin Shop, 2 Polwarth Crescent, Edinburgh
Scotland. T. (0131) 229 3007. - Num / Jew /
Instr -   066138
Ellis Antiques, Donald, 7 Bruntsfield Pl, Edinburgh EH10
4HN. T. (0131) 2294720. - Furn / China / Silv - 066139
Fideolo, Tom, 49 Cumberland St., Edinburgh Scotland.
T. (0131) 557 2444. - Paint -   066140
Forrest & Co Antiques, E. B., 3 Barcley Terrace, Edin-
burgh Scotland. T. (0131) 229 3156. - China / Jew /
Silv -   066141
Fyfe's Antiques, 41 Thistle St., Edinburgh Scotland.
T. (0131) 225 4287. - Paint / Furn / China -   066142
Georgian Antiques, 10 Pattison St, Edinburgh Scotland.
T. (0131) 553 7286, Fax (0131) 5536299. - Ant /
Furn -   066143
Gladrags, 17 Henderson Row, Edinburgh Scotland.
T. (0131) 557 1916. - Tex -   066144
Goodwin's Antiques, 15-16 Queensferry St., Edinburgh
Scotland. T. (0131) 225 4717. - Jew / Silv - 066145
Hand in Hand, 3 North West Circus Pl., Edinburgh Scot-
land. T. (0131) 226 3598. - Tex -   066146
Herrald Antiques, 38 Queen St., Edinburgh Scotland.
T. (0131) 225 5939. - Furn / Tex -   066147
Innes Gallery, 67 George St., Edinburgh EH2.
T. (0131) 226 4151, Fax (0131) 2264151.
- Paint -   066148
Jackson, Kenneth, 66 Thistle St., Edinburgh EH3 6Q0.
T. (0131) 225 9634. - Furn -   066149
Jacksonville Antiques Warehouse, 108A Causewayside,
Edinburgh Scotland. T. (0131) 667 0616. - Furn /
Naut -   066150
Letham, 20 Dundas St., Edinburgh EH3 6HZ.
T. (0131) 556 6565. - Ant / Paint / Furn / Orient / China /
Jew / Silv / Glass / Mod -   066151
Letham, David, 65 Queen Charlotte St., Edinburgh EH6
7ET. T. (0131) 554 6933. - Ant / Furn -   066152
MacAdam, Wiliam, 86 Pilrig St., Edinburgh Scotland.
T. (0131) 553 1364. - Glass -   066153
Macintosh & Co, William, 499 Lawnmarket, Edinburgh
Scotland. T. (0131) 225 6113. - Furn -   066154
Mathieson, John & Co., John, 48 Frederick St., Edin-
burgh Scotland. T. (0131) 225 6798. - Paint /
Graph -   066155
Mulherron Antiques, 83 Grassmarket, Edinburgh Scot-
land. T. (0131) 226 5907. - Furn / Tex -   066156
Nelson, John O., 22-24 Victoria St., Edinburgh EH1 2JW.
T. (0131) 2254413. - Paint / Graph -   066157
Now and Then, 7 and 9 West Crosscauseway, Edinburgh
Scotland. T. (0131) 668 2927. - Furn / Instr - 066158

Open Eye Gallery, 75/79 Cumberland, Edinburgh Scotland. T. (0131) 557 1020. - Paint / China / Jew - *066159*

Parry, H., 330 Lawnmarket, Edinburgh Scotland. T. (0131) 225 7615. - Furn / China / Silv - *066160*

Quadrant Antiques, 5 North West Circus Pl., Stockbridge, Edinburgh Scotland. T. (0131) 226 7282. - Ant / Furn / Instr - *066161*

Royal Mile Curios, 363 High St., Edinburgh Scotland. T. (0131) 226 4050. - Jew / Silv - *066162*

Scott, James, 43 Dundas St., Edinburgh Scotland. T. (0131) 556 8260. - Ant - *066163*

Scottish Gallery, 16 Dundas St, Edinburgh EH2 3DF. T. (0131) 5581200, Fax (0131) 2262312. - Paint / China / Jew - *066164*

Shackleton, Daniel, 17 Dundas St., Edinburgh Scotland. T. (0131) 557 1115. - Paint / Graph - *066165*

Stockbridge Antiques and Fine Art, 8 Deanhaugh St, Edinburgh Scotland. T. (0131) 332 1366. - Paint / China / Glass - *066166*

This and That Antiques and Bric-a-Brac, 22 Argyle Pl., Edinburgh Scotland. T. (0131) 229 6069. - Furn / China / Silv - *066167*

Thrie Estaits, 49 Dundas St., Edinburgh Scotland. T. (0131) 556 7084. - Furn / China / Glass - *066168*

Unicorn Antiques, 65 Dundas St., Edinburgh EH3. T. (0131) 556 7176. - Lights / Glass / Lights - *066169*

West Bow Antiques, 102 West Bow, Edinburgh Scotland. T. (0131) 226 2852. - Furn / China / Glass - *066170*

Whyte, John, 116b Rose St., Edinburgh Scotland. T. (0131) 225 2140. - Jew / Silv / Instr - *066171*

Whytock & Reid, Sunbury House, Belford Mews, Edinburgh EH4 3DN. T. (0131) 226 4911, Fax (0131) 2264595. - Furn / Tex - *066172*

Wild Rose Antiques, 15 Henderson Row, Edinburgh Scotland. T. (0131) 5571916. - Ant - *066173*

Young, Aldric, 49 Thistle St., Edinburgh EH2 1DY. T. (0131) 226 4101. - Ant / Paint / Furn - *066174*

Young Antiques, 36 Bruntsfield Pl., Edinburgh Scotland. T. (0131) 229 1361. - Furn / China / Tex - *066175*

Egham (Surrey)

Fisher, 94 High St., Egham Surrey. T. (01932) 849624. - Ant - *066176*

Pastimes, 86 High St.,, Egham Surrey. T. (01784) 436290. - Ant - *066177*

Elgin (Grampian)

West End Antiques, 35 High St., Elgin Scotland. T. (01343) 547531. - Ant / Jew / Silv - *066178*

Ellesmere (Shropshire)

White Lion Antiques, Market St., Ellesmere SY12 0AN. T. (01691) 622335. - Furn / China / Instr - *066179*

Ely (Cambridgeshire)

Mrs Mills Antiques, 1a Saint Mary's St., Ely Cmabs. T. (01353) 664268. - Ant / China / Jew - *066180*

Waterside Antiques, The Wharf, Ely Cambs. T. (01353) 667066. - Ant - *066181*

Empingham (Leicestershire)

Churchgate Antiques, 13 Church St., Empingham Leics. T. (0178) 086528. - Paint / Graph / Furn - *066182*

Old Bakery Antiques, Church St., Empingham Leics. T. (0178) 086243. - Furn / China - *066183*

Emsworth (Hampshire)

Tiffins Antiques, 12 Queen St., Emsworth Hants. T. (01243) 372497. - Ant / Lights / Instr - *066184*

Endmoor (Cumbria)

Calvert Antiqes, Sycamore House, Endmoor Cumbria. T. (015395) 67597. - Furn / Instr - *066185*

Enfield (Greater London)

Enfield Corner Cupboard, 61 Chase Side, Enfield Middx. T. (0181) 363 6493. - Furn / China / Silv - *066186*

Kimbell, Richard, Country World, Cattlegate Rd., Enfield Middx. T. (0181) 364 6661. - Furn - *066187*

La Trouvaille, 1A Windmill Hill, Enfield Middx. T. (0181) 367 1080. - Ant / Graph / Furn - *066188*

Epping (Essex)

Epping Galleries, 64-66 High St., Epping Essex. T. (01992) 573023. - Furn / Instr / Music - *066189*

Epping Saturday Market, Rear of 64-66 High St., Epping Essex. T. (01992) 573023. - Ant - *066190*

Epsom (Surrey)

Fogg Antiques, 75 South St., Epsom Surrey. T. (01372) 726931. - Furn - *066191*

Errol (Tayside)

Errol Antiques, The Cross, Errol Scotland. T. (01821) 642391. - Paint / Furn - *066192*

Greycroft Antiques, Greycroft, Station Rd., Errol Scotland. T. (01821) 642221. - Furn / China - *066193*

Eton (Berkshire)

Antiquus, 17 High St., Eton Berks. T. (01753) 831039. - Furn / China / Tex - *066194*

Barnett, Roger, 91 High St., Eton Berks. T. (01753) 867785. - Ant - *066195*

Cavendish Fine Arts, 127-128 High St., Eton Berks. T. (01753) 860850. - Furn / China / Glass - *066196*

Eton Gallery Antiques, 116 High St., Eton SL4 6AN. T. (01753) 865147. - Paint / Furn / Instr - *066197*

Eyre & Greig, 20 High St., Eton Berks. T. (01753) 859562. - Paint / Furn / Glass - *066198*

Hayden Antiques, Shirley, 79 High St., Eton Berks. T. (01753) 833085. - Paint / Furn / China / Lights - *066199*

Manley, J., 27 High St., Eton Berks. T. (01753) 865647. - Paint / Graph - *066200*

Martin, Peter J., 40 High St., Eton Berks. T. (01753) 864901. - Furn - *066201*

Mostly Boxes, 92 High St., Eton Berks. T. (01753) 858470. - Ant / Furn - *066202*

Oliver, Tony L., Longclose House, Common Rd., Eton Berks. T. (01753) 862637. - Mil - *066203*

Partnership, 80 High St., Eton Berks. T. (01753) 860752. - Furn - *066204*

Stafford Antiques, Ulla, 41 High St., Eton SL4 6BD. T. (01753) 859625. - Furn / Orient / China - *066205*

Studio 101, 101 High St., Eton Berks. T. (01753) 863333. - Furn / Silv - *066206*

Times Past Antiques, 59 High St., Eton Berks. T. (01753) 857018. - Furn / China / Silv / Instr - *066207*

Turks Heas Antiques, 98 High St., Eton. T. (01753) 863939. - Jew / Silv / Glass - *066208*

Eversley (Hampshire)

Kingsley Barn Antique Centre, Church Ln., Eversley Hants. T. (01734) 328518. - Furn - *066209*

Evesham (Worcestershire)

Magpie Antiques and Antiques, 2 Port St, and 61 High St, Evesham Herefs & Worcs. T. (01386) 41031. - Ant / Furn / Silv - *066210*

Yesterday, 79 Port St., Evesham Herefs & Worcs. T. (01386) 48068. - China / Tex / Jew - *066211*

Ewell (Surrey)

Token House Antiques, 7 Market Parade, High St., Ewell Surrey. T. (0181) 393 9654. - Furn / China / Glass - *066212*

Ewhurst (Surrey)

Cranleigh Antiques, Milkhill, The Street, Ewhurst Surrey. T. (01483) 277318. - Furn - *066213*

Exeter (Devon)

Antique Centre on the Quay, The Quay, Exeter Devon. T. (01392) 214180. - Ant - *066214*

Bruford & Son, Wm., 1 Bedford St., Exeter Dvon. T. (01392) 54901. - Jew / Silv - *066215*

Fagin Antiques, Old Whiteways, Cider Factory, Hele, Exeter Devon. T. (01392) 882062. - Furn / Naut - *066216*

Gold and Silver Exchange, Eastgate House, Princesshay, Exeter Devon. T. (01392) 217478. - Jew - *066217*

Micawber Antiques, 25-26 Gandy St., Exeter Devon. T. (01392) 52200. - Ant / China / Lights - *066218*

Mortimer, Brian, 87 Queen St., Exeter Devon. T. (01392) 79994. - Ant / China / Jew - *066219*

Nathan Antiques, John, 153-154 Cowick St., Exeter Devon. T. (01392) 78216. - Jew / Silv / Instr - *066220*

Pirouette, 5 West St., Exeter Devon. T. (01392) 432643. - Tex - *066221*

Priory Antiques, 19-20 Friernhay St., Exeter Devon. T. (01392) 495928. - Furn - *066222*

Quay Gallery Antiques Emporium, 43 The Quay, Exeter Devon. T. (01392) 213283. - Furn / China / Silv - *066223*

Wadham, Peter, 5 Cathedral Close, Exeter Devon. T. (01392) 439741. - Graph / Furn / Glass - *066224*

Exmouth (Devon)

Boase & Vaughan Antiques and Jewellery, 5 High St., Exmouth Devon. T. (01395) 271528. - Jew / Silv - *066225*

Treasures, 32-34 Exeter Rd., Exmouth Devon. T. (01395) 273258. - Ant - *066226*

Eye (Suffolk)

Corner Shop, Castle St., Eye Suffolk. T. (01379) 870614. - Ant - *066227*

Fairford (Gloucestershire)

Blenheim, Market Pl., Fairford GL7 4AB. T. (01285) 712094. - Furn / Instr - *066228*

Cirencester Antiques, High St., Fairford Suffolk. T. (01285) 713774. - Furn - *066229*

Gloucester House Antiques, Market Pl., Fairford Glos. T. (01285) 712790, Fax (01285) 713324. - Furn / China / Dec - *066230*

Fakenham (Norfolk)

Fakenham Antique Centre, 14 Norwich Rd., Fakenham Norfolk. T. (01328) 862941. - Ant - *066231*

Market Place Antiques, 28 Upper Market Pl., Fakenham Norfolk. - Ant / China / Jew - *066232*

Rivett Antiques and Bygones, Sue, 6 Norwich Rd., Fakenham Norfolk. T. (01328) 862924. - Ant - *066233*

Falkirk (Central)

Finlay, James, 178 Grahams Rd., Falkirk Scotland. T. (01324) 31505. - Ant / Furn - *066234*

Falmouth (Cornwall)

Cunningham Antique, E., 5 Webber St., Falmouth Cornwall. T. (01326) 313207. - Ant - *066235*

Maggs, John, 54 Church St., Falmouth Cornwall. T. (01326) 313153. - Graph - *066236*

Rosina's, 4 High St., Falmouth Cornwall. T. (01326) 311406. - Tex / Music - *066237*

Waterfront Antiques Market, 4 Quay St., Falmouth Cornwall. T. (01326) 311491. - Furn / China / Silv - *066238*

Fareham (Hampshire)

Elizabethans, 58 High St., Fareham PO16 7BG. T. (01329) 234964. - Ant / Furn / Jew - *066239*

Faringdon (Oxfordshire)

A. and F. Partners, 20 London St., Faringdon Oxon. T. (01367) 2420078. - Furn - *066240*

Faringdon Gallery, 21 London St., Faringdon Oxon. T. (01367) 2422030. - Paint - *066241*

La Chaise Antique, 30 London St., Faringdon SN7 7AA. T. (01367) 240427, Fax (01367) 241001. - Ant / Furn - *066242*

Farnborough (Greater London)

Farnborough Antiques, 10 Church Rd., Farnborough BR6 7DB. T. (01689) 854286. - Furn / Sculp - *066243*

Farnborough (Hampshire)

Martin & Parke, 97 Lynchford Rd., Farnborough Hants. T. (01252) 515311. - Furn / Naut - *066244*

Farndon (Cheshire)

Meadowcroft Antiques, Stephen, 65 High St., Farndon Cheshire. T. (01829) 270377. - Furn - *066245*

Farnham (Surrey)

Bits and Pieces, 82 West St., Farnham Surrey. T. (01252) 722355. - Furn / Mod - *066246*

Bourne Mill Antiques, Guildford Rd., Farnham Surrey. T. (01252) 716663. - Ant / Paint / Furn - *066247*

Casque and Gauntlet Antiques, 55/59 Badshot Lea Rd, Farnham Surrey. T. (01252) 20745. - Mil - *066248*

Christopher's Antiques, 39a West St., Farnham Surrey. T. (01252) 713794. - Furn - *066249*

Farnham Antique Centre, 27 South St., Farnham Surrey. T. (01252) 724475. - Ant - *066250*

Heytesbury, Farnham Surrey. T. (01252) 850893. - Furn /
Tex -   *066251*

Jordan, P. and B., 90 West St., Farnham Surrey.
T. (01252) 716272. - Paint / Furn / China -   *066252*

Maltings Monthly Market, Bridge Sq., Farnham Surrey.
T. (01252) 726234. - Ant -   *066253*

Putnam, R. and M., 60 Downing St., Farnham Surrey.
T. (01252) 715769. - Paint / Furn / China -   *066254*

Village Pine, 32 West St., Farnham Surrey.
T. (01252) 726660. - Furn -   *066255*

Weijand Fine Oriental Carpets, Karel, Lion and Lamb
Courtyard, Farnham Surrey. T. (01252) 726215.
- Tex -   *066256*

Wrecclesham Antiques, 47 Wresslesham Rd., Farnham
Surrey. T. (01252) 716468. - Furn / Instr -   *066257*

Farnham Common (Buckinghamshire)
A Thing of Beauty, 5 Broadway, Farnham Common
Bucks. T. (01753) 642099. - Ant / Furn -   *066258*

Farningham (Kent)
Beasley, P. T., Forge Yard, High St., Farningham Kent.
T. (01322) 862453. - Furn / Tex -   *066259*

Faversham (Kent)
Gunpowder House Antiques, 78 Lower West St., Faversham Kent. T. (01795) 534208. - Ant -   *066260*

Squires Antiques, 3 Jacob Yard, Preston St., Faversham
Kent. T. (01795) 531503. - Ant -   *066261*

Felixstowe (Suffolk)
McCulloch Antiques, John, 1a Hamilton Rd., Felixstowe
Suffolk. T. (01394) 283126. - Paint / Furn /
Instr -   *066262*

Felpham (West Sussex)
Botting, Susan and Robert, 38 Firs Av., Felpham Sussex
West. T. (01243) 584515. - Paint -   *066263*

Felsted (Essex)
Argyll House Antiques, Argyll House, Station Rd., Felsted
Essex. T. (01371) 820682. - Furn / China -   *066264*

Feock (Cornwall)
Strickland & Dorling, Come-to-Good, Feock Cornwall.
T. (01872) 862394. - Furn / China / Jew -   *066265*

Fernhurst (West Sussex)
Hamilton, Steelagh, 9b Midhurst Rd., Fernhurst Sussex
West. T. (01428) 653253. - Paint / Furn -   *066266*

Filey (North Yorkshire)
Cairncross & Sons, 31 Bellevue St., Filey Yorks North.
T. (01723) 513287. - Mil -   *066267*

Filey Antiques, 1 Belle Vue St., Filey Yorks North.
T. (01723) 513440. - Ant / Furn / Jew -   *066268*

Finchingfield (Essex)
Tate, Andrew, Great Wincey Farm, Finchingfield Essex.
T. (01371) 810004. - Furn -   *066269*

Finedon (Northamptonshire)
Burnett Antiques, Jean, 37 High St., Finedon Northants.
T. (01933) 681882. - Ant -   *066270*

Chapman, M. C., 3-3a Church St., Finedon NN9 5NA.
T. (01933) 681260. - Furn / Instr -   *066271*

Finedon Antiques, 3 Church St., Finedon Northants.
T. (01933) 681260. - Ant -   *066272*

Noton Antiques, 1 High St., Finedon Northamb.
T. (01933) 680973. - Ant -   *066273*

Quaker Lodge Antiques, 28 Church St., Finedon Nor-
thambs. T. (01933) 680371. - Ant / Furn -   *066274*

Thorpe Antiques, 51 High St., Finedon Northants.
T. (01933) 680196. - Furn -   *066275*

Fishguard (Dyfed)
Hermitage Antiques, 10 West St., Fishguard Wales.
T. (01348) 873037. - Ant / Jew / Mil -   *066276*

Manor House Antiques, Main St., Fishguard Wales.
T. (01348) 873260. - Ant / China -   *066277*

Flimwell (Sussex)
Lower, Graham, Stonecrouch Farmhouse, Flimwell Sussex East. T. (0158) 087535. - Furn -   *066278*

Flore (Northamptonshire)
Madeira, V. and C., The Huntershields, Flore Northants.
T. (01327) 40718, Fax (01327) 349263.
- Furn -   *066279*

Fochabers (Grampian)
Antiques and Interior Design, 64 High St., Fochabers
Scotland. i. (01343) 549313. - Furn / China -   *066280*

Granny's Kist, 22 The Square, Fochabers Scotland.
T. (01343) 820838. - Furn -   *066281*

Pringle Antiques, High St., Fochabers Scotland.
T. (01343) 820362. - Ant / Furn / China -   *066282*

Folkestone (Kent)
Amos, Richard, 37 Cheriton High St., Folkestone Kent.
T. (01303) 275449. - Ant -   *066283*

Lord Antiques, Alan, 71 Tontine St., Folkestone CT20
IJR. T. (01303) 253674. - Furn -   *066284*

Marrin & Sons, G. and D. I., 149 Sandgate Rd., Folkestone Kent. T. (01303) 253016, Fax (01303) 850956.
- Paint / Graph / Draw -   *066285*

Fordham (Cambridgeshire)
Phoenix Antiques, 1 Carter St., Fordham CB7 5NG.
T. (01638) 720363. - Furn / China / Instr -   *066286*

Fordingbridge (Hampshire)
Collier, Mark, 24 High St., Fordingbridge SP6 1AX.
T. (01425) 652555, Fax (01425) 656886.
- Ant -   *066287*

Quatrefoil, Burgate, Fordingbridge SP6 1LX.
T. (01425) 653309. - Furn / Sculp -   *066288*

Forres (Grampian)
Low Antiques, Michael, 45 High St., Forres Scotland.
T. (01309) 673696. - Ant -   *066289*

Fortrose (Highland)
Black Isle Antiques, Fortrose IV10. T. (01381) 20407.
- China -   *066290*

Four Elms (Kent)
Treasures, The Cross Rds., Four Elms Kent.
T. (0173) 270363. - China / Jew / Silv -   *066291*

Yew Tree Antiques, The Cross Rds., Four Elms Kent.
T. (01732) 70215. - China / Tex / Jew -   *066292*

Four Oaks (Warwickshire)
Allen Watch and Clockmaker, M., 76A Walsall Rd, Four
Oaks West Mids. T. (0121) 3086117. - Instr -   *066293*

Taylor, Robert, Windy Ridge, Worcester Ln., Four Oaks
West Mids. T. (0121) 3084209. - Toys -   *066294*

Fowlmere (Cambridgeshire)
Mere Antiques, High St., Fowlmere Cambs.
T. (01763) 208477. - Furn / China / Instr -   *066295*

Framlingham (Suffolk)
Bed Bazaar, 29 Double St., Framlingham Suffolk.
T. (01728) 723756, Fax (01728) 724626.
- Furn -   *066296*

Goodbreys, 29 Double St., Framlingham Suffolk.
T. (01728) 723756. - Paint / Furn / China -   *066297*

Freshwater (Isle of Wight)
Aladdin's Cave, 147-149 School Green Rd., Freshwater
I. of Wight. T. (01983) 752934. - China / Tex -   *066298*

Frinton on Sea (Essex)
Dickens Curios, 151 Connaught Av., Frinton on Sea
CO13 9AH. T. (01255) 674134. - Furn / Num /
Jew -   *066299*

Frinton Antiques, 5 Old Rd., Frinton on Sea Essex.
T. (01255) 671894. - Furn / China / Silv -   *066300*

Friockheim (Tayside)
Barclay, M. J. and D., 29 Gardyne St., Friockheim DD11
4SQ. T. (012412) 265. - Ant / Furn / China -   *066301*

Frome (Somerset)
Sutton & Sons, 15 and 33 Vicarage St, Frome Somerset.
T. (01373) 462062/462526. - Ant / Furn / Instr - *066302*

Gainsborough (Lincolnshire)
Carrick Antiques, G., 130 Trinity St, Gainsborough Lincs.
T. (01427) 611393. - Ant / Naut -   *066303*

Van Hefflin, 12 High St., Kriton Lindsey, Gainsborough
Lincs. T. (01652) 648044. - Jew / Instr -   *066304*

Galston (Southclyde)
Galleries de Fresnes, Cessnock Castle, Galston Lincs.
T. (01563) 820314. - Ant -   *066305*

Gants Hill (Greater London)
Antique Clock Repair Shoppe, 26 Woodford Av., Gants
Hill Essex. T. (0181) 550 9540. - Graph / Instr -   *066306*

Gargrave (North Yorkshire)
Antiques at Forge Cottage, 22-24 High St., Gargrave
Yorks North. T. (01756) 749796. - Ant -   *066307*

Blackburn, H., 9 East St., Gargrave Yorks North.
T. (01756) 749796. - Paint / Furn / China -   *066308*

Dickinson, Bernard, Estate Yard, West St., Gargrave
Yorks North. T. (01756) 748257. - Furn -   *066309*

Gargrave Gallery, 48 High St., Gargrave Yorks North.
T. (01756) 749641. - Ant -   *066310*

Myers Galleries, High St, Gargrave BD23 3LX.
T. (01756) 749587. - Furn / China -   *066311*

Gateshead (Tyne and Wear)
Boadens of Hexham, 28 The Boulevard, Gateshead Tyne
& Wear. T. (0191) 460 0358. - Paint / China /
Jew -   *066312*

Metro Antiques, 31 The Boulevard, Antique Village, Metrocentre, Gateshead Tyne & Wear. T. (0191) 460 0340.
- Graph / Furn / China -   *066313*

Sovereign Antiques, 35 The Boulevard, Antique Village,
Metrocentre, Gateshead Tyne & Wear.
T. (0191) 460 9604. - Graph / Jew / Silv -   *066314*

Gedney (Lincolnshire)
Johnston, Paul, Old Red Lion, Gedney PE12 0DB.
T. (01406) 362414. - Furn -   *066315*

Gillingham (Kent)
Dickens Antiques, 42 Sturdee Av., Gillingham Kent.
T. (01634) 850950. - Furn / Jew -   *066316*

Gilwern (Gwent)
Gilwern Antiques, Main Rd, Gilwern NP7 0AS.
T. (01873) 830276. - Ant -   *066317*

Glasgow (Strathclyde)
Albany Antiques, 1347 Argyle St., Glasgow G3 8AD.
T. (0141) 339 4267. - Furn / China / Naut -   *066318*

Bath Street Antiques Galleries, 203 Bath St., Glasgow
Scotland. T. (0141) 248 4220. - Ant -   *066319*

Butler's Funiture Galleries, 24-26 Millbrae Rd., Langside, Glasgow Scotland. T. (0141) 632 9853.
- Furn -   *066320*

Forrest, James, 53 West Nile St., Glasgow Scotland.
T. (0141) 221 0494. - Jew / Silv / Instr -   *066321*

Heritage House Antiques, Unit 6a, Yorkhill Quay, Glasgow Scotland. T. (0141) 334 4924. - Ant /
Furn -   *066322*

Kerr Antiques, Caroline, 103 Niddrie Rd., Queens Park,
Glasgow Scotland. T. (0141) 4230022. - Ant -   *066323*

King's Court Antique Centre, Units 1-6, King's Court,
King St., Glasgow. T. (0141) 423 7216. - Ant -   *066324*

Lovatt, 100 Torrisdale St., Glasgow Scotland.
T. (0141) 423 6497. - Ant / Naut -   *066325*

Megahy, Jean, 481 Great Western Rd., Glasgow Scotland. T. (0141) 334 1315. - Ant / Furn / Orient -   *066326*

Mercat-Hughes, 85 Queen St., Glasgow Scotland.
T. (0141) 204 0851. - Furn / China / Instr -   *066327*

Muirhead Moffat, 182 West Regent St., Glasgow Scotland. T. (0141) 226 3406. - Furn / Silv / Instr -   *066328*

Nice Things Old And New, 1010 Pollokshaws Rd, Glasgow Scotland. T. (0141) 649 3826. - Ant -   *066329*

Nithsdale, 100 Torrisdale St, Glasgow Scotland.
T. (0141) 424 0444. - Ant -   *066330*

Pettigrew & Mail, 7 The Loaning, Glasgow Scotland.
T. (0141) 639 2989. - Paint -   *066331*

Rose R.L., 19 Waterloo St., Glasgow Scotland.
T. (0141) 248 3313. - Tex -   *066332*

Russell & Son, Frank, Unit 104, 1 Rutherglen Rd., Glasgow Scotland. T. (0141) 647 9608. - Ant -   *066333*

Stenlake & McCourt, 1 Overdale St., Langside, Glasgow
Scotland. T. (0141) 632 2304. - Ant -   *066334*

Victorian Village, 53 West Regent St., Glasgow Scotland.
T. (0141) 332 0808. - Ant -   *066335*

Virginia Antique Galleries, 3133 Virginia St, Glasgow Scotland. T. (0141) 552 2573. - Ant -　　*066336*
West of Scotland Antique Centre, 539 Victoria Rd., Queens Park, Glasgow Scotland. T. (0141) 422 1717. - Ant -　　*066337*
Wright, Tim, 147 Bath St., Glasgow Scotland. T. (0141) 221 0364. - Graph / China -　　*066338*
Yesteryear, 158 Albert Dr., Glasgow Scotland. T. (0141) 429 3966. - Ant -　　*066339*

Glastonbury (Somerset)
Abbey Antiques, 51 High St., Glastonbury Scotland. T. (01458) 831694. - Furn / Glass -　　*066340*
Abbots House, 4 Benedict St., Glastonbury Scotland. T. (01458) 832123. - China / Jew / Silv -　　*066341*
Antiques Fair, Market Pl., Glastonbury Scotland. T. (01458) 832939. - Ant / Furn / Dec -　　*066342*
Antiques Market, Town Hall, Glastonbury Scotland. T. (01963) 862478. - Ant -　　*066343*
Lace and Linen Shop, 15 High St., Glastonbury Scotland. T. (01458) 834522. - Paint / Tex / Jew -　　*066344*
Monarch Antiques, 15 High St., Glastonbury Scotland. T. (01458) 832498. - Ant -　　*066345*

Glossop (Derbyshire)
Antiques for All, Old Chapel, 1 Shrewsbury St., Glossop Derbys. T. (01457) 866960. - Furn / China / Glass -　　*066346*
Derbyshire Clocks, 104 High St. West, Glossop Derbys. T. (01457) 862677. - Instr -　　*066347*
Glossop Antique Centre, Brookfield, Glossop Derbys. T. (01457) 863904. - Ant -　　*066348*
Old Cross Gallery, 16 Henry St, Glossop Derbys. T. (01457) 854052. - Paint / Furn -　　*066349*

Gloucester (Gloucestershire)
Bartrick, Steven D., Antique Centre, Severn Rd., Gloucester GL1 2LE. T. (01452) 529716. - Paint -　　*066350*
Cook & Son, E.J., Antique Centre, Severn Rd., Gloucester Glos. T. (01452) 529716. - Paint / Furn / Instr -　　*066351*
Farr, Antique Centre, Severn Rd., Gloucester Glos. - China / Silv / Instr -　　*066352*
Gloucester Antique Centre, Severn Rd., Gloucester Glos. T. (01452) 529716, Fax (01452) 307161. - Ant -　　*066353*
Kent, David, 300 Barton St., Gloucester Glos. T. (01452) 304396. - Naut -　　*066354*
Medcalf, Paul, Antique Centre, Severn Rd., Gloucester Glos. T. (01452) 415186. - Paint / Graph -　　*066355*
Military Curios, Southgate St., Gloucester Glos. T. (01452) 527716, Fax (01452) 527716. - Mil -　　*066356*

Godalming (Surrey)
Cry for the Moon, 31 High St., Godalming Surrey. T. (01483) 426201, Fax (01483) 860117. - Jew / Silv -　　*066357*
Goldthrope, P. and J., Bicton Croft, Deanery Rd., Godalming Surrey. T. (01483) 414356. - Paint -　　*066358*
Heath-Bullock, 8 Meadrow, Godalming GU7 3HN. T. (01483) 422562, Fax (01483) 426077. - Paint / Furn -　　*066359*
Olde Curiosity Shoppe, 99 High St., Godalming Surey. T. (01483) 415889. - China / Jew / Silv -　　*066360*
Priory Antiques, 29 Church St., Godalming GU7 1EL. T. (01483) 421804. - Ant -　　*066361*
White, David, 34 Meadrow, Godalming Surrey. T. (01483) 420957. - Furn -　　*066362*

Gosforth (Tyne and Wear)
Causey Antique Shop, Causey St., Gosforth Tyne & Wear. - Ant / Silv -　　*066363*
H. and S. Collectables, 149 Salters Rd., Gosforth Tyne & Wear. T. (0191) 284 6626. - Ant / China / Instr -　　*066364*
Harrison, Anna, Grange Park, Great North Rd., Gosforth Tyne & Wear. T. (0191) 284 3202. - Paint / Furn / China -　　*066365*
MacDonald, 2 Ashburton Rd., Gosforth Tyne & Wear. T. (0191) 284 4214. - Paint -　　*066366*

Gosport (Hampshire)
Cooper, E.T., 20 Stoke Rd., Gosport Hants. T. (01705) 585032. - Furn / China / Silv -　　*066367*

Peter Pan's Bazaar, 105 Forton Rd., Gosport PO12 4TQ. T. (01705) 524254. - Instr -　　*066368*
Peter Pan's of Gosport, 105c Forton Rd., Gosport Hants. T. (01705) 524254. - Jew / Toys -　　*066369*

Goudhurst (Kent)
Old Saddlers Antiques, Church Rd., Goudhurst TN17 1BH. T. (01580) 211458. - Paint / Furn / China -　　*066370*

Grampound (Cornwall)
Pine and Period Furniture, Fore St., Grampound Cornwall. T. (01726) 883117. - Furn -　　*066371*
Radnor House, Fore St., Grampound Cornwall. T. (01726) 882921. - Furn -　　*066372*

Grantham (Lincolnshire)
Grantham Clocks, 30 Lodge Way, Grantham Lincs. T. (01476) 61784. - Instr -　　*066373*
Grantham Furniture Emporium, 4-6 Wharf Rd., Grantham Lincs. T. (01476) 62967. - Furn -　　*066374*
Nadin, Harold, 109 London Rd., Grantham Lincs. T. (01476) 63562. - Ant / Furn -　　*066375*
Redmile, William, 15 Elmer St., Grantham Lincs. T. (01476) 64074. - Ant -　　*066376*

Grasmere (Cumbria)
Aladdin's Cave, Helm House, Langdale Rd., Grasmere Cumbria. T. (015394) 35774. - Ant / Furn -　　*066377*
Stables, College St., Grasmere Cumbria. T. 35453. - Graph / China / Silv -　　*066378*

Grassington (North Yorkshire)
Fairings, Lucy Fold, Grassington Yorks. North. T. (01756) 752755. - Furn / China -　　*066379*

Gravesend (Kent)
Copperfield, 33 Darnley Rd., Gravesend Kent. T. (01474) 535200. - Furn -　　*066380*
Martin, Greg, 116 Wrotham Rd., Gravesend Kent. T. (01474) 566067. - Ant -　　*066381*

Grays (Essex)
Grays, 6 London Rd, Grays Essex. T. (01375) 374883. - Ant / Furn / Jew -　　*066382*

Great Bardfield (Essex)
Golden Sovereign, Old Police House, High St., Great Bardfield Essex. T. (01371) 810507. - Furn / Silv / Glass -　　*066383*

Great Bookham (Surrey)
Bookham Galleries, Leatherhead Rd., Great Bookham Surrey. T. (01372) 452668. - Furn -　　*066384*
Davis, Roger A., 19 Dorking Rd., Great Bookham Surrey. T. (01372) 457655. - Instr -　　*066385*

Great Chesterford (Essex)
Mortimer & Son, C. and J., School St, Great Chesterford CB10 1NN. T. (01799) 30261. - Paint / Furn -　　*066386*

Great Malvern (Hereford and Worcester)
Carlton Antiques, 43 Worcester Rd., Great Malvern Herefs & Worcs. T. (01684) 573092. - Furn -　　*066387*
Church Walk Antiques, 5 Church Walk, Great Malvern Herefs & Worcs. T. (01684) 565192. - Furn / Jew / Silv -　　*066388*
Coates of Malvern, Joan, 26 Saint Ann's Rd., Great Malvern Herefs & Worcs. T. (01684) 575509. - Furn / Silv -　　*066389*
Gray, Units 24 & 26, Great Malvern Herefs & Worcs. T. (01684) 560038, Fax (01684) 893639. - Ant / Naut -　　*066390*
Great Malvern Antiques, 6 Abbey Rd., Great Malvern Herefs & Worcs. T. (01684) 575490. - Paint / Furn -　　*066391*
Lismore, 3 Edith Walk, Great Malvern Herefs & Worcs. T. (01684) 568610. - Paint -　　*066392*
Malvern Arts, 43 Worcester Rd., Great Malvern Herefs & Worcs. T. (01684) 575889. - Paint -　　*066393*
Malvern Studios, 56 Cowleigh Rd., Great Malvern Herefs & Worcs. T. (01684) 574913. - Furn -　　*066394*
Miscellany Antiques, 18 and 20 Cowleigh Rd, Great Malvern Herefs & Worcs. T. (01684) 566671, Fax (01684) 560562. - Furn / China / Jew -　　*066395*

Treasures of Childhood Past, 43 Wyche Rd., Great Malvern Herefs & Worcs. T. (01684) 560010. - Toys -　　*066396*
Whitmore, Teynham Lodge, Chase Rd, Great Malvern Herefs & Worcs. T. (01684) 40651. - Num -　　*066397*

Great Missenden (Buckinghamshire)
Gemini Antiques, 68a High St., Great Missenden Bucks. T. (0124 06) 6203. - Ant -　　*066398*
Pine Merchants, 52 High St., Great Missenden Bucks. T. (0124 06) 2002. - Furn -　　*066399*

Great Shefford (Berkshire)
Ivy House Antiques, Wantage Rd., Great Shefford RG16 7DA. T. (0148 839) 549. - Ant / Furn -　　*066400*

Great Urswick (Cumbria)
Wood, Lilian, Midtown House, Great Urswick Cumbria. T. (01229) 56297. - Paint -　　*066401*

Great Wakering (Essex)
Times Past, 195 High St., Great Wakering Essex. T. (01702) 219752. - Furn -　　*066402*

Great Waltham (Essex)
Stores, On A 130, Great Waltham Essex. T. (01245) 360277. - Furn -　　*066403*

Great Yarmouth (Norfolk)
Barry's Antiques, 35 King St., Great Yarmouth Norfolk. T. (01493) 842713. - Paint / China / Jew / Instr -　　*066404*
Ferrow, 6-7 Hall Quay, Great Yarmouth Norfolk. T. (01493) 855391. - Ant -　　*066405*
Folkes, 74 Victoria Arcade, Great Yarmouth Norfolk. T. (01493) 851354. - Ant / Jew -　　*066406*
Haven, 6-7 Hall Quay, Great Yarmouth Norfolk. T. (01493) 855391. - Paint / Draw -　　*066407*
Howkins, Peter, 39-41 and 135 King St, Great Yarmouth Norfolk. T. (01493) 844639. - Furn / China / Jew / Glass -　　*066408*
Wheatley S, 16 Northgate St., Great Yarmouth Norfolk. T. (01493) 857219. - Ant / Jew -　　*066409*

Greenlaw (Borders)
Greenlaw Antiques, Town Hall, Greenlaw Scotland. T. (0136 16) 220. - Ant -　　*066410*

Greyabbey (Co. Down)
Antique Shop, 9 Main St., Greyabbey BT22 2NE. T. (012477) 38333. - Ant -　　*066411*
B.B. Antiques, 5-7 Main st., Greyabbey N. Ireland. T. (01232) 654145. - Furn / Tex -　　*066412*
Greyabbey Timecraft, 18 Main St., Greyabbey N. Ireland. T. (01247) 88416, Fax (012477) 88250. - Jew / Instr -　　*066413*
Old Cross Antiques, 3-5 Main St., Greyabbey BT22 2NE. T. (012477) 88346. - Furn / China / Silv -　　*066414*
Priory Antiques, 3-5 Main St., Greyabbey N. Ireland. T. (012477) 88346. - Furn / Tex / Jew / Silv -　　*066415*

Greystoke (Cumbria)
Pelican Antiques, Church Rd., Greystoke CA11 0TW. T. (018533) 477. - Ant -　　*066416*
Roadside Antiques, Watsons Farm, Greystoke Hill, Greystoke Cumbria. T. (017684) 83279. - Furn / China / Jew / Instr / Glass -　　*066417*

Grimsby (Humberside)
Bell Antiques, 68 Harold St., Grimsby Humberside South. T. (01472) 695110. - Furn -　　*066418*
Goodman, 47 Pasture St, Grimsby Humberside South. T. (01472) 341301. - Furn / Jew -　　*066419*
Simon, 7 Saunders St., Grimsby Humberside South. T. (01472) 360740. - Furn / Jew -　　*066420*

Guildford (Surrey)
Antiques Centre, 22 Haydon Pl., Guildford GU1 4LL. T. (01483) 67817. - Ant -　　*066421*
Bijoux Jewellers, 12 Epsom Rd., Guildford Surrey. T. (01483) 32992. - Jew / Silv -　　*066422*
Denning, 1 Chapel St., Guildford Surrey. T. (01483) 39595. - Tex / Jew / Silv -　　*066423*
Horological Workshops, 204 Worplesdon Rd., Guildford GU2 6UY. T. (01483) 576496. - Instr -　　*066424*

Guilsborough (Northamptonshire)

Goodwin, Nick, The Firs, Nortoft Rd., Guilsborough
Northhants. T. (01280) 813115, Fax (01280) 813115.
- Furn - 066425

Guisborough (Cleveland)

Atrium Antiques, 12 Chaloner St., Guisborough TS14
6QD. T. (01287) 632777. - Ant / Furn / Jew / Silv /
Instr - 066426

Haddenham (Buckinghamshire)

Wellby, H.S., Malt House, Church End, Haddenham
Bucks. T. (01844) 290036. - Paint - 066427

Haddington (Lothian)

Elm House Antiques, The Sands, Church St., Haddington
Scotland. T. (0162 082) 3413. - Furn / China - 066428
Leslie & Leslie, Haddington Scotland.
T. (0162 082) 2241, Fax (0162 082) 2241.
- Ant - 066429

Hadleigh (Suffolk)

Randolph, 97 and 99 High St, Hadleigh IP7 5EJ.
T. (01473) 823789. - Ant / Furn / China / Instr - 066430
Rhodes, Isobel, 69-73 Angel St., Hadleigh Suffolk.
T. (01473) 823754. - Furn - 066431
Sutcliffe, Gordon, 11 High St., Hadleigh Suffolk.
T. (01473) 823464. - Furn / China - 066432
Tara's Hall, Victoria House, Market Pl., Hadleigh Suffolk.
T. (01473) 824031. - Tex / Jew - 066433

Hadlow (Kent)

Pedlar's Pack, The Square, Hadlow TN11 0DA.
T. (01732) 851296. - Ant / Furn / China / Jew /
Glass - 066434

Halesworth (Suffolk)

Ash Tree Antiques, Ash Tree Farm, Wissett, Halesworth
Suffolk. T. (01986) 872867. - Furn / China - 066435
Blyth Bygones, 8 Station Rd., Halesworth Suffolk.
T. (01986) 873397. - Ant / Furn - 066436
Number Six Antiques, Chediston St., Halesworth Suffolk.
T. (01986) 875492. - Furn / China / Glass - 066437

Halifax (West Yorkshire)

Balme, Ken, 10/12 Keighley Rd, Ovenden, Halifax Yorks.
West. T. (01422) 344193. - Ant / Glass - 066438
Boulevard Reproductions, 369 Skircoat Green Rd., Hali-
fax Yorks. West. T. (01422) 368628. - Furn - 066439
Brear, Jean, 19 Causeway Head, Burnley Rd., Halifax
Yorks. West. T. (01422) 366144. - Ant / Paint - 066440
Collectors Old Toy Shop and Antiques, 89 Northgate, Ha-
lifax Yorks. West. T. (01422) 822148. - Ant /
Instr - 066441
Halifax Antiques Centre, Queens Rd., Halifax Yorks.
West. T. (01422) 366657. - Ant - 066442
Hewitt, Muir, Queens Rd, Halifax Yorks. West.
T. (01422) 366657. - Furn / China / Lights - 066443
Hillside Antiques, Denholme Gate Rd., Hipperholme, Ha-
lifax Yorks. West. T. (01422) 202744. - Furn / China /
Glass - 066444
North Bridge Antiques, 5 North Bridge, Halifax Yorks.
West. T. (01422) 358474. - Naut - 066445
Scott & Varey, 10 Prescott St., Halifax Yorks. West.
T. (01422) 366928, Fax (01422) 340277. - Ant / Furn /
Instr - 066446

Halstead (Essex)

Halstead Antiques, 71 Head St., Halstead Essex.
T. (01787) 473265. - Ant / Glass - 066447
Townsford Mill Antiques Centre, The Causeway, Hals-
tead Essex. T. (01787) 474451. - Ant - 066448

Handcross (West Sussex)

Handcross Antiques, High St., Handcross Sussex West.
T. (01444) 400784. - Furn - 066449

Harefield (Greater London)

Jay's Antique Centre, 25-29 High St., Harefield Middx.
T. (01895) 824738. - Ant / Jew - 066450

Harlington (Bedfordshire)

Willow Farm Pine Centre, Willow Farm, Harlington Beds.
T. (01525) 872052. - Furn - 066451

Harpenden (Hertfordshire)

Andrews, Meg, 20 Holly Bush Lane, Harpenden AL5 4AT.
T. (01582) 460107, Fax 768627. - Orient / Tex - 066452
Knights, 38 Station Rd., Harpenden Herts.
T. (01582) 460564. - Paint / Graph - 066453

Harpole (Northamptonshire)

Inglenook, 23 High St., Harpole Northants.
T. (01604) 830007. - Ant / Furn / Jew - 066454

Harrietsham (Kent)

Peppitt, Judith, Chegworth Manor Farm, Chegworth,
Harrietsham Kent. T. (01622) 859313. - Paint - 066455

Harrogate (North Yorkshire)

Ann-tiquities, 12 Cheltenham Parade, Harrogate Yorks.
North. T. (01423) 503567. - Tex - 066456
Antiques and Collectables, 37/39 Cheltenham Crescent,
Harrogate Yorks. North. T. (01423) 521897. - Furn /
Jew / Silv / Instr - 066457
Armstrong, 10-11 Montpellier Parade, Harrogate Yorks.
North. T. (01423) 506843. - Furn / Glass - 066458
Bentley, Bill, 16 Montpellier Parade, Harrogate HG1 2TG.
T. (01423) 564084. - Furn - 066459
Bloomers, 41 Cheltenham Crescent, Harrogate Yorks.
North. T. (01423) 569389. - Tex - 066460
Daffern, John, 38 Forest Lane Head, Starbeck, Harro-
gate Yorks. North. T. (01423) 889832. - Furn / China /
Sculp / Instr - 066461
Derbyshire Antiques, 27 Montpellier Parade, Harrogate
Yorks. North. T. (01423) 503115. - Furn - 066462
Dragon Antiques, 10 Dragon Rd., Harrogate Yorks. North.
T. (01423) 562037. - Ant / China / Glass - 066463
Fox, 83 Knaresborough Rd., Harrogate Yorks. North.
T. (01423) 888116. - Furn - 066464
Garth, 2 Montpellier Mews, Harrogate Yorks. North.
T. (01423) 530573. - Paint / Furn - 066465
Ginnel, Harrogate Antique Centre, Harrogate HG1 2RB.
T. (01423) 508857. - Ant - 066466
Grove Collectors Centre, Grove Rd., Harrogate Yorks.
North. T. (01423) 561680. - Ant - 066467
Haworth, 26 Cold Bath Rd., Harrogate Yorks. North.
T. (01423) 521401. - Furn / Instr - 066468
Kendal-Greene, R.B., 2A Chudleigh Rd, Harrogate Yorks.
North. T. (01423) 562497. - Ant - 066469
Lawes, David, 125 Cold Bath Rd, Harrogate Yorks. North.
T. (01423) 568428. 066470
London House, 9 Montpellier Parade, Harrogate Yorks.
North. T. (01423) 567167. - Tex - 066471
Love, David, 10 Royal Parade, Harrogate HG1 2SZ.
T. (01423) 565797. - Ant / Furn / China - 066472
Lumb & Sons, Charles, 2 Montpellier Gardens, Harrogate
HG1 2TF. T. (01423) 503776, Fax (01423) 530074.
- Furn - 066473
Mason, D., 7-8 Westmoreland St., Harrogate Yorks.
North. T. (01423) 567305. - Jew / Instr - 066474
McTague of Harrogate, 17-19 Cheltenham Mount, Har-
rogate Yorks. North. T. (01423) 567086. - Paint /
Graph - 066475
Montpellier Gallery, 12 Montpellier St., Harrogate Yorks.
North. T. (01423) 500460, Fax (01423) 528400.
- Paint / Furn / Sculp - 066476
Montpellier Mews, Montpellier St., Harrogate Yorks.
North. T. (01423) 530484. - Ant - 066477
Ogden of Harrogate, 38 James St., Harrogate HG1 1RQ.
T. (01423) 504123, Fax (01423) 522283. - Jew /
Silv - 066478
Omar, 8 Crescent Rd., Harrogate HG1 2RS.
T. (01423) 503675. - Tex - 066479
Paraphernalia, 38A Cold Bath Rd, Harrogate Yorks.
North. T. (01423) 567968. - Ant / China - 066480
Peters, Paul M., 15a Bower Rd., Harrogate Yorks. North.
T. (01423) 560118. - Ant / China / Instr - 066481
Phillips, Elaine, 1-2 Royal Parade, Harrogate Yorks.
North. T. (01423) 569745. - Furn - 066482
Pianorama, 1,3 and 5 Omega St, Harrogate Yorks. North.
T. (01423) 567573. - Music - 066483
Shaw Bros., 21 Montpellier Parade, Harrogate Yorks.
North. T. (01423) 567466. - China / Jew / Silv - 066484
Singing Bird Antiques, 19 Knaresborough Rd., Harrogate
Yorks. North. T. (01423) 888292. - Furn / China /
Silv - 066485
Smith's, Dragon Rd., Harrogate Yorks. North.
T. (01423) 503217. - Ant - 066486

Sutcliffe Galleries, 5 Royal Parade, Harrogate Yorks.
North. T. (01423) 562976, Fax (01423) 528729.
- Paint - 066487
Thorntons of Harrogate, 1 Montpellier Gardens, Harro-
gate HG1 2TF. T. (01423) 504118. - Paint / Furn / Chi-
na / Instr / Mil - 066488
Traditional Interiors, Library House, Regent Parade, Har-
rogate Yorks. North. T. (01423) 560452.
- Furn - 066489
Walker, 6 Montpellier Gardens, Harrogate Yorks. North.
T. (01423) 567933. - Paint / Furn - 066490
Warner, Christopher, 15 Princes St., Harrogate HG1 1NG.
T. (01423) 503617. - Jew / Silv - 066491
Weatherell's of Harrogate, 29 Montpellier Parade, Harro-
gate Yorks. North. T. (01423) 507810,
Fax (01423) 520005. - Furn - 066492
Windmill Antiques, Montpellier St, Harrogate Yorks.
North. T. (01423) 530502. - Furn - 066493

Harrow (Greater London)

Mann, Kathleen, 49 High St., Harrow HA1 3HT.
T. (0181) 4221892. - Furn / Dec - 066494
Winston Galleries, 68 High St., Harrow Middx.
T. (0181) 4224470. - Ant / Furn / China / Silv - 066495

Harston (Cambridgeshire)

Antique Clocks, 1 High St., Harston Cambs.
T. (01223) 870264. - Instr - 066496

Hartley (Kent)

Hartley Antiques, Yew Cottage, Hartley Green, Hartley
Kent. T. (01474) 702330. - China / Jew / Silv /
Glass - 066497

Hartley Wintney (Hampshire)

Abbott, Nicholas, High St., Hartley Wintney Hants.
T. (01252) 842365. - Furn - 066498
Airdale Antiques, Deva, High St., Hartley Wintney Hants.
T. (01252) 843538. - Furn - 066499
Andwells, High St., Hartley Wintney Hants.
T. (01252) 842305. - Furn - 066500
Antique House, 22 High St., Hartley Wintney Hants.
T. (01252) 844499. - Paint / Graph / Furn - 066501
Cedar Antiques, High St., Hartley Wintney Hants.
T. (01252) 843252, Fax (01252) 845235. - Furn /
Instr - 066502
Clisby at Andwells, Bryan, High St., Hartley Wintney
Hants. T. (01252) 716436. - Instr - 066503
Deva, High St., Hartley Wintney Hants.
T. (01252) 843538, Fax (01252) 842946.
- Furn - 066504
Harris, Colin, High St., Hartley Wintney Hants.
T. (01252) 843538. - Ant / Furn - 066505
Just the Thing, High St., Hartley Wintney Hants.
T. (01252) 843393. - Furn / China - 066506
Lazarus, David, High St., Hartley Wintney Hants.
T. (01252) 842287. - Furn - 066507
Old Forge Antiques, Old Forge Cottage, Hartley Wintney
Hants. T. (01252) 842287. - Ant / Paint - 066508
Phoenix Green Antiques, London Rd., Hartley Wintney
Hants. T. (01252) 844430. - Furn - 066509
Porter & Son, A.W., High St., Hartley Wintney Hants.
T. (01252) 842676, Fax (01252) 842064. - Jew / Silv /
Instr - 066510
Revell, Sheila, High St., Hartley Wintney Hants.
T. (01252) 843538. - Ant / Furn - 066511

Harwich (Essex)

Mayflower Antiques, 105 High St, Harwich CO12 3AP.
- Instr - 066512

Haslemere (Surrey)

Avery, Allen, 1 High St., Haslemere Surrey.
T. (01428) 643883. - Furn - 066513
Glover, J.K., Grayswood, Haslemere Surrey.
T. (01428) 642184. - Art - 066514
Surrey Clock Centre, 3 Lower St., Haslemere Surrey.
T. (01428) 651313. - Instr - 066515
Wood's Wharf Antiques Bazaar, 56 High St., Haslemere
GU27 2LA. T. (01428) 642125, Fax (01428) 725045.
- Furn - 066516

Haslingden (Lancashire)

Brown, P.J., 8 Church St., Haslingden Lancs.
T. (01706) 224888. - Ant / Naut - 066517

Clifton House Antiques, 198 Blackburn Rd., Haslingden
BBÜ 5HW. T. (01706) 214895. - Ant -   066518
Fielding, 176, 178 and 180 Blackburn Rd, Haslingden
Lancs. T. (01706) 214254. - Furn / Instr /
Glass -   066519
Norgrove, P.W., 38 Bury Rd., Haslingden Lancs.
T. (01706) 211995. - Instr -   066520

Hastings (Sussex)
Abbey Antiques, 364 Old London Rd., Hastings Sussex
East. T. (01424) 429178. - Paint / Furn / China /
Tex -   066521
George Street Antiques Centre, 47 George St., Hastings
Sussex East. T. (01424) 429339. - Ant -   066522
Hallstand, 23 Courthouse St., Hastings Sussex East.
- Furn / China / Jew -   066523
Nakota Curios, 12 Courthouse St., Hastings Sussex East.
T. (01424) 438900. - Furn / China / Jew -   066524
Radcliffe, J., 40 Cambridge Rd., Hastings Sussex East.
T. (01424) 426361. - Ant -   066525

Hatfield Broad Oak (Essex)
Tudor Antiques, B183, close to M11 and A120, Hatfield
Broad Oak Essex. T. (01279) 718557. - Furn / China /
Glass -   066526

Hatfield Heath (Essex)
Barn Gallery, Parvilles Farm, Hatfield Heath Essex.
T. (01279) 730114. - Paint / Graph -   066527

Hatherleigh (Devon)
Hatherleigh Antiques, 15 Bridge St, Hatherleigh Devon.
T. (01837) 810159. - Furn -   066528

Havant (Hampshire)
Antiques and Nice Things, 40 North St., Havant Hant.
T. (01705) 484935. - Paint / Graph / Furn / China /
Jew -   066529

Haverfordwest (Dyfed)
Oliver, Gerald, 14 Albany Terrace, Saint Thomas Green,
Haverfordwest SA61 1RH. T. (01437) 762794. - Ant /
Furn -   066530
Pine Design Workshop, 19 Bridgend Sq., Haverfordwest
Wales. T. (01437) 765676. - Furn -   066531

Hawes (North Yorkshire)
Sturman, Main St., Hawes Wales. T. (01969) 667742.
- Paint / Furn / China -   066532

Hawkhurst (Kent)
Quayles Emporium, Septimus, Ockley Rd., Hawkhurst
Kent. T. (01580) 752222. - Ant -   066533

Haworth (West Yorkshire)
Haworth Antiques, Lees Mill, Lees Ln., Haworth Yorks.
West. T. (01535) 643535. - Ant / Naut -   066534

Hay-on-Wye (Powys)
Antiques Market, 6 Market St., Hay-on-Wye Wales.
T. (01497) 820175. - Ant -   066535
Corner Shop, 5 Saint John's Pl., Hay-on-Wye Wales.
T. (01497) 820045. - Paint / Graph -   066536
Hebbards of Hay, 7 Market St., Hay-on-Wye Wales.
T. (01497) 820413. - China -   066537
Le Bailly, Tamara, 5 Market St., Hay-on-Wye Wales.
T. (01497) 821157. - Ant / Furn -   066538
Wigington, 1 Heolydwr, Hay-on-Wye Wales.
T. (01497) 820545. - Ant / Furn -   066539

Haydon Bridge (Northumberland)
Haydon Bridge Antiques, 3 Shaftoe St., Haydon Bridge
Northumbs. T. (01434) 684200. - Paint / Furn -   066540
Haydon Gallery, 3 Shaftoe St., Haydon Bridge Nor-
thumbs. T. (01434) 648200. - Paint / Sculp -   066541
Revival Beds, Oddfellows Workshop, Haydon Bridge Nor-
thumbs. T. (01434) 684755. - Furn -   066542

Hayfield (Derbyshire)
Allcroft, Michael, 1 Church St., Hayfield Derbys.
T. (01663) 742684. - Furn -   066543

Hayle (Cornwall)
Copperhouse Gallery, 14 Fore St., Hayle Cornwall.
T. (01736) 752787. - Paint -   066544

Haywards Heath (West Sussex)
Burkinshaw, David, Sugworth Farmhouse, Borde Hill,
Haywards Heath Sussex West. T. (01444) 459747.
- Furn -   066545
Penman, Caroline, POB 114, Haywards Heath RH16
2YU. T. (01444) 482514, Fax 483412.   066545a
Ramm, 43 Sussex Rd., Haywards Heath Sussex West.
T. (01444) 451393. - Ant -   066546

Hazel Grove (Cheshire)
Gay's Antiques, 34 London Rd., Hazel Grove Cheshire.
T. (0161) 4835532. - Furn -   066547

Heacham (Norfolk)
Robinson, Peter, 7 Lynn Rd., Heacham PE31 7EP.
T. (01485) 70228. - Furn / China -   066548

Headcorn (Kent)
Lampard, Penny, 31-33 High St., Headcorn TN27 9NE.
T. (01622) 890682. - Furn / China -   066549

Heanor (Derbyshire)
Bygones, 23c Derby Rd., Heanor Derbys.
T. (01773) 768503. - Paint / Graph / Furn /
China -   066550

Heath and Reach (Bedfordshire)
Brindleys, Woburn Rd., Heath and Reach Beds.
T. (01525) 237750. - Paint / Furn / China -   066551
Charterhouse Gallery, 26 Birds Hill, Heath and Reach
Beds. T. (01525) 23379. - Paint -   066552
Heath Antique Centre, Woburn Rd., Heath and Reach
Beds. T. (01525) 237831. - Ant -   066553
Helton Antiques, 28 Birds Hill, Heath and Reach Beds.
T. (0152) 523 474. - Ant / Naut -   066554

Hebden Bridge (West Yorkshire)
Cornucopia Antiques, 9 West End, Hebden Bridge Yorks.
West. T. (01422) 844497. - Ant / Furn -   066555
Larkhall, 39 Market St., Hebden Bridge Yorks. West.
- Ant / Furn -   066556

Helmshore (Lancashire)
Gregory's Antique Pine, Albert Mill, Helmshore Lancs.
T. (01706) 220049. - Furn -   066557

Helmsley (North Yorkshire)
Westway Cottage Restored Pine, 28 Bond St., Helmsley
Yorks. North. T. (01439) 70172. - Furn -   066558
York Cottage Antiques, 7 Church St., Helmsley Yorks.
North. T. (01439) 70833. - Furn / China /
Glass -   066559

Hemel Hempstead (Hertfordshire)
Abbey, 97 High St., Hemel Hempstead HP1 3AH.
T. (01442) 64667. - Paint / Furn / Jew / Silv -   066560
Antique and Collectors Market, Market Pl., Hemel
Hempstead Herts. T. (01442) 242831. - Ant -   066561
Cherry Antiques, 101-103 High St., Hemel Hempstead
Herts. T. (01442) 64358. - Ant / Furn / China -   066562

Hempstead (Essex)
Beaumont, Michael, Hempstead Hall, Hempstead Herts.
T. (01440) 730239. - Furn -   066563

Henfield (West Sussex)
Alexander, Post House, Small Dole, Henfield Sussex
West. T. (01273) 493121. - Furn -   066564

Henley-in-Arden (Warwickshire)
Arden Gallery, 54 High St., Henley-in-Arden B95 5AN.
T. (01564) 792520. - Paint -   066565
Chadwick Gallery, Doctors Lane, Henley-in-Arden
Warks. T. (01564) 794820. - Paint / Graph -   066566
Colmore, 52 High St., Henley-in-Arden Warks.
T. (01564) 792938. - Paint -   066567
Lacy, 56 High St., Henley-in-Arden Warks.
T. (01564) 793073. - Paint / Graph -   066568
Marsh, Jasper, 3 High St., Henley-in-Arden Warks.
T. (01564) 792088. - Furn / Orient / China -   066569

Henley-on-Thames (Oxfordshire)
Friday Street Antique Centre, 2 and 4 Friday St, Henley-
on-Thames Oxon. T. (01491) 574104. - Ant -   066570

Keene, Barry M., 12 Thameside, Henley-on-Thames
Oxon. T. (01491) 577119. - Paint / Graph / Sculp /
Draw -   066571
Kingston, Richard J., 95 Bell St., Henley-on-Thames
RG9 2BD. T. (01491) 574535. - Ant / Furn / China /
Silv -   066572
Rhino Antiques, 20 Market Pl., Henley-on-Thames Oxon.
T. (01491) 411162. - Ant -   066573
Ryland, B.R., 75 Reading Rd., Henley-on-Thames RG9
1AX. T. (01491) 573663. - Ant / Furn / Instr -   066574
Thames Gallery, Thameside, Henley-on-Thames Oxon.
T. (01491) 572449. - Paint / Silv -   066575
Thames Oriental Rug Company, 48/56 Reading Rd, Hen-
ley-on-Thames Oxon. T. (01491) 574676.
- Tex -   066576

Hereford (Hereford and Worcester)
Brown, I. and J.L., 58-59 Commercial Rd., Hereford HR1
2BP. T. (01432) 358895, Fax (01432) 275338.
- Furn -   066577
Hereford Antique Centre, 128 Widemarsh St., Hereford
Herefs & Worcs. T. (01432) 266242. - Ant -   066578
Richards & Son, G.E., 57 Blueschool St., Hereford HR1
2AR. T. (01432) 267840. - Ant -   066579
Waring, 43 Saint Owen St., Hereford Herefs& Worcs.
T. (01432) 276241. - Furn / Jew / Silv -   066580

Hertford (Hertfordshire)
Beckwith & Son, Saint Andrew St, Hertford SG14 IHZ.
T. (01992) 582079. - Ant -   066581
Horton, Robert, 13 Castle St., Hertford SG14 1ER.
T. (01992) 587546. - Ant / Furn / Instr -   066582
Rochford, Michael, 25 Saint Andrew St., Hertford Herts.
T. (01992) 584385. - Ant / Furn -   066583
Village Green Antiques, 6 and 8 Old Cross, Hertford
Herts. T. (01992) 587698. - Ant / Furn / China -   066584

Hessle (Humberside)
Antique Parlour, 21 The Weir, Hessle Humberside North.
T. (01482) 643329. - Ant -   066585

Heswall (Merseyside)
Rosenberg, C., 120-122 Telegraph Rd., Heswall Merseyside. T. (0151) 342 1053. - China / Jew / Silv -   066586

Hexham (Northumberland)
Boaden, Arthur, 29-30 Market Pl., Hexham Northumbs.
T. (01434) 603187. - Ant / Paint / Furn / Jew -   066587
Caris, Gordon, 16 Market Pl., Hexham Northumbs.
T. (01434) 602106. - Instr -   066588
Hallstile Antiques, 17 Hallstile Bank, Hexham Nor-
thumbs. T. (01434) 602239. - Paint / Furn / China /
Silv / Instr -   066589
Hedley, J.A. and T., 3 Saint Mary's Chare, Hexham NE46
1NQ. T. (01434) 602317. - Furn / China / Silv /
Glass -   066590
Hexham Antiques, 6 Rear Battle Hill, Hexham Nor-
thumbs. T. (01434) 603851. - Paint / Furn / China /
Instr -   066591
Turn of the Century Antiques, 8 Market St., Hexham Nor-
thumbs. T. (01434) 607621. - Furn / China /
Glass -   066592
Violin Shop, 31a Hencotes, Hexham Northumbs.
T. (01434) 607897. - Music -   066593
Walker, John, Stable Bldgs., Station Rd., Hexham Nor-
thumbs. T. (01434) 608520. - Ant / Naut -   066594

High Wycombe (Buckinghamshire)
Brown, Church Lane, High Wycombe Bucks.
T. (01494) 524537. - Furn -   066595
Burrell, Kitchener Works, Kitchener Rd., High Wycombe
Bucks. T. (01494) 523619. - Furn -   066596

Highbridge (Somerset)
Dyte, T.M., 1 Huntspill Rd., Highbridge Somerset.
T. (01278) 786495. - Naut -   066597
Kelly, Terence, Huntspill Court, W. Huntspill, Highbridge
Somerset. T. (01278) 785052. - Furn -   066598
Treasure Chest, 19 Alstone Lane, Highbridge Somerset.
T. (01278) 787267. - Ant / Furn -   066599

Hinckley (Leicestershire)
House Things Antiques, 44 Mansion St., Hinckley Leics.
T. (01455) 618518. - Furn -   066600

Hindhead (Surrey)

Albany, 8-10 London Rd., Hindhead Surrey.
T. (01428) 605528. - Furn / China -　066601
Bowdery, M.J., 12 London Rd., Hindhead Surrey.
T. (01428) 606376. - Furn -　066602
Oriel, 3 Royal Parade, Tilford Rd., Hindhead Surrey.
T. (01428) 606281. - Paint / Furn -　066603
Second Hand Rose, Portsmouth Rd., Bramshott Chase,
Hindhead Surrey. T. (01428) 604880. - Paint /
Furn -　066604
What Not Antiques, Crossways Rd, Grayshot, Hindhead
Surrey. T. (01428) 604871. - Ant / Furn -　066605

Hindon (Wiltshire)

Monkton, High St., Hindon Surrey. T. (0174) 789235.
- Furn / Instr -　066606

Hitchin (Hertfordshire)

Bexfield, 13-14 Sun St., Hitchin Herts.
T. (01462) 432641. - Furn / China / Jew / Silv -　066607
Countrylife Gallery, 41-43 Portmill Ln., Hitchin Herts.
T. (01462) 433267. - Paint -　066608
Gander, Michael, 10 Bridge St., Hitchin Herts.
T. (01462) 432678. - Furn -　066609
Hitchin Antiques Gallery, 37 Bridge St., Hitchin Herts.
T. (01462) 434525. - Ant / Paint / Furn / Jew /
Instr -　066610
Perry, R.J., 38 Bridge St., Hitchin Herts.
T. (01462) 434525. - Ant / Furn -　066611
Phillips of Hitchin, The Manor House, Hitchin SG5 1JW.
T. (01462) 432067, Fax (01462) 441368.
- Furn -　066612

Hollinwood (Lancashire)

Fernlea, 305 Manchester Rd., Hollinwood Lancs.
T. (0161) 682 0589. - Ant / Naut -　066613
O'Brien & Son, R.J., 291-293 Manchester Rd., Hollin-
wood Lancs. T. (0161) 683 4717. - Ant / Furn / Music /
Naut -　066614

Holme (Cumbria)

JBW Antiques, Green Farm, Duke St., Holme Cumbria.
T. (01524) 781377. - Furn / China / Silv / Mil -　066615

Holmfirth (West Yorkshire)

Andrew Spencer Bottomley, Coach House, Huddersfield
Rd., Holmfirth Yorks. West. T. (01484) 685234,
Fax (01484) 681551. - Mil -　066616
Chapel House Fireplaces, Saint Georges Rd, Holmfirth
Yorks. West. T. (01484) 682275.　066617

Holsworthy (Devon)

Victoria Antiques, Victoria Hill, Holsworthy Devon.
T. (01409) 253815. - Furn -　066618

Holt (Norfolk)

Collectors Cabin, 7 Cromer Rd., Holt Norfolk.
T. (01263) 712241. - Ant -　066619
In the Picture, 16 Chapel Yard, Holt Norfolk.
T. (01263) 713720, Fax (01263) 822097.
- Graph -　066620
Scott, Richard, 30 High St., Holt Norfolk.
T. (01263) 712479. - Ant / China -　066621

Honiton (Devon)

Antique Centre Abingdon House, 136 High St., Honiton
Devon. T. (01404) 42108. - Ant -　066622
Barrymore & Co., J., 73-75 High St., Honiton Devon.
T. (01404) 42244. - Jew / Silv -　066623
Bramble Cross Antiques, Exeter Rd., Honiton Devon.
T. (01404) 47085. - Furn / Instr -　066624
Butler, Roderick, Marwood House, Honiton Devon.
T. (01404) 42169. - Furn -　066625
Button-Stephens, Christopher J., 59 High St., Honiton
EX14 8PW. T. (01404) 42640. - Ant -　066626
Fountain Antiques, 132 High St., Honiton Devon.
T. (01404) 42074. - Ant / Furn -　066627
Gilmore, Elizabeth, 126 High St., Honiton Devon.
T. (01404) 43565. - Paint / Furn -　066628
Honiton Antique Toys, 38 High St., Honiton Devon.
T. (01404) 41194. - Toys -　066629
Honiton Fine Art, 189 High St., Honiton Devon.
T. (01404) 45942. - Paint / Draw -　066630
Honiton Junction, 159 High St., Honiton Devon.
T. (01404) 43436. - Furn -　066631

Honiton Lace Shop, 44 High St., Honiton Devon.
T. (01404) 42416, Fax (01404) 47797. - Tex -　066632
Huggett & Son, L.J., Stamps Bldg., King St., Honiton
EX14 8AG. T. (01404) 42043. - Furn -　066633
Lombard, 14 High St., Honiton EX14 8PU.
T. (01404) 42140. - Ant / Furn / China -　066634
Otter Antiques, 69 High St., Honiton Devon.
T. (01404) 42627. - Silv -　066635
Pilgrim Antiques, 145 High St., Honiton Devon.
T. (01404) 41219. - Furn / Instr -　066636
Sexton, Kenneth, 140 High St., Honiton Devon.
T. (01404) 44224. - Paint / Furn -　066637
Upstairs, Downstairs, 12 High St., Honiton Devon.
T. (01404) 44481. - Paint / Furn / China / Instr -　066638
Wickham, 191 High St., Honiton Devon.
T. (01404) 44654. - Furn -　066639
Woodhead, Geoffrey M., 53 High St., Honiton Devon.
T. (01404) 42969. - Ant -　066640

Horncastle (Lincolnshire)

Boam, Clare, 22-38 North St, Horncastle Lincs.
T. (01507) 522381. - Ant / Furn -　066641
Horncastle Antiques, 23 North St., Horncastle Lincs.
T. (01507) 524415. - Furn -　066642
Kitching, Robert, 9-11 West St., Horncastle Lincs.
T. (01507) 522120. - Ant / Instr -　066643
Lincolnshire Antiques Centre, Bridge St., Horncastle
Lincs. T. (01507) 527794. - Ant -　066644
Seaview Antiques, 47a East St., Horncastle Lincs.
T. (01507) 523287. - Furn -　066645
Shaw, Lawrence, 77 East St, Horncastle Lincs.
T. (01507) 527638. - Furn / Furn -　066646
Staines, 25 Bridge St., Horncastle Lincs.
T. (01507) 527976. - Paint / Furn / Instr -　066647
Talisman, 51/53 North St, Horncastle Lincs.
T. (01507) 526893. - Furn -　066648
Warehouse, Bank St., Horncastle Lincs.
T. (01507) 524569. - Furn -　066649

Horndean (Hampshire)

Goss and Crested China Centre, 62 Murray Rd., Hornde-
an Hants. T. (01705) 597440. - China -　066650

Hornsea (Humberside)

Padgett, 19 Hull Rd., Hornsea Humberside North.
T. (01964) 534086. - Instr -　066651

Horrabridge (Devon)

Ye Olde Saddlers Shoppe, Horrabridge Devon.
T. (01822) 852109. - Ant / Furn / Instr -　066652

Horsham (West Sussex)

Lampard & Sons, L.E., 23-31 Springfield Rd., Horsham
Sussex West. T. (01403) 254012. - Furn -　066653

Horwich (Greater Manchester)

Butterworth, Alan, Unit 6, Union Mill, Albert St, Horwich
Lancs. T. (01204) 68094. - Furn / Naut -　066654

Hoylake (Merseyside)

Clock Shop, 7 The Quadrant, Hoylake Merseyside.
T. (0151) 632 1888. - Jew / Instr -　066655
Hoylake Antique Centre, 128-130 Market St., Hoylake
Merseyside. T. (0151) 632 4231. - Paint / Furn / China /
Silv -　066656
Market Antiques, 80 Market St., Hoylake Merseyside.
T. (0151) 632 4059. - Ant / Paint / Furn / China /
Silv -　066657

Huddersfield (West Yorkshire)

Berry Brow, 90/92 Dodds Royd, Woodhead Rd, Hudders-
field Yorks. West. T. (01484) 663320. - Ant / Furn /
China -　066658
Dyson, D.W., Wood Lea, Shepley, Huddersfield Yorks.
West. T. (01484) 607331. - Mil -　066659
Fillans, 2 Market Walk, Huddersfield Yorks. West.
T. (01484) 531609. - Jew / Silv -　066660
Heritage Antiques, 10 Byram Arcade, Huddersfield
Yorks. West. T. (01484) 514667. - Ant -　066661
Huddersfield Antiques, 170 Wakefield Rd, Huddersfield
Yorks. West. T. (01484) 539747. - Ant / Naut -　066662
Second Childhood, 20 Byram Arcade, Huddersfield
Yorks. West. T. (01484) 530117. - Toys -　066663

Hughenden Valley (Buckinghamshire)

Pine Reflections, Holly Cottage, Boss Lane, Hughenden
Valley Bucks. T. (0124 024) 3598. - Furn -　066664

Hungerford (Berkshire)

Ashley, 129 High St., Hungerford RG17 0DL.
T. (01488) 682771. - Ant / Furn -　066665
Below Stairs, 103 High St., Hungerford RG17 0NB.
T. (01488) 682317. - Furn / Lights -　066666
Bow House Antiques, 3-4 Faulkner St., Hungerford
Berks. T. (01488) 683198. - Furn -　066667
Dolls and Toys of Yesteryear, 3-4 Faulkner Sq., Hunger-
ford Berks. T. (01488) 683198. - Toys -　066668
Fire Place, Hungerford Old Fire Station, Charnham St.,
Hungerford RE17 0EP. T. (01488) 683420.
- Ant -　066669
Hastie, Robert and Georgina, 35a High St., Hungerford
Berks. T. (01488) 682873. - Furn / Tex / Instr -　066670
Hungerford Arcade, High St., Hungerford Berks.
T. (01488) 683701. - Ant / Furn -　066671
King, Roger, 111 High St., Hungerford Berks.
T. (01488) 682256. - Paint / Furn / China -　066672
Medalcrest, 29-30 Charnham St., Hungerford Berks.
T. (01488) 684157. - Furn / Instr -　066673
Old Malthouse, 15 Bridge St., Hungerford RG17 0EG.
T. (01488) 682209. - Furn / China / Instr -　066674
Riverside Antiques, Charnham St, Hungerford Berks.
T. (01488) 682314. - Ant / Furn -　066675
Styles, 12 Bridge St., Hungerford Berks.
T. (01488) 683922. - Silv -　066676
Victoria's Bedroom, 4 Bridge St., Hungerford Berks.
T. (01488) 682523. - Furn -　066677
Youll, 27-28 Chantham St., Hungerford Berks.
- Ant -　066678

Hunstanton (Norfolk)

Delawood, 10 Westgate, Hunstanton Norfolk.
T. (01485) 532903. - Ant / Furn -　066679
Old Bakery Antiques, 1 Church St., Hunstanton Norfolk.
T. (01485) 210396. - Ant / Paint -　066680
Woodhouse, R.C., 10 Westgate, Hunstanton Norfolk.
T. (01485) 532903. - Instr -　066681

Huntingdon (Cambridgeshire)

Antique Centre, George St., Huntingdon Cambs.
T. (01480) 435100. - Ant -　066682

Hursley (Hampshire)

Hursley Antiques, Hursley Hants. T. (01962) 775488.
- Furn -　066683

Hurst (Berkshire)

Shepherd, Peter, Penfold, Lodge Rd., Hurst Berks.
T. (01734) 340755. - Glass -　066684

Hurst Green (East Sussex)

Pigeon House Antiques, 52 London Rd., Hurst Green
TN19 7PN. T. (01580) 860474. - Furn / Dec -　066685

Hurstpierpoint (West Sussex)

Clock Shop, 36 High St., Hurstpierpoint Sussex West.
T. (01273) 832081. - Instr -　066686
Julian Antiques, 124 High St., Hurstpierpoint Sussex
West. T. (01273) 832145. - Furn / Sculp / Instr -　066687
Miller, Michael, 8 Cuckfield Rd., Hurstpierpoint Sussex
West. T. (01273) 834567. - Ant / Mil -　066688

Hyde (Cheshire)

Bunting, Peter, 238 Higham Ln, Hyde Cheshire.
T. (0161) 368 5544. - Furn -　066689

Hythe (Kent)

Den of Antiquity, 35 Dymchurch Rd., Hythe Kent.
T. (01303) 267162. - China / Jew / Silv / Instr -　066690
Hythe Antique Centre, 5 High St., Hythe Kent.
T. (01303) 269643. - Paint / Furn / China -　066691
Kennedy, 148 High St., Hythe Kent. T. (01303) 269323.
- Paint -　066692
Malthouse Arcade, High St., Hythe Kent.
T. (01303) 260103. - Furn / Jew -　066693
Radio Vintage, 250 Seabrook Rd, Hythe Kent.
T. (01303) 230693.　066694
Samovar Antiques, 158 High St., Hythe Kent.
T. (01303) 264239. - Ant / Tex / Instr -　066695

Traditional Furniture, 248 Seabrook Rd, Hythe Kent.
T. (01303) 239931. - Furn -   *066696*

Ickleton (Cambridgeshire)
Abbey Antiques, 18 Abbey St., Ickleton CB10 1SS.
T. (01799) 30637. - Ant -   *066697*

Ilford (Essex)
Belgrave Antiques, 77 Belgrave Rd., Ilford Essex.
T. (0181) 554 8032. - Paint / Furn -   *066698*
Flowers Antiques, 733 High Rd., Ilford Essex.
T. (0181) 599 9959. - Furn / China / Glass -   *066699*

Ilkeston (Derbyshire)
Matsell, 52 King St., Ilkeston Derbys. T. (01602) 302446.
- Furn -   *066700*

Ilkley (West Yorkshire)
Burrows & Raper, 37 The Grove, Ilkley Yorks. West.
T. (01943) 817631. - Furn / China / Silv -   *066701*
Cooper & Son, J.H., 33-35 Church St., Ilkley LS29 0DS.
T. (01943) 608020. - Furn / China / Silv -   *066702*
Richardson, Keith, 26 Leeds Rd., Ilkley Yorks. West.
T. (01943) 600045. - Furn / Jew / Glass -   *066703*
Shaw, Jack, Old Grammar School, Skipton Rd, Ilkley
Yorks. West. T. (01943) 609467. - Furn / Silv -   *066704*
Simon, 25 Church St., Ilkley Yorks. West.
T. (01943) 602788. - Furn / Instr -   *066705*

Ilminster (Somerset)
Best, Ray, North Street House, Ilminster TA19 0DG.
T. (01460) 52194. - Ant / Furn / China -   *066706*
County Antiques Centre, 21-23 West St., Ilminster Som-
erset. T. (01460) 54151. - Ant -   *066707*
Hutchison, James, 5 West St., Ilminster Somerset.
- Paint / Furn / China / Glass -   *066708*
Moolham Mill Antiques, Moolham Lane, Ilminster TA19
0PD. T. (01460) 52834. - Furn -   *066709*
West End House Antiques, 34-36 West St., Ilminster
Somerset. T. (01460) 52793. - Paint / Furn /
China -   *066710*

Inchture (Tayside)
Moreton, C.S., Inchmartine House, Inchture Scotland.
T. (01828) 86412. - China / Tex -   *066711*

Ingatestone (Essex)
Meyers, 66 High St., Ingatestone Essex.
T. (01277) 355335. - Paint / Furn -   *066712*

Inverness (Highland)
Attic, 17 Huntly St., Inverness IV3 5PR.
T. (01463) 243117. - China / Tex / Jew -   *066713*

Ipswich (Suffolk)
Abbott, A., 757 Woodbridge Rd., Ipswich Suffolk.
T. (01473) 728900. - Furn / Jew / Instr -   *066714*
Adams, Tony, 175 Spring Rd., Ipswich Suffolk.
- Ant -   *066715*
Ashley, 20A Fore St, Ipswich Suffolk. T. (01473) 251696.
- Ant / Furn / China / Instr -   *066716*
Atfield & Daughter, 17 Saint Stephens Lane, Ipswich IP1
1DP. T. (01473) 251158. - Furn / China / Instr /
Mil -   *066717*
Bruce, Paul, Frobisher Rd., Ipswich Suffolk.
T. (01473) 255400, Fax (01473) 233656. - Ant / Paint /
Furn -   *066718*
Cordell, Sonia, 13 Saint Peters St., Ipswich IP1 1FX.
T. (01473) 219508. - Ant / Jew / Silv -   *066719*
Country Bygones and Antiques, 13c Saint Peters St.,
Ipswich Suffolk. T. (01473) 253683. - Paint / Graph /
China / Silv -   *066720*
Croydon & Sons, 50-56 Tavern St., Ipswich Suffolk.
T. (01473) 256514, Fax (01473) 231565. - Furn / Chi-
na / Jew / Silv -   *066721*
Edwardian Shop, 556 Spring Rd., Ipswich Suffolk.
T. (01473) 7216576. - Furn -   *066722*
Fortescue, 27 Saint Peters St., Ipswich Suffolk.
T. (01473) 251342. - Paint -   *066723*
Gazeley, John, 17 Fonnereau Rd., Ipswich Suffolk.
T. (01473) 252420. - Paint / Graph -   *066724*
Hubbard, 16 Saint Margarets Green, Ipswich Suffolk.
T. (01473) 226033. - Ant / Furn -   *066725*
Hyland House Antiques, 45 Felixstowe Rd., Ipswich Suf-
folk. T. (01473) 210055. - Ant / Furn -   *066726*

Major, 6 Saint Helens St., Ipswich Suffolk.
T. (01473) 221190. - Paint / Furn / Instr -   *066727*
Orwell Galleries, 1 Upper Orwell St., Ipswich Suffolk.
T. (01473) 221190. - Furn -   *066728*
Orwell Paint Strippers, 427 Wherstead Rd., Ipswich Suf-
folk. T. (01473) 680091. - Furn -   *066729*
Smith, Tom, 33A Saint Peter's St, Ipswich Suffolk.
T. (01473) 210172. - Furn / Naut -   *066730*
Spring Antiques, 436 Spring Rd., Ipswich Suffolk.
T. (01473) 725606. - China / Jew / Silv / Instr -   *066731*
Thompson's, 418 Norwich Rd., Ipswich Suffolk.
T. (01473) 47793. - Furn -   *066732*
Wall, C.A., 11 Saint Peter's St., Ipswich.
T. (01473) 214366. - Furn -   *066733*
Weir, Gerald, 7-11 Vermont Rd., Ipswich Suffolk.
T. (01473) 252606. - Furn -   *066734*

Iron Bridge (Shropshire)
Dickenson, Bill, 11 Tontine Hill, Iron Bridge Shrops.
T. (01952) 433783. - Ant / China -   *066735*
Ironbridge Antique Centre, Dale End, Iron Bridge Shrops.
T. (01952) 433784. - Paint / Furn / China / Jew -   *066736*
Whitelaw, Peter, 11 Tontine Hill, Iron Bridge Shrops.
T. (01952) 433783. - Ant / China -   *066737*

Isleworth (Greater London)
Crowther of Syon Lodge, London Rd, Isleworth TW7
5BH. T. (0181) 560 7978, Fax (0181) 568 7572.
- Sculp / Dec -   *066738*
Yistelworth, 13 Shrewsbury Walk, Isleworth Middx.
T. (0181) 847 5429. - Paint / Furn / China -   *066739*

Iver (Buckinghamshire)
Yester-Year, 12 High St., Iver Bucks. T. (01753) 652072.
- Furn / China / Glass -   *066740*

Ixworth (Suffolk)
Cousins & Ew., 27 High St., Ixworth IP31 2HJ.
T. (01359) 30254. - Ant / Naut -   *066741*
Ixworth Antiques, 17 High St., Ixworth Suffolk.
T. (01359) 31691. - Furn / Silv -   *066742*

Jedburgh (Borders)
Mainhill Gallery, Ancrum, Jedburgh Scotland.
T. (0183 5) 3 518. - Paint / Graph -   *066743*
Turner, R. and M., 34/36 High St, Jedburgh TD8 6AG.
T. (01835) 63445. - Furn / Paint / China / Instr -   *066744*

Jesmond (Tyne and Wear)
Hugall, Geoffrey, 19 Clayton Rd., Jesmond Tyne & Wear.
T. (0191) 281 8408. - Ant / Furn / China -   *066745*
Humble, Owen, 11-12 Clayton Rd., Jesmond Tyne &
Wear. T. (0191) 281 4002. - Ant / Furn   *066746*
Osborne Art and Antique, 18c Osborne Rd., Jesmond
Tyne & Wear. T. (0191) 281 6380. - Paint / Graph /
Draw -   *066747*
Walker, W. and J., 231 Jesmond Rd., Jesmond Tyne &
Wear. T. (0191) 281 7286. - Furn / Instr -   *066748*

Keighley (West Yorkshire)
Barleycote Hall Antiques, 2 Janet St, Keighley Yorks.
West. T. (01535) 644776. - Paint / Furn / China / Tex /
Jew -   *066749*
Keighleys of Keighley, 153 East Parade, Keighley Yorks.
West. T. (01535) 663439. - Furn / China / Jew /
Silv -   *066750*
Real Macoy, 2 Janet St., Keighley Yorks. West.
T. (01535) 644776. - Tex -   *066751*
Richardson, D., 72 Haworth Rd., Crossroads, Keighley
Yorks. West. T. (01535) 644982. - Ant / Naut -   *066752*

Kelvedon (Essex)
Kelvedon Antiques, 90 High St., Kelvedon CO5 9AA.
T. (01376) 570557. - Furn -   *066753*
Kelvedon Antiques Centre, 139 High St., Kelvedon Es-
sex. T. (01376) 570896. - Ant -   *066754*
Miller, 46 High St., Kelvedon Essex. T. (01376) 570098,
Fax (01376) 572186. - Furn -   *066755*
Ratcliff, G.T., Coggeshall Rd, Kelvedon CO5 9PH.
T. (01376) 570234, Fax (01376) 571764.
- Furn -   *066756*
Sykes, Thomas, 16 High St., Kelvedon Essex.
T. (01376) 571969. - Paint / Furn -   *066757*

Templar Antiques, 6 Peter's House, High St., Kelvedon
Essex. T. (01376) 572101. - Paint / Graph / Furn /
Glass -   *066758*
Times Past, 110 High St., Kelvedon Essex.
T. (01376) 571858. - Ant / Furn / Mod -   *066759*

Kempston (Bedfordshire)
Queen Adelaide Gallery, 79 High St., Kempston Beds.
T. (01234) 854083. - Paint / Graph -   *066760*
Rogers, Eva, Spinney Lodge, Rodge Rd., Kempston
Beds. T. (01234) 854823. - Ant -   *066761*

Kendal (Cumbria)
Below Stairs, 78 Highgate, Kendal Cumbria.
T. (01539) 741278. - China / Silv / Instr / Glass - *066762*
Cottage Antiques, 80 Highgate, Kendal Cumbria.
T. (01539) 722683. - Ant / Furn -   *066763*
Kendal Studios Antiques, 2-3 Wildman St, Kendal LA9
6EN. T. (01539) 723291. - Paint / Graph /
China -   *066764*
Silver Thimble, 39 All Hallows Lane, Kendal Cumbria.
T. (01539) 731456. - China / Jew / Silv / Glass - *066765*

Kenilworth (Warwickshire)
Allen, 38 Castle Hill, Kenilworth Warks.
T. (01926) 851435. - Paint / Graph / Tex / Fra -   *066766*
Castle Gallery, 32 Castle Hill, Kenilworth Warks.
T. (01926) 58727. - Paint / Draw -   *066767*
Paull, Janice, 125 Warwick Rd., Kenilworth Warks.
T. (01926) 55253. - Graph / China -   *066768*

Kennington (Kent)
Knight, Peter, Mill House, Kennington TN24 4EL.
T. (01233) 623009. - Ant -   *066769*

Kentisbeare (Devon)
Sextons, Dulford Cottage, Kentisbeare Devon.
T. (0188) 46429. - Furn -   *066770*

Kessingland (Suffolk)
Kessingland Antiques, 36A High St, Kessingland Suffolk.
T. (01502) 740562. - Ant / Furn / Jew / Instr -   *066771*

Keswick (Cumbria)
And So To Bed, Lake Rd., Keswick Cumbria.
T. (0176 87) 74881. - Furn -   *066772*
Young & Son, John, 12-14 Main St., Keswick Cumbria.
T. (0176 87) 73434. - Furn -   *066773*

Kettering (Northamptonshire)
Albion Antiques, 36 Duke St., Kettering Northants.
T. (01536) 516220. - Furn -   *066774*
Antiques Warehouse, 53-56 Havelock St., Kettering
Northhants. T. (01536) 411394. - Furn / China /
Naut -   *066775*
Brook, Alexis, 74 Lower St., Kettering NN16 8DL.
T. (01536) 513854. - Ant -   *066776*
Dragon Antiques, 85 Rockingham Rd., Kettering Nor-
thants. T. (01536) 517017. - Paint / Orient -   *066777*
Ward, C.W., 40 Lower St., Kettering NN16 8DT.
T. (01536) 513537. - Ant / Furn / China / Glass - *066778*

Kibworth Beauchamp (Leicestershire)
Vendy, 17 Fleckney Rd., Kibworth Beauchamp Leics.
T. (0153) 796133. - Ant / Furn -   *066779*

Kidderminster (Hereford and Worcester)
B.B.M. Jewellery and Antiques, 8-9 Lion St., Kiddermin-
ster Herefs & Worcs. T. (01562) 744118. - Ant / Num /
Jew -   *066780*
Gorst Hall Restoration, Gorst Hall, Barnetts Ln., Kidder-
minster Herefs & Worcs. T. (01562) 515880.
- Furn -   *066781*
Hi-Felicity, 1 Comberton Rd., Kidderminster Herefs &
Worcs. T. (01562) 742549. - Furn -   *066782*

Kidwelly (Dyfed)
Country Antiques, 31 Bridge St., Kidwelly Wales.
T. (01554) 890328. - Furn / Tex -   *066783*
Country Antiques, Old Castle Mill, Kidwelly SA17 4UU.
T. (01554) 890534. - Ant / Furn -   *066784*

Kilbarchan (Southclyde)
Gardner's, Kibblestone Rd., Kilbarchan Scotland.
T. (0150 57) 2292. - Ant -   *066785*

McDougall, Marjorie and Sandy, 10 The Cross, Kilbarchan Scotland. T. (0150 57) 2229. - Furn / Tex - *066786*

Killamarsh (Derbyshire)
Havenplan's Architectural Emporium, Old Station, Station Rd., Killamarsh Derbs. T. (01742) 489972. - Ant / Furn - *066787*

Killin (Central)
Gauld, Maureen H., Cameron Bldgs., Main St., Killin Scotland. T. (01567) 820475. - Ant / Paint / Silv - *066788*

Killinghall (North Yorkshire)
Norwood House Antiques, 88 Ripon Rd., Killinghall Yorks. North. T. (01423) 506468. - Furn / China / Silv / Instr - *066789*

Kilmacolm (Southclyde)
Kilmacolm Antiques, Stewart Pl, Kilmacolm Scotland. T. (0150) 5873149. - Paint / Furn / Jew - *066790*

Kilmarnock (Southclyde)
MacInnes, 5a David Orr St, Kilmarnock Scotland. T. (01563) 26739. - Ant - *066791*
QS Antiques, Troon Rd, Kilmarnock Scotland. T. (01292) 74377. - Furn / Naut - *066792*

Kimpton (Hertfordshire)
Annick, 28 High St., Kimpton Herts. T. (01438) 832491. - Ant / Paint / Furn - *066793*

Kineton (Warwickshire)
Jeremy Venables, Old Mill, Mill Ln., Kineton Warks. T. (01926) 640971. - Furn - *066794*

King's Lynn (Norfolk)
Clayton, Tim, 23 Chapel St., King's Lynn Norfolk. T. (01553) 772329. - Paint / Furn / Jew / Instr - *066795*
Glenmore, 28 Tower St., King's Lynn Norfolk. T. (01553) 766532. - Ant / Furn - *066796*
Norfolk Galleries, Railway Rd., King's Lynn Norfolk. T. (01553) 765060. - Furn - *066797*
Old Curiosity Shop, 25 Saint James St., King's Lynn Norfolk. T. (01553) 766591. - Paint / Furn / Tex / Jew - *066798*
Old Granary Antiques, King Straithe Ln, Off Queens St, King's Lynn Norfolk. T. (01553) 775509. - Ant / China / Jew / Silv - *066799*
Silverton, 23 Chapel St., King's Lynn Norfolk. T. (01553) 772329. - Paint / Furn / China / Instr - *066800*
Tower Gallery, Middleton Tower, King's Lynn Norfolk. T. (01553) 840203. - Ant / Paint / Furn / China - *066801*

Kings Langley (Hertfordshire)
Frenches Farm Antiques, Tower Hill, Chipperfield, Kings Langley Herts. T. (01923) 265843. - Furn / China - *066802*

Kingsbridge (Devon)
Avon House Antiques, 13 Church St., Kingsbridge Devon. T. (01548) 853718. - Ant - *066803*

Kingston-upon-Thames (Surrey)
Glencorse, 321 Richmond Rd, Kingston-upon-Thames KT2 5PP. T. (0181) 541 0871. - Paint / Furn - *066804*
Glydon & Guess, 14 Apple Market, Kingston-upon-Thames Surrey. T. (0181) 546 3758. - Jew / Silv - *066805*

Kingswear (Devon)
Southwick, David L.H., Beacon Lodge, Beacon Ln., Kingswear Devon. T. (01803) 752533, Fax (01803) 752535. - Orient - *066806*

Kingussie (Highland)
Mostly Pine, Gynack Cottage, High St., Kingussie PH21 1HZ. T. (01540) 661838. - Furn - *066807*

Kinross (Tayside)
Miles, 16 Mill St., Kinross Scotland. T. (01577) 864858. - Furn / China - *066808*

Kinver (Staffordshire)
Antique Centre, 128 High St., Kinver Staffs. T. (01384) 877441. - Furn / China / Instr / Glass / Music - *066809*

Kirkby Lonsdale (Cumbria)
Adamson, Alexander, Tearnside Hall, Kirkby Lonsdale Cumbria. T. (015242) 71989. - Furn / China / Glass - *066810*

Kirkby Stephen (Cumbria)
Haughey, Market St, Kirkby Stephen CA17 4QN. T. (0176 83) 71302. - Furn - *066811*
Hill, David, 36 Market Sq., Kirkby Stephen Cumbria. T. (0176 83) 71598. - Furn / Instr - *066812*
Mortlake, 32-34 Market St., Kirkby Stephen Cumbria. T. (0176 83) 71666. - Furn - *066813*

Kirkbymoorside (North Yorkshire)
Crown Square Antiques, 3 Crown Sq., Kirkbymoorside Yorks. North. T. (01751) 33295. - Furn - *066814*

Kirkcudbright (Dumfries and Galloway)
Chapel Antiques, Chapel Farm, Kirkcudbright Scotland. T. (01557) 22281. - Furn / China / Silv - *066815*
Osborne, 41 Castle St., Kirkcudbright Scotland. T. (01557) 30441. - Ant - *066816*

Kirton (Lincolnshire)
Kirton Antiques, 3 High St., Kirton PE20 1DR. T. (01205) 722595, Fax (01205) 722895. - Furn / Naut - *066817*

Knaresborough (North Yorkshire)
Aagaard, Robert, Frogmire House, Stockwell Rd., Knaresborough HG5 0JP. T. (01423) 864805. - Ant - *066818*
Bowkett, 9 Abbey Rd., Knaresborough Yorks. North. T. (01423) 866112. - Ant / Furn - *066819*
Cheapside Antiques, 4 Cheapside, Knaresborough Yorks. North. T. (01423) 867779. - Furn / China - *066820*
Emporium, Market Flat Ln, Knaresborough Yorks. North. T. (01423) 868539. - Ant / Furn - *066821*
Holgate, Milton J., 36 Gracious St., Knaresborough Yorks. North. T. (01423) 865219. - Furn / Instr - *066822*
Kelly, 96 High St., Knaresborough Yorks. North. T. (01423) 862041. - Lights - *066823*
Northern Kilim Centre, 24 Finkle St., Knaresborough Yorks. North. T. (01423) 868219. - Tex - *066824*
Pictoriana, 88 High St., Knaresborough Yorks. North. T. (01423) 866116. - Furn - *066825*
Reece, Gordon, Finkle St., Knaresborough Yorks. North. T. (01423) 866502. - Furn / Tex - *066826*
Reflections, 23 Waterside, Knaresborough Yorks. West. T. (01423) 862005. - Paint / Furn - *066827*
Shaw, Charles, 2 Station Rd., Knaresborough Yorks. North. T. (01423) 867715. - Ant / Paint / Furn - *066828*
Swadforth House, Gracious St., Knaresborough Yorks. North. T. (01423) 864698. - Ant - *066829*

Knebworth (Hertfordshire)
Hamilton & Tucker, Park Lane, Knebworth Herts. T. (01438) 811995. *066830*

Knowle (West Midlands)
Chadwick Antiques, Chadwick End, Knowle B93 0BP. T. (01564) 782096. - Ant / Furn - *066831*

Knutsford (Cheshire)
Bedale, David, 5-7 Minshull St, Knutsford Chshire. T. (01565) 653621. - Ant / Furn - *066832*
Cranford Clocks, 12 Princess St., Knutsford Cheshire. T. (01565) 633331. - Instr - *066833*
Cranford Galleries, 10 King St., Knutsford WA16 6DL. T. (01565) 633646. - Ant / Paint - *066834*
Glynn, 92 King St., Knutsford Cheshire. T. (01565) 634418. - Furn - *066835*
Lion Gallery and Bookshop, 15a Minshull St., Knutsford Cheshire. T. (01565) 652915. - Graph - *066836*
Twenty-Two Antiques, 22 King St., Knutsford Cheshire. T. (01565) 633655. - Ant / Furn / China - *066837*

Lake (Isle of Wight)
Lake Antiques, Sandown Rd., Lake I. of Wight. T. (01983) 406888. - Ant / Furn / Instr - *066838*

Lampeter (Dyfed)
Barn Antiques, 2 Market St., Lampeter Wales. T. (01570) 423526. - Furn - *066839*

Lancaster (Lancashire)
Articles Antiques, 134/136 Greaves Rd, Lancaster Lancs. T. (01524) 39312. - Furn / China / Glass - *066840*
Assembly Rooms Market, King St., Lancaster Lancs. T. (01524) 66627. - Ant - *066841*
G.B. Antiques, Wyresdale Rd, Lancaster Lancs. T. (01524) 844734, Fax (01524) 844735. - Furn / China / Silv / Glass - *066842*
G.W. Antiques, 47 North Rd., Lancaster Lancs. T. (01524) 32050. - Furn - *066843*
Lancaster Leisure Park Antiques, Wyresdale Rd., Lancaster Lancs. T. (01524) 844734. - Ant - *066844*
Lancastrian Antiques, 66 Penny St., Lancaster Lancs. T. (01524) 843764. - Ant - *066845*
Studio Arts Gallery, 6 Lower Church St., Lancaster Lancs. T. (01524) 68014, Fax (01524) 844422. - Paint / Graph - *066846*
Vicary Antiques, 18a Brook St., Lancaster Lancs. T. (01524) 843322. - Paint / Graph / Furn / China / Tex - *066847*

Landbeach (Cambridgeshire)
Garner, P.R., 104 High St., Landbeach Cambs. T. (01223) 860470. - Furn / China / Naut - *066848*

Langford (Nottinghamshire)
Baker, T., Langford House Farm, Langford Notts. T. (01636) 704026. - Furn - *066849*

Langholm (Dumfries and Galloway)
Antique Shop, High St., Langholm Scotland. T. (0138 73) 80238. - Paint / China / Jew / Glass - *066850*

Langley Burrell (Wiltshire)
Fairfax, Harriet, Langley Green, Langley Burrell Wilts. T. (01249) 652030. - Ant - *066851*

Langport (Somerset)
King's House Antiques, King's House, Bow St., Langport Somerset. T. (01458) 250350. - Ant - *066852*

Largs (Southclyde)
Narducci, 11 Waterside St., Largs Scotland. T. (01475) 672612. - Ant / Naut - *066853*

Laugharne (Dyfed)
Speed, Neil, The Strand, Laugharne Wales. T. (01994) 427412. - Ant / Furn - *066854*

Launceston (Cornwall)
Tamar, 5 Church St., Launceston PL15 8AW. T. (01566) 774233. - Paint / Furn / China / Glass - *066855*

Lavenham (Suffolk)
Antiques, 14a High St., Lavenham Suffolk. T. (01787) 248524. - Tex / Jew - *066856*
Baker, J. and J., 12-14 Water St., Lavenham Suffolk. T. (01787) 247610. - Ant / Paint / Furn / China - *066857*
Motts of Lavenham, 8 Water St., Lavenham Suffolk. T. (01449) 736637. - Furn / China - *066858*
Smith, Tom, 36 Market Pl., Lavenham Suffolk. T. (01787) 247463. - Furn / China - *066859*

Laxfield (Suffolk)
Mangate Gallery, Old Vicarage, Laxfield Suffolk. T. (01986) 798524. - Furn - *066860*

Layer-de-la-Haye (Essex)
Pugh, Layer Fields House, Field Farm Rd., Layer-de-la-Haye Essex. T. (01206) 738170. - China - *066861*

Leamington Spa (Warwickshire)
Goodwin & Sons, John, Blackdown Mill, Blackdown, Leamington Spa Warks. T. (01926) 450687. - Paint / Furn - *066862*
Hague, 2 Regent St., Leamington Spa Warks. T. (01926) 337236. - Furn - *066863*
Hooper, David, 20 Regent St., Leamington Spa Warks. T. (01926) 429679. - Ant - *066864*
Leamington, 20 Regent St., Leamington Spa Warks. T. (01926) 429679. - Ant - *066865*

Olive Green, 12 Station Approach, Avenue Rd., Leamington Spa Warks. T. (01860) 613610. - Paint / Furn / China - 066866

Spa Antiques, 4 Windsor St., Leamington Spa Warks. T. (01926) 422927. - Furn - 066867

Trading Post, 39 Chandos St., Leamington Spa Warks. T. (01926) 421857. - Ant / Jew - 066868

Yesterdays, 21 Portland St., Leamington Spa Warks. T. (01926) 450238. - Graph / Furn / China - 066869

Lechlade (Gloucestershire)

Antiques Etcetera, High St., Lechlade Glos. T. (01367) 252567. - Ant / Furn / China / Glass - 066870

Bell, Cottar's Barn, Downington, Lechlade Glos. T. (01367) 252255. - Paint / Graph - 066871

Campbell, Gerard, Maple House, Market Pl., Lechlade Glos. T. (01367) 252267. - Paint / Instr - 066872

D'Arcy, High St., Lechlade Glos. T. (01367) 252471. - Furn / China - 066873

Lechlade Antiques Arcade, 5-7 High St., Lechlade Glos. T. (01367) 252832. - Ant - 066874

Little Barrow Antiques, High St., Lechlade Glos. T. (01367) 253140. - Furn / China / Glass - 066875

Serle, Mark A., 6 Burford St., Lechlade Glos. T. (01367) 253145. - Furn / Mil - 066876

Whitby, Peter, Ashleigh House, High St., Lechlade Glos. T. (01367) 252347. - Furn / China - 066877

Ledbury (Hereford and Worcester)

Nash, John, 17c High St., Ledbury Herefs & Worcs. T. (01531) 5714, Fax (01531) 5050. - Furn - 066878

Serendipity, The Tythings, Preston Court, Ledbury HR8 2LL. T. (0153184) 380. - Ant - 066879

Shaw-Cooper, Susan, 155 The Homend, Ledbury HR8 1LY. T. (01531) 634687. - Furn / Silv - 066880

Leeds (West Yorkshire)

Aladdin's Cave, 19 Queens Arcade, Leeds Yorks. West. T. (0113) 2457903. - Jew - 066881

Antique Exchange, 400 Kirkstall Rd., Leeds Yorks. West. T. (0113) 2743513. - Furn - 066882

Batty's, 3 Stanningley Rd., Leeds Yorks. West. T. (0113) 2639011. - Furn - 066883

Bishop House Antiques, 169 Town St., Rodley, Leeds Yorks. West. T. (0113) 2563071. - Ant / China / Glass - 066884

Boston Pine, Globe Mills, Back Row, Leeds Yorks. West. T. (0113) 2428007. - Furn - 066885

Coins International and Antiques, 1-2 Melbourne St., Leeds. T. (0113) 2434230, Fax (0113) 345544. - Num / Jew / Silv - 066886

Geary, 114 Richardshaw Ln, Leeds Yorks. West. T. (0113) 2564122. - Furn - 066887

Goldsmith, William, 23 County Arcade, Leeds Yorks. West. T. (0113) 2451345. - Graph / Jew / Instr - 066888

Kirkstall Antiques, 366 Kirkstall Rd., Leeds Yorks. West. T. (0113) 2757367. - Ant / Furn - 066889

Oakwood Gallery, 613 Roundhay Rd, Leeds Yorks. West. T. (0113) 2401348. - Paint / Graph - 066890

Originals, 193 Meanwood Rd., Leeds Yorks. West. T. (0113) 2431613. - Ant - 066891

Parker, 6 Grange Croft, Leeds Yorks. West. T. (0113) 2662302. - Paint - 066892

Piano Shop, 39 Holbeck Ln., Leeds Yorks West. T. (0113) 2443685. - Music - 066893

Smith, Bryan, 26-28 Chapeltown, Leeds Yorks. West. T. (0113) 2555815. - Paint / Furn / China / Glass - 066894

Thirkill, 107 West End Ln, Leeds Yorks. West. T. (0113) 2589160. - Paint / Furn / Music - 066895

Waterloo Antiques Centre, Waterloo House, Crown St., Leeds. T. (0113) 423194. - Ant - 066896

Windsor House Antiques, 18-20 Benson St., Leeds LS7 1BL. T. (0113) 2444666, Fax 426394. - Ant / Paint / Furn - 066897

Year Dot, 15 Market St. Arcade, Leeds Yorks. West. T. (0113) 2460860. - Furn / China / Jew / Instr - 066898

Leedstown (Cornwall)

Glasby & Son, A.W., Leedstown Cornwall. T. (01736) 850303. - Furn / China / Instr - 066899

Leek (Staffordshire)

Antiques and Objets d'Art, 70 Saint Edwards St., Leek Staffs. T. (01538) 382587. - Paint / Furn / China / Silv / Glass - 066900

Anvil, Cross St Mill, Leek Staffs. T. (01538) 371657. - Ant - 066901

Aspley, Compton Mill, Compton, Leek Staffs. T. (01538) 373396. - Ant / Furn - 066902

Chapman, Sylvia, 4 Saint Edward St., Leek Staffs. T. (01538) 399116. - Ant / China / Glass - 066903

Cox, Cyril, 76/78 Saint Edward St, Leek Staffs. T. (01538) 399924. - Ant - 066904

Directmoor, Albany House, Abbey Green Rd., Leek Staffs. T. (01538) 387474, Fax (01538) 371307. - Paint / Furn - 066905

England's Gallery, 1 Ball Haye Terrace, Leek Staffs. T. (01538) 373451. - Paint / Graph - 066906

Gemini Trading, Limes Mill, Abbotts Rd., Leek Staffs. T. (01538) 387834, Fax (01538) 399819. - Furn - 066907

Gilligans, 59 Saint Edward St., Leek Staffs. T. (01538) 384174. - Furn - 066908

Grosvenor Antiques, Overton Bank House, Leek Staffs. T. (01538) 385669. - Furn / Instr - 066909

Haynes, Roger, 31 Compton, Leek Staffs. T. (01538) 385161. - Furn - 066910

Johnson's, Park Works, Park Rd., Leek Staffs. T. (01538) 386745. - Furn - 066911

Molland, 40 Compton, Leek Staffs. T. (01538) 372553. - Ant - 066912

Leicester (Leicestershire)

Antiques Complex, Saint Nicholas Pl., Leicester. T. (0116) 533343, Fax (0116) 533347. - Ant - 066913

Betty's, 9 Knighton Fields Rd. West, Leicester. T. (0116) 839048. - Paint / Furn - 066914

Birches, 18 Francis St, Leicester. T. (0116) 703235. - Ant - 066915

Boulevard, Old Dairy, Western Blvd., Leicester. T. (0116) 541201. - Ant / Furn / Jew / Silv - 066916

Corry's, 24/26 Francis St, Leicester. T. (0116) 703794. - Paint / Furn / China / Jew / Silv - 066917

Letty's, 6 Rutland St., Leicester. T. (0116) 626435. - China / Jew / Silv - 066918

Montague Antiques, 60 Montague Rd., Leicester. T. (0116) 706485. - Ant / Furn / China / Silv / Glass - 066919

Moores & Son, Walter, 89 Wellington St., Leicester LE1 6HJ. T. (0116) 551402. - Furn - 066920

Oxford Street Antique Centre, 16-26 Oxford St., Leicester. T. (0116) 553006, Fax (0116) 555863. - Ant - 066921

Smith, E., Saint Nicholas Pl, Leicester. T. (0116) 533343, Fax (0116) 533347. - Paint / Furn / Instr - 066922

Smith, Hammond, 32 West Av., Claredon Park, Leicester. T. (0116) 709020. - Paint / Graph - 066923

Leigh (Kent)

Woodburn, Anthony, Orchard House, High St., Leigh Kent. T. (01732) 832258, Fax (01732) 838023. - Instr - 066924

Leigh (Lancashire)

Leigh Coins, 4 Queens St., Leigh Lancs. T. (01942) 607947. - Ant / Jew - 066925

Leigh-on-Sea (Essex)

Buchan, K.S., 135 The Broadway, Leigh-on-Sea Essex. T. (01702) 79440. - Ant / Furn - 066926

Castle Antiques, 72 The Broadway, Leigh-on-Sea Essex. T. (01702) 75732. - Furn / China / Silv / Mil - 066927

Collectors' Paradise, 993 London Rd., Leigh-on-Sea Essex. T. (01702) 73077. - Instr - 066928

Pall Mall Antiques, 104c-d Elm Rd., Leigh-on-Sea Essex. T. (01702) 77235. - Ant / China / Glass - 066929

Past and Present, 81 and 83 Broadway West, Leigh-on-Sea Essex. T. (01702) 79101. - Ant - 066930

Streamer, J., 86 Broadway, Leigh-on-Sea Essex. T. (01702) 72895. - Furn / Jew / Silv - 066931

Tilly's Antiques, 1801 London Rd., Leigh-on-Sea SS9 2ST. T. (01702) 557170. - Ant / Furn / Toys - 066932

Wrenn, Richard, 113/115 Broadway West, Leigh-on-Sea SS9 2BU. T. (01702) 710745. - Furn / China / Jew / Silv / Glass - 066933

Leighton Buzzard (Bedfordshire)

Ball, David, 59 North St., Leighton Buzzard Beds. T. (01525) 382954. - Ant / Paint / Furn - 066934

Leiston (Suffolk)

Leiston Furniture Warehouses, High St., Leiston Suffolk. T. (01728) 831414. - Furn - 066935

Leiston Trading Post, 13a High St, Leiston Suffolk. T. (01728) 830081. - Ant / Furn - 066936

Leominster (Hereford and Worcester)

Barometer Shop, New St., Leominster Herefs & Worcs. T. (01568) 613652. - Instr - 066937

Chapman, 2 Bridge St., Leominster Herefs & Worcs. T. (01568) 615803. - Furn / Instr - 066938

Eddy, P. and S.N., 22 Etnam St., Leominster Herefs & Worcs. T. (01568) 612813. - Ant / Furn - 066939

Farmers Gallery, 28 Broad St., Leominster Herefs & Worcs. T. (01568) 611413. - Paint / Graph - 066940

Hammond, J., 38 Broad St., Leominster Herefs & Worcs. T. (01568) 614876. - Furn - 066941

Hubbard, Golden Lion, Bridge St., Leominster Herefs & Worcs. T. (01568) 614362. - Furn - 066942

Jennings of Leominster, 30 Bridge St., Leominster HR6 8DX. T. (01568) 612946. - Paint / Furn / Instr - 066943

La Barre, 116 South St., Leominster Herefs & Worcs. T. (01568) 614315. - Furn - 066944

Leominster Antiques, 87 Etnam St., Leominster Herefs & Worcs. T. (01568) 613217. - Paint / Furn - 066945

Leominster Antiques Market, 14 Broad St., Leominster Herefs & Worcs. T. (01568) 612189. - Ant - 066946

Mayfield, 13 South St., Leominster Herefs & Worcs. T. (01568) 612127. - Paint / Furn - 066947

Letchmore Heath (Hertfordshire)

Barlow, Anne, 1 Letchmore Cottages, Letchmore Heath Herts. T. (01923) 85270. - Ant - 066948

Leuchars (Fife)

Earlshall Castle, Leuchars Scotland. T. (01334) 839205. - Mil - 066949

Lewes (East Sussex)

Bird, John, Norton House, Iford, Lewes Sussex East. T. (01273) 483366. - Paint / Furn - 066950

Charleston Antiques, 4 Lansdown Pl., Lewes Sussex East. T. (01273) 477916. - Furn - 066951

Cliffe Antiques Centre, 47 Cliffe High St., Lewes Sussex East. T. (01273) 473266. - Ant - 066952

Cliffe Gallery, 39 Cliffe High St., Lewes Sussex East. T. (01273) 471877. - Furn / China / Jew / Glass - 066953

Dennison & Son, H.P., 22 High St., Lewes BN7 2LN. T. (01273) 480655. - Furn - 066954

Drawing Room, 53 High St., Lewes Sussex. T. (01273) 478560. - Furn - 066955

Felix Gallery, Sun St/Lancaster St, Lewes Sussex. T. (01273) 472668. - Furn / China / Silv - 066956

Green, Renée and Roy, Ashcombe House, Lewes Rd., Lewes Sussex. T. (01273) 474794. - Furn - 066957

Lewes Antiques Centre, 20 Cliffe High St , Lewes Sussex. T. (01273) 476148. - Furn / China / Instr / Glass - 066958

Pastorale Antiques, 15 Malling St., Lewes Sussex. T. (01273) 473259, Fax (01273) 473259. - Furn - 066959

Sautter, Mary, 6 Station St., Lewes Sussex. T. (01273) 474842. - Furn / Instr - 066960

Southdown Antiques, 48 Cliffe High St., Lewes BN7 2AN. T. (01273) 472439. - Ant / China / Silv - 066961

Trevor, 110 High St., Lewes BN7 1XY. T. (01273) 471975. - Furn - 066962

Lichfield (Staffordshire)

Antique Shop, 31 Tamworth St., Lichfield Staffs. T. (01543) 268324. - Paint / Graph / Furn / China / Silv - 066963

Cordelia and Perdy's, 53 Tamworth St., Lichfield Staffs. T. (01543) 263223. - Ant / Naut - 066964

Jordan, James A., 7 The Corn Exchange, Lichfield Staffs. T. (01543) 416221, Fax (0121) 522 2004. - Instr - 066965

Limpsfield (Surrey)
Limpsfield Watercolours, High St., Limpsfield Surrey. T. (01883) 717010. - Paint - 066966

Lincoln (Lincolnshire)
Brewer, Michael, 5 Drury Lane, Lincoln Lincs. T. (01522) 545854. - Paint / Furn / China / Silv - 066967
Castle Gallery, 61 Steep Hill, Lincoln Lincs. T. (01522) 535078. - Paint - 066968
Designs on Pine, 27 The Strait, Lincoln Lincs. T. (01522) 529252. - Furn - 066969
Doyle, 24 Steep Hill, Lincoln Lincs. T. (01522) 542226. - Paint / Furn / Instr - 066970
Dring, C. and K.E., 111 High St., Lincoln Lincs. T. (01522) 540733. - Furn / China / Instr / Naut - 066971
Eastgate Antique Centre, 6 Eastgate, Lincoln Lincs. T. (01522) 544404. - Paint / Furn / China / Jew / Silv - 066972
Hansord & Son, David J., 32 Steep Hill, Lincoln Lincs. T. (01522) 530044. - Ant / Furn / Instr - 066973
Harlequin Gallery, 22 Steep Hill, Lincoln Lincs. T. (01522) 522589. - Paint - 066974
Lambert, Dorrian, 64 Steep Hill, Lincoln Lincs. T. (01522) 545916. - Furn / China / Instr - 066975
Lincoln Fine Art, 33 The Strait, Lincoln Lincs. T. (01522) 533029. - Paint / China / Draw - 066976
Mansions, 5a Eastgate, Lincoln Lincs. T. (01522) 513631. - Ant / Tex - 066977
Pullen, Richard, 28 The Strait, Lincoln Lincs. T. (01522) 537170. - Jew / Silv - 066978
Rowletts of Lincoln, 338 High St., Lincoln LN5 7DQ. T. (01522) 524139. - Num / Jew - 066979
Strait Antiques, 5 The Strait, Lincoln Lincs. T. (01522) 523130. - Ant / Furn / China - 066980
Usher & Son, James, 6 Silver St., Lincoln Lincs. T. (01522) 527547. - Jew / Silv - 066981
20th Century Frocks, 65 Steep Hill, Lincoln Lincs. T. (01522) 545916. - Tex - 066982

Lingfield (Surrey)
Lingfield Antiques, 4 East Grinstead Rd., Lingfield Surrey. T. (01342) 834501. - Ant / Furn / China / Silv - 066983

Linlithgow (Lothian)
Heritage Antiques, 222 High St., Linlithgow Scotland. T. (01506) 847460. - Furn / China / Jew / Silv / Glass - 066984

Linslade (Bedfordshire)
Linslade Antiques, 1 New Rd., Linslade Beds. T. (01525) 378348. - Ant / Furn / China / Silv / Instr - 066985

Liss (Hampshire)
du Cros, J., Farnham Rd., West Liss, Liss Hants. T. (01730) 895299. - Furn - 066986
Pine Collection, 71 Station Rd., Liss Hants. T. (01730) 893743. - Furn - 066987
Plestor Barn Antiques, Farnham Rd., Liss Hants. T. (01730) 893922. - Furn / China / Naut - 066988

Little Brickhill (Buckinghamshire)
Baroq Antiques, Watling St., Little Brickhill Bucks. T. (0152 52) 3 7750. - Paint / Furn / China - 066989

Little Haywood (Staffordshire)
Jalna, Coley Lane, Little Haywood ST18 0UP. T. (01889) 881381. - Furn - 066990

Littlebourne (Kent)
Warren, Jimmy, 28 The Hill, Littlebourne Kent. T. (01227) 721510. - Furn - 066991

Litton Cheney (Dorset)
Whillock, F., Court Farm, Litton Cheney Dorset. T. (01308) 482457. - Graph - 066992

Liverpool (Merseyside)
Boodle & Dunthorne, Boodles House, Lord St., Liverpool L2 9SQ. T. (0151) 227 2525. - Jew / Silv / Instr - 066993
Delta Antiques, 175/177 Smithdown Rd, Liverpool Merseyside. T. (0151) 734 4277. - Furn - 066994
Edward, 45a Whitechapel, Liverpool Merseyside. T. (0151) 236 2909. - Jew / Silv - 066995
Kensington Tower Antiques, 170 Kensington, Liverpool Merseyside. T. (0151) 260 9466, Fax (0151) 260 9130. - Ant / Naut - 066996
Liverpool Militaria, 48 Manchester St., Liverpool Merseyside. T. (0151) 236 4404. - Orient / Mil - 066997
Lyvor & Boydell, 15 Castle St., Liverpool Merseyside. T. (0151) 236 3256. - Paint / Graph - 066998
Maggs, 26-28 Fleet St., Liverpool Merseyside. T. (0151) 708 0221. - Ant - 066999
Pryor & Son, E., 110 London Rd., Liverpool L3 5NL. T. (0151) 709 1361. - Ant / China / Jew / Silv - 067000
Ryan-Wood, 102 Seel St., Liverpool L1 4BL. T. (0151) 709 7776. - Ant / Paint / Furn / China / Silv - 067001
Stefani, 497 Smithdown Rd., Liverpool Merseyside. T. (0151) 734 1933. - China / Jew / Silv - 067002
Swainbanks, 170 Kensington, Liverpool Merseyside. T. (0151) 260 9466, Fax (0151) 260 9130. - Ant / Naut - 067003
Theta Gallery, 29 and 31 Parliament St, Liverpool Merseyside. T. (0151) 708 6375. - Ant / Furn / Instr - 067004

Llandeilo (Dyfed)
Ash, Jim and Pat, 5 Station Rd., Llandeilo Wales. T. (01558) 823726. - Furn - 067005

Llandovery (Dyfed)
Dyfri Antiques, 11 High St., Llandovery Wales. T. (01550) 20602. - Ant / China - 067006
Ovell, 1 Kings Rd., Llandovery Wales. T. (01550) 20928. - Graph / China / Jew - 067007

Llandudno (Gwynedd)
Antique Shop, 24 Vaughan St., Llandudno Wales. T. (01492) 875575. - Furn / China / Jew / Silv / Glass - 067008
Madoc Antiques and Art Gallery, 48 Madoc St., Llandudno Wales. T. (01492) 879754. - Paint / Furn / China / Silv / Instr - 067009

Llanelli (Dyfed)
Alice's Antiques, 24 Upper Park St., Llanelli Wales. T. (01554) 773045. - Ant / Paint / Silv - 067010

Llangollen (Clwyd)
Gallagher, M., Hall St., Llangollen Wales. T. (01978) 860655. - Ant - 067011
Longford, J. and R., 12 Bridge St., Llangollen Wales. T. (01978) 860182. - Ant / Paint / Furn / China / Silv - 067012
Oak Chest, 1 Oak St., Llangollen Wales. T. (01978) 860095. - Jew / Silv - 067013
Passers Buy, Chapel St/Oak St, Llangollen Wales. T. (01978) 860861. - Furn / China / Silv - 067014

Llanrwst (Gwynedd)
Snowdonia Antiques, Station Rd., Llanrwst LL26 0EP. T. (01492) 640789. - Furn / Instr - 067015

Llanwrda (Dyfed)
Maclean, Tiradda, Llansadwrn, Llanwrda Wales. T. (01550) 777509. - Furn - 067016

London
Aaron, 34 Bruton St., London W1X 7DD. T. (0171) 499 9434, Fax (0171) 499 0072. - Ant / Orient / Tex - 067017
Aaron, Didier, 21 Ryder St, London SW1Y 6PX. T. (0171) 8394716, Fax (0171) 9306699. - Paint / Furn - 067018
Abbott, 109 Kirkdale, London SE26. T. (0181) 699 1363. - Furn - 067019
Abbott & Holder, 30 Museum St., London WC1. T. (0171) 637 3981. - Paint - 067020
Aberdeen House Antiques, 75 Saint Mary's Rd., London W5 5RH. T. (0181) 567 5194. - Paint / Furn / China / Silv / Glass - 067021
Acanthus, 171 Arthur Rd., London SW19. T. (0181) 944 8404. - Furn / China / Glass / Music - 067022
Ackermann & Johnson, 27 Lowndes St., London SW1. T. (0171) 235 6464. - Paint - 067023
Acorn, 111 Rosendale Rd., London SE21. T. (0181) 761 3349. - Paint / Furn / China / Jew / Silv - 067024
Acquisitions, 4-6 Jamestown Rd., London NW1 7BY. T. (0171) 485 4955, Fax (0171) 267 4261. - Ant - 067025
Adams, 18-20 Ridgway, London SW19. T. (0181) 946 7047. - Furn / Silv - 067026
Adams, 47 Chalk Farm Rd., London NW1. T. (0171) 267 9241. - Furn - 067027
Adams, Norman, 8/10 Hans Rd, London SW3 1RX. T. (0171) 589 5266, Fax (0171) 589 1968. - Ant / Furn - 067028
A.D.C. Heritage, 2 Old Bond St., London W1X 3TD. T. (0181) 995 3066, Fax (0181) 747 4794. - Silv - 067029
Addison Fine Art, 57 Addison Av., London W11. T. (0171) 603 2374. - Paint - 067030
Addison Ross, 40 Eaton Terrace, London SW1. T. (0171) 730 1536. - Paint - 067031
After Noah, 121 Upper St., London N1. T. (0171) 359 4281, Fax (0171) 359 4281. - Ant - 067032
Age of Elegance, 61 Sheen Lane, London SW14. T. (0181) 876 0878. - China / Tex / Jew / Glass - 067033
Agnew's, 43 Old Bond St., London W1X 4BA. T. (0171) 629 6176, Fax (0171) 629 4359. - Paint / Graph / Sculp / Draw - 067034
Agnew's, 3 Albemarle St., London W1. T. (0171) 629 6176, Fax (0171) 629 4359. - Paint / Graph / Sculp / Draw - 067035
Ahuan, 17 Eccleston St., London SW1. T. (0171) 730 9382. - Orient - 067036
Al-Mashreq, 110 Kensington Church St., London W8. T. (0171) 229 5453. - Orient - 067037
Albert and Victoria Antiques, Station Approach, Station Rd., London E4. T. (0181) 529 6361. - Ant / Tex - 067038
Alexander & Berendt, 1A Davies St, London W1Y 1LL. T. (0171) 499 4775, Fax (0171) 724 0999. - Ant / Furn - 067039
Alfies Antique Market, 13-25 Church St., London NW8. T. (0171) 723 6066. - Ant - 067040
Alice's, 86 Portobello Rd., London W11. T. (0171) 229 8187, Fax (0171) 792 2456. - Ant - 067041
All in One Antiques, 1 Church St., London NW8. T. (0171) 724 3746. - Ant - 067042
Allen, Peter, 17-17a Nunhead Green, London SE15. T. (0171) 732 1968. - Furn - 067043
Allsopp, John, 26 Pimlico Rd., London SW1W. T. (0171) 730 9347. - Furn - 067044
Alton, 72 Church Rd., London SW13. T. (0181) 748 0606. - Ant - 067045
Amazing Grates, 61-63 High Rd., London N2 8AB. T. (0181) 883 9590. - Ant - 067046
Amell, Verner, 4 Ryder St., London SW1Y. T. (0171) 925 2759. - Paint - 067047
Amor, Albert, 37 Bury St., London SW1Y 6AU. T. (0171) 930 2444, Fax (0171) 930 9067. - China - 067048
Anchor, 26 Charing Cross Rd., London WC2H 0DG. T. (0171) 836 5686. - Orient / China - 067049
Andipa, Maria, 162 Walton St., London SW3. T. (0171) 589 2371. - Ico - 067050
Andy's All Pine, 70 Russell Rd, London W14. T. (0171) 602 0856, Fax (0171) 602 8655. - Furn - 067051
Angel Arcade, 116-118 Islington High St., London N1. - Ant - 067052
Anglo-Persian Carpet, 6 South Kensington Station Arcade, London SW7 2NA. T. (0171) 589 5457, Fax (0171) 589 2592. - Tex - 067053
Annie's Antique Clothes, 10 Camden Passage, London N1. T. (0171) 359 0796. - Tex - 067054
Anno Domini Antiques, 66 Pimlico Rd., London SW1W 8LS. T. (0171) 730 5496. - Furn / Tex / Glass - 067055
Antiquarius, 131/141 King's Rd, London SW3. T. (0171) 351 5353, Fax (0171) 351 5350. - Ant - 067056
Antique and Modern Furniture, 160 Earls Court Rd., London SW5. T. (0171) 373 2935. - Furn - 067057

Bernheimer

LONDON · MUNICH

Old Master and 19th Century Paintings
French Furniture
Chinese Ceramics

Konrad O. Bernheimer Ltd	Konrad O. Bernheimer Kunsthandel
By appointment only	Promenadeplatz 13
1 Mount Street	D-80333 München
London W1Y 5AA	Tel. 49-89-22 66 72
Tel: 0171-495 7028 / Fax: 7027	Fax: 49-89-22 60 37

Antique Carpets Gallery, 150 Wandsworth Bridge Rd., London SW6. T. (0171) 371 9619. - Tex - 067058

Antique City, 98 Wood St., London E17. T. (0181) 520 4032. - Ant - 067059

Antique Home, 104A Kensington Church St, London W8 G3. T. (0171) 229 5892. - Furn - 067060

Antique Shop, 9 Fortis Green, London N2. T. (0181) 883 7651. - Ant / Paint / Furn / China - 067061

Antique Trader, 357 Upper St., London N1. T. (0171) 359 2019, Fax (0171) 226 9446. - Furn - 067062

Antique Warehouse, 175D Bermondsey St, London SE8. T. (0181) 469 0295. - Furn - 067063

Antique Warehouse, 175d Bermondsey St., London SE1. T. (0171) 407 5960. - Furn - 067064

Antiques and Things, 91 Eccles Rd., London SW11. T. (0171) 350 0597. - Furn / China / Tex / Glass - 067065

Antiques Pavilion, 175 Bermondsey St., London SE1. T. (0171) 403 2021. - Furn - 067066

Antiques 132, 132 Chiswick High Rd., London W4. T. (0181) 995 0969. - Furn / China - 067067

Antiquites, 227 Ebury St., London SW1. T. (0171) 730 5000. - Furn - 067068

Antiquus, 90-92 Pimlico Rd., London SW1W. T. (0171) 730 8681. - Paint / Tex / Glass - 067069

Antrobus, Philip, 11 New Bond St., London W1. T. (0171) 493 4557, Fax (0171) 495 2120. - Jew - 067070

Apple Market Stalls, Covent Garden Market, London WC2. T. (0171) 836 9136. - Ant - 067071

Apter Fredericks, 265-267 Fulham Rd., London SW3 6HY. T. (0171) 352 2188, Fax (0171) 376 5619. - Furn - 067072

Arbras, 292 Westbourne Grove, London W11. T. (0171) 229 6772. - Ant - 067073

Architectural Antiques, 351 King St., London W6 9NH. T. (0181) 741 7883, Fax (0181) 741 1109. - Ant / Furn - 067074

Argyll Etkin, 48 Conduit St., London W1. T. (0171) 437 7800. - Ant - 067075

Arieta, Valerie, 97b Kensington Church St., London W8. T. (0171) 243 1074. - Ant / Eth - 067076

Armelin, Karin, 592 King's Rd., London SW6. T. (0171) 736 0375. - Graph / Furn - 067077

Armour-Winston, 43 Burlington Arcade, London W1V 4AE. T. (0171) 493 8937. - Jew - 067078

Armoury of Saint James' Military Antiquarians, 17 Picadilly Arcade, London SW1. T. (0171) 493 5082. - Mil - 067079

Art Furniture, 158 Camden St, London NW1 9PA. T. (0171) 267 4324. - Furn / Mod - 067080

Artemis Fine Arts, Duke St., London SW1. T. (0171) 930 8733. - Paint / Graph - 067081

Ashcroft, Nan S., 10a Daleham Gardens, London NW3. T. (0171) 794 6658. - Glass - 067082

Asprey, 165-169 New Bond St., London W1. T. (0171) 493 6767, Fax (0171) 491 0384. - Furn / Jew / Silv / Instr - 067083

Asprey, Maurice, 41 Duke St., London SW1Y 6DF. T. (0171) 930 3921, Fax (0171) 321 0769. - Jew / Silv - 067084

Astarte Gallery, Shop 5 Grosvenor Sq, London W1. T. (0171) 409 1875, Fax (0171) 409 1875. - Ant / Paint / Graph / Furn / Jew - 067085

Astleys, 109 Jermyn St., London SW1. T. (0171) 930 1687. - China - 067086

At the Sign of the Chest of Drawers, 281 Upper St., London N1. T. (0171) 359 5909. - Furn - 067087

Atkins, Gary, 107 Kensington Church St., London W8. T. (0171) 727 8737, Fax (0171) 792 9010. - Furn / China - 067088

Atlantic Bay Carpets, 7 Sedley Pl., London W1R 1HH. T. (0171) 355 3301, Fax (0171) 355 3760. - Tex - 067089

Auld, Ian, 1 Gateway Arcade, London N1 0PG. T. (0171) 359 1440. - China / Eth / Silv - 067090

Austin & Sons, G., 11-23 Peckham Rye, London SE15. T. (0171) 639 3163. - Paint / Furn / China / Silv / Glass - 067091

Axia Art Consultants, 121 Ledbury Rd., London W11. T. (0171) 727 9724. - Orient / China / Tex - 067092

B. & T. Antiques, 79 Ledbury Rd., London W11. T. (0171) 229 7001. - Paint / Furn / Silv - 067093

Badger, 12 Saint Mary's Rd., London W5. T. (0181) 567 5601. - Furn / China / Instr - 067094

Badger, 320-322 Creek Rd., London SE10. T. (0181) 853 1394. - Ant / Furn - 067095

Baillache, Serge, 189 Westbourne Grove, London W11. T. (0171) 229 2270. - Furn - 067096

Baker, Greg, 34 Brook St., London W1Y 1YA. T. (0171) 629 7926, Fax (0171) 495 3872. - Orient - 067097

Baldwin & Sons, A.H., 11 Adelphi Terrace, London WC2. T. (0171) 930 6879, Fax (0171) 930 9450. - Num - 067098

Banbury Fayre, 6 Pierrepont Arcade, London N1. T. (0181) 852 5675. - Ant / Naut - 067099

Bangs, Christopher, London SW11. T. (0171) 223 5676, Fax (0171) 223 4933. - Ant - 067100

Barbagallo, Sebastiano, 294-304 Saint James Rd., London SE1. T. (0171) 231 3680, Fax (0171) 232 1385. - Orient - 067101

Barclay Samson, 39 Inglethorpe St., London SW6. T. (0171) 381 4341, Fax (0171) 610 0434. - Paint / Graph - 067102

Bardawill, Eddy, 106 Kensington Church St., London W8. T. (0171) 221 3967, Fax (0171) 221 5124. - Furn - 067103

Barham, 83 Portobello Rd., London W11. T. (0171) 727 3845. - Paint / Furn / Silv / Instr / Glass - 067104

Barham, P.R., 111 Portobello Rd., London W11 2QB. T. (0171) 727 3397, Fax (0171) 243 1719. - Furn / Orient / Silv / Instr - 067105

Barley, Robert, 48 Fulham High St., London SW6 3LQ. T. (0171) 736 4429. - Ant / Furn / Lights - 067106

Barnes, R.A., 26 Lower Richmond Rd., London SW15 1JP. T. (0181) 789 3371. - Paint / Furn / Orient / China - 067107

Barnet, 79 Kensington Church St., London W8. T. (0171) 376 2817. - Furn - 067108

Barometer Fair, Pied Bull Yard, Bury Pl., London WC1A 2JR. T. (0171) 404 4521. - Instr - 067109

Bartlett, Nigel A., 67 Saint Thomas St., London SE1. T. (0171) 378 7895, Fax (0171) 378 0388. - Ant - 067110

Baumkotter, 63a Kensington Church St., London W8. T. (0171) 937 5171. - Paint - 067111

Baxter & Sons, H.C., 53 Stewarts Grove, London SW3 6PH. T. (0171) 352 9826. - Furn - 067112

B.C. Metalcrafts, 69 Tewkesbury Gardens, London NW9. T. (0181) 204 2446, Fax (0181) 206 2871. - Lights / Instr - 067113

Beagle, 303 Westbourne Grove, London W11. T. (0171) 229 9524. - Orient - 067114

Beare, John and Arthur, 7 Broadwick St., London W1. T. (0171) 437 1449. - Music - 067115

Beaver Coin Room, 57 Philbeach Gardens, London SW5 9ED. T. (0171) 373 4553, Fax (0171) 373 4555. - Num - 067116

Bedford, William, 46 Essex Rd., London N1. T. (0171) 226 9648, Fax (0171) 226 6225. - Furn - 067117

Beech, Nicholas, 787-789 Wandsworth Rd., London SW8. T. (0171) 720 8552. - Furn - 067118

Beer, John, 191-199 Archway Rd., London N6. T. (01242) 576080. - Furn - 067119

Beetles, Chris, 10 Ryder St., London SW1Y 6QB. T. (0171) 839 7551. - Paint - 067120

Belgrave Carpet Gallery, 91 Knightsbridge, London SW1. T. (0171) 235 2541. - Tex - 067121

Belgrave Gallery, 22 Mason's Yard, Duke St., London SW1. T. (0171) 930 0294. - Paint / Sculp - 067122

Benardout & Benardout, 18 Grosvenor St., London W1. T. (0171) 355 4531, Fax (0171) 491 9710. - Tex - 067123

Bennett, Paul, 48A George St., London W1. T. (0171) 935 1555. - Silv - 067124

Bensiglio, S., 41 The Ridings, London W5. T. (0181) 997 2140. - Tex - 067125

Bentley & Co, 19 Burlington Arcade, London W1. T. (0171) 495 3783. - Jew - 067126

Beresford-Clark, 558 King's Rd., London SW6. T. (0171) 731 5079. - Paint / Furn / Tex - 067127

Bermondsey Antique Market, Bermondsey St, London SE1. T. (0171) 351 5353, Fax (0171) 351 5350. - Ant - 067128

Bermondsey Antique Warehouse, 173 Bermondsey St., London SE1. T. (0171) 407 2566, Fax (0171) 924 3121. - Ant - 067129

Bernheimer, 1 Mount St, London W1Y 5AA. T. (0171) 4957028, Fax 4957027. - Furn / Orient - 067130

Berwald Oriental Art, 101 Kensington Church St, London W8 7LN. T. (0171) 2290800, Fax 2291101. - Orient - 067131

Beverley, 30 Church St., London NW8. T. (0171) 262 1576. - Mod - 067132

Biddulph, Peter, 35 Saint George St., London W1R 9FA. T. (0171) 491 8621. - Music - 067133

Big Ben Antique Clocks, New King's Rd, London SW6 4AA. T. (0171) 736 1770, Fax (0171) 384 1957. - Instr - 067134

Binder, D. and A., 34 Church St., London NW8. T. (0171) 723 0542, Fax (0171) 724 0837. - Ant - 067135

Bingham, Tony, 11 Pond St., London NW3 2PN. T. (0171) 794 1596, Fax (0171) 433 3662. - Paint / Music - 067136

Bishops Park Antiques, 53-55 Fulham High St., London SW6. T. (0171) 736 4573. - Furn - 067137

Bizarre, 24 Church St., London NW8. T. (0171) 724 1305, Fax (0171) 724 1316. - Mod - 067138

Black Cat, 202 High St., London SE20. T. (0181) 778 4230. - Ant / Furn - 067139

Black, David, 96 Portland Rd., London W11 4LN. T. (0171) 727 2566, Fax (0171) 229 4599. - Tex - 067140

Blackburn, Norman, 32 Ledbury Rd., London W11. T. (0171) 229 5316. - Graph - 067141

Blairman & Sons, H., 119 Mount St., London W1Y 5HB. T. (0171) 493 0444, Fax (0171) 495 0766. - Ant / Paint / Furn / China - 067142

Blake, K.N. and P., 8 High St., London E11.
T. (0181) 989 2317. - Paint / Furn -　　067143
Blanchard & Allan, 86/88 Pimlico Rd, London SW1W.
T. (0171) 823 6310, Fax (0171) 823 6303. - Furn /
Lights -　　067144
Bloom, Anne, 10a New Bond St, London W1.
T. (0171) 4911213, Fax (0171) 4090777. - Jew / Fra /
Silv -　　067145
Bloom & Son, N., 124 New Bond St, The Bond Street An-
tiques Centre, London W1Y 9AE. T. (0171) 6295060,
Fax (0171) 4932528.　　067146
Blunderbuss, 29 Thayer St., London W1.
T. (0171) 486 2444. - Mil -　　067147
Bly, John, 27 Bury St., London SW1Y.
T. (0171) 930 1292. - Paint / Furn / China / Silv /
Glass -　　067148
Bolour, Y. and B., 53-79 Highgate Rd., London NW5.
T. (0171) 485 6262, Fax (0171) 267 7351.
- Tex -　　067149
Bond Street Antique Centre, 124 New Bond St., London
W1Y 9AE. T. (0171) 351 5353, Fax (0171) 351 5350.
- Ant -　　067150
Bond Street Silver Galleries, 111-112 New Bond St.,
London W1. T. (0171) 493 6180. - Silv -　　067151
Bonrose, 207-211 Kensington Church St., London W8.
T. (0171) 221 3139. - Furn / China / Silv / Instr -　　067152
Boodle & Dunthorne, 58 Brompton Rd., London SW3.
T. (0171) 584 6363. - Jew -　　067153
Bookham Galleries, 164 Wandsworth Bridge Rd., London
SW6. T. (0171) 736 5125. - Furn / Tex -　　067154
Books and Things, 292 Westbourne Grove, London W11
2PS. T. (0171) 370 5593. - Ant -　　067155
Booth, Joanna, 247 King's Rd., London SW3.
T. (0171) 352 8998, Fax (0171) 376 7350. - Graph /
Tex -　　067156
Bord, M., 16 Charing Cross Rd., London WC2.
T. (0171) 836 0631. - Num -　　067157
Bornoff, Claude, 20 Chepstow Cnr, London W2.
T. (0171) 229 8947. - Furn / China -　　067158
Bourdon-Smith, J.H., 24 Mason's Yard, Duke St., London
SW1Y 6BU. T. (0171) 839 4714. - Silv -　　067159
Boutique Fantasque, 13 Pierrepont Row, London N1.
T. (0125) 126 2287. - Paint / Graph / Furn / China /
Jew -　　067160
Bowmoore, 77 Peterborough Rd., London SW6.
T. (0171) 736 4111. - Paint -　　067161
Brandt, 771 Fulham Rd., London SW6.
T. (0171) 731 6835. - Orient -　　067162
Bridge, Christine, 78 Castelnan, London SW13.
T. (0181) 741 5501, Fax (0181) 741 5501. - China /
Sculp / Glass -　　067163
Briggs, F.E.A., 73 Ledbury Rd., London W11.
T. (0171) 727 0909. - Furn / Tex -　　067164
Brisigotti, 44 Duke St., London SW1Y 6DD.
T. (0171) 839 4441. - Paint -　　067165
Brocklehurst, Aubrey, 124 Cromwell Rd., London SW7
4ET. (0171) 373 0319. - Instr -　　067166
Brook, Beverley, 29 Grove Rd., London SW13.
T. (0181) 878 5656. - China / Silv / Glass -　　067167
Brower, David, 113 Kensington Church St., London W8.
T. (0171) 221 4155. - Furn / China / Instr -　　067168
Brown, Alasdair, 560 King's Rd., London SW6.
T. (0171) 736 8077. - Furn -　　067169
Brown, I. and J.L., 632-636 King's Rd, London SW6.
T. (0171) 736 4141, Fax (0171) 736 9164.
- Furn -　　067170
Browse & Darby, 19 Cork St., London W1.
T. (0171) 734 7984. - Paint / Sculp / Draw -　　067171
Bruford & Heming, 28 Conduit St., London W1R 9TA.
T. (0171) 499 7644, Fax (0171) 493 5879. - Jew /
Silv -　　067172
Buck & Payne, 5 Camden Passage, London N1.
T. (0171) 226 4326. - Furn -　　067173
Bull, John, 139A New Bond St, London W1.
T. (0171) 629 1251, Fax (0171) 495 3001.
- Ant -　　067174
Bunzl, Tony, 344 King's Rd., London SW3.
T. (0171) 352 3697, Fax (0171) 352 1792.
- Furn -　　067175
Burdon, Alyson, 4 Anley Rd., London W14.
T. (0171) 602 1973. - Tex -　　067176

Burlington Gallery, 10 Burlington Gardens, London W1.
T. (0171) 734 9228, Fax (0171) 494 3770.
- Graph -　　067177
Burlington Paintings, 12 Burlington Gardens, London
W1X 1LG. T. (0171) 734 9984, Fax (0171) 494 3770.
- Paint -　　067178
Burne, W.G.T., 11 Elystan St., London SW3 3NT.
T. (0171) 589 6074, Fax (0181) 944 1977.
- Glass -　　067179
Burness, Victor, 241 Long Ln., London SE1.
T. (01732) 454591. - Instr / Naut -　　067180
Bushwood, 317 Upper St., London N1.
T. (0171) 359 2095, Fax (0171) 704 9578. - Ant / Furn /
Instr -　　067181
Butchoff, 229 and 233 Westbourne Grove, London W11.
T. (0171) 221 8174, Fax (0171) 792 8923. - Paint /
Furn -　　067182
Butler & Wilson, 189 Fulham Rd., London SW3.
T. (0171) 352 3045. - Jew -　　067183
Button Queen, 19 Marylebone Lane, London W1M 5FF.
T. (0171) 935 1505. - Ant -　　067184
Caelt, 182 Westbourne Grove, London W11.
T. (0171) 229 9309, Fax (0171) 243 0215.
- Paint -　　067185
Camden Art Gallery, 22 Church St., London NW8.
T. (0171) 262 3613, Fax (0171) 723 2333. - Paint /
Furn -　　067186
Camden Passage Antiques Centre, 12 Camden Passage,
London N1. T. (0171) 359 0190. - Ant -　　067187
Cameo Gallery, 38 Kensington Church St., London W8.
T. (0171) 938 4114, Fax (0171) 376 0686. - Furn /
Sculp / Glass -　　067188
Camerer Cuss & Co., 17 Ryder St., London SW1Y.
T. (0171) 930 1941. - Instr -　　067189
Campbell, Lucy B., 123 Kensington Church St., London
W8. T. (0171) 727 2205. - Graph -　　067190
Campion, 71 White Hart Ln., London SW13.
T. (0181) 878 6688. - Furn / Tex / Jew -　　067191
Capital Clocks, 190 Wandsworth Rd., London SW8 2JU.
T. (0171) 720 6372. - Instr -　　067192
Capon, Patrick, 350 Upper St., London N1.
T. (0171) 354 0487. - Instr -　　067193
Carrington & Co., 170 Regent St., London W1R 6BQ.
T. (0171) 734 3727. - Jew / Silv / Instr -　　067194
Carritt, David, 15 Duke St., London SW1Y 6DB.
T. (0171) 930 8733, Fax (0171) 839 5009.
- Paint -　　067195
Casimir, Jack, 23 Pembridge Rd., London W11 3HG.
T. (0171) 727 8643. - Ant -　　067196
Cassio, 68 Ledbury Rd., London W11.
T. (0171) 727 0678. - Furn -　　067197
Cavendish, Odile, 14 Lowndes St., London SW1X 9EX.
T. (0171) 243 1668, Fax (0171) 235 4371. - Paint /
Furn / Orient -　　067198
Cavendish, Rupert, 98 Waterford Rd., London SW6.
T. (0171) 384 2642, Fax (0171) 731 8302. - Furn /
Mod -　　067199
Cavendish, Rupert, 610 King's Rd., London SW6 2DX.
T. (0171) 731 7041, Fax (0171) 731 8302. - Paint /
Furn -　　067200
Cazalet, L., 24 Davies St., London W1.
T. (0171) 491 4767. - Graph -　　067201
Centaur Gallery, 82 Highgate High St., London N6.
T. (0181) 340 0087. - Paint / Graph / Sculp /
Eth -　　067202
Chancery Antiques, 357a Upper St., London N1 0PD.
T. (0171) 359 9035. - Orient -　　067203
Chanticleer, 6 Tilton St, London W11.
T. (0171) 385 0919. - Ant / Orient -　　067204
Chapman, Peter, 10 Theberton St., London N1 0QX.
T. (0171) 226 5565, Fax (0181) 348 4846. - Paint /
Graph / Furn / Draw -　　067205
Charge, Graham, 305 Westbourne Grove, London W11.
T. (0171) 229 7907. - Furn -　　067206
Charleville Gallery, 7 Charleville Rd., London W14.
T. (0171) 385 3795. - Tex -　　067207
Chaucer, 45 Pimlico Rd., London SW1.
T. (0171) 730 2972. - Paint / Graph / Sculp -　　067208
Chelsea Antique Market, 245A and 253 King's Rd, Lon-
don SW3 5EL. T. (0171) 352 5689. - Ant -　　067209
Chelsea Bric-a-Brac Shop, 16 Hartfield Rd., London
SW19. T. (0181) 946 6894. - Ant / Furn -　　067210

Chelsea Coins, Fulham Rd., London SW10 9PQ.
T. (0181) 870 5501. - Num -　　067211
Cheneviere, Antoine, 94 Mount St., London W1Y.
T. (0171) 491 1007. - Paint / Furn -　　067212
Chenil, 181-183 King's Rd., London SW3.
T. (0171) 351 5353, Fax (0171) 351 5350.
- Ant -　　067213
Chiswick Antiques, 97 Northfield Av, London W13.
T. (0181) 579 3071. - Furn / China / Silv /
Glass -　　067214
Christie, J., 26 Burlington Arcade, London W1.
T. (0171) 629 3070, Fax (0171) 409 3631. - Sculp /
Jew / Silv -　　067215
Christopher, 173 Saint John's Hill, London SW11.
T. (0171) 978 5132. - Furn -　　067216
Church Street Antiques, 8 Church St., London NW8.
T. (0171) 723 7415. - Furn -　　067217
Ciancimino, 99 Pimlico Rd., London SW1W 8PH.
T. (0171) 730 9950, Fax (0171) 730 5365. - Ant /
Furn -　　067218
City Clocks, 31 Amwell St., London EC1.
T. (0171) 278 1154. - Instr -　　067219
Clark, Gerald, 1 High St., London NW7.
T. (0181) 906 0342. - Furn / Paint / China -　　067220
Clay, John, 263 New King's Rd., London SW6 4RB.
T. (0171) 731 5677. - Furn / Silv / Instr -　　067221
Clock Clinic, 85 Lower Richmond Rd., London SW15
1EU. T. (0181) 788 1407, Fax (0181) 780 2838.
- Instr -　　067222
Clunes, 9 West Pl., London SW19 4UH.
T. (0181) 946 1643. - Ant / China -　　067223
Coats, 4 Kensington Church Walk, London W8.
T. (0171) 937 0983. - Tex -　　067224
Coats, Dick, 32 Grantham Rd., London W4.
T. (0181) 995 9733. - Paint / Sculp -　　067225
Cobra & Bellamy, 149 Sloane St., London SW1.
T. (0171) 730 2823. - Jew -　　067226
Cochrane, Fergus, 570 King's Rd., London SW6 2DY.
T. (0171) 736 9166. - Lights -　　067227
Cohen, Edward, 40 Duke St., London SW1.
T. (0171) 839 5180. - Paint -　　067228
Cohen & Pearce, 84 Portobello Rd., London W11.
T. (0171) 229 9458, Fax (0171) 229 9653.
- Orient -　　067229
Colefax and Fowler, 39 Brook St., London W1Y 2JE.
T. (0171) 493 2231. - Paint / Furn / Tex -　　067230
Coleman, Garrick D., 5 Kensington Court, London W8.
T. (0171) 937 5524. - Furn -　　067231
Coleman, Simon, 40 White Hart Ln., London SW13.
T. (0181) 878 5037. - Furn -　　067232
Collingwood & Co., 171 New Bond St., London W1Y
9PB. T. (0171) 734 2656, Fax (0171) 629 5418. - Jew /
Silv / Instr -　　067233
Collino, Julie, 15 Glendower Pl., London SW7.
T. (0171) 584 4733. - Paint / Furn / China -　　067234
Collins, Peter, 92 Waterford Rd., London SW6.
T. (0171) 736 4149. - Furn -　　067235
Colnaghi & Co., P. and D., 14 Old Bond St., London W1.
T. (0171) 491 7408. - Paint / Graph / Sculp /
Draw -　　067236
Commemoratives, 3 Pierrepont Arcade, London N1.
- China / Glass -　　067237
Connaught Brown, 2 Albemarle St., London W1.
T. (0171) 408 0362. - Paint -　　067238
Connaught Galleries, 44 Connaught St., London W2.
T. (0171) 723 1660. - Paint -　　067239
Connoisseur Gallery, 14-15 Halkin Arcade, London
SW1X. T. (0171) 245 6431. - Orient -　　067240
Cooke, Mary, 121a Kensington Church St., London W8.
T. (0171) 792 8077. - Silv -　　067241
Cooper, 768 Fulham Rd., London SW6.
T. (0171) 731 3421. - Paint / Sculp -　　067242
Coote, Belinda, 29 Holland St., London W8.
T. (0171) 937 3924. - Furn / China / Tex -　　067243
Corner Cupboard, 679 Finchley Rd., London NW2.
T. (0171) 435 4870. - Furn / China / Jew / Silv /
Glass -　　067244
Corner Portobello, 282, 284, 288 and 290 Westbourne
Grove, London W11. T. (0171) 727 2027. - Ant / Jew /
Silv -　　067245
Cornucopia, 12 Upper Tachbrook St., London SW1.
T. (0171) 828 5752. - Tex / Jew -　　067246

Corrigan, 114 Islington High St., London N1. T. (0171) 704 0678. - Furn - 067247
Courtney, Richard, 112-114 Fulham Rd., London SW3. T. (0171) 370 4020. - Furn - 067248
Covent Garden Flea Market, Jubilee Market, Covent Garden, London WC2. T. (0171) 836 2139. - Ant - 067249
Craven Gallery, 30 Craven Terrace, London W2. T. (0171) 402 2802. - Furn / China / Silv / Glass - 067250
Crispin, Ian, 95 Lisson Grove, London NW1. T. (0171) 402 6845. - Ant / Naut - 067251
Cronan, Sandra, 18 Burlington Arcade, London W1. T. (0171) 491 4851, Fax (0171) 493 2758. - Jew - 067252
Crotty & Son, J., 74 New King's Rd., London SW6. T. (0171) 731 4209. - Ant / Lights - 067253
Crouch End Antiques, 47 Park Rd, London N8. T. (0181) 348 7652. - Furn - 067254
Csaky's, 20 Pimclico Rd., London SW1W. T. (0171) 730 2068. - Ant / Furn - 067255
Cura Antiques, 34 Ledbury Rd., London W11. T. (0171) 229 6880. - Paint / Furn / China / Sculp - 067256
Curios, 130c Junction Rd., London N19. T. (0171) 272 5603. - Ant - 067257
Curious Grannies, 2 Middleton Rd., London E8. T. (0171) 254 7074. - Ant / Jew / Music - 067258
d'Orsai, Sebastian, 39 Theobalds Rd., London WC1. T. (0171) 405 6663. - Paint - 067259
Daggett, 153 Portobello Rd., London W11. T. (0171) 229 2248. - Paint / Furn / Tex / Fra / Instr - 067260
Dale, John, 87 Portobello Rd., London W11. T. (0171) 727 1304. - Ant - 067261
Dale, Peter, 11-12 Royal Opera Arcade, London SW1. T. (0171) 930 3695. - Mil - 067262
Dare, George, 9 Launceston Pl., London W8 5RL. T. (0171) 937 7072. - Paint - 067263
Davar, Zal, 344 King's Rd., London SW3. T. (0171) 351 5730, Fax (0171) 352 1792. - Furn - 067264
Davidson Brothers, 33 Camden Passage, London N1. T. (0171) 226 7491. - Ant / Furn - 067265
Davidson, Michael, 52 and 54 Ledbury Rd, London W11. T. (0171) 229 6088. - Furn - 067266
Davies, 44A Kensington Church St, London W8. T. (0171) 937 9216, Fax (0171) 938 2032. - China - 067267
Davies, A.B., 18 Brook St., London W1. T. (0171) 629 1053. - Jew / Silv - 067268
Davies, Barry, 1 Davies St., London W1. T. (0171) 408 0207. - Orient - 067269
Davighi, N., 117 Shepherd's Bush Rd., London W6. T. (0171) 603 5357. - Ant / Lights - 067270
Davis, Kenneth, 15 King St., London SW1Y. T. (0171) 930 0313, Fax (0171) 976 1306. - Silv - 067271
Day, Richard, 173 New Bond St., London W1. T. (0171) 629 2991, Fax (0171) 493 7569. - Graph - 067272
Day, Shirley, 91b Jermyn St., London SW1Y 6JB. T. (0171) 839 2804, Fax (0171) 839 3334. - Orient - 067273
de Biolley, Jehanne, 29 Conduit St., London W1R. T. (0171) 495 4257. - Orient - 067274
Dean's Antiques, 52-53 Camden Passage, London N1. T. (0171) 354 9940. - Ant - 067275
Delehar, Peter, 146 Portobello Rd., London W11. T. (0171) 727 9860. - Instr - 067276
Delieb, 31 Woodville Rd., London NW11 9TP. T. (0181) 458 2083. - Silv - 067277
Delightful Muddle, 11 Upper Tachbrook St., London SW1. - Ant / China / Tex / Glass - 067278
Demas, 31 Burlington Arcade, London W1. T. (0171) 493 9496. - Jew - 067279
Denham, John, 50 Mill Ln., London NW6 1NJ. T. (0171) 794 2635. - Paint / Graph / Draw - 067280
Dennier, Guy, 48A Lower Sloane St, London SW1. T. (0171) 823 4121. - Paint / Furn / China / Lights - 067281
Dennis, Richard, 144 Kensington Church St., London W8 4BN. T. (0171) 727 2061. - China - 067282
Denny, Colin, 18 Cale St., London SW3 3QU. T. (0171) 584 0240. - Naut - 067283
Denton, 156 Kensington Church St., London W8. T. (0171) 229 5866, Fax (0171) 792 1073. - Glass - 067284
Desmonde, Kay, 17 Kensington Church Walk, London W8. T. (0171) 937 2602. - Toys - 067285
Deutsch, H. and W., 111 Kensington Church St., London W8 7LN. T. (0171) 727 5984. - China / Sculp / Silv - 067286
Di Michele, E. and A., 36 Ledbury Rd., London W11. T. (0171) 229 1823. - Furn - 067287
Dickson, Robert, 263 Fulham Rd., London SW3 6HY. T. (0171) 351 0330. - Furn - 067288
Dining Room Shop, 62/64 White Hart Ln, London SW13. T. (0181) 878 1020. - Furn - 067289
Dixon, 471 Upper Richmond Rd. West, London SW14. T. (0181) 878 6788. - Furn / China / Jew / Silv - 067290
Dodo, 286 Westbourne Grove, London W11. T. (0171) 229 3132. - Ant - 067291
Dolls House Toys, 29 The Market, London WC2 8RE. T. (0171) 379 7243. - Toys - 067292
Dolphin Arcade, 155-157 Portobello Rd., London W11. T. (0171) 727 4883. - Ant / China / Jew / Silv - 067293
Dolphin Coins, 2c England's Lane, London NW3. T. (0171) 722 4116, Fax (0171) 483 2000. - Num - 067294
Dome, 75 Upper St., London N1. T. (0171) 226 7227, Fax (0171) 704 2960. - Furn - 067295
Donay, 35 Camden Passage, London N1. T. (0171) 359 1880. - Ant - 067296
Douch, A., 28 Conduit St., London W1. T. (0171) 493 9413. - Jew / Silv / Glass - 067297
Douwes, 38 Duke St., London SW1 6DF. T. (0171) 8395795, Fax 8395904. 067298
Dragons of Walton Street, 23 Walton St., London SW3. T. (0171) 589 3795, Fax (0171) 584 4670. - Furn - 067299
Drummond, Nicholas, 6 Saint John's Wood Rd., London NW8 8RE. T. (0171) 286 6452. - Paint - 067300
Ealing Gallery, 78 Saint Mary's Rd., London W5. T. (0181) 840 7883. - Paint - 067301
East-Asia, 103 Camden High St., London NW1. T. (0171) 388 5783, Fax (0171) 387 5766. - Orient - 067302
Eccles Road Antiques, 60 Eccles Rd., London SW11 1LX. T. (0171) 228 1638. - Ant / Furn - 067303
Ede, Charles, 20 Brook St., London W1Y 1AD. T. (0171) 493 4944. - Arch - 067304
Edelstein, Annamaria, 94 Jermyn St., London SW1. T. (0171) 930 5300. - Draw - 067305
Editions Graphiques Gallery, 3 Clifford St., London W1X. T. (0171) 734 3944. - Ant - 067306
Edmonds, D.H., 27 Burlington Arcade, London W1. T. (0171) 495 3127. - Jew / Silv / Instr - 067307
Edmunds, Andrew, 44 Lexington St., London W1 3LH. T. (0171) 437 8594, Fax (0171) 439 2551. - Graph / Draw - 067308
Edwards, Charles, 582 King's Rd., London SW6. T. (0171) 736 8490, Fax (0171) 371 5436. - Paint / Furn / Tex - 067309
Edwards, Christopher, 62 Pimlico Rd., London SW1W. T. (0171) 730 4025, Fax (0171) 823 6873. - Furn - 067310
Eimer, Christopher, London NW11. T. (0181) 458 9933, Fax (0181) 455 3535. - Num - 067311
Eldridge, 99-101 Farringdon Rd, London EC1R. T. (0171) 837 0379. - Furn - 067312
Elliott & Snowdon, 61A Ledbury Rd, London W11. T. (0171) 229 6900. - Ant - 067313
Elson, E. D., Coins, 8 The Arches, Villiers Street, London WC2. T. (0171) 930 0711. - Num - 067314
Ermitage, 14 Hay Hill, London W1. T. (0171) 499 5459, Fax (0171) 499 5459. - Jew / Silv - 067315
Eskenazi, 10 Clifford St, London W1X 1RB. T. (0171) 4935464, Fax (0171) 4993136. - Orient / Sculp - 067316
Essie, 62 Piccadilly, London W1. T. (0171) 493 7766. - Tex - 067317
Facade, 196 Westbourne Grove, London W11. T. (0171) 727 2159. - Furn / Lights - 067318
Fagiani, A., 30 Wagner St., London SE15. T. (0171) 732 7188. - Furn - 067319
Fairfax, 568 King's Rd., London SW6. T. (0171) 736 5023, Fax (0171) 736 5023. - Ant - 067320
Fairman, Jack, 218 Westbourne Grove, London W11. T. (0171) 229 2262, Fax (0171) 229 2263. - Tex - 067321
Farrelly, S., 634 Streatham High St., London SW16. T. (0181) 764 4028. - Ant - 067322
Farrelly, Stephen, 152 Fleet Rd., London NW3. T. (0171) 485 2089. - Ant / Paint / Furn / China - 067323
Faustus, 90 Jermyn St., London SW1. T. (0171) 930 1864. - Graph / Jew - 067324
Ferrant, D.J., 21a Camden Passage, London N1. T. (0171) 359 2597. - Ant / Furn / Sculp / Instr - 067325
Few, Ted, 97 Drakefield Rd., London SW17. T. (0181) 767 2314. - Paint / Sculp - 067326
Fielden, Brian, 3 New Cavendish St., London W1. T. (0171) 935 6912. - Furn / Instr - 067327
Finchley Fine Art Galleries, 983 High Rd, London N12 8QR. T. (0181) 446 4848. - Paint / Graph / Furn / China / Instr - 067328
Fine Art Society, 148 New Bond St., London W1. T. (0171) 629 5116. - Paint / Sculp / Draw - 067329
Finney, Michael, 11 Camden Passage, London N1. T. (0171) 226 9280. - Paint - 067330
Five Five Six Antiques, 556 King's Rd., London SW6 2DZ. T. (0171) 731 2016. - Paint / Furn - 067331
Fleamarket, 7 Pierrepont Row, London N1. T. (0171) 226 8211. - Furn / Num / China / Jew / Mil - 067332
Fleur de Lys Gallery, 227a Westbourne Grove, London W11. T. (0171) 727 8595, Fax (0171) 727 8595. - Paint - 067333
Floyd, George, 592 Fulham Rd., London SW6. T. (0171) 736 1649. - Furn - 067334
Fluss & Charlesworth, 1 Lauderdale Rd., London W9. T. (0171) 286 8339. - Furn - 067335
Fortnum & Mason, 181 Piccadilly, London W1 1ER. T. (0171) 734 8040. - Furn - 067336
Foster, Michael, 118 Fulham Rd., London SW3 6HU. T. (0171) 373 3636. - Furn - 067337
Fowle, A. and J., 542 Streatham High St., London SW16. T. (0181) 764 2896. - Ant / Furn - 067338
Fox, Judy, 81 Portobello Rd., London W11. T. (0171) 229 8130, Fax (0171) 229 6998. - Furn / China - 067339
Fox, Judy, 176 Westbourne Grove, London W11. T. (0171) 229 8130, Fax (0171) 229 6998. - Furn / China - 067340
Franklin, N. and I., 11 Bury St., London SW1Y. T. (0171) 839 3131, Fax (0171) 839 3132. - Silv - 067341
Franklin's Camberwell, 161 Camberwell Rd., London SE5. T. (0171) 703 8089. - Ant - 067342
Franks, J.A.L., 7 New Oxford St., London WC1A 1BA. T. (0171) 405 0274, Fax (0171) 430 1259. - Ant - 067343
Franks, J.A.L., 7 Allington St., London SW1. T. (0171) 834 8697. - Ant - 067344
Franses, S., 82 Jermyn St., London SW1. T. (0171) 976 1234. - Tex - 067345
Franses, Victor, 57 Jermyn St., London SW1. T. (0171) 493 6284, Fax (0171) 629 1144. - Sculp / Tex - 067346
Fredericks & Son, C., 92 Fulham Rd., London SW3 6HR. T. (0171) 589 5847, Fax (0171) 589 7893. - Furn - 067347
Freedman, Gerald, London SW6. T. (0171) 736 8666. - Orient / China - 067348
Freeman, J., 85a Portobello Rd., London W11. T. (0171) 221 5076, Fax (0171) 221 5329. - Silv - 067349
Freeman, Vincent, 1 Camden Passage, London N1. T. (0171) 226 6178, Fax (0171) 226 7231. - Furn / Music - 067350
Fritz-Denneville, H., 31 New Bond St., London W1. T. (0171) 629 2466, Fax (0171) 408 0604. - Paint / Graph / Draw - 067351
Frost & Reed, 16 Old Bond St, London WIX 3DB. T. (0171) 629 2457, Fax (0171) 499 0299. - Paint / Graph / Draw - 067352
Furniture Cave, 533 King's Rd., London SW10. T. (0171) 352 4229. - Furn - 067353

Furniture Vault, 50 Camden Passage, London N1. T. (0171) 354 1047. - Furn - 067354
Gage, Deborah, 38 Old Bond St., London W1X 3AE. T. (0171) 493 3249, Fax (0171) 495 1352. - Ant / Paint - 067355
Galerie Moderne, 10 Halkin Arcade, London SW1X. T. (0171) 245 6907. - China / Glass - 067356
Gallery Downstairs, 92 Rossiter Rd., London SW12. T. (0181) 673 5150. - Paint / Graph / Draw - 067357
Gallery Kaleidoscope, 66 Willesden Ln., London NW6. T. (0171) 328 5833. - Paint / Graph / China / Sculp - 067358
Gallery of Antique Costume, 2 Church St, London NW8 8ED. T. (0171) 723 9981. - Tex - 067359
Gallery on Church Street, 12 Church St., London NW8. T. (0171) 723 3389, Fax (0171) 723 3389. - Paint / Graph / Mod - 067360
Gallery 25, Motcombe St, London SW1X. T. (0171) 235 5178. - Furn / Glass - 067361
Game Advice, 23 Holmes Rd., London NW5. T. (0171) 485 4226. - Toys - 067362
Garrard & Co., 112 Regent St., London W1A 2JJ. T. (0171) 734 7020. - Jew / Silv / Instr - 067363
Garratt, Stephen, 60 Addison Rd., London W14. T. (0171) 603 0681. - Paint - 067364
Garrick, Philip, 42 Ledbury Rd., London W11. T. (0171) 243 0500. - Furn / Sculp - 067365
Garrow, Marilyn, 6 The Broadway, London SW13. T. (0181) 392 1655. - Tex - 067366
General Trading, 144 Sloane St., London SW1x 9BL. T. (0171) 730 0411. - Graph / Furn / China - 067367
Georgian Village Antique Centre, 30 Islington Green, London N1. T. (0171) 225 1571. - Ant - 067368
Georgian Village Antiques Market, 100 Wood St., London E17 3HX. T. (0181) 520 6638. - Ant / China / Jew / Instr - 067369
Georgiana's Antiques, 134 Palmerston Rd., London E17. T. (0181) 520 7015. - Furn / China - 067370
German, Michael C., 38B Kensington Church St., London W8. T. (0171) 937 2771. - Mil - 067371
Get Stuffed, 105 Essex Rd., London N1 2SL. T. (0171) 226 1364. - Ant - 067372
Gibbs, Christopher, 8 Vigo St., London WIX 1LG. T. (0171) 439 4557. - Paint / Furn / Sculp - 067373
Gibson, Thomas, 44 Old Bond St., London W1. T. (0171) 499 8572, Fax (0171) 495 1924. - Paint - 067374
Gifford-Mead, N.J.A., 533 King's Rd., London SW10. T. (0171) 352 9904. - Furn - 067375
Gill, David, 60 Fulham Rd., London SW3. T. (0171) 589 5946. - Paint / Furn / China / Draw - 067376
Gillingham, G. & F., 62 Menelik Rd, London NW2 3RH. T. (0171) 4355644, Fax (0171) 4355644. - Furn - 067377
Godden, Geoffrey, Kensington Church St, London W8. T. (0171) 727 4573. - China - 067378
Godson & Coles, 310 King's Rd., London SW3. T. (0171) 352 8509. - Furn - 067379
Good Fairy Open Air Market, 100 Portobello Rd., London W11. T. (0171) 720 9341. - Ant / Jew / Silv - 067380
Goode & Co., Thomas, 19 South Audley St., London W1Y 6BN. T. (0171) 499 2823. - Furn / China / Glass - 067381
Gould, Gillian, 49 Albemarle St., London W1. T. (0171) 493 4633. - Naut - 067382
Gould & Gonnermann, Betty and Julian, 408-410 Archway Rd., London N6. T. (0181) 340 4987. - Furn - 067383
Graham, 104 Islington High St., London N1 8EG. T. (0171) 354 2112. - Ant / Paint / Furn / China / Silv - 067384
Graham, Gavin, 47 Ledbury Rd., London W11. T. (0171) 229 4848, Fax (0171) 792 9697. - Paint - 067385
Graham, Joss, 10 Eccleston St., London SW1. T. (0171) 730 4370. - Furn / Orient / Tex / Jew - 067386
Graham-Stewart, 293a Westbourne Grove, London W11. T. (0171) 229 6959. - Eth - 067387
Graham & Green, 4 Elgin Crescent, London W11. T. (0171) 727 4594. - Furn / Orient / Tex - 067388
Graham & Oxley, 101 Kensington Church St., London W8. T. (0171) 229 1850. - China - 067389
Graus, 39-42 New Bond St, London W1. T. (0171) 629 6680, Fax (0171) 629 3361. - Ant / Jew / Instr - 067390
Gray, Marion, 33 Crouch Hill, London N4. T. (0171) 272 0372. - Furn - 067391
Grays Antique Market, 58 Davies St., London W1Y 1LB. T. (0171) 629 7034. - Ant - 067392
Grays Portobello, 138 Portobello Rd., London W11. T. (0171) 221 3069, Fax (0171) 724 0999. - Ant - 067393
Green, 117 Kensington Church St., London W8. T. (0171) 229 9618. - Paint / Furn / China / Tex / Silv - 067394
Green Parrot, 2 Turnpin Ln., London SE10. T. (0181) 858 6690. - Furn / China - 067395
Green, Richard, 44 Dover St., London W1. T. (0171) 493 3939, Fax (0171) 629 2609. - Paint - 067396
Green & Stone, 259 King's Rd., London SW3. T. (0171) 352 0837. - Paint / Draw - 067397
Greenwich Antiques, 14-15 King William Walk, London SE10. T. (0181) 858 7557, Fax (0181) 293 4135. - Ant / Furn - 067398
Greenwich Antiques Market, Greenwich High Rd., London SE10. - Ant - 067399
Greenwich Gallery, 9 Nevada St., London SE10 9JL. T. (0181) 305 1666. - Paint - 067400
Greenwood, Judy, 657 Fulham Rd., London SW6 5PY. T. (0171) 736 6037. - Furn / Tex - 067401
Greeton, Keith, Unit 14 Northcote Rd, London SW11. T. (0171) 228 6850. - Ant - 067402
Gregory, Bottley and Lloyd, 8-12 Rickett St., London SW6 1RU. T. (0171) 381 5522, Fax (0171) 381 5512. - Cur - 067403
Gregory, Martyn, 34 Bury St., London SW1Y 6AU. T. (0171) 839 3731, Fax (0171) 930 0812. - Paint - 067404
Gridley, Gordon, 41 Camden Passage, London N1. T. (0171) 226 0643. - Ant / Paint / Furn / Instr - 067405
Griffin, Simon, 28 Old Bond St., London W1. T. (0171) 491 7367. - Silv - 067406
Grosvenor Antiques, 27 Holland St., London W8 4NA. T. (0171) 937 8649. - China - 067407
Grosvenor Prints, 28/32 Shelton St, London WC2H 9HP. T. (0171) 836 1979, Fax (0171) 379 6695. - Graph - 067408
Grove, 102 Fulham Rd., London SW3. T. (0171) 581 1589, Fax (0181) 207 4413. - Paint / Furn / Instr - 067409
Guinevere, 574/580 King's Rd, London SW6. T. (0171) 736 2917, Fax (0171) 736 8267. - Ant - 067410
Gumb, Linda, 9 Camden Passage, London N1 8EA. T. (0171) 354 1184. - Ant / Tex - 067411
Gunter, 4 Randall Av., London NW2. T. (0181) 452 3997. - Paint - 067412
Hadji Baba, 34a Davies St., London W1Y 1LD. T. (0171) 499 9363, Fax (0171) 493 5504. - Orient / Tex - 067413
Hadleigh, 30A Marylebone High St, London W1. T. (0171) 935 4074. - Jew / Silv - 067414
Hahn & Son, 47 Albermarle St., London W1X. T. (0171) 493 9196. - Paint - 067415
Halcyon Days, 4 Royal Exchange, London EC3. T. (0171) 629 8811, Fax (0171) 409 0280. - Ant / Furn / China - 067416
Halcyon Days, 14 Brook St., London W1Y 1AA. T. (0171) 629 8811, Fax (0171) 409 0280. - Graph / Furn / China - 067417
Hales, Robert, 131 Kensington Church St., London W8 7LP. T. (0171) 229 3887. - Eth / Mil - 067418
Hall, Robert, 140 Sutherland Av., London W9. T. (0171) 286 0809, Fax (0171) 289 3287. - Orient - 067419
Halliday's, 28 Beauchamp Pl., London SW3 1NJ. T. (0171) 589 5534, Fax (0171) 589 2477. - Ant / Furn - 067420
Hamilton, 186 Willifield Way, London NW11. T. (0181) 455 7410. - Paint / Sculp - 067421
Hamilton, Rosemary, 44 Moreton St., London SW1. T. (0171) 828 5018. - Furn / China - 067422
Hamilton, Ross, 95 Pimlico Rd., London SW1W. T. (0171) 730 3015. - Paint / Furn / China - 067423
Hamilton's Corner, 407A Kingston Rd, London SW20. T. (0181) 540 1744. - Furn / Naut - 067424
Hampstead Antique Emporium, 12 Heath St., London NW3. T. (0171) 794 3297. - Ant - 067425
Hancocks & Co., New Bond St, London W1X 2HP. T. (0171) 493 8904, Fax (0171) 493 8905. - Jew / Silv - 067426
Handford, William, 517 King's Rd., London SW10. T. (0171) 351 2768. - Ant - 067427
Harbottle, Patricia, Stand 16, 107 Portobello Rd., London W11. T. (0171) 731 1972. - Glass - 067428
Harcourt Antiques, 5 Harcourt St., London W1H IDS. T. (0171) 723 5919. - China - 067429
Hardy & Co., James, 235 Brompton Rd., London SW3. T. (0171) 589 5050, Fax (0171) 823 8760. - Jew / Silv - 067430
Hares, 498 King's Rd., London SW10. T. (0171) 351 1442. - Furn - 067431
Harold's Place, 148 South Ealing Rd., London W5. T. (0181) 579 4825. - China - 067432
Harrington, David, 27 Berkeley St., London W1. T. (0171) 495 3194, Fax (0171) 409 3175. - Paint - 067433
Harris, Jonathan, 63-66 Hatton Garden, London EC1. T. (0171) 242 9115, Fax (0171) 831 4417. - Jew - 067434
Harris, Jonathan, 54 Kensington Church St., London W8. T. (0171) 937 3133. - Furn - 067435
Harris, Nicholas, 564 King's Rd., London SW6 2DY. T. (0171) 371 9711, Fax (0171) 371 9537. - Silv - 067436
Harris & Son, S.H., 17-18 Old Bond St., London W1. T. (0171) 499 0352. - Jew / Silv - 067437
Harrods, Brompton Rd, London SW1. T. (0171) 730 1234. - Ant / Paint / Furn - 067438
Hart, Rosemary, 4 Gateway Arcade, London N1. T. (0171) 359 6839. - Silv - 067439
Hart & Rosenberg, 2-3 Gateway Arcade, London N1 0PG. T. (0171) 359 6839. - Furn / Orient / China - 067440
Hartnoll, Julian, 14 Mason's Yard, Duke St., London SW1. T. (0171) 839 3842. - Paint / Graph / Draw - 067441
Harvey-Lee, Elizabeth, 1 Belton Rd., London NW2. T. (0181) 459 7623. - Graph - 067442
Harvey & Co., W.R., 5 Old Bond St., London W1X 3TA. T. (0171) 499 8385, Fax (0171) 495 0209. - Ant / Paint / Furn / Instr - 067443
Harvey & Gore, 4 Burlington Gardens, London W1X 1LH. T. (0171) 493 2714, Fax (0171) 493 0324. - Ant / Jew / Silv - 067444
Harwood, 24 Lower Richmond Rd., London SW15. T. (0181) 788 7444. - Paint / Graph / Furn / Tex - 067445
Haslam & Whiteway, 105 Kensington Church St., London W8. T. (0171) 229 1145. - Ant / Furn - 067446
Hatcher, Sherry, 5 Gateway Arcade, London N1. T. (0171) 226 5679. - Silv / Glass - 067447
Haughton, Brian, Old Bond St, London W1X 1LE. T. (0171) 734 5491. - China - 067448
Hawkins, Brian, 73 Upper St., London N1. T. (0171) 359 3957. - Furn - 067449
Hayhurst, Jeanette, 32A Kensington Church St, London W8. T. (0171) 938 1539. - Glass - 067450
Hazlitt, Gooden and Fox, 38 Bury St., London SW1. T. (0171) 930 6422. - Paint / Sculp / Draw - 067451
Hearth and Home, 13 Chalk Farm Rd., London NW1. T. (0171) 485 9687. - Ant / Furn - 067452
Heather Antiques, 14 Camden Passage, London N1. T. (0171) 226 2412. - Silv - 067453
Helius Antiques, 487-493 Upper Richmond Rd., London SW14. T. (0181) 876 5721. - Ant / Furn - 067454
Henham, Martin, 218 High Rd., London N2. T. (0181) 444 5274. - Paint / Furn / China - 067455
Hennell, 12 New Bond St., London W1Y 0HE. T. (0171) 629 6888. - Jew / Silv / Instr - 067456
Heraz, 25 Motcomb St., London SW1X. T. (0171) 245 9497. - Tex - 067457
Heritage Antiques, 112 Islington High St., London N1. T. (0171) 226 7789. - Furn - 067458
Hermitage Antiques, 97 Pimlico Rd., London SW1W 8PH. T. (0171) 730 1973, Fax (0171) 730 6586. - Paint / Furn - 067459

Hershkowitz, Robert, 94 Queen's Gate, London SW7.
T. (0171) 373 8994. - Pho -   *067460*

Hicks, 2 and 4 Leopold Rd, London SW19.
T. (0181) 944 7171. - Paint -   *067461*

Hillyers, 301 Sydenham Rd., London SE26.
T. (0181) 778 6361. - Furn / China / Silv /
Glass -   *067462*

Hirsh, 10 Hatton Garden, London EC1.
T. (0181) 405 6080. - Jew / Silv -   *067463*

Hirst, 59 Pembridge Rd., London W11 3HN.
T. (0171) 727 9364. - Furn -   *067464*

Hobson, Claire, 19 South Audley St., London W1.
T. (0171) 499 2823. - China -   *067465*

Hobson, Platon, 34 Belsize Park Gardens, London NW3.
T. (0171) 722 3703. - Paint / Furn / Tex -   *067466*

Hodsoll, Christopher, 91 Pimlico Rd., London SW1W
8PH. T. (0171) 730 3370, Fax (0171) 730 1516.
- Paint / Furn / Tex -   *067467*

Holland & Holland, 31 and 33 Bruton St, London W1X
8JS. T. (0171) 499 4411. - Graph / Mil -   *067468*

Hollingshead & Co., 783 Fulham Rd., London SW6.
T. (0171) 736 6991. - Ant -   *067469*

Hollywood Road Gallery, 12 Hollywood Rd., London
SW10. T. (0171) 351 1973. - Paint / Graph   *067470*

Holmes, 24 Burlington Arcade, London W1.
T. (0171) 629 8380. - Jew / Silv -   *067471*

Holmes, 29 Old Bond St, London W1X 3AB.
T. (0171) 493 1396. - Jew / Silv -   *067472*

Holmes, D., 47c Earls Court Rd., London W8 6EY.
T. (0171) 937 6961. - Furn -   *067473*

Holt & Co., R., 98 Hatton Garden, London EC1.
T. (0171) 405 0197, Fax (0171) 430 1279.
- Orient -   *067474*

Home to Home, 355c Archway Rd., London N6.
T. (0181) 340 8354. - Furn -   *067475*

Hope and Glory, 131a Kensington Church St., London
W8. T. (0171) 727 8424. - China / Glass -   *067476*

Hoppen, Stephanie, 17 Walton St., London SW3 2HX.
T. (0171) 589 3678. - Paint / Draw -   *067477*

Horne, Jonathan, 66b-c Kensington Church St., London
W8 4BY. T. (0171) 221 5658, Fax (0171) 792 3090.
- China -   *067478*

Hornsey, Adrian, 160 Chiswick High Rd., London W4.
T. (0181) 995 4166. - Ant -   *067479*

Hornsey, Adrian, 220 Westbourne Grove, London W11.
T. (0171) 221 2571, Fax (0171) 221 2612. - Ant /
Furn -   *067480*

Hotspur, 14 Lowndes St., London SW1.
T. (0171) 235 1918. - Furn -   *067481*

Hotz, Dennis, 9 Cork St., London W1.
T. (0171) 287 8324, Fax (0171) 287 9713. - Ant /
Sculp -   *067482*

House of Buckinham, 113-117 Farringdon Rd., London
EC1R. T. (0171) 278 2013. - Furn / Instr -   *067483*

House of Mirrors, 597 King's Rd., London SW6.
T. (0171) 736 5885. - Ant -   *067484*

House of Steel Antiques, 400 Caledonian Rd., London
N1 1DN. T. (0171) 607 5889. - Ant / Furn -   *067485*

How, 28 Albemarle St., London W1X 3FA.
T. (0171) 408 1867. - Silv -   *067486*

Howard, 8 Davies St., London W1Y 1LJ.
T. (0171) 629 2628. - Furn -   *067487*

Howard, Valerie, 131E Kensington Church St, London
W8. T. (0171) 792 9702. - China -   *067488*

Howe, Christopher, 36 Bourne St., London SW1W.
T. (0171) 730 7987, Fax (0171) 730 0157. - Furn /
Lights -   *067489*

HRW Antiques, 4a Kings Av., London SW4 8BD.
T. T.(0171) 978 1026, Fax (0171) 498 6376. - Ant /
Furn -   *067490*

Hudes, Eric, 142 Portobello Rd., London W11.
T. (0171) 727 4643. - Orient / China -   *067491*

Hunter, Sally, 11-12 Halkin Arcade, Motcomb St., London
SW1. T. (0171) 235 0934. - Ant -   *067492*

Huntley, Diana, 8 Camden Passage, London N1 3ED.
T. (0171) 226 4605. - China / Glass -   *067493*

Hurford, Peter, 618-620 King's Rd., London SW6 2DU.
T. (0171) 731 4655. - Ant / Furn -   *067494*

Iconastas, 5 Piccadilly Arcade, London SW1Y.
T. (0171) 629 1433. - Ico -   *067495*

Inglis, Brand, 9 Halkin Arcade, Motcomb St., London
SW1X 8JT. T. (0171) 235 6604, Fax (0171) 259 6211.
- Silv -   *067496*

Inheritance, 8-10 Gateway Arcade, London N1.
T. (0171) 226 8305. - China / Jew / Instr -   *067497*

Innes, Malcolm, 172 Walton St., London SW3 2JL.
T. (0171) 584 0575, Fax (0171) 589 1066.
- Paint -   *067498*

Iona Antiques, London W8 6HZ. T. (0171) 602 1193,
Fax (0171) 371 2843. - Paint -   *067499*

Islington, 12 and 14 Essex Rd, London N1.
T. (0171) 226 6867. - Furn -   *067500*

J. and B. Antiques, 67 Portobello Rd., London W11.
T. (01295) 711689. - China -   *067501*

Jaffa, John, 28 Old Bond St, London W1.
T. (0171) 499 4228. - Silv -   *067502*

James, P.L., 681 Fulham Rd., London SW6.
T. (0171) 736 0183. - Furn -   *067503*

James & Son, Anthony, 88 Fulham Rd., London SW3
6HR. T. (0171) 584 1120, Fax (0171) 823 7618. - Ant /
Furn -   *067504*

Japanese Gallery, 23 Camden Passage, London N1 8EA.
T. (0171) 226 3347. - Furn / Orient / China -   *067505*

Japanese Gallery, 66d Kensington Church Rd., London
W8. T. (0171) 229 2934. - Orient -   *067506*

Jay, Melvyn, 64a Kensington Church St., London W8.
T. (0171) 937 6832. - Furn / China / Silv / Instr -   *067507*

Jazzy Art Deco, 67 Camden Rd., London NW1.
T. (0171) 267 3342. - Furn / Mod -   *067508*

Jefferson, Patrick, 572 King's Rd., London SW6.
T. (0171) 371 9088. - Ant / Furn -   *067509*

Jeremy, 29 Lowndes St., London SW1.
T. (0171) 823 2923. - Furn / Glass -   *067510*

Jesse, John, 160 Kensington Church St., London W8
4BN. T. (0171) 229 0312, Fax (0171) 229 4732.
- Sculp / Jew / Silv / Glass -   *067511*

Jessop, 67 Great Russell St., London WC1.
T. (0171) 831 3640, Fax (0171) 831 3956.
- Instr -   *067512*

Jetts, Peter, 564 King's Rd., London SW6.
T. (0171) 371 9711. - Silv -   *067513*

Jewell, S. and H., 26 Parker St., London WC2B 5PH.
T. (0171) 405 8520. - Furn -   *067514*

John, C., 70 South Audley St., London W1Y.
T. (0171) 493 5288, Fax (0171) 409 7030.
- Tex -   *067515*

Johnson Walker & Tolhurst, 64 Burlington Arcade, London W1. T. (0171) 629 2615. - Jew / Silv -   *067516*

Jones, 194 Westbourne Grove, London W11.
T. (0171) 229 6866, Fax (0171) 229 6866.
- Lights -   *067517*

Jones, Annabel, 52 Beauchamp Pl., London SW3.
T. (0171) 589 3215. - Jew / Silv -   *067518*

Jones, Howard, 43 Kensington Church St., London W8.
T. (0171) 937 4359. - China / Jew -   *067519*

Jones, R. and J., 6 Bury St., London SW1Y 6AB.
T. (0171) 925 2079. - Paint / China -   *067520*

Jones & Son, W., 295 Westbourne Grove, London W11.
T. (0171) 727 7051. - Furn -   *067521*

Jorgen, 40 Lower Richmond Rd, London SW15.
T. (0181) 789 7329. - Furn -   *067522*

Joseph & Pearce, 63-66 Hatton Garden, London EC1.
T. (0171) 405 4604, Fax (0171) 242 1902.
- Jew -   *067523*

Joslin, Richard, 150 Addison Gardens, London W14 0ER.
T. (0171) 603 6435, Fax (0171) 603 6435.
- Paint -   *067524*

Jubilee Antiques, 70 Cadogan Pl., London SW1X.
T. (0171) 823 1034. - Ant / Furn -   *067525*

Jubilee Photographica, 10 Pierrepont Row, London N1.
T. (0171) 607 5462. - Instr -   *067526*

Julian Antiques, 54 Duncan St., London N1.
T. (0171) 833 0835. - Sculp / Instr -   *067527*

Junk Shop, 9 Greenwich St., London SE10.
T. (0181) 305 1666. - Furn -   *067528*

Juran & Co., Alexander, 74 New Bond St., London W1Y
9DD. T. (0171) 629 2550. - Tex -   *067529*

Just a Second Antiques, 27 Battersea Rise, London
SW11. T. (0171) 223 5341. - Ant / Furn / China /
Silv -   *067530*

Just Desks, 20 Church St., London NW3.
T. (0171) 723 7976, Fax (0171) 402 6416.
- Furn -   *067531*

Kaplan, Lewis M., 50 Fulham Rd., London SW3.
T. (0171) 589 3108. - Furn / Jew / Glass -   *067532*

Kate House, 139 Lower Richmond Rd., London SW15.
T. (0181) 785 9944. - Ant / Furn / China / Tex -   *067533*

Keen, Cassandra, Shop 18, 30 Islington Green, London
N1. T. (0171) 226 1571. - Furn -   *067534*

Keil, John, 154 Brompton Rd., London SW31HX.
T. (0171) 589 6454. - Furn -   *067535*

Kemp, Peter, 170 Kensington Church St., London W8
4BN. T. (0171) 229 2988, Fax (0171) 229 2988.
- Orient / China -   *067536*

Kendal, 91A Heath St, London NW3. T. (0171) 435 4351.
- Paint / Graph / Furn / China -   *067537*

Kendall, Beryl, 2 Warwick Pl., London W9.
T. (0171) 286 9902. - Paint -   *067538*

Kennedy, 9A Vigo St, London W1. T. (0171) 439 8873,
Fax (0171) 437 1201. - Tex -   *067539*

Kennedy, Robin, 29 New Bond St., London W1Y 9HD.
T. (0171) 408 1238. - Orient -   *067540*

Kensington Antiques Centre, 58-60 Kensington Church
St., London W8. T. (0171) 376 0425. - Ant -   *067541*

Kensington Fine Arts, 46 Kensington Church St., London
W8. T. (0171) 937 5317. - Paint -   *067542*

Kerr, Thomas, 11 Theberton St., London N1.
T. (0171) 226 0626. - Paint / Furn -   *067543*

Ketley, Carol, 30-31 Islington Green, London N1.
T. (0171) 359 5529. - China / Glass -   *067544*

Kettle, Thomas, 53a Neal St., London WC2.
T. (0171) 379 3579. - Jew / Instr -   *067545*

Kihl, Richard, 164 Regents Park Rd., London NW1.
T. (0171) 586 5911, Fax (0171) 586 2960.
- Glass -   *067546*

Kilim Warehouse, 28A Pickets St, London SW12 8QB.
T. (0181) 675 3122, Fax (0181) 675 8494.
- Tex -   *067547*

King, Dominic, 85 Ebury St., London SW1W.
T. (0171) 824 8319. - Glass -   *067548*

King, Eric, 11 Crondace Rd., London SW6 4BB.
T. (0171) 731 2554. - Ant / Furn -   *067549*

Kirkdale Pianos, 251 Dartmouth Rd., London SE26.
T. (0181) 699 1928. - Music -   *067550*

Kirsch, 292 Westbourne Grove, London W11.
T. (0171) 372 7617. - Furn -   *067551*

Klaber & Klaber, 2a Bedford Gardens, London W8 7EH.
T. (0171) 727 4573, Fax (0171) 435 9459.
- China -   *067552*

Knightsbridge Coins, 43 Duke St., London SW1.
T. (0171) 930 7597. - Num -   *067553*

Kreckovic, L. and E., 62 Fulham High St., London SW6.
T. (0171) 736 0753. - Furn -   *067554*

Kyle, Susan, Vault 68, London WC2A.
T. (0171) 242 1708. - Ant -   *067555*

L'Acquaforte, 49A Ledbury Rd, London W11.
T. (0171) 221 3388. - Paint / Graph / Draw -   *067556*

Lacquer Chest, 71 Kensington Church St., London W8.
T. (0171) 937 1306. - Furn -   *067557*

Lacy, 203 Westbourne Grove, London W11.
T. (0171) 229 6340. - Paint / Fra -   *067558*

Lacy, 38 Ledbury Rd., London W11 2AB.
T. (0171) 229 9105. - Paint / Graph / Dec / Fra -   *067559*

Lamont, Tunnel Av Antique Warehouse, London SE10.
T. (0181) 305 2230, Fax (0181) 305 1805. - Ant /
Furn -   *067560*

Lamp Gallery, 355 New King's Rd., London SW6.
T. (0171) 736 6188. - Lights -   *067561*

Lampard & Son, S., 32 Notting Hill Gate, London W11.
T. (0171) 229 5457. - Jew / Silv / Instr -   *067562*

Lane, 123 New Bond St., London W1Y 9AE.
T. (0171) 499 5020, Fax (0171) 495 2496.
- Paint -   *067563*

Langford, 535 King's Rd., London SW10.
T. (0171) 351 4881, Fax (0171) 352 0763.
- Naut -   *067564*

Langfords, Vaults 8/10, London WC2A 1QS.
T. (0171) 351 4881, Fax (0171) 405 6401.
- Silv -   *067565*

Lassalle, Judith, 7 Pierrepont Arcade, London N1.
T. (0171) 607 7121. - Graph / Toys -   *067566*

Laurie, John, 352 Upper St., London N1.
T. (0171) 226 0913, Fax (0171) 226 4599.
- Silv -   *067567*

Laurie, Peter, 28 Greenwich Church St., London SE10.
T. (0181) 853 5777. - Instr / Mil / Cur -   *067568*

Lavender, D.S., 16b Grafton St., London W1X.
T. (0171) 629 1782. - Ant / Jew -   *067569*

Lavian, Joseph, 53-79 Highgate Rd., London NW5 1TL.
T. (0171) 485 7955, Fax (0171) 267 9222.
- Tex -   067570

Lee, Ronald A., 1-9 Bruton Pl., London W1X 7AD.
T. (0171) 629 5600. - Paint / Furn / Instr -   067571

Lefevre, 30 Bruton St., London W1. T. (0171) 493 2107.
- Paint -   067572

Leger, 13 Old Bond St., London W1. T. (0171) 629 3538.
- Paint -   067573

Leicester Galleries, 5 Ryder St, London SW1Y 6PY.
T. (0171) 9306059, Fax (0171) 9304678. - Paint /
Graph -   067574

Leigh, Joan, 153 Portobello Rd., London W11.
T. (0171) 727 6848. - Mod -   067575

Lemkow, Sara, 12 Camden Passage, London N1.
T. (0171) 359 0190. - Ant / Lights -   067576

Leslie, Stanley, 15 Beauchamp Pl., London SW3 1NQ.
T. (0171) 589 2333. - Silv -   067577

Lev, 97A Kensington Church St, London W8 7LN.
T. (0171) 727 9248. - Jew / Silv -   067578

Levene, M.P., 5 Thurloe Pl., London SW7 2RR.
T. (0171) 589 3755. - China / Silv -   067579

Lewin, David, 82D Portobello Rd, London W11.
T. (0171) 229 2023. - Furn -   067580

Lewis, Arthur S., c/o Harrods, Brompton Rd., London
SW1. T. (0171) 730 1234. - Instr / Music -   067581

Lewis, M. and D., 83 Ledbury Rd., London W11.
T. (0171) 727 3908. - Furn / China -   067582

Lewis, M. and D., 84 Pimlico Rd., London SW1W.
T. (0171) 730 1015. - Furn / China -   067583

Lewis, M. and D., 212 Westbourne Grove, London W11.
T. (0171) 229 0466. - Furn / China -   067584

Lewis, M. and D., 172 Westbourne Grove, London W11.
T. (0171) 727 3908. - Furn / China -   067585

Lewis, Michael, 16 Essex Rd., London N1.
T. (0171) 359 7733. - Furn -   067586

Li, Wan, 355 Upper St., London N1. - Orient /
China -   067587

Liberty, 210-220 Regent St., London W1R 6AH.
T. (0171) 734 1234. - Furn -   067588

Libra Antiques, 131d Kensington Church St., London
W8. T. (0171) 727 2990. - China -   067589

Lieber, Ian, 29 Craven Terrace, London W2.
T. (0171) 262 5505. - Paint / Furn / China /
Jew -   067590

Lighthouse, 75-77 Ridgway, London SW19.
T. (0181) 946 2050. - Furn / Lights -   067591

Linden & Co., Vault 7, London WC2. T. (0171) 242 4863,
Fax (0171) 405 9946. - Silv -   067592

Lindsay, 99 Kensington Church St., London W8.
T. (0171) 727 2333. - Ant / China -   067593

Lineham & Sons, Eric, 62 Kensington Church St., London
W8. T. (0171) 937 9650. - China / Silv / Instr -   067594

Lion, Witch and Lampshade, 89 Ebury St., London SW1.
T. (0171) 730 1774. - Lights -   067595

Lipitch, J., 177 Westbourne Grove, London W11.
T. (0171) 229 0783. - Furn / China / Sculp -   067596

Lipitch, Michael, 98 Fulham Rd., London SW3.
T. (0171) 589 7327, Fax (0171) 823 9106.
- Furn -   067597

Lipitch, Peter, 120/124 Fulham Rd, London SW3.
T. (0171) 373 3328, Fax (0171) 373 8888.
- Furn -   067598

Little Curiosity Shop, 24 The Green, London N21.
T. (0181) 886 0925. - Ant / China / Jew / Silv -   067599

Little Winchester Gallery, 36a Kensington Church St.,
London W8 4BX. T. (0171) 937 8444. - Paint -   067600

London Architectural Salvage, Mark St, London EC2A
4ER. T. (0171) 739 0448, Fax (0171) 729 6853.
- Ant -   067601

London Militaria Market, Angel Arcade, Camden Passage, London N1. T. (0162882) 2503. - Mil -   067602

London Silver Vaults, 53-65 Chancery Ln., London WC2.
T. (0171) 242 3844. - Jew / Silv / Instr -   067603

Long, Stephen, 348 Fulham Rd., London SW10 9UH.
T. (0171) 352 8226. - Ant / Furn / China -   067604

Longmire, Paul, 12 Bury St., London SW1Y 6AB.
T. (0171) 930 8720, Fax (0171) 930 1898. - Jew /
Silv -   067605

Lotinga, Heather, Stand 4, 80 Islington High St, London
N1. T. (0171) 223 6272, Fax (0181) 892 4387.
- Ant -   067606

Loveless, Clive, 29 Kelfield Gardens, London W10.
T. (0181) 969 5831. - Tex -   067607

Lubbock Coins, 315 Regent Street, London W1R 7YB.
T. (0171) 580 9922, 323 0670. - Num -   067608

Lunn, 86 New King's Rd., London SW6.
T. (0171) 736 4638. - Tex -   067609

Lyons, John, 18 South Hill Park, London NW3.
T. (0171) 794 3537. - China / Glass / Mod -   067610

M. and L.Silver, 2 Woodstock St., London W1.
T. (0171) 499 5392. - Silv -   067611

Maas, 15a Clifford St., London W1X 1RF.
T. (0171) 734 2302, Fax (0171) 287 4836. - Paint /
Draw -   067612

MacConnal-Mason, 14 Duke St., London SW1Y 6DB.
T. (0171) 839 7693. - Paint -   067613

MacConnal-Mason, 15 Burlington Arcade, London W1Y
9AB. T. (0171) 499 6991. - Paint -   067614

Magpies, 152 Wandsworth Bridge Rd., London SW6.
T. (0171) 736 3738. - Furn / China / Glass -   067615

Magus, 187 Westbourne Grove, London W11.
T. (0171) 229 0267. - Paint / Furn / Sculp -   067616

Magus, 4 Church St., London NW8. T. (0171) 724 1278.
- Furn / Orient / China / Glass -   067617

Mahboubian, 65 Grosvenor St., London W1X.
T. (0171) 493 9112. - Ant -   067618

Main Street Antiques, 24 Woolwich Rd., London SE10.
T. (0181) 305 1971. - Furn -   067619

Major, C.H., 154 Kensington Church St., London W8
4BN. T. (0171) 229 1162, Fax (0171) 221 9676.
- Furn -   067620

Malik, David, Unit 5 Britannia Way, London NW10.
T. (0181) 965 4232, Fax (0181) 965 2401.
- Lights -   067621

Mall Antiques Arcade, 359 Upper St., London N1.
T. (0171) 354 2839. - Ant -   067622

Mall Galleries, The Mall, London SW1.
T. (0171) 930 6844, Fax (0171) 839 7830.
- Paint -   067623

Mallett, 2 Davies St., London W1Y 1L5.
T. (0171) 629 2444, Fax (0171) 499 2670. - Ant / Furn /
Instr -   067624

Mallett & Son, 141 New Bond St., London W1Y 0BS.
T. (0171) 499 7411, Fax (0171) 495 3179. - Ant / Paint /
Furn / Instr -   067625

Mammon, C. and T., 31 and 64 Chancery Lane, London
WC2. T. (0171) 405 2397. - Silv -   067626

Mammon, J., Vault 30, London WC2A 1QS.
T. (0171) 242 4704. - Silv -   067627

Manheim, D.M. and P., London N6. T. (0181) 340 9211.
- China -   067628

Mankowitz, Daniel, 16 Pembridge Sq., London W2.
T. (0171) 229 9270, Fax (0171) 792 2141. - Furn /
Tex -   067629

Manners, E. & H., E. and H., 66a Kensington Church St.,
London W8. T. (0171) 229 5516, Fax (0171) 229 5516.
- China -   067630

Mansell, William C., 24 Connaught St., London W2.
T. (0171) 723 4154. - Jew / Silv / Instr -   067631

Mansour, 46-48 Davies St, London W1Y 1LD.
T. (0171) 499 0510. - Orient / Arch -   067632

Map House, 54 Beauchamp Pl., London SW3.
T. (0171) 589 4325, Fax (0171) 589 1041.
- Graph -   067633

Marchant & Son, S., 120 Kensington Church St., London
W8 4BH. T. (0171) 229 5319. - Orient -   067634

Mark, 9 Porchester Pl., London W2. T. (0171) 262 4906,
Fax (0171) 224 9416. - Rel / Ico -   067635

Marks, 49 Curzon St., London W1Y 7RE.
T. (0171) 499 1788. - China / Silv -   067636

Marlborough Fine Art, 6 Albemarle St., London W1X 2BY.
T. (0171) 629 5161, Fax (0171) 629 6338.
- Paint -   067637

Marriott, Michael, 588 Fulham Rd., London SW6 5NT.
T. (0171) 736 3110. - Graph / Furn -   067638

Marsh & Son, A.V., Vale House, Kingston Vale, London
SW15. T. (0181) 546 5996. - Furn -   067639

Martin, C.J., 85 The Vale, Southgate, London N14.
T. (0181) 882 1509. - Num -   067640

Martin, Robin, 44 Ledbury Rd., London W11.
T. (0171) 727 1301. - Ant / Furn / Instr -   067641

Martin-Taylor, David, 56 Fulham High St., London SW6
3LQ. T. (0171) 731 4135, Fax (0171) 371 0029. - Furn /
Cur -   067642

Maryan & Daughters, Richard, 177 Merton Rd., London
SW19. T. (0181) 542 5846. - Ant -   067643

Mason, Paul, 149 Sloane St., London SW1X 9BZ.
T. (0171) 730 3683. - Paint / Fra / Naut -   067644

Massada Antiques, 45 New Bond St., London W1.
T. (0171) 493 4792. - Jew / Silv -   067645

Mathaf, 24 Motcomb St., London SW1X 8JU.
T. (0171) 235 0010. - Paint / Orient -   067646

Mathon, 38 Cheyne Walk, London SW3.
T. (0171) 352 5381. - Paint / Sculp -   067647

Matthiesen, 7-8 Mason's Yard, Duke St., London SW1Y
6BU. T. (0171) 930 2437, Fax (0171) 930 1387.
- Paint -   067648

Maude, Richard, 22 Parkfields, London SW15 6NH.
T. (0181) 788 2991. - Instr -   067649

May, J. and J., 40 Kensington Church St., London W8
4BX. T. (0171) 937 3575. - Paint / China / Tex -   067650

Mayfair Carpet Gallery, 41 New Bond St., London W1.
T. (0171) 493 0126. - Tex -   067651

Mayfair Coin Company, 117 Regent St., London W1R
7HA. T. (0171) 734 0086. - Num -   067652

Mayfair Gallery, 36 Davies St., London W1Y.
T. (0171) 491 3435, Fax (0171) 491 3437. - Graph /
Glass -   067653

Mayflower Antiques, 117 Portobello Rd., London W11.
T. (0171) 727 0381. - Ant / Furn / Instr / Music -   067654

Maynard, Mark, 651 Fulham Rd., London SW6.
T. (0171) 731 3533. - Furn -   067655

Mayorcas, 38 Jermyn St., London SW1Y 6DN.
T. (0171) 629 4195. - Tex -   067656

Mazure & Co., J., 90 Jermyn St., London SW1Y.
T. (0171) 839 3101. - Ant -   067657

McClenaghan-Gilhooly, 125 Camden Mews, London
NW1. T. (0171) 485 7755. - Furn -   067658

McDonald, Joy, 50 Station Rd., London SW13.
T. (0181) 876 6184. - Ant / Furn -   067659

McKay, R.I., 88/90 Hatton Garden, London EC1.
T. (0171) 405 7544, Fax (0171) 404 5586.
- Jew -   067660

McKenna & Co, 28 Beauchamp Pl., London SW3.
T. (0171) 584 1966, Fax (0171) 225 2893. - Jew /
Silv -   067661

McLennan, Rodd, 24 Holbein Pl., London SW1.
T. (0171) 730 6330. - Furn -   067662

McVeigh & Charpentier, 498 King's Rd., London SW10.
T. (0171) 937 6459. - Ant / Furn -   067663

McWhirter, 22 Park Walk, London SW10.
T. (0171) 351 5399, Fax (0171) 352 9821. - Ant /
Furn -   067664

Melton's, 27 Bruton Pl., London W1. T. (0171) 409 2938.
- Graph / Tex / Lights -   067665

Mendez, Christopher, 58 Jermyn St., London SW1Y 6LP.
T. (0171) 491 0015, Fax (0171) 495 4949.
- Graph -   067666

Mendoza & Wissinger, 166 Bermondsey St., London
SE1. T. (0171) 407 5795. - Paint / Furn -   067667

Mercury, 1 Ladbroke Rd., London W11 3PA.
T. (0171) 727 5106. - China / Glass -   067668

Merola, 178 Walton St., London SW3.
T. (0171) 589 0365, Fax (0171) 373 4297.
- Jew -   067669

Michael Coins, 6 Hillgate St., London W8.
T. (0171) 727 1518. - Num -   067670

Middleton, Arthur, 12 New Row, London WC2.
T. (0171) 836 7042, Fax (0171) 497 9386.
- Instr - *067671*

Miles, Richard, 8 Holbein Pl., London SW1 8NL.
T. (0171) 730 1957, Fax (0171) 824 8865. - Furn /
Orient - *067672*

Milne Henderson, 112 Clifton Hill, London NW8 0JS.
T. (0171) 328 2171, Fax (0171) 624 7274.
- Orient - *067673*

Milne, Nigel, 16c Grafton St., London W1X 3LF.
T. (0171) 493 9646, Fax (0171) 495 6010. - Jew /
Fra - *067674*

Milne & Moller, 35 Colville Terrace, London W11.
T. (0171) 727 1679. - Paint / Sculp - *067675*

Mitchell, Laurence, 13 Camden Passage, London N1.
T. (0171) 359 7579. - China - *067676*

Mitchell, Paul, 99 New Bond St., London W1.
T. (0171) 493 8732. - Fra - *067677*

Mitchell & Son, John, 160 New Bond St., London W1.
T. (0171) 493 7567. - Paint / Draw - *067678*

Moggach, Ian, 723 Fulham Rd., London SW6.
T. (0171) 731 4883. - Furn - *067679*

Moira, 22-23 New Bond St., London W1.
T. (0171) 629 0160. - Jew - *067680*

Money, Lennox, 93 Pimlico Rd., London SW1.
T. (0171) 730 3070. - Furn / Orient / Tex - *067681*

Monk & Son, D.C., 132-134 Kensington Church St., London W8 4BH. T. (0171) 229 3727. - China - *067682*

Morley & Co., Robert, 34 Engate St., London SE13.
T. (0181) 318 5838, Fax (0181) 297 0720.
- Music - *067683*

Morrison, Guy, 91 Jermyn St, London SW1.
T. (0171) 839 1454. - Paint - *067684*

Morse & Son, Terence, Westbourne Grove, London W11.
T. (0171) 229 9380, Fax (0171) 792 3284.
- Furn - *067685*

Morse & Son, Terence, 237 Westbourne Grove, London
W11. T. (0171) 229 4059, Fax (0171) 792 3284.
- Furn - *067686*

Moss, 2 Prebend Gardens, London W4 1TW.
T. (0181) 994 2099. - Paint / Graph - *067687*

Moss, Sydney L., 51 Brook St., London W1Y 1AU.
T. (0171) 629 4670, Fax (0171) 491 9278.
- Orient - *067688*

Mould, Anthony, 173 New Bond St., London W1Y 9PB.
T. (0171) 491 4627. - Paint - *067689*

Mr Brooks, Temple, 12 Mill Ln., London NW6.
T. (0181) 452 9696. - Instr - *067690*

Mrs Crick, M.E., 166 Kensington Church St., London W8.
T. (0171) 229 1338, Fax (0171) 792 1073. - Ant /
Glass - *067691*

Mrs Monro, 16 Motcomb St., London SW1.
T. (0171) 235 0326. - Ant / Furn / China / Furn - *067692*

M.S.M. Antiques, 533 King's Rd., London SW10.
T. (0171) 352 7305. - Furn - *067693*

Mulder, Frederick, 83 Belsize Park Gardens, London
NW3 4NJ. T. (0171) 722 2105, Fax (0171) 483 4228.
- Graph - *067694*

Nahum, Peter, 5 Ryder St., London SW1 6PY.
T. (0171) 930 6059. - Paint / Sculp / Draw - *067695*

Nanking Porcelain, 84 Portobello Rd., London W11.
T. (0171) 229 9458. - Orient - *067696*

Nanwani & Co., 2 Shopping Arcade, London EC3V 3LA.
T. (0171) 623 8232, Fax (0171) 283 2548. - Orient /
Jew - *067697*

Napier, Sylvia, 554 King's Rd., London SW6.
T. (0171) 371 5881. - Furn / Orient - *067698*

Nels, Paul, 6-8 Sedley Pl., London W1.
T. (0171) 629 1909. - Tex - *067699*

Nevill, Guy, 251A Fulham Rd, London SW3 6HY.
T. (0171) 351 4292. - Paint - *067700*

New Century, 69 Kensington Church St., London W8.
T. (0171) 937 2410. - Furn / China - *067701*

New Grafton Gallery, 49 Church Rd., London SW13.
T. (0181) 748 8850. - Paint / Draw - *067702*

Newhart, London NW3. T. (0171) 722 2537,
Fax (0171) 722 4335. - Paint - *067703*

Ning, 58 Cambridge St., London SW1.
T. (0171) 834 3292. - Furn / China - *067704*

Noble, Avril, 2 Southampton St., London WC2.
T. (0171) 240 1970. - Graph - *067705*

Noortman, 40-41 Old Bond St., London W1X 3AF.
T. (0171) 491 7284. - Paint - *067706*

North London Clock Shop, 72 Highbury Park, London N5
2XE. T. (0171) 226 1609. - Instr - *067707*

Northcote Road Antiques Market, Northcote Rd., London
SW11. T. (0171) 228 6850. - Ant - *067708*

Nortonbury, BCM Box 5345, London WC1.
T. (01984) 31668. - Silv - *067709*

Number Nineteen, 19 Camden Passage, London N1.
T. (0171) 226 1126. - Ant / Furn - *067710*

Nye, Pat, 105 Portobello Rd., London W11.
T. (0181) 948 4314. - China / Tex - *067711*

O'Shea, 89 Lower Sloane St., London SW1W 8DA.
T. (0171) 730 0081, Fax (0171) 730 1386.
- Graph - *067712*

Oakstar, Clarendon Rd., London W11.
T. (0171) 630 1822. - Graph / Furn - *067713*

Oddiquities, 61 Waldram Park Rd., London SE23.
T. (0181) 699 9574. - Ant / Lights - *067714*

Ogden, Richard, 28-29 Burlington Arcade, London W1.
T. (0171) 493 9136. - Jew - *067715*

Okolski, Z.J., 14 Princes Av., London W3.
T. (0181) 992 7032. - Paint - *067716*

Old Church Galleries, 320 King's Rd., London SW3.
T. (0171) 351 4649. - Graph - *067717*

Old Cinema Antique, 160 Chiswick High Rd., London W4
1PR. T. (0181) 995 4166. - Ant - *067718*

Old Dairy, 164 Thames Rd., London W4.
T. (0181) 994 3140. - Furn - *067719*

Old Father Time Clock Centre, 101 Portobello Rd., London W11. T. (0181) 546 6299. - Instr - *067720*

Old Haberdasher, 139 Portobello Rd., London W11.
T. (0181) 907 8684. - Tex - *067721*

Old London Galleries, 4 Royal Opera Arcade, London
SW1. T. (0171) 930 7679. - Graph - *067722*

Old Pine, 594 King's Rd., London SW6.
T. (0171) 736 5999. - Furn - *067723*

Old Tool Chest, 41 Cross St., London N1.
T. (0171) 359 9313. - Ant - *067724*

Old World Trading, 565 King's Rd., London SW6.
T. (0171) 731 4708, Fax (0171) 731 1291. - Ant /
Furn - *067725*

Olimpia Theodoli, 55 Cambridge St, London SW1V4PS.
T. (0171) 8397805. - Graph / Fra / Pho / Draw - *067726*

Oliver-Sutton, 34c Kensington Church St., London W8.
T. (0171) 937 0633. - China - *067727*

Omell, 22 Bury St., London SW1Y 6AL.
T. (0171) 839 4274. - Paint - *067728*

Oola Boola Antiques, 166 Tower Bridge Rd., London
SE1. T. (0171) 403 0794, Fax (0171) 403 8405. - Furn /
Naut - *067729*

Oosthuizen, Jacqueline, Georgian Village, London N1.
T. (0171) 226 5393. - China / Jew - *067730*

Oosthuizen, Jacqueline, 23 Gale St., London SW3.
T. (0171) 352 6071. - China / Jew - *067731*

Oriental Bronzes, 96 Mount St., London W1.
T. (0171) 493 0309, Fax (0171) 629 2665.
- Orient - *067732*

Original Remember When, 6-7 Rocks Ln., London
SW13. T. (0181) 878 2817. - Furn - *067733*

Ormonde, 156 Portobello Rd., London W11.
T. (0171) 229 9800. - Orient / China - *067734*

Ossowski, A. and M., 83 Pimlico Rd., London SW1W
8PH. T. (0171) 730 3256. - Ant - *067735*

Osterley, 595 King's Rd., London SW6.
T. (0171) 731 0334. - Furn - *067736*

Page, A. and H., 66 Gloucester Rd., London SW7.
T. (0171) 584 7349. - Jew / Silv - *067737*

Page, Kevin, 214 and 6 Camden Passage, London N1
8ED. T. (0171) 226 8558. - Orient - *067738*

Park Galleries, 20 Hendon Lane, London N3.
T. (0181) 346 2176. - Paint / Graph - *067739*

Park Walk Gallery, 20 Park Walk, London SW10.
T. (0171) 351 0410. - Paint / Draw - *067740*

Parker, 28 Pimlico Rd., London SW1. T. (0171) 730 6768,
Fax (0171) 259 9180. - Paint / Graph - *067741*

Parkin, Michael, 11 Motcomb St., London SW1.
T. (0171) 235 1845, Fax (0171) 245 9846. - Paint /
Graph / Draw - *067742*

Partridge, 144-146 New Bond St., London W1.
T. (0171) 629 0834, Fax (0171) 495 6266. - Paint /
Furn / Silv - *067743*

Patterson, W.H., 19 Albemarle St., London W1X 3HA.
T. (0171) 629 4119. - Paint - *067744*

Pauw, M., 606 King's Rd., London SW6 2DX.
T. (0171) 731 4022, Fax (0171) 731 7356. - Ant / Furn /
Lights - *067745*

Pawsey & Payne, 90 Jermyn St., London SW1.
T. (0171) 930 4221, Fax (0171) 839 1903.
- Paint - *067746*

Pearl Cross, 35 Saint Martin's Court, London WC2N 4AL.
T. (0171) 836 2814. - Jew / Silv / Instr - *067747*

Pelham Galleries, 24-25 Mount St., London W1Y 5RB.
T. (0171) 629 0905, Fax (0171) 485 4511. - Ant / Furn /
Tex / Instr / Music - *067748*

Pembridge Art Gallery, 57 Pembridge Rd., London W11.
T. (0171) 792 2717. - Paint / Furn / Sculp - *067749*

Penny Farthing Antiques, 177 Bermondsey St., London
SE1. T. (0171) 407 5171. - Furn / Instr / Naut - *067750*

Period Brass Lights, 9a Thurloe Pl., London SW7.
T. (0171) 589 8305. - Lights - *067751*

Perovetz, H., 50/52 Chancery Ln, London WC2.
T. (0171) 405 8868, Fax (0171) 242 1211.
- Silv - *067752*

Petherton Antiques, 124 Petherton Rd., London N5.
T. (0171) 226 6597. - Paint / Graph / Furn / China /
Silv - *067753*

Petrou, Peter, 195 Westbourne Grove, London W11.
T. (0171) 229 9575. - Furn / Sculp - *067754*

Pflugh, Johnny von, 289 Westbourne Grove, London
W11. T. (0181) 740 5306. - Paint / Instr - *067755*

Philip & Son, Trevor, 75a Jermyn St., London SW1.
T. (0171) 930 2954, Fax (0171) 321 0212.
- Instr - *067756*

Phillips, Henry, 2 Campden St., London W8.
T. (0171) 727 4079. - Furn - *067757*

Phillips, Ronald, 26 Bruton St., London W1X 8LH.
T. (0171) 493 2341, Fax (0171) 495 0843.
- Furn - *067758*

Phillips, S.J., 139 New Bond St, London W1A 3DL.
T. (0171) 6296261, Fax (0171) 4956180. - Jew / Silv /
Instr - *067759*

Phillips & Son, E.S., 99 Portobello Rd., London W11.
T. (0171) 229 2113, Fax (0171) 229 1963.
- Ant - *067760*

Philp, 59 Ledbury Rd., London W11. T. (0171) 727 7915.
- Paint / Furn / Sculp / Draw - *067761*

Piccadilly Gallery, 16 Cork St., London W1.
T. (0171) 629 2875, Fax (0171) 499 0431. - Paint /
Draw - *067762*

Piermont, 7 Wades Hill, London N21. T. (0181) 886 2486.
- Furn / China / Jew / Silv - *067763*

Pine Mine, 100 Wandsworth Bridge Rd., London SW6.
T. (0171) 736 1092. - Furn - *067764*

Pitcher, Nicholas S., 29 New Bond St., London W1Y.
T. (0171) 499 6621. - Orient - *067765*

Place, Peter, 632-636 King's Rd, London SW6.
T. (0171) 736 9945. - Paint / Eth - *067766*

Polak, 21 King St., London SW1. T. (0171) 839 2871.
- Paint - *067767*

Portobello Antique, 133 Portobello Rd., London W11.
T. (0171) 221 0344. - Furn / China / Silv - *067768*

Portobello Antique Store, 79 Portobello Rd., London
W11. T. (0171) 221 1994. - Ant / Silv - *067769*

Potter, Jonathan, 125 New Bond St, London W1X 9FE.
T. (0171) 491 3520, Fax (0171) 491 9754.
- Graph - *067770*

Poulter & Son, H.W., 279 Fulham Rd., London SW10
9PZ. T. (0171) 352 7268. - Ant - *067771*

Powell & Mathers, 571 King's Rd., London SW6.
T. (0171) 371 7837. - Furn - *067772*

Preston & Isbell, Anthony and Sally, 555 King's Rd., London SW6. T. (0171) 371 8301. - Furn - *067773*

Prides of London, 15 Paultons House, London SW3.
T. (0171) 586 1227. - Ant / Furn - *067774*

Priest, Michael, 27a Motcomb St., London SW1X.
T. (0171) 235 7241. - Paint / Furn - *067775*

Print Room, 37 Museum St., London WC1.
T. (0171) 430 0159. - Graph - *067776*

Pruskin, 73 Kensington Church St., London W8.
T. (0171) 937 1994. - Paint / Graph / Furn / China /
Silv - *067777*

Purple Shop, 15 Flood St., London SW3 5ST.
T. (0171) 352 1127. - China / Jew - *067778*

Pyms, 9 Mount Str, Mayfair, London W1Y 5AD.
T. (0171) 629 2020, Fax (0171) 629 2060.
- Paint - *067779*

Quest, 90 Northfields Av., London W13.
T. (0181) 840 2349. - Ant / Furn - 067780
Rabi, 94 Mount St., London W1Y. T. (0171) 499 8886.
- Orient / Tex - 067781
Raffles, 40/42 Church St, London NW8.
T. (0171) 724 6384. - Ant - 067782
Randalls, 46/52 Church Rd, London SW13.
T. (0181) 748 1858. - Furn / Tex / Jew - 067783
Rankin, George, 325 Bethnal Green Rd., London E2.
T. (0171) 739 1840, Fax (0171) 729 5023. - Num /
Jew - 067784
Rapscallion, 25 Shrubbery Rd., London SW16.
T. (0181) 769 8078. - Ant - 067785
Rare Carpets Gallery, 496 King's Rd., London SW10.
T. (0171) 351 3296, Fax (0171) 376 4876.
- Tex - 067786
Red Lion Market, 165/169 Portobello Rd, London W11.
T. (0171) 221 7638. - Ant - 067787
Redford, William, 99 Mount St., London W1Y 5AD.
T. (0171) 629 1165. - Ant / Furn / China - 067788
Reeves, Paul, 32B Kensington Church St, London W8.
T. (0171) 937 1594. - Furn - 067789
Regent Antiques, 9-10 Chester Court, Albany St., Lon-
don NW1 4BU. T. (0171) 935 6944,
Fax (0171) 935 7814. - Ant / Furn - 067790
Reindeer, 81 Kensington Church St., London W8.
T. (0171) 937 3754. - Furn - 067791
Relcy, 9 Nelson Rd., London SE10. T. (0181) 858 2812.
- Paint / Furn / Instr / Naut - 067792
Relic Antiques, 5 Angel Arcade, London N1.
T. (0171) 359 9558, Fax (0171) 388 2691. - Ant /
Furn - 067793
Relic Antiques Trade Warehouse, 127 Pancras Rd., Lon-
don NW1. T. (0171) 387 6039, Fax (0171) 388 2691.
- Ant - 067794
Rendall, Lesley, 69 Pimlico Rd., London SW1W.
T. (0171) 730 7206. - Furn - 067795
Rendlesham, 498 Kings Rd., London SW10.
T. (0171) 351 1442. - Furn - 067796
Reubens, 44 Honour Oak Park, London SE23.
T. (0181) 291 1786. - Instr / Mil - 067797
Reverie, 24 Cheval Pl., London SW7. T. (0171) 589 0133.
- Furn / Tex / Dec / Lights - 067798
Rex Antiques, 63 Ledbury Rd., London W11.
T. (0171) 229 6203. - Furn - 067799
Rezai, A., 123 Portobello Rd., London W11.
T. (0171) 221 5012. - Tex - 067800
Richards & Sons, David, 12 New Cavendish St., London
W1M. T. (0171) 935 3206, Fax (0171) 324 4423.
- Silv - 067801
Richardson & Kailas, 65 Rivermead Court, London SW6.
T. (0171) 371 0491. - Ico - 067802
Richmond Gallery, 8 Cork St., London W1.
T. (0171) 437 9422, Fax (0171) 734 7018.
- Paint - 067803
Risky Business, 44 Church St, London NW8.
T. (0171) 724 2194, Fax (0171) 724 2194.
- Furn - 067804
Robinson, Jonathan, 29 New Bond St., London W1Y
1AR. T. (0171) 493 0592. - Orient - 067805
Roderick, 23 Vicarage Gate, London W8.
T. (0171) 937 8517. - Instr - 067806
Roger, Joan, 17 Uxbridge St., London W8 7TQ.
T. (0171) 603 7627. - Graph / Furn / China - 067807
Roger's Antiques Gallery, 65 Portobello Rd., London
W11. T. (0171) 351 5353, Fax (0171) 351 5350.
- Ant - 067808
Rogers de Rin, 76 Royal Hospital Rd., London SW3 4HN.
T. (0171) 352 9007, Fax (0171) 351 9407. - Ant / Furn /
China - 067809
Rookery Farm Antiques, 12 Camden Passage, London
N1. T. (0171) 359 0190. - Furn - 067810
Rose, Geoffrey, 77 Pimlico Rd., London SW1W 8PH.
T. (0171) 730 3004. - Furn - 067811
Rose, R.E., 731 Sidcup Rd., London SE9.
T. (0181) 859 4754. - Instr - 067812
Ross, Marcus, 14/16 Pierrepont Row, London N1.
T. (0171) 359 8494. - Ant / Furn / China - 067813
Rothman, 103-105 Pimlico Rd., London SW1W.
T. (0171) 730 2558, Fax (0171) 730 3329. - Furn /
Instr - 067814
Royal Exchange Art Gallery, 14 Royal Exchange, London
EC3. T. (0171) 283 4400. - Paint - 067815

Rupert's, 151 Northfield Av., London W13.
T. (0181) 567 1368. - Instr - 067816
Rutland, 32a Saint George St., London W1.
T. (0171) 499 5636. - Paint - 067817
S. and H. Antiques, 7 Church St., London NW8.
T. (0171) 724 7118. - Paint / China / Silv /
Glass - 067818
Sabin, 82 Campden Hill Rd., London W8 7AA.
T. (0171) 937 0471. - Graph / Draw - 067819
S.A.G. Art Galleries, 589 Garratt Ln., London SW18.
T. (0181) 944 1404, Fax (0181) 947 8174. - Paint /
Graph - 067820
Sainsbury & Mason, 145 Ebury St, London SW1W.
T. (0171) 730 3393, Fax (0171) 730 8334. - Paint /
Furn / Orient / Glass - 067821
Saint James's Art Group, 91 Jermyn St., London SW1.
T. (0171) 321 0233. - Paint - 067822
Saint Peters Organ Works, Saint Peters Close, London
E2. T. (0171) 739 4747. - Music - 067823
Sampson, Alistair, 156 Brompton Rd., London SW3 1HW.
T. (0171) 589 5272, Fax (0171) 823 8142. - Paint /
Furn / China / Cur - 067824
San Fairy, Ann, 110 Salmon Ln., London E14.
T. (0171) 987 5771. - Ant - 067825
Sanaiy, 57 Pimlico Rd., London SW1.
T. (0171) 730 4742, Fax (0171) 259 9194.
- Tex - 067826
Sandberg, Patrick, 140-142 Kensington Church St., Lon-
don W8. T. (0171) 229 0373, Fax (0171) 792 3467.
- Graph / Furn / Instr - 067827
Sanders & Sons, Robin, 590 Fulham Rd., London SW6
5UA. T. (0171) 736 0586. - Paint / Furn / China /
Glass - 067828
Santos, A.V., 1 Campden St., London W8 7EP.
T. (0171) 727 4872, Fax (0171) 229 4801.
- Orient - 067829
Sarti, G., 186 Westbourne Grove, London W11 2RH.
T. (0171) 221 7186. - Paint / Furn - 067830
Sattin, Gerald, 14 King St., London SW1Y 6QU.
T. (0171) 493 6557, Fax (0171) 493 6557. - China /
Silv / Glass - 067831
Saunders, Charles, 255 Fulham Rd., London SW3.
T. (0171) 351 5242. - Furn / Lights - 067832
Scallywag, 224 Clapham Rd., London SW9 0QE.
T. (0171) 735 2444, Fax (0171) 735 0787.
- Furn - 067833
Scarisbrick & Bate, 111 Mount St., London W1.
T. (0171) 499 2043, Fax (0171) 499 2897.
- Furn - 067834
Schell, Christine, 15 Cale St., London SW3.
T. (0171) 352 5563. - Silv - 067835
von Schilgen, 21 Holland Park Gardens, London W14
5PL. T. (0171) 6027423. 067836
Schredds, 107 Portobello Rd., London W11.
T. (0181) 348 3314, Fax (0181) 341 5971. - China /
Silv - 067837
Schuster, Thomas E., 14 Maddox St., London W1R 9PL.
T. (0171) 491 2208, Fax (0171) 491 9872.
- Ant - 067838
Scope Antiques, 64-66 Willesden Ln., London NW6 7SX.
T. (0171) 328 5833. - Ant / Furn / Silv - 067839
Seaby, B.A., 7 Davies St., London W1.
T. (0171) 495 2590, Fax (0171) 491 1595. - Ant /
Num - 067840
Seager, Arthur, 25a Holland St., London W8.
T. (0171) 937 3262. - Furn / China - 067841
Seago, 22 Pimlico Rd., London SW1. T. (0171) 730 7502,
Fax (0171) 730 9179. - Sculp - 067842
Seale, Jeremy, 56 White Hart Ln., London SW13.
T. (0181) 876 1041. - Paint / Graph / Furn - 067843
Searle & Co., 1 Royal Exchange, London EC3.
T. (0171) 626 2456. - Jew / Silv - 067844
Select Antiques Gallery, 219 Kensington Church St.,
London W8. T. (0171) 727 4783. - Furn - 067845
Seligmann, M. and D., 37 Kensington Church St., Lon-
don W8. T. (0171) 937 0400. - Furn / China - 067846
Senior, Mark, 240 Brompton Rd., London SW3.
T. (0171) 589 5811. - Paint - 067847
Sensation, 66 Fulham High St., London SW6 6DU.
T. (0171) 736 4135, Fax (0171) 371 5486. - Ant / Furn /
China / Silv - 067848
Sewell, Jean, 3 Campden St., London W8 7EP.
T. (0171) 727 3122. - China - 067849

Seyfried, David, 759 Fulham Rd., London SW6.
T. (0171) 731 4230. - Furn / Tex - 067850
Shaikh & Son, 16 Brook St., London W1.
T. (0171) 629 3430. - Tex - 067851
Sheen, 370 Upper Richmond Rd., London SW14.
T. (0181) 878 1100. - Paint / Graph - 067852
Sheppard & Cooper, 11 Saint George St., London W1R
9DF. T. (0171) 629 6489, Fax (0171) 495 2905. - Ant /
Glass - 067853
Sherlock, George, 588 King's Rd., London SW6.
T. (0171) 736 3955, Fax (0171) 371 5179. - Ant /
Furn - 067854
Shield & Allen, 584 and 586 Kings' Rd, London SW6.
T. (0171) 736 7145, Fax (0171) 736 0029. - Ant / Paint /
Furn - 067855
Shrubsole, S. J., 43 Museum St., London WC1A 1LY.
T. (0171) 405 2712. - Silv - 067856
Siden, G. T., 69 Compayne Gardens, London NW6 3DB.
T. (0171) 624 9045. - Draw - 067857
Silver Belle, 48 Church St., London NW8.
T. (0171) 723 2908. - China / Silv - 067858
Silver Mouse Trap, 56 Carey St., London WC2.
T. (0171) 405 2578. - Jew / Silv - 067859
Silverman, B., Vault 26, 53-65 Chancery Lane, London
WC2A. T. (0171) 242 3269. - Silv - 067860
Simon, Julian, 70 Pimlico Rd., London SW1 8LS.
T. (0171) 730 8673, Fax (0171) 823 6116.
- Paint - 067861
Simon, Tracy, 18 Church St., London NW8.
T. (0171) 724 5890, Fax (0171) 2620275.
- Ant - 067862
Simons, Jack, Vault 35, 53-65 Chancery Lane, London
WC2. T. (0171) 242 3221. - Silv - 067863
Simply Capital, 33 Victoria Rd., London F18.
T. (0181) 530 6229. - Furn - 067864
Simpson, Michael, 11 Savile Row, London W1.
T. (0171) 437 5414, Fax (0171) 287 5967.
- Paint - 067865
Simpsons, 100 Blythe Rd., London W14.
T. (0171) 6038625. - Ant - 067866
Sims, Robin, 7 Camden Passage, London N1.
T. (0171) 226 2393. - Ant / Furn - 067867
Sinai, 221 Kensington Church St., London W8.
T. (0171) 229 6190. - Orient / Tex / Silv - 067868
Sitch, W., 48 Berwick St., London W1.
T. (0171) 437 3776. - Lights - 067869
Skeel, Keith, 94/98 Islington High St, London N1.
T. (0171) 359 9894. - Ant - 067870
Skeel, Keith, 7-9 Elliotts Pl., London N1.
T. (0171) 226 7012. - Furn - 067871
Skrebowski, Justin, 82E Portobello Rd, London W11.
T. (0171) 792 9742. - Paint / Graph / Draw - 067872
Sladmore, 32 Bruton Pl., London W1X 7AA.
T. (0171) 499 0365. - Sculp - 067873
Slater, David, 170 Westbourne Grove, London W11.
T. (0171) 727 3336. - Ant - 067874
Smith, Colin and Gerald Robinson, 105 Portobello Rd.,
London W11. T. (0181) 994 3783. - Silv - 067875
Smyth, Peta, 42 Moreton St., London SW1V 2PB.
T. (0171) 630 9898. - Tex - 067876
Somerville, Stephen, 32 Saint George St., London W1R
9FA. T. (0171) 493 8363. - Paint / Graph /
Draw - 067877
Somlo, 7 Piccadilly Arcade, London SW1.
T. (0171) 499 6526. - Instr - 067878
Sotheran's, 80 Pimlico Rd., London SW1W 8PL.
T. (0171) 730 8756. - Graph - 067879
South Audley Antiques, 36 South Audley St., London
W1Y 5DH. T. (0171) 4993178, Fax (0171) 355 3548.
- Ant / Paint / Furn / China / Glass - 067880
Spatz, 4 Castlehaven Rd., London NW1.
T. (0171) 482 3785. - Tex - 067881
Spatz, 48 Monmouth St., London WC24.
T. (0171) 379 0703. - Tex - 067882
Speelman, Alfred, 129 Mount St., London W1.
T. (0171) 499 5126. - Orient - 067883
Speelman, Edward, 175 Piccadilly, London W1V 0NP.
T. (0171) 493 0657. - Paint - 067884
Spencer, Charles, 24a Ashworth Rd., London W9.
T. (0171) 286 9396. - Paint / Graph - 067885
Spero, Simon, 109 Kensington Curch St., London W8.
T. (0171) 727 7413. - Paint / China - 067886

Spink & Son Ltd

London's Oldest Fine Art
and Antique Dealers
(Established 1666)

English Paintings
and Watercolours

•

Jewellery

•

Furniture

•

Chinese & Japanese
Works of Art

•

South East Asian,
Indian & Islamic Art

•

Textiles

•

Coins, Banknotes
and Bullion

•

Orders, Decorations,
Medals & Militaria

•

Numismatic Books

BY APPOINTMENT TO
HER MAJESTY THE QUEEN
MEDALLISTS
SPINK & SON LTD. LONDON

BY APPOINTMENT TO
H.R.H. THE DUKE OF EDINBURGH
MEDALLISTS
SPINK & SON LTD. LONDON

BY APPOINTMENT TO
H.R.H. THE PRINCE OF WALES
MEDALLISTS
SPINK & SON LTD. LONDON

SPINK

5 King St, St. James's
London, SW1Y 6QS

Tel: 0171-930 7888
Fax: 0171-839 4853
Internet: http://spinkandson.co uk

Spice, 2 Wandon Rd., London SW6. T. (0171) 736 4619.
- Furn - *067887*

Spink, John, 14 Darlan Rd., London SW6.
T. (0171) 731 8292. - Paint - *067888*

Spink & Son, 5 King St, St. James's, London SW1Y 6QS.
T. (0171) 9307888, Fax 8394853. - Ant / Paint / Num /
Jew / Silv - *067889*

Spread Eagle Antiques, 8 Nevada St., London SE10 9JL.
T. (0181) 305 1666. - Graph / China / Tex / Cur - *067890*

Spread Eagle Antiques, 1 Stockwell St., London SE10.
T. (0181) 305 1666. - Ant / Furn - *067891*

Spyer, Gerald, 28 Motcomb St., London SW1X 8LB.
T. (0171) 235 3348, Fax (0171) 823 2234.
- Furn - *067892*

Stage Door Prints, Charing Cross Rd, London WC2.
T. (0171) 240 1683. - Graph - *067893*

Stair & Co., 14 Mount St., London W1.
T. (0171) 499 1784, Fax (0171) 629 1050. - Ant / Paint /
Furn / Lights / Instr - *067894*

Stanton, Louis, 299 and 301 Westbourne Grove, London
W11 2QA. T. (0171) 727 9336, Fax (0171) 7275424.
- Ant / Furn / Sculp / Tex / Instr - *067895*

Steel, Jeremy and Guy, 8 Princes Arcade, Jermyn St.,
London SW1. T. (0171) 287 2528. - Jew - *067896*

Stefani, 179 Kingston Rd., London SW19.
T. (0181) 542 4696. - Paint / China / Jew / Silv - *067897*

Stephenson, Robert, 1 Elystan St., London SW3 3NT.
T. (0171) 225 2343. - Tex - *067898*

Stern, 46 Ledbury Rd., London W11 2AB.
T. (0171) 229 6187. - Paint - *067899*

Stewart, Lauri, 36 Church Ln., London N2.
T. (0181) 883 7719. - Paint / Graph - *067900*

Stobo, Constance, 31 Holland St., London W8.
T. (0171) 937 6282. - China - *067901*

Stockspring, 114 Kensington Church St., London W8.
T. (0171) 727 7995. - Orient / China - *067902*

Stodel, Jacob, 116 Kensington Church St., London W8
4BH. T. (0171) 221 2652, Fax (0171) 229 1293. - Ant /
Furn / China - *067903*

Stodel, S. and J., 53-65 Chancery Lane, London WC2.
T. (0171) 405 7009, Fax (0171) 2426366.
- Silv - *067904*

Stone, Alan, 3 Wadham Rd., London SW15.
T. (0181) 8701606. - Ant - *067905*

Stoppenbach & Delestre, 25 Cork St., London W1X 1HB.
T. (0171) 734 3534. - Paint / Sculp / Draw - *067906*

Storey, Harold T., 3 Cecil Court, Charing Cross Rd., London WC2. T. (0171) 836 3777. - Graph - *067907*

Stouts Antiques Market, 144 Portobello Rd., London
W11. T. (0171) 7273649, Fax (01923) 897618.
- Ant - *067908*

Strand Antiques, 166 Thames Rd., London W4.
T. (0181) 994 1912. - Paint / Furn / China / Jew /
Silv - *067909*

Strand Numismatics-Coins-Stamps-Medals, 2 Southampton St., London WC2E 7HA. T. (0171) 240 1970.
- Num - *067910*

Streather, Pamela, 4 Studio Pl., London SW1X 8EW.
T. (0171) 235 3450. - Paint / Furn - *067911*

Strike One, 33 Balcombe St., London NW1.
T. (0171) 224 9719. - Instr - *067912*

Style, Camden Passage, London N1. T. (0171) 359 7867.
- China / Glass / Mod - *067913*

Sugar Antiques, 8 – 9 Pierrepoint Arcade, London N1.
T. (0171) 354 9896. - Jew / Instr - *067914*

Sukmano, 133 Kensington Church St., London W8.
T. (0171) 229 4323. - Orient - *067915*

Swan Fine Art, 120 Islington High St., London N1.
T. (0171) 226 5335. - Paint - *067916*

Swann, Olivr, 170 Walton St, London SW3.
T. (0171) 581 4229. - Paint / Naut - *067917*

Symes, Robin, 3 Ormond Yard, London SW1.
T. (0171) 9309856. - Ant - *067918*

Tara Antiques, 6 Church St., London NW8.
T. (0171) 724 2405. - Paint / Furn / Sculp / Silv - *067919*

Taylor, 4 Royal Arcade, Old Bond St., London W1.
T. (0171) 493 4111. - Paint - *067920*

Teignmouth & Son, Pamela, 108 Kensington Church St.,
London W8. T. (0171) 229 1602. - Furn - *067921*

Telfer-Smollett, M. and C., 88 Portobello Rd., London
W11. T. (0171) 727 0117. - Furn / Orient - *067922*

Teltscher, F., 17 Crawford St., London W1H 1PF.
T. (0171) 935 0525. - Paint - *067923*

Temple, 6 Clarendon Cross, London W11.
T. (0171) 727 3809, Fax (0171) 727 1546.
- Ico - *067924*

Terrace Antiques, 10 South Ealing Rd., London W5 4QA.
T. (0181) 5675194. - Paint / Furn / China / Silv /
Glass - *067925*

Terry Antiques, 160 Chiswick High Rd., London W4.
T. (0181) 995 4166. - Furn - *067926*

Tessiers, 26 New Bond St., London W1.
T. (0171) 629 0458, Fax (0171) 629 5110. - Ant / Jew /
Silv - *067927*

Themes and Variations, 231 Westbourne Grove, London
W11. T. (0171) 727 5531. - Furn / China / Tex / Jew /
Lights / Glass - *067928*

This and That, 50-51 Chalk Farm Rd., London NW1.
T. (0171) 267 5433. - Furn - *067929*

Thomson-Albany, Bill, 1 Bury St., London SW1.
T. (0171) 839 6119. - Paint - *067930*

Thomson, Murray, 152 Kensington Church St., London
W8. T. (0171) 727 1727, Fax (0171) 727 1825.
- Furn - *067931*

Thornhill Galleries, 76 New King's Rd., London SW6.
T. (0171) 736 5830. - Ant - *067932*

Thornhill Galleries, 78 Deodar Rd., London SW15.
T. (0181) 8742101. - Ant - *067933*

Through the Looking Glass, 563 King's Rd., London
SW6. T. (0171) 736 7799. - Ant - *067934*

Through the Looking Glass, 137 Kensington Church St.,
London W8. T. (0171) 221 4026. - Glass - *067935*

Tillman, William, 30 Saint James's St., London SW1A.
T. (0171) 839 2500. - Furn - *067936*

Tillou, Peter, 39 Duke St., London SW1.
T. (0171) 930 9308, Fax (0171) 930 2088. - Paint /
Mil - *067937*

Tobias and the Angel, 68 White Hart Ln., London SW13.
T. (0181) 878 8902. - Furn / Tex - *067938*

Tociapski, Igor, 39 Ledbury Rd., London W11.
T. (0171) 229 8317. - Instr - *067939*

Tomkinson, 87 Portobello Rd., London W11.
T. (0171) 727 1304. - Glass - *067940*

Toth, Ferenc, 598A King's Rd, London SW6.
T. (0171) 731 2063, Fax (0171) 6021771. - Ant /
Furn - *067941*

Totteridge Gallery, 61 Totteridge Ln., London N20.
T. (0181) 4467896. - Paint - *067942*

Toubian, 180 Kensington Church St., London W8.
T. (0171) 221 6476. - Ant - *067943*

Tower Antiques, 463 Harrow Rd., London W10.
T. (0181) 969 0535. - Paint / Graph / Furn - *067944*

Tower Bridge Antiques Warehouse, 159/161 Tower Bridge Rd, London SE1. T. (0171) 403 3660. - Furn /
Naut - *067945*

Townsend, 81 Abbey Rd., London NW8 0AE.
T. (0171) 624 4756. - Ant / Glass - *067946*

Toynbee-Clarke, 95 Mount St., London W1.
T. (0171) 499 4472, Fax (0171) 4951204. - Paint /
Furn - *067947*

Tracy, Simon, 18 Church St., London NW8.
T. (0171) 724 5890, Fax (0171) 262 0275.
- Furn - *067948*

Trader Antiques, 484 Green Ln., London N13.
T. (0181) 886 9552. - Ant / Furn / Glass - *067949*

Tradition-Military Antiques, 5a Sheperd St., London W1.
T. (0171) 493 7452. - Mil - *067950*

Trafalgar Galleries, 35 Bury St., London SW1Y 6AY.
T. (0171) 839 6466. - Paint - *067951*

Trafalgar Square Collectors Centre, 7 Whitcomb St.,
London WC2. T. (0171) 930 1979. - Num - *067952*

Tron, David, 275 King's Rd., London SW3 5EN.
T. (0171) 352 5918. - Furn - *067953*

Trove, 71 Pimlico Rd., London SW1W 8NE.
T. (0171) 730 6514. - Ant / Paint / Furn / Sculp - *067954*

Truscott, Christina, 77 Portobella Rd, London W11.
T. (0171) 7275263. - Orient - *067955*

Tsar Architectural, 487 Liverpool Rd., London N7.
T. (0171) 609 4238. - Ant - *067956*

Tulissio de Beaumont, 277 Lillie Rd., London SW6.
T. (0171) 385 0156. - Ant / Sculp / Lights - *067957*

Turn On Lighting, 116/118 Islington High St, London N1
8EG. T. (0171) 359 7616. - Lights - *067958*

Turpin, M., 27 Bruton St., London W1X 7DB.
T. (0171) 493 3275, Fax (0171) 2446254.
- Furn - *067959*

Twentieth Century, 14 Blandfield Rd., London SW12.
T. (0181) 675 6511. - Mod - *067960*

Ullman, A. R., 10 Hatton Garden, London EC1N 8AH.
T. (0171) 405 1877. - Jew / Silv - *067961*

Under Two Flags, 4 Saint Christopher's Pl., London
W1M. T. (0171) 935 6934. - Mil - *067962*

Underhill, Leigh, 100 Islington High St., London N1.
T. (0171) 226 5673. - Paint / Graph / Sculp /
Draw - *067963*

Valcke, Francois, 610 King's Rd., London SW6 2DX.
T. (0171) 736 6024, Fax (0171) 7318302. - Paint /
Graph / Draw - *067964*

Vale Antiques, 245 Elgin Av, London W9.
T. (0171) 328 4796. - Ant - *067965*

Vale Stamps and Antiques, 21 Tranquil Vale, London
SE3. T. (0181) 852 9817. - China / Jew - *067966*

Valls, Rafael, 11 Duke St., London SW1Y 6BN. T. (0171) 930 1144, Fax (0171) 976 1596. - Paint - 067967
Van Beers, Jan, 34 Davies St., London W1Y. T. (0171) 408 0434. - Orient / China - 067968
Van Haeften, Johnny, 13 Duke St., London SW1Y 6DB. T. (0171) 930 3062, Fax (0171) 839 6303. - Paint - 067969
Van Vredenburgh, Eric, 37 Bury St., London SW1. T. (0171) 839 5818. - Orient / Sculp - 067970
Vandekar Antiques, 174 Kensington Church St., London W8. T. (0171) 229 7100. - Orient - 067971
Vane House Antiques, 15 Camden Passage, London N1. T. (0171) 359 1343. - Furn - 067972
Vaughan, 158-160 Wandsworth Bridge Rd., London SW6. T. (0171) 731 3133. - Furn / Lights - 067973
Venners Antiques, 7 New Cavendish St., London W1M. T. (0171) 935 0184. - China - 067974
Victoriana Dolls, 101 Portobello Rd., London W11. T. (01737) 249525. - Toys - 067975
Vigo Carpet Gallery, 6a Vigo St., London W1X 1AH. T. (0171) 439 6971, Fax (0171) 439 2353. - Tex - 067976
Vigo-Sternberg Galleries, 37 South Audley St., London W1Y 5DH. T. (0171) 629 8307, Fax (0171) 6299591. - Tex - 067977
Village Time, 43 The Village, Charlton, London SE7. T. (0181) 858 2514. - Jew / Instr - 067978
Vintage Cameras, 256 Kirkdale, London SE26. T. (0181) 7785416. - Instr - 067979
Virginia Antiques, 98 Portland Rd., London W11. T. (0171) 727 9908. - Tex - 067980
Wace, Rupert, 107 Jermyn St., London SW1Y. T. (0171) 495 1623. - Orient / Arch - 067981
Wainwright, David, 251 Portobello Rd., London W11. T. (0171) 792 1988. - Eth - 067982
Walker-Bagshawe, 73 Walton St., London SW3. T. (0171) 589 4582. - Paint / Furn - 067983
Walker, W. E., 277/279 Camden High St, London NW1 7BX. T. (0171) 485 6210. - Paint / Furn / China - 067984
Wallace Antiques, 56 Tranquil Vale, London SE3. T. (0181) 852 2647. - Furn - 067985
Wallwitz, Angela Gräfin von, 18 Clareville Grove, London SW7 5AR. T. (0171) 3732502, Fax (0171) 3705110. - China - 067986
Walpole Gallery, 38 Dover St., London W1. T. (0171) 499 6626. - Paint - 067987
Walter, William, 53-65 Chancery Lane, London WC2A 1QS. T. (0171) 242 3248. - Ant / Silv - 067988
Wandle, 202 Garratt Ln., London SW18. T. (0181) 870 5873. - Ant - 067989
Ward Antiques, 267 Woolwich Rd., London SE7. T. (0181) 305 0963. - Furn - 067990
Waroujian, M. L., 110-112 Hammersmith Rd., London W6 7JP. T. (0181) 748 7509. - Tex - 067991
Warren, Leigh, 566 King's Rd., London SW6. T. (0171) 736 2485. - Ant - 067992
Wartski, 14 Grafton St., London W1X 4DE. T. (0171) 493 1141. - Jew / Silv - 067993
Waterhouse & Dodd, 110 New Bond St., London W1. T. (0171) 491 9293. - Paint / Draw - 067994
Wearn, R., 322 King's Rd., London SW3. T. (0171) 352 3918. - Ant / Furn - 067995
Weaver, Trude, 71 Portobello Rd., London W11. T. (0171) 229 8738. - Furn / Tex - 067996
Web, A. M., 93 Portobello Rd., London W11. T. (0171) 727 1485. - Instr / Music - 067997
Weiss Gallery, 1B Albemarle St, London W1. T. (0171) 409 0035. - Paint - 067998
Weiss, Peter K., 53-65 Chancery Lane, London WC1V. T. (0171) 2428100. - Instr - 067999
Welbeck Gallery, 18 Thayer St., London W1. T. (0171) 935 4825. - Graph / Mil - 068000
Wellington Antiques, 2-5 Wellington Close, London W11. T. (0171) 221 4950. - Furn - 068001
Wellington Gallery, 1 St. John's Wood High St., London NW8. T. (0171) 586 2620. - Paint / China / Silv / Glass - 068002
West, Mark J., 39B High St, London SW19. T. (0181) 946 2811. - Furn / China / Glass - 068003
West, Mark J., 15 Georgian Village, London N1. T. (0171) 359 8686. - Ant / Glass - 068004
Westenholz, Piers von, 76-78 Pimlico Rd., London SW1W. T. (0171) 824 8090. - Furn - 068005
Weston, William, 7 Royal Arcade, London W1. T. (0171) 493 0722, Fax (0171) 491 9240. - Graph - 068006
Whiteway & Waldron, 305 Munster Rd., London SW6. T. (0171) 381 3195. - Rel / Glass - 068007
Whitfield, Robert, Tunnel Av, London SE10. T. (0181) 305 2230, Fax (0181) 305 1805. - Furn - 068008
Whitworth & O'Donnell, 282 Lewisham High St., London SE13. T. (0181) 690 1282. - Jew - 068009
Whyte, Philip, 32 Bury St., London SW1Y. T. (0171) 321 0353, Fax (0171) 321 0350. - Instr - 068010
Wibroe, Neil, 185 Westbourne Grove, London W11. T. (0171) 229 6334. - Furn - 068011
Wiggins & Sons, Arnold, 4 Bury St., London SW1Y 6AB. T. (0171) 925 0195, Fax (0171) 839 6928. - Fra - 068012
Wildenstein & Co., 147 New Bond St, London W1Y 0NX. T. (0171) 629 0602, Fax (0171) 493 3924. - Paint / Draw - 068013
Wilkins & Wilkins, 1 Barrett St., London W1. T. (0171) 935 9613. - Paint - 068014
Wilkinson, 5 Catford Hill, London SE6 4NU. T. (0181) 314 1080. - Glass - 068015
Wilkinson, 1 Grafton St., London W1. T. (0171) 495 2477. - Glass - 068016
Williams & Son, 2 Grafton St., London W1. T. (0171) 4934985, Fax (0171) 409 7363. - Paint - 068017
Wilson, O. F., Old Chruch St, London SW3 6EJ. T. (0171) 352 9554. - Ant / Furn - 068018
Winchmore Antiques, 14 The Green, Winchmore Hill, London N21. T. (0181) 882 4800. - Ant - 068019
Wingfield Sparting Art, 35 Sibella Rd., London SW4. T. (0171) 622 6301. - Paint / Graph - 068020
Wise, Mary, 27 Holland St., London W8. T. (0171) 937 8649. - Orient / China - 068021
Wissinger & Mendoza, George and Antanio, 166 Bermondsey St., London SE1. T. (0171) 407 5795. - Paint / Furn - 068022
Witch Ball, 51A Blackbird Hill, London NW9. T. (0181) 200 4937. - Furn - 068023
Witch Ball, Charing Cross Rd, London WC2. T. (0171) 836 2922. - Graph - 068024
World Famous Portobello Market, 1-3 Elgin Crescent, London W11. T. (0171) 221 4964. - Ant - 068025
World Famous Portobello Market, 177 Portobello Rd., London W11. T. (0171) 221 4964. - Ant - 068026
Wray, Christopher, 600-606 King's Rd., London SW6 2DX. T. (0171) 736 8434, Fax (0171) 731 3507. - Lights - 068027
Wren Antiques, 49b Church Rd., Barnes, London SW13 9HH. T. (0181) 741 7841. - Paint / Furn / Instr - 068028
Wrigglesworth, Lind, 34 Brook St., London W1Y. T. (0171) 408 0177. - Tex - 068029
Wright, Clifford, 104-106 Fulham Rd., London SW3 6HS. T. (0171) 589 0986, Fax (0171) 589 3565. - Ant / Furn - 068030
Wynards Antiques, 5 Ladbroke Rd., London W11 3PA. T. (0171) 221 7936. - Ant / Furn - 068031
Wynter, Harriet, 50 Redcliffe Rd., London SW10 9NJ. T. (0171) 352 6494, Fax (0171) 352 9312. - Instr - 068032
W.13 Antiques, 10 The Avenue, Ealing, London W13. T. (0181) 998 0390. - Ant / Furn / China - 068033
Yesterday Child, 118 Islington High St., London N1. T. (0171) 354 1601, Fax (01908) 583403. - Toys - 068034
Yesterday's Antiques, 315 Upper Richmond Rd. West, London SW14. T. (0181) 876 7536. - Furn - 068035
York Arcade, 80 Islington High St., London N1. T. (0171) 833 2640. - Ant - 068036
Young, Robert, 68 Battersea Bridge Rd., London SW11. T. (0171) 228 7847, Fax (0171) 585 0489. - Furn / China - 068037
Young & Stephens, 1 Burlington Gardens, London W1X 1LD. T. (0171) 499 7927, Fax (0171) 4938905. - Jew - 068038
Zadah Gallery, 29 Conduit St., London W1. T. (0171) 4932622. - Tex - 068039
Zebrak, 284 Westbourne Grove, London W11. T. (01273) 202929, Fax (01273) 321021. - Jew / Silv / Instr - 068040
139 Antiques, 139 Green Lanes, London N16. T. (0171) 354 2466. - Ant / Furn - 068041
309 Antiques, 309 Old Kent Rd., London SE1. T. (0171) 237 3600. - Ant - 068042

Long Buckby (Northamptonshire)

Antique Coffee Pot, 15 High St., Long Buckby Northants. T. (01327) 843849. - Furn - 068043
Thompson, R. E., 17 Church St., Long Buckby Northants. T. (01327) 842242. - Furn / Instr / Naut - 068044

Long Crendon (Buckinghamshire)

Hollington Antiques, 87 Bicester Rd., Long Crendon Bucks. T. (01844) 208294. - Ant / Paint / China / Glass / Draw - 068045

Long Eaton (Derbyshire)

Goodacre, Thrumpton Av., Meadow Lane, Long Eaton Derbys. T. (01602) 734387. - Instr - 068046
Miss Elany, 2 Salisbury St., Long Eaton Derbys. T. (01602) 734835. - Ant / Music - 068047

Long Hanborough (Oxfordshire)

Hallett, David A., 125 and 127 Main Rd, Long Hanborough Oxon. T. (01993) 882767. - Furn / Tex / Cur - 068048

Long Melford (Suffolk)

Antique Clocks, Hall St, Long Melford Suffolk. T. (01787) 880040. - Instr - 068049
Ashley Gallery, Belmont House, Hall St., Long Melford C10 9JF. T. (01787) 375434. - Paint / Furn / China / Tex / Draw - 068050
Carling, Roger & Tess Sinclair, Coconut House, Hall St., Long Melford Suffolk. T. (01787) 312012. - Ant / Furn / Tex / Instr - 068051
Chater-House Gallery, Foundry House, Hall St., Long Melford Suffolk. T. (01787) 379831. - Furn / Music - 068052
Cooper, Bruno, Hall St, Long Melford Suffolk. T. (01787) 312613. - Paint / Furn / Sculp - 068053
Enchanted Aviary, 63 Hall St., Long Melford Suffolk. T. (01787) 378814. - Ant - 068054
Long Melford Antiques Centre, Chapel Maltings, Long Melford Suffolk. T. (01787) 379287. - Ant - 068055
Lyall, Alexander, Belmont House, Hall St., Long Melford Suffolk. T. (01787) 375434. - Furn - 068056
Magpie Antiques, Hall St., Long Melford Suffolk. T. (01787) 310581. - Furn / China - 068057
Marney, Patrick, Gate House, Melford Hall, Long Melford Suffolk. T. (01787) 880533. - Instr - 068058
Melford Fine Arts, Little Saint Mary's, Long Melford Suffolk. T. (0178725) 312174. - Ant - 068059
Neptune Antiques, Hall St., Long Melford IP4 1LB. T. (01787) 375787, Fax (01787) 375242. - Furn - 068060
Raine Bell, Little Saint Marys, Long Melford Suffolk. T. (01787) 880040. - Paint / Furn - 068061
Seabrook Antiques, Hall St, Long Melford Suffolk. T. (01787) 379638, Fax (01787) 311788. - Furn - 068062
Simpson, Oswald, Hall St., Long Melford Suffolk. T. (01787) 377523. - Furn - 068063
Suthburgh Antiques, Red House, Hall St., Long Melford Suffolk. T. (01787) 374818. - Furn / Instr - 068064
Tudor Antiques, Little Saint Mary's, Long Melford CO10 9HY. T. (01787) 375950. - Furn / Silv / Instr - 068065
Village Clocks, Little Saint Mary's, Long Melford Suffolk. T. (01787) 375896. - Instr - 068066
Ward Antiques, Hall St., Long Melford CO10 9JQ. T. (01787) 378265, Fax (01787) 378265. - Furn - 068067

Long Stratton (Norfolk)

Old Coach House, Ipswich Rd., Long Stratton Norfolk. T. (01508) 30942. - Paint / Furn - 068068

Long Sutton (Lincolnshire)

Northam, E. and J., 15 High St., Long Sutton Lincs. T. (01406) 363191. - Ant / Silv / Lights / Glass - 068069
Trade Antiques, 7 Market St., Long Sutton Lincs. T. (01406) 363758. - Naut / Instr - 068070

Longridge (Lancashire)

Charnley Fine Arts, Preston Rd, Longridge Lancs.
T. (01772) 782800. - Paint - 068071
Folly, 21 Inglewhite Rd., Longridge Lancs.
T. (01772) 784786. - Furn - 068072
Joy's Shop, 83 Berry Lane, Longridge Lancs.
T. (01772) 782083. - Furn / China / Jew /
Lights - 068073
Kitchenalia, 36 Inglewhite Rd., Longridge Lancs.
T. (01772) 785411. - Furn / China - 068074

Looe (Cornwall)

Dowling & Bray, Fore St., Looe PL13 1AE.
T. (01503) 262797. - Ant / Furn - 068075
Martin, Tony, Fore St., Looe Cornwall.
T. (01503) 262734. - Paint / Furn / Silv / Glass - 068076
West Quay Curios, 6 The Quay, Looe Cornwall.
T. (01503) 264411. - Ant - 068077

Lostwithiel (Cornwall)

Bragg, John, 35 Fore St., Lostwithiel PL22 0BN.
T. (01208) 872827. - Furn - 068078
Old Palace Antiques, Old Palace, Quay St., Lostwithiel
PL22 0BS. T. (01208) 872909. - Ant / Furn - 068079

Loughborough (Leicestershire)

Copperfield Antiques, 221a Derby Rd., Loughborough
Leics. T. (01509) 232026. - Paint / Furn /
China - 068080
Lowe, 37-40 Church Gate, Loughborough LE11 1UE.
T. (01509) 212554. - Graph / Furn / China /
Instr - 068081

Loughton (Essex)

Morris, Pearl, Loughton Essex. T. (0181) 5087177.
- Ant - 068082

Low Fell (Tyne and Wear)

Jewett N., 639/643 Durham Rd, Low Fell Tyne & Wear.
T. (0191) 487 7636. - Furn / China / Glass - 068083

Lowestoft (Suffolk)

Taylor, W., 13 Saint Peters St., Lowestoft Suffolk.
T. (01502) 573374. - Ant / Paint / Furn - 068084
Windsor Gallery, 167 London Rd. South, Lowestoft Suf-
folk. T. (01502) 512278. - Paint - 068085

Lubenham (Leicestershire)

Leicestershire Sporting Gallery, 62 Main St., Lubenham
LE16 9DG. T. (01858) 465787. - Paint / Furn - 068086
Stevens & Son, 61 Main St., Lubenham Leics.
T. (01858) 463521. - Ant / Furn - 068087

Ludlow (Shropshire)

Antique Corner, 12 Old St., Ludlow Shrops.
T. (01584) 873176. - Furn - 068088
Architectural Antiques, 140 Corve St., Ludlow Shrops.
T. (01584) 876207. - Ant / Lights - 068089
Bayliss, D. W. and A. B., 22 Old St., Ludlow Shrops.
T. (01584) 873634. - Furn / Silv - 068090
Cave, R. G., 17 Broad St., Ludlow Shrops.
T. (01584) 873568. - Furn / Instr - 068091
Corve Galleries, 12 Corve St., Ludlow Shrops.
T. (01584) 873420, Fax (01562) 825249. - Ant /
Furn - 068092
Curiosity Shop, 127 Old St., Ludlow Shrops.
T. (01584) 875927. - Paint / Furn / Mil - 068093
Ginger, G. & D., 5 Corve St., Ludlow Shrops.
T. (01584) 876939. - Furn - 068094
Marler, Jane, Dawes Mansion, Church St., Ludlow
Shrops. T. (01584) 874160. - Paint / Graph - 068095
Mitre House Antiques, Corve Bridge, Ludlow Shrops.
T. (01584) 872138. - Ant / Furn / Instr - 068096
Pepper Lane Antique Centre, Pepper Lane, Ludlow
Shrops. T. (01584) 876494. - Paint / Furn / China /
Jew / Silv / Glass - 068097
Saint Leonards Antiques, Corve St., Ludlow Shrops.
T. (01584) 875573. - Paint / Furn / China / Tex /
Jew - 068098
Taylor, M. and R., 53 Broad St., Ludlow Shrops.
T. (01584) 874169. - Ant / Furn / Tex - 068099
Teme Valley Antiques, 1 The Bull Ring, Ludlow Shrops.
T. (01584) 874686. - Paint / Furn / China / Silv /
Glass - 068100

Lurgan (Co. Armagh)

Gardiner, Charles, 48 High St., Lurgan N. Ireland.
T. (01762) 323934. - Ant / Furn / Instr - 068101

Luton (Bedfordshire)

Bargain Box, 4 and 6a Adelaide St., Luton Beds.
T. (01582) 423 809. - Ant - 068102
Bernadette's Antiques, 19a Ardelaide St., Luton Beds.
T. (01582) 21469. - Ant - 068103
Denton, J., Rear of 440 Dunstable Rd., Luton Beds.
T. (01582) 582726. - Furn / Naut - 068104
Foye Gallery, 15 Stanley St., Luton Beds.
T. (01582) 38487. - Paint / Graph / Draw - 068105
Knight's Gallery, 59-61 Guildford St., Luton Beds.
T. (01582) 36266. - Paint - 068106

Lydford (Devon)

Skeaping Gallery, Townend House, Lydford Devon.
T. (0182) 282383. - Paint - 068107

Lymington (Hampshire)

Captain's Cabin Antiques, 1 Quay St., Lymington Hants.
T. (01590) 672912. - Paint / Furn / China /
Naut - 068108
Corfield Antiques, 120 High St., Lymington SO4 9AQ.
T. (01590) 673532. - Furn / Paint / China / Mil - 068109
Lymington Antiques Centre, 76 High St., Lymington
Hants. T. (01590) 670934. - Ant - 068110

Lytchett Minster (Dorset)

Old Button Shop, Lytchett Minster Dorset.
T. (01202) 622169. - Ant - 068111

Lytham (Lancashire)

Clifton Antiques, 8 Market Sq., Lytham Lancs.
T. (01253) 736356. - Furn / Jew / Silv - 068112

Macclesfield (Cheshire)

Bolton, Paula, 38/85 Chestergate, Macclesfield Cheshi-
re. T. (01625) 433033, Fax (01625) 430033. - Paint /
Furn / Jew / Silv - 068113
Brooks, Philip, 6 West Bank Rd., Upton, Macclesfield
Cheshire. T. (01625) 426275. - Paint / Graph - 068114
Cheshire Antiques, 88-96 Chestergate, Macclesfield
Cheshire. T. (01625) 423268. - Furn / China /
Glass - 068115
Copperfield, Robert, 5-7 Chester Rd., Macclesfield
Cheshire. T. (01625) 511233. - Paint / Furn / Tex /
Eth - 068116
Gatehouse Antiques, 72 Chestergate, Macclesfield.
T. (01625) 426476. - Ant / Furn / Jew / Silv /
Glass - 068117
Hidden Gem, 3 Chester Rd., Macclesfield Cheshire.
T. (01625) 828348. - Ant / Paint - 068118
Hills Antiques, Grosvenor Centre, Macclesfield Cheshire.
T. (01625) 420777. - Furn / Num - 068119
Massey & Son, D. J., 47 Chestergate, Macclesfield
Cheshire. T. (01625) 616133. - Jew - 068120

Maentwrog (Gwynedd)

Harvey-Owen Antiques, Old School, Maentwrog Wales.
T. (0176) 685310. - Ant - 068121

Maidenhead (Berkshire)

Jaspers, 36 Queen St., Maidenhead Berks.
T. (01628) 36459. - Paint / Graph - 068122
Miscellanea, 71 Saint Marks Rd., Maidenhead Berks.
T. (01628) 23058. - Ant / Furn - 068123
Widmerpool House Antiques, Boulters Lock, Maidenhead
Berks. T. (01628) 23752. - Paint / Furn / China / Silv /
Glass - 068124

Maidstone (Kent)

Charles, 3 Market St., Maidstone Kent.
T. (01622) 682882. - Naut - 068125
Salmagundi, 63 Charlton St., Maidstone Kent.
T. (01622) 726859. - Ant - 068126
Sutton Valence Antiques, Unit 4, Haslemere, Maidstone
Kent. T. (01622) 675332. - Furn - 068127

Maldon (Essex)

Abacus Antiques, 105 High St., Maldon CM9 7EP.
T. (01621) 850528. - Ant - 068128

Antique Rooms, 63D High St., Maldon CM9 7EB.
T. (01621) 856985. - Paint / Furn / China / Silv /
Glass - 068129
Beardall, Clive, 104B High St, Maldon Essex.
T. (01621) 857890. - Furn - 068130
Maldon Antiques and Collectors Market, Maarket Hill,
Maldon CM9 7PZ. T. (017872) 22826. - Ant - 068131

Malmesbury (Wiltshire)

Antiques, 56 High St., Malmesbury Wilts.
T. (01666) 823089. - Paint / China - 068132
Britten, Andrew, 48 High St., Malmesbury Wilts.
T. (01666) 823376. - Furn / China / Glass - 068133
Cross Hayes Antiques, 19 Bristol St., Malmesbury SN6
0AY. T. (01666) 824260, Fax (01666) 823020.
- Furn - 068134
Dovetail Antiques, 67/69 High St, Malmesbury SN16
9AG. T. (01666) 822191. - Furn - 068135
Kadwell, J. P., Silver St., Malmesbury Wilts.
T. (01666) 823589. - Ant - 068136
Relic Antiques, Brillscote Farm, Lea, Malmesbury Wilts.
T. (01666) 822332. - Furn / Dec - 068137

Malpas (Cheshire)

Evans, Stewart, Church St., Malpas Cheshire.
T. (01948) 860214. - Ant / Furn - 068138

Malton (North Yorkshire)

Malton Antique Market, 2 Old Maltongate, Malton Yorks
North. T. (01653) 692732. - Ant / Furn / China /
Glass - 068139
Maw, Matthew, 18 Castlegate, Malton Yorks North.
T. (01653) 694638. - Furn / Naut - 068140
Talents Fine Arts, 7 Market Pl., Malton Yorks North.
T. (01653) 600020. - Paint / Graph - 068141

Malvern Link (Hereford and Worcester)

Kimber and Son, 6 Lower Howsell Rd., Malvern Link
WR14 1SS. T. (01684) 574339. - Ant / Furn - 068142

Malvern Wells (Hereford and Worcester)

Gandolfi House, 211-213 Wells Rd., Malvern Wells Herefs & Worcs. T. (01684) 569747. - Paint / Graph /
Furn - 068143

Manchester (Greater Manchester)

Abstract Antiques, 16 Lloyd St., Manchester Lancs.
- Furn / China / Glass - 068144
Albion Antiques, 643 Stockport Rd, Manchester Lancs.
T. (0161) 225 4957. - Furn - 068145
Antique Fireplaces, 1000 Stockport Rd, Manchester
Lands. T. (0161) 431 8075. - Ant - 068146
A S Antique Galleries, 26 Broad St., Salford, Manche-
ster Lancs. T. (0161) 737 5938, Fax (0161) 7376626.
- Ant / Furn / Sculp / Silv / Lights - 068147
Authentiques, 373 Bury New Rd, Manchester Lancs.
T. (0161) 773 9601, Fax (0161) 7259579. - Paint /
Graph / Furn / China / Silv - 068148
Baron Antiques, 13 Clifton Rd., Manchester Lancs.
T. (0161) 773 9929, Fax (0161) 9290299. - Furn / Chi-
na / Instr / Naut - 068149
Boodle & Dunthore, 1 King St., Manchester Lancs.
T. (0161) 833 9000. - Jew / Silv / Instr - 068150
Cathedral Jewellers, 26 Cathedral St., Manchester
Lancs. T. (0161) 832 3042. - Jew - 068151
Chestergate Antiques, 1034 Stockport Rd, Manchester
Lancs. T. (0161) 224 7795. - Furn / Instr - 068152
Christabelle's Antiques, 973 Stockport Rd, Manchester
Lancs. T. (0161) 225 4666. - Ant - 068153
Didsbury Antiques, 21 Range Rd, Manchester Lancs.
T. (0161) 227 9979. - Paint / Furn / China - 068154
Family Antiques, 405/407 Bury New Rd, Manchester
Lancs. T. (0161) 798 0036. - Ant - 068155
Fulda Gallery, 19 Vine St, Manchester Lancs.
T. (0161) 792 1962. - Paint - 068156
Garson & Co., 47 Houldsworth St., Manchester M1 2ES.
T. (0161) 236 9393, Fax (0161) 2364211. - Paint /
Instr - 068157
Ginnel, 16 Lloyd St., Manchester M2 5ND.
T. (0161) 833 9037. - Furn / China / Glass - 068158
Haworth, M. and N., Saint Ann's Sq, Manchester Lancs.
T. (0161) 834 2929, Fax (0161) 8394714.
- Num - 068159

Manchester Antique Company, 95 Lapwing Ln., Manchester Lancs. T. (0161) 434 7752. - Furn -   *068160*
Quentin, Paul, 626 Manchester Rd, Manchester Lancs. T. (0161) 766 6673. - Ant / Mil -   *068161*
Royal Exchange Shopping Centre, Saint Ann's Sq., Exchange St., Manchester Lancs. T. (0161) 8343731. - Ant -   *068162*
Saint James Antiques, 41 South King St., Manchester Lancs. T. (0161) 834 9632. - Paint / Jew -   *068163*
Village Antiques, 416 Bury New Rd, Manchester Lancs. T. (0161) 773 3612. - Furn / China / Glass -   *068164*

Manningtree (Essex)
Forty Nine, High St., Manningtree Essex. T. (01206) 396170. - Ant -   *068165*
Freestone, F., 29 Colchester Rd., Manningtree Essex. T. (01206) 392998. - Ant / Furn / Instr -   *068166*

Mansfield (Nottinghamshire)
Antiques Warehouse, 375 Chesterfield Rd. North, Mansfield Notts. T. (01623) 810480. - Furn -   *068167*
Fair Deal Antiques, 138 Chesterfield Rd. North, Mansfield Notts. T. (01623) 653768. - Furn / Naut -   *068168*
Mansfield Antiques, 49-51 Ratcliffe Gate, Mansfield Notts. T. (01623) 27475. - Furn -   *068169*
Sheppards Antiques, 122-124 Chesterfield Rd. North, Mansfield Notts. T. (01623) 631691. - Ant / Furn -   *068170*

Manton (Leicestershire)
Smith, David, 20 Saint Mary's Rd., Manton Leics. T. (0137) 285244. - Ant / Furn / Silv / Glass -   *068171*

Margate (Kent)
Furniture Mart, Grotto Hill, Margate CT9 2BV. T. (01843) 220653. - Ant / Naut -   *068172*
Manor House Antiques and Furniture, 45/46 Arlington Sq, Margate Kent. T. (01843) 295025. - Furn / China -   *068173*

Market Bosworth (Leicestershire)
Corner Cottages Antiques, 5 Market Pl., Market Bosworth Leics. T. (01455) 290344. - Paint / Furn / China / Silv / Instr -   *068174*
Country Antiques, 4 Main St., Market Bosworth Leics. T. (01455) 291303. - Furn -   *068175*

Market Deeping (Lincolnshire)
Portland House Antiques, 23 Church St., Market Deeping Leics. T. (01778) 347129. - Furn / China / Glass -   *068176*

Market Harborough (Leicestershire)
Abbey Antiques, 17 Abbey St., Market Harborough Leics. T. (01858) 462282. - Furn -   *068177*
Kimbell, Richard, Riverside Industrial Estate, Market Harborough LE16 7PT. T. (01858) 433444, Fax (01858) 467627. - Furn -   *068178*
Stamp & Sons, J., 15 Kettering Rd., Market Harborough Leics. T. (01858) 462524. - Furn -   *068179*
Watts, 64 Saint Marys Rd., Market Harborough Leics. T. (01858) 432314. - Tex -   *068180*

Market Rasen (Lincolnshire)
Harwood Tate, Church Mill, Caistor Rd., Market Rasen Leics. T. (01673) 843579. - Furn / Instr -   *068181*

Market Weighton (Humberside)
Dyson & Sons, C. G., 51 Market Pl., Market Weighton Humberside North. T. (01430) 872391. - Paint / Jew / Silv / Instr -   *068182*
Grannie's Attic, Kiplingcotes Station, Market Weighton Humberside North. T. (01430) 810284. - Ant -   *068183*
Houghton Hall Antiques, Cliffe Rd, Market Weighton YO4 3RE. T. (01430) 873234. - Paint / Furn / China -   *068184*
Plantenga, Pieter, 49 Home Rd., Market Weighton Humberside North. T. (01430) 872473. - Furn -   *068185*

Marlborough (Wiltshire)
Antique and Book Collector, Katharine House, The Parade, Marlborough Wilts. T. (01672) 514040. - Paint / Graph / Furn / China / Silv / Glass -   *068186*
Cook, High Trees House, Savernake Forest, Marlborough Wilts. T. (01672) 513017, Fax (01672) 514455. - Paint / Furn -   *068187*

Cracknell, Nigel, 138 High St., Marlborough SN8 1HN. T. (01672) 512912. - Furn -   *068188*
Kime, Robert, Upper Farm, Fosbury, Marlborough Wilts. T. (0126 489) 268. - Furn -   *068189*
Lacewing Fine Art Gallery, 124 High St., Marlborough SN8 1LZ. T. (01672) 514580. - Paint -   *068190*
Marlborough Parade Antique Centre, The Parade, Marlborough Wilts. T. (01672) 515331. - Ant -   *068191*
Principia Arts and Sciences, 5 London Rd., Marlborough SN8 1PH. T. (01672) 512072, Fax (01672) 512072. - Ant -   *068192*
Stuart, 4 London Rd., Marlborough Wilts. T. (01672) 513593. - Ant -   *068193*
Turner, Annmarie, 22 Salisbury Rd., Marlborough Wilts. T. (01672) 515396. - Paint / Furn -   *068194*

Matching Green (Essex)
Stone Hall Antiques, Down Hall Rd., Matching Green Essex. T. (01279) 731440. - Furn -   *068195*

Mathon (Hereford and Worcester)
Mathon Gallery, Mathon Court, Mathon Herefs & Worcs. T. (01684) 892242. - Paint / Sculp -   *068196*

Matlock (Derbyshire)
J.H.S. Antiques, 25 Wolds Rise, Matlock Derbys. T. (01629) 584624. - Paint / Furn -   *068197*

Mayfield (Sussex)
Gravener, Wm. J., High St., Mayfield TN20 6AA. T. (01435) 873389. - Furn / Instr -   *068198*

Melbourn (Cambridgeshire)
Hardiman, P. N., 62 High St., Melbourn Cambs. T. (01353) 260093. - Ant / Furn -   *068199*

Melksham (Wiltshire)
Dann Antiques, New Broughton Rd, Melksham Wilts. T. (01225) 707329, Fax (01225) 790120. - Furn -   *068200*
Jaffray, Alan, 16 Market Pl., Melksham SN12 6EX. T. (01225) 702269, Fax (01225) 790413. - Furn -   *068201*

Menston (West Yorkshire)
Antiques, 101 Bradford Rd., Menston Yorks West. T. (01943) 877634. - Ant / Furn / China / Tex / Silv -   *068202*
Park Antiques, 2 North View, Main St., Menston Yorks West. T. (01943) 872392. - Furn -   *068203*

Meonstoke (Hampshire)
Trivess, W. D., Heathfield House, Meonstoke Hants. T. (01489) 877326. - Graph -   *068204*

Merrow (Surrey)
Pine Shop, 174 Epsom Rd., Merrow Surrey. T. (01483) 572533. - Furn -   *068205*

Merstham (Surrey)
Old Smithy Antique Centre, 7 High St., Merstham RH1 3BA. T. (01737) 642306. - Ant -   *068206*

Merton (Devon)
Barometer World, Quicksilver Barn, Merton Devon. T. (01805) 443. - Instr -   *068207*

Mevagissey (Cornwall)
Barron, J., Fore St., Mevagissey Cornwall. T. (01726) 842172. - Ant -   *068208*

Middleham (North Yorkshire)
White Boar Antiques and Books, Kirkgate, Middleham Yorks North. T. (01969) 23901. - Furn / China / Silv / Instr / Glass -   *068209*

Middlesbrough (Cleveland)
Bradley, 327 Linthorpe, Middlesbrough Cleveland. T. (01642) 850518. - Naut -   *068210*

Middleton (Lancashire)
G.G. Exports, 25 Middleton Rd., Middleton Lancs. T. (01524) 851565. - Ant / Furn / Naut -   *068211*

Midhurst (West Sussex)
Churchhill Clocks, West St, Midhurst Sussex West. T. (01730) 813891. - Instr -   *068212*

Eagle House Antiques Market, Market Sq., Midhurst GU29 9NJ. T. (01730) 812718. - Ant -   *068213*
Foord, POB 14, Midhurst Sussex West. T. (0179) 86351. - Furn -   *068214*
Midhurst Antiques Market, Knockhundred Row, Midhurst Sussex West. T. (01730) 814231. - Ant -   *068215*
Midhurst Walk, West St., Midhurst Sussex West. T. (01730) 813207. - Ant -   *068216*
West Street Antiques, West St., Midhurst Sussex West. T. (01730) 815232. - Paint / Furn / China / Tex / Jew -   *068217*

Midsomer Norton
Somervale Antiques, 6 Radstock Rd., Midsomer Norton Avon. T. (01761) 412686. - Glass -   *068218*

Milburn (Cumbria)
Netherley Cottage Antiques, Milburn Cumbria. T. (017683) 61403. - Ant / Paint / Furn / China -   *068219*

Milford (Surrey)
Andrews, Michael, Portsmouth Rd., Milford Surrey. T. (01483) 420765. - Furn -   *068220*

Milford Haven (Dyfed)
Milford Haven Antiques, Robert St., Milford Haven Wales. T. (01646) 692152. - Ant -   *068221*

Milton Keynes (Buckinghamshire)
Temple, Stockwell House, Wavendon, Milton Keynes Bucks. T. (01908) 583597. - Furn / Lights -   *068222*

Milton Lilbourne (Wiltshire)
Gentle, Rupert, Manor House, Milton Lilbourne SN9 5LQ. T. (01672) 63344. - Ant / Paint / Furn -   *068223*

Milverton (Somerset)
Milverton Antiques, Fore St., Milverton Somerset. T. (01823) 400597. - Furn / China / Instr -   *068224*

Minchinghampton (Gloucestershire)
Vosper, J. F., 20 High St., Minchinghampton GL6 9BN. T. 882480. - Ant / Furn / China / Silv / Glass -   *068225*
Wright, Mick and Fanny, The Trumpet, West End, Minchinghampton Glos. T. 883027, Fax (01453) 883027. - Ant / Instr -   *068226*

Minster (Kent)
Lamb, Michael, 2 Church St., Minster Kent. T. (01843) 821666. - Ant / Naut -   *068227*

Mirfield (West Yorkshire)
Brooke, David, 9A Pratt Lane, Mirfield Yorks West. T. (01924) 492483. - Ant / Furn / Silv -   *068228*

Modbury (Devon)
Bell Inn Antiques, 3 Broad St., Modbury Devon. T. (01548) 830715. - Ant / Paint / China / Jew / Silv -   *068229*
Fourteen A, 14A Broad St, Modbury Devon. T. (01548) 830732. - Ant / Tex / Jew -   *068230*
Wild Goose Antiques, 34 Church St., Modbury PL21 0QR. T. (01548) 830715. - Ant / Paint / China / Jew / Silv -   *068231*
Ye Little Shoppe, 1B Broad St, Modbury Devon. T. (01548) 830732. - Furn / China -   *068232*

Moffat (Dumfries and Galloway)
Harthope House Antiques, Church Gate, Moffat Scotland. T. (01683) 20710. - Ant / Furn / Jew -   *068233*

Mold (Clwyd)
Mold Antiques and Interiors, Old Chapel, 91 Wrexham St., Mold Wales. T. (01352) 752979. - Paint / Furn / China -   *068234*

Monmouth (Gwent)
Freeman, Carol, The Gallery, Nailers Ln., Monmouth Wales. T. (01600) 772252. - Ant -   *068235*

Montacute (Somerset)
Lewis, Gerald, Old Estate Yard, Montacute TA15 6XP. T. (01935) 825435. - Furn / Instr -   *068236*
Montacute Antiques, 12 South St., Montacute Somerset. T. (01935) 824786. - Paint / Furn / China / Glass -   *068237*

Montrose (Tayside)

Harper-James, 25-27 Baltic St., Montrose Scotland.
T. (01674) 671307. - Ant / Furn / China / Jew /
Silv - *068238*

Monyash (Derbyshire)

Robinson, A., Chapel St., Monyash Derbys.
T. (0162981) 2926. - Furn / China - *068239*

Morecambe (Lancashire)

Magpies Nest, Unit 4, Queen St, Morecambe Lancs.
T. (01524) 423328. - China / Mil / Glass - *068240*
Vescovi, Luigino, 1 and 3 Back Avondale Rd, Morecam-
be Lancs. T. (01524) 416732. - Ant - *068241*

Moreton-in-Marsh (Gloucestershire)

Antique Centre, London House, High St., Moreton-in-
Marsh Glos. T. (01608) 51084. - Paint / Graph / Furn /
Jew / Silv - *068242*
Astley House Fine Art, Astley House, High St., Moreton-
in-Marsh Glos. T. (01608) 50601, Fax (01608) 51777.
- Paint - *068243*
Avon Gallery, 21 Old Market Way, Moreton-in-Marsh
Glos. T. (01608) 50614. - Graph - *068244*
Brett, Simon, Creswyke House, High St., Moreton-in-
Marsh GL56. T. (01608) 50751, Fax (01608) 51791.
- Ant / Furn - *068245*
Chandlers Antiques, High St., Moreton-in-Marsh Glos.
T. (01608) 51347. - Ant / Furn / China / Silv /
Glass - *068246*
Grimes House Antiques, High St., Moreton-in-Marsh
Glos. T. (01608) 51029. - Furn / China - *068247*
Lemington House Antiques, Oxford St., Moreton-in-
Marsh Glos. T. (01608) 51443. - Furn / China /
Glass - *068248*
Nielsen, M. K., Seaford House, High St., Moreton-in-
Marsh Glos. T. (01608) 50448. - Ant / Paint / Furn /
China - *068249*
Parker, Elizabeth, High St., Moreton-in-Marsh Glos.
T. (01608) 50917. - Paint / Furn / China / Instr - *068250*
Roberts, Peter, High St., Moreton-in-Marsh Glos.
T. (01608) 50698. - Furn - *068251*
Sampson, Anthony, Dale House, Moreton-in-Marsh Glos.
T. (01608) 50763. - Furn - *068252*
Windsor House Antiques Centre, High St., Moreton-in-
Marsh Glos. T. (01608) 50993. - Ant - *068253*

Moretonhampstead (Devon)

Old Brass Kettle, 2-4 Ford St., Moretonhampstead Devon. T. (01647) 40334. - Furn / China - *068254*

Mousehole (Cornwall)

Vanity Fayre, Commercial Rd., Mousehole Cornwall.
- Furn / China / Instr - *068255*

Much Hadham (Hertfordshire)

Careless Cottage Antiques, High St., Much Hadham
Herts. T. (0127) 9842007. - Ant / Furn / China /
Glass - *068256*

Much Wenlock (Shropshire)

Cruck House Antiques, 23 Barrow St., Much Wenlock
Shrops. T. (01952) 727165. - Ant / Paint / Furn - *068257*
Wenlock, 3 The Square, Much Wenlock Shrops.
T. (01952) 728232. - Paint - *068258*

Nailsworth (Gloucestershire)

Hand, 3 Bridge St., Nailsworth Glos. T. (0145383) 4967.
- Paint / Graph - *068259*

Nantwich (Cheshire)

Adams Antiques, 57 Welsh Row, Nantwich Cheshire.
T. (01270) 625643. - Furn / Lights / Instr /
Naut - *068260*
Armitage, Tim, 99 Welsh Row, Nantwich Cheshire.
T. (01270) 626608. - Ant - *068261*
Boyer, Rex, Nantwich Cheshire. T. (01270) 625953.
- Furn - *068262*
Chapel Antiques, 47 Hospital St., Nantwich Cheshire.
T. (01270) 629508. - Furn / China / Instr /
Glass - *068263*
Farthings Antiques, 50 Hospital St., Nantwich Cheshire.
T. (01270) 625117. - Furn / China / Silv / Glass - *068264*
Gibson, Roderick, 2 Chapel Court, Hospital St., Nantwich
Cheshire. T. (01270) 625301. - Furn - *068265*

Lions and Unicorns, 33 Hospital St., Nantwich Cheshire.
T. (01270) 628892. - Furn / China / Tex - *068266*
Love Lane Antiques, Love Ln., Nantwich Cheshire.
T. (01270) 626239. - Ant - *068267*
Nantwich Art Deco and Decorative Arts, 87 Welsh Row,
Nantwich Cheshire. T. (01270) 624876. - China /
Lights - *068268*
Pillory House, 18 Pillory St., Nantwich Cheshire.
T. (01270) 623524. - Ant / Furn - *068269*
Richardson Antiques, 89 Hospital St., Nantwich Cheshi-
re. T. (01270) 625963. - Furn / China - *068270*
Wyche House Antiques, 50 Welsh Row, Nantwich Ches-
hire. T. (01270) 627179. - Furn / China / Silv /
Glass - *068271*

Naphill (Buckinghamshire)

Foster, A. and E., Little Heysham, Forge Rd., Naphill
HP14 4SU. T. (01494) 562024. - Ant - *068272*

Narberth (Dyfed)

Barn Court Antiques, 12 High St., Narberth Wales.
T. (01834) 861421. - Paint / Furn / China / Silv /
Glass - *068273*

Nelson (Lancashire)

Blakey, Colin, 115 Manchester Rd., Nelson Lancs.
T. (01282) 64941. - Furn / Instr - *068274*
Britton, 34 Scotland Rd., Nelson Lancs.
T. (01282) 697659. - Ant / Jew - *068275*
Brooks Antiques, 7 Russell St., Nelson Lancs.
T. (01282) 698148. - Furn - *068276*
Margaret's Antique Shop, 79a Scotland Rd., Nelson
Lancs. - Ant - *068277*

Neston (Cheshire)

Vine House Antiques, Parkgate Rd., Neston Cheshire.
T. (0151) 3362423. - Furn / Silv / Glass - *068278*

Newark-on-Trent (Nottinghamshire)

Castle Gate Antiques Centre, 55 Castle Gate, Newark-
on-Trent Notts. T. (01636) 700076. - Ant - *068279*
D. and G. Antiques, 11 Kings Rd., Newark-on-Trent
Notts. T. (01636) 702782. - Paint / Furn / China /
Glass - *068280*
D. and V. Antiques, 4A Northgate, Newark-on-Trent
Notts. T. (01636) 71888. - Furn / Lights / Instr - *068281*
Limb Antiques, R. R., 31-35 Northgate, Newark-on-Trent
Notts. T. (01636) 74546. - Ant / Music - *068282*
Newark Antique Warehouse, Kelham Rd., Newark-on-
Trent Notts. T. (01636) 74869. - Ant - *068283*
Newark Antiques Centre, Regent House, Lombard St.,
Newark-on-Trent Notts. T. (01636) 605504.
- Ant - *068284*
Portland Antiques, 20 Portland St., Newark-on-Trent
Notts. T. (01636) 701478. - Ant / Naut - *068285*
Sarsby, Roger & Michael Picering, Mill Farm, Kirklington,
Newark-on-Trent Notts. T. (01636) 813394.
- Paint - *068286*
Second Time Around, Regent House, Lombard St., Ne-
wark-on-Trent Notts. T. (01636) 605504.
- Instr - *068287*
Spratt Antiques, Jack, Unit 5, George St., Newark-on-
Trent Notts. T. (01636) 707714, Fax (01636) 640595.
- Furn - *068288*
Wade-Smith & Read, 1-3 Castlegate, Newark-on-Trent
Notts. T. (01636) 73792. - Furn - *068289*

Newbury (Berkshire)

Baker Antiques, John, 20 George St, Newbury Berks.
T. (01635) 298744. - Furn - *068290*
Griffons Court, Highclere, Newbury Berks.
T. (01635) 253247. - Paint / Furn - *068291*

Newby Bridge (Cumbria)

Shire Antiques, Post House, High Newton, Newby Bridge
Cumbria. T. (015395) 31431. - Furn - *068292*
Townhead Antiques, Newby Bridge Cumbria.
T. (015395) 31321, Fax (015395) 30019. - Furn / Chi-
na / Jew / Silv / Instr - *068293*

Newcastle Emlyn (Dyfed)

Castle Antiques, Market Sq., Newcastle Emlyn Wales.
T. (01239) 710420. - Ant / Furn / China / Instr - *068294*

Newcastle-under-Lyme (Staffordshire)

Antique Market, The Stones, Newcastle-under-Lyme
Staffs. T. (0171) 6244848. - Ant - *068295*
Errington Antiques, 63 George St., Newcastle-under-
Lyme Staffs. T. (01782) 632822. - Ant / Furn / Orient /
Lights - *068296*
Hood & Broomfield, 29 Albert St., Newcastle-under-
Lyme Staffs. T. (01782) 626859. - Paint - *068297*
Midwinter, Richard, 13 Brunswick St., Newcastle-under-
Lyme Staffs. T. (01782) 712483. - Paint / Furn / China /
Tex - *068298*

Newcastle-upon-Tyne (Tyne and Wear)

Antiques Centre, 8-10 Saint Mary's Pl., Newcastle-
upon-Tyne Tyne & Wear. T. (0191) 232 3821.
- Ant - *068299*
Davidson, 94 and 96 Grey St, Newcastle-upon-Tyne NE1
6AG. T. (0191) 232 2551. - Jew / Silv - *068300*
Dean Gallery, 42 Dean St., Newcastle-upon-Tyne Tyne &
Wear. T. (0191) 232 1208. - Paint - *068301*
Intercoin, 99 Clayton St., Newcastle-upon-Tyne Tyne &
Wear. T. (0191) 232 2064. - Num / Jew / Silv - *068302*
Owen, 14 Shields Rd., Byker, Newcastle-upon-Tyne
Tyne & Wear. T. (0191) 265 4332. - Jew - *068303*
Shiner, 123 Jesmond St., Newcastle-upon-Tyne Tyne &
Wear. T. (0191) 281 6474. - Ant - *068304*
Spicer, 75 Grainger Market, Newcastle-upon-Tyne Tyne
& Wear. T. (0191) 232 5057. - Jew - *068305*
Warner Fine Art, 208 Wingrove Rd., Fenham, Newcastle-
upon-Tyne Tyne & Wear. T. (0191) 273 8030. - Paint /
Graph - *068306*

Newhaven (Sussex)

Newhaven Flea Market, 28 South Way, Newhaven Sus-
sex East. T. (01273) 517207. - Ant - *068307*
Russell, Leonard, 21 Kings Av, Newhaven Sussex East.
T. (01273) 515153. - China - *068308*

Newmarket (Suffolk)

Equus Art Gallery, Sun Ln., Newmarket Suffolk.
T. (01638) 560445. - Paint / Graph / Sculp - *068309*
Godfrey, Jemima, 5 Rous Rd., Newmarket Suffolk.
T. (01638) 663584. - Ant / Tex / Jew - *068310*
Newmarket Gallery, 156 High St., Newmarket Suffolk.
T. (01638) 661183. - Paint / Graph / Draw - *068311*

Newnham-on-Severn (Gloucestershire)

Cottonwood, Old House, Lower High St., Newnham-on-
Severn Glos. T. (01594) 516633. - Furn - *068312*
Cottonwood, High St., Newnham-on-Severn Glos.
T. (01594) 516633. - Furn - *068313*

Newport (Essex)

Brown House Antiques, High St., Newport Essex.
T. (01799) 40238. - Furn - *068314*
Newport Gallery, High St., Newport CB11 3QZ.
T. (01799) 40623. - Paint / Graph - *068315*

Newport (Gwent)

Antiques of Newport, 82 Chepstow Rd., Newport Wales.
T. (01633) 259935. - Furn / China / Jew / Silv - *068316*
Beechwood Antiques, 418 Chepstow Rd., Newport
Wales. T. (01633) 279192. - Ant - *068317*

Newport (Isle of Wight)

Heath, Mike, 3-4 Holywood St., Newport I. of Wight.
T. (01983) 525748. - Ant - *068318*
Rose Antiques Centre, 87 Pyle St., Newport I. of Wight.
T. (01983) 528850. - Furn / China / Jew / Silv - *068319*
Watts, Chris, Heylesbury, Worsley Rd., Newport I. of
Wight. T. (01983) 298963, Fax (01983) 290571.
- Paint / Furn / Instr - *068320*

Newport (Shropshire)

Worth's, 34 Saint Marys St., Newport Shrops.
T. (01952) 810122. - Ant / Naut - *068321*

Newry (Co. Down)

Downshire House Antiques, 62 Downshire Rd., Newry N.
Ireland. T. (01693) 66689. - Ant / Furn / China - *068322*
McCabe, 11-12 Saint Mary's St., Newry N. Ireland.
T. (01693) 62695. - Ant / Furn / China - *068323*

Newton Abbott (Devon)
Newton Abbot Antiques Centre, 55 East St., Newton Abbott Devon. T. (01626) 54074. - Ant -   *068324*
Old Treasures, 126a Queen St., Newton Abbott TQ12 2EV. T. (01626) 67181. - China / Jew / Glass -   *068325*

Newton Stewart (Dumfries and Galloway)
Pathbrae Antiques, 20 Albert St., Newton Stewart Scotland. T. (01671) 3429. - China / Jew / Silv -   *068326*

Newtonmore (Highland)
Antique Shop, Main St., Newtonmore Scotland.
  T. (01540) 673272. - Furn / China / Silv / Glass - *068327*

Newtownabbey (Co. Antrim)
New Abbey Antiques, Caragh Lodge, Glen Rd., Newtownabbey BT37 0RY. T. (01232) 862036, Fax 853281.
- Ant / Furn -   *068328*

North Petherton (Somerset)
Kathleen's Antiques, 60 Fore St., North Petherton Somerset. T. (01278) 662535. - Paint / Furn / China / Silv /
Instr -   *068329*

North Shields (Tyne and Wear)
Coulson, Peter, 8-10 Queen Alexandra Rd., North Shields Tyne & Wear. T. (0191) 257 9761. - Ant / Instr - *068330*
May's, Maggie, 49 Kirton Park Terrace, North Shields Tyne & Wear. T. (0191) 257 0076. - Ant / Paint / Furn /
China -   *068331*

North Walsham (Norfolk)
Anglia Antique Exporters, Station Yard, Norwich Rd, North Walsham Norfolk. T. (01692) 406266. - Furn /
Naut -   *068332*
Bates & Sons, Eric, Melbourne House, Bacton Rd., North Walsham Norfolk. T. (01692) 403221. - Ant /
Furn -   *068333*
North Walsham Antique Gallery, 29 Grammar School Rd., North Walsham Norfolk. T. (01692) 405059.
- Furn / China / Silv / Glass -   *068334*

Northallerton (North Yorkshire)
Antique and Art, 7 Central Arcade, Northallerton Yorks North. T. (01609) 772051. - Paint / Graph / China / Silv /
Glass -   *068335*
Collectors Corner, 145-146 High St., Northallerton Yorks North. T. (01609) 777623. - Ant -   *068336*

Northampton (Northamptonshire)
Adne and Naxos, 71-73 Kingsthorpe Rd., Northampton Northants. T. (01604) 710740. - Furn -   *068337*
Buley Antiques, 164 Kettering Rd., Northampton Northants. T. (01604) 31588. - Ant -   *068338*
Cave, F. and C. H., 111 Kettering Rd., Northampton NN1 4BA. T. (01604) 38278. - Ant / Furn -   *068339*
Jones, Michael, 1 Gold St., Northampton Northants.
  T. (01604) 32548. - Jew / Silv / Instr -   *068340*
Nostalgia Antiques, 190 Kettering Rd., Northampton Northants. T. (01604) 33823. - Ant / Instr - *068341*
Penny's Antiques, 83 Kettering Rd., Northampton Northants. T. (01604) 32429. - Furn / China / Naut - *068342*
Regent House, Royal Terrace, Northampton Northants.
  T. (01604) 37992. - Furn -   *068343*
Savage & Son, R. S. J., Alfred St., Northampton Northants. T. (01604) 20327. - Paint / Graph - *068344*

Northchapel (West Sussex)
Callingham, D. and A., Northchapel Sussex West.
  T. (0142) 878379. - Furn -   *068345*
Callingham, N. and S., London Rd, Northchapel Sussex West. T. (0142) 878379. - Furn -   *068346*
Mason, J., Rose Villa, London Rd., Northchapel Sussex West. T. (01428) 707500. - Instr -   *068347*

Northfleet (Kent)
Northfleet Hill Antiques, 36 The Hill, Northfleet Kent.
  T. (01474) 321521. - Furn -   *068348*

Northleach (Gloucestershire)
Harding, Keith, Oak House, High St., Northleach GL54 3EU. T. (01451) 60181, Fax (01451) 861133. - Instr /
Music -   *068349*
Northleach Gallery, The Green, Northleach.
  T. (01451) 60519. - Graph -   *068350*

Northop Mold (Clwyd)
Morris & Co, James H., Old Village School, The Green, Northop Mold CH7 6BD. T. (0135) 286768. - Furn /
Instr -   *068351*

Norwich (Norfolk)
Albrow & Sons, 10 All Saints Green, Norwich Norfolk.
  T. (01603) 622569. - China / Jew / Silv / Glass - *068352*
Allchin, William, 22-24 Saint Benedict St., Norwich Norfolk. T. (01603) 660046, Fax (01603) 660046. - Furn /
Lights -   *068353*
Bank House Gallery, 71 Newmarket Rd., Norwich Norfolk. T. (01603) 633380, Fax (01603) 633387.
- Paint -   *068354*
Brett & Sons, Arthur, 40-44 Saint Giles St., Norwich NOR 16E. T. (01603) 628171, Fax (01603) 630245. - Furn /
China / Sculp -   *068355*
Cathedral Gallery, 93 Upper St., Norwich Norfolk.
  T. (01603) 624800. - Graph -   *068356*
Cloisters Antiques Fair, Saint Andrew's Plain, Norwich Norfolk. T. (01603) 628477, Fax (01603) 762182.
- Ant -   *068357*
Country and Eastern, 8 Redwell St., Norwich Norfolk.
  T. (01603) 623107. - Furn / Tex -   *068358*
Crome Gallery, 34 Elm Hill, Norwich Norfolk.
  T. (01603) 622827. - Paint / Graph -   *068359*
D'Amico Antiques, 20 Highland Rd., Norwich Norfolk.
  T. (01603) 52320. - Furn / Instr -   *068360*
Dennett, Clive, 66 Saint Benedicts St., Norwich Norfolk.
  T. (01603) 624315. - Num -   *068361*
Fairhurst Gallery, 13 Bedford St., Norwich Norfolk.
  T. (01603) 614214. - Paint / Fra -   *068362*
Hallam, Michael, 17 Magdalen St., Norwich Norfolk.
  T. (01603) 413692. - Paint / Furn / China - *068363*
Haugh, Roderic, Fairhurst Gallery, Bedford St, Norwich Norfolk. T. (01603) 614214. - Furn -   *068364*
Howkins, John, 1 Dereham Rd., Norwich Norfolk.
  T. (01603) 627832, Fax (01603) 666626.
- Furn -   *068365*
Jarrett, G., 12-14 Old Palace Rd., Norwich Norfolk.
  T. (01603) 625847. - Ant -   *068366*
Levine, Leona, 35 St Giles St, Norwich NR2 1HL.
  T. (01603) 628709. - Silv -   *068367*
Maddermarket Antiques, 18c Lower Goat Ln., Norwich Norfolk. T. (01603) 620610. - Jew / Silv - *068368*
Mandell's Gallery, Elm Hill, Norwich Norfolk.
  T. (01603) 626892, Fax (01603) 767471.
- Paint -   *068369*
Movie Shop, 11 Saint Gregory's Alley, Norwich Norfolk.
  T. (01603) 615239. - Ant / Furn / China / Tex - *068370*
Ninety-One, 91 Upper Saint Giles St., Norwich Norfolk.
- Furn -   *068371*
Queen of Hungary Antiques, 49 Saint Benedicts St., Norwich Norfolk. T. (01603) 625082. - Furn - *068372*
Saint Michael at Plea Antiques, Bank Plain, Norwich Norfolk. T. (01603) 619129. - Ant -   *068373*
Sebley, Owald, 20 Lower Goat Lane, Norwich Norfolk.
  T. (01603) 626504. - Jew / Silv -   *068374*
This and That, 56 Bethel St., Norwich Norfolk.
  T. (01603) 632201. - Ant / Furn -   *068375*
Tillett, James & Ann, 12-13 Tombland, Norwich Norfolk.
  T. (01603) 624914. - Jew / Silv / Instr - *068376*
Tillett & Co, Thomas, 17 Saint Giles St., Norwich Norfolk.
  T. (01603) 625922. - Jew / Silv -   *068377*
Tooltique, 54 Waterloo Rd., Norwich Norfolk.
  T. (01603) 414289. - Ant -   *068378*
Turner, Malcolm, 15 Saint Giles St., Norwich Norfolk.
  T. (01603) 627007. - China / Silv -   *068379*
Yesteryear, 24D Magdalen St, Norwich Norfolk.
  T. (01603) 622908. - Paint / Paint / Furn - *068380*

Nottingham (Nottinghamshire)
Antiques and General Trading, 145 Lower Parliament St., Nottingham Notts. T. (0115) 9585971.
- Furn -   *068381*
Breck, 726 Mansfield Rd, Nottingham Notts.
  T. (0115) 9605263. - Furn / China -   *068382*
Golden Cage, 99 Derby Rd., Nottingham.
  T. (0115) 9411794. - Tex -   *068383*
Granny's Attic, 308 Carlton Hill, Carlton, Nottingham Notts. T. (0115) 9265204. - Ant / Furn / Toys - *068384*
Hockley Coins, 170 Derby Rd., Nottingham Notts.
  T. (0115) 9790667. - Num -   *068385*

Kemp, Melville, 79-81 Derby Rd., Nottingham NG1.
  T. (0115) 9417055, Fax (01602) 417055. - China /
Jew / Silv / Glass -   *068386*
Lustre Metal Antiques, Meadow Ln, Nottingham NG7 3GD. T. (0115) 863523. - Ant / Silv -   *068387*
Mitchell, Anthony, 11 Albemarle Rd., Nottingham.
  T. (0115) 623865. - Paint -   *068388*
Nottingham Antique Centre, London Rd, Nottingham Notts. T. (0115) 9504504, 9505548. - Furn / China /
Instr -   *068389*
Pegasus Antiques, 62 Derby Rd., Nottingham Notts.
  T. (0115) 9474220. - Paint / Furn / Jew / Silv - *068390*
Pembleton, S., 306 Carlton Hill, Carlton, Nottingham Notts. T. (0115) 9265204. - Ant -   *068391*
Pollock, Mike, 31 Lees Rd, Nottingham.
  T. (0115) 504027. - Instr -   *068392*
Potter, David and Carole, 76 Derby Rd., Nottingham Notts. T. (0115) 9417911. - Furn / China / Instr /
Glass -   *068393*
Smith, Val, 170 Derby Rd., Nottingham Notts.
  T. (0115) 9781194. - Ant / Num / Jew -   *068394*
Station Pine Antiques, 103 Carrington St., Nottingham Notts. T. (0115) 9582710. - Furn -   *068395*
Top Hat Antiques Centre, 66-72 Derby Rd., Nottingham Notts. T. (0115) 9419143. - Paint / Graph / Furn /
China -   *068396*
Trident Arms, 74 Derby Rd., Nottingham Notts.
  T. (0115) 9474137, Fax (0115) 414199. - Mil - *068397*

Oakham (Leicestershire)
Fine Art of Oakham, 4 High St., Oakham Leics.
  T. (01572) 755221, Fax (01572) 770047.
- Paint -   *068398*
Gallery Antiques, 17 Mill St., Oakham Leics.
  T. (01572) 755094. - Furn / China / Silv - *068399*
Grafton, 153 Brooke Rd., Oakham Leics.
  T. (01572) 757266. - Paint / Graph -   *068400*
Oakham Antiques, 16 Melton Rd., Oakham Leics.
  T. (0166) 479571. - Paint / Graph / Furn / Silv /
Glass -   *068401*
Old House Gallery, 13-15 Market Pl., Oakham Leics.
  T. (01572) 755538. - Paint / Graph / China - *068402*
Swans Antique Centre, 27 Mill St., Oakham Leics.
  T. (01572) 724364. - Ant / Furn / China / Tex /
Jew -   *068403*
Warrington, Paul, 46 High St., Oakham Leics.
  T. (01572) 722414. - Furn -   *068404*

Oakley (Hamshire)
Hutchins, E. H., 48 Pardown, East Oakley, Oakley RG23 7OZ. T. (01256) 780494. - Ant / Furn -   *068405*

Oban (Southclyde)
Mclan Gallery, 10 Argyll Sq., Oban Scotland.
  T. (01631) 66755. - Paint -   *068406*
Oban Antiques, 35 Stevenson St., Oban Scotland.
  T. (01631) 66203. - Ant / Furn -   *068407*

Odiham (Hampshire)
Monaltrie, 76 High St., Odiham Hants.
  T. (01256) 702660. - Furn / Silv -   *068408*
Odiham Gallery, 78 High St., Odiham Hants.
  T. (01256) 703415. - Tex -   *068409*

Okehampton (Devon)
Jones, Alan, Fatherford Farm, Okehampton Devon.
  T. (01837) 52970. - Ant / Paint / Furn - *068410*

Oldham (Lancashire)
Heritage Antiques, 123 Milnrow Rd, Oldham Lancs.
  T. (01706) 842385. - Ant -   *068411*
Howell, Charles, 2 Lord St., Oldham Lancs.
  T. (0161) 624 1479. - Jew / Silv / Instr - *068412*
Simpson & Sons, H. C., 37 High St., Oldham Lancs.
  T. (0161) 624 7187. - Jew / Silv -   *068413*
Valley Antiques, Soho St., Oldham Lancs.
  T. (0161) 624 5030. - Ant / Furn / China - *068414*
Waterloo Antiques, 16 Waterloo St., Oldham Lancs.
  T. (0161) 624 5975, Fax 8061) 6245975. - Furn /
Jew -   *068415*

Ollerton (Nottinghamshire)
Hamlyn Lodge, Station Rd., Ollerton Notts.
  T. (01623) 823600. - Ant -   *068416*

Olney (Buckinghamshire)

Market Square Antiques, Market Sq., Olney Bucks.
T. (01234) 712172. - Paint / China / Silv / Instr /
Glass - 068417

Martin, Alan, Clickers Yard, Olney Bucks.
T. (01234) 712446. - Instr - 068418

Olney Antique Centre, Rose Court, Market Pl., Olney
Bucks. T. (01234) 712172. - Furn / China / Tex /
Jew - 068419

Overland, John, Rose Court, Market Pl., Olney Bucks.
T. (01234) 712351. - Furn / Instr - 068420

Unsworth 28, Robin, 1 Weston Rd., Olney Bucks.
T. (01234) 711210. - Furn / Instr - 068421

Ombersley (Hereford and Worcester)

Stables Antiques, Blacksmith Cottage, Ombersley Herefs
& Worcs. T. (01905) 620353. - Ant / Furn /
China - 068422

Ormskirk (Lancashire)

Grice, Alan, 106 Aughton St., Ormskirk Lancs.
T. (01695) 572007. - Furn - 068423

Revival Pine Stripping, 181 Southport Rd., Ormskirk
Lancs. T. (01695) 578308. - Furn - 068424

Orpington (Greater London)

Antica, 48 High St., Orpington Kent. T. (01689) 851181.
- Ant - 068425

Orwell (Cambridgeshire)

West Farm Antiques, High St., Orwell Cambs.
T. (01223) 207464. - Ant / Furn - 068426

Osbournby (Lincolnshire)

Audley House Antiques, North St, Osbournby NG34 0DR.
T. (0152) 95473. - Furn - 068427

Oswestry (Shropshire)

Antique Shop, King St., Oswestry Shrops.
T. (01691) 653011. - Ant - 068428

Oswald Road Antique and Reproduction Centre, Oswald
Rd., Oswestry Shrops. T. (01691) 670690.
- Ant - 068429

Otley (West Yorkshire)

Martin-Clifton Antiques, 28 Westgate, Otley Yorks West.
T. (01943) 851117. - Furn / China / Instr - 068430

Oundle (Northamptonshire)

Quinn Galleries, 36 Market Pl., Oundle Northants.
T. (01832) 273744. - Paint / Furn / Tex - 068431

Outwell (Cambridgeshire)

Haylett, A.P. and M.A., 393 Wisbech Rd., Outwell Cambs.
T. (01945) 772427. - Furn / China - 068432

Oxford (Oxfordshire)

Davis, Reginald, 34 High St., Oxford OX1 4AN.
T. (01865) 248347. - Jew / Silv - 068433

Jeremy's, 98 Cowley Rd, Oxford Oxon.
T. (01865) 241011. 068434

Legge, Christopher, 25 Oakthorpe Rd, Oxford OX2 7BD.
T. (01865) 57572, Fax (01865) 54877. - Tex - 068435

Leigh, Laurie, 36 High St., Oxford OX1 4AN.
T. (01865) 244197. - Instr / Music - 068436

Little, Roger, White Lodge, Osler Rd, Oxford Oxon.
T. (01865) 62317. - China - 068437

Magna Gallery, 41 High St., Oxford Oxon.
T. (01865) 245805. - Graph - 068438

Number Ten, 10 North Parade, Oxford.
T. (01865) 512816. - Furn / China - 068439

Oxford Antique Trading Company, 40-41 Park End St.,
Oxford. T. (01865) 793927. - Ant - 068440

Oxford Antiques Centre, 27 Park End St., Oxford.
T. (01865) 251075. - Paint / Furn / Tex / Jew /
Silv - 068441

Oxford Architectural Antiques, Old Depot, Nelson St., Je-
richo, Oxford. T. (01865) 53310. - Ant - 068442

Payne & Son, 131 High St., Oxford OX1 4DH.
T. (01865) 243787. - Jew / Silv - 068443

Rowell, 12 Turl St., Oxford OX1. T. (01865) 242187.
- Jew / Silv - 068444

Saywell, A. J., 15 Hollybush Row, Oxford Oxon.
T. (01865) 248889. - Num - 068445

Oxted (Surrey)

Treasures, 151 Station Rd., Oxted Surrey.
T. (01883) 713301. - Furn / China / Jew / Silv - 068446

Padiham (Lancashire)

Crowther, C., 47 Higham Hall Rd, Padiham.
T. (01282) 774418. - Ant - 068447

Padstow (Cornwall)

Mayflower Antiques, 15 Duke St., Padstow PL28 8AB.
T. (01841) 532308. - China / Jew / Silv - 068448

Painswick (Gloucestershire)

Craig Carrington Antiques, Brook House, Painswick GL6
6SE. T. (01452) 813248. - Furn - 068449

Painswick Antique Centre, New St., Painswick Glos.
T. (01452) 812431. - Ant / Furn / Jew - 068450

Regent Antiques, Dynevor House, New St., Painswick
Glos. T. (01452) 812543. - Furn - 068451

Weavers Cottage Antiques, Friday St, Painswick Glos.
T. (01452) 812609. - Furn - 068452

Paisley (Strathclyde)

Heritage Antiques, Walker St., Paisley Scotland.
T. (01506) 825579. - Ant / Furn / Naut - 068453

Parkstone (Dorset)

Wiffen's Antiques, 95-101 Bournemouth Rd, Parkstone
Dorset. T. (01202) 736567. - Paint / Furn / China / Silv /
Instr - 068454

Pateley Bridge (North Yorkshire)

Cat in the Window Antiques, 22 High St., Pateley Bridge
Yorks North. T. (01423) 711343. - Paint / Furn / China /
Jew / Silv - 068455

Loomes, Brian, Calf Haugh Farm, Bewerley, Pateley
Bridge HG3 5HW. T. (01423) 711163. - Instr - 068456

Pattishall (Northamptonshire)

King, F., Foster Booth Rd., Pattishall Northants.
T. (01327) 830326. - Paint / Furn - 068457

Paulerspury (Northamptonshire)

Antique Galleries, Watling St., Paulerspury Northants.
T. (0132) 733238. - Furn / Instr - 068458

Peasenhall (Suffolk)

Peasenhall Art and Antiques Gallery, The Street, Peasenhall Suffolk. T. (0172) 879224. - Paint / Furn - 068459

Peel (Isle of Man)

Horn, Dorothea, 18A Michael St, Peel I. of Man.
T. (01624) 842170. - Paint / Furn / China / Jew /
Silv - 068460

Pembroke Dock (Dyfed)

Jones, Glyn, 11-13 Bush St., Pembroke Dock Wales.
T. (01646) 621732. - Furn - 068461

Pembroke Antique Centre, The Hall, Hamilton Terrace,
Pembroke Wales. T. (01646) 687017. - Ant - 068462a

Penarth (South Glamorgan)

Corner Cupboard Antiques, 4a Station Approach, Penarth
Wales. T. (01222) 705392. - Ant - 068463

Stanwell, 36 Windsor Terrace, Penarth Wales.
T. (01222) 706906. - Paint / China / Jew / Silv - 068464

Penkridge (Staffordshire)

Golden Oldies, 1 and 5 Crown Bridge, Penkridge Staffs.
T. (01785) 714722. - Paint / Furn - 068465

Penn (Buckinghamshire)

Country Furniture Shop, 3 Hazlemere Rd, Penn Bucks.
T. (0149) 4812244. - Furn - 068466

Penn Barn, By the Pond, Elm Rd., Penn Bucks.
T. (01494) 815691. - Paint - 068467

Wigram, Francis, Cottars Barn, Elm Rd., Penn Bucks.
T. (0149) 4813266. - Furn / China - 068468

Penrith (Cumbria)

Antiques of Penrith, 4 Corney Sq., Penrith CA11 7PX.
T. (01768) 62801. - Ant - 068469

Arcade Antiques and Jewellery, 11 Devonshire Arcade,
Penrith Cumbria. T. (01768) 67754. - Furn /
Jew - 068470

Corney House Antiques, 1 Corney Pl., Penrith Cumbria.
T. (01768) 67665. - Furn / China - 068471

Gallery, 54 Castlegate, Penrith Cumbria.
T. (01768) 65538. - Paint - 068472

James, Joseph, Corney Sq., Penrith CA11 7PX.
T. (01768) 62065. - Furn / Furn / China / Silv - 068473

Penrith Coin and Stamp Centre, 37 King St., Penrith
CA11 7AY. T. (01768) 64185. - Num / Jew - 068474

Pollock, Jane, 4 Castlegate, Penrith Cumbria.
T. (01768) 67211. - Furn / China / Silv - 068475

Penryn (Cornwall)

Broad Street Gallery, 9 Broad St., Penryn Cornwall.
T. (01326) 377216. - Paint / Graph - 068476

Original Choice, 15 Church Rd., Penryn Cornwall.
T. (01326) 375092. - Ant - 068477

Robertson, Leon, 7 The Praze, Penryn Cornwall.
T. (01326) 372767. - Ant - 068478

Penzance (Cornwall)

Ashbrook, Ken, Leskinnick Pl., Penzance Cornwall.
T. (01736) 65477. - Furn - 068479

Catherine and Mary Antiques, Bread St, Penzance Cornwall. T. (01736) 51053. - Furn / Tex / Jew - 068480

Chapel Antiques, 10 Chapel St., Penzance Cornwall.
T. (01736) 63124. - Furn / Instr - 068481

Daphne's Antiques, 17 Chapel St., Penzance Cornwall.
T. (01736) 61719. - Paint / Furn / Jew / Glass - 068482

Humphrys, Brian, 1 Saint Clare St., Penzance TR18 2PB.
T. (01736) 65154. - Furn / Silv / Instr - 068483

Kirk, Barbara and David, 51 Chapel St., Penzance Cornwall. T. (01736) 64507. - Graph / China / Jew /
Glass - 068484

Little Jem's, 56 Chapel St., Penzance Cornwall.
T. (01736) 51400. - Paint / Tex / Jew / Instr - 068485

New Generation Antiques Market, 61-62 Chapel St.,
Penzance Cornwall. T. (01736) 63267. - Paint / Furn /
China / Jew / Silv - 068486

Old Posthouse, 9 Chapel St., Penzance TR18 4AJ.
T. (01736) 60320. - Ant - 068487

Pinewood Studio, 46 Market Jew St., Penzance Cornwall. T. (01736) 68793. - Furn - 068488

Sanders, Tony, 14 Chapel St., Penzance Cornwall.
T. (01736) 66620. - Paint / Furn / China / Silv /
Glass - 068489

Vive Antiques, 52 Chapel St., Penzance Cornwall.
T. (01736) 330100. - Furn - 068490

Perranporth (Cornwall)

Saint George's Antiques, 33 Saint George's Hill, Perranporth Cornwall. T. (01872) 572947. - Paint / Furn / China / Glass - 068491

Pershore (Hereford and Worcester)

Hansen Chard Antiques, 126 High St., Pershore Herefs &
Worcs. T. (01386) 553423. - Instr - 068492

Look-In Antiques, 134b High St., Pershore Herefs &
Worcs. T. (01386) 556776. - Paint / Furn / China / Jew /
Silv - 068493

Penoyre Antiques, 9 and 11 Bridge St, Pershore Herefs
& Worcs. T. (01386) 553522. - Paint / Furn - 068494

S.W. Antiques, Abbey Showrooms, Newlands, Pershore
Herefs & Worcs. T. (01386) 555580,
Fax (01386) 556205. - Furn - 068495

Perth (Tayside)

Ainslie's Antique Warehouse, Unit 3, 13 Gray St., Perth
Scotland. T. (01738) 36825. - Ant - 068496

Atholl Antiques, 80 Princess St., Perth Scotland.
T. (01738) 20054. - Ant - 068497

Deuchar & Son, A. S., 10-12 South St., Perth PH2 8PG.
T. (01738) 26297. - Ant / Furn / China / Silv - 068498

Forsyth Antiques, 2 Saint Pauls Sq, Perth Scotland.
T. (01738) 22173. - Jew / Silv - 068499

Gallery One, 1-2 Saint Paul's Sq., Perth Scotland.
T. (01738) 24877. - Paint / Furn / Jew / Glass - 068500

George Street Gallery, 38 George St., Perth Scotland.
T. (01738) 38953. - Paint / Graph - 068501

Hardie Antiques, 25 Saint John St., Perth Scotland.
T. (01738) 33127. - Jew / Silv - 068502

Henderson, 5 North Methven St., Perth Scotland.
T. (01738) 24836. - Ant / Num / China / Jew - 068503

Murray, Ian, 21 Glasgow Rd., Perth PH2 0NZ.
T. (01738) 37222. - Ant - 068504

Robertson & Cox, 60 George St., Perth PH1 5JL.
T. (01738) 26300. - Ant / Paint / Furn / China - 068505

Tay Street Gallery, 70 Tay St., Perth Scotland.
T. (01738) 20604. - Paint / Graph / Furn -　　068506

Peterborough (Cambridgeshire)
Fitzwilliam Antiques Centre, Fitzwilliam St., Peterborough Cambs. T. (01733) 65415. - Ant -　　068507
Lewis, Ivor and Patricia, 30 Westwood Park Rd., Peterborough Cambs. T. (01733) 344567. - Furn /
China -　　068508
Smith, G., 1379 Lincoln Rd, Peterborough Cambs.
T. (01733) 571630. - Ant / Furn / Instr -　　068509

Petersfield (Hampshire)
Barn, Station Rd., Petersfield Hants. T. (01730) 62958.
- Ant / Naut -　　068510
Cull Antiques, 62 Station Rd., Petersfield Hants.
T. (01730) 263670. - Furn -　　068511
Elmore, 5 Charles St., Petersfield Hants.
T. (01730) 262383. - Paint / Furn / China /
Glass -　　068512

Petworth (West Sussex)
Amini, Majid, Church St., Petworth Sussex West.
T. (01798) 43344. - Tex -　　068513
Bacchus Gallery, Lombard St., Petworth Sussex West.
T. (01798) 42844, Fax (01798) 42634. - Glass - 068514
Baskerville Antiques, Saddlers House, Saddlers Row,
Petworth Sussex West. T. (01798) 42067,
Fax (01798) 43956. - Furn / Instr -　　068515
Bassett, Nigel, Swan House, Market Sq., Petworth Sussex West. T. (01798) 44121. - Ant -　　068516
Bragge, Lesley, Fairfield House, High St., Petworth Sussex West. T. (01798) 42324. - Furn / China / Tex /
Silv -　　068517
Cooper, Philip, The Nook, Golden Sq., Petworth Sussex West. T. (01798) 42033. - Furn -　　068518
Cracknell, Nigel, Lombard St., Petworth Sussex West.
T. (01798) 44188. - Furn -　　068519
Frith Antiques, New St., Petworth Sussex West.
T. (01798) 43155. - Furn -　　068520
Granville Antiques, High St., Petworth Sussex West.
T. (01798) 43250. - Paint / Furn -　　068521
Griffin Antiques, Church St, Petworth Sussex West.
T. (01798) 43306, Fax (01798) 42367. - Furn - 068522
Grove House Antiques, Middle St., Petworth Sussex
West. T. (01798) 43151. - Furn / Tex -　　068523
Hockley, William, East St., Petworth Sussex West.
T. (01798) 43172. - Furn / China -　　068524
Hopkins, John, Trumpers Corner, East St., Petworth Sussex West. T. (01798) 43104. - Furn / Glass - 068525
Humphry Antiques, North St., Petworth Sussex West.
T. (01798) 43053. - Furn / Sculp -　　068526
Madison Gallery, Swan House, Market Sq., Petworth
Sussex West. T. (01798) 43638. - Paint / Furn - 068527
Morris, John G., Market Sq., Petworth GU28 0AH.
T. (01798) 42305. - Furn / Instr -　　068528
Petworth Antique Market, East St., Petworth GU28 0AB.
T. (01798) 42073. - Ant -　　068529
Streeter & Daughter, Ernest, Lombard St, Petworth Sussex West. T. (01798) 42239. - Jew / Silv -　　068530
Tutt, J. C., Angel St., Petworth Sussex West.
T. (01798) 43221. - Furn -　　068531
Wakelin, Michael and Helen Linfield, 10 New St., Petworth Sussex West. T. (01798) 42417. - Paint /
Furn -　　068532
Wilkinson, T. G., New St., Petworth Sussex West.
T. (01798) 44443. - Paint / Furn -　　068533
Wood, Jeremy, East St., Petworth Sussex West.
T. (01798) 43408. - Paint / Graph -　　068534

Pevensey (Sussex)
Old Mint House, High St., Pevensey Sussex East.
T. (01323) 762337, Fax (01323) 762337. - Ant / Furn /
China / Instr -　　068535

Pevensey Bay (East Sussex)
Murray-Brown, Silverbeach, Norman Rd., Pevensey Bay
Sussex East. T. (01323) 764298. - Paint /
Graph -　　068536

Pickering (North Yorkshire)
Antiques and Things, South Gate, Pickering Yorks North.
T. (01751) 76142. - Ant / Tex / Toys -　　068537

Hague, John, 18 Hallgarth, Pickering Yorks North.
T. (01751) 72829. - Paint / Graph / Furn /
China -　　068538
Reynolds, C. H., 122 Eastgate, Pickering Yorks North.
T. (01751) 72785. - Ant -　　068539

Pinner (Greater London)
Artbry's Antiques, 44 High St., Pinner HA5 5PW.
T. (0181) 8680834. - Paint / Furn / Instr / Glass - 068540

Pitlochry (Tayside)
Blair Antiques, 14 Bonnethill Rd., Pitlochry Scotland.
T. (01796) 472624. - Paint / Furn / Tex / Silv /
Instr -　　068541

Pittenweem (Fife)
Pittenweem Antiques and Fine Art, 15 East Shore, The
Harbour, Pittenweem Scotland. T. (01333) 312054.
- Paint / Furn / China -　　068542

Plaitford (Hampshire)
Plaitford House Gallery, Plaitford Hants.
T. (01794) 22221. - Paint / Sculp -　　068543

Plymouth (Devon)
Annterior Antiques, 22 Molesworth Rd, Plymouth Devon.
T. (01752) 558277. - Furn -　　068544
Antique Fireplace Centre, 30 Molesworth Rd, Plymouth
Devon. T. (01752) 559441. - Ant -　　068545
Barbican Antiques Centre, 82-84 Vauxhall St, Plymouth
PL4 0EX. T. (01752) 266927. - Ant -　　068546
Jones, Alan, Applethorn Slade Farm, Plymouth Devon.
T. (01752) 338188. - Furn / Instr -　　068547
M. & A. Antique Exporters, 42/44 Breton Side, Plymouth
PL4 0AU. T. (01752) 665419, Fax 80752) 228058.
- Ant / Furn / Naut -　　068548
Scott-Masson, Anne-Marie, Devil's Point, Plymouth Devon. T. (01752) 664413. - Furn -　　068549
Secondhand Rose, 22 Weston Park Rd, Plymouth Devon.
T. (01752) 221715. - Furn / China -　　068550
Taylor, Brian, 24 Molesworth Rd, Plymouth Devon.
T. (01752) 569061. - Furn / Orient / Instr -　　068551
Upstairs Downstairs, Camden St, Plymouth Devon.
T. (01752) 261015. - Ant / Tex -　　068552

Polegate (East Sussex)
Price, Graham, Unit 4, Dittons Rd, Polegate Sussex East.
T. (01323) 487167, Fax (01323) 483904.
- Furn -　　068553

Pontypridd (Mid Glamorgan)
Pontypridd Antiques, Old Bakery, Shepherd St., Pontypridd Wales. T. (01443) 407616. - Furn /
China -　　068554

Port Erin (Isle of Man)
Spinning Wheel, Church Rd., Port Erin I. of Man.
T. (01624) 833137. - Furn / China / Jew / Silv /
Instr -　　068555

Portadown (Co. Armagh)
Moyallon Antiques, 54 Moyallon Rd., Portadown N. Ireland. T. (01762) 831615. - Ant / Furn / China - 068556

Porthcawl (Mid Glamorgan)
Harlequin Antiques, Dock St., Porthcawl Wales.
T. (01656) 785910. - Ant -　　068557

Portrush (Co. Antrim)
Alexander, 108 Dunluce Rd., Portrush N. Ireland.
T. (01265) 822783. - Paint / Furn / China / Silv - 068558

Portscatho (Cornwall)
Curiosity Antiques, Portscatho Cornwall.
T. (01872) 580411. - Ant -　　068559

Portslade (West Sussex)
Marks, Peter, 1/11 Church Rd, Portslade BN4 1LB.
T. (01273) 415471. - Ant / Naut -　　068560
Powell, J., 20 Wellington Rd., Portslade Sussex West.
T. (01273) 411599. - Ant / Furn / Instr -　　068561
Semus, Peter, Warehouse, Gladstone Rd., Portslade Sussex West. T. (01273) 420154, Fax (01273) 430355.
- Ant / Furn / Repr -　　068562

Portsmouth (Hampshire)
Affordable Antiques, 89 Albort Rd, Portsmouth Hants.
T. (01705) 293344. - Furn -　　068563
Amos, Tony, 239 Albert Rd, Portsmouth Hants.
T. (01705) 736818. - Ant / Naut -　　068564
Dodson, R. C., 85-87 Fawcett Rd, Portsmouth Hants.
T. (01705) 829481. - Ant -　　068565
Fleming, A., Clock Tower, Castle Rd, Portsmouth Hants.
T. (01705) 822934. - Ant / Furn / China / Jew /
Silv -　　068566
Gallery, 11 and 19 Marmion Rd, Portsmouth Hants.
T. (01705) 822016. - Furn -　　068567
Leslie's, 107 Fratton Rd., Portsmouth Hants.
T. (01705) 825952. - Jew -　　068568
Oldfield, 76 Elm Grove, Portsmouth Hants.
T. (01705) 838042, Fax (01705) 838042. - Paint /
Graph -　　068569
Portsmouth Stamp Shop, 184 Chichester Rd, Portsmouth
Hants. T. (01705) 663450. - Num -　　068570
Pretty Chairs, 189/191 Highland Rd, Portsmouth Hants.
T. (01705) 731411. - Furn -　　068571
Times Past, 141 Highland Rd, Portsmouth Hants.
T. (01705) 822701. - Ant / Naut -　　068572
Wessex, 77 Carmarthen Av., Portsmouth Hants.
T. (01705) 376518, Fax (01705) 201479.
- Instr -　　068573

Pottersbury (Northamptonshire)
Reindeer, 43 Watling St., Pottersbury NN12 7QD.
T. (01908) 542407, Fax (01908) 542121. - Paint / Furn /
Sculp / Instr -　　068574

Poynton (Cheshire)
Harper, Overdale, Woodford Rd., Poynton Cheshire.
T. (01625) 879105. - Paint / Graph -　　068575

Pratt's Bottom (Kent)
Jennings, Celia, 3 Mount Pleasant Cottages, Pratt's Bottom Kent. T. (01689) 853250. - Ant -　　068576

Prestbury (Cheshire)
Prestbury Antiques, 4 Swanwick House, The Village,
Prestbury Cheshire. T. (01625) 827966. - Paint / Furn /
China / Silv / Glass -　　068577

Preston (Lancashire)
Antique and Reproduction Clocks, 73 Friargate, Preston
Lancs. T. (01772) 58465. - Instr -　　068578
Antique Centre, 56 Garstang Rd., Preston Lancs.
T. (01772) 882078, Fax (01772) 885115.
- Ant -　　068579
Barronfield, 47 Friargate, Preston Lancs.
T. (01772) 563465. - Paint -　　068580
Blackburn, Jack, 41 New Hall Ln., Preston Lancs.
T. (01772) 791117. - Ant -　　068581
Duckworth, 45 New Hall Lane, Preston Lancs.
T. (01772) 794336. - Furn -　　068582
Guy's, Peter, 26-30 New Hall Lane, Preston Lancs.
T. (01772) 703771, Fax (01772) 703771.
- Furn -　　068583
Preston Antique Centre, The Mill, New Hall Ln., Preston
Lancs. T. (01772) 794498, Fax (01772) 651694.
- Ant -　　068584
Swag, 24 Leyland Rd, Preston Lancs.
T. (01772) 744970. - Furn / China / Toys -　　068585
Treasure, Frederick, 56 Garstang Rd., Preston Lancs.
T. (01772) 736801. - Furn -　　068586
Wade, Ray, 111 New Hall Ln., Preston Lancs.
T. (01772) 792950, Fax (01772) 651415. - Paint / Furn /
China -　　068587

Prestwick (Southclyde)
Yer Granny's Attic, 176 Main St., Prestwick Scotland.
T. (01292) 76312. - Ant -　　068588

Princes Risborough (Buckinghamshire)
Bell Street Antiques Centre, 20/22 Bell St, Princes Risborough Bucks. T. (0184) 443034. - Furn /
China -　　068589
White House Antiques, 33 High St., Princes Risborough
Bucks. T. (0184) 446976. - Furn -　　068590

Puckeridge (Hertfordshire)
Saint Quen, Old Cambridge Rd, Puckeridge Herts.
T. (01920) 821336. - Paint / Furn / China / Dec /
Instr - 068591

Pulborough (West Sussex)
Mulberry House Galleries, Codmore Hill, Pulborough
Sussex West. T. (01798) 872463. - Paint /
Graph - 068592

Purley (Greater London)
Addison, Michael, 28-30 Godstone Rd., Purley Surrey.
T. (0181) 668 6714. - Furn - 068593

Pwllheli (Gwynedd)
Adams, Rodney, 10 Penlan St., Pwllheli LL53 5DH.
T. (01758) 613173. - Furn / Instr - 068594

Queniborough (Leicestershire)
Green, J., 1 Coppice Lane, Queniborough LE7 8DR.
T. (01533) 606682. - Furn - 068595

Quorn (Leicestershire)
Mill on the Soar Antiques, 1/3 High St, Quorn Leics.
T. (01509) 414218. - Furn - 068596
Quorn Pine, Leicester Rd, Quorn Leics.
T. (01509) 416031. - Furn - 068597

Radlett (Hertfordshire)
Hasel-Britt, 157 Watling St., Radlett WD7 7NQ.
T. (01923) 854477. - Ant / China - 068598
Old Hat, 64 Watling St., Radlett Herts.
T. (01923) 855753. - Ant / Paint / Furn / China - 068599

Rainford (Merseyside)
Stock, Colin, 8 Mossborough Rd., Rainford Merseyside.
T. (0174) 4882246. - Furn - 068600

Ramsbury (Wiltshire)
Inglenook, 59 High St., Ramsbury Wilts.
T. (01672) 20261. - Furn / Instr - 068601

Ramsey (Cambridgeshire)
Abbey Antiques, 63 Great Whyte, Ramsey Cambs.
T. (01487) 814753. - Furn / China - 068602
Yesteryear Antiques, 79/81 High St, Ramsey Cambs.
T. (01487) 815006. - Paint / Graph / Furn - 068603

Ramsey (Isle of Man)
Allom & Co, P. G., 3 Parliament St., Ramsey I. of Man.
T. (01624) 812490. - Jew / Silv - 068604

Ramsgate (Kent)
Ash House, 18 Hereson Rd., Ramsgate Kent.
T. (01843) 595480. - Ant / Furn - 068605
De Tavener Antiques, 24 Addington St., Ramsgate Kent.
T. (01843) 582213. - Instr - 068606
Granny's Attic, 2 Addington St., Ramsgate Kent.
T. (01843) 588955. - Ant - 068607
Thanet, 45 Albert St., Ramsgate Kent.
T. (01843) 597336. - Furn - 068608

Raveningham (Norfolk)
Cannell, M. D., Castell Farm, Raveningham Norfolk.
T. (0150) 846441. - Furn - 068609

Rayleigh (Essex)
Bruschweiler, F. G., 41-67 Lower Lambricks, Rayleigh
SS6 7EH. T. (01268) 773761, Fax (01268) 773318.
- Furn - 068610

Reading (Berkshire)
Bye, Ann, 88 London St., Reading RG1 4SJ.
T. (01734) 582029. - Furn - 068611
Leatherland, P. D., 68 London St., Reading Berks.
T. (01734) 581960. - Furn / China / Instr - 068612
Reading Emporium, 1a Merchant's Pl., Reading Berks.
T. (01734) 590290. - Ant - 068613

Redbourn (Hertfordshire)
J.N. Antiques, 86 High St., Redbourn Herts.
T. (01582) 793603. - Paint / Furn / China - 068614
Wharton, Tim, 24 High St., Redbourn Herts.
T. (01582) 794371. - Furn - 068615

Redhill (Surrey)
Lawrence & Sons, F. G., 89 Brighton Rd., Redhill RH1
6PS. T. (01737) 764196. - Furn - 068616

Redruth (Cornwall)
Penandrea Gallery, 12 Higher Fore St., Redruth Cornwall.
T. (01209) 213134. - Paint / Graph - 068617
West End Antiques Market, 3 West End, Redruth Corn-
wall. T. (01209) 217001. - Paint / Graph / Furn / China /
Silv - 068618
Winkworth, Richard, Unit 6, Station Rd., Redruth Corn-
wall. T. (01209) 216631. - Furn / China / Glass - 068619

Reepham (Norfolk)
Chimes, Market Pl., Reepham Norfolk.
T. (01603) 870480. - Ant / Furn / Instr - 068620

Reigate (Surrey)
Bourne Gallery, 31/33 Lesbourne Rd, Reigate Surrey.
T. (01737) 241614. - Paint - 068621
Heath, 15 Flanchford Rd., Reigate Surrey.
T. (01737) 244230. - Furn / China - 068622
Noller, Bertram, 14a London Rd., Reigate Surrey.
T. (01737) 242548. - Furn / Glass - 068623
Showcase, 27 Croydon Rd., Reigate Surrey.
T. (01737) 222305. - Ant - 068624

Rhos-on-Sea (Clwyd)
Clwyd Coins and Stamps, 12 Colwyn Crescent, Rhos-
on-Sea Wales. T. (01492) 540610. - Num - 068625
Hyde, Shelagh, 11 Rhos Rd., Rhos-on-Sea Wales.
T. (01492) 548879. - Ant / Furn / China / Glass - 068626
North Wales Coins Ltd., 8 Abbey Dr., Rhos-on-Sea.
T. (01492) 4 8904. - Num - 068627

Richmond (North Yorkshire)
Brown, 2 New Rd., Richmond Yorks North.
T. (01748) 824095. - Paint / Furn / China / Silv - 068628

Richmond (Surrey)
Antique Mart, 72-74 Hill Rise, Richmond TW10 6UB.
T. (0181) 940 6942. - Furn - 068629
Antiques Arcade, 22 Richmond Hill, Richmond Surrey.
T. (0181) 940 2035. - Paint / Graph / Furn /
China - 068630
Brookville, 222 Sandycombe Rd., Richmond Surrey.
T. (0181) 940 6230. - Furn - 068631
Court Antiques, 12/14 Brewer's Lane, Richmond Surrey.
T. (0181) 940 0515. - Ant / Furn / Jew / Silv - 068632
Dukes Yard Antique Market, 1A Duke St, Richmond Sur-
rey. T. (0181) 332 1051. - Ant - 068633
Evans, Mollie, 82 Hill Rise, Richmond TW10 6UB.
T. (0181) 948 0182. Ant / Furn / China / Sculp /
Tex - 068634
Gooday, Peter and Debbie, 20 Richmond Hill, Richmond
TW10 6QX. T. (0181) 940 8652. - Paint / Graph / Furn /
China / Jew - 068635
Goslett, Roland, 139 Kew Rd., Richmond Surrey.
T. (0181) 9404009. - Paint - 068636
Hill Rise Antiques, 26 Hill Rise, Richmond TW10 6UA.
T. (0181) 3322941. - Furn / Silv - 068637
Horton's, 2 Paved Court, The Green, Richmond Surrey.
T. (0181) 332 1775. - Paint / Jew / Silv - 068638
Lawson, F. & T., 13 Hill Rise, Richmond Surrey.
T. (0181) 940 0461. - Paint / Furn - 068639
Layton, 1 Paved Court, The Green, Richmond TW9 1LZ.
T. (0181) 940 2617. - Furn / Silv - 068640
Lion Antiques, 16 Brewers Lane, Richmond Surrey.
T. (0181) 9408069. - Jew / Silv - 068641
Marryat, 88 Sheen Rd., Richmond Surrey.
T. (0181) 332 0262. - Paint / Furn / China / Silv - 068642
Palmer, 10 Paved Court, Richmond Surrey.
T. (0181) 948 2668. - Paint / Graph - 068643
Piano Nobile Fine Paintings, 26 Richmond Hill, Rich-
mond Surrey. T. (0181) 940 2435, Fax (0181) 9402435.
- Paint / Sculp - 068644
Richmond Traders, 28, 30/31 Hill Rise, Richmond Sur-
rey. T. (0181) 948 4638. - Ant - 068645
Rowan, 4 Worple Way, Richmond Surrey.
T. (0181) 332 1167. - Paint / Furn / Instr - 068646

Rickmansworth (Hertfordshire)
McCrudden, 23 Station Rd., Rickmansworth Herts.
T. (01923) 772613. - Paint / Graph - 068647

Ridgewell (Essex)
Ridgewell Crafts and Antiques, On A604, Ridgewell Essex. T. (0144) 085272. - Furn / China / Instr - 068648

Ringwood (Hampshire)
Davies, Barbara, 30A Christchurch Rd, Ringwood Hants.
T. (01202) 872268. - Furn / China - 068649
Millers, 86 Christchurch Rd., Ringwood BH24 1DR.
T. (01425) 472062, Fax (01425) 472727. - Ant / Furn /
Mil - 068650
Palmer, P. E., 132 Christchurch Rd., Ringwood Hants.
T. (01425) 472640. - Ant / Furn / Jew - 068651
Pine Company, 104 Christchurch Rd., Ringwood Hants.
T. (01425) 476705, Fax (01425) 480467.
- Furn - 068652
Robinson, Glen, 82 Christchurch Rd., Ringwood Hants.
T. (01425) 480450. - Furn / China - 068653

Ripley (Surrey)
Cedar House Gallery, High St, Ripley Surrey.
T. (01483) 211221. - Paint - 068654
Hartley, J., 186 High St., Ripley Surrey.
T. (01483) 224318. - Furn - 068655
Manor House, High St., Ripley Surrey.
T. (01483) 223350. - Ant - 068656
Ripley Antiques, 67 High St., Ripley GU23 6AQ.
T. (01483) 224981. - Furn - 068657
Sage, Green Cottage, High St., Ripley GU23 6BB.
T. (01483) 224396, Fax (01483) 211996. - Ant / Paint /
Furn - 068658
Welling, Anthony, Broadway Barn, High St., Ripley GU23
GAQ. T. (01483) 225384. - Ant / Furn - 068659

Ripon (North Yorkshire)
Balmain, 13 High Skellgate, Ripon Yorks North.
T. (01765) 601294. - Paint / Furn / China / Silv - 068660
Pinetree Antiques, 44 North St., Ripon Yorks North.
T. (01765) 602905. - Furn - 068661
Rose, 13 Kirkgate, Ripon Yorks North.
T. (01765) 690118. - Paint / Furn / China /
Glass - 068662
Sigma Antiques and Fine Art, Water Skellgate, Ripon
Yorks North. T. (01765) 603163, Fax (01765) 690933.
- Paint / Furn / China / Jew / Silv - 068663
Skellgate Curios, 2 Low Skellgate, Ripon Yorks North.
T. (01765) 601290. - Ant / Jew / Silv / Cur - 068664
Yesteryear, 6-7 High Skellgate, Ripon Yorks North.
T. (01765) 607801. - Ant / Furn / Jew / Silv - 068665

Riverhead (Kent)
Amherst, 23 London Rd., Riverhead Kent k7000 (0732)
455047. T. 455047. - Furn / China / Silv - 068666
Mandarin Gallery, 32 London Rd., Riverhead Kent.
T. (01732) 457399. - Paint / Furn / China - 068667

Robertsbridge (Sussex)
de Montfort, 49 High St., Robertsbridge TN32 5AN.
T. (01580) 880698. - Ant / Furn / Orient / Tex - 068668

Rochdale (Greater Manchester)
Owen, 191 Oldham Rd., Rochdale OH6.
T. (01706) 48138. - Paint / Furn / Silv / Instr /
Mil - 068669

Rochester (Kent)
Cottage Style Antiques, 24 Bill Street Rd., Rochester
Kent. T. (01634) 717623. - Ant - 068670
Droods, 62 High St., Rochester Kent. T. (01634) 829000.
- Ant - 068671
Iles, Francis, Rutland House, High St, Rochester Kent.
T. (01634) 843081. - Paint - 068672
Langley, 153 High St., Rochester Kent.
T. (01634) 811802. - Furn - 068673
Memories, 128 High St., Rochester Kent.
T. (01634) 811044. - Paint / Furn / China - 068674
Vines, 18 Crow Ln., Rochester Kent. T. (01634) 815796.
- Ant / Furn / China - 068675

Rolvenden (Kent)
Falstaff Antiques, 63-67 High St., Rolvenden TN17 4LP.
T. (01580) 241234. - Furn / China / Silv / Glass - 068676
Kent Cottage Antiques, 39 High St., Rolvenden Kent.
T. (01580) 241719. - Furn / China / Jew / Silv - 068677
Walters, J.D. & R.M., 10 Regent St., Rolvenden Kent.
T. (01580) 241563. - Furn - 068678

Romsey (Hampshire)
Bell Antiques, 8 Bell St., Romsey Hants.
T. (01794) 514719. - Furn / China / Jew / Silv /
Glass - 068679
Cambridge Antiques, 5 Bell St., Romsey Hants.
T. (01794) 512885. - Paint / Graph / Furn /
China - 068680
Creighton, 23-25 Bell St., Romsey Hants.
T. (01794) 522758. - Ant - 068681
Old Cottage Things, Broxmore Park, Romsey Hants.
T. (01794) 884538. - Ant / Furn - 068682
Romsey Medal and Collectors Centre, 5 Bell St., Romsey
Hants. T. (01794) 512069, Fax (01794) 830332.
- Num / China / Mil - 068683

Ross-on-Wye (Hereford and Worcester)
Baileys, Engine Shed, Ross-on-Wye Herefs & Worcs.
T. (01989) 63015, Fax (01989) 768172. - Ant - 068684
Fryer, Fritz, 12 Brookend St., Ross-on-Wye Herefs &
Worcs. T. (01989) 67416. - Lights - 068685
Green, Robert, 12 Brookend St., Ross-on-Wye Herefs &
Worcs. T. (01989) 67504. - Furn / China / Tex / Silv /
Glass - 068686
Lloyd, Robin, 23-24 Brookend St., Ross-on-Wye HR9
7EE. T. (01989) 62123. - Ant / Furn - 068687
Old Pine Shop, Gloucester Rd., Ross-on-Wye Herefs &
Worcs. T. (01989) 64738. - Furn - 068688
Relics, 19 High St., Ross-on-Wye Herefs & Worcs.
T. (01989) 64539. - Jew / Silv / Instr - 068689
Trecilla, 36 High St., Ross-on-Wye HR9 5HD.
T. (01989) 63010. - Furn / China / Silv / Instr /
Mil - 068690

Rotherham (South Yorkshire)
Appleyard, Roger, Fitzwilliam Rd, Rotherham Yorks
South. T. (01709) 367670, Fax (01709) 829395.
- Ant - 068691
Mason, John, 36 High St., Rotherham Yorks South.
T. (01709) 382311. - Jew / Silv - 068692
Shaw, John, Old Methodist Chapel, Rotherham Yorks
South. T. (01709) 522340. - Ant - 068693
South Yorkshire Antiques, 88-94 Broad St., Rotherham
Yorks South. T. (01709) 526514. - Ant / Furn - 068694
Turnor, Philip, 94a Broad St., Rotherham Yorks South.
T. (01709) 524640. - Furn / Naut - 068695

Rottingdean (Sussex)
Jupiter Antiques, Rottingdean Sussex East.
T. (01273) 302865. - China - 068696
Trade Wind, 15a Lille Crescent, Rottingdean BN2 7GF.
T. (01273) 301177. - Furn / Silv - 068697

Royston (Hertfordshire)
Royston Antiques, 29 Kneesworth St., Royston SG8 5AB.
T. (01763) 243876. - Ant / Furn / China - 068698

Ruddington (Nottinghamshire)
Rodgers, Arthur and Ann, 7 Church St., Ruddington
Notts. T. (01602) 216214. - Graph / Furn /
China - 068699

Rugeley (Staffordshire)
Winter, Eveline, 1 Wolseley Rd., Rugeley WS15 2QH.
T. (01889) 583259. - Ant / China - 068700

Rushden (Northamptonshire)
Sherwood, D. W., 59 Little St., Rushden Northants.
T. (01933) 53265. - Ant - 068701
Shire Antiques, 111 High St. South, Rushden Northants.
T. (01933) 315567. - Ant / Naut - 068702

Ruthin (Clwyd)
Castell Delmar Antiques, Wrexham Rd., Ruthin Wales.
T. (01824) 704484. - Furn / Naut - 068703
Old Tyme Antiques, 21 Clwyd St., Ruthin Wales.
T. (01824) 702902. - China / Jew / Silv / Instr - 068704
Percival, R. and S.M., 65 Clwyd St., Ruthin Wales.
T. (01824) 704454. - Furn - 068705

Ryde (Isle of Wight)
Hayter's, 19-20 Cross St., Ryde PO33 2AD.
T. (01983) 563795. - Furn - 068706
Royal Victoria Arcade, Union St., Ryde I. of Wight.
T. (01983) 564661. - Ant - 068707
Uriah's Heep, Union St, Ryde PO33 2LQ.
T. (01983) 564661. - Ant / China / Tex / Jew /
Silv - 068708

Rye (East Sussex)
Bragge & Sons, Landgate House, Rye TN31 7LH.
T. (01797) 223358. - Paint / Furn - 068709
Gasson, Herbert Gordon, Lion Galleries, Lion St., Rye
TN31 7LB. T. (01797) 222208. - Ant / Furn /
China - 068710
Landgate Antiques, 22 Landgate, Rye Sussex East.
T. (01797) 224746. - Furn / Sculp / Instr - 068711
Lingard, Ann, 18-22 Rope Walk, Rye Sussex East.
T. (01797) 223486. - Furn - 068712
Lingard, Ann, 17 Tower St., Rye Sussex East.
- Furn - 068713
Rye Antiques, 93 High St., Rye Sussex East.
T. (01797) 222259. - Furn / Jew / Silv - 068714

Saffron Walden (Essex)
Lankester, Market Hill, Saffron Walden Essex. - Ant /
Graph / Furn / China - 068715
Lankester, Old Sun Inn, Church St., Saffron Walden
CB10 1HQ. T. (01799) 522685. - Ant / Graph / Furn /
China - 068716
Littlebury, 58/60 Fairycroft Rd, Saffron Walden Essex.
T. (01799) 527961, Fax (01799) 527961. - Instr /
Cur - 068717
Summer, Jane, 9 Market Sq., Saffron Walden Essex.
T. (01672) 870727. - Furn / Jew - 068718

Saint Agnes (Cornwall)
Agnes Ago Antiques, 1B Churchtown, Saint Agnes Cornwall. T. (0187) 2553820. - Furn / China - 068719

Saint Albans (Hertfordshire)
By George Antiques Centre, 23 George St., Saint Albans
Herts. T. (01727) 53032. - Ant - 068720
Clock Shop, 161 Victoria St., Saint Albans AL1 3TA.
T. (01727) 56633. - Instr - 068721
Dolphin Antiques, Garden Cottage, Dolphin Yard, Saint
Albans Herts. T. (01727) 863080. - Paint / Furn / China /
Glass - 068722
James of Saint Albans, 11 George St., Saint Albans
Herts. T. (01727) 56996. - Ant / Furn - 068723
Leaside Antiques, Shop 5 George St, Saint Albans Herts.
T. (01727) 40653. - Furn / China / Silv - 068724
Oriental Rug Gallery, 27 Verulam Rd., Saint Albans
Herts. T. (01727) 41046. - Orient / Tex - 068725
Saint Albans Antique Market, Town Hall, Chequer St.,
Saint Albans Herts. T. (01727) 44957. - Ant - 068726
Stevens, 41 London Rd., Saint Albans Herts.
T. (01727) 57266. - Furn / China - 068727
Wharton, Stuart, 1 George St., Saint Albans Herts.
T. (01727) 59489, Fax (01727) 55474. - Jew /
Silv - 068728

Saint Andrews (Fife)
Bygones, 68 South St., Saint Andrews Scotland.
T. (01334) 75849. - Furn / Silv - 068729
Old Saint Andrews, 9 Albany Pl., Saint Andrews KY16
9HH. T. (01334) 77840, Fax (01334) 77135. - Ant /
Jew / Silv - 068730
Old Saint Andrews Gallery, 10 Golf Pl., Saint Andrews
Scotland. T. (01334) 77840. - Ant - 068731
Saint Andrews Fine Art, 84a Market St., Saint Andrews
Scotland. T. (01334) 74080. - Paint / Draw - 068732

Saint Annes-on-Sea (Lancashire)
Stamford, 29 The Crescent, Saint Annes-on-Sea Lancs.
T. (01253) 728385. - Furn / Instr - 068733
Victorian Shop, 19 Alexandria Dr., Saint Annes-on-Sea
Lancs. T. (01253) 725700. - Ant - 068734

Saint Austell (Cornwall)
Ancient and Modern, 32-34 Polkyth Rd., Saint Austell
Cornwall. T. (01726) 73983. - Ant / Paint / Jew /
Instr - 068735
Chesterton, Margaret, 33 Pentewan Rd., Saint Austell
PL25 5BU. T. (01726) 72926. - Paint / Furn / China /
Jew / Instr - 068736
Furniture Store, 37/39 Truro Rd, Saint Austell Cornwall.
T. (01726) 63178. - Paint / Furn / China / Glass - 068737

Saint Helier (Jersey)
Cooper, John, 16 The Market, Saint Helier C. I.
T. (01534) 23600. - Ant - 068738
Grange Gallery, 39 New St., Saint Helier C. I.
T. (01534) 20077. - Paint / Graph - 068739
Rae, Lance and Marcus, Savile St., Saint Helier C. I.
T. (01534) 32171. - Ant / Paint / Furn / Silv /
Instr - 068740
Saint Helier Galleries, 9 James St., Saint Helier C. I.
T. (01534) 67048. - Paint / Draw - 068741
Selective Eye Gallery, 50 Don St., Saint Helier C. I.
T. (01534) 25281. - Paint / Graph - 068742
Shepherd's, 4 Wharf St, Saint Helier C. I.
T. (01534) 601081. - Ant - 068743
Thesaurus, 3 Burrard St., Saint Helier JE2 4WS.
T. (01534) 37045. - Ant / Paint - 068744
Thomson, Joan, 39 Don St., Saint Helier C. I.
T. (01534) 80603. - Furn / Tex - 068745
Union Street Antique Market, 8 Union St., Saint Helier C.
I. T. (01534) 73805. - Ant - 068746

Saint Ives (Cambridgeshire)
Broadway Antiques, 31 The Broadway, Saint Ives
Cambs. T. (01480) 461061. - Ant / Furn - 068747
Knight & Sons, B. R., Quay Court, Bull Ln., Saint Ives
PE17 4AR. T. (01480) 68295. - Ant / Paint / China /
Jew / Glass - 068748

Saint Ives (Cornwall)
Read, Mike, Wheal Whidden, Carbis Bay, Saint Ives
Cornwall. T. (01736) 798219. - Instr - 068749

Saint Lawrence (Jersey)
I.G.A. Old Masters, 5 Kimberley Grove, Rue de Haut,
Saint Lawrence C. I. T. (01534) 24226.
- Paint - 068750

Saint Leonards-on-Sea (East Sussex)
Aarquebus Antiques, 46 Norman Rd., Saint Leonards-
on-Sea Sussex East. T. (01424) 433267. - Furn / Jew /
Silv / Naut - 068751
Banner, 56 Norman Rd., Saint Leonards-on-Sea Sussex
East. T. (01424) 420050. - Furn / China - 068752
Chapel Antiques, 1 London Rd., Saint Leonards-on-Sea
Sussex East. T. (01424) 440025. - Paint / Furn / China /
Glass - 068753
Filsham Farmhouse Antiques, 111 Harley Shute Rd.,
Saint Leonards-on-Sea Sussex East.
T. (01424) 433109. - Furn / Instr / Naut - 068754
Galleon Antiques, 18 Gensing Rd., Saint Leonards-on-
Sea Sussex East. T. (01424) 714881. - Ant - 068755
Galleon Antiques, 70 Sedlescombe Rd., Saint Leonards-
on-Sea Sussex East. T. (01424) 424145.
- Orient - 068756
Galleria Fine Arts, 77 Norman Rd., Saint Leonards-on-
Sea Sussex East. T. (01424) 722317. - Ant /
Furn - 068757
Lang, John, 65 Norman Rd., Saint Leonards-on-Sea
Sussex East. T. (01424) 714848. - Ant - 068758
Monarch Antiques, 6 Grand Parade, Saint Leonards-on-
Sea Sussex East. T. (01424) 445841,
Fax (01424) 445841. - Furn - 068759
Nunn, K., 1 London Rd., Saint Leonards-on-Sea Sussex
East. T. (01424) 431093. - Ant / Mil - 068760

Saint Margaret's Bay (Kent)
Impressions and Alexandra's Antiques, 1-3 The Drove-
way, Saint Margaret's Bay Kent. T. (01304) 853102.
- Furn / China / Jew - 068761

Saint Neots (Cambridgeshire)
John, Peter, 38 Saint Mary's St, Saint Neots Cambns.
T. (01480) 216297. - Jew - 068762
Tavistock Antiques, Cross Hall Manor, Eaton Ford, Saint
Neots Cambs. T. (01480) 472082. - Furn - 068763

Saint Peter Port (Guernsey)
Channel Islands Galleries, Trinity Sq, Saint Peter Port C.
I. T. (01481) 723247. - Paint / Graph - 068764
Grange Antiques, 7-8 The Grange, Saint Peter Port C. I.
T. (01481) 721480. - Furn / China / Jew / Silv - 068765
Pine Collection, 17 Mansell St., Saint Peter Port C. I.
T. (01481) 726891. - Furn - 068766
Proctor, David, 12 Mansell St., Saint Peter Port C. I.
T. (01481) 726808. - Ant / Furn / Instr - 068767

Saint James's Gallery, 18-20 The Bordage, Saint Peter Port C. I. T. (01481) 720070. - Paint / Furn / China - 068768

Saint Sampson (Guernsey)
Old Curiosity Shop, Commercial Rd., Saint Sampson C. I. T. (01481) 45324. - Paint / Furn / China / Silv / Glass - 068769

Salcombe (Devon)
A-B Gallery, 67 Fore St., Salcombe Devon. T. (01548) 842764. - Paint / Graph - 068770

Salisbury (Wiltshire)
Amos, Joan, 7a Saint John St., Salisbury Wilts. T. (01722) 330888. - Furn / China - 068771
Antique and Collectors Market, 37 Catherine St., Salisbury SP1 2DH. T. (01722) 326033. - China / Silv / Glass - 068772
Avonbridge Antiques and Collectors Market, United Reformed Church Hall, Fisherton St., Salisbury Wilts. - Ant - 068773
Boston, Derek, 223 Wilton Rd., Salisbury SP2 7TY. T. (01722) 322682. - Furn / China - 068774
Bradley, Robert, 71 Brown St., Salisbury Wilts. T. (01722) 333677. - Furn - 068775
Castle Galleries, 81 Castle St., Salisbury Wilts. T. (01722) 333734. - Ant / Num - 068776
Hastie, Ian G., 46 Saint Ann St., Salisbury Wilts. T. (01722) 322957. - Ant / Furn - 068777
Hurst, Edward, Paynes Hill, Salisbury Wilts. T. (01722) 320595. - Furn - 068778
Micawber's, 53 Fisherton St., Salisbury SP2 7ST. T. (01722) 333822. - Ant - 068779
Newsam, T. J., 49 Saint Ann St., Salisbury Wilts. T. (01722) 411059. - Instr - 068780
Wadge, Chris, 142 Fisherton St., Salisbury Wilts. T. (01722) 334467. - Instr - 068781

Saltburn (Cleveland)
Endeavour Antiques, Vicotira Terrace, Saltburn TS12 1HN. T. (01287) 622385. - Ant / China / Jew - 068782

Saltcoats (Southclyde)
Narducci, 57 Raise St., Saltcoats Scotland. T. (01294) 61687. - Ant / Naut - 068783

Samlesbury (Lancashire)
Samlesbury Hall, Preston New Rd., Samlesbury Lancs. T. (01254) 812229. - Ant - 068784

Sandhurst (Berkshire)
Berkshire Metal Finishers, Swan Lane Trading Estate, Sandhurst Berks. T. (01252) 873475, Fax (01252) 875434. - Silv - 068785

Sandhurst (Kent)
Forge Antiques and Restorations, Rye Rd., Sandhurst Kent. T. (01580) 850308. - Furn / China - 068786

Sandwich (Kent)
Delf, 14 New St., Sandwich Kent. T. (01304) 617684. - Ant / Paint / Graph / China - 068787
Delf, 36 Harnet St., Sandwich Kent. T. (01304) 612779. - Furn - 068788
Empire Antiques, Strand St, Sandwich Kent. T. (01304) 614474, Fax (01304) 451375. - Furn / Naut - 068789
Hythe, 47a Strand St., Sandwich Kent. T. (01304) 614971. - Graph / Furn / Jew / Silv - 068790
Noah's Ark Antique Centre, King St., Sandwich Kent. T. (01304) 611144. - Paint / Furn / China / Jew / Silv - 068791
Porter, James, 5 Potter St., Sandwich Kent. T. (01304) 612218. - Furn - 068792
Wilson, Nancy, Monken Qay, Strand St., Sandwich Kent. T. (01304) 612345. - Ant / Furn / Instr - 068793

Sawbridgeworth (Hertfordshire)
Herts and Essex Antique Centre, Station Rd, Sawbridgeworth Herts. T. (01279) 722044. - Ant - 068794

Saxmundham (Suffolk)
Antiques and Country Things, 49 North Entrance, High St., Saxmundham IP17 1AS. T. (01728) 604171. - Ant / Furn / Jew - 068795

Scarborough (North Yorkshire)
Browns, 6 Seamer Rd. Corner, Scarborough Yorks North. T. (01723) 377112. - Paint / Furn / China - 068796
Hanover Antiques, 10 Hanover Rd., Scarborough Yorks North. T. (01723) 374175. - Ant / Mil - 068797
Shuttleworths, 7 Victoria Rd., Scarborough Yorks North. T. (01723) 366278. - Ant / Furn - 068798

Scarthoe (Humberside)
Scarthoe Antiques, 38 Louth Rd., Scarthoe DN32 0BX. T. (01472) 77394. - China / Jew / Silv - 068799

Scunthorpe (Humberside)
Guns and Tackle, 25A Ashby High St, Scunthorpe Humberside South. T. (01724) 865445. - Mil - 068800
Mill Antiques, 249 Ashby High St., Scunthorpe Humberside South. T. (01724) 865445. - Ant / Instr - 068801

Seaford (East Sussex)
Alexander, Molly, Crouch Lane, Seaford Sussex East. T. (01323) 896577. - Ant / Paint - 068802
Alexander, Richard, Crouch Lane, Seaford Sussex East. T. (01323) 896577. - Paint / Orient - 068803
Courtyard Antiques Market, 13, 15, 17 High St, Seaford Sussex East. T. (01323) 892091. - Ant - 068804
Old House, 13, 15, 17 High St, Seaford BN25 3PD. T. (01323) 892091. - Furn / China / Glass - 068805
Seaford's Barn Collectors Market, Church Lane, Seaford BN25 2UA. T. (01323) 890010. - Ant - 068806
Steyne House Antiques, 35 Steyne Rd., Seaford Sussex East. T. (01323) 895088. - Furn / China - 068807

Seaton (Devon)
Etceteras Antiques, Beer Rd., Seaton Devon. T. (01297) 21965. - Ant - 068808

Sedbergh (Cumbria)
Hollett & Son, R.F.G., 6 Finkle St., Sedbergh Cumbria. T. (015396) 20298, Fax (015396) 21396. - Ant / Paint / Graph - 068809
Sedbergh Antiques and Collectables, 59 Main St., Sedbergh Cumbria. T. (015396) 21276. - Furn / China / Tex - 068810
Stable Antiques, 15-16 Back Ln., Sedbergh LA10 5AQ. T. (015396) 20251. - Furn / China / Silv - 068811

Sedlescombe (Sussex)
Holmes House Antiques, The Green, Sedlescombe Sussex East. T. (01424) 870450. - Paint / Furn / Silv - 068812
Kinloch, C., Bulmer House, The Green, Sedlescombe Sussex East. T. (01424) 870364. - Toys - 068813

Selkirk (Borders)
Heatherlie Antiques, 6/8 Heatherlie Terrace, Selkirk Scotland. T. (01750) 20114. - Ant / Furn / China - 068814

Settle (North Yorkshire)
Folly Antiques, The Folly, Chapel St., Settle Yorks North. - Furn / China / Jew / Silv - 068815
Milnthorpe, H. I., Kirkgate, Settle Yorks North. T. (01729) 823046. - Furn / China - 068816
Milnthorpe & Daughters, Mary, Market Pl., Settle Yorks North. T. (01729) 822331. - Jew / Silv - 068817
Nanbooks, Roundabout, Duke St., Settle BD24 9DJ. T. (01729) 823324. - Ant / China - 068818
Precious, Roy, High St, Settle Yorks North. T. (01729) 823946. - Ant / Paint / Furn / China - 068819
Thistlethwaite, E., Market Sq., Settle Yorks North. T. (01729) 822460. - Furn - 068820
Well Cottage Antiques, High St, Settle Yorks North. T. (01729) 823593. - Furn / China - 068821

Sevenoaks (Kent)
Antiques Centre, 120 London Rd., Sevenoaks Kent. T. (01732) 452104. - Ant - 068822
Bradbourne, 4 Saint John's Hill, Sevenoaks Kent. T. (01732) 460756, Fax (01732) 460756. - Paint / Furn / China / Jew / Glass - 068823
Stead, Myold, 120 London Rd., Sevenoaks Kent. T. (01732) 452040. - Paint / Furn / Silv / Lights / Glass - 068824
Ward, Sheldon, 57 Saint John's Hill, Sevenoaks Kent. T. (01732) 455311. - Furn - 068825

Shaftesbury (Dorset)
Gold Hill Antiques and Collectibles, Gold Hill, Shaftesbury Dorset. T. (01747) 54050. - Ant - 068826

Shardlow (Derbyshire)
Shardlow Antiques Warehouse, 24 The Warf, Shardlow Derbys. T. (01332) 792899. - Furn - 068827

Sheffield (South Yorkshire)
A. and C. Antiques, 239 Abbeydale Rd., Sheffield. T. (0114) 589161. - Ant / Jew - 068828
Anita's Holme Antiques, 144 Holme Lande, Sheffield. T. (0114) 336698. - Ant - 068829
Chimney Piece Antique Fires, 262 South St, Sheffield. T. (0114) 346085. 068830
Cobwebs, 208 Whitham Rd, Sheffield. T. (0114) 681923. - Paint / Furn / China / Jew - 068831
Dronfield, 375-377 Abbeydale Rd., Sheffield. T. (0114) 550172. - China / Glass - 068832
Ellis's, 144 Whitham Rd., Sheffield. T. (0114) 662920. - Tex - 068833
Fillibuster & Booth, 749 Eccleshall Rd., Sheffield. T. (0114) 682653. - Ant / Paint - 068834
Findley, 314 Langsett Rd., Sheffield. T. (0114) 346088. - Naut - 068835
Fulwood, 7 Brooklands Av., Sheffield. T. (0114) 307387. - Ant / Paint / Furn - 068836
Fun Antiques, 72 Abbeydale Rd., Sheffield Yorks South. T. (0114) 553424. - Ant - 068837
Gilbert & Sons, 16 Abbeydale Rd., Sheffield. T. (0114) 552043. - Naut - 068838
Green, G. H., 334 Abbeydale Rd, Sheffield. T. (0114) 550881. - Furn - 068839
Hibbert Bros., 117 Norfolk St., Sheffield. T. (0114) 722038. - Paint - 068840
Hinson, 290 Glossop Rd., Sheffield. T. (0114) 722082. - Ant / Paint - 068841
James, Peter, 112 and 114 London Rd., Sheffield. T. (0114) 700273. - Furn - 068842
Jameson & Son, A.E., 257 Glossop Rd., Sheffield S70 2QZ. T. (0114) 723846. - Ant / Furn / China / Mil - 068843
Oriental Rug Shop, 763 Abbeydale Rd., Sheffield. T. (0114) 552240, 589821, Fax (0114) 509088. - Tex - 068844
Paraphernalia, 66/68 Abbeydale Rd, Sheffield. T. (0114) 550203. - Ant / Furn - 068845
Porter, 205 Whitham Rd., Sheffield. T. (0114) 685751. - Graph - 068846
Pot-Pourri, 647 Ecclesall Rd, Sheffield. T. (0114) 669790. - Jew / Silv - 068847
Salt, N.P. and A., Units 1-2, Barmouth Rd., Sheffield. T. (0114) 582672. - Ant / Furn / Toys / Naut - 068848
Turn of the Century, 48-50 Barber Rd., Crookesmoor, Sheffield. T. (0114) 670947. - Paint / Furn / Instr - 068849
Ward, Paul, 8 Burnell Rd., Sheffield. T. (0114) 335980. - Ant / Furn - 068850

Shefford (Bedfordshire)
Secondhand Alley, 2-4 High St., Shefford Beds. T. (01462) 814747. - Ant / Naut - 068851

Shenfield (Essex)
Chart House, 33 Spurgate, Hutton Mount, Shenfield Essex. T. (01277) 225012. - Naut - 068852

Shepperton (Surrey)
Rickett & Co., Church Sq., Shepperton Surrey. T. (01932) 243571. - Ant / Lights / Instr - 068853

Shepshed (Leicestershire)
Hadfield, G. K., Tickow Ln, Shepshed Leics. T. (01509) 503014, Fax (01509) 600136. - Instr - 068854

Sherborne (Dorset)
Antique Market, Digby Hall, Sherborne Dorset. T. (01258) 840224. - Ant - 068855
Antiques of Sherborne, The Green, Sherborne DT9 3HZ. T. (01935) 816549. - Ant / Paint / Furn / Tex - 068856
Burton, Jasper, 23 Cheap St., Sherborne Dorset. T. (01935) 814434. - Ant / Furn - 068857
Castleton Country Furniture, Long St., Sherborne Dorset. T. (01935) 812195. - Furn - 068858

Dodge & Son, 28-33 Cheap St., Sherborne Dorset.
T. (01935) 815151. - Paint / Furn / China /
Instr - 068859
Greystoke, Swan Yard, off Cheap St., Sherborne Dorset.
T. (01935) 812833. - Ant / China / Silv - 068860
Heygate Browne, South St., Sherborne Dorset.
T. (01935) 815487. - Furn / China - 068861
Nook, South St., Sherborne Dorset. T. (01935) 813987.
- Ant / Furn / China / Glass - 068862
Sherborne Antique Centre, Mattar Arcade, 17 Newlands,
Sherborne Dorset. T. (01935) 813464. - Paint / Furn /
Tex / Jew / Silv - 068863
Swan Gallery, 51 Cheap St., Sherborne Dorset.
T. (01935) 814465. - Paint / Graph - 068864

Shere (Surrey)
Yesterdays Pine, Gomshall Lane, Shere Surrey.
T. (0148) 6413198. - Furn - 068865

Sheringham (Norfolk)
Denis, Rose, 20 High St., Sheringham Norfolk.
T. (01263) 823 699. - Jew / Silv - 068866
Dorothy's Antiques, 23 Waterbank Rd., Sheringham Nor-
folk. T. (01263) 822319. - Furn / China / Instr /
Glass - 068867
Parriss, 20 Station Rd., Sheringham Norfolk.
T. (01263) 822661. - Jew / Silv / Instr - 068868
Westcliffe Gallery, 2-8 Augusta St., Sheringham Norfolk.
T. (01263) 824320. - Paint / Furn / Draw - 068869

Shipley (West Yorkshire)
Bell & Son, R., 37 Briggate, Shipley Yorks West.
T. (01274) 582602. - Ant - 068870
Price-Less Antiques, 2 Gaisby Ln., Shipley Yorks West.
T. (01274) 581760. - Ant / China - 068871

Shipston-on-Stour (Warwickshire)
Fine-Lines, 31 Sheep St., Shipston-on-Stour Works.
T. (01608) 662323. - Paint / Draw - 068872
Grandfather Clock Shop, West St, Shipston-on-Stour
Warks. T. (01608) 662144. - Furn / Instr - 068873
Time in Hand, 11 Church St., Shipston-on-Stour Warks.
T. (01608) 662578. - Instr - 068874

Shoreham (Kent)
Porcelain Collector, 29 High St., Shoreham TN14 7TD.
T. (01959) 523416. - Ant / Furn / China / Sculp /
Silv - 068875

Shoreham-by-Sea (West Sussex)
Tudor Cottage Antiques, Upper Shoreham Rd., Shore-
ham-by-Sea Sussex West. T. (01273) 453554.
- Ant - 068876

Shrewsbury (Shropshire)
Collectors' Gallery, 6-7 Castle Gates, Shrewsbury
Shrops. T. (01743) 272140. - Num - 068877
Expressions, 17 Princess St., Shrewsbury Shrops.
T. (01743) 351731. - Paint / Graph / Furn / Repr /
Jew - 068878
Hutton, 18 Princess St., Shrewsbury Shrops.
T. (01743) 245810. - Furn / China / Jew / Silv /
Glass - 068879
Little Gem, 18 Saint Mary's St., Shrewsbury SY1 1ED.
T. (01743) 352085. - Ant / Jew / Silv - 068880
Manser & Son, F.C., 53-54 Wyle Cop, Shrewsbury SY1
1XJ. T. (01743) 351120, Fax (01743) 271047. - Furn /
Orient / Jew / Silv - 068881
Raleigh House, 23 Belle Vue Rd., Shrewsbury Shrops.
T. (01743) 359552. - Furn / China / Jew / Silv /
Glass - 068882
Shrewsbury Antique Centre, The Square, Shrewsbury
Shrops. T. (01743) 247704. - Ant - 068883
Shrewsbury Antique Market, Frankwell Quay Ware-
house, Shrewsbury Shrops. T. (01743) 350916.
- Ant - 068884
Tiffany Antiques, Unit 3, 15 Princess House, Shrewsbury
Shrops. T. (01270) 257425. - China / Silv - 068885
Wyle Cop Antiques and Reproductions, Old School, off
Wyle Cop, Shrewsbury Shrops. T. (01743) 231180.
- Furn / Instr - 068886

Sible Hedingham (Essex)
Churchgate Antiques, 150 Swan St., Sible Hedingham
Essex. T. (01787) 62269. - Furn - 068887

Hedingham Antiques, 100 Swan St., Sible Hedingham
Essex. T. (01787) 60360. - Furn / China / Silv /
Glass - 068888
Pinn & Sons, W. A., 124 Swan St., Sible Hedingham Es-
sex. T. (01787) 61127. - Furn / Instr - 068889

Sidmouth (Devon)
Gainsborough House Antiques, 12 Fore St., Sidmouth
Devon. T. (01395) 514394. - Furn / China / Silv /
Mil - 068890
Hartnell, Dorothy, 21 Fove St, Sidmouth Devon.
T. (01395) 515291. - Paint / Furn / China - 068891
Lantern Shop, 4 New St., Sidmouth Devon.
T. (01395) 516320. - Paint / Furn / China /
Lights - 068892
Sidmouth Antique Market, 132 High St., Sidmouth De-
von. T. (01395) 577981. - China / Glass - 068893
Vintage Toy and Train Museum, Market Pl, Sidmouth De-
von. T. (01395) 515124. - Toys - 068894

Skegness (Lincolnshire)
Crowson, G. H., 50 High St., Skegness Lincs.
T. (01754) 764360. - Ant / Jew - 068895
Romantiques, 87 Roman Bank, Skegness Lincs.
T. (01754) 767879. - Furn / China / Jew / Instr - 068896

Skipton (North Yorkshire)
Adamson, Newmarket St., Skipton Yorks North.
T. (01756) 791355. - Mil - 068897
Corn Mill Antiques, High Corn Mill, Chapel Hill, Skipton
Yorks North. T. (01756) 792440. - Paint / Graph / Furn /
China - 068898

Smeeth (Kent)
Moate, Richard, Wentworth, Plain Rd., Smeeth Kent.
I. (01303) 813241. - Furn - 068899

Smethwick (West Midlands)
Grannies Attic Antiques, 437 Bearwood Rd., Smethwick
West Mids. T. (0121) 4294180. - Ant / Paint / Furn / Chi-
na / Tex - 068900

Snodland (Kent)
Aaron, 90 High St., Snodland Kent. T. (01634) 241748.
- Paint / Furn / Orient / China / Instr - 068901

Solihull (West Midlands)
Hassall, Geoffrey, 20 New Rd., Solihull West Mids.
T. (0121) 705 0068. - Furn - 068902
Renaissance, 18 Marshall Lake Rd, Solihull West Mids.
T. (0121) 745 5140. - Ant - 068903

Somerton (Somerset)
Gardiner, John, Monteclefe House, Somerton Somerset.
T. (01458) 72238. - Ant / Furn - 068904
London Cigarette Card, West St., Somerton Somerset.
T. (01458) 73452. - Graph / Fra - 068905
Valetta House Antiques, West St., Somerton Somerset.
T. (01458) 74015. - Ant / Furn - 068906

South Brent (Devon)
Andrade, Philip, White Oxen Manor, Rattery, South Brent
TQ10 9JXC. T. (01364) 72454. - Furn / China - 068907
Wootton, L. G., 2 Church St., South Brent Devon.
T. (01364) 72553. - Instr - 068908

South Harting (West Sussex)
Holmes, Julia, South Gardens Cottage, South Harting
Sussex West. T. (01730) 825040. - Graph - 068909

South Molton (Devon)
Architectural Antiques, West Ley, Alswear Old Rd., South
Molton Devon. T. (01769) 573342,
Fax (01769) 574363. - Ant - 068910
Furniture Market, 14a Barnstaple St., South Molton De-
von. T. (01769) 573401. - Furn / Silv / Glass - 068911
Great Western Pine, 99 East St., South Molton Devon.
T. (01769) 572689. - Furn - 068912
Lace Shop, 33 East St., South Molton Devon.
T. (01769) 573184. - Tex - 068913
Memory Lane Antiques, 100 East St., South Molton De-
von. T. (01769) 574288. - Ant / Furn / China / Jew /
Silv - 068914
Mole, 32 East St., South Molton Devon.
T. (01769) 573845. - Graph - 068915

South Molton Antiques, 103 East St., South Molton De-
von. T. (01769) 573478. - Ant / Furn / Naut - 068916
Tredant, J. R., 50-50a South St., South Molton Devon.
T. (01769) 573006. - Ant - 068917
Tredantiques, 19 Broad St., South Molton Devon.
T. (01769) 573841. - Ant / Furn - 068918

South Shields (Tyne and Wear)
Curiosity Shop, 16 Frederick St., South Shields Tyne &
Wear. T. (0191) 456 5560. - Ant / Paint / Furn /
Jew - 068919

South Walsham (Norfolk)
Pratt & Son, Leo, South Walsham Norfolk.
T. (0160) 549204. - Ant / Furn / China / Glass - 068920

Southampton (Hampshire)
Alfred, 280 Shirley Rd., Southampton S01 3HL.
T. (01703) 774772. - Ant / Paint / Furn / China /
Glass - 068921
Campbell, Meg, 10 Church Lane, Highfield, Southamp-
ton Hants. T. (01703) 557636. - Silv - 068922
Cottage Antiques, 9 Northam Rd., Southampton Hants.
T. (01703) 221546. - Ant / Furn - 068923
Gazelles Art Deco Interiors, 31 Northam Rd, Southamp-
ton Hants. T. (01703) 235291. - Mod - 068924
Leslie, R. K., 23 Northam Rd., Southampton SO2 0NZ.
T. (01703) 224784. - Furn / China / Jew / Silv /
Instr - 068925
Moody, L., 70 Bedford Pl., Southampton Hants.
T. (01703) 333720. - Furn / China / Silv - 068926
Parkhouse & Wyatt, 96 Above Bar, Southampton Hants.
T. (01703) 226653. - Jew / Silv - 068927
Relics Antiques, 54 Northam Rd., Southampton Hants.
T. (01703) 221635. - Ant - 068928
Wellington Antiques, 109 Saint Denys Rd., Southampton
Hants. T. (01703) 553022. - Furn / China /
Instr - 068929

Southborough (Kent)
Baines, Henry, 14 Church Rd., Southborough Kent.
T. (01892) 532099. - Furn - 068930

Southend-on-Sea (Essex)
Kickshaws, 20 Alexandra St., Southend-on-Sea Essex.
T. (01702) 353630. - Ant - 068931
Lonsdale Antiques, 86 Lonsdale Rd, Southend-on-Sea
Essex. T. (01702) 462643. - Ant / Paint / China /
Jew - 068932
Redding, 98 London Rd., Southend-on-Sea Essex.
T. (01702) 354647. - Ant / Paint - 068933

Southport (Merseyside)
Anderson, 14 Wesley St., Southport Merseyside.
T. (01704) 540024. - Instr - 068934
Decor Galleries, 52 Lord St., Southport Merseyside.
T. (01704) 535134. - Furn / Dec - 068935
Fine Pine, 19 Market St., Southport Merseyside.
T. (01704) 538056. - Furn - 068936
Molloy, 6-8 Saint James St., Southport Mersyside.
T. (01704) 535024. - Furn - 068937
Oldfield Cottage Antiques, 97 East Bank St., Southport
Merseyside. T. (0161) 6282646. - Furn / China /
Tex - 068938
Osiris Antiques, 104 Shakespeare St., Southport Mer-
seyside. T. (01704) 500991. - Tex / Jew / Mod - 068939
Pinocchio, 2 & 2A Portland St, Southport Merseyside.
T. (01704) 535028. - Furn / Toys - 068940
Spinning Wheel, 1 Liverpool Rd, Southport Merseyside.
T. (01704) 68245. - Ant - 068941
Studio 41, 340 Liverpool Rd, Southport Merseyside.
T. (01704) 579132. - Paint - 068942
Sutcliffe, Tony & Anne, 37a Linaker St., Southport Mer-
seyside. - Furn - 068943
Sutcliffe, Tony & Anne, 130 Cemetery Rd., Southport
Mersyside. T. (01704) 537068. - Furn - 068944
Walne, H. S., 183 Lord St., Southport Merseyside.
T. (01704) 532469. - Jew / Silv - 068945
Weldon, 567 Lord St., Southport Merseyside.
T. (01704) 532191. - Furn / Num / Jew / Silv /
Instr - 068946
White Elephant, 22 Kew Rd., Southport PR8 4HH.
T. (01704) 60525. - Ant - 068947

Southwell (Nottinghamshire)

Stroud, 3-7 Church St., Southwell NG25 0HQ.
T. (01636) 815001. - Paint / Furn / Instr -   068948

Sowerby Bridge (West Yorkshire)

Memory Lane, 69 Wakefield Rd., Sowerby Bridge Yorks
West. T. (01422) 833223. - Furn / Toys -   068949
Talking Point Antiques, 66 West St., Sowerby Bridge
Yorks West. T. (01422) 834126. - Ant / China -   068950

Spalding (Lincolnshire)

Dean, Weston Saint Mary's, Spalding Lincs.
T. (01406) 370429. - Ant -   068951

Spilsby (Lincolnshire)

Shaw, High St., Spilsby Lincs. T. (01790) 52317.
- Ant -   068952
Spilsby, 29 Halton Rd., Spilsby Lincs. T. (01790) 52148.
- Jew / Silv -   068953

Stafford (Staffordshire)

Browse, 127 Lichfield Rd., Stafford Staffs.
T. (01785) 41097. - Furn -   068954

Staines (Surrey)

Dunster, K. W., 23 Church St., Staines TW18 4EN.
T. (01784) 453297. - Ant / Furn / Jew / Instr -   068955
Melville, Margaret, Market Sq, Staines Surrey.
T. (01784) 455395. - Paint -   068956

Stalham (Norfolk)

Stalham Antique Gallery, High St., Stalham NR12 9AH.
T. (01692) 580636. - Paint / Furn / China /
Glass -   068957

Stamford (Lincolnshire)

Cox, Robin, 35-36 Saint Peter's St., Stamford PE9 2PF.
T. (01780) 64592. - Furn / Sculp -   068958
Saint Mary's Galleries, 5 Saint Mary's Hill, Stamford
Lincs. T. (01780) 64159. - Paint / Tex / Jew -   068959
Sinclair, John, 11-12 Saint Mary's St., Stamford Lincs.
T. (01780) 65421. - Furn -   068960
Stamford Antiques Centre, Exchange Hall, Broad St.,
Stamford Lincs. T. (01780) 62605. - Ant -   068961
Thomas, Andrew, 10 North St, Stamford PE9 2YN.
T. (01780) 62236, Fax (01780) 62236. - Ant /
Furn -   068962

Stanford Dingley (Berkshire)

Eliot, Stanford Dingley Berks. T. (01734) 744649.
- Ant -   068963

Stanford-le-Hope (Essex)

Barton House Antiques, Wharf Rd., Stanford-le-Hope Essex. T. (01375) 672494. - Furn / China / Glass -   068964

Stansted (Essex)

Linden House Antiques, 3 Silver St., Stansted Essex.
T. (01279) 812372. - Furn -   068965
Valmar, Croft House, High Lane, Stansted Essex.
T. (01279) 813201, Fax (01279) 816962.
- Furn -   068966

Staunton Harold (Leicestershire)

Ropers Hill Antiques, Ropers Hill Farm, Staunton Harold
Leics. T. (01530) 413919. - Ant / Silv -   068967

Steeton (North Yorkshire)

Owls Antiques, 1-3 Station Rd., Steeton Yorks West.
T. (01535) 652614. - Ant / China -   068968

Steyning (West Sussex)

Fileman, David R., Squirrels, Bayards, Steyning Sussex
West. T. (01903) 813229. - Ant -   068969
Penfold, 30 High St., Steyning Sussex West.
T. (01903) 815595. - Ant / Paint / Graph -   068970

Stillington (North Yorkshire)

Pond Cottage Antiques, Brandsby Rd., Stillington Yorks
North. T. (01347) 810796. - Ant / Furn -   068971

Stirling (Central)

Paterson, Elizabeth, 52 1/2 Spittal St., Stirling Scotland.
T. (01786) 823779. - Furn / China -   068972

Stock (Essex)

Sabine Antiques, 38 High St., Stock Essex.
T. (01277) 840553. - Furn / China / Glass -   068973

Stockbridge (Hampshire)

Hofman, George, Brookside, High St., Stockbridge
Hants. T. (01264) 810570. - Ant / Furn -   068974
Lane, High St., Stockbridge Hants. T. (01264) 810435.
- Furn / China / Silv / Glass -   068975
Mulberry House Antiques, High St., Stockbridge.
T. (01264) 810357. - Furn -   068976
Stockbridge Antiques, High St., Stockbridge Hants.
T. (01264) 810829. - Furn / China / Silv / Glass - 068977
Viney, Elizabeth, High St, Stockbridge S020 6HF.
T. (01264) 810761. - Ant / Furn -   068978

Stockbury (Kent)

Steppes Hill Farm Antiques, Hill Farm, South St., Stock-
bury ME9 7RB. T. (01795) 842205. - Ant / China /
Silv -   068979

Stockport (Cheshire)

Antique Furniture Warehouse, Units 3-4, Cooper St,
Stockport Cheshire. T. (0161) 4298590. - Paint / Furn /
China / Instr -   068980
Bright, 6 Portland Grove, Stockport Cheshire.
T. (0161) 4429334. - Furn / China / Glass -   068981
E.R. Antiques Centre, 122 Wellington St., Stockport
Cheshire. T. (0161) 4296646. - Paint / China / Jew /
Glass -   068982
Flintlock Antiques, 28 and 30 Bramhall Ln, Stockport
Cheshire. T. (0161) 4809973. - Graph / Furn /
Instr -   068983
Halcyon, 435 Buxton Rd., Stockport Cheshire.
T. (0161) 4395038. - Furn / China / Glass -   068984
Highland Antiques, 65A Wellington Rd, Stockport Ches-
hire. T. (0161) 476 6669, Fax (0161) 4766669.
- Orient / Silv -   068985
Hole in the Wall Antiques, 370 Buxton Rd, Stockport
Cheshire. T. (0161) 4836603. - Furn -   068986
Imperial Antiques, 295 Buxton Rd, Stockport SK2 7NR.
T. (0161) 4833322. - China / Silv -   068987
Nostalgia, 61 Shaw Heath, Stockport Cheshire.
T. (0161) 4777706. - Ant -   068988
Page, 424 Buxton Rd, Stockport Cheshire.
T. (0161) 4839202. - Furn / Silv -   068989
Zippy Antiques, Units 2-3, Cooper St, Stockport Cheshi-
re. T. (0161) 4777953. - Furn / China -   068990

Stoke-on-Trent (Staffordshire)

Ann's Antiques, 24 Leek Rd, Stoke-on-Trent Staffs.
T. (01782) 503991. - Paint / Furn / China / Jew - 068991
Antiques Workshop, 43-45 Hope St, Stoke-on-Trent
Staffs. T. (01782) 273645. - Ant / Furn -   068992
Castle Antiques, 113 Victoria St, Stoke-on-Trent Staffs.
T. (01782) 625168. - Furn / Instr -   068993
Five Towns Antiques, 17 Broad St, Stoke-on-Trent
Staffs. T. (01782) 272930. - Ant / China -   068994
Potteries Antique Centre, Waterloo Rd, Stoke-on-Trent
Staffs. T. (01782) 201455. - Paint / Furn / China / Jew /
Instr -   068995
Steele, W. G., 20 Piccadilly, Hanley, Stoke-on-Trent
Staffs. T. (01782) 213216. - Jew -   068996
Tinder Box, 61 Lichfield St, Stoke-on-Trent Staffs.
T. (01782) 261368. - Furn / Jew / Lights -   068997

Stokesley (North Yorkshire)

Three Tuns Antiques, 2 Three Tuns Wynd, Stokesley TS9
5DQ. T. (01642) 711377. - Ant / Furn / China / Jew /
Silv -   068998

Storrington (West Sussex)

Thakeham, Rock Rd, Storrington Sussex West.
T. (01903) 745464. - Furn -   068999

Stourbridge (West Midlands)

Oldswinford Gallery, 106 Hagley Rd, Stourbridge West
Mids. T. (01384) 395577. - Paint / Graph -   069000
S.O.S. Militaria, 32 Park St., Stourbridge West Mids.
T. (01384) 379652. - Mil -   069001

Stow-on-the-Wold (Gloucestershire)

Acorn Antiques, Sheep St., Stow-on-the-Wold Glos.
T. (01451) 831519. - Furn / China / Glass -   069002

Ashton Dodkin, 7a Talbot Court, Stow-on-the-Wold Glos.
T. (01451) 870067. - Furn / China / Silv -   069003
Baggott, Church St., Stow-on-the-Wold GL54 1BB.
T. (01451) 830370, Fax (01451) 832174. - Ant / Paint /
Furn / Lights / Instr -   069004
Baggott, Duncan J., Sheep St, Stow-on-the-Wold GL54
1AA. T. (01451) 830662, Fax (01451) 832174. - Ant /
Paint / Furn -   069005
Baggott, Duncan J., Woolcomber House, Stow-on-the-
Wold GL54 1AA. T. (01451) 830662,
Fax (01451) 832174. - Ant / Paint / Furn / Instr /
Cur -   069006
Brand, Colin, Tudor House, Sheep St., Stow-on-the-Wold
Glos. T. (01451) 831760. - Furn / China / Instr - 069007
Bryden, P., Sheep St., Stow-on-the-Wold Glos.
T. (01451) 830840. - Furn / Silv -   069008
Caspall, J. and J., Sheep St., Stow-on-the-Wold GL54
1AA. T. (01451) 831160. - Ant / Furn -   069009
Clark, Annarella, 11 Park St., Stow-on-the-Wold Glos.
T. (01451) 830535. - Furn / China -   069010
Clark, Christopher, The Fosse Way, Stow-on-the-Wold
GL54 1JS. T. (01451) 830476, Fax (01451) 830300.
- Furn -   069011
Cotswold Antiques Centre, The Square, Stow-on-the-
Wold Glos. T. (01451) 831585. - Ant -   069012
Cotswold Galleries, The Square, Stow-on-the-Wold
GL54 1AB. T. (01451) 830586. - Paint -   069013
Country Life Antiques, Grey House, The Square, Stow-
on-the-Wold GL54 1AF. T. (01451) 831564. - Paint /
Furn / Instr -   069014
Curiosity Shop, The Square, Stow-on-the-Wold Glos.
T. (01451) 831586. - Furn / Instr -   069015
Davies, John, Church St., Stow-on-the-Wold Glos.
T. (01451) 831698, Fax (01451) 832477.
- Paint -   069016
Fosse Gallery, Manor House, The Square, Stow-on-the-
Wold Glos. T. (01451) 831319. - Paint -   069017
Fosse Way Antiques, The Square, Stow-on-the-Wold
Glos. T. (01451) 830776. - Ant / Paint / Furn / China /
Glass -   069018
Hockin, Keith, The Square, Stow-on-the-Wold Glos.
T. (01451) 831058. - Furn -   069019
Huntington, Old Forge, Church St., Stow-on-the-Wold
Glos. T. (01451) 830842, Fax (01451) 832211. - Furn /
Tex -   069020
Little Elms Antiques, The Square, Stow-on-the-Wold
Glos. T. (01451) 870089. - Furn -   069021
Martin House Antiques, Sheep St., Stow-on-the-Wold
Glos. T. (01451) 831217. - China -   069022
No. 2 Park Street Antiques, 2-3 Park St., Stow-on-the-
Wold Glos. T. (01451) 832311. - Ant / Paint / Furn /
China -   069023
Nutter, Simon W., Wraggs Row, Fosse Way, Stow-on-
the-Wold CL54 1JT. T. (01451) 830658.
- Furn -   069024
Oriental Gallery, 1 Digbeth St., Stow-on-the-Wold Glos.
T. (01451) 830944, Fax (01451) 870126.
- Orient -   069025
Park House Antiques, Park St., Stow-on-the-Wold Glos.
T. (01451) 830159. - Paint / Furn / China / Tex /
Toys -   069026
Preston, Antony, The Square, Stow-on-the-Wold Glos.
T. (01451) 831586. - Furn / Instr -   069027
Priest, Malt House, Digbeth St., Stow-on-the-Wold Glos.
T. (01451) 830592. - Graph / Furn -   069028
Saint Breock Gallery, Digbeth St., Stow-on-the-Wold
GL54 1BN. T. (01451) 830424. - Paint / Paint /
Furn -   069029
Samarkand Galleries, 2 Brewery Yard, Sheep St., Stow-
on-the-Wold Glos. T. (01451) 832322,
Fax (01451) 832322. - Tex -   069030
Stow Antiques, The Square, Stow-on-the-Wold Gloos.
T. (01451) 830377, Fax (01451) 870018.
- Furn -   069031
Talbot Court Galleries, Talbot Court, Stow-on-the-Wold
Glos. T. (01451) 832169. - Graph -   069032
Touchwood International, 9 Park St., Stow-on-the-Wold
Glos. T. (01451) 870800, Fax (01451) 870800. - Furn /
China / Sculp -   069033
Vanbrugh House Antiques, Park St., Stow-on-the-Wold
Glos. T. (01451) 830797. - Graph / Furn / Instr /
Music -   069034

Stradbroke (Suffolk)
Palmer, Mary, Cottage Farm, Stradbroke Suffolk.
T. (01379) 388100. - Furn / Glass - 069035

Stratford-upon-Avon (Warwickshire)
Abode, 40 Sheep St., Stratford-upon-Avon Warks.
T. (01789) 68755. - Furn - 069036
Arbour Antiques, Sheep St, Stratford-upon-Avon CV37
6EF. T. (01789) 293453. - Mil - 069037
Art Deco Ceramics, 4 Sheep St., Stratford-upon-Avon
Warks. T. (01789) 297249. - China / Lights - 069038
Bateman, Jean A., 41 Sheep St., Stratford-upon-Avon
Warks. T. (01789) 298494. - Jew / Glass - 069039
Bow Cottage Antiques, 4 Sheep St., Stratford-upon-Avon
Warks. T. (01789) 297249. - Ant / Paint / Graph / China /
Silv - 069040
Burman, 5 Trinity St., Stratford-upon-Avon Warks.
T. (01789) 295164. 069041
Harrison, Tim, Hotton Rock, Stratford-upon-Avon Warks.
T. (01789) 292921. - Furn / Naut - 069042
Howard, 44a Wood St., Stratford-upon-Avon Warks.
T. (01789) 205404. - Jew / Silv - 069043
Jazz, Shop 2 Rother St, Stratford-upon-Avon Warks.
T. (01789) 298362. - Furn / China / Jew /
Lights - 069044
Lions Den, 31 Henley St., Stratford-upon-Avon Warks.
T. (01789) 415802, Fax (01789) 415853. - Paint /
China - 069045
Loquens, The Minories, Rother St., Stratford-upon-Avon
Warks. T. (01789) 297706. - Paint - 069046
Rich Designs, 4 Sheep St., Stratford-upon-Avon Warks.
T. (01789) 261612. - China - 069047
Stratford Antique Centre, Ely St., Stratford-upon-Avon
Warks. T. (01789) 204180. - Ant - 069048
Wigington, James, 276 Alcester Rd., Stratford-upon-
Avon CV37 9QX. T. (01789) 261418,
Fax (01789) 261600. - Ant / Mil - 069049

Streatley (Berkshire)
Vine Cottage Antiques, High St., Streatley Berks.
T. (01491) 872425. - Ant / Furn - 069050

Streetly (West Midlands)
Hardwick, 317b Chester Rd., Streetly WS9 0PH.
T. (0121) 3531489. - Furn / China / Jew / Silv - 069051

Stretton (Cheshire)
Antiques Etc., Shepcroft House, London Rd., Stretton
Cheshire. T. (01925) 730431. - Furn / Instr - 069052

Stretton-on-Fosse (Warwickshire)
Astley House Fine Art, Old School, CV23 Stretton-on-
Fosse Warks. T. (01608) 50601, Fax (01608) 51777.
- Paint - 069053

Stroud (Gloucestershire)
Gnome Cottage Antiques, 55-57 Middle St., Stroud GN5
1DZ. T. (01453) 763669. - Ant / Graph / Furn / China /
Glass - 069054
R.J.D. Fine Arts, 12 Wallbridge, Stroud Glos.
T. (01453) 764878. - Paint - 069055
Shabby Tiger Antiques, 18 Nelson St., Stroud GL5 2HN.
T. (01453) 759175. - Ant / Paint / Furn / Dec - 069056

Studley (Warwickshire)
Prospect Antiques, Chester House, Alcester Rd., Studley
Warks. T. (0152) 7852494. - Furn / Orient /
China - 069057

Sturminster Newton (Dorset)
Quarter Jack Antiques, Bridge St., Sturminster Newton
Dorset. T. (01258) 72558. - Furn / China /
Glass - 069058
Toll House, Bagber Lane, Sturminster Newton Dorset.
T. (01258) 72296. - Ant / Furn / Instr - 069059
Tribe & Son, Tom, Bridge St., Sturminster Newton Dor-
set. T. (01258) 72311. - Instr - 069060

Sudbury (Suffolk)
Antique Clocks, 72 Melford Rd., Sudbury Suffolk.
T. (01787) 375931. - Instr - 069061
Napier House, Church St., Sudbury Suffolk.
T. (01787) 375280. - Furn - 069062

Sunderland (Tyne and Wear)
Smith, Peter, 12-14 Borough Rd., Sunderland SR1 1EP.
T. (0191) 5673537, Fax (0191) 5142286. - Instr /
Naut - 069063

Sundridge (Kent)
Sundridge Gallery, 9 Church Rd., Sundridge Kent.
T. (01959) 564104. - Paint / Tex - 069064
Wilson, Colin, 99-103 Main Rd., Sundridge Kent.
T. (01959) 562043. - Furn - 069065

Sunninghill (Berkshire)
Antiques of Ascot, 3c High St., Sunninghill Berks.
T. (01344) 872282. - Ant - 069066

Surbiton (Surrey)
House of Mallett, 77 Brighton Rd., Surbiton Surrey.
T. (0181) 3903796. - Ant / Furn / China - 069067
Newlove, B. M., 139-141 Ewell Rd., Surbiton Surrey.
T. (0181) 3998857. - Paint / Furn / China /
Instr - 069068
Tauber, Laurence, 131 Ewell Rd., Surbiton Surrey.
T. (0181) 3900020. - Ant - 069069

Sutton (Surrey)
Warrender & Co, S., 4-6 Cheam Rd., Sutton Surrey.
T. (0181) 643 4381. - Jew / Silv / Instr - 069070

Sutton Bridge (Lincolnshire)
Bridge Antiques, 30-32 Bridge Rd., Sutton Bridge Lincs.
T. (01406) 350704. - Naut - 069071
Old Barn, New Rd., Sutton Bridge Lincs.
T. (01406) 350435. - Furn / Naut - 069072

Sutton Coldfield (West Midlands)
Coulborn & Sons, Thomas, 64 Birmingham Rd., Sutton
Coldfield B72 1QP. T. (0121) 354 3974. - Ant / Furn /
Instr - 069073
Cutler, Stancie, Town Hall, Sutton Coldfield West Mids.
T. (01270) 624288. - Ant / Furn - 069074
Driffold, 78 Birmingham Rd., Sutton Coldfield West
Mids. T. (0121) 355 5433. - Paint - 069075
Kelford, 14a Birmingham Rd., Sutton Coldfield West
Mids. T. (0121) 354 6607. - Ant / Furn / China / Jew /
Silv - 069076
Osborne, 91 Chester Rd, Sutton Coldfield West Mids.
T. (0121) 355 6667. - Furn / Instr - 069077
Parry, H. and R.L., 23 Maney Corner, Sutton Coldfield
West Mids. T. (0121) 354 1178. - Ant / Paint / China /
Jew / Silv - 069078

Sutton Valence (Kent)
Sutton Valence Antiques, North St., Sutton Valence
ME17 3AP. T. (01622) 843333. - Ant / Furn / China /
Silv / Naut - 069079

Swaffham (Norfolk)
Cranglegate Antiques, Market Pl., Swaffham PE37 7LE.
T. (01760) 721052. - Ant - 069080
Swaffham Antiques Supplies, 66-68 London St., Swaff-
ham Norfolk. T. (01760) 721697. - Ant / Naut - 069081

Swaffham Prior (Cambridgeshire)
Firmin, Rodney, Lowfield, Lower End, Swaffham Prior
CB5 0HT. T. (01638) 742881. - Instr - 069082

Swafield (Norfolk)
Straithe Lodge Gallery, Straithe Lodge, Swafield Norfolk.
T. (01692) 402669. - Paint / Graph - 069083

Swanage (Dorset)
Georgian Gems, 28 High St., Swanage Dorset.
T. (01929) 424697. - Jew / Silv - 069084
Old Forge Antiques, 273a High St., Swanage Dorset.
T. (01929) 423319. - Ant - 069085

Swansea (West Glamorgan)
Allan, James, 22 Park St., Swansea Wales.
T. (01792) 652176. - Jew - 069086
Antique Emporium, 76 Saint Helens Rd., Swansea
Wales. T. (01792) 654697. - Ant - 069087
Bygone Antiques, 37-39 Saint Helens Rd., Swansea
Wales. T. (01792) 468248. - Furn / China / Tex - 069088
Chugg, Keith, Gwydr In, Swansea Wales.
T. (01792) 472477. - Ant / Furn / Music - 069089

Clydach Antiques, 83 High St, Swansea Wales.
T. (01792) 843209. - Ant - 069090
Davies, Philip, 130 Overland Rd, Swansea Wales.
T. (01792) 361766. - Paint / Graph - 069091
Elizabeth Antiques, 504 Mumbles Rd., Swansea Wales.
T. (01792) 361909. - Ant / Jew - 069092
Hughes, Eynon, Henrietta St, Swansea Wales.
T. (01792) 651446. - Furn / Instr - 069093
Hulbert, Anne and Colin, 17 Approach Rd, Swansea
Wales. T. (01792) 653818. - Ant / Naut - 069094
Magpie, 57 Saint Helens Rd., Swansea Wales.
T. (01792) 648722. - Furn / China - 069095
Scurlock, Kim, 25 Russell St., Swansea Wales.
T. (01792) 643085. - Furn - 069096
Swansea Antique Centre, 21 Oxford St., Swansea Wales.
T. (01792) 466854. - Ant - 069097

Swindon (Wiltshire)
Antiques and All Pine, 11 Newport St., Swindon SN1
3DX. T. (01793) 520259. - Ant / Furn / China /
Jew - 069098
Marlborough Sporting Gallery, 6 Milton Rd., Swindon
Wilts. T. (01793) 421458, Fax (01793) 421640.
- Paint / Graph - 069099
Smith, Allan, 162 Beechcroft Rd., Swindon Wilts.
T. (01793) 822977. - Instr - 069100

Swinton (Greater Manchester)
Ambassador House, 273 Chorley Rd., Swinton Lancs.
T. (0161) 7943806. - Ant - 069101

Tarporley (Cheshire)
Arden, Brendy, 67 High St., Tarporley Cheshire.
T. (01829) 733026. - Furn - 069102

Tattershall (Lincolnshire)
Lindum, Tattershall Thorpe, Tattershall Lincs.
T. (01562) 342454. - China - 069103
Wayside Antiques, Market Pl., Tattershall LN4 4LQ.
T. (01562) 342436. - Ant - 069104

Taunton (Somerset)
Barrett, Philip, Cheddon Fitzpaine, Taunton Somerset.
T. (01823) 451248. - Paint / Graph / Furn /
China - 069105
Joshua Antiques, Paul St., Taunton Somerset.
T. (01823) 332874. - Furn - 069106
Selwoods, Marys St, Taunton Somerset.
T. (01823) 272780. - Furn - 069107
Staplegrove Lodge Antiques, Staplegrove Lodge, Taun-
ton Somerset. T. (01823) 331153. - Ant / Furn / China /
Silv - 069108
Taunton Antiques Market, 27/29 Silver St, Taunton Som-
erset. T. (01823) 289327, Fax (0171) 3515350.
- Ant - 069109

Tavistock (Devon)
King Street Curios, 5 King St., Tavistock Devon. - Ant /
Furn / China - 069110
Pendar, 8 Drake Rd., Tavistock Devon.
T. (01822) 617642. - Ant / Furn - 069111

Teddington (Greater London)
Crisp, J. W., 166 High St., Teddington Middx.
T. (0181) 9774309. - Paint / Furn / China - 069112

Teignmouth (Devon)
Charterhouse Antiques, 1B Northumberland Pl, Teign-
mouth Devon. T. (01626) 54592. - Paint / Furn / China /
Jew / Silv - 069113
Extence Antiques, 2 Wellington St., Teignmouth Devon.
T. (01626) 777353. - Furn / Jew / Silv / Instr - 069114
Old Passage, 13a Bank St., Teignmouth Devon.
T. (01626) 772634. - China / Tex / Silv / Glass - 069115

Telford (Shropshire)
Haygate Gallery, 40 Haygate Rd, Telford Shrops.
T. (01952) 248553. - Ant / Paint - 069116
Pugh, Bernie, 120 High St., Wellington, Telford Shrops.
T. (01952) 256184. - Ant - 069117
Telford Antiques Centre, High St, Telford Shrops.
T. (01952) 256450. - Ant - 069118

Templecombe (Somerset)

Yewtree Antiques, Park House, High St., Templecombe
Somerset. T. (01963) 70505. - Ant -   *069119*

Tenby (Dyfed)

Bull, Andrey, 15 Upper Frog St., Tenby Wales.
T. (01834) 843114. - Ant / Furn / Jew / Silv -   *069120*
Clareston, Warren St., Tenby Wales. T. (01834) 843350.
- Furn / China / Silv -   *069121*

Tenterden (Kent)

Garden House Antiques, 118 High St., Tenterden Kent.
T. (01580) 763664. - Paint / Furn / China -   *069122*
Lace Basket, 1a East Cross, Tenterden Kent.
T. (01580) 763923. - Tex -   *069123*
McMaster, John, 5 Sayers Sq., Tenterden TN30 6BW.
T. (01580) 762941. - Furn / Silv -   *069124*
Tenterden Antiques Centre, 66 High St., Tenterden Kent.
T. (01580) 765885. - Ant -   *069125*

Tetbury (Gloucestershire)

Antique Interiors, 35 Long St., Tetbury Glos.
T. (01666) 504043. - Furn -   *069126*
Balmuir House Antiques, 14 Long St., Tetbury Glos.
T. (01666) 503822. - Paint / Furn -   *069127*
Breakspeare, 36 Long St., Tetbury Glos.
T. (01666) 503122. - Furn / Instr -   *069128*
Breakspeare, 57 Long St., Tetbury Glos.
T. (01666) 503122. - Furn / Instr -   *069129*
Bristow, J. and M., 28 Long St., Tetbury GL8 8AQ.
T. (01666) 502222. - Ant / Furn / Instr -   *069130*
Chest of Drawers, 24 Long St., Tetbury Glos.
T. (01666) 502105. - Furn / China -   *069131*
Country Homes, 61 Long St., Tetbury Glos.
T. (01666) 502342. - Furn -   *069132*
Day, Ann & Roger, 5 New Church St., Tetbury Glos.
T. (01666) 502413. - Furn / China -   *069133*
Dolphin Antiques, 48 Long St., Tetbury Glos.
T. (01666) 504242. - Ant / China -   *069134*
Elgin House Antiques, 1 New Church St., Tetbury Glos.
T. (01666) 504068. - Furn -   *069135*
Hampton Gallery, 10 New Church St., Tetbury Glos.
T. (01666) 502971. - Mil -   *069136*
Nash, Paul, Cherington House, Tetbury GL8 8SN.
T. (01285) 841215. - Furn -   *069137*
Old George, 3 The Chipping, Tetbury GL8 8EU.
T. (01666) 503405. - Paint / Furn / China / Tex /
Lights -   *069138*
Old Mill Market Shop, 12 Church St., Tetbury Glos.
T. (01666) 503127. - Ant -   *069139*
Porch House Antiques, 42 Long St., Tetbury Glos.
T. (01666) 502687. - Paint / Furn / China -   *069140*
Primrose Antiques, 45 Long St., Tetbury Glos.
T. (01666) 502440. - Furn -   *069141*
Rudge, 46 Long St., Tetbury Glos. T. (01666) 503546.
- Furn -   *069142*
Upton Lodge Galleries, 6 Long St., Tetbury Glos.
T. (01666) 503416. - Furn -   *069143*
Yeo Antiques, 6 Westonbirt, Tetbury GL8 5QG.
T. (01666) 880388. - Ant / Furn / China -   *069144*

Tewkesbury (Gloucestershire)

Abbey Antiques, 62 Church St., Tewkesbury Glos.
T. (01684) 292378. - Ant / Naut -   *069145*
Berkeley, 132 High St., Tewkesbury Glos.
T. (01684) 292034. - Furn / China / Tex / Silv /
Glass -   *069146*
Gainsborough House Antiques, 81 Church St., Tewkes-
bury Glos. T. (01684) 293072. - Furn / China /
Glass -   *069147*
Taylor, F.W., 71 Church St., Tewkesbury GL20 5RX.
T. (01684) 295990. - Furn / China / Silv / Glass -   *069148*
Tewkesbury Antique Centre, Tolsey Ln, Tewkesbury
Glos. T. (01684) 294091. - Ant -   *069149*

Teynham (Kent)

Jackson-Grant, 133 London Rd., Teynham Kent.
T. (01795) 522027. - Furn -   *069150*

Thame (Oxfordshire)

Rosemary and Time, 42 Park St., Thame Oxon.
T. (0184) 4216923. - Instr -   *069151*
Thame Antique Galleries, 11-12 High St., Thame Oxon.
T. (0184) 4212725. - Paint / Furn -   *069152*

Thames Ditton (Surrey)

Curzon, David, 1 High St., Thames Ditton Surrey.
T. (0181) 3987860. - Paint -   *069153*
Fern Cottage Antique Centre, 28/30 High St., Thames
Ditton KT7 0RY. T. (0181) 3982281. - Ant -   *069154*

Thatcham (Berkshire)

Jackdaw, Bluecoat School, Thatcham Berks.
T. (01635) 865901. - Ant -   *069155*
Kimbell, Richard, Turnpike Rd, Thatcham Berks.
T. (01635) 874822. - Furn -   *069156*

Thaxted (Essex)

Thaxted Galleries, 1 Newbiggen St., Thaxted CM6 2QS.
T. (01371) 830350. - Furn / Lights -   *069157*
Turpin's, 4 Stoney Lane, Thaxted Essex.
T. (01371) 830495. - Furn -   *069158*

Thirsk (North Yorkshire)

Cottage Antiques and Curios, 1 Market Pl., Thirsk Yorks
North. T. (01845) 522536. - Furn / China / Silv /
Glass -   *069159*
Ogleby, B., 35-37 The Green, Thirsk Yorks North.
T. (01845) 524120. - Furn -   *069160*

Thornhill (Dumfries and Galloway)

Thornhill Gallery Antique Centre, 47-48 Drumlanrig St.,
Thornhill Scotland. T. (01848) 30566. - Ant -   *069161*

Thornton Heath (Surrey)

Corner Cabinet, 446 Whitehorse Rd., Thornton Heath
Surrey. T. (0181) 684 3156. - Ant / Furn -   *069162*

Thrapston (Northamptonshire)

Roe, John, Unit 14, Cottingham Way, Thrapston Northants. T. (01832) 732937. - Ant / Jew / Naut -   *069163*

Thundersley (Essex)

Bramley, 180 Kiln Rd., Thundersley Essex.
T. (01702) 551800. - Furn / China / Jew / Silv /
Glass -   *069164*

Thurso (Highland)

Thurso Antiques, Sinclair St, Thurso Scotland.
T. (01847) 63291. - Paint / Num / China / Jew /
Silv -   *069165*

Tilston (Cheshire)

Well House Antiques, Well House, Tilston Cheshire.
T. (01829) 250332. - China / Silv / Glass -   *069166*

Tingewick (Buckinghamshire)

Lennard, Main St, Tingewick Buck. T. (01280) 848371.
- Furn -   *069167*
Marshall, Tim, Main St., Tingewick Bucks.
T. (01280) 848546. - Furn / Instr -   *069168*
Tingewick Antiques Centre, Main St., Tingewick Bucks.
T. (01280) 847922. - Paint / Furn / China /
Instr -   *069169*

Tintern (Gwent)

Abbey Antiques, On A488 opp. Tintern Abbey, Tintern
Wales. T. (01291) 689233. - Furn / Jew / Silv / Instr /
Naut -   *069170*

Tisbury (Wiltshire)

Marnier, Edward, 17 High St., Tisbury Wilts.
T. (01747) 871074. - Paint / Furn / Tex -   *069171*
Pearson, Carols, 2-4 High St., Tisbury SP3 6PS.
T. (01747) 870710. - Paint / Furn / China -   *069172*

Titchfield (Hampshire)

Gaylords, 75 West St., Titchfield Hants.
T. (01329) 843402. - Furn / Instr / Naut -   *069173*
Manley, Pamela, 6 and 8 South St, Titchfield Hants.
T. (01329) 42794. - China / Sculp / Jew / Silv -   *069174*
Titchfield Antiques, 13-15 South St., Titchfield Hants.
T. (01329) 845968. - Paint / Silv / Glass / Mod -   *069175*

Tiverton (Devon)

Bygone Days Antiques, 40 Gold St., Tiverton Devon.
T. (01884) 252832. - Paint / Furn -   *069176*
Chancery Antiques, 8-10 Barrington St., Tiverton Devon.
T. (01884) 252416. - Furn -   *069177*

Toddington (Bedfordshire)

Cobblers Hall Antiques, 119/121 Leighton Rd, Todding-
ton LU5 6AR. T. (0152) 552890. - China -   *069178*

Todmorden (Lancashire)

Todmorden Fine Art, 27 Water St., Todmorden Yorks
West. T. (01706) 814723. - Paint -   *069179*

Tonbridge (Kent)

Barden House Antiques, 1-3 Priory St, Tonbridge Kent.
T. (01732) 350142. - Ant -   *069180*
Roberts, Derek, 25 Shipbourne Rd., Tonbridge TN10
3DN. T. (01732) 358986, Fax (01732) 770637. - Instr /
Music -   *069181*

Topsham (Devon)

Allnutt, 13 Fore St., Topsham Devon. T. (01392) 874224.
- China / Silv / Glass -   *069182*

Torquay (Devon)

Birbeck, 45 Abbey Rd., Torquay Devon.
T. (01803) 297144. - Ant / Paint / Graph /
Draw -   *069183*
Gold Shop, 24 Torwood St., Torquay Devon. - Jew /
Silv -   *069184*
Rocking Horse Pine, 3 Laburnum Row, Torquay Devon.
T. (01803) 296983. - Furn -   *069185*
Sheraton House, 1 Laburnum Row, Torquay Devon.
T. (01803) 293334. - Furn -   *069186*
Spencer, 187 Union St., Torquay Devon.
T. (01803) 296598. - Ant -   *069187*
Stodgell, Colin, 45 Abbey Rd., Torquay Devon.
T. (01803) 292726. - Paint -   *069188*
Torre, 266 Higher Union St., Torquay Devon.
T. (01803) 292184. - Ant -   *069189*

Totnes (Devon)

Bogan House Antiques, 43 High St., Totnes Devon.
T. (01803) 862075. - Graph / Silv / Glass -   *069190*
Pyke, Beverley J., Gothic House, Bank Ln., Totnes De-
von. T. (01803) 864219. - Paint -   *069191*

Towcester (Northamptonshire)

Clark, 215 Watling St., Towcester Northants.
T. (01327) 52957. - Paint -   *069192*
Green, Ron, 209, 227-239 Watling St, Towcester NN12
7BX. T. (01327) 50387. - Paint / Furn -   *069193*
Jones, John & Jennifer, 2 Watling St., Towcester Nor-
thants. T. (01327) 51898. - Paint / Furn / China /
Naut -   *069194*
Nicholas, R. & M., 161 Watling St., Towcester Northants.
T. (01327) 50639. - China / Silv / Glass -   *069195*
Shelron, 9 1/2 Brackley Rd., Towcester Northants.
T. (01327) 50242. - Ant -   *069196*

Tregony (Cornwall)

Clock Tower Antiques, 57 Fore St., Tregony Cornwall.
T. (0187) 253225. - Ant / Furn / China -   *069197*

Trenance (Cornwall)

South West Coins, Trenance TR8 4DS.
T. (0106374) 063 74 327. - Num -   *069198*

Tring (Hertfordshire)

Bly, John, 50 High St., Tring Herts. T. (01442) 823030.
- Ant / Furn -   *069199*
Country Clocks, 3 Pendley Bridge Cottages, Tring Sta-
tion, Tring HP23 5QU. T. (01442) 825090.
- Instr -   *069200*
Farrelly, 50 High St., Tring Herts. T. (01442) 891905.
- Furn -   *069201*

Truro (Cornwall)

Bennett, Alan, 24 New Bridge St., Truro TR1 2AA.
T. (01872) 73296. - Paint / Graph / Furn / China /
Jew -   *069202*
Pydar Antiques and Gallery, Pydar St, Truro.
T. (01872) 510485. - Paint / Graph / Furn / China /
Silv -   *069203*
Winkworth, Richard, Calenick St., Truro Cornwall.
T. (01872) 40901. - Furn / China / Glass -   *069204*

Tunbridge Wells (Kent)

Aaron, 77 Saint Johns Rd., Tunbridge Wells Kent.
T. (01634) 241748. - Paint / Graph / Furn / China /
Instr -   *069205*

Amadeus Antiques, 32 Mount Ephraim, Tunbridge Wells Kent. T. (01892) 544406. - Ant / Furn / China -   069206
Annexe Antiques, 33 The Pantiles, Tunbridge Wells Kent. T. (01892) 547213. - Paint / China / Mil / Glass / Toys-   069207
Antique Pine Shop, 2 Mount Sion, Tunbridge Wells Kent. T. (01892) 511591. - Ant / Furn / China -   069208
Chapel Place Antiques, 9 Chapel Pl., Tunbridge Wells Kent. T. (01892) 546561. - Furn / China / Jew / Silv / Toys-   069209
Clare Gallery, 21 High St., Tunbridge Wells TN1 1AA. T. (01892) 538717. - Paint -   069210
Collectables, 53 Colebrook Rd., Tunbridge Wells Kent. T. (01892) 539085. - Ant -   069211
Corn Exchange Antiques, 29 The Pantiles, Tunbridge Wells Kent. T. (01892) 539652. - Paint / Furn / China / Silv / Instr -   069212
County Antiques, 94 High St., Tunbridge Wells Kent. T. (01892) 530767. - Ant -   069213
Cowden, 24 Mount Ephraim Rd., Tunbridge Wells Kent. T. (01892) 520752. - Ant / Furn -   069214
Glassdrumman Antiques, Antique Centre, Union Sq., Tunbridge Wells Kent. T. (01892) 533708. - Furn / China / Jew / Silv / Glass -   069215
Graham, 1 Castle St., Tunbridge Wells Kent. T. (01892) 526695. - Paint -   069216
Hadlow, 1 The Pantiles, Tunbridge Wells Kent. T. (01825) 830368. - Instr / Toys -   069217
Neville, Howard, 21 The Pantiles, Tunbridge Wells Kent. T. (01892) 511461. - Ant / Furn / Sculp -   069218
Pantiles Antiques, 31 The Pantiles, Tunbridge Wells Kent. T. (01892) 531291. - Ant / Paint / Furn / China -   069219
Pantiles Spa Antiques, 4-6 Union House, The Pantiles, Tunbridge Wells Kent. T. (01892) 541377. - Furn / China / Jew / Instr / Music -   069220
Rare Chairs, 37 Quarry Rd., Tunbridge Wells Kent. T. (01892) 521783. - Ant / Toys -   069221
Relf, 132/134 Camden Rd, Tunbridge Wells Kent. T. (01892) 538362. - Furn -   069222
Russell, Patricia, 43 Mount Ephraim, Tunbridge Wells Kent. T. (01892) 523719. - Furn / China / Jew / Silv / Glass -   069223
Strawson, 33, 39 and 41 The Pantiles, Tunbridge Wells TN2 5TE. T. (01892) 530607. - Furn / Silv / Glass -   069224
Thompson, John, 27 The Pantiles, Tunbridge Wells Kent. T. (01892) 547215. - Paint / Furn / China / Glass -   069225
Tunbridge Wells Antique Centre, Union Sq, Tunbridge Wells Kent. T. (01892) 533708. - Ant -   069226
Up Country, 68 Saint Johns Rd., Tunbridge Wells Kent. T. (01892) 523341. - Furn -   069227
Wood, Alan, 33 The Pantiles, Tunbridge Wells Kent. T. (01892) 547213. - China -   069228

Tutbury (Staffordshire)
Town and Country Antiques, 40 Monk St., Tutbury Staffs. T. (01283) 520556. - Furn / Tex -   069229
Tutbury Mill Antiques, 6 Lower High St., Tutbury Staffs. T. (01283) 815999. - Furn -   069230

Twickenham (Greater London)
Ailsa, 32 Crown Rd., Twickenham Middx. T. (0181) 891 2345. - Paint / Furn / Sculp / Silv / Glass -   069231
Alberts, 113 London Rd., Twickenham Middx. T. (0181) 891 3067. - Graph / Mil -   069232
Marble Hill Gallery, 70/72 Richmond Rd, Twickenham TW1 3BE. T. (0181) 892 1488. - Paint / Furn / China -   069233
Morley, David, 371 Richmond Rd., Twickenham Middx. T. (0181) 892 2986. - Ant -   069234
Phelps, 133-135 Saint Margaret's Rd., Twickenham TW1 1RG. T. (0181) 8921778, Fax (0181) 923661. - Furn / Naut -   069235
Shenton, Rita, 148 Percy Rd., Twickenham Middx. T. (0181) 894 6888, Fax (0181) 8938766. - Instr -   069236
Wilcox, Neil, 113 Strawberry Vale, Twickenham Middx. T. (0181) 892 5858. - Glass -   069237

Twyford (Hampshire)
Twyford Antiques, High St., Twyford Hants. T. (01962) 713484. - Furn / Instr -   069238

Tynemouth (Tyne and Wear)
Renaissance Antiques, 11 Front St., Tynemouth Tyne & Wear. T. (0191) 259 5555. - Furn / China / Silv / Naut -   069239
Sharp, Ian, 23 Front St., Tynemouth Tyne & Wear. T. (0191) 296 0656. - Paint / Furn / China -   069240
Strain, David F., 66 Front St., Tynemouth Tyne & Wear. T. (0191) 259 2459. - Ant / Furn -   069241

Uckfield (Sussex)
Barness Gallery, 8 Church St., Uckfield Sussex East. T. (01825) 762066. - Paint -   069242
Bowlby, Nicholas, Owl House, Poundgate, Uckfield Sussex East. T. (01892) 653722. - Paint / Draw -   069243
Deverall, Ivan R., Duval House Cambridge Way, Uckfield Sussex East. T. (01825) 762474. - Graph -   069244
Georgian House Antiques, 222 High St., Uckfield Sussex East. T. (01825) 765074. - Furn -   069245
Ringles Cross Antiques, Ringless Cross, Uckfield Sussex East. T. (01825) 762909. - Furn / Orient -   069246

Ulverston (Cumbria)
A1A Antiques, 59B Market St, Ulverston Cumbria. T. (01229) 869745. - Paint / Furn / Instr -   069247
Elizabeth & Son, Market Hall, Ulverston Cumbria. T. (01229) 52763. - Jew / Silv / Glass -   069248

Upminster (Essex)
Old Cottage Antiques, Old Cottage, Corbets Tey, Upminster Essex. T. (01708) 222867. - Ant / Furn / China / Silv -   069249

Uppermill (Greater Manchester)
Queen Anne Gallery, High St., Uppermill Lancs. T. (01457) 874537. - Furn / Tex -   069250

Uppingham (Leicestershire)
Bay House Antiques, 33 High St., Uppingham Leics. T. (01572) 821045. - Paint / Furn / China / Glass -   069251
Clutter, 14 Orange St., Uppingham Leics. T. (01572) 823745. - Furn / China / Tex / Silv / Glass -   069252
Garner, John, 51-53 High St., Uppingham Leics. T. (01572) 823607, Fax (01572) 821654. - Paint / Graph / Furn -   069253
Gilbert, Ayston Rd., Uppingham Leics. T. (01572) 823486. - Ant -   069254
Martin Antiques, Marie-Ange, 43 High St., Uppingham Leics. T. (01572) 821359. - Paint / Furn / Silv -   069255
Roberts, T. J., 39/41 High St, East, Uppingham Leics. T. (01572) 821493. - Paint / Furn / China -   069256
Royall Antiques, E. and C., Printers Yard, High St, Uppingham Leics. T. (0185) 883. - Paint / Furn / China / Sculp / Silv -   069257
Tattersall's, 14b Orange St., Uppingham Leics. T. (01572) 821171. - Tex -   069258

Upton-upon-Severn (Hereford and Worcester)
Highway Gallery, 40 Old St., Upton-upon-Severn Herefs & Worcs. T. (01684) 592645. - Paint -   069259

Usk (Gwent)
Castle Antiques, 41 Old Market St., Usk NP5 1AL. T. (01291) 672424. - Ant / China -   069260

Uxbridge (Greater London)
Antiques Warehouse, 34-36 Rockingham Rd., Uxbridge UB8 2TZ. T. (01895) 256963. - Ant / Naut -   069261
Barnard, Thomas, 11 Windsor St., Uxbridge Middx. T. (01895) 258054. - Paint -   069262

Waddesdon (Buckinghamshire)
Collectors' Corner, 106 High St., Waddesdon Bucks. T. (01296) 651563. - Ant / China / Jew / Silv -   069263

Wadebridge (Cornwall)
Saint Breock Gallery, Saint Breock Churchtown, Wadebridge PL27 7JS. T. (01208) 812543. - Ant / Paint / Furn -   069264

Victoria Antiques, 21 Molesworth St., Wadebridge Cornwall. T. (01208) 814160. - Furn -   069265

Wakefield (West Yorkshire)
Taylor, Robin, 36 Carter St., Wakefield Yorks West. T. (01924) 381809. - Paint -   069266
Tuckwell, D. K., 45 Regent St., Wakefield Yorks West. T. (01924) 377467. - Ant -   069267

Walkerburn (Borders)
Townhouse Antiques, Walkerburn Scotland. T. (0189) 687694. - Furn / China / Tex -   069268

Wallasey (Merseyside)
Arbiter, 10 Atherton St, Wallasey Merseyside. T. (0151) 639 1159. - Paint / Orient / Eth / Draw -   069269
Decade Antiques, 62 Grove Rd., Wallasey Merseyside. T. (0151) 6396905. - Paint / Furn / Tex -   069270

Wallingford (Oxfordshire)
de Albuquerque, Michael & Jane, 12 High St., Wallingford Oxon. T. (01491) 832322. - Furn -   069271
Lamb Arcade, High St., Wallingford Oxon. T. (01491) 835048. - Ant -   069272
MGJ Antiques, 1A Saint Martins St, Wallingford Oxon. T. (01491) 834336. - Jew -   069273
Ottrey, Mike, 16 High St., Wallingford Oxon. T. (01491) 836429. - Paint / Furn -   069274
Second Time Around Antiques, 6 Saint Peters St., Wallingford Oxon. T. (01491) 839345. - Furn / China / Silv / Instr -   069275
Summers & Son, David, 6 High St., Wallingford OX10 0BP. T. (01491) 836284, Fax (01491) 833443. - Furn -   069276

Wallington (Surrey)
Manor Antiques, 75A Manor Rd, Wallington Surrey. T. (0181) 6695970. - Ant -   069277

Walsall (West Midlands)
Nicholls, 57 George St., Walsall. T. (01922) 641081. - Jew -   069278
Past and Present, 66 George St., Walsall West Mids. T. (01922) 611151. - Furn / China / Tex -   069279
Rutter, Jon & Kate, 309 Bloxwich Rd., Walsall West Mids. T. (01922) 92323. - Ant -   069280
Walsall Antiques Centre, 7A Digbeth Arcade, Walsall West Mids. T. (01922) 725163, Fax (01922) 725163. - Ant -   069281

Walton-on-Thames (Surrey)
Becker, Susan, Walton-on-Thames Surrey. T. (01932) 227820. - China / Glass -   069282
Boathouse Gallery, The Towpath, Manor Rd., Walton-on-Thames Surrey. T. (01932) 242718. - Paint / Graph -   069283

Walton-on-the-Hill (Surrey)
Caldwell, Ian, 9a Tadworth Green, Dorking Rd., Walton-on-the-Hill Surrey. T. (01737) 813969. - Furn - 069284

Wansford (Cambridgeshire)
Old House Antiques, 16 London Rd., Wansford Cambs. T. (01780) 783999. - Lights -   069285
Sydney House Antiques, 14 Elton Rd., Wansford Cambs. T. (01780) 782786. - Furn -   069286
Wansford Antiques and Oriental Pottery, 10 London Rd., Wansford Cambs. T. (01780) 783253. - Furn / China -   069287

Wareham (Dorset)
Heirlooms, 21 South St., Wareham Dorset. T. (01929) 554207. - Jew / Silv -   069288

Wargrave (Berkshire)
Millgreen Antiques, 86 High St, Wargrave Berks. T. (01734) 402955. - Furn / China / Glass -   069289
Wargrave Antiques, 66 High St., Wargrave Berks. T. (01734) 402914. - Furn -   069290

Warminster (Wiltshire)
Antique Warehouse, 61 East St., Warminster Wilts. T. (01985) 219460. - Ant / Naut -   069291
Bishopstrow, 55 East St., Warminster Wilts. T. (01985) 212683. - Furn / China / Silv -   069292

Britannia Antiques Exports, 61 East St., Warminster
Wilts. T. (01985) 219360. - Ant - *069293*
Century Antiques, 10 Silver St., Warminster Wilts.
T. (01985) 217031. - Ant - *069294*
Choice Antiques, 4 Silver St., Warminster Wilts.
T. (01985) 218924. - Ant - *069295*
Houghton, Peter, 33 Silver St., Warminster Wilts.
T. (01985) 213451. - Paint / Furn / Instr - *069296*
Hurley, Emma, 9 Silver St., Warminster Wilts.
T. (01985) 219726. - Furn / Tex - *069297*
Obelisk Antiques, 2 Silver St., Warminster Wilts.
T. (01985) 846646, Fax (01985) 219901.
- Furn - *069298*
Welch, K. & A., A1 Church St, Warminster BA12 8PG.
T. (01985) 214687. - Furn / Naut - *069299*

Warrington (Cheshire)
Rocking Chair Antiques, Unit 3, Saint Peter's Way, Warrington Cheshire. T. (01925) 52409. - Furn - *069300*

Warwick (Warwickshire)
Apollo Antiques, Birmingham Rd., Warwick Works.
T. (01926) 494746, Fax (01926) 401477. - Paint / Furn /
Sculp - *069301*
Bray, H. H., 9 Jury St., Warwick Works.
T. (01926) 492791. - China / Jew / Silv - *069302*
Goodwin & Sons, John, Unit F and M Budbrooke Rd,
Warwick Warks. T. (01926) 491191,
Fax (01926) 491191. - Furn - *069303*
Lane, Russell, 2-4 High St., Warwick Warks.
T. (01926) 494494. - Furn / China / Jew / Silv - *069304*
Morley, Patrick & Gillian, 62 West St., Warwick Warks.
T. (01926) 494464, Fax (01926) 400531. - Furn /
Sculp / Tex - *069305*
Pacne, Martin, 30 Brook St., Warwick Warks.
T. (01926) 494498. - Silv - *069306*
Pine Design, 33 The Saltisford, Warwick Warks.
T. (01926) 494666. - Furn - *069307*
Reeve, James, 9 Church St., Warwick Warks.
T. (01926) 498113. - Ant / Furn / China - *069308*
Smith Street Antiques Centre, 7 Smith St., Warwick
Warks. T. (01926) 497864. - Ant - *069309*
Spencer, Don, 36a Market Place, Warwick Warks.
T. (01926) 499857. - Furn - *069310*
Vintage Antique Market, 36 Market Pl., Warwick Warks.
T. (01926) 491527. - Furn / China / Glass - *069311*
Warwick Antique Centre, 20-22 High St., Warwick
Warks. T. (01926) 495704. - Ant - *069312*
Warwick Antiques, 16-18 High St., Warwick CV34 4AP.
T. (01926) 492482, Fax (01926) 493867.
- Ant - *069313*
Westgate Antiques, 28 West St., Warwick Warks.
T. (01926) 494106. - Furn / Silv - *069314*

Washington (Tyne and Wear)
Carr, Harold J., Field House, Rickleton, Washington Tyne
& Wear. T. (0191) 388 6442. - Ant / Furn - *069315*

Washington (West Sussex)
Chanctonbury, Clematis Cottage, Washington RH20 4AP.
T. (01903) 892233. - Ant / Furn / China / Glass - *069316*
Sandhill Barn Antiques, Sandhill Barn, Washington RH20
4AJ. T. (01903) 892210. - Furn - *069317*

Watchet (Somerset)
Clarence House Antiques, 41 Swain St., Watchet Somerset. T. (01984) 31389. - Ant / Furn - *069318*

Watford (Hertfordshire)
Copper Kettle Antiques, 172 Bushey Mill Ln., Watford
Herts. T. (01923) 248877. - Ant / Paint / Furn /
Instr - *069319*

Watlington (Oxfordshire)
Cross Antiques, 37 High St., Watlington Oxon.
T. (01491) 612324. - Furn / Furn - *069320*
Orton, Stephen, Antiques Warehouse, Shirburn Rd., Wat-
lington Oxon. T. (01491) 613752, Fax (01491) 613875.
- Furn - *069321*

Watton (Norfolk)
Clermont Antiques, Clermont Hall, Watton Norfolk.
T. (01953) 882189. - Furn - *069322*

Wedmore (Somerset)
Coach House Gallery, Church St., Wedmore Somerset.
T. (01934) 712718. - Paint / Furn / China / Silv /
Glass - *069323*

Wednesbury (West Midlands)
Wilkins, Brett, 81 Holyhead Rd., Wednesbury West Mids.
T. (0121) 502 0720. - Furn / Naut - *069324*

Weedon (Northamptonshire)
Helios & Co., 25/27 High St, Weedon Northants.
T. (01327) 40264. - Furn - *069325*
Rococo Antiques, 5 New St., Weedon Northants.
T. (01327) 41288. - Ant - *069326*
Thirty-Eight Antiques, 14 Royal Ordance Depot, Weedon
Northants. T. (01327) 40766, Fax (01327) 40808.
- Furn - *069327*
Village Antique Market, 62 High St., Weedon Northants.
T. (01327) 42015. - Ant - *069328*

Wellingborough (Northamptonshire)
Antqiues and Bric-a-Brac Market, Market Sq., Town
Centre, Wellingborough Northants. T. (01905) 611321.
- Ant - *069329*
Park Gallery, 16 Cannon St., Wellingborough Northants.
T. (01933) 222592. - Graph - *069330*
Perkins, Finedon Rd, Wellingborough Northants.
T. (01933) 228812. - Paint / Furn - *069331*

Wellington (Somerset)
Lewis, Michael & Amanda, 8 North St., Wellington Som-
erset. T. (01823) 667430. - Tex - *069332*
Oxenhams, 74 Mantle St., Wellington Somerset.
T. (01823) 662592. - Ant - *069333*

Wells (Somerset)
Berryman, Shelagh, 15 Market Pl., Wells Somerset.
T. (01749) 676203. - Ant / Instr / Music - *069334*
House, Bernard G., Market Pl., Wells Somerset.
T. (01749) 672607. - Furn / Instr - *069335*
Lovejoys, Queen St., Wells Somerset.
T. (01749) 670706, Fax (01275) 333302. - Paint / Furn /
China - *069336*
Nowell, Edward A., 12 Market Pl., Wells BA5 2RB.
T. (01749) 672415, Fax (01749) 670508. - Furn / Jew /
Silv / Instr - *069337*
Nowell, Marcus, 21 Market Pl., Wells Somerset.
T. (01749) 678051. - Furn - *069338*

Wells-next-the-Sea (Norfolk)
Church Street Antiques, 2 Church St., Wells-next-the-
Sea Norfolk. T. (01328) 711698. - Ant / Tex /
Jew - *069339*
Wells Antique Centre, Old Mill, Maryland, Wells-next-
the-Sea Norfolk. T. (01328) 711433. - Ant - *069340*

Welshpool (Powys)
Anderson & Son, F. E., 5-6 High St., Welshpool Wales.
T. (01938) 553340. - Paint / Furn / China / Silv /
Glass - *069341*
Horley, 19 High St., Welshpool Wales.
T. (01938) 552421. - Ant / Paint - *069342*
School House Antiques, 21 High St., Welshpool Wales.
T. (01938) 554858. - Paint / Furn / Silv - *069343*
Waterloo Antiques, Salop Rd., Welshpool Wales.
T. (01938) 553999. - Paint / Furn / China - *069344*

Wembley (Greater London)
Kelaty, L., Kelaty House, First Way, Wembley Middx.
T. (0181) 903 9998. - Tex - *069345*

Wendover (Buckinghamshire)
Antiques at Wendover, 25 High St, Wendover Bucks.
T. (01296) 625335. - Ant / Furn / Silv / Lights - *069346*
Bowood Antiques, Bowood Lane, Wendover HP22 6PY.
T. (01296) 622113. - Furn / China / Tex - *069347*
Turner, Sally, Hogarth House, High St., Wendover Bucks.
T. (01296) 624402. - Ant / Furn - *069348*
Wendover Antiques, 1 South St., Wendover Bucks.
T. (01296) 622078. - Paint / Graph / Furn / Silv - *069349*

West Bridgford (Nottinghamshire)
Bridgford Antiques, 2A Rushworth Av, West Bridgford
Notts. T. (01602) 821835. - Ant / Paint / Furn - *069350*

Cotton, Joan, 5 Davies Rd., West Bridgford NG2 5JE.
T. (01602) 813043. - Ant / China / Jew / Silv /
Glass - *069351*
Moulton's, 5 Portland Rd., West Bridgford Notts.
T. (01602) 814354. - Ant - *069352*

West Haddon (Northamptonshire)
Antiques, 9 West End, West Haddon Northants.
T. (01788) 510772. - Furn - *069353*
Country Pine Shop, Romney Bldg., Northampton Rd.,
West Haddon Northants. T. (01788) 510430.
- Furn - *069354*
Hopwell, Paul, 30 High St., West Haddon Northants.
T. (01788) 510636. - Paint / Furn / Instr - *069355*

West Kirby (Merseyside)
Horswill, Helen, 62 Grange Rd., West Kirby L48 1PJ.
T. (0151) 6258660. - Furn - *069356*
Oliver Antiques, 62 Grange Rd., West Kirby Merseyside.
T. (0151) 6252803. - Ant - *069357*
Trentini, 79 Banks Rd., West Kirby Merseyside.
T. (0151) 6252122. - Ant - *069358*
Victoria Cottage Antiques, 6 Village Rd., West Kirby Mer-
seyside. T. (0151) 6257517. - Graph / Furn /
China - *069359*

West Malling (Kent)
Old Clock Shop, 63 High St., West Malling Kent.
T. (01732) 843246. - Instr - *069360*
Pataky, Victoria, 3 The Colonnade, West Malling Kent.
T. (01732) 843646. - Ant - *069361*
Scott House Antiques, Scott House, High St., West Mal-
ling ME 19 6QH. T. (01732) 841380. - Ant / Furn / Chi-
na / Silv / Instr - *069362*
Smith, Andrew, 89 High St., West Malling Kent.
T. (01732) 843087. - China / Jew / Silv / Instr - *069363*

West Peckham (Kent)
Langold, Oxon Heath, West Peckham TN11 0DA.
T. (01732) 810577. - Furn - *069364*
Persian Rugs, Vines Farm, Matthews Lane, West Peck-
ham Kent. T. (01732) 850228. - Tex - *069365*

Westbury (Wiltshire)
Booth, 30 Edenvale Rd., Westbury Wilts.
T. (01373) 823271. - Graph - *069366*
Coggins, Ray, 1 Fore St., Westbury Wilts.
T. (01373) 826574. - Furn - *069367*

Westcliff-on-Sea (Essex)
David, Jean & John, 587 London Rd., Westcliff-on-Sea
Essex. T. (01702) 339106, Fax (01268) 560536.
- Furn / China / Instr / Mil - *069368*
It's About TIme, 863 London Rd., Westclliff-on-Sea Es-
sex. T. (01702) 72574. - Furn / Instr - *069369*

Westcott (Surrey)
Westcott Antiques, The Studio, Parsonage Lane, West-
cott Surrey. T. (01306) 881900. - Furn - *069370*
Westcott Gallery, 4 Guildford Rd., Westcott Surrey.
T. (01306) 876261. - Paint - *069371*

Westerham (Kent)
Apollo Galleries, 19-21 Market Sq, Westerham Kent.
T. (01959) 562200. - Ant / Paint / Furn / China / Silv /
Instr - *069372*
Brazil Antiques, 2 The Green, Westerham Kent.
T. (01959) 563048. - Furn - *069373*
Castle Antiques Centre, 1 London Rd., Westerham Kent.
T. (01959) 562492. - Ant - *069374*
Hook, Anthony J., 3 The Green, Westerham Kent.
T. (01959) 562161. - Furn - *069375*
London House Antiques, 4 Market St., Westerham Kent.
T. (01959) 564479. - Paint / Furn / Sculp - *069376*
McNair, Hugh, 1 Fullers Hill, Westerham Kent.
T. (01959) 562970. - Furn / Silv / Toys - *069377*
Mistral Galleries, 12 Market Sq., Westerham Kent.
T. (01959) 564477. - Paint / Furn / China - *069378*
Old Hall, 24 Market Sq., Westerham Kent.
T. (01959) 563114. - Furn / China / Sculp - *069379*
Sargeant, Denys, 21 The Green, Westerham TN16 1AX.
T. (01959) 562130. - Glass - *069380*
Taylor-Smith, 4 The Grange, High St., Westerham TN16
1AH. T. (01959) 563100. - Ant / Paint / Furn / China /
Glass - *069381*

Weston-super-Mare (Avon)

Bay Tree House Antiques, Stevens Lane, Lympsham, Weston-super-Mare Avon. T. (01934) 750367.
- Furn -   069382
D.M. Restorations, 3 Laburnum Rd., Weston-super-Mare Avon. T. (01934) 631681. - Furn -   069383
Harwood, 13 West St., Weston-super-Mare BS23 1JR. T. (01934) 629874. - Ant / Jew / Instr -   069384
Moorland Antiques, 134 Moorland Rd., Weston-super-Mare Avon. T. (01934) 632361. - Ant -   069385
Toby's Antiques, 47 Upper Church Rd., Weston-super-Mare Avon. T. (01934) 623555. - Ant / Furn -   069386
Winters, 62 Severn Rd., Weston-super-Mare Avon. T. (01934) 620118. - Ant / Furn / Instr -   069387

Wetherby (West Yorkshire)

Mitchell-Hill, 2 Church St., Wetherby Yorks West. T. (01937) 585929. - Paint -   069388

Weybridge (Surrey)

Church House Antiques, 42 Church St., Weybridge Surrey. T. (01932) 842190. - Paint / Furn / Jew -   069389
Clock Shop Weybridge, 64 Church St., Weybridge Surrey. T. (01932) 840407. - Instr -   069390
Cross, Edward, 128 Oatlands Dr., Weybridge Surrey. T. (01932) 851093. - Paint -   069391
Hatch, 49 Church St., Weybridge Surrey. T. (01932) 846782. - Ant / Furn / Instr -   069392
Jandora, 112 Oatlands Dr, Weybridge Surrey. T. (01932) 851858. - Graph / Furn / China / Silv / Toys -   069393
Not Just Silver, 16 York Rd., Weybridge Surrey. T. (01932) 842468. - Paint / Furn / China / Silv - 069394
Saunders, R., 71 Queen's Rd., Weybridge KT13 9SQ. T. (01932) 842601. - Ant / Furn / China / Silv / Instr -   069395
Weybridge Antiques, 43 Church St., Weybridge Surrey. T. (01932) 852503. - Paint / Furn -   069396

Weymouth (Dorset)

Finesse Fine Art, 9 Coniston Crescent, Weymouth Dorset. T. (01305) 770463, Fax (01305) 761459.
- Lights -   069397
North Quay Antique Centre, North Quay, Weymouth Dorset. T. (01305) 779313. - Ant -   069398
Park Antiquities, Park St., Weymouth Dorset. T. (01305) 787666. - Ant / Furn / China -   069399
Treasure Chest, 29 East St., Weymouth DT4 8BN. T. (01305) 772757. - Ant / Paint / Num / China / Silv -   069400

Whaley Bridge (Derbyshire)

Nimbus, Chapel Rd, Whaley Bridge Derbys. T. (01663) 734248. - Instr -   069401

Whalley (Lancashire)

Abbey Antique Shop, 43 and 45 King St, Whalley BB6 9SP. T. (01254) 823139. - Furn / China / Glass - 069402
Davies, 32 King St., Whalley Lancs. T. (01254) 823764. - Furn / Jew / Instr -   069403

Wheathampstead (Hertfordshire)

Collins, Corner House, Wheathampstead AL4 8AP. T. (0158) 2833111. - Furn -   069404

Whitby (North Yorkshire)

Aird-Gordon, 15 Baxtergate, Whitby. T. (01947) 601515. - Furn / China / Jew / Glass -   069405
Bazaar, 7 Skinner St., Whitby Yorks North. T. (01947) 602281. - Ant / Furn / Jew -   069406
Bobbins, Wesley Hall, Church St., Whitby Yorks North. T. (01947) 600585. - Ant / Lights -   069407
Caedmon House, 14 Station Sq., Whitby Yorks North. T. (01947) 602120. - Ant / China / Jew / Toys - 069408
Coach House Antiques, Coach Rd., Sleights, Whitby YO22 5BT. T. (01947) 810313. - Ant / Paint / Furn / Jew / Silv -   069409
Mount Antiques, Khyber Pass, Whitby YO21 3HD. T. (01947) 604516. - Paint / Furn -   069410

Whitchurch (Buckinghamshire)

Deerstalker Antiques, 28 High St., Whitchurch HP22 4JT. T. (01296) 641505. - Ant -   069411

Whitchurch (Hampshire)

Regency House Antiques, 14 Church St., Whitchurch RG28 7AB. T. (01256) 892149. - Ant / Furn / Instr -   069412

Whitchurch (Shropshire)

Civic Antiques, Dairy Farm, Heath Rd, Whitchurch Shrops. T. (01948) 2626, Fax (01948) 3604.
- Furn -   069413
Dodington Antiques, 15 Dodington, Whitchurch SY13 1EA. T. (01948) 663399. - Ant / Furn / Instr -   069414
Whitney, Robert, Withinlee, Alport Rd., Whitchurch Shrops. T. (01948) 4084. - Furn -   069415

White Colne (Essex)

Compton-Dando, Berewyk Hall, White Colne Essex. T. (01787) 222200, Fax (01787) 222945.
- Furn -   069416
Fox & Pheasant Antique Pine, White Colne Essex. T. (01787) 223297. - Furn -   069417

White Roding (Essex)

White Roding Antiques, Ivydene, Chelmsford Rd., White Roding Essex. T. (01279) 876376. - Furn / Naut -   069418

Whitefield (Lancashire)

Donn, Henry, 138/142 Bury New Rd, Whitefield Lancs. T. (0161) 7668819. - Paint -   069419

Whitley Bay (Tyne and Wear)

Bric-a-Brac, 195 Park View, Whitley Bay NE25 8EH. T. (0191) 252 6141. - Ant -   069420
Northumbria Pine, 54 Whitley Rd., Whitley Bay Tyne & Wear. T. (0191) 252 4550. - Furn -   069421
Treasure Chest, 2 and 4 Norham Rd, Whitley Bay Tyne & Wear. T. (0191) 2512052. - Ant -   069422

Whitstable (Kent)

Laurens, 2 Harbour St., Whitstable Kent. T. (01227) 261940. - Furn -   069423
Magpie, 8 Harbour St., Whitstable Kent. T. (01227) 771666. - Ant -   069424
Tankerton Antiques, 136 Tankerton Rd., Whitstable Kent. T. (01227) 266490. - Furn / China / Glass - 069425

Whitwell (Hertfordshire)

Boosey, Simon, Tun House, Whitwell Herts. T. (01438) 871563. - Tex -   069426

Wickham Market (Suffolk)

Crafer, The Hill, Wickham Market Suffolk. T. (01728) 747347. - Furn / China / Jew / Silv / Glass -   069427
Webb, Roy, 179 High St., Wickham Market Suffolk. T. (01728) 746077. - Furn / Instr -   069428

Wigan (Lancashire)

de Rouffignac, Colin, 57 Wigan Ln., Wigan Lancs. T. (01942) 37927. - Paint / Furn / Jew -   069429
Robinson, John, 172-176 Manchester Rd., Wigan Lancs. T. (01942) 47773. - Ant -   069430
Roby, John, 12 Lord St., Wigan Lancs. T. (01942) 30887. - Ant / Furn -   069431
Whatnot Antiques, 90 Wigan Lane, Wigan Lancs. T. (01942) 491880. - Ant -   069432

Wigton (Cumbria)

Jackson, S., 71 High St., Wigton Cumbria. T. (0169) 7345034. - Ant -   069433

Williton (Somerset)

Venn, Edward, 52 Long St., Williton Somerset. T. (01984) 32631. - Furn / Instr -   069434

Wilmslow (Cheshire)

Bosson, Peter, 10B Swan St, Wilmslow SK9 1HE. T. (01625) 525250. - Instr -   069435
Chapel Antiques, 59 Chapel Ln., Wilmslow Cheshire. T. (01625) 548061. - Paint / Furn / China -   069436

Wilton (Wiltshire)

Brook, Ian J., 26 North St., Wilton SP2 0HJ. T. (01722) 743392. - Paint / Furn -   069437
Earle, 47 North St., Wilton Wilts. T. (01722) 743284. - Ant -   069438

Lynch, Pamela, 18 West St., Wilton Wilts. T. (01722) 744113. - Paint / Furn -   069439
Romain & Sons, A. J., 11 and 13 North St, Wilton Wilts. T. (01722) 743350. - Furn -   069440

Wimborne Minster (Dorset)

Antiquatat Antiques, Old Civic Centre, Hanham Rd., Wimborne Minster Dorset. T. (01202) 887496. - China / Silv / Instr -   069441
Barnes House Antiques, West Row, Wimborne Minster Dorset. T. (01202) 886275. - Ant -   069442
J.B. Antiques, 10A West Row, Wimborne Minster Dorset. T. (01202) 882522. - Furn -   069443
T.W. Antiques, 12 West Row, Wimborne Minster Dorset. T. (01202) 888958. - Furn -   069444
Victoriana Antiques, 3 Leigh Rd., Wimborne Minster Dorset. T. (01202) 886739. - Ant / China / Jew / Glass -   069445
West Borough Antiques, 36 West Borough, Wimborne Minster Dorset. T. (01202) 841167. - Ant / China -   069446

Wincanton (Somerset)

Sainsbury, Barry M., 17 High St., Wincanton Somerset. T. (01963) 32289. - Paint / Furn / China / Glass - 069447

Winchcombe (Gloucestershire)

Kenulf Fine Arts, 5 North St., Winchcombe Glos. T. (01242) 603204. - Paint / Graph / Furn / China -   069448
Lindsay, Muriel, Queen Anne House, High St., Winchcombe GL54 5LJ. T. (01242) 602319. - Ant / Glass -   069449
Prichard, 16 High St., Winchcombe Glos. T. (01242) 603566. - Furn -   069450

Winchester (Hampshire)

Bell, 67b Parchment St., Winchester Hants. T. (01962) 860439. - Paint / Graph -   069451
Blanchard, J. W., 12 Jewry St., Winchester SO23 8PE. T. (01962) 854547, Fax (01962) 842572. - Ant / Furn -   069452
Burns & Graham, 4 Saint Thomas St., Winchester Hants. T. (01962) 853779. - Furn -   069453
Marsh, Gerald E., 32a The Square, Winchester Hants. T. (01962) 844443. - Instr -   069454
Pine Cellars, 39 Jewry St., Winchester Hants. T. (01962) 867014. - Furn -   069455
Printed Page, 2-3 Bridge St., Winchester Hants. T. (01962) 854072, Fax (01962) 862995.
- Graph -   069456
Roofe, Mary, 67 Parchment St., Winchester SO23 8AT. T. (01962) 840613. - Furn -   069457
Skipwith, W. G., 5 Parchment St., Winchester Hants. T. (01962) 852911. - Paint / Graph / Furn - 069458
Spencer, Samuel, 39 Jewry St., Winchester Hants. T. (01962) 867014. - Ant -   069459
Thompson, 20a Jewry St., Winchester Hants. T. (01962) 866633. - Paint / Furn / Naut -   069460
Todd & Austin, 2 Andover Rd., Winchester SO23 7BS. T. (01962) 869824. - Ant -   069461
Webb, 6 and 8 Romsey Rd, Winchester Hants. T. (01962) 842273. - Paint / Furn -   069462

Windermere (Cumbria)

Birdcage Antiques, College Rd., Windermere Cumbria. T. (015394) 45063. - Ant / China / Lights / Glass -   069463
Century Antiques, 13 Victoria St., Windermere Cumbria. T. (015394) 44126. - Ant / Furn / Instr -   069464
Thornton, Joseph, 4 Victoria St., Windermere Cumbria. T. (015394) 42930. - Ant / Paint / Furn / Instr - 069465

Windsor (Berkshire)

Addison Bros., 25 King's Rd., Windsor Berks. T. (01753) 863780. - Furn -   069466
Bousfield, Guy, 58 Thames St., Windsor Berks. T. (01753) 864575. - Furn -   069467
Compton, 42 Thames St., Windsor Berks. T. (01753) 830100. - Ant / Furn / China / Jew / Silv -   069468
Dee's Antiques, 89a Grove, Windsor Berks. T. (01753) 865627. - Ant -   069469

Grove Gallery, 89 Grove Rd., Windsor Berks.
T. (01753) 865954. - Paint / Graph -   *069470*
O'Connor Bros., 59 Saint Leonards Rd., Windsor SL4
3BX. T. (01753) 866732. - Ant / Furn -   *069471*

Wingham (Kent)
Bridge Antiques, 97 High St., Wingham Kent.
T. (01227) 720445. - Furn / Silv / Instr / Toys - *069472*
Old College Antiques, 31 High St., Wingham Kent.
T. (01227) 720783. - Ant / Paint / Furn -   *069473*
Silvesters, 33 High St., Wingham Kent.
T. (01227) 720278. - Furn / China / Dec / Silv /
Glass -   *069474*

Winslow (Buckinghamshire)
Winslow Antiques Centre, 15 Market Sq., Winslow
Bucks. T. (01296) 714540, Fax (01296) 714928.
- Ant -   *069475*

Wisbech (Cambridgeshire)
Attic Gallery, 88 Elm Rd., Wisbech Cambs.
T. (01945) 583734. - Silv -   *069476*
Crofts, Peter A., High Rd., Elm, Wisbech Cambs.
T. (01945) 584614. - Ant / Furn / China / Jew /
Silv -   *069477*
Wilding, R., Lanes End, Gadds Ln., Wisbech Cambs.
T. (01945) 588204. - Furn -   *069478*

Witney (Oxfordshire)
Country Pine Antiques, 14A West End, Witney Oxon.
T. (01993) 778584. - Furn -   *069479*
Country Pine Antiques, 47A High St, Witney Oxon.
T. (01993) 778772. - Furn -   *069480*
Greenway, Colin, 90 Corn St., Witney OX8 7BU.
T. (01993) 705026. - Ant / Furn -   *069481*
Pout, Ian, 99 High St., Witney Oxon. T. (01993) 702616.
- Ant / Furn -   *069482*
Relics, 35 Bridge St., Witney Oxon. T. (01993) 704611.
- Ant / Naut -   *069483*
Scaramanga, Anthony, 108 & 49 Newland St, Witney
Oxon. T. (01993) 703472. - Paint / Furn /
China -   *069484*
Wilings, Joan, 158 Corn St., Witney Oxon.
T. (01993) 704749. - Furn / Glass -   *069485*
Windrush Antiques, 107 High St., Witney Oxon.
T. (01993) 772536. - Furn / China -   *069486*
Witney Antiques, 96/100 Corn St, Witney OX8 7BU.
T. (01993) 703902, Fax (01993) 779852. - Furn /
Instr -   *069487*

Wittersham (Kent)
Old Corner House Antiques, 6 Poplar Rd., Wittersham
Kent T. (01797) 270236. - Ant / Paint / Furn /
China -   *069488*

Wiveliscombe (Somerset)
Carousel Pig, 9 High St., Wiveliscombe Somerset.
T. (01984) 24556. - Ant / Furn / Tex -   *069489*
Heads 'n' Tails, 41 Church St., Wiveliscombe Somerset.
T. (01984) 23097, Fax (01984) 24445. - Ant - *069490*
Lee, Peter, 1 Silver St., Wiveliscombe Somerset.
T. (01984) 24055. - Ant / Furn / China -   *069491*

Woburn (Bedfordshire)
Large, George, 13-14 Market Pl., Woburn Beds.
T. (01525) 290658. - Ant -   *069492*
Questor, 13-14 Market Pl., Woburn Beds.
T. (01525) 290658. - Furn / China / Jew -   *069493*
Sykes, Christopher, Old Parsonage, Woburn Beds.
T. (01525) 290259. - Ant -   *069494*
Woburn Abbey Antiques Centre, Woburn Beds.
T. (01525) 290350. - Furn -   *069495*
Woburn Fine Arts, 12 Market Pl., Woburn Beds.
T. (01525) 290624. - Furn -   *069496*

Woburn Sands (Buckinghamshire)
Haydon House Antiques, Haydon House, Station Rd.,
Woburn Sands Bucks. T. (01908) 582447. - Paint /
Furn -   *069497*
Neville's, 50 Station Rd, Woburn Sands MK17 8RZ.
T. (01908) 584827. - Paint / Furn -   *069498*

Woking (Surrey)
Baker, Keith, 42 Arnold Rd., Woking Surrey.
T. (01483) 767425. - Ant -   *069499*

Chattel, 156 High St., Woking Surrey. T. (01483) 771310.
- Furn / Instr -   *069500*
Manor Antiques, 2 New Shops, High St., Woking Surrey.
T. (01483) 750366, Fax 750366. - Ant / Furn / China /
Glass -   *069501*
Venture, High St., Woking Surrey. T. (01483) 772103.
- Ant / Furn -   *069502*
Wych House Antiques, Aberdeen House, Wych Hill, Wo-
king Surrey. T. (01483) 764636. - Paint / Furn - *069503*

Wolverhampton (West Midlands)
Antiquities, 75-76 Dudley Rd., Wolverhampton West
Mids. T. (01902) 459800. - Ant -   *069504*
Broad Street Gallery, 16 Broad St., Wolverhampton West
Mids. T. (01902) 24977. - Paint / Graph -   *069505*
Collectors' Paradise, 56a Worcester St., Wolverhampton
West Mids. T. (01902) 20315. - Ant / Mil -   *069506*
Gemini Antiques, 18a Upper Green, Tettenhall, Wolver-
hampton West Mids. T. (01902) 742523.
- Ant -   *069507*
Golden Oldies, 5 Saint George's Parade, Wolverhampton
West Mids. T. (01902) 22397. - Paint / Furn - *069508*
Martin-Quick, 323 Tettenhall Rd., Wolverhampton WV6
0JZ. T. (01902) 754703, Fax (01902) 756889. - Ant /
Furn / Naut -   *069509*
Pendeford House Antiques, 1 Pendeford Av, Wolver-
hampton West Mids. T. (01902) 756175. - Ant / Paint /
Furn / China / Instr -   *069510*
Red Shop, 7 Hollybush Ln, Wolverhampton West Mids.
T. (01902) 342915. - Furn -   *069511*
Second Thoughts, 1-3 Coalway Rd, Wolverhampton
West Mids. T. (01902) 337748. - Paint / Graph / Furn /
China / Glass -   *069512*
Wakeman & Taylor, 140b Tettenhall Rd., Wolverhampton
West Mids. T. (01902) 751166. - Furn -   *069513*

Woodbridge (Suffolk)
Antique Furniture Warehouse, Old Maltings, Crown Pl.,
Woodbridge Suffolk. T. (01394) 387222. - Ant /
Furn -   *069514*
Bagatelle, 40 Market Hill, Woodbridge Suffolk.
T. (01394) 380204. - Paint / Graph / Furn / China /
Glass -   *069515*
Carter, Simon, 23 Market Hill, Woodbridge IP12 4LX.
T. (01394) 382242. - Paint / Furn / China /
Draw -   *069516*
Gibbins, David, 21 Market Hill, Woodbridge IP12 4LX.
T. (01394) 383531. - Furn / China -   *069517*
Hamilton, 5 Church St., Woodbridge IP12 1DH.
T. (01394) 387222. - Furn -   *069518*
Hurst, Anthony, 13 Church St., Woodbridge IP12 1DL.
T. (01394) 382500. - Furn -   *069519*
Jackson, Jenny, 30 Market Hill, Woodbridge IP12 4LU.
T. (01394) 380667. - Ant / Furn / Tex -   *069520*
Lambert's Barn, 24a Church St., Woodbridge Suffolk.
- Furn -   *069521*
Manson, Edward, 8 Market Hill, Woodbridge Suffolk.
T. (01394) 380235. - Instr -   *069522*
Melton Antiques, Kingdom Hall, Melton Rd, Woodbridge
Suffolk. T. (01394) 386232. - Ant / Furn / Silv - *069523*
Meysey-Thompson, Sarah, 10 Church St., Woodbridge
Suffolk. T. (01394) 382144. - Furn / China /
Tex -   *069524*
Voss, A. G., 24 Market Hill, Woodbridge.
T. (01394) 385830. - Furn / Instr -   *069525*

Woodbury (Devon)
Woodbury Antiques, Church St., Woodbury Devon.
T. (01395) 32727. - Furn -   *069526*

Woodchurch (Kent)
Treasures of Woodchurch, 1-3 The Green, Woodchurch
Kent. T. (01233) 860249. - Furn / China -   *069527*

Woodford Green (Greater London)
Blake, P. and K. N., 403 High Rd., Woodford Green Es-
sex. T. (0181) 504 9264. - Furn -   *069528*
Lev Galerie, 1 The Broadway, Woodford Green Essex.
T. (0181) 505 2226. - Paint / China / Silv -   *069529*

Woodhall Spa (Lincolnshire)
Underwoodhall Antiques, Broadway Centre, Woodhall
Spa Lincs. T. (01526) 353815. - Ant / Paint / Furn /
China -   *069530*

V.O.C. Antiques, 27 Witham Rd., Woodhall Spa Lincs.
T. (01526) 352753. - Paint / Furn / China -   *069531*

Woodhouse Eaves (Leicestershire)
Paddock Antiques, Old Smithy, Brand Hill, Woodhouse
Eaves leics. - Graph / Furn / China -   *069532*

Woodstock (Oxfordshire)
Span Antiques, 6 Market Pl., Woodstock Oxon.
T. (01993) 811332. - Ant -   *069533*
Thistle House Antiques, 14 Market Pl., Woodstock Oxon.
T. (01993) 811736. - Paint / Furn / China -   *069534*
Woodstock Antiques, 11 Market St., Woodstock Oxon.
T. (01993) 811494. - Paint / Graph / Furn /
China -   *069535*

Woolacombe (Devon)
Woolacombe Bay Antiques, 1 Bay Mews, South St.,
Woolacombe Devon. T. (01271) 870167. - Furn /
Instr -   *069536*

Woolhampton (Berkshire)
Bath Chair, Woodbine Cottage, Bath Rd., Woolhampton
Berks. T. (01734) 712 225. - Ant / Furn -   *069537*
Old Bakery, Bath Rd., Woolhampton RG7 5RE.
T. (01734) 712116. - Ant / Furn -   *069538*
Old Post House Antiques, Bath Rd., Woolhampton Berks.
T. (01734) 712294. - Ant / Furn -   *069539*

Woolpit (Suffolk)
Heather, J. C., Old Crown, Woolpit Suffolk.
T. (01359) 40297. - Furn -   *069540*

Worcester (Hereford and Worcester)
Alma Street Warehouse, Alma St., Worcester Herefs &
Worcs. T. (01905) 27493. - Furn / Furn -   *069541*
Antique Warehouse, 74 Droitwich Rd, Worcester Herefs
& Worcs. T. (01905) 27493. - Ant / Furn -   *069542*
Antiques and Curios, 50 Upper Tything, Worcester Her-
efs & Worcs. T. (01905) 25412. - Ant -   *069543*
Antiques and Interiors, 41 Upper Tything, Worcester Her-
efs & Worcs. T. (01905) 29014. - Paint / Furn / Jew /
Silv -   *069544*
Bygones, 55 Sidbury, Worcester WR1 2HU.
T. (01905) 23132. - Furn / China / Jew / Silv /
Glass -   *069545*
Bygones by the Cathedral, Cathedral Sq., Worcester Her-
efs & Worcs. T. (01905) 25388. - Paint / Furn / China /
Jew / Silv -   *069546*
Gray's Antiques, 49 and 50 Upper Tything, Worcester
Herefs & Worcs. T. (01905) 724456. - Ant /
Furn -   *069547*
Heirlooms, 46 Upper Tything, Worcester Herefs & Worcs.
T. (01905) 23332. - Ant / Graph / China -   *069548*
Hodge, Jean, Peachley Manor, Hallow Lane, Worcester
Herefs & Worcs. T. (01905) 640255. - Ant /
Furn -   *069549*
Hodge, Sarah, Peachley Manor, Hallow Lane, Worcester
Herefs & Worcs. T. (01905) 640255. - Ant /
Furn -   *069550*
Lees, M., Tower House, Severn St., Worcester Herefs &
Worcs. T. (01905) 26620. - Furn / China -   *069551*
Original Choice, 56 The Tything, Worcester Herefs &
Worcs. T. (01905) 613330. - Ant -   *069552*
Saint Georges Antiques, 3B Barbourne Rd, Worcester
Herefs & Worcs. T. (01905) 25915. - Ant -   *069553*
Tolley's Galleries, 26 College St., Worcester WR1 2LS.
T. (01905) 26632. - Orient / Tex -   *069554*
Tything Antique Market, 49 The Tything, Worcester Her-
efs & Worcs. T. (01905) 610597. - Ant -   *069555*
W.H.E.A.P. Antiques, 17 Bromyard Rd., Worcester Herefs
& Worcs. T. (01905) 427796. - Ant / Naut -   *069556*
Worcester Antiques Centre, Reindeer Court, Mealchea-
pen St., Worcester Herefs & Worcs. T. (01905) 610680.
- Furn / China / Jew / Silv -   *069557*

Wortham (Suffolk)
Falcon Gallery, Honeypot Farm, Wortham Suffolk.
T. (01379) 783312. - Paint -   *069558*

Worthing (West Sussex)
Biscoe, A., 122 Montague St., Worthing Sussex West.
T. (01903) 202489. - Furn / China / Jew / Silv /
Instr -   *069559*

Cheriton Antiques, 21 New Broadway, Tarring Rd., Worthing Sussex West. T. (01903) 235463. - Furn / China / Glass - 069560

Chloe Antiques, 61 Brighton Rd., Worthing Sussex West. T. (01903) 202697. - Ant / Furn / Jew / Silv / Glass - 069561

Godden, Geoffrey, 19a Crescent Rd., Worthing BN11 1RT. T. (01903) 235958. - China - 069562

Rococo Antiques, 21 Warwick Rd., Worthing Sussex West. T. (01903) 235896. - Ant - 069563

Steyne Antique Gallery, 29 Brighton Rd., Worthing Sussex West. T. (01903) 200079. - Ant / Furn / China / Instr - 069564

Warner & Son, Robert, 1-13 South Farm Rd., Worthing Sussex West. T. (01903) 232710, Fax (01903) 217515. - Furn - 069565

Wilson Antiques, 57/59 Broadwater Rd, Worthing Sussex West. T. (01903) 202059. - Furn - 069566

Wotton-under-Edge (Gloucestershire)
Bell Passage Antiques, 36-38 High St., Wickwar, Wotton-under-Edge Glos. T. (01454) 294251. - Paint / Graph / Furn / China / Glass - 069567

Wrington (Avon)
Flint, Sir William Russell, Georgian House, Broad St., Wrington Avon. T. (01934) 863149. - Paint / Graph - 069568

Wroughton (Wiltshire)
Wroughton Antique Centre, 23 High St., Wroughton Wilts. T. (01793) 813232. - Ant - 069569

Wroxham (Norfolk)
Brooke, T.C.S., The Grange, Wroxham Norfolk. T. (01603) 782644. - Ant / Furn / China / Tex / Silv - 069570

Wymeswold (Leicestershire)
Bryan-Peach, N., 28 Far St., Wymeswold Leics. T. (01509) 880425. - Furn / Instr - 069571

Wymondham (Norfolk)
King, Market Pl., Wymondham NR18 0AX. T. (01953) 604758. - Ant / Furn / China / Jew / Silv - 069572

Standley, M.E. & J.E., Warehouse, Chandlers Hill, Wymondham Norfolk. T. (01953) 602566. - Furn - 069573

Turret House, 27 Middleton St., Wymondham Norfolk. T. (01953) 603462. - Instr - 069574

Wymondham Antique Centre, 1 Town Green, Wymondham Norfolk. T. (01953) 604817. - Ant - 069575

Yarm (Cleveland)
Snowden, Ruby, 20 High St., Yarm Cleveland. T. (01642) 785363. - Furn / China / Jew / Silv / Glass - 069576

Yarmouth (Isle of Wight)
Marlborough House Antiques, Saint James Sq., Yarmouth I. of Wight. T. (01983) 760498. - Graph / Furn / China / Jew / Silv - 069577

Yatton (Avon)
Glenville Antiques, 120 High St., Yatton BS19 4DH. T. (01934) 832284. - Ant / China / Glass - 069578

Yazor (Hereford and Worcester)
Russell, M. & J., Old Vicarage, Yazor Herefs & Worcs. T. (0198) 122674. - Furn - 069579

Yeovil (Somerset)
Fox & Co., 30 Princes St., Yeovil Somerset. T. (01935) 72323. - Ant / Num / Mil - 069580

Hamblin, John, Unit 3, 15 Oxford Rd., Yeovil Somerset. T. (01935) 71154. - Furn - 069581

York (North Yorkshire)
Barker Court Antiques and Bygones, 44 Gillygate, York Yorks North. T. (01904) 622611. - China / Glass - 069582

Bishopsgate Antiques, 23-24 Bishopsgate St., York Yorks North. T. (01904) 623893. - Ant - 069583

Bobbins, 31-33 Goodramgate, York Yorks North. T. (01904) 653597. - Ant / Furn / China / Instr - 069584

Cattle, Barbara, 45 Stonegate, York YO1 2AW. T. (01904) 623862. - Jew / Silv - 069585

Coulter Galleries, 90 Tadcaster Rd., York Yorks. North. T. (01904) 702101. - Paint - 069586

Danby Antiques, 61 Hewarth Rd., York Yorks North. T. (01904) 415280. - Furn - 069587

French Fine Arts, 1 Goodramgate, York Yorks North. T. (01904) 654266. - Paint - 069588

Himsworth, Robert K., 28 The Shambles, York Yorks North. T. (01904) 625089. - Jew - 069589

Holgate Antiques, Holgate Rd., York Yorks North. T. (01904) 30005. - Ant / Furn - 069590

Morrison, Son, Robert, 131 The Mount, York YO2 2DA. T. (01904) 655394. - Ant / Furn / China / Instr - 069591

Newgate Antiques Centre, 14 Newgate, York Yorks North. T. (01904) 679844. - Ant - 069592

Saint John Antiques, 26 Lord Mayor's Walk, York Yorks North. T. (01904) 644263. - Furn - 069593

Thacker's, 42 Fossgate, York Yorks North. T. (01904) 633077. - Furn - 069594

Yates, Inez M.P., 5 The Shambles, York YO1 2LZ. T. (01904) 654821. - Paint / Furn / China / Jew - 069595

York Antiques Centre, 2 Lendal, York Yorks North. T. (01904) 641445. - Ant - 069596

Yoxall (Staffordshire)
Armson's, The Hollies, Yoxall DE13 8NH. T. (01543) 472352. - Furn / Naut - 069597

Heron & Son, H. W., 1 King St., Yoxall DE13 8NF. T. (01543) 472266. - Paint / Furn / China / Glass - 069598

Yoxford (Suffolk)
Red House Antiques, Red House, Old High Rd., Yoxford. T. (0172877) 615. - Paint / Furn / China - 069599

Suffolk House Antiques, High St., Yoxford. T. (0172877) 8122. - Paint / Furn / China / Instr - 069600

Uruguay

Montevideo
Adelphi, Bartolomé Mitre 1372, 11000 Montevideo. T. (02) 96 33 36. 069601

Alvaro, Rodriguez, Rincón 650, 11000 Montevideo. T. (02) 95 12 91. 069602

Alvez, Mirta Bazzi de, Bartolomé Mitre 1372, 11000 Montevideo. T. (02) 95 74 70. 069603

Antigüedades, Bacacay 1338, 11000 Montevideo. T. (02) 95 22 47. 069604

Armu's Antiques, Rincón 622, 11000 Montevideo. T. (02) 95 94 16. 069605

Barbacana, Bartolomé Mitre 1337, 11000 Montevideo. T. (02) 95 90 14. 069606

Barbery, Lia, Bacacay 1331, 11000 Montevideo. T. (02) 96 30 62, Fax 96 16 66. 069607

Bay & Vidal, Av. Uruguay 996, 11100 Montevideo. T. (02) 985 339. - Num - 069608

Cabral, Jorge, Bartolomé Mitre 1385, 11000 Montevideo. T. (02) 95 96 70. 069609

Cantú, Monica Crosa de, P.F. Berro 631, 11300 Montevideo. T. (02) 71 46 38. 069610

Carmen, Tristán Narvaja 1655, 11200 Montevideo. T. (02) 40 04 45, 72 20 62. 069611

Cerisola, Martinez José, San Josey 978, 11100 Montevideo. T. (02) 98 43 35. 069612

Déjà-vu, Rincón 650, 11000 Montevideo. T. (02) 95 12 91. 069613

Delbondo, Leandri, Juncal 1410, 11000 Montevideo. T. (02) 91 21 53. 069614

Delbono, Juan, Bartolomé Mitre 1332, 11000 Montevideo. T. (02) 95 28 81. 069615

Don Quijote, Sergio N. Furas, Colonia 1215-1217, 11200 Montevideo. T. (02) 90 87 49, 92 14 76. - Furn / China / Glass - 069616

Doskal, Pza. Independencia 729, 11000 Montevideo. T. (02) 90 14 56. 069617

El Altillo, Bacacay 1337, 11000 Montevideo. T. (02) 96 31 11. 069618

El Frances, Maldonado 1029, 11000 Montevideo. T. (02) 91 22 67. 069619

El Prado, Mercedes 1783, 11200 Montevideo. T. (02) 40 09 11. 069620

El Rastro, Tristán Narvaja 1659, 11200 Montevideo. T. (02) 49 05 64. 069621

El Rincón, Tacuarembó 1442, 11200 Montevideo. T. (02) 48 14 00. 069622

El Sótano, Avda. 18 de Julio 2259, 11200 Montevideo. T. (02) 48 24 03. 069623

Erenberg, Fany S. de, Soriano 909, 11100 Montevideo. T. (02) 90 42 10. 069624

Eugenio e Hijo, Colonia 911, 11100 Montevideo. T. (02) 91 57 54. 069625

Fuchs, Daniel, Bartolomé Mitre 1379, 11000 Montevideo. T. (02) 95 02 10. 069626

Galindos, San José 1191, 11100 Montevideo. T. (02) 90 35 54. 069627

Gannuso, Ruggiero, Tristán Narvaja 1739, 11200 Montevideo. T. (02) 40 98 07. 069628

Guili, Convención 1494, 11100 Montevideo. T. (02) 98 01 31. 069629

Karausz, Daniel, J.C. Gómez 1429, 11000 Montevideo. T. (02) 95 77 02. 069630

Kolen, F., Bartolomé Mitre 1386, 11000 Montevideo. T. (02) 95 95 11, 96 21 75. 069631

Krauthamer, Frida, Bartolomé Mitre 1393, 11000 Montevideo. T. (02) 95 58 79. 069632

La Fontaine, Sarandi 635, 11000 Montevideo. T. (02) 96 01 58, 96 03 67. 069633

Lago, R., Mercedes 1783, 11200 Montevideo. T. (02) 40 09 11. 069634

Las Artes, Tristán Narvaja 1645, 11200 Montevideo. T. (02) 40 31 12. 069635

Las Artes, Carlos Roxlo 1379/81, 11200 Montevideo. T. (02) 48 69 51. - Ant / Furn / Glass - 069636

Lopez, Bartolomé Mitre 1410, 11000 Montevideo. T. (02) 95 81 42. 069637

Louvre, Sarandi 652, 11000 Montevideo. T. (02) 96 26 86/87. 069638

Martinez, Avda. Uruguay 1032 bis, 11000 Montevideo. T. (02) 90 45 69. 069639

Miscellaneous, Bartolomé Mitre 1393, 11000 Montevideo. T. (02) 95 58 79. 069640

Misia, Paca, Bartolomé Mitre 1383, 11000 Montevideo. T. (02) 96 95 69. 069641

Mundo Antiguo, Tristán Narvaja 1618, 11200 Montevideo. T. (02) 40 95 39. 069642

Naftalina, Bartolomé Mitre 1388, 11000 Montevideo. T. (02) 95 64 26. 069643

Nigro, Horacio F., Canelones 1146, 11100 Montevideo. T. (02) 98 08 24. 069644

Obelar, Tristán Narvaja 1673, 11200 Montevideo. T. (02) 48 85 76, 48 06 45. - Ant - 069645

Portobello Road, Bartolomé Mitre 1368, 11000 Montevideo. - Ant - 069646

Ramses, Sarandi 699, 11000 Montevideo. T. (02) 95 77 21. - Ant / Furn - 069647

Rilax, Juncal 1317, 11000 Montevideo. T. (02) 96 17 26. 069648

Roble Center, Avda. Gral. Rivera 2004, 11200 Montevideo. T. (02) 40 50 03. 069649

Roferber, Tristán Narvaja 1774, 11200 Montevideo. T. (02) 41 95 72. 069650

Santopietro, Ejido 1317 bis, 11100 Montevideo. T. (02) 90 41 81. 069651

Savvas Thrasyvoulos, Michael, Rio Branco 1317, 11100 Montevideo. T. (02) 90 35 33. - Ant / Num / Jew / Mil - 069652

Seoane, Roald, Payasandú 1762, 11200 Montevideo. T. (02) 40 03 28. 069653

Solange, Ciudadela 1224, 11000 Montevideo. T. (02) 92 26 58. 069654

Torrejon, Bartolomé Mitre 1329, 11000 Montevideo. T. (02) 95 05 15. - Furn / Mil / Glass - 069655

Urubras, Avda. D. Fernández 1899, 11200 Montevideo. T. (02) 49 08 35. 069656

Valiño Fernández, Jorge, Bartolomé Mitre 1324, 11000 Montevideo. T. (02) 96 27 11. 069657

Viejo Paris, Tristán Narvaja 1614, 11200 Montevideo. T. (02) 48 91 19. 069658

Vieux Paris, Avda. 18 de Julio 976, 11100 Montevideo. T. (02) 90 70 14. - Ant / Jew - 069659

Vitorio, Joyas, Uruguay 951 bis, 11100 Montevideo. T. (02) 91 51 81. - Ant / Glass - 069660

Zira, Tristán Narvaja 1695, 11200 Montevideo.
T. (02) 48 24 61. - Ant -   *069661*
Zubia, Eduardo, Bartolomé Mitre 1329, 11000 Montevideo. T. (02) 95 05 15.   *069662*

Punta del Este
Adelphi, Gal. Torre Gorlero, Loc. 018, 20100 Punta del Este. T. (042) 42110.   *069663*
Lago, R., Torre Gorlero, Loc. 031, 20100 Punta del Este. T. (042) 42113.   *069664*
Miscellaneous, Calle 29 y Gorlero, Loc. 30, 20100 Punta del Este. T. (042) 43260.   *069665*

U.S.A.

Abington (Pennsylvania)
Abington Antique Shop, 1165 Old York Rd., 19001 Abington, PA 19001. T. 884-3204. - Ant / Paint / Furn / China / Jew / Silv / Mil / Glass -   *069666*

Adamstown (Pennsylvania)
Black Angus, Rte. 272, Adamstown, PA 19501.
T. (215) 484-4385.   *069667*
Johnson, Tex, 40 Willow St., Adamstown, PA 19501.
T. (215) 484-4005.   *069668*

Afton (Minnesota)
Afton Antique Shop, Afton, MN 55001. T. (612) 436-7798.   *069669*

Akron (Ohio)
Stagecoach Antiques, 439 W. Market St., Akron, OH 44303. T. (216) 762-5422. - Ant -   *069670*

Alameda (California)
Lynn's, 2807 Encinal Ave., Alameda, CA 94501.
T. (415) 5232383.   *069671*

Albany (New York)
Central Antique Exchange, 184 Washington Ave, 12210 Albany, NY 12200. T. (518) 462-3156. - Ant / Paint / Furn / Num / China / Sculp / Dec / Jew / Silv / Lights / Instr / Glass -   *069672*

Albion (New York)
Fischer, 14049 W County H. Rd., Albion, NY 14411.
T. (716) 589-7559.   *069673*

Albuquerque (New Mexico)
Alameda Antique Shop, 9306 4th St. NW, Albuquerque, NM 87114. T. (505) 898-3161. - Ant -   *069674*
Antique Work Shop, 7322 NW 4th St., Albuquerque, NM 87107. T. (505) 898-0348. - Ant / Furn / China / Tex / Dec / Jew / Fra / Silv / Lights / Instr / Glass -   *069675*
Art + Antiques, 120 Morningside, Albuquerque, NM 87108. T. (505) 255-0266. - Ant / Fra -   *069676*
Covered Wagon, 4010 Romero St. NW, Albuquerque, NM 87104. - Paint / Graph / Furn / Sculp -   *069677*
Eddie's Antique Shop, 119 S.E. Darmouth Pl., Albuquerque, NM 87106. - Ant / Furn / China / Lights -   *069678*
El Mercado, 2038 South Plaza NW, Albuquerque, NM 87104. T. (505) 242-4784. - Ant -   *069679*
Old Town Indian Trading Post, 208 San Felipe NW, Albuquerque, NM 87104. - Graph / China / Tex / Dec / Jew / Silv -   *069680*
Treasure House, 2012 South Plaza NW, Albuquerque, NM 87104. T. (505) 242-7204. - China / Dec / Jew -   *069681*
Workshop Originals, POB 7062, Albuquerque, NM 87104. T. (505) 242-2048. - Paint / Graph / Furn / Orient / China / Sculp / Tex / Arch / Eth / Dec / Jew / Glass -   *069682*
Yucca Art Gallery, 1919 Old Town Rd. NW, Albuquerque, NM 87100. T. (505) 247-8931. - Paint / Sculp / Jew -   *069683*

Alexandria (Virginia)
Apothecary Shop, 105 S. Fairfax St., Alexandria, VA 22314. T. (703) 836-3713. - Ant -   *069684*
Lee, Virginia, Virginia, 606 West View Terrace, Alexandria, VA 22301. - Ant -   *069685*

Silverman, 110 N Saint Asaph St., Alexandria, VA 22314. T. (703) 836-5363. - Ant / Paint / Furn / Jew / Silv -   *069686*
Woldman & Woldman, POB 19839, Alexandria, VA 22320. T. (703) 548-3122.   *069687*

Alpine (New Jersey)
Rabenou, K., POB 501, Alpine, NJ 07620. T. (201) 768-2161. - Ant / Orient / Tex / Arch / Eth / Jew / Mil / Glass -   *069688*

Amherst (Massachusetts)
Baker, Kay, North and East Pleasant Sts., Amherst, MA 01002. T. (413) 549-0890.   *069689*
French, R. & R., 657 S. Pleasant.St., Amherst, MA 01002. T. (413) 253-2269. - Ant / Furn / China -   *069690*

Amherst (New Hampshire)
Bradford Roberts, H., Green Trim Farm, Old Manchester Rd., Amherst, NH 03031. T. (603) 673-6688.   *069691*

Anaheim (California)
Evie, 555 S Harbor Blvd., Anaheim, CA 92805.
T. (714) 535-0110. - Ant / Furn / China / Lights / Glass -   *069692*
Hodges, 3050 W Ball Rd., Anaheim, CA 92804. - Ant / Orient / Lights / Glass -   *069693*

Andover (Massachusetts)
New England Gallery, 356 N Main St., Andover, MA 01810. T. (617) 475-2116.   *069694*

Ann Arbor (Michigan)
Drouyor, Gertrude & Wendell, 5097 Jackson Ave., Ann Arbor, MI 48103. - Ant -   *069695*
Lotus Gallery, 119 E Liberty, Ann Arbor, MI 48104.
T. (313) 665-6322. - Orient -   *069696*

Ardmore (Oklahoma)
Southern Vending, 7 W Broadway, POB 1116, Ardmore, OK 73401. - Ant -   *069697*

Ardmore (Pennsylvania)
Milione, Amalia F., 2713 Haverford Rd., Ardmore, PA 19003. T. (215) 896-5770. - Tex -   *069698*

Arlington (Virginia)
Arlington Antique Shop, POB 311, Arlington, VA 22210.
T. (703) 522-8500. - Instr / Mil -   *069699*
Mil, Dor, POB 693, Courthouse Station, Arlington POB 693, Courthouse Station, VA 22216. T. (703) 243-8455.   *069700*

Arvada (Colorado)
Demko, Eugene, 5710 Everett St., Arvada, CO 80002.
T. (303) 421-6567. - Ant / China / Glass -   *069701*

Ashby (Massachusetts)
The Country Bed Shop, RR1, Richardson Rd., Box 65, Ashby, MA 01431. T. (508) 386-7550.   *069702*

Ashland (Massachusetts)
Beaudoin, Ruth M., 98 Main St., Ashland, MA 01721.
T. (617) 881-1273. - Ant -   *069703*

Ashland (Ohio)
Cake, Johnny, 802 E Main St., Ashland, OH 44805.
T. (419) 322-1041. - Ant / Paint / Graph / Num / China / Sculp / Tex / Eth / Jew / Fra / Silv / Lights / Instr / Mil / Glass -   *069704*
Myers, Rd. 5, POB 41, Ashland, OH 44805.   *069705*

Ashley Falls (Massachusetts)
Ashley Falls Antiques Shop, Rte 7A, Ashley Falls, MA 01222. - Furn / China -   *069706*
Lewis & Wilson, Rte. 7A, Ashley Falls, MA 01222.
T. (413) 229-3330. - Furn -   *069707*

Aspen (Colorado)
Shaw Gallery, 525 E Cooper, Aspen, CO 81611.
T. (303) 925-2873.   *069708*

Atglen (Pennsylvania)
Schiffer, 77 Lower Valley Rd, Atglen, PA 19310.
T. (215) 593-1777, Fax (215) 593-2002. - Ant -   *069709*

Atlanta (Georgia)
Accent on Designs, 3107 Early St. NW, Atlanta, GA 30305. T. (404) 237-4332.   *069710*
Adams, Jaqueline, 2300 Peachtree Rd. NW, Atlanta, GA 30309. T. (404) 355-8123.   *069711*
Albert, Y., & Son, 2303 Peachtree Rd. NE, Atlanta, GA 30309. T. (404) 355-0944. - Tex -   *069712*
Antique Paintings, 631 Miami Circle NE, Atlanta, GA 30324. T. (404) 264-0349.   *069713*
Antique Shop of Paris, 631 Miami Circle NE, Atlanta, GA 30324. T. (404) 231-1238.   *069714*
Architectural Accents, 2711 Piedmont Rd. NE, Atlanta, GA 30305. T. (404) 266-8700.   *069715*
Arnett, William & Robert, 3603 Knollwood Dr. NW, Atlanta, GA 30305. T. (404) 266-1151. - Ant / Orient / China / Sculp / Arch / Eth -   *069716*
Art Gallery, 4407 Roswell Rd. NE, Atlanta, GA 30342.
T. (404) 851-9808.   *069717*
Atlanta Antiques Exchange, 1185 Howell Mill Rd., Atlanta, GA 30318. T. (404) 351-0727. - Ant / Paint / Furn / Silv -   *069718*
Atlanta Camera Exchange, 2682 Weigelia Rd. NE, Atlanta, GA 30345. T. (404) 325-9367.   *069719*
Atlanta Fairgrounds Antique Market, 2000 Lakewood Av. SW, Atlanta, GA 30344. T. (404) 624-4322.   *069720*
Atlanta Flea Market, 5360 Peachtree Industrial Blvd., Atlanta, GA 30341. T. (404) 458-0456.   *069721*
Aunt Teeks, 1166 Euclid Av. NE, Atlanta, GA 30307.
T. (404) 525-0630.   *069722*
Barrington, 631 Miami Circle NE, Atlanta, GA 30324.
T. (404) 231-8595.   *069723*
Big Chandelier, 761 Miami Circle NE, Atlanta, GA 30324.
T. (404) 266-8437.   *069724*
Bittersweet, 45 Bennett St. NW, Atlanta, GA 30309.
T. (404) 351-6594.   *069725*
Boomerang, 1145 Euclid Av. NE, Atlanta, GA 30307.
T. (404) 577-8158.   *069726*
Boone, 2050 Hills Av. NW, Atlanta, GA 30318.
T. (404) 351-6409.   *069727*
British American Antiques, 800 Miami Circle NE, Atlanta, GA 30324. T. (404) 231-4454.   *069728*
Browne, W. E., 443 Peachtree St., Atlanta, GA 30308.
T. (404) 874-4416. - Ant / Paint / China / Silv -   *069729*
Bull and Bear Antiques, 1189 Howell Mill Rd. NW, Atlanta, GA 30318. T. (404) 355-6697.   *069730*
Burroughs, 631 Miami Circle NE, Atlanta, GA 30324.
T. (404) 264-1616.   *069731*
Canterbury Antiques, 660 Miami Circle NE, Atlanta, GA 30324. T. (404) 231-4048.   *069732*
Carolyn's Corner, 1189 Howell Mill Rd. NW, Atlanta, GA 30318. T. (404) 351-4972.   *069733*
Century Shop, 1189 Howell Mill Rd. NW, Atlanta, GA 30318. T. (404) 351-8022.   *069734*
Chandelier, Maurice, 715 Miami Circle NE, Atlanta, GA 30324. T. (404) 237-5402.   *069735*
Circa, 25 Bennett St. NW, Atlanta, GA 30309.
T. (404) 351-1702.   *069736*
Consignment Shop, 1185 Howell Mill Rd. NW, Atlanta, GA 30318. T. (404) 351-6025.   *069737*
Curios by Christina, 780 N Highland Av. NE, Atlanta, GA 30312. T. (404) 872-3018.   *069738*
Currey & Co., 45 Bennett St. NW, Atlanta, GA 30309.
T. (404) 351-1844.   *069739*
Decorative Crafts, 10 A-4 Atlanta Merchandise Mart, 240 Peachtree St., Atlanta, GA 30303. - Paint / Furn / Num / Instr / Mil -   *069740*
Elaine's, 3174 Peachtree Rd. NE, Atlanta, GA 30305.
T. (404) 233-5751.   *069741*
Elliott, J. H., 537 NE Peachtree St., Atlanta, GA 30308.
T. (404) 872-8233. - Ant / Furn / China / Silv -   *069742*
Embassy Antiques, 418 Woodward Av. SE, Atlanta, GA 30312. T. (404) 577-1516.   *069743*
Feimster, Alberta, 209 Edgewood Av. SE, Atlanta, GA 30303. T. (404) 589-9601.   *069744*
Furniture Exchange, 646 Lindbergh Way, Atlanta, GA 30324. T. (404) 233-2100.   *069745*
Gables, 711 Miami Circle NE, Atlanta, GA 30324.
T. (404) 231-0734.   *069746*
Garret, Frank, 2300 Peachtree Rd. NW, Atlanta, GA 30309. T. (404) 355-2224.   *069747*
Gentlemans Quarters Antiques, 2267 Peachtree Rd. NE, Atlanta, GA 30309. T. (404) 352-8877.   *069748*

Godwin, 715 Miami Circle NE, Atlanta, GA 30324.
T. (404) 231-4262. *069749*
Gryphon, 715 Miami Circle NE, Atlanta, GA 30324.
T. (404) 231-0040. *069750*
Harwell-Steffler, 1409 N Highland Av. NE, Atlanta, GA
30306. T. (404) 872-7551. *069751*
Highland Antiques, 1039 N Highland Av. NE, Atlanta, GA
30306. T. (404) 874-1716. *069752*
Holland & Company, 351 Peach Tree Hills Ave NE, Atlanta, GA 30305. *069753*
Howell Mill Antiques Mall, 1189 Howell Mill Rd. NW, Atlanta, GA 30318. T. (404) 351-0309. *069754*
Junque & Stuff, 674 11th St. NW, Atlanta, GA 30318.
T. (404) 873-5090. *069755*
Keishian, Dan, 458 E Paces Ferry Rd. NE, Atlanta, GA
30305. T. (404) 266-8863. *069756*
Kennedy, 2050 Hills Av. NW, Atlanta, GA 30318.
T. (404) 351-4464. - Ant - *069757*
Kichline, 287 The Prado NE, Atlanta, GA 30309.
T. (404) 892-1994. *069758*
Kipling, 3234 Roswell Rd. NW, Atlanta, GA 30305.
T. (404) 261-4196. *069759*
Lamp Arts, 1199 Howell Mill Rd. NW, Atlanta, GA 30318.
T. (404) 352-5211. *069760*
Le Garage Antiques, 2159 Piedmont Rd. NE, Atlanta, GA
30324. T. (404) 892-4705. *069761*
Major Furniture, 1158 Euclid Av. NE, Atlanta, GA 30307.
T. (404) 524-1931. *069762*
Major Furniture, 488 Flat Shoals Av. SE, Atlanta, GA
30316. T. (404) 522-2093. *069763*
Marcella Fine Rugs, 3162 Piedmont Rd. NE, Atlanta, GA
30305. T. (404) 261-2706. *069764*
Marche d'Or, 480 E Paces Ferry Rd. NE, Atlanta, GA
30305. T. (404) 237-7011. *069765*
Mardsen, Jane J., 2300 Peachtree Rd. NW, Atlanta, GA
30309. T. (404) 355-1288. *069766*
McLure-Faller, 2087 Piedmont Rd. NE, Atlanta, GA
30324. T. (404) 872-3991. *069767*
Melosi, 2300 Peachtree Rd. NW, Atlanta, GA 30309.
T. (404) 352-5451. *069768*
Mitchell, Ronald, 2159 Piedmont Rd. NE, 30300 Atlanta,
GA 30324. T. (404) 892-4705. *069769*
Moog, H., 2271 Peachtree Rd. NE, 30300 Atlanta, GA
30309. T. (404) 351-2200. *069770*
Morehouse, 715 Miami Circle NE, Atlanta, GA 30324.
T. (404) 237-0599. *069771*
Morgan & Allen, 2300 Peachtree Rd. NW, Atlanta, GA
30309. T. (404) 355-5799. *069772*
Morring, Robert, 2295 Peachtree Rd. NE, Atlanta, GA
30309. T. (404) 351-7256. *069773*
O'Karma Jones, 540 14th St. NW, Atlanta, GA 30318.
T. (404) 874-9461. *069774*
Oxford Antiques, 204 14th St. NW, Atlanta, GA 30318.
T. (404) 874-5566. *069775*
Perry, Charles, POB 12468, Atlanta, GA 30355.
T. (404) 364-9731. - China - *069776*
Photographs by Historic Photographica, 2682 Weigelia
Rd. NE, Atlanta, GA 30345. T. (404) 325-9367. *069777*
Pine Cottage, 1189 Howell Mill Rd. NW, Atlanta, GA
30318. T. (404) 351-7463. *069778*
Pine-Wicker Heirloom, 709 Miami Circle NE, Atlanta, GA
30324. T. (404) 233-6333. *069779*
Red Baron's Antiques, 6450 Roswell Rd., Atlanta, GA
30328. T. (404) 252-3770. - Ant / Paint / Furn / Sculp /
Lights - *069780*
Reeves, Robert, 49 S Prado, Atlanta, GA 30309.
T. (404) 874-1755. *069781*
Regallo, 652 Miami Circle NE, Atlanta, GA 30324.
T. (404) 237-4899. *069782*
Richter, 87 West Paces Ferry Rd. NW, Atlanta, GA
30305. T. (404) 262-2070. *069783*
Saint Charles Emporium, 1060 Saint Charles Av. NE, Atlanta, GA 30306. T. (404) 873-2084. *069784*
Scan Des, 2140 Peachtree Rd. NW, Atlanta, GA 30309.
T. (404) 350-0155. *069785*
Scavenger, Hunt, 3438 Clairmont Rd. NE, Atlanta, GA
30319. T. (404) 634-4948. *069786*
Scudder, 800 Miami Circle NE, Ste 100, Atlanta, GA
30324. T. (404) 231-4820. *069787*
Second Hand, 628 North Highland Av. NE, Atlanta, GA
30306. T. (404) 875-6773. *069788*
Sharon, Bennett, 3 Peachtree Av. NE, Atlanta, GA 30305.
T. (404) 233-0124. *069789*

Sterling Touch, 1050 Northside Dr. NW, Atlanta, GA
30318. T. (404) 873-4826. *069790*
Thames Valley Antiques, 631 Miami Circle NE, Atlanta,
GA 30324. T. (404) 262-1541. *069791*
Trudgeon, K. A., 4010 Peachtree Rd. NE, Atlanta, GA
30319. T. (404) 239-9333. *069792*
Twickenham, 631 Miami Circle NE, Atlanta, GA 30324.
T. (404) 261-0951. *069793*
Word, William, 707 Miami Circle NE, Atlanta, GA 30324.
T. (404) 233-6890. *069794*
Wrecking Bar, 292 Moreland Av. NE, Atlanta, GA 30307.
T. (404) 525-0468. *069795*
Wynfield House Warehouse, 349 Peachtree Hills Av. NE,
Atlanta, GA 30305. T. (404) 364-0524. *069796*
20th Century Antiques, 1044 N Highland Av. NE, Atlanta,
GA 30306. T. (404) 892-2065. *069797*

Atlas (Michigan)
Reid, Maurice E., 8470 Perry Rd., Atlas, MI 48411.
T. (313) 636-2240. - Furn - *069798*

Auburndale (Florida)
Attic Gallery, 205 Batow Ave., Auburndale, FL 33823.
T. (813) 967-2267, 293-7525. *069799*

Austerlitz (New York)
Courcier, Suzanne, & Robert W. Wilkins, Rte. 22, Austerlitz, NY 12017. T. (518) 392-5754. - Furn - *069800*
Herron, Robert, Rte 22, 12017 Austerlitz, NY 12017.
T. (518) 392-5478. - Ant / Furn - *069801*

Austin (Texas)
Country Store Gallery, 1304 Lavaca St., Austin, TX
78701. T. (512) 476-1663, 476-2019. - Ant / Paint /
Fra - *069802*
House of Antique, 509 W 12 St., Austin, TX 78701.
T. (512) 477-7125. - Furn / China / Silv / Glass - *069803*
Powell, James, 715 West Ave., Austin, TX 78701.
T. (512) 477-9939. - Furn / Tex - *069804*
Whirligig, POB 834, Austin, TX 78767. T. (512) 327-
3182. *069805*

Baldwin (New York)
Quest Antiques, 871 Merrick Rd., Baldwin, NY 11510.
T. (516) 623-8351. *069806*

Baltimore (Maryland)
Antique Shop, 827 N Howard St., Baltimore, MD 21201.
T. (301) 837-5991. - Ant / Paint / Orient / China /
Silv - *069807*
Ayers & Frazier, 330 Tunbridge Rd., Baltimore, MD
21212. T. (301) 332-1330. *069808*
Brass Towne, 219 W Mulberry St., Baltimore, MD
21201. T. (301) 539-8284. - Ant - *069809*
Eicker, 618 Warwick Rd., Baltimore, MD 21229.
- Ant - *069810*
Ford, John, 2601 N Charles St., Baltimore, MD 21218.
T. (301) 467-9400. - Ant / Furn / Orient / China / Arch /
Dec - *069811*
Harris, Jacob, 875 N Howard St., Baltimore, MD 21201.
T. (301) 837-2045. - Ant - *069812*
Lobe, N.B., 4303 Old Court Rd., Baltimore, MD 21208.
- Ant - *069813*
London Shop, 1500 Bolton St., Baltimore, MD 21217.
T. (301) 523-3330. - Paint / Graph / Furn / China /
Sculp / Tex / Dec / Jew / Silv / Lights / Instr / Glass --
069814
Margolet, B., 885 N Howard St., Baltimore, MD 21201.
T. (301) 772-2804. - Ant / Paint / Graph / Furn / Furn /
China / Tex / Dec / Jew / Silv - *069815*
Pimlico, 3350 W Belvedere Av., Baltimore, MD 21215.
T. (301) 367-4472. - Num - *069816*
Purnell, 309 Cathedral St., Baltimore, MD 21201.
T. (301) 685-6033/34. - Paint / Graph / Orient / China /
Repr / Rel / Mul / Draw - *069817*
Runkles, Hanson H., 318 S Monroe St., Baltimore, MD
21223. - Ant - *069818*
Rush, Cecil Archer, 1410 Northgate Rd., 21200 Baltimore, MD 21218. T. (301) 323-7767. - Orient / Sculp /
Eth - *069819*
Sunnyfields, 6305 Falls Rd., Baltimore, MD 21209.
T. (301) 823-6666. - Ant / Dec - *069820*
Talkin, H.N., 8106 Woodhaven Rd., Baltimore, MD
21237. - Ant - *069821*

Thayne, 881 N. Howard St., Baltimore, MD
21201. *069822*
Windsor Galleries, 1013 N Charles St., Baltimore, MD
21201. T. (301) 539-2691. - Ant / Paint / Orient / China /
Sculp / Tex / Arch / Eth / Mil / Rel / Glass - *069823*

Banning (California)
The W's Antiques, 4092 W. Ramsey St., Banning, CA
92220. T. (714) 849-7100. - Ant - *069824*

Barnesville (Georgia)
Fleewoochi Farms Antiques, I-75, Exit Johnstonville Rd.,
Barnesville, GA 30204. T. (404) 358-0382.
- Ant - *069825*

Barrington (Illinois)
Silver Vault, POB 421, Barrington, IL 60010.
T. (312) 381-7063. - Ant / Silv - *069826*

Bascom (Ohio)
Rainey, Rte. 18, Bascom, OH 44809. - Ant / Furn /
Lights / Glass - *069827*

Basking Ridge (New Jersey)
Whistler Gallery, Basking Ridge POB 362, NJ 07920.
T. (201) 766-6222. - Ant - *069828*

Bath (Maine)
Yesterday Shop, 27 Washington St., Bath, ME 04530.
T. (207) 443-4203. - Ant / China / Jew / Glass - *069829*

Baton Rouge (Louisiana)
Fetzer & Co., 711 Jefferson Hwy., Baton Rouge, LA
70806. T. (504) 927-7420. - Ant / Paint / Furn / Orient /
China / Tex / Dec - *069830*
Lafayette Gallery, 348 Lafayette St., Baton Rouge, LA
70801. T. (504) 383-7763. - Ant / Paint / Furn / China /
Sculp - *069831*

Battle Creek (Michigan)
Blaske, Edmund R., 1509 National Security Tower, Battle
Creek, MI 49014. - Ant - *069832*

Bayville (New York)
Meyerson, Ronnie, 23 Oak Point Dr. N, Bayville, NY
11709. T. (516) 628-1461. - Draw - *069833*

Beaumont (Texas)
Cropper, 1495 Calder St., Beaumont, TX 77701. *069834*
Lyn's Antiques, 2579 Calder Ave., Beaumont, TX 77702.
- Furn - *069835*

Bedford (New Hampshire)
Bell Hill Antiques, Rt. 101 and Bell Hill Rd., Bedford, NH
03102. T. (603) 472-5580. *069836*

Bedford Hills (New York)
Howard, 38 Robinson Av., Bedford Hills, NY 10507.
T. (914) 241-3989. - Paint - *069837*

Belchertown (Massachusetts)
Loving Cup, Main St., Belchertown, MA 01007.
T. (413) 323-7482. - Ant / Paint / Furn / China / Lights /
Instr / Glass - *069838*

Belfast (Maine)
Howell, Avis, 21 Pearl St., Belfast, ME 04915.
T. (207) 338-3302. *069839*

Bell Gardens (California)
Ediphos, Bell Gardens, CA 90201. - Jew - *069840*

Belle Chasse (Louisiana)
Schlief, V. B., 201 Schlief Dr., Belle Chasse, LA 70037.
T. (504) 394-3087. - Ant - *069841*

Bellevue (Washington)
Kharouba, 10203 Main St., Bellevue, WA 98004.
T. (206) 454-7400. - Jew - *069842*
Old and Elegant Distributing, 10203 Main St., Bellevue,
WA 98004. T. (206) 455-4660. - Ant / Jew - *069843*

Bellingham (Washington)
Leaf, Cheryl, 2828 Northwest Ave., Bellingham, WA
98225. - Ant - *069844*

Bellmore (New York)
Exquisite Antiques, 2938 Merrick Rd., Bellmore, NY
11710. T. (516) 781-7305. - China / Glass -   *069845*

Benecia (California)
Dials, 190 W J St., Benecia, CA 94510. T. (707) 745-
2552.   *069846*

Bennington (Vermont)
Fonda's Antiques, Pownal Rd., Bennington, VT 05201.
- Ant -   *069847*
Four Corners East Antiques, 307 North St., Bennington,
VT 05201. T. (802) 442-2612. - Paint / Furn -   *069848*
Matteson, South St. Rte 7, Bennington, VT 05201.
T. (802) 442-6242. - Ant / Furn -   *069849*

Berkeley (California)
Bradley, 1182 Solano Av., Berkeley, CA 94706.
T. (415) 527-3454. - Ant / Paint / Orient / China / Sculp /
Arch -   *069850*
Bruce, Robert, 2910 Telegraph Ave., Berkeley, CA
94705. T. (415) 845-7424.   *069851*
Carol's Antiques, 2808 A Adeline St., Berkeley, CA
94703. T. (415) 483-7582. - Ant -   *069852*
Finlinson, Jim, 3023 Adeline St., Berkeley, CA 94703.
T. (415) 848-0463. - Ant / Paint / Furn -   *069853*

Berryville (Virginia)
Talio, U.S. S 340, Berryville, VA 22611. T. (703) 955-
1740. - Paint / Furn -   *069854*

Berwyn (Illinois)
Rusnak, 6338 W. 26th St., Berwyn, IL 60402.
T. (312) 788-4086. - Ant / Paint / Furn / Dec /
Lights -   *069855*

Beverly Hills (California)
Barakat, 429 N Rodeo Dr., Beverly Hills, CA 90210.
T. (213) 859-8408. - Arch -   *069856*
Geary, 351 N Beverly Dr., Beverly Hills, CA 90210.
T. (213) 273-4741. - Graph / Sculp / Jew / Silv - *069857*
Jade Collector, 8484 Wilshire Blvd., Beverly Hills, CA
90211. T. (213) 652-0020, Fax (213) 653-9951.
- Orient -   *069858*
Klein, Frances, 310 N. Rodeo Dr., Beverly Hills, CA
90210. T. (213) 273-0155. - Jew -   *069859*
Lapa, Frank A., POB 2002, Beverly Hills, CA 90213.
- Num -   *069860*
Michael, 430 N Rodeo Dr., Beverly Hills, CA 90210.
T. (213) 273-3377. - Ant -   *069861*
Orgell, David, 320 N Rodeo Dr., Beverly Hills, CA 90210.
T. (213) 272-3355. - Jew / Silv -   *069862*
Provence de Pierre Deux, 436 N Rodeo Dr., Beverly Hills,
CA 90210. T. (213) 550-7265   *069863*
Royal-Athena Galleries, 332 N Beverly Dr., Beverly Hills,
CA 90210. T. (213) 550-1199, Fax (213) 550-1395.
- Num / Orient / Sculp / Arch / Eth / Lights -   *069864*
Szymanski, POB 936, Beverly Hills, CA 90213.
T. (213) 681-1114. - Ant / Paint / Furn / Sculp / Fra / Ico /
Draw -   *069865*
Zehil, Robert, 445 N Rodeo Dr., Beverly Hills, CA 90210.
T. (213) 858-0824. - Paint / Furn / Jew / Silv /
Lights -   *069866*

Binghamton (New York)
Cone House Antiques, 9 Church St., Binghamton, NY
13901. T. (607) 722-5445.   *069867*
Oxen Hill Antiques, 35 Andrews Av., Binghamton, NY
13904. T. (607) 723-0841. - Ant -   *069868*

Birdsboro (Pennsylvania)
Fred and Dottie's Antiques, 221, Birdsboro, PA 19508.
T. (215) 582-1506. - Ant -   *069869*

Birmingham (Alabama)
Adams, Mary, 1822 29th Av.S, Birmingham, AL 35209.
- Ant -   *069870*
Iron Art, 2901 Cahaba Rd., Birmingham, AL 35223.
T. (205) 879-0529. - Ant / Furn -   *069871*
King's House, 2418 Montevallo Rd., Birmingham, AL
35223. T. (205) 871-5787.   *069872*
Westbury, 3412 Westbury Pl., Birmingham, AL 35223.
T. (205) 967-3079.   *069873*
Wren's Nest Antiques, 948 41st St., Birmingham, AL
35208. T. (205) 786-9264. - Ant -   *069874*

Birmingham (Michigan)
Modern Studio of Interiors, 217 Pierce St., Birmingham,
MI 48011. - Ant / Furn / China / Tex / Dec / Lights /
Glass -   *069875*

Blandford (Massachusetts)
Sage House Antiques, Rte 23, Blandford, MA 01008.
T. (413) 848-2843.   *069876*

Bloomfield Hills (Michigan)
Frederick, David, 869 W. Long Lake, Bloomfield Hills, MI
48013. - Ant -   *069877*

Bloomington (Illinois)
Fredericks, 3 Towanda Rd., Bloomington, IL 61701.
T. (309) 447-1302.   *069878*

Blowing Rock (North Carolina)
Lamp Post Antiques, Main Street, Blowing Rock, NC
28605. T. (704) 295-3868. - Furn -   *069879*

Bluffton (Ohio)
Reichenbach, 562 N. Main St., Bluffton, OH
45817.   *069880*

Bluffton (South Carolina)
Stock Farm Antiques, 25 Miles North of Savannah Hwy.
46, Bluffton, SC 29910. T. (803) 757-2511. - Furn /
Repr -   *069881*

Boca Raton (Florida)
Ming Furniture, 4400 N Federal Hwy., Boca Raton, FL
33431. T. (305) 368-9109. - Furn / Orient -   *069882*

Boise (Idaho)
Galerie des Refusées, 4829 Sorrento Dr., Boise, ID
83704. T. (208) 322-7759. - Paint -   *069883*
Riebe, Helen, 2910 Good St., Boise, ID 83702.   *069884*

Boston (Massachusetts)
A Kings's Collection, 102 Waltham St., Boston, MA
02118. T. (617) 482-1111.   *069885*
Alberts-Langdon, 126 Charles St., Boston, MA 02114.
T. (617) 523-5954. - Orient -   *069886*
Anderson, & Co., John B., 40 Wareham St., Boston, MA
02118. T. (617) 542-1515.   *069887*
Araby Rug Imperium, 667 Boylston St., Boston, MA
02116. T. (617) 267-0012. - Tex -   *069888*
Art Collector, 382 Commonwealth Av., Boston, MA
02215. T. (617) 424-9008.   *069889*
Aunt Rose's Antiques, 131 Jersey St., Boston, MA
02215. T. (617) 262-0259.   *069890*
Autrefois Antiques, 125 Newbury St., Boston, MA
02116. T. (617) 424-8823.   *069891*
Avery, M C., 229 Berkeley St., Boston, MA 02116.
T. (617) 262-6617.   *069892*
Bee, Kay, 1122 Boyle St., Boston, MA 02129.
T. (617) 266-4487.   *069893*
Belgravia, 222 Newbury St., Boston, MA 02116.
T. (617) 267-1915.   *069894*
Brodney, 811 Boylston St., Boston, MA 02116.
T. (617) 536-0500. - Ant / Paint / Graph / Orient / China /
Sculp / Jew / Silv / Rel -   *069895*
Brookline Village Antiques, 1 Design Center Pl, Boston,
MA 02210. T. (617) 542-2853.   *069896*
Calantropo, Paul S., 387 Washington St., Boston, MA
02108. T. (617) 426-4259.   *069897*
Camden Passage, 120 Brookline Av., Boston, MA
02215. T. (617) 421-9899.   *069898*
Comenos, 81 Arlington St., Boston, MA 02116.
T. (617) 423-9365, Fax (617) 423-6675. - Ant / Paint /
Furn / Fra / Ico -   *069899*
Cove Hollow Antiques, Westin Hotel, Copley Pl, Boston,
MA 02116. T. (617) 266-7850.   *069900*
Divine Decadence, 535 Columbus Av., Boston, MA
02118. T. (617) 266-1477.   *069901*
Eugene Galleries, 76 Charles St, Boston, MA 02114.
T. (617) 227-3062. - Ant / Paint / Graph / Num / Orient /
Repr / Sculp / Eth / Dec / Fra -   *069902*
Eyges, Ray K., 38 Newbury St., Boston, MA 02116.
T. (617) 247-8400.   *069903*
Firestone & Parson, 1 Newbury St., Boston, MA 02117.
T. (617) 266-1858. - Jew / Silv -   *069904*
Forty River Street Antiques, 40 River St., Boston, MA
02126. T. (617) 227-9261.   *069905*

Freedman, David C., 333 Washington St., Boston, MA
02108. T. (617) 227-4294.   *069906*
Global Antiques, 23 Commonwealth Ave., Boston, MA
02116. T. (617) 698-2218.   *069907*
Gravert, George, 122 Charles St., Boston, MA 02114.
T. (617) 227-1593. - Ant / Paint / Furn / Orient / China /
Arch / Dec / Lights / Instr / Glass -   *069908*
Grogan & Co, 890 Commonwealth Av., Boston, MA
02215. T. (617) 566-4100.   *069909*
Grossman, 51 Charles St., Boston, MA 02114.
T. (617) 523-1879. - Ant / Graph / Furn / Num / China /
Dec / Silv / Lights / Glass -   *069910*
Hershoff, Seymoor, 333 Washington St., Boston, MA
02108. T. (617) 227-4294.   *069911*
Hilary House, 86 Chestnut St., Boston, MA 02108.
T. (617) 523-7118. - Ant / Paint / Graph / Furn / Orient /
China / Dec / Silv / Lights / Glass -   *069912*
Knollwood, 517 Columbus Av., Boston, MA 02118.
T. (617) 536-8866.   *069913*
Lowe, Samuel L., 80 Charles St., Boston, MA 02114.
T. (617) 742-0845. - Ant / Paint / Graph / Furn / China /
Instr -   *069914*
Marcoz, 660 Summer St., Boston, MA 02210.
T. (617) 357-0211.   *069915*
Marcoz, 177 Newbury St., Boston, MA 02116.
T. (617) 262-0780.   *069916*
Marika's Antiques, 130 Charles St., Boston, MA 02114.
T. (617) 523-4520. - Ant / Paint / Furn / Orient / China /
Sculp / Eth / Dec / Jew / Silv / Instr / Glass -   *069917*
Montambeau, Mildred E., 46 Gloucester St., Boston,
02115.   *069918*
Newbury Street Jewelry and Antiques, 255 Newbury St.,
Boston, MA 02116. T. (617) 236-0038.   *069919*
Norumbega, 297 Auburn St., Boston, MA 02166.
T. (617) 527-5554. - Num -   *069920*
Nostalgia Factory, 324 Newbury St., Boston, MA 02115.
T. (617) 236-8754.   *069921*
Odeon, 562 Tremont St., Boston, MA 02118.
T. (617) 542-4412.   *069922*
Postar, William, 129 Charles St., Boston, MA 02114.
- Ant -   *069923*
Ruppert, C. A., 121 Charles St., Boston, MA 02114.
T. (617) 523-5033.   *069924*
Seidler, 333 Washington St., Boston, MA 02108.
T. (617) 227-5790.   *069925*
Shreve, Crump & Low, 330 Boylston St., Boston, MA
02116. T. (617) 267-9100. - Ant / Paint / Graph / Furn /
Orient / China / Dec / Silv / Lights / Instr / Glass - *069926*
Small Pleasures, 142 Newbury St., Boston, MA 02116.
T. (617) 267-7371.   *069927*
Studio 106, 106 Waltham St., Boston, MA 02118.
T. (617) 482-5207.   *069928*
Tiger Lily Antiques, 152 Mount Vernon St., Boston, MA
02132. T. (617) 723-8494.   *069929*
Trade Winds, 141 Newbury St., Boston, MA 02116.
T. (617) 267-5044. - Ant / Paint / Graph / Furn / China /
Repr / Dec / Silv / Lights / Instr -   *069930*
Vose, Robert C., 238 Newbury St., Boston, MA 02116.
T. (617) 536 6176. - Paint -   *069931*
Wenham Cross, 232 Newbury St., Boston, MA 02116.
T. (617) 236-0409.   *069932*
Women's Educational and Industrial Union, 356 Boylston
St., Boston, MA 02116. T. (617) 536-5651.   *069933*
Zulalian, 1680 Beacon St., Boston, MA 02146.
T. (617) 277-4686. - Ant / Tex -   *069934*

Bowling Green (Ohio)
Adams, 478 S Church St., Bowling Green, OH 43402.
- Ant / China / Glass -   *069935*
Barnett, 11954 E.Gypsy Lane Rd., Bowling Green, OH
43402. T. (419) 352-5194.   *069936*
Yesteryear's Antique Shoppe, 230 Clay St., Bowling
Green, OH 43402.   *069937*

Boyertown (Pennsylvania)
Boyertown Antiques, R.D.4, Weisstown and Funk Rds.,
Boyertown, PA 19512. T. (215) 367-2452. - Furn /
Instr -   *069938*
Ye Olde Ram Run, Hill Church Rd., Boyertown, PA
19512. T. (215) 367-2875. - Ant -   *069939*

Branford (Connecticut)
C+R Antiques, 62 Knollwood Dr., Branford, CT 06405.
T. (203) 488-9860.   069940

Brewster (Massachusetts)
Freeman Perry House Antiques, Rte 6A, Brewster, MA
02631. T. (617) 896-5323.   069941
Grant, Barbara, Rte 6A, Brewster, MA 02631. - Furn /
China / Jew / Glass -   069942
Howes, Donald B., Rte 6A, Brewster, MA 02631.
T. (617) 896-3502.   069943
Kingsland Manor Antiques, Rte 6A, Brewster, MA 02631.
T. (617) 385-9741. - Furn -   069944
Red Jacket Antiques, Rte 6A, Brewster, MA 02631.
T. (617) 896-3608, 255-0864. - Furn / China -   069945

Bridgehampton (New York)
Sterling & Hunt, POB 300, Bridgehampton, NY 11932.
T. (516) 537-1096. - Ant / Paint -   069946

Bridgeport (Connecticut)
Greens Farms Antiques, 3142 Fairfield Ave, Bridgeport,
CT 06605. - Ant / Furn / China -   069947

Bridgewater (Massachusetts)
Harvest Hill Antiques, 450 Plymouth St., Bridgewater,
MA 02324. T. (617) 697-7160.   069948

Brilliant (Ohio)
Green, 610 Powell Av., Brilliant, OH 43913.
- Ant -   069949

Bristol (Rhode Island)
Babbitt House, 328 Hope St, Bristol, RI 02809.
T. (401) 253-8763. - Ant -   069950

Brockton (Massachusetts)
Gerber, B. I., 386 Pleasant St., Brockton, MA 02401.
T. (617) 586-2547. - Ant / Furn / Orient / China / Jew /
Fra / Silv / Lights / Glass / Cur -   069951

Bronxville (New York)
Shepard, Bob, 81 Pondfield Rd., Bronxville, NY 10708.
T. (914) 779-8700.   069952

Brookline (Massachusetts)
Nissman & Abromson, 286 Clinton Rd, Brookline, MA
02146. T. (617) 735-0467, Fax (617) 277-
1925.   069953

Brunswick (Maine)
Robbins, M. H., Bath Rd., Brunswick, ME 04011.
T. (207) 729-3473. - Ant / Paint / Furn / China /
Glass -   069954

Brunswick (Ohio)
Brunswick Antiques, 808 Pearl Rd., Brunswick, OH
44212.   069955

Bryan (Ohio)
Criswell, 535 Center St., Bryan, OH 43506.   069956

Buckingham (Pennsylvania)
Edna's Antique Shop, Rtes 263 and 413, Buckingham,
PA 18912. T. (215) 794-7261. - Ant -   069957

Buena Park (California)
Antique Shop, Knotts Berry Farm, Buena Park, CA
90620. T. (714) 527-8484.   069958

Buffalo (New York)
Anderson, David, 1 Barcher Pl., Buffalo, NY 14216.
T. (716) 834-2579. - Paint / Graph / Sculp / Tex / Fra /
Pho / Draw -   069959
Buffalo Goodwill Industries, 153 N Division St., Buffalo,
NY 14203. T. (716) 854-7686. - Ant / Paint / Furn /
Num / Tex / Jew / Instr -   069960
D'Arcangelo, 1740 Main St., Buffalo, NY 14208.
T. (716) 885-1146. - Ant / Paint / Furn / Repr / Sculp /
Fra / Mil -   069961
Dick's Antiques, 238 Grimsby Rd., Buffalo, NY 14223.
T. (716) 882-2300. - Furn / China / Jew / Silv / Lights /
Glass -   069962
Mileham, Tom, 148 Elmwood St., Buffalo, NY 14201.
T. (716) 884-4550. - Ant -   069963
Tillou, Dana, 417 Franklin St., Buffalo, NY 14202.
T. (716) 854-5285. - Paint / Furn -   069964

Burgoon (Ohio)
Ellenberger, Burgoon, OH 43407.   069965

Burlingame (California)
Hotmann, 1386 Hillside Circle, Burlingame, CA 94010.
- Ant / China / Glass -   069966
Kerwin, 1107 California Dr, Burlingame, CA 94010.
T. (415) 340-8400. - Graph -   069967

Burlington (Vermont)
Allen, Ethan, 1625 Williston Rd., Burlington, VT 05401.
T. (802) 863-3764. - Ant / Furn -   069968

Burton (Ohio)
Western Reserve Antiques, 14352 N. Cheshire, Burton,
OH 44021. T. (216) 834-1577. - Furn -   069969

Butte (Montana)
Tony's Antique Store, 209 E Park St., Butte, MT 59701.
T. (406) 723-6337. - Ant -   069970

Buzzards Bay (Massachusetts)
Old House, 291 Head of the Bay Rd., Buzzards Bay, MA
02532. T. (617) 759-4942. - Ant / Furn / China /
Glass -   069971

Caledonia (New York)
Feeley, G.D., 2 Spring St., Caledonia, NY 14423.
- Ant -   069972

Calvert (Texas)
Boll Weevil, Hwy 6, Calvert, TX 77837. T. (409) 364-
2835. - Furn / Jew -   069973

Cambridge (Massachusetts)
Bernheimer, 52c Brattle St., Cambridge, MA 02138.
T. (617) 547-1177. - Ant / Orient / Arch / Eth / Jew /
Rel -   069974
Hubley & Co., F.B., 364 Broadway, Cambridge, MA
02139. T. (617) 876-2030. - Ant -   069975
Hurst, 53 Mount Auburn St., Cambridge, MA 02138.
T. (617) 491-6888. - Eth -   069976

Camp Hill (Pennsylvania)
House of Curios, 2106 Market Pl, Camp Hill, PA 17011.
T. (717) 763-0774. - Ant / Paint / Graph / China / Lights /
Cur -   069977

Canandaigua (New York)
Harvest Mill, 40 Parrish St., Canandaigua, NY 14424.
T. (716) 394-5907. - Furn -   069978

Canfield (Ohio)
Brick, William, 27 W. Main St., Canfield, OH 44406.
T. (216) 533-5661. - Ant / Paint / Furn / China /
Dec -   069979

Canonsburg (Pennsylvania)
Rolling Hills Farm Antiques, RD1, Canonsburg POB 101,
PA 15317. T. (412) 746-2794.   069980

Canton (Massachusetts)
Cline, 876 Pleasant St., Canton, MA 02021.
T. (617) 828-1679. - Ant / Paint / Num / Mil -   069981

Canton (Ohio)
Dornhecker, 414 Schneider Rd. SE, Canton, OH 44720.
- Cur -   069982
Tally-Ho Studio, 639 Park Av. SW, Canton, OH 44706.
T. (216) 452-4488. - Ant / Graph / Glass / Cur -   069983

Carmel (California)
Bowen & Bossier, San Carlos and 7th St., Carmel, CA
93921. T. (408) 624-1169.   069984
Carmel Antiques, Dolores and 7th St, Carmel, CA 93921.
T. (408) 624-7760. - Ant -   069985
Carmel Bay Comp., Corner of Ocean and Lincoln, Car-
mel, CA 93921. T. (408) 624-3868.   069986
Carmel Stamp and Coin Shop, Ocean and Dolores, Car-
mel, CA 93921. T. (408) 624-3951. - Num -   069987
David & Arthur Antiques, Lincoln Ave., Carmel, CA
93921. - Ant / Paint / Graph / Furn / China / Tex / Jew /
Silv / Lights / Instr / Mil / Glass -   069988
Harrinton-Brown, Corner Sixth and Lincoln, Carmel, CA
93921. T. (408) 624-3054. - Paint / Graph / Sculp /
Jew -   069989

Interior Traditions, Between 5th and 6th on S. Carlos,
Carmel, CA 93921. T. (408) 625-2300.   069990
Karges, William A., 26352 Carmel Rancho Lane, POB
222091, Carmel, CA 93923. T. (408) 625-
4226.   069991
Langer, Dolores St., Carmel, CA 93921. T. (408) 624-
2102.   069992
Luciano Antiques, POB 5686, Carmel, CA 93921.
T. (408) 624-9396. - Ant -   069993
Oriental Fine Art, Pine Inn, Carmel, CA 93921.
T. (408) 624-3646. - Furn -   069994

Carmel (Indiana)
Acorn Farm Antiques, 15466 Oak Rd., Carmel, IN
46032. T. (317) 846-2383. - Ant / Paint / Furn / Orient /
China / Jew / Silv / Glass -   069995

Carolina (Rhode Island)
Scudder, James E., Rte. 112, Carolina, RI 02812.
T. (401) 364-7228. - Ant / Furn / Orient / Glass -   069996

Carpinteria (California)
Floyd, Jan, 3900 N Via Real, Carpinteria, CA 93013.
T. (805) 684-4302. - Furn -   069997

Carrollton (Ohio)
Thomas, 311 Fourth St. NE, Carrollton, OH 44615.
- Ant / Furn / China / Glass -   069998

Cedar Grove (New Jersey)
Korby, Marion, 447 Pompton Av., Cedar Grove, NJ
07009. T. (201) 239-2188. - Ant -   069999

Cedar Rapids (Iowa)
Koehn, Agnes, 5100 Johnson Ave SW, Cedar Rapids, IA
52404. T. (319) 364-6594.   070000
Mahurans', 1917 B Ave NE, Cedar Rapids, IA 52402.
T. (319) 365-0027. - Ant / China / Glass -   070001

Celina (Ohio)
Dell, 404 E. Livingston St., Celina, OH 45822. - Ant /
Furn / China / Instr -   070002

Centerbrock (Connecticut)
Carde, June & Ben, Old Bull House, Main St., Centerb-
rock, CT 06409. T. (203) 767-0022. - Furn /
Orient -   070003

Centreville (Maryland)
Young, Gary E., 128 S Commerce, Centreville, MD
21617.   070004

Ceres (California)
Opal, 3040 9th St., Ceres, CA 95307.   070005

Chadds Ford (Pennsylvania)
Chadds Ford Gallery, Rte 1 and Rte 100, Chadds Ford
POB 179, PA 19317. T. (215) 459-5510. - Paint /
Repr -   070006

Chagrin Falls (Ohio)
Millside, 89 N. Main St., Chagrin Falls, OH
44022.   070007

Chapel Hill (North Carolina)
Chinaberry Hill, Turkey Farm Rd., Chapel Hill, NC 27514.
T. (919) 929-2553. - Orient / China -   070008
Daniel, Elizabeth R., 2 Gooseneck Rd, Chapel Hill, NC
27514. T. (919) 968-3041.   070009
Gooseneck Antiques, 2 Gooseneck Rd., Chapel Hill, NC
27514. T. (919) 968-3041. - Ant / Paint / Furn /
China -   070010
Whitehall Shop, 1215 E. Franklin St., Chapel Hill, NC
27514. T. (919) 942-3179. - Ant / Paint / Furn / Orient /
China / Repr / Tex / Arch / Jew / Lights / Instr / Glass --
                                                      070011

Chappaqua (New York)
Johnstone, Philip D., 11 Brook Ln, Chappaqua, NY
10514. T. (914) 238-4068. - Ant -   070012

Chardon (Ohio)
Bostwick, 310 South St., Chardon, OH 44024.   070013

Charleston (South Carolina)
Austin, Elizabeth, 165 King St., Charleston, SC 29400.
T. (803) 722-8227. - Furn / Silv -   070014

Birlant, George C., & Co., 191 King St., Charleston, SC 29401. - Ant / Furn / China / Repr / Silv / Lights / Glass - *070015*

British Antique Importers, Market Pl, Charleston, SC 29401. *070016*

Century House Antiques, 77 Church St., Charleston, SC 29401. *070017*

Coles & Co., 84 Wentworth St., Charleston, SC 29401. T. (803) 723-2142. - Ant / Paint / Furn - *070018*

Colonial Antique Shop, 193 King St, Charleston, SC 29401. *070019*

Garden Gate Antiques, 96 King St, Charleston, SC 29401. T. (803) 722-0308. - Furn / China - *070020*

Gibson, John & Co., Inc., 183 King St, Charleston, SC 29401. T. (803) 722-0909. - Furn - *070021*

Livingston & Sons, 2137 Savannah Hwy., Charleston, SC 29407. *070022*

Patla, Jack, 181 King St., Charleston, SC 29401. T. (803) 723-2314. - Ant - *070023*

Red Toril, 197 King St., Charleston, SC 29401. T. (803) 723-0443. *070024*

Schindler, 200 King St., Charleston, SC 29401. T. (803) 722-0853. - Ant / China - *070025*

Charlotte (North Carolina)
Lee, 1601 E Seventh St, Charlotte, NC 28204. T. (704) 376-5360. - Furn / Jew / Silv - *070026*

Treasures Unlimited, 6401 Morrison Blvd., Charlotte, NC 28211. T. (704) 366-7272. - Ant / Furn / China / Silv - *070027*

Charlottesville (Virginia)
Caperton, Bernard M., 1113 W Main St., Charlottesville, VA 22903. T. (804) 293-2383. - Ant / Paint / Graph / Furn / Orient / China / Arch / Eth / Jew / Silv / Lights / Instr / Glass / Cur / Mul / Draw - *070028*

Lionbridge, POB 5231, Charlottesville, VA 22905. T. (804) 977-2785/86, 971-7100. - Paint / Furn / China / Silv / Instr / Glass - *070029*

Woods, Ann, 1211 W Main St., Charlottesville, VA 22903. T. (804) 295-6108. - Ant / Dec - *070030*

1740 House Antiques, Rte 250 W, Charlottesville, VA 22901. T. (804) 977-1740. - Furn - *070031*

Chatfield (Ohio)
Almendinger, POB 77, Chatfield, OH 44825. *070032*

Chatham (Massachusetts)
Johnstone, 265 Old Harbor Rd., Chatham, MA 02633. T. (617) 945-0367. *070033*

Chatham (New York)
Rasso, Richard & Betty, Rte 295 and Frisbee St., Chatham, NY 12060. T. (518) 392-4501. *070034*

Skevington-Back, Arnold's Mills Rd, Chatham, NY 12037. T. (518) 392-9056. *070035*

Chattanooga (Tennessee)
Clements, 5520 Hwy. 153, Chattanooga, TN 37443. T. (615) 842-4177, 842-5992. - Furn / China - *070036*

Chelsea (Michigan)
Kala Farm Antiques, 2156 Manchester Rd., Chelsea, MI 48118. *070037*

Cherry Valley (California)
Moore, Herbert, 40238 Brookside Ave, Cherry Valley, CA 92223. - Ant / Furn - *070038*

Chesapeake (Virginia)
Melton, 4201 Indian River Rd, Chesapeake, VA 23325. T. (804) 420-8911, 420-5117. *070039*

Cheshire (Massachusetts)
Cheshire Village Antiques, Rte 8, Cheshire, MA 01225. T. (413) 743-4385. *070040*

Chester (Massachusetts)
Chester Gallery, Rte 20, Chester, MA 01011. T. (413) 354-6378. *070041*

Chesterton (Indiana)
Coffee Creek Antiques, 601 S. Calumet Rd, Chesterton, IN 46304. T. (219) 926-3018. - Ant - *070042*

Chestnut Hill (Pennsylvania)
Hutchinson, Martha, 10 E Hartwell Ln, Chestnut Hill, PA 19118. - Ant - *070043*

Chevy Chase (Maryland)
Keshishian & Sons, Mark, 4505 Stanford St., Chevy Chase, MD 20815. T. (301) 951-8880. *070044*

Mendelsohn, 6826 Wisconsin Ave, Chevy Chase, MD 20015. - Ant - *070045*

Chicago (Illinois)
A A Coins, 2349 W 95th St., Chicago, IL 60643. T. (312) 239-1461. - Num - *070046*

A Antiques and Interiors, 1006 S. Michigan, Chicago, IL 60605. T. (312) 939-9449. - Ant / Furn / Dec - *070047*

Antiques Limited, Merchandise Mart Plaza, Chicago, IL 60654. *070048*

Baker, Frederick, 1230 W Jackson Blvd., Chicago, IL 60607. T. (312) 243-2980. - Paint / Graph - *070049*

Beloian, Leon, 6245 N. Broadway, Chicago, IL 60660. *070050*

Ben's Stamp and Coin Company, 31 N. Clark St., Chicago, IL 60602. T. (312) 346-3443. - Num - *070051*

Bucheit, Mira, 449 N Wells St, Chicago, IL 60610. T. (312) 527-4080. *070052*

Callard, 100 E. Walton Pl., Chicago, IL 60611. - Ant - *070053*

Cavalier, 4412 N. Ashland, Chicago, IL 60640. T. (312) 561-5957. - Ant / Paint / Graph / China / Lights / Instr - *070054*

Coach House, 60 W Erie St., Chicago, IL 60610. T. (312) 787-3457. - Ant - *070055*

Decorative Crafts, Merchandise Mart Plaza, Chicago, IL 60654. - Graph / Repr / Sculp / Fra / Lights / Instr - *070056*

Di Salvo, E.V., & Co., 55 E. Washington St., Chicago, IL 60602. T. (312) 726-1974. - Jew - *070057*

Edgeworth, C. Richard, 5000 N Marine Dr., Chicago, IL 60640. T. (312) 728-4445. - Paint / Draw - *070058*

Feigen, Richard L., & Co., 325 W Huron St., Chicago, IL 60610. T. (312) 787-0500, Fax (312) 787-7261. - Ant / Paint - *070059*

Fell, Joseph-W., 3221 N Clark St., Chicago, IL 60657. T. (312) 549-6076. - Tex - *070060*

Finkelman, M. Y., 5 S. Wabash, Chicago, IL 60603. *070061*

Fly By Nite Antiques and Gallery, 714 N. Wells St, Chicago, IL 60610. T. (312) 664-8136. - Ant / Paint / Graph / Furn / China / Sculp / Dec / Jew / Silv / Lights / Instr / Glass / Cur - *070062*

Gallo, Pia, POB 11678, Chicago, IL 60611. T. (312) 348-5840. - Graph *070063*

Gold, Stella, 4630 W. Harrison, Chicago, IL 60644. T. (312) 378-0920. - Num - *070064*

Hamlet, 1412 N Wells St., Chicago, IL 60610. T. (312) 642-4444. - Graph / China / Sculp / Dec / Jew / Silv / Glass - *070065*

Hanzel, 1120 South Michigan Ave, Chicago, IL 60605. T. (312) 922-6234, Fax (312) 922-6972. - Ant / Furn - *070066*

Hynes, 5932 N Virginia Ave, Chicago, IL 60659. T. (312) 878-1147. - Paint - *070067*

Kind, Phyllis, 313 W Superior St, Chicago, IL 60610. T. (312) 642-6302. *070068*

Lincoln Gallery, 3039 N Lincoln Ave, Chicago, IL 60657. T. (312) 248-3647. *070069*

Marshall, Field & Co., 111 N State St, Chicago, IL 60690. T. (312) 781-1000. - Ant / Paint / Graph / Furn / Num / Orient / Repr / China / Sculp / Tex / Eth / Jew / Fra / Silv - *070070*

Matsumoto, Kakuro, 226 S Wabash Ave, Chicago, IL 60604. - Ant / Orient / China - *070071*

Norton, Richard, 612 Merchandise Mart Plaza, Chicago, IL 60654. T. (312) 644-9359. - Ant / Furn / China / Repr / Dec / Lights / Instr - *070072*

Owen, W. C., 1520 Merchandise Mart Plaza, Chicago, IL 60654. - Paint / Repr - *070073*

Serwer, Barbara, Chicago POB 14824, IL 60614. T. (312) 528-6456. - Graph - *070074*

Williams, Taylor B., 1624 N La Salle Dr., Chicago, IL 60614. T. (312) 266-0908. - Furn - *070075*

Chickasha (Oklahoma)
Fran's Antiques, 1328 S 14th St, Chickasha, OK 73018. T. (405) 224-7111. *070076*

Christiana (Pennsylvania)
Irion Company, 1 S Bridge St., Christiana, PA 17509. T. (215) 593-2153. *070077*

Cincinnati (Ohio)
Albrecht, Gloria J., 8849 Kenwood Rd, Cincinnati, OH 45200. T. (513) 891-0531. - Furn - *070078*

Aronoff, Samuel, 4923 Whetsel Ave, Cincinnati, OH 45227. T. (513) 561-6900. - Ant / Paint / Furn / Orient / China / Sculp / Tex / Arch / Dec / Lights / Rel - *070079*

Buckeye Hill Antiques, 8765 Montgomery Rd, Cincinnati, OH 45236. T. (513) 891-6128. - Ant / Orient / China - *070080*

Closson, 401 Race St, Cincinnati, OH 45202. T. (513) 762-5500. - Ant / Paint / Graph / Furn / Orient / China / Tex / Fra / Silv / Lights / Instr - *070081*

Creekwood, 9257 Montgomery Rd, Cincinnati, OH 45242. T. (513) 791-8459. - Ant / Furn - *070082*

Federation Antiques, 2030 Madison Rd, Cincinnati, OH 45208. T. (513) 321-2671. - Furn - *070083*

General Store, 818 Elm St, Cincinnati, OH 45200. T. (513) 721-4445. - Ant / Paint / Graph / Furn / Num / China / Repr / Tex / Arch / Dec / Jew / Fra / Lights / Instr / Mil / Glass - *070084*

Leonhard, Ran, Mary, 3668 Erie Ave, Cincinnati, OH 45208. T. (513) 871-5604. - Paint / Sculp - *070085*

Okura, Frank M., 1133 Vine St, Cincinnati, OH 45210. T. (513) 721-7299. - Graph / Orient / China / Jew - *070086*

Springs Antiques, 3871 Cooper, Cincinnati, OH 45210. T. (513) 791-7935. - Ant / Furn / Mil / Glass - *070087*

Trivet, 917 Race St, Cincinnati, OH 45202. - Ant - *070088*

Circleville (Ohio)
Summer House Craft Shop, Rte 4, 7 Miles East on Rte 56, Circleville, OH 43113. *070089*

Claverack (New York)
Dunn, Michael, Route 23B, Box B, Claverack, NY 12513. T. (518) 851-7052, Fax (518) 851-7564. *070090*

Dunn, Michael & Jane, Rte 23B, Box B, Claverack, NY 12513. T. (518) 851-7052. - China - *070091*

Clayton (New Jersey)
Den of Antiquity, 213 N. Delsea Dr., Clayton, NJ 08312. - Ant / China / Glass - *070092*

Cleveland (Ohio)
Ambrose, 1867 Prospect, Cleveland, OH 44115. T. (216) 771-4874. - Ant / Paint / Orient / China / Jew / Mil - *070093*

Brookside, 5801 Train Ave, Cleveland, OH 44102. *070094*

Brownstone, 10728 Carnegie Ave, Cleveland, OH 44106. T. (216) 791-0679. - Ant - *070095*

Clutterboxe, 4126-4128 Lorain Ave, Cleveland, OH 44102. T. (216) 631-7788. *070096*

Federal Brand Enterprises, 5940 Pearl Rd, Cleveland, OH 44130. - Num - *070097*

Feldman, Arthur L., 488 The Arcade, Cleveland, OH 44114. T. (216) 861-3580. - Graph / Mul - *070098*

Greater Cleveland Antiques, 5940 Pearl Rd, Cleveland, OH 44130. - Ant / Num - *070099*

Greenwald, June, 3096 Mayfield, Cleveland, OH 44118. T. (216) 932-5535. - Ant / Furn / China / Jew / Glass - *070100*

Gwynby, 2482 Fairmount Blvd, Cleveland, OH 44106. T. (216) 229-2526. - Ant - *070101*

Holzheimer, 10901 Carnegie Ave, Cleveland, OH 44106. T. (216) 791-9292. - Ant / Paint / Furn - *070102*

Lakewood, 15500 Edgewater Dr., Cleveland, OH 44107. - Num - *070103*

Narosny, Anne, 2118 S. Taylor St, Cleveland, OH 44118. *070104*

Sender, 10800 Carnegie Ave, Cleveland, OH 44106. T. (216) 721-2155. - Ant / Paint / Furn - *070105*

Skeffington, Abigail, 7806 Lorain St, Cleveland, OH 44102. *070106*

Cleveland (Tennessee)
May, J., 2706 Parkwood Trail N.W., Cleveland, TN
37311. T. (615) 476-8392. - Furn -   070107

Cliffside Park (New Jersey)
Vintage Years Antiques, 619 Palisade Ave, Cliffside Park,
NJ 07010. T. (201) 945-6035. - Furn / Orient / China /
Jew / Mod -   070108

Clifton (New Jersey)
Antiques Dealer, 1115 Clifton Ave, Clifton, NJ 07013.
T. (201) 779-1600.   070109

Clinton (New Jersey)
Paddy-Wak Antiques, 19 1/2 Old Rte 22, Clinton, NJ
08829. T. (201) 735-9770.   070110

Closter (New Jersey)
Brewer, Harvey W., Closter POB 322, NJ 07624.
T. (201) 768-4414.   070111

Coatesville (Pennsylvania)
Howe, Don, 360 Harmony St, Coatesville, PA 19320.
T. (215) 384-3615. - Ant / Furn -   070112

Cogan Station (Pennsylvania)
Roan, Bob, Chuck & Rich, RD2, Cogan Station, PA
17728. T. (717) 494-0170.   070113

Colchester (Connecticut)
Liverant, Nathan, & Son, 48 S. Main St., Colchester, CT
06415. T. (203) 537-2409. - Ant / China -   070114

Cold Spring Harbor (New York)
Jacobsen, Valdemar F., 5 Main St., Cold Spring Harbor,
NY 11724. T. (516) 692-7775.   070115

Colerain (Ohio)
Litten, U.S. 250 16 Miles South of Cadiz, Colerain, OH
43916. - Ant -   070116

Collingswood (New Jersey)
Schmidt, Anthony C., 112 E Linden Av., Collingswood,
NJ 08108. T. (609) 858-4719. - Paint -   070117

Coloma (Michigan)
Millstone Shop, 6162 Martin Rd., Coloma, MI 49038.
- Ant / Furn / Arch / Fra / Lights / Glass -   070118

Colorado Springs (Colorado)
Augustin, 618 N Tejon, Colorado Springs, CO 80903.
T. (303) 634-8863. - Ant / Orient -   070119
Beroni, 645 Glen Eyre Circle, Colorado Springs, CO
80904. - Ant / Dec -   070120
Bryan & Scott, 112 114 N. Tejon St., Colorado Springs,
CO 80902. - Jew -   070121
Cobweb, 2624 W Colorado Av., Colorado Springs, CO
80904. T. (303) 634-5494. - Ant / Paint / Furn / China /
Silv / Lights / Instr / Glass -   070122
Hibbitt, 720 N Nevada, Colorado Springs, CO 80902.
T. (303) 473-0464. - Ant / Paint / Orient / China /
Sculp -   070123

Colton (California)
Trash and Treasures, 12400 Reche Canyon Rd, Colton,
CA 92324.   070124

Columbia (South Carolina)
Safran, 930 Gervais St., Columbia, SC 29201.
T. (803) 252-7927. - Ant / Furn -   070125

Columbus (Ohio)
Antieks, 37 W. Kossuth St., Columbus, OH 43206.
T. (614) 444-4488. - Furn -   070126
Church on the Lane Antiques, Inc., 1251 Grandview
Ave., Columbus, OH 43212. T. (614) 488-3606, 488-
8755.   070127
Edmundson, Jean, 1202 Wilson Ave, Columbus, OH
43206.   070128
Hallam, 3860 N High St., Columbus, OH 43206. - Ant /
China -   070129
North, P.H., 81 Bullitt Park Pl, Columbus, OH 43209.
- Ant / Paint / Graph / Orient / Arch -   070130

Colusa (California)
Gertrude's Antiques, 840 Oak St., Colusa, 95932.
- Ant -   070131

Concord (New Hampshire)
Hamel, Douglas H., R.F.D. 10, POB 100, Concord, NH
03301. T. (603) 798-5912. - Furn -   070132

Conneaut (Ohio)
Ferguson, 282 E. Main Rd, Conneaut, OH
44030.   070133

Conshohocken (Pennsylvania)
Sharpe, Matthew and Elisabeth, Spring Mill, Conshohoc-
ken, PA 19428. T. (215) 828-0205. - Ant / Furn /
China -   070134

Corning (New York)
Hunter, Betty, R.D.1, Caton Rd., Corning, NY 14830.
- Ant / Furn -   070135
King, Margaret S., 10 E. First St., Corning, NY 14830.
T. (607) 962-0876. - Ant -   070136

Cornwall (Connecticut)
Holmes, Carter Rd., Cornwall, CT 06754. T. (203) 672-
6427. - Ant / Paint / Mil -   070137

Corona del Mar (California)
Hearthstone, 2711 E Coast Hwy, Corona del Mar, CA
92625. T. (714) 673-7065.   070138

Coronado (California)
Oriental Arts, 1204-1206 Orange Ave., Coronado, CA
92118. T. (714) 435-5451. - Paint / Arch / Fra /
Mil -   070139

Cortland (Ohio)
Chapman, Ruth, Rte. 2, Cortland, 44410. T. (216) 637-
1414. - Ant / Furn / China / Lights / Glass -   070140

Costa Mesa (California)
Charles & Charles, 365 Clinton Ave., Costa Mesa, CA
92626. - Ant / Paint / Furn / China / Repr / Tex / Fra /
Lights / Instr / Rel / Glass / Cur -   070141
Yankee Peddler, 2134 Newport Blvd., Costa Mesa, CA
92627. T. (714) 642-9256.   070142

Cross River (New York)
Yellow Monkey Antiques, Rte 35, Cross River, NY 10518.
T. (914) 763-5848.   070143

Culver City (California)
McLaughlin, 3814 Willat St., Culver City, CA 90230.
- Ant / Furn / Lights -   070144

Cumberland (Rhode Island)
Antiques, Sneech Pond Rd., Cumberland, RI 02864.
T. (401) 333-5371.   070145

Cummaquid (Massachusetts)
Cummaquid Antiques, Historic Rte. 6A, Cummaquid, MA
02637. T. (617) 363-2492. - Furn / Instr -   070146

Dallas (Texas)
Antique House, 3903 Lemmon Av., Dallas, TX
75219.   070147
Berge Boghossian, 2714 Fairmount St., Dallas, TX
75201. T. (214) 741-5512. - Tex -   070148
Cameron, POB 7326, Dallas, TX 75200. T. (214) 352-
0497. - Ant / Paint / Furn / Orient / China / Sculp /
Lights / Glass -   070149
Chelsea Square, 3126 Routh St., Dallas, Tx
75201.   070150
Fairmount Antiques, 2706 Fairmount St., Dallas, TX
75201. T. (214) 742-7957. - Ant / Paint / Furn / China /
Lights / Glass -   070151
Ferrell, William, 2913 Fairmount St., Dallas, TX 75201.
T. (214) 651-8861. - Paint / Furn / China -   070152
Heirloom House, 2521 Fairmount St., Dallas, TX 75201.
T. (214) 748-2087. - Paint / Graph / Furn / Orient / Chi-
na / Sculp / Tex -   070153
Jackson, Leon C., 6209 Hillcrest Av., Dallas, TX 75205.
T. (214) 521-9929. - Mil -   070154
Jolliffe, Fairmont Hotel, Dallas, TX 75221.
- Orient -   070155
Kahn, Ralph H., 4152 Sahdy Bend, Dallas, TX
75244.   070156
Neiman-Marcus, Main St., Dallas, TX 75201.
T. (214) 741-6911. - Ant / Orient / China / Dec / Silv /
Lights / Glass -   070157

O'Brien, 6011 Mercedes, Dallas, TX 75206.
T. (214) 823-5923. - Ant -   070158
Olla Podrida, 12215 Coit Rd., Dallas, TX 75251. - Ant /
Graph / Orient / China / Sculp / Jew / Silv / Cur -   070159
Samuels, 43-46 Lover's Ln., Dallas, TX 75225.
T. (214) 739-0029. - Ant -   070160
Spinning Wheel Antiques, 2708 Fairmount St., Dallas,
TX 75201. - Ant / Paint / Graph / Furn / Orient / China /
Dec / Instr / Glass -   070161

Danbury (Connecticut)
Ethan Allen Antique Gallery, Ethan Allen Dr, Danbury, CT
06810. T. (203) 743-8500.   070162

Dania (Florida)
Art World International, 69 N Federal Hwy., Dania, FL
33004. T. (305) 923-3001. - Ant -   070163
Arthur, 51 N Federal Hwy., Dania, FL 33004. - Ant /
Instr -   070164
Cameo Antiques, 18 N Federal Hwy., Dania, FL 33004.
T. (305) 929-0101.   070165
Ely, 246 S Federal Hwy., Dania, FL 33004. T. (305) 922-
5590. - Ant / Orient / Lights / Glass -   070166
English Accent Antiques, 57 N Federal Hwy, Dania, FL
33004. T. (305) 923-8383. - Ant / Paint / China / Jew /
Silv / Glass -   070167
Hirsch, 75 N Federal Hwy., Dania, FL 33004.   070168
Rapaport, Walter, 1531 Jackson St., Dania, FL 33020.
T. (305) 927-6878. - Ant -   070169
Trimble, 30 N. Federal Hwy., Dania, FL 33004.
T. (305) 524-9274. - Ant -   070170

Danielson (Connecticut)
M + C Antiques, Welsh St. & Blackrock Av., Danielson,
CT 06239. T. (203) 774-5552.   070171

Danville (Kentucky)
Riffemoor, Hwy. 34, Danville, KY 40422. T. (606) 236-
6582. - Ant / Paint / Furn / Orient / China / Repr / Sculp /
Tex / Dec / Silv / Lights / Instr -   070172

Dayton (Ohio)
Somerset House Antiques, 1858 Emerson Ave., Dayton,
OH 45406. - Ant / Furn / China / Glass -   070173
Towpath Antiques, 5357 Indian Ripple Rd., Dayton, OH
45440. - Ant / Furn / China / Eth / Instr / Glass -   070174
Woodford Fonda, 4263 Catalpa Dr., Dayton, OH
45405.   070175

Dayton (Tennessee)
Reynolds, 214 E Main Ave, Dayton, TN 37321.
T. (615) 775-2005.   070176

Deansboro (New York)
Sanders, Arthur H., S Main St., Deansboro, NY 13328.
T. (315) 841-8774. - Fra / Paint -   070177

Dearborn (Michigan)
Loren, 1000 N. York, Dearborn, MI 48128.
- Lights -   070178

Dedham (Massachusetts)
Antique Shop, 622 High St., Dedham, MA 02026.
T. (617) 329-0984. - Ant / Furn -   070179
Century Shop, 626 High St., Dedham, MA
02026.   070180
Scott, 175 Court St., Dedham, MA 02026.   070181

Deep River (Connecticut)
Winthrop Corners, R.F.D. 1, Rte. 80, Deep River, CT
06417. T. (203) 526-9462. - Ant -   070182

Deerfield (Massachusetts)
Deerfield Inn, Deerfield, MA 01342. - Ant -   070183

Delaware (Ohio)
Oberlander, Mounted Rte 9, 2 Miles South Rte. 23, Dela-
ware, OH 43015.   070184
Zeller, Rte. 4, Delaware, OH 43015.   070185

Delaware Water Gap (Pennsylvania)
Clausen, Rosa, POB 14, Delaware Water Gap, PA 18327.
T. (717) 421-2089. - China -   070186

Dennison (Ohio)
Maitland, 13 N Third St., Dennison, OH 44621.   070187

Denver (Colorado)

Artis's Center, 315 Columbine St., Denver, CO 80206.
T. (303) 333-1201. - China / Tex / Dec / Jew /
Glass - *070188*
Centaur Gallery, 1162 Speer Blvd., Denver, CO 80204.
T. (303) 222-4334. *070189*
Gustermann, 1420 Larimer Sq., Denver, CO 80202.
T. (303) 629-6927. - Jew / Silv - *070190*
Pick, Donald, 550 E 12th Ave, Ste 1908, Denver, CO
80203. - Ant / Paint / Sculp / Jew - *070191*
Rosvall, 1238 S. Broadway, Denver, CO 80210. - China /
Glass - *070192*
Trianon Art Gallery, 335 14th St., Denver, CO 80202.
- Ant / Paint / Graph / Furn / Orient / China / Sculp / Tex /
Dec / Silv / Lights / Instr / Mil / Glass - *070193*
Ye Olden Days Antiques, 4209 W. 38th, Denver, CO
80212. - Ant / Glass - *070194*

Deposit (New York)

Axtell, 1 River St., Deposit, NY 13754. T. (607) 467-
2353. *070195*

Des Moines (Iowa)

Fine Art Investments, 4223 Chamberlain Dr., Des Moines, IA 50312. T. (515) 277-3174. *070196*

Detroit (Michigan)

Clayton, Ruby, 326 Withington St., Detroit, MI
48220. *070197*
Du Mouchelle, Joseph, 409 E. Jefferson Ave., Detroit,
MI 48226. T. (313) 963-6255. - Ant / Paint / Furn /
Orient / China / Glass / Jew - *070198*
Goodman, Freda K., 2900 E. Jefferson, Detroit, Mi
48124. *070199*
Huber, R.E., 2731 W. Grand Blvd., Detroit, MI 48208.
T. (313) 874-0458. - Ant - *070200*
Scheff, Flo, 24310 Berkley St., Detroit, MI 48237.
- Ant - *070201*
Wiest, Margaret C., 2900 E Jefferson Av., Detroit, MI
48207. T. (313) 259-1223. - Ant / Paint / Graph /
Orient / Silv - *070202*

Dixon (Illinois)

Huber, Robert & Marianne, 1012 Timber Trail, Dixon, IL
61021. T. (815) 652-4196, Fax (815) 652-4754.
- Eth - *070203*

Dorset (Vermont)

Anglophile Antiques, Rte. 30, POB 815, Dorset, VT
05251. T. (802) 362-1621. - Ant / China / Silv - *070204*
Ramsey & Pope, Rte. 30, Dorset, VT 05251.
T. (802) 867-2268. - Furn - *070205*

Dothan (Alabama)

Antique Corner, Quality Inn Carousel, 231 North at By-
Pass., Dothan, AL 36301. T. (205) 792-5181. *070206*

Douglas (Michigan)

Button, W.Russell, 955 Center St., Douglas, MI 49406.
T. (616) 857-2194. - Ant - *070207*

Douglas Hill (Maine)

Jones, Douglas Hill, ME 04024. T. (207) 787-3370.
- Ant / China / Glass - *070208*

Douglasville (Pennsylvania)

Merrit, R.D. 2, Rte. 422, Douglasville, PA 19518.
T. (215) 689-9541. - Ant / Furn / China / Silv /
Glass - *070209*

Dover (Ohio)

Allenbaugh, R.G. & Charlotte, 419 S Tuscarawas Av., Dover, OH 44622. T. (216) 343-5783. *070210*
Hisrich, 324 E. 20th St., Dover, OH 44622. *070211*

Downingtown (Pennsylvania)

Bradley, Phillip H., E. Lancaster Ave., Downingtown, PA
19335. T. (215) 269-0427. - Ant / Furn - *070212*
Pook, Ronald, 463 E Lancaster Pike, Downingtown, PA
19335. T. (215) 269-0695. - Furn - *070213*

Doylestown (Pennsylvania)

Robertson & Thornton, Rte. 202 at Mill Rd., Doylestown,
PA 18901. - Ant - *070214*

Duncansville (Pennsylvania)

Patton, 1504 Third Ave., Duncansville, PA 16635.
T. (814) 695-0812. - Ant - *070215*

Durango (Colorado)

Brass and Copper Shop, 835 Main Av., Durango, CO
81301. *070216*

Durham (North Carolina)

American International Antiques and Furniture, 301 S.
Duke St., Durham, NC 27701. T. (919) 682-
3694. *070217*
Tranquil Corners Antiques, 5634 Chapel Hill Blvd , Dur-
ham, NC 27707. T. (919) 493-3769, 942-6600.
- Ant - *070218*

Duxbury (Massachusetts)

Duxbury, 590 Washington St., Duxbury, MA 02332.
- Ant / Paint / Furn / China - *070219*

East Arlington (Vermont)

Silversmiths, POB 157, East Arlington, VT 05252.
T. (801) 375-6307. - Silv - *070220*

East Aurora (New York)

Meibohm, Walter, 478 Main St., East Aurora, NY
14052. *070221*
Mulberry Place Antiques, 1450 Porterville Rd., East Aurora, NY 14052. T. (716) 652-1589. - Ant - *070222*

East Chatham (New York)

Rasso, Richard & Betty Ann, East Chatham, NY 12060.
T. (518) 392-4501. - Furn - *070223*

East Haddam (Connecticut)

Howard & Dickinson, Main St., Rte. 149, East Haddam,
CT 06423. T. (203) 873-9990. - Furn - *070224*

East Lyme (Connecticut)

Huber, Stephen & Carol, 82 Plants Dam Rd., East Lyme,
CT 06333. T. (203) 739-0772. - Furn - *070225*

Edgerton (Ohio)

Chapman, 318 Michigan Ave., Edgerton, OH 43517.
- Ant / Jew / Lights / Glass - *070226*

El Paso (Texas)

Reddy, Juanita, 4204 Buckingham Dr., El Paso, TX
79900. T. (215) 925 1132. - Ant / China /
Glass - *070227*

Elmira (New York)

Henderson, 1107 Pennsylvania Ave., Elmira, NY 14904.
- Lights - *070228*

Elmont (New York)

Tac Antiques, 355 Hill Ave., Elmont, NY 11003.
T. (516) 775-0115. *070229*

Elmore (Ohio)

Old Barn Antique Shop, Rte. 1, 1 1/2 Miles East, Elmore,
OH 43416. *070230*

Elverson (Pennsylvania)

Stallfort, R.D. 1, Elverson, PA 19520. T. (215) 286-5882.
- Ant - *070231*

Elwood (Indiana)

Decor Original, R.R. 3, Elwood, IN 46036. - Ant / Furn /
China / Dec / Lights / Glass - *070232*

Elyria (Ohio)

Eschke, Gloria, 1647 Grafton Rd., Elyria, OH
44035. *070233*

Encino (California)

Malter, 16661 Ventura Blvd. Ste 518, Encino, CA 91316.
T. (818) 784-7772, 784-2181. - Num - *070234*
Malter, Joel L., 17005 Ventura Blvd., Encino, CA 91436.
T. (818) 784-7772, 784-2181, Fax (818) 784-4726.
- Num / Arch / Jew / Instr - *070235*

Englewood (New Jersey)

Old Stone House, 488 Grand Ave., Englewood, NJ
07631. T. (201) 568-2524. - Ant / Furn - *070236*

Ephrata (Pennsylvania)

Lausch, 22 Steinmetz, Ephrata, (Penns.) 17522.
T. (717) 733-2659. - Ant - *070237*

Erie (Pennsylvania)

Veenschoten, John C., 4205 W 38th St., Erie, PA 16506.
T. (814) 833-7996. - Paint / Graph / Furn - *070238*

Esperance (New York)

Curran & Curran, Creek Rd., R.R.I Box 229, Esperance,
NY 12066. T. (518) 875-6788. *070239*

Essex (Connecticut)

Bealey, Francis, 3 S Main St., Essex, CT 06426.
T. (203) 767-0220. - Furn - *070240*
Hastings House Antiques, Essex Sq, Essex, CT 06426.
T. (203) 767-0014. - Ant / Furn - *070241*

Essex (Massachusetts)

Landry, L.A., 164 Main St., Essex, MA 01929.
T. (617) 768-6233, 526-1588. - Ant / Paint / Furn /
Orient / China / Repr / Sculp / Silv / Lights / Instr / Glas-
s - *070242*
Score, Stephen, 159 Main St., Essex, MA 01929.
T. (617) 768-6252. - Tex - *070243*

Essex Fells (New Jersey)

Holt, Henry B., POB 6, 07021 Essex Fells, NJ 07021.
T. (201) 228-0853. - Ant - *070244*

Etna Green (Indiana)

Amy's Antiques, S Walnut St, Etna Green, IN 46524.
T. (219) 858-9276. - Ant - *070245*

Eureka Springs (Arkansas)

Garrett, 35 Spring St., Eureka Springs, AR 72632.
T. (501) 253-9481. *070246*

Evanston (Illinois)

Harvey, 1231 Chicago, Evanston, IL 60200. *070247*
Milliman, Richard, 3309 Central, Evanston, IL 60201.
T. (312) 328-3232, Fax (312) 328-8802. - Paint /
Graph / Orient / Sculp / Mod / Draw - *070248*

Exeter (New Hampshire)

Mills, 91 Front St, Exeter, NH 03833. T. (603) 772-3054.
- Ant / Paint / Graph - *070249*

Fairfield (Connecticut)

Bok, James, 1954 Post Rd., Fairfield, CT 06430.
T. (203) 255-6500, 255-0007. - Furn - *070250*
Gagarin, Patty, Banks North Rd., Fairfield, CT 06430.
T. (203) 259-7332. *070251*

Fallbrook (California)

Roberta's Antiques, 3137 S. Mission Rd., Fallbrook, CA
92028. *070252*
Skunk Hollow Shops, 2809 So. Mission Rd., Fallbrook,
CA 92028. T. (619) 728-2816. - Ant / Paint - *070253*

Falls Church (Virginia)

Bromwell, 414 S Washington St., Falls Church, VA
22046. T. (703) 534-7323. - Ant / Silv - *070254*

Falls Village (Connecticut)

Ferguson-Schmidt, Main St., Falls Village, CT 06031.
T. (203) 824-5825. - China - *070255*

Falmouth (Massachusetts)

Bourne, Carlton M., 86 E. Riddle Hill Rd., Falmouth, MA
02540. - Ant - *070256*
Garland, 204 Palmer Ave., Falmouth, MA 02540.
T. (617) 548-1755. - Ant / Furn - *070257*

Faribault (Minnesota)

Rue, Mae, 9th Ave S, Faribault, MN 55021. T. (507) 334-
7846. *070258*

Farmington (Connecticut)

Blankley, Cogan Lillian, 22 High St., Farmington, CT
06032. T. (203) 677-9259. - Ant - *070259*

Farmington (Kentucky)

Merida, Frederick A., Farmington POB 53, KY 42040.
T. (502) 345-2713. - Ant / Paint / Furn / China / Eth /
Draw - *070260*

Farmington (Maine)
Veilleux, Tom & Sandra, POB 63, Farmington, ME
04938. T. (207) 778-3719. - Paint -   070261

Fayette (Alabama)
Smith, James St., Fayette, AL 35555. - Ant /
Glass -   070262

Fayetteville (New York)
Colony Shop, Fayetteville Rd., Fayetteville, NY 13066.
T. (315) 422-2181. - Ant -   070263

Findlay (Ohio)
Redman, 1414 Tiffin Rd, Findlay, OH 45840.   070264

Fitzwilliam (New Hampshire)
Lewan, William, Old Troy Rd., Fitzwilliam, NH 03447.
T. (603) 585-3365. - Ant / Furn -   070265
Murphy, Alicia F., Lower Troy Rd., Fitzwilliam, NH
03447. T. (603) 585-7719. - Ant -   070266

Flemington (New Jersey)
Art Exchange, Deer Trail, R.D.6, Flemington, NJ 08822.
T. (201) 782-5481.   070267

Flora (Illinois)
Dunigan, 210 E South St., Flora, IL 62839. - Ant /
Instr -   070268

Florida (New York)
Wagner, RD 1, Florida, NY 10921. T. (914) 651-
4172.   070269

Flourtown (Pennsylvania)
Trump & Co., 666 Bethlehem Pike, Flourtown, PA
19031. T. (215) 233-1805. - Ant / Furn -   070270

Flushing (New York)
Newman, Steve, 137-69 75 Rd., Flushing, NY 11367.
T. (718) 793-7981. - Sculp -   070271

Forest (Mississippi)
McMullan, Mary E., 210 East Fourth St., Forest, MS
39074. T. (601) 469-1354.   070272

Forest Hills (New York)
Balaban, Bernice, POB 411, Forest Hills, NY 11375.
- Graph / China / Dec -   070273

Forney (Texas)
Clements, POB 727, Forney, TX 75126. T. (214) 226-
1520. - Ant -   070274

Fort Lauderdale (Florida)
Circa Antiques, POB 33303, Fort Lauderdale, FL 33303.
T. (305) 758-3020. - Furn -   070275
Reiss, Jason, 703 E. Las Olas Blvd., Fort Lauderdale, FL
33301. T. (305) 467-1031. - Ant -   070276

Fort Lee (New Jersey)
Kohn, POB 347, Fort Lee, NY 07024. T. (201) 947-1099.
- Silv -   070277

Fort Mill (South Carolina)
Fu-Ming-Fair Gallery, 2786 Dogwood Hills Court, Fort
Mill, SC 29715. - Orient -   070278

Fort Morgan (Colorado)
Robison, 227 W. Beaver Ave., Fort Morgan, CO 80701.
T. (303) 867-5379. - Ant -   070279

Fort Washington (Pennsylvania)
Meetinghouse Antique Shop, 509 Bethlehem Pike, Fort
Washington, PA 19034. T. (215) 646-5126.   070280

Fort Wayne (Indiana)
Beck, Don, POB 15305, Fort Wayne, IN 46885. - Ant /
Orient / Sculp / Mil -   070281
Letha, 7213 Baer Rd., Fort Wayne, IN 46809.
T. (219) 747-2322.   070282

Fort Worth (Texas)
Baker, Norma, 3311 W 7th St., Fort Worth, TX 76107.
T. (817) 335-1152.   070283
Estate Galleries, 2824 W Seventh St., Fort Worth, TX
76107. T. (817) 336-3296. - Ant / Furn -   070284
Neiman-Marcus, Antiques Dept., Camp Bowie Bldg.,
Fort Worth, TX 76100.   070285

Fostoria (Ohio)
Scherger, 204 W. Jackson St., Fostoria, OH
44830.   070286

Framingham (Massachusetts)
Faini, 35 Shawmut Terr., Framingham, MA 01701.
T. (617) 875-5402.   070287

Frankfort (Maine)
Birmingham, Mary Irene, Rte. 1A, Frankfort, ME 04438.
T. (207) 223-4406, 223-4441. - Ant -   070288

Franklin (Massachusetts)
Johnston, 789 W Central St., Franklin, MA 02038.
T. (617) 528-0942.   070289

Franklin (Tennessee)
Cinnamon Hill, High Meadow Dr., Franklin, TN 37046.
T. (615) 790-0833. - Furn -   070290

Franktown (Colorado)
Ayers, Hwy. 83, Franktown, CO 80116. T. (303) 688-
3827. - Ant / Furn / China / Glass -   070291

Frederick (Maryland)
Cahn, Harold B., 108 W. 3rd St., Frederick, MD 21701.
T. (301) 662-5787. - Paint / Furn / China / Silv - 070292
Dronenburg, 200 W. Patrick St., Frederick, MD 21701.
T. (301) 663-9013. - Ant / China / Glass -   070293

Fredericksburg (Virginia)
Virginians, 1501 Caroline St., Fredericksburg, VA 22401.
T. (703) 373-8896. - Ant / Furn / China / Lights - 070294

Freeport (New York)
Dorida, 134 Meister Blvd., Freeport, NY 11520.
T. (516) 623-7866. - Jew -   070295

Fremont (Nebraska)
Smith, 807 W Fourth St., Fremont, NE 68025. - Ant /
Furn / Glass -   070296

Fresh Meadows (New York)
Frame Art, 185-17 Union Turnpike, Fresh Meadows, NY
11366. T. (212) 454-1630. - Ant / Paint / Graph /
Orient / China / Repr / Sculp / Tex / Dec / Fra / Silv / Lights / Rel / Glass / Cur / Mod / Pho / Mul / Draw -   070297

Gaithersburg (Maryland)
Craft Shop, 405 S. Frederick Ave., Gaithersburg, MD
20877. T. (301) 926-3000. - Ant / Furn / China / Repr /
Tex / Lights / Glass -   070298

Galion (Ohio)
Herndon, 945 S. Market Street, Galion, OH
44833.   070299

Gardiner (Maine)
Morrell, 106 Highland Ave., Gardiner, ME 04345.
T. (507) 582-4797.   070300
Tuttle, R.F.D.4,POB 16, Gardiner, ME 04345.
T. (207) 582-4496. - Furn -   070301

Gatlinburg (Tennessee)
Morton, 377 Parkway, Gatlinburg, TN 37738.
T. (615) 436-5504. - Ant / Furn / Glass -   070302
Zarnon, Cherokee Orchard Rd., Gatlinburg, TN 37738.
T. (615) 436-6359. - Ant -   070303

Geneva (Illinois)
Grunwald, 315 W State St., Geneva, IL 60134.
T. (312) 232-8040. - Ant / Paint / Sculp / Jew /
Silv -   070304

Georgetown (Kentucky)
Wag'n Tongue, 137 E Main St., Georgetown, KY 40324.
T. (502) 863-1275, 863-1592. - Ant -   070305

Georgetown (Massachusetts)
Hills, 34 E Main St., Georgetown, MA 01830.
- Ant -   070306

Georgetown (Ohio)
Bullock, R.F.D. 3, State Rd. 221, Georgetown, OH
45121.   070307

Germantown (Tennessee)
Anderson-Mulkins, 9336 Hwy. 72, Germantown, TN
38138. T. (901) 853-2766. - Ant -   070308
Babcock, 2262 Germantown Rd., Germantown, TN
38138. T. (901) 754-7950. - Ant / Paint / Furn / Orient /
China / Repr / Tex / Dec / Silv / Lights / Instr / Glass / Cu-
r -   070309

Glassboro (New Jersey)
Ternay, Delsea Dr., Glassboro, NJ 08028. T. (609) 881-
4527. - Ant / Jew -   070310

Glastonbury (Connecticut)
William, 24 Hopewell Rd., Glastonbury, CT 06033.
T. (203) 633-4474. - Ant -   070311

Glen Ellyn (Illinois)
Lacock, Patricia, 526 Crescent, Glen Ellyn, IL
60137.   070312

Glencoe (Illinois)
It's about time, 375 Park Ave., Glencoe, IL 60022.
T. (312) 835-2012. - Instr -   070313
Nebenzahl, Kenneth, Glencoe, IL 60022. T. (312) 835-
0515, Fax (312) 835-0519. - Graph -   070314

Glendale (California)
Period Furniture, 612 E. Glenoaks Blvd., Glendale, CA
91207. T. (213) 241-2031. - Ant / Furn -   070315

Glenside (Pennsylvania)
Okies, 224 Bickley Rd., Glenside, PA 19038. - Ant /
China -   070316

Gloversville (New York)
Brickwood, R.D.1, POB 378, Gloversville, NY 12078.
T. (518) 725-0230. - China -   070317
Kretser, Howard L., 103 Prospect Ave., Gloversville, NY
12078. T. (518) 725-9060. - Ant -   070318

Golden (Colorado)
Fisher, 13325 W 15 Dr., Golden, CO 80401. T. (303) 237-
3710. - Paint / Graph / Draw -   070319

Gorham (Maine)
Greenleaf, 173 Main St., Gorham, ME 04038.   070320

Grafton (Vermont)
Village Pump Antiques, Rte 121, Grafton, VT 05146.
- Ant -   070321

Granby (Connecticut)
Knotty Pine Antiques Shop, 186 Hartford Av., Granby, CT
06026. T. (203) 653-2274. - Furn -   070322

Granby (Massachusetts)
Darr, P.T., 507 E State St., Granby, MA 01033.
T. (413) 467-9634. - Ant -   070323

Grand Canyon (Arizona)
Harvey, Fred, Grand Canyon National Park, Grand Ca-
nyon, AZ 86023. T. (602) 638-2631. - Paint / China /
Tex / Jew -   070324

Grand Rapids (Michigan)
Marshall, 100 56th W., Grand Rapids, MI 49508.
- Ant -   070325
Moch, Joseph A., 479 Diamond Ave. NE, Grand Rapids,
MI 49503.   070326
Van Claires, 330 E. Fulton St., Grand Rapids, MI
49502.   070327
Wishing Well Antiques, 1829 Eastbrook St. SE, Grand
Rapids, MI 49508.   070328

Great Barrington (Massachusetts)
Antiques at the Red Horse, 117 State Rd., Great Barrington, MA 01230. T. (413) 528-2637.   070329
Barnbrook, 72 Stockbridge Rd., Great Barrington, MA
01230. T. (413) 528-4423.   070330
Corashire, Rtes 7 and 23 at Belcher Sq., Great Barrington, MA 01230. T. (413) 528-0014.   070331

Great Falls (Montana)
Brighten Up Shop, 618 Central Ave., Great Falls, MT
59401. - Glass -   070332
Merrie, 2612 Second Av S, Great Falls, MT 59405.
T. (406) 452-4420.   070333

Great Neck (New York)
Showcase, 113 Middle Neck Rd, Great Neck, NY 11021.
T. (516) 487-7815. - Ant / Jew -   *070334*

Greenlane (Pennsylvania)
Colonial House Antiques, Corner Rts. 29 and 63, Green-
lane, PA 18054. T. (215) 234-4113.   *070335*

Greensboro (North Carolina)
Byerly, 4311 Wiley Davis Rd., Greensboro, NC 27407.
T. (919) 299-6510. - Ant / Paint / Furn / China /
Glass -   *070336*
Faison, Caroline, 18 Battleground Court, Greensboro, NC
27408. - Ant -   *070337*
Salomon, 16061, Greensboro, NC 27406. T. (919) 275-
5660. - Silv -   *070338*
Zenke, Otto, 215 S Eugene St., Greensboro, NC 27401.
T. (919) 275-8487. - Art / Paint / Furn / Tex / Dec / Silv /
Lights / Instr / Glass -   *070339*

Greentown (Ohio)
Stevens, J.A., 9677 N. Cleveland St., Greentown, OH
44630. - Ant / Paint / Furn / China / Silv / Mil -   *070340*

Greenville (Alabama)
Solomon, 215 College St., Greenville, AL 36037.
T. (205) 382-3224. - Ant -   *070341*

Greenville (Delaware)
Borton, POB 3944, Greenville, DE 19807. T. (302) 388-
7687, 655-4924.   *070342*

Greenville (Ohio)
Jack's Antique Shop, 718 Gray Ave., Greenville, OH
45331. - Ant / Graph -   *070343*
Red Barn Antiques, 140 13th St., Greenville, OH 45331.
T. (513) 548-4292. - Ant -   *070344*
Thomas, 747 Garden Wood Dr., Greenville, OH 45331.
T. (513) 548-9644.   *070345*

Gresham (Oregon)
Dawn, 650 N.W. 5th St., Gresham, OR 97030.
- Ant -   *070346*

Grosse Pointe (Michigan)
Johnston, 1022 Bishop Rd., Grosse Pointe, MI 48236.
T. (313) 885-3446. - China -   *070347*

Grosse Pointe Farms (Michigan)
C M Gallery, 18226 Mack Av., Grosse Pointe Farms, MI
48236. - Ant -   *070348*

Groton (Massachusetts)
1810 House Antiques, 27 Hollis St., POB 276, Groton,
MA 01450. T. (617) 448-6046.   *070349*

Haddam (Connecticut)
Hobart House, Route 154, POB 128, Haddam, CT 06438.
T. (203) 345-2015. - Art / Tex / Silv -   *070350*

Haddonfield (New Jersey)
By Hand Fine Craft Gallery, 142 Kings Hwy. E, Haddon-
field, NJ 08033. T. (609) 429-2550.   *070351*
Sanski, 50 Tanner St., Haddonfield, NJ 08033.
T. (609) 429-2511. - Paint / Sculp -   *070352*

Hagerstown (Maryland)
Beaver Creek Antique Shop, Beaver Creek Rd., Hagers-
town, MD 21740. T. (301) 739-0792. - Ant -   *070353*

Halltown (Mississippi)
Cameron, 18 Miles West of Springfield on 1 b. 44, Hall-
town, MS 65664. - Ant / Furn / China / Lights /
Glass -   *070354*

Hamden (Connecticut)
Murdock, Margaret B., 192 Eramo Terrace, Hamden, CT
06518. T. (203) 248-7832. - Furn / China /
Glass -   *070355*
Pari, Joseph, 3846 Whitney Ave., Hamden, CT 06518.
T. (203) 248-4951. - Ant -   *070356*

Hamilton (Ohio)
Rentschler, Thomas B., 1030 New London Rd., Hamilton,
OH 45013. T. (513) 863-8633. - Furn -   *070357*

Hammonton (New Jersey)
Gurelia, James, 847 S. White Horse Pike, Hammonton,
NJ 08037. T. (609) 561-5562. - Ant -   *070358*

Hampton (New Hampshire)
Webber, H.G., 495 Lafayette Rd., Hampton, NH 03842.
T. (603) 926-3349. - Ant -   *070359*

Hancock (New Hampshire)
Cobbs, Old Dublin Rd., Hancock, NH 03449.
T. (603) 525-4053. - Furn -   *070360*
Hardings, Depot St., Hancock, NH 03449. T. (603) 525-
3518. - Ant / Furn -   *070361*

Hanover (New Hampshire)
Marie-Louise Antiques, Lyme Rd., Hanover, NH 03755.
T. (603) 643-4276. - Ant -   *070362*

Hanover (Pennsylvania)
Rudisill, John C., 800 Broadway, Hanover, PA 17331.
T. (717) 632-3195. - Ant -   *070363*

Harrisburg (Pennsylvania)
Alpert, Samuel, 1416 Green St., Harrisburg, PA 17102.
T. (717) 233-2488. - Ant / Furn / China / Glass -   *070364*
Benney, George & Helen, 100 N 67th St., Harrisburg, PA
17111. T. (717) 564-1002. - Ant / China /
Glass -   *070365*

Hartford (Connecticut)
Koda, P., 790 Wetherfield Ave, Hartford, CT 06114.
T. (203) 247-7671. - Furn -   *070366*
Lux, Bond, Green & Stevens, 15 Pratt, Hartford, CT
06103. T. (203) 278-3050. - Ant / Jew -   *070367*

Harwich (Massachusetts)
Windsong Antiques, 243 Bank St., Harwich, MA 02645.
T. (617) 432-1994. - Ant -   *070368*

Harwich Port (Massachusetts)
Flying Horse Antiques, Rte 28, Harwich Port, MA 02646.
T. (617) 432-0030.   *070369*
Ox Bow Antiques, 133 Bank St., Harwich Port, MA
02646. - Ant / China / Glass -   *070370*

Harwington (Connecticut)
Davis, POB 262, Harwington, CT 06791. T. (203) 485-
9182. - China -   *070371*

Hastings (Michigan)
Le Duc Mansion, Hastings, MI 49058. T. (616) 437-
4052. - Dec -   *070372*

Hastings (Minnesota)
Simmons, Carroll B., Hastings, MN 55033. T. (612) 437-
4052. - Ant -   *070373*

Haverhill (Massachusetts)
Lynch & Graham, 426 Water St., Haverhill, MA 01830.
T. (617) 374-8031. - Ant -   *070374*

Haverhill (New Hampshire)
Pine Cone Antiques, On the Commen, Dartmouth Hwg.,
Rte. 10, Haverhill, NH 03765. T. (802) 898-5983, 429-
3423. - Ant -   *070375*

Hebron (Nebraska)
Yost, 845 Lincoln Ave, Hebron, NE 68370. - Ant / China /
Lights -   *070376*

Hemlock (Michigan)
Scherzler, 12675 Trinklin Rd., Hemlock, MI 48626.
- Ant / Glass -   *070377*

Hendersonville (North Carolina)
Brownings, First and Main, Hendersonville, NC 28739.
- Furn / Tex -   *070378*

Hickory (North Carolina)
Renaissance Gallery, 254 First Ave., N.W., Hickory, NC
28601. T. (704) 322-2688. - Ant -   *070379*

Hickory (Pennsylvania)
Wilson, Gailey B., & Son, Main St., Hickory, PA 15340.
T. (412) 356-2203. - Ant / China -   *070380*

Hicksville (Ohio)
Antique Shop, 204 1/2 E High St., Hicksville, OH 43526.
- Ant -   *070381*

Higganum (Connecticut)
Muir, Bryce George, Nelson Pl, Killingworth Rd., Higga-
num, CT 06441. T. (203) 345-4741. - Furn -   *070382*

Highland Falls (New York)
Heberling, Glen A., 58 Church St., Highland Falls, NY
10928. T. (914) 446-3866. - Paint / Graph / Repr /
Draw -   *070383*

Highland Park (Illinois)
Pollack, Frank & Barbara, 1214 Green Bay Rd., Highland
Park, IL 60035. T. (312) 433-2213. - Paint /
Furn -   *070384*

Hillsboro (Ohio)
Gable House Antiques, 240 E. Main St., Hillsboro, OH
45133.   *070385*

Hillsboro (Texas)
Victorian Shop, 110 W. Elm St., Hillsboro, TX 76645.
- Ant -   *070386*

Hillsborough (North Carolina)
Hillsborough House of Antiques, Daniel Boone Complex,
Hillsborough, NC 27278. T. (919) 732-8882.   *070387*

Hillsdale (New York)
Pax Antiques, Hillsdale Rd., Rte 23, Hillsdale, NY 12028.
T. (518) 325-3974.   *070388*

Hilton Head Island (South Carolina)
Harbour Town Antiques, POB 3242, Hilton Head Island,
SC 29928. T. (803) 671-5999, 671-5777.
- Ant -   *070389*

Hingham (Massachusetts)
Pierce, 721 Main St., Hingham, MA 02043. T. (617) 749-
6023, Fax (617) 746-6685. - Ant / Paint / Sculp / Jew /
Pho / Draw -   *070390*

Hinsdale (Illinois)
Longley, 53 S Washington St, Hinsdale, IL 60521.
T. (312) 887-1975. - Ant / Furn / China / Silv -   *070391*

Hixson (Tennessee)
Clement, 7022 Dayton Pike, Hixson, TN 37343.
T. (615) 842-4177. - Ant -   *070392*

Holland (Michigan)
Lantern Antiques, 542 Elm Dr., Holland, MI
49423.   *070393*
Old Dutch Antique Shop, 361 Lane Ave, Holland, MI
49423.   *070394*

Hollywood (Florida)
Capital Antique Shoppe, 921 E Hawthorne Circle, Hollywood, FL 33021. - Ant -   *070395*

Holmes (New York)
Red Wheel Antiques, Bowen Rd., Holmes, NY 12531.
T. (914) 878-6873.   *070396*

Honolulu (Hawaii)
Bushido, 936 Maunakea St., Honolulu, HI 96817.
T. (808) 536-5693, Fax (808) 521-1994.   *070397*
Micklautz, Ferdinand, Kilohana Square, 1016 E Kapahulu
Av., Honolulu, HI 96816. T. (808) 735-4503.   *070398*
Ting, Lan, 1120 Maunakea St., Suite 191, Honolulu, HI
96817. T. (808) 528-1158, Fax (808) 528-
0851.   *070399*
Young, John, 3161 Poka Pl, Honolulu, HI 96816. - Ant /
Paint / Orient / Arch / Eth -   *070400*

Hope Hull (Alabama)
Sullivan, Wasden Rd, Hope Hull, AL 36043.   *070401*

Hope Valley (Rhode Island)
Hawthorn Cottage, Main St., Rte. 138, Hope Valley, RI
02832. T. (401) 539-2891, 539-2914. - Ant -   *070402*

Hopewell (New Jersey)
Cox, 21 E Broad St., Hopewell, NJ 08525. T. (609) 466-
1614.   *070403*

McGrail, Elisabeth, 11 E. Broad St., Hopewell, NJ
08525. T. (609) 466-0934. - Ant -   070404

Hopewell (New York)
Round Mountain Antiques, W Hook Rd., Hopewell, NY
12533. T. (914) 896-9351.   070405

Hopkinton (Massachusetts)
Heritage Antiques, 216 Wood St., Hopkinton, MA 01748.
T. (617) 435-4031.   070406

Hopkinton (New Hampshire)
Meadow Hearth Antiques, Briar Hill Rd., Hopkinton, NH
03301. T. (603) 746-3947.   070407

Horsehead (New York)
Stoney Knoll Antiques, 382 E Franklin St., Horsehead,
NY 14845. T. (607) 739-4108.   070408

Houston (Texas)
Antique Brokers, 1716 Westheimer Rd., Houston, TX
77006. T. (713) 522-7415. - Ant -   070409
Chappell Jordan, 2222 Westheimer Rd., Houston, TX
77006. T. (713) 523-0133. - Furn / Instr -   070410
Connally & Altermann, 3461 W Alabama, Houston, TX
77027. T. (713) 840-1922. - Paint -   070411
Corrigan, 2035 W Gray, Houston, TX 77019.
T. (713) 524-2107. - China / Dec / Jew / Silv / Lights /
Instr / Glass -   070412
DuBose-Rein, 1700 Bissonnet, Houston, TX 77005.
T. (713) 526-4916. - Paint / Graph / China / Sculp /
Tex -   070413
Duckworth, Doris, 2323 Woodhead St., Houston, TX
77019. T. (713) 523-4118. - Ant / Paint / Furn / Orient /
China / Tex / Dec / Silv / Lights / Instr / Glass -   070414
Gillespie, 3802 Drew St., Houston, Tx 77004.   070415
Goldman, Sam, 1909 Huldy, Houston, TX 77019.
T. (713) 528-7014. - Ant -   070416
Gundry, J.A., 2910 Ferndale, Houston, TX 77098.
T. (713) 524-6622. - Ant -   070417
Guzzardi, Josephine D., 907 Harold, Houston, TX 77006.
T. (713) 524-4574. - Ant / Paint -   070418
Heath & Brown, 609 Tuam Av., Houston, TX 77006.
T. (713) 529-0011. - Ant / Paint / Orient / China / Sculp /
Tex / Dec / Instr / Glass -   070419
House of Glass, 3319 Louisiana St., Houston, TX 77006.
T. (713) 528-5289. - Ant / Furn / Orient / China / Repr /
Dec / Lights / Instr / Glass -   070420
King Thomasson, 1213 1/2 Berthea St., Houston, TX
77006. T. (713) 529-9768. - Furn -   070421
Mostert, Dorothy, 404 Avondale, Houston, TX 77006.
T. (713) 523-9165. - Ant / Furn / China / Glass -   070422
Norbert, 3601 Main St., Houston, TX 77002.
T. (713) 524-9134. - Ant / Paint / Graph / Furn / China /
Sculp / Tex / Dec / Lights / Instr / Mil / Rel / Glass --   070423
Pearson, 2217 Woodhead, Houston, TX 77019.
T. (713) 528-3750. - Ant -   070424
Peyton Place Antiques, 819 Lovett Blvd., Houston, TX
77006. T. (713) 523-4841. - Ant / Paint / Graph / Furn /
Orient / China / Tex / Dec / Lights / Instr / Glass - 070425
Sanders, 315 Fairview, Houston, TX 77006.
T. (713) 522-0539. - Ant -   070426
This Old House of Forget-Me-Nots, 315 Westheimer Rd.,
Houston, TX 77006. T. (713) 524-9784. - Ant / Furn /
Lights / Glass / Mod -   070427
Trash and Treasure Shop, 1716 Westheimer Rd., Hou-
ston, TX 77006. T. (713) 522-7415. - Ant -   070428

Howard City (Michigan)
Buggy Wheel, 5 Miles W. on M. 46, Howard City, MI
49329. - Ant -   070429
Haack's Antique Shop, 129 Muencher St., Howard City,
MI 49329.   070430

Howell (Michigan)
Nectar Nook Farm Antiques, 1401 S Hughes Rd., Howell,
MI 48843.   070431

Hudson (Michigan)
Reece & Merritt, Sr., 311 Tiffin St., Hudson, MI
49247.   070432

Hudson (Ohio)
Knapp & Farley, 135 Boston Mills Rd., Hudson, OH
44236. T. (216) 653-6141. - Ant / Paint / Furn /
Lights -   070433
Wooden Bridge Antiques, 2821 Woodbridge Rd., Hud-
son, OH 44236. T. (216) 653-6596.   070434

Huntsville (Alabama)
Antiquity Shoppe, 1011 Locust Ave. S.E., Huntsville, AL
35801. - Ant -   070435

Hurley (New York)
Van Deusen House Antiques, 11 Main St., Hurley, NY
12443. T. (914) 331-8852. - Ant / Orient -   070436

Hyannis (Massachusetts)
Stone, H., 659 Main St., Hyannis, MA 02601.
T. (617) 775-3913. - Ant -   070437

Independence (Missouri)
Moore, LaVonne & Sidney, 135 E Hwy. 24, Independence, MO 64050. T. (816) 252-8348. - Furn -   070438

Independence (Ohio)
Mariwynne Shop, 7481 Brecksville Rd., Independence,
OH 44131. T. (216) 524-1608. - Ant -   070439

Indian River (Michigan)
Carriage Trade Antiques, 6288 South Av., Indian River,
MI 49749. - Ant -   070440

Indianapolis (Indiana)
Ewing, 7718 Michigan Rd. N.W., Indianapolis, IN
46268.   070441
Folkways Antiques, 7714B N. Michigan Rd., Indianapolis, IN 46268.   070442
Four Corners Antiques, 3406 N. Shadeland Ave., Indianapolis, IN 46226.   070443
Red Barn Galleries, 325 E 106 St., Indianapolis, IN
46280. - Ant / Paint -   070444

Indianola (Mississippi)
Antique Mall, 5 Miles North of Town, Indianola, MS
38751. T. (601) 887-2522.   070445

Ipswich (Massachusetts)
Nason, Clyde, 75 High St., Ipswich, MA 01938.
T. (617) 356-3811. - Ant -   070446

Jackson (Michigan)
Wayne, 935 S Gorham, Jackson, MI 49203.   070447

Jackson (Mississippi)
Cheek, Joanne, 4025 Dogwood Dr., Jackson, MS
39211. T. (601) 982-7428. - Furn -   070448
Willians, John, 4074 N State St., Jackson, MS 39206.
T. (601) 362-6510.   070449

Jacksonville (Florida)
Coburg, 2005 Dellwood Av., Jacksonville, FL 32204.
T. (904) 356-5213. - Ant / Paint / Furn / China / Silv /
Mod -   070450
Cummer, 829 Riverside Av., Jacksonville, FL 32204.
T. (904) 356-6857.   070451
Lamp Post Antiques, 3955 Riverside Ave, Jacksonville,
FL 32205. - Ant -   070452
Reddi-Arts, 1038 Kings Ave., Jacksonville, FL 32207.
T. (904) 398-3161. - Graph / Fra -   070453

Jamaica Plain (Massachusetts)
Origins, 111 Perkins St., Jamaica Plain, MA 02130.
T. (617) 524-4280. - Orient / Sculp / Arch / Eth - 070454

Jamestown (New York)
Galeria, 341-343 E. Third St., Jamestown, NY 14701.
T. (716) 485-1711. - Ant / Paint / Graph / China / Repr /
Sculp / Fra / Mod -   070455
Wellman Brothers, 130 S Main St., Jamestown, NY
14701. T. (716) 664-4006. - Ant / Paint / Graph / Furn /
Orient / China / Sculp / Tex / Dec / Lights / Rel / Glass / I-
co --   070456

Jeromesville (Ohio)
Delagrange, 12 N High, Jeromesville, OH 44840.
T. (419) 368-8971. - Furn -   070457
Momchilov, Charles, 42 W Main, Jeromesville, OH
44840. T. (419) 368-6244. - Furn -   070458

Jewett City (Connecticut)
Walton, John, POB 307, Jewett City, CT 06351.
T. (203) 376-0862. - Ant -   070459

Johnson City (New York)
Bartlett, Betty, 110 Main St., Johnson City, NY 13790.
T. (607) 729-9651. - Furn / China / Silv / Glass - 070460

Kalamazoo (Michigan)
Kramer, Cora, 611 Axtell St., Kalamazoo, MI
49001.   070461

Kanab (Utah)
Johnston, Andrew T., Kanab, UT 84741.   070462

Kansas City (Missouri)
Allen, 8102 Evanston Av., Kansas City, MO 64138.
- Ant / Furn / Lights -   070463
Au Marché, 320 Ward Parkway, Kansas City, MO 64112.
T. (816) 821-7997. - Ant / Furn / Silv -   070464
Brookside Antiques, 6219 Oak, Kansas City, MO
64113.   070465
Old World Antiques, 1715 Summit, Kansas City, MO
64108. T. (816) 472-0815. - Ant / Paint / Furn / Orient /
China / Sculp / Tex / Dec / Jew / Silv / Lights / Instr --
      070466

Keene (New Hampshire)
Pregent, 142 Marlboro St., Keene, NH 03431.
T. (603) 352-6736.   070467

Kenilworth (Illinois)
Federalist Antiques, 523 Park Dr, Kenilworth, IL 60043.
T. (312) 256-1791. - Ant -   070468

Kennebunkport (Maine)
Old Fort Inn and Antiques, Old Fort Ave, Kennebunkport,
ME 04046. T. (207) 967-5353.   070469

Kennett Square (Pennsylvania)
Campbell, Judy & Bill, 160 East Doe Run Road, Kennett
Square, PA 19348. T. (212) 347-6756.   070470
Johnstone-Fong, 1600 East Street Rd, Kennett Square,
PA 19348. T. (215) 793 3176. - Ant / Orient -   070471
Willowdale, 101 East Street Rd, Kennett Square, PA
19348. T. (215) 444-5377. - Ant -   070472

Kensington (California)
Sweet, Belinda, 190 Stanford Ave, Kensington, CA
94708. T. (415) 526-8689. - Orient -   070473

Kensington (Maryland)
Potomac Trading Post, 3610 University Blvd, Kensington,
MD 20795. - Ant / Mil -   070474

Kent (Connecticut)
Forrer, Edward E., Rte 7, Kent, CT 06757. T. (203) 927-
3612. - Ant -   070475
Goode Hill Antiques, Rte 7, North of Town, Kent, CT
06757. T. (203) 927-3872.   070476
Holmes, Harry, Rte 7 and Carter Rd, Kent, CT 06757.
T. (203) 927-3420.   070477
Side Door Antiques, Main St, Rt. 7, Kent, CT 06757.
T. (203) 927-3288. - Ant -   070478

Kenton (Ohio)
Hilton, Ruth, 46 Broadway, Kenton, OH 43326. 070479
Young, 621 S. Detroit Ave, Kenton, OH 43326. 070480

Killingworth (Connecticut)
Scranton, Lewis W., Roast Meat Hill, Killingworth, CT
06417. T. (203) 663-1060. - Furn -   070481

Kingston (New York)
Brossard, Eugene, CPOB 1544, Kingston, NY 12401.
T. (914) 338-2172. - Ant / Paint / Fra / Glass /
Pho -   070482
Johnston, Fred J., Van Lueven Mansion Main St, Kings-
ton, NY 12401. - Furn -   070483

Kingston (Rhode Island)
Antiques at Potter House, Potter Ln, Kingston, RI 02881.
T. (401) 783-5734.   070484

Kirksville (Missouri)
Husted, 915 N. Osteopathy Ave, Kirksville, MO 63501.
T. (816) 665-2392.   070485

Knoxville (Iowa)
Carter, 406 N. Kent St, Knoxville, IA 50138.
- Ant -   *070486*

Kutztown (Pennsylvania)
Schick, Janet, 244 Pennsylvania Ave, Kutztown, PA
19530. T. (215) 683-6250. - Ant -   *070487*

La Jolla (California)
Adler, Allan, 1268 Prospect St., La Jolla, CA 92037.
- Ant / Paint / Graph / Furn / China / Sculp / Dec / Jew / S-
ilv / Glass -   *070488*
Gallery Eight, 7464 Girard Av., La Jolla, CA 92037.
T. (619) 454-9781. - Furn / China / Dec / Lights / Glass /
Mod -   *070489*
Ladner-Young, 414 La Canada, La Jolla, CA 92037.
- Ant -   *070490*

La Porte (Indiana)
Burger, W. T., 1105 Washington St., La Porte, IN 46350.
T. (219) 362 2168. - Ant / Paint / Orient / Pho - *070491*

La Vergne (Tennessee)
Champ's Antiques, Old Jefferson Pike, La Vergne, TN
37086. T. (615) 793 54 34. - Ant / Furn / Glass - *070492*

La Verne (California)
Steven's Antiques, 2157 5th St., La Verne, CA 91750.
- Ant / Jew -   *070493*

Lafayette (Indiana)
Price, 921 S 9th St., Lafayette, IN 47905. T. (714) 423-
1926.   *070494*

Lafayette (New Jersey)
Pumleye, Rte 15 near Post Office, Lafayette, NJ 07848.
T. (201) 383-2114. - Ant / Paint / Furn / Num / Lights /
Mil -   *070495*

Laguna Beach (California)
Ancient Art, 860 Glenneyre St, Laguna Beach, CA
92651. T. (714) 494-2478.   *070496*
Nicholson, 362 N Coast Hwy, Laguna Beach, CA 92651.
T. (714) 494-4820. - Ant -   *070497*
Warren, 1910 S. Coast Hwy, Laguna Beach, CA 92652.
T. (714) 494-6505. - Orient -   *070498*
Yeakel, Carl, 1099 S. Coast Hwy, Laguna Beach, CA
92651. T. (714) 494-5526. - Ant / Paint / Graph / Furn /
China / Arch / Jew / Fra / Silv / Lights / Glass - *070499*

Lahaina (Hawaii)
Gallery, 716 Front St., Lahaina, HI 96761. T. (808) 661-
0696. - Ant / Orient / China / Dec / Jew / Glass - *070500*

Lahaska (Pennsylvania)
Lahaska Antique Courte, Rte 202, Lahaska, PA 18931.
T. (215) 794-7884. - Ant -   *070501*
Lippincott, Rte 202, Lahaska, PA 18931. T. (215) 794-
7734. - Ant / Furn -   *070502*

Laingsburg (Michigan)
Found Object, 11600 Woodbury Rd, Laingsburg, MI
48848. - Ant / Furn / Arch / Dec -   *070503*

Lake Bluff (Illinois)
Macalister, Paul R., POB 157, Lake Bluff, IL 60044.
- Instr -   *070504*

Lake City (Michigan)
Guest, 415 N. Main St, Lake City, MI 49651.   *070505*

Lake Elsinore (California)
Chimes, Lake Elsinore, CA 92330. T. (714) 674-3456.
- Ant -   *070506*

Lake Forest (Illinois)
Country House, 179 East Ave, Lake Forest, IL 60045.
T. (312) 234-0244. - Ant / Furn / China / Lights /
Glass -   *070507*
Lake Forest Antiquarians, POB 841, Lake Forest, IL
60045. T. (312) 234-1990. - Silv -   *070508*
Spruce, POB 949, Lake Forest, Il 60045.   *070509*

Lake Leelanau (Michigan)
Nautic Antiques, Saint Mary's at Meinrad St, Lake Lee-
lanau, MI 49653. - Ant / Furn / Arch -   *070510*

Lakeville (Connecticut)
Carriage Step Antiques, Wells Hill Rd, Lakeville, CT
06039. T. (203) 435-2953.   *070511*
Gunther, M., Main St, Lakeville, CT 06039. T. (203) 435-
9581. - Ant / Furn / China / Repr / Dec / Lights - *070512*

Lambertville (New Jersey)
Artfull Eye, 10-12 N Union St., Lambertville, NJ 08530.
T. (609) 397-8115.   *070513*
Rago, David, 17 S Main St, Lambertville, NJ 08530.
T. (609) 397-9374.   *070514*

Lancaster (Pennsylvania)
Figari, J., 319 N Queen St, Lancaster, PA 17603.
T. (717) 392-6843. - Ant -   *070515*
Janet's Antiques, 145 Strasborg Pike, Lancaster, PA
17602. T. (717) 397-9723.   *070516*
Kimmich, Jessie, 2389 New Holland Pike, Lancaster, PA
17601. T. (717) 656-7871. - Ant -   *070517*
Valley, Heather, 1461 Hunsicker Rd, Lancaster, PA
17601. T. (717) 299-0900.   *070518*

Lanesboro (Massachusetts)
Amber Springs Antiques, 29 S Main St, Lanesboro, MA
01237. T. (413) 442-1237.   *070519*
Walden, Main St, Lanesboro, MA 01237. T. (413) 499-
0312.   *070520*

Lansdowne (Pennsylvania)
Harbach & Culver, POB 19050, Lansdowne, PA 19050.
T. (215) 622-6434. - Glass -   *070521*

Lansing (Michigan)
Thomason, Edna & Robert, 4511 S Logan St, Lansing,
MI 48910.   *070522*

Lapeer (Michigan)
Dillon, 181 Myers Rd, Lapeer, MI 48446. - Ant /
Furn -   *070523*

Larchmont (New York)
Post Road Gallery, 2128 Boston Post Rd, Larchmont, NY
10538. T. (914) 834-7568, Fax (914) 834-9245. - Ant /
Paint / Furn / Sculp -   *070524*

Lawton (Michigan)
Dutch Cupboard, 112 S Main St, Lawton, MI 49065.
- Ant / Paint / Furn / China / Tex / Glass -   *070525*

Lebanon (New Hampshire)
Hayward, Rte 4, Lebanon, NH 03766. T. (603) 448-
2052.   *070526*

Leland (Michigan)
Van Ness, Margaret, 302 S Main St, Leland, MI 49654.
- Ant / Lights / Mil / Glass -   *070527*

Lenox (Massachusetts)
Crazy Horse Antiques, Main St., Lenox, MA 01240.
T. (413) 637-1634. - Ant -   *070528*
Flint, Charles L., 81 Church St, Lenox, MA 01240.
T. (413) 637-1634. - Furn -   *070529*

Lerna (Illinois)
Carriage House Antiques, RR 1, Lerna, IL 62440.
T. (217) 345-7186.   *070530*

Leslie (Georgia)
Perry, Malcolm W., 11. S. 280, Leslie, GA 31764.
T. (912) 874-5570. - Ant -   *070531*

Lexington (Kentucky)
Boone, 4996 Old Versailles Rd, Lexington, KY 40504.
T. (606) 254-5335. - Furn / China -   *070532*
Faulkner, Zec, 113 Walton Ave, Lexington, KY 40508.
T. (606) 252-1309. - Furn -   *070533*
Gribbin, E. L., 429 N. Broadway, Lexington, KY
40508.   *070534*
Heinsmith, 868 E High St, Lexington, KY 40502.
T. (606) 259-0755. - Ant -   *070535*
Iliff, Nancy A., POB 7122, Lexington POB 7122, KY
40502. T. (606) 266-7873. - Ant -   *070536*
McGurk, Donald, Central Av, Lexington, KY 40502.
T. (606) 253-0137. - Tex -   *070537*

Lima (Ohio)
Ashcroft, Donna, 1008 W. Wayne, Lima, OH
45805.   *070538*
Edith's Antiques, 316 S. Dana, Lima, OH 45804. - Ant /
Furn / China / Lights / Instr / Glass -   *070539*
Old Country Store, 1196 Greely Chapel Rd, Lima, OH
45806. - Ant / Furn / China / Instr / Glass -   *070540*
Ray, E. B., 1760 W Wayne St., Lima, OH 45805. - Ant /
Num -   *070541*

Limington (Maine)
Stuart, Robert O., Jo Joy Rd, Limington, ME 04049.
T. (207) 793-2342, 793-8533. - Furn -   *070542*

Lincoln (Nebraska)
Coach House Antiques, 135 N 26 St., Lincoln, NE
68503.   *070543*

Lincoln Park (Michigan)
Park Coin Shop, 3022 Fort, Lincoln Park, MI 48146.
T. (313) 381-0103. - Num -   *070544*

Lisbon (Connecticut)
Blum, Jerome, Ross Hill Rd, Lisbon, CT 06351.
T. (203) 376-0300. - Ant / Furn / China -   *070545*
Friedland, Joan W., Ross Hill Rd, Lisbon, CT 06351.
T. (203) 376-9680. - Ant / Paint / Furn / Tex / Dec /
Lights -   *070546*

Lisbon (Ohio)
Barnes, R. E., 501 E Lincoln Way, Lisbon, OH
44432.   *070547*
Day, Rte. 45, Lisbon-Salem Rd, Lisbon, OH
44432.   *070548*

Litchfield (Connecticut)
Williams, Thomas D. & Constance R., POB 1028, Litch-
field, CT 06759. T. (203) 567-8794. - Ant -   *070549*
Willians, Thomas D. & Constance R., Brush Hill Rd.,
Litchfield, CT 06759. T. (203) 567-8794.
- China -   *070550*

Little Compton (Rhode Island)
Clark, Meeting House Ln, Little Compton, RI 02837.
T. (401) 635-2392. - Ant / Repr -   *070551*

Littleton (Massachusetts)
Blue Cape Antiques, 620 Great Rd., Littleton, MA
01460.   *070552*

Livonia (Michigan)
Kegler, 35800 E. Ann Arbor Terrace, Livonia, MI 48150.
- Ant / China / Lights / Instr / Glass -   *070553*
Riegal, 33910 Plymouth Rd, Livonia, MI 48150.
T. (313) 427-2700. - Ant -   *070554*

Lodi (Ohio)
Presznick, Rte. 1, Lodi, OH 44254. - Glass -   *070555*

London (Ohio)
Antique House, 198 S. Main St., London, OH 43140.
- Ant -   *070556*
Bangham, 118 N. Main St., London, OH 43140.   *070557*

Long Beach (California)
Belkin, Ron, 3801 E 4th St., Long Beach, CA 90814.
T. (213) 439-9833. - Ant -   *070558*
Market Street Antiques, 1340 Market St., Long Beach,
CA 90805. - Ant -   *070559*
Oak Haven Antiques, 321 W Pacific Coast Hwy, Long Be-
ach, CA 90806. T. (213) 591-4008.   *070560*
Potter, Tom, 1036 Atlantic Ave, Long Beach, CA 90813.
T. (213) 437-1595. - Ant -   *070561*

Long Island City (New York)
Judson, 49-20 Fifth St., Long Island City, NY 11101.
Fax 937-5860. - Ant -   *070562*

Long Valley (New Jersey)
Marshall, Ruth, Rte. 24, Long Valley, NJ 07853.
T. (201) 876-3258. - Ant / China / Fra / Lights /
Glass -   *070563*

Longmont (Colorado)
Paul's Antiques, 931 Main St., Longmont, CO 80501.
T. (303) 776-1866. - Furn / Ant -   *070564*

Lorain (Ohio)
Lehmann-Fisher, 160 Foster Park Rd, Lorain, OH
44053. 070565

Los Altos (California)
Oriental Corner, 280 Main St., Los Altos, CA 94022.
T. (415) 941-3207, Fax (415) 941-3297.
- Orient - 070566

Los Angeles (California)
Antique Guild, 3225 Helms Ave., Los Angeles, CA
90034. 070567
Antique Mart of Los Angeles, 809 N La Cienega Blvd.,
Los Angeles, CA 90069. T. (213) 652-1282. - Ant /
Paint / Orient / China / Sculp / Silv / Mil - 070568
Asia Import Company, 6669 Hollywood Blvd., Los Ange-
les, CA 90028. - Orient - 070569
Baldacchino, 919 N. La Cienega Blvd., Los Angeles, CA
90069. T. (213) 657-6810. - Ant / Furn / China / Mil /
Sculp / Repr / Dec / Lights - 070570
Byrnes, James B., 7820 Mulholland Dr., Los Angeles, CA
90046. T. (213) 851-0128. 070571
Charles & Charles, 8886 Venice Blvd., Los Angeles, CA
90034. - Ant / Paint / Furn / China / Repr / Tex / Fra /
Lights / Instr / Rel / Glass / Cur - 070572
Corbell & Co., 1535 S. Sepulveda, Los Angeles, CA
90025. - Orient / Repr / Jew / Silv - 070573
Crow, Dennis G., POB 691571, Los Angeles, CA 90069.
T. (213) 650-0430, Fax (213) 656-2483. 070574
Dennis en, 612 N. Robertson Blvd., Los Angeles, CA
90069. T. (213) 652-0855. - Ant / Furn / Sculp / Tex /
Arch / Dec / Fra / Lights - 070575
Dubas, Cyril, 11131 Rose Av., Los Angeles, CA 90034.
T. (213) 838-3336. - Ant - 070576
Ellio, Craoo, 731 N. La Cienega Blvd., Los Angeles, CA
90069. T. (213) 652-1688. - Ant / Paint / Furn / China /
Sculp / Dec / Lights / Glass - 070577
English Heritage, 8424 Melrose Pl., Los Angeles, CA
90060. T. (213) 655-5946. - Silv - 070578
Etcetera, 336 N. Lafayette Park Pl., Los Angeles, CA
90026. - Ant / Paint / Graph / Furn / China / Dec /
Lights / Glass - 070579
French Antique Shoppe, 737 N La Cienega Blvd., Los
Angeles, CA 90069. T. (213) 652-1666. - Ant / Paint /
Furn / China / Sculp / Dec / Fra / Lights / Instr / Mil / Rel /
Glass - 070580
Henderson, R. W., 153 S. Western Ave., Los Angeles, CA
90004. 070581
Hing, Jin, 412 Bamboo Ln, Los Angeles, CA
90012. 070582
Ingersoll, Thomas, 805 N. La Cienega Blvd., Los Ange-
les, CA 90069. T. (213) 652-7677. - Ant / Orient / Chi-
na / Silv - 070583
Jean's Antiques, 4616 Eagle Rock Blvd., Los Angeles,
CA 90041. T. (213) 257-8653. - Ant / Furn / Orient /
Glass - 070584
La Belle Epoque, 10942 Weyburn Av., Los Angeles, CA
90024. T. (213) 208-8449. - Mod - 070585
Laemmle, Walter, 735 N. La Cienega Blvd., Los Angeles,
CA 90069. T. (213) 652-2671. - Ant - 070586
Lil-Job-Lou, 8040 W. 3rd St., Los Angeles, CA 90048.
T. (213) 651-3838. - Ant / Jew - 070587
Maison Francaise Antiques, 8420 Melrose Pl., Los Ange-
les, CA 90069. 070588
McMullen, 146 N Robertson Blvd., Los Angeles, CA
90048. T. (213) 652-9492, Fax (213) 652-2877.
- Orient - 070589
Mehditach, Joseph, 1257 1/2 N. New Hampshire, Los
Angeles, CA 90029. 070590
Museum Antiques, 8417 Melrose Pl., Los Angeles, CA
90065. - Ant - 070591
Nelson, John J., 8472 Melrose Pl., Los Angeles, CA
90069. - Ant - 070592
Nob Hill AntiqÜes, 8627 Melrose, Los Angeles, CA
90069. 070593
Pollock, Charles, 8478 Melrose Pl., Los Angeles, CA
90069. T. (213) 651-5852. - Ant - 070594
Smith & Houchins, 921 N. La Cienega Blvd., Los Ange-
les, CA 90069. T. (213) 652-0308. - Ant / Paint /
Graph / Furn / China / Repr / Sculp / Dec / Silv / Lights / I-
nstr / Rel / Glass - 070595
Space, 6015 Santa Monica Blvd, Los Angeles, CA
90038. - Paint / Graph / Sculp / Draw - 070596

Stendahl, 7055-7065 Hillside Av., Los Angeles, CA
90068. T. (213) 876-7740. - Arch / Eth - 070597
Stuart, David, 748 N. La Cienega Blvd., Los Angeles, CA
90069. T. (213) 652-7422. - Paint / Graph / Sculp /
Arch / Eth - 070598
Talbot, Renée, 8400 Melrose Pl, Los Angeles, CA 90069.
T. (213) 653-7792. - Ant / Paint / Graph / Furn / China /
Dec / Lights / Instr - 070599
Tennant, 725 N La Cienega Blvd., Los Angeles, CA
90069. T. (213) 659-3610. - Ant / Paint /
China - 070600
Tiberio-Art Deco, 458 N. Robertson, Los Angeles, CA
90048. T. (213) 659-5777. - Graph / Furn / Sculp /
Jew / Glass / Mod - 070601
Tile Elon, 8678 Melrose St., Los Angeles, CA 90069.
T. (213) 655-8484, 659-3373. - Ant - 070602
Wertz Brothers, 11879 Santa Monica Blvd., Los Angeles,
CA 90025. 070603
Zeitlin & Ver Brugge, 815 N La Cienega Blvd., 90000
Los Angeles, CA 90069. T. (213) 652-0784, 655-7581.
- Paint / Graph / Pho / Draw - 070604

Los Gatos (California)
Montgomery, 262 E. Main St., Los Gatos, CA 95030.
T. (408) 354-1825. - Ant / Paint / Sculp - 070605
Opera House Antiques, 140 W Main St., Los Gatos, CA
95030. T. (408) 354-3484. - Ant - 070606
Pearl Antiques, 108 N. Santa Cruz Ave., Los Gatos, CA
95030. T. (408) 354-7177. - Ant - 070607
Powers, Brian Michael, 5 University Av., Los Gatos, CA
95030. T. (408) 354-8180. 070608

Louisville (Kentucky)
Bittner, 731 E. Main St., Louisville, KY 40202.
T. (502) 584-6349. - Ant / Paint / Furn / China / Repr /
Tex - 070609
Century Shop, 1703 Bardstown Rd., Louisville, KY
40205. T. (502) 451-7692. - Ant / Paint / Furn / China /
Arch / Silv / Lights / Rel / Glass - 070610
Glassclock Interiors, 155 Chenoweth Ln, Louisville, KY
40207. T. (502) 895-0212. - Ant - 070611
Schumann, 4545 Taylorsville Rd., Louisville, KY 40220.
T. (502) 491-0134. - Ant - 070612

Lowell (Michigan)
Crawberry Urn Shop, 208 E. Main St., Lowell, MI 49331.
- Ant / China / Lights - 070613

Ludlow Falls (Ohio)
Landes, Harold & Carole, Rte. 1, 1 Mile South of Pleasant Hill, Ludlow Falls, OH 45339. 070614

Lusby (Maryland)
Fehr, Cynthia, Star Rte. 2, Box 27, Lusby, MD 20657.
- Ant - 070615

Lynn (Massachusetts)
Walfield, Leo, 59 Union St., Lynn, MA 01902.
T. (617) 595-3859. - Ant - 070616

Lynnfield (Massachusetts)
Hart-Tapley, 172 Chesnut St., Lynnfield, MA 01940.
T. (617) 334-4184. 070617

Lyons (New York)
Lyons Den, 57 Cherry St., Lyons, NY 14489.
T. (315) 946-9294. - Ant - 070618

Lyons (Ohio)
Hoefer, Lawrence H., 2 Miles North of Hwy 20, Lyons,
OH 43533. 070619

Macon (Georgia)
Paul, Mary, 5211 Bloomfield Rd, Macon, GA
31206. 070620

Madison
International Coin Exchange, 891 Boston Post Rd., Ma-
dison, CT 06440. T. (203) 245-2719. - Num - 070621
Schafer, 82 Bradley Rd., Madison, CT 06443.
T. (203) 245-4173. 070622

Madison (Indiana)
Historic Shrewsbury House Antiques, 301 W First St.,
Madison, IN 47250. T. (812) 265-4481. - Ant / Furn /
China / Silv / Glass - 070623

Maitland
Dunn, POB 965-MR, Maitland, FL 32751.
- Num - 070624

Malaga
Scotland Run Antiques, Rte. 40, Malaga, NJ 08328.
T. (609) 694-3322. - Ant - 070625

Malibu
Lewis, Dorothy, POB 1052, Malibu, CA 90265.
T. (213) 456-6874. - Ant / Orient / Sculp / Arch / Eth /
Jew / Rel / Ico - 070626

Manchester (Connecticut)
Bailey, 24 Wyneding Hill Rd., Manchester, CT 06040.
- Ant - 070627

Manchester (New Hampshire)
Harrington, 1466 Hooksett Rd, Manchester, NH 03106.
T. (603) 485-3092. - Ant / Furn / China / Jew /
Glass - 070628

Manchester (Vermont)
Brewster, Bonnet St, Rte 30, Manchester, VT 05255.
T. (802) 362-1579. - Ant / Jew / Silv - 070629
Paraphernalia Antiques, Rte 7, Manchester, VT 05254.
T. (802) 362-2421. 070630

Manhasset (New York)
Coronnet Coin Shop, 336 Plandome Rd., Manhasset, NY
11030. T. (516) 627-5909. - Num - 070631

Manhattan Beach (California)
Husk, POB 3446, Manhattan Beach, CA 90266.
T. (310) 372-1757, Fax (310) 372-1757. 070632

Mankato (New Mexico)
Bargain Center, 731 S. Front St., Mankato, NM 56001.
- Ant / Furn / China - 070633
Stutzman, 403 N Broad St., Mankato, NM 56001. - Ant /
China - 070634

Manlius (New York)
Cooper, Andrew, POB 42, Manlius, NY 13104.
T. (315) 861-7196. - Num - 070635
Fanlight, 4574 Meadowridge Rd., Manlius, NY 13104.
T. (315) 682-6551. - Ant / Paint / Furn / Orient /
China - 070636

Mansfield (Ohio)
Shangri-La Antiques, 37 Brinkerhoff Ave., Mansfield, OH
44906. - Ant - 070637
Woodhall, 163 Penn Ave., Mansfield, OH 44905.
T. (419) 525-0447. - Ant - 070638

Marblehead (Massachusetts)
Budrose, Ph. A., 10 Greystone Rd., Marblehead, MA
01945. T. (617) 631-3221. - Ant / Paint / Furn /
Jew - 070639
Jarnell, A. J., 162 Front St., Marblehead, MA 01945.
- Ant - 070640

Marietta (Georgia)
Boxwood Cottage, 597 Rose Lane St. NW, Marietta, GA
30060. T. (404) 427-6839. - Ant / Paint / Furn / China /
Tex / Instr - 070641

Marietta (Ohio)
Calico Bonnet, 102 Front St., Marietta, OH
45750. 070642
Roy, 149 Franklin St., Marietta, OH 45750. 070643

Marietta (Pennsylvania)
Gleason, Hovey & Evelyn, 114 E. Market St., Marietta,
PA 17547. T. (717) 426-946. - Furn - 070644
Hartman, Harry B., 14 E. Front St., Marietta, PA 17547.
T. (717) 426-1474. - Ant / Furn - 070645

Marion (Iowa)
Antiques by the Bullards, 260 7th Av, Marion, IA 52302.
T. (319) 377-6007. - Furn / Orient / Eth / Glass - 070646

Marion (Massachusetts)
Captain Hadley House Antiques, 345 Front St., Marion,
MA 02738. T. (617) 748-0482. - Ant / Paint / Furn /
Orient / China / Tex / Arch / Jew / Silv / Instr / Glass --
070647

Heirlooms, 369 Wareham Rd., Marion, MA 02738.
T. (617) 748-1663. - Ant -   070648

Marion (New York)
Drave, Raymond & Alice, 134 N. Main St., Marion, NY
14505. T. (315) 926-4401. - Ant -   070649

Marlboro (Massachusetts)
Pratt, Wayne, 257 Forest St., Marlboro, MA 01752.
T. (617) 481-2917. - Furn -   070650

Marlboro (New Jersey)
Grandma's Treasures, State Hwy 79, Marlboro, NJ
07746. T. (201) 462-2381. - Ant -   070651

Marlborough (New Hampshire)
Herb Farm Antiques, RFD Jaffrey Rd., Rte. 124, Marlborough, NH 03455. T. (603) 876-4080. - Ant -   070652
Longacre, Thomas R., Rte. 124, Marlborough, NH
03455. T. (603) 8764080. - Furn -   070653

Martin (Michigan)
Hogeboom, Eva A., 1037 W. Allegan St., Martin, MI
49070.   070654

Mason (Ohio)
Mason Antique Shop, 207 W. Church St., Mason, OH
45040. - Ant / Furn / China / Glass -   070655

Massillon (Ohio)
Markham, 12441 Lincoln St. N. W., Massillon, OH
44646.   070656

Mattapoisett (Massachusetts)
Valladoa, Rte 6, Mattapoisett, MA 02739. T. (617) 758-
3381.   070657

Mattawan (Michigan)
Lesterhouse, William, 112 Front, Mattawan, MI 49071.
- Ant / Paint / Furn / Orient / China / Tex / Dec / Silv / Lig-
hts -   070658

Maxville
Nichols, 5 Antiques Court, Maxville, MT 59850.   070659

Maysville (Kentucky)
River City Antiques, 222 Limestone St., Maysville, KY
41056. T. (606) 564-9379. - Furn -   070660

Mazomanie
American Antiques, 505 Commercial St, Mazomanie, WI
53560. T. (608) 767-2608.   070661

McArthur (Ohio)
Federoff, Main St., McArthur, OH 45651.   070662

McClure (Ohio)
Gerdes, Charles, Rte. 1, 241st Rd. S., McClure, OH
43534.   070663

McConnelsville (Ohio)
Ehrenfeld, 165 S. 10th St., McConnelsville, OH
43756.   070664

McLean (Virginia)
Evans Farm Inn Country Store, 1696 Chain Bridge Rd.,
McLean, VA 22101. T. (703) 356-8000. - Ant / Furn /
China / Repr / Dec / Jew / Fra / Silv / Lights / Glass --
                                                         070665
Time and Strike, 6216 Old Dominion Dr., McLean, VA
22101. T. (703) 534-1777. - Furn / Instr -   070666

Medfield (Massachusetts)
Rudisill, 3 Lakewood Dr., Medfield, MA 02052.
T. (617) 359-2261.   070667

Memphis (Tennessee)
Alan, 1613 Union Av., Memphis, TN 38104. T. (901) 276-
5475. - Tex -   070668
Goldsmith, Oak Court, Memphis, TN 38143.
T. (901) 766-2361. - Tex -   070669

Mendenhall (Pennsylvania)
Borton, Sally, Kennett Pike, Rt.52, Mendenhall, PA
19357. T. (215) 388-7687.   070670

Mendon (Michigan)
Huff, Barbara, Mendon, MI 49072. - Ant / Jew -   070671

Menlo Park (California)
Rafferty, Mary, 871 Santa Cruz Av, Menlo Park, CA
94025. T. (415) 321-6878.   070672

Mentor (Ohio)
Hahn, 7639 Salida Rd., Mentor, OH 44060. T. (216) 257-
6562. - Furn -   070673
Old Country Store Antiques, 8607 Rte. 20, Mentor, OH
44060.   070674

Meridian (Mississippi)
A. and I. Place Antiques, 2021 24th Ave., Meridian, MS
39301. T. (601) 483-9281. - Furn / China -   070675

Miami (Florida)
A and M Antiques and Gallery, 94-79 S Dixie Hwy., Mia-
mi, FL 33156. T. (305) 667-4214. - Paint /
Graph -   070676
Balogh, 242 Miracle Mile Coral Gables, Miami, FL
33134. T. (305) 445-2644. - Ant / Jew / Silv /
Glass -   070677
Collectors Corner, 2665 S. W. 22nd St., Miami, FL
33145. T. (305) 443-2227. - Ant -   070678
Decor, 9446 Hardin Ave, Miami, FL 33154. T. (305) 866-
0905. - Ant / Paint / Furn / Orient / Silv -   070679
Kranzler, H., 2393 Coral Way, Miami, FL 33134.
T. (305) 444-3306. - Ant / Furn / China / Jew /
Silv -   070680
Midori, 3390 Mary St., Miami, FL 33133. T. (305) 443-
3399. - Orient -   070681
Oriental Accessory House, 2365 Coral Way, Miami, FL
33134.   070682
Ye Olde Mantel Shoppe, 3800 NE Second Av., Miami, FL
33137. T. (305) 576-0225. - Ant / Sculp -   070683

Middleboro (Massachusetts)
Heritage Antiques, 15 Prospekt St., Middleboro, MA
02346. T. (617) 947-7277.   070684

Middleburg (Virginia)
Carousel Antiques, 110 W Washington St., Middleburg,
VA 22117. T. (703) 687-6636. - Ant / Furn / China /
Silv -   070685
Chase, POB 1215, Middleburg, VA 22117. T. (703) 687-
6973. - Ant -   070686
Sporting Gallery, POB 146, Middleburg, VA 22117.
T. (703) 687-6447. - Ant -   070687

Middleton
Webber, Max, 47 East St., Middleton, MA 01949.
T. (617) 774-1785. - Ant / Furn / Tex -   070688

Middletown
Lindeman, 121 S. Main St., Middletown, OH 45042.
- Ant / Glass -   070689

Middletown (New York)
Stepping Stone Inn Antiques, RD 3, Middletown, NY
10940. T. (914) 361-3211.   070690

Middletown (Ohio)
Banzhaf, 211 Arlington Ave., Middletown, OH
45042.   070691
Long, 3809 Central Av., Middletown, OH 45042. - Ant /
China / Glass -   070692
Sheard, 4104 Grand Ave., Middletown, OH 45042.
- Ant / Lights -   070693

Midland (Michigan)
D. and B. Antique Glassware, 2708 Rodd St., Midland,
MI 48640. - Ant / Glass -   070694

Midlothian (Virginia)
Gates Antiques, 12700 Old Buckingham Rd., Midlothian,
VA 23113. T. (804) 794-8472. - Ant / Furn /
China -   070695

Midway (Kentucky)
Lehmann & Sons, D., US Rte 62, Midway, KY 40347.
T. (606) 846-4513. - Furn -   070696
Rawlings, 311 S. Winter, Midway, KY 40347.
T. (606) 846-4550. - Furn -   070697

Milan (Illinois)
Old Toll Gate Antiques, 600 North Av., Milan, IL 61264.
T. (309) 787-2392.   070698

Milan (Ohio)
Coulter, Joan, 123 Center St., Milan, OH 44846.
T. (419) 499-4061. - Ant / Furn / China -   070699
Samaha, G. W., Public Sq., Milan, OH 44846.
T. (419) 499-4044.   070700

Mill Valley (California)
Gorham, John S., 357 Miller Avenue, Mill Valley, CA
94941.   070701

Millbrook
Millbrook Antiques Mall, Franklin Av., Millbrook, NY
12545. T. (914) 677-9311.   070702

Millbrook (New York)
Tompkins, John C. R., Shunpike Rd., Millbrook, NY
12545. T. (914) 677-3026. - Ant / Furn -   070703

Millburn (New Jersey)
Keyman, Sol & Dorothy, 49 Walnut Av., Millburn, NJ
07041. T. (201) 379-1977. - Furn -   070704
Nussbaum, Sheila, 358 Millburn Av., Millburn, NJ
07041. T. (201) 467-1720. - Jew -   070705

Milwaukee (Wisconsin)
Astor Galleries, 2630 N. Downer Ave., Milwaukee, WI
53211.   070706
Bader, Alfred, 924 E Juneau Av, Milwaukee, WI 53202.
T. (414) 277-0730, Fax (414) 277-0709.   070707
Braun, Richard, 3327 W. National Ave., Milwaukee, WI
53215.   070708
Graf, 3018 W. Lincoln Ave., Milwaukee, WI
53215.   070709
House of Oak, 914 S. 101st St., Milwaukee, WI
53214.   070710
Kondos, Peter J., E Wisconsin Av at N Water, Milwaukee,
WI 53202. T. (414) 272-8000. - Paint / Graph /
Sculp -   070711
Levinger, 1499 N Farwell Av., Milwaukee, WI 53202.
T. (414) 273-5920. - Paint / Graph / Furn / Num / Orient /
China / Dec / Jew / Silv / Lights / Instr / Glass -   070712
Milwaukee Antique Center, 341 N Milwaukee St., Mil-
waukee, WI 53202.   070713
Town and Country Shop, 8836 N. Port Washington Rd.,
Milwaukee, WI 53217. T. (414) 352-6570. - Ant / Furn /
China / Silv -   070714
Victorian Shop, 2630 N. Downer Ave., Milwaukee, WI
53211. T. (414) 962-0272. - Ant / Furn / China / Jew /
Glass -   070715

Minneapolis (Minnesota)
Asian Fine Arts, 825 Second Av., Minneapolis, MN
55402. - Orient -   070716
Erickson, 2735 Nicollet Ave., Minneapolis, MN 55408.
T. (612) 827-2911. - Furn -   070717
Fiterman, Dolly, 100 University Av. S.E., Minneapolis,
MN 55414. T. (612) 623-3300, Fax (612) 623-
0203.   070718
Fjelde & Co., 3020 W. 50th St., Minneapolis, MN
55410.   070719
Gabbert, 3501 W 69th St., Minneapolis, MN 55410.
- Ant / Furn -   070720
Hansen, 6945 Park Ave., Minneapolis, MN 55423.
T. (612) 869-5774. - Ant -   070721
Oredson, Oliver, 4921 Abbott Ave. S., Minneapolis, MN
55410.   070722
Temple, 6721 Portland Av. S, Minneapolis, MN 55423.
T. (612) 861-4025.   070723

Mobile (Alabama)
Adams, Kathryn, 352 N Gould Av., Mobile, AL 36612.
- Ant / Furn / China / Glass -   070724
Appleseed Antiques, 1502 Wolfridge Rd., Mobile, AL
36618. T. (205) 342-6690.   070725
Chilton, 938-944 Conti St., Mobile, AL 36604.
T. (205) 432-3036.   070726
Plantation Antique Galleries, 3750 Government Blvd.,
Mobile, AL 36609. T. (205) 478-8900.   070727

Monmouth (Illinois)
Carpenter, M. C., 414 E. 2nd Ave., Monmouth, IL 61462.
T. (309) 734-6605. - Ant -   070728

Monroe (Michigan)
Fountain, 1974 N. Monroe St., Monroe, MI 48161.
- Ant / Furn / China / Fra / Lights / Instr / Glass -   070729

Montecito (California)
Morrey, 1225 Coast Village Rd., Montecito, CA 93108.
T. (805) 969-4464. - Ant -   070730

Monterey (California)
House of Crispo, 425 Cannery Row, Monterey, CA
93940. T. (408) 373-8467.   070731

Monterey (Massachusetts)
Ledgehurst, Tyringham Rd., Monterey, MA 01245.
T. (413) 528-3170.   070732

Montgomery
Herron House Antiques, 422 Herron St, Montgomery, AL
36104.   070733

Montgomery (New York)
Historic Importants, 198 Corbett Rd, Montgomery, NY
12549. T. (914) 457-3765.   070734

Montgomery (Ohio)
DuPriest, 10275 Montgomery Rd., Montgomery, OH
45242. - Ant / Paint / Furn / Fra / Lights / Glass / Pho /
Draw -   070735

Montgomeryville
Burmese Cruet, POB 432, Montgomeryville, PA 18936.
T. (215) 855-5388. - Glass -   070736

Montvale
Antique Mall, Chestnut Ridge, Shopping Center, 30
Chestnut Rd., Montvale, NJ 07645.   070737

Morristown (New Jersey)
Wiley, Katharine, 17 Georgian Rd., Morristown, NJ
07960. T. (201) 538-6243. - Ant -   070738

Morrisville (New York)
Bury Farm, Rte 20, Morrisville, NY 13408. T. (315) 684-
3208. - Ant -   070739

Mount Morris
Willis House Antiques, 408 Bruce Ln, Mount Morris, IL
61054. T. (815) 734-4588.   070740

Mount Vernon (Iowa)
Mount Vernon Antiques, Mount Vernon, IA 04320.
T. (319) 293-4431.   070741

Mount Vernon (New York)
West Chester Exchange, 78 W. First St., Mount Vernon,
NY 10550. T. (914) 668- 0447. - Ant / Furn -   070742

Mount Vernon (Ohio)
Palmer, Frank R., 606 N. Main St., Mount Vernon, OH
43050. - Ant / Paint / Orient / China / Tex / Jew / Silv /
Lights -   070743
Shoemaker, 106 Wooster Ave., Mount Vernon, OH
43050.   070744

Mountainside (New Jersey)
Dutch Oven Antiques, 1260 Hwy 22, Mountainside, NJ
07092. T. (201) 233-1567. - Ant / Furn / Tex -   070745
Maxwell, D., 885 Mountain Ave., Mountainside, NJ
07092. T. (201) 232-0226. - Ant -   070746

Mullica Hill (New Jersey)
Raintree Antiques, 32 N. Main St., Mullica Hill, NJ
08062. T. (609) 478-4100.   070747
Schumann, Robert & Ann, 74 N. Main St., Mullica Hill,
NJ 08062. T. (609) 478-2553.   070748

Murfreesboro (Arkansas)
Caddo, POB 669, Murfreesboro, AR 71958. T. (501) 285-
3736. - Ant / Arch / Eth -   070749

Murfreesboro (Tennessee)
Immigrant Trail Antiques, Rte. 2, Murfreesboro, TN
37130. - Ant / Furn / China -   070750

Muskegon (Michigan)
Attic, 238 Houston, Muskegon, MI 49441.   070751
Town and Country Antiques, POB 5023, Muskegon, MI
49445.   070752

Muskogee (Oklahoma)
Antiques, 2212 W. Shawnee St., Muskogee, OK 74401.
T. (918) 687-4447. - Ant -   070753
Archie's Antiques, 825 N. K. St., Muskogee, OK 74401.
- Ant / Furn / China / Lights / Glass -   070754
Johnson, 901 S. 32nd St., Muskogee, OK 74401.
T. (918) 687-6791. - Furn / China / Glass -   070755

Myrtle Beach (South Carolina)
Four Seasons Interiors, N. Kings Hwy. at 76th Ave.,
Myrtle Beach, SC29577. T. (803) 449-5330.
- Ant -   070756

Nags Head (North Carolina)
Seaside Art Gallery, POB 1, Nags Head, NC 27959.
- Paint / Graph / Orient / Sculp / Rel / Ico / Draw --
     070757

Nantucket (Massachusetts)
Maitino, 31 N Liberty St., Nantucket, MA 02554.
T. (617) 228-2747. - Furn -   070758

Naples (Florida)
Davis, Lee, 360 S Ninth St., Naples, FL 33940.
T. (813) 261-2552. - Ant / Paint / Furn / Orient / China /
Tex / Lights -   070759

Nashville (Tennessee)
Anderson, Evelyn, Westgate Center, Hwy. 100, Nashville,
TN 37205. T. (615) 352-6770. - Ant / Furn / China /
Tex / Dec -   070760
Bradford, 4100 Hillsboro Rd., Nashville, TN 37215.
- Ant -   070761
Farm House Antiques, Otter Creek Rd., Nashville, TN
37220. T. (615) 832-1611. - Ant -   070762
Harpeth, 4102 Hillsboro Rd., Nashville, TN 37215.
T. (615) 297-4300. - Ant / Furn / China / Silv -   070763
Leland, Ted, 3301 West End Av., Nashville, TN 37203.
T. (615) 383-2421. - Furn -   070764
Trace Tavern Antiques, 8456 Hwy 100, Nashville, TN
37221. T. (615) 646-5600. - Furn -   070765

Natural Bridge (Virginia)
Antiques by Bradford, Hwy 130, Natural Bridge, VA
24578. T. (703) 291-2217. - Furn -   070766

Needham (Massachusetts)
Stewart, 190 Nehoiden St., Needham, MA 02192.
T. (617) 444-0124. - Ant -   070767

Nelson (New Hampshire)
Backes, Peter B. Flint, Old Stoddard Rd., Nelson, NH
03457. T. (603) 847-9015. - Ant -   070768

Nevada City (California)
Art and Antique Dealer, POB 370, Nevada City, CA
95959. T. (916) 786-7313. - Jew -   070769

New Bedford (Massachusetts)
Brookside, 24 N Water St., New Bedford, MA 02740.
T. (617) 993-4944.   070770

New Boston (Michigan)
Escher, 19224 Craig, New Boston, MI 48164.
T. (313) 753-4112. - Instr -   070771

New Brunswick (New Jersey)
Gaslight Antiques, 280 George St, New Brunswick, NJ
08901. T. (201) 247-8341. - China -   070772

New Canaan (Connecticut)
English Heritage Antiques, 13 South Av., New Canaan,
CT 06840. T. (203) 966-2979.   070773
Findlay, Mimi, 10 Father Peter's Ln, New Canaan, CT
06840. T. (203) 966-4617. - Furn -   070774
Markurt, 5 South Av, New Canaan, CT 06840.
T. (203) 966-8839.   070775

New Carlisle (Ohio)
Pillar & Scroll, 312 S. Adams St., New Carlisle, OH
45344.   070776

New Era (Michigan)
Lewis, Stony Lake Rd., New Era, MI 49446. - Ant / China / Lights / Glass -   070777

New Hampton (New York)
Four Winds Antiques, Rte. 17, New Hampton, NY 10958.
T. (914) 374-2381. - Ant / Paint / Furn -   070778

New Haven (Connecticut)
Ahlberg, Edwin C., 441 Middletown Av., New Haven, CT
06513. T. (203) 624-9076. - Furn -   070779
Antiques Market, 881 Whalley Ave., New Haven, CT
06515. T. (203) 389-5440.   070780
Ark Antiques, POB 3133, New Haven, CT 06515.
T. (203) 387-3754. - Jew / Silv -   070781
Colville, Thomas, 58 Trumbull St, New Haven, CT
06511. T. (203) 787-2816. - Ant / Draw -   070782
Kasowitz, 895 Whalley Ave., New Haven, CT 06515.
T. (203) 389-2514.   070783
Littlefield, 3 Magnolia Ave., New Haven, CT 06516.
T. (203) 933-1062.   070784

New Hope (Pennsylvania)
Ingham Springs Antiques, Rte. 202 at Ingham Springs,
New Hope, PA 18938. T. (215) 862-0818.
- Furn -   070785
Old Hope Antiques, Rte. 202, New Hope, PA 18938.
T. (215) 862-5055. - Furn -   070786
Olde Hope, 6465 Route 202, New Hope, PA 18938.
T. (215) 862-5055.   070787
Pink House, Rt. 179, New Hope, PA 18938. T. (215) 862-
5947. - Ant / Furn / China / Repr -   070788
Purcell, Francis J., 88 N Main St., New Hope, PA 18938.
T. (215) 862-9100. - Ant -   070789
Queripel, 93 W Bridge St, New Hope, PA 18938.
T. (215) 862-5830. - Furn -   070790
Robertson, R.D.1, New Hope, PA 18938. T. (215) 297-
5068. - Furn -   070791
Ronley, River Rd. N, Rt. 32, New Hope, PA 18938.
T. (215) 862-2427. - Ant / Paint / Furn / China / Lights /
Glass -   070792
Stanley, Joseph, 181 W Bridge St., New Hope, PA
18938. T. (215) 862-9300. - Paint / Furn /
China -   070793

New Ipswich (New Hampshire)
Glavey, Estelle M., Rtes. 123 and 124, New Ipswich, NH
03071. - Ant / Paint / Furn / Orient / Tex / Glass -   070794

New London (New Hampshire)
Drake, Priscilla, Main St., New London, NH
03257.   070795
Lauridsen, Laurids, 1 Mile from Rte. 11 on Knight's Hill,
New London, NH 03257. T. (603) 526-6407.
- Furn -   070796
Mad Eagle, Rte. 11, New London, NH 03257.
T. (603) 526-4880. - Ant -   070797

New Orleans (Louisiana)
A-E-Antiques, 305 Chartres St., New Orleans, LA 70130.
T. (504) 525-0327. - Ant / Paint / Sculp / Sculp / Tex /
Mil -   070798
Adriaan, 618 Conti, New Orleans, LA 70130.   070799
Antique Coin Appraisal Service, 437 Royal St., New Or-
leans, LA 70130. T. (504) 522-3305. - Num -   070800
Blackamoor, 3433 Magazine St., New Orleans, LA
70115. T. (504) 897-2711.   070801
Borenstein, E. Lorenz, 511 Royal St., New Orleans, LA
70130. T. (504) 523-0549. - Arch / Eth -   070802
Cohen, James H. & Sons, 437 Royal St., New Orleans,
LA 70130. T. (504) 522-3305. - Num / Mil -   070803
Davis, 3964 Magazine St., New Orleans, LA 70115.
T. (504) 897-0780. - Arch / Eth -   070804
Dellwen, 3954 Magazine St., New Orleans, LA
70115.   070805
Dickson, 729 Royal St., New Orleans, LA 70130. - Ant /
Furn / Orient / China / Tex / Dec / Jew / Silv / Lights / Ins-
tr / Rel / Glass -   070806
Eighteenth Century Antique Shop, 2109 Magazine St.,
New Orleans, LA 70130.   070807
English Antiques, 5533 Magazine St., New Orleans, LA
70115. T. (504) 891-3803. - Ant / Paint -   070808
French Antique Shop, 225 Royal St., New Orleans, LA
70130. T. (504) 524-9861. - Ant / Paint / Furn / Sculp /
Lights -   070809
Good, Joan, 807 Royal St., New Orleans, LA 70116.
- Ant / Paint -   070810

DIDIER AARON, Inc.
32 East 67th Street
New York, N. Y. 10021
Tel. (212)988 5248
fax (212) 737 3513
18TH & 19TH CENTURY
FURNITURE ART OBJECTS
OLD MASTER 19TH C. PAINTINGS

Granet, Arnold M., 225 Royal St., New Orleans, LA
70130. *070811*
Herman, J. & Son, 321 Royal St., New Orleans, LA
70130. T. (504) 525-6326. - Paint / Graph / Furn / Jew /
Silv / Lights / Instr - *070812*
Lazard, 3146 Calhoun, New Orleans, LA 70125.
T. (504) 861-2581. - Num - *070813*
Manheim, B., 403-409 Royal St., New Orleans, LA
70130. T. (504) 524-0846. - Ant - *070814*
Moss, 411 Royal St., New Orleans, LA 70130.
T. (504) 722-3981. - Furn / Jew - *070815*
Nahan, 540 Royal St., New Orleans, LA 70130.
T. (504) 524-8696. - Paint / Graph - *070816*
New Orleans Silversmiths, 600 Chartres St., New Or-
leans, LA 70130. T. (504) 523-7874. - Ant / Jew /
Silv - *070817*
Old Bottons, 404 Chartres St., New Orleans, LA 70130.
- Ant / Num / Orient / Jew - *070818*
Petit Soldier Shop, 528 Royal St., New Orleans, LA
70130. - Graph / Mil - *070819*
Rau, M. S., 630 Royal St., New Orleans, LA 70176.
T. (504) 523-5660, Fax (504) 566-0057. - Ant / Paint /
Furn / Orient / China / Repr / Sculp / Dec / Jew / Fra / Sil-
v / Lights / Instr / Mil / Glass / Mod - *070820*
Renaissance, 1101 First St., New Orleans, LA 70130.
T. (504) 529-2286. - Ant / Furn / China / Repr /
Silv - *070821*
Roth, Richard J., 618 Chartres St., New Orleans, LA
70130. T. (504) 522-3395. - Ant / Paint / Num / China /
Silv / Glass - *070822*
Rothschild, 229 Royal St., New Orleans, LA 70130.
T. (504) 523-6815. - Ant - *070823*
Royal Antiques, 307-309 Royal St., New Orleans, LA
70130. T. (504) 524-7033. - Ant - *070824*
Royal Company, 325 Royal St., New Orleans, LA 70130.
T. (504) 522-4552. - Ant - *070825*
Sloss, Nina, 6008 Magazine St., New Orleans, LA
70100. *070826*
Stern, Henry, 329 Royal St., New Orleans, LA 70130.
T. (504) 522-8687. - Ant / Paint / Graph / Furn / Orient /
China / Lights / Instr - *070827*
Waldhorn, 343 Royal St., New Orleans, LA 70130.
T. (504) 581-6379. - Ant / Furn / China / Jew /
Silv - *070828*
Winn, 4122 Magazine St., New Orleans, LA 70115.
- Ant / Furn / China / Fra / Instr / Glass - *070829*
Zwarr, Charles S., 1716 Milan St., POB 50994, New Or-
leans, LA 70115. T. (504) 899-2666. - Paint / Orient /
Instr / Ico - *070830*
305 Shop, 305 Chartres St., New Orleans, LA 70130.
T. (504) 525-0327. - Ant - *070831*

New Rochelle (New York)
Klein, Luce A., 310 North Ave., New Rochelle, NY
10801. T. (914) 576-2383. *070832*

New York
A A A A Antiques, 207 E 84 St., New York, NY 10028.
T. (212) 249-8108. *070833*
A B C Carpet, 888 Broadway, New York, NY 10003.
T. (212) 473-3000. *070834*
A D C Heritage, 965 Madison Av., New York, NY 10021.
T. (212) 734-5666. *070835*
A la Francaise, 125 E 57 St., New York, NY 10022.
T. (212) 223-2728. *070836*
A la Vieille Russie, 781 Fifth Av., New York, NY 10022.
T. (212) 752-1727. - Ant / Paint / Furn / China / Jew /
Silv / Instr - *070837*
Aaron, 1050 Second Av., New York, NY 10022.
T. (212) 644-5868. *070838*

Aaron, Didier, 32 E 67 St., New York, NY 10021.
T. (212) 988-5248, Fax (212) 737-3513. - Ant - *070839*
Abe, 815 Broadway, New York, NY 10003. T. (212) 260-
6424. *070840*
Abemayor, 125 E 57 St., New York, NY 10022.
T. (212) 371-4592. - Sculp - *070841*
Aberbach, 980 Fifth Av, New York, NY 10021.
T. (212) 988-1100. - Paint / Graph - *070842*
Abraham, Eleanor, 125 E 57 St, New York, NY 10022.
T. (212) 688-1667, Fax (212) 688-1667. *070843*
Accents Unlimited, 2211 Broadway, New York, NY
10024. T. (212) 799-7490. *070844*
Accents Unlimited, 360 Amsterdam Av., New York, NY
10024. T. (212) 580-8404. *070845*
Ackerman, 50 E. 57th St., New York, NY 1022.
T. (212) 752-5292. - Ant / Paint / Furn / China /
Lights - *070846*
Adelaide Boutique, 1658 Third Av., New York, NY 10128.
T. (212) 860-2161. *070847*
Agostino, 808 Broadway, New York, NY 10003.
T. (212) 533-3355. *070848*
Albino, William, 55 E 11 St., New York, NY 10003.
T. (212) 677-8820. *070849*
Aldega & Gordon, 137 W 66 St, New York, NY 10021.
T. (212) 988-2965, Fax (212) 517-8799. - Paint /
Graph - *070850*
Alessandro, Danny, 1159 2nd Ave., New York, NY
10021. T. (212) 421-9228. - Ant / Repr - *070851*
Alex Gallery, 11 E 57 St., New York, NY 10022.
T. (212) 486-3434, Fax (212) 223-4409. *070852*
Alexander, 34 E 10 St., New York, NY 10003.
T. (212) 228-7304. *070853*
Alexander., Marvin, 315 E. 62nd St., New York, NY
10021. T. (212) 838-2320. - Ant / Lights - *070854*
Alice's Antiques, 552 Columbus Ave, New York, NY
10024. T. (212) 874-3400. *070855*
Alice Underground, 481 Broadway, New York, NY 10013.
T. (212) 431-9067. *070856*
Allied International Products, 401 W 56 St., New York,
NY 10019. Fax (212) 697-6134. - Ant - *070857*
Altman, B., 361 5th Ave., New York, NY 10016.
T. (212) 689-7000. - Ant / Furn / Repr - *070858*
Altman, Robert, 1148 Second Ave, New York, NY 10021.
T. (212) 832-3490. *070859*
Altomare, Iris, 33-52 Crescent St., New York, NY
11106. *070860*
Amdur, Judith, 1148 Lexington Ave, New York, NY
10021. *070861*
America Hurrah, 766 Madison Av., New York, NY 10021.
T. (212) 535-1930, Fax (212) 249-9718. - Tex - *070862*
American Antiquo Firearms, 1359 Broadway, New York,
NY 10018. T. (212) 594-5390. *070863*
American Brilliant Cut Glass Company, 660 Bergen St,
New York, NY 11238. T. (212) 389-6777, 229-3420.
- Glass - *070864*
American Heritage Antiques, 213 W 22 St., New York,
NY 10011. T. (212) 242-0441. - Paint / Furn - *070865*
American Pastime, 240 Lafayette St., New York, NY
10012. T. (212) 966-8954. *070866*
Anand India Shop of Handicrafts and Arts, 30 Rockefel-
ler Plaza, Shop 11, New York, NY 10020. T. (212) 247-
2054. - Ant / Jew - *070867*
Ancient Art of the New World, 42 E 76 St., New York, NY
10021. T. (212) 737-3766. - Eth - *070868*
Ancient World Arts, 50 W 76 St., New York, NY 10023.
T. (212) 724-9455. - Arch - *070869*
Ann-Morris, 239 E 60 St., New York, NY 10022.
T. (212) 755-3308. *070870*
Ann's Art and Antique Gallery, 161 Ninth Av, New York,
NY 10011. T. (212) 675-9415. - Ant - *070871*
Antik Haus, 31 Bedford St., New York, NY 10014.
T. (212) 633-8642. *070872*
Antiquaire and The Connoisseur, 36 E 73 St., New York,
NY 10021. T. (212) 517-9176, Fax (212) 988-5674.
- Ant / Paint / Furn / China / Tex / Arch / Dec / Jew / Fra /
Rel / Draw - *070873*
Antiquarium, 948 Madison Av., New York, NY 10021.
T. (212) 734-9776. - Ant / Arch / Jew / Glass - *070874*
Antique Accents, 1159 Second Ave, New York, NY
10021. T. (212) 755-6540. - Ant - *070875*
Antique Boutique, 227 E 59 St., New York, NY 10022.
T. (212) 752-1680. *070876*

Antique Boutique, 712 Broadway, New York, NY 10003.
T. (212) 460-8830. *070877*
Antique Buff, 321 1/2 Bleecker St., New York, NY
10014. T. (212) 243-7144. *070878*
Antique Cache, 1050 Second Av., New York, NY 10022.
T. (212) 752-0838. *070879*
Antique City, 51 E Houston St., New York, NY 10012.
T. (212) 219-2069. *070880*
Antique Company of New York, 605 Park Av., Apt. 12A,
New York, NY 10021. T. (212) 758-2363. - Ant / Furn /
China / Jew / Lights - *070881*
Antique Fair, 28 E 12 St., New York, NY 10003.
T. (212) 255-1511. *070882*
Antique Indaica, 45 Essex St, New York, NY 10002.
T. (212) 674-1770. - Ant - *070883*
Antique Loft, 514 W 24 St., New York, NY 10011.
T. (212) 243-8625. *070884*
Antique Porcelain Company, 605 Park Av., Apt. 12A,
New York, NY 10021. - China - *070885*
Antique Rug Studio, 601 W 54 St., New York, NY 10019.
T. (212) 315-4308. *070886*
Antiques by Patrick, 77 E 10 St., New York, NY 10003.
T. (212) 254-8336. *070887*
Antiques Corner, 52 W 47 St., New York, NY 10036.
T. (212) 869-1411. *070888*
Antiques Market, 137 Ludlow St., New York, NY 10002.
T. (212) 674-9805. *070889*
Antorino, T.J., 152 E 70 St., New York, NY 10021.
T. (212) 628-4330. *070890*
Arader, Graham W., 29 E 72 St., New York, NY 10021.
T. (212) 628-3668. - Paint / Graph - *070891*
Ares, 961 Madison Ave, New York, NY 10021.
T. (212) 988-0190, Fax (212) 744-6961.
- Jew - *070892*
Ariadne Galleries, 970 Madison Av, New York, NY
10021. T. (212) 772-3388. - Num / Arch - *070893*
Arion, 1065 Madison Ave, New York, NY 10028.
T. (212) 772-1230. - Ant / China - *070894*
Art Asia, 1088 Madison Ave., New York, NY 10028.
T. (212) 249-7250. - Ant / Paint / Furn / Orient / China /
Repr / Sculp / Jew / Rel - *070895*
Art Trading, 305 E 61 St., Ste 101, New York, NY 10021.
T. (212) 752-2057. - China - *070896*
Artisan Antiques, 81 University Pl, New York, NY 10003.
T. (212) 353-3970. *070897*
Arts and Antiques, 200 E 57 St., New York, NY 10022.
T. (212) 644-3771. *070898*
Arts Land Carving, 21 Allen St., New York, NY 10002.
T. (212) 219-2016. *070899*
As-Is Antiques, 561 Hudson St., New York, NY 10014.
T. (212) 866-1891. *070900*
Asian Antique Center, 1050 Second Ave, New York, NY
10022. T. (212) 832-1330. *070901*
Asprey, 725 Fifth Ave, New York, NY 10022.
T. (212) 688-1811. - Jew - *070902*
Atlantic Importers Company, 90 University Pl, New York,
NY 10003. T. (212) 242-2158. - Ant - *070903*
Atlantic Importers of Antiques, 99 University Pl, New
York, NY 10003. T. (212) 674-8577. *070904*
Attic Treasures, 530 W 23 St., New York, NY 10011.
T. (212) 243-2684. *070905*
Back Pages Antiques, 125 Greene St., New York, NY
10012. T. (212) 460-5998. *070906*
Balot, Georges, 67 E 11 St., New York, NY 10003.
T. (212) 473-2925. *070907*
Bardith, 901 Madison Ave., New York, NY 10021.
T. (212) 737-3775. *070908*
Bargin Basement, 163 E 87 St., New York, NY 10128.
T. (212) 996-5593. *070909*
Baron, Clifford, 1050 Second Ave, New York, NY 10022.
T. (212) 752-4376. - Jew / Cur - *070910*
Barr-Gardner, 125 E 57 St., New York, NY 10022.
T. (212) 838-2415. - Ant - *070911*
Barry of Chelsea, 154 Ninth Ave, New York, NY 10011.
T. (212) 242-2666. *070912*
Bart, Betty Jane, 1225 Madison Ave, New York, NY
10128. T. (212) 410-2702. *070913*
Baruch Steinitz, Bernard, 125 E 57 St., New York, NY
10022. T. (212) 832-3711. - Ant / Furn - *070914*
Baudinet-Hubbard, 45 E 30 St., New York, NY 10016.
T. (212) 684-4475. *070915*
Beaujard, Jean Paul, 209 E. 76th St., New York, NY
10021. *070916*

Beggarstaff, 200 E. 63rd St., New York, NY 10021.
T. (212) 753-1378. - Ant / Furn / Lights -   070917
Beige, 119 Greenwich Ave, New York, NY 10014.
T. (212) 619-5488.   070918
Bell, Mike, 60 E 10 St., New York, NY 10003.
T. (212) 598-4677.   070919
Bellechasse Antiques, 125 E 57 St., New York, NY
10022. T. (212) 826-6680.   070920
Bellini, Philip, 423 W 55 St., New York, NY 10019.
T. (212) 581-3033.   070921
Benedict Bros. & Co., 80 Wall St., New York, NY 10005.
T. (212) 944-6467. - Num -   070922
Berenson, Ellen, 179 E 87 St., New York, NY 10128.
T. (212) 410-1771. - Ant / Paint / Furn / Orient / China /
Tex / Dec / Lights / Draw -   070923
Berkey, Addison, 318 E 51 St., New York, NY 10022.
T. (212) 935-5125. - Furn / Orient -   070924
Berkley, 899 First Ave., New York, NY 10022.
T. (212) 355-4050. - Furn / Repr -   070925
Berman, 221 W 82 St., New York, NY 10024.
T. (212) 362-0669. - Arch / Eth -   070926
Berman, Aaron, 660 E 19 St., New York, NY 11230.
T. (212) 757-7630. - Ant -   070927
Bernice, Richard, 5 E. 64th St., New York, NY
10021.   070928
Bernstein, David, 12 E 86 St., Ste 831, New York, NY
10028. T. (212) 898-5898. - Tex / Eth -   070929
Berry-Hill, 743 Fifth Ave, New York, NY 10022.
T. (212) 371-6777. - Paint -   070930
Beshar & Co., 611 Broadway, New York, NY 10012.
T. (212) 718-1400. - Tex -   070931
Best of Everything Collection, 148 E 70 St., New York,
NY 10021. T. (212) 472-0191.   070932
Better Times Antiques, 500 Amsterdam Ave., New York,
NY 10024. T. (212) 496-9001. - Furn -   070933
Bigel, Ruth, 743 Madison Av., New York, NY 10021.
T. (212) 988-3116. - Furn -   070934
Bijan Royal, 60 E 11 St., New York, NY 10003.
T. (212) 228-3757.   070935
Bittner, Marvin, 7410 35th Ave, New York, NY 11372.
T. (212) 898-3396. - Ant / China -   070936
Bizarre Bazaar Antiques, 125 E 57 St., New York, NY
10022. T. (212) 688-1830.   070937
Black, Bertha, 80 Thompson St., New York, NY 10012.
T. (212) 966-7116.   070938
Blantree & Co., 725 Fifth Av., New York, NY 10022.
T. (212) 223-2445.   070939
Blau, Doris Leslie, 15 E. 57th St., New York, NY 10022.
T. (212) 759-3715. - Tex -   070940
Blau, Vojtech, 800B Fifth Ave, New York, NY 10021.
T. (212) 249-4525. - Tex -   070941
Bloomrosen, 547 W 27 St., New York, NY 10001.
T. (212) 695-6578.   070942
Blum, 1050 Second Av., New York, NY 10022.
T. (212) 759-2055.   070943
Blumka, 101 E 81 St, New York, NY 10028. T. (212) 734-
3222. - Ant / Furn -   070944
Blumka II, 23 E 67 St., New York, NY 10021.
T. (212) 879-5611, Fax 772-1432. - Ant -   070945
Boerner, C.G., 61 E 77 St, New York, NY 10021.
T. (212) 772-7330. - Graph / Draw -   070946
Boisson, Judi, 4 E 82 St., New York, NY 10028.
T. (212) 734-5844.   070947
Boscardin, 1050 Second Av., New York, NY 10022.
T. (212) 980-3268.   070948
Brascomb & Schwab, 309 E Fifth St., New York, NY
10003. T. (212) 777-5363.   070949
Brass Antique Shoppe, 32 Allen St., New York, NY
10002. T. (212) 925-6600. - Ant -   070950
Braswell & Chase, 639 1/2 Hudson St., New York, NY
10014. T. (212) 727-7995.   070951
Brill, Stanley S., 110-20 71st Ave, New York, NY 11375.
- Ant -   070952
Brooks, Daniel, 150 E 77 St., New York, NY 10021.
T. (212) 861-3556.   070953
Brooks, Robert L., 235 E 53 St., New York, NY 10022.
- Mil / Glass -   070954
Broomer, A.R., 125 E 57 St., New York, NY 10022.
T. (212) 421-9530. - China -   070955
Brower, David, 1050 Second Av., New York, NY 10022.
T. (212) 755-2921.   070956
Brown, Iris, 253 E 57 St., New York, NY 10022.
T. (212) 593-2882.   070957

Burke, 979 Third Av., New York, NY 10022. T. (212) 308-
7551.   070958
Burlington, 1082 Madison Av., New York, NY 10028.
T. (212) 861-9708.   070959
Caldonia Antiques, 1685 Third Av., New York, NY 10128.
T. (212) 534-3307.   070960
Campbell, Vivian, 408 W. 20th, New York, NY 10011.
- Ant / Paint / Graph / Sculp / Mod / Pho / Draw -   070961
Cano, 721 Fifth Av, New York, NY 10022. T. (212) 832-
8172, Fax (212) 370-9250. - Arch -   070962
Capo Dacqua, 123 Fourth Av., New York, NY 10003.
T. (212) 353-9681.   070963
Carl, Victor, 55 E 13 St., New York, NY 10003.
T. (212) 673-8740.   070964
Caro, Frank, 41 E 57 St., New York, NY 10022.
T. (212) 753-2166. - Paint / Orient / Arch -   070965
Chait, Ralph M., 12 E 56 St., New York, NY 10022.
T. (212) 758-0937, Fax (212) 319-0471. - Orient /
Arch -   070966
Chan, 273 Fifth Av., New York, NY 10016. T. (212) 686-
8668.   070967
Charles & Co., The Plaza, 5 Ave at 59th St., New York,
NY 10019. T. (212) 421-7307.   070968
Charterhouse Antiques, 115 Greenwich Av., New York,
NY 10011. T. (212) 243-4726.   070969
Cheap Jack's, 841 Broadway, New York, NY 10003.
T. (212) 777-9564.   070970
Chelsea Mews Antiques, 415 W. 21st St., New York, NY
10011. - Ant -   070971
Chen & Chen, 64A Bayard St, New York, NY 10013.
T. (212) 226-1158.   070972
Cherchez Antiques and Potpourri, 862 Lexington Av.,
New York, NY 10021. T. (212) 737-8215.   070973
Cheriff, Charles, 84 University Pl., New York, NY 10003.
T. (212) 675-6131. - Ant / Furn / China / Sculp / Lights /
Instr / Glass -   070974
China House of Arts, 1100 Madison Av., New York, NY
10028. T. (212) 794-9652.   070975
China Importing Company, 28 E 10 St., New York, NY
10003. T. (212) 995-0800.   070976
Chinese Arts and Antiques, 848 Broadway, New York, NY
10003. T. (212) 473-7684.   070977
Chinese Porcelain Company, 475 Park Av, New York, NY
10022. T. (212) 838-7744, Fax (212) 838-4922.
- Orient / China -   070978
Chodoff, Christopher, 400 E 59 St., New York, NY 10022.
T. (212) 355-7110.   070979
Christofle Silver, 55 E. 57th St., New York, NY 10022.
T. (212) 688-0535. - Silv -   070980
Circa 1890, 265 E. 78th St., New York, NY 10021.
T. (212) 734-7388. - Ant -   070981
Circle Gallery, 725 Fifth Av, New York, NY 10022.
T. (212) 980-5455. - Jew -   070982
Claiborne, 136 W 18 St., New York, NY 10011.
T. (212) 727-7219.   070983
Cleopatra Antiques and Jewelry, 10A W 47th St, New
York, NY 10036. T. (212) 575-9616. - Ant /
Jew -   070984
Coates, Ruth, 530 E 19th St, New York, NY 11226.
- Ant -   070985
Cobweb, 116 W Houston St., New York, NY 10012.
T. (212) 505-1558.   070986
Coen, Joel D., 39 W 55 St., New York, NY 10019.
T. (212) 246-5025. - Num -   070987
Coin Galleries, 123 W 57 St., New York, NY 10019.
T. (212) 582-5955. - Num -   070988
Colnaghi, 21 E 67 St, New York, NY 10021. T. (212) 772-
2266. - Paint / Draw -   070989
Colville, Thomas, 1000 Madison Av, New York, NY
10021. T. (212) 879-9259. - Paint / Draw -   070990
Connor-Rosenkranz, 251 E 84 St., New York, NY 10028.
T. (212) 517-3710. - Sculp -   070991
Corallo, 86 Bowery, New York, NY 10013. T. (212) 966-
3749. - Jew -   070992
Corporate Art Associates, 270 Lafayette St, New York,
NY 10012. T. (212) 941-9685. - Paint -   070993
Cotswold, 1566 Second Av., New York, NY 10028.
T. (212) 472-0701.   070994
Covered Bridge Antiques, 60 First Av., New York, NY
10009. T. (212) 674-1675.   070995
Crider, Norman, 725 Fifth Av., New York, NY 10022.
T. (212) 832-6958.   070996

Criswick, 325 E 41th St, New York, NY 10017.
T. (212) 490-2337. - Paint -   070997
Cross Keys Antiques, 64 E 13 St., New York, NY 10003.
T. (212) 473-2087.   070998
Cullen, Richard L., 229 E 11 St., New York, NY 10003.
T. (212) 460-8758.   070999
Cumming, Rose, 232 E 59 St, New York, NY 10022.
- Ant / Paint / Graph / Furn / Orient / China / Sculp / Tex /
Dec / Lights / Rel / Glass -   071000
C.W.W. Toys, 69 Thompson St., New York, NY 10012.
T. (212) 941-9129.   071001
Cyn Thai Arts and Antiques, 505 Fifth Av, New York, NY
10017. T. (212) 697-0792. - Eth -   071002
D'Auria, P., 155 Canal St., New York, NY 10013. - Jew /
Silv -   071003
Daedalus Ancient Art, 41 E 57 St., New York, NY 10022.
T. (212) 758-6007, Fax 832-0448. - Arch -   071004
Dalva Brothers, 44 E 57 St., New York, NY 10022.
T. (212) 758-2297. - Paint / Furn / China / Sculp / Tex /
Instr -   071005
Dampierre, Florence de, 79 Greene St., New York, NY
10012. T. (212) 966-1357.   071006
Davis, 29 W 47 St., New York, NY 10036. T. (212) 819-
0985.   071007
Dawson, Howard, 117 Greenwich Av., New York, NY
10014. T. (212) 675-7580.   071008
Deak & Co., 29 Broadway, New York, NY 10004.
T. (212) 425-6789. - Num -   071009
Dealers Den, 578 5th Ave, New York, NY 10036.
T. (212) 575-8180.   071010
Deco Deluxe, 125 E 57 St., New York, NY 10022.
T. (212) 751-3326. - Mod -   071011
Deco Jewels, 375 W Broadway, New York, NY 10012.
T. (212) 941-1468.   071012
Deglin, Didi, 75-28 Juniper Blvd.S, New York, NY 11379.
T. (212) 894-7773.   071013
Delbanco, 9 E 82 St., New York, NY 10028. T. (212) 861-
5936. - Paint -   071014
Delorenzo, 958 Madison Av., New York, NY 10021.
T. (212) 249-7575.   071015
Den of Antiquity, 108 MacDougal St., New York, NY
10012. T. (212) 475-6888. - Ant / Jew -   071016
Depression Modern, 135 Sullivan St., New York, NY
10012. T. (212) 982-5699.   071017
Deux, Pierre, 369 Bleecker St., New York, NY 10014.
T. (212) 243-7740. - Ant -   071018
Devenish & Co., 929 Madison Av, New York, NY 10021.
T. (212) 535-2888. - Ant / Furn -   071019
Dickinson, Simon, 14 E 73 St, New York, NY 10021.
T. (212) 772-8083, Fax (212) 772-8186.   071020
Dildarian, 595 Madison Av., New York, NY 10022.
T. (212) 288-4948. - Tex -   071021
Dixon, Prentice J., 1036 Lexington Av., New York, NY
10021. T. (212) 249-0458.   071022
Doge, 215 E 58 St., New York, NY 10022. T. (212) 758-
2770.   071023
Donahue, J. Barry, 118 E 82 St., New York, NY
10028.   071024
Dorar, 95 Canal St., New York, NY 10002. T. (212) 966-
3301, Fax 966-2490. - Ant -   071025
Doyle, William, 175 E 87 St, New York, NY 10028.
T. (212) 427-2730, Fax (212) 369-0892. - Ant / Paint /
Furn / China / Tex / Jew / Silv / Lights -   071026
Draper & Draper, 200 Lexington Av., New York, NY
10016. T. (212) 679-0547.   071027
Drey, Paul, 11 E 57 St, New York, NY 10022.
T. (212) 753-2551, Fax (212) 838-0339. - Ant / Paint /
Sculp / Draw -   071028
Dubrow, POB 128, New York, NY 11361. T. (212) 767-
9758. - Furn -   071029
Duncan, David, 232 E 59 St., New York, NY 10022.
T. (212) 688-0666.   071030
Dynasty Gallery, 111 E 56 St., New York, NY 10022.
T. (212) 758-2763.   071031
Eagles Antiques, 1097 Madison Av., New York, NY
10028. T. (212) 772-3266. - Furn -   071032
East Side House Settlement, 337 Alexander Ave, New
York, NY 10454. T. (212) 292-7392. - Ant -   071033
Eccentrix, 529 Broome St., New York, NY 10013.
T. (212) 941-5917.   071034
Eclectiques, 483 Broome St., New York, NY 10013.
T. (212) 966-0650.   071035

Edelman, Louis, 1140 Broadway at 26th St, New York, NY 10001. T. (212) 683-4266. - Paint / Fra - *071036*

Edo, 67 E 11 St., New York, NY 10003. T. (212) 254-2508. *071037*

Ellington, 93 University Pl., New York, NY 10003. T. (212) 686-6247. - Ant / Paint / Paint / Furn / Orient / China / Repr / Silv / Instr- *071038*

Elliott, 155 E 79 St., New York, NY 10021. T. (212) 861-2222. *071039*

Ellsworth, R.H., 960 Fifth Ave., New York, NY 10021. T. (212) 535-9249. - Orient- *071040*

Emporium Antique Shop, 20 W 64 St., New York, NY 10023. T. (212) 724-9521. *071041*

Engel, Paul, 515 West End Ave., New York, NY 10022. - Ant - *071042*

Evergreen Antiques, 1249 Third Av., New York, NY 10021. T. (212) 744-5664. *071043*

Evergreen Antiques, 120 Spring St., New York, NY 10012. T. (212) 966-6458. *071044*

Faber Donoughe, 201 W 89 St., New York, NY 10024. T. (212) 873-5882. - Sculp- *071045*

Fair, Anthony, 146 E 74 St., New York, NY 10021. T. (212) 772-6338. - Graph / Draw - *071046*

Fairfield, 1166 Second Ave., New York, NY 10021. - Ant / Paint / Furn / China / Instr- *071047*

Far Eastern Antiques and Arts, 799 Broadway, New York, NY 10003. T. (212) 460-5030. *071048*

Far Eastern Arts, 225 Fifth Av., New York, NY 10010. T. (212) 889-3414. - Ant / Furn / Orient / China / Repr / Sculp / Tex / Arch / Eth / Dec / Jew / Mil / Rel / Cur-- *071049*

Farhadi, Nuri, 920 Third Av., New York, NY 10022. T. (212) 355-5462. - Orient / Sculp - *071050*

Farhadi & Anavian, 920 Third Av., New York, NY 10022. T. (212) 752-1930. - Ant / Orient / China / Arch - *071051*

Farley, Philippe, 157 E 64 St., New York, NY 10021. T. (212) 472-1622. - Ant - *071052*

F.D.R. Drive, 109 Thompson St., New York, NY 10012. T. (212) 966-4827. *071053*

Feigen, Richard L., & Co., 49 E 68 St., New York, NY 10021. T. (212) 628-0700, Fax 249-4574. - Paint / Sculp / Draw - *071054*

Feinberg, Michael, 225 Fifth Av., New York, NY 10010. T. (212) 532-0311. - Ant / Repr / Jew / Silv- *071055*

Felicie, 141 E 56 St., New York, N.Y. 10022. T. (212) 752-7567. - Paint / Graph / Tex / Mod / Draw - *071056*

Ferber, Benjamin, 351 E. 54th St., New York, NY 10022. - Ant / Paint / Furn - *071057*

Fifty-50, 793 Broadway, New York, NY 10003. T. (212) 777-3208. *071058*

Finchera, Lou, 50 University Pl., New York, NY 10003. *071059*

Findlay, Mimi, 177 E 87 St., New York, NY 10128. T. (212) 410-5920. *071060*

Fine Arts of Ancient Lands, 12 E 86 St, New York, NY 10028. T. (212) 249-7442. - Arch - *071061*

Fischzang, Isi, 29 W 47th St, New York, NY 10036. T. (212) 757-9465. *071062*

Fisher, Laura, 1050 Second Ave., New York, NY 10022. T. (212) 838-2596. *071063*

Fitch-Febvrel, 5 E 57 St, New York, NY 10022. T. (212) 688-8522. - Graph - *071064*

Flores, 67 E 11 St., New York, NY 10003. T. (212) 979-5461. *071065*

Flores And Iva Antiques, 799 Broadway, New York, NY 10003. T. (212) 673-1866. *071066*

Flying Cranes Antiques, 1050 Second Ave., New York, NY 10022. T. (212) 223-4600, Fax (212) 223-4601. - Orient - *071067*

Ford, Rita, 19 E 65, New York, NY 10021. T. (212) 535-6717. *071068*

Ford & Co., Laurence W., 578 Fifth Ave, New York, NY 10036. T. (212) 869-8600. - Jew - *071069*

Fortuna Fine Arts, 984 Madison Av, New York, NY 10021. T. (212) 794-7272, Fax (212) 794-7275. - Ant / Num - *071070*

Fortunoff, 681 Fifth Av., New York, NY 10022. T. (212) 758-6660. - Jew / Silv - *071071*

Foster, Gordon, 1322 Third Av, New York, NY 10021. T. (212) 744-4922. *071072*

Frankel, E. & J., 25 E 77 St, New York, NY 10021. T. (212) 879-5733, Fax (212) 879-1998. *071073*

Franklin, Malcolm, 15 E 57 St., New York, NY 10022. T. (212) 308-3344. - Instr - *071074*

Freeman & Son, I., 12 E 52 St., New York, NY 10022. T. (212) 759-6900. - Ant / Furn / China / Repr / Dec / Jew / Silv / Lights - *071075*

French & Co., 17 E 65 St., New York, NY 10021. T. (212) 535-3330, Fax 772-1756. - Ant - *071076*

Fried, Bernice, 1050 Second Ave., New York, NY 10022. *071077*

Funt, Patricia, 50 E 78 St., New York, NY 10021. T. (212) 772-2482. *071078*

Furgang, Sam, 137 Ludlow St., New York, NY 10002. T. (212) 475-5496. *071079*

Gagosian, 980 Madison Av, New York, NY 10021. T. (212) 744-2313. *071080*

Galerie Metropol, 927 Madison Av., New York, NY 10021. T. (212) 772-7401. - Ant / Paint / Furn / Mod - *071081*

GAllery 47, 1050 Second Ave., New York, NY 10022. T. (212) 888-0165. *071082*

Gander & White, 159 E 63 St., New York, NY 10021. T. (212) 888-1916. *071083*

Gem Antiques, 1088 Madison Av., New York, NY 10028. T. (212) 535-7399. - China - *071084*

Geneva Galleries, 1050 Second Ave., New York, NY 10022. T. (212) 355-3103. *071085*

George, David, 165 E 87 St., New York, NY 10028. T. (212) 860-3034. - Furn / Orient / China - *071086*

Georgian Manor Antiques, 305 E 61th St., New York, NY 10021. T. (212) 593-2520. *071087*

Gerena, Joseph G., 12 E 86 St., Ste 627, New York, NY 10028. T. (212) 650-0117. - Orient / Arch / Eth - *071088*

Gestas, Gilbert, 1015 Lexington Av., New York, NY 10021. T. (212) 744-5925. - Paint / Furn - *071089*

Ghiordian Knot, 136 E 57 St., New York, NY 10022-2707. T. (212) 371-6390. - Ant - *071090*

Giallo, Vito, 966 Madison Av., New York, NY 10021. T. (212) 535-9885. *071091*

Gingold, Robert, 95 E 10 St., New York, NY 10003. T. (212) 475-4008. *071092*

Ginsberg, Cora, 819 Madison Av, Apt 1A, New York, NY 10021. T. (212) 744-1352. - Tex - *071093*

Ginsburg, Benjamin, 815 Madisor Ave., New York, NY 10021. T. (212) 744-1352. - Ant / Paint / Graph / Furn / China / Fra / Silv / Lights / Instr - *071094*

Globe Overseas Company, 301 E. 63rd St., New York, NY 10021. - Ant / Furn / China / Lights - *071095*

Glover Price, 59 E 79 St., New York, NY 10021. T. (212) 772-1740. *071096*

Gluckselig, Kurt, 1050 Second Av., New York, NY 10022. T. (212) 758-1805. - Ant / Paint / Furn / China / Sculp / Tex / Eth / Lights / Rel / Glass / Draw - *071097*

Godel & Co., 969 Madison Av., New York, NY 10021. T. (212) 288-7272. *071098*

Goffman, Judy & Alan, 18 E 77 St., New York, NY 10021. T. (212) 744-5190. - Paint - *071099*

Gold Dolphin, 109 Lexington Av., New York, NY 10016. T. (212) 679-7455. *071100*

Gold Dust Memories, 386 Second Ave., New York, NY 10010. T. (212) 677-2590. *071101*

Good Old Things, 155 Lexington Av., New York, NY 10016. T. (212) 686-0788. *071102*

Gordon, John, 313 W. 57th St., New York, NY 10019. T. (212) 832-2255. - Ant / Paint / Furn / Num / Sculp / Eth / Pho - *071103*

Gorevic & Son, 635 Madison Av., New York, NY 10022. T. (212) 753-9319. *071104*

Gracie, & Sons, Charles R., 979 3rd Ave., New York, NY 10022. T. (212) 753-5350. - Ant / Furn / Orient - *071105*

Grafstein, James, 236 E. 60th St., New York, NY 10022. *071106*

Gramercy, 841 Broadway, New York, NY 10003. T. (212) 477-5656. *071107*

Gramercy Galleries, 52 E. 13th St., New York, NY 10003. T. (212) 477-5656. - Ant / Paint / Furn / China / Lights - *071108*

Greenspon, William, 465 West End Av., New York, NY 10024. T. (212) 787-2727. - Sculp - *071109*

Gross, Stephen, 400 Lafayette St., New York, NY 10003. T. (212) 777-8944. - Furn - *071110*

Guild Antiques II, 1095 Madison Av., New York, NY 10028. T. (212) 472-0830. - Furn / Orient / China - *071111*

Gunther-Watson, 107 E. 63rd St., New York, NY 10021. T. (212) 758-0286. - Ant / Num / Sculp / Tex / Instr- *071112*

Haber, Robert, 16 W 23 St., New York, NY 10010. T. (212) 243-3656, Fax (212) 727-9669. - Arch - *071113*

Hall, Michael, 49 E 82 St, New York, NY 10028. T. (212) 249-5053, Fax 249-5735. - Sculp / Ant / Paint / Dec / Draw - *071114*

Halpern, Renate, 325 E 79 St., New York, NY 10021. T. (212) 988-9316. - Tex - *071115*

Hancock, Eleanor T., 202 Riverside Dr., New York, NY 10025. T. (212) 866-5267. - Eth - *071116*

Hannan, Olive, 68-60 108th St. Forest Hills, New York, NY 11375. - Ant - *071117*

Harmer Rooke, 32 E 57 St., New York, NY 10022. T. (212) 751-1900. - Num - *071118*

Harootunian, O., & Sons, 315 E 62 St., New York, NY 10021. T. (212) 755-8222. - Tex - *071119*

Harris, B., & Sons, 25 E 61 St., New York, NY 10021. T. (212) 755-6455. *071120*

Harris, I.M., & Co., 667 Madison Av., Room 904, New York, NY 10022. T. (212) 755-6459. - Silv - *071121*

Hebrew Religious Articles, 45 Essex St., New York, NY 10002. T. (212) 674-1770. *071122*

Heidenberg, Lillian, 50 W 57 St, New York, NY 10019. T. (212) 586-3808. - Paint / Graph / Sculp / Tex / Mul / Draw - *071123*

Hellman, Nina, 35 Harris Rd., New York, NY 10536. T. (212) 232-7288. *071124*

Herrup & Wolfner, 12 E 86 St., New York, NY 10028. T. (212) 737-9051. - Tex - *071125*

Herrup & Wolfner, 328 Clinton St., New York, NY 11231. T. (212) 875-5295. - Tex - *071126*

Hill-Stone, New York POB 273, Gracie Station, NY 10028. T. (212) 249-1397, Fax (212) 861-4513. - Graph / Draw - *071127*

Hillman-Gemini, 743 Madison Av, New York, NY 10021. T. (212) 734-3262. *071128*

Hirschl & Adler, 21 E 70 St, New York, NY 10021. T. (212) 535-8810. - Ant / Paint / Graph / Sculp - *071129*

Hlinka, Peter, New York POB 310, NY 10028. T. (212) 369-1660. - Ant / Num / Mil - *071130*

Hoffman Gampetro, 125 E 57 St., Gallery 68, New York, NY 10022. T. (212) 755-1120. - China / Jew / Silv - *071131*

Hoffman, Jean, 236 E 80 St., New York, NY 10021. - Ant / Furn / Orient / China / Tex / Dec / Jew / Fra / Silv / Instr / Glass / Pho - *071132*

Hoffman, Ronald, 1050 Second Av., Shop 89, New York, NY 10022. *071133*

Horowicz, Nathan, 1050 Second Av., New York, NY 10022. T. (212) 755-6320. *071134*

House of Screens, 219 E 89 St., New York, NY 10028. - Orient - *071135*

Howell, Clinton, Pound Ridge, Box 254, New York, NY 10576. T. (914) 764-5168. *071136*

Hudson House Antiques, 555 Hudson St., New York, NY 10014. T. (212) 463-0350, 645-0353. *071137*

Hyde Park Antiques, 836 Broadway, New York, NY 10003-4899. T. (212) 477-0033, Fax (212) 477-1781. - Ant / Paint / Furn / China / Lights - *071138*

Isak, 1050 Second Av., New York, NY 10022. T. (212) 751-1133. *071139*

Jackson, Edwin, 306 E. 61st St. 2nd fl., New York, NY 10021. T. (212) 759 8210. *071140*

Jacobs Antiques, 810 Broadway, New York, NY 10003. T. (212) 673-4254. *071141*

Jacoby, Margot, 250 W. 94th St., New York, NY 10025. - Jew - *071142*

Jaffe, Sidney, 21 Allen St., New York, NY 10002. T. (212) 226-5965. *071143*

Janet, Christophe, 58 E 79 St., New York, NY 10021. T. (212) 734-0734. - Paint - *071144*

Janos and Ross, 110 East End Avenue, New York, NY 10028. T. (212) 988-0407. - Ant - *071145*

Jares, Jerry, 192 Columbus Av., New York, NY 10023. T. (212) 799-2095. *071146*

Jezebel, 630 Ninth Av., New York, NY 10036.
T. (212) 582-1045. *071147*
J.M.S. & Eva, 400 E 58 St., New York, NY 10022.
T. (212) 593-1113. *071148*
Johnson, Margot, 18 E 68, New York, NY 10021.
T. (212) 794-2225. *071149*
Joia Interiors, 149 E 60 St., New York, NY 10022.
T. (212) 759-1224. *071150*
Josie & Paul, 125 E 57 St., Gallery 8, New York, NY
10022. T. (212) 838-6841. - Jew - *071151*
Joslin, Douglas Le Roy, 102 Christopher St., New York,
NY 10014. T. (212) 2425713. *071152*
Judd & Judd, 419 E. 57th St., New York, NY 10022.
- Graph / Furn - *071153*
Kable, Claudia, 106 Macdougal St., New York, NY
10012. T. (212) 475-2114. *071154*
Kahane, Andrew, 42 E 76 St., New York, NY 10021.
T. (212) 861-5001, Fax 861-0788. - Orient - *071155*
Kander Group, 8 E 12 St., New York, NY 10003.
T. (212) 727-8080. *071156*
Kang, 24 E 81 St, New York, NY 10028. T. (212) 734-
1490, Fax (212) 734-6653. *071157*
Kaplan, Howard, 827 Broadway, New York, NY 10003.
T. (212) 674-1000. *071158*
Kaplan, Howard, 400 Bleecker St., New York, NY 10014.
T. (212) 741-2181. *071159*
Kaplan, Leo, 967 Madison Av., New York, NY 10021.
T. (212) 249-6766. - Glass - *071160*
Kapner, John Lee, 100 La Salle St., New York, NY
10027. T. (212) 666-4999. - Ant / Furn / China / Dec /
Lights / Instr / Glass - *071161*
Kapoor Curios + Art Palace, 1050 Second Ave., New
York, NY 10022. T. (212) 7553350. *071162*
Kassai, R. & P., 1050 Second Av., New York, NY 10022.
T. (212) 838-7010. *071163*
Kay, Frank, 232 E. 59th St., New York, NY 10022.
T. (212) 758 0917. - China - *071164*
Kelly, Sarah Hunter, 134 E. 71st St., New York, NY
10021. T. (212) 288 10004. *071165*
Kelter-Malcé, 361 Bleecker St., New York, NY 10014.
T. (212) 989-6760. *071166*
Kemp, Karl & Assoc., 29 E 10 St., New York, NY 10003.
T. (212) 254-1877. *071167*
Kennedy, 40 W 57 St, New York, NY 10019.
T. (212) 514-9600. - Paint - *071168*
Keno, Leigh, 19 E 74 St., New York, NY 10021.
T. (212) 734-2381. - Furn - *071169*
Kensington Place Antiques, 80 E 11 St., New York, NY
10003. T. (212) 533-7652. - Ant / Furn / Dec /
Instr - *071170*
Kentshire, 37 E 12 St., New York, NY 10003.
T. (212) 673-6644. *071171*
Kerne, Rene, 322 Bleecker St., New York, NY 10014.
T. (212) 727-3455. *071172*
Khayam, 1050 Second Av., New York, NY 10022.
T. (212) 751-0009. - Ant - *071173*
Kilian, Joseph H., 353 E 78 St., New York, NY 10021.
T. (212) 879-6332. - Silv - *071174*
Killen, David, 1777 First Av., New York, NY 10128.
T. (212) 860-4121. *071175*
Kimcherava, 290 Lafayette St., New York, NY 10012.
T. (212) 219-8136. *071176*
King, R.J., 370 Bleecker St., New York, NY 10014.
T. (212) 645-6978. *071177*
Klobe, Molly, 225 W 86 St, New York, NY 10024.
T. (212) 769-1725, Fax (212) 769-1725. *071178*
Kollitus, Constantine, 440 West 34th Street, New York,
NY 10001. T. (212) 7360947. - Silv - *071179*
Komor, Mathias, 19 E 71 St., New York, NY 10021.
T. (212) 879-3840. - Ant / Orient - *071180*
Koreana Art & Antiques, 963 Madison Av., New York, NY
10021. T. (212) 249-0400. *071181*
Korn, Betty, 1050 Second Av., New York, NY 10022.
T. (212) 759-3507. *071182*
Kretz, Gertrude „Magnificent Antiques", 3230 55th St.
Woodside, New York, NY 11377. T. (212) 278 1071.
- Ant / Paint / China - *071183*
Krex, Ira, Antiques, 240 East 56 St., New York, NY
10022. T. (212) 838-4310, 593-0805. - Ant / Furn / Chi-
na / Sculp / Lights / Instr - *071184*
Krishna Gallery, 125 E 57 St., Gallery 23, New York, NY
10022. T. (212) 688-7243. - Orient - *071185*

Krugier, Jan, 41 E 57 St., New York, NY 10022.
T. (212) 755-7288, Fax (212) 980-6079. *071186*
Kumar, Navin, 1001 Madison Av., New York, NY 10021.
T. (212) 734-4075. - Ant / Paint / Furn / Orient / Sculp /
Tex / Arch / Eth / Dec / Jew / Silv / Mil / Rel / Glass / Cur --
071187
Kurland- Zabar, 19 E 71 St., New York, NY 10021.
T. (212) 517-8576. - Furn / Silv - *071188*
Kwartler, Alice, 125 E 57 St., Gallery 26, New York, NY
10022. T. (212) 752-3590. - Silv - *071189*
L'Antiquaire & The Connoisseur, 36 E 73 St, New York,
NY 10021. T. (212) 517-9176. - Ant / Paint / Furn / Chi-
na / Sculp / Arch / Lights / Draw - *071190*
L'Art de Vivre, 978 Lexington Av., New York, NY 10021.
T. (212) 734-3510. *071191*
L'Ibis Gallery, 23 E 67 St, New York, NY 10021.
T. (212) 734-9229. - Arch - *071192*
La Raia Dom, 1050 Second Av., New York, NY 10022.
T. (212) 751-1983. *071193*
Lally, J.J., & Co., 42 E 57 St., New York, NY 10022.
T. (212) 371-3380. - Orient - *071194*
Lands Beyond, 1218 Lexington Ave., New York, NY
10028. T. (212) 249 6275. - Eth - *071195*
Lane, Eileen, 150 Thompson St., New York, NY 10012.
T. (212) 475-2988. *071196*
Lane, Raymond E., 305 E 61st St., New York, NY 10021.
T. (212) 752-2057, (212) 687-7576, Fax (212) 557-
1038. *071197*
Larsen, 1 Jane St., New York, NY 10014. T. (212) 645-
6434. *071198*
Lavezzo Inc., 205 E. 55th St., New York, NY 10022.
T. (212) 753 0896. - Ant - *071199*
Lawrence, Michael, 816 Broadway, New York, NY
10003. T. (212) 529-8444. *071200*
Loah's Gallery, 1050 Second Av., New York, NY 10022.
T. (212) 838-5590. *071201*
Lehr, Janet, 891 Park Av., New York, NY 10021.
T. (212) 288-6234. - Ant - *071202*
Lenox Court, 972 Lexington Av., New York, NY 10021.
T. (212) 772-2460. - Furn - *071203*
Leo Antiques, 2190 Broadway, New York, NY 10024.
T. (212) 799-6080. *071204*
Leonard, C.M., 1577 York Av., New York, NY 10028.
T. (212) 861-6821. *071205*
Leonard, D., & Gerry Trent, 950 Madison Ave., New York,
NY 10021. T. (212) 7379511. - Mod - *071206*
Levy, Bernard & S. Dean, 24 E 84 St., New York, NY
10028. T. (212) 628-7088. - Furn - *071207*
Limited Additions, 1050 Second Ave., New York, NY
10022. T. (212) 421-8132. *071208*
Limited Editions, 253 E. 72nd St., New York, NY 10021.
T. (212) 249 5563. - Ant / Furn / China / Dec / Lights /
Instr - *071209*
Lindenbaum, J., 1050 Second Av., New York, NY 10022.
T. (212) 751-4293. *071210*
Lindsay, 517 W 35 St., New York, NY 10001.
T. (212) 465-8800. *071211*
Linlo House, Inc., 1019 Lexington Ave., NY New York,
10021. T. (212) 288 1848. - Ant / Furn / China /
Lights - *071211a*
Little Shop of Antiques, 230 E 80 St., New York, NY
10021. T. (212) 861-6656. *071212*
Lord & Taylor, 424 5th Ave., New York, NY 10018.
T. (212) 947 3300. - Ant / Paint / Furn / Orient / Sculp /
Tex / Dec / Jew / Silv / Lights / Instr / Glass - *071213*
Lost City Art, 275 Lafayette St., New York, NY 10012.
T. (212) 941-8025. *071214*
Lotrow, Bernard, 475 Amsterdam Ave., New York, NY
10024. T. (212) 362 4665. - Ant - *071215*
Love, Harriet, 412 W Broadway, New York, NY 10013.
T. (212) 966-2280. *071216*
Lovelia Enterprises, New York POB 1845, Grand Central
Stat., NY 10017. T. (212) 490-0930. - Repr /
Tex - *071217*
Lubin, 30 W 26 St., New York, NY 10001. T. (212) 254-
1080. - Ant / Furn / China / Tex / Silv / Lights / Instr /
Glass - *071218*
Lucas, Phyllis, 981 Second Av, New York, NY 10022.
T. (212) 753-1441. - Ant / Paint / Graph / Orient / Repr /
Fra / Draw - *071219*
Lucy Anna Folk Art, 502 Hudson St., New York, NY
10014. T. (212) 645-9463. *071220*

Lune, 125 E 57 St., Galleries 71 & 87, New York, NY
10022. T. (212) 752-7732. - Ant / Paint - *071221*
Luther, H.M., 999 Madison Av., New York, NY 10021.
T. (212) 439-7919. - Furn - *071222*
Luther, H.M., 61 E 11 St., New York, NY 10003.
T. (212) 505-1485. *071223*
Lynn's Place, 571 Second Av., New York, NY 10016.
T. (212) 213-2989. *071224*
Madalynne Galleries, 1070 3rd Ave., New York, NY
10021. T. (212) 751 3820. *071225*
Madison Antiques, 1225 Madison Av., New York, NY
10128. T. (212) 348-2150. *071226*
Madison Galleries, 840 Broadway, New York, NY 10003.
T. (212) 529-5020. *071227*
Magner, D., 275 Lafayette St., New York, NY 10012.
T. (212) 966-2194. *071228*
Magni Import Co., 40 E 12 St., New York, NY 10003.
T. (212) 677-5652. *071229*
Magriel, Paul, 85 East End Avenue, New York, NY
10028. T. (212) 7375925. - Graph - *071230*
Malina, G., 680 Madison Av., New York, NY 10021.
T. (212) 593-0323. - Orient - *071231*
Man-Tiques, 1050 Second Av., New York, NY 10022.
T. (212) 759-1805. *071232*
Manhattan Art & Antiques Center, 1050 2nd Ave., New
York, NY 10022. - Ant / Paint / Furn / Num / Orient / Chi-
na / Sculp / Tex / Arch / Eth / Dec / Jew / Fra / Silv / Light-
s / Instr / Mil / Rel / Glass / Cur / Ico / Draw - *071233*
Manheim, D.M. & P., 305 E 61 St., New York, NY 10021.
T. (212) 758-2986. *071234*
Manic, Robert, 125 E 57 St., Gallery 15, New York, NY
10022. T. (212) 735-6650. - Jew - *071235*
Maqam, 19 W 55 St., Ste. 6A, New York, NY 10019.
T (212) 077 0003. - Ant - *071236*
Marco Polo Antiques, 1135 Madison Av., New York, NY
10128. T. (212) 734-3775. *071237*
Marine and Collections, 125 E 57 St., Gallery 84, New
York, NY 10022. T. (212) 755-0782. - Paint / Orient /
China - *071238*
Marquit, Andrea, 300 E 57 St., New York, NY 10022.
T. (212) 980-1717. - Paint / Sculp / Pho / Mul /
Draw - *071239*
Martell, 53 E 10 St., New York, NY 10003. T. (212) 777-
4360. *071240*
Martin, Mary-Anne, 23 E 73 St, New York, NY 10021.
T. (212) 288-2213, Fax (212) 861-7656. - Paint /
Graph / Draw - *071241*
Martin, Paul, 833 Broadway, New York, NY 10003.
T. (212) 982-5050. *071242*
Maslow, Louis & Son, 979 3rd Ave., New York, NY
10022. - Furn - *071243*
Mathieson, Joel, 190 Avenue of the Americas, New York,
NY 10013. T. (212) 966-7332. *071244*
Mattia, Louis, 980 Second Av., New York, NY 10022.
T. (212) 753-2176. *071245*
Mavec, J., & Co., 52 E 76 St., New York, NY 10021.
T. (212) 517-8822. - Jew / Silv - *071246*
Mazoh & Co, Stephen, 67 E 93 St., New York, NY 10128.
T. (212) 289-0606, Fax (212) 289-5991. - Paint /
Draw - *071247*
McNeil, Elise, 509 Madison Av., New York, NY 10022.
T. (212) 753-7153. *071248*
M.E. Collection, 12 W 57 St., New York, NY 10019.
T. (212) 315-3010. *071249*
Merrin, 724 Fifth Av, New York, NY 10019. T. (212) 757-
2884. - Arch / Eth - *071250*
Metro, 80 E 11 St., New York, NY 10003. T. (212) 673-
3510. - Furn / Sculp / Rel - *071251*
Metropol, Galerie, 927 Madison Av., New York, NY
10021. T. (212) 7727-401. - Ant / Paint / Furn /
Mod - *071252*
Metropolitan Antiques Pavilion, 110 W 19 St, New York,
NY 10011. T. (212) 463-0200, Fax (212) 463-7099.
- Graph - *071253*
Meyans, Susana, 1050 Second Av., New York, NY
10022. T. (212) 888-0728. *071254*
Michael's Antiques & Jewelry, 1050 Second Av., New
York, NY 10022. T. (212) 838-8780. *071255*
Midtown Antiques, 812 Broadway, New York, NY 10003.
- Ant / Furn / Dec / Lights - *071256*
Miller, Steve, 17 E 96 St., New York, NY 10128.
T. (212) 348-5219. - Paint / Sculp - *071257*

Milne, Judy & James, 524 E 73 St., New York, NY
10021. T. (212) 472-0107. *071258*
Mirviss, Joan B., POB 1095, New York, NY 10023.
T. (212) 799-4021. - Orient - *071259*
Mitchell, Ellin, 535 Park Av., New York, NY 10021.
T. (212) 688-9861. - Ant / Furn - *071260*
Mokotoff, 584 Broadway, New York, NY 10012.
T. (212) 941-1901. - Orient - *071261*
Monde Magique, 125 E 57 St., Gallery 47, New York, NY
10022. T. (212) 755-4120. - Ant - *071262*
Monleon, Leonore, 1050 Second Av., New York, NY
10022. T. (212) 838-0825. *071263*
Montaperto, Angelo L., 262 Mott St., New York, NY
10012. T. (212) 226-4991. *071264*
Mood Indigo, 181 Prince St., New York, NY 10012.
T. (212) 254-1176. *071265*
Morceaux Choisis, 1050 Second Av., New York, NY
10022. T. (212) 888-0657. *071266*
Moriah, 699 Madison Av., New York, NY 10021.
T. (212) 751-7090. *071267*
Moss, Alan, 88 Wooster St., New York, NY 10012.
T. (212) 219-1663. *071268*
Moss, Alan, 20 E 17 St., New York, NY 10003.
T. (212) 243-4176. *071269*
Moss, Charlotte, & Co., 131 E 70 St., New York, NY
10021. T. (212) 772-3320. - Furn - *071270*
Mottahedeh & Co., 225 Fifth Av., New York, NY 10010.
T. (212) 685-3050. - China - *071271*
Myers, Robert J., Lenox Hill, New York POB 442, NY
10021. T. (212) 249-8085. - Num / Arch - *071272*
Nacht, Bernard, & CO., 29 W 47 St., New York, NY
10036. T. (212) 398-1673. - Jew - *071273*
Nadler, 643 Park Av., New York, NY 10021. T. (212) 570-
4927. *071274*
Naga, 145 E 61 St., New York, NY 10021. T. (212) 593-
2788, Fax 308-2451. - Orient - *071275*
Nassau, Lilian, 220 E 57 St., New York, NY 10022.
T. (212) 759-6062. - Ant / Furn / China - *071276*
Natale, Peter de, 170 Broadway, New York, NY 10038.
- Jew - *071277*
Naumann, Otto, 4 E 74 St., New York, NY 10021.
T. (212) 734-4443, Fax (212) 535-0617.
- Paint - *071278*
Neikrug, 224 E 68 St., New York, NY 10021.
T. (212) 288-7741. - Pho - *071279*
Nelson & Nelson, 1050 Second Av., New York, NY
10022. T. (212) 980-5191. *071280*
Nesle, 151 E 57 St., New York, NY 10022. T. (212) 755-
0515. - Ant / Repr / Lights - *071281*
Newel, 425 E 53 St., New York, NY 10022. T. (212) 758-
1970. - Ant / Furn - *071282*
Night Gallery, 328 W 44 St., New York, NY 10036.
T. (212) 315-3165. *071283*
Nusraty, 215 W 10 St., New York, NY 10014.
T. (212) 691-1012. *071284*
Oaksmiths, 1321 Second Av., New York, NY 10021.
T. (212) 535-1451. *071285*
Objets Plus, 315 E 62 St., New York, NY 10021.
T. (212) 832-3386. *071286*
Old Horizons Antiques, 176 Bleecker St., New York, NY
10014. T. (212) 675-7431. *071287*
Old Print Center, 981 Second Av., New York, NY 10022.
T. (212) 755-1516. - Graph - *071288*
Old Print Shop, 150 Lexington Av, New York, NY 10016.
T. (212) 686-2111. - Paint / Graph - *071289*
Old Versailles, 315 E 62 St., New York, NY 10021.
T. (212) 421-3663. *071290*
Oliphant & Co., 360 E 55 St., New York, NY 10022.
T. (212) 935-6324. - Paint - *071291*
Olivieri, 306 E 61 St., New York, NY 10021. T. (212) 838-
7281. - Ant / Furn / Dec - *071292*
Oriental Decorations, 260 E 72 St., New York, NY 10021.
T. (212) 535-3278. *071293*
Orientations Gallery, 125 E 57 St, Gallery 22, New York,
NY 10022. T. (212) 371-9006, Fax (212) 371-9388.
- Orient - *071294*
Ottin, Michael, 305 E 61 St., New York, NY 10021.
T. (212) 355-1922. *071295*
Pace, 32 E 57 St., New York, NY 10022. T. (212) 421-
3688. - Arch / Eth - *071296*
Paladin Trading, 305 E 61 St., New York, NY 10021.
T. (212) 644-3949. *071297*

Palimpsest, 163A E 87 St., New York, NY 10028.
T. (212) 831-1198. - Paint / Graph / Furn / Sculp / Instr /
Glass - *071298*
Pan-Asia Gallery, 145 E 72 St., New York, NY 10021.
T. (212) 472-1737. - Orient - *071299*
Pan, L. S., 635 Riverside Dr., New York, NY 10031.
T. (212) 862-5883. *071300*
Panache Antiques, 525 Hudson St., New York, NY
10014. T. (212) 242-5115. *071301*
Pantry & Hearth, 121 E 35 St., New York, NY 10016.
T. (212) 889-0026. *071302*
Papp, Florian, 962 Madison Av., New York, NY 10021.
T. (212) 288-6770. - Ant / Furn / China - *071303*
Paracelso, 414 W Broadway, New York, NY 10012.
T. (212) 966-4232. *071304*
Park Temple, 125 E 57 St., Gallery 13, New York, NY
10022. T. (212) 752-1706. - Jew - *071305*
Parrish, Susan, 390 Bleecker St., New York, NY 10014.
T. (212) 645-5020. *071306*
Partridge, Gail, 96 Morton St., New York, NY 10014.
T. (212) 645-7088. *071307*
Pascoe & Solomon, 1122 Madison Av., New York, NY
10028. T. (212) 535-5200. - Ant - *071308*
Pasquale, Joy de, 117 E 77 St., New York, NY 10021.
T. (212) 737-6714. *071309*
Pillowry, 19 E 69 St., New York, NY 10021. T. (212) 628-
3844. *071310*
Pine Country Antiques, 42 E 12 St., New York, NY
10003. T. (212) 529-3480. *071311*
Pines, Sylvia, 1102 Lexington Av., New York, NY 10021.
T. (212) 744-5141. *071312*
Pinkus, E. Antiques, Inc., 420 West End Ave., New York,
NY 10024. T. (212) 724 7045. - Ant / Paint / Graph /
Furn / China - *071313*
Piston's, 1050 – 2ND AVE., New York, NY 10022.
T. (212) PL 3 8322. - Ant - *071314*
Place des Antiquaires, 125 E 57 St., New York, NY
10022. T. (212) 758-2900. *071315*
Place on Second Avenue Antiques, 175 2nd Ave., New
York, NY 10003. T. (212) 475 6597. - Ant /
Furn - *071316*
Pony Circus Antiques, 476 Broadway, New York, NY
10013. T. (212) 925-7589. *071317*
Portela, Juan, 138 E 71 St., New York, NY 10021.
T. (212) 650-0085. - Paint / Furn / Tex - *071318*
Posner Antiques, 2216 Avenue L., New York, NY 11210.
T. (212) 3770035. - Ant - *071319*
Potts, Trevor, 1011 Lexington Av., New York, NY 10021.
T. (212) 737-0909. - Paint / Furn - *071320*
Primavera Gallery, 808 Madison Av., New York, NY
10021. T. (212) 288-1569. - Ant / Graph / Furn / China /
Tex / Jew / Silv / Lights / Instr / Glass / Draw - *071321*
Provence de Pierre Deux, La, 353 Bleecker St., New
York, NY 10014. T. (212) 6754054. *071322*
Pryor, Bob, 1023 Lexington Av., New York, NY 10021.
T. (212) 688-1516. - Ant / Cur - *071323*
Quorum Antiques, 125 E 57 St., Gallery 58, New York,
NY 10022. T. (212) 752-3354. - China / Glass - *071324*
Rafael Gallery, 1020 Madison Ave., New York, NY
10021. T. (212) 7448660. - Tex *071325*
Raphael, M., 1050 Second Av., New York, NY 10022.
T. (212) 838-0178. - Silv - *071326*
Reflections, 232 E 78 St., New York, NY 10021.
T. (212) 472-8989. *071327*
Regal Collection, 5 W 56 St., New York, NY 10022.
T. (212) 582-7696. *071328*
Renée Antiques, 8 E 12 St., New York, NY 10003.
T. (212) 929-6870. - Ant / Furn / China / Sculp / Lights /
Glass - *071329*
Reymer-Jourdan, 43 E 10 St., New York, NY 10003.
T. (212) 674-4470. *071330*
Roberts, Peter, 134 Spring St., New York, NY 10012.
T. (212) 226-4777. *071331*
Robinson, James, 15 E 57 St., New York, NY 10022.
T. (212) 752-6166. - Jew - *071332*
Roedler, Stephen, 433 E. 51st St., New York, NY
10022. *071333*
Rondina, Joseph, 27 E. 62nd St., New York, NY 10021.
T. (212) 758 2182. - Ant / Graph / Furn / Orient / China /
Lights / Instr - *071334*
Roselle's Antiques, 158 E. 30th St., New York, NY
10016. T. (212) 864 0773. *071335*

Rosenau, Siegfried, 25 E. 83rd St., New York, NY 10028.
- Ant / Furn / China - *071336*
Rosenberg & Stiebel, 32 E 57 St, New York, NY 10022.
T. (212) 753-4368. - Ant / Paint / Furn / China / Sculp /
Draw - *071337*
Rosenblatt Ltd., Minna, 816 Madison Ave., New York, NY
10002. *071338*
Rosselli, John, 255 E 72 St., New York, NY 10021.
- Ant / Furn / Orient / China / Repr / Lights - *071339*
Rothschild, Sigmund, 27 W 67 St., New York, NY 10023.
T. (212) 873-5522. *071340*
Royal Antiques, 46 E. 11th St., New York, NY 10003.
T. (212) 533 6390. *071341*
Royal-Athena Galleries, 153 E 57 St., New York, NY
10021. T. (212) 355-2034, Fax 688-0412. - Num /
Orient / Sculp / Arch / Eth / Draw - *071342*

Royal Athena Galleries, 153 E 57 St, New York, NY
10022. T. (212) 355-2034. - Num / Orient / Sculp /
Arch / Eth / Draw - *071343*
Royal Marks Gallery, 29 E. 64th St., New York, NY
10021. T. (212) 861 3400. - Ant / Furn / China / Arch /
Jew / Glass / Cur - *071344*
R.S. Antiques, 13 Christopher St., New York, NY 10014.
T. (212) 924-5777. *071345*
Rudert, Anton, Jr., 30 E. 42nd St., New York, NY 10017.
T. (212) 661 0595. *071346*
Rug Loft, The, 845 Lexington Av., New York, NY 10021.
- Tex - *071347*
Ruseau, Don, Inc., 413 E. 53rd St., New York, NY 10022.
T. (212) 753 0876. - Ant / Furn - *071348*
Russissimoff, 125 E 57 St., Gallery 27, New York, NY
10022. T. (212) 752-1284. - Furn / Sculp - *071349*
Sack, Florence, 813 Broadway, New York, NY 10003.
T. (212) 777-2967. *071350*
Sack, Israel, 15 E 57 St., New York, NY 10022.
T. (212) 753-6562. - Furn - *071351*
Safani, 960 Madison Av., New York, NY 10021.
T. (212) 570-6360. - Ant / Arch - *071352*

Salander-O'Reilly, 20 E 79 St., New York, NY 10021.
T. (212) 879-6606, Fax (212) 744-0655. - Paint /
Sculp / Fra / Mod / Draw - 071353
Salvage Barn, 523 Hudson St., New York, NY 10014.
T. (212) 929-5787. 071354
Sands, Nicholas J., POB 893, New York Lenox Hill Sta-
tion, NY 10021. - Paint / Graph / Sculp / Mul /
Draw - 071355
Sanford & Patricia Smith, 1045 Madison Ave., New
York, NY 10021. - Ant / Paint / Furn / Sculp / Eth - 071356
Saphire Galleries, 15 W 55 St., New York, NY 10019.
T. (212) 247-8110. 071357
Schaeffer, 983 Park Av, New York, NY 10028.
T. (212) 535-6410. - Paint / Graph - 071358
Schaeffer, Martha, 500 E 77 St., Suite 512, New York,
NY 10162. T. (212) 794-9712. - Ant - 071359
Schiller & Bodo, 19 E 74 St, New York, NY 10021.
T. (212) 772-8627, Fax (212) 535-5943. - Paint /
Sculp - 071360
Schlesch, Arne V. and Jose Juarez Garza, 158 East 64th
St., New York, NY 10021. T. (212) 8383923. 071361
Schneider, Max & Son, 225 E. 24th St., New York, NY
10010. T. (212) 369 2065. - Ant - 071362
Schoellkopf, George E., 1065 Madison Av., New York, NY
10028. T. (212) 879-3672. - Ant / Paint / Furn /
Tex - 071363
Schorsch, David A., 30 E 76 St., New York, NY 10021.
T. (212) 439-6100. - Paint / Furn / Sculp / Tex - 071364
Schultz, Frederick, 41 E 57 St, New York, NY 10022.
T. (212) 758-6007, Fax (212) 832-0448. 071365
Schutz, Matthew, 1025 Park Av., New York, NY 10028.
T. (212) 876-4195. 071366
Second Childhood, 283 Bleecker St., New York, NY
10014. T. (212) 989-6140. 071367
Second Coming, 72 Greene St., New York, NY 10012.
T. (212) 431-4424. 071368
Seidenberg, David, 836 Broadway, New York, NY
10003. 071369
Settel, Joyce, 124 E 93 St., New York, NY 10128.
T. (212) 996-0641. 071370
Shepherd, 21 E 84 St, New York, NY 10028.
T. (212) 861-4050, 744-3392, Fax (212) 772-1314.
- Paint / Sculp / Fra / Draw - 071371
Shickman, H., 980 Madison Av, New York, NY 10021.
T. (212) 249-3800. - Paint / Graph / Sculp /
Draw - 071372
Shrubsole, S. J., 104 E 57 St., New York, NY 10022.
T. (212) 753 8920. - Silv - 071373
Siegel, Paul, 808 Broadway, New York, NY 10003.
T. (212) 533 5566. - Ant - 071374
Silberman, Fred, 83 Wooster St., New York, NY 10012.
T. (212) 925-9470. 071375
Silver Eagle Gallery, 1050 Second Av., New York, NY
10022. T. (212) 751-3213. 071376
Simon, 230 Fifth Av., New York, NY 10001. T. (212) 779-
7306. 071377
Simpson Merton, D., 1063 Madison Av, New York, NY
10028. T. (212) 988-6290. - Paint / Sculp / Arch /
Eth - 071378
Skala, Jan, 1 W 47 St., New York, NY 10036.
T. (212) 246-2942, 246-2814. - Jew / Instr - 071379
Small Pleasures, 1050 Second Av., New York, NY
10022. T. (212) 688-8510. 071380
Smith, A., 235 E 60 St., New York, NY 10022.
T. (212) 888-6337. 071381
Smith Antiques, Niall, 344B Bleecker St., New York, NY
10014. 071382
Smith, Dene, 160 East 65th St., New York, NY 10021.
T. (212) 8796071. 071383
Smith, Sanford & Patricia, 1045 Madison Ave., New
York, NY 10021. T. (212) 9293121. - Ant - 071384
Smith & Watson, 305 E. 63rd St., New York, NY 10021.
- Ant / Furn / Instr - 071385
Solomon, Malvina, 1122 Madison Av., New York, NY
10028. T. (212) 535-5200. 071386
Something Else Antiques & Needle Arts, 182 Ninth Av.,
New York, NY 10011. T. (212) 924-0006. 071387
Sonnabend, 420 W Broadway, New York, NY 10012.
T. (212) 966-6160. - Paint / Sculp / Pho / Draw - 071388
Sotheby Parke-Bernet, 980 Madison Av., New York, NY
10021. T. (212) 472 3400. - Ant / Paint / Furn / Num /
China / Sculp / Tex / Eth / Jew / Silv / Instr / Glass -- 071389

Sp Antiques, 378 Bleecker St., New York, NY 10014.
T. (212) 633-6792. 071390
Staal, F., 5 E 57 St., New York, NY 10022. T. (212) 758-
0664. - Furn / China / Jew - 071391
Stack's Coin Co., 123 W. 57th St., New York, NY 10019.
T. (212) 582 2580. - Num - 071392
Staghorn, 362 Third Av., New York, NY 10016.
T. (212) 689-0858. 071393
Stair & Co., 942 Madison Av., New York, NY 10021.
T. (212) 517-4400. - Ant / Paint / Furn / China / Dec /
Lights / Instr - 071394
Stanger, Estelle, 2508 Broadway, New York, NY 10025.
T. (212) 749-0393. 071395
Stark, 979 Third Av., New York, NY 10022. T. (212) 752-
9000. - Tex - 071396
Starr, Jana, 236 E 80 St., New York, NY 10021.
T. (212) 861-8256. 071397
Steinberg, Barbara, 964 Lexington Av., New York, NY
10021. T. (212) 439-9600. - Paint / Furn - 071398
Steinhacker, Paul, 151 E 71 St., New York, NY 10021.
T. (212) 879-1245. - Orient / Arch / Eth - 071399
Steinitz & Fils, Bernard, 125 E 57 St., Gallery 10, New
York, NY 10022. T. (212) 838-6841. - Furn - 071400
Stephenson, Garrick C., 625 Madison Av., New York, NY
10022. T. (212) 753-2570, Fax 832-4893. - Ant / Furn /
Dec / Silv - 071401
Stern, Henrietta C., Inc., 160 E. 89th St., New York, NY
10028. T. (212) 759 1291. - Ant / Furn / China / Dec /
Lights - 071402
Stievelman, Harriet, 880 Madison Av., New York, NY
10021. T. (212) 744-3005. 071403
Stingray-Hornsby, 59 E 78 St., New York, NY 10021.
T. (212) 532-0609. - Furn - 071404
Stockwell, David, 643 Park Av., New York, NY 10021.
T. (212) 879-2173. 071405
Stone, Eve & Son, 125 E 57 St., New York, NY 10022.
T. (212) 935-3780. 071406
Stradlings, 1225 Park Av., New York, NY 10028.
T. (212) 534-8135. - China / Glass - 071407
Strasser, Irma, 1050 Second Av., New York, NY 10022.
T. (212) 753-0885. 071408
Strasser, Tibor, 1050 Second Av., New York, NY 10022.
T. (212) 759-2513. 071409
Stroheim & Romann, 155 E. 56th St., New York, NY
10022. - Tex - 071410
Studio Seventy Five, 821 Park Av., New York, NY 10021.
T. (212) 535-4775. 071411
Subkoff, George, 835 Broadway, New York, NY 10003.
T. (212) 673-7280. 071412
Sulaiman, Diane, 515 E 72 St., New York, NY 10021.
T. (212) 534-8983. 071413
Sunjay Arts & Antiques, 1050 Second Av., New York, NY
10022. T. (212) 371-6835. 071414
Sutton Jewelers, 996 1st Ave., New York, NY 10022.
- Jew - 071415
Sutton Place Mews Antiques, 36 E 10 St., New York, NY
10003. T. (212) 473-0196. 071416
Tauber, Oscar, 3135 Johnson Av., New York, NY 10463.
T. (212) 548-8611. - Graph / Repr - 071417
Tavakoli, Hamid, 151 W 30 St., New York, NY 10001.
T. (212) 967-7847. 071418
Taylor, Valery, 10 Waterside Plaza, New York, NY 10010.
T. (212) 213-5314. - Ant - 071419
Tearston, Sylvia, 1053 3rd Ave., New York, NY 10021.
- Ant / Paint / Graph / Furn / China / Dec - 071420
Tell, Arthur, 360 E. 12nd St., New York, NY 10021.
T. (212) 758 3370. - Ant / China - 071421
Tender Buttons, 143 E 62 St., New York, NY 10021.
T. (212) 758-7004. 071422
Tepper Galleries, 110 E 25 St., New York, NY 10010.
T. (212) 677-5300, Fax (212) 673-3686. 071423
Throckmorton, 153 E 61 St, New York, NY 10021.
T. (212) 223-1059, Fax (212) 223-1937. - Ant /
Arch - 071424
Tibet West, 19 Christopher St., New York, NY 10014.
T. (212) 255-3416. 071425
Tiller & King, 1058 Madison Av., New York, NY 1028.
T. (212) 988-2861. - Furn / Orient / China - 071426
Topalian, Malcolm F., 281 Fifth Av., New York, NY
10010. T. (212) 684-0735. 071427
Toyobi, POB 1036, Ansonia Station, New York, NY
10023. T. (212) 873-1593. - Orient - 071428

Trace, Jonathan, Peekskill Hollow Road, Putnam Valley,
New York, NY 10579. T. (212) 5287963. 071429
Treasures & Gems, 250 E 90 St., New York, NY 10128.
T. (212) 410-7360. 071430
Treasures & Pleasures, 1050 Second Av., New York, NY
10022. T. (212) 750-1929. 071431
Treganowan, Ernest, Inc., 306 E. 61st St., New York, NY
10021. T. (212) 755 1050. - Repr / Tex - 071432
Trent, D. Leonard & Gary, 950 Madison Av., New York,
NY 10021. T. (212) 879-1799, 737-9511. 071433
Tudor Rose Antiques, 28 E 10 St., New York, NY 10003.
T. (212) 677-5239. 071434
Twentieth Century Antiques, 760 Madison Av., New York,
NY 10021. T. (212) 988-5181. 071435
Underground Antiques, 269 W. 4th St., New York, NY
10014. T. (212) 7411164. - Furn - 071436
Unique Handicraft Corp., 801 Broadway, New York, NY
10003. T. (212) 533-5810. 071437
Universe Antiques, 832 Broadway, New York, NY
10003. 071438
Upstairs Downtown Antiques, 12 W 19 St., New York, NY
10011. T. (212) 989-8715. 071439
Urban Archaeology Co., 285 Lafayette St., New York, NY
10012. T. (212) 431-6969. 071440
Ursus Prints, 981 Madison Av., New York, NY 10021.
T. (212) 772-8787. - Graph / Draw - 071441
Utilla, Richard, 244 E. 60th St., New York, NY
10022. 071442
Vandekar of Knightsbridge, Earle D., 15 E 57 St., New
York, NY 10022. T. (212) 308-2022, Fax 308-2105.
- Ant / Furn / Orient / China / Lights / Glass - 071443
Vang Olson, Mimi, 545 Hudson St., New York, NY
10014. T. (212) 675-5410. 071444
Vartanian + Sons, Inc., 680 Fifth Ave., New York, NY
10019. T. (212) 2456633. 071445
Vercel, Felix, 17 E 64 St, New York, NY 10021.
T. (212) 744-3131. - Paint / Sculp - 071446
Vernay & Jussel, 625 Madison Av., New York, NY
10022-1808. T. (212) 308-1906, Fax (212) 308-1944.
- Ant / Furn / Instr - 071447
Versailles Antiques & Interiors, 509 Madison Av., New
York, NY 10022. T. (212) 688-9447. 071448
Vestige Antiques, 289 Dekalb Avenue, New York, NY
11205. T. (212) 6389213. - Ant - 071449
Victor Carl, 55 E 13 St., New York, NY 10011.
T. (212) 673-8740. 071450
Victoria Falls, 451 W Broadway, New York, NY 10012.
T. (212) 254-2433. 071451
Victoria, Frederick P., 154 E 55 St., New York, NY
10022. T. (212) 755-2549. - Ant / Paint / Furn / China /
Tex / Furn - 071452
Victoria Galleries, 106 Greenwich Ave., New York, NY
10011. T. (212) 929 5909. - Ant / Paint / Paint / Graph /
Graph / Furn / Num / Orient / China / Jew / Silv / Lights /
Instr - 071453
Village East Antiques, 159 Second Av., New York, NY
10003. T. (212) 533-1510. 071454
Village Fair Inc., 15 E 18 St., New York, NY 10003.
T. (212) 260-4842. 071455
Vive la France Inc., 104 W 14 St., New York, NY 10011.
T. (212) 627-1416. 071456
Voth Antiques, Duane, 1050 Second Ave., New York, NY
10022. 071457
Walker, John, 125 E 57 St., Gallery 66, New York, NY
10022. T. (212) 758-6600. - Furn / Orient /
Sculp - 071458
Wall Street Fine Arts, 139 Fulton St., New York, NY
10038. T. (212) 766-8157. 071459
Wally's, 332 W 46 St., New York, NY 10036.
T. (212) 757-0339. 071460
Wan & Co., C. T., 1050 2nd Ave., New York, NY
10022. 071461
Warshaw, Karen, 167 E 74 St., New York, NY 10021.
T. (212) 439-7870. 071462
Waves, 32 E 13 St., New York, NY 10003. T. (212) 989-
9284. 071463
Weber, Edith, & Co., 125 E 57 St., Gallery 29, New York,
NY 10022. T. (212) 688-4331. - Jew - 071464
Weber, William, 49 E 10 St., New York, NY 10003.
- Furn - 071465
Weber, William, 49 E 10 St., New York, NY 10003.
T. (212) 228-0040. 071466

Weinbaum, David, 1159 2nd Ave., New York, NY 10021.
T. (212) 755 6540. - Ant / Furn / China -   071467
Weisbrod, Michael B., 987 Madison Av., New York, NY
10021. T. (212) 734-6350. - Paint / Orient / China /
Tex / Glass -   071468
Weiss, Beatrice, 219 W. 37th St., New York, NY 10018.
T. (212) 594 9040.   071469
Welcome Home Antiques, 556 Columbus Av., New York,
NY 10024. T. (212) 362-4293.   071470
Wender, L.J., 3 E 80 St, New York, NY 10021.
T. (212) 734-3460, Fax (212) 427-4945.
- Orient -   071471
Wendover, 6 W 20 St., New York, NY 10011.
T. (212) 924-6066.   071472
Werther, Sandra, 23 E 74 St., New York, NY 10021.
T. (212) 734-0910. - Paint -   071473
Western European Fine Arts Corp., 42 E. 12th St., New
York, NY 10003. - China -   071474
White, Julian, 957 Madison Av., New York, NY 10021.
T. (212) 249-8181.   071475
Wicker Garden, 1318 Madison Av., New York, NY 10128.
T. (212) 410-7000.   071476
Wigmore, D., 121 E 71 St., New York, NY 10021.
T. (212) 794-2128. - Paint -   071477
Wilner, Eli, & Co., 1525 York Av., New York, NY 10028.
T. (212) 744-6521. - Fra -   071478
Winston, Charles J. & Co. Inc., 41 E. 53rd St. 515 Ma-
dison Ave., New York, NY 10021. T. (212) PL 3 3312.
- Ant / Orient / China / Lights / Instr / Glass -   071479
Wise, John, Ltd., 15 E. 69th St., New York, NY 10021.
T. (212) RE 4 2228. - Arch / Eth -   071480
Wood & Hogan, Inc., 305 E. 63rd St., New York, NY
10021. T. (212) 355 1335. - Ant / Furn -   071481
Woodard, Thomas K., 835 Madison Av., New York, NY
10021. T. (212) 794-9404. - Tex -   071482
Wooden Indian Antiques, 60 W 15 St., New York, NY
10011. T. (212) 243-8590.   071483
Wook Kim, 175 East 87th Street, New York, NY 10028.
T. (212) 4271642.   071484
Wooster Gallery, 86 Wooster St., New York, NY 10012.
T. (212) 219-2190.   071485
Worldwide Antiques Import & Export Co., 45 E. 11th St.,
New York, NY 10003. T. (212) 751 3995. - Ant / Orient /
China -   071486
Yates, David & Constance, POB 580, Lenox Hill Station,
New York, NY 10021. T. (212) 879-7758,
Fax (212) 794-4680.   071487
Yesterdays, 2 W 32 St., New York, NY 10001.
T. (212) 319-0817, 564-3244.   071488
1065 Madison Av. Antiques, 1065 Madison Av., New
York, NY 10028. T. (212) 472-8834.   071489
280 Lafayette, 284 Lafayette St., New York, NY 10012.
T. (212) 941-5825.   071490

Newark (Delaware)
Walters, Paris M., 134 Capitol Trail, Newark, DE 19711.
T. (302) 737 5853. - Ant / Paint / Graph / Furn / Sculp /
Lights -   071491

Newark (New Jersey)
Antique Porcelain Company, 155 Washington St., Ste.
304, Newark, NJ 07102. - China -   071492
Scheiner, George & Son, 429 Broad St., Newark, NJ
07102. T. (201) 621 8311. - Ant / Furn -   071493

Newark (Ohio)
Hoffman's Antiques, 129 S. Fourth St., Newark, OH
43055. T. (614) 345-8550.   071494

Newburgh (New York)
Balmville Antiques, 34 Balmville Rd., Newburgh, NY
12550. T. (914) 561-2710. - Furn -   071495
Besso, Ida F., 164 West St., Newburgh, NY 12550.
T. (914) 561 3377. - Ant -   071496

Newbury (Massachusetts)
Brown, F. Thurlow, 165 High Rd., Newbury, MA 01950.
- Ant -   071497

Newburyport (Massachusetts)
Eaton, Peter, 39 State St., Newburyport, MA 01950.
T. (617) 465 2754. - Furn -   071498

Newcomerstown (Ohio)
Harding, Mrs. Thelma, R.F.D.1 5 miles N. on Hwy., Newcomerstown, OH 43832.   071499
Heller, John S., 784 N. Cross St., Newcomerstown, OH
43832. T. (614) 498-7126. - Ant -   071500

Newfane (Vermont)
British Clockmaker, West St., Newfane, VT 05345.
T. (802) 365-7770. - Ant / Instr -   071501

Newport (Rhode Island)
Norton, 415 Thames St., Newport, RI 02840.
T. (401) 849-4468. - Orient -   071502
Orche Point Gallery, Carriage House, Ruggles Avenue,
Newport, RI 02840. T. (401) 8474359. - Paint -   071503

Newport Beach (California)
Antiques and Nautical, 430 W Coast Hwy., Newport Be-
ach, CA 92663. T. (714) 642-7945.   071504
Beverly and Partner, 1800 West Coast Hwy., Newport
Beach, CA 92663. T. (714) 5487187.   071505

Newport News (Virginia)
Brill's Antique Shop, 10527 Jefferson Ave., Newport
News, VA 23601. T. (804) 596 5333. - Ant -   071506

Newton (Iowa)
Damman's Antiques, 1420 1st St. North, Newton, IA
50208. - Ant / Glass -   071507

Newton (Massachusetts)
Any Old Thing, 28 Yord Rd., Newton, MA 02168.
T. (617) 3326747, 7340234.   071508

Newton Lower Falls (Massachusetts)
Gregorian, Arthur T., 2284 Washington St., Newton Lo-
wer Falls, MA 02162. T. (617) 244-2553.
- Ant -   071509

Newton Upper Falls (Massachusetts)
O'Neill, Eugene, Antique Gallery, Echo Bridge Mall, 381
Elliot St., Newton Upper Falls, MA 02164.
T. (617) 9655965.   071510

Newtown (Connecticut)
Ladderback Antiques, RD2, Huntingtown Rd., Newtown,
CT 06470. T. (203) 4264621.   071511
Poverty Hollow Antiques, Poverty Hollow Road, New-
town, CT 06470. T. (203) 4262388.   071512

Newtown (Pennsylvania)
Ren, 14 S State St., Newtown, PA 18940. T. (215) 968-
5511. - Ant / China / Jew / Fra / Silv / Lights -   071513
Ren's Antiques, 14 S State St., Newtown, PA 18940.
T. (215) 968-5511, 968-3636.   071514

Niles (Illinois)
Bradford Exchange, 9333 Milwaukee Av., Niles, IL
60648. T. (616) 966-2770.   071515

Norfolk (Virginia)
Colonial Antiques, 119 W 21 St., Norfolk, VA 23517.
T. (804) 622-7236.   071516

Norristown (Pennsylvania)
Allen, R. D. 3, Norristown, PA 19401. T. (215) 272-3341.
- Ant / Paint / Furn / Fra -   071517

North Andover (Massachusetts)
Hammond, Roland B., 169 Andover St., North Andover,
MA 01845. T. (617) 682-9672. - Ant / Furn / Silv /
Instr -   071518

North Belgrade (Maine)
Totem Pole Antiques, Route 8, North Belgrade, ME
04959. T. (207) 4652085.   071519

North Bethesda (Maryland)
Sloan, C. G., & Co., 4920 Wyaconda Rd., North Bethes-
da, MD 20852. T. (301) 468-4911. - Ant / Paint /
Graph / Furn / Orient / China / Sculp / Tex / Dec / Jew / S-
ilv / Instr / Ico / Draw -   071520
Sloan, C.G., & Co., 4920 Wyaconda Rd., North Bethesda,
MD 20852. T. (301) 468-4911. - Ant / Paint / Graph /
Furn / Orient / China / Sculp / Tex / Dec / Jew / Silv / Inst-
r / Ico / Draw -   071521

North Conway (New Hampshire)
Plusch, Richard M., Rtes. 16 & 302, North Conway, NH
03860. - Furn / Tex / Silv / Instr / Glass -   071522

North Edgecomb (Maine)
Partridge, Jack, Rte. 1, North Edgecomb, ME 04556.
T. (207) 882-7745. - Paint / Furn -   071523

North Hollywood (California)
Altobelli, 4419 Lankershim Blvd., North Hollywood, CA
91602. T. (213) 763-5151. - Jew / Silv -   071524
Helen Williams, 12643 Hortense St., North Hollywood,
CA 91604. I. (213) 761 2756. - Ant / China /
Rel -   071525
House of Jonathon, North Hollywood POB 47, CA 91603.
- Ant / Paint / Furn -   071526
Williams, Helen, 12643 Hortense St., North Hollywood,
CA 91604. T. (213) 761-2756. - Ant / China /
Rel -   071527

North Ridgeville (Ohio)
Antique Mall, 7474 Avon Belden, North Ridgeville, OH
44039.   071528

North Scituate (Rhode Island)
Peters, Lynda D., R.F.D. 4, Box 283, North Scituate, RI
02857. T. (401) 934-1472. - Furn -   071529

Northampton (Massachusetts)
Walters & Benisek, One Amber Lane, Northampton, MA
01060. T. (413) 586-3909, (219) 533-9416.   071530

Northborough (Massachusetts)
Claflin, Marjorie, 206 South St., Northborough, MA
01532. T. (617) 393 2270. - Ant -   071531

Northbridge (Massachusetts)
House of James Ant., 163 Sutton St., Northbridge, MA
01534. T. (617) 2342766.   071532

Northeast Harbor (Maine)
Pine Bough Antiques, Main St., Northeast Harbor, ME
04662. T. (207) 2765079. - Ant / Tex -   071533

Northridge (California)
Weston, Edward, 19355 Business Center Dr, Northridge,
CA 91324. T. (818) 885-1044, Fax (818) 885-1021.
- Ant / Paint / Graph / Furn / Orient / China -   071534

Norton (Massachusetts)
Blanche's Old House, 9 Smith St., Rt. 140, Norton, MA
02766. T. (617) 2854747.   071535

Norwalk (Connecticut)
Moore, Gates, River Road, Norwalk, CT 06850.
T. (203) 847 3231. - Lights -   071536

Norwich (Ohio)
Kemble, Roland & Marilyn, 55 N Sundale Rd., Norwich,
OH 43767. T. (614) 872-3507. - Furn -   071537

Oakhurst (New Jersey)
Copper Kettle Antiques, 251 Monmouth Rd., Oakhurst,
NJ 07755. T. (201) 531-1699.   071539

Oakland (California)
Witt, Frank de, 5374 Manila Ave., Oakland, CA 94618.
- Dec -   071540

Odin (Illinois)
Lincoln Trail Antiques, Odin POB 295, IL 62870.
T. (618) 775-8255. - Instr -   071541

Ogunquit (Maine)
Clipper Ship Antiques and Guest House, Route 1, Ogun-
quit, ME 03907. T. (207) 6469735.   071542
Mathews, G. D., 112 Shore Rd., Ogunquit, ME 03907.
T. (207) 646 2537.   071543
Zankowich, M., U. S. Rte. 1, Ogunquit, ME 03907.
T. (207) 646 3529. - Ant / Jew -   071544

Oil City (Pennsylvania)
Szabat's, 228 Plummer St., Oil City, PA 16301.
T. (814) 646 6351. - Ant -   071545

Oklahoma City (Oklahoma)
Don Juan Antiques, 4401 N. E. 36th St., Oklahoma City, OK 73111. T. (405) 424 3795. - Ant / Paint / Graph / Furn / Orient / China / Tex / Silv / Lights / Instr - 071546
Pickard, 7108 N Western Av, Oklahoma City, OK 73116. T. (405) 842-5828. - Paint / Graph / Sculp / Eth - 071547
Wilks, Norman, Art Gallery, 3839 63rd St., Oklahoma City, OK 73116. - Ant / Paint / China / Dec / Lights - 071548

Olathe (Kansas)
Hourglass, The, 11515 Blackbob Rd., Olathe, KS 66061. T. (913) 8883020. - Instr - 071549

Old Greenwich (Connecticut)
New England Shop, 254 Sound Beach Ave., Old Greenwich, CT 06870. T. (203) 637 0326. - Ant - 071550

Old San Juan (Puerto Rico)
don Roberto, Inc., 205 Calle Cristo, Old San Juan, PR 00903. T. (809) 7240194. - Ant / Arch / Rel - 071551

Old Saybrook (Connecticut)
House of Pretty Things, 49 Sherwood Terrace, Old Saybrook, CT 06475. T. (203) 388-5920. - Ant / China / Glass - 071552

Oldwick (New Jersey)
Melody Cottage Antiques, At the crossroads, Oldwick, NJ 08858. T. (201) 439-2519. 071553
Tewksbury Antiques, Crossroads, P.O. Box 131, Oldwick, NJ 08858. T. (201) 4392221. - Ant / Paint / Graph / Furn / China / Tex / Silv / Lights - 071554

Oley (Pennsylvania)
Heist, R. and K., R. D. 2, Oley, PA 19547. T. (215) 689 9242. - Ant / Furn / Lights / Glass - 071555

Ontario (New York)
Old Mill Antiques, 858 Ridge Rd., Ontario, NY 14519. T. (315) 524 9555. - Ant - 071556

Orange (California)
Sherry's Antiques, 605 W Chapman, Orange, CA 92668. T. (714) 639-6401. - Ant - 071557

Orange (Virginia)
The Piedmont Shoppe, Rte. 15 N., Orange, VA 22960. T. (703) 672 2880. - Ant / Paint / Furn / China / Repr / Sculp / Sculp / Jew / Fra - 071558

Orlando (Florida)
A & T Antiques, 1620 N. Orange Avenue, Orlando, FL 32804. 071559

Orleans (Massachusetts)
Pleasant Bay Antiques, Route 28, Orleans, MA 02662. T. (617) 2550930. 071560

Ormond Beach (Florida)
Surfview Ant. + Unique Nauticals, 2120 Ocean Shore Blvd., Ormond Beach, FL 32074. T. (904) 6721853. - Ant - 071561

Ossining (New York)
Salloch, William, Pines Bridge Rd., Ossining, NY 10562. T. (914) 941-8363. 071562

Osterville (Massachusetts)
The Old House, Main Street, Osterville, MA 02655. T. (617) 428 6028. - Ant / Furn / Dec - 071563

Ottumwa (Iowa)
Brown's Antique Shop, 1620 East Main St., Ottumwa, IA 52501. T. (515) 6846026. 071564

Oxford (Maryland)
Americana Antique + Art Gallery, Morris St., Oxford, MD 21654. T. (301) 2265680. 071565

Oxford (Michigan)
Old Colonial Shop, 103 S. Washington St., Oxford, MI 48051. 071566

Oyster Bay (New York)
Abbe, James, 45 W Main St., Oyster Bay, NY 11771. T. (516) 922-3325. - Ant / Paint - 071567

Pacific Grove (California)
Trotter's London Tower, 225 Forest Ave., Pacific Grove, CA 93950. T. (408) 3733505. - Ant - 071568

Palm Beach (Florida)
Amore, Joseph A., 148 Australian Ave., Palm Beach, FL 33480. T. (407) 833 1084. - Ant / Paint / Graph - 071569
Douglas Lorie, Inc., 334 Worth Avenue, Palm Beach, FL 33480. T. (407) 655 0700. - Ant / China / Silv / Glass - 071570
The Meissen Shop, 329 Worth Av., Via Roma, Palm Beach, FL 33480. T. (407) 832-2504. - China - 071571

Palos Verdes (California)
Gallery, 27 Malaga Cove Plaza, Palos Verdes, CA 90274. T. (213) 375-2212. - Ant / Orient / China / Repr / Tex / Jew - 071572

Paoli (Pennsylvania)
Irion Company, 44 N Valley Rd., Paoli, PA 19301. T. (215) 644-7516. 071573

Park Ridge (Illinois)
Galleries of Europe, Inc., 514 Austin Ave., Park Ridge, IL 60068. T. (312) 823 2466. - Ant / Paint / Jew / Silv - 071574

Pasadena (California)
Antiques Showcase, 17 S. Sierra Madre Blvd., Pasadena, CA 91107. T. (818) 7935798. - Ant - 071575
Arnold's Antiques, 865 E Del Mar Blvd., Pasadena, CA 91106. - Ant - 071576
Oriental Gift Box, Huntington Sheraton Hotel, Pasadena, CA 91108. - Orient - 071577
Plummer's Antiques, 180 S Lake Av., Pasadena, CA 91101. - Ant - 071578
Port O'Call, 540 S Lake Av., Pasadena, CA 91101. T. (818) 793-7732. - Graph / Furn - 071579
West World Imports, Antiques, 171 E California Av., Pasadena, CA 91101. T. (818) 449-8565. - Ant - 071580

Pasadena (Texas)
A & L Picture Framing Shop, 137 W. Southmore Ave., Pasadena, TX 77502. T. (713) 472 2055. - Fra - 071581

Pascoag (Rhode Island)
Carrol Antiques, Jane, 94 Church St., Rt.100, Pascoag, RI 02859. T. (401) 568-4521. 071582

Passaic (New Jersey)
Jan, Jill & Jon, 170 Main Av., Passaic, NJ 07055. T. (201) 777-4670. - Ant / Paint / Furn / Orient / China / Jew / Silv / Lights / Glass / Ico - 071583

Pearland (Texas)
Cole's Antique Village, 1016 N. Main St., Pearland, TX 77581. 071584

Peekskill (New York)
Trace, Timothy, Red Mill Rd, Peekskill, NY 10566. T. (914) 528-4074. - Ant - 071585

Pell City (Alabama)
Kilgroe's Antiques, 2212 3rd Ave. North, Pell City, AL 35125. T. (205) 338 7923. - Ant / Furn / Orient / China - 071586

Pensacola (Florida)
Cleland, 412 E Zarragossa, Pensacola, FL 32501. T. (904) 432-9933. - Furn - 071587
Diamond House, 9 E. Garden St., Pensacola, FL 32501. T. (904) 432 2838. - Paint / Jew - 071588

Peoria (Illinois)
Grissom, Betty, 602 W Maywood Av., Peoria, IL 61604. T. (309) 685-0841. 071589

Perrysburg (Ohio)
Poole, J.M., 106 Louisiana Av., Perrysburg, OH 43551. T. (419) 874-8605. - Furn - 071590

Philadelphia (Pennsylvania)
Antique Fair, 2218-2220 Market St., Philadelphia, PA 19103. T. (215) 563-3682. - Ant - 071591
Attic Galleries, 1330 E Washington Lane, Philadelphia, PA 19138. T. (215) LI8-2434. - Ant / Paint / China / Lights / Instr / Glass - 071592
au bon goût, 1700 Locust St., Philadelphia, PA 19103. T. (215) 545 4045. - Ant / Graph / Furn / China / Repr / Dec / Lights / Glass - 071593
Bullard, Alfred, 1604 Pine St., Philadelphia, PA 19103. T. (215) 735-1879. - Ant / Furn / China / Glass - 071594
Burke, Harry, N.E.Cor, Chestnut St 1919, Philadelphia, PA 19103. T. (215) 564 1869. - Ant / Paint / Graph / Orient / China / Sculp / Jew / Silv / Glass - 071595
Caldwell, J. E. Co., Chestnut and Juniper Sts., Philadelphia, PA 19107. T. (215) 563 3300. - Silv - 071596
Chait, Harold H., 101 S Eighth St., Philadelphia, PA 19106. T. (215) 922-1961. - Ant - 071597
Chelsea Silverplating Co., 920 Pine St., Philadelphia, PA 19107. T. (215) WA 5 1132. - Ant / Silv - 071598
David, David, 260 S 18 St., Philadelphia, PA 19103. T. (215) 735-2922. - Paint - 071599
Escourt, Ted, Antiques & Bric-Brac, 6228 Germantown Ave., Philadelphia, PA 19144. T. (215) 848 4146. - Ant - 071600
Finkel M., & Daughter, 936 Pine St., Philadelphia, PA 19107. T. (215) 627-7797. - Ant / Paint / Furn / Sculp - 071601
Fiorillo, Michael, 1120 Pine St., Philadelphia, PA 19107. T. (215) 923 3173. - Ant / Paint / Furn - 071602
Frack, J. A., 1029 Pine St., Philadelphia, PA 19107. T. (215) 923 4062. - Ant / Furn / Repr - 071603
Gallery of Fine Arts & Antiques, 1506 Lombard St., Philadelphia, PA 19146. 071604
Glazer, James and Nancy, 2209 Delancey Pl., Philadelphia, PA 19103. T. (215) 732-8788. 071605
Hesperia Art, 2219 Saint James Pl., Philadelphia, PA 19103. T. (215) 567-6533. - Num / Arch - 071606
Jaipaul, 1610 Locust St., Philadelphia, PA 19103. T. (215) 735-7303. - Ant / Orient - 071607
Joe's Antique Shop, 918 Pine St., Philadelphia, PA 19107. T. (215) 922 2879. 071608
Kohn & Kohn, 1112 Pine St., Philadelphia, PA 19107. T. (215) 627 3909. - Ant / Graph / Furn / China - 071609
Leather Bucket, 84 Bethlehem Pike, Philadelphia, PA 19118. T. (215) 242-1140. - Ant - 071610
Maqam, Gravers Lane, Philadelphia POB 4312, PA 19118. T. (215) 438-7873. - Orient / Tex - 071611
Maranca, Albert, 1100 Pine St., Philadelphia, PA 19107. 071612
Mario's Antique Shop, 1020 Pine St., Philadelphia, PA 19107. T. (215) 922 0230. - Ant / Furn - 071613
Moenning, W. and Son, 2039 Locust St., Philadelphia, PA 19103. T. (215) 567 498. - Ant - 071614
Morettini, Louis J., 262 S. 20th St., Philadelphia, PA 19103. 071615
Murray, Jay P., 2019 Rittenhouse Sq., Philadelphia, PA 19103. 071616
Neal, D. B., 1712 Rittenhouse Square, Philadelphia, PA 19103. T. (215) 545 5930. - Ant / China - 071617
Neri, Charles, 313 South St., Philadelphia, PA 19147. 071618
Nesco, M.J., 1002 Pine St., Philadelphia, PA 19107. 071619
Philly Coin Company, 1804 Chestnut St., Philadelphia, PA 19103. T. (215) 503-7341. - Num - 071620
Reese's Antiques, 928 Pine St., Philadelphia, PA 19107. T. (215) 922 0796. - Ant - 071621
Schaffer, Irwin, 1032 Pine St., Philadelphia, PA 19107. T. (215) 923 2949. - Ant - 071622
Schwarz, Frank S., & Son, 1806 Chestnut St., Philadelphia, PA 19103. T. (215) 563-4887. - Ant / Paint / Furn / Silv - 071623
Shapiro, Adeline, 1506 Lombard St., Philadelphia, PA 19146. T. (215) 545-7425. - Ant - 071624
Simons, Seal, 473 W. Ellet St., Philadelphia, PA 19119. T. (215) 247 2062. - China / Jew - 071625
Switt, I., 130 S. 8th St., Philadelphia, PA 19106. T. (215) 922 3830. - Ant / Silv - 071626
Syderman, Harry, 6279 Souder St., Philadelphia, PA 19149. T. (215) 535 0112. - Ant - 071627
The Hodge-Podge, 9645 James St., Philadelphia, PA 19114. T. (215) 732 1194. - Ant - 071628
Wilson, Edward G., 1802 Chestnut St., Philadelphia, PA 19103. T. (215) 563 7369. - Ant / Furn / Orient / China / Jew / Silv - 071629

Zulli, J., 918 Pine St., Philadelphia, PA 19107.
T. (215) 922 2879. - Ant -   071630

Phoenix (Arizona)

Reddy's Corner Antiques, 1602 E. Jefferson St., Phoenix, AZ 85034. - Ant / China / Jew / Glass -   071631
Spinning Wheel, 1102 E. McDowell Rd., Phoenix, AZ 85006. - Ant / China / Jew / Silv / Glass -   071632
The Antiquary, 3044 N. 24th St., Phoenix, AZ 85015.   071633

Pierceton (Indiana)

Beebe's Antique Shop, First St., Pierceton, IN 46562.
T. (219) 594 2244. - Ant / Paint / Furn / Jew / Lights / Glass -   071634

Pine City (New York)

Bedrosian, Mrs., 1317 Pennsylvania Ave., Pine City, NY 14871. - Tex -   071635

Pinehurst (Noth Carolina)

Crown & Griffin, Pinehurst, NC 28374. T. (919) 295-5401. - Ant / Paint / Furn / Orient / China / Jew / Silv / Glass -   071636

Pittsburgh (Pennsylvania)

Dillner Galleries, 2748 W. Liberty Ave., Pittsburgh, PA 15216.   071637
Four Winds Gallery, 5512 Walnut St., Pittsburgh, PA 15238. T. (412) 682-5092. - Ant / Paint / Graph / China / Sculp / Tex / Arch / Eth / Jew / Mul -   071638
George, Margery B., Pittsburgh POB 8155, PA 15217.
T. (412) 422-7307. - Ant -   071639
Kunziar, John E., 2915 Brownsville Rd., Pittsburgh, PA 15227.   071640
Morewood Galleries, Centre & Morewood, Pittsburgh, PA 15213.   071641
Snuggery Farm of Sewickley, Camp Meeting Rd., Pittsburgh, PA 15200. T. (412) 7413276. - Ant / Furn -   071642

Pittsfield (New Hampshire)

Cadarette, Jo Ann, R.F.D. 2, Pittsfield, NH 03263.
T. (603) 435-6615. - Furn -   071643

Plainwell (Michigan)

Barber's Antiques, 418 Park St., Plainwell, MI 49080.   071644

Plattsburgh (New York)

Gordon, Philip & Shirley, 41 Prospect Av., Plattsburgh, NY 12901. T. (518) 561-3383. - Ant / Jew / Silv / Lights / Glass -   071645
Shoremont Antiques, 444 Margaret St., Plattsburgh, NY 12901. - Ant -   071646

Pleasant Valley (New York)

Beckwith Antiques, A., Route 44, Pleasant Valley, NY 12569. T. (914) 635-3217.   071647

Pleasantville (New York)

Fisher, Mary, 33 Bedford Rd., Pleasantville, NY 10570.   071648

Pluckemin (New Jersey)

Country Antique Shop, Routes 202 and 206, Pluckemin, NJ 07978. T. (201) 658-3759.   071649

Plymouth (Indiana)

Boggs, Georgia C., R.R. 1, Plymouth, IN 46563.
T. (219) 936-2619. - Ant / Orient / Glass -   071650

Plymouth (Massachusetts)

Plymouth Antique Center, 26 Union St., Plymouth, MA 02360. T. (617) 7460076.   071651

Point Pleasant (Pennsylvania)

Time & Tide, River Rd. Rte. 32, Point Pleasant, PA 18950. T. (215) 297 5854. - Ant / Instr -   071652

Pomfret Center (Connecticut)

Meadow Rock Farm Antiques, Route 169, Pomfret Center, CT 06259. T. (203) 9287896. - Paint / Furn -   071653

Pomona (California)

Armstrong's, 150 E. Third St., Pomona, CA 91766.
T. (714) 623 6464. - China -   071654

Pontiac (Michigan)

Gabler, Helen Antiques, 2045 Dixie Highway, Country Fair Antique Flea Market, Pontiac, MI 48055.
- Ant -   071655
Shoppe of Antiquity, 7766 Highland Rd., Pontiac, MI 48054. T. (313) OR 3 0301. - Ant / Furn / China / Arch / Glass -   071656

Poolesville (Maryland)

The Springs Antiques, Sugarland Rd., Poolesville, MD 28037. T. (301) 948 5540. - Ant / Paint / Silv -   071657

Port Chester (New York)

Berner's, 16 N. Main, Port Chester, NY 10573.
- Jew -   071658

Port Huron (Michigan)

Ophelia's Surprise-Shop, 4992 Gratiot Rd., Port Huron, MI 48060. - Ant / Furn / China / Jew / Silv - 071659

Port Washington (New York)

NKB Antiques, 3 Carlton Ave., Port Washington, NY 11050. T. (516) 883-4184.   071660

Portland (Maine)

Eisenhart & Co., P. T., 17 W. Commonweal Dr., Portland, ME 04103.   071661
Harmon's Antique Attic, 584 Congress St., Portland, ME 04101.   071662
Nelson, Andrew, Monument Sq., Portland POB 453, ME 04112. T. (207) 775-1135. - Jew / Silv / Instr - 071663
Vose-Smith Antiques, 646 Congress, Portland, ME 04101.   071664

Portland (Michigan)

The Buggy Wheel, 220 Lincoln St., Portland, MI 48875.   071665

Portland (Oregon)

Aigner's Diamond Loan Brokers, 299 S. W. Alder St., Portland, OR 97204. T. (503) 233 4659. - Jew - 071666
Alder Street Clock Shop, 251 S. W. Alder St., Portland, OR 97204. T. (503) 227 3651. - Instr -   071667
Candelier Shop, 1007 S. E. 12th Ave., Portland, OR 97214. T. (503) 2 6654. - Ant / Orient / China / Jew / Rel -   071668
Cathy's Antique Shop, 2425 NW Lovejoy St., Portland, OR 97210. T. (503) 223-1767. - Ant / Orient / China / Silv / Glass -   071669
Gerson's Stamps & Coins, 522 S. W. Yamhill St., Portland, OR 97204. T. (503) 228 5233. - Num -   071670
Goodwill Industries of Oregon, 1831 S. E. 6th Ave., Portland, OR 97214. - Ant -   071671
Hollyhock Cottage Antiques Shop, 2914 N. E. 50th Ave., Portland, OR 97213. T. (503) 287 1358. - Ant - 071672
Lamb, Jerry, 1323 N. W. 23rd Ave., Portland, OR 97210.
T. (503) 227 6077. - Ant / Paint / Graph / Furn / Orient / China / Repr / Sculp / Tex / Dec / Silv / Lights -   071673
Lamplighters, 2937 E Burnside, Portland, OR 97214.
T. (503) 235-5157. - Ant -   071674
Orientale Motif Shop, 725 N. W. 23rd Ave., Portland, OR 97210. T. (503) CA 3 4978. - Ant / Paint / Graph / Furn / Num / Orient / China / Tex / Arch / Eth / Dec / Jew / Instr / Mil / Rel -   071675
Russell, Lorraine S., 1323 N. W. 23rd St., Portland, OR 97222. T. (503) 227 6077. - Ant -   071676

Pottstown (Pennsylvania)

Penn Wick, Ridge Road, R.D. 4, Pottstown, PA 19464.
T. (215) 4696903. - Ant -   071677

Pound Ridge (New York)

Brown & CO., Trinity Pass, Pound Ridge, NY 10576.
T. (914) 7648392. - Ant -   071678
Roberts, Alan Y., Scotts Corners, Pound Ridge, NY 10576. T. (914) 764-5427. - Ant -   071679

Prescott (Arizona)

Friendship House, 28 White Star Rd., Prescott, AZ 86301. - Ant -   071680

Princeton (New Jersey)

Milholland & Olson, Inc., 8 Stockton St., Princeton, NJ 08540. T. (609) 924 2175. - Ant -   071681

Prosperity (Pennsylvania)

Stout, June, 1-79 Exit 4, 221 N. at Ruff Creek, Prosperity, PA 15329. T. (412) 627-6885. - Ant -   071682

Providence (Rhode Island)

Spectrum-India, 262 Thayer St., Providence, RI 02906.
- Paint / Graph / Sculp / Tex / Dec / Jew -   071683

Putnam Valley (New York)

Allen, Mark & Marjorie, R.D.1, Box 11, Putnam Valley, NY 10579. T. (914) 528-8989. - Furn -   071684
Trace, Jonathan, Peekskill Hollow Rd., Putnam Valley, NY 10579. T. (914) 528-7963. - Silv -   071685

Quarryville (Pennsylvania)

England, Victor, POB 245, Quarryville, PA 17566.
T. (717) 786-4013, Fax (717) 786-7954.   071686

Quincy (Michigan)

Wentworth, D., 11 E. Jefferson St., Quincy, MI 49082.
- Ant -   071687

Raleigh (North Carolina)

Craig & Tarlton, 122 Glenwood Av., Raleigh, NC 27603.
T. (919) 828-2559. - Ant / Paint / Sculp -   071688

Randallstown (Maryland)

Speert, GLoria C., 9802 Southall Rd., Randallstown, MD 21133. - Ant -   071689

Randolph (Vermont)

Colonial House Antiques, 1 mile from exit 4, 1-89, Randolph, VT 05061.   071690

Reading (Michigan)

Ye Old Yoke Antiques, 119 Silver St., Reading, MI 49274. - Ant / Furn / China / Lights / Glass -   071691

Reading (Pennsylvania)

Troutman, Emily S., 325 N. 6th St., Reading, PA 19601.
T. (215) 374 0181. - Glass -   071692

Red Bank (New Jersey)

The Antiques Center, 217 W. Front St., Red Bank, NJ 07701. T. (201) 741 5331. - Ant -   071693

Red Wing (Minnesota)

Teahouse Antiques, 927 W Third St., Red Wing, MN 55066. T. 388- 3669. - Ant -   071694

Redondo Beach (California)

Wind Bells Cottage Antiques, 720 8th St. Hermosa Beach, Redondo Beach, CA 90254. T. (213) FR 4 1582.
- Ant / China / Dec / Jew / Silv / Glass -   071695

Rehoboth (Massachusetts)

Mendes, 52 Blanding Rd., Rehoboth, MA 02769.
T. (617) 3367381.   071696

Riceboro (Georgia)

Low Country Antiques, Hwy. 17, Riceboro, GA 31323.   071697

Richland (Michigan)

Plomp, Bernard G., 8023 Church St., Richland, MI 49083. T. (616) 629-4268. - Ant / Furn -   071698

Richmond (Illinois)

Richmond Antique Hub, Rte. 12, Box 441, Richmond, IL 60071. T. (815) 6784218. - Ant -   071699

Richmond (Massachusetts)

Sayman, Wynn A., Old Fields, Richmond, MA 01254.
T. (413) 698-2272, Fax (413) 698-3282.
- China -   071700

Richmond (Virginia)

Antique Warehouse, 1310 E Cary St., Richmond, VA 23219. T. (415) 643-1310. - Furn -   071701
Hampton House, Inc., 5720 Grove Avenue, Richmond, VA 23226. - Ant -   071702
Mayo, 5705 Grove Av., Richmond, VA 23226.
T. (804) 288-2109. - Paint / Graph -   071703

071704–071784

ART and ANTIQUE DEALERS, NUMISMATICS
San Francisco / U.S.A.

Reese's Antiques, 207 E. Main St., Richmond, VA
23219. T. (804) 644 0781. - Ant -   071704
Richmond Art Company, 101 E Grace St., Richmond, VA
23219. T. (804) 644 0733. - Ant -   071705
Wright, J. O., 821 W. Cary St., Richmond, VA 23220.
T. (804) 648 0977. - Ant -   071706
Zincone & Son, 3027 W. Cary St., Richmond, VA 23221.
T. (804) 355 2782. - Ant -   071707

Ridgefield (Connecticut)
Eve's Antiques, 709 Danbury Rd., Ridgefield, CT 06877.
- Ant -   071708

Ripley (New York)
Odell's Antique Shop, E. Main Rd., Ripley, NY 14775.
T. (716) 736 2942. - Ant -   071709

Rochester (New York)
Nova Finishing, 1922 South Av, Rochester, NY 14620.
- Furn -   071710
Wolfard's Galleries of Fine Arts, 9 S Goodman St., Ro-
chester, NY 14607. T. (716) 271 0846. - Paint / Graph /
Orient / China / Sculp / Glass -   071711

Rock City Falls (New York)
Saratoga Antiques Center, Route 29, Rock City Falls, NY
12863. T. (518) 885-7645.   071712

Rockport (Massachusetts)
Polack, Louis, 16 South St., Rockport, MA 01966.
T. (617) 546 2745. - Ant / Furn / China -   071713
Salt Box, The Antiques Shop, 16 South St., Rockport,
MA 01966. T. (617) 5462745. - Ant -   071714

Rockville (New York)
Bogart, Joan, Rockville POB 265, NY 11571.
T. (516) 764-0529. - Ant -   071715

Romeo (Michigan)
Top of the Hill Antiques, 253 Chandler St., Romeo, MI
48065.   071716

Roscoe (New York)
Cain's Antiques, Rockland Rd., Roscoe, NY 12776.
T. (914) 498-4303. - Furn / Eth -   071717

Roseville (Michigan)
Cook's Lamp Shop, 27427 Gratiot Ave., Roseville, MI
48066. - Lights -   071718

Roslyn Harbor (New York)
Artmar Antiques, 1362 Old Northern Blvd., Roslyn Harbor, NY 11576. T. (516) 484-4409.   071719

Round Pond (Maine)
Foster, Robert L., Round Pond, ME 04564.
- Ant -   071720

Roxbury (Connecticut)
Wiese, I.M., Roxbury Station, Rte. 67, Roxbury, CT
06783. T. (203) 354-8911, 264-5309. - Furn - 071721

Roxobel (North Carolina)
Tyler, John E., Roxobel, NC 27872. T. (919) 344 - 5241.
- Ant / Paint / Graph / Furn -   071722

Royal Oak (Maryland)
Oak Creek Sales, Rte. 329 between Easton & St. Mi-
chaels, Royal Oak, MD 21662. T. (301) 7459193.
- Ant -   071723

Royal Oak (Michigan)
Lampcraft, Inc., 4308 N. Woodward Ave., Royal Oak, MI
48072. - Lights -   071724

Rumson (New Jersey)
Roosevelt, Mary Jane, 109 E River Rd., Rumson, NJ
07760. T. (201) 842-3159.   071725

Rutherford Heights (Pennsylvania)
Benney's Antique Shop, 100 North 67th St, Rutherford
Heights, PA 17111. T. (717) 564-1002.   071726

Rutland (Vermont)
Eagle's Nest Antiques, 53 Prospect St., Rutland, VT
05701. T. (802) 773-2418.   071727

Rye (New York)
Hubbell, Ruth, Windcrest Rd., Rye, NY 10580.
T. (914) 967-7275.   071728

Sacramento (California)
Lovell's Windo – Art, 2114 P Street, Sacramento, CA
95814. T. (916) 452-1749, 443-5789. - Lights /
Glass -   071729

Saddle River (New Jersey)
Kyllo Antiques, Richard C., 158 W. Saddle River Rd.,
Saddle River, NJ 07458. T. (201) 327-7343.   071730
Samp Mill Farm, 109 W. Saddle River Rd., Saddle River,
NJ 07458. T. (201) 3276252. - Furn -   071731

Sadsburyville (Pennsylvania)
Sadsbury House, Rte. 30 and Octororo Rd., Sadsbury-
ville, PA 19369. T. (215) 857-3372. - Ant / Paint / Furn /
Num / Orient / China / Sculp / Silv / Mil -   071732

Sag Harbor (New York)
Little Barn Antiques, Sage and Madison Sts., Sag Harbor,
NY 11963. T. (516) 725-3034.   071733

Saginaw (Michigan)
Diekman's Antiques, 1172 Burbank Pl., Saginaw, MI
48603. - Ant -   071734
Tuke, Arthur T. & Theresa C., 1846 W. Michigan Ave.,
Saginaw, MI 48602.   071735

Saint Albans (Vermont)
Century Co., Saint Albans, VT 05478. - Mil -   071736

Saint Johns (Michigan)
Irrer Antiques, 201 W. McConnell, Saint Johns, MI
48779. - Ant / Furn / China / Lights / Glass - 071737

Saint Louis (Missouri)
Bennet Antiques, 146 S. Maple Ave., Saint Louis, MO
63119. - Ant / China / Glass -   071738
Braun Galleries, 10315 Clayton Rd., Saint Louis, MO
63131.   071739
Fellenz, William B., 437 N. Euclid Ave., Saint Louis, MO
63108. T. (314) 367 0214. - Ant -   071740
Gibson Antiques, 3545 Arsenal St., Saint Louis, MO
63118. - Ant / Furn / China / Instr / Glass - 071741
Good-Fellow Antiques, 7178 Manchester Ave., Saint
Louis, MO 63143. - Ant / Paint / China / Glass - 071742
Graves, Clark, 132 N Meramec Av., Saint Louis, MO
63105. T. (314) 725-2695. - Ant -   071743
Hammond, 1939 Cherokee St., Saint Louis, MO 63118.
T. (314) 776-4737. - Ant / Paint / Graph / Furn / China /
Sculp / Tex / Dec / Silv / Cur -   071744
Harris House Antiques, 20 N. Gore, Saint Louis, MO
63119.   071745
Homemaker Furniture & Antique Shop, 2124 Cherokee
St., Saint Louis, MO 63118. T. (314) 776 - 4267. - Ant /
Furn -   071746
Opel, Catherine, 9201 Big Bend Blvd., Saint Louis, MO
63119.   071747
Selkirk, B.J. & Co, 4166 Olive St, Saint Louis, MO
63108. T. (314) 533-1700, Fax (314) 533-1704.
- Ant -   071748
Ten Eyck Antique Auctions Ltd., 7438 Leadale, Saint
Louis, MO 63133.   071749
Ziern Galleries, Inc., 10333 Clayton Rd., Saint Louis, MO
63131. T. (314) 993 0809. - Ant / Paint / Furn / China /
Tex / Jew / Silv / Glass -   071750

Saint Michael's (Maryland)
Ayres, Nina A. Lanham, Talbot & Mulberry Sts., Saint Mi-
chael's, MD 21663. T. (301) 7455231. - Paint / Furn /
China / Tex / Silv -   071751

Saint Paul (Minnesota)
Chappell, Sharen, Saint Paul POB 9091, MN 55109.
T. (612) 777-8910. - Orient -   071752
Hudgins Gallery, 250 W. 7th Street, Saint Paul, MN
55102. T. (612) 2224388. - Furn / Orient -   071753
Johannsen, Mr. + Mrs. H., 1692 Charlton St., Saint Paul,
MN 55118. T. (612) 4511175. - Ant / Furn -   071754
Riesberg, Robert J., 343 Salem Church Rd., Saint Paul,
MN 55118. T. (612) 457-1772. - Ant -   071755
Twin City Stamp & Coin, 404 St. Peter St., Saint Paul,
MN 55102. T. (612) 224 6227. - Eth -   071756

Saint Petersburg (Florida)
Rebel's Rest Ant., 2048 Illinois Ave., NE, Saint Peter-
sburg, FL 33703. T. (813) 5227745. - Furn / Num /
China -   071757

Saint Thomas (Virgin Islands)
Circe Gallery, Palm Passage, Saint Thomas, VI 00802.
T. (809) 774-6514. - Ant / Eth / Jew -   071758

Salem (New York)
Eden Galleries, Halls Pond Rd., R.D. 2, Salem, NY
12865. T. (518) 854-7844. - Ant / Paint / Furn /
China -   071759

Salem (Ohio)
Wilson, Esther, 1171 E. State St., Salem, OH 44460.
- Ant -   071760

Salisbury (Connecticut)
Carrell, Russell, Rte. 44, Salisbury, CT 06068.
T. (203) 435-9301. - Ant -   071761

San Anselmo (California)
Kaufman, 540 San Anselmo Av., San Anselmo, CA
94960. T. (415) 456-7890. - Ant -   071762

San Antonio (Texas)
Antique Gallery, 4211 McCullough, San Antonio, TX
78212. - Ant / Orient / China / Jew / Silv /
Glass -   071763
Gas Light Antique Shop, 1525 McCullough Ave., San An-
tonio, TX 78212. - Ant -   071764
Horse of a Different Color, 140 W. Sunset Rd., San Anto-
nio, TX 78209. - Ant -   071765
Libby's, 1807 McCullough Ave., San Antonio, TX 78212.
T. (512) 732 2791. - Ant / Furn / China / Dec / Lights /
Glass -   071766
Miss Robertson's Shop, Menger Hotel 202 Alamo Plaza,
San Antonio, TX 78205. T. (512) 226 4091. - Ant / Chi-
na / Dec / Jew / Silv / Instr / Glass -   071767
Pagenkopf, M., 1820 Nacogdoches Rd., San Antonio, TX
78209. T. (512) 826-8222. - Ant / Furn / Jew / Silv /
Glass -   071768
Wilson, Charlotte, POB 120084, San Antonio, TX 78212.
T. (210) 828-9767.   071769

San Diego (California)
A. and B. Antique Shop, P. O. Box 5352, San Diego, CA
92105. T. (619) 283 2594. - Ant / China /
Glass -   071770
Connoisseur, 3165 Adams Av., San Diego, CA 92116.
T. (619) 284-1132. - Ant / Paint -   071771
House of Heirlooms, 801 University Ave., San Diego, CA
92103. T. (619) 2980502. - Ant -   071772
Lamplighter Antiques, 3020 Adams Ave., San Diego, CA
92116. - Ant -   071773

San Fernando (California)
Waninger, Bert, P.O.Box 1248, San Fernando, CA 91341.
T. (213) 368-6172.   071774

San Francisco (California)
Antique Exchange, 1211 Sutter St., San Francisco, CA
94109.   071775
Antiques Gallery, 412 Jackson St., San Francisco, CA
94111. T. (415) 986-0823. - Furn -   071776
Antonio's Antiques, 701 Bryant St., San Francisco, CA
94107. T. (415) 781-1737. - Furn -   071777
Argentum The Leopard's Head, 414 Jackson St., San
Francisco, CA 94111. T. (415) 296-7757.   071778
Baktiari, 2843 Clay St., San Francisco, CA 94115.
T. (415) 346-0437. - Tex -   071779
Bauer, Erik B., 1878 Union St., San Francisco, CA
94123.   071780
Beaver, 1637 Market St., San Francisco, CA 94103.
T. (415) 863-4344. - Ant -   071781
Bernstein & Co, S., 1 Daniel Burnham Ct, San Francisco,
CA 94109. T. (415) 346-9193, Fax (415) 346-
9136.   071782
Biordi Art Imports, 412 Columbus Av., San Francisco, CA
94133. T. (415) 392 8096. - Paint / China / Lights / Rel /
Glass -   071783
Blue Heaven Imports, 1021 Market St., San Francisco,
CA 94103. T. (415) 431 2429. - Jew -   071784

Caruso, Gilbert, 1400 Green St., San Francisco, CA 94109. T. (415) 673 8912. - Ant / Paint / Furn / Orient / China / Repr / Sculp / Arch / Eth / Dec / Rel -   *071785*

Challiss House, 3 Henry Adams St., San Francisco, CA 94103. T. (415) 863-1566. - Furn -   *071786*

Challiss House, 463 Jackson St., San Francisco, CA 94111. T. (415) 397-6999. - Furn -   *071787*

Clark, Mark, 760 Market St, San Francisco, CA 94102. T. (415) 296-8495. - Ant / Num / Arch / Eth -   *071788*

Coffee Cuntatut Gallery, 2030 Union St., San Francisco, CA 94123. - Paint / China -   *071789*

Conquuare, Evelyne, 550 15 St., San Francisco, CA 94103. T. (415) 552-6100/01. - Ant -   *071790*

Corwith, H. P., Ltd., 1833 Union St., San Francisco, CA 94123. T. (415) 567-7252. - Paint / Sculp / Dec / Fra / Instr / Mod -   *071791*

Craftsman's Guild, 300 De Haro St, San Francisco, CA 94107. T. (415) 431-5425. - Graph / Furn / China / Lights / Glass -   *071792*

Daibutsu, 3028 Filmore St., San Francisco, CA 94123. T. (415) 567 1530. - Ant / Orient -   *071793*

Davis, Jeffrey, & Co., 37 Presidio Av., San Francisco, CA 94115. T. (415) 921-1200. - Ant -   *071794*

Denenberg, 257 Grant Av, San Francisco, CA 94108. T. (415) 788-8411. - Paint -   *071795*

Dillingham & Co., 470 Jackson St., San Francisco, CA 94111. T. (415) 989-8777. - Paint / Furn / China / Dec -   *071796*

Domergue, Robert, & Co., 560 Jackson St., San Francisco, CA 94133. T. (415) 781-4034. - Furn -   *071797*

Doughty, John, 619 Sansome St., San Francisco, CA 94111. T. (415) 398-6849. - Furn -   *071798*

Drum & Co., 415 Jackson St., San Francisco, CA 94111. T. (415) 788-5118. - Paint / Furn -   *071799*

Every Era Antiques, 3599 Sacramento St., San Francisco, CA 94118. T. (415) 346 0313. - Ant -   *071800*

Fenton Antiques, Louis D., 432 Jackson St., San Francisco, CA 94111. T. (415) 398-3046. - Ant -   *071801*

Fillipello Antiques, Inc., 1632 Market St, San Francisco, CA 94102. T. (415) 6263372. - Ant -   *071802*

Ford, Eleanor, 1878 Union St., San Francisco, CA 94125.   *071803*

Foster-Gwin, 425 Jackson St., San Francisco, CA 94111. T. (415) 397-4986. - Furn -   *071804*

Fox's, St. Francis Hotel Union Sq., San Francisco, CA 94119. T. (415) 989-5409. - Ant / Orient / Jew -   *071805*

Frankel Antiques, 746 Clement St., San Francisco, CA 94118.   *071806*

Frizzell, Virginia, 872 North Point Street, San Francisco, CA 94109. T. (415) 474 2644. - Ant / Furn / China / Tex / Dec / Fra / Silv / Glass -   *071807*

Gaylord, Charles William, 2151 Powell St., San Francisco, CA 94133. T. (415) 392-6085. - Ant -   *071808*

Gump's, 250 Post St., San Francisco, CA 94108. T. (415) 982-1616. - Paint / Graph / Furn / Orient / China / Sculp / Silv -   *071809*

Hardy, Ed, 750 Post St., San Francisco, CA 94109. T. (415) 771-6644. - Furn -   *071810*

Heynemann, John, Oriental and European Fine Arts, 357 Arguello Blvd., San Francisco, CA 94118. T. (415) 752 2288. - Ant / Paint / Graph / Orient / Eth -   *071811*

Hill, David, 553 Pacific Av., San Francisco, CA 94133. T. (415) 677-9770.   *071812*

House of Sung, 3661 Sacramento St., San Francisco, CA 94118. T. (415) 922-4422. - Ant / Furn -   *071813*

Hunt, 405 Jackson St., San Francisco, CA 94111. T. (415) 989-9531. - Furn -   *071814*

International Art Gallery, 1581 Webster St, San Francisco, CA 94115. T. (415) 567-4390. - Graph / Orient -   *071815*

Kimura, 1933 Ocean Av, San Francisco, CA 94127. T. (415) 585-0052. - Orient -   *071816*

Knolle, 411 Vermont St., San Francisco, CA 94107. T. (415) 563-7717. - Ant -   *071817*

Kuromatsu, 722 Bay St., San Francisco, CA 94109. T. (415) 474 4027. - Ant / Orient -   *071818*

La Salle Gallery Inc., 2083 Union St., San Francisco, CA 94123.   *071819*

Lang, J.M., 361 Sutter St., San Francisco, CA 94108.   *071820*

Lyons, 2700 Hyde St, San Francisco, CA 94109. T. (415) 441-2202. - Graph -   *071821*

MacKenzie, John A., 209 Post St., San Francisco, CA 94108.   *071822*

Modern Furniture Classics, 53 Page and 32 Rose, San Francisco, CA 94102. T. (415) 553-4500.   *071823*

Old and Rare Prints, 209 Corbett Av, San Francisco, CA 94114. T. (415) 621-3565. - Graph -   *071824*

Oriental Porcelain Gallery, 2702 Hyde St., San Francisco, CA 94109. T. (415) 776-5969. - Ant / Orient / China -   *071825*

Pantechnicon, 1849 Union St., San Francisco, CA 94123. T. (415) 922 1104. - Ant / Paint / Furn / Orient -   *071826*

Pearson, Bill & Margaret, 3315 Sacramento St., Suite 355, San Francisco, CA 94118. - Eth -   *071827*

Percy, Alan and John Doughty Antiques, 619 Sansome St. Jackson Sq., San Francisco, CA 94111. T. (415) 3986849. - Ant -   *071828*

Pertersen's Antiques, 1866-68 Union St., San Francisco, CA 94123. T. (415) 567 6260. - Ant -   *071829*

Pugsley & Son, P. G., 4900 California St., San Francisco, CA 94118. - Ant / Paint / Furn / Dec / Lights / Mod -   *071830*

San Francisco Antique Furniture & Woodworks, 3030 17th St, San Francisco, CA 94110. T. (415) 431-2465.   *071831*

Sanuk, 1810 Union St., San Francisco, CA 94123. T. (415) 563-0270, Fax (415) 563-1429.   *071832*

Sean's Antiques, 2501 Irving St, San Francisco, CA 94122. T. (415) 731-0758. - Ant / Furn -   *071833*

Shepherd, Norman, 458 Jackson St., San Francisco, CA 94111. T. (415) 362-4145. - Ant -   *071834*

Shibata, 3028 Filmore St., San Francisco, CA 94123. T. (415) 567-1530. - Orient -   *071835*

Shiota, T. Z., 3131 Fillmore St., San Francisco, CA 94123. T. (415) 929-7979. - Ant / Graph / Orient / China -   *071836*

Stein, Daniel, 701 Sansome St., San Francisco, CA 94111. T. (415) 956-5620. - Furn / Instr -   *071837*

Therien & Co., 411 Vermont St., San Francisco, CA 94107. T. (415) 956-8850. - Furn / Orient -   *071838*

Thomson, Claire, 3232 Sacramento St., San Francisco, CA 94115. T. (415) 567-9898. - Furn -   *071839*

Titanic Art Deco Gallery, 1810 Union St., San Francisco, CA 94123. T. (415) 563-0555. - Furn / Mod -   *071840*

Ukiyo-e Gallery, 4736 17 St., San Francisco, CA 94117. T. (415) 731-5971. - Orient -   *071841*

Vingo, Joseph, 872 North Point St., San Francisco, CA 94109. T. (415) 928-0771. - Ant / Furn / China -   *071842*

Wofsy, Alan, 1109 Geary Blvd, San Francisco, CA 91409. T. (415) 292-6500, Fax (415) 547-1623. - Paint -   *071843*

Wong, Wylie, 1055 Washington St., San Francisco, CA 94108. T. (415) 433-7389. - Orient -   *071844*

San Gabriel (California)
Brackett's Fine Antiques, 8956 Huntington Dr., San Gabriel, CA 91775. - Furn / China / Glass -   *071845*

San Jose (California)
Brookings, J.J., 330 Commercial St., San Jose, CA 95112. T. (408) 287-3311. - Ant -   *071846*

Classic Antiques, 2210 Lincoln Ave., San Jose, CA 95125. T. (408) 264-0604. - Ant -   *071847*

San Juan Capistano (California)
Durenberger, G. R., 31431 Camino Capistrano, San Juan Capistano, CA 92675. T. (714) 493 1283. - Ant / Furn -   *071848*

San Mateo (California)
Kovacs, Frank L., POB 25300, San Mateo, CA 94402. T. (415) 574-2028, Fax (415) 574-1995. - Num / Arch -   *071849*

Sandwich (Massachusetts)
Dillingham House Antiques, Rte. 130, 71 Main St., Sandwich, MA 02563. T. (617) 8880999. - Ant -   *071850*

The Brown Jug, 155 Main St., Sandwich, MA 02563. T. (617) 888-0940. - Glass -   *071851*

Santa Ana (California)
Hansen, Herb, 210 W 19 St., Santa Ana, CA 92706. - Ant -   *071852*

Santa Barbara (California)
Arlington, 819 Anacapa St., Santa Barbara, CA 93101. - Ico -   *071853*

Decker, Burton A., 20 E. Cota St., Santa Barbara, CA 93101. T. (805) 962 4615. - Ant -   *071854*

Le Papillon, 1637 East Valley Road, Santa Barbara, CA 93103. T. (805) 969 3142. - Ant -   *071855*

Santa Cruz (California)
Hall's Surry House Antiques, 708 Water St., Santa Cruz, CA 95060. T. (408) 4232475. - Ant -   *071856*

Santa Fe (New Mexico)
Dewey-Kofron, 74 E San Francisco St., Santa Fe, NM 87501. T. (505) 982-8632. - Ant / Paint / Furn / China / Sculp / Tex / Arch / Eth / Jew / Silv / Rel -   *071857*

Doodlet's, Santa Fe, NM 87501. - Ant / Paint / Graph / Furn / China / Arch / Dec / Jew / Lights / Rel / Glass --   *071858*

Hansen Galleries, 923 Paseo de Peralta, Santa Fe, NM 87501.   *071859*

Harvey, Fred, 100 San Francisco St., Santa Fe, NM 87501. - Ant / China / Repr / Sculp / Tex / Arch / Eth / Dec / Jew / Silv / Rel -   *071860*

Kachina House, 610 Canyon Rd., Santa Fe, NM 87501. - Paint / China / Tex / Arch -   *071861*

Madtson, Don J., 806 Old Santa Fe Trail, Santa Fe, NM 98501. T. (505) 982 4102. - Ant / Paint / Graph / Furn / Orient / China / Sculp / Arch / Jew / Lights / Instr / Glass -   *071862*

Packard's Chaparral Trading Post, On the Plaza, Santa Fe, NM 87501. T. (505) 983 9241. - Paint / China / Sculp / Tex / Arch / Dec / Jew / Silv -   *071863*

Padilla & Heinemann, 7 Montoya Circle, Santa Fe, NM 87501. T. (505) 988-3739.   *071864*

Peters, Gerald, 439 Camino del Monte Sol, Santa Fe, NM 87504-0908. T. (505) 988-8961. - Paint / Graph / Sculp / Mod -   *071865*

Shop of the Rainbow Man, 107 E Palace Av., Santa Fe, NM 87501. T. (505) 982-0791. - Ant -   *071866*

Santa Monica (California)
Anderson, E. S., 135 Entrada Dr., Santa Monica, CA 90402.   *071867*

Argentum The Leopard's Head, 216 26th St., Santa Monica, CA 90402. T. (213) 458-3432.   *071868*

Chait, I.M., 2409 Wilshire Blvd, Santa Monica, CA 90403. T. (213) 828-8537, Fax (213) 828-5181. - Ant / Furn / Arch / Eth / Jew -   *071869*

Ganz, Whitney, 1109 Montana Av., Santa Monica, CA 90403. T. (310) 576-2666.   *071870*

Gould, Richard, Antiques Ltd., 216 26th St., Santa Monica, CA 90402. T. (213) 395 0724. - Ant / China / Lights -   *071871*

Japan Gallery, 2718 Wilshire Blvd., Santa Monica, CA 90403. T. (213) 453-6406. - Orient -   *071872*

Mukashiya, K.K., 2717 Wilshire Blvd., Santa Monica, CA 90403. T. (213) 453-4736. - Orient -   *071873*

Potpourri Shop, 1322 18th St., Santa Monica, CA 90404. - Ant -   *071874*

Samuels & Co, Spencer A., 1040 4 Str, Santa Monica, Ca 90403. T. (310) 395-0124, Fax (310) 395-8364. - Ant / Paint -   *071875*

Saranac (Michigan)
Little Brown Jug, 64 Pleasant St., Saranac, MI 48881.   *071876*

Sarasota (Florida)
Hang-up, 3850 S Osprey Av., Suite 100, Sarasota, FL 34239. T. (813) 953-5757. - Paint / Graph / Repr / Sculp / Jew / Fra / Mul -   *071877*

Saratoga (California)
Corinthian Studios, 20506 Saratoga-Los Gatos Rd., Saratoga, CA 95070. T. (408) 867-4630. - Silv -   *071878*

McKenzie House, 14554 Big Basin Way, Saratoga, CA 95070. T. (408) 8671341. - Furn / Eth -   *071879*

Saugatuck (Michigan)
Gothic Cottage Antiques, 3442 Holland Rd., Saugatuck, MI 49453. T. (616) 8572908.   *071880*

Kollen, Ben, Country Store, 120 Butler St., Saugatuck, MI 49453. T. (616) 857 8601. - Ant / Furn / Silv / Glass -   *071881*

White House Curio Shop, 106 Mason St, Saugatuck, MI
49453. T. (616) 857-2404. - Ant -   071882

Sausalito (California)
Imari Imports, 40 Filbert Ave, Sausalito, CA 94965.
T. (415) 332-0245, Fax (415) 332-3621.
- Orient -   071883
The Arts & Crafts Shop of the West Coast, 1417 Bridge-
way, Sausalito, CA 94965. T. (415) 331-2554. 071884

Savage (Maryland)
Antique Gallery Ltd., The, Foundry St., Savage, MD
20863. T. (202) 7924538. - Furn / Instr -   071885

Savannah (Georgia)
An English Accent, 509 Lincoln St., Savannah, GA
31401.   071886
Kimble Antiques, Caroline, 230 W. Bay St., Savannah,
GA 31401.   071887
Pink House Antiques and Paintings, 23 Abercorn St., Sa-
vannah, GA 31412. - Ant / Paint / Furn / Orient / China /
Tex / Dec / Fra / Silv / Instr / Glass / Draw -   071888
Smith Antiques, Arthur, 1 West Jones St., Savannah, GA
31401.   071889
White Bluff Furniture & Antiques, 5701 White Bluff Rd.,
Savannah, GA 31405.   071890
Williams Interiors, 447 Bull St., Savannah, GA 31401.
- Ant / Paint / Graph / Furn / China / Lights / Instr --
                                                    071891

Schenectady (New York)
Frances Antiques, Mary, 302 Front St., Schenectady, NY
12305. T. (518) 377-9806, 393-6536.   071892
Hagar Antiques, Bell, 1608 Union St., Schenectady, NY
12309. T. (518) 346-3646.   071893
Ona Curran Antiques, 2336 Cayuga Road, Schenectady,
NY 12309. T. (518) 3723653. - Furn -   071894
Skype's Gallery, 140 N Broadway, Schenectady, NY
12305. T. (518) 372-1870. - Paint / Graph / Furn / Chi-
na / Tex / Dec / Lights / Instr / Glass -   071895

Scottsdale (Arizona)
Hill, John C., 6990 E Main St, Second Floor, Scottsdale,
AZ 85251. T. (602) 946-2910.   071896
House of the Six Directions, Indian Art, 7051 Fifth Ave.,
Scottsdale, AZ 85251. T. (602) 946-1316. - Ant /
Paint / Graph / Sculp / Arch / Eth / Jew / Rel -   071897
J.H. Armer Interior Design, 6926 Main St., Scottsdale,
AZ 85251. T. (602) 9472407. - Furn -   071898
Marco P., 3940 N Marshall Way, Scottsdale, AZ 85251.
T. (602) 946-2046, Fax (602) 946-2279.   071899
Marsha's Antiques, 7121 Fifth Av., Scottsdale, AZ
85251. - Ant -   071900
Ye Olde Curiosity Shoppe, 7245 E. 1st Ave., Scottsdale,
AZ 85251. T. (602) 947 3062. - Ant / China /
Fra -   071901

Seaford (New York)
Spindel, Michael, POB 390, Seaford, NY 11783.
T. (516) 541-5027. - Orient -   071902

Seal Beach (California)
Audrey's Antiques, 132 Main St., Seal Beach, CA 90740.
T. (213) 430 7213. - Ant / Jew / Silv -   071903

Searsport (Maine)
Captain's House, The, Rte. 1, Searsport, ME 04974.
T. (207) 5486344. - Furn / Orient -   071904

Seattle (Washington)
Admiralty House Antiques, 2141 California Ave., S. W.,
Seattle, WA 98116. T. (206) WE 5 4195;MU 2 0594.
- Ant / Furn / China / Dec / Silv / Lights / Instr / Mil / Glas-
s -   071905
Bamboo Hut, 1914 3rd Ave., Seattle, WA 98101.
T. (206) 622 4090. - Num / Instr / Mil -   071906
Barker, 22456 Pacific Hwy. S, Seattle, WA 98188.
T. (206) 878-4161. - Ant / Furn / China / Tex / Jew / Silv /
Glass -   071907
Carriage House Galleries, 5611 University Way N. E.,
Seattle, WA 98105. T. (206) 523 4960. - Ant / Paint /
Furn / China / Sculp / Dec / Jew / Lights / Instr /
Glass -   071908
Chelsea Cottage Antiques, 3622 N.E. 45th St., Seattle,
WA 98105.   071909

Corona Decor Co., 260 E 39 Av., Seattle, WA 98102.
T. (206) 325-0972. - Ant / Repr / Tex / Dec / Fra / Rel /
Ico -   071910
Crane Gallery, 1203b Second Av., Seattle, WA 98101.
T. (206) 622-7185. - Orient -   071911
Davis, William L., 1300 Fifth Av., Seattle, WA 98101.
T. (206) 622-0518. - Ant / Furn / Orient / China / Repr /
Dec / Silv / Lights / Instr -   071912
Flury & Co, Lois, 322 First Av. S, Seattle, WA 98104.
T. (206) 587-0260, Fax (206) 382-3519.   071913
Fox's Shop Inc.- Olympic Shop – Fox's Jade Shop, 1341
5th Ave. Olympic Hotel, Seattle, WA 98101.
T. (206) 623 - 2528. - Ant / Furn / China / Jew - 071914
Gunderson, 527 Pine St., Seattle, WA 98101.
T. (206) 624 1531. - Ant -   071915
Honeychurch, 1008 James St., Seattle, WA 98104.
T. (206) 622-1225. - Orient -   071916
Janison, Bernard, Joshua Green Bldg. 1425 4th Ave.,
Seattle, WA 98101. - Num -   071917
Kagedo, 520 First Av. S, Seattle, WA 98104.
T. (206) 467-9077. - Orient / Jew -   071918
Market Coins, 19 Lower Pike Place Market, Seattle, WA
98101. T. (206) 227603. - Num -   071919
Nimba, 8041 32 Av. NW, Seattle, WA 98107.
T. (206) 783-4296. - Ant / Sculp / Sculp / Arch /
Eth -   071920
Old Fire House, 213 1st Ave. S., Seattle, WA 98104.
- Ant / Lights / Mil -   071921
Queen Anne Gifts & Antiques, Lower Level, Pike Place
Market Stall No. 12, Seattle, WA 98110. - Ant / Dec /
Silv / Glass -   071922
Ye Olde Curiosity Shop, 601 Alaskan Way, Pier 51,
Seattle, WA 98104. T. (206) 682-5844. - Ant / Graph /
Orient / China / Repr / Sculp / Dec / Jew / Mil / Glass / C-
ur -   071923

Seekonk (Massachusetts)
Leonard's, 600 Taunton Av., Seekonk, MA
02771.   071924

Seekonok (Massachusetts)
American Art Search, 400 Jacob Hill Rd., Seekonok, MA
02771. T. (617) 336-5627.   071925
Antiques at Hearthstone House, 15 Fall River Av., Seeko-
nok, MA 02771. T. (617) 336-6273. - Ant /
Furn -   071926
Leonard's, 600 Taunton Av., Seekonok, MA 02771.
T. (617) 336-8585. - Ant / Furn -   071927

Sewickley (Pennsylvania)
The Antiquarian Shop, 421 Broad St., Sewickley, PA
15143. T. (412) 741 6100. - Ant / Paint / Sculp - 071928

Shaker Heights (Ohio)
Shaker Square Antiques, 12733 Larchmere Blvd.,
Shaker Heights, OH 44120. T. (216) 921-0581. 071929

Sharon (Vermont)
Columns Antique Shop, The, Rte. 14, Sharon, VT 05065.
T. (802) 763-7040.   071930

Shawnee Mission (Kansas)
Lanne, 6711 Antioch Rd. Meriam, Shawnee Mission, KS
66202. T. (913) 432 3882. - Ant -   071931
Mean, Cleo, 7701 W. 61st St. Overland Park, Shawnee
Mission, KS 66202. T. (913) 432 3516.
- Glass -   071932

Shawnee-on-Delaware (Pennsylvania)
Sittig, Charlotte and Edgar, Shawnee-on-Delaware, PA
18356. T. (717) 421 5632. - Ant -   071933

Sheffield (Massachusetts)
Dovetail, Rte. 7, Sheffield, MA 01257. T. (413) 229 2628.
- Furn / Instr -   071934
Fifty King Antiques, Route 7, Sheffield, MA 01257.
T. (413) 229-8900. - Paint / Furn -   071935
Hamilton, Josephine, S Main St., Sheffield, MA 01257.
T. (413) 229-8737. - Ant -   071936
Spring, Lois W., Ashley Falls Rd. Rte. 7-A, Sheffield, MA
01257. T. (413) 229 2542. - Ant / Furn / Silv -   071937
Twin Fires Antiques, Berkshire School Rd., Sheffield, MA
01257. T. (413) 229-8307.   071938

Shelbyville (Kentucky)
Wakefield-Scearce, 525 Washington St., Shelbyville, KY
40065. T. (502) 633-4382. - Ant / Furn / China /
Silv -   071939

Sherman Oaks (California)
L'Imagerie, 15030 Ventura Blvd., Sherman Oaks, CA
91403. T. (818) 3449713. - Graph / Repr -   071940
Orlando Gallery, 14553 Ventura Blvd., Sherman Oaks,
CA 91403. T. (818) 789-6012. - Paint / Sculp / Arch /
Eth / Rel / Pho / Draw -   071941

Shreveport (Louisiana)
Manning's Antiques, 6235 Greenwood Rd., Shreveport,
LA 71109. T. (318) 635 0911. - Ant / Furn / China / Silv /
Glass -   071942
May's Antiques, 2713 Fairfield Ave., Shreveport, LA
71104. T. (318) 422 6297. - Ant -   071943
Mosley Manor Antiques, 628 Stoner Avenue, Shreveport,
LA 71101.   071944

Shutesbury (Massachusetts)
Smith, Kay, off Rte. 202, Shutesbury, MA 01072.
T. (413) 256 6965. - Ant / Furn / Orient / Instr - 071945

Silver Spring (Maryland)
Hecht & Co., Silver Spring, MD 20900.
T. (301) 587 1500. - Num -   071946

Simsbury (Connecticut)
Hawkshead Antiques, 56 Country Rd., Simsbury, CT
06070. T. (203) 6589841.   071947

Sinclair (Wyoming)
Budd's, 204 N 9th St., Sinclair, WY 82334. - Ant / China / Glass -   071948

Sinking Spring (Pennsylvania)
Fegley, J. Russell, State Hill Rd., Sinking Spring, PA
19608. T. (215) 678 2035. - Ant -   071949

Sioux City (Iowa)
The Victorian Shop, 3720 6th Ave., Sioux City, IA 51106.
- Ant / China / Glass -   071950

Skokie (Illinois)
Prestige Art Galleries, 3909 Howard St., Skokie, IL
60076. T. (312) 679-2555. - Paint -   071951

Smithtown (New York)
GBI Antiques, 94 Croft Lane, Smithtown, NY 11787.
T. (516) 724-7781. - Paint / Furn / Sculp -   071952

Sodus Point (New York)
Heritage House, Bay St., Sodus Point, NY 14555.
T. (315) 483 9813. - Ant -   071953
White Pillars, Bay St., Sodus Point, NY 14555.
T. (315) 484 4508. - Ant -   071954

Solebury (Pennsylvania)
Whitley, Robert, Laurel Rd., Solebury, PA 18963.
T. (215) 297-8452. - Ant / Furn / Repr / Sculp /
Arch -   071955

South Attleboro (Massachusetts)
Leonard Antiques, George, 707 Washington St., South
Attleboro, MA 02703. T. (617) 3997004.   071956

South Easton (Massachusetts)
Joes Antiques, The, 688 Washington St., South Easton,
MA 02375. T. (617) 2387516.   071957

South Egremont (Massachusetts)
Bird Cage Antiques, Rte. 23, South Egremont, MA
01258. T. (413) 528 3556. - Ant -   071958
Red Barn Antiques, Main St., Route 23, South Egremont,
MA 01258. T. (413) 5383230.   071959
Smithy Antiques, Sheffield Rd. and Rt. 23, South Egre-
mont, MA 01258. T. (413) 5281417.   071960
Snyder, Elliott & Grace, Rte. 41, Box 598, South Egre-
mont, MA 01258. T. (413) 528-3581. - Furn -   071961

South Essex (Massachusetts)
Landry, L.A., 94 Main St, South Essex, MA 01981.
T. (617) 768-6233. - Ant -   071962

South Orleans (Massachusetts)
Pleasant Bay Antiques, Rte. 28, Main Rd. Between Chatham and Orleans, South Orleans, MA 02662.
T. (617) 255 0930. - Ant / Furn / Orient -   071963

South Salem (New York)
Russel, John Keith, Spring St., South Salem, NY 10590.
T. (914) 763-8144. - Furn -   071964
Schorsch, David A., South Salem POB 413, NY 10590.
T. (914) 234-9556. - Furn -   071965

Southampton (New York)
Windmill, Antique Galleries, 715 Hampton Rd., Southampton, NY 11968. T. (516) 283 1542. - Ant /
Furn -   071966

Southboro (Massachusetts)
Toomey's Haven Antiques, 89 Framingham Rd., Southboro, MA 01772. T. (617) 4856910.   071967

Southbury (Connecticut)
Richmond, Howard and Priscilla, Rte. 6, Southbury, CT
06488. T. (203) 264 8168. - Furn -   071968

Southfield (Michigan)
Schneider, Lila, 15692 Pennsylvania Ave., Southfield, MI
48075. - Jew -   071969

Southport (Connecticut)
Eyck – Emerich, Ten Antiques, 351 Pequot Ave., Southport, CT 06490. T. (203) 2592559. - Furn / China /
Glass -   071970
Guthman, Pat, 342 Pequot Rd., Southport, CT 06490.
T. (203) 259-5743.   071971
Richardson, J.B., 362 Pequot Av., Southport, CT 06490.
T. (203) 259-1903, 226-0358. - Furn -   071972

Sparta (New Jersey)
Century House, 24 Main St., Sparta, NJ 07871.
T. (201) 729-5420. - Ant / Furn / Glass -   071973

Spartanburg (South Carolina)
Chestnut Galleries, 144 Chestnut St, Spartanburg, SC
29302. T. (803) 585 9576. - Ant / Furn / China /
Tex -   071974
Dennis, Ann S., 13 Montgomery Dr., Spartanburg, SC
29302. T. (803) 585-3084. - Furn -   071975
Hicklin, Robert M., 509 E Saint John St., Spartanburg,
SC 29302. T. (803) 583-9847. - Paint -   071976

Spokane (Washington)
McCormick Antiques, Kay, South 1224 Grand Blvd., Spokane, WA 99202. T. (509) 747-2523.   071977
McLeod's Antiques, E. 2118 Sprague Ave., Spokane, WA
99202. T. (509) 535-6032.   071978

Springfield (Illinois)
Eastnor Gallery of Antiques, 700 E. Miller, Springfield, IL
62702. T. (217) 5230998, 7877729. - Ant /
Furn -   071979

Springfield (Pennsylvania)
Marple, 816 W Springfield Rd., Springfield, PA 19064.
T. (215) 543-3809. - Ant -   071980

Springfield (Vermont)
Summer Hill Shop, 80 Summer Hill, Springfield, VT
05156. T. (802) 885 3294. - Ant / Graph / Furn /
Glass -   071981

Springfield (Virginia)
Minh van Nguyen, 7420 Highland Street, Springfield, VA
22150.   071982

Stamford (Connecticut)
Antiques Et Cetera, 3020 High Ridge Rd., Stamford, CT
06903. T. (203) 3229288.   071983
Avis & Rockwell Gardiner, 60 Mill Road, Stamford, CT
06903. T. (203) 3221129. - Ant -   071984
Gardiner, Avis & Rockwell, 60 Mill Rd., Stamford, CT
06903. T. (203) 322-1129. - Ant / Paint /
Graph -   071985
Weed House Antiques, 1415 High Ridge Rd., Stamford,
CT 06903. T. (203) 322-7246.   071986

Stanfordville (New York)
Country Fare Antiques, Route 82, Stanfordville, NY
12581. T. (914) 868-7107.   071987

Staunton (Virginia)
Mint Spring Antiques, Rte. 2, Box 282, Staunton, VA
24401. T. (703) 337-2164.   071988

Stockton (California)
Smith's Trading Post, 1416 N. „D" St., Stockton, CA
95205. - Ant / Mil -   071989

Stone Ridge (New York)
Thumbprint, Tongore Rd., Stone Ridge, NY 12484.
T. (914) 687-9318.   071990

Stonersville (Pennsylvania)
Fred and Dottie's Antiques, Stonersville, PA 19556.
T. (215) 582 8870. - Ant -   071991

Stony Ridge (Ohio)
Ridge Antiques, Stony, Route 20, Stony Ridge, OH
43463.   071992

Stowe (Vermont)
Green Antiques, Main St., Stowe, VT 05672.
T. (802) 253-4369. - Paint / Furn / China / Repr /
Silv -   071993

Studio City (California)
Adler, Allan, 3263 Oakdell Rd., Studio City, CA 91604.
- Ant / Paint / Graph / Furn / China / Sculp / Dec / Jew / Silv / Glass -   071994
Appraisal Company, Antiques and Art, 4205 Alcove Av.,
Studio City, CA 91604.   071995

Sturgis (Michigan)
Yesh's Antiques, E. City Limits on Rte. 12, Sturgis, MI
49091.   071996

Sudbury (Massachusetts)
Woodvine Antiques, 254 Old Sudbury Rd., Sudbury, MA
01776. T. (617) 4432374.   071997

Suffern (New York)
North Hill Antiques, Suffern POB 455, NY 10901.
T. (914) 357-4484. - Silv -   071998

Sugar Hill (New Hampshire)
Lynn, Eleanor M. & Monahan, Elizabeth A., Rte. 117, Sugar Hill, NH 03585. T. (603) 8235550. - Furn -   071999

Summit (New Jersey)
Blair, Catherine, 83 Summit Av., Summit, NJ 07901.
T. (201) 273-5771.   072000
Summit Auction Rooms, 47 Summit Ave., Summit, NJ
07901.   072001

Surfside (Florida)
Mankin, Surfside POB 546146, FL 33154. T. (305) 861-9743. - Orient -   072002

Sutton Center (Massachusetts)
Polly's Antiques, Corn. Boston + Singletary Ave., Sutton
Center, MA 01527. T. (617) 8652654.   072003

Syracuse (New York)
Dixon, Jeannette H., 917 Valley Dr., Syracuse, NY
13207. - Ant -   072004
Egy, Lester, 1039 Euclid Av., Syracuse, NY 13210. - Ant /
Glass -   072005
Jacobsen, Charles W., 401 S Salina St., Syracuse, NY
13202. T. (315) 422-7832. - Tex -   072006
Kenyon, Henrietta M., 3401 James St., Syracuse, NY
13206. - Ant -   072007
Syracuse Stamp & Coin Company, 122 E Washington
St., Syracuse, NY 13202. - Num -   072008
Worfel, J. Sons, 934 Oak St, Syracuse, NY 13208.
T. (315) 479-6431. - Furn -   072009

Tacoma (Washington)
Meier's House of Clocks, 525 Tacoma Mall, Tacoma, WA
98409. T. (206) 246-7450. - Instr -   072010
Old Tacoma Antique Shop, 2223 N. 30th St., Tacoma,
WA 98403. T. (206) MA 7 2743. - Ant / Furn / China /
Jew / Silv / Glass -   072011

South Tacoma Coin Co., 5225 S. Tacoma Ave., Tacoma,
WA 98408. T. (206) 472 8920. - Num -   072012
The Glass Rooster, 3709 6th Ave., Tacoma, WA 98406.
T. (206) 752 7347. - Ant / Paint / Graph / Furn / China /
Arch / Dec / Jew / Instr / Mil / Glass -   072013

Tampa (Florida)
Village Antique Center Inc., 4323 El Prado Blvd., Tampa,
FL 33609. T. (813) 837-2631.   072014

Taos (New Mexico)
Don Fernando Curio & Gift Shop, P. O. Box 1187, Taos,
NM 87571. T. (505) 758 3791; 758 2401. - Ant /
Cur -   072015
The Market, E. Kit Carson Rd., P. O. Box 1111, Taos, NM
87571. T. (505) 758 3195. - Furn / China / Sculp / Tex /
Dec / Jew / Lights / Rel -   072016

Tarboro (North Carolina)
Miriam's Oriental Rugs, 905 Main St., Tarboro, 27886
NC. T. (919) 823 4964.   072017

Taylor (Michigan)
Buterbaugh, Dorothy, 16663 Ziegler, Taylor, MI 48180.
- Ant / Glass -   072018

Tempe (Arizona)
Reverie Antiques, 516 S. Mill, Tempe, AZ 85251. - Ant /
Furn / Pho -   072019

Temperance (Michigan)
Stark Antiques, Lester, 4532 St. Anthony Road, Temperance, MI 48182.   072020

Toledo (Ohio)
Cheshire Cat Antiques & Art Gallery, 2215 Collingwood
Blvd., Toledo, OH 43620.   072021
Goldie's Antiques, 2154 Alvin St., Toledo, OH 43607.
- Ant -   072022
Town Gallery, 1811 Adams St., Toledo, OH 43624.
- Paint / Graph / Orient / China / Sculp / Tex / Arch / Eth /
Dec / Fra -   072023

Tolland (Massachusetts)
Good & Hutchinson, Rte. 57, Tolland, MA 01257.
T. (413) 258 4555. - Paint / Furn -   072024
Whitney, Marie, Antiques, Granville Rd., Tolland, MA
01034. T. (413) 258 4538. - China -   072025

Topanga (California)
Caskey-Lees Gallery, Box 1637, Topanga, CA 90290.
T. (310) 455-2886.   072026

Torrington (Connecticut)
Barredo's Antiques, 2496 South Main St., Torrington, CT
06790. T. (203) 4820627, 4898716.   072027
Good Old Days Antiques, 262 New Harwinton Rd., Torrington, CT 06790. T. (203) 4826866.   072028

Towaco (New Jersey)
Weaver, Frank, Jacksonville Rd., Towaco, NJ 07082.
T. (201) 334 5335. - Furn -   072029

Traverse City (Michigan)
Baynton, Elmer, 37a High St., Traverse City, MI
49684.   072030

Trenton (New Jersey)
Pitasky's Inc., 8 Diane Dr., Trenton, NJ 08628.
- Ant -   072031
Robinson, Dorothy N., Trenton POB 180, OH 45373.
T. (609) 392-2878. - Silv -   072032

Troy (Ohio)
Colonial House Antiques, 1755 W.Swailes Rd., 45373
Troy, 45373. T. (513) 335-3468.   072033

Tuckahoe (New York)
Ox Bow, 281 White Plains Rd., Tuckahoe, NY 10707.
T. (914) 961 8060. - Ant -   072034

Tucson (Arizona)
Kopper Key Coin Co., 6441 Calle de Estevan, Tucson, AZ
85718. - Num -   072035
Thunderbird Shop, 40 W Broadway, Tucson, AZ 85701.
T. (602) 623-1371. - Eth / Jew / Rel -   072036

Tulsa (Oklahoma)

Barber, 3421 E Fifth Pl., Tulsa, OK 74112. T. (918) 834-1544, 834-6640. - Ant - 072037

Berry's, 4817 S. Victor Ave., Tulsa, OK 74105. - Ant - 072038

Golden Eagle Antiques, 3844 S. Atlanta Pl., Tulsa, OK 74105. T. (918) 743 1805. - Ant - 072039

O'Shea, Dan, 2050 Utica Sq., Tulsa, OK 74114. T. (918) 747-5187. - Ant / Paint / Graph / Furn / Arch / Lights - 072040

Porry's Antiques, 8312 E. 11th St., Tulsa, OK 74112. - Ant / Furn / Orient / China / Sculp / Tex / Eth / Silv / Lights / Glass - 072041

Sharp's 1860 Antiques, 1860 East 15th St., Tulsa, OK 74104. T. (918) 939-1121. 072042

Stone's Antiques, 3920 S. Lewis Pl., Tulsa, OK 74105. T. (918) 742 6082. - Ant - 072043

Tuscaloosa (Alabama)

Blossom Top Farm, Jug Factory Rd., Tuscaloosa, AL 35401. T. (205) 3455224. 072044

Tustin (California)

Dwaine Galleries, 220 El Camino Real, Tustin, CA 92680. T. (714) 8388115. - Ant - 072045

Tyler (Texas)

Dickerson, Shirley, 1205 S. Chilton Ave., Tyler, TX 75701. T. (214) 5951320. - Ant - 072046

Tyringham (Massachusetts)

Tyringham Galleries, Tyringham, MA 01264. T. (413) 243-0654,243-3260. - Ant / Paint / Graph / Furn / Orient / China / Sculp / Mul - 072047

Union (Maine)

Ebenezer Alden House, The, Union, ME 04862. T. (207) 7852881. - Ant / Paint / Furn - 072048

Union City (Michigan)

Radebaugh's Plantation Antiques, 120 Calhoun St., R2, Box 218, Union City, MI 49094. - Ant / Paint / Furn / China / Lights / Mil / Glass - 072049

Union City (Tennessee)

Doss, John & Naomi, 625 N. First St., Union City, TN 38261. T. (901) 885 3994. - Ant / Furn / Lights - 072050

Uniontown (Maryland)

Woodwards, The, 3443 Uniontown Rd., Uniontown, MD 21157. T. (301) 8766554. - Ant / Furn - 072051

Upper Black Eddy (Pennsylvania)

McCarty, Ann, River Rd. Rte. 32, P. O. Box 424, Upper Black Eddy, PA 18972. T. (215) 982 5796. - Ant / Furn - 072052

Upperville (Virginia)

Golden Horse Shoe, The, Rte. 50, Upperville, VA 22176. T. (703) 5923470. - Furn - 072053

Upton (Massachusetts)

Boulder Farm Ant., Grove and Menden Streets, Upton, MA 01568. T. (617) 5293948. 072054

Trask Farm Antiques, Mendon St., Upton, MA 01568. T. (617) 5293000. 072055

Utica (New York)

Johnny's Swap Shop, Corner of South & Steuben Sts., Utica, NY 13501. T. (315) 732-2427. - Ant / Graph / Furn / Num / China / Tex / Jew / Lights / Instr / Glass -- 072056

Uxbridge (Massachusetts)

Wildcares Antiques, Henry St., Uxbridge, MA 01569. T. (617) 4730068. 072057

Vancouver (Washington)

Jadgestone Gallery, 10922 NE Saint Johns Rd, Vancouver, WA 98686. T. (206) 573-2580, Fax (206) 573-4834. 072058

Versailles (Kentucky)

Kelly, Charles W., Kelwood Farm, Dry Ridge Rd., Versailles, KY 40383. T. (606) 873-8358. - Furn - 072059

Vevay (Indiana)

Lost Cause Antique Galleries, Main at Main Cross, Vevay, IN 47043. T. (812) 427-2900. - Ant / Paint / Graph / Orient / China / Sculp / Tex / Lights - 072060

Victoria (Texas)

Donoghue, Christy, 2424 N Navarro St., Victoria, TX 77901. T. (512) 573-7895. - Ant / Paint / Furn / Sculp / Jew / Lights - 072061

Vienna (Ohio)

Tara Antiques, 4340 Warren Sharon Rd., P.O.Box 274, Vienna, OH 44473. T. (216) 856-2301. 072062

Villanova (Pennsylvania)

Gordon, Elinor, 812 Lancaster Pike, P. O. Box 211, Villanova, PA 19085. T. (215) 525 0981. - Ant / Orient / China - 072063

Wadsworth (Ohio)

Collector's Corner, 1435 Ridgewood Rd., Wadsworth, OH 44281. - Ant - 072064

Wake Forest (North Carolina)

Minta Holding Folk, Corner White and Owen Sts., Wake Forest, NC 27587. T. (919) 556-3778, 556-4328. - Ant / Furn / China / Lights - 072065

Wakefield (Massachusetts)

Marks, Marjorie, 194 Main St., Wakefield, MA 01880. 072066

Wakefield (Rhode Island)

Dove & Distaff, 472 Main St., Wakefield, RI 02879. T. (401) 783-5714. - Furn - 072067

Under the Stairs Antiques, 19 Whitford St., Wakefield, RI 02879. T. (401) 789 6367. - Ant - 072068

Wales (Massachusetts)

Memory Lane Antiques, 1733 House, Main St., Wales, MA 01081. T. (617) 7547201, 2457006. 072069

Walker Valley (New York)

Walker Valley Antiques, Jeronimo Rd.off Rte 52, Walker Valley, NY 12588. T. (914) 944-3916. 072070

Wallingford (Vermont)

Country House Antiques, Rte. 7, Wallingford, VT 05773. T. (802) 4462344. - Furn - 072071

Wallkill (New York)

Hartmann's Antiques, The, Hoagburg Hill Rd., Wallkill, NY 12589. T. (914) 895-2270. 072072

Windy Hill Antiques, Tillson Lake Rd., Wallkill, NY 12589. T. (914) 895-3664. 072073

Walnut (California)

Antiquarians, The, 2050 N. Broadway, Walnut, CA 94596. T. (213) 9332327. - Furn / Instr - 072074

Walpole (New Hampshire)

Lamothe, A. K., Main St., Walpole, NH 03608. - Ant - 072075

Walworth (New York)

Pierce, Frank & Justine, 893 Ontario Center Rd., Walworth, NY 14568. T. (315) 524 9329. - Ant / Instr - 072076

Warrenton (Missouri)

The Wonder Shop, 712 Steinhagen Rd., Warrenton, MO 63383. T. (314) 456 2173. - Ant / Furn / China - 072077

Washington (District of Columbia)

Adams, Davidson & Co., 3233 P. St. NW, Washington, DC 20007. T. (202) 965 3800. - Ant / Paint / Graph / Sculp - 072078

Arpad Antiques, Inc., 3222 O St., NW, Washington, DC 20007. T. (202) 337 3424. - Ant / Paint / Furn / Orient / China / Sculp / Tex / Arch / Silv / Lights / Instr / Glass / Ico - 072079

Atlantic Gallery of Georgetown, 1055 Thomas Jefferson St NW, Washington, DC 20007. T. (202) 337-2299. - Paint / Graph - 072080

Attica, 5804 Augusta Lane, Washington, DC 20016. 072081

Bush, G.K.S., 2828 NW Pennsylvania Av., Washington, DC 20007. T. (202) 965-0653. - Furn - 072082

Duncan & Duncan, 1509 NW Connecticut Av., Washington, DC 20036. T. (202) 232-4884. - Ant / Paint / Graph / Furn / China / Repr / Sculp / Tex / Dec / Jew / Lights - 072083

Early American Shop, 1317-1319 Wisconsin Av. NW, Washington, DC 20007. T. (202) 333 5843. - Ant / Graph - 072084

Fehr, Cynthia, 3214 NW O St., Washington, DC 20007. T. (202) 338-5090. - Ant / Paint / Furn / Orient / China / Tex / Silv / Lights / Glass - 072085

Guarisco, 2828 Pennsylvania Av NW, Washington, DC 20007. T. (202) 333-8533. - Paint - 072086

Hecht & Co., 7th & F.St. N.W., Washington, DC 20004. T. (202) 628 5100. - Ant - 072087

Jade House, 3050 K St. NW, Washington, DC 20007. T. (202) 944-4128. - Orient - 072088

Keshishian, Mark, & Sons, 6930 Wisconsin Av NW, Washington, DC 20015. - Tex - 072089

Marston, Luce, 1314 NW 21 St., Washington, DC 20037. T. (202) 775-9460. 072090

Martin's, 1304 Wisconsin Ave. N.W., Washington, DC 20007. T. (202) 338 6144. - Ant / Paint / Furn / Orient / Dec / Silv / Glass - 072091

Nonomura Studios, 3432 Connecticut Av. NW, Washington, DC 20008. T. (202) 363-4025. - Graph / Orient / China / Fra / Lights - 072092

Old Print Gallery, 1220 31 St NW, Washington, DC 20007. T. (202) 965-1818. - Graph - 072093

On the Hill, 701 North Carolina Ave. S.E., Washington, DC 20003. - Ant - 072094

Ponolor, 2029 Q 3t. NW, Washington, DC 20008. T. (202) 328-9190. - Paint - 072095

Shogun Gallery, 1083 Wisconsin Av. NW, Washington, DC 20007. T. (202) 965-5454. - Orient - 072096

Taggart & Jorgensen, 3241 P St NW, Washington, DC 20007. T. (202) 298-7676, Fax (202) 333-3087. - Paint - 072097

Trocadero, 1501 Connecticut Av. NW, Washington, DC 20036. T. (202) 234-5656. - Orient - 072098

Washington (Georgia)

Antique Studio, 306 S. Alexander Ave., Washington, GA 30673. - Ant - 072099

Washington (Pennsylvania)

Richardson, T. W., 127 E. Chestnut St., Washington, PA 15301. T. (412) 222 2164. - Ant - 072100

Washington (Washington, DC)

Affrica, 2010 1/2 R St NW, Washington, DC 20009. T. (202) 745-7272. 072101

Waterbury (Connecticut)

Beasleys Antiques, 230 Frost Rd., Waterbury, CT 06705. T. (203) 7547768. 072102

Shirt + Dom's Antiques, 1405 Highland Ave., Waterbury, CT 06708. T. (203) 7566493. 072103

Waterbury (Vermont)

Upland Acres Antiques, Blush Hill, Rt.D, Waterbury, VT 05676. T. (802) 244-7197. 072104

Waterford (Virginia)

Akre, Anne B., Loudoun County 45 mls. from Washington D.C., Waterford, VA 22190. T. (703) 882 3404. - Ant / Paint / Furn / Silv - 072105

Waterloo (New York)

Cohen, Barbara N., 115 E Main St., Waterloo, NY 13165. T. (315) 539-3032. - Ant / Paint / Furn / China / Tex / Dec / Instr - 072106

Waupun (Wisconsin)

Hallocks, The Donald Wm., 222 Carrington St., Waupun, WI 53963. T. (414) 3242209. - Glass / Furn / Silv - 072107

Wausau (Wisconsin)

Little Green House, 630 2nd St., Wausau, WI 54401. T. (715) 845 6189. - Ant - 072108

Wayzata (Minnesota)
The Gold Mine Antiques, 332 S. Broadway, Wayzata, MN 55391. T. (612) 473 7719. - Ant - *072109*

Weatherford (Texas)
Jones, Lilian, 402 Garner Rd., Weatherford, TX 76086. - Ant - *072110*

Welch (Minnesota)
Hunt Antiques, Sarah, 6 Old Deerfield Rd., Welch, MN 55089. T. (612) 3883997. *072111*

Wellesley (Massachusetts)
Dana, Richard M., Inc., 43 Central St., Wellesley, MA 02181. T. (617) 237 2730. - Jew / Silv - *072112*
Spivack's Antiques, 54 Washington St., Wellesley, MA 02181. T. (617) 235 1700. - Ant / Paint / Furn / China / Sculp / Lights - *072113*

Wells (Maine)
Jorgensen, R., Box 382, Rte. 1, Wells, ME 04090. T. (207) 646-9444. *072114*
MacDougall-Gionet, Rte. 1, Box 278, RFD 2, Wells, ME 04090. T. (207) 646 3531. - Ant / Paint / Furn / Orient / China / Tex / Glass - *072115*
The Farm, Mildram Rd., Wells, ME 04090. T. (207) 9852656. - Paint / Furn / Tex / Lights / Instr - *072116*

West Chester (Pennsylvania)
Chalfant, H.L., 1352 Paoli Pike, West Chester, PA 19380. T. (215) 696-1862. - Furn - *072117*
Matlat, Elizabeth L., 1300 Wilmington Pike Rte. 202, 322, West Chester, PA 19380. T. (215) 399-0455. - Ant - *072118*

West Dennis (Massachusetts)
Trotting Park Antiques, 185 Main St. Rte. 28, Cape Cod, West Dennis, MA 02670. T. (617) 398 3762. - Ant / Furn - *072119*

West Friendship (Maryland)
Matthews, Robert T., 2400 Pfefferkorn Rd., West Friendship, MD 21794. - Ant / Lights / Glass - *072120*

West Salem (Wisconsin)
Old Salem House, Inc., 99 Jefferson St., West Salem, WI 54669. T. (608) 7861675. - China / Lights / Glass - *072121*

West Sullivan (Maine)
Gray, Charlotte, Rte. 1, West Sullivan, ME 04689. T. (207) 422 - 6716. - Ant - *072122*

West Townsend (Massachusetts)
Delamey, John & Barbara, 473 Main St., West Townsend, MA 01474. T. (617) 597-2231. - Instr - *072123*

Westfield (New York)
Bertram, Dorothea F., 53 S. Portage St., Westfield, NY 14787. T. (716) 326 2551. - Ant - *072124*
Candle-Lite Antiques Shoppe, 143 E. Main St., Westfield, NY 14787. T. (716) 326 3861. - Ant - *072125*
Militello, 31 Jefferson St., Westfield, NY 14787. T. (716) 326-2587. - Ant / Furn / China / Fra / Lights / Glass - *072126*
Mollards Antiques, 120 E. Main St., Westfield, NY 14787. T. (716) 326 3521. - Ant / Glass - *072127*
The Brass Eagle, 21 Pearl St., Westfield, NY 14787. T. (716) 326 3464. - Ant - *072128*
The Leonards, 2 E Main Rd., Westfield, NY 14787. T. (716) 326-2210. - Ant - *072129*

Westmoreland (New Hampshire)
Hampshire Dunes Antiques, Route 63, Westmoreland, NH 03467. T. (603) 3994478. *072130*

Weston (Connecticut)
Cobb's Mill, Weston Rd., Weston, CT 06880. T. (203) 227 3106. - Ant / Graph - *072131*

Weston (Massachusetts)
Weston Antique Exchange, 584 Boston Post Rd., Weston, MA 02193. T. (617) 8934337. *072132*

Weston (Vermont)
Gay Meadow Farm Antiques, Inc., Trout Club Rd., Weston, VT 05161. T. (802) 8246386. - Furn - *072133*

Westport (Connecticut)
Sachs, Michael S., Westport POB 2837, CT 06880. T. (203) 227-1058. - Paint / Graph - *072134*
Three Bears Ant. Shop, 79 Newtown Turnpike, Westport, CT 06880. T. (203) 2277219. *072135*
Wassung, J., 15 Baker Ave., Westport, CT 06880. T. (203) 227 2153. - Silv - *072136*

Weymouth (Massachusetts)
Marshall 1700 House, 231 Washington St., Weymouth, MA 02188. - Furn / Orient / Repr / Dec - *072137*

White Marsh (Maryland)
Foley's Antiques, 10807 Railroad Ave., White Marsh, MD 21162. T. (301) 335-3313. *072138*

Whitehall (Michigan)
The Box, 8198 Whitehall Rd., Whitehall, MI 49461. - Ant - *072139*

Whitestone (New York)
Kindler, Joan & Larry, 15-02 150 ST., Whitestone, NY 11357. T. 767-2260. *072140*

Wichita (Kansas)
Antique Shop, 1356 N Topeka, Wichita, KS 67214. - Ant - *072141*
Antiques Plus, 2130 North Market, Wichita, KS 67214. *072142*
Bunny Antiques & Gifts, 1851 South Broadway, Wichita, KS 67211. *072143*

Williamsburg (Virginia)
Keepsake Antiques Collection, Duke of Gloucester St., Merchant Square, Williamsburg, VA 23185. T. (804) 220-0400. *072144*
Shaia, Merchants Sq., Williamsburg, VA 23187. T. (804) 220-0400. - Tex - *072145*
TK Oriental Antiques, 1654 Jamestown Rd., Williamsburg, VA 23187. T. (804) 229-7720. - Paint / Furn / Orient / China - *072146*

Williamsfield (Ohio)
Karen's Antiques, 7163 Beaver Rd., Williamsfield, OH 44093. T. (216) 293-5171. - Ant - *072147*

Williamson (New York)
Nortier, Tina & Nelson, 4209 E. Main St., Williamson, NY 14589. T. (315) 589 2043. - Ant / Furn / China / Lights / Instr *072148*

Williamsville (New York)
Williamsville Antiques, 94 Caesar Blvd., Williamsville, NY 14221. T. (716) 633-4889. *072149*

Wilmette (Illinois)
Print Mint Gallery, 1147 Greenleaf Av., Wilmette, IL 60091. T. (312) 256-4140. - Graph / Orient / Repr / Sculp / Fra / Mul - *072150*

Wilmington (Delaware)
Stockwell, David, 3701 Kennett Pike, Wilmington, DE 19807. T. (302) 655-4466. - Furn - *072151*
The Horse, 5810 Kennett Pike Centerville, Wilmington, DE 19807. T. (302) 656 2096. - Ant - *072152*

Wilson (North Carolina)
Boone's Antiques, Inc., Wilson, NC 27893. T. (919) 237 1508. - Ant / Paint / Furn / China / Tex - *072153*
Langston, Bobby, Hwy. 301 S, Wilson, NC 27893. T. (919) 237-8224. - Furn - *072154*
Rackley, Lucinda, 100 W, Wilson, NC 27893. T. (919) 237-0408. - Ant / Furn / China - *072155*
Walston, Stuart, Inc., 417 W. Nash St., Wilson, NC 27893. T. (919) 243 4900. - Ant - *072156*

Wilton (Connecticut)
Meyer, Philip E., 39 Old Range Rd., Wilton, CT 06897. T. (203) 762 5059. - Ant / Orient / China / Dec - *072157*
Toby House, 526 Danbury Rd. Rte. 9, Wilton, CT 06897. T. (203) 762 7824. - Ant / Furn / China / Glass - *072158*

Vallin Galleries, 516 Danbury Rd., Wilton, CT 06897. T. (203) 762 7441. - Ant / Paint / Furn / Orient / China / Sculp - *072159*

Winchester (Kentucky)
Todd's Antique Shop, 530 S. Maple St., Winchester, KY 40391. - Ant - *072160*

Windham (Connecticut)
Clark, Isaac, Rte. 14, Box 237, Windham, CT 06280. T. (203) 423-5685. - Ant - *072161*
Cole, Betty, Windham, CT 06380. T. (203) 423 4163. - Ant - *072162*

Windsor (Vermont)
Covered Bridge Antiques, Rte. 2, Windsor, VT 05089. - Ant - *072163*

Winnetka (Illinois)
Coledonian, Inc., 562 Lincoln Ave., Winnetka, IL 60093. T. (312) 446-0912. - Ant / Graph / Furn / China / Instr - *072164*
Fallen Oakes, PO Box 617, Winnetka, IL 60093. T. (312) 446-3540. - Furn - *072165*
Pick Galleries, Inc., 886 Linden Ave., Winnetka, IL 60093. T. (312) 446 7444. - Ant / Furn - *072166*

Winslow (Arizona)
Dauwalter's, 322 E. 3rd St., Winslow, AZ 86047. - Ant - *072167*

Winter Park (Florida)
Ferris, 216 N Park Av., Winter Park, FL 32789. - Ant - *072168*

Winterport (Maine)
Bean, Richard & Patricia, Rte. 1A, Winterport, ME 04496. T. (207) 2235536. - Furn - *072169*
Riverside Antiques, RFD1, Route 1A, Winterport, ME 04496. T. (207) 2235536. *072170*

Wolcott (New York)
Furnace Village Antiques, West Fort Bay Rd., Wolcott, NY 14590. T. (315) 594 5734. - Ant - *072171*

Wolfeboro (New Hampshire)
Marden, Richard G., Wolfeboro POB 524, NH 03894. T. (603) 569-3209. - China - *072172*
Reed, Ralph K., 3 mls. off Rte. 28 on Pleasant Valley Rd., Wolfeboro, NH 03894. T. (603) 569 1897. - Ant / Furn - *072173*

Woodbury (Connecticut)
British Country Antiques, Rte. 6, Woodbury, CT 06798. T. (203) 263-5100. - Ant / Furn - *072174*
County Bazaar, 451 S Main St., Woodbury, CT 06798. T. (203) 263-2228. - Paint / Furn / Eth - *072175*
Crossways Antiques, Main St., Woodbury, CT 06798. T. (203) 263 4100. - Ant - *072176*
Dunton, David, Exit 15, Interstate 84, Woodbury, CT 06798. T. (203) 263-5355. - Furn - *072177*
Half-House Antiques, Flanders Rd., Woodbury, CT 06798. T. (203) 2634416. *072178*
Hammitt, Kenneth, Inc., Main St., Woodbury, CT 06798. T. (203) 263-5676. - Ant / Paint / Furn / Tex / Lights - *072179*
Homestead Antiques, Rte. 6 and Flanders Rd., Woodbury, CT 06798. T. (203) 263 2464. - Ant - *072180*
Mill House Antiques, Rte. 6, Woodbury, CT 06798. T. (203) 2633446. - Ant - *072181*
Murphy, Gerald, 60 Main St. S, Woodbury, CT 06798. *072182*
Nelson, Peter A., 881 S Main St., Woodbury, CT 06798. T. (203) 263-5881. - Furn - *072183*
Walin, Robert S. Antiques, Flanders Rd., Woodbury, CT 06798. T. (203) 2634416. - Ant - *072184*
West, Madeline, War Memorial, Main St., Woodbury, CT 06798. *072185*

Woodside (California)
Fine Prints, POB 620145, Woodside, CA 94062. T. (415) 851-4627. - Graph / Sculp - *072186*

Woodstock (New York)
Tomlinson, Terry Ann, Antiques, Inc., Woodstock, NY 12498. T. (914) 6796554. - Furn / Tex - *072187*

Woodstock (Vermont)
Ross, Elsa, A.S.I.D. the Green, Woodstock, VT 05901.
T. (802) 4571700. - Furn / Dec -   072188

Worcester (Massachusetts)
Butler Antiques, 299 Plantation St., Worcester, MA
01604. T. (617) 7994994.   072189

Farmelo, Andrew E., 170 Main St., Worcester, MA
01608. T. (617) 799 7074.   072190

Wrentham (Massachusetts)
King Philip Antiques, Route 1a, Wrentham, MA 02093.
T. (617) 3843857. - Ant -   072191

Wurtsboro (New York)
Wurtsboro Wholesale Antic, Sullivan St., Wurtsboro POB
386, NY 12790. T. (914) 888-4411. - Ant / Paint / Furn /
Orient / China / Arch / Rel -   072192

Wyckoff (New Jersey)
Brenwasser, Donald, 509 Wellington Drive, Wyckoff, NJ
07481. T. (201) 891 7032. - Paint / Graph / Sculp /
Arch / Eth -   072193

Wynnewood (Pennsylvania)
Jerrehian Brothers, 1011 Cedar Grove Rs., Wynnewood,
PA 19096. T. (215) 8968800. - Tex -   072194

Wyoming (Rhode Island)
Smith, Brad, Junction of Rte. 138 and 112, Wyoming, RI
02898. T. (401) 539 2870. - Ant / Paint / Furn /
Glass -   072195

Yardley (Pennsylvania)
Prickett, C. L., 930 Stonyhill Rd., Yardley, PA 19067.
T. (215) 493 4284. - Ant / Furn -   072196

Yarmounth Port (Massachusetts)
Gray Goose Antiques, Route 6 A, Yarmounth Port, MA
02675. T. (617) FO 2 3046. - Ant / Furn -   072197

Yarmouth (Maine)
Schwind, W. M., Jr., 17 East Main St., Yarmouth, ME
04096. T. (207) 8469458. - Paint / Furn / Repr - 072198

York (Pennsylvania)
Ettline, Paul L., 3790 E. Market St., York, PA 17402.
T. (717) 755 3927. - Ant -   072199

Kindig, Joe Jr. & Son, 325 W. Market St., York, PA
17401. T. (717) 848 2760. - Ant -   072200

Ypsilanti (Michigan)
Gillentines Antique Shop, 507 Osband, Ypsilanti, MI
48197.   072201

Schmidt, A. S. & Sons, 5138 W. Michigan Ave., Ypsilanti,
MI 48197. T. (313) 434 2660. - Ant / Paint /
Instr -   072202

Yucaipa (California)
Bellcrest Antiques, 32223 Ave. E., Yucaipa, CA 92399.
- Ant / Glass -   072203

Knoll Haven Antiques, 31558 Yucaipa Blvd., Yucaipa, CA
92399. T. (714) 792 4200. - Ant / Furn / Orient / Tex /
Lights / Instr -   072204

Zanesville (Ohio)
Jim's Antiques, 3215 Old Falls Rd., Zanesville, OH
43701. - Ant -   072205

Zeeland (Michigan)
Kollen, Ben, 141 E. Main St., Zeeland, MI 49464.
T. (616) 772 1140. - Ant / Furn / Silv / Glass -   072206

Zionsville (Indiana)
Brown's Antique Shop, 315 N. 5th St., Zionsville, IN
46077.   072207

Venezuela

Caracas (D.F.)
Antigüedades del Rey, Av. Solano las Declicias de SG,
Caracas.   072208

Galeria Groszman, Calle Humbolt SG Edf. Tachira, Caracas. - Furn -   072209

Galleries International, Abbie Vischschoonmaker, Local
P. A. B. 2, Paseo las Mercedes, Caracas.
T. (02) 92 37 08.   072210

Yugoslavia

Beograd (Srbija)
Milenkovic, 8 Rue Koche Kapetana, 11000 Beograd.
T. (011) 43 73 40, Fax 43 73 40.   072211

Novi Sad (Srbija)
Vojvodina, Maksima Gorkijk 24, 21000 Novi
Sad.   072212

ALLGEMEINES KÜNSTLERLEXIKON
Die Bildenden Künstler aller Zeiten und Völker

(General dictionary of artists. Artists of the world throughout all ages)

Edited by K.G. Saur Publishers. Founded and co-edited by Günter Meißner
1991ff. c. 78 volumes. c. 700 pages per volume. Half leather-bound with dust cover.
DM 398.00 per volume
ISBN 3-598-22740-X

◆ A total of nearly 500,000 artist entries with c. 7,000 articles per volume

◆ Precise biographical and bibliographical information on representatives of the fine arts

◆ No comparable work exists whose information on artists throughout the world and
from every age is as extensive, up-to-date, and authoritative as that in the **Allgemeines Künstlerlexikon**

◆ For further information, please send for our brochure, our 32-page sample booklet
or a volume on approval.

K•G•Saur Verlag
Postfach 701620 · D-81316 München · Tel. (089) 7 69 02-232 · Fax (089) 7 69 02-150/250
E-mail: 100730.1341@compuserve.com

Page / Seite

Galleries
Galerien
Galeries
Gallerie
Galerías

Das Register zum *Thieme-Becker*, *Vollmer* und zum *Allgemeinen Künst-lerlexikon* – jetzt inklusive der vollständigen Lexikonartikel aus dem *Allgemeinen Künstlerlexikon!*

Allgemeines Künstlerlexikon – Internationale Künstlerdatenbank

AKL – World Biographical Dictionary of Artists

3. CD-ROM-Ausgabe 1996
DM 2.400,–*
(DM 498,–* für Bezieher der Buchausgabe *Allgemeines Künstlerlexikon*)
(DM 796,–* für Bezieher der *IKD II*)

Die dritte erheblich erweiterte Ausgabe enthält nun neben den Strukturdaten aus den 37 Bänden des *Thieme-Becker* und den 6 Bänden des *Vollmer* die Struktur-daten und die **vollständigen Texteinträge** aus den ersten 12 Bänden des *Allgemeinen Künstlerlexikons*.
Maler, Graphiker, Bildhauer, Architekten – die Vertreter der bildenden Künste aller Kulturräume der Erde von der Antike bis zur Gegenwart können hier nach den verschiedensten Kriterien gesucht und ihre biographischen Daten abgerufen werden.

* unverbindliche Preisempfehlung

Bitte fordern Sie einen ausführlichen Prospekt bei uns an!

K•G•Saur Verlag
Postfach 701620 · D-81316 München · Tel. (089) 7 69 02-0
Fax (089) 7 69 02-150 · E-mail: 100730.1341@compuserve.com

Angola

Luanda

Grafica Portugal Ltda., Rua Serpa Pinto 85-97, Luanda Caixa Postal 1290. - Graph - 072213

Argentina

Buenos Aires

Adriana, Indik, Viamonte 611, 1053 Buenos Aires. T. (01) 393-9184. 072214
Alberto, Elia, Azcuénaga 1739, Buenos Aires, 1128. T. (01) 803-0496. 072215
Allegretta, Tacuari 715, 1071 Buenos Aires. T. (01) 334-6321. - Graph - 072216
Alto Nivel, Defensa 1287, 1143 Buenos Aires. T. (01) 362-8932. - Paint - 072217
Alvaro Castagnino, Florida 939, 1005 Buenos Aires. T. (01) 311-3279. 072218
Alvini, Florida 943, 1005 Buenos Aires. T. (01) 311-2220. 072219
AMC Gallery, Avda. Alvear 1777, 1014 Buenos Aires. T. (01) 42-6416. 072220
Angelis, Horacio N. de, Via Monte 1819, 1056 Buenos Aires. T. (01) 41 87 48. 072221
Angelus, Suipacha 834, 1008 Buenos Aires. T. (01) 311-8213. 072222
Art-Gallery, Florida 683, 6 0, Buenos Aires. T. (01) 39 29 522. 072223
Arte Nuevo, Florida 939, 1 0, Buenos Aires. T. (01) 31 32 79. 072224
Arthea, Esmeralda 1037, Buenos Aires. T. (01) 325 723. 072225
Arthea, Charcas 961, Buenos Aires. T. (01) 31 98 74. 072226
Asociación Estimulo de Bellas Artes, Córdoba 701, Buenos Aires. T. (01) 32 32 11. 072227
Atica, Paraguay 414, 1057 Buenos Aires. T. (01) 32 14 15. 072228
Austral, 48No633, La Plata, Buenos Aires. T. (01) 346 08. 072229
Bachiaz, Enrique, Cachi 351, 1437 Buenos Aires. T. (01) 91-5629. - Graph - 072230
Benzacar, Ruth, Florida 1000, 1005 Buenos Aires. T. (01) 313-8480. 072231
Bodo, Pte. José Uriburu 1645, 1114 Buenos Aires. T. (01) 804 63 71. 072232
Bolañez, Carlos, Avda. Bredo 1964, 1239 Buenos Aires. T. (01) 921 46 31. - Graph - 072233
Brites, Angel, Hubac 6965, 1439 Buenos Aires. T. (01) 687 25 75. - Graph - 072234
C. & P., Estados Unidos 404, 1101 Buenos Aires. T. (01) 361 99 50. 072235
Capalbo, Miguel A., Carlos Calvo 409, 1102 Buenos Aires. T. (01) 362 04 27. 072236
„Casa America", Av. de Mayo 979, Buenos Aires. T. (01) 38 20 65. 072237
Casa Veltri, Juncal 1642, Buenos Aires. T. (01) 44 41 74. - Paint / Graph - 072238
Casado, Jorge, Cda. De Gómez 5257, Buenos Aires. T. (01) 601 23 02. - Graph - 072239
Cascales, Rodalfo, Piedras 1032, 1070 Buenos Aires. T. (01) 26 15 86. 072240
Cativiela, Hermanos, Pepirí 750, 1437 Buenos Aires. T. (01) 91 03 86. - Graph - 072241
Centoira, Montevideo 1780, 1018 Buenos Aires. T. (01) 41 60 87. 072242
Céspedes, Martina, Bolívar 660, 1066 Buenos Aires. T. (01) 30 21 27. 072243
Chanes Santiago, Beazley 3944, 1437 Buenos Aires. T. (01) 91 85 55. - Graph - 072244
Christel K., Arenales 1239, 1061 Buenos Aires. T. (01) 812 39 17. 072245
Compagnoni, Carlos, Av. Congreso 2393, 1428 Buenos Aires. T. (01) 70 94 75. - Graph - 072246
Danysh Galería, Arroya 858, 1007 Buenos Aires. T. (01) 393 08 03. 072247
Demartino, Francisco N., Viel 442, 1424 Buenos Aires. T. (01) 99 17 21. 072248
Dery, Avda. San Pedro 4049, 1406 Buenos Aires. T. (01) 69 84 62. - Graph - 072249
Donela, Condorca 1240, 1416 Buenos Aires. T. (01) 582 3923. - Graph - 072250
Durruty, Marcos D., Luis Sáenz Peña 1955, 1135 Buenos Aires. T. (01) 23 20 48. - Graph - 072251
Dynasty, Florida 970, Buenos Aires. T. (01) 31 17 73. - Paint / Graph / Sculp - 072252
Eugemar, Varela 265, 1406 Buenos Aires. T. (01) 613 04 25. - Graph - 072253
Ferrari, Enrique de, Sánchez de Loria 2322, 1241 Buenos Aires. T. (01) 91 94 72. - Graph - 072254
Foto Club Buenos Aires, San José 181, 1076 Buenos Aires. T. (01) 38 7890, 37 2182. - Pho - 072255
Galería del Pasador, Arenales 1239, 1061 Buenos Aires. T. (01) 41 96 55. 072256
Galería Jorcas, Esmeralda 781, 1035 Buenos Aires. T. (01) 322 49 26. 072257
Galeria del Retiro, Marcelo T. de Alvear 636, 1058 Buenos Aires. T. (01) 311 25 27. - Paint - 072258
Galeria el Circulo, Florida 846, 10, Buenos Aires. T. (01) 33 18 20. - Paint / Graph - 072259
Galeria el Sol, Esmeralda 911, Buenos Aires. T. (01) 31 75 07;32 07 70. - Tex - 072260
Galeria le Passé, Charcas 664, Buenos Aires. T. (01) 32 97 62. - Paint - 072261
Galeria Rose Marie, Florida 433, Buenos Aires. T. (01) 49 51 58. 072262
Galeria Studio, Libertad 1269-1271, Buenos Aires. T. (01) 41 16 16, 42 20 46. - Graph - 072263
Galeria van Riel, Florida 659, Buenos Aires. T. (01) 31 12 82. - Paint / Graph - 072264
Galeria Velazquez, Maipú 932, 1376 Buenos Aires. T. (01) 311 0583. - Paint - 072265
Galerie du Nord, Rua Libertad 1389, Buenos Aires. T. (01) 41 08 19. - Paint - 072266
Garbarino, Eugenio, Uspallata 833, 1268 Buenos Aires. T. (01) 362 64 35. - Graph - 072267
Gómez-Roberto, Carlos, Marcelo T. de Alvear 829, 1058 Buenos Aires. T. (01) 311 17 77. 072268
Gordon, M.T. de Alvear 930, Buenos Aires. 072269
Gradiva, Reconquista 962, Buenos Aires. T. (01) 31 88 50. 072270
Graf-Plan, Miralla 3555, 1439 Buenos Aires. T. (01) 601 48 13. - Graph - 072271
Grandes Galerías Tokio, Avda. Rivadavia 6843, 1406 Buenos Aires. T. (01) 613 26 22. 072272
Gruskin, Benjamín, Suipacha 855, 1008 Buenos Aires. T. (01) 311 79 42. 072273
Helft, Jorge S., Defensa 1344, 1143 Buenos Aires. T. (01) 361 54 85. 072274
Il Mobile, Suipacha 945, 1008 Buenos Aires. T. (01) 312 25 34. 072275
Imagen, Paraguay 867, Buenos Aires. T. (01) 31 69 67. 072276
Impresora Alloni, Barco del Centenera 1436, 1424 Buenos Aires. T. (01) 92 76 50. - Graph - 072277
Jasen, Carlos, Tres Arroyos 200, 1414 Buenos Aires. T. (01) 855 80 76. - Graph - 072278
La Perricholi, Paraguay 589, 1057 Buenos Aires. T. (01) 312 37 24. 072279
Lagard, Suipacha 1216, 1011 Buenos Aires. T. (01) 393-7822. 072280
Lirolay S. C. A., Paraguay 794, Buenos Aires, 1057. T. (01) 32 00 12. - Paint / Sculp - 072281
Lublin, Julia, M.T. de Alvear 636, 1058 Buenos Aires. T. (01) 311 25 27, 312 20 58, Fax 334 81 45. 072282
Mantova, G. de Asencio 3465, Buenos Aires. T. (01) 91 10 68. - Graph - 072283
Marier, Av. Cabildo 1057, 1426 Buenos Aires. T. (01) 785 29 09. 072284
Martín, Aurelio, Posadas 1563, 1112 Buenos Aires. T. (01) 804 21 07. 072285
Martínez, Jacques, Florida 948, 1005 Buenos Aires. T. (01) 311 40 28. 072286
Menguenedijian, Zareh, Juncal 1238, 90, Buenos Aires. T. (01) 41 34 18. - Paint - 072287
Migliori, Eduardo, Solis 543, 1078 Buenos Aires. T. (01) 38 42 57. - Graph - 072288
„Mimo", Florida 973 Local 22, Buenos Aires. - Paint - 072289
Momofer, Ercilla 5521, 1408 Buenos Aires. T. (01) 682 83 65. - Graph - 072290
Montdor, Jorge, Esmeralda 587, 1007 Buenos Aires. T. (01) 322 36 03. 072291
Palatina, Arroyo 821, 1007 Buenos Aires. T. (01) 22 6620. 072292
Perelstein, Julio, Marcelo T. de Alvacar 865, 1058 Buenos Aires. T. (01) 311 22 65. 072293
Pizarro Crespo, Josefina, Malabia 2791, 120, Buenos Aires. T. (01) 72 05 50. - Paint - 072294
Praxis International Art, Arenales 1311, 1061 Buenos Aires. T. (01) 812 62 54, 812 86 47, Fax 814 11 56. 072295
Raznovich, Berta, Av. Directorio 2406, 1406 Buenos Aires. T. (01) 612 75 86. 072296
Rodriguez, R.H., Ascasubi 232, 1286 Buenos Aires. T. (01) 38 42 57. - Graph - 072297
Rubbers, Suipacha 1175, 1008 Buenos Aires. T. (01) 42-4682, 44-6010. - Paint - 072298
Rubio, Viamonte 458, Buenos Aires. T. (01) 32 51 52. 072299
Saudades, Libertad 1278, Buenos Aires. T. (01) 42 13 74. - Paint - 072300
Scheinshon, Amenábar 2052, 1428 Buenos Aires. T. (01) 782 36 78. 072301
Solano, Hilda, Carlos Calvo 447, 1102 Buenos Aires. T. (01) 23 75 52. 072302
Soudan, Arenales 868, 1061 Buenos Aires. T. (01) 393 15 00. 072303
Sousa, Aldo de, Florida 860, 1005 Buenos Aires. T. (01) 313 60 11. 072304
Stanford, Ayacucho 1945, 1112 Buenos Aires. T. (01) 804 52 54. 072305
Suipacha, Suipacha 1248, 1011 Buenos Aires. T. (01) 322 15 66. 072306
Tartaroglu, Leonor, Beazley 3765, 1437 Buenos Aires. T. (01) 91 78 13. - Graph - 072307
Touson, Margot, Zabala 3075, 1426 Buenos Aires. T. (01) 552 19 54. 072308
Traba, Francisco, Arroyo 852, 1007 Buenos Aires. T. (01) 393 42 22. 072309
Ursomarzo, Federico D., Marcelo T. de Alvear 1420, 1060 Buenos Aires. T. (01) 41 96 36. 072310
Valmont, Avda. Quintana 171, Buenos Aires, 1014. T. (01) 22-6588. - Paint - 072311
Van Eyck, Suipacha 1176, 1008 Buenos Aires. T. (01) 393 31 85. 072312
Van Riel, Talcahuano 1257, 1014 Buenos Aires. T. (01) 41 83 59. - Paint - 072313
Veinchelbaum, Isidoro, Ramón L. Falcón 2804, 1406 Buenos Aires. T. (01) 613 70 25. 072314
Ver Bo, Arenales 979, 1061 Buenos Aires. T. (01) 393 07 57. 072315
Vermeer, Suipacha 1168, 1008 Buenos Aires. T. (01) 393 51 02. - Paint - 072316
Villagarcía, Sergio A., Av. Córdoba 1335, 1055 Buenos Aires. T. (01) 42 61 77. 072317
Wildenstein, Cordoba 618, Buenos Aires. T. (01) 322-0628. - Paint / Sculp / Sculp - 072318
Witcomb, Esmeralda 870, Buenos Aires. T. (01) 32 44 24. - Paint / Paint - 072319
Wough Carmen, Florida 948, 1 0C, Buenos Aires. T. (01) 21 40 28. 072320
Zurbaran, Cerrito 1522, 1010 Buenos Aires. T. (01) 22 77 03. - Paint - 072321
Zylberberg, Pinkus, Paraguay 758, 1057 Buenos Aires. T. (01) 311 29 66. 072322

Australia

Balgowlah (New South Wales)

Rainsford Fine Art, 21 New St., 2093 Balgowlah, 2093. T. 94 41 41. - Paint - 072323

Ballarat (Victoria)

Antiques and Art Gallery, 14 Armstrong St. N, 3350 Ballarat, 3350. T. (053) 31 14 72. - Paint - 072324

Brisbane (Queensland)

Hughes, Ray, 11 Enoggera Terrace, Red Hill, 4000 Brisbane. T. (07) 369 3757. 072325

Carlton (New South Wales)
The Saints Gallery, 10 Jubilee Av., 2218 Carlton, 2218.
T. 587 93 58. 072326

Collingwood (Victoria)
Australian Galleries, 35 Derby St., 3066 Collingwood,
3066. T. 417 4303, Fax 419 7769. - Paint / Graph /
Sculp / Fra - 072327

Melbourne (Victoria)
Abrahams, Christine, 27 Gipps St., Richmond, Mel-
bourne, Vic. 3121. T. (03) 428 6099. - Paint / Graph /
China / Sculp / Tex / Eth / Jew / Pho / Draw - 072328
Artists Space, 150 Park Street, North Fitzroy, Melbourne,
Vic. 3068. T. (03) 4892749. - Paint / Graph / Repr /
Pho / Draw - 072329
Deans, 368 Lonsdale St., Melbourne, Vic. 3000. - Repr /
Fra - 072330
Deutscher, 68 Drummond St., Carlton, Melbourne, Vic.
3053. T. (03) 6635044. 072331
Distelfink, 432 Burwood Rd., Hawthorn, Melbourne, Vic.
3122. T. (03) 8182555. 072332
East and West Art, 665 High St., East Kew, Melbourne,
Vic. 3102. T. (03) 8596277. - Ant / Paint / Graph / Furn /
Orient / China / Sculp / Arch / Dec / Jew / Draw - 072333
Editions Galleries, Roseneath Pl., Melbourne, Vic. 3205.
T. (03) 6998600. 072334
Eltham Gallery, 559 Main Rd., Eltham, Melbourne, Vic.
3095. T. (03) 4391467. 072335
Girgis & Klym, 342 Brunswick St., Fitzroy, Melbourne,
Vic. 3065. T. (03) 4172327. - Paint / Sculp / Mod / Pho /
Draw - 072336
Gould, 270 Torrak Rd., South Yarra, Melbourne, Vic.
3141. T. (03) 2414701. 072337
Greythorn, 2 Tannock St., Balwyn North, Melbourne, Vic.
3104. T. (03) 8579920. 072338
Hawthorn Gallery, 556 Glenferrie Rd. Hawthorn, Mel-
bourne, Vioc. 3000. T. (03) 812092. - Paint /
Fra - 072339
Ivanyi, Andrew, 262 Toorak Rd., South Yarra, 3000 Mel-
bourne, 3141. T. (03) 241 8366. 072340
Kew Gallery, 26 Cotham Rd., Kew, Melbourne, Vic.
3101. T. (03) 8615181. 072341
Kozminsky, 421 Bourke St., 3000 Melbourne, 3000.
T. (03) 670 1277. - Paint - 072342
Leveson, 130 Faraday St., Carlton, Melbourne, Vic.
3053. T. (03) 3471919. 072343
Luba Bilu Gallery, 142 Greville St., Melbourne, Vic.
3181. T. (03) 5292433, Fax (03) 5213442. 072344
Moorabbin Art Gallery, 342 South Rd., Moorabbin, Mel-
bourne, Vic. 3189. T. (03) 5552191. 072345
Niagara Galleries, 245 Punt Rd., Richmond, Melbourne,
Vic. 3121. T. (03) 4293666. - Paint / Sculp /
Draw - 072346
Pinacotheca, 10 Waltham Pl., Richmond, Melbourne,
Vic. 3121. T. (03) 4283066. 072347
Pizzi, Gabrielle, 141 Flinders Ln., Melbourne, Vic. 3000.
T. (03) 6542944, Fax (03) 6507087. 072348
Powell Street Gallery, 20 Powell St., South Yarra, Mel-
bourne, Vic. 3141. T. (03) 2665519. 072349
Powell Street Graphics, 20a Powell St., South Yarra,
Melbourne, Vic. 3141. T. (03) 2663127. 072350
Print Council of Australia, 105 Collins St., Melbourne,
Vic. 3000. T. (03) 6542460. - Graph - 072351
Realities Gallery, 35 Jackson St., Toorak, Melbourne,
Vic. 3142. T. (03) 2413312. 072352
Rivergum Art Gallery, 189 Yarra St., Warrandyte, Mel-
bourne, Vic. 3113. T. (03) 8443948, 7120220. 072353
Roar Studios, 115 Brunswick St., Fitzroy, Melbourne,
Vic. 3065. T. (03) 4199975. 072354
Saint Martins Theater Foyer Gallery, St. Martins Lane,
South Yarra, Melbourne, Vic. 3141. T. (03) 2672477.
- Paint - 072355
Spectrum Gallery, 184 Belmore Rd., Balwyn North, Mel-
bourne, Vic. 3103. T. (03) 8575718. 072356
Stuart Gerstman Galleries, 29 Gipps St., Richmond, Mel-
bourne, Vic. 3121. T. (03) 4285479,
Fax (03) 4280754. 072357
The Jade Gallerie, Dr. A. Cymons, Sth. Cross Centre,
Melbourne, Vic. 3000. T. (03) 638437. - Ant / Orient /
China / Jew - 072358
The Pentax Brummels Gallery of Photography, 95 Toorak
Rd. South Yarra, Melbourne, Vic. 3141. 072359

Tolarno Galleries, 98 River St., South Yarra, Melbourne,
Vic. 3141. T. (03) 8278381, Fax (03) 8274746. - Paint /
Graph / Sculp / Mod / Draw - 072360
Visibility, 642 Station St., North Carlton, Melbourne,
VGic. 3054. T. (03) 3877432. 072361
Wiregrass Gallery, Station Ent., Eltham, Melbourne, Vic.
3095. T. (03) 4398139. - Paint - 072362
Young Originals Gallery, 110 Punt Rd., Windsor, Mel-
bourne, Vic. 3181. T. (03) 5292924. 072363

Mona Vale (New South Wales)
Gallery Six, Bungan St., 2103 Mona Vale, 2103.
T. 99 10 39. 072364

Moorebank (New South Wales)
Au Goût Artistique, 105-119 Longstaff Av., 2170 Moore-
bank, 2170. T. 601 44 88. 072365

Newtown (New South Wales)
King Street Gallery, 613 King St., Newtown, NSW 2042.
T. 517 2969. - Paint / Sculp - 072366
terrapotta, 8 King St., Newtown, 2042. T. 516 3151.
- Sculp - 072367

North Sydney (New South Wales)
Byrne, Noella, 242 Miller St., 2060 North Sydney, 2060.
T. 92 65 89. 072368
Hawk, 370 Pacific Hwy., Crows Nest, 2060 North Syd-
ney, 2065. T. 436 2350. - Paint - 072369

Parkville (Victoria)
Paton, Melbourne Univ. Union, 3052 Parkville, 3052.
T. (065) 347 38 11. 072370

Ramsgate (New South Wales)
Dorff, von, 280 Rocky Point Rd., 2217 Ramsgate, 2217.
T. 529 60 26. 072371

Rylstone (New South Wales)
O.P. Books, P.O.Box 78, 2849 Rylstone, 2849.
T. (063) 79 11 82, Fax 79 10 86. 072372

Surry Hills (New South Wales)
Design Partners, 45 Corben St., 2010 Surry Hills, 2010.
T. 212 19 04. 072373

Sutherland (New South Wales)
Box Road Bazaar, 61 East Parade, 2232 Sutherland,
2232. T. (02) 545 16 88. 072374

Sydney (New South Wales)
Abbia Gallery, 123 George St., Sydney, NSW 2000.
T. (02) 272 737. 072375
Aboriginal Art Centre, 7 Walker Lane, Paddington, Syd-
ney, NSW 2021. T. (02) 357 68 39. 072376
Aboriginal Arts and Crafts, 40 Harrington St., Sydney,
NSW 2000. T. (02) 247 9625. 072377
A.J.D.'s Gallery, 104 Longueville Rd., Sydney, NSW
2000. T. (02) 428 1344. 072378
Allegro Gallery, 1 Porters Rd., Kenthurst, Sydney, NSW
2156. T. (02) 654 1386. 072379
Anna Art Studio and Gallery, 94 Oxford St., Paddington,
Sydney, NSW 2021. T. (02) 331 11 49. 072380
Art Gallery of New South Wales, Art Gallery Rd., Domain,
Sydney, NSW 2000. T. (02) 225 17 00. 072381
Artarmon Galleries, 479 Pacific Hwy., Artarmon, Sydney,
NSW 2064. T. (02) 427 03 22. - Paint / Sculp /
Draw - 072382
Artstok, Cremore Plaza, Sydney, NSW 2000.
T. (02) 909 3884. 072383
Atherton Gallery, Old Northern Rd., Sydney, NSW 2000.
T. (02) 634 5791. 072384
Australian Centre for Photography, 257 Oxford St., Pad-
dington, Sydney, NSW 2021. T. (02) 332 1455,
331 6253. 072385
Australien Galleries, 15 Roylston St. Paddington, Sydney,
NSW 2021. T. (02) 360 5177, Fax 360 2361. 072386
Avianca Folk Art, 76 Paddington St., Sydney, NSW 2000.
T. (02) 333 860. 072387
Balmain Studio, 218 Darling Bal., Sydney, NSW 2000.
T. (02) 824 194. 072388
Barbizon, 148-152 Spit Rd., Mosman, Sydney, NSW
2088. T. (02) 969 35 54. 072389
Blackland Gallery, 436 George St., Sydney, NSW 2000.
T. (02) 201 50 ext. 390. 072390

Bloomfield, 118 Sutherland St., Paddington, Sydney,
NSW 2021. T. (02) 326 21 22. 072391
Boronia, 768 Military Rd., Mosman, Sydney, NSW 2088.
T. (02) 969 2100. - Paint - 072392
Bridges Gallery, 20 Kingsford Rd., Sydney, NSW 2000.
T. (02) 449 1080. 072393
Burning Log Galleries, 623 Old Northern Rd., Dural, Syd-
ney, NSW 2000. T. (02) 651 2502. 072394
Burwood Galleries, 24 Burwood St., Sydney, NSW 2000.
T. (02) 741 121. 072395
Bush Hut Gallery, 137 River Rd., Sydney, NSW 2000.
T. (02) 428 4146. 072396
C.B. Art Gallery, 12 Falcon St., Sydney, NSW 2000.
T. (02) 439 7964. 072397
Central Street Gallery, 1 Central St., Sydney, NSW 2000.
T. (02) 26 31 16. 072398
Chapman, Mavis, 7 Bay St., Sydney, NSW 2000.
T. (02) 328 1739. 072399
Chelsea Art Gallery, 331 Barrenjoey Rd., Sydney, NSW
2000. T. (02) 997 2131. 072400
Chester Hill Gallery, 96 Waldron Rd., Sydney, NSW
2000. T. (02) 644 4838. 072401
Chin Hua Galleries, 243 Sussex St., Sydney, NSW 2000.
T. (02) 298 479. 072402
Cook, James, 30 Cronulla St., Sydney, NSW 2000.
T. (02) 523 01 92. 072403
Coventry, Chandler, 38 Hargrave St., Sydney, NSW
2000. 072404
Crowther, B., 137 River Rd., Sydney, NSW 2000.
T. (02) 428 4146. 072405
Doddi, 191 Ramsgate Rd., Sydney, NSW 2000.
T. (02) 529 5788. 072406
Englund, Patricia, 2 Casade St., Sydney, NSW 2000.
T. (02) 358 4987. 072407
Erskine Street Gallery, 64 Erskine St., Sydney, NSW
2000. T. (02) 296 227. 072408
Fairfield Gallery, 15a Railway Parade, Sydney, NSW
2000. T. (02) 727 6801. 072409
Firenze Art Gallery, 21 Falcon St., Sydney, NSW 2000.
T. (02) 439 75 42. 072410
Forest Gallery, 61a The Centre, Darley St., Forestville,
Sydney, NSW 2000. T. (02) 451 84 19,
452 37 24. 072411
Gallerie, 190 Military Rd., Sydney, NSW 2000.
T. (02) 90 61 08. 072412
Gallery A Exhibitions, 21 Gipps St., Paddington, Sydney,
NSW 2021. T. (02) 31 97 20. - Paint / Sculp /
Pho - 072413
Gizas, 125 King St., Sydney, NSW 2000.
T. (02) 519 65 13. 072414
Glen Galleries, 10 Surf Rd., Cronulla, Sydney, NSW
2000. T. (02) 523-5233. 072415
Halina Art Gallery, 361 Liverpool Rd, Ash, Sydney, NSW
2000. T. (02) 797 69 02. 072416
Hambly, Kevin, 10 Jubilee Ave., Sydney, NSW 2000.
T. (02) 587 49 24. 072417
Harrington Street Gallery, 17 Meagher St., Chippendale,
Sydney, NSW 2008. T. (02) 699 7378. - Paint /
Draw - 072418
Hogarth, 7 Walker Lane, Paddington, Sydney, NSW
2021. T. (02) 357 68 39. 072419
Holdsworth Galleries, 86 Holdsworth St., Woollahra,
Sydney, NSW 2025. T. (02) 32 13 64. - Paint / Sculp /
Lights - 072420
Hughes, Ray, 270 Devonshire St. Surry Hills, Sydney,
NSW 2010. T. (02) 698 3200. 072421
Hung-Hoi, 57 Darlinghurst Rd., Sydney, NSW 2000.
T. (02) 357 37 68. 072422
Kabuki Gallery, 17 Glenmore Rd., Sydney, NSW 2000.
T. (02) 31 29 26. 072423
Kellner, Stephen, 72 Carrington Rd., Sydney, NSW 2000.
T. (02) 389 74 63. 072424
Kenwick Galleries, 14a Hannah St., Sydney, NSW 2000.
T. (02) 84 78 00. 072425
Kirk Gallery, 422 Cleveland St., Surrey Hills, Sydney,
NSW 2010. T. (02) 698 17 98. 072426
Kunama Galleries, 373 Alfred St., Sydney, NSW 2060.
T. (02) 929 35 76. 072427
Lane, Peter, 14 Martin Pl., Sydney, NSW 2000.
T. (02) 235 01 36. - Paint - 072428
Macquarie Galleries, 40 King St., Sydney, NSW 2000.
T. (02) 29 57 87. - Paint / Graph / China / Sculp /
Draw - 072429

Mariner's Art Gallery, 64 Erskine St., Sydney, NSW 2000. T. (02) 29 62 27. *072430*

Messis, 374 Oxford St., Sydney, NSW 2000. T. (02) 389 37 53. *072431*

Montrose Galleries, 4 Brady St., Mosman, Sydney, NSW 2088. T. (02) 969 58 79. *072432*

Mori, 56 Catherine St., Sydney, NSW 2040. T. (02) 560 47 04, Fax (02) 560 92 15. *072433*

Native Art Gallery, 13 Gurner St., Paddington, Sydney, NSW 2021. T. (02) 331 48 27. *072434*

New Guinea Primitive Arts, 428 George St., Sydney, NSW 2000. T. (02) 232 47 37. *072435*

Norfolk Gallery, 46 Norfolk St., Paddington, Sydney, NSW 2021. T. (02) 31 38 41. *072436*

Ocean Art Gallery, 376 Barrenjoey Rd., Newport Beach, Sydney, NSW 2106. T. (02) 997 64 35. *072437*

Old Bakery Gallery, 22 Rosenthal Av., Lane Cove, Sydney, NSW 2066. T. (02) 428 45 65. *072438*

Parker, 39 Argyle St., Sydney, NSW 2000. T. (02) 27 99 79. *072439*

Pickwick Gallery, Corner Harbord and Wattle Rds., Sydney, NSW 2000. T. (02) 939 74 31. *072440*

Picture Show Art Gallery, 37 Eastwood St., Sydney, NSW 2000. T. (02) 85 31 65. *072441*

Pitt Stop Gallery, 362 Pitt St., Sydney, NSW 2000. T. (02) 26 56 11. *072442*

Potters' Gallery, 2/68 Alexander St., Crows Nest, Sydney, NSW 2065. T. (02) 436 1184. *072443*

Purnama Gallery, 245 Oxford St., Darlinghurst, Sydney, NSW 2010. T. (02) 357 68 80. *072444*

Rocks Gallery, The, 75a George St., Sydney, NSW 2000. T. (02) 27 68 86. *072445*

Roslyn Oxley9, Soudan Lane (off 27 Hampden St), Paddington, Sydney, NSW 2021. T. (02) 3316253, Fax 3315609. - Paint - *072446*

Royce Galleries, 80 George St., Sydney, NSW 2000. T. (02) 27 68 86. *072447*

Sarah's Gallery, 29 Carousel Cntr., Bondi Jn., Sydney, NSW 2022. T. (02) 389 34 50. *072448*

Savill, 156 Hargrave St., Paddington, Sydney, NSW 2021. T. (02) 327 8311. - Paint - *072449*

Scott, L., 194 Old Canterbury Rd., Sydney, NSW 2000. T. (02) 797 87 85. *072450*

Stadia Graphics Gallery, 85 Elizabeth St., 1st Fl., Sydney, NSW 2021. T. (02) 326 2637. - Graph / Draw - *072451*

Stanley Hill Galleries, 549 Royal Arc., Sydney, NSW 2000. T. (02) 235 76 59. *072452*

Stern, Barry, 28 Glenmore Rd., Paddington, Sydney, NSW 2000. T. (02) 31 76 76. *072453*

Styles Gallery, 50 Hunter St., Sydney, NSW 2000. T. (02) 233 2628. - Paint - *072454*

That Glebe Gallery, 35e Ross St., Glebe, Sydney, NSW 2037. T. (02) 660 38 72. *072455*

Thirty Victoria Street, 30 Victoria St., Potts Point, Sydney, NSW 2011. T. (02) 357 3755. *072456*

Upstairs Gallery, 323 Church St., Sydney, NSW 2000. T. (02) 633 42 07. *072457*

Vivian Art Gallery, 309 Forest Rd., Hurstville, Sydney, NSW 2220. T. (02) 579 4383. *072458*

Wagner, 39 Gurner St., Paddington, Sydney, NSW 2021. T. (02) 357 6069. *072459*

Wahroonga Gallery, 3 Redleaf Ave., Sydney, NSW 2000. T. (02) 48 23 99. *072460*

Watters, Frank, 109 Riley St., Sydney, NSW 2010. T. (02) 31 25 56. - Paint / Graph / Sculp - *072461*

Thornbury (Victoria)

Northcote Pottery, 85 A Clyde St., 3071 Thornbury, 3071. T. 484 45 80. *072462*

Warrandyte

Potters Cottage, Jumoing Creek Rd., 3113 Warrandyte, 3113. T. 884 3078. *072463*

Williamstown (Victoria)

Access Studio, Rear 69 Stevedore St., Williamstown, Vic. 3016. *072464*

Austria

Baden bei Wien

Kleine Galerie am Hauptplatz, 2500 Baden bei Wien. - Graph - *072465*

Kosak, Christine, Kaiser Franz-Ring 13, 2500 Baden bei Wien. *072466*

Scherz, Angela, Beethovengasse 2, 2500 Baden bei Wien. *072467*

Badgastein (Salzburg)

Greyer, Margita, Bismarckstr 14, 5640 Badgastein. T. (06434) 2652, Fax 2652. - Paint - *072468*

Bleiburg (Kärnten)

Falke-Galerie, Loibach, Schulweg 17, 9150 Bleiburg. T. (04235) 3600, Fax 3600. *072469*

Bludenz (Vorarlberg)

Seebacher, Josefine Maria, Dr., Lindenweg 26, 6714 Bludenz. T. (05552) 22 98. - Paint / Graph / Sculp - *072470*

Bregenz (Vorarlberg)

Albert, Herbert, Anton Schneider-Str. 20, 6900 Bregenz. T. (05574) 25192. *072471*

Künstlerhaus Palais Thum + Taxis, Gallusstr 10a, 6900 Bregenz. T. (05574) 42751, Fax 44029. *072472*

Brixlegg (Tirol)

Schloß Galerie, Schloß Lipperheide, 6230 Brixlegg. T. (05337) 3318. - Ant / Paint / Graph / China / Sculp / Tex / Glass / Mod / Ico / Draw - *072473*

Döllach (Kärnten)

Lindsberger, Josef, Schloß Großkirchheim, 9843 Döllach. T. (04825) 23 10 06. *072474*

Dornbirn (Vorarlberg)

Alber, Herbert, Dr. Waibel-Str. 6, 6850 Dornbirn. T. (05572) 67791. *072475*

Feldkirch (Vorarlberg)

Hirn, Gerold, Dr, Ardetzenbergstr 60, 6800 Feldkirch. T. (05522) 73618, Fax 79990. - Paint / Graph / Sculp - *072476*

Grafenwörth (Niederösterreich)

Lang, Seebarn 100, 3484 Grafenwörth. T. (02738) 2413. - Paint / Graph / Jew - *072477*

Graz (Steiermark)

Adnatz, Wilhelm-Raabe-Gasse 4, 8010 Graz. T. (0316) 61 79 82. *072478*

Artelier, Eisengasse 3, 8020 Graz. T. (0316) 55036, Fax 57 31 34. *072479*

Bleich-Rossi, Bürgergasse 4, 8010 Graz. T. (0316) 83 27 13-0, Fax 83 27 13-4. *072480*

Bleich-Rossi, Gabriella, Peinlichgasse 8, 8010 Graz. T. (0316) 834587, Fax 834588. *072481*

Carneri-Galerie, Carnerig. 34, 8010 Graz. T. (0316) 64 982. - Paint - *072482*

Forum Stadtpark, Stadtpark 1, 8010 Graz. T. (0316) 82 77 34, 82 53 69, Fax (0316) 8253696. - Pho - *072483*

Fromme Contempora, Altstadt-Passage, Herrengasse 7, 8010 Graz. T. (0316) 830254, Fax 830244. - Graph / China / Sculp / Tex / Jew / Glass / Pho - *072484*

Galerie am Rosenberg, Hochsteingasse 131, 8010 Graz. T. (0316) 67 22 64, 787 30. *072485*

Galerie an der Mur, Kaiser Franz-Josef-Kai 22, 8010 Graz. T. (0316) 73 277. *072486*

Galerie H, Lastenstr. 11, 8020 Graz. - Pho - *072487*

Kiss, Rudolf, Prof., Merangasse 45, 8010 Graz. T. (0316) 31 091. *072488*

Klement, Münzgrabenstr. 10, 8010 Graz. T. (0316) 77 425. *072489*

Moser, Hans-Sachs-Gasse 14, Passage, I.Stock, 8010 Graz. T. (0316) 82982123, 830110 (Antiquariat), 825696 (Galerie u. Antiquitäten), Fax 83011020. - Paint / Graph / Draw - *072490*

Stiegengalerie, Sporgasse 21, 8010 Graz. T. (0316) 789 82. *072491*

Grödig (Salzburg)

Galerie Slavi, Kellerstr. 31, 5082 Grödig. T. (06246) 4448, Fax 4497. - Paint / Graph / China / Draw / Draw - *072492*

Gumpoldskirchen (Niederösterreich)

Oegg, Magret, Wiener Str 26, 2352 Gumpoldskirchen. T. (02252) 62433, Fax (02252) 63820. *072493*

Hall (Tirol)

Lami, Monika Maria, Burg Hasegg, 6060 Hall. T. (05223) 3127. *072494*

Hallstatt (Oberösterreich)

Mistlberger, Wilfried, Seestr. 117, 4830 Hallstatt. T. (06134) 594. *072495*

Zauner, Maria-Alice, Sumatingerweg 179, 4830 Hallstatt. T. (06134) 510. *072496*

Hermagor (Kärnten)

Walker, Judith, 10. Oktober-Str 7, 9620 Hermagor. T. (04282) 2102, Fax (04282) 35014. *072497*

Hirschegg (Vorarlberg)

Willand, Detlef, Wäldelestr. 1, 6992 Hirschegg. T. (05517) 6216. *072498*

Horn (Niederösterreich)

Thurnhof, Wiener Str. 2, 3580 Horn. T. (02982) 3333. *072499*

Imst (Tirol)

Public Art Gallery – Gebhard Schatz, Pfarrgasse 8, 6460 Imst. T. (05412) 64317, Fax 64317. *072500*

Innsbruck (Tirol)

Bloch, Peter, Prandtauerufer 2, 6020 Innsbruck. *072501*

Bloch, Thomas, Friedrich-Str. 5, 6020 Innsbruck. T. (0512) 21 21 34. *072502*

Flora, Thomas, Herzog Friedrich-Str. 5, 6020 Innsbruck. T. (0512) 57 74 02. *072503*

Galeothek 2 – Galerie der Wandlung, Sennstr. 14, 6020 Innsbruck. T. (0512) 58 68 04. - Paint - *072504*

Galerie-Cafe 44, Maria-Theresienstr. 44/I, 6020 Innsbruck. T. (0512) 58 61 60, Fax 580 18 96. *072505*

Galerie im Europahaus, Bruneckerstr 2e, 6020 Innsbruck. T. (0512) 561748, Fax 561788. *072506*

Galerie-Stadtturm, Herzog-Friedrich-Str. 21, 6020 Innsbruck. T. (0512) 58154. *072507*

Hofinger, Tempelstr. 5, 6010 Innsbruck. T. (0512) 57 71 82, Fax 57 22 06. - Paint / Graph / Repr / Fra - *072508*

Maier, Josef, Sparkassenplatz 2/II, 6020 Innsbruck. T. (0512) 58 08 29. - Paint / Graph / Sculp - *072509*

Oberweger, Innrain 25/5, 6020 Innsbruck. T. (0512) 579768. *072510*

Schuler, Wolfgang, Maria Theresien-Str. 10, 6020 Innsbruck. T. (0512) 58 10 17. *072511*

Stadtturmgalerie, Herzog-Friedrich-Str. 21, 6020 Innsbruck. T. (0512) 57 81 54. *072512*

Theresien Galerie, Maria-Theresien-Str. 10, 6020 Innsbruck. T. (0512) 21017. *072513*

Thoman, Elisabeth & Klaus, Adamgasse 7a, 6020 Innsbruck. T. (0512) 575785, Fax 575786. *072514*

Trautner, Josef, Pfarrgasse 6, 6020 Innsbruck. T. (0512) 213 23. - Paint - *072515*

Unterberger, Fr., Burggraben 10, 6020 Innsbruck. T. (0512) 320 88. - Paint / Graph / Orient / Repr / Fra - *072516*

Kirchdorf (Oberösterreich)

Schloß Neupernstein, Pernsteiner Str. 40, 4560 Kirchdorf. T. (07582) 396 73. *072517*

Kitzbühel (Tirol)

Maier, Ferdinand, Traunsteinerweg 2, 6370 Kitzbühel. T. (05356) 4204. *072518*

Zeitkunst, Hammerschmiedstr. 5, 6370 Kitzbühel. T. (05356) 4805. - Paint - *072519*

Klagenfurt (Kärnten)

Bernthaler, Kurt Ewald, Linsengasse 52, 9020 Klagenfurt. T. (0463) 55122, Fax 5512213. *072520*

Carinthia, Alter Platz 30, 9010 Klagenfurt. T. (0463) 51 25 06, Fax 588 01 15, 04212/4306. - Paint / Graph / Repr / Lights - *072521*

GALERIE WELZ

Kunst des 20. Jahrhunderts, Kunstverlag · Salzburg, Sigmund-Haffner-Gasse 16,
Tel.: (06 62) 84 17 71-0 · Fax: (06 62) 84 17 71 20 · Postanschrift: A-5010 Salzburg, Postfach 123

Mayr, Ilse, Khevenhüllerstr. 23, 9020 Klagenfurt.
- Paint / Graph - 072522
Schnitzer, Günter, Dr., St. Veiter Str 1, 9020 Klagenfurt.
T. (0463) 512486, Fax 502475. - Paint / Graph / Sculp /
Draw - 072523
Slama, Hans, Karfreitstr. 1, 9020 Klagenfurt.
T. (0463) 55 63 81. - Paint / Graph / Fra - 072524
Walker, Judith, Lidmanskygasse 8, 9020 Klagenfurt.
T. (0463) 500950, 21305, Fax (0463) 500950. 072525

Kollerschlag (Oberösterreich)
Kollerschlag Kunst-, Produktions- und Vertriebsgesellschaft, 4154 Kollerschlag. 072526

Krems an der Donau (Niederösterreich)
Bildergalerie beim Steinertor, Brauhofgarten, 3500
Krems an der Donau. T. (02732) 37 70. 072527
Galerie Rabe, Wachtbergstr. 42, 3500 Krems an der Donau. T. (02732) 82980. - Paint / Graph / Sculp / Fra /
Pho - 072528
Galerie Stadtpark, Wichnerstr, 3500 Krems an der Donau. T. (02732) 84705, Fax 81276. - Paint / Graph /
Sculp / Pho / Draw - 072529
Hoffelner, Gernot, Dr., Bahnhofpl. 12, 3500 Krems an
der Donau. T. (02732) 82717. 072530
Maringer, Karl Heinz, Dr., Göglstr. 3, 3500 Krems an der
Donau. T. (02732) 74741, Fax 74741. 072531
Wolfsberger, Günter, Steiner Landstr 74, 3500 Krems an
der Donau. T. (02732) 61312. 072532

Kufstein (Tirol)
Schön, Josefgang, Kinkstr. 10, 6330 Kufstein.
T. (05372) 64535. 072533

Lieboch (Steiermark)
Galerie von Gogg, Dorfstr. 1, 8501 Lieboch.
T. (03136) 31 05. 072534

Lienz (Tirol)
Galerie Gaudens Pedit, Bürgeraustr 31, 9900 Lienz.
T. (04852) 668510, Fax 668519. - Paint / Graph /
Sculp / Draw - 072535
Galerie Rondula, Beim Stadtsaal-Südtirolerplatz, 9900
Lienz. T. (04852) 2780, 5400. 072536

Linz (Oberösterreich)
Aigner, Fritz, Waltherstr. 10, 4020 Linz.
T. (0732) 27 50 04. 072537
Eder, Richard, Knabenseminarstr. 41, 4040 Linz.
T. (0732) 231 97 45. Paint / Graph / Draw - 072538
Eigl, Alois, Dametzstr. 25, 4020 Linz. T. (0732) 77 02 70,
Fax 78 56 12. - Paint / Graph / Repr / Fra - 072539
Figl, Felice, Dinghoferstr 44, 4020 Linz.
T. (0732) 669640. 072540
Fischnaller, Paul, Hofgasse 12, 4020 Linz.
T. (0732) 27 42 84. 072541
Galerie am Taubenmarkt, Landstr. 7, 4010 Linz.
T. (0732) 77 17 86. 072542
Galerie für Naive Kunst, Bismarckstr 10, 4020 Linz.
T. (0732) 777404. - Paint / Sculp - 072543
Galerie für zeitgenössische Kunst, Klammstr. 4, 4020
Linz. T. (0732) 79 49 54, Fax 79 49 54. - Paint / Graph /
Sculp / Fra - 072544
Gaulinger, Siegfried, Linke Brückenstr. 19, 4020 Linz.
T. (0732) 315 00. - Paint / Graph / Repr / Fra - 072545
Hofkabinett, Hofgasse 12, 4020 Linz. T. (0732) 27 42 84.
- Paint / Graph - 072546
Khemeter, Franz, Wiener Str. 380, 4020 Linz.
- Paint - 072547
Kleine Galerie, Herrenstr. 17, 4020 Linz.
T. (0732) 273 51 02. 072548
Kozierowski, Alexander, Knabenseminarstr. 6, 4040 Linz.
T. (0732) 23 80 77. 072549

Kunststücke, Spittelwiese 15, 4020 Linz.
T. (0732) 794679, Fax 794679. - Graph / Fra - 072550
Mühlviertler Künstlergilde, Ursulinenhof, Landstr 31,
4020 Linz. T. (0732) 794120. - Paint / Graph / Sculp /
Jew - 072551
Schrey, Norbert, Spittelwiese 2, 4020 Linz.
T. (0732) 27 63 77. 072552
Studio Galerie, Waltherstr. 26, 4020 Linz.
T. (0732) 272 56 52. 072553

Lustenau (Vorarlberg)
Hollenstein, Pontenstr. 20, 6890 Lustenau.
T. (05577) 45 42. - Paint / Graph / Pho / Draw - 072554
Neufeld Verlag & Galerie, Schillerstr. 7, 6890 Lustenau.
T. (05577) 84657, Fax 84657-20. - Paint / Graph /
Repr / Sculp / Fra - 072555

Maria Enzersdorf (Niederösterreich)
Riefel, Hauptstraße 8, 2344 Maria Enzersdorf.
T. (02236) 87 02 75. - Paint - 072556

Mauerkirchen (Oberösterreich)
Menschik, Rosemarie Franziska, Untermarkt 15, 5270
Mauerkirchen. T. (07724) 2158. 072557

Melk (Niederösterreich)
Brocza, Rudolf, Linzer Str. 15, 3390 Melk.
T. (02752) 3603. 072558

Millstatt (Kärnten)
Dürmoser, Ingeborg, Mirnockstr. 203, 9872 Millstatt.
T. (04766) 2681. 072559

Mödling (Niederösterreich)
Arcade, Hauptstr 79, 2340 Mödling. T. (02236) 860457,
Fax (0222) 5235905. 072560
Rull, Elfriede, Schrannenpl. 3, 2340 Mödling. 072561
Weiss, H., Dr-Rieger-Str 10, 2340 Mödling.
T. (02236) 44672, Fax 23086. - Graph - 072562

Münster (Tirol)
Gechösser, Marianne, Schloß Lipperheide 4, 6232 Münster. T. (05337) 3318. 072563

Mürzzuschlag (Steiermark)
Heifler, Karl, Wienerstr. 39, 8680 Mürzzuschlag.
- Paint - 072564

Pörtschach am Wörther See
Fromme Contempora, Hauptstr 143, 9210 Pörtschach
am Wörther See. T. (04272) 3728. - China / Tex / Jew /
Glass - 072565

Potzneusiedl (Burgenland)
Egermann, Gerhard, 2473 Potzneusiedl.
T. (02145) 2249. 072566

Salzburg
Academia, Residenz, 5010 Salzburg. T. (0662) 845185,
Fax 620609. - Paint / Graph / China / Sculp / Jew / Fra /
Glass / Draw / Eth - 072567
Altnöder, Sigmund-Haffner-Gasse 3/1, 5020 Salzburg.
T. (0662) 841435, Fax (0662) 841435. - Paint / Graph /
Sculp / Draw - 072568
Anif, Neutorstr 22, 5020 Salzburg.
T. (0662) 46882. 072569
Contemporary Art, Ignaz Rieder Kai 9, 5020 Salzburg.
T. (0662) 623423, Fax 620609. - Paint / Sculp /
Draw - 072570
Dürnberger, Josef, Malerweg 5, 5020 Salzburg.
T. (0662) 877384. 072571
Galerie im StudentInnenhaus, Wiener-Philharmoniker-
Gasse 2, 5020 Salzburg. T. (0662) 841327,
Fax 8413276. 072572

Galerie Linzergasse, Linzergasse, 5020 Salzburg.
T. (0662) 879119, Fax (0662) 879119. - Paint / Graph /
China / Sculp / Glass / Draw - 072573
Galerie Weihergut, Linzerg 25, 5020 Salzburg.
T. (0662) 879119, Fax 879119. - Paint / Graph / Sculp /
Glass / Draw - 072574
Heinze, Giselakai 15, 5020 Salzburg. T. (0662) 872272,
Fax 872272. - Paint / Graph / Sculp / Mod /
Draw - 072575
Klos, Jana, Maxglaner Hauptstr 12, 5020 Salzburg.
T. (0662) 827838. 072576
Kutscha, Getreidegasse 22, 5020 Salzburg.
T. (0662) 843746/15, Fax (0662) 846852. - Paint /
Graph / China / Sculp - 072577
Matern, Peter, Linzer Gasse 5, 5024 Salzburg.
T. (0662) 873795, Fax (0662) 873795. - Paint / Graph /
Draw - 072578
Müller, Johannes, Hildmannpl 1A, 5020 Salzburg.
T. (0662) 846338, Fax 846338. - Graph - 072579
Prem, S. & J., Goldgasse 16, 5020 Salzburg.
T. (0662) 845181. - Paint / Repr - 072580
Ropac, Thaddaeus, Kaigasse 40, 5020 Salzburg.
T. (0662) 841561, Fax (0662) 841565. - Paint / Graph /
Sculp / Draw - 072581
Sailer, Wiener Philharmoniker Gasse 3, 5020 Salzburg.
T. (0662) 846483, Fax (0662) 8425609. 072582
Salis, Goldgasse 13, 5020 Salzburg. T. (0662) 845434,
Fax (0662) 840146. - Paint - 072583
Schlager, Ingeborg, Bristol Passage, Makartpl 4, 5020
Salzburg. T. (0662) 885696, Fax (0662) 641690. - Ant /
Jew / Silv / Glass / Ico - 072584
Seywald, Sigmund-Haffner-Gasse 7, 5020 Salzburg.
T. (0662) 840426, Fax 840426. - Paint / Graph / Repr /
Sculp / Draw - 072585
Vereinigung zur Förderung Volksnaher Kunst, Waagplatz
1a, 5020 Salzburg. T. (0662) 45004. - Paint /
Graph - 072586
Welz, Sigmund-Haffner-Gasse 16, Postfach 123, 5010
Salzburg. T. (0662) 841771-0, Fax 84177120. - Paint /
Graph / Orient / Repr / Sculp / Fra / Draw - 072587
Wichmann, Horst P., Nonntaler Hauptstr 21, 5020 Salzburg. T. (0662) 842393. - Paint / Sculp - 072588

Sankt Florian (Oberösterreich)
Liedl, Klaus, Weilling 3, 4490 Sankt Florian.
T. (07224) 5353. - Sculp - 072589

Sankt Johann (Tirol)
Briem, Anna, Gasteiger Str. 5, 6380 Sankt Johann.
T. (05352) 2111, 5350. 072591
Galerie im Fellerhaus, Kaiserstr. 7, 6380 Sankt Johann.
T. (05352) 5350. 072592

Sankt Kanzian (Kärnten)
Freund, neben der Sternwarte, 9122 Sankt Kanzian.
T. (04239) 211. - Paint / Graph - 072593

Sankt Pölten (Niederösterreich)
Maringer, Schreinergasse 4, 3100 Sankt Pölten.
T. (02742) 54277, Fax 54198. - Paint / Graph - 072594

Sankt Veit an der Glan (Kärnten)
Atelier 43, Boteng 111, 9300 Sankt Veit an der Glan.
T. (04212) 6780, Fax 214878. 072595

Schärding (Oberösterreich)
Galerie am Stein, Lamprechtstr. 16, 4780 Schärding.
T. (07712) 5130. - Paint / Graph / Sculp / Pho / Mul /
Draw - 072596
Heindl, Josef, Linzertor 2-3, 4780 Schärding.
T. (07712) 3035, Fax 4708. 072597
Palfinger, Otto, Ob. Stadtpl. 21, 4780 Schärding.
T. (07712) 2477. 072598

Weidenholzer, Erna, Unterer Stadtpl. 7, 4780 Schärding.
T. (07712) 2537. 072599

Schörfling (Oberösterreich)
Galerie Zwach Dorschvilla, Weyregger Str 11, 4861
Schörfling. T. (07662) 2261, Fax 2261. - Paint / Graph /
Sculp / Fra - 072600

Schruns (Vorarlberg)
Oberweger, Werner, Alte Montjola 22, 6780 Schruns.
T. (05556) 737 92. 072601

Schwaz (Tirol)
Angerer, Vomperbach 311, 6130 Schwaz.
T. (05242) 71208. - Paint / Graph / Sculp - 072602

Stoob
Hametner, Franz, Kircheng. 16, 7344 Stoob.
T. (02612) 2961. 072603

Telfs
Gundolf, Martin, Prof., Wiesenweg 16, 6410 Telfs.
T. (05262) 62981. 072604

Traun (Oberösterreich)
Krasensky, Elfriede, Linzer Str. 2, 4050 Traun.
T. (07229) 2406. 072605

Trausdorf (Burgenland)
Egger, Ralf, Flugplatzstr. 12, 7061 Trausdorf.
T. (02682) 55 36. - Paint / Graph / Draw - 072606

Tribuswinkel (Niederösterreich)
Skarics, Ingrid, Grenzgasse 30, 2512 Tribuswinkel.
T. (02252) 20 05. 072607

Untergrub (Niederösterreich)
Ziolkowski, Horst, 2013 Untergrub. - Paint / Graph /
Sculp - 072608

Vöcklabruck (Oberösterreich)
Nagl, Regine, Vorstadt 8, 4840 Vöcklabruck.
T. (07672) 4567. 072609

Wels (Oberösterreich)
Glück, Gabriele, Ringstr. 2, 4600 Wels.
T. (07242) 30 64. 072610
Kellner, Johann, Dr. Koß-Str. 1, 4600 Wels.
T. (07242) 76 92. 072611
Nöttling & Fasser, Anzengruberstr. 6-10, 4600 Wels.
T. (07242) 69 67. - Paint / Graph / Repr / Fra - 072612

Wien
Basic, Luka, Gaullachergasse 14, 1160 Wien.
T. (0222) 408 39 74. 072613
Berger, Devy Franz, Grabnerstraße 60, 1060
Wien. 072614
Blutsch, Eduard, Weißgerberlände 38, 1030 Wien.
T. (0222) 712 42 97. - Paint / Fra - 072615
Böck, Anton, Währinger Str. 27, 1090 Wien.
T. (0222) 405 02 46, Fax (0222) 405 02 46. - Paint /
Fra - 072616
Cen am Kohlmarkt, Kohlmarkt 7/2, 1010 Wien.
T. (0222) 533 10 57. - Ant / China / Repr / Sculp / Dec /
Lights / Rel / Glass / Ico - 072617
Chobot, Manfred & Dagmar, Domgasse 6, 1010 Wien.
T. (0222) 5125332, Fax 512 20 38. - Paint - 072618
City-Galerie, Stallburggasse 2, 1010 Wien.
T. (0222) 5133717. 072619
Czerni, Graf, Friedr.-Schmidt-Platz 4, 1010
Wien. 072620
Czikelj, Maximilian, Döblinger Hauptstr. 69, 1190 Wien.
T. (0222) 36 88 77. 072621
Dättel, Rudolf, Zimmermanngasse 8, 1080 Wien.
T. (0222) 402 91 07. 072622
Dorotheer Galerie, Dorotheergasse 6, 1010 Wien.
T. (0222) 512 92 66. - Paint / Graph / Sculp - 072623
Ebeseder, Alois, Babenbergstr. 3, 1010 Wien.
T. (0222) 57 03 53. - Paint / Graph / Repr - 072624
Eibl, Cornelia, Dr., Hüttelbergstr. 26, 1140 Wien. 072625
Entzmann & Sohn, Reinhold, Seilerstätte 21, 1010 Wien.
T. (0222) 512 18 90. - Paint / Graph / Fra /
Draw - 072626
Erbens, Wolfgang, Grimmgasse 36, 1150 Wien.
T. (0222) 83 48 343. 072627

GIESE & SCHWEIGER

Kunsthandel, Gesellschaft mbH.
Akademiestr. 1, 1010 Wien I
Tel. 513 18 43, 513 18 44
Fax 513 93 74

**Gemälde des 19. und 20.
Jahrhunderts**

Franke, Jens, Rotenturmstr. 14, 1010 Wien.
T. (0222) 512 78 84. 072628
Gabriel, Erich, Seilerstätte 19, 1010 Wien.
T. (0222) 512 78 02, Fax 513 84 11. - Paint / Graph /
Sculp / Fra / Mul / Draw - 072629
Galerie am Opernring, Opernring 17, 1010 Wien.
T. (0222) 587 97 24, 587 32 99. 072630
Galerie am Rabensteig, Rabensteig 3, 1010 Wien.
T. (0222) 5337374. 072631
Galerie am Rennweg, Rennweg 11/13, 1030 Wien.
T. (0222) 7151360. - Paint - 072632
Galerie am Salzgries, Salzgries 19, 1010 Wien.
T. (0222) 5336959, Fax 5336959. 072633
Galerie am Schottenfeld, Schottenfeldg. 63, 1070 Wien.
T. (0222) 96 17 53. 072634
Galerie am Stubentor, Zedlitzgasse 3, 1010 Wien.
T. (0222) 513 92 60. 072635
Galerie Ariadne, Bäckerstr. 6, 1010 Wien.
T. (0222) 512 94 79. 072636
Galerie Austria, Liliengasse 2, 1010 Wien.
T. (0222) 512 32 97. - Paint / Graph - 072637
Galerie Contact, Singerstr. 17, 1010 Wien.
T. (0222) 512 98 80, Fax 51298804, (02236) 46151.
- Paint / Graph / Sculp / Draw - 072638
Galerie Flutlicht, Harmoniegasse 2, 1090 Wien.
T. (0222) 31 73 75. 072639
Galerie Gras, Grünangergasse 6, 1010 Wien.
T. (0222) 512 81 06. 072640
Galerie Herzog im Pferdestall, Getreidemarkt 17, 1060
Wien. T. (0222) 587 26 52. - Paint / Graph - 072641
Galerie Image, Ruprechtspl. 4-5, 1010 Wien.
T. (0222) 535 42 84, Fax 535 42 84. - Graph /
Repr - 072642
Galerie in der Biberstraße, Biberstr. 4, 1010 Wien.
T. (0222) 5122374, Fax 5126463/75. 072643
Galerie Metropol, Dorotheergasse 12, 1010 Wien.
T. (0222) 5132208, Fax 513 99 63. - Ant / Paint /
Graph / Draw - 072644
Galerie nächst St. Stephan, Grünangergasse 1, 1010
Wien. T. (0222) 512 12 66, 513 92 96, Fax 513 43 07.
- Graph / Sculp - 072645
Galerie Pavillon – Kunst im Salettl Wien, Hartäckerstr.
80, 1190 Wien. T. (0222) 4792222. - Paint / Sculp /
Cur / Draw - 072646
Galerie Phönix, Sterngasse 2, 1010 Wien.
T. (0222) 5128428. 072647
Galerie Prisma, Franziskanerpl. 1, 1010 Wien.
T. (0222) 5128237, 513320316. - Paint - 072648
Galerie Sanct Lucas, Josefspl 5, 1010 Wien. 072649
Galerie Sonnenfels, Sonnenfelsg 11, 1010 Wien.
T. (01) 5133919, Fax 5133919. - Arch / Eth - 072650
Galerie Station 3, Mariahilferstr 82, 1070 Wien.
T. (0222) 5265501, Fax (0222) 52655011. - Paint /
Graph / Sculp / Jew / Pho / Mul / Draw - 072651
Galerie Ulysses, Opernring 21, 1010 Wien.
T. (0222) 5871226, Fax (0222) 5872199.
- Paint - 072652
Galerie Walfischgasse, Walfischgasse 12, 1010 Wien.
T. (0222) 5123716. 072653
Galerie 10, Getreidemarkt 10, 1010 Wien.
T. (0222) 5875744, Fax 5870767. - Paint / Graph /
Draw - 072654
Galerie 16, Ottakringer Str. 107, 1160 Wien.
T. (0222) 46 34 57. 072655
Galerie 23, Karl Krestan-Gasse 10, 1230 Wien.
T. (0222) 675 01 56. 072656
Galerie 3, Schwarzingergasse 8/23, 1020 Wien.
T. (0222) 9195851, Fax 0222/214 78 31. - Paint /
Graph - 072657

Galerie 7, Siebensterngasse 17, 1070 Wien.
T. (0222) 933 45 13. 072658
Gerersdorfer, Währinger Str 12, 1090 Wien.
T. (0222) 3108484, Fax 310 84 85. - Paint / Graph /
Sculp / Tex / Jew / Fra / Draw - 072659
Gerold & Co., Graben 31, 1011 Wien.
T. (0222) 533 50 14, Fax 533 50 14 12. - Paint /
Graph - 072660
Giese & Schweiger, Akademiestr 1, 1010 Wien.
T. (0222) 5131843, Fax 5139374. - Paint / Graph /
Mod - 072661
Gogl, M., Domgasse 3, 1010 Wien.
T. (0222) 52 61 12. 072662
Gregoritsch, Lucia, Dr., Walfischgasse 11/11, 1010
Wien. 072663
Gril, Cajetan, Grünangergasse 8, 1010 Wien.
T. (0222) 5132270, Fax 5122313. - Graph - 072664
Grill, Cajetan, Grünangergasse 8, 1010 Wien.
T. (0222) 513 22 70, Fax 512 23 13. - Paint - 072665
Haider, Bianca-Maria, Schlösselgasse 24/2, 1080 Wien.
T. (0222) 43 43 86. 072666
Hassfurther, Wolfdietrich, Hohenstaufengasse 7, 1010
Wien. T. (0222) 53509850, Fax (0222) 535098575.
- Ant / Paint / Graph / Glass / Mod / Draw - 072667
Hieke, Ursula, Dr., Grünangergasse 12, 1010 Wien.
T. (0222) 5133259. - Paint - 072668
Hilger, Dorotheergasse 5/1, 1010 Wien.
T. (0222) 512 53 15, Fax 513 91 26. 072669
Hofgalerie, Spiegelg 14, 1010 Wien. T. (0222) 5126350,
Fax 5121406. - Paint - 072670
Hofstätter, Ingrid, Bräunerstr. 7, 1010 Wien.
T. (0222) 512 32 55, Fax 512 16 61. - Paint / Jew /
Glass - 072671
Holzer, Werner, Hermanngasse 25, 1070 Wien.
T. (0222) 96 19 27. 072672
Holzer, Werner, Siebensterngasse 32, 1070 Wien.
T. (0222) 52615068, Fax (0222) 5237218. 072673
Honegger, Franz, Josefsgasse 4-6, 1080 Wien. 072674
Hummel, Julius, Bäckerstr. 14, 1010 Wien.
T. (0222) 512 12 96, Fax 512 12 96. - Paint / Graph /
Furn / Sculp - 072675
Insam, Grita, Köllnerhofgasse 6a, 1010 Wien.
T. (0222) 512 53 30, Fax 512 61 94. - Paint / Sculp /
Pho / Draw - 072676
Junker, Dorotheerstr 12, 1010 Wien. T. (0222) 5132208,
Fax 5139963. 072677
Kaiser, Am Gestade 5, 1013 Wien. T. (0222) 5355222,
Fax 5353915. 072678
Kalb, Kurt, Rennweg 2, 1030 Wien. T. (0222) 715 22 50.
- Paint / Graph - 072679
Keil, Robert, Dr., Gloriettegasse 13, 1130 Wien.
T. (0222) 8765574, Fax (0222) 8775034. - Paint /
Draw - 072680
Kleine Galerie, Neudeggergasse 8, 1080 Wien.
T. (0222) 402 31 25. - Paint / Graph / Sculp - 072681
Klute, Franziskaner Pl. 6, 1010 Wien. T. (0222) 5135322,
5208674. 072682
Knoll, Hans, Esterházygasse 29, 1060 Wien.
T. (0222) 587 50 52, Fax 587 59 66. - Paint / Graph /
Sculp / Pho / Mul / Draw - 072683
Körber, Edith, Alser Str 26, 1090 Wien.
T. (0222) 4053280, Fax 4053280. - Paint / Fra /
Graph - 072684
Kokorian, Spiegelgasse 19, 1010 Wien.
T. (0222) 5127163. 072685
Kosian, Silvia, Stiftgasse 11, 1070 Wien.
T. (0222) 937 88 24. 072686
Kotzian, Eva, Lobkowitzpl. 3, 1010 Wien.
T. (0222) 512 13 38. 072687
Kovacek, Michael, Spiegelgasse 12, 1010 Wien.
T. (0222) 5129954, Fax 5132166. - Glass /
Paint - 072688
Krinzinger, Ursula, Seilerstätte 16, 1010 Wien.
T. (0222) 513 30 06, Fax 513 30 06 33. 072689
Kunst-Depot, Himmelpfortgasse 10, 1010 Wien.
T. (0222) 513 52 02. - Paint / Sculp / Jew - 072690
Kunst & Form, Sonnenfelsgasse 8, 1010 Wien.
T. (0222) 513 13 21. 072691
Lang Wien, Seilerstätte 16, 1010 Wien.
T. (0222) 5122 0190, Fax 512 02 37. - Paint / Graph /
Jew / Instr - 072692
Leitinger, Olga, Schottenfeldg. 63, 1070 Wien.
T. (0222) 96 17 53. 072693

Linke, Margaretha, Nußdorfer Str. 53, 1090
Wien. *072694*

Lonsky, Ilse, Ignazgasse 3, 1120 Wien.
T. (0222) 85 12 25. *072695*

Maegle, Rudolf, Freyung 1, 1010 Wien.
T. (0222) 5354361, Fax (0222) 5354361. - Paint /
Graph / Sculp / Draw - *072696*

GALERIE MAEGLE
IM PALAIS HARRACH

An- u. Verkauf von Gemälden
Aquarellen des 19. u. 20. Jhdts.
Dekorative und künstl. Graphik

Freyung 3
A 1010 Wien
Tel. u. Fax 02 22/5 35 43 61 und 5 35 45 90

Management Club, Galerie, Kärntnerstr. 8, 1000 Wien.
T. (0222) 512 79 35. - Paint / Draw - *072697*

Michnowski, Erna, Berggasse 25, 1090 Wien.
T. (0222) 31 12 17. *072698*

Mündel, Ferry, Blumauergasse 9, 1020 Wien.
T. (0222) 214 74 34. - Paint / Graph - *072699*

Netusil, Ferdinand, Bäckerstr. 6, 1010 Wien.
T. (0222) 5129479. *072700*

Neue Galerie Wien, Rotenturmstr. 27, 1010 Wien.
T. (0222) 5336131. *072701*

Nevidal, Hans, Kohlgasse 11, 1050 Wien.
T. (0222) 5452831. - Paint / Graph / Furn / Repr / Sculp /
Eth / Dec / Jew / Fra / Rel / Cur / Pho / Mul / Draw --
072702

Novotny, Franz Karl, Wichtelgasse 12, 1160
Wien. *072703*

Ogrisegg, Eva, Himmelpfortgasse 10, 1010
Wien. *072704*

Otto, Taborstr. 33, 1020 Wien. T. (0222) 21467138.
- Paint - *072705*

Otto, Märzstr. 64, 1150 Wien. T. (0222) 9823608.
- Paint - *072706*

Otto, Seilergasse 1, 1010 Wien. T. (0222) 5125910,
5138039. - Paint - *072707*

Otto, Floridsd. Hauptstr. 14, 1210 Wien.
T. (0222) 2703737. - Paint - *072708*

Otto, Hietz. Hauptstr. 22, 1130 Wien. T. (0222) 8778330.
- Paint - *072709*

Otto, Meidl. Hauptstr. 49, 1120 Wien. T. (0222) 830152.
Paint - *072710*

Otto, Favoritenstr. 99, 1100 Wien. T. (0222) 6040159.
- Paint - *072711*

Otto, Währinger Str. 79, 1180 Wien. T. (0222) 43 13 92.
- Paint - *072712*

Otto, Mariahilfer Str. 24, 1070 Wien. T. (0222) 5231066.
- Paint / Paint - *072713*

Otto, Landstr. Hauptstr. 81, 1030 Wien.
T. (0222) 7133476. - Paint - *072714*

Otto, Lobkowitzpl. I, 1010 Wien. T. (0222) 5125801,
Fax 877 75 00 12. - Paint - *072715*

Otto, Lainzer Str. 53, 1131 Wien. T. (0222) 8777500,
Fax (0222) 877750012. - Paint - *072716*

Pabst, Michael, Habsburger Gasse 10, 1010 Wien.
T. (0222) 5337014. - Paint / Graph / Sculp - *072717*

Pakesch, Peter, Ungargasse 27, 1030 Wien.
T. (0222) 7137456, Fax 71 37 45 64. - Paint / Sculp /
Draw - *072718*

Pakesch, Peter, Ballgasse 6, 1010 Wien.
T. (0222) 5124814. - Paint / Sculp / Draw - *072719*

Pallamar, Friederike, Dorotheergasse 7, 1010 Wien.
T. (0222) 5125228. - Paint - *072720*

Peithner & Lichtenfels, Pressgasse 30, 1040 Wien.
T. (0222) 5873729. *072721*

Perny, Peter, Seilerstätte 28, 1010 Wien.
T. (0222) 51 32 097. *072722*

Petritsch, Roswitha, Rotgasse 3, 1010 Wien.
T. (0222) 5353082, 7698639, Fax 7698824. - Paint /
Draw / Sculp - *072723*

Planer, Leopold, Ratschkygasse 16, 1120 Wien. *072724*

Planer, Leopold, Quellenstr. 115, 1100 Wien. *072725*

Planer, Leopold, Erlgasse 26, 1120 Wien.
072726

Prokopetz, Ingrid, Neubaugasse 2, 1070 Wien.
T. (0222) 93 76 70, 96 30 14. *072727*

Reisch, Günther, Linzer Str. 373, 1140 Wien.
T. (0222) 94 12 60. *072728*

Ruberl, Richard, Himmelpfortg 11, 1010 Wien.
T. (0222) 5131992, Fax 5137709. - Paint /
Graph - *072729*

Schaffler, Heide, Thaliastr. 49, 1160 Wien.
T. (0222) 4931753. *072730*

Schaumberger, Elisabeth, Rabensteig 3, 1010
Wien. *072731*

Scherzer, Egon, Schottenring 14, 1010 Wien.
T. (0222) 5334406. - Paint / Graph / Repr / Fra - *072732*

Schwerer, Margaretha, Opernring 17, 1010 Wien.
T. (0222) 57 97 24. *072733*

Squire, Maria Magdalena, Spiegelgasse 4, 1010 Wien.
T. (0222) 512 13 99. *072734*

Stalzer, Andreas, Barnabitengasse 6, 1060 Wien.
T. (0222) 5879934. *072735*

Steinek, Heinrich, Himmelpfortgasse 22, 1010 Wien.
T. (0222) 5128759, Fax 3103930, 5128759. - Paint /
Draw - *072736*

Sternat, Reinhold, Dr., Lobkowitzpl 1, 1010 Wien.
T. (0222) 5121871, Fax (0222) 5138517. - Paint /
Graph / Furn / Mod - *072737*

Suppan, Martin, Seilerstätte 3, Palais Coburg, 1010
Wien. T. (0222) 535 53 52, Fax 513 74 74. - Paint /
Furn - *072738*

Tichatschek, Dietmar, Palmgasse 8, 1150 Wien.
T. (0222) 83 31 64. *072739*

Tuchlauben Galerie, Tuchlauben 22, 1010 Wien.
T. (0222) 5330455. *072740*

Un'Art Galerie am Spittelberg, Gutenberggasse 18/III,
1070 Wien. T. (0222) 6153504. - Paint / Graph / Sculp /
Pho / Draw - *072741*

United Art Gallery, Leopoldsg. 9, 1020 Wien.
T. (0222) 332 87 02. - Paint / Graph / China / Repr /
Sculp / Jew / Pho / Draw - *072742*

V & V Galerie, Bauernmarkt 19, 1010 Wien.
T. (0222) 5356334, Fax 5356334. - Sculp /
Jew - *072743*

Verkauf, Helga, Rauchgasse 39, 1120 Wien.
T. (0222) 812 23 48, 812 38 77. - Paint / Graph / Tex /
Mod / Draw - *072744*

Wickenburg-Galerie, Wickenburggasse 4, 1080 Wien.
T. (0222) 408 18 26. *072745*

Widauer, Heinz, Goldeggasse 9, 1040 Wien. *072746*

Winter, Hubert, Sonnenfelsg 8, 1010 Wien.
T. (0222) 5129285, Fax 5129285. *072747*

Wissmann, Harald, Margaretenstr. 39, 1040 Wien.
T. (0222) 56 74 99. *072748*

Wolfrum, Augustinerstr 10, 1010 Wien.
T. (0222) 51253980, Fax 5121557. - Paint / Graph /
Repr / Fra / Pho / Draw - *072749*

Zacke, Schulerstr. 15, 1010 Wien. T. (0222) 5122223,
Fax (0222) 5132704. - Orient - *072750*

Zambo-Curtze, Heike, Dr., Seilerstätte 15, 1010 Wien.
T. (0222) 5129375, Fax 5134943. *072751*

7ehetbauer-Engelhart, Ulrike, Max-Emanuel-Str. 7, 1180
Wien. T. (0222) 4792377. - Jew - *072752*

Wischathal (Niederösterreich)

Galerie im Bauernhof, 2013 Wischathal.
T. 617 72. *072753*

Zwettl (Niederösterreich)

Viertelgalerie-Waldviertel, Zwettler Kunstverein, Gal-
genbergstr. 16, 3910 Zwettl. T. (02822) 5 31 52.
- Paint / Graph - *072754*

Barbados

Bridgetown

Studio Art Gallery, Speedbird House, Fairchild St.,
Bridgetown. T. 427-5463. *072755*

Christ Church

Bertalan, Marine Gardens, Christ Church. T. 427-
0714. *072756*

Saint John, Stella, Enterprise Rd., Christ Church. T. 428-
9305. *072757*

Talma Mill Art Gallery, Enterprise Rd., Christ Church.
T. 428-9383. *072758*

Saint Michael

Dayrell's Art Gallery, Dayrell's Plantation, Saint Michael.
T. (08) 437-9400. *072759*

Devonish, Pelican Village, Saint Michael. T. (08) 427-
5235. *072760*

Garrison, Letchworth House, Saint Michael. T. (08) 429-
3670. *072761*

Pelican Art Gallery, c/o Barbados Arts Council, Pelican
Village, Saint Michael. T. (08) 426-4385. *072762*

Belgium

Aalst (Oost-Vlaanderen)

Apostelken, t', O.L. Vrouwplein, 9300 Aalst.
- Paint - *072763*

Borghmans, Galerij, Geraardbergsestraat 28, 9300
Aalst. T. (053) 21 04 15. - Paint - *072764*

Callebaut, Ponststr 37, 9300 Aalst.
T. (053) 21 29 20. *072765*

Gallery S 65, Tragel 7, 9300 Aalst. T. (053) 770164,
Fax (053) 770787. - Paint - *072766*

Muylaert-Hofman, Nieuwstr 36, 9300 Aalst.
T. (053) 78 71 12. *072767*

Path, Leo de Bethuneln 59, 9300 Aalst.
T. (053) 77 22 97. *072768*

Smet, L. de, Hoogstr 11, 9300 Aalst.
T. (053) 21 05 60. *072769*

Smiks, Dr De Cockstr 5, 9300 Aalst.
T. (053) 77 37 38. *072770*

Van de Velde, Tragel 7, 9300 Aalst.
T. (053) 78 75 47. *072771*

Van de Velde, C Haeltermanstr 77, 9300 Aalst.
T. (053) 70 04 65. *072772*

Aalter (Oost-Vlaanderen)

Frame Belgium, Brugstr 188, 9880 Aalter.
T. (051) 748060, Fax 748060. *072773*

Aartselaar (Antwerpen)

Slootmaeckers, Kapellestr 212, 2630 Aartselaar.
T. (031) 8874161. *072774*

Afsnee (Oost-Vlaanderen)

Kouterloo, Galerij, Molenstraat 3, 9051 Afsnee.
T. (091) 21 27 29. - Paint - *072775*

Antwerpen

Arln, Verlatstr 12, 2000 Antwerpen. T. (03) 2386875.
- Paint - *072777*

Alkader, Abdijstr. 62, 2020 Antwerpen. T. (03) 237 56 65.
- Paint - *072778*

Alting, Catrin, Schuttershofstr 30, 2000 Antwerpen.
T. (03) 233 26 12. *072779*

Anto, Raapstr 18-20, 2000 Antwerpen.
T. (03) 232 15 50. *072780*

Antwerp Art Info, Bervoetsstr. 45, 2000 Antwerpen.
T. (03) 233 35 90. - Paint / Graph / Sculp / Eth / Mul /
Draw - *072781*

Arc, E., E Banningstr 15, 2000 Antwerpen.
T. (03) 237 09 51. *072782*

Art Gallery, Sonja Mertens, Ballaerstr 10, 2018 Antwerpen. T. (03) 237 53 40. *072783*

Art Touché, Lge Brilstr 8, 2610 Antwerpen.
T. (03) 232 88 13. *072784*

Artiges & Zonen, Belgiëlei 76, 2018 Antwerpen.
T. (03) 239 78 80. - Paint - *072785*

Artro, Leopoldpl 1, 2000 Antwerpen.
T. (03) 233 81 62. *072786*

Bam, Montebellostr. 17, 2018 Antwerpen.
T. (03) 237 57 27. - Paint - *072787*

BBL Galerij, de Keyserlei 14, 2018 Antwerpen.
T. (03) 658 28 93. *072788*

Beernaert, J.G., Kerkstr. 51, 2008 Antwerpen.
T. (03) 324 23 14. - Paint - *072789*

Beers, H., I Brantstr 71, 2018 Antwerpen.
T. (03) 238 40 34. *072790*

Bogarts, Lge Beeldekensstr 73, 2060 Antwerpen.
T. (03) 236 54 32. *072791*

Bongers, H., Kielpark 160, 2020 Antwerpen. T. (03) 237 74 49. 072792
Bozar Galerie, Minderbroederstr 18-20, 2000 Antwerpen. T. (03) 234 25 79. 072793
Brabo, Melkmarkt 25a, 2000 Antwerpen. T. (03) 232 62 33. - Paint - 072794
Buytaert, Jeanne, Jan van Rijswijcklaan 204, 2020 Antwerpen. T. (03) 238 66 99. - Paint - 072795
Cami, Jezuitenrui 9, 2000 Antwerpen. T. (03) 232 23 23. - Paint - 072796
Campo, Carine, Leopoldstr. 53, 2000 Antwerpen. T. (03) 232 62 70, Fax 233 82 80. - Paint / Sculp - 072797
Claassens, A., Desguinlei 84, 2018 Antwerpen. T. (03) 238 63 59. 072798
Contact, J., Bresstr 10, 2018 Antwerpen. T. (03) 216 31 38. 072799
Contact J, Bresstr. 10, 2018 Antwerpen. T. (03) 216 31 38. - Mod - 072800
Crucitti, Paolo, Appelmansstr 17, 2018 Antwerpen. T. (03) 232 11 03. 072801
D'Huyvetter, L., I Brantstr 44, 2018 Antwerpen. T. (03) 238 08 58. 072802
Dajak, Anselmostr. 93, 2018 Antwerpen. T. (03) 237 51 26. - Paint - 072803
Defour, J., Huybrechtsstr 27, 2008 Antwerpen. T. (03) 235 11 33. 072804
Den Tijd, Scheldestr 21, 2000 Antwerpen. T. (03) 238 79 75. 072805
Dujardin, R.M., 2 Ch. de Costerin, 2050 Antwerpen. T. (03) 219 14 43. - Paint - 072806
Dyck, Antoon van, Klapdorp 89-91, 2000 Antwerpen. T. (03) 231 14 62. 072807
Europa Galerij, Oude Koornmarkt 69, 2000 Antwerpen. T. (03) 234 21 52. 072808
Eykelberg, Jan, Bolwerkstr. 8, 2018 Antwerpen. T. (03) 2386260. - Paint - 072808a
Gärtner & Co, Steenhouwersvest 18, 2000 Antwerpen. T. (03) 231 17 61. - Paint / Graph / Sculp / Mod - 072809
Galerij BBL, 14 de Keyserlei, 2018 Antwerpen. T. (03) 233 81 06. 072810
Galerij De Zwarte Panter, Hoogstr 70-72, 2000 Antwerpen. T. (03) 233 13 45. 072811
Galerij 58, Lge Herentalsestr 58, 2018 Antwerpen. T. (03) 231 04 69. 072812
Gallery De Lelie, Stoofstr. 9, 2000 Antwerpen. T. (03) 231 16 81, 236 77 85. - Sculp / Pho / Draw - 072813
Galt, John, Guldenberg 1, 2000 Antwerpen. T. (03) 226 39 67. 072814
G.C. Art Selections, Kloosterstr. 58, 2000 Antwerpen. T. (03) 238 26 40. - Paint - 072815
Goya, Coquilhatstr 43-45, 2000 Antwerpen. T. (03) 248 29 63, Fax 238 51 58. 072816
Gramo, Huidevettersstr. 20-24, 2000 Antwerpen. T. (03) 225 22 05. - Paint - 072817
Haest, Lamberta, Lge Doornikstr 27, 2000 Antwerpen. T. (03) 233 12 70. 072818
Henau, St. Jozefstr. 10, 2018 Antwerpen. T. (03) 239 77 58. - Paint - 072819
Hispantics, Coquilhatstr 43-45, 2000 Antwerpen. T. (03) 237 45 73. 072820
Hoste, L., De Beuckerstr 18, 2018 Antwerpen. T. (03) 216 09 21. 072821
Isabella Brant, Isabella Brantstr 71, 2000 Antwerpen. T. (03) 238 40 34. 072822
Jozefien, Reyndersstr. 45, 2000 Antwerpen. T. (03) 232 35 88. - Paint - 072823
Klaver, de, Volkstr 70, 2000 Antwerpen. T. (03) 216 38 63. 072824
Kunsthandel den Tijd, Scheldestr. 21, 2000 Antwerpen. T. (03) 238 79 75. - Paint / Graph / Sculp / Mul / Draw - 072825
Lelie, de, Stoofstr. 9, 2000 Antwerpen. T. (03) 231 16 81. - Graph - 072826
Lens, Mechelsesteenweg 146, 2018 Antwerpen. T. (03) 237 68 57. 072827
Lobo Press, Lange Lozannastr. 152, 2018 Antwerpen. T. (03) 238 39 63. - Paint - 072828
Mattysses, A., Italiëlei 115, 2000 Antwerpen. T. (03) 231 30 45. 072829
Mollaert, Casteleinstr 29e, 2000 Antwerpen. T. (03) 238 71 37. 072830
Montevideo, Peter Benoitstr. 40, 2018 Antwerpen. T. (03) 216 30 28. - Paint - 072831
Nine Arts Gallery, Lge Lozanastr 238, 2018 Antwerpen. T. (03) 238 84 77. 072832
Nova Platea 20, Kte Nieuwstr 20, 2000 Antwerpen. T. (03) 231 66 16. 072833
Ophelia, St-Jacobsmarkt 10, 2000 Antwerpen. T. (03) 226 44 85. 072834
Orpheus, Stoofstr. 9, 2000 Antwerpen. T. (03) 231 16 81. - Paint - 072835
Paolo, Appelmansstr. 17, 2000 Antwerpen. T. (03) 232 11 03. - Paint - 072836
Papasideris, Lge Leemstr 73, 2018 Antwerpen. T. (03) 232 06 39. 072837
Parbleu, Verbrande-Entrepotstr 9, 2000 Antwerpen. T. (03) 238 36 92. 072838
Promart, Oude Leeuwenrui 50, 2000 Antwerpen. - Paint - 072839
Quintus, Lge Lozannastr 152, 2018 Antwerpen. T. (03) 238 39 63. 072840
Ronge, J., Rolwagenstr 60, 2018 Antwerpen. T. (03) 239 30 12. 072841
Roos, de, Minderbroedersrui 66, 2000 Antwerpen. T. (03) 231 72 40. 072842
Sant, de, St Jorispt 37, 2000 Antwerpen. T. (03) 232 31 61. 072843
Schuddeboom, J., Groenendaalln 346, 2030 Antwerpen. T. (03) 542 57 32. 072844
Sebregts, L., Vrijheidstr 58, 2000 Antwerpen. T. (03) 238 00 22. 072845
Sky is the Limit, The, Kloosterstr 68, 2000 Antwerpen. T. (03) 238 66 26. 072846
Star Arts Gallery, Vlaamse Kaai 35, 2000 Antwerpen. T. (03) 238 33 33. 072847
Strecker, W., Lamorinierestr 201, 2018 Antwerpen. T. (03) 239 43 57. 072848
Stynen, H., Coquilhatstr 45, 2000 Antwerpen. T. (03) 237 45 73, Fax 238 51 58. 072849
Szwajcer, Micheline, Verlatstr 12, 2000 Antwerpen. T. (03) 237 11 27. 072850
Szymon, Oude Koornmarkt 68, 2000 Antwerpen. T. (03) 231 04 42. 072851
't Verlengde, Volkstr 59, 2000 Antwerpen. T. (03) 237 47 63. 072852
Terninckgalerij, Terninckstr 20, 2000 Antwerpen. T. (03) 233 86 94. 072853
Teugels, W.-J., Museumstr 12, 2000 Antwerpen. T. (03) 238 89 21. 072854
Timmermans, M., Plantin 56 en Moretuslei, 2018 Antwerpen. T. (03) 230 78 40. 072855
Tollhuis 70, 2621 Schelle Tolhuisstr. 70, 2000 Antwerpen. T. (03) 887 60 90. - Paint / Paint - 072856
Torfs, L., Lge Leemstr 21, 2018 Antwerpen. T. (03) 449 90 60. 072857
Van den Branden, G., Lge Koepoortstr 41, 2000 Antwerpen. T. (03) 233 56 83. 072858
Van der Planken, Rubenslei 17, 2018 Antwerpen. T. (03) 233 54 58, Fax 231 6580. 072859
Van Hoof, Francis, Reyndersstr. 12-16-18, 2000 Antwerpen. T. (03) 231 85 55, Fax 231 88 67. - Paint / Graph / Sculp / Dec / Lights - 072860
Vandaag, Leopoldpl. 11, 2000 Antwerpen. T. (03) 233 39 88. - Paint - 072861
Vanriet, J., Louizastr 22, 2000 Antwerpen. T. (03) 232 47 76. 072862
Veran, Lange Lozanastr. 152, 2018 Antwerpen. T. (03) 238 39 63. - Paint - 072863
Vermoeide Model, Het, Lijnwandmarkt 2, 2000 Antwerpen. T. (03) 233 52 61. 072864
Walschap, L., Mechelsesteenweg 10, 2000 Antwerpen. T. (03) 232 93 41. - Paint - 072865
Wieuw, de, Scheldestr. 53-55, 2000 Antwerpen. T. (03) 237 23 23. - Paint - 072866
Zeno X Gallery, Leopold de Waelpl 16, 2000 Antwerpen. T. (03) 216 16 26, Fax 216 16 26. 072867
Zwanepand, Vlasmarkt 18-20, 2000 Antwerpen. T. (03) 232 29 75. 072868
Zwarte Panter, De, Hoogstr. 70-72, 2000 Antwerpen. T. (03) 233 13 45. - Paint - 072869
121 Art Gallery, Mechelsesteenweg 121, 2018 Antwerpen. T. (03) 218 68 73. 072870
20 Nova Platea, Korte Nieuwstr. 20, 2000 Antwerpen. T. (03) 231 66 16. - Paint - 072871

Aspelare (Oost-Vlaanderen)

Prieels, G., Geraardbergsestw 296, 9404 Aspelare. T. (054) 33 86 77. 072872

Assenede (Oost-Vlaanderen)

Boeve, Margaretha de, Holleken 15, 9960 Assenede. T. (09) 44 65 80. - Paint - 072873

Balen (Antwerpen)

Imro, Olmensebn. 136, 2490 Balen. T. (014) 81 61 20. - Paint - 072874

Bazel (Oost-Vlaanderen)

Wissekerke, Kon Astridplein 17, 9150 Bazel. T. (030) 743466. 072875

Beersel (Vlaams Brabant)

Teirlinck, Herman, Uwenberg 14, 1650 Beersel. T. (02) 3724557. 072876

Berchem (Antwerpen)

Amap, Coosemansstr 87, 2600 Berchem. T. (03) 218 54 36. 072877
Caeyers, M., A Sterckstr 4, 2600 Berchem. T. (03) 230 14 45. 072878
Defoer, Eliane, J Ratinckxstr 1-7, 2600 Berchem. T. (03) 49 53 64, 40 08 85. 072879
Den Tijd, Waterloostr 59, 2600 Berchem. T. (03) 239 10 75. 072880
Hanssens, R., Apollostr 81, 2600 Berchem. T. (03) 321 66 38. 072881
Mariman, L., St-Hubertusstr 111, 2600 Berchem. T. (03) 218 95 82. 072882
Schraenen, G., Uitbreidingsstr. 552, 2600 Berchem. T. (03) 235 85 96. - Paint - 072883
Verdyck, H., Potvlietln 72, 2600 Berchem. T. (03) 235 53 66. 072884

Beringen (Limburg)

Rustique Art Gallery, Molenaarstr 68, 3580 Beringen. T. (011) 341486. 072885

Beveren (Oost-Vlaanderen)

Clerck, H.N. de, Gaverlanddam 5, 9120 Beveren. T. (031) 7757796. 072886
Moore, Kloosterstr 44, 9120 Beveren. T. (031) 7552019, Fax 755 27 60. 072887
Pietstaut, Pietstautstr 83, 9120 Beveren. T. (031) 7753427. 072888
Vijver, van de, Bosdamlaan 5, 9120 Beveren. T. (031) 757059. 072889

Beverlo (Limburg)

Douven, Luc, Molenaarsstr. 68, 3581 Beverlo. T. (011) 341486. - Paint - 072890

Bissegem (West-Vlaanderen)

Haenens, Marc, d', Meensestr 341, 8501 Bissegem. T. (056) 35 08 70. 072891

Boechout (Antwerpen)

Corthals, J., Schransstr 114, 2530 Boechout. T. (031) 3225092. 072892
Pee, van, O. L. Vrouwplein 13, 2530 Boechout. - Paint - 072893

Bonheiden (Antwerpen)

Ado, Boerenkrijglaan 21, 2820 Bonheiden. T. (015) 20 18 77. 072894

Boom (Antwerpen)

Vergult, R., Leliestr 7, 2850 Boom. T. (03) 888 89 33. 072895

Borgerhout (Antwerpen)

Felbier, M., Langstr. 74, 2140 Borgerhout. T. (031) 236 96 21. 072896
Melsen, J., St.-Lucasstr. 11, 2140 Borgerhout. T. (031) 236 96 82. 072897
Prenen, A., Kroonstr. 63, 2140 Borgerhout. T. (031) 236 65 34. 072898

Bornem (Antwerpen)

Helan-Arts, Luipegem 77, 2880 Bornem. T. (03) 889 01 69. 072899
West, J., Sleutelbloemenln 25, 2880 Bornem. T. (03) 889 61 14. 072900

Borsbeek (Antwerpen)
Van den Meersch, Singel 6, 2150 Borsbeek.
T. (03) 3227162. *072901*

Brasschaat (Antwerpen)
Galerie Tableaux, Leopoldslei 7, 2930 Brasschaat.
T. (031) 652 02 24. *072902*
Global Art Promotion, Bloemenlei 14, 2930 Brasschaat.
T. (031) 652 07 45. *072903*
Van Loon, L., Het Innemen 98, 2930 Brasschaat.
T. (031) 651 57 66. *072904*

Bree (Limburg)
Kunstgalerij RB, Hoogstr 192, 3960 Bree.
T. (011) 47 13 47. *072905*

Brugge (West-Vlaanderen)
Amphora Finippon, Oudstrijdersln 14, 8200 Brugge.
T. (050) 38 83 42. *072906*
Arabesk Gallery, Katelijnestr 21, 8000 Brugge.
T. (050) 33 08 82. *072907*
Art Gallery, Wollestr 21, 8000 Brugge.
T. (050) 33 58 22. *072908*
Broes, Koen, Simon Stevinpl. 12, 8000 Brugge.
T. (050) 33 37 74. - Furn - *072909*
Bruges la morte, Johan Vansteenkiste, Krom Genthof
1B, 8000 Brugge. T. (050) 33 89 56,
Fax 33 97 24. *072910*
Bruynseraede, J., Blankenbergsestw 12, 8000 Brugge.
T. (050) 31 34 35. *072911*
Callewaert, Carlos, Genthof 19, 8000 Brugge.
T. (050) 33 21 74. *072912*
De Lege Ruimente, Blockstr 32 B, 8000 Brugge.
T. (050) 33 98 61, 38 63 77. *072913*
Dieperinck, Hoefijzering 20, 8000 Brugge.
T. (050) 33 50 89. *072914*
Galerij T'Leerhuys, Groeninge 35, 8000 Brugge.
T. (050) 33 03 02. *072915*
Garnier, Korte Zilverstraat 8, 8000 Brugge.
T. (050) 33 01 96. - Graph / Sculp / Arch - *072916*
Guy Art, Fort Lapin 37, 8000 Brugge.
T. (050) 33 21 59. *072917*
Huidevetterhuis, Huidevetterspl. 10, 8000 Brugge.
- Paint / Sculp - *072918*
Koen Broes, Simon Stevinplein 12, 8000 Brugge.
T. (050) 33 37 74. *072919*
Korrekelder, Kraanplein 7, 8000 Brugge.
T. (050) 33 03 83. - Paint - *072920*
Michot, Marc, Groene Rei 3, 8000 Brugge.
T. (050) 33 97 20. - Orient / China - *072921*
Muze, de, Philipstockstr 14, 8000 Brugge.
T. (050) 34 59 14. *072922*
Promart Ziverpoort, Zuidzandstr 2, 8000 Brugge.
T. (050) 31 98 34. *072923*
Storms, Rik, Katelijnestr 47, 8000 Brugge.
T. (050) 33 25 47, Fax 34 03 37. *072924*

Bruxelles
Abac Gallery, 31 Rue de la Madeleine, 1000 Bruxelles.
T. (02) 513 12 84. - Paint - *072925*
ABC-Galerie, 53 Rue Lebeau, 1000 Bruxelles.
T. (02) 511 32 53. - Paint - *072926*
Afassa, Keltenln 30, 1040 Bruxelles.
T. (02) 736 91 34. *072927*
Aguimme, Lugo C. de, 88 Rue de Ruysbroeck, 1000
Bruxelles. T. (02) 513 74 06. *072928*
Al Farahnick, 88 Rue de Namur, 1000 Bruxelles.
T. (02) 511 33 63. - Paint - *072929*
Alaerts, J.-P., 5 Rue Coppens, 1000 Bruxelles.
T. (02) 511 11 29. - Ant / Paint / Furn / Sculp - *072930*
Alcantara, Waversestw 286, 1050 Bruxelles.
T. (02) 648 07 27. - Paint / Graph - *072931*
Alexander's Gallery, 9 Pl. du Grand Sablon, 1000 Bruxel-
les. T. (02) 527 57 76. - Paint - *072932*
Alfican, 2 Pl du Grand Sablon, 1000 Bruxelles.
T. (02) 511 68 74. *072933*
Amaryllis, Gentsesteenweg 1108, 1082 Bruxelles.
T. (02) 465 67 09. *072934*
Amilys, 27 Rue des Minimes, Sablon, 1000 Bruxelles.
T. (02) 513 77 70, Fax 3210-86 73 00. - Paint - *072935*
Anubis, 223 Rue Gray, 1050 Bruxelles. T. (02) 649 75 15.
- Paint - *072936*
Apollo Galeries, 25 Gal du Roi, 1000 Bruxelles.
T. (02) 512 51 81. *072937*

Arcade Mauve, L', 20 Rue de la Samaritaine, 1000 Bru-
xelles. T. (02) 511 11 61. *072938*
Argile, 5a Rue de Neuchâtel, 1060 Bruxelles.
T. (02) 534 02 99. *072939*
Art Bizarre, 150 Rue Blaes, 1000 Bruxelles.
T. (02) 514 27 82. *072940*
Art Contact, 10 Pl. du Petit Sablon, 1000 Bruxelles.
T. (02) 514 08 82. - Paint / Sculp - *072941*
Artiges, C., & Fils, 10 Rue Gray, 1040 Bruxelles.
T. (02) 648 90 39. - Paint - *072942*
Artiscope, 35 Blvd. St.-Michel, 1040 Bruxelles.
T. (02) 735 52 12, Fax 735 95 15. - Paint / Graph /
Sculp / Draw - *072943*
Atelier 18, 18 Rue du Président, 1050 Bruxelles.
T. (02) 511 93 49. *072944*
Atelier 340, Drève de Rivieren 340, 1090 Bruxelles.
T. (02) 424 24 12. - Sculp - *072945*
Ateliers de Jolymont, 70 Rue Middelbourg, 1170 Bruxel-
les. T. (02) 673 94 90. - Paint - *072946*
Autre Musée, 4 Rue St. Michel, 1000 Bruxelles.
T. (02) 219 16 03. - Paint - *072947*
Autre Musée, L', 122 Rue du Viaduc, 1050 Bruxelles.
T. (02) 640 18 33. *072948*
Bailly, Le, 63 Rue du Bailli, 1050 Bruxelles.
T. (02) 538 70 58. *072949*
Bande des Six Nez, 179 Chaussée de Wavre, 1050 Bru-
xelles. T. (02) 513 72 58. - Paint - *072950*
Baronian, Albert, 8 Rue Villa-Hermosa, 1000 Bruxelles.
T. (02) 512 09 78. - Paint / Graph / Sculp / Mul /
Draw - *072951*
Bastien, J., 61 Rue de la Madeleine, 1000 Bruxelles.
T. (02) 513 25 63. *072952*
Berko, 36 Pl. du Grand Sablon, 1000 Bruxelles.
T. (02) 511 15 76. - Paint - *072953*
Berryer, S., 20-22 Av L Lepoutre, 1050 Bruxelles.
T. (02) 343 75 44. *072954*
Bilinelli, Lucien, 169 Chaussée de Charleroi, 1060 Bru-
xelles. T. (02) 538 16 41. *072955*
Brachot, Isy, 62a Av Louise, 1050 Bruxelles.
T. (02) 511 05 25. *072956*
Brussels Art Gallery, Pletinckxstr 14, 1000 Bruxelles.
T. (02) 502 18 30. *072957*
Carniere, de, 30 Av Jeanne, 1050 Bruxelles.
T. (02) 646 00 23. *072958*
Cheval de Verre, 12-14 Rue Ste.-Anne, 1000 Bruxelles.
T. (02) 513 97 14. - Paint / Graph / China / Sculp /
Glass - *072959*
Cloots, Christiane, 34 Rue Ravenstein, 1000 Bruxelles.
T. (02) 512 44 88. *072960*
Cloots, Christiane, 423 A Louise, 1050 Bruxelles.
T. (02) 648 60 55. *072961*
Colmant, Christine, 94 c Av Louise, 1050 Bruxelles.
T. (02) 511 17 27, Fax 511 88 51. *072962*
Contrast Gallery, 69 Av Louise, 1050 Bruxelles.
T. (02) 537 14 87. *072963*
Daniel, André, 15 Rue de l'Hôpital, 1000 Bruxelles.
T. (02) 512 36 72. *072964*
Debras-Bical, 36 Rue de la Victoire, 1060 Bruxelles.
T. (02) 538 54 66. *072965*
Derom, Patrick, 1 Rue aux Laines, 1000 Bruxelles.
T. (02) 5140882, Fax 5141158. - Paint - *072966*

Dieleman, 21 Pl. du Grand Sablon, 1000 Bruxelles.
T. (02) 512 31 20, 512 22 86, Fax 512 31 29.
- Sculp - *072967*

Dierickx, 161 Chaussée de Charleroi, 1060 Bruxelles.
T. (02) 5376984. - Paint / Sculp / Eth / Cur - *072968*
Disque Rouge, 15 Rue Piers, 1080 Bruxelles.
T. (02) 425 59 09. - Paint / Graph / Sculp /
Draw - *072969*
Echancrure, 563 Av Brugmann, 1180 Bruxelles.
T. (02) 346 35 19, Fax 344 31 08. *072970*
Ecuyer, 187-189 Av Louise, 1050 Bruxelles.
T. (02) 6473544. - Paint / Sculp - *072971*
Egmont, D', Petit Sablon 11, 1000 Bruxelles.
T. (02) 512 83 64. *072972*
Encadrement/Framing, 146 Rue Washington, 1050 Bru-
xelles. T. (02) 648 05 93. - Paint - *072973*
Epsilon, 178a Av. Blucher, 1180 Bruxelles.
T. (02) 374 64 58. - Paint - *072974*
Escalier, L', 41 Rue Duquesnoy, 1000 Bruxelles.
T. (02) 513 54 29. *072975*
Espace Libre, 348 Ch de Waterloo, 1060 Bruxelles.
T. (02) 538 98 30. *072976*
Esthète, 230 Ch de Charleroi, 1060 Bruxelles.
T. (02) 537 64 97. *072977*
Europa Gallery, 17 Sq Ambiorix, 1000 Bruxelles.
T. (02) 733 14 50. *072978*
Fefler & Coufo, 59 Rue de Stassart, 1050 Bruxelles.
T. (02) 512 11 21. *072979*
Fein Arts Gallery, 62 Rue Jeu de Balle, 1000 Bruxelles.
T. (02) 514 54 16. *072980*
Ficheroulle Art Gallery, 36 Rue Veydt, 1050 Bruxelles.
T. (02) 538 38 38. *072981*
Folio-The Graphic House, Woluwe Shopping Center,
1200 Bruxelles. T. (02) 772 15 14. - Graph - *072982*
Fondation Goyens de Heusch pour l'Art Belge Contem-
porain, 15 Pl du Grand Sablon, 1000 Bruxelles.
T. (02) 513 37 24. *072983*
Fondations Deglumes, 9 Rue Ablée Cuypers, 1040 Bru-
xelles. T. (02) 733 88 75. - Paint - *072984*
Forni, Ruben, 35 Rue St-Jean, 1000 Bruxelles.
T. (02) 513 16 08. *072985*
Franco, Filippo, 272 Av. Molière, 1180 Bruxelles.
T. (02) 347 34 11. - Paint - *072986*
Frenne, Michel, de, 7 Rue E. Allard, 1000 Bruxelles.
T. (02) 512 46 15. - Paint - *072987*
Fydjy's, 56 Av Louise, 1050 Bruxelles. T. (02) 513 87 17.
- Paint - *072988*
Galerie Albert Ier, 45 Rue de la Madeleine, 1000 Bruxel-
les. T. (02) 512 19 44. - Paint - *072989*
Galerie Alpha, 4 Rue de la Longue-Haie, 1050 Bruxelles.
T. (02) 511 00 93. *072990*
Galerie Art du XXème Siècle, 26 Pl de la Justice, 1000
Bruxelles. T. (02) 513 57 44. *072991*
Galerie Camomille, 30 Rue Vilain XIV, 1050 Bruxelles.
T. (02) 649 23 68, Fax 731 90 09. - Paint / Graph /
Draw - *072992*
Galerie Carrette, 257 Ch de Charleroi, 1060 Bruxelles.
T. (02) 534 03 25. *072993*
Galerie Château Malou, 45 Ch de Stockel, 1200 Bruxel-
les. T. (02) 762 27 67. *072994*
Galerie de Pret d'Oeuvres d'Art, 45 Chaussée de Stok-
kel, 1200 Bruxelles. T. (02) 762 21 05, 761 27 67.
- Paint - *072995*
Galerie des Beaux-Arts, 20-22 Rue Ravenstein, 1000
Bruxelles. T. (02) 513 67 77, Fax 513 67 76. *072996*
Galerie des Lyres, 64 Rue Defacqz, 1050 Bruxelles.
T. (02) 537 69 48. *072997*
Galerie du Vieux Marché, 174 Rue Blaes, 1000 Bruxel-
les. T. (02) 513 22 63. *072998*
Galerie KA, 133 Rue Keyenveld, 1050 Bruxelles.
T. (02) 511 25 73. *072999*
Galerie L'Oeil, 7 Rue Ravenstein, 1000 Bruxelles.
T. (02) 512 86 83. - Paint / Graph / Sculp - *073000*
Galerie Larousse, 4 Sq Larousse, 1190 Bruxelles.
T. (02) 347 47 48. *073001*
Galerie Max, 19 Rue de l'Hopital, 1000 Bruxelles.
T. (02) 511 24 70. *073002*
Galerie Montjoie, 21 Rue Ernest-Allard, 1000 Bruxelles.
T. (02) 512 98 59. - Paint - *073003*
Galerie Sephiha, 21 Rue Tasson Snel, 1060 Bruxelles.
T. (02) 537 61 94. - Pho - *073004*
Galerie X, 7 Rue des Champs Elysées, 1050 Bruxelles.
T. (02) 512 46 35. - Paint - *073005*
Gallery 45, 45 Rue V. Allard, 1180 Bruxelles.
T. (02) 376 11 68. - Paint - *073006*

Galuchat, 182 Av Louise, 1050 Bruxelles.
T. (02) 647 45 40. *073007*
Gavilan, 9 Pl Dumon, 1150 Bruxelles. T. (02) 731 70 59,
Fax 762 28 27. *073008*
Geerinckx, B., 33 Rue des Minimes, 1000 Bruxelles.
T. (02) 513 58 93. - Paint - *073009*
Gokelaere & Janssen, 35 Rue de Livourne, 1050 Bruxel-
les. T. (02) 538 56 60. *073010*
Group 2, 8 Rue Blanche, 1000 Bruxelles.
T. (02) 539 23 09. *073011*
Guimiot, Philippe, 138 Av. Louise, 1050 Bruxelles.
T. (02) 640 69 48. - Paint - *073012*
Hallet, Pierre, 33 Rue E Allard, 1000 Bruxelles.
T. (02) 512 25 23. *073013*
Haumont, Marie-Christine, 20-22 Av Brugmann, 1060
Bruxelles. T. (02) 345 16 02, Fax 345 24 06. *073014*
Hermes, 5 Petite Rue des Minimes, 1000 Bruxelles.
T. (02) 511 11 23. - Paint - *073015*
Het Steen, 32 Rue des Pierre, 1000 Bruxelles.
T. (02) 511 44 73. *073016*
Hoffsumer, M., 146 Av. G. Demey, 1160 Bruxelles.
T. (02) 660 64 11. - Paint - *073017*
Horizons Modern Art Gallery, 59 Rue de la Madeleine,
1000 Bruxelles. T. (02) 512 86 42. - Paint - *073018*
Hôtel de Ville de Saint-Gilles, 39 Pl van Meenen, 1060
Bruxelles. T. (02) 536 02 11, Fax 536 02 02. *073019*
Hufkens, Xavier, 8 Rue Saint-Georges, 1050 Bruxelles.
T. (02) 646 63 30, Fax 646 93 42. *073020*
Hutse, Louis, 21 Rue Uyttenhove, 1090 Bruxelles.
T. (02) 426 27 11. *073021*
Huysser, Willy d', 35 Pl du Grand Sablon, 1000 Bruxel-
les. T. (02) 511 37 04. *073022*
Hyperion Art, 19a, ave. Marnix, 1000 Bruxelles.
T. (02) 511 71 57. - Graph - *073023*
Ideos, 225 Deschanellaan, 1030 Bruxelles.
T. (02) 241 95 74. *073024*
International Center of Naïve Art, 27 Rue du Minimes,
Sablon, 10000 Bruxelles. T. (02) 513 17 70,
Fax 3210 867300. *073025*
Janssens Galerie, 4 Rue de la Longue Haie, 1050 Bru-
xelles. T. (02) 511 00 93. - Paint / Sculp - *073026*
Jonckheere, Georges de, 55 Blvd de Waterloo, 1000
Bruxelles. T. (02) 5129948, 5121554. - Paint - *073027*
Kaya, 53 Rue des Epéronnier, 1000 Bruxelles.
T. (02) 511 95 07. *073028*
Keitelman, M., 9 Rue de la Paille, 1000 Bruxelles.
T. (02) 511 35 80, Fax 512 96 40. - Paint - *073029*
Kunst in Huis Kunstuitleen, Gallaitstr 80, 1030 Bruxelles.
T. (02) 216 00 80, Fax 216 01 20. *073030*
L'Angle Aigu, 96, av Louise, 1050 Bruxelles.
T. (02) 5 12 84 80. *073031*
„L'Atelier" Galerie D'Exposition, 51, rue du Commerce,
1000 Bruxelles. T. (02) 11 20 65. *073032*
Laminne, de, 33 Rue de Rollebeek, 1000 Bruxelles.
T. (02) 511 72 83. - Paint / Paint - *073033*
Lancelle, E., Quai au Foin 33, 1000 Bruxelles.
T. (02) 219 96 912. - Paint / Furn - *073034*
Lannoy, Yonnal, Steenstr 32, 1000 Bruxelles.
T. (02) 511 44 73. *073035*
Lanzenberg, Fred, 9 Av des Klauwaerts, 1050 Bruxelles.
T. (02) 647 30 15. *073036*
Le Gatti, 3 Gal de Ruysbroeck, 1000 Bruxelles.
T. (02) 502 03 36. *073037*
Le Sacre du Printemps, 12 Rue de la Congue Haie, 1050
Bruxelles. T. (02) 511 70 31. *073038*
Ledune, Guy- Contemporary Art, 20 Rue E Picard, 1050
Bruxelles. T. (02) 346 11 14, Fax 343 88 80. *073039*
Liverpool Gallery, 26 Av de Stalingrad, 1000 Bruxelles.
T. (02) 502 13 02, Fax 502 13 17. *073040*
Lorelei, 21 Pl. du Grand-Sablon, 1000 Bruxelles.
T. (02) 513 52 19. - Paint - *073041*
Mahaux, P., 14 Rue Watteeu, 1000 Bruxelles.
T. (02) 512 24 06. - Paint - *073042*
Main, La, 215 Rue de la Victoire, 1060 Bruxelles.
T. (02) 538 54 66. *073043*
Majerus, Pierre, 64 Av. de la Chasse, 1040 Bruxelles.
T. (02) 733 87 33. - Glass - *073044*
Meert, Greta & André Rihoux, 55 Quai au foin, 1000 Bru-
xelles. T. (02) 22 19 14 22, Fax 91 21 85 17. *073045*
Mets, de, 86 Rue de Haerne, 1040 Bruxelles.
T. (02) 647 56 79. - Num - *073046*
Monochrome Gallery, 94C Av Louise, 1050 Bruxelles.
T. (02) 512 44 50. *073047*

Montjoie, 21 Rue E. Allard, 1000 Bruxelles.
T. (02) 512 98 59. - Paint - *073048*
Nouvel Art Galerie, 33 Rue F. Neuray, 1050 Bruxelles.
T. (02) 345 28 71. - Paint - *073049*
Nuances, 277 Chaussée de Charleroi, 1060 Bruxelles.
T. (02) 539 22 96. - Paint - *073050*
Occase, L', 188 Chaussée d'Ixelles, 1050 Bruxelles.
T. (02) 648 19 02. *073051*
Office Provincial des Artisanats et Industries d'Art du
Brabant, 61 Rue du Marché aux Herbes, 1000 Bruxel-
les. T. (02) 513 07 05, 512 96 80. *073052*
Passage 44, 44 Passage, 1000 Bruxelles.
T. (02) 214 41 11. *073053*
Peeters, E., Langedijk 1, 1190 Vorst.
T. (02) 66 35 25. *073053a*
Piontek, 150 Rue Blaes, 1000 Bruxelles.
T. (02) 514 27 82. - Graph - *073054*
Polar, Pascal, 185 Ch de Charleroi, 1060 Bruxelles.
T. (02) 537 81 36. *073055*
Présences, 132a Av Louise, 1050 Bruxelles.
T. (02) 648 82 75. *073056*
Présences, 423 Av. Louise, 1050 Bruxelles.
T. (02) 648 60 55. - Paint - *073057*
Presences, 34 Rue Ravenstein, 1000 Bruxelles.
T. (02) 512 44 88. - Paint - *073058*
Quadro, 177 Rue Vanderkindere, 1180 Bruxelles.
T. (02) 344 96 15. *073059*
Racines, 5 Rue Ravenstein, 1000 Bruxelles.
T. (02) 511 10 49. - Paint / Graph / Sculp - *073060*
Regent Galerie, 8 Rue Pletinckx, 1000 Bruxelles.
T. (02) 511 79 58. *073061*
Rona, A.M., 23 Rue des Champs Elysées, 1050 Bruxel-
les. T. (02) 640 57 05. *073062*
Run Art Gallery, 26 Rue des Renaids, 1000 Bruxelles.
T. (02) 513 53 74. *073063*
Salon d'Art, Le, 81 Rue Hôtel-des-Monnaies, 1060 Bru-
xelles. T. (02) 537 65 40. - Paint / Graph / Pho /
Draw - *073064*
Scholz, C. von, 30 Rue Vilain XIV, 1050 Bruxelles.
T. (02) 649 23 68. *073065*
Simonson, 38-40 Rue de l'Aqueduc, 1060 Bruxelles.
T. (02) 538 31 58. - Paint - *073066*
Sisley, 27-29 Rue St.-Jean, 1000 Bruxelles.
T. (02) 511 40 36, 511 46 69. - Paint - *073067*
Tempera, 40 Av Brugman, 1180 Bruxelles.
T. (02) 343 41 41. *073068*
Temps d'Un Regard, 3 Rue Thérésienne, 1000 Bruxelles.
T. (02) 514 00 43. - Paint - *073069*
Thomas, Philippe, 64 Rue de Neufchâtel, 1060 Bruxel-
les. T. (02) 537 97 80. - Paint - *073070*
Timpermann, 18 Pl Stéphanie, 1050 Bruxelles.
T. (02) 511 28 55. *073071*
Toio Art Gallery, 200 Chaussée de Charleroi, 1060 Bru-
xelles. T. (02) 537 69 51. - Paint - *073072*
Triangl, 21 Rue Hôtel des Monnaies, 1060 Bruxelles.
T. (02) 537 83 93. - Paint - *073073*
Tzwern-Aisinber, 36 Rue aux Laines, 1000 Bruxelles.
T. (02) 511 84 49, Fax 511 98 10. *073074*
Van Laethem, Jef, 53 Rue de la Grande Haie, 1040 Bru-
xelles. T. (02) 735 88 83. *073075*
Vieille Galerie d'Art, La, 12 Rue des Six Jeunes Hom-
mes, 1000 Bruxelles. T. (02) - Paint - *073076*
Wachters, Sabine, 36 Rue Bosquet, 1060 Bruxelles.
T. (02) 534 14 41, Fax 534 13 04. *073077*
X + Plus Gallery, 7 Rue des Champs Elysées, 1050 Bru-
xelles. T. (02) 512 46 35. *073078*
Yannick, David, 26 Blvd. de Waterloo, 1000 Bruxelles.
T. (02) 513 16 10. - Paint - *073079*
Yu-I Institut, 386 Av. Henri, 1200 Bruxelles.
T. (02) 734 65 32. - Paint - *073080*
Zen Gallery, Rue E. Allard, 23, 1000 Bruxelles.
T. 02 5119510, Fax 052 373950. - Furn / Orient /
China - *073081*
Zinzen, 20 Pl. J. van der Elst, 1180 Bruxelles.
T. (02) 376 15 15, 345 83 84. - Paint - *073082*

Charleroi (Hainaut)
Galerie Monte Carlo, 66 Av de l'Europe, 6000 Charleroi.
T. (071) 31 86 44. *073083*
Lisart, Elian, 21 Rue de Dampremy, 6000 Charleroi.
T. (071) 32 80 18. - Paint / Paint / Fra - *073084*
XXe Siècle, Galerie du, av. de l'Europe 48, 6000 Charle-
roi. - Paint - *073085*

Damme (West-Vlaanderen)
Indigo, Kerkstr 15, 8340 Damme.
T. (050) 37 03 31. *073086*

Deerlijk (West-Vlaanderen)
Galerij ter Ponte, Pontstraat, 202-204, 8540 Deerlijk.
T. (056) 77 83 83. - Paint - *073087*
Henri, 55 Pontstr, 8540 Deerlijk.
T. (056) 71 10 14. *073088*

Deinze (Oost-Vlaanderen)
Galerij M.A.S., E. Clauslaan 65, 9800 Deinze.
T. (091) 76 11 71. - Paint - *073089*

Denderleeuw (Oost-Vlaanderen)
Bani, F., Kasteelstr 24, 9470 Denderleeuw.
T. (053) 666585. *073090*

Dendermonde (Oost-Vlaanderen)
Buck, J. de, Kasteelstr 8, 9200 Dendermonde.
T. (052) 22 22 92. *073091*
Palet Kunstgalerij, Franz Courtensstr. 4, 9200 Dender-
monde. T. (052) 21 46 10. - Paint - *073092*
Pand, Het, Oude Vest 16-24, 9200 Dendermonde.
T. (052) 21 00 23. *073093*
Strooper, J. de, Dijkstr 8, 9200 Dendermonde.
T. (052) 22 35 71. *073094*

Dessel (Antwerpen)
Minnen, H., Broekstr 125, 2480 Dessel.
T. (014) 37 81 98. *073095*

Deurle (Oost-Vlaanderen)
Bosgalm, Dorpsstr 31, 9831 Deurle.
T. (091) 825104. *073096*
Pieters, Guy, Rode Beukendreef 29, 9831 Deurle.
T. (091) 828284. - Paint - *073097*
Wachters, Sabine, Pontstr 41, 9831 Deurle.
T. (091) 829357. *073098*

Deurne (Antwerpen)
Beernaert, Grapheusstr 39, 2100 Deurne.
T. (03) 324 23 14. *073099*
D.M. Kunstgalerij, F Craeybeckxln 7-9, 2100 Deurne.
T. (03) 325 73 42. *073100*
Kunstkamer Manebrugge, Manebruggestr. 247, 2100
Deurne. T. (03) 321 09 81. - Paint / Graph / Orient /
Sculp / Arch / Eth / Mod / Ico - *073101*
Ponsaerts, F., Eyendijkstr 28, 2100 Deurne.
T. (03) 324 76 54. *073102*
Pro-Sales, Kerkelveldln 41, 2100 Deurne.
T. (03) 325 62 01. *073103*
Rivierenhof, Turnhoutsebn 242, 2100 Deurne.
T. (03) 325 55 55. *073104*
Vanderboom, Boekenberglei 268, 2100 Deurne.
T. (03) 21 42 22. - Paint - *073105*
Vermin, W., F Versmissenln 6, 2100 Deurne.
T. (03) 325 34 51. *073106*

Diest (Vlaams Brabant)
Esschius, Begijnhofpt 1, 3290 Diest. T. (013) 311529.
- Paint - *073107*
Koninckx, S., F Moonsstr 18, 3290 Diest.
T. (013) 335965. *073108*
Uten Galerij, Ketelstr 15, 3290 Diest.
T. (013) 310174. *073109*

Dilbeek (Vlaams Brabant)
Kunst in Huis, Kamerijklaan z/N, 1700 Dilbeek.
T. (02) 4656015. *073110*
Westrand, Kamerijklaan, 1700 Dilbeek.
T. (02) 4656015. *073111*

Drongen (Oost-Vlaanderen)
Dronghene, Kunstschip, Solvijnsdreef 24, 9031 Drongen.
T. (091) 82 58 92. - Paint - *073112*

Duffel (Antwerpen)
Domein de Locht, 2570 Duffel. - Paint - *073113*

Durbuy (Luxembourg)
Hanotiau, Roger, 111 Rue Cromte d'Ursel, 6940 Durbuy.
T. (086) 21 21 77. *073114*

Eeklo (Oost-Vlaanderen)
Steur, de, Molenstr 16, 9900 Eeklo.
T. (091) 77 38 26.   073115

Ekeren (Antwerpen)
Elst, W., Oorderseweg 7, 2180 Ekeren.
T. (031) 541 66 89.   073116
Hof de Bist, Veltwijcklaan 252, 2180 Ekeren.
T. (031) 236 78 95. - Paint -   073117
De Leeuw, Jan, De Beukelaerln 12, 2180 Ekeren.
T. (031) 5410459.   073118

Erps-Kwerps (Vlaams Brabant)
Van der Ven, K., Keizerdelle 17, 3071 Erps-Kwerps.
T. (02) 759 42 14.   073119

Essen (Antwerpen)
Oude Pastorij, Essendonk 3, 2910 Essen.
T. (03) 667 29 88.   073120

Etikhove (Oost-Vlaanderen)
Ladeuze, Ladeuze 3, 9680 Etikhove.
T. (055) 31 10 93.   073121

Geel (Antwerpen)
Bal, A. de, & Zn., Rijn 72, 2440 Geel.
T. (014) 58 85 44.   073122

Genk (Limburg)
El Greco, Hasseltweg 392, 3600 Genk.
T. (011) 22 35 87.   073123
Galerij De White Room, Eikenlaan 53, 3600
Genk.   073124
Maten, de, Shopping Center 1, 3600 Genk.
T. (011) 35 57 16. - Paint / Repr -   073125

Gent (Oost-Vlaanderen)
Art Center, Geldmunt 18, 9000 Gent.
T. (09) 2232663.   073126
Art Work, Grauwpoort 10, 9000 Gent. T. (09) 2240277,
2219202.   073127
Beckers, J., J Breydelstr 24, 9000 Gent.
T. (09) 2238918.   073128
Beckers, J. & K., A Baeyensstr 122, 9000 Gent.
T. (09) 2281009.   073129
Bekaert, P., Visserij, 9000 Gent.
T. (09) 2235365.   073130
Bouckaert, Katherina, Korte Dalsteel 18, 9000 Gent.
T. (09) 2236193. - Paint / Graph -   073131
Buck, S. & H. de, Zuid-Stationsstr. 25-27, 9000 Gent.
T. (09) 2251081. - Paint / Jew -   073132
Buylo, M., Bagattenstraat 154, 9000 Gent.
T. (09) 2231235. - Paint -   073133
Cooremeter, Galerij, Graslei 12, 9000 Gent.
T. (09) 2250965. - Paint -   073134
Count, S., Rekelingstraat 1, 9000 Gent. T. (09) 2253127.
- Paint -   073135
Declerq, Joost, Geward 23, 9000 Gent.
T. (09) 2255616.   073136
Derave, Onderstr 65, 9000 Gent.
T. (09) 2230406.   073137
Eyck, Jan van, Kalandeberg 6, 9000 Gent.
T. (09) 2236021. - Paint / Graph / Sculp -   073138
Fas, Onderstr 21, 9000 Gent. T. (09) 2242712.   073139
Foncke, Richard, St Jansvest 18, 9000 Gent.
T. (09) 2238128.   073140
Foncke, Richard, St. Jansvest 18, 9000 Gent.
T. (09) 2238128. - Paint / Graph / Sculp / Draw -   073141
Fortlaan 17, Fortln 17, 9000 Gent. T. (09) 2220033,
Fax 21 63 27.   073142
Galerie Mathieu, Serpentstr 22-24, 9000 Gent.
T. (09) 2307700.   073143
Galerie Napoleon, Kouterdreef 1, 9000 Gent.
T. (09) 2255869.   073144
Gele Zaal, Nonnemeerstr. 26, 9000 Gent.
T. (09) 2353700. - Mod -   073145
Gouden Pluim, De, Vrijdagmarkt 12, 9000 Gent.
T. (09) 2256905.   073146
Gravensteen, Ter, Burgstr. 6, 9000 Gent.
T. (09) 2243584. - Paint / Graph / Furn -   073147
Houwen, Joris, Bij St-Jacobs 17, 9000 Gent.
T. (09) 2237696. - Paint -   073148
Kaleidoskoop, Nederkouter 45, 9000 Gent.
T. (09) 2255130. - Jew -   073149

Lignea, J Breydelstr 32, 9000 Gent.
T. (09) 2334252.   073150
Mahieu, Serpentstr 22-24, 9000 Gent. T. (09) 2307700,
2250122.   073151
P-Art, Woordstr 20, 9000 Gent. T. (09) 2333661.   073152
Promart Heuvelpoort, Hofbouwln 8, 9000 Gent.
T. (09) 2225516.   073153
Resonans, Zuidstationstr 20, 9000 Gent.
T. (09) 2252381.   073154
Ric Urmel Gallery, Visserij 41, 9000 Gent.
T. (09) 2254818.   073155
Roos, Rosa, Kraanlei 13, 9000 Gent.
T. (09) 2256854.   073156
Sennesael/De Wulf, Predikherenlei 13, 9000 Gent.
T. (09) 2258032.   073157
Stenbock-Fermor, St-Pieterspln 21, 9000 Gent.
T. (09) 2200118.   073158
Van Denmeersschaut, D., Ottogracht 5, 9000 Gent.
T. (09) 2334545.   073159
Van Langenhove, St-Jorriskaai 6a, 9000 Gent.
T. (09) 2236534.   073160
Walry's Art Gallery, Burgstr 14, 9000 Gent.
T. (09) 2258469.   073161
Wolfaert-Masson, Baudelostr 71, 9000 Gent.
T. (09) 2333638.   073162
XXIst Century, Recollettenlei 17, 9000 Gent.
T. (09) 2235447.   073163
XYZ Fotogalerie, Brabantdam 110, 9000 Gent.
T. (09) 2240776.   073164

Gentbrugge (Oost-Vlaanderen)
Dizein, Galerij, Jef van der Meulenstraat 13, 9050 Gentbrugge. - Paint -   073165

Gosselies (Hainaut)
Vivart, 32, rue de la Ferté, 6041 Gosselies.
T. (071) 35 72 18. - Paint -   073166

's Gravenwezel (Antwerpen)
Atelier 22, De Dreef van Hertebos, 2970 's Gravenwezel.
T. (031) 658 87 26.   073167

Grobbendonk (Antwerpen)
Het Karmijn, Kroonspaadje 25, 2280 Grobbendonk.
T. (014) 50 06 80.   073168

Haasdonk (Oost-Vlaanderen)
Poortje, 'T, Zandstr 74, 9120 Haasdonk.
T. (031) 775 66 51.   073169
Van Meirvenne, A., Perstr 40b, 9120 Haasdonk.
T. (031) 775 87 67.   073170

Hallaar (Antwerpen)
Galerij Kerkstoel, Leopoldlei 41, 2220 Hallaar.
- Paint -   073171

Hamme (Oost-Vlaanderen)
Kinders-Salembier, de, Zouavenstr. 2a, 9220 Hamme.
T. (052) 47 73 68. - Paint / Repr -   073172
Oude Galerij, D', Dendermondsestw 17, 9220 Hamme.
T. (052) 47 04 45.   073173

Hamont-Achel (Limburg)
Wouters, Bosstr 136, 3930 Hamont-Achel.
T. (011) 44 52 34.   073174

Hasselt (Limburg)
A & A, Luc Theuwis, Thonissenln 42, 3500 Hasselt.
T. (011) 24 14 23.   073175
Bartok Studio, Vismarkt 1-3, 3500 Hasselt.
T. (011) 22 94 73. - Paint -   073176
Dessers, Janine, Ridderstr 4, 3500 Hasselt.
T. (011) 22 60 10.   073177
Hasselt Art Gallery, Maastrichterstw 277, 3500 Hasselt.
T. (011) 22 47 52.   073178
Hermans, E., Guffensln 50, 3500 Hasselt.
T. (011) 22 74 45.   073179
Il Ventuno, Kuringerstw 190, 3500 Hasselt.
T. (011) 25 22 27.   073180
I.M.D., Galerij, Havermarkt 32, 3500 Hasselt.
T. (011) 22 54 01. - Paint -   073181
Kunst in Huis, Kunstlaan 5, 3500 Hasselt.
T. (011) 22 99 31.   073182
Kunstgang Art Gallery, Zuivelmarkt 50, 3500 Hasselt.
T. (011) 24 13 91.   073183

't Pandje, 3, Paardsdemerstraat, 3500 Hasselt.
T. (011) 22 38 37. - Paint -   073184

Heist-Op-Den-Berg (Antwerpen)
Galerij Mylene, Aarschotsesteenweg 44, 2220 Heist-Op-
Den-Berg. T. (015) 24 47 80. - Paint -   073185
Pact Art Gallery, Westerlosteenweg 32, 2220 Heist-Op-
Den-Berg. T. (015) 24 67 97. - Paint / Sculp -   073186

Hekelgem (Vlaams Brabant)
Kultureelcentrum „Affligem", 1790 Hekelgem.
- Paint -   073187

Herentals (Antwerpen)
Kriek, Lierseweg 64, 2200 Herentals.
T. (014) 21 89 24.   073188
Kunstkamer, Molenvest 28, 2200 Herentals.
T. (014) 21 72 05, 21 31 50.   073189

Heusden (Limburg)
Quidrousse, H., Graaf de Theuxln. 5, 3550 Heusden.
T. (011) 42 92 74. - Paint -   073190

Hingene (Antwerpen)
Zoutkeet, De, Klein Mechelen 73, 2880 Hingene.
T. (031) 89 11 28.   073191

Hoboken (Antwerpen)
Galerij Hobo, Krügerstr 75, 2660 Hoboken.
T. (031) 827 35 29.   073192

Hoegaarden (Vlaams Brabant)
Bullecom, Klein Overlaar 77, 3320 Hoegaarden.
T. (016) 766481.   073193

Jambes (Namur)
Detour, 162 Av. Bourg. Jean-Materne, 5100 Jambes.
T. (081) 24 64 42. - Paint -   073194

Kalmthout (Antwerpen)
IBC, Missiehuislaan 8, 2920 Kalmthout.
T. (031) 66 66 18.   073195

Kapellen (Antwerpen)
Baele, S., Klinkaardstr 149, 2950 Kapellen.
T. (03) 664 63 32.   073196
Veldeman-Snoekx, Lindendr 32, 2950 Kapellen.
T. (03) 664 96 87.   073197
Vos, Alda, Hoogboomstw 113, 2950 Kapellen.
T. (03) 664 40 30.   073198

Kluisbergen (Oost-Vlaanderen)
Art-Center Beukenhof, Van Vlaanderenstr 9, 9690 Kluis-
bergen. T. (055) 388387.   073199
Kultuur 69, 9690 Kluisbergen. Paint -   073200
Malpertuis, Ommegangstr 18, 9690 Kluisbergen.
T. (055) 388866.   073201

Knesselare (Oost-Vlaanderen)
Galerie Claire, Urselweg 51, 9910 Knesselare.
T. (091) 740608.   073202

Knokke (West-Vlaanderen)
Abado, Sparrendr 85a, 8300 Knokke.
T. (050) 61 18 71.   073203
Berko, Kustlaan 163, 8300 Knokke. T. (050) 60 57 90,
Fax 61 53 81. - Paint -   073204
Booser, Luc de, Golvenstr. 7, 8300 Knokke.
T. (050) 61 56 34. - Paint / Sculp / Draw -   073205
Dajak, Zeedijk 518, 8300 Knokke.
T. (050) 61 34 41.   073206
Erasmus, Kustlaan 1, 8300 Knokke. T. (050) 61 06 66.
- Paint / Graph -   073207
Fayt, Christian, Kustlaan 94, 8300 Knokke.
T. (050) 60 25 09.   073208
Frame's Gallery, Lippenslaan 188, 8300 Knokke.
T. (050) 62 10 68, Fax 62 10 68.   073209
Franck, Elisabeth, Kustlaan 124, 8300 Knokke.
T. (050) 60 68 81.   073210
Gaeli, Taborastr 10, 8300 Knokke.
T. (050) 60 83 09.   073211
Galerie des Artistes, Zeedijk 616, 8300 Knokke.
T. (050) 60 94 46. - Paint -   073212
Galerie Pantheon, Kustlaan 335, 8300 Knokke.
T. (050) 61 40 68. - Paint / Jew -   073213

Galerie Presences, Elisabethlaan 1, 8300 Knokke.
T. (050) 60 74 48. *073214*
Galerij Hedendaags, Kerkstraat 37-39, 8300 Knokke.
T. (050) 51 32 22. - Paint - *073215*
Galerij Horizon, Zeedijk 726-731, 8300 Knokke.
T. (050) 60 41 74. *073216*
Golds International, Elisabethln 21, 8300 Knokke.
T. (050) 61 59 16. *073217*
Huysser, D', Kustlaan 146b, 8300 Knokke.
T. (050) 62 00 71. *073218*
Jamar, J., Phillippartpad 1, 8300 Knokke.
T. (050) 51 56 63. *073219*
Jipian, Kustlaan 128, 8300 Knokke.
T. (050) 61 14 12. *073220*
Kunst in Huis, Meerlaan 30, 8300 Knokke.
T. (050) 60 03 93. *073221*
Pieters, Guy, Zeedijk 742, 8300 Knokke.
T. (050) 61 28 00, Fax 61 56 07. - Paint - *073222*
Simoens, André, Kustlaan 130, 8300 Knokke.
T. (050) 61 00 87. - Paint / Sculp - *073223*
Van Lear, Vera, Elisabethlaan 160, 8300 Knokke.
T. (050) 61 56 46, Fax 60 37 06. *073224*
Wachters, Sabine, Golvenstr 11, 8300 Knokke.
T. (050) 61 58 35, Fax 62 03 30. *073225*
Weckx, Sparredr 76, 8300 Knokke.
T. (050) 60 47 98. *073226*
Zwarte Maan, Breartstr 13-15a, 8300 Knokke.
T. (050) 41 78 10. *073227*

Kontich (Antwerpen)
Walter, Sijs, Broekbosstr 8, 2550 Kontich.
T. (031) 457 76 96. *073228*

Kortrijk (West-Vlaanderen)
An – Hyp, Grote Markt 42, 8500 Kortrijk.
T. (066) 21 55 94. - Paint - *073229*
Couttenier, V., Voorstr 22a, 8500 Kortrijk.
T. (056) 20 23 89. *073230*
Epoque, Gentsesteenweg 24-26, 8500 Kortrijk.
T. (056) 21 01 02. - Paint / Furn / Sculp / Tex /
Jew – *073231*
Kanaal, Art Foundation, Groeningstr 37, 8500 Kortrijk.
T. (056) 20 38 44, Fax 21 60 77. *073232*
Standaard Galerij, Leiestraat 12, 8500 Kortrijk.
T. (056) 22 10 89. - Paint - *073233*

Kruishoutem (Oost-Vlaanderen)
Veranneman, Vandevoordeweg 2, 9770 Kruishoutem.
T. (091) 835287. *073234*

Kuurne (West-Vlaanderen)
Depypere, Michel, Kerkstr. 59, 8520 Kuurne.
T. (056) 71 13 40. - Paint - *073235*
Marckok, Brugsestw 64, 8520 Kuurne.
T. (056) 35 63 43. *073236*

La Louvière (Hainaut)
Tendances Contemporaines, 64 Rue du Moulin, 7100 La
Louvière. T. (064) 22 32 65. - Paint - *073237*

Lasne-Chapelle-St. Lambert (Brabant Wallon)
Beaumont, 18 Rue Haute, 1380 Lasne-Chapelle-St.
Lambert. T. (02) 6333840. - Paint / Graph - *073238*
International Art Gallery, 16 Rue Bois Lionnet, 1380
Lasne-Chapelle-St. Lambert. T. (02) 6331806. *073239*
Naif, 140 Rue Lasne, 1380 Lasne-Chapelle-St. Lambert.
T. (02) 6541933. *073240*

Lebbeke (Oost-Vlaanderen)
Elias, Hendrik, Rooienstraat 78, 9280 Lebbeke.
T. (053) 21 44 35. - Ant / Paint / Graph / China / Sculp /
Eth / Glass / Cur - *073241*

Leopoldsburg (Limburg)
Maesen-Douven, Hospitalstr. 10, 3970 Leopoldsburg.
T. (011) 34 13 44. - Paint - *073242*
Naegels, M., Antwerpsestw. 16, 3970 Leopoldsburg.
T. (011) 34 14 47. - Paint / Repr - *073243*

Leuven (Vlaams Brabant)
Belarte, Kortestr 3, 3000 Leuven.
T. (016) 222622. *073244*
Galerie Embryo, Naamsestraat 49, 3000 Leuven.
T. (016) 235640. - Paint - *073245*

Galerie Transit, Tiensevest 39, 3000 Leuven.
T. (16) 226244. *073246*
Gamma Galerij, Naamsestr 7, 3000 Leuven.
T. (016) 205445. *073247*
Perspektief, Naamsestr 17, 3000 Leuven.
T. (016) 227914. *073248*

Lichtaart (Antwerpen)
Artepik Lichtaart, Provincie Antwerpen, 2460 Lichtaart.
T. (014) 56 428. - Sculp - *073249*

Liège
Bellartes, 45 Rue de l'Université, 4000 Liège.
T. (04) 2232741. *073250*
Cercle Royal des Beaux-Arts, 1a Rue Soeurs de Hasque,
4000 Liège. T. (04) 2234391. - Paint - *073251*
Crals, Jean, Passage Cathédrale 30, 4000 Liège.
- Paint - *073252*
Ecritures 82, bd 'Avroy 82, 4000 Liège. - Paint - *073253*
Galerie Art Actuel, 5 Rue sur les Foulons, 4000 Liège.
T. (04) 2224265, Fax 2231950. - Paint - *073254*
Galerie Cyan, 48-50 Rue Cathédrale, 4000 Liège.
T. (04) 2223227. *073255*
Galerie d'Art Moderne et Contemporain, 48-50 Rue Ca-
thédrale, 4000 Liège. T. (04) 2223222,
2224652. *073256*
Galerie Evasion, 10f Cour Saint-Rémy, 4000 Liège.
T. (04) 2235573. - Paint - *073257*
Galerie Le Prado, 15 Rue du Mouton Blanc, 4000 Liège.
T. (04) 2225331. *073258*
Gustin, Valère, 7 Rue Bonne Fortune, 4000 Liège.
T. (04) 2236491. - Paint - *073259*
La Galerie, 4 Rue Chapelle des Clercs, 4000 Liège.
T. (04) 2231808. *073260*
Liehrmann, 4 Blvd Piercot, 4000 Liège.
T. (04) 2235893. *073261*
Sacré, 6 Rue Hongrée, 4000 Liège.
T. (04) 2236274. *073262*

Lier (Antwerpen)
Konvent, Galerij, Vredebergstraat 22, 2500 Lier.
- Paint - *073263*
Lierse Kunstgalerij, Fl Van Cauwenberghstraat 15, 2500
Lier. T. (03) 480 2840. *073264*
Publi Ropart, H Geeststr 4, 2500 Lier.
T. (03) 480 52 79. *073265*
Schaeckbert, Zimmerplein 12, 2500 Lier.
T. (03) 80 66 40. *073266*

Linkebeek (Vlaams Brabant)
Menuiserie, La, 6 Pl Communale, 1630 Linkebeek.
T. (02) 3749506. *073267*

Lokeren (Oost-Vlaanderen)
Di Art, Vrijheidspln 1, 9160 Lokeren.
T. (091) 48 06 42. *073268*
Rembrandt, Markt 54, 9160 Lokeren.
T. (091) 48 15 55. *073269*
Vuyst, de, Markstr. 22-54, 9160 Lokeren.
T. (09) 3485440, Fax 09 3489218. - Paint / Graph /
Sculp / Mod / Ico / Mul / Draw - *073270*

Maarke-Kerkem (Oost-Vlaanderen)
Houdenmuyse, Bossenaer 2, 9680 Maarke-Kerkem.
T. (055) 31 60 74. *073271*

Maaseik (Limburg)
Den Peroun, Boomgaardstr 2, 3680 Maaseik.
T. (011) 56 75 26. *073272*

Maldegem (Oost-Vlaanderen)
Forma International, Kon Albertln 46c, 9990 Maldegem.
T. (050) 71 77 29. *073273*

Malmédy (Liège)
Galerie Ponsart, 1 Rue de Commerce, 4960 Malmédy.
T. (080) 33 05 27. - Paint / Repr / Sculp / Fra - *073274*

Mechelen (Antwerpen)
Alkader, Steenweg 34, 2800 Mechelen.
T. (015) 20 03 22. *073275*
Belcieurop, Battelsestw 340, 2800 Mechelen.
T. (015) 29 07 12, Fax 21 98 15. *073276*
Galerie 28, Guldenstr 9, 2800 Mechelen. *073277*

Galerij Louiza, Louizastr 29, 2800 Mechelen.
T. (015) 41 74 16. *073278*
Klimroos, de, Hanswijkstr 11, 2800 Mechelen.
T. (015) 41 30 06. *073279*
Op de Beeck, J., Sint-Kaelijnestr 22, 2800 Mechelen.
T. (015) 290155, 246297. *073280*
Vier Winden, Frederick de Merodestraat 51, 2800 Me-
chelen. - Paint - *073281*

Mechelen-aan-de-Maas (Limburg)
Makc, Rijksweg 254, 3630 Mechelen-aan-de-Maas.
T. (011) 76 59 86. *073282*

Meerhout (Antwerpen)
Lucas, Molsebaan 33-37, 2450 Meerhout.
T. (014) 30 04 75. - Paint / Furn / Jew - *073283*

Meerle (Antwerpen)
Van den Heuvel, C., Hazenweg 9, 2328 Meerle.
T. (03) 315 77 04. *073284*

Melle (Oost-Vlaanderen)
Distel, Kalverhagestr 26, 9090 Melle.
T. (091) 52 14 07. *073285*

Melsele (Oost-Vlaanderen)
Svara, Heirbn 132, 9120 Melsele.
T. (03) 775 27 48. *073286*

Menen (West-Vlaanderen)
Athena, Hogeweg 326, 8930 Menen. T. (056) 51 26 01.
- Paint / Graph / Sculp / Draw - *073287*

Merchtem (Vlaams Brabant)
Uyl, Den, Holbeek 52, 1785 Merchtem.
T. (052) 359435. *073288*

Merksem (Antwerpen)
Akkermans, Bredabaan 960, 2170 Merksem.
- Paint - *073289*
Alkader, Bredabn 334, 2170 Merksem.
T. (031) 6459245. *073290*
Gorsen, R., Moeshofstr 91, 2170 Merksem.
T. (031) 6458240. *073291*

Middelkerke (West-Vlaanderen)
Rubens, Zeedijk 110, 8430 Middelkerke.
T. (059) 30 51 99. *073292*

Mol (Antwerpen)
Oude Post, Galerij, Markt, 2400 Mol. - Paint - *073293*
Vreven, René, Groot Kapellen 28, 2400 Mol.
T. (014) 31 74 36. *073294*

Mons (Hainaut)
Galerie 7, 7 Rue du 11 Novembre, 7000 Mons.
T. (065) 33 50 98. - Paint - *073295*

Montigny-le-Tilleul (Hainaut)
Ephemere, 33 Pl. du Try, 6110 Montigny-le-Tilleul.
T. 51 00 60. - Paint - *073296*

Moortsele (Oost-Vlaanderen)
Galerij 't Muziekpalet, Moortselestr 70, 9860 Moortsele.
T. (091) 62 55 13. *073297*

Mortsel (Antwerpen)
Bosmans, L., Boechoutselei 97, 2640 Mortsel.
T. (031) 455 21 40. *073298*
„La Mano", Studio, Pieter Reypenslei 56, 2640 Mortsel.
- Paint - *073299*

Muizen (Antwerpen)
Buelens, Tr., Trianonln 4, 2812 Muizen.
T. (015) 513155. *073300*

Namur (Namur)
Art de Namur, 21 Blvd. Ad' Aquam, 5000 Namur.
T. (081) 22 73 66. - Ant / Paint / Furn / Orient / China /
Ico - *073301*
Centre Fel. Rops, 18, rue des Brasseurs, 5000 Namur.
T. (081) 71 35 89. - Paint - *073302*
La Ruche, Galerie, rue du Collège 9, 5000 Namur.
T. (081) 51 19 69. - Paint - *073303*
Rops' Center, 18 Rue des Brasseurs, 5000 Namur.
T. (081) 22 09 44. - Paint - *073304*

Nederzwalm-Hermelgem (Oost-Vlaanderen)
Hof Ten Doeyer, Beekmeersstr., 9636 Nederzwalm-Hermelgem. T. (055) 49 79 89. - Graph -   *073305*

Nieuwkerken-Waas (Oost-Vlaanderen)
Maris, D., Ster 64, 2770 Nieuwkerken-Waas.
T. 776 87 35.   *073306*

Nijlen (Antwerpen)
Peuter, P. de, Bergsgoorstr 7, 2560 Nijlen.
T. (03) 481 80 83.   *073307*

Ninove (Oost-Vlaanderen)
Geniep, 't, Geraardbergsestr 60, 9400 Ninove.
T. (054) 33 38 02.   *073308*
Penseeltje, Preulegem 8, 9400 Ninove.
T. (054) 33 92 44.   *073309*

Oelegem (Antwerpen)
Fyens, Kantonbn 15, 2520 Oelegem.
T. (031) 383 21 85.   *073310*

Oostduinkerke (West-Vlaanderen)
Korre, de, Dorpstr. 36, 8670 Oostduinkerke.
- Paint -   *073311*

Oosteeklo (Oost-Vlaanderen)
Wauter, William, Antwerpse Heirweg 5, 9968 Oosteeklo.
T. (091) 73 70 06.   *073312*

Oostende (West-Vlaanderen)
Dialoog '92, Zwaluwenstr 131, 8400 Oostende.
T. (059) 701419.   *073313*
Kunsthuis Loosvelt, Romestr 41, 8400 Oostende.
T. (059) 705273.   *073314*
Magnus Fine Arts, Romestr 20, 8400 Oostende.
T. (059) 809214, Fax (059) 2829836.   *073315*
Van Middelem, Luc, Romestr 6, 8400 Oostende.
T. (059) 510239.   *073316*
De Peperbusse, Prins Boudewijnst 7, 8400 Oostende.
T. (059) 702880.   *073317*
Piretti, Monacoplein, 8400 Oostende.
T. (059) 512183.   *073318*
Robert & Partners, Prinsenlaan 27, 8400 Oostende.
T. (059) 515076.   *073319*

Oostende (West-Vlaanderen)
Fine Arts, Vlaanderenstr 68, 8400 Oostende.
T. (059) 70 67 36.   *073320*

Oostrozebeke (West-Vlaanderen)
Visschere, De, Stationstraat 18-26, 8780 Oostrozebeke.
- Paint -   *073321*

Otegem (West-Vlaanderen)
Deweer Art Gallery, Tiegemstr. 6 a, 8553 Otegem.
T. (056) 64 48 93, Fax 64 76 85. - Paint -   *073322*

Oud-Turnhout (Antwerpen)
Waterschoot, A., Stw op Turnhout 6, 2360 Oud-Turnhout.
T. (014) 41 20 23.   *073323*

Oudenaarde (Oost-Vlaanderen)
Galerij Tivoli, Tivolistraat 171, 9700 Oudenaarde.
T. (055) 31 50 47. - Paint -   *073324*
Gallery Kerkgate, Kerkgate 35, 9700 Oudenaarde.
T. (055) 45 64 83.   *073325*
Herreman, Marcel, Aalststr 17, 9700 Oudenaarde.
T. (055) 31 30 79.   *073326*
Liberte, Markt 25-26, 9700 Oudenaarde.
T. (055) 31 10 36.   *073327*
Van Parma, Margaretha, Kasteelstraat 11, 9700 Oudenaarde. T. (055) 31 87 43.   *073328*
Vos, J. de, Tivolistr 169, 9700 Oudenaarde.
T. (055) 31 50 49.   *073329*

Plainevaux (Liège)
Galerie Vega, 5 Rue de Strivay, Neupré, 4122 Plainevaux. T. (041) 80 22 70, Fax 41 80 43 11.
- Paint -   *073330*

Polleur (Lie ge)
Modern Art Galerie, Château Fays, 4800 Polleur.
T. (087) 22 21 26. - Paint -   *073331*

Pulderbos (Antwerpen)
Art Forum, Nachtegaaldr 14, 2242 Pulderbos.
T. (03) 484 52 50.   *073332*

Rhode-Saint-Genèse (Brabant Wallon)
Finck, Odette, 11 Av. du Manoir, 1640 Rhode-Saint-Genèse. T. (02) 3581298. - Paint -   *073333*

Riemst (Limburg)
Nibema, Galerij, Steenweg 102, 3770 Riemst.
- Paint -   *073334*

Rijkhoven (Limburg)
Artfarm, Bosselaar 2, 3740 Rijkhoven. T. (011) 491791.
- Paint -   *073335*

Roeselare (West-Vlaanderen)
Eleckhoutte, van, Bruggesteenurg 296, 8800 Roeselare.
T. (051) 20 01 23. - Paint -   *073336*
Man, de, Ardoorsestw 15, 8800 Roeselare.
T. (051) 22 91 98.   *073337*
Tempo, Noordstraat 137, 8800 Roeselare.
T. (051) 20 70 57. - Paint -   *073338*
Tilkin-Mandelhove, Galerij, Westlaan 417, 8800 Roeselare. - Paint -   *073339*
V.A.N., Van Mahieustraat 25-27, 8800 Roeselare.
- Paint -   *073340*

Ronse (Oost-Vlaanderen)
Princekouter, Galerij, Opgeeisteenstraat 126, 9600 Ronse. T. (055) 215481. - Paint -   *073341*
St. Hermes, Galerij, Plein A, Delhaye 3, 9600 Ronse.
T. (055) 214472.   *073342*

Ruddervoorde (West-Vlaanderen)
Brunet, Westkantstr 38, 8040 Ruddervoorde.
T. (050) 27 66 33.   *073343*

Schelderode
Kunstforum, Lange Weide 2, 9820 Schelderode.
T. (091) 62 59 58, Fax 62 47 75. - Paint / Graph / Sculp / Sculp / Jew -   *073344*

Schelle (Antwerpen)
Scherpenstein, Provinciale Steenweg 20, 2627 Schelle.
T. (031) 87 46 43.   *073345*
Tolhuis, Tolhuisstr 70, 2627 Schelle.
T. (031) 87 60 90.   *073346*

Schilde (Antwerpen)
Lommaert, L., De Pont 14, 2970 Schilde.
T. (031) 383 04 82.   *073347*
Van Dijk, F., Waterstr 60, 2970 Schilde
T. (031) 383 44 80.   *073348*

Schoten (Antwerpen)
Adamantis, Kastanjedr 2, 2900 Schoten.
T. (031) 658 81 99.   *073349*
Bauters, P., Paalstr 343, 2900 Schoten.
T. (031) 658 87 26.   *073350*
Benoit, P., Hagenlei 15, 2900 Schoten.
T. (031) 658 35 10.   *073351*
Deken, de, Braamstr 53, 2900 Schoten.
T. (031) 658 63 90.   *073352*
Galerie Stilleven, Lariksdreef 46, 2900 Schoten. *073353*
Garbis, G., Deuzeldln 58, 2900 Schoten.
T. (031) 645 71 83.   *073354*
Rigazzi, J., Terheidedr 31, 2900 Schoten.
T. (031) 663 20 95.   *073355*
Schijndael, V Frislei 56, 2900 Schoten.
T. (031) 58 19 98.   *073356*

Sinaai-Waas (Oost-Vlaanderen)
Sterck, M., Wijnveld 205, 9112 Sinaai-Waas.
T. (031) 772 38 23.   *073357*

Sint-Amandsberg (Oost-Vlaanderen)
Kunstgalerij DM, Dendermondsesteenweg 259, 9040 Sint-Amandsberg. T. (091) 28 56 68.   *073358*
Oude Vlaamse Galerij, R. Steppestr. 40, 9040 Sint-Amandsberg. T. (091) 33 63 56. - Paint -   *073359*

Sint-Gillis-Waas (Oost-Vlaanderen)
Bals, H., Oude Molenstr 106, 9170 Sint-Gillis-Waas.
T. (03) 707 05 23.   *073360*

Sint-Martens-Latem (Oost-Vlaanderen)
Artemis, Nelemeersstr 55, 9830 Sint-Martens-Latem.
T. (091) 82 56 59.   *073361*
Bekaert, P., Voordeln 13, 9830 Sint-Martens-Latem.
T. (091) 82 61 82.   *073362*
Buysse, George, Galerij, Nelemeerstr. 57, 9830 Sint-Martens-Latem. T. (091) 82 47 04. - Paint / Furn / Sculp -   *073363*
Deurle Dorp, Dorpsstr 52, 9830 Sint-Martens-Latem.
T. (091) 82 56 49.   *073364*
Flanders Gallery, Kortrijksestw 20, 9830 Sint-Martens-Latem. T. (091) 82 38 84.   *073365*
Galerij Latem Molen, Molenstr 1a, 9830 Sint-Martens-Latem. T. (091) 21 27 29, Fax 21 06 06.   *073366*
Kerkenhoek, Dorp 2, 9830 Sint-Martens-Latem.
T. (091) 82 63 99.   *073367*
Pieters, Guy, Rode Beukendreef 29, 9830 Sint-Martens-Latem. T. (091) 82 82 84. - Paint -   *073368*
Vos, Oscar de, Latemstr. 94, 9830 Sint-Martens-Latem.
T. (091) 82 68 38, Fax 21 06 06. - Paint -   *073369*
XXth Art Gallery, Ph. Serck, Eikeldreef 33, 9830 Sint-Martens-Latem. T. (091) 82 45 49.   *073370*

Sint-Niklaas (Oost-Vlaanderen)
Het Einde, Eindestr 26, 9100 Sint-Niklaas.
T. (03) 772 11 93.   *073371*
La Linea, Regentiestr 29, 9100 Sint-Niklaas.
T. (03) 778 15 27.   *073372*
Labyrint Gallery, Grote Markt 73, 9100 Sint-Niklaas.
T. (03) 766 24 54.   *073373*
Piessens, F., Plezantstr 282, 9100 Sint-Niklaas.
T. (03) 776 39 19.   *073374*
Vael, R., De Meerleerstr 107, 9100 Sint-Niklaas.
T. (03) 777 36 97.   *073375*
Van Goethem, J., Truweelstr 34, 9100 Sint-Niklaas.
T. (03) 777 72 28.   *073376*

Sint-Pauwels (Oost-Vlaanderen)
Griffioen, Potterstr 2, 9170 Sint-Pauwels.
T. (031) 777 51 09.   *073377*

Sint-Truiden (Limburg)
Palet, Breendonkstr 12, 3800 Sint-Truiden.
T. (011) 68 51 15.   *073378*
Tilbury's Art Gallery, Minderbroederstr 18, 3800 Sint-Truiden. T. (011) 68 97 79.   *073379*

Soignies (Hainaut)
Capricorne, 10 Rue de Mons, 7060 Soignies.
T. (067) 33 46 81.   *073380*

Spa (Liège)
Spa Art Gallery – Paul Piront, 1 Chemin Préfayhai, 4900 Spa. T. (087) 77 49 33, Fax 77 49 28.   *073381*

Steenokkerzeel (Vlaams-Brabant)
Punt, de, Driesstr 15, 1820 Steenokkerzeel.
T. (016) 751 71 73.   *073382*

Temse (Oost-Vlaanderen)
Meersman, Doornstr 252, 9140 Temse.
T. (03) 771 15 90.   *073383*
Pauw, G. de, Elsstr 8a, 9140 Temse.
T. (03) 771 16 31.   *073384*
Van den Berghe, J., F Beeckxln 20, 9140 Temse.
T. (03) 771 16 58.   *073385*

Tiegem (West-Vlaanderen)
Sisse, de, Meulenwijk, 8573 Tiegem. - Paint -   *073386*

Tielrode (Oost-Vlaanderen)
Mals, C., Lijsterbesln 3, 9140 Tielrode.
T. (03) 771 33 13.   *073387*

Tielt (West-Vlaanderen)
Degrijse, Ghislaine, Galerij, Rameplein 22, 8700 Tielt.
T. (051) 400418. - Paint -   *073388*

Tienen (Vlaams Brabant)
Kabbeek, Gilainstr 13, 3300 Tienen.
T. (016) 812128.   *073389*
Riland, Grote Bergstr 26, 3300 Tienen.
T. (016) 812350.   *073390*

Tongeren (Limburg)
t' Palet, Maastrichterstraat 27, 3700 Tongeren.
T. (012) 23 17 94. 073391

Turnhout (Antwerpen)
Kunst in Huis, Warandestr 42, 2300 Turnhout.
T. (014) 41 94 94. 073392

Verlaine (Liège)
Vieux Tibunal, 6 Rue Trixchelette, 4537 Verlaine.
T. (041) 59 57 59. 073393

Verviers (Liège)
Primaver, Spintay 79, 4800 Verviers. T. (087) 33 92 32.
- Paint - 073394

Veurne (West-Vlaanderen)
Galerij Aspekt, Zuidstraat 70, 8630 Veurne.
T. (058) 311 88. - Paint - 073395
Kunst onder de Toren, St-Niklaaspleintje, 8630 Veurne.
T. (058) 23 34 42. 073396

Vrasene (Oost-Vlaanderen)
Tilleman, U., Provinciale Baan 36, 9120 Vrasene.
T. (03) 775 98 50. 073398

Waasmunster (Oost-Vlaanderen)
Branzinni, Fortenstr 111, 9250 Waasmunster.
T. (052) 46 30 90, Fax 03/778 03 25, 091/
23 73 46. 073399

Wakken (West-Vlaanderen)
Wever, de, Molenstr 40, 8720 Wakken.
T. (056) 60 70 05. 073400

Wannegem-Lede (Oost-Vlaanderen)
Hermelyn, Dorp 7, 9772 Wannegem-Lede.
T. (091) 836411. 073401

Waregem (West-Vlaanderen)
Galerij Aksent, Molenstraat 47, 8790 Waregem.
T. (056) 60 20 25. - Paint - 073402
Kunst in Huis, Schakelweg 8, 8790 Waregem.
T. (056) 60 35 00. 073403

Waremme (Liège)
Galerie Evasion, 42 Av Joachim, 4300 Waremme.
T. (019) 32 53 88. 073404

Watou (West-Vlaanderen)
Katteman, Helleketelbos, 8978 Watou.
T. (057) 38 83 68. 073405

Wechelderzande (Antwerpen)
Drie Berken, Pulsebaan 80, 2275 Wechelderzande.
T. (031) 312 14 31. - Paint - 073406

Westerlo (Antwerpen)
Van Looy, W., Abdijstr 10, 2260 Westerlo.
T. (014) 54 46 44. 073407

Westkerke (West-Vlaanderen)
Studio Kyndt, Gistelsteenweg 35, 8460 Westkerke.
- Paint / Graph - 073408

Wetteren (Oost-Vlaanderen)
Kijk, Kerkstr 23, 9230 Wetteren.
T. (091) 69 10 35. 073409

Wijnegem (Antwerpen)
Roo, H. de, Turnhoutsebn 383, 2110 Wijnegem.
T. (031) 353 24 27. 073410

Wilrijk (Antwerpen)
Cort, J. de, Kon Albertstr 41-43, 2610 Wilrijk.
T. (031) 827 03 55. 073411
Heeffer, Lissette, St Bavostr 35, 2610 Wilrijk.
T. (031) 827 08 29. 073412
Mija, Sporthalpln 122, 2610 Wilrijk.
T. (031) 828 00 69. 073413

Wommelgem (Antwerpen)
Immerseel, Immerseelstr 39, 2160 Wommelgem.
T. (031) 353 84 90. 073414

Zandhoven (Antwerpen)
Ibou & Partners, Hofeinde 3, 2240 Zandhoven.
T. (03) 484 55 11. 073415

Universal Art Galleries, Kasteelstr 9, 2240 Zandhoven.
T. (03) 484 65 56. 073416

Zele (Oost-Vlaanderen)
Boerenhof, Lokerenbaan 250, 9240 Zele.
T. (052) 44 63 98. 073417

Zomergem (Oost-Vlaanderen)
Galerij Gudrun, Nico Devoldere, Grote Baan 22e, 9930
Zomergem. T. (091) 72 84 98. 073418

Zottegem (Oost-Vlaanderen)
Volkwin, Wijnhuizestr 127, 9620 Zottegem.
T. (091) 60 58 90. 073419

Zulte (West-Vlaanderen)
Coorevits, J., Nachtegaalstr 3, 9870 Zulte.
T. (091) 88 70 71. 073420

Bolivia

La Paz
Los Amigos del Libro, Mercado 1307, La Paz. T. 227 94.
- Ant / Ant - 073421

Brazil

Belo Horizonte (Minas Gerais)
Galeria Guinard, Av. Alfredo Balena, 586, 30000 Belo
Horizonte. 073422

Blumenau (Santa Catarina)
Galeria de Arte Açu-Açu, Rua Namy Beeke, 99, 89100
Blumenau. T. (0473) 22 2247. - Ant / Paint / Graph /
Furn / China / Sculp / Tex / Jew / Instr / Cur / Mod / Mul /
Draw - 073423

Juiz de Fora (Minas Gerais)
Galeria Celina, Rua Halfeld, 8, 2.0, 36100 Juiz de
Fora. 073424

Porto Alegre (Rio Grande do Sul)
Galeria de Arte Leopoldina, Av. Independência, 925,
90000 Porto Alegre. 073425
Galeria de Artes Delphus, Av. Cristóvão Columbo, 1103,
90000 Porto Alegre. - Fra / Paint - 073426

Recife (Pernambuco)
Galeria 88, Patio de São Pedro, 50000 Recife. 073427

Rio de Janeiro (Rio de Janeiro)
Boghici, Jean, R. Nascimento Silva 223, Ipanema,
20000 Rio de Janeiro, 20000. 073428
Bonino, Galeria, Rua Barata Ribeiro 578, 20000 Rio de
Janeiro, 22051. T. (021) 235 7831. - Paint / Graph /
Sculp / Draw - 073429
„Escada", Av. Gen. San Martin, 1.219, 20000 Rio de
Janeiro. 073430
Galeria IBEU, Av. N. S. de Copacabana 690-2, 20000 Rio
de Janeiro, 22050. T. (021) 255 42 68. 073431
Hollanda, Luiz Buarque de & Paulo Bittencourt, Rue de
Palmeiras 19, 20000 Rio de Janeiro.
T. (021) 26 65 837. 073432
Maison de France, Av. Pdte. Antonio Carlos 58/4, 20000
Rio de Janeiro, 20000. T. (021) 220 34 29, 220 36 29,
220 38 29. 073433
Place des Arts, Av. N. S. Copacabana 313, 22021 Rio de
Janeiro. T. (021) 257 1818. 073434
Pontual, Mauricio, Rua Maria Angelica 7, 22461 Rio de
Janeiro. T. (021) 286 29 97. - Paint - 073435
Saracini, Av Armando Lombardi, 205/112, 22640-020
Rio de Janeiro. T. (021) 4937976, Fax (021) 4932950.
- Paint / Graph / Sculp / Draw - 073436

Santos (Sâo Paulo)
Galeria de Arte, Jorge Tiberiça, 5, 11100 Santos.
T. (0132) 4 2608, 4 6877. 073437
Kiart, Av. São Francisco, 194, 11100 Santos. 073438

São Paulo
Arco Arte Contemporanea, Alameda Tiete 46, 1417 São
Paulo. T. (011) 853 34 32, Fax 36 69 90. 073439

Bonfiglioli, Alberto, Rua Augusta 2.995, São
Paulo. 073440
Casa e Jardim, Avda. Santo Amaro 3493, São Paulo.
T. (011) 61 29 15, 34 43 44. - Graph / Repr /
Sculp - 073441
Documenta, R. Padre Joao Manoel 811, São Paulo.
T. (011) 81 37 66. 073442
Galeria de Arte KLM, Av. S. Luis, 120, São Paulo.
T. (011) 257 4011. 073443
Galeria Teatro Anchieta, Rua Dr. Villa Nova 245 Eq. An-
gélica, São Paulo. 073444
Gouvêa, Renato Magalhães, Rua Pelotas, 475, São Pau-
lo, 04012. T. (011) 70 5555. - Ant / Paint / Paint /
Graph / Graph / Furn / China / Sculp / Sculp / Silv / Cur /
Mod - 073445
Mirante das Artes Galeria, Rua Estados Unidos, 1494,
São Paulo. 073446
Multipla, Ave. Morumbi 7990 Brooklin, 04703 São Pau-
lo. T. (011) 2417115, 2410157. - Paint / Graph / Sculp /
Mul / Tin - 073447
„Ouro Velho", Rua Augusta, 1.371, loja 1, São
Paulo. 073448
„Paiol", Rua Amaral Gurgel, 164, São Paulo. 073449
Pinacoteca do Estado, Avenida Tiradentes, 141, São
Paulo, 01101. T. (011) 6329. - Ant - 073450
Seta, Rua Antonio Carlos, 282 Trav. Augusta, São
Paulo. 073451
Strina, Luisa, R. Padre Joao Manoel 974a, São Paulo,
01411. T. (011) 280 2471, 646 391. - Paint / Graph /
Sculp / Draw - 073452

Bulgaria

Plovdiv
Chudožestvena galerija, Ul Vasil Kolarov 15, 4000 Plovdiv. T. (032) 22 42 20. 073453

Canada

Beaconsfield (Québec)
Heidersdorf, E., 480 Beaconsfield, Beaconsfield.
T. (514) 695-6503. 073454

Calgary (Alberta)
Canadian Art Galleries, 801 Tenth Av. SW, Calgary, Alta.
T2R 0B4. T. (403) 290-0203. - Paint / Graph / Sculp /
Fra - 073455
Canerva Art, 3627 61st. Ave., Calgary, S.W. 073456
Chinook Art Gallery, Chinook Centre, MacLeod Trail, Cal-
gary. T. (403) 255-6233. - Paint / Graph / Sculp /
Fra - 073457
Lynn, John, 1236 73rd Ave. S. W., Calgary. 073458
Mona Lisa, 1606 7th St. S. W., Calgary. T. (403) 262-
2488. - Paint / Graph / Fra - 073459
Unisource Art Gallery, 223 Tenth St. NW, Calgary, T2N
1V5. T. (403) 242-4294. - Paint / Graph - 073460

Edmonton (Alberta)
Canadiana Galleries, 10414 Jasper Ave., Edmonton.
T. (403) 423-4221. - Graph / Repr / Sculp - 073461
Morgan, T. H., 11024 127th St., Edmonton. T. (403) 422-
4858. - Paint / Graph / Fra - 073462
West End Gallery, 12308 Jasper Av., Edmonton, T5N
3K5. T. (403) 488 4892. - Paint / Graph - 073463

Fonthill (Ontario)
The Windpoppy Art Gallery, 1412 Church St., Fonthill,
LOS 1EQ. T. (905) 892-6262. 073464

Halifax (Nova Scotia)
Leonowens, Anna, 5163 Duke St., Halifax, N.S. B3J 3J6.
T. (902) 422-7381. - Paint / Graph - 073465
Manuge, 1674 Hollis St., Halifax, B3J 1V7.
T. (902) 423 6315. - Paint / Graph - 073466

Lachine (Québec)
Artistica Inc., 401, rue des Erables, Lachine, H8S 2P8.
T. (514) 364-6090. - Repr / Fra - 073467

Markham (Ontario)

The Electric Gallery, 226 Steelcase Rd. W.,, Markham, L3R 1B3. T. (416) 925-4441. - Paint - *073468*

Montreal (Québec)

Artlenders, 318 Victoria Ave., Montreal. T. (514) 484-4691. - Paint / Graph - *073469*

Atelier J. Lukacs, 1504 Sherbrooke St. W, Montreal, H3G 1L3. T. (514) 933-9877. - Paint / Sculp - *073470*

Bennett's, 232 Laurier Blvd. W., Montreal. T. (514) 271-8285. - Fra - *073471*

Boutique Soleil, 430 Bonsecours, Montreal. T. (514) 866-9019. - Repr / Sculp - *073472*

Canadian Guild of Crafts Quebec, 2025 Peel St. XXX 87A, H3A 1T6, Montreal. T. (514) 849-6091. *073473*

Continental Gallery, 1450 Drummond St., Montreal. T. (514) 842-1072. - Paint / Graph / Sculp - *073474*

Desroches, Bernard, 1444 Sherbrooke St. W, Montreal, H3G 1K4. T. (514) 842-8648. - Paint / Sculp / Draw - *073475*

Dominion Gallery, 1438 Sherbrooke St. W, Montreal, P.Q. H3G 1K4. T. (514) 845-7471, 845-7833. - Paint / Sculp - *073476*

Gemst, 5380 Sherbrooke St. W., Montreal. T. (514) 488-5104. - Graph - *073477*

Graff, 963 Rue Rachel Est, Montreal, P.Q. H2J 2J4. T. (514) 526-2616. *073478*

Kadar, Paul, 7431 Ostell Crescent, Montreal. T. (514) 733-5533. - Paint - *073479*

Kastel, Paul, 1366 Greene Ave., Westmount, Montreal. T. (514) 933-8735. - Paint / Graph - *073480*

Klinkhoff, Walter, Gallery Inc., 1200 Sherbrooke St. W., Montreal, H3A 1H6. T. (514) 288-7306. - Paint / Graph - *073481*

Le Gobelet, 8401 St. Laurent, Montreal. T. (514) 381-0469. *073482*

Metro Art Centre, Inc., Alexis Nihon Plaza, Montreal. T. (514) 935-8614. *073483*

Morency, Galerie, 1564 St. Denis St., Montreal. T. (514) 845-6894. - Paint / Fra - *073484*

Nova, 2100 Rue Crescent, Montreal, H3G 2B8. T. (514) 845-1221. - Paint / Sculp - *073485*

Rolland, 2350 Guy St., Montreal. T. (514) 932-9739. - Paint / Fra - *073486*

Royal Art Galleries, 1420 Sherbrooke St. W., Montreal. T. (514) 845-4383. - Paint / Sculp - *073487*

Singer Picture & Frame, Inc., 6220 Somerled St., Montreal. T. (514) 482-0243. - Paint / Fra - *073488*

Tremblay, Laurent, 4809 rue Marquette, Montreal. T. (514) 521 87 86. *073489*

Unique, 5800 St. Hubert, Montreal. T. (514) 271-7067. *073490*

Universal Art Studio, 5395 Rosedale, Montreal. T. (514) 486-1981. - Paint - *073491*

Valentin, Jean-Pierre, 1434 Sherbrooke St. W, Montreal, P.Q. H3G 1K4. T. (514) 849-3637, Fax 849-4684. - Paint - *073492*

West End Art Gallery, 1358 Greene Av., Westmount, Montreal, H3Z 2B1. T. (514) 933-4314. *073493*

Yajima, 307 W Ste. Catherine St., Suite 515, Montreal, H2X 2A3. T. (514) 842-2676. - Pho - *073494*

Niagara Falls (Ontario)

Niagara Falls Art Gallery and Kurelek Collection, Queen Elizabeth Way, Niagara Falls, L2E 6S5. T. (905) 356-1514. - Paint / Graph / Sculp - *073495*

Oakville (Ontario)

Brand, Britta, 83 Reynolds St., Oakville, L6J 3K3. T. (905) 844-9534, 845-4697. - Paint / Graph / Sculp - *073496*

Ottawa (Ontario)

Gallery 93, 93 Sparks St., Ottawa. *073497*

Koyman's Art, 320 Queen, Ottawa. T. (613) 234-4658. *073498*

Nicholas Art Gallery, 5 Nicholas, Ottawa. T. (613) 232-6515. - Paint / Graph / Sculp / Fra - *073499*

Robertson, 162 Lautier Ave. West, Ottawa. T. (613) 235-6426. - Paint / Sculp / Fra - *073500*

Wallack, 203 Bank St., Ottawa, Ont. K2P 1W7. T. (613) 235-4339. - Paint / Graph / Sculp / Fra / Draw - *073501*

Streetsville (Ontario)

Gelder's Fine Arts, 133 Queen St. S., Streetsville. T. (905) 826-1243. - Paint - *073502*

Toronto (Ontario)

A. C. T., 424 Wellington St. West, Toronto. *073503*

A J's Fine Framing, 372 Danforth Av., Toronto. T. (416) 466-7860. - Paint - *073504*

A Moment in Time, 620 Richmond W, Toronto. T. (416) 367-9770. - Paint - *073505*

A Space, 183 Bathurst, Toronto. T. (416) 364-3227. - Paint - *073506*

Absolutley Art, 836 Yonge, Toronto. T. (416) 960-5638. - Paint - *073507*

Access Fine Arts, 66 Portland, Toronto. T. (416) 861-0606. - Paint - *073508*

Aimis, Evelyn, 14 Hazelton Av., Toronto, Ont. M5R 2E2. T. (416) 961-0878. *073509*

Ainsley, Sandra, 2 First Canadian Pl., Toronto. T. (416) 362-4480. - Paint - *073510*

Aird, John B., 900 Bay, Toronto. T. (416) 928-6772. - Paint - *073511*

Airmen's Gallery, 295 King W, Toronto. T. (416) 593-0157. - Paint - *073512*

Alexander, 154 King E, Toronto. T. (416) 363-8814. - Paint - *073513*

Algonquians Sweet Grass Gallery, 668 Queen W, Toronto. T. (416) 368-1336. - Paint - *073514*

Allen, 331 Queen E, Toronto. T. (416) 366-3195. - Paint - *073515*

Allery, 322 1/2 Queen W, Toronto. T. (416) 593-0853. - Paint - *073516*

Alter Natives, 30 Saint Andrew, Toronto. T. (416) 593-6891. - Paint - *073517*

Alvin Tan, 55 Avenue Rd., Toronto. T. (416) 920-6226. - Paint - *073518*

Animation Celection, 183 Avenue Rd., Toronto. T. (416) 928-2357. - Paint - *073519*

Animation Gallery, 1977 Queen E, Toronto. T. (416) 691-4105. - Paint - *073520*

Arctic Bear, 125 Yorkville, Toronto. T. (416) 967-7885. - Paint - *073521*

Arctic Experience Gallery, 189 Hughson S, Toronto. T. (905) 522-9443. - Paint - *073522*

Ares, 1351 Main E, Toronto. T. (905) 547-2417. - Paint - *073523*

Armen, 16 Wellesley W, Toronto. T. (416) 924-5375. - Paint - *073524*

Art and Fashion, 2213 Bloor W, Toronto. T. (416) 766-5528. - Paint - *073525*

Art Collection Canada, 315 Queen W, Toronto. T. (416) 977-4456. - Paint - *073526*

Art Dialogue Gallery, 80 Spadina Av., Toronto. T. (416) 368-3534. - Paint - *073527*

Art-Fac Masterpiece Gallery, 295 King W, Toronto. T. (416) 593-0157. - Paint - *073528*

Art Form, 12a Hugo, Toronto. T. (416) 766-4362. - Paint - *073529*

Art Gallery of Ontario and the Grange, 317 Dundas W, Toronto. T. (416) 977-0414. - Paint - *073530*

Art House, 101 Richmond W, Toronto. T. (416) 864-9858. - Paint - *073531*

Art Imperial Gallery, 130 McCaul, Toronto. T. (416) 596-1064. - Paint - *073532*

Art Master Galleries, 1172 Eglinton W, Toronto. T. (416) 785-7880. - Paint - *073533*

Art of Glass, 35 E Beaver Creek, Toronto. T. (905) 764-0777. - Paint - *073534*

Art One, 1 First Canadian Pl., Toronto. T. (416) 368-3575. - Paint - *073535*

Art Stalf's Gallery, 3367 Yonge, Toronto. T. (905) 476-1080. - Paint - *073536*

Artefect, 51 Bathurst, Toronto. T. (416) 369-0272. - Paint - *073537*

Arterie, 1611 Queen E, Toronto. T. (416) 463-3636. - Paint - *073538*

Artia, 153 Christie, Toronto. T. (416) 531-7443. - Paint - *073539*

Arts Channel, 622 Richmond W, Toronto. T. (416) 367-2787. - Paint - *073540*

Artworks, Fairview Mall, Toronto. T. (416) 498-8130. - Paint - *073541*

Ashtons, 267 Queens E, Toronto. T. (416) 366-6846. - Paint - *073542*

Astley, James, & Co., 82 Castle Frank Rd., Toronto. T. (416) 922-3294. - Paint - *073543*

Atelier Fine Arts, 588 Markham, Toronto. T. (416) 532-9244. - Paint - *073544*

Atelier G.F., 512 Lansdowne, Toronto. T. (416) 588-7390. - Paint - *073545*

Bau-Xi, 340 Dundas St., Toronto, Ont. M5T 1G5. T. (416) 977-0600. *073546*

Beach Gallery, 2339 Queen E, Toronto. T. (416) 691-6744. - Paint - *073547*

Beckett, 142 James S, Toronto. T. (905) 525-4266. - Paint - *073548*

Belli, Flavio, 52 McCaul St., Toronto, M5T 1V9. T. (416) 598-1368. - Paint - *073549*

Benitz & Benitz, 120 Carlton, Toronto. T. (416) 926-1632. - Paint - *073550*

Biggs, 15165 Yonge, Toronto. T. (416) 727-6308. - Paint - *073551*

Bikan, 117 Kendal, Toronto. T. (416) 922-9411. - Graph - *073552*

Birganart, 333 Danforth Av., Toronto. T. (416) 461-6809. - Paint - *073553*

Black Creek Art Studios, 425 Alliance, Toronto. T. (416) 762-2888. - Paint - *073554*

BMW Gallery, 21 Adelaide St. W, Toronto. T. (416) 365-1088. - Paint - *073555*

Bolduc, D., 58 Wade, Toronto. T. (416) 533-3263. - Paint - *073556*

Braem & Minnetti, 1262 Yonge, Toronto. T. (416) 923-7437. - Paint - *073557*

Bremner, 60 Bullock Rd., Toronto. T. (905) 294-1104. - Paint - *073558*

Bren Art, 388 Carlow Av., Toronto. T. (416) 461-7537. - Paint - *073559*

Bridgestone, 276 Dundas E, Toronto. T. (416) 961-9780. - Paint - *073560*

Buckingham Fine Art, 144 Main St., Toronto. T. (905) 479-3747. - Paint - *073561*

Bystriansky, Luba, 699 Queen W, Toronto. T. (416) 594-3436. - Paint - *073562*

Canadian Art Wholesalers, 5170 Dixie, Toronto. T. (905) 624-9244. - Paint - *073563*

Central Art Wholesalers, 3105 Unity De., Toronto. T. (905) 828-6806. - Paint - *073564*

Century Art, 321 Davenport, Toronto. T. (416) 944-3475. - Paint - *073565*

China Arts, 421 Dundas W, Toronto. T. (416) 596-7466. - Paint - *073566*

Circle Gallery, 83 Yorkville, Toronto. T. (416) 961-5806. - Paint - *073567*

City Streets Gallery, 339 Dundas E, Toronto. T. (416) 363-0466. - Paint - *073568*

Cold City Gallery, 30 Duncan, Toronto. T. (416) 593-5332. - Paint - *073569*

Collected Works, 1579 Bayview Av., Toronto. T. (416) 485-3839. - Paint - *073570*

Collins & Chandler, 181 Avenue Rd., Toronto. T. (416) 922-8784. - Paint - *073571*

Connoisseur Art Gallery, 350 Dundas W, Toronto. T. (416) 340-9669. - Paint - *073572*

Contemporary Fine Art Services, 413 Dundas E, Toronto. T. (416) 366-9770. - Paint - *073573*

Corkin, Jane, 179 John St., Toronto, M5T 1X4. T. (416) 979-1980. *073574*

Costin & Klintworth, 80 Spadina Av., Toronto. T. (416) 363-7800. - Paint - *073575*

Cutts, Christopher, 23 Morrow, Toronto. T. (416) 532-5566. - Paint - *073576*

Dadashi, 3417 Yonge, Toronto. T. (416) 482-6040. - Paint - *073577*

Danforth Picture Frames, 2513 Danforth Av., Toronto. T. (416) 694-4126. - Paint - *073578*

Darroch, 987 1/2 Pape, Toronto. T. (416) 421-1124. - Paint - *073579*

David's Framing, 89 Collier, Toronto. T. (416) 964-6140. - Paint - *073580*

Davis, Geraldine, 225 Richmomnd W, Toronto. T. (416) 595-5225. - Paint - *073581*

Del Bello, 363 Queen St. W, Toronto, Ont. M5V 2A4. T. (416) 593-0884, Fax 593-8729. - Paint / Graph - *073582*

Della Scala, 77 Front E, Toronto. T. (416) 362-6755.
- Paint - *073583*

Deveau, Robert, 299 Queen E, Toronto. T. (416) 364-6271. - Paint - *073584*

Dickinson, 3377 Yonge, Toronto. T. (416) 322-3377.
- Paint - *073585*

Dorset, 33 Belmont, Toronto. T. (416) 961-0511.
- Paint - *073586*

Dream 21, Toronto POB 219, Station M. T. (416) 239-2163. - Paint - *073587*

Dresdnere, 12 Hazelton, Toronto. T. (416) 923-4662.
- Paint - *073588*

Dzo, 1160 Queen W, Toronto. T. (416) 530-0768.
- Paint - *073589*

Ebony Treasures, 207 Queens Quay W, Toronto.
T. (416) 360-8702. - Sculp - *073590*

Ebony Treasures, 104 Yorkville, Toronto. T. (416) 966-4061. - Sculp - *073591*

El-Baz, Jacob, 17 Hazelton Av., Toronto, M5R 2E1.
T. (416) 968-1990. - Paint / Graph - *073592*

Elder, Norman, 140 Bedford Rd., Toronto. T. (416) 920-0120. *073593*

Elite Art Supplies, 120 Dynamic Dr., Toronto.
T. (416) 299-9613. - Paint - *073594*

Engel, Walter, 350 Lonsdale Rd., Suite 201, Toronto, M5P 1R6. T. (416) 487-8868. - Paint / Graph / Sculp - *073595*

Eskimo Art Gallery, 458 Queen's Quay W, Toronto.
T. (416) 591-9004. - Sculp - *073596*

Eskimo Art Innuit Gallery, 9 Prince Arthur Av., Toronto.
T. (416) 921-9985. - Paint / Sculp - *073597*

Famous Art and Custom Framing, 1536 Danforth Av., Toronto. T. (416) 469-4488. - Paint - *073598*

Feheley, 45 Avenue Rd., Toronto. T. (416) 323-1373. *073599*

Fintona, 525 Queen E, Toronto. T. (416) 601-0042.
- Paint - *073600*

First Edition, 491 Bloor W, Toronto. T. (416) 925-5055.
- Paint - *073601*

Four Corners, 5322 Yonge, Toronto. T. (416) 221-0653.
- Paint - *073602*

Frame Concepts-Masterangelo Gallery, 876 Yonge, Toronto. T. (416) 923-7600. - Paint - *073603*

Frame Designs, 1727 Bayview Av., Toronto.
T. (416) 485-5177. - Paint - *073604*

Frame Place, 387 Jane, Toronto. T. (416) 762-9669.
- Paint - *073605*

Frame Shoppe and Gallery, 1710 Avenue Rd., Toronto.
T. (416) 789-0419. - Paint - *073606*

Framing Experience, 3009 Kingston Rd., Toronto.
T. (416) 267-1450. - Paint - *073607*

Framing Spectrum Gallery, 1462 Kingston Rd., Toronto.
T. (416) 691-6099. - Paint - *073608*

Friedland, 122 Scollard St., Toronto, M5G IR2.
T. (416) 961-4900. - Paint / Graph / Graph - *073609*

Fringe, 1179a King W, Toronto. T. (416) 535-2323.
- Paint - *073610*

Gabor, 587 Markham, Toronto. T. (416) 534-1839.
- Paint - *073611*

Galerie Heritage, 137 Yorkville, Toronto. T. (416) 967-1675. - Paint - *073612*

Galerie Sherway, Sherway Gardens, Toronto.
T. (416) 622-6809. - Paint - *073613*

Gallerie Beaux Arts, 2064 Avenue Rd., Toronto.
T. (416) 322-0995. - Paint - *073614*

Gallery Boutique, 626 Yonge, Toronto. T. (416) 921-4616. - Paint - *073615*

Gallery Incollaboration, 25 Bellair, Toronto. T. (416) 515-8080. - Paint - *073616*

Gallery O, 589 Markham St., Toronto, M6G 2L7.
T. (416) 5342141. - Paint / Graph - *073617*

Gallery One, 121 Scollard, Toronto. T. (416) 929-3103.
- Paint - *073618*

Gallery Wall, 783 Queen E, Toronto. T. (416) 778-5044.
- Paint - *073619*

Gallery 133, 74 Bathurst, Toronto. T. (416) 361-6099.
- Paint - *073620*

Gallery 306, 80 Spadina Av., Toronto. T. (416) 363-7253.
- Paint - *073621*

Gallery 44, 183 Bathurst, Toronto. T. (416) 363-5187.
- Paint - *073622*

GalleryBrougham, 1613 Hwy. 7, Brougham, Toronto.
T. (905) 683-7010. - Paint - *073623*

Gamma Art International, 62 Wellesley W, Toronto.
T. (416) 966-3616. - Paint - *073624*

Garo, 4a Baldwin, Toronto. T. (416) 591-1710.
- Paint - *073625*

George, Mary, 136 Hillsdale E, Toronto. T. (416) 483-4353. - Paint - *073626*

Gilbert & Coles, 160 Pears, Toronto. T. (416) 921-9145.
- Paint - *073627*

Glass Art Gallery, 21 Hazelton, Toronto. T. (416) 968-1823. - Glass - *073628*

Glass Chimney Art and Antiques, 1661 Eglinton W, Toronto. T. (416) 783-9423. - Glass - *073629*

Godard, Mira, 22 Hazelton, Toronto. T. (416) 964-8197.
- Paint - *073630*

Godard, Mira, 22 Hazelton Av., Toronto, Ont. M5R 2E2.
T. (416) 964-8197. - Paint / Graph / Sculp - *073631*

Gottlieb, Arnold, 80 Spadina Av., Toronto. T. (416) 359-0103. - Paint - *073632*

Grange, 71 McCaul, Toronto. T. (416) 581-8813.
- Paint - *073633*

Graphis, 78 Hilton, Toronto. T. (416) 537-9777.
- Graph - *073634*

Gutenberg, 664 Yonge St., Toronto. T. (416) 925-3535. *073635*

Han, 1032 Saint Clair W, Toronto. T. (416) 656-4315.
- Paint - *073636*

Harbour Arctic Bear, 1 Harbour Sq., Toronto.
T. (416) 360-0677. - Paint - *073637*

Harrop, 345 Steeles, Toronto. T. (905) 878-8161.
- Paint - *073638*

Harumi, 135 Danforth Av., Toronto. T. (416) 463-7928.
- Paint - *073639*

Heavenly Goose Gallery, 1058 Gerrard E, Toronto.
T. (416) 463-4135. - Paint - *073640*

Hennock, Jim A., 185 Queen E, Toronto. T. (416) 363-7757. - Paint - *073641*

Hickl-Szabo, 66 Avenue Rd., Toronto. T. (416) 962-4140.
- Paint - *073642*

Hildebrando, 1078 Queen W, Toronto. T. (416) 535-0184.
- Paint - *073643*

Hollander York, 33 Hazelton, Toronto. T. (416) 923-9275.
- Paint - *073644*

Homeculture, 3 Southvale Dr., Toronto. T. (416) 421-7573. - Paint - *073645*

Idee, 883 Queen W, Toronto. T. (416) 362-3380.
- Paint - *073646*

Images Art Gallery, 3345 Yonge, Toronto. T. (416) 481-9584. - Paint - *073647*

Imaginus Print Shop, 3221 Yonge, Toronto. T. (416) 483-1970. - Graph - *073648*

In the Making, 207 Queen's Quay W, Toronto.
T. (416) 366-9381. - Paint - *073649*

Incurable Collector, 1945 Queen E, Toronto. T. (416) 694-9485. - Paint - *073650*

Innuit Gallery, 9 Prince Arthur Av., Toronto, Ont. M5R 1B2. T. (416) 921-9985, Fax 921-9530. - Paint / Graph / Sculp / Fra - *073651*

International Gallery, 119 Isabella Street, Toronto, M4Y JP2. T. (416) 924-6678. - Paint / Paint / Graph / Graph / Sculp / Sculp - *073652*

Island Gallery, 137 Yonge, Toronto. T. (416) 603-0319.
- Paint - *073653*

Jackdaw, 20 Maud, Toronto. T. (416) 368-3395.
- Paint - *073654*

Jackson, 119 Yorkville, Toronto. T. (416) 967-9166.
- Graph - *073655*

Jackson, Stuart, 119 Yorkville, Toronto. T. (416) 967-9166. - Paint - *073656*

Jacobson & Associates, 41 Spadina Rd., Toronto.
T. (416) 925-1384. - Paint - *073657*

Jared Sable Gallery, 33 Hazelton Ave., Toronto.
T. (416) 961 01 11. *073658*

Kamen, Leo, 80 Spadina Av., Toronto. T. (416) 365-9515.
- Paint - *073659*

Karney, 11 Yorkville, Toronto. T. (416) 964-1122.
- Paint - *073660*

Karwah, 289 Dundas W, Toronto. T. (416) 598-0043.
- Paint - *073661*

Kaspar, 27 Prince Arthur, Toronto. T. (416) 968-2536.
- Paint - *073662*

Ken, 1179 Finch W, Toronto. T. (416) 665-8022.
- Paint - *073663*

Kernerman, Barry, 100 Canyon, Toronto. T. (416) 630-5870. - Paint - *073664*

Kingsmount, 1879 Gerrard E, Toronto. T. (416) 463-6762. - Paint - *073665*

Kinsman, Robinson, 112 Scollard, Toronto. T. (416) 964-2374. - Paint - *073666*

Kiondo, 67 Mowat, Toronto. T. (416) 533-9959.
- Sculp - *073667*

Klonaridis, 80 Spadina Av., Toronto. T. (416) 360-7800.
- Paint / Sculp - *073668*

Knight, 476 Bedford Park, Toronto. T. (416) 781-9940.
- Paint - *073669*

Korper, Olga, 17 Morrow, Toronto. T. (416) 538-8220.
- Paint - *073670*

KS Art and Crafts, 1286 Weston, Toronto. T. (416) 243-0233. - Paint - *073671*

La Parete, 1071 Bathurst, Toronto. T. (416) 533-8292.
- Paint - *073672*

Laing, 194 Bloor St. W., Toronto. T. (416) 922-7762.
- Paint / Sculp - *073673*

Lake, D., 237 King E, Toronto. T. (416) 863-9930.
- Paint - *073674*

Lamanna, Carmen, 788 King St. W, Toronto, M5V 1N6.
T. (416) 363-8787. - Paint / Graph / Sculp / Pho / Mul / Draw - *073675*

Legault, Irene, 130 Avenue Rd., Toronto. T. (416) 923-8084. - Paint - *073676*

Let's Frame It, 754 Mount Pleasant, Toronto.
T. (416) 482-5667. - Paint - *073677*

Libby's of Toronto, 463 E King St., Toronto, M5A 1L6.
T. (416) 364-3730. - Paint - *073678*

Light Spectrum, 473a Church, Toronto. T. (416) 921-7149. - Paint - *073679*

Lipman Marci, 231 Avenue Rd., Toronto. T. (416) 922-7061. - Paint - *073680*

Living Art, 8440 Hwy. 27, Toronto. T. (905) 856-1909.
- Paint - *073681*

Lonti Ebers, 114 Hazelton, Toronto. T. (416) 961-5363.
- Paint - *073682*

Lord of Fantasy Egyptian Art Show, 595 Bay, Toronto.
T. (416) 593-1827. - Paint - *073683*

Lourie, 100 Front W, Toronto. T. (416) 368-1312.
- Paint - *073684*

Lukacs, J., 238 Davenport, Toronto. T. (416) 923-8908.
- Paint - *073685*

Lumu, 174 Spadina Av., Toronto. T. (416) 369-0814.
- Paint - *073686*

Madison Gallery, 80 Spadina Av., Toronto. T. (416) 365-7332. - Paint - *073687*

Madison Gallery, 334 W Dundas St., Toronto, M5T 1G5.
T. (416) 977-4060, 977-4017. - Paint / Graph - *073688*

Manfred Gallery, 87 Avenue Rd., Toronto. T. (416) 925-9324. - Paint - *073689*

Map Room, Marine Arts and Wildlife Galleries, 18 Birch Av., Toronto, M4V 1C8. T. (416) 922-5153. - Ant / Paint / Graph / Sculp / Tex / Instr / Draw - *073690*

Marble Arch Gallery, 3329 Yonge, Toronto. T. (416) 440-1995. - Paint - *073691*

Marine Arts Gallery, 18 Birch Av., Toronto. T. (416) 922-5153. - Paint - *073692*

Markham, 7665 Kennedy, Toronto. T. (905) 479-0918.
- Paint - *073693*

Marshall, Christine, R.R. 3, Caledon E, Toronto.
T. (905) 880-0116. - Paint - *073694*

Master Framers Gallery, 597a Annette, Toronto.
T. (416) 769-8390. - Paint - *073695*

Masterpiece Gallery, 295 King W, Toronto. T. (416) 593-0157. - Paint - *073696*

Mazelow Gallery, 3463 Yonge St., Toronto, M4N 2N3.
T. (416) 481-7711, 481-3876. - Paint / Graph / Sculp / Fra - *073697*

McConnell, Eileen, 40 Maple, Toronto. T. (416) 963-9308. - Paint - *073698*

McCready, 192 Davenport, Toronto. T. (416) 961-6665.
- Paint - *073699*

McMichael, Toronto. T. (905) 893-1121. - Paint - *073700*

Media Montage, 96 Spadina Av., Toronto. T. (416) 363-9563. - Paint - *073701*

Mercer Union, 333 Adelaide W, Toronto. T. (416) 977-1412. - Paint - *073702*

Midway Films, 146 Douglas Dr., Toronto. T. (416) 55-7400. - Paint - *073703*

Mitchell, David M., 358 Berkeley, Toronto. T. (416) 960-9336. - Paint - *073704*
Moos, Walter A., 136 Yorkville Av., Toronto, Ont. M5R 1C2. T. (416) 922-0627. - Paint / Graph / Sculp - *073705*
Morrow Gallery, 21 Morrow, Toronto. T. (416) 588-6843. - Paint - *073706*
Nature Store, 207 Queen's Quay W, Toronto. T. (416) 867-1790. - Paint - *073707*
Neville, 1945 Avenue Rd., Toronto. T. (416) 781-6667. - Paint - *073708*
New Bronx Art Space, 443 Adelaide W, Toronto. T. (416) 601-1628. - Paint - *073709*
Office Elan Art Services, 3637 Beechollow Cr., Toronto. T. (905) 624-1914. - Paint - *073710*
Ontario Crafts Council, 35 McCaul, Toronto. T. (416) 977-3551. - Paint - *073711*
Open Studio, 520 King W, Toronto. T. (416) 368-8238. - Paint - *073712*
Pacific Art Services, 1620 Midland, Toronto. T. (416) 752-5360. - Paint - *073713*
Pao & Moltke, 21 Avenue Rd., Toronto. T. (416) 925-6197. *073714*
Partisan Gallery, 1200 Queen W, Toronto. T. (416) 532-9681. - Paint - *073715*
Pende, 15 Forest Wood, Toronto. T. (416) 782-3005. - Paint - *073716*
Phillip, Don Mills Centre, Toronto. T. (416) 447-1301. - Paint - *073717*
Picture Frame Factory, 240 Adelaide, Toronto. T. (416) 977-3921. - Paint - *073718*
Picture Frame Shop, 117 Danforth Ave., Toronto. T. (416) 461-4543. - Fra - *073719*
Picture Only Us, 1592 Bayview Av., Toronto. T. (416) 483-8246. - Paint - *073720*
Plews, 114 Avenue Rd., Toronto. T. (416) 961-3739. - Paint - *073721*
Ponova, 191 Gerrard E, Toronto. T. (416) 968-2231. - Paint - *073722*
Poole, Nancy, 16 Hazelton Ave., Toronto, M5R 2E2. T. (416) 964-9050. - Paint / Graph / China / Sculp / Eth - *073723*
Posterity Graphics, 438 Queen E, Toronto. T. (416) 861-1851. - Graph - *073724*
Posters ETC, 382 Eglinton W, Toronto. T. (416) 481-2152. - Graph - *073725*
Presence, 567 Mount Pleasant, Toronto. T. (416) 486-1066. - Paint - *073726*
Preservation Gallery, 177 King, Toronto. T. (905) 468-4431. - Paint - *073727*
Prestige Gallery, 2555 Dixie, Toronto. T. (905) 270-3243. - Paint - *073728*
Prime Gallery, 52 McCaul, Toronto. T. (416) 593-5750. - Paint - *073729*
Prince Arthur Galleries, 33 Prinve Arthur Ave., Toronto, M5R 1B2. T. (416) 967 9148. *073730*
Prinsep, Valentine, 441 Sackville, Toronto. T. (416) 923-6200. - Paint - *073731*
Printziples Fine Art, 1470 Yonge, Toronto. T. (416) 920-1957. - Paint - *073732*
Profile Art, 33 Elm Grove, Toronto. T. (416) 534-8864. - Paint - *073733*
Progressive Editions, 418 Queen E, Toronto. T. (416) 860-0983. - Graph - *073734*
Public Access, 67a Portland, Toronto. T. (416) 979-0466. - Paint - *073735*
Rafelman, Marcia, 466 Saint Clair E, Toronto. T. (416) 482-0944. - Paint - *073736*
Red Head Gallery, 96 Spadina Av., Toronto. T. (416) 863-1654. - Paint - *073737*
Reid, Jack, 1875 Steeles W, Toronto. T. (905) 457-2078. - Paint - *073738*
Rembrandt Art Gallery, 3025 Bathurst St., Toronto. T. (416) 781-6580. - Paint / Draw - *073739*
Rich and Famous Gallery, 126 Cumberland, Toronto. T. (416) 929-2357. - Paint - *073740*
R.M. Studio Gallery, 2498 Yonge, Toronto. T. (416) 482-7207. - Paint - *073741*
Roberts, 641 Yonge St., Toronto, M4Y 1Z9. T. (416) 924-8731. - Paint / Sculp - *073742*
Rochon, 80 Spadina Av., Toronto. T. (416) 367-8057. - Paint - *073743*
Rogerson, 14 Greenbriar, Toronto. T. (416) 223-8361. - Paint - *073744*
Roth, Sheila, 276 Avenue Rd., Toronto. T. (416) 920-0112. - Paint - *073745*
Ryerson, 80 Spadina Av., Toronto. T. (416) 368-2235. - Paint - *073746*
S A G E, 2007 Lawrence Av. W, Toronto. T. (416) 247-0664. - Paint - *073747*
Sable-Castelli, 33 Hazelton Ave., Toronto, Ont. M5R 2E3. T. (416) 961 0011. *073748*
Sabrina's Art and Gift, 23 Norlang, Toronto. T. (416) 467-6574. - Paint - *073749*
Safrance & Associates, 305 Church, Toronto. T. (905) 842-4151. - Paint - *073750*
Scrimshaw & Co., 12 Lakeshore Rd. W, Toronto. T. (905) 844-6283. - Paint - *073751*
Sevan Art Gallery, 480 Yonge, Toronto. T. (416) 920-8809. - Paint - *073752*
Shelley Lambe, 2 Matilda, Toronto. T. (416) 778-0700. - Paint - *073753*
Shiell, Miriam, 16a Hazelton, Toronto. T. (416) 925-2461. - Paint - *073754*
Show Gallery, 978 Queen W, Toronto. T. (416) 533-4276. - Paint - *073755*
Simpson, S.L., 515 Queen W, Toronto. T. (416) 362-3738. - Paint - *073756*
Smith, Louise, 33 Prince Arthur, Toronto. T. (416) 924-1096. - Paint - *073757*
Smith, W.H., 220 Yonge, Toronto. T. (416) 979-9376. - Paint - *073758*
Spiro's Gallery, 2547 Warden, Toronto. T. (416) 497-6665. - Paint - *073759*
Sporting Art Gallery, 18 Birch Av., Toronto. T. (416) 922-5133. - Paint - *073760*
Stalf's Oil Painting Ltd., 3409 Yonge St., Toronto, M4N 2M6. T. (416) 486-1080. - Paint / Fra - *073761*
Steiner, 114 Florence Av., Toronto. T. (416) 865-9377. - Paint - *073762*
Studio QB, 1 Yonge, Toronto. T. (416) 368-1941. - Paint - *073763*
Terrance & Sulymko, 488 Castlefield, Toronto. T. (416) 481-8170. - Paint - *073764*
The Guild Shop, 140 Cumberland Street, Toronto, M5R 1A8. T. (416) 921-1721. - Graph / China / Sculp / Jew - *073765*
Thebes, 613 King W, Toronto. T. (416) 363-3956. - Paint - *073766*
THOM Fine Art, POB 38040, Toronto. T. (416) 487-8466. - Paint - *073767*
Thom, Frederick W., 194 W Bloor St., Toronto, M5S 1T8. T. (416) 921 3622. - Paint / Paint - *073768*
TLC Art Services, POB 99521, Toronto. T. (416) 696-8056. - Paint - *073769*
Toniara, 1715 Lakeshore Rd. W, Toronto. T. (416) 822-5079. - Paint - *073770*
Toronto Photographers Workshop, 80 Spadina Av., Toronto. T. (416) 362-4242. - Pho - *073771*
Tralli, 1952 Gerrard E, Toronto. T. (416) 699-1870. - Paint - *073772*
Tralli's Art, 1952 Gerrard St. E., Toronto. T. (416) 699-1870. - Sculp - *073773*
Trypillia, 2285 Bloor W, Toronto. T. (416) 766-0113. - Paint - *073774*
Twenty-First Century Gallery, 111 Davisville Av., Toronto, M4S 1G6. T. (416) 487-3883. *073775*
Up the Wall, 132 Ava Rd., Toronto. T. (416) 783-3007. - Paint - *073776*
Van der Veen, Geert, 97 Marlborough Av., Toronto, Ont. M5R 1X5. T. (416) 921-3504. - Paint / Graph / Sculp - *073777*
Vernacular, 1166 Yonge, Toronto. T. (416) 961-6490. - Paint - *073778*
Victoria Art Gallery, 1967 Queen E, Toronto. T. (416) 698-1967. - Paint - *073779*
Visual Arts Ontario, 439 Wellington W, Toronto. T. (416) 591-8883. - Paint - *073780*
Waddington, 33 Hazelton Ave., Toronto, Ont. M5R 2E3. T. (416) 925 2461. *073781*
Waddington McLean & Co., 189 Queen E, Toronto. T. (416) 362-1678. - Paint - *073782*
Wagman, Stanley, & Son, 111 Avenue Rd., Toronto. T. (416) 964-1047. - Paint - *073783*
Waleeds, 630 Yonge, Toronto. T. (416) 324-9160. - Paint - *073784*
Welcome-in Gallery and Framing, 217 Queen E, Toronto. T. (416) 364-0475. - Paint - *073785*
Westmount Gallery, 4143 Dundas W, Toronto. T. (416) 239-5427. - Paint - *073786*
White, Albert, 80 Spadina Av., Toronto, Ont. M5V 2J3. T. (416) 865-1021. - Paint / Graph / Sculp / Arch / Eth / Draw - *073787*
Wild Wolves, 5 King Rd. W, Toronto. T. (905) 859-5355. - Paint - *073788*
Wildlife, 18 Birch Av., Toronto. T. (416) 922-5153. - Paint - *073789*
Windebank, Ronald, 21 Avenue Rd., Toronto. T. (416) 962-2862. - Paint - *073790*
Workscene Gallery Artists Co-Operative, 183 Bathurst, Toronto. T. (416) 362-7548. - Paint - *073791*
Wyget Woods Gallery, 20 Ride Rd., Toronto. T. (506) 854-2173. - Paint - *073792*
Wynick & Tuck, 80 Spadina Av., Toronto. T. (416) 364-8716. *073793*
Yaneff International Gallery, 119 Isabella St., Toronto, M4Y 1P2. T. (416) 924-6678. - Paint / Graph / Sculp - *073794*
Ydessa Hendeles Art Foundation, 778 King W, Toronto. T. (416) 941-9400. - Paint - *073795*
Young Fox Gallery, 209 Queen E, Toronto. T. (416) 368-2502. - Paint - *073796*
YYZ Artists Outlet, 1087 Queen W, Toronto. T. (416) 531-7869. - Paint - *073797*
Zohar, 284 Forest Hill, Toronto. T. (416) 483-4499. - Paint - *073798*
20th Century, 23 Beverley, Toronto. T. (416) 598-2172. - Paint - *073799*
291 Gallery, 80 Spadina Av., Toronto. T. (416) 364-5541. - Paint - *073800*

Vancouver (British Columbia)

Araki, 470-999 Canada Pl., Vancouver. T. (604) 641-1343. - Paint - *073801*
Art Emporium, 2928 Granville Street, Vancouver, V6H 3J7. T. (604) 738-3510. - Paint / Graph / Fra - *073802*
Art Image Gallery, 5888 Cambie, Vancouver. T. (604) 327-7554. - Paint - *073803*
Art Works Gallery, 400 Smithe, Vancouver. T. (604) 688-3301. - Paint - *073804*
Atelier Gallery, 3084 Granville St., Vancouver. T. (604) 732-3021. - Paint - *073805*
Barr, 1854 W First, Vancouver. T. (604) 732-5613. - Graph - *073806*
Bau-Xi Gallery, 3045 Granville St., Vancouver. T. (604) 733-7011. - Paint - *073807*
Berndette, 103-1200 Lonsdale N Van, Vancouver. T. (604) 980-7216. - Paint - *073808*
Bikadi, 307-876 W 16, Vancouver. T. (604) 879-8884. - Paint - *073809*
Blackmore, Jo, 3886 W 37, Vancouver. T. (604) 266-6949. - Paint - *073810*
Bond, 319 W Hastings Van, Vancouver. T. (604) 688-5227. - Paint - *073811*
Buschlen-Mowatt, 111-1445 W Georgia, Vancouver. T. (604) 682-1234. - Paint - *073812*
Cameo Framing and Gallery, 1990 W Fourth, Vancouver. T. (604) 731-4211. - Paint - *073813*
Canada West Antique Company, 3607 W Broadway, Vancouver. T. (604) 733-3212. - Paint - *073814*
Canadian Images, 308-1280 Nicola, Vancouver. T. (604) 689-4065. - Paint - *073815*
Catriona Jeffries, 304-550 Burrard, Vancouver. T. (604) 683-2415. - Paint - *073816*
Cavalier Art Galleries, 125-9040 Blundell Rmd, Vancouver. T. (604) 273-3222. - Paint - *073817*
C.C. Arts Centre, 20 E Pender, Vancouver. T. (604) 669-2601. - Paint - *073818*
Chan, 525 Main St., Vancouver. T. (604) 684-6851. - Paint - *073819*
Circle Craft Co-Op, 1666 Johnston, Vancouver. T. (604) 669-8021. - Paint - *073820*
City Art Gallery, 1112 Davie, Vancouver. T. (604) 684-6034. - Paint - *073821*
Contemporary Art Gallery, 555 Hamilton St., Vancouver, V6B 2R1. T. (604) 687-1345. *073822*

Craft House, 1386 Cartwright, Vancouver. T. (604) 687-7270. - Paint - 073823

Creekhouse, 3-1551 Johnston, Vancouver. T. (604) 681-5016. - Paint - 073824

Crown Gallery, 1017 Cambie, Vancouver. T. (604) 684-5407. - Paint - 073825

Davie Art Shop, 1242 Davie, Vancouver. T. (604) 683-3415. - Paint - 073826

Denbigh, 169 W Seventh, Vancouver. T. (604) 876-3303. - Paint - 073827

Disco Art Mart, 10-4429 Kingsway, Vancouver. T. (604) 431-9215. - Paint - 073828

Downstairs Gallery, 260-1425 Marine W Van, Vancouver. T. (604) 926-3525. - Paint - 073829

Eagle Aerie Gallery, 350 Campbell Tofino, Vancouver. T. (604) 725-3235. - Paint - 073830

Equinox Gallery, 1525 West 8th Ave., Vancouver. T. (604) 736 24 05. 073831

Executive Gallery, 4971B N Third, Vancouver. T. (604) 278-4581. - Paint - 073832

Farquhar Place Gallery, 4396 W Tenth, Vancouver. T. (604) 224-4811. - Paint - 073833

Federation of Canadian Artists, 952 Richmonds, Vancouver. T. (604) 681-8534. - Paint - 073834

First Choice Gallerie and Frame Shoppe, 144-8115 120 St., Vancouver. T. (604) 596-6010. - Paint - 073835

Folkart, 3715 W Tenth, Vancouver. T. (604) 228-1011. - Paint - 073836

Framagraphic, 1116 W Broadway, Vancouver. T. (604) 738-0017. - Paint - 073837

Frame-Your-Own, 3306 Cambie, Vancouver. T. (604) 876-5232. - Paint - 073838

Framing Experience, 4-1926 W Fourth, Vancouver. T. (604) 732-3097. - Paint - 073839

Fraser, Alex, 2027 W. 41st St., Vancouver. T. (604) 266-6010. 073840

Gallery, 2901 W Broadway, Vancouver. T. (604) 731-1214. - Paint - 073841

Gallery of B.C. Ceramics, 1359 Cartwright, Vancouver. T. (604) 669-5645. - China - 073842

Gallery 88, 6007 W Boulevard, Vancouver. T. (604) 263-4428. - Paint - 073843

Georgia Art Gallery, 3536 E Hastings, Vancouver. T. (604) 294-0100. - Paint - 073844

Grosvenor Gallery, 330-885 Dunsmuir, Vancouver. T. (604) 684-4295. - Paint - 073845

Grunt, 209 E Sixth, Vancouver. T. (604) 875-9516. - Paint - 073846

Hall of Frames, 6128 Fraser, Vancouver. T. (604) 322-4910. - Paint - 073847

Harrison, 2932 Granville St., Vancouver, B.C. V6H 3J7. T. (604) 732-5217, 732-0911. - Paint / Graph / Fra - 073848

Harrison, 2022 Park Royal, South Mall, Vancouver, B.C. VFT 1A1. T. (604) 926-2615. - Paint / Graph / Fra - 073849

Heffel, 2247 Granville St., Vancouver, B.C. V6H 3G1. T. (604) 732-6505, Fax 752-4245. 073850

Horizons West Fine Art Gallery, 2235 Granville St., Vancouver. T. (604) 732-6621. - Paint - 073851

Image Art and Framing, 9616 Cameron Bby., Vancouver. T. (604) 421-6663. - Paint - 073852

Image Frames, 7329 Kingsway Bby., Vancouver. T. (604) 522-2514. - Paint - 073853

Image Galleries, 456 W Broadway, Vancouver. T. (604) 879-7731. - Paint - 073854

Images for a Canadian Heritage, 164 Water, Vancouver. T. (604) 685-7046. - Paint - 073855

Imagistics Art Services, 403-343 Railway, Vancouver. T. (604) 687-8020. - Paint - 073856

Impressions Art Gallery and Framing, 236-9855 Austin Bby., Vancouver. T. (604) 420-7707. - Paint - 073857

In Graphic Detail, 1000 Parker, Vancouver. T. (604) 253-8311. - Graph - 073858

Inuit Gallery of Vancouver, 345 Water, Vancouver. T. (604) 688-7323. - Eth - 073859

Island Studio 1551, 1551 Duranleau, Vancouver. T. (604) 669-1551. - Paint - 073860

Kerrisdale, 8859 Selkirk, Vancouver. T. (604) 263-3253. - Paint - 073861

Kupczynski, A-2243 Granville St., Vancouver. T. (604) 734-5673. - Paint - 073862

Mammoth, 320-380 W First, Vancouver. T. (604) 872-2115. - Paint - 073863

Marcus, Richard, 320-380 W First, Vancouver. T. (604) 872-2115. - Paint - 073864

Marik, 49 Powell, Vancouver. T. (604) 689-4850. - Eth - 073865

Metrotown Gallery, 4800 Kingsway Bby., Vancouver. T. (604) 439-1626. - Paint - 073866

Mexico-Arte, 2248 W Fourth, Vancouver. T. (604) 731-5374. - Paint - 073867

Mido, 2960 W Fourth, Vancouver. T. (604) 736-1321. - Paint - 073868

Newsmall & Sterling, 1440 Old Bridge, Vancouver. T. (604) 681-6730. - Glass - 073869

Or Gallery Society, 110-314 W Hastings, Vancouver. T. (604) 683-7395. - Paint - 073870

Osterson, 113-505 Burrard, Vancouver. T. (604) 684-4585. - Paint - 073871

Pacific Picture People, 215-1080 Mainland, Vancouver. T. (604) 681-4767. - Paint - 073872

Pacific Rim Art and Design, 209-1050 Kingsway, Vancouver. T. (604) 876-6767. - Paint - 073873

Panache, 3030 Granville, Vancouver. T. (604) 732-1206. - Paint - 073874

Paperworks Gallery, 1650 Johnston, Vancouver. T. (604) 687-8914. - Graph - 073875

Park & Mason, 777 Dunsmuir, Vancouver. T. (604) 685-4438. - Paint - 073876

Petley, Jones, 2245 Granville, Vancouver. T. (604) 732-5353. - Paint - 073877

Rae, Dorian, 3151 Granville St., Vancouver. T. (604) 732-6100. - Paint - 073878

Ramsay, John, 1065 Cambie, Vancouver. T. (604) 685-5570. - Paint - 073879

Regis Pictures & Frames Fried, 5305 W. Bwd., Vancouver, V6M 3W4. T. (604) 263-4933. - Graph / Graph / Repr / Fra - 073880

Riviera Art, 2235 Granville St., Vancouver. T. (604) 732-6621. - Paint - 073881

Robinson, Frankie, 3055 Granville St., Vancouver. T. (604) 634-6568. - Paint - 073882

Rocky Mountain Art Galleries, 3060 W Broadway, Vancouver. T. (604) 734-1100. - Paint - 073883

Rogell, 323-611 Alexander, Vancouver. T. (604) 253-6672. - Paint - 073884

Sayell, Graham, 2416 Granville St., Vancouver. T. (604) 738-3521. - Paint - 073885

Scott, Marion, 671 Howe, Vancouver. T. (604) 685-1934. - Paint - 073886

Soho Art Gallery, 4534 Main, Vancouver. T. (604) 874-0032. - Paint - 073887

Terriffic Picturiffic Company, 2529 Kingsway, Vancouver. T. (604) 430-4115. - Paint - 073888

Uno Langmann, 2117 Granville St., Vancouver. T. (604) 736-8825. - Paint - 073889

Video Inn, 261 Powell, Vancouver. T. (604) 688 43 36. 073890

VP Art Studios, 396A W Fifth, Vancouver. T. (604) 872-2335. - Paint - 073891

Westbridge, 1683 Chestnut, Vancouver. T. (604) 736-1014. - Paint - 073892

Western Front, 303 E Eighth Av., Vancouver, V5T 1S1. T. (604) 876 93 43. 073893

Williams, Joyce, 346 W Pender, Vancouver. T. (604) 688-7434. - Paint - 073894

Windfish Gallery, 3632 W Fourth, Vancouver. T. (604) 738-7115. - Paint - 073895

Wynans, Frans, 7-8-550 Beatty, Vancouver. T. (604) 685-0936. - Paint - 073896

Victoria (British Columbia)

Leaf Hill Galleries Ltd., 47 Bastion Sq., Victoria. T. (604) 384-1311. - Paint / Fra - 073897

Lowe, Stephen, 637 Humboldt St., Victoria, V8W 1AG. T. (604) 384-3912. - Paint - 073898

Willowdale (Ontario)

Upstairs Gallery, 69 Banstock Dr., Willowdale, M2K 2H7. T. (416) 222-2349. - Paint / Graph / Sculp - 073899

Windsor (Ontario)

Fabry, 2451 Dougall Rd., Windsor. T. (519) 966-2078. - Paint / Graph / Repr / Sculp / Fra - 073900

Winnipeg (Manitoba)

Fleet Galleries Ltd., 173 McDermot St. E., Winnipeg, R3B 0S1. T. (204) 942-8026. - Paint / Graph / China / Sculp / Fra - 073901

Little Gallery, 396 Notre Dame, Winnipeg. - Paint / Fra - 073902

One, One, One, University of Manitoba Man., Winnipeg. T. (204) 474 95 59. 073903

Upstairs Gallery, 266 Edmonton St., Winnipeg, R3C 1R9. T. (204) 943-2734. - Paint / Graph / Eth / Draw - 073904

Winnipeg Art Gallery, 300 Memorial Blvd., Winnipeg, Man. R3C 1V1. T. (204) 786-6641, Fax 788-4998. 073905

China, Republic

Taipei

Chang, W. C., East and West Book Co. Ltd., P. O. Box 1655, Taipei. T. (02) 381-8589, Telex: 22192 Neworld. - Graph / Fra - 073906

Egyetti Ltd., 13 Lane 128 Chung Shan N. Rd., Sec. 2, P.O.Box 68-1705, Taipei. T. (02) 571-1701, 581-3624, 571-9902. - Sculp - 073907

Hwa Guan Enterprise Inc., 7, St. 26, Tien-Mou 1 Rd., P.O.Box 52-73, Taipei. T. (02) 871-8658. - Paint / Fra - 073908

Lung Men Art Gallery, Apollo Bldg., 3rd. Fl. 281-1 Chung Hsioa E Rd. Sec. 4, Taipei. T. (02) 781-3979, 781-4398, 752-9456. - Paint / Sculp / Draw - 073909

Nan In Ting Gallery, 124-11 Fulin Rd., Shihlin, Taipei. T. (02) 88 20 66. - Paint / Graph - 073910

Taiwan Variety & Novelty Supplies, 2 Alley 11, Lane 174 Sec. 2, Pa-Teh Rd., 10401 Taipei. T. (02) 771 6801, 771 8541. - Paint / Repr / Jew / Draw - 073911

Colombia

Barranquilla (Atlantico)

Quintero, Cra. 51B, 80-65, Barranquilla. T. 35 92 10. - Paint - 073912

Bogotá

Buchholz, Galeria, Calle 59-13-13, Bogotá. T. 359 558. - Sculp / Draw - 073913

Callejón, Avenida 82, No. 11-18, Bogotá. T. 256 21 20. - Paint / Graph / Graph - 073914

Casa Negret, Calle 81, 8-70, Bogotá. T. 212 00 16, 212 36 72. - Paint - 073915

La Medusa, Calle 95, No. 15-48 Apt. Aero No. 90067, Bogotá. - Paint / Sculp - 073916

„La Paleta", Museo de Reproducciones, Carrera 24, No. 53-90, Bogotá. T. 35 47 07. - Paint - 073917

Meindl, Adalbert, Carrera 7 No. 27-38, Bogotá. T. 283 16 02, 283 16 42. - Paint / Graph / Sculp - 073918

Perez, Luis, Calle 81 Nr. 8-72, Bogotá. T. 211 54 03. - Paint / Sculp - 073919

Sandiego, Carrera 7, No. 72-22, Bogotá. T. 249 51 84. 073920

Velásquez, Garcés, Carrera 5a, No 26-92 Apt. Aéreo 28936, Bogotá. T. 284 59 75, 284 55 93. - Paint / Graph / Sculp - 073921

Ibagué (Tolima)

Taller, Carrera 3 8-80, Ibagué. T. 63 35 02. - Paint - 073922

Croatia

Hlebine

Generalić, Josip, Gajeva 75, 48323 Hlebine. T. 048 836071. 073923

Czech Republic

Březnice

Městské muzeum a galerie Ludvíka Kuby, Zámek, 262 72 Březnice. T. (0306) 982153, 982453. *073924*

Brno

Dům Umění města Brna, Malinovského 2, 60107 Brno. T. (05) 242 27, 226 59. - Paint - *073925*

Ostrava

Galerie Studio Della, Dr. Smerala 5, 73067 Ostrava. T. (069) 22 65 51. *073926*

Praha

ARTIA, Ve Smečkách 30, Praha. T. (02) 24 60 41. *073927*
Galerie Centrum, ul. 28 Října, Praha. *073928*
Galerie Karolina, Železná ul., Praha. *073929*
Galerie Platýz, Národní tř 37, 100 00 Praha. T. (02) 22 43 29. - Paint / Graph / Sculp - *073930*
Galerie Vodičkova, Vodičkova ul., Praha. *073931*
Galerie Zlatá lilie, Malé nám, Praha. T. (02) 227001. - Paint / Graph / Sculp - *073932*
Peithner-Lichtenfels, Michalská 12, 11000 Praha 1. T. (02) 24227680, Fax 24227680. *073933*
Staatliche Galerie am Bethlehemsplatz, Praha. - Paint / Graph / Sculp - *073934*

Denmark

Århus (Jütland)

Nellemann & Thomsen, Skanderborgvej 104-106, 8260 Århus. T. 11 47 11. - Paint - *073935*

Charlottenlund

Grothe, Knud, Jaegersborg Allé 11, 2920 Charlottenlund. T. 31 63 53 43. - Paint - *073936*

Esbjerg

Meyer, Jyllandsgade 30, 6700 Esbjerg. T. 292 30. - Paint - *073937*

Gentofte

Galerie 93, Gentofteg. 93, 2820 Gentofte. T. 31 65 22 93. - Paint / Graph - *073938*

Hellerup

Galleri Prag, Strandvejen 114, 2900 Hellerup. T. 31 62 30 71. - Paint - *073939*

Holte

Aeblegården, Søllerødvej 15, 2840 Holte. T. 80 33 50. - Paint - *073940*
Neo-Grafik, Skovlytoften 6, 2840 Holte. T. 4245 52 02. - Paint - *073941*

Karlslunde

Edition Copenhagen, Navergangen 12, 2690 Karlslunde. T. 42 15 33 08, 42 15 23 52, Fax 42 15 38 03. - Paint - *073942*

København

A Galerie, Vesterbrog. 171, Frederiksberg, 1800 København. T. 31 23 12 65. - Paint - *073943*
Amager Kunsthandel, Amagerbrogade 247, 1000 København. T. 50 81 63. *073944*
Ambrosia, Kompagnistr. 2, 1208 København K. T. 33 32 30 48. - Paint - *073945*
Andersen, Mikael, Bregade 63, 1260 København. T. 33 33 05 12, Fax 33 15 43 93. *073946*

Asbæk, Bredgade 20, 1260 København K. T. 33154004, Fax 33131610. - Paint / Graph / Sculp / Draw - *073947*
Balderskilde Gallerie, Vermundsg. 9, 1000 København. T. 31 83 47 47. *073948*
Banks Gallery, Fiolstr. 28, 1171 København K. T. 33 14 50 62. - Paint - *073949*
Bech, Nordre Fasanvej 18, 1000 København. T. 31 86 68 55, Fax 50 18 58 80. - Paint - *073950*
Bechager, Nørre Farimagsg. 72, 1364 København. T. 33 11 01 47. *073951*
Bie & Vadstrup, Bülowsv. 7 a, Frederiksberg, 1870 København. T. 31 31 16 31. *073952*
Bilø, Arne, & Co., Gaunøvej 19, 2700 København. T. 31 60 38 60. - Paint - *073953*
Binger, Palaeg 6, 1261 København K. T. 33 14 44 56. - Paint - *073954*
Bloch, H., Strandgade 55, 1401 København K. T. 31 54 74 00. - Paint - *073955*
Bork, Store Regneg. 2, 1110 København. T. 33 93 97 71. - Paint / Graph / Sculp / Mod - *073956*
Bredgade Kunsthandel, Esplanaden 14, 1263 København. T. 33 93 50 41. - Paint / Graph / Sculp - *073957*
Bregade Kunsthandel, Bredg. 67-69, 1260 København K. T. 33 13 50 41. - Graph - *073958*
Center Art, Admiralg. 20, 1066 København K. T. 33 15 13 72. - Paint - *073959*
Chapé, Nørrebrog. 36, 1000 København. T. 31 35 90 30. - Paint - *073960*
Christensen, Børge, Solbjerg Have 17, 2000 København. T. 31 87 42 35. - Paint - *073961*
Christensen, Reinhold, Gl. Kongev. 161, 1850 København V. T. 31 23 18 37. - Paint - *073962*
Clausen, Toldbodgade 9, 1253 København K. T. 33 15 41 54. - Paint - *073963*
Connoisseur, Svanemøllevej 44, 2100 København Ø. T. 42 80 78 86. - Paint - *073964*
Darrell, Pilestr. 37, 1112 København K. T. 33 11 55 67. - Paint - *073965*
Drescher, Sølvgade 14, 1307 København K. T. 33 12 65 09. *073966*
Edeling, Gl. Mønt 39, 1117 København K. T. 33 14 17 55. - Paint / Graph / Sculp / Draw - *073967*
Falkersby, Finn Lauge, Svinget 17, 1000 København. T. 31 54 61 82. - Paint - *073968*
Galerie Admiralgade 20, Admiralg. 20, 1066 København K. T. 33 15 13 72. - Paint - *073969*
Galerie Gammel Strand, Gl. Strand 44, 1202 København K. T. 15 83 01. - Paint / Graph / Sculp - *073970*
Galerie J & B, Allégade 8, 1000 København. T. 31 22 20 20. - Paint - *073971*
Galerie Jerome, Hovedvagtsg. 2, 1103 København K. T. 33 12 47 33. - Paint - *073972*
Galerie Laaland, Rosenlundv. 1, 1000 København. T. 53 86 95 65. *073973*
Galerie Metal, Nybrog. 26, 1203 København K. T. 33 14 55 40. - Paint - *073974*
Galerie Mosede Gamle Skole, Mosede Byg. 2, 1000 København. T. 42 61 01 20. *073975*
Galerie Sankt Gertrud, Hyskenstrade 9, 1207 København K. T. 33 13 33 53. - Paint - *073976*
Galerie Victoria, St. Strandstr. 20, 1255 København K. T. 33 15 47 66. - Paint - *073977*
Galleri Knabro, Knabrostr. 15, 1210 København K. T. 33 14 25 24. - Paint - *073978*
Galleri 33, Nørrebrog. 33, 1000 København. T. 31 35 33 91. - Paint - *073979*
Galleri 99, Amagerbrog. 99, 2300 København. T. 31 55 17 30. - Paint - *073980*
Gallerihuset, Studiestr. 19, 1455 København K. T. 33 15 35 52, 33 93 69 20. - Paint - *073981*
Gerly, Vandkunsten 13, 1467 København K. T. 33 11 11 99. - Paint - *073982*
Green Art, Rosengrd. 9, 1174 København K. T. 33 11 04 05. - Paint - *073983*
Hansen, Sv., Plalaeg. 4, 1000 København. T. 33 91 00 20. - Paint - *073984*
Hartman Hansen, Ole, Vesterled 10, 1000 København. T. 29 11 02. - Paint - *073985*
Heede & Moestrup, Gothersgade 29, 1123 København K. T. 33146474, Fax 33143499. - Paint / Graph / Sculp - *073986*
Hjarsbaek, Poul, Sankt Kongensg. 32, 1264 København K. T. 33 12 95 74. - Paint - *073987*
Hjortberg, J.K., Classensg. 36, 1000 København. T. 26 00 95. - Paint - *073988*
Horsten Antique, Holbergsgade 11, 1057 København K. T. 33 12 79 29. - Paint - *073989*
Husets Galleri, Rådhusstraede 13, 1466 København K. T. 33 14 26 65, 33 13 59 49. - Ant / Paint - *073990*
Jensen, Pilestr. 47, 1112 København K. T. 33 11 70 67. - Paint - *073991*
Krog, Peter, Bredg. 4, 1260 København. T. 33 12 45 55. *073992*
Kunstkredsen for Grafik og Skulptur, Gl. Strand 44, 1202 København K. T. 15 83 01. - Paint - *073993*
Kvindegalleriet, Bådsmandsstr. 43, 1000 København. T. 31 95 10 92. - Paint - *073994*
Larsen, Vald., Aboul. 21, 1000 København. T. 31 37 10 00. - Paint - *073995*
Limkilde, T., Bredg. 28, 1260 København K. T. 33 13 17 91. - Paint - *073996*
Lithoart Galerie, Ordrupv. 103, 1000 København. T. 31 64 44 26. *073997*
Mortensen, Chr. Winthersv. 25A, 1860 København V. T. 31 31 48 90. - Paint - *073998*
Nielsen, Ruth Aargaard, Vendsysselv. 11, 1000 København. T. 87 53 07. - Paint - *073999*
Österbro's Kunsthandel, Viborggade 2, 1000 København. T. OB 907. *074000*
O.P. Reproduktioner-Posters, Strøget Nyg. 6, 1000 København. T. 14 94 78. - Paint - *074001*
Ottesen, Susanne, Gothersgade 49, 1264 København K. T. 33 15 52 44. - Paint / Graph / Sculp - *074002*
Oxe, Peder, Gråbrødretorv 8, 1000 København. T. 33 13 17 73. - Paint - *074003*
Palmer, Folke Bernadottesallé 31, 1000 København. T. 33 14 11 21. - Paint - *074004*
Palsager, Allan, Nørre Farimagsg. 72, 1364 København K. T. 11 01 47. - Paint - *074005*
Point, Alicia, Dr. Abildgaardsallé 15, 1955 København V. T. 31 35 81 09. - Paint - *074006*
Rubin & Magnussen, Ll. Kirkestr. 3, 1072 København K. T. 33 12 44 80. - Paint - *074007*
Sander, Gl. Kongev. 82, 1850 København V. T. 31 24 84 68. - Paint - *074008*
Scannex Art, Købmagerg. 50, 1004 København K. T. 33 14 76 80. - Paint / Graph / Repr / Fra - *074009*
Søvaenget, Vesterlundv. 55, 1000 København. T. 86 83 70 00. *074010*
Stalke, Vesterbrog. 15 a, 1620 København. T. 31 21 15 33. *074011*
Stoltze, Inger, Hellerupv. 41, 1000 København. T. 31 61 18 42. *074012*
Tiro, Store Strandstr. 21, 1255 København K. T. 33 91 41 31. - Paint - *074013*
Trap, Vesterbrogade 111, 1620 København V. T. 31 31 90 38. - Paint - *074014*
Vendsborg, Skt. Pedersstr. 27, 1453 København K. T. 12 19 26. - Paint - *074015*
Weinberger, Galleri, Valkendorfsg. 13, 1151 København K. T. 33 93 45 44, Fax 33 93 45 49. - Paint - *074016*
Zeidler, Elin, Store Kongensgade 14, 1264 København K. T. 12 64 86. - Paint - *074017*
Zenit Galleri, Sølvgade 22, 1307 København K. T. 33 11 44 31. - Paint - *074018*

Lyngby (Kopenhagen)

Bunch, Lyngby Torv 5, 2800 Lyngby. T. 42 88 19 83. - Paint - *074019*

Nykøbing

Catalpa, Kongensg. 19, 4800 Nykøbing F. T. 54 85 98 46. - Paint / Graph / Draw - *074020*

Odense

Aigens, Ingvar, Munkerisvej 41, 5230 Odense. - Paint - *074021*
Galleri Torso, Vintapperstr. 57, 5000 Odense C. T. 6613 4466, 6594 2495, Fax 6594 1095. - Paint / Graph / Sculp - *074022*
Kunsthallen Brandts Klaedefabrik, Brandts Passage 37, 5000 Odense. T. 66137897, Fax 66137310. *074023*
Westing Galerie, Dronningensgade 19, 5000 Odense. T. 11 46 47. - Paint / Graph / Sculp - *074024*

Rebild pr. Skorping
Roldjoj, 9520 Rebild pr. Skorping. T. 39 12 62. - Paint /
Graph - 074025

Roskilde
Galleri Sankt Agnes, Sankt Olsgade 7, 4000 Roskilde.
T. 42 36 88 74. - Paint - 074026

Rungsted Kyst
Wiin, Sophienbergvej 61, 2960 Rungsted Kyst.
T. 57 04 02. - Paint - 074027

Silkeborg
Galerie Moderne, Torvet 1, 8600 Silkeborg. T. 82 31 05.
- Paint / Graph - 074028
Søvaenget, Vesterlundvej 55, 8600 Silkeborg.
T. 83 70 00. - Paint - 074029

Soendersoe
Doré, Vestergade 16, 5471 Soendersoe.
T. 841 050. 074030

Sorø
Stubtoft, Søgade 6, 4180 Sorø. T. 63 37 36.
- Paint - 074031

Vedbaek
Hotel Marina, Vedbaeck Strandvej 391, 2950 Vedbaek.
T. 89 17 11. 074032

Egypt

Cairo (El Qahira)
L'Atelier du Care, 2, rue Karim el Dawla, nr. Groppies,
Cairo. - Paint / Graph - 074033

El Salvador

México (D.F.)
Editiones de Obras Seriadas S.A. de C.V., Moliere 48,
Me'1xico. T. (05) 2028708, 2029547. 074034
Galeria de Arte Contemporaneo, Montes Urales Sur 780,
Me'1xico. T. (05) 2028588. 074035
Galeria de Pinturas, Hamburgo 165B, 06600 Me'1xico.
T. (05) 2071848, 2077934. 074036
Galeria Rodriguez Caramaza, Horacio 1132, 11560 Mé-
xico. T. (05) 2503737. 074037
Galeria 930, Homero 930, 11560 México.
T. (05) 5311813, 5311241. 074038

Finland

Helsinki (Uudenmaan lääni)
Artegrafica, Museokatu 3, 00100 Helsinki.
T. (09) 442 072, Fax 499 898. - Paint / Graph / Fra /
Mod / Draw - 074039
Bronda, Kasarmikatu 44, 00130 Helsinki.
T. (09) 626 494. 074040
City Galleria, Iso Roobertinkatu 3, 00120 Helsinki.
T. (09) 60 55 64, 60 76 69. 074041
D'Arte, Aleksanterinkatu 19, 00100 Helsinki.
T. (09) 63 10 50, Fax 37 32 69. 074042
Donner, Merikatu 1, 00140 Helsinki.
T. (09) 66 45 47. 074043
Forsblom, Kaj, Bulevardi 22 B, 00120 Helsinki.
T. (09) 64 02 11, Fax 64 88 55. 074044
Galerie Artek, Pohj. Esplanadi 25b, 00100 Helsinki.
T. (09) 66 99 89. - Paint / Graph / Repr / Sculp - 074045
Galerie Oljemark, Sandelsinkatu 10, 00260 Helsinki.
T. (09) 49 36 39. 074046
Galleria Kokko, Lapinlahdenkatu 12, 00180 Helsinki.
T. (09) 694 08 64. 074047
Galleria Sculptor, Yrjönkatu 11, 00120 Helsinki.
T. (09) 64 69 03, 64 92 77. 074048
Hörhammer, Yrjönkatu 31, 001 00 Helsinki.
T. (09) 694 47 44. - Paint / Graph - 074049
Kellarigalleria, Fredrikinkatu 49, 00100 Helsinki.
T. (09) 60 71 17. 074050

Kluuvin, Unioninkatu 28 B, 00100 Helsinki.
T. (09) 169 2411. 074051
Lindblom, Martti, Töölönkatu 8, 00260 Helsinki.
T. (09) 40 83 36, 40 91 16. 074052
Mikkola & Rislakki, Tollberginkatu 1E1 pl 54, 00181 Hel-
sinki. T. (09) 613 33 33, Fax 613 33 33. 074053
Munkinseudun Galleria, Ulvilantie 9, 00350 Helsinki.
T. (09) 55 81 54. 074054
Pikasso, Caloniuksenkatu 6c, 00100 Helsinki.
T. (09) 40 76 45. 074055
Pinx, Tunturikatu A 19, 00100 Helsinki. T. (09) 493 615.
- Paint / Graph / Sculp - 074056
Seven Art, Yrjönkatu 27-29, 00100 Helsinki.
T. (09) 694 98 69. 074057
Strindberg, Sven P., Esplanaadikatu 33, 00100 Helsinki.
T. (09) 62 55 81, 62 84 04. - Paint / Graph / Sculp /
Fra - 074058
Taide Art, Bulevardi 5, 00120 Helsinki.
T. (09) 640 567. 074059
Taidekauppa P. Grahn, Kalevankatu 16, 00100 Helsinki.
T. (09) 60 50 77. - Paint - 074060
Taidemaalariliiton Galleria, Fabianinkatu 4, 00130 Hel-
sinki. T. (09) 66 02 31. 074061

Jämsä (Keski-Suomen lääni)
Valkama, Jorma-Tapio, Kämmekkäpolku 25, 42100
Jämsä. T. (014) 2744. 074062

Jyväskylä (Keski-Suomen lääni)
Galleria Sirius, Asemakatu 9, 40100 Jyväskylä.
T. (014) 61 09 06. 074063
Keski-Suomen Taidegalleria, Kauppakatu 41b, 40100
Jyväskylä. T. (014) 61 20 11. 074064
Kulta Galleria Ailio, Kauppakatu 27, 40100 Jyväskylä.
T. (014) 61 50 51. 074065

Kajaani (Oulun lääni)
Sisustus Artsi, Valikatu 19, 87100 Kajaani.
T. (08) 27223. 074066

Kosula (Kuopion lääni)
Ateljee Karhuluostari, Kosula. T. (017) 75 32 17. 074067

Kouvola (Kymen lääni)
Galleria 5, Salpausselänkatu 28, 45100 Kouvola.
T. (05) 10783. 074068

Kuopio (Kuopion lääni)
Galleria Preesens, Hapelähteenkatu 5, 70100 Kuopio.
T. (017) 14 24 15. 074069
Kuopion Taidegalleria, Kuninkaankatu 27, 70100 Kuopio.
T. (017) 12 13 41. 074070
Lotta Galleria, Minna Canthinkatu 23, 70100 Kuopio.
T. (017) 11 97 36. - Paint - 074071
Ramun Kehys, Suokatu 9, 70100 Kuopio.
T. (017) 11 57 16. 074072

Lahti (Hämeen lääni)
Galleria Nuovo, Mariankatu 16, 15110 Lahti.
T. (03) 21 03 77. 074073
Häme-Galleria, Hämeenkatu 26, 15140 Lahti.
T. (03) 10 22 65. 074074
Kotitaidenäyttely Halmeila, Vuorikatu 20a, 15110 Lahti.
T. (03) 51 70 81. 074075
Simolan Taide ja Kehys, Hollolankatu 10, 15110 Lahti.
T. (03) 43318. 074076

Laukaa (Keski-Suomen lääni)
Laukaan Taidekeskus Art-Gallerie, Laukaantie 16,
41340 Laukaa. T. (014) 83 16 17. 074077

Leppävirta (Mikkelin lääni)
Komet, 79100 Leppävirta. T. (017) 40486. 074078

Lohja (Uudenmaan lääni)
Galleria Taide Apaja, Sammonkatu 11, 08100 Lohja.
T. (019) 14994. 074079

Oulu (Oulun lääni)
Auran Galleria, Tuureporinkatu 12, 90100 Oulu.
T. (08) 33 34 52. 074080
Bellarte Taidesalonki, L Rantakatu 5, 90100 Oulu.
T. (08) 33 62 00. 074081

Pori (Turun ja Porin lääni)
Galleria Taide-Eloranta, Yrjönkatu 25, 28130 Pori.
T. (03) 41 22 50. 074082

Raahe (Oulun lääni)
Neliö-Galleria, Ouluntie 26, 92100 Raahe.
T. (08) 22 01 00. 074083

Raisio (Turun ja Porin lääni)
Raision Taidegalleria, Kauppakatu 1, 21200 Raisio.
T. (02) 78 52 65. 074084

Riihimäki (Hämeen lääni)
Taula ja Kehys, Hämeenkatu 6, 11100 Riihimäki, 11100.
- Paint / Fra - 074085

Rovaniemi (Lapin lääni)
Lapin Taulu- ja Kehysliike, Kansankatu 4, 96100 Rovaniemi. T. (016) 31 29 97. 074086

Sysmä (Mikkelin lääni)
Vanha Kerttu, Sysmäntie 29, 19700 Sysmä.
T. (014) 171717. 074087

Tampere (Hämeen lääni)
Art Leonardo, Hämeenkatu 19, 33200 Tampere.
T. (03) 14 00 30. 074088
Galleria Saskia, Kauppakatu 14a, 33210 Tampere.
T. (03) 30812. 074089
Lepokorpi, Juhani, Pajapuronkatu 6, 33820 Tampere.
T. (03) 65 40 44. 074090
Nyström, Rautatienkatu 15, 33100 Tampere.
T. (03) 23 66 56. 074091
Pyhältö, Ipi & Pekka, Tuuliikinkatu 17, 33730 Tampere.
T. (03) 64 66 41. 074092
Taidegalleria Grafiikka, Rautatienkatu 15, 33100 Tampe-
re. T. (03) 36656. 074093
Taidegrafiikka & Sisustus, Pajupuronkatu 6, 33100 Tam-
pere. T. (03) 65 40 44. 074094
Taldesalonki Husa, Hämeenkatu 18 IV kerros, Tampere.
T. (03) 289 42. - Paint / Graph / Sculp - 074095

Tornio (Lapin lääni)
Raja-Galleria, Saarenpäänkatu 39, 95430 Tornio.
T. (016) 40897. 074096

Turku (Turun ja Porin lääni)
Art-Idee, Kauppiaskatu 16, 20100 Turku.
T. (02) 31 90 88. 074097
Auran Galleria, Tuureporinkatu 12, 20100 Turku.
T. (02) 33 34 52. 074098
Bellarte Taidesalonki, Läntinen Rantakatu 5, 20100 Tur-
ku. T. (02) 33 62 00. 074099
Brahen Galleria, Linnankatu 3a, 20110 Turku.
T. (02) 31 55 83. 074100
Forsblom, Kaj, Yliopistokatu 10, 20110 Turku.
T. (02) 31 16 14, Fax 51 51 71. 074101
Galerie Grafiart, Yliopistonkatu 10, 20110 Turku.
T. (02) 31 16 14. 074102
Galerie Titanik, Itainen Rantakatu 8, 20000 Turku.
T. (02) 62 33 90. 074103
Gallerie 1, Aurakatu 1, 20100 Turku.
T. (02) 50 01 26. 074104
Nurmi, J.A., Kristiinankatu 6, 20000 Turku.
T. (02) 51 16 33. 074105
Rantagalleria, Läntinen Rantakatu 27, 20100 Turku.
T. (02) 33 39 69. 074106
Turun Taidesalonki, Kauppiaskatu 16, 20100 Turku.
T. (02) 31 90 88. 074107
Villa Carlo Taidetalo, Ruissalo 41, 20100 Turku.
T. (02) 58 90 72. 074108
Villa Roman Ateljeet, Ruissalo 63, 20100 Turku.
T. (02) 58 90 25. 074109

Vaasa/Vasa (Vaasan lääni)
Art Amy Galerie, Vaasanpuistikko 18, 65100 Vaasa/Va-
sa. T. (06) 17 48 66. 074110
Puisto Galleria, Hovioikeudenpuistikko 5, 65100 Vaasa/
Vasa. T. (06) 11 01 13. 074111
Taide- ja Kehysliike, Kauppapuistikko 8, 65100 Vaasa/
Vasa. T. (06) 12 05 95. 074112

Vantaa (Uudenmaan lääni)
Myy-Galleria, Löydöspolku 2c, 01600 Vantaa.
T. (09) 53 13 12. 074113

France

Agde (Hérault)
Monnet, C., 5 Av Victor Hugo, 34300 Agde.
T. 0467211307.   *074114*

Agen (Lot-et-Garonne)
Artothèque, 28 Rue Richard-Coeur-de-Lion, 47000
Agen. T. 0553474429.   *074115*
Brodoux, Germaine, 70 Rue Montesquieu, 47000 Agen.
T. 0553663067.   *074116*
Galerie Anton, 87 Rue Montesquieu, 47000 Agen.
T. 0553474070.   *074117*

Agon-Coutainville (Manche)
Galerie des Arts, 4bis Rue Alexis-Lemoine, 50230 Agon-
Coutainville. T. 0233457397.   *074118*

Aigues-Mortes (Gard)
Galerie Z, 4 Pl Saint-Louis, 30220 Aigues-Mortes.
T. 0466536198. - China / Glass -   *074119*
Jardins o Soleil, 17 Rue République, 30220 Aigues-Mor-
tes. T. 0466538825.   *074120*

Aiguillon (Lot-et-Garonne)
Galerie du Château, Cours Alsace-Lorraine, 47190 Aiguillon. T. 0553881811.   *074121*

Aix-en-Provence (Bouches-du-Rhône)
Amis des Arts, 26 Cours Mirabeau, 13100 Aix-en-Pro-
vence. T. 0442267144.   *074122*
Art'Hélios, Villa Magbelle-Roquefavour, CD 65, Les Mil-
les, 13100 Aix-en-Provence. T. 0442244499,
Fax 0442397987.   *074123*
Bleue comme une Orange, 45 Rue Mignet, 13100 Aix-
en-Provence. T. 0442234763.   *074124*
Casadisagne, 2 Rue Jaubert, 13100 Aix-en-Provence.
T. 0442219785.   *074125*
Des Chevalets Un Poète, 6110 Rte Avignon-Puyricard,
Lignane, 13090 Aix-en-Provence.
T. 0442923110.   *074126*

Féraud, Suzanne, 7 Rue Loubon, 13100 Aix-en-Proven-
ce. T. 0442965392.   *074127*
Galerie du Festival, 24 Rue Gaston-de-Saporta, 13100
Aix-en-Provence. T. 0442234253,
Fax 0442216030.   *074128*
Galerie Lacydon, 14 Rue Emeric-David, 13100 Aix-en-
Provence. T. 0442272200.   *074129*
Galerie Manuel, 4 Rue Manuel, 13100 Aix-en-Provence.
T. 0442275940.   *074130*
Galerie Montigny, 19 Rue Lucas-de-Montigny, 13100
Aix-en-Provence. T. 0442965152,
Fax 0442232892.   *074131*
Galerie Parallèle, 1 Rue Matheron, 13100 Aix-en-Pro-
vence. T. 0442960874.   *074132*
Galerie Portalis, 28 Rue Portalis, 13100 Aix-en-Proven-
ce. T. 0442932066.   *074133*
Galerie Ramus, 10 Pl Ramus, 13100 Aix-en-Provence.
I. 0442260795.   *074134*
Galerie Susini, 19 Cours Sextius, 13100 Aix-en-Proven-
ce. T. 0442273529.   *074135*
Moscato, Simone, 22 Rue Gaston de Saporta, 13100
Aix-en-Provence. T. 0442210751.   *074136*
Passé Présent, 23 Rue Couronne, 13100 Aix-en-Proven-
ce. T. 0442263844.   *074137*
Piluso, Karina, 30 Rue Puits-Neuf, 13100 Aix-en-Pro-
vence. T. 0442239430.   *074138*

Aix-les-Bains (Savoie)
Aixessoires, 6 Rue Casino, 73100 Aix-les-Bains.
T. 0479884801.   *074139*
Art'Image Galerie, 5 Rue Casino, 73100 Aix-les-Bains.
T. 0479615250.   *074140*

Ajaccio (Corse)
Artco, 9 Rue Notre-Dame, 20000 Ajaccio.
T. 0495510720.   *074141*
Bassoul, 4 Cours Grandval, 20000 Ajaccio.
T. 0495214050. - Paint / Fra -   *074142*
Convergences, 6 Rue Roi-de-Rome, 20000 Ajaccio.
T. 0495214140.   *074143*

Galerie, 27 Cours Napoléon, 20000 Ajaccio.
T. 0495214747. - Paint / Graph -   *074144*
Galerie du Point à la Ligne, 20 Rue Bonaparte, 20000
Ajaccio. T. 0495510583.   *074145*
Galerie Regard, 55 Rue Cardinal-Fesch, 20000 Ajaccio.
T. 0495510402. - Paint / Graph / Repr / Dec -   *074146*

Albertville (Savoie)
Bottini, Marie-France, 9 Rue Félix-Chautemps, 73200
Albertville. T. 0479328240.   *074147*

Albi (Tarn)
Art Cadre, 9 Pl Archevêché, 81000 Albi. T. 0563471004.
- Paint / Furn / Repr / Fra -   *074148*
Centre d'Art Cimaise et Portique, 8 Rue Jules-Verne,
81000 Albi. T. 0563471423, Fax 0563541310. *074149*
Dutilleul, 25 Pl Sainte-Cécile, 81000 Albi.
I. 0563544864, Fax 0563472041.   *074150*
Forum des Images, 12 Lices Georges-Pompidou, 81000
Albi. T. 0563548333, Fax 0563548696.   *074151*
Galerie d'Accueil du Vieil Alby, 11 Rue Plancat, 81000
Albi. T. 0563540457.   *074152*
Nadine'Art, 13 Rue Puech-Bérenguier, 81000 Albi.
T. 0563389876.   *074153*
Tableau de Bord, 2 Rue Croix-Blanche, 81000 Albi.
T. 0563384930.   *074154*

Alençon (Orne)
Goupil, Jacques, 34 Rue Granges, 61000 Alençon.
T. 0233266329.   *074155*

Alès (Gard)
Galerie L'Arche, 9 Rue Albert-1er, 30100 Alès.
T. 0466528236.   *074156*

Amboise (Indre-et-Loire)
Galerie La Martinerie, 7 Rampe Château, 37400 Amboise. T. 0547573751.   *074157*

Amélie-les-Bains-Palalda (Pyrénées-Orientales)
Espace Beaulieu, 43bis Rue Thermes, 66110 Amélie-les-Bains-Palalda. T. 0468839549. - Paint - 074158
Orangerie, 71 Av Vallespir, 66110 Amélie-les-Bains-Palalda. T. 0468398262. - Paint - 074159

Amiens (Somme)
Art Dufour, 24 Rue Dusevel, 80000 Amiens.
T. 0322918565, Fax 0322925879. 074160
Boiservice, 11 Rue Henriette-Dumuin, 80000 Amiens.
T. 0322913069. 074161
Café Saint-Michel, 22 Rue Metz-l'Evêque, 80000
Amiens. T. 0322713217. 074162
Euridice, 14 Rue Cormont, 80000 Amiens.
T. 0322923513. 074163
Fardel, 3 Pl Aguesseau, 80000 Amiens.
T. 0322979701. 074164
Martelle, 3 Rue Vergeaux, 80000 Amiens.
T. 0322920376. 074165
Sergeant, Hubert, 16 Rue Cormont, 80000 Amiens.
T. 0322925913. 074166
Vent et Marées Expo, 12 Rue Majots, 80000 Amiens.
T. 0322929979. 074167

Ancenis (Loire-Atlantique)
Cuisnier, Génica, 61 Rue Aristide-Briand, 44150 Ancenis. T. 40988021. 074168

Ancy-le-Franc (Yonne)
Lerein, Guy, Rue Arbres, 89160 Ancy-le-Franc.
T. 0386751005. 074169

Andernos-les-Bains (Gironde)
Galerie L'Estey, 153 Blvd République, 33510 Andernos-les-Bains. T. 0556822308. 074170

Angers (Maine-et-Loire)
Atelier, 9 Rue Toussaint, 49100 Angers. T. 41887410.
- Paint / Graph / Draw - 074171

Angoulême (Charente)
Fond Régional d'Art Contemporain (F.R.A.C.), 15 Rue
Cloche-Verte, 16000 Angoulême. T. 0545928701,
Fax 0545959416. 074172
Galerie d'Argence, 19 Rue Tison-d'Argence, 16000 Angoulême. T. 0545951582, Fax 0545697436. 074173
Galerie Marengo, 26 Pl Marengo, 16000 Angoulême.
T. 0545950149. 074174
Galerie M.R., 38 Rue Genève, 16000 Angoulême.
T. 0545929014, Fax 0545947404. 074175

Annecy (Haute-Savoie)
Art'Chipel, 24 Pl Sainte-Claire, 74000 Annecy.
T. 0450456525. 074176
Chabanian-le-Baron, 20 Rue Perrière, 74000 Annecy.
T. 0450457842, Fax 0450457846. 074177
Galerie Le Sagittaire, 9 Rue Royale, 74000 Annecy.
T. 0450450023. 074178
Galerie Nemours, 1 Passage Nemours, 74000 Annecy.
T. 0450457113. 074179
Galerie Voyage de l'Oeil, 29 Rue Vaugelas, 74000 Annecy. T. 0450451652. 074180
Losserand, Jacques, 4 Rue Camille-Dunant, 74000 Annecy. T. 0450512687, Fax 0450511408. 074181
Mélanson, Chantal, 10 Passage Cathédrale, 74000 Annecy. T. 0450452278. 074182
Nadir, 15 Rue Filaterie, 74000 Annecy.
T. 0450452060. 074183

Annemasse (Haute-Savoie)
Villa du Parc Centre d'Expositions, 12 Rue Genève,
74100 Annemasse. T. 0450388461,
Fax 0450872892. 074184

Annonay (Ardèche)
Art et Fact, 13 Rue Franki-Kramer, 07100 Annonay.
T. 0475697409. 074185
Méaux-Rougemont, Andrée, 7 Rue Recluzière, 07100
Annonay. T. 0475335147. 074186

Antibes (Alpes-Maritimes)
Atelier 13, 13 Av Grand-Cavalier, 06600 Antibes.
T. 0493345205. 074187

Fil d'Ariane, 25 Cours Masséna, 06600 Antibes.
T. 0493345119. 074188
Galerie d'Art Albert-1er, 7 Blvd Albert-1er, 06600 Antibes. T. 0493348669. - Paint - 074189
Galerie Fersen, 27 Rue De Fersen, 06600 Antibes.
T. 0493342517. - Paint / Graph / Cur / Draw - 074190
Galerie Les Cyclades, 18 Rue Petit-Four, 06600 Antibes.
T. 0493349620, Fax 0493342114. 074191
Pams, Geneviève & Jean-Marie, 25 Cours Masséna,
06600 Antibes. 074192
Urbani, Claude, 11 Imp Aubernon, 06600 Antibes.
T. 0493344256. 074193

Arc-et-Senans (Doubs)
Galerie des Salines Royales, 33 Grande Rue, 25610 Arc-et-Senans. T. 0381574108. 074194

Arcachon (Gironde)
Galerie Art Addict, 209 Blvd Plage, 33120 Arcachon.
T. 0556830372. 074195
Galerie Art's Painting, 193 Blvd Plage, 33120 Arcachon.
T. 0556830241. 074196
Galerie d'Art, 193 Blvd Plage, 33120 Arcachon.
T. 0556837251. 074197
Galerie Grangilles, 276bis Blvd Plage, 33120 Arcachon.
T. 0556830642. 074198
Galerie 17, 17 Rue Maréchal-de-Lattre-de-Tassigny,
33120 Arcachon. T. 0556832931. 074199
Héraud, Patrick, 209 Blvd Plage, 33120 Arcachon.
T. 0556832409. 074200
Thomas-Dubarry, 282 Blvd Plage, 33120 Arcachon.
T. 0556834382. 074201

Argenteuil (Val-d'Oise)
Lelong, 98ter Blvd Héloise, 95100 Argenteuil.
T. 0130769293, Fax 0130769490. 074202

Arles (Bouches-du-Rhône)
Galerie Réattu, 2 Rue Réattu, 13200 Arles.
T. 0490932496. 074203
Galerie Saint-Jean-Chrysmart, 1 Pl Constantin, 13200
Arles. T. 0490937824. 074204
Galerie 13, 1 Pl Docteur-Félix-Rey, 13200 Arles.
T. 0490933212. 074205
Rose des Vents, 18 Rue Diderot, 13200 Arles.
T. 0490961585. - Paint - 074206

Armentières (Nord)
Legrand, Nadine, 21 Rue Jean-Jaurès, 59280 Armentières. T. 0320774451. - Paint - 074207

Arromanches-les-Bains (Calvados)
Mézerac, Arnaud de, 22 Rue Maréchal-Joffre, 14117 Arromanches-les-Bains. T. 0231921305. 074208

Arzon (Morbihan)
Atelier, 55 Rue Fontaines, 56640 Arzon. T. 0297537073.
- Paint - 074209
Main d'Or, 7 Quai Voiliers, Bât E, 56640 Arzon.
T. 0297537305. 074210

Asnières-sur-Seine (Hauts-de-Seine)
Atelier 182, 182 Rue Bourguignons, 92600 Asnières-sur-Seine. T. 0141320203. 074211

Aubais (Gard)
Nick, H. & D., Chemin Gardie, 30250 Aubais.
T. 0466802363, Fax 0466802364. - China /
Glass - 074212

Aubervilliers (Seine-Saint-Denis)
Aladjem, Sabitaï, 27 Rue Henri-Barbusse, 93300 Aubervilliers. T. 0148331254. 074213

Aubusson (Creuse)
A. C. T. A. L. Picturemass, 1 Pl Maurice-Dayras, 23200
Aubusson. T. 0555838628. 074214

Aucamville (Tarn-et-Garonne)
Temps Lumière, 5 Rue Vent-Autan, 82600 Aucamville.
T. 0563025614. 074215

Auge-Saint-Médard (Charente)
Scheurer Pajot, Patrick, Le Bourg Auge, 16170 Auge-Saint-Médard. T. 0545216328. 074216

Augea (Jura)
Mathieu Coron, Andrée, Chemin Château, 39190 Augea.
T. 0384489192. 074217

Augny (Moselle)
Deporama, 2 Rue Orly, 57157 Augny.
T. 0387383948. 074218

Auray (Morbihan)
Foch, 2 Rue Maréchal-Foch, 56400 Auray.
T. 0297241711. 074219
Vent de Soleil, 17 Rue Château, 56400 Auray.
T. 0297566911. 074220

Aurillac (Cantal)
Cadres Décors, 4 Rue Forgerons, 15000 Aurillac.
T. 0471485901. 074221
Caseneuve, Christiane, 20 Rue Fargues, 15000 Aurillac.
T. 0471488531. 074222
Didier, Marty, 10 Pl Square, 15000 Aurillac.
T. 0471648166. 074223

Autun (Saône-et-Loire)
Bailly, Gabrielle, 12 Petite-Rue-Chauchien, 71400 Autun. T. 0385526960. 074224
Richen, Philippe, Pass Couvert, 71400 Autun.
T. 0385522457. 074225

Auxerre (Yonne)
Arc en Ciel, 41 Rue Paris, 89000 Auxerre.
T. 0386522978, Fax 0386521534. 074226

Auxonne (Côte-d'Or)
Vuillemot-Morel, Jean-Marc, 8 Rue Redoutey, 21130
Auxonne. T. 0380373251, Fax 0380373688.
- Paint - 074227

Avallon (Yonne)
Atrium IV, 28 Rue Saint-Martin, 89200 Avallon.
T. 0386344762. 074228

Avignon (Vaucluse)
Agape Barbarak, 74 Rue Lices, 84000 Avignon.
T. 0490852518. 074229
Ardéco, Rue Escaliers-Sainte-Anne, 84000 Avignon.
T. 0490857525. 074230
Calades, 41 Rue Joseph-Vernet, 84000 Avignon.
T. 0490868221, Fax 0490868221. 074231
Charton, Roland, 15 Rue des Trois-Faucons, 84000 Avignon. T. 0490823979. 074232
Dionée, 37 Rue Bonneterie, 84000 Avignon.
T. 0490852563. 074233
Kouyaté, 25 Av Monclar, 84000 Avignon.
T. 0490854015, Fax 0490854114. 074234
Marina, 14 Rue Campane, 84000 Avignon.
T. 0490861381. 074235
Mesme, 18 Rue Balance, 84000 Avignon.
T. 0490863743. 074236
Sardinoux, Pierre, 15 Pl Crillon, 84000 Avignon.
T. 0490868760. 074237
Tempora Galerie, 43 Rue Vieux-Sextier, 84000 Avignon.
T. 0490823531. 074238

Avranches (Manche)
Galerie Doublet, 61 Rue Constitution, 50300 Avranches.
T. 0233580391. 074239

Azay-le-Rideau (Indre-et-Loire)
Corps de Garde, 4 Rue Château, 37190 Azay-le-Rideau.
T. 0547454065. 074240
Guéguen, Alain, 116 Rte Langeais, 37190 Azay-le-Rideau. T. 0547453244, Fax 0547454502. 074241

Bages (Aude)
Etang d'Art, Rue Ancien-Puits, 11100 Bages.
T. 0468428111. 074242

Bagnères-de-Bigorre (Hautes-Pyrénées)
Atelier Renaissance, 10 Blvd Carnot, 65200 Bagnères-de-Bigorre. T. 0562954375. 074243

Bagnères-de-Luchon (Haute-Garonne)
Oréades, 69 All Etigny, 31110 Bagnères-de-Luchon.
T. 0561790666. - Paint - 074244
Oréades, 4 Pl Mengué, 31110 Bagnères-de-Luchon.
T. 0561793830. - Paint - 074245

Bagneux (Hauts-de-Seine)
Galerie Sud, 10 Av Victor-Hugo, 92220 Bagneux.
T. 0146645211.   *074246*

Bar-le-Duc (Meuse)
P'tit Michaux, 15 Rue Minimes, 55000 Bar-le-Duc.
T. 0329456606.   *074247*

Barbizon (Seine-et-Marne)
Anabel's Galerie, 78 Grande Rue, 77630 Barbizon.
T. 0360664617, Fax 0360692396.   *074248*
Entrée des Artistes, 52 Grande Rue, 77630 Barbizon.
T. 0360692121, Fax 0360664813.   *074249*
Galerie Artès, 2 Rue 23-Août, 77630 Barbizon.
T. 0360662393.   *074250*
Galerie d'Art de Barbizon, 64 Grande Rue, 77630 Barbi-
zon. T. 0360662242.   *074251*
Galerie du Musée, 83 Grande Rue, 77630 Barbizon.
T. 0360662991.   *074252*
Galerie Got, 21 Grande Rue, 77630 Barbizon.
T. 0360692212.   *074253*
Galerie Triade, 6 Rue du 23 Août, 77630 Barbizon.
Fax (1) 60662026.   *074254*
Tarasiève, Suzanne, 10bis Rue du 23 Août, 77630 Barbi-
zon. T. 0160692312.   *074255*

Barcelonette (Alpes-de-Haute-Provence)
Briatte, Francis, Imm Les Gentianettes, 04400 Barcelonette. T. 0492813425.   *074256*

Bastia (Corse)
Artis, 21 Rue Général-Cabuccia, 20200 Bastia.
T. 0495321415.   *074257*
Galerie Catani, 7 Blvd Paoli, 20200 Bastia.
T. 0495316716, Fax 0495316716.   *074258*

Bayonne (Pyrénées-Atlantiques)
Ateliers du Cloître, 21 Rue Luc, 64100 Bayonne.
Fax 59255184.   *074259*
Galerie de la Nuit, 1 Quai Am-Jauréguiberry, 64100
Bayonne. T. 0559598707.   *074260*
Galerie Expression Artistique Marengo, 30 Rue Marengo,
64100 Bayonne. T. 0559593964.   *074261*
Grenier des Arts, 2 Rue Lafaurie-Detchepare, 64100
Bayonne. T. 0559633228.   *074262*
Jakin, 7 Quai Lesseps, 64100 Bayonne.
T. 0559551673.   *074263*

Bayonville-sur-Mad (Meurthe-et-Mosel-le)
Alvarez, Robert, Grande Rue, Manoir du Mad, 54890
Bayonville-sur-Mad. T. 0383818042.   *074264*

Bazouges-sur-le-Loir (Sarthe)
Salle d'Exposition, 9 Rue Juive, 72200 Bazouges-sur-le-
Loir. T. 0243453037.   *074265*

Beaulieu-sur-Mer (Alpes-Maritimes)
Bizet, Raymond, 1 Av Blumdell-Maples, 06310 Beaulieu-sur-Mer. T. 0493010131.   *074266*
Galerie Les Iris, 10 Blvd Maréchal-Joffre, 06310 Beaulieu-sur-Mer. T. 0493010520.   *074267*

Beaumont-en-Auge (Calvados)
Jardin des Arts, Pl Eglise, 14950 Beaumont-en-Auge.
T. 0231641919.   *074268*

Beaune (Côte-d'Or)
Bonlieu, Inès, 12 Pl La-Halle, 21200 Beaune.
T. 0380249075, Fax 0380229303.   *074269*
Galerie de l'Hôtel de Saulx, 13 Pl Fleury, 21200 Beaune.
T. 0380246834, Fax 0380242128.   *074270*
Galerie des Ducs, 6 Pl Beurre, 21200 Beaune.
T. 0380246957.   *074271*
Galerie du Cloître, 1 Rue Enfer, 21200 Beaune.
T. 0380249547.   *074272*
Galerie Titren, 3 Rue Edouard-Fraisse, 21200 Beaune.
T. 0380247807.   *074273*
Galerie 23, 23 Rue Maufoux, 21200 Beaune.
T. 0380242027.   *074274*
Lauer, Paul, 7 Rue Thiers, 21200 Beaune.
T. 0380240019, Fax 0380247366. - Paint /
Sculp -   *074275*

Beauvais (Oise)
Rueé vers l'Art, 25 Rue 27 Juin, 60000 Beauvais.
T. 0344451221. - Paint -   *074276*

Bécherel (Ille-et-Vilaine)
Galerie-Librairie Saphir, 7 Rue Fbg-Berthault, 35190 Bécherel. T. 0299668360.   *074277*

Bègles (Gironde)
Galerie Imago, 58 Av Maréchal-de-Lattre-de-Tassigny,
33130 Bègles. T. 0556493472.   *074278*

Belfort (Territoire-de-Belfort)
Cheloudiakoff, 21 Fbg France, 90000 Belfort.
T. 0384226416. - Paint / Graph / Sculp / Fra -   *074279*
Galerie Azur, 154 Av Jean-Jaurès, 90000 Belfort.
T. 0384210462. - Paint / Graph / Sculp / Fra -   *074280*
Galerie du Vieux Belfort, 8 Pl Grande-Fontaine, 90000
Belfort. T. 0384280680, Fax 0384227140. - Paint /
Graph / Fra -   *074281*
Lion d'Art, 1 Rue Etuve, 90000 Belfort.
T. 0384218446.   *074282*

Bergerac (Dordogne)
Espace Rêverie, Rte Agen, 24100 Bergerac.
T. 0553271264.   *074283*
Galerie Pictura, 33 Rue Fontaines, 24100 Bergerac.
T. 0553234816.   *074284*

Besançon (Doubs)
Barthélémy, J., 8 Rue Liberté, 25000 Besançon, BP 125,
25014 Besançon Cédex. T. 0381808031. - Paint /
Graph -   *074285*
Espace Besançon Planoise, 8 Pl 8-Septembre, 25000
Besançon. T. 0381828216, Fax 0381830617.   *074286*
Galerie des Quais, 27 Quai Strasbourg, 25000 Besan-
çon. T. 0381835957.   *074287*
Galerie du Théâtre, 12 Rue Chifflet, 25000 Besançon.
T. 0381831723, Fax 0381823934. - Paint /
Graph -   *074288*
Galerie Fauçonnet, 93 Grande Rue, 25000 Besançon.
T. 0381810877.   *074289*
Galerie La Cimaise, 10 Rue Préfecture, 25000 Besan-
çon. T. 0381810485.   *074290*
Galerie Médicis, 9 Pl Victor-Hugo, 25000 Besançon.
T. 0381828585.   *074291*
Galerie Traje, 40bis Rue Charles-Nodier, 25000 Besan-
çon. T. 0381814403.   *074292*
Mathieu, 87 Rue Belfort, 25000 Besançon.
T. 0381881907.   *074293*

Bessoncourt (Territoire-de-Belfort)
Bourquin, René, 11 Rue Eglantines, 90160 Bessoncourt.
T. 0384299395, Fax 0384299123. - Furn -   *074294*

Béthune (Pas-de-Calais)
Galerie d'Art, 169 Rue Sadi Carnot, 62400 Béthune.
T. 0321568282.   *074295*

Béziers (Hérault)
Galerie Clemenceau, 44 Av Georges-Clemenceau,
34500 Béziers. T. 0467493620,
Fax 0467493640.   *074296*
Galerie de la Madeleine, 36 Pl Madeleine, 34500 Bé-
ziers. T. 0467499494 703) 67499440.   *074297*
Galerie Vincent, 23 Rue Tourventouse, 34500 Béziers.
T. 0467283287.   *074298*
Pastre, Pierre, 24 Rue Duchartre, 34500 Béziers.
T. 0467762549, Fax 0467623929.   *074299*

Biarritz (Pyrénées-Atlantiques)
Bouscayrol, 7 Rue Cent-Gardes, 64200 Biarritz.
T. 0559241161.   *074300*
Drouet, Fabrice, 8 Av Jaulerry, 64200 Biarritz.
T. 0559246455.   *074301*
Lys de France, 1 Pl Bellevue, 64200 Biarritz.
T. 0559243465.   *074302*
Osmanthus, 6 Av Jaulerry, 64200 Biarritz.
T. 0559247004, Fax 0559249172.   *074303*

Bièvres (Essonne)
Moulin de Vauboyen, Porte de Châtillon, 91570 Bièvres.
T. 0169410121. - Paint -   *074304*

Biot (Alpes-Maritimes)
Galerie Ghiglione, 6 Chemin Bachettes, 06410 Biot.
T. 0493655560.   *074305*
Galerie International du Verre, Chemin Combes, 06410
Biot. T. 0493650300. - Glass -   *074306*
G.R.'Art Editions, 495 Blvd de la Mer, 06410 Biot.
T. 0493657414.   *074307*
Palette du Roy, 7 Rte Valbonne, 06410 Biot.
T. 0493651422.   *074308*
Pierini, Robert, 9 Chemin Plan, 06410 Biot.
T. 0493650114.   *074309*
Reflets d'Art, 18 Rue Saint-Sébastien, 06410 Biot.
T. 0493651810.   *074310*

Biscarrosse (Landes)
Galerie Municipale, 60 Av 14-Juillet, 40600 Biscarrosse.
T. 0558780320.   *074311*

Blois (Loir-et-Cher)
Art Cadre, 18 Rue Denis-Papin, 41000 Blois.
T. 0254748010.   *074312*
Blois Artistique, 3 Rue Emile-Laurens, 41000 Blois.
T. 0254785859.   *074313*
Briau, Jacques, 11 Rue Prêche, 41000 Blois.
T. 0254746780. - Paint / Sculp / Cur -   *074314*
Côté Sel Côté Cour, 5 Rue Grenier-à-Sel, 41000 Blois.
T. 0254561708.   *074315*
Marge, 2 Pl Château, 41000 Blois. T. 0254781805.
- Paint / Sculp -   *074316*

Bondy (Seine-Saint-Denis)
Picard, Jean-Dominique, 63 Av Galliéni, 93140 Bondy.
T. 0148028783.   *074317*

Bonifacio (Corse)
Galerie du Mercadial, 19 Rue Saint-Dominique, 20169
Bonifacio. T. 0495730592.   *074318*
Galerie du Mercadial, 43 Quai Comparetti, 20169 Boni-
facio. T. 0495731757.   *074319*

Bordeaux (Gironde)
Aguas, Jean Christophe, 44 Rue Leyteire, 33000 Bor-
deaux. T. 0556921483.   *074320*
A.R.P.A., 17 Rue de Candale, 33000 Bordeaux.
T. 0556918812. - Pho -   *074321*
Arrêt sur l'Image, 13 Rue Buffon, 33000 Bordeaux.
T. 0556485636, Fax 0556485639.   *074322*
Art Espace Pluriel, 16 Rue Conrad-Gaussen, 33000 Bor-
deaux. T. 0556810454, Fax 0556011417.   *074323*
Baguette de Bois, 116 Cours-Aristide-Briand, 33000
Bordeaux. T. 0556913786.   *074324*
Bako, Omar, 11 Rue Bahutiers, 33000 Bordeaux.
T. 0556526433.   *074325*
Bédélire, 249 Rue Sainte-Catherine, 33000 Bordeaux.
T. 0556314639, Fax 0557959050.   *074326*
Boeuf Galerie, 33 Rue Bouviers, 33800 Bordeaux.
T. 0556959797.   *074327*
Bouscayrol, 22 Rue Condillac, 33000 Bordeaux.
T. 0556526678.   *074328*
Dominantes, 8bis Rue Montesquieu, 33000 Bordeaux.
T. 0556810112.   *074329*
Dumont, Jean-François, 54bis Rue Ducau, 33000 Bor-
deaux. T. 0556012620.   *074330*
Dutilleul, 8 Cours Albret, 33000 Bordeaux.
T. 0556793179.   *074331*
Espace BD, 33 Pass Galerie Bordelaise, 33000 Bor-
deaux. T. 0556481109, Fax 0556446905.   *074332*
Essences Primitives, 61 Rue Borie, 33000 Bordeaux.
T. 0556512151.   *074333*
Galerie, 12 Rue Devise, 33000 Bordeaux.
T. 0556448821.   *074334*
Galerie Art Céleste, 53 Rue Ayres, 33000 Bordeaux.
T. 0556481576.   *074335*
Galerie Atelier 80, 80 Cours Martinique, 33000 Bor-
deaux. T. 0556446855.   *074336*
Galerie Condillac, 24 Rue Condillac, 33000 Bordeaux.
T. 0556790431.   *074337*
Galerie d'Art Contemporain Zographia, 62 Rue Borie,
33000 Bordeaux. T. 0556444582. - Paint / Sculp /
Draw -   *074338*
Galerie du Triangle, 1 Rue Etables, 33000 Bordeaux.
T. 0556915777.   *074339*
Galerie Interface, 105 Rue Fondaugège, 33000 Bor-
deaux. T. 0556481936. - Paint -   *074340*

Galerie L'Encadr'Heure, 20 Pl Gambetta, 33000 Bordeaux. T. 0556510801. *074341*
Galerie Le Troisième Oeil, 17 Rue des Remparts, 33000 Bordeaux. T. 0556443223, Fax 0556517455. *074342*
Galerie Plexus, 10 Rue Argentiers, 33000 Bordeaux. T. 0556818990. *074343*
Galerie St'Art, 16 Rue Ferrère, 33000 Bordeaux. T. 0556011738. *074344*
Imagine Arts Espaces Matières, 16 Rue Parlement-Sainte-Catherine, 33000 Bordeaux. T. 0556511822. *074345*
Maréchal, Roland, 5 Rue Jean-Jacques-Bel, 33000 Bordeaux. T. 0556791534, Fax 0556529406. *074346*
Mas, Yannick, 2 Pl Camille-Pelletan, 33000 Bordeaux. T. 0556917782. *074347*
Montaut, 87 Rue Course, 33000 Bordeaux. T. 0556819638. *074348*
Mosaïques, 59 Av Arès, 33200 Bordeaux. T. 0556243120. *074349*
Sarkissian, Serge, 15 Rue Devise, 33000 Bordeaux. T. 0556522957. *074350*
Tanoutamon, 58 Rue Remparts, 33000 Bordeaux. T. 0556520746. *074351*
Varga Darlet, 22 Rue Bouffard, 33000 Bordeaux. T. 0556517819. *074352*

Bouleurs (Seine-et-Marne)
Criss, Any, 8 Rue Mont, 77580 Bouleurs. T. 64637266. *074353*

Boulogne-Billancourt (Hauts-de-Seine)
Galerie de l'Ouest, 10 Rue Thiers, 92100 Boulogne-Billancourt. T. 0146216600. *074354*
Galerie Les Palettes, 101 Blvd Jean-Jaurès, 92100 Boulogne-Billancourt. T. 0149090962. *074355*

Boulogne-sur-Mer (Pas-de-Calais)
Galerie de Villiers, 10 Pl Godefroy-de-Bouillon, 62200 Boulogne-sur-Mer. T. 0321802445. *074356*

Bourg-de-Péage (Drôme)
W.H., 11 Rue Docteur-Eynard, 26300 Bourg-de-Péage. T. 0475025889, Fax 0475052310. *074357*

Bourg-en-Bresse (Ain)
Guinot, Philippe, 12 Rue Docteur-Hudellet, 01000 Bourg-en-Bresse. T. 0474236202, Fax 0474222779. *074358*

Bourges (Cher)
Coeur, Jacques, 19 Blvd Juranville, 18000 Bourges. T. 0248704077, Fax 0248706880. *074359*
Galerie d'Art Contemporain, 9 Rue Edouard-Branly, 18000 Bourges. T. 0248247870. *074360*

Bourgneuf-en-Retz (Loire-Atlantique)
Amisse-Grasset, Suzanne, Saint-Laurent, 44580 Bourgneuf-en-Retz. T. 40219521. *074361*

Brantôme (Dordogne)
Auchère-Merle, Marie-Hélène, 19 Rue Victor-Hugo, 24310 Brantôme. T. 0553058613. - Paint - *074362*

Brest (Finistère)
Art Déco Création, 20 Rue Yves-Collet, 29200 Brest. T. 0298442962. *074363*
Gilbert, P., 15 Rue Navarin, 29200 Brest. T. 0298445983. *074364*
Océane, 40 Rue Château, 29200 Brest. T. 0298443360. *074365*
Saluden, Anne, 26 Rue Traverse, 29200 Brest. T. 0298442581. - Paint - *074366*

Brie-Comte-Robert (Seine-et-Marne)
Galerie Laétitia, 102 Rue du Gén Leclerc, 77170 Brie-Comte-Robert. T. 0164050118. - Paint / Sculp - *074367*

Brive-la-Gaillarde (Corrèze)
Atelier, 10 Rue Lieutenant-Colonel-Faro, 19100 Brive-la-Gaillarde. T. 0555241530. - Paint / Graph / Fra - *074368*
Galerie Chris, 6 Rue Gambetta, 19100 Brive-la-Gaillarde. T. 0555741041, Fax 0555848878. - Paint - *074369*
Valette, Jean-Max, 34 Rue Corrèze, 19100 Brive-la-Gaillarde. T. 0555242958. - Paint / Fra - *074370*

Bruges (Gironde)
New Art 33, 76 Av Charles-de-Gaulle, 33520 Bruges. T. 0556575791, Fax 0556575792. *074371*

Bussières (Saône-et-Loire)
Château Grand Bussières, Grand Bussières, 71960 Bussières. T. 0385377962. *074372*

Cabourg (Calvados)
Duval-Wenta, Simone, 8 Av République, 14390 Cabourg. T. 0231915398. *074373*
Galerie du Chevalier, Promenade Marcel-Proust, 14390 Cabourg. T. 0231910714. *074374*

Caen (Calvados)
Boukhezer, Gérard, 33 Rue Montoir-Poissonnerie, 14000 Caen. T. 0231444938. - Paint - *074375*
Cadrerie d'Art, 5 Rue Caponière, 14000 Caen. T. 0231851106. *074376*
Leloutre, Joël, 6 Pl Jean-Letellier, 14000 Caen. T. 0231862799. *074377*
Martinot-Lagarde, Catherine, 5 Rue Maurice-Souriau, 14000 Caen. T. 0231955990. *074378*
Romain, Christian, 28 Rue Froide, 14000 Caen. T. 0231862324. *074379*

Cagnes-sur-Mer (Alpes-Maritimes)
Galerie Solidor, Pl Château, 06800 Cagnes-sur-Mer. T. 0492028505. *074380*

Cahors (Lot)
Galerie Amada, 81 Rue Château-du-Roi, 46000 Cahors. T. 0565220802. *074381*

Calais (Pas-de-Calais)
Atout Coeur, 38 Rue Royale, 62100 Calais. T. 0321965303. *074382*
Channel Scène Nationale de Calais, 13 Blvd Gambetta, 62100 Calais. T. 0321467710. *074383*
Hélios, 60 Rue Royale, 62100 Calais. T. 0321342082, Fax 0321342292. *074384*

Calvi (Corse)
Almar, Rue Millie, 20260 Calvi. T. 0495653981. *074385*

Cambrai (Nord)
Maison Falleur, 39 Rue Saint-Georges, 59400 Cambrai. T. 0327818429. - Paint - *074386*

Cannes (Alpes-Maritimes)
Alliance Copie Texte, 20 Rue Serbes, Résidence Le Gray d'Albion, 06400 Cannes. T. 0493999849. *074387*
Asquinazi, Marcel, 132 Rue d'Antibes, 06400 Cannes. T. 0493396295. *074388*
Ballester, Frédéric, Cormoran 1, 13 Rue Victor-Cousin, 06400 Cannes. T. 0492980822, Fax 0492980825. *074389*
Becker, Joachim, 7 Rue Bivouac-Napoléon, 06400 Cannes. T. 0493382048. - Paint / Graph / Sculp / Draw - *074390*
Galerie Arpe, 4 Blvd Croisette, 06400 Cannes. T. 0493391715. *074391*
Galerie Art Présent, 85bis Rue Félix-Faure, 06400 Cannes. T. 0493389013. *074392*
Galerie d'Art du Gray d'Albion, 17 Blvd Croisette, Résidence Le Gray d'Albion, 06400 Cannes. T. 0493399604, Fax 0493680531. *074393*
Galerie de Cannes, 111 Rue Antibes, 06400 Cannes. T. 0493990792. *074394*
Galerie de la Colombe, 3 Rue Notre-Dame, 06400 Cannes. T. 0493388398. *074395*
Galerie du Carlton, Blvd Croisette, 06400 Cannes. T. 0493380181. - Paint / Graph / Sculp - *074396*
Galerie Festival, 2 Rond-Point Duboys-d'Angers, 06400 Cannes. T. 0493992085. - Paint - *074397*
Galerie Vecchio, 26 Rue Commandant-André, 06400 Cannes. T. 0492980600, Fax 0492980150. *074398*
Galerie Victoria, 14 Rue Macé, 06400 Cannes. T. 0493388783. *074399*
Galerie 17, 18 Rue Macé, 06400 Cannes. T. 0492980728, Fax 0492989104. *074400*
Gantois, 105 Rue Antibes, 06400 Cannes. T. 0493385701. - Paint - *074401*

Gervis, Daniel, 24 Rue d'Antibes, 06400 Cannes. T. 0492984990, Fax 0492984993. - Paint / Graph / Sculp / Draw - *074402*
Granoff, Katia, 29 Rue Commandant-André, Résidence Villa Royale, 06400 Cannes. T. 0493396608. *074403*
Grey, 19 Rue Notre-Dame, 06400 Cannes. T. 0493685819. - Paint / Graph / China / Sculp / Tex / Draw - *074404*
Mengin, 8 Rue Florian, 06400 Cannes. T. 0493992867, Fax 0493395784. - Paint / Graph / Sculp - *074405*
Nissen, Sylvie, 58 Blvd Croisette, 06400 Cannes. T. 0493387040. - Paint / Sculp / Cur - *074406*
Robin, 101 Rue d'Antibes, 06400 Cannes. T. 0493993211. *074407*

Capbreton (Landes)
Chevalet Poète, Résidence Mille-Sabords, 40130 Capbreton. T. 0558418383. *074408*

Carcassonne (Aude)
Galerie A.D.A.P.A., 31 Rue Antoine-Armagnac, 11000 Carcassonne. T. 0468479293. *074409*
Galerie Truphémus, Pl Saint-Nazaire, 11000 Carcassonne. T. 0468720965. *074410*
Sourillan International, 1bis Rue Saint-Jean, 11000 Carcassonne. T. 0468473045. *074411*
Tilché, Jean-Marc, 46 Rue Trivalle, 11000 Carcassonne. T. 0468473636, Fax 0468724747. *074412*

Carennac (Lot)
Galerie du Prieuré, Bourg, 46110 Carennac. T. 0565109463. *074413*

Carnac (Morbihan)
Besseiche, Daniel, 52 Av Druides, 56340 Carnac. T. 0297522667. *074414*
Grassin, Jean, Pl Port-en-Dro, 56342 Carnac. T. 0297529363, Fax 0297528390. - Paint / Graph / Draw - *074415*
Lauro, Stéphane, 22 Av Miln, 56340 Carnac. T. 0297528982. *074416*
Tournemine, Tatiana, 78 Av Druides, 56340 Carnac. T. 0297521607, Fax 0297528639. *074417*

Carpentras (Vaucluse)
Cézanne, 68 Rue David-Guillabert, 84200 Carpentras. T. 0490605674. *074418*
Trait d'Union, 4 Pl Général-de-Gaulle, 84200 Carpentras. T. 0490603747. *074419*

Cassis (Bouches-du-Rhône)
Espace Réduit, 3 Rue Four, 13260 Cassis. T. 0442017925. *074420*
Galerie d'Art L'Infini, 5 Rue Adolphe-Thiers, 13260 Cassis. T. 0442011280. *074421*
Galerie du Port, 16 Quai Baux, 13260 Cassis. T. 0442013065. *074422*
Galerie Marina, 1 Rue Brémond, 13260 Cassis. T. 0442010724. *074423*

Castelnau-le-Lez (Hérault)
Centre d'Art Regard Majeur, 232 Av Europe, 34170 Castelnau-le-Lez. T. 0467799030, Fax 0467799484. *074424*
Espace Mally, Imp Amans, 34170 Castelnau-le-Lez. T. 0467720123. *074425*
Mas du Diable, 34170 Castelnau-le-Lez. T. 0467720246. *074426*

Castelnaudary (Aude)
Reby, Didier, 7 Rue 11-Novembre-1918, 11400 Castelnaudary. T. 0468233289. *074427*

Castillonnès (Lot-et-Garonne)
Galerie des Cornières, 3 Pl Cornières, 47330 Castillonnès. T. 0553368159, Fax 0553368162. *074428*

Castres (Tarn)
Esperluette, 63 Blvd Pierre-Mendès-France, 81100 Castres. T. 0563724773. *074429*

Cauterets (Hautes-Pyrénées)
In Art Véritas, Rés. Petit-Vignemale Av Gare, 65110 Cauterets. T. 0562926161. *074430*

Cavaillon (Vaucluse)
Art Cadre, 63 Av Gabriel-Péri, 84300 Cavaillon.
T. 0490761916. *074431*

Cébazat (Puy-de-Dôme)
Favier, Georges, 24 Rue Joseph-Castaigne, 63118 Cébazat. T. 0473230365. *074432*

Céret (Pyrénées-Orientales)
Catalane, 30 Blvd Mar-Joffre, 66400 Céret.
Fax 68872183. - Paint - *074433*
Pannetier, Dominique, 7 Blvd Mar-Joffre, 66400 Céret.
T. 0468871278. - Paint - *074434*
Terre de Sienne, 9 Av Michel-Aribaux, 66400 Céret.
T. 0468874443. - Paint - *074435*

Cernay (Haut-Rhin)
Galerie des Prés, Rue Artisans, 68700 Cernay.
T. 0389754468. *074436*

Challans (Vendée)
Galerie des Ormeaux, 17 Rue Sables, 85300 Challans.
T. 0251681037. *074437*

Chalon-sur-Saône (Saône-et-Loire)
Branchard, Alexandre, 13 Rue Blé, 71100 Chalon-sur-Saône. T. 0385930025. *074438*
Châtelet, 1 Rue Châtelet, 71100 Chalon-sur-Saône.
T. 0385487956. *074439*
Erel, 4 Rue Poulets, 71100 Chalon-sur-Saône.
T. 0385933940. *074440*
Saint-Jean, 32 Quai Messagerie, 71100 Chalon-sur-Saône. T. 0385485614. *074441*

Chambéry (Savoie)
Art Alp Décor, 1 Pl Maché, 73000 Chambéry.
T. 0479693017. *074442*
Boidet, Philippe, Carré-Curial, 73000 Chambéry.
T. 0479854887. *074443*
Demeter, 4 Rue Métropole, 73000 Chambéry.
T. 0479336163. *074444*
Galerie de Lans, 3 Rue de Lans, 73000 Chambéry.
T. 0479856843. *074445*

Chamonix-Mont-Blanc (Haute-Savoie)
Galerie Mont Blanc, 65 Av Michel-Croz, 74400 Chamonix-Mont-Blanc. T. 0450531650,
Fax 0450532501. *074446*

Champagné (Sarthe)
Mairie, le Moulin Rte Réveillon, 72470 Champagné.
T. 0243890932. *074447*

Champigny-sur-Marne (Val-de-Marne)
Ateliers du Parc, 634 Rue Bernau, 94500 Champigny-sur-Marne. T. 0148810831, Fax 0147062643. *074448*

Chantilly
Caverne des Arts, 5 Rue Creil, 60500 Chantilly.
T. 0344572421. - Paint - *074449*
Rêves et Regards, 60 Rue Connétable, 60500 Chantilly.
T. 0344582203. - Paint - *074450*

Charenton-le-Pont (Val-de-Marne)
Actée, 114 Rue Paris, 94220 Charenton-le-Pont.
T. 0143963052. *074451*
Adéquation Services, Rue Nouveau-Bercy, 94220 Charenton-le-Pont. T. 0149778438,
Fax 0143963431. *074452*
Cadres Décor, 22 Rue Paris, 94220 Charenton-le-Pont.
T. 0143784779. - Fra - *074453*

Charleville-Mézières (Ardennes)
Cadr'Art, 51 Cours Aristide-Briand, 08000 Charleville-Mézières. T. 0324332731. *074454*
Spitz, Jean-Marie, 29 Rue Théâtre, 08000 Charleville-Mézières. T. 0324333335. *074455*

Chartres (Eure-et-Loir)
Camaïeu, 26 Pl Cygne, 28000 Chartres.
T. 0237365151. *074456*
Galerie d'Art, 6 Rue Serpente, 28000 Chartres.
T. 0237216111, Fax 0237217419. *074457*

Château-Chalon (Jura)
Agoldapie, Rue Roche, 39210 Château-Chalon.
T. 0384852364, Fax 0384852124. *074458*

Lorimer, N., Rue Eglise, 39210 Château-Chalon.
T. 0384852459. *074459*

Château-Gontier-Bazouges (Mayenne)
Centre Culturel le Carré, Chapelle Geneteil, Rue Général-Lemonnier, 53200 Château-Gontier-Bazouges.
T. 0243078896. *074460*

Châteauroux (Indre)
Atelier Ocre d'Art, 51 Rue Indre, 36000 Châteauroux.
T. 0254221955. *074461*
Lafond, 73 Rue Grande, 36000 Châteauroux.
T. 0254342227. *074462*

Châtillon (Rhône)
Grand A, 1 Sentier Remparts, 69380 Châtillon.
T. 0478380. *074463*

Chaumont (Haute-Marne)
Salon des Expositions, 1 Rue Frères-Mistarlet, 52000 Chaumont. T. 0325323985. *074464*

Chazelles-sur-Lyon (Loire)
Néel, Albert, 16 Rue Emile-Rivoire, 42140 Chazelles-sur-Lyon. T. 0477543261. *074465*

Chelles (Seine-et-Marne)
Cadres Décor, 12 Av Résistance, 77500 Chelles.
T. 64264099. *074466*

Chennevières-sur-Marne (Val-de-Marne)
Peintres d'Aujourd'hui, Centre Commercial Pince-Vent, 94430 Chennevières-sur-Marne.
T. 0145949288. *074467*

Cherbourg (Manche)
Galerie de la Marine, 3bis Rue Christine, 50100 Cherbourg. T. 0233530768. *074468*
Galerie des Beaux-Arts, Ecole des Beaux-Arts, 109 Av Paris, 50100 Cherbourg. T. 0233433374. *074469*

Chinon (Indre-et-Loire)
Atelier 25, 25 Rue Jean-Jacques-Rousseau, 37500 Chinon. T. 0547931796. *074470*

Clairac (Lot-et-Garonne)
Feille, 5 Imp Clocher, 47320 Clairac. T. 0553843200,
Fax 0553790821. *074471*

Clamecy (Nièvre)
Petite Galerie, 6 Rue La-Monnaie, 58500 Clamecy.
T. 0386279688. *074472*

Clapiers (Hérault)
Leenhardt, Claude, 24 Rue Château, 34830 Clapiers.
T. 0467591001. *074473*

Clermont-Créans (Sarthe)
Atelier d'Art Drussant, Château Sénéchal, 72200 Clermont-Créans. T. 0243456746. *074474*

Clermont-Ferrand (Puy-de-Dôme)
A:B:C: du Cadre, 38 Rue Fontgiève, 63000 Clermont-Ferrand. T. 0473377338. *074475*
Artco-Muzac, 10 Rue Terrasse, 63000 Clermont-Ferrand. T. 0473908289, Fax 0473902119. *074476*
Artéfact, 53 Rue Blatin, 63000 Clermont-Ferrand.
T. 0473938557. *074477*
Cadr'express, Marché Saint-Pierre, 63000 Clermont-Ferrand. T. 0473312464. *074478*
Chabannes, Cyril, 21 Rue Gras, 63000 Clermont-Ferrand. T. 0473377499. *074479*
Cusset, Gérard, 5 Rue Sidonie-Apollinaire, 63000 Clermont-Ferrand. T. 0473912357. *074480*
Doigt dans l'Oeil, 8 Rue Fontgiève, 63000 Clermont-Ferrand. T. 0473310772. *074481*
Espace Photo, 18 Rue Fontgiève, 63000 Clermont-Ferrand. T. 0473313838. *074482*
Favier, Georges, 4 Rue Saint-Pierre, 63000 Clermont-Ferrand. T. 0473374433. *074483*
Galerie, 12 Rue Oratoire, 63000 Clermont-Ferrand.
T. 0473904705. *074484*
Galerie AA, 9 Rue Chaussetiers, 63000 Clermont-Ferrand. T. 0473913523. *074485*

Galerie d'Art Salvany, 27 Rue Blatin, 63000 Clermont-Ferrand. T. 0473342300, Fax 0473341401. *074486*
Galerie de Tableaux, 15 Rue Philippe-Marcombes, 63000 Clermont-Ferrand. T. 0473920632,
Fax 0473908749. *074487*
Galerie Gastaud, 7 Rue Terrail, 63000 Clermont-Ferrand.
T. 0473928410. *074488*
Galerie 17, 17 Rue Chaussetiers, 63000 Clermont-Ferrand. T. 0473372002. *074489*
Jury, Jean, 12 Rue Pascal, 63000 Clermont-Ferrand.
T. 0473919571. *074490*
Moennard, Sarah, 79 Rue Blatin, 63000 Clermont-Ferrand. T. 0473340665. *074491*
Sten's, 12 Rue Treille, 63000 Clermont-Ferrand.
T. 0473905145. *074492*
Trocmez, Bertrand, 11 Rue Philippe-Marcombes, 63000 Clermont-Ferrand. T. 0473909797,
Fax 0473904481. *074493*

Collioure (Pyrénées-Orientales)
Blend, Barry, 19 Rue Arago, 66190 Collioure.
T. 0468825782. - Paint - *074494*
Snodgrass, Kenneth, 8 Rue Rière, 66190 Collioure.
T. 0468825532. - Paint - *074495*

Colmar (Haut-Rhin)
Andlauer, Pierre, 5 Rue Mercière, 68000 Colmar.
T. 0389231838. *074496*
Galerie Art et Collection, 5 A Rue Marchands, 68000 Colmar. T. 0389237143. - Paint / China / Toys - *074497*
Galerie Jade, 1 Rue Tanneurs, 68000 Colmar.
T. 0389231234, Fax 0389241475. *074498*
Galerie JCB, 17 et 28 Grand-Rue, 68000 Colmar.
T. 0389413391, Fax 0389413975. *074499*
Mannsfeld, 7 Rue Tanneurs, 68000 Colmar.
T. 0389230628. *074500*

Compiègne
Athena, 14 Rue Lombards, 60200 Compiègne.
T. 0344403102. - Paint - *074501*
Galerie du Palais, 8 Rue Dahomey, 60200 Compiègne.
T. 0344403204. - Paint - *074502*

Concarneau (Finistère)
Depoid, H., 2 Blvd Alfred-Guillou, 29110 Concarneau.
T. 0298973091. *074503*
Reney, 30 Rue Vauban, 29110 Concarneau.
T. 0298974019. *074504*
Sabatier, 20bis Av Docteur-Nicolas, 29110 Concarneau.
T. 0298509895. *074505*
Trannoi, 11 Rue Saint-Guénolé, 29110 Concarneau.
T. 0298973544. *074506*
Ville Ouverte, 25 Rte Quimper, 29110 Concarneau.
T. 0298508686. *074507*

Conches-en-Ouche (Eure)
Artistes Régionaux Tradition (A.R.T.), 43 Pl Carnot, BP 12, 27190 Conches-en-Ouche.
T. 0232309292. *074508*
Thoumyre, François, 2 Rue Saint-Etienne, 27190 Conches-en-Ouche. T. 0232300438. - Paint - *074509*

Conteville (Eure)
Pottier, Chrystèle, Friches, 27210 Conteville.
T. 0232560022. *074510*

Cordes (Tarn)
Cimaise, Grand'Rue, 81170 Cordes.
T. 0563560439. *074511*
Gaudrin, Michel, Pl Halle, 81170 Cordes.
T. 0563561228. *074512*

Cormatin (Saône-et-Loire)
Chavanne, Henriette, Ancienne Filaterie, 71460 Cormatin. T. 0385501569. *074513*

Courchevel (Savoie)
Besseiche, Daniel, Espace Diamant Imm Grandes-Alpes, 73120 Courchevel. T. 0479083983,
Fax 0479080457. *074514*
Chabanian le Baron, Rue Verdons, 73120 Courchevel.
T. 0479084605. *074515*

Courcy (Manche)
Normandy Expo, 8 La Hastonnière, 50200 Courcy.
T. 0233478034.   074516

Coutances (Manche)
Astrolabe, 9 Rue Saint-Nicolas, 50200 Coutances.
T. 0233077355.   074517

Crest (Drôme)
Rekow, Lydie, Peyrambert, 26400 Crest.
T. 0475254633, Fax 0475252172.   074518

Crevant (Indre)
Galerie Le Gué, Le Gué, 36140 Crevant.
T. 0254301329.   074519

Croix (Nord)
Galerie de l'Egalité, 27 Rue Favreuil, 59170 Croix.
T. 0320253797. - Paint -   074520

Crozant (Creuse)
Grenier, Bourg, 23160 Crozant. T. 0555898336. 074521

Crozon (Finistère)
Finistère, 48 Blvd Plage, 29160 Crozon.
T. 0298270740.   074522
Vandenberghe, Philippe, 2 Rue Cap-de-la-Chèvre,
29160 Crozon. T. 0298262687.   074523

Dannemarie (Haut-Rhin)
Demontrond, Paul, 10 Pl Hôtel-de-Ville, 68210 Dannemarie. T. 0389250030.   074524

Dax (Landes)
Ducasse, Charles, 108 Av Saint-Vincent-de-Paul, 40100
Dax. T. 0558740020.   074525

Deauville (Calvados)
Apesteguy, Anne, Rue Casino, 14800 Deauville.
T. 0231886513, Fax 0231882361.   074526
Art Prestige, 61 Rue Désiré-le-Hoc, 14800 Deauville.
T. 0231815752, Fax 0231815218.   074527
Ateliers d'Artistes, 51 Av République, 14800 Deauville.
T. 0231982810.   074528
Bocquel, Claire, 97 Rue Eugène-Colas, 14800 Deauville.
T. 0231989564, Fax 0231989564.   074529
Espace Deauville, 2 Av Lucien-Barrière, 14800 Deau-
ville. T. 0231882100.   074530
Malaurent, J., 7 Rue Hoche, 14800 Deauville.
T. 0231874697.   074531
Rendez-Vous des Arts, 75 Rue Eugène-Colas, Résid
Desmoulins, 14800 Deauville. T. 0231989440. 074532
Royal Galerie, 3 Rue Désiré-le-Hoc, 14800 Deauville.
T. 0231876464.   074533
Tour, Marthe de la, Englesqueville-en-Auge, 14800
Deauville. T. 0231652120. - Paint / Cur -   074534

Decazeville (Aveyron)
Bou, Marie-Hélène, 1 Rue Maréchal-Foch, 12300 Decazeville. T. 0565635757.   074535

Dieppe (Seine-Maritime)
Galerie du Bout du Quai Villy, 20 Rue Parmentier, 76200
Dieppe. T. 0235062393.   074536
Galerie Montador, 4 Rue Bains, 76200 Dieppe.
T. 0235826303.   074537
Galerie Telloë, 3 Rue Commandant-Fayolle, 76200 Diep-
pe. T. 0235824707.   074538

Dieulefit (Drôme)
Galerie S, All Promenades, 26220 Dieulefit.
T. 0475463028. - Paint / Sculp -   074539
Girard, Frank, 34 Rue Bonnefoy, 26220 Dieulefit.
T. 0475468272.   074540
Pouchain, Jacques, Quai Roger-Morin, 26220 Dieulefit.
T. 0475463122.   074541

Dijon (Côte-d'Or)
Adeline Déco, 23 Rue Condorcet, 21000 Dijon.
T. 0380418871. - Toys -   074542
Ancet, Jean-Claude, 5 Pl Théâtre, 21000 Dijon.
T. 0380675103.   074543
Cadre Noir, 6 Pl Ducs-de-Bourgogne, 21000 Dijon.
T. 0380308974.   074544
Coin du Miroir, 16 Rue Quentin, 21000 Dijon.
T. 0380307523.   074545

Dazy, Christian, 16 Pl Ducs-de-Bourgogne, 21000 Dijon.
T. 0380364140, Fax 0380663832.   074546
Galerie Arcanes, 25 Rue Am-Roussin, 21000 Dijon.
T. 0380589631.   074547
Galerie du Théâtre, 10 Pl Théâtre, 21000 Dijon.
T. 0380666920, Fax 0380364174.   074548
Galerie Oniris, 44 Rue Am-Roussin, 21000 Dijon.
T. 0380300820.   074549
Galerie Vauban, 3 Rue Vauban, 21000 Dijon.
T. 0380302699. - Paint / Fra -   074550
Galerie 6, 6 Rue Auguste-Comte, 21000 Dijon.
T. 0380716846. - Paint / Graph / Draw -   074551
Goudot, Didier, 15 Rue Michelet, 21000 Dijon.
T. 0380308896, Fax 0380589082.   074552
Laroche, Passage Darcy, 21000 Dijon.
T. 0380589182.   074553
Tiercin, Christian, 38 Rue Charrue, 21000 Dijon.
T. 0380307656.   074554

Dinan (Côtes-d'Armor)
Galerie del'Art, 12 Les Combournaises, 22100 Dinan.
T. 0296854979.   074555
Galerie du Phonographe, 2 Rue Apport, 22100 Dinan.
T. 0296393838.   074556
Galerie Saint-Sauveur, 12 Rue Apport, 22100 Dinan.
T. 0296852662, Fax 0296394390.   074557

Dinard (Ille-et-Vilaine)
Besseiche, Daniel, 6 Blvd Président-Wilson, 35800 Di-
nard. T. 0299465115.   074558
Galerie d'Art du Prince Noir, 70bis Av Georges V, 35800
Dinard. T. 0299462999.   074559
Galerie du Phonographe, 7 Rue Maréchal-Leclerc,
35800 Dinard. T. 0299466066.   074560
Galerie Gay, 39 Rue Levavasseur, 35800 Dinard.
T. 0299461073.   074561
Galerie Saphir, 38 Rue Maréchal-Leclerc, 35800 Dinard.
T. 0299468685.   074562
Galerie Séraphine, 11 Rue Levavasseur, 35800 Dinard.
T. 0299469488. - Paint / Eth -   074563
Galerie Vendôme, 6bis Rue Maréchal-Leclerc, 35800 Di-
nard. T. 0299468484.   074564
Galerie Vue sur Mer, 15 Rue Levavasseur, 35800 Dinard.
T. 0299881499.   074565
Gayet, Martine, Digue-de-L'Ecluse, 35800 Dinard.
T. 0299468781.   074566
Le Tertre, Ronan, 71 Blvd Féart, 35800 Dinard.
T. 0299461749.   074567
Motte, Alexandre, 16 Rue Maréchal-Leclerc, 35800 Di-
nard. T. 0299160347.   074568
Peintres de Plein Vent, 15 Rue Maréchal-Leclerc, 35800
Dinard. T. 0299467262.   074569

Dole (Jura)
Atelier d'Arlequin, 22 Pl Nationale, 39100 Dole.
T. 0384724219.   074570
Galerie de l'Arbitraire, 4 Rue Gouvenon, 39100 Dole.
T. 0384710651.   074571

Dossenheim-sur-Zinsel (Bas-Rhin)
Schitter, René, 18 Rue Herrenstein, 67330 Dossenheim-
sur-Zinsel. T. 0388700405, Fax 0388703444.
- Repr -   074572

Douai (Nord)
Iglou Art Esquimau, 35 Rue N-D-des-Wetz, 59500
Douai. T. 0327882914. - Paint -   074573
Maison, 15 Rue Pierre-Dubois, 59500 Douai.
T. 0327870087. - Paint -   074574
Rivages, 10 Quai Desbordes, 59500 Douai.
T. 0327990249. - Paint -   074575

Douarnenez (Finistère)
Hippocampe, 47 Rue Duguay-Trouin, 29100 Douarnen-
ez. T. 0298921140.   074576
Nausicaa, 3 Rue Jean-Jaurès, 29100 Douarnenez.
T. 0298929191.   074577

Douchy-les-Mines (Nord)
Centre d'Art Photographique Artothèque, Pl Nations,
59282 Douchy-les-Mines. T. 0327435650,
Fax 0327313193. - Paint -   074578

Dracy-le-Fort (Saône-et-Loire)
Fraisse, Janie, Pl Mairie, 71640 Dracy-le-Fort.
T. 0385445550, Fax 0385444345.   074579

Draguignan (Var)
Galerie d'Art Alvarès, 21 Rue Labat, 83300 Draguignan.
T. 0494681782, Fax 0494470700. - Paint / Graph /
Sculp -   074580

Dun-le-Palestel (Creuse)
Johnson-Feugère, Rue Sabots, 23800 Dun-le-Palestel.
T. 0555891654.   074581

Eaubonne (Val-d'Oise)
Galerie de Mézières, 16 Av Europe, 95600 Eaubonne.
T. 0134165643. - Paint / Dec / Cur -   074582

Echiré (Deux-Sèvres)
Aubisse, G., Logis de Beaulieu, 79410 Echiré.
T. 0549257199. - Paint -   074583

Enghien-les-Bains (Val-d'Oise)
Guirgis, 1ter Rue Libération, 95880 Enghien-les-Bains.
T. 0134129628.   074584
Henot, Marc, 14 Rue Mora, 95880 Enghien-les-Bains.
T. 0134126996. - Paint -   074585
Tropisme, 4 Rue Mora, 95880 Enghien-les-Bains.
T. 0139641852.   074586

Ensisheim (Haut-Rhin)
Vonesch, Roland, 9 Rte Ungersheim, 68190 Ensisheim.
T. 0389810155, Fax 0389264856.   074587

Epernay (Marne)
Galerie I.M., 20 Rue Cuissotte, 51200 Epernay.
T. 0326552016.   074588

Equeurdreville (Manche)
Duval, 45 Rue Paix, 50120 Equeurdreville.
T. 0233938628. - Paint -   074589

Etampes (Essonne)
Galerie de l'Encadrement, 21 Rue Saint-Antoine, 91150
Etampes. T. 0164945718.   074590

Evian-les-Bains (Haute-Savoie)
Daumarie, Jacques, Av Anna-de-Noailles, 74500 Evian-
les-Bains. T. 0450708496.   074591
Galerie Atalante, 29 Rue Nationale, 74500 Evian-les-
Bains. T. 0450752961.   074592
Galerie du Théâtre, 1 Pl Port, 74500 Evian-les-Bains.
T. 0450755099.   074593

Evigny (Ardennes)
Atelier des Arts, Rue Derrière, 08090 Evigny.
T. 0324370369.   074594

Evry (Essonne)
Art Coopération, 8 Pl Aunettes, 91000 Evry.
T. 0160792122.   074595
Carlier, Centre Commercial Agora, 91000 Evry.
T. 0160790556.   074596

Fabrègues (Hérault)
Galerie Iris, RN 113, Zone Artisanale C. Campanelles,
34690 Fabrègues. T. 0467851928, Fax 0467852458.
- Paint / Dec / Fra / Glass / Naut -   074597

Ferney-Voltaire (Ain)
Salon Voltaire, 30 Grand-Rue, 01210 Ferney-Voltaire.
T. 0450429747.   074598

Figeac (Lot)
Galerie 2B, 6 Pl Champollion, 46100 Figeac.
T. 0565347676.   074599

Fillinges (Haute-Savoie)
Strauss, Jacques, Bonnaz, 74250 Fillinges.
T. 0450364214.   074600

Fontaine-de-Vaucluse (Vaucluse)
Zubrycki, Château Vieux, 84800 Fontaine-de-Vaucluse.
T. 0490202294.   074601

Fontaine-lès-Dijon (Côte-d'Or)
Ariltone, 5 A Rue Docteur-Majnoni-D'Intignano, 21121
Fontaine-lès-Dijon. T. 0380575951.   074602

Fontainebleau (Seine-et-Marne)
Infini, 48 Rue France, 77300 Fontainebleau.
T. 64227373. *074603*

Fontenay-le-Comte (Vendée)
Luminaires de Prestige, 67 Rue Tiraqueau, 85200 Fontenay-le-Comte. T. 0251690322. - Dec - *074604*
Perce-Oreilles Productions, 4 Rue Gaston-Guillemet,
85200 Fontenay-le-Comte. T. 0251697169. *074605*

Fontvieille (Bouches-du-Rhône)
Galerie de Fontvieille, 101 Av Frédéric-Mistral, 13990
Fontvieille. T. 0490547676. *074606*
Galerie Saint-Michel, 159 Rte Nord, 13990 Fontvieille.
T. 0490547461. *074607*

Fougères (Ille-et-Vilaine)
Art et Décoration, 1 Blvd Maréchal-Leclerc, 35300 Fougères. T. 0299993098. *074608*

Fréjus (Var)
Centre de Rencontre des Arts Occitans, Centre Commer-
cial Muscadière, 83600 Fréjus.
T. 0494444298. *074609*
Mahe Rihn, 531 Av Provence, 83600 Fréjus.
T. 0494442600. *074610*

Fresnes (Val-de-Marne)
Maison d'Art Contemporain Chailloux, 3 Rue Julien-
Chailloux, 94260 Fresnes. T. 0146685831. *074611*

Gaillac (Tarn)
Blanc, Robert, 23 Rue Jean-Jaurès, 81600 Gaillac.
T. 0563574653. *074612*

Gaillard (Haute-Savoie)
Barchini, C., 2 Rue Vallard, 74240 Gaillard.
T. 0450870707. *074613*

Gallargues-le-Montueux (Gard)
Galerie Courte-Echelle, Rue Poujade, 30660 Gallargues-
le-Montueux. T. 0466737554. *074614*

Ganges (Hérault)
Galerie Associative Caliope, 16 Plan Ormeau, 34190
Ganges. T. 0467735674. *074615*

Gap (Hautes-Alpes)
Espace Dhyana, 5 Rue Valentin-Chabrand, 05000 Gap.
T. 0492524522. *074616*

Gargilesse-Dampierre (Indre)
Art Collection International, Dampierre, 36190 Gargilesse-Dampierre. T. 0254477247. *074617*

Gassin (Var)
Galerie Deï Barri, Pl Deï-Barri, 83580 Gassin.
T. 0494561352. - Paint / Sculp - *074618*

Gennevilliers (Hauts-de-Seine)
Obsis, 70 Av Gabriel-Péri, 92230 Gennevilliers.
T. 0147932087. *074619*

Givors (Rhône)
Grand Lyon, 30 Rue Joseph-Longarini, 69700 Givors.
T. 0478731213. *074620*

Gordes (Vaucluse)
Epicurieux, Pl Château, 84220 Gordes.
T. 0490721065. *074621*
Lainé, Pascal, Pl Château, 84220 Gordes.
T. 0490720090. *074622*
Luberon, Pl Monument, 84220 Gordes.
T. 0490720031. *074623*

Gosnay (Pas-de-Calais)
Galerie des Chartreuses, 5 Rte Nationale, 62199 Gosnay. T. 0321536366. *074624*

Gramat (Lot)
Galerie Sillage, 6 Av Louis-Conte, 46500 Gramat.
T. 0565331434. *074625*

Granville (Manche)
Emergences, 34 Rue Lecampion, 50400 Granville.
T. 0233900553. *074626*

Galerie du 20ème Siècle, 3 Rue Georges-Clemenceau,
50400 Granville. T. 0233614141. - Paint / Graph /
Sculp - *074627*
Gautier, 116 Rue Couraye, 50400 Granville.
T. 0233507014. *074628*

Grasse (Alpes-Maritimes)
Galerie Rosal, 18 Rue Paul-Goby, 06130 Grasse.
T. 0493361132. - Paint / Sculp - *074629*

Grenoble (Isère)
Aalto, Gandit, 19 Rue Voltaire, 38100 Grenoble.
T. 0476511029. *074630*
Aristoloches, 10 Rue Guétal, 38000 Grenoble.
T. 0476468711. *074631*
Giroud, Robert, 1 Rue Lakanal, 38000 Grenoble.
T. 0476562889. - Graph - *074632*
Pléiade, 22 Blvd Edouard-Rey, 38000 Grenoble.
T. 0476465303. - Paint - *074633*

Grignan (Drôme)
Durgnat, René, 2 Rue Planette, 26230 Grignan.
T. 0475465543. *074634*

Gruissan (Aude)
Galerie Cap au Large, 9 Passage Marchands, 11430
Gruissan. T. 0468490132. *074635*

Guebwiller (Haut-Rhin)
Doigts d'Or, 95 Rue République, 68500 Guebwiller.
T. 0389765772. - Paint / Graph / Fra - *074636*

Guérande (Loire-Atlantique)
Atelier d'Art, 1 Pl Saint-Aubin, 44350 Guérande.
T. 40620911. *074637*
Galerie du Chien Assis, 7 Rue Saint-Michel, 44350 Gué-
rande. T. 40247965. *074638*
Galerie Saint-Michel, 26 Rue Saint-Michel, 44350 Gué-
rande. T. 40247844. *074639*

Guingamp (Côtes-d'Armor)
Franjac, Paule, 36 Rue Notre-Dame, 22200 Guingamp.
T. 0296440797, Fax 0296437983. *074640*
Galerie Le Parc, 1 Rue Maréchal-Foch, 22200 Guin-
gamp. T. 0296444216, Fax 0296437109. *074641*

Gurgy (Yonne)
Wiegersma, Tjerk, Château Guillebaudon, 89250 Gurgy.
T. 0386406300. *074642*

Hallivillers (Somme)
Joubert, Anne, 21 Rue de l'Eglise, 80250 Hallivillers.
T. 0322094589. *074643*

Hénin-Beaumont (Pas-de-Calais)
Salle d'Exposition Espace Lumière, 39 Rue Elie-Gruyelle,
62110 Hénin-Beaumont. T. 0321491442. *074644*

Hessenheim (Bas-Rhin)
Riviera, 19 Rue Baldenheim, 67390 Hessenheim.
T. 0388853576. *074645*

Homécourt (Meurthe-et-Moselle)
Galerie Gouverneur, 2 Rue Basse-Soulieu, 54310 Homécourt. Fax 82229144. *074646*

Honfleur (Calvados)
Art Conseil International, 16 Rue Lingots, 14600 Honf-
leur. Fax 31899089. *074647*
Banque de l'Image, 35 Rue Dauphin, 14600 Honfleur.
T. 0231988670. *074648*
Besseiche, Daniel, 34 Quai Sainte-Catherine, 14600
Honfleur. T. 0231890482, Fax 0231895834. *074649*
Boudin, Arthur, 6 Pl Hôtel-de-Ville, 14600 Honfleur.
T. 0231800666. *074650*
Brainin, Michel, 8 Rue Homme-de-Bois, 14600 Honfleur.
T. 0231895860. *074651*
Brunner, Katia, 46 Rue Dauphin, 14600 Honfleur.
T. 0231988510. *074652*
Centhor, 24 Pl Hamelin, 14600 Honfleur.
T. 0231893433. *074653*
Fleuron, 2 Rue Dauphin, 14600 Honfleur.
T. 0231892068. *074654*
Forum des Arts, 16 Rue Lingots, 14600 Honfleur.
T. 0231895850. *074655*

Galerie Arts de l'Enclos, 2 Rue Saint-Antoine, 14600
Honfleur. T. 0231891913. *074656*
Galerie aux Impressionnistes, 22 Rue Ville, 14600 Honf-
leur. T. 0231892999. *074657*
Galerie de l'Obélisque, 32 Pl Pierre-Berthelot, 14600
Honfleur. T. 0231894902. *074658*
Galerie de la Plaisance, 50 Quai Sainte-Catherine,
14600 Honfleur. T. 0231894922. *074659*
Galerie des Lingots, 32 Rue Lingots, 14600 Honfleur.
T. 0231894806. *074660*
Galerie du Dauphin, 43 Rue Dauphin, 14600 Honfleur.
T. 0231899423, Fax 0231894494. *074661*
Galerie du Vieux Bassin, 66 Quai Sainte-Catherine,
14600 Honfleur. T. 0231890425. *074662*
Galerie Hamelin, 32 Pl Hamelin, 14600 Honfleur.
T. 0231988842. *074663*
Galerie Hélios, 17 Rue Dauphin, 14600 Honfleur.
T. 0231895858. *074664*
Galerie Impression, 12 Rue Dauphin, 14600 Honfleur.
T. 0231894240. *074665*
Galerie Mouce, 58 Quai Sainte-Catherine, 14600 Honf-
leur. T. 0231988732. *074666*
Granoff, Katia, 9 Quai Saint-Etienne, 14600 Honfleur.
T. 0231890403, Fax 0231895507. *074667*
Grège, Robert, 14 Rue Haute, 14600 Honfleur.
T. 0231894113. *074668*
Homme de Bois, Pl Alphonse-Allais, 14600 Honfleur.
T. 0231893404. *074669*
Jardin des Arts, 2 Rue Montpensier, 14600 Honfleur.
T. 0231899111. *074670*
Jauneaux, Madeleine, 70 Quai Sainte-Catherine, 14600
Honfleur. T. 0231893366. *074671*
Jauneaux, Suzanne, 6 Pl Sainte-Catherine, 14600 Honf-
leur. T. 0231892766. *074672*
Mondial de l'Art, 20 Pl Pierre-Berthelot, 14600 Honfleur.
T. 0231894557. *074673*
Motte, J., 70 Quai Sainte-Catherine, 14600 Honfleur.
T. 0231893366. - Paint - *074674*
Pastuszkiewicz, Alexandra, 56 Quai Sainte-Catherine,
14600 Honfleur. T. 0231893127. *074675*
Piel, Michel, 34 Pl Pierre-Berthelot, 14600 Honfleur.
T. 0231898359. *074676*
Point d'Or, 15 Cours Fossés, 14600 Honfleur.
T. 0231893471. *074677*
Robert, J.C., 25 Rue Dauphin, 14600 Honfleur.
T. 0231890060. *074678*
Rustinoff, Vladimir, 13 Rue Logettes, 14600 Honfleur.
T. 0231895306. *074679*
Signatures, 4 Rue Dauphin, 14600 Honfleur.
T. 0231895045. *074680*

Horbourg-Wihr (Haut-Rhin)
Galerie du Rhin, 10 Rue Synagogue, 68000 Horbourg-
Wihr. T. 0389415706. *074681*

Hossegor (Landes)
Galerie, 132 Av Paul-Lahary-Soorts, 40150 Hossegor.
T. 0558439949. *074682*

Hyères (Var)
Fossard, Eliane, 76 Av Gambetta, 83400 Hyères.
T. 0494359827. *074683*
Galerie Alfil, 6 Pl Massillon, 83400 Hyères.
T. 0494656620. *074684*
Galerie des Remparts, 2 Rue Rempart, 83400 Hyères.
T. 0494355292. *074685*

Illkirch-Graffenstaden (Bas-Rhin)
Chelly, 29 Rte Lyon, 67400 Illkirch-Graffenstaden.
T. 05369641. *074686*

Irancy (Yonne)
Hosotte, Georges, Pl Eglise, 89290 Irancy.
T. 0386423789. *074687*

Issoire (Puy-de-Dôme)
Galerie de l'Historial, 3 Rue Fer, 63500 Issoire.
T. 0473890441. *074688*

Issoudun (Indre)
Bouniol, Denise, 32 Rue 4-Août, 36100 Issoudun.
T. 0254215177. *074689*
Demaret, Marc, 32 Rue 4-Août, 36100 Issoudun.
T. 0254215177. *074690*

Issy-les-Moulineaux (Hauts-de-Seine)
Kamien, Frances, 7 Rue Jean-Pierre-Timbaud, 92130 Issy-les-Moulineaux. T. 0146456004. *074691*

Ivry-sur-Seine (Val-de-Marne)
Khim Art, 25 Rue Pierre-Curie, 94200 Ivry-sur-Seine. Fax (1) 49600296. *074692*

Jard-sur-Mer (Vendée)
Galeries des Islattes, 1 Rue Commandant-Guilbaud, 85520 Jard-sur-Mer. T. 0251336557. *074693*

Jarny (Meurthe-et-Moselle)
Gagneré, Guy, 13 Rue Verdun, 54800 Jarny.
T. 0382331203. *074694*

Joigny (Yonne)
Atelier Cantoisel, 32 Rue Montant-au-Palais, 89300 Joigny. T. 0386620865, Fax 0386624638. *074695*

Keskastel (Bas-Rhin)
Maison de l'Art, 20 Rue Faubourg, 67260 Keskastel.
T. 0388002629. *074696*

Kingersheim (Haut-Rhin)
Wustmann, Annie, 116 Fbg Mulhouse, 68260 Kingersheim. T. 0389571516. *074697*

L'Arbresle (Rhône)
Coeur, Jacques, 20 Rue Gabriel-Péri, 69210 L'Arbresle.
T. 0474267005. - Paint / Sculp / Glass - *074698*

L'Etrat (Loire)
Bruyère, Jean, Château-La-Bertrandière, 42580 L'Etrat.
T. 0477747620. *074699*

L'Isle-Adam (Val-d'Oise)
Galerie Conti, 3 Rue Pâtis, 95290 L'Isle-Adam.
T. 0134080372. *074700*

L'Isle-sur-la-Sorgue (Vaucluse)
Archipel Galerie, 5 Pl Rose-Goudard, 84800 L'Isle-sur-la-Sorgue. T. 0490384880. *074701*
Baron Samedi, 10 Rue Docteur-Tallet, 84800 L'Isle-sur-la-Sorgue. T. 0490384701. *074702*
Bonias, 17 Rue République, 84800 L'Isle-sur-la-Sorgue. T. 0490385638, Fax 0490385681. *074703*
Ceruse, 3bis Quart Clovis-Hugues, 84800 L'Isle-sur-la-Sorgue. T. 0490381762. *074704*
Lacydon, L'Orée-de-l'Ile, 84800 L'Isle-sur-la-Sorgue.
T. 0490383374. *074705*
Limon, Martine, 3 lot Jardins-de-l'Isle, 84800 L'Isle-sur-la-Sorgue. T. 0490385741. *074706*
Riches Heures, Résidence Orée-de-l'Ile, 84800 L'Isle-sur-la-Sorgue. T. 0490383980. *074707*
Roussillon, L'Orée-de-l'Ile, 84800 L'Isle-sur-la-Sorgue.
T. 0490385602. *074708*
Tour des Cardinaux, 4 Rue Ledru-Rollin, 84800 L'Isle-sur-la-Sorgue. T. 0490208419. *074709*

La Baule (Loire-Atlantique)
Art Galerie, 36 Av Louis-Lajarrige, 44500 La Baule.
T. 0460620. *074710*
Baconnais, Jean, 60 Av Maréchal-de-Lattre-de-Tassigny, 44500 La Baule. T. 0460600606. *074711*
Bellanger, A., 14 Blvd René-Dubois, 44500 La Baule.
T. 40608242. *074712*
Billy, Marcel, 32 Esplanade François-André, 44500 La Baule. T. 40604575, Fax 40609797. *074713*
Dany, Lucas, 136 Av Général-de-Gaulle, 44500 La Baule. T. 40605213, Fax 40110879. *074714*
Galerie Alexandre, 3 Av Pierre-Loti, 44500 La Baule.
T. 40242833. *074715*
Galerie d'Art G.W.H., 41 Esplanade François-André, 44500 La Baule. T. 40608802. *074716*
Galerie Epreuves d'Artistes, 22 Av Louis-Lajarrige, 44500 La Baule. T. 40609875, Fax 40119320. *074717*
Galerie Esclarmonde, 18 Av Pavie, 44500 La Baule.
T. 40420132. *074718*
Galerie Phoënix, 34 Av Louis-Lajarrige, 44500 La Baule. T. 40603030. *074719*
Galerie 13, Esplanade François-André, 44500 La Baule.
T. 40600797. *074720*
Goinard, M.C., 32 Esplanade François-André, 44500 La Baule. T. 40110608. *074721*

Le Tac, Monique, 20 Av Ibis, 44500 La Baule.
T. 40609604. *074722*
Morvillo, Isabelle, 23 Av Louis-Lajarrige, 44500 La Baule. T. 40604000. *074723*

La Bégude-de-Mazenc (Drôme)
Association Culturelle Terre des Arts, Galerie Mistral, Av Aristide-Briand, 26160 La Bégude-de-Mazenc.
T. 0475462590. *074724*
Emiliani, Michèle, Quart Manotière, 26160 La Bégude-de-Mazenc. T. 0475462410, Fax 0475462765. *074725*
Galerie d'Ophélie, Châteauneuf de Mazenc, 26160 La Bégude-de-Mazenc. T. 0475462777. *074726*

La Celle-Dunoise (Creuse)
Rameix, Christophe, Bourg, 23800 La Celle-Dunoise.
T. 0555892394. *074727*

La Chapelle-Saint-Luc (Aube)
Accession à l'Art, 26 Rue Marcel-Defrance, 10600 La Chapelle-Saint-Luc. T. 0325719187, Fax 0325719246.
- Paint - *074728*

La Ciotat (Bouches-du-Rhône)
Lou Pichot Village, 9 Pl Sadi-Carnot, 13600 La Ciotat.
T. 0442714484. *074729*

La Colle-sur-Loup (Alpes-Maritimes)
Canus, Evelyne, 60 Av Foch, 06480 La Colle-sur-Loup.
T. 0493326328, Fax 0493325500. *074730*
Clef des Champs, 60 Rue Maréchal-Foch, 06480 La Colle-sur-Loup. T. 0493329399. *074731*
Consortium International des Arts, 890 Blvd Pierre-Sauvaigo, 06480 La Colle-sur-Loup.
T. 0493328800. *074732*
Galerie Rive Gauche, 75 Av Maréchal-Foch, 06480 La Colle-sur-Loup. T. 0493327998. - Paint / Furn / Dec / Cur - *074733*
Résidence du Village, 3 Rue Max-Barel, 06480 La Colle-sur-Loup. T. 0493320000. *074734*

La Crèche (Deux-Sèvres)
Vanuxem, Roland, 109 Chemin Miséré, 79260 La Crèche. T. 0549255082. *074735*

La Flotte (Charente-Maritime)
Galerie Marine, 13 Rue Général-de-Gaulle, 17630 La Flotte. T. 0546095590. *074736*
Jamault, Laurent, 23 Rue Marché, 17630 La Flotte.
T. 0546092866, Fax 0546092856. *074737*

La Grande-Motte (Hérault)
New Galerie, Quai Honneur, Le Forum, Loc 16, 34280 La Grande-Motte. T. 0467568534. *074738*

La Roche-Bernard (Morbihan)
Beuthner, Manfred, 5 Pl Bouffay, 56130 La Roche-Bernard. T. 0299906293. *074739*

La Roche-Guyon (Val-d'Oise)
Art'Ure, 4 Rue Général-Leclerc, 95780 La Roche-Guyon. T. 0134797208, Fax 0134797205. *074740*

La Roche-sur-Yon (Vendée)
Galerie Entre-Temps, 8 Rue Thiers, 85000 La Roche-sur-Yon. T. 0251462933. *074741*

La Rochelle (Charente-Maritime)
Alain Encadreur, 41 Rue Minage, 17000 La Rochelle.
T. 0546410146. *074742*
Atelier d'Eve, 11 Quai Valin, 17000 La Rochelle.
T. 0546411190. *074743*
Dars, André, 21 Quai Valin, 17000 La Rochelle.
T. 0546417726, Fax 0546419488. *074744*
Galerie du Cloître Saint-Michel, 5 Rue Saint-Michel, 17000 La Rochelle. T. 0546412636,
Fax 0546505872. *074745*
Galerie du Temple, 8 Rue Ferté, 17000 La Rochelle.
T. 0546419709. *074746*
Galerie Louis d'Argenville, 23 Av Mulhouse, 17000 La Rochelle. T. 0546418434. *074747*
Galerie Saint-Nicolas, 16 Rue Saint-Nicolas, 17000 La Rochelle. T. 0546412020. *074748*
Sanguine, 2 Pl Hôtel-de-Ville, 17000 La Rochelle.
T. 0546415391. *074749*

La Roque-d'Anthéron (Bouches-du-Rhône)
Coquelicots, 7bis Rue Albert-Camus, 13640 La Roque-d'Anthéron. T. 0442505051, Fax 0442505061. *074750*

La Trinité-sur-Mer (Morbihan)
Art et Mer, 42 Cours Quais, 56470 La Trinité-sur-Mer.
T. 0297558086. *074751*
Océane, Embarquadère Cours Quais, 56470 La Trinité-sur-Mer. T. 0297558943. *074752*

Labastide-Rouairoux (Tarn)
Fabrique du Pré, Le Pré-Malet-La-Mouline, 81270 Labastide-Rouairoux. T. 0563982914. *074753*

Lachapelle-aux-Pots
Ehgner, Solange, 15 Rue Crapaudière, 60650 Lachapelle-aux-Pots. T. 0344805260. *074754*

Lambersart (Nord)
Weppe, 89 Rue A.-Bonte, 59130 Lambersart.
T. 0320923254. - Paint - *074755*

Landerneau (Finistère)
Carré Noir, 8 Rue Henri-Bourhis, 29220 Landerneau.
T. 0298213213. *074756*
Croissant de Lune, 12 Rue Saint-Thomas, 29220 Landerneau. T. 0298214282. *074757*

Landévennec (Finistère)
Art de Landevennec, Rue Abbaye, 29146 Landévennec.
T. 0298277213. *074758*

Laon (Aisne)
Athanor, 10 Rue Change, 02000 Laon. T. 0323207070.
- Paint - *074759*

Laval (Mayenne)
Atelier, 43 Av Robert-Buron, 53000 Laval.
T. 0243532125. *074760*
Encadrement Thébault, 71 Grande-Rue, 53000 Laval.
T. 0243532925. *074761*
Itinéraires, 33 Rue Pont-de-Mayenne, 53000 Laval.
T. 0243566857. *074762*
Méduane, 1 Rue Chapelle, 53000 Laval.
T. 0243530469. *074763*

Le Bugue (Dordogne)
Galerie Tanagra, Grande Rue, 24260 Le Bugue.
T. 0553034248. *074764*

Le-Buisson-de-Cadouin (Dordogne)
Guilmet, Danièle, Pl Abbaye, 24480 Le-Buisson-de-Cadouin. T. 0553634135. *074765*

Le Cannet (Alpes-Maritimes)
Atelier des Techniques d'Art, 272 Rue Saint-Sauveur, 06110 Le Cannet. T. 0493695307. *074766*

Le Castellet (Var)
Castel'Art, 8 Rue Congrégation, 83330 Le Castellet.
T. 0494326658. *074767*
Dame du Castellet, 8 Rue Congrégation, 83330 Le Castellet. T. 0494326830. *074768*
Galerie Julien, 4 Pl Jeu-de-Paume, 83330 Le Castellet.
T. 0494326948. - Paint - *074769*
Galerie Palangka, 1 Pl Fontaine, 83330 Le Castellet.
T. 0494327204. *074770*
Galerie Peinture, 21 Rue Aube, 83330 Le Castellet.
T. 0494326616. - Paint - *074771*

Le Chesnay (Yvelines)
Galerie 78, 324 Centre Commercial Parly II, 78150 Le Chesnay. T. 0139540615. *074772*

Le Croisic (Loire-Atlantique)
Galerie du Croisic, 19 Quai Port Ciguet, 44490 Le Croisic. T. 40230077. *074773*
Triangle Blanc, 14 Quai Petite-Chambre, 44490 Le Croisic. T. 40157416. *074774*

Le Havre (Seine-Maritime)
Atelier Saint-Michel, 30 Av Résistance, 76600 Le Havre.
T. 0235434814. *074775*
Baudet, Eric, 121 Av Foch, 76600 Le Havre.
T. 0235423244. *074776*

Galerie Alfa, 149 Rue Victor-Hugo, 76600 Le Havre.
T. 0235226550. - Paint / Sculp / Fra - *074777*
Galerie d'Art de l'Estuaire, 88 Rue Docteur-Vigné, 76600
Le Havre. T. 0235412230. *074778*
Galerie Malouvier, 77 Rue Louis-Brindeau, 76600 Le
Havre. T. 0235425107. - Paint / Furn - *074779*
Galerie Saint-Philibert, 15 et 17 Pl Halles, 76600 Le
Havre. T. 0235213945. - Furn - *074780*
Hamon, Jacques, 44 Pl Hôtel-de-Ville, 76600 Le Havre.
T. 0235424230, Fax 0235229098. - Paint / Graph /
Furn / Draw - *074781*
Marc, Jean, 53 Rue Emile-Zola, 76600 Le Havre.
T. 0235420533. - Fra - *074782*
Multiple, 304 Rue Aristide-Briand, 76600 Le Havre.
T. 0235241887. *074783*
Orange, 259 Blvd François-1er, 76600 Le Havre.
T. 0235432266. *074784*
Slotine Perkowsky, 119 Blvd Strasbourg, 76600 Le Hav-
re. T. 0235417498. *074785*
Taormina, 174 Rue Victor-Hugo, 76600 Le Havre.
T. 0235433747. *074786*
Turlure, Emilienne, 20 Rue Robert-de-la-Villehervé,
76600 Le Havre. T. 0235434171. *074787*

Le Mans (Sarthe)
Espace Montoise, 21 Rue Montoise, 72000 Le Mans.
T. 0243282173. *074788*
Galerie d'Arcadie, 6 Rue Poules, 72000 Le Mans.
T. 0243230823. *074789*
Galerie Jaune, 42 Rue Docteur-Leroy, 72000 Le Mans.
T. 0243875646. *074790*
Nouveaux Décors, 7 Rue Vicotr-Bonhommet, 72000 Le
Mans. T. 0243248779. *074791*
Univers'Art, 6bis Pl Saint-Pierre, 72000 Le Mans.
T. 0243243179. *074792*

Le Palais (Morbihan)
Entre-Port, 1 Rue Manutention, 56360 Le Palais.
T. 0297314909. *074793*
Wild Crayons, 2 Pl Bigarre, 56360 Le Palais.
T. 0297315899. *074794*

Le Poët-Laval (Drôme)
Commanderie, Vieux Village, 26160 Le Poët-Laval.
T. 0475462131. *074795*

Le Port-Marly (Yvelines)
Mihailescu, Ursula, 6 Rue Jean-Jaurès, 78560 Le Port-
Marly. T. 0139160443. - Paint - *074796*

Le Portel (Pas-de-Calais)
Galerie d'Art et d'Essais, 29 Blvd Général-de-Gaulle,
62480 Le Portel. T. 0321339001. *074797*

Le Puy-en-Velay (Haute-Loire)
Cadrerie, 9 Blvd République, 43000 Le Puy-en-Velay.
T. 0471095730. *074798*
Guilhaumet, Roger, 26 Blvd Saint-Louis, 43000 Le Puy-
en-Velay. *074799*

Le Raincy (Seine-Saint-Denis)
Weider, 31 Av Résistance, 93340 Le Raincy.
T. 0143813499. *074800*

Le Touquet-Paris-Plage (Pas-de-Calais)
Carlier, 15 Av Verger, 62520 Le Touquet-Paris-Plage.
T. 0321051131. *074801*
Dorval, Av Phares, Résidence Prince-de-Galles, 62520
Le Touquet-Paris-Plage. T. 0321057542,
Fax 0321057550. *074802*
Ermitage, Pl Hermitage, 62520 Le Touquet-Paris-Plage.
T. 0321055149. *074803*
Galerie de Villiers, 18 Rue Saint-Jean, 62520 Le Tou-
quet-Paris-Plage. T. 0321050448. *074804*
Galerie Demay Debève, Av Phares, Résidence Prince-
de-Galles, 62520 Le Touquet-Paris-Plage.
T. 0321055730. *074805*
Galerie du Touquet, Av Phares, Résidence Prince-de-
Galles, 62520 Le Touquet-Paris-Plage.
T. 0321053289. *074806*
Goradis, Av Phares, Résidence Prince-de-Galles, 62520
Le Touquet-Paris-Plage. T. 0321055719,
Fax 0321059474. *074807*
Nettis, 16 All Quatre Saisons, 62520 Le Touquet-Paris-
Plage. T. 0321053432. *074808*

Spilliaert, 4 Av Saint-Jean, 62520 Le Touquet-Paris-Plage. T. 0321054000, Fax 0321052786. *074809*
Touquet Fine Art, 1 Pl Hermitage, 62520 Le Touquet-Paris-Plage. T. 0321055178. *074810*

Le Vigan (Gard)
Wolgensinger, Marlène, 15 Pl Quai, 30120 Le Vigan.
T. 0466810889. *074811*

Les Andelys (Eure)
Tuffier, Thierry, 22 Rue Marcel-Lefèvre, 27700 Les An-
delys. T. 0232540957, Fax 0232545044.
- Paint - *074812*

Les Baux-de-Provence (Bouches-du-Rhône)
Baux-Arts, Rue Trincat, 13520 Les Baux-de-Provence.
T. 0490543950. *074813*
Galerie de la Méditerranée, Rue Calade, 13520 Les
Baux-de-Provence. T. 0490544272. *074814*
Galerie du Musée, Rue Eglise-à-Ancienne-Mairie, 13520
Les Baux-de-Provence. T. 0490544942. *074815*
Galerie YR, Rue Calade, 13520 Les Baux-de-Provence.
T. 0490543949, Fax 0490545128. *074816*

Les Eyzies-Tayac-Sireuil (Dordogne)
La Barque Bleue, Bourg, 24620 Les Eyzies-Tayac-Sireuil. T. 0553353012. *074817*

Les Rousses (Jura)
Person, Laurent, 123 Rte Porte-de-France, 39400 Les
Rousses. T. 0384603479, Fax 0384603885. *074818*

Les Sables-d'Olonne (Vendée)
Galerie Climat, 21 Promenade Am-Lafargue, 85100 Les
Sables-d'Olonne. T. 0251320762. *074819*

Les Vans (Ardèche)
C Cédille, Rue Courte, 07140 Les Vans.
T. 0475373499. *074820*

Leucate (Aude)
Maison d'Art Le Simourgh, 42 Av Languedoc, 11370
Leucate. T. 0468457015. *074821*

Levallois-Perret (Hauts-de-Seine)
Arte Viva, 25 Rue Trébois, 92300 Levallois-Perret.
T. 0147376637. *074822*
François, Gabriel, 83 Rue Paul-Vaillant-Couturier, 92300
Levallois-Perret. T. 0142708384. *074823*

Lichtenberg (Bas-Rhin)
Walch, R., 21 Rue Château, 67340 Lichtenberg.
T. 0388899241. *074824*

Lille (Nord)
Arts Palettes, 6 Rue Mourmant, 59000 Lille.
T. 0320129712, Fax 0320307123. - Paint - *074825*
Carré, Rue Archives, La Halle au Sucre, 59000 Lille.
T. 0320317116. - Paint - *074826*
Claeyssens, Paule, 53bis Blvd Liberté, 59800 Lille.
T. 0320143102, Fax 0320143103. - Paint - *074827*
Collégiale, 4 Rue Collégiale, 59000 Lille.
T. 0320063869. - Paint - *074828*
Delattre, 8 Rue Chats-Bossus, 59800 Lille.
T. 0320780828. - Paint - *074829*
Dequeker, Michelle, 5 Rue Monnaie, 59800 Lille.
T. 0320555780. - Paint - *074830*
Espace Droulet, 41 Rue Boucher-de-Perthes, 59800
Lille. T. 0320151997. - Paint - *074831*
Estampille, 7 Pl Lion-d'Or, 59800 Lille. T. 0320741656.
- Paint / Graph - *074832*
François, 37 Rue Lepelletier, 59800 Lille.
T. 0320554091, Fax 0320513865. - Paint - *074833*
Galerie des Estampes, 43 Rue Monnaie, 59800 Lille.
T. 0320317397. - Paint - *074834*
Galerie 31, Rue Monnaie, 59800 Lille. T. 0320310072.
- Paint - *074835*
Gontier Leroux, 18 Rue Bartholomé-Masurel, 59800
Lille. T. 0320131812, Fax 0320131887. *074836*
Hollevout and so, 29 Rue Royale, 59800 Lille.
T. 0320064577. - Paint - *074837*
Incartade, 37 Rue Basse, 59800 Lille. T. 0320311719.
- Paint - *074838*

L'Art pour l'Art, 29 Rue Colson, 59800 Lille.
T. 0320542747. - Paint - *074839*
Mic Art Galerie, 76 Rue Grand, 59000 Lille.
T. 0320210840, Fax 0320210839. - Paint - *074840*
Mischkind, Raphaël, 7 Rue Jean-Sans-Peur, 59800 Lille.
T. 0320573049, Fax 0320301804. - Paint - *074841*
Schèmes Galerie, 27 Hôpital-Militaire, 59800 Lille.
T. 0320543707. - Paint - *074842*
Spilliaert, 5 Rue Fossés, 59800 Lille. T. 0320542743.
- Paint - *074843*
Storme, Jacqueline, 37 Av du Peuple-Belge, 59000 Lille.
T. 0320510121, Fax 0320519944. - Paint /
Graph - *074844*
Touquet, 49 Rue Réaumur, 59800 Lille. T. 0320211122.
- Paint - *074845*
Veljkovic, Stevan, 9 Rue Trois-Mollettes, 59800 Lille.
T. 0320555926. - Paint - *074846*
Villiers, 47 Rue Esquermoise, 59800 Lille.
T. 0320549005. - Paint - *074847*

Limoges (Haute-Vienne)
Alandier, 1 Imp Louis-Bourdery, 87000 Limoges.
T. 0555337677. *074848*
Champaloux, Emile, 4 Rue Monte-à-Regret, 87000 Li-
moges. T. 0555342600. *074849*
Christel, 15 Blvd Louis-Blanc, 87000 Limoges.
T. 0555342356. *074850*
Jayat, Jean, 50 Rue François-Chénieux, 87000 Limoges.
T. 0555775657. *074851*
La Galerie, 12 Rue Lansecot, 87000 Limoges.
T. 0555321144. *074852*
Marie-Reine, 14 Rue Gondinet, 87000 Limoges.
T. 0555324050. *074853*
Nombre d'Or, 21 Rue Tanneries, 87000 Limoges.
T. 0555332566. *074854*
Ouvrageurs de la Pierre au Bois, 15 Rue Canal, 87000
Limoges. T. 0555331411. *074855*
Vagualame, 7 Rue Lansecot, 87000 Limoges.
T. 0555328792. *074856*

Lisieux (Calvados)
Galerie du Paradis, 4 Rue Paradis, 14100 Lisieux.
T. 0231626656. *074857*
Le Roy, Sabine, 10 Rue Henry-Chéron, 14100 Lisieux.
T. 0231629254. *074858*

Lissac-sur-Couze (Corrèze)
Syndicat Intercommunal d'Aménagement du Causse,
Salle d'Expositions Moulin, 19600 Lissac-sur-Couze.
T. 0555858750. *074859*

Livarot (Calvados)
Le Brun, Guy, 27 Rue Lisieux, 14140 Livarot.
T. 0231631109. *074860*

Loches (Indre-et-Loire)
Crépin France Art, 37600 Loches.
T. 0547593841. *074861*

Locronan (Finistère)
Arts et Couleurs, 4 Rue Moal, 29136 Locronan.
T. 0298518170. *074862*
Manoir la Tour Saint-Maurice, 20 Rue Saint-Maurice,
29136 Locronan. T. 0298917033. *074863*

Lorient (Morbihan)
Art Expo, 12bis Pass Blavet, 56100 Lorient.
T. 0297212447. *074864*
Carré d'Art, 2 Rue du Couëdic, 56100 Lorient.
T. 0297849614. *074865*
Contemporain Espace l'Orient, 13bis Rue Edouard-
Beauvais, 56100 Lorient. T. 0297217873. *074866*
Le Lieu, 11bis Pl Anatole-le-Braz, 56100 Lorient.
Fax 97211802. *074867*
Lemoigne, Lea, 21 Rue Belle-Fontaine, 56100 Lorient.
T. 0297219533. *074868*
Palette, 12 Pl Anatole-le-braz, 56100 Lorient.
T. 0297643699. *074869*
Saint-Louis, 18 Rue de Turenne, 56100 Lorient.
T. 0297641258. *074870*

Loudéac (Côtes-d'Armor)
Le Bouffo, Magdeleine, Venelle Victor-Boner, 22600
Loudéac. T. 0296280735. *074871*

Louviers (Eure)
Dubosc, 36bis Rue Pierre-Mendès-France, 27400 Louviers. T. 0232252510. *074872*

Lumio (Corse)
Boutet, Lionel, Rte Calvi, Clos des Fleurs, 20260 Lumio. T. 0495607708. - Paint - *074873*

Luxé (Charente)
Galerie Aurore, Domaine d'Echoisy, Le Galiment, 16230 Luxé. T. 0545203737. *074874*

Lyon (Rhône)
Athisma, 10 Rue du Boeuf, 69005 Lyon. T. 0472409033.
- Paint / Graph / Sculp / Draw - *074875*
Aux Arts, 9 Blvd Brotteaux, 69006 Lyon.
T. 0478526634. *074876*
Betton, Jacqueline, 44 Rue Sala, 69002 Lyon.
T. 0478381717. *074877*
Buchin, Christian, 82 Rue Vendôme, 69006 Lyon.
T. 0472741078. *074878*
Chalvin, Yves, 25 Rue Auguste-Comte, 69002 Lyon.
T. 0478382146, Fax 0478928887. *074879*
Chartier, Alice, 18 Rue Auguste-Comte, 69002 Lyon.
T. 0478370388, Fax 0478382573. *074880*
Charveriat, Jean, 133 Rue de Créqui, 69006 Lyon.
T. 0478526316. - Paint - *074881*
Chomarat, Gérard, 4 Pl Ambroise-Courtois, 69008 Lyon.
T. 0478002679. *074882*
Descours, Michel, 44 Rue Auguste-Comte, 69002 Lyon.
T. 0478373454, Fax 0472419067. - Paint / Sculp /
Draw - *074883*
Dettinger Mayer, 4 Pl Docteur-Gailleton, 69002 Lyon.
T. 0472410780, Fax 0478928346. *074884*
Dhikéos, Gabriel-Michel, 24 Rue Auguste Comte, 69002 Lyon. T. 0478377556. *074885*
Dhikéos, Pierre, 16 Rue Sainte-Hélène, 69002 Lyon.
T. 0478376643. *074886*
Ecl'Art, 26 Quai Claude-Bernard, 69007 Lyon.
T. 0478586014. *074887*
E.L.A.C. – Espace Lyonnais d'Art Contemporain, Centre Echange Lyon-Perrache, 69002 Lyon. T. 0478423303, Fax 0478425083. *074888*
Espace Affiches de Lyon, 5 Rue François-Dauphin, 69002 Lyon. T. 0478423663, Fax 0478380204.
- Graph / Repr / Fra - *074889*
Espace Poisson d'Or, 10 Rue Juiverie, 69005 Lyon.
T. 0478272065. *074890*
Favre Cochet, 51 Rue Auguste-Comte, 69002 Lyon.
T. 0478424037. *074891*
Ferré, Sylvie, 34 Quai Saint-Antoine, 69002 Lyon.
T. 0478929805, Fax 0472409594. *074892*
Galerie Addenda, 24 Rue Boeuf, 69005 Lyon.
T. 0478425018. *074893*
Galerie Appia, 2 Av Général Brosset, 69006 Lyon.
T. 0472744663. *074894*
Galerie Arterra, 29 Rue Remparts-d'Ainay, 69002 Lyon.
T. 0472419471. *074895*
Galerie Atelier La Trinité, 6 Rue Saint-Georges, 69005 Lyon. T. 0472409506. - Paint - *074896*
Galerie Bellecour, 12 Rue Charles Bienner, 69002 Lyon.
T. 0478378046, Fax 0472419512. - Paint / Graph /
Sculp / Draw - *074897*
Galerie Caracalla, 12 Rue du Boeuf, 69005 Lyon.
T. 0478370314. - Paint / Graph / Draw - *074898*
Galerie de l'Estampe, 32 Rue Auguste-Comte, 69002 Lyon. T. 0478378826. - Graph - *074899*
Galerie de l'Olympe, 58 Rue Auguste-Comte, 69002 Lyon. T. 0478372562. *074900*
Galerie de Sèze, 21 Rue Sèze, 69006 Lyon.
T. 0472742481. *074901*
Galerie des Brotteaux, 93 Blvd Belges, 69006 Lyon.
T. 0478242525, Fax 0478520287. *074902*
Galerie des Remparts-d'Ainay, Rue Remparts-d'Ainay, 69002 Lyon. T. 0478383969. *074903*
Galerie Dorée, 1 Rue Marius-Gonin, 69005 Lyon.
T. 0478420798. *074904*
Galerie du Vieux Lyon, 5 Pl Gouvernement, 69005 Lyon.
T. 0478426704. *074905*
Galerie Fleurieu, 8 Rue Fleurieu, 69002 Lyon.
T. 0478429447. *074906*
Galerie Foch, 40 Av Maréchal-Foch, 69006 Lyon.
T. 0478930000, Fax 0478894969. *074907*

Galerie Hermès, 49 Rue Auguste-Comte, 69002 Lyon.
T. 0472419795. *074908*
Galerie L'Amateur, 20 Rue Remparts-d'Ainay, 69002 Lyon. T. 0472410580. *074909*
Galerie L'Oeil Ecoute, 4 Rue Quarantaine, 69005 Lyon.
T. 0472417390, Fax 0472400759. *074910*
Galerie Le Réverbère 2, 38 Rue Burdeau, 69001 Lyon.
T. 0472000672. *074911*
Galerie Malaval, 1 Rue Prés Edouard Herriot, 69001 Lyon. T. 0472611756, Fax 0478603295. *074912*
Galerie Nelson, 5 Rue Bonnefoi, 69003 Lyon.
T. 0472611756, Fax 0478603295. *074913*
Galerie Saint-Georges, 22 Rue Saint-Georges, 69005 Lyon. T. 0478377273. - Paint / Graph - *074914*
Galerie Saint-Hubert, 7 Av Général-Brosset, 69006 Lyon.
T. 0478520051, Fax 0478247076. - Paint /
Sculp - *074915*
Galerie Saint-Vincent, 61 Quai Saint-Vincent, 69001 Lyon. T. 0478286592, Fax 0472078944. - Paint /
Sculp - *074916*
Galerie Vrais Rêves, 6 Rue Dumenge, 69004 Lyon.
T. 0478306542, Fax 0478308077. - Paint / Graph /
Sculp / Pho / Draw - *074917*
Galerie 32, 14 Rue Auguste Comte, 69002 Lyon.
T. 0478422542. - Graph - *074918*
Georges, Alain, 47 Rue Auguste-Comte, 69002 Lyon.
T. 0478420731, Fax 0478382364. *074919*
Guardi, 6 Rue Fleurieu, 69002 Lyon.
T. 0472410507. *074920*
Guedj, Célia B., 9 Rue Monnaie, 69002 Lyon.
T. 0478383141, Fax 0478383146. *074921*
Hoppenot, Hubert, 3 Rue Remparts-d'Ainay, 69002 Lyon. T. 0478928330. *074922*
Jacquet, Gérard, 60 Rue Auguste-Comte, 69002 Lyon.
T. 0472402885. *074923*
Juste à Côté, 47 Rue Cuvier, 69006 Lyon.
T. 0478525121. - Furn - *074924*
Laurent, Valérie, 11 Rue Auguste-Comte, 69002 Lyon.
T. 0472402811. *074925*
Loulou Cinéma, 58 Rue Saint-Jean, 69005 Lyon.
T. 0478428628. *074926*
Marouska, 39 Rue Sainte-Hélène, 69002 Lyon.
T. 0472410424. *074927*
Masséna Collection, 69 Rue Masséna, 69006 Lyon.
T. 0478520204. - China / Glass - *074928*
Mazarini, 6 Pl Baleine, 69005 Lyon. T. 0472409949, Fax 0478377855. *074929*
Michel, Hélène, 17 Rue Auguste Comte, 69002 Lyon.
T. 0478372196. - Paint - *074930*
Milton Fox, 57 Rue Mercière, 69002 Lyon.
T. 0478373076, Fax 0478373076. *074931*
Monier, Nicole, 90 Rue Duguesclin, 69006 Lyon.
T. 0472443042. *074932*
Montheillet, Pierre, 224 Rue Duguesclin, 69003 Lyon.
T. 0478608795. - Paint - *074933*
Moulin, Françoise, 38 Rue Franklin, 69002 Lyon.
T. 0478428617. *074934*
Ollave, 9 Av Doyenné, 69005 Lyon.
T. 0478425115. *074935*
Peintres de Demain, Centre Commercial Part-Dieu, 69003 Lyon. T. 0472618819,
Fax 0478622462. *074936*
Poinard, Andrée, 42 Rue Saint-Jean, 69005 Lyon.
T. 0478379808. *074937*
Raphaël, B., 57 Av Félix-Faure, 69003 Lyon.
T. 0478950222, Fax 0478627976. *074938*
Romeuf, Jean, 33 Rue Auguste-Comte, 69002 Lyon.
T. 0478426693. *074939*
Rouss'Art, 14 Rue Roussy, 69004 Lyon.
T. 0472002992. *074940*
Saint-Hubert, 7 Av Général-Brosset, 69006 Lyon.
T. 0478520051. *074941*
Sandrelle, 101 Rue Béchevelin, 69007 Lyon.
T. 0472800409, Fax 0472800446. *074942*
Solo, 9 Rue Vaubecour, 69002 Lyon. T. 0478420100, Fax 0478420145. *074943*
Vannoni, 27 Rue Tramassac, 69005 Lyon.
T. 0478929904. *074944*
Vernay-Carron, Georges, 99 Cours Emile-Zola, 69100 Lyon. T. 0478940069, Fax 0472449770. *074945*

Lyons-la-Forêt (Eure)
Hirsch, Serge, Rue Hôtel-de-Ville, 27480 Lyons-la-Forêt.
T. 0232495108. *074946*
Noblet, Jean-Pascal, Rue Hôtel-de-Ville, 27480 Lyons-la-Forêt. T. 0232498103. *074947*

Maîche (Doubs)
Bouton, Jean-Marie, 2 Rue Scierie, 25120 Maîche.
T. 0381641001. *074948*

Mâcon (Saône-et-Loire)
Amandier, 22 Rue Dufour, 71000 Mâcon.
T. 0385409267. *074949*
Galerie des Ursulines, 2 Pl de la Baille, 71000 Mâcon.
T. 0385383238. - Paint / Sculp - *074950*
Sel d'Argent, 31 Rue Philibert-Laguiche, 71000 Mâcon.
T. 0385393106. *074951*

Mandelieu (Alpes-Maritimes)
Aquaréel, 272 Av Henry-Clews, 06210 Mandelieu.
T. 0493932182. *074952*
Galerie Anaïs, Av Jean-Monnet, 06210 Mandelieu.
T. 0493497352. *074953*
Galerie Image In, Rallye Centre Commercial, 06210 Mandelieu. T. 0493935939. *074954*

Marcq-en-Barœul (Nord)
Septentrion Galerie Peinture, Chemin Ghesles, 59700 Marcq-en-Barœul. T. 0320463580, Fax 0320033932.
- Paint - *074955*

Marignane (Bouches-du-Rhône)
Deleuil, Huguette, 5 Pl République, 13700 Marignane.
T. 0442887885. *074956*

Marly-le-Roi (Yvelines)
Marly Encadrements, 12 Grande Rue, 78160 Marly-le-Roi. Fax (1) 39162642. *074957*
Paccard, Nadia, 30 Grande Rue, 78160 Marly-le-Roi.
T. 0139584792. - Graph - *074958*

Marsanne (Drôme)
Espace 515, Rue Comte-de-Poitiers, 26740 Marsanne.
T. 0475903041. *074959*

Marseille (Bouches-du-Rhône)
Agora, 3 Rue Edmond-Rostand, 13006 Marseille.
T. 0491531292. *074960*
Andréa's Gallery, 10 Pl Alexandre-Labadie, 13001 Marseille. T. 0491623154, Fax 0491500601. *074961*
A.R.C.A. (Action Régionale pour la Création Artistique), 61 Cours Julien, 13006 Marseille. T. 0491421801, Fax 0491429641. - Paint / Graph / Sculp /
Draw - *074962*
Arthotèque Antonin Artaud, 9 Chemin Notre-Dame Consolation, 13013 Marseille. T. 0491063805. *074963*
Artiphore, 44 Rue Tilsit, 13006 Marseille.
T. 0491484162. *074964*
Atelier, 144 Rue Loubon, 13003 Marseille.
T. 0491843209. *074965*
Atelier Cézanne, 56 Rue Sainte, 13001 Marseille.
T. 0491555778. *074966*
Au Domaine des Arts, 60 Blvd Chave, 13005 Marseille.
T. 0491489112. *074967*
Avanti Rapido, 73 Rue Palud, 13006 Marseille.
T. 0491543147. *074968*
Berthier, Jean, 104 Rue Paradis, 13006 Marseille.
T. 0491375348. *074969*
Brès, Martin, 60 Rue Grignan, 13001 Marseille.
T. 0491330292, Fax 0491555314. - Paint /
Graph - *074970*
Briard, Claude, 125 Rue Breteuil, 13006 Marseille.
T. 0491378414. *074971*
Cadrerie, 23 Rue Docteur-Fiolle, 13006 Marseille.
T. 0491370609. - Paint - *074972*
Carnova, 104 Rue Paradis, 13006 Marseille.
T. 0491375481. *074973*
Castell Art, 31 Av Jules-Cantini, 13006 Marseille.
T. 0491790502. *074974*
Darisio, Angel, 22 Rue Panier, 13002 Marseille.
T. 0491910606. *074975*
Dell'Aria, Ignace, 138 Blvd Baille, 13005 Marseille.
T. 0491798779. - Paint - *074976*
Drago, Christiane, 28 Rue Saint-Savournin, 13001 Marseille. T. 0491420462. *074977*

Editions Lacydon, 27 Cours Honoré d'Estienne d'Orves,
13001 Marseille. T. 0491547705. - Paint -   *074978*
Editions Méditerranéennes du Prado, Galerie La Litho-
graphie, 10 Pl aux Huiles, 13001 Marseille.
T. 0491544000.   *074979*
Galerie Athanor, 84 Rue Grignan, 13001 Marseille.
T. 0491338346.   *074980*
Galerie d'Art La Poutre, 206 Rue Paradis, 13006 Mar-
seille. T. 0491371093. - Paint / Sculp / Dec / Fra /
Pho -   *074981*
Galerie de la Cathédrale, 26 Rue Cathédrale, 13002
Marseille. T. 0491560676.   *074982*
Galerie de la Méditerranée, 82 Rue Rome, 13006 Mar-
seille. T. 0491556758, Fax 0491542234.   *074983*
Galerie de Marseille, 68 A Rue Sainte, 13001 Marseille.
T. 0491333377, Fax 0491333990.   *074984*
Galerie du Pharos, 28 Pl aux Huiles, 13001 Marseille.
T. 0491332223.   *074985*
Galerie du Port, 19 Rue Sainte, 13001 Marseille.
Fax 91541524.   *074986*
Galerie du Sud, 32 Rue Saint-Jacques, 13006 Marseille.
T. 0491817464. - Paint -   *074987*
Galerie du Tableau, 37 Rue Sylvabelle, 13006 Marseille.
T. 0491570534.   *074988*
Galerie Gelsi, 105 Rue Paradis, 13006 Marseille.
T. 0491371740. - Paint -   *074989*
Galerie Got, 153 Rue Breteuil, 13006 Marseille.
T. 0491374491.   *074990*
Galerie Horizon, 333 Promenade Corniche-John-Kenne-
dy, 13007 Marseille. T. 0491762603,
Fax 0491772306.   *074991*
Galerie Hyaline, 13 Rue Vian, 13006 Marseille.
T. 0491424794.   *074992*
Galerie Jouvène, 39 Rue Paradis, 13001 Marseille.
T. 0491333201. - Paint -   *074993*
Galerie Léoni, 14 Rue Edmond-Rostand, 13006 Marseil-
le. T. 0491571684.   *074994*
Galerie Levana, 160 Rue Breteuil, 13006 Marseille.
T. 0491374232.   *074995*
Galerie Pythéas, 51 Rue Vallon-Montebello, 13006 Mar-
seille. Fax 91813386.   *074996*
Galerie Trolleybus, 104 Rue Breteuil, 13006 Marseille.
T. 0491534201.   *074997*
Galeries Andréozzi, 19 Rue Edmond-Rostand, 13006
Marseille. T. 0491812602, Fax 0491535396.   *074998*
Panalba International, 26 Quai Rive-Neuve, 13001 Mar-
seille. T. 0491335767.   *074999*
Porcher, Fernand, 20 Rue Saint-Saëns, 13001 Marseille.
T. 0491337794, Fax 0491334476. - Ant / Paint / Mul /
Draw / Tin -   *075000*
Silvestre, Jean-Pierre, 131 Rue Paradis, 13006 Marseil-
le. T. 0491812940, Fax 0491814969.   *075001*
Sordini, 51 Rue Sainte, 13001 Marseille.
T. 0491555999.   *075002*
Stammegna, Marc, 74 Rue Breteuil, 13006 Marseille.
T. 0491374605, Fax 0491812946. - Paint -   *075003*
Vis à Vis, 38 Rue Fort-Notre-Dame, 13007 Marseille.
T. 0491332080.   *075004*

Martigues (Bouches-du-Rhône)
Atelier Métal, 4 Quai Brescon, 13500 Martigues.
T. 0442803190.   *075005*
Galerie Psyché Collodion, 5 Rue Cordonniers, 13500
Martigues. T. 0442801486.   *075006*

Maussane-les-Alpilles (Bouches-du-Rhône)
Aillaud-Serre, 57 Av Vallée-des-Beaux, 13520 Maus-
sane-les-Alpilles. T. 0490545146.   *075007*

Meaux (Seine-et-Marne)
Galerie du Vieux Chapitre, 10 Imp Maciet, 77100 Meaux.
T. 0360239767, Fax 0364339780.   *075008*
Garnier, Marie-Thérèse, 62 Rue Saint-Rémy, 77100
Meaux. T. 0360251988.   *075009*

Megève (Haute-Savoie)
Galerie Consortium International des Arts, 55 Rue Saint-
François-de-Sales, 74120 Megève.
T. 0450587954.   *075010*
Galerie Consortium International des Arts, 100 Rue
Saint-François-de-Sales, 74120 Megève.
T. 0450212246.   *075011*

Galerie d'Art de l'Alpage, 112 Rue Saint-François-de-
Sales, 74120 Megève. T. 0450919232.   *075012*
Gauthier, Danielle, 40 Rue Saint-Jean, 74120 Megève.
T. 0450587673.   *075013*
Salley, Eric, 132 Rue Arly, 74120 Megève.
T. 0450213919.   *075014*

Melun (Seine-et-Marne)
Arts et Bijoux, 19 Blvd Gambetta, 77000 Melun.
T. 64521750.   *075015*
Fulda, Constance, 15 Rue Four, 77000 Melun.
T. 64398837.   *075016*
Galerie de l'Escalier, 41 Rue Saint-Aspais, 77000 Melun.
T. 64394027.   *075017*

Ménerbes (Vaucluse)
Nicolaï, Geneviève, Pl Albert-Roure, 84560 Ménerbes.
T. 0490724322.   *075018*

Mennetou-sur-Cher (Loir-et-Cher)
Galerie Act, 21 Grande Rue, 41320 Mennetou-sur-Cher.
T. 0254980172.   *075019*

Menton (Alpes-Maritimes)
Eau Bleue, 1 Rue Saint-Charles, 06500 Menton.
T. 0492100303, Fax 0492100500.   *075020*
Galerie Mongibello, 21 Rue Saint-Michel, 06500 Men-
ton. T. 0493284878, Fax 0493352266.   *075021*

Méry-sur-Marne (Seine-et-Marne)
Brunet, Francis, 4 Rte Courcelles, 77730 Méry-sur-
Marne. T. 0360236791.   *075022*

Métabief (Doubs)
Dazy, Christian, 15 Rue Village, 25370 Métabief.
T. 0381492717.   *075023*

Metz (Moselle)
Art Cadre des Trinitaires, 2 Rue Boucherie-Saint-Geor-
ges, 57000 Metz. T. 0387747071. - Paint / Graph /
Fra -   *075024*
Art Fonctionnel, 11 Rue Lasalle, 57000 Metz.
T. 0387365737, Fax 0387362576.   *075025*
Art Gambetta, 4 Rue Gambetta, 57000 Metz.
T. 0387380054, Fax 0387626898.   *075026*
Cercle Bleu, 11 Pl Cathédrale, 57000 Metz.
T. 0387761616.   *075027*
Cimaise d'Or, 5 En Nicolairue, 57000 Metz.
T. 0387756400, Fax 0387763959. - Paint / Sculp /
Glass -   *075028*
Faux-Mouvement, 8 Pl Chambre, 57000 Metz.
T. 0387361822, Fax 0387373829.   *075029*
Galerie Art du Temps, 33 Rue Jardins, 57000 Metz.
T. 0387747565.   *075030*
Galerie Arts Multiples, 42 Rue Saint-Marcel, 57000
Metz. T. 0387354901.   *075031*
Galerie d'Art Cour Carrée, 23 Rue Parmentiers, 57000
Metz. T. 0387361777.   *075032*
Galerie La Malle des Indes, 15 Pl Chambre, 57000 Metz.
T. 0387751438. - Paint / Graph -   *075033*
Galerie La Signature, 13 Rue Fabert, 57000 Metz.
T. 0387754227, Fax 0387747110.   *075034*
Galerie Parcours, 2 Rue Tanneurs, 57000 Metz.
T. 0387362553.   *075035*
Galerie Perspective, 7 Rue Tanneurs, 57000 Metz.
T. 0387751500.   *075036*
Galerie Saint-Martin, 6 Pl Saint-Martin, 57000 Metz.
T. 0387761129.   *075037*
Palette Messine, 16 Pl Charrons, 57000 Metz.
T. 0387762111.   *075038*
Roger, Andres Roland, 35 A Rue Jardins, 57000 Metz.
T. 0387363478, Fax 0387363487.   *075039*
Schmitt, 22 Rue Wilson, 57000 Metz. T. 0387663358.
- Paint / Graph / Fra -   *075040*
Simon, 11 En Fournirue, 57000 Metz. T. 0387750295.
- Paint / Graph / Fra -   *075041*
Thiam, 30 Rue Clercs, 57000 Metz.
T. 0387752889.   *075042*

Meyrals (Dordogne)
Magis, Pascal, Les Plantes, 24220 Meyrals.
T. 0553303362.   *075043*

Meyzieu (Rhône)
Agopian, Madeleine, 93 Rue République, 69330 Mey-
zieu. T. 0478314273. - Paint / Graph -   *075044*

Migennes (Yonne)
T.I.A. (France I), 8 Av Roger-Salengro, 89400 Migennes.
T. 0386926934.   *075045*

Milhaud (Gard)
Galerie Esca, 76 Rte Nîmes, 30540 Milhaud.
T. 0466742327.   *075046*

Millau (Aveyron)
Galerie, 23 Blvd Sadi-Carnot, 12100 Millau.
T. 0565600612. - Fra -   *075047*

Mirabel (Tarn-et-Garonne)
Licorne, Bourg, 82440 Mirabel. T. 0563311625.   *075048*

Mirepeisset (Aude)
Lauduique, Patrice, Condamine, 11120 Mirepeisset.
T. 0468461444.   *075049*

Mirmande (Drôme)
Héritier, Carmen, Village, 26270 Mirmande.
T. 0475630363.   *075050*
Sapet, Rue Boulanger, 26270 Mirmande.
T. 0475630271.   *075051*

Moissac (Tarn-et-Garonne)
Espace Montauriol, Galerie Cloître, 2 Pl Durand-de-Bre-
don, 82200 Moissac. T. 0563044000.   *075052*

Monceaux (Orne)
Pontgirard, manoir du Pontgirard, 61290 Monceaux.
T. 0233736436. - Paint -   *075053*

Monflanquin (Lot-et-Garonne)
Graniou, Christian, Pl Arcades, 47150 Monflanquin.
T. 0553365314.   *075054*

Monsempron-Libos (Lot-et-Garonne)
Sauret, 1bis Rue Liberté, 47500 Monsempron-Libos.
T. 0553711869.   *075055*

Mont-Dauphin (Hautes-Alpes)
Arthé, Rue Catinat, 05600 Mont-Dauphin.
T. 0492452942.   *075056*

Mont-de-Marsan (Landes)
Centre d'Art Contemporain, 1bis Rue Saint-Vincent-de-
Paul, 40000 Mont-de-Marsan.
T. 0558755584.   *075057*
Pavillon des Arts, 4 Pl Charles-de-Gaulle, 40000 Mont-
de-Marsan. T. 0558460507.   *075058*

Montargis (Loiret)
Galerie Métamorphose, 7 Rue Dévidet, 45200 Montargis. T. 0238851799.   *075059*

Montauban (Tarn-et-Garonne)
Afrikaans Baaz'Art, 23 Rue Soubirous-Bas, 82000 Montauban. T. 0563203786.   *075060*

Montbazon (Indre-et-Loire)
Artgument, 47 Rue Nationale, 37250 Montbazon.
T. 0547731304.   *075061*

Montbéliard (Doubs)
Malriat, Fernand, 106 Fbg Besançon, 25200 Montbé-
liard. T. 0381912261.   *075062*
Montagnon, Jeanney Sylvie, 8 Quai Tanneurs, 25200
Montbéliard. T. 0381917986.   *075063*
Puysatier, 13 Rue Schliffe, 25200 Montbéliard.
T. 0381911863.   *075064*

Montboucher-sur-Jabron (Drôme)
Editions du Marronnier, ZA Fontgrave, 26740 Montbou-
cher-sur-Jabron. T. 0475460500.   *075065*

Montbrison (Loire)
Galerie Les Tournesols, 1 Rue Paradis, 42600 Montbrison. T. 0477587470, Fax 0477582309.   *075066*

Montfort-l'Amaury (Yvelines)
Coville, Pierre, 10 Rue Moutière, 78490 Montfort-
l'Amaury. T. 0134860002.   *075067*

Montigny-lès-Metz (Moselle)

Galerie Perspective, 17 Rue Pierre-de-Coubertin, 57158
Montigny-lès-Metz. T. 0387634992. *075068*
Monceau Art Fondation, 2bis All Parc-des-Couvents,
57158 Montigny-lès-Metz. T. 0387639496. *075069*

Montluçon (Allier)

Ecritures, 20 Rue d'Alembert, 03100 Montluçon.
T. 0470059850. *075070*

Montmorency (Val-d'Oise)

Fleur et le Blason, 23 Rue Carnot, 95160 Montmorency.
T. 0134122652. *075071*

Montpellier (Hérault)

Artothèque, 1 Rue Joubert, 34000 Montpellier.
T. 0467606166. *075072*
Carré Sainte-Anne, 2 Rue Philippy, 34000 Montpellier.
T. 0467608242. *075073*
Cool'Heures, All Jules Milhau, Centre Commercial Le
Triangle, 34000 Montpellier. T. 0467920800. - Paint /
China / Glass - *075074*
Espace Photo Angle Corum, Esplanade Charles-de-Gaul-
les, 34000 Montpellier. T. 0467791509. *075075*
Galerie d'Art Massane, 4 Rue Massane, 34000 Montpel-
lier. T. 0467608109. - Paint / Graph / Repr /
Fra - *075076*
Galerie d'Art Reno, 12 Rue Saint-Firmin, 34000 Mont-
pellier. T. 0467663730. *075077*
Galerie de l'Ancien Courrier, r Rue Ancien-Courrier,
34000 Montpellier. T. 0467607188. *075078*
Galerie de l'Ecusson, 11 Rue Ancien-Courrier, 34000
Montpellier. T. 0467528014. *075079*
Galerie J.P.F., 10 Rue Sainte-Anne, 34000 Montpellier.
T. 0467605755, Fax 0467607142. *075080*
Galerie Place des Arts, 8 Rue Argenterie, 34000 Mont-
pellier. T. 046/660508, Fax 0467604785.
- Glass - *075081*
Galerie Structures, 12 Rue Palais des Guilhem, 34000
Montpellier. T. 0467661512. *075082*
Glénat, 5 Rue Aiguillerie, 34000 Montpellier.
T. 0467663440. - Graph - *075083*
Librairie La Marge, 9 Rue Docteur-Lachapelle, 34080
Montpellier. T. 0467757858. - Graph - *075084*
Trintignan, Hélène, 21 Rue Saint-Guilhem, 34000 Mont-
pellier. T. 0467605718. - Paint / Graph - *075085*
Wimmer, 8 Rue Monnaie, 34000 Montpellier.
T. 0467662218. *075086*

Montreuil (Seine-Saint-Denis)

Noir d'Ivoire, 24 et 65 Rue Marceau, 93100 Montreuil.
T. 0148709390. - Orient - *075087*

Montreuil-Bellay (Maine-et-Loire)

Rançon, Louis, 87 Rue Douves, 49260 Montreuil-Bellay.
T. 41387104. *075088*

Morlaix (Finistère)

Dedalus, 24 Rue Ange-de-Guernisac, 29210 Morlaix.
T. 0298632216. *075089*
Heurtel, Jean, 26 Rue Ange-de-Guernisac, 29210 Mor-
laix. T. 0298632216. *075090*

Mougins (Alpes-Maritimes)

Galerie de Mougins, Mougins Village, 06250 Mougins.
T. 0493901908. - Paint / Sculp - *075091*
Galerie di Crescendo, 54 Pl Commandant-Lamy, 06250
Mougins. T. 0492920255. - Paint / Sculp /
Jew - *075092*
Galerie Gray d'Albion, 68 Pl Commandant-Lamy, 06250
Mougins. T. 0492920600. *075093*
Galerie 38, 35 Rue Lombards, 06250 Mougins.
T. 0493752640. *075094*

Moulins (Allier)

Galerie des Artisans, 83, rue Allier, 03000 Moulins.
T. 0470467834. *075095*

Mulhouse (Haut-Rhin)

A.M.C., 7 Rue Alfred Engel, 68100 Mulhouse.
T. 0389456395. *075096*
Berné, 16 Rue Sauvage, 68100 Mulhouse.
T. 0389451588. *075097*
Braun, 15 Rue Landser, 68100 Mulhouse.
T. 0389565805, Fax 0389460890. *075098*

Courant d'Art, 19 Rue Arsénal, 68100 Mulhouse.
T. 0389663377. - Graph / Repr / Fra - *075099*
Galerie Concorde, 1 Pl Concorde, 68100 Mulhouse.
T. 0389456454. *075100*
Galerie des Tanneurs, 17 Rue Tanneurs, 68100 Mul-
house. T. 0389458888. *075101*
Galerie Euros, 20 Rue Franciscains, 68100 Mulhouse.
T. 0389563077. *075102*
Marbach, 10 Rue Tanneurs, 68100 Mulhouse.
T. 0389462635. *075103*
Meichler, 9 Rue Couvent, 68100 Mulhouse.
T. 0389564750. *075104*

Nançay (Cher)

Galerie Le Débuché, 2 Rue Château, 18330 Nançay.
T. 0248518507. *075105*

Nancy (Meurthe-et-Moselle)

Bize, Hervé, 19 Rue Gambetta, 54000 Nancy.
T. 0383301731, Fax 0383301717. *075106*
Delhomme Art Suite, 129 Rue Saint-Dizier, 54000 Nan-
cy. T. 0383321620. *075107*
Galerie Art International, 17 Rue Amerval, 54000 Nancy.
T. 0383350683. *075108*
Galerie de la Carrière, 26 Rue Héré, 54000 Nancy.
T. 0383325373, Fax 0383325423. *075109*
Galerie Ovadia, 14 Grande Rue, 54000 Nancy.
T. 0383379332. *075110*
Galerie Raugraff, 14 Rue Raugraff, 54000 Nancy.
T. 0383356595. *075111*
Galerie 91, 91 Grande Rue, 54000 Nancy.
T. 0383378500. *075112*
Harcos, Ladislas, 33 Rue Stanislas, 54000 Nancy.
T. 0383353545. - Paint / Dec - *075113*
Jaeckin, André, 18 Rue J.B. Thierry Solet, 54000 Nancy.
T. 0383923008. - Paint / Graph / Sculp / Tex - *075114*
Lillebonne, 14 Rue Cheval Blanc, 54000 Nancy.
T. 0383355774. *075115*
Thinus, Emmanuel, 93 Grande Rue, 54000 Nancy.
T. 0383351348. - Paint - *075116*
Wingerter, I., 87 Grande Rue, 54000 Nancy.
T. 0383350933. - China / Jew / Cur - *075117*

Nandy (Seine-et-Marne)

Art et Passion, 1 Rue Arqueil, 77176 Nandy.
T. 0360636050. *075118*

Nantes (Loire-Atlantique)

Absidial, 38 Quai Versailles, 44000 Nantes.
T. 40354382. *075119*
Anti-Reflets, 2 Pl Aristide-Briand, 44000 Nantes.
T. 40892369. *075120*
Arcadim, 21 Rue Strasbourg, 44000 Nantes.
T. 0251820169. *075121*
Art Concept, 3 Rue Provence, 44000 Nantes.
T. 40143191, Fax 40745383. *075122*
Art Espace, 45 Blvd Jean-XXIII, 44100 Nantes.
T. 40943098. - Paint / Graph - *075123*
Artothèque Galerie de Prêt, 24 Quai Fosse, 44000 Nan-
tes. T. 40431278, Fax 40698908. *075124*
Atelier Mézzotint, 14 Rue Carmélites, 44000 Nantes.
T. 40481495, Fax 40355488. *075125*
Bernier, 11 Rue Maréchal-Joffre, 44000 Nantes.
T. 40742034. - Paint - *075126*
Bernier, Renée, 11 Av Bascher, 44000 Nantes.
T. 40742034. *075127*
Bourlaouën, 1 Rue Roi-Albert, 44000 Nantes.
T. 40470409. *075128*
Fradin, Jean, 14bis Rue Alger, 44100 Nantes.
T. 40731956. *075129*
Fradin, Jean-Christian, 4 Pl Edouard-Normand, 44000
Nantes. T. 40082629, Fax 51723770. *075130*
Galerie Arlogos, 16 Blvd Gabriel-Guisthau, 44000 Nan-
tes. T. 40082788, Fax 40201048. *075131*
Galerie Art Comparaison, 18 Pass Pommeraye, 44000
Nantes. T. 40893131. - Paint / Sculp / Glass - *075132*
Galerie Convergence, 18 Rue Jean-Jaurès, 44000 Nan-
tes. T. 40201148. *075133*
Galerie de la Découverte, 1 Rue Briord, 44000 Nantes.
T. 40354691. *075134*
Galerie du Martray, 8 Rue Sarrazin, 44000 Nantes.
T. 40120924, Fax 40764639. *075135*
Galerie du Palais, 3 Pl Aristide-Briand, 44000 Nantes.
T. 40482342. - Paint - *075136*

Galerie Hilligot, 3bis Rue Copernic, 44000 Nantes.
T. 40691216. *075137*
Galerie Humbert, 4 Pl Saint-Pierre, 44000 Nantes.
T. 40471415. *075138*
Galerie Images'in, 21 Rue Strasbourg, 44000 Nantes.
T. 40487776, Fax 40481354. *075139*
Galerie Images'in, 16 Rue Budapest, 44000 Nantes.
T. 0251720082. *075140*
Galerie Much, 3 Rue Piron, 44000 Nantes.
T. 40730934. *075141*
Galerie Plessis, 21 Rue Crébillon, 44000 Nantes.
T. 40692100, Fax 51823859. *075142*
Galerie Suffren, 1 Rue Suffren, 44000 Nantes.
T. 40693637. *075143*
Grafis, 36 Rue Verdun, 44000 Nantes.
T. 0251820025. *075144*
Luneau, Michel, 17 Rue Mercoeur, 44000 Nantes.
T. 40200864, Fax 40200867. *075145*
Moyon-Avenard, Pass Pommeraye, 44000 Nantes.
T. 40487508. *075146*
Petit Jaunais, 7 Rue Saint-Pierre, 44000 Nantes.
T. 0251822156. *075147*
Rayon Vert, 13 Av Sainte-Anne, 44100 Nantes.
T. 40718827. *075148*
Seston, Paule, 128 Rue Hauts-Pavés, 44000 Nantes.
T. 40404561. *075149*
Sourdille, Catherine, 9 Rue Voltaire, 44000 Nantes.
T. 40734498. *075150*
Zoo, 1 Rue Santeuil, 44000 Nantes.
T. 40730391. *075151*

Narbonne (Aude)

Espace Gauthier, 2bis Rue Armand-Gauthier, 11100 Nar-
bonne, T. 0468655275. *075152*
Galerie Irénée, 17bis Rue Chennebier, 11100 Narbonne.
T. 0468904169. *075153*

Navarrenx (Pyrénées-Atlantiques)

37ème Marine, Pl Casernes, 64190 Navarrenx.
T. 0559660712. *075154*

Nérac (Lot-et-Garonne)

Editions Vers les Arts, 79 Av Georges-Clemenceau,
47600 Nérac. T. 0553653613,
Fax 0553653164. *075155*

Neufchâtel-Hardelot (Pas-de-Calais)

Dupuis, Joël, 4 Pl Bournonville, Hardelot-Plage, 62152
Neufchâtel-Hardelot. T. 0321336538,
Fax 0321326542. *075156*
Galerie Alternance, 448 Av François-1er, Hardelot-Plage,
62152 Neufchâtel-Hardelot. T. 0321876566. *075157*

Neuilly-sur-Seine (Hauts-de-Seine)

Fil des Galeries, 71 et 73 Rue Chézy, 92200 Neuilly-sur-
Seine. T. 0147227244. *075158*
MVD Gravures, 7 Rue Berteaux-Dumas, 92200 Neuilly-
sur-Seine. T. 0147223751. *075159*

Nevers (Nièvre)

Arts et Communications, 1bis Rue Vertpré, 58000 Ne-
vers. T. 0386571225. *075160*
Galerie du Puits du Bourg, 46bis Blvd Maréchal-Juin,
58000 Nevers. T. 0386576031. *075161*
Galerie Saint-Cyr, 18 Rue Cathédrale, 58000 Nevers.
T. 0386574565. - Paint / Graph / Sculp / Cur - *075162*

Nice (Alpes-Maritimes)

Air de Paris, 18 Rue Barillerie, 06300 Nice.
T. 0493623362, Fax 0493853200. *075163*
Art et l'Affiche, 17 Rue Alfred-Mortier, 06000 Nice.
T. 0493623655. - Repr - *075164*
Artepolis, 6 Rue Paradis, 06000 Nice.
T. 0493888434. *075165*
Atelier, 3 Rue Saint-François-de-Paule, 06300 Nice.
T. 0493858888, Fax 0493852422. *075166*
Atelier Carina, 3 Rue de France, 06000 Nice.
T. 0493889339. - Paint - *075167*
Boco, Brigitte, 14 Rue Droite, 06300 Nice.
T. 0493804343. *075168*
Boutique Ferrero, 24 Rue de France, 06000 Nice.
T. 0493874150. - Paint / Graph - *075169*
Chapuis, 62 Blvd Risso, 06300 Nice. T. 0493555313.
- Graph - *075170*

Colt Gallery, 21 Rue Ponchettes, 06300 Nice.
T. 0493138623, Fax 0493138622. *075171*
Debarn, Raph, 22bis Blvd Stalingrad, 06300 Nice.
T. 0493566222, Fax 0493568118. *075172*
Duh-Four, 11bis Rue Pertinax, 06000 Nice.
T. 0493852404. *075173*
Dury, Christian, 31 Rue Droite, 06300 Nice.
T. 0493625057. *075174*
E.M.H., 1 Rue Alphonse-Karr, 06000 Nice.
T. 0493821047. *075175*
Galerie Art'Nold, 20 Rue Saint-François-de-Paule,
06300 Nice. T. 0493854577,
Fax 0493850656. *075176*
Galerie Art'7, 7 Promenade des Anglais, 06000 Nice.
T. 0493888229. - Paint / Graph / Sculp - *075177*
Galerie Chevalier, 17 Rue Benoît-Bunico, 06000 Nice.
T. 0493800494, Fax 0493806120. *075178*
Galerie Chifflet, 63 Rue France, 06000 Nice.
T. 0493873168. *075179*
Galerie de la Gare, 49 Av Thiers, 06000 Nice.
Fax 93871321. *075180*
Galerie des Maîtres Contemporains, 39 Rue Gioffredo,
06000 Nice. T. 0493139495. *075181*
Galerie du Château, Espace Graphique, 14 Rue Droite,
06300 Nice. Fax 93859436. *075182*
Galerie du Comté, 7 Av Suède, 06000 Nice.
T. 0493883188. *075183*
Galerie du Palais-Royal, 35 Rue France, 06000 Nice.
T. 0493823055. *075184*
Galerie Ferrero, 2 Rue Congrès, 06000 Nice.
T. 0493883444, Fax 0493887475. - Paint / Graph /
Sculp / Pho - *075185*
Galerie Ferrero, 7 Promenade Anglais, 06000 Nice.
T. 0493821702. *075186*
Galerie Gye-Jacquot, 1 Rue Rivoli, 06000 Nice.
T. 0493821332. *075187*
Galerie Kristina, 16 Rue Liberté, 06000 Nice.
T. 0493882577. *075188*
Galerie Krivy, 15 Rue Ponchettes, 06300 Nice.
T. 0493924919. *075189*
Galerie Le Chanjour, 11 Quai Deux-Emmanuel, 06000
Nice. T. 0493899797. *075190*
Galerie Lézarts, 2 Rue Défly, 06000 Nice.
T. 0493808093. *075191*
Galerie Longchamp, 8 Av Verdun, 06000 Nice.
T. 0493822428, Fax 0493161393. *075192*
Galerie Racine, 4 Av Suède, 06000 Nice.
T. 0493870681. *075193*
Galerie Saint-Michel, 48 Rue de France, 06000 Nice.
T. 0493880301. *075194*
Galerie Sintitulo, 64 Blvd Risso, 06300 Nice.
T. 0492040272, Fax 0492040291. *075195*
Galerie Villaréal, 5 Blvd Gambetta, 06000 Nice.
T. 0493861040. *075196*
Garden-Gallery, 4 Av de Suède, 06000 Nice.
T. 0493870772. *075197*
Gassin, Lola, 6 Rue Terrasse, 06000 Nice.
T. 0493855656. *075198*
Hervieu, Paul, 26 Rue Pastorelli, 06000 Nice.
T. 0493800210. - Paint / Graph - *075199*
Iris Bleu, 5 Rue Rossetti, 06000 Nice.
T. 0493850996. *075200*
Lesné-Falsetti, 11 Rue Colonna-d'Istria, 06000 Nice.
T. 0493926965. *075201*
Magliano, 38 Av Galliéni, 06000 Nice.
T. 0493926165. *075202*
Méditerranée, 40 Rue Smolett, 06300 Nice.
T. 0493269210. *075203*
Mercier-Münch, Mireille, 6bis Rue France, 06000 Nice.
T. 0493820993, Fax 0493160675. *075204*
Montauti, Siegfried, 40 Rue de France, 06000 Nice.
T. 0493873334. - Paint / Graph / Repr / Fra - *075205*
Oh Couleur de l'Art, 22 Rue Emmanuel-Philibert, 06300
Nice. T. 0493552575. *075206*
Otmezguine, Jane, 25 Av Notre-Dame, 06000 Nice.
T. 0493924249. *075207*
Perrin, Jacqueline, 14 Av Saint-Jean-Baptiste, 06000
Nice. T. 0493925747, Fax 0493925746. - Paint / Furn /
Cur - *075208*
Quadrige, 21 Rue France, 06000 Nice.
T. 0493877440. *075209*
Roger, Anne, 26 Rue Saint-François-de-Paule, 06300
Nice. T. 0493625757. *075210*

Sapone, Antonio, 25 Blvd Victor-Hugo, 06000 Nice.
T. 0493885427. - Paint - *075211*
Soardi, 8 Rue Désiré-Niel, 06000 Nice. T. 0493139897,
Fax 0493623330. *075212*
Traverso, Joseph, 51 Av Maréchal-Lyautey, 06000 Nice.
T. 0493626633. *075213*
Vrais Faux de Bernard Feldain, 12 Rue Paradis, 06000
Nice. T. 0493162576. *075214*

Niort (Deux-Sèvres)
Espace 31, 31 Av Paris, 79000 Niort.
T. 0549280444. *075216*
Galerie Royale, 8 Rue Basse, 79000 Niort.
T. 0549246581. *075217*

Nîmes (Gard)
Artothèque Sud, 9 Rue Emile-Jamais, 30900 Nîmes.
T. 0466760201. *075218*
Camaïeu, 1bis Rue Pierre-Semard, 30000 Nîmes.
T. 0466218781. *075219*
Espace Bronze, 24 Rue Aspic, 30000 Nîmes.
T. 0466761516. *075220*
Galerie de la Fontaine, 12 B Quai Fontaine, 30900
Nîmes. T. 0466217425. *075220a*
Galerie des Arts, 10 Rue Emile-Jamais, 30900 Nîmes.
T. 0466217663. *075221*
Galerie du Sud, 30 Rue Agau, 30000 Nîmes.
T. 0466360504. *075222*
Image de Marque, 8 Imp Viala, 30000 Nîmes.
Fax 66680603. *075223*
Image en Plus, 5 Rue Marchands, 30000 Nîmes.
T. 0466760393. *075224*
Papespa's, 22 Rue Cerisiers, 30000 Nîmes.
T. 0466233990, Fax 0466623466. *075225*
Ribelin, 64 Blvd Gambetta, 30000 Nîmes.
Fax 66676979. *075226*
Vidal, 22 Rue Littré, 30000 Nîmes.
T. 0466360737. *075227*

Noailhac (Corrèze)
Atelier de Vigreyos, Château La Coste, 19500 Noailhac.
T. 0555254203. *075228*

Noirmoutier-en-l'Ile (Vendée)
Bourreau Ravier, 19 Grande Rue, 85330 Noirmoutier-en-
l'Ile. T. 0251391714. - Paint - *075229*
Galerie du Château, 7 Rue Cure, 85330 Noirmoutier-en-
l'Ile. T. 0251391827. *075230*
Galerie du Port, 6 Quai Jean-Bart, 85200 Noirmoutier-
en-l'Ile. T. 0251399949. *075231*
Galerie L'Intemporelle, 1 Rue Marché, 85200 Noirmoutier-en-l'Ile. T. 0251394040. *075232*
Galerie Phidias, 1 Rue Grand-Four, 85200 Noirmoutier-
en-l'Ile. T. 0251395354. *075233*
Martin-L'Houtellier, 4 Rue Piet, 85200 Noirmoutier-en-
l'Ile. T. 0251393392. *075234*

Nonant (Calvados)
Art du Temps, Le Bourg, 14400 Nonant.
T. 0231213449. *075235*

Olivet (Loiret)
Haure, Christian, La Grange de l'Orbellière, 487 Rue Ivoy,
45160 Olivet. T. 0238564811. *075236*

Orléans (Loiret)
Boutique aux Chimères, 10 Rue Fauchets, 45000 Or-
léans. T. 0238536249. *075237*
F.R.A.C. du Centre, 12 Rue Tour-Neuve, 45000 Orléans.
T. 0238625200. *075238*
Fraquet, Madeleine, 6 Rue Pensées, 45000 Orléans.
T. 0238546838. *075239*
Nirvana, 3 Rue Louis-Roguet, 45000 Orléans.
T. 0238779732, Fax 0238539692. *075240*
Oulan Bator, 20 Rue Curés, 45000 Orléans.
T. 0238543392. *075241*
Squ'Art, 211 Rue Bourgogne, 45000 Orléans.
T. 0238533272. *075242*

Ornans (Doubs)
Galerie Saint-Laurent, 25 Rue Pierre-Vernier, 25290 Or-
nans. T. 0381571673. *075243*

Orvault (Loire-Atlantique)
Galerie d'Art de la Grée, 18 Rte Basse-Indre, 44700 Or-
vault. T. 40630363. *075244*

Oyonnax (Ain)
Ex-Libris, 3 Rue Brunet, 01100 Oyonnax.
T. 0474736497. *075245*

Paimpol (Côtes-d'Armor)
Le Nost, Alain, 2 Rue Georges-Brassens, 22500 Paimpol. T. 0296205846. *075246*

Pamiers (Ariège)
Angé, Annie, 9 Rue Blanche, 09100 Pamiers.
T. 0561675980. *075247*

Paradou (Bouches-du-Rhône)
Coerten, Jacques, Rte Saint-Roch, Moulin de Paradou,
13520 Paradou. T. 0490544311. *075248*

Paris
Aaron, Didier, 118 Rue Fbg-Saint-Honoré, 75008 Paris.
T. 0147424734, Fax 0142662417. - Paint / Graph /
Furn / Orient / Dec / Draw - *075249*
Accrosonge, 17 Rue Sainte-Croix-la-Bretonnerie, 75004
Paris. T. 0142774631, Fax 0148870139.
- Eth - *075250*
Actis Casa Bella, 19 Rue Miromesnil, 75008 Paris.
T. 0142669929. - Paint - *075251*
ADAC, 21 Rue Saint-Paul, 75004 Paris. T. 0142779626.
- Paint - *075252*
Adler, 11 Rue Miromesnil, 75008 Paris. T. 0140060382,
Fax 0142665602. *075253*
Affich' et Vous, 42 Av Félix-Faure, 75015 Paris.
T. 0143586365. *075254*
Afghane, 13 Rue Descartes, 75005 Paris.
T. 0144070153. *075255*
Agartha, 40 Rue Seine, 75006 Paris. T. 0146332930,
Fax 0146339452. *075256*
A.H. Fine Arts, 32 Av Matignon, 75008 Paris.
T. 0140070637, Fax 0140070638. *075257*
Aigle Impérial, 3 Rue Miromesnil, 75008 Paris.
T. 0142652733. - Paint - *075258*
Aigouy & Roujon, 4 Rue Agar, 75016 Paris.
T. 0145250198. *075259*
Ainsi Soient-Ils, 39 Rue Charonne, 75011 Paris.
T. 0148054247. *075260*
Aittouares, 10 Rue Grange-Batelière, 75009 Paris.
T. 0145234113, Fax 0142070390. - Ant / Paint /
Graph / Sculp / Draw - *075261*
Aittouares, 35 Rue Seine, 75006 Paris. T. 0140518746.
- Ant / Paint / Graph / Sculp / Draw - *075262*
Akagni, 57 Quai Grands-Augustins, 75006 Paris.
T. 0143268252. - Paint - *075263*
Albert 1er, 37bis Rue Jean-Goujon, 75008 Paris.
T. 0142562251. - Paint - *075264*
Albertine, 9 Rue Maître-Albert, 75005 Paris.
T. 0143293920. - Paint / Draw - *075265*
Aleph, 38 Rue Université, 75007 Paris. T. 0142612905.
- Paint - *075266*
Alexandre, 13 Rue Miromesnil, 75008 Paris.
T. 0140070052. - Paint - *075267*
Alexandre, 73 Rue Seine, 75006 Paris. T. 0143265322,
Fax 0143298029. *075268*
Alexandre, 57 Rue Bourgogne, 75007 Paris.
T. 0147538841. *075269*
Alias, 6 Rue Coutures-Saint-Gervais, 75003 Paris.
T. 0148040014, Fax 0148040136. *075270*
Alibert, Lisette, 26 Pl Vosges, 75003 Paris.
T. 0148874550. - Paint - *075271*
Alinéa, 13 Rue Abbaye, 75006 Paris. T. 0143265110.
- Paint - *075272*
Almorial, 13 Rue Dupont-des-Loges, 75007 Paris.
T. 0145552425. - Paint - *075273*
Alphecca, 20 Rue Mogador, 75009 Paris.
T. 0142800334, Fax 0142820476. - Paint - *075274*
A.L.T. Production, 63 et 68 Blvd Voltaire, 75011 Paris.
T. 0143557755, Fax 0143381624. - Paint / Graph /
Repr - *075275*
Alyskewycz, Jorge, 14 Rue Tallandiers, 75011 Paris.
T. 0148065923. - Paint - *075276*
Amate, Moreno & Garcia, 4 Rue Ferdinand-Duval, 75004
Paris. T. 0142783773. - Paint - *075277*

Il était une fois

3, Quai Malaquais, 75006 Paris
Tél. 01 43 26 86 06
Fax 01 43 26 62 08

Arenthon...

Ambassade du Brésil, 28 Rue La-Boétie, 75008 Paris. T. 0145634655. - Paint - *075278*
Ame, 28 Av Laumière, 75019 Paris. T. 0142033664. *075279*
Amyot, 60 Rue Saint-Louis-en-l'Ile, 75004 Paris. T. 0144072341, Fax 0144072348. *075280*
Amyot, Elisabeth, 20 Rue Saint-Louis-en-l'Ile, 75004 Paris. T. 0143267430. - Paint - *075281*
Ancely, Jacques, 34 Rue Drouot, 75009 Paris. T. 0145232025. - Paint - *075282*
Annapurna, 56 Rue Paradis, 75010 Paris. T. 0142465736. - Paint - *075283*
Antarés, 218 Blvd Raspail, 75014 Paris. T. 0143223194. - Graph - *075284*
Antiope, 57 Rue Saint-Louis-en-l'Ile, 75004 Paris. T. 0146335095. - Paint - *075285*
Antipodes, 3 Rue Beaux-Arts, 75006 Paris. T. 0143294568. - Arch / Eth / Jew - *075286*
Antiquités et Art d'Asie, 4 Av Bugeaud, 75116 Paris. T. 0145537748, Fax 0147550252. - Orient - *075287*
Antoinette, 7 Rue Jacob, 75006 Paris. T. 0143268485. - Paint - *075288*
Apartelier, 47 Rue Censier, 75005 Paris. Fax (1) 45356261. *075289*
Apologue, 4 Rue Braque, 75003 Paris. T. 0142745804, Fax 0142743950. *075290*
Apomixie, 19 Rue Guénégaud, 75006 Paris. T. 0146330302, Fax 0143297615. *075291*
Appel, Hélène, 75 Rue Saint-Dominique, 75007 Paris. T. 0145512817. - Paint / Graph - *075292*
Applicat, 16 Rue Seine, 75006 Paris. T. 0143253924, Fax 0140468676. *075293*
Arc en Seine, 31 Rue Seine, 75006 Paris. T. 0143291102, Fax 0143299766. - Paint / Graph / Furn / Sculp - *075294*
Arcade Colette, 17 Rue Valois, 75001 Paris. T. 0142860538. *075295*
Arcelin Saxe, 14 Rue Poissy, 75005 Paris. T. 0143290618. - Paint - *075296*
Archéologie, 40 Rue Bac, 75007 Paris. T. 0145486160, Fax 0145487525. *075297*
Arches et Toiles, 98 Rue Lepic, 75018 Paris. T. 0142518458. *075298*
Archétype, 17 Rue Francs-Bourgeois, 75003 Paris. T. 0142721815. - Graph / Draw - *075299*
Arditti, 15 Rue Miromesnil, 75008 Paris. T. 0142656120. - Paint - *075300*
Aréa, 10 Rue Picardie, 75003 Paris. T. 0142726866. *075301*
Aronthon, 3 Quai Malaquais, 75006 Paris. T. 0143268606, Fax 0143266208. - Graph - *075302*
Ariane, 112 Rue Croix-Nivert, 75015 Paris. T. 0142502133, Fax 0148425928. *075303*
Ariane, 103 Rue Croix-Nivert, 75015 Paris. T. 0145310952. *075304*
Aricchi, Akie, 26 Rue Keller, 75011 Paris. T. 0140216457. *075305*
Ariel, 140 Blvd Haussmann, 75008 Paris. T. 0145621309. - Paint / Sculp - *075306*
Ariel Rive Gauche, 21 Rue Guénégaud, 75006 Paris. T. 0143545701. - Paint - *075307*
Armonie, 8 Rue Chauveau-Lagarde, 75008 Paris. T. 0142664743. *075308*
Arnaud, Florence, 10 Rue Saintonge, 75003 Paris. T. 0142770179. - Graph / Draw - *075309*
Arnoux, 27 Rue Guénégaud, 75006 Paris. T. 0146330466, Fax 0146332540. - Ant / Paint / Graph / Sculp / Draw - *075310*
Art Actuel, 22 Rue Chauchat, 75009 Paris. T. 0142471011, Fax 0142470465. *075311*
Art Actuel, 6 Rue Lisbonne, 75008 Paris. T. 0145220166, Fax 0142937601. *075312*
Art Cadre, 47 Cours Vincennes, 75020 Paris. T. 0143728064, Fax 0143261007. - Paint / Graph / Sculp / Fra / Draw - *075313*
Art Cadre Dauphine, 24 Rue Dauphine, 75006 Paris. T. 0143265621. - Paint / Graph / Sculp / Fra / Draw - *075314*
Art Club, 1 Rue Pierre-Lescot, 75001 Paris. T. 0140260216, Fax 0140262107. *075315*
Art Concorde, 36 Rue Penthièvre, 75008 Paris. T. 0145620044, Fax 0142257938. - Graph - *075316*
Art Conseil, 14 Rue Taillandiers, 75011 Paris. T. 0148065906, Fax 0148065926. *075317*
Art Conseil International, 46 Av George-V, 75008 Paris. T. 0147202405. *075318*
Art des Isles, 8 Rue Charlot, 75003 Paris. T. 0148047753. *075319*
Art du Bristol, 112 Rue Fbg-Saint-Honoré, 75008 Paris. T. 0142650463. - Paint - *075320*
Art en Mouvement, 17 Rue Duvivier, 75007 Paris. T. 0145550316, Fax 0147057407. *075321*
Art Estampe, 67 Blvd Général-Martial-Valin, 75015 Paris. T. 0140607797, Fax 0140607339. - Graph - *075322*
Art et Art, 204 Blvd Saint-Germain, 75007 Paris. T. 0145442405. *075323*
Art et Communication, 6 Rue Lanneau, 75005 Paris. T. 0143261355. *075324*
Art et Créations, 102 Rue Noilet, 75017 Paris. T. 0142295748. *075325*
Art et Regard, 45 Rue Cambronne, 75015 Paris. T. 0147343007. *075326*
Art Expo, 33 Rue Saint-Paul, 75004 Paris. T. 0142786367, Fax 0142782139. *075327*
Art Facts, 145 Rue Pelleport, 75020 Paris. T. 0143586204, Fax 0143586283. *075328*
Art International, 12 Rue Ferrandi, 75006 Paris. T. 0145488428. - Paint - *075329*
Art K, 2 Av Champaubert, 75015 Paris. T. 0140560069. *075330*
Art Linéa, 16 Rue Linois, 75015 Paris. T. 0145758666. *075331*
Art Matignon, 14 Av Matignon, 75008 Paris. T. 0142256477. - Paint - *075332*
Art Mel, 63 Rue Fbg-Saint-Honoré, 75008 Paris. T. 0142666116, Fax 0149249594. *075333*
Art Modeste, 43 Rue Poitou, 75003 Paris. T. 0140279282. - Paint - *075334*
Art Mouvement, 34 Rue Keller, 75011 Paris. T. 0149299419. - Paint - *075335*
Art Mural, 77 Av Gobelins, 75013 Paris. T. 0145351460. - Paint - *075336*
Art of this Century, 63 Blvd Raspail, 75006 Paris. Fax (1) 42228775. *075337*
Art Pluralis, 5 Rue Champ-de-Mars, 75007 Paris. T. 0145502967. - Paint / Graph / Fra - *075338*
Art Présent, 79 Rue Quincampoix, 75003 Paris. T. 0140278025. *075339*
Art Public, 36 Rue Serpente, 75006 Paris. T. 0140460242. *075340*
Art's Sagot International, 123 Rue Pompe, 75016 Paris. Fax (1) 47550350. *075341*
Art Sanjo, 17 Rue Bonaparte, 75006 Paris. T. 0144070045, Fax 0144070046. *075342*
Art Service, 115 Rue Saint-Martin, 75004 Paris. T. 0142741910, Fax 0142746382. - Paint - *075343*
Art-Vie, 69 Rue Entrepreneurs, 75015 Paris. T. 0145796060. *075344*
Art Yomiuri France, 5 Quai Conti, 75006 Paris. T. 0143261535. - Paint - *075345*
Art 204, 204 Blvd Saint-Germain, 75007 Paris. T. 0142222629, Fax 0145484848. - Paint / Graph / Sculp / Draw - *075346*
Art 29, 29 Rue Guénégaud, 75006 Paris. T. 0143252404. - Paint - *075347*
Art 3, 26 Pl Vosges, 75003 Paris. T. 0142718608. *075348*
Art 50, 50 Rue Verneuil, 75007 Paris. T. 0140159950. *075349*
Art 97, 97 Rue Vieille-du-Temple, 75003 Paris. T. 0142775121. *075350*
Artabo, 3 Rue Saint-Sabin, 75011 Paris. T. 0148051407. *075351*
Artcanal, 107 Rue Saint-Dominique, 75007 Paris. T. 0147538771. - Paint - *075352*
Artchipel, 53 Rue Orsel, 75018 Paris. T. 0142513900. *075353*
Artco Europe, 49 Rue Saintonge, 75003 Paris. T. 0142789000. *075354*
Artcodis, 5 Rue Charonne, 75011 Paris. T. 0147008049, Fax 0147006018. *075355*
Artcurial, 9 Av Matignon, 75008 Paris. T. 0142991616. - Paint - *075356*
Arte Mundi France, 134 Blvd Haussmann, 75008 Paris. T. 0145631278, Fax 0145633431. *075357*
Arteca France, 10 Rue Thérèse, 75001 Paris. T. 0142962141. *075358*
Artel, 25 Rue Bonaparte, 75006 Paris. T. 0143549377. - Paint / Sculp / Fra / Ico - *075359*
Artes Magnus France, 16 Pl Vosges, 75004 Paris. T. 0148872948. - Paint - *075360*
Artfrance, 36 Av Matignon, 75008 Paris. T. 0143591789, Fax 0145638483. - Paint - *075361*
Arti, 14 Rue Perche, 75003 Paris. T. 0140278785. *075362*
Artina, 3 Rue Beaux-Arts, 75006 Paris. T. 0143264476. - Paint - *075363*
Artisanat Réalité, 5 Rue Le-Goff, 75005 Paris. T. 0143545959. *075364*
Artmeudon, 42 Av Junot, 75018 Paris. Fax (1) 42232614. *075365*
Arts Contemporains, 55 Rue Roquette, 75011 Paris. Fax (1) 40218384. *075366*
Arts d'Aujourd'hui, 2 Rue Pont-Neuf, 75001 Paris. T. 0142213575. *075367*
Arts et Editions, 21 Quai Voltaire, 75007 Paris. T. 0142610130. *075368*
Arts Plastiques Modernes, 41 Rue Seine, 75006 Paris. T. 0143295055. - Sculp - *075369*
Artuel, 31 Rue Guénégaud, 75006 Paris. T. 0143269243. *075370*
Artveler, 17 Rue Van-Loo, 75016 Paris. T. 0140500680. *075371*
Arver Space, 24 Rue Saint-Ambroise, 75011 Paris. Fax (1) 43571558. *075372*
Askéo, 19 Rue Debelleyme, 75003 Paris. T. 0142771777, Fax 0142772777. *075373*
Association Lil Orsay, 77 Rue Lille, 75007 Paris. T. 0145449010. *075374*
A.T.B., 72 Rue Saint-Honoré, 75001 Paris. T. 0142367131, Fax 0142368498. *075375*
Atelier des Peintres du Marais, 72 Rue François-Miron, 75004 Paris. T. 0142724221. - Paint - *075376*
Atelier Matignon, 33ter Av Matignon, 75008 Paris. T. 0142666387. *075377*
Atelier Original, 2 Pl Porte-Maillot, Palais des Congrès, 75017 Paris. T. 0140682249. *075378*
Atelier Saint-Joseph, 4 Rue Poinsot, 75014 Paris. T. 0143200384. *075379*
Atelier Vert, 84 Rue Ouest, 75014 Paris. T. 0143206280. - Paint - *075380*
Atelier 87, 87 Blvd Ney, 75018 Paris. T. 0142648428. *075381*
Atlantide des 5 Sens, 3 Rue Sauval, 75001 Paris. T. 0142333595. *075382*
Atlantis Gallery, 33 Rue Seine, 75006 Paris. T. 0143268962, Fax 0146336944. - Paint - *075383*
Attali, Jean-Hubert, 18 Rue Saint-Antoine, 75004 Paris. T. 0142760186. *075384*
Au Coeur Couronné, 44 Rue Chevalier-de-La-Barre, 75018 Paris. T. 0142574246. *075385*
Aubry, Christine, 24 Rue Seine, 75006 Paris. T. 0143269131. - Paint - *075386*
Aubry, Claude, 2 Rue Beaux-Arts, 75006 Paris. T. 0143262727, Fax 0140510207. - Paint - *075387*
Auffret, Marie-Josèphe, 42 Rue Frémicourt, 75015 Paris. T. 0145670959. - Paint / Graph / Draw - *075388*
Aurore, 70 Rue Dutot, 75015 Paris. T. 0147348911. - Paint - *075389*
Aurus, 88 Rue Quincampoix, 75003 Paris. T. 0142746242, Fax 0142746241. *075390*
Aux Etoiles de Marie, 46 Rue Chevalier-de-La-Barre, 75018 Paris. T. 0142235050. *075391*
Avant Musée, 2 Rue Brisemiche, 75004 Paris. T. 0148874581, Fax 0142770955. *075392*
Aveline, 20 Rue Cirque, 75008 Paris. T. 0142666029, Fax 0142664591. - Paint - *075393*
Bacquier-Reiner, 7 Rue Bonaparte, 75006 Paris. T. 0143267488. *075394*
Baillon, Elisabeth, 19 Rue Molière, 75001 Paris. T. 0140200406. - Paint - *075395*

Galerie
Charles et André Bailly
25, quai Voltaire - 75007 Paris
Tél. : (33) 01 42 60 56 47
Fax : (33) 01 42 60 54 92

Bailly, Charles & André, 25 Quai Voltaire, 75007 Paris.
T. 0142603647. - Paint - 075396
Bailly, Jacques, 41 Blvd Lannes, 75016 Paris.
T. 0140728536. - Paint - 075397
Bailly, Jacques, 36 Av Matignon, 75008 Paris.
T. 0143590918, Fax 0145635671. - Paint - 075398
Bailly, Laury, Louvre des Antiquaires, 2 Pl Palais-Royal,
75001 Paris. T. 0142615686. 075399
Baladine, 100 Av Daumesnil, 75012 Paris.
T. 0143070519. - Paint / China - 075400
Ballesteros, Ernesto, 119 Rue Montreuil, 75011 Paris.
T. 0143678053. 075401
Balsan, 33 Rue Monge, 75005 Paris. T. 0143549093.
- Paint - 075402
Barberousse, Michel, 70 Quai Hôtel-de-Ville, 75004 Pa-
ris. T. 0142721644. - Paint - 075403
Barbéry, Jean-Louis, 2 Rue Grands-Degrés, 75005 Pa-
ris. T. 0143253376. - Graph / Draw - 075404
Barbier Boltz, Jacques & Caroline, 7 et 8 Rue Pecquay,
75004 Paris. T. 0140278414,
Fax 0140278115. 075405
Barbizon, 71 Rue Saints-Pères, 75006 Paris.
T. 0142221812, Fax 0142226974. - Paint - 075406
Barès, 7 Rue Saints-Pères, 75006 Paris. T. 0142606583.
- Ant / Paint / Graph / Draw - 075407
Barlier, Francis, 36 Rue Penthièvre, 75008 Paris.
T. 0149530005, Fax 0145634737. - Paint / Graph /
Sculp / Draw - 075408
Baron, Marie-Anne, 6 Rue Lille, 75007 Paris.
T. 0140159760. - Orient / Dec - 075409
Baroni, Jean-François, 12 Rue Louvois, 75002 Paris.
T. 0140200473, Fax 0140200207. - Paint - 075410
Barre, Jean-Yves du, 6 Rue Saint-Claude, 75003 Paris.
T. 0148049948. 075411
Barrère, Jacques, 36 Rue Mazarine, 75006 Paris.
T. 0143265761, Fax 0146340283. - Paint / China /
Orient - 075412
Barthe, 35 Blvd Strasbourg, 75010 Paris.
T. 0148244073. - Paint - 075413
Basmadjian, Garig, 90 Blvd Raspail, 75006 Paris.
T. 0142220097, Fax 0142227691. - Paint / Graph /
Draw - 075414
Bassereau, N., 14 Rue Saint-Jean, 75017 Paris.
T. 0142289446. - Graph / Draw - 075415

Bastille, Franka Berndt, 12 Rue Saint-Sabin, 75011 Pa-
ris. T. 0143553193. - Paint - 075416
Bateau Lavoir, 18 Rue Seine, 75006 Paris.
T. 0143251387. - Paint / Graph / Draw - 075417
Baulat, Paul, 18 Rue Montpensier, 75001 Paris.
T. 0142960934. - Paint - 075418
Baxter, 15 Rue Dragon, 75006 Paris. T. 0145490134.
- Paint / Graph / Draw - 075419
Bayser, Bruno de, 69 Rue Sainte-Anne, 75002 Paris.
T. 0147034987, Fax 0142605932. 075420
Beaubourg, 52 Rue Temple, 75004 Paris.
T. 0142784320, Fax 0142786534. 075421
Beaubourg, 23 Rue Renard, 75004 Paris.
T. 0142712050, Fax 0142711926. - Paint / Graph /
Sculp / Draw - 075422
Beaubourg, Gana, 3 Rue Pierre-au-Lard, 75004 Paris.
T. 0142710045, Fax 0142710223. - Paint - 075423
Beaumer Rosenberg, 5 Quai Montebello, 75005 Paris.
T. 0144072796, Fax 0143545280. 075424
Beauséjour, 35 Blvd Beauséjour, 75016 Paris.
T. 0145279706. - Paint - 075425
Beaux-Arts Matignon, 6 Av Delcassé, 75008 Paris.
T. 0142891632. 075426
Bellanger, Patrice, 198 Blvd Saint-Germain, 75007 Pa-
ris. T. 0145441915, Fax 0142840229. 075427
Belle et Belle, 8 Rue Seine, 75006 Paris.
T. 0143257724. - Paint - 075428
Belle Gabrielle, 3 Rue Norvins, 75018 Paris.
T. 0146063567. - Paint - 075429
Bellechasse, 10 Rue Bellechasse, 75007 Paris.
T. 0155558369. - Paint - 075430
Bellechasse, 55 Rue Bellechasse, 75007 Paris.
T. 0145519297. 075431
Bellefroid, 8 Rue Debelleyme, 75003 Paris.
T. 0140279622. 075432
Bellier, Jean-Claude, 32 Av Pierre-1er-de-Serbie, 75008
Paris. T. 0147201913, Fax 0147206509. - Paint /
Sculp / Pho / Draw - 075433
Bellier, Nicole, 25 Rue Charonne, 75011 Paris.
T. 0148055693. - Paint - 075434
Bellint, 28bis Blvd Sébastopol, 75004 Paris.
T. 0142780191. - Paint / Graph / Sculp - 075435
Benézit, Henri, 20 Rue Miromesnil, 75008 Paris.
T. 0142655456. - Paint - 075436
Benézit, M., 29 Rue Seine, 75006 Paris. T. 0143545665.
- Paint / Graph - 075437
Bercovy, Martine, 5 Rue Charonne, 75011 Paris.
T. 0148070779. - Paint / Graph - 075438
Berès, Huguette, 25 Quai Voltaire, 75007 Paris.
T. 0142612791, Fax 0149279588. - Paint / Graph /
Orient - 075439
Bergerot, 32 Rue Charonne, 75011 Paris.
T. 0147003235, Fax 0140218295. 075440
Berggruen & Cie, 70 Rue Université, 75007 Paris.
T. 0142220212, Fax 0142225743. - Paint /
Furn - 075441
Berko, Louvre des Antiquaires, 2 Pl Palais-Royal, 75001
Paris. T. 0142601940, Fax 0142601941. - Ant /
Paint - 075442

Berna, Suzel, 18 Rue Tournelles, 75004 Paris.
T. 0148873033, Fax 0148873023. - Paint / Sculp /
Pho - 075443
Bernard, Claude, 5 Rue Beaux-Arts, 75006 Paris.
T. 0143269707. 075444
Bernheim-Jeune, 83 Rue Fbg-Saint-Honoré, 75008 Pa-
ris. T. 0142666031. - Ant / Paint / Graph /
Draw - 075445
Bernheim-Jeune, 27 Av Matignon, 75008 Paris.
T. 1 42666031, Fax 1 42666503. - Ant / Paint / Graph /
Draw - 075446
Bernheim, Marcel, 18 Av Matignon, 75008 Paris.
T. 0142652223, Fax 0142652716. - Paint - 075447
Bernier, 4 Rue Jacques-Callot, 75006 Paris.
T. 0143265458. - Paint - 075448
Bert, Louvre des Antiquaires, 2 Pl Palais-Royal, 75001
Paris. T. 0142615850, Fax 0142615849. - Ant /
Paint - 075449
Berthet-Aittouares, 29 Rue Seine, 75006 Paris.
T. 0143265309, Fax 0143269566. 075450
Besseiche, Daniel, 91 Rue Fbg-Saint-Honoré, 75008 Pa-
ris. T. 0144713532. 075451
Beuque, Antoine van de, 15 Pl Vauban, 75007 Paris.
T. 0144183004, Fax 0144183005. 075452
Beyrie, Catherine & Stéphane de, 5 Rue Saintonge,
75003 Paris. T. 0142744727. - Paint - 075453
Beyrie, Maria de, 23 Rue Seine, 75006 Paris.
T. 0143257615. - Paint - 075454
Bideau, Yannick, 30 Rue Varenne, 75007 Paris.
T. 0142221603. - Paint - 075455
Biren, André, 11 Rue Cassette, 75006 Paris.
T. 0142842050, Fax 0142842889. 075456
Birtschansky, Pierre, 156 Blvd Haussmann, 75008 Paris.
T. 0145628886, Fax 0142894197. - Paint - 075457
Black New Arts, 35 Rue Hermel, 75018 Paris.
T. 0142526285. - Paint - 075458
Blanc, Anne, 158 Rue Valois, 75001 Paris.
T. 0142869485. - Paint - 075459
Blanche, 22 Rue Mazarine, 75006 Paris.
T. 0143542929, Fax 0143293591. 075460
Bled, Maud, 20 Rue Jacob, 75006 Paris.
T. 0143294651. - Paint - 075461
Bloch, Denis, 52 Rue Université, 75007 Paris.
T. 0142222526, Fax 0145487373. - Graph - 075462
Blondel, Alain, 50 Rue Temple, 75004 Paris.
T. 0142718586, Fax 0148043397. - Paint /
Sculp - 075463
Blondel, Alain, 4 Rue Aubry-le-Boucher, 75004 Paris.
T. 0142786667, Fax 0142784790. - Paint /
Sculp - 075464
Boldyreff, Natalie, 91 Rue Saint-Honoré, 75001 Paris.
T. 0142360737. 075465
Bomsel, Ariane, 1 Rue Séguier, 75006 Paris.
T. 0143258904. - Paint - 075466
Bonafous-Murat, Arsène, 15 Rue Echaudé, 75006 Paris.
T. 0146334231. - Paint / Graph / Draw - 075467
Bongard, Isabelle, 4 Rue Rivoli, 75004 Paris.
T. 0142781344, Fax 0142781390. 075468
Bonnaud, Jacques, 8 Rue Nesles, 75006 Paris.
T. 0143250206. - Paint - 075469

BOUQUINERIE DE L'INSTITUT S.A.

12, rue de Seine   **PARIS 6e**   *Téléphone 01.43.26.63.49*

Achat   **Vente**

Oeuvres graphiques modernes originales et de reproduction

Affiches modernes   **Livres illustrés modernes**

Boogaerts, 44 Rue Vieille-du-Temple, 75004 Paris.
T. 0142744468.   075470
Boomrang, Louvre des Antiquaires, 2 Pl Palais-Royal,
75001 Paris. Fax (1) 49260581.   075471
Bosc, Jean-Louis, Louvre des Antiquaires, 2 Pl Palais-
Royal, 75001 Paris. T. 0142601948. - Ant / Paint /
Graph / Draw -   075472
Bosquet, 44 Av Bosquet, 75007 Paris. T. 0145515586.
- Paint -   075473
Bouché, Bernard, 123 Rue Vieille-du-Temple, 75003 Pa-
ris. T. 0142726003, Fax 0142726051.   075474
Bouisson, Agnès, 72 Rue Saint-Honoré, 75001 Paris.
T. 0142367131. - Amants -   075475
Boulakia, Fabien & Cie, 20 Rue Bonaparte, 75006 Paris.
Fax 43259192. - Paint / Graph -   075476
Boulakia Rive Droite, 30 Rue Miromesnil, 75008 Paris.
T. 0147425551. - Paint / Graph -   075477
Boulanger, Jacqueline, 1 Av Corbera, 75012 Paris.
T. 0146289719. - Paint -   075478
Boulet, Michelle, 14 Rue La-Boétie, 75008 Paris.
T. 0149240063, Fax 0149240100.   075479
Boulle, Louvre des Antiquaires, 2 Pl Palais-Royal, 75001
Paris. T. 0142615743. - Paint -   075480
Bouqueret-Lebon, 69 Rue Turenne, 75003 Paris.
T. 0140279221.   075481
Bouquinerie de l'Institut, 12 Rue de Seine, 75006 Paris.
T. 0143266349. - Graph -   075482

BOUQUINERIE DE L'INSTITUT
MAZO, LEBOUC S.A.

12, rue de Seine
Paris-6ᵉ
Tél.: 01.43.26.63.49

Bourdon, Lucien, 79 Blvd Raspail, 75006 Paris.
T. 0145480139. - Paint -   075483
Bousbaa, Attia, 1bis Rue Saint-Gilles, 75003 Paris.
T. 0142744545.   075484
Boutersky, Jacques, Louvre des Antiquaires, 2 Pl Palais-
Royal, 75001 Paris. T. 0142615796. - Paint / Graph /
Draw -   075485
Boutet de Monvel, François, 94 Rue Martyrs, 75018 Pa-
ris. T. 0142572925. - Paint / Graph / Draw -   075486
Boutique des Amants, 13 Av Théophile-Gautier, 75016
Paris. T. 0142308969.   075487
Boutique Musée, 19 Rue Saint-Louis-en-l'Ile, 75004 Pa-
ris. T. 0140460696, Fax 0140460763.   075488
Boyer, 38bis Rue Fontaine, 75009 Paris.
T. 0148742174.   075489
Brachot-Amélio, 4 Rue Jacques-Callot, 75006 Paris.
T. 0143265458, Fax 0146340398.   075490
Brame & Lorenceau, 68 Blvd Malesherbes, 75008 Paris.
T. 0145221689, Fax 0145220167. - Paint / Sculp /
Draw -   075491

Brasil Inter Art Galerie, 30 Rue Charonne, 75011 Paris.
T. 0148072017, Fax 0140219849.   075492
Bréhéret, René, 9 Quai Malaquais, 75006 Paris.
T. 0142607474. - Paint / Draw -   075493
Breton, 16 Rue Dauphine, 75006 Paris. T. 0143541490,
Fax 0143290478. - Paint -   075494
Briance, Jean, 23 Rue Guénégaud, 75006 Paris.
T. 0143268551. - Paint -   075495
Brichler, 15 Rue Chaptal, 75009 Paris.
T. 0142829667.   075496
Brimaud, Carole, 103 Rue Réaumur, 75002 Paris.
T. 0140260065, Fax 0140265848.   075497
Broomhead, Michel, 46 Rue Seine, 75006 Paris.
T. 0143253470. - Paint -   075498
Broutta, Michèle, 31 Rue Bergers, 75015 Paris.
T. 0145779371, Fax 0140590432. - Graph / Sculp /
Draw -   075499
Brownstone, Gilbert & Cie, 26 Rue Saint-Gilles, 75003
Paris. T. 0142784321, Fax 0142740400. - Paint /
Graph / Sculp / Draw -   075500
Brullé, Pierre, 25 Rue Tournon, 75006 Paris.
T. 0143251873, Fax 0144070055.   075501
BSMD, 42bis Rue Boursault, 75017 Paris.
T. 0145221511.   075502
Bucher, Jeanne, 53 Rue Seine, 75006 Paris.
T. 0143262232, Fax 0143294704. - Paint / Graph /
Sculp / Draw -   075503
Buci, A.J., 65 Rue Saint-André-des-Arts, 75006 Paris.
T. 0143262329. - Paint -   075504
Burawoy, Robert, 12 Rue Le-Regrattier, 75004 Paris.
T. 0143546736, Fax 0140469229. - Paint /
Orient -   075505
Burrus, Claire, 16 Rue Lappe, 75011 Paris.
T. 0143553690, Fax 0147002603. - Paint / Graph /
Sculp / Pho -   075506
Bussière, Jannel, 16 Rue Norvins, 75018 Paris.
T. 0146069461, Fax 0142544653.   075507
Butman, Alexander, 4 Pl Vendôme, 75001 Paris.
T. 0140159283, Fax 0140150548. - Paint -   075508
Butte Montmartre, 1 Rue Saules, 75018 Paris.
T. 0142574915. - Paint -   075509
Cachoux, Michel, 16 Rue Guénégaud, 75006 Paris.
T. 0143258586.   075510
Cadet Roussel, 92 Rue Grenelle, 75007 Paris.
T. 0142220105. - Paint -   075511
Cadot, Farideh, 77 Rue Archives, 75003 Paris.
T. 0142780836, Fax 0142786361. - Paint / Sculp /
Pho -   075512

Cahiers d'Art
14 Rue du Dragon
75006 - Paris
Tel: 01.45.48.76.73
Fax: 01.45.44.98.50

Cadre Noir, 21bis Av Motte Picquet, 75007 Paris.
T. 0145551363. - Graph -   075513
Cahiers d'Art, 14 Rue du Dragon, 75006 Paris.
T. 0145487673, Fax 0145449850   075513a
Cailac, Paule, 13 Rue Seine, 75006 Paris.
T. 0143269888. - Paint / Graph / Draw -   075514
Caille Matignon, Martin, 75 Rue Fbg-Saint-Honoré,
75008 Paris. T. 0142666071, Fax 0147425548.
- Paint -   075515
Cailleux, 136 Rue Fbg-Saint-Honoré, 75008 Paris.
T. 0143592524, Fax 0142259511. - Paint / Graph /
Draw -   075516
Callithos, 46 Rue Université, 75007 Paris.
T. 0142860059, Fax 0142860069. - Paint /
Graph -   075517
Callu Mérite, 17 Rue Beaux-Arts, 75006 Paris.
T. 0146330418, Fax 0140518221. - Paint -   075518
Camera Obscura, 12 Rue Ernest-Cresson, 75014 Paris.
T. 0145456708.   075519
Camus, Roger, 34 Rue Claude-Decaen, 75012 Paris.
T. 0143441402.   075520
Candillier, André, 26 Rue Seine, 75006 Paris.
T. 0143545924. - Graph -   075521
Caplain Matignon, 29 Av Matignon, 75008 Paris.
T. 0142650463.   075522
Caractère, 99 Rue Saint-Maur, 75011 Paris.
T. 0143572153. - Dec -   075523
Carlebach, K. Emmanuel, 157 Rue Saint-Martin, 75003
Paris. T. 0142715566.   075524
Carlhian, 35 Rue Charonne, 75011 Paris.
T. 0147007928.   075525
Carlier-Desbordes, Evelyne, 9 Rue Médicis, 75006 Paris.
T. 0143252553. - Paint -   075526
Carlimpex Reproduction, 33 Rue Ponthieu, 75008 Paris.
T. 0142255251. - Repr -   075527
Carol, 25 Rue Drouot, 75009 Paris.
T. 0148242027.   075528
Carpentier, 46 Rue Bac, 75007 Paris. T. 0142227958.
- Paint -   075529
Carré, 16 Rue Filles-du-Calvaire, 75003 Paris.
T. 0142747373.   075530
Carré (Galerie des Orfèvres), 23 Pl Dauphine, 75001 Pa-
ris. T. 0143268130. - Paint / Graph / Draph -   075531
Carré d'Or, 46 Av George-V, 75008 Paris.
T. 0140701100, Fax 0140709681. - Jew /
Silv -   075532
Carré, Louis, 10 Av Messine, 75008 Paris.
T. 0145625707, Fax 0142256389. - Paint / Sculp /
Draw -   075533
Casini, Philippe, 13 Rue Chapon, 75003 Paris.
T. 0148040034. - Paint / Graph / Sculp / Draw - 075534
Cassé, Carmen, 10 Rue Malher, 75004 Paris.
T. 0142784314. - Graph -   075535
Castel, Jeanne, 3 Rue Cirque, 75008 Paris.
T. 0143597124. - Paint / Sculp -   075536
Castiglione, 9 Rue Castiglione, 75001 Paris.
T. 0142608791, Fax 0142602796. - Paint -   075537
Castille, 8 Rue Miromesnil, 75008 Paris.
T. 0140070366.   075538
Cath'Art, 13 Rue Sainte-Croix-la-Bretonnerie, 75004 Pa-
ris. T. 0148048010.   075539

Catto Animation France, 53 Rue Vieille-du-Temple, 75004 Paris. T. 0148045459, Fax 0148045610. *075540*

Causans, Etienne de, 25 Rue Seine, 75006 Paris. T. 0143265448, Fax 0143257338. - Paint - *075541*

Cazeau-Berandière, 16 Av Matignon, 75008 Paris. T. 145630900, Fax 145630990. - Paint - *075541a*

Centrale des Tableaux, 256 Rue Marcadet, 75018 Paris. T. 0142295533, Fax 0142294942. - Paint / Repr - *075542*

Centre Européen d'Art, 39bis Av Victor-Hugo, 75016 Paris. T. 0145022288, Fax 0145022290. *075543*

Centre Régional des Oeuvres Universitaires, et Scolaires de Paris (CROUS), 11 Rue Beaux-Arts, 75006 Paris. T. 0143541099. *075544*

Cercle des Arts, 199 Rue Grenelle, 75007 Paris. T. 0144180507, Fax 0144180459. *075545*

Cercle des Collectionneurs d'Art Contemporain, 55 Rue Quincampoix, 75003 Paris. T. 0142785803. *075546*

Cernuschi, Ursula, 75 Rue Oberkampf, 75011 Paris. T. 0148055523. - Paint / Graph - *075547*

Cervantes, 29 Rue Saint-Roch, 75001 Paris. T. 0142602529. *075548*

Cézanne, Philippe, Louvre des Antiquaires, 2 Pl Palais-Royal, 75001 Paris. T. 0142615711, Fax 0142616938. - Paint / Sculp - *075549*

Chabin, 4 Rue Mont-Cenis, 75018 Paris. T. 0142643083. - Paint - *075550*

Chamak, Chantal, 18 Rue Provence, 75009 Paris. T. 0142466694, Fax 0142463930. - Paint - *075551*

Chammard, Monique de, 54 Av La-Motte-Picquet, 75015 Paris. T. 0147344738. *075552*

Champfleury, 17 Rue Nantes, 75019 Paris. T. 0142011931. - Paint - *075553*

Champs Bleus, 4 Rue Candolle, 75005 Paris. T. 0143375752. *075554*

Champvallins, Jacqueline de, 83 Rue Javel, 75015 Paris. T. 0145778833, Fax 0145775867. - Graph - *075555*

Chardin, 18 Av Matignon, 75008 Paris. T. 0142650079. - Paint - *075556*

Charpentier, Françoise, 52 Rue Saint-Louis-en-l'Ile, 75004 Paris. T. 0143545886. - Paint - *075557*

Chaye, Simon, 125 Gal Valois, 75001 Paris. T. 0142962910. - Paint - *075558*

Cheneau, Christian, 127 Rue Vieille-du-Temple, 75003 Paris. T. 0142741848, Fax 0142741729. *075559*

Cheneau, Christian, 30 Rue Lisbonne, 75008 Paris. T. 0145633606. - Paint / Graph / Sculp - *075560*

Chereau, 40 Rue Université, 75007 Paris. T. 0142964058. *075561*

Cheval de Sable, 17 Rue François-Miron, 75004 Paris. T. 0148871967. *075562*

Chez Valentin, 9 Rue Charonne, 75011 Paris. T. 0143573328. *075563*

Chisseaux Rive Gauche, 33 Av La-Bourdonnais, 75007 Paris. T. 0145554917. - Ant - *075564*

Chock, Déborah, 85 Blvd Macdonald, Cité des Sciences, 75019 Paris. T. 0140343122, Fax 0140348494. *075565*

Chomette, Michèle, 24 Rue Beaubourg, 75003 Paris. T. 0142780562. - Paint / Graph / Sculp / Draw - *075566*

Chourlet, Céline, 4 Pl Vosges, 75004 Paris. T. 0142760409. *075567*

Christie's France, 6 Rue Paul-Baudry, 75008 Paris. T. 0140768585, Fax 0142562601. - Ant - *075568*

Cimaise de Paris, 74 Rue Notre-Dame-des-Champs, 75006 Paris. T. 0143252321. - Paint - *075569*

Ciné-images, 68 Rue Babylone, 75007 Paris. T. 0145512750. - Graph / Repr - *075570*

Cinédoc, 45 Passage Jouffroy, 75009 Paris. T. 0148247136. - Graph / Repr - *075571*

Clair, François, 12 Blvd Capucines, 75009 Paris Paris. T. 0140734848. - Paint - *075572*

Clarac-Serou, Max, 19 Rue Dragon, 75006 Paris. Fax (1) 45480326. - Paint - *075573*

Classi, 5 Av Opéra, 75001 Paris. T. 0142860232, Fax 0142860243. *075574*

Claude, Bernard, 5-9 Rue Beaux-Arts, 75006 Paris. T. 0143269707. - Paint / Graph / Sculp / Draw - *075575*

Claude & Lima, 17 Rue Saint-Paul, 75004 Paris. T. 0142779802. - Furn / Orient / Dec - *075576*

GALERIE CAZEAU-BERAUDIERE

Tableaux impressionistes et modernes

16, avenue Matignon - 75008 PARIS
Tél.: 01 45 63 09 00
Fax: 01 45 63 09 90

Clivages, 5 Rue Sainte-Anastase, 75003 Paris. T. 0142724002. *075577*

Coard, 12 Rue Jacques-Callot, 75006 Paris. T. 0143269973. - Paint - *075578*

Coatalem, 93 Rue Fbg-Saint-Honoré, 75008 Paris. T. 0142661717. *075579*

Cochin, Marie-Thérèse, 49 Rue Quincampoix, 75004 Paris. T. 0148049416, Fax 0148049283. *075580*

Cohen-Boulakia, Fabien, 49 Rue Tour, 75016 Paris. T. 0145033485. *075581*

Cohen, Gloria, 26 Rue Bonaparte, 75006 Paris. T. 0146346200, Fax 0143264404. *075582*

Cohen, Joël, 136 Rue Pipcus, 75012 Paris. T. 0143440970. *075583*

Coin de Montcalm, 28 Rue Montcalm, 75018 Paris. T. 0142586327. *075584*

Colas, Christine, 12 Rue Sainte-Anastase, 75003 Paris. T. 0148047300, Fax 0148047746. *075585*

Colin, Christiane, 33 Quai Bourbon, 75004 Paris. T. 0146331403. - Paint - *075586*

Colin-Maillard, 11 Rue Miromesnil, 75008 Paris. T. 0142654670, Fax 0142654362. - Paint - *075587*

Colle-Gobeau, 23 Rue Jean-Mermoz, 75008 Paris. T. 0142894964. - Ant / Paint - *075588*

Colline, 48 Rue Chevalier-de-La-Barre, 75018 Paris. T. 0142644665. *075589*

Colnaghi, 108-112 Rue Fbg-Saint-Honoré, 75008 Paris. T. 0142661451, Fax 0142662395. - Paint / Sculp / Draw - *075590*

Colonne, 4 Pl Vendôme, 75001 Paris. T. 0142606234. - Paint - *075591*

Compagnie Promotion Artistique, 45 Rue Villiers-de-l'Isle-Adam, 75020 Paris. T. 0140336725, Fax 0140336728. *075592*

Comptoir du Timbre d'Art, 7 Rue Trois-Frères, 75018 Paris. T. 0142622248. *075593*

Concorde Art International, 4 Pl Concorde, 75008 Paris. Fax (1) 49249385. *075594*

Confluences, 190 Blvd Charonne, 75020 Paris. T. 0142491560. - Paint - *075595*

Connoisseurs Gallery, 28 Rue Mazarine, 75006 Paris. T. 0144073557. *075596*

Contrejour, 96 Rue Daguerre, 75014 Paris. T. 0143214188, Fax 0143204945. *075597*

Corianne, 32 Av Rapp, 75007 Paris. T. 0145558849. *075598*

Corre, Caroline, 53 Rue Berthe, 75018 Paris. T. 0142553776, Fax 0146060628. *075599*

Correspondances, 38 Rue Penthièvre, 75008 Paris. T. 0145631283. *075600*

Couderc, Christine, 6 Rue Bûcherie, 75005 Paris. T. 0139234441. - Paint - *075601*

Coulon, Jean, 32 Av Matignon, 75008 Paris. T. 0142665080. - Paint - *075602*

Couvrat-Desvergnes, 15 Rue Beaux-Arts, 75006 Paris. T. 0143542808. - Paint - *075603*

Couvrat-Desvergnes, Thierry, 12 Rue Guénégaud, 75006 Paris. T. 0143297270. - Paint - *075604*

CR Galerie, 103 Rue Vieille-du-Temple, 75003 Paris. T. 0142760542. *075605*

Créations Mogador, 20 Rue Mogador, 75009 Paris. T. 0145266917. - Paint - *075606*

Crète, Guy, 121 Rue Vieille-du-Temple, 75003 Paris. T. 0142662122. - Paint - *075607*

Crété, Guy, 121 Rue Vieille-du-Temple, 75004 Paris. T. 0142728225, Fax 0142728230. *075608*

Creuze, Raymond, 12 Rue Beaujon, 75008 Paris. T. 0145637872, Fax 0145614218. *075609*

Creuzevault, Colette, 58 Rue Mazarine, 75006 Paris. T. 0143266785, Fax 0143252570. - Paint / Graph / Sculp / Mul / Draw - *075610*

Crousel-Robelin, 40 Rue Quincampoix, 75004 Paris. T. 0142773887, Fax 0142775900. - Paint / Sculp / Pho - *075611*

C.S.T., 16 Rue Sédillot, 75007 Paris. T. 0147053636. *075612*

Cybele, 65bis Rue Galande, 75005 Paris. T. 0143541626. - Paint - *075613*

Cymaise, 174 Rue Fbg-Saint-Honoré, 75008 Paris. T. 0142895020 k703 (1) 45639978. - Paint - *075614*

Cyril Varet Créations, 67 Av Daumesnil, 75012 Paris. T. 0144758888, Fax 0144758889. *075615*

D'Orient et d'Ailleurs, 13 Rue Bonaparte, 75006 Paris. T. 0143269253. *075616*

Daffos & Estournel, 5 Rue Echaudé, 75005 Paris. T. 0143269710. - Paint - *075617*

Damase, Jacques, 61 Rue Varenne, 75007 Paris. T. 0147055504, Fax 0145513371. - Paint / Graph / Sculp / Draw - *075618*

Dambier-Masset, 5 Rue Beaux-Arts, 75006 Paris. T. 0146330252, Fax 0143260705. *075619*

Darial, 22 Rue Beaune, 75007 Paris. T. 0142612063. *075620*

Daumesnil, 13 Rue Docteur-Goujon, 75012 Paris. T. 0143434357. - Paint - *075621*

Daune, Alain, 14 Av Matignon, 75008 Paris. T. 0143599490. - Paint - *075622*

Davidov, Lina, 210 Blvd Saint-Germain, 75007 Paris. T. 0145489987. *075623*

Déa, 30 Rue Bonaparte, 75006 Paris. T. 0146346900, Fax 0144072676. - Paint - *075624*

Debaigts, Jacques, 28 Rue Poissy, 75005 Paris. T. 0143257173. - Paint - *075625*

Debret, 28 Rue La-Boétie, 75008 Paris. T. 0145634655. - Paint - *075626*

Decker Heftler, Sylviane de, 4 Rue Perronet, 75007 Paris. T. 0145444028, Fax 0145491750. *075627*

Défense d'Afficher, 3 Rue Norvins, 75018 Paris. T. 0146067902. *075628*

Delamare, Daniel, 36 Av Matignon, 75008 Paris. T. 0142891418, Fax 0142562483. *075629*

Delaunay, 7 Rue Isby, 75008 Paris. T. 0143874600. - Paint - *075630*

Delestre, François, 36 Rue Laffitte, 75009 Paris. T. 0148240501, Fax 0148240612. *075631*

Delh, Richard, 34 Av Hoche, 75008 Paris. T. 0142251382, Fax 0142563884. *075632*

Delorme, 21 Rue Miromesnil, 75008 Paris. T. 0142662520. *075633*

Delpire, 13 Rue Abbaye, 75006 Paris. T. 0143265110. - Paint - *075634*

Demeure, 26 Rue Mazarine, 75006 Paris. T. 0143260274. - Paint - *075635*

Démons et Merveilles, 45 Rue Jacob, 75006 Paris. T. 0142962611. *075636*

Depretz, Bernard, 5 Rue Artois, 75008 Paris. T. 0142563775. *075637*

Derry, Benjamin, 26 Rue Jardins-Saint-Paul, 75004 Paris. T. 0142771575. - Paint - *075638*

Desbois, Christian, 14 Av La-Bourdonnais, 75007 Paris. Fax (1) 45560616. *075639*

Désir d'Art, 74 Av Champs-Elysées, Gal Claridge, 75008 Paris. T. 0149539444, Fax 0142890080. *075640*

Develon, Yves, 11 Rue Charles-V, 75004 Paris. T. 0142780055, Fax 0148040108. - Eth - *075641*

Di Meo, 9 Rue Beaux-Arts, 75006 Paris. T. 0146345482, Fax 0143548865. - Paint / Sculp - *075642*

Diegoni, Christine, 47ter Rue Orsel, 75018 Paris. T. 0142646948. *075643*

Différences, 11 Rue Roi-Doré, 75003 Paris. T. 0148873813, Fax 0148878166. *075644*

Digard, Alain, 11 Rue Guénégaud, 75006 Paris. T. 0143548903. - Paint - *075645*

Dimpoulos, 36 Rue Laos, 75015 Paris. T. 0143062308. - Paint / Graph / Sculp - *075646*

Dinet, Etienne, 30 Rue Lisbonne, 75008 Paris. T. 0142564326. - Paint - *075647*

Dionne, 19bis Rue Saints-Pères, 75006 Paris. T. 0149260306, Fax 0140200931. *075648*

Dizian, 11 Rue Saint-Maur, 75011 Paris. T. 0143707026. *075649*

Dmochowski, 43 Rue Quincampoix, 75004 Paris.
T. 0142777773. *075650*
Documents, 53 Rue Seine, 75006 Paris. T. 0143545068.
- Mod - *075651*
Donguy, J. & J., 57 Rue Roquette, 75011 Paris.
T. 0147001094. - Paint - *075652*
Donna, Pierrette di, Louvre des Antiquaires, 2 Pl Palais-
Royal, 75001 Paris. T. 0142960148. - Paint - *075653*
Dorfmann, Patricia, 61 Rue Verrerie, 75004 Paris.
T. 0142775541. *075654*
Doria, 16 Rue Seine, 75006 Paris. T. 0143547349,
Fax 0143256872. *075655*
Dorval, Claude, 22 Rue Keller, 75011 Paris.
T. 0148063567, Fax 0148062558. *075656*
Down Town, 33 Rue Seine, 75006 Paris.
T. 0146338241. *075657*
Dreyfus, Raymond, 3 Rue Beaux-Arts, 75006 Paris.
T. 0143260920. - Paint / Graph / Sculp / Mul /
Draw - *075658*
Dreyfus, Solange, 78 Blvd Sébastopol, 75003 Paris.
T. 0147716774. - Paint - *075659*
Drouant International, 23 Av Marceau, 75116 Paris.
T. 0147235590. - Paint - *075660*
Drouart, 14-16 Rue Grange-Batelière, 75009 Paris.
T. 0147705290, Fax 0148009372. - Paint - *075661*
Drouot, 2 Rue Drouot, 75009 Paris.
T. 0142469009. *075662*
Dubois, Colette, 420 Rue Saint-Honoré, 75001 Paris.
T. 0142601344. - Paint - *075663*
Dubois, Eric, 9 Rue Saint-Paul, 75004 Paris.
T. 0142740529. - Eth / Tin - *075664*
Dulon, 5 Rue Jacques-Callot, 75006 Paris.
T. 0143255000. - Paint - *075665*
Dumonteil, Pierre-Michel, 38 Rue Université, 75007 Pa-
ris. T. 0142612338, Fax 0142611461. - Ant / Paint /
Repr / Sculp - *075666*
Dumoussaud, Daniel, 13 Rue Grange-Batelière, 75009
Paris. T. 0142466855. - Paint - *075667*
Duputel, 20 Rue Beaune, 75007 Paris. T. 0142974792.
- Paint - *075668*
Durand-Dessert, L. & M., 28 Rue Lappe, 75011 Paris.
T. 0148069223. - Paint / Sculp - *075669*
Durand, Lucien, 19 Rue Mazarine, 75006 Paris.
T. 0143262535. - Paint / Sculp - *075670*
Durand, Lucien, 36 Av Bosquet, 75007 Paris.
T. 0145557092. - Paint / Sculp - *075671*
Durand Ruel & Cie, 37 Av Friedland, 75008 Paris.
T. 0145610933, Fax 0145636268. - Paint - *075672*
Duret Dujarric Paris, 21 Rue Miromesnil, 75008 Paris.
T. 0149249199, Fax 0149249173. *075673*
Dutilleul, 24 Pl Vosges, 75003 Paris. T. 0142722181,
Fax 0142722455. - Paint - *075674*
Dutko, Jean-Jacques, 13 Rue Bonaparte, 75006 Paris.
T. 0143269613, Fax 0143292191. - Paint - *075675*
Eclipse, 11 Rue Beaux-Arts, 75006 Paris.
T. 0146338355. - Ant / Arch / Eth / Jew - *075676*
Edition Diffusion Mazel, 154 Rue Temple, 75003 Paris.
T. 0142728607. *075677*
Editions de l'Ermitage, 33 Rue Henri-Barbusse, 75005
Paris. T. 0143547144, Fax 0146338903.
- Graph - *075678*
Editions de la Chapelière, 2 Rue Juste-Métivier, 75018
Paris. T. 0146068295. *075679*
Editions de la Fenêtre, 67 Rue Gergovie, 75014 Paris.
T. 0145412162. - Graph - *075680*
Editions du Beau Livre de France, 22 Rue Colonnes-du-
Trône, 75012 Paris. T. 0143078874,
Fax 0143075337. *075681*
Editions F.B., 85 Blvd Pasteur, 75015 Paris.
T. 0143354495. *075682*
Editions Futura, 43 Rue Sainte-Anne, 75001 Paris.
T. 0142602871, Fax 0142604718. *075683*
EFFA, 84 Av Champs-Elysées, 75008 Paris.
T. 0145626030. - Paint - *075684*
Ehgner, Catherine, 26 Rue Charonne, 75011 Paris.
T. 0140218765. - Paint - *075685*
Ejumeau, 78 Av Suffren, 75015 Paris. T. 0140659497.
- Paint - *075686*
Elbaz, Jacques, 1 Rue Alger, 75001 Paris.
Fax (1) 40209809. *075687*
Eléonore, 18 Rue Miromesnil, 75008 Paris.
T. 0142651781. - Jew / Silv - *075688*

Elsay, 45 Rue La-Rochefoucauld, 75009 Paris.
T. 0145260577, Fax 0140239746. *075689*
Elstir, 6 Rue Chaise, 75007 Paris. T. 0145481495,
Fax 0145483662. - Paint / Sculp / Draw - *075690*
Elysée-Miromesnil, 18 Rue Miromesnil, 75008 Paris.
T. 0147425080. - Paint - *075691*
Elysée-Montaigne, 26 Av Champs-Elysées, 75008 Paris.
T. 0142895101, Fax 0142895103. *075692*
Elysées George V, 47 Av George-V, 75008 Paris.
T. 0147203994. *075693*
Empreintes, 16 Rue Carmes, 75005 Paris.
T. 0146330090. *075694*
En Attendant les Barbares, 50 Rue Etienne-Marcel,
75002 Paris. T. 0142333787. *075695*
Enseigne des Arts, 7 Rue Gomboust, 75001 Paris.
T. 0140159779. - Paint - *075696*
Eolia, 10 Rue Seine, 75006 Paris.
T. 0143263654. *075697*
Epoca, 60 Rue Verneuil, 75007 Paris. T. 0145484866,
Fax 0145448582. *075698*
Epona, 80 Rue Quincampoix, 75003 Paris.
T. 0142773690, Fax 0142771494. *075699*
Epry, Nichols, 9 Rue Dareau, 75014 Paris.
T. 0145803800, Fax 0145806076. *075700*
Ergastère, 7 Rue Miromesnil, 75008 Paris.
T. 0142665892, Fax 0142665907. *075701*
Ermitage, 30 Rue Voûte, 75012 Paris. T. 0143437330,
Fax 0143439774. *075702*
Esders, Viviane, 40 Rue Pascal, 75013 Paris.
T. 0143311010. - Paint - *075703*
Espace Archide, 170bis Rue Fbg-Saint-Antoine, 75012
Paris. T. 0143721753. *075704*
Espace Commines, 17 Rue Commines, 75003 Paris.
T. 0142775326. *075705*
Espace Confort et Vision, 95 Rue Passy, 75016 Paris.
T. 0146474780. - Paint - *075706*
Espace Photographique de Paris, 1 Rue Pierre-Lescot,
75001 Paris. T. 0140268712. - Pho - *075707*
Espace Temps, 27 Rue Saint-Dominique, 75007 Paris.
T. 0145511839. - Paint / Glass - *075708*
Espace Temps, 27 Rue Saint-Paul, 75004 Paris.
T. 0142780881. - Paint / Glass - *075709*
Estève, 3 Rue Jacques-Callot, 75006 Paris.
T. 0140331910. - Paint - *075710*
Eterso, 74 Rue Perche, 75003 Paris. T. 0142726520,
Fax 0142726562. *075711*
Etude et Commerce International, 14 Rue Saussaies,
75008 Paris. T. 0142662811. *075712*
Europa, 22 Rue Jardins-Saint-Paul, 75004 Paris.
T. 0142776404. *075713*
Everarts, 8 Rue Argenson, 75008 Paris T. 0142655488.
- Paint - *075714*
Eyris, 5 Rue Nicolas-Appert, 75011 Paris.
T. 0143389869, Fax 0143389540. *075715*
Fabius Frères, 152 Blvd Haussmann, 75008 Paris.
T. 0145623918, Fax 0145625307. - Paint / Graph /
Draw - *075716*
Fabre, 6 Rue Pont-de-Lodi, 75006 Paris.
T 0143254263. - Paint - *075717*
Façade, 10 Rue Beaubourg, 75003 Paris.
T. 0148870220. - Paint / Graph / Sculp / Draw - *075718*
Falcone, Pierre, 42 Av Montaigne, 75008 Paris.
T. 0147230295, Fax 0140701847. - Paint /
Graph - *075719*
Farley, Philippe, 7 Rue Aguesseau, 75008 Paris.
T. 0142746756. - Paint - *075720*
Farnier, Anne-Marie, 11 Rue Saints-Pères, 75006 Paris.
T. 0142602825. *075721*
Faure, Florence, 6 Rue Bonaparte, 75006 Paris.
Fax (1) 40518288. *075722*
Fay, 6 Rue Saint-Merri, 75004 Paris.
T. 0142299432. *075723*
Felli, Jean-Marie, 15 Rue Guénégaud, 75006 Paris.
T. 0143542841. *075724*
Felman, Jacqueline, 8 Rue Popincourt, 75011 Paris.
T. 0147008771. - Paint / Graph / Sculp / Draw - *075725*
Fels, Mathias & Cie, 138 Blvd Haussmann, 75008 Paris.
T. 0142652134. - Paint / Sculp - *075726*
Fenêtre, 3 Quai Tournelle, 75005 Paris. T. 0143545115,
Fax 0143545189. *075727*
Ferrara, 7 Rue Charlemagne, 75004 Paris.
T. 0148876404. *075728*

Ferrière, 78 Rue Saint-Louis-en-l'Ile, 75004 Paris.
T. 0146347418. - Paint - *075729*
Ferronnerie, 40 Rue Folie-Méricourt, 75011 Paris.
T. 0148065084. *075730*
Ferry, Nicole, 57 Quai Grands-Augustins, 75006 Paris.
T. 0146335245. *075731*
Fiat, Dominique, 80 Rue Quincampoix, 75003 Paris.
T. 0142714873. *075732*
Field, Jere, 18 Rue Miromesnil, 75008 Paris.
T. 0142652498. - Paint - *075733*
Figure, 27 Blvd Saint-Germain, 75005 Paris.
T. 0143296785. *075734*
Finard, Alain, 7 Rue Beaune, 75007 Paris.
T. 0142612395, Fax 0140200192. - Paint - *075735*
Findlay, Wally, 2 Av Matignon, 75008 Paris.
T. 0142257074, Fax 0142564045. - Paint - *075736*
Findlay, Wally, 48 Av Gabriel, 75008 Paris.
T. 0142257074. - Paint - *075737*
Fischbacher, 33 Rue Seine, 75006 Paris.
T. 0143268487, Fax 0143264887. - Paint /
Graph - *075738*
Fischer-Kiener, 46 Rue Verneuil, 75007 Paris.
T. 0142611782, Fax 0142601337. - Paint / Graph /
Sculp / Draw - *075739*

J. FISCHER – CH. KIENER

Dessins – Peintures
Sculptures

46, rue de Verneuil,
75007 PARIS
Tél.: 01.42.61.17.82
Fax: 01.42.60.13.37

Flak, 8 Rue Beaux-Arts, 75006 Paris. T. 0146337777,
Fax 0146332757. - Paint / Sculp / Mul / Draw - *075740*
Flament, Christiane, 113 Rue Cherche-Midi, 75006 Pa-
ris. T. 0142221309. - Graph / Draw - *075741*
Flaviand, 6 Rue Seine, 75006 Paris. T. 0143548026.
- Paint - *075742*
Flay, Jennifer, 7 Rue Debelleyme, 75003 Paris.
T. 0148874002, Fax 0148873422. *075743*
Fletcher, 116 Rue Vieille-du-Temple, 75003 Paris.
T. 0140290112. - Paint - *075744*
Flora, 10 Rue La-Vacquerie, 75011 Paris.
T. 0144641170. - Paint / Sculp - *075745*
Fondation Paul Ricard, 35 Av Franklin-Roosevelt, 75008
Paris. T. 0142669141. - Paint - *075746*
Fontana, 12 Rue Brisemiche, 75004 Paris.
T. 0142776428. *075747*
Forum des Arts, Forum des Halles, 11 Grande Galerie,
75001 Paris. T. 0140265390. - Paint / Sculp / Mod /
Mul / Draw - *075748*
Four, Robert, 28 Rue Bonaparte, 75006 Paris.
T. 0143293060, Fax 0143253395. - Paint - *075749*
Fournier, Louvre des Antiquaires, 2 Pl Palais-Royal,
75001 Paris. T. 0147039 / 8. *075750*
Fournier, Jean, 44 Rue Quincampoix, 75004 Paris.
T. 0142773231, Fax 0148873465. - Paint /
Sculp - *075751*
Fragments, Village Saint-Paul, 13 Rue Saint-Paul,
75004 Paris. T. 0142743283. *075752*
Framond, 3 Rue Saints-Pères, 75006 Paris.
T. 0142607477, Fax 0149270163. - Paint - *075753*
France Art, 66 Av Champs-Elysées, 75008 Paris.
T. 0144357019. *075754*
France Huot, Alibert, 4 Rue Rémusat, 75016 Paris.
T. 0142885948. *075755*
François, Liliane, 15 Rue Seine, 75006 Paris.
T. 0143269432. - Paint - *075756*
François-Miron, 39 Rue François-Miron, 75004 Paris.
T. 0142747614, Fax 0142746104. *075757*
Françoise P., 57 Rue Sainte-Anne, 75002 Paris.
T. 0142601001. *075758*
De Francony, 47 Rue Paradis, 75010 Paris.
T. 0148010865. - Paint - *075759*
Frank, 14 Rue Pyramides, 75001 Paris. T. 0142606513.
- Paint / Graph - *075760*

Fregnac, 50 Rue Jacob, 75006 Paris. T. 0142608631.
- Paint - *075761*
Frégnac, Philippe, 50 Rue Jacob, 75006 Paris.
T. 0142608631. - Paint - *075762*
Froment & Putman, 33 Rue Charlot, 75003 Paris.
T. 0142760350, Fax 0142728750. *075763*
Furstenberg, 8 Rue Jacob, 75006 Paris. T. 0143258958.
- Graph - *075764*
Gabert, Pascal, 80 Rue Quincampoix, 75003 Paris.
T. 0148049484. *075765*
Gaguech, Patrick, 3 Rue Jacques-Coeur, 75004 Paris.
T. 0142760707. - Paint - *075766*
Gaillard, Agathe, 3 Rue Pont-Louis-Philippe, 75004 Pa-
ris. T. 0142773824, Fax 0142777836. - Pho - *075767*
Galanis, 8 Rue Duras, 75008 Paris. T. 0142654096.
- Paint / Sculp - *075768*
Galarté, 13 Rue Mazarine, 75006 Paris. T. 0143259084,
Fax 0143545893. - Paint - *075769*
Galatée, 132 Blvd Montparnasse, 75014 Paris.
- Paint - *075770*
Galerie, 9 Rue Guénégaud, 75006 Paris. T. 0143548585,
Fax 0146330469. *075771*
Galerie A.B., 63 Passage Jouffroy, 75009 Paris.
T. 0142470517. - Paint / Graph / Sculp / Draw - *075772*
Galerie A.R., 14 Rue Crussol, 75011 Paris.
T. 0143384627. *075773*
Galerie Contemporaine, 3 Rue Joseph-de-Maistre,
75018 Paris. T. 0146060128. - Paint - *075774*
Galerie d'Art, 23 Rue Rodier, 75009 Paris.
T. 0142855971. *075775*
Galerie d'Orient, 159 Av Wagram, 75017 Paris.
T. 0146221657. - Paint - *075776*
Galerie d'Orsay, 34 Av Matignon, 75008 Paris.
T. 0145631936. *075777*
Galerie de Castelnou, 20 Rue Abbé-Grégoire, 75006 Pa-
ris. T. 0142220839. *075778*
Galerie de Florence, 15 Rue Saint-Paul, 75004 Paris.
T. 0142787131. *075779*
Galerie de France, 52 Rue Verrerie, 75004 Paris.
T. 0142743800, Fax 0142743467. - Paint / Graph /
Sculp - *075780*
Galerie de l'Académie, 6 Rue Seine, 75006 Paris.
Fax (1) 43548026. - Paint / Sculp - *075781*
Galerie de l'Arcade, 2 Pl Vosges, 75004 Paris.
T. 0140278234. *075782*
Galerie de l'Assemblée, 9 Pl Palais-Bourbon, 75007 Pa-
ris. T. 0147051330. - Paint - *075783*
Galerie de l'Echaudé, 1 Rue Echaudé, 75006 Paris.
T. 0143252021, Fax 0143253746. *075784*
Galerie de l'Ecluse, 8 Rue Eugène-Varlin, 75010 Paris.
T. 0142057369. *075785*
Galerie de l'Empereur, 61 Rue Bonaparte, 75006 Paris.
T. 0143268710. *075786*
Galerie de l'Etoile, 22 Rue Dumont-d'Urville, 75016 Pa-
ris. T. 0140677266, Fax 0140677809. *075787*
Galerie de l'Odéon, 11 Rue Odéon, 75006 Paris.
T. 0143265550. *075788*
Galerie de l'Olympe, 55 Blvd Batignolles, 75008 Paris.
T. 0142933646. - Paint - *075789*
Galerie de la Grange, 8 Rue Grange-Batelière, 75009
Paris. T. 0148241109. - Paint - *075790*
Galerie de la Place Beauvau, 94 Rue Fbg-Saint-Honoré,
75008 Paris. T. 0142656698, Fax 0149249382.
- Paint - *075791*
Galerie de la Présidence, 90 Rue Fbg-Saint-Honoré,
75008 Paris. T. 0142654960, Fax 0149249427.
- Paint - *075792*
Galerie de la Scala, 68 Rue La-Boétie, 75008 Paris.
T. 0145632012, Fax 0142894963. - Paint / Sculp /
Draw - *075793*
Galerie de la Sorbonne, 52 Rue Ecoles, 75005 Paris.
T. 0143255210. *075794*
Galerie de Messine, 1 Av Messine, 75008 Paris.
T. 0145622504. *075795*
Galerie de Monbrison, 2 Rue Beaux-Arts, 75006 Paris.
T. 0146340520. - Arch / Eth - *075796*
Galerie de Navarre, 3 Rue Cirque, 75008 Paris.
T. 0142561413, Fax 0143590550. *075797*
Galerie de Nesle, 8 Rue Nesle, 75006 Paris.
T. 0143252541, Fax 0143250000. *075798*
Galerie de Paris, 6 Rue Pont-de-Lodi, 75006 Paris.
T. 0143254263. - Sculp - *075799*

Galerie de Poche, 3 Rue Bonaparte, 75006 Paris.
T. 0143297623. - Paint - *075800*
Galerie de Rohan, 2 Rue Rohan, 75001 Paris.
T. 0142613424, Fax 47034774. - Paint - *075801*
Galerie de Sèvres, 59 Rue Notre-Dame-des-Champs,
75006 Paris. T. 0143257980. - Paint - *075802*
Galerie de Varenne, 61 Rue Varenne, 75007 Paris.
T. 0147055504. - Paint / Graph - *075803*
Galerie de Villiers, 3 Rue Monceau, 75008 Paris.
T. 0145611227. - Paint - *075804*
Galerie de Villiers, 15 Rue Miromesnil, 75008 Paris.
T. 0142658754. - Paint - *075805*
Galerie de Villiers, 5 Av Villiers, 75017 Paris.
T. 0146220077. - Paint - *075806*
Galerie de Villiers, Village Suisse, 78 Av Suffren, 75015
Paris. T. 0145660652. *075807*
Galerie de Villiers, 32 Rue Pasquier, 75008 Paris.
T. 0142651503, Fax 0140170313. *075808*
Galerie des Ambassades, 4 Av Matignon, 75008 Paris.
T. 0142251735, Fax 0143599890. - Paint - *075809*
Galerie des Arts, 29 Rue Lille, 75007 Paris.
T. 0142616007. *075810*
Galerie des Arts Quotidiens, 17 Rue Halles, 75001 Paris.
T. 0140263379, Fax 0140410493. *075811*
Galerie des Colonnes, 90 Rue Château, 75014 Paris.
T. 0143271186. - Paint - *075812*
Galerie des Femmes, 74 Rue Seine, 75006 Paris.
T. 0143295075. - Paint - *075813*
Galerie des Grands Augustins, 15 Rue Grands-Augu-
stins, 75006 Paris. T. 0143268900,
Fax 0143268802. *075814*
Galerie des Indépendants, 7 Pl Vosges, 75004 Paris.
T. 0142775003, Fax 0142773136. - Paint - *075815*
Galerie des Isles, 160 Blvd Montparnasse, 75014 Paris.
T. 0143354343. - Paint - *075816*
Galerie des Lyons, 9 Rue Beaune, 75007 Paris.
T. 0142611681. *075817*
Galerie des Orfèvres, 66 Quai Orfèvres, 75001 Paris.
T. 0143268130. - Paint / Graph - *075818*
Galerie des Saints-Pères, 11 Rue Saints-Pères, 75006
Paris. T. 0142602594. - Paint / Graph / Arch - *075819*
Galerie des Tuileries, 186 Rue Rivoli, 75001 Paris.
T. 0142604731. *075820*
Galerie Du Carousel, 11 Quai Voltaire, 75007 Paris.
T. 0142611075. - Paint - *075821*
Galerie du Centre, 5 Rue Pierre-au-Lard, 75004 Paris.
T. 0142773792, Fax 0142772631. *075822*
Galerie du Cercle, 23 Rue Pépinière, 75008 Paris.
T. 0143874543. *075823*
Galerie du Cherche-Midi, 17 Rue Dupin, 75006 Paris.
T. 0142227479. - Paint - *075824*
Galerie du Chevalier et des Collectionneurs, 42 Rue
Chevalier-de-la-Barre, 75018 Paris. T. 0142648493,
Fax 0142574013. - Paint - *075825*
Galerie du Cobra, 5 Rue Visconti, 75006 Paris.
T. 0143264259. - Paint - *075826*
Galerie du Cygne, 5 Rue Princesse, 75006 Paris.
T. 0143260059, Fax 0140510632. - Paint /
Graph - *075827*
Galerie du Dôme, 205 Blvd Raspail, 75014 Paris.
T. 0143218294. *075828*
Galerie du Dragon, 19 Rue Dragon, 75006 Paris.
T. 0145482419, Fax 0145480326. - Paint /
Sculp - *075829*
Galerie du Fbg-Saint-Honoré, 172 Rue Fbg-Saint-Hono-
ré, 75008 Paris. T. 0142898450. *075830*
Galerie du Fleuve, 6 Rue Seine, 75006 Paris.
T. 0143260896, Fax 0143282891. - Paint / Graph /
Sculp / Mul / Draw - *075831*
Galerie du Haut Pavé, 3 Quai Montebello, 75005 Paris.
T. 0143545879. - Paint / Sculp - *075832*
Galerie du Jour, 6 Rue Jour, 75001 Paris.
T. 0142334340. *075833*
Galerie du Lethe, 1 Rue Jacob, 75006 Paris.
T. 0146332517. - Paint - *075834*
Galerie du Luxembourg, 4 Rue Aubry-le-Boucher, 75004
Paris. T. 0142786667. - Paint - *075835*
Galerie du Montparnasse, 185 Av Maine, 75014 Paris.
T. 0145425002. - Paint - *075836*
Galerie du Moulin de la Galette, 81 Rue Lepic, 75018
Paris. T. 0142557682. - Paint - *075837*
Galerie du Musée, 16 Rue Parc-Royal, 75003 Paris.
T. 0148876090, Fax 0148875453. *075838*

Galerie du Palais-Royal, 18 Rue Montpensier, 75001 Pa-
ris. T. 0142960934. *075839*
Galerie du Parc-Royal, 20 Rue Francs-Bourgeois, 75003
Paris. T. 0142715607. - Paint - *075840*
Galerie du Pavillon Royal, 16 Rue Birague, 75004 Paris.
T. 0140290131. *075841*
Galerie du Portrait-OK, 42 Rue La-Tour-d'Auvergne,
75009 Paris. T. 0142852720. *075842*
Galerie du Prévôt, 8 Rue Prévôt, 75004 Paris.
T. 0142773248. - Paint / Sculp - *075843*
Galerie du Ressort, 12 Rue Lille, 75007 Paris.
T. 0149260489, Fax 0149260490. *075844*
Galerie du Temple, 31 Rue Temple, 75004 Paris.
T. 0148871572. *075845*
Galerie du Vent d'Automne, 12 Rue Rennequin, 75017
Paris. T. 0140530684. *075846*
Galerie du Village, 48 Rue Chevalier-de-La-Barre,
75018 Paris. T. 0142644665. - Paint - *075847*
Galerie du 5ème Art, 60 Rue Fbg-Saint-Antoine, 75012
Paris. T. 0143439800. *075848*
Galerie Eclipse, 29 Rue Penthièvre, 75008 Paris.
T. 0142569300. *075849*
Galerie G, 19 Rue Abbé-Grégoire, 75006 Paris.
T. 0145481022. - Paint - *075850*
Galerie GNG, 3 Rue Visconti, 75006 Paris.
T. 0143266471. *075851*
Galerie H.M., 185 Blvd Saint-Germain, 75007 Paris.
T. 0142220114. - Paint - *075852*
Galerie La Hune Brenner, 14 Rue Abbaye, 75006 Paris.
T. 0143255406, Fax 0140468481. *075853*
Galerie MC, 46 Rue Seine, 75006 Paris. T. 0143253470,
Fax 0140517664. *075854*
Galerie R.A., 7 Rue Turbigo, 75001 Paris.
T. 0142364574. - Paint - *075855*
Galerie SR, 16 Rue Tocqueville, 75017 Paris.
T. 0140549017, Fax 0140549067. *075856*
Galerie 10, 10 Rue Beaux-Arts, 75006 Paris.
T. 0143251072. - Paint - *075857*
Galerie 12, 12 Rue Chaligny, 75012 Paris.
T. 0143075343. *075858*
Galerie 15, 15 Rue Guénégaud, 75006 Paris.
T. 0146330438. - Paint - *075859*
Galerie 16, 16 Rue Raymond-Losserand, 75006 Paris.
T. 0143209894. - Paint - *075860*
Galerie 19, 19 Rue Penthièvre, 75008 Paris.
T. 0147420427. *075861*
Galerie 1900-2000, 9 Rue Penthièvre, 75008 Paris.
T. 0147429306. - Paint - *075862*
Galerie 1900-2000, 8 Rue Bonaparte, 75006 Paris.
T. 0143258420, Fax 0146347452. - Paint / Sculp /
Draw - *075863*
Galerie 26, 31 Rue Penthièvre, 75008 Paris.
T. 0142894617. *075864*
Galerie 26, 26 Pl Vosges, 75003 Paris. T. 0140270090,
Fax 0140279056. *075865*
Galerie 27, 27 Rue Seine, 75006 Paris. T. 0143547854,
Fax 0143540684. - Paint / Graph / Sculp /
Draw - *075866*
Galerie 28, 28 Rue Alésia, 75014 Paris.
T. 0143272936. *075867*
Galerie 38, 38 Rue Seine, 75006 Paris. T. 0143260065.
- Paint - *075868*
Galerie 8, 8 Rue Beaux-Arts, 75006 Paris.
T. 0143259901. *075869*
Galerie 9, 9 Rue Jacob, 75006 Paris. T. 0143268383,
Fax 0143264039. - Paint / Dec - *075870*
Galeries 54, 54 Rue Fbg-Saint-Honoré, 75008 Paris.
T. 0142665175. *075871*
Galfard, Eric, 2 Rue Messine, 75008 Paris.
T. 0145624560. *075872*
Galland, Anne-Marie, 50 Rue Hôtel-de-Ville, 75004 Pa-
ris. T. 0142778344. *075873*
Gand, Philippe, 8 Rue Saint-Merri, 75004 Paris.
T. 0148049071, Fax 0148049072. *075874*
Garcia, Maud, Village Suisse, 78 Av Suffren, 75015 Pa-
ris. T. 0147839303, Fax 0147832610. - Eth /
Jew - *075875*
Garnier, Maurice & Cie, 6 Rue Marie-Pape-Carpentier,
75006 Paris. T. 0145442343. - Paint - *075876*
Garnier, Serge, 12 Blvd Courcelles, 75017 Paris.
T. 0147630646. - Paint - *075877*
Garoche, Marie-Jane, 33 Rue Seine, 75006 Paris.
T. 0143268962. - Paint - *075878*

KARSTEN GREVE

5 RUE DEBELLEYME
F-75003 PARIS

Tél. (1) 42 77 19 37, Fax (1) 42 77 05 58

Gary-Roche, 18 Rue Le-Peletier, 75009 Paris.
T. 0147703216, Fax 0142868291. - Paint - *075879*
Gasnier-Kamien, 43 Rue Blancs-Manteaux, 75004 Paris.
T. 0148045005. - Paint - *075880*
Gastaud & Caillard, 6 Rue Debelleyme, 75003 Paris.
T. 0142742295. *075881*
Gastou, Yves, 12 Rue Bonaparte, 75006 Paris.
T. 0146347217, Fax 0143296299. - Paint / Graph /
Sculp / Draw / Dec - *075882*
Gastou, Yves, 12 Rue Bonaparte, 75006 Paris.
T. 0146347217, Fax 0143296299. - Dec - *075883*
Gattegno, A., 13-15 Rue Grande-Chaumière, 75006 Pa-
ris. T. 0143266318. - Fra - *075884*
Gaubert, Pierre, 80 Rue Miromesnil, 75008 Paris.
T. 0143870988. - Paint / Graph / Sculp / Draw - *075885*
Gautier, Jacques, 36 Rue Jacob, 75006 Paris.
T. 0142608433. - Paint - *075886*
Gavardie, Ivana de, 10 Rue Beaux-Arts, 75006 Paris.
T. 0143545523. *075887*
Gérard, Nicole, 28 Rue Jacob, 75006 Paris.
T. 0143262643. - Ant / Paint / Furn / Dec - *075888*
Gervis, Daniel, 14 Rue Grenelle, 75007 Paris.
T. 0145444190, Fax 0145491898. - Paint / Graph /
Sculp / Draw - *075889*
Ghanassia, Danielle, 44 Av New-York, 75016 Paris.
T. 0147203364, Fax 0147206823. *075890*
Gillet, Michel, 54 Av La-Bourdonnais, 75007 Paris.
T. 0147537273, Fax 0145569003. *075891*
Gimaray, Arlette, 12 Rue Mazarine, 75006 Paris.
T. 0146347180. *075892*
Giovanni, Louvre des Antiquaires, 2 Pl Palais-Royal,
75001 Paris. T. 0142615673. - Paint / Graph /
Draw - *075893*
Girand, François, 76 Rue Seine, 75006 Paris.
T. 0143260761. - Paint / Graph - *075894*
Girard, 7 Rue Campagne-Première, 75014 Paris.
T. 0143220116. *075895*
Godjo Bastille, 26 Rue Taillandiers, 75011 Paris.
T. 0148066475, Fax 0148066061. *075896*
Gomes, Henriette, 6 Rue Cirque, 75008 Paris.
T. 0142254249. - Paint - *075897*
Gosselin, François, 25 Quai Grands-Augustins, 75006
Paris. T. 0143267619. - Paint / Graph - *075898*
Gossieaux, Martine, 56 Rue Université, 75007 Paris.
T. 0145444855, Fax 0142840017. *075899*
Got, 52 Rue Jacob, 75006 Paris.
T. 0142034278. *075900*
Grands Papiers, 1 Rue Séguier, 75006 Paris.
T. 0143258904. *075901*
Granoff, Katia, 13 Quai Conti, 75006 Paris.
T. 0143544192, Fax 0146337790. - Paint - *075902*
Graphes, 13 Rue Buci, 75006 Paris. T. 0146335757.
- Pho - *075903*
Gravier, Philippe, 6 Av Delcassé, 75008 Paris.
T. 0142891632. *075904*
Gravure, 41 Rue Seine, 75006 Paris. T. 0143260544.
- Graph - *075905*
Gravure Actuelle, 53 Rue Seine, 75006 Paris.
T. 0143255352, Fax 0143299387. - Graph - *075906*

Greiner, Daniel, 14 Gal Véro-Dodat, 75001 Paris.
T. 0142334330, Fax 0142334319. - Paint / Sculp /
Draw - *075907*
Greve, Karsten, 5 Rue Debelleyme, 75003 Paris.
T. 0142771937, Fax 0142770558. - Paint / Sculp /
Draw - *075908*
Grillon, 44 Rue Seine, 75006 Paris. T. 0146330344.
- Paint / Graph / Draw - *075909*
Grimaud, 27 Rue Charlot, 75003 Paris. T. 0142722853.
- Paint - *075910*
Grise, 19 Rue Saint-Paul, 75004 Paris. T. 0142724625.
- Paint - *075911*
Grondin-Thibault, 33 Rue Galilée, 75016 Paris.
T. 0144435407. *075912*
Grosman, Alexander, 12 Rue Francis-de-Pressensé,
75014 Paris. T. 0145450930, Fax 0145457231.
- Paint / Sculp - *075913*
Gualtieri, Fernando, 132 Blvd Montparnasse, 75014 Pa-
ris. T. 0143202225. *075914*
Gudea, 22 Rue Bonaparte, 75006 Paris. T. 0146337862,
Fax 0146334230. - Arch - *075915*
Guénégaud, 31 Av Matignon, 75006 Paris.
T. 0146331851. - Paint - *075916*
Guérard, Cathérine, 82 Rue Saint-Louis-en-l'Ile, 75004
Paris. T. 0146337311. *075917*
Guigné, 89 Rue Fbg-Saint-Honoré, 75008 Paris.
T. 0142666688. - Paint / Sculp - *075918*
Guigue, 11 Rue Saint-Gilles, 75003 Paris.
T. 0148040495. - Furn - *075919*
Guillet, 8 Av Trudaine, 75009 Paris. T. 0148789825.
- Paint - *075920*
Guillois, Alain, Louvre des Antiquaires, 2 Pl Palais-Royal,
75001 Paris. T. 0142615655. *075921*
Guillon-Laffaille, Fanny, 4 Av Messine, 75008 Paris.
T. 0145635200, Fax 0145619291. *075922*
Guiot, Roberts, 18 Av Matignon, 75008 Paris.
T. 0142666584, Fax 0149240793. - Paint /
Graph - *075923*
Gutharc-Ballin, 47 Rue Lappe, 75011 Paris.
T. 0147003210, Fax 0140217274. - Paint / Graph /
Sculp / Draw - *075924*
Haboldt & Cie, 137 Rue Fbg-Saint-Honoré, 75008 Paris.
T. 0142898463, Fax 0142895881. - Paint /
Draw - *075925*
Hahn, Joseph, 10 Rue Louvois, 75002 Paris.
T. 0147034255, Fax 0147034234. - Paint - *075926*
Hanse, Norbert, 38-40 Av Victor-Hugo, 75016 Paris.
T. 0145018840. - Paint / Graph / Sculp / Draw - *075927*
Hansen, 265 Rue Saint-Honoré, 75001 Paris.
T. 0142600808. - Paint - *075928*
Haranchipy, Nicole, 11 Rue Londres, 75009 Paris.
T. 0145260423. *075929*
Hartbye's, 16 Rue Le-Regrattier, 75004 Paris.
T. 0146346377, Fax 0140510281. *075930*
Haut-Pavé, 3 Quai Montebello, 75005 Paris.
T. 0143545879. - Paint - *075931*
Hautecoeur, 172 Rue Rivoli, 75001 Paris.
T. 0142613078, Fax 0142868008. - Paint /
Graph - *075932*
Hautôt, Pierre, 36 Rue Bac, 75007 Paris.
T. 0142611015. *075933*

Heim, Jacques, 86 Rue Fbg-Saint-Honoré, 75008 Paris.
T. 0142680084. *075934*
Heim, Philippe, 38 Rue Penthièvre, 75008 Paris.
T. 0145611636. *075935*
Hénault, 3 Pl Pyramides, 75001 Paris. T. 0142604754.
- Paint - *075936*
Henry Bussière Art's, 26 Rue Mazarine, 75006 Paris.
T. 0143547811, Fax 0143548243. *075937*
Héraud, 24 Av Matignon, 75008 Paris. T. 0142663162.
- Paint - *075938*
Herbert, Sabine, 86bis Rue Vieille-du-Temple, 75003
Paris. T. 0142726766. - Paint - *075939*
Herold, Thessa, 7 Rue Thorigny, 75003 Paris.
T. 0142787868, Fax 0142787869. *075940*
Herzog, Lucette, 157 Rue Saint-Martin, 75003 Paris.
T. 0148873994. - Graph - *075941*
Hesdin, Philippe de, 46 Rue Bac, 75007 Paris.
T. 0145481329. *075942*
Heyraud-Bresson, 56 Rue Université, 75007 Paris.
T. 0142225809. - Paint - *075943*
Heyraud, Michèle, 79 Rue Quincampoix, 75003 Paris.
T. 0148870206. - Paint - *075944*
Hiri, Guy-Max, 44 Rue Francs-Bourgeois, 75003 Paris.
T. 0142786260, Fax 0142784414. *075945*
Holmsky, Marie de, 80 Rue Bonaparte, 75006 Paris.
T. 0143290890, Fax 0145005997. - Paint /
Dec - *075946*
Homme et la Ville, 102 Rue Cherche-Midi, 75006 Paris.
T. 0145448071. *075947*
Homme Objet, 192 Rue Courcelles, 75017 Paris.
T. 0143804741. *075948*
Hopkins-Thomas, 2 Rue Miromesnil, 75008 Paris.
T. 0142655105, Fax 0142669028. - Paint - *075949*
Horizon, 21 Rue Bourgogne, 75007 Paris.
T. 0145555827. - Paint / Graph / Draw - *075950*
Hosokawa, Chizuko, 12 Rue Sainte-Anne, 75001 Paris.
T. 0142960509. - Paint - *075951*
Hoss, Marwan, 12 Rue Alger, 75001 Paris.
T. 0142963796. - Paint / Graph / Sculp / Draw - *075952*
Hubbard, Rizzo, 37 Rue Lappe, 75011 Paris.
T. 0147009112, Fax 0147009111. *075953*
Huguenin, Jean-Michel, 27 Rue Guénégaud, 75006 Pa-
ris. T. 0143547856. *075954*
Hussenot, Ghislaine, 5bis Rue Haudriettes, 75003 Paris.
T. 0148876081, Fax 0148870501. - Paint / Graph /
Sculp / Pho / Draw - *075955*
Ibanez, Rogelio, 12 Passage Molière, 75003 Paris.
T. 0142720945. - Paint - *075956*
IGA Boutique, 20 Quai Louvre, 75001 Paris.
T. 0140390869. *075957*
Ikuo, 11 Rue Grands-Augustins, 75007 Paris.
T. 0143295639. - Paint - *075958*
Il Campiello, 98 Blvd Montparnasse, 75014 Paris.
Fax (1) 40470942. *075959*
Ile de France, 29 Rue Université, 75007 Paris.
T. 0142224163. - Paint - *075960*
Imagerie, 9 Rue Dante, 75005 Paris. T. 0143251866,
Fax 0143251808. - Graph / Orient / Eth / Dec /
Draw - *075961*
Images d'Artistes, 85 Rue Rambuteau, 75001 Paris.
T. 0142363048, Fax 0142363045. *075962*
Imbert, Didier, 19 Av Matignon, 75008 Paris.
T. 0147660131. - Paint - *075963*
Impressions 21, 21 Rue Turenne, 75004 Paris.
T. 0148040448. *075964*
Inard, 179 Blvd Saint-Germain, 75007 Paris.
T. 0145446688 k703 (1) 40510281. - Tex - *075965*
Instants F Desjours, 17 Quai Fleurs, 75004 Paris.
Fax (1) 44071802. *075966*
Institut International d'Art Moderne, 24 Rue Aumale,
75009 Paris. T. 0145263574. - Paint - *075967*
Inter Tableaux, 22 Rue Miromesnil, 75008 Paris.
T. 0142658639. *075968*
International Projet, 37 Rue Lappe, 75011 Paris.
T. 0149234408. *075969*
Istria-Damez, 5 Rue Saussaies, 75008 Paris.
T. 0142650533. - Paint - *075970*
Jacob, 28 Rue Jacob, 75006 Paris.
T. 0146339066. *075971*
Jacomo-Santiveri, 104 Rue Bac, 75007 Paris.
T. 0145481900. - Paint - *075972*
Jadis et Naguère, 166 Rue Fbg-Saint-Honoré, 75008
Paris. T. 0143594052, Fax 0145629354. *075973*

GALERIE LOUISE LEIRIS

47, rue de Monceau · 75008 Paris · Tel. 01.45.63.28.85 et 01.45.63.37.14

A. BEAUDIN, G. BRAQUE, Juan GRIS,
S. HADENGUE, E. de KERMADEC, Elie LASCAUX,
H. LAURENS, F. LEGER, André MASSON,
MANOLO, PICASSO, Suzanne ROGER, Y. ROUVRE

Fondateurs: D. H. Kahnweiler – Louise Leiris. Direction: Maurice Jardot – Quentin Laurens

Jannel Galerie, 59 Rue du Chevalier-de-La-Barre, 75018 Paris. T. 0144920259. - Paint - *075974*

Janos, 107 Rue Quincampoix, 75003 Paris. T. 0142711565. *075975*

Jansen, Flora, 44 Rue Bac, 75007 Paris. T. 0145485252, Fax 0142228839. *075976*

Jaquester, 153 Rue Saint-Martin, 75003 Paris. T. 0142781666. - Paint - *075977*

Jardin de Flore, 24 Pl Vosges, 75004 Paris. T. 0142776190. *075978*

Jean, 24 Rue Tournelles, 75004 Paris. T. 0142716176. *075979*

Jean, Antoinette, 65 Rue Saint-André-des-Arts, 75006 Paris. T. 0143262329, Fax 0146347335. *075980*

Jean César Présente, 10 Rue Hautefeuille, 75006 Paris. T. 0144071865. *075981*

Jehau, Jean-Yves, 33 Quai Voltaire, 75007 Paris. T. 0142611400. - Paint - *075982*

JGM Galerie, 8bis Rue Jacques-Callot, 75006 Paris. T. 0143261205. - Paint / Sculp / Draw - *075983*

Jonas, 12 Rue Seine, 75006 Paris. T. 0143265028, Fax 0143296566. - Paint / Graph / Draw - *075984*

De Jonckheere, Louvre des Antiquaires, 2 Pl Palais-Royal, 75001 Paris. T. 0142602082. - Paint - *075985*

De Jonckheere, 100 Rue Fbg-Saint-Honoré, 75008 Paris. T. 0142666949, Fax 0142661342. - Paint - *075986*

Jones, David, 8 Rue Rossini, 75009 Paris. T. 0145230165, Fax 0145233879. *075987*

Jordan, Bernard, 54 Rue Temple, 75003 Paris. T. 0142723984. - Paint - *075988*

Joubert, Jean-Pierre, 18 Av Matignon, 75008 Paris. T. 0142650079, Fax 0147426381. - Ant / Paint / Graph / Sculp / Draw - *075989*

Jousse-Séguin, 32 Rue Charonne, 75011 Paris. T. 0147003235. - Paint - *075990*

Julien, Anne, 14 Rue Seine, 75006 Paris. T. 0143256566. *075991*

J.Y.B. International Art Trading, 174 Blvd Saint-Germain, 75006 Paris. T. 0142843361, Fax 0142227632. *075992*

K Art, 45 Rue Amelot, 75011 Paris. T. 0140210932. *075993*

Kamer & Cie, 34 Rue Seine, 75006 Paris. T. 0143254689. - Paint - *075994*

Kamouh, Pierre, 13 Rue Keller, 75011 Paris. T. 0140216556. - Paint - *075995*

Karsenty, Jean-Louis, Village Suisse, 78 Av Suffren, 75015 Paris. T. 0145677208. *075996*

Kartir, 11 Rue Bonaparte, 75006 Paris. T. 0143269028. - Tex - *075997*

Katlas Editions, Galerie des Indépendants, 7 Pl Vosges, 75004 Paris. T. 0142775003, Fax 0142773136. *075998*

Katsura, 39 Rue Cherche-Midi, 75006 Paris. T. 0142226065, Fax 0142222799. *075999*

Kellermann, Michel, 55 Rue Varenne, 75007 Paris. T. 0142221124. - Paint - *076000*

Kieffer, 46 Rue Saint-André-des-Arts, 75006 Paris. T. 0143264711. - Paint - *076001*

Kinge, Samy, 54 Rue Verneuil, 75007 Paris. T. 0142611907. - Paint / Graph - *076002*

Kiras, 10 Rue Bonaparte, 75006 Paris. T. 0143296693. - Paint - *076003*

Kitsch, 3 Rue Bonaparte, 75006 Paris. T. 0143297623. *076004*

Klein-Roncari, 16 Rue Seine, 75006 Paris. T. 0143296393. - Paint - *076005*

Koralewski, 92 Rue Quincampoix, 75003 Paris. T. 0142774893. *076006*

Koryo, 8 Rue Perronnet, 75007 Paris. T. 0142223789. - Paint - *076007*

Kostel, 51 Rue Archives, 75003 Paris. T. 0148870330. *076008*

Kouki, Village Saint-Paul, 19 Rue Lions-Saint-Paul, 75004 Paris. T. 0148875670, Fax 0148875675. - Furn - *076009*

Kraftchik, Jean-Claude, 47 Rue Lyon, 75012 Paris. T. 0143467821, Fax 0143470947. *076010*

Krief, 50 Rue Mazarine, 75006 Paris. T. 0143293237, Fax 0143269981. - Paint - *076011*

Kugel, Jacques, 279 Rue Saint-Honoré, 75008 Paris. T. 0142608623, Fax 0142610672. - Paint - *076012*

Laage, Salomon, 57 Rue Temple, 75004 Paris. T. 0142781171. - Paint / Graph / Sculp / Pho / Mul / Draw - *076013*

Labatut, 199bis Blvd Saint-Germain, 75007 Paris. T. 0145489771. *076014*

Laburthe-Tolra, 12 Av Franklin-Roosevelt, 75008 Paris. T. 0145610192. *076015*

Lacourière & Frelaut, 11 Rue Foyatier, 75018 Paris. T. 0146061770. - Paint - *076016*

Ladoucette, Marc de, 28 Rue Bézout, 75014 Paris. T. 0140470506. *076017*

Lagarde, Michel, 2 Pl Thorigny, 75003 Paris. T. 0148870366. *076018*

Lahumière, 88 Blvd Courcelles, 75017 Paris. T. 0147630395, Fax 0140530078. - Paint / Graph / Sculp - *076019*

Lalandre, Claude, 15 Rue Seine, 75006 Paris. T. 0140460228, Fax 0146339138. *076020*

Lambert, 14 Rue Saint-Louis-en-l'Ile, 75004 Paris. T. 0143251421. - Paint - *076021*

Lambert, Yvon, 108 Rue Vieille-du-Temple, 75003 Paris. T. 0142710933, Fax 0142718747. - Ant / Paint / Sculp / Draw - *076022*

Lammelin, Jean, 15 Rue Dauphine, 75006 Paris. T. 0144071203. - Paint - *076023*

Lancry, 33 Rue Miromesnil, 75008 Paris. T. 0142661646, Fax 0142661630. - Paint / Graph / Sculp / Draw - *076024*

Landrot, 5 Rue Jacques-Callot, 75006 Paris. T. 0143267113. - China - *076025*

Langlois, Suzy, 266 Blvd Saint-Germain, 75007 Paris. T. 0145512039. - Paint - *076026*

Langloys, Regis, 169 Rue Saint-Honoré, 75001 Paris. T. 0142605694. - Paint / Graph / Sculp - *076027*

Lansberg, Pascal, 36 Rue Seine, 75006 Paris. T. 0140518434, Fax 0143298607. *076028*

Larmes d'Eros, 58 Rue Amelot, 75011 Paris. T. 0143383343. *076029*

Lauma, Louvre des Antiquaires, 2 Pl Palais Royal, 75001 Paris. T. 0142601930. - Paint / Graph / Draw - *076030*

Laure, Dany, 1 Rue Jouvenet, 75016 Paris. T. 0142249433. *076031*

Laurent, Juliette, 54bis Av La-Motte-Picquet, 75015 Paris. T. 0147342773. *076032*

Lavau, 18 Av Raphaël, 75016 Paris. T. 0145030834. - Paint - *076033*

Lavignes-Bastille, 27 Rue Charonne, 75011 Paris. T. 0147008818. - Paint - *076034*

Lavrov, Georges, 42 Rue Beaubourg, 75003 Paris. T. 0142727119. *076035*

Le Breton, Catherine, 27 Rue Varenne, 75007 Paris. T. 0142227855. - Paint - *076036*

Le Duc, Marie-Laure, 54 Rue Fbg-Saint-Honoré, 75008 Paris. T. 0147422509. - Ant / Paint - *076037*

Le Moine, Annick, 21 Av Maine, 75015 Paris. T. 0142224701. *076038*

Léar, 54 Rue Fbg-Saint-Honoré, 75008 Paris. T. 0147427794. *076039*

Lebon, Baudoin, 38 Rue Sainte-Croix-de-la-Bretonnerie, 75004 Paris. T. 0142720910. - Paint - *076040*

Lecomte, Guy, 49 Av La-Motte-Picquet, 75015 Paris. T. 0147347302, Fax 0147341665. *076041*

Lecomte, Marcel, 17 Rue Seine, 75006 Paris. T. 0143268547. - Graph - *076042*

Leegenhock, J.O., 23 Quai Voltaire, 75007 Paris. T. 0142963608. *076043*

Lefèbvre, Arnaud, 30 Rue Mazarine, 75006 Paris. T. 0143265067, Fax 0144070519. *076044*

Lefèvre Warmé, Louvre des Antiquaires, 2 Pl Palais-Royal, 75001 Paris. T. 0142615736. - Paint / Graph / Draw - *076045*

Lefor-Openo, 29 Rue Mazarine, 75006 Paris. T. 0146338724. - Paint / Graph / Sculp - *076046*

Lefortier, 54 Rue Fbg-Saint-Honoré, 75008 Paris. T. 0142654374. - Tex - *076047*

Lehalle, 3 Rue Augereau, 75007 Paris. T. 0145558099, Fax 0147538884. *076048*

Leiris, Louise, 47 Rue Monceau, 75008 Paris. T. 0145632056, Fax 0145637613. - Paint / Graph / Sculp - *076049*

Lelong, 12 et 13 Rue Téhéran, 75008 Paris. T. 0145631319, Fax 0142893433. - Paint / Sculp - *076050*

Leloup, Hélène & Philippe, 9 Quai Malaquais, 75006 Paris. T. 0142607591, Fax 0142614594. - Orient / Sculp / Arch / Eth - *076051*

Lemand, Claude, 16 Rue Littré, 75006 Paris. T. 0145492095. *076052*

Lemoine, Jacqueline, 32 Rue Saint-Louis-en-l'Ile, 75004 Paris. T. 0143257335. - Paint - *076053*

Léonardo, 62 Rue Hautpoul, 75019 Paris. T. 0142401311. *076054*

Lescot, Pierre, 153 Rue Saint-Martin, 75003 Paris. T. 0148878171. - Paint - *076055*

Lesieutre, Alain, Louvre des Antiquaires, 2 Pl Palais-Royal, 75001 Paris. T. 0142615713. *076056*

Letailleur, Alain, 50 Rue Seine, 75006 Paris. T. 0146332517, Fax 0146330209. - Paint - *076057*

Lettrée, Anne, 204 Blvd Saint-Germain, 75007 Paris. Fax (1) 42843778. *076058*

Levasseur & Fils, 232 Rue Rivoli, 75001 Paris. T. 0142607759. - Paint / Furn - *076059*

Levet, J.C., 51 Rue Saint-Louis-en-l'Ile, 75004 Paris. T. 0143543647, Fax 0140517792. *076060*

Lévy-Cerquant, Dona, 19 Rue Petites-Ecuries, 75010 Paris. T. 0142469602. *076061*

Lévy, Denise, 12 Av Paul-Doumer, 75016 Paris. T. 0147277732. - Paint - *076062*

Lévy, Etienne, 42 Rue Varenne, 75007 Paris. T. 0145446550, Fax 0145490538. - Paint - *076063*

Levy & Cie, 14 Av Paul-Doumer, 75016 Paris. T. 0147277732. *076064*

Leymarie, M., 4 Rue Miromesnil, 75008 Paris. T. 0142659617, Fax 0147424834. - Paint - *076065*

Liaisons Beaux-Arts, 22 Rue Delambre, 75014 Paris. T. 0143354261, Fax 0143203007. *076066*

Lima, Denise de, 51 Rue Bonaparte, 75006 Paris. T. 0143269006. - Paint / Graph / Draw - *076067*

Lithographie, 31 Av Matignon, 75008 Paris. T. 0142663442. - Paint / Graph / Sculp - *076068*

Lito A.T., 30 Rue Blancs-Manteaux, 75004 Paris. T. 0148873899, Fax 0142777469. *076069*

Locatoile, 39 Rue Vieille-du-Temple, 75004 Paris. T. 0142784818. *076070*

Locus Solus, 21 Villa Riberolle, 75020 Paris. T. 0143563551. *076071*

Loeb, Albert, 12 Rue Beaux-Arts, 75006 Paris. T. 0146330687. - Paint / Sculp - *076072*

Loft, 3 Rue Beaux-Arts, 75006 Paris. T. 0146331890, Fax 0143545614. - Paint / Graph / Sculp / Draw - *076073*

Lorenz, Sylvana, 13 Rue Chapon, 75000 Paris. T. 0148045302, Fax 0148047338. - Paint - *076074*

Lorette, M.G., 34 Rue Saint-Louis-en-l'Ile, 75004 Paris. T. 0143266463. *076075*

Lucernaire, 53 Rue Notre-Dame-des-Champs, 75006 Paris. T. 0145445734. - Paint - *076076*

Lühl, Jan & Hélène, 19 Quai Malaquais, 75006 Paris. T. 0142607697. - Paint / Graph / Orient - *076077*

Luhl, J.& H., 19 Quai Malaquais, 75006 Paris. T. 0142607697. - Paint - *076078*

Lussan, Régine, 7 Rue Odéon, 75006 Paris. T. 0146333750. - Paint / Graph / Sculp / Fra / Draw - *076079*

Lustman, Claudine, 111 Rue Quincampoix, 75003 Paris. T. 0142773800. *076080*

Lutèce Edition, 22 Rue Georges Bizet, 75016 Paris. T. 0147206595, Fax 0147206345. - Paint - *076081*

Lyons, Olivier des, 9 Rue Beaune, 75007 Paris. T. 0142611681, Fax 0149487001. - Paint - *076082*

Ma Galerie, 12 Rue Ancienne-Comédie, 75006 Paris. T. 0143256767. *076083*

Maeght, 12 Rue Saint-Merri, 75004 Paris. T. 0142784344. *076084*

Maeght, Adrien, 42 Rue Bac, 75007 Paris. T. 0145481955, Fax 0145484515. - Paint / Graph - *076085*

Magelan, 37 Rue Richard-Lenoir, 75011 Paris. T. 0143483310, Fax 0143483373. *076086*

Mailliet, Gérard, 15 Rue Miromesnil, 75008 Paris. T. 0142656120, Fax 0142652225. - Paint - *076087*

Main d'Or, 64 Rue Saint-Louis-en-l'Ile, 75004 Paris. T. 0143260201, Fax 0146335754. *076088*

Maine Durieu, 57 Quai Grands-Augustins, 75006 Paris. T. 0143268252, Fax 0143256058. *076089*

Maison de la Lithographie, 110 Blvd Courcelles, 75017 Paris. T. 0142272016. - Graph - *076090*

Maison des Beaux-Arts, 11 Rue Beaux-Arts, 75006 Paris. T. 0140331099. - Paint - *076091*

Makassar-Paris, Louvre des Antiquaires, 2 Pl Palais-Royal, 75001 Paris. T. 0140200425, Fax 0143737812. *076092*

Makassar France, 112 Rue Fbg-Saint-Honoré, 75008 Paris. T. 0142662795. *076093*

Malingue, Daniel, 26 Av Matignon, 75008 Paris. T. 0142666033, Fax 0142660380. - Paint / Sculp - *076094*

Mamias, Marie, 95 Rue Vieille-du-Temple, 75003 Paris. T. 0142744092. *076095*

Mancheron, Roger, Louvre des Antiquaires, 2 Pl Palais-Royal, 75001 Paris. T. 0142602026. - Paint / Graph / Draw - *076096*

Manic, Louvre des Antiquaires, 2 Pl Palais-Royal, 75001 Paris. T. 0142615812, Fax 0142970014. - Ant / Ico / Sculp / Jew - *076097*

Manière, Diane, 11 Rue Pastourelle, 75003 Paris. T. 0142770426. - Paint - *076098*

Mann, 7 Rue Guénégaud, 75006 Paris. T. 0144070202, Fax 0144070203. *076099*

Mansart, 5 Rue Payenne, 75003 Paris. T. 0148874103. *076100*

Mantoux-Gignac, 55 Rue Archives, 75003 Paris. T. 0142784037. *076101*

Marbeau, 4 Rue Miromesnil, 75008 Paris. T. 0142662286. *076102*

Marcault, Michèle, 11 Rue Ormesson, 75004 Paris. T. 0140299400, Fax 0140299414. *076103*

Marceau, 48 Av Marceau, 75008 Paris. T. 0147202128. - Paint / Sculp - *076104*

Marcus, Claude, 20 Rue Chauchat, 75009 Paris. T. 0147709123, Fax 0145232041. - Paint - *076105*

Margaron, Alain, 5 Rue Perche, 75003 Paris. T. 0142742052. *076106*

Marquardt, Nikki Diana, 9 Pl Vosges, 75004 Paris. T. 0142782100, Fax 0142788673. - Paint / Sculp / Mul - *076107*

Marquet de Vasselot, 18 Rue Charlot, 75003 Paris. T. 0142760031, Fax 0142720421. *076108*

Martel-Greiner, 71 Blvd Raspail, 75006 Paris. T. 0145481305. - Glass - *076109*

Martin-Caille, Bruno, 34 Rue Fbg-Saint-Honoré, 75008 Paris. T. 0142652750, Fax 0140170440. - Paint / Graph - *076110*

Martin-Ishihara, 62 Rue Boétie, 75008 Paris. T. 0145610401, Fax 0142561995. - Paint - *076111*

Marumo, C., 243 Rue Saint-Honoré, 75001 Paris. T. 0142600866, Fax 0140159604. - Paint - *076112*

Mas, Colette, 48 Rue La-Fayette, 75009 Paris. T. 0148247777. - Paint / Graph - *076113*

Masselin, Perrine, 5 Rue Mayet, 75006 Paris. T. 0145665218. *076114*

Massol, Jacques, 12 Rue La-Boétie, 75008 Paris. T. 0142659365. - Paint - *076115*

Matignon, 32 Av Matignon, 75008 Paris. T. 0142662012. - Paint / Graph - *076116*

Matignon, 18 Av Matignon, 75008 Paris. T. 0142666032, Fax 0142664874. - Paint / Graph / Draw - *076117*

Matignon Fine Art, 12 Rue La-Boétie, 75008 Paris. T. 0142664803. *076118*

Matignon Saint-Honoré, 34 Av Matignon, 75008 Paris. T. 0143593531, Fax 0145612039. - Paint - *076119*

Maxé, Véronique, 33 Av Matignon, 75008 Paris. T. 0147420252, Fax 0142662834. - Sculp - *076120*

Mazo Lebouc, 15 Rue Guénégaud, 75006 Paris. T. 0143263984. - Graph - *076121*

M.D.C., 40 Rue Université, 75007 Paris. T. 0142860302. *076122*

Méchiche, Jean-Luc, 182 Rue Fbg-Saint-Honoré, 75008 Paris. T. 0145632011, Fax 0142259134. - Paint - *076123*

Médiart, 107 Rue Quincampoix, 75003 Paris. T. 0142784493. *076124*

Médicis, Louvre des Antiquaires, 2 Pl Palais-Royal, 75001 Paris. T. 0142610192. *076125*

Médicis 26, 26 Pl Vosges, 75003 Paris. T. 0148871188. *076126*

Meissirel, Christian, 91 Blvd Malesherbes, 75008 Paris. T. 0142259885, Fax 0142259887. - Paint - *076127*

Mémoires Africaines, 76 Av Champs-Elysées, 75008 Paris. T. 0145626828. *076128*

Mendrisse, 13 Rue Blancs-Manteaux, 75004 Paris. T. 0142745506. *076129*

Menthon, Lise & Henri de, 4 Rue Perche, 75003 Paris. T. 0142726208. *076130*

Di Méo, 9 Rue Beaux Arts, 75006 Paris. T. 0143541098. - Paint - *076131*

Mercuri, J., 119 Rue Vieille-du-Temple, 75003 Paris. T. 0148873366, Fax 0148873396. *076132*

Mermoz, 6 Rue Cirque, 75008 Paris. T. 1 42258480, Fax 1 40750390. - Orient / Sculp / Arch / Eth - *076133*

Métaphore, 12 Rue Boucharon, 75010 Paris. T. 0142386312. - Paint - *076134*

Météo, 4 Rue Saint-Nicolas, 75012 Paris. T. 0143422020, Fax 0143423020. *076135*

Métropolis, Village Saint-Paul, 5bis Rue Saint-Paul, 75004 Paris. T. 0142775871. *076136*

Meyer, 17 Rue Beaux-Arts, 75006 Paris. T. 0143548574. - Eth - *076137*

Meyer, Josette, 54 Rue Fbg-Saint-Honoré, 75008 Paris. T. 0147429644. *076138*

Meyer, Marion, 19 Rue Galande, 75006 Paris. T. 0146330438, Fax 0140469141. - Paint - *076139*

Meyer, Michel, 24 Av Matignon, 75008 Paris. T. 0142666295, Fax 0149240788. - Ant / Furn / Lights / Instr - *076140*

Michel, 17 Quai Saint-Michel, 75005 Paris. T. 0143547775. *076141*

Michel, R.-G., 17 Quai Saint-Michel, 75005 Paris. T. 0143547775. - Graph / Draw - *076142*

Mifsud, Louis-Philippe, 117 Blvd Mortier, 75020 Paris. T. 0143616651. - Paint - *076143*

M.I.L.D., 69 Rue Mouffetard, 75005 Paris. T. 0143314533, Fax 0145359458. *076144*

Millet, René, 4 Rue Miromesnil, 75008 Paris. T. 0144510590, Fax 0144510591. *076145*

Gabrielle OHL

artiste peintre

10, rue des Halles
F-75001 PARIS - Tél.: 01.42.36.01.45

- Peinture à l'huile - Encres de Chine
- Collages - Vitraux
- Gouaches

Mairie du 1ᵉʳ arrondissement, Paris
Encre de Chine 8F.

Minerve, 52 Rue Jacob, 75006 Paris. T. 0142613666.
- Paint - 076146
Minet, Annie, 4 Rue Maître-Albert, 75005 Paris.
T. 0143541061. - Paint - 076147
Minotaure, 2 Rue Beaux-Arts, 75006 Paris.
T. 0143253537, Fax 0143546293. 076148
Mirabeau, 1 Rue Balard, 75015 Paris. T. 0145782528.
- Paint - 076149
Miromesnil, 12 Rue Miromesnil, 75008 Paris.
T. 0147427000. - Paint - 076150
Mitaine, François, 60 Rue Mazarine, 75006 Paris.
T. 0140517060. 076151
Moatti, Alain, 77 Rue Saints-Pères, 75006 Paris.
T. 0142229104, Fax 0145448617. - Paint /
Draw - 076152
Modern Art Gallery, 71 Rue Quincampoix, 75003 Paris.
T. 0142784302. 076153
Moirignot, 90 Blvd Raspail, 75006 Paris.
T. 0142220097. - Paint - 076154
Moisan, Martine, 6 Gal Vivienne, 75001 Paris.
T. 0142974665. - Paint / Graph / Sculp / Draw - 076155
Mollet-Viéville, Ghislain, 52 Rue Crozatier, 75012 Paris.
T. 0140020740, Fax 0140020750. - Paint - 076156
Mona Lisa, 32 Rue Varenne, 75007 Paris.
T. 0145481725. - Paint - 076157
Monbrison, Naïla de, 6 Rue Bourgogne, 75007 Paris.
T. 0147051115, Fax 0140629365. 076158
De Monceau, 17 Av Messine, 75008 Paris.
T. 0142258932. 076159
Monde de l'Art, 33 Rue Guénégaud, 75006 Paris.
T. 0143542240, Fax 0143545021. 076160
Monde de l'Art, 18 Rue Paradis, 75010 Paris.
T. 0142464344, Fax 0142464353. 076161
Mondineu, Guy, 11 Rue Neuve-Popincourt, 75011 Paris.
T. 0143384681. - Paint - 076162
Monegier du Sorbier, 14 Rue Beaune, 75007 Paris.
T. 0142616900. - Paint - 076163
Montaigne, 36 Av Montaigne, 75008 Paris.
T. 0147233225. - Paint - 076164
Montbel, Eric de, 55 Rue Charlot, 75003 Paris.
T. 0142787916, Fax 0142787917. 076165
Montenay, 31 Rue Mazarine, 75006 Paris.
T. 0143548530. - Paint - 076166
Montpensier, 23 Rue Montpensier, 75001 Paris.
T. 0142868770, Fax 0142868771. 076167
Moreau Gobard, Yvonne, 5 Rue Saints-Pères, 75006 Paris. T. 0142608825. 076168
Morlet, 29 Rue Philippe-de-Girard, 75010 Paris.
T. 0146071304, Fax 0146073357. - Graph - 076169
Mostini, 18 Rue Seine, 75006 Paris. T. 0143253218.
- Paint - 076170
Mostini, Jacques, 23 Rue Basfroi, 75011 Paris.
T. 0144939360, Fax 0144939364. 076171
Mougin, 30 Rue Lille, 75007 Paris.
T. 0140200833. 076172
Moussion, Jacqueline, 110 Rue Vieille-du-Temple,
75003 Paris. T. 0142716200. - Paint - 076173
Moyse, Jacques, 89 Blvd Pasteur, 75015 Paris.
T. 0143200224. 076174
Mugnier, Yves, 18 Rue Palestine, 75019 Paris.
T. 0142030393. - Paint - 076175

Mur du Nomade, 28 Rue Bonaparte, 75006 Paris.
T. 0146330260. - Paint - 076176
Musée Galerie de la Seita, 12 Rue Surcouf, 75007 Paris.
T. 0145566017. - Ant / Paint - 076177
Museum Collection, 14 Rue Castiglione, 75001 Paris.
T. 0142974311. 076178
Nadalini, Gianpaolo, 7 Rue Budé, 75004 Paris.
T. 0146346353, Fax 0146346088. - Paint /
Sculp - 076179
Naïfs du Monde Entier, 8 Rue Pas-de-la-Mule, 75003
Paris. T. 0142787157. - Paint - 076180
Naïfs et Primitifs, 33 Rue Dragon, 75006 Paris.
T. 0142228615. - Paint / Eth - 076181
Nahon, Pierre, 52 Rue Temple, 75004 Paris.
T. 0142788690. 076182
Namy-Caulier, Martine, 43 Rue Verneuil, 75007 Paris.
T. 0142602037. 076183
Namy-Caulier, Martine, 36 Rue Saints-Pères, 75007 Paris. T. 0145445527, Fax 0145449344. 076184
Narbon, 6 Rue Raffet, 75016 Paris. T. 0145276102.
- Paint - 076185
Nast à Paris, 10 Rue Alger, 75001 Paris. T. 0147033474,
Fax 0147033695. 076186
Nataf, Louvre des Antiquaires, 2 Pl Palais-Royal, 75001
Paris. T. 0142602223, Fax 0142602229.
- Paint - 076187
Natkin-Berta, 124 Rue Vieille-du-Temple, 75003 Paris.
T. 0142744216, Fax 0142745853. 076188
Navarra, Enrico, 34 Rue Bac, 75007 Paris.
T. 0142617320, Fax 0142869653. 076189
Navarra, Enrico, 16 Rue Seine, 75007 Paris.
T. 0142843210, Fax 0145489588. 076190
Nelson, 40 Rue Quincampoix, 75004 Paris.
T. 0142717456. 076191
Néotu, 25 Rue Renard, 75004 Paris. T. 0142789183,
Fax 0142782627. 076192
Nichido, 61 Rue Fbg-Saint-Honoré, 75008 Paris.
T. 0142666286, Fax 0142669197. - Paint - 076193
Nieszawer, Nadine, 14 Rue Provence, 75009 Paris.
T. 0142460024, Fax 0142467212. - Paint - 076194
Nieszawer, Nadine, 3ter Rue Rosiers, 75004 Paris.
T. 0142788161, Fax 0142780280. 076195
Nisenbaum, Charles, 32 Av Matignon, 75008 Paris.
T. 0142666267. - Paint - 076196
Nochy, Marthe, 93 Rue Seine, 75006 Paris.
T. 0143263176. - Paint - 076197
Noir d'Ivoire, 19 Rue Mazarine, 75006 Paris.
T. 0143549766. - Eth - 076198
Noir d'Ivoire, 6 Rue Visconti, 75006 Paris.
T. 0143549766. - Eth - 076199
Noir Ebène, 5 Rue Bréa, 75006 Paris. T. 0146347293.
- Ant / Furn / Mod - 076200
Noire et Blanche, 18 Rue Keller, 75011 Paris.
T. 0148078118. - Pho - 076201
Noirmont, Jérôme de, 36 Av Matignon, 75008 Paris.
T. 0142898900, Fax 0142898903. 076202
Nord-Est, 3 Rue Turenne, 75004 Paris.
T. 0142775683. 076203
Norre, Loraine, 6 Rue Beaune, 75007 Paris.
T. 0142616847, Fax 0149279601. 076204

Nouveaux Territoires, 87 Blvd Ney, 75018 Paris.
T. 0142232263. 076205
Nouvel Essor, 40 Rue Saints-Pères, 75007 Paris.
T. 0145489402, Fax 0145487735. - Graph - 076206
Nouvelle Gravure, 42 Rue Seine, 75006 Paris.
T. 0146330192. - Graph - 076207
Nouvelles Images, 6 Rue Dante, 75005 Paris.
T. 0143256243. 076208
Nouvellet, Olivier, 19 Rue Seine, 75006 Paris.
T. 0143294315. - Paint / Graph / Sculp / Draw - 076209
Nunki, 12 Rue Tocqueville, 75017 Paris.
T. 0142276084. 076210
Nvision Grafix France, 16 Av Friedland, 75008 Paris.
T. 0145614308, Fax 0145612627. 076211
Obadia, Nathalie, 8 Rue Normandie, 75003 Paris.
T. 0142746768, Fax 0142746866. 076212
Odermatt, Hervé, 71 Rue Fbg-Saint-Honoré, 75008 Paris. - Paint - 076213
Oeil de Boeuf, 11 Rue La-Reynie, 75004 Paris.
T. 0142783666. 076214
Oeil Sévigne, 14 Rue Sévigne, 75004 Paris.
T. 0142777459. - Paint - 076215
Of'Art, 8 Rue Récamier, 75004 Paris.
T. 0145448810. 076216
Olga Soé, 77 Blvd Voltaire, 75011 Paris.
T. 0148078830. 076217
Opéra Galerie Art, 6 Rue Monsigny, 75002 Paris.
T. 0142614651. 076218
Oréades, 52 Rue Moscou, 75008 Paris. T. 0143875920,
Fax 0143879920. - Ant / Paint / Draw - 076219
Orient-Occident, 5 Rue Saints-Pères, 75006 Paris.
T. 0142607765, Fax 0142600855. - Orient / Sculp /
Arch / Eth - 076220
Origami, 138 Blvd Montparnasse, 75014 Paris.
T. 0143204914, Fax 0143354114. 076221
ORKF, 50 Rue Etienne-Marcel, 75002 Paris.
Fax (1) 42331904. 076222
Orsay, 73bis Quai Orsay, 75007 Paris. T. 0144648154.
- Paint - 076223
Orsoni, Denise, 9 Rue Valois, 75001 Paris.
T. 0142963230. - Paint - 076224
Ostier, Janette, 26 Pl Vosges, 75003 Paris.
T. 0148872857, Fax 0148874494. - Paint /
Graph - 076225
Otsuka Europe, 15 Rue Boissy-d'Anglas, 75008 Paris.
T. 0142652061. 076226
Ouaiss, Jacques, Louvre des Antiquaires, 2 Pl Palais-Royal, 75001 Paris. T. 0142615699. 076227
Oudin, Alain, 47 Rue Quincampoix, 75004 Paris.
T. 0142718365. - Paint - 076228
Oz, 15 Rue Keller, 75011 Paris. T. 0147006623,
Fax 0147004463. 076229
Pailhas, Roger, 36 Rue Quincampoix, 75004 Paris.
T. 0148047131. 076230
Palette d'Or, 8 Blvd Voltaire, 75011 Paris.
T. 0147001472. 076231
Palix, 13 Rue Keller, 75011 Paris. T. 0148063670,
Fax 0147000121. 076232
Papierski, Daniel, 55 Rue Didot, 75014 Paris.
T. 0145406392. - Paint - 076233

Papierski, Daniel, 5 Rue Labrouste, 75015 Paris.
T. 0145406392, Fax 0145391948. - Paint /
Graph - *076234*
Papillon, Claudine, 59 Rue Turenne, 75003 Paris.
T. 0140299880. - Paint - *076235*
arat, Pierre, 76 Rue Vieille-du-Temple, 75003 Paris.
T. 0142774424. - Paint - *076236*
Pardo Tableaux, 160 Blvd Haussmann, 75008 Paris.
T. 0145625540. - Paint - *076237*
Paris American Art, 4 Rue Bonaparte, 75006 Paris.
T. 0143267985, Fax 0143543380. - Fra - *076238*
Paris Art Gallery, 1 Rue Jacob, 75006 Paris.
T. 0143262629, Fax 0146332022. *076239*
Parnasse 167, 167 Blvd Montparnasse, 75006 Paris.
T. 0146332374. *076240*
Passage de Retz, 9 Rue Charlot, 75003 Paris.
T. 0148043799, Fax 0142723945. *076241*
Passali, 27 Blvd Voltaire, 75011 Paris.
T. 0148051513. *076242*
Passebon, Pierre, 39 Rue Bourdonnais, 75001 Paris.
T. 0142364456, Fax 0140419886. - Ant /
Furn - *076243*
Patras, Jean-Marc, 9 Rue Saint-Anastase, 75003 Paris.
T. 0142722204. - Paint - *076244*
Patrice-Auzeral, Louvre des Antiquaires, 2 Pl Palais-
Royal, Paris. T. 0142615693. *076245*
Pavillon Royal, 16 Rue Birague, 75004 Paris.
T. 0140290131. - Paint - *076246*
Paviot, Alain, 5 Rue Marché-Saint-Honoré, 75001 Paris.
T. 0142606808. - Paint - *076247*
Peintres de Demain, 16 Passage Main-d'Or, 75011 Pa-
ris. T. 0148066740. - Paint - *076248*
Peintres de Demain, 23 Blvd Madeleine, 75001 Paris.
T. 0149260522, Fax 0149260515. *076249*
Peintres sans Frontières, 2 Av Moderne, 75019 Paris.
T. 0142380582, Fax 0142004225. - Paint /
Repr - *076250*
Peinture Fraîche, 29 Rue Bourgogne, 75007 Paris.
T. 0145510085. *076251*
Pellegrin, Jacques, 19 Rue Annonciation, 75016 Paris.
T. 0142886473, Fax 0142309436. - Paint - *076252*
Peron, Daniel, 21 Pass Véro-Dodat, 75001 Paris.
T. 0142368860. - Paint - *076253*
Perquis, 12 Rue Popincourt, 75011 Paris.
T. 0143382258. - Paint - *076254*
Perreau-Saussine, F., 11 Quai Voltaire, 75007 Paris.
T. 0142611075, Fax 0142615949. *076255*
Perrin, Jacques, 98 Rue Fbg-Saint-Honoré, 75008 Paris.
T. 0142650138, Fax 0149240408. - Ant /
Furn - *076256*
Perrin, Jacques, 3 Quai Voltaire, 75007 Paris.
T. 0142604312, Fax 0142613261. - Paint / Furn /
Lights / Draw - *076257*
Petit, André-François, 196 Blvd Saint-Germain, 75007
Paris. T. 0145446483, Fax 0145443204.
- Paint - *076258*
Petite, 8 Rue Cochin, 75005 Paris.
T. 0143263378. *076259*
Petite Galerie, 35 Rue Seine, 75006 Paris.
T. 0143263751. *076260*
Pétridès, Gilbert, 63 Rue Fbg-Saint-Honoré, 75008 Pa-
ris. T. 0142664232, Fax 0142652584. - Paint - *076261*
Peyre, Elyette, 5 Rue Visconti, 75006 Paris.
T. 0143264259, Fax 0143264389. *076262*
Peyrole, Jean, 14 Rue Sévigné, 75004 Paris.
T. 0142777459. - Paint - *076263*
Peyroulet, Gilles, 7 Rue Debelleyme, 75003 Paris.
T. 0142746920. *076264*
Phal, 9 Rue Vignon, 75008 Paris.
T. 0147425379. *076265*
Phénix, 9 Rue Guénégaud, 75006 Paris. T. 0143250013,
Fax 0143251353. *076266*
Philip, 14 Rue Sainte-Anastase, 75003 Paris.
T. 0148045822, Fax 0148049954. *076267*
Picturalissime, 16 Rue Odéon, 75006 Paris.
T. 0143290991, Fax 0140469027. *076268*
Pièce Unique, 4 Rue Jacques-Callot, 75006 Paris.
T. 0143265458. *076269*
Pierre Michel D., 70 Rue Gay-Lussac, 75005 Paris.
T. 0143296520. *076270*
Piltzer, Gérald, 78 Av Champs-Elysées, 75008 Paris.
T. 0142894359. *076271*

Pissarro, Lionel & Sandrine, 6 Rue Beaux-Arts, 75006
Paris. T. 0146337411, Fax 0146330734. - Paint /
Sculp / Draw - *076272*
Pittiglio, 157 Rue Pyrénées, 75020 Paris.
T. 0143731236. *076273*
Pixi et Cie, 95 Rue Seine, 75006 Paris. T. 0143251012.
- Paint / Graph / Sculp / Draw - *076274*
Pochade, 11 Rue Guénégaud, 75006 Paris.
T. 0143548903, Fax 0143297511. *076275*
Point Cardinal, 3 Rue Jacob, 75006 Paris.
T. 0140333208. - Paint / Graph / Sculp - *076276*
Point de Vue, 91 Rue Saint-Honoré, 75001 Paris.
T. 0142335090, Fax 0145085652. *076277*
Point Rouge, 45 Rue Penthièvre, 75008 Paris.
T. 0142561090. *076278*
Polaris, 8 Rue Saint-Claude, 75003 Paris.
T. 0142722127. - Paint - *076279*
Pomme d'Or, 21 Rue Saint-Jacques, 75005 Paris.
T. 0143545713. *076280*
Pons, 38 Rue Sainte-Croix-la-Bretonnerie, 75004 Paris.
T. 0142714670, Fax 0142714762. *076281*
Poo, Ivi, 25 Rue Dauphine, 75006 Paris. T. 0143298708,
Fax 0140517702. *076282*
Portal Gallery, 18 Rue Montpensier, 75001 Paris.
T. 0147039085. *076283*
Posters Gallery, 58 Rue Auteuil, 75016 Paris.
T. 0142248962. - Repr - *076284*
Pothuau, Virginie de, 40 Rue Jacob, 75006 Paris.
T. 0142603985. *076285*
Praz Delavallade, 10 Rue Saint-Sabin, 75011 Paris.
T. 0143385260, Fax 0143384502. - Paint / Graph /
Sculp / Draw - *076286*
Prazan-Fitoussi, 25 Rue Guénégaud, 75006 Paris.
T. 0146347761, Fax 0146347762. *076287*
Prestige, 3 Rue Saules, 75018 Paris.
T. 0142513899. *076288*
Primitif, 5 Rue Jacques-Callot, 75006 Paris.
T. 0143252164. - Paint - *076289*
Princesse, 18 Rue Princesse, 75006 Paris.
T. 0143252518. - Paint - *076290*
Prints, 57 Quai Grands-Augustins, 75006 Paris.
T. 0146335245. - Paint - *076291*
Private View, 233 Rue Convention, 75015 Paris.
T. 0145302352. *076292*
Protée, 38 Rue Seine, 75006 Paris. T. 0143252195,
Fax 0140460402. - Paint / Graph / Sculp - *076293*
Prouté, Paul, 74 Rue Seine, 75006 Paris.
T. 0143268980, Fax 0143258341. - Graph /
Draw - *076294*

Paul PROUTÉ S.A.

Estampes Originales · Dessins

74, rue de Seine (6e)

Tél. 01.43.26.89.80
Fax 01.43.25.83.41

Punchinello, 6 Rue Arras, 75005 Paris.
T. 0143541631. *076295*
Pym, Gordon & Fils, 1 Rue Keller, 75011 Paris.
T. 0147002198. - Paint - *076296*
Queyras, 29 Rue Guénégaud, 75006 Paris.
T. 0146337974. - Paint - *076297*
Queyrel, 34 Rue Mazarine, 75006 Paris.
T. 0146347041. *076298*
Quiguer, Donya, 31 Rue Vieille-du-Temple, 75004 Paris.
T. 0148047255. *076299*
Raffray, P., 4 Rue Miromesnil, 75008 Paris.
T. 0142659617. - Paint - *076300*
Rambaud, Gérard, 14 Rue Tournelles, 75004 Paris.
T. 0148047370, Fax 0148047279. *076301*
Rambert, 4 Rue Beaux-Arts, 75006 Paris.
T. 0143293490, Fax 0143250163. - Paint / Graph /
Sculp / Draw - *076302*
Raph, 12 Rue Pavée, 75004 Paris. T. 0148878036.
- Paint - *076303*

Ray, Michel, 157 Rue Saint-Martin, 75003 Paris.
T. 0140270322. *076304*
Reber, Elisabeth, 52 Rue Verrerie, 75004 Paris.
T. 0142724633. - Paint - *076305*
Rec, 7 Rue Charlemagne, 75004 Paris.
T. 0142773363. *076306*
Reflets du Temps, 46 Rue Sainte-Anne, 75002 Paris.
T. 0142600153, Fax 0142601757. *076307*
Regards, 11 Rue Blancs-Manteaux, 75004 Paris.
T. 0142771961, Fax 0142775711. - Paint / Sculp /
Draw - *076308*
Regency, 45 Rue Bac, 75007 Paris. T. 0145483310,
Fax 0145485926. *076309*
René, Denise, 22 Rue Charlot, 75003 Paris.
T. 0148877394, Fax 0148877395. - Paint / Graph /
Sculp / Tex / Silv - *076310*
René, Denise, 196 Blvd Saint-Germain, 75007 Paris.
T. 0142227757, Fax 0145448918. *076311*
Renoncourt, 33 Quai Voltaire, 75007 Paris.
T. 0142611400. *076312*
Renou & Poyet, 164 Rue Fbg-Saint-Honoré, 75008 Paris.
T. 0143593595, Fax 0143389547. - Paint - *076313*
Resche, J.E., 20 Rue Seine, 75006 Paris.
T. 0143294403. - Paint - *076314*
Resche, Sylvie, 53 Rue Seine, 75006 Paris.
T. 0143269348, Fax 0143269004. *076315*
Richebourg, R., 5 Rue Dupuis, 75003 Paris.
T. 0142717600, Fax 0142717700. *076316*
Riedel, Jean-Claude, 12 Rue Guénégaud, 75006 Paris.
T. 0146332573, Fax 0143296945. - Paint /
Sculp - *076317*
Robert, Roland, 6 Rue Saint-Marc, 75002 Paris.
T. 0142361558. *076318*
Robin, Anne, 18 Rue Charlot, 75003 Paris.
T. 0148872285, Fax 0148876842. *076319*
Robin-Leadouze, 2 Av Matignon, 75008 Paris.
T. 0142892683, Fax 0142892703. - Paint / Graph /
Sculp / Draw - *076320*
Robin, Pierre, 10 Rue Jacques-Callot, 75006 Paris.
T. 0146346207. *076321*
Roger-Binet, Patrick, 138 Rue Saint-Honoré, 75001 Pa-
ris. T. 0142602151. - Paint - *076322*
Rohwedder, 6 Rue Roi-Doré, 75003 Paris.
T. 0140278263. - Paint - *076323*
Roi Fou, 182 Rue Fbg-Saint-Honoré, 75008 Paris.
T. 0145638259, Fax 0145635891. - Paint / Cur /
Mod - *076324*
Romagny, 13 Rue Thorigny, 75003 Paris.
T. 0142773810, Fax 0142773580. *076325*
Romanet, André, 30-32 Rue Seine, 75006 Paris.
T. 0143264670, Fax 0140517608. - Paint - *076326*
Ropac, Thaddaeus, 7 Rue Debelleyme, 75003 Paris.
T. 0142729900, Fax 0142726166. *076327*
Roquefeuil, Hélène de, 10 Rue Arquebusiers, 75003 Pa-
ris. T. 0142786758, Fax 0142784868. *076328*
Roquefeuil, Hélène de, 70 Rue Amelot, 75011 Paris.
T. 0143571632, Fax 0143571394. *076329*
Di Rosa, 43 Rue Poitou, 75003 Paris. T. 0140279282,
Fax 0140270284. *076330*
Rossignol, Gérard, 3 Rue Bonaparte, 75006 Paris.
T. 0143267261. *076331*
Rouif, Abel, 133 Rue Rome, 75017 Paris.
T. 0142272375. - Paint / Sculp / Glass - *076332*
Rouillon, Jean-Paul, 27 Rue Seine, 75006 Paris.
T. 0143267300. - Graph - *076333*
Rouland, Lambert, 7 Rue Saint-Sabin, 75011 Paris.
T. 0140218764. *076334*
Rouland, Lambert, 62 Rue La-Boétie, 75008 Paris.
T. 0145635152, Fax 0142895924. *076335*
Roussard, André, 7 et 13 Rue Mont-Cenis, 75018 Paris.
T. 0146063046. - Paint - *076336*
Route de la Soie, 14 Rue Lacépède, 75005 Paris.
T. 0143378839. *076337*
Royer, Alain, 45 Rue Montreuil, 75011 Paris.
T. 0143724255. - Paint / Graph - *076338*
Royer, Elisabeth, 5 Blvd Raspail, 75007 Paris.
T. 0144395400, Fax 0144395402. - Paint /
Graph - *076339*
Rudnicki, Patrick, 38 Rue Berri, 75008 Paris.
T. 0142872041. - Paint - *076340*
Ryaux, 67 Rue Sainte-Anne, 75002 Paris.
T. 0142603747, Fax 0142603141. *076341*

Sadoun, Michèle, 108 Rue Fbg-Saint-Honoré, 75008 Pa-
ris. T. 0142663272. - Paint - 076342
Sadoun, Michèle, 32 Rue Picardie, 75003 Paris.
T. 0142783297. - Paint - 076343
Sagittaire Import, 26 Rue Malar, 75007 Paris.
T. 0145512221, Fax 0147530201. 076344
Sagot-Le-Garrec, 10 Rue Buci, 75006 Paris.
T. 0143264338, Fax 0143297747. - Graph /
Draw - 076345
Saint-Charles de Rose, Pascal J.M., 15 Rue Keller,
75011 Paris. T. 0147001154. 076346
Saint-Honoré, 69 Rue Fbg-Saint-Honoré, 75008 Paris.
T. 0142663663, Fax 0142669265. - Paint - 076347
Saint-Jacques, 328 Rue Saint-Jacques, 75005 Paris.
T. 0140510681. 076348
Saint-Loui's Posters, 23 Rue Saint-Louis-en-l'Ile, 75004
Paris. T. 0140469165. 076349
Saint-Merri, 9 Rue Saint-Merri, 75004 Paris.
T. 0142773912. 076350
Saint-Paul, 35 Rue Saint-Paul, 75004 Paris.
T. 0142727407. - Paint - 076351
Saint-Placide, 41 Rue Saint-Placide, 75006 Paris.
T. 0145485958. - Paint - 076352
Saint-Roch, 10 Rue Saint-Roch, 75001 Paris.
T. 0140200152. - Paint - 076353
Saint-Séverin, 4 Rue Prêtres-Saint-Séverin, 75005 Pa-
ris. T. 0143547208. - Paint - 076354
Salaun, Joël, 9 Rue Mont-Thabor, 75001 Paris.
T. 0142613184. - Paint - 076355
Samagra, 52 Rue Jacob, 75006 Paris. T. 0142868619.
- Paint / Graph / Sculp / Draw - 076356
Samarcande, 13 Rue Saints-Pères, 75006 Paris.
T. 0142608317. - Orient / Sculp / Arch - 076357
Samia Saouma, 16 Rue Coutures-Saint-Gervais, 75003
Paris. T. 0142784044, Fax 0142786400. - Pho / Paint /
Sculp - 076358
Samovar, 16 Rue Brémontier, 75017 Paris.
T. 0142673420. 076359
Samuel, Claude, 69 Av Daumesnil, 75012 Paris.
T. 0153170111, Fax 0153170708. 076360
San Carlo, 57 Rue Saint-Jacques, 75005 Paris.
T. 0144071431. 076361
Sanguine, 106 Rue Tour, 75016 Paris. T. 0145041090,
Fax 0145030865. 076362
Sani, Gladys, Louvre des Antiquaires, 2 Pl Palais-Royal,
75001 Paris. T. 0142615692. - Paint / Graph /
Draw - 076363
Santoni & Cerveau, 15 Quai Saint-Michel, 75005 Paris.
T. 0143547573. - Paint - 076364
Sao, 1 Rue Saint-Benoît, 75006 Paris. T. 0142963260.
- Eth - 076365
Saphir, 84 Blvd Saint-Germain, 75005 Paris.
T. 0143265422. 076366
Saphir, 69 Av Villiers, 75017 Paris. T. 0144402684,
Fax 0143802349. 076367
Sarah B., 113 Rue Château, 75014 Paris.
T. 0145385848, Fax 0145385853. 076368
Sarver, 6 Rue Trésor, 75004 Paris.
T. 0148049927. 076369
Sarver, 99 Rue Quincampoix, 75003 Paris.
T. 0148045051. 076370
Sassi, Etienne, 14 Av Matignon, 75008 Paris.
T. 0142256477. - Paint - 076371
Satellite, 7 Rue François-de-Neufchâteau, 75011 Paris.
T. 0143798020. 076372
Sauveur Bismuth, 73 Quai Tournelle, 75005 Paris.
T. 0143292131, Fax 0143293151. 076373
Saxo, 270 Rue Fbg-Saint-Martin, 75010 Paris.
T. 0142051332. - Paint / Graph - 076374
Sayegh, John, 178 Rue Fbg-Saint-Honoré, 75008 Paris.
T. 0142257621, Fax 0145620299. 076375
Scarbo, 93 Rue Saint-Honoré, 75001 Paris.
T. 0145088642. 076376
Scavongelli, Luciano, 27 Rue Penthièvre, 75008 Paris.
T. 0142894601, Fax 0142890441. - Paint / Graph /
Draw - 076377
Scavongelli, Luciano, 84 Rue Quincampoix, 75003 Paris.
T. 0142783532. - Paint - 076378
Schauer, 153 Rue Saint-Martin, 75003 Paris.
T. 0148878171. 076379
Schehade, Brigitte, 44 Rue Tournelles, 75004 Paris.
T. 0142779674, Fax 0148874361. 076380

Schmidt, Valérie, 41 Rue Mazarine, 75006 Paris.
T. 0143547191. - Paint - 076381
Schmit, Manuel, 396 Rue Saint-Honoré, 75001 Paris.
T. 0142603636, Fax 0149279716. - Paint /
Sculp - 076382
Schmit, Robert, 396 Rue Saint-Honoré, 75001 Paris.
T. 0142603636, Fax 0149279716. - Paint / Sculp /
Draw - 076383
Schmitt, Michel, 84 Av Breteuil, 75015 Paris.
T. 0143062890. - Paint - 076384
Schöffer de Lavandeyra, Eléonore, 15 Rue Hégésippe-
Moreau, 75018 Paris. T. 0145226792. 076385
Schoffel, Alain, 21 Rue Guénégaud, 75006 Paris.
T. 0143541383. - Paint - 076386
Schottle, Rudiger, 5 Rue Grenier-Saint-Lazare, 75003
Paris. T. 0144598206. - Paint - 076387
Scot, 7 Rue Miromesnil, 75008 Paris.
T. 0147426898. 076388
Scremini, Clara, 39 Rue Charonne, 75011 Paris.
T. 0143552121, Fax 0143555355. 076389
Sculptures, 11 Rue Visconti, 75006 Paris.
T. 0146341375. - Sculp - 076390
Seconde Modernité, 80 Rue Taitbout, 75009 Paris.
T. 0142819142. - Paint - 076391
Segoura, Maurice, 20 Rue Fbg-Saint-Honoré, 75008 Paris.
T. 0142651103, Fax 0142651608. - Paint /
Draw - 076392
Segoura, Michel, 11 Quai Voltaire, 75007 Paris.
T. 0142611923, Fax 0142600198. - Paint - 076393
Séguier, 10 Rue Séguier, 75006 Paris.
T. 0143257323. 076394
Seltzer-Lejeune, 100 Rue Folie-Méricourt, 75011 Paris.
T. 0143553209, Fax 0143553558. 076395
Sens Art, 3 Rue Fénelon, 75010 Paris. T. 0145262382,
Fax 0145261591. 076396
Sensitive, 264 Rue Saint-Jacques, 75005 Paris.
T. 0143547832. - Paint - 076397
Sentou Galerie, 18 Rue Pont-Louis-Philippe, 75004 Pa-
ris. T. 0142774479. 076398
Sépia Galerie d'Art, 31 Rue Vieille-du-Temple, 75004
Paris. T. 0140290696, Fax 0140290693. 076399
Séraphine, 22 Rue Odéon, 75006 Paris. T. 0146334924.
- Paint - 076400
Seroussi, Nathalie, 34 Rue Seine, 75006 Paris.
T. 0146340584, Fax 0146330337. 076401
Serret, Marc, 21 Rue Drouot, 75009 Paris.
T. 0148243115. 076402
Serret & Fabiani, 71 Rue Fbg-Saint-Honoré, 75008 Pa-
ris. T. 0142666619. 076403
SIAM, 8 Rue Jacques Callot, 75006 Paris.
Fax (1) 46334483. 076404
Simourgh, 17 Rue Saint-Roch, 75001 Paris.
T. 0142601654. - Paint - 076405
Singe Blanc, 15 Rue Saint-Jacques, 75005 Paris.
T. 0143261470, Fax 0140468536. - Orient - 076406
Sistu, Gianna, 29 Rue Université, 75007 Paris.
T. 0142220881, Fax 0145449385. 076407
Smagghe, Véronique, 24 Rue Charlot, 75003 Paris.
T. 0142728340. 076408
Société Art Location, 68 Rue La-Boétie, 75008 Paris.
T. 0145611736. 076409
Société Internationale d'Art Contemporain, 36 Av Mon-
taigne, 75008 Paris. T. 0147233235,
Fax 0147233243. 076410
Sorbier des Oiseleurs, 70 Rue Vieille-du-Temple, 75003
Paris. T. 0148876972. 076411
Sordello, M., 25 Rue Penthièvre, 75008 Paris.
T. 0140750159, Fax 0140750159. 076412
Sous Sol, 12 Rue Petit-Musc, 75004 Paris.
T. 0142724672. 076413
Speyer, Darthea, 6 Rue Jacques-Callot, 75006 Paris.
T. 0143547841. 076414
Sphynx, 104 Rue Fbg-Saint-Honoré, 75008 Paris.
T. 0142659096. - Paint - 076415
Spira, Thierry, 19 Rue Guénégaud, 75006 Paris.
T. 0146331819, Fax 0146332021. 076416
Spiridon, 12 Rue Crozatier, 75012 Paris. T. 0143970971.
- Paint - 076417
Stadler, Rodolphe, 51 Rue Seine, 75006 Paris.
T. 0143269110. - Paint - 076418
Stal, Dominique, 8 Rue Sainte-Lucie, 75015 Paris.
T. 0145787903. 076419

Stardom, 2 Rue Voltaire, 75011 Paris. T. 0143563504,
Fax 0143563501. 076420
Steinitz, Baruch Bernard, 75 Rue Fbg-Saint-Honoré,
75008 Paris. T. 0147423194, Fax 0149249116.
- Paint / Sculp / Dec - 076421
Stella Graphics, 35 Rue Boileau, 75016 Paris.
T. 0140718420, Fax 0140718421. 076422
Stern, Frédéric-Robert, 11 Rue Faustin-Hélie, 75116 Pa-
ris. T. 0145031184. 076423
Strouk Art 333, 25 Rue Renard, 75004 Paris.
T. 0148049460, Fax 0148049466. 076424
Strouk, Marcel, 21-23 Rue Saint-Merri, 75004 Paris.
T. 0148049460. - Paint - 076425
Studio de l'Image, 14 Rue Carmes, 75005 Paris.
T. 0143548873, Fax 0143298504. 076426
Sud, 23 Rue Archives, 75004 Paris. T. 0142784237.
- Paint - 076427
Sun, 32 Av George-V, 75008 Paris. T. 0147206578,
Fax 0147206692. - Paint / Graph - 076428
Sybille, 42 Rue Université, 75007 Paris. T. 0142961675.
- Paint - 076429
Synthèse, 116 Rue Rennes, 75006 Paris.
T. 0145482337. - Paint / Graph - 076430
Syrus, 25 Rue Saint-Paul, 75004 Paris. T. 0148049781,
Fax 0148040103. 076431
Talabardon, Bertrand, 44 Rue Sainte-Anne, 75002 Paris.
Fax 0147033916, 0147033951. 076432
Talvi, 16 Rue Thorigny, 75003 Paris. T. 0140279950,
Fax 0140279955. 076433
Tamenaga, 18 Av Matignon, 75008 Paris.
T. 0142666194. - Paint - 076434
Tanakaya, 4 Rue Saint-Sulpice, 75006 Paris.
T. 0143257291, Fax 0143257291. - Graph /
Orient - 076435
Targa, 10 Rue Sainte-Anastase, 75003 Paris.
T. 0140270034, Fax 0140270036. 076436
Tassel, Jean-Max, 15 Quai Voltaire, 75007 Paris.
T. 0142610201, Fax 0142612563. - Paint - 076437
Teisseire, A., 13 Av Mozart, 75016 Paris.
T. 0145270868. - Paint / Graph / Fra - 076438
Templon, Daniel, 30 Rue Beaubourg, 75003 Paris.
T. 0142760240, Fax 0142774536. - Paint /
Sculp - 076439
Tendances, 105 Rue Quincampoix, 75003 Paris.
T. 0142786179, Fax 0142781275. - Paint / Graph /
Sculp / Mul / Draw - 076440
Terres de l'Est, 4 Rue Frédéric-Sauton, 75005 Paris.
T. 0144073858. 076441
Texbraun, 12 Rue Mazarine, 75006 Paris.
T. 0146334784. - Paint - 076442
Théorème, Louvre des Antiquaires, 2 Pl Palais-Royal,
75001 Paris. T. 0140159323. - China - 076443
Thibaud, Dany, 52 Rue Labrouste, 75015 Paris.
T. 0142507211. - Paint - 076444
Thomas, Hadrien, 3 Rue Plâtre, 75004 Paris.
T. 0142760310. - Paint - 076445
Thomas I.S., 46 Av Suffren, 75015 Paris.
T. 0145671346, Fax 0145673316. 076446
Thomire Roux, Louvre des Antiquaires, 2 Pl Palais-Roy-
al, 75001 Paris. T. 0142615700, Fax 0142615701.
- Paint - 076447
Thompson, Michel, 23 Rue La Reynie, 75001 Paris.
T. 0142337387. 076448
Thorigny, 13 Rue Thorigny, 75003 Paris. T. 0148876065,
Fax 0148878727. 076449
Thouard, Jeannie, 21 Rue Bonaparte, 75006 Paris.
T. 0143254243. 076450
Tibourg, 15 Rue Bourg-Tibourg, 75004 Paris.
T. 0142770928. - Paint - 076451
Tiger Galerie, 33 Rue Mazarine, 75006 Paris.
T. 0143256559. 076452
Timsit, Corinne, 9 Rue Mazarine, 75006 Paris.
T. 0143543200, Fax 0143541592. 076453
Toit du Monde, 33 Rue Berthe, 75018 Paris.
T. 0142237643. 076454
Touchaleaume, Eric, 54 Rue Mazarine, 75006 Paris.
T. 0143268996, Fax 0143293629. 076455
Tour, Jean, 68 Quai Hôtel-de-Ville, 75004 Paris.
T. 0140270666. 076456
Tourbillon, Louvre des Antiquaires, 2 Pl Palais-Royal,
75001 Paris. T. 0142615658. 076457
Tournelle, 3 Rue Haut-Pavé, 75005 Paris.
T. 0143546857. - Paint - 076458

Tournié, Françoise, 10 Rue Roi-de-Sicile, 75004 Paris.
T. 0142781318. - Ant / Paint - *076459*
Tourtour, 20 Rue Quincampoix, 75004 Paris.
T. 0148878248. - Paint - *076460*
Transit, 36 Rue Saints-Pères, 75007 Paris.
T. 0145445527. - Paint - *076461*
Íransoxiane, 6 Rue Christine, 75006 Paris.
T. 0143266233. *076462*
Transparence, 42 Rue Caulaincourt, 75018 Paris.
T. 0142237445. *076463*
Treger, Richard, 47 Rue Mazarine, 75006 Paris.
T. 0146338160. - Paint - *076464*
Triangle, 36 Rue Penthièvre, 75008 Paris.
T. 0142894554, Fax 0142891258. *076465*
Trigano, Patrice, 4bis Rue Beaux-Arts, 75006 Paris.
T. 0146341501. - Paint / Sculp / Pho / Draw - *076466*
Trigone, 3 Rue Tardieu, 75018 Paris.
T. 0142648351. *076467*
Troisième Oeil, 98 Rue Vieille-du-Temple, 75003 Paris.
T. 0148043025, Fax 0148040998. *076468*
Troubetzkoy, 1 Av Messine, 75008 Paris.
T. 0145626602, Fax 0142259939. - Repr - *076469*
Turquin, Eric, 69 Rue Sainte-Anne, 75002 Paris.
T. 0147034878, Fax 0142605932. *076470*
Un Autre Regard, 20 Rue Jardins-Saint-Paul, 75004 Pa-
ris. T. 0142772251, Fax 0142772239. *076471*
Un Sourire de Toi, 10 Rue Moulin-Joly, 75011 Paris.
T. 0147004323. *076472*
Univers Bronze, 29 Rue Penthièvre, 75008 Paris.
T. 0142565030. - Paint - *076473*
Univers Sept, 26 Rue Charonne, 75011 Paris.
T. 0140218464. *076474*
Uraeus, 24 Rue Seine, 75006 Paris. T. 0143269131.
- Sculp / Arch / Eth - *076475*
Urubamba, 4 Rue Bûcherie, 75005 Paris.
T. 0143540824, Fax 0143299180. - Paint / Graph /
Sculp / Eth / Draw - *076476*
Uzzan, Philippe, 11 Rue Thorigny, 75003 Paris.
T. 0144598300, Fax 0144598301. *076477*
Vachet, Louvre des Antiquaires, 2 Pl Palais-Royal,
75001 Paris. T. 0142615756. *076478*
Valdo, 19 Rue Penthièvre, 75008 Paris. T. 0142659055.
- Paint - *076479*
Valleix, 7 Rue Oberkampf, 75011 Paris.
T. 0143558509. *076480*
Vallet, François, 19 Blvd Voltaire, 75011 Paris.
T. 0148070098. *076481*
Vallois, 20 Rue Seine, 75006 Paris.
T. 0143258259. *076482*
Vallois, 36 Rue Seine, 75006 Paris.
T. 0143295115. *076483*
Vallois, Georges-Philippe, 38 Rue Seine, 75006 Paris.
T. 0146346107, Fax 0143251880. - Paint / Sculp /
Mod - *076484*
Valluet, Christine, 14 Rue Guénégaud, 75006 Paris.
T. 0143268338. *076485*
Valmay, Akka, 22 Rue Seine, 75006 Paris.
T. 0143546675, Fax 0143250132. *076486*
Valtat, Denise, 59 Rue La-Boétie, 75008 Paris.
T. 0143592740. - Paint - *076487*
Van M., 39 Rue Notre-Dame-de-Lorette, 75009 Paris.
T. 0149700777. *076488*
Vanuxem, 134 Rue Fbg-Saint-Honoré, 75008 Paris.
T. 0143597218. *076489*
Varine-Gincourt, 110 Blvd Courcelles, 75017 Paris.
T. 0142272016. *076490*
Varnier, 4 Rue Beaux-Arts, 75006 Paris. T. 0146345709.
- Paint - *076491*
Vaury, Madeleine, 16 Rue Seine, 75006 Paris.
T. 0143541528. - Paint - *076492*
Veinstein, Alain, 30 Rue Lappe, 75011 Paris.
T. 0147001520, Fax 0147001793. *076493*
Vendôme, 8 Rue Jacob, 75006 Paris. T. 0143262917,
Fax 0143296902. - Paint / China / Glass - *076494*
Vendôme, 12 Rue Paix, 75002 Paris. T. 0142617391,
Fax 0140200520. - Paint / Sculp - *076495*
Vent d'Ouest, 180 Rue Saint-Martin, 75003 Paris.
T. 0142760060. *076496*
Verberke, Dominique, 34 Rue Guynemer, 75006 Paris.
T. 0145483934. *076497*
Vercel, Félix, 9 Av Matignon, 75008 Paris.
T. 0142562519, Fax 0145633327. - Paint - *076498*

Verkamer, 3bis Rue Beaux-Arts, 75006 Paris.
T. 0146331890. - Paint - *076499*
Verneuil Saints-Pères, 13 Rue Saints-Pères, 75006 Pa-
ris. T. 0142602830. - Paint - *076500*
Victor Hugo, 3 Rue Mesnil, 75016 Paris.
T. 0147045307. *076501*
Vidal, Aline, 70 Rue Bonaparte, 75006 Paris.
T. 0143260868. *076502*
Vidal, Bernard, 10 Rue Trésor, 75003 Paris.
T. 0142760605. - Paint - *076503*
Vidal, Michel, 56 Rue Fbg-Saint-Antoine, 75012 Paris.
T. 0143422271, Fax 0143421510. - Paint / Graph /
Sculp / Draw - *076504*
Vidal Saint-Phalle, 10 Rue Trésor, 75004 Paris.
T. 0142760605, Fax 0142760533. *076505*
Vieille du Temple, 23 Rue Vieille-du-Temple, 75004 Pa-
ris. T. 0140299752, Fax 0142713975. *076506*
Vierny, Dina, 36 Rue Jacob, 75006 Paris.
T. 0142602318, Fax 0142860087. - Ant / Paint /
Graph / Sculp / Draw - *076507*
Vieux Paris Artistique, 17 Rue Maubeuge, 75009 Paris.
T. 0148781554. - Paint - *076508*
Village Voice, 6 Rue Princesse, 75006 Paris.
T. 0143633647. - Paint - *076509*
Villain, Jean-Paul, 29 Rue Miromesnil, 75008 Paris.
T. 0142653719. - Paint / Graph / Sculp / Draw - *076510*
Villepoix, Anne de, 11 Rue Tournelles, 75004 Paris.
T. 0142783224, Fax 0142783216. *076511*
Vincent, Emile, 29 Quai Tournelle, 75005 Paris.
T. 0140518544. *076512*
Vincy, Lara, 47 Rue Seine, 75006 Paris. T. 0143267251,
Fax 0140517888. - Paint - *076513*
Virtuoses de la Réclame, 5 Rue Saint-Paul, 75004 Paris.
T. 0142720786. - Repr / Graph - *076514*
Visat, Suzanne, 6 Rue Bourbon-le-Château, 75006 Paris.
T. 0143265262. - Paint - *076515*
Visconti, 37 Rue Seine, 75006 Paris.
T. 0143265261. *076516*
Vision Nouvelle, 45 Rue Archives, 75003 Paris.
T. 0140279678. - Paint - *076517*
Vitesse, 48 Rue Berri, 75008 Paris.
Fax (1) 42254813. *076518*
Vitoux, Pierre-Marie, 3 Rue Ormesson, 75004 Paris.
T. 0148048100, Fax 0148045699. *076519*
Vivas, Alesandro, 11bis Rue Perche, 75003 Paris.
T. 0148872366, Fax 0148872362. *076520*
Voir, 16 Rue Guénégaud, 75006 Paris.
T. 0146339746. *076521*
Voldère, Florence de, Louvre des Antiquaires, 2 Pl Pa-
lais-Royal, 75001 Paris. T. 0140159326.
- Paint - *076522*
Volmar, Ror, 6 Rue Miromesnil, 75008 Paris.
T. 0142660960, Fax 0142660628. - Paint /
Sculp - *076523*
Vos, Jacques de, 7 Rue Bonaparte, 75006 Paris.
T. 0143298894, Fax 0140469545. - Furn / Sculp /
Lights - *076524*
Vos, Jacques de, 34 Rue Seine, 75006 Paris.
T. 0143262926. - Paint / Graph / Sculp / Draw - *076525*
V.R.G. Saint-Germain, 23 Rue Jacob, 75006 Paris.
T. 0143262917. - Paint / Graph / China / Sculp / Jew /
Glass - *076526*
Weil Seligmann, Lucie, 6 Rue Bonaparte, 75006 Paris.
T. 0143547195. *076527*
Weiller, 5 Rue Gît-le-Coeur, 75006 Paris.
T. 0143264768. - Paint - *076528*
Weiller, Patrick, 76 Rue Notre-Dame-des-Champs,
75006 Paris. T. 0146345969,
Fax 0143296860. *076529*
Weinman, Christine, 20 Rue Jardins-Saint-Paul, 75004
Paris. T. 0142789087. - Paint - *076530*
Wiegersma, 75 Rue Fbg-Saint-Honoré, 75008 Paris.
T. 0147421202. - Paint - *076531*
Wildenstein, 57 Rue Boétie, 75008 Paris.
T. 0145630100, Fax 0145614653. *076532*
Wisen, 102 Rue Fbg-Saint-Honoré, 75008 Paris.
T. 0142666944. - Ant / China - *076533*
Woo Mang & Partners, 43 Rue Folie-Méricourt, 75011
Paris. T. 0148054535. *076534*
Wyrs, Jacques, 31 Rue Maire, 75003 Paris.
T. 0142773271. - Paint - *076535*
Xippas, Renos, 108 Rue Vieille-du-Temple, 75003 Paris.
T. 0140270555, Fax 0140270716. *076536*

Yoshi, 8 Av Matignon, 75008 Paris. T. 0143597346.
- Paint - *076537*
Zabriskie, Virginia, 37 Rue Quincampoix, 75004 Paris.
T. 0142723547, Fax 0140279966. - Sculp /
Pho - *076538*
Zimmermann, Jean, 11 Rue Perchamps, 75016 Paris.
T. 0142245647. *076539*
Zone et Phase, 30 Rue Lappe, 75011 Paris.
T. 0148065125, Fax 0148064941. *076540*
Zurcher, 19 Rue Abbé-Grégoire, 75006 Paris.
T. 0145481022. - Paint - *076541*
20ème Siècle, 22 Rue Lille, 75007 Paris.
T. 0142860393. *076542*
7 Fois 7, Village Suisse, 75015 Paris.
T. 0143068396. *076543*

Parthenay (Deux-Sèvres)

Galerie Art 2000, 23 Rue Jean-Jaurès, 79200 Parthenay. T. 0549642609. *076544*

Pau (Pyrénées-Atlantiques)

Carrier, Alain, 7 Pl Georges-Clemenceau, 64000 Pau.
T. 0559839999. *076545*
Henry, 16 Rue Lamothe, 64000 Pau.
T. 0559271214. *076546*
Taylor, 7 Rue Alexander-Taylor, 64000 Pau.
T. 0559277151, Fax 0559271904. *076547*

Penne-d'Agenais (Lot-et-Garonne)

Galerie de la Cité, Rue 14-Juillet, 47140 Penne-d'Agenais. T. 0553413451. *076548*

Pérols (Hérault)

Lasalle, Claude, Centre Commercial Plein-Sud, 34470
Pérols. T. 0467201019. *076549*

Perpignan (Pyrénées-Orientales)

Architecture, 11 Rue Bastion-Saint-Dominique, 66000
Perpignan. Fax 68348090. - Paint - *076550*
Art et Loisir, 13 Rue Marché-de-Gros, 66000 Perpignan.
T. 0468350692. - Fra - *076551*
Atelier 45, 6 Rue Tour-de-Mir, 66000 Perpignan.
T. 0468612103. - Fra - *076552*
Droit de Regard, 6 Rue Révolution-Française, 66000
Perpignan. T. 0468511576. - Paint - *076553*
Marion, 8 Av Palmiers, 66000 Perpignan.
T. 0468353575. - Paint - *076554*
Ruiz la Caverne, Hélène, 58 Rue Saint-Jacques, 66000
Perpignan. T. 0468053573. - Paint - *076555*
Ruiz, Maurice, 7 Pl Eglise, 66000 Perpignan.
T. 0468965346. - Paint - *076556*
Serra, Yvette & Marie-Françoise, 8 Pl Gambetta, 66000
Perpignan. T. 0468350480. - Paint - *076557*
Sud Cadre, Chemin Del-Vives, 66000 Perpignan.
T. 0468639693. - Fra - *076558*

Perros-Guirec (Côtes-d'Armor)

Galerie Le Linkin, 65 Rue Anatole-Le-Braz, 22700 Perros-Guirec. T. 0296230424. *076559*
Maison du Littoral, Sent Douaniers, 22700 Perros-Guirec. T. 0296916277. *076560*

Pessac (Gironde)

Art à l'Affiche, Centre Commercial Tuileranne, 33600
Pessac. T. 0556360390, Fax 0556360390. *076561*
Art Connexion, 66 Av Magellan, 33600 Pessac.
T. 0556071914, Fax 0556071920. *076562*

Pézenas (Hérault)

Flipo, Emmanuel, 7 Rue Orfèvres, 34120 Pézenas.
T. 0467980602. *076563*
Galerie Feille, 11 Rue Foire, 34120 Pézenas.
T. 0467988450, Fax 0467982561. *076564*
Galerie Feille, 9 Rue de la Foire, 34210 Pézenas.
T. 0467988328. *076565*

Pinsac (Lot)

Société d'Investissement et de Restauration (S.I.R.), Terregaye, 46200 Pinsac. T. 0565326534. *076566*

Pithiviers (Loiret)

Alibert, Lisette, 36 Mail Ouest, 45300 Pithiviers.
T. 0238306000. *076567*

Poitiers (Vienne)
Boncenne, 1 Rue Boncenne, 86000 Poitiers.
T. 0549418349. *076568*
Bonnafoux, Dolorès, 37 Pl Charles-de-Gaulle, 86000
Poitiers. T. 0549883437. *076569*

Poligny (Jura)
Triangle de Verre, Av Wladimir-Gagneur, 39800 Poligny.
T. 0384372877. *076570*

Pont-Aven (Finistère)
Galerie de Pont-Aven, 13 Rue du Port, 29123 Pont-Aven.
T. 0298061102. - Paint - *076571*
Gyral, 3 Rue Emile-Bernard, 29930 Pont-Aven.
T. 0298060293. *076572*
Holding, D. L., Pl Paul-Gaugin, 29930 Pont-Aven.
T. 0298060212, Fax 0298061813. *076573*

Pont-Saint-Esprit (Gard)
Héloise, 10 Rue Jean-Jacques, 30130 Pont-Saint-Esprit.
T. 0466390437. *076574*

Pontarlier (Doubs)
Art et Lithographies, 5 Rue République, 25300 Pontarlier. T. 0381468910. - Paint / Graph / Fra - *076575*

Pontault-Combault (Seine-et-Marne)
Cadres Décor, Centre Commercial Carrefour, 77340 Pon-
tault-Combault. T. 0360285849. *076576*

Pontivy (Morbihan)
Le Bonhomme, Jean-Paul, 31 Rue Pont, 56300 Pontivy.
T. 0297252996. *076577*

Pontoise (Val-d'Oise)
12 19, 24 Pl Moineaux, 95300 Pontoise.
T. 0130322117. *076578*

Portbail (Manche)
Harambat, Guy, 42 Rue Philippe-Lebel, 50580 Portbail.
T. 0233049790. *076579*

Porto-Vecchio (Corse)
Galerie Mila, 6 Rue Jean-Jaurès, 20137 Porto-Vecchio.
T. 0495705716. *076580*

Pouilly-sur-Loire (Nièvre)
Rêverie, 6 Rue Joyeuse, 58150 Pouilly-sur-Loire.
T. 0386390787. *076581*

Pujols (Lot-et-Garonne)
Galerie Ex Arte, Bourg, 47300 Pujols.
T. 0553015621. *076582*

Quiberon (Morbihan)
Art Plus, 44 Rue Surcouf, 56170 Quiberon.
T. 0297501129. *076583*
Astrid, 1 Blvd Goulvars, Résid. Le Conguel, 56170 Qui-
beron. T. 0297303623. *076584*
Galerie d'Ys, 11 Rue Port-maria, Résid. Beau-Rivage,
56170 Quiberon. T. 0297303546. *076585*
Galerie 2B, 37 Blvd Chanard, 56170 Quiberon.
T. 0297502317, Fax 0297305489. *076586*
Laporte, Georges, 10 Quai Houat, 56170 Quiberon.
T. 0297502045, Fax 0297503672. *076587*
Matin Clair, 25 Rue Port-maria, 56170 Quiberon.
T. 0297504241. *076588*
Nello, 27 Rue Port-Maria, 56170 Quiberon.
T. 0297304294. *076589*
Phidias, 36 Rue Saint-Clément, 56170 Quiberon.
T. 0297503607. *076590*
Poulet, Jean, 7 Quai Houat, 56170 Quiberon.
T. 0297305893. *076591*
Serot, 1 Quai Océan, 56170 Quiberon.
T. 0297503127. *076592*

Quimper (Finistère)
Seize, 16 Rue Am-Ronarc'h, 29000 Quimper.
T. 0298554743. *076593*

Ramonville-Saint-Agne (Haute-Garonne)
Daudet, Alain, 65 Av Tolosane, 31520 Ramonville-Saint-
Agne. T. 0561735417. *076594*

Reims (Marne)
Aerts, P.M., 111 Rue Ledru-Rollin, 51100 Reims.
T. 0326061508. - Paint / Draw - *076595*

Brasseur, Martine, 4 Rue Tambour, 51100 Reims.
T. 0326404272, Fax 0326476548. *076596*
Centre Application et Etude, 9 Rue Thiers, 51100 Reims.
Fax 26475041. *076597*
Dewez, Martine, 24 Rue Colbert, 51100 Reims.
T. 0326479997. - Paint / Graph - *076598*
Peltriaux, 15 Rue Vieux-Coq, 51100 Reims.
T. 0326872687. *076599*
Petite Galerie, 18 Rue Colbert, 51100 Reims.
T. 0326472400. *076600*
Rêve d'Affiches, 32bis Rue Colbert, 51100 Reims.
T. 0326881806. *076601*
Vision du Temps, 26 Rue Etape, 51100 Reims.
T. 0326500439. *076602*

Rennes (Ille-et-Vilaine)
Artialis Galerie, 17 Rue Chapitre, 35000 Rennes.
T. 0299302463. *076603*
Criée – Halle d'Art Contemporain, Pl Honoré-Commeu-
rec, 35000 Rennes. T. 0299781820. *076604*
Cristill, 9 Rue Pré-Botté, 35000 Rennes.
T. 0299791489. *076605*
Divet, 4 Rue Saint-Guillaume, 35000 Rennes.
T. 0299796132. *076606*
Dutertre, Joseph, 22 Rue du Capitaine Alfred Dreyfus,
35000 Rennes. T. 0299794426. *076607*
Galerie d'Antrain, 32 Rue Antrain, 35700 Rennes.
T. 0299630009. *076608*
Galerie du Chapitre, 4 Rue du Chapitre, 35000 Rennes.
T. 0299792672. - Paint / Dec / Fra - *076609*
Galerie 13, 13 Pl Lices, 35000 Rennes.
T. 0299676320. *076610*
Galerie 27, 27 Rue Nantaise, 35000 Rennes.
T. 0299672929. *076611*
Haller, Yves, 13 Rue Chapitre, 35000 Rennes.
T. 0299792437. *076612*
Ikkon, 35 Rue Carnot, 35000 Rennes, BP 1112, 35014
Rennes Cedex. T. 0299841166. *076613*
Jobbé-Duval, 5 Rue Bertrand, 35000 Rennes.
T. 0299387210. *076614*
Massicot, 9 Rue Horloge, 35000 Rennes.
T. 0299790581. *076615*
Ombre et Lumière, 3 Rue Monnaie, 35000 Rennes.
T. 0299781988. *076616*
Oniris, 38 Rue Antrain, 35700 Rennes.
T. 0299364606. *076617*

Restinclières (Hérault)
Amilien, H., 11 Rte Nationale 110, 34160 Restinclières.
T. 0467865323. *076618*

Revel (Haute-Garonne)
Aguado, Tyrone, 6 Rue Jean-Moulin, 31250 Revel.
T. 0561832628, Fax 0562189730. *076619*
Lobéto, Christian, 15 Rue Jean-Moulin, 31250 Revel.
T. 0561838349. *076620*

Reviers (Calvados)
Galerie de Beaupré, 4 Rue Moulins, 14470 Reviers.
T. 0231379976. *076621*

Riez (Alpes-de-Haute-Provence)
Nomadic Zone Gallery, 5 Pl Colonne, 04500 Riez.
T. 0492777936. *076622*

Riom (Puy-de-Dôme)
Galerie de l'Horloge, 7 Rue Horloge, 63200 Riom.
T. 0473631783. *076623*
Passelard, François, 73 Rue du Commerce, 63200 Riom.
T. 0473380352. *076624*

Ris-Orangis (Essonne)
Galerie Jardins des Arts, 73 Rte Grigny, 91130 Ris-Orangis. T. 0169258520. *076625*

Roanne (Loire)
Galerie des 4 Coins, 20 Av Gambetta, 42300 Roanne.
T. 0477674925. *076626*
Prebet, Jean-Pierre, 20 Av Gambetta, 42300 Roanne.
T. 0477708338, Fax 0477230842. *076627*

Romans-sur-Isère (Drôme)
Flirey Art, 15bis Rue Flirey, 26100 Romans-sur-Isère.
T. 0475710342. - Paint / Sculp - *076628*

Vernier, 10 Côte Cordeliers, 26100 Romans-sur-Isère.
T. 0475028375. *076629*
Vignon, Marie, 6 Rue Félix-Faure, 26100 Romans-sur-
Isère. T. 0475021852. *076630*

Rosny-sous-Bois (Seine-Saint-Denis)
Jabes, 19bis Av Jean-Jaurès, 93110 Rosny-sous-Bois.
T. 0148949402. *076631*

Roubaix (Nord)
Tuileries, 105 Rue Lannoy, 59100 Roubaix.
T. 0320738863, Fax 0320739212. - Paint - *076632*

Rouen (Seine-Maritime)
Atelier Saint-Romain, 28 Rue Saint-Romain, 76000
Rouen. T. 0235887617. - Paint / Graph - *076633*
Bayeul, Chantal, 4 Rue Saint-Romain, 76000 Rouen.
T. 0235981333. - Paint / Sculp - *076634*
Boudin, Gérard, 25 Pl Lieutenant-Aubert, 76000 Rouen.
T. 0235719732. - Fra - *076635*
Bourdier, Anne, 45 Rue Bons-Enfants, 76000 Rouen.
T. 0235717000. *076636*
Complément d'Objet, 20 Rue Georges-d'Amboise,
76000 Rouen. Fax 35985911. *076637*
Comptoir Rouennais, 4 Pl Pucelle-d'Orléans, 76000
Rouen. T. 0235703927. *076638*
Cour d'Albane, 84 Rue Saint-Romain, 76000 Rouen.
T. 0235704500. - Paint - *076639*
Duchoze, Daniel, 21 Rue Vieux-Palais, 76000 Rouen.
T. 0235073413, Fax 0235894774. *076640*
Galerie Caviart, 21 Rue Etoupée, 76000 Rouen.
T. 0235985909. *076641*
Galerie Doré, 3 Pl 39ème-Régiment-d'Infanterie, 76000
Rouen. T. 0235701703. *070042*
Galerie Géricault, 111 Blvd Yser, 76000 Rouen.
T. 0235715159. - Paint / Fra - *076643*
Galerie Helios, 37 Rue Damiette, 76000 Rouen.
T. 0235708517. *076644*
Galerie Mandragore, 52 Rue Bouvreuil, 76000 Rouen.
T. 0235711718. *076645*
Goudenhooft, Denis, 20 Rue Georges-d'Amboise, 76000
Rouen. T. 0235980714. *076646*
Hermann, Liliane, 202 Rue Martainville, 76000 Rouen.
T. 0235153910. *076647*
Hue, Bertrand, 17 Rue Père-Adam, 76000 Rouen.
T. 0235077424. *076648*
Lernon, 7 Rue Damiette, 76000 Rouen.
T. 0235893686. *076649*
Lespinasse, François, 220 Rue Martainville, 76000
Rouen. T. 0235893815. - Paint / Sculp - *076650*
Maîtres Verriers, 35A Rue Jean-Lecanuet, 76000 Rouen.
T. 0235154735. *076651*
N.P.B. Création, 30 Rue Grand-Point, 76000 Rouen.
T. 0235071557. *076652*
Rustinoff, Vladimir, 170 Rue Eau-de-Ropec, 76000
Rouen. T. 0235702247, Fax 0235899744. *076653*

Roussillon (Vaucluse)
Artisane, pl Poste, 84420 Roussillon.
T. 0490056314. *076654*
Courthaudon, Jean-Claude, Pl Castrum, 84420 Roussil-
lon. T. 0490056299. *076655*
Meyer, Pl Abbé-Avon, 84420 Roussillon.
T. 0490056666. *076656*

Royan (Charente-Maritime)
Arnoux, Serge, 215 Av Pontaillac, 17200 Royan.
T. 0546393600. *076657*
Galerie Briand, 86 Blvd Aristide-Briand, 17200 Royan.
T. 0546055823, Fax 0546059773. *076658*
Galerie Voûtes du Port, 11 Quai Am-Meyer, 17200
Royan. T. 0546392052. *076659*

Rueil-Malmaison (Hauts-de-Seine)
Galerie Saint Rémy, 19 Rue Hervet, 92500 Rueil-Malmaison. T. 0147323627. *076660*

Saâcy-sur-Marne (Seine-et-Marne)
Duc Ateliers, 36 Av Citry-Montménard, 77730 Saâcy-
sur-Marne. T. 0360236333, Fax 0360235370. *076661*

Saint-Amand-Montrond (Cher)
Berry, Jean de, 25 Rue Nationale, 18200 Saint-Amand-
Montrond. T. 0248962272. *076662*

Saint-Ambroix (Gard)
Espace Art, Rue Fbg-Paradis, Rte Aubenas, 30500
Saint-Ambroix. T. 0466242263. *076663*

Saint-Bertrand-de-Comminges (Haute-Garonne)
Art et Culture en Haut Comminges, Pl Basilique, 31510
Saint-Bertrand-de-Comminges.
T. 0561883098. *076664*

Saint-Briac-sur-Mer (Ille-et-Vilaine)
Galerie Le Vieux Moulin, 2 Rue Vieux-Moulin, 35800
Saint-Briac-sur-Mer. T. 0299880494. - Paint - *076665*

Saint-Brice (Charente)
Galerie France-Art, Garde Epée, 16100 Saint-Brice.
T. 0545812792. *076666*

Saint-Brieuc (Côtes-d'Armor)
Atelier du Passe Partout, 11 Rue Maréchal-Foch, 22000
Saint-Brieuc. T. 0296614839. - Fra - *076667*
Athéna, 5 Pl Glais-Bizoin, 22000 Saint-Brieuc.
T. 0296620474. *076668*
Galerie Flore, 10 Rue Saint-Gouéno, 22000 Saint-Brieuc. T. 0296331320. *076669*

Saint-Cast-le-Guildo (Côtes-d'Armor)
Galerie de l'Aquilon, 44 Rue Rioust, Villes Audrains,
22380 Saint-Cast-le-Guildo. T. 0296418339. *076670*

Saint-Céneri-le-Gérei (Orne)
Katiane, Le Bourg, 61250 Saint-Céneri-le-Gérei.
T. 0233267167. - Paint - *076671*

Saint-Céré (Lot)
Casino, Av Jean-Mouliérat, 46400 Saint-Céré.
T. 0565381960. *076672*

Saint-Claude (Jura)
Galerie Ophrys, 6 Rue Reybert, 39200 Saint-Claude.
T. 0384450492. - Paint / Sculp - *076673*

Saint-Cloud (Hauts-de-Seine)
Socag, 3 Parc Béarn, 92210 Saint-Cloud.
T. 0146024511, Fax 0146022576. *076674*

Saint-Cyr-au-Mont-d'Or (Rhône)
Galeries Vrais Rêves, 3 Imp Lassalle, 69450 Saint-Cyr-au-Mont-d'Or. Fax 78434703. *076675*

Saint-Cyr-les-Colons (Yonne)
Art et la Vigne, Grande Rue Préhy, 89800 Saint-Cyr-les-Colons. T. 0386414770. *076676*

Saint-Denis (Seine-Saint-Denis)
Galerie Indigo, 6 Rue Boulangerie, 93200 Saint-Denis.
T. 0142436919. *076677*
Galerie Librairie Australienne, 7 Rue Samson, 93200
Saint-Denis. T. 0148099459. *076678*

Saint-Dié (Vosges)
Ecole de Dessin, 20 Rue 10ème RCB, 88100 Saint-Dié.
T. 0329562604. - Paint / Graph / Draw - *076679*
Galerie Efal, 3 Rue Orient, Pl Marché, 88100 Saint-Dié.
T. 0329561456. - Paint / Cur - *076680*

Saint-Dizier (Haute-Marne)
Maison du Cadre, 1 Quai Robespierre, 52100 Saint-Dizier. T. 0325051420. *076681*

Saint-Emilion (Gironde)
Galerie d'Art de Saint-Emilion, Rue Cadenne, 33330
Saint-Emilion. T. 0557744394. *076682*

Saint-Etienne (Loire)
Galerie Clément, 13 Rue Michelet, 42000 Saint-Etienne.
T. 0477325012. *076683*
Galerie L, 38 Rue Pointe-Cadet, 42000 Saint-Etienne.
T. 0477378363. *076684*
Galerie Le Cocotier, 26 Rue Benoît-Malon, 42000 Saint-Etienne. T. 0477335454. *076685*
Galerie Les Tournesols, 1 Pl Maxime-Gorki, 42000
Saint-Etienne. T. 0477418077,
Fax 0477418084. *076686*
Galerie Saint-Uzel, 41 Rue Paul-Bert, 42000 Saint-Etienne. T. 0477416030. *076687*

Géode, 1 Rue Elise-Gervais, 42000 Saint-Etienne.
T. 0477322071. *076688*
In Extremis, 11 Rue Charité, 42000 Saint-Etienne.
T. 0477479588. *076689*
Thonney, 13 Rue Michelet, 42000 Saint-Etienne.
T. 0477325459. - Graph / Repr - *076690*

Saint-Gatien-des-Bois (Calvados)
Besseiche, Daniel, Chemin Mue, 14130 Saint-Gatien-des-Bois. T. 0231648600, Fax 0231648585. *076691*

Saint-Gély-du-Fesc (Hérault)
Galerie Reno, 40 All Ecureuils, 34980 Saint-Gély-du-Fesc. T. 0467848860. *076692*

Saint-Germain-en-Laye (Yvelines)
Galerie des Coches, 12 Rue Coches, 78100 Saint-Germain-en-Laye. T. 0130615528. - Paint / Graph /
Fra - *076693*
Galerie Garance, 17 Rue Coches, 78100 Saint-Germain-en-Laye. T. 0130615861. *076694*

Saint-Gilles-Croix-de-Vie (Vendée)
Galerie Nuances, 7 Rue Général-de-Gaulle, 85800
Saint-Gilles-Croix-de-Vie. T. 0251553350. *076695*

Saint-Hilaire-du-Harcouët (Manche)
Bailleul, Patrick, 21 Rue Waldeck-Rousseau, 50600
Saint-Hilaire-du-Harcouët. T. 0233493392. *076696*

Saint-Jean-de-Luz (Pyrénées-Atlantiques)
Alma, Maison Louis-XIV, 8 Pl Louis-XIV, 64500 Saint-Jean-de-Luz. Fax 59261283. *076697*
Benoît, Bastien, Quartier Infante, 64500 Saint-Jean-de-Luz. T. 0559267637. *076698*
Galerie de la Colombe, 16 Rue Tourasse, 64500 Saint-Jean-de-Luz. T. 0559512701. *076699*
Galerie Portal, 17 Rue Tourasse, 64500 Saint-Jean-de-Luz. T. 0559267067. *076700*
Galilea, René, 16 Rue Tourasse, 64500 Saint-Jean-de-Luz. T. 0559512699. *076701*
Proulx, Albert, 8 Blvd Thiers, 64500 Saint-Jean-de-Luz.
T. 0559260393. *076702*
Velez-Guimont, Marie-Carmen, 29 Blvd Thiers, 64500
Saint-Jean-de-Luz. T. 0559267389,
Fax 0559512544. *076703*

Saint-Julien-du-Sault (Yonne)
Atelier du Chapitre, 1 Pl Mairie, 89330 Saint-Julien-du-Sault. T. 0386633485. *076704*

Saint-Julien-en-Genevois (Haute-Savoie)
Sphinx d'Or, 4 Le Mail, 74160 Saint-Julien-en-Genevois.
T. 0450350507. - Draw - *076705*

Saint-Julien-Molin-Molette (Loire)
Archéologues du Futur, Montée Usines, 42220 Saint-Julien-Molin-Molette. T. 0477515625. *076706*

Saint-Laurent-d'Aigouze (Gard)
Porquier, Philippe, Rue Robert-Florentin, 30220 Saint-Laurent-d'Aigouze. T. 0466889057,
Fax 0466889063. *076707*

Saint-Malo (Ille-et-Vilaine)
Acanthe, 84 Av Pasteur, 35400 Saint-Malo.
T. 0299401701. *076708*
Enfance et l'Art, 9 Rue Cordiers, 35400 Saint-Malo.
T. 0299565657. *076709*
Guinemer, André, 13 Rue Jacques Cartier, 35400 Saint-Malo. T. 0299408302. *076710*
Librairie Le Septentrion, 2 Pl Brevet, 35400 Saint-Malo. T. 0299546346, Fax 0299561893. *076711*
Petit, Pierre, 1 Pl Jean-de-Châtillon, 35400 Saint-Malo.
T. 0299402978. *076712*
Sklerijenn, 3 Rue Harpe, 35400 Saint-Malo.
T. 0299405621. *076713*

Saint-Martin-de-Fontenay (Calvados)
Cadre Noir, 4 Rte Harcourt, 14320 Saint-Martin-de-Fontenay. T. 0231799956. *076714*

Saint-Martin-de-Ré (Charente-Maritime)
Galerie de l'Amateur d'Art, 1 Petite Rue Marché, 17410
Saint-Martin-de-Ré. T. 0546092614. *076715*
Galerie de Thoiras, 9 Av Victor-Bouthillier, 17410 Saint-Martin-de-Ré. T. 0546092543. - Furn - *076716*
Imagerie, 1 Quai Poithevinière, 17410 Saint-Martin-de-Ré. T. 0546091472. *076717*
Maréchal, Roland, 15 Cours Pasteur, 17410 Saint-Martin-de-Ré. T. 0546093120. *076718*

Saint-Maur-des-Fossés (Val-de-Marne)
Epreuve d'Artiste, 78 Blvd Créteil, 94100 Saint-Maur-des-Fossés. T. 0148862001,
Fax 0148862430. *076719*

Saint-Médard-en-Jalles (Gironde)
Atelier de Marie, 102 Av Montesquieu, 33160 Saint-Médard-en-Jalles. T. 0556958523. *076720*

Saint-Nazaire (Loire-Atlantique)
Galerie de Peinture Regards, 17 Rue Port, 44600 Saint-Nazaire. T. 40225207. *076721*
Galerie des Franciscains, Rue Croisic, 44600 Saint-Nazaire. T. 40663781. *076722*
Galerie Pygmalion, 80 Rue Jean-Jaurès, 44600 Saint-Nazaire. T. 40222953. *076723*

Saint-Omer (Pas-de-Calais)
Galerie d'Art Contemporain, 36 Rue Gambetta, 62500
Saint-Omer. T. 0321885380. *076724*

Saint-Ouen (Seine-Saint-Denis)
Abstraction Figuration, 140 Rue Rosiers, 93400 Saint-Ouen. T. 0140109123. *076725*
Aflalo, Pilar, 108 Rue Rosiers, 93400 Saint-Ouen.
T. 0140112748. *076726*
Art-Cadral, 140 Rue Rosiers, 93400 Saint-Ouen.
T. 0140118801. *076727*
Deschamps, Pierre, 152 Rue Rosiers, 93400 Saint-Ouen. T. 0140101351. *076728*
Dupré, Maurice, 85 Rue Rosiers, 93400 Saint-Ouen.
T. 0140115467. *076729*
Eisenberg, Henry, 140 Rue Rosiers, Stand 31, 93400
Saint-Ouen. T. 0140116567. *076730*
Estades, Michel, 142 Rue Rosiers, 93400 Saint-Ouen.
T. 0140113260. *076731*
Galerie Pluriel, 75 Rue Rosiers, 93400 Saint-Ouen.
T. 0140101694. *076732*
Tesi, Pierre, 110 Rue Rosiers, 93400 Saint-Ouen.
T. 0140111183. *076733*
Turion, Patrick, Marché Vernaison, All 8, Stand 198,
93400 Saint-Ouen. T. 0140111633. *076734*

Saint-Paul (Alpes-Maritimes)
Atelier de la Courtine, 83 B Rue Grande, 06570 Saint-Paul. T. 0493327720. *076735*
Atelier de la Tour, Rue Grande, 06570 Saint-Paul.
T. 0493320451. *076736*
Clair Obscur, 14 Rue Grande, 06570 Saint-Paul.
T. 0493326808. *076737*
Consortium International des Arts, 92 Rue Grande,
06570 Saint-Paul. T. 0493326392. *076738*
Consortium International des Arts, Chemin Sainte-Claire,
06570 Saint-Paul. T. 0493327749,
Fax 0493320100. *076739*
Dame à la Licorne, 4 Montée l'Eglise, 06570 Saint-Paul.
T. 0493328204, Fax 0493328121. *076740*
Galerie Aparte, 37 Rue Grande, 06570 Saint-Paul.
T. 0493327472, Fax 0493327403. *076741*
Galerie du Bresc, 2 Rue Bresc, 06570 Saint-Paul.
T. 0493328932. *076742*
Galerie J'Aime, 33 Rue Grande, 06570 Saint-Paul.
T. 0493329942, Fax 0493329040. *076743*
Galerie Le Capricorne, 15 Rue Grande, 06570 Saint-Paul. T. 0493328765. *076744*
Galerie Vendôme, 18 Grande Rue, 06570 Saint-Paul.
T. 0493320160. *076745*
Galerie Walter, 77 Rue Grande, 06570 Saint-Paul.
T. 0493326032. *076746*
Galerie X, 10 Pl Tilleul, 06570 Saint-Paul.
T. 0493329459. *076747*
Gollong, Frédéric, Rue Pontis Le Pontis, 06570 Saint-Paul. T. 0493329210. - Paint - *076748*

Hervieu, Paul, La Placette, Rue Grande, 06570 Saint-Paul. T. 0493329069. - Paint / Graph - 076749

Ile en Terre, 5 Rue Grande, 06570 Saint-Paul. T. 0493328691. 076750

International Fine Art Club France, Pl Grande Fontaine, 06570 Saint-Paul. T. 0493320848. 076751

Issert, Catherine, Rond-Point Sainte-Claire, 06570 Saint-Paul. T. 0493329692. 076752

Orangeraie, 838 Rte La Colle, 06570 Saint-Paul. T. 0493320276. 076753

Orangeraie, Pl Général-de-Gaulle, 06570 Saint-Paul. T. 0493329600, Fax 0493329026. 076754

Rustinoff, Vladimir, 13 Rue Grande, 06570 Saint-Paul. T. 0493325454. 076755

Salle, Alexandre de la, Chemin des Trious, 06570 Saint-Paul. T. 0493329241. - Paint / Sculp / Pho / Draw - 076756

Saint-Paul-Trois-Châteaux (Drôme)
Angle, 12 Rue Notre-Dame, 26130 Saint-Paul-Trois-Châteaux. T. 0475047303. 076757

Erlecke, 3 Pl Esplan, 26130 Saint-Paul-Trois-Châteaux. T. 0475049102. 076758

Saint-Quentin (Aisne)
Desprey-Pollet, 31 Rue Victor-Basch, 02100 Saint-Quentin. T. 0323623705, Fax 0323625509. - Paint - 076759

Saint-Rémy-de-Provence (Bouches-du-Rhône)
Arts 04, 4 Av Frédéric-Mistral, 13210 Saint-Rémy-de-Provence. T. 0490925981. 076760

Donation Mario Prassino, 3 Rue Jean-de-Nostredame, 13210 Saint-Rémy-de-Provence. T. 0490923513. 076761

Grand-Magasin, 24 Rue Commune, 13210 Saint-Rémy-de-Provence. T. 0490921879, Fax 0490923576. 076762

Lézard'Ailleurs, 12 Blvd Gambetta, 13210 Saint-Rémy-de-Provence. T. 0490924744. 076763

Saint-Tropez (Var)
Filipovic, Andrija, 179 Passerelle Port, 83990 Saint-Tropez. T. 0494970937. 076764

Galerie Carane, 4 Rue Aire-du-Chemin, 83990 Saint-Tropez. T. 0494978713. 076765

Galerie Cupillard, 1 Rue Commandant-Guichard, 83990 Saint-Tropez. T. 0494976843, Fax 0494976935. 076766

Sié, Henri, 4 Rue Clocher, 83990 Saint-Tropez. T. 0494970964, Fax 0494548302. 076767

Sainte-Croix-du-Mont (Gironde)
Galerie Atelier 33, 33410 Sainte-Croix-du-Mont. T. 0556620167. 076768

Saintes (Charente-Maritime)
Galerie d'Art, 8 Pl Bassompierre, 17100 Saintes. T. 0546740205. 076769

Salies-de-Béarn (Pyrénées-Atlantiques)
Galerie, 10 Cours Jardin-Public, 64270 Salies-de-Béarn. T. 0559381109. 076770

Oustaouï dou Saleys, Rue Eglise, 64270 Salies-de-Béarn. T. 0559380603. 076771

Sallèles-d'Aude (Aude)
Indigo, Quai Alsace, 11590 Sallèles-d'Aude. T. 0468469437. 076772

Salles-sur-Garonne (Haute-Garonne)
Marques, Gérard, Rte Saint-Julien, La Comère, 31390 Salles-sur-Garonne. T. 0561876213. 076773

Salon-de-Provence (Bouches-du-Rhône)
Chevalet d'Eon, 25 Rue Moulin-d'Isnard, 13300 Salon-de-Provence. T. 0490562906. - Paint - 076774

Tabouret, Patrice, 44 Rue Horloge, 13300 Salon-de-Provence. T. 0490566613. 076775

Sarlat-la-Canéda (Dordogne)
Shasmoukine, Gorodka, 24200 Sarlat-la-Canéda. T. 0553310200. 076776

Sarrebourg (Moselle)
Boyrié, 2 Rue Victor-Hugo, 57400 Sarrebourg. T. 0387230811. 076777

Sarzeau (Morbihan)
Maison des Artisans d'Art, Rue Adrien-Régent, 56370 Sarzeau. T. 0297418238. 076778

Saumur (Maine-et-Loire)
Bouvet Ladubay, 28 Rue Jean-Ackermann, 49400 Saumur. T. 41501968. 076779

Sausset-les-Pins (Bouches-du-Rhône)
Galerie Berlioz, 1 Av Clément-Monnier, 13960 Sausset-les-Pins. T. 0442450980. 076780

Sauvian (Hérault)
Art'G, 28 Rue Honoré-de-Balzac, 34410 Sauvian. T. 0467324111. 076781

Savenay (Loire-Atlantique)
Robin, Jean, 10 Blvd Acacias, 44260 Savenay. T. 40569212. - Paint / Repr / Dec / Pho - 076782

Scharrachbergheim (Bas-Rhin)
Galerie Edition du Faisan, 111 Imp Lavoir, 67310 Scharrachbergheim. T. 0388506012. 076783

Seignosse (Landes)
Galerie, Rte Saubion, 40510 Seignosse. T. 0558728073. 076784

Sens (Yonne)
Bianchini, Paul, 5 Rue Jules Verne, 89100 Sens. T. 0386952720, Fax 0386642709. - Pho / Mul - 076784a

Galerie Abélard, 15 Rue Abélard, 89100 Sens. T. 0386954979. 076785

Galerie d'Abraham, 16bis Rue République, 89100 Sens. T. 0386951425. 076786

Sète (Hérault)
Art 7, 22 Rue Montmorency, 34200 Sète. T. 0467741887. 076787

Boyé, Paul, 31 Rue Paul-Bousquet, 34200 Sète. T. 0467537888. 076788

Comptoir Un Port Exposé, 5 Quai Vauban, 34204 Sète Cedex. T. 0467461089, Fax 0467461091. 076789

Espace Saint-Louis, 28 Grand'Rue Mario-Roustan, 34200 Sète. T. 0467748560. 076790

Galerie Beau Lézard Sud, 6 Quai Léopold-Suquet, 34200 Sète. T. 0467742770. 076791

Galerie Clo, 2 Rue Général-de-Gaulle, 34200 Sète. T. 0467460206. 076792

Galerie 13, 13 Grand'Rue Mario-Roustan, 34200 Sète. T. 0467740948. 076793

Sèvres (Hauts-de-Seine)
Audibert, 2 Rue Ville-d'Avray, 92310 Sèvres. T. 0145078718. 076794

Sierentz (Haut-Rhin)
Galerie Action, 44 Rue Rogg-Haas, 68510 Sierentz. T. 0389. 076795

Soufflenheim (Bas-Rhin)
Galerie de l'Archange, 9 Rue Haguenau, 67620 Soufflenheim. T. 0388867050. 076796

Souillac (Lot)
Daly Déco, 4 Pl Toiles, 46200 Souillac. T. 0565370252. 076797

Strasbourg (Bas-Rhin)
Aktuaryus, 23 Rue Nuée-Bleue, 67000 Strasbourg. T. 0388323938. - Paint / Graph / Sculp / Fra - 076798

Asperger, 4 Pl Austerlitz, 67000 Strasbourg. T. 0388369528, Fax 0388251942. 076799

Buck, Nicole, 4 Rue Orfèvres, 67000 Strasbourg. T. 0388226309. - Paint / Sculp - 076800

Chenkier, Marcel, 10 Rue des Dentelles, 67000 Strasbourg. T. 0388328276. - Paint - 076801

Eichwald, Huguette, 47 Rue Finkwiller, 67000 Strasbourg. T. 0388250189. - Paint / Fra - 076802

Espace Suisse, 6 Rue Charpentiers, 67000 Strasbourg. T. 0388325036. - Paint / Sculp - 076803

Finnegan's, 2 A Rue Saint-Marc, 67000 Strasbourg. T. 0388255575. 076804

Galerie Artal, 10 Rue Bain-aux-Plantes, 67000 Strasbourg. T. 0388328754. 076805

Galerie Brûlée, 6 Rue Brûlée, 67000 Strasbourg. T. 0388210404. 076806

Galerie Edition du Faisan, 19 Rue Thiergarten, 67000 Strasbourg. T. 0388221184. 076807

Galerie J., 10 Rue Tonneliers, 67000 Strasbourg. T. 0388220555. 076808

Galerie Mikaël, 12 Rue Moulins, 67000 Strasbourg. T. 0388235248. 076809

Galerie Oberlin, 19 Rue Francs-Bourgeois, 67000 Strasbourg. T. 0388324583, Fax 0388210587. 076810

Galerie Park, 6 Quai Bateliers, 67000 Strasbourg. T. 0388329276. 076811

Galerie Saint-Martin, 17 A Rue Moulins, 67000 Strasbourg. T. 0388225075. 076812

Galerie Saint-Pétersbourg, 16 Rue Austerlitz, 67000 Strasbourg. T. 0388241183. 076813

Galerie Sum Qui Sum, 20 Pl Cathédrale, 67000 Strasbourg. T. 0388221117. - Paint / Graph / Fra - 076814

Goralsky, Pierre-Henri, 1 Rue Chaîne, 67000 Strasbourg. T. 0388756288. 076815

Lacan, 31 Quai Bateliers, 67000 Strasbourg. T. 0388257852. - Paint / Graph / Sculp - 076816

Maison d'Art Alsacienne, 1 Rue Vieux-Marché-aux-Poissons, 67000 Strasbourg. T. 0388324039. 076817

Oberlin, 19 Rue Francs-Bourgeois, 67000 Strasbourg Cedex. T. 0388324583. 076818

Palette d'Or, 18 Rue Dôme, 67000 Strasbourg. T. 0388327910, Fax 0388326488. 076819

Petrouchka, 32 Grand'Rue, 67000 Strasbourg. T. 0388759802, Fax 0388759883. 076820

Rauscher, 14 Rue Dentelles, 67000 Strasbourg. T. 0388327448. - Paint / Sculp - 076821

Rendez-vous, 5 Rue Adolphe-Wurtz, 67000 Strasbourg. T. 0388257109. 076822

Rezvanian, K., 6 Rue Travail, 67000 Strasbourg. T. 0388222734. - Paint - 076823

Tanlay (Yonne)
Alexandre, Christian, 2 Pl Général-de-Gaulle, 89430 Tanlay. T. 0386758147. 076824

Tarascon-sur-Ariège (Ariège)
Galerie Athéna, 16 Rue Barry, 09400 Tarascon-sur-Ariège. T. 0561051953. 076825

Tarbes (Hautes-Pyrénées)
Expression, 10 Rue Massey, 65000 Tarbes. T. 0562345956. 076826

Zeller, Michel, 25 Pl Foirail, 65000 Tarbes. T. 0562344814. 076827

Thiais (Val-de-Marne)
Galerie d'Art, Centre Commercial Belle-Epine, 94320 Thiais. T. 0146861132. - Paint - 076828

Thiers (Puy-de-Dôme)
Centre d'Art Contemporain du Creux de l'Enfer, 85 Av Joseph-Claussat, 63300 Thiers. T. 0473802656, Fax 0473802808. 076829

Chevalet, 28 Rue Coutellerie, 63300 Thiers. T. 0473803896. 076830

Thionville (Moselle)
Art s'affiche, 9 Sq Hôtel-de-Ville, 57100 Thionville. T. 0382821457. 076831

Bolognini, 17 Av Albert-1er, 57100 Thionville. T. 0382530222. 076832

Grand Aigle, 23 Rue Lazare-Hoche, 57100 Thionville. T. 0382539209. 076833

Thonon-les-Bains (Haute-Savoie)
Galerie Espace, 1bis Av Léman, 74200 Thonon-les-Bains. T. 0450266427, Fax 0450262172. 076834

Patrice-Alexis, 11 Rue Saint-Sébastien, 74200 Thonon-les-Bains. T. 0450701167. 076835

Petersen, Galise, Pl Château, 74200 Thonon-les-Bains. T. 0450717897, Fax 0450819233. 076836

Toulenne (Gironde)
Héraud, Patrick, Château Rougemont, 33210 Toulenne. T. 0556622073. 076837

Toulon (Var)

Boeuf, Robert, 49 Rue Jean-Jaurès, 83000 Toulon.
T. 0494092800, Fax 0494930093. *076838*

Bureau Expertise Toulonnais, 12 Rue Garibaldi, 83000
Toulon. Fax 94919762. *076839*

Espace Castillon, 15 Rue Castillon, 83000 Toulon.
T. 0494421588. *076840*

Estades, Michel, 22 Rue Henri-Seillon, 83000 Toulon.
T. 0494894998. - Paint - *076841*

Galerie du Vieux Toulon, 2 Pl Gustave-Lambert, 83000
Toulon. T. 0494628685. *076842*

Galerie Mazarine, 4 Av Colbert, 83000 Toulon.
T. 0494935544. *076843*

Lecomte-Durouil, Marc, 49 Rue Lamalgue, 83000 Toulon. T. 0494411905, Fax 0494311682. *076844*

New Arts Gallery, 6 Rue Notre-Dame, 83000 Toulon.
T. 0494922593. *076845*

Rossi, 18 Rue Revel, 83000 Toulon. T. 0494623020.
- Paint - *076846*

Toulouse (Haute-Garonne)

A Foyer Décor, 48 Av Saint-Exupéry, 31400 Toulouse.
T. 0561209536. *076847*

Alla Prima, 1bis Rue Pargaminières, 31000 Toulouse.
T. 0561136038. *076848*

Art Mural, 8 Rue Bayard, 31000 Toulouse.
T. 0561625506. *076849*

Art Présent Espace, 7 Rue Rempart-Saint-Etienne,
31000 Toulouse. T. 0561219028. *076850*

Arts et Formes, 34 Rue Metz, 31000 Toulouse.
T. 0561530083. *076851*

Betti, Roger, 9 Rue Fermat, 31000 Toulouse.
T. 0561550077. *076852*

Boudet, Simone, 42 Rue Roquelaine, 31000 Toulouse.
T. 0561627519. *076853*

Cahiers de l'Atelier, 42 Rue Couteliers, 31000 Toulouse.
T. 0562264700. *076854*

Clar, Jacqueline, 27 Rue Bouquières, 31000 Toulouse.
T. 0561328361, Fax 0561554480. *076855*

Courtiade, Françoise, 7 Rue Clémence-Isaure, 31000
Toulouse. T. 0561220674. *076856*

Difarco, 11 Pl Saint-Pierre, 31000 Toulouse.
T. 0561218787. *076857*

Dupont, Eric, 25 Rue Croix-Baragnon, 31000 Toulouse.
T. 0561258585. *076858*

Dutilleul, 14 Pl Esquirol, 31000 Toulouse.
T. 0561238094. *076859*

Editions Universelles, 13 Blvd Lazare-Carnot, 31000
Toulouse. T. 0561227530. *076860*

Galerie Art Sud, 17 Rue Peyras, 31000 Toulouse.
T. 0561233727. *076861*

Galerie Auriel, 54 Rue Pharaon, 31000 Toulouse.
T. 0561529121. *076862*

Galerie Bayard, 33 Rue Bayard, 31000 Toulouse.
T. 0561990083. *076863*

Galerie BL, 1ter Rue Languedoc, 31000 Toulouse.
Fax 61330726. *076864*

Galerie Européenne des Beaux-Arts, 44 Rue Rempart-
Saint-Etienne, 31000 Toulouse. T. 0561233545,
Fax 0561137736. *076865*

Galerie Inard, 39 Rue Metz, 31000 Toulouse.
T. 0561225859, Fax 0561239034. *076866*

Galerie L'Atelier, 2 Rue Canard, 31000 Toulouse.
T. 0561539155. *076867*

Galerie Le Biblion, 29 Rue Croix-Baragnon, 31000 Toulouse. T. 0561527928. *076868*

Galerie Municipal du Château-d'Eau, 17 Pl Laganne,
31300 Toulouse. T. 0561426172,
Fax 0561420270. *076869*

Galerie Protée, 13 Rue Croix-Baragnon, 31000 Toulouse.
T. 0561538444, Fax 0561550244. *076870*

Galerie Sollertis, 12 Rue Regans, 31000 Toulouse.
T. 0561554332, Fax 0561253413. *076871*

Galvani, 18 Pl Dupuy, 31000 Toulouse. T. 0561629779,
Fax 0561629771. *076872*

Girard, Jacques, 20 Rue Blanchers, 31000 Toulouse.
T. 0561233595. *076873*

Grand Bazar, 6 Rue Rempart-Villeneuve, 31000 Toulouse. T. 0561238570, Fax 0561120590. *076874*

Kandler, 14 Rue Bayard, 31000 Toulouse.
T. 0561638511. *076875*

Leborgne, Benoît, 1ter Rue Languedoc, 31000 Toulouse.
T. 0561554260. *076876*

Meurisse, Pierre-Jean, 56 Rue Tourneurs, 31000 Toulouse. T. 0561210081. *076877*

Oréades, 39 Rue Pharaon, 31000 Toulouse.
T. 0561539989. - Paint - *076878*

Sourillan, 20 Av Honoré-Serres, 31000 Toulouse.
T. 0561992200, Fax 0561992300. - Paint /
Cur - *076879*

Viguerie, Eliane, 14 Rue Ozenne, 31000 Toulouse.
T. 0561527540, Fax 0561255093. *076880*

Tourgéville (Calvados)

Galerie, La Fromagerie, 14800 Tourgéville.
T. 0231873111, Fax 0231873177. *076881*

Tours (Indre-et-Loire)

Atelier d'Onze Heures, 38bis Rue Bernard-Palissy,
37000 Tours. T. 0547614301. *076882*

Atelier du Change, 9 Rue Châteauneuf, 37000 Tours.
T. 0547612383. - Graph - *076883*

Cadre d'Or, 2 Pl Grand-Marché, 37000 Tours.
T. 0547646146. - Graph / Fra - *076884*

Carré Davidson, 17 Rue Cérisiers, 37000 Tours.
T. 0547391981. *076885*

Gaëtan, 86 Rue Commerce, 37000 Tours.
T. 0547052271. *076886*

Galerie d'Exposition, Rue Maures, 37000 Tours.
T. 0547053781. *076887*

Galerie Harmonies, 97 Rue Colbert, 37000 Tours.
T. 0547611263. *076888*

Galerie La Martinerie, 20 Rue Scellerie, 37000 Tours.
T. 0547054113. *076889*

Galerie Opaline, 45 Rue Scellerie, 37000 Tours.
T. 0547644647. *076890*

Galerie Saint-Pierre du Puillier, 32 B Rue Briçonnet,
37000 Tours. T. 0547200543. *076891*

Galerie 21, 58 Rue Scellerie, 37000 Tours.
T. 0547649334. *076892*

Lachenaud, Jean-Luc, 36 Rue François-Richer, 37000
Tours. T. 0547375102. *076893*

Montreau, Chantal, 2 Pl Grand-Marché, 37000 Tours.
T. 0547646146. - Paint - *076894*

Oeil Fertile, 89 Rue Scellerie, 37000 Tours.
T. 0547661204. *076895*

Rein, Michel, 56bis Rue Rempart, 37000 Tours.
T. 0547667372. *076896*

Tangram, 42 Rue Scellerie, 37000 Tours.
T. 0547055408. *076897*

Toiles, 9bis Rue Jules-Charpentier, 37000 Tours.
T. 0547382404. *076898*

Tresses (Gironde)

Castellon, Adora, 51 Av Branne, 33370 Tresses.
T. 0556212393. *076899*

Trets (Bouches-du-Rhône)

Attrait, 13 Pl Garibaldi, 13530 Trets. T. 0442615913,
Fax 0442292871. *076900*

Trouville-sur-Mer (Calvados)

Nadar, 21 Rue Victor-Hugo, 14360 Trouville-sur-Mer.
T. 0231983232. *076901*

Troyes (Aube)

Akhenaton, 30 Rue Georges-Clémenceau, 10000
Troyes. T. 0325735761. - Paint - *076902*

Cayon, 80 Rue Urbain IV, 10000 Troyes. T. 0325738500.
- Paint - *076903*

Galerie Turenne, 38 Rue Turenne, 10000 Troyes.
T. 0325733533, Fax 0325731172. - Paint / Fra /
Glass - *076904*

Prod'Homme, Jean-René, 1 Rue Urbain, 10000 Troyes.
T. 0325432682. - Paint / Fra - *076905*

Tulle (Corrèze)

Galerie des Portes Chanac, 6 Rue Portes-Chanac, 19000
Tulle. T. 0555264929. *076906*

Ussel (Corrèze)

Galerie Saint-Boniface, 3 Rue Saint-Boniface, 19200
Ussel. T. 0555729410. *076907*

Uzès (Gard)

Dumas, Xavier, 19 Pl Herbes, 30700 Uzès.
T. 0466031172. *076908*

Vaison-la-Romaine (Vaucluse)

Chema, 39 Av Victor-Hugo, 84110 Vaison-la-Romaine.
T. 0490288221. *076909*

Danielou, Roland, 22 Pl Montfort, 84110 Vaison-la-Romaine. T. 0490362524. *076910*

Galerie du Vieux Marché, Pl Vieux-Marché, 84110 Vaison-la-Romaine. T. 0490361605. *076911*

Montfort, 2 Pl Montfort, 84110 Vaison-la-Romaine.
T. 0490361738. *076912*

Valençay (Indre)

Valençay Art Galerie, 54051374, 3 Pl Halle, 36600 Valençay. T. 0254051375. *076913*

Valence (Drôme)

Arts Verts, 1 Rue Jonchère, 26000 Valence.
T. 0475565650. - Paint - *076914*

Coulet, Jean-François, 22 Rue d'Athènes, 26000 Valence. T. 0475435133, Fax 0475557538. - Paint - *076915*

Editions Trans International, 471 Av Victor-Hugo, 26000
Valence. T. 0475401094. *076916*

Galerie Lacydon, 4 Rue Poncet, 26000 Valence.
T. 0475416207. *076917*

Galerie Université, 53 Grande Rue, 26000 Valence.
T. 0475420317. *076918*

Sapet, 58 Rue Bouffier, 26000 Valence.
T. 0475420211. *076919*

Valenciennes (Nord)

Galerie L'Aquarium, 8 Rue Ferrand, 59300 Valenciennes. T. 0327332202, Fax 0327452425. *076920*

Maison du Cadre, 6 Pl Neuf-Bourg, 59300 Valenciennes.
T. 0320913657. - Paint - *076921*

Vallauris (Alpes-Maritimes)

Consortium International des Arts, 52 Av Georges-Clemenceau, 06220 Vallauris. T. 0493631370,
Fax 0493632427. *076922*

Editions d'Art Sassi-Milici, 65bis Av Georges-Clemenceau, 06220 Vallauris. T. 0493643440. *076923*

Galerie de la Colombe, 33 Av Georges-Clemenceau,
06220 Vallauris. T. 0493646650. - Paint - *076924*

Galerie Valdoria, 59 Av Georges-Clemenceau, 06220
Vallauris. T. 0493646576, Fax 0493648276. *076925*

Galerie Vincent, 65 Av Georges-Clemenceau, 06220 Vallauris. T. 0493640307. *076926*

Madoura, Av des Anciens-Combattants, 06220 Vallauris.
T. 0493646639. - Paint / Graph / China / Sculp /
Tex - *076927*

Marais, Jean, Av Martyrs-Résistance, 06220 Vallauris.
T. 0493638574. - Graph / China - *076928*

Valentin, Gilbert, Av Pablo-Picasso, Les Archanges,
06220 Vallauris. T. 0493637628,
Fax 0493636959. *076929*

Valognes (Manche)

Kasuo, Iwamura, 61 Rue Religieuses, 50700 Valognes.
T. 0233402572. - Paint - *076930*

Vannes (Morbihan)

Adam, Jacques, 11 Rue Saint-Salomon, 56000 Vannes.
T. 0297472210, Fax 0297425969. *076931*

Arcadia, 6 Rue Saint-Nicolas, 56000 Vannes.
T. 0297470859. *076932*

Galerie Bleue, 8 Rue Chanoines, 56000 Vannes.
T. 0297542423. *076933*

La Méridienne, 26 Rue Chanoines, 56000 Vannes.
T. 0297425890. *076934*

Le Bonhomme, Jean-Paul, 21 Rue Halles, 56000 Vannes. T. 0297475528. *076935*

Made Décoration, 61 Rue Vincin, 56000 Vannes.
T. 0297635969. *076936*

Nota Bene, 18 Rue Saint-Salomon, 56000 Vannes.
T. 0297475956. *076937*

Riquelme, Patrick, 19 Rue Noé, 56000 Vannes.
T. 0297470266. *076938*

Vélizy-Villacoublay (Yvelines)

Epreuve d'Artiste, Rue André-Citroën, 78140 Vélizy-Villacoublay. T. 0139466750, Fax 0134659862. *076939*

Vence (Alpes-Maritimes)

Centre d'Art Vaas, 14 Traverse Moulins, 06140 Vence.
T. 0493582942, Fax 0493583083. *076940*

GALERIE MADOURA

LE PLAN   06220 VALLAURIS   Téléphone 04.93.64.66.39

SCULPTURES · CERAMIQUES · TAPISSERIES

Céramiques éditées de

PICASSO
EN EXCLUSIVITÉ

Dessins   Peintures
Gravures   MADOURA BOUTIQUE   Sculptures

Chave, Alphonse, 13 Rue Isnard, 06140 Vence.
T. 0493580345. - Paint / Sculp -   076941
Chave, Alphonse, 20 Rue Isnard, 06140 Vence.
T. 0493581273.   076942
Galerie Beaubourg, 2618 Rte Grasse, Château Notre-
Dame-Fleurs, 06140 Vence. T. 0493245200.   076943
Nature Art et Life League, 232 Blvd Lattre, 06140 Ven-
ce. T. 0493581326, Fax 0493580900.   076944

Verberie (Oise)
Vigoureux, Philippe, 9 Rue Juliette-Adam, 60410 Verberie. T. 0344405334. - Paint -   076945

Verdun (Meuse)
Terre ou Art, 5 Rue Dame-Zabée, 55100 Verdun.
T. 0329837285.   076946

Véretz (Indre-et-Loire)
Tunnel, 11 La Rue Vieille, 37270 Véretz.
T. 0547503590.   076947

Vern-sur-Seiche (Ille-et-Vilaine)
Abbaye Galerie, 5 Hameau L'Abbaye, 35770 Vern-sur-
Seiche. T. 0299627663, Fax 0299004846.   076948

Versailles (Yvelines)
Accroche-Coeur, 15 Rue Paroisse, 78000 Versailles.
T. 0139538123.   076949
Aquarelle Dessin Sculpture, 24 Rue Henri-Simon, 78000
Versailles. T. 0139023285. - Paint / Sculp /
Draw -   076950
Lefebvre, Michel, 38 Rue Paroisse, 78000 Versailles.
T. 0139504484. - Paint / Graph -   076951
Mailliet, Gérard, 4 Rue Baillage, 78000 Versailles.
T. 0139539321.   076952
Rufin, Sylvie, 65 Rue Royale, 78000 Versailles.
T. 0130219369.   076953

Verson (Calvados)
Hirondel, 14 Rue Pichauvin, 14790 Verson.
T. 0231268751.   076954

Vesoul (Haute-Saône)
Salle des Ursulines, 13 Rue Salengro, 70000 Vesoul.
T. 0384760782.   076955

Vétheuil (Val-d'Oise)
Galerie d'Art, 6 Rue Eglise, 95510 Vétheuil.
T. 0134782188.   076956

Veyrier-du-Lac (Haute-Savoie)
Platini, Sylvie, 1 Rue Tournette, 74290 Veyrier-du-Lac.
T. 0450601608.   076957

Vézelay (Yonne)
Cabalus, Rue Saint-Pierre, 89450 Vézelay.
Fax 86332066.   076958

Galerie d'Art Saint-Pierre, 68 Grande Rue Saint-Pierre,
89450 Vézelay. T. 0386332796.   076959
Leiber, 14 Rue Saint-Etienne, 89450 Vézelay.
T. 0386333390, Fax 0386332957.   076960

Vianne (Lot-et-Garonne)
Galerie Bastide, Rue Résistance, 47230 Vianne.
T. 0553651609.   076961

Vic-la-Gardiole (Hérault)
G.A.L.A., Chemin Cresses, 172 Lot Laval, 34110 Vic-la-
Gardiole. T. 0467781906.   076962

Vichy (Allier)
Art Contemporain, 25 Rue Lucas, 03200 Vichy.
T. 0470975851, Fax 0470975577.   076963
Casino, 12 Pass Noyer, 03200 Vichy.
T. 0470318483.   076964
H.A.D, 23 Gal Source-Hôpital, 03200 Vichy.
T. 0470317336.   076965
Hexagone des Arts, 20 Rue Montaret, 03200 Vichy.
T. 0470310637.   076966
Kermabon, Ginette, 22 Rue Maréchal-Foch, 03200 Vi-
chy. T. 0470982876.   076967
Lesec, Marie-Laure, 25 Rue Lucas, 03200 Vichy.
T. 0470975851.   076967a
Parc, 2 Gal Source-Hôpital, 03200 Vichy.
T. 0470976997.   076968
Patio Albert 1er, 14 Rue Ravy-Breton, 03200 Vichy.
T. 0470974456.   076969

Vierzon (Cher)
Galerie Foch, 13 Pl Maréchal-Foch, 18100 Vierzon.
T. 0248714591.   076971

Villars-les-Dombes (Ain)
Galerie 21, Rue Gilbert-Boullier, 01330 Villars-les-Dombes. T. 0474982666.   076972

Villefranche-sur-Mer (Alpes-Maritimes)
Galerie Artis, Promenade Mariniers, 06230 Villefranche-
sur-Mer. T. 0493019373.   076973
Palette, Quai Amiral-Courbet, 06230 Villefranche-sur-
Mer. T. 0493017392. - Paint / Graph / Repr -   076974

Villefranche-sur-Saône (Rhône)
Centre Rencontre Arts Nouvelles Expressions, 118 Rue
Corlin, 69400 Villefranche-sur-Saône.
T. 0474682756.   076975
Galerie 102, 98 Rue Nationale, 69400 Villefranche-sur-
Saône. T. 0474654472.   076976

Villemandeur (Loiret)
Nouvelles Images, Lombreuil, 45700 Villemandeur.
T. 0238962662, Fax 0238963200.   076977

Villemomble (Seine-Saint-Denis)
Galerie La Régence, 59 Av Raincy, 93250 Villemomble.
T. 0148947755, Fax 0148941288.   076978
Galerie 157, 157 Grande Rue, 93250 Villemomble.
T. 0148546837, Fax 0148549437.   076979

Villeneuve-lès-Avignon (Gard)
Desterne, Joëlle, 7 Rue Porte-Rouge, 30400 Villeneuve-
lès-Avignon. T. 0490258506.   076980

Villeneuve-Loubet (Alpes-Maritimes)
Giraudo, Jean-Pierre, 2 All Calernet, 06270 Villeneuve-
Loubet. T. 0493737448, Fax 0492130187.   076981

Villeneuve-sur-Lot (Lot-et-Garonne)
Anagui, 17 Rue Girondins, 47300 Villeneuve-sur-Lot.
T. 0553417419, Fax 0553708050.   076982
Atelier 51, 7bis Rue Jean-Jacques-Rousseau, 47300
Villeneuve-sur-Lot. T. 0553492699.   076983
Gajac, 19 Rue Penne, 47300 Villeneuve-sur-Lot.
T. 0553402033.   076984
Toiles de Magellan, 27 Rue Etienne-Marcel, 47300 Vil-
leneuve-sur-Lot. T. 0553367070.   076985

Villepreux (Yvelines)
Maison Saint-Vincent, 1 Rue Pierre-Curie, 78450 Villepreux. T. 0130561063.   076986

Vincennes (Val-de-Marne)
Art Kahn, 45 Rue Raymond-du-Temple, 94300 Vincen-
nes. T. 0148086290.   076987
CBN Créations, 1 B Rue Eglise, 94300 Vincennes.
T. 0148086290. - Paint / Fra -   076988
Frémeaux & Assoc, 27 Rue Raymond-du-Temple, 94300
Vincennes. T. 0143749024, Fax 0143652422. 076989
Gallion, 51 Rue Robert-Giraudineau, 94300 Vincennes.
T. 0143287137.   076990

Vitré (Ille-et-Vilaine)
Bouet, Françoise, 30 Rue Beaudrairie, 35500 Vitré.
T. 0299746045.   076991

Voiron (Isère)
Art du Temps, 14 Grande Rue, 38500 Voiron.
T. 0476930532. - Paint -   076992
G'YS, 13 Av Dugueyt-Jouvin, 38500 Voiron.
T. 0476058414. - Paint -   076993
Tréma, 1 Pl Porte-de-la-Buisse, 38500 Voiron.
T. 0476661500. - Paint -   076994

Vouvant (Vendée)
Galerie Art'Monic, Pl Eglise, 85120 Vouvant.
T. 0251008000.   076995

Wimereux (Pas-de-Calais)
Dupuis, Joël, 63 Rue Carnot, 62930 Wimereux.
T. 0321329485.   076996

Galerie du Rayon Vert, 13 Rue Digue-der-Mer, 62930
Wimereux. T. 0321333321. - Paint / Glass - *076997*

Wittenheim (Haut-Rhin)
Kelcolor, 14 A Rue Saint-Cloud, 68270 Wittenheim.
T. 0389530916. *076998*

Yutz (Moselle)
Daub, 111 Rte Nationale, 57110 Yutz.
T. 0382562357. *076999*

Yvoire (Haute-Savoie)
Equinoxe Groupe Artisanat Contemporain, Rue Princi-
pale, 74140 Yvoire. T. 0450728077. *077000*
Galerie Fert, Chef Lieu, 74140 Yvoire.
T. 0450728479. *077001*

French Guiana

Kourou
Pierre, Anne, 51 Allée Diamant, 97310 Kourou.
T. (594) 321471, Fax (594) 325966. *077002*

French Polynesia

Papeete
NOA NOA, Bard. Pomaré, Papeete. T. 273 47. - Paint /
Sculp - *077003*
Winkler & J. Jacques Laurent, rue Jeanne d'Arc, Pa-
peete. T. 281 77. - Paint / Graph / Sculp - *077004*

Germany

Aachen (Nordrhein-Westfalen)
Ahlmann, K., & U. Schmitz, Heinrichsallee 9, 52062 Aa-
chen. T. (0241) 26206. *077005*
Appel, Oppenhoffallee 161, 52066 Aachen.
T. (0241) 50 65 55. - Graph / Fra / Pho - *077006*
Bernardi, A. de, Adalbertstr. 67, 52062 Aachen.
T. (0241) 4703440, Fax (0241) 47034426. - Paint /
Paint / Graph / Fra - *077007*
Beumers, Manfred, Jakobstr. 37, 52064 Aachen.
T. (0241) 333 95. - Ant / Paint / Graph / Furn - *077008*
Galerie am Elisengarten, Hartmannstr. 6, 52062 Aachen.
T (0241) 376 75. *077009*
Galerie art direct, Hartmannstr. 6, 52062 Aachen.
T. (0241) 265 89. *077010*
Galerie Art et Décoration, Kleinmarschierstr. 11-15,
52062 Aachen. T. (0241) 36351. *077011*
Galerie 33, Wirichsbongardstr. 6, 52062 Aachen.
T. (0241) 27507, Fax (0241) 27530. - Paint / Graph /
Fra - *077012*
Graphik Galerie, Heinrichsallee 17, 52062 Aachen.
T. (0241) 238 28. *077013*
Grenzland-Galerie, Theaterstr. 71, 52062 Aachen.
T. (0241) 3 53 16. - Paint / Fra - *077014*
Grobusch, Münsterpl. 10, 52062 Aachen.
T. (0241) 37665. *077015*
Kohl, Hubert, Harscampstr. 76, 52062 Aachen.
T. (0241) 331 89. *077016*
Korneliusgalerie, Korneliusstr. 14e, 52076 Aachen.
T. (0241) 3743. *077017*
Küppers, I., Adalbertsteinweg 74, 52070 Aachen.
T. (0241) 50 21 11. *077018*
Kunstladen, Pontstr. 38, 52062 Aachen.
- Graph - *077019*
Milwe, Von der, Kleinkölnstr. 1, 52062 Aachen.
T. (0241) 26407, 26151. *077020*
Petzold, H., Hartmannstr. 6, 52062 Aachen.
T. (0241) 376 75. *077021*
Rautenberg, E., Hohenstaufenallee 22, 52064 Aachen.
T. (0241) 727 03. *077022*
Rop-Kässbohrer, G. de, Kapuzinergraben 28, 52062 Aa-
chen. T. (0241) 316 16. *077023*
Schneider, W., Heinrichsallee 17, 52062 Aachen.
T. (0241) 238 28. *077024*

Schoenen, Wilhelmstr 103, 52070 Aachen.
T. (0241) 504561, Fax 902061. - Paint / Graph / Repr /
Fra / Draw - *077025*
Schwanen, Peterstr. 77-79, 52062 Aachen.
T. (0241) 278 74. - Paint / Sculp / Draw - *077026*
Severin-Rautenberg, Hohenstaufenallee 18-22, 52064
Aachen. T. (0241) 727 03. - Paint / Draw - *077027*

Aalen (Baden-Württemberg)
Galerie im Atelier, Langertstr 44, 73431 Aalen. *077028*
Wellandgalerie, Treppacher Str 10, 73434 Aalen.
T. (07361) 6373. - Paint / Graph / Repr / Fra /
Draw - *077029*

Achern (Baden-Württemberg)
Schnurr, Dieter, Neulandstr 2a, 77855 Achern.
T. (07841) 21084. *077030*

Ahausen (Niedersachsen)
Ahauser Bilderstübchen, Birkenstr. 207, 27367 Ahausen.
T. (04269) 55 21. - Paint - *077031*

Ahrensburg (Schleswig-Holstein)
Mohr, E., Klaus Grothstr. 33, 22926 Ahrensburg.
T. (04102) 550 21. *077032*

Ahrenshoop (Mecklenburg-Vorpommern)
Bunte Stube, Dorfstr. 24, 18347 Ahrenshoop.
T. (038220) 238, Fax (038220) 80472. - Paint / Graph /
Repr / China / Jew / Glass / Draw - *077033*

Albbruck (Baden-Württemberg)
Drei Waldshut Galerie, Bohland, 79774 Albbruck.
T. (07753) 706. - Ant / Paint / Graph - *077034*

Albstadt (Baden-Württemberg)
Paulus-Galerie, Paulusstr. 3, 72461 Albstadt.
T. (07431) 6625, Fax (07431) 4821. - Paint / Graph /
Repr - *077035*

Allensbach (Baden-Württemberg)
Siedler-Witting, Ilse, Richard-Dilgerstr. 8, 78476
Allensbach. *077036*

Allmendingen (Baden-Württemberg)
Feucht, R.G., Hauptstr. 18, 89602 Allmendingen.
T. (07391) 12 76, Fax (07391) 83 24. - Paint / Graph /
Sculp / Jew / Cur / Draw - *077037*

Alpirsbach (Baden-Württemberg)
Alpirsbacher Galerie, Ambrosius-Blarer-Pl. 1, 72275 Al-
pirsbach. T. (07444) 670, Fax (07444) 1510. *077038*

Altdorf bei Nürnberg (Bayern)
Galerie am Markt, Unterer Markt 4, 90518 Altdorf bei
Nürnberg. T. (09187) 2903. *077039*

Altenberge (Nordrhein-Westfalen)
Ellering, Burkhard, Zum Borndal 14, 48341 Altenberge.
T. (02505) 1863. - Paint / Fra - *077040*

Altenstadt (Hessen)
Quanz, Bahnhofstr. 2, 63674 Altenstadt.
T. (06047) 55 88, Fax (06047) 2742. - Graph / Repr /
Fra - *077041*

Amorbach (Bayern)
Kreuzer, Maria, Johannisturmstr. 7, 63916 Amorbach.
T. (09373) 1756. - Paint / Graph / Sculp / Glass - *077042*

Andernach (Rheinland-Pfalz)
Galerie am Rathaus, Hochstr. 37, 56626 Andernach.
T. (02632) 49 38 94. - Paint - *077043*

Angelburg (Hessen)
Blank, Am Stöckenberg 10, 35719 Angelburg.
T. (06464) 70 66. - Paint / Graph - *077044*

Archsum/Sylt (Schleswig-Holstein)
Schmücking, Bobtäärp 17, 25980 Archsum/Sylt.
T. (04654) 567, Fax (04654) 567. - Paint / Graph /
Sculp - *077045*

Arnsberg (Nordrhein-Westfalen)
Nawrath, Heinz hr +, Müggenbergring 1, 59755 Arnsberg. T. (02931) 1239. - Paint / Graph / Fra - *077046*

Schulte, P.J., Mendener Str. 8, 59755 Arnsberg.
T. (02931) 78 85. *077047*
Thomas, A., Hauptstr. 28, 59755 Arnsberg. *077048*

Arolsen (Hessen)
Hoppek, Gabriele, Uplandstr.1, 34454 Arolsen. *077049*

Aschaffenburg (Bayern)
Dering, Elisabeth, Karlstr. 1, 63739 Aschaffenburg.
T. (06021) 155 38. - Paint / Graph / Draw - *077050*
Galerie am Nachmittag, Grünewaldstr. 12, 63739
Aschaffenburg. T. (06021) 26893. *077051*
Galerie Bild & Rahmen, Erthalstr. 16, 63739 Aschaffen-
burg. T. (06021) 155 58, Fax (06021) 155 58. - Graph /
Repr / Fra - *077052*
Galerie Dalbergstraße, Dalbergstr. 37, 63739 Aschaffen-
burg. T. (06021) 72 24. - Paint / Graph / Sculp - *077053*
Galerie Viola, Dalbergstr. 5, 63739 Aschaffenburg.
T. (06021) 240 29, Fax (06021) 24039. - Graph /
Fra - *077054*
Keller, Grünewaldstr. 7, 63739 Aschaffenburg.
T. (06021) 203 22. *077055*
Stiftsgalerie, Dalbergstr. 5, 63739 Aschaffenburg.
T. (06021) 22426. *077056*

Augsburg (Bayern)
Art-Line, Blücherstr 35, 86165 Augsburg.
T. (0821) 272780, Fax (0821) 2727813.
- Paint - *077057*
Beck, Helga, Frohsinnstr 18, 86150 Augsburg. *077058*
Bessler, Maximilianstr 36, 86150 Augsburg.
T. (0821) 33498. - Paint / Graph / Fra - *077059*
Fischer, Arminstr 5, 86199 Augsburg. T. (0821) 91744.
- Jew / Silv / Glass - *077060*
Galerie im Brechthaus, Auf dem Rain 7, 86150 Augs-
burg. T. (0821) 516545. - Paint / Graph / Sculp - *077061*
Galerie im Kolping-Bildungszentrum, Frauentorstr 29,
86152 Augsburg. T. (0821) 325800,
Fax (0821) 3258010. - Paint - *077062*
Galerie im Richard-Wagner-Hof, Georg-Brach-Str 43,
86152 Augsburg. T. (0821) 3491110. *077063*
Private Kunsträume Augsburg, Friedberger Str 11,
86161 Augsburg. *077064*
Rehklau, Alte Gasse 11, 86152 Augsburg.
T. (0821) 515401. - Paint - *077065*
Schröder, Schlossermauer 10, 86150 Augsburg.
T. (0821) 153474, Fax (0821) 158700. *077066*
Treppenhaus-Galerie, Annastr 19, 86150 Augsburg.
T. (0821) 32500. *077067*
Winkler, Günter, Zeuggasse 5, 86150 Augsburg.
T. (0821) 151346, Fax (0821) 151980. - Paint /
Jew - *077068*

Aukrug (Schleswig-Holstein)
Floristische Galerie Bünzen, Bünzer Str. 3, 24613 Aukrug. T. (04873) 785. *077069*

Bad Aibling (Bayern)
Regensburger, Max I., Kirchzeile 10, 83043 Bad Aibling.
T. (08061) 2581, Fax (08061) 5071. - Graph / Orient /
Jew / Draw - *077070*

Bad Bergzabern (Rheinland-Pfalz)
Galerie n + f, Weinstr. 12, 76887 Bad Bergzabern.
T. (06343) 3988. - Paint / Graph - *077071*
Gilde Galerie, Altes Rathaus, 76887 Bad Bergzabern.
T. (06343) 8506. - Paint / Graph / China / Jew / Pho /
Draw - *077072*

Bad Bocklet (Bayern)
Galerie am Grünen Markt, Balthasar-Neumann-Str. 2,
97708 Bad Bocklet. T. (09708) 69 93. - Paint / Graph /
China / Sculp / Fra / Pho / Draw - *077073*

Bad Driburg (Nordrhein-Westfalen)
Galerie Glas-Werkstatt, Gottfried-Büren-Weg 45, 33014
Bad Driburg. T. (05253) 3779. - Glass - *077074*

Bad Harzburg (Niedersachsen)
Glötzer, Reinh., Bilderstube, Badestr. 3, 38667 Bad
Harzburg. *077075*
Rathausgalerie, Forstwiese 5, 38667 Bad Harzburg.
T. (05322) 74110, 74119. - Paint - *077076*

Bad Hersfeld (Hessen)

Hess, Werner, Ludwig-Braun-Str. 2a, 36251 Bad Hersfeld. T. (06621) 754 34. - Ant / Furn -   *077077*

Schneider, Wallengasse 6, 36251 Bad Hersfeld.
T. (06621) 770 61.   *077078*

Schultes, R., Dudenstr. 6, 36251 Bad Hersfeld.
T. (06621) 731 37.   *077079*

Bad Homburg vor der Höhe (Hessen)

Art Galerie Ansichtssache, Louisenstr 3, 61348 Bad Homburg vor der Höhe. T. (06172) 21111.   *077080*

Blaszczyk, M., Ludwigstr, 61348 Bad Homburg vor der Höhe. T. (06172) 29398. - Paint / Graph / Fra /
Draw -   *077081*

Die Bilderstube, Louisenstr 22, 61348 Bad Homburg vor der Höhe. T. (06172) 22660. - Paint -   *077082*

Galerie Junge Kunst, Kaiser-Friedrich-Promenade 15, 61348 Bad Homburg vor der Höhe. T. (06172) 21105.
- Paint / Graph / Furn / Orient / Cur / Pho -   *077083*

Krause, Christof, Ober-Eschbacher Str 101, 61352 Bad Homburg vor der Höhe. - Sculp -   *077084*

New Art Consulting, Haingasse 10, 61348 Bad Homburg vor der Höhe. T. (06172) 46056, Fax (06172) 25832.
- Paint / Graph / Sculp / Mul / Draw -   *077085*

Retter, Rind'sche Stiftstr 38, 61348 Bad Homburg vor der Höhe. T. (06172) 21121, Fax (06172) 21151.
- Paint / Sculp / Fra -   *077086*

Scheffel, Ferdinandstr 19, 61348 Bad Homburg vor der Höhe. T. (06172) 82133, Fax (06172) 28968. - Paint /
Graph / Sculp / Draw -   *077087*

Bad Kissingen (Bayern)

Galerie Art Forum, Frühlingstr 6a, 97688 Bad Kissingen.
T. (0971) 99556. - Paint / Sculp -   *077088*

Galerie in Laudensack's Parkhotel, Kurhausstr. 23, 97688 Bad Kissingen.   *077089*

Galerie Moderna, Salinenstr. 26, 97688 Bad Kissingen.
T. (0971) 996 56. - Paint / Graph / Sculp /
Draw -   *077090*

Hirnickel, E., Salinenstr. 26, 97688 Bad Kissingen.
T. (0971) 996 56. - Ant / Paint / Sculp -   *077091*

Bad Kreuznach (Rheinland-Pfalz)

Galerie Zapp, Ledderhoser Weg 77, 55543 Bad Kreuznach.   *077092*

Bad Münstereifel (Nordrhein-Westfalen)

Klein, Zum Rosental 16, 53902 Bad Münstereifel.
T. (02257) 7651, Fax (02257) 4176. - Paint / Graph /
Sculp / Pho / Mul / Draw -   *077093*

Lammel, Wertherstr. 22, 53902 Bad Münstereifel.
T. (02253) 8086. - Paint / Graph / Sculp / Fra /
Draw -   *077094*

Teufel, Heinz, An der Hüh 2, 53902 Bad Münstereifel.
T. (02257) 1240, Fax (02257) 3264. - Paint / Graph /
Sculp / Draw -   *077095*

Bad Nauheim (Hessen)

Galerie Isi, Kurpark-Kolonnade 4, 61231 Bad Nauheim.
T. (06032) 68 48. - Paint / Graph / Sculp /
Draw -   *077096*

Galerie Remise, Mittelstr. 23, 61231 Bad Nauheim.
T. (06032) 315 33. - Paint -   *077097*

Rademacher, Gutenbergstr. 62, 61231 Bad Nauheim.
T. (06032) 32210. - Paint / Graph / Sculp /
Glass -   *077098*

Bad Neuenahr-Ahrweiler (Rheinland-Pfalz)

Galerie Bel Art, Kreuzstr. 8a, 53474 Bad Neuenahr-Ahrweiler. T. (02641) 29829. - Paint / Graph / China /
Fra -   *077099*

Bad Oeynhausen (Nordrhein-Westfalen)

Usakowska-Wolff, Urszula, Maschweg 28, 32549 Bad Oeynhausen. T. (05731) 29536, Fax (05731) 29676.
- Paint / Graph / Draw -   *077100*

Bad Pyrmont (Niedersachsen)

Guttmann, Galerie, Wandelhalle, 31812 Bad Pyrmont.
T. (05281) 60 68 66, Fax 60 99 71. - Paint / Graph /
Sculp -   *077101*

Picturae & Form, Arolser Str. 12, 31812 Bad Pyrmont.
T. (05281) 608246, Fax (05281) 609731.
- Paint -   *077102*

Bad Rappenau (Baden-Württemberg)

Steiner, Schloss Babstadt, 74906 Bad Rappenau.
T. (07264) 597. - Paint / Graph / Sculp / Pho /
Draw -   *077103*

Bad Salzuflen (Nordrhein-Westfalen)

Das Atelier, Parkstr. 14, 32105 Bad Salzuflen.
T. (05222) 6441.   *077104*

Fachwerk, Pfarrkamp 8, 32108 Bad Salzuflen. - Paint /
Draw -   *077105*

Junghanns, Rolf, Turmstr. 21, 32105 Bad Salzuflen.
T. (05222) 409 16. - Paint / Fra -   *077106*

Bad Schwalbach (Hessen)

Kuma, Brunnenstr. 47, 65307 Bad Schwalbach.
T. (06124) 3979.   *077107*

Bad Soden (Hessen)

Paul, Henri S., Königsteiner Str 79, 65812 Bad Soden.
T. (06196) 23595, Fax (06196) 27176. - Paint / Graph /
Fra -   *077108*

Sander, Jürgen, Alleestr 6, 65812 Bad Soden.
T. (06196) 21767. - Paint / Graph / Repr / Fra -   *077109*

Bad Tölz (Bayern)

Weber, Jakob, Marktstr. 31, 83646 Bad Tölz.
T. (08041) 95 68. - Paint -   *077110*

Bad Vilbel (Hessen)

Galerie im Amtsgericht, Friedrich-Ebert-Str., 61118 Bad Vilbel. T. (06101) 800 90. - Paint -   *077111*

Bad Waldsee (Baden-Württemberg)

Kleine Galerie am Elisabethenbad, Badstr. 16, 88339 Bad Waldsee. T. (07524) 80 08. - Paint / Paint -   *077112*

Bad Wildbad (Baden-Württemberg)

Endres, Am Kurplatz, 75323 Bad Wildbad.   *077113*

Bad Wildungen (Hessen)

Galerie Bild & Rahmen, Lindenstr. 26, 34537 Bad Wildungen. T. (05621) 723 27. - Paint / Graph / Repr / Fra /
Glass -   *077114*

Bad Wörishofen (Bayern)

Faust, Arthur, Kneippstr. 18, 86825 Bad Wörishofen.
T. (08247) 55 70.   *077115*

Galerie Alexander, Bgm.-Stöckle-Str. 10, 86825 Bad Wörishofen. T. (08247) 31536. - Paint / Graph -   *077116*

Bad Zwischenahn (Niedersachsen)

Edition Galerie Moderne, Am Delf 37, 26160 Bad Zwischenahn. T. (04403) 5429, Fax 63450. - Paint /
Graph -   *077117*

Baden-Baden (Baden-Württemberg)

Amorc-Kunstkabinett, Stolzenbergstr. 15, 76532 Baden-Baden. T. (07221) 66041, Fax (07221) 66044.
- Paint -   *077118*

Apfelbaum-Galerie, Kaiser-Wilhelm-Str. 10, 76530 Baden-Baden. T. (07221) 314 82. - Paint / Graph / Sculp /
Mul -   *077119*

Elwert, J., Lichtentaler Str 40, 76530 Baden-Baden.
T. (07221) 24464, Fax (07221) 29474. - Paint / Graph /
Repr / Dec / Fra -   *077120*

Fischer, Suzanne, Stephanienstr. 14, 76481 Baden-Baden. T. (07221) 271437, (07221) 71307. - Paint /
Graph / Sculp / Draw -   *077121*

Galerie Kleiner Prinz, Rheinstr. 191, 76532 Baden-Baden. T. (07221) 61985, Fax (07221) 17965.
- Paint -   *077122*

Gesellschaft der Freunde junger Kunst, Stephanienstr. 16, 76530 Baden-Baden. T. (07221) 26261.
- Graph -   *077123*

Pages, Frank, Sophienstr. 4/Kreuzstr., 76530 Baden-Baden. T. (07221) 25755, Fax (07221) 29880. - Paint /
Sculp -   *077124*

RA-Collection, Jagdhausstr. 28, 76530 Baden-Baden.
T. (07221) 25445. - Ant / Graph -   *077125*

Weber, Peter, Eichstr 12, 76530 Baden-Baden.
T. (07221) 25571. - Paint / Graph -   *077126*

Wirnitzer, Elfriede, Lilienmattstr. 6, Haus Lauschan, 76530 Baden-Baden. T. (07221) 26725. - Graph /
Sculp / Draw -   *077127*

Badenweiler (Baden-Württemberg)

Krohn, Luise, Dr., Hintere Au 1, 79410 Badenweiler.
T. (07632) 290. - Paint / Sculp / Draw -   *077128*

Baiersbronn (Baden-Württemberg)

Root, Ruhesteinstr. 523, 72270 Baiersbronn.
T. (07447) 07449/538. - Paint / Graph / Glass -   *077129*

Baldham (Bayern)

Krempl, Claudia, Baldhamer Str. 26, 85598 Baldham.
T. (08106) 32601. - Paint -   *077130*

Balingen (Baden-Württemberg)

Pollermann, Christel, Ebertstr. 3, 72336 Balingen.
T. (07433) 7206. - Paint -   *077131*

Bamberg (Bayern)

Galerie Hainpark, Hainstr. 27, 96047 Bamberg.
T. (0951) 210 92. - Paint -   *077133*

Galerie im Hause H. Grünthal-Möbel, Nürnberger Str. 243, 96050 Bamberg. T. (0951) 2 81 81.   *077134*

Galerie Kunst im Licht, Rheinstr. 16, 96052 Bamberg.
T. (0951) 79090, Fax (0951) 7909198. - Paint -   *077135*

Grimm-Beickert, Annelie, Obere Königstr 3, 96052 Bamberg. T. (0951) 23597.   *077135a*

Kunst im Gang, Im Bauernfeld 18, 96049 Bamberg.
T. (0951) 57182. - Paint -   *077136*

Kunstgalerie Böttingerhaus, Judenstr., 96049 Bamberg.
T. (0951) 23027, 55727, Fax (0951) 202813. - Ant /
Paint / Graph / Furn / Sculp / Tex / Fra / Mul -   *077137*

Kunstkontor, Obere Brücke 5, 96047 Bamberg.
T. (0951) 23027, 55727, Fax (0951) 202813. - Paint /
Graph -   *077138*

Sommer, Pfahlplätzchen 6, 96049 Bamberg.
T (0951) 536 01.   *077139*

studio M, Amalienstr. 27, 96047 Bamberg.
T. (0951) 203940, Fax (0951) 200602. - Paint / Graph /
Sculp / Draw -   *077140*

Bautzen (Sachsen)

Galerie Budissin, Kurt-Pchalek-Str. 22, 02625 Bautzen.
T. (03591) 42223. - Paint / Graph / China / Tex / Jew /
Glass / Draw -   *077141*

Bayreuth (Bayern)

Galerie, Maxstr. 32, 95444 Bayreuth.
T. (0921) 630 09.   *077142*

Galerie an der Stadtkirche, Kämmereigasse 4, 95444 Bayreuth. T. (0921) 53109. - Paint / Graph / Sculp /
Jew / Draw -   *077143*

Galerie Ophir, Brandenburger Str. 36, 95448 Bayreuth.
T. (0921) 206 16.   *077144*

Meyer, Marianne, Mosinger Str 7, 95445 Bayreuth.
T. (0921) 43925.   *077145*

Steingraeber & Söhne, Steingraeber Passage 1, 95444 Bayreuth. T. (0921) 64049, Fax (0921) 58272. - Paint /
Graph / Sculp -   *077146*

Weithauer, Gert, Ludwigstr. 4, 95444 Bayreuth.
T. (0921) 64656. - Paint / Graph / Repr / Fra -   *077147*

Bensheim (Hessen)

Böhler, Wolfgang, Marktpl. 6, 64625 Bensheim.
T. (06251) 39600. - Paint / Graph -   *077148*

Galerie 78, Ludwigstr. 78, 64625 Bensheim.
T. (06251) 734 05. - Paint / Graph -   *077149*

Berg (Rheinland-Pfalz)

Witzleben, von, Ludwigstr. 100, 76768 Berg.
T. (07273) 1016/17, Fax 2475. - Paint / Graph /
Repr -   *077150*

Bergheim (Nordrhein-Westfalen)

Schmiedel, Karlheinz, Mandelweg 7, 50127 Bergheim.
T. (02271) 94538. - Paint / Graph / China / Sculp / Silv /
Glass / Pho -   *077151*

Bergisch Gladbach (Nordrhein-Westfalen)

Galerie am Brunnen, Schloßfeldweg 58-60, 51429 Bergisch Gladbach. T. (02202) 540 66. - Paint / Graph / China / Sculp / Draw -   *077152*

Bergkamen (Nordrhein-Westfalen)

Galerie Sohle 1, Jahnstr. 31, 59192 Bergkamen.
T. (02307) 8676. - Paint -   *077153*

Berlin

Aboriginal Art Gallery, Lützeritzstr 3, 13351 Berlin.
T. (030) 4528398. *077154*

Ägyptische Galerie Papyri, Kaiser-Friedrich-Str 4a,
10585 Berlin. T. (030) 3411270. - Paint - *077155*

Aktiv, Holsteinische Str 48, 12163 Berlin.
T. (030) 7931129. *077156*

Alom, van, Meierottostr 1, 10719 Berlin.
T. (030) 8832505. - Paint / Sculp / Eth / Draw - *077157*

Ararat Curiosity Shop, Bergmannstr 99a, 10961 Berlin.
T. (030) 6935080, Fax (030) 6930229. *077158*

Arndt & Partner, Rosenthaler Str 40/41, 10178 Berlin.
T. (030) 2833738, Fax (030) 2833738. *077159*

Art 5 III, Motzstr 9, 10777 Berlin. T. (030) 2165332,
Fax (030) 2165332. *077160*

Baguette Galerie, Westfälische Str 27, 10709 Berlin.
T. (030) 8915560. *077161*

Barthel, Gunar, Fasanenstr 12, 10623 Berlin.
T. (030) 3137430, 3133137, Fax (030) 3123819.
- Paint / Graph - *077162*

Bassenge, Gerda, Erdener Str 5a, 14193 Berlin.
T. (030) 8912909, Fax 8918025. - Graph - *077163*

Bellevue, Flensburger Str 13, 10557 Berlin.
T. (030) 3922561. *077164*

Berinson, Niebuhrstr 2, 10629 Berlin. T. (030) 8826464,
Fax (030) 8813863. - Pho - *077165*

Berliner Häuser im Siebdruck, Breitscheidplatz, 10789
Berlin. T. (030) 2612978. *077166*

Biermann, Edda, Bundesplatz, 10715 Berlin.
T. (030) 8548025, Fax (030) 8548832. *077167*

Binhold, Kurfürstendamm 48-49, 10707 Berlin.
T. (030) 8813855, Fax (030) 8836389. *077168*

Block, René, Schaperstr 11, 10719 Berlin.
T. (030) 2113145, Fax 2176432. *077169*

Bremer, Fasanenstr 37, 10719 Berlin.
T. (030) 8814908. *077170*

Brennecke, Pestalozzistr 11, 10625 Berlin.
T. (030) 3123949, Fax 3129481. - Paint - *077171*

Brodhag & Wörn, Meierottostr 1, 10719 Berlin.
T. (030) 8811896. *077172*

Brückmann, Ursula, Stuttgarter Platz 15, 10627 Berlin.
T. (030) 3248910. *077173*

Brusberg, Kurfürstendamm 213, 10719 Berlin.
T. (030) 8827682, Fax (030) 8815389. - Paint / Graph /
Sculp / Draw - *077174*

Büsch, Glockenturmstr 20a, 14055 Berlin.
T. (030) 3041513, Fax (030) 3236898. - Paint / Graph /
Sculp / Draw - *077175*

Busche, Wielandstr 34, 10629 Berlin. T. (030) 8819009,
Fax (030) 8618876. *077176*

Busmann, Ortrun, Karlsruher Str 4, 10711 Berlin.
T. (030) 8912776. *077177*

Contemporary Fine Arts, Tauroggener Str 15, 10589 Berlin. T. (030) 3446338, Fax (030) 3446794. *077178*

Coppi, Leo, Wallstr 90, 10179 Berlin. T. (030) 2044129,
Fax (030) 2044129. *077179*

Diehl, Volker, Niebuhrstr 2, 10629 Berlin.
T. (030) 8818280, Fax (030) 8824798. - Paint /
Graph - *077180*

Dietrich, Horst, Giesebrechtstr 19, 10629 Berlin.
T. (030) 3245345, Fax (030) 3243151. - Paint / Graph /
Draw - *077181*

Dinkler, Marina, Niebuhrstr 77, 10629 Berlin.
T. (030) 8819677. - Paint / Graph / Pho / Draw - *077182*

dirty windows gallery, U-Bhf. Kurfürstendamm, 10719
Berlin. T. (030) 7829675, Fax (030) 7829675. *077183*

Dogenhaus Galerie, Auguststr 63, 10117 Berlin.
T. (030) 2833765, Fax (030) 294989. - Paint / Graph /
Sculp - *077184*

Dreher, Anselm, Pfalzburger Str 80, 10719 Berlin.
T. (030) 8835249, 7965572, Fax (030) 8816531.
- Paint / Graph / Sculp / Mul - *077185*

Droysen Keramikgalerie, Babelsberger Str 5, 10715 Berlin. T. (030) 8532093, Fax (030) 8542306.
- China - *077186*

Eglau, Johanna, Witzlebenplatz 5, 14057 Berlin.
T. (030) 3222267. *077187*

Ermer, Knesebeckstr 97, 10623 Berlin.
T. (030) 3126684. - Paint / Sculp / Pho / Draw - *077188*

Extra, Bleibtreustr 41, 10623 Berlin.
T. (030) 8821612. *077189*

Fahnemann, Fasanenstr 61, 10719 Berlin.
T. (030) 8839897, Fax 8824572. - Paint / Graph /
Sculp / Pho - *077190*

Fedorowskij, Natan, Leibnizstr 60, 10629 Berlin.
T. (030) 3247823, Fax (030) 3249858. *077191*

Fiebig, Lutz, Linienstr 117, 10115 Berlin.
T. (030) 28599333, Fax 28599334. *077192*

Fischer, Carmerstr 14, 10623 Berlin. T. (030) 3131371,
Fax 3131860. *077193*

Fischer, Klaus, Motzstr 9, 10777 Berlin.
T. (030) 2158273, Fax (030) 2168717. - Paint / Graph /
Sculp - *077194*

Fischer-Reinhardt, Thea, Fasanenstr 29, 10719 Berlin.
T. (030) 8824057. - Paint / Sculp - *077195*

Fort Knox Design, Suarezstr 8, 14057 Berlin.
T. (030) 3224021, Fax (030) 3255102. - Paint / Sculp /
Fra - *077196*

Fotogalerie am Mommseneck, Mommsenstr 45, 10629
Berlin. T. (030) 3275375. *077197*

Fragile Gesellschaft, Haubachstr 6, 10585 Berlin.
T. (030) 3422373. *077198*

Franck & Schulte, Mommsenstr 56, 10629 Berlin.
T. (030) 3240044, Fax (030) 3451596. - Paint / Sculp /
Pho / Mul / Draw - *077199*

front art, Kollwitzstr 64, 10435 Berlin. T. (030) 4411828,
Fax (030) 4411828. *077200*

Fuchs, Michael, Linienstr 55, 10629 Berlin.
T. (030) 8819448, Fax (030) 8819448. *077201*

Gärtner, Uhlandstr 20-25, 10623 Berlin.
T. (030) 8835385, Fax (030) 8835385. - Paint / Graph /
Paint / Sculp / Fra - *077202*

Galerie Aedes, Stadtbahnbogen 600, 10115 Berlin.
T. (030) 312 25 98. *077203*

Galerie am Chamissoplatz, Chamissoplatz 6, 10965 Berlin. T. (030) 6925381, Fax (030) 6915782. *077204*

Galerie am Gendarmenmarkt, Mohrenstr 30, 10117 Berlin. T. (030) 20230, Fax (030) 23824521. - Paint /
Graph / Sculp / Mod - *077205*

Galerie am Havelufer, Imchenpl. 2, 14089 Berlin.
T. (030) 3655281. - Paint / Graph - *077206*

Galerie am Savignyplatz, Carmerstr 10, 10623 Berlin.
T. (030) 3136564. - Paint / Graph - *077207*

Galerie am Strausberger Platz, Strausberger Platz 4,
10243 Berlin. T. (030) 4275832. - Paint / Graph / Repr /
Sculp - *077208*

Galerie am Südwestkorso, Südwestkorso 65, 12161
Berlin. T. (030) 8218859. *077209*

Galerie Augustus, Auguststr 61, 10117 Berlin.
T. (030) 2833284. *077210*

Galerie Avantgarde, Leibnizstr 60, 10629 Berlin.
T. (030) 3247823, Fax (030) 3249858. *077211*

Galerie B. & D., Auguststr 61, 10117 Berlin.
T. (030) 2833288, Fax (030) 2833289. *077212*

Galerie Berlin Küttner Ebert, Friedrichstr 58, 10117 Berlin. T. (030) 2002400, 2384111,
Fax (030) 2384111. *077213*

Galerie der Berliner Graphikpresse und bibliophiles Antiquariat, Brunnenstr 165, 10119 Berlin.
T. (030) 2818106, Fax (030) 2818106. - Paint / Graph /
Sculp / Draw - *077214*

Galerie Eigen + Art, Auguststr 26, 10117 Berlin.
T. (030) 2806605, Fax (030) 2806616. - Paint - *077215*

Galerie Eylau 5, Eylauer Str 5, 10965 Berlin.
T. (030) 7863024, 3053236, Fax (030) 3052782. *077216*

Galerie für Holographie, Europa-Center, 10789 Berlin.
T. (030) 2614490, Fax (030) 3446379. *077217*

Galerie G, Meinekestr 26, 10719 Berlin.
T. (030) 8835527. - Paint - *077218*

Galerie Glaswerk, Kantstr 138, 10623 Berlin.
T. (030) 3139762, Fax (030) 3129321. - Glass - *077219*

Galerie im Rathaus, Tempelhofer Damm 165, 12099
Berlin. T. (030) 756 02 78. *077220*

Galerie Inselstrasse 13, Inselstr 13, 10179 Berlin.
T. (030) 2791808, Fax (030) 2798083566. - Paint /
Graph - *077221*

Galerie Jain, Schillerstr 106, 10115 Berlin.
T. (030) 3138809. *077222*

Galerie Lietzow, Knesebeckstr. 32, 10623 Berlin.
T. (030) 8812895, Fax (030) 8854392. - Paint / Graph /
Sculp / Glass / Pho / Draw - *077223*

Galerie Malschule, Kopenhagener Str 8, 13407 Berlin.
T. (030) 4969006. *077224*

Galerie Mönch im Antiquariat Skowronska, Schustehrusstr 28, 10585 Berlin. T. (030) 3482583. *077225*

Galerie Mutter Fourage, Chausseestr 15a, 14109 Berlin.
T. (030) 8052311. - Paint / Graph / Sculp - *077226*

Galerie neuger/riemschneider, Goethestr 73, 10625 Berlin. T. (030) 3120860, Fax (030) 3130933. - Paint /
Sculp / Pho / Mul - *077227*

Galerie no name, Sybelstr 37, 10629 Berlin.
T. (030) 3243495. *077228*

Galerie November, Bleibtreustr 7, 10623 Berlin.
T. (030) 313 75 00, 321 35 29. - Paint / Graph /
Sculp - *077229*

Galerie O Zwei, Oderberger Str 2, 10435 Berlin.
T. (030) 6097526, Fax (030) 6097526. - Paint - *077230*

Galerie Orbis Pictus, Bayerische Str. 3, 10707 Berlin.
T. (030) 8812392. *077231*

Galerie Parzival, Linienstr 213, 10119 Berlin.
T. (030) 2833228, Fax (030) 2833228. *077232*

Galerie re, Friedrichstr 58, 10117 Berlin.
T. (030) 2086870. *077233*

Galerie Rotunde im Alten Museum, Bodestr. 1-3, 10178
Berlin. T. (030) 20355409, Fax (030) 20355409.
- Paint / Graph / Sculp / Draw - *077234*

Galerie S, Maximilianstr 12a, 13187 Berlin.
T. (030) 4787523, Fax (030) 4723825. - Paint / Graph /
China / Repr / Fra / Lights - *077235*

Galerie Sievi, Gneisenaustr 112, 10961 Berlin.
T. (030) 6932997, Fax (030) 6933136. *077236*

Galerie Sophien-Edition, Sophienstr 24, 10178 Berlin.
T. (030) 2828233, Fax (030) 2828233. *077237*

Galerie Sophienstraße 8, Sophienstr 8, 10317 Berlin.
T. (030) 5251739. *077238*

Galerie Spandow, Fischerstr 28, 13597 Berlin.
T. (030) 3331414. - Paint / Graph / Sculp /
Draw - *077239*

Galerie Unwahr, Invalidenstr 116, 10115 Berlin.
T. (030) 6115510. *077240*

Galerie vier, Nollendorfstr 11, 10777 Berlin.
T. (030) 2172887. *077241*

Galerie Wohnmaschine, Tucholskystr 34-36, 10117 Berlin. T. (030) 2820795, Fax (030) 2824223. - Paint /
Graph / Sculp / Pho / Mul / Draw - *077242*

Gebauer und Günther, Torstr 220, 10115 Berlin.
T. (030) 2808110, Fax (030) 2808109. *077243*

Geitel, Marianne, Bleibtreustr 38/39, 10623 Berlin.
T. (030) 881 46 57. - Jew - *077244*

Giesler, Manfred, Großbeerenstr 56f, 10963 Berlin.
T. (030) 7865968, Fax (030) 7866184. - Paint - *077245*

Gleditsch 45, Gleditschstr 45, 10781 Berlin.
T. (030) 2162233. *077246*

Gleser, Kurfürstendamm 48, 10707 Berlin.
T. (030) 8617000, 8826050. *077247*

Goldsworthy, Rupert, Brunnenstr 44, 10115 Berlin.
T. (030) 6860698, Fax (030) 6860698. *077248*

Grob, Marianne, Blücherstr 42, 10961 Berlin.
T. (030) 6933814, Fax (030) 6936228. *077249*

Gutsch, Knesebeckstr 29, 10623 Berlin.
T. (030) 8826739. *077250*

Haas, Michael, Niebuhrstr 5, 10629 Berlin.
T. (030) 8827006, Fax (030) 8824694. - Paint / Graph /
Draw - *077251*

Hänel, Frank, Stargarder Str 18, 10437 Berlin.
T. (030) 4447268, Fax (030) 4449991. - Paint / Graph /
Sculp / Pho / Mul / Draw - *077252*

Hartmann, Günther, Prof. Dr., Bahnhofstr 38, 12207 Berlin. T. (030) 7725001. *077253*

Hartmann & Noé, Knesebeckstr 32, 10623 Berlin.
T. (030) 8812895, Fax (030) 8854392. *077254*

Helikon, Klausenerplatz 5, 14059 Berlin.
T. (030) 3224822. *077255*

Herbert, Inge, Koloniestr 10, 13357 Berlin.
T. (030) 4944402. *077256*

Hesselbach, Kurfürstendamm 35, 10719 Berlin.
T. (030) 8836137, Fax (030) 8837797. *077257*

Hetzler, Max, Schillerstr 94, 10625 Berlin.
T. (030) 3152261, Fax (030) 3131963. *077258*

Hulsch, Carlos, Emster Str 43, 10719 Berlin.
T. (030) 8822842, Fax (030) 8822844. *077259*

Jahnhorst & Preuss, Fasanenstr 29, 10709 Berlin.
T. (030) 8831117, Fax (030) 8831117. - Paint /
Sculp - *077260*

Janssen, Pariser Str 45, 10719 Berlin.
T. (030) 8811590. *077261*

GALERIE LUDWIG LANGE

Wielandstr. 26 (am Kurfürstendamm)
10707 Berlin, Telefon: 030/8812926

Schwerpunkt:
Deutsche Plastik des
19. u. 20. Jahrhunderts

Jungnitz, Winfried, Mühlenstr 1, 10243 Berlin.
  T. (030) 7074371. *077262*
Koch, Hans Horst, Kurfürstendamm 216, 10719 Berlin.
  T. (030) 8826360, Fax (030) 8824066. *077263*
Kohnert, Jacob, Krumme Str 35-36, 10627 Berlin.
  T. (030) 3234064. - Paint - *077264*
Kondeyne, Inga, Rosenthaler Str 40/41, 10178 Berlin.
  T. (030) 6156634, Fax (030) 6156634. *077265*
Krafünf, Krausnickstr 5, 10115 Berlin.
  T. (030) 2832826. *077266*
Krause, Dieter, Seelenbinderstr 24, 12555 Berlin.
  T. (030) 6527135. *077267*
Kunsthaus am Moritzplatz, Oranienstr 46, 10969 Berlin.
  T. (030) 6145577, Fax (030) 6141791. - Paint / Graph /
  Sculp / Fra / Pho / Draw - *077268*
Kunsthaus Miro, Siefersheimer Str 11a, 12559 Berlin.
  T. (030) 6598402, Fax (030) 2000920. *077269*
Kunstraum, Luckauer Str 1, 10969 Berlin.
  T. (030) 6154427. *077270*
La Girafe, Glogauer Str. 24, 10999 Berlin. *077271*
Ladengalerie, Kurfürstendamm 64, 10707 Berlin.
  T. (030) 881 42 14. - Paint / Graph / Sculp - *077272*
Lange, Ludwig, Wielandstr 26, 10707 Berlin.
  T. (030) 8812926, Fax 8811535. - Paint / Graph / Chi-
  na / Sculp - *077273*
Lasard, Loulou, Crellestr 42a, 10827 Berlin.
  T. (030) 7844444, Fax (030) 7844444. *077274*
Lauterbach, Hans, Bötzowstr 31, 10407 Berlin.
  T. (030) 4264455. *077275*
Liechtenfeld, Galina Gloria von, Fügener Weg 28, 12209
  Berlin. T. (030) 7113388, Fax (030) 7113388. - Paint /
  Graph / Orient / Pho / Mul - *077276*
Liesenfeld, Marcus, Willibald-Alexis-Str 20, 10965 Ber-
  lin. T. (030) 6929270. *077277*
Linneborn, Parkstr 7-9, 13187 Berlin.
  T. (030) 4826080. *077278*
Maass, Wilfriede, Schönfließer Str 2I, 10439 Berlin.
  T. (030) 4457004. - Paint / Graph / China - *077279*
Magnet, Gustav-Freytag-Str 5a, 10827 Berlin.
  T. (030) 7822289. *077280*
Mainz, Zossener Str 40, 10961 Berlin.
  T. (030) 69409277/78, Fax 69409279. - Paint / Graph /
  Sculp / Mul / Draw - *077281*
manufactura scenografia, Martin-Luther-Str 8, 10777
  Berlin. T. (030) 2143730. *077282*
Martins, Liliana Monica, Königsberger Str 33a, 12207
  Berlin. T. (030) 7738216, Fax (030) 7736768. *077283*
Meinhold, Marion, Friedrichstr 133, 10117 Berlin.
  T. (030) 2813550. *077284*
MIRO, Marienfelder Chaussee 133, 12349 Berlin.
  T. (030) 76296265, Fax (030) 7435547. *077285*
Modern Graphics, Oranienstr 22, 10999 Berlin.
  T. (030) 6158810. *077286*
Moegelin, Edda, Zerndorfer Weg 63, 13465 Berlin.
  T. (030) 4016758. *077287*
Mösch, Bleibtreustr 15-16, 10623 Berlin.
  T. (030) 8838300, Fax (030) 8838300. - Graph /
  Mul - *077288*
Nesic, Milan, Pfalzburger Str 76, 10719 Berlin.
  T. (030) 8822803. *077289*
Neue Räume, Lindenstr 39, 10969 Berlin.
  T. (030) 2514812, Fax (030) 2521390. - Paint - *077290*
New Art Gallery, Kantstr 13, 10623 Berlin.
  T. (030) 3124186, Fax (030) 3121089. - China - *077291*
Niemann, Bodo, Knesebeckstr 30, 10623 Berlin.
  T. (030) 8822620, Fax (030) 8812792. - Paint / Graph /
  Sculp / Pho / Draw - *077292*
Nierendorf, Hardenbergstr 19, 10623 Berlin.
  T. (030) 8325013, Fax 3129327. - Paint / Graph /
  Sculp / Draw - *077293*

Noack, Michael, Crellestr 33, 10827 Berlin.
  T. (030) 7874012. *077294*
Nothelfer, Georg, Uhlandstr 184, 10623 Berlin.
  T. (030) 8814405, 8825443, Fax (030) 8818610.
  - Paint / Graph / Sculp / Mul / Draw - *077295*
Oldenburg, Jörg, Kohlfurter Str 8, 10999 Berlin.
  T. (030) 6154213. *077296*
Pels-Leusden, Fasanenstr 25, 10719 Berlin.
  T. (030) 8859150, Fax 8824145. - Paint / Graph /
  Sculp / Draw - *077297*
Peter, Johannes, Friedrichstr 206, 10969 Berlin.
  T. (030) 2511941. *077298*
Petersen, J., Herderstr 5, 10623 Berlin.
  T. (030) 3134508, 3128787, Fax (030) 3133362.
  - Paint / Graph / Sculp - *077299*
Pfundt, Bregenzer Str 16, 10707 Berlin.
  T. (030) 8831311. *077300*
Pillango, Elberfelder Str 31, 10555 Berlin.
  T. (030) 3928224. - Paint / Graph - *077301*
Poll, Eva, Lützowpl 7, 10785 Berlin. T. (030) 2617091,
  Fax (030) 2617092. - Paint / Graph / Sculp / Pho /
  Draw - *077302*
Pommersfelde, Knesebeckstr 97, 10623 Berlin.
  T. (030) 3138005. - Paint / Graph / Sculp / Pho /
  Draw - *077303*
Poster Galerie 200, Kurfürstendamm 200, 10719 Berlin.
  T. (030) 8821959, 8825737, Fax (030) 8825628.
  - Graph / Sculp - *077304*
Raab, Potsdamer Str 58, 10785 Berlin.
  T. (030) 2619218, Fax (030) 2629217. - Paint /
  Draw - *077305*
Redmann, Katharina-Heinroth-Ufer 1, 10787 Berlin.
  T. (030) 2619425, Fax (030) 2619525. - Paint / Graph /
  Sculp / Cur / Draw - *077306*
Reinke, Nassauische Str 57, 10717 Berlin.
  T. (030) 8738043. *077307*
Richter, Hans W., Flensburger Str 11, 10557 Berlin.
  T. (030) 3933265. *077308*
Rössiger & Lindemuth, Schützenstr 53, 12165 Berlin.
  T. (030) 7918488, Fax (030) 7932237. *077309*

Rosenthal studio-haus, Kurfürstendamm 226, 10719
  Berlin. T. (030) 8817051/52. - China - *077310*
Rothe, Martin, Schildhornstr 21, 12163 Berlin.
  T. (030) 7926663. *077311*
Saborowski, Peter, Friedrichstr 120, 10117 Berlin.
  T. (030) 2817311. *077312*
Sakschewski, Katzbachstr 2, 10965 Berlin.
  T. (030) 7854530. *077313*
Schäfer, Kurt, Fasanenstr 41a, 10719 Berlin.
  T. (030) 8851804, Fax (030) 8851805. *077314*
Schauwecker, Jasna, Klausener Platz 22, 14059 Berlin.
  T. (030) 3227119. *077315*
Schirmacher, Ingeborg, Königin-Luise-Str 48, 14195
  Berlin. T. (030) 8324560. *077316*
Schmidt, Karin, Mariendorfer Damm 432, 12107 Berlin.
  T. (030) 7427268. *077317*
Schneider, Tinatin, Tiroler Str 68, 13187 Berlin.
  T. (030) 4720935. *077318*
Schoen & Nalepa, Pariser Str 56, 10719 Berlin.
  T. (030) 8824124, 8826501, Fax (030) 8823379.
  - Paint - *077319*
Schrade, R. & N. Denkel, Wilhelmsaue 137, 10715 Ber-
  lin. T. (030) 8616461. *077320*
Schultz, Michael, Mommsenstr 32, 10629 Berlin.
  T. (030) 3241591, Fax 3231575. - Paint - *077321*
Schultz, Reinhard, Oranienburger Str 45, 110117 Berlin.
  T. (030) 2832476. *077322*
Schumacher, Marianne, Königstr. 44, 12105 Berlin.
  T. (030) 7050244. *077323*
Schwichtenberg, Tina, Märkisches Ufer 30, 10179 Ber-
  lin. T. (030) 2792766. *077324*
Seibert-Philippen, Gisela, Giesebrechtstr 15, 10629 Ber-
  lin. T. (030) 8836446. - Jew - *077325*
Sonne, Nikolaus, Kantstr 138, 10623 Berlin.
  T. (030) 3122355, Fax (030) 3123539. - Paint / Graph /
  Pho / Mul / Draw - *077326*
Sperlich, Lothar, Blissestr 54, 10713 Berlin.
  T. (030) 8226180. *077327*

KUNSTHANDEL WOLFGANG WERNER
BREMEN · BERLIN

Gemälde, Skulpturen und Graphik des 19. und 20. Jahrhunderts

Fasanenstraße 72
10719 Berlin
Telefon 0 30 - 882 76 16

Rembertistraße 1a
28203 Bremen
Telefon 04 21 - 32 74 78

Springer, Fasanenstr 13, 10623 Berlin.
T. (030) 3127063, Fax (030) 3131308. - Paint / Graph /
Sculp - *077328*
Struck, Nicolaus, Spandauer Str 29, 10178 Berlin.
T. (030) 2427261, Fax (030) 2427261. *077329*
studio-galerie-berlin, Frankfurter Allee 36a, 10247 Ber-
lin. T. (030) 2910850. *077330*
Tafelski, Schillerstr 63, 10627 Berlin.
T. (030) 3240130. *077331*
Tammen & Busch, Fidicinstr 40, 10965 Berlin.
T. (030) 6945248, Fax (030) 6915782. *077332*
Taube, Pariser Str 54, 10719 Berlin. T. (030) 8835694.
- Paint / Graph / Sculp / Pho / Draw - *077333*
Theis, Neufertstr 6, 14059 Berlin. T. (030) 3212322,
Fax (030) 3224103. - China - *077334*
Thiede, Wolfgang, Meierottostr 1, 10719 Berlin.
T. (030) 8819024. *077335*
Tode, R. Q., Dudenstr 36, 10965 Berlin.
T. (030) 7865186. *077336*
Treykorn, Savignyplatz 13, Passage, 10623 Berlin.
T. (030) 3124275. - Jew - *077337*
vierte Etage, Bregenzer Str 10, 10707 Berlin.
T. (030) 8834354, Fax (030) 8834354. *077338*
Vostell, Rafael, Niebuhrstr 2, 10629 Berlin.
T. (030) 8852280, Fax (030) 8817677. *077339*
Waszkowiak, Friedrichstr 127, 10117 Berlin.
T. (030) 2190460. - Paint / Graph / Sculp / Pho / Mul /
Draw - *077340*
Weber, Christof, Stierstr 8, 12159 Berlin.
T. (030) 8513289, Fax (030) 8513531. - Paint /
Graph - *077341*
Weinand, Oranienplatz 5, 10999 Berlin.
T. (030) 6142545. - Furn / Tex / Dec / Glass - *077342*
Weiss, Andreas, Nollendorfstr 11-12, 10777 Berlin.
T. (030) 2172484, Fax (030) 2172887. *077343*
Weiss, Barbara, Potsdamer Str 93, 10785 Berlin.
T. (030) 262428, Fax (030) 2651652. *077344*
Werner, Wolfgang, Fasanenstr 72, 10719 Berlin.
T. (030) 8827616, Fax 8815387. - Paint / Graph /
Sculp - *077345*
Westphal, Fasanenstr 68, 10719 Berlin.
T. (030) 8821162, Fax (030) 8831761. - Paint /
Sculp - *077346*
Wewerka, Pariser Str 55, 10785 Berlin.
T. (030) 2619734, Fax (030) 2619734. - Paint / Graph /
Sculp - *077347*
Wewerka, Homeyerstr 32, 13156 Berlin.
T. (030) 4826662, Fax 4829261. *077348*
Wolf, Großbeerenstr 36, 10965 Berlin. T. (030) 7864378/
7867310. *077349*
Wolff, Reinhard, Lietzenburger Sgtr 92, 10719 Berlin.
T. (030) 8822808. *077350*
Zellermayer, Ludwigkirchstr 6, 10719 Berlin.
T. (030) 8824537, Fax (030) 8837316. - Paint / Graph /
Sculp - *077351*
Zellermayer-Lorenzen, Thielallee 30a, 10719 Berlin.
T. (030) 8311797, Fax (030) 883731. - Paint / Graph /
Sculp / Pho / Draw - *077352*
Zielke, Johannes, Gipsstr 7, 10119 Berlin.
T. (030) 2829802, Fax (030) 2829793. - Paint / Sculp /
Mul / Draw - *077353*
Zwinger Galerie, Dresdener Str 125, 10999 Berlin.
T. (030) 6154605, Fax (030) 6155888. - Paint - *077354*

Bernau (Brandenburg)
Galerie der Bildenden Künste, Bürgermeisterstr. 4,
16321 Bernau. T. (03338) 8068. *077355*

Bernkastel-Kues (Rheinland-Pfalz)
Galerie im Geburtshaus des Nikolaus von Kues, Niko-
lausufer 49, 54470 Bernkastel-Kues. *077356*
Galerie im Landshut, Gestade 11, 54470 Bernkastel-
Kues. T. (06531) 30 19. - Paint - *077357*

Biberach (Baden-Württemberg)
Assfalg, Siegfried, Steigstr. 7, 88400 Biberach.
T. (07351) 90 83. - Graph - *077358*
Reichle, Brigitte, Sennhofgasse 5, 88400 Biberach.
T. (07351) 14422. - Paint / Graph / Sculp - *077359*

Biebergemünd (Hessen)
Galerie Oly, Bahnhofstr. 9, 63599 Biebergemünd.
T. (06050) 303. - Paint / Graph / Sculp / Mul - *077360*

Biedenkopf (Hessen)
Glas-Galerie, Hospitalstr. 21, 35216 Biedenkopf.
T. (06461) 21 00. - Glass - *077361*

Bielefeld (Nordrhein-Westfalen)
Baumgarte, Samuelis, Obernstr 28, 33602 Bielefeld.
T. (0521) 173532, Fax (0521) 173521. *077362*
Galerie Artists Unlimited, August-Bebel-Str. 94-96,
33602 Bielefeld. T. (0521) 63178. - Paint - *077363*
Galerie David, Beckhausstr. 229, 33611 Bielefeld.
T. (0521) 86961, Fax (0521) 84336. - Paint / Graph /
Sculp - *077364*
Galerie David, Marktstr. 2-4, 33602 Bielefeld.
T. (0521) 179233, Fax (0521) 84336. - Paint / Graph /
Sculp - *077365*
Kokerbeck, W., Hauptstr. 92, 33647 Bielefeld.
T. (0521) 44 16 55. - Paint - *077366*
Nonnenbruch, Splittenbrede 11, 33613 Bielefeld.
T. (0521) 88 79 70. *077367*
Nonnenbruch, Splittenbrede 11, 33613 Bielefeld.
T. (0521) 88 79 70. - Graph / Repr / Dec / Fra /
Draw - *077368*
Osthoff, Berthold, Humboldtstr. 40, 33615 Bielefeld.
T. (0521) 790 37. - Paint / Fra - *077369*
Reinermann & Co., Hügelstr. 8, 33613 Bielefeld.
- Paint / Fra - *077370*
Salustowicz, Izabella, Voltmannstr. 121 a, 33619 Biele-
feld. T. (0521) 88 96 53. - Paint - *077371*
Stieghorst, Rainer, Striegauer Str. 11, 33719 Bielefeld.
T. (0521) 201 76 23, Fax 208 80 88. *077372*
Teutloff, Lutz, Skulpturengarten, Am Südhang 19-21,
33739 Bielefeld. T. (0521) 893708,
Fax 893708. *077373*
Weinland, Dr. Wolf, Goldbach 10, 33615 Bielefeld.
T. (0521) 7 14 62. *077374*

Bietigheim-Bissingen (Baden-Württemberg)
Bayer, Pforzheimer Str. 30, 74321 Bietigheim-Bissingen.
T. (07142) 43753, Fax 45174. - Paint / Graph / Sculp /
Draw - *077375*
Galerie im Unteren Tor, Hauptstr 17, 74321 Bietigheim-
Bissingen. T. (07142) 41309, Fax 41534. - Paint /
Graph / Fra / Draw - *077376*
Saußele, Lore, Ulrichstr. 7, 74321 Bietigheim-Bissingen.
T. (07142) 527 56. *077377*

Billerbeck (Nordrhein-Westfalen)
Galerie am Dom, Markt 2, 48727 Billerbeck.
T. (02543) 222, 8180. *077378*

Bitburg (Rheinland-Pfalz)
Galerie Haus Beda, Bedapl.1, 54634 Bitburg.
T. (06561) 96450. - Paint - *077379*
Zimmer, Heinrich, Trierer Str. 40, 54634 Bitburg.
T. (06561) 31 92. *077380*

Bocholt (Nordrhein-Westfalen)
Art Galerie, Osterstr. 53, 46397 Bocholt.
T. (02871) 124 83. - Graph - *077381*
Galerie Am Finkenbusch, Langenbergstr. 17 und Nordstr.
20, 46397 Bocholt. T. (02871) 153 94. *077382*
Wissing, Karl, Robert-Bosch-Str 6, 46375 Bocholt.
T. (02871) 13804, Fax 184624. - Paint / Fra - *077383*

Bochum (Nordrhein-Westfalen)
Ahlheim, U., Oberstr. 108, 44892 Bochum.
T. (0234) 29 39 05. *077384*
Akzente, Kemnader Str 1, 44797 Bochum.
T. (0234) 470109. *077385*
Berswordt-Wallrabe, H.L.A. von, Schloßstr 1aa, 44795
Bochum. T. (0234) 43997. *077386*
Claubergs Galerie der Experimente, Bongardstr. 6,
44787 Bochum. T. (0234) 169 76. - Paint / Graph /
Sculp - *077387*
Galerie Grashalme, Marthastr. 23, 44791 Bochum.
T. (0234) 58 04 53, 51 08 36. - Paint / Graph - *077388*
Galerie Haus Laer, Höfestr. 45, Gut Haus Laer, 44803
Bochum. T. (0234) 38 30 44. - Ant / Paint / Graph /
Fum / Repr / Rel / Pho / Draw - *077389*
Galerie Januar, Eislebener Str. 9, 44892 Bochum.
T. (0234) 280621. *077390*
Galerie Kunst & Glas, Massenbergstr. 1, 44787 Bochum.
T. (0234) 68 15 88. *077391*
Galerie m, Haus Weitmar, 44787 Bochum.
T. (0234) 439 97, Fax 43997. - Paint / Graph / Sculp /
Pho / Mul / Draw - *077392*
Galerie Neue Ansichten, Huestr 34, 44787 Bochum.
T. (0234) 18276. *077393*
Galerie Vernissage, Massenbergstr 9, 44787 Bochum.
T. (0234) 66528. *077394*
Godehardt, F., Huestr. 34, 44787 Bochum.
T. (0234) 18276. *077395*
Haus der Kunst, Am Varenholt 123, 44797 Bochum.
T. (0234) 79 11 01. - Paint / Graph / Repr / Fra /
Draw - *077396*
Hebler, Unicenter Querenburg 283, 44801 Bochum.
T. (0234) 70 10 27. - Graph / Mul - *077397*
Hutterloh, Auf dem Helwe 2, 44892 Bochum.
T. (0234) 9210181. *077398*
Knappmann-Thon, L., Alte Bahnhofstr. 56, 44892 Bo-
chum. T. (0234) 29 35 05. *077399*
Kückels + Hartmann, Nordring 47, 44787 Bochum.
T. (0234) 1 30 62, 3 29 82. - Paint / Graph - *077400*
Kunst- und Bücherscheune, Lennershofstr. 156, 44801
Bochum. T. (0234) 70 43 91. *077401*
Kunsthaus Samoticha, Gerberstr 1, 44787 Bochum.
T. (0234) 13201. *077402*
Laackman, Andreas, Huestr. 13, I.F.U., 44787 Bochum.
T. (0234) 38 30 88. *077403*
Magic Art Gallery, Kortumstr. 34, 44787 Bochum.
T. (0234) 15051. - Repr / Fra - *077404*
Perspective Art Gallery, Kortumstr 97, 44787 Bochum.
T. (0234) 12424. *077405*
Pinx, Castroper Str 38, 44791 Bochum.
T. (0234) 58 38 99. *077406*
Reich, W., Brunsteinstr. 1, 44789 Bochum.
T. (0234) 30 91 57. *077407*
Schwarz Edition, Unterm Kolm 4a, 44797 Bochum.
T. (0234) 79 15 83. - Graph / Mul - *077408*
Situation Kunst -Haus Weitmar-, Schloßstr. 1a, 44795
Bochum. T. (0234) 45 21 94. *077409*
Studio Jaeschke, Westerholtstr. 15, 44801 Bochum.
T. (0234) 70 37 66. - Paint / Graph - *077410*
Wrobel-Schwarz, M., Stadtgärtnering 35, 44866 Bo-
chum. T. (0234) 889940. *077411*

Bodenmais (Bayern)
Keddi-Leimberger, Bahnhofstr. 60, 94249 Bodenmais.
T. (09920) 240, 15 25. - Paint - *077412*

Böblingen (Baden-Württemberg)
Galerie am Marktplatz, Altvaterstr. 23b, 71032
Böblingen. *077413*

Galerie Eisenmann, Tübinger Str. 81, 71032 Böblingen.
T. (07031) 487-0, Fax 27 88 60 (78-1000). *077414*
Galerie in der Jahnstrasse, Jahnstr. 51, 71032 Böblingen. T. (07031) 26233. - Paint / Graph / Sculp - *077415*

Bonn (Nordrhein-Westfalen)
A.K.G. Auktionen-Kunsthandel-Galerie, Prinz-Albert-Str. 1, 53113 Bonn. T. (0228) 21 90 90, Fax 8986.
- Paint - *077417*
Bonner Kunsthaus, Bonner Talweg 70, 53113 Bonn.
T. (0228) 21 17 70. - Paint / Graph / Sculp / Draw - *077418*
Chenz, H. Ch., China Galerie, Bertha-von-Suttner-Platz 4, 53111 Bonn. T. (0228) 65 85 70. *077419*
Cramer, Barbara, Poppelsdorfer Allee 58a, 53115 Bonn.
T. (0228) 63 44 65. *077420*
Dierkes, G., Meßdorfer Str. 215, 53123 Bonn.
T. (0228) 64 63 60. *077421*
Firla, S., Thomas-Mann-Str. 15, 53111 Bonn.
T. (0228) 69 13 85. *077422*
Galerie Marco, Händelstr. 12, 53115 Bonn.
T. (0228) 65 12 08, Fax 69 79 33. - Paint / Sculp - *077423*
Gerstenberg, A., Sternpassage, 53111 Bonn.
T. (0228) 634988, 653044, 657199. *077424*
Hennemann, Marianne, Poppelsdorfer Allee 17, 53115 Bonn. T. (0228) 223769, Fax (0228) 216507. - Paint / Graph / Repr / Sculp / Fra / Mul / Draw - *077425*
Hilo Pictures, Kaiserpl. 10, 53111 Bonn.
T. (0228) 65 01 00, Fax 10199. - Paint - *077426*
Hübers, K. H., Brunnenallee 4, 53173 Bonn.
T. (0228) 36 47 46. *077427*
Kessel, Dieter, Friesdorfer Str. 23, 53173 Bonn.
T. (0228) 31 02 30, Fax 31 02 22. - Paint / Sculp / Fra - *077428*
Kleinschmidt, J., Bonner Talweg 28a, 53113 Bonn.
T. (0228) 21 97 68. *077429*
Kunstraum MI Posselt, Kurfürstenstr 50, 53115 Bonn.
T. (0228) 220781, Fax 220781. - Paint / Graph / Sculp / Mul / Draw - *077430*
Kurek, Stanislaw, Bonner Str. 23, 53173 Bonn.
T. (0228) 31 42 60. *077431*
Lempert, Herbert Fritz, Dr., Prinz-Albert-Str. 38, 53113 Bonn. T. (0228) 21 07 61, Fax 21 22 59. - Graph / Repr - *077432*
Lessenich, Meßdorfer Str. 215, 53123 Bonn.
T. (0228) 64 38 81. - Graph - *077433*
Löhrl in Syndikat Halle, Thomas-Mann-Str. 41, 53111 Bonn. *077434*
Lux, K. W. Dr., Im Eichholz 1, 53127 Bonn.
T. (0228) 28 29 36. *077435*
Multimedia-Galerie, Moltkestr. 72, 53173 Bonn.
T. (0228) 36 22 44. *077436*
Netzhammer, M., Beethovenallee 45, 53173 Bonn.
T. (0228) 36 38 52. *077437*
Ossenpohl, Brunnenallee 15, 53173 Bonn.
T. (0228) 36 47 46. *077438*
Pudelko, Heinrich-von-Kleist-Str. 11, 53113 Bonn.
T. (0228) 224230, Fax (0228) 210804. - Paint / Graph - *077439*
Reichl, E. & H., Ostpreußenstr. 8, 53119 Bonn. *077440*
Reul, M., Giersbergstr 37, 53229 Bonn.
T. (0228) 481105. *077441*
Rosenzweig, M. & D., Hausdorffstr. 86, 53129 Bonn.
T. (0228) 23 81 89. *077442*
Ruchti, Graurheindorfer Str. 23, 53111 Bonn.
T. (0228) 63 53 63. - Paint / Graph - *077443*
Spindler, M.J., Poppelsdorfer Allee 42, 53115 Bonn.
T. (0228) 69 39 00, Fax 693900. - Paint - *077444*
Steinmetz, Bernhard-Michael, Ermekeilstr. 25, 53113 Bonn. T. (0228) 21 51 01, Fax 26 11 14. - Paint / Graph / Sculp / Pho / Mul / Draw - *077445*
Stemmeler, Ch., Endenicher Str. 305, 53121 Bonn.
T. (0228) 61 47 51. *077446*
Suliak, B., Dürenstr. 3, 53173 Bonn.
T. (0228) 35 76 67. *077447*
Wagner, Brigitte, Wolkenburgweg 6, 53227 Bonn.
T. (0228) 462536/461167,
Fax (0228) 469051. *077447a*

Bordesholm (Schleswig-Holstein)
Galerie Leviathan, Alte Landstr. 1, 24582 Bordesholm.
T. (04322) 2041. - Paint - *077448*

KUNSTHANDEL WOLFGANG WERNER
BREMEN · BERLIN

Gemälde, Skulpturen und Graphik des 19. und 20. Jahrhunderts

Fasanenstraße 72
10719 Berlin
Telefon 0 30 - 882 76 16

Rembertistraße 1a
28203 Bremen
Telefon 04 21 - 32 74 78

Bottrop (Nordrhein-Westfalen)
Galerie am Rathaus, Kirchhellener Str. 28, 46236 Bottrop. T. (02041) 22920. *077449*
Galerie 7, Böckenhoffstr. 7, 46236 Bottrop.
T. (02041) 239 20. - Paint / Graph / Sculp / Jew - *077450*
Multi-Media-Contact Galerie, Böckenhoffstr. 7, 46236 Bottrop. *077451*

Bovenden (Niedersachsen)
Buch- und Kunsthandlung Prisma, Rathauspl. 23, 37120 Bovenden. T. (0551) Göttingen 819 03. - Paint / Graph - *077452*

Braunfels (Hessen)
Koch, Rose-Marie, Nelkenweg 2, 35619 Braunfels.
T. (06442) 46 38. - Paint / Graph / China / Sculp / Draw - *077453*

Braunschweig (Niedersachsen)
BBK-Galerie/Torhaus-Galerie, Humboldtstr. 34, 38106 Braunschweig. T. (0531) 34 61 66. - Paint - *077454*
Bilder-Etage, Am Ringerbrunnen, 38100 Braunschweig.
T. (0531) 44387. - Paint - *077455*
Buch & Kunst, Kasernenstr. 12, 38102 Braunschweig.
T. (0531) 34 73 32. - Paint - *077456*
Fehlisch, Neuer Weg 2, 38100 Braunschweig.
T. (0531) 43095. - Paint / Draw - *077457*
Galerie Kreuzweg Neun, Augualstr. 5, 38100 Braunschweig. T. (0531) 60044. *077458*
Jaeschke, Horst, Schuhstr. 42, 38100 Braunschweig.
T. (0531) 443 87. - Paint / Graph / Repr / Fra - *077459*
Kemenate Galerie, Ölschlägern 18, 38100 Braunschweig. T. (0531) 444 66. - China / Jew - *077460*
Malerwinkel, Ziegenmarkt 4a, 38100 Braunschweig.
T. (0531) 40947. - Paint - *077461*
Schmücking, R., Lessingpl. 12, 38100 Braunschweig.
T. (0531) 449 60, Fax 44960. - Paint / Graph / Sculp - *077462*
Seelmann, Paul, Bindestr. 1, 38106 Braunschweig.
T. (0531) 33 20 71. *077463*
Tautz, S.B., Daimlerstr. 12, 38112 Braunschweig. *077464*
Veltheim, Hennebergstr. 3, 38102 Braunschweig.
- Glass - *077465*
Wohnstudio Extra, Schützenstr. 4, 38100 Braunschweig. T. (0531) 170 96. - Paint / Graph / Furn / Sculp / Dec / Fra / Lights / Glass - *077466*

Breisach (Baden-Württemberg)
Galerie Schloss Rimsingen, Oberrimsingen, 79206 Breisach. T. (07667) 31 35. - Paint - *077467*

Bremen
Art'n Card, Am Dobben 69, 28203 Bremen.
T. (0421) 767 13. - Repr / Fra / Pho / Mul - *077468*
Atelier, Harzburger Str. 10, 28205 Bremen.
T. (0421) 49 21 26. *077469*
Atelierhof, Alexanderstr. 9b, 28203 Bremen.
T. (0421) 77703. - Paint - *077470*
Bertram, Contrescarpe 45, 28195 Bremen.
T. (0421) 32 10 93, Fax 32 45 26. - Paint / Sculp - *077471*
Borgward, Monica, Parkstr 73, 28209 Bremen.
T. (0421) 3479035. - Glass - *077472*
Bremer Bank, Domshof 8-9, 28195 Bremen. *077473*
Emigholz, Hans, Wachmannstr. 35, 28209 Bremen.
- Paint / Fra - *077474*

Galerie Beim Steinernen Kreuz, Beim Steinernen Kreuz 1, 28203 Bremen. T. (0421) 70 15 15, Fax 72171.
- Paint / Mul / Draw - *077475*
Galerie Bismarck, Bismarckstr. 12, 28203 Bremen.
T. (0421) 772 78, Fax 77078. - Paint / Graph / Sculp / Draw - *077476*
galerie gruppe grün, Fedelhören 32, 28203 Bremen.
T. (0421) 32 65 72. - Paint / Graph / Sculp - *077477*
Galerie im Hofmeierhaus, Oberneulander Landstr. 153, 28355 Bremen. T. (0421) 25 66 52. *077478*
Galerie im Kulturzentrum Schlachthof, Findorffstr. 51, 28215 Bremen. T. (0421) 35 30 75. *077479*
Galerie im Park, Züricher Str 40, 28325 Bremen.
T. (0421) 4081846. *077480*
Galerie im Winter, Richard-Wagner-Str 32, 28209 Bremen. T. (0421) 342294. - Paint / Sculp - *077481*
Galerie Kunsthandwerk, Wüstestätte 10, 28195 Bremen.
T. (0421) 32 58 01. *077482*
Galerie Plakatkunst, Hillmannplatz, 28195 Bremen.
T. (0421) 13808. - Graph - *077483*
Galerie Siuta, Stavendamm 8, 28195 Bremen.
T. (0421) 32 68 88. *077484*
Galerie 22, Bismarckstr. 22, 28203 Bremen.
T. (0421) 70 19 27. *077485*
Gerling, Rolf-Peter, Händelstr. 11, 28209 Bremen.
- Graph / Graph - *077486*
Graphik & Buch, St.-Pauli-Str 44, 28203 Bremen.
T. (0421) 74793. - Graph / Draw - *077487*
Harting, Friedrich, Hamburger Str. 119, 28205 Bremen.
- Paint - *077488*
Hertz, Cornelius, Richard-Wagner-Str. 22, 28209 Bremen. T. (0421) 34 16 70. - Paint / Graph / Sculp - *077489*
Hoffmüller, Münchener Str. 146, 28215 Bremen.
T. (0421) 35 53 43. - Paint - *077490*
Kalk, K., Lahnstr. 33, 28199 Bremen.
T. (0421) 592993. *077491*
Kirsch, Silvia, Wüstestätte 8, 28195 Bremen.
T. (0421) 32 76 82. - Jew - *077492*
Kleine Galerie in der Stadtbibliothek Gröpelingen, Lissaer Str. 7, 28237 Bremen. T. (0421) 61 83 270.
- Paint - *077493*
Kunsthandel Wolfgang Werner, Rembertistr 1a, 28203 Bremen. T. (0421) 327478, Fax 325949. - Paint / Graph / Sculp - *077494*
Lagerhaus Bremen-Ostertor, Schildstr. 12-19, 28203 Bremen. T. (0421) 70 21 68. *077495*
Leuwer, Franz, Bischofsnadel 15, 28195 Bremen.
T. (0421) 32 32 05. - Ant / Furn - *077496*
Mönch, Oberneulander Landstr. 153, 28355 Bremen.
T. (0421) 25 66 52. *077497*
Oertel, Peter, St.-Pauli-Str. 44, 28203 Bremen.
T. (0421) 74793. - Paint - *077498*
Ohse, Rolf, Contrescarpe 36, 28203 Bremen.
T. (0421) 32 75 50, Fax 336 54 83. - Paint / Graph - *077499*
Rabus, Katrin, Plantage 13, 28215 Bremen.
T. (0421) 356568, Fax (0421) 371963. - Paint / Graph / Sculp / Draw - *077500*
Roche, Fedelhören 30, 28203 Bremen.
T. (0421) 32 37 47. *077501*
Ropers, W.M., Schnoor 26, 28195 Bremen.
T. (0421) 32 61 86. *077502*
Schröder, Brigitte von, Am Distelkamp 2, 28357 Bremen. T. (0421) 27 07 08. *077503*

Schröder & Leisewitz, Carl-Schurz-Str. 39-41, 28209 Bremen. T. (0421) 34 40 83, Fax 344083. - Paint - 077504
Schulz, Johannes, Fedelhören 81, 28203 Bremen. T. (0421) 327050, Fax 321700. 077505
Securitas Galerie, Am Wall 121, 28195 Bremen. T. (0421) 30850, Fax (0421) 3085300. 077506
Vilsen, Hermann-Böse-Str. 29, 28209 Bremen. T. (0421) 349 91 25. - Paint / Graph / Sculp / Fra - 077507
Waller, Birgit, Am Kapellenberg 5, 28759 Bremen. T. (0421) 62 16 66. 077508
Wattenberg, H., Römerstr. 16, 28203 Bremen. T. (0421) 74337. 077509
Ziemann, Außer der Schleifmühle 40, 28203 Bremen. T. (0421) 32 44 32, Fax 32 38 28. - Paint / Graph / Sculp - 077510

Bremerhaven (Bremen)
Design Labor Bremerhaven, Karlsburg 9, 27568 Bremerhaven. T. (0471) 460 01. - Graph - 077511
Häfen, Gustav von, Bürgermeister-Smidt-Str. 117, 27568 Bremerhaven. - Paint / Fra - 077512
Kabinett für aktuelle Kunst, Karlsburg 4, 27568 Bremerhaven. T. (0471) 42763. 077513
Teyssen, Hafenstr. 87, 27576 Bremerhaven. T. (0471) 466 39. - Paint / Graph / Repr / Jew / Fra - 077514

Bretten (Baden-Württemberg)
Fuhr, V., Pforzheimer Str 9, 75015 Bretten. T. (07252) 6112. 077515
Goppelsröder, Uta, Melanchthonstr 32, 75015 Bretten. T. (07252) 86398, Fax 87239. - Paint / Graph / China / Sculp / Jew / Glass - 077516

Brilon (Nordrhein-Westfalen)
Dry Mounting, Im Kissen, 59929 Brilon. T. (02961) 80 01. 077517

Brücken (Rheinland-Pfalz)
Genesis, Paulengrunder Str. 16a, 66904 Brücken. T. (06386) 400. 077518

Brüggen (Nordrhein-Westfalen)
Galerie 2000, Genroherstr 54, 41379 Brüggen. T. (02163) 6149. 077519

Brühl (Nordrhein-Westfalen)
Galerie, Mühlenstr 39, 50321 Brühl. T. (02232) 13210. 077520
Link, M., Uhlstr 41-45, 50321 Brühl. T. (02232) 44817. 077521
Morstein, R., Wallstr 66, 50321 Brühl. T. (02232) 43688. 077522
Opitz, H.M., Mühlenstr 79, 50321 Brühl. T. (02232) 13210. 077523
Winterscheid-Barth, Heike, Köln-Str 69-71, 50321 Brühl. T. (02232) 43772. 077524

Buchenbach (Baden-Württemberg)
Galerie im Höllental, Höllentalstr. 16, 79256 Buchenbach. T. (07661) 48 66. - Graph - 077525

Buchholz in der Nordheide (Niedersachsen)
Jolka, Seppenser Mühlenweg 102, 21244 Buchholz in der Nordheide. T. (04181) 7396. - Paint / Graph / China / Draw - 077526

Bückeburg (Niedersachsen)
Das Atelier, Adolf-Holst-Str. 10, 31675 Bückeburg. 077527
Harmening, Peter, Herderstr. 19, 31675 Bückeburg. T. (05722) 57 70. - Paint / Graph / Sculp - 077528

Bühl (Baden-Württemberg)
Zucker, Otto, Grabenstr 6a, 77815 Bühl. - Paint / Fra - 077529

Büsingen (Baden-Württemberg)
Hochleitner, Josef F., Höhenstr 36, 78266 Büsingen. T. (07734) 6778. - Paint / Sculp / Mod - 077530

Büsum (Schleswig-Holstein)
Galerie Manjana, Werftstr. 10-14, 25761 Büsum. T. (04834) 3056. - Paint / Graph / Sculp / Pho - 077531

Burg (Schleswig-Holstein)
Burg-Galerie, Breite Str 41, 23769 Burg. T. (04371) 1222. - Ant / Paint / China / Sculp / Jew / Glass - 077532

Burgdorf (Niedersachsen)
Galerie in der Stadtsparkasse, Marktstr. 59, 31303 Burgdorf. 077533

Buseck (Hessen)
Weppler, H., Am Rinnerborn 45, 35418 Buseck. T. (064 08) 3700. 077534

Buxtehude (Niedersachsen)
Galerie in der Mühle, Ritterstr. 16, 21614 Buxtehude. 077535

Calw (Baden-Württemberg)
Wohlleben, R. & M., Asternweg 5, 75365 Calw. T. (07051) 12617. - Paint / Graph / Fra / Lights / Glass / Draw - 077536

Castrop-Rauxel (Nordrhein-Westfalen)
Krankenhausgalerie, Grutholzallee 21, 44577 Castrop-Rauxel. 077537
Rathausgalerie, Europaplatz 1, 44575 Castrop-Rauxel. T. (02305) 1061, Fax 18440. - Paint / Furn / Draw - 077538

Celle (Niedersachsen)
Bergmann, Kirchweg 29, 29223 Celle. T. (05141) 54983. 077539
Galerie L'Auberge, Winsener Str. 10, 29223 Celle. 077540
Schubert, Barbara, Neue Str. 32, 29221 Celle. 077541

Chemnitz (Sachsen)
„bbb" Bärbels Bunte Bude Volkskunstgalerie, Zwickauerstr. 238, 09116 Chemnitz. 077542
Galerie am Luxor, Hartmannstr 15, 09113 Chemnitz. T. (0371) 34586. - Paint / Graph / Repr / Draw - 077543
Galerie D 19, Karl-Liebknecht-Str 19, 09111 Chemnitz. T. (0371) 429829. 077544
Galerie Hermannstrasse, Hermannstr. 3, 09111 Chemnitz. T. (0371) 40 31 10. - Paint / Graph / China / Sculp / Jew / Glass / Pho - 077545
Galerie in Lehmann's Café, Markersdorfer Str 112, 09123 Chemnitz. T. (0371) 226216. - Paint / Graph / Tex / Pho - 077546
Galerie Oben, Innere Klosterstr 1, 09111 Chemnitz. T. (0371) 61266, Fax 61266. - Paint / Graph / Sculp / Jew / Pho / Mul - 077547
Galerie Schmidt-Rottluff, Markt 1, 09111 Chemnitz. T. (0371) 61107. - Paint / Graph / China / Repr / Sculp / Tex / Jew / Fra / Glass / Draw - 077548
Kunstkreis Rosenkranzq, Max-Planck-Str 46b, 09114 Chemnitz. T. (0371) 32380. 077549
Weise, Hartmannstr 7c, 09111 Chemnitz. T. (0371) 671619, Fax (0371) 671263. 077550

Clausthal-Zellerfeld (Niedersachsen)
Keller, Christel, Reichenberger Str. 13, 38678 Clausthal-Zellerfeld. T. (05323) 19 82. 077551

Cloppenburg (Niedersachsen)
Galerie der Landessparkasse, Stadtmitte, 49661 Cloppenburg. 077552

Cottbus (Brandenburg)
Kunsthandlung am Altmarkt, Altmarkt 29, 03046 Cottbus. T. (0355) 25 020. - Paint / Graph / China / Sculp / Tex / Jew / Glass / Pho / Draw - 077553

Creglingen (Bayern)
Jungblut, Edith, Creglingen, 97991 Creglingen. T. (07933) 7576, Fax (07933) 7576. 077554

Cremlingen (Niedersachsen)
Galerie für Visuelle Erlebnisse, Nordstr. 31, 38162 Cremlingen. 077555

Cuxhaven (Niedersachsen)
Galerie Artica, Westerwischweg 46a, 27474 Cuxhaven. T. (04721) 234 25. 077556
Galerie K, Weidenstieg 4, 27474 Cuxhaven. T. (04721) 34877, Fax 6200. - Paint / Graph / Sculp / Mul / Draw - 077557
Kelleratelier, Kleine Hardewiek 12, 27472 Cuxhaven. T. (04721) 3 33 36. - Paint - 077558

Daaden (Rheinland-Pfalz)
Knautz, Brunhild, Ströther Weg 16, 57567 Daaden. T. (02743) 6102. - Paint / Graph - 077559

Dachau (Bayern)
Eberle, Gottesackerstr. 8a, 85221 Dachau. 077560
Rauchfang, Mittermayerstr. 20, 85221 Dachau. T. (08131) 66 95. - Graph - 077561

Dahn (Rheinland-Pfalz)
Galerie N, Marktstr, Altes Rathaus, 66994 Dahn. T. (06391) 1394, Fax (06391) 769. - Mul - 077562

Darmstadt (Hessen)
Barber, Wilfried, Lucasweg 6, 64287 Darmstadt. 077563
Beckers, Rheinstr 99, 64295 Darmstadt. T. (06151) 899704, Fax 899706. 077564
Bilderkabinett Darmstadt, Wilhelm-Leuschner-Str 22, 64293 Darmstadt. T. (06151) 20878, Fax (06151) 294951. - Paint / Graph / Sculp - 077565
Darmstädter Galerie, Luisenstr. 24, 64283 Darmstadt. T. (06151) 208 99. - Paint / Orient / Jew / Draw - 077566
Galerie arte, Elisabethenstr. 30, 64283 Darmstadt. T. (06151) 215 76. - Ant / Paint / Furn / China / Sculp / Tex / Jew / Silv / Glass / Mod / Toys - 077567
Galerie Garten, Richard-Wagner-Weg 33, 64287 Darmstadt. T. (06151) 74797. 077568
Galerie im Keller-Klub, Schloß, 64283 Darmstadt. T. (06151) 241 10. 077569
Galerie im Schuppen, Arheilger Woogstr. 17, 64291 Darmstadt. T. (06151) 37 33 08. - Paint / China - 077570
Galerie Perspektive, Alte Sackgasse 4, 64297 Darmstadt. T. (06151) 71 35 78. 077571
Hennig, Charlotte, Rheinstr. 18, 64283 Darmstadt. T. (06151) 246 17. - China / Jew / Glass - 077572
Kappler, Herdweg 46, 64285 Darmstadt. T. (06151) 623 21, Fax 62427. - Paint / Graph / Sculp / Mul / Draw - 077573
Kellergalerie Schloß Darmstadt, im Kellerclub, Schloß, 64283 Darmstadt. T. (06151) 241 10. - Paint / Graph / Sculp - 077574
Langheinz, F., Schulstr. 10, 64283 Darmstadt. T. (06151) 242 64. - Repr / Fra - 077575
Netuschil, Adelungstr. 16, 64283 Darmstadt. T. (06151) 249 39, Fax 29 52 80. - Paint / Graph / Sculp / Draw - 077576
Sander, Prinz-Christians-Weg 16, 64287 Darmstadt. T. (06151) 44442. - Paint - 077577
Schloss, Sibylle, Heidelberger Landstr. 280, 64297 Darmstadt. T. (06151) 550 04. - Jew - 077578
Thieme & Pohl, Donnersbergring 22, 64295 Darmstadt. T. (06151) 319981, Fax 319983. - Paint / Graph / Sculp / Pho / Mul / Draw - 077579
Wolf, Gerhard, Friedensplatz, 64283 Darmstadt. T. (06151) 221 66. 077580
Wullkopf, Doris, Dieburger Str. 111, 64287 Darmstadt. T. (06151) 782160, Fax 782159. - Paint / Graph / Sculp - 077581

Dassel (Niedersachsen)
Solling Galerie Deitersen, Am Mooranger 1, Deitersen, 37586 Dassel. T. (05564) 8682. 077582

Datteln (Nordrhein-Westfalen)
Mertins, Jürgen, Provinzialstr. 51, 45711 Datteln. T. (02363) 668 67, Fax 77 19 26. - Paint / Graph / Pho / Draw - 077583

Deggendorf (Bayern)
Hartl, Georg L., Stadtpl. 5, 94469 Deggendorf. T. (0991) 331 21. - Paint / Orient / Sculp - 077584

Deinste (Niedersachsen)
Art Studio 1, Am Schafsteich 1, 21717 Deinste.
T. (04149) 235. - Paint / Graph / Sculp -   077585

Delmenhorst (Niedersachsen)
DEL-Bilderstudio, City-Center, 27749 Delmenhorst.
T. (04221) 17852.   077586

Denklingen (Bayern)
Buchholz, Godula, Unter der Halde 1, 86920 Denklingen.
T. (08869) 08243/1257. - Paint / Graph / Furn / Sculp /
Cur / Draw -   077587

Dessau (Sachsen-Anhalt)
Galerie Schlosstraße, Schloßstr. 10, 06844 Dessau.
T. (0340) 3739.   077588

Detmold (Nordrhein-Westfalen)
Busche, H., Hornsche Str. 26, 32756 Detmold.
T. (05231) 288 96. - Paint / Graph / Repr / Jew / Fra /
Draw -   077589
Die Galerie, Krumme Str. 28, 32756 Detmold.
T. (05231) 35136.   077590

Dettingen unter Teck (Baden-Württemberg)
Uhlig & Polz, Kirchheimer Str. 85, 73265 Dettingen unter
Teck. T. (070 21) 83515.   077591

Deutsch Evern (Niedersachsen)
Kohlstedt, Angelika, Am Petersberg 18, 21407 Deutsch
Evern. T. (04131) 797 86. - Paint -   077592

Diepholz (Niedersachsen)
Die Galerie, Steinstr. 4, 49356 Diepholz.
T. (05441) 4319.   077593

Dießen am Ammersee (Bayern)
Fritz-Winter-Atelier, Forstanger 15a, 86911 Dießen am
Ammersee. T. (08807) 45 59, Fax 45 59.
- Paint -   077594

Dietzenbach (Hessen)
Wagner, Karl-Heinz, Schäfergasse 16, 63128 Dietzen-
bach. T. (06074) 234 38. - Paint / Graph /
Sculp -   077595

Diez (Rheinland-Pfalz)
Walbröhl & Co., Felkestr. 48, 65582 Diez.
T. (06432) 36 01.   077596

Dillenburg (Hessen)
Lebeau, R., Hauptstr. 56, 35683 Dillenburg.
T. (02771) 21699.   077597

Dinkelsbühl (Bayern)
Fricker, Jürgen H., Hechtzwinger, 91550 Dinkelsbühl.
T. (09851) 36 53. - Paint / Graph / Sculp -   077598
Reichstadt-Schabert, Segringerstr. 39, 91550 Dinkels-
bühl. T. (09851) 3123.   077599

Dorfen (Bayern)
Münzenloher, Franz, Furth 1, 84405 Dorfen.
T. (08081) 571, Fax (08081) 1840.   077600

Dormagen (Nordrhein-Westfalen)
Brausen, Hans, Kölner Str. 114, 41539 Dormagen.
T. (02133) 5604.   077601
Kurth, K., Meerbuscher Str. 47, 41540 Dormagen.
T. (02133) 62350.   077602

Dornburg (Hessen)
Schardt, R., Friedenstr 16, 65599 Dornburg.
T. (06436) 1306.   077603

Dornstetten (Baden-Württemberg)
Markt-Galerie, Marktplatz 6 + 7, 72280 Dornstetten.
T. (07443) 3369.   077604

Dortmund (Nordrhein-Westfalen)
Galerie Ambiente, Blickstr 251, 44227 Dortmund.
T. (0231) 770234, Fax (0231) 771926. - Paint / Graph /
Repr / Sculp / Pho / Draw -   077605
Galerie Colonnette, Am Surck 4, 44225 Dortmund.
T. (0231) 77 97 31.   077606

Galerie Hamburg-Münchener, Hohe Str. 28, 44139 Dort-
mund. T. (0231) 182040, Fax 1820468.
- Graph -   077607
Galerie im Gartenhaus, Lotenkamp 3, 44329 Dortmund.
T. (0231) 89862.   077608
Galerie im Hof, Kaiserstr. 46, 44135 Dortmund.
T. (0231) 57 20 35.   077609
Galerie Signal Versicherungen, Joseph-Scherer-Str. 3,
44139 Dortmund. T. (0231) 1352045, Fax 135392045.
- Paint -   077610
Galerie Torhaus Rombergpark, Am Rombergpark, 44225
Dortmund. T. (0231) 542-23194.   077611
Galerie Unikat, Wunnenbergstr. 23, 44229 Dortmund.
T. (0231) 73 13 51.   077612
Henrichsen, Kampstr. 45, 44137 Dortmund.
T. (0231) 14 29 70.   077613
Junge Galerie, Eichlinghofer Str. 22, 44227
Dortmund.   077614
Künstlerhaus, Sunderweg 1, 44147 Dortmund.
T. (0231) 82 03 04. - Paint -   077615
Lamers, Hansastr. 44, 44137 Dortmund.
T. (0231) 57 37 36.   077616
Malten, Helga, Kleppingstr. 28, 44135 Dortmund.
T. (0231) 57 19 66, Fax 522983. - Graph / Sculp / Tex /
Jew -   077617
Postergalerie, Brückstr. 20, 44135 Dortmund.
T. (0231) 52 76 54. - Graph / Repr / Fra / Pho -   077618
Purschke, Wunnenbergstr. 23, 44229 Dortmund.
T. (0231) 73 13 51.   077619
Schneider, Leopoldstr. 10, 44147 Dortmund.
T. (0231) 983 31 18. - Paint -   077620
Studio Galerie, Hirschweg 13, 44269 Dortmund.
T. (0231) 48934. - Paint / Graph / China / Repr / Fra /
Draw -   077621
Türke, Gerda, Johannesstr. 8a, 44137 Dortmund.
T. (0231) 145545. - Paint / Sculp -   077622
Utermann, Betenstr 12, 44137 Dortmund.
T. (0231) 571021, Fax 525026. - Paint / Graph /
Sculp -   077623
Wolnin, Manfred, Hagener Str. 221, 44229 Dortmund.
T. (0231) 73 72 46. - Graph -   077624
Wortkötter, Paul, Gnadenort 3-5, 44135 Dortmund.
T. (0231) 811749. - Ant / Paint / Graph / Furn / China /
Jew / Fra / Silv / Instr -   077625

Dossenheim (Hessen)
Bühler, Ute, & Hanno Böttcher, Richard-Wagner-Str. 11,
69221 Dossenheim. T. (062 21) 864271.
- Paint -   077626

Dresden (Sachsen)
Antik & Design, Dornblüth Str. 9, 01277 Dresden.
T. (0351) 35596, Fax (0351) 35596. - Ant / Paint /
Graph / Furn -   077627
Art+Forum, Rothenburger Str 24, 01099 Dresden.
T. (0351) 571322.   077628
Blaue Fabrik, Prießnitzstr. 44-48 Hof, 01099 Dresden.
T. (0351) 57 41 43, 502 28 07.   077629
Farbtick, Hans-Peter Fischer, Bergmannstr. 21, 01309
Dresden. T. (0351) 33 51 43.   077630
Französisches Kulturzentrum, Kreuzstr. 2, 01067 Dres-
den. T. (0351) 4951478, Fax (0351) 4954108.
- Paint -   077631
Galerie Adlergasse, Adlergasse 14, 01067 Dresden.
T. (0351) 2568411, Fax (0351) 4328968. - Paint /
Graph / Lights -   077632

Galerie am Blauen Wunder, Pillnitzer Landstr. 2, 01326
Dresden. T. (0351) 37020. - Paint / Graph / Sculp / Pho /
Draw -   077633
Galerie am Damm, Peter Eisermann, Dammstr. 2, 01326
Dresden.   077634
Galerie Autogen, Rähnitzgasse 25, 01097 Dresden.
T. (0351) 5022147, Fax (0351) 5022147. - Paint /
Graph / Sculp / Pho / Mul / Draw -   077635
Galerie Dresden Hilton, An der Frauenkirche 5, 01067
Dresden. T. (0351) 484 16 98.   077636
Galerie Finkenstein, Bautzner Landstr 7, 01324 Dres-
den. T. (0351) 36835, Fax (0351) 36835.   077637
Galerie Hieronymus, Angelika Makolies, Malerstr. 21,
01326 Dresden. T. (0351) 37 53 33.   077638
Galerie im Hotel Dresdner Hof, An der Frauenkirche 5,
01067 Dresden.   077639
Galerie Königstraße, Dr. Manfred Heirler, Königstr. 11,
01097 Dresden. T. (0351) 57 82 04   077640
Galerie Kunst der Zeit, Gisela Lincke, Wilsdruffer Str. 7,
01067 Dresden. T. (0351) 4952408.   077641
Galerie Malkasten, An der Frauenkirche 10, 01067 Dres-
den. T. (0351) 495 15 71.   077642
Galerie Mitte, Fetscherpl 7, 01307 Dresden.
T. (0351) 4590052, Fax (0351) 4590052. - Paint /
Graph / Pho / Draw -   077643

Galerie Mosaik, Leipziger Str. 56, 01127 Dresden.
T. (0351) 57 59 79priv. *077644*
Galerie Niederwald, Niederwaldstr. 20, 01309 Dresden.
T. (0351) 3360254. - Paint - *077645*
Galerie Nord, Leipziger Str 54/56, 01127 Dresden.
T. (0351) 55178. - Paint / Graph / Sculp / Draw - *077646*
Galerie Ränitzgasse der Landeshauptstadt Dresden,
Rähnitzgasse 8, 01097 Dresden.
T. (0351) 51456. *077647*
Galerie Süd, Herzberger Str. 30, 01239 Dresden.
T. (0351) 274 21 30. *077648*
Hochschulgalerie, Brühlsche Terrasse 1, 01067 Dresden. T. (0351) 4459415, Fax (0351) 4952023. *077649*
Hübner & Thiel, Pulsnitzer Str 10, 01099 Dresden.
T. (0351) 5670156, Fax (0351) 8013335. - Paint /
Graph / Repr / Sculp / Draw - *077650*
Kühl, Johannes, Zittauer Str. 12, 01099 Dresden.
T. (0351) 55588. - Paint - *077651*
Kühne, R., Bautzner Landstr 7, 01324 Dresden.
T. (0351) 36835. *077652*
Kulturetage Prohlis, Herzberger Str. 30, 01239
Dresden. *077653*
Kunst & Design, Reimann, Lahmannring 19, 01324
Dresden. *077654*
Lehmann, Gebr., Görtlitzer Str 21, 01099 Dresden.
T. (0351) 8011783, Fax (0351)8014905. - Paint /
Graph / Sculp / Draw - *077655*
Nestler-Design, Loschwitzer Str. 58, 01309 Dresden.
T. (0351) 32945, 30190. *077656*
Segor, R., Dr., Boltenhagener Str 20, 01109 Dresden.
T. (0351) 586679. *077657*
Sillack, M., Königsbrücker Landstr. 63, 01109 Dresden.
T. (0351) 584001, Fax (0351) 584001. *077658*
Spieltour Press Verlag, Rothenburger Str 22, 01099
Dresden. T. (0351) 51928. *077659*
Teufel-Holze, Prellerstr 31, 01309 Dresden.
T. (0351) 3360642, Fax (0351) 3360642. *077660*
Wendland, H., Prießnitzstr 21, 01099 Dresden.
T. (0351) 8010684. *077661*

HERBERT EGENOLF
Japanische Holzschnitte,
jap. ill. Bücher, Zeichnungen

Citadellstr. 14, D-40213 Düsseldorf
Tel. 02 11/32 05 50, Fax 13 12 91

USA: c/o Veronica Miller
P. O. Box 1439, Venice, CA 90294
Tel./Fax (310) 581-99 32

Düren (Nordrhein-Westfalen)
Galerie Treppe, Yorckstr. 3, 52351 Düren.
T. (02421) 732 88. - Paint - *077662*
Gilson, Ernst, Kölnstr. 55, 52351 Düren.
T. (02421) 14219. - Ant / Paint / Graph / China /
Fra - *077663*
Heidbüchel, B., Yorckstr. 3, 52351 Düren.
T. (02421) 73288. *077664*
Vetter, Oberstr. 10-12, 52349 Düren. T. (02421) 14638,
10461, Fax (02421) 10616. *077665*
Ziehn & Dickmeis, Kölnstr. 65, 52351 Düren.
T. (02421) 15128, Fax (02421) 15705. - Paint / Graph /
Repr / Sculp / Jew / Rel / Glass / Draw - *077666*

Düsseldorf (Nordrhein-Westfalen)
Achenbach Art Consulting, Kaiserswerther Markt 16,
40489 Düsseldorf. T. (0211) 4089031,
Fax (0211) 4790331. - Paint / Graph / Sculp / Pho /
Mul - *077667*
Ackens, Carl, Oststr. 162, 40210 Düsseldorf.
T. (0211) 36 43 43. - Paint - *077668*
Adler, Dorit, Angeraue 14, 40489 Düsseldorf.
T. (0211) 74 05 64. - Paint / Graph / Sculp - *077669*
Art Consulting, Habsburgerstr. 10, 40547 Düsseldorf.
T. (0211) 58 80 41. *077670*
Art Galerie, Ratinger Str. 23, 40213 Düsseldorf.
T. (0211) 329791, Fax (0211) 555988. - Paint / Graph /
Sculp - *077671*
Art Galerie Leuchter & Peltzer, Ratinger Str 23, 40213
Düsseldorf. T. (0211) 329791,
Fax (0211) 132091. *077672*
Artax, Kölner Str. 26, 40211 Düsseldorf.
T. (0211) 36 55 56, 35 85 64, Fax 35 78 24. - Paint /
Graph / Sculp / Pho / Mul / Draw - *077673*
Artis-Galerie in Firma Heinzelmann, Herderstr. 16,
40237 Düsseldorf. T. (0211) 672047. - Tex - *077674*
Atelier-Galerie, Am Mühlenturm 6, 40489 Düsseldorf.
T. (0211) 40 77 46. - Paint / Graph / Sculp / Fra - *077675*
Bartoldus, Erika, Rochusstr. 58, 40479 Düsseldorf.
T. (0211) 357000. - Paint - *077676*
Begasse, Gabriele, Ludenberger Str. 33, 40629 Düsseldorf. T. (0211) 675218. *077677*
Beletage, Galerie im Studio, Schillerstr. 7, 40237 Düsseldorf. T. (0211) 684800, Fax (0211) 6803160.
- Paint - *077678*
Blaeser, Norbert, Bilker Str 5, 40213 Düsseldorf.
T. (0211) 323180, Fax 328887. - Paint / Graph / Sculp /
Draw - *077679*
Blau, Siegfried, Hohe Str. 16, 40213 Düsseldorf.
T. (0211) 131456, Fax (0211) 322717. - Paint / Graph /
China / Repr / Sculp / Tex / Dec / Fra / Glass / Cur / Pho /
Mul / Draw - *077680*
Bodewig, Hans, Humboldtstr. 17, 40237 Düsseldorf.
T. (0211) 661125. - Paint / Tex - *077681*
Boerner, C.G., Kasernenstr 13, 40213 Düsseldorf.
T. (0211) 131805, Fax (0211) 132177. - Graph /
Draw - *077682*
Bröhan, Torsten, Graf-Recke-Str 30, 40239 Düsseldorf.
T. (0211) 678086, Fax (0211) 672012. - Mod - *077683*
Bugdahn & Kalmer, Mühlengasse 3, 40213 Düsseldorf.
T. (0211) 329140, Fax (0211) 329147. *077684*
Citadellchen, Citadellstr. 27, 40213 Düsseldorf.
T. (0211) 325253. *077685*
Clemens, W., Neusser Str. 115, 40219 Düsseldorf.
T. (0211) 396571, Fax (0211) 592729. - Paint / Graph /
Sculp - *077686*
Conrads, Poststr. 3 40213 Düsseldorf.
T. (0211) 3230720, Fax (0211) 3230722. - Paint /
Sculp / Pho - *077687*
CO10 Galerie, Citadellstr. 10, 40213 Düsseldorf.
T. (0211) 327571. *077688*
Dielemann, Königsallee 30, 40212 Düsseldorf.
- Paint - *077689*
Dinnendahl, Anne, Alte Landstr. 88, 40489 Düsseldorf.
T. (0211) 402118. *077690*
Dünnebacke, Gisela, Graf-Adolf-Str. 18, 40212 Düsseldorf. T. (0211) 13 13 68. - Paint - *077691*
Egenolf, Herbert, Citadellstr. 14, 40213 Düsseldorf.
T. (0211) 320550, Fax 131291. - Graph - *077691a*
EP-Galerie, Marienstr. 10, 40212 Düsseldorf.
T. (0211) 360706, Fax (0211) 351953. - Paint / Graph /
Sculp / Draw - *077692*

Esser, Günther, Schumannstr 55, 40237 Düsseldorf.
T. (0211) 662449. - Paint - *077693*
Fesel, Karin, Prinz-Georg-Str. 104, 40479 Düsseldorf.
T. (0211) 460201, Fax (0211) 480530. - Paint / Graph /
Sculp / Draw - *077694*
Fischer, Konrad, Platanenstr. 7, 40233 Düsseldorf.
T. (0211) 685908, Fax (0211) 689780. - Paint / Graph /
Sculp - *077695*
Förster, Sabrina, Poststr 3, 40213 Düsseldorf.
T. (0211) 323413, Fax (0211) 328218. - Draw - *077696*
Fricke, M. & R., M. & R., Poststr 3, 40213 Düsseldorf.
T. (0211) 323234, Fax (0211) 329569. - Paint - *077697*
Galerie am Dreieck, Münsterstr. 11, 40477 Düsseldorf.
T. (0211) 48 23 19. *077698*
Galerie am Stadtgeschichtlichen Museum, Citadellstr.
25, 40213 Düsseldorf. T. (0211) 327867. *077699*
Galerie Amir, Königsallee 102, 40215 Düsseldorf.
T. (0211) 37 18 31. *077700*
Galerie an der Börse, Klosterstr. 29, 40211 Düsseldorf.
T. (0211) 351575, 351295. *077701*
Galerie Art 204, Rethelstr. 139, 40237 Düsseldorf.
T. (0211) 676501, Fax (0211) 675967. - Paint / Graph /
Fum / Mul / Draw - *077702*
Galerie Beethovenstrasse, Beethovenstr. 3, 40233 Düsseldorf. T. (0211) 689409, Fax (0211) 686453. - Paint /
Graph / Sculp - *077703*
Galerie des Arts, Haroldstr. 32, 40213 Düsseldorf.
T. (0211) 329625, Fax (0211) 329625. - Paint / Graph /
China / Sculp / Fra / Mul / Draw - *077704*
Galerie Eichenwand, Rathelbeckstr. 246, 40627 Düsseldorf. T. (0211) 20 82 70. *077705*
Galerie für Design, Hüttenstr. 40, 40215
Düsseldorf. *077706*
Galerie im Hotel Niko, Immermannstr., 40210 Düsseldorf. - Paint - *077707*
Galerie Mode & Art, Hohe Str. 6, 40213 Düsseldorf.
T. (0211) 32 48 42. *077708*
Galerie Orfèvre, Bastionstr. 31, 40213 Düsseldorf.
T. (0211) 325328. *077709*
Galerie Winkelmann, Neubrückstr. 12, 40213 Düsseldorf. T. (0211) 324387, 329301, Fax (0211) 132267.
- Paint / Graph / Sculp - *077710*
Gmyrek, Wolfgang, Mühlengasse 5, 40213 Düsseldorf.
T. (0211) 327770, Fax (0221) 133993. - Paint / Sculp /
Pho / Draw - *077711*
Hamma, J.C., Lantzallee 36, 40474 Düsseldorf.
T. (0211) 435 07 00. *077712*
Hartmann, Brehmstr. 86, 40239 Düsseldorf.
T. (0211) 631581, Fax (0211) 614892. - Paint - *077713*
Heuser, Margret, Gartenstr 41, 40479 Düsseldorf.
T. (0211) 4931741, Fax 4931738. - Paint / Graph /
Sculp - *077714*

GALERIE MARGRET HEUSER

Gartenstraße 41 · 40479 Düsseldorf
Telefon 02 11/4 93 17 41
Fax 02 11/4 93 17 38

Gemälde · Aquarelle · Graphik
Plastik
Brücke, Blauer Reiter, Bauhaus

Hölzl, Cora, Mutter-Ey-Str. 5, 40213 Düsseldorf.
T. (0211) 326412, 490958, Fax (0211) 131235.
- Paint - *077715*
Holz, Ellen, Bastionstr. 15, 40213 Düsseldorf.
T. (0211) 32 31 33. - Paint / Graph / Sculp /
Draw - *077716*
Hünermann, Hete A.M., Ratinger Tor 2, 40213 Düsseldorf. T. (0211) 325483, Fax (0211) 326339. - Paint /
Graph / Sculp / Draw - *077717*
ID Galerie, Kölner Str 26, 40211 Düsseldorf.
T. (0211) 356319. - Paint / Sculp / Pho / Mul /
Draw - *077718*
Kleinsimlinghaus, Aderstr. 26, 40215 Düsseldorf.
T. (0211) 37 17 70. - Paint / Graph / Sculp / Pho / Mul /
Draw - *077719*

Kollektion-Pergel-Galerie, Talstr. 40, 40217 Düsseldorf.
T. (0211) 37 41 41. - Paint / Graph / Furn /
Sculp - *077720*
Kraushaar, Gabi, Platanenstr. 11, 40233 Düsseldorf.
T. (0211) 6790991, Fax (0211) 6790991. - Paint /
Graph / Sculp / Pho - *077721*
Künstler-Verein Malkasten, Jacobistr. 6, 40211 Düssel-
dorf. T. (0211) 35 64 71. - Paint / Graph - *077722*
Kunstforum Reinhard Franz, Neuburgstr. 18, 40629
Düsseldorf. *077723*
Lahm, Wilhelm, Ludwigstr. 16, 40229 Düsseldorf.
- Paint / Fra - *077724*
Langenkamp, Tabea, Düsseldorfer Str. 25a, 40545 Düs-
seldorf. T. (0211) 572644, Fax (0211) 579763.
- Paint - *077725*
Lingenauber, Eckard, Schwerinstr. 38, 40477 Düssel-
dorf. T. (0211) 494202, Fax (0211) 494202.
- Paint - *077726*
Ludorff, Königsallee 22, 40212 Düsseldorf.
T. (0211) 326566, Fax (0211) 323589. - Paint /
Graph - *077727*
Maier-Hahn, Eiskellerberg 1-3, 40213 Düsseldorf.
T. (0211) 323644, 555187, Fax (0211) 134468.
- Paint / Sculp - *077728*
Mayer, Hans, Grabbeplatz 2, 40213 Düsseldorf.
T. (0211) 132135, Fax (0211) 132948. - Paint - *077729*
Mensendiek, Ingrid, Gerresheimer Landstr. 82, 40627
Düsseldorf. T. (0211) 202190, 201931,
Fax (0211) 254234. - Paint / Graph / Sculp / Glass /
Mod - *077730*
Neumann, Michael, Orangeriestr 6, 40213 Düsseldorf.
T. (0211) 325550, Fax (0211) 324625. - Paint / Graph /
Sculp - *077731*
Niepel, Orangeriestr. 6, 40213 Düsseldorf.
T. (0211) 13 16 66. - Paint / Sculp - *077732*
Paffrath, G., Königsallee 46, 40212 Düsseldorf.
T. (0211) 326405, Fax (0211) 320216. - Paint - *077733*
Parduhn, Ute, Kaiserswerther Markt 6a, 40489 Düssel-
dorf. T. (0211) 400655, Fax (0211) 40670. - Paint /
Draw - *077734*
Peiffer, Bismarckstr. 61, 40210 Düsseldorf.
T. (0211) 36 52 61. *077735*
Rehbock & Co., Hans, Berliner Allee 34-36, 40212 Düs-
seldorf. T. (0211) 36 01 10. *077736*
Remmert & Barth, Bilker Str 20, 40213 Düsseldorf.
T. (0211) 327436, Fax (0211) 322259. - Paint / Graph /
Sculp / Draw - *077737*
Remus, Ruth, Lakronstr. 75, 40625 Düsseldorf.
T. (0211) 28 95 84. *077738*
Rutz, Anita, Schäferstr. 10, 40479 Düsseldorf.
T. (0211) 44 44 42. *077739*
Scheelen, Heinz, Akazienstr. 37, 40627 Düsseldorf.
T. (0211) 20 19 29. - Paint - *077740*
Schoeller, Poststr. 2, 40213 Düsseldorf.
T. (0211) 326532, Fax (0211) 135290. - Paint / Graph /
Sculp / Mul / Draw - *077741*
Schübbe, Christa, Neubrückstr. 6, 40213 Düsseldorf.
T. (0211) 32 85 89. - Paint - *077742*
Schumacher, Postfach 230147, 40087 Düsseldorf.
T. (0211) 672063, Fax 672065. - Paint / Graph / Repr /
Jew / Mul - *077743*
Schwarzer, Klaus, Hüttenstr. 90, 40215 Düsseldorf.
T. (0211) 323658, 374553. - Paint - *077744*
Sels, Clara Maria, Poststr. 3, Atelierhaus, 40213 Düssel-
dorf. T. (0211) 32 80 20, Fax (0211) 32 80 26. *077745*
Söhn, Gerhart, Robert-Reinick-Str. 2, 40474 Düsseldorf.
T. (0211) 4380092, Fax (0211) 4350889.
- Graph - *077746*
Spinrath, Rosenstr. 6, 40479 Düsseldorf.
T. (0211) 44 59 81. - Paint - *077747*
Steinkuhl, Christel, Bilker Str. 22, 40213 Düsseldorf.
T. (0211) 32 98 78. - Paint / Graph / Sculp / Jew /
Lights / Rel - *077748*
Strelow, Hans, Luegpl. 3, 40545 Düsseldorf.
T. (0211) 555503, Fax (0211) 576308. - Paint / Graph /
Sculp / Pho / Draw - *077749*
Strittmatter, Steffi, Hohe Str. 33, 40213 Düsseldorf.
T. (0211) 32 32 35. *077750*
Swetec, Franz, Kasernenstr. 13-IV, 40213 Düsseldorf.
T. (0211) 32 42 47. - Paint - *077751*
Tondorf, Paul, Königstr. 5, 40212 Düsseldorf.
T. (0211) 32 96 66. - Paint / Tex - *077752*

Trouville, An St. Swidbert 12, 40489 Düsseldorf.
T. (0211) 40 16 96. - Paint - *077753*
Valenta, Hans, Prof., Kaiser-Wilhelm-Ring 34, 40545
Düsseldorf. T. (0211) 57 04 32. *077754*
Vieler & Bänder, Neubrückstr. 6+14, 40213 Düsseldorf.
T. (0211) 32 63 61. - Paint / Graph / Sculp / Fra - *077755*
Vömel, Alex, Königsallee 30, 40212 Düsseldorf.
T. (0211) 327422, Fax (0211) 135267. - Paint / Graph /
Sculp - *077756*
Volmer, Königsallee 44, 40212 Düsseldorf.
T. (0211) 32 72 75. - Ant / Paint / Furn / Repr /
Dec - *077757*
Voss, Südstr. 9, 40213 Düsseldorf. T. (0211) 134982,
Fax (0211) 133400. - Paint - *077758*
Walther, Poststr. 7, 40101 Düsseldorf. T. (0211) 28261.
- Paint / Graph - *077759*
Wehrens, Horst, Oststr. 13, 40211 Düsseldorf.
T. (0211) 36 34 38. *077760*
Winkelmann, Neubrückstr. 12, 40213 Düsseldorf.
T. (0211) 32 93 01, Fax 13 22 67. - Paint - *077761*
Wittrock, Wolfgang, Sternstr. 42, 40479 Düsseldorf.
T. (0211) 491 10 35, Fax (0211) 498 10 58. - Paint /
Graph / Sculp - *077762*
Wolf, Bismarckstr. 50, 40210 Düsseldorf.
T. (0211) 13 22 68, Fax (0211) 13 22 69. - Paint /
Graph / Sculp - *077763*
Wunschik, Hubertus, Dianastr. 13, 40223 Düsseldorf.
T. (0211) 309710, Fax (0211) 309710. - Paint / Graph /
Sculp / Pho / Mul / Draw - *077764*
Zimmer, Oberbilker Allee 27, 40215 Düsseldorf.
T. (0211) 332919, Fax (0211) 314381. - Paint - *077765*

Duisburg (Nordrhein-Westfalen)
Artwork Galerien, Lenzmannstr. 16, 47051 Duisburg.
T. (0203) 20710. - Pho - *077766*
Collet, H., Tilsiter Ufer 4, 47279 Duisburg.
T. (0203) 249 11. - Paint / Sculp / Fra - *077767*
Galerie Frühling, Wallstr. 36, 47051 Duisburg. *077768*
Galerie Sammlung Ostarhem Volkram Anton Scharf,
Paschacker 2, 47228 Duisburg. T. (0203) 6 02 35.
- Paint / Graph - *077769*
Genner, August, & Co., Sonnenwall 39, 47051 Duisburg.
T. (0203) 257 77. - Paint / Graph / Repr / Fra - *077770*
Idos, Galerie, Iduna Schnepf, Paschacker 2, 47228 Duis-
burg. T. (0203) 60235. - Paint / Graph / Sculp - *077771*
Künstler- u. Atelierhaus, Goldstr. 15, 47051
Duisburg. *077772*
Luther, Mülheimer Str. 199, 47058 Duisburg.
T. (0203) 33 51 72. - Paint / Graph / China / Sculp / Fra /
Draw - *077773*
Mercatorgalerie, Mercatorstr. 90, 47051 Duisburg.
T. (0203) 264 53. *077774*
Orober, Bismarckpl. 3, 47051 Duisburg. T. (0203) 7165/
67. *077775*
Pesch & Pieper, Kalkweg 175, 47229 Duisburg.
T. (0203) 72 01 09. - Paint / Graph - *077776*

Durmersheim (Baden-Württemberg)
Dollenbacher, E., Auerstr. 44, 76448 Durmersheim.
T. (07245) 29 06. - Paint - *077777*

Eberbach (Baden-Württemberg)
Galerie B, Bahnhofstr 21, 69412 Eberbach.
T. (06271) 2412. *077778*
Polygraphicum, Backgasse 1, 69412 Eberbach.
T. (06271) 1387. *077779*

Eberdingen (Baden-Württemberg)
Stierle, Hanns Peter, Martinstr. 22, 71735 Eberdingen.
T. (07042) 124 91. - Paint / Graph / Draw - *077780*

Ebsdorfergrund (Hessen)
Galerie im Grund, Raingasse 9, 35085 Ebsdorfergrund.
T. (06424) 37 52. - Paint / Graph / Sculp - *077781*

Eckental (Bayern)
Fister, Eckentaler Str. 10, 90542 Eckental.
T. (09126) 4910. *077782*

Eckernförde (Schleswig-Holstein)
NEMO – Kunst in Nordeuropa, Bootshaus am Südstrand,
24340 Eckernförde. T. (04351) 712500, Fax 712501.
- Paint / Graph / Furn / Sculp - *077783*
Studio Capricornus, Domstag 30, 24340 Eckernförde.
T. (04351) 41538. *077784*

Edewecht (Niedersachsen)
Galerie La Voilà, Hauptstr. 132, 26188
Edewecht. *077785*
Micro Hall Art Center, Heidedamm 6, 26182 Edewecht.
T. (04486) 2697, Fax (04486) 6485. - Graph / Pho /
Draw - *077786*
Röhrig, Heidi, Verbindungsweg 35, 26188
Edewecht. *077787*

Egling (Bayern)
Bleymaier, E. A., Schallkofen, 82544 Egling.
T. (08176) 7403. *077788*

Ehingen, Donau (Baden-Württemberg)
Galerie Schloß Mochental, Schloß Mochental, 89584
Ehingen, Donau. T. (07375) 418/19, Fax (07375) 467.
- Ant / Paint / Graph / Repr / Sculp / Mul / Draw - *077789*

Eichendorf (Bayern)
Galerie coArt, Exing 32, 94428 Eichendorf.
T. (09952) 753, Fax (09952) 1228. *077790*

Eisenach (Thüringen)
Fotogalerie im Hause Bohl, Ulrich Kneise, Karlstr. 32,
99817 Eisenach. T. (03691) 3472/72078. - Paint /
Graph / Repr / Pho - *077791*

Eitorf (Nordrhein-Westfalen)
Galerie Icontro, Asbacher Str/Ecke Schümmerichstr.,
53783 Eitorf. T. (02243) 80697, 82088. *077792*

Ellwangen (Baden-Württemberg)
Raible, Aloys, Marktplatz 12, 73479 Ellwangen.
T. (07961) 2281. *077793*

Elmshorn (Schleswig-Holstein)
Galerie Raum + Kunst, In der Burg Vossloch, Haase's
Park, 25335 Elmshorn. T. (04121) 6238. *077794*
Kunstverein, Torhaus, 25335 Elmshorn.
T. (04121) 24677. *077795*

Eltville (Hessen)
Münd, Balduinstr 19, 65343 Eltville. T. (06123) 3245.
- Paint / Graph / Repr / Fra - *077796*
Ribbentrop, Walluferstr 61, 65343 Eltville.
T. (06123) 63626, Fax (06123) 4314. *077797*

Emmerich (Nordrhein-Westfalen)
Galerie De Wette Telder, Steinstr. 15, 46446 Emmerich.
T. (02822) 702 59. - Paint / Graph - *077798*

Emsdetten (Nordrhein-Westfalen)
Ems Galerie, Emsstr 19, 48282 Emsdetten.
T. (02572) 84700. *077799*

Enger (Nordrhein-Westfalen)
Urban, Bahnhofstr 62, 32130 Enger. T. (05224) 4253,
Fax (05224) 4253. - Paint / Graph - *077800*

Erftstadt (Nordrhein-Westfalen)
Palme, Karl-Arnold-Str. 38, 50374 Erftstadt.
T. (022 35) 59 42. - Paint / Graph / Draw - *077801*

Erfurt (Thüringen)
Galerie am Fischmarkt, Fischmarkt 7, 99094 Erfurt.
T. (0361) 6422188, Fax (0361) 6463092.
- Paint - *077802*
Galerie Johannesstraße 178, Johannesstr 178, 99084
Erfurt. - Graph - *077803*

Erlangen (Bayern)
Barthelmeß, Eugen, Heuwaagstr. 12, 91054 Erlangen.
T. (09131) 2 14 50. - Paint / Graph / Fra - *077804*
Csonth, Istvan, Paulistr. 4, 91054 Erlangen.
T. (09131) 211 14. *077805*
Galerie im Gässla, Im Gässla 2, 91058 Erlangen.
T. (09131) 60 27 34, Fax (09131) 60 27 34.
- Paint - *077806*
KVE-Galerie, Marktpl. 1, 91052 Erlangen.
T. (09131) 26867. - Graph - *077807*
Palais Stutterheim, Marktpl. 1, 91054 Erlangen.
- Paint - *077808*
Prapone, D. & G.-M. Bauer, Neue Str. 44, 91054 Erlan-
gen. T. (09131) 20 48 99. *077809*
Rudolph, E., Dompfaffstr. 42, 91056 Erlangen.
T. (09131) 437 35. - Graph - *077810*

Eschborn (Hessen)

Kunstgalerie Apollon, Hauptstr 23, 65760 Eschborn.
T. (06196) 481520, Fax (06196) 43882. - Paint /
Fra –   *077811*

Eschweiler (Nordrhein-Westfalen)

Jantzen, Hanni, Pumpe 2, 52249 Eschweiler.   *077812*
Kazarian, Aleke, Langwahn 96, 52249 Eschweiler.
T. (02403) 25560. - Paint / Fra –   *077813*

Esens (Niedersachsen)

Petersen, H.-Chr., Westerstr. 17, 26427 Esens.
T. (04971) 13 83. - Paint / Graph / Draw –   *077814*

Essen (Nordrhein-Westfalen)

AKS Holographie-Galerie, Potsdamer Str. 10, 45145 Essen. T. (0201) 70 45 62.   *077815*
Essener Forum bildender Künstler, Alfredistr. 2, 45127
Essen. T. (0201) 22 65 38. - Paint / Graph /
Sculp –   *077816*
Essener Glasgalerie, Annastr. 74, 45130 Essen.
T. (0201) 773612, Fax (0201) 791010. - Glass - *077817*
Ester, Margret, Humboldtstr. 301, 45149 Essen. *077818*
Galerie Aviva, Bungertstr. 21, 45239 Essen.
T. (0201) 49 47 45, Fax (0201) 49 47 45.   *077819*
Galerie im Hof, Neukircher Str. 1, 45239 Essen.
T. (0201) 491403, Fax (0201) 493105. - Paint - *077820*
Galerie KK, Rüttenscheider Str. 73, 45130 Essen.
T. (0201) 78 82 66.   *077821*
Galerie 25, Eduard-Lucas-Str. 25, 45131 Essen.
T. (0201) 41 06 16. - Paint / Graph / Sculp / Fra - *077822*
Galerie 33, Vereinstr. 21, 45127 Essen.
T. (0201) 23 98 97. - Paint / Graph -   *077823*
Gramolla, B., Freiheit 2, 45128 Essen.
T. (0201) 23 03 27.   *077824*
Heimeshoff, Moltkepl. 5, 45138 Essen.
T. (0201) 263742. - Paint / Graph / Sculp -   *077825*
Heimeshoff, Kennedypl. 5, 45127 Essen.
T. (0201) 230490, Fax (0201) 235949. - Paint / Graph /
Sculp –   *077826*
Honnef, Ursula, Jürgengang 18, 45138 Essen.
T. (0201) 28 14 73. - Paint –   *077827*
Husmann, Claus, Dr., Heierbusch 22, 45133 Essen.
T. (0201) 42 03 72. - Paint –   *077828*
Kiefer, K., Rüttenscheider Str. 73, 45130 Essen.
T. (0201) 78 82 66.   *077829*
Klein, Hans, Lindenallee 73-75, 45127 Essen.
T. (0201) 22 63 28, Fax (0201) 28 91 65. - Paint /
Graph / Repr / Fra –   *077830*
Kruft, G., Annastr. 74, 45130 Essen.
T. (0201) 77 36 12.   *077831*
Kunsthaus Essen, Rubezahlstr. 33, 45134 Essen.
T. (0201) 443313, Fax (0201) 472241. - Paint - *077832*
Marre & Dahms, Gerlingstr. 47, 45127 Essen.
T. (0201) 22 44 00, Fax (0201) 22 45 00.
- Paint –   *077833*
Naiv Art Studio, Bochumer Landstr. 216, 45276 Essen.
T. (0201) 53 59 06. - Paint / Sculp –   *077834*
Neher, Moltkepl. 61, 45027 Essen. T. (0201) 266990,
Fax (0201) 2669943 - Paint / Graph –   *077835*
Neuffer, In der Borbeck 48-50, 45239 Essen.
T. (0201) 49 47 01, Fax (0201) 49 45 58.
- Paint -   *077836*
Ranke-Heinemann, Johannes, Schnutenhausstr. 44,
45136 Essen.   *077837*
Reimus, Dagmar, Velberter Str. 81, 45239 Essen.
T. (0201) 40 84 40, Fax (0201) 40 83 62. - Paint /
Sculp / Draw –   *077838*
Schmidt, H., Kleiststr. 4, 45128 Essen.
T. (0201) 23 43 68.   *077839*
Schütte, Bornstr. 15, 45127 Essen. T. (0201) 202510,
Fax (0201) 207848. - Paint / Graph / Sculp /
Draw –   *077840*

Esslingen (Baden-Württemberg)

Galerie im Heppächer, Im Heppächer 3, 73728 Esslingen. T. (0711) 356412, Fax (0711) 356412. - Paint /
Graph / Sculp / Fra / Pho / Mul / Draw –   *077841*
Galerie in der Baden-Württembergischen Bank, Ritterstr,
73728 Esslingen.   *077842*
Galerie Kreissparkasse, Bahnhofstr 8, 73728
Esslingen.   *077843*
Köder, Waldemar, Berliner Str 5, 73728 Esslingen.
- Paint / Graph / Repr / Fra –   *077844*
Künstlergilde, Hafenmarkt 2, 73728 Esslingen.
T. (0711) 3969010. - Paint –   *077845*
Kunsthaus Huggele, Küferstr 52, 73728 Esslingen.
T. (0711) 359036. - Ant / Paint / Graph / Furn / Repr /
Fra –   *077846*
Kunstkabinett, Unterer Metzgerbach 9, 73728 Esslingen.
T. (0711) 356177, Fax (0711) 75956. - Paint /
Graph -   *077847*
Schaller, Oberer Metzgerbach 26, 73728 Esslingen.
T. (0711) 356337, Fax (0711) 3508058.
- Paint -   *077848*
Volksbank-Galerie, Fabrikstr 5, 73728 Esslingen.
T. (0711) 39090, Fax (0711) 3909367.   *077849*
Zeisel-Audy, P., Rotenackerstr 43, 73732 Esslingen.
T. (0711) 373060.   *077850*

Ettenheim (Baden-Württemberg)

Treiber, Linda, Münstertalstr. 34, 77955 Ettenheim.
T. (07822) 54 64. - Paint / Graph / Sculp /
Draw -   *077851*

Ettlingen (Baden-Württemberg)

Fuchs, G., Markstr. 16, 76275 Ettlingen.
T. (07243) 793 33. - Paint –   *077852*

Euskirchen (Nordrhein-Westfalen)

Hausen, Luisa, Wilhelmstr. 67, 53879 Euskirchen.
T. (02251) 2969.   *077853*
Rathaus-Galerie, Baumstr. 13, 53879 Euskirchen.
T. (02251) 712 50, Fax (02251) 543 55. - Paint / Graph /
Sculp / Fra –   *077854*

Eutin (Schleswig-Holstein)

Galerie Schwedenkate, Krete 6, 23701 Eutin.
T. (04521) 4580.   *077855*

Fahrdorf, Holstein (Schleswig-Holstein)

Lütt Galerie, Strandholm 2, 24253 Fahrdorf, Holstein.
T. (04333) 33989.   *077856*

Feldkirchen-Westerham (Bayern)

Atelier am Berg, Am Berg 26, 83620 Feldkirchen-Westerham. T. (08063) 7711. - Paint –   *077857*

Felsberg (Hessen)

Ahle Schiere, Melsunger Str. 22, 34587
Felsberg.   *077858*

Filderstadt (Baden-Württemberg)

Galerie und Edition Michael Domberger, Hölderlinstr. 4-6, 70794 Filderstadt. T. (0711) 77 20 40,
Fax (0711) 777 58 70.   *077859*

Fischen (Bayern)

Poggi, Obermühlegg 2, 87538 Fischen. T. (08326) 699.
- Paint / Graph / Sculp –   *077860*

Flensburg (Schleswig-Holstein)

Danielsen, Rote Str. 18, 24937 Flensburg.
T. (0461) 12862.   *077861*
Galerie am Museum, Rathausstr 20, 24937 Flensburg.
T. (0461) 26701.   *077862*
Galerie Trapez, Norderstr. 89, 24939 Flensburg.
T. (0461) 29939.   *077862a*

Galerie United Status, Fruerlunder Str. 44, 24943
Flensburg.   *077863*
Kruse, E., Rote Str. 22, 24937 Flensburg.
T. (0461) 220 63. - Paint / Repr-   *077864*
Liebmann, Peter, Norderstr. 89, 24939
Flensburg.   *077865*

Flintbek (Schleswig-Holstein)

Hartz, Anke, Bergkoppel 19, 24220 Flintbek.
T. (04347) 39 60. - Paint –   *077866*

Forstinning (Bayern)

Galerie S, Buchenstr. 10, 85661 Forstinning.
T. (08121) 18 88. - Graph –   *077867*

Frankfurt am Main (Hessen)

Achenbach, Hedderichstr 108-110, 60596 Frankfurt am
Main. T. (069) 621024, Fax (069) 611282.   *077869*
Adeniran, Diesterwegstr 10, 60594 Frankfurt am Main.
T. (069) 612776.   *077870*
Aichelmann, U., Uhlandstr 48, 60314 Frankfurt am Main.
T. (069) 442566.   *077871*
AL Galerie, Mainzer Landstr 695, 65934 Frankfurt am
Main. T. (069) 397725.   *077872*
Appel & Fertsch, Corneliusstr 30, 60325 Frankfurt am
Main. T. (069) 749377, Fax (069) 7410669. - Paint /
Sculp –   *077873*
Aquiles, Hanauer Landstr 3, 60314 Frankfurt am Main.
T. (069) 444010.   *077874*
Art to use, Eschersheimer Landstr 5-7, 60322 Frankfurt
am Main. T. (069) 599110, Fax (069) 595054.
- Graph -   *077875*
Artelier, Niddastr 66-68, 60329 Frankfurt am Main.
T. (069) 253061, Fax (069) 251735.   *077876*
Asian Trade Center, Kaiserhofstr 10, 60313 Frankfurt am
Main. T. (069) 296599.   *077877*
Atelier 695, Mainzer Landstr 695, 65934 Frankfurt am
Main. T. (069) 397725.   *077878*
Ausstellungsraum, Alte Mainzer Gasse 4-6, 60311
Frankfurt am Main. T. (069) 60500868.   *077879*
Bellen, E., Wallstr 23, 60594 Frankfurt am Main.
T. (069) 64604301.   *077880*
Berger, Berger Str 84, 60316 Frankfurt am Main.
T. (069) 440600.   *077881*
Besler, Holzgraben 11b, 60313 Frankfurt am Main.
T. (069) 285777, 296608.   *077882*
Bild & Kunst 410, Eschersheimer Landstr 410, 60433
Frankfurt am Main. T. (069) 511180, Fax (069) 524162.
- Paint / Graph / Fra / Mod –   *077883*
Das Bilderhaus, Hermannstr 41, 60318 Frankfurt am
Main. T. (069) 557058.   *077884*
Brieke, Tilsiter Str 10, 60487 Frankfurt am Main.
T. (069) 793020. - Pho –   *077885*
CMC-Art, Christiana Crueger, Offenbacher Landstr 7,
60599 Frankfurt am Main. T. (069) 612712,
Fax (069) 612712. - Paint / Graph –   *077886*
Creative Support, Konstanzer Str 3, 60386 Frankfurt am
Main. T. (069) 419106.   *077887*
Detterer, Martina, Hanauer Landstr 20-22, 60314 Frankfurt am Main. T. (069) 491613, Fax (069) 492922.
- Mul –   *077888*
Durhammer, Klingerstr 8, 60313 Frankfurt am Main.
T. (069) 289293.   *077889*
Ehrler, W., Fahrgasse 23, 60311 Frankfurt am Main.
T. (069) 283357.   *077890*
Eurasia-Galeria, Egenolffstr 396, 60316 Frankfurt am
Main. T. (069) 439329.   *077891*
Exler, Fahrgasse 6, 60311 Frankfurt am Main.
T. (069) 283818.   *077892*
Fach, Joseph, Fahrgasse 8, 60311 Frankfurt am Main.
T. (069) 287761, Fax 285844. - Paint / Graph / Sculp /
Mod –   *077893*

1947 ——————————— **50 JAHRE** ——————————— **1997**

GALERIE FRANKFURTER KUNSTKABINETT HANNA BEKKER VOM RATH
Zeitgenössische Kunst und Klassische Moderne

**BRAUBACHSTRASSE 14–16 (PARKHAUS RÖMER) D-60311 FRANKFURT / MAIN
TELEFON (0 69) 28 10 85 · TELEFAX (0 69) 28 06 87
Di.–Fr. 11–18 Uhr Sa. 11–14 Uhr**

Fichter, H.W., Arndtstr 49, 60325 Frankfurt am Main.
T. (069) 746741, Fax (069) 747946.   077894

Filupeit, Peter-Bied-Str 42, 65929 Frankfurt am Main.
T. (069) 3300850, Fax (069) 33008530.
- Graph -   077895

Fischer, Nikolaus, Braubachstr 32, 60311 Frankfurt am
Main. T. (069) 292447, Fax (069) 2977978. - Paint /
Graph / Draw -   077896

Fluxus Plakatgalerie, Leipziger Str 11b, 60487 Frankfurt
am Main. T. (069) 774521. - Graph -   077897

forme, Mainluststr 8, 60329 Frankfurt am Main.
T. (069) 251490.   077898

Forum Frankfurter Sparkasse, Töngesgasse 40, 60255
Frankfurt am Main. T. (069) 21702234, 21702058,
Fax (069) 287507. - Paint -   077899

Frankfurter Kunstkabinett Hanna Bekker vom Rath,
Braubachstr 14-16, 60311 Frankfurt am Main.
T. (069) 281085, Fax 280687. - Paint / Sculp /
Draw -   077900

Frankfurter Westend Galerie, Arndtstr 12, 60325 Frankfurt am Main T. (069) 746752, Fax (069) 7411453.
- Paint / Graph / Sculp / Draw -   077901

Frick, D., Im Trutz Frankfurt 32, 60322 Frankfurt a Main.
T. (069) 551913.   077901a

Friedmann-Guinness Gallery, Braubachstr 32, 60311
Frankfurt am Main. T. (069) 296246,
Fax (069) 280157.   077902

Gärtner, Michael, Kaiserhofstr 16, Schweizer Str 67,
60313 u 60594 Frankfurt am Main. T. (069) 281672,
624614, Fax (069) 289531.   077903

Galerie ak, Gartenstr 47, 60596 Frankfurt am Main.
T. (069) 622104, Fax (069) 6032207. - Paint / Graph /
Sculp / Draw -   077904

Galerie Aurum, Oppenheimer Landstr 42, 60596 Frankfurt am Main. T. (069) 627726. - Paint -   077905

Galerie Bernauer Berg, Textorstr 58, 60594 Frankfurt
am Main. T. (069) 628744, Fax (069) 628744.
- Paint -   077906

Galerie Königsforum, Auf der Körnerwiese 2, 60323
Frankfurt am Main. T. (069) 592508, 5963277. 077907

Galerie Plakart, Oeder Weg 43, 60318 Frankfurt am
Main. T. (069) 595449. - Graph -   077908

Galerie Spectrum, Frauenlobstr 76, 60487 Frankfurt am
Main.   077909

Galerie & Edition Artelier, Niddastr 66-68, 60329 Frankfurt am Main. T. (069) 253061.   077910

Galerie Vetro, Oeder Weg 29, 60322 Frankfurt am Main.
T. (069) 551279, Fax (069) 592221. - Glass -   077911

Galleria, Berliner Str 66, 60311 Frankfurt am Main.
T. (069) 281461. - Paint -   077912

Galleria Scandinavia, Hamburger Allee 37, 60486 Frankfurt am Main. T. (069) 771645.   077913

Gering, Ulrich, Textorstr 91, 60596 Frankfurt am Main.
T. (069) 625116, Fax (069) 629504. - Paint / Graph /
Draw -   077914

Gierig, Timm, Weckmarkt 17, 60311 Frankfurt am Main.
T. (069) 287111, Fax (069) 283687. - Paint / Graph /
Sculp / Draw -   077915

Giessen, Julius, Hochstr 48, 60313 Frankfurt am Main.
T. (069) 287679. - Paint / Graph / Repr / Fra /
Draw -   077916

Grässlin, Bärbel, Bleichstr 48, 60313 Frankfurt am Main.
T. (069) 280961/2, Fax (069) 294277. - Paint / Graph /
Sculp -   077917

Graphisches Kabinett im Westend, Barckhausstr 6,
60325 Frankfurt am Main. T. (069) 728015.   077918

Gres, Koselstr 5, 60318 Frankfurt am Main.
T. (069) 599202, Fax 5973375. - Paint / Graph / China /
Sculp / Fra / Draw -   077919

Günther, K., Auf der Körnerwiese 19, 60322 Frankfurt
am Main. T. (069) 553292.   077920

Haarscharf, Basaltstr, 60487 Frankfurt am
Main.   077921

Hänel, Frank, Braubachstr 26, 60311 Frankfurt am
Main. T. (069) 294664, 552609, 4693537, 415544,
Fax (069) 295873. - Paint / Graph / Sculp / Pho /
Draw -   077922

Hagemeier, Joachim, Neue Mainzer Str 60, 60311
Frankfurt am Main. T. (069) 294121, Fax (069) 289965.
- Paint -   077923

Harder, J., Auf der Kuhr 40, 60435 Frankfurt am Main.
T. (069) 544782.   077924

Hartje, K.C., Holbeinstr 33, 60596 Frankfurt am Main.
T. (069) 628695.   077925

Heil, I, Hochstr 47, Merianstr 23, 60313 u 60316
Frankfurt am Main. T. (069) 291900, 288718,
492824.   077926

Herber, Fahrgasse 21, 60311 Frankfurt am Main.
T. (069) 2979741.   077927

Heussenstamm'sche Stiftung, Barckhausstr 1-3, 60325
Frankfurt am Main. T. (069) 724667. - Paint /
Graph -   077928

Himmighoffen, Schillerstr 28, Steinkleestr 15, 60313
Frankfurt am Main. T. (069) 284066, 542054,
Fax (069) 541523. - Paint / Graph / Repr / Fra - 077929

Hoeppner, Hans, Bockenheimer Landstr 2-4, 60323
Frankfurt am Main. T. (069) 724420. - Paint /
Graph -   077930

Huber-Nising, Saalgasse 6, 60311 Frankfurt am Main.
T. (069) 20213, Fax 289130. - Paint / Graph -   077931

IKON, Deutschherrnufer 32, 60594 Frankfurt am Main.
T. (069) 615026.   077932

Japan Art Galerie, Braubachstr 9, 60311 Frankfurt am
Main. T. (069) 282839.   077933

Jessen, P., Eichthaler Str 5, 60435 Frankfurt am Main.
T. (069) 5488257.   077934

Klier, A., Töngesgasse 7, 60311 Frankfurt am Main.
T. (069) 282781.   077935

Knabe, Francoise, Weckmarkt 7-9, 60311 Frankfurt am
Main. T. (069) 282847, 281070, Fax (069) 20250.
- Paint / Graph / Sculp -   077936

Koch, W.A. & Sabine, Fürstenbergerstr 162, 60322
Frankfurt am Main. T. (069) 555337, Fax (069) 551063.
- Graph -   077937

Kraus, G., Zehnmorgenstr 5, 60433 Frankfurt am Main.
T. (069) 523073.   077938

Krause, Helmut, Postfach 160454, 60067 Frankfurt am
Main. T. (06105) 74306, Fax 74190. - Ant /
Paint -   077939

Künstlerhaus Mousonturm, Waldschmidtstr 4, 60316
Frankfurt am Main. T. (069) 4058950,
Fax (069) 40589540. - Paint / Graph / Sculp /
Pho -   077940

Kunst und Rahmen Atelier, Alt-Rödelheim 17, 60489
Frankfurt am Main. T. (069) 787174.   077941

Kunsthandlung Rötzel, Berliner Str 42 u 20, 60311
Frankfurt am Main. T. (069) 282548, Fax (069) 287385.
- Paint / Graph / Repr / Fra / Rel -   077942

L.A. Galerie, Domstr 6, 60311 Frankfurt am Main.
T. (069) 288687, Fax (069) 280912. - Paint /
Pho -   077943

Land in Sicht, Rotteckstr 13, 60316 Frankfurt am Main.
T. (069) 443095, Fax (069) 4909266. - Ant -   077944

Loehr, Dorothea, Alt Niederursel 41, 60439 Frankfurt am
Main. T. (069) 57 58 55. - Paint / Graph / Sculp / Pho /
Mul / Draw -   077945

Lüpke, Klaus, Braubachstr 37, 60014 Frankfurt am
Main. T. (069) 291134, Fax (069) 294792. - Paint /
Graph / Sculp / Fra -   077946

Lugert, Peter, Siesmayerstr 9, 60323 Frankfurt am Main.
T. (069) 752337.   077947

Lunsford, C., Kurfürstenstr 3, 60486 Frankfurt am Main.
T. (069) 775443.   077948

Majchrzak, C., Königsteiner Str 69, 65929 Frankfurt am
Main. T. (069) 333354.   077949

Mellendijk und De Sehm, Fahrgasse 87, 60311 Frankfurt
am Main. T. (069) 284342.   077950

Metropolis, Schillerpassage, Frankfurt am Main.
T. (069) 1310466.   077951

Meyer-Ellinger, Brönnerstr. 22, 60313 Frankfurt am
Main. T. (069) 292994, Fax (069) 296297. - Paint /
Graph / Sculp -   077952

Miller, von, Braubachstr 33, 60311 Frankfurt am Main.
T. (069) 292519, Fax (069) 292519. - Paint / Sculp /
Tex / Eth -   077953

modern art galerie, Brückenstr 32, 60594 Frankfurt am
Main. T. (069) 627878.   077954

Morbe, Thomas, De-Neufville-Str 7, 60599 Frankfurt am
Main. T. (069) 656201. - Orient / Arch / Eth / Jew / Silv /
Cur -   077955

Museumsgalerie, Bornwiesenweg 14, 60322 Frankfurt
am Main. T. (069) 550077, Fax (069) 590894. - Graph /
Repr / Sculp / Jew -   077956

Neuendorf, Beethovenstr 71, 60325 Frankfurt am Main.
T. (069) 748066, Fax (069) 746947. - Paint / Sculp /
Draw -   077957

Oevermann, Kristine, Dr., Krögerstr 6, 60313 Frankfurt
am Main. T. (069) 295708, Fax (069) 289909. - Paint /
Graph / Sculp / Draw -   077958

Ostertag, Hans, Siesmayerstr 9, 60323 Frankfurt am
Main. T. (069) 748808. - Paint / Graph / Sculp /
Draw -   077959

Ostheimer – v. Miller, Braubachstr 33, 60311 Frankfurt
am Main. T. (069) 292519. - Paint / Sculp /
Eth -   077960

Otto, Manfred, Schwanthaler Str 53, 60596 Frankfurt
am Main. T. (069) 617350, Fax (069) 616826.
- Paint -   077961

Pabst, Helmut, Saalgasse 26, 60311 Frankfurt am Main.
T. (069) 2977353.   077962

Paraskevova, J., Dr., Diesterwegstr 29, 60594 Frankfurt
am Main. T. (069) 628845.   077963

Poller, Thomas, Neue Mainzer Str 60, 60311 Frankfurt
am Main. T. (069) 285269, Fax (069) 288869. - Paint /
Sculp -   077964

Portikus, Schöne Aussicht 2, 60311 Frankfurt am Main.
T. (069) 60500830, Fax 60500831. - Paint / Pho /
Draw / Sculp -   077965

Poster-Galerie, Hasengasse 2, 60311 Frankfurt am
Main. T. (069) 294252.   077966

Prestel, F.A.C., Braubachstr 30-32, 60311 Frankfurt am
Main. T. (069) 284744. - Paint / Graph / Sculp - 077967

Raphael, Domstr 6, 60311 Frankfurt am Main.
T. (069) 291338, Fax 2977532. - Paint / Graph /
Fra -   077968

DR. EWALD RATHKE

KUNST XX. JAHRHUNDERT
60323 FRANKFURT AM MAIN
ROSSERTSTRASSE 4
FERNSPRECHER (069) 72 22 55
FAX (069) 72 22 56

Rathke, Ewald, Dr, Rossertstr 4, 60323 Frankfurt am Main. T. (069) 722255, Fax 722256. - Paint / Graph - 077969

raum für kunst, Saalgasse 22, 60311 Frankfurt am Main. T. (069) 287729, Fax 287729. 077970

Reichard, Bernusstr 18, 60487 Frankfurt am Main. T. (069) 706860, Fax (069) 708771. - Paint / Graph / Sculp / Mod - 077971

Richert, Dieter P., Im Trutz Frankfurt 13, 60313 Frankfurt am Main. T. (069) 283381. - Paint / Tex / Fra / Rel / Ico / Draw - 077972

Ritter-Moritz, Beatrix, Flörsheimer Str 9, 60326 Frankfurt am Main. T. (069) 734533. - Paint / Graph / Draw - 077973

Rothe, Maria, Barckhausstr 6, 60325 Frankfurt am Main. T. (069) 722717, Fax (069) 728320. - Paint - 077974

Rothenstein, Auf der Kuhr 40, 60435 Frankfurt am Main. T. (069) 644782. - Paint / Graph / Draw - 077975

Rumscheidt, S., Eschersheimer Landstr 410, 60433 Frankfurt am Main. T. (069) 511180. 077976

Ruppel, K., Schweizer Str 44, 60594 Frankfurt am Main. T. (069) 611279. - Paint / Fra - 077977

Schneider, J.P., Roßmarkt 23, 60311 Frankfurt am Main. T. (069) 281033, 281034, Fax (069) 287416. - Paint / Sculp / Draw - 077978

Schütz, Schöne Aussicht 6, 60311 Frankfurt am Main. T. (069) 299170, Fax (069) 295200. - Paint / Graph - 077979

Schwind, Braubachstr 24, 60311 Frankfurt am Main. T. (069) 287072, Fax (069) 287804. - Paint - 077980

Siebert, Fritz, Berliner Str 68, 60311 Frankfurt am Main. T. (069) 284685, Fax (069) 541523. - Paint / Graph / Repr / Dec / Fra / Lights - 077981

Simon, U., Dr., Sachsenhäuser Landwehrweg 60, 60598 Frankfurt am Main. T. (069) 682441. 077982

Slutzky, Bernd, Friedrichstr 8, 60323 Frankfurt am Main. T. (069) 723940, Fax (069) 172799. - Paint / Graph / Sculp - 077983

Soosten, Karsko von, Klingerstr 8, 60313 Frankfurt am Main. T. (069) 287456. 077984

Stepping, I., Oppenheimer Landsstr 42, 60596 Frankfurt am Main. T. (069) 627726. 077985

Stolzenberg, Kurt G., Große Seestr 63, 60486 Frankfurt am Main. T. (069) 701379. 077986

Sworowski, Hans, Gartenstr 47, 60596 Frankfurt am Main. T. (069) 622104, Fax (069) 6032207. - Paint - 077987

Tabrizian, Ali Asghar, Westhafen 5, 60327 Frankfurt am Main. T. (069) 231581. - Tex - 077988

Teutschbein, Weckmarkt 7, 60311 Frankfurt am Main. T. (069) 288516. 077989

Urlass, Rüdiger, Fahrgasse 19, 60311 Frankfurt am Main. T. (069) 295727, 284932, Fax (069) 284932. 077990

U4 frAnKfuRT, Berger Str 329, 60385 Frankfurt am Main. T. (069) 466970. - Paint - 077991

Viertel, Wolfhard, Braubachstr 12, 60311 Frankfurt am Main. T. (069) 293903, Fax (069) 293578. - Paint - 077992

Voges und Deisen, Weberstr 23, 60318 Frankfurt am Main. T. (069) 557454, 551028. 077993

Voll, Kurfürstenstr 8a, 60486 Frankfurt am Main. T. (069) 173845. 077994

Vonderbank, Goethestr 11, 60313 Frankfurt am Main. T. (069) 282490, Fax (069) 296148. - Paint / Graph / Repr / Fra - 077995

Vonderbank, Goethestr 11, 60313 Frankfurt am Main. T. (069) 282490, Fax (069) 296148. 077996

Werkstatt der Phantasie, Schwanthaler Str 10, 60594 Frankfurt am Main. T. (069) 615980. - Graph - 077997

Westpoint, Grünburgweg 25, 60322 Frankfurt am Main. T. (069) 173845. 077998

Wild, E.M., Bettinastr 30, 60325 Frankfurt am Main. T. (069) 7410823, Fax (069) 7411881. - Paint / Graph / Sculp / Lights - 077999

Wilhelm, Otto, Gellertstr 24, 60389 Frankfurt am Main. T. (069) 454472. - Paint - 078000

Woeller-Paquet, T., Schneckenhofstr 10, 60596 Frankfurt am Main. T. (069) 623819. 078001

Frankfurt/Oder (Brandenburg)

Galerie Gallus, Rosa-Luxemburg-Str. 43a, 15230 Frankfurt/Oder. T. (0335) 22979. - Paint / Graph / China / Jew / Glass / Draw - 078002

Haus der Künste, St. Spiritus, Lindenstr. 4 7, 15230 Frankfurt/Oder. T. (0335) 22393. 078003

Frechen (Nordrhein-Westfalen)

Erdtmann, M., Hauptstr. 132, 50226 Frechen. T. (02234) 159 09. 078004

Kewenig, Jule, Mauritiusstr 102/4, 50226 Frechen. T. (02234) 12039, Fax (02234) 53786. 078005

Kewenig, Jule, Mauritiusstr. 102-104, 50226 Frechen. T. (02234) 12039, Fax (02234) 53786. - Paint / Graph / Sculp / Pho / Mul / Draw - 078006

Frei-Laubersheim (Rheinland-Pfalz)

Apollon Galerie, Scharrenberg 2, 55546 Frei-Laubersheim. T. (06709) 701. - Paint - 078007

Freiberg (Sachsen)

Schiffner, Klaus, Korngasse 4, 09599 Freiberg. T. (03731) 47454, Fax (03731) 47454. 078008

Freiberg am Neckar (Baden-Württemberg)

Gundel, Karin, Hertzstr 5, 71691 Freiberg am Neckar. 078009

Freiburg (Baden-Württemberg)

Art Club Kunstforum, Schwarzwaldstr. 30, 79102 Freiburg. T. (0761) 725 48. - Paint - 078010

Baumgarten, Mühlenstr 2, 79102 Freiburg. T. (0761) 35298, Fax (0761) 35212. - Paint / Graph / Sculp / Draw - 078011

BBK Werkstatt, Metzgerau 4, 79098 Freiburg. T. (0761) 344 99. - Paint - 078012

BBK-Werkstatt Mehlwaage, Metzgerau 4, 79098 Freiburg. T. (0761) 34499. - Paint - 078013

Blau, Dorfstr 10, 79280 Freiburg. T. (0761) 407898, Fax 408860. - Furn / Sculp / Draw - 078014

Blendwerk Galerie, Marienstr. 13, 79098 Freiburg. T. (0761) 35095, Fax (0761) 35095. - Repr / Fra - 078015

Correa, Ruta, Goethestr 3, 79100 Freiburg. T. (0761) 74163, Fax (0761) 702624. - Paint / Graph / Sculp / Pho / Mul / Draw - 078016

E-Werk Freiburg, Hallen für Kunst, Ferdinand-Weiss-Str 6a, 79106 Freiburg. T. (0761) 280322. - Paint - 078017

Eberwein, Gerberau 5a, 79098 Freiburg. T. (0761) 34921, Fax (0761) 283453. - Paint / Graph / China / Repr / Sculp - 078018

Friedrich, Kurt, Friedrichstr. 27, 79098 Freiburg. T. (0761) 377 68. - Paint / Fra - 078019

Galerie G, Reichsgrafenstr 10, 79102 Freiburg. T. (0761) 77657, Fax (0761) 706378. - Paint / Draw - 078020

Galerie Pro Arte, Schwabentorpl 6, 79098 Freiburg. T. (0761) 37768, Fax (0761) 286602. - Paint / Graph / Sculp / Draw - 078021

Hass, Barbara, Adlerstr. 7, 79098 Freiburg. T. (0761) 22831, 30643. 078022

Kaiser, M.G., Mühlenstr. 2, 79102 Freiburg. T. (0761) 345 74. 078023

Kleine Galerie, Gerberau 15, 79098 Freiburg. 078024

Limmer, Maria-Theresia-Str 15, 79102 Freiburg. T. (0761) 75999, Fax (0761) 78592. - Paint / Graph / Sculp / Draw - 078025

Rombach, Bertoldstr. 10, 79098 Freiburg. T. (0761) 49 09 434, Fax (0761) 49 09 413. - Paint - 078026

raum für kunst

A N N M A R I E   T A E G E R

Saalgasse 22
60311 Frankfurt/Main
Telephon + Fax
069/28 77 29

Öffnungszeiten
Di – Fr 14 – 18 Uhr
Sa 11 – 14 Uhr
und nach tel.
Vereinbarung

Schiessel, Sebastian-Kneipp-Str. 28, 79104 Freiburg.
T. (0761) 248 41. - Paint / Graph / Sculp -   078027
Selz, Gudrun, Dr., Reichsgrafenstr. 10, 79102 Freiburg.
T. (0761) 77657, Fax (0761) 706378. - Paint -   078028
Straetz, Salzstr. 15, 79098 Freiburg. T. (0761) 365 85.
- Graph / Graph / Repr / Fra -   078029
VP Galerie, Neunlindenstr. 35, 79106 Freiburg.
T. (0761) 50 69 76. - Paint / Graph / Sculp / Pho / Mul /
Draw -   078030

Freiensteinau (Hessen)

Galerie Künstlerhaus, Hoher Vogelsberg R5, 36399 Frei-
ensteinau. T. (06666) 640. - Paint / Graph / Sculp /
Draw -   078031

Freising (Bayern)

Hartl, Hans, Dr., Amtsgerichtsgasse 3, 85354 Freising.
T. (08161) 50650, Fax (08161) 50912. - Paint / Graph /
Repr / Sculp / Draw -   078032

Freudenstadt (Baden-Württemberg)

Altendorf, Irmeli & Wolfgang, Wittlensweiler, 72250
Freudenstadt. T. (07441) 7864, Fax 951031. - Paint /
Graph -   078033
Bilder-Lang I. Widmann Nachf., Reichsstr. 29, 72250
Freudenstadt. T. (07441) 2938, Fax (07441) 83932.
- Paint / Graph / Repr / Fra -   078034
Friedrich, Schulstr. 35, 72250 Freudenstadt.
T. (07441) 29 35.   078035

Friedberg (Bayern)

Külmer, Renate von, Thomas-Mann-Str. 23, 86316
Friedberg. T. (0821) 635 40. - Paint -   078036

Friedberg (Hessen)

Draier, Görbelheimer Mühle 1, 61169 Friedberg.
T. (06031) 24 29. - Paint -   078037
Hoffmann, Görbelheimer Mühle, 61169 Friedberg.
T. (06031) 24 43. - Paint / Sculp / Mul / Draw -   078038
Limpert, U., & E. Reuter, Engelsgasse 1, 61169 Fried-
berg. T. (06031) 41 88. - China -   078039

Friedrichshafen (Baden-Württemberg)

Lutzer, Bernd, Zeppelinstr. 7, 88045 Friedrichshafen.
T. (07541) 22713. - Paint / Graph / Mul / Draw -   078040

Friesenheim (Baden-Württemberg)

Otto, Renate, Mühlgasse 13, 77948 Friesenheim.
T. (078 21) 67804. - Paint / Graph / Sculp -   078041

Fronhausen (Hessen)

Schenk zu Schweinsberg, Ekkehard, Giessener Str.4,
35112 Fronhausen. T. (06426) 63 43.   078042

Fürstenfeldbruck (Bayern)

Klostergalerie, Fürstenfeld 3, 82256 Fürstenfeldbruck.
T. (08141) 4514, 43718, Fax (08141) 42670.
- Paint -   078043

Fürth (Bayern)

Frauenknecht, Nürnberger Str. 3, 90762 Fürth.
- Paint -   078044

Fulda (Hessen)

Bilder-Fuchs, Abtstor 41, 36037 Fulda. T. (0661) 723 43.
- Paint -   078045
Galerie Bohemica, Franz-Schubert-Str. 1, 36043 Fulda.
T. (0661) 37377.   078046
Galerie zum kleinen Mann, Peterstor 10, 36037 Fulda.
T. (0661) 217 57.   078047
Raab, Mittelstr. 29, 36037 Fulda. - Paint /
Graph -   078048

Gadebusch (Mecklenburg-Vorpommern)

Galerie am Schloßberg, Postfach 41, 19201
Gadebusch.   078049

Ganderkesee (Niedersachsen)

Roeschen, Kehnmoorweg 21a, 27777 Ganderkesee.
T. (04222) 2595. - Paint / Graph / Sculp / Draw - 078050

Garbsen (Niedersachsen)

M & R Galerie Kolbien, Steinbockgasse 6, 30823
Garbsen.   078051

Garching bei München (Bayern)

Poster-Galerie-München, Carl-von-Linde-Str 33, 85748
Garching bei München. T. (089) 3205026,
Fax (089) 3203567. - Graph -   078052

Garmisch-Partenkirchen (Bayern)

Corneli, Am Kurpark 16, 82467 Garmisch-Partenkirchen.
T. (08821) 27 34. - Paint -   078053

Garrel (Niedersachsen)

Galerie L.K., Garrelerstr. 31, 49681 Garrel.
T. (04471) 3602.   078054

Gau-Bischofsheim (Rheinland-Pfalz)

Galerie Jottwedee im Geiserhof, Bergstr. 4, 55296 Gau-
Bischofsheim. T. (06135) 31 37.   078055

Gauting (Bayern)

Behringer, D., Germeringerstr 23, 82131 Gauting.
T. (089) 8507980.   078056

Geisenheim (Hessen)

English Gallery, Römerberg 2, 65366 Geisenheim.
T. (067 22) 507 26. - China -   078057

Gelnhausen (Hessen)

Oly-Galerie, Am Ziegelturm 12, 63571 Gelnhausen.
T. (06051) 3959.   078058

Gelsenkirchen (Nordrhein-Westfalen)

Maennig, Reinersweg 9, 45894 Gelsenkirchen.
T. (0209) 39 70 60. - Ant / Paint / Graph / Furn / China /
Sculp / Glass / Mod / Pho / Mul / Draw -   078059

Gera (Thüringen)

Galerie am Markt, Markt 12a, 07545 Gera.
T. (0365) 22412, Fax (0365) 22412. - Paint / Graph /
China / Sculp / Tex / Jew / Fra / Glass / Draw -   078060

Germering (Bayern)

Galerie InterArt, Kleinfeldstr. 30a, 82110 Germering.
T. (089) 8404241, Fax 8404222. - Paint / Graph /
Sculp / Draw -   078060a

Gevelsberg (Nordrhein-Westfalen)

Appelt, Doris, Neustr. 4 1/2, 58285 Gevelsberg.
T. (02332) 14584. - Graph / China / Jew / Fra -   078061

Gießen (Hessen)

Farben-Schmidt, Neuenweg 7, 35390 Gießen.   078062
Macarel, Seltersweg 55, 35390 Gießen.
T. (0641) 742 22.   078063
Rätzel, Georg, Grünberger Str. 11, 35390 Gießen.
T. (0641) 32440, Fax (0641) 33454.   078064
Schäfer, K.G., Gartenstr 13, 35390 Gießen.
T. (0641) 33999, Fax 390439. - Paint / Graph / Sculp /
Mul / Draw -   078065

Gladbeck (Nordrhein-Westfalen)

Junge Galerie, Hochstr 51-53, 45964 Gladbeck.
T. (02143) 63390, Fax (02043) 57691. - Paint -   078066

Gmund (Bayern)

Duensing, Tölzer Str. 2, 83703 Gmund.
T. (08022) 754 23, 745 80.   078067

Göppingen (Baden-Württemberg)

Mauch, Brigitte, Mittenfeldstr. 54, 73035 Göppingen.
T. (07161) 49750. - Paint / Graph / Repr /
Draw -   078068

Göttingen (Niedersachsen)

Ahlers, Düstere Str 20, 37073 Göttingen.
T. (0551) 57056, Fax (0551) 56187. - Paint / Graph /
Sculp / Pho / Mul / Draw -   078069
Galerie Apex, Burgstr. 46, 37073 Göttingen.
T. (0551) 468 86. - Paint / Graph / China -   078070
Galerie unikate, Burgstr. 25, 37073 Göttingen.
T. (0551) 47473.   078071
Galerie 19, Jüdenstr. 19, 37073 Göttingen.
T. (0551) 57456, Fax (0551) 45905. - Graph / Repr /
Fra -   078072
Harlekin-Galerie, Burgstr. 38a, 37073 Göttingen.
T. (0551) 48 46 99.   078073
Kommunikations- und Aktionszentrum Göttingen Junges
Theater GmbH, Hospitalstr. 1, 37073 Göttingen.
T. (0551) 551 23. - Paint / Graph / Sculp / Cur - 078074

Künstlerhaus mit Galerie, Gotmarstr. 1, 37073 Göttin-
gen. T. (0551) 46890. - Paint / Graph / Draw -   078075
L'Art Galerie, Kurze Geismarstr. 33, 37073 Göttingen.
T. (0551) 57456, Fax (0551) 45905. - Paint / Graph /
Repr / Fra / Fra -   078076
Nottbohm, Friedrich, Kurze Geismarstr. 31, 37073 Göt-
tingen. T. (0551) 57456, Fax (0551) 45905. - Paint /
Graph / Repr / Sculp / Jew / Fra / Glass / Draw - 078077
Piper, Hans-A., Theaterstr. 22, 37073 Göttingen.   078078
Polnische Galerie, Jüdenstr. 8, 37073 Göttingen.
T. (0551) 575 33.   078079
Wohnstift, Charlottenburger Str. 19, 37085
Göttingen.   078080

Gommern (Sachsen-Anhalt)

Galerie in Gommern, M.-Schwantes-Str. 13, 39245
Gommern. T. (039200) 676.   078081

Goslar (Niedersachsen)

Galerie in der Kemenate, Hokenstr. 6, 38640 Goslar.
T. (05321) 23697. - Paint / Graph / Sculp / Silv - 078082
Krebs & Tippach GmbH, Petersilienstr. 3, 38640 Goslar.
T. (05321) 226 76. - Graph / Graph -   078083
Stubengalerie, Abzuchtstr. 4, 38640 Goslar.
T. (05321) 409 57. - Paint / Graph / Sculp -   078084

Gottmadingen (Baden-Württemberg)

Galerie Harlekin, 78244 Gottmadingen.   078085

Graben-Neudorf (Baden-Württemberg)

Notheis, B., Mannheimer Str. 91, 76676 Graben-Neu-
dorf. T. (07255) 906 26. - Paint -   078086

Grafenau (Baden-Württemberg)

Schlichtenmaier, Schloß Dätzingen, 71117 Grafenau.
T. (07033) 41394, Fax (07033) 44923. - Paint / Graph /
Sculp / Draw -   078087

Grafenrheinfeld (Bayern)

Hulsch, Carlos, c/o Dr. Schwabe, Unterer Dorfgraben 38,
97506 Grafenrheinfeld. T. (09723) 70 55. - Paint /
Graph / Sculp -   078088

Greifswald (Mecklenburg-Vorpommern)

Greifen-Galerie, Fleischerstr. 17a, 17489 Greifswald.
T. (03834) 2638.   078089

Grenzach-Wyhlen (Baden-Württemberg)

Schmidt, Heinrich, Rheinstr. 37, 79639 Grenzach-Wyh-
len. T. (07624) 8380, Fax (07624) 4921.
- Paint -   078090

Grevenbroich (Nordrhein-Westfalen)

Randolff, Talstr. 104, 41516 Grevenbroich.
T. (02181) 2044.   078091
Trendframe, Braunsberger Str. 15, 41516 Grevenbroich.
T. (02181) 9807.   078092

Griesheim (Hessen)

Swetec, Franz, Friedrich-Ebert-Str. 48, 64347 Griesheim. T. (06155) 783 91.   078093

Grömitz (Schleswig-Holstein)

Ostsee-Galerie, Op de Horst 12, 23743 Grömitz.
T. (04562) 1018. - Paint -   078094

Grönenbach (Bayern)

Galerie Grönenbach, Silcherstr. 15, 87730 Grönenbach.
T. (08334) 10 01. - Paint / Graph / Sculp /
Draw -   078095

Gronau (Nordrhein-Westfalen)

Almsick, Georg van, Merschstr. 21, 48599 Gronau.
T. (02562) 10 61/63. - Paint / Graph / China / Sculp /
Jew / Fra / Ico -   078096

Groß-Gerau (Hessen)

Kleine Galerie, Oppenheimer Str. 20, 64521 Groß-Gerau.
T. (06152) 7727.   078097

Groß-Umstadt (Hessen)

Galerie im Hof, Friedr.-Ebert-Str. 5, 64823 Groß-Um-
stadt. T. (06078) 4973. - Paint / Graph / Draw -   078098
Hoenisch, Schwanengasse 2, 64823 Groß-
Umstadt.   078099

H. Janssen – dennoch gewaschen, 1983

GALERIE BROCKSTEDT

20er Jahre	E. Barlach	**Spanische Realisten**
DADA	Marc Chagall	Francisco Lopez
Neue Sachlichkeit	Otto Dix	Maria Moreno
Konstruktivismus	Otto Freundlich	I. Quintanilla
	Hundertwasser	
	Horst Janssen	
	Paul Joostens	
	E. Nolde	
	R. Oelze	
	Chr. Schad	
	Schröder-Sonnenstern	

Magdalenenstr. 11 – 20148 Hamburg – Tel. 0 40/4 10 40 91 – Fax: 0 40/4 10 14 26

Gross Vollstedt (Schleswig-Holstein)
Lüder, Am Sportpl. 2, 24802 Gross Vollstedt.
T. (04305) 658. - Paint / Graph / Fra -   *078100*

Großhansdorf (Schleswig-Holstein)
Hamer, Hoisdorfer Landstr. 38, 22927 Großhansdorf.
T. (04102) 65748. - Graph / Draw -   *078101*

Großostheim (Bayern)
Oettl, Barbara, Schwarzwaldstr. 9b, 63762 Großostheim.
T. (06026) 51 79. - Graph -   *078102*

Großpösna (Sachsen)
Müller, Bärbel, Damaschkestr. 47, 04463 Großpösna.
T. (04297) 2777, Fax (04297) 2777. - Graph -   *078103*

Grünkraut (Baden-Württemberg)
Galerie der Raiffeisenbank, 88287 Grünkraut.   *078104*

Grünstadt (Rheinland-Pfalz)
Kunst am Taubengarten, Taubengartenhohl 4, 67269 Grünstadt. T. (06359) 2528. - Paint / Graph / Sculp / Draw -   *078105*

Grünwald (Bayern)
Galerie Geiselgasteig, Robert-Koch-Str 9, 82031 Grünwald. T. (089) 6492546, 6492313. - Ant / Furn / Tex / Dec -   *078106*
Galerie im Video Zentrum, Bavariafilmpl 7, 82031 Grünwald. T. (089) 64992231, Fax (089) 64992952. - Paint -   *078107*
Griebert, Peter, Ricarda-Huch-Str 4, 82031 Grünwald. T. (089) 6413054. - Paint -   *078108*
Müller-Raß, Eva, Wilhelm-Humser-Str 7, 82031 Grünwald. T. (089) 6415739, Fax (089) 6415740.   *078109*

Günzburg (Bayern)
Atelier am Kappenzipfel, Kappenzipfel 19, 89312 Günzburg. T. (08221) 33414. - Paint / Graph / Sculp / Fra / Draw -   *078110*

Gütersloh (Nordrhein-Westfalen)
Friedemann, Friedrichstr. 7, 33330 Gütersloh.
T. (05241) 29810. - Paint / Graph / Sculp / Draw -   *078111*
Kurze, Bernd R., Spiekergasse 12, 33330 Gütersloh.
T. (05241) 279 71. - Paint / Graph / China / Repr / Sculp / Jew / Glass / Glass / Draw -   *078112*

Gummersbach (Nordrhein-Westfalen)
Leidig, Schürweg 6, 51643 Gummersbach.
T. (02261) 25091. - Draw -   *078113*

Gunzenhausen (Bayern)
Markgraf, Wagstr 2, 91710 Gunzenhausen.
T. (09831) 8484. - Ant / Paint / Graph / Fra -   *078114*

Haan (Nordrhein-Westfalen)
Franicevic, A., Neuer Markt 15, 42781 Haan.
T. (02129) 6451.   *078115*
Oster, Kurt, Kaiserstr 34, 42781 Haan.
T. (02129) 51857.   *078116*
Rech, Manfred, Graf-Engelbert-Str 5, 42781 Haan.
T. (02129) 7820. - Paint -   *078117*

Scholzen, Werner, Jahnstr 12, 42760 Haan.
T. (02129) 52783, Fax (02129) 53982. - Ant / Paint / Orient / China / Sculp -   *078118*

Hagen (Nordrhein-Westfalen)
Cercle d'Art Orthodoxe du Sud-Est, Bolohstr. 39, 58093 Hagen. T. (02331) 520 60.   *078119*
Fischer, H., Hindenburgstr. 20, 58095 Hagen.
T. (02331) 14821. - Graph -   *078120*
Galerie Nova, Lange Str. 39, 58089 Hagen.
T. (02331) 331788, Fax (02331) 337904. - Paint / Graph / Sculp -   *078121*
Galerie Vossloh, Voßloh 1, 58135 Hagen.
T. (02331) 45443. - Ant / Paint / Furn / Repr / Sculp / Fra -   *078122*
Gey, Hans-Werner, Lützowstr. 50a, 58095 Hagen.
T. (02331) 238 86. - Paint / Sculp -   *078123*
Hagenring Galerie, Emilienpl. 11, 58097 Hagen.
T. (02331) 28779. - Paint -   *078124*
Produzentengalerie, Bismarckstr. 4, 58089 Hagen.
- Paint / Draw -   *078125*
Schlieper, Michael, Böhmerstr. 18, 58095 Hagen.
T. (02331) 22022, Fax (02331) 22096. - Paint -   *078126*

Haiger (Hessen)
Weber, Rolf, Bahnhofstr 33, 35708 Haiger.
T. (02773) 4548.   *078127*

Haigerloch (Baden-Württemberg)
Galerie Die schwarze Treppe, Hohenbergstr. 8-10, 72401 Haigerloch. I. (07474) 84 09. - Paint / Graph / Sculp / Pho / Draw -   *078128*
Galerie im Schloss, Schloßfeld 9, 72401 Haigerloch.
T. (07474) 69380, Fax (07474) 69381. - Paint / Graph / China / Sculp / Jew / Glass / Draw -   *078129*
Kulthaus, Kätzling 2, 72401 Haigerloch. T. (07474) 2319, Fax (07474) 2336. - Tex / Arch / Eth -   *078130*

Haimhausen (Bayern)
Reichold, G., Weiherstr. 4, 85778 Haimhausen.
T. (08133) 6270, Fax (08133) 8310. - Paint / Jew / Draw -   *078131*

Hallbergmoos (Baden-Württemberg)
Schnittger, Ute, Weidenweg 5, 85399 Hallbergmoos.
T. (08169) 0811/8632. - Paint / Graph / Repr / Fra -   *078132*

Halle (Sachsen-Anhalt)
Galerie Junge Kunst, Alter Markt 31, 06108 Halle.   *078133*
Galerie Moritzburg, Friedemann-Bach-Platz 5, 06108 Halle. T. (0345) 37031.   *078134*
Gross, Christa, Fundgrube am Eselsbrunnen, Alter Markt 33, 06108 Halle. T. (0345) 35536. - Ant / Paint / Graph / China / Tex / Jew / Pho -   *078135*
Jugendclub am Steg, Steg 2, 06110 Halle.
T. (0345) 26381. - Pho -   *078136*

Halstenbek
Brande, Dockenhudener Ch 227, 25469 Halstenbek.
T. (01401) 45815.   *078137*

Hamburg
Abdul, Großmarkt 54 6110 20459, Hamburg.
T. (040) 344973.   *078138*
Abrahams, Poststr 36, 20354 Hamburg. T. (040) 352657, Fax (040) 342895.   *078139*
Ahrens, Colonnadenstr 72, 20354 Hamburg.
T. (040) 343805.   *078140*
Aida, Magdalenenstr. 18, 20148 Hamburg.
T. (040) 45 26 75. - Furn -   *078141*
Aktien Galerie, Rathausstr. 12, 20095 Hamburg.
T. (040) 323948.   *078142*
Ambiente, Elbe-Einkaufszentrum, 22609 Hamburg.
T. (040) 8007744.   *078143*
Amica, Große Bleichen 21, 20354 Hamburg.
T. (040) 34 02 50.   *078144*
AMSA-Galerie, Mittelweg 44, 20149 Hamburg.
T. (040) 457433, Fax (040) 446036. - Paint -   *078145*
Art Studio, Fischmarkt 8, 22767 Hamburg.
T. (040) 3192684.   *078146*
art & bookGalerie, Grindelallee 132, 20146 Hamburg.
T. (040) 44 79 36, Fax 410 29 06. - Paint / Graph / Repr / Fra / Pho / Draw -   *078147*
Atelier Mensch, Fischmarkt 12, 22767 Hamburg.
T. (040) 312455.   *078148*
Azadi, Siawosch, Deichstr. 24, 20459 Hamburg.
T. (040) 34 32 12.   *078149*
Barlach, Hans, Willistr. 11, 22299 Hamburg.
T. (040) 475066, Fax (040) 489642. - Paint / Sculp / Draw -   *078150*
BAT Kunst Foyer, Esplanade 39, 20354 Hamburg.
T. (040) 41512539, Fax (040) 4151729.
- Paint -   *078151*
Becker, Jürgen, Admiralitätstr 71, 20459 Hamburg.
T. (040) 365544, Fax (040) 365444. - Paint / Graph / Sculp / Pho / Mul / Draw -   *078152*
Bilderland, Kieler Str 565, 22525 Hamburg.
T. (040) 5403011.   *078153*
Bingemer, Caspar, Bismarckstr. 56, 20259 Hamburg.
T. (040) 408510, Fax (040) 4903483. - Paint / Graph / Sculp / Draw -   *078154*
Bock u. Sohn, Louis, Große Bleichen 34, 20354 Hamburg. T. (040) 34 41 13. - Paint -   *078155*
Böhrs, Richard, Colonnaden 30, 20354 Hamburg.
T. (040) 35 27 80. - Paint / Graph / Repr / Fra -   *078156*
Brill, Hohe Bleichen 26-28, 20354 Hamburg.
T. (040) 351637.   *078157*
Brockstedt, Magdalenenstr 11, 20148 Hamburg.
T. (040) 4104091, Fax 4101426. - Paint / Graph / Sculp -   *078158*
CELS Galerie, Colonnaden 72, 20354 Hamburg.
T. (040) 343805, Fax (040) 352524.   *078159*
Chapel Art Center, Bebelallee 153, 22297 Hamburg.
T. (040) 518630, 53805111, Fax (040) 516225. *078160*
Commeter, Hermannstr 37, 20095 Hamburg.
T. (040) 326321, Fax (040) 321993.   *078161*
Cosmix, Rosenhofstr 13, 20357 Hamburg.
T. (040) 4303139, Fax (040) 4303139.   *078162*
Crone, Ascan, Isestr. 121, 20149 Hamburg.
T. (040) 479067, Fax (040) 479060. - Paint / Graph -   *078163*

Deichtorhallen, Deichtorstr 1-2, 20095 Hamburg.
T. (040) 323763, Fax (040) 323661. - Paint /
Sculp - *078164*
Dirks, H.-H., Friedrich-Ludwig-Jahn-Str. 7, 21073 Hamburg. T. (040) 77 77 82. *078165*
Dörrie/Priess, Admiralitätstr 71, 20459 Hamburg.
T. (040) 364131, Fax 362877. - Paint / Graph / Sculp /
Mul / Draw - *078166*
Dörrie & Priess, Admiralitätstr 71, 20459 Hamburg.
T. (040) 364131. *078167*
Dresdner Bank Kunstetage, Mühlenkamp 5, 22303 Hamburg. T. (040) 35013077, Fax (040) 35013079.
- Paint / Graph / Draw - *078168*
Dröscher, Elke, Grotiusweg 79, 22587 Hamburg.
T. (040) 810581, Fax (040) 818166. - Paint - *078169*
Eksymä-Frenz, Rehwechsel 2, 21224 Hamburg.
T. (040) 7967268. *078170*
Elbdörfer Galerie, Osdorfer Landstr. 233, 22549 Hamburg. T. (040) 800 34 74. *078171*
Ellefsen, U., Bunatwiete 12, 21073 Hamburg.
T. (040) 765 10 87. *078172*
Essen, G.-W., Alexander-Zinn-Str. 25, 22607 Hamburg.
T. (040) 82 64 74. *078173*
Finckenstein, Charlotte Gräfin Finck von, Elbchaussee 31, 22765 Hamburg. T. (040) 3903011,
Fax (040) 3903011. *078174*
Galerie Abriß, Bernhard-Nocht-Str. 42, 20359 Hamburg.
T. (040) 319 14 20. *078175*
Galerie an der Staatsoper, Große Theaterstr. 32, 20354 Hamburg. T. (040) 34 25 16. *078176*
Galerie Antik, Hofweg 15, 22085 Hamburg.
T. (040) 2291001. *078177*
Galerie Artgebiet, Ifflandstr 69, 22087 Hamburg.
T. (040) 2291694. *078178*
Galerie B, Dorotheenstr 125, 22299 Hamburg.
T. (040) 472501. *078179*
Galerie Basta, Großheidestr. 21, 22303 Hamburg.
T. (040) 2792130, Fax (040) 4919683. *078180*
Galerie Condor, Volksdorfer Damm 33, 22359 Hamburg.
T. (040) 6039816, Fax (040) 6036158. - Paint / Graph /
Sculp - *078181*
Galerie d'histoire, Dammtorstr. 12, 20354 Hamburg.
T. (040) 34 31 31. *078182*
Galerie Deichstrasse, Deichstr 28, 20459 Hamburg.
T. (040) 365151, Fax (040) 362819. *078183*
Galerie der Gedok, Koppelstr. 66, 22527 Hamburg.
T. (040) 6305744, Fax (040) 6323985. *078184*
Galerie Felix, Bismarckstr. 44, 20259 Hamburg.
T. (040) 491 75 02. - Paint / Graph / Sculp - *078185*
Galerie Hauptsache Keramik, Danziger Str. 40, 20099 Hamburg. T. (040) 243898, Fax (040) 243898. - China /
Sculp - *078186*
Galerie Hoheluft, Hoheluftchaussee 71, 20253 Hamburg.
T. (040) 420 65 35. *078187*
Galerie in Eppendorf, Lehmweg 46, 20251 Hamburg.
T. (040) 47 01 57. - Graph / Sculp / Fra / Mod /
Draw - *078188*
Galerie in Flottbek, Alexander-Zinn-Str. 25, 22607 Hamburg. T. (040) 82 64 74. *078189*
Galerie Kammer-Studio, Münzpl. 11, 20097 Hamburg.
T. (040) 232651. *078190*
Galerie Kunststück, Eimsbütteler Chaussee 23, 20259 Hamburg. T. (040) 4302443, Fax (040) 4395660.
- Paint - *078191*
Galerie L, Elbchaussee 31, 22765 Hamburg.
T. (040) 3903011, Fax (040) 3903011. - China / Sculp /
Glass - *078192*
Galerie Lapislazuli, Grindelallee 24, 20146 Hamburg.
T. (040) 4105593. *078193*
Galerie M Hamburg, Holstestr 2, 22767 Hamburg.
T. (040) 826169. *078194*
Galerie Maritim, Martin-Luther-Str. 21, 20459 Hamburg.
T. (040) 364312, Fax (040) 363367. *078195*
Galerie Moderne Grafik, Karstadt, Mönckebergstr. 16/I,
20095 Hamburg. T. (040) 33 99 01. - Graph - *078196*
Galerie Möbel perdu, Fettstr. 7a, 20357 Hamburg.
T. (040) 439 11 63. - Paint - *078197*
Galerie Morganti, Wandsbeker Chaussee 3, 22089 Hamburg. T. (040) 2513003. *078198*
Galerie Morgenland, Sillemstr. 79, 20257 Hamburg.
T. (040) 490 46 22. *078199*
Galerie Passepartout, Quarree 8-10, 22041 Hamburg.
T. (040) 652 90 46. *078200*

Galerie Passepartout, Hoheluftchaussee 71, 20253 Hamburg. T. (040) 420 65 35. *078201*
galerie prospect placate, Pinneberger Chaussee 62, 22523 Hamburg. T. (040) 573586, Fax (040) 574383.
- Graph / Mil / Cur / Mod - *078202*
Galerie Sankt Gertrude, Gertrudenkirchhof 4-6, 20095 Hamburg. T. (040) 33 60 50. - Paint / Graph - *078203*
Galerie-Treff, Gerhart-Hauptmann-Platz 48, 20095 Hamburg. T. (040) 33 14 80. *078204*
Galerie-Treff, Gerhart-Hauptmann-Pl 48, 20095 Hamburg. T. (040) 331480. *078205*
Galerie Vorsetzen, Seilerstr 29, 20359 Hamburg.
T. (040) 3191867, Fax (040) 3174352. - Paint - *078206*
Galerie Weisses Haus, Heilwigstr. 52, 20249 Hamburg.
T. (040) 47 90 51. - Sculp / Mul - *078207*
Galerie zur alten Schmiede, Nienstedtener Str 13, 22609 Hamburg. T. (040) 823448. *078208*
Galerie 13, Taubenstr 13, 20359 Hamburg.
T. (040) 3171888. *078209*
Galerie7/8 Barmherzigkeit, Sternstr 115, 20357 Hamburg. T. (040) 4390497. *078210*
Gehrke, Thomas, Martin-Luther-Str 21, 20459 Hamburg.
T. (040) 3743290, 775909, Fax (040) 3743291.
- Paint / Graph / Sculp / Draw - *078211*
Gemälde-Centrum, Hoisberg 2a, 22359 Hamburg.
T. (040) 603 17 35. - Paint - *078212*
Gerbhardt, Magdalenenstr 41, 20148 Hamburg.
T. (040) 457803. *078213*
Glass Expressions, Robert Butt, Mundsburger Damm 54, 22087 Hamburg. T. (040) 220 33 65. *078214*
Glassblowers Gallery am Michel, Krayenkamp 13, 20459 Hamburg. T. (040) 37 16 72. - Glass - *078215*
Hamburger Galerie für Neue Medien, Mundsburger Damm 6, 22087 Hamburg. T. (040) 227 85 80. *078216*
Hans, Mathias F., Jungfernstieg 34, 20354 Hamburg.
T. (040) 353009. - Paint - *078217*
Hauptmann, Colonnaden 96, 20354 Hamburg.
T. (040) 34 60 86. - Paint / Graph / Sculp - *078218*
Henning, Karl, Dr., Wexstr. 35, 20355 Hamburg.
T. (040) 32 25 85. - Ant / Paint / Graph / Furn / Orient /
Sculp / Tex - *078219*
Herold, Loogepl 1, 20249 Hamburg.
T. (040) 478060. *078220*
Herrmann, Hohe Bleichen 5, 20354 Hamburg.
T. (040) 342211. *078221*
Hochhuth, Walter D., Poststr 11, 20354 Hamburg.
T. (040) 342211, Fax 352020. - Paint / Graph / Mod /
Sculp - *078222*
Hoffmann, Bebelallee 129, 22297 Hamburg.
T. (040) 51161760. *078223*
Holstein, Karl, Alsterchaussee 11, 20149 Hamburg.
T. (040) 450371, 438969, 366185. - Paint /
Draw - *078224*
Horstmann, Rainer, Dr., Hofweg 69, 22085 Hamburg.
T. (040) 270 04 28. - Paint / Graph / Sculp - *078225*
Huelsmann, F.K.A., Hohe Bleichen 15, 20354 Hamburg.
T. (040) 342017, Fax 354534. - Graph - *078226*
hy-editions, Glashüttenstr 3, 20357 Hamburg.
T. (040) 4304189, Fax (040) 4307934. *078227*
Jensen, Eppendorfer Baum 39a, 20249 Hamburg.
T. (040) 48 18 60. - Paint - *078228*
Jürgensen, Bei den Mühren 90, 20457 Hamburg.
T. (040) 374522. *078229*
Justus & Partner, Rutsch 2, 22587 Hamburg.
T. (040) 865007. *078230*
Kabul, Wandsbeker Chaussee 114, 22089 Hamburg.
T. (040) 2002062. *078231*

Kammer, Böhmersweg 9, 20148 Hamburg.
T. (040) 459427, Fax (040) 4104873. - Paint / Graph /
Sculp / Fra / Mul / Draw - *078232*
Klose, Gustav, Steinstr. 13, 20095 Hamburg.
Fax (040) 327196. *078233*
Klosterfelde, Helga Maria, Admiralitätsstr 71, 20459 Hamburg. T. (040) 37500754, Fax 37500753. *078234*
KM 235 Galerie, Eppendorfer Weg 235, 20251 Hamburg.
T. (040) 489598. *078235*
Kramer, Große Elbstr 146, 22767 Hamburg.
T. (040) 3893334, Fax (040) 869803. *078236*
Kröbel, H., Bogenstr. 68, 20253 Hamburg.
T. (040) 422 34 39. *078237*
Kuball, Ralf-Matthias, Hohe Bleichen 22, 20354 Hamburg. T. (040) 35 27 35. *078238*
Künstlerhaus, Weidenallee 10b-10c, 20357 Hamburg.
T. (040) 41 89 61, 44 29 01, 45 70 20. *078239*
Kunst im Holz, Hackmackbogen 90, 21035 Hamburg.
T. (040) 7358516. *078240*
Kunstgerecht, Zimmerstr 17, 22085 Hamburg.
T. (040) 222228. *078241*
Kunsthaus, Steinstr 19a, 20095 Hamburg.
T. (040) 335803. - Paint - *078242*
Kunsthaus, Klosterwall 15, 20095 Hamburg.
T. (040) 335803, Fax 321732. - Paint - *078243*
Kunstraum Falkenstein, Grotiusweg 79, 22587 Hamburg. T. (040) 810581, Fax (040) 818166. - Paint /
Graph / Sculp - *078244*
Kunstraum Fleetinsel, Admiralitätstr. 71, 20459 Hamburg. T. (040) 3743200. - Pho - *078245*
Lehmann, M., Harburger Ring 17, 21073 Hamburg.
T. (040) 7664567. - Graph / Repr / Fra - *078246*
Leiss, Hilde, Großer Burstah 36, 20457 Hamburg.
T. (040) 36 55 74. - Jew - *078247*
Levy, Magdalenenstr 54, 20148 Hamburg.
T. (040) 459188, Fax (044) 447225. - Paint / Graph /
Sculp / Fra / Mul - *078248*
Liedigk, Thomas, Rothenbaumchaussee 207, 20149 Hamburg. T. (040) 456139, Fax (040) 4105929.
- Paint / Graph / Sculp / Pho / Draw - *078249*
Lindemann, Oberstr 135, 20149 Hamburg.
T. (040) 452742. *078250*
Lindemann, Max, Eppendorfer Landstr. 59, 20249 Hamburg. T. (040) 480 11 66. - Paint / Graph / Repr /
Fra - *078251*
Lochte, Mittelweg 164, 20148 Hamburg.
T. (040) 457851. - Graph / Repr / Fra - *078252*
Loeper, Gabriele von, Mittelweg 152, 20148 Hamburg.
T. (040) 453292, Fax (040) 442996. - Paint / Graph /
Sculp / Fra - *078253*
Master's Galerie, Große Bleichen 21, 20354 Hamburg.
T. (040) 34 04 47. *078254*
Mewes, Lehmweg 51, 20251 Hamburg.
T. (040) 481126. *078255*
Multiple Art, Heegbargstr. 31, 22391 Hamburg.
T. (040) 602 60 77. - Mul - *078256*
Munro, Vera, Heilwigstr 64, 20249 Hamburg.
T. (040) 484552, 372550, Fax (040) 472550.
- Paint - *078257*
Museumsgalerie Krokodil, Palmerstr. 30, 20535 Hamburg. T. (040) 250 89 54, Fax (040) 250 39 61.
- Paint - *078258*
Null-Commanix Galerie, Paulinenstr. 14, 20359 Hamburg. T. (040) 430 23 51. *078259*
Ohm, August, Röntgenstr. 57, 22335 Hamburg.
T. (040) 59 87 46. - Paint - *078260*

PRODUZENTENGALERIE HAMBURG
TEL. 0 40 / 37 82 32 · Fax 0 40 / 36 33 04

Oltmanns, Heilwigstr 101, 20249 Hamburg.
T. (040) 483984. *078261*

Opus Art, Landwehrstr. 25, 22087 Hamburg.
T. (040) 251 38 85. - Paint - *078262*

Osterwalder's Art Office Gallery, Isestr 37, 20144 Hamburg. T. (040) 486109, Fax (040) 2277719. *078263*

Pentiment, Internationale Akademie für Kunst und Gestaltung an der Fachhochschule Hamburg, Arngartstr 24, 22087 Hamburg. T. (040) 291884163,
Fax (040) 291883374. *078264*

Peter, E., Blankeneser Hauptstr. 141, 22587 Hamburg.
T. (040) 86 15 83, Fax (040) 86 94 98. - Paint / Graph /
Sculp - *078265*

Piorr, Beim Amsinckpark 18, 22529 Hamburg.
T. (040) 56 76 80. *078266*

Poster-Galerie, Große Bleichen 31, 20354 Hamburg.
T. (040) 34 68 50. - Graph / Repr / Sculp / Fra - *078267*

PPS-Galerie, F.C. Gundlach, Feldstr., Hochhaus 1, 20095 Hamburg. T. (040) 431 17 00. - Pho - *078268*

Prager & Prinz, Neue ABC-Str. 8, 20354 Hamburg.
T. (040) 34 48 82. - Graph - *078269*

Produzentengalerie Hamburg, Michaelisbrücke 3, 20459 Hamburg. T. (040) 378232, Fax 363304. - Paint /
Sculp / Pho / Mul - *078270*

Prospettive d'Arte, Sierichstr. 132, 22299 Hamburg.
T. (040) 4601979. *078271*

Quittenbaum, Sülldorfer Kirchenweg 51, 22587 Hamburg. T. (040) 868491, Fax (040) 865484. *078272*

Richter, Markt 1, 21509 Hamburg. T. (040) 7101411,
Fax (040) 7101786. *078273*

Riemenschneider, Saseler Chaussee 95a, 22391 Hamburg. T. (040) 536 74 56. - Paint / Graph - *078274*

Rogalsky, Wandsbeker Allee 62, 22041 Hamburg.
T. (040) 68 20 16. - Paint / Fra - *078275*

Rose, Dirk, Großer Burstah 36, 20457 Hamburg.
T. (040) 365636. *078276*

Rüsch, Andreas, Fabricusstr. 121, 22177 Hamburg.
T. (040) 642 72 64. *078277*

Saturnus, Bremer Str 30, 21073 Hamburg.
T. (040) 7655501. *078278*

Schäfer, Waltraut, Fuhlsbüttler Str. 230, 22307 Hamburg. T. (040) 691 63 42. - Paint / Sculp /
Draw - *078279*

Schnabel, Eppendorfer Landstr 95, 20249 Hamburg.
T. (040) 485427, Fax (040) 479081. *078280*

Schönewald, Ursula, Mundsburger Damm 2, 22087 Hamburg. T. (040) 2291668,
Fax (040) 2278802. *078281*

Schröter, Gr Burstah 29, 20457 Hamburg.
T. (040) 364218. *078282*

Stelow, Ingo, Hallerpl 8, 20146 Hamburg.
T. (040) 444265. *078283*

Studio Galerie, Beim Schlump 13a, 20144 Hamburg.
T. (040) 452448, Fax (040) 457362. - Paint / Graph /
Sculp - *078284*

Sturm, von, Grosse Flottbeker Str. 30, 22607 Hamburg.
T. (040) 89 39 71. *078285*

Tolksdorf, Wilma, Admiralitätstr 71, 20459 Hamburg.
T. (040) 37722253, Fax (040) 362031. - Paint / Graph /
Draw - *078286*

Uhlenhorst, Averhoffstr 24, 22085 Hamburg.
T. (040) 2204255. *078287*

Unikat, Eulenkrugstr 68, 22359 Hamburg.
T. (040) 6032826. *078288*

Waluga, Wildschwanbrook 93, 22145 Hamburg.
T. (040) 6785015. *078289*

Weißer Raum, Admiralitätstr. 71, 20459 Hamburg.
T. (040) 36 66 65, Fax (040) 36 28 50. *078290*

Werdermann art, Grubesallee 1, 22143 Hamburg.
T. (040) 67777056. *078291*

Weßel, K., Reventlowstr. 66, 22605 Hamburg.
T. (040) 899 12 55. - Paint - *078292*

Westenhoff, Klauspeter, Magdalenenstr 21, 20148 Hamburg. T. (040) 440293, Fax (040) 457985.
- Paint - *078293*

Westermann, Parkberg 24, 22397 Hamburg.
T. (040) 6071024. *078294*

Westwerk, Admiralitätstr. 74, 20459 Hamburg.
T. (040) 36 39 03. *078295*

Wiechern, Gardy, Alter Steinweg 1, 20459 Hamburg.
T. (040) 364661, Fax (040) 364661. - Paint / Graph /
Sculp - *078296*

Wiegel, K., August-Krogmann-Str. 205, 22159 Hamburg.
T. (040) 643 67 99. *078297*

Zen Galerie, Wexstr. 35, 20355 Hamburg.
T. (040) 352585, Fax (040) 8663550. - Paint / Graph /
Orient - *078298*

Zwang, Christian, Paulinenallee 28, 20259 Hamburg.
T. (040) 43 29 39. - Paint / Graph / Fra / Draw - *078299*

Hameln (Niedersachsen)
adp Galerie, Lohstr. 37, 31785 Hameln. - Paint / Graph /
Sculp / Draw - *078300*

Fahrenhorst, Christel, Bäckerstr. 31, 31785 Hameln.
T. (05151) 422 60, 425 99. - Paint - *078301*

Fargel, C., Bäckerstr. 55, 31785 Hameln.
T. (05151) 2 49 01. - Paint / Graph / Repr / Fra - *078302*

Jung, Albert, Lohstr. 7, 31785 Hameln.
T. (05151) 36 13. *078303*

Nehls, Günter David, Gänsefüße 3, 31785 Hameln.
T. (05151) 37 81. - Paint / Graph - *078304*

Schloss-Atelier-Galerie, Schloss Hastenbeck, 31785 Hameln. - Paint - *078305*

Hamm (Nordrhein-Westfalen)
Kley, Werler Str 304, 59069 Hamm. T. (02381) 5483,
Fax 58480. - Paint / Graph - *078306*

Maximilianpark, Grenzweg 76, 59071 Hamm. *078307*

Mensing, Josef, Ostendorfstr 10, 59069 Hamm.
T. (02381) 5018. - Paint / Graph / Sculp / Fra - *078308*

Schmohr, Kunststudio, Bahnhofstr, 59065 Hamm.
T. (02381) 26028. - Paint / Graph - *078309*

Hamminkeln (Nordrhein-Westfalen)
Galerie Schloss Ringenberg, Schloßstr. 8, 46499 Hamminkeln. T. (02852) 41 61. - Paint / Graph / Repr /
Sculp - *078310*

Hanau (Hessen)
Galerie Thekla, Friedrich-Ebert-Anlage 11b, 63450 Hanau. T. (06181) 937750, Fax (06181) 33038.
- Sculp - *078311*

Galerie 88, Gustav-Adolf-Str. 9, 63452 Hanau.
T. (06181) 857 88, Fax (06181) 83027. - Paint / Graph /
China / Sculp / Mul / Draw - *078312*

Hanauer Kunstkabinett, Burgallee 65, 63454 Hanau.
T. (06181) 21632, Fax (06181) 257064. - Paint /
Graph / Repr / Sculp / Fra / Draw - *078313*

Hild, Parkpromenade 5, 63454 Hanau.
T. (06181) 849 94. *078314*

Reus, Nürnberger Str. 15, 63450 Hanau.
T. (06181) 81029, Fax (06181) 82164. - Paint / Graph /
Fra / Glass - *078315*

Hann Münden (Niedersachsen)
Kleine Galerie Münden, Lange Str. 2, 34346 Hann Münden. T. (05541) 8785, Fax 5655. - Paint / Sculp / Jew /
Fra / Ico / Mul / Draw - *078316*

Hannover (Niedersachsen)
Ars Mundi Collection, Bödekerstr. 13, 30161 Hannover.
T. (0511) 348 43 43. *078317*

Atelier Block 16, An der Strangriede 50b, 30167 Hannover. T. (0511) 71 41 99. - Paint - *078318*

avanti Galerie, Lange Laube 19, 30159 Hannover.
T. (0511) 184 43. - Graph - *078319*

Barz, Bertramstr. 4a, 30165 Hannover.
T. (0511) 3502933, Fax (0511) 3502933. - Paint /
Sculp / Pho - *078320*

Baubo Kultur Werkstatt, Seilerstr. 15-17, 30171 Hannover. T. (0511) 28 22 62. *078321*

Bauer, J.H., Holzmarkt 4, 30159 Hannover.
T. (0511) 324485, Fax 324452. - Paint / Graph / Fra /
Draw - *078322*

Beckmann, Erich, Georgstr. 48, 30159 Hannover.
T. (0511) 323074, Fax (0511) 329922. - Paint / Furn /
Orient / China / Sculp / Jew / Ico - *078323*

Bilderetage, Luisenstr. 1, 30159 Hannover.
T. (0511) 32 58 89. - Paint - *078324*

Bödeker, E., Wietzendiek 10, 30657 Hannover.
T. (0511) 65 22 64. *078325*

Böer, Claudia, Berliner Allee 54, 30175 Hannover.
T. (0511) 3632212, Fax (0511) 327191. - Paint /
Graph / Sculp / Fra / Pho / Mul / Draw - *078326*

Böwig, Wolf, Friedrichstr. 2a, 30169 Hannover.
T. (0511) 32 07 02, 81 55 25, Fax (0511) 32 46 30.
- China - *078327*

Borkowski, Borchersstr 23, 30559 Hannover.
T. (0511) 527374. - Paint - *078328*

Cartoonage Galerie und Versand, Wedekindstr 32,
30161 Hannover. T. (0511) 990560, Fax 9905620.
- Draw - *078329*

Effective Accessoires, Friesenstr. 13, 30161 Hannover.
T. (0511) 31 40 84 / 85. *078330*

Galerie am Tiergarten 62, Am Tiergarten 62, 30559 Hannover. T. (0511) 52 30 66/68, Fax (0511) 52 30 69.
- Sculp - *078331*

Galerie Artforum, Ballhofstr. 8, 30159 Hannover.
T. (0511) 363 22 00, 42 47 98, Fax (0511) 42 10 70.
- Paint / Aquarelle / Sculp / Draw - *078332*

Galerie der Aquarelle, Rückerstr. 1, 30169 Hannover.
T. (0511) 153 85. - Paint - *078333*

Galerie Kanaa, Am Marstall 19, 30159 Hannover.
T. (0511) 363 17 15. - Tex - *078334*

Galerie Kö 24, Königsworther Str. 24, 30167 Hannover.
T. (0511) 17783, Fax (0511) 17743. *078335*

Galerie Kunst & Raum, Seelhorststr. 6, 30175 Hannover.
T. (0511) 28 17 71, 34 43 30. *078336*

Galerie Refugium, Volgersweg 19, 30175 Hannover.
T. (0511) 34 50 48. - Paint / Graph / Graph / China /
Sculp / Draw - *078337*

Galerie Schwarzer Bär 6, Schwarzer Bär 6, 30449 Hannover. T. (0511) 44 14 40, Fax (0511) 45 35 72. *078338*

Galerie VVK, Schwarzer Bär 6, 30449 Hannover.
T. (0511) 44 14 40, Fax (0511) 45 35 72. *078339*

Galerie 28, Passerelle 28, 30159 Hannover.
T. (0511) 3681044, Fax 3681121. *078340*

GEDOK-Galerie, Odeonstr. 2, 30159 Hannover.
T. (0511) 13 14 04. - Paint / Graph / China / Sculp / Tex /
Jew - *078341*

Glashart, Am Marstall 23, 30159 Hannover.
T. (0511) 32 40 00. - Paint - *078342*

Glashoff, Nordfeldstr. 29, 30459 Hannover.
T. (0511) 41 66 67, 42 31 93. *078343*

Horn, M., Sonnenweg 19, 30171 Hannover.
T. (0511) 51 12 51, 81 23 78. - Paint - *078344*

Kater-Delitz, Wilma, Vahrenwalder Str. 54, 30165 Hannover. - Paint - *078345*

Kempin, Hermann, Marienstr. 62, 30171 Hannover.
T. (0511) 81 72 89, Fax (0511) 819392. 078346
Koch, Jürgen, Königstr. 50, 30175 Hannover.
T. (0511) 34 20 06, Fax (0511) 388 03 60. - Paint /
Graph / Sculp - 078347
Koch, W., Volgersweg 19, 30175 Hannover.
T. (0511) 34 50 48. - Paint / Graph / Sculp /
Draw - 078348
Kühl, Christoph, Kaiser-Wilhelm-Str. 1, 30559 Hannover.
T. (0511) 523751, Fax (0511) 9525453. - Paint /
Graph / Sculp / Fra / Draw - 078349
Lessentin, Heinz, Ferdinand-Wallbrecht-Str. 24, 30163
Hannover. 078350
Marghescu, Marika, Kirchröder Str. 40, 30625 Hannover.
T. (0511) 559694, Fax (0511) 559049. - Paint - 078351
Menges & Söhne, Königstr. 51, 30175 Hannover.
T. (0511) 34 35 22. 078352
Mühlnikel, S., Marienstr. 85, 30171 Hannover.
T. (0511) 85 19 71. 078353
Nitzsche, Frank, Friesenstr. 51, 30161 Hannover.
T. (0511) 31 21 88. 078354
Rosenbach, Detlev, Walderseestr 24, 30177 Hannover.
T. (0511) 669348, Fax (0511) 621285. - Paint / Graph /
Sculp - 078355
Rykel & Kühnast, Knochenhauerstr. 21, 30159 Hannover.
T. (0511) 32 09 89. 078356
Sandmann & Haak, Theodor-Lessing-Platz 3, 30159
Hannover. T. (0511) 32 48 03, Fax (0511) 329327.
- Paint - 078357
Schulze, Theodor, Osterstr. 24, 30159 Hannover.
T. (0511) 326234, Fax (0511) 3681458.
- Paint - 078358
Stübler, Langensalzastr. 1a, 30169 Hannover.
T. (0511) 880066, Fax (0511) 9805177. - Paint /
Graph / Sculp - 078359
Stula, D., Wiesenstr. 24, 30169 Hannover.
T. (0511) 88 53 14. 078360
Ulrichs, Timm, Sodenstr. 6, 30161 Hannover.
T. (0511) 31 28 23. - Paint / Graph / Sculp / Pho / Mul /
Draw - 078361
Vollmeyer, Körtingstr. 6, 30161 Hannover.
T. (0511) 39 34 21, Fax (0511) 39 33 10.
- Paint - 078362
Wesemann, W., Steinhuder Str. 21, 30459 Hannover.
T. (0511) 42 14 12. 078363
Wiedemann, Marktstr. 45, 30159 Hannover.
T. (0511) 134 43. 078364
Wiehering, R., Kötnerholzweg 13, 30451 Hannover.
T. (0511) 210 16 96. - Paint - 078365
Zörnig + Mock, Marienstr. 18, 30171 Hannover.
T. (0511) 81 49 95, Fax 283 44 59. 078366

Hanstedt (Niedersachsen)
Romantische Galerie Overbeck, Küsterhaus, 21271 Hanstedt. T. (04184) 76 08. 078367

Haßloch (Rheinland-Pfalz)
Kastenholz-Galerie, Kirchgasse 27, 67454
Haßloch. 078368

Hattersheim (Hessen)
Atelier Die Scheune, Mainzer Landstr. 48, 65795 Hattersheim. T. (06190) 55 74. - Paint / Graph /
Sculp - 078369

Hattingen (Nordrhein-Westfalen)
Meyer-Christiansen & Kämpgen, Heggerstr. 35, 45525
Hattingen. T. (02324) 202292. - Paint - 078370

Heide (Schleswig-Holstein)
Schumacher, Dieter, Süderstr 14, 25746 Heide.
T. (0481) 61010, Fax (0481) 61045. - Fra - 078371

Heidelberg (Baden-Württemberg)
Baumann, H., Hauptstr. 135, 69117 Heidelberg.
T. (06221) 16 34 19. - Paint - 078372
Calumet-Nuzinger, St.-Anna-Gasse 11, 69117 Heidelberg. T. (06221) 161670, Fax (06221) 181204.
- Paint - 078373
Edition Staeck, Ingrimstr. 3, 69117 Heidelberg.
T. (06221) 24753, Fax (06221) 10230. - Paint /
Sculp - 078374

GALERIA PALATINA
Galerie + Edition GmbH

Landkarten · Stadtansichten
Alte und moderne Kunst

Hildastr. 12 · 69115 Heidelberg
Tel. 06221/168588 · Fax 164631

Galeria Palatina, Hildastr 12, 69115 Heidelberg.
T. (06221) 168588, Fax 164631. 078375
Galerie Diego's Collection, Familia-Center, 69115 Heidelberg. T. (06221) 30 37 26. 078376
Galerie G, Uferstr. 4, 69120 Heidelberg.
T. (06221) 48 41 20. - Paint / Graph / Sculp - 078377
Galerie K, Ladenburger Str. 21, 69120 Heidelberg.
T. (06221) 463 62. - Paint - 078378
Galerie Kohlhof, Kohlhof 9, 69117 Heidelberg.
T. (06221) 16 25 01. - Paint / Sculp - 078379
Galerie Neuropa, Bauamtsgasse 6, 69117 Heidelberg.
T. (06221) 163666. - Paint / Graph / Sculp / Pho /
Mul - 078380
Galerie T., Kettengasse 23, 69117 Heidelberg.
T. (06221) 2 77 63. 078381
Galerie 33, Brückenstr. 33, 69120 Heidelberg.
T. (06221) 41 07 78. 078382
Ginilewicz, Dossenheimer Landstr. 83, 69121 Heidelberg. T. (06221) 41 34 37. - Paint - 078383
Greiser, Olaf, Schröderstr. 14, 69120 Heidelberg.
T (06221) 40 15 07. 078384
Hassbecker, Haspelgasse 12, 69117 Heidelberg.
T. (06221) 24466. - Paint / Graph - 078385
H.S. Galerie, Berliner Str. 109a, 69121 Heidelberg.
T. (06221) 47 36 06. - Mul - 078386
Kammerer, U., Neugasse 5, 69117 Heidelberg.
T. (06221) 213 96. 078387
Lux, Michael, Akademiestr 1, 69117 Heidelberg.
T. (06221) 23851. - Ant / China / Jew - 078388
Melnikow, M., Theaterstr. 11, 69117 Heidelberg.
T. (06221) 18 36 26. - Paint - 078389
Michael, Uwe, Neuenheimer Landstr 36, 69120 Heidelberg. T. (06221) 46024/25. - Paint - 078390
Mohr, M., Plöck 77, 69117 Heidelberg.
T. (06221) 243 74. - Paint - 078391
Sacksofsky, Uwe, Oberer Rainweg 27, 69118 Heidelberg. T. (06221) 80 32 57, Fax (06221) 80 36 83.
- Paint / Graph / Sculp / Draw - 078392
Sole d'Oro, Hauptstr. 172, 69117 Heidelberg.
T. (06221) 2 14 80. - Paint / Graph - 078393
Stefan, Untere Str. 18, 69117 Heidelberg.
T. (06221) 287 37. 078394
Tenner, Erna, Hauptstr. 194, 69117 Heidelberg.
T. (06221) 262 52. - Graph - 078395
Terbrüggen, Birgit, Bauamtsgasse 12, 69117 Heidelberg. T. (06221) 184350, Fax (06221) 29282.
- Paint - 078396
Vogel, Hauptstr 25, 69117 Heidelberg. T. (06221) 22821,
Fax 162142. - Paint / Graph / Sculp / Fra / Mul - 078397
Welker, W., Hauptstr. 106, 69117 Heidelberg.
T. (06221) 226 12. - Paint / Graph / Repr / Fra - 078398
Winterberg, Arno, Hildastr 12, 69115 Heidelberg.
T. (06221) 22631, Fax 164631. - Paint / Graph / Sculp /
Draw - 078399

Heidenheim an der Brenz (Baden-Württemberg)
Galerie Türmle, Grabenstr 26, 89522 Heidenheim an der
Brenz. 078400
Galerie Zeitlupe, Hintere Gasse 30, 89522 Heidenheim
an der Brenz. T. (07321) 23183. - Paint / Graph /
Sculp / Jew / Glass / Draw - 078401

Heilbronn (Baden-Württemberg)
Endwerk Galerie, Wilhelmstr 24, 74072 Heilbronn.
T. (07131) 84577, Fax (07131) 177694. - Paint /
Graph / Sculp / Fra - 078402

Rieker, Manfred, Weinsberger Str 3, 74019 Heilbronn.
T. (07131) 162666, Fax (07131) 173202. - Paint /
Sculp / Mul / Draw - 078403
Seiler, Hafenmarktplatz 8, 74072 Heilbronn.
T. (07131) 85737. - Graph / Repr / Fra - 078404
Vogel, Rathausgasse 5, 74072 Heilbronn.
T. (07131) 84473, Fax (07131) 76272. - Paint / Graph /
Sculp / Fra / Lights - 078405

Heiligenhaus (Nordrhein-Westfalen)
Foto, Jürgen, Kirchpl 6, 42579 Heiligenhaus.
T. (02126) 68212. 078406
Müller, H.-J., Gohrstr 10, 42579 Heiligenhaus.
T. (02126) 23466/67. 078407

Heimbach (Nordrhein-Westfalen)
Dorsel, F., In den Wingerten 15, 52396 Heimbach.
T. (02446) 36 36. 078408

Heinsberg (Nordrhein-Westfalen)
de Bernardi, R., Liecker Str 20, 52525 Heinsberg.
T. (02452) 3766, Fax (02452) 23660. - Graph - 078409
Galerie und Atelier Altes Rathaus, Waldfeuchterstr 145,
52525 Heinsberg. T. (02452) 7368. 078410
Mülstroh, Klaus, Roermonder Str 30, 52525 Heinsberg.
T. (02452) 7698. - Graph / Orient / Glass - 078411

Helgoland (Schleswig-Holstein)
Knauß, Maren, Siemensterrasse 140, 27498 Helgoland.
T. (04725) 78 66. - Graph - 078412

Helmstedt (Niedersachsen)
Galerie 333, Südertor 10, 38350 Helmstedt. 078413

Hemmingen (Niedersachsen)
GPK-Galerie, Gutenbergstr 21, 30966 Hemmingen.
T. (0511) 420017. - Paint - 078414

Hemsbach (Baden-Württemberg)
Altstadt-Galerie, Bachgasse 26, 69502 Hemsbach.
T. (06201) 44767. 078415

Herford (Nordrhein-Westfalen)
Eickhoff, Berliner Str. 10, 32052 Herford.
T. (05221) 550 44. - Paint / Draw - 078416

Herne (Nordrhein-Westfalen)
Haus am Grünen Ring, Wilhelmstr. 37, 44649 Herne.
T. (02323) 163242, Fax (02323) 162100. - Paint /
Graph / Draw - 078417
Klecks-Herne, Neustr. 25, 44623 Herne.
T. (02323) 57262, Fax (02323) 53278. - Paint / Sculp /
Lights - 078418
Lindquist, H., Mont-Cenis-Str. 1, 44623 Herne.
T. (02323) 582 37. - Paint - 078419
Wurm-Schleimer, M., Hauptstr. 153, 44652 Herne.
T. (02323) 712 97. - Paint / Graph - 078420

Heroldstatt (Baden-Württemberg)
Frenzel, Fridolin, Lange Str. 6, 72535 Heroldstatt.
T. (07389) 228. 078421

Herrenberg (Baden-Württemberg)
Györfi, G. & S., Schuhgasse 2, 71083 Herrenberg.
T. (07032) 5730. - Paint - 078422

Herten (Nordrhein-Westfalen)
Galerie Trend Art, Richterstr 103, 45701 Herten.
T. (02366) 43553, 55519. - Paint / Graph / Sculp /
Draw - 078423

Herzogenrath (Nordrhein-Westfalen)
Brücken-Gemälde-Galerie, Südstr. 182, 52134 Herzogenrath. T. (02406) 22 49. - Paint - 078424

Heubach (Baden-Württemberg)
Stephan, Josef, Im Bürglesbühl 271, 73540
Heubach. 078425

Heuchelheim (Hessen)
Perspektive, Ausstellungs & Kunstwerkstatt, Wilhelmstr.
14, 35452 Heuchelheim. T. (0641) 67133.
- Paint - 078426

Heusenstamm (Hessen)
Rekus, Irene, Ludwigstr. 7, 63150 Heusenstamm.
T. (06104) 5764. - Paint / Graph - *078427*

Hilden (Nordrhein-Westfalen)
Galerie am Stadtpark, Benrather Str. 34, 40721 Hilden.
T. (02103) 546 86. *078428*

Hildener Auktionshaus und Galerie, Klusenhof 12,
40723 Hilden. T. (02103) 602 00. - Ant / Paint / Graph /
Furn / Num / Orient / China / Silv / Instr - *078429*

Keramikwerkstatt und Galerie für Kunsthandwerk,
Schwanenstr. 12, 40721 Hilden. T. (02103) 518 77.
- China - *078430*

Michels, Eichenstr. 120, 40721 Hilden.
T. (02103) 55512. *078431*

Schmidt, Klaus-J., Erlenweg 3, 40723 Hilden.
T. (02103) 613 13. - Paint / Graph / Sculp /
Draw - *078432*

Waldbröl, Ursula, Heerstr. 52, 40721 Hilden. *078433*

Hildesheim (Niedersachsen)
Galerie, Markt, 31134 Hildesheim.
T. (05121) 13 16 86. *078434*

Meine Kleine Galerie, Gallbergstieg 115, 31137 Hildesheim. T. (05121) 655 30. - Paint / Graph / Sculp /
Draw - *078435*

Hille (Nordrhein-Westfalen)
Hüsing, Wolfgang, Lübbecker Str. 242, 32479 Hille.
T. (05703) 10 95. - Paint - *078436*

Hilter (Niedersachsen)
Galerie Kuckucksmühle, Münsterstr. 70, 49176 Hilter.
T. (05409) 37446, Fax (05409) 38252. - Paint / Graph /
Repr / Fra - *078437*

Hochheim (Hessen)
Galerie in der Weststadt, Danziger Allee 72, 65239
Hochheim. T. (06146) 2170. *078438*

Hockenheim (Baden-Württemberg)
Arayan, Ludwigstr. 48, 68766 Hockenheim.
T. (06205) 88 16. - Paint - *078439*

Höhr-Grenzhausen (Rheinland-Pfalz)
Künstlerhof-Galerie, Im Silbertal 4a, 56203 Höhr-Grenz-
hausen. T. (02624) 20 52. - Paint / Graph / Sculp / Pho /
Draw - *078440*

Höxter (Nordrhein-Westfalen)
Kunstkabinett, Julius Henze, Marktstr. 5, 37671 Höxter.
T. (05271) 22 71. - Paint / Graph - *078441*

Hof (Bayern)
Bauer, Ludwigstr 39, 95028 Hof.
T. (09281) 3975. *078442*

Galeriehaus, Sophienberg 28, 95028 Hof.
T. (09281) 87210. - Paint / Graph / Sculp - *078443*

Ganz-Friedrich, H., Sophienstr 15, 95028 Hof.
T. (09281) 3176. - Paint - *078444*

Hofbieber (Hessen)
Kunststation Kleinsassen, An der Milseburg 2, 36145
Hofbieber. *078445*

Hofheim (Hessen)
Ernst, Rolf August, Im Klingen 5a, 65719 Hofheim.
T. (06192) 22138. *078446*

Pelkmann, C., Wilhelmstr 6, 65719 Hofheim.
T. (06192) 22233. *078447*

Holzgerlingen (Baden-Württemberg)
Schwedler, Horst, Schwalbenweg 4, 71088 Holzgerlingen. T. (07031) 412 28. - Paint - *078448*

Holzkirchen, Oberbayern (Bayern)
Weber, Hans, Roggersdorfer Str 27, 83607 Holzkirchen,
Oberbayern. T. (08024) 8285. *078449*

Homburg (Saarland)
Beck, Monika, Am Schwedenhof, 66424 Homburg.
T. (06841) 6527. - Paint / Graph / Sculp / Pho / Mul /
Draw - *078450*

Galerie Homburg, Kasernenstr 16, 66424 Homburg.
T. (06841) 62636. - Paint / Graph / Sculp / Fra - *078451*

Hude (Niedersachsen)
Galerie Klostermühle, Klostermühle, 27798 Hude.
T. (04408) 597. - Paint - *078452*

Hünfelden (Hessen)
Präsenz Galerie Edition, Gnadenthal, 65597 Hünfelden.
T. (06438) 81266, Fax (06438) 81270. - Paint /
Graph - *078453*

Hürtgenwald (Nordrhein-Westfalen)
Spriewald, Raffelsbrand, 52393 Hürtgenwald.
T. (02429) 1239, Fax (02429) 2190. - Fra - *078454*

Hürth (Nordrhein-Westfalen)
Die Kleine Galerie, Hürth-Park, Einkaufszentrum, 50354
Hürth. T. (02233) 78764. *078455*

Husum (Schleswig-Holstein)
Husumer Bilderstube, Schiffbrücke 10, 25813 Husum.
T. (04841) 61006. *078456*

Kloss, R., Joseph-Haydn-Weg 8, 25813 Husum.
T. (04841) 73576. *078457*

Idar-Oberstein (Rheinland-Pfalz)
Retzler, E. & P. Weglinski, Hauptstr. 536, 55743 Idar-
Oberstein. T. (06781) 23720. *078458*

Idstein (Hessen)
Galerie Mandos, Markptpl 12, 65510 Idstein.
T. (06126) 51784, 52431. *078459*

Kleist, Am Löherpl, 65510 Idstein. T. (06126) 6752,
Fax (06126) 55102. *078460*

Igensdorf (Bayern)
Frey, 91338 Igensdorf. *078461*

Ingelheim (Rheinland-Pfalz)
Kleine Galerie, Bahnhofstr 123, 55218 Ingelheim.
T. (06132) 4413, Fax (06132) 76472. *078462*

Wermann, Binger Str 91 a, 55218 Ingelheim.
T. (06132) 2236. - Paint - *078463*

Ingolstadt (Bayern)
Nemec, V., Neubaustr 2, 85049 Ingolstadt.
T. (0841) 33696, Fax (0841) 17113. - Paint /
Graph - *078464*

Inzlingen (Baden-Württemberg)
Galerie Altes Rathaus, Dorfstr. 36, 79594 Inzlingen.
T. (076 21) 822 92. *078465*

Irsee (Bayern)
Michelfelder, Klosterring 9, 87660 Irsee.
T. (08341) 15463, Fax (08341) 13314. - Paint / Graph /
Draw - *078466*

Iserlohn (Nordrhein-Westfalen)
Ballauf, K., Laarstr. 5, 58636 Iserlohn.
T. (02371) 243 72. *078467*

Galerie im Parktheater, 58636 Iserlohn.
T. (02371) 142 38. - Paint - *078468*

Villa Wessel, Gartenstr. 31, 58636 Iserlohn.
T. (02371) 142 38. - Paint - *078469*

Isernhagen (Niedersachsen)
Galerie Isernhagen, Dorfstr. 12, 30916 Isernhagen.
T. (0511) 872 21. - Paint / Sculp / Pho / Draw - *078470*

Jeroch, Gabriele, Burgwedeler Str. 53, 30916 Isernhagen. T. (0511) 73 39 12. - Paint - *078471*

Koch, Irisweg 15, 30916 Isernhagen.
T. (0511) 61 33 03. *078472*

Lüpfert, Turnierweg 11, 30916 Isernhagen.
T. (0511) 736178, Fax (0511) 777067. - Paint / Graph /
Sculp / Draw - *078473*

Ismaning (Bayern)
Galerie im Schlosspavillon, Schloßstr. 1, 85737 Isma-
ning. T. (089) 96 68 52, 96 42 39. - Paint /
Graph - *078474*

Isny (Baden-Württemberg)
Galerie Gut Neuhaus, Gut Neuhaus, 88316 Isny.
T. (07562) 8855, Fax (07562) 155986. - Paint - *078475*

Itzehoe (Schleswig-Holstein)
Kunstkabinett Peter Gerbers, Breite Str. 2, 25524 Itzehoe. T. (04821) 37 44. - Paint / Sculp - *078476*

Jarplund-Weding (Schleswig-Holstein)
Galerie Altholzkrug, Altholzkrug 24, 24941 Jarplund-
Weding. *078477*

Jena (Thüringen)
Galerie des Jenaer Kunstvereins, Zwätzengasse 16,
07743 Jena. T. (03641) 26754, Fax (03641) 26754.
- Paint / Sculp / Pho / Draw - *078478*

Galerie im Stadthaus, Unterm Markt 14, 07743 Jena.
T. (03641) 24604. - Paint / Graph / China / Sculp / Jew /
Pho / Draw - *078479*

Kneipengalerie, Oberlauengasse 10, 07743
Jena. *078480*

Jerxheim (Niedersachsen)
Jerxheimer Kunstverein, Bahnhofstr. 33, 38381
Jerxheim. *078481*

Jockgrim (Rheinland-Pfalz)
Zehnthaus, 76751 Jockgrim. - Paint / Graph /
Sculp - *078482*

Jork (Niedersachsen)
Ritter, Hans-Dieter, Höhen 21, 21635 Jork.
T. (04162) 26 96. *078483*

Jüchen (Nordrhein-Westfalen)
Studio Damm, Marienweg 17, 41363 Jüchen.
T. (02182) 56 56. - Sculp / Jew / Silv / Rel - *078484*

Wolf, Schloß Dyck, 41363 Jüchen. - Paint - *078485*

Kaarst (Nordrhein-Westfalen)
Domin, Giemesstr. 16, 41564 Kaarst.
T. (021 01) 60 47 79. - China - *078486*

Gallery 44, Hasselstr. 60, 41564 Kaarst.
T. (02131) 64723, 67029, Fax (02131) 667819.
- Paint / Graph / Sculp / Mul / Draw - *078487*

Gross, Am Maubishof 31, 41564 Kaarst.
T. (021 01) 693 27. *078488*

Kaiserslautern (Rheinland-Pfalz)
Accent Galerie am Schillerplatz, Schillerstr. 5-7, 67655
Kaiserslautern. T. (0631) 63751, Fax (0631) 64207.
- Paint / Graph / Draw - *078489*

Behr, A.A., Mannheimer Str. 37, 67655 Kaiserslautern.
- Paint / Repr / Fra - *078490*

Boschert, Hermann, Eisenbahnstr. 20, 67655 Kaiserslautern. T. (0631) 932 98. - Paint - *078491*

Goebels, Marisa, Otterberger Str. 51, 67659 Kaiserslautern. - Paint - *078492*

Heer, W., Königstr. 29, 67655 Kaiserslautern.
T. (0631) 18342. *078493*

Jung, Fackelstr. 30, 67655 Kaiserslautern.
T. (0631) 645 55. *078494*

Matzdorf, F., Riesenstr. 15, 67655 Kaiserslautern.
T. (0631) 63434. *078495*

Röder, Steinbruchstr. 9, 67659 Kaiserslautern. *078496*

Wack, Morlauterer Str. 80, 67657 Kaiserslautern.
T. (0631) 72 773. - Paint / Graph / Sculp / Pho / Mul /
Draw - *078497*

Kakenstorf (Niedersachsen)
Kunsthaus Nordheide, Stückhöhen 17, 21255 Kakens-
torf. T. (04186) 8197, Fax (04186) 5528.
- Paint - *078498*

Kamen (Nordrhein-Westfalen)
Galerie im VHS-Haus, Kirchpl 4, 59174 Kamen.
T. (02307) 148450. *078499*

Lewerenz, Weiße Str 25, 59174 Kamen. *078500*

Kampen (Schleswig-Holstein)
Eckert, Iris, Haus Hansen-Wai 30, 25999 Kampen.
T. (04651) 41460. - Paint / Graph / Mul - *078501*

Eglau, Alte Dorfstr., 25999 Kampen. T. (04651) 41102. - Paint / Graph - 078502
Peerlings, J., Kurhausstr. 7, 25999 Kampen. T. (04651) 4940, Fax (04651) 46468. - Paint / Graph - 078503
Pels-Leusden, 25999 Kampen. T. (04651) 41374, Fax 46507. - Paint / Graph / Sculp / Draw - 078504

Karlsbad (Baden-Württemberg)

Galerie Hummelstall, Friedr.-Dietz-Str. 2, 76307 Karlsbad. - Paint - 078505

Karlsruhe (Baden-Württemberg)

Altstadt-Galerie-Durlach, Zunftstr. 10, 76227 Karlsruhe. 078506
Art-Atrium, Kreuzstr. 33, 76133 Karlsruhe. T. (0721) 356113. - Paint - 078507
Art contact, Gartenstr. 1, 76133 Karlsruhe. T. (0721) 37 62 66. 078508
Bücherschiff, Kaiserstr. 186, 76133 Karlsruhe. T. (0721) 210 44, Fax (0721) 29315. - Ant / Paint / Graph / Furn - 078509
Büchle, E., Kreuzstr. 19, 76133 Karlsruhe. T. (0721) 69 93 87, 75 16 27. 078510
Burhenne, H., Scheffelstr. 68, 76135 Karlsruhe. T. (0721) 84 26 81. - Paint - 078511
Degeler, Karlstr. 23, 76113 Karlsruhe. T. (0721) 296 60. - Paint - 078512
Dorer, J., Erbprinzenstr. 19, 76133 Karlsruhe. T. (0721) 257 57. - Paint - 078513
Fischer-Zöller, M., Beiertheimer Allee 48, 76137 Karlsruhe. T. (0721) 320 08. - Paint - 078514
Flammann, Winfried, Tulpenstr. 5, 76199 Karlsruhe. T. (0721) 885420, Fax (0721) 885429. - Paint / Graph / Sculp / Pho / Mul / Draw - 078515
Galerie Akademiestraße, Akademiestr. 27, 76133 Karlsruhe. T. (0721) 27416, Fax (0721) 22594. - Paint / Graph / Eth / Fra / Pho / Mul / Draw - 078516
Galerie art-contact, Gartenstr. 1, 76133 Karlsruhe. T. (0721) 376266, Fax (0721) 376266. - Paint - 078517
Galerie drei 5, Weinbrennerstr. 15, 76135 Karlsruhe. 078518
Galerie Im Oberviertel 19, Im Oberviertel 19, 76229 Karlsruhe. T. (0721) 48650. - Eth - 078519
Gräff, Armin, Waldstr 20, 76133 Karlsruhe. T. (0721) 28060. - Paint / Graph / Repr / Fra - 078520
Hansen, M., Herrenstr. 44, 76133 Karlsruhe. T. (0721) 232 47. - Paint - 078521
Hartmann, Weinbrennerstr. 32, 76135 Karlsruhe. T. (0721) 84 21 91. - Paint - 078522
Hess, Dietrich, Kaiserstr. 36, 76133 Karlsruhe. T. (0721) 69 81 24. 078523
Hilbur, Scheffelstr. 68, 76135 Karlsruhe. T. (0721) 272 81. 078524
Hotz, Marlisa, Albert-Schweitzer-Str. 46, 76139 Karlsruhe. T. (0721) 68 24 26. - Paint - 078525
Künstlerhaus-Galerie, Am Künstlerhaus 47, 76131 Karlsruhe. T. (0721) 37 33 76. - Graph - 078526
Meyer, Karlheinz, Ernststr. 88, 76131 Karlsruhe. T. (0721) 612111, Fax (0721) 616578. - Paint / Graph / Sculp / Draw - 078527
Modern Art Gallery, Waldstr. 73, 76133 Karlsruhe. T. (0721) 22741, Fax (0721) 27177. - Paint - 078528
Papala, Herbert, Bahnhofstr. 12, 76137 Karlsruhe. T. (0721) 288 11. - Paint - 078529
Pavlik, E., Dr., Adlerstr. 20, 76133 Karlsruhe. T. (0721) 69 52 76. - Paint - 078530
Rösch, An der Stadtmauer 10, 76227 Karlsruhe. T. (0721) 495519. - Paint / Sculp - 078531
Rottloff, Sophienstr. 105, 76135 Karlsruhe. T. (0721) 84 32 25. - Paint - 078532
Schneider-Sato, Hardy, Zunftstr. 9, 76227 Karlsruhe. T. (0721) 42574, Fax (0721) 497104. - Paint / Graph / Repr / Sculp / Fra / Draw - 078533
Schork, G., Karlsruher Str. 41, 76139 Karlsruhe. T. (0721) 68 11 89. - Paint - 078534
Usine, Rheinstr. 65, 76185 Karlsruhe. T. (0721) 59 27 94. - Paint - 078535
Witzleben, von, Baumeisterstr. 4, 76137 Karlsruhe. T. (0721) 37 73 42, Fax 37 48 97. - Paint - 078536
Zlotos, M., Amalienstr. 39, 76133 Karlsruhe. T. (0721) 221 26. - Paint - 078537

Kassel (Hessen)

Fotoforum Galerie, Menzelstr. 13, 34121 Kassel. 078538
Galerie Eule, Wolfsschlucht 8a, 34117 Kassel. T. (0561) 127 40. - Paint / Graph / Sculp / Ico - 078539
Galerie im Orangeriecafe, An der Karlsaue 20b, 34121 Kassel. 078540
Galerie Studio Kausch, Friedrich-Ebert-Str. 177, 34119 Kassel. T. (0561) 751 58. - Paint / Graph / Repr / Sculp / Pho / Draw - 078541
Heinzel, B., Opernstr. 9, 34117 Kassel. T. (0561) 158 79. 078542
Krüger, Karl-Heinz, Heinrich-Heine-Str. 1a, 34121 Kassel. T. (0561) 213 21. - Paint / Sculp / Fra / Rel / Ico - 078543
Kunstkabinett Kassel, Bei den Weidenbäumen 42, 34128 Kassel. T. (0561) 88 02 03. - Paint / Graph - 078544
Lometsch, Kölnische Str. 5, 34117 Kassel. T. (0561) 14358, Fax (0561) 772017. - Repr - 078545
Meru, Lassallestr. 11, 34004 Kassel. T. (0561) 777108, Fax (0561) 16467. - Paint - 078546
Missler, Pestalozzistr. 12, 34119 Kassel. T. (0561) 77 65 25. 078547
No-Institute, Bodelschwinghstr. 17, 34119 Kassel. T. (0561) 77 16 45. - Paint - 078548
Puri, Rolandstr. 3, 34131 Kassel. T. (0561) 32436, Fax (0561) 35168. - Paint / Graph / Repr / Fra - 078549
Sander, Siegfried, Schönfelder Str 3, 34121 Kassel. T. (0561) 24494, Fax 26049. - Paint / Graph / Repr / Sculp / Pho / Mul / Draw - 078550
Schmitz, Martin, Pferdemarkt 1a, 34117 Kassel. T. (0561) 18292, Fax (0561) 713041. - Paint - 078551
Waldmann, Peter, Friedrich-Ebert-Str. 114, 34119 Kassel. T. (0561) 78 05 65. 078552

Kelsterbach (Hessen)

Palme, Karlsbader Str. 12 b, 65451 Kelsterbach. T. (06107) 48 70. - Paint / Graph - 078553

Kempten (Bayern)

Berger, Hildegard, Fürstenstr 7, 87439 Kempten. - Paint - 078554
Felle, M., Dr., Poststr 7, 87435 Kempten. T. (0831) 27585, Fax (0831) 28036. - Paint - 078555
Galleria Müßiggengelzunfthaus, Vogtstr 21, 87435 Kempten. T. (0831) 17340, Fax (0831) 21316. 078556
Kemptener Kunstkabinett, Salzstr 12, 87435 Kempten. T. (0831) 24168. 078557

Kevelaer (Nordrhein-Westfalen)

Dierkes, Luxemburger Platz 1, 47623 Kevelaer. T. (02832) 64 31. - Paint - 078558
Janssen, H., Hoogeweg 16, 47623 Kevelaer. T. (02832) 2281, Fax (02832) 3902. - Paint / Graph / Sculp / Fra / Rel - 078559
Janssen, H., Busmannstr. 2, 47623 Kevelaer. T. (02832) 6966, Fax (02832) 3902. - Paint / Graph / Sculp / Fra / Rel - 078560
Kocken, Willi, Hauptstr. 21, 47623 Kevelaer. T. (02832) 781 36. - Paint / Graph / Fra - 078561

Kiel (Schleswig-Holstein)

Brunswiker Pavillon, Brunswiker Str. 13, 24103 Kiel. T. (0431) 554650, Fax (0431) 51691. - Paint / Pho / Draw - 078562
Buchert, Inge, Europaplatz 2, 24103 Kiel. T. (0431) 955 11. - Jew - 078563
Fischer, Ringstr. 51, 24114 Kiel. - Paint - 078564
Galerie am Eichhof, Eichhofstr. 24a, 24116 Kiel. T. (0431) 54 29 75. 078565
Galerie Hinterhaus, Wilhelminenstr. 19, 24103 Kiel. T. (0431) 55 40 11. 078566
Galerie in der Kieler Spar- und Leihkasse, Lorentzendamm 28-30, 24103 Kiel. 078567
Koch, Carsten, Holstentörnpassage, 24103 Kiel. T. (0431) 333025, Fax (0431) 333025. - Paint / Graph / Fra / Pho / Mul / Draw - 078568
Künstlerhaus Kiel, Schönkirchener Str. 48, 24149 Kiel. T. (0431) 287 73, 20 28 68. - Paint / Graph / China / Sculp / Pho / Mul / Draw - 078569
Möbius, Manfred, Esmarchstr. 58, 24105 Kiel. T. (0431) 81893. - Ant / Paint / Graph / Furn / China / Silv / Glass - 078570
Pörksen, Kai, Holtenauer Str. 131, 24118 Kiel. T. (0431) 817 62. - Paint / Graph / Sculp / Rel - 078571
Schwarz, Willi, Ringstr. 44, 24103 Kiel. T. (0431) 67 36 70. 078572
Sfeir-Semler, Dänische Str 30-32, 24103 Kiel. T. (0431) 96162, Fax (0431) 94753. - Paint / Graph / Sculp / Draw - 078573

Kindsbach (Rheinland-Pfalz)

Wagner, T.E., Kaiserstr. 35, 66862 Kindsbach. T. (06371) 151 44. 078574

Kirchheim (Baden-Württemberg)

Kleine Galerie, Flachstr. 5, 73230 Kirchheim. T. (07021) 710 19. 078575
Kunstkabinett, Alleenstr. 8, 73230 Kirchheim. T. (07021) 6023, Fax (07021) 75956. - Paint / Graph - 078576

Kirchheimbolanden (Rheinland-Pfalz)

Waldherr, Neue Allee 11, 67292 Kirchheimbolanden. T. (06352) 3729, Fax (06354) 4109. - Paint / Graph / Sculp / Fra / Draw - 078577

Kirchnüchel (Schleswig-Holstein)

Galerie Kirchnüchel, Am Bungsberg, 23714 Kirchnüchel. T. (04528) 583, 688. 078578

Kleinostheim (Bayern)

Die Galerie, Bahnhofstr. 38, 63801 Kleinostheim. T. (06027) 5515. 078579

Kleve (Nordrhein-Westfalen)

Dönisch-Seidel, Bresserbergstr 35, 47533 Kleve. T. (02821) 23726, Fax (02821) 13429. 078580
Fotogalerie in der Schwanenburg, Schlossberg 1, 47533 Kleve. T. (02821) 69702, Fax (02821) 13179. - Pho - 078581
Kellergalerie 195, Nymeger Str 56, 47533 Kleve. T. (02821) 25564. - Paint / Graph - 078582

Knappenrode (Sachsen)

Braunkohlenwerk Glückauf, Kulturhaus, 02979 Knappenrode. 078583

Koblenz (Rheinland-Pfalz)

Die Galerie, Florinspfaffengasse 5, 56068 Koblenz. T. (0261) 16727. - Paint / Graph / Sculp - 078584
Galerie am Görresplatz, Josef-Görres-Platz 7, 56068 Koblenz. T. (0261) 352 38. 078585
Galerie Markenbildchen, Markenbildchenweg 13, 56068 Koblenz. T. (0261) 36652. - Paint / Graph / Sculp - 078586
Görg, Rathauspassage 6, 56068 Koblenz. T. (0261) 154 87. - Paint - 078587
Laik, Jean-Marc, Altenhof 9, 56068 Koblenz. T. (0261) 171 41. 078588
Wutzke, Volker, Schloßstr. 9-11, 56068 Koblenz. T. (0261) 35781, Fax (0261) 35615. - Paint - 078589

Köln (Nordrhein-Westfalen)

Agentur Pol-Art, Gottfried-Keller-Str. 3, 50931 Köln. T. (0221) 40 23 21. 078594
APC Galerie, Maastrichter Str 26, 50672 Köln. T. (0221) 520063, Fax (0221) 520087. - Paint / Graph / Sculp - 078595
Art Agentur Köln, Venloer Str. 461, 50825 Köln. T. (0221) 544100, 541400, Fax (0221) 543977. - Paint / Sculp / Mul / Draw - 078596

Baukunst-Galerie

Theodor-Heuss-Ring 7
D - 5 0 6 6 8   K ö l n
Telefon 02 21/77 13-335
Telefax 02 21/7 71 33 80

Art und Unart, Meerfeldstr. 27, 50737 Köln.
T. (0221) 599 18 66. - Paint -   *078597*
Artcom, Mozartstr. 39, 50674 Köln. T. (0221) 24 74 43.
- Paint -   *078598*
Artothek, Am Hof 50, 50667 Köln.
T. (0221) 221 23 32.   *078599*
Atelier Katz, Venloer Str 463, 50825 Köln.
T. (0221) 541769.   *078600*
Atelier Roonstraße, Roonstr. 78, 50674 Köln.
T. (0221) 242485, Fax (0221) 561841. - Paint / Graph /
Sculp / Pho / Mul / Draw -   *078601*
Atelier 109, Dürener Str. 109, 50931 Köln.
T. (0221) 400 90 14/15.   *078602*
Baecker, Inge, Zeughausstr 13, 50667 Köln.
T. (0221) 2570401, Fax (0221) 2577012. - Paint /
Graph / Sculp / Pho / Draw -   *078603*
Bar-Gera, Poststr. 2, 50676 Köln. T. (0221) 218788,
Fax (0221) 230863. - Paint -   *078604*
Barthel & Tetner, Sankt Apern-Str 17, 50667 Köln.
T. (0221) 255559.   *078605*
Baukunst-Galerie, Theodor-Heuss-Ring 7, 50668 Köln.
T. (0221) 7713335, Fax 7713380. - Paint / Graph /
Sculp -   *078606*

KUNST
NACH 1950

ZEITGENÖSSISCHE
KUNST

GALERIE
BOISSERÉE

KÖLN SEIT 1838
J. & W. BOISSERÉE GMBH
GF: JOHANNES SCHILLING
DRUSUSGASSE 7 - 11
D - 50667 KÖLN
TEL. 0221 / 2 57 85 19
FAX 0221 / 2 57 85 50
MONTAGS GESCHLOSSEN

Belgisches Haus, Cäcilienstr. 46, 50667 Köln.
T. (0221) 218216, 217196, 218857,
Fax (0221) 242956. - Paint / Graph / China / Sculp /
Tex -   *078607*
Berndt, Albertusstr 9-11, 50667 Köln.
T. (0221) 2574831, Fax (0221) 2574910. - Paint /
Graph / Sculp / Pho / Mul / Draw -   *078608*
Beuse, R., Ebertpl, 50668 Köln.
T. (0221) 134441.   *078609*
BilderSchreck, Königswinterstr 1, 50939 Köln.
T. (0221) 417885.   *078610*

Binhold, Hohe Str. 96, 50667 Köln. T. (0221) 214222,
2578971, Fax (0221) 254401. - Paint / Sculp - *078611*
Bismarck, Kamekestr. 14, 50672 Köln.
T. (0221) 56 10 27.   *078612*
Blüher, Joachim, Dr., Gertrudenstr 7, 50667 Köln.
T. (0221) 2575401, Fax (0221) 2576533. - Paint /
Graph / Draw / Pho -   *078612a*
Böhm, Maria & Josef, Bazaar de Cologne, 50672 Köln.
T. (0221) 2583474.   *078613*
Boisserée, Drususgasse 7-11, 50667 Köln.
T. (0221) 2578519, Fax 2578550. - Paint / Graph /
Fra -   *078614*
Boisserée, S., Unter den Ulmen, 50968 Köln.
T. (0221) 387721.   *078615*
Bolz, Karin, Hansaring 77, 50670 Köln.
T. (0221) 134626, Fax (0221) 131965. - Paint - *078616*
Bootz, Th., Klosterstr. 124a, 50931 Köln.
T. (0221) 40 63 05. - Paint -   *078617*
Borgmann, Thomas, Apostelnstr 19, 50667 Köln.
T. (0221) 256676, Fax (0221) 256593. - Paint / Sculp /
Draw -   *078618*
Born Fine Art Galerie, Bobstr. 9, 50676 Köln.
T. (0221) 235777, Fax (0221) 213022. - Paint /
Graph -   *078619*
Bozionek, M., Gereonswall 8, 50668 Köln.
T. (0221) 122994.   *078620*
Buchholz, Neven-DuMont-Str 17, 50667 Köln.
T. (0221) 2576251, Fax (0221) 253351. - Paint / Sculp /
Pho / Mul -   *078621*
Buchmann, Lupusstr 22, 50670 Köln.
T. (0221) 730650.   *078622*
Campana, Luis, Friesenplatz 13, Köln.
T. (0221) 2571570, Fax (0221) 256213.   *078623*
Capitain, Gisela, Apostelnstr. 19, 50667 Köln.
T. (0221) 256676, Fax (0221) 256593. - Paint / Graph /
Mul / Draw -   *078624*
CCA Galleries, Braugasse 14h, 50859 Köln.
T. (02234) 71836, Fax (02234) 4156. - Paint / Graph /
Repr / Sculp / Fra -   *078625*
CCAA Glasgalerie Köln, Auf dem Berlich 24, 50667 Köln.
T. (0221) 2576191, Fax (0221) 2576192.
- Glass -   *078626*
Chapel Art Center, Jülicher Str 26, 50674 Köln.
T. (0221) 2402168, Fax (0221) 351334. - Paint /
Graph / Sculp / Tex -   *078627*
Clasen, Olaf, St.-Apern-Str 17-21, 50667 Köln.
T. (0221) 252104, Fax (0221) 251978. - Paint / Graph /
Sculp / Draw -   *078628*
Dege & B. Plein, U., Sankt Martin, 51143 Köln.
T. (0221) 256204.   *078629*
Die Weisse Galerie, Albertusstr 26, 50667 Köln.
T. (0221) 254725, Fax (0221) 254822. - Paint / Graph /
Furn / Sculp / Draw -   *078630*
Dieckmann, L., Stenzelbergstr 17, 50939 Köln.
T. (0221) 444909. - Paint -   *078631*
Dieda, Maybachstr 96, 50670 Köln.
T. (0221) 1390216.   *078632*
Dielen-Galerie, Boltensternstr. 111, 50735 Köln.
T. (0221) 76 16 10. - Paint / Graph -   *078633*
Dreiseitel, Aachener Str 1013, 50858 Köln.
T. (0221) 483888, Fax 4844452. - Paint / Graph /
Sculp / Draw -   *078634*
Edel, K., Neumarkt 1c, 50667 Köln. T. (0221) 43 23 27,
Fax (0221) 46 66 56. - Paint / Orient -   *078635*

Eichhorst, D., Gertrudenstr. 15, 50667 Köln.
T. (0221) 2571390. - Paint -   *078636*
Falck, Ottopl 7, 50679 Köln. T. (0221) 810923. *078636a*
Feuerle & Ruiz de Villa, Hansaring 77, 50670 Köln.
T. (0221) 123050, Fax (0221) 121293.   *078637*
Fiedler, Ulrich, Lindenstr 19, 50674 Köln.
T. (0221) 2401338, Fax (0221) 249601. - Furn /
Mod -   *078638*
Flügel, M. u. P., Kurische Str 39, 50997 Köln.
T. (0221) 21927.   *078639*
Friebe, Anna, Im Hasengarten 33, 50996 Köln.
T. (02236) 64802, Fax (02236) 68771. - Paint - *078640*
Friedrich, K., Mathildenstr. 19, 50679 Köln.
T. (0221) 81 32 23. - Paint -   *078641*
Fuchs, B., Salzburger Weg 4, 50858 Köln.
T. (0221) 487882.   *078642*
Fuhrmann, I., An der Bottmühle 16, 50678 Köln.
T. (0221) 32 31 03.   *078643*
Funken, Albertusstr. 4, 50667 Köln. T. (0221) 2571234,
Fax (0221) 2571435. - Paint / Graph -   *078644*
Galerie am Buttermarkt/Produzentinnen Galerie, Butter-
markt 23, 50667 Köln. T. (0221) 258 12 06. - Paint /
Graph / Sculp / Tex / Pho / Draw -   *078645*
Galerie am Markt, Kölner Str 232, 50859 Köln.
T. (0221) 10234.   *078646*
Galerie arting, Brüsseler Str. 29, 50674 Köln.
T. (0221) 24 56 65, Fax (0221) 24 56 65.
- Paint -   *078647*
Galerie Axiom, Hans-Driesch-Str. 7, 50935 Köln.
T. (0221) 43 82 40. - Paint / Graph / Sculp -   *078648*
Galerie Claude, Deutzer Freiheit 103, 50679 Köln.
T. (0221) 81 34 94. - Paint -   *078649*
Galerie der Handwerkskammer, Heumarkt 12-14, 50667
Köln. T. (0221) 202 21. - Paint -   *078650*
Galerie der Nomaden, Apostelnstr. 28, 50667 Köln.
T. (0221) 257 81 63.   *078651*
Galerie der Spiegel, Bonner Str 328, 50968 Köln.
T. (0221) 385799, Fax (0221) 386206. - Paint / Graph /
Sculp -   *078652*
Galerie des Beaux-Arts, Heumarkt 55-57, 50667 Köln.
T. (0221) 2582208. - Paint / Graph -   *078653*
Galerie Die Maske, Albertusstr. 13-17, 50667 Köln.
- Pho -   *078654*
Galerie für naive Kunst, Roteichenweg 5, 51069 Köln.
T. (0221) 68 83 38. - Paint / Sculp -   *078655*
Galerie Glockengasse, Glockengasse 4711, 50667 Köln.
T. (0221) 23 47 11.   *078656*
Galerie IGS Multimedia, Mittelstr. 52-54, 50672 Köln.
T (0221) 257 60 30, 257 36 36, Fax 257 34 97. - Paint /
Graph / Sculp -   *078656a*
Galerie im alten Kloster, Gütergasse 33, 51143 Köln.
T. (0221) 839 85. - Paint -   *078657*
Galerie Imago, Wiethasestr. 22, 50933 Köln.
T. (0221) 40 31 20.   *078658*
Galerie in C, Hohenstaufenring 53, 50674 Köln.
T. (0221) 21 16 17, Fax (0221) 21 16 17.
- Paint -   *078659*
Galerie in der Isenburg, Johann-Bensberg-Str. 67,
51067 Köln. - Paint -   *078660*
Galerie Lichtblick, Steinbergerstr. 21, 50733 Köln.
T. (0221) 72 91 49, Fax (0221) 52 49 89. - Pho - *078661*
Galerie ON, Jülicher Str 27, 50674 Köln.
T. (0221) 2406135, Fax (0221) 2406034.   *078662*
Galerie Orangerie Reinz, Helenenstr 2, 50667 Köln.
T. (0221) 2575038, Fax 2575132. - Paint -   *078663*
Galerie Orangerie-Reinz, Helenenstr 2, 50667 Köln.
T. (0221) 2575038, Fax (0221) 2575132. - Paint /
Graph / Sculp -   *078664*
Galerie Skala, Lindenstr 21, 50674 Köln.
T. (0221) 210041, Fax (0221) 242786.   *078665*
Galerie und Edition Hundertmark, Brüsseler Str 29,
50674 Köln. T. (0221) 237944, Fax 249146. - Paint /
Graph / Sculp -   *078666*
Glöckner, Claudia, Mommsenstr 65, 50935 Köln.
T. (0221) 2576130, Fax 254863. - Graph /
Draw -   *078667*

GALERIE ORANGERIE
REINZ

COLOGNE

HELENENSTR. 2 · D-50667 KÖLN · TEL 02 21-2 57 50 38 · FAX 02 21-2 57 51 32

---

galerie gmurzynska

goethestraße 65a · d-50968 köln
telefon 02 21 / 37 64 40 · fax 02 21 / 37 87 30

Gmurzynska, Goethestr 65a, 50968 Köln.
T. (0221) 376440, Fax 378730. - Paint - *078668*
Göddertz, G., Mauritiuswall 62, 50676 Köln.
T. (0221) 23 05 90. - Paint - *078669*
Greve, Karsten, Wallrafpl 3, 50667 Köln.
T. (0221) 2580478, Fax 2580479. - Paint / Sculp /
Draw - *078670*
Grunert, Tanja, Venloer Str 19, 50672 Köln.
T. (0221) 562006, Fax (0221) 515181. - Paint / Graph /
Sculp / Pho - *078671*
Gün, I., Ludwigstr. 15, 50667 Köln. T. (0221) 257 65 97,
257 66 55. *078672*
Hansen, R. u H., Kaesenstr 19, 50677 Köln.
T. (0221) 326757. *078673*
Hensel & Wiegers, Gertrudenstr 21, 50667 Köln.
T. (0221) 2578166, Fax (0221) 255911. *078674*
Hetzler, Max, Venloer Str. 21, 50672 Köln.
T. (0221) 52 75 41, Fax (0221) 52 51 01. *078675*
Hohenthal und Bergen, Bismarckstr 60, 50672 Köln.
T. (0221) 5103410, Fax (0221) 5103419. *078676*
Hohmann, Kölner Ladenstadt, 50667 Köln.
T. (0221) 21 96 06. *078677*
Holtmann, Heinz, Richartzstr 10, 50667 Köln.
T. (0221) 2578607, 2578716, Fax 2578724. *078678*
Hoppe, G., Hohe Str 41, 50667 Köln.
T. (02219 255334. *078679*
Hua Yue, Luxemburger Str. 311, 50674 Köln.
T. (0221) 44 40 25. *078680*
Hülchrath Galerie, Hulchrather Str. 6, 50670 Köln.
T. (0221) 72 00 78. - Paint - *078681*
Ihsen, Brigitte, St.-Apern-Str 40, 50667 Köln.
T. (0221) 2583560, Fax (0221) 2580750. *078682*
Iliev, Domstr 95, 50668 Köln. T. (0221) 1392454,
Fax 1392455. *078682a*
in focus, Marzellenstr 9, 50667 Köln. T. (0221) 1300341,
Fax (0221) 1300341. - Pho - *078683*
Inter Art Galerie Reich, Neue Langgasse 2, 50667 Köln.
T. (0221) 2576297, Fax (0221) 2582489. - Paint /
Graph / Sculp - *078684*

Jablonka, Venloer Str 21, 50672 Köln. T. (0221) 526867,
Fax (0221) 525569. - Paint / Sculp / Pho / Mul - *078685*
Jahns, Wolfgang, Trierer Str. 19, 50676 Köln.
T. (0221) 32 89 78. *078686*
Jarzyk, Béla, Im Klapperhof 33, 50670 Köln.
T. (0221) 9127053, Fax (0221) 91270521. *078687*
Jaschinski, A., Tempelstr. 16, 50679 Köln.
T. (0221) 81 27 68. *078688*
Jöllenbeck, Maastrichter Str 53, 50672 Köln.
T. (0221) 515852, Fax (0221) 519275. - Paint / Graph /
Sculp / Pho / Mul / Draw - *078689*
Johnen, J., Kamekestr 21, 50672 Köln.
T. (0221) 524505, Fax (0221) 527596. - Paint - *078690*
Kamp, M., Zeppelinstr 2, 50667 Köln.
T. (0221) 2581812. *078691*
KAOS Galerie, Genter Str. 6, 50672 Köln.
T. (0221) 2583560. *078692*
Kicken, Rudolf, Bismarckstr. 50, 50672 Köln.
T. (0221) 515005, Fax (0221) 519858. - Paint - *078693*
Klein, H.G., St. Apern-Str 2, 50667 Köln.
T. (0221) 2576133, Fax (0221) 2583264. - Ant / Paint /
Graph / Silv - *078694*
Köhrmann, Gerd, Yorckstr. 3, 50733 Köln.
T. (0221) 76 11 44. - Paint / Graph / Sculp /
Draw - *078695*
Kolon, Bismarckstr 70, 50672 Köln. T. (0221) 517001,
Fax (0221) 519055. - Paint / Graph / Sculp / Mul /
Draw - *078696*
Koppelmann, Ingrid, Mettfelder Str 34, 50996 Köln.
T. (0221) 519165, Fax (0221) 351334. *078697*
Korndörfer, Sülzburgstr 172, 50937 Köln.
T. (0221) 412922. *078698*
Krämer, H., Dürener Str. 109, 50931 Köln.
T. (0221) 400 90 14. *078699*
Krause, Hermann, Thürmchenswall 6, 50668 Köln.
T. (0221) 12 43 15, Fax (0221) 13 17 15.
- Graph - *078700*
Kreihausgalerie R. Schröder, St.-Apern-Str 17-21,
50667 Köln. T. (0221) 2570041,
Fax (0221) 2570089. *078701*

Krings-Ernst Galerie, Goltsteinstr 106, 50968 Köln.
T. (0221) 382048, Fax (0221) 342370. - Paint / Graph /
Sculp / Pho / Mul / Draw - *078702*
Krips, Maximilian, Brüsseler Str 78, 50672 Köln.
T. (0221) 5101688, Fax (0221) 519702.
- Graph - *078703*
Krombholz, Gabriele, Dürener Str 121, 50931 Köln.
T. (0221) 409535. - Paint - *078704*
Kühn, Marianne, Roteichenweg 5, 51069 Köln.
T. (0221) 688338. *078705*
Kuhn Galerie, Lützowstr. 13, 50674 Köln.
T. (0221) 24 67 26. - Paint / Graph / Arch / Mul - *078706*
Kunst-Station Sankt Peter Köln, Jabachstr. 1, 50676
Köln. T. (0221) 23 67 14, Fax (0221) 21 45 64. - Ant /
Paint - *078707*
Kunst & Psyche, Dr. Lenhardt GmbH, Ebertplatz 9,
50668 Köln. T. (0221) 72 71 25. *078708*
Kunsthandlung Goyert, Hahnenstr 18, 50667 Köln.
T. (0221) 2570330, Fax (0221) 2570339. - Paint /
Graph / Fra / Draw - *078709*
Kunsthaus am Museum, Drususgasse 1-5, 50667 Köln.
T. (0221) 9258620, Fax (0221) 92586230. *078710*
Kunsthaus am Museum-Studio, Drususgasse 1-5,
50667 Köln. T. (0221) 252057, Fax (0221) 236077,
2578558. - Paint - *078711*
Kunstlicht, Herbigstr. 8, 50825 Köln. T. (0221) 550 72 55.
- Paint - *078712*
Kunstraum Fuhrwerkswaage, Bergstr. 79, 50739 Köln.
T. (0221) 02236/61049. - Paint / Sculp / Draw - *078713*
Kunstverein Buttermarkt, Buttermarkt 23, 50667 Köln.
T. (0221) 258 12 06. *078714*
Kunstzentrum Wachsfabrik, Industriestr. 170, 50735
Köln. T. (0221) 02236/63770. *078715*
la linea, Auf dem Berlich 26, 50667 Köln.
T. (0221) 2574953, Fax (0221) 2574951. - Paint /
Graph / Sculp / Pho / Mul / Draw - *078716*
Lachmann, Alex, St.-Apern-Str 17-21, 50667 Köln.
T. (0221) 2574953, Fax (0221) 2574951. - Paint /
Graph / Sculp / Pho / Mul / Draw - *078717*
Lempertz, Neumarkt 3, 50667 Köln. T. (0221) 9257290,
Fax 9257296. - Paint / Sculp - *078718*
Limbach, A., Eigelstein 118, 50668 Köln.
T. (0221) 13 79 75. *078719*
Limbach Jingles, Obenmarspforten, 50667 Köln.
T. (0221) 2582202. *078720*
Lindenthal, Friedrich-Schmidt-Str 20a, 50935 Köln.
T. (0221) 401092. *078721*
Logo, Kempener Str 54, 50733 Köln.
T. (0221) 7325266. *078722*
Lukas & Hoffmann, Albertusstr 4, 50667 Köln.
T. (0221) 2574653, Fax (0221) 2574753. *078723*
M & M Galerie, Richmodstr. 4, 50667 Köln.
T. (0221) 25 58 25. *078724*
Magers, Philomene, Maria-Hilf-Str 17, 50677 Köln.
T. (0221) 318843, Fax (0221) 318677. - Paint / Graph /
Sculp / Pho / Mul - *078725*
Maier, Ferdinand, Neusser Str 8, 50670 Köln.
T. (0221) 726075, Fax (0221) 729030. *078726*
Malchow, Wittgensteinstr. 18, 50931 Köln.
T. (0221) 40 42 82. *078727*
Maulbecker, H. u M., Volkhovener Weg 81, 50767 Köln.
T. (0221) 796415. *078728*
Mautsch, Janine, Eifelstr 19, 50677 Köln.
T. (0221) 322733, Fax (0221) 323500. *078729*
Mendoza-Velaslo, Neumarkt 18a, 50667 Köln.
T. (0221) 2577128. *078730*
Mondorf, Willi, Bergisch Gladbacher Str. 83, 51065 Köln.
T. (0221) 86 30 95. *078731*
Montezuma-Galerie, Andreaskloster 14, 50667 Köln.
T. (0221) 13 51 36. *078732*
Moog, Eike, Albertusstr. 9-11, 50667 Köln.
T. (0221) 2574916, 2574839. - Paint / Graph /
Orient - *078733*
Müller, Alfred Otto, Sternengasse 1, 50676 Köln.
T. (0221) 231513. - Paint / Sculp / Fra - *078734*
Müller-Brunert, Marspfortengasse 8, 50667 Köln.
T. (0221) 2578894, Fax (0221) 696621. - Paint /
Graph / China - *078735*
Müller, Ha.Jo., Brüsseler Platz 15, 50674 Köln.
T. (0221) 520763. - Paint - *078736*
Mueller, Ulrich, 50939 Köln. T. (0221) 414864,
Fax (0221) 4201116. *078737*
NADA, Körnerstr. 77, 50823 Köln. T. (0221) 51 76 41.
- Paint / Furn - *078738*

KARSTEN GREVE

WALLRAFPLATZ 3 · 50667 KÖLN

TEL. 02 21/2 58 04 78 · FAX 02 21/2 58 04 79

Nagel, Christian, UFA-Palast, Hohenzollernring 22-24, 50672 Köln. T. (0221) 2570591, Fax (0221) 2570592.
- Paint - *078739*
Naive-Kunst-Galerie, Roteichenweg 5, 51069 Köln.
T. (0221) 688338, Fax (0221) 688338. - Paint - *078740*
Navarrete, Paloma, Spichernstr 63a, 50672 Köln.
T. (0221) 5102787, Fax (0221) 5102787. *078741*
Neumärker, Carsten, Antwerpener Str 49, 50672 Köln.
T. (0221) 5104382, Fax (0221) 5104383. *078742*
Nilius, Joachim, Vorgebirgstr 37, 50677 Köln.
T. (0221) 383360, Fax (0221) 382459. - Paint /
Graph - *078743*
Opitz, Walter-Flex-Str 2, 50996 Köln.
T. (0221) 351597. *078744*
Orientgalerie, Brückenstr, 50667 Köln.
T. (0221) 2581964. *078745*
Osper, Knut, Pfeilstr. 29, 50672 Köln. T. (0221) 9257100,
Fax (0221) 92571010. - Paint / Graph / Fra / Mod / Ico /
Draw - *078746*
Parmentier, H., Palmstr. 21, 50672 Köln.
T. (0221) 253790. *078747*
Paszti-Bott, Thürmchenswall 70, Köln.
T. (0221) 1390549. *078748*
Pesch-Galerie-Atrium, Kaiser-Wilhelm-Ring 22, 50672
Köln. T. (0221) 161 30. *078749*
Petite Galerie 72, Marzellenstr. 72-74, 50668 Köln.
T. (0221) 13 73 95. - Paint - *078750*
Pfennigs, M., Nüssenberger Str. 18, 50829 Köln.
T. (0221) 50 19 68. - Paint - *078751*
Poster- Galerie, An der Hahnepooz, 50674 Köln.
T. (0221) 2574419. *078752*
Projekt Oberbuschweg, Ober Buschweg 32, 50999
Köln. *078753*
Querengässer, Thomas A., Lindenstr 21, 50674 Köln.
T. (0221) 210041, Fax (0221) 242786. *078754*
Räderscheidt, Gisèle, Landsbergstr. 45, 50678 Köln.
T. (0221) 31 37 83. - Paint - *078755*
Raum für Malerei, Alteburger Str. 79, 50678 Köln.
T. (0221) 38 83 95. - Paint - *078756*
Reckermann, W. und H., Albertusstr 16, 50667 Köln.
T. (0221) 2574868, Fax (0221) 2574867. - Paint /
Graph / Sculp - *078757*
Rehbein, Thomas, Wormserstr. 21, 50677 Köln.
T. (221) 344434, Fax (221) 344296. *078758*
Ricke, Rolf, Volksgartenstr 10, 50667 Köln.
T. (0221) 315717, Fax (0221) 327043. - Paint / Sculp /
Draw - *078759*
Rivet, Volksgartenstr 10, 50667 Köln.
T. (0221) 319254. *078759a*
Röpke, Andreas, St.-Apern-Str 17-21, Köln.
T. (0221) 255559, Fax (0221) 255742. *078760*
Roesinger, Ch. E., Alteburger Str 111, 50678 Köln.
T. (0221) 382958, Fax (0221) 381625. - Paint - *078761*
Saghari, K., Hansestr. 51, 51149 Köln.
T. (0221) 30 00 31. *078762*
Scheibler, Maria-Hilf-Str 17, 50677 Köln.
T. (0221) 311011, Fax (0221) 3319615. *078763*
Schellmann, Jörg, Alsdorfer Str 1-3, 50933 Köln.
T. (0221) 5461020, Fax (0221) 5461030. *078764*
Schenk, Brigitte, Hohenzollernring 46, 50672 Köln.
T. (0221) 9250901, Fax (0221) 9250902. *078765*
Schilling, Breite Str 2, 50667 Köln. T. (0221) 2578538,
Fax (0221) 2578550. *078766*
Schipper & Krome, Neusserstr 28, 50670 Köln.
T. (0221) 727915, Fax (0221) 722816. - Paint / Graph /
Sculp / Draw - *078767*
Schlote, Im Klapperhof 33, 50670 Köln.
T. (0221) 125995. *078768*
Schmidt, Adriana, Albertusstr 26, 50667 Köln.
T. (0221) 253610, Fax (0221) 2570903. - Paint /
Graph / Sculp - *078769*
Schmidt, Sabine, Hohenzollernring 22-24, 50672 Köln.
T. (0221) 2578441, Fax (0221) 2580979. *078770*
Schneiderei, Gereonswall 8, Köln. T. (0221) 122994,
Fax (0221) 727592. *078771*
Schönewald, P., & R. Beuse, Ebertplatz-Passage, 50668
Köln. T. (0221) 13 44 41. - Paint - *078772*
Schröder, Renate, Albertusstr 26, 50667 Köln.
T. (0221) 2582758, Fax (0221) 2582748.
- Paint - *078773*

Schüppenhauer, Christel, Bismarckstr 60, 50672 Köln.
T. (0221) 513075, Fax (0221) 518001. - Paint / Graph /
Sculp / Pho - *078774*
Schweins, Otto, Wormser Str 23, 50677 Köln.
T. (0221) 343932, Fax (0221) 343932. *078775*
Seegert, Hochwaldstr. 12, 50935 Köln.
T. (0221) 43 03 198. *078776*
Seippel, Flandrische Str 6, 50674 Köln.
T. (0221) 255834, Fax (0221) 252265. - Paint / Graph /
Sculp / Mul / Draw - *078777*
Seyhan, M., Hohenstaufenring 10, 50674 Köln.
T. (0221) 24 74 74. *078778*
Smend, Mainzer Str 31, 50678 Köln. T. (0221) 312047/
48, Fax (0221) 325134. - Paint - *078779*
Sprenger, G., Breniger Str. 5, 50969 Köln.
T. (0221) 36 69 03. - Paint - *078780*
Sprüth, Monika, Wormser Str 23, 50677 Köln.
T. (0221) 380415/16, Fax (0221) 380417. *078781*
Staacke, Lütticher Str 53, 50674 Köln.
T. (0221) 529182. *078782*
Stein, Manfred, Stadtwaldgürtel 13, 50935 Köln.
T. (0221) 406 05 16. - Sculp - *078783*
Stenvert-Mittrowsky, Antonia, Johanniterstr 2a, 50859
Köln. T. (02234) 70304, Fax 709385. - Paint - *078784*
Stoll multiple-art, Mauritiussteinweg 64, 50676 Köln.
T. (0221) 23 18 99. *078785*
Stolz, Am Römerturm 15, 50667 Köln.
T. (0221) 2575144, Fax (0221) 2575145. - Paint /
Graph / Sculp - *078786*
Studio Kunsthaus am Museum, Drususgasse 1-5, 50667
Köln. T. (0221) 9258620, Fax 92586230. - Paint /
Glass - *078787*
Stützer, Carla, Kamekestr 21, 50672 Köln.
T. (0221) 518214, Fax (0221) 511192. - Paint / Graph /
Sculp / Mul / Draw - *078788*
Tengelmann, Am Mönchhof 1, 50667 Köln.
T. (0221) 43 22 04. *078789*
Teutloff, Lutz, Albertusstr 55, 50667 Köln.
T. (0221) 2570100, Fax 2570110. - Paint - *078790*

LUTZ TEUTLOFF GALERIE

Albertusstraße 55, 50667 Köln

T.: 02 21-25 70 100
F.: 02 21-25 70 110

Theisen, U., Auf dem Berlich 13, 50667 Köln.
T. (0221) 257 80 10. *078791*
Thoma, Peter, Norbertstr. 15, 50670 Köln.
T. (0221) 135493. - Paint - *078792*
Tittel, Roswitha, Gilbachstr 24, 50672 Köln.
T. (0221) 526184. - Paint - *078793*
Tobies & Chr. Silex, R., Bernhardstr 97, Köln.
T. (0221) 387358. *078794*
TransArt Exhibition Service, Sankt-Apern-Str 17-21,
50667 Köln. T. (0221) 2574937, Fax 254657. *078795*
Tress, Horst, Postfach 660114, 50708 Köln.
T. (0221) 714261, Fax 7127584. *078796*
Ucher, A., Großer Griechenmarkt 39, 50676 Köln.
T. (0221) 215956, Fax (0221) 215668. - Paint /
Graph - *078797*
Ungers, Sophia, Schaafenstr 43, 50676 Köln.
T. (0221) 2401289, Fax (0221) 2406151. *078798*
Vahlkamp, H., Marzellenstr. 72, 50668 Köln.
T. (0221) 13 73 95. *078799*
Voosen, C., & H. Wohlgemuth, Kattenbug 2, 50667 Köln.
T. (0221) 13 52 81. *078800*
Wasserturm Edition, Birkenstr. 9, 50996 Köln.
T. (0221) 35 37 58. *078801*
Wegner, J., Leonhard-Tietz-Str. 4, 50676 Köln.
T. (0221) 21 19 29. - Paint - *078802*
Werle, Dietmar, Köln. T. (0221) 515790,
Fax (0221) 511389. *078803*

GALERIE MICHAEL WERNER

Gertrudenstr. 24-28, 50667 Köln
Tel. 02 21 / 9 25 46 20
Fax 02 21 / 9 25 46 22

MICHAEL WERNER INC.

21 East 67 Street
New York, N.Y. 10021
USA
Tel. 212 - 9 88 16 23
Fax 212 - 9 88 17 74

Werner, Michael, Gertrudenstr 24-28, 50667 Köln.
T. (0221) 9254620, Fax 9254622. - Paint / Furn / Pho /
Draw - *078804*
Westernhagen, Bismarckstr 33, 50672 Köln.
T. (0221) 561637, Fax (0221) 561637. *078805*
Wilbrand, Dieter, Lindenstr 20, 50674 Köln.
T. (0221) 244904, Fax (0221) 237592. - Paint / Graph /
Sculp / Draw - *078806*
Wilkens, Maria, Aachener Str 23, 50674 Köln.
T. (0221) 252590, Fax (0221) 252638. - Paint / Graph /
Mul - *078807*
Zwirner, Rudolf, Albertusstr. 18, 50667 Köln.
T. (0221) 2574841, Fax (0221) 2574876.
- Paint - *078808*
ZZZ Die Letzten, Klosterstr. 92, 50931 Köln.
T. (0221) 406 09 83. - Paint - *078809*
235 Media, Postfach 19 03 60, 50500 Köln.
T. (0221) 52 38 28, Fax (0221) 52 27 41.
- Paint - *078810*

Königsberg (Bayern)

Bittenbrünn, Briegelstr 3, 97486 Königsberg.
T. (09525) 521. *078811*

Königstein (Hessen)

Galerie im Haus Bender, Gerichtstr 12, 61462 Königs-
tein. T. (06174) 24555. - Paint / Graph / Sculp /
Draw - *078812*
Herzer, Hildegard, Schwalbenweg 5, 61462 Königstein.
T. (06174) 23281. - Paint - *078813*

Kolbermoor (Bayern)

Lehle, Wilhelm-Zerr-Str. 46, 83059 Kolbermoor.
T. (08031) 954 64. - Paint - *078814*

Konstanz (Baden-Württemberg)

Grashey, Schützenstr. 14, 78462 Konstanz.
T. (07531) 16614. - Paint / Graph / Sculp /
Draw - *078815*
Heureiter, Ringstr. 109, 78465 Konstanz.
T. (07531) 07533/6882. - Paint / Mul - *078816*
Knittel, Neuhauser Str. 13, 78464 Konstanz.
T. (07531) 646 44. *078817*
Orek, Wessenbergstr. 32, 78462 Konstanz.
T. (07531) 211 17. - Paint / Graph / Orient / Eth / Jew /
Glass - *078818*
Repphun, Kreuzlinger Str. 39, 78462 Konstanz.
T. (07531) 246 65. - Paint / Graph / Sculp / Fra /
Ico - *078819*
Scheureck, Kurt, Reutestr. 81, 78467 Konstanz. *078820*

Kornwestheim (Baden-Württemberg)

Agethen, Atelier, Ulrichstr. 17, 70806
Kornwestheim. *078821*
Geiger, Roland, Enzstr. 9, 70806 Kornwestheim.
T. (07154) 72 23, Fax 16662. - Paint / Graph / Sculp /
Fra - *078822*

Korschenbroich (Nordrhein-Westfalen)

Galerie am Hufeisen, Nöhlenweg 7, 41352 Korschen-
broich. T. (02161) 644654. *078823*
Otten, H., Donatusstr. 21, 41352 Korschenbroich.
T. (02161) 64 00 95. *078824*

Kraichtal (Baden-Württemberg)

Galerie im Amtshaus, Neuenwegstr. 8, 76703 Kraichtal.
T. (07250) 606 23, Fax 695 64. - Paint - *078825*

Krefeld (Nordrhein-Westfalen)

Beckershof, Kemmerhofstr. 319, 47802 Krefeld. *078826*

Fochem, Christian, Wallstr. 14, 47798 Krefeld. T. (02151) 66679, 59 74 46. - Paint / Graph / Sculp / Mul / Draw - 078827
Graf, Illa, Angerhausenstr. 11-13, 47798 Krefeld. T. (02151) 296 64. 078828
Hanssen, Breite Str. 21, 47798 Krefeld. T. (02151) 292 30. - Paint - 078829
Hoves, Eberhard, Evertsstr. 35, 47798 Krefeld. T. (02151) 60 26 57. - Paint / Graph / Fra - 078830
Hülser Bildergalerie, Klever Str. 19, 47839 Krefeld. 078831
Königs, Heinz, Dreikönigenstr. 26, 47799 Krefeld. T. (02151) 214 31. - Paint / Fra - 078832
Krüll, Luisenstr. 99, 47799 Krefeld. T. (02151) 2 21 06. - Paint / Graph / Sculp / Fra - 078833
Kunst-Spektrum GKK und Artothek, St.-Anton-Str. 90, 47798 Krefeld. T. (02151) 77 90 37. - Paint / Graph / Sculp / Pho / Draw - 078834
Linner Galerie, Margaretenstr. 24, 47809 Krefeld. T. (02151) 57 34 30. 078835
Ludwig, Oelschlägerstr. 65-67, 47798 Krefeld. T. (02151) 31 05 40, Fax 31 05 20. - Paint / Graph / Sculp / Mul / Draw - 078836
Meditativ Art Galerie, Kuhdyk 20, 47802 Krefeld. T. (02151) 56 17 19. - Paint - 078837
Peerlings, Friedrichstr. 49, 47798 Krefeld. T. (02151) 699 66, 297 43, Fax 28524. - Paint / Graph - 078838
Peerlings, Friedrichstr 49, 47798 Krefeld. T. (02151) 29743, Fax 28524. 078839
Schönewald & Beuse, Uerdinger Str. 342, 47800 Krefeld. T. (02151) 59 02 33/4, Fax 59 17 64. - Paint / Graph / Mul - 078840
Schröer, Friedrich-Ebert-Str. 14, 47799 Krefeld. T. (02151) 59 96 09. - Paint / Graph / Sculp - 078841
Steinbach & Sohn, Hans, Rheinstr. 38 und 39, 47799 Krefeld. T. (02151) 2 65 34. - Paint / Graph / Repr / Fra - 078842
Treppengalerie, Marktstr. 59, 47798 Krefeld. T. (02151) 228 70. 078843
Weber, Meta, Evertsstr. 45, 47798 Krefeld. - Paint - 078844
Zerres, Peter, Carl-Wilhelm-Str 27-29, 47798 Krefeld. T. (02151) 601393, Fax (02151) 601393. 078845

Kronach (Bayern)
Fränkische Galerie, Festung Rosenberg, 96317 Kronach. T. (09261) 95251. - Ant - 078846
Franken Galerie, Kulmbergstr. 20, 96317 Kronach. T. (09261) 91952. - Graph - 078847
KKV-Galerie am Kloster, Klosterstr., 96317 Kronach. T. (09261) 31 65. - Paint - 078848
Ludwig, Martin, Stadtgraben 15, 96317 Kronach. T. (09261) 51361. 078849
Städtische Galerie am Rathaus, Marktpl. 5, 96317 Kronach. T. (09261) 972 08, Fax 972 89. - Paint - 078850

Kronberg (Hessen)
Flachsmann, Hildegard, Kellergrundweg 22, 61476 Kronberg. T. (06173) 79333. 078851
Galerie Satyra, Steinstr 1, 61476 Kronberg. T. (06173) 2500. 078852
Hellhof, Königsteiner Straße 2, 61476 Kronberg. T. (06173) 4724. - Paint / Graph - 078853
Opper, Uwe, Tanzhausstr 1, 61476 Kronberg. T. (06173) 1718. 078854

Kyllburg (Rheinland-Pfalz)
Kellergalerie, H.-D. Mues, Schulstr. 9, 54655 Kyllburg. T. (06563) 8123. 078855

Ladenburg (Baden-Württemberg)
märz galerien, Rheingaustr. 34, 68526 Ladenburg. T. (06203) 10 08 30. 078856
Maul, Emil G., Kirchenstr. 18, 68526 Ladenburg. 078857
Menrad, W., Hauptstr. 29, 68526 Ladenburg. T. (06203) 141 32. - Paint - 078858

Lage, Lippe (Nordrhein-Westfalen)
Stanke, Doris, Paulinenstr 23, 32791 Lage, Lippe. T. (05232) 63524. - Paint / Graph / Sculp - 078859

Lahnau (Hessen)
Schmidt, F., Brunnenstr. 3, 35633 Lahnau. T. (06441) 612 24. 078860

Lahr (Baden-Württemberg)
Die Treppe, Weiherstr 1-3 S2, 77933 Lahr. T. (07821) 23018. - Paint / Graph / Sculp / Mul / Draw - 078861
Wild, Rathauspl 6, 77933 Lahr. T. (07821) 23847, Fax (07821) 271631. - Ant / Paint / Graph - 078862

Lamspringe (Niedersachsen)
Internationale Künstlerwerkstatt, Hindenburgstr. 10, 31195 Lamspringe. T. (05183) 10 11. 078863

Landshut (Bayern)
Maulberger, Grasgasse 325, 84028 Landshut. T. (0871) 26803. - Paint - 078864
Schönberger, Papiererstr 3, 84034 Landshut. T. (0871) 670606, Fax (0871) 62104. 078865

Landstuhl (Rheinland-Pfalz)
Burg-Galerie, Weiherstr. 2, 66849 Landstuhl. T. (06371) 158 54. 078866
Kerp, W., Kaiserstr. 8, 66849 Landstuhl. T. (06371) 129 93. - Paint - 078867
Naffong, Ziegelhütte, 66849 Landstuhl. T. (06371) 38 31. 078868

Langen (Hessen)
von Kupsch, Im Buchenhain 5, 63225 Langen. T. (06103) 72243. - Paint / Graph / Sculp - 078869

Langenchursdorf (Sachsen)
Galerie K 58, Holzhäuser Str, 09337 Langenchursdorf. - Paint / Graph / Sculp - 078870

Langenfeld (Nordrhein-Westfalen)
Kröner, Ewald, Wasserschloss Graven, 40764 Langenfeld. T. (02173) 6811. 078871

Langenhagen (Niedersachsen)
Depelmann, Walsroder Str 305, 30855 Langenhagen. T. (0511) 733693, Fax 723629. - Graph / Sculp / Mul / Draw - 078872

Langerwehe (Nordrhein-Westfalen)
Tolbiac, Schönthaler Str. 76, 52379 Langerwehe. 078873

Lauda-Königshofen (Baden-Württemberg)
Galerie das auge, Rathausstr. 23, 97922 Lauda-Königshofen. T. (09343) 4760, 3077. - Paint / Graph 078874
Kreativ-Studio, Kirchstr. 4, 97922 Lauda-Königshofen. T. (09343) 21 35, 56 99. - Paint / Graph / Repr - 078875

Lauf (Bayern)
Engelmann, C.-D., Neuhäuser Str 5, 91207 Lauf. T. (09123) 14991, Fax 81170. - Paint - 078876

Leichlingen (Nordrhein-Westfalen)
Galerie Balker Mühle, Am Gemeindeberg 11, 42799 Leichlingen. T. (02175) 9382. - Paint - 078877

Leinfelden-Echterdingen (Baden-Württemberg)
Lucas, Kolumbusstr 25, 70771 Leinfelden-Echterdingen. T. (0711) 792121, Fax (0711) 7978844. - Paint / Graph / Repr - 078878

Leipzig (Sachsen)
Ausstellungszentrum der Universität Leipzig, Goethestr 2, 04109 Leipzig. T. (0341) 286453, Fax (0341) 286453. - Paint / Graph / Sculp / Draw - 078879
Beck, Michael, Naunhofer Str 24, 04299 Leipzig. T. (0341) 8622550, Fax 8622803. 078880
Galerie am Sachsenplatz, Katharinenstr. 11, 04109 Leipzig. T. (0341) 29 22 31. - Paint / Graph / Sculp / Draw - 078881
Galerie Augen-Blick, Beethovenstr 17, 04107 Leipzig. T. (0341) 286447. - Paint - 078882
Galerie-Cafe Barbakane in der Moritzbastei, Universitätsstr 9, 04109 Leipzig. T. (0341) 292932. - Paint / Graph - 078883
Galerie-Cafe Vis-a-Vis, Rudolf-Breitscheid-Str 33, 04105 Leipzig. T. (0341) 292718. - Paint - 078884
Galerie der Hochschule für Graphik und Buchkunst Leipzig, Wächterstr 11, 04107 Leipzig. T. (0341) 3913211. - Paint - 078885
Galerie Eigen + Art, Barfußgäßchen 2-8, 04109 Leipzig. T. (0341) 9607886, Fax 9607886. - Paint / Graph / Pho / Mul / Draw - 078886
Galerie im Hörsaalgebäude der Universität Leipzig, Universitätsstr, 04109 Leipzig. T. (0341) 286453, 7197319. - Paint - 078887
Galerie im Institut für Kultur und wissenschaftlich-technologische Information der Republik Polen, Brühl 9, 04109 Leipzig. T. (0341) 282064. - Paint - 078888
Galerie Kolonie Ost, Kapellenstr 10, 04315 Leipzig. - Paint - 078889
Galerie Pikanta, Viertelsweg 47, 04157 Leipzig. T. (0341) 584496. - Paint / Graph - 078890
Galerie Quadriga, Querstr 27, 04103 Leipzig. T. (0341) 295115. - Paint / Graph / Fra - 078891
Galerie Sehens-Wert, Einertstr. 3, 04315 Leipzig. T. (0341) 66497. - Paint - 078892
Galerie StöckArt, Stöckartstr 4, 04277 Leipzig. - Paint - 078893
Galerie Theaterpassage, Goethestr 2, 04109 Leipzig. T. (0341) 200725. - Paint / Graph / China / Sculp - 078894
Galerie Wort und Werk, Markt 9, 04109 Leipzig. T. (0341) 295621. 078895
Galerie Zone, Sternwartenstr 39, 041039 Leipzig. - Paint - 078896
Graphik-Galerie des Leipziger Antiquariats, Ritterstr 4, 04109 Leipzig. T. (0341) 209155. - Graph - 078897
Kleine Galerie Süd, Karl-Liebknecht-Str 84, 04275 Leipzig. T. (0341) 315102, Fax (0341) 315102. - Paint / Graph / Repr / Jew / Fra / Pho - 078898
Klubgalerie im Leibniz-Klub, Elsterstr 35, 04109 Leipzig. T. (0341) 294533. - Paint - 078899

Lemgo (Nordrhein-Westfalen)
Rosteck, Stift St. Marien, 32657 Lemgo. T. (05261) 4077, Fax 17358. - Ant / Paint / Furn / China - 078900

Lennestadt (Nordrhein-Westfalen)
Föhrdes, Clemens, Hangstr. 4, 57368 Lennestadt. T. (02721) 22 64. 078901

Lenningen (Baden-Württemberg)
Schlattstall, Lautermühle, 73252 Lenningen. T. (07026) 2450. - Paint / Graph - 078902

Lenting (Bayern)
Kurz, Lothar, Bahnhofstr. 10, 85101 Lenting. T. (08456) 1488. - Paint / Graph - 078903

Leverkusen (Nordrhein-Westfalen)
Künstlerbunker, Karlstr. 9, 51379 Leverkusen. 078904
Lommel, I., Dr., Bergische Landstr. 22, 51375 Leverkusen. T. (0214) 50 45 36. 078905

Lilienthal (Niedersachsen)
Kühn, Hauptstr 39, 28865 Lilienthal. T. (04298) 1368. - Paint - 078906
Niels Stensen Haus, Worpshauser Landstr 55, 28865 Lilienthal. T. (04298) 544. - Paint / Graph / Sculp / Rel / Pho - 078907

Limburg an der Lahn (Hessen)
Galerie auf der Treppe, Fleischgasse 10, 65549 Limburg an der Lahn. T. (06431) 25966, Fax 6280. - Graph / Jew / Fra / Draw - 078908
Kohl, F., Rütsche 15, 65549 Limburg an der Lahn. T. (06431) 23211. 078909
Kotte, Frank-Hans, Fischmarkt/Rütsche 15, 65549 Limburg an der Lahn. T. (06431) 23211. - Paint / Graph / Fra / Draw - 078910
Marten, R., Limburger Str 13, 65555 Limburg an der Lahn. T. (06431) 57129. - Paint - 078911
Topp, Hans-Jürgen, Grabenstr 31, 65549 Limburg an der Lahn. T. (06431) 6490, Fax 24172. - Paint / Graph / Repr / Sculp / Fra - 078912

Lindau, Bodensee (Bayern)

Galerie M am Markt, Marktplatz 4, 88131 Lindau, Bodensee. T. (08382) 5999. - Paint / Graph / China / Sculp / Jew / Silv / Glass / Draw - *078913*
Galerie zur Fischerin, Ludwigstr 50, 88131 Lindau, Bodensee. *078914*
Galerienpassage, Rathaus-Krummgasse, 88131 Lindau, Bodensee. T. (08382) 28459. - Paint / China / Sculp - *078915*
Holbein, Brougierstr. 6, 88131 Lindau, Bodensee. T. (08382) 4507. *078916*

Lindenberg im Allgäu (Bayern)

Galerie der Volksbank, Kreuzhofstr 2, 88161 Lindenberg im Allgäu. T. (08381) 8060, Fax 80663. - Paint / Graph - *078917*

Linz am Rhein (Rheinland-Pfalz)

Galerie Haus Hegarda, Zum Ziegenbusch, 53545 Linz am Rhein. T. (02644) 1818. *078918*

Lippstadt (Nordrhein-Westfalen)

Ferlemann, W., Cappelstr. 55, 59555 Lippstadt. T. (02941) 581 88. *078919*
Trost, Stiftstr. 10, 59555 Lippstadt. T. (02941) 31 54. - Paint / Graph - *078920*

Lohmar (Nordrhein-Westfalen)

Steuber, H. & J., Meisenweg 6, 53797 Lohmar. T. (02246) 58 64. *078921*

Lohra (Hessen)

Wolter, Martin, Scheunengalerie Wera Wolter, 35102 Lohra. T. (06462) 06462/1234. - Paint - *078922*

Ludwigsburg (Baden-Württemberg)

Kleine Galerie, Marktpl. 5, 71634 Ludwigsburg. T. (07141) 233 72. - Paint - *078923*

Ludwigshafen am Rhein (Rheinland-Pfalz)

Kleinhenz, Hans-Dieter, Heinigstr 31, 67059 Ludwigshafen am Rhein. T. (0621) 514024, Fax (0621) 514029. - Ant / Paint / Graph / Furn / China / Sculp / Jew / Silv / Glass / Mod / Ico - *078924*
Lauterhahn, Im Hengstpark 3, 67071 Ludwigshafen am Rhein. T. (0621) 679915. - Paint - *078925*
Scharpf, Hemshofstr 54, 67063 Ludwigshafen am Rhein. *078926*

Lübbecke (Nordrhein-Westfalen)

Tantius, Hans-Gerd, Andreasstr 6, 32312 Lübbecke. T. (05741) 31877, Fax 318799. - Paint / Graph / Repr / Sculp / Fra / Rel - *078927*

Lübeck (Schleswig-Holstein)

Galerie Werkkunstschule, Mengstr. 64, 23552 Lübeck. - Paint - *078928*
Heiden, Heino, Galerie, Dr.-Julius-Leber-Str. 25, 23552 Lübeck. T. (0451) 7 88 03. - Paint / Graph - *078929*
Koch-Westenhoff, Margot, Hüxstr. 29, 23552 Lübeck. T. (0451) 72808, Fax (0451) 7063359. - Paint / Sculp - *078930*
Kunstgalerie-Atelier Signos, Wallstr. 26, 23560 Lübeck. - Paint - *078931*
Kunsthaus Lübeck, Königstr 20, 23552 Lübeck. T. (0451) 75700, Fax 73755. - Paint / Graph / Sculp / Glass / Mul / Draw - *078932*
Linde, Metta, Dr.-Julius-Leber-Str. 49, 23552 Lübeck. T. (0451) 78851, Fax (0451) 7063306. - Paint / Graph / Sculp / Draw - *078933*
Nitsche, Peter, Dr., Fleischhauerstr. 67-71, 23552 Lübeck. T. (0451) 72951, 72051, Fax (0451) 75631. - Paint / Graph / Sculp - *078934*
Overbeck-Gesellschaft, Königstr. 11, 23552 Lübeck. T. (0451) 74760. *078935*
Schauerte, gen. Lueke, P., Beckergrube 19, 23552 Lübeck. T. (0451) 764 79. - Paint / Graph / Sculp - *078936*

Lüdenscheid (Nordrhein-Westfalen)

Friebe, Parkstr 54, 58509 Lüdenscheid. T. (02351) 38924, Fax (02351) 27066. - Paint / Graph / Sculp / Pho / Mul / Draw - *078937*

Hoffmeister, Liebigstr. 9, 58511 Lüdenscheid. T. (02351) 23372, Fax (02351) 26739. - Paint / Sculp / Pho / Mul / Draw - *078938*
Holub, Reinhard, Knapper Str. 59, 58507 Lüdenscheid. T. (02351) 202 32. *078939*
Nina's Bildermarkt, Wilhelmstr. 38, 58511 Lüdenscheid. T. (02351) 234 76. - Paint - *078940*
Riedel, B., Wikingerweg 16, 58509 Lüdenscheid. T. (02351) 262 80. *078941*
Schmidt, U., Wilhelmstr. 1, 58511 Lüdenscheid. T. (02351) 254 30. *078942*

Lüdinghausen (Nordrhein-Westfalen)

Noran, Hermannstr. 11-13, 59348 Lüdinghausen. T. (02591) 4869, Fax (02591) 22565. - Paint / Graph / Repr / Sculp / Fra / Glass / Pho - *078943*

Lüneburg (Niedersachsen)

Findorff, Ursula, Bardowicker Str. 3, 21335 Lüneburg. T. (04131) 3 15 72. - Paint / Graph / Repr / Fra - *078944*
Galerie im Centre, Grapengießerstr. 46, 21335 Lüneburg. T. (04131) 4 33 63. - Graph - *078945*
Meyer, A., Rosenstr. 9, 21335 Lüneburg. - Paint / Graph / Repr - *078946*

Lünen (Nordrhein-Westfalen)

Galerie Kiliansmühle, Münsterstr. 290, 44534 Lünen. T. (02306) 55080, Fax (02306) 55080. - Paint / Graph - *078947*
Heseler, W., Lange Str. 65, 44532 Lünen. T. (02306) 1 21 50. - Paint - *078948*
Heseler, Walter, Lange Str. 65, 44532 Lünen. T. (02306) 121 50. - Paint - *078949*
Röttger, Dietrich, Dortmunder Str. 33, 44536 Lünen. T. (02306) 13280, Fax (02306) 24776. - Paint / Graph / Sculp / Eth - *078950*

Magdeburg (Sachsen-Anhalt)

Burg-Galerie, Ernst-Reuter-Allee 23, 39104 Magdeburg. T. (0391) 31027. *078951*
Fischer, Holger, Feuerbachstr. 1, 39104 Magdeburg. T. (0391) 5613023. - Paint / Graph / Sculp / Mul / Draw - *078952*
Galerie Himmelreich, Himmelreichstr. 2, 39104 Magdeburg. T. (0391) 30114, Fax (0391) 30114. - Paint / Graph / China / Sculp / Tex / Jew / Glass / Draw -- *078953*
Mauritius, Max-Josef-Metzger-Str. 2, 39104 Magdeburg. T. (0391) 34 43 39. *078954*
Rahn, R., Breiter Weg 255, 39104 Magdeburg. T. (0391) 32918. *078955*
Trigon, Feuerbachstr. 1, 39104 Magdeburg. T. (0391) 561 30 23. - Paint / Graph / Sculp / Mul / Draw - *078956*

Magstadt (Baden-Württemberg)

Braitmaier, Brunnenstr. 14, 71106 Magstadt. - Graph / Sculp - *078957*

Maintal (Hessen)

ZK-Galerie, Kennedystr. 29, 63477 Maintal. T. (06181) 49 30 66. - Paint / Fra - *078958*

Mainz (Rheinland-Pfalz)

Druckhaus, Weberstr. 9, 55130 Mainz. T. (06131) 810 00. *078959*
Edition GD, Klosterstr. 1, 55124 Mainz. T. (06131) 42523. - Paint - *078960*
Galerie Brückenturm, Rheinstr., 55116 Mainz. T. (06131) 122522, Fax (06131) 123087. - Paint - *078961*
Galerie Grosse Bleiche, Große Bleiche 47, 55116 Mainz. T. (06131) 23 47 47, Fax (06131) 23 47 48. - Paint / Graph / Sculp / Pho / Mul / Draw - *078962*
van der Koelen, Dorothea, Dr., Hinter der Kapelle 54, 55128 Mainz. T. (06131) 34664, 834380, Fax 369076. - Paint / Graph / Sculp / Mul / Draw - *078963*
Krabler, J. & M., Hintere Bleiche 7, 55116 Mainz. T. (06131) 22 74 37. *078964*
Kunstkreis Novo, Kantstr. 2, 55122 Mainz. T. (06131) 386 30. - Paint / Graph / Sculp - *078965*
Kunstverein Eisenturm, Rheinstr. 59, 55116 Mainz. *078966*
Rehberg, Dagmar, Uferstr. 17, 55116 Mainz. T. (06131) 22 46 05. - Sculp / Draw - *078967*

Vulkan-Galerie zeitgenössischer Kunst, Leibnizstr. 44, 55118 Mainz. T. (06131) 67 19 00, Fax (06131) 67 19 43. - Paint / Graph / Sculp / Draw - *078968*
Weber, Augustinerstr. 43, 55116 Mainz. T. (06131) 2246 93. - Graph - *078969*

Malente (Schleswig-Holstein)

Glasgalerie Malente, Janussallee 18, 23714 Malente. T. (04523) 4955. *078970*
Musisches Zentrum und Galerie, Grebiner Weg 8a, 23714 Malente. T. (04523) 1407. - Paint / Graph / Tex / Pho - *078971*

Mannheim (Baden-Württemberg)

Antonitsch, J., Augustaanlage 3, 68165 Mannheim. T. (0621) 41 13 07. - Paint - *078972*
Atelier Galerie, Germaniastr. 4, 68199 Mannheim. T. (0621) 85 37 04. - Paint / Graph / Sculp - *078973*
Augenladen, Heinrich-Lanz-Str. 29, 68165 Mannheim. T. (0621) 40 67 29. - Paint / Graph - *078974*
Bamberger, Friedrichspl. 5, Hanse-Merkur-Haus, 68159 Mannheim. T. (0621) 20814. *078975*
Bausback, Franz, N 3, 9, 68161 Mannheim. T. (0621) 25808, Fax (0621) 105957. - Paint / Graph / Sculp / Tex - *078976*
Contemporary Art, R 3, 1, 68161 Mannheim. T. (0621) 10 51 65. - Paint - *078977*
Fahlbusch, Friedrichspl. 6, 68165 Mannheim. T. (0621) 406126, 677999, Fax (0621) 672074. *078978*
Falzone & Huthmacher, Augustaanlage 30, 68165 Mannheim. T. (0621) 44 88 59. - Paint - *078979*
Friebe, Karin, Sophienstr. 8, 68165 Mannheim. T. (0621) 41 27 06. - Paint / Graph / Sculp - *078980*
Galerie am kleinen Markt, Rheinhäuser Str. 24b, 68165 Mannheim. T. (0621) 44 44 90. - Paint - *078981*
Galerie Artec, Gontardstr. 5, 68163 Mannheim. T. (0621) 81 87 70. - Paint - *078982*
galerie und buch, Seckenheimer Str. 33, 68165 Mannheim. T. (0621) 44 89 72, Fax (0621) 44 32 95. - Graph - *078983*
Galerie und Kreathek, Seckenheimer Str. 33, 68165 Mannheim. T. (0621) 40 28 08. *078984*
Grafic & Arts, N 1, Stadthaus, 68161 Mannheim. T. (0621) 15 38 43. - Graph - *078985*
Gruber, P 6, Plankenhof-Passage, 68159 Mannheim. T. (0621) 1561019, Fax (0621) 3126. - Paint - *078986*
Harms, Molly, Hortenpassage, Friedrichspl. 5, 68159 Mannheim. T. (0621) 25132. - Paint / Graph - *078987*
Inuit Galerie, Augusta Anlage 3, 68159 Mannheim. T. (0621) 41 13 07. - Paint / Graph / Sculp / Eth / Draw - *078988*
Kazinikas, Jokubas, P 2,8, 68161 Mannheim. T. (0621) 2 35 31. - Graph / Sculp / Tex - *078989*
Kreathek, Friedrichstr. 14, 68199 Mannheim. T. (0621) 85 40 51. *078990*
Lauter, Margarete, Dr. Harro, Friedrichsplatz 14, 68165 Mannheim. T. (0621) 406066, Fax (0621) 406067. - Paint / Graph / Sculp / Mul / Draw - *078991*
märz galerien, Beethovenstr. 18, 68165 Mannheim. T. (0621) 41 22 37. *078992*
Panetta, Fausto, Augusta-Anlage 54-56, 68159 Mannheim. T. (0621) 44 84 41, 89 19 35. - Paint / Graph / Sculp / Draw - *078993*
Pertsch, Armin, Augusta-Anlage 38, 68159 Mannheim. T. (0621) 44 17 56. - Paint - *078994*
Placard Galerie, Wolfgang Dahm, Q 2, 5, 68161 Mannheim. T. (0621) 29 18 45, Fax (0621) 15 44 71. *078995*
R, Rheindammstr. 50, 68163 Mannheim. T. (0621) 82 29 91. - Paint / Graph / Sculp - *078996*
Rist, B., Mosbacher Str. 37, 68259 Mannheim. T. (0621) 71 23 80. - Paint - *078997*
Rödel, R., Rheindamm 50, 68163 Mannheim. T. (0621) 82 29 91. - Paint - *078998*
Rudloff, H., Dr., O 7, 2, 68161 Mannheim. T. (0621) 10 51 61, Fax (0621) 10 20 96. - Paint / Graph - *078999*
Schreiber, J., Dürerstr. 130, 68163 Mannheim. T. (0621) 41 13 81, Fax (0621) 41 51 37. - Paint / Sculp - *079000*
Stahl, Karl-Theodor, P 7, 16-17, 68165 Mannheim. T. (0621) 220 22. - Paint / Graph - *079001*

Vogel, Kurfürstenarkade N 6, 68161 Mannheim.
T. (0621) 153155, Fax (0621) 24245. - Paint / Graph /
Sculp / Fra - 079002
Zimmermann, Otto-Georg, Germaniastr. 4, 68199 Mann-
heim. T. (0621) 85 37 04. 079003

Marbach am Neckar (Baden-Württem-
berg)
Galerie in der Wendelinskapelle, Marktstr 2, 71672 Marbach am Neckar. T. (07144) 16605. - Paint / Graph /
Jew / Fra / Draw - 079004

Marburg (Hessen)
Galerie der Stadtsparkasse, Barfüßerstr 50, 35037
Marburg. 079005
Heide, Anna-Maria, Bunsenstr 1, 35037 Marburg.
T. (06421) 68357. - Paint / Graph / Sculp / Mul - 079006

March (Baden-Württemberg)
Galerie Regio, Dorfstr 4, 79232 March. T. (07665) 3067.
- Paint / Graph / Sculp - 079007

Markt Schwaben (Bayern)
Grohmann, Friedrich, Adalbert-Stifter-Weg 17, 85570
Markt Schwaben. T. (08121) 6767, Fax 48369. - Dec /
Fra / Draw - 079008

Bilderschienen
Versandkatalog 8
F.GROHMANN
Adalbert-Stifter-Weg 17,
85570 Markt Schwaben
Tel. (0 81 21) 67 67,
Fax 4 83 69

Marl (Nordrhein-Westfalen)
Lorra & Giese, Korthausen 7, 45770 Marl.
T. (02365) 82414. - Paint / Graph / Sculp /
Draw - 079009

Marsberg (Nordrhein-Westfalen)
Klein, F.-B. & E., Vitusstr. 7, 34431 Marsberg.
T. (02992) 02994/444. 079010

Meckenheim, Rheinland (Nordrhein-
Westfalen)
Dietz, Sieglinde, Dechant-Kreiten-Str 21, 53340 Mek-
kenheim, Rheinland. T. (02225) 5758,
Fax (02225) 15729. - Paint / Graph / Sculp - 079011

Meerane (Sachsen)
Galerie Art-In, Marienstr. 22, 08393 Meerane.
T. (03764) 56261. - Paint / Graph / China / Sculp /
Glass / Draw - 079012

Meerbusch (Nordrhein-Westfalen)
Buch- u. Kunstkabinett, Kirchplatz 1-5, 40670 Meer-
busch. T. (02132) 3530. - Paint / Sculp / Draw - 079013
Bumm, Ilse E., Gustav-van-Beek-Allee 30, 40670 Meer-
busch. T. (02132) 6134, Fax (02132) 6501.
- Paint - 079014
B9 Gemälde, Moerser Str 74, 40667 Meerbusch.
T. (02132) 5449, Fax 5449. - Paint - 079015
Failenschmid, M., Xantener Str. 9, 40670 Meerbusch.
T. (02132) 88 60. 079016
Galerie Ilverich, Alte Schule, 40668 Meerbusch.
T. (02132) 3378, Fax (02132) 1791. - Paint / Graph /
Sculp / Pho / Mul / Draw - 079017
Mück, Moerser Str. 84, 40667 Meerbusch.
T. (02132) 3798. 079018
Sorina, Dorfstr. 26, 40667 Meerbusch. 079019

Meersburg (Baden-Württemberg)
Galerie Winzergasse 7, Winzergasse 7, 88709 Meers-
burg. T. (07532) 9343. - Paint / Sculp / Draw - 079020
Müller-Ortloff, Edith, & Töchter, Neues Schloß, alter An-
bau, 88709 Meersburg. T. (07532) 6476. - Tex /
Rel - 079021

Mehring (Bayern)
Kleine Galerie, Meisterweg 3, 84561 Mehring.
T. (08677) 49 18. - Graph / Draw - 079022

Meinerzhagen (Nordrhein-Westfalen)
G & S, Siepener Weg 10, 58540 Meinerzhagen.
T. (02354) 5098. 079023

Meldorf (Schleswig-Holstein)
Galerie Dom-Café, Südermarkt 4, 25704 Meldorf.
T. (04832) 14 44. - Paint / Graph - 079024

Mellrichstadt (Bayern)
Galerie Eigen Art, Franziska-Streitel-Pl. 1, 97638 Mell-
richstadt. T. (09776) 7237. - Paint / Graph - 079025

Melsungen (Hessen)
Galerie an der Kirche, Burgstr. 6, 34212
Melsungen. 079026

Meppen (Niedersachsen)
Galerie Bild und Form, Einsteinstr. 2, 49716 Meppen.
T. (05931) 8233. 079027

Merseburg (Sachsen-Anhalt)
Riemke, Obere Burgstr. 9, 06217 Merseburg.
T. (03461) 21 49 62. - Paint / Graph - 079028

Mettmann (Nordrhein-Westfalen)
Schlüter, E. & W., Hammer Str. 1, 40822 Mettmann.
T. (02104) 285 55. 079029
Schlüter, Ferdinand, Weststr. 5, 40822 Mettmann.
T. (02104) 747 14. 079030
Schübbe, Christa, Hasselerstr. 85, 40822 Mettmann.
T. (02104) 53348. - Paint / Graph / Sculp - 079031
Stil, Beratungsagentur, Lindenstr. 9, 40822 Mettmann.
T. (02104) 15634, Fax (02104) 12883. 079032

Miltenberg (Bayern)
Gülden Cron, Hauptstr. 163, 63897 Miltenberg.
T. (09371) 28 85. - Paint - 079033

Minden, Westfalen (Nordrhein-Westfa-
len)
Fischer, Rosemarie, Moltkestr 7, 32427 Minden, Westfa-
len. T. (0571) 25109, Fax (0571) 25109.
- Graph - 079034
Lübking, Dorothea, Königstr 247, 32427 Minden, West-
falen. T. (0571) 28826. 079035
Ragab, Said, Marienstr 29, 32427 Minden,
Westfalen. 079036

Modautal (Hessen)
Galerie Neutsch, Neutsch 15, 64397 Modautal.
T. (06167) 12 62. 079037

Möhnesee (Nordrhein-Westfalen)
Druckgrafik Kätelhön, Hermann-Kätelhön-Str. 8, 59519
Möhnesee. T. (02924) 391. - Paint - 079038

Möhrendorf (Bayern)
Zimmermann, E. & W., Am Nussbuck 15, 91096 Möhrendorf. T. (09131) 21 92. - Paint / Graph - 079039

Mömbris (Bayern)
Pötzelberger, Haagstr. 22, 63776 Mömbris.
T. (06029) 16 79. - China - 079040

Mönchengladbach (Nordrhein-
Westfalen)
Carat, Kleistr. 10, 41061 Mönchengladbach.
T. (02161) 18 15 35. - Paint / Graph / Mod /
Draw - 079041
Cohnen, Carl, Hindenburgstr. 160, 41061 Mönchenglad-
bach. T. (02161) 156 55. - Ant / Paint / Furn /
Sculp - 079042
Commercial Art Studio Harald Hansen, Mennrath 27a,
41179 Mönchengladbach. T. (02161) 205 76. - Paint /
Sculp / Draw - 079043
Gärtner, Stresemannstr. 60, 41236 Mönchengladbach.
T. (02161) 470 00. - Paint / Graph / Sculp - 079044
Galerie Augenblick, Von-Galen-Str. 105, 41236 Mön-
chengladbach. T. (02161) 462 44. - Paint / Graph /
Sculp - 079045
Galerie 2000, Hauptstr. 55, 41236 Mönchengladbach.
T. (02161) 413 71. - Paint - 079046

Jungbluth, Horst, Hauptstr. 160, 41236 Mönchenglad-
bach. T. (02161) 42 09 71. - Graph - 079047
Kunstkabinett E. Vischer, Bismarckstr. 59, 41061 Mön-
chengladbach. T. (02161) 2 65 77. - Paint / Graph /
Repr / Fra - 079048
Löhrl, Christa und Dietmar, Kaiserstr. 58/60, 41061
Mönchengladbach. T. (02161) 200762,
Fax (02161) 208661. - Paint / Graph / Sculp / Fra / Mul /
Draw - 079049
Strunk-Hilgers, Straßburger Allee 39, 41199 Mönchen-
gladbach. T. (02161) 601362, Fax (02161) 605823.
- Paint / Graph - 079050
Zimmermann & Franken, Lürriper Str. 228, 41065 Mön-
chengladbach. T. (02161) 66 44 27, 44960, Fax 48412.
- Paint / Graph / Orient / Sculp / Eth / Mul / Draw -- 079051

Moers (Nordrhein-Westfalen)
Kugel, Friedrichstr. 18, 47441 Moers. T. (02841) 21853.
- Graph - 079052
Zimmermann, Elke, Wörthstr. 7, 47441 Moers.
- Paint - 079053

Moisburg (Niedersachsen)
Esteburg, Buxtehuder Str. 7, 21647 Moisburg. - Paint /
Graph / Sculp - 079054

Moos, Bodensee (Baden-Württemberg)
Gielen, Böhringer Str 8, 78345 Moos, Bodensee.
T. (07732) 4438. 079055

Moosinning (Bayern)
Billesberger, Siegfried, Billesberger Hof, 85452 Moosin-
ning. T. (08123) 1477, Fax (08123) 8399.
- Draw - 079056

Mühltal (Hessen)
Lattemann, Papiermüllerweg 7, 64367 Mühltal.
T. (06151) 148588. - Paint / Graph / China / Sculp /
Draw - 079057

Mülheim an der Ruhr (Nordrhein-West-
falen)
Alte Post, Viktoriapl 1, 45468 Mülheim an der
Ruhr. 079058
Kunst-Kabinett, Bleichstr 16, 45468 Mülheim an der
Ruhr. T. (0208) 31806. - Sculp - 079059
MK Kunst Galerie, Am Schloß Broich 31, 45479 Mülheim
an der Ruhr. T. (0208) 429198. 079060
Neumann, Dora, Wallstr 7, 45468 Mülheim an der Ruhr.
T. (0208) 472279. - Paint / Fra - 079061
Sonntag, Isabe von, Bleichstr 16, 45468 Mülheim an der
Ruhr. T. (0208) 31806. 079062
Wickerath, Franz, Klöttschen 50a, 45468 Mülheim an
der Ruhr. T. (0208) 472166. - Paint - 079063

Müllheim (Baden-Württemberg)
Harnapp, Dr., Marzellerweg 7, 79379 Müllheim, Baden.
T. (07631) 30 16. - Paint - 079064

München (Bayern)
A.-Paul-Weber-Kabinett, Dall'Armistr. 57, 80638 Mün-
chen. T. (089) 17 04 17, 17 04 77. - Paint /
Graph - 079067
Abercron, von, Maximilianstr 22, 80539 München.
T. (089) 226420, Fax (089) 226746. - Paint / Graph /
Sculp - 079068
ACA Galleries, Maximilianstr 29, 80539 München.
T. (089) 29161200, Fax 29161201. - Paint - 079069
ad artem, Pütrichstr. 4, 81667 München.
T. (089) 48 59 97. - Paint / Graph / Draw - 079070
A.D.A.M.S-VW Kunst- u Handelsgesellschaft mbH, Schel-
lingstr 24, 80799 München. T. (089) 281328. 079071
Ahlers, Dachauer Str 163, 80636 München.
T. (089) 187210. 079072
Albrecht, Susanne, Klenzestr 38, 80469 München.
T. (089) 268689, Fax (089) 2605292. - Paint / Graph /
Sculp / Draw - 079073
Alvensleben, von, Arcisstr 58, 80799 München.
T. (089) 2715656, Fax (089) 2730772. - Paint /
Graph - 079074
Architekturgalerie, Türkenstr 30, 80333 München.
T. (089) 282807. - Draw - 079075
Arco & Flotow, Brennerstr 10/V, 80333 München.
T. (089) 284089, Fax (089) 285696. 079076

Arnoldi-Livie, Galeriestr. 2b, 80539 München.
T. (089) 22 59 20, Fax (089) 22 63 21. - Paint -   079077
ars vita Junsthandelsges mbH, Nadistr 16, 80809 München. T. (089) 3516826.   079078
ART-CONSULT Kunsthandel GmbH, Dachauer Str 7a, 80335 München. T. (089) 593565.   079079
Art Galerie, Oettingenstr 24, 80538 München.
T. (089) 223060, Fax (089) 223060.   079080
Art-Inform, Bavariaring 10, 80336 München.
T. (089) 5380340.   079081
Art und be Galerie, Georgenstr 28, 80799 München.
T. (089) 337262, Fax (089) 337242. - China / Pho -   079082
Artcurial, Maximilianstr 10, 80539 München.
T. (089) 294131, Fax (089) 2913867. - Graph / Sculp -   079083
Arte Galerie N, Luisenstr 68, 80798 München.
T. (089) 7255291.   079084
Artothek, St.-Jakobs-Platz 15, 80331 München.
T. (089) 23352988.   079085
Arts & Antiques Edition, Postfach 400128, 80701 München. T. (089) 349830, Fax (089) 349834.   079086
Autoren Galerie 1, Pündtterpl 6, 80803 München.
T. (089) 395132, Fax (089) 396788. - Paint -   079087
Balogh, Dr., Theatinerstr. 35, 80333 München.
T. (089) 227214, Fax (089) 3618502. - Paint -   079088
Bantele, Häberlstr. 5, 80337 München. T. (089) 53 52 54.
- Glass -   079089
Bartsch & Chariau, Galeriestr 2, 80539 München.
T. (089) 295557, Fax (089) 2904789. - Draw -   079090
Bastian, Andreas, Bazeillesstr. 19, 81603 München.
T. (089) 481590, Fax (089) 4471494. - Paint / Graph / Sculp / Mul -   079091
Bayer, Konrad, Prälat-Zistl-Str. 20, 80331 München.
T. 01728969606, (089) 264709. - Paint -   079092

GALERIE KONRAD BAYER

Wilhelm Bode   Sommertag am Starnberger See

Landschaftsmalerei
1850 – 1900

—

Malerei um 1900
SCHOLLE
NEU-DACHAU
SECESSION
JUGEND

GALERIE KONRAD BAYER · PRÄLAT-ZISTL-STR. 20
80331 MÜNCHEN · AM VIKTUALIENMARKT
GEÖFFNET n. V. · 089-26 47 09 · oder 01 72-89 69 606

Beil 506 J., Ottostr 3, 80333 München.
T. (089) 557276.   079093
Bender, Renate, Hohenzollernstr 122, 80796 München.
T. (089) 27290531, Fax (089) 27290536.
- Paint -   079094

Berr, Ernst, Lenbachpl. 7, 80333 München.
T. (089) 221245, Fax (089) 205126. - Paint / Graph -   079095
Biedermann, Maximilianstr 25, 80539 München.
T. (089) 297257, Fax 292237. - Eth / Draw / Paint -   079096

galerie biedermann

Gemälde, Zeichnungen, Skulpturen
19. u. 20. Jhd.
Zeitgenössische Kunst

Maximilianstraße 25
80539 München
Telefon 0 89 / 29 72 57
Fax 0 89 / 29 22 37

Biehler, M., Georgenstr 28, 80799 München.
T. (089) 337262.   079097
Bierl, Sadie, Lindwurmstr 173, 80337 München.
T. (089) 774338, (08065) 563, Fax (089) 772087.
- Paint -   079098
Binder, Andreas, Isartalstr 34, 80469 München.
T. (089) 763020, Fax (089) 763283.   079099
Blau, Daniel, Maximilianstr 26, 80539 München.
T. (089) 297474, Fax (089) 295848.   079100
von Braunbehrens, Ainmillerstr 2, 80801 München.
T. (089) 390339, 331230, Fax (089) 334316. - Paint / Graph / Sculp -   079101
Brincken, Klaus von, Salvatorstr 2, 80333 München.
T. (089) 298815, Fax (089) 222983. - Graph -   079102
Brochier, Klenzestr 32, 80469 München.
T. (089) 267926, Fax (089) 264406. - Paint -   079103
Brück, H.G., Mannhardtstr. 7, 80538 München.
T. (089) 294752, Fax (089) 294752. - Paint / Graph -   079104
Brunner, Käthe, Stauffenbergstr. 3, 80797 München.
T. (089) 30 38 47. - Paint / Graph -   079105
Bühler, Hans-Peter, Dr., König-Marke-Str. 1, 80804 München. T. (089) 363647,
Fax (089 36100645.   079106
CCC-Cartoon-Caricature-Contor, Rosmarinstr 4, 80939 München. T. (089) 3233669, Fax 3226859.
- Graph -   079107
Clegg-Littler, Galeriestr 2a, 80539 München.
T. (089) 2913898.   079108
Collage e.V., Oberföhringer Str. 156, 81925 München.
T. (089) 9579506.   079109
Deschler, Maximilian, Wirtstr 9, 81539 München.
T. (089) 6923675. - Paint / Graph / Draw -   079110
Dietz, Klaus, Oettingenstr. 62, 80538 München.
T. (089) 226505, Fax (089) 226505. - Graph -   079111
Dittmar, P., Rablstr 45, 81669 München.
T. (089) 4488105.   079112
Dörfel, Karl, Heiglhofstr. 8, 81377 München.
T. (089) 71 60 81. - Paint / Graph / Furn / Repr / Pho / Draw -   079113
Dritsoulas, S., Theresienstr 9, 80333 München.
T. (089) 284647.   079114
Dube-Heynig, A., Dr, Schumannstr 3, 81679 München.
T. (089) 479295.   079115
Dube-Heynig, Annemarie, Dr., Schumannstr 3, 81679 München. T. (089) 479295, Fax (089) 6885534.
- Paint / Graph / Sculp / Tex / Draw -   079116
Dürr, Bernd, Oberföhringer Str 12, 81679 München.
T. (089) 985228, Fax (089) 981146. - Paint / Graph / Sculp / Draw -   079117
Dürr, Christoph, Maximilianstr 25, 80539 München.
T. (089) 225110, Fax (089) 188722.   079118
Edition de Beauclair, Gabelsbergerstr. 17, 80333 München. T. (089) 281500, Fax (089) 286063. - Paint / Graph / Tex / Draw -   079119
Eichinger, Widenmayerstr. 2, 80538 München.
T. (089) 292616, Fax (089) 2285478. - Paint / Graph / Sculp -   079120
Ettl, German, Thierschstr. 1, 80538 München.
T. (089) 22 32 49. - Paint -   079121
Fassnacht, Emeran, Josephspitalstr. 15, 80331 München. T. (089) 592336, 605708.   079122

FernOst-Galerie, Kreuzstr 1, 80331 München.
T. (089) 2606766.   079123
Fetscherin, Hans, Dr., Mareesstr. 9, 80638 München.
T. (089) 172760, Fax (089) 172256. - Paint / Graph / Sculp -   079124
Fine Art Gallery, Nymphenburgerstr. 166, 80634 München. T. (089) 13 12 16, Fax (089) 13 19 39. - Paint / Graph / Sculp -   079125
First Glas Galerie, Heßstr. 58, 80798 München.
T. (089) 523 62 08. - Paint -   079126
FOE 156Collage e.V., Oberföhringer Str 156, 81925 München. T. (089) 9579506.   079127
Foraum Bereiteranger, Bereiteranger 15, 81541 München. T. (089) 655413, Fax (089) 656997.   079128
Frank-Osayamwen, H., Georgenstr. 49, 80799 München. T. (089) 2716217.   079129
Frank, R., Schellingstr. 130, 80797 München.
T. (089) 1292393.   079130
Fresen, Dr., Ottostr. 13, 80333 München.
T. (089) 592170. - Paint -   079131
Friedrich, Six, Cuv illiésstr 15, 81679 München.
T. (089) 9828882, Fax (089) 9827212. - Paint / Graph / Fra -   079132
Fritz-Denneville, H., Georgenstr. 15, 80799 München.
T. (089) 347411.   079133
Füssl & Jakob, Odeonsplatz 15, 80539 München.
T. (089) 22 70 08, Fax (089) 2904278. - Paint -   079134
Fusban, Daniel, Georgenstr 70, 80799 München.
T. (089) 2722848.   079135
Galerie Acade, Prannerstr. 5, 80333 München.
T. (089) 22 41 26.   079136
Galerie am Gasteig, Steinstr. 54, 81667 München.
T. (089) 480 24 44. - Paint -   079137
Galerie am Haus der Kunst, Franz-Josef-Strauß-Ring 4, 80539 München. T. (089) 222315,
Fax (089) 2800044.   079138
Galerie am kloster, Sankt-Anna-Str 17, 80538 München. T. (089) 223603. - Paint -   079139
Galerie am Markt, Westenriederstr 14, 80331 München. T. (089) 224407.   079140
Galerie am Schlachthof, Reifenstuelstr. 16, 80469 München. T. (089) 76 87 81.   079141
Galerie Anaïs, Sedanstr 22-24, 81667 München.
I. (089) 4801020.   079142
Galerie Ayan, Lenbachplatz 7, 80333 München.
T. (089) 295611, Fax (089) 298547. - Orient -   079143
Galerie b 15, Baaderstr. 15, 80469 München.
T. (089) 202 10 10. - Paint -   079144
Galerie Biro, Ziebland 19, München.
T. (089) 2730686.   079145
Galerie Blue Dog, Maximilianspl 12a, 80333 München. T. (089) 224432.   079146
Galerie B.O.A., Gabelsbergerstr. 17, 80333 München.
- Paint -   079147
Galerie Brunner, Stauffenbergstr 3, 80797 München.
T. (089) 303847.   079148
Galerie der bayerischen Landesbank, Maximilianspl 9, 80333 München. T. (089) 21715038,
Fax 21711329.   079149
Galerie der Künstler im BBK München, Maximilianstr 42, 80538 München. T. (089) 220463. - Paint / Graph / Sculp / Pho / Draw -   079150
Galerie DIN A 4, Brienner Str. 11, 80333 München.
T. (089) 280 05 44.   079151
Galerie Drächslhaus, Drächslstr. 6, 81541 München.
- Paint / Graph / Draw -   079152
Galerie Etcetera, Wurzerstr. 12, 80539 München.
T. (089) 22 60 68. - Paint / Graph -   079153
Galerie Forum 1, Nymphenburger Str 151, 80636 München. T. (089) 163101.   079154
Galerie Française, Kardinal-Döpfner-Str. 4, 80333 München. T. (089) 283600, Fax (089) 282666.
- Paint -   079155
Galerie für angewandte Kunst, Pacellistr 8, 80333 München. T. (089) 2901470. - Jew -   079156
Galerie für Schiffsmodelle, Bachbauerstr 7, 81241 München. T. (089) 8888293.   079157
Galerie Goethe 53, Goethestr. 53, 80336 München.
- Paint -   079158
Galerie Golf, Theresienstr 154, 80333 München.
T. (089) 5420918.   079159
Galerie Gronert, reichenbachstr 22, 80469 München.
T. (089) 2014547.   079160

Galerie Gronert, Schäfflerstr 18, 80333 München.
T. (089) 226170, Fax (089) 2014579. *079161*
Galerie Handwerk, Max-Joseph-Str 4, 80333 München.
T. (089) 595584. *079162*
Galerie Havermann, Maaswsg 3, 80805 München.
T. (089) 36100163. *079163*
Galerie im BBV-Haus, Thomas-Dehler-Str 25, 81737 München. T. (089) 67872104. *079164*
Galerie im Hotel Astoria, Nikolaistr. 9, 80802 München.
T. (089) 39 50 91. *079165*
Galerie in der Prannerstrasse, Prannerstr 7, 80333 München. T. (089) 299067, Fax (089) 223544.
- Graph - *079166*
Galerie Musik-Knobloch, Lenbachplatz 9, 80333 München. T. (089) 598166. *079168*
Galerie Nymphenburg, Mareesstr. 5, 80638 München.
T. (089) 17 17 76. - Paint - *079169*
Galerie Objekte, Kurfürstenstr. 17, 80799 München.
T. (089) 271 13 45, Fax (089) 271 13 45. - Paint / China / Glass / Pho / Mul - *079170*
Galerie O.S. 11, Damenstiftstr 11, 80331 München.
T. (089) 2607227. *079171*
Galerie Pritschow, Theresienhöhe 6, 80339 München.
T. (089) 5024165. *079172*
Galerie Ruetz, Kapuzinerstr 33, 80469 München.
T. (089) 2015418. *079173*
Galerie und Buchhandlung im Süddeutschen Verlag,
Sendlinger Str. 80, 80331 München.
T. (089) 260 74 84. - Paint / Graph - *079174*
Galerie Winokurow, Montsalvatstr 4, 80804 München.
T. (089) 3617192. *079175*
Galerie X, Lindwurmstr. 173, 80337 München.
T. (089) 774338, Fax (089) 772087. - Tex / Jew - *079176*
Galerie 71, Kaiserstr. 71, 80801 München.
T. (089) 342111. *079177*
Galerie 87, Westendstr 87, 80339 München.
T. (089) 5025049. *079178*
Gallerie an der Finkenstrasse, Wittelsbacherpl. 2, 80333 München. T. (089) 28 25 48, Fax (089) 28 86 45.
- Paint - *079179*
Gemälde-Cabinett Unger, Brienner Str. 7, 80333 München. T. (089) 22 75 15, 22 03 26, 29 84 04.
- Paint - *079180*
Gemälde-Cabinett Unger, Steinsdorfstr. 10, 80538 München. T. (089) 22 03 26, 22 75 15, 29 84 04. *079181*
Gemäldegalerie Krupan, Pfisterstr 73, 80331 München.
T. (089) 221482. - Paint - *079182*
Gemini, Herrnstr. 13, 80539 München. T. (089) 22 40 46, Fax (089) 28 37 17. *079183*
Goedecker, Gabelsbergerstr. 19, 80333 München.
T. (089) 28 57 40. - Paint / Sculp - *079184*
Gögger, Christian, Seitzstr 15, 80538 München.
T. (089) 296500, Fax (089) 220602. - Paint / Graph / Sculp / Pho / Draw - *079185*
Götze, Gerhard, Beetzstr. 7, 81679 München.
T. (089) 47 23 07. - Paint - *079186*
Gräf, Friedrich, Chamissostr 12, 81925 München.
T. (089) 982009. - Paint / Paint - *079187*
Graf, R., Reichenbachstr. 16, 80469 München.
T. (089) 26 63 40. *079188*
Grohmann, Hans, Peter-Schlemihl-Str 17, 81377 München. T. (089) 7144173, Fax (089) 7194282.
- Paint - *079189*
Gronert, Kurt, Reichenbachstr. 22, 80469 München.
T. (089) 201 45 47. - Paint - *079190*
Gross, Barbara, Thierschstr 51, 80538 München.
T. (089) 296272, Fax (089) 295510. - Paint / Graph / Sculp / Mul / Draw - *079191*
Grünwald, Michael D., Dr., Römerstr. 26, 80803 München. T. (089) 34 75 62, Fax (089) 34 83 91. - Paint / Sculp / Draw - *079192*
Gunzenhauser, Maximilianstr 10, 80539 München.
T. (089) 223030, Fax (089) 299544. - Paint / Graph / Sculp / Draw - *079193*
Haeusgen, Ursula, Maximilianstr 38, 80539 München.
T. (089) 346299, Fax (089) 345395. *079194*
Häusler, Hohenlohestr 27, 80637 München.
T. (089) 155720. *079195*
Hahn, Mauerkircherstr 102, 81925 München.
T. (089) 985524, Fax (089) 4704860. *079196*
Haider, Ottostr 13, 80333 München.
T. (089) 596815. *079197*

Hampel, Holger J., Prinzregentenstr 68, 81675 München. T. (089) 473067, Fax 479899. *079198*
Hansen, Christophstr. 4, 80538 München.
T. (089) 22 39 71. - Paint / Graph - *079199*
Hanssler, Westenriederstr. 8a, 80331 München.
T. (089) 292525. *079200*
Hartl, Georg L., Ludwigstr. 11, 80539 München.
T. (089) 28 38 54. *079201*
Hartmann, Richard P., Franz-Joseph-Str. 20, 80801 München. T. (089) 347967, Fax (089) 349694. - Paint / Graph / Sculp - *079202*
Hasenclever, Michael, Cuvilliesstr 5, 81679 München.
T. (089) 99750070, Fax (089) 99750069. *079202a*
Haus der Begegnung, Rumfordstr. 21, 80469 München.
T. (089) 29 29 40. - Paint / Graph - *079203*
Das Haus der Gemälde, Maximilianstr 21, 80539 München. T. (089) 299595. - Paint - *079204*
Hauser, Schellingstr. 17, 80799 München.
T. (089) 28 11 59. - Paint / Graph - *079205*
Heitsch, Françoise, Elsässer Str 13, 81667 München.
T. (089) 481200, Fax (089) 918519. *079206*
Hell, Am Platzl 3, 80331 München. T. (089) 226695, Fax (089) 291278. *079207*
Helms, Sabine, Kaulbachstr 35, 80539 München.
T. (089) 285657, Fax 283313. - Paint / Draw - *079208*

Henrich, R., Theresienstr. 58, 80333 München.
T. (089) 28 23 06. *079209*
Henseler, Galeriestr. 2a, 80539 München.
T. (089) 22 11 76. *079210*
Hermanns, Am Platzl 4, 80331 München.
T. (089) 292745, Fax (089) 296863. *079211*
Hermeyer, Wilhelmstr. 3, 80801 München.
T. (089) 39 61 96, 39 24 94, Fax (089) 33 54 17.
- Paint / Graph / Sculp - *079212*
Herzer, Heinz, Maximilianstr 43, 80538 München.
T. (089) 297729, Fax (089) 297730. - Paint / Graph / Sculp - *079213*
Heseler, Walter, Residenzstr 27, 80333 München.
T. (089) 220834, 299661, Fax (089) 227169. - Paint / Graph / Sculp - *079214*
Hierling, Joseph, Kurfürstenstr 17, 80799 München.
T. (089) 2731000. - Paint / Graph / Sculp - *079215*
Hilton Art Gallery, Am Tucherpark 7, 80538 München.
T. (089) 384 52 89. - Paint / Graph / Draw - *079216*
Hinrichs, E., Boosstr. 14, 81541 München.
T. (089) 65 21 41. - Paint - *079217*
Hohenthal & Littler, Galeriestr 2a, 80539 München.
T. (089) 2913898, Fax (089) 2285100. *079218*
Holzinger, Galeriestr. 2, 80539 München.
T. (089) 292487. - Paint / Sculp / Cur - *079219*
Iliu, Julia F., Barerstr 46, 80799 München.
T. (089) 2800688. *079220*
Jahn, Fred, Maximilianstr 10, 80539 München.
T. (089) 220714, 220117, Fax 221541. - Paint / Graph / China / Eth / Jew / Glass / Draw - *079221*
Jaspers, Maximilianstr 8, 80539 München.
T. (089) 2289377, Fax (089) 2730834. *079222*
Jeanne, Prannerstr 5, 80333 München. T. (089) 297570, Fax (089) 223587. - Paint / Graph / Fra / Draw - *079223*
Johnssen, Carol, Königinstr 27, 80539 München.
T. (089) 283646, Fax (089) 2805256. - Paint - *079224*
Kamm, H., & B. Lindermayr, Sonnenstr. 9, 80331 München. T. (089) 555596. *079225*
Kampl, Mathias, Isartalstr 34, 80469 München.
T. (089) 765890, Fax (089) 7256463. *079226*
Karl & Faber, Amirapl 3, 80333 München.
T. (089) 221865/66, Fax 2283350. - Paint / Graph / Sculp - *079227*

Keller, Dany, Buttermelcherstr 11, 80469 München.
T. (089) 226132, Fax 295508. - Paint / Graph / Sculp / Pho / Draw - *079228*
Kelz-Simon, D., Griegstr. 59, 80807 München.
T. (089) 353551. - Paint / Graph - *079229*
Klein-Kunstkeller Neuhausen, Elvirastr. 17a, 80636 München. T. (089) 33 39 33. - Paint - *079230*
Klewan, Klenzestr 23, 80469 München.
T. (089) 2021606, Fax (089) 2021618. - Paint / Graph / Mul / Draw - *079231*
Klüser, Bernd, Georgenstr 15, 80799 München.
T. (089) 332179, Fax (089) 392541. - Paint - *079232*
Kneiding, Jürgen, Holbeinstr. 12, 81679 München.
T. (089) 47 73 78. *079233*
Köck, Beichstr 5, 80802 München. T. (089) 337538, Fax 337538. - Paint / Graph - *079234*
Koestler, B., Maximilianstr 28, 80539 München.
T. (089) 221508. - Paint / Graph - *079235*
Koropp, E. M., Theatinerstr. 40-42, 80333 München.
T. (089) 229542. *079236*
Koropp, Elionore, Theatinerstr. 42, 80333 München.
T. (089) 22 95 42. - Graph - *079237*
Künstlerwerkstatt Lothringerstrasse, Lothringerstr 13, 81667 München. T. (089) 4486961. - Sculp / Pho - *079238*
Kugler-Eder, A., Prinzregentenpl. 17, 80331 München.
T. (089) 478416. *079239*
Kunst im Tal, Talstr. 32, 80331 München.
T. (089) 292907. *079240*
Kunst in der Bayerischen Vereinsbank, Palais Preysing, Prannerstr. 2, 80333 München. T. (089) 21326143, Fax 21325996. - Paint / Graph / Sculp / Draw - *079241*
kunstpublik, Konradstr 10a, 80801 München.
T. (089) 345350. *079242*
Kunstsalon Franke, Briennerstr 7, 80333 München.
T. (089) 225133, 297359, Fax (089) 223926. *079242a*
Ladengalerie Lothringerstrasse, Lothringerstr 13, 81667 München. T. (089) 4486961. - Pho - *079243*
Langemann, M., Nusselstr. 49, 81245 München.
T. (089) 83 86 43. *079244*
LCD & Co., Isoldenstr 22, 80804 München.
- Paint - *079245*
Lea, Klaus, Blütenstr 1, 80799 München.
T. (089) 2724179. *079246*
Leger, Helmut, Herzogstr 41, 80803 München.
T. (089) 393930, Fax (089) 334033. - Paint / Graph / Fra / China - *079247*
Leidel, Promenadepl 10, 80333 München.
T. (089) 298808. *079248*
Limbacher, Konradstr 10, 80801 München.
T. (089) 3455350, Fax (089) 396732. *079249*
I intel, Thomas von, Residenzstr 10, 80333 München.
T. (089) 221875, Fax (089) 292174. *079250*
Lörch, Rose, Grünwalderstr 53, 81547 München.
T. (089) 6927966. - Paint - *079251*
Loo, Otto van de, Maximilianstr 27, 80539 München.
T. (089) 226270, Fax (089) 2285599. - Paint / Graph / Sculp - *079252*
Maciuga, P.-Chr., Römerstr. 26, 80803 München.
T. (089) 39 85 04. - Paint - *079253*
Mahler & Partner, Maximilianstr 21, 80539 München.
T. (089) 299595. *079254*
Malura, Oswald, Hohenzollernstr. 16, 80801 München.
T. (089) 39 85 87. - Paint / Graph - *079255*
Manis Gallery, Holzstr. 20, 80469 München.
T. (089) 266857. *079256*
Margelik, Gabriella, Steinheilstr. 12, 80333 München.
T. (089) 52 82 96. - Paint / Graph - *079257*
Marquardt, Tottenbachstr 16, 80538 München.
T. (089) 292991, Fax (089) 224107. *079258*
Meier, Gisela, Prannerstr 4, 80333 München.
T. (089) 226340, Fax 2289481. - Paint - *079259*
Meißner, K.H., Pütrichstr. 4, 81667 München.
T. (089) 485997. *079260*
Menth, Adelgundenstr 6, 80538 München.
T. (089) 2283840. *079261*
Michler, R., Herzogspitalstr 10, 80331 München.
T. (089) 2603614, Fax (089) 268738. - Graph - *079262*
Modern Art Gallery, Amalienstr. 46, 80799 München.
T. (089) 284280, 284639, Fax (089) 284639. - Paint / Graph / Fra - *079263*
Mosel und Tschechow, Winterstr 7, 81543 München.
T. (089) 6515621, Fax (089) 669350. - Paint - *079264*

Galerie Gisela Meier
[redacted]
München
Gemälde 19. Jahrhundert
Prannerstraße 4
D-80333 München
Telefon (089) 22 63 40
Telefax (089) 228 94 81

Nasty, J., Schleißheimer Str. 2, 80333 München. T. (089) 523 18 41. - Paint - *079265*
Nehmann, Wilhelm, Rosenheimer Str. 46, 81669 München. T. (089) 486994. *079266*
Neithardt, Heinrich, Ainmillerstr. 35/III, 80801 München. T. (089) 36 89 36. - Graph / Repr - *079267*
Notwehr, Blumenstr 23, 80331 München. T. (089) 2605761. *079268*
Nowak, Schillerstr. 7, 80336 München. T. (089) 591660. *079269*
Obermüller, A., Schloßstr. 5, 81675 München. T. (089) 476384. *079270*
Orny, L. & H., Herzog-Heinrich-Str. 15, 80336 München. T. (089) 532015. *079271*
Osram-Galerie, Hellabrunner Str 1, 81536 München. T. (089) 62132503, Fax (089) 62132016. - Paint - *079272*
Östler, Thomas-Wimmer-Ring 3, 80539 München. T. (089) 2289264, Fax 220377. - Paint / Sculp / Tex - *079273*
Ott, E., Türkenstr. 61, 80799 München. T. (089) 272 50 94. - Paint - *079274*
Otto, Sendlinger Str 45, 80331 München. T. (089) 2608485. *079275*
Otto-Galerie, Augustenstr 45, 80333 München. T. (089) 529392, Fax (089) 1784033/34. - Paint / Furn / Sculp / Silv - *079276*
Otto, Rudolf, Schrammerstr 3, 80333 München. T. (089) 223818. *079277*
Paal, Baaderstr 84, 80469 München. T. (089) 2015240, Fax (089) 2015260. *079278*
Pabst, Michael hr, Stollbergstr 11, 80539 München. T. (089) 292939, Fax (089) 296687. - Paint / Graph / Sculp - *079279*
Pfefferle, Rumfordstr 29, 80469 München. T. (089) 292015, Fax (089) 2285324. - Paint - *079280*
Pfefferle, Maximilianstr 16, 80539 München. T. (089) 297969, Fax (089) 2913571. - Paint - *079281*
Pfetten, W. Freiherr von, Georgenstr. 123, 80797 München. T. (089) 188630. - Paint - *079282*
Pollmer, Alexander, Landsberger Str 3, 80339 München. T. (089) 505546, Fax (089) 374729. - Orient / Eth - *079283*
Poster-Gallery-Munich, Thomas-Dehler-Str 10, 81737 München. T. (089) 6378387, Fax (089) 6378324. *079284*
Poster-Gallery-Munich, Münchener Freiheit 7, 80802 München. T. (089) 345672, Fax (089) 347962. *079285*
Poster-Gallery-Munich, Sendlinger Str 26, 80331 München. T. (089) 265702, Fax (089) 2605380. *079286*
Poster-Gallery-Munich, Hanauer Str 68, 80993 München. T. (089) 1401404, Fax (089) 1401427. *079287*
Pressmar, J., Planeggerstr 33, 81241 München. T. (089) 834 61 72. - Paint - *079288*
Preysing, W. Graf, Königinstr 37, 80539 München. T. (089) 285801. - Orient / Jew - *079289*
Produzentengalerie, Adelgundenstr 6, 80538 München. T. (089) 174659, 2283840. - Paint / Graph / Sculp / Pho / Draw - *079290*
Ratfisch, H., Bereiteranger 15, 81541 München. T. (089) 65 64 45. - Paint - *079291*
Reile, M., Wörthstr 7, 81667 München. T. (089) 4470881, Fax (089) 9827378. *079292*
Reith, Schäfflerstr. 5, 80333 München. T. (089) 29 69 29. *079293*
Reuther, C., Seestr. 4, 80802 München. T. (089) 39 17 11. - Paint - *079294*
Rieder, Maximilianstr 22, 80539 München. T. (089) 294517, Fax (089) 223451. - Paint / Graph / Sculp / Draw - *079295*
Ritthaler, Albert, Bismarckstr 2, 80803 München. T. (089) 399959, Fax (089) 391113. - Paint / Glass / Mod - *079296*
Rössler, Reifenstuelstr 16, 80469 München. T. (089) 768781, Fax (089) 7212765. - Paint - *079297*
Roubaud, S., Franz-Joseph-Str 9, 80801 München. T. (089) 397157. - Paint - *079298*
Roucka, Feilitzschstr. 14, 80802 München. T. (089) 348559, 348030. *079299*
Ruf, Oberanger 35, 80331 München. T. (089) 265272, 266597. - Paint / Graph / Sculp - *079300*
Rutzmoser, Ludwigstr 7, 80539 München. T. (089) 2809117. - Paint / Graph / Jew / Fra - *079301*
Sachs, Karin, Buttermelcherstr 16, 80469 München. T. (089) 2011250, 6010060, Fax (089) 2021560. - Paint / Sculp / Pho / Draw - *079302*
Sachse, Artur, Leonrodstr. 6, 80634 München. T. (089) 162400. - Paint / Orient - *079303*
Scharnowski, Günter, Lechelstr 58, 80997 München. T. (089) 8114006. - Paint - *079304*
Scheidwimmer, Xaver, Barerstr 3, 80333 München. T. (089) 594979, Fax 557187. - Paint - *079305*
Schmalreck, A., Dr., Germaniastr. 3, 80802 München. T. (089) 34 61 34. *079306*
Schoeller, T., Corneliusstr. 23, 80469 München. T. (089) 201 65 78. *079307*
Schöninger, H., Karlspl. 25, 80331 München. T. (089) 592148. *079308*
Schöninger, H., Karlspl. 25, 80335 München. T. (089) 59 21 48. - Paint / Graph / Sculp / Fra - *079309*
Schöttle, Rüdiger, Martiusstr 7, 80802 München. T. (089) 333686, Fax (089) 342296. - Paint / Graph / Sculp / Pho / Mul - *079310*
Schott, Alexander, St.-Anna-Str 29, 80538 München. T. (089) 297436. - Graph - *079311*
Schuler, Ottostr. 13, 80333 München. T. (089) 595356. *079312*
Schweden, Oliver, Damenstiftstr 11, 80331 München. T. (089) 2607333, Fax (089) 2607227. *079313*
Schweinsteiger, Ilse, Neufahrner Str. 18, 81679 München. T. (089) 989945, Fax (089) 981652. - Paint / Graph / Draw - *079314*
Schwertl, Theresienstr. 77, 80333 München. T. (089) 52 56 15. - Ant / Paint / Graph - *079315*
Seifert-Binder, Inge, Keplerstr. 1, 81679 München. T. (089) 47 73 04. - Paint / Graph / Sculp - *079316*
Setzer, O., Ostpreußenstr. 43, 81927 München. T. (089) 930 28 30, Fax 9294018. - Paint / Fra / Draw - *079317*
Seufert-Stock, H., Artilleriestr 5, 80636 München. T. (089) 183349. - Paint - *079318*
Singer, A. & M., Widenmayerstr. 42, 80538 München. T. (089) 223453. *079319*
Soin, Leopoldstr. 116, 80802 München. T. (089) 334040, 7603585, Fax 346000. *079320*
Spaeth, von, Theresienstr 19, 80333 München. T. (089) 2809132, Fax (089) 2809132. - Glass - *079321*
Spektrum, Türkenstr 37, 80799 München. T. (089) 284590, Fax (089) 284627. - Paint - *079322*
Spielvogel, Gudrun, Oettingenstr 22, 80538 München. T. (089) 291738, Fax (089) 291507. - Paint - *079323*
Stadtviertel Neuhausen, Hirschbergstr 9, 80634 München. T. (089) 1689810. *079324*
Stölzle, Prannerstr. 5, 80333 München. T. (089) 297366. *079325*
Storms, Walter, Ismaninger Str 51, 81675 München. T. (089) 41902828, Fax 41902829. - Paint / Graph / Sculp / Draw - *079326*
Studio Bruckmann, Nymphenburger Str 84, 80636 München. T. (089) 185871. *079327*
Studio Edition Günter Stöberlein, Niethammerstr. 15, 80997 München. T. (089) 811 52 89, 18 82 22. - Paint / Graph - *079328*
Taiping, Gabelsbergerstr. 17, 80333 München. *079329*
Tanit, Maximilianstr 36, 80539 München. T. (089) 292233, Fax (089) 295792. - Paint / Graph / Pho / Mul / Draw - *079330*

DEUTSCHER
EXPRESSIONISMUS
KLASSISCHE MODERNE
GALERIE THOMAS
MAXIMILIANSTR. 25
80539 MÜNCHEN
TEL. 0 89/22 27 41
FAX 0 89/29 14 04
THOMAS

Telkamp, Karoline, Maximilianstr 6, 80539 München. T. (089) 226283. *079331*
Thomas, Maximilianstr 25, 80539 München. T. (089) 222741, Fax 291404. - Paint / Graph / Sculp - *079332*
Thomsen, B. u E., Angertorstr 5, 80469 München. T. (089) 2605620. *079333*
Toth, R. u J.Dr., Viktoriastr 6, 80803 München. T. (089) 392021. *079334*
Universal Arts Galerie Studio, Orffstr 35a, 80637 München. T. (089) 134245. *079335*
Vertes, von, Neuturmstr. 1, Hotel Rafael, 80331 München. T. (089) 22 27 77, Fax 220070. - Paint - *079336*
Vogdt, Stefan A., Kurfürstenstr. 5, 80799 München. T. (089) 2716857, Fax (089) 272 12 68. *079337*
Vornehm, H., Plinganser Str. 42, 81369 München. T. (089) 77 42 45. - Paint - *079338*
Waldrich, Theresienstr 19, 80333 München. T. (089) 281909. - Paint / Glass - *079339*
Walser, Rupert, Fraunhoferstr 19, 80469 München. T. (089) 2011515, Fax (089) 2021312. - Paint / Graph / Sculp / Pho / Mul / Draw - *079340*
Waßermann, Baaderstr 56b, 80469 München. T. (089) 2023032, Fax (089) 2023038. - Paint / Pho - *079341*
Weiss, Isolde, Söllereckstr. 12, 81545 München. T. (089) 64 63 53. - Paint - *079342*
Wilhelm, C., Pestalozzistr. 5, 80469 München. T. (089) 268671. *079343*
Wittenbrink, Bernhard & Hanna, Jahnstr 18, 80469 München. T. (089) 2605580, Fax (089) 2605868. - Paint / Graph / Sculp / Pho / Draw - *079344*
Wolf, E., Steirerstr. 30, 81247 München. T. (089) 8117028. *079345*
Zorn, Askolf W., Fallmerayerstr 9a, 80796 München. T. (089) 3081023. - Paint / Ico - *079346*

Münster (Nordrhein-Westfalen)

Art consult, Rothenburg 16, 48143 Münster. T. (0251) 44400, Fax 56283. - Paint - *079347*
Brinckmann, Ludwig, Spiekerhof 34, 48143 Münster. - Paint / Fra - *079348*
Clasing, Prinzipalmarkt 37, 48143 Münster. T. (0251) 4 41 65, Fax 518911. - Paint / Sculp / Fra - *079349*
Etage, Prinzipalmarkt 37, 48143 Münster. T. (0251) 454 42, Fax 518911. - Paint / Sculp / Fra - *079350*
Frye & Sohn, Hörsterstr. 47-48, 48143 Münster. T. (0251) 466 62. - Paint - *079351*
Galerie am Kalkmarkt, Münzstr., 48143 Münster. *079352*
Gesellschaft Kunst und Creation, Engelstr. 68, 48143 Münster. T. (0251) 530 50, Fax 530 51 95. - Ico - *079353*
Hanses, Sprakeler Str. 6, 48159 Münster. *079354*
Hüning, Bernhard, Grevener Str. 343, 48159 Münster. T. (0251) 21 56 40, 21 16 68, Fax 215640. - Graph - *079355*
Humbert, Ermlandweg 14, 48159 Münster. T. (0251) 21 21 46. - Paint / Graph / Sculp - *079356*

Kunsthandlung Klosterbusch, Klosterbusch 12, 48167
Münster. T. (0251) 61 56 83. - Graph -   *079357*

Nettels, Th., Spiegelturm 3, 48143 Münster.
T. (0251) 4 62 93. - Paint / Fra -   *079358*

Ostendorff, Gerd, Nachf., Prinzipalmarkt 11, 48143
Münster. T. (0251) 574 04. - Paint / Graph -   *079359*

Pohl, Carl, Hansaplatz 1, 48155 Münster. - Paint /
Fra -   *079360*

Pohlkötter, Bernhard, Rothenburg 38, 48143 Münster.
T. (0251) 445 11. - Paint / Graph / Repr / Fra -   *079361*

Schemm, Josef, Ludgeristr. 58, 48143 Münster.   *079362*

Schnake, Beelertstiege 5, 48143 Münster.
T. (0251) 51 83 63, Fax 51 83 64. - Paint / Graph /
Sculp -   *079363*

Steins, Hansjürgen, Bahnhofstr. 14, 48143 Münster.
T. (0251) 5 84 41. - Paint -   *079364*

Torhausgalerie, Hindenburgplatz 78, 48143
Münster.   *079365*

Nauheim (Hessen)

Groth, Winfrid, Rüsselsheimer Str 5, 64569 Nauheim.
T. (06152) 64124. - Paint / Graph / Repr / Sculp /
Fra -   *079372*

Naumburg (Sachsen-Anhalt)

Kockler, A., Steinweg 32, 06618 Naumburg.
T. (03445) 31 25. - Graph -   *079373*

Neckargemünd (Baden-Württemberg)

Palette, Bahnhofstr. 9, 69151 Neckargemünd.
T. (06223) 66 29. - Paint -   *079374*

Nettersheim (Nordrhein-Westfalen)

Galerie für Natur- und Jagdkunst, Brunnenstr. 13, 53947
Nettersheim. - Paint / Graph / Draw -   *079375*

Nettetal (Nordrhein-Westfalen)

Galcrie Burg Ingenhoven, Burgstr. 10, 41334
Nettetal.   *079376*

Galerie Esch, Hochstr. 16, 41334 Nettetal.   *079377*

Galerie in der Diele, Friedrichstr. 5, 41334 Nettetal.
T. (02153) 02157/6017. - Ant / Graph / Draw -   *079378*

Galerie Stadtsparkasse, Doerkes-Platz 1, 41334
Nettetal.   *079379*

Neu-Isenburg (Hessen)

Galerie la Coupole, Friedensallee 98, 63263 Neu-Isenburg. T. (06102) 273 36, Fax 47 36. - Paint -   *079380*

Gessmann, Schulstr.2, 63263 Neu-Isenburg.
T. (06102) 225 80, 237 96. - Paint / Graph /
Draw -   *079381*

Neu-Ulm (Bayern)

Aena Privat-Galerie, Griesmayerstr. 7, 89233 Neu-Ulm.
T. (0731) 71 23 09. - Paint -   *079382*

Neu Wulmstorf (Niedersachsen)

Blieske, Christine, Elchpfad 6, 21629 Neu Wulmstorf.
T. (040) 700 51 50, Fax 7008069. - Graph / China /
Repr / Ico -   *079383*

Neubeuern (Bayern)

Alex' Antiques-Galerie, Winkl 25, 83115 Neubeuern.
T. (08035) 47 76.   *079384*

Studio Rindle, Fraithenstr. 1, 83115 Neubeuern.
- Paint -   *079385*

Neubrandenburg (Mecklenburg-Vorpommern)

Galerie Friedländer Tor, Friedländer Tor, 17033 Neubrandenburg. T. (0395) 2695. - Paint / Graph / China /
Sculp / Tex / Jew / Draw -   *079386*

Neuenkirchen, Lüneburger Heide (Niedersachsen)

Falazik, Ruth, Tiefe Str. 4, 29643 Neuenkirchen, Lüneburger Heide. T. (05195) 366. - Paint / Graph / Sculp /
Draw -   *079387*

Neuhaus an der Pegnitz (Bayern)

Lehmann, H. & P. Meng, Burgstr. 3, 91284 Neuhaus an
der Pegnitz. T. (09156) 1399.   *079388*

Neulingen (Baden-Württemberg)

Künstlergilde Buslat e. V., Schloß Bauschlott, 75245
Neulingen. T. (07237) 302, 7194, Fax 1083. - Paint /
Graph -   *079389*

Neumünster (Schleswig-Holstein)

Zielke, Cranachstr. 17, 24539 Neumünster.
T. (04321) 244 67. - Paint -   *079390*

Neunkirchen, Saar (Saarland)

Galerie im Bürgerhaus, Marienstr 2, 66538 Neunkirchen, Saar. T. (06821) 202561, Fax 21530.
- Paint -   *079391*

Neunkirchen, Siegerland (Nordrhein-Westfalen)

Schütz, G., Kirchbergweg 3, 57290 Neunkirchen, Sie-
gerland. T. (02735) 3739.   *079392*

Neuss (Nordrhein-Westfalen)

Bilder-Etage, Kurt-Huber-Str. 78, 41466 Neuss.
T. (02131) 250 73.   *079393*

Grünewald, Kurt, Promenadenstr. 17, 41460 Neuss.
- Paint -   *079394*

Höhne, H., Osterather Str. 15, 41460 Neuss.
T. (02131) 59 31 76.   *079395*

Klöden, K., Oberstr. 78, 41460 Neuss. T. (02131) 250 73.
- Paint -   *079396*

Kowallik, Brigitta, Klarissenstr 10, 41460 Neuss.
T. (02131) 24832, Fax (02131) 278114. - Paint /
Graph -   *079397*

Neustadt am Rübenberge (Niedersachsen)

Fotogalerie Bordenau, Bäckergasse 2, 31535 Neustadt
am Rübenberge. T. (05032) 5781. - Pho -   *079398*

Schlehn, Empeder Str 9, 31535 Neustadt am Rübenberge. T. (05032) 64601.   *079399*

Neustadt an der Aisch (Bayern)

Galerie in der Sparkasse, Sparkassenpl 1, 91413 Neustadt an der Aisch.   *079400*

Schmelzer, Hermann, Markgrafenstr 5a, 91413 Neustadt
an der Aisch. T. (09161) 2287. - Paint / Graph /
Sculp -   *079401*

Neustadt an der Weinstraße (Rheinland-Pfalz)

Boschert, H., Walter-Bruch-Str 7, 67434 Neustadt an
der Weinstraße. T. (06321) 88624.   *079402*

Galerie am Bach, Klemmhof, 67433 Neustadt an der
Weinstraße. T. (06321) 31255.   *079403*

Müller, M., Landschreibereistr 7, 67433 Neustadt an der
Weinstraße. T. (06321) 32053.   *079404*

Palatia Galerie Biffar, Mandelring 66, 67433 Neustadt an
der Weinstraße. T. (06321) 83039.   *079405*

Weinstrassen-Atelier, Erika-Köth-Str 67-69, 67435 Neustadt an der Weinstraße. T. (06321) 66066. - Paint /
Graph -   *079406*

Neustrelitz (Mecklenburg-Vorpommern)

refugium, Hohenzieritzer Str 13, 17235 Neustrelitz.
T. (03981) 206484, Fax (03981) 206485. - Paint /
Graph / Sculp / Draw -   *079407*

Neuwied (Rheinland-Pfalz)

Failer, Marktstr., am Hallenbad, 56564 Neuwied.
T. (02631) 25750. - Paint / Graph / Fra -   *079408*

Nideggen (Nordrhein-Westfalen)

Haser, K.-H., Mühlbachstr. 7, 52385 Nideggen.
T. (02427) 62 12.   *079409*

Nieblum (Schleswig-Holstein)

Klinger, Kertelheinallee 1, 25938 Nieblum.
T. (04681) 1711.   *079410*

Nieder-Olm (Rheinland-Pfalz)

Kleine Galerie Eckes, Ludwig-Eckes-Allee 6, 55268 Nie-
der-Olm. T. (06136) 35 237, Fax 35697. - Paint /
Graph / Pho / Draw -   *079411*

Niederkrüchten (Nordrhein-Westfalen)

Aeffner, Thomas, Schlehenweg 30, 41372 Niederkrüchten. T. (02163) 4162.   *079412*

Galerie HKV, Laarer Weg 16, 41372 Niederkrüchten.
T. (02163) 823 51. - Paint / Graph / Draw -   *079413*

Nienburg, Weser (Niedersachsen)

Bauer & Thurau, Georgstr 6, 31582 Nienburg,
Weser.   *079414*

Nordenham (Niedersachsen)

Galerie Edition Care, Saarstr. 28, 26954 Nordenham.
T. (04731) 52 52. - Paint / Graph -   *079415*

Norderney (Niedersachsen)

Galerie am Kurplatz, Kurplatz, 26548 Norderney.
- Paint / Sculp -   *079416*

Norderstedt (Schleswig-Holstein)

Bilder-Rahmen-Center, Ulzburger Str. 6, 22859 Norderstedt. T. (040) 527 70 65, Fax 5312704.
- Paint -   *079418*

Menssen, Ulzburger Str. 308, 22846 Norderstedt.
T. (040) 5228822, Fax 5228822. - Paint / Graph / Repr /
Sculp / Fra -   *079419*

Nordkirchen (Nordrhein-Westfalen)

Schlossgalerie, Schloß 8, 59394 Nordkirchen.
T. (02596) 34 70. - Paint -   *079420*

Northeim (Niedersachsen)

Bunde, Kurt, Hinter der Kapelle 12, 37154 Northeim.
T. (05551) 8100. - Paint / Sculp / Fra -   *079421*

Nottuln (Nordrhein-Westfalen)

Stiftsgalerie, Kirchstr. 9, 48301 Nottuln.
T. (02502) 10 66.   *079422*

Nürnberg (Bayern)

Art In, Allersberger Str 167a, 90461 Nürnberg.
T. (0911) 476655, Fax (0911) 476655. - Paint -   *079423*

Augustiner-Galerie, Weinmarkt 14, 90403 Nürnberg.
T. (0911) 226126, Fax 2419083. - Paint /
Graph -   *079424*

Barthelmeß, Kaiserstr. 32, Vordere Ledergasse 4-6,
90403 Nürnberg. T. (0911) 22 72 42, 22 45 58. - Paint /
Graph / Repr / Fra -   *079425*

Bauer & Bloessl, Füll 14, 90403 Nürnberg.
T. (0911) 22 29 28, Fax 551443. - Paint / Graph /
Sculp -   *079426*

Berger, J., Mittagstr. 13a, 90451 Nürnberg.
T. (0911) 63 21 89. - Paint -   *079427*

Bode, Klaus D., Elbinger Str 11, 90491 Nürnberg.
T. (0911) 5109200, Fax (0911) 5109108.   *079428*

Defet, Hansfried, Gerhart-Hauptmann-Str. 35, 90431
Nürnberg. T. (0911) 96128-15, Fax (0911) 96128-
40.   *079429*

Douth, P., Mögeldorfer Hauptstr. 51, 90482 Nürnberg.
T. (0911) 54 17 43. - Paint -   *079430*

Dürr, Bernd, Hallpl 2, 90402 Nürnberg.
T. (0911) 204040, Fax (0911) 209090. - Paint / Graph /
Sculp / Draw -   *079431*

Galerie Artificial, Hummelsteiner Weg 76, 90459 Nürnberg. T. (0911) 44 06 66.   *079432*

Galerie Decus, Obere Schmledgasse 24, 90403 Nürn
berg. T. (0911) 22 29 75.   *079433*

Galerie Die Christengemeinschaft, Krelingstr. 26, 90408
Nürnberg. T. (0911) 35 25 20. - Paint / Graph / Sculp /
Draw -   *079434*

Galerie Glasnost, Krugstr 16, Rückgebäude, 90419
Nürnberg. T. (0911) 397949,
Fax (0911) 339677.   *079435*

Galerie im Kuno, Wurzelbauerstr. 35, 90409 Nürnberg.
T. (0911) 55 33 87.   *079436*

Galerie Sima, Hochstr. 33, 90429 Nürnberg.
T. (0911) 26 34 09.   *079437*

Galerie Sorko, Hessestr 8, 90443 Nürnberg.
T. (0911) 267496. - Paint / Graph / Orient /
Draw -   *079438*

Herzle, Lindengasse 42, 90419 Nürnberg.
T. (0911) 33 99 99. - Paint -   *079439*

Hesselmann, Evelyn, Wilhelm-Spaeth-Str. 10, 90461
Nürnberg. T. (0911) 47 15 25. - Paint -   *079440*

Höfler, Berliner Platz 2, 90489 Nürnberg.
T. (0911) 55 01 28. - Paint / Graph -   *079441*

Horlbeck, Pillenreuther Str. 44, 90459
Nürnberg.   *079442*

Institut für moderne Kunst in der Schmidt Bank-Galerie, Lorenzer Pl 29, 90402 Nürnberg. T. (0911) 227623.
- Paint / Graph / Sculp - *079443*
Karlicek, Werner, Albrecht-Dürer-Str. 17, 90403 Nürnberg. *079444*
Kielkowski, Z., Weinmarkt 12a, 90403 Nürnberg. T. (0911) 241 80 80. *079445*
Kunstquartier, Bauerngasse 32, 90443 Nürnberg.
- Paint - *079446*
Maximum Galerie, Färberstr. 11, 90402 Nürnberg.
- Paint - *079447*
Nickel & Zadow, Plobenhofstr. 4, 90403 Nürnberg. T. (0911) 209752, Fax (0911) 2418903. - Paint / Graph / Repr / Fra - *079448*
Nürnberger, D., Torwartstr. 29, 90480 Nürnberg. T. (0911) 40 62 22. *079449*
Nürnberger Galerie für Naive Kunst, Burgstr. 21, 90403 Nürnberg. T. (0911) 22 29 99, Fax 222-455. - Paint / Repr / Fra / Glass / Draw - *079450*
Orth, Rathenauplatz 2, 90489 Nürnberg. T. (0911) 58 85-0. *079451*
Poster-Galerie, Hallpl. 37, 90402 Nürnberg.
T. (0911) 22 17 22. - Graph - *079452*
Rosenthal Studio Haus, Königstr. 5, 90402 Nürnberg.
T. (0911) 22 18 61. *079453*
Sankt Lorenz Galerie, Karolinenstr. 14, 90402 Nürnberg. T. (0911) 20 81 49. *079454*
Schmidt, G., Adam-Klein-Str. 112, 90431 Nürnberg. T. (0911) 326 36 42. *079455*
Schrag, Heinrich, Königstr. 15, 90402 Nürnberg. T. (0911) 20 46 08. - Graph / Repr / Fra / Draw - *079456*
Voigt, Obere Wörthstr. 1, 90403 Nürnberg.
T. (0911) 22 65 86, Fax 20 38 86. *079457*
Voigt, Schustergasse 10, 90403 Nürnberg.
T. (0911) 205 92 97. - Fra - *079458*
Weigl, Innere Laufer Gasse 27, 90403 Nürnberg.
T. (0911) 22 36 50, Fax 24 10 60. - Graph - *079459*
Wormser, Karl, An der Fleischbrücke 2, 90403 Nürnberg. T. (0911) 20 37 47. - Paint / Tex - *079460*

Nürtingen (Baden-Württemberg)
Galerie Die Treppe, Breitäckerstr. 6, 72622 Nürtingen.
T. (07022) 34874, 31277, Fax 42772. *079461*

Nußloch (Baden-Württemberg)
Ohrnberger, N., Gartenstr. 3, 90443 Nußloch.
T. (06224) 101 79, 166 65. - Paint - *079462*

Ober-Ramstadt (Hessen)
Galerie und Handwerkshaus Goldene Nudel, Nieder-Ramstädter-Str 48, 64372 Ober-Ramstadt.
T. (06154) 4493, 3939. *079463*

Oberaudorf (Bayern)
Galerie der Sammlung Berthold-Sames, Sudelfeldstr. 31, 83080 Oberaudorf. T. (08033) 1319. - Graph / Sculp - *079464*

Oberbiberg (Bayern)
Gemälde-Galerie Marsie, Waldstr. 2, 82041 Oberbiberg.
T. (089) 613 41 93. - Paint - *079465*

Oberbillig (Rheinland-Pfalz)
Reeh, H. & K., Lerchenweg 2b, 54331 Oberbillig.
T. (06501) 12297. *079466*

Oberhausen, Rheinland (Rheinland-Pfalz)
Gentsch, Alb., Wörthstr 8-10, 46045 Oberhausen, Rheinland. T. (0208) 801057, Fax (0208) 803615.
- Paint / Repr / Fra - *079467*
Stadtsparkasse Oberhausen, Marktstr 97, 46045 Oberhausen, Rheinland. *079468*

Oberkirch (Baden-Württemberg)
Link, B., Stadtgartenstr 6, 77704 Oberkirch.
T. (07802) 7788. - Paint - *079469*

Obernburg (Bayern)
Kleine Galerie, Kapellengasse 6, 63785 Obernburg.
T. (06022) 72177. - Paint / Graph / Draw - *079470*

Oberursel (Hessen)
Braas-Galerie, Frankfurter Landstr 2-4, 61440 Oberursel. T. (06171) 6330. *079471*

Galerie L9, Liebfrauenstr 9, 61440 Oberursel.
T. (06171) 53986. - Paint / Graph / Sculp - *079472*
Priamos, Im Oelgarten 6, 61440 Oberursel.
T. (06171) 56134, 54323. - Ico - *079473*
Wolf-Bütow, Eva, Liebfrauenstr 9, 61440 Oberursel.
T. (06171) 53986. *079474*

Oberwesel (Rheinland-Pfalz)
Loreley Galerie, Liebfrauenstr. 41, 55430 Oberwesel.
T. (06744) 7404, Fax (06744) 7494. *079475*

Öhningen (Baden-Württemberg)
Atelier Janz, Stiegerstr. 4, 78337 Öhningen.
T. (07735) 639, Fax 639. - Paint / Graph / Sculp / Draw - *079476*

Offenbach (Hessen)
Atelier unterm Dach, Kaiserstr. 40, 63065 Offenbach.
T. (069) 800 48 18. *079477*
Hant, Bismarckstr. 171, 06065 Offenbach. *079478*
Huber, Volker, Berliner Str. 218, 63067 Offenbach.
T. (069) 81 45 23, Fax 88 01 55. - Paint / Graph / Sculp / Mul / Draw - *079479*
Hügelow, Manfred, Kaiserstr. 94, 63065 Offenbach.
T. (069) 88 07 96, Fax 88 08 49. - Graph - *079480*
Kindel, H. P., Kaiserstr. 61, 63065 Offenbach.
T. (069) 88 68 75. *079481*
Opis, Emil-Peter, Aschaffenburger Str. 65, 63073 Offenbach. T. (069) 89 70 73. *079482*
Rosenberg, Ludwigstr. 134, 63067 Offenbach.
T. (069) 88 00 51. - Paint - *079483*
Travel-Art, Hospitalstr. 18, 63065 Offenbach.
T. (069) 81 10 96. *079484*

Offenburg (Baden-Württemberg)
Werkstattgalerie Alte Wäscherei, Wilhelm-Bauer-Str., 77652 Offenburg. *079485*

Oldenburg (Niedersachsen)
Art-Plakat-Kunsthandel, Gaststr. 21, 26122 Oldenburg.
T. (0441) 76756, Fax 72997. - Graph - *079486*
bbk-Galerie, Peterstr. 1, 26121 Oldenburg.
T. (0441) 25280. - Paint - *079487*
Galerie d'Or, Herbartgang, 26122 Oldenburg.
T. (0441) 121 92. - Jew - *079488*
Galerie Forum Kunst-Handwerk, Staulinie 1/Lappangasse 4, 26122 Oldenburg. T. (0441) 15445. *079489*
Galerie in der Mühle, Cloppenburger Str. 428, 26133 Oldenburg. T. (0441) 482 58. *079490*
Galerie Jacob, Achternstr. 42-43, 26122 Oldenburg.
T. (0441) 277 11, Fax 14456. - Paint - *079491*
Galerie O, Bloherfelder Str. 141, 26129 Oldenburg.
T. (0441) 59 12 82. - Paint / Graph / Draw - *079492*

Olfen (Nordrhein-Westfalen)
Atelier Ulla Zymner, Am Hohen Ufer 27, 59399 Olfen.
T. (02595) 630. - Paint / Graph / Sculp / Draw - *079493*

Osnabrück (Niedersachsen)
Clasing, Rolandstr. 21, 49074 Osnabrück.
T. (0541) 252 57. - Sculp - *079494*
Este, Markt 9a, 49074 Osnabrück. T. (0541) 224 90.
- Paint - *079495*
Gäng, Alfred, Iburger Str. 21, 49082 Osnabrück.
- Paint - *079496*
Galerie Schwarz-Weiss, Alte Münze 25, 49074 Osnabrück. T. (0541) 27906. - Paint - *079497*
Gildewart-Galerie, Große Gildewart 27, 49074 Osnabrück. T. (0541) 258456, Fax 23995. - Paint - *079498*
Illmer, Hasestr. 58, 49074 Osnabrück. T. (0541) 295 92.
- Graph / China / Dec / Fra - *079499*

Osterholz-Scharmbeck (Niedersachsen)
Galerie Gut Sandbeck, Sandbeckstr., 27711 Osterholz-Scharmbeck. T. (04791) 586 24. - Graph - *079500*

Oststeinbek
Maier-Busse, Dorfstr 31, 22113 Oststeinbek.
T. (040) 7388914. *079501*

Ottersberg (Niedersachsen)
Fischerhuder Galerie, In der Bredenau 1A, 28870 Ottersberg. T. (04205) 7657. - Paint / Graph / Sculp / Draw - *079502*

Galerie C, Wilhelmshauser Str. 4, 28870 Ottersberg.
T. (04205) 04293/70 87. *079503*
Grünspan, Grellenbrook 10, 28870 Ottersberg.
T. (04205) 1262. *079504*

Paderborn (Nordrhein-Westfalen)
Asmuth, Dorit, Nesthauser Str. 35, 33106 Paderborn.
T. (05251) 05254/5381. - Paint - *079505*
Galerie Double You, Karl-Schurz-Str 35, 33100 Paderborn. *079506*
Galerie Edition G, Zum Rottberg 97, 33106 Paderborn.
T. (05251) 6303. - Paint - *079507*
Janssen, Grube 9, 33098 Paderborn.
T. (05251) 25444. *079508*
Plakatgalerie, Marienstr. 18, 33098 Paderborn.
T. (05251) 265 70. - Graph - *079509*

Panker (Schleswig-Holstein)
Galerie im Torhaus, Torhaus, 24321 Panker.
T. (04381) 66 86. - Paint - *079510*

Passau (Bayern)
Galerie am Steinweg, Steinweg 2, 94032 Passau.
- Paint - *079511*
Galerie im Scharfrichterhaus, Milchgasse 2, 94032 Passau. T. (0851) 24 83. - Paint - *079512*

Peine (Niedersachsen)
Gillmeister, Breite Str. 8, 31224 Peine.
T. (05171) 170 26, Fax 17025. - Paint / Graph / Sculp / Mul / Draw - *079513*

Pfaffenhofen an der Ilm (Bayern)
Eckert Ateliergalerie, Dorfstr 20, 85276 Pfaffenhofen an der Ilm. T. (08441) 672. - Paint / Graph - *079514*
Pennarz, Rainer, Gundamsried, Alte Schule, 85276 Pfaffenhofen an der Ilm. T. (08441) 72952, Fax (08441) 83875. - Paint / Graph - *079515*

Pfarrkirchen (Bayern)
Galerie Artica, Lindenstr. 9, 84347 Pfarrkirchen.
T. (08561) 4494, Fax 71281. - Paint / Graph / Draw - *079516*

Pforzheim (Baden-Württemberg)
Schaffrath-Larché, Dilsteiner Str. 12, 75173 Pforzheim.
T. (07231) 258 00. - Paint - *079517*
Wehr, I., Lammstr. 3, 75172 Pforzheim.
T. (07231) 10 27 67. *079518*

Pfullingen (Baden-Württemberg)
Henderson, Römerstr 96, 72793 Pfullingen.
T. (07121) 790633, Fax 790688. *079519*

Pfungstadt (Hessen)
Kaleidoskop Galerie, Raiffeisenstr. 15, 64319 Pfungstadt. T. (06157) 37 53. *079520*

Pinneberg (Schleswig-Holstein)
Brande, Dockenhudener Chaussee 227, 25421 Pinneberg. T. (04101) 458 15. *079521*
Schaar, Lindenstr. 35, 25421 Pinneberg.
T. (04101) 20 79 87. *079522*

Plön (Schleswig-Holstein)
Galerie am See, Rosenstr. 8, 24306 Plön.
T. (04522) 92 25. - Paint / Graph / Draw - *079523*

Pocking (Bayern)
Kirchner, Bernd H.D., Lindenberg 5, 82343 Pocking.
T. (08531) 1498, Fax 1616. - Sculp - *079524*

Poing (Bayern)
Galerie Hartl, Hohenzollernstr. 24, 85586 Poing.
T. (08121) 71818. - Paint / Graph - *079525*

Potsdam (Brandenburg)
Galerie, Kleine Gasse 3, 14467 Potsdam.
T. (0331) 21320. *079526*
Galerie am Neuen Palais, Straße am Neuen Palais, 14467 Potsdam. T. (0331) 97 21 65. - Paint / Graph / Sculp - *079527*
Galerie Posthofstrasse, Posthofstr. 5, 14467 Potsdam.
T. (0331) 24149. *079528*
Galerie Trapez, Charlottenstr. 27, 14467 Potsdam.
T. (0331) 2801251, Fax 2801251. - Paint / Graph / Sculp / Pho / Draw - *079529*

Jordan, Erich, Hermann-Elflein-Str. 8/9, 14467 Potsdam.
T. (0331) 21355.   *079530*
Potsdam-Galerie am Staudenhof, Am Alten Markt 10,
14467 Potsdam. T. (0331) 21373. - Paint -   *079531*
Samtleben, Brandenburger Str. 66, 14467 Potsdam.
T. (0331) 24075, Fax 24075. - Paint / Graph /
Pho -   *079532*
Staudenhof-Galerie, Am Alten Markt 10, 14467 Pots-
dam. T. (0331) 213 73. - Paint / Graph / China / Sculp /
Tex / Pho / Draw -   *079533*

Prerow (Mecklenburg-Vorpommern)
Sommergalerie, D. Wolff, Hauptstrandaufgang, 18375
Prerow. T. (038233) 348.   *079534*

Pullach (Bayern)
Otto, Schillerstr 16, 82049 Pullach. T. (089) 7932225,
Fax (089) 7933135. - Paint -   *079535*

Quedlinburg (Sachsen-Anhalt)
Galerie Lyonel-Feininger, Finkenherd 5a, 06484 Quedlinburg. T. (03946) 2238.   *079536*

Quickborn, Kreis Pinneberg (Schleswig-Holstein)
Petersen, Hans, Marienhöhe 124, 25451 Quickborn,
Kreis Pinneberg. T. (04106) 5721. - Paint -   *079537*

Radebeul (Sachsen)
Kleine Galerie Radebeul, Hauptstr. 20, 01445 Radebeul.
T. 74449.   *079538*

Radevormwald (Nordrhein-Westfalen)
Hardt, Sieplenbusch 1, 42477 Radevormwald.
T. (02195) 8058/59.   *079539*
Krauskopf, G., Kaiserstr. 98, 42477 Radevormwald.
T. (02195) 2601.   *079540*

Radolfzell (Baden-Württemberg)
Vayhinger, Liggeringer Str. 7, 78315 Radolfzell.
T. (07732) 100 55, Fax 12570. - Paint / Graph / Sculp /
Draw -   *079541*

Rangendingen-Höfendorf (Baden-Württemberg)
Edition Automobile, Kesslerstr 21, 72414 Rangendin-
gen-Höfendorf. T. (07471) 1597, Fax 8197. - Paint /
Graph / Repr -   *079542*

Rastatt (Baden-Württemberg)
Modern Graphics, Lochfeldstr. 30, 76437 Rastatt.
T. (07222) 827 34. - Graph -   *079543*

Ratingen (Nordrhein-Westfalen)
Galerie Les Beaux Arts, Lintorfer Markt 6, 40885 Ratin-
gen. T. (02102) 371 36, Fax 39184. - Paint / Graph /
Sculp / Fra / Draw -   *079544*
Riedel, Allscheidt 16, 40883 Ratingen.
T. (02102) 678 14, Fax 66976. - Ant / Paint / Graph /
Jew / Fra / Lights -   *079545*

Ravensburg (Baden-Württemberg)
A.R.S. Art Gallery, Zeppelinstr 7, 88212 Ravensburg.
T. (0751) 13162, Fax (0751) 13162.   *079546*
Hölder, Doris, Eichelstr. 10, 88212 Ravensburg.
T. (0751) 165 56. - Graph -   *079547*
Kunsthandlung, Untere Breite Str. 14, 88212 Ravens-
burg. T. (0751) 14868. - Paint -   *079548*

Recklinghausen (Nordrhein-Westfalen)
Gesterkamp, Herzogswall 10, 45657 Recklinghausen.
T. (02361) 23891. - Sculp / Draw -   *079549*
Künstlerhaus Kenkmannshof, Unterstr. 14, 45659 Reck-
linghausen. T. (02361) 22025, 18 39 75. - Paint /
Graph -   *079550*

Rees (Nordrhein-Westfalen)
Galerie Schloß Sonsfeld, Schloß Sonsfeld, 46459 Rees.
T. (02851) 268. - Ico -   *079551*

Regensburg (Bayern)
Bäumler, P., Obere Bachgasse 9, 93047 Regensburg.
T. (0941) 56 02 63. - Paint / Graph / Sculp -   *079552*
Bezenka, Helmut, Kurt-Tucholsky-Weg 8, 93051 Re-
gensburg. T. (0941) 99 09 75, Fax 99 76 03.
- Paint -   *079553*

Blaeser, Norbert, Neue Waag-Gasse 2, 93047 Regens-
burg. T. (0941) 561217, Fax 561212. - Paint / Graph /
Sculp -   *079554*
Galerie Bild und Rahmen, Wahlenstr. 20, 93047 Regens-
burg. T. (0941) 57886.   *079555*
Galerie im Donau-Einkaufszentrum, 93047
Regensburg.   *079556*
Michl, M. J., Untere Bachgasse, 93047 Regensburg.
T. (0941) 557 96. - Paint / Fra -   *079557*
Studio-Galerie, Donaueinkaufszentrum Laden 28, 93047
Regensburg. T. (0941) 459 69. - Paint / Graph / Fra /
Draw -   *079558*

Reinbek
Kröger, Schulstr 6, 21465 Reinbek.
T. (040) 7224184.   *079559*

Remagen (Rheinland-Pfalz)
Bahnhof Rolandseck, Bahnhof, 53424 Remagen.
T. (02642) 7365, Fax 8381. - Graph -   *079560*
Galerie Rolandshof, 53424 Remagen. T. (02642) 02288/
7564.   *079561*
Unika Gemälde-Center, Mainzer Str. 87, 53424 Rema-
gen. T. (02642) 02288/8061. - Paint / Graph / Sculp /
Fra / Mul / Draw -   *079562*

Remscheid (Nordrhein-Westfalen)
Altstadt Galerie, Kölner Str. 14, 42897 Remscheid.
T. (02191) 68798, Fax 66 31 55. - Paint / Graph / Mul /
Draw -   *079563*
Herget, Hildegard, Buchenstr. 1, 42855
Remscheid.   *079564*
Müller, Georg, Alleestr. 71, 42853 Remscheid.
T. (02191) 259 10. - Paint / Graph / Repr / Fra / Glass /
Draw -   *079565*
Tarillion, Josef, Sieper Str. 16, 42855 Remscheid.
T. (02191) 484 31. - Paint -   *079566*
Werkstattgalerie, Hindenburgstr. 122, 42853 Rem-
scheid. T. (02191) 763 57. - Paint / Graph / Sculp / Mul /
Draw -   *079567*

Remseck (Baden-Württemberg)
Galerie Schloß Remseck, Am Schloßberg, 71686 Remseck. T. (07146) 63 21. - Paint / Orient / Sculp - *079568*

Remshalden (Baden-Württemberg)
Galerie im Atelier, Obere Hauptstr. 8, 73630
Remshalden.   *079569*
Galerie Meissen Art, Kanalstr. 10, 73630 Remshalden.
T. (07181) 73505, Fax 74933. - China -   *079570*
Hollmann, Wolfgang, Kanalstr. 10, 73630 Remshalden.
T. (07181) 749 73, Fax 749 33. - Graph / Fra / Glass /
Cur / Draw -   *079571*
Kinter, Hirschgasse 15, 73630 Remshalden.   *079572*

Reutlingen (Baden-Württemberg)
Fauser, Urbanstr 26, 72764 Reutlingen.
T. (07121) 40314, 40287, Fax (07121) 47320.
- Paint -   *079573*
Galerie am Ledergraben, Lederstr. 98, 72764 Reutlin-
gen. T. (07121) 365 92, Fax 32 06 94. - Graph /
Fra -   *079574*
Reutlinger Kunstkabinett, Nürtingerhofstr. 7, 72764
Reutlingen. T. (07121) 30 02 88. - Ant / Paint / Graph /
Furn / Jew / Instr -   *079575*

Rheda-Wiedenbrück (Nordrhein-Westfalen)
Artes, Berliner Str 52, 33378 Rheda-Wiedenbrück.
T. (05242) 410720.   *079576*

Rheinfelden (Baden-Württemberg)
Baioui, Müssmattstr 29, 79618 Rheinfelden.
T. (07623) 62545.   *079577*

Rheinsberg (Brandenburg)
Galerie-Zopf, Am Markt 1, 16831 Rheinsberg.
T. (033931) 373 61. - Paint / Graph / China / Jew /
Glass -   *079578*

Rödermark (Hessen)
Schöning, Rudolf, Jägerstr. 19, 63322 Rödermark.
T. (06074) 98289.   *079579*

Rohr (Bayern)
Dahlen, Paul, Lorettostr. 23, 93352 Rohr. T. (08783) 400.
- Graph -   *079580*

Rosbach (Hessen)
Kunstgalerie Rodheim, An der Mergel 16, 61191 Rosbach. T. (06007) 496, Fax 8551. - Paint -   *079581*
Kunstgalerie Rodheim, An der Mergel 16, 61191 Rosbach. T. (06007) 496. - Graph / Draw -   *079582*

Rosenheim (Bayern)
Weiss, Hildegard, Brünnsteinstr. 1, 83026 Rosenheim.
T. (08031) 45513. - Paint / Repr -   *079583*

Rostock (Mecklenburg-Vorpommern)
Galerie am Meer, Am Strom 68, 18119 Rostock.
T. (0381) 52436. - Graph / China / Tex / Jew / Glass /
Draw -   *079584*
Refugium, Am Berg 13, 18055 Rostock.
T. (0381) 4907160.   *079585*

Rotenburg (Niedersachsen)
Galerie Wiese, Verdener Str. 38, 27356 Rotenburg.
T. (04261) 84267, Fax 84267. - Paint -   *079586*

Rothenburg ob der Tauber (Bayern)
Geissendörfer, Ernst, Obere Schmiedgasse 1, 91541 Ro-
thenburg ob der Tauber. T. (09861) 2005, Fax 2009.
- Graph -   *079587*

Rottach-Egern (Bayern)
Beck, Michael, Ganghoferstr. 15, 83700 Rottach-Egern.
T. (08022) 27 96 18. - Paint / Graph -   *079588a*
Binhold, Enzianstr. 7, 83700 Rottach-Egern.
T. (08022) 658 25. - Paint -   *079588*
Hyna, Seestr. 17, 83700 Rottach-Egern.
T. (08022) 58 70, Fax 24230. - Paint / Graph /
Sculp -   *079589*
Marx, Werner, Seestr. 24, 83700 Rottach-Egern.
T. (08022) 21 72. - Graph -   *079590*
Richter, G.A., Pitscherweg 2, 83700 Rottach-Egern.
T. (08022) 52 22, Fax 26591. - Paint / Graph / Sculp /
Fra / Pho / Draw -   *079591*
Schott, Seestr. 43, 83700 Rottach-Egern.
T. (08022) 52 84. - Paint -   *079592*

Rottendorf (Bayern)
Galerie am Grasholz, Am Grasholz 6 h, 97228 Rottendorf. T. (09302) 437. - Graph -   *079593*

Rottweil (Baden-Württemberg)
Forum Kunst Rottweil, Friedrichspl. 2, 78628 Rottweil.
T. (0741) 49 42 19. - Graph -   *079594*

Saalfeld, Saale (Thüringen)
Galerie das bunte Lädchen, Saalstr. 11, 07318 Saalfeld,
Saale. T. (03671) 2531. - Paint / Graph / China / Sculp /
Tex / Jew / Glass / Pho / Draw -   *079595*
Saale-Galerie, Brudergasse 9, 07318 Saalfeld, Saale.
T. (03671) 510176, Fax 274. - Paint / Graph / China /
Repr / Sculp / Jew / Fra / Pho / Draw -   *079596*

Saarbrücken (Saarland)
abs Galerie, Kaiserstr. 2a, 66111 Saarbrücken.
- Graph -   *079597*
Altstadtgalerie, St. Johanner Markt 20, 66111 Saarbrük-
ken. T. (0681) 39 96 67, Fax 33242. - Paint / Graph /
Draw -   *079598*
Andreescu-Bernhardt, Despina, Fröschengasse 14,
66111 Saarbrücken. T. (0681) 35871.   *079599*
Elitzer, Ernst, Fürstenstr. 17, 66111 Saarbrücken.
T. (0681) 3 33 90. - Paint / Graph / Repr / Fra -   *079600*
Ernst, Albert J., Im Flürchen 59, 66133 Saarbrücken.
T. (0681) 815767, 06805/7172, Fax 06805/21571.
- Paint / Sculp -   *079601*
EuRo-Kunst, Saargemünder Str. 10, 66119 Saarbrücken.
T. (0681) 555 65, Fax 53649. - Paint / Paint / Graph /
Sculp -   *079602*
Galerie Nouvelle, Kaltenbachstr. 15, 66111 Saarbrük-
ken. T. (0681) 34495.   *079603*
Galerie Sankt Johann, St. Johanner Markt 22, 66111
Saarbrücken. T. (0681) 334 73. - Paint / Graph / China /
Sculp / Fra / Mul -   *079604*
Genso, E., Fröschengasse 12, 66111 Saarbrücken.
T. (0681) 30618.   *079605*

Hammad, S., Kappenstr. 14, 66111 Saarbrücken.
T. (0681) 37 13 34. *079606*
Hees, van, Kaiserstr. 28a, 66111 Saarbrücken.
T. (0681) 3 43 77. - Paint / Graph / Tex - *079607*
Rabe, Eberhard, Lohmeyerstr. 26, 66119 Saarbrücken.
T. (0681) 58 41 62, Fax 53487. - Paint / Graph / Sculp /
Pho / Mul / Draw - *079608*
Schröder, Weinbergweg 34, 66119 Saarbrücken.
T. (0681) 0681/53106. - Paint / Sculp - *079609*
Seekatz, Bahnhofstr. 34, 66111 Saarbrücken.
T. (0681) 241 69. - Paint / Repr / Fra - *079610*
Weinand-Bessoth, Gerberstr. 7, 66111 Saarbrücken.
T. (0681) 335 53. - Paint / Graph - *079611*

Saarlouis (Saarland)
Fritzen, H., Silberherzstr. 6, 66740 Saarlouis.
T. (06831) 2426. *079612*
Scharwath, Helga, Dr., Silberherzstr. 17, 66740 Saar-
louis. T. (06831) 21 14. *079613*
Walzinger, A. & A., Pavillonstr. 45, 66740 Saarlouis.
T. (06831) 495 41, Fax 49544. - Paint / Draw - *079614*

Salach (Baden-Württemberg)
Holographie Hofmann, Schmidtackerstr. 13, 73084 Sa-
lach. T. (07162) 44064, Fax 43900. *079615*

Salzhausen (Niedersachsen)
Albrecht, Schmiedestr. 9, 21376 Salzhausen.
T. (04172) 8527. *079616*

Sande (Niedersachsen)
Schlieper, Kirchstr. 47, 26452 Sande. T. (04422) 0T4360.
- Paint / Graph / Sculp / Draw - *079617*
Wolff, Wilfried, Sanderahmer Str. 33a, 26452 Sande.
T. (04422) 4000, Fax 4000. - Paint / Graph /
Draw - *079618*

Sandhausen (Baden-Württemberg)
Heller, M. & H., Allmendstr. 31, 69207 Sandhausen.
T. (06224) 33 17. - Paint - *079619*

Sankt Augustin (Nordrhein-Westfalen)
Radicke, J., Eisenachstr. 33, 53757 Sankt Augustin.
T. (02241) 33 57 73. - Paint / Graph / Sculp /
Draw - *079620*

Sankt Julian (Rheinland-Pfalz)
Kleiner Kunstbahnhof, Bahnhofstr. 10, 66887 Sankt Julian. - Paint / China / Draw - *079621*

Sankt Peter-Ording (Schleswig-Hol-
stein)
Schiel, Dorfstr. 27, 25826 Sankt Peter-Ording.
T. (04863) 3105. *079622*

Sassnitz (Mecklenburg-Vorpommern)
Hartwich, Hauptstr. 30, 18546 Sassnitz.
T. (038392) 22390. - Paint / Graph / Furn / China /
Sculp / Mul / Draw - *079623*

Scheeßel (Niedersachsen)
Meyerhof, Zevener Str., 27383 Scheeßel.
T. (04263) 8551. - Paint / Graph / Draw - *079624*

Schmallenberg (Nordrhein-Westfalen)
Grawe, Oststr 22, 57392 Schmallenberg.
T. (02972) 2844. - Paint / Fra - *079625*

Schmitten (Hessen)
Pigge, Ursula, Zum Feldberg 8, 61389 Schmitten.
T. (06084) 3670. - Ant / Paint / Graph / Orient / Eth /
Silv / Lights - *079626*

Schorndorf (Baden-Württemberg)
Galerie Spectrum, Vorstadtstr. 10, 73614 Schorndorf.
T. (07181) 615 95. - Paint / Graph - *079627*

Schramberg (Baden-Württemberg)
Galerie Villa Uechtritz, Hammergraben 62, 78713
Schramberg. *079628*
Podium Kunst, Erhard-Junghans-Str. 48, 78713 Schram-
berg. T. (07422) 4713. - Paint - *079629*

Schriesheim (Baden-Württemberg)
Bahnmüller, Zentgrafenstr. 13, 69198 Schriesheim.
- Paint - *079630*

Schwabach (Bayern)
La Nouvelle Galerie, Nördliche Ringstr. 4, 91126 Schwa-
bach. T. (09122) 13960, Fax 13960. - Ant /
Paint - *079631*

Schwäbisch Gmünd (Baden-Württem-
berg)
D'ovado Schmuckgalerie, Türlensteg 22, 73525 Schwä-
bisch Gmünd. T. (07171) 651 83. - Jew - *079632*
Kraforst, Hans, Kappelgasse 3, 73525 Schwäbisch
Gmünd. T. (07171) 27 34. - Paint / Graph / Repr / Sculp /
Fra - *079633*
Kunstforum Schwäbisch Gmünd, Parlerstr. 5, 73525
Schwäbisch Gmünd. T. (07171) 307 00. *079634*
Maier, Konrad, Rinderbacher Gasse 23, 73525 Schwä-
bisch Gmünd. T. (07171) 661 77. - Paint - *079635*

Schwäbisch Hall (Baden-Württemberg)
Galerie am Markt, Am Markt 7, 74523 Schwäbisch Hall.
T. (0791) 751325, Fax 751305. - Paint - *079636*

Schwalmstadt (Hessen)
Willingshäuser Gemäldekabinett, Industriestr. 1a, 34613
Schwalmstadt. T. (06691) 29 88, 29 44, Fax 242 24.
- Ant / Paint / Graph / Sculp - *079637*

Schwarzenbach a d Saale (Bayern)
Richter, Anton, Färberstr. 7, 95126 Schwarzenbach a d
Saale. T. (09284) 75 42. - Paint / Graph - *079638*

Schwedt (Brandenburg)
Galerie im Ermelerspeicher, Lindenallee, 16303
Schwedt. T. (03332) 23245. *079639*

Schweich (Rheinland-Pfalz)
Galerie in der Synagoge, 54338 Schweich. *079640*

Schweinfurt (Bayern)
Oberhofer, Peter, Graben 20, 97421 Schweinfurt.
T. (09721) 219 57. - Paint / Repr / Fra - *079641*
Rückert-Buchhandlung, Keßlergasse 9, 97421 Schwein-
furt. T. (09721) 218 72. - Graph / Repr - *079642*

Schwelm (Nordrhein-Westfalen)
Basiner, Kölner Str. 9, 58332 Schwelm.
T. (02336) 186 52. - Paint - *079643*

Schwerin (Mecklenburg-Vorpommern)
Galerie Schwerin, Arsenalstr. 14, 19053 Schwerin.
T. (0385) 57 17 13. - Paint / Graph / China / Tex /
Jew - *079644*

Schwetzingen (Baden-Württemberg)
Rothe, Dreikönigstr. 6, 68723 Schwetzingen.
T. (06202) 48 80. - Paint - *079645*

Seebruck (Bayern)
Chiemsee-Galerie, Ludwig-Thoma-Str 9, 83358 See-
bruck. T. (08667) 7791. - Paint - *079646*

Seeheim-Jugenheim (Hessen)
Böhler, Wolfgang, Ludwigstr 4a, 64342 Seeheim-Jugenheim. T. (06257) 3624. *079647*

Seesen (Niedersachsen)
Galerie 77, Lautenthalerstr. 77, 38723 Seesen.
T. (05381) 50 15. - Paint / Fra - *079648*

Seevetal (Niedersachsen)
Glasgalerie Hittfeld, Kirchstr 1, 21218 Seevetal.
T. (04105) 53444, Fax (04105) 52364. - Glass - *079649*
Hitfeld, Kirchstr 1, 21218 Seevetal. T. (04105) 53444.
- Glass - *079649a*
Metzner, Bernd, Am Felde 28, 21217 Seevetal.
T. (04105) 768 62 92. - Pho - *079650*

Seligenstadt (Hessen)
Blehle, Karl, Steinheimer Str. 12, 63500 Seligenstadt.
T. (06182) 33 23. *079652*
Galerie im Kloster, Klosterhof 2, 63500 Seligenstadt.
T. (06182) 36 58. *079653*
Kunstforum Seligenstadt, Galerie im Alten Haus, Frank-
furter Str., 63500 Seligenstadt.
T. (06182) 25667. *079654*
Selm (Nordrhein-Westfalen)
Cappenberger Remise, Cappenberger Damm 203,
59379 Selm. *079655*

Senftenberg (Brandenburg)
Galerie am Schloss, Steindamm, 01968 Senftenberg.
T. (03573) 73527, Fax 2628. - Paint - *079656*

Siegburg (Nordrhein-Westfalen)
Grunschel, K. & R., Siegfeldstr. 15a, 53721 Siegburg.
T. (02241) 65215. *079657*
Wasserwerk Galerie Lange, Wahnbachtalstr. 17, 53721
Siegburg. T. (02241) 674 44. - Paint - *079658*

Siegen (Nordrhein-Westfalen)
Galerie S, Weidenauer Str 167, 57076 Siegen.
T. (0271) 706287. - China - *079659*
Neuser, H., Obergraben 29, 57072 Siegen.
T. (0271) 53705. *079660*
Nohl, Ruth, Kölner Str 44, 57072 Siegen.
T. (0271) 55108. - Graph - *079661*
Schindler, F., Hagener Str 137, 57072 Siegen.
T. (0271) 45081, 45082. *079662*
Siebel, K., Marburger Str 26, 57072 Siegen.
T. (0271) 51330. *079663*

Simmern (Rheinland-Pfalz)
Galerie im Alten Rathaus, Kirchgasse 5, 55469 Sim-
mern. T. (06761) 7799. *079664*

Sindelfingen (Baden-Württemberg)
Galerie Tendenz, Rathauspl 4, 71063 Sindelfingen.
T. (07031) 878170, Fax 873580. - Paint /
Graph - *079665*

Sinsheim (Baden-Württemberg)
Deberle, Johann, Burghäldeweg 13, 74889 Sinsheim.
- Paint - *079666*
Herrmann, Am Zehnt 7, 74889 Sinsheim.
T. (07261) 1684. - Paint / Graph - *079667*
Schwald, G., Waibstadter Str 19, 74889 Sinsheim.
T. (07261) 4292. - Paint - *079668*

Sinzheim (Baden-Württemberg)
Galerie B, Bergstr 19, 76547 Sinzheim.
T. (07221) 85585. - Paint / Glass - *079669*

Sögel (Niedersachsen)
Forum Form, Jagdschloß Clemenswerth, 49751
Sögel. *079670*

Soest (Nordrhein-Westfalen)
Mahler, Aldegrever Wall 28b, 59494 Soest. *079671*
Streiter, Franz, Marktstr 20, 59494 Soest.
T. (02921) 13956. *079672*

Solingen (Nordrhein-Westfalen)
Alfermann, Armin, Benrather Str. 36a, 42697 Solingen.
T. (0212) 763 73. - Paint / Graph - *079673*
Galerie art-eck, Gräfrather Markt, 42627 Solingen.
- Graph - *079674*
Galerie im Heidestübchen, Hermann-Löns-Weg 107,
42697 Solingen. *079675*
Galerie Solinger Künstler, Wuppertaler Str. 160, 42653
Solingen. - Paint / Draw - *079676*
Müllenmeister, K.J., Börsenstr 69, 42657 Solingen.
T. (0212) 809004, Fax 809617. - Paint - *079677*

Sommerhausen (Bayern)
Galerie beim Roten Turm, Rathausgasse 20, 97286
Sommerhausen. T. (09333) 489. - Graph /
China - *079678*

Sontheim (Baden-Württemberg)
Galerie an der Brenz, Sontheimer Str. 18, 89567 Sontheim. T. (07325) 61 25, Fax 4495. - Graph - *079679*

Speyer (Rheinland-Pfalz)
Weingärtner, Galerie, Korngasse 34, 67346 Speyer. T. (06232) 75136. - Ant / Paint / Graph / Orient / China / Fra / Paint / Graph / Fra - 079680

Stadthagen (Niedersachsen)
Weilandt, Adalbert, Obernstr. 13, 31655 Stadthagen. 079683

Starnberg (Bayern)
Bayer, Konrad, Postfach 2142, 82311 Starnberg. T. 01728969606, (08151) 3903, Fax 78664. - Paint - 079684

Gebhardt, Alexander, Dinardstr. 10, 82319 Starnberg. T. (08151) 3220. - Paint - 079685

Weihs, Helga, Kirchpl. 7, 82319 Starnberg. T. (08151) 65 70, Fax 6570. - Paint / Graph / Repr / Sculp / Jew / Rel / Draw - 079686

Steinenbronn (Baden-Württemberg)
Wenger, Brigitte, Stuttgarter Str. 96, 71144 Steinenbronn. T. (07157) 34 90. - Sculp / Tex / Jew / Mul - 079687

Stolberg (Nordrhein-Westfalen)
Pitz, L., Wilhelm-Pitz-Str 15, 52223 Stolberg. T. (02402) 16073. 079688

Stollberg (Sachsen)
Bilder-Knauf, Gretlestr 3, 09366 Stollberg. 079689

Stralsund (Mecklenburg-Vorpommern)
Hanse Galerie, Badenstr. 5, 18439 Stralsund. T. (03831) 292889. - Paint / Graph / China / Sculp / Tex / Jew / Glass / Pho / Draw - 079690

Strande (Schleswig-Holstein)
Weberkate, Dänischenhagener Str. 7, 24229 Strande. - Graph - 079691

Stuttgart (Baden-Württemberg)
AL Galerie, Mittlere Str 8, 70597 Stuttgart. T. (0711) 767183, Fax 7671814. 079692

American Poster Galerie, Kleiner Schloßplatz, 70173 Stuttgart. T. (0711) 29 79 54. - Graph - 079693

Architektur-Galerie am Weissenhof, Am Weißenhof 30, 70191 Stuttgart. T. (0711) 257 14 34. 079694

Bauer-Osthus, Trossinger Str. 6, 70619 Stuttgart. T. (0711) 47 45 58. 079695

Baum, Erich, Fraasstr. 26, 70184 Stuttgart. T. (0711) 24 34 17. - Paint - 079696

Beck, Richard, Happoldstr. 571, 70469 Stuttgart. 079697

Beyer, Wolfgang, Birkenwaldstr. 40, 70191 Stuttgart. - Paint / Fra - 079698

Bildhauergarten, Tuchmachergasse 6, 70372 Stuttgart. T. (0711) 56 00 09. - Sculp - 079699

Bischoff, Walter, Hölderlinstr 57, 70193 Stuttgart. T. (0711) 2264880, (07835) 1453, Fax (07835) 3434. - Paint / Graph / Sculp / Draw - 079700

Braun, Klaus, Christophstr. 40-42, 70180 Stuttgart. T. (0711) 640 59 89, Fax 6074236. - Paint - 079701

Brunnenwiesen Galerie, Brunnenwiesen 42, 70619 Stuttgart. T. (0711) 47 87 08, Fax 47 87 08. - Paint / Graph - 079702

Bühler, Wagenburgstr 4, 70184 Stuttgart. T. (0711) 240507, Fax (0711) 2361153. - Paint / Graph / Sculp - 079703

Döbele, Lautenschlagerstr 3, 70173 Stuttgart. T. (0711) 2262131, Fax (0711) 2265057. - Paint / Graph / Sculp / Draw - 079704

Dorn, Gertrud, Planckstr. 123, 70184 Stuttgart. T. (0711) 46 32 80. - Paint / Graph / Sculp / Draw - 079705

Duppel, Armin, Alexanderstr. 51, 70182 Stuttgart. T. (0711) 24 52 18. - Paint - 079706

Edition Camu, Im Schellenkönig 56, 70184 Stuttgart. - Paint / Draw - 079707

Erdmannsdörfer, Gisela, Staufeneckstr. 15, 70469 Stuttgart. T. (0711) 85 28 90. - Paint / Graph / Sculp - 079708

Fischer, Torstr. 23, 70173 Stuttgart. T. (0711) 24 41 63, Fax 264562. - Paint / Graph - 079709

Fischinger, Peter, Esslinger Str. 20, 70182 Stuttgart. T. (0711) 245982, Fax (0711) 6492437. - Paint / Graph / Fra - 079710

Galerie am Jakobsbrunnen, Tuchmachergasse 6, 70372 Stuttgart. T. (0711) 56 00 09. - Graph - 079711

Galerie für Möbel, Weißenburgstr. 31,, 70180 Stuttgart. 079712

Galerie Gespräch, Reinsburgstr. 93, 70197 Stuttgart. 079713

Galerie im Augustinum, Florentiner Str. 20, 70619 Stuttgart. 079714

Galerie im Rudolf-Steiner-Haus, Zur Uhlandshöhe 10, 70188 Stuttgart. T. (0711) 164310. - Paint - 079715

Galerie im Werkstatthaus, Gerokstr. 7, 70188 Stuttgart. T. (0711) 24 18 49. - Paint / Graph / Pho - 079716

Galerie in der Walpenreute, Walpenreute 10, 70469 Stuttgart. T. (0711) 856 73 44. 079717

Galerie Kultur unterm Turm, Eberhardstr. 61a, 70173 Stuttgart. T. (0711) 216 34 34. - Paint - 079718

Galerie Kunsthöfle, Badstr. 23, 70372 Stuttgart. T. (0711) 74786. - Paint - 079719

Galerie Landesgirokasse, Königstr. 3, 70144 Stuttgart. T. (0711) 1243864, Fax 1243699. - Paint - 079720

Galerie Manus Presse, Lieschingstr. 6, 70567 Stuttgart. T. (0711) 71 30 36/37, Fax 71 76 18. - Paint / Graph / Draw - 079721

Galerie Oase, Hallschlag 23, 70376 Stuttgart. T. (0711) 54 60 80. - Graph / Jew / Draw - 079722

Galerie Quovadis, Weißenburgstr. 31, 70180 Stuttgart. T. (0711) 60 22 04, Fax 74 87 88. - Furn / Dec / Lights / Mul - 079723

Galerie unterm Turm, Eberhardstr. 61, 70173 Stuttgart. 079724

Galerie Zeitkunst, Traubenstr. 47, 70176 Stuttgart. T. (0711) 29 26 56. 079725

Galerie 103, Reinsburgstr. 114, 70197 Stuttgart. T. (0711) 62 21 90. 079726

Galeriering im Kolpinghaus, Waiblinger Str. 27, 70372 Stuttgart. T. (0711) 56 14 61. - Paint / Graph / Sculp / Rel - 079727

Galetzki, Günter, Unter dem Birkenkopf 14, 70197 Stuttgart. T. (0711) 65 09 54. - Paint / Graph - 079728

GEDOK, Gruppe Stuttgart e.V., Hölderlinstr. 17, 70174 Stuttgart. T. (0711) 29 78 12. - Paint / Graph - 079729

Gemäldegalerie am Schloßgarten, Königstr. 1, 70173 Stuttgart. T. (0711) 22 31 22. 079730

Glauner, E., & M. Marazzi, Rienzistr. 17, 70597 Stuttgart. T. (0711) 765 51 41. - Arch / Jew - 079731

Gmeiner, Annette, Esslinger Str. 22, 70182 Stuttgart. T. (0711) 244715, Fax (0711) 2261456. - Paint / Graph / Sculp / Mul / Draw - 079732

Götz, Baumwiesenweg6, 70569 Stuttgart. T. (0711) 6872030, Fax 1316024. 079733

Haderek, Tilly, Römerstr. 1, 70178 Stuttgart. T. (0711) 609040, Fax (0711) 604915. - Paint / Graph - 079734

Harthan, Angelika, Haußmannstr. 20, 70188 Stuttgart. T. (0711) 232333, Fax (0711) 6404213. - Paint / Draw - 079735

Hermann-Metzger-Galerie, Brückenstr. 27, 70376 Stuttgart. T. (0711) 54 44 58. 079736

Herrmann, Peter, Kreuznacher Str 15a, 70372 Stuttgart. T. (0711) 551638, Fax (0711) 551350. 079737

Holografie-Galerie, Kleiner Schloßplatz 5, 70173 Stuttgart. T. (0711) 226 37 27. 079738

Holzwarth, Heidi, Reinsburgstr. 103, 70197 Stuttgart. T. (0711) 615 95 68, Fax 615 95 81. - Paint / Graph / Sculp / Draw - 079739

Hoss, Haußmannstr. 124a, 70188 Stuttgart. T. (0711) 26 26 139. - Graph / Repr - 079740

Inter-Art Galerie, Römerstr. 65, 70180 Stuttgart. T. (0711) 649 32 86. - Paint / Graph / Sculp / Draw - 079741

Jahn, Fred, Weberstr. 39, 70182 Stuttgart. T. (0711) 236 46 45, Fax 2364646. - Paint / Graph / Sculp / Eth / Draw - 079742

Julius, Charlottenstr. 12, 70182 Stuttgart. T. (0711) 24 07 09. - Paint - 079743

KA Galerie für Schmuck, Bebelstr. 27, 70193 Stuttgart. T. (0711) 636 53 38. 079744

Kaess-Weiss, Grüneisenstr. 19, 70184 Stuttgart. T. (0711) 232627, Fax (0711) 248165. - Paint / Graph / Furn / Pho - 079745

Kaiser, Walter, Im Unteren Kienle 42, 70184 Stuttgart. T. (0711) 24 76 48. 079746

Künstlergruppe Experiment, Weberstr. 104, 70182 Stuttgart. T. (0711) 24 64 51. - Paint / Graph / Sculp / Lights - 079747

Künstlerhaus Stuttgart, Reuchlinstr. 4b, 70178 Stuttgart. T. (0711) 61 76 52, Fax 61 31 65. - Paint - 079748

Kunstinstitut, Reinsburgstr. 93, 70197 Stuttgart. T. (0711) 62 00 13. - Paint - 079749

Lindemanns, H., Nadlerstr. 10, 70173 Stuttgart. T. (0711) 23 34 99, Fax 236 96 72. - Pho - 079750

Löffler, Gisela, Esslinger Str. 20, 70182 Stuttgart. - Pho - 079751

March, Brigitte, Solitudestr. 254, 70499 Stuttgart. T. (0711) 8874535, 8875875, Fax (0711) 88743. - Paint / Graph / Sculp / Pho / Mul / Draw - 079752

Mayer & Mayer Galerie für Photographie, Schloßstr 83, 70176 Stuttgart. T. (0711) 622026, Fax (0711) 617909. 079753

Mueller-Roth, Christophstr. 40-42, 70180 Stuttgart. T. (0711) 6493950, Fax (0711) 6400337. - Paint / Graph / Sculp / Mul / Draw - 079754

Neubauer, Günter, Böckinger Str 20a, 70437 Stuttgart. T. (0711) 841632. 079755

Rau, Eberhard, Dr., Olgastr. 39, 70182 Stuttgart. 079756

Regenbogengalerie, Eberhardstr. 35, 70173 Stuttgart. T. (0711) 24 16 24, 24 24 39, Fax 242439. - Paint / Graph / Fra - 079757

Schaller, Marienstr. 3, 70178 Stuttgart. T. (0711) 162650, Fax (0711) 2261677. - Paint / Graph / Repr / Sculp / Fra - 079758

Schmidt, Adriana, Katharinenstr. 21b, 70182 Stuttgart. T. (0711) 23 55 82, Fax (0711) 640 85 18. 079759

Schurr, Alexanderstr. 153, 70180 Stuttgart. T. (0711) 60 54 64, Fax (0711) 649 37 04. - Paint / Graph / Sculp / Draw - 079760

Schwarz, Augsburger Str. 356, 70327 Stuttgart. T. (0711) 33 13 13. - Paint - 079761

Schwerpunkt-Galerie Leibniz-Gymnasium, Klagenfurter Str. 75, 70469 Stuttgart. T. (0711) 81 57 30, 81 68 13. - Paint - 079762

Senatore, Schmidener Str. 60, 70372 Stuttgart. T. (0711) 56 22 40. 079763

Sonnenberg Galerie, Laustr. 17, Eingang Sonnenbühl, 70597 Stuttgart. 079764

Strauss, Billie, Werfmershalde 16,, 70190 Stuttgart. T. (0711) 28 38 08, 07021/52204, Fax 53242. 079765

Tamp, Horst, Colmarer Str. 10, 70435 Stuttgart. T. (0711) 87 44 25. 079766

Valentien, Gellertstr 6, 70184 Stuttgart. T. (0711) 246242, Fax (0711) 246241. - Paint / Graph / Sculp / Draw - 079767

Wahlandt, Edith, Werastr. 6, 70182 Stuttgart. T. (0711) 24 23 55, Fax (0711) 291816. - Paint / Graph / Sculp - 079768

Walz & Wetter, Bogenstr. 25, 70569 Stuttgart. 079769

Wehr, Rainer, Alexanderstr. 53, 70182 Stuttgart. T. (0711) 24 26 72. - Paint / Sculp / Fra / Pho - 079770

Wehrle, Reinhard, Am Kräherwald 171, 70193 Stuttgart. T. (0711) 29 48 57. - Paint - 079771

Weissert, Friedrich, Reinsburgstr 134, 70197 Stuttgart. T. (0711) 625639. 079772

Werkstatt Galerie, Friederike Glück, Reinsburgstr. 154, 70197 Stuttgart. T. (0711) 65 06 34. 079773

Wilhelm, Beatrix, Friedenstr. 12, 70190 Stuttgart. T. (0711) 26 40 25. 079774

Witthoeft, Traubenstr. 51, 70176 Stuttgart. 079775

Suhl (Thüringen)
Galerie im Steinweg, Steinweg 33, 98527 Suhl. T. (03681) 22079. 079776

Sundern (Nordrhein-Westfalen)
Schmitt, W., Tyskerströtken 2, 59846 Sundern. T. (02933) 2961. 079777

Sylt-Ost (Schleswig-Holstein)
Hof-Galerie, Serkwai 1, Morsum, 25980 Sylt-Ost.
T. (04651) 1761/2, Fax 1035. - Sculp -   *079778*
Papillon, Friedrichstr. 16, 25980 Sylt-Ost.
T. (04651) 73 60. - Paint / Sculp -   *079779*
Pfauenhof Archsum, Norderende 20, 25980 Sylt-Ost.
T. (04651) 04654/278. - Paint -   *079780*
Schwarz, H. & H., Am Tipkenhoog 3, 25980 Sylt-Ost.
T. (04651) 31475.   *079781*

Taching (Bayern)
Galerie auf dem Lande, Lehmberg 7, 83373 Taching.
- Paint -   *079782*

Tangermünde (Sachsen-Anhalt)
Guth, K., Kirchstr. 59, 39590 Tangermünde.
T. (039322) 2025.   *079783*

Taunusstein (Hessen)
Galerie Derix, Platter Str. 94, 65232 Taunusstein.
T. (06128) 84201. - Paint / Graph / Sculp /
Glass -   *079784*
Matuschek, Aarstr. 96, 65232 Taunusstein.
T. (06128) 42579.   *079785*

Tegernsee (Bayern)
Weiler, Dieter, Prof. Dr., Olaf-Gulbransson-Weg 25,
83684 Tegernsee. T. (08022) 31 11, Fax 4182.
- Paint -   *079786*

Thedinghausen (Niedersachsen)
Franck, Katharina, Werder Dorfstr 2, 27321 Thedinghau-
sen. T. (04204) 5098, Fax (04204) 5098.
- Mul -   *079787*

Traben-Trarbach (Rheinland-Pfalz)
Brückentor-Galerie, Brückenstr., Brückentor, 56841 Tra-
ben-Trarbach. T. (06541) 6011, Fax 6013. - Paint /
Graph / Mod -   *079788*
Zimmer, U., Bahnstr. 27, 56841 Traben-Trarbach.
T. (06541) 1535, Fax 5127. - Paint -   *079789*

Trier (Rheinland-Pfalz)
Die kleine Hofgalerie, Saarstr. 61, 54290 Trier.   *079790*
Galerie am Stadion, Kloschinskystr. 96, 54292 Trier.
T. (0651) 22866.   *079791*
Galerie der editions trèves, Weberbach, 54290 Trier.
T. (0651) 42505, Fax 300699. - Paint -   *079792*
Kaschenbach, Peter, Fleischstr. 50, 54290 Trier.
T. (0651) 734 87. - Paint / Graph / Repr / Eth / Jew /
Fra -   *079793*
Nohn, Markus, Paulinstr 32, 54292 Trier.
T. (0651) 24032, Fax (0651) 24062.   *079794*
Sauerwein, Hans, Edition und Kunstversand, Eurener Str.
193A, 54294 Trier. - Paint / Graph -   *079795*
Veit, Brückenstr. 24, 54290 Trier.
T. (0651) 744 35.   *079796*

Troisdorf (Nordrhein-Westfalen)
Donath, Inge, Hippolytusstr. 6, 53840 Troisdorf.
T. (02241) 734 93.   *079797*

Tübingen (Baden-Württemberg)
Dacic, Ingrid, Im Schönblick 12, 72076 Tübingen.
T. (07071) 63435, Fax (07071) 67797. - Paint / Graph /
Toys / Draw -   *079798*
Galerie am Haagtor, Ammergasse 23, 72070 Tübingen.
T. (07071) 523 73. - Paint -   *079799*
Galerie an der A.O.K., Rottenburger Str. 4, 72070
Tübingen.   *079800*
Galerie des Künstlerbundes, Metzgergasse, 72070
Tübingen.   *079801*
Galerie Druck & Buch, Nauklerstr 7, 72070 Tübingen.
T. (07071) 25554, Fax 21135.   *079802*
Galerie Tabula, Mühlstr. 18, 72074 Tübingen.
T. (07071) 248 50, Fax 23015. - Paint / Graph -   *079803*
Gottschick, Uhlandstr. 10a, 72072 Tübingen.
T. (07071) 344 23, Fax 37680. - Paint / Graph / China /
Sculp / Jew / Fra / Mul / Draw -   *079804*
Schmidt, Neuhaldenstr. 17, 72074 Tübingen.
T. (07071) 83724, Fax 87799. - Paint -   *079805*
Tangente-Jour, Münzgasse 17, 72070 Tübingen.
T. (07071) 245 72. - Paint / Graph -   *079806*

Überlingen (Baden-Württemberg)
Mathias, Gotthold B., Münsterstr 10, 88662 Überlingen.
T. (07551) 63413. - Paint / Graph -   *079807*

Uettingen (Bayern)
Jäger, Haus Tusculum, 97292 Uettingen.
T. (09369) 82 81. - Paint -   *079808*

Uetze (Niedersachsen)
Galerie an der Mühle, Liegnitzer Str. 11, 31311 Uetze.
T. (05173) 467. - Paint / Graph / China -   *079809*

Ulm (Baden-Württemberg)
Abendgalerie, König-Wilhelm-Str 1, 89073 Ulm.
T. (0731) 27232, 54131, Fax 6020027.   *079810*

Abendgalerie
Werner Küppers

König-Wilhelm-Straße 1
89073 Ulm
Tel. 07 31/2 72 32 und 5 41 31
Fax 07 31/6 02 00 27

Geöffnet:
Mi–Fr   17–20 Uhr
Sa   11–14 Uhr

Ehinger-Schwarz, Marktplatz 20, 89073 Ulm.
T. (0731) 14430, Fax (0731) 144350.   *079811*
Eichhorn, Manfred, Herrenkellergasse 10, 89073 Ulm.
T. (0731) 64610. - Paint / Graph / Repr -   *079812*
Fischerplatz – Galerie, Fischergasse 21, 89073 Ulm.
T. (0731) 63349, Fax (0731) 619159. - Ant / Paint /
Graph / Furn / Sculp / Tex / Silv / Draw -   *079813*
Galerie im Kornhauskeller, Hafengasse 19, 89073 Ulm.
T. (0731) 619576. - Paint / Graph -   *079814*
Galerie Plus, Gideon-Bacher-Str, 89073 Ulm.   *079815*
Galerie Samt und Seide, Herrenkellergasse 15, 89073
Ulm.   *079816*
Holm, Hafenbad 11, 89073 Ulm. T. (0731) 65497,
Fax (0731) 6022398. - Paint -   *079817*
Künstlergilde, Postfach 2609, 89016 Ulm.
T. (0731) 47181. - Graph -   *079818*
Kunstschalter.ulm, Schülinstr 11, 89073 Ulm.
T. (0731) 23447, Fax (0371) 23447.   *079819*

Unkel (Rheinland-Pfalz)
Oltmanns, Scheurener Str 25, 53572 Unkel.
T. (02224) 78691, Fax 72348. - Paint / Graph /
Sculp -   *079820*

Vahlbruch (Niedersachsen)
Galerie Meiborssen, Meiborssen Nr. 5, 37647 Vahlbruch.
T. (05535) 88 51. - Paint / Graph / China / Sculp /
Pho -   *079821*

Vaihingen (Baden-Württemberg)
Linea Galerie, Wassermanngasse 5, 71665 Vaihingen.
- Draw -   *079822*

Vastorf (Niedersachsen)
Galerie Merlin Verlag, Gifkendorf 38, 21397 Vastorf.
T. (04137) 7207, Fax 7948. - Paint / Graph /
Draw -   *079823*

Velbert (Nordrhein-Westfalen)
Fischer, G., Bonsfelder Str. 99, 42555 Velbert.
T. (02124) 02052/807 78.   *079824*
Fuchs, Günter, Zum Hardenberger Schloß 1-3, 42553
Velbert. T. (02124) 406 12. - Graph / Draw -   *079825*
Obach, Friedrichstr. 120, 42551 Velbert.
T. (02124) 538 62.   *079826*

Verden (Niedersachsen)
Pro Art Galerie, Grosse Fischerstr 2, 27283 Verden.
T. (04231) 3666, Fax 3668. - Ant / Paint / Graph /
Furn -   *079827*

Verl (Nordrhein-Westfalen)
Dingwerth, Postfach 1134, 33398 Verl. T. (05246) 41 02.
- Graph -   *079828*

Versmold (Nordrhein-Westfalen)
Werkstatt-Galerie, Ravensberger Str.10, 33775 Versmold. T. (05423) 418 22. - Graph -   *079829*

Viersen (Nordrhein-Westfalen)
Art Partner, Petersstr 7a, 41747 Viersen.
T. (02162) 24171, Fax 24171. - Paint / Fra -   *079830*
Galerie Kunst Parterre, Oberstr. 2, 41749 Viersen.
T. (02162) 80864, 77059, Fax 81385. - Paint / Graph /
Sculp / Mul / Draw -   *079831*
Galerie 2a, Königsallee 2a, 41747 Viersen.
- Paint -   *079832*

Vilgertshofen (Bayern)
Atelier-Galerie Punkt 5, Wessobrunnerstr. 5, 86946 Vil-
gertshofen. T. (08194) 1522. - Paint / Sculp /
Draw -   *079833*

Villingen-Schwenningen (Baden-Württemberg)
Keller, Helmar, Paradiesgasse 2, 78050 Villingen-
Schwenningen. T. (07721) 271 70. - Paint / Graph / Chi-
na / Repr / Sculp / Jew / Fra / Glass -   *079834*
Rettich, Louise, Rietstr. 21, 78050 Villingen-Schwennin-
gen. T. (07721) 247 16. - Paint -   *079835*
Schlenker, Felix, Prof., Stöckenweg 7, 78056 Villingen-
Schwenningen. T. (07721) 61790. - Paint / Graph /
Sculp -   *079836*

Vorderweidenthal (Rheinland-Pfalz)
Porträt-Galerie, Berwartsteinstr 5, 76889 Vorderweiden-
thal. T. (06398) 1555. - Paint / Graph / Repr -   *079837*

Wachtberg (Nordrhein-Westfalen)
Turm-Galerie-Bonn, 53343 Wachtberg.
T. (0228) 34 08 11, Fax 857089. - Paint / Graph /
Sculp -   *079838*

Wackernheim (Rheinland-Pfalz)
Gerlach, B. u. H., Rosenweg 1, 55263 Wackernheim.
T. (06132) 5567.   *079839*
Hutten-Ostermayer, Kleine Hohl 2, 55263 Wackernheim.
T. (06132) 57319.   *079840*

Waiblingen (Baden-Württemberg)
Kleine Galerie, Schmidener Str. 2, 71332 Waiblingen.
T. (07151) 549 75, Fax 56 21 32. - Paint -   *079841*

Waibstadt (Baden-Württemberg)
Galerie Aspekte, Hauptstr 59, 74915 Waibstadt.
T. (07263) 4777.   *079842*

Waldbröl (Nordrhein-Westfalen)
Schneider, G., Nümbrechter Str. 4, 51545 Waldbröl.
T. (02291) 35 90.   *079843*

Waldbronn (Baden-Württemberg)
Neuhoff, G., Esternaystr. 48, 76337 Waldbronn.
T. (07243) 691 75. - Paint -   *079844*

Waldenbuch (Baden-Württemberg)
Imkon, Hauptstr. 11, 71111 Waldenbuch.
T. (07157) 8018, Fax 8018. - Paint / Graph / Repr /
Sculp / Dec / Ico / Draw -   *079845*
Mayer, Hannelore, Beethovenstr. 3, 71111 Waldenbuch.
T. (07157) 33 34. - Paint -   *079846*

Waldshut-Tiengen (Baden-Württemberg)
Atelier Aureus, Wallstr. 18, 79761 Waldshut-Tiengen.
T. (07741) 61 13.   *079847*
Galerie Kargados, Tannenstr. 48, 79761 Waldshut-Tien-
gen. T. (07741) 07751/4768.   *079848*
Langenfeld, Eschbacher Str. 24, 79761 Waldshut-Tien-
gen. T. (07741) 27 41. - Paint -   *079849*
Schloss-Galerie, Schloßplatz 1, 79761 Waldshut-Tien-
gen. T. (07741) 4733.   *079850*

Walldorf (Baden-Württemberg)
Görlach, B., Hauptstr. 47, 69190 Walldorf.
T. (06227) 99 00. - Paint -   *079851*

Walldürn (Baden-Württemberg)
Englert, O., Hornbacher Str. 29, 74731 Walldürn.
T. (06282) 74 41. - Paint -   *079852*

Walsrode (Niedersachsen)
Hohmann, Hannoversche Str. 2, 29664 Walsrode.
T. (05161) 55 17, Fax 73708. - Paint -   *079853*

Warendorf (Nordrhein-Westfalen)
Budde, Wolfgang, Splieter Straße, 48231 Warendorf.
- Sculp -   *079854*

Wasserburg (Bayern)
Galerie im Ganserhaus, Schmidzeile 8, 83512 Wasser-
burg. T. (08071) 4484. - Paint / Graph / Sculp / Pho /
Mul / Draw -   *079855*

Wathlingen (Niedersachsen)
Kilian, Peter, Kirchstr 17, 29339 Wathlingen.
T. (05144) 8838. - Paint / Graph / Repr / Fra / Glass /
Draw -   *079856*

Wedel (Schleswig-Holstein)
Galerie Nr. 77, Elbstr. 77, 22880 Wedel.   *079857*
Jacob, Martin, Bündtwiete 1, 22880 Wedel.
T. (04103) 34 30. - Paint / Repr -   *079858*

Weil am Rhein (Baden-Württemberg)
Galerie, Am Mühlenrain, 79576 Weil am Rhein.
T. (07621) 774 04.   *079859*
Jogerst, A. Dr., Gartenstr. 4, 79576 Weil am Rhein.
T. (07621) 711 22. - Paint -   *079860*
Stahlberger, Pfädlistr 4, 79576 Weil am Rhein.
T. (07621) 74650, Fax (07621) 78834. - Sculp /
Draw -   *079861*

Weimar (Thüringen)
ACC Galerie Weimar, Burgplatz 1, 99423 Weimar.
T. (03643) 62970, Fax (03643) 502280.
- Paint -   *079862*
Cranach-Haus Weimar, Markt 12, 99423 Weimar.
T. (03643) 37 68. - Paint / Graph / Sculp -   *079863*
Galerie Goethe trifft Nina, Burgpl. 1, 99423 Weimar.
T. (03643) 62970, Fax 502280. - Paint / Graph / Sculp /
Pho / Draw -   *079864*
Hebecker, Marienstr 1, 99423 Weimar.
T. (03643) 510526, Fax (03643) 510526.   *079865*
Lesecafé Gratis, Weimarhallenpark, Asbachstr. 1, 99423
Weimar. T. (03643) 61984.   *079866*

Weingarten, Württemberg (Baden-Württemberg)
Böser, D., Bahnhofstr 1, 76356 Weingarten, Württem-
berg. T. (0751) 2890. - Paint -   *079867*
Galerie im Jugendstilhaus, Wilhelmstr 46, 88250 Wein-
garten, Württemberg.   *079868*
Galerie in Kunstverlag Weingarten, Lägelerstr 31,
88250 Weingarten, Württemberg. T. (0751) 41039,
Fax (0751) 48735. - Paint / Graph -   *079869*

Weinheim (Baden-Württemberg)
Altstadt Galerie, Marktplatz 3, 69469 Weinheim.
T. (06201) 15848. - Graph / China / Jew -   *079870*
Galerie in der Volksbank, Bismarckstr 1, 69469
Weinheim.   *079871*

Weißenhorn (Bayern)
Mahler-Schrapp, Grafik-edition, Josef Haydnstr. 10,
89264 Weißenhorn. - Paint / Graph -   *079872*

Wennigsen (Niedersachsen)
image art, Sedanstr 7, 30974 Wennigsen.
T. (05103) 2513, Fax 7724.   *079873*

Werl (Nordrhein-Westfalen)
Galerie am Hellweg, Unionstr. 8, 59457 Werl.
T. (02922) 822 22. - Paint -   *079874*

Wesel (Nordrhein-Westfalen)
Lipski, Johann-Sigismund-Str. 3, 46483 Wesel.
T. (0281) 295 12. - Paint -   *079875*

Westensee (Schleswig-Holstein)
Habeck, Dr., Gut Westensee, 24259 Westensee.
T. (04305) 620, Fax 979912. - Paint -   *079876*

Westerland (Schleswig-Holstein)
Georg's Galerie, Strandstr. 16, 25980 Westerland.
T. (04651) 7360.   *079877*
Meierhenrich, Angelika, Neue Str. 3, 25980 Westerland.
T. (04651) 1885.   *079878*

Westerstede (Niedersachsen)
Hobby-Kunstgalerie, Ihauserstr. 39, 26655 Westerstede.
T. (04488) 1567.   *079879*

Wiernsheim (Baden-Württemberg)
Galerie Auto & Kunst, Dreilindenweg 9, 75446 Wierns-
heim. T. (07044) 60 25.   *079880*

Wiesbaden (Hessen)
Atelier Moehring, Martinstr. 6, 65189
Wiesbaden.   *079881*
Beisac, de, Taunusstr. 38, 65183 Wiesbaden.
T. (0611) 52 21 41.   *079882*
Bronzegalerie, Wilhelmstr. 56, 65183 Wiesbaden.
T. (0611) 37 33 41.   *079883*
Buschlinger, Ulrike, Adolfsallee 47, 65185 Wiesbaden.
T. (0611) 371570, Fax (0611) 302591. - Paint / Sculp /
Pho / Draw -   *079884*
Emil, Grabenstr. 4, 65183 Wiesbaden.
T. (0611) 37 25 90. - Graph -   *079885*
Friedrichs-Dehlsen, I., Walter-Gieseking-Str. 29, 65193
Wiesbaden. T. (0611) 56 26 45.   *079886*
Galerie Casa-Nova, Nerostr. 36, 65183
Wiesbaden.   *079887*
Galerie Cicero, Kirchgasse 50, 65183 Wiesbaden.
T. (0611) 30 31 20.   *079888*
Galerie Eremitage, Sonnenberger Str. 9, 65193 Wiesba-
den. T. (0611) 52 30 06.   *079889*
Galerie in der Vorstadt, Auringer Str. 9, 65207 Wiesba-
den. T. (0611) 61376. - Graph -   *079890*
Galerie P.a.b.l.o., Luisenstr. 4, 65185 Wiesbaden.
T. (0611) 30 23 98, 37 90 28.   *079891*
Haasner, Saalgasse 38, 65183 Wiesbaden.
T. (0611) 514 22, Fax 514 22. - Paint / Graph / Sculp /
Pho / Draw -   *079892*
Hafemann, Oranienstr. 48, 65185 Wiesbaden.
T. (0611) 37 45 09. - Paint -   *079893*
Harlekin Art, Wandersmannstr. 2b + 39, 65205 Wiesba-
den. T. (0611) 740 01, Fax 71 41 06. - Paint / Graph /
Pho / Mul / Draw -   *079894*
Heinemann, Taunusstr. 39, 65183 Wiesbaden.
T. (0611) 52 29 56. - Ant / Paint / Furn / Sculp -   *079895*
Hörner, H.-J., Saalgasse 1, 65183 Wiesbaden.
T. (0611) 37 53 19.   *079896*
Keul & Sohn, Taunusstr. 33-35, 65183 Wiesbaden.
T. (0611) 52 26 61. - Paint -   *079897*

Galerie
Keul & Sohn

Gemälde 19. Jahrhundert
Antike Möbel – Kunstgewerbe

Wiesbaden, Taunusstraße 33–35
Tel.: 52 26 61

Matuschek, Walkmühlstr. 12a, 65195 Wiesbaden.
T. (0611) 40 40 95.   *079898*
Neubert, Hans K., Berliner Str. 260, 65205 Wiesbaden.
- Paint -   *079899*
Nied, Pavillon am Bahnhofsvorpl., 65183 Wiesbaden.
T. (0611) 71 91 03, 70 10 03. - Paint / Graph / Repr /
Sculp -   *079900*
Ostendorff, Mauergasse 16, 65183 Wiesbaden.
T. (0611) 30 14 31. - Graph / Fra / Draw -   *079901*
Reichard, Hermann, Taunusstr. 18, 65183 Wiesbaden.
T. (0611) 519 27. - Graph / Fra -   *079902*
Ressel, Schöne Aussicht 24, 65193 Wiesbaden.
T. (0611) 52 45 94, Fax 52 62 94. - Paint -   *079903*
Schäfer, Kurt, Faulbrunnenstr 11, 65183 Wiesbaden.
T. (0611) 304721, Fax (0611) 333361. - Paint / Graph /
Repr / Fra -   *079904*
Scharwächter, Eugen, & Heinz Döring, Taunusstr. 24,
65183 Wiesbaden. T. (0611) 52 32 51. - Ant -   *079905*

Schwaedt, Arthur, Rheinstr. 43, 65185 Wiesbaden.
T. (0611) 30 14 89. - Graph / Repr -   *079906*
Simon, Herbert, Taunusstr. 34, 65183 Wiesbaden.
T. (0611) 59 92 10. - Paint / Graph / Sculp /
Lights -   *079907*
Stolanova-Hamara, Lichtenbergstr. 9, 65191 Wiesba-
den. T. (0611) 56 21 87.   *079908*
Swatosch & Kerner GmbH, Rheingaustr. 26, 65201
Wiesbaden. T. (0611) 225 66. - Paint -   *079909*
Thurow, Helga, An den Quellen 4, 65183 Wiesbaden.
T. (0611) 30 60 37. - Paint -   *079910*
Witkowski, Taunusstr. 24, 65183 Wiesbaden.
T. (0611) 59 04 65.   *079911*
Witzel, Erhard, Kaiser-Friedrich-Ring 63, 65185 Wiesba-
den. T. (0611) 87696, Fax 87696. - Paint -   *079912*
Zuta, B., Rathauspassage, 65183 Wiesbaden.
T. (0611) 30 22 36. - Graph / Sculp -   *079913*

Wiesenbach (Baden-Württemberg)
arte'rie, Hebelstr. 9, 69257 Wiesenbach.
T. (06223) 407 60. - Paint / Graph / Sculp /
Draw -   *079914*

Wiesloch (Baden-Württemberg)
Engelhorn, Helmut, Hauptstr. 132, 69168 Wiesloch.
- Paint -   *079915*

Wilhelmshaven (Niedersachsen)
Bistro-Galerie, Gökerstr. 112, 26384 Wilhelmshaven.
- Paint / Graph / Draw -   *079916*

Willebadessen (Nordrhein-Westfalen)
Hofgalerie, Bahnhofstr. 14, 34439 Willebadessen.
- Paint / Graph -   *079917*

Willich (Nordrhein-Westfalen)
Temporäre Galerie, Schloßweg, 47877 Willich.
T. (02154) 949263, Fax 949101. - Paint -   *079918*

Wilnsdorf (Nordrhein-Westfalen)
Jordan, Ingrid, Breitenbachsfeld 7, 57234 Wilnsdorf.
T. (02739) 39 28 14. - Paint / Graph / Sculp / Mul /
Draw -   *079919*

Winnenden (Baden-Württemberg)
Galerie im Rathaus, Torstr. 10, 71364 Winnenden.
T. (07195) 66610.   *079920*

Witten (Nordrhein-Westfalen)
Galerie Backstube, Hauptstr. 25, 58452 Witten. - Paint /
Graph / Sculp / Draw -   *079921*
Galerie Fachwerkhof, Alte Straße 25, 58452 Witten.
T. (02302) 303 98. - Paint -   *079922*

Wittenberg (Sachsen-Anhalt)
Galerie Bücherscheune, Elke Stiegler, Schulstr. 112,
06886 Wittenberg. T. (03491) 82979. - Ant / Paint /
Repr / Glass / Mul -   *079923*

Wolfenbüttel (Niedersachsen)
Galerie am Holzmarkt, Holzmarkt 12-13, 38300 Wolfenbüttel. T. (05331) 265 89. - Paint / Fra -   *079924*

Wolfsburg (Niedersachsen)
Galerie in der Porschehütte, Sauerbruchstr., 38440
Wolfsburg. T. (05361) 232 00. - Paint / Graph / Sculp /
Pho / Draw -   *079925*
Galerie Theater, Twetge 28, 38440 Wolfsburg.   *079926*

Worpswede (Niedersachsen)
Bollhagen, Osterweder Str. 21, 27726 Worpswede.
T. (04792) 2241. - Paint / Graph / Sculp / Pho /
Draw -   *079927*
Die Galerie, Bergstr 25, 27726 Worpswede.
T. (04792) 7137, Fax 7224. - Paint -   *079928*
Galerie Atlantis, Auf der Domenhorst 13, 27726
Worpswede.   *079929*
Galerie in der Lindenallee 25, Lindenallee 25, 27726
Worpswede. T. (04792) 845.   *079930*
Girschner, Alfred, Findorffstr. 1, 27726 Worpswede.
T. (04792) 77 38.   *079931*
Grosse Kunstschau, Lindenallee 3, 27726 Worpswede.
T. (04792) 13 02.   *079932*
Hoffmann, Carl-Vinnen-Weg 7, 27726 Worpswede.
T. (04792) 7190.   *079933*

Kunst-Treff Worpswede, Hembergstr. 2a, 27726 Worpswede. T. (04792) 2078. - Paint / Sculp / Jew / Glass - *079934*
Kunstzentrum Alte Molkerei, Osterweder Str. 21, 27726 Worpswede. T. (04792) 22 91. *079935*
Laves, Bergstr. 11, 27726 Worpswede. T. (04792) 79 18. *079936*
Lichtbild-Galerie, Neu-Bergedorfer Damm 44a, 27726 Worpswede. T. (04792) 4135. - Sculp / Pho - *079937*
Lux, Adorjan, Bremer Landstr. 3, 27726 Worpswede. T. (04792) 2303, Fax 4489. - Paint - *079938*
Schmuckgalerie 2 AC, Osterwederstr. 21, 27726 Worpswede. - Jew - *079939*

Würselen (Nordrhein-Westfalen)
Galerie am Dobach, Dobacher Str. 45, 52146 Würselen. T. (02405) 922 33. - Paint / Graph / Draw - *079940*

Würzburg (Bayern)
Galerie am Main, Untere Johannitergasse 4-6, 97070 Würzburg. *079941*
Galerie im Schildhof, Im Schildhof, 97070 Würzburg. T. (0931) 17721, Fax 17736. - Paint - *079942*
Müller, Franz Xaver, Kardinal-Faulhaber-Platz 2, 97070 Würzburg. T. (0931) 526 24. - Paint / Graph / Repr / Fra - *079943*
Pfeiffer, Petra, Reuerergasse 6, 97070 Würzburg. T. (0931) 548 27. - Paint / Graph - *079944*
Villinger, Radegundis, Kaiserstr. 13, 97070 Würzburg. T. (0931) 588 86, 938 26, Fax 93826. - Paint / Graph / Sculp / Jew / Draw - *079945*
Werkkunstgalerie, Rathaus, Südflügel, 97070 Würzburg. T. (0931) 121 89. - Paint - *079946*
Werkstatt-Galerie, Semmelstr. 42, 97070 Würzburg. T. (0931) 139 08. - Graph / Fra - *079947*

Wuppertal (Nordrhein-Westfalen)
Backstubengalerie, Schreinerstr. 7, 42105 Wuppertal. *079948*
Brusten, Annelie, Annelie, Parsevalstr. 13, 42285 Wuppertal. T. (0202) 857 22, 42 45 66. - Paint / Sculp / Pho / Draw - *079949*
City-Galerie, Werth 48, 42275 Wuppertal. T. (0202) 52 09 02. *079950*
Galerie Palette, Sedanstr. 68-68a, 42281 Wuppertal. T. (0202) 50 67 69. - Paint - *079951*
Galerie 32, Jägerhofstr. 43, 42119 Wuppertal. T. (0202) 42 33 23. - Paint - *079952*
Galerie 59, Hochstr. 59, 42105 Wuppertal. T. (0202) 31 22 39. *079953*
Gelhard, Gräfrather Str. 36, 42329 Wuppertal. T. (0202) 73 32 87. - Ant / Paint / Graph / China / Sculp / Glass / Tin - *079954*
Kocks, Aschenweg 5, 42103 Wuppertal. T. (0202) 46 48 66. - Fra - *079955*
Krause, G., Concordienstr. 9, 42275 Wuppertal. T. (0202) 59 44 49. *079956*
Kunstraum Wuppertal, Friedrich-Ebert-Str. 191, 42117 Wuppertal. *079957*
Mumbeck, Bernd, Luisenstr. 104, 42103 Wuppertal. T. (0202) 31 16 26. *079958*
Pavillon Galerie, Wormserstr. 53, 42119 Wuppertal. T. (0202) 424566. - Paint - *079959*
Pavillongalerie, Wormser Str. 53, 42119 Wuppertal. T. (0202) 42 45 66. - Paint / Sculp / Pho / Draw - *079960*
Putty, Hans, Sophienstr. 1, 42103 Wuppertal. T. (0202) 31 31 13. - Paint - *079961*
Rieder, B., Gustavstr. 13, 42329 Wuppertal. T. (0202) 78 11 78. *079962*
Schmidt & Green, Herbringhausen 10, 42399 Wuppertal. T. (0202) 612061, Fax 613740. *079963*
Schwarzkopf, Emil, Bredde 99, 42275 Wuppertal. T. (0202) 66 33 61. *079964*
Simon, Friedrich-Ebert-Str. 32, 42103 Wuppertal. T. (0202) 31 22 31. *079965*
Stöhr, H. & Wilma, Jägerhofstr. 43, 42119 Wuppertal. T. (0202) 42 33 23. - Paint - *079966*
Wicher, Helga, Gräfrather Str 43a, 42327 Wuppertal. T. (0202) 738217, Fax 738440. - Paint / Graph - *079967*

Xanten (Nordrhein-Westfalen)
Galerie an de Marspoort, Marsstr. 78, 46509 Xanten. T. (02801) 10 57. *079968*

Galerie Oase-Haus der Begegnung, Scharnstr. 48, 46509 Xanten. T. (02801) 45 60. - Paint / Graph / Sculp - *079969*
Hinskes-Kocea, Marsstr. 45, 46509 Xanten. T. (02801) 25 75. - Paint / Graph - *079970*

Zell (Baden-Württemberg)
Bischoff, Walter, Meyershofenstr 39, 77736 Zell. T. (07835) 1453, Fax 3434. - Paint / Graph / Sculp / Draw - *079971*
Galerie am Brühl, Gresgen 29, 79669 Zell. *079972*

Zwickau (Sachsen)
Galerie am Domhof, Robert-Schumann-Haus, Domhof 2, 08056 Zwickau. T. (0375) 25687. - Paint - *079973*
Gutenberg Buchhandlung OHG Kozok & Unger, Galerie & Buch „Peter Breuer", Hauptstr. 22, 08056 Zwickau. T. (0375) 25992, Fax (0375) 25429. - Graph / Jew / China - *079974*
Städtische Galerie Peter Breuer, Hauptstr. 22, 08056 Zwickau. T. (0375) 25992. - Paint / Graph / China / Tex / Jew / Glass / Draw - *079975*

Zwingenberg, Bergstr. (Hessen)
Schumacher, Schulstr. 10, 64673 Zwingenberg, Bergstr. T. (06251) 736 28. *079976*

Greece

Athinai
Athens Gallery, 4 Glykonos St, 106 75 Athinai. T. (01) 71 39 38. *079977*
Bernier, Jean, Marasli 51, 10676 Athinai. T. (01) 723 56 57, Fax 722 61 89. - Paint / Graph / Sculp / Pho / Mul / Draw - *079978*
Bontzidis, Victor, 35 Marasli St., 106 76 Athinai. T. (01) 714208. - Paint - *079979*
Contemporary Graphics, 8 Haritos St, 106 75 Athinai. T. (01) 73 26 90. *079980*
Kourt, Athanassios, 37 Skoufa St., 106 73 Athinai. T. (01) 613113. - Paint - *079981*
New Forms Art Gallery, 9 Od. Valaoritou, 106 71 Athinai. T. (01) 36 16 165. - Paint / Graph / Sculp - *079982*
Ora, Odos Xenofontos 7, 105 57 Athinai. T. (01) 32 29 178, 32 30 698. *079983*
Paletta, 14 Voulis & Karag. Serbias,, 105 63 Athinai. T. (01) 23 34 30. - Paint / Graph / Repr / Fra - *079984*
Papadopoulos, Maria, Xenokratous 33, 10676 Athinai. T. (01) 722 97 33. *079985*
Poliplano, Odos Lykavittou 16, 106 73 Athinai. T. (01) 36 37 859. - Ant / Paint / Furn / China - *079986*
Spanos, 32, rue Hippocratus, 106 79 Athinai. T. (01) 61 43 32. *079987*
To Trito Mati, 21B Loukianou St, 114 75 Athinai. T. (01) 729 733. *079988*
Tounta, Ileana, Contemporary Art Center, 48 Armatolon & Klefton, 114 71 Athinai. T. (01) 64 39 466/473, Fax 64 42 852. *079989*
Zoumboulaktis Galerie, Kriezotou 7, 106 71 Athinai. - Ant / Paint / Furn / Sculp / Tex / Dec / Jew / Rel / Ico / Mul / Draw - *079990*
Zygos Gallery, Od. Iofontos 33, 116 34 Athinai. T. (01) 722 92 72/19, Fax 723 46 77. - Paint / Sculp / Jew / Mul / Draw - *079991*

Chalkis (Euboea)
Hatzigianni, Nikos, 341 00 Chalkis. - Paint / Graph - *079992*

Patras (Peleponnisos)
Epikentro, 16 Norman St, 262 23 Patras. T. (061) 43 26 88, Fax 42 84 10. *079993*

Skiathos
Archipelagos, 370 02 Skiathos. T. (0424) 0427/22163. - Ant / Paint / Furn / Num / China / Tex / Dec / Jew / Silv / Lights / Glass / Ico / Mul - *079994*

Thessaloniki
Kaligos, 95, A Papanastasiou St, 544 53 Thessaloniki. T. (031) 92 03 58. *079995*

Guadeloupe

Pointe-à-Pitre
Mas, Christian, 33bis Rue Henri-IV, 97110 Pointe-à-Pitre. T. (590) 915269, Fax (590) 832728. - Paint / Sculp - *079996*
Thyan, 25 Rue Sadi-Carnot, 97110 Pointe-à-Pitre. T. (590) 839665. - Paint / Sculp / Draw - *079997*

Saint-François
Alamanda, 2bis Av Europe, 97118 Saint-François. T. (590) 886332. *079998*
Little Gallery, 13 La Coursive-Marina, 97118 Saint-François. T. (590) 886522. *079999*

Saint-Martin
Art en Ciel, 10 B Coin-Mairie-Marigot, 97150 Saint-Martin. T. (590) 290309. *080000*
Mahogany et Gingerbread, Port La-Royale-Marina, 97150 Saint-Martin. T. (590) 877321. *080001*
Valentin, 112 Lot Amandiers, 97150 Saint-Martin. T. (590) 870894. *080002*

Terre-de-Haut
Cotten, Martine, Bourg, 97137 Terre-de-Haut. T. (590) 995537. *080003*
Galerie de la Baie, Mouillage, 97137 Terre-de-Haut. T. (590) 995462. *080004*

Guatemala

Guatemala City
Tuncho Granados Liberia Guatemala, 10 Calle 6-56, Zona 1, Apartado Postal 13, Guatemala City. T. 2 11 81, 2 47 36, 2 72 69. *080005*

Haiti

Port-au-Prince
Nader, 256-258 Rue du Magasin de l'Etat, POB 962, Port-au-Prince. T. 200 33, 200 69. - Paint / Graph / Sculp - *080006*

Hong Kong

Hong Kong
Chang, Robert, 127 Tai Shan Gallery, Prince Edward Road 9 AIF, Hong Kong. *080007*
Chinese Arts Gallery, 17-21 Hankow Rd., Shop K Kowloon, Hong Kong. T. 3-669645. *080008*
Gallery 69, 69 Wyndham Road, Hong Kong. T. 5241487. *080009*
Hanart, 40 Hollywood Rd., Hong Kong. T. 5-410941. - Paint - *080010*
Jackson, Sally, Ocean Terminal, Deck 2, 277 Tathong Pl., Hong Kong. T. 67 25 24. - Paint - *080011*
Kenneth Art Gallery, No. 9 Chungking Arcade Nathan Rd., T.S.T., Hong Kong. T. 3-669493. *080012*
Maple, 51 Queen's Rd., Room 102, Central, Hong Kong. T. 5-234771. - Paint - *080013*
Moon and Sun Art Gallery, 63 Mody Rd., Kowloon, Hong Kong. T. K-7227841, K-670 626. - Paint / Orient - *080014*
Nishiki, 304 The Podium, Exchange Sq., Central, Hong Kong. T. 5-8452551. - Paint - *080015*
Specialty Trading Galleries Co., Kowloon Central, Hong Kong P.O.B. 3086. *080016*
Tih Gallery, C. C., 146 Prince's Bldg., Hong Kong. T. 5-228913. *080017*
To, Dominic C. H., 15 Babington Path, Flats A-2, P. O. Box 8889, Hong Kong. T. H 4 5-4486980. - Paint / Graph - *080018*
Wattis, 20 Hollywood Rd., Hong Kong. *080019*

Kowloon (Hong Kong)
Creative Illusions, 144 A Boundary St. Overseas Court 3rd Fl., Kowloon. T. 36 84 33, 39 04 54. - Paint / Graph - *080020*

Hungary

Budapest
Artbureau Budapest, Münnich Ferenc u. 31, 1051 Budapest. - Paint / Graph / China / Sculp / Glass / Draw - *080021*
Budapest Galeria Kiallitohaza, Lajos u. 158, 1036 Budapest. T. (01) 88 67 71. *080022*
Budapest Kiallitoterem, Szabadsajto ut 5, 1056 Budapest. T. (01) 17 10 01. *080023*
Dorottya utcai Kialitoterem, Dorottya u. 8, 1051 Budapest. T. (01) 18 38 90. *080024*
Duna Galeria, Rajk Laszlo u. 95, 1033 Budapest. T. (01) 40 91 86. *080025*
Eri, Endrödi Sándor St. 10a, 1022 Budapest. T. (01) 361 115 6329, Fax 361 115 6329. - Paint - *080026*
Fenyes Adolf Terem, Rakoczi ut 30, 1072 Budapest. T. (01) 22 58 18. *080027*
Figura Galeria, Vitkovics Mihaly u. 6, 1052 Budapest. T. (01) 37 61 80. *080028*
Foto Galeria, Vaci u. 7, 1052 Budapest. T. (01) 18 30 05. - Pho - *080029*
Generalart Galeria, Nepkoztarsasag u. 8, 1061 Budapest. T. (01) 12 00 47. - Paint / Graph / Sculp - *080030*
Gulacsy Galeria, Furj u. 4a, 1124 Budapest. T. (01) 26 00 81. *080031*
Jozsefvarosi Kiallitoterem, Jozsef krt. 70, 1085 Budapest. T. (01) 34 01 59. *080032*
Knoll Galéria, Liszt Ferenc tér 10, 1061 Budapest. T. (01) 14 20 444, Fax 14 20 444. *080033*
Obuda Galeria, Fö ter. 1, 1033 Budapest. T. (01) 80 33 40. *080034*
Qualitas Galeria, Becsi u. 2, 1052 Budapest. T. (01) 18 44 38, Fax 118 44 38. *080035*
Studio Galeria, Bajcsy Zs. u. 52, 1054 Budapest. T. (01) 11 98 82. *080036*
Varga Imre Kiallitas, Laktanya u. 7, 1033 Budapest. - Sculp - *080037*
Varszinhaz Galeria, Szinhaz u. 1-3, 1014 Budapest. *080038*
Vigado Galeria, Vigado ter. 2, 1051 Budapest. T. (01) 18 70 70. *080039*

Iceland

Hafnarfjördur
Gallory Hafnarborg, Strandgata 34, 220 Hafnarfjördur. T. 50080. *080040*

Reykjavik
Borg, Austurstraeti 3, 101 Reykjavik. T. (91) 11664. *080041*
Borg, Pósthússtraeti 9, 101 Reykjavik. T. (91) 24211. *080042*
Borg, Sidumula 32, 108 Reykjavik. T. (91) 67 90 65. *080043*
Fridriksson, Fridrik Thor, Sudurgata, Reykjavik, 101. T. (91) 15442. *080044*
Gallery Art-Hún, Stangarhylur 7, 110 Reykjavik. T. (91) 67 35 77. *080045*
Gallery Asmundur, Freyjugata 41, 101 Reykjavik. T. (91) 14055. *080046*
Gallery FIM, Gardastraeti 6, 101 Reykjavik. T. (91) 25060. *080047*
Gallery Jens, Stigahilö 45-47, 105 Reykjavik. T. (91) 36778. *080048*
Gallery Kirkjumunir, Kirkjustraeti 10, 101 Reykjavik. T. (91) 15030. *080049*
Gallery Pyrit, Vesturgata 3, 101 Reykjavik. T. (91) 20376. *080050*
Gallery 11, Skólavörönstigur 4a, 101 Reykjavik. T. (91) 11138. *080051*
Gallery 8, Austurstraeti 8, 101 Reykjavik. T. (91) 18080. *080052*
Hladvarpinn-Gallery, Vesturgata 3b, 101 Reykjavik. T. (91) 19055. *080053*
List, Skipholt 50b, 105 Reykjavik. T. (91) 84020. *080054*
Nordic House, Hringbraut, Reykjavik, 101. *080055*

Nyhöfn, Hafnarstraeti 18, 101 Reykjavik. T. (91) 12230. *080056*
Rikey, Ingim, Hverfisgata 59, 101 Reykjavik. *080057*

India

Bombay (Maharashtra)
Artists Centre, 6 Rampart Row, Bombay. - Paint / Graph / Sculp - *080058*
Chemould, c/o Jehangir Art Gallery, 161 B Mahatma Gandhi Rd, 1st F, Bombay, 400023. T. (022) 244356. - Ant / Paint / Graph / Repr / Sculp / Fra - *080059*
Pundole, 705-369 D. Naoroji Rd, Bombay, 400023. T. (022) 2048473. - Paint / Graph / Sculp / Fra - *080060*
Taj Art Gallery, Taj Mahal Hote, GF, Apollo Bunder, Bombay. T. (022) 219101. - Paint / Graph / Sculp - *080061*

Delhi (Delhi)
Kumar, Virendra, Ashok Hotel, Delhi, 110021. T. 37 01 01/21 60. *080062*
Kumar, Virendra, 11 Sundar Nagar Market, Delhi, 110003. T. 61 88 75, 61 11 13. *080063*

Madras (Madras)
Cholomandal, Artists' Village, Madras, 600 041. *080064*

New Delhi
Chanakya, 114 Yashwant Pl, New Delhi. *080065*
Dhoomi Mal Gallery, 8A Connaught Pl, New Delhi. T. (011) 3320839. - Paint / Graph / Sculp - *080066*

Iran

Shiraz
Derissi, Moshir Fatemi Av., Shiraz. T. 321 88. *080068*

Tabriz
Ossouli, Admin. Générale de la Culture et des Arts, Tabriz. *080069*

Teheran
Khanéh Aftab, 1/154 Av. Roosevelt Litho, Teheran. *080070*
Seyhoun, Abbasse Abad, Av. Vozara, 4ème Av. 27, Teheran. *080071*
Sulivan Gallery, 136 Fakhrerazy Ave, Enghelab Av., Teheran. T. (021) 64 97 51. - Paint / Graph / Furn / Repr / Sculp / Dec / Fra / Mod - *080072*
Takhté-Djamchid, Av. Takhté-Djamchid, Av. Bandaré Pahlavi 30, Teheran. *080073*
Zinat Serai, 233, Ave. Soraya, Teheran. T. (021) 822 170. *080074*

Ireland

Blackrock (Co. Dublin)
Lyndsay, Roy, 7 Rockville Rd., Blackrock. T. (01) 88 30 63. - Paint - *080075*

Cork (Co. Cork)
Waters, J. & Sons, 114 Oliver Plunkett St., Cork. T. (021) 232 91. - Fra - *080076*

Dalkey (Co. Dublin)
James Gallery, 7 Railway Rd., Dalkey. T. (01) 85 87 03. - Paint - *080077*

Dublin (Co. Dublin)
Artist Studio Gallery, Marley Craft Centre, Rathfarnam, Dublin 16. T. (01) 98 75 61. - Paint - *080078*
Ashe Wellesley, 25 South Frederick St., Dublin 2. T. (01) 679 6439. - Paint - *080079*
Bower, Annabel, 33 Kildare St., Dublin 2. T. (01) 61 17 40. - Paint - *080080*
Caldwell, Tom, 31 Upper Fitzwilliam St., Dublin 2. T. (01) 68 86 29. - Paint - *080081*
Chester Beatty, 20 Shrewsbury Rd, Dublin 4. T. (01) 69 23 86. *080082*
Combridge, 24 Suffolk St., Dublin 2. T. (01) 77 46 52. - Paint / Sculp - *080083*

Crafts Council of Ireland Gallery, 59 South William St., Dublin 2. T. (01) 79 73 83. - Paint - *080084*
Davis, Gerald, 11 Capel St., Dublin 1. T. (01) 72 69 69, Fax (01) 73 30 80. - Paint - *080085*
Dowling, Oliver, 19 Kildare St., Dublin 2. T. (01) 766 573. - Paint / Graph / Sculp / Mod / Draw - *080086*
European Fine Arts Gallery, 6 Lower Merrion St., Dublin 2. T. (01) 76 25 06. - Paint / Graph - *080087*
Gallagher, R.H.A., 15 Ely Pl., Dublin 2. T. (01) 61 25 58. - Paint - *080088*
Gallery of Photography, 37 Wellington Quay, Dublin 2. T. (01) 71 46 54. - Pho - *080089*
George Gallery, 22 South Frederick St., Dublin 2. T. (01) 679 3429. - Paint - *080090*
Gorry, James A., 20 Molesworth St., Dublin 2. T. (01) 679 53 19. - Paint - *080091*
Graphic Studio Dublin, Under the Arch, Cope St., Dublin 2. T. (01) 679 8021. - Graph - *080092*
Hoyan, P., Molesworth Pl., Dublin 2. T. (01) 76 52 88. - Paint - *080093*
Kennedy, 12 Harcourt St., Dublin 2. T. (01) 75 17 49. - Paint - *080094*
Kerlin, 38 Dawson St., Dublin 2. T. (01) 77 91 79, Fax (01) 77 96 52. - Paint - *080095*
Legge, 9 Chelmsford Ln., Dublin 6. T. (01) 96 23 99. - Paint - *080096*
Linders, Eve, 11 Upper Mount St., Dublin 2. T. (01) 76 23 31. - Paint - *080097*
MacKenzie & McCarthy, 38 Molesworth St., Dublin 2. T. (01) 76 71 37. - Paint - *080098*
Milmo-Penny, 55 Ailesbury Rd., Dublin 2. T. (01) 69 34 86, Fax (01) 83 04 14. - Paint - *080099*
O'Connor, Cynthia, & Co., 17 Duke St., Dublin 2. T. (01) 679 2177. - Paint - *080100*
Oisin, 10 Marino Mart, Fairview, Dublin 3. T. (01) 33 34 56. - Paint / Graph / Sculp - *080101*
Oriel, 17 Clare St., Dublin 2. T. (01) 76 34 10. - Paint - *080102*
Pym, Grace, 18 Duke St., Dublin 2. T. (01) 77 04 16. - Paint - *080103*
Solomon, 59 South William St., Dublin 2. T. (01) 679 4237. - Paint - *080104*
Taylor, 6 Dawson St., Dublin 2. T. (01) 77 60 89. - Paint - *080105*
Temple Bar Gallery and Studio, 4 Temple Bar, Dublin 2. T. (01) 71 00 73. - Paint - *080106*
Wyvern, 22 Wicklow St., Dublin 2. T. (01) 679 9046. - Paint - *080107*

Dun Laoghaire (Co. Dublin)
Framework Gallery, 55 Upper Georges St., Dun Laoghaire. T. (01) 80 57 56. - Paint - *080108*
Joyce, T.J., & Sons, 25 Patrick St., Dun Laoghaire. T. (01) 84 37 26. - Paint / Sculp - *080109*

Galway (Co. Galway)
Kenny, High St., Cross St., Salthill, Galway. T. (091) 62739, 61014, 61021. - Paint - *080110*
Kinvara Press, Cloosh-Kinvara, Galway. - Graph / Sculp - *080111*

Howth (Co. Dublin)
Howth Harbour Gallery, 6 Abbey St., Howth. T. (01) 39 33 66. - Paint - *080112*
Tramway, 1 Harbour Rd., Howth. T. (01) 39 33 66. - Paint - *080113*

Kilcock (Co. Kildare)
Kilcock Art Gallery, School St., Kilcock. T. (01) 28 76 19. - Paint - *080114*

Limerick (Co. Limerick)
Riverrun Gallery, Honan's Quay, Limerick. T. (061) 402 77. - Paint - *080115*
Woulfe, Angela, 16 Pery Sq., Limerick. T. (061) 31 01 64. - Paint - *080116*

Mullingar (Co. Westmeath)
Whyte, Jill, Castle St., Mullingar. T. (044) 486 62. - Paint - *080117*

Thurles (Co. Tipperary)
Bank of Ireland Gallery, Liberty Sq., Thurles. T. (0504) 215 11. - Paint - *080118*

Israel

Bet Shmesh

Artis, Givat Sharet 102, 99000 Bet Shmesh, 99000. T. 915 415, Fax 911 419. - Graph / Repr / Sculp / Pho / Draw - 080119

Haifa

Goldman, 93b Hanassi Av., 34642 Haifa. T. (04) 370 480. - Paint / Graph / Sculp - 080120
Mount Carmel Art Gallery, 24A Jerusalem St., 33 103 Haifa. T. (04) 66 19 23, Fax 972-4-671525. - Paint / Graph / Repr / Ico / Draw - 080121

Jerusalem

Collector, Jerusalem Hilton Hotel, POB Box 4075, 91 040 Jerusalem. T. (02) 53 38 90, 24 42 18. - Paint / Graph / Sculp - 080122
Debel, Ruth, Ein Kerem, PO Box 984, 91 009 Jerusalem. T. (02) 417785. - Paint / Sculp - 080123
Engel, 13 Shlomzion Hamalka, 91000 Jerusalem. T. (02) 223 523. 080124
Ezry Gallery, 18 King David St., 91000 Jerusalem. T. (02) 22 31 03. - Paint / Graph / Sculp - 080125
Gilat, Sara, 4 Pinzker St., 91000 Jerusalem. T. (02) 64121. 080126
Gimel, 17 Shlomzion Hamalkha, 91000 Jerusalem. T. (02) 227 636. 080127
Iran Bazar, 3, Ben Yehuda St., 91000 Jerusalem. T. (02) 22 58 24. 080128
Rina, 90 a Herzi Blvd., Beth Hakerem, 91000 Jerusalem. T. (02) 5 60 78. - Paint / Graph / Sculp - 080129
safrai galleries, 19 King David St., 94101 Jerusalem. T. (02) 25 48 85, Fax 24 03 87. - Paint / Graph / Sculp - 080130
Soussana, Jacques, 37 P. Koenig St. Talpioth, 91041 Jerusalem. T. (02) 78 26 78, Fax 78 24 26. 080131
The Gate Gallery, Marketin Center Ltd. Jaffa Gate, 91000 Jerusalem. T. (02) 39787. 080132
The Old City Art Gallery, 1, Hayehudim St., 91000 Jerusalem. T. (02) 282 233. 080133
Urdang, Bertha, 7 Bialik St., 91000 Jerusalem. T. (02) 526 078. 080134

Tel Aviv

Bineth Gallery, 15 Frishman, Tel Aviv. T. (03) 5238910. 080135
Dugith, 43 Frishman St, Tel Aviv. T. (03) 227586. - Paint - 080136
Givon, Noemi, 35 Gordon St, Tel Aviv, 63414. T. (03) 5225427, Fax (03) 5232310. 080137
Gordon Gallery, 95 Ben Yehuda St, 63401 Tel Aviv. T. (03) 5244862, Fax (03) 5240935. - Paint / Graph / Sculp / Draw - 080138
Hadassa, K., 33 Frug St, 63417 Tel Aviv. T. (03) 5224022. - Paint / Graph / Sculp - 080139
Julie, M., 7 Glikson St, Tel Aviv, 63141. T. (03) 295473. 080140
Kedem Gallery, 1 Shimon Haburski St, Old Yaffo, Tel Aviv. T. (03) 829424. 080141
Kibbutz Art Gallery, 25 Dov Hoz St, 63416 Tel Aviv. T. (03) 232533. 080142
Kishon, Sara, 31 Frug St, Tel Aviv, 63417. T. (03) 225069. 080143
Levy, Sara, 10 Pineles St, Tel Aviv, 62265. T. (03) 450202. 080144
Ofakim Art Gallery, 40 Harechesh St, Tel Aviv. T. (03) 5410417. - Paint - 080145
Old Jaffa Gallery, 14 Mazal Arie, Tel Aviv, 68036. T. (03) 829675. - Paint / Graph / Sculp - 080146
Orit Art Gallery, 103 Rothschild Blvd, Tel Aviv. T. (03) 5229061. 080147
Richter, Horace, 24 Simtat-Mazal-Arieh, Tel Aviv. T. (03) 5229045. - Paint / Graph / Tex / Jew / Mul / Draw - 080148
R.I.G. Arts, 5 Druyanov St, Tel Aviv. T. (03) 5057186. - Graph - 080149
Rosenfeld, 147 Dizengoff St, Tel Aviv. T. (03) 5229044. - Paint - 080150
Tiroche, Jean, Mifratz Shlomo St, Old Jaffa, Tel Aviv. T. (03) 823154. - Paint / Sculp - 080151
Ugarit Gallery, 25 Gordon St, Tel Aviv, 63414. T. (03) 5220414, 5241033. 080152

Italy

Acquaviva delle Fonti (Bari)

Tenaglio, Rocco, Via Dante Alighieri 4, 70021 Acquaviva delle Fonti. T. (080) 76 80 12. 080153

Alassio (Savona)

Galleria Buca del Muretto, Balconata Café Roma, 17021 Alassio. T. (0182) 401 88. 080154
Galliata, Piazza Partigiani 10, 17021 Alassio. T. (0182) 453 05. 080155

Alessandria

Vigato, Graziano, Via Ghilini 30, 15100 Alessandria. T. (0131) 44 41 90. 080156

Ardea (Roma)

Raccolta, Manzu, 00071 Ardea. T. (06) 916 10 22. - Paint / Sculp - 080157

Arezzo

La Chimera, Via Anfiteatro 7, 52100 Arezzo. T. (0575) 217 04. 080158
Vasari, G., Via Cesalpino 14, 52100 Arezzo. T. (0575) 239 16. 080159

Asagio (Vicenza)

Barbierato, Via Bonato 11, 36017 Asagio. T. (0424) 63915, Fax (0424) 64028. 080160

Asolo (Treviso)

Galleria al Pozzo, Piazza di Roma 59, 31011 Asolo. T. (0423) 55100. 080161
Galleria d'Arte Antica Regina Cornaro, Via Regina Cornaro 214, 31011 Asolo. T. (0423) 527 85. - Ant - 080162

Asti

La Giostra, Via G. Verdi 22, 14100 Asti. T. (0141) 563 02. 080163

Avezzano (L'Aquila)

La Trozzella, Corso della Libertà 54b, 67051 Avezzano. T. (0863) 3 11 59. - Paint / Graph / Sculp - 080164

Bari

Altraimmagine, Corso Vitt. Emanuele II 114, 70122 Bari. T. (080) 523 24 19. 080165
Arte Spazio, Via Suppa 12, 70122 Bari. T. (080) 232 468. 080166
Boccuzzi, V., Via Gimma 203, 70123 Bari. T. (080) 524 10 16. 080167
Bonomo, Marilena, Via Nicolò dell'Arca 19, 70121 Bari. T. (080) 521 01 45, Fax (080) 521 75 08. - Paint - 080168
Campanile, Via Principe Amedeo 101, 70122 Bari. T. (080) 521 22 19. 080169
Centrosei, Via XXIV Maggio 13/15, 70121 Bari. T. (080) 659314. 080170
Den Hertog, Via Andrea da Bari 117, 70121 Bari. T. (080) 524 63 11. - Fra - 080171
Fante di Fiori, Via Cairoli 17, 70122 Bari. T. (080) 213 881. 080172
Gagliano, A., Viale Repubblica 74, 70125 Bari. T. (080) 536 62 46. 080173
Galleria David, Via Piccinni 103, 70122 Bari. T. (080) 523 52 42. - Paint - 080174
L'Approdo, Corso Vitt. Emanuele II 152, 70122 Bari. T. (080) 523 51 66. 080175
La Spirale, Via Roberto da Bari 14, 70122 Bari. T. (080) 523 71 38. 080176
La Vernice, Piazza Massari 6, 70122 Bari. T. (080) 523 29 06. 080177
Le Muse, Via Piccinni 142/A, 70122 Bari. T. (080) 523 26 32. 080178
Milano, Ester, Via Gimma 93, 70122 Bari. T. (080) 523 71 33. 080179
Milella & Sansonetti, Via Quintano Sella 150, 70122 Bari. T. (080) 521 77 76. 080180
Panchetta, Corso Cavour 24, 70121 Bari. T. (080) 339176. - Paint - 080181
Patscot, M., Via Filippo Turati 5, 70125 Bari. T. (080) 41 77 66. 080182
Putignano, Via Putignano 209, 70122 Bari. T. (080) 524 56 00. 080183
Tropico del Cancro, Via Putignani 116, 70122 Bari. T. (080) 521 21 68. 080184
Unione, Via XXIV Maggio 9, 70121 Bari. T. (080) 523 22 60. 080185
Zelig, Via Cardassi 66, 70121 Bari. T. (080) 54 49 19. 080186

Barletta (Bari)

Salvemini, R., Vicolo Ospizio 1, 70051 Barletta. T. (0883) 51 81 98. 080187
Tobo Arte Diffusione, Corso Vitt. Emanuele 132, 70051 Barletta. T. (0883) 51 87 96. 080188

Bedizzole (Brescia)

Allemandi, E., Via Silvio Pellico 6, 25081 Bedizzole. T. (030) 64 47 95. 080189

Bergamo

Caruggio, Via S. Orsola 18, 24100 Bergamo. T. (035) 21 40 34. 080190
Centro 2B, Viale Vitt. Emanuele 47, 24100 Bergamo. T. (035) 217171. 080191
Galleria della Torre, Piazza V. Veneto 1, 24100 Bergamo. T. (035) 23 87 77. 080192
Galleria Permanente d'Arte, Piazza Dante 1, 24100 Bergamo. T. (035) 24 85 34. - Graph - 080193
Galleria 38, Via Tiraboschi 48, 24100 Bergamo. T. (035) 238652. 080194
Galleria 9 Colonne, Viale Papa Giovanni 120, 24100 Bergamo. T. (035) 22 52 22. 080195
La Garitta, Via T. Tasso 6, 24100 Bergamo. T. (035) 24 99 72. 080196
Scaccabarozzi, Giorgio, Viale Vittorio Emanuele 52b, 24100 Bergamo. T. (035) 21 73 73. - Paint / Furn / Sculp - 080197
Steffanoni, Vitali, Via Matris Domini 10, 24100 Bergamo. T. (035) 23 44 15. - Paint / Graph / Fra - 080198

Biella (Vercelli)

Circolo degli Artisti, Via Nazario Sauro 2/9, 13051 Biella. T. (015) 287 94. 080199
Dialoghi, Via C. Colombo 4, 13051 Biella. T. (015) 34017. 080200
Galleria il Quadro, Via Italia 48, 13051 Biella. T. (015) 29765, Fax (015) 29765. 080201
Galleria Mercurio, Via Italia 25, 13051 Biella. T. (015) 298 72. 080202
Graffio, Via Italia 39, 13051 Biella. T. (015) 209 59. - Paint - 080203
L'uomo e L'arte, Via Losana 13, 13051 Biella. T. (015) 22757. 080204
Ronda Omar Aprile, Salita di Riva 3, 13051 Biella. T. (015) 34 017. 080205

Bologna

Al Crocicchio, Via Santo Stefano 30, 40125 Bologna. T. (051) 23 30 54. 080206
Asinelli, Via Castel Tialto 2, 40125 Bologna. T. (051) 267 095. 080207
Brighenti, Gino, Via Guido Reni 4, 40125 Bologna. T. (051) 23 61 01. 080208
Caminetto, Via Marescalchi 2, 40123 Bologna. T. (051) 23 33 13. 080209
Circolo Artistico, Via Clavature 8, 40126 Bologna. T. (051) 229490. - Paint - 080210
Duemila, Via M. d'Azeglio 50, 40123 Bologna. T. (051) 228944. 080211
Fabjbasaglia, Via Farini 26, 40124 Bologna. T. (051) 23 49 22. 080212
Forni, Via Farina 26, 40124 Bologna. T. (051) 231589, Fax (051) 224486. 080213
Foscherari, Via Goidaniche 1/D, 40124 Bologna. T. (051) 275226. 080214
Galleria d'Arte Maggiore, Via d'Azeglio 15, 40123 Bologna. T. (051) 23 58 43. 080215
Galleria d'Arte Studio '900, Via del Carro 6b, 40126 Bologna. T. (051) 26 30 99. - Paint / Graph / Sculp - 080216
Galleria del Vicolo Quartirolo, Vicolo Quartirolo 3, 40121 Bologna. T. (051) 22 67 95. 080217
Galleria Nuova Trianon, Via Santo Stefano 10, 40125 Bologna. T. (051) 26 42 20. 080218

Galleria San Petronio, Via S. Vitale 7, 40125 Bologna.
T. (051) 92 71 35. *080219*
Galleria Saragozza, Via Saragozza 115, 40135 Bologna.
T. (051) 41 39 34. *080220*
Galleria 9 Colonne, Via Indipendenza 20, 50100 Bologna. *080221*
Il Giardino dell'Arte, Via S. Vitale 7 A, 40125 Bologna.
T. (051) 22 06 42. *080222*
L'Ariete, Via Marsili 7, 40124 Bologna.
T. (051) 33 12 02. *080223*
La Loggia, Via S. Stefano 15, 40125 Bologna.
T. (051) 23 76 52. - Paint - *080224*
Marescalchi, Via Mascarella 116, 40126 Bologna.
T. (051) 240352. *080225*
Mascarella, Via Mascarella 31, 40126 Bologna.
T. (051) 24 54 68. *080226*
La Meridiana, Via Massarenti 464, 40138 Bologna.
T. (051) 53 42 51. *080227*
Nanni, Paolo, Via S. Stefano 15, 40125 Bologna.
T. (051) 23 76 52. *080228*
Neon, Via Solferino 41 A, 40124 Bologna.
T. (051) 332783. *080229*
Pepoli, Via Toschi 2/1, 40124 Bologna.
T. (051) 275274. *080230*
Pignattari, Via Pignattari 1, 40124 Bologna.
T. (051) 220942. - Paint - *080231*
S. Vitale 19, Via San Vitale 19, 40125 Bologna.
T. (051) 26 18 79. *080232*
Sagittario, II, Via Cesare Battisti 24, 40123 Bologna.
T. (051) 26 64 84. *080233*
San Luca, Via Castiglione 2, 40124 Bologna.
T. (051) 22 49 62. *080234*
Severiarte, Via Rialto 4 A/B, 40124 Bologna.
T. (051) 26 84 84, Fax 26 84 84. *080235*
Spazio, Via Carbonesi 6, 40123 Bologna.
T. (051) 22 01 84, Fax 22 01 84. *080236*
Stamparte, Via Morandi 4, 40124 Bologna.
T. (051) 22 19 13, Fax (051) 269412. - Graph / Mul /
Draw - *080237*
Studio Cavalieri, Via Guerrazzi 18, 40125 Bologna.
T. (051) 26 12 19. *080238*
Studio Cristofori, Via Val d'Aposa 7/2, 40123 Bologna.
T. (051) 22 82 57. *080239*
Studio d'Arte Grafica, Piazza dei Tribunali 5, 40124 Bologna. T. (051) 23 34 08. - Paint / Graph - *080240*
Studio Felsina, Via S. Stefano 14/c, 40125 Bologna.
T. (051) 231332. - Paint / Sculp - *080241*
Studio G 7, Via Val d'Aposa 7c, 40123 Bologna.
T. (051) 26 64 97, Fax (051) 266497. *080242*
Studio 5, Via Tovaglie 14/3, 40100 Bologna.
T. (051) 58 43 63. *080243*
Tenza, Via Alessandrini 5/A-B, 40126 Bologna.
T. (051) 25 19 01. *080244*
Trimarchi, Via Val d'Aposa 5A, 40123 Bologna.
T. (051) 22 85 65. *080245*

Bolzano
Capitolare, Piazza Domenicani 20, 39100 Bolzano.
T. (0471) 323 44. *080246*
Galerie am Dominikanerplatz, Dominikanerpl 18, 39100 Bolzano. T. (0471) 219 66. *080247*
Goethe, Via della Mostra 1, 39100 Bolzano.
T. (0471) 97 54 61, Fax (0471) 970260. - Paint / Graph /
Sculp - *080248*
Il Sole, Via Goethe 44, 39100 Bolzano.
T. (0471) 246 64. *080249*
Vintler Galerie, Galleria Vintler 10, 39100 Bolzano.
T. (0471) 97 45 58. *080250*

Bormio e Bagni Nuovi (Sondrio)
„En-Plein-Air", 23032 Bormio e Bagni Nuovi.
T. (0342) 916 66. *080251*

Bovezza (Brescia)
Moreschi, V., Via Castello 1, 25073 Bovezza.
T. (030) 271 26 39. *080252*

Brescia
Arici, A., Corso Magenta 26, 25121 Brescia.
T. (030) 56018. *080253*
Armondi, Corso Palestro 37B, 25121 Brescia.
T. (030) 29 55 50. *080254*
Banco, Via Luigi Apollonio 68, 25100 Brescia.
T. (030) 56 27 5. *080255*

Bistro, Piazza della Loggia 11r, 25100 Brescia.
T. (030) 29 01 28. - Paint - *080256*
Busi, E., Via S. Faustino 83b, 25122 Brescia.
T. (030) 42085. *080257*
Campana, Via A. Monti 4, 25121 Brescia.
T. (030) 51110. - Graph / Fra - *080258*
Campana, Mario & C., Corso Palestro 43A, 25122 Brescia. T. (030) 41143. *080259*
Ciferri, A., Via Paganora 21, 25121 Brescia.
T. (030) 57453. *080260*
De Martino, A., Via Battaglie 36b, 25122 Brescia.
T. (030) 53027. *080261*
Galleria A. A. B., Via Gramsci 17, 25100 Brescia.
T. (030) 452 22. *080262*
Galleria Contemporanea, Via Fratelli Bandiera 17, 25122 Brescia. T. (030) 240 04 40. *080263*
Galleria dell' Incisione, Via Bezzecca 4, 25128 Brescia.
T. (030) 30 46 90. *080264*
Galleria Tre Archi, Contrada S. Chiara 13, 25100 Brescia. T. (030) 49369. - Paint - *080265*
Galleria 9 Colonne, Via XX Settembre 48, 25000 Brescia.
T. (030) 28 90 26. - Paint - *080266*
Minini, Massimo, Via L. Apollonio 68, 25128 Brescia.
T. (030) 383034, Fax (030) 392446. *080267*
Mor, Luigi, Contrada Bassiche 7/c, 25122 Brescia.
T. (030) 71 53 03. - Paint - *080268*
Multimedia, Via Calzavellia 20, 25121 Brescia.
T. (030) 42202, Fax (030) 43224. *080269*
Paini, C., Via Moretto 53C, 25121 Brescia.
T. (030) 29 22 08. *080270*
Piccola Galleria U.C.A.I., Via Pace 12/a, 25100 Brescia.
T. (030) 455 51. - Paint / Sculp - *080271*
Pitocchetto, T., Via Marsala 15, 25122 Brescia.
T. (030) 44060. *080272*
San Michele, Via A. Gramsci 10, 25100 Brescia.
T. (030) 29 49 78. - Paint - *080273*
Schreiber, Gianfranco, Via Granuci 8, 25100 Brescia.
T. (030) 29 30 79. - Paint / Graph / Sculp / Mul - *080274*

Brindisi
Mediterranean, Via Mazzini 13, 72100 Brindisi.
T. (0831) 232 79. *080275*

Busto Arsizio (Varese)
Boscolo, Manuela, Via Mazzini 48, 21052 Busto Arsizio.
T. (0331) 32 10 43, Fax (0331) 625111. *080276*
Italiana Arte, Via General Biancardi 9, 21052 Busto Arsizio. T. (0331) 631135, Fax (0331) 631135.
- Paint - *080277*

Cagliari
Arte Duchamp, Via Marche 9, 09100 Cagliari.
T. (070) 497 533. *080278*
Galleria dell'antico, Via Puccini 49, 09100 Cagliari.
T. (070) 493462. *080279*
Il Pennellaccio, Via Cocco Ortu 63/A, 09100 Cagliari.
T. (070) 48 93 38. *080280*
Il Pozzo, Via G. Mameli 103, 09100 Cagliari.
T. (070) 66 00 39. - Paint / Furn - *080281*
La Contemporanea, Via Azuni 30, 09100 Cagliari.
T. (070) 562 95. *080282*
Simula, Alberto, Portico S. Antonio 3, 09100 Cagliari.
T. (070) 596 48. - Paint / Graph - *080283*

Caldaro (Bolzano)
Albrecht, Pianizza di Sopra 50, 39052 Caldaro.
T. (0471) 514 21. - Paint / Sculp / Draw - *080284*

Caltanissetta
Cavallotto, Corso V. Emanuele 133, 93100 Caltanissetta.
T. (0934) 20081. - Paint / Graph - *080286*

Campello sul Clitunno (Perugia)
Meneghetti, T., Borgo S. Benedetto 28, 06042 Campello sul Clitunno. T. (0743) 52 15 85. *080287*

Campi Bisenzio (Firenze)
Desireau, Via Po 56, 50013 Campi Bisenzio.
T. (555) 89 15 04. *080288*

Cantù (Como)
Galleria Pianella, Via Vergani 7, 22063 Cantù.
T. (031) 70 54 82. - Paint - *080289*

Capri (Napoli)
Bowinkel, Uberto, Via Camerelle 49, 80073 Capri.
T. (081) 837 06 81. - Graph / Repr / Fra / Cur /
Pho - *080290*

Casale di Scodosia (Padova)
Missaglia, Nevio, Via Roma 31, 35040 Casale di Scodosia. T. (049) 87084. - Sculp - *080291*

Casalmaggiore (Cremono)
Galleria d'Orlane, Piazza Turati 11, 26041 Casalmaggiore. T. (0375) 43318. - Paint / Sculp - *080292*

Caserta
Centro Artistico, Via Majelli 32, 81100 Caserta.
T. (0823) 230 85. - Paint / Graph / Sculp - *080293*
Le Muse, Corso Trieste 200, 81100 Caserta.
T. (0823) 32 60 54. - Paint - *080294*
Oggetto, Corso Trieste 175, 81100 Caserta.
T. (0823) 329187. - Paint - *080295*

Cassano delle Murge (Bari)
Valerio, G., Via per Mercadante, 70020 Cassano delle Murge. T. (080) 76 37 11. *080296*

Cassino (Frosinone)
Aedes, Via G. di Blasio 19, 03043 Cassino.
T. (0776) 27 78 10. *080297*
Grilli de Angelis, G., Via degli Eroi 76, 03043 Cassino.
T. (0776) 21752. *080298*

Castel di Sangro (L'Aquila)
Gapas, Piazza Plebiscito, 67031 Castel di Sangro.
T. (0864) 80106. - Paint - *080299*

Castiglione del Lago (Perugia)
Gallery Trio, Via Fiorentina 14, 06061 Castiglione del Lago. T. (075) 95 36 94. *080300*

Catania (Sicilia)
Allia, Melo, Via Tomaselli 29, 95124 Catania.
T. (095) 275265. *080301*
Cavallotto, Corso Sicilia 89-91, 95131 Catania.
T. (095) 310600. - Paint / Graph - *080302*
Sicilia-Arte U. C. A. I., Via Crociferi 34, 95124 Catania.
T. (095) 27 29 38. *080303*

Cellatica (Brescia)
Arser, Via Badia 72, 25060 Cellatica.
T. (030) 32 22 10. *080304*

Chianciano Terme (Siena)
Morosini, Piazza Italia 52, 53042 Chianciano Terme.
T. (0578) 35 51. *080305*

Chiari (Brescia)
L'Incontro, Via Ventisei Aprile 46, 25032 Chiari.
T. (030) 71 25 37. *080306*

Chirionago (Venezia)
Totem Gallery, Via Miranese 426, 30030 Chirionago.
T. (041) 91 30 76, Fax (041) 913076. *080307*

Città della Pieve (Perugia)
Fondazione Arrigo Fora, Via Loc Canale, 06062 Città della Pieve. T. (0578) 29 86 13. *080308*

Città di Castello (Perugia)
Galleria delle Arti, Via Albizzini 21, 06012 Città di Castello. T. (075) 855 89 18, Fax (075) 8553000. *080309*

Como
La Colorna, Via Manzoni 12, 22100 Como.
T. (031) 26 61 31. - Paint - *080310*
Galleria Cavour, Piazza Cavour 27, 22100 Como.
T. (031) 26 41 66. - Paint - *080311*
Galleria del Francobello, Via Bellini 8, 22100 Como.
T. (031) 27 72 20. *080312*
Galleria Internazionale, Via Grimaldi 1, 22100 Como.
T. (031) 238 55. *080313*
Solenghi, Giuseppe, Via Rubini 3, 22100 Como.
T. (031) 26 82 27. *080314*

Concesio (Brescia)
Asa Centro Artistico Culturale, Viale Europa 174, 25062 Concesio. T. (030) 275 15 87. *080315*

Corciano (Perugia)
Patrizia, Via A. Gramsci 6, 06073 Corciano.
T. (075) 790730. *080316*

Cortina d'Ampezzo (Belluno)
Cristallo Galleria, Via Poste Vecchie 21, 32043 Cortina
d'Ampezzo. T. (0436) 60332. *080317*
Hausamann, Largo delle Poste, 32043 Cortina d'Ampez-
zo. T. (0436) 37 14. *080318*
Medea, Corso Italia 15, 32043 Cortina d'Ampezzo.
T. (0436) 26 53. - Paint - *080319*

Cosenza
La Bussola, Piazza Fera 9/10, 87100 Cosenza.
T. (0984) 25638. *080320*

Crema (Cremona)
Belluti, Gianfranco, Via Borletto 1, 26013 Crema.
T. (0373) 41 12 21. - Paint / Sculp - *080321*

Cremona
Gruppo Renzo Botti, Corso Campi 30, 26100 Cremona.
T. (0372) 293 44. *080322*

Cuneo
Ranno, Corso Nizza 25, 12100 Cuneo.
T. (0171) 46 94. *080323*

Deruta (Perugia)
Antichità Cà Muse, Via Mancini 11, 06053 Deruta.
T. (075) 971 17 89. *080324*

Desenzano del Garda (Brescia)
Lido, Via da Molin 45, 25015 Desenzano del Garda.
T. (030) 914 12 15. *080325*
Zacchi, A., Piazza Malvezzi, 25015 Desenzano del Gar-
da. T. (030) 914 15 08. *080326*

Ferrara
Alba, Corso Porta Pl 82/A, 44100 Ferrara.
T. (0532) 49854, Fax (0532) 49854. *080327*
La Linea, Via Cavour 89, 44100 Ferrara.
T. (0532) 21 719. *080328*

Firenze
Acantuhus, 18 Via S. Niccolo', 50125 Firenze.
T. (055) 2342878. *080329*
Accademia Riaci, 4 Via dei Conti, 50123 Firenze.
T. (055) 212791. *080330*
Acquario Edizioni D'Arte, 41 Via Corsi, 50123 Firenze.
T. (055) 415545. *080331*
Aglaia, Borgo S. Jacopo 48r, 50125 Firenze.
T. (055) 210934. *080332*
Alfani Viviana & Figli, Sdrucciolo de' Petti 11R, 50125
Firenze. T. (055) 283709, 225558. *080333*
Archivi Alinari, 6 Via Nazionale, 50123 Firenze.
T. (055) 210202. *080334*
Arno, Via Vigna Nuova 73, 50123 Firenze.
T. (055) 29 43 43. - Paint / Graph - *080335*
Arte Antica e Moderna, Borgo S. Frediano 53, 50124 Fi-
renze. T. (055) 219021. *080336*
Arte III, 22 Via G. della Bella, 50124 Firenze.
T. (055) 220678, 2335096. *080337*
Artia Studio, 38r Via Palmieri, 50122 Firenze.
T. (055) 282815. *080338*
Bacarelli, Benvenuto, Via dei Fossi 33, 50123 Firenze.
T. (055) 21 54 57. - Paint - *080339*
Baicchi M., 3b/r Via Chiantgiana, 50126 Firenze.
T. (055) 6820668. *080340*
Baroni J.M., 9 Borgo Ognissanti, 50123 Firenze.
T. (055) 282977. *080341*
Bazzanti, Pietro, Lungarno Corsini 44r, 50123 Firenze.
T. (055) 21 56 49. - Sculp - *080342*
Bezuga Stamperia, 22/24r Via Pandolfini, 50122 Firen-
ze. T. (055) 2479693. *080343*
Bigi-Arte, Via Targioni Tozzetti 32, 50144 Firenze.
T. (055) 36 16 27. *080344*
Bottega Cimabue, Borgo Allegri 1, 50122 Firenze.
T. (055) 24 17 67. *080345*
Bottega D'Arte il Duomo, 9r Via Ricasoli, 50122 Firenze.
T. (055) 211863. *080346*
La Bottega dei Grassi Nesi, Via dei Pollaiolo, 510142 Fi-
renze. T. (055) 715775, 7398751. *080347*
Bottega delle Stampe, 56r Borgo S. Jacopo, 50125 Fi-
renze. T. (055) 295396. *080348*

Bruschi, Alberto, Via Santo Spirito 40, 50125 Firenze.
T. (055) 21 03 74. - Paint / Furn / Sculp - *080349*
Cancelli, Via Terme 17r, 50123 Firenze.
T. (055) 21 30 87. *080350*
Carini, Via S. Niccolo 90, 50123 Firenze.
T. (055) 234 24 10, Fax (055) 9122646. *080351*
Cavour, 148a Via Cavour, 50129 Firenze.
T. (055) 2398836. *080352*
Centro Culturale il Bisonte, 13r Via Giard Serristori,
50125 Firenze. T. (055) 2479816. *080353*
Centro Storico, 20r Via Pietrapiana, 50121 Firenze.
T. (055) 241186. *080354*
Centro Tormabuoni, Via Tornabuoni 5, 50123 Firenze.
T. (055) 2396045, 280062. *080355*
Centro Tornabuoni, Via Tornabuoni 5, 50123 Firenze.
T. (055) 239 60 45, Fax (055) 280062. - Paint /
Graph - *080356*
Centro Tornabuoni, Via Tornabuoni 5, 50123 Firenze.
T. (055) 2302906, Fax (055) 280062. - Paint / Graph /
Fra - *080357*
Cherubini G., 402 Via di Brozzi, 50145 Firenze.
T. (055) 308236. *080358*
Davanzati, Borgo degli Albizi 67r, 50122 Firenze.
T. (055) 243864. *080359*
Dei Benci di Paladini Romano L., 30r Via Benci, 50122
Firenze. T. (055) 243273. *080360*
Edizioni Saf, 30a Via Steccuto, 50141 Firenze.
T. (055) 411168. *080361*
Erebi, Via Fortezza 6, 50129 Firenze.
T. (055) 48 02 22. *080362*
Falteri R., 20 Via Benci, 50122 Firenze.
T. (055) 243704. *080363*
Fasone, 8r Via Maggio, 510125 Firenze.
T. (055) 213087. *080364*
Faustini, Via Pepi 6, 50122 Firenze.
T. (055) 24 14 37. *080365*
Florence, Via Borgognissanti, 50123 Firenze.
T. (055) 21 36 71. *080366*
Forlai, Borgo Croce 54, 50121 Firenze.
T. (055) 234 35 89. *080367*
Frascione, Dr. Vittorio, Corso Italia 26, 50125 Firenze.
- Ant - *080368*
Fratelli Alinari, 15 lg. F. III Alinari, 50123 Firenze.
T. (055) 288228. *080369*
Frilli, A., Via Fossi 4, 50123 Firenze.
T. (055) 21 02 12. *080370*
Galleria Cavour, Via Cavour 148, 50129 Firenze.
T. (055) 239 88 36. *080371*
Galleria Cavour, Via Romana 12, 50129 Firenze.
T. (055) 233 77 73. *080372*
Galleria dei Benci, Via Benci 30, 50122 Firenze.
T. (055) 24 32 73. *080373*
Galleria Orlando, Via Romana 12, 50125 Firenze.
T. (055) 233 77 73. *080374*
Galleria Ottaviani, Borgognissanti 36, 50123 Firenze.
T. (055) 29 60 06. - Sculp - *080375*
Galleria Santa Trinita, Via Tornabuoni 3, 50123 Firenze.
T. (055) 216598. *080376*
Galzerino N., 113a Via G. Orsini, 50126 Firenze.
T. (055) 686657. *080377*
Gentili Innocenti, G., Borgo S. Croce 10, 50122 Firenze.
T. (055) 24 08 77, Fax (055) 240877. *080378*
I Capolavori, Lungarno Acciaiuoli 54, 50123 Firenze.
T. (055) 239 86 65. *080379*
Il Bisonte, Via S. Niccolo 24/28r, 50125 Firenze.
T. (055) 2342585, Fax (055) 2346768. *080380*
Il Cesello, Via dei Magazzini 5/7, 50122 Firenze.
T. (055) 28 24 66. - Sculp - *080381*
Il Duomo, Via Ricasoli 9, 50122 Firenze.
T. (055) 21 18 63. *080382*
Il Faro, Via S. Egidio 33, 50122 Firenze.
T. (055) 247 98 36. *080383*
Il Mirteto, Via Maggio 7, 50125 Firenze.
T. (055) 214917. *080384*
Inclub, 76 Via Capo di Mondo, 50136 Firenze.
T. (055) 666151. *080385*
Ken's, Via Lambertesca 17, 50122 Firenze.
T. (055) 239 65 87. *080386*
L'Affiche Illustree', Via dei Servi 69R, 50122 Firenze.
T. (055) 289187. *080387*
L'Affiche Illustree', Via Guelfa 14R, 50129 Firenze.
T. (055) 289963. *080388*

La Barca, Via Bufalini 37, 50122 Firenze.
T. (055) 28 29 78. *080389*
La Piramide, Via Martelli 5, 50129 Firenze.
T. (055) 280764, 282865. *080390*
La Scala, Via della Scala, 50123 Firenze.
T. (055) 26 36 47. - Paint - *080391*
La Stanzina, Via Fossi 51r, 50123 Firenze.
T. (055) 28 98 26. *080392*
La Strozzina, Piazza Strozzi, 50123 Firenze.
T. (055) 21 14 81. *080393*
Lapiccirella, Leonardo, Via Tornabuoni 3, 50123 Firenze.
T. (055) 21 65 98. - Paint - *080394*
Le Muse, Via Cavour 31, 50129 Firenze.
T. (055) 29 45 05. *080395*
Libri D'Arte, 68r Borgo S. Jacapo, 50125 Firenze.
T. (055) 2396696. *080396*
Linea Arte Contemporanea, 35r Via Palmieri, 50122 Fi-
renze. T. (055) 2347027. *080397*
Maccolini, A., Via Ricasoli 95r, 50122 Firenze.
T. (055) 272812. *080398*
Marco Villani e C. Bottega D'Arte, 49r Via Neri, 50122
Firenze. T. (055) 287583. *080399*
Marselli, Via Ginori 51, 50129 Firenze. T. (055) 282142.
- Graph / Fra - *080400*
Masini, Piazza Goldoni 6r, 50123 Firenze.
T. (055) 29 40 00. - Paint - *080401*
Mecacci A., 127r Borgo Ognissanti, 50123 Firenze.
T. (055) 216616. *080402*
Menghelli, Via Pepi 3/5r, 50122 Firenze.
T. (055) 24 49 98. *080403*
Mentana, Piazza Mentana 2r, 50122 Firenze.
T. (055) 21 19 85. - Paint - *080404*
Meyer B.A., 15r Via fra' P. Sarpi, 50136 Firenze.
T. (055) 677612 *080405*
Michaud, Corsini 4, 50123 Firenze.
T. (055) 29 86 95. *080406*
Michelucci, Giancarlo, Via Montebello 23, 50123 Firen-
ze. T. (055) 29 50 24. - Paint / Graph / China / Sculp /
Glass - *080407*
Mossa G., 73r Borgo Albizi, 50122 Firenze.
T. (055) 2476637. *080408*
Naldini Virgilio Riproduzioni, 23 Via Villani, 50124 Firen-
ze. T. (055) 2336095. *080409*
Nencioni Vanda, 34r Via Condotta, 50122 Firenze.
T. (055) 281202. *080410*
Nencioni Vanda, Via Condotta 34R, 50122 Firenze.
T. (055) 215345. *080411*
Palazzo Vecchio, Vacchereccia 3, 50122 Firenze.
T. (055) 21 41 94. - Paint - *080412*
Pallavicini, Via Serragli 19, 50124 Firenze.
T. (055) 29 51 12. *080413*
Pananti, Piazza S. Croce 8, 50122 Firenze.
T. (055) 24 49 31. *080414*
Paolieri U., 23 Via Villani, 50124 Firenze.
T. (055) 220504. *080415*
Par Avion, 84r Via Vigne Nuova, 50123 Firenze.
T. (055) 2396190. *080416*
Par Avion – Art Shop, 12r Via Federighi, 50123 Firenze.
T. (055) 289532. *080417*
Parronchi, Via dei Fossi 18/20r, 50123 Firenze.
T. (055) 21 51 09, Fax (055) 294097. *080418*
Parronchi A., 18r Via Fossi, 50123 Firenze.
T. (055) 294097. *080419*
Perrotta C., 27r Via Vigna Vecchia, 50122 Firenze.
T. (055) 2284826. *080420*
Poggiali & Forconi, Via della Scala 35A, 50123 Firenze.
T. (055) 28 77 48. *080421*
Il Ponte, 44 Via Mezzo, 50121 Firenze.
T. (055) 240617. *080422*
Ponte Vecchio, 18r Borgo S. Jacopo, 50125 Firenze.
T. (055) 214307. *080423*
Raffaelli Gianni e C., 7r Via Pisana, 50143 Firenze.
T. (055) 2280004. *080424*
Raffaello, Florence, Viale Petrarca 88, 50124 Firenze.
T. (055) 2280442. *080425*
Saf Edizioni, Via dello Steccuto 30A, 50141 Firenze.
T. (055) 411168, Fax (055) 411168. *080426*
Salome', 70 Via Campuccio, 50125 Firenze.
T. (055) 221481, 2298507. *080427*
Santa Reparata, 41 Via S. Reparata, 50129 Firenze.
T. (055) 214365. *080428*
Santacroce, Piazza S. Croce 13, 50122 Firenze.
T. (055) 24 29 35. - Paint / Graph / Sculp - *080429*

Santo Ficara, Via Ghibellina 101, 50122 Firenze.
T. (055) 28 70 61, Fax (055) 213383.   080430
Schema, Via Vigna Nuova 17, P.O.Box 6324, 50123 Firenze. T. (055) 28 40 90, Fax (055) 8712107. - Ant /
Graph / Sculp -   080431
Schwicker-Tosi, Piazza Pitti 40r, 50125 Firenze.
T. (055) 21 18 51.   080432
Spagnoli, Renzo, Piazza Mentana 4A, 50122 Firenze.
T. (055) 28 27 09, 21 41 91.   080433
Spazio Tempo, Piazza Peruzzi 15r, 50122 Firenze.
T. (055) 21 86 78, 28 05 90, Fax (055) 287590. 080434
Spinetti, Chiasso Armagnati 2, 50122 Firenze.
T. (055) 239 60 43. - Paint -   080435
Stefanini, Aurelio, Via Cavour 31, 50129 Firenze.
T. (055) 21 39 78, Fax (055) 213978.   080436
Studio D. di de Nicola, 26r Via Benci, 50122 Firenze.
T. (055) 2341549.   080437
Teorema, Via del Corso 21r, 50122 Firenze.
T. (055) 29 53 45.   080438
Tornabuoni, 74r Via Tornabuoni, 50123 Firenze.
T. (055) 284720.   080439
Varart, 47 Via Oriolo, 47r Via Oriuolo, 50122 Firenze.
T. (055) 284265, 213827.   080440
Villa Medicea della Petraia, Via Castello, 50141 Firenze.
T. (055) 451208.   080441
Viviane e Vincenzo Stampe d'Arte di Alfani Viviana, 11
Sdrucciolo Pitti, 50125 Firenze.
T. (055) 283709.   080442
Vivita, Borgo degli Albizi 16, 50122 Firenze.
T. (055) 247 98 51, 248 00 13,
Fax (055) 2479851.   080443
Vivita, Borgo S. Frediano 69, 50124 Firenze.
T. (055) 28 48 51.   080444
Zambini, Piazza S. Croce 8, 50122 Firenze.
T. (055) 24 08 72.   080445

Foggia
Galleria dell'Artista, Via Arpi 74, 71100 Foggia.
T. (0881) 79111. - Paint -   080446

Foligno (Perugia)
Innocenti, Antonietta, Piazza S. Francesco 16, 06034
Foligno. T. (0742) 59091.   080447
Perna, Corso Cavour 39, 06034 Foligno.
T. (0742) 56340.   080448

Forte dei Marmi (Lucca)
La Polena, Viale a Mare 23, 55042 Forte dei Marmi.
T. (0584) 801 61. - Paint -   080449

Frosinone
Evangelisti, M., Via Moro 156, 03100 Frosinone.
T. (0775) 87 40 42.   080450
L'Orsa Maggiore, Via Minghetti 27, 03100 Frosinone.
T. (0775) 85 73 41.   080451

Frossasco (Torino)
Riva, Attilio, Via de Vitis 5, 10060 Frossasco.
T. (0121) 35 29 64.   080452

Gallarate (Varese)
Sagittario, Grampa Andreina, Via Posporta 2, 21013 Gallarate. T. (0331) 79 31 46. - Paint -   080453

Gargnano (Brescia)
Calla di Mattka, Via S. Rocco 11, 25084 Gargnano.
T. (0365) 72678.   080454

Genova
Araghi, 18r Vicolo Falamonica, 16123 Genova.
T. (010) 293535.   080455
Arius, 33r Via Rolando, 16151 Genova.
T. (010) 6450225.   080456
Arius, 136r Viale Brig. Partigiane, 16129 Genova.
T. (010) 592723.   080457
Arte Casa, 68r Via Giustiniani, 16123 Genova.
T. (010) 281520.   080458
Arte Club, Via Loggia Spinola 8R, 16123 Genova.
T. (010) 58 18 75.   080459
Arte Verso, Vico dei Garibaldi 39A, 16123 Genova.
T. (010) 20 35 46.   080460
Barrel Stampe Antiche, Via Granello 15R da Via XX Settembre, 16121 Genova. T. (010) 540251.   080461
Boccadasse, Via Aurora 1, 16146 Genova.
T. (010) 36 10 37.   080462

Bors Art, 48 Via Sestri, 16154 Genova. T. (010) 622881,
6509016.   080463
Borsart, 48 Via Sestri, 16154 Genova.
T. (010) 622851.   080464
Il Capolinea, 35r Viale Franchini, 16167 Genova.
T. (010) 321841.   080465
Carlevaro, Piazza De Marini 22r, 16123 Genova.
T. (010) 29 18 72.   080466
Centro D'Arte la, Maddalena, 12r Piazza Maddalena,
16124 Genova. T. (010) 281785.   080467
Centro D'Arte le Prigioni, 45 Via Vigna, 16154 Genova.
T. (010) 624607.   080468
Cesarea, Via Cesarea 105r, 16121 Genova.
T. (010) 580 116.   080469
Chisel, Salita S. Caterina 6, 16123 Genova.
T. (010) 58 14 14, Fax (010) 5531459. - Paint - 080470
Citifin, Piazza Dante 18, 16121 Genova.
T. (010) 53 22 53. - Paint -   080471
Clemente L., 94r Via XX Settembre, 16121 Genova.
T. (010) 580151.   080472
Colombo Gallery, 183r Via Rimassa, 16129 Genova.
T. (010) 580732.   080473
Comelli R., 35 Passeg. A. Garibaldi, 16167 Genova.
T. (010) 3726183.   080474
Comelli R., 11r Via Mille, 16147 Genova.
T. (010) 3770729.   080475
Contemporanea, Corso Buenos Aires 46C, 16129 Genova. T. (010) 566 290. - Paint -   080476
Il Crocicchio, Via del mercato 2, 16014 Genova.
T. (010) 780085.   080477
Dallai, 11r Piazza de Marini, 16123 Genova.
T. (010) 298338.   080478
Devoto, Vico del Fieno 13r, 16123 Genova.
T. (010) 20 27 57, Fax (010) 202757.   080479
Ellequadro Documenti Arte Contemporanea, 29r Vicolo
Fallamonica, 16123 Genova. T. (010) 295855.   080480
Enrico Gallerie D'Arte, 11r Via Garibaldi, 16167 Genova.
T. (010) 2470150.   080481
Esposizione Rubinacci, 8 Via Garibaldi, 16167 Genova.
T. (010) 291539.   080482
Esposizioni Rubinacci, 8 Via Garibaldi, 16167 Genova.
T. (010) 293857.   080483
FE.INT.E.R.CART, 1 Via Cadamosto, 16159 Genova.
T. (010) 443322.   080484
Fontane Marose 4, 4 Piazza Fontane Marose, 16123 Genova. T. (010) 542623, 5704831.   080485
Galleria d'Arte, Via B. Bisagno 6, 16133 Genova.
T. (010) 561178.   080486
Galleria D'Arte Giordano, Via Conservatori del Mare 5/2,
16123 Genova. T. (010) 206906.   080487
Galleria D'Arte Laura Son, Via S. Vincenzo 190R, 16121
Genova. T. (010) 587781.   080488
Galleria D'Arte R. Rotta, Via XX Settembre 181, 16121
Genova. T. (010) 564454.   080489
Galleria Galliani, Piazza S. Matteo 16/1, 16123 Genova.
T. (010) 200790.   080490
La Galleria Sestri – Arte, 17r Via Cat Rossi, 16154 Genova. T. (010) 16154.   080491
Galleria Tavorone, Piazzetta Tavarone 9R, 16123 Genova.
T. (010) 204939.   080492
Galliani S., 16 Piazza S. Matteo, 16123 Genova.
T. (010) 200800.   080493
Grana R., 2 Piazza Fossatello, 16124 Genova.
T. (010) 208975.   080494
Gualco C., 1 Vicolo dei Garibaldi, 16167 Genova.
T. (010) 200485.   080495
Guidi, 6r Vicolo Falamonica, 16123 Genova.
T. (010) 298522.   080496
Guidi G., 19r Via Chiossone, 16123 Genova.
T. (010) 202475.   080497
Il Vicolo, Salita Pollaiuoli 37r, 16123 Genova.
T. (010) 2471298, Fax (010) 297909.   080498
Interarte, Via XX Settembre 233, 16121 Genova.
T. (010) 54 13 83. - Paint -   080499
Investart, 121r Via Fischi, 16121 Genova.
T. (010) 5705703.   080500
Investart, 43r Piazetta Dante, 16121 Genova.
T. (010) 587021.   080501
Investart, 121r Via Fieschi, 16121 Genova.
T. (010) 561996.   080502
Katia, 7r S. Dinegro, 16123 Genova.
T. (010) 5535235.   080503

L'Akuba, Via Montevideo 37/r, 16129 Genova.
T. (010) 36 06 80. - Paint -   080504
L'Artemodello di Pollicino Amalia, 31r S. S. Caterina,
16123 Genova. T. (010) 581377.   080505
Locus Solus, 3 Piazza Fontane Marose, 16123 Genova.
T. (010) 5702807, 5702808.   080506
Martini e Ronchetti, Via Roma 9, 16121 Genova.
T. (010) 58 69 62.   080507
Martini & Ronchetti, 9 Via Roma, 16121 Genova.
T. (010) 586962.   080508
Mengoni P., 8 Campetto, 16123 Genova.
T. (010) 299290.   080509
Nettuno, 9r Piazza Nettuno, 16146 Genova.
T. (010) 3771832.   080510
Nuovo Fondaco, 3r Vicolo Vigne, 16124 Genova.
T. (010) 208429.   080511
Oneto Gift di G.B. Oneto, 75r Via S. Lorenzo, 16123 Genova. T. (010) 291543.   080512
Oneto Gift di G.B. Oneto, 75r Via S. Lorenzo, 16123 Genova. T. (010) 2470632.   080513
Orti Sauli, 51 Viale Sauli, 16121 Genova.
T. (010) 532903, 532904, 583712, 583742.   080514
Orti Sauli, Viale Sauli 51, 16121 Genova.
T. (010) 58 37 12, Fax (010) 583742.   080515
La Polena, Largo XII Ottobre 24, 16121 Genova.
T. (010) 562339.   080516
La Polena, 26 Piazza Catteneo, 16128 Genova.
T. (010) 204497.   080517
Portobello Road Casa D'Aste, 4 Piazza de Ferrari, 16121
Genova. T. (010) 281048.   080518
Portobello Rood Case D'Aste, 4 Piazza de Ferrari, 16121
Genova. T. (010) 281513.   080519
Il Punto, 1 Piazza Colombo, 16121 Genova.
T. (010) 585822.   080520
Ravecca, 49r Via Ravecca, 16128 Genova.
T. (010) 294056.   080521
Rotta, Via XX Settembre 181, 16123 Genova.
T. (010) 56 44 54. - Paint / Graph -   080522
Rovani, 100r Via Gianelli, 16166 Genova.
T. (010) 331651.   080523
Rubinacci Esposizione, 8 Via Garibaldi, 16167 Genova.
T. (010) 203720.   080524
Rubinacci Galleria D'Arte, 7 Via Garibaldi, 16167 Genova. T. (010) 298758, 2770028.   080525
S. Sebastiano, 59r Via S. Sebastiano, 16123 Genova.
T. (010) 593685.   080526
San Andrea, Via Cairoli 8, 16124 Genova.
T. (010) 29 08 45.   080527
San Lorenzo – Galleria D'Arte, Via S. Lorenzo 75R,
16123 Genova. T. (010) 2470632, 291543.   080528
Studio B 2, 1 Via S. Luca, 16124 Genova.
T. (010) 593685.   080529
Studio Ghiglione, Piazza S. Matteo 6A/R-6B/R, 16123
Genova. T. (010) 207887, 208707,
Fax (010) 292295.   080530
Studio Leonardi, 8a Campetto, 16123 Genova.
T. (010) 298029.   080531
Tirotta, 36r Via Volturno, 16129 Genova.
T. (010) 16129.   080532
Tirotta O., 67r Via Malta, 16121 Genova.
T. (010) 564579.   080533
Unimedia, Vico Garibaldi 1, 16123 Genova.
T. (010) 20 04 85. - Paint -   080534
Vela, Via Caprettari 18, 16123 Genova. T. (010) 29 25 77.
- Paint -   080535
Il Vicolo, 8 Piazza Pollaiuoli, 16123 Genova.
T. (010) 293717.   080536
Il Vicolo, 8 S. Pollaiuoli, 16123 Genova.
T. (010) 297909.   080537

Ghedi (Brescia)
Bozzoni, F., Via Carlo Alberto 36, 25016 Ghedi.
T. (030) 90 17 65.   080538

Gioia del Colle (Bari)
Bianco, G., Piazza Plebiscito 21, 70023 Gioia del Colle.
T. (080) 83 06 651.   080539

Grosseto
Centro delle Arti, Piazza S. Michele 2, 58100 Grosseto.
T. (0564) 290 14.   080540
Galleria d'Arte Moderna, Via Garibaldi 7, 58100 Grosseto. T. (0564) 271 94.   080541

Galleria d'Arte Modigliani, Via Montanara 6, 58100
Grosseto. T. (0564) 268 15. *080542*

Gubbio (Perugia)
Alunno, Camelia E., Via Leonardo da Vinci 85, 06024
Gubbio. T. (075) 927 77 76. *080543*

Guidizzolo (Mantova)
Soraya, Via Fabio Filzi 2, 46040 Guidizzolo.
T. (0376) 810 75. *080544*

Lecce
Artestudio 36, Via C. Battisti 23 A, 73100 Lecce.
T. (0832) 45598. *080545*
Il Sedile, Piazza S. Oronzo, 73100 Lecce.
T. (0832) 24 43. - Paint / Graph - *080546*
Studio Gi, Via T. Tasso 12, 73100 Lecce.
T. (0832) 404 50. - Paint / Graph / Sculp - *080547*

Lecco (Como)
Giuli, Via Leonardo da Vinci 9, 22053 Lecco.
T. (0341) 374126. *080548*
Visconti, Via Visconti 18, 22053 Lecco.
T. (0341) 36 93 94. *080549*

Legnano (Milano)
La Cornice, Via Palestro 7, 20025 Legnano.
T. (0331) 486 61. - Paint - *080550*
Cozzi, Giovanni, Corso Sempione 127, 20025 Legnano.
T. (0331) 544 39. - Paint / Graph / Sculp - *080551*
Galleria del Mobile Antico, Via de Gasperi 36, 20025
Legnano. T. (0331) 48 684. - Paint - *080552*

Lenno (Como)
Bolaffio, Via degli Ulivi 9, 22016 Lenno.
T. (03 44) 551 46. - Graph - *080553*

Limone Piemonte (Cuneo)
Il Tarlo, Via Roma 71, 12015 Limone Piemonte.
T. (0171) 92 61 15. *080554*

Livorno
Bottega d'Arte, Via Indipendenza 12, 57100 Livorno.
T. (0586) 261 37. - Paint - *080555*
Giraldi, Piazza Grande, 57100 Livorno.
T. (0586) 38391. *080556*
La Saletta, Via della Madonna 34, 57100 Livorno.
T. (0586) 233 50. *080557*
Libreria Belforte, Via Grande 91/93, 57100 Livorno.
T. (0586) 223 79. *080558*
Peccolo, Roberto, Piazza Repubblica 12, 57123 Livorno.
T. (0586) 88 85 09. - Paint - *080559*
Rotini, Via Indipendenza 28-32, 57126 Livorno.
T. (0586) 89 97 89. *080560*
Sears Gallery, Via Roma 66, 57100 Livorno.
T. (0586) 30486. *080561*

Lodi (Milano)
Galleria il Gelso, Via Corso Adda 5, 20075 Lodi.
T. (0371) 42 09 81. *080562*

Lucca
Galleria dei Servi, Via S. Croce 58, 55100 Lucca.
T. (0583) 45986. *080563*
Galleria San Croce, Via S. Croce 57, 55100 Lucca.
T. (0583) 42209. *080564*
Vangelisti Casa d'Arte, Piazza dei Servi 11, 55100 Luc-
ca. T. (0583) 45135. *080565*

Macerata
Arte Studio Macerata, Corso della Repubblica 29, 62100
Macerata. T. (0733) 470 19. - Paint - *080566*
Cicconi, Franco, Via S. Maria della Porta 36, 62100 Ma-
cerata. T. (0733) 49309. - Paint / Eth - *080567*
L'Arco, Via Crispi 36, 62100 Macerata. T. (0733) 21 14.
- Graph - *080568*

Mantova
Il Chiodo, Via Oberdan 24, 46100 Mantova.
T. (0376) 32 27 53, Fax (0376) 322753. *080569*
L'Inferriata, Sottoportico Lattonai 4, 46100 Mantova.
T. (0376) 36 63 67. - Paint / Graph / Sculp - *080570*

Martina Franca (Taranto)
Studio Carrieri, Via Principe Umberto 49, 74015 Martina
Franca. T. (080) 70 17 59. *080571*

Matera
La Scaletta, Via Sette Dolori 10, 75100 Matera.
T. (0835) 2 38 97. - Paint - *080572*
Studio Arti Visive, Via Margherita 41, 75100 Matera.
T. (0835) 214 31. - Paint / Graph / Sculp - *080573*

Merate (Como)
Studio Casati, Via Sant' Ambrogio 61, 22055 Merate.
T. (039) 53163. *080574*

Milano
A Arte – Studio Invernizzi, 12 Via Scarlatti, 20124 Mila-
no. T. (02) 29402855. *080575*
A. Z. Galleria D'Arte, 19 Via Bigli, 20121 Milano.
T. (02) 76022647. *080576*
Accademia, Via Fiori Chiari 2, 20121 Milano.
T. (02) 86 69 89. *080577*
A.C.I., 1 Via Dracone, 20126 Milano.
T. (02) 2579686. *080578*
Ada Zunino, Via Turati 8, 20121 Milano.
T. (02) 29002913. *080579*
Ala S., 3 Via Mamelli, 20129 Milano. T. (02) 7610077,
745468. *080580*
Ala, Salvatore, Piazza Umanitaria 2, 20122 Milano.
T. (02) 540 06 12. - Paint / Sculp / Draw - *080581*
Albatros, 20 Via Vanzetti, 20133 Milano.
T. (02) 7490885. *080582*
Albatros, 18 Via Pinio, 20129 Milano. T. (02) 2043487,
2046947. *080583*
Albergo Auriga Hotel, 7 Via Pirelli, 20124 Milano.
T. (02) 66985258. *080584*
Albertoni F., 234 Via Lorenteggio, 20147 Milano.
T. (02) 4158681. *080585*
Alchimia, Foro Bonaparte 55, 20121 Milano.
T. (02) 805 27 13, Fax (02) 862557. *080586*
Angolare, Via Clerici 13, 20121 Milano. T. (02) 899 188.
- Paint - *080587*
Angolare Studio D'Arte, 4 Via Urbano III, 20123 Milano.
T. (02) 8377609, 8376239, 8377690,
8376307. *080588*
Annovazzi A., 10 Via Poliziano, 20154 Milano.
T. (02) 341083. *080589*
Annunciata, Via Manzoni 46, 20121 Milano.
T. (02) 796026, 796027, Fax (02) 76009767. - Paint /
Graph / Sculp - *080590*
Appiani Arte Trentadue, Via Appiani 1, 20121 Milano.
T. (02) 6554044, Fax (02) 6570337. *080591*
Arcadia Arte del Nostro Tempo di Zanetti, Franca e C., 7
Via Maroncelli, 20154 Milano. T. (02) 653765. *080592*
Arcadia di Raschella Enzo e C., 64 Via Canonica, 20154
Milano. T. (02) 33103626. *080593*
Area Studio di Giongo, 20 Via Masotto, 20133 Milano.
T. (02) 70126479. *080594*
Ariete Graphica, Via S. Andrea 5, 20121 Milano.
T. (02) 70 99 44. - Paint / Sculp - *080595*
Ars Italica, Via Marconi 3A, 20123 Milano.
T. (02) 87 65 33. *080596*
Art and Publishing A P, 3 Piazza Massaia, 20123 Mila-
no. T. (02) 8057851. *080597*
Art Bridge, Via Vigevano 3, 20144 Milano.
T. (02) 4239523, Fax 312 31 10. *080598*
Art Company di Angiulli, Vincenzo e C., 55 Ripa Piazetta
Ticinese, 20143 Milano. T. (02) 89404277. *080599*
Art Consultant, 6 Via Cerva, 20122 Milano.
T. (02) 76014226, 76014228, 76014237. *080600*
Arte Borgogna, 2 Via Pietro Mascagni, 20122 Milano.
T. (02) 780884. *080601*
Arte Borgogna, Corso Porta Vigentina 27, 20122 Milano.
T. (02) 58 30 54 20, Fax 76 00 33 30. - Paint /
Graph - *080602*
Arte Borgogna, Via Borgogna 7, 20122 Milano.
T. (02) 76004826, Fax (02) 76003330. *080603*
Arte Borgogna di Gianni Schubert e C., 14 Via Serbelloni,
20122 Milano. T. (02) 783779. *080604*
Arte Borgognadi Schubert Gianni, 14 Via Serbelloni,
20122 Milano. T. (02) 76004826. *080605*
Arte Centro, Via Brera 11, 20121 Milano.
T. (02) 86 58 88, Fax (02) 86462213. - Paint / Graph /
Sculp - *080606*
Arte Centro Due, 31 Via Annunciata, 20121 Milano.
T. (02) 29000071. *080607*
Arte Contemporanea, 33 Via Castaldi, 20124 Milano.
T. (02) 29406019, 29406404. *080608*

Arte Oro di Minardi Salvatore e Silvio, 9 Via Ozanam,
20129 Milano. T. (02) 29521142. *080609*
Arte Struktura, Via Mercato 1, 20121 Milano.
T. (02) 805446, Fax (02) 875884. *080610*
Arte Studio Milano, 50 Via Gluck, 20125 Milano.
T. (02) 6697388. *080611*
Arte & Altro, Via Pisoni 2, 20121 Milano.
T. (02) 65 33 93, Fax (02) 8051307. *080612*
Arte 92, Via Moneta 1A, 20123 Milano. T. (02) 8052347,
8053110, Fax (02) 5464562. *080613*
Artema, 14 Via S. Marco, 20121 Milano.
T. (02) 6575220, 6575420. *080614*
Artestampa di Grandi, Fernando, 7 Via Tirso, 20141 Mi-
lano. T. (02) 57401010. *080615*
Artestudio BST, 10 Via Maroncelli, 20154 Milano.
T. (02) 29002028. *080616*
Artitalia, 117 Via Lod. il Moro, 20143 Milano.
T. (02) 8911744, 8910209. *080617*
Associazione Studio Borromei, 12 Piazza Borromeo,
20123 Milano. T. (02) 8052349. *080618*
Ateneo, 16 Via Castaldi, 20124 Milano.
T. (02) 29526884. *080619*
Austoni, Maria Luisa, Via Pontaccio 17, 20121 Milano.
T. (02) 805 25 94. *080620*
Avida Dollars, Via Laghetto 2, 20122 Milano.
T. (02) 7600 3979. *080621*
Baldacci, Paolo, Via Bagutta 8, 20121 Milano.
T. (02) 76 01 59 69, Fax (02) 76001897. *080622*
Baldacci Paolo Arte Antica e Moderna, 8 Via Bagutta,
20121 Milano. T. (02) 76015969, 76001897. *080623*
Bartolomucci A., 28a Viale C. da Forli', 20133 Milano.
T. (02) 40091571. *080624*
Bella Valeria Stampe, 2 Via S. Cecilia, 20122 Milano.
T. (02) 76004413, 76006505. *080625*
Belvedere, Valeria, Via Senato 6, 20121 Milano.
T. (02) 79 56 26, Fax (02) 76020266. *080626*
Bergamini, Corso Venezia 16, 20121 Milano.
T. (02) 76002346, 798871, Fax (02) 798871.
- Paint - *080627*
Bianco G.B., 7 Via Bellezza, 20136 Milano.
T. (02) 58315786. *080628*
Binozzi R., 3 Via Dante, 20123 Milano.
T. (02) 875768. *080629*
Biraghi Ettore, 13 Via Negroli, 20133 Milano.
T. (02) 7386027. *080630*
Bixio, 2 Via Bixio, 20129 Milano.
T. (02) 29516638. *080631*
Blu, Via Senato 18, 20121 Milano. T. (02) 792404,
Fax (02) 782398. - Paint / Graph / Sculp - *080632*
Blu', 18 Via Senato, Milano. T. (02) 76022404,
76020028. *080633*
„Bohème", Viale Piave 38, 20129 Milano.
T. (02) 22 40 87. - Paint - *080634*
Bolzani, Corso Matteotti 20, 20121 Milano.
T. (02) 78 10 26. - Paint / Fra - *080635*
Bolzani Cornici e Stampe, 20 Corso Matteotti, 20121 Mi-
lano. T. (02) 76014221. *080636*
Bonaparte, Via P. della Francesca 47, 20154 Milano.
T. (02) 3496290. *080637*
Bonaparte Arte Contemporanea di, Nicol Luciani, 12 Via
S. Marco, 20121 Milano. T. (02) 29001267,
29004809. *080638*
Bordone, Via Telesio 13, 20145 Milano.
T. (02) 48 01 53 65, Fax (02) 48015365. *080639*
Bosoni L., 5/7 Via S. Lucia, 20122 Milano.
T. (02) 58300952. *080640*
Bottega dei Vasai, Corso S. Gottardo 14, 20136 Milano.
T. (02) 837 60 16, Fax (02) 58102028. *080641*
Bottega delle Stampe, Via Osti 3, ang. Corso Porta Ro-
mana 23, 20122 Milano. T. (02) 58307458. *080642*
Brera 3 Studio d'Art, Via Brera 3, 20121 Milano.
T. (02) 8057049, Fax (02) 8057049. - Paint / Graph /
Sculp - *080643*
Brerarte, Piazza S. Marco 1, 20121 Milano.
T. (02) 655 50 40. *080644*
Brini R., 11 Via Bergamo, 20135 Milano.
T. (02) 5468089. *080645*
Buraschi F., 23 Via Padova, 20131 Milano.
T. (02) 2613026. *080646*
Buratti S., 10 Via S. M. alla Porta, 20123 Milano.
T. (02) 86450007. *080647*
Cadario, Via Annuciata 7, 20121 Milano.
T. (02) 66 25 88. - Paint - *080648*

Cafiso, Piazza S. Marco 1, 20121 Milano.
T. (02) 654864/ 6570211, Fax (02) 6596546.   *080649*
Cairola, Via Senato 45, 20121 Milano. T. (02) 79 42 86.
- Graph -   *080650*
Cammarella L., 4 Via S. Damiano, 20122 Milano.
T. (02) 76023058.   *080651*
Cannaviello, E., Via Cusani 10, 20121 Milano.
T. (02) 86 46 12 54, Fax (02) 862857.   *080652*
Capitani, 45 Via Manzoni, 20121 Milano.
T. (02) 29000406, 653091.   *080653*
Cardenas, Monica de, Via F. Vigano 4, 20124 Milano.
T. (02) 29 01 00 68, Fax (02) 29005784.   *080654*
Cardi, Piazza S. Erasmo 3, 20121 Milano.
T. (02) 29003235, Fax (02) 29003382.   *080655*
Cardillo R., 31 Via Novara, 20147 Milano.
T. (02) 4043138.   *080656*
Carini, Via V. Hugo 3, 20123 Milano.
T. (02) 87 56 17.   *080657*
Carini D., 4 Via Battistotti Sassi, 20133 Milano.
T. (02) 70126465.   *080658*
Carpeni' R., 5 Via Binda, 20143 Milano.
T. (02) 89122203.   *080659*
Carrano M., 12 Via Imbonati, 20159 Milano.
T. (02) 66805245.   *080660*
Case, Via Plinio 29, 20129 Milano. T. (02) 29 51 76 53,
Fax (02) 29526374.   *080661*
Le Case D'Arte di Leccese Pasquale, 8 Via Gorani,
20123 Milano. T. (02) 8054071.   *080662*
Casoli, Via P. Lambertenghi 3, 20159 Milano.
T. (02) 6880353, 6880355, Fax (02) 6880353.   *080663*
Casoli, Corso Monforte 23, 20122 Milano.
T. (02) 76 02 32 38.   *080664*
Cavallini e Maria Cilena, Piero, Via Ariberto 17, 20123
Milano. T. (02) 832 35 21, Fax (02) 8323521.   *080665*
Cavellini, Piero, Via Brera 30, 20121 Milano.
T. (02) 806098.   *080666*
La Caverna di Ali' Baba di Maronnat Chantal, 3 Via Bon-
vesin de la Riva, 20129 Milano.
T. (02) 70108346.   *080667*
Celestini, Via S. Andrea 11, 20121 Milano.
T. (02) 70 90 09. - Paint -   *080668*
Centenari, Via Emanuele 92, Milano.
T. (02) 874608.   *080669*
Centro Arte Mige, 8 Via Maloja, 20158 Milano.
T. (02) 6888407.   *080670*
Centro D'Arte e Cultura la Pleiade, 5 Via Tulipani, 20146
Milano. T. (02) 4154931.   *080671*
Centro D'Arte il Biscione, 45 Via Pianell, 20125 Milano.
T. (02) 6428520.   *080672*
Centro D'Arte Mercurio, 21 Viale Bianca Maria, 20122
Milano. T. (02) 780119.   *080673*
Centro Domus Arte, 2 Via Pisoni, 20121 Milano.
T. (02) 6592768, 6598227.   *080674*
Centro Steccata 2, Via P. Maroncelli 10, 20154 Milano.
T. (02) 29 00 61 74, Fax (02) 29006174.   *080675*
Centro Tilbaldi, 15 Via Teulie', 20136 Milano.
T. (02) 58316480.   *080676*
Chisel, Via Senato 24, 20121 Milano. T. (02) 78 15 08,
Fax (02) 76009061. Paint -   *080677*
Ciovasso, Via Ciovasso 4, 20121 Milano.
T. (02) 87 09 51.   *080678*

City Art – International, 57 Via Boncompagni, 20139 Mi-
lano. T. (02) 57403870, 57403701.   *080679*
Colanzi D., 1 Via Orso, 20121 Milano.
T. (02) 877231.   *080680*
Colombari, Via solferino 37, 20121 Milano.
T. (02) 29 00 11 89, Fax (02) 29001375.   *080681*
Colombari Galleria di Colombari R. e P., 37 Via Solferino,
20121 Milano. T. (02) 29001189.   *080682*
Colombari Galleria di Colombari R. & P., 37 Via Solferino,
20121 Milano. T. (02) 29001375.   *080683*
Colorenero di Floriana de, Stefani e C., 6 Viale Caldara,
20122 Milano. T. (02) 5512001.   *080684*
Compagnia dei Fotografi di Scurria, Mario & C., 8 Via
Slataper, 20125 Milano. T. (02) 69001354.   *080685*
Compagnia del Disegno, Via del Carmine 11, 20121 Mi-
lano. T. (02) 86 46 35 10, Fax (02) 8053374.   *080686*
Compagnia del Disegno di, Alain Toubas & C., 11 Via
Carmine, 20121 Milano. T. (02) 8053374,
86463510.   *080687*
Consilvio G., 37 Ripa Piazetta Ticinese, 20143 Milano.
T. (02) 8360288.   *080688*
Consulart, 14 Via Cerva, 20122 Milano.
T. (02) 76005632.   *080689*
Consulenza d'Arte, Via Passione 7, 20122 Milano.
T. (02) 76 00 07 74, Fax (02) 76000813.   *080690*
Contatto Europa, Via Fiori Chiari 2-4, 20121 Milano.
T. (02) 805 23 39, Fax (02) 8052339.   *080691*
Cortina, Via Turati 3, 20121 Milano. T. (02) 29 00 28 08,
Fax (02) 29002808.   *080692*
Cortina Art, Piazza Cavour 1, 20121 Milano.
T. (02) 667703. - Paint -   *080693*
Cotugno M., 19 Via Varesina, 20156 Milano.
T. (02) 324249.   *080694*
Damy, Ken, Via Brera 30, 20121 Milano. T. (02) 80 60 98.
- Pho -   *080695*
Daverio, Philippe, Via Montenepoleone 6A, 20121 Mila-
no. T. (02) 76001748, Fax (02) 76021507. - Paint /
Sculp -   *080696*
De Carlo, Massimo, Via Bocconi 7, 20136 Milano.
T. (02) 58 31 61 40, Fax (02) 58316356.   *080697*
De Simone M., 60 Forobuanaparte, 20121 Milano.
T. (02) 86462202.   *080698*
De Simone M., 60 Foro Buonaparte, 20121 Milano.
T. (02) 874141.   *080699*
Del Barcon, 54 Alz. Nav. Grande, 20144 Milano.
T. (02) 89409992.   *080700*
Del Naviglio, 45 Via Manzoni, 20121 Milano.
T. (02) 6551538, 6552371.   *080701*
Dell'Ariete, 5 Via S. Andrea, 20121 Milano.
T. (02) 76003944.   *080702*
Dell'Incisione, 33 Via Spiga, 76000766, 76005993
Milano.   *080703*
Delle Ore, 18 Via Fibri Chiari, 20121 Milano.
T. (02) 8693333.   *080704*
Di Pettinaroli, Raimondi, Corso Venezia 6, 20121 Milano.
T. (02) 702412.   *080705*
Di Pietro A., 135a Via Primaticcio, 20147 Milano.
T. (02) 48302935.   *080706*
Diagramma, Via Pontacclo 12A, 20121 Milano.
T. (02) 87 42 37. - Paint -   *080707*

Diecidue Arte, Via Bramante 39, 20154 Milano.
T. (02) 8393041, Fax (02) 8358167.   *080708*
Dilmos, Piazza San Marco 1, 20121 Milano.
T. (02) 29 00 24 37, Fax (02) 29002350.   *080709*
Il Discanto, 7 Via Turati, 20121 Milano.
T. (02) 29003557.   *080710*
Il Discanto di Consciani, Luciano, 7 Via Settala, 20124
Milano. T. (02) 29403142.   *080711*
Donzelli A., 18/12 pl. Farina, 20125 Milano.
T. (02) 6880888.   *080712*
Dradi G., 12 Corso Plebisciti, 20129 Milano.
T. (02) 740686.   *080713*
Edizioni del Cappello, 9 Via Losanna, 20154 Milano.
T. (02) 315323, 3450598.   *080714*
Edizioni dello Scarabeo di Munafo' R. – Romeo A.M. &
C., 3 Via Vettabbia, 20122 Milano.
T. (02) 58310093.   *080715*
Eidac, Via Ronchi 39, 20134 Milano.
T. (02) 2159895.   *080716*
Elleti, 14 Via Finocchiaro Aprile, 20124 Milano.
T. (02) 6554440.   *080717*
Ennesse Studio, Corso di Porta Ticinese 65, 20123 Mila-
no. T. (02) 837 48 24.   *080718*
EOS, Via E. Tazzoli 11, 20154 Milano. T. (02) 29 00 0 41,
Fax (02) 6590688.   *080719*
Erha, Via Segantini 71, 20143 Milano.
T. (02) 58 10 36 32, Fax (02) 58103651.   *080720*
Esposti Annibale, Via Mincio 18, 20139 Milano.
T. (02) 5391024.   *080721*
Ethnoarte di Comensoli, Maria Ros e Rossi Gianfranco, 4
Via Marsaia, 20121 Milano. T. (02) 6598466.   *080722*
Eunomia Galleria D'Arte, 2a Via Bossi, 20121 Milano.
T. (02) 8056292.   *080723*
Eustachi, 33 Via Eustachi, 20129 Milano.
T. (02) 29512395.   *080724*
Fac-simile, Via Morigi 8, 20123 Milano. T. (02) 8056504,
Fax (02) 8055158.   *080725*
Farsetti Arte, Portichetto di Via Manzoni, 20121 Milano.
T. (02) 79 42 74.   *080726*
Ferrari, Gian, Via Gesù 19, 20121 Milano.
T. (02) 76005250, Fax (02) 781555. - Paint -   *080727*
Ferrari, Gian, Via Breda 30, 20121 Milano.
T. (02) 86461690, Fax (02) 801019. - Paint -   *080728*
Ferrari M., 8 Via Anfossi, 20135 Milano.
T. (02) 59902295.   *080729*
Filippin, Via Statuto 21, 20121 Milano.
T. (02) 29 00 45 07, Fax (02) 6554946.   *080730*
Filippin L., 21 Via Statuto, 20121 Milano.
T. (02) 29004507, 6554946.   *080731*
Fonte d'Abisso Arte, Via del Carmine 7, 20121 Milano.
T. (02) 86 46 44 07, Fax (02) 860313.   *080732*
Franco Semenzato, 7 Corso Matteotti, 20121 Milano.
T. (02) 76014502.   *080733*
Galleria Arcadia Nuova, Via S. Carpeforo 3/3, 20121 Mi-
lano. T. (02) 86461000.   *080734*
Galleria Baguttino, Via Bagutta 24, 20121 Milano.
T. (02) 70 26 09. - Paint -   *080735*
Galleria Bixio 2, Via N. Bixio 2, 20129 Milano.
T. (02) 29 51 66 38, Fax (02) 221970.   *080736*
Galleria del Barcon, Alzaia Naviglio Grande 54, 20144
Milano. T. (02) 839 99 92. - Paint -   *080737*
Galleria dell'Incisione, Via della Spiga 33, 20121 Milano.
T. (02) 70 59 93. - Paint / Graph / Sculp -   *080738*
Galleria delle Ore, Via Fiori Chiari 18, 20121 Milano.
T. (02) 869 33 33. - Paint / Graph / Sculp -   *080739*
La Galleria di, Patrizia Pisani & C., 24 Via S. Marco,
20121 Milano. T. (02) 29000290.   *080740*
Galleria di Porta Ticinese, Corso di Porta Ticinese 87,
20123 Milano. T. (02) 839 43 74.   *080741*
Galleria Salamon, Via S. Damiano 2, 20122 Milano.
T. (02) 76013142, 76022230,
Fax (02) 76004938.   *080742*
Galleria Strasburgo 2, Strasburgo 2, 20122 Milano.
T. (02) 79 66 21.   *080743*
Gallerie Via Borromei, 12 Piazza Borromeo, 20123 Mila-
no. T. (02) 8900980.   *080744*
Gallery House di, Olivieri Simona, 51 Via Moscova,
20121 Milano. T. (02) 29004955.   *080745*
Gallery Night, Foro Buonaparte 60, 20121 Milano.
T. (02) 7200 3342, Fax (02) 76014598.   *080746*
Gariboldi, Enrico, Largo Richini 4, 20122 Milano.
T. (02) 58304384, Fax (02) 220751.   *080747*

Gastaldelli, Piazza Castello 22, 20121 Milano.
T. (02) 863867, Fax (02) 863867. - Paint -   *080748*

Gavioli, Via Durini 1, 20122 Milano. T. (02) 76000024.
- Paint -   *080749*

Geri, Via Bagutta 13, 20121 Milano.
T. (02) 76000785.   *080750*

Gianferrari Arte Contemporanea, 30 Via Brera, 20121
Milano. T. (02) 86461690, 801019.   *080751*

Gierre, 2 Via Fusaro, 20146 Milano.
T. (02) 4691812.   *080752*

Gilli R., 17 Via Gesu, 20121 Milano.
T. (02) 794087.   *080753*

Ginevra Cadre D'Art, 8 Via Caronti, 20133 Milano.
T. (02) 7384671.   *080754*

Giorgi, Alberto, Viale Abruzzi 67, 20131 Milano.
T. (02) 29 51 83 60, Fax (02) 2049897.   *080755*

Grafica Azeta di, Michela Levi e C., 106/1 Via Cilea,
20151 Milano. T. (02) 3536554.   *080756*

Grafica Uno – Upiglio G., Via Marco Bruto 24, 20138 Milano. T. (02) 715339.   *080757*

Grafiche Tassotti di, Giorgio Tassotii & Figli, 3 pl. de
Agostini, 20146 Milano. T. (02) 472141.   *080758*

Greve, Karsten, Via S. Spirito 13, 20121 Milano.
T. (02) 783840, Fax 783866.   *080759*

Grisanti, Ezio, Viale Certosa 153, 20151 Milano.
T. (02) 308 74 87.   *080760*

Grossetti, Carlo, Via Pisoni 2, 20123 Milano.
T. (02) 653393.   *080761*

Guaitamacchi J., 43 Ripa Piazzetta Ticinese, 20143 Milano. T. (02) 89405877.   *080762*

Guenzani, Claudio, Via Eustachi 10, 20129 Milano.
T. (02) 29 40 92 51, Fax (02) 29408080.   *080763*

Hoesch R., 8 Viale Argonne, 20133 Milano.
T. (02) 715451.   *080764*

Idea Books, Via Vigevano 41, 20144 Milano.
T. (02) 8373949, 8360395, 8390284,
Fax (02) 8357776.   *080765*

Il Cannocchiale, Via Brera 4, 20121 Milano.
T. (02) 86 75 18. - Paint -   *080766*

Il Castello, Via Brera 16, 20121 Milano. T. (02) 862913,
877962. - Paint -   *080767*

Il Mercante, Via Brera 29, 20121 Milano.
T. (02) 879148.   *080768*

Immagine, 53 Corso Piazzetta Ticinese, 20143 Milano.
T. (02) 58102270.   *080769*

Immobiliare il Forte di Boldrini, Elena & C., 40 gall. Manzoni, 20121 Milano. T. (02) 795928.   *080770*

Inga-Pin, Luciano, Via Pontaccio 12A, 20121 Milano.
T. (02) 874237, Fax (02) 874237.   *080771*

Inghilleri F., 7 Via Marco de Marchi, 20121 Milano.
T. (02) 6555399.   *080772*

Isola di Milano, Via Volturno 35, 20124 Milano.
T. (02) 60 68 15. - Paint -   *080773*

Istituto Grafico' Italiano, 21 Via Menotti, 20129 Milano.
T. (02) 29530058.   *080774*

Istituto Seledi Promozione Arte Contemporanea, 27 Via
Comelico, 20135 Milano. T. (02) 55188151.   *080775*

Jannone, Antonia, Corso Garibaldi 125, 20121 Milano.
T. (02) 29 00 29 30, Fax (02) 29400447.   *080776*

Japanese Works of Art, 21 Via M.te Napoleone, 20121
Milano. T. (02) 794115, 794869.   *080777*

L'Affiche, 6 Via Unione, 20122 Milano.
T. (02) 804978.   *080778*

L'Affiche di A. Mei Gentilicci e C., 11 Via Nirone, 20123
Milano. T. (02) 862866.   *080779*

L'Affiche Due, Via Unione 6, 20122 Milano.
T. (02) 804978.   *080780*

L'Agrifoglio, Via Montenapoleone 21, 20121 Milano.
T. (02) 70 90 66. - Paint -   *080781*

L'Agrifoglio di Montuoro, Isabella, 12 Via Fiori Chiari,
20121 Milano. T. (02) 72001519.   *080782*

L'Ambrosiana Galleria D'Arte, 1 Via Cardinale Federico,
20123 Milano. T. (02) 804209.   *080783*

L'Eroica, Via S. Simpliciano 5, 20121 Milano.
T. (02) 86460141, Fax (02) 8690598.   *080784*

L'Oro di Noma, Corso di Porta Ticinese 76, 20123 Milano. T. (02) 837 96 83, Fax (02) 6572901.   *080785*

La Nave, Via C.M. Maggi 6, 20154 Milano.
T. (02) 349 04 59.   *080786*

La Nuova Sfera, Via S. Marco 16, 20121 Milano.
T. (02) 6595209. - Paint -   *080787*

La Torre, Via Fatebenefratelli 13, 20121 Milano.
T. (02) 6575669, Fax (02) 655669.   *080788*

Laminage Ribot di Margarethe Bacher & C., 12 Via Ta-
naro, 20128 Milano. T. (02) 27203054.   *080789*

Lattuada, Via Annunciata 31, 20121 Milano.
T. (02) 29 00 00 71, Fax (02) 8050137.   *080790*

Lazzardo di Corsi, Adriano, 40 Via Cenisio, 20154 Milano. T. (02) 33604514.   *080791*

Le Arcate, Via Manzoni 41, 20121 Milano.   *080792*

Le Case d'Arte, Viale Col di Lana 14, 20136 Milano.
T. (02) 89400628, 58103402,
Fax (02) 8370407.   *080793*

Linati Stampatore in Milano, 8 Via Copernico, 20125 Milano. T. (02) 6886010.   *080794*

Lorenzelli Arte, Via S. Andrea 19, 20121 Milano.
T. (02) 783035, Fax (02) 76005692.   *080795*

Lucia A.C., 57 Ripa Piazetta Ticinese, 20143 Milano.
T. (02) 89400121.   *080796*

M'Arte, 3 Via Poerio, 20129 Milano.
T. (02) 794034.   *080797*

M'arte, Via Carlo Poerio 3, 20129 Milano.
T. (02) 794034, Fax (02) 48196171.   *080798*

Macor di Corti, Giuseppe & C., 14 Via de Marchi Gherini,
20128 Milano. T. (02) 2563039.   *080799*

Maestri Incisori, Piazza S. Erasmo 3, 20121 Milano.
T. (02) 6886010.   *080800*

Il Magnifico, 2 Via Baracchini, 20124 Milano.
T. (02) 72002797.   *080801*

Mainetti, U., Galleria Unione 3, 20122 Milano.
T. (02) 86 27 97. - Paint -   *080802*

Il Mappamondo, 2 Via Borgonuovo, 20121 Milano.
T. (02) 29002435.   *080803*

Marconi, Giò, Via Tadino 15, 20124 Milano.
T. (02) 29 40 43 73, Fax (02) 29405573.   *080804*

Marin, Luciano, Via Alserio 13, 20159 Milano.
T. (02) 66 80 32 21.   *080805*

Mark Print, 78 Viale Sarca, 20125 Milano.
T. (02) 66100250.   *080806*

Master Fine Art, Via Manzoni 43, 20121 Milano.
T. (02) 655 17 61.   *080807*

Master International Art, 43 Via Manzoni, 20121 Milano.
T. (02) 6555833, 6571805, 6572617.   *080808*

Master International Art, 43 Via Manzoni, 20121 Milano.
T. (02) 6551761, 6551762, 654889, 654921.   *080809*

Master International Art, 31 Via Manzoni, 20121 Milano.
T. (02) 6555499.   *080810*

Matelli Arti Grafiche, 34 Via Spartaco, 20135 Milano.
T. (02) 55195770.   *080811*

Mazzoleni Arte, Via Morone 6, 20121 Milano.
T. (02) 79 50 26, Fax (02) 76002650. - Sculp / Eth /
Cur -   *080812*

Medea, Foro Bonaparte 68, 20121 Milano.
T. (02) 879402. - Paint -   *080813*

Mediarte Invest, 8 Via Cadamosto, 20129 Milano.
T. (02) 29405005.   *080814*

Menotti, 26 Via Menotti, 20129 Milano.
T. (02) 29400447.   *080815*

Mercante di Stampe, 29 Corso Venezia, 20121 Milano.
T. (02) 76004402.   *080816*

Mercato del Sale, Via Orti 16, 20122 Milano.
T. (02) 551 12 50, Fax (02) 5511250.   *080817*

Meretti G., 31 Corso Vercelli, 20144 Milano.
T. (02) 48007523, 4697363, 4987363.   *080818*

Messina F., 34 Via M.A. Colonna, 20149 Milano.
T. (02) 39210290.   *080819*

Milano, 13 Via Manin, 20121 Milano.
T. (02) 29000352.   *080820*

Milano, Via Manin 13, 20121 Milano. T. (02) 29000352,
Fax (02) 29003523. - Paint / Graph / Glass /
Pho -   *080821*

Milenium, Via Marsala 11, 20121 Milano.
T. (02) 65 42 29, Fax 655 48 41. - Ant / Graph / Repr /
Sculp / Draw -   *080822*

Miniature Artistiche Marinella, 6 Viale Aretusa, 20148
Milano. T. (02) 40090911.   *080823*

Moderna Seno di Paolo Seno & C., 11 Via Ciovasso,
20121 Milano. T. (02) 72004503.   *080824*

Modigliani Artistica Culturale, 11 Via M. Bianchi, 20149
Milano. T. (02) 4694493.   *080825*

Molino delle Armi, 27 Via Crocefisso, 20122 Milano.
T. (02) 58312768, 58308433.   *080826*

Molino delle Armi, 27 Via Crocefisso, 20122 Milano.
T. (02) 58313503.   *080827*

Mondial Art, 11 Via Sibari, 20141 Milano.
T. (02) 5391715, 5392454, 57401910.   *080828*

Montenapoleone, Via Montenapoleone 6a, 20121 Milano. T. (02) 79 95 93. - Paint -   *080829*

Morone, 6 Via Morone, 20121 Milano.
T. (02) 76003994.   *080830*

Morone 6, Via Morone 6, 20121 Milano.
T. (02) 76 00 39 94, Fax (02) 76003994.   *080831*

Morone 6, Via Morone 6, 20121 Milano.
T. (02) 799591.   *080832*

Motta T., 3 Via Caposile, 20137 Milano.
T. (02) 5513585.   *080833*

Mucchi & Petrus, 8 Via Garigliano, 20159 Milano.
T. (02) 6887559.   *080834*

Mu.Di.Ma., Via Tadino 26, 20124 Milano.
T. (02) 29 40 96 33, Fax (02) 29401455.   *080835*

Multipla Edizioni D'Arte di Paolo Cocorocchia, 59 Via
Marcchi, 20124 Milano. T. (02) 6701523.   *080836*

Murnik, Via Giulianova 1, 20123 Milano. T. (02) 80 60 30,
Fax (02) 878392.   *080837*

Museum, 20 Via Noccolini, 20154 Milano.
T. (02) 33600558.   *080838*

My Art, 8 Via Festa Perdono, 20122 Milano.
T. (02) 58316295.   *080839*

Naviglio, Via Manzoni 45, 20121 Milano.
T. (02) 655 15 38, Fax (02) 6552371. - Paint / Graph /
Sculp -   *080840*

Nicholls P., 41 Via Manzoni, 20121 Milano.
T. (02) 6575874.   *080841*

Nuages Grafica, Via S. Spirito 5, 20121 Milano.
T. (02) 76014437, Fax (02) 76014437.   *080842*

Nuova Arte, 70 Foro Buonaparte, 20121 Milano.
T. (02) 72022839, 89010577, 89010631.   *080843*

Nuova Artelite, 5 Via Fontana, 20122 Milano.
T. (02) 5457991.   *080844*

Nuova Cadario, Via Annunciata 7, 20121 Milano.
T. (02) 662 558.   *080845*

Nuova Sooquadro di Savi, Pieralberto, 13 Via V. Colonna,
20149 Milano. T. (02) 48003995.   *080846*

Nuovo-Aleph, Corso Garibaldi 95, 20121 Milano.
T. (02) 655 21 00.   *080847*

Nuovo Sagittario, Via Monte di Pietà 1, 20121 Milano.
T. (02) 86 46 08 74, Fax (02) 4585557.   *080848*

Nus di M.R., Andreani e P. Rizzi, 5 Via Carmagnola,
20159 Milano. T. (02) 66802294.   *080849*

Old Britannia, Piazza Biancamano 2, 20121 Milano.
T. (02) 66 26 67. - Paint -   *080850*

Olivieri G., 1 Piazza Mirabello, 20121 Milano.
T. (02) 29005930.   *080851*

Pace, Piazza S. Marco 1, 20121 Milano.
T. (02) 659 01 47, Fax (02) 6592307.   *080852*

Pace di Gimmi, Stefanini, 1 Piazza S. Marco, 20121 Milano. T. (02) 6590147.   *080853*

Palazzoli, Luca, Via S. Primo 4, 20121 Milano.
T. (02) 78 23 98.   *080854*

Palmisano, Via Volta 20, 20121 Milano.
T. (02) 655 44 89, Fax (02) 6554857.   *080855*

Parrella L.A., 24 Viale Vittorio Veneto, 20124 Milano.
T. (02) 6572246.   *080856*

Patelli, Nicola, Via Perugino 8, 20135 Milano.
T. (02) 546 10 20.   *080857*

Patrizia, Via Giuseppe Pozzone 5, 20121 Milano.
T. (02) 87 87 06.   *080858*

Pero, Via Visconti di Modrone 40, 20122 Milano.
T. (02) 794 580.   *080859*

Pilat, Bianca, Via P. Custodi 4, 20136 Milano.
T. (02) 89 40 12 50, Fax (02) 8373204. - Paint -   *080860*

Le Pleiadi, 10 Via Bossi, 20121 Milano.
T. (02) 72022723, 72022734.   *080861*

Plinius, via Plinio 39, 20129 Milano.
T. (02) 20 94 47.   *080862*

Plura, Via Salvini 1, 20122 Milano.
T. (02) 70 12 87.   *080863*

Plura Edizioni di Arioli, Roberto, 59 Via Paruta, 20127
Milano. T. (02) 26300291.   *080864*

Il Ponte Casa D'Aste, 12 Via Pontaccio, 20121 Milano.
T. (02) 72003749.   *080865*

Il Ponte di Alibrandi, Vincenzo, 3 Corso S. Gottardo,
20136 Milano. T. (02) 8379370, 8322296.   *080866*

Ponte Rosso, 2 Via Brera, 20121 Milano.
T. (02) 86461053.   *080867*

Progetto Volpini, Via Palermo 1, 20121 Milano.
T. (02) 875063, Fax (02) 55193390.   *080868*

Rabuffetti S., 2 Via Spiga, 20121 Milano.
T. (02) 76005901, 76008265, 76022447.   *080869*

Ravagli M.L., 14 Via Cavallotti, 20122 Milano. T. (02) 784491. 080870
Ravagli R., 3 Via Osti, 20122 Milano. T. (02) 58307458. 080871
Reggiani, Via S. Gregorio 27, 20124 Milano. T. (02) 29531990, Fax (02) 29406531. 080872
Reggio A., 51 Via Meda, 20141 Milano. T. (02) 8464921. 080873
Revival, 52 Foro Buonaparte, 20121 Milano. T. (02) 877724. 080874
La Rinascente, Via Durini 24, 20122 Milano. - Paint / Graph - 080875
Riviere J., 7 Via Fiori Chiari, 20121 Milano. T. (02) 86461751. 080876
Rizzardi, Via Solferino 56, 20121 Milano. T. (02) 657 05 63, Fax (02) 6570563. - Paint - 080877
Ruggerini & Zonca, Via Ciovasso 4, 20121 Milano. T. (02) 72 00 33 77, Fax (02) 72003369. 080878
Sacerdoti, Edmondo, Via S. Andrea 17, 20121 Milano. T. (02) 79 51 51. - Paint - 080879
Saffioti L., 28 Corso Genova, 20123 Milano. T. (02) 89409310. 080880
Sala C., 25 Via Solferino, 20121 Milano. T. (02) 653418. 080881
San Barnaba di del Sole, Patrizia, 39 Via S. Barnaba, 20122 Milano. T. (02) 5459385. 080882
San Carlo, Via Manzoni 46, 20121 Milano. T. (02) 794218, 795490, Fax (02) 783578. 080883
San Fedele, Piazza S. Fedele, 20121 Milano. T. (02) 80 44 41. - Paint / Graph / Sculp - 080884
Sant'Erasmo, Via S. Paolo 13, 20121 Milano. T. (02) 877069, 876426, Fax (02) 72002334. 080885
Schmidlin, Via Molino delle Armi 31, 20123 Milano. T. (02) 89 40 16 87. 080886
Schubert, Alberto, Via Monte Napoleone, 20121 Milano. T. (02) 76001626. - Paint / Graph / Sculp - 080887
Schubert Galleria, 13 Via Bagutta, 20121 Milano. T. (02) 798251. 080888
Scotti, Michaele, Via Molino delle Armi 15, 20123 Milano. T. (02) 58 31 42 93, Fax (02) 58314293. 080889
Sei del Carmine 6, Piazza del Carmine 6, 20121 Milano. T. (02) 87 98 66, Fax (02) 867614. 080890
Selene di Ciuffani, Constanzo, 5 Via Tadino, 20124 Milano. T. (02) 29526385. 080891
Semenzato, Franco, 25 Via Sant Eufemia, 20122 Milano. T. (02) 809191, 809192. 080892
Senato, 45 Via Senato, 20121 Milano. T. (02) 76008976. 080893
Senato, Via Senato 45, 20121 Milano. T. (02) 70 89 76. 080894
Senen Arts, 11 Via Fiori Oscuri, 20121 Milano. T. (02) 864491. 080895
Seno, Paolo, Via Ciovasso 11, 20121 Milano. T. (02) 86463908, 8692868, Fax (02) 72004503. - Paint / Graph / Sculp - 080896
Serena Fine Art, 15 Via Cappuccio, 20123 Milano. T. (02) 877135. 080897
Seven Arts, 11 Via Fiori Oscuri, 20121 Milano. T. (02) 865265, 8052250. 080898
Shop Art, Viale Affori 19, 20161 Milano. Fax (02) 645095. 080899
Sianesi, Via Durini 25, 20122 Milano. T. (02) 76000989. - Paint / Graph / Sculp - 080900
Sigma Arte, 4 lg. Richini, 20122 Milano. T. (02) 58304384. 080901
Sigma Arte, 31 Via Lomellina, 20133 Milano. T. (02) 719053. 080902
Silbernagl Montenapoleone, 4 Via Borgospesso, 20121 Milano. T. (02) 781792, 76014944. 080903
Sitbon, Martine, Corso di Porta Vigentina 6, 20122 Milano. T. (02) 58301145, Fax (02) 58300460. 080904
Soldano A., 81a Via A. Sforza, 20141 Milano. T. (02) 89512274, 89512281. 080905
Soletti, Bruna, Piazza Sant'Alessandro 6, 20123 Milano. T. (02) 860 789. 080906
Solo Arte di Pintor, Antonietta, 18 Corso S. Gottardo, 20136 Milano. T. (02) 58105377. 080907
La Spatola, 16 Via Gianferrari, 20159 Milano. T. (02) 6880006. 080908
Spazio Immagine, Via S. Damiano 4, 20122 Milano. T. (02) 76023058, Fax (02) 76014684. 080909
Spazio Temporaneo, Via Solferino 56, 20121 Milano. T. (02) 659 80 56. 080910
Spazio 92, Via Vela 8, 20133 Milano. T. (02) 29 40 92 84. 080911
La Spirale, 1 Via Marradi, 20123 Milano. T. (02) 8693279. 080912
La Spirale Edizioni D'Arte, 16 Via S. Agnese, 20123 Milano. T. (02) 8056685. 080913
Square Gallery, Piazza della Libertà 8, 20121 Milano. T. (02) 79 82 68. 080914
Stamperia D'Arte di Losio G., Via S. Pellico 25, 20121 Milano. T. (02) 33501618. 080915
Stanza del Borgo, Via G. Puccini 5, 20121 Milano. T. (02) 870544. - Paint / Graph / Sculp / Fra / Draw - 080916
Steffanoni, Via Monti 32 /A Saffi, 20123 Milano. T. (02) 43 21 70. 080917
Stein, Christian, Via Lazzaretto 15, 20124 Milano. T. (02) 670 47 54, Fax (02) 6696637. - Paint - 080918
Stein, Christian, 1 Via Amedei, 20123 Milano. T. (02) 8900867. 080919
Stein, Christian, 15 Via Lazzaretto, 20124 Milano. T. (02) 66982444. 080920
Stein, Christian, 15 Via Lazzaretto, 20124 Milano. T. (02) 6696637, 6704754. 080921
Studio A, Via Nirone 11, 20123 Milano. T. (02) 80 73 80. 080922
Studio Clive Foster, Via De Togni 29, 20123 Milano. T. (02) 877014. 080923
Studio Copernico, 10 Via Copernico, 20125 Milano. T. (02) 6887563, 69000490. 080924
Studio d'Ars, Via S. Agnese 12, 20123 Milano. T. (02) 80 79 57. - Paint - 080925
Studio D'Arte Grafica, 11 Via Marsala, 20121 Milano. T. (02) 6572810. 080926
Studio D'Arte Sintesi, 11 Via Goldoni, 20129 Milano. T. (02) 798899. 080927
Studio d'arte 111, Via Gesù 7, 20121 Milano. T. (02) 76004596. 080928
Studio Maddalena Carioni, Viale Cassiodoro 16, 20145 Milano. T. (02) 46 28 24. - Paint - 080929
Studio Marconi, Via Tadino 15, 20124 Milano. T. (02) 225543, Fax (02) 202655. 080930
Studio Oggetto, Ford Buonaparte 60, 20121 Milano. T. (02) 874141, Fax (02) 72023534. 080931
Studio Panigati, Via della Signora 5, 20155 Milano. T. (02) 70 42 84. 080932
Studio Pianon, 23 Corso Monforte, 20122 Milano. T. (02) 794695. 080933
Studio Sant'Andrea, Via Sant'Andrea 21, 20121 Milano. T. (02) 78 16 34. 080934
Studio Soldano Nino, Corso di Porta Ticinese 65, 20123 Milano. T. (02) 837 48 24. - Paint / Sculp - 080935
Studio Venticinque, Via Vigevano 25, 20144 Milano. T. (02) 58 10 98 82, Fax (02) 58312782. 080936
Sugarte, 48 Corso Magenta, 20123 Milano. T. (02) 48008895. 080937
Swart, Via Montegrappa, 20124 Milano. T. (02) 668 42 48. 080938
Swart Gallery – Duemondi, 1 Via Rosales, 20124 Milano. T. (02) 6599272. 080939
Le Tamerici, 13 Via Prati, 20145 Milano. T. (02) 312077, 33600318, 33600319. 080940
Tavaglione G., 27 Via Ausonio, 20123 Milano. T. (02) 8361227. 080941
Taverna C., 5 Via Santo Spirito, 20121 Milano. T. (02) 781847. 080942
La Tavolozza, 22 Via Grazioli, 20161 Milano. T. (02) 6459401. 080943
Tega, Via Senato 24, 20121 Milano. T. (02) 76006473, Fax (02) 799707. - Paint - 080944
Tega di Tega, Giulio & C., 24 Via Senato, 20121 Milano. T. (02) 799707. 080945
Tesio Gallery, 4 Via Schiaparelli, 20125 Milano. T. (02) 6080145, 6887164. 080946
Il Timpano, 1 Via Visconti di Modrone, 20122 Milano. T. (02) 76000908. 080947
Toninelli, Via S. Andrea 8, 20121 Milano. T. (02) 79 23 69. - Paint / Graph / Sculp - 080948
Top Art, Via San Marco, 20121 Milano. T. (02) 5473551, Fax (02) 55302215. 080949
Top Graphic, Via G. Modena 15, 20129 Milano. T. (02) 204 62 56. 080950
Torchio di Porta Romana, 17 Via Altaguardia, 20135 Milano. T. (02) 58306889. 080951
Torcular, 37 Via Bixio, 20129 Milano. T. (02) 29405741. 080952
Toselli, Via del Carmine 9, 20121 Milano. T. (02) 8050434, Fax (02) 72022717. 080953
Transart, Via Sacchi 3, 20121 Milano. T. (02) 89 99 50. - Paint / Graph / Sculp - 080954
Transepoca, Via Col di Lana 12, 20136 Milano. T. (02) 89 40 95 04, Fax (02) 89409504. 080955
Treves di Colonna, Carletto, 1 Via Palermo, 20121 Milano. T. (02) 870694. 080956
Trimarchi, Via Cappuccio 21, 20123 Milano. T. (02) 890 06 52, Fax (02) 89010435. 080957
Turati Arte, 6 Via Turati, 20121 Milano. T. (02) 29006192, 29006205. 080958
Turchetto/Plurima, Via Mercadante 3, 20124 Milano. T. (02) 669 74 44. 080959
Tuttobello A., 2 Via Correnti, 20123 Milano. T. (02) 86454282. 080960
Untitled e Artra, Via Conchetta 20, 20136 Milano. T. (02) 8376489. 080961
Valsecchi, Massimo, Via S. Marta 11, 20123 Milano. T. (02) 86 45 25 32. 080962
Veder, Via Cirillo 10, 20145 Milano. T. (02) 349 01 70. 080963
Velasquez, Via Pisanello 1, 20146 Milano. T. (02) 45 42 03. 080964
Verlato, Via Tazzoli 11, 20154 Milano. T. (02) 29 00 00 41, Fax (02) 6590688. 080965
Il Vertice, Via Visconti di Modrone 29, 20122 Milano. T. (02) 70 86 13. 080966
Viafarini, Via Farini 35, 20159 Milano. T. (02) 69001524, Fax (02) 66804473. 080967
Vinciana, 13 Via Maroncelli, 20154 Milano. T. (02) 29001116. 080968
Viola R., 2 gall. Strasburgo, 20122 Milano. T. (02) 796621. 080969
Vismara Arte, Piazza S. Marco 1, 20121 Milano. T. (02) 29 00 03 67, Fax (02) 29000367. 080970
ZA.MA, 11 Via Traiano, 20149 Milano. T. (02) 39263350. 080971
Zecchillo Abbatangelo C., 9 Via Friuli, 20135 Milano. T. (02) 5450418, 55194510. 080972
Zuffellato Ugo, 14 Via Cenisio, 20154 Milano. T. (02) 33105407. 080973
2 RC, Via Marco de' Marchi 1, 20121 Milano. T. (02) 650 603. 080974
70 di Bitetti, Eugenio Michele, 27 Via Moscova, 20121 Milano. T. (02) 6597809. 080975

Modena

Artestudio, Via Castel Maraldo 5, 41100 Modena. T. (059) 21 41 61. - Paint / Graph / Sculp / Mul / Draw - 080976
Benassati, Via C. Battisti 60A, 41100 Modena. T. (059) 22 66 30. 080977
Fronte d'Abisso, Via Fonte d'Abisso 23, 41100 Modena. T. (059) 222050, Fax (059) 221717. 080978
Govi, Rua Frati Minori 14, 41100 Modena. T. (059) 21 75 41. - Paint - 080979
Palazzetto, Via Emilia Ovest 737, 41100 Modena. T. (059) 33 81 74. 080980
Sala Mostre Del Centro Studi L. A. Muratori, Via Castel Maraldo 19, 41100 Modena. T. (059) 21 41 61. - Paint / Graph / Sculp / Mul - 080981

Moncalieri (Torino)

Galleria d'Arte Cavour, Piazza Vittorio Emanuele 1, 10024 Moncalieri. T. (011) 640 81 57. 080982
Pezzato, L., Via S. Croce 20, 10024 Moncalieri. T. (011) 640 82 94. 080983

Montecatini Terme e Tettuccio (Pistoia)

Bottega d'Arte, Via F. d'Azeglio 12, 51016 Montecatini Terme e Tettuccio. T. (0572) 35 52. 080984
Flori, Via Verdi 2, 51016 Montecatini Terme e Tettuccio. T. (0572) 2318. 080985
Le Chiavi d'Oro, Viale Rosseli 2/c, 51016 Montecatini Terme e Tettuccio. T. (0572) 72645. - Paint / Fum / Jew / Silv / Instr - 080986

Monterotondo (Roma)

Grafica Campioli, Via V. Bellini 46, 00015 Monterotondo. T. (06) 900 04 56. 080987

Monza (Milano)

Agrati, Via Pesa del Lino, 20052 Monza. T. (039) 2 42 18.
- Paint - 080988

Napoli

Aben Stamperia di Febbraio Fabio, 2b Via de Marco,
80137 Napoli. T. (081) 5990031. 080989
Alabardieri Gallery di Minervini F. & C., 28 Via Alabardie-
ri, 80121 Napoli. T. (081) 402067. 080990
Amelio, Lucio, 58 Piazza Martiri, 80121 Napoli.
T. (081) 422023. 080991
Amelio, Lucio, Piazza dei Martiri 58, 80121 Napoli.
T. (081) 422023, Fax (081) 406486. - Paint / Sculp /
Pho / Mul / Draw - 080992
American Studies Center, Via Andrea d'Isernia 36,
80122 Napoli. T. (081) 30 75 62. - Paint - 080993
Annichini R., 248 Via Arenaccia, 80141 Napoli.
T. (081) 7513623. 080994
Antiquarte, 6 Via V. Colonna, 80121 Napoli.
T. (081) 422086. 080995
Arte Antica, Via Domenico Morelli V 6, 80121 Napoli.
T. (081) 418157. - Paint - 080996
Arte Antica, 9 Via Ferrigni, 80121 Napoli.
T. (081) 7646897. 080997
La Barcaccia, 10a Via V. Colonna, 80121 Napoli.
T. (081) 418471. 080998
Bowinkel E., 24 Piazza Martiri, 80121 Napoli.
T. (081) 7644344. 080999
Caiafa R., 54 Viale Poggio, 80131 Napoli.
T. (081) 7435994. 081000
Candela S., 29b Via d'Ambrosio, 80141 Napoli.
T. (081) 5990267. 081001
Centro Arte Contemporanea, 13 Via Alvino, 80127 Napo-
li. T. (081) 5565987. 081002
Centro Artistico Galleria dei Mille, 14 Vicolo Belledonne
Chiala, 80121 Napoli. T. (081) 407279. 081003
Il Cerchio – Quadri e Cornici, 131 Via Morghen, 80129
Napoli. T. (081) 5569645. 081004
Cilea, 239 Via Cilea, 80127 Napoli.
T. (081) 640541. 081005
D'Ambra R., 38c Viale Colli Aminei, 80131 Napoli.
T. (081) 7414650. 081006
D.E.S.CA., 10 Via Mianella, 80145 Napoli.
T. (081) 7548001. 081007
Ediarte, 129 Via S. Giac. dei Capri, 80131 Napoli.
T. (081) 7702828. 081008
Il Fante di Quadri, 33 Via Alvino, 80127 Napoli.
T. (081) 5563262. 081009
Firma D'Autore di Hay Walter, 331 Via Posillipo, 80123
Napoli. T. (081) 7690725. 081010
Framart Studio, 62 Via Nuova S. Rocco Pc. soleado,
80131 Napoli. T. (081) 7414321. 081011
Framart Studio, 62 Nuova S. Rocco (Pc. Soleado), 10131
Napoli. T. (081) 7414427. 081012
Galleria di S. Carlo, Via Chiatamone 57, 80121 Napoli.
Fax (081) 741917. - Paint - 081013
Ganzerli, Via Camillo de Nardis 24, 80127 Napoli.
T. (081) 649292. 081014
Giacometti L., 129 Via Ruoppolo, 80128 Napoli.
T. (081) 5797769. 081015
Giosi, Via Chiatamone 6A, 80121 Napoli.
T. (081) 7645074. - Paint - 081016
La Gravure, Via C. Poerio 86, 80121 Napoli.
T. (081) 764 26 30. - Graph - 081017
Grossi L., 7 Via C. de Cesare, 80125 Napoli.
T. (081) 425246. 081018
Il Centro, Via Carducci 28, 80121 Napoli.
T. (081) 411692. - Paint / Graph - 081019
Il Diagramma 32, Via F. Crispi 32, 80121 Napoli.
T. (081) 68 10 22. 081020
Il Triangolo, Viale Colli Aminei 381, 80131 Napoli.
T. (081) 430069. - Paint - 081021
L'Ariete di Rosario Todaro, 147b/c Via Manzoni, 80123
Napoli. T. (081) 644006. 081022
L'Opera, 16 Via Mille, 80121 Napoli.
T. (081) 400612. 081023
L'Ottocento, Via D. Morelli 28, 80121 Napoli.
T. (081) 7643521, Fax (081) 265970. 081024
L'Ottocento di Russo, Nocola e Luciano, 28 Via D. Mo-
relli, 80121 Napoli. T. (081) 7644496. 081025
Le Petit Price Ediz Arte, 7 Via D. Morelli, 80121 Napoli.
T. (081) 7647696, 7647697, 7647698. 081026

Le Petit Prince Ed Arte, 7 Via D. Morelli, 80121 Napoli.
T. (081) 2451348, 2451349, 2451350. 081027
Le Petit Prince Ed Arte, 15 Via D. Morelli, 80121 Napoli.
T. (081) 2451347. 081028
Lia Rumma, 12 Via Gaetani Vannella, 80121 Napoli.
T. (081) 7644213. 081029
Lo Spazio, Piazza Medaglie d'Oro 46, 80129 Napoli.
T. (081) 5784927. 081030
Manzo, Via V. Gaetani 2, 80121 Napoli. T. (081) 41 18 03.
- Paint - 081031
Manzoni L'Aquila, 8 Via G. de Bonis, 80123 Napoli.
T. (081) 5753520. 081032
Maresca, Alberto, Via S. Lucia 121, 80132 Napoli.
T. (081) 23 63 69. - Paint - 081033
Maresca Art Gallery, Via S. Lucia 121, Via Terracina 115,
80132 Napoli. T. (081) 2451017, 2301053,
Fax (081) 231055. 081034
Maresca Art Gallery, 115 Via Terrachina, 80125 Napoli.
T. (081) 2301055. 081035
Marusini, 107 Via Caserta al Bravo, 80144 Napoli.
T. (081) 7365274. 081036
Mazzini di Gallina, Giuseppe, 3 Piazza Mazzini, 80138
Napoli. T. (081) 5498991. 081037
Mediterranea, Via Carlo de Cesare 60, 80132 Napoli.
T. (081) 41 74 13, Fax (081) 416821. - Paint - 081038
Modigliani, 24 Vicolo Florentine Chiala, 80122 Napoli.
T. (081) 662205. 081039
Moresco Centro D'Arte Dante, 3/4/5 Via V. Bellini, 80135
Napoli. T. (081) 5499694. 081040
Morra G., 20 Via Calabritto, 80121 Napoli.
T. (081) 7643737. 081041
Nell'Incanto, 29 Via Cilea, 80127 Napoli.
T. (081) 5584417. 081042
Officine Grafiche del Sud, 25 Via Righi, 80125 Napoli.
T. (081) 5700861. 081043
Rea S., 9 Via Colombo, 80133 Napoli.
T. (081) 5511950. 081044
Rinaldini a., 4 Via B. Croce, 80134 Napoli.
T. (081) 5517036. 081045
Rumma, Lia, Via Vannella Gaetani 12, 80121 Napoli.
T. (081) 7643619, Fax (081) 7644213. 081046
Serio R., 14 Via Oberdan, 80134 Napoli.
T. (081) 5523193. 081047
Settembrini G., 86 Via C. Poerio, 80121 Napoli.
T. (081) 7642630. 081048
Sindaco N., 107 Via Caserta al Bravo, 80144 Napoli.
T. (081) 7386662. 081049
Studio Morra, Via Calabritto 20, 80121 Napoli.
T. (081) 40 20 25. 081050
Trisorio, Pasquale, Riviera di Chiaia 215, 80121 Napoli.
T. (081) 41 43 06, Fax (081) 412969. 081051
Vittoriana, 15 Via Caravita, 80134 Napoli.
T. (081) 5512804. 081052

Nichelino (Torino)

Passeretti, Via S.F. d'Assisi 5, 10042 Nichelino.
T. (011) 62 45 16. 081053

Noci (Bari)

Faro Arte, Piazza Garibaldi 29, 70015 Noci.
T. (080) 897 15 92. 081054

Noicattaro (Bari)

Lo Scrigno, Via Oberdan 6, 70016 Noicattaro.
T. (080) 66 31 81. 081055

Novara

Galleria gli Araldi, Via dei Caccia 5, 28100 Novara.
T. (0321) 23026. 081056
La Cruna, Portici Duomo 4, 28100 Novara.
T. (0321) 25620. - Paint / Graph - 081057
Uxa, Via Gautieri 5, 28100 Novara. T. (0321) 2 49 37.
- Paint - 081058

Omegna (Novara)

Spirano, Silvio, Via Cattaneo 16, 28026 Omegna.
T. (0323) 61805. 081059

Padova (Belluno)

Arte Sacra, Via del Santo 53, 35100 Padova.
T. (049) 224 14. 081061
Baldacci & Porro Arte Moderna, Passaggio San Fermo 3,
35137 Padova. T. (049) 8762776,
Fax (049) 8761130. 081061a

Bordin, Alessandro, Via Umberto 10, 35100 Padova.
T. (049) 3 61 30. - Paint - 081062
Callegari, Roberto, Via Davila 8, 35137 Padova.
T. (049) 875 58 03. 081063
Gallerie d'Arte Antica, Via Altinate 45, 35100 Padova.
T. (049) 394 74. - Paint / Graph / Sculp / Fra - 081064
Il Liocorno, Via San Fermo 32, 35100 Padova.
T. (049) 24908. - Sculp - 081065
Il Sigillo, Via E. Filiberto 1, 35100 Padova.
T. (049) 30831. - Graph - 081066

Palazzolo sull'Oglio (Brescia)

La Roggia, Via Torre del Popolo 11, 26036 Palazzolo sul-
l'Oglio. T. (030) 740 14 18. 081067
Studio F22, Piazza Zamara 22, 25036 Palazzolo sull'O-
glio. T. (030) 731027. 081068

Palermo (Sicilia)

Flaccovio, Salvatore F., Via Ruggiero Settimo 37, 90139
Palermo. T. (091) 247322. - Paint / Graph - 081069
La Persiana, Via della Libertà, 90141 Palermo.
T. (091) 611 11 53. - Paint - 081070
Porta Quinta, Via Mazzini 9, 90139 Palermo.
T. (091) 56 84 51. 081071
Sarno, Via Emerico Amari 148, 90139 Palermo.
T. (091) 58 18 48. - Paint - 081072

Parma

Angelo d'Oro, Borgo Onorato 4, 43100 Parma.
T. (0521) 337 45. - Paint / Graph / China / Arch /
Mod - 081073
Aurea Parma, Via al Duomo 5, 43100 Parma.
T. (0521) 38908. - Graph - 081074
Camattini, Via Garibaldi 13, 43100 Parma.
T. (0521) 33235. 081075
Galleria del Teatro, Piazza Garibaldi via Mameldi, 43100
Parma. T. (0521) 28 51 18. - Paint / Graph / Sculp - 081076
Galleria della Steccata, Via Dante 3, 43100 Parma.
T. (0521) 28 51 18. - Paint / Graph / Sculp - 081077
Niccoli, Via B. Longhi 6, 43100 Parma.
T. (0521) 28 26 69, Fax (0521) 230338. 081078
Parma, Via Macedonio Melloni 5, 43100 Parma.
T. (0521) 349 33. - Paint - 081079
San Andrea, Via Cavestro 6, 43100 Parma.
T. (0521) 671 52. 081080

Pavia

Gavazzi, Pavia, Via dei Mille 92, 27100 Pavia.
T. (0382) 230 33. 081081

Perugia

Cecchini, Corso Vannucci 66, Palazzo Baldeschi, 06121
Perugia. T. (075) 25853. - Paint / Graph / Sculp /
Fra - 081082
Spazio Arte, Via della Nespola 8A, 06122 Perugia.
T. (075) 61441. 081083

Pesaro

Altomani & C., Via Baviera 20, Palazzo Barignani, 61100
Pesaro. T. (0721) 69237. 081084
Mancini, Franca, Via Mazzolari 20, 61100 Pesaro.
T. (0721) 68853, Fax (0721) 35553. 081085

Pescara

de Domizio, Lucrezia, Via delle Caserme 44, 65100 Pes-
cara. T. (085) 888954. 081086
Verrocchio, Giuliano, Viale Regina Margherita 3, 65100
Pescara. T. (085) 219 72. - Paint / Graph /
Sculp - 081087

Piacenza

Art & Craft, Via Mandelli 4, 29100 Piacenza.
T. (0523) 37052. 081088
Atelier Romano, Via Campagna 22, 29100 Piacenza.
T. (0523) 248 15. - Paint - 081089
Braga, Via Cavour 46, 29100 Piacenza.
T. (0523) 31768. 081090
Conte Singarella, Via Garibaldi 62, 29100 Piacenza.
T. (0523) 20252. - Paint / Furn - 081091
Studio Coin, Via Cittadella 2/a, 29100 Piacenza.
T. (0523) 28948. - Paint - 081092

Pieve di Cadore (Belluno)

Del Quadro, Via Carducci, 32044 Pieve di Cadore.
T. (0435) 4570. - Paint / Graph / Sculp - 081093

Pisa

Bagno di Nerone, Piazza Buonamici 3, 56100 Pisa.
T. (050) 50 04 60. - Graph -   *081094*
La Molla, Corso Italia 12-14, 56100 Pisa.
T. (050) 425 64. - Paint -   *081095*
Macchi, Alfredo, Borgo Largo 43, 56100 Pisa.
T. (050) 225 92. - Paint / Graph / Sculp -   *081096*

Pistoia

Caselli, Umberto, Via Bastione Mediceo 21, 51100 Pistoia. T. (0573) 32912.   *081097*
La Torre, Via Palestro 25, 51100 Pistoia.
T. (0573) 366259.   *081098*

Policoro (Matera)

Luciana, Via Giustino Fortunato, 75025 Policoro.
T. (0835) 97 10 29. - Paint -   *081099*

Pordenone

Etching, Viale Franco Martelli 25A, 33170 Pordenone.
T. (0434) 27785, Fax (0434) 27785.   *081100*
Il Camino, Via Mazzini 51, 33170 Pordenone.
T. (0434) 281 51. - Ant / Paint / Graph -   *081101*
Sagittaria, Via Concordia 7, 33170 Pordenone.
T. (0434) 238 36.   *081102*

Porto Cervo (Sassari)

Rizziero Arte, Via della Passeggiata, 07020 Porto Cervo.
T. (0789) 94624.   *081103*

Porto Rotondo (Sassari)

Mantovano, Antonio, Piazza S. Marco, 07020 Porto Rotondo. T. (0789) 34124. - Jew -   *081104*

Prato (Firenze)

Ballerini, Via L. Muzzi 47, 50047 Prato.
T. (0574) 259 28. - Paint -   *081105*
Farsetti Arte, Viale della Repubblica, 50047 Prato.
T. (0574) 57 24 00, Fax (0574) 574132.
- Paint -   *081106*
Metastasio, Via B. Cairoli 62, 50047 Prato.
T. (0574) 336 97. - Paint -   *081107*
Mirabili, Via O. Vannucchi, 50047 Prato.
T. (0574) 59 17 19, Fax (0574) 583182.   *081108*

Rapallo (Genova)

Galleria d'Arte Patané, Via Rossetti 10, 16035 Rapallo.
T. (0185) 548 77.   *081109*
Motivi d'Arte, Via Marsala 5, 16035 Rapallo.
T. (0185) 501 20. - Paint -   *081110*

Ravenna

Svmilllta, Via Dagolini 43-45, 48100 Ravenna.
T. (0544) 34779, Fax (0544) 34149.   *081111*

Reggio Emilia

Libreria Prandi, Viale Timavo 75, 42100 Reggio Emilia.
T. (0522) 349 73. - Graph -   *081112*

Riccione (Forli)

Medas, Via Cattolica 8, 47036 Riccione.
T. (0541) 4 03 19.   *081113*
Tavolozza, Viale Ceccarini 37, 47036 Riccione.
T. (0541) 433 52. - Paint -   *081114*

Riva del Garda (Trento)

La Firma, Via A. Maffei 6, 38066 Riva del Garda.
T. (0464) 540 80. - Paint -   *081115*

Roma

A.A.M. Coop Architettura Arte Moderna, 12 Via Vantaggio, 00186 Roma. T. (06) 3219151.   *081116*
Acta International, 83 Via Panisperna, 00184 Roma.
T. (06) 4742005.   *081117*
Affabile S., 27 Piazza Pollarola, 00186 Roma.
T. (06) 68804191.   *081118*
Agenzia D'Arte Moderna, 3 Piazza Popolo, 00187 Roma.
T. (06) 3220338, 3220538.   *081119*
Agenzia D'Arte Moderna Roma, 3 Piazza Popolo, 00187
Roma. T. (06) 3218918, 3610975.   *081120*
Agostinelli, Via D. Barolomeo 42, 00126 Roma.
T. (06) 521 99 86, 521 90 58,
Fax (06) 5218407.   *081121*
Agostinelli F.LLI, Via D. Bartolomeo 42 – Dragona,
00126 Roma. T. (06) 5219986, 5219058,
Fax (06) 5218407.   *081122*

AL- FA Gallery, 15 Via Panetteria, 00187 Roma.
T. (06) 3789715.   *081123*
Alessandri R., 9 Via Margutta, 00187 Roma.
T. (06) 3614006.   *081124*
Alifieri E., 2 Via corso, 00186 Roma.
T. (06) 3610504.   *081125*
Alpha Laser, 105 Via Revoltella, 00152 Roma.
T. (06) 538833, 58238230.   *081126*
Amenta L., 140e Via Giulia, 00186 Roma.
T. (06) 6875641.   *081127*
Andre' Arte contemporanea, Via Giulia 175A, Roma.
T. (06) 6877343.   *081128*
Antiquaria, Dr. M. Alessandro, Corso Vittorio Emanuele
141, 00186 Roma. T. (06) 65 18 67. - Paint / Graph /
Sculp / Fra -   *081129*
Antiquaria S. Angelo, Via Banco di S. Spirito 61, 00186
Roma. T. (06) 6865944.   *081130*
Antiquarius di Bifolco Stefano e C., 63 Corso Rinascimento, 00186 Roma. T. (06) 68802941.   *081131*
Apollodoro, Piazza Mignanelli 17, 00187 Roma.
T. (06) 678 75 57.   *081132*
Arco Farnes, Via Giulia 180, 00186 Roma.
T. (06) 6896829, Fax (02) 6862282.   *081133*
Arco Farnese, 180 Via Giulia, 00186 Roma.
T. (06) 6865145, 6896829.   *081134*
Art Center, 9 Piazza Za. di Spagna, 00187 Roma.
T. (06) 6789138.   *081135*
Art Gallery Bosi, 28 Via XX Settembre, 00187 Roma.
T. (06) 4819256, 4821689.   *081136*
Art & Design, Via di S. Giacomo 18, 00186 Roma.
T. (06) 678 69 63. - Ant / Paint / Dec / Glass /
Cur –   *081137*
Art.Center, 9 Piazza Za di Spagna, 00187 Roma.
T. (06) 6792482.   *081138*
Arte Colosseo di Mengoli, Angela, 58 Via S. Giov. Laterano, 00184 Roma. T. (06) 7096404.   *081139*
Arte Corso, 259 Via Corso, 00186 Roma.
T. (06) 6795363.   *081140*
Arte Cortina, 14a/15 Via Gesu'e Maria, 00187 Roma.
T. (06) 3219667.   *081141*
Arte in Cornice di Sonni Edoardo, Viale Libia 10, 00199
Roma. T. (06) 86216017.   *081142*
Arte – Per, 27 Via Tor Millina, 00186 Roma.
T. (06) 68802146.   *081143*
Arte 2000, 557 Via Staz. Cesano – Cesano, 00060 Roma. T. (06) 3038950.   *081144*
Artistica Romana, 11 Via Kossuth, 00149 Roma.
T. (06) 55285012.   *081145*
Artivisive di Sylvia Franchi, Via Sistina 121, 00187 Roma. T. (06) 48 38 85.   *081146*
Astrolabio Art, Via del Babuino 144, 00187 Roma.
T. (06) 678 01 80. - Paint -   *081147*
Athena Arte, 2 Via Mascherino, 00193 Roma.
T. (06) 6865615.   *081148*
Badiali L., 4 Via S. Eligio, 00186 Roma.
T. (06) 68801953.   *081149*
Balestra A., 50 Via Modena, 00184 Roma.
T. (06) 4821595.   *081150*
Banchi Nuovi, Via dei Banchi Nuovi 37, 00186 Roma.
T. (06) 68805554, Fax (02) 68805554.   *081151*
Belletti S., 27 Via Crociferi, 00187 Roma.
T. (06) 6789870.   *081152*
Blasi L., 76 Via Dossi, 00137 Roma. T. (06) 8280865,
8273483.   *081153*
Bono E., Via Terme Diociezano, 00185 Roma.
T. (06) 4742671.   *081154*
Bonomo, Alessandra, Piazza Apollonia 3, 00153 Roma.
T. (06) 581 05 79, Fax (02) 6884440.   *081155*
Bor – Art, 71 Via Val Maira, 00141 Roma.
T. (06) 8124836.   *081156*
Bor – Art, 77 Via Val Maira, 00141 Roma.
T. (06) 88327011.   *081157*
La Borgognona, 525 Via Corso, 00186 Roma.
T. (06) 3610258.   *081158*
Borgognona, Via del Corso 525, 00186 Roma.
T. (06) 361 0258. - Graph -   *081159*
Borzi, Ennio, Piazza Trilussa 41, 00153 Roma.
T. (06) 581 86 85, Fax (06) 5836724.   *081160*
Bosi Art Center, 2e Via Morgagni, 00161 Roma.
T. (06) 44230412.   *081161*
Bottega D'Arte il Saggiatore, 83b Via Margutta, 00187
Roma. T. (06) 3207709.   *081162*

La Botticella, 19 pl. Flaminio, 00196 Roma.
T. (06) 3202735.   *081163*
Broccoletti R., 27 Via Angelini, 00149 Roma.
T. (06) 5565861.   *081164*
Bruno L., 3 Via della Robbia, 00153 Roma.
T. (06) 5781644.   *081165*
Burckhardt, Piazza S. Salvatore in Lauro 13, 00186 Roma. T. (06) 65 97 37. - Paint / Graph -   *081166*
Ca' D'Oro, 81 Piazza di Spagna, 00187 Roma.
T. (06) 6791331, 6796417, 6797550.   *081167*
Camelu' di, Catherine Bonvalet, 43 Via Fornaci, 00165
Roma. T. (06) 39367236.   *081168*
Campaiola G., 1c Via Vantaggio, 00186 Roma.
T. (06) 3612352.   *081169*
Carpine, Via delle Mantellate 30, 00165 Roma.
T. (06) 656 88 78.   *081170*
Casa D'Arte la Grandiva, 119 Via Babuino, 00187 Roma.
T. (06) 6793334, 6793353, 69920294.   *081171*
Casa della Cornice, 19 Via Castani, 00172 Roma.
T. (06) 2310603.   *081172*
Casa Editrice C.I.D.A. di Remo Piperno, 26 Via F. Fiorini,
00152 Roma. T. (06) 5826422.   *081173*
Casali, Piazza della Rotonda 81A-82, 00186 Roma.
T. (06) 6783515, 6873705.   *081174*
Casciano A., 71 Via S. F. a Ripa, 00153 Roma.
T. (06) 5884240.   *081175*
Castagnari M., 57 Via Babuino, 00187 Roma.
T. (06) 3207618.   *081176*
Castellani G., 5 Via Sestio Calvino, 00174 Roma.
T. (06) 71510002.   *081177*
Castellani G., 27 Viale Giulio Agricola, 00174 Roma.
T. (06) 71510001.   *081178*
La Centrale dell'Arte, 16 Via Carrozze, 00187 Roma.
T. (06) 6790011.   *081179*
Centro D'Arte Edizioni la Vite, 18 Corso Vitt. Eman. II,
00186 Roma. T. (06) 6991144.   *081180*
Centro Luigi di Sarro, Viale G. Cesare 71, 00192 Roma.
T. (06) 3243642.   *081181*
Centro Persia, 151 Via Anastasio II, 00165 Roma.
T. (06) 39377380, 39377385.   *081182*
Certel di Romano Petrucci, 169 Via Babuino, 00187 Roma. T. (06) 3614148.   *081183*
Cesaroni P., 7 Via Albalonga, 00183 Roma.
T. (06) 77205005.   *081184*
Chistolini P., 1 Via Ceneda, 00183 Roma.
T. (06) 70476752.   *081185*
Ciambrelli C.F., 143 Via Coronari, 00186 Roma.
T. (06) 68801024.   *081186*
Ciccarelli S., 32b Via Grottoni, 00149 Roma.
T. (06) 5501718.   *081187*
Cinquegrana G., 19 Viale Mura Aurelie, 00165 Roma.
T. (06) 6390346.   *081188*
Citifin, Via Po 8, 00182 Roma. T. (06) 849 71.
- Paint -   *081189*
Clemente A., 49 Via Nazionale, 00184 Roma.
T. (06) 4818821.   *081190*
Clemente A., 6 Corso Vitt. Eman. II, 00186 Roma.
T. (06) 6796528.   *081191*
Il Club dell'Arte e della Cultura di Tosi T. & C., 220 Via
Coronari, 00186 Roma. T. (06) 68801529.   *081192*
Coccia, Mara, Via del Corso 530, 00187 Roma.
T. (06) 3210290.   *081193*
Condotti, Via Condotti 85, 00187 Roma.
T. (06) 679 1196.   *081194*
Consorti, Via Margutta 52A, 00187 Roma.
T. (06) 3614053. - Paint / Graph -   *081195*
Cooperativa Grafica, 40 Via F. P. Cantelli, 00166 Roma.
T. (06) 2288950.   *081196*
Coronari di Dall'Aglio, Laura, 59 Via Coronari, 00186 Roma. T. (06) 6869917.   *081197*
Costa B., 4 Via Ciciliano, 00156 Roma.
T. (06) 4072756.   *081198*
La Cour, 21a Via Vantaggio, 00186 Roma.
T. (06) 3614125.   *081199*
Creazioni Artistiche Baglio, 68 Via Casale S. Basilio,
00156 Roma. T. (06) 4101697.   *081200*
Credit Art, 89 Via Babuino, 00187 Roma.
T. (06) 3230610.   *081201*
Crescenzo, Giuliana de, Via Principessa Clotilde 5,
00186 Roma. T. (06) 322 54 55, Fax (06) 3220588.
- Paint / Graph / Sculp / Draw -   *081202*
D'Amico A., 81 Via Margutta, 00187 Roma.
T. (06) 3207710.   *081203*

D'Ascanio, Anna, Via del Babuino 29, 00187 Roma.
T. (06) 6785920/6783897, Fax (06) 6793821.   *081204*

Damy, Ken, Via Archimede 67-69, 00197 Roma.
- Pho -   *081205*

Data Arte, 53 Via Garibaldi, 00153 Roma.
T. (06) 5896229.   *081206*

De Benedetti A., 96 Via Nemorense, 00199 Roma.
T. (06) 86206813.   *081207*

De Bernardins L., 7 Via Pigna, 00186 Roma.
T. (06) 6795929.   *081208*

De' Florio Arte, 13 Via Scala, 00153 Roma.
T. (06) 5894741.   *081209*

De Lullo M., 8 Via Paglia, 00153 Roma.
T. (06) 5885510.   *081210*

De Mata, Antonio, Via Babuino 55, 00187 Roma.
T. (06) 68 08 39. - Paint -   *081211*

De Santis B., 197 Via Giulia, 00186 Roma.
T. (06) 68803542.   *081212*

Dè Serpenti, Via Dè Serpenti 32, 00184 Roma.
T. (06) 487 22 25, Fax (06) 4815625.   *081213*

Decleva, Uberto, Via Pegaso 12, 00128 Roma.
T. (06) 607 08 64. - Paint / Graph -   *081214*

Degli Artisti, 46 Piazza Barberini, 00187 Roma.
T. (06) 486838.   *081215*

Del Cortile, Via del Babuino 51, 00187 Roma.
T. (06) 678 57 24, Fax (02) 6785724. - Paint -   *081216*

Del Vicolo, 17 Vicolo Penitenza, 00165 Roma.
T. (06) 6877032.   *081217*

Del Zio F., 9b Via Collatina, 00177 Roma.
T. (06) 2186764.   *081218*

Della Pigna, 13 Via Pigna, 00186 Roma.
T. (06) 6781525.   *081219*

Della Tartaruga, 85a Via Sistina, 00187 Roma.
T. (06) 6788956.   *081220*

Deniarte, Via Marianna Dionigi 43, 00193 Roma.
T. (06) 3232868, 3232265.   *081221*

Di Cave, Guiliana, Via dei Pastini 23, 00186 Roma.
T. (06) 678 02 97. - Graph -   *081222*

Di Marco I., 63/65 Via T. Prisco, 00181 Roma.
T. (06) 78344702.   *081223*

Di Stefano R., 22 Lungotevere Mellini, 00191 Roma.
T. (06) 3208148, 3242836.   *081224*

Di Summa G., 9 Via F. Massimo, 00192 Roma.
T. (06) 3241730, 3241731.   *081225*

Diacono M., 22 Via Ripetta, 00186 Roma.
T. (06) 3218081.   *081226*

Domestici M.M., 27 Via Colonette, 00186 Roma.
T. (06) 3227162.   *081227*

Don Chisciotte, Via Brunetti 21, 00186 Roma.
T. (06) 3224515. - Paint / Graph -   *081228*

Due CI, 3 Piazza Mignanelli, 00187 Roma.
T. (06) 6781173, 6783808,6787566.   *081229*

E.B.S. Editoriale, 47 Viale Shakespeare, 00144 Roma.
T. (06) 5921107, 5921408.   *081230*

Echeoni E., 338 Viale Alessandrino, 00172 Roma.
T. (06) 2300193.   *081231*

Edarcom Europa, 15 Via Macedoni, 00179 Roma.
T. (06) 7802620, 7856890, 7886663,
7887152.   *081232*

Edieuropa, Via del Corso 525, 00186 Roma.
T. (06) 3610189, 3610246, Fax (06) 3610246.   *081233*

Edieuropa Gallerie D'Arti, 7 Via Pallacorda, 00186 Roma.
T. (06) 3610246.   *081234*

Editrice Latina Promozioni Artistiche e Culturali, 41c Via
Latina, 00179 Roma. T. (06) 70452088,
70452846.   *081235*

Eidos di, Andre' Sylvie, 175a Via Giulia, 00186 Roma.
T. (06) 6877343.   *081236*

Elisep di C. Sinibaldi & E. Simon & C., 183e Via Nazionale, 00184 Roma. T. (06) 4744959.   *081237*

E.R.A. di Adriana Muccifora, 43 Via Tritone, 00187 Roma. T. (06) 6797277.   *081238*

Esedra, 95 Via Torino, 00184 Roma.
T. (06) 4818660.   *081239*

Esmeralda, 23 Via Condotti, 00187 Roma.
T. (06) 69920094.   *081240*

Esposito E., 228 Via Merulana, 00185 Roma.
T. (06) 4872826.   *081241*

Esposizione Arte, 251 Via Nazionale, 00184 Roma.
T. (06) 4744998.   *081242*

Etrusculudens, Via Barge 39, 00166 Roma.
T. (06) 6243465. - Paint -   *081243*

Euroart, 42 Via Ripetta, 00186 Roma.
T. (06) 3204529.   *081244*

Euroarte, 4 Via Stamira, 00162 Roma. T. (06) 44236516,
44244405.   *081245*

Fabian M., 14 Via Fra Mauro, 00176 Roma.
T. (06) 291930.   *081246*

Fabiani M., 27 Via P. Anicio, 00178 Roma.
T. (06) 7802458.   *081247*

Faella G., 36 Via D. Bartolomeo, 00126 Roma.
T. (06) 5215844.   *081248*

Fauro, 120 Via Monserrato, 00186 Roma.
T. (06) 6867747.   *081249*

Ferranti L., 17 Via Specchi, 00186 Roma.
T. (06) 68307871.   *081250*

Ferranti, Ugo, Via Tor Millani 26, 00186 Roma.
T. (06) 654 21 46, Fax (06) 6542146.   *081251*

Ferri A., 30 Via Milazzo, 00185 Roma.
T. (06) 4940848.   *081252*

Ferri Cappiello M.T., 10 Via Aleardi, 00185 Roma.
T. (06) 70497793.   *081253*

Fidi Arte Moderna di Fiume Fausto e C., 49 Via Brunetti,
00186 Roma. T. (06) 3612051.   *081254*

Finarte, Via Quattro Fontane 20, 00184 Roma.
T. (06) 463564. - Paint / Graph -   *081255*

Fine Arts Shop, Via Sistina 19, 00187 Roma.
T. (06) 4743156.   *081256*

Fioroni G., 66/68 Via S. Franc. di Sales, 00165 Roma.
T. (06) 6833623.   *081257*

Fontana di Pandolfini, Sergio e C., 12 Via D. Fontana,
00185 Roma. T. (06) 70497592.   *081258*

La Fontanella, 88 Ig. Fontan di Borghese, 00186 Roma.
T. (06) 6871347.   *081259*

Fontanella Borghese, Via della Fontanella di Borghese
31, 00186 Roma. T. (06) 6876127, 6873741,
Fax (06) 6876127.   *081260*

Forsyte Grafica, 179 Via Archimede, 00197 Roma.
T. (06) 8080742.   *081261*

Forum Arte, Corso Vitt. Emanuele 326, 00186 Roma.
T. (06) 654 13 58, Fax (06) 6540477.   *081262*

Gall D'Arte Mod. Toninelli, 86 Piazza di Spagna, 00187
Roma. T. (06) 6793488.   *081263*

Galleria AAM, Via del Vantaggio 12, 00186 Roma.
T. (06) 3619151, Fax 70 19 12 47.   *081264*

Galleria d'Arte Gregoriana, Via Gregoriana 54/B, 00187
Roma. T. (06) 68 28 22. - Paint -   *081265*

Galleria degli Artisti, Piazza Barberini 46, 00187 Roma.
T. (06) 48 68 38. - Paint -   *081266*

Galleria dei Greci, Via dei Greci 6, 00187 Roma.
T. (06) 679 60 97, Fax (06) 6789413. - Paint / Graph /
Draw -   *081267*

Galleria del Cortile, Via del Babuino 51, 00187 Roma.
T. (06) 6785724, Fax (06) 6785724.   *081268*

Galleria dell'oca, Via dell'Oca 41, 00186 Roma.
T. (06) 3610410, Fax (02) 6785901.   *081269*

Galleria Giulia, Via Giulia 148, 00186 Roma.
T. (06) 6861443, Fax (06) 68802061. - Paint / Graph /
Sculp -   *081270*

Galleria Il Ponte, Via Sant'Ignazio 6, 00186 Roma.
T. (06) 679 61 14, Fax (06) 6796114.   *081271*

Galleria San Simeone, Piazzetta San Simeone 26, 00186
Roma. T. (06) 656 43 41. - Paint / Furn -   *081272*

Galleria 2RC, Via dei Delfini 16, 00186 Roma.
T. (06) 792811, Fax (06) 5783445.   *081273*

Gallerie Internazionale Peter Santana, 108/109 Via Giulia, 00186 Roma. T. (06) 6875413.   *081274*

Gallerie Internazionali Peter Santana, 08 Via Giulia,
00186 Roma. T. (06) 6893690.   *081275*

Gasparrini, Via della Fontanella di Borghese 43, 00186
Roma. T. (06) 6892150. - Paint -   *081276*

Gasparrini C., 19 Ig. Fontanella di Borghese, 00186 Roma. T. (06) 6876542.   *081277*

G.F. Arte di Licastro, Francesco, 1d Via Vantaggio,
00186 Roma. T. (06) 3200985.   *081278*

La Giara, 53 Via Coronari, 00186 Roma.
T. (06) 68804783.   *081279*

Giulia, 148 Via Giulia, 00186 Roma. T. (06) 6861443,
68802061.   *081280*

Gjokaj M., 40 Via Moro, 00153 Roma.
T. (06) 5809668.   *081281*

Godel, Piazza Poli 45, 00187 Roma. T. (06) 68 87 16.
- Paint -   *081282*

Grafica Ricambi di Tomasello Paolo, 14 Via Baris da Trani, 00153 Roma. T. (06) 5882002.   *081283*

Grafiche Tassotti, Via S. F. Lazzaro 103, 00136 Roma.
T. (0424) 566105, 566112.   *081284*

La Grandiva, 5 Via Fontanella, 00187 Roma.
T. (06) 3230098.   *081285*

Graphis Arte Jolly, 52 Via Babuino, 00187 Roma.
T. (06) 6797326.   *081286*

Hermes, Via Margutta 54, 00187 Roma.
T. (06) 68 70 55.   *081287*

Hulsmann, Eva, Via Tacchini 13, 00197 Roma.
T. (06) 80 36 60. - Ant -   *081288*

Il Campo, Via Minerva 5, 00186 Roma.
T. (06) 6781505.   *081289*

Il Gabbiano, Via della Frezza 51, 00186 Roma.
T. (06) 3227049, 3227251, Fax (06) 3220401.
- Paint -   *081290*

Il Millennio, Via Margutta 51A, 00187 Roma.
T. (06) 322 41 56, Fax (06) 3224489.   *081291*

Il Narciso, Via Alibert 25, 00187 Roma.
T. (06) 320 77 00.   *081292*

Il Polittico, Via dei Banchi Vecchi 135, 00186 Roma.
T. (06) 683 25 74, Fax (06) 6832574.   *081293*

Il Segno, Via Capo le Case 4, 00187 Roma.
T. (06) 679 13 87.   *081294*

Incontro d'Arte, Via del Vantaggio 17A, 00186 Roma.
T. (06) 361 22 67, Fax (06) 3612267.   *081295*

Intergrafica, 30 Via Scrofa, 00186 Roma.
T. (06) 68308754.   *081296*

Italarte, 11 Ig. Pallaro, 00186 Roma. T. (06) 6865776,
68805859.   *081297*

Italarte Fine Print, 57 Via Pozzo Cornacchie, 00186 Roma. T. (06) 68307355.   *081298*

Italiana D'Arte Moderna Palazzo Margutta, 55 Via Margutta, 00187 Roma. T. (06) 3207683.   *081299*

Janin G., 26 via Sistina, 00187 Roma.
T. (06) 4885416.   *081300*

Jartrakor, Via dei Pianellari 20, 00186 Roma.
T. (06) 6867824. - Sculp / Draw -   *081301*

L'Albatros, Via del Babuino 169, 00187 Roma.
T. (06) 6798738. - Paint / Graph / Sculp -   *081302*

L'Angolo, 7 Via Orto napoli, 00192 Roma.
T. (06) 3207674.   *081303*

L'Antonina, 23 Piazza Mignanelli, 00187 Roma.
T. (06) 6795830.   *081304*

L'Arcadia, 70a Via Babuino, 00187 Roma.
T. (06) 6791023.   *081305*

L'Ippocastano di, Janin Giancarlo, 28 Via Cossa, 00193
Roma. T. (06) 3215045.   *081306*

L'Isola, 5 Via Gregoriana, 00187 Roma. T. (06) 6784678,
6790029, 6785477.   *081307*

La Feluca, Via Frattina 38, 00187 Roma.
T. (06) 679 00 21. - Paint / Graph -   *081308*

La Margherita, Via Giulia 108, 00186 Roma.
T. (06) 65 54 13.   *081309*

La Nuova Pesa, Via del Corso 530, 00187 Roma.
T. (06) 361 08 92, Fax (06) 3222873.   *081310*

La Vetrata, Via Tagliamento 4, 00198 Roma.
T. (06) 8840393. - Paint / Graph -   *081311*

Lampronti, Cesare, Via del Babuino 67 e 182, 00187 Roma. T. (06) 6795800.   *081312*

Le Jardin des Arts, Via del Vantaggio 1A, 00186 Roma.
T. (06) 3611445. - Paint / Graph / Sculp -   *081313*

Liberatore R., 26 Via S. Ippolito, 00162 Roma.
T. (06) 44232444.   *081314*

Lo Presti A.P., 27 Via G. da Castelbolognese, 00127 Roma. T. (06) 5894006.   *081315*

Lodolo Pasialis R., 77 Via Acherusio, 00199 Roma.
T. (06) 86207481.   *081316*

Lombardi E., 70 Via Babuino, 00187 Roma.
T. (06) 6792010.   *081317*

Maino M.P., 125 Via Flaminia, 00196 Roma.
T. (06) 3203565.   *081318*

Malanga G., 48 Via Tomassini, 00168 Roma.
T. (06) 3013335.   *081319*

Mantovano, Antonio, Piazza di Spagna 60/A, 00187 Roma. T. (06) 6792284. - Jew -   *081320*

Marchetta G., 149 Via Sistina, 00187 Roma.
T. (06) 4740915.   *081321*

Marguttina, 50 Via Margutta, 00187 Roma.
T. (06) 3614052.   *081322*

Mariani G., 4 Via Vivanti, 00144 Roma.
T. (06) 5204522.   *081323*

Marino, Piazza Mignanelli 25, 00186 Roma.
T. (06) 678 91 38. - Paint / Graph / Sculp -   *081324*

Marino G., 43 Piazza Navona, 00186 Roma.
T. (06) 6875394. 081325
Mario dei Fiori, Via Mario dei Fiori 24 c, 00187 Roma.
T. (06) 6780833. - Paint - 081326
Martinoja, Angelo, Via del Babuino 107/a, 00187 Roma.
T. (06) 679 82 63. - Paint - 081327
Mazzoni C., 25 Via Alibert, 00187 Roma.
T. (06) 3207700. 081328
Mediarte Invest, 101 Via Cadlolo, 00136 Roma.
T. (06) 3496331. 081329
Medusa Gallery, Via del Babuino 124, 00187 Roma.
T. (06) 679 65 46. - Paint / Graph / Sculp / Pho / Mul /
Draw - 081330
La Mente e Immagine, 8 Via Caio Mario, 00192 Roma.
T. (06) 3223392. 081331
MGP Arte Contemporanea di, Maria Giovanna Patteri,
177 Via Arta Terme, 00188 Roma. T. (06) 33614217,
33614405. 081332
Miano G., 8 Via Tripoli, 00188 Roma.
T. (06) 86325854. 081333
Minnucci M.L., 1 Via Balestrari, 00186 Roma.
T. (06) 68307034. 081334
Mirabilia, 83 Via S. Giov. Laterano, 00184 Roma.
T. (06) 70450453. 081335
Mirko's Gold Inter, 36 Via F. Romagnoli, 00137 Roma.
T. (06) 86802244. 081336
Miscetti, Stefania, Via delle Mantellate 14, 00165 Roma.
T. (06) 68805880, Fax (06) 68805880. 081337
Mizzoni G., 22 Via Coronari, 00186 Roma.
T. (06) 68803853. 081338
Molica G., 46a Via Crescenzio, 00193 Roma.
T. (06) 68308423. 081339
Molica, Pino, Via Crescenzio 46A, 00193 Roma.
T. (06) 68 30 84 23, Fax (06) 68308423. 081340
Monachesi L., 51 Via Babuino, 00187 Roma.
T. (06) 6785724. 081341
Moncada, Valentina, Via Margutta 54, 00187 Roma.
T. (06) 3208209, Fax (06) 3207956. 081342
Mondo Arte, Via dei Gracchi 291B, 00192 Roma.
T. (06) 321 29 03, Fax (06) 3217931. 081343
Il Mondo dell'Arte, 193 Via Castani, 00171 Roma.
T. (06) 2314864. 081344
Monti Associazione Culturale, 41 Via Ripetta, 00186 Ro-
ma. T. (06) 3225759. 081345
MR Arte Contemporanea, Via Garibaldi 53-54, 00153
Roma. T. (06) 589 97 07, Fax (06) 5896229. 081346
Mucciaccia L., 40 Via Greci, 00187 Roma.
T. (06) 6787425. 081347
Muccifora Bianchelli, 19 Via Cuccagna, 00186 Roma.
T. (06) 6875822. 081348
Muri A., 30 Via Isola Bella, 00141 Roma.
T. (06) 82000885. 081349
M.2.M, 107 Via Germanico, 00192 Roma.
T. (06) 3241673. 081350
Navona Club, Piazza De Massimi 6, 00186 Roma.
T. (06) 68804552, 68805454. 081351
Nesbitt, Celilia Federici, Via Stevenson 24, 00162 Roma.
T. (06) 8901963. 081352
Nordecchla P., 25 Piazza Navona, 00186 Roma.
T. (06) 6869318. 081353
Numero, Via Principessa Clotilde 1, 00196 Roma.
T. (06) 359 89 92. 081354
Obelisco, Via Sistina 146, 00187 Roma. T. (06) 465917.
- Paint / Graph / Sculp - 081355
Oddi Baglioni, Via Gregoriana 34, 00187 Roma.
T. (06) 679 79 06, Fax (06) 6788424. 081356
Odyssia, Via Ludovisi 16, 00817 Roma. T. (06) 46 52 81.
- Paint / Sculp - 081357
Oikos, 33/37 Via Valsarvaranche, 00141 Roma.
T. (06) 8123465. 081358
Orichio F., 18 Via S. Costanza, 00198 Roma.
T. (06) 8558900. 081359
Orlandini E., 20 Via Baccina, 00184 Roma.
T. (06) 6780368. 081360
P. 21 Arte, 21 Via Stelletta, 00187 Roma.
T. (06) 68806504. 081361
Pacitti N.A., 59 Via Banchi Vecchi, 00186 Roma.
T. (06) 68806391. 081362
Palmieri, Virginia & Figli, 80 Via Vittoria, 00122 Roma.
T. (06) 6796310. 081363
Pamphilj, Doria, Piazza Collegio Romano 1a, 00186 Ro-
ma. T. (06) 679 43 65. - Paint - 081364

Panatta Fratelli, 117 Via Crispi, 00187 Roma.
T. (06) 6795948. 081365
Panatta R., 19 Via Sistina, 00187 Roma.
T. (06) 4743156. 081366
Pandolfini S., 24a Via Agnello, 00184 Roma.
T. (06) 6797795. 081367
Parametro, Via Margutta 8, 00187 Roma.
T. (06) 679 43 17. 081368
Paris, Via Margutta 53bis, 00187 Roma. T. (06) 875069.
- Paint - 081369
Patrone L., 49 Piazza Farnese, 00186 Roma.
T. (06) 6833750, 6872500, 6872501,
68805827. 081370
Peace Ful Planet, 60 Corso Rinascimento, 00186 Roma.
T. (06) 6830756. 081371
Perazzini E., 13 Via S. Vincenzo, 00187 Roma.
T. (06) 6784406. 081372
Peretti, Ferdinando, Via Governo Vecchio 120, 00186
Roma. T. (06) 652563. - Paint - 081373
Perrera A., 118 Via Babuino, 00187 Roma.
T. (06) 6792069. 081374
Picchi M.S., 7 Via M. Clementi, 00193 Roma.
T. (06) 3201495. 081375
Pieroni, 144 Pia Vitt. Eman. II, 00186 Roma.
T. (06) 4940892, 4940893. 081376
Pieroni, Mario, Via Panisperna 203, 00184 Roma.
T. (06) 465706, Fax (06) 4820179. 081377
Pierucci P., 187 Viale reg. Margherita, 00198 Roma.
T. (06) 8554769. 081378
Pinacoteca Arte Moderna, 158 Via 4 Fontane, 00184 Ro-
ma. T. (06) 4885226. 081379
Planita, Via di Ripetta 22, 00186 Roma.
T. (06) 321 80 81, Fax (06) 4453906. 081380
Poggi, Sandro, Via di Parione 16, 00186 Roma.
T. (06) 654 88 81. 081381
Pont des Arts, 7 Via Angeletto, 00184 Roma.
T. (06) 483424. 081382
Popoli P., 102 Via Margutta, 00187 Roma.
T. (06) 6786960. 081383
Primo Piano, Via Panisperna 203, 00184 Roma.
T. (06) 488 03 09, Fax (06) 4881894. 081384
Il Professionista, 167 Via S. F. a. Ripa, 00153 Roma.
T. (06) 5894847. 081385
Promoart, 257 Via Emanuele Filiberto, 00185 Roma.
T. (06) 70475413. 081386
Publicast, 101 Via Arcione, 00187 Roma.
T. (06) 69922320. 081387
Il Punto, Via del Mascherino 40, 00193 Roma.
T. (06) 6875481. 081388
Il Punto Centro Arte Contemporanea, 96e Via de Carolis,
00136 Roma. T. (06) 3451997, 3497855. 081389
La Quercia di Annamarie Valente, 7 lg. Bacone, 00137
Roma. T. (06) 86896762. 081390
Quintini G., 2 Vicolo Sforza Cesarini, 00186 Roma.
T. (06) 6877940. 081391
Raponi M., 3 Via E. Romagnoli, 00137 Roma.
T. (06) 8272279, 8277038. 081392
La Rassegna, via Monti di Creta 29-31, 00167 Roma.
T. (06) 6232555. - Paint - 081393
Ribaudo F., 64 Via Purificazione, 00187 Roma.
T. (06) 4743677, 4881350. 081394
Rive Gauche, Via Margutta 1b, 00187 Roma.
T. (06) 361 04 47. - Paint / Graph - 081395
Romana Quadri, Via Scortiacabove, 00156 Roma.
T. (06) 4112908. 081396
Romano, Licia, Via del Babuino 141, 00187 Roma.
T. (06) 679 11 98. - Paint / Sculp - 081397
Rondanini, Piazza Rondanini 48, 00186 Roma.
T. (06) 6543259. 081398
Rossi Lecce Marco, Via della Minerva 5, 00186 Roma.
T. (06) 678 15 05, Fax (06) 6794272. 081399
Rubinarte, 88 Via Trevis, 00147 Roma.
T. (06) 5138353. 081400
Rucellai, 56 Via Fontan di Borghese, 00186 Roma.
T. (06) 6832177. 081401
Sala 1, Piazza di Porta S. Giovanni 10, 00185 Roma.
T. (06) 700 86 91, Fax (06) 7591663. 081402
Salini N., 51a Via Margutta, 00187 Roma.
T. (06) 3207610. 081403
La Salita, 15 Via Ibernesi, 00184 Roma.
T. (06) 6786941. 081404
Sambuco C., 30 Via Pelliccia, 00153 Roma.
T. (06) 5816614. 081405

Sargentini, Fabio, Via del Paradiso 41, 00186 Roma.
T. (06) 686 98 46, Fax (06) 6869846. 081406
Schneider, Prof. R. E., Rampa Mignanelli 10, 00187 Ro-
ma. T. (06) 678 40 19. - Paint / Graph / Sculp /
Draw - 081407
Schneider R.E., 10 rampa Mignanelli, 00187 Roma.
T. 6784019. 081408
Sconci S., 25 Via Chismaio, 00199 Roma.
T. (06) 86218476. 081409
Selfart, 29 Via Bragaglia, 00123 Roma. T. (06) 3789128,
3789158. 081410
Selfart, 29m Via Bragaglia, 00123 Roma.
T. (06) 3788442. 081411
Senior, Via del Babuino 114, 00187 Roma.
T. (06) 679 15 56. - Paint - 081412
Serafini, Via Condotti 85, 00186 Roma.
T. (06) 6794092. 081413
Sestieri L., 18 Via Alibert, 00187 Roma.
T. (06) 6785766. 081414
Simonato I., 164 Corso Trieste, 00198 Roma.
T. (06) 8606253. 081415
Sistina, Via Sistina 149, 00187 Roma. T. (06) 480915.
- Paint - 081416
Sonni E., 10 Viale Libia, 00199 Roma.
T. (06) 86216017. 081417
Sparaci, Silvio, 142a Via Robinie, 00172 Roma.
T. (06) 2313275. 081418
Sperone, Gian Enzo, Via di Pallacorda 15, 00186 Roma.
T. (06) 6893525, Fax (06) 6893527. 081419
Spicchi dell'Est, Piazza S. Salvatore Lauro 15, 00186
Roma. T. (06) 68805610, Fax (06) 68307465. 081420
Sprovieri, Piazza del Popolo 3, 00187 Roma.
T. (06) 3610975, Fax (06) 3220338. 081421
Stagni Fides, 43 Via Brunetti, 00186 Roma.
T. (06) 3612055. 081422
Stoico Galleria Arte Antica e Moderna, 45 Via Lucio E.
Seiano, 00174 Roma. T. (06) 71510357. 081423
Studio Arco D'Alibert, 42 Via Brunetti, 00186 Roma.
T. (06) 3226145. 081424
Studio Bocchi, Piazza dei Ricci 129, 00186 Roma.
T. (06) 686 25 19. 081425
Studio Condotti 85, Via Condotti 85, 00187 Roma.
T. (06) 679 40 92. - Paint / Graph / Sculp - 081426
Studio D'Arte A 2, 29 Via Babuino, 00187 Roma.
T. (06) 6785920. 081427
Studio D'Arte F. Russo, 15a Via Alibert, 00187 Roma.
T. (06) 6789949. 081428
Studio D'Arte F. Russo, 15 Via Alibert, 00187 Roma.
T. (06) 69920692. 081429
Studio di Val Cervo, 561 Via Marcigliana, 00138 Roma.
T. (06) 87120443, 87120508. 081430
Studio Durante, Via del Babuino 179, 00187 Roma.
T. (06) 321 94 29, Fax (06) 3219429. 081431
Studio Erre, 22 Via S. Giacomo, 00187 Roma.
T. (06) 6791637. 081432
Studio S, Via della Penna 59, 00186 Roma.
T. (06) 361 20 86. 081433
Studio S Arte Contemporanea, 59 Via Penna, 00186 Ro-
ma. T. (06) 3612086. 081434
Studio Soligo, Via del Babulno 51, 00187 Roma.
T. (06) 678 43 28, Fax (06) 3214640. 081435
Studio 5, Via Belisario 8, 00187 Roma.
T. (06) 474 471 33, Fax (06) 4744028. 081436
Studio 5 di Carla Tofone, 8 Via Belisario, 00187 Roma.
T. (06) 4744028. 081437
Tanca G. – Stampe Antiche, Sal. dei Crescenzi 10/11/12
Senato-Pantheon, 00186 Roma. T. (06) 6875272,
68803328. 081438
Tartaglia A., 33 Via Gasperina, 00040 Roma.
T. (060) 7231576. 081439
Tartaglia P., 14 Via Centauri, 00133 Roma.
T. (06) 2001238. 081440
Tartaglia P., 98c/d Via XX Settembre, 00187 Roma.
T. (06) 4884234. 081441
Tell G., 13 Via C. Porta, 00153 Roma.
T. (06) 5803783. 081442
Il Tetto 87, 53 Via Margutta, 00187 Roma.
T. (06) 3207978. 081443
Todi T., 17 Via Margutta, 00187 Roma. T. (06) 3242596,
3242598. 081444
Todi T., 103 Via Margutta, 00187 Roma.
T. (06) 3242599. 081445

Tofone C., 8 Via Belisario, 00187 Roma.
T. (06) 4747133. *081446*

Toninelli, Piazza di Spagna 86, 00187 Roma.
T. (06) 6780810. - Paint / Graph / Sculp - *081447*

Trasselli F., 166 Via Nomentana, 00162 Roma.
T. (06) 86209871. *081448*

Trifalco, 22a Via Vantaggio, 00153 Roma.
T. (06) 3610236. *081449*

Trifalco, Via del Vantaggio 22A, 00186 Roma.
T. (06) 361 02 36. *081450*

Ughetti F., 24a Vicolo Cinque, 00153 Roma.
T. (06) 5884309. *081451*

Ugolini M., 5 Via Fortuny, 00196 Roma.
T. (06) 3218304. *081452*

Ugolini, Milena, Via Vittoria 60, 00187 Roma.
T. (06) 679 58 09, Fax (06) 6791724. *081453*

Valentinetti B., 19 lg. Fontan di Borghese, 00186 Roma.
T. (06) 6875346. *081454*

Vangelli de Cresci R., 35 Via Margutta, 00187 Roma.
T. (06) 3207592. *081455*

VE.CO.ART., 2 Viale Milizie, 00192 Roma.
T. (06) 3211739, 3221040. *081456*

Vespignani Netta, 89 Via Babuino, 00187 Roma.
T. (06) 3207724. *081457*

Vespignani, Netta, Via del Babuino 89, 00187 Roma.
T. (06) 3207725, Fax (06) 3230610. *081458*

La Vetrina, Via dei Coronari 57, 00187 Roma.
T. (06) 654 08 66. - Paint - *081459*

Videoarte, 21 Via Cavallini, 00193 Roma.
T. (06) 3207180. *081460*

Vigna Antoniniana Stamperia D'Arte di Valter Rossi & C., 70 Viale Baccelli, 00153 Roma.
T. (06) 5754158. *081461*

Violi G., 28 Via Campo Carleo, 00184 Roma.
T. (06) 6797369. *081462*

Virgilio, Carlo, Via della Lupa 10, 00186 Roma.
T. (06) 687 10 93, Fax (06) 6871093. - Graph / Graph - *081463*

Vision 3 G di Fattini Teresa Eugenia in Botti e C., 31 Via Fontan di Borghese, 00186 Roma.
T. (06) 6876127. *081464*

Vitolo, Paolo, Via Gregoriana 4, 00178 Roma.
T. (06) 679 04 94, Fax (06) 6840251. *081465*

Zanini, Via del Babuino 41A, 00187 Roma.
T. (06) 678 35 74. - Paint / Graph - *081466*

Rovereto (Trento)
Delfino, Via Roma 7, 38068 Rovereto.
T. (0464) 24234. *081467*

Rovigo
Alexandra, Corso del Popolo 36, 45100 Rovigo.
T. (0425) 259 46. - Paint / Graph - *081468*

Garofolo, Via Cavour 17, 45100 Rovigo.
T. (0425) 231 41. *081469*

Rudiano (Brescia)
Contemporanea, Piazza Martiri Libertà 13, 25030 Rudiano. T. (030) 706 00 55. *081470*

Salerno
Il Catalogo, Via A. M. de Luca 14, 84100 Salerno.
T. (089) 296 66. - Paint - *081471*

La Seggiola, Corso Vitt. Emanuele 171, 84100 Salerno.
T. (089) 233 10. - Paint - *081472*

Tafuri, Clemente, Via Principati 8, 84100 Salerno.
T. (089) 23 32 99. *081473*

Salò (Brescia)
Carmine, Piazza Vittoria 9, 25087 Salò.
T. (0365) 22183. *081474*

Zanca, B., Complesso Gasparo, 25087 Salò.
T. (0365) 40153. *081475*

Salsomaggiore Terme (Parma)
Alfieri, G., Viale Romagnosi 5, 43039 Salsomaggiore Terme. T. (0524) 77219. *081476*

Berna, Via Berzieri 3, 43039 Salsomaggiore Terme.
T. (0524) 722 79. *081477*

Old Britannia, Via Romagnosi 22, 43039 Salsomaggiore Terme. T. (0524) 742 41. - Paint - *081478*

San Donato Milanese (Milano)
Metanopoli, Via Triulziana 2, 20097 San Donato Milanese. - Paint - *081479*

Sanremo (Imperia)
Cose d'Altri Tempi, Via Roma 44, 18038 Sanremo.
T. (0184) 837 67. *081480*

La Tavolozza, Corso Inglesi 56, 18038 Sanremo.
T. (0184) 752 43. - Paint - *081481*

Santa Margherita Ligure (Genova)
Casabella, Via dell'Arco 30, 16038 Santa Margherita Ligure. T. (0185) 87577. - Paint - *081482*

Piras, Nicola, Via Algeria 9, 16038 Santa Margherita Ligure. T. (0185) 28 61 37. - Paint - *081483*

Saronno (Varese)
Il Chiostro, Via Carcano 5, 21047 Saronno.
T. (02) 962 27 17, Fax (02) 9622717. *081484*

Sassari
Galleria 2 D, Viale Italia 50/C, 07100 Sassari.
T. (079) 247 68. - Paint - *081485*

La Catena, Via Alghero 56, 07100 Sassari.
T. (079) 398 76. - Paint - *081486*

Savona
Santandrea, Piazzetta dei Consoli 3, 17100 Savona.
T. (019) 826553. - Paint / Sculp - *081487*

Settimo Torinese (Torino)
Arte Oggi, Via Torino 11, 10036 Settimo Torinese.
T. (011) 801 40 80. *081488*

Siena
Nuovo Aminta, Via del Cavallerizzo 1, 53100 Siena.
T. (0577) 422 02. *081489*

Sirmione (Brescia)
Piccolo San Michele, Piazza Castello 22, 25019 Sirmione. T. (030) 91 64 05. *081490*

Sondrio
Maspes e Romegialli, Via Beccaria 21, 23100 Sondrio.
T. (0342) 220 61. - Graph - *081491*

Numero Uno, Via Quadrio 7, 23100 Sondrio.
T. (0342) 2 26 49. - Paint / Graph - *081492*

Sorrento (Napoli)
Mandara, O., Piazza Tasso 21, 80067 Sorrento.
T. (081) 78 16 49. *081493*

Spoleto (Perugia)
Astrolabio, Via Saffri 26, 06049 Spoleto.
T. (0743) 49417. *081494*

Fontanarte, Piazza Mercato 21, 06049 Spoleto.
T. (0743) 49873. *081495*

Galleria d'Arte 1631, Via dell'Arringo 2, 06049 Spoleto.
T. (0743) 44391. - Paint / Furn / China / Sculp - *081496*

La Cappuccina, Via degli Abeti 1, 06049 Spoleto.
T. (0743) 47516. - Paint / Furn - *081497*

Profili, Piazza Mercato 13, 06049 Spoleto.
T. (0743) 44040. *081498*

Taranto
Magna Graecia, Via Duomo 196, 74100 Taranto.
T. (099) 68 78 74. - Paint - *081499*

San Cataldo, Via Duomo 198, 74100 Taranto.
T. (099) 40 45 58. - Paint - *081500*

Teramo
Legnini, C., Via G. Annunzio 74a, 64100 Teramo.
T. (0861) 39 34. *081501*

Rizziero Arte, Via Irelli 9, 64100 Teramo.
T. (0861) 247782, Fax (0861) 244744. *081502*

Terracina (Latina)
La Scuderia, Via Posterula, 04019 Terracina.
T. (0773) 72 48 60. - Paint - *081503*

Thiene (Vicenza)
Torchio Nuovo, Via Zanella 37, 36016 Thiene.
T. (0445) 34 84 8. *081504*

Todi (Perugia)
Extra Moenia, Piazza Garibaldi 7, 06059 Todi.
T. (075) 894 48 67. *081505*

Torino
Accademia, Via Accademia Albertina 3, 10123 Torino.
T. (011) 88 54 08. - Paint / Graph / Sculp - *081506*

Accademia, 3e Via Acc. Albertina, 10123 Torino.
T. (011) 885408. *081507*

Ai Tre Torch, 14 Corso Cairoli, 10123 Torino.
T. (011) 8395458. *081508*

Angeloro D., 34 Corso pr. Oddone, 10152 Torino.
T. (011) 4362876, 4367516. *081509*

Antichi Maestri Pittori, Via Doria 190, 10123 Torino.
T. (011) 8127587, 8127612. *081510*

Area, 14 Via Rocca, 10123 Torino.
T. (011) 883655. *081511*

A.R.M.A.C., 32 Via Canonico Tancredi, 10156 Torino.
T. (011) 2733148. *081512*

Art In, 147 Corso Francia, 10238 Torino.
T. (011) 745840. *081513*

Arte Club di Robiolio Bose C. & C., 39 Via Rocca, 10123 Torino. T. (011) 836331. *081514*

Arte Figurativa, 27 Via Bertola, 10122 Torino.
T. (011) 5176377. *081515*

Arteincornice, 11c Via Vanchiglia, 10124 Torino.
T. (011) 885071. *081516*

Artestudio di Bausano E. & C., 13 Via Montebello, 10124 Torino. T. (011) 8177052. *081517*

Arx, 4 Piazza Savoia, 10122 Torino. T. (011) 4310728, 4369700. *081518*

Associazione Artifex, 68 Via Valprato, 10155 Torino.
T. (011) 2484221. *081519*

Aversa, Roberto & Co, Via Carlo Alberto 24, 10123 Torino. T. (011) 532662, Fax (011) 532662.
- Paint - *081520*

Balocco, Carla, Via Barbaroux, 10122 Torino.
T. (011) 54 83 07. *081521*

Berman, Via Arcivescovado 9/18, 10121 Torino.
T. (011) 53 74 30. - Graph - *081522*

Bertola, Lauro, Via Silvio Pellico 29/a, 10125 Torino.
T. (011) 68 97 12. - Paint - *081523*

Biasutti, Gianpietro, Via Juvarra 18, 10122 Torino.
T. (011) 54 09 93, Fax (011) 5400993. *081524*

Bottisio, Corso Matteotti 2A, 10121 Torino.
T. (011) 54 48 21. - Paint - *081525*

Bourlot – di C. Birocco Libri e stampe antiche, Piazza S. Carlo 183, 10123 Torino. T. (011) 537405. *081526*

Il Calamo, Via della Rocca 4, 10123 Torino.
T. (011) 8174808. - Graph - *081527*

Caretto, Girogio, Via Maria Vittoria 10, 10123 Torino.
T. (011) 53 72 74. - Paint - *081528*

Cassiopea, Via Cavour 8, 10123 Torino.
T. (011) 53 01 96. *081529*

Centro Arte, 4 Corso Palestro, 10122 Torino.
T. (011) 5620772. *081530*

Centro del Dipinto, Corso Lecce 72, 10143 Torino.
T. (011) 74 75 55. *081531*

Chado' Fiorio – dal 1933, Coro Pr. Oddone 66, 10152 Torino. T. (011) 4363070. *081532*

Christiani, Giancarlo, Via Porta Palatina 3, 10122 Torino. T. (011) 436 07 15. *081533*

Cittadella, Via Bertola 31/l, 10121 Torino.
T. (011) 51 48 89. *081534*

Colombari, Paolo & Rossella, Via Giolitti 8, 10123 Torino. T. (011) 513044. *081535*

Cosmo Graf, 67 Via Zumaglia, 10145 Torino.
T. (011) 7496865. *081536*

Cristina, 31 Via M. Vittoria, 10147 Torino.
T. (011) 837900. *081537*

Cristina, Via Maria Vittoria 31, 10123 Torino.
T. (011) 83 79 00. *081538*

Cutica, Via Maria Vittoria 1, 10123 Torino.
T. (011) 54 27 36. - Graph / Num - *081539*

D'arte Martano, Via Principe Amadeo 29, 10123 Torino.
T. (011) 8177987, Fax (011) 876782. *081540*

Dantesca, Piazza Carlo Felice 19, 10123 Torino.
T. (011) 535897, 541512, Fax (011) 530305. - Paint / Graph - *081541*

Davico, Galleria Subalpina 30, 10123 Torino.
T. (011) 5629152. - Paint / Graph / Sculp - *081542*

Davico di Silvano Gherlone e C., 30 gall Subalpina, 10123 Torino. T. (011) 5629152. *081543*

Di Rivera, Mirella, Via Maria Vittoria 31, 10123 Torino.
T. (011) 83 75 60. *081544*

Di Silvano Gherlone, Davico, Galleria Subalpina 30, 10123 Torino. T. (011) 5629152. *081545*

Documenta Palazzo Villanis, Via Santa Maria 2, 10122 Torino. Fax (011) 515304. *081546*

Espace, 28h Via Rocca, 10123 Torino.
T. (011) 8178559. *081547*
Esperide, Via Lagrange 34, 10123 Torino.
T. (011) 561 13 70. *081548*
Esposito, F., Via Berthollet 43, 10125 Torino.
T. (011) 6690148. - Graph / Num - *081549*
Febbo I., 81 Via Mongineyro, 10141 Torino.
T. (011) 3852124. *081550*
Flash Art, 69 Via Borgaro, 10149 Torino.
T. (011) 259437. *081551*
Fogliato Fratelli, Via Mazzini 9, 10123 Torino.
T. (011) 887733. - Paint - *081552*
Folco, Natalia & Guido, Corso Cairoli 4, 10123 Torino.
T. (011) 812 54 35. *081553*
Fossati, F., Via Vanchiglia 24, 10124 Torino.
T. (011) 87 84 65. *081554*
Free Art, Via dei Mille 42, 10123 Torino.
T. (011) 8395397, Fax (011) 8398905. *081555*
Galleria Carlo Alberto, Via Carlo Alberto 12, 10123 Tori-
no. T. (011) 54 15 85. *081556*
Galleria d'Arte Antica Bodda, Via Cavour 28, 10123 Tori-
no. T. (011) 512762. - Paint - *081557*
Galleria D'Arte Nuova Gissi, Piazza Solferino 2, 10121
Torino. T. (011) 534473, 538625. *081558*
Galleria La Rocca, Via della Rocca 4, 10123 Torino.
T. (011) 87 46 44. - Paint / Mul - *081559*
Gallerie Patrizia Caretto, 11 Via M. Vittoria, 10147 Tori-
no. T. (011) 887756. *081560*
Gissi, G., Piazza Soliferno 2, 10121 Torino.
T. (011) 534473. *081561*
Grafica Internazionale Studio Sardi, 23 Corso Re Umbe-
rto, 10128 Torino. T. (011) 543891. *081562*
Grafica Monzoni di Fas Antonio, 27g Via Manzoni,
10122 Torino. T. (011) 545051. *081563*
Guernica Arte, 68 Via Valprato, 10155 Torino.
T. (011) 235602. *081564*
Guernica Arte, Via Gioberti 40, 10128 Torino.
T. (011) 533418. *081565*
Guerriero R., 68 Via Verolengo, 10149 Torino.
T. (011) 2160540. *081566*
Il Rospo, Via di Nanni Dante 24A, 10138 Torino.
T. (011) 44 32 55. *081567*
Il Torchio, Corso Moncalieri 3/G, 10131 Torino.
T. (011) 87 22 53. *081568*
In Arco, 1 Piazza Via Venete, 10124 Torino.
T. (011) 8171393, 8122927. *081569*
L'Acquaforte, 29 Via pr. Amedeo, 10123 Torino.
T. (011) 8174314. *081570*
L'Affiche, Via C. Alberto 30D, 10123 Torino.
T. (011) 561 22 63. *081571*
L'Approdo, Via Bogino 17, 10123 Torino.
T. (011) 839 78 04. - Paint / Graph / Sculp - *081572*
L'Ariete, Via Bava 4, 10124 Torino.
T. (011) 8172122. *081573*
L'Arte Antica, 9 Via Volta, 10122 Torino.
T. (011) 549041, 5625834. *081574*
L'Immagine, 1 Via Cermaia, 10121 Torino.
T. (011) 5629831. *081575*
La Bussola, Via Po 9B, 10123 Torino. T. (011) 51 89 94.
- Paint - *081576*
La Bussola Galleria d'arte moderna, Via Po 9b, 10124
Torino. T. (011) 8170558. *081577*
La Conchiglia, Via Garibaldi 35, 10122 Torino.
T. (011) 53 83 56. *081578*
La Giara, Via degli Stampatori 9, 10122 Torino.
T. (011) 561 22 63. *081579*
La Parisina, Corso Moncalieri 47, 10133 Torino.
T. (011) 6505464. *081580*
La Polena, Via Amendola 7, 10121 Torino.
T. (011) 52 15 16. - Paint - *081581*
La Tavolozza, Corso de Gasperi 35, 10100 Torino.
T. (011) 587110. - Paint / Graph / Sculp - *081582*
La Telaccia, Via Pietro Santarosa 12, 10122 Torino.
T. (011) 5628220. *081583*
La Tesoriera, Corso Francia 268, 10146 Torino.
T. (011) 776 21 47. - Paint / Graph / Sculp - *081584*
Le Immagini, Via Rocca 3, 10123 Torino.
T. (011) 83 67 65. *081585*
Mantra, Via Federico Ozanam 7, 10123 Torino.
T. (011) 8127150. *081586*
Marin, Via Lagrange 1, 10123 Torino.
T. (011) 54 16 57. *081587*

Masoero F., 13 Via G. di Barolo, 10124 Torino.
T. (011) 885933. *081588*
Menabo', 53 Via Cibrario, 10144 Torino.
T. (011) 4374364. *081589*
Menzio, Eva, Via Cavour 41, 10123 Torino.
T. (011) 887175, 8171078, Fax (011) 871078. *081590*
Micró, Piazza Vittorio Veneto 10, 10123 Torino.
T. (011) 88 26 02. *081591*
Narciso, Piazza Carlo Felice 18, 10121 Torino.
T. (011) 54 31 25. - Paint / Sculp - *081592*
Nigra, Mario, Via Borgo Dora 35, 10152 Torino.
T. (011) 740584, 5213913. *081593*
Notizie, Via Assetta 17, 10128 Torino.
T. (011) 54 66 68. *081594*
La Nuova Bussola, 9 Via Po, 10124 Torino.
T. (011) 8127530. *081595*
Nuova Galleria Bottisio, Corso Matteotti 2/a, 10121 Tori-
no. T. (011) 54 48 21. *081596*
Nuova Gissi, Piazza Solferino 2, 10121 Torino.
T. (011) 538625, 534473. - Paint / Graph /
Sculp - *081597*
Palbert, Corso Vitt. Emanuele 28, 10123 Torino.
T. (011) 8127431. *081598*
Peola, Alberto, Via della Rocca 29, 10123 Torino.
T. (011) 812 44 60. *081599*
Persano, Giorgio, Piazza Vitorio Veneto 9, 10124 Torino.
T. (011) 835527, Fax (011) 8174402. - Paint - *081600*
Petrecca, R., Via L. Galvani 5, 10144 Torino.
T. (011) 4732328. *081601*
Piemonte Artistico e Culturale, Via Roma 264, 10121 To-
rino. T. (011) 542737. - Paint - *081602*
Pirra, S., Corso Vitt Emanuele II 82, 10121 Torino.
T. (011) 54 33 93. *081603*
Pozzallo, Flavio, Via Cavour 17/a, 10123 Torino.
T. (011) 51 50 25. - Furn / China / Sculp - *081604*
Pregliasco – Stampe, Via Acc. Albertina 3/Bis, 10123
Torino. T. (011) 8177114. *081605*
Principe Eugenio Arte ed Antiquariato, 17 Via Cavour,
10123 Torino. T. (011) 5624209. *081606*
Recalcati F., 73b Corso S. Maurizio, 10124 Torino.
T. (011) 8123468. *081607*
Remolino, Matteo, Via Guastalla 11, 10124 Torino.
T. (011) 83 61 50, Fax (011) 836150. *081608*
Ricci R., 10 Via Giola, 10121 Torino.
T. (011) 541298. *081609*
Rimoldi, Giovanni & C., Via Santa Maria 2, 10122 Torino.
T. (011) 51 53 04. *081610*
La Rocca, 4 Via Rocca, 10123 Torino.
T. (011) 8174644. *081611*
Rosini M., 27 Via Chiesa Salute, 10147 Torino.
T. (011) 2296612. *081612*
Salamon, Via Cosseria 6, 10128 Torino.
T. (011) 669 22 26, Fax (011) 3121761. - Paint / Graph /
Sculp / Pho / Mul / Draw - *081613*
Salamon L'Arte Moderna, 4 Via S. Quintino, 10121 Tori-
no. T. (011) 5613170. *081614*
Salzano, Giancarlo, Piazza Carignano 2, 10123 Torino.
T. (011) 54 51 65. *081615*
Sant'Agostino, Corso Tassoni 56, 10142 Torino.
T. (011) 4377577, 4377770. *081616*
Sapori Spoleta, Paolo, Via Cavour 17/a, 10123 Torino.
T. (011) 515711. *081617*
Soave – Libreria Antiquaria, Via Po 48, 10123 Torino.
T. (011) 8178957. *081618*
Spazi D'Essenza Contemporanea, 1 Via Cercenasco,
10121 Torino. T. (011) 616125. *081619*
Stamperia del Borgo, Borgo Medioevale Parco del Valen-
tino, 10126 Torino. T. (011) 6692929. *081620*
Stein, Christian, Piazza San Carlo 206, 10121 Torino.
T. (011) 535574/5628140, Fax (011) 518140.
- Paint - *081621*
Stenger, Edmee, 9 Piazza Solferino, 10121 Torino.
T. (011) 541708, 5172355. *081622*
Studio Arte 2000, 52 Via Sacchi, 10128 Torino.
T. (011) 5818083. *081623*
Studio D'Arte Pictor, 9/Bis Via Garibaldi, 10122 Torino.
T. (011) 5622969. *081624*
Studio D'Arte Sangregorio, 34 Via Domodossola, 10145
Torino. T. (011) 7711605. *081625*
Studio Fornaresio, 68 Via Valprato, 10155 Torino.
T. (011) 238018. *081626*
Studio Pegaso – Galleria D'Arte, 86 Via Baltimora,
10137 Torino. T. (011) 396109. *081627*

Studio 16/e, Via Cardinal Maurizio 16/e, 10131 Torino.
T. (011) 269417. *081628*
Studio 46, Via Maria Vittoria 46, 10123 Torino.
T. (011) 88 59 68. - Paint / Graph / Sculp / Pho /
Draw - *081629*
Sul Po, Lungo Po Cadorna 1, 10124 Torino.
T. (011) 8123300. *081630*
Torre, Luciano, Via Accademia Albertina 3, 10123 Tori-
no. T. (011) 877857. *081631*
Torredimare L., 17 Via Cavour, 10123 Torino.
T. (011) 532603. *081632*
Tucci Russo, Via Gattinara 7, 10153 Torino.
T. (011) 812 66 40, Fax (011) 8126076. *081633*
Tuttagrafica, Piazza Carlo Emanuele II 19G, 10123 Tori-
no. T. (011) 8174383. - Paint / Graph / Num /
Sculp - *081634*
Viretti, M., Via Principe d'Acaja 33, 10138 Torino.
T. (011) 4343595. *081635*
Voena, 36 Via dei Mille, 10123 Torino.
T. (011) 889884. *081636*
Weber, Alberto, Via S. Francesca da Paola 4, 10123 Tori-
no. T. (011) 839 74 93, Fax (011) 8123519. *081637*
Zabert, Gilberto, Piazza Maria Teresa 3, 10123 Torino.
T. (011) 878627, Fax (011) 878627. - Paint - *081638*
Zanotti A., 18 Via Saluzzo, 10125 Torino.
T. (011) 6698722. *081639*
Zizzi A., 242 Via Genova, 10127 Torino.
T. (011) 6647838. *081640*
Zolino J., 37 Via Cavour, 10123 Torino.
T. (011) 837866. *081641*

Trento
Galleria 9 Colonne, Via Cavour 39, 38100 Trento.
T. (0461) 98 62 96. *081642*
Studio Raffaelli, Via Travai 22, 38100 Trento.
T. (0461) 98 25 95, Fax (0461) 237790. *081643*

Treviglio (Bergamo)
Ferrari, Corso Matteotti 14, 24047 Treviglio.
T. (0363) 433 95. *081644*

Treviso
Città di Treviso, Piazza S. Leonardo, 31100 Treviso.
T. (0422) 546 13. - Paint - *081645*
Di Vincenzo, Via Manin 36, 31100 Treviso.
T. (0422) 54 37 83. - Paint - *081646*
Galleria Giraldo, Piazza dei Signori 4, 31100 Treviso.
T. (0422) 528 20. - Paint - *081647*
La Cave, Via Pescheria 37, 31100 Treviso.
T. (0422) 519 97. - Paint - *081648*
Trevisoarte, Via Campana 15, 31100 Treviso.
T. (0422) 54 37 83. - Paint / Furn - *081649*

Trieste
Cappella, Via Franca 17, 34123 Trieste.
T. (040) 764 327. *081650*
Cartesius, Via Marconi 16, 34133 Trieste.
T. (040) 76 15 82. *081651*
Geremy, Via Cadorna 2 d, 34124 Trieste.
T. (040) 63 04 84. *081652*
Tommaseo, Via del Monte 2, 34122 Trieste.
T. (040) 691 87. - Paint / Graph / Sculp / Pho / Mul /
Draw - *081653*
Torbandena, Via di Torbandena 1B, 34121 Trieste.
T. (040) 60598. - Paint / Graph - *081654*

Udine
Galleria del Girasole, Salita al Castello 1, 33100 Udine.
T. (0432) 205825. - Paint / Graph / Sculp - *081655*
Marchetti & C., Via Bonaldo Stringher 25/3, 33100
Udine. T. (0432) 29 91 29. - Paint / Graph / Furn /
Orient / China - *081656*
Plurima, Via E. Valvason, 33100 Udine.
T. (0432) 50 22 36. *081657*

Urbino (Pesaro e Urbino)
Galleria dell'Aquilone, Portici Garibaldi 68, 61029 Urbino. T. (0722) 20 23. - Paint / Graph / Sculp - *081658*

Varese
Bilancia, Via Speroni 14, 21100 Varese.
T. (0332) 28 01 81. - Paint / Graph / China / Repr /
Sculp - *081659*
Bluart, Via Manin 30, 21100 Varese.
T. (0332) 820826. *081660*

Galleria Internazionale, Via Veratti 9, 21100 Varese.
T. (0332) 232 411. - Paint / Sculp / Ico / Draw - 081661
Zabert, Gilberto, Corte Vecchio Broletto 2, 21100 Varese.
T. (0332) 240 667. - Paint - 081662

Venezia
Antichita' La Torre, 49c Via Spalti – Mestre, 30173 Venezia. T. (041) 940591. 081663
Arab Art di Hashi Mohamed, 364 Via Miranese – Mestre, 30171 Venezia. T. (041) 917437. 081664
Art, 3876 Castello, 30122 Venezia.
T. (041) 5225895. 081665
B. & S. Art, 1996a S. Marco, 30124 Venezia.
T. (041) 5229315. 081666
Bac Art Studio, 1069 S. Polo, 30125 Venezia.
T. (041) 5231108. 081667
Barossi, Paolo, S. Marco 2084, 30124 Venezia.
T. (041) 70 39 88. - Paint - 081668
Bianchini, Pietro, S. Marco 4778, 30124 Venezia.
T. (041) 523 15 86. - Paint / Furn - 081669
Bottega d'Arte, S. Marco 689, 30100 Venezia.
T. (041) 5226975. - Paint / Graph - 081670
Bottega D'Arte Ca'Venier dei Leoni, 710 Dorsoduro, 30123 Venezia. T. (041) 5205996. 081671
Brunello S., 22 Piazzetta Bruno – Mestre, 30174 Venezia.
T. (041) 981141. 081672
Bugno & Samueli, Campo S. Fantin 1996A, 30124 Venezia. T. (041) 5231305, Fax (041) 5230360. 081673
Capricorno, S. Marco F. 1994, 30124 Venezia.
T. (041) 5206920. 081674
Cassini, Giocondo, Via 22 Mazzo 2424, 30124 Venezia.
T. (041) 31815. - Graph - 081675
Continl, 2765 S. Marco, 30124 Venezia.
T. (041) 5204942, 5207525, 5208381. 081676
Contini – Arte Italia, 11 Via Ferro Mestre, 31074 Venezia. T. (041) 970621, 981611, 980863. 081677
Del Cavallino, 1725 S. Marco, 30124 Venezia.
T. (041) 5210488. 081678
Dogi, 47 Via A. da Mestre – Mestre, 30174 Venezia.
T. (041) 970060. 081679
Fidesarte, 7 Via Padre Giuliani – Mestre, 30174 Venezia.
T. (041) 950539. 081680
Fidesarte, Via P. Giuliani 7, 30174 Venezia.
T. (041) 950354, Fax (041) 950539. 081681
Follini I., 1105a S. Marco, 30124 Venezia.
T. (041) 5235220. 081682
Fulgenzi G., 3740 S. Marco, 30124 Venezia.
T. (041) 5205068. 081683
Galleria al Pozzo, Corto Legrenzi 7, 30170 Venezia.
T. (041) 950722. 081684
Galleria del Cavallino, S. Marco 1725, 30124 Venezia.
T. (041) 521 0488, Fax (041) 5210642. - Paint / Graph / Sculp / Pho / Mul - 081685
Galleria San Vidal, Campo San Vidal, 30100 Venezia.
T. (041) 523 4602. - Paint / Sculp - 081686
Gasparini V., 25 Via Rosa – Mestre, 30171 Venezia.
T. (041) 980840. 081687
Graziussi, S. Marco 1998, 30124 Venezia.
T. (041) 85 081. 081688
Guarnieri Andrea, 3 Via Cappuccina, 30172 Venezia.
T. (041) 951972. 081689
Ikona Gallery, Dorsoduro 48, 30123 Venezia.
T. (041) 5205854. - Pho - 081690
Il Traghetto, Via XXII Marzo 2407, 30100 Venezia.
T. (041) 211 88. - Paint - 081691
Imagine Venezia London, 3921 Dorsoduro, 30123 Venezia. T. (041) 5229288. 081692
L'Occhio, 181 Dorsoduro, 30123 Venezia.
T. (041) 5226550. 081693
Luce Arte Moderna, 1922a S. Marco, 30124 Venezia.
T. (041) 5222949. 081694
Luna, 1856 S. Polo, 30125 Venezia.
T. (041) 5244022. 081695
Master International Art, C7o Chiesa S. Bartolomeo, 30124 Venezia. T. (041) 5226556, 5226829. 081696
Mazzucchi F., 1771 S. Marco, 30124 Venezia.
T. (041) 5207045. 081697
Meeting, 58 Mestrina – Mestre, 30172 Venezia.
T. (041) 987794. 081698
Min.Ar.Ve, 6039 Castello, 30122 Venezia.
T. (041) 5203143. 081699
Minima Degan, Bruno, 92 Via Verdi – Mestre, 30171 Venezia. T. (041) 962964. 081700

Moderna' 'Il Traghetto', 2460 S. Marco, 30124 Venezia.
T. (041) 5221188. 081701
Moderna Novello di Novello G.E.C., 30124, 30124 Venezia. T. (041) 5285599. 081702
Morra, Lella & Gianni, Giudecca 699, 30123 Venezia.
T. (041) 528 80 06. - Graph - 081703
Nardi, Sergio, Piazza S. Marco 69, 30124 Venezia.
T. (041) 522 57 33. - Jew - 081704
Naviglio, S. Marco 1652, 30124 Venezia.
T. (041) 522 76 34. 081705
Naviglio Venezia, S. Marco 1652, 30124 Venezia.
T. (041) 27634. 081706
Nuovo Spazio 2, 41 Via Piraghetto – Mestre, 30171 Venezia. T. (041) 920054. 081707
Orfino, Via Verdi 88, 30171 Venezia. T. (041) 95 74 24.
- Paint / Graph - 081708
Prova D'Artista, 1994b S. Marco, 30124 Venezia.
T. (041) 5224812. 081709
Puntidivista, S. Marco 2566, 30124 Venezia.
T. (041) 523 49 36. - Paint / Furn - 081710
Rava' T., 2324 Dorsoduro, 30124 Venezia.
T. (041) 5239732. 081711
Ravagnan, Piazza S. Marco 50A, 30124 Venezia.
T. (041) 520 30 21, Fax (041) 5203021. - Paint / Graph / Sculp - 081712
Ravagnan Arte, 5188 S. Marco, 30124 Venezia.
T. (041) 5206004. 081713
San Bartolomeo, S. Bartolomeo 5536, 30124 Venezia.
T. (041) 522 64 36. - Jew - 081714
San Giorgio, Via Ca'Savorgnan 12, 30170 Venezia.
T. (041) 980392. - Paint / Graph / Sculp - 081715
San Stefano, S. Marco – Campo S. Stefano 2953, 30100 Venezia. T. (041) 345 18. - Paint / Sculp - 081716
Santo Stefano, 2953 S. Marco, 30124 Venezia.
T. (041) 5234518. 081717
Scarpa, Pietro, Via S. Marco 2089, 30124 Venezia.
T. (041) 522 71 99. - Graph / Draw - 081718
Schola S. Zaccaria, 4683b Castello, 30122 Venezia.
T. (041) 5234343. 081719
Stamperia Calcografica, 2219a S. Croce, 30135 Venezia. T. (041) 5240772. 081720
Studio D'Arte Barnabo', 3074 S. Marco, 30124 Venezia.
T. (041) 5200673. 081721
Totem Gallery di Gatta, Claudio & C., 426 Via Miranese – Mestre, 30171 Venezia. T. (041) 913076. 081722
Totem-Il Canale, Accademia 878B, 30123 Venezia.
T. (041) 522 3641, Fax (041) 913076. - Paint / Graph - 081723
Venice Commitee – World Monuments Fund, 63 S. Marco, 30124 Venezia. T. (041) 5237614. 081724
Venice Design, 1243 S. Marco, 30124 Venezia.
T. (041) 5238530, 5239083. 081725
Venice Design, 1243 S. Marco, 30124 Venezia.
T. (041) 5239082. 081726
Venice Design, 3146 S. Marco, 30124 Venezia.
T. (041) 5207915. 081727
Venice Design, 3146 S. Marco, 30124 Venezia.
T. (041) 5239082. 081728
Verticale, 30 Via Fapanni – Mestre, 30174 Venezia.
T. (041) 975469. 081729
Viancini, Ettore, S. Marco 1659, 30100 Venezia.
T. (041) 210 31. - Paint / Sculp - 081730

Venezia Mestre
Barovier, Marino, Calle delle Botteghe 3127, 30124 Venezia Mestre. T. (041) 5236748,
Fax (041) 5236748. 081731
Frezzato, Gianni, Via Mestrina 58, 30171 Venezia Mestre. T. (041) 98 77 94. - Paint / Graph - 081732

Verbania Intra (Novara)
Corsini, Via S. Vittore 22, 28044 Verbania Intra.
T. (0323) 43377. 081733
Lanza, Via Canna 4, 28044 Verbania Intra.
T. (0323) 42557. 081734

Vercelli
Gianolio, Corso della Liberta 90, 13100 Vercelli.
T. (0161) 24 00. 081735

Verona
Cortina, Via Carlo Cattaneo 8, 37100 Verona.
T. (045) 388 21. - Paint - 081736

Ferrari, Via C. Cattaneo 14, 37121 Verona.
T. (045) 597040. - Paint - 081737
Frà Giocondo, Piazza dei Signori 4, 37100 Verona.
T. (045) 32545. - Paint - 081738
Galleria Cinquetti, Via Cattaneo 1, 37121 Verona.
T. (045) 59 56 96, Fax (045) 6080600. 081739
Galleria dello Scudo, Via Scudo di Francia 2, 37100 Verona. T. (045) 59 01 44. - Paint / Graph - 081740
Galleria Meneguali, Via A. Massalongo 1, 37121 Verona.
T. (045) 59 48 68. 081741
Ghelfi, Via Roma 7, 37100 Verona. T. (045) 32889.
- Paint / Graph - 081742
Giò, Via Teatro Filarmònica 8, 37100 Verona.
T. (045) 590122. - Paint - 081743
L'Incontro, Via IV Novembre 25, 37100 Verona.
T. (045) 916568. - Paint - 081744
Novelli, Via Oberdan 15, 37100 Verona. T. (045) 230 86.
- Paint - 081745
Studio la Città, Vicolo Samaritana 10, 37121 Verona.
T. (045) 800 07 28. - Paint / Graph / Sculp - 081746
Studio la Città, Via Dietro Filippini 2, 37121 Verona.
T. (045) 59 75 49, Fax (045) 597029. 081747

Vicenza
Ghelfi Libri e quadri, Corso Palladio 13, 36100 Vicenza.
T. (0444) 272 60. - Paint / Graph / Sculp - 081748

Vico Equense (Napoli)
Galleria d'Arte Sonya, Via Roma 20, 80069 Vico Equense. T. (081) 879 94 08. - Paint / Graph - 081749
La Scogliera, Via Nicotera 13, 80069 Vico Equense.
T. (081) 879 87 93. - Paint - 081750
Lincar, Charles, Corso Filangieri 44, 80069 Vico Equense. T. (081) 879 88 16. - Paint / Num / Repr / Fra / Mil - 081751

Vigevano (Pavia)
Stopino, Bruno, Via del Popolo 16, 27029 Vigevano.
T. (0381) 85664. - Paint / Graph / Furn - 081752

Jamaica

Montego Bay
Lester Art Gallery, Belmont, St. James, Montego Bay POB 590, W.F. T. 1387. - Paint / Repr / Fra - 081753

Japan

Fukuoka
Centro Culturale Italiano, 1-121-8, Imaizumi, Chuo-ku, Fukuoka 810. - Paint - 081754
Da Vinci Gallery, Nr. 2 Prince Bldg., 2-9-29 Daimyo, Chuo-ku, Fukuoka 810. T. (092) 714-3517. 081755
Fujikawa Galleries Inc., 2-9, Daimyo Chuo-Ku, Fukuoka.
T. (092) 7714778. - Paint / Graph / Sculp - 081756

Gifu
Atrandom, 7-16, Kanazono-cho, Gifu-shi, Gifu 500.
T. 46-1686. - Paint / Graph - 081757

Hiroshima
Suzukawa, 9-5 Hondori Naka-ku, Hiroshima 730.
T. (0829 2472011. - Paint / Graph - 081758

Kanagawa-shi (Kanagawa-ken)
Ueda Yugawara, 773-109 Miyagami, Yugawara-machi, Kanagawa-shi 259-03. T. 62-0033. 081759

Kanazawa
Art Salon Yutaka, 1-3-10 Katamachi, Kanazawa 920.
T. (0762) 321341. 081760

Kobe
Motomachi Gallery, 1-7-2 Motomachi-dori Chuo-ku, Kobe 650. T. (078) 3312359. - Paint / Graph / Sculp - 081761
Tor Road Gallery, Miwaboshi Bldg 3F, 3-12-16 Kitanagasa-dori Chuo-ku, Kobe 650. T. (078) 3211574. 081762

Kyoto
Aoiya, Sakai-Machi Shijo St., Kyoto. - Paint / Graph / Repr / Sculp / Fra - 081763

Galerie 16, Sakurano-cho, Sanjo-Teramachi, Nakagyo-ku, Kyoto 604. T. (075) 221-6438.   *081764*

Gallery Beni, Kyoto Grand Height 1F 47-5/Entomi-cho Shogoin', Kyoto. T. (075) 751-0591.   *081765*

Gallery Coco, Hollyhock Bldg. 2F Sanjodori Jingumichci, Higashi-iru, Kyoto 605. T. (075) 752-9081.
- Paint -   *081766*

Gallery Heian, Nishigawa Sanjo-agaru Teramachi-dori, Nakagyo-ku, Kyoto. T. (075) 231-0694.   *081767*

Gallery Oike, Gokomati-Kado /Oike Nakagyo-ku, Kyoto 604. T. (075) 211-1995.   *081768*

Gallery Ushio, Higashiyama Nishi iru Shinmonzen-dori/ Higashiyama-ku, Kyoto.   *081769*

Gasendo, Kawara-machi-dori, Goja-agaru, Shimokyo-ku, Kyoto. - Paint / Repr / Fra -   *081770*

Inaba Cloisonne Co., Higashiyama-ku Sanjo Shirakawa-bashi, Kyoto 605. T. (075) 761-1161.   *081771*

Mikumo Wood-Block Hand Print Co., Ltd., Shijo Kakas-hinmichi, Nishi-Iro, Kyoto. - Graph / Graph -   *081772*

Nishimura, Harukichi, Sanjo Teramachi Nakagyo-ku, Kyoto 604. T. (075) 211-2849. - Graph -   *081773*

Shibunkaku, Furumonzen-dori, Yamato-oji, Higashi-iru, Higashiyama-ku, Kyoto 605. T. (075) 531 0001,
Fax 561 4386.   *081774*

Uchida Art Co., Kumanojinga-Higashi, Sakyo-ku, Kyoto 606. T. (075) 761 0345, 761 0349. - Paint / Graph / Repr / Sculp / Fra -   *081775*

Yamada Art Gallery, 253 Umemo-tocho, Shinmonzen St., Higashi-yama-ku, Kyoto. T. (075) 561-5382. - Paint / Graph / Sculp -   *081776*

Zokyudo, Oike Kawaramachi Nishi, Nakagyo-ku, Kyoto 604. T. (075) 255-2232. - Paint / Draw -   *081777*

Kyushy

Fujikawa Galleries, Inc., 9, 2-Chome, Daimyo, Fukuoka, Kyushy. T. 77-4778. - Paint / Graph / Sculp -   *081778*

Meito

B & M Gallery, 622 Tsutsujigaoka, 465 Meito 465. T. (052) 771 7370, Fax 772 5800. - Paint / Draw -   *081779*

Miki

Yuyudo Art Gallery, 1-51 Otsuka 2-chome Hyogo, 673 Miki 673-04. T. (081) 273 73. - Paint -   *081780*

Nagoya (Aichi-ken)

Akira Ikeda Gallery, 17-30, Nishiki 2-chome, Naka-ku, Nagoya. T. (052) 211-6119.   *081785*

Galerie Humanité, Nikko Shoken Bldg, B2F, 3-2-3 Sakae Naka-ku, Nagoya 460. T. (052) 2518640. - Paint / Graph / Sculp / Draw -   *081786*

Garando Gallery, White Bldg 4F, 3-15-32 Nishiki Naka-ku, Nagoya 460. T. (052) 9518839.   *081786a*

Hasegawa Art, Inosis Bldg B1, 2-2-1 Shinsakae Naka-ku, Nagoya 460. T. (052) 2422864.   *081786b*

Kohji Ogura, 2-15-15 Nishiki, Naka-ku, Nagoya 460. T. (052) 204 7376, Fax 204 3705.   *081787*

Maruzen, 2-Ban 7-Go 3-chome, Sakae, Naka-ku, Nago-ya. T. (052) 261-2251. - Paint / Graph / Repr / Arch / Fra -   *081788*

Oise Gallery, 3-2-16 Taiko Nakamura-ku, Nagoya 453. T. (052) 4510565. - Paint / Graph -   *081788a*

Takagi Gallery, 1-17-17 Nishiki, Naka-ku, Nagoya 460. T. (052) 201 4777, Fax 201 4771.   *081789*

Venux Gallery, 3-6 Shin-ei-cho, Naka-ku, Nagoya-shi, Nagoya. T. (052) 961-0591.   *081790*

Osaka

Daiwa Bussan Co., 40, 2-Chome, Minamihonmachi, Higashi-Ku, Fukutake Bldg., Osaka. T. (06) 261-8871.   *081791*

Dan, 2-2-1 chome Edobori Nishi-ku, Osaka 550. T. (06) 447-0005. - Paint / Draw -   *081792*

Ebisubashi Gallery, 1-9-3 Dotonbori, Minami-ku, Osaka, 542. T. (06) 2114001, 2117692. - Paint / Sculp / Repr -   *081793*

Edobori Gallery, 1-11-4 Edobori, Nishiku, Osaka 550. T. (06) 4415377, Fax 4415388. - Paint / Repr / Sculp -   *081794*

Fujikawa Galleries, 1-7 Kawaramachi, Chuo-ku, Osaka. T. (06) 231 4536, Fax (06) 231 1490. - Paint / Graph / Sculp -   *081795*

Fukuzumi Art, Korai new Bldg B1, 2-1-10 Koraibashi Chuo-ku, Osaka 541. T. (06) 2320608.   *081796*

Galerie RA, Matsushita IMP Bldg. 2F, 1-3-7, Shiromi, Chuo-ku, Osaka 540. T. (06) 943 5373, Fax 943 5374.
- Paint / Sculp -   *081797*

Gallery Fukuda, Do-Bldg, 2-6-8, Nishitenman Kita-ku, Osaka-shi, Osaka 530. T. (06) 3641069. - Paint / Graph / Sculp / Draw -   *081798*

Gallery Fukuda, Dojima Bldg, 2-6-8 Nishitenda Kita-ku, Osaka 530. T. (06) 3641069. - Paint / Repr / Sculp -   *081799*

Gallery Kasahara, Kincho Tosabori Bldg 1F, 1-4-11 Tosa-bori Nishi-ku, Osaka 550. T. (06) 4471851.
- Paint -   *081800*

Gallery Nii, Fujimura Yamato Seimei Bldg B1F, 4-2-14 Fushimichou Chuo-ku, Osaka 541. T. (06) 2223023.
- Paint / Graph -   *081801*

Gallery Umeda Co., Ltd., 2-3-9 Sonezaki, Kita-ku, Osaka 530. T. (06) 364-5071. - Paint / Sculp -   *081802*

Hokuyu Automatic Co. Ltd, 12-1-2 Sonezaki-Ue, Kita-ku Kokudo Bldg., Osaka 530. - Paint / Graph / Sculp -   *081803*

Imabashi Gallery, Fujinami Bldg, 2-21 Imabashi, Higashi-ku, Osaka 541. T. (06) 203-4583. - Graph -   *081804*

Kagawa Gallery, Murakami Bldg 1F, 1-1-29 Kitahama Chuo-ku, Osaka 541. T. (06) 2010828.   *081805*

Kansai, 12-3 chome, Dozima kami, Kita-ku, Osaka. T. (06) 341-0868. - Paint / Graph / Sculp -   *081806*

Kawasumi, Nihon-Seimei-Nishi-Kani 4 5-chome, Ima-hashi, Higashi-ku, Osaka. T. (06) 202-5081. - Paint / Sculp -   *081807*

Laurier Fine Art, 5-11 Fushimi-cho Higashi-ku, Osaka 541. T. (06) 2271323.   *081808*

Mitsukoshi, 2-63 Komabashi, Higashi-ku, Osaka.   *081809*

Osaka Main Gallery, 2-3-9 Sonezaki, Kita-ku, Osaka. T. (06) 364-5071.   *081810*

Sogo, 1 Shinsaibashi, Minami-ku, Osaka.   *081811*

Space Gallery, 4-4-1 Fushimichou Chuo-ku, Osaka 541. T. (06) 2292637.   *081812*

Takamiya Gallery, Rajkumen Bldg, 1-8-11 Kyoumachi-bori Nishi-ku, Osaka 550. T. (06) 4455220.   *081813*

Takii Garoh, 11-8 Nishi Temna 4-chome, Kita-ku, Osaka 530. T. (06) 365-1653.   *081814*

Tusjiume, 4-55 Hiranomachi, Higashi-Ku, Osaka. T. (06) 231 3941. - Paint -   *081815*

Umeda, 2-3-9, Sonezaki, Kita-ku, Osaka 530. T. (06) 364-5071. - Paint -   *081816*

Yamaguchi Gallery, 2-3-9 Dojima, Kita-ku, Osaka 530. T. (06) 345 3203, Fax 345 2770. - Paint / Graph / Sculp / Draw -   *081817*

Yamaki Art Gallery, Dai Bldg 1F, 3-6-32 Nakanoshima Kita-ku, Osaka. T. (06) 4460123. - Paint -   *081817a*

Yamamoto Gallery, Nishitenma Bldg 112, 4-9-2 Nishi-tenma Kita-ku, Osaka 530. T. (06) 3615209.   *081818*

Yamashita Gallery, Nishitenma Bldg, 4-9-2 Nishitenma Kita-ku, Osaka 530. T. (06) 3651304. - Paint / Graph -   *081819*

Yodo Gallery, Wataya Bldg 2F, 3-2-6 Dojima Kita-ku, Osaka 530. T. (06) 3651304. - Paint / Graph -   *081820*

Yodo Gallery, 5-3-92-223, Nakanoshima, Kita-ku, Osaka 530. T. (06) 447 2288.   *081821*

Saitama

Iruma Garoh, 867-6, Shimokawara, Keroyama- cho, Iru-ma-gun, 350-04 Saitama 350-04. T. 94-0714. *081823*

Tokyo

Ai, 1-8-17 Ginza, Chuo-ku, Tokyo. T. (03) 35640579.   *081824*

Akiyama, 15, 4-chome, Nihonbashi, Homcho, Chuo-ku, Tokyo. - Paint / Graph / Sculp -   *081825*

Aoki Gallery, Shimada Bldg 3-5-16, Ginza Chuo-ku, To-kyo 104. T. (03) 35356858. - Paint / Graph -   *081826*

Art Collection House, WHOM Bldg., 5-19 Jinnan 1-cho-me, Shibuya-ku, Tokyo 150. T. (03) 3770-0913, Fax 3770-9567.   *081827*

Art Front Gallery, Daikanyama Edge, 3,4F, 28-10 Saru-gaku-cho, Shibuya-ku, Tokyo 150. T. (03) 3476 4868, Fax 3476 1779.   *081828*

Art Gallery Kaigado, Hotel Imperial, 1-1, Uchis. cho 1-chome, Chiyoda-ku, Tokyo.   *081829*

Atagoyama Gallery, Iseman Bldg. 3F 8-8-17 Ginza, Chuo-ku, Tokyo 104. T. (03) 3571 5508, Fax 3571 5382. - Paint / Graph / Sculp / Draw -   *081830*

Bancho Gallery, 9F Iijima Bldg., 6-4-8, Ginza, Chuo-ku, Tokyo 104. T. (03) 3571-8121.   *081831*

Bijutsu Saloon Hamanoya, 6-chome, Ginza, Chuo-ku, Tokyo. T. (03) 3571-0033.   *081832*

Brain Trust Inc., 28 Mori Bldg.,16-13,Nishiazabu 4-cho-me, Minato-ku, Tokyo. T. (03) 3406 3291. - Paint / Graph / China / Sculp -   *081833*

Bungei Shunju, 5, Ginza, Chuo-ku, Tokyo. - Paint / Graph -   *081834*

Bustamante, Sergio, Roppongi 5-16-22, Mani Bldg., Mi-nato-ku, Tokyo 106. T. (03) 3588-9115/6, Fax 3588-9117. - Sculp -   *081835*

Canon Salon, 9-9, 5-chome Ginza, Chuoku, Tokyo. - Paint -   *081836*

CBA Gallery, 4th Fl. Tomono Honsha Bldg., 12-4 Ginza 7-chome, Chuo-ku, Tokyo 104. T. (03) 3541-4039, Fax 3541-4087.   *081837*

Chikyudo, 8-chome, Ginza, Tokyo.   *081838*

Chuo Koron, 7th fl. Chuo Koron Bldg., 2-1 Kyobashi, Tokyo.   *081839*

Daimaru Gallery, 9-1 Marunouchi 1-chome, Chiyoda-ku, Tokyo 100. T. (03) 3212-8011.   *081840*

Decor, 8-5, Ginza 6-chome, Chuo-ku, Tokyo. T. (03) 3572-9685.   *081841*

Ebiya Co., 2-18 Nihonbashi Muro-machi 3-chome, Chuo-ku, Tokyo 103. T. (03) 3241-6543.   *081842*

Enderle, Ichiko Building, Yotsuya 1-5 Shinjuku-ku, Tokyo 160. T. (03) 3352-2481. - Ant / Orient -   *081843*

Formes Gallery, 3-3-6 Ginza, Chuo-ku, Tokyo. T. (03) 35613686, 35641606.   *081844*

Formes Gallery, New Melsa 7F, 5-7-10 Ginza Chuo-ku, Tokyo 104. T. (03) 35715061.   *081845*

Frannell Gallery, Okura Hotel Annex, 10-4 Tora- nomon 2-chome, Minato-ku, Tokyo 105. T. (03) 3538-2751.   *081846*

Fuji Aoki Gallery, Dai-2 Saiki Bldg 1F, 1-15-12 Uchi-Kanda Chiyoda-ku, Tokyo. T. (03) 32917364.   *081847*

Fuji Television Gallery, 3-1 Kawadacho, Shinjuku-ku, To-kyo 162. T. (03) 33570660, Fax (03) 33588238. - Paint / Graph / Sculp -   *081848*

Fujikawa Galleries, 8-6 Ginza, Chuo-ku, Tokyo 104. T. (03) 3574-6820, Fax (03) 3574-6206. - Paint / Graph / Sculp -   *081849*

Fuma Gallery, Aoyanagi Bldg 9F, 8-8-15 Ginza Chuo-ku, Tokyo 104. T. (03) 35713531.   *081850*

Galerie Arche, 4-1-16-302, Roppongi, Minato-ku, Tokyo. T. (03) 3583-0819   *081851*

Galerie Ginsen, 5-6-8 Ginza Chuo-ku, Tokyo. T. (03) 3572 5038.   *081852*

Galerie Nichido, 5-3-16, Ginza Chuo-ku, Tokyo 104. T. (03) 35712553, Fax 3289 4446. - Paint / Graph / Sculp / Fra -   *081853*

Galerie Saikodo, Ginza Boeki Bldg 8F, 2-7-18 Ginza Chuo-ku, Tokyo 104. T. (03) 5640711. - Paint -   *081854*

Galerie Saison, 1-12-1 Kyobashi Chuo-ku, Tokyo 104. T. (03) 5612984, 5613765.   *081855*

Galerie Shinkura, Hotel New Otani 4, Kioi-cho, Tokyo. T. (03) 3239-0548. - Paint / Graph -   *081856*

Galerie Taimei, Nikkei Bldg. 1F, 3-5 Ginza 7-chome, Chuo-ku, Tokyo 104. T. (03) 3574-7225, Fax 3573 5737.   *081857*

Galerie Vivant, Daini Yanagiya Bldg. 3F 10-12 Ginza 7 chome, Chuo-ku, Tokyo. T. (03) 3574-6725.   *081858*

Galerie Yoshii, 8-2-8 Ginza Chuo-ku, Tokyo. T. (03) 3571-0412, 3572-5727. - Paint -   *081859*

Galleria Grafica Tokio, Kato Bldg. 7-8-9 Ginza, Chuo, To-kyo 104. T. (03) 3573-7732. - Paint / Graph -   *081860*

Gallery, 11-6 Akasaka 1-chome Minato-ku, Tokyo 107. T. (03) 3585-4816. - Ant / Orient / China / Sculp / Tex / Jew -   *081861*

Gallery Ann Art, Ishii Bldg, 3-20-3 Tamagawa Setagaya-ku, Tokyo 158. T. (03) 37002030.   *081862*

Gallery Asunaro, Kiyonaga Bldg 2F, 3-4-8 Ginza Chuo-ku, Tokyo 104. T. (03) 35620476.   *081863*

Gallery Hasegawa, Chiyoda Ginza Bldg 2F, 6-7-19 Ginza Chuo-ku, Tokyo 104. T. (03) 32890350.   *081864*

Gallery Hiro, Iwatsuki Bldg, 6-7-16 Ginza Chuo-ku, To-kyo 104. T. (03) 5740545. - Paint / Repr / Sculp -   *081865*

Gallery Hirota Bijutsu, Zenya Bldg 1F, 7-3-15 Ginza Chuo-ku, Tokyo 104. T. (03) 35711288.   081866
Gallery Iida, 8-6-23 Ginza Chuo-ku, Tokyo 104. T. (03) 35723746.   081867
Gallery Kabutoya, 8-8-7 Ginza Chuo-ku, Tokyo 104. T. (03) 35716331, 5714305. - Paint -   081868
Gallery Kasuku, 15-1 Minami Motomachi Shinjuku-ku, Tokyo 160. T. (03) 33572920.   081869
Gallery Kojima, Puzzle Aoyama 1F, 3-38-11 Jingumae Shibuya-ku, Tokyo 150. T. (03) 34044876. - Paint / Repr -   081870
Gallery Kokusai, 7-8-14 Ginza Chuo-ku, Tokyo 104. T. (03) 5716765. - Paint / Graph -   081871
Gallery Mikimoto, 4-5-5 Ginza Chuo-ku, Tokyo 104. T. (03) 5354611. - Paint / Graph / Sculp -   081872
Gallery Piazza, Harajuku Piazza Bldg., 4-26-18, Jiugumae, Tokyo. T. (03) 3403-5161.   081873
Gallery Sanyo, Ginza Ohno Bldg 1F, 4-1-17 Tsukiji Chuo-ku, Tokyo 104. T. (05) 5433709. - Paint / Repr / Sculp -   081874
Gallery Shimomura, Imperial Hotel Carcade 1-1, Uchisaiwai-cho/1-chome, Tokyo.   081875
Gallery Ueda, Asahi Bldg, 6-6-7 Ginza, Chuo-ku, Tokyo 104. T. (03) 3574 7553, Fax 3572 0704. - Paint / Graph / Sculp / Draw -   081876
Gallery Wada, Mikamikogyo Watanabe Kyodo Bldg 1F, 1-8-8 Ginza Chuo-ku, Tokyo 104. T. (03) 3561 4207.   081877
Gallery Wadachi, Fuso Bldg 4F, 1-7-16 Ginza Chuo-ku, Tokyo 104. T. (03) 35630886.   081878
Gallery 21, 4-17, 3-chome Ginza, Chuo-ku, Tokyo 104. T. (03) 3567-2816.   081879
Gingyo Gallery, 10-2 8-chome Ginza, Chuo-ku, Tokyo. T. (03) 3571-0586. - Paint -   081880
Ginza Art Gallery, Nagasaki-Center Bldg. 2F 8-9-16 Ginza, Chuo-ku, Tokyo 104. T. (03) 3572-7688.   081881
Gion Gallery, 8-4-24 Ginza, Chuo-ku, Tokyo. T. (03) 3573-3124.   081882
Green Collections, Axis Bldg. 5-17-1 Roppongi, Minato-Ku, Tokyo. T. (03) 3587 0316.   081883
Green Collections, 110, 111 Palace Aoyama 6-1-6 Minamiaoyama, Minato-ku, Tokyo. T. (03) 3400-1182. - Paint / Graph / Sculp / Draw -   081884
Hagurodo, Yushima-High-Town 2F, 4-6-11 Yushima, Bunkyo-ku, Tokyo. T. (03) 3815-0431.   081885
Heisando Co., 2-4, I Chome, Shiba Park, Minato-Ku, Tokyo 105. T. (03) 3434-0588. - Paint / Sculp -   081886
Hibiya Yamagata Gallery, Hibiya Park Bldg. B1, 1-1 Yuraku-cho, Chiyoda-ku, Tokyo. T. (03) 3271-9222. 081887
Hiiragi Gallery, Gallery Center Bldg., 3-2, Ginza 6-chome, Chuo-ku, Tokyo. T. (03) 3573-5180. - Paint -   081888
Hiro Gallery, Iwatsuki Bldg, 6-7-16, Ginza Chuo-ku, Tokyo 104. T. (03) 3574 0545, Fax 3574 0359. - Paint / Graph / Sculp / Draw -   081889
Hoyu Gallery, Toraya Bldg. 4F, 7-10-20 Nishi-Shinjuku, Shinjuku-ku, Tokyo. T. (03) 3363-7096.   081890
Ichibanboshi Gallery, 3-6-9 Nihonbashi Chuo-ku, Tokyo 103. T. (03) 32722525.   081891
Iida Bijutsu, 6-10-10 Ginza Chuo-ku, Tokyo 104. T. (03) 35737277. - Paint -   081892
Iida Gallery, 8-6-23 Ginza, Chuo-ku, Tokyo. T. (03) 3572-3746. - Paint -   081893
Ikeda Bijutsu Gallery, Watanabe Bldg. 1-8-8 Ginza, Chuo-ku, Tokyo 104. T. (03) 3657 5080, Fax 3567 5083. - Paint / Graph / Sculp / Draw - 081894
Interface, 7-5-56 Akasaka, Minato-ku, Tokyo 107. T. (03) 3587-1307. - Ant / Paint / Graph / Orient / Repr / Dec / Fra / Draw -   081895
Isetan Gallery, 14-1, Shinjuku, 3-chome Shinjuku-ku, Tokyo 160. T. (03) 3225-2793.   081896
Ishii Sanryudo Gallery, 1-8-15 Ginza, Chuo-ku, Tokyo. T. (03) 3563-3251.   081897
Ishiro, 2 Senoh Bldg., 4F, 3-1-4, Azabudai, Minato-ku, Tokyo 106. T. (03) 35822934, Fax 35822997. - Ant / Paint / Graph / Draw -   081898
Isseido Gallery, 1-29-7 Jiyugaoka, Meguto-ku, Tokyo. T. (03) 3717-6660.   081899
Japan International Corp., 2nd Fl., Shuwa Roppongi Bldg., 3-14-12, Roppongi, Minato, Tokyo 106. T. (03) 3404-7473, Fax 3404-2816.   081900
Jiyugaoka Gallery, 1-25-12 Jiyugaoka, Meguro-ku, Tokyo. T. (03) 3723-5367.   081901

Kaigado Art Gallery, Hotel Okura Arcade, 2-10-4 Toranomon, Minato-ku, Tokyo 105. T. (03) 3584-3896.   081902
Kaigado Art Gallery, Galerie Arai Co. Ltd., Imperial Hotel Arcade, 1 Uchisaiwai-cho, Chiyoda-ku, Tokyo. T. (03) 3503-7988/9.   081903
Kamakura, 7-10-8 Ginza, Chuo-ku, Tokyo 104. T. (03) 3574-8307, Fax (03) 3574-8377. - Paint -   081904
Kaneda, Dei Bldg, 6-3-6 Ginza, Chuo-ku, Tokyo. T. (03) 3574-6388.   081905
Kaneko Art Gallery, Sansei Bldg. 1F 3-7-13 Kyobashi, Chuo-ku, Tokyo 104. T. (03) 3564 0455, Fax 3564 3318. - Paint / Graph / Sculp / Draw - 081906
Katsura Gallery, 8-10-15 Ginza Chuo-ku, Tokyo 104. T. (03) 5746990. - Paint -   081907
Keio Gallery, 1-4 Nishi Shinjuku 1-chome, Shinjuku-ku, Tokyo 160. T. (03) 3342-2111.   081908
Keio Umeda Gallery, Ginza-Nogakudo Bldg. 6-5-15 Ginza, Chuo-ku, Tokyo. T. (03) 3574-7261.   081909
Kikuchi, Sanraku Bldg. 2F 6-5-16 Ginza, Chuo-ku, Tokyo.   081910
Kimura, Keiko, 18-12, 2-chome, Naka-machi, Meguro-ku, Tokyo 153. T. (03) 3719-2908. - Graph / Pho / Mul / Draw -   081911
Kinokuniya Gallery, 17-7 Shinjuku 3-chome, Shinjuku-ku, Tokyo 160. T. (03) 3354-7401, Fax 3354-0405.   081912
Kiriyama, Kitaya Bldg. 2-26-34, Minami Aoyama, Minato-ku, Tokyo 107.   081913
Kite Museum, Taimeiken Bldg., 12-10, 1-chome, Nihonbashi, Chuo-ku, Tokyo 103. T. (03) 3271-2465. - Paint -   081914
Kokusai Gallery, 7-8-14 Ginza, Chuo-ku, Tokyo. T. (03) 3571-6765.   081915
Konohana Gallery, 19-7 Higashiyama-machi, Itabashi-ku, Tokyo 174. T. (03) 3955-1509.   081916
Kou Gallery, Gallery Center Bldg., 3-2, Ginza 6-chome, Chuo-ku, Tokyo. T. (03) 3572-3818. - Paint -   081917
Kunugi, 7-3, Ginza, Chuo-ku, Tokyo.   081918
Lunami, 2-5-2 Ginza, Chuo-ku, Tokyo. T. (03) 3561 6076.   081919
Mainichi, 3-7-16 Kanda Ogawa-cho, Chiyoda-ku, Tokyo 101. T. (03) 3233-7377.   081920
Marlborough Fine Art, Akasaka Center Bldg., 1-3-12 Moto Akasaka, Minato-ku, Tokyo 107. T. (03) 3404-8001.   081921
Maruzen Gallery, 3-3-10 Nihombashi, Chuo-ku, Tokyo.   081922
Miki Gallery, Maruchu Bldg., 2nd Fl., 1-8-4 Shinbashi, Minato-ku, Tokyo 105. T. (03) 3537-0865.   081923
Mikomoto Gallery, B1, Ginza Bldg. 2-9-14 Ginza, Chuo-ku, Tokyo 104. T. (03) 3563-1607, Fax 3563 1608.   081924
Mitsukoshi Gallery, 4-1 Nihonbashi, Muro-machi 1 chome, chuo-ku, Tokyo 103. T. (03) 3241-3311.   081925
Mitsukoshi Gallery, 29-1 Shinjuku 3-chome, Shinjuku, Tokyo 160. T. (03) 3354-1111.   081926
Miyuki Gallery, 4-4, 6-chome, Ginza, Chuo-ku, Tokyo 104. T. (03) 3571 1771. - Paint / Graph / Sculp / Silv / Draw -   081927
Modern Art Co., 11-14, Tamagawadai 1-chome Setagaya-ku, Tokyo 158. T. (03) 3700-7352. - Paint / Graph / Repr / Fra -   081928
Mudo Gallery, Gallery Center Bldg 7F, 6-3-2 Ginza Chuo-ku, Tokyo 104. T. (03) 5722426. - Paint / Graph -   081929

Mukaï, Tsukamoto Fudosan Bldg 6F, 5-5-11 Ginza Chuo-ku, Tokyo 104. T. (03) 35713292. - Paint / Repr / Sculp -   081930
Muramatsu, 7-1 Ginza, Chuo-ku, Tokyo.   081931
Mureta Gallery, 6-6, Shiroganedai, 5-chome Minato-ku, Tokyo 108. T. (03) 3442-0762, Fax 3442-8537.   081932
Muromachi, Nihon Bldg, 2-6-2 Ohtemachi Chiyoda-ku, Tokyo 100. T. (03) 32423177.   081933
Nabisu, 1-5-2, Ginza, Chuo-ku, Tokyo. T. (03) 3561-2962.   081934
Nagasawa Gallery, Makishido Bldg 7F, 8-5-13 Ginza Chuo-ku, Tokyo 104. T. (03) 35746877.   081935
Nahan Galleries, 2-2-6 Roppongi, Monato-Ku, Tokyo 106. T. (03) 3589-4411.   081936
Nantenshi, Kimura Bldg 1F, 3-6-5 Kyobashi Chuo-ku, Tokyo 104. T. (03) 35633511. - Paint / Graph / Sculp -   081937
Nantenshi Soko Gallery, 1-17-4 Shinkiba, Koto-ku, Tokyo 136. T. (03) 5569 6762, Fax 5569 6764. - Paint / Graph / Sculp / Draw -   081938
Nihonbashi Gallery, 3-8-6 Nihonbashi Chuo-ku, Tokyo 103. T. (03) 2715995, 2718626. - Paint -   081939
Nikkei Gallery, 8th fl., Nikkei Bldg., Ohte-machi, Chiyoda-ku, Tokyo. T. (03) 3270-0251.   081940
Nikon Salon, Ginza 5-6, 3-chome, Chuo-ku, Tokyo 104. T. (03) 3567-5757. - Paint -   081941
Nippon, 3-1-4 Nihonbashi, Chuo-ku, Tokyo. T. (03) 3271-0011.   081942
Nishi-Ginza Gallery, Ono Shoko Bldg., 6-4-7 Ginza, Chuo-ku, Tokyo 104. T. (03) 3572-1726.   081943
Nurihiko Gallery, 1 Nurihiko Bldg., 2-9-2 Kyobashi, Chuo-ku, Tokyo 104. T. (03) 3564-5807, Fax 3561-6329.   081944
Odakyo Gallery, 1-3 Nishi Shinjuku 1-chome, Shinjuku-ku, Tokyo 160. T. (03) 3342-1111.   081945
Ohashi Hall, Ohashi Bldg. 1F, 1-59-1 Yoyogi, Shibuya-ku, Tokyo. T. (03) 3370-1030.   081946
Okabe, behind Wako, 4-4-5 Ginza, Tokyo.   081947
Okamotoya, 12 Shiba-Toranomon, Minato-ku, Tokyo. T. (03) 3591-2231.   081948
Okura Shuko Kan, 2-10-3 Toranomon in front of Hotel Okura, Tokyo 105.   081949
Oriental Art Gallery, 5, 1-chome, Ginza, Chuo-ku, Tokyo. T. (03) 3561-8033.   081950
Osaka Formes Gallery, Gal. Center Bldg, 3-2, Ginza 6-chome, Chuo-ku, Tokyo. T. (03) 35710833. - Paint -   081951
Pentax Gallery, 21-20, 3-chome, Nishi-Azabu Minato-ku, Tokyo 106. T. (03) 3401-2186, 3478-3071. - Fra -   081952
Petit Gallery, Hotel New Otani, 4 Kioi-cho, Chiyoda-ku, Tokyo 102. T. (03) 3239-0845.   081953
Rikugien, Nakamura Bld 2F, 5-9-13, Ginza, Chuo-ku, 104 Tokyo.   081954
Rurien Gallery, 4-6-10 Ginza, Chuo-ku, Tokyo. T. (03) 3561-5490.   081955
Sankeido Ltd., 1, 4-chame, Nihonbashi Muramachi, Chuo-Ku, Tokyo. T. (03) 3241 1003. - Paint -   081956
Satani, Daini Asahi Bldg B1,4-2-6 Ginza Chuo-ku, Tokyo 104. T. (03) 5646733. - Paint / Graph / Sculp -   081957
Sayegusa, 3-5-7 Ginza Chuo-ku, Tokyo. T. (03) 35678531. - Paint / Graph / Sculp -   081958
Seibu Gallery, 21-1 Udagawa-cho, Shibuya-ku, Tokyo 150. T. (03) 3462-0111.   081959
Seibu Gallery, 1-28-1 Minami Ikebukuro, Toshima-ku, Tokyo 171. T. (03) 3981-0111.   081960
Seijyu Gallery, 2-3-19 Ginza Chuo-ku, Tokyo 104. T. (03) 35635235.   081961
Seiza, Sennari Bldg. 1F, 5-6-20 Minami-Aoyama, Minato-ku, Tokyo 3. T. (03) 3407-5337.   081962
Shibuya Gallery, Shibuya Bldg. 8-1 Ginza, 7-chome, Chuo-ku 104, Tokyo. T. (03) 3461-4336.   081963
Shinobazu Gallery, Fuji Bldg, 1-5-3 Yaesu Chuo-ku, Tokyo 103. T. (03) 32713810.   081964
Shinseido, 5-4-30 Minamiaoyama, Minato-ku, Tokyo 107. T. (03) 34988383.   081965
Shirota Gallery, 7-10-8 Ginza, Tokyo 104. T. (03) 3572 7971, Fax 3572 7972. - Paint / Graph / Sculp / Draw -   081966
Shiseido, 8-3, Ginza 8-chome, Chuo-ku, Tokyo 104. T. (03) 3572-2121.   081967
Showa, Kyoritsu Bldg, Higashi Ginza, Tokyo.   081968

YAYOI GALLERY
SADAO OGAWA

7-6-16, Ginza
Chuo-Ku, Tokyo

Telephone 35 71-32 20
Fax 35 74-09 03

MODERN JAPANESE ART
19 & 20th Centuries European Art

Shunpudo Gallery, 6-10, 1-chome Kyobashi, Chuo-ku, Tokyo. T. (03) 3563-5455. - Paint - 081969

Shunsei Gallery, Kuya Bldg 2F, 6-7-19 Ginza Chuo-ku, Tokyo 104. T. (03) 35747688. 081970

Sodosha, 7, 1-chome Kanda Ogawamachi Chiyoda-ku, Tokyo 101. T. (03) 3294-6411, Fax 3294-6415. 081971

Soko Tokyo Gallery, 1-17-4 Shinkiba, Koto-ku, Tokyo 136. T. (03) 5569 6641, Fax 03 5569 6640. - Paint / Graph / Sculp / Draw - 081972

Soumeido, Soumeido Bldg, 4-5-2 Aobadai Meguro-ku, Tokyo 153. T. (03) 34651014. 081973

Spark Gallery, Ogura Bldg. 3F, 2-12-4 Nishiazabu, Mina-to-ku, Tokyo 106. T. (03) 5499 0226, Fax 5485 5246. 081974

Station Gallery, Fuji Bldg. 1F, 1-5-3 Yaesu, Chuo-ku, Tokyo. T. (03) 3271-3810. 081975

Sumisho Art Gallery, UN Bldg., 3F, 2-15 Yurakucho, 1-chome, Chiyoda-ku, Tokyo 100. T. (03) 3593-0777, Fax (03) 3593-0848. 081976

Sun Motoyama, Ginza 6, Chome 6-7, Tokyo. T. (03) 3537 0003/8. 081977

Suzuki Gallery, Simojo Bldg, 5F, 3-2-12 Kyobashi Chuo-ku, Tokyo 104. T. (03) 32812020, Fax 32815528. - Paint - 081978

Taiga, 3-15-16 Shinjuku Shinjuku-ku, Tokyo 160. T. (03) 33527731. 081979

Taigado Gallery, 1-16 Nishi-Shinjuku, Shinjuku-ku, Tokyo. T. (03) 3343-6841. 081980

Takagen Gallery, 6-9-7 Ginza, Chuo-ku, Tokyo. T. (03) 3571-5053. 081981

Takahashi, 403, 2-Chome, Shin-machi, Setagaya-ku, Tokyo. T. (03) 3420-0458. 081982

Tamenaga, 2-4, Ginza 7, Chuo-ku, Tokyo. T. (03) 3573-5368. - Paint / Graph / Sculp - 081983

Tanaka, D., 11-5, 5-chome, Minami-Aoyama, Minato-ku, Tokyo. T. (03) 3400-9550 081984

Tanisho, Iijima Bldg. 2 Go-Kan, 4-8, Ginza, 6-chome, Chuo-ku, Tokyo 104. T. (03) 3574-6633/34. - Paint - 081985

Tokoro Gallery, 1-6-2 Ginza, Chuo-ku, Tokyo 104. T. (03) 3563 3696, Fax 3535 2667. - Paint / Graph / Sculp / Draw - 081986

Tokyo Gallery, Shuwa Bldg 2F, 8-6-18 Ginza Chuo-ku, Tokyo 104. T. (03) 35711808. - Paint / Graph / Sculp - 081987

Tokyo Station Gallery, 1-9-1 Marunouchi, Chiyoda-ku, Tokyo 100. T. (03) 3312 2763, Fax 03 3212 2058. 081988

Tomoyuki & Eriko Hasumi, 4-7-3 Nakameguro, Meguro-ku, Tokyo 701. T. (03) 5704 3425, Fax 5704 3426. - Paint - 081989

Toppan, 1-6 Kanda Surugadai,Chiyoda-ku, Tokyo. 081990

Transworld Art Business, K Bldg, 12-5 Sakuragaoka, Shibuya-ku, Tokyo 150. T. (03) 37801286, Fax 37801287. 081991

Tsubaki Modern Gallery, 3-15-16 Shinjyuku, Shinjyuku-ku, Tokyo 160. T. (03) 3352 7731. 081992

Ueda Gallery SC, Asahi Bldg B1, 6-6-7 Ginza Chuo-ku, Tokyo. T. (03) 5747553, 5747554. - Paint / Graph / Sculp / China - 081993

Universe, 5-13-3, Ginza, Chuo-ku, Tokyo. T. (03) 3542-1311. 081994

Universe, in front of Kabuki Theater, 5-13-3 Ginza, Tokyo. 081995

Von Gallery, Konparu Bldg 5F, 8-7-5 Ginza Chuo-ku, Tokyo 104. T. (03) 5722438. - Paint / Sculp - 081996

Watanabe, S., Color Print Co., 6-19, Ginza, 8-chome, Ginza, Chuo-ku, Tokyo. T. (03) 3571-4684. - Graph / Repr - 081997

Watari, 3-7-6 Jingumae, Shibuya-ku, Tokyo 150. T. (03) 3405-7005. - Paint - 081998

Wildenstein Tokyo Co., Ltd., 3-1-1 Marunouchi, Chiyo-da-Ku, Tokyo. - Paint / Sculp - 081999

Yabumoto, S., 7th Fl., Gallery Center Bldg 3-2, Ginza 6-chome Chuo-ku, Tokyo 104. T. (03) 3572-2748, Fax 03 3289-2527. - Paint / Graph / Repr / Sculp - 082000

Yamato Gallery, Yamato Bldg., 7-9-17 Ginza, Tokyo. 082001

Yanagawa Art Store, 5-4-27 Minami-Aoyama, Minato-ku, Tokyo 107. T. (03) 3407 2244, Fax 3407 7943. 082002

Yayoi Gallery, 7-6-16, Ginza, Chuo-ku,, Tokyo 104. T. (03) 35713220, Fax 35740903. - Paint - 082003

Yomogi Gallery, 7-2-11 Ginza, Chuo-ku, Tokyo. T. (03) 3574-6011. 082004

Yoseido Gallery, 5-5-15 Ginza Chuo-ku, Tokyo 104. T. (03) 3571-1312, 3571-2471. - Graph - 082005

Yoseido Reflection Gallery, 3rd Fl., Abe Bldg. 5-5-9 Gin-za, Chuo-ku, Tokyo 104. T. (03) 3571-4493. 082006

Zeit Foto Salon, Yagicho Bldg. 5F, Chuo-ku, 1-7-2 Ni-honbashi-Muromachi, Tokyo 103. T. (03) 3246 1370, Fax 3279 3224. - Pho - 082007

3 Gallery, Ginza San-ban gal, Sunny Bldg. 3F, 3-4-16 Ginza, Chuo-ku, Tokyo. T. (03) 3567-5545. 082008

Kenya

Nairobi
New Stanley Hotel Gallery, New Stanley Hotel, Nairobi. T. (02) 332333. - Paint - 082009

Watatu Gallery, Consolidated House, 1st Fl, Standard St., Nairobi. T. (02) 228737. 082010

Korea, Republic

Seoul
Bogo Trading Co., Korea World Trade Cnt./R 3207 159-1, Samsung-Dong, Seoul. T. (02) 551-3241-6, Fax 551-3247. 082011

Hu Gallery, 343-10 Seokyo-Dong, Mapo-ku, Seoul, 121. T. (02) 393-9714. - Paint / Graph / Sculp / Pho / Draw - 082012

Tong-In, 16 Kwanhun-dong, Chongno-gu, Seoul, 110. T. (02) 723 4827, 725 9094. - Ant / Paint / Furn / Orient / China / Repr / Sculp / Jew / Silv - 082013

Lebanon

Beirut
L'Amateur, rue Hamra, Capucins, Beirut POB 11-982. T. (961) 342 930, 345 384. - Paint / Graph / Orient / Chi-na / Sculp / Fra - 082014

The House of Art, Beirut B. P. 7178. T. (961) 30 08 91. 082015

Liechtenstein

Balzers
Marte, Annemarie, Egerta 271, 9496 Balzers. T. (075) 42860. 082016

Eschen
Galerie Benissimo, Fallsgasse 261, 9492 Eschen. T. (075) 31534, Fax 35233. 082017

Nissl, Stieg 413, 9492 Eschen. T. (75) 2321379, Fax 2322080. 082018

Tangente, Haldeng 510, 9492 Eschen. T. (075) 3732817, Fax 3734949. - Paint / Graph / Sculp / Draw - 082019

Nendeln
Altesse, Churerstr. 69, 9491 Nendeln. T. (075) 320 85/ 325 23. 082020

Schaan
Brigand Trading, Im Bretscha 21, 9494 Schaan. T. (075) 21326. 082021

Galerie am Lindenplatz, Landstr. 1-3, 9494 Schaan. T. (075) 294 95. 082022

Galerie am Lindenplatz, 9494 Schaan. T. (075) 2333646, Fax (075) 2333647. - Paint / Graph / Sculp - 082023

Galerie Sonnegg, Im Kresta 36, 9494 Schaan. T. (075) 52 13 09. 082024

Karst, Jean, Landstr 65, 9494 Schaan. T. (075) 2322935, Fax (075) 2323103. - Paint / Furn / China / Fra / Instr / Glass / Cur / Mod - 082025

Triesen
Kunst & Rahmen, Landstr. 179, 9495 Triesen. T. (075) 200 94. 082026

Vaduz
Antik-Galerie Vaduz, Herrengasse 25, 9490 Vaduz. T. (075) 245 79/221 69. 082027

Art Studio, Austr 19, 9490 Vaduz. T. (075) 2328939, Fax 2328939. 082028

Haas, Städtle 20, 9490 Vaduz. T. (075) 234 14. - Paint / Graph - 082029

Perspective, Kirchstr. 1, 9490 Vaduz. 082030

Lithuania

Vilnius
Kunstgalerie Siena, Verkiu 109, 2021 Vilnius. T. (02) 720524. - Paint / Graph / Sculp / Eth - 082031

Luxembourg

Luxembourg
Art Gallery & Art Shop, 6 Av. du X Septembre, 2550 Lu-xembourg. T. (0352) 452460, Fax (0352) 458346. - Paint / Graph / Sculp / Mul - 082032

Gredt, Lea, 1 B Rue Beaumont, 1219 Luxembourg. T. (0352) 41148, Fax 21156. 082033

Kutter, 17, rue des Bains, Luxembourg. T. (0352) 235 71. - Paint / Graph - 082034

Malaysia

Kuala Lumpur (Selangor)
Art Galleries & Dealers, Balai S.L.N., 173 A Mdn. T. Abdul Rahman, Kuala Lumpur. *082035*
Chinese Art House, 182 Jalan T. Abdul Rahman, Kuala Lumpur. *082036*
Malaysia Emporium Sy'kat, Art Galleries, 38 Jalan T. Abdul Rahman, Kuala Lumpur. *082037*

Penang
Galerie de Mai, Bangunan Tung Hing 54/3 Burmah Road, Penang. *082038*

Martinique

Fort-de-France
Artibijoux, 89 Rue Victor-Hugo, 97200 Fort-de-France. T. (596) 631062. - Paint / Sculp / Jew - *082039*

Les Trois-Ilets
Saint Soleil, Marina Pointe-du-Bout, Bâtiment Vermeil, 97229 Les Trois-Ilets. T. (596) 660989. *082040*

Mexico

Acapulco (Guerrero)
Galeria Tasende, Costera Miguel Aleman y V. Yanez Pinzon, Acapulco. T. 410 04. - Paint / Sculp - *082041*

Guadalajara (Jalisco)
Casa de la Cultura Jalisciense, Calz. Independencia Sur y Constitugentes, Guadalajara. T. 12 30 32, 12 44 49. *082042*
„Elena", Caseta de Cristal No. 2, Condominio, Guadalajara. *082043*

México (D.F.)
Acuarelas de Mexico SA, 101 ZP 18 Vermont 34, México. T. 5361186. *082051*
Art Centrum, Seneca 114, 11540 México. T. (05) 2551159. *082051a*
Art Forum S.A., Bosque Duraznos 65-301, 11000 México. T. (05) 5965964, 5966434. *082052*
Art Galeria Dolores, 2 ZP 1, México. T. 5121801. *082053*
Arte de Coleccionistas, Paseo de la Reforma 325-10 A, México. T. 25 90 60 ext. 91. - Paint / Graph / Sculp – *082054*
Arte Internacional, Gante 6-3, México. T. 5127226. *082055*
Arvil Gráfica, Cda. Hamburgo 9, 06600 México. T. 525 34 29. - Graph - *082056*
Arvil S.A., Cerrada de Hamburgo 7, 06600 México. T. (05) 2089045, 5116527. - Paint / Graph / Sculp / Mod / Pho / Draw - *082057*
Aura Galerias, Amberes 38, México. T. (05) 5254344. *082058*
Avril Grafica, Campos Elíseos 65, 11550 México. T. 531 4039. *082059*
Chumacero Lourdes Gómez Luna de, Esocolmo 30, México. T. 5140646. *082060*
Coloniart, Estocolmo 37, México. T. 5144799. *082061*
Comercial Partow S.A., Anatole France 115, México. T. (05) 2800091, 2800229. *082062*
Cristobal, Cda. Hamburgo 165B, 06600 México. T. 207 1848, 207 7934. - Paint - *082063*
Del Circulo, Hamburgo 112, México. T. 528 76 33. *082064*
El Angel, Rio Po 130, México. *082065*
„El Presidente", Hamburgo 135, México. *082066*
Excelsior, Reforma 18, México. *082067*
Galeria Alexandra, A.France 130, 11550 México. T. (05) 2802516. *082068*
Galeria Artdicre, Versalles 56D, México. T. (05) 5666635, 5355156. *082068a*
Galeria Arte Nucleo, Edgar Allen Poe 308, 11560 México. T. (05) 2543732, 5316875. *082068b*
Galeria Artistica Shalom, Seneca 114, 11540 México. T. (05) 2027334. *082069*

Galeria Atil, Moliere 97, 11550 México. T. (05) 2546319. *082070*
Galeria Barandiaran, Division del Norte 1276, México. T. 5752735. *082071*
Galeria Burgos, Orient 55 No 244 ZP 13, México. T. 6961761. *082072*
Galeria Coyoacàn, Fernándes Leal 58 ZP 21, México. T. 6890210. *082073*
Galeria Cramen S.A. de C.V., Calderon de la Barca 72, 11560 México. T. (05) 2551520, 2551539. *082074*
Galeria David, Av Nino Perdido 539-B ZP 13, México. T. 5387608. *082075*
Galeria de Arte Alejandro Jiménez Gil, Czda Tlalpan 2191, México. T. 5441660. *082076*
Galeria de Arte Maren y Libreria, Hamburgo No 175 Loc-A-ZP 6, México. T. 5333904. *082077*
Galeria de Arte Mexicanos de R.L., Milan 18, 06600 México. T. (05) 7051014, 7051139, 7055516. *082078*
Galeria de Arte Misrachi S. A., Genova 20, Zona Rosa, México, 06600. T. (05) 5334551. - Paint / Graph / Sculp – *082079*
Galeria de Arte Novedades, Balderas 87, México. *082080*
Galeria de Arte Plaza Comermex, Blvd Avila Camacho 1, 06400 México. T. (05) 5406388. *082080a*
Galeria de Arte Rafael Matos, Montes Urales Sur 730c, 11000 México. T. (05) 2024218, 2021567. *082080b*
Galeria de Arte Victor Navarro, Gutemberg 186, 11590 México. T. (05) 2029352, 2029365. *082081*
Galeria de la Escuela Mexicana, Higuera 57, México. T. 5544265. *082082*
Galeria de los 7+Knoll, Hamburgo 239, México. T. 5116070. *082083*
Galeria del Circulo, Hamburgo 112, México. T. 514 22 03, 528 76 33. - Graph - *082084*
Galeria del Club de Periodistas de Mexico, Filomena Mata 8, México. *082085*
Galeria del Deportivo Israelita, Av. Manuel Avila Camancho 620, México. T. 557 30 00 ext. 135. - Paint / Graph / Sculp - *082086*
Galeria Del Prado, Revillagigedo 10, 06000 México. T. (05) 5124002. *082087*
Galeria Delbos, Hamburgo 75, México. T. 5112543. *082088*
Galeria Derene, Div del Norte 148, 03100 México. T. (05) 6878602. *082089*
Galeria Fabio, Allende 32, 04000 México. T. (05) 5547961. *082090*
Galeria Foto Impacto, Bosque Duraznos 65-2A, 11000 México. T. (05) 5965639. *082091*
Galeria Juan Martin, Dickens 33B, México. T. (05) 5403815. *082092*
Galeria Kashan, Paseo Reforma 408-1, 06600 México. T. (05) 5259375. *082092a*
Galeria Kin, Amargura 12, San Angel, México. T. 5480367. *082093*
Galeria Kin S.A. de C.V., Altavista 92, 01000 México. T. (05) 5508641. *082094*
Galeria Lai, Rio Panuco 41, México. T. 5352840. *082095*
Galeria Lai-Rio, Panuco 41, 03300 México. T. (05) 5352840. *082096*
Galeria Mer-Kup, Moliere 328-C, 06000 México. T. (05) 5207327. - Paint / Graph - *082097*
Galeria Praxis, Arquimedes 175, 11570 México. T. (05) 2548813. *082097a*
Galeria Pintura Joven de Mexico, Rio Marne 18, México. T. 5359386. *082098*
Galeria Ponce S de RL, Belgrado 5 ZP 6, México. T. 5119743. *082099*
Galeria Teresa Haas SA, Genova 2-201 ZP 6, México. T. 5116134. *082100*
Galeria Val Rey, Paseo de la Reforma 412-A ZP 6, México. T. 5110697. *082101*
Galerias C. D. I., Boulev. M. Avila Camacho 620 Lomas de Sotelo, México. *082102*
Galerias Central de Arte, Av. Juarez 4, México. - Paint / Graph / Repr / Sculp / Draw – *082103*
Galerias Coyoacán, M A de Quevedo 532-C, México. T. 5541369. *082104*
Galerias del Zócalo, Monte de Piedad 5-A ZP 1, México. T. 5125895. *082105*
Galerias Enrique, Polanco 8D, 11560 México. T. (05) 2555371. *082106*

Galerias La Granja, Bolivar 16, México. T. 512 96 11, 521 39 00. *082107*
Galerias Piazza, Ejercito Nal 57, 03300 México. T. (05) 5310337. *082108*
Galerias Roberto Guerra, Gante 6-1, 06700 México. T. (05) 5102043. *082109*
Galerias Roberto Guerrero, Gante 6-1, México. T. 5102043. *082110*
Galerias Rubens SA, Independencia 68-4-ZP 1, México. T. 5183176. *082111*
Galerias Tabriz S.A. de C.V., Homero 333, 11570 México. T. (05) 5316964. *082112*
Gamez Sánchez Tomás, Rio Tiber 64 ZP 5, México. T. 5287536. *082113*
Hagerman Mosquera Eduardo, Bosque Duraznos 69, 11000 México. T. (05) 5962206, 5962246. *082114*
Hemer Osker Galerias, Lafayette 137, México. T. 2500919. *082115*
Inter Art S.A. de C.V., Campos Eliseos 65, 11560 México. T. (05) 5317742, 5317800. *082116*
Juarez, Heriberto, Cda. V. Guerrero 5, 10600 México. T. 546 82 20, 595 68 68. - Sculp - *082117*
La Galeria 100, Taine 417, 11560 México. T. (05) 2551159. *082118*
Lanai, Hamburgo 151, México. T. 5113332. - Paint / Graph / Sculp / Dec / Mod / Draw – *082119*
Lourdes, Paseo de la Reforma 264, México. T. 514 63 79. *082120*
Marcos Artisticos, Torojil 172, México. T. 5563096. *082121*
Martin, Juan, Amberes 17, México. T. 5287602. *082122*
Mestre Ventura Ricardo, Morelos 42, México. T. 5120886. *082123*
Misrachi, Génova 20, México. T. 5334551. *082124*
Moctezuma Morales Carlos, Amsterdam 240, México. T. 5743877. *082125*
o, Gob. Rafael Rebollar 43, Col. San Miguel Chapultepec, México, 00660. T. 515 16 36, 272 55 29, 273 12 61, Fax 272 55 83. *082126*
Orozco, Gabriela, Cda. Salamanca 17, 06700 México. T. 511 87 34, 514 69 52. - Paint / Graph - *082127*
Pecanins, Hamburgo 103, México. T. 514 06 21. *082128*
Pecanins, Durango 186, Col. Roma, México, 06700 DF. T. 514 06 21, 528 94 13. *082129*
Pintura Joven, Rio Marne 18, México. T. 5352298. *082130*
Quadra, Enrique de la, Monte Ararat 220-4, México, 11000. T. 540 41 58. *082131*
Romero Zazueta Enrique, Polanco 8, 11580 México. T. (05) 2502614. *082132*
Rosano la Galeria, Altavista 58, México. T. 548 47 60. *082133*
Sala de Arte José Guadalupe Posada, Avda. Hidalgo 23, México. *082134*
Sala de Exhibicion, Niza 45-2 Piso A ZP 6, México. T. 5146632. *082135*
Sala Velasquez, Independencia 68, México. *082136*
Salazar Jose, Rio Rhin 13, México. T. 5468209. *082137*
Shapiro, Estela, Varsovia 23, México, 06600. T. 5250123. - Sculp - *082138*
Taller de Grafica Mexicana, Hamburgo 112-B, México. T. 398 0055, 398 0380. - Graph - *082139*
Taller de Grafica Popular, Reforma 18, México. *082140*
Teity Galeria de Arte, Altavista 106, 01000 México. T. (05) 5487097. *082141*
Teorema Obra Grafica, Hamburgo 214 Local 2 ZP 6, México. T. 5118280. *082142*
Trapote Crispin Escultor, Av Insurgentes Sur 1658, México. T. 5101175, 5246747. *082143*
Turok-Wassermann, Rio AmaZonas 17, Col. Cuauhtemoc, México. *082144*

Mexico (MO)
Galerias Garagui, Juanacatián 272, 65265 Mexico. T. (314) 5115923. *082145*
Martinez Castaneda Raymundo, Camino del Desierto, de los Leones 31-202 ZP 20, 65265 Mexico. T. (314) 5508794. *082146*
Ponce, Belgrado 5, 65265 Mexico. T. (314) 5112298. *082147*

Monterrey (Nuevo León)
„Elena", Hidalgo 2724 Pte., Monterrey. *082148*

„Forma", Padre Mier 845 Pte., Monterrey. *082149*
Galeria de Arte Moderna, Hidalgo 1808 Pte., Monterrey.
- Paint / Graph / Sculp - *082150*
Unidad Cultural la Ciudadela, Juarez Norte 507,
Monterrey. *082151*

Puebla (Puebla)
Bazar de los Sapos, S. A., 7 Oriente No. 401, Casa de la
Cupula, Puebla. T. 244 97, 110 82. *082152*

San Miguel de Allende (Guanajuato)
Galeria San Miquel I, Plaza Principal 14, San Miguel de
Allende. T. 204 54. - Paint / Graph / Sculp /
Tex - *082153*
Parroquia, Plaza Principal, San Miguel de
Allende. *082154*

Xalapa (Veracruz)
Galeria del Teatro del Estado, Universidad Veracruzana,
Xalapa. *082155*

Monaco

Monte Carlo
Atrium du Casino, Pl du Casino, 98000 Monte Carlo.
T. 93 30 69 31. *082156*
Blanc et Noir, 9, rue Comte-Félix-Gastaldi, 98000 Monte
Carlo. - Paint - *082157*
Continental, Le, place des Moulins, 98000 Monte Carlo.
T. 93 30 69 59. - Paint - *082158*
Forum Art Gallery, 39 Av. Princesse-Grace, 98000 Monte
Carlo. T. 93 30 12 42. - Paint / Graph / Sculp / Tex / Ico /
Draw - *082159*
Galerie des Arts Contemporains, 23 Bd des Moulins,
98000 Monte Carlo. T. 93 30 69 59. *082160*
Karsenty, 51, bd. du Jardin-Exotique, 98000 Monte Car-
lo. T. 93 30 37 63. - Paint / Fra - *082161*
Lanteri et Fils, 26, rue des Remparts et 3, rue de Lorète,
98000 Monte Carlo. T. 93 30 31 01. - Fra - *082162*
Point, Le, 1-5 Av. de Grande Bretagne, 98000 Monte
Carlo. T. 93 50 68 17. - Paint / Sculp - *082163*
Trianon, 6 Blvd. des Moulins, 98000 Monte Carlo.
T. 93 25 11 22. - Paint - *082164*
Vismara, 25 Bd Albert 1er, 98000 Monte Carlo.
T. 93 30 96 27. *082165*

Netherlands

Alkmaar (Noord-Holland)
Drie Kronen, Luttik Oudorp 114, 1811 MZ Alkmaar.
T. (072) 5116311. - Paint / Graph - *082166*
Lansen, J., Laat 158, 1811 EM Alkmaar. *082167*

Amersfoort (Utrecht)
Galerie Rosart, P.J. Toelstralaan 2, 3818 KT Amersfoort.
T. (033) 4622326. - Paint - *082168*
Harmen, Zuidsingel 73, 3811 HD Amersfoort.
T. (033) 52 082. *082169*
Kapelhuis, Breestr. 1, 3811 BH Amersfoort.
T. (033) 4631984. - Paint - *082170*
Zonnehof, Zonnehof 8, 3811 ND Amersfoort.
T. (033) 4633034. - Paint - *082171*

Amstelveen (Noord-Holland)
Aemstelle, Amsterdamseweg 511, 1181 BS Amstelveen.
T. (020) 643 24 94. - Paint / Graph / Furn - *082172*
Bekaerh Portretenzo, Kzr. Karelweg 72, 1185 HW Am-
stelveen. T. (020) 641 22 65. - Paint - *082173*
Hulst, Emmy van der, Nieuwe Karselaan 10, 1182 BR
Amstelveen. T. (020) 641 31 24. - Paint - *082174*
Oude Dorp Potterie, Het, Dorpsstr. 29, 1182 JA Amstel-
veen. T. (020) 647 24 03. - Paint - *082175*

Amsterdam
Abeille, Transvaalkade 2, 1092 JH Amsterdam.
T. (020) 692 63 77. *082176*
Amazone Studio, Keizersgracht 678, 1017 ET
Amsterdam. *082177*
American Graffiti, Berenstr. 20, 1016 GH Amsterdam.
- Paint - *082178*

Amsterdam Apollo Hotel, Apollolaan 2, 1077 BA Amster-
dam. T. (020) 673 59 22. *082179*
Andrae, B.J., 2e Rozendwarstr. 14-16, 1016 PE Amster-
dam. T. (020) 627 19 05. - Paint - *082180*
Andriesse, Paul, Prinsengracht 116, 1015 EA Amster-
dam. T. (020) 623 62 37. *082181*
Art, Singel 100, 1015 AD Amsterdam.
T. (020) 625 77 64. - Paint - *082182*
Art Affairs, Wittenburgergracht 313, 1018 ZL Amster-
dam. T. (020) 620 64 33. *082183*
Art Rages, Spiegelgracht 2A, 1017 JR Amsterdam.
T. (020) 627 36 45. - Paint - *082184*
Art & Architecture, J. Verhulststr. 109, 1071 MZ Amster-
dam. T. (020) 675 18 92. - Paint - *082185*
Art Unlimited, Keizersgracht 510, 1017 EJ Amsterdam.
T. (020) 624 84 19, Fax 23 65 24. *082186*
Art Works, Herengracht 229-31, 1016 BG Amsterdam.
T. (020) 624 19 80. - Paint - *082187*
Art Yard, Singel 26, 1015 AA Amsterdam.
T. (020) 618 16 35. *082188*
Artering Gallerij, Brouwersgracht 180, 1013 HC Amster-
dam. T. (020) 622 47 52. - Paint - *082189*
Artes, Prinsengracht 768, 1017 LE Amsterdam.
T. (020) 622 24 98. - Paint - *082190*
Arti et Amicitiae/Artigalerie, Rokin 112, 1012 LB Am-
sterdam. T. (020) 623 35 08. - Paint - *082191*
Artindex, J. Obrechtstr. 55 hs, 1071 KJ Amsterdam.
T. (020) 676 99 61. - Paint - *082192*
Aschenbach, Bilderdijkstr 165c, 1053 KP Amsterdam.
T. (020) 685 35 80, Fax 683 35 29. *082193*
Asselijn, Lange Leidsedwarsstr. 198-200, 1017 NR Am-
sterdam. T. (020) 624 90 30, 623 32 32. - Paint /
Graph / Draw - *082194*
Baldinger, Artuur, Jodenbreestr. 16, 1011 NK Amster-
dam. T. (020) 623 22 39. - Paint - *082195*
Balolu, Herzengracht 340, 1016 GG Amsterdam.
T. (020) 627 35 20. - Paint - *082196*
Baudelaire, Entrepotdok 62, 1018 AD Amsterdam.
T. (020) 624 77 62. - Paint - *082197*
Bettini, Marti & Brummelkamp, Kerkstr 127-129, 1017
GE Amsterdam. T. (020) 622 99 63,
Fax 625 11 89. *082198*
Bidenbach, G., Prins Hendrijklaan 8, 1075 BB Amster-
dam. T. (020) 679 66 32. - Paint - *082199*
Biederberg, S., OZ Voorburgwal 223, 1012 EX Amster-
dam. T. (020) 624 54 55. - Paint - *082200*
Biervliet, Amstel 176A, 1017 AE Amsterdam.
T. (020) 623 49 77. *082201*
Binnen, Keizersgracht 82, 1015 CT Amsterdam.
T. (020) 625 96 03. - Paint - *082202*
Binnenland, 2e Weteringdwarsstr 51-53, 1017 SR Am-
sterdam. T. (020) 622 73 83. *082203*
Bloem, De, Bloemstr. 26, 1016 LB Amsterdam.
T. (020) 625 21 71. - Paint - *082204*
Boeddha, Kaija, Hartenstr. 1, 1016 BZ Amsterdam.
T. (020) 626 92 12. - Paint - *082205*
Borgerd Fine Arts, Weteringschans 69, 1017 RX Amster-
dam. T. (020) 638 56 26. - Paint - *082206*
Bres, De, Kerkstr. 179, 1017 GT Amsterdam.
T. (020) 623 16 05. - Paint - *082207*
Breughel, Pieter, Kalverstr. 7, 1012 NX Amsterdam.
T. (020) 623 00 26. - Paint / Graph / Sculp - *082208*
Brouwersgracht Tweedriacht, Brouwersgracht 238,
1013 HE Amsterdam. T. (020) 622 08 45.
- Paint - *082209*
Buri, Da Costakade 174, 1053 XE Amsterdam.
T. (020) 665 48 48, 683 55 80. - Paint / Graph /
Draw - *082210*
Casa Decor, Koninginneweg 69, 1075 CH Amsterdam.
T. (020) 664 60 73, Fax 02155/25593. - Ant - *082211*
Cassirer, Paul, Keizersgracht 109, 1015 CJ Amsterdam.
T. (020) 6248337. - Paint - *082212*
Cheiron, PC Hooftstr 153, 1071 BT Amsterdam.
T. (020) 664 58 13. *082213*
Cirelli, Rechtboomssloot 26, 1011 EB Amsterdam.
T. (020) 627 62 68. *082214*
Coelho, René, Singl 137, 1000 Amsterdam.
T. (020) 623 71 01. - Paint - *082215*
Collection d'Art, Keizersgracht 516, 1017 EJ Amster-
dam. T. (020) 6221511. - Paint / Graph / Sculp / Tex /
Mul / Draw - *082216*
Collection International, Hendrik Jacobszstr 14, 1075 PD
Amsterdam. T. (020) 6797878, Fax 6796464. *082217*

Couzijn, Simon, Prinsengracht 578, 1017 KR Amster-
dam. T. (020) 623 26 54. - Paint - *082218*
Daane, C., Kerkstr 127-29, 1017 GE Amsterdam.
T. (020) 622 99 63. *082219*
Delaive, Keizersgracht 467-69, 1017 DK Amsterdam.
T. (020) 625 90 87. *082220*
Den Bieman de Haas, Elisabeth, Passeerdersgracht 19,
1016 XG Amsterdam. *082221*
Dérive Gauche, Kerkstr 105, 1017 GD Amsterdam.
T. (020) 624 59 65. *082222*
Design Studio, Prinsengracht 397, 1016 HL Amsterdam.
T. (020) 624 38 05. *082223*
Dijkstra, Laagte Kadk 4, 1018 BA Amsterdam.
T. (020) 623 14 88. - Paint - *082224*
Dorate, A., Kribbestr 15, 1079 WK Amsterdam.
T. (020) 646 50 58. *082225*
Douwes, Stadhouderskade 40, Amsterdam, 1071 ZD.
T. (020) 6643262, Fax 6640154. - Paint / Graph / Chi-
na / Lights - *082226*
Drie Hendricken, De, Bloemgracht 89, 1016 KH Amster-
dam. - Paint / Graph - *082227*
Eendt, d', Spuistr. 270-272, 1012 VW Amsterdam.
T. (020) 626 57 77, 624 30 64. - Paint / Graph - *082228*
Emmering, S., N.Z. Voorburgwal 304, 1012 RV Amster-
dam. T. (020) 6231476, Fax (020) 6245487.
- Graph - *082229*
Expeditie, De, F. Halsstr. 9hs, 1072 BJ Amsterdam.
T. (020) 679 47 45. - Paint - *082230*
Fagel, Prinzengracht 723, 1017 JW Amsterdam.
T. (020) 671 77 77. *082231*
Farber, Barbara, Keizersgracht 265, 1016 EC Amster-
dam. T. (020) 627 63 43, Fax 627 80 91. *082232*
Fetter & Zonen, Gasthuismolensteeg 5, 1016 AM Am-
sterdam. T. (020) 623 09 92. *082233*
Fijnaut, Keizersgracht 536, 1017 EK Amsterdam.
T. (020) 622 84 92. *082234*
First Blossom Sticht, Laurierstr 41, 1016 PH Amster-
dam. T. (020) 638 23 05. *082235*
Forum, Singel 157-163, 1012 VK Amsterdam.
T. (020) 626 52 07. - Paint - *082236*
Fotogallery F 32, Singel 266, 1016 AC Amsterdam.
T. (020) 627 17 75. *082237*
Galerie A, Kleine Gartmanplantsoen 12, 1017 RR Am-
sterdam. T. (020) 622 70 65. *082238*
Galerie A, Joh Verhulststr 53 bv, 1071 MS Amsterdam.
T. (020) 671 40 87. *082239*
Galerie Amsterdam, Warmoesstr. 101, 1012 HZ Amster-
dam. T. (020) 624 74 08. - Paint - *082240*
Galerie Cricri, Alex Boerstr. 4, 1071 KX Amsterdam.
T. (020) 679 84 01. - Paint - *082241*
Galerle de Witte Voet, Kerkstr. 149, 1017 GG Amster-
dam. T. (020) 625 84 12. - Paint / Tin - *082242*
Galerie Drie 05, Overtoom 305, 1054 JL Amsterdam.
T. (020) 616 54 27. - Paint / Graph / Sculp /
Draw - *082243*
Galerie Espace, Keizersgracht 548, 1017 EL Amsterdam.
T. (020) 624 08 02. - Paint - *082244*
Galerie Hommage, Kerkstr. 142, 1017 GR Amsterdam.
T. (020) 620 02 72. - Paint - *082245*
Galerie Inart, Paulus Potterstr. 22-24, 1017 DA Amster-
dam. T. (020) 664 18 81. - Paint - *082246*
Galerie Josine, Bokhoven, Prinsengracht 154, 1016 HA
Amsterdam. T. (020) 623 65 98. - Paint - *082247*
Galerie K318, Keizersgracht 318, 1016 EZ Amsterdam.
T. (020) 625 70 04. - Paint - *082248*
Galerie Mathilde, Kerkstr 168, 1017 GS Amsterdam.
T. (020) 623 79 23. *082249*
Galerie Paladjin, Singel 26, 1015 AA Amsterdam.
T. (020) 622 08 65. - Paint - *082250*
Galerie Petit, N.Z. Voorburgwal 270, 1012 RS Amster-
dam. T. (020) 626 75 05. - Paint / Graph /
Draw - *082251*
Galerie Picasso, Haarlemmerstr 27, 1051 KN Amster-
dam. T. (020) 638 12 31. *082252*
Galerie Plein 7, Da Costaplein 7hs, 1053 ZV Amsterdam.
T. (020) 618 33 88. - Paint - *082253*
Galerie Ra, Vijzelstr. 80, 1017 HL Amsterdam.
T. (020) 626 51 00. - Jew - *082254*
Galerie Reflex, Weteringschans 83, 79a, 1017 RZ Am-
sterdam. T. (020) 6272832. - Paint - *082255*
Galerie Regalo, Herengracht 300, 1016 CD Amsterdam.
T. (020) 620 59 95. - Paint - *082256*

Galerie Serv, Lekstr. 80-1, 1079 EV Amsterdam.
T. (020) 644 60 31. - Paint - 082257
Galerie WFK, Kerkstr. 143, 1017 GG Amsterdam.
T. (020) 622 36 67. - Paint - 082258
Galerie XY, 23 Laurierdwarsstr. 42, 1016 PZ Amsterdam.
T. (020) 625 02 82. - Paint - 082259
Galerie Zuid, Joh. Verhulststr. 101, 1071 MX Amsterdam. T. (020) 672 56 64. - Paint - 082260
Gallery Nine, P. Jacobszstr. 21-23, 1012 HL Amsterdam.
T. (020) 627 10 97. - Paint - 082261
Ge Ce Ge, Zuiderakerweg 51B, 1069 MD Amsterdam.
T. (020) 619 98 00. - Paint - 082262
Gelder, Van, Planciusstr. 9A, 1013 MD Amsterdam.
T. (020) 627 74 19. - Paint - 082263
Gieles, H., Nieuwe Keizersgracht 41, 1018 VC Amsterdam. T. (020) 623 72 92. - Paint - 082264
Gottlieb, Molsteg 1, 1012 SM Amsterdam.
T. (020) 624 96 53. - Paint - 082265
Groote Meer, De, Nieuwe Kerkstr. 18, 1018 EB Amsterdam. T. (020) 626 56 48. - Paint - 082266
Haar met Speiden, Oosterspoorplein 1, 1093 JW Amsterdam. T. (020) 694 81 02. - Paint - 082267
Hamer, Leliegracht 38, 1015 DH Amsterdam.
T. (020) 626 73 94. - Paint - 082268
Heijdenrijk, Rokin 105, 1012 KM Amsterdam.
T. (020) 624 48 47. - Fra - 082269
Hellingman, Des Presstr. 4, 1075 NX Amsterdam.
T. (020) 662 22 62. - Paint - 082270
Hilton Gallery, Apollolaan 138-140, 1077 BG Amsterdam. T. (020) 678 07 80. - Paint - 082271
Houthakker, Bernard, Rokin 98, 1012 KZ Amsterdam.
T. (020) 623 39 39, Fax 27 35 48. - Rel / Draw - 082272
Icon Gallery, Spiegelgracht 31, 1017 JP Amsterdam.
T. (020) 627 84 43. 082273
Image, Reestr. 19, 1016 DM Amsterdam.
T. (020) 620 51 15. - Paint - 082274
Imago, Nieuwe Zijdsvoorburgwal 371, 1012 RM Amsterdam. T. (020) 627 70 46. - Paint - 082275
Interart Prom, Hazenstr. 20, 1016 SP Amsterdam.
T. (020) 620 81 00, 638 49 70. - Paint - 082276
Israêl, Prinsengracht 690, 1017 KZ Amsterdam.
T. (020) 624 35 62. - Paint - 082277
Jansen, H., Kerkstr. 301, 1017 GZ Amsterdam.
T. (020) 625 22 89. - Paint - 082278
Jaski Art Gallery, Nieuwe Spiegelstr. 27 + 30, 1017 DB Amsterdam. T. (020) 620 39 39. - Paint - 082279
Jester Art Gallery, Leidsestr. 57 I/II, 1017 NV Amsterdam. T. (020) 638 27 04. - Paint - 082280
Joosten, M., Keizersgracht 318/1, 1016 EZ Amsterdam.
T. (020) 625 70 04. - Paint - 082281
Jurka, Singel 28, 1015 AA Amsterdam.
T. (020) 626 67 33. - Paint / Graph / Sculp /
Pho - 082282
Kamp, Keizersgracht 670, 1017 ET Amsterdam.
T. (020) 626 26 40, 626 67 62. - Paint / Graph /
Sculp - 082283
Kappa, Keizersgracht 690, 1017 EV Amsterdam.
T. (020) 625 47 03. - Paint - 082284
Kaufman, Inna, Rokin 124, 1012 LC Amsterdam.
T. (020) 638 27 36. - Paint - 082285
Keramik in Kunst, Kerkstr. 376, 1017 JB Amsterdam.
T. (020) 624 61 09. - Paint - 082286
Knubben, George, Prinsengracht 578, 1017 KR Amsterdam. T. (020) 624 76 91. - Paint / Graph / Orient /
Sculp - 082287
Koch, Gebr., F. Bolstr. 333, Hotel Okura, 1072 LH Amsterdam. T. (020) 673 65 08. - Paint - 082288
Kooring, C.M., Spiegelgracht 14-16, 1017 JR Amsterdam. T. (020) 623 65 38. - Paint - 082289
Kornblit, Yaki, Nassaukade 162-163, 1053 LL Amsterdam. T. (020) 616 9133, Fax 612 0286. 082290
Krikhaar, Herman Th. W., Spuistr. 330, 1012 VX Amsterdam. T. (020) 626 71 66. - Paint / Graph / Sculp /
Draw - 082291
Krimpen, van, Prinsengracht 629, 1016 HV Amsterdam.
T. (020) 622 93 75. - Paint / Sculp / Pho / Draw - 082292
Kuhler Glasgalerie, Prinsengracht 134, 1015 EB Amsterdam. T. (020) 638 02 30. - Paint - 082293
Kunst Allerlei, Noordermarkt 9, 1015 MV Amsterdam.
T. (020) 625 72 69. - Paint - 082294
Kunst & Beterschap, Sloterweg 1301, 1066 CL Amsterdam. T. (020) 614 03 43. - Paint - 082295

Kunstbemiddeling, Keizersgracht 318, 1016 EZ Amsterdam. T. (020) 626 12 14. - Paint - 082296
Kwartijn, Reestraat 5, 1016 DM Amsterdam.
T. (020) 622 07 35. - Paint - 082297
Lambiek, Kerkstr. 78, 1017 GN Amsterdam.
T. (020) 626 75 43. - Paint - 082298
Langenberg, K. Prinsengracht 44, 1013 GT Amsterdam.
T. (020) 623 63 37. - Paint - 082299
Lieve Hemel, Vijzelgracht 6-8, 1017 HR Amsterdam.
T. (020) 623 00 60, Fax 27 26 63. - Paint / Graph /
Sculp - 082300
Linka, Prinsengracht 690, 1017 KZ Amsterdam.
T. (020) 624 35 62. - Paint - 082301
Living Room, The, Laurierstr. 70, 1016 PN Amsterdam.
T. (020) 625 84 49. - Paint - 082302
Loa, Bloemgracht 121, 1016 KK Amsterdam.
T. (020) 631 47 32. 082303
Loerakker, Keizersgracht 380, 1016 GA Amsterdam.
T. (020) 622 17 32. - Paint - 082304
Lotus, Singel 417, 1012 WP Amsterdam.
T. (020) 622 23 13. - Paint - 082305
Lughien, Reestr. 17, 1016 DM Amsterdam.
T. (020) 625 31 93. - Paint - 082306
Modern African Art, Prinsengracht 472, 1017 KG Amsterdam. T. (020) 620 66 96. - Paint - 082307
Mokum, O.Z. Voorburgwal 334, 1012 GH Amsterdam.
T. (020) 624 39 58. - Paint - 082308
Momentary Modern, Warmoesstr. 12, 1012 JD Amsterdam. T. (020) 626 93 53, Fax 638 17 44. 082309
Monet, Rokin 97, 1071 EE Amsterdam.
T. (020) 676 33 04. - Paint / Graph / Sculp - 082310
Multi Art Points, Herengracht 270, 1016 BW Amsterdam. T. (020) 622 63 82. 082311
Munchhausen, Baroness von, 2e C. Huyensstr. 67, 1054 CR Amsterdam. T. (020) 612 67 97. - Paint - 082312
Nederlandsche Kunstkoopersbond, Keizersgracht 542, 1017 EL Amsterdam. 082313
Novanta Nove, Keizersgracht 717, 1017 DX Amsterdam. T. (020) 627 07 97. - Paint - 082314
Onrust, Prinsengracht 627, 1016 HV Amsterdam.
T. (020) 638 04 74. - Paint - 082315
Oscar, Nieuwer Voorburgwal 306, 1012 RV Amsterdam. T. (020) 620 62 50. - Paint - 082316
Otten, Prinsenstr. 4, 1015 DC Amsterdam.
T. (020) 625 06 76. - Paint - 082317
Papillon, Le, Amstelpark 13, 1083 HZ Amsterdam.
T. (020) 642 86 32. - Paint - 082318
Peperbus, De, Vyzelgracht 22, 1017 HS Amsterdam.
T. (020) 623 66 90. 082319
Prestige Art Gallery, Reguliersbreestr. 46, 1017 CN Amsterdam. T. (020) 624 01 04. - Paint - 082320
Print Gallery, Prinsengracht 628, 1017 KT Amsterdam.
T. (020) 622 42 65. - Graph - 082321
Printshop, Prinsengracht 845, 1017 KB Amsterdam.
T. (020) 625 16 56. - Graph - 082322
Richartz, C., Dr., Nic Maesstraat 22, 1071 RA Amsterdam. T. (020) 671 33 11. - Graph - 082323
Rijbroeck, Strawinskylaan 65, WTC Gebouw, 1077 XN Amsterdam. T. (020) 675 30 30. - Paint - 082324
Ronen Kunst Import, Weissenbruchstr. 17, 1058 KL Amsterdam. T. (020) 615 56 10, Fax 614 26 48.
- Paint - 082325
Rosenthal, J. J., Michelangelostraat 32, 1077 CC Amsterdam. T. (020) 672 46 20. - Paint - 082326
Rueb, Banstraat 4, 1071 ZP Amsterdam.
T. (020) 6767566, Fax (020) 6755700. - Paint - 082327
Schlichte Bergen, P.C. Hooftstr. 53, 1071 BN Amsterdam. T. (020) 6751701, 6769344, Fax (020) 6734786.
- Paint / Draw - 082328
Schlichte Bergen, Velazquezstr 8, 1077 NH Amsterdam. T. (020) 6769344, 6751701, Fax (020) 6734786.
- Paint / Draw - 082329
Selly, De, Nieuwe Teertuinen 16, 1013 LV Amsterdam.
T. (020) 625 09 90. - Paint - 082330
Siau, Keizersgracht 267, 1016 EC Amsterdam.
- Paint - 082331
Signaal OKK, Zieseniskade 23-24, 1017 RT Amsterdam. T. (020) 624 75 33. - Paint - 082332
Spa, Guido de, 2e Weteringdwarsstr. 34, 1017 SW Amsterdam. T. (020) 622 15 28. - Paint - 082333
Sparts, Utrechtsestr. 139, 1017 VM Amsterdam.
T. (020) 627 44 82, Fax 638 00 37. - Paint / Graph /
Sculp / Mul / Draw - 082334

Spiegeling, Spiegelgracht 34, 1017 JS Amsterdam.
T. (020) 620 06 50. - Paint / Graph - 082335
Steendrukkerij Amsterdam, Lauriergracht 80, 1016 RM Amsterdam. T. (020) 624 14 91. - Paint - 082336
Steltman, Spuitstr. 330, 1012 VX Amsterdam. - Ant /
Paint / Graph / Furn - 082337
Studio 2000 Art Gallerij, Keizersgracht 699, 1017 DW Amsterdam. T. (020) 638 26 74. - Paint - 082338
Swart, Van Breestraat 23, 1071 ZE Amsterdam.
T. (020) 676 47 36. - Paint / Draw - 082339
Teutenberg, Singel 105, 1012 VG Amsterdam.
T. (020) 625 77 36. - Paint - 082340
Theeboom, Singel 210, 1016 AB Amsterdam.
T. (020) 624 88 28. - Paint - 082341
Thielen, A., 1e Lindendwstr. 2, 1015 LG Amsterdam.
T. (020) 625 93 31. - Paint - 082342
Thorbecke Sticht, Zykan-H-weg 23, 1037 RR Amsterdam. T. (020) 670 30 30. 082343
Valeton & Henstra, Nes 39, 1012 KC Amsterdam.
T. (020) 620 14 54. - Paint - 082344
Verver, J., Prinsengracht 136-138, 1015 EB Amsterdam. T. (020) 626 85 62. - Paint - 082345
Vlaams Cultureel Centrum de Brakke Grond, Nes 45, 1012 KD Amsterdam. T. (020) 622 90 14.
- Paint - 082346
Voetboog, De, Voetboogstr 16, 1012 XL Amsterdam.
T. (020) 626 01 69. 082347
Welters, Fons, Bloemstr 140, 1016 LJ Amsterdam.
T. (020) 6227193. - Paint - 082348
Wending, Rubensstr. 60, 1077 MV Amsterdam.
T. (020) 617 86 30. - Paint - 082349
Wetering, Lijnbaansgracht 288, 1017 RM Amsterdam.
T. (020) 623 61 89. 082350
Yin & Yang, Reguliersdwarsstr. 82 + 84, 1017 BN Amsterdam. T. (020) 620 49 69/77. - Paint - 082351
Zedde, van der, de Clercqstraat 85, 1053 AG Amsterdam. T. (020) 638 50 87. 082352
Zee Aan, Adm. de Ruyterweg 158, 1056 GN Amsterdam. T. (020) 683 63 93. - Paint - 082353
3 Gratiên, De, Weteringstr 39, 1017 SM Amsterdam.
T. (020) 624 19 45. 082354

Arnhem (Gelderland)

Kunstcentrum De Gele Rijder, Korenmarkt 43, 6811 GW Arnhem. T. (026) 3511300. - Paint / Graph / Sculp /
Pho / Draw - 082355
Peter, Rijnstr 71, 6811 EZ Arnhem.
T. (026) 4456318. 082356

Beekbergen (Gelderland)

Konstkabinet, Het, Arnhemseweg 625, 7361 TR Beekbergen. T. (055) 5061539. - Paint / Sculp - 082357

Bennekom (Gelderland)

Kijkdoos, De, Dorpsstr. 12, 6721 JK Bennekom.
T. (0318) 413005. - Paint - 082358

Bergen (Noord-Holland)

Kunstenaarscentrum, Plein 7, 1861 JX Bergen.
T. (072) 5894195. - Paint - 082359
Vanderveen, Ayenseweg 18, 5854 PT Bergen. 082360

Blaricum (Noord-Holland)

Lier, van, Torenlaan 57b, 1261 GC Blaricum.
T. (035) 5383418. - Paint / Graph / Sculp - 082361

Borne (Overijssel)

Polder, Abr. ten Catestr. 25, 7622 EG Borne.
T. (074) 2662584. - Paint / Graph - 082362

Bussum (Noord-Holland)

Scherpel, G. J., Brediusweg 45, 1401 AC Bussum.
T. (035) 6916683. - Paint - 082363

Delft (Zuid-Holland)

Fiets, de, Oude Delft 195, 2611 HD Delft.
T. (015) 2131849. - Ant / Paint / Sculp / Glass /
Draw - 082364
Inkt, Choorstr. 29, 2611 JE Delft. T. (015) 2138650.
- Paint - 082365
Kunstcentrum Delft, Kruisstr. 71, 2611 ML Delft.
T. (015) 2123636. - Paint - 082366
Pennings, W., Oude Delft 216, 2611 HJ Delft.
T. (015) 2122315. - Paint - 082367

Seele, Oude Delft 111a, 2611 BE Delft.
T. (015) 2122464. 082368
Terra, Nieuwstr 7, 2611 HK Delft.
T. (015) 2147072. 082369
Trits Sieraden, Nieuwstr 11-13, 2611 HK Delft.
T. (015) 2132697. 082370
Zaal, De, Koornmarkt 4, 2611 EE Delft.
T. (015) 2145913. 082371

Den Helder (Noord-Holland)
Marin, Parnassia 12, 1787 CD Den Helder.
T. (0223) 644150. - Paint / Graph / Draw - 082372

Deventer (Overijssel)
Tambaran, Bergstr 34, 7411 ET Deventer.
T. (0570) 615077. 082373

Doesburg (Gelderland)
Gooijer Fine Art, Eerkstr. 4, 6984 AE Doesburg.
T. (0313) 479250, Fax 479585. - Paint / Graph / Sculp /
Glass / Draw - 082374

Doorn (Utrecht)
Galerie Nieuwe Weg, Sterkenburgerlaan 4, 3941 BD
Doorn. T. (0343) 412627. - Paint / Graph - 082375

Dordrecht (Zuid-Holland)
Galerie 56-58, Nieuwestr. 56-58, 3311 XR Dordrecht.
T. (078) 6146121. - Paint - 082376
„In der Vergulde Lampet", Blindeliedengasthuissteeg 2,
3400 Dordrecht. - Paint / Graph / Sculp - 082377
Kijck over den Dijck, Noordendijk 144, 3311 RR Dord-
recht. T. (078) 6130187. 082378
Witt, Groenmarkt 45, 3311 BD Dordrecht.
T. (078) 6148158. - Paint - 082379

Eck en Wiel (Gelderland)
Beerenburght, de, Wielseweg 31, 4024 BJ Eck en Wiel.
T. (0344) 692195, 691760. 082380

Ede (Gelderland)
Galerie 51, Parkweg 51, 6717 HM Ede.
T. (0318) 633152. - Graph / Draw - 082381
Simonis & Buunk, Notaris Fischerstr. 30-32, 6711 BD
Ede. T. (0318) 614825. - Paint - 082382

Eemnes (Utrecht)
Impression Art Gallery, Hasselaarlaan 8, 3755 AW Eemnes. T. (035) 5316174. - Paint - 082383

Eindhoven (Noord-Brabant)
Bies, A. H., Boschdijk 221a, 5612 HC Eindhoven.
T. (040) 2431377. - Paint - 082385
Goma, Boschdijk 223a, 5612 HC Eindhoven.
T. (040) 2436962, 2431377. - Paint - 082386
Herberge, De, St Lambertusstraat 42, 5615 PH Eindho-
ven. T. (040) 228445. 082387
J.A.J.A. Gemälde, Marconilaan 6, 5621 AA Eindhoven.
T. (040) 2432081, Fax 2456692. 082387a
Leolux, Stratumsedijk 34, 5611 NE Eindhoven.
T. (040) 2116388. - Paint - 082388
Schoots, Willy, Willemstr. 27, 5611 HB Eindhoven.
T. (040) 2449705. - Graph / Sculp - 082389
Verspaget, N. M., Heezerweg 278d, 5643 KL Eindhoven.
T. (040) 212001. - Paint - 082390

Elspeet (Gelderland)
Kalb, Joseph, Schapendrift 164, 8075 BA
Elspeet. 082391

Emmen (Drenthe)
Muzeval, De, Boermarkeweg 43, 7822 HM Emmen.
T. (0591) 619200. - Paint - 082392

Enschede (Overijssel)
Galerie, Markt 17, 7511 GB Enschede. T. (053) 4310041.
- Paint / Graph / China / Sculp / Tex / Pho / Draw --
082393
Tardy, Wooldriksweg 28, 7512 AS Enschede.
- Paint - 082394

Epse-Gorssel (Gelderland)
Lenten, Kletterstr 25-27, 7214 DP Epse-
Gorssel. 082395

Finsterwolde (Groningen)
Waalkens, Hoofdweg 39, 9684 CB Finsterwolde.
T. (0597) 331426. - Paint / Graph / Sculp / Pho /
Draw - 082396

Groningen
Locations, Oude Boteringstr 74, 9712 GN Groningen.
T. (050) 3124502. 082397
Magazijn, Helperwestsingel 16, 9721 BE Groningen.
T. (050) 5257838. 082398
Wiek XX, Nw. Boteringestr. 9, 9712 PE Groningen.
T. (050) 3131987. - Paint - 082399
Wiek XX, Korenstr. 7, 9712 LX Groningen.
T. (050) 3131987. - Paint - 082400

Grootschermer (Utrecht)
Jonk, Nic, Haviksdijkje 5, 1843 JG Grootschermer.
T. (0299) 671560. 082401

Den Haag (Zuid-Holland)
Akkolades, Waldeck Pymontkade 882, 2518 JT Den
Haag. T. (070) 345 55 79. - Paint - 082402
All Arte, 2e Schuytstr. 37, 2517 XC Den Haag.
T. (070) 360 00 81. - Paint - 082403
Art Propos Sticht, Maziestr. 13a, 2514 GT Den Haag.
T. (070) 345 64 88. - Paint - 082404
Art & Kraft, F. Hendrikplein 4, 2582 AT Den Haag.
T. (070) 354 11 46. - Paint - 082405
Artefact, Bankastr. 101, 2585 EJ Den Haag.
T. (070) 350 45 01. - Paint - 082406
Arti et Gaudia, Boekhorststr. 121, 2512 CN Den Haag.
T. (070) 380 38 36. - Paint - 082407
Arti et Industriae, Denneweg 7, 2514 CB Den Haag.
T. (070) 365 37 76. - Paint - 082408
Artline, Toussaintkade 67-68, 2513 CN Den Haag.
T. (070) 345 26 45, Fax 361 78 21. - Ant / Paint / Graph /
Sculp / Draw - 082409
Baks, Nobelstr. 1, 2513 BC Den Haag.
T. (070) 345 66 04. - Paint - 082410
Beaux-Arts, Noordeinde 113a, 2514 GE Den Haag.
T. (070) 360 58 91. - Paint - 082411
Beelen, Paul, Noordeinde 96, 2514 GM Den Haag.
T. (070) 365 28 58. - Paint - 082412
Bekij het Maar, Prinsegracht 14, 2512 GA Den Haag.
T. (070) 363 73 88. - Paint - 082413
Bouwman, Ivo, Jan van Nassaustraat 80, 2596 BW Den
Haag. T. (070) 3283660, Fax (070) 3283881.
- Paint - 082414
Cramer, G., Javastr. 38, 2585 AP Den Haag.
T. (070) 3630758, Fax (070) 3630759. - Paint - 082415
Delta 98, P. Heinstr. 98, 2518 CL Den Haag.
T. (070) 356 21 54. - Paint - 082416
Dubio, Wagenstr. 108, 2512 AZ Den Haag.
T. (070) 363 51 34. - Paint - 082417
Elshout, J.A.P. van der, A. Paulownastr. 27, 2518 BA Den
Haag. T. (070) 363 71 92. - Paint - 082418
Galerie Edison, Javastr. 16, 2585 AN Den Haag.
T. (070) 363 50 00. - Paint / Graph / Orient / China /
Sculp / Tex / Pho / Mul / Draw - 082419
Galerie Het Kunstcentrum, Molenstr. 16, 2513 BK Den
Haag. T. (070) 346 36 97. - Paint / Graph / Sculp /
Draw - 082420
Galerie Westeinde, Westeinde 203, 2512 GZ Den Haag.
T. (070) 389 29 93. - Paint - 082421
Galerie 2005, Ln. v. Roosend 10, 2514 BD Den Haag.
T. (070) 360 00 35. - Paint - 082422
Grafiekwinkel, Grote Halstr. 3, 2513 AX Den Haag.
T. (070) 356 37 88. - Graph - 082423
Grafiekwinkel Inkt., Prinsegracht 16, 2514 AP Den Haag.
T. (070) 310 63 36. - Graph - 082424
Haagse Kunstring, Denneweg 64, 2514 CJ Den Haag.
T. (070) 364 75 85. - Paint - 082425
Happy Hands, Thompsonplaan 10, 2565 LA Den Haag.
T. (070) 346 14 76. - Paint - 082426
Heijdenrijk, A. J., Noordeinde 134, 2514 GP Den Haag.
- Fra - 082427
Hoogsteder, Lange Vijverberg 15, 2513 AC Den Haag.
T. (070) 3615575, Fax (070) 3617074. - Paint - 082428
Impression, Prins Hendrikstr. 159, 2518 HP Den Haag.
T. (070) 363 73 44. - Paint - 082429
Island Gallery, Gedempte Gracht 9, 2512 AK Den Haag.
T. (070) 310 67 81. - Paint - 082430
Koch, Gr., Hoogstr. 7, 2513 AN Den Haag.
T. (070) 346 33 05. - Paint / Graph - 082431

Konstkabinet, Noordeinde 159, 2514 GG Den Haag.
T. (070) 346 28 86. - Paint - 082432
Kouw, C. J. J., Surinamestr. 32, 2585 GK Den Haag.
T. (070) 346 17 86. - Paint - 082433
Kranendonk, van, Westeinde 29, 2512 GS Den Haag.
T. (070) 365 04 06. - Paint - 082434
Laar, M. v.d., Westeinde 203, 2512 GZ Den Haag.
T. (070) 364 01 51. - Paint - 082435
Lijn 3, Ln. v. Meerdervoort 295, 2563 AE Den Haag.
T. (070) 310 71 10. - Paint - 082436
Maranta, Elandstr. 81, 2513 GM Den Haag.
T. (070) 365 82 85. - China / Draw - 082437
Metsers, G.L., Molenstr. 35, 2513 BJ Den Haag.
T. (070) 345 05 75. - Paint - 082438
Munster, J. van, Koon. Emmakade 55, 2518 RL Den
Haag. T. (070) 365 82 85. - Paint - 082439
North Sea, Gevers Deijnootweg 990-91, 2586 BZ Den
Haag. T. (070) 354 42 44. - Paint - 082440
Nouvelles Images, Westeinde 22, 2512 HD Den Haag.
T. (070) 346 19 98. - Paint / Graph / Sculp /
Draw - 082441
Nova Spectra, Laan van Meerdervoort 41, 2517 AD Den
Haag. T. (070) 365 52 33. - Paint / Graph /
Sculp - 082442
Nystad, S., Ruychrocklaan 442, 2597 EJ Den Haag.
T. (070) 324 50 24. - Paint - 082443
Orez Mobiel, Paviljoensgracht 68-70, 2512 BR Den
Haag. T. (070) 364 54 16. - Paint - 082444
Ornis, Javastr 17, 2585 AB Den Haag.
T. (070) 364 21 57. 082445
Parmentier, Bezuidenhoutseweg 86a, 2594 AX Den
Haag. T. (070) 385 87 18. - Paint - 082446
Pigeon, Le, Bezuidenhoutseweg 106b, 2594 AZ Den
Haag. 082447
Point to Comm, Rubensstr. 207, 2526 MA Den Haag.
T. (070) 380 76 78. - Paint - 082448
Pulchri, L. Voorhout 15, 2514 EA Den Haag.
T. (070) 365 71 78, 346 17 35. - Paint - 082449
Ronkes Agerbeek, K. Molenstr. 11a, 2513 BM Den Haag.
T. (070) 356 19 02. - Paint - 082450
Ruach, Papestr. 31, 2513 AV Den Haag.
T. (070) 345 16 54. - Paint - 082451
Seasons Galleries, Toussaintkade 70, 2513 CL Den
Haag. T. (070) 345 48 81. - Paint / Graph / Sculp /
Draw - 082452
Serendipity, P. Heinstr. 40, 2518 CH Den Haag.
T. (070) 392 45 93. - Paint - 082453
Smelik & Stokking Galleries, Noordeinde 150, 2514 GP
Den Haag. T. (070) 364 07 68. - Paint / Graph / Sculp /
Draw - 082454
Statengalerie, v. Boetzelaelaan 116, 2581 AN Den Haag.
T. (070) 354 21 53. - Paint - 082455
Sticht, Fluwelen Burgwal 18, 2511 CJ Den Haag.
T. (070) 361 68 97. - Paint - 082456
Takayama, Maliestr. 22, 2514 CA Den Haag.
T. (070) 365 79 65. - Paint - 082457
Trendens, Vos in Tuinstr. 8, 2514 BX Den Haag.
T. (070) 363 34 60. - Paint - 082458
Iwee Pauwen, De, A. Paulownastr. 83-85a, 2518 BC
Den Haag. T. (070) 346 41 84. - Paint - 082459
Van den Doel, Rob, Anna Paulownastr. 105a, 2518 BD
Den Haag. T. (070) 364 62 39, Fax 361 76 12.
- Paint - 082460
Veeneman, Martin, Noordeinde 100, 2514 GM Den
Haag. T. (070) 365 75 83. - Graph - 082461
Verboon, Leo, Paviljoensgracht 68-70, 2512 BR Den
Haag. T. (070) 346 54 16. - Paint / Graph /
Sculp - 082462
Viagalerie, Noordeinde 14, 2514 GH Den Haag.
T. (070) 365 04 65. - Paint - 082463
Voorst van Beest, P.B. van, Anna Paulownastr. 107,
2518 AD Den Haag. T. (070) 364 43 34.
- Paint - 082464
Voorst van Beest, P.B. van, Laan van Meerdervoort 5a,
2517 AA Den Haag. T. (070) 364 43 34.
- Paint - 082465
Wiegel, Ln. v. Meerdervoort 79, 2517 AH Den Haag.
T. (070) 345 56 36. - Paint - 082466
Wisselink, L., P. Heinstr. 61, 2518 CC Den Haag.
T. (070) 346 83 17. - Paint - 082467
World Pictures Art, Grote Hertoginnenlaan 274, 2517 EZ
Den Haag. T. (070) 360 76 15. - Ant - 082468

Yeramian, J., Mauritskade 65, 2514 HG Den Haag.
T. (070) 365 04 80. - Paint -   082469

Haaren (Noord-Brabant)
Hüsstege, Driehoeven 12, 5076 BB Haaren.
T. (0411) 621264. - Ant / Paint / Graph / Furn / Sculp /
Dec / Ico -   082470

Haarlem (Noord-Holland)
Galerie Klein Heiligland, Distelblom, Klein Heiligland 46,
2011 RH Haarlem. T. (023) 5313448. - Paint -   082471
Galerie Zijlstraat, Zijlstr. 31, 2011 TK Haarlem.
T. (023) 5321529, 5327341. - Paint / Graph / Sculp /
Tex / Glass / Draw -   082472
Heerkens Thijssen, Wagenweg 6, 2012 ND Haarlem.
T. (023) 5312725. - Ant / Paint / Graph / Furn / China /
Sculp / Dec / Silv / Glass / Cur / Draw -   082473
Van, Hagestraat 18, 2011 CV Haarlem.
T. (023) 5334361.   082474

Harlingen (Friesland)
Blauwe Hand, De, Grote Brede Plaats, 8861 BB Harlin-
gen. T. (0517) 143195. - Paint / Graph / Sculp -   082475

Heemstede (Noord-Holland)
Galerie De Bleeker, Bleekersvaart 18, 2101 CB Heemstede. T. (023) 5285980. - Paint -   082476

Heerlen (Limburg)
Galerie des Arts, Honigmanstraat 33, 6411 LJ Heerlen.
T. (045) 5719902. - Paint -   082477

's-Hertogenbosch (Noord-Brabant)
Hüsstege, Verwersstr. 28, 5211 HW 's-Hertogenbosch.
I. (073) 6142863. - Paint -   082478
Kruithuis, Citadellaan 7, 5211 XA 's-Hertogenbosch.
T. (073) 6122188. - Paint -   082479

Heusden (Noord-Brabant)
Tegenbosch, Lambert, Putterstr. 48, 5256 AN Heusden.
T. (0416) 662772. - Paint -   082480

Hilversum (Noord-Holland)
Expositiecentrum Gooiland, Emmastraat 2, 1214 CA Hil-
versum. T. (035) 6292835. - Paint -   082481
Sirag, Peter, Langestr. 59c, 1211 GW Hilversum.
T. (035) 612931. - Paint -   082482

Hoensbroek (Limburg)
Ruyters, Ger, Hommerterweg 72, 6431 EX Hoensbroek.
T. (045) 5213501. - Paint -   082483

Hoorn (Noord-Holland)
An de Frachtwage, West 50, 1621 AW Hoorn.
T. (0229) 218368.   082484
Galerie De Krijtkring, Appelsteeg 6, 1621 BD Hoorn.
T. (0229) 219261. - Paint -   082485

Laren (Noord-Holland)
Broerse, Ina, Brink 4, 1251 KV Laren. T. (035) 5310053.
- Paint -   082486
Enneking, Fred, Hoog Hoefloo 35, 1251 EC Laren.
T. (035) 5387639. - Paint -   082487
Vischschoonmaker, Abbie, Zevenend 2, 1251 RN Laren.
T. (035) 5383806.   082488

Leende (Noord-Brabant)
Dutch Art Studio, Narcislaan 5, 5595 EE Leende.
T. (040) 2061660. - Paint -   082489

Leeuwarden (Friesland)
Hulsen, van, Nieuwestad 99, 8911 CL Leeuwarden.
T. (058) 2124904, 2130096, 2152300. - Paint / Graph /
Fra -   082490

Leiden (Zuid-Holland)
Oude Rijn, Stille Mare 4, 2312 DH Leiden.
T. (071) 5146330. - Paint / Sculp -   082491
Sint Lucas Society, Rapenburg 83, 2311 GK Leiden.
T. (071) 5125514. - Fra -   082492

Lunteren (Gelderland)
Galerie Aan de Kippenlijn, Spoorstr. 2-4, 6740 AA Lunte-
ren Postbus 40. T. (0318) 482227, 483421. - Paint /
Graph / China / Repr / Sculp / Jew / Glass / Draw --
     082493

Maastricht (Limburg)
Hack-Rutten, Gerard, Wolfstr. 10, 6211 GN Maastricht.
T. (043) 3215684. - Graph / Repr -   082494
Henn, St Nicolaasstr 26c, 6211 NN Maastricht.
Fax 27 53 05.   082495
Noortman, Vrijthof 49, 6211 LE Maastricht.
T. (043) 3216745. - Paint / Draw -   082496
Reiff, Wanda, Rechtstr 43, 6221 EH Maastricht.
T. (043) 3219108.   082497
Rijn, Jacques van, O.L. Vrouweplein 28, 6211 HD Maas-
tricht. T. (043) 312233. - Paint / Jew / Sculp -   082498

Middelburg (Zeeland)
Cleene Catte, De, Lange Geere 18, 4331 LX Middelburg.
T. (0118) 626353.   082499
Roelant, Koepoortstr. 10, 4331 SL Middelburg.
T. (0118) 633309. - Paint / Graph / China / Glass / Cur /
Draw -   082500

Mijnsherenland (Zuid-Holland)
Visser, Victor, Laan van Moerkerken 65, 3271 AJ Mijnsherenland. T. (0186) 601726.   082501

Naarden (Noord-Holland)
Van Wisselingh, E.J., Valkeveenselaan 46, 1411 GT
Naarden. T. (035) 6943708, Fax 6949358. - Paint /
Draw -   082502

Nijmegen (Gelderland)
Delta Art Gallery, Oranjesingel 2a, 6501 BK Nijmegen.
T. (024) 3602270, Fax 3602823. - Paint / Graph /
Sculp / Tex / Jew / Mul -   082503
Kunstcentrum Hollandsche Spoorweg, Kannenmarkt 6,
5611 KC Nijmegen. T. (024) 3511300. - Paint / Graph /
Sculp / Pho / Draw -   082504

Nuenen (Noord-Brabant)
Biggelarij, de, Wettenseind 12, 5674 AA Nuenen.
T. (040) 2832529. - Paint / Graph -   082505
Galerie t'Weefhuis, Lucas van Hauthemlaan 1, 5671 CJ
Nuenen. T. (040) 2832782. - Paint -   082506
Smits, Joop, Lijsterbesstr. 7, 5671 AE Nuenen.
T. (040) 2833542. - Paint -   082507

Oosterbeek (Gelderland)
POK, Evert van Wilpweg 6, 6862 ZJ Oosterbeek. 082508

Rijswijk (Zuid-Holland)
Galerie Arti-Shock, Schoolstr. 26, 2282 RD Rijswijk.
- Paint -   082509

Rotterdam (Zuid-Holland)
Art Space, Beatrijsstr. 55, 3021 RC Rotterdam.
T. (010) 476 20 87. - Paint -   082510
Artline, Watertorenweg 641, 3063 Rotterdam.
T. (010) 453 25 38.   082511
Barley & Groats, Oudedijk 207, 3061 AT Rotterdam.
T. (010) 412 79 25.   082512
Basstylja, Blaustr. 22, 3086 JM Rotterdam.
T. (010) 480 52 63. - Paint -   082513
Braggiotti, 's-Landswerf 220, 3063 GG Rotterdam.
T. (010) 412 60 95. - Paint -   082514
Delta, Oude Binnenweg 113, 3012 JB Rotterdam.
T. (010) 413 17 07. - Paint / Sculp -   082515
Doelen, de, Kruisstr 2, 3012 CT Rotterdam.
T. (010) 414 29 11.   082516
Duo-Duo, Mathenesserln 304, 3021 HW Rotterdam.
T. (010) 477 85 29.   082517
Evers, Oostmaasln. 139, 3063 AR Rotterdam.
T. (010) 452 76 73, 425 80 57. - Paint -   082518
Galerie Aelbrecht, Aelbrechtskolk 2, 3024 RE Rotterdam.
T. (010) 477 16 37, 477 56 06.   082519
Galerie Brutto Gusto, Oostkousdijk 12a, 3024 CM
Rotterdam.   082520
Galerie Delta, Oude Binnenweg 113, 3012 JB Rotter-
dam. T. (010) 413 17 07. - Paint -   082521
Galerie Galerie, Passerelstr. 30, 3023 ZD Rotterdam.
T. (010) 476 68 08. - Paint -   082522
Galerie 'T Venster, Oude Binnenweg 113, 3012 JB
Rotterdam.   082523
Galerie 2000, Westersingel 30, 3014 GR Rotterdam.
T. (010) 436 30 18.   082524
Hers, Scheepstimmermanln. 35, 3016 AE Rotterdam.
T. (010) 436 51 40. - Paint -   082525

Koch, Gebr., Lijnbaan 78, 3012 ER Rotterdam.
T. (010) 413 59 92. - Paint -   082526
Leemans, A., Benthuizerstr. 77A, 3036 CE Rotterdam.
T. (010) 466 52 37. - Paint -   082527
Lijst-in, Coolsingel 12, 3011 AD Rotterdam.
T. (010) 414 60 18. - Paint -   082528
Maas, Oudedijk 159, 3061 AB Rotterdam.
T. (010) 412 40 48. - Paint / Graph / Sculp -   082529
Midland, Tweede Middellandstr. 16B, 3021 BN Rotter-
dam. T. (010) 476 54 56. - Paint -   082530
Modus, Bergw. 245A, 3037 EL Rotterdam.
T. (010) 465 46 74. - Paint -   082531
Mourik, Van, Witte de Withstr 19a, 3012 BL Rotterdam.
T. (010) 411 82 28, Fax 411 82 28.   082532
Phoebus, Eendrachtsweg 61, 3012 LG Rotterdam.
T. (010) 414 51 51. - Paint -   082533
Raadt, Srd., Watergeusstr. 115 B, 3025 HN Rotterdam.
T. (010) 425 64 27. - Paint -   082534
Rotta, E. de Withstr. 55, 3012 BS Rotterdam.
T. (010) 414 00 08. - Paint -   082535
Schouwburg, Schouwburgplein 25, 3012 CL Rotterdam.
T. (010) 413 89 22. - Paint -   082536
Semar, Schiedamseweg 91, 3026 AE Rotterdam.
T. (010) 425 82 29. - Paint -   082537
Snoei, W. de. Withstr. 17A, 3012 BL Rotterdam.
T. (010) 414 08 77. - Paint -   082538
Solidair, Middenhoefstr. 11, 3022 ER Rotterdam.
T. (010) 425 49 86. - Paint -   082539
Stralen, H. van, Voorhaven 34, 3024 RN Rotterdam.
T. (010) 477 80 78. - Paint -   082540
Studio Eline, Kleiweg 271B, 3051 XN Rotterdam.
T. (010) 461 00 47. - Paint -   082541
Tudelu, W. de Withstr. 41A, 3012 BM Rotterdam.
T. (010) 411 99 33. - Paint -   082542
Tudelu, Bentincklaan 57C, 3039 KJ Rotterdam.
T. (010) 466 50 67. - Paint -   082543
Veem, Het, W. de Withstr. 44, 3012 BR Rotterdam.
T. (010) 414 88 74. - Paint -   082544
Waning, Van, Jan, Westersingel 35, 3014 GS Rotterdam.
T. (010) 436 01 98, Fax 436 75 18. - Paint / Graph /
Sculp / Fra / Silv -   082545
Waterleau, Waterloustr. 163A, 3062 TM Rotterdam.
T. (010) 414 64 03. - Paint -   082546

Schipluiden (Zuid-Holland)
Konstkabinet, Vlaardingsekade 57, 2636 BD Schipluiden. T. (015) 3808311. - Paint -   082547

Slootdorp (Noord-Holland)
Art & Project, Postbus 9, 1774 ZG Slootdorp.
T. (0227) 577375. - Paint / Sculp / Draw -   082548

Soest (Utrecht)
Drie Ringen, De, Kerkstr. 11b, 3764 CR Soest.
T. (035) 6012169. - Paint -   082549

't Gooi (Utrecht)
Westrenen, Tuurdijk 16, 3997 MS 't Gooi.
T. (030) 6011671.   082550

Tilburg (Noord-Brabant)
Galerie Kokon, Stationsstr. 38, 5038 ED Tilburg.
T. (013) 5436732. - Paint -   082551

Toldijk (Gelderland)
Leeman, J. C., Zutphen-Emmerikseweg 59, 7227 DJ
Toldijk. T. (0575) 451826.   082552

Ulft (Gelderland)
Galerie bij de Boeken, Pastor Vernooystr 1, 7071 BR
Ulft.   082553

Utrecht
Art Lease Nederland, Oudegracht 63, 3511 AD Utrecht.
T. (030) 2322026. - Paint -   082554
Dekker, D., Oudegracht 230a, 3511 NT Utrecht.
T. (030) 2332158. - Paint -   082555
Elsen, Marianne van der, Lynmarkt 32, 3511 KJ Utrecht.
T. (030) 2342066. - Paint -   082556
Ex Parte, Minrebroederstr. 6, 3512 GT Utrecht.
T. (030) 2311921. - Paint -   082557
Flatland, L. Nieuwstr. 7, 3512 PA Utrecht.
T. (030) 2315181. - Paint -   082558
Galerie Quintessens, Nieuwegracht 53, 3512 LE Utrecht.
T. (030) 2322351. - Paint / Sculp / Draw -   082559

Hart Voor Hout, Wittevrouwenstr. 42, 3512 CV Utrecht.
T. (030) 2340587. - Paint - 082560
Horizon, Wittevrouwenstr. 8, 3512 CT Utrecht.
T. (030) 2319517. - Paint - 082561
Huis van Beeldende Kunst, Koningslaan 37, 3583 GH Ut-
recht. T. (030) 2515395. - Paint - 082562
Jas, Nachtegaalstr. 3, 3581 AA Utrecht.
T. (030) 2317675. - Paint - 082563
Kunstliefde, Genootschap, Nobelstraat 12a, 3512 EN Ut-
recht. T. (030) 2314218. - Paint - 082564
Leolux, Hammerskjöldhof 28, 3527 HE Utrecht.
T. (030) 2938149. - Paint - 082565
Overbeek, H. van, Oudegr. 90, 3511 AV Utrecht.
T. (030) 2322108. - Paint - 082566
Quintessens, Nieuwegracht 53, 3512 LE Utrecht.
T. (030) 2322351. - Paint - 082567
Raster, Oudegracht 204, 3511 NR Utrecht.
T. (030) 2310906. - Paint - 082568
Reiger, De, Burg Reigerstr. 3, 3581 KJ Utrecht.
T. (030) 2317815. - Paint - 082569
Sepia, Twynstr 30, 3511 ZL Utrecht.
T. (030) 2343152. 082570
Vogelpot, Oudegracht 268, 3511 NW Utrecht.
T. (030) 2328256. - Paint - 082571
Weijer, J. H. Th. van de, Minrebroederstraat 22, 3512
GT Utrecht. T. (030) 227105. - Paint - 082572
Witte Vrouwen, Bemuurde Weerd 5 oostzijde, 3514 AN
Utrecht. T. (030) 2733380. - Paint - 082573
Y'Art & P, Willemstr. 26, 3511 RK Utrecht.
T. (030) 2322260. - Paint - 082574

Velp (Gelderland)

Albricht, Hobbemalaan 3, 6881 CT Velp.
T. (026) 3611876. - Paint - 082575

Vlissingen (Zeeland)

Marquis, Nieuwendijk 15, 4380 AB Vlissingen Postbus
5050. T. (0118) 416588. 082576

Wassenaar (Zuid-Holland)

„Heuff" Kunstzaal, Hoflaan 7, 2242 EL Wassenaar.
T. (070) 5112185. - Furn / Tex - 082577
Smith, Leslie, Hertelaan 15, 2243 EK Wassenaar.
T. (070) 5179075, 5179079. - Paint - 082578

Weurt (Gelderland)

Tweeling, de, Jonkerstraat 1-3, 6551 DC Weurt.
T. 8024) 6777752. - Paint / Graph / China / Sculp / Pho /
Draw - 082579

Zeist (Utrecht)

Wortmann, J. R., Slotlaan 128, 3701 GR Zeist.
T. (030) 6923285. - Ico - 082580

New Caledonia

Nouméa

Galeria, 3 Rue Général-Gallieni, Nouméa.
T. (687) 271985. 082581
Galerie Cadr'in, 81 Rue Charleroi, Nouméa.
T. (687) 252442. 082582

New Zealand

Auckland (Auckland)

John Leech Gallery, 106 Albert Street, Auckland.
T. (09) 735 044. - Paint / Graph / Fra / Repr - 082583
Kitchener Gallery, 24 Kitchener St., Auckland.
T. (03) 608584 082584
Moller, N. L., & Co., 313 Queen St. Auckland, Auckland.
T. (09) 37 09 39. - Paint / Repr / Sculp / Fra - 082585
Snaps Gallery, 30 Airedale St., Auckland.
082586

Christchurch

Canterbury Society of Arts, 66 Gloucester St., Christ-
church, 1. T. (03) 667261, 667167. 082587
Canterbury Society of Arts Gallery, 66 Gloucester St.,
Christchurch. T. (03) 66 72 61, 66 71 67.
- Paint - 082588
Fisher, H., & Son, 691 Colombo Str., Christchurch.
T. (03) 611 61. - Paint / Graph / Repr / Fra - 082589

Dunedin (Otago)

Abernethy, Joseph, 251 George St., Dunedin.
T. (024) 779 290. - Paint / Graph / Repr - 082590
Lapierre, 434 High St., Dunedin. 082591

Invercargill (Otago)

Anderson Park Art Gallery, Invercargill POB 755. 082592

Paraparaumu Beach

McGregor Wright, 181 Raumati Rd., Paraparaumu Beach. T. (058) 84 958. - Paint / Graph / Repr /
Fra - 082593

Surfdahe

Treebeard Art Gallery, 8 Miami Av., Surfdahe.
- Paint - 082594

Wellington

Dowling, G. W., Halley's Lane, Wellington.
T. (04) 84 72 93. - Graph / Repr / Fra - 082595
Webster, G., & Co., 44 Manners St., Wellington.
T. (04) 85 41 36, Fax (04) 85 41 38. - Paint / Graph /
Repr / Fra - 082596

Norway

Arendal (Aust-Agder)

Arendals Kunsthandel, Nedre Tyholmsv. 10, 4800 Are-
ndal. - Paint / Fra - 082597

Moss

Galleri F 15, POB 1033, 1501 Moss. T. 69271033,
Fax 69275410. 082598

Oslo

Abel, Kristian IV's G. 15, Oslo. T. 22 20 52 02.
- Paint - 082599
Albin Upp, Briskebyv. 42, 0259 Oslo. T. 22 55 71 92.
- Paint - 082600
Artes Galleri, Riddervolds G. 9, 0258 Oslo.
T. 22 55 93 77, Fax 22 43 48 49. - Paint - 082601
Astrup, Ingeborg, Bjørnv. 42, 0387 Oslo. T. 22 14 72 82.
- Paint - 082602
Bellman, Frognerv. 31, 0263 Oslo. T. 22 44 95 11.
- Paint - 082603
Berntsen, Kaare, Universitetsg. 12, 0164 Oslo.
T. 22 20 34 29, Fax 22 11 01 08. - Paint - 082604
Bildeforum Wiik, Haugesg. 15, Oslo.
T. 22 15 22 30. 082605
Blomqvist, Tordenskiolds G. 5, 0160 Oslo.
T. 22 41 26 31. - Paint - 082606
Casa Arte, Trondheimsv. 178, Oslo. T. 22 15 58 78.
- Paint - 082607
Christensen, Haaken A., Lille Frogner Allé 6, 0263 Oslo.
T. 22 55 91 97. - Paint - 082608
Christie's, Riddervoldsg. 10b, 0258 Oslo. T. 22 44 12 42.
- Paint - 082609
Danielsen, A., & Co., Drammensv. 40, 0255 Oslo.
T. 22 44 42 55, 22 44 85 86. - Paint - 082610
Dobloug, St. Olavsgt. 13, 0165 Oslo.
T. 22 11 30 96. 082611
Føyner, Gimleterr. 4, 0264 Oslo. T. 22 56 11 93.
- Paint - 082612
Frysja Senter, Kjelsåsv. 141, 0491 Oslo.
T. 22 15 80 83. 082613
Gabrielsen, E., Grensen 8, 0159 Oslo. T. 22 42 79 49.
- Paint - 082614
Galleri Aktuell Kunst, Youngstorget, 0028 Oslo.
T. 22 42 95 98. - Paint - 082615
Galleri Arctandria, Frognerv. 4a, 0257 Oslo.
T. 22 43 69 83. 082616
Galleri D 40, Drammensv. 40, 0255 Oslo. T. 22 44 85 86,
22 55 14 60. 082617
Galleri Graffiti, Parkv. 25, 0350 Oslo. T. 22 46 27 02.
- Paint - 082618
Galleri K, Bjørn Farmanns G. 6, 0271 Oslo.
T. 22 55 35 88. - Paint - 082619
Galleri KB, Universitetsgt. 12, 0164 Oslo.
T. 22 203429. 082620
Galleri LNM, Kongens gate 2, 0351 Oslo.
T. 22 42 15 78. 082621
Galleri Nordstrand, Nordstrandv. 36, 1163 Oslo.
T. 22 28 79 27. 082622

Galleri Orbit, Maridalsv. 3, 0178 Oslo.
T. 22 11 33 06. 082623
Galleri Palladio, Nedre Slottsg. 5, 0157 Oslo.
T. 22 41 05 10. 082624
Galleri Tonne, Fr. Nansenspl., 0160 Oslo. T. 22 33 35 60.
- Paint - 082625
Galleri 27, Pilestr. 27, 0164 Oslo. T. 22 20 30 47. 082626
Galleri 33, Thv. Meyers G. 33c, 0555 Oslo.
T. 22 38 55 15. - Paint - 082627
Gallerie J2, Josefinesg. 2, 0351 Oslo. T. 22 56 81 73.
- Paint - 082628
Gallerikroken, Meyersg. 81, 0552 Oslo.
T. 22 35 51 96. 082629
Galtung, Bygdøy Allé 51, 0265 Oslo.
T. 22 44 79 21. 082630
Hammerlunds, Tordenskioldsgt. 3, 0160 Oslo.
T. 22 42 36 26, 22 41 27 44. - Paint / Graph /
Sculp - 082631
Heer, Seilduksg. 4, 0553 Oslo. T. 22 38 54 32.
- Paint - 082632
Holst Halvorsen, Elisenbergv. 4, 0265 Oslo.
T. 22 55 85 87. - Paint - 082633
Huset, Teaterg. 1, Oslo. T. 22 20 99 66. - Paint - 082634
JMS Kunst, Niels Juels G. 50, 0257 Oslo. T. 22 55 32 51.
- Paint - 082635
Jørgen, Maries G. 7b, 0368 Oslo. T. 22 44 95 95.
- Paint - 082636
Kampen, Norderhovg. 30, 0654 Oslo. T. 22 67 49 46.
- Paint - 082637
Kortfolaget, Ö. Aker V. 101, 0596 Oslo. T. 22 64 25 50,
22 64 25 51. - Paint - 082638
Kulø, Erry, Harbitzalléen 2 b, 0275 Oslo.
T. 22 73 12 16. 082639
Kunst-utsmykning, Oscars G. 88, 0256 Oslo.
T. 22 44 51 32. - Paint - 082640
Kunstklubben, Postboks 8843, 0181 Oslo.
T. 22 42 95 98. - Paint - 082641
Kunstnernes Informasjonskontor, Kongensgt. 3, 0153
Oslo. T. 22 33 59 93. - Paint - 082642
Kunstnerringen, Skovv. 8, 0257 Oslo. T. 22 44 12 71.
- Paint - 082643
Leding, Hjalmar, Fr. Stangs G. 46b, 0264 Oslo.
T. 22 44 10 42. - Paint - 082644
Magnussen, C., Herslebs G. 2b, 0561 Oslo.
T. 22 35 51 76. - Paint - 082645
Majorstuen Ramme og Kunst, Industrig. 40, 0357 Oslo.
T. 22 46 02 99. - Paint - 082646
Mittet & Co., Kongens G. 15, 0153 Oslo. T. 22 41 55 56.
- Paint - 082647
Monique, Torgg. 35, 0183 Oslo. T. 22 11 15 64.
- Paint - 082648
Mørch, Jan, Frognerveien 48b, 0266 Oslo.
T. 22 43 45 40. - Draw - 082649
Munchforlaget, Behrens G. 8, 0257 Oslo. T. 22 55 77 30/
32. - Paint - 082650
Nouvelle Art, Bjerkebakken, 0756 Oslo. T. 22 50 43 09.
- Paint - 082651
Ny Kunstformidling, Riddervoldsg. 12, 0258 Oslo.
T. 22 44 63 78, 56 11 34. 082652
Olsen, Kjell, Kr. Ang. G. 19, 0164 Oslo. T. 22 20 22 41.
- Paint - 082653
Paletten Galleri, Torgg. 21, 0183 Oslo. T. 22 20 03 60.
- Paint - 082654
Plakat Palakat, Torgg. 35, 0183 Oslo. T. 22 11 15 64.
- Graph - 082655
Rammesnekker'n Kunst og Rammeforretning, Daele-
nengg. 12, 0567 Oslo. T. 22 35 51 04. - Paint - 082656
RR Interiør, Thereses G. 51, 0354 Oslo. T. 22 46 83 51.
- Paint - 082657
Samleren, Hedgehaugsv. 14a, Oslo. T. 22 56 84 56.
- Paint - 082658
Scarabé, Sofiesg. 14, 0170 Oslo. T. 22 56 94 58. 082659
Smith-Hald, Løska, Riddervoldsg. 9, 0258 Oslo.
T. 22 55 93 77. 082660
Solberg, Esaias, Dronningens G. 27, Oslo.
T. 22 41 63 49. - Paint - 082661
Tegnerforbundet, Rådhusgt. 17, 0158 Oslo.
T. 22 42 38 06, Fax 22 41 19 87. - Paint - 082662
Tjøme, J., Tollbug. 25, 0157 Oslo. T. 22 41 55 21.
- Paint - 082663
Vognremissen Galleri, Karl-Johans-G. 11, 0154 Oslo.
T. 22 33 26 04. 082664

082665 – 082747

Wang, Kristian Augusts Gate 1, 0164 Oslo.
T. 22 11 51 70. 082665

Stavanger (Rogaland)
Floor, Carl A/S, Prostebakken 3, 4000 Stavanger.
- Graph / Repr - 082666
Stavanger Faste Galleri, Madlavn, 33, 4001 Stavanger.
T. 51 53 09 00. 082667

Pakistan

Lahore
Ferozsons, 60 Shara-e-Quaid-i-Azam, Lahore.
T. 30 11 96/98. - Graph / Repr - 082668

Peru

Lima
Art Center, Instituto Centro de Arte, Alameda Ricardo
Palma 246, Miraflores, Lima. T. 25 60 97, 45 94 11.
- Paint - 082669
Borkas, Las Camelias 851, San Isidro, Lima.
T. 40 84 15. 082670
Camino Brent, Enrique, Burgos 170, San Isidro,
Lima. 082671
Galeria de Arte Sol, Las Lilas 150, Lince, Lima.
T. 71 10 29. 082672
Galeria Forum, Av. Larco 1150, Miraflores, Lima.
T. 46 13 13. 082673
Garden Sala de Arte, R. Rivera Navarrete 450,
Lima. 082674
Leyva, General Varela 596, Miraflores, Lima. T. 45 50 48,
45 65 93. - Paint - 082675
Trapecio, Av. Larco 743, Miraflores, Lima.
T. 45 08 42. 082676

Philippines

Las Piñas
Kristiregi Galleries, 271 Manila South Rd, LAS Bldg, Las
Pin'4as. T. (02) 8010506, 8010283. 082677

Makati
Alliance Franchaise Gallery, 220 Gil Puyat Ave, Makati.
T. (02) 880402. 082678
Art Lab, 466 EDSA, Makati. T. (02) 8171219. 082679
Auction House Galleries, Ayala Center, Makati.
T. (02) 8171236. 082680
Finale Art File, Pasay Road, Sunvar Plaza, Makati.
T. (02) 8151813. 082681
Frame House Makati, Amorsolo St Creekside Bldg, Ma-
kati. T. (02) 8173671. 082682
Galleria Aurora, 19 Ponce St, Makati.
T. (02) 8150464. 082683
Gintong Sining Inc., Goldcrest Vill, Makati Cinema Squa-
re, Makati. T. (02) 856436. 082684
Luz Gallery, Makati Ave L.V. Locsin Bldg., Makati.
T. (02) 8156906. 082685
Traditions East Gallery, Amorsolo St, 2/F Milelong Cen-
ter, Makati. T. (02) 878284. 082686

Mandaluyong
Galleria Duemila, Building A, SM Megamall EDSA, Ortig-
as Center, Mandaluyong. T. (02) 6336687. 082687
Genesis, Building A, SM Megamall EDSA, Ortigas Center,
Mandaluyong. T. (02) 6338137, 6338138. 082688
Genesis, 718 Shaw Boulevard, Banco del Oriente Center,
Mandaluyong. T. (02) 794806. 082689
Kawilihan Art Gallery, 241 Shaw Blvd, Mandaluyong.
T. (02) 781153. 082690
Pacheco Art Gallery, Bldg A, SM Megamall EDSA, Ortigas
Center, Mandaluyong. T. (02) 6342422. 082691
West Gallery, Bldg A, SM Megamall EDSA, Ortigas Cen-
ter, Mandaluyong. T. (02) 6341284. 082692

Manila
Archipelago Galleries, 1310 A. Mabin Ermita, Manila.
T. 586794. 082693

Contreras Sculpture, SM Megamall EDSA, Ortigas Cen-
ter, Manila. T. (02) 6341283. 082694
Cultural Center of the Philippines Art Galleries, Roxas
Blvd, CCP Complex, Manila. T. (02) 8321125,
8313415. 082695
Design Center of the Philippines Gallery, Roxas Blvd,
CCP Complex, Manila. T. (02) 8323645,
8337881. 082696
Emperor Arts + Antiques, Harrison Plaza 2nd Fl. Shop.
City, A. Mabini St., Malate, Manila. T. 521 7481. - Ant /
Paint / Orient / China - 082697
Finale Art File, SM Megamall EDSA, Ortigas Center, Ma-
nila. T. (02) 6342410, 6342411. 082698
Galleria de las Islas, 744 Calle Real del Palacio, Manila.
T. (02) 407318. 082699
Gallery of Modern Art, 3320 V. Mapa St, Sta. Mesa, Ma-
nila. T. (029 623574, 607559. 082700
Greater Manila Art Gallery, 1311 A. Mabini St, Manila.
T. (02) 504144. 082701
Hiraya Gallery, 530 United Nations Ave, Manila.
T. (02) 594223. 082702
Kanlungan ng Sining, T.M. Kalaw St, Rizal Park, Manila.
T. (02) 587411. 082703

Muntinlupa
Madrigal Center, Commerce Ave, Ayala-Alabang, Mun-
tinlupa. T. (02) 8420127. 082704

Parañaque
Kulay-Diwa Art Galleries, 25 Lopez Ave, Lopez Village,
Parañaque. T. (02) 8277735, 8197377. 082705

Pasay City
Galleria Duemila, 210 Loring St, Pasay City.
T. (02) 8339815, 8319990. 082706

Pasig
Lopez Museum Gallery, Tektite Rd, Chronicle Bldg, Pa-
sig. T. (02) 6735418, 6735409. 082707

Quezon City
Ateneo Art Gallery, Katipunan Road, Loyola Heights,
Quezon City. T. (02) 998721, 982541. 082708
Galleria Bernice L, 126 9th Str, Quezon City.
T. (02) 7218636, 7214994. 082709
Gallerie Dominique, 201-202 Eastbridge, 2/F SM City,
North EDSA, Quezon City. T. (02) 995842,
998472. 082710
Galleries of Fine Arts, 82 Katipunan Rd, White Plains,
Quezon City. T. (02) 7217852. 082711
Heritage Art Center, 43 Hillside Loop, Blue Ridge, Que-
zon City. T. (02) 787257, 7224212. 082712
Liongoren Art Gallery, 111 New York St, Cubao, Quezon
City. T. (02) 981625. 082713
Mariposa Workshop Gallery, 28 Mariposa St, Cubao,
Quezon City. T. (02) 7221246. 082714
West Gallery, 48 West Ave, Quezon City. T. (02) 980297,
977132. 082715

Poland

Białystok
Salon Sztuki Współczesnej-Antyki, Pl Kościuszki 17, 15-
421 Białystok. T. 272 06. - Paint / Paint / Sculp / Tex /
Jew / Glass / Ico - 082716

Chełm
Galeria 72, ul. Lubelska 55, 22-100 Chełm.
T. 2693. 082717

Częstochowa
Salon Sztuki Współczesnej – Antyki, Al. N.M. Panny 40/
42, 42 200 Częstochowa. T. 437 26. - Paint / Paint /
Tex / Jew / Glass / Ico - 082718

Gdynia (Gdańsk)
Galeria Świętojańska, ul Świętojańska 44, 81-391 Gdy-
nia. - Paint / Graph / Sculp / Tex / Jew / Glass /
Ico - 082719
Galeria Sztuki Współczesnej, ul Świętojańska 44, 81-
393 Gdynia. 082720

Katowice
Salon Sztuki Współczesnej, ul Wieczorka 8, 40-013 Ka-
towice. T. 53 94 70. - Paint / Graph / Sculp / Tex / Jew /
Glass / Ico - 082721

Kraków
Galeria B, ul. Solskiego 21, 31-020 Kraków. T. 22 31 14.
- Graph - 082722
Galeria „DESA", ul Św. Jana 3, 31-017 Kraków.
T. 22 98 91. - Paint / Graph / Sculp / Tex / Jew / Glass /
Ico - 082723
Galeria Kramy Dominikańskie, ul. Stolarska 8-9, 31-043
Kraków. T. 22 70 41. - Paint / Graph / Sculp / Tex / Jew /
Glass - 082724
Galeria Pawilon, Osiedle Kościuszkowskie 5, 31-858
Kraków. T. 44836. 082725

Łódź
Salon Sztuki Współczesnej, ul. Piotrkowska 113, 90-430
Łódź. - Paint / Graph / Sculp / Tex / Jew / Glass /
Ico - 082726

Lublin
Arcus, ul Narutowicza 10, POB 212, Lublin, 20-
950. 082727
Labirynt 2 BWA, ul Grodzka 3, 20-112 Lublin. T. 25947.
- Paint / Graph / Sculp - 082728

Nowa Huta
Galeria Sztuki Współczesnej, Os. Ogrodowe 10, 31-915
Nowa Huta. - Paint / Graph / Sculp - 082729

Olsztyn
Salon Sztuki Współczesnej-Antyki, ul Dąbrowszczaków
1, 10-538 Olsztyn. - Paint / Graph / Sculp / Tex / Jew /
Glass / Ico - 082730

Opole
Salon Sztuki Współczesnej-Antyki, Rynek 22, 45-015
Opole. - Paint / Graph / Tex / Jew / Glass / Ico - 082731

Poznań
Akumulatory 2, ul Zwierzyniecka 7, 60-813 Poznań.
T. (061) 22 25 05. - Mul - 082732
Galeria Współczesna, ul Armii Czerwonej 63, 61-806
Poznań. - Paint / Graph / Sculp / Tex / Jew / Glass /
Ico - 082733
Karenska, Anna, Wroniecka 17, 61-763 Poznań.
T. (061) 52 08 85, Fax 52 78 17. 082734

Przemyśl
Salon Sztuki Współczesnej, Rynek 15, 37-700 Przemyśl.
- Paint / Graph / Tex / Jew / Glass / Ico - 082735

Sopot (Gdańsk)
Biuro Wystaw Artystycznych, Pawiliony wystawowe przy
molo, 80-827 Sopot. 082736

Szczecin
Antykwariat i Galeria Sztuki Współczesnej, Pl Żołnierza
5, 70-551 Szczecin. 082737
Galeria „Gryl", Pl Żołnierza 5, 70-561 Szczecin. - Paint /
Graph / Sculp / Tex / Jew / Glass / Ico - 082738
„Klub", Pl Żołnierza 2, 70-561 Szczecin. 082739

Toruń
Biuro Wystaw Artystycznych, Stary Rynek 6, 87-100
Toruń. 082740

Warszawa
Antykwariat DESA, Rynek Starego Miasta 4/6, 00-272
Warszawa. T. (022) 31 16 81. - Paint / Graph / Furn /
Orient / Sculp / Tex - 082741
Dom Artysty Plastyka, ul. Mazowiecka 11a, 00-052 War-
szawa. T. (022) 27 31 35. - Draw - 082742
Galeria Foksal CBWA, ul. Foksal 1/4, 00-366 Warszawa.
T. (022) 27 73 14. - Paint / Graph / Sculp - 082743
Galeria Fotografii Hybrydy CKS, ul. Kniewskiego 7/9, 00-
019 Warszawa. T. (022) 27 37 63. - Pho - 082744
Galeria Kordegarda, ul Krakowskie Przedmieście 15/17,
00-171 Warszawa. T. (022) 20 02 31. - Paint - 082745
Galeria Koszykowa DESA, ul. Koszykowa 62, 00-673
Warszawa. T. (022) 21 96 65. - Paint / Graph / China /
Tex / Jew / Glass - 082746
Galeria Muzeum Techniki, ul Żelazna 51-53, 00-848
Warszawa. T. (022) 20 47 10. 082747

Galeria Nowogrodzka DESA, ul Nowogrodzka 25, 00-511 Warszawa. T. (022) 28 28 37. - Jew / Glass - *082748*

Galeria Nowy Świat DESA, ul Nowy Świat 23, 00-029 Warszawa. T. (022) 26 35 01. - Paint / Graph / Sculp / Tex / Jew / Glass / Ico - *082749*

Galeria Pokaz, ul Krakowskie Przedmieście 20/22, 00-325 Warszawa. - Graph / Draw - *082750*

Galeria RR Klub Riviera-Remont, ul Waryńskiego 12, 00-631 Warszawa. T. (022) 25 74 97. - Mul - *082751*

Galeria Rzeźby, ul. Marchlewskiego 36, 00-141 Warszawa. T. (022) 20 78 72. - Sculp - *082752*

Galeria Sztuki Alicji i Bożeny Wahl, ul Mierosławskiego 9, 01-527 Warszawa. T. (022) 39 08 56. - Paint / China / Sculp - *082753*

Galeria Test, ul Marszałkowska 34/50, 00-554 Warszawa. T. (022) 28 66 83. - Paint / Graph - *082754*

Galeria Zachęta, pl Małachowskiego 3, 00-916 Warszawa. T. (022) 27 58 54. - Paint / Sculp / Mod / Draw - *082755*

Galeria Zapiecek DESA, ul Zapiecek 1, 00-274 Warszawa. T. (022) 31 99 18. - Paint / Graph / Sculp / Tex / Jew / Glass - *082756*

Mała Galeria Zpaf, Plac Zamkowy 8, 00-277 Warszawa. T. (022) 312 339. - Pho - *082757*

Wrocław

Antykwariat i Salon Plastyki Współczesnej, Pl. Kościuszki 16, 50-027 Wrocław. T. 53 99 22. *082758*

Galeria Sztuki Współczesnej, ul Kościuszki 16, 50-027 Wrocław. T. 372 80. *082759*

Galeria Wrocławska, Pl Nankiera 8, Domek Romański, 50-140 Wrocław. T. 447 840. - Pho - *082760*

Mały Salon BWA, ul Świdnicka 41, 50-028 Wrocław. T. 44 84 85. - Paint / Graph / Sculp / Pho - *082761*

Permafo, Rynek-Ratusz 24, 50-101 Wrocław. *082762*

Zakopane (woj. Nowy Sącz)

Biuro Wystaw Artystycznych, ul Krupówski 41, 34-500 Zakopane. T. 2792. - Paint / Graph / Sculp / Tex - *082763*

Portugal

Alcobaca (Estremadura)

Casa Alcobaça, Praça D. Afonso Henriques 6 e 7, 2460 Alcobaca. T. 424 08. - Paint / Sculp - *082764*

Cascais (Estremadura)

Arraia, Joaquim Jose, Rua Frederico Arouca 93, 2750 Cascais. *082765*

Estoril

Canguru, Av. Bombeiros Voluntarios 6, 2765 Estoril. - Sculp - *082766*

Lisboa

Assoc. Portuguesa de Arte Fotografica, Rua das Chagas 17, 1200 Lisboa. T. (01) 36 76 59. - Pho - *082767*

Audlmagem, Largo Trindade Coelho 3 e4, 1200 Lisboa. T. (01) 371 675. - Pho - *082768*

Centro de Arte, Sociedade Tipográfica, Rua de D. Estefânia 195 D, 1000 Lisboa. T. (01) 54 32 80, Fax 57 79 26. *082769*

Comicos, Rua Tenente Raul Cascais 1B, 1900 Lisboa. T. (01) 67 77 94, Fax 397 02 51. - Paint - *082770*

Cortez, Alda, Largo Santos 1F, 1200 Lisboa. T. (01) 67 10 53, Fax 67 88 05. *082771*

Diferença, Comunição visual, Rua S. Filipe Nery 42, 1, 1200 Lisboa. T. (01) 65 75 36. *082772*

Dinastia, Rua da Escola Politecnica 183 R/C, 1200 Lisboa. T. (01) 66 89 73. - Paint - *082773*

Fonseca, Graça, Rua da Emenda 26, 1200 Lisboa. T. (01) 347 70 37, Fax 347 83 12. *082774*

Galeria 111, Campo Grande 113A, 1700 Lisboa. T. (01) 76 74 06. *082775*

Galerie Sesimbra, Rua Castilho 77, 1000 Lisboa. *082776*

Mamede, S., Rua Escola Politécnica 167, 1200 Lisboa. T. (01) 67 32 55, 66 86 91. - Paint - *082777*

Matias, Manuel, Av. 5 de Ourubro 351, 1., E., Lisboa. *082778*

Modulo, Calcada dos Mestres 34a, 1000 Lisboa. T. (01) 68 55 70, Fax 68 55 70. - Paint / Graph / Pho - *082779*

Moira, R. Nova da Piedade 33, 1200 Lisboa. T. (01) 67 02 94, Fax 397 02 77. *082780*

Nasoni, Avda. Columbano Bordalo Pinheiro 9B, 1000 Lisboa. T. (01) 7266 992, 7268 939, 7268 940, Fax 7266 924. *082781*

Quadrum, Galerie de Arte, rua Alberto de Oliveira, 52, 1700 Lisboa. T. (01) 77 97 23. *082782*

Roberto, Rua Almeida e Sousa 44 B, Lisboa. *082783*

Sam-Mamede, Rua da Escola Politecnica 163, 1200 Lisboa. T. (01) 67 32 55. - Paint - *082784*

Sociedade Nacional de Belas Artes, Rua Barata Salgueiro 36, Lisboa. T. (01) 412 93. - Paint / Sculp - *082785*

Tempo, R. Nova de S. Mamede 17, 1200 Lisboa. T. (01) 683 308. *082786*

Yela, Rua Rodrigo da Fonseca, 103-B, 1000 Lisboa. T. (01) 68 03 99. *082787*

Portimao

Galeria Portimao, Rua Santa Isabel 5, 8500 Portimao. T. (082) 229 65. - Paint / Graph / Sculp / Tex / Draw - *082788*

Porto

Alvarez, Rua da Alegria 117, Porto. T. (02) 236 96. - Paint / Graph - *082789*

„Candelbro", Rua da Conceiçao 3, 4000 Porto. T. (02) 224 49. - Graph - *082790*

Dois, Avda. da Boavista 707, Porto. T. (02) 65771. *082791*

Galeria Atlantica, Rua Galeria de Paris 71, 4000 Porto. T. (02) 200 08 40, Fax 32 53 02. - Paint - *082792*

Galeria Nasoni, Rua Galeria de Paris 80, 4000 Porto. T. (02) 32 05 59, 32 54 75, Fax 325 302. - Paint - *082793*

Galerie Fluxus, R. do Rosário 125-129, 4000 Porto. T. (02) 201 10 74, 200 69 09, Fax 200 10 42. *082794*

Modulo, Av. da Boavista 854, 4100 Porto. T. (02) 69 47 42. - Paint / Graph / Sculp / Pho - *082795*

Oliveira, Pedro, Cal. de Mouchique 3, 4000 Porto. T. (02) 200 23 34, Fax 200 23 34. *082796*

Silva e C., Mario, Lda., Rua D. Manuel II.20, 4000 Porto. *082797*

Réunion

Saint-Denis

Art Lacaze, 10 Rue Nice, 97400 Saint-Denis. T. (262) 216088. *082798*

Cadre Noir, 77 Rue Labourdonnais, 97400 Saint-Denis. T. (262) 214488. *082799*

Charmerie, 27 Av Victoire, 97400 Saint-Denis. T. (262) 202896. *082800*

Samarkand, 16 Rue Sainte-Anne, 97400 Saint-Denis. T. (767) 413580. *082801*

Saint-Paul

Braud, Stéphane, Forum Saint-Gilles-les-Bains, 97460 Saint-Paul. T. (262) 240101. *082802*

Osmose, Chemin Eperon, 97460 Saint-Paul. T. (262) 556573. *082803*

Saint-Pierre

Vincent, Chemin Archambaud 400, 97410 Saint-Pierre. T. (262) 273273. *082804*

Romania

Alba Iulia (judetul Alba)

Galeria de Artà, Bd. 6 Martie, Bloc M 9-10, 2500 Alba Iulia. T. (0968) 21500. - Paint - *082805*

Arad (judetul Arad)

Galeria de Artà, Str. Vasile Alecsandri 1, 2900 Arad. - Paint - *082806*

Galeria de Artà, Bd. Revolutie nr. 90, 2900 Arad. T. (0966) 16071. *082807*

Bacau (judetul Bacau)

Galeria de Artà, Str. Nicolae Bàlcescu 12, 5500 Bacau. T. (0931) 45618. - Paint - *082808*

Baia Mare (judetul Maramures)

Galeria de Artà, Bd. Bucuresti Nr. 6, 4800 Baia Mare. T. (0994) 12025. *082809*

Baile Felix

Galeria de Artà, Hotel Muresul, 3700 Baile Felix. T. (0991) 34072. *082810*

Birlad (judetul Vaslui)

Galeria de Artà, Str. Victoriei 12, 6400 Birlad. T. (0984) 16655. - Paint - *082811*

Bistrita (judetul Bistrita-Nasaud)

Galeria de Artà, Piata Libertatii Nr. 1, 4400 Bistrita. T. (0996) 15979. *082812*

Botosani (judetul Botosani)

Galeria de Artà, Str. Republicii 10, 5800 Botosani. T. (0985) 11417. - Paint - *082813*

Braila (judetul Braila)

Galeria de Artà, Pta. Lenin 1, 6100 Braila. T. (0946) 43247. - Paint - *082814*

Brasov (judetul Brasov)

Galeria de Artà, B-dul Victoriei 10, 2200 Brasov. T. (0921) 17451. - Paint - *082815*

Galeria de Artà, Str. 7 Noiembrie 1, 2200 Brasov. T. (0921) 43762. - Paint - *082816*

Bucuresti

Complexul Hanul cu Tei, Str. Blànari 5-7, 7000 Bucuresti. T. (01) 616 23 40. - Paint - *082817*

Galeria de Artà Arcade, Str. Selari 13, 7000 Bucuresti. T. (01) 615 85 78. - Paint - *082818*

Galeria de Artà Càminul Artei, Str. Biserica Enei 16, 7000 Bucuresti. T. (01) 614 18 18. - Paint - *082819*

Galeria de Artà Dalles, B-dul Bàlcescu 19, 7000 Bucuresti. T. (01) 615 14 45. - Paint - *082820*

Galeria de Artà Gara de Nord, B-dul Gàrii de Nord 6-8, 7000 Bucuresti. T. (01) 66659 69 95. - Paint - *082821*

Galeria de Artà Magheru 3, B-dul Magheru 22, 7000 Bucuresti. T. (01) 66659 75 80. - Paint - *082822*

Galeria de Artà Magheru 4, B-dul Magheru 20, 7000 Bucuresti. T. (01) 66659 75 80. - Paint - *082823*

Galeria de Artà Orizont 5+6, B-dul Bàlcescu 23a, 7000 Bucuresti. T. (01) 615 89 17. - Paint - *082824*

Galerià de Artà 1 Mai, B-dul I Mai 113, 7000 Bucuresti. T. (01) 6665 44 43. - Paint - *082825*

14 galerii de artà, Str. Lipscani, 70000 Bucuresti. - Paint - *082826*

Buzau (judetul Buzau)

Galeria de Artà, Str. Col Buzoianu 12, 5100 Buzau. - Paint - *082827*

Calarasi (judetul Talomita)

Galeria de Artà, Str. Cornisei, Bloc P3, 8500 Calarasi. T. (0911) 16123. - Paint - *082828*

Cluj-Napoca

Galeria de Artà Nr. 1, Str. Napoca 2-4, 3400 Cluj-Napoca. - Paint - *082829*

Galeria de Artà Nr. 2, Str. Napoca 2-4, 3400 Cluj-Napoca. - Paint - *082830*

Galeria de Artà Nr. 3, Piata Libertàtii nr. 14, 3400 Cluj-Napoca. T. (0951) 11332. *082831*

Constanta (judetul Constanta)

Galeria de Artà, Bd. Stefan cel Mare 15, 8700 Constanta. T. (0916) 14980. *082832*

Craiova (judetul Dolj)

Galeria de Artà, Str. Oltet 2-4, 1100 Craiova. T. (0941) 16051. - Paint - *082833*

Deva (judetul Hunedoara)

Galeria de Artà Nr. 1, B-dul Decebal bl. 8, 2700 Deva. T. (0956) 11341. *082834*

Galeria de Artà Nr.2, Str. Victoriei nr. 1, 2700 Deva. T. (0956) 11341. *082835*

Focsani (judetul Vrancea)
Galeria de Artà, B-dul Unirii 57a, 6800 Focsani.
T. (0939) 21465. - Paint -   082836

Galati (judetul Galati)
Galeria de Artà, Str. Republicii 19-21, 6200 Galati.
- Paint -   082837

Giurgiu (judetul Giurgiu)
Galeria de Artà, Piata Unirii nr. 1, bloc 92, 8375 Giurgiu.
T. (0912) 15375.   082838

Iasi
Galeria de Artà Cupola, Str. Cuza Vodà 2, 6600 Iasi.
- Paint -   082839
Galeria de Artà Nr. 1, Str. Làpusneanu 7-9, 6600 Iasi.
- Paint -   082840
Galeria de Artà Nr. 2, Str. Lapušneanu nr. 7-9, 6600
Iasi.   082841

Lugoj (judetul Timis)
Galeria de Artà PRO-ARTE, Str. Gh. Gheorghiu-Dej 3,
1800 Lugoj. T. (0963) 13886. - Paint -   082842

Mamia
Galeria de Artà, Complex Perla, 8741 Mamia.
T. (0918) 31551.   082843

Medias (judetul Sibiu)
Galeria de Artà, Str. Ludwig Roth nr. 13, 3125
Medias.   082844

Miercurea Ciuc (judetul Harghita)
Galeria de Artà, Str. Petöfi nr. 29, 4100 Miercurea Ciuc.
T. (0958) 12094.   082845

Oradea (judetul Bihor)
Galeria de Artà, Bd. Republicii 13, 3700 Oradea.
T. (0991) 11437. - Paint -   082846

Piatra Neamt (judetul Neamt)
Galeria de Artà, Str. Republicii Bl. A1, 5600 Piatra Neamt. T. (0936) 11928.   082847

Pitesti (judetul Arges)
Galeria de Artà Metopa, Piata Vasile Milea 4, 0300 Pitesti. T. (0976) 36050. - Paint -   082848

Ploiesti (judetul Prahova)
Galerie de Artà, Str. 16 Februarie 4, 2000 Ploiesti.
T. (0971) 46336. - Paint -   082849

Resita (judetul Caras-Severin)
Galeria de Artà AGORA, Bd. Republicii 8, 1700 Resita.
T. (0964) 33056. - Paint -   082850
Galeria Paleta, Bd. Lenin – Complex – 23 August, 1700
Resita. T. (0964) 15781.   082851

Rîmnicu Vîlcea (judetul Vilcea)
Galeria de Artà, Bd. Lenin, Bloc N-Zona Centralá, 1000
Rîmnicu Vîlcea. T. (0947) 13301. - Paint -   082852

Satu Mare (judetul Satu Mare)
Galeria de Artà, Str. Eliberàrii nr. 10, 3900 Satu Mare.
T. (0997) 14579.   082853
Galeria de Artà, Str. Piata 25 Octombrie nr. 12, 3900 Sa-
tu Mare. T. (0997) 12521.   082854

Sfintu Gheorghe (judetul Covasna)
Galeria de Artà, Str. Lenin 3, 2200 Sfintu Gheorghe.
T. (0923) 15266. - Paint -   082855

Sibiu (judetul Sibiu)
Galeria de Artà, Bd. Bàlcescu 31, 2400 Sibiu.
- Paint -   082856
Galeria Sirius, Bd. Bàlcescu nr. 16, 2400 Sibiu.
T. (0924) 12051.   082857

Sighisoara (judetul Mures)
Galeria de Artà, Bd. Gh. Gheorghiu-Dej nr. 16, 3050 Sighisoara. T. (0950) 72613.   082858

Slatina (judetul Olt)
Galeria de Artà, B-dul Al. I. Cuza 1, 0500 Slatina.
T. (0944) 13477. - Paint -   082859

Suceava (judetul Suceava)
Galeria de Artà, Str. Stefan cel Mare nr. 26, 5800 Suceava. T. (0987) 16288.   082860

Timisoara (judetul Timis)
Galeria de Artà CETATE, Calea Aradului 2, 1900 Timisoa-
ra. T. (0961) 36091. - Paint -   082861
Galeria de Artà PRO-DOMO, Str. Alba Iulia 9, 1900 Timi-
soara. T. (0961) 37841. - Paint -   082862
Galeria Helios, Bd. 30 Decembrie nr. 6, 1900 Timisoara.
T. (0961) 36091. - Graph -   082863

Tirgoviste (judetul Dimbovita)
Galeria de Artà, Bd. Libertatii, Bloc B1, 0200 Tirgoviste.
T. (0926) 34734. - Paint -   082864

Tîrgu Jiu (judetul Gorj)
Galeria de Artà, B-dul Traiani 27, 1400 Tîrgu Jiu.
T. (0929) 17921. - Paint -   082865

Tîrgu Mures (judetul Mures)
Galeria de Artà, Piata Eroilor Sovietici nr. 1, 4300 Tîrgu
Mures. T. (0954) 33147.   082866

Tulcea (judetul Tulcea)
Galeria de Artà, Str. Isaccei, Bloc 1, 8800 Tulcea.
T. (0915) 12011. - Paint -   082867

Turnu Severin
Galeria de Artà Apolodor, Str. Karl Marx nr. 3, 1500 Tumu
Severin. T. (0978) 15503.   082868

Vaslui (judetul Vaslui)
Galeria de Artà, Str. Stefan cel Mare 95, Bloc B 2, 6500
Vaslui. T. (0983) 11782. - Paint -   082869

Russia

Moskva

Aidan-galerya, pl Novopeschanaya 23/7, 123317 Mos-
kva. T. (095) 9435348. - Paint / Graph / Sculp - 082870
Aktsiya, ul Bolshaya Nikitskaya 21/18, 101000 Moskva.
T. (095) 2917509. - Ant / Paint / Graph -   082871
Akvarius, ul Bibliotechnaya 29 kv 5, 141400 Moskva.
T. (095) 5704800, 1519370. - Paint / Graph /
Sculp -   082872
Albatros, ul 5-aya Parkovaya 21A, 105215 Moskva.
T. (095) 3675372, 3675654. - Paint / Graph /
Sculp -   082873
Alma-mater, Lavrushenski per 15, 109017 Moskva.
T. (095) 2318409. - Paint / Graph -   082874
Arbat-34, ul Arbat 34, 121002 Moskva.
T. (095) 2414329. - Ant / Paint / Graph -   082875
Art Galereya Manezh, Manezhnaya pl 1, 103009 Mos-
kva. T. (095) 2028252. - Paint / Graph / Sculp - 082876
Art-modern, ul Ordynka 39, 109004 Moskva.
T. (095) 2331551. - Paint / Graph / Sculp -   082877
Asti, ul Tverskaya 5, 119309 Moskva. T. (095) 2033773,
Fax 2003210. - Paint / Graph / China / Eth /
Jew -   082878
Bagira, Krymski val 8 kor 2, 117049 Moskva.
T. (095) 2303054. - Paint / Graph -   082879
Belyaevo, ul Profsoyuznaya 100, 117485 Moskva.
T. (095) 3358322. - Paint / Graph -   082880
Bomond, Kutuzovski prosp 31, 121002 Moskva. - Paint /
Graph -   082881
Dar, ul Malaya Polyanka 7/7 korp5, 109180 Moskva.
T. (095) 2386554. - Paint / Graph -   082882
Dom Nashchokina, Vorotnikovski per 12, 123056 Mos-
kva. T. (095) 2991178, 2994774. - Paint /
Graph -   082883
Dominanta, prosp Mira 85, 125097 Moskva.
T. (095) 2076698. - Paint / Graph -   082884
Ekspo-88, ul Zabelina 1, 101000 Moskva.
T. (095) 9257242. - Paint / Graph / Sculp -   082885
Ensi, prosp Mira 14, 125250 Moskva. T. (095) 2081403.
- Paint / Ant -   082886
Fargo, Spiridonevski per 10, 121980 Moskva. - Paint /
Graph -   082887
Feniks, Kutuzovski prosp 3, 121248 Moskva. - Paint /
Graph -   082888
Forma, ul Lublinskaya 1, Moskva. T. (095) 1770411,
Fax 1770444. - Paint -   082889

Futura Klassik, ul Gilyarovskogo 58, Moskva.
T. (095) 2816885. - Paint / Graph / Sculp -   082890
Galereya Amerikanskogo Biznes Tsentra, Berezhkovska-
ya nab 2, 121059 Moskva. T. (095) 9418963. - Paint /
Graph / Sculp -   082891
Galereya Gelmana, ul M Polyanka 7/7, 109180 Moskva.
T. (095) 2388492. - Paint / Graph / Sculp -   082892
Galereya Kariny Shanshievoi, Krymski val 10, 117049
Moskva. T. (095) 2388392, Fax 2388392. - Paint /
Graph / Sculp -   082893
Galereya Mezhdunarodnogo universiteta, Leningradski
prosp 17, 125057 Moskva. T. (095) 2503481. - Paint /
Graph / Eth -   082894
Galereya nochnykh khudozhnikov, Truzhennikov per 2 kv
71, Moskva. T. (095) 2031722. - Paint / Graph - 082895
Galereya Olgi Khlebnikovoi, Krymski val 10/14, 117049
Moskva. T. (095) 1253078, Fax 3674420. - Paint /
Graph / Sculp -   082896
Galereya Soyuza Khudozhnikov Rossii, ul Usievicha 13,
125057 Moskva. T. (095) 1512441. - Paint / Graph /
Sculp -   082897
Galereya XL, ul Bolshaya Sadovaya 6, 103009 Moskva.
T. (095) 2695126, Fax 2695126. - Paint / Graph /
Sculp -   082898
Gelos, 1-i Botkinski proezd 2/6, 125252 Moskva.
T. (095) 9461171, 9460977. - Paint / Graph -   082899
Geoid, Kashirskoe shosse 70 korp 3, 115561 Moskva.
T. (095) 3201675, Fax 3201695. - Paint -   082900
Gerold Enterpraiz, ul Geroev Panfilovtsev 10/13, 123480
Moskva. T. (095) 4928235, Fax 4940147. - Paint /
Graph -   082901
Inter Art Ring, ul Profsoyuznaya 100, 117485 Moskva.
T. (095) 3358322. - Paint / Graph -   082902
Inter galereya, ul M Filyovskaya 32, 121433 Moskva.
T. (095) 1415455. - Paint / Graph / Sculp -   082903
Interkolor, ul Shekhova 24/2, 123056 Moskva.
T. (095) 2091385. - Paint / Graph / Sculp -   082904
Istoki, Soyuzny prosp 15A, 111396 Moskva.
T. (095) 3010348. - Graph / Eth -   082905
Katalog, Moskva. T. (095) 2006747. - Ant / Paint / Graph /
Sculp -   082906
Koloniya, Krimski val 10, 117049 Moskva.
T. (095) 2381666. - Paint -   082907
Kovcheg, ul Nemchinova 12, 127434 Moskva.
T. (095) 9770044. - Paint / Graph / Sculp -   082908
Krosna, ul Novy Arbat 11, 121019 Moskva.
T. (095) 2915138. - China -   082909
Kuntsevo, ul Kremenchugskaya 22, 121357 Moskva.
T. (095) 4451650. - Graph / China -   082910
L-Galereya, ul Oktyabrskaya 26, 127018 Moskva.
T. (095) 2892491. - Paint / Graph / Sculp / Pho - 082911
Le Sha-Art Alyans, Lavrushenski per 15, 109017 Mos-
kva. T. (095) 2330323. - Paint / Graph -   082912
Lez Oread, Krimski val 10, 117049 Moskva.
T. (095) 2380217, 2386066. - Paint / Graph /
Sculp -   082913
MArs, ul Malaya Filyovskaya 32, 121433 Moskva.
T. (095) 1462029; 1466335. - Paint / Graph /
Sculp -   082914
Modius, Moskva. T. (095) 1446064; 3968770,
Fax 2459621. - Paint / Graph / Sculp -   082915
Moscow Fine Art, ul Arbat 38, 121002 Moskva.
T. (095) 2411267. - Paint / Graph / Sculp -   082916
Moskovskaya galereya, ul kuznetski Most 11, 103031
Moskva. T. (095) 9254264. - Paint / Graph -   082917
Moskovskaya Kollektsiya, Shchetinski per 10, 113184
Moskva. T. (095) 2383968, Fax 9450768. - Ant / Paint /
Graph / Sculp -   082918
Moskovskaya Palitra, ul Povorskaya 35, 121069 Mos-
kva. T. (095) 2989503. - Paint / Graph / Sculp - 082919
Moskovskaya Studiya, Lavrushenski per 15, 109017
Moskva. T. (095) 2314364, Fax 1627604.
- Graph -   082920
Murtuz, ul Gertsena 22, 103009 Moskva.
T. (095) 2903139. - Paint / Graph / Sculp / Eth - 082921
Na Solyanke, ul solyanka 1/2, 109028 Moskva.
T. (095) 9215572. - Paint / Graph -   082922
Nagornaya, ul Remizova 14, 113186 Moskva.
T. (095) 1236569. - Paint / Graph -   082923
Neo-Shag, ul Arbat 53, 121069 Moskva.
T. (095) 2417586, 9560757. - Paint / Graph -   082924
Neskuchny Sad, Leninski prosp 2a, 117296 Moskva.
T. (095) 2304430. - Paint / Graph -   082925

Novaya Galereya, Moskva. T. (095) 1571450. - Paint /
Graph - 082926
Novy Kovcheg, ul 3-ya Parkovaya 33, 105425 Moskva.
T. (095) 1654943. - Graph - 082927
Obraz, Kutuzovski prosp 45, 121248 Moskva.
T. (095) 1489182, 4454972. - Ico - 082928
Olga, Krasnopresnenskaya nab 12, 123610 Moskva.
T. (095) 2556173. - Paint / Graph - 082929
Pan-dan, Moskva. T. (095) 2670320. - Paint / Graph /
Sculp - 082930
Peresvetov pereulok, Peresvetov per 4 korp 1, 103301
Moskva. T. (095) 2752228. - Paint / Graph - 082931
Predmet, ul Verkhnyaya Maslovka 18, Moskva.
T. (095) 2134286. - Eth - 082932
Rama-Art-Galeri, ul Dmitriya ulyanova 24, 117039 Mos-
kva. T. (095) 1246151. - Paint / Graph - 082933
Raut, Simferopolski prosp 6, Moskva. T. (095) 1132236.
- Paint / Graph - 082934
Re-Art-Gallery, ul Bolshaya Nikitskaya 19, 103009 Mos-
kva. T. (095) 2905371. - Paint / Graph - 082935
Renessans, Krymski val 10/14, 117049 Moskva.
T. (095) 2301161. - Paint / Graph / Sculp - 082936
Ridzhina, Moskva. T. (095) 2508571, 1247632,
Fax 2081653. - Paint / Graph / Sculp - 082937
Rosizo Galereya, Petrovka 28/2, 103051 Moskva.
T. (095) 9281455, 2001808, Fax 9219291. - Eth /
China - 082938
Roza Azora, Maly Vlasevski per 5, Moskva.
T. (095) 2414438, Fax 2177828. - Paint / Graph /
Sculp - 082939
Russkaya galereya, ul Vozdvizhenka 5, 121019 Moskva.
T. (095) 2986563. - Paint / Graph / Sculp - 082940
Russkaya ikona, Arbatski per 2, 121069 Moskva.
T. (095) 2024100. - Ico - 082941
Russkaya kollektsiya, ul Usievicha 3, 125315 Moskva.
T. (095) 1510758. - Paint / Graph / Eth - 082942
Sart, ul Krasina 27 korp2, 123056 Moskva.
T. (095) 2519817. - Paint / Graph / Sculp - 082943
Segodnya, ul Novy Arbat 19, 121002 Moskva.
T. (095) 2033344. - Paint / Graph - 082944
Slavyanski dom, Gancharnaya nab 3, 109172 Moskva.
T. (095) 9156821. - China - 082945
Sovart, Krymski val 10, 117049 Moskva.
T. (095) 2388536. - Paint / Graph / Sculp - 082946
ST-Art, Krymski val 10, 117049 Moskva.
T. (095) 2381933. - Paint / Graph / Sculp / Eth - 082947
Stanbet, Krymski val 9, 117049 Moskva.
T. (095) 2371088. - Paint / Graph - 082948
Tsentr Russkoi kultury, ul Staraya Basmannaya 15,
103069 Moskva. T. (095) 2654649. - Eth - 082949
Tsentr sovremennogo iskusstva, ul Bolshaya Jakimanka
6, 109180 Moskva. T. (095) 2384422. - Paint / Graph /
Sculp - 082950
TV-Galereya, ul Bolshaya Yakimanka 6, 109180 Moskva.
T. (095) 2384422, 2386729. - Paint / Graph /
Sculp - 082951
Universal Art, ul Neglinnaya 29-14, Moskva.
T. (095) 2024609. - Paint / Graph - 082952
Usadba, Starosadski per 5 stroenie 2, 103062 Moskva.
T. (095) 9287618. - Paint / Graph / Sculp - 082953
Velta, Dmitrovski proezd 16/19, 125442 Moskva.
T. (095) 2112272. - Paint / Graph / Sculp - 082954
Vlada, Rublyovskoe shosse 38 kv 2, Moskva.
T. (095) 3720467, 2116718, Fax 4857309. - Paint /
Graph - 082955
Vostochnaya galereya, ul Shmelyova 10, 103045 Mos-
kva. T. (095) 2081167, 2084204. - Paint /
Graph - 082956
Yakut-Galereya, ul Dolgorukovskaya 5, 103000 Moskva.
T. (095) 9733452. - Paint / Graph - 082957
Yuneya, ul Sadovo-Chernogryazskaya 11-2, 103064
Moskva. T. (095) 2085548. - 082958
Yunion, ul Smolenskaya 6, 119121 Moskva.
T. (095) 2417036, 2471136. - Graph - 082959
Zamoskvoreche, Serpukhovskoi val 24 korp 2, 117449
Moskva. T. (095) 9563009, 9523008, Fax 9542300.
- Paint / Graph - 082960
Zero, Moskva. T. (095) 2144262. - Paint /
Graph - 082961

Sankt-Peterburg

Akvilon, Konnogvardeiski bulv 4, Sankt-Peterburg.
T. (812) 3112909, Fax (812) 3152003. - Paint /
Graph - 082962
Andreevski dom, 8-ja liniya 43, Sankt-Peterburg.
T. (812) 2180614. - Paint / Graph / China / Eth - 082963
Anna, Nevski prosp 57, 191186 Sankt-Peterburg.
T. (812) 3100777. 082964
Ariadna Art Gallery, Konnogvardeiski bulv 11 kv 17,
Sankt-Peterburg. T. (812) 3116997. - Paint /
Jew - 082965
Art-Kollegiya, Ligovski prosp 64, Sankt-Peterburg.
T. (812) 1649564, Fax (812) 2712934. - Paint /
Graph - 082966
Borei Art, Liteiny prosp 58, 191104 Sankt-Peterburg.
T. (812) 2733693. - Paint / Graph / Sculp - 082967
Elena, Morskaya nab 15, Sankt-Peterburg.
T. (812) 3560313. - Paint / Graph - 082968
Gala, Nevski prosp 73/2, 191011 Sankt-Peterburg.
T. (812) 2341756. - Paint / Graph - 082969
Galereya Garmoniya, Kamehhoostrovski prosp 26/28,
Sankt-Peterburg. T. (812) 2350814. - Graph / Paint /
Sculp - 082970
Galereya 10-10, ul Pushkinskaya 10 kv 10, Sankt-Peter-
burg. T. (812) 3152832, Fax (812) 2305074. - Paint /
Graph / Sculp - 082971
Galereya 102, Nevski prosp 102, 191025 Sankt-Peter-
burg. T. (812) 2736842. - Paint / Graph / Sculp - 082972
Garmoniya-Adam, Kamennoostrovski proezd 26, Sankt-
Peterburg. T. (812) 2350814. - Paint / Graph - 082973
Gildiya Masterov, Nevski prosp 82, 191011 Sankt-Peter-
burg. T. (812) 2790979. - China / Sculp / Eth - 082974
Golubaya gostinaya, ul Bolshaya Morskaya 38, 191186
Sankt-Peterburg. T. (812) 3157414. - Paint / Graph /
Sculp - 082975
Grifon, ul Bolshaya Morskaya 33, 191186 Sankt-Peter-
burg. T. (812) 3152057. - Eth - 082976
Hiron, ul 3-ya Sovetskaya 8, Sankt-Peterburg.
T. (812) 1133207. - Paint / Graph / Sculp - 082977
Initsiativa, Nevski prosp 104, 191025 Sankt-Peterburg.
T. (812) 2720906, Fax (812) 2796111. - Paint /
Graph - 082978
Krunk, Solyanoi per 14, Sankt-Peterburg.
T. (812) 2733830, Fax (812) 2727286. - Paint / Graph /
Sculp - 082979
Lavka drevhostei, Morskaya nab 10, Sankt-Peterburg.
T. (812) 3556229. - Paint / Eth - 082980
Lavka khudozhnikov, Nevski prosp 8, 191186 Sankt-Pe-
terburg. T. (812) 3126193. - Paint / Graph /
Sculp - 082981
LenArt, Fontanki nab 34, 191187 Sankt-Peterburg.
T. (812) 2757510, Fax (812) 2755096. - Paint /
Graph - 082982
Navikula Arts, Truda pl 4, Sankt-Peterburg.
T. (812) 2198100, Fax (812) 3121913. - Paint / Graph /
Sculp - 082983
Okraina, Industrialny proezd 15, Sankt-Peterburg.
T. (812) 5240831. - Paint - 082984
Palitra, Nevski prosp 166, 193036 Sankt-Peterburg.
T. (812) 2771216. - Paint - 082985
Petropol, ul Millionnaya 27, 191186 Sankt-Peterburg.
T. (812) 3153414. - Eth - 082986
Peyzazh, 6-aya Liniya 11, Sankt-Peterburg.
T. (812) 2135296, Fax (812) 2134278. - Paint - 082987
Russkoe iskusstvo, ul Saltykova-Shchedrina 53, Sankt-
Peterburg. T. (812) 2756960, 2756968. - China /
Eth - 082988
Sankt-Peterburgski khudozhnik, Nevski prosp 31,
191011 Sankt-Peterburg. T. (812) 3148081, 1105005.
- Paint / Graph - 082989
Shkola Sidlina, Grafiki per 7, Sankt-Peterburg.
T. (812) 1132245, 2495053. - Paint / Graph - 082990
S.P.A.S., ul Sestroretckaya 8, Sankt-Peterburg.
T. (812) 3392349. - Paint - 082991
Vasilevski ostrov, Sredni proezd 31, 199053 Sankt-Pe-
terburg. T. (812) 2132835. - Paint / China /
Eth - 082992
Vityaz, Nevski prosp 20, 191186 Sankt-Peterburg.
T. (812) 3124936. 082993
Vzglyad, Aleksandra Nevskogo pl 1, Sankt-Peterburg.
T. (812) 2771716. - Paint / Graph - 082994
Zerkalo, ul Nekrasova 11, Sankt-Peterburg. - Paint /
Graph - 082995

Saint Pierre and Miquelon

Saint-Pierre

Ravenel, 5bis Rue Maître-George-Lefevre, 97500 Saint-
Pierre. T. (508) 414978, Fax (508) 413115. 082996

Singapore

Singapore

Alpha Gallery, 211 Upper Bukit Timah Rd., Singapore.
T. 467 28 12. - Paint / Sculp / Mod - 082997
Centre of Fine Arts, 311 Plaza Singapura, Singapore.
T. 336 06 62. 082998
Chan Mooi Fah, 5125 Golden Mile Shopping Centre, Sin-
gapore. T. 2581560. 082999
Chan Pui Kee, 86 Neil Rd., Singapore, 0208.
T. 223 48 06. 083000
Chen Wen Hsi Gallery, 167 Singapore Handicraft Centre,
Singapore. T. 2355373. 083001
Collector's Gallery, 304 Orchard Towers, Singapore.
T. 235 08 17. - Paint - 083002
Decor Arts International, 22 Pasir Panjang Rd., Singapo-
re, 0511. T. 271 75 97. 083003
Gallery Asia, 81 Victoria Str., Singapore, 0718.
T. 338 52 92, 336 01 44. 083004
Gallery of Fine Art, 237 Orchard Towers, Singapore.
T. 2353398. 083005
Gim Lin Gallery, 259 Lucky Plaza, Singapore.
T. 7373424. 083006
Han Heng Siang, 413 River Valley Rd., Singapore.
T. 2357283. 083007
Jurong Hand Centre, 15 Blk., 110 Ying Sheng Rd., Sin-
gapore. T. 653329. 083008
Mandarin Galleries, F2/F3/F4 Mandarin Hotel Shopping
Arcade, Singapore. T. 7370125. 083009
Michelangelo, 207 Orchard Towers, Singapore.
T. 7379731. 083010
Modern Art Gallery, 325 Sims Ave, Singapore.
T. 497434. 083011
Paul Art Gallery, 9 Penang Rd. 01-14a, Supreme House,
Singapore, 09 223. T. 31217. 083012
Raphael Art Gallery, 121 Far East Shopping Centre, Sin-
gapore. T. 2353076. 083013
Regal Arts + Crafts, 24 Outram Park, Singapore, 0316.
T. 2207891. 083014
Rick House, 219 Shaw Centre, Singapore.
T. 7376002. 083015
Sentasa Art Centre, Bek.4 Charlton Hill, Sentosa, Singa-
pore. T. 625492. 083016
Shoppers' Choice, G-90 Lucky Plaza, Singapore.
T. 2350889. 083017
Sun Craft, 108 Tanglin Shopping Centre, Singapore.
T. 7371308. 083018
Talent Arts Gallery, 106 Golden Bridge, Singapore.
T. 2226205. 083019
Tang Chou Art Gallery, 333 Blk., 24 Outram Pk., Singa-
pore. T. 2205576. 083020
The Old + New Gallery, Tangling Shopping Centre 02-32
2nd Fl., 19 Tangling Rd., Singapore, 1024.
T. 7376105. 083021
Unique Art and Crafts, 136 Far East Shopping Centre,
Singapore. T. 2354230. 083022
Yip Po Wang Art Gallery, 223 Far East Shopping Centre,
Singapore. T. 2356349. 083023
Yue Chu Tang Art Gallery, Block 22, Outram Park, Nr 02-
287, Singapore 0316. T. 2275123,
Fax 2275389. 083024

Slovakia

Bratislava

Dielo, Trnavska ul. 112, 826 33 Bratislava.
T. (07) 22 58 63, 22 02 13. - Paint / Graph / China / Tex /
Glass / Pho - 083025

Slovenia

Ljubljana

Galerija Equrna, Gregorc'7ic'7eva 3, 1000 Ljubljana.
T. (061) 223932.   *083026*
Galerija S'7kuc, Stari trg 21, 1000 Ljubljana.
T. (061) 225632.   *083027*
Mestna Galerija, Mestni trg 3, 1000 Ljubljana.
T. (061) 212896.   *083028*
Moderna Galerija, Toms'7ic'7eva 14, 1000 Ljubljana.
T. (061) 219759.   *083029*
Narodna Galerija, Prez'7ihova 1, 1000 Ljubljana.
T. (061) 219759.   *083030*

Maribor

Umetnostna Galerija, Strossmayerjeva 6, 2000 Maribor.
T. (062) 211771.   *083031*

Murska Sobota

Galerija MS, Kocljeva 7, 9000 Murska Sobota.
T. (069) 21008.   *083032*

Piran

Obalne Galerije Piran, Tartinijev trg 3, 6330 Piran.
T. (066) 73753.   *083033*

South Africa

Cape Town (Cape Province)

Derry, William, 99 Plein St., Cape Town. T. (021) 2 96 59.
- Paint / Graph / Repr / Fra -   *083034*
Wolpe, 27 Castle St., Cape Town, 8001. T. (021) 23-
5214.   *083035*

Durban (Natal)

Coppin Johnson, 150 West St., Durban, 4001.
T. (031) 377538. - Paint / Graph / Sculp / Fra -   *083036*

East London (Cape Province)

Art Centre, 192 Oxford St., East London.
T. (0431) 27 100. - Paint / Graph -   *083037*

George

Strydom, Matthys, 79 Market Str, George, 6530.
T. (0441) 744027/8.   *083038*

Johannesburg (Tvl.)

Editions Graphiques, 183 Sixth Av., Johannesburg,
2192. T. (011) 440-2477. - Graph / Sculp -   *083039*
Gallery 21, 34 Harrison St., Johannesburg, 2001.
T. (011) 838 66 30. - Paint / Graph / Sculp /
Draw -   *083040*
Guenther, Egon, 4 Krans St., Linksfield,
Johannesburg.   *083041*
Whippmann, S Gallery, 107 B Eloff St., Johannesburg.
T. (011) 23 76 88, 22 38 35.   *083042*

Pretoria (Tvl.)

Ivan Solomon Gallery, 420 Church St., Pretoria, 0002.
T. (012) 28 38 11 ext. 316. - Paint / Graph / Sculp / Jew /
Pho / Draw -   *083043*

Sandton (Transvaal)

Little Gallery, 88 Linden Rd., Sandown, Sandton.
T. 33 83 98. - Paint -   *083044*

Tulbagh

Silberberg, Church St., Tulbagh, 6820. T. (02362) 100.
- Paint / Graph / Sculp -   *083045*

Spain

Alayor (Baleares)

Galeria, Sant Joan 8, 07730 Alayor.   *083046*

Albacete

Alfar, Marqués de Villores 30, 02003 Albacete.   *083047*
Cáncora, Concepción 32, 02001 Albacete.   *083048*
Galeria Verona, Rosario 22, 02001 Albacete.   *083049*
Yarara, Sant Antón 5, 02001 Albacete.   *083050*

Albarracin (Teruel)

Goya, Azagra 10, 44100 Albarracin.   *083051*

Alcoy (Alicante)

Capitol, José Antonio 58, 03800 Alcoy.   *083052*
Emecé, La Alameda 59, 03800 Alcoy.   *083053*
Galeria San Jorge, Alameda 4, 03800 Alcoy.   *083054*

Alcudia (Baleares)

Italia, Italia 9, 03003 Alcudia. T. (971) 12 00 91.
- Paint -   *083055*

Algeciras (Cadiz)

Bellotti, Magda, Fray Tomás del Valle 7, 11202 Algeci-
ras. T. (956) 66 02 04, Fax 63 37 54. - Paint -   *083056*

Alhaurin el Grande (Malaga)

Pizarro, San Sebastián 44, 29120 Alhaurin el
Grande.   *083057*

Alicante (Alicante)

Amics, Pl. Santísima Faz 5, 03002 Alicante.   *083058*
Decoradora, Mayor 18, 03002 Alicante. T. (96) 21 30 27,
21 38 94, 20 14 24. - Paint / China / Repr / Fra - *083059*
Devesa, Tte. Cor. Chapuli s/n, 03001 Alicante.   *083060*
Galeria Italia, Italia 9, 03002 Alicante.
T. (96) 512 00 91.   *083061*
Galeria 11, Belando, 11, 03001 Alicante.
T. (96) 520 87 65.   *083062*
Goya, Sala, P. del Dr. Gadea 11, 03009 Alicante.
T. (96) 22 08 48.   *083063*
Juanes, Juan de, Ramón y Cajal 3, 03001 Alicante.
T. (96) 520 25 54.   *083064*
Litoral, Castaños, 14, 30001 Alicante.
T. (96) 21 30 86.   *083065*
Naya, La, General Sanjurjo 3, 03002 Alicante.   *083066*
Once, Belando 11, 03004 Alicante.   *083067*
Xaloc, Villa Vieja, 03000 Alicante.   *083068*

Almagro (Ciudad Real)

Fucares, San Francisco 2, 13270 Almagro.
T. (926) 86 09 02.   *083069*

Almeria (Almeria)

Argar, General Tamayo 7, 04004 Almeria.   *083070*
Galeria Rebecca, Dr. Gómez Ulla 4, 04001 Almeria.
T. (951) 26 29 22.   *083071*
Haruy, Galeria, Mendez Nuñez, 6, 04001 Almeria.
T. (951) 23 64 80.   *083072*
Meca, Regocijos 87, 04003 Almeria.   *083073*

Almuñécar (Granada)

Lecrin, 18690 Almuñécar.   *083074*

Altea (Alicante)

Art Lanuza, Condes de Altea 14, 03590 Altea.   *083075*
Sol, El, Conde de Altea 56 bis, 03590 Altea.   *083076*

Andoain (Guipuzcoa)

Leizaran, Mayor 53, 20140 Andoain.   *083077*

Aoiz (Navarra)

Bilaketa, Medidía 18, 31430 Aoiz.   *083078*

Aranda de Duero (Burgos)

A ua Crag, Arias de Miranda 3, 09400 Aranda de Duero.
T. (947) 50 77 06.   *083079*

Arcos de la Frontera (Cádiz)

Arx Arcis, Marqués Torresoto 11, 11630 Arcos de la
Frontera.   *083080*

Arenys de Mar (Barcelona)

Blaudemar, Iglesia 15, 08350 Arenys de Mar.
T. (93) 792 39 38.   *083081*

Arrecife (Lanzarote)

Aljibe-El Almacen, José Betancort 33, 35500 Arrecife.
T. (928) 81 24 16/17. - Paint -   *083082*

Aviles (Oviedo)

Amaga, José M. Pedregal 4, 33400 Aviles.   *083083*
Casa Verde, La, La Ferrería 4, 33400 Aviles.   *083084*
Hericar, General Franco 46, 33400 Aviles.   *083085*

Badajoz

Acuarela, La Bomba 16, 06004 Badajoz.   *083086*

Badalona (Barcelona)

Deulofen, Gral. Primo de Rivera 64, 08900
Badalona.   *083087*
Trazos, San Pedro 17, 08911 Badalona.
T. (93) 389 18 47.   *083088*
Voramar, Pje. Jovellar 1, 08911 Badalona.   *083089*

Bañolas (Gerona)

Galeria Banyoles, Mayor 3, 17820 Bañolas.   *083090*

Barcelona

Academia, Muntaner 514, 08022 Barcelona.   *083091*
Actual, Comercio 31, 08003 Barcelona.
T. (93) 319 99 75.   *083092*
Aguirre, Daniel, Via Augusta 76, 08007
Barcelona.   *083093*
Alcolea, Fernando, Pl. Sant Gregori Taumaturg 7, 08021
Barcelona. T. (93) 209 27 79.   *083094*
Amagatotis, De la Liebre 2, 08002 Barcelona.
T. (93) 302 38 38.   *083095*
Amat, Virrei, Avda. Borbón 72, 08016 Barcelona.
T. (93) 340 91 97.   *083096*
Ambit, Consell de Cent 282, 08007 Barcelona.
T. (93) 301 70 40. - Paint -   *083097*
Anar i Tornar, Buen Pastor 5, 08021 Barcelona.
T. (93) 209 82 99.   *083098*
Anglada, Viladomat 271, 08029 Barcelona.
T. (93) 410 09 26.   *083099*
Aribau, Galeria, Aribau, 320, 08006 Barcelona.
T. (93) 200 41 44.   *083100*
Arnau, Provenza, 376, 08037 Barcelona.
T. (93) 257 89 51.   *083101*
Art, Consejode Ciento 284, 08007 Barcelona.
T. (93) 318 23 83.   *083102*
Art Canuda, Canuda 4, 08006 Barcelona.
T. (93) 317 83 30.   *083103*
Art Petritxol, Petritxol 8, 08002 Barcelona.
T. (93) 317 49 52.   *083104*
Art 85, Vía Augusta 120 pral., 08006 Barcelona. *083105*
Arte Moderno, Petritxol 11, 08002 Barcelona. *083106*
Artgrafic, Balmes 54, 08007 Barcelona.
T. (93) 302 45 22.   *083107*
Artraval, Consejo de Ciento 64, 08015 Barcelona.
T. (93) 423 61 37.   *083108*
Artual, Comercio 31, 08003 Barcelona.
T. (93) 319 99 75.   *083109*
Athenea, Luis Antúnez 13-15, 08006 Barcelona.
T. (93) 218 54 37.   *083110*
Augusta, Paseo de Gracia, 98, 08008 Barcelona.
T. (93) 215 32 11. - Paint -   *083111*
Balari, Juan J., Bruc 144, 08004 Barcelona.
T. (93) 207 45 56. - Ant / Paint -   *083112*
Barbie, Juan Sebastián Bach 14, 08021 Barcelona.
T. (93) 201 08 88.   *083113*
Barcinova, P.S. Gervasio 57 bis, 08022 Barcelona.
T. (93) 211 00 05.   *083114*
Bargalló, Sala, Muntaner, 87-89, 08036 Barcelona.
T. (93) 254 14 52.   *083115*
Barna, San Eusebio 57, 08006 Barcelona.
T. (93) 200 57 99.   *083116*
Barna, Rio, Avda. Diagonal 511, 08029
Barcelona.   *083117*
Beardsley, Petritxol 12, 08002 Barcelona.
T. (93) 301 11 97.   *083118*
Bel Air, Córsega 286, 08008 Barcelona.
T. (93) 237 75 88.   *083119*
Berini, Pl. Comercial 3, 08003 Barcelona.
T. (93) 310 54 43.   *083120*
Bernat, Vincent, Córcega 239, 08036 Barcelona.
T. (93) 322 24 71.   *083121*
Bertsch, Aragón 233, 08007 Barcelona.   *083122*
Binomi, Sant Lluís 63, 08024 Barcelona.
T. (93) 210 81 01. - Graph -   *083123*
Bisbe, Rosa, Ganduxer 20, 08021 Barcelona.
T. (93) 201 65 90. - Paint / Sculp / Jew / Mul /
Draw -   *083124*
Bon Pastor, Alfarras 7-9, 08030 Barcelona.   *083125*
Bona-Nova, Obispo Sivilla, 27, 08022 Barcelona.
T. (93) 212 31 60.   *083126*
Calaix de Sastre, Baños Viejos 5, 08003
Barcelona.   *083127*
Carstens, Thomas, C. Josep Anselm Clavé 4, 08002
Barcelona. T. (93) 302 59 89.   *083128*

Caso, de, Calvet 58, 08021 Barcelona.
T. (93) 209 02 06. *083129*
Chevere, Rbla. del Prat 14, 08012 Barcelona.
T. (93) 217 63 59. *083130*
Comas, Paseo de Gracia 114, 08008 Barcelona.
T. (93) 218 33 50. *083131*
Contraluz, Aribau 231, 08021 Barcelona.
T. (93) 209 05 99. *083132*
Costa, Tapineria 4, 08002 Barcelona. *083133*
Costa, Benet, Comercio 29, 08003 Barcelona.
T. (93) 310 16 84. *083134*
Dau Al Set, Consejo de Ciento 333, 08007 Barcelona.
T. (93) 301 12 36, 301 13 86. - Paint / Sculp /
Draw - *083135*
Diagonal Art, Rosellón 254, 08037 Barcelona.
T. (93) 216 08 64, Fax 215 78 37. - Paint / Graph /
Sculp / Mul / Draw - *083136*
Diagonal Bertrand, Avda. Diagonal 379, 08008 Barcelo-
na. T. (93) 238 08 39. *083137*
Diagonalart, Rosellón 254, 08037 Barcelona.
T. (93) 216 08 64. - Paint / Graph / China / Sculp /
Mul - *083138*
Drassanes, Pg. Josep Carner 26, 08004 Barcelona.
T. (93) 301 77 75. *083139*
Dube, Gerona 122, 08009 Barcelona.
T. (93) 258 20 01. *083140*
Duna Sala D'Art, Amargós 6, 08000 Barcelona.
T. (93) 318 01 07. *083141*
Españolas, Rosellón 238, 08008 Barcelona.
T. (93) 215 32 87. *083142*
Estrany, Antoni, P. Mercader 18, 08008 Barcelona.
T. (93) 215 70 51, Fax 487 35 52. *083143*
Flat, Mestre Nicolau 18, 08021 Barcelona.
T. (93) 200 41 34. *083144*
Foga 2, Párroco Ubach 29, 08021 Barcelona.
T. (93) 209 35 78. *083145*
Fort Pascual, Apartado 9319, 08080 Barcelona.
T. (93) 217 00 56. *083146*
Galeria Barcelona, Pça. Doctor Letamendi 34, 08007
Barcelona. T. (93) 323 38 52. *083147*
Galeria Catalònia, Av. Roma 139, 08011
Barcelona. *083148*
Galeria Cezanne, Santa Amelia 51, 08034 Barcelona.
T. (93) 204 98 56. *083149*
Galeria Ciento, Consejo de Ciento 347, 08007 Barcelo-
na. T. (93) 215 63 65. *083150*
Galeria Cinquecento, Tuset 15, 08006 Barcelona.
T. (93) 209 29 15. *083151*
Galeria Eude, Calle Consejo de Ciento 278, 08011 Bar-
celona. T. (93) 317 78 73. - Paint / Graph / Pho / Mul /
Draw - *083152*
Galeria Fort, Riera de Sant Miquel 30, 08006
Barcelona. *083153*
Galeria Génesis, Consell de Cent 325, 08007 Barcelona.
T. (93) 302 33 42. *083154*
Galeria Greca, Ganduxer 45, 08021 Barcelona.
T. (93) 201 04 70. *083155*
Galeria Leonardo da Vinci, Cucurulla 9, 08002
Barcelona. *083156*
Galeria Surrealista Vaillerte, Montcada 19, 08003 Barce-
lona. T. (93) 310 33 11. *083157*
Galeria Theseus, Ganduxer 28, 08021 Barcelona.
T. (93) 200 87 26. *083158*
Galerie Eude, Consejo de Ciento 278, 08007 Barcelona.
T. (93) 317 78 73, Fax 317 78 73. *083159*
Gaudi, Sala, Consejo de Ciento, 337, 08007 Barcelona.
T. (93) 318 41 76. *083160*
Gespa, Más Alto de San Pedro 25, 08000
Barcelona. *083161*
Gothsland, Consejo de Ciento 331, 08007 Barcelona.
T. (93) 302 48 36, 302 48 91. *083162*
Gracia, Mayor de Gracia 116, 08012 Barcelona. *083163*
Graf, Mama, Alta de San Pedro 17, 08003 Barcelona.
T. (93) 318 05 15. *083164*
Gràfica Quatre, Petritxol 4, 08002 Barcelona.
T. (93) 302 56 89. *083165*
Grifé y Escoda, Avda. Diagonal 484, 08036 Barcelona.
T. (93) 228 78 61. - Ant / Paint / Furn / China / Sculp /
Tex / Dec / Lights / Glass - *083166*
Grito, José Anselmo Clavé 4, 08002 Barcelona.
T. (93) 302 59 89. - Paint - *083167*
Gu, Vidriera 15, 08003 Barcelona.
T. (93) 319 79 31. *083168*

Hamm, Camila, Rosellón 197, 08036 Barcelona.
T. (93) 218 22 11. *083169*
Hivernacle, Parque Ciudadela, 08003 Barcelona.
T. (93) 410 22 91. *083170*
Ingres, Córcega 239, 08010 Barcelona.
T. (93) 230 49 12. *083171*
Interamericana, Barquillo 13, 28004 Barcelona.
T. (93) 521 93 70. *083172*
Jaimes, Passeig de Gracia 64, 08007 Barcelona.
T. (93) 215 36 26, 215 18 89. - Paint - *083173*
Joanot, La Granada 19-21, 08006 Barcelona. *083174*
Karalaz, Petritxol 18, 08002 Barcelona.
T. (93) 318 83 95. *083175*
Keting, Balanqueria 9, 08003 Barcelona.
T. (93) 310 67 58. *083176*
Kreisler, Valencia 262, 08007 Barcelona.
T. (93) 215 74 05. *083177*
La Pinacoteca, Paseo de Gracia, 34, 08007 Barcelona.
T. (93) 318 17 43. - Paint - *083178*
Laietana, Pau Claris 127, 08009 Barcelona. *083179*
Lassaletta, Ignacio de, Rambla de Cataluña 47, 08007
Barcelona. T. (93) 301 05 90, 301 06 36.
- Paint - *083180*
Lleonart, Paja 6, 08002 Barcelona. T. (93) 301 76 26.
- Paint - *083181*
Llorens, Rosellón 236-238, 08008 Barcelona.
T. (93) 215 32 87. *083182*
Lluria, de, Roger de Lauria 114, 08037
Barcelona. *083183*
Look, Balmes 155-157, 08006 Barcelona. *083184*
Maeght, Montcada, 25, 08003 Barcelona.
T. (93) 3104245, Fax 3106809. - Paint / Graph /
Sculp - *083185*
Maple Syrup, Verdaguer i Callís 8, 08003 Barcelona.
T. (93) 315 19 17. *083186*
Marabello, Maria del, Gran Via de les Corts Catalanes
662, 08010 Barcelona. T. (93) 412 56 51,
Fax 268 25 75. *083187*
Marcs, Jesús, Balmes 260, 08006 Barcelona.
T. (93) 237 86 82, 217 29 32. *083188*
Matisse, Balmes, 86, 08008 Barcelona.
T. (93) 216 06 14. *083189*
Mercader, Robert, Mallorca 603-609, 08026
Barcelona. *083190*
Metras, René, Consejo Ciento, 331, 08007 Barcelona.
T. (93) 302 05 39. - Paint / Graph - *083191*
Metronom, Fusina 9, 08003 Barcelona.
T. (93) 310 61 62. *083192*
Miret, Petritxol 7, 08002 Barcelona.
T. (93) 317 38 85. *083193*
Montfalcón, Boters 4, 08002 Barcelona.
T. (93) 301 13 25. - Graph / Repr / Fra - *083194*
Mundi Art, Rocafort 142, 08015 Barcelona. *083195*
Muñoz, Mayte, Valencia, 263, 08007 Barcelona.
T. (93) 215 74 40. *083196*
Muntaner, Domenech, S. Antoni M. Claret 167, 08025
Barcelona. *083197*
Nonell, Juan Sebastiàn Bach 16, 08021 Barcelona.
T. (93) 201 69 11. *083198*
Noucents, Paseo de Gracia 55, 08007 Barcelona.
T. (93) 215 64 63. *083199*
Oriol, Provenza 264, 08008 Barcelona.
T. (93) 215 21 13. *083200*
Pedrera, La, Provenza 265, 08008 Barcelona. *083201*
Pergamon, Duque de la Victoria12, 08002 Barcelona.
T. (93) 318 06 35. *083202*
Petritxol Art, Petritxol 8, 08002 Barcelona.
T. (93) 317 49 52. *083203*
Piscolabis, Rbla. Cataluña 49, 08007 Barcelona. *083204*
Poligrafa, Balmes 54, 08007 Barcelona.
T. (93) 301 91 00. - Paint - *083205*
Populart, Montcada 22, 08003 Barcelona.
T. (93) 310 78 49. *083206*
Prats, Joan, Rambla Cataluña, 54, 08007 Barcelona.
T. (93) 216 02 90. - Paint / Graph / Sculp /
Draw - *083207*
Ramon, Artur, Palla 23, 08002 Barcelona.
T. (93) 302 59 70-74. *083208*
Riera, Salvador, Consell de Cent 333, 08007 Barcelona.
T. (93) 488 22 26, 488 32 77, Fax 488 35 70. *083209*
Rovira, Sala, Rambla de Cataluña, 62, 08007 Barcelona.
T. (93) 215 20 92. *083210*
Ruiz, Anna, Provenza 304, 08000 Barcelona. *083211*

Sala Dalmau, Consell de Cent 349, 08007 Barcelona.
T. (93) 215 45 92, Fax 487 85 03. *083212*
Sala Gaspar, Consejo de Ciento 323, 08007 Barcelona.
T. (93) 318 87 40. - Paint / Graph / Repr / Sculp /
Fra - *083213*
Sala Nonell, Juan Sebastian Bach 16, 08021 Barcelona.
T. (93) 201 69 11. - Ant / Paint - *083214*
Sala Parés, Petritxol 5, 08002 Barcelona.
T. (93) 318 70 20. - Paint / Sculp / Fra / Rel - *083215*
Sala Vayreda, Rambla de Cataluña, 116, 08008 Barcelo-
na. T. (93) 218 2960. - Paint - *083216*
Sala Vincon, Paseig de Gracia 96, 08008 Barcelona.
T. (93) 215 6050. *083217*
Salvat, María, Muntaner 239, 08021 Barcelona.
T. (93) 201 25 05, Fax 201 03 96. *083218*
Sambró, Miquel, Rec 65, 08003 Barcelona.
T. (93) 31 96 314. - Paint / Graph / Sculp - *083219*
Sanlley, Vilaseca 2, 08024 Barcelona. *083220*
Sant Jordi, Manila 42, 08034 Barcelona.
T. (93) 204 33 39. *083221*
Santaló, Roglan, Santaló 26, 08021 Barcelona.
T. (93) 209 79 80. *083222*
Sarda i Sarda, Avda. Pau Casals 4, 08021 Barcelona.
T. (93) 414 38 46, Fax 414 05 53. *083223*
Sarda, Ramon, París 207, 08008 Barcelona.
T. (93) 237 18 30. *083224*
Sargadelos, Provenza, 274, 08008 Barcelona.
T. (93) 215 01 79. *083225*
Saro, Helena de, Alicante 4, 08017 Barcelona.
T. (93) 211 86 57, 418 16 77. *083226*
Silverstein, Lino, C. Antigua de San Juan 3, 08003 Bar-
celona. T. (93) 319 24 39. - Paint - *083227*
Subex, Mallorca 253, 08008 Barcelona.
T. (93) 215 81 87. *083228*
Taché, Carlos, Consell de Cent 290, 08007 Barcelona.
T. (93) 318 18 87, Fax 301 24 74. *083229*
Talleres Picasso, Plata 5, 08002 Barcelona.
T. (93) 315 18 54. *083230*
Tartessos, Canuda 35, 08002 Barcelona.
T. (93) 301 81 81. *083231*
Tavern, Tavern 38, 08021 Barcelona.
T. (93) 202 07 97. *083232*
Trade Art, Riera de San Miguel 30, 08000 Barcelona.
T. (93) 217 00 56. *083233*
Transformadors, Ausias Marc 60, 08010 Barcelona.
T. (93) 246 63 56. *083234*
Trece, Rambla de Cataluna, 49, 08007 Barcelona.
T. (93) 352 13 34. - Paint - *083235*
Vayreda, Rbla. Cataluña 116, 08008 Barcelona.
T. (93) 218 29 60. *083236*
Vinçon, Paseo de Gracia 96, 08008 Barcelona.
T. (93) 215 60 50. *083237*
Xami, San Juanistas 8, 08006 Barcelona.
T. (93) 217 11 93. *083238*
Xoc, Paseo Fabra y Puig 325, 08031 Barcelona. *083239*
4 Gats, Monte Sión 3 bis, 08002 Barcelona. *083240*

Benicasim (Castellon)

Galeria Torreón, Playa Torréon 1, 12560 Benicasim.
T. (964) 30 00 88. *083241*

Benidorm (Alicante)

Caballete, El, Ctra. de Pego, 03500 Benidorm. *083242*
Velázquez, Del Rosario 9, 03500 Benidorm. *083243*

Berga (Barcelona)

Astral, C. de los Angeles 6, 08600 Berga. *083244*

Bilbao (Vizcaya)

Aritza, Galeria, Marques del Puerto, 14, 48008 Bilbao.
T. (94) 415 94 10. - Paint / Graph / China / Repr / Sculp /
Mul - *083245*
Bay-Sala, Galeria, Licenciado Poza, 14, 48011 Bilbao.
T. (94) 443 54 47. *083246*
Caledonia, Ercilla 11, 48009 Bilbao. *083247*
Tavira, Alameda Mazarredo 15, 48001 Bilbao.
T. (94) 424 61 50. *083248*
Vanguardia, Alameda de Mazzaredo 19, 48001 Bilbao.
T. (94) 423 76 91. - Paint / Sculp / Pho / Draw - *083249*
Windsor, Juan de Ajuriaguerra 14, 48009 Bilbao.
T. (94) 423 89 89. - Paint - *083250*

Blanes (Gerona)
Celler d'Art, Pedro Roure 12, 17300 Blanes.
T. (972) 33 20 25. 083251
Rusc d'Art, Pl. Catalunya 12, 17300 Blanes. 083252
Silva, Av. Joaquín Ruyra 17, 17300 Blanes. 083253

Burgos
Escorpio, Laín Calvo 15, 09003 Burgos. 083254
Mainel, Vitoria, 27, 09004 Burgos.
T. (947) 201 277. 083255
Rua 2, Pza. José Antonio 4, 09003 Burgos. 083256
Siena, Villa Pilar 2, 09006 Burgos. 083257
Tagra, Vitoria, 13, 09004 Burgos.
T. (947) 209 148. 083258

Cáceres
Brocense, El, Dr. Marañon s/n, 10002 Cáceres. 083259
Morales, Divino, Pl. Concepción 3, 10003
Cáceres. 083260

Cadaques (Gerona)
Amistat, L', Pl. Dr. Tremols 1, 17488 Cadaques. 083261
Cledalike, Pl. Iglesia 1, 17488 Cadaques. 083262
Galeria Cadaques, Hort d'en Sanes 9, 17488 Cadaques.
T. (972) 25 82 44. - Paint / Graph / Sculp / Pho / Mul /
Draw - 083263
Galeria Poal, C. Poal s/n, 17488 Cadaques. 083264
Galeria Port Lligat, Port Lligat s/n, 17488
Cadaques. 083265
Llumera, Sa, Del CII 4, 17488 Cadaques. 083266
Lozano, Carlos, Carrer Les Voltes 9bis, 17488 Cada-
ques. T. (972) 25 82 30. - Paint - 083267
Nota Bene, Poal 16, 17488 Cadaques. T. (972) 25 80 92,
25 86 34. - Paint / Graph / Sculp / Jew / Pho /
Draw - 083268
Ramos, Helena, Puerto Alguer s/n, 17488 Cadaques.
T. (972) 15 92 48. - Paint / Graph / Sculp / Pho - 083269
Taller Galeria Fort, Horta d' en Sanes 11, 17488 Cada-
ques. T. (972) 25 85 49. - Graph - 083270
Uno, Playa Poal 1, 17488 Cadaques. 083271

Cádiz
Casa Rodríguez, Enrique de las Marinas, 1, 11003 Cá-
diz. T. (956) 21 31 04. - Paint / Sculp - 083272
Melkart, Galería, Rosario, 12, 11005 Cádiz. 083273

Calafell (Tarragona)
Dama, Angel Guimerà 16, 43820 Calafell.
T. (977) 69 01 49. 083274

Calella (Barcelona)
Calleart, San Juan 55, 08370 Calella. 083275

Callosa de Ensarriá (Alicante)
Galeria Arrabal, Arrabal 13, 03510 Callosa de Ensarriá.
T. (965) 88 07 68. - Ant / Paint / Graph / Sculp - 083276

Camproden (Gerona)
Delta, Sant Antonio 5, 17 867 Camproden. 083277
Forn, El, Valencia 7, 17867 Camproden. 083278

Canet de Mar (Barcelona)
Cap i Cua, Gram 11, 08360 Canet de Mar. 083279

Cartagena (Murcia)
Maiquez, Isidoro, Jara, 18-2., 30201 Cartagena.
T. (968) 506 117. 083280
Zurbarán, Carmen, 56, 30201 Cartagena.
T. (968) 500 236. 083281

Castellón de la Plana
Bernard, E., Mijares 9-5, 12001 Castellón de la Plana.
T. (964) 25 50 93. 083282
Braulio, Avda. Rey D. Jaime, 23, 12001 Castellón de la
Plana. T. (964) 210 354. 083283
Canem, Antonio Maura 6, 12001 Castellón de la
Plana. 083284
Canem, Poeta Guimera, 2, 12001 Castellón de la Plana.
T. (964) 211 510. 083285
Casino Antiguo, Puerta del Sol 1, 12001 Castellón de la
Plana. 083286
Derenzi, Colón 34, 12001 Castellón de la Plana. 083287
Enarros, Avda. de Lidon, 18, 12001 Castellón de la
Plana. 083288
Pictograma, Gaibiel 8, 12003 Castellón de la
Plana. 083289

Terra, Galeria, Vera, 13, 12001 Castellón de la Plana.
T. (964) 231 924. 083290
Tretze, Enseñanza 13, 12001 Castellón de la
Plana. 083291
Vermell, Pl. de la Paz 9, 12001 Castellón de la
Plana. 083292

Castro del Rio (Cordoba)
Mirazhara, Ctra. Badajoz-Granada km 314, 14840 Castro del Rio. 083293

Ciudadela (Menorca)
Antígona, Nueve de Julio, 07760 Ciudadela. 083294
Galeria Cala Bruch, Cala Bruch, Playa, 07760
Ciudadela. 083295
Galeria Sant Josep, Santa Clara 9, 07750
Ciudadela. 083296
Lletra Menuda, Obispo Villa 36, 07760
Ciudadela. 083297
Retxa, 9 de Julio 15, 07760 Ciudadela. 083298

Coin (Malaga)
Galeria Alameda, Alameda 4, 29100 Coin. 083299

Córdoba
Céspedes, Alfonso XII 4, 14002 Córdoba. 083300
Studio 52, Ronda los Tejares 15, 14008
Córdoba. 083301

Corralejo (Las Palmas)
Las Chimeneas, Avda. Maritima 71, 35660
Corralejo. 083302

Cubellas (Barcelona)
Galeria Adrià, San Antonio 101, 08880
Cubellas. 083303

Cuenca
Machetti, Lope de Vega, 12, 16002 Cuenca.
T. (966) 212 480. 083304
Sala Alta, Pl. de la Merced 4, 16001 Cuenca.
T. (966) 21 36 13. 083305

Denia (Alicante)
Avima, Temple Sant Telmo, 03700 Denia. 083306
Elia, Magallanes, 4, 03700 Denia.
T. (965) 78 03 09. 083307
Galeria San Antonio, Generalísimo 55, 03700
Denia. 083308
Mona, Callejón Morand 8, 03700 Denia.
T. (965) 578 71 70. - Paint / China - 083309
Montgo, Avda. Jose Antonio, 38, 03700 Denia.
T. (965) 78 17 46. 083310

Eibar (Guipuzcoa)
Kezka, Pl. Guipuzcoa, 20600 Eibar.
T. (943) 642 458. 083311

El Ferrol del Caudillo (La Coruna)
Arboreda, Dr. Fleming, Edificio Altamira, 15401 El Ferrol
del Caudillo. 083312

Elche (Alicante)
Galeria Lloc d'Art, 03203 Elche.
T. (965) 545 89 43. 083313
Sorolla, Sagasta 7, 03203 Elche. 083314
Studio, Dr. Caro, 45, 03201 Elche. T. (965) 45 60 91 -
92. 083315

Elda (Alicante)
Sorolla, Sala de Arte, Zorilla, 4, 03600 Elda.
T. (965) 38 31 61. 083316

Esparraguera (Barcelona)
D'Act 77, Hospital 7, 08292 Esparraguera. 083317

Figueres (Girona)
Art-3, Pujada del Castell 41, 17600 Figueres.
T. (972) 50 35 16. 083318
Ediciones Tristan, Pere III 36, 17600 Figueres.
T. (972) 51 02 94, Fax 67 24 68. 083319
Fajol, Josep, Juan Maragall 14, 17800
Figueres. 083320
Rhodas, Galeria, La Sauca, 21, 17600 Figueres.
T. (972) 503 721. 083321

Foz (Lugo)
O Fetizo, Avda. General Franco 38, 27780 Foz. 083322
Solloso, Reinante 4, 27780 Foz. 083323

Fraga (Huesca)
Viladrich, Miguel, San José de Calasanz 12, 22520 Fra-
ga. T. (974) 47 25 33. 083324

Fuenterrabia (Guipuzcoa)
Hernández, Hidalgo, Juan de Laborda 6, 20280
Fuenterrabia. 083325
Mensu, Zuloaga 16, 20280 Fuenterrabia.
T. (943) 62 38 20. - Paint / Sculp / Draw - 083326
Movellan, G., Zuloaga 2, 20280 Fuenterrabia. 083327
Pórtico, Juan de Laborda, 6, 20280 Fuenterrabia.
T. (943) 643 288, 642 837. 083328
Sala Municipal, Maxtin de Arzu, 20280
Fuenterrabia. 083329
Topara, Pl. de las Armas s/n, 20280
Fuenterrabia. 083330

Gandia (Valencia)
Charpa, Nogueres 14, 46700 Gandia.
T. (96) 287 40 15. 083331
Jose Lull, Estudio, San Francisco de Borja, 81, 46700
Gandia. T. (96) 287 11 91. - Graph - 083332

Gijon (Asturias)
Altamira, Arte, Merced, 27, 33201 Gijon.
T. (985) 351 333. 083333
Atalaya, Merced, 45, 33201 Gijon.
T. (985) 342 507. 083334
Bellas Artes, P. Begoña 7, 33201 Gijon. 083335
Cornion, Merced 45, 33201 Gijon.
T. (985) 34 25 07. 083336
Durero, Covadonga 26, 33201 Gijon. 083337
Fragata, La, Paseo Begoña 26, 33207 Gijon. 083338
Galeria van Dyck, Menéndez Valdés 21, 33201
Gijon. 083339
Monticelli, Galeria, Jovellanos 1, 33202 Gijon.
T. (985) 341 151. 083340
Pinole, Nicanor, Jovellanos 23, 33201 Gijon. 083341
Tioda, Instituto 9, 33201 Gijon. 083342
Vicent, Dindura 4, 33201 Gijon. 083343

Girona
Aguilar, Fidel, Rbla. de la Libertat 1, 17004
Girona. 083344
Artística, L', Ctra. Barcelona 31, 17001 Girona.
T. (972) 21 44 50. - Paint / Fra - 083345
Artística, L', Santa Clara 37, 17001 Girona.
T. (972) 20 26 78. - Paint / Fra - 083346
Capuccino, Hortea 11, 17002 Girona.
T. (972) 20 71 23. 083347
Caramany, Palau de, Santo Domingo, 1, 17004 Girona.
T. (972) 213 564. 083348
Cec, Isaac el, Forza 8, 17004 Girona.
T. (972) 20 31 26. 083349
Claustra, El, Nueva 9, 17001 Girona.
T. (972) 20 31 26. 083350
Croquis, S.Juan Bautista de la Salle 6, 17002
Girona. 083351
Espais, Bisbe Lorenzana 31-33, 17002 Girona.
T. (972) 20 23 64. 083352
Expoart, Hortas 22, 17001 Girona.
T. (972) 21 64 55. 083353
Fontana d'Or, Ciudadanos 19, 17004 Girona.
T. (972) 20 98 36. 083354
Galeria Fòrum, Albareda 3-5, 17004 Girona.
T. (972) 21 54 45, 21 09 91. 083355
Girona Art, Maestro Francisco Civil 8, 17005
Girona. 083356
Jané Sebastià, Forza 1, 17004 Girona.
T. (972) 21 68 62. 083357
Nummulit, Norte 7-9, 17004 Girona. 083358
Penyora, La, C. Nueva del Teatro 3, 17004 Girona.
T. (972) 21 89 48. 083359
Sant Jordi, Norte 7, 17001 Girona. 083360

Granada
Cartel, Pedro A. Alarcón 15, 18005 Granada. 083361
Casa de los Tiros, Pavaneras 19, 18009
Granada. 083362
Juste, Julio, Arteaga 3, 18010 Granada.
T. (958) 27 01 95. 083363

Laguada, Puentezuelas 44, 18002 Granada.
T. (958) 26 04 95.   083364
Melia, Angel Ganivet, 7, 18009 Granada.
T. (958) 227 400.   083365
Palacio de la Madraza, Oficios 14, 18001
Granada.   083366
Sajonia, Pl. Isabel Católica 4, 18009 Granada.   083367
Sánchez, Acera de Darro 98, 18005 Granada.   083368
Xaven, Recogidas 41, 18002 Granada.   083369

Granollers (Barcelona)
BM Espai, C. Nueva 19, 08400 Granollers.
T. (93) 870 63 32.   083370
Galeria AB, Viñamata 55, 08400 Granollers.
T. (93) 870 73 52.   083371
Mima, Joan Prim 52, 08400 Granollers.   083372
Quatre, El, Santa Esperanza 4, 08400 Granollers.
T. (93) 870 79 85.   083373

Hospitalet (Barcelona)
AAM, Baron de Malda, 15, 08901 Hospitalet. - Paint /
Graph -   083374

Huelva (Huelva)
Fernández, Camino, San Jose, 3, 21006 Huelva.
T. (955) 216 599.   083375

Huesca
Art, S', Coso Alto 43, 22003 Huesca.   083376
S'Art, Loreto, 4, 22003 Huesca.
T. (974) 220 272.   083377

Ibiza (Ibiza)
Art i Marcs, Avda. España 2, 07800 Ibiza.   083378
Lanzenberg, Fred, Gral. Balanzart, 17, 07800
Ibiza.   083379
Skyros, José Verdera 8, 07800 Ibiza.   083380
Voort, Carl van der, Pl. de Vila, 13, 07800 Ibiza.
T. (971) 30 06 49, 30 60 24.   083381

Igualada (Barcelona)
Ara, D', Del Vidrio 8, 08700 Igualada.   083382

Inca (Baleares)
Cunium, La Estrella 10, 07300 Inca.   083383
Espirafoes, Av. Obispo Llopart 127, 07300 Inca.   083384
Fiol, Calle Mayor, 07300 Inca.   083385

Jaca (Huesca)
Galeria Carola, Obispo 3, 22700 Jaca.   083386

Jaén
Cica, San Clemente 11, 23003 Jaén.   083387
Jabalcruz, P de la Estación 2, 23007 Jaén.   083388

Javea (Alicante)
Galeria Mediterranea, Cristo del Mar 13ps, 03730
Javea.   083389
Galeria Ronda Sur, Ronda Sur 49, 03730 Javea.   083390

Jerez de la Frontera (Cádiz)
Daza, Francisco, Tornería Ed. St. Miguel, 11403 Jerez
de la Frontera.   083391
Isabelita, Clavel, 11, 11402 Jerez de la Frontera.
T. (956) 24 28 52. - Paint -   083392
Plom, San Cristobal, 12, 11403 Jerez de la Frontera.
T. (956) 343 722, 346 711.   083393
Tragaluz, Almenillas 5, 11403 Jerez de la
Frontera.   083394

La Bisbal (Gerona)
DN Galeria, L'Aigueta 79, 17100 La Bisbal.   083395
Taller Vila Clara, 6 de Octubre 19, 17100 La
Bisbal.   083396

La Coruña
Arracada, Zapatería 4, 15001 La Coruña.
T. (981) 20 92 70.   083397
Fratelli, Boquete S. Andrés 51, 15003 La
Coruña.   083398
Lume, Fernando Macías 3, 15004 La Coruña.   083399
Terraza, La, P.A. Méndez Núñez, 15006 La
Coruña.   083400

La Escala (Gerona)
Massanet, Joan, Ave. Maria, s/n., 17130 La
Escala.   083401

La Laguna (Tenerife, Islas Canarias)
Conca, Pl. la Concepción, 38201 La Laguna.   083402

La Unión (Murcia)
Jayam, Pz. J. Costa Ed. Mery, 30360 La Unión.   083403

Las Arenas (Vizcaya)
Vanguardia, Urquijo 16, 48930 Las Arenas.
T. (94) 464 04 84. - Paint -   083404

Las Palmas de Gran Canaria
Attür, Pl. de Santa Ana 2, 35001 Las Palmas de Gran
Canaria. T. (928) 31 29 56. - Paint -   083405
Balos, Colon, 4, 35001 Las Palmas de Gran Canaria.
T. (928) 319 139.   083406
Estoril, Triana 35, 35002 Las Palmas de Gran
Canaria.   083407
Galeria Los Balcones, Los Balcones 17, 35001 Las Pal-
mas de Gran Canaria. T. (928) 3100.   083408
Novarro, Radach, Avda. de Trajano 1, 35000 Las Palmas
de Gran Canaria. T. (928) 76 28 12.   083409
Vegueta, Colón 12, 35001 Las Palmas de Gran Canaria.
T. (928) 70 02 17.   083410
Vegueta, Los Balcones 17, 35001 Las Palmas de Gran
Canaria. T. (928) 31 83 00. - Paint -   083411
Yurfa, Perdomo 26, 35002 Las Palmas de Gran
Canaria.   083412

Las Rozas (Madrid)
Burgo Centro, Ctra. El Escosial km 12, 28230 Las Rozas.
T. (91) 637 66 62.   083413
Yamoka, Kijashi, De la Capilla s/n, 28200 Las Rozas.
T. (91) 890 5749.   083414

León
Arte Inversión, Rep. Argentina 5, 24004 León.
T. (987) 25 19 00.   083415
Arte Lancia, Lancia 21, 24004 León.
T. (987) 21 43 63.   083416
Ausaga, Alferez Provisional, 2, 24001 León.
T. (987) 221 424.   083417
Ausaga Durán, Padre Isla 62, 24008 León.   083418
Bernesca, Roa de la Vega 8, 24002 León.
T. (987) 221 528. - Paint -   083419
Centro Arte, Ramiro II 4, 24004 León.
T. (987) 25 84 12.   083420
Maese, Nicolas, Garcia I, 11, 24003 León.
T. (987) 213 001.   083421
Palat, De la Sal 6, 24003 León.   083422
Provincia, Puerto de la Reina, 1, 24003 León.
T. (987) 216 533.   083423
Santos Estudio Taller, Comp. Santo Domingo 7, 24002
León. T. (987) 23 90 03. - Paint -   083424
Sardon, Juan Madrazo 25, 24002 León.
T. (987) 23 57 34.   083425

Lérida
Altisent, P. de Ronda 9, 25002 Lérida.   083426
Rusinoz, Hambert Torras 16, 25008 Lérida.
T. (973) 24 90 20.   083427
Terra Ferma, Obispo Ruano 15, 25006 Lérida.   083428

Linares (Jaén)
Eduma, Isaac Peral 34, 23700 Linares.   083429

Llanes (Asturias)
Barón de San Carlos, Nemesio Sabrino 1, 33500
Llanes.   083430

Lleida
Petit, Sebastià, Comtes d'Urgell 12, 25003 Lleida.
T. (973) 222738, Fax (973) 222738. - Draw -   083431

Lloret de Mar (Gerona)
Maragall, Joan, Casino de Lloret, 17310 Lloret de
Mar.   083432

Logroño (La Rioja)
Berruet, Calvo Sotelo 27, 26002 Logroño.   083433
Galeria Atenea, Gran Vía 36, 26002 Logroño.   083434
Oscura, Cámara, Portales 43, 26006 Logroño.   083435

Lorca (Murcia)
Thais, Residencia San Mateu, 30800 Lorca.   083436

Lugo (Lugo)
Galeria Nova Rua, C. Nueva 114, 27001 Lugo.
T. (982) 24 25 10.   083437
Prisma, Dr. Castro 22, 27001 Lugo.   083438

Madrid
Aachen Gallery, Jovellanos 3, 28014 Madrid.
T. (91) 450 20 88.   083439
Aboleng 50, Santa Engracia 50, 28004 Madrid.
T. (91) 593 04 81, 593 36 91.   083440
Acuarela, Lombia 5, 28009 Madrid.   083441
Adysa, Larra, 16, 28004 Madrid.
T. (91) 445 9148.   083442
Aele, Puigcerdá 2, 28001 Madrid.
T. (91) 275 66 79.   083443
Afinsa, Lagasca 18, 28001 Madrid. T. (91) 542 60 97,
578 04 44, Fax 575 96 28.   083444
Aizpuru, Juana de, Barquillo 44, 28004 Madrid.
T. (91) 410 55 61, Fax 319 52 86.   083445
Albatros Galeria, Serrano 6, 28001 Madrid.
T. (91) 564 12 98.   083446
Albéniz, De la Paz 11, 28012 Madrid.
T. (91) 522 02 00.   083447
Alcaraz Gonzalez, Francisco, Prim, 17, 28004 Madrid.
T. (91) 222 16 97. - Paint -   083448
Alcolea, Claudio Coello 30, 28001 Madrid.
T. (91) 435 23 47.   083449
Alcon, Infanta 27, 28004 Madrid.
T. (91) 221 35 68.   083450
Aldea, General Diez Porlier 85, 28006 Madrid.   083451
Alfama, Serrano 7, 28001 Madrid.
T. (91) 276 00 88.   083452
Alfelzar, Lagasca 36, 28004 Madrid.
T. (91) 276 71 32.   083453
Alvar, Almirante 11-1, 28004 Madrid.
T. (91) 532 73 32.   083454
Amadis, J. Ortega y Gasset, 71, 28006 Madrid.
T. (91) 401 13 00.   083455
Ambito, Emilio Carrere 3, 28015 Madrid.   083456
Analcai, Viriato 57, 28010 Madrid.   083457
Andrade, Carmen, General Pardiñas 35, 28001 Madrid.
T. (91) 276 83 21.   083458
Andrómeda, Serrano 5, 28001 Madrid.
T. (91) 431 38 33.   083459
Angel Romero, San Pedro 5, 28014 Madrid.
T. (91) 429 32 08. - Paint -   083460
Ansorena, Alcalá 54, 28014 Madrid.
T. (91) 531 63 53.   083461
Arauna, Olivia, Claudio Coello 19, 28001 Madrid.
T. (91) 435 18 08, Fax 276 87 19. - Paint /
Sculp -   083462
Arce's, Fernán González 26, 28009 Madrid.   083463
Arfirenze, Clara del Rey 46, 28002 Madrid.   083464
Art 0, José Abascal 20, 28003 Madrid.   083465
Artaller, Ferraz 33, 28008 Madrid.   083466
Arte en Europa, M. Villamejor 3, 28006 Madrid.
T. (91) 435 42 63.   083467
Arte Puerta de Alcalá, Alcalá 67, 28005 Madrid.
T. (91) 276 52 77.   083468
Arte 16, Diego de Leòn 16, 28006 Madrid.   083469
Arte 43, Atocha 43, 28012 Madrid.   083470
Arteara Galeria, Paseo Pintor Rosales 8, 28008 Madrid.
T. (91) 248 03 53, Fax 248 12 18. - Paint /
Sculp -   083471
Artechamartín, Mantuano 51, 28002 Madrid.
T. (91) 413 55 64.   083472
Artemadrid, Independencia 2, 28013 Madrid.
T. (91) 242 36 32.   083473
Balboa 13, Galeria, Nuñez de Balboa, 13, 28001 Madrid.
T. (91) 275 0418.   083474
Barchet, A., General Oraa 19, 28006 Madrid.   083475
Bardazoso, Villanueva 22, 28001 Madrid.   083476
Barrios, Concha, Claudio Coello 17, 28001 Madrid.
T. (91) 275 14 39.   083477
Bat, Ríos Rosas 12, 28003 Madrid.
T. (91) 442 38 82.   083478
BD Galeria, Villanueva 5, 28001 Madrid.
T. (91) 435 06 27.   083479
Bennassar, Barceló 15-6, 28004 Madrid.
T. (91) 446 50 72.   083480
Biosca, Génova, 11, 28004 Madrid. T. (91) 419 33 93.
- Paint -   083481

Blanco, García J., Fundadores 19, 28028 Madrid. 083482
Botticelli, Bravo 33, 28006 Madrid. 083483
Buades, Gran Via 16, 28013 Madrid. T. (91) 522 25 62, 522 31 12. 083484
Canal de Isabel II, Santa Engracia 125, 28003 Madrid. T. (91) 445 10 00. 083485
Cano, Sala, P. del Prado, 26, 28014 Madrid. T. (91) 420 05 20. 083486
Cardani Art Search, Prof Waksman, 12, 28036 Madrid. T. (91) 4588279, Fax 4588974. - Paint / Sculp - 083487
Cardani, Daniel, Prof Waksman, 12, 28036 Madrid. T. (91) 4588279, Fax 4588974. - Paint / Sculp - 083488
Cassy, Menor, Príncipe de Vergara 17, 28001 Madrid. 083489
Cayon, Augusto Figueroa 4, 28004 Madrid. 083490
Cellini, Barbara de Braganza 8, 28004 Madrid. T. (91) 308 11 56. 083491
Centro Naîf, Béjar 11, 28028 Madrid. T. (91) 255 97 39. 083492
Centro Washington Irving, Marqués de Villamagna 8, 28001 Madrid. 083493
Cid, Núñez de Balboa 119, 28006 Madrid. 083494
Cisne, El, Eduardo Dato 17, 28010 Madrid. T. (91) 410 07 22. 083495
Club Pueblo, Sala Exposiciones, Huertas, 73, 28014 Madrid. 083496
Club 24, Claudio Coello 24, 28001 Madrid. T. (91) 435 97 30. 083497
Collage, Villanueva 22, 28001 Madrid. 083498
Columela, Lagasca 3, 28001 Madrid. T. (91) 577 75 03. 083499
Conde, Infantas 19, 28001 Madrid. T. (91) 522 98 54. 083500
Dacal, Claudio Coello 16, 28001 Madrid. T. (91) 435 71 07. 083501
Diago, Lucas, Argensola 30, 28004 Madrid. 083502
Diart, Bárbara de Braganza 2, 28004 Madrid. T. (91) 419 57 57. - Paint - 083503
Diez, Augusto Figueroa 10, 28004 Madrid. 083504
Duayer, Alcántara 7 y 9, 28006 Madrid. T. (91) 564 01 32. 083505
Durán, Antonia, Castello 19, 28001 Madrid. T. (91) 577 21 83, Fax 230 41 72. 083506
Duran, Fernando, Conde de Aranda 11, 28001 Madrid. T. (91) 575 68 57, Fax 577 51 44. - Paint / Graph / Sculp / Draw - 083507
Duran, Pedro S. A., Serrano, 12 y 30, 28001 Madrid. T. (91) 276 30 00, 226 54 17. 083508
Durán, Ramón, Villanueva, 35, 28001 Madrid. T. (91) 276 4338. 083509
Edition Emilio Alvarez, Arturo Soria 187, 28043 Madrid. T. (91) 0413 6178. 083510
Edurne, Marqués de Villamejor 3, 28006 Madrid. T. (91) 435 42 63. - Paint - 083511
Egam, Villanueva, 29, 28001 Madrid. T. (91) 435 31 61. 083512
El Coleccionista, Claudio Coello, 23, 28001 Madrid. T. (91) 431 03 82. 083513
Escali, M., Paseo Moret 9, 28008 Madrid. T. (91) 275 50 32. 083514
Esfinge, Serrano 88, 28006 Madrid. T. (91) 456 41 75. 083515
Esfinge, Orense 6, 28014 Madrid. 083516
Espalter, Marques de Cubas, 23, 28014 Madrid. T. (91) 429 0784-3. 083517
Espel-Wasart, Miguel, Pl. de la Independencia 8, 28001 Madrid. T. (91) 429 92 26. - Paint - 083518
Establecimientos Maragall, S. A., Po Eduardo Dato, 17, 28010 Madrid. T. (91) 223 80 53. - Paint - 083519
Estampa, Argensola 6, 28004 Madrid. T. (91) 308 30 30, Fax 308 30 31. - Paint / Graph / Sculp / Fra / Cur / Mod / Mul / Draw - 083520
Estiarte, Almagro 44, 28010 Madrid. T. (91) 308 15 69, 308 15 70. 083521
Eureka, Caballero de Gracia 21, 28013 Madrid. T. (91) 222 98 19. 083522
Europalia 85, Ayala 27, 28001 Madrid. 083523
Fauna's, Montalban 11, 28014 Madrid. T. (91) 522 60 02. - Paint - 083524
Faycosa, Gen. Ram. de Madrid 8-10, 28028 Madrid. 083525

Fernández, A. Barbero, Príncipe de Vergara 17, 28001 Madrid. 083526
Fernández, E., Avda. Lemos s/n, 28029 Madrid. 083527
Figuras, Augusto Figueroa 20, 28004 Madrid. 083528
Fila 15, Jesús del Valle 34, 28004 Madrid. 083529
Fomento de las Artes, General Ramírez de Madrid 8, 28020 Madrid. T. (91) 270 12 05. 083530
Fortes Boza, M., Serrano 63, 28006 Madrid. 083531
Frame, General Pardiñas 69, 28006 Madrid. T. (91) 411 02 86. 083532
Fresneda de Miguel, Príncipe de Vergara 36, 28001 Madrid. T. (91) 577 06 56. 083533
Fúcares, Conde de Xiguena 12-1, 28004 Madrid. T. (91) 419 04 931. 083534
Galeria Almirante, C. Almirante 5, 28004 Madrid. T. (91) 532 74 74, Fax 575 96 28. 083535
Galeria Arte del Louvre, Serrano 5, 28001 Madrid. 083536
Galeria Blasco de Garay, Blasco de Garay 38, 28015 Madrid. 083537
Galeria Casarrubuelos, Casarrubuelos 5, 28015 Madrid. 083538
Galeria Emilio Navarro, Gral. Arrando 5, 28010 Madrid. T. (91) 593 15 32. 083539
Galeria Galileo Galilei, Galileo 100, 28015 Madrid. T. (91) 234 74 57. 083540
Galeria Gaudí, García de Paredes 76, 28010 Madrid. T. (91) 410 52 88. 083541
Galeria Infantas, Infantas 19, 28004 Madrid. T. (91) 521 61 02. - Paint / Graph / Furn / Sculp / Fra - 083542
Galeria, La, Prado 13, 28014 Madrid. T. (91) 429 34 37. 083543
Galeria Miguel Angel, Miguel Angel 31, 28010 Madrid. 083544
Galeria Novart, Monte Esquina 46, 28010 Madrid. T. (91) 419 79 68. 083545
Galeria Paul Klee, Claudio Coello 21, 28001 Madrid. 083546
Galeria Tesarte, Potosí 2, 28016 Madrid. T. (91) 458 71 40. 083547
Galeria 57, Columela 3, 28001 Madrid. T. (91) 577 53 97, Fax 577 82 55. 083548
Galerie Theo, Marqués de la Ensenada 2, 28004 Madrid. T. (91) 308 23 59/60, Fax 308 23 61. - Paint - 083549
Galerie Weber, Alexandery Cobo, C. Doc. Fourquet 12, 28012 Madrid. T. (91) 539 45 17. 083550
Galerie 57, Columela 3, 28001 Madrid. T. (91) 577 53 97, Fax 577 82 55. 083551
Gamarra y Garrigues, Villanueva 21, 28001 Madrid. T. (91) 435 98 63. - Paint - 083552
Gavar, Almagro 32, 28004 Madrid. T. (91) 410 45 77. 083553
Gene, Fernando el Católico 62, 28015 Madrid. T. (91) 244 58 44. 083554
Gómez, Fernán, Luna 28, 28004 Madrid. T. (91) 532 10 07. 083555
Grassy, Gran Vía 1, 28001 Madrid. T. (91) 532 10 07. 083556
Greco, El, Príncipe de Vergara 204, 28002 Madrid. T. (91) 563 84 33. 083557
Grifé y Escoda, Alcalá 30-32, 28014 Madrid. T. (91) 232 05 05. 083558
Gris, Juan, Villanueva 22, 28001 Madrid. T. (91) 275 04 27. - Paint - 083559
Heller, Claudio Coello, 13, 28001 Madrid. T. (91) 435 91 02. 083560
Hernando, Pérez, Claudio Coello 18, 28001 Madrid. 083561
Iberia Mart, Orense 34, 28020 Madrid. 083562
Ideas de Arte, Corredora San Pablo, 28004 Madrid. 083563
Ingres, Sala de Arte, Espalter, 13, 28014 Madrid. T. (91) 467 83 67. 083564
Interforma, Paseo Castellana 174, 28046 Madrid. 083565
Iris Antiques, Av. Monforte Lemos 101, 28029 Madrid. T. (91) 730 7098. 083566
Ispahan, Serrano 6, 28001 Madrid. 083567
Jaldo, Menéndez Pelayo 39, 28009 Madrid. 083568
Jorge Juan, Galeria, Jorge Juan, 11, 28001 Madrid. T. (91) 4036821. 083569

Kreisler Dos, Calle de Prim 13, 28004 Madrid. T. (91) 522 0534. - Paint / Graph / Sculp / Mod / Mul / Draw - 083570
Kreisler, Jorge, C/ Prim 13, 28004 Madrid. T. (91) 522 05 34, Fax 522 06 85. - Paint / Graph - 083571
La Kabala, Conde de Aranda, 10, 28001 Madrid. T. (91) 435 87 81. 083572
Lázaro, Carlos III, 3, 28013 Madrid. T. (91) 241 6032. 083573
Levy, López de Hoyos 38, 28006 Madrid. T. (91) 261 00 16. 083574
Linea, Caracas 8, 28010 Madrid. T. (91) 410 46 39. - Paint - 083575
López, Otero, Carlos III 3, 28013 Madrid. 083576
Macarrón, Jovellanos, 2, 28014 Madrid. T. (91) 222 6494/5/6/7. 083577
Machon, Antonio, Conde de Xiquena 8, 28004 Madrid. T. (91) 232 40 93. - Paint - 083578
Magerit, Montesa 26, 28010 Madrid. T. (91) 402 71 94. 083579
Manso, Domíguez J., Barquillo 44, 28004 Madrid. 083580
Manzanares, M. Cuevas, Cavarrubias 7, 28010 Madrid. 083581
Máquina Española, Marqués de Valdavia 3, 28012 Madrid. T. (91) 468 26 12, 468 24 08. 083582
March, Juan, Castello 77, 28006 Madrid. T. (91) 435 42 40. 083583
Marciano, Fabian, Infantas 42, 28004 Madrid. 083584
Martin, Victor, Caracas 7 bis, 28010 Madrid. T. (91) 410 00 00. 083585
Martínez, Marcos, Orfilia 3, 28010 Madrid. T. (91) 261 00 16. 083586
Mateos Muñoz, San Rafael 10, 28023 Madrid. 083587
Melgar, Alfredo, Lope de Vega 47, 28014 Madrid. T. (91) 416 98 44. 083588
Minas, Las, Bailén 16, 28005 Madrid. 083589
Mínima, Pl. de las Salesas 7, 28004 Madrid. 083590
Montaner Subis, Moratín 33, 28014 Madrid. 083591
Monzòn, Velázquez 119, 28006 Madrid. 083592
Mordó, Juana, Villanueva 7, 28001 Madrid. T. (91) 435 84 42, Fax 575 16 26. - Paint / Graph / Sculp - 083593
Moriarty, Almirante 5, 28004 Madrid. T. (91) 479 61 61, Fax 531 97 40. - Paint - 083594
Muedra, V. Venedito, Juan Bravo 4, 28006 Madrid. 083595
Multiarte, Claudio Alcolea 28, 28001 Madrid. 083596
Mundiarte, Julián Romea, 7, 28003 Madrid. T. (91) 254 17 10, 254 67 65. - Sculp / Mul - 083597
Muñoz, Mayte, Manuel Silvela 2, 28010 Madrid. T. (91) 446 69 86. 083598
Muriedas, Gomez Acebo, Villanueva 29, 28001 Madrid. 083599
Mutiple 4-17, General Mola, 17, 28001 Madrid. T. (91) 226 0822, 226 0582. 083600
Navarro, Leandro, Amor de Dios 1, 28014 Madrid. T. (91) 429 89 55. - Paint - 083601
Nieto Viso, Goya 54, 28001 Madrid. 083602
Noes, Martín de los Heros 15, 28008 Madrid. T. (91) 542 79 86. 083603
Novart, Monte Esquina, 28010 Madrid. T. (91) 419 79 68. 083604
Orejón, Marín, Espalter 13, 28014 Madrid. 083605
Orfila, Galeria, Calle Orfila, 3, 28004 Madrid. T. (91) 419 88 64. 083606
Ovidio, Covarrubias 28, 28010 Madrid. T. (91) 445 6795. 083607
Peironcely, Don Ramón de la Cruz 17, 28003 Madrid. T. (91) 435 46 10. 083608
Populart, Huertas 22, 28004 Madrid. 083609
Priet, Masha, Travesía de Belén 2, 28004 Madrid. T. (91) 419 53 71. 083610
Prinz, Brita, Alfonso XII 8, 28014 Madrid. T. (91) 522 18 21. - Graph - 083611
Quirós, Serrano 77, 28006 Madrid. T. (91) 415 62 04. 083612
Quixote, Plaza de Espana, 11, 28008 Madrid. T. (91) 247 55 64. - Paint / Graph / Sculp - 083613
Quorum, Costanilla de los Angeles 13, 28013 Madrid. T. (91) 248 62 34. - Paint - 083614
Ralea, La, Fuentes 6, 28013 Madrid. T. (91) 542 59 78. 083615

Rayuela, Claudio Coello, 19, 28001 Madrid.
T. (91) 275 3146. *083616*
Redor, Villalar 7, 28001 Madrid. T. (91) 275 67 76.
- Paint - *083617*
Reinaldo, A. Canete, Avda. Marqués Corbera 67, 28017
Madrid. *083618*
Rembrandt, Orense 35, 28020 Madrid.
T. (91) 455 5988. *083619*
Ribera Decaro Delia, Alcalá 115, 28009 Madrid. *083620*
Rojo y Negro, Plaza de las Salesas 2, 28004 Madrid.
T. (91) 419 58 33. *083621*
Sala Berriobena, Zorilla, 23, 28014 Madrid.
T. (91) 222 26 86. - Paint / Graph / Sculp - *083622*
Sala de Arte, Cuchilleros 5, 28007 Madrid.
T. (91) 266 54 21. *083623*
Sala Monzon, Velazquez, 119, 28006 Madrid.
T. (91) 261 1732. *083624*
Salas Toison, Arenal, 5, 28013 Madrid.
T. (91) 232 16 16. *083625*
Salquer, General Arrando 12, 28010 Madrid.
T. (91) 445 73 15. *083626*
Sammer Galleries, Pl. Independencia 9, 28013 Madrid.
T. (91) 231 02 57, 231 76 97. *083627*
Sanz Hernández Sampelayo, D. Ramón de la Cruz 17,
28001 Madrid. *083628*
Sargadelos, Zurbano, 46, 28010 Madrid.
T. (91) 410 4830. *083629*
Scarpellini Corrity, García Paredes 76, 28010
Madrid. *083630*
Seiquer, General Arrando 12, 28010 Madrid.
T. (91) 445 73 15. - Paint - *083631*
Sen, Nuñez de Balboa 37, 28001 Madrid.
T. (91) 435 52 02. - Paint / Graph / Sculp - *083632*
Serie-Diseno, S.A., Don Ramon de la Cruz, 27, 28001
Madrid. T. (91) 431 05 93. *083633*
Serrano 19, Galeria, Serrano, 19, 28001 Madrid.
T. (91) 275 29 49. *083634*
Sokoa, Claudio Coello, 25, 28001 Madrid.
T. (91) 275 7239. *083635*
Soledad, Lorenzo, Orfila 5, 28010 Madrid.
T. (91) 308 28 87/88, Fax 308 68 30. *083636*
Soto Mesa, San Pedro 1, 28014 Madrid.
T. (91) 429 40 89. - Paint - *083637*
Soto, Rodríguez, Montalbán 11, 28014 Madrid. *083638*
Stampa, Argensola 6, 28004 Madrid. T. (91) 308 30 31-
0. *083639*
Sumer, Juan de Urbieta 61, 28007 Madrid.
T. (91) 551 10 73, 551 81 70. *083640*
Suner Español, Núñez de Balboa 37, 28001
Madrid. *083641*
Taboada Fernández Cid, Núñez Balboa 13, 28001
Madrid. *083642*
Talleres de Arte Granda, Serrano, 56, 28001 Madrid.
T. (91) 275 90 15. *083643*
Tebas, Ruiz, 3, 28010 Madrid. T. (91) 221 4582. *083644*
Término, Rafael Calvo 15, 28010 Madrid.
T. (91) 419 46 65. *083645*
Theografic, Bárbara de Braganza 8, 28004 Madrid.
T. (91) 308 11 59. *083646*
Toisón, Arenal, 5, 28013 Madrid.
T. (91) 232 1616. *083647*
Torculo, Claudio Coello 17, 28001 Madrid.
T. (91) 275 86 86. - Paint - *083648*
Torres-Begue, Fernan Gonzalez, 31, 28009 Madrid.
T. (91) 274 10 38. *083649*
Trazos, San Bernardo 100, 28015 Madrid.
T. (91) 447 78 91. *083650*
Veiga, Princesa 47, 28008 Madrid. T. (91) 542 07 90.
- Jew - *083651*
Veiga, Goya 57, 28001 Madrid. T. (91) 521 55 06,
577 07 44. - Mul - *083652*
Vijando, F., Ramón de la Cruz 17, 28001
Madrid. *083653*
Williams, Villar 3, 28001 Madrid. *083654*
Xeito, General Pardiñas 108, 28006 Madrid.
T. (91) 262 43 28. *083655*
Yerba, Monte Esquinza 25, 28010 Madrid.
T. (91) 410 33 90. *083656*
Ynguanzo, Antonio Maura 12, 28014 Madrid.
T. (91) 531 54 10. - Paint - *083657*
Zama, Fuencarral 91, 28004 Madrid. *083658*
Zenhio, Marqués de Urquijo 18, 28008 Madrid.
T. (91) 247 11 48. *083659*

Zurbano, Andrade, General Pardiñas 35, 28001
Madrid. *083660*
17 Galeria, Claudio Coello 17, 28001 Madrid. *083661*
24 Galeria, Claudio Coello 24, 28001 Madrid.
T. (91) 435 97 30. *083662*

Mahón (Menorca, Baleares)
Bastió, Bastión 5, 07409 Mahón. *083663*
Cos 4, Cos de Gracia 4, 07702 Mahón. *083664*
Cristanal y Granadina, Isabel II 1, 07701 Mahón. *083665*
Dalt i Baix, San Jorge, 31, 07409 Mahón.
T. (971) 36 48 75, 36 05 30. *083666*
Rufana, Ctra. San Clemente, 07703 Mahón. *083667*
Tobermory, Isabel 41, 07409 Mahón. *083668*

Málaga (Malaga)
Bacardi, Cortijo, Polígono Industrial Santa Teresa, 29006
Málaga. T. (952) 33 02 00. *083669*
Benedito, Nino de Guevara 2, 29008 Málaga. *083670*
Galeria Don Carlos, El Condado, 29018 Málaga. *083671*
Galeria Pedro Pizarro, Alamos 45, 29012 Málaga.
T. (952) 22 02 86. *083672*
Julián, Carmen de, Pl. de la Merced 21, 29012
Málaga. *083673*
Malacke, Paseo del Reding 21, 29016 Málaga. *083674*
Miramar Arte, Avda. Pries 20, 29016 Málaga. *083675*
Taller de Grabado, Beatas 13, 29008 Málaga. *083676*

Malpartida de Cáceres (Cáceres)
Wewerka, Carretera 26, 10910 Malpartida de
Cáceres. *083677*

Manresa (Barcelona)
Chelsea, San Miguel 37, 08240 Manresa. *083678*
Galeria d'Art, Era Firmat 12-14, 08240
Manresa. *083679*
Reves, El, Calle Nueva 8, 08240 Manresa. *083680*
Sánchez, Sergio, Era Firmat 12-14, 08240 Manresa.
T. (93) 874 05 07. *083681*
Xipell, A. Guimera, 38, 08240 Manresa.
T. (93) 873 26 84, 873 22 96. *083682*

Marbella (Málaga)
Cantero, Martin, San Juan de Dios 3, 29600
Marbella. *083683*
Hollander Gallery, Ampara Calvo, Hotel Don Pepe, 29600
Marbella. T. (952) 82 39 78. - Paint / Graph - *083684*
Showroom, Edif. Marino i 1, 29600 Marbella. *083685*
Vilches, Manuela, Ctra. Cádiz km 179, 29600 Marbella.
T. (952) 86 14 47. *083686*

Martorell (Barcelona)
Setze, El, A. Clavé 16, 08760 Martorell. *083687*

Mataro (Barcelona)
Mimesis, Carrero 27-29, 08301 Mataro. *083688*
Minerva, Barcelona 13, 08301 Mataro.
T. (93) 79644. *083689*
Mon Regal, El Torrent 26, 08302 Mataro. *083690*
Tertre, Alamos 6, 08301 Mataro. T. (93) 790 5026,
790 3096. *083691*

Medinaceli (Soria)
Arco Romano, Portillo 1, 42240 Medinaceli.
T. (975) 85. *083692*

Mérida (Badajoz)
Rivolta, Comandante Castejon 21, 06800
Mérida. *083693*

Molina de Segura (Murcia)
Zen, General Aranda 2, 30500 Molina de
Segura. *083694*

Montjuic
Expoart, Abat Escarré 8, 17007 Montjuic. T. 21 64 65.
- Paint - *083695*

Moraira (Alicante)
Galerie, La, Castillo 12, 03724 Moraira. *083696*

Motril (Granada)
Galeria Motril, Comedias 16, 18600 Motril. *083697*

Murcia
Agora, Pza. de Fontes 4, 30001 Murcia. *083698*

Ahora, Jaime I 7, 30008 Murcia.
T. (968) 26 92 86. *083699*
Arteplas, Licenciado Carcales 14, 30001
Murcia. *083700*
Chys, Galeria, Traperia, 11, 30001 Murcia.
T. (968) 213 412. *083701*
Clave, Sagasta 6, 30004 Murcia. *083702*
Meca, Enrique Vilar 9, 30008 Murcia. *083703*
Medina, Pedro, Platería 9, 30004 Murcia. *083704*
Taba, Alfonso x el Sabio 3, 30008 Murcia. *083705*
Vidal Espinosa, Avda. Jose Antonio, 21, 30001 Murcia.
T. (968) 237 831. *083706*
Yerba, Vinadel, 6, 30004 Murcia.
T. (968) 210 015. *083707*
Zero, Pl. de la Cruz, 4, 30003 Murcia.
T. (968) 215 066. *083708*

Navacerrada (Madrid)
Nolde, Pl. de las Españoles, 28491 Navacerrada.
T. (91) 856 7986. *083709*

Oliva (Valencia)
Fonda, La, Purísima 25, 46780 Oliva. *083710*

Olot (Gerona)
Armengol, Francisco, Pl. Parroco Ferrer, 6, 17800 Olot.
T. (972) 260 460. *083711*
Art i Traca, Sastres 111-15, 17800 Olot. *083712*
Clarà, P. Barcelona 1, 17800 Olot. *083713*
Cràter d'Art, Civillers 34, 17800 Olot. *083714*
Sant Lluic, Esplayers, 1, 17800 Olot. T. (972) 260 356,
261 455. *083715*
Vayreda, Solà, Vilanova 2, 17800 Olot. *083716*
Voltes, Les, Santo Tomàs 4, 17800 Olot. *083717*
4 Cantos, Sant Ferriol 23, 17800 Olot. *083718*

Orense
Rey, Mary Chelo, Card. Quiroga 25, 32003
Orense. *083719*
Souto, Pl. Nueva 2, 32003 Orense. *083720*
Zorelle, Parque San Lázaro 1, 32003 Orense. *083721*

Orihuela (Alicante)
Juanes, Juan de, Pl. Condesa Vía Manuel 1, 03300 Orihuela. T. (965) 530 88 24. *083722*

Orotava, La (Teneriffe)
Anepa, La, Las Rosales 13, 38300 Orotava, La. *083723*

Oviedo (Asturias)
Benedet, Arguelles, 37, 33003 Oviedo. T. (985) 213 206,
242 234. *083724*
Diego, Carmen de, Covadonga 30, 33002
Oviedo. *083725*
Gainsborough, Galeria, Ventura Rodriguez, 33004
Oviedo. *083726*
Lancia, Maetmático Pedrayes 6, 33005 Oviedo. *083727*
Murillo, Marques de Pidal, 17, 33004 Oviedo. *083728*
Nogal, Galeria, Asturias, 12, 33004 Oviedo.
T. (985) 242 503, 244 081. *083729*
Norte, Matemático Pedrayes 6, 33005 Oviedo. *083730*
Shalom-Art, Covadonga, 30, 33002 Oviedo.
T. (985) 210 012. *083731*
Vetusta, Avda. Galicia 9, 33005 Oviedo. *083732*

Palafrugell (Gerona)
Emporda, Quatre Cosas, 1, 17200 Palafrugell.
T. (972) 300 872. *083733*
Palafrugell Art, Bailén 1, 17220 Palafrugell. *083734*

Palamós (Gerona)
Gavina, Notarios 16, 17230 Palamós. *083735*
Tramontan, Avda. Generalisimo, 61, 17230 Palamós.
T. (972) 314 485. *083736*

Palma de Mallorca (Baleares)
Altaír, San Jaime 15 a, 07012 Palma de Mallorca.
T. (971) 71 10 04, Fax 71 95 40. - Paint / Graph /
Sculp - *083737*
Art Fama, Santa Catalina de Siena, 4-B, 07002 Palma
de Mallorca. T. (971) 22 13 07. *083738*
Art Viu, Palacio Real 4, 07001 Palma de
Mallorca. *083739*
Auba, L', Barón de Pinopar 4, 07012 Palma de
Mallorca. *083740*

Barrier, Brigitte, Apuntadores 38, 07012 Palma de
Mallorca. 083741
Bearn, Galeria, Concepion 6, 07012 Palma de Mallorca.
T. (971) 72 28 37. - Paint - 083742
Byblos, Avda. Argentina 16, 07013 Palma de
Mallorca. 083743
Ca'n Marquès, Palacio Real 3, 07001 Palma de Mallor-
ca. T. (971) 71 78 28. 083744
Cano, Ferran, Carrer de la Paz 3, 07012 Palma de Mal-
lorca. T. (971) 71 40 67, Fax 72 56 17. 083745
Center Galeries d'Art, Sindicato 34-2, 07012 Palma de
Mallorca. T. (971) 71 76 25. 083746
Dera, San Jaime, 6, 07012 Palma de Mallorca.
T. (971) 21 01 04. 083747
Dibuixos, San Pedro Nolasco 13 a, 07001 Palma de
Mallorca. 083748
Estudio, Guaita Juan, Luis Fábregas 10, 07014 Palma
de Mallorca. 083749
Fluxà, Lluc, Ribera 4, 07012 Palma de Mallorca.
T. (971) 71 90 90. 083750
Galeria Jaime III, Avda. Jaime III 25, 07001 Palma de
Mallorca. 083751
Galeria Maneu Moncadas, Moncadas 2, 07012 Palma
de Mallorca. T. (971) 71 13 24. 083752
Galeria Privat, Apuntadores 38, 07012 Palma de Mallor-
ca. T. (971) 71 29 72. 083753
L'Angel Blau, San Bernardo, 12, 07001 Palma de Mal-
lorca. T. (971) 21 60 96. 083754
Mas, Antonia, Concepció 3 b, 07012 Palma de
Mallorca. 083755
Mir, Joaquin, Concepción, 3, 1., 07012 Palma de Mallor-
ca. T. (971) 22 77 28. 083756
Nadal, Moncadas 9-11, 07012 Palma de
Mallorca. 083757
Palau Solleric, St. Gaietà 10, 07012 Palma de Mallorca.
T. (971) 72 20 92. 083758
Retall, Es, Montesion 5, 07001 Palma de
Mallorca. 083759
Rubines, Padre Molina 18, 07003 Palma de
Mallorca. 083760
Sala Pelaires, Pelaires 23 b, 07001 Palma de Mallorca.
T. (971) 22 36 96. - Paint - 083761
Tres d'Ors, Concepción 3 b, 07012 Palma de Mallorca.
T. (971) 74 77 28. 083762
Universo, Muntaner 13-15, 07003 Palma de
Mallorca. 083763
4 Gats, San Sebastián, 2 y 7, 07001 Palma de Mallorca.
T. (971) 72 64 93. 083764

Pamplona (Navarra)
Art'5, Conde de Rodezno, 5, 31003 Pamplona.
T. (948) 233 007. 083765
Bohemios, Avda. Carlos III, 51, 31004 Pamplona.
T. (948) 249 197. 083766
Cuadro, del, Mayor 54, 31001 Pamplona. 083767
Echauri, Fermín, Navas de Tolosa 13, 31002
Pamplona. 083768
Galeria Monet, Iturrama 35, 31007 Pamplona.
T. (948) 26 64 72. 083769
Nudo, Dormitaleria 9, 31001 Pamplona.
T. (948) 22 78 07. 083770
Nueva Imagen, Gorriti 26, 31003 Pamplona. 083771
Pintzel, Abejeras 6, 31007 Pamplona. 083772

Piedralaves (Avila)
Tani, Rosales 61, 05440 Piedralaves. 083773

Playa de Aro (Gerona)
Galeria d'Art 3 i 5, Carretera Palamós 12, 17250 Playa
de Aro. 083774
3 i 5, Ctra. de Palamós 12, 17250 Playa de Aro. 083775

Pollensa (Baleares)
Bennassar, Pl. Major 6, 07460 Pollensa.
T. (971) 53 35 14. - Paint / Graph / Repr / Sculp / Fra /
Mul - 083776
Blauart, Joan XIII 104, 07470 Pollensa.
T. (971) 53 16 49. 083777
Ca Mestre Paco, Ctra. del Port Crever, 07460
Pollensa. 083778
Galeria d'Art, Del Mar Cant. Pg. Vives, 07460 Pollensa.
T. (971) 53 14 69. 083779
Norai, Ctra. Pollensa, 07640 Pollensa.
T. (971) 53 16 79. 083780

Pruna, Antonio Maura 16, 07460 Pollensa. 083781

Pontevedra
Altamira, Charino, 14, 36002 Pontevedra.
T. (986) 859 910. - Ant / Paint / Furn - 083782
Laberinto, Oliva 23-1, 36001 Pontevedra. 083783
Torrado, Sala, Oliva, 22, 36001 Pontevedra.
T. (986) 852 584. 083784
Van Gogh, Arzobispo Malver, 59, 36002 Pontevedra.
T. (986) 850 250, 850 254. 083785

Pozancos (Guadalajara)
Pau, Carmen, Del Monte s/n, 19265 Pozancos. 083786

Prat Llobregat, El (Barcelona)
Bages, Josep, Casanova 82, 08820 Prat Llobregat,
El. 083787

Puerto de la Cruz (Tenerife)
Colombe, La, Ctra. El Botánico 2, 38400 Puerto de la
Cruz. Fax 38 73 82. - Paint - 083788

Rentería (Guipuzcoa)
Sala Gaspar, Sancho Enea 16, 20100 Rentería. 083789

Reus (Tarragona)
Anquin's, Galeria, San Juan, s/n. Edificio Catalunya,
43004 Reus. T. (977) 312 759, 310 848. 083790
Anquin's II, Campoamor s/n, 43202 Reus. 083791
Rebull, Arrabal Sta. Ana 36, 43201 Reus.
T. (977) 34 26 52. 083792

Sabadell (Barcelona)
Calaixera de l' Avia, San Francisco 15, 08202
Sabadell. 083793
Comellas, Convent 110, 08202 Sabadell. 083794
Dies, Els, C. del Sol 55, 08201 Sabadell. 083795
Gabarró Art, Rbla. de Sabadell 82, 08021 Sabadell.
T. (93) 726 57 85. 083796
Gisbert Art, Del Sol 3, 08201 Sabadell. 083797
Interlecte, Pedregar 10, 08202 Sabadell. 083798
Quasar, Pl. Mayor 38, 08202 Sabadell. 083799
Sala d'Art Negre, Pl. Mayor 38, 08202 Sabadell.
T. (93) 726 56 38. 083800
Tot Art, San Pedro 21, 08201 Sabadell. 083801

Salamanca
Artis, Zamora, 24, 37002 Salamanca.
T. (923) 215 049. 083802
Iris, Avda. Alemania 17, 37007 Salamanca. 083803
Miranda, Toro 27, 37002 Salamanca. 083804
Unamona, Pl. de la Fuente 24, 37002
Salamanca. 083805
Varron, Pasaje Azafranal s/n, 37001 Salamanca.
T. (923) 21 42 85. - Paint - 083806
Winker, Azafranal 27, 37001 Salamanca. 083807

Salt (Gerona)
Sete Cel, Mayor 163, 17190 Salt. 083808

San Cugat del Valles (Barcelona)
Art de Vallès, Avda. Alfonso Sala 25, 08190 San Cugat
del Valles. 083809
Canals, De la Cruz 16, 08190 San Cugat del Valles.
T. (93) 675 49 02. 083810
Febo, Rbla. Ribatallada 6, 08190 San Cugat del Valles.
T. (93) 674 19 55. 083811
Rusiñol, Santiago Rusiñol 52, 08190 San Cugat del Val-
les. T. (93) 675 47 51. 083812

San Feliú de Guixols (Gerona)
Rutlla, La, Rutlla 14, 17220 San Feliú de
Guixols. 083813

San José (Baleares)
Can Berri, Pl. Iglesia S. Agustí, 07830 San José. 083814
Palio, El, Pedro Escanellas 2, 07830 San José. 083815
Sargantana, Pedro Escanellas 2, 07930 San
José. 083816

San Juan de la Peña (Huesca)
Short, San Miguel, 07240 San Juan de la Peña. 083817

San Lorenzo de El Escorial (Madrid)
Floridablanca, Galeria, Floridablanca, 12, 28200 San Lorenzo de El Escorial. T. (91) 896 0021. 083818

Mellado, Juan Toledo 22, 28200 San Lorenzo de El Escorial. T. (91) 896 00 59. 083819
Westermann, Silvia, De la Capilla 6, 28200 San Lorenzo
de El Escorial. T. (91) 891 19 91. 083820

San Pedro Alcántara (Malaga)
Galeria, La, Pl. La Libertad s/n, 29670 San Pedro
Alcántara. 083821

San Pol de Mar (Barcelona)
Espai, L', Calle Nueva 36, 08395 San Pol de
Mar. 083822

San Sebastián (Guipuzcoa)
Alga, Embeltran 4, 20003 San Sebastián. 083823
Altxerri, Avda. Libertad 6, 20004 San Sebastián. 083824
Arteleku, B. Martutene Polig. 28, 20014 San Sebastián.
T. (943) 45 36 62. 083825
Botticelli, Oyarzun 5, 33490 San Sebastián. 083826
Dieciseis, Pl. del Buen Pastor 16, 20005 San Sebastián.
T. (943) 46 69 16. - Paint - 083827
Echeberria -2, Zubieta 20, 20007 San Sebastián.
T. (943) 42 89 23, 46 19 78. 083828
Estudio, Galeria, Avda. Sancho el Sabio, 17, 20010 San
Sebastián. T. (943) 46 05 14. 083829
Musikarte, San Martín 17, 20005 San
Sebastián. 083830
Pez, El, Arrasate 13, 20005 San Sebastián.
T. (943) 42 21 71. 083831
16 Galleria, Pl. del Buen Pastor 16, 20005 San
Sebastián. 083832

Santa Cruz de Tenerife (Islas Canarias)
Arte, Callao de Lima 39, 38002 Santa Cruz de
Tenerife. 083833
Garoe, Villalba Hervas 8-1, 38002 Santa Cruz de
Tenerife. 083834
I Arte, Vicente Ferrer 93, 38002 Santa Cruz de Tenerife.
T. (922) 27 01 73. 083835
Lavaderos, Los, Trasera Hotel Mencey, 38001 Santa
Cruz de Tenerife. 083836
Lázaro, Magda, Numancia 24, 38004 Santa Cruz de Te-
nerife. T. (922) 28 22 44. 083837
Leyendecker, Rbla. General Franco 86, 38004 Santa
Cruz de Tenerife. T. (922) 28 00 53, Fax 24 39 50.
- Paint - 083838
Rodriguez, Felix, Teobaldo Power 20-22, 38002 Santa
Cruz de Tenerife. T. (922) 27 80 67. 083839
Vesan, Santa Rosalía 54, 38002 Santa Cruz de
Tenerife. 083840

Santa Eulalia (Ibiza)
Elefante, El, Santa Gertrudis, 07840 Santa
Eulalia. 083841
Elliot Gallery, The, San Carlos, 07840 Santa
Eulalia. 083842
Owl and Pussicat, The, P. Santa Eulalia del Río, 07840
Santa Eulalia. 083843

Santa Gertrudis (Baleares)
Moli, Es, ctra. San Miguel Km 1300, 07814 Santa
Gertrudis. 083844

Santander (Cantabria)
Dintel, Santa Clara 8, 39001 Santander. 083845
Novelo, Pza. Príncipe 1, 39003 Santander. 083846
Palacete Embarcadero, Zona Marítima, 39071
Santander. 083847
Siboney, Castelar 7, 39004 Santander. T. (942) 31 10 03.
- Paint / Graph / Sculp - 083848
Silio, Fernando, Eduardo Benot 8, 39003
Santander. 083849
Simancas, Cádiz 8, 39002 Santander. 083850
Sur, San Jose, 20, 39003 Santander.
T. (942) 226 813. 083851
Trazos, Dos, Francisco de Quevedo, 15, 39001 Santan-
der. T. (942) 224 750. 083852
Trazos Tres, C. Daoíz y Velarde 1, 39003 Santander.
T. (942) 21 17 87, 21 17 07. 083853
Velazquez, San Jose, 17-1., 39003 Santander.
T. (942) 216 786, 230 327. 083854

Santiago de Compostela (La Coruña)
Citania, La Rosa 22, 15701 Santiago de
Compostela. 083855

Oraguaney, Monteros Ríos 29-1, 15706 Santiago de
Compostela. 083856
Sargadelos, Calle Nueva 16, 15705 Santiago de
Compostela. 083857
Tenda, Gelmirez, 2, 15704 Santiago de Compostela.
T. (981) 58 25 20. 083858
Torques, Algalia de Abaixo, 39, 1., 15704 Santiago de
Compostela. T. (981) 599 385. 083859

Segovia
Enebro, Marqués del Arco 26, 40003 Segovia. 083860
La Casa del Siglo XV, Juan Bravo, 32, 40001 Segovia.
T. (911) 43 45 31. 083861
Ladreda 25, Gobernador Fernandez Jimenez, 6, 40001
Segovia. 083862

Sepúlveda (Segovia)
Rincòn del Arte, Plaza Generalisimo 3, 40300
Sepúlveda. 083863

Sevilla
Aizpuru, Juana de, Zaragoza 26, 41001 Sevilla.
T. (954) 22 85 01. 083864
Alvaro, Gloria 9, 41004 Sevilla. T. (954) 21 37 96.
- Paint / Sculp / Draw - 083865
Azcue Galeria, C/. San Isidoro, 9, 41004 Sevilla.
T. (954) 21 59 61. 083866
Casa Damas, Asunción 43, 41011 Sevilla.
T. (954) 272 421. 083867
Fulton, John, P. de la Alianza, 11, 41004 Sevilla.
T. (954) 214 48 97. 083868
Galeria Promo Arte, Mariano de Cavia 4, 41001 Sevilla.
T. (954) 422 73 41. 083869
Guadalquivis, Castellar 71, 41003 Sevilla. 083870
Haurie, Galeria, Guzman el Bueno, 7, Acc.3, 41001 Se-
villa. T. (954) 22 57 26. 083871
Lienzo & Papel, Conde de Barajas 23, 41002 Sevilla.
T. (954) 438 91 55, 422 36 97. 083872
Melchor, Pl. Santa Cruz, 10 Pl de Alfaro, 2, 41004 Sevil-
la. T. (954) 21 22 28. 083873
Mesa, Magdalena, Cuna, 11, 41004 Sevilla. 083874
Montparnasse, Galeria, Don Remondo, 5, 41004 Sevilla.
T. (954) 21 27 34. 083875
Ortiz, Rafael, Mármoles 12, 41004 Sevilla.
T. (954) 21 48 74. - Paint - 083876
Roldán, A., Sierpes 32, 41004 Sevilla. 083877
Sorolla, Canalejas 6, 41001 Sevilla. T. (954) 22 46 62,
Fax 95-421 94 86. - Paint - 083878

Simancas (Valladolid)
Casa Vieja, La, Galeria Arte, 47130 Simancas. 083879

Sitges (Barcelona)
Agora 3, P. de la Ribera, 08870 Sitges. T. (93) 894 0338.
- Paint / Sculp - 083880
Art Ginesta, Ctra. Barna-Sitges km 23, 08860
Sitges. 083881
Cau de la Carreta, El, Carreta 20, 08870 Sitges. 083882
Escala d'Art, L', Parellada 54, 08870 Sitges. 083883
Foz, San Bartolomé 15, 08870 Sitges. 083884
Mediterráneo, Avda. Sofía 3, 08870 Sitges.
T. (93) 894 51 34. 083885
Ríos, Yolanda, Mayor 22-24, 08870 Sitges.
T. (93) 894 04 75. 083886

Son Servera (Baleares)
Galeria Sa Pleta Freda, Sa Pleta Freda, 07550 Son
Servera. 083887

Soria
Emilia, Pl. de la Iglesia, 42240 Soria. 083888

Talavera de la Reina (Toledo)
Cerdán, Puento Nuevo 4, 45600 Talavera de la
Reina. 083889

Tarragona
Arimany, Rbla. Nueva 20, 43003 Tarragona.
T. (977) 23 78 41. 083890
Contratalla, Santa Ana 16, 43003 Tarragona. 083891
Forum, Santa Ana 18, 43003 Tarragona. 083892
Sala d'Art 32, Pl. Cedazos 42, 43003 Tarragona. 083893
Tinglado 2, Muelle de la Costa, 43003 Tarragona.
T. (977) 22 40 98. 083894

Tarrasa (Barcelona)
Amics de les Arts, Calle Teatro 2, 08221 Tarrasa.
T. (93) 783 51 37, 785 92 31. - Paint / Mod - 083895
Sala Muncunill, Pl. Didó-La Rasa s/n, 08221 Tarrasa.
T. (93) 789 16 15. - Paint / Graph / Sculp / Mod / Pho /
Draw - 083896
Trajecte, Puerte Nueva 27, Portal Nou 17bis, 08221 Tar-
rasa. T. (93) 786 23 10. - Graph - 083897

Terrassa (Barcelona)
Casamada, Soler, Calva Sotelo, 5, 08224
Terrassa. 083898
Galeria Aida, Cardaire 36, 08220 Terrassa.
T. (93) 784 34 05. 083899
Lloveras, San Pedro 13, 08221 Terrassa. 083900
Soler, Casamada, Camí Fondo 5, 08221
Terrassa. 083901
Tobella, Arxiu, Placeta Zaragoza 12, 08227
Terrassa. 083902

Toledo
Selección, Puerta Llana 4, 45000 Toledo. 083903
Tolmo, Santa Isabel, 14, 45002 Toledo.
T. (925) 22 75 07. 083904

Torrelavega (Santander)
Espi, Alonso Astulez, 5, 39300 Torrelavega.
T. (942) 890 516. 083905
Pincel, Alba, Ctra. Bilbao 15, 39300
Torrelavega. 083906
Puntal 2, Juan XIII 10, 39300 Torrelavega. 083907

Torremolinos (Málaga)
Galeria Andalucia, Barrío Andaluz 7, 29620
Torremolinos. 083908
Galeria de Arte 25, La Nogalera 106, 29620
Torremolinos. 083909
Güerri, Gimeno, La Nogalera 107, 29620
Torremolinos. 083910
Hollander Gallery, Amparo Calvo, Hotel Pez Espada,
29620 Torremolinos. T. (952) 38 03 00. - Paint /
Graph - 083911

Tortosa (Tarragona)
Bosch y Curto Disseny, Despuig 14, 43500
Tortosa. 083912
Gamma, Portal de Romeu 1, 43500 Tortosa. 083913

Tossa de Mar (Gerona)
Arxa d'Art, Enrique Granados 6, 17320 Tossa de
Mar. 083914

Valencia
Adelantado, Luis, Paz 33, 46003 Valencia.
T. (96) 351 01 97. 083915
A.G.S. Cerámicas, Zeluán 4, 46009 Valencia. 083916
Alamar, Juan M., Cirilo Amorós 55, 46004 Valencia.
T. (96) 351 39 90. 083917
Artis, Pso. Ruzafa 20, 46007 Valencia. 083918
Arts, Galeria, Mar 29, 46003 Valencia. T. (96) 332 23 72.
- Paint - 083919
Benlliure, Cirilo Amorós 5, 46004 Valencia. 083920
Berruete, Avda. Ponce de Léon s/n, 34005
Valencia. 083921
Centre del Carme, Museo 2, 46003 Valencia.
T. (96) 386 30 00. 083922
Cuatro, Olivo 4, 46003 Valencia.
T. (96) 351 00 63. 083923
Dart, Dávila, Pérez Pujol 10, 46002 Valencia. 083924
Delirio Gráfico, Císcar 10, 46005 Valencia. 083925
Ebanis, Cirilo Amorós 50, 46004 Valencia. 083926
Espais, Blanquerías 23, 46003 Valencia. 083927
Estil, Isabel la Catolica 23, 46004 Valencia.
T. (96) 352 15 12. - Paint / Graph / Sculp / Fra /
Draw - 083928
Fandos y Leonarte, Aparisi y Guijarro 8, 46003 Valencia.
T. (96) 331 87 97. 083929
Farinetti, Paz 17, 46003 Valencia. 083930
Gabernia, Isabel la Catolica 16, 46004 Valencia.
T. (96) 351 88 65. 083931
Galeria, Ribera 10, 46002 Valencia. 083932
Galeria Bachiller, Bachiller 25, 46010 Valencia.
T. (96) 369 70 11. 083933
Galeria Bréton, de los Herreros 4, 46003 Valencia.
T. (96) 394 06 21, Fax 394 14 79. 083934

Galeria Cavallers de Neu, Cavallers 19, 46001
Valencia. 083935
Galeria Colour Art Photo, Calle Lepanto 25, 1. fl., 46008
Valencia. T. (96) 331 53 00, Fax 332 33 42. 083936
Galeria del Palau, Palau 10, 46003 Valencia.
T. (96) 331 72 48. - Paint - 083937
Galeria Nave 10, Nave 10, 46010 Valencia.
T. (96) 352 33 45. 083938
Galeria Punto, Av. Barón de Cárcer 37, 46001 Valencia.
T. (96) 351 07 24, Fax 394 05 92. - Paint / Graph /
Sculp - 083939
Galeria Temple, Gobernador Viejo 26, 46003 Valencia.
T. (96) 332 20 95, Fax 332 20 95. - Paint - 083940
Galeria Temple, Gobernador Viejo 26, 46003 Valencia.
T. (96) 332 20 95, Fax 332 20 95. 083941
Galeria Viciana, Viciana 5, 46003 Valencia.
T. (96) 331 32 60. 083942
Galerias San Vicente, Pizarro 5, 46004 Valencia.
T. (96) 352 77 99. 083943
Garcia, Rita, Bretón de los Herreros 6, 46003 Valencia.
T. (96) 352 75 14. 083944
Goya – 2, Maestro Gozalbo, 6, 46005 Valencia.
T. (96) 373 1735. 083945
Lezama, Salvador 9-20, 46003 Valencia.
T. (96) 332 31 71. 083946
Lioscol, Pizarro 21, 46004 Valencia. 083947
Línea Valencia, En Sala 9, 46002 Valencia.
T. (96) 351 14 00. 083948
Lucas, Pascual, Jofrens 6, 46001 Valencia. 083949
My Name's Lolita Arts, Pl. Correo Viejo 3, 46001 Valen-
cia. T. (96) 331 98 48. 083950
Novel, Mar 29, 46010 Valencia. 083951
Palau, del, Palacio 10, 46005 Valencia. 083952
Parallel 39, Paz 23-1, 46003 Valencia. 083953
Parpallo, Larender 5, 46003 Valencia.
T. (96) 332 30 77. 083954
Pascual Lucas, Jofrens 6, 46001 Valencia.
T. (96) 331 56 55. 083955
Pizarro 8, Galeria, Pizarro 8, 46004 Valencia.
T. (96) 352 57 90. 083956
Postpas, Bolsería 21, 46001 Valencia.
T. (96) 331 28 37. 083957
Railowski, Gravador Esteve 34, 46004 Valencia.
T. (96) 351 72 18. - Pho - 083958
Sala Braulio, Pascual y Genis, 3, 46002 Valencia.
T. (96) 321 3213. 083959
Salvatierra, Puchol, Conde de Alava 32, 46004 Valencia.
T. (96) 352 98 19. 083960
San Vicente, Pizarro 8, 46004 Valencia. 083961
Segrelles del Pilar, Cirilo Amoros, 65, 46004 Valencia.
T. (96) 322 77 66. 083962
Siena, Sorolla 23, 46004 Valencia. 083963
Subastas, Cirilo Amoros, 55, 46004 Valencia.
T. (96) 322 9575. 083964
Thema, Jaime Roig 12, 46010 Valencia.
T. (96) 360 96 38. 083965
Theo, Galeria, Nave, 46003 Valencia.
T. (96) 51 19 33. 083966
Toscana, Cirilo Amoros, 55, 46005 Valencia.
T. (96) 322 5164. 083967
Val, I 30, Galeria, Almirante, 1, 46003 Valencia.
T. (96) 331 8866. 083968
Valencia 2000, Caballero 26, 46001 Valencia. 083969
Valle Orti, Vidal, Avellanos, 22, 46003 Valencia.
T. (96) 322 1758. 083970
Ventana, La, Pintor López 3, 46003 Valencia.
T. (96) 332 13 81. 083971
Visor, Corretgeria 26, 46001 Valencia. T. (96) 332 23 99.
- Pho - 083972
Xiner, Serranos, 8, 46003 Valencia.
T. (96) 331 2699. 083973
Zaguàn, Juristas 5, 46001 Valencia.
T. (96) 332 29 35. 083974
27 Galeria, Cirilo Amorós 27, 46004 Valencia.
T. (96) 352 10 92. 083975
4 Galeria, Olivo 4, 46003 Valencia.
T. (96) 351 00 63. 083976

Valladolid
Berruguete, Alonso, Ruiz Hernández 14, 47002
Valladolid. 083977
Castilla, Pl. de la Universidad, 2, 47002 Valladolid.
T. (983) 227 360. 083978

Creativo de Artes, Pl. de Val 5 bis, 47003 Valladolid.
T. (983) 30 55 66. - Graph / Repr / Draw -   083979
Durango, Carmen, Pza. Tur Palau 13, 47002
Valladolid.   083980
Evelio Gayubo, López Gómez 8, 47002 Valladolid.
T. (983) 39 70 25. - Paint -   083981
Galeria Velazquez, Ramón y Cajal 12, 47011 Valladolid.
T. (983) 25 02 85.   083982
Graf, Mama, Bailarín Vicente Escudero12, 47005
Valladolid.   083983
Grisalla, Detras de San Andres, 2, 47002 Valladolid.
T. (983) 232 245.   083984
IGSA, Plaza del Val 5, 47003 Valladolid.
T. (983) 30 65 29. - Ant / Paint / Jew / Draw -   083985
Imán, Teresa Gil 19, 47002 Valladolid. T. (983) 30 65 29.
- Graph / Repr / Draw -   083986
Lanusse, Regalado 9, 47002 Valladolid.   083987
Olenka, Lopez Gomez, 18, 47002 Valladolid.
T. (983) 229 705.   083988
Rafael, Miguel Iscar 11, 47001 Valladolid.   083989
Siena, López Gómez 8, 47002 Valladolid.   083990

Vendrell, El (Tarragona)
Art Escofet, Jaime Ramón 9, 43700 Vendrell, El. 083991
Ur, Galeria, Paseo Castelar 11, 43700 Vendrell, El.
T. (977) 66 03 37.   083992

Ventalló (Gerona)
Galeria La Bassa, La Bassa s/n, 17473 Ventalló. 083993

Vic (Barcelona)
Ahir, Pl. de la Catedral, 08500 Vic.   083994
Articolor, Pl. del Paraíso 2, 08500 Vic.   083995
Ausart, Sant Miquel del Sants, 8, 08500 Vic.
T. (93) 885 4878.   083996
Carme, El, Rbla. Devalladas 35, 08500 Vic.   083997
Clariana, Dos Soles 4, 08500 Vic.   083998
Culi, Padre Coll 16, 08500 Vic.   083999
Galeria d'Art, Pg. Generalitat 58, 08500 Vic.
T. (93) 855 56 07.   084000
Gusany, Verdaguer 14, 08500 Vic.
T. (93) 885 32 61.   084001
Tralla, La, Riera 7, 08500 Vic.   084002

Vigo (Pontevedra)
Abracadabra, Rep. Argentina 24, 36201 Vigo.   084003
Androx Arte, Via Norte 22, 36204 Vigo.   084004
Cerralbo, M. de, Pl. Compostela 19-20, 36201
Vigo.   084005
Laxeiro, Urzaiz 32, 36201 Vigo.   084006
Lepina, Abel, Pl. Constitución 6, 36201 Vigo.   084007

Vilanova i la Geltrú (Barcelona)
Montparnasse, Rbla. Principal 45, 08800 Vilanova i la
Geltrú.   084008
Prisma, Santa Madrona 37, 08800 Vilanova i la
Geltrú.   084009
Valenti, Ctra. Barna-Vilanova, 08800 Vilanova i la Geltrú.
T. (93) 893 15 58.   084010
Vell i Nou, San Pablo 16, 08800 Vilanova i la
Geltrú.   084011
Vilanova, Sala d'Arte, Escolapis, 2, 08800 Vilanova i la
Geltrú. T. (93) 893 3625.   084012

Vilassar de Mar (Barcelona)
Roma, Sant Josep 13, 08340 Vilassar de Mar.   084013

Villareal (Castellon)
Cuatro, Desamparador 2, 12540 Villareal.   084014
Estudi, San Luis Gonzaga 15, 12540 Villareal.   084015

Villaviciosa (Asturias)
Algalia, Agua 26, 33300 Villaviciosa.   084016

Vitoria (Alava)
Artelarre, San Francisco, 18, 01001 Vitoria.
T. (945) 26 32 27.   084017
Céramo, Correría 38, 01001 Vitoria.
T. (945) 28 78 82.   084018
Eder Arte, San Antonio, 18, 01005 Vitoria.
T. (945) 23 06 97.   084019
Galeria Renoir, Postas 18-1, 01006 Vitoria.   084020
Galeria Rubens, Manuel Iradier 9 a, 01006
Vitoria.   084021
Portalón, El, Correría 151, 01001 Vitoria.   084022

Trayecto, Ramiro de Maeztu 10, 01008 Vitoria.
T. (945) 13 25 42.   084023

Zaragoza
Alfama, San Clemente 18, 50001 Zaragoza.
T. (976) 23 64 76.   084024
Ambigú, Gran Via 11, 50005 Zaragoza.
T. (976) 23 45 81.   084025
Atrium, Residencial Paraíso 4, 50003 Zaragoza.
T. (976) 22 01 83.   084026
Bailo, Victor, Fuenclara, 2, 50008 Zaragoza.
T. (976) 226 464, 222 829.   084027
Bellas Artes, Pl. de los Sitios 6, 50001
Zaragoza.   084028
Borsao, Cuatro de Agosto 23, 50003 Zaragoza.
T. (976) 39 57 19.   084029
Costa 3, Costa, 3, 50000 Zaragoza. T. (976) 23 85 67.
- Paint -   084030
Decor Art, Cuatro de Agosto 2, 50003 Zaragoza.
T. (976) 29917.   084031
Galeria de Arte Costa 3, Costa 3, 50003 Zaragoza.
T. (976) 216 42 54.   084032
Galeria Renoir, San Clemente 6, 50001
Zaragoza.   084033
Goya, Pl. del Pilar 16, 50001 Zaragoza.   084034
Itxaso, Dato 13-15, 50005 Zaragoza.   084035
Libros, Fuenclara 2, 50003 Zaragoza.
T. (976) 22 64 64.   084036
Luzán, P. Independencia 10, 50004 Zaragoza.
T. (976) 23 20 05.   084037
Marcos, Miguel, Ciprés s/n, 50003 Zaragoza.
T. (976) 29 63 66, Fax 29 39 42. - Paint / Sculp /
Draw -   084038
Muriel, Giménez Soler 7, 50009 Zaragoza.   084039
Spectrum, Concepción Arenal 19-13, 50005 Zaragoza.
T. (976) 35 94 73. - Paint -   084040
Tlaloc, Temple 10, 50003 Zaragoza.   084041
Zeus, Pas. San Clemente 6-8, 50004 Zaragoza.   084042

Zarauz (Guipuzcoa)
Euromar, Avda. de Navarra, 20800 Zarauz.
T. (943) 831 186.   084043
Kayua, Avda. Generalisimo, 10, 20800 Zarauz.
T. (943) 830 103.   084044
Salas Municipales de Arte Sanz-Enea, Avda. Navarra-
Villa Sanz-Enea, 20800 Zarauz.   084045
Teilatupe, Avda. Navarra Vila Sanz, 20800
Zarauz.   084046
Zazpi, Kale Nagusia 21, 20800 Zarauz.   084047

Sweden

Gävle
„Svarta Katten", Nedre Bergsgatan 11, 802 22 Gävle.
T. (026) 11 62 60. - Paint -   084048

Göteborg
Art Now Gallery, Götaborgsgatan 32, 412 33 Göteborg.
T. (031) 16 06 86.   084049
Börjesson, D., Västra Hamngatan 15, 411 17 Göteborg.
T. (031) 13 31 77. - Paint / Graph / Sculp -   084050
Galerie 69, Kungsportsavenyn 43, 411 36 Göteborg.
T. (031) 20 12 83. - Paint -   084051
Galleribolage, Götabegsgatan 3, 411 34 Göteborg.
T. (031) 11 23 00. - Paint / Graph / Sculp -   084052
Wallin & Eriksson, Götaplatsen 9, 412 56 Göteborg.
T. (031) 18 31 86. - Paint / Sculp -   084053
Wetterling Gallery, Kungsportsavenyn 8, 41136 Göte-
borg. T. (031) 13 12 13, Fax 13 21 75.   084054

Halmstad
Mjellby Art Centre, The Halmstad Group Foundation,
Halmstadgruppens Museum, 30591 Halmstad.
T. (035) 31619, Fax (035) 32262.   084055

Helsingborg
Eskils Kleine Gallerie, Per Eskils gata 27, 25260
Helsingborg.   084056
Galleri 1 + 1, Drottninggatan 29, 252 21 Helsingborg.
T. (042) 14 73 65. - Paint / Graph / Sculp -   084057
Konstgarden, Bruksgatan 17, 252 23 Helsingborg.
T. (042) 21 46 73. - Paint / Graph / Sculp -   084058

Karlstad
Gripen, Norrastrandgatan 6, 652 24 Karlstad.
T. (054) 18 42 50. - Paint / Graph / Sculp -   084059

Kungsbacka
Tre Fiskar, S. Torggatan 5-7, 434 00 Kungsbacka.
T. (0300) 114 73. - Paint -   084060

Linköping
Ugglan, Box 323, 581 03 Linköping. T. (013) 10 33 22.
- Paint / Graph -   084061

Lund
Anders Tornberg Gallery, Kungsgt. 4, 223 50 Lund.
T. (046) 12 84 80, Fax (046) 143637.   084062
Tornberg, Anders, Kungsgatan 4, 22350 Lund.
T. (046) 12 84 80, Fax 14 36 37. - Paint / Graph / Sculp /
Mul / Draw -   084063

Malmö
Adlers, Bengt, Drottningtorget 1, 211 25 Malmö.
T. (040) 12 08 99, Fax 97 64 74.   084064
Leger, Lilla Torg, 20010 Malmö. T. (040) 72 730.   084065
Qualite, Rodins Väg 4, 217 55 Malmö. - Paint /
Graph -   084066
Rooseum – Center for Contemporary Art, Gasverksgatan
22, Box 6186, 20011 Malmö. T. (040) 12 17 16,
Fax 30 45 61.   084067
Wallner, Fersensväg 4, 200 10 Malmö. T. (040) 23 56 56,
Fax (040) 23 56 57.   084068

Nälden
Konstförmedlingen, Näldenvägen 6, 830 44 Nälden.
- Paint / Graph -   084069

Skurup
Edition Hylteberga, 27400 Skurup. T. 47000,
Fax 42333.   084070

Stockholm
Ahlner, Österlänggatan 22, 111 31 Stockholm.
T. (08) 20 74 06. - Paint / Graph -   084071
Amells Konsthandel, Regeringsg. 52, 111 56 Stockholm.
T. (08) 11 41 91, Fax 11 09 87. - Paint -   084072
Apollo Antik & Konsthandel, Tegnérg. 5, 111 40 Stock-
holm. T. (08) 21 90 98. - Paint -   084073
Arnault, Jean Claude, Sigtunagatan 14, 11322
Stockholm.   084074
Aronowitsch, Sturegatan 24, 114 36 Stockholm.
T. (08) 663 80 89. - Paint / Graph / Sculp -   084075
Art & Form, Sveav. 77, 113 50 Stockholm.
T. (08) 34 60 55. - Paint -   084076
Artema, Stora Nyg. 46, 104 65 Stockholm.
T. (08) 20 95 95, 21 56 30. - Paint -   084077
Axlund, Stortorget 5, 111 29 Stockholm.
T. (08) 11 70 10. - Paint -   084078
Belenins Belart, Birg. Jarlsg. 2, 114 34 Stockholm.
T. (08) 11 60 52, 11 60 54. - Paint -   084079
Bengtsson & Osterman, Svartmansg. 16, 111 57 Stock-
holm. T. (08) 791 82 50. - Paint -   084080
Bergman, Hornsg. 4, 117 20 Stockholm.
T. (08) 44 40 42, 44 40 72. - Paint -   084081
Bild & Ram, St. Nygatan 38, 10090 Stockholm.
T. (08) 20 67 80. - Paint -   084082
Blås & Knåda, Hornsg. 26, 117 20 Stockholm.
T. (08) 41 77 67. - Paint -   084083
Blasius, Arsenalsg. 1, 111 47 Stockholm.
T. (08) 20 01 71. - Paint -   084084
Bohman, Lars, Karlav. 16, 114 31 Stockholm.
T. (08) 20 78 07, 20 78 34, Fax 21 23 66.
- Paint -   084085
Bohman, Sven, Adolf Fredriks Kyrkog. 15, 111 37 Stock-
holm. T. (08) 21 31 81, 21 25 04. - Paint -   084086
Boibrino, Strandv. 7C, 114 56 Stockholm.
T. (08) 667 36 60. - Paint -   084087
Boj, Hornsg. 42, 117 21 Stockholm. T. (08) 40 75 88.
- Paint -   084088
Bonerud, Hans, Folkungag. 100, 116 30 Stockholm.
T. (08) 41 34 00, 41 09 00. - Glass -   084089
Bukowski, Arsenalsgt. 8, 111 47 Stockholm.
T. (08) 10 25 95, Fax 11 46 74. - Ant -   084090
Couleur Konsthandel, Nybrog. 14, 115 23 Stockholm.
T. (08) 660 68 03. - Paint -   084091
Cupido, Svartmang. 27, 111 29 Stockholm.
T. (08) 20 00 38. - Paint -   084092

Decorum, Folkungag. 91, 116 30 Stockholm. T. (08) 20 40 91. - Paint - *084093*
Dehlin, Västerlångg. 42, 111 29 Stockholm. T. (08) 33 34 38, 21 73 72. - Paint - *084094*
Doktor Glas, Kungsträdgården 4, 111 47 Stockholm. T. (08) 11 17 52. - Glass - *084095*
Doret, Kornhamastorg 59, 111 27 Stockholm. T. (08) 21 11 74. - Paint - *084096*
Ekelund/Johan Galleries, Karlavägen 68, 10090 Stockholm. T. (08) 667 82 30, Fax 758 22 70. *084097*
Elva, Strandv. 11, 114 56 Stockholm. T. (08) 663 37 67, 663 37 88. - Sculp - *084098*
Engström, Karlapl. 9A, 114 60 Stockholm. T. (08) 660 29 29, 661 64 88. - Paint - *084099*
Expo Art International, Järnvägsg. 58, 163 60 Stockholm. T. (08) 98 03 30. - Paint - *084100*
Färgo och Form, Stureg. 36A, 114 36 Stockholm. T. (08) 667 19 19. - Paint - *084101*
Frameland, Drottningg. 71D, 111 60 Stockholm. T. (08) 10 73 27, 11 68 38. - Paint - *084102*
Futura Grafikhuset, Karlaplan 14, 10055 Stockholm. T. (08) 660 70 20. - Paint / Graph / Orient - *084103*
Galerie Bleue, Kommendörsg. 12, 114 38 Stockholm. T. (08) 660 83 41. - Paint / Graph / Sculp - *084104*
Galerie Konstruktiv Tendens, Nybrog. 69, 114 40 Stockholm. T. (08) 661 13 65, 661 50 65. - Paint - *084105*
Galerie MB, Kammakarg. 42, 111 60 Stockholm. T. (08) 11 05 05. - Paint - *084106*
Galerie Micro, Hornsg. 40, 117 21 Stockholm. T. (08) 40 03 07. - Paint - *084107*
Galerie Morgan, Köpmang. 12, 10090 Stockholm. T. (08) 20 07 19, 20 90 62. - Paint - *084108*
Galerie Q, Karlav. 17, 114 31 Stockholm. T. (08) 20 47 45, 20 94 44. - Paint - *084109*
Galerie S:t Nikolaus, Svartmang. 27, 111 29 Stockholm. T. (08) 10 09 74. - Paint - *084110*
Galleri Dialog, Triewaldsg. 5, 111 29 Stockholm. T. (08) 20 40 91. - Paint - *084111*
Galleri Fleming, Flemingg. 11, 112 26 Stockholm. T. (08) 50 63 25. - Paint - *084112*
Galleri Glasbruket, Katarinav. 19, 116 45 Stockholm. T. (08) 44 46 11. - Glass - *084113*
Galleri JC, Eriksbergsg. 13, 114 30 Stockholm. T. (08) 10 90 80. - Paint - *084114*
Galleri Klara, Beridarebanan 1, 111 51 Stockholm. T. (08) 11 08 03. - Paint - *084115*
Galleri Konstruktiv Tendens, Nybrog. 69, 114 40 Stockholm. T. (08) 661 13 65. - Paint - *084116*
Galleri LR, Västerlångg. 36 B, 111 29 Stockholm. T. (08) 20 08 08. - Paint - *084117*
Galleri Max, Grev Tureg 25, 114 38 Stockholm. T. (08) 660 74 62. - Paint - *084118*
Galleri Off Side/HG5, Hälsingengatan 5, 113 23 Stockholm. T. (08) 34 01 69, Fax T 34 01 69. - Paint / Graph / Sculp - *084119*
Galleri S, Västerlångg. 11-13, 111 29 Stockholm. T. (08) 20 13 81. - Paint - *084120*
Galleri XIII, Strandv. 13, 114 56 Stockholm. T. (08) 660 72 42, 661 06 66. - Paint - *084121*
Galleri 1 L., L. Nygatan 10, 10090 Stockholm. T. (08) 10 27 18. - Paint - *084122*
Galleri 17, Strandv. 17, 114 56 Stockholm. T. (08) 663 48 28. - Paint - *084123*
Gallerie Lars, Tokel Knutssonsg. 31, 116 51 Stockholm. T. (08) 668 67 23. - Paint - *084124*
Gallerie Selectum, Sibyllegatan 31, 114 42 Stockholm. T. (08) 663 61 69. - Paint - *084125*
Grafikhuset Futura, Karlapl. 14, Växel, 115 22 Stockholm. T. (08) 660 70 20. - Graph - *084126*
Grafioteket, Västerlångg. 14, 111 29 Stockholm. T. (08) 20 50 04. - Graph - *084127*
Grafiska Sällskapet, Roslagsg. 33, 113 54 Stockholm. T. (08) 30 86 24. - Graph - *084128*
Grafiska Sällskapet Galleriet, Rödbodtorget, 111 52 Stockholm. T. (08) 21 68 46. - Paint - *084129*
Greven Galerie, Grevg. 8, 114 46 Stockholm. T. (08) 667 54 10. - Paint - *084130*
Gröna Paletten, Odeng. 52, 113 51 Stockholm. T. (08) 30 85 39. - Paint - *084131*
Gummesons, Strandvägen 17, 114 56 Stockholm. T. (08) 662 15 37, 783 66 15. - Paint / Graph / Sculp - *084132*
Händer, Hornsg. 36, 117 20 Stockholm. T. (08) 40 03 47. - Paint - *084133*
Hässelby Slott, Box 520, 162 15 Stockholm. T. (08) 89 34 12. - Paint - *084134*
Hagman, H. Lars, Hornsg. 42-44, 117 21 Stockholm. T. (08) 42 47 64. - Paint - *084135*
Heinbrandt, Norrlandsg. 21, 113 27 Stockholm. T. (08) 20 75 72, 20 63 57. - Paint - *084136*
Heinbrandt, Störtloppsv. 14, 10090 Stockholm. T. (08) 88 49 83. - Paint - *084137*
Heland & Grafiska Sällskapet, Kungsträdgarden 3, 111 47 Stockholm. T. (08) 10 10 09. - Paint / Graph / Arch - *084138*
Holm & Samuelsson, N. Mälarstr. 26, 10090 Stockholm. T. (08) 52 51 10. - Paint - *084139*
Hultberg, Kungsg. 9-11, Box 7709, 103 95 Stockholm. T. (08) 10 39 57, Fax 20 02 98. - Paint - *084140*
Humlan, Stureg. 30, 114 36 Stockholm. T. (08) 663 91 40. - Paint - *084141*
Katten, Vita, Bondeg. 48, 116 33 Stockholm. T. (08) 40 47 77. - Paint - *084142*
Klostergalleriet, Österlångg. 41, 111 31 Stockholm. T. (08) 21 39 82. - Paint - *084143*
Konst & Ram, S:t Eriksg. 83, 113 32 Stockholm. T. (08) 30 89 46. - Paint - *084144*
Konstföreningarnas Inköpscentral, Hornsg. 46, 117 21 Stockholm. T. (08) 40 80 24. - Paint - *084145*
Konstförmedlarna, Pustegr. 6, 117 20 Stockholm. T. (08) 44 29 56. - Paint - *084146*
Konstfrämjandet, Västerlångg. 1, 111 29 Stockholm. T. (08) 11 79 01. - Paint - *084147*
Konstfrämjandet, Syssloman 16, 102 24 Stockholm. T. (08) 54 19 70. - Paint - *084148*
Konstfrämjandet i Stockholms Län., L. Nygatan 10, 10090 Stockholm. T. (08) 27 70 06. - Paint - *084149*
Konstnärshuset, Smålandsg. 7, 111 46 Stockholm. T. (08) 20 40 72. - Paint - *084150*
Kosta Boda Djurgården, Djurgårdsbrunnsv. 59, 115 25 Stockholm. T. (08) 662 96 10. - Paint - *084151*
Lejonet, Själagårdsg. 21, 111 31 Stockholm. T. (08) 11 00 92. - Paint - *084152*
Lilja, Regenringsg. 42, 111 56 Stockholm. T. (08) 21 87 76. - Paint - *084153*
Liljevalchs, Djurgårdsvägen 60, 115 21 Stockholm. T. (08) 14 46 35. - Paint - *084154*
Lilla Galleriet, St. Gråmunkegr. 3, 111 27 Stockholm. T. (08) 11 57 60. - Paint / Graph / Sculp - *084155*
Lillklara-Grafik, Västerlångg. 57, 111 29 Stockholm. T. (08) 20 07 43. - Graph - *084156*
Lindbom, Nybrog. 61, 114 40 Stockholm. T. (08) 662 84 97. - Paint - *084157*
Linnäus, Stureg. 32, 114 36 Stockholm. T. (08) 663 80 71. - Paint - *084158*
Löwendahl, B. & B., Odengatan 23, 11424 Stockholm. T. (08) 11 90 42. - Paint - *084159*
Lorentzon, Hantverkarg. 38, 112 21 Stockholm. T. (08) 51 22 71, Fax 512271. - Paint / Graph / Sculp / Draw - *084160*
LP Reproduktioner Trading, Västerlångg. 36, 111 29 Stockholm. T. (08) 20 05 61. - Paint - *084161*
Lucidor, Hornsg. 36, 117 20 Stockholm. T. (08) 40 67 86. - Paint - *084162*
Margren, Norrtullsg. 9, 113 29 Stockholm. T. (08) 31 17 44, 31 11 59. - Paint - *084163*
Merkur Konst & Ram, Adolf Fredriks Kyrkog. 15, 111 37 Stockholm. T. (08) 21 98 00. - Paint - *084164*
Metallum Konsthantverksgruppen, Hornsg. 30, 117 20 Stockholm. T. (08) 40 13 23. - Paint - *084165*
Mira Galleri, Upplandsg. 7, 111 23 Stockholm. T. (08) 21 81 08, 21 32 06. - Paint - *084166*
Moser & Klang, Östermalmstorg 4, 114 42 Stockholm. T. (08) 661 31 10, 661 24 10. - Paint - *084167*
Munken, Storkyrkobr. 11, 111 28 Stockholm. T. (08) 10 55 35. - Paint - *084168*
New Art, Skepparg. 78, 114 59 Stockholm. T. (08) 660 50 90. - Paint - *084169*
New Art Workshop, Bältg. 1, 114 59 Stockholm. T. (08) 660 50 90. - Paint - *084170*
Nilsson & Knall, Hornsg. 26A, 117 20 Stockholm. T. (08) 41 25 80. - Paint - *084171*
Nordenhake, Fredsg. 12, 111 52 Stockholm. T. (08) 21 18 92, 21 03 06, Fax 10 96 41. - Paint - *084172*
Nutida, Strandv. 21, 114 56 Stockholm. T. (08) 660 60 06. - Paint - *084173*
Nybro Galleriet, Nybrogatan 6, 10090 Stockholm. T. (08) 660 42 00. - Paint - *084174*
Nybrogalleriet, Nybrog. 6, 114 34 Stockholm. T. (08) 660 42 00. - Paint - *084175*
Östermalm, Karlavägen 72a, 114 59 Stockholm. T. (08) 667 45 81, 663 77 35. - Paint / Graph - *084176*
Olofsson, Sven, Berguddsv. 7, 162 40 Stockholm. T. (08) 38 25 24. - Paint - *084177*
Olsson, Gunnar, Sturegatan 28, 114 44 Stockholm. T. (08) 662 28 68, Fax 661 18 85. - Paint - *084178*
Origo, Hornsg. 34, 117 20 Stockholm. T. (08) 43 02 59. - Paint - *084179*
Ossian, Dalag. 48, 113 24 Stockholm. T. (08) 32 10 05. - Paint - *084180*
PA Konst & Rau, Östjötag. 22, 116 25 Stockholm. T. (08) 41 34 21. - Paint - *084181*
Pictorama, Regeringsg. 83, 111 39 Stockholm. T. (08) 11 77 58. - Paint - *084182*
Primitiv & Modern Konst, Riddarg. 3, 114 35 Stockholm. T. (08) 11 05 95. - Paint - *084183*
Puckeln, Hornsg. 26, 117 20 Stockholm. T. (08) 41 23 23. - Paint - *084184*
Q Cards Posters, Karkav. 17, 114 31 Stockholm. T. (08) 20 25 02. - Paint - *084185*
Ramis, Malmgårdsv. 51, 116 38 Stockholm. T. (08) 43 50 90. - Paint - *084186*
RB Konsthandel, Karlav. 58, 114 49 Stockholm. T. (08) 660 29 00, 663 60 03. - Paint - *084187*
Resnard, Box 14237, 104 40 Stockholm. T. (08) 716 03 02. - Paint - *084188*
Ressle, Grevgatan 61, 114 59 Stockholm. T. (08) 660 41 40, Fax 665 32 20. - Paint - *084189*
Ringens Konst & Ramar, Ringv. 108, 116 61 Stockholm. T. (08) 43 15 14. - Paint - *084190*
Rocade, Skepparg. 29, 114 52 Stockholm. T. (08) 660 99 70. - Paint - *084191*
S:t Eriks Ramateljé, S:t Eriksg. 79, 113 32 Stockholm. T. (08) 31 01 89. - Paint - *084192*
Saleks, Storkyrkobr. 8, 111 28 Stockholm. T. (08) 21 03 63. - Paint - *084193*
Scandinavian Art Trade System, Fyrskeppsv. 60, 121 54 Stockholm. T. (08) 48 16 55. - Paint - *084194*
Sergel Galleriet, Sergelstorget 12, 111 57 Stockholm. T. (08) 796 00 35. - Paint - *084195*
Sjöström, Hans Göran, Artillerig. 57, 102 43 Stockholm. T. (08) 661 30 36. - Paint - *084196*
Skärgårdsgallerieti, Österlångg.31, 111 31 Stockholm. T. (08) 21 25 65. - Paint - *084197*
Skaj, Lästmakarg. 6, 111 44 Stockholm. T. (08) 10 76 80. - Paint - *084198*
Skoglund, Erik, Jakobsbgsg. 8, 111 44 Stockholm. T. (08) 20 40 48. - Paint - *084199*
Skulptörförbundet, Pustegr. 6, 117 20 Stockholm. T. (08) 43 52 80. - Paint - *084200*
Stortorgets Konsthandel, Stortorget 14, 111 29 Stockholm. T. (08) 20 95 33, 20 75 39. - Paint - *084201*
Strandgalleriet, Strandv. 5B, 114 51 Stockholm. T. (08) 663 83 25. - Paint - *084202*
Suomi Galleri, Birger Jarlsg. 35, 111 45 Stockholm. T. (08) 11 16 55. - Paint - *084203*
Sveagalleriet, Sveavägen 41, Box 1305, 111 83 Stockholm. T. (08) 22 75 88, 21 62 00. - Paint / Graph / Sculp - *084204*
Svensson, Kurt, Tomtebog. 17, 113 39 Stockholm. T. (08) 31 86 84, 31 14 67. - Paint - *084205*
Tersäus, Pustegr. 6, 117 20 Stockholm. T. (08) 42 04 82. - Paint - *084206*
Textilgruppen-Textilkonst, Hornsg. 6, 117 20 Stockholm. T. (08) 43 30 72. - Paint - *084207*
Thorden, Edward, Götabergsgatan 18, 411 34 Stockholm. T. (08) 20 06 20. - Paint / Graph / Sculp - *084208*
Tornvall, Karlavägen 68, 11459 Stockholm. T. (08) 667 32 30, Fax 662 05 14. *084209*
Tyresö, Västangr. 10, 10090 Stockholm. T. (08) 742 72 90. - Paint - *084210*
Ungas Salong, Hornsg. 8, 117 20 Stockholm. T. (08) 44 20 37. - Paint - *084211*
Värderingar, Arbin Lars, Grev Magnig. 13, 114 55 Stockholm. T. (08) 660 83 62. - Paint - *084212*
Victors Konsthandel, Jakobsbergsg. 11, 111 44 Stockholm. T. (08) 21 34 80. - Paint - *084213*

Wetterling, Kungsträdgården 3, 111 47 Stockholm.
T. (08) 810 10 09, Fax 87 91 74 82. - Paint -   084214

Sundsvall
Dahlin, Bengt, Mosjön, 855 90 Sundsvall. - Paint /
Repr -   084215

Uppsala
Wallin, Johan, Svartbäcksgatan 30, 752 47 Uppsala.
T. (018) 13 44 30. - Paint / Graph / Sculp -   084216

Switzerland

Aarau (Aargau)
Ad Opticus, Laurenzentorgasse 7, 5000 Aarau.   084217
Auf dem Rain Galerie, Rain 34, 5000 Aarau.
T. (064) 24 30 26.   084218
Edler, Rain 15, 5000 Aarau. T. (064) 24 20 22.   084219
Galerie Bianchi & Haberstich, Kronengasse 2, 5000 Aa-
rau. T. (064) 22 39 59.   084220
Galerie 6, Milchgasse 35, 5000 Aarau. T. (064) 22 07 45.
- Paint / Graph -   084221
Kunstraum Aarau im Kiff, Tellistr 118, 5001
Aarau.   084222
Werkstatt-Galerie, Vordere Vorstadt 21, 5000 Aarau.
T. (064) 24 75 16.   084223
Zum goldige Nüüteli, Golattenmattgasse 3, 5000 Aarau.
T. (064) 24 40 74.   084224
Zum Stadtturm, Zwischen den Toren 18, 5000 Aarau.
T. (064) 24 69 53.   084225
Zur Zinne, Rathausgasse 9, 5000 Aarau.
T. (064) 24 76 26. - Paint -   084226

Aarburg (Aargau)
Bären Galerie, Städtchen 16, 4663 Aarburg.
T. (062) 41 68 40.   084227

Aarwangen (Bern)
Galerie 89, Gewerbezentrum Hard, Bützbergstr 17, 4912
Aarwangen. T. (062) 9225673, Fax 9231219.   084228

Adetswil (Zürich)
Schmid, Yvette, Egglen, 8345 Adetswil. T. (01) 9392706,
Fax 9392706.   084229

Adligenswil (Luzern)
Sankt Martinskeller, Buggenacher Str. 20, 6043 Adli-
genswil. T. (041) 370 40 72.   084230

Adliswil (Zürich)
Dür, Irma, Poststr 7, 8134 Adliswil. T. (01) 710 55 00,
Fax 7105500.   084231
Werkladen-Galerie Krone 16, Kronenstr. 16, 8134 Adlis-
wil. T. (01) 710 02 01.   084232

Aesch (Basel-Land)
Fuchs, Delly, Römerstr 52, 4147 Aesch.
T. (061) 7515844. - Paint -   084233
Galerie Claire, Im Häslirain 83, 4147 Aesch.
T. (061) 7515595.   084234

Aeugst am Albis (Zürich)
Galerie Aeugstherthal, 8914 Aeugst am Albis.
T. (01) 361 29 89.   084235

Affoltern am Albis (Zürich)
Seewadel Galerie, Seewadelstr. 27, 8910 Affoltern am
Albis. T. (01) 761 69 76.   084236

Agarn (Valais)
Kunstgalerie Zur Kastanienallee, 3951 Agarn.
T. (027) 4733236.   084237

Aigle (Vaud)
Au Louvre, 16 Rue de la Gare, 1860 Aigle.
T. (024) 4662456.   084238
L'Echoppe du Cloître, 2 Rue Farel, 1800 Aigle.
T. (024) 4661128.   084239
Galerie Farel, 1 Pl. du Marché, 1860 Aigle.
T. (024) 4665307.   084240

Allschwil (Basel-Land)
Novum-Galerie, Binningerstr. 94, 4123 Allschwil.
T. (061) 481 63 97.   084241

Altdorf (Uri)
ARTAxerces, Kornmattstr., 6460 Altdorf.
T. (041) 8710198.   084242
Bistro, Gitschenstr. 4, 6460 Altdorf. T. (041) 8709516.
- Paint -   084243
Galerie Holzwurm, Schmiedgasse, 6460 Altdorf.
T. (041) 870 62 38.   084244

Altendorf (Schwyz)
Galerie zur Fazion, Fazion, 8852 Altendorf.
T. (055) 4421803.   084245

Altenrhein (Sankt Gallen)
Bodensee-Galerie, Gozenrüti 4, 9423 Altenrhein.
T. (071) 8553868.   084246

Altstätten (Sankt Gallen)
Altstadtgalerie, Obergasse 17, 9450 Altstätten.
T. (071) 7551708.   084247
Rhy, Churerstr. 20, 9450 Altstätten.
T. (071) 7552233.   084248

Altwis (Luzern)
Galerie Altwis, Unterdorf 63, 6286 Altwis.
T. (041) 917 32 28. - Paint / Graph / Repr / Sculp /
Fra -   084249

Andwil (Sankt Gallen)
Engeler, Glasmalerei-Glasgestaltung, Postpl 9, 9204 An-
dwil. T. (071) 3851226, Fax 3851252.   084250

Anières (Genève)
Art & Sculpture, 297a Rte. d'Hermance, 1247 Anières.
T. (022) 751 11 08.   084251

Appenzell (Appenzell Innerrhoden)
Appezöllertröckli, Gaiser Str. 3, 9050 Appenzell.
T. (071) 7873202, Fax 7875471. - Paint -   084252
Galerie Bleiche, Bleichestr. 8, 9050 Appenzell.
T. (071) 7871183.   084253
Galerie Pappelhof, Gaiser Str. 4 a, 9050 Appenzell.
T. (071) 7871006.   084254
Galerie Ziel, Zielstr. 3, 9050 Appenzell.
T. (071) 7874455.   084255
Mettler, Dölf, Lehn, 9050 Appenzell. T. (071) 7872353,
7873785. - Paint -   084256

Arbon (Thurgau)
Forma, Kapellgasse 5, 9320 Arbon. T. (071) 4463040.
- Paint -   084257
Galerie zum Schweizerhaus, Neugasse 6, 9320 Arbon.
T. (071) 4464020, Fax 4466091.   084258
König, Josef, Bahngasse 1, 9320 Arbon.
T. (071) 4465051.   084259

Arisdorf (Basel-Land)
Galerie Arisdorf, Hauptstr. 89, 4422 Arisdorf.
T. (061) 83 23 33. - Ant / Paint / Graph / Furn / Sculp /
Fra / Mul / Draw -   084260

Arlesheim (Basel-Land)
Galerie im Dach, Hollenweg 46, 4144 Arlesheim.
T. (061) 701 78 35.   084261
Galerie & Blueme zu de 17 Sunnestrahle, Eremitagestr.
14, 4144 Arlesheim. T. (061) 701 72 17.   084262
Galerie 4, Dorfgasse 18, 4144 Arlesheim.
T. (061) 701 99 44.   084263

Arosa (Graubünden)
Presente, Dorfplatz, 7050 Arosa.
T. (081) 3774052.   084264

Ascona (Ticino)
AION Witnesses of Time, Palazzo Otello, 6612 Ascona.
T. (091) 7915548, Fax 7915549. - Num / Orient /
Arch -   084265
Frido, Maurice, Via B. Berner 12, 6612 Ascona.
T. (091) 7916030.   084266
Galleria AAA, Carrà dei Nasi 18, 6612 Ascona.
T. (091) 7911144. - Paint / Graph -   084267

Galleria Aryana, Pass. della Carrà, 6612 Ascona.
T. (091) 7916663.   084268
Galleria Borgo, Via B. Berno, 6612 Ascona.
T. (091) 7913645.   084269
Galleria Sacchetti, Via B. Berno, Postfach 538, 6612 As-
cona. T. (091) 7912079, Fax 7913683.   084270
Hugelmann-Tièche, F., Vicolo S. Pietro 9, 6612
Ascona.   084271
Kohler, Via Orelli 4, 6612 Ascona.
T. (091) 7911357.   084272
Kurfis, Josef, Via Collegio 28, 6612 Ascona.
T. (091) 7917110.   084273
Noack, Via Moscia 61, 6612 Ascona.
T. (091) 7916335.   084274
La Perla, Vic. Olive 6, 6612 Ascona.
T. (091) 7918182.   084275
Schmid, Roger, Sentiero Vigne 47, 6612 Ascona.
T. (091) 7921761.   084276
Selmi, Vincenzo, Via Locarno 23, 6612 Ascona.
T. (091) 7911713.   084277
Serodine, Via S. Pietro 9, 6612 Ascona.
T. (091) 7911861.   084278

Astano (Ticino)
Etter, Helmut, Casa Lucertola, 6999 Astano.
T. (091) 6081706.   084279

Aubonne (Vaud)
Ferry, 5 Rue Trévelin, 1170 Aubonne.
T. (021) 808 51 92.   084280

Aurigeno (Ticino)
Bovien, Ursula, Castello Ciappui 9, 6671 Aurigeno.
T. (091) 7531831.   084281
Galerie-Atelier Ca-Selva, Haus Ca-Selva, 6671 Aurigeno.
T. (091) 7531844.   084282

Auvernier (Neuchâtel)
Numaga 2, 24 Grand-Rue, 2012 Auvernier.
T. (032) 7314490. - Paint / Orient / Sculp / Arch / Eth /
Jew / Draw -   084283

Avenches (Vaud)
Galerie au Paon, 10 Rue de Lausanne, 1580 Avenches.
T. (026) 6752540.   084284
Galerie du Château, Rue du Château, 1580 Avenches.
T. (026) 6753303.   084285

Baar (Zug)
Z-Galerie, Dorfstr. 6a, 6340 Baar. T. (041) 761 13 33.
- Paint -   084286

Baden (Aargau)
Antiquitäten & Gegenwartskunst, Zürcherstr 7, 5400 Ba-
den. T. (056) 2220285, Fax 2228986. - Paint -   084287
Atelier-Galerie Wameling-Richon, Obere Halde 24, 5400
Baden. T. (056) 2225481.   084288
Atelier Sven Spiegelberg, Obere Halde 20, 5400 Baden.
T. (056) 2220786.   084289
Galerie im Amtshimmel, Rathausgasse 3, 5400 Baden.
T. (056) 20 82 67. - Paint -   084290
Galerie Villa, Sonnmattstr. 28, 5400 Baden.
T. (056) 2211651.   084291
Gallery M, Bäderstr 19, 5400 Baden.
T. (056) 2211636.   084292
Rickli, Zürcherstr. 210, 5400 Baden.
T. (056) 2221066.   084293
Sampl, Ursula & Wolfgang, Züricherstr. 7, 5400 Baden.
T. (056) 22 02 85. - Paint -   084294
Steiner, Heinz, Untere Halde 5, 5400 Baden.
T. (056) 2228685.   084295
Stiftung H. Trudel-Haus, Obere Halde 36, 5400 Baden.
T. (056) 2226418. - Paint / Graph -   084296

Bätterkinden (Bern)
Galerie zur Krone, Bahnhofstr. 1, 3315 Bätterkinden.
T. (032) 6654840. - Paint -   084297
Schaer, Kurt, Bahnhofstr. 1, 3315 Bätterkinden.
T. (032) 6654840.   084298

Ballens (Vaud)

Galerie de Ballens, 1144 Ballens.
T. (021) 809 54 35. *084299*

Balsthal (Solothurn)

Rössli, 4710 Balsthal. *084300*

Basadingen (Thurgau)

Elliott, Chris, Hauptstr., 8254 Basadingen.
T. (052) 6571379. - Paint - *084301*

Basel (Basel-Stadt)

Analytica Art Galerie, Hermann-Albrecht-Str. 17, 4058
Basel. *084302*
Atelier Fanal, Sankt Alban-Tal 39, 4052 Basel.
T. (061) 272 13 54. *084303*
Ausstellungsraum Klingental, Kasernenstr. 23, 4058 Basel. T. (061) 681 66 98. *084304*
von Bartha, Schertlinggasse 16, 4051 Basel.
T. (061) 271 63 84, Fax (061) 271 03 05. - Paint /
Sculp / Glass / Mod - *084305*
Basels 1. Kuriositätengeschäft, Spalenberg 12, 4051
Basel. T. (061) 261 93 23. *084306*
Beyeler, Ernst, Bäumleing 9, 4001 Basel.
T. (061) 2725412, Fax 2719691. - Paint / Graph /
Sculp - *084307*
Braitmaier, Werner, Petersgraben 73, 4051 Basel.
T. (061) 261 53 21. *084308*
Breitmaier, Werner, Petersgraben 73, 4051 Basel.
T. (061) 261 53 21. *084309*
Buchmann, Sankt Alban-Rheinweg 52, 4006 Basel.
T. (061) 2729988. *084310*
Cahn, Herbert A., Dr, Malzg 23, 4052 Basel.
T. (061) 2716755, Fax 2715733. *084311*
Conrad, L.F. & O., Nadelberg 32, 4001 Basel.
T. (061) 261 85 37. - Paint / Graph / Sculp /
Draw - *084312*
Detraz, Gérard, Schlettstadterstr. 21, 4055 Basel.
T. (061) 321 66 94. *084313*
Egli, René, Blotzheimerstr. 19, 4055 Basel.
T. (061) 321 68 67. *084314*
Filiale Basel, Kannenfeldstr 22, 4056 Basel.
T. (061) 3210900. *084315*
Fuchs, Nadelberg 18, 4051 Basel. T. (061) 2614744,
Fax 2614744. - Graph - *084316*
La Galeria, Glockengasse 4, 4051 Basel.
T. (061) 261 03 49. *084317*
Galerie am Fischmarkt, Fischmarkt 1, 4051 Basel.
T. (061) 261 76 70. *084318*
Galerie Art Connection, Socinstr. G0, 4053 Basel.
T. (061) 272 52 30. *084319*
Galerie Art-Vision, Kannenfeldstr. 32, 4056 Basel.
T. (061) 382 62 26. *084320*
Galerie Carzaniga + Ueker AG, Gemsberg 8, 4051 Basel.
T. (061) 2617451, Fax 2617402. *084321*
Galerie d'Analytica Art, Hermann-Albrecht-Str. 17, 4002
Basel. T. (061) 681 76 66, 681 76 55. - Paint / Graph /
Orient / Sculp / Mod - *084322*
Galerie d'Art Moderne, Auf der Lyss 16, 4051 Basel.
T. (061) 261 21 08. *084323*
Galerie Demenga, Henric-Petri-Str. 19, 4051 Basel.
T. (061) 272 45 62, Fax (061) 272 44 00. - Paint /
Graph / Sculp / Tex / Fra / Glass / Mul / Draw - *084324*
Galerie Ethno-Art, Schnabelgasse 1, 4051 Basel.
T. (061) 2622250. - Eth / Orient / Jew - *084325*
Galerie Filiale, Mörsbergerstr. 52, 4057 Basel.
T. (061) 692 59 06. - Paint / Sculp / Draw - *084326*
Galerie Freie, Freie Str. 35, 4001 Basel.
T. (061) 261 24 96. *084327*
Galerie für naive Kunst, Webergasse 35, 4058 Basel.
T. (061) 681 52 44. *084328*
Galerie Guillaume Daeppen, Kirchg 2, 4058 Basel.
T. (061) 6930479. *084329*
Galerie Hinterhuus, Mathäusstr. 7, 4057 Basel.
T. (061) 691 55 30. *084330*
Galerie Le Cadre, Biascastr. 38, 4059 Basel.
T. (061) 361 37 35. *084331*
Galerie Münsterberg, Münsterberg 8, 4051 Basel.
T. (061) 272 04 44. - Graph - *084332*

Galerie Noodlebärg, Nadelberg 23, 4051 Basel.
T. (061) 261 32 40. *084333*
Galerie Orly Basel, St. Johanns-Vorstadt 33, 4056 Basel.
T. (061) 322 07 28, Fax 3220728. - Paint / Graph /
Sculp - *084334*
Galerie Pro Arte, Blumenrain 24, 4051 Basel.
T. (061) 261 51 21. *084335*
Galerie Riehentor, Spalenberg 52, 4051 Basel.
T. (061) 2618340. - Paint / Graph / Sculp - *084336*
Galerie Sevogel, Sevogelstr. 76, 4052 Basel.
T. (061) 312 26 59. *084337*
Galerie Varia, Rümelinspl. 6, 4051 Basel.
T. (061) 261 45 51, Fax (061) 261 35 57. - Orient / Eth /
Jew - *084338*
Galerie Vorstadt 78, Sankt Johanns-Vorstadt 78, 4056
Basel. T. (061) 462 56 57. - Paint / Graph - *084339*
Galerie Zum Isaak, Münsterpl. 16, 4051 Basel.
T. (061) 261 77 11. *084340*
Galleria Artis, Schönaustr. 48, 4058 Basel.
T. (061) 691 15 92. *084341*
Gass, Margrit, Sankt-Alban-Rheinweg, 4052 Basel.
T. (061) 2729080. *084342*
Geiger, Ludwig, Gotthardstr. 71, 4002 Basel.
T. (061) 302 16 19, Fax (061) 302 16 20.
- Paint - *084343*
Goetz, Steinentorstr. 15, 4010 Basel. T. (061) 272 57 26,
Fax (061) 272 39 83. *084344*
Gogniat, Simone, Unterer Heuberg 2, 4051 Basel.
T. (061) 2619239, Fax 2619239. *084345*
Graf & Schelble, Spalenvorstadt 14, 4003 Basel.
T. (061) 2610911, Fax 2610951. - Paint / Graph /
Sculp / Mul / Draw - *084346*
Grill, Ivan M., Webergasse 35, 4058 Basel.
T. (061) 681 52 44. - Paint - *084347*
Hilt, Freiestr 88, 4051 Basel. T. (061) 2720922,
Fax 2740661. - Paint / Graph / Sculp - *084348*
Hilt Galerie St Alban, St. Alban-Vorstadt 52, 4052 Basel.
T. (061) 2720627, Fax 2740661. - Paint / Graph /
Sculp / Eth - *084349*
Hofer, Peter, Burgunderstr. 5, 4051 Basel.
T. (061) 271 56 14. *084350*
Indekor, Marktpl. 36, 4051 Basel. - Paint - *084351*
Jäggi, W., Freie Str 32, 4001 Basel. T. (061) 2615200,
Fax 2615205. *084352*
Jakob, Ernst, Güterstr 189, 4053 Basel.
T. (061) 3615080. *084353*
Katz, David, Dufourstr. 5, 4052 Basel. T. (061) 272 73 51,
Fax (061) 272 73 51. *084354*
Katzen-Galerie, St.-Alban-Vorstadt 88, 4052 Basel.
T. (061) 272 03 55. *084355*
Kaufmann, Elisabeth, St.-Alban-Vorstadt 33, 4052 Basel. T. (061) 2720840, Fax 2721752. - Paint / Graph /
Sculp / Draw - *084356*
Knöll, Niklaus, Herbergsg. 4, 4003 Basel.
T. (061) 261 60 06. - Paint / Fra - *084357*
Knöll, Thomas, Utengasse 52, 4058 Basel.
T. (061) 6922988, Fax 6922942. *084358*
Krieg, Hans-Peter, Allschwilerstr. 24, 4055 Basel.
T. (061) 302 78 24. - Paint / Graph / Fra - *084359*
Kübli, Martin, Leonhardsberg 14, 4051 Basel.
T. (061) 261 03 15, Fax (061) 261 03 57. *084360*
Kuhn, Claude, Blumenrain 12, 4051 Basel.
T. (061) 261 40 10. - Paint - *084361*
Kunsthaus St. Alban, Gellertstr. 1, 4052 Basel.
T. (061) 311 55 70. - Paint / Graph / Sculp - *084362*
Labyrinth, Nadelberg 17, 4001 Basel. T. (061) 261 57 67.
- Paint / Graph / Draw - *084363*
Lang, Clodette, Strassburgerallee 104, 4055 Basel.
T. (061) 381 88 45. *084364*
Laszlo, Carlo, Sonnenweg 24, 4052 Basel.
T. (061) 311 06 07. *084365*
Lilian, Andrée, Socinstr. 60, 4051 Basel.
T. (061) 2722600, 232600. - Paint - *084366*
Linder, Gisèle, Elisabethenstr 54, 4051 Basel.
T. (061) 2728377, Fax 2722728. - Paint / Graph /
Sculp / Mul / Draw / Pho - *084367*
Littmann, Klaus, Elisabethenstr. 44, 4051 Basel.
T. (061) 272 87 67. - Paint - *084368*

Lüdin, Paul, Riehenstr. 6, 4058 Basel. T. (061) 681 73 75.
- Paint / Graph / Repr / Sculp / Fra / Draw - *084369*
Mäder, Franz, Claragraben 45, 4005 Basel.
T. (061) 691 89 47. - Paint / Graph / Sculp - *084370*
Mesmer, St. Johanns-Vorstadt 78, 4004 Basel.
T. (061) 322 56 57. *084371*
Münzer, Adolf, Hammerstr. 92, 4057 Basel.
T. (061) 6914681. *084372*
Neugebauer, Anita, St.-Alban-Vorstadt 10, 4052 Basel.
T. (061) 272 21 57. - Paint - *084373*
Palladion, Rennweg 51, 4052 Basel. T. (061) 3123400,
3120344. *084374*
Pep & No Name Gallery, Güterstr. 153, 4053 Basel.
T. (061) 361 20 65, Fax 3612065. - Paint / Pho - *084375*
Raeber, Edith, St.-Alban-Anlage 68, 4052 Basel.
T. (061) 311 26 38. *084376*
Reinhard, B. + J., Heuberg 12, 4051 Basel.
T. (061) 2619920. *084377*
Rusterholz Kunstauktionen, Hammerstr. 108, 4057 Basel. T. (061) 691 14 14, Fax (061) 691 14 61. - Paint /
Graph / Mul / Draw - *084378*
Sandia, Auf der Lyss 20, 4051 Basel.
T. (061) 261 04 59. *084379*
Schmid, Karl, Rosshofgasse 11, 4051 Basel.
T. (061) 261 28 27. *084380*
Schmidt, Ernesto, Gerbergasse 53, 4001 Basel.
T. (061) 261 10 08. *084381*
Schmücking, Sattelg 2, 4051 Basel. T. (061) 2613705,
Fax 2613705. - Paint / Graph / Sculp - *084382*
Seckinger, Cachet Hansueli, Münsterberg 13, 4051 Basel. T. (061) 272 35 94. *084383*
Ségal, M. & G., Aeschengraben 14-16, 4051 Basel.
T. (061) 272 39 08, Fax (061) 272 29 84. *084384*
Stampa, Spalenberg 2, 4051 Basel. T. (061) 2617910,
Fax 2617919. *084385*
Suter & Suter, Lautengartenstr. 23, 4010 Basel. *084386*
Thaler, Werner, Lindenberg 17, 4058 Basel.
T. (061) 692 98 28. - Paint - *084387*
Thorens, Daniel Blaise, Aeschenvorstadt 15, 4051 Basel. T. (061) 2717211, Fax (061) 2717206.
- Paint - *084388*
Thorens, Daniel Blaise, Aeschenvorstadt 15, 4051 Basel. T. (061) 271 72 11, Fax (061) 271 72 06.
- Paint - *084389*
Totentanz, Totentanz 17-18, 4004 Basel.
T. (061) 261 34 25. *084390*
Triebold, Rittergasse 22, 4051 Basel. T. (061) 272 35 35,
Fax (061) 272 33 00. - Paint / Sculp - *084391*
Vogelsperger, Grenzacherstr 481, 4058 Basel.
T. (061) 6016650. - Graph - *084392*
Walter, Fabian, Wallstr 13, Postfach, 4010 Basel.
T. (061) 2713877, Fax 2713887. *084393*
Wenger, Christine, Rütimeyerstr. 3, 4054 Basel.
T. (061) 281 15 68. *084394*
Wüthrich, Tony, Vogesenstr 29, 4056 Basel.
T. (061) 3219192. *084395*
Zangbieri, Kohlenberggasse 21, 4011 Basel.
T. (061) 281 66 55. *084396*
Zellweger, Harry, Martinsgasse 9, 4051 Basel.
T. (061) 2613736, Fax 2613735. - Paint / Sculp /
Draw - *084397*
Zschokke, Bea, Glaserbergstr. 9, 4056 Basel.
T. (061) 462 81 81. - Paint - *084398*
Zürrer, W., Herrengrabenweg 75, 4054 Basel.
T. (061) 302 53 69. *084399*

Belfaux (Fribourg)

Post-Scriptum Galerie, 1782 Belfaux.
T. (026) 4751940. *084400*

Bellevue (Genève)

Salle Colovracum, 1293 Bellevue. T. (022) 9598820.
- Paint - *084401*

Bellinzona (Ticino)

Castel Arte, P. Collegiata 1, 6501 Bellinzona.
T. (091) 8256710. *084402*
Civica Galleria d'Arte, Villa dei Cedri, 6500
Bellinzona. *084403*
Forme e Colori, Via Camminata 3, 6500 Bellinzona.
T. (091) 8262369. *084404*

GALERIE KORNFELD · BERN

KUNST DES 19. UND 20. JAHRHUNDERTS
GRAPHIK UND HANDZEICHNUNGEN ALTER MEISTER

AUKTIONEN – AUSSTELLUNGEN – LAGER – VERLAG

LAUPENSTRASSE 41 · 3008 BERN · TELEFON (031) 381 46 73
FAX (031) 382 18 91

Belmont-sur-Lausanne (Vaud)
Fondation Deutsch, 12 Rte Mont de Lavaux, 1092 Belmont-sur-Lausanne. T. (021) 7283625. *084405*

Bern
Aebli, Marlyse, Tannenweg 7, 3012 Bern.
T. (031) 302 77 87. - Paint - *084406*
Altstadt-Galerie, Kramgasse 7, 3011 Bern.
T. (031) 311 23 81. - Ant / Paint / Paint / Graph / Furn /
Repr - *084407*
American Gallery, Nydeggstalden 20, 3011 Bern.
T. (031) 311 44 86, Fax 3726306. - Paint / Fra - *084408*
Angst, Frlmà, Dr., Gerechtigkeitsgasse 33, 3011 Bern.
T. (031) 311 24 72. - Paint - *084409*
ARCUM-B, Breiteweg 28, 3006 Bern.
T. (031) 312 11 44. *084410*
Arlequin, Gerechtigkeitsgasse 51, 3011 Bern.
T. (031) 311 39 46. - Paint - *084411*
Art + Vision, Junkerngasse 34, 3011 Bern.
T. (031) 3113191. - Graph - *084412*
Art'Café, Gurtengasse 3, 3013 Bern. T. (031) 332 72 40.
- Paint - *084413*
Art Deco, Rathausgasse 55, 3011 Bern.
T. (031) 311 58 59. *084414*
Bagnoud, Agathe, Postgasse 50, 3011 Bern.
T. (031) 311 64 98. - Paint - *084415*
Baumann, Berne de, Aarbergergasse 16/18, 3011 Bern.
T. (031) 311 68 66/21 17 47. *084416*
Berner Galerie, Rathausgasse 20, 3011 Bern.
T. (031) 3114335. *084417*
Brand, Joachim, Herzogstr. 23, 3014 Bern.
T. (031) 331 70 60. *084418*
Brügger, Christine, Kramgasse 31, Postfach 329, 3011
Bern. T. (031) 3119021, Fax 3121650. *084419*
Campagna Rosenberg, Laubeggstr. 27+29, 3006 Bern.
T. (031) 352 86 33. *084420*
Cellector's Gallery, Nydeggstalden 38, 3011 Bern.
T. (031) 311 64 24. - Paint - *084421*
Duinmeyer, Eddy, Nydeggstalden 32, 3011 Bern.
T. (031) 311 90 91. *084422*
Fine Art, Kramgasse 29, 3011 Bern.
T. (031) 312 28 38. *084423*
Foto Galerie, Rathausgasse 22, 3011 Bern.
T. (031) 311 43 35. *084424*
Friedrich, Erika & Otto, Junkerngasse 39, 3011 Bern.
T. (031) 311 78 03. - Paint / Sculp / Draw - *084425*
Fries, Liesbeth, Nydeggstalden 32, 3011 Bern.
T. (031) 311 57 75. *084426*
Galerie am Kreis, Muristr. 51, 3006 Bern.
T. (031) 352 35 60. *084427*
Galerie Art + Vision, Junkerngasse 34, 3011 Bern.
T. (031) 3113191. - Graph - *084428*
Galerie Fröhlich, Helvetiastr 19a, 3005 Bern.
T. (031) 3520688. *084429*
Galerie Illusoria, Schwarztorstr 70, 3007 Bern.
T. (031) 3817731, Fax (031) 3817731. - Paint / Graph /
Repr / Sculp / Cur / Pho / Draw - *084430*
Galerie im Kramgass-Chäller, Kramgasse 10, 3011 Bern.
T. (031) 312 51 50. *084431*
Galerie Nydegg, Mattenenge 7, 3001 Bern.
T. (031) 311 34 00. *084432*

Galerie Rigassi, Münstergasse 62, 3011 Bern.
T. (031) 311 69 64, Fax (031) 312 58 78. *084433*
Galerie Rosenbergstrasse, Rosenbergstr. 42, 3006 Bern.
T. (031) 352 70 05. *084434*
Galerie Vita, Taubenstr 32, 3001 Bern. T. (031) 3120308.
- Paint / Graph / China / Sculp / Jew / Cur / Mod -- *084435*
Galerie Zum Bärengraben, Nydeggasse 17, 3011 Bern.
T. (031) 311 44 44. *084436*
Gehrig, Roland, Morgenstr. 70, 3018 Bern.
T. (031) 991 34 67. - Paint - *084437*
Gerber, Toni, Gerechtigkeitsgasse 62, 3011 Bern.
I. (031) 311 I 36 50. *0044306*
Haldemann, Margit, Brunngasse 14, 3000 Bern 7.
T. (031) 311 56 56, Fax 3115656. - Paint / Graph /
Sculp / Mul / Draw - *084439*
Hans-Huber-Galerie, Marktgasse 59, 3011 Bern.
T. (031) 312 14 14. - Paint / Graph - *084440*
Hofer, Münstergasse 56, 3011 Bern.
T. (031) 3117897. *084441*
Ikonen-Galerie, Kramgasse 67, 3011 Bern.
T. (031) 312 16 60. *084442*
Kaynak, Kramgasse 35, 3011 Bern.
T. (031) 311 01 11. *084443*
Kogal, Burkhard, Kramgasse 53, 3011 Bern.
T. (031) 311 89 19. - Paint / Graph / Num - *084444*
Kollbrunner, Marktgasse 14, 3011 Bern.
T. (031) 311 21 44. *084445*
Kornfeld, Laupenstr 41, 3008 Bern. T. (031) 3814673,
Fax 3821891. - Paint / Graph / Sculp / Draw - *084446*
Krebs, Martin, Münstergasse 43, 3011 Bern.
T. (031) 3117370. *084447*
Kulli, Susanne, Nydeggstalden 30, 3011 Bern.
T. (031) 3120640, Fax (031) 3121463. *084448*
Kunstkeller Bern, Gerechtigkeitsgasse 40, 3011 Bern.
T. (031) 3118630, Fax 3118630. - Paint / Graph / Repr /
Sculp - *084449*
Kunstklause, Seftigenstr 65, 3007 Bern.
T. (031) 3716259. - Paint - *084450*
Liz Antiquitäten, Rathausgasse 39, 3011 Bern.
T. (031) 311 11 77. *084451*
Loebgalerie, Münstergasse 45, 3011 Bern.
T. (031) 312 74 40. *084452*
Look & Like, Kramgasse 19, 3011 Bern.
T. (031) 311 55 47, Fax (031) 311 55 80. - Paint /
Repr - *084453*
Mäder, Max, Kramgasse 54, 3011 Bern.
T. (031) 311 62 35, Fax (031) 311 76 32. *084454*
Maurer, Catherine, Nydeggstalden 24, 3011 Bern.
T. (031) 3119332, Fax (031) 3119332. *084455*
Müller, Verena, Junkerngasse 1, 3011 Bern.
T. (031) 311 41 72. *084456*
Nussbaum, Walter, Mühlenplatz 14, 3011 Bern.
T. (031) 311 35 39. - Paint - *084457*
Amano L. Pauli & R. Amacher, Münstergasse 42, 3011
Bern. T. (031) 311 04 03. *084458*
Pia, Francesca, Münstergasse 6, 3011 Bern.
T. (031) 311 73 02, 22 48 72. - Paint / Graph / Sculp /
Fra / Mul / Draw - *084459*

Pulitzer & Knöll, Kramgasse 62, 3011 Bern.
T. (031) 311 56 91, 22 93 33. - Paint / Graph /
Fra - *084460*
QUADRO-Kunstverleih, Gerechtigkeitsgasse 60, 3011
Bern. T. (031) 312 38 21. *084461*
Rathaus Galerie, Gerechtigkeitsgasse 79, 3011 Bern.
T. (031) 311 51 94. *084462*
Sanske Stähli, Kramgasse 67, 3011 Bern.
T. (031) 3121371. *084463*
Schaedeli, Heidi, Gerechtigkeitsgasse 30, 3011 Bern.
T. (031) 3111104. *084464*
Scherer & Sohn, Otto, Kramgasse 26, 3011 Bern.
T. (031) 311 73 69. *084465*
Schindler, Bernhard, Münstergasse 36, 3011 Bern.
T. (031) 3115071, Fax (031) 3118558. - Paint / Graph /
Sculp / Pho / Mul / Draw - *084466*
Schneiter, Victor, Quartierg. 10, 3013 Bern.
T. (031) 332 54 47. - Paint - *084467*
Schwab, Kurt, Spitalackerstr 26, 3013 Bern.
T. (031) 332 96 16. *084468*
Stuker, Jürg, Alter Aargauerstalden 30, 3006 Bern.
T. (031) 352 00 44, Fax (031) 352 78 13. *084469*
Suti Galerie und Edition, Gerberngasse 15, 3011 Bern.
T. (031) 3110966, 3312007. - Paint / Graph / Sculp /
Draw - *084470*
Trag-Art, Gerechtigkeitsg 9, 3011 Bern.
T. (031) 3116449, Fax 3116538. *084471*
Vitrine, Gerechtigkeitsg 73, 3000 Bern 8.
T. (031) 3118570, Fax 3118269. - Tex / Glass - *084472*
Voirol, Paul, Kramgasse 74, 3007 Bern.
T. (031) 311 20 88. *084473*
Werkgalerie am Läuferplatz, Läuferpl. 9, 3011 Bern.
T. (031) 311 63 01. - China - *084474*
Zähringer Galerie + Kleinkunsthalle, Badgasse 1, 3011
Bern. T. (031) 3110882. *084475*
Zähringerhof, Badgasse 1, 3011 Bern.
T. (031) 311 08 82. - Paint / Graph / Sculp - *084476*
Zeller, Michèle, Kramgasse 20, 3000 Bern 13.
T. (031) 3119388, Fax 3123242. - Jew / Fra /
Draw - *084477*

Berneck (Sankt Gallen)
Galerie am Rathausplatz, Rathauspl. 2, 9442 Berneck.
T. (071) 7446106. *084478*

Bevaix (Neuchâtel)
Gabus, Pierre-Yves, 6 Rue de la Fontaine, 2022 Bevaix.
T. (032) 8461609, Fax 8462637. *084479*
Galerie Pro Arte, 22 Rte. de Neuchâtel, 2022 Bevaix.
T. (032) 8461316. *084480*

Bex (Vaud)
Galerie de l'Avançon, 3 Rte. de Gryon, 1880 Bex.
T. (024) 4633452. *084481*

Biasca (Ticino)
Odeonart, Via San Gottardo, 6710 Biasca.
T. (091) 8622660. *084482*

Biel (Bern)
Alte Krone, Obergasse 1, 2500 Biel. T. (032) 3234012.
- Paint - *084483*

FINE ART GALLERY FOR WATERCOLOURS

GALERIE AQUARELLE ✛

C.ROESSINGER RUE DES ALPES 46, CH-2502 BIEL/BIENNE
SWITZERLAND   TEL (032) 323 10 57   FAX (032) 322 23 71
Schweizer Aquarelle und Zeichnungen (besonders 18. + 19. Jahrh.)
Fine European watercolours and drawings, open by appointment only.
Belles aquarelles et dessins anciens; nous ouvrons sur rendez-vous.

Flury, Max, Zentralstr. 12, 2501 Biel. T. (032) 3224505,
Fax 3226865. - Graph / Fra -   *084484*
Galerie Aquarelle, Alpenstr 46, 2502 Biel.
T. (032) 3231057, Fax 3222371. - Paint / Graph /
Draw -   *084485*
Galerie d'Art & d'Horlogerie, Untergasse 48, 2503 Biel.
T. (032) 3232341.   *084486*
Galerie Foto-Foyer 3, Obergässli 3, 2502 Biel.
T. (032) 3235547. - Pho / Paint / Mul -   *084487*
Galerie-Théatre 3, Kellertheater, Obergässli 3, 2502
Biel. T. (032) 3235547.   *084488*
Galleria, Aarbergstr 121 A, 2502 Biel.
T. (032) 3231223.   *084489*
Kunstverein, Centre PasqART, 2500 Biel.
T. (032) 3225586. - Paint -   *084490*
Lüthi, Paul, Untergasse 38, 2500 Biel. T. (032) 3228555.
- Paint / Graph / Repr / Fra -   *084491*
Michel, Lotti, Pianostr. 51, 2500 Biel.
T. (032) 3650593.   *084492*
Muck, Jurastr. 41, 2500 Biel. T. (032) 3420164.
- Paint -   *084493*
Patzer, Lilian, BP 408, 2501 Biel. T. (032) 3656748.
- Paint / Graph -   *084494*
Steiner, Silvia, Seevorstadt 57, 2502 Biel.
T. (032) 3234056. - Paint / Graph / Sculp /
Draw -   *084495*

Binningen (Basel-Land)
Schlossmatt, Parkstr. 16, 4102 Binningen.
T. (061) 421 66 91.   *084496*

Birsfelden (Basel-Land)
von Sterndorff, Rheinstr. 4, 4127 Birsfelden.
T. (061) 311 09 92. - Paint -   *084497*

Bischofszell (Thurgau)
Stäcker, Peter, Neugasse 2, 9220 Bischofszell.
T. (071) 4225544, Fax 4225543.   *084498*

Bissone (Ticino)
Casa Tencalla, Pl. Borromini 11, 6816 Bissone.
T. (091) 6497342.   *084499*

Blonay (Vaud)
Kellenberger, Eric, 22 Ch. Planaz, 1807 Blonay.
T. (021) 943 44 44, Fax 9437777. - Graph / Mod /
Mul -   *084500*

Bôle (Neuchâtel)
Galerie l'Enclume, 9 Rue de la Gare, 2014 Bôle.
T. (032) 8425814, Fax 8425814. - Ant / Ant / Paint /
Paint -   *084501*

Bonstetten (Zürich)
Galerie für Gegenwartskunst, Im Burgwies 2, 8906 Bon-
stetten. T. (01) 700 32 10. - Paint -   *084502*
Seiler, Anton, Islisbergstr. 21, 8906 Bonstetten.
T. (01) 700 19 19.   *084503*

Le Brassus (Vaud)
Vuilleumier, Stéphan, 12 Rue de la Gare, 1348 Le Bras-
sus. T. (021) 845 66 85.   *084504*

Bremgarten (Aargau)
Galerie am Bogen, Am Bogen 4/6, 5620 Bremgarten.
T. (056) 6334953, Fax 6334957. - Instr -   *084505*
Galerie Antonigasse, Antonigasse 16, 5620 Bremgarten.
T. (056) 6331280.   *084506*

Brig (Valais)
Galerie Zur Matze, Schlossgasse, 3900 Brig.
T. (027) 9231901.   *084507*
Jodok, Alte Simplonstr. 26, 3900 Brig.
T. (027) 9236229.   *084508*

Brugg (Aargau)
Galerie Falkengasse, Falkengasse 9, 5200 Brugg.
T. (056) 441 83 31, Fax 441 78 84. - Paint / Sculp /
Draw -   *084509*
Zimmermannhaus, Vorstadt 19, 5200 Brugg.
T. (056) 441 96 01.   *084510*

Bubikon (Zürich)
Pulver, Otto, Ebmattstr. 7, 8608 Bubikon.
T. (052) 2431355.   *084511*

Buchs (Aargau)
Kleiner, Lochmattweg 37, 5033 Buchs. T. (064) 22 33 20,
Fax 24 36 83. - Ant / Paint / China / Sculp / Silv / Glass /
Draw -   *084512*

Bülach (Zürich)
Altstadt Galerie, Gerbegasse 5, 8180 Bülach.
T. (01) 861 00 54.   *084513*
Galerie Kreuz, Bahnhofstr. 1, 8180 Bülach.
T. (01) 860 24 78.   *084514*
Galerie Sigristenkeller, Hans-Haller-G 4, 8180 Bülach.
T. (01) 8604710. - Paint / Graph / Sculp - *084515*

Büren zum Hof (Bern)
Herzog, Georges, Limpachstr. 17, 3313 Büren zum Hof.
T. (031) 767 82 96.   *084516*

Bützberg (Bern)
Waldmann, F., Im Oberfeld 8, Thunstetten, 4922 Bütz-
berg. T. (062) 9631447. - Paint / Num -   *084517*

Bulle (Fribourg)
Galerie Trace Ecart, 44 Rue de Gruyères, 1630 Bulle.
T. (026) 9124737.   *084518*

Burgdorf (Bern)
Bertram, Kirchbühl 4, 3400 Burgdorf. - Paint / Graph /
Sculp / Pho / Mul / Draw -   *084519*
Fink, Eduard, Metzgergasse 18, 3400 Burgdorf.
T. (034) 4226044, 4224711.   *084520*
Galerie ist, Kirchbühl 16, 3400 Burgdorf.
T. (034) 4228056. - Paint / Graph / Sculp - *084521*
Galerie Lorraine 7, Lorraine 7, 3400 Burgdorf.
T. (034) 4227097.   *084522*
Kunstraum Burgdorf, Friedeggstr 5, 3401 Burgdorf.
T. (034) 4231188, Fax 4227252.   *084523*
Maxe's Kunsthandel, Neuengasse 1, 3400 Burgdorf.
T. (034) 4228511.   *084524*
Münger, Esther, Kirchbühl 4, 3400 Burgdorf.
T. (034) 4225639.   *084525*

Bursins (Vaud)
Galerie les Deux-Fontaines, 1183 Bursins.
T. (021) 824 15 64.   *084526*

Bussigny-près-Lausanne (Vaud)
Ateliers, II Rue des Alpes, 1030 Bussigny-près-Lausanne. T. (021) 701 45 84.   *084527*

Le Cachot (Neuchâtel)
Ferme du Grand-Cachot-de-Vent, Vallée de la Brévine,
2405 Le Cachot. T. (032) 9361261.   *084527a*

Campione d'Italia (Ticino)
Lodi, Silvano, Viale Marco 32, 6911 Campione d'Italia.
T. (091) 6496827. - Paint -   *084528*
Tonino Art Gallery, Via Volta 3, 6911 Campione d'Italia.
T. (091) 6499697.   *084529*

Carona (Ticino)
Wendy, Via Fontanella, 6914 Carona.
T. (091) 6063983.   *084530*

Carouge (Genève)
Art Gallery Rita Gallmann, 6 Rue du Centenaire, Postfach
1707, 1227 Carouge. T. (022) 3421069.
- Paint -   *084531*
Brand, Marianne, 20 Rue Ancienne, 1227 Carouge.
T. (022) 343 35 65. - Paint -   *084532*
Delafontaine, 24 Rue Jacques-Dalphin, 1227 Carouge.
T. (022) 342 11 50, Fax 342 53 29.   *084533*
Galerie Carougeoise de la Fontaine, 24 Rue Jacques-
Dalphin, 1227 Carouge. T. (022) 3421150.   *084534*
Galerie de la Cour, 18 Rue Jacques-Dalphin, 1227 Ca-
rouge. T. (022) 342 41 97. - Paint -   *084535*
Galerie des Platanes, Rue Vautier 37-39, 1227 Carouge.
T. (022) 342 14 49, Fax 343 23 61. - Paint - *084536*
Galerie St. Victor, Rue Saint-Victor 33, 1227 Carouge.
T. (022) 3001743.   *084537*
Galerie 1990, 46 Rue Jacques-Dalphin, 1227 Carouge.
T. (022) 300 21 15.   *084538*
SMA Galerie, 12 Rue du Marché, 1227 Carouge.
T. (022) 3438055.   *084539*

Carouge/Genf (Genève)
Atelier Rose Azur, 6 Rue Centenaire, 1227 Carouge/
Genf. T. (022) 3421069. - Paint -   *084540*

Cartigny (Genève)
Centre de Recontres de Cartigny, 21 Rue du Temple,
1236 Cartigny. T. (022) 756 12 10. - Paint - *084541*

Castagnola (Ticino)
Galleria San Michele, Strada di Gandria 70, 6976 Ca-
stagnola. T. (091) 9412432.   *084542*
Thyssen-Bornemisza, Villa Favorita, 6976 Castagnola.
T. (091) 9721741, Fax 9716151.   *084543*

Chalais (Valais)
Galerie des Chevaliers de la Tour, 3966 Chalais.
T. (027) 4583704.   *084544*

Cham (Zug)
Lander, Zugerstr. 53, 6330 Cham.
T. (041) 781 18 18.   *084545*

Chambésy (Genève)
Vecteur, 11 Ch. des Cornillons, 1292 Chambésy.
T. (022) 758 26 06. - Paint -   *084546*

Château-d'Oex (Vaud)
Art Suisse, Les Arcades, 1837 Château-d'Oex.
T. (026) 9247403.   *084547*
Galerie Paltenghi, 1837 Château-d'Oex.
T. (026) 9246801, Fax 9246801.   *084548*

La Chaux-de-Fonds (Neuchâtel)
Art-Cité, 23 Rue Numa Droz, 2300 Chaux-de-Fonds.
T. (032) 9681208, Fax 9681208.   *084549*
Ducommun, Louis, 14 Rue des Granges, 2300 La
Chaux-de-Fonds. T. (032) 9681704.   *084550*
L'Eplattenier, 25 a Courvoisier, 2300 La Chaux-de-
Fonds.   *084551*
Eve, Jean d', 96 Av. Léopold-Robert, 2300 La Chaux-de-
Fonds. T. (032) 9130123.   *084552*
Galerie d'Art, Ruelle Robert 132, 2300 La Chaux-de-
Fonds. T. (032) 9268225.   *084553*
Galerie d'Horlogerie Ancienne, Rue des Musées 26,
2300 La Chaux-de-Fonds. T. (032) 9138526. *084554*
Galerie de l'Atelier, 4 Rue du Versoix, 2300 La Chaux-
de-Fonds. T. (032) 9685664.   *084555*
Galerie de l'Echoppe, 41 Rue Jardinière, 2301 La
Chaux-de-Fonds. T. (032) 9137500.   *084556*
Galerie du Club 44, Serre 64, 2300 La Chaux-de-Fonds.
T. (032) 9134544.   *084557*
Galerie du Manoir, 25a Rue Fritz-Courvoisier, 2300 La
Chaux-de-Fonds. T. (032) 9681552.   *084558*

Michelotti, Armando, 4 Rue du Versoix, 2300 La Chaux-de-Fonds. T. (032) 9685664.   *084559*
Steudler-Antiquites, 2 Blvd. des Endroits, 2300 La Chaux-de-Fonds. T. (032) 9265249. - Ant / Furn / Orient / China -   *084560*

Chernex (Vaud)
Galerie Art-Top, Rte. de l'Arzillière, 1822 Chernex. T. (021) 964 53 97.   *084561*
Galerie du Chaudronnier, 1822 Chernex.   *084562*

Chexbres (Vaud)
Aeschlimann, Richard, Rte. de Vevey, 1605 Chexbres. T. (021) 946 22 69.   *084563*
Plexus Galerie, Grand-Rue, 1605 Chexbres. T. (021) 946 28 30. - Paint -   *084564*

Chiasso (Ticino)
Cons Arc, 15 Via Sildini, 6830 Chiasso. T. (091) 6837949.   *084565*
Fotografia Oltre, Via Bossi 13, 6830 Chiasso. T. (091) 6828655.   *084566*
Mosaico, Via Emilio Bossi 32, 6830 Chiasso. T. (091) 6824821. - Paint -   *084567*
Quadrarte, Via Soldini 2 a, 6830 Chiasso. T. (091) 6837840.   *084568*

Chur (Graubünden)
Bilderbank Chur, Bankstr 8, 7000 Chur. T. (081) 2525085, Fax 2525293. - Graph / Dec / Fra / Pho / Sculp -   *084569*
Crameri, A., Am Regierungspl. 40, 7000 Chur. T. (081) 2523326. - Graph / Fra -   *084570*
Galerie zur Kupfergasse, Calunastr. 28, 7000 Chur. T. (081) 2529190.   *084571*
Studio 10, Rabengasse 10, 7002 Chur. T. (081) 2520919. - Paint / Graph / Sculp / Pho / Draw -   *084572*
Werkstatt-Atelier Stampa, Reichsgasse 45/47, 7000 Chur. T. (081) 2526426.   *084573*

Clarens (Vaud)
Olsommer, Carlo & Jacqueline, 28 Rue du Sac, 1815 Clarens. T. (021) 964 74 50.   *084574*

Concise (Vaud)
Prise Gaulaz, Rte. de Provence, 1426 Concise. T. (024) 4341180.   *084575*

Coppet (Vaud)
Galerie Les Hirondelles, 86 Rte. de Suisse, 1296 Coppet. T. (022) 776 26 65.   *084576*

Corcelles-le-Jorat (Vaud)
Galerie Châtel-Rose, Au Grossan, 1082 Corcelles-le-Jorat.   *084577*

Cormondrèche (Neuchâtel)
Muller, Marie-Louise, 52 Grand-Rue, 2036 Cormondrèche. T. (032) 7313294.   *084578*

Cortaillod (Neuchâtel)
Jonas, Petit-Cortaillod 21, 2016 Cortaillod. T. (032) 8425121.   *084579*

Corteglia (Ticino)
Galleria Rosso-Blu, 6851 Corteglia. T. (091) 6468403.   *084580*

Courrendlin (Jura)
Galerie du Cenacle, 17 Rue Chavon Dedos, 2764 Courrendlin. T. (032) 4355985.   *084581*

Court (Bern)
Galerie de l'Empreinte, 1 Rue Centrale, 2738 Court. T. (032) 4979497.   *084582*

Crans-sur-Sierre (Valais)
Galerie des Neiges, Pl. de la Poste, 3963 Crans-sur-Sierre.   *084583*
Galerie 2300, Restaurant de Cry d'Err, 3963 Crans-sur-Sierre. T. (027) 4812410.   *084584*

Cureglia (Ticino)
Ca de Neri, 6944 Cureglia. T. (091) 9661971.   *084585*

Davos Platz (Graubünden)
Galerie Promenade, Promenade 114, 7270 Davos Platz. T. (081) 4161500, Fax 46 51 03. - Paint / Graph -   *084586*
Galerie Regina, Talstr. 44, 7270 Davos Platz. T. (081) 4165181.   *084587*
Kunstraum, Promenade 70, 7270 Davos Platz. T. (081) 4136441.   *084588*
Wazzau, Iris, Promenade 79, 7270 Davos Platz. T. (081) 4133106, Fax 4136554. - Paint / Graph / Sculp -   *084589*

Delémont (Jura)
Bovée, Paul, Arcades de l'Hôtel-de-Ville, 2800 Delémont. T. (032) 4234191.   *084590*
Galerie Nouss Carnal, 4 Pl. Brûlée, 2800 Delémont. T. (032) 4227142.   *084591*
Grands Magasins la Placette, 27 Av. de la Gare, 2800 Delémont. T. (032) 4224222.   *084592*
Michel, Pierre, Chemin de Vorbourg 75, 2800 Delémont. T. (066) 223673.   *084593*

Derendingen (Solothurn)
Galerie Hotel Linde, 4552 Derendingen. T. (032) 6823525.   *084594*

Detligen (Bern)
Aktionsgalerie Bern, Oltigen, 3036 Detligen. T. (031) 8256303. - Paint / Graph / Sculp -   *084595*

Dierikon (Luzern)
Neue Galerie, Schlössli Götzenthal, 6036 Dierikon. T. (041) 450 10 58.   *084596*

Disentis/Mustér (Graubünden)
Art-Deco, Casa Postidliun, 7180 Disentis/Mustér. T. (081) 9475050.   *084597*

Döttingen (Aargau)
Kunsthaus am Rebberg 5, Rebbergstr. 5, 5312 Döttingen. T. (056) 245 10 05. - Paint / Fra -   *084598*

Domat/Ems (Graubünden)
Büro für Bild und Text, Rieven 17, 7013 Domat/Ems. T. (081) 6335133, Fax 6332252. - Paint -   *084599*

Dübendorf (Zürich)
Galerie im Bettli, Bettlistr. 35, 8600 Dübendorf. T. (01) 20 14 45.   *084600*
Galerie im Schörlihus, Im Schörlihus, 8600 Dübendorf. T. (01) 821 20 22.   *084601*
Gallery One, Überlandstr. 220, 8600 Dübendorf. T. (01) 820 27 20.   *084602*
Gysin, Bob, Oberdorfstr. 113, 8600 Dübendorf. T. (01) 821 52 66, Fax 8215272. - Paint / Graph -   *084603*
Obere Mühle, Oberdorfstr. 15, 8600 Dübendorf. T. (01) 820 17 46.   *084604*

Dulliken (Solothurn)
Schenker, Jacob, Büchsweg 3, 4657 Dulliken. T. (062) 35 46 29.   *084605*

Ebikon (Luzern)
Rogers, Anthony, Luzernerstr. 6, 6030 Ebikon. T. (041) 420 11 85.   *084606*

Ebmatingen (Zürich)
Baehler, Steinmueri 24a, 8123 Ebmatingen. T. (01) 980 19 53, Fax 980 38 49. - Graph -   *084607*

Ebnat-Kappel (Sankt Gallen)
Kunstwerkstatt, Ebnater Str 23, 9642 Ebnat-Kappel. T. (071) 9932313, Fax 9933913. - Paint / Lights / Sculp -   *084608*

Echandens-Denges (Vaud)
Galerie d' Arfi, Pl de l'Ancien-Collège 1, 1026 Echandens-Denges. T. (021) 801 45 28, Fax 8014528. - Paint / Sculp -   *084609*
Galerie Le Vieux Bourg, 20 Vieux-Bourg, 1026 Echandens-Denges. T. (021) 801 70 71.   *084610*

Ecublens (Vaud)
Galerie du Pressoir de Bassenges, Rue de Bassenge, 1024 Ecublens. T. (021) 691 96 98.   *084611*

Eglisau (Zürich)
Galerie am Platz, Obergasse 23, 8193 Eglisau. T. (01) 867 00 41. - Paint / Graph / Sculp -   *084612*

Embrach (Zürich)
Galerie Am Irchel, Dorfstr 18, 8424 Embrach. T. (01) 8650303.   *084613*
Galerie Zum alten Amtshaus, Oberdorfstr., 8424 Embrach. T. (01) 865 02 08.   *084614*
Werkgalerie Alte Mühle, Obermühlweg 193, 8424 Embrach. T. (01) 865 40 29.   *084615*
Woods, Arthur, Dorfstr 75, 8424 Embrach. T. (01) 8650853.   *084616*

Erlenbach (Zürich)
Arteca, Seestr. 34, 8703 Erlenbach. T. (01) 910 72 11.   *084617*
Hiller's, Bahnhofstr. 4, 8703 Erlenbach. T. (01) 910 02 29.   *084618*

Erzenholz (Thurgau)
Oberli, Amei, 8500 Erzenholz. T. (01) 219775.   *084619*

Eschenz (Thurgau)
Wochenend-Galerie Schwelle, Kirchgasse 56, 8264 Eschenz.   *084620*

Etagnières (Vaud)
Rosset, Villa Milou, 1037 Etagnières. T. (021) 91 35 61.   *084621*

Faido (Ticino)
Meyerhans, Annelies, 6760 Faido. T. (091) 8661506.   *084622*

Feldmeilen (Zürich)
Galerie Vontobel, General-Wille-Str. 144, 8706 Feldmeilen. T. (051) 925 11 41.   *084623*
Schwabach, Schwabachstr. 50, 8706 Feldmeilen.   *084624*

Ferlens (Vaud)
Galerie Quadry, En Busigny, 1076 Ferlens. T. (021) 903 28 95.   *084625*

Fislisbach (Aargau)
Küng, Elisabeth, Alte Birmensdorferstr. 3, 5442 Fislisbach. T. (056) 493 35 25.   *084626*

Flawil (Sankt Gallen)
BW Classic-Galerie, Riedernstr. 21, 9230 Flawil. T. (071) 3935575.   *084627*
Galerie Arte Nuova, Riedernstr. 21, 9230 Flawil. T. (071) 3935545. - Paint -   *084628*

Fleurier (Neuchâtel)
Galerie du Château de Motiers, 2114 Fleurier. T. (038) 7611754.   *084629*

Forch (Zürich)
Dietliker, Robert, Zelglistr. 1, 8127 Forch. T. (01) 918 05 61.   *084630*

Frauenfeld (Thurgau)
Art Trading, Hungerbuelstr. 22, 8500 Frauenfeld. T. (052) 7214727. - Paint -   *084631*
Galerie am Kreuzplatz, Zürcherstr. 124, 8500 Frauenfeld. T. (052) 7221788. - Graph -   *084632*
Galerie Hess – Kunstsammlung zur Krone, Zürcherstr. 183, 8500 Frauenfeld. T. (052) 7213604. - Paint -   *084633*
Galerie Laubgasse, Laubgasse 45, 8500 Frauenfeld. T. (052) 7215707.   *084634*
Hess, Langwiesstr. 26, 8500 Frauenfeld. T. (052) 7213604.   *084635*

Freienbach (Schwyz)
Galerie Steinbruch, Kantonsstr. 22, 8807 Freienbach. T. (055) 784 22 56, Fax 785 07 35. - Paint / Sculp -   *084636*

Fribourg
Arcurial Suisse, Villars-les-Joncs, 1700 Fribourg. T. (026) 4814877. - Graph / Furn / China / Sculp / Tex / Jew / Mul -   *084637*
Espace du Pertuis, 23 Grand Fontaine, 1700 Fribourg. T. (026) 4752433. - Paint -   *084638*

Galerie de l'Arcade, Rue de la Samaritaine 34, 1700 Fribourg. T. (026) 3228513. *084639*
Galerie de la Cathedrale, 2 Rue du Pont-Suspendu, 1700 Fribourg. T. (026) 3224696. *084640*
Galerie La Margelle, 6 Rue des Epouses, 1700 Fribourg. T. (026) 3223322. *084641*
Hilde, F., 3 Rue Grimoux, 1700 Fribourg. T. (026) 3223544. - Paint - *084642*
Hofstetter, J.-J., 23 Rue de la Samaritaine, 1700 Fribourg. T. (026) 3232403. *084643*
Mara, 25 Rue d'Or, 1700 Fribourg. T. (026) 3222810, 6841510. - Paint / Graph / Sculp / Tex - *084644*

Frick (Aargau)
Galerie Geissgasse 7, Geissgasse 7, 5262 Frick. T. (064) 61 18 00. *084645*

Gais (Aargau)
Ebner, Willy, Zwislen 136, 9056 Gais. T. (071) 7932686. *084646*

Gempen (Solothurn)
Galerie Campus, Hauptstr. 19, 4145 Gempen. T. (061) 701 73 41. *084647*

Genève
Analix, 25, rue de l'Arquebuse, 1204 Genève. T. (022) 3291709, Fax 3295401. *084648*
Arcade Chausse-Coqs, 16 Rue Chausse-Coqs, 1204 Genève. T. (022) 320 06 30. *084649*
Art & Public, 35, rue des Bains, 1205 Genève. T. (022) 7814666, Fax (022) 7814715. *084650*
Arta Art, 24 Rue Saint Léger, 1204 Genève. T. (022) 311 13 77. - Paint - *084651*
Atelier Galerie, 2 Rue de l'Encyclopédie, 1201 Genève. T. (022) 344 64 51. *084652*
Au Pinceau Magique, 15 Rue Necker, 1201 Genève. T. (022) 731 75 70. *084653*
Benador, Jacques, 7 Rue Hôtel-de-Ville, 1204 Genève. T. (022) 3116136, Fax 3113205. - Paint / Sculp - *084654*
Blancpain & Stepczynski, 16bis Blvd. Helvétique, 1207 Genève. T. (022) 7351010, Fax (022) 7354277. *084655*
Bonnier, 4, rue St.-Laurent, 1207 Genève. T. (022) 7358735, Fax 7861489. *084656*
Bronze Gallery, 12 Rue Kléberg, 1201 Genève. T. (022) 732 63 33. - Paint / Sculp / Jew - *084657*
Bungener Galerie, 13 Rue F.-Hodler, 1207 Genève. T. (022) 735 15 06. *084658*
Cabinet d'Art Contemporain, 7 Rue Bellot, 1206 Genève. T. (022) 346 56 09. - Paint - *084659*
Calart, 4 bis Rue Prévost-Martin, 1205 Genève. T. (022) 3204050, Fax (022) 3212081. - Paint / Graph / Sculp / Mul / Draw - *084660*
Centre d'Art Contemporain, 10 Rue des Vieux-Grenadiers, 1205 Genève. T. (022) 3291842, Fax (022) 3291886. - Ant - *084661*
Centre d'art en l'Ile, 1 Pl de l'Ile, 1204 Genève. T. (022) 3121230, Fax 3121232. - Paint - *084662*
Cigarini, Romano, 1 Rue Rôtisserie, 1204 Genève. T. (022) 329 29 33. - Paint - *084663*
Cluny, 21 Rue des Glacis-de-Rive, 1207 Genève. T. (022) 735 15 24. *084664*
Comte, Roland, 25 Rue Montchoisy, 1207 Genève. T. (022) 736 05 89. - Paint - *084665*
Couleurs du Temps, 24 Rue de la Cité, 1204 Genève. T. (022) 321 74 13. - Paint - *084666*
Cramer, Patrick, 13, Chantepoulet, 1201 Genève. T. (022) 7325432, Fax 7314731. - Graph / Sculp - *084667*
Cramer, Patrick, Chantepoulet 13, 1201 Genève. T. (022) 7325432, Fax 7314731. *084668*
Decolony, 16bis Blvd. Helvétique, 1207 Genève. T. (022) 736 34 04. *084669*
Editart, 17 Av. Pictet-de-Rochemont, 1207 Genève. T. (022) 7369603, Fax (022) 7369703. - Paint / Graph / Sculp / Mul / Draw - *084670*
Engelberts, Edwin, 3 Grand-Rue, 1204 Genève. T. (022) 3116192, Fax 3116192. - Paint / Graph - *084671*
Espace Noga Hilton, 19 Quai du Mont-Blanc, 1201 Genève. T. (022) 731 98 11. *084672*
Espace Penta, Av Louis-Casai 75-77, 1216 Genève. T. (022) 798 47 00, Fax 7987758. - Paint - *084673*

Faure, Jean-Jacques, 4 Rue Georges Leschot, 1205 Genève. T. (022) 320 87 59. *084674*
Foëx, 5 Cour St.-Pierre, 1204 Genève. T. (022) 781 03 22. - Paint - *084675*
Foëx, 1, rue de l'Évêché, 1204 Genève. T. (022) 3112687, Fax (022) 3112783. *084676*
Galerie A. Blodé, 52 Blvd. de St. Georges, 1205 Genève. T. (022) 3288928. *084677*
Galerie Andata-Ritorno, 37 Rue du Stand, 1204 Genève. T. (022) 329 60 69. *084678*
Galerie Cour-du-Cygne, 12 Grand-Rue, 1204 Genève. T. (022) 328 57 83. *084679*
Galerie Cour Saint-Pierre, 25 Rue du Perron, 1204 Genève. T. (022) 328 57 83. *084680*
Galerie de l'Hôtel-de-Ville, 16 Rue Hôtel-de-Ville, 1204 Genève. T. (022) 321 56 21. *084681*
Galerie de la Corraterie, 18 Rue Corraterie, 1204 Genève. T. (022) 328 88 80. - Paint - *084682*
Galerie de Saint-Jean, 92 Rue de Saint-Jean, 1201 Genève. T. (022) 732 32 52. *084683*
Galerie des Chaudronniers, 2 bis Pl. Bourg-de-Four, 1204 Genève. T. (022) 3204061. *084684*
Galerie Diorama, 2 Rue Jargonnant, 1207 Genève. T. (022) 786 81 21. *084685*
Galerie du Cygne, 12 Grand-Rue, 1204 Genève. T. (022) 329 51 29. *084686*
Galerie du Parc, 24 Av. Dumas, 1206 Genève. T. (022) 347 30 37. - Paint - *084687*
Galerie du Théâtre, 2-4 Pl. Neuve, 1204 Genève. T. (022) 328 50 33. - Paint - *084688*
Galerie Faust, 25 Grand-Rue, 1204 Genève. T. (022) 328 18 50. *084689*
Galerie Ferrero, 9 Rue Hôtel-de-Ville, 1204 Genève. T. (022) 310 51 33. *084690*
Galerie Forum 2000, 35 Rue de la Terrassière, 1207 Genève. T. (022) 7368686, Fax 7867358. *084691*
Galerie Grand-Rue, 25 Grand-Rue, 1204 Genève. T. (022) 3117685. - Paint / Graph - *084692*
Galerie Interart, 33 Grand-Rue, 1204 Genève. T. (022) 312 24 60. *084693*
Galerie La Regie, 19 Rue Montbrillant, 1201 Genève. T. (022) 740 04 01. *084694*
Galerie Le Bois Sacré, 92 Rue de Saint-Jean, 1201 Genève. T. (022) 738 20 11. *084695*
Galerie les Salles du Palais, 2bis Pl. du Bourg-de-Four, 1204 Genève. T. (022) 3204061. - Paint / Draw - *084696*
Galerie Liotard, 37 Rue J.-Et.-Liotard, 1202 Genève. T. (022) 3445011, Fax 3443222. - Paint / Fra / Pho - *084697*
Galerie Loanne, 23 Rue de la Navigation, 1201 Genève. T. (022) 738 25 50. *084698*
Galerie Ruine, 15 Rue Vollandes, 1207 Genève. T. (022) 736 60 37. - Paint - *084699*
Galerie Shirley, 14 Rue des Gares, 1201 Genève. T. (022) 734 97 03. - Graph - *084700*
Galerie Trois, 2 Pl. Taconnerie, 1204 Genève. T. (022) 328 45 07. *084701*
Galerie Verdaine, 1 Rue Verdaine, 1204 Genève. - Paint - *084702*
Galerie 1990, 46 Rue Jaques Dalphin, 1227 Genève. T. (022) 300 21 15. *084703*
Girardin, Gilbert, 7 Blvd. Théâtre, 1204 Genève. T. (022) 3293960, 3113383. *084704*
Granges, Pl. du Bourg-de-Four, 1204 Genève. T. (022) 329 40 55. - Paint - *084705*
Héritage, 3 Rue Pierre Fatio, 1204 Genève. T. (022) 786 96 30. - Paint - *084706*
Hirsch, Claude, 24 Rue St Léger, 1204 Genève. T. (022) 3111377. *084707*
Horngacher, François, 34 Pl. du Bourg-de-Four, 1204 Genève. T. (022) 3113186, 299930. *084708*
Huber, Pierre, CP 349, 1211 Genève. T. (022) 7814666, Fax 7814715. *084709*
Jardin des Arts, 32 Rue Rothschild, 1202 Genève. T. (022) 731 15 37. - Paint - *084710*
Koller, 2 Rue de l'Athénée, 1205 Genève. T. (022) 3210385, Fax (022) 3287872. - Paint - *084711*
Krugier, Jan, 29-31 Grand-Rue, 1204 Genève. T. (022) 3105719, Fax 3105712. - Paint / Sculp - *084712*

Letu, Bernard, Rue Calvin 2, 1204 Genève. T. (022) 3104757, Fax 3108492. - Paint / Graph - *084713*
Liofard, 37 Rue Liotard, 1202 Genève. T. (022) 3445011, Fax 3443222. - Paint / Fra / Pho - *084714*
Literart, 15 Blvd. Georges-Favon, 1204 Genève. T. (022) 321 40 80. - Paint / Graph - *084715*
Meier, Anton, 2, Rue de l'Athénée, 1205 Genève. T. (022) 3111450, Fax 3113407. - Paint / Graph / Sculp / Draw - *084716*
Meyrat, Sonia, 25 Rte. Bout-du-Monde, 1206 Genève. T. (022) 346 65 05. - Paint - *084717*
Miroir aux Alouettes, 15 Rue 31. Décembre, 1207 Genève. T. (022) 786 63 66. - Paint - *084718*
Morard, Claude, 22 Ch. de Briquet, 1201 Genève. T. (022) 733 66 50. *084719*
Motte, 21 Rue des Glacis-de-Rive, 1207 Genève. T. (022) 735 09 33. *084720*
Objets d'art joaillerie, 4 Rue du Mont-Blanc, 1201 Genève. T. (022) 732 30 86. *084721*
Odermatt-Cazeau, 38 Grand-Rue, 1204 Genève. T. (022) 312 04 10. - Paint - *084722*
Reymondin, 3 Grand-Rue, 1204 Genève. T. (022) 3212490. *084723*
Selano, Benedetto, 24 Av. Pictet-de-Rochemont, 1207 Genève. T. (022) 786 60 26. *084724*
Skopia, 9, rue des Vieux-Grenadiers, 1205 Genève. T. (022) 3216161. *084725*
Tonon, Paola & Gemma, 52 Blvd. Saint-Georges, 1205 Genève. T. (022) 328 82 21. - Paint - *084726*
Turetsky, Rosa, 25, Grand-Rue, 1204 Genève. T. (022) 3103105, Fax (022) 3103105. *084727*
Un-Deux-Trois, 5 Rue Muzy, 1207 Genève. T. (022) 7861675, Fax 7861611. - Graph - *084728*
Varenne, Daniel, 8 Rue Toepffer, 1206 Genève. T. (022) 7891675, Fax (022) 7891688. - Paint - *084729*
Videomixmedia, 5 Rue de Savoie, 1207 Genève. T. (022) 7355961. *084730*
Voutat, C.N., 16 Rue de Hôtel-du-Ville, 1204 Genève. T. (022) 3115621, Fax (022) 3115621. - Paint - *084731*
Weber, 13 Rue de Monthoux, 1201 Genève. T. (022) 7326450, Fax 7384305. - Graph - *084732*
Zannettacci, Sonia, 4 Rue Henri-Fazy, 1204 Genève. T. (022) 321 99 75. - Paint - *084733*

Genolier (Vaud)
Au Temps qui Passe, 1 Rte. de Coinsins, 1261 Genolier. T. (022) 366 25 15, Fax 366 37 02. *084734*
Degal, Simone, Rte. Trélex, 1261 Genolier. T. (022) 366 29 79. *084735*

Gipf-Oberfrick (Aargau)
Galerie Hofstatt, Im Hof 11, 5264 Gipf-Oberfrick. T. (064) 61 42 35. *084736*

Gland (Vaud)
Galerie de la Louve, 9 Rue du Nord, 1196 Gland. T. (022) 3644550. *084737*

Glarus (Glarus)
Kunsthaus, Im Volksgarten, 8750 Glarus. T. (055) 6402535, Fax 6402519. *084738*
Tschudi, Lill, Eichenstr. 26, 8750 Glarus. T. (055) 6406360. - Paint / Graph / Sculp / Draw - *084739*

Glattfelden (Zürich)
Gottfried Keller Zentrum, Gottfried-Keller-Str 8, 8192 Glattfelden. T. (01) 8672804, 8672232. *084740*
Löwen-Galerie, Juchstr. 9, 8192 Glattfelden. T. (01) 867 05 62. *084741*

Goldach (Sankt Gallen)
UNION-Forum für Architektur und Kunst, Unionstr. 9/11, 9403 Goldach. T. (071) 8454440, Fax 8454441. - Paint / Graph / Furn / Pho / Mul / Draw - *084742*

Gondiswil (Bern)
Internationale Photographieförderung, Mühlegasse, 4955 Gondiswil. Fax 781468. *084743*

Gossau (Sankt Gallen)
Bürgli-Galerie, Bahnhofstr. 8, 9200 Gossau. T. (071) 3853135. - Paint / Graph / Sculp - *084744*

Gottlieben (Thurgau)
Art-Galerie, Krongasse 5, 8274 Gottlieben.
T. (071) 6691421.   084745

Grand-Lancy (Genève)
Galerie Ferme de la Chapelle, 39 Rte. Chapelle, 1212
Grand-Lancy. T. (022) 342 94 38.   084746

Le Grand-Saconnex (Genève)
Galerie du Perron – Borel, 5 Chemin Taverney, 1218 Le
Grand-Saconnex. T. (022) 7886380. - Paint /
Sculp -   084747

Grandson (Vaud)
Dougoud, Willy, Corcelettes, 1422 Grandson.
T. (024) 4452250.   084748
Galerie d'Art de Grandson, Rue Basse 29, 1422 Grand-
son. T. (024) 4453822.   084749

Greifensee (Zürich)
Galerie Am Greifensee, Breitistr. 1, 8606
Greifensee.   084750

Grenchen (Solothurn)
Bernard, Lötschbergweg 5, 2540 Grenchen.
T. (032) 6525658. - Paint / Graph / Sculp /
Draw -   084751
Con Tempo Galerie, Schützengasse 9, 2540 Grenchen.
T. (032) 6525380.   084752
Galerie Brechbühl, Kirchstr. 38, 2540 Grenchen.
T. (032) 6521957. - Paint / Graph / Sculp -   084753
Grossen, Centralstr. 102, 2540 Grenchen.
T. (032) 6520050.   084754
Kunsthaus, Freierstr. 2, 2540 Grenchen.
T. (032) 6525022. - Paint -   084755
Lechner, Gerald B., Kirchstr. 38, 2540 Grenchen.
T. (032) 6521957.   084756

Greppen (Luzern)
Galerie Oberhus, Oberhus, 6404 Greppen.
T. (041) 390 47 19.   084757
Galerie Zum Rigi-Keller, Dorfstr. 15, 6404 Greppen.
T. (041) 390 43 49.   084758

Grindelwald (Bern)
Gydis, Hauptstr., 3818 Grindelwald. T. (033) 8534358,
8531580, Fax 8232740. - Paint -   084759

Grüningen (Zürich)
Action Galerie, Im Stedtli 858, 8627 Grüningen.
T. (01) 935 28 25.   084760
Fehr, Marlysa, Im Stedli, 8627 Grüningen.
T. (01) 935 28 25.   084761

Gstaad (Bern)
Galerie Francis, Parkstr., 3780 Gstaad.
T. (033) 7446420.   084762
Marci, Georges, Chalet Saggârah, 3780 Gstaad.
T. (033) 7445551. - Paint -   084763
Saccarah, Châlet Saccarah, 3780 Gstaad.
T. (033) 7445551.   084764

Gümligen (Bern)
Mäder, Walchstr. 9, 3073 Gümligen.
T. (031) 951 62 52.   084765

Gümmenen (Bern)
Galerie Alter Bären, 3205 Gümmenen.
T. (031) 751 10 59.   084766

Guntershausen (Thurgau)
Galerie Zur Alten Pressi, Hauptstr. 4, 8357 Guntershau-
sen. T. (052) 3654244.   084767
Magnin, Silvia, Hauptstr. 25, 8357 Guntershausen.
T. (052) 3855675. - Paint -   084768

Häggenschwil (Sankt Gallen)
Bären Galerie, Unter Dorf 5, 9312 Häggenschwil.
T. (071) 2985191, Fax 2985140.   084769

Haldenstein (Graubünden)
Knapp, Claudia, Im Ährenfeld, 7023 Haldenstein.
T. (081) 2845149.   084770

Hedingen (Zürich)
China, Rainstr. 24, 8908 Hedingen.
T. (01) 761 57 55.   084771

Heiden (Aargau)
Galerie im Werd, Hasenbühlweg 2, 9410 Heiden.
T. (071) 8911111.   084772
Kursaal-Galerie, Seeallee 3, 9410 Heiden.
T. (071) 8912222. - Paint / Graph -   084773

Heimberg (Bern)
Galerie Riegelhaus, Kilchstutz 3, 3627 Heimberg.
T. (033) 4373060.   084774

Herisau (Aargau)
Galerie Windegg, Windegg 4, 9100 Herisau.
T. (071) 3521868. - Paint -   084775
Niggli, Ida, Sandbühl, 9100 Herisau.
T. (071) 3331244.   084776
Tanner Farben, Oberdorfstr. 31, 9100 Herisau.
T. (071) 3516160.   084777

Hermance (Genève)
Galerie Centrale, 19 Rue Centrale, 1248 Hermance.
T. (022) 751 15 33. - Paint -   084778
Galerie d'Hermance, 546 Rte. d'Hermance, 1248 Her-
mance. T. (022) 751 22 82. - Paint / Graph -   084779
Galerie d'Hermance, 546 Rte d'Hermance, 1248 Her-
mance. T. (022) 7512282. - Paint / Sculp -   084780
Galerie Francis, Auberge d'Hermance, 12 Rue du Midi,
1248 Hermance. T. (022) 751 13 68.   084781
Gay, Susy, 19 Rue Centrale, 1248 Hermance.
T. (022) 751 15 33. - Paint -   084782

Herrenschwanden (Bern)
Galerie Altes Schulhaus, Bernstr. 39, 3037 Herren-
schwanden. T. (031) 302 24 45. - Paint -   084783

Herrliberg (Zürich)
Galerie Vogtei, Pfarrgasse 41, 8704 Herrliberg.
T. (01) 915 27 34, Fax 9152734. - Paint / Graph / Chi-
na / Sculp -   084784

Herzogenbuchsee (Bern)
Dorfgalerie, Ringstr. 4, 3360 Herzogenbuchsee.
T. (062) 9612841.   084785
Kornhaus-Galerie, 3360 Herzogenbuchsee.
T. (062) 9632110. - Paint -   084786

Hochdorf (Luzern)
Galerie Ad Hoc, Hauptstr. 35, 6280 Hochdorf.
T. (041) 910 21 51. - Paint / Graph / Sculp -   084787

Hochfelden (Zürich)
Wirth, Marie-Louise, Martins-Mühle, 8182 Hochfelden.
T. (01) 8603327, Fax 8611305. - Sculp -   084788

Horgen (Zürich)
Burkhardt, Helga, Seebrünneliweg 3, 8810 Horgen.
T. (01) 725 48 16. - Paint / Graph / Fra -   084789
Galerie Arte 2, Stockenstr 2, 8810 Horgen.
T. (01) 7260676.   084790
Galerie Carina, Zugerstr. 28, 8810 Horgen.
T. (01) 725 52 58.   084791
Galerie du Relais, Seestr. 163, 8810 Horgen.
T. (01) 201 28 11.   084792
Kunst im Haus zur Mühle, Bergwerkstr. 64, 8810
Horgen.   084793
Murbach, Gottfried, Seestr. 295, 8810 Horgen.
T. (01) 725 0701.   084794
Schneider, Heidi, Löwengasse 48, 8810 Horgen.
T. (01) 720 30 53, Fax 720 79 73. - Graph / China /
Jew / Glass -   084795

Hüttwilen (Thurgau)
Galerie im Riegelhaus, Mitteldorf, 8536 Hüttwilen.
T. (052) 7471532. - Paint / Graph / Draw -   084796

Hunzenschwil (Aargau)
RZ-Galerie, Untere Schoren, 5502 Hunzenschwil.
T. (064) 47 01 27.   084797

Huttwil (Bern)
Mery, Mühleweg 12, 4950 Huttwil.
T. (062) 9622561.   084798

Interlaken (Bern)
Bhend, Papeterie, Centralstr. 27, 3800 Interlaken.
T. (033) 8223236. - Graph / Fra -   084799

Galerie Artemia, Centralstr. 6, 3800 Interlaken.
T. (033) 8220156.   084800
Galerie Interlaken, Kursaal, 3800 Interlaken.
T. (033) 8224852. - Paint / Graph -   084801
Rainbow, Marktgasse 54, 3800 Interlaken.
T. (033) 8224482. - Paint -   084802
Schmidt, Rachel, Waldeggstr. 20/3, 3800 Interlaken.
T. (033) 8231916. - Paint -   084803
Spectrum, Steindlerstr. 19 H, 3800 Interlaken.
T. (033) 8229646. - Paint -   084804
Tantra Galerie, Jungfraustr. 29, 3800 Interlaken.
T. (033) 8227414. - Paint / Orient -   084805

L'Isle (Vaud)
Au Violon d'Ingres, En Chabiez, 1148 L'Isle.
T. (021) 864 54 25.   084806

Ittenthal (Aargau)
Verena Voeglin & Walter Zimmerli, Hauptstr. 39, 4337
Ittenthal.   084807

Kaiserstuhl (Aargau)
Nepomuk, Hauptgasse 93, 8434 Kaiserstuhl.
T. (01) 858 05 32, Fax 37 13 44. - Paint / Graph / Repr /
Sculp / Fra -   084808

Kilchberg (Basel-Land)
Fossati, 4496 Kilchberg. T. (061) 991 32 97.
- Paint -   084809

Kilchberg (Zürich)
Artidea, Seestr. 150, 8802 Kilchberg.
T. (01) 715 24 24.   084810
Galerie im Krankenhaus Sanitas, Grütstr. 60, 8802 Kilch-
berg. T. (01) 716 61 61, Fax 716 69 69. - Paint - 084811

Kirchberg (Bern)
Kunstforum Kirchberg desinfarkt, Eystr 66, 3422 Kirchberg. T. (034) 457467, Fax 457467.   084812

Kirchberg (Sankt Gallen)
Galerie Flora, Florastr. 7, 9533 Kirchberg.
T. (071) 9311402.   084813
Galerie Häne, Rätenbergstr. 15, 9533 Kirchberg.
T. (071) 9311430.   084814

Klosters (Graubünden)
Alex's Art Galerie, Talstr 1, 7250 Klosters.
T. (081) 4223637, Fax 4223816.   084815
Galerie Allegra, Alte Bahnhofstr. 3, 7250 Klosters.
T. (081) 4225167, 4223692, Fax 69 36 92. - Paint /
Graph -   084816
Galerie 63, Doggilochstr. 28, 7250 Klosters.
T. (081) 4222704, 4221614.   084817

Kloten (Zürich)
Gymnata, Hohstr. 3, 8302 Kloten.
T. (01) 8143388.   084818
Schmuck Galerie, Gerbegasse 6, 8302 Kloten.
T. (01) 813 38 55.   084819
Wullschleger, John R., Gerbegasse 6, 8302 Kloten.
T. (01) 813 38 55. - Paint / Graph / Jew -   084820

Köniz (Bern)
Könizer Galerie, Stapfenstr 45, 3098 Köniz.
T. (031) 9711769. - Paint / Graph -   084821

Kreuzlingen (Thurgau)
Galerie Raffaello, Stählistr. 57, 8280 Kreuzlingen.
T. (071) 6725120.   084822
Kunstraum, Brückenstr. 14, 8280 Kreuzlingen.
T. (071) 6721279. - Paint / Draw -   084823
Latzer, Romanshornerstr 82, 8280 Kreuzlingen.
T. (071) 6882311. - Paint / Graph -   084824
Lauer, Kurt, Finkenstr. 24, 8280 Kreuzlingen.
T. (071) 6726154. - Paint -   084825
Signer, Werner, Haus Avantgarde, 8280 Kreuzlingen.
T. (071) 6724383. - Paint -   084826

Kriegstetten (Solothurn)
Pisoni, Hotel Kreuz, 4566 Kriegstetten.
T. (032) 6756002.   084827

Kriens (Luzern)
Galerie Krienbach, Schachenstr. 9, 6010 Kriens.
T. (041) 320 48 42.   084828

Galerie Kunstkeller, Schachenstr. 9, 6010 Kriens.
T. (041) 320 48 42. *084829*
Stern-Galerie, Güterstr.2, 6010 Kriens.
T. (041) 320 67 34. *084830*

Küsnacht (Zürich)
Aebi-Lang, Bruno, Traubenweg 12, 8700 Küsnacht.
T. (01) 910 01 11. - Paint - *084831*
Atelier zur Eule, Zürichstr. 143, 8700 Küsnacht.
T. (01) 910 05 38. *084832*
Benkert, Roswitha, Seestr. 55, 8700 Küsnacht.
T. (01) 910 52 07. *084833*
Galerie Am Bach, Am Bach 7, 8700 Küsnacht.
T. (01) 910 86 67. *084834*
Galerie im Höchhus, Seestr. 123, 8700
Küsnacht. *084835*
Kunststube Küsnacht, Seestr. 160, 8700 Küsnacht.
T. (01) 910 45 72. *084836*
Maurer, Im Düggel 3, 8700 Küsnacht. *084837*
Minigalerie, Traubenweg 12, 8700 Küsnacht.
T. (01) 910 01 11. *084838*
Weber, Heidi, Seestr. 13a, 8700 Küsnacht.
T. (01) 383 64 70. - Paint / Graph / Sculp / Tex - *084839*

Lachen (Schwyz)
Living-Art, Hafenstr. 2, 8853 Lachen.
T. (052) 4426206. *084841*

Lamone (Ticino)
Birth Gramm, Strada Cantonale Ostarietta, 6814 Lamone. T. (091) 9664656. *084842*

Le Landeron (Neuchâtel)
Schneider, 32 Ville, 2524 Le Landeron.
T. (032) 7513821, Fax 7511421. - Paint / Graph /
Sculp - *084843*

Langendorf (Solothurn)
Breiter, Rüttenenstr 68, 4513 Langendorf.
T. (032) 6220904, 6235954. *084844*

Langenthal (Bern)
Bensaid Saber, M., Melchnaustr. 124, 4900 Langenthal.
T. (062) 9232154. - Paint - *084845*
Galerie Leuebrüggli, Jurastr. 38, 4900 Langenthal.
T. (062) 9223047. *084846*
Weder, J., Försterstr. 4a, 4900 Langenthal.
T. (062) 9223655. - Paint - *084847*

Langnau am Albis (Zürich)
Galerie Elfrizzo, Irgelstr. 2, 8135 Langnau am Albis.
T. (01) 713 38 77. *084848*
Schutzbach, Christian, Weldstr. 4, 8135 Langnau am Albis. T. (01) 713 00 33. *084849*

Langnau im Emmental (Bern)
Stöckli Keller, Hansenstr. 1, 3550 Langnau im Emmental. T. (034) 4021589. - Paint - *084850*

Laufenburg (Aargau)
Galerie Marktgasse, Marktgasse 163, 4335 Laufenburg.
T. (064) 64 18 84. *084851*

Lausanne (Vaud)
A L'Emeraude, 12 Pl St. François, 1002 Lausanne.
T. (021) 3129583, Fax 3207530. *084852*
Aparté, 18 Rue Curtat, 1003 Lausanne.
T. (021) 625 09 11. *084853*
Au Foyer d'Autrefois, 3 Rue de la Mercerie, 1003 Lausanne. T. (021) 323 44 27. *084854*
Berset, Marika, 90 Av. du Léman, 1005 Lausanne.
T. (021) 728 24 28. *084855*
Collis Art International, 18 Av. d'Ouchy, 1006 Lausanne.
T. (021) 617 42 59. - Paint - *084856*
Espace d'Art Contemporain, 3 Allée Ernest-Ansermet,
1003 Lausanne. T. (021) 312 25 21. *084857*
Espace Flon, 6 Côtes de Montbenon, 1003 Lausanne.
T. (021) 312 39 21. *084858*
Focus Gallery, 16 Côtes-de-Montbenon, 1003 Lausanne.
T. (021) 323 74 09. *084859*
Fontannaz, Serge, Rue St.-Laurent 8, 1003 Lausanne.
T. (021) 3126482. *084860*
Galerie Aurum, 1 Pl. Pépinet, 1003 Lausanne.
T. (021) 323 44 22. *084861*

Galerie Basta, 4 Rue Petit Rocher, 1003 Lausanne.
T. (021) 625 52 34. *084862*
Galerie d'Etraz, Rue d'Etraz 1, 1003 Lausanne.
T. (021) 3222101. *084863*
Galerie de l'Academie, Rue Centrale 31, 1003 Lausanne.
T. (021) 320 07 60. *084864*
Galerie de la Cité, 1 Ruelle du Lapin-Vert, 1005 Lausanne. T. (021) 320 92 98. *084865*
Galerie Espace 16/25, Cité-Derrière 12, 1005 Lausanne.
T. (021) 323 76 28. *084866*
Galerie Filambule, 18 bis Rue de Terreaux, 1003 Lausanne. T. (021) 323 12 23. *084867*
Galerie Florimont, Av. de Florimont 4, 1006 Lausanne.
T. (021) 3233450, Fax 3233450. - Paint / Sculp / Jew /
Glass - *084868*
Galerie Humus, 18 bis Rue des Terreaux, 1003 Lausanne. T. (021) 323 21 70. *084869*
Galerie Image Plus, 27 Rue du Petit-Chêne, 1003 Lausanne. T. (021) 312 51 21. *084870*
Galerie L'Entracte, 4 Lion d'Or, 1003 Lausanne.
T. (021) 3125775, Fax 3127775. - Paint / Graph /
Sculp - *084871*
Galerie L'Eplattenier, 17 Port-Franc, 1003 Lausanne.
T. (021) 312 12 09. *084872*
Galerie Mouettes, 1 Av. des Alpes, 1006 Lausanne.
T. (021) 323 93 16. *084873*
Galerie Point 3, 3 Rue Caroline, 1003 Lausanne.
T. (021) 312 17 68. *084874*
Galerie Port Franc, 17 Rue du Port Franc, 1003 Lausanne. T. (021) 323 12 14. *084875*
Gismondi, 1 Ch. Beau-Rivage, 1006 Lausanne.
T. (021) 616 24 14. *084876*
Junod, Pl. St.-François 8, 1003 Lausanne.
T. (021) 320 45 00. *084877*
Knapp, 28 Rue Pré du Marché, 1004 Lausanne.
T. (021) 3122320, Fax 3122320. *084878*
Lehmann, Rachel, 19 Rue de Genève, 1003 Lausanne.
T. (021) 311 24 48. *084879*
Leonardo, 1 Av des Alpes, 1006 Lausanne.
T. (021) 3239316, Fax 3239316. *084880*
Librairie-Galerie, 2 Pl. St.-François, 1002 Lausanne.
T. (021) 323 77 17. *084881*
Nando, 5 Grand-St.-Jean, 1003 Lausanne.
T. (021) 312 67 40. - Paint - *084882*
Noblesse Oblique, Enning 6, 1003 Lausanne.
T. (021) 320 03 86. *084883*
Pauli, Alice, 9 Rue du Port-Franc, 1003 Lausanne.
T. (021) 3128762, Fax (021) 3110149. - Paint - *084884*
Planque, Claudine, esc. de Billens 1, 1003 Lausanne.
T. (021) 323 69 54. - Paint - *084885*
Rivas, Ramon, 25 Rue St.-Martin, 1003 Lausanne.
T. (021) 323 41 43. *084886*
Rivolta, Jacqueline, 1 Rue de la Mercerie, 1003 Lausanne. T. (021) 3123572, Fax (021) 6170711. - Paint /
Graph / Sculp / Draw - *084887*
Roy, Patrick, 16 Côtes-de-Montbenon, 1003 Lausanne.
T. (021) 3237409, Fax 3231555. *084888*
Steiner, René, 17 Av. de la Gare, 1003
Lausanne *084889*
Les Trouvailles, 13 Rue du Pré-du-Marché, 1004 Lausanne. T. (021) 312 04 82. *084890*
Vallotton, Paul, 2 Av J.-J.-Mercier, Postfach, 1002 Lausanne. T. (021) 3129166, Fax (021) 3208463. - Paint /
Draw - *084891*
Vaterlaus, Nando, Rue Grand-St.-Jean 5, 1003 Lausanne. T. (021) 3226740. - Paint - *084892*
Vieille Fontaine, 9-13 Rue Cheneau-de-Bourg, 1003
Lausanne. T. (021) 3234787, Fax 3112823. - Ant /
Orient / Cur - *084893*
Wartensleben, Elisabeth, 4 Av. Jurigoz, 1006 Lausanne.
T. (021) 616 13 26. *084894*

Lenzburg (Aargau)
Art Atelier Aquatinta, Stadtgässli 2, 5600 Lenzburg.
T. (062) 8914686, Fax 8914686. - Paint / Graph /
Sculp / Fra - *084896*
Galerie in der Stadtbibliothek, Kirchgasse 2, 5600 Lenzburg. T. (064) 51 40 41. - Paint / Graph /
Sculp - *084897*
Galerie Rathausgasse, Rathausgasse 32, 5600 Lenzburg. T. (062) 8913818, Fax 3600291.
- Paint - *084898*

Lenzerheide (Graubünden)
Art Gallery Lai, Plaz da Posta, 7078 Lenzerheide.
T. (081) 3851014, Fax 3851019. *084899*
Casa Lai, Via Principala 56, 7078 Lenzerheide.
T. (081) 3844441. - Paint - *084900*

Leuk (Valais)
Kastanienallee, Rathausplatz, 3953 Leuk.
T. (027) 4731867. *084901*

Leukerbad (Valais)
Kulturzentrum St. Laurent, 3954 Leukerbad.
T. (027) 4705111. *084902*

Liestal (Basel-Land)
Galerie Bilboquet, Mühlegasse 8, 4410 Liestal.
T. (061) 921 41 28. *084903*
Glatt, Brigitta, Fraumattstr. 11, 4410 Liestal.
T. (061) 901 15 34. *084904*
Kunsthalle Palazzo, Poststr. 2, 4410 Liestal.
T. (061) 9215062, 9211413, Fax (061) 921 19 30.
- Paint - *084905*
Rotstab, Mühlegasse 6, 4410 Liestal.
T. (061) 921 38 39. *084906*

Littau (Luzern)
Creatio-Glas-Studio, Luzernerstr. 88, 6014 Littau.
T. (041) 250 31 71. - Glass - *084907*

Locarno (Ticino)
Câ dal Portic, Vicolo della Motta 12, 6600 Locarno.
T. (091) 7510621, Fax 7510004. - Sculp - *084908*
Castrovillari, Egidio, Via della Motta, 6600
Locarno. *084909*
Città Vecchia Galleria, Via della Motta 2, 6600 Locarno.
T. (091) 7511727. *084910*
Flaviana, Via Varenna 45-47, 6600 Locarno.
T. (091) 7512208. *084911*
Galleria L, Via Sempione 17, 6600 Locarno.
T. (091) 7434119. *084912*
Galleria SPSAS, Sentiero del Tazzino, Pal. Martini, 6600
Locarno. T. (091) 7511507. *084913*
Galleria Ugas, Pzza. di San Antonio 14, 6600 Locarno.
T. (091) 7521853. *084914*
Studio d'Arte Verbano, Via delle Corporazioni 5, 6600
Locarno. T. (091) 7515488. *084915*
Sutter, Federico, Sentiero del Roccolo 11, 6605 Locarno.
T. (091) 7516715. *084916*

Le Locle (Neuchâtel)
Atelier du Lion d'Or, 20 Grand-Rue, 2400 Le Locle.
T. (032) 9316454. *084917*

Lohn (Solothurn)
Kunst im Lärchenhof, Alte Bernstr. 26, 4573 Lohn.
T. (032) 6771780. - Sculp - *084918*

Lucens (Vaud)
Koller, Château de Lucens, 1522 Lucens. *084919*

Lütisburg (Sankt Gallen)
Galerie Fäderehalter, Tuffertschwil 990, 9235 Lütisburg.
T. (071) 9311954. *084920*

Lugano (Ticino)
Anfitrite, Via Pessina 22, 6900 Lugano.
T. (091) 9220967. *084921*
Bader-Koller, Edith, Via C. Cantù 3, 6900 Lugano.
T. (091) 9239360, Fax 9239350. - Arch /
Draw - *084922*
Bottega delle stampe e delle cornici, P. Indipendenza 1,
6900 Lugano. T. (091) 9226821. *084923*
Coray, Pieter, Via Nassa/Contrada Sassello 2, 6900 Lugano. T. (091) 9227556, Fax 9220971. - Sculp /
Sculp - *084924*
La Cornice, Via Giacometti 1, 6900 Lugano.
T. (091) 9231583. *084925*
Dabbeni, Felice & Angela, Corso Pestalozzi 5, 6900 Lugano. T. (091) 9232980, Fax 9231211. *084926*
Giorgio Dannecker & Paola Garbini, Via Marconi 3a,
6900 Lugano. T. (091) 9228341, 9231880. - Paint /
Sculp - *084927*
Design Arredamenti, Via Carducci 1, 6900 Lugano.
T. (091) 9227447. *084928*

Evan, Via Pessina 9, 6900 Lugano.
T. (091) 9234224. *084929*
Galerie 800, Via Cattedrale 11, 6900 Lugano.
T. (091) 9234538. *084930*
Galleria d'Arte, Via Ginevra 4, 6900 Lugano.
T. (091) 9227589. *084931*
Galleria dell'Angelo, Piazza Cioccaro 11, 6900 Lugano.
T. (091) 9229858. *084932*
Galleria La Colonna, Via Nassa 29, 6900 Lugano.
T. (091) 9233819. *084933*
Galleria Palladio, Via Nassa 30, 6900 Lugano.
T. (091) 9234861. *084934*
Galleria Poltera, Via Castagnola 21e, 6900 Lugano.
T. (091) 9413686. *084935*
Galleria Pro Arte, P. Cioccaro 8, 6900 Lugano.
T. (091) 9227603. *084936*
Gallerie l'Incontro, Via Ferri 2, 6900 Lugano.
T. (091) 9234069. *084937*
Gübelin, Via Nassa 7, 6900 Lugano.
T. (091) 9237802. *084938*
Kremmos, Via Nassa 66, 6900 Lugano.
T. (091) 9234159. *084939*
Ortelius, Via Cattedrale 12, 6900 Lugano.
T. (091) 9237403. *084940*
Owens, Salita Chiattone 18, 6900 Lugano.
T. (091) 9237088. *084941*
Papiri, Adriana, Via Ginevra 4, 6900 Lugano.
T. (091) 9227589. *084942*
Passardi, Gabriele, C. Pestalozzi 25, 6900 Lugano.
T. (091) 9451288. *084943*
Stabile Posta, Via Vegezzi, 6900 Lugano.
T. (091) 9227444. *084944*

Lutry (Vaud)
Galerie Au Tracasset, 19 Rue du Voisinand, 1095 Lutry.
T. (021) 7911631. *084945*
Galerie Pomone, 15 Rue Friporte, 1095 Lutry.
T. (021) 7912884. *084946*
Galerie Tango, 8 Rue de l'Horloge, 1095 Lutry.
T. (021) 7915677. *084947*

Luzern
Architekturgalerie, Denkmalstr 15, 6006 Luzern.
T. (041) 4107481, Fax (041) 4202092. *084948*
Arlecchino, Habsburgerstr. 23, 6003 Luzern.
T. (041) 210 64 41. *084949*
Atelier Simone Erni, Waldstätterstr 18, 6003 Luzern.
T. (041) 2105144, Fax 2104184. - Paint / Graph / Repr /
Draw - *084950*
Bader, Haldenstr 2, 6006 Luzern. T. (01) 4106210,
Fax 4106310. *084951*
Burkard Galerie + Auktion, Schützenstr. 6, 6003 Luzern.
T. (041) 2405022, 2403188,
Fax (041) 240 82 52. *084952*
Editions Aujourd'hui, Abendweg 9, 6006 Luzern.
T. (041) 347 87 38. - Graph - *084953*
Foto-Forum, Weggisgasse 28, 6004 Luzern.
T. (041) 410 34 80. - Pho - *084954*
Galerie Ambiance, Cysatstr. 15, 6004 Luzern.
T. (041) 410 38 78. *084955*
Galerie Apropos, Sentimattstr.6, 6003 Luzern.
T. (041) 240 15 78. *084956*
Galerie Baslerhof, Baslerstr. 75, 6003 Luzern.
T. (041) 240 20 27. *084957*
Galerie Diebold-Schilling, Diebold-Schilling-Str. 1, 6004
Luzern. T. (041) 610 26 74. *084958*
Galerie du Quai, Schweizerhofquai 4, 6004 Luzern.
T. (041) 410 66 77. - Paint - *084959*
Galerie H+B, Pilatusstr. 20, 6002 Luzern.
T. (041) 210 03 01. - Paint / Graph / Draw - *084960*
Galerie im Rothenburgerhaus, St. Leodegarstr. 13, 6006
Luzern. T. (041) 410 52 41. - Paint / Graph - *084961*
Galerie Kornschütte, Kornmarkt 3, 6004 Luzern.
T. (041) 410 28 75. *084962*
Galerie Meile, Rosenberghöhe 4a, 6004 Luzern.
T. (041) 4203318, Fax 4202169. *084963*
Galerie Partikel, Denkmalstr. 15, 6004 Luzern.
T. (041) 410 62 14. - Paint / Graph / Sculp - *084964*
Galerie Schmid & Partner, Furrengasse 13, 6004 Luzern.
T. (041) 410 21 16. *084965*
Galerie West, Baselstr. 56, 6003 Luzern.
T. (041) 240 87 33. *084966*

Galerie 87, Waldstätterstr 18, 6003 Luzern.
T. (041) 2105121, Fax 2104184. - Paint / Graph / Repr /
Sculp / Draw - *084967*
Gloggner, Paul C., Hochbühlstr 1, 6003 Luzern.
T. (041) 2402223, Fax 2408282. - Paint /
Draw - *084968*
Grob, Marianne, Löwengraben 15, 6004 Luzern.
T. (041) 410 58 96. *084969*
Hofmann, Fritz, Habsburgerstr. 35, 6003 Luzern.
T. (041) 210 17 33. - Ant / Paint / Graph - *084970*
Kesselturm, Kesselgasse 3, 6003 Luzern.
T. (041) 2400778, Fax 2400778. *084971*
Kleiner, Postfach 1449, 6000 Luzern 15.
T. (041) 3721074, Fax 3721073. *084972*
Kupferstich Boutique, Weinmarkt 17, 6004 Luzern.
T. (041) 410 23 83. - Graph - *084973*
Lötscher, Hannelore, Haldenstr 25, 6006 Luzern.
T. (041) 4108530, Fax 3774484. - Paint / Graph /
Sculp / Draw - *084974*
Müller, Hugo, Berglistr. 46, 6002 Luzern.
T. (041) 240 55 51. - Paint / Graph - *084975*
O. T. Galerie, Zürichstr. 43, 6004 Luzern.
T. (041) 410 50 91. *084976*
Poster Kunst Galerie, Moosstr. 15, 6003 Luzern.
T. (041) 210 67 87. *084977*
Pro Art Galerie, Industriestr. 9, 6005 Luzern.
T. (041) 360 79 40. *084978*
Rosengart, Angela, Adligenswilerstr 8, 6006 Luzern.
T. (041) 410 31 86, Fax 4103181. - Paint - *084979*
Rotenfluh, Sepp, Murbacherstr. 25, 6005 Luzern.
T. (041) 210 87 80. *084980*
Sieber, Hans Holbeingasse 4, 6004 Luzern.
T. (041) 4106040. - Paint - *084981*
Twerenbold Söhne, Passage zum Stein, 6004 Luzern.
T. (041) 410 11 18. *084982*
Wey & Co., Haldenstr. 11, 6006 Luzern.
T. (041) 410 55 07, Fax (041) 410 19 49. - Ant / Paint /
China / Sculp / Jew / Rel / Glass / Ico - *084983*
Willen, Pfisterg 3, 6003 Luzern. T. (041) 2400560,
Fax 2400563. *084984*
Zum Hof, Stiftstr. 4, 6006 Luzern. T. (041) 410 39 86.
- Paint - *084985*

Lyss (Bern)
Kistler, Bernstr. 11, 3250 Lyss.
T. (032) 3844433. *084987*

Mägenwil (Aargau)
Oldani, Hans-Rudolf, Eckwilerstr. 5, 5506 Mägenwil.
T. (064) 56 17 53. *084988*

Männedorf (Zürich)
Bischofberger, Verenaweg 9, 8708 Männedorf.
T. (01) 920 20 70. *084989*
Collector's Corner, Dorfgasse 46, 8708 Männedorf.
T. (01) 9203801, Fax 9203801. *084990*
Novel Art, Seestr 410, 8708 Männedorf.
T. (01) 9211555, Fax 9211556. - Orient - *084991*

Martigny (Valais)
Fondation Louis Moret, 31 Chemin des Barrières, 1920
Martigny. T. (027) 7222347. *084992*
Fondation Pierre Gianadda, 59 Rue du Forum, 1920
Martigny. T. (027) 7223978, Fax 7223163. *084993*
Galerie Latour Cadrama, 1 Pl de Rome, 1920 Martigny.
T. (027) 7224475. *084994*

Massagno (Ticino)
Galleria Temi d'Arte, Via Stazio 7, 6900 Massagno.
T. (091) 9668863. *084995*

Matten bei Interlaken (Bern)
Galerie Am Höhenweg, Klostergässli 15, 3800 Matten
bei Interlaken. T. (033) 8229895. *084996*
Kämpf, Willy, Hauptstr. 57, 3800 Matten bei Interlaken.
T. (033) 8226305. *084997*

Maur (Zürich)
Guckloch Galerie, Badeanstaltstr. 0, 8124 Maur.
T. (01) 980 22 48. - Mul - *084998*

Meggen (Luzern)
Gemeindegalerie, Benzeholz, 6045 Meggen.
T. (041) 377 13 65. - Paint - *084999*

Meilen (Zürich)
Galerie La Charpenna, Grübstr., 8706 Meilen.
T. (01) 9152147, 9233202. *085000*
Gottschalk & Ash International, Ormisstr. 72, 8706 Mei-
len. T. (01) 923 38 32. *085001*
Komatzki, Dorfstr. 140, 8706 Meilen. T. (01) 9234512,
Fax (01) 9236158. - Graph - *085002*
Vontobel, General-Wille-Str. 144, 8706 Meilen.
T. (01) 925 51 11. *085003*

Meinier (Genève)
Galerie du Château, 19 Rte. de Corsige, 1252 Meinier.
T. (022) 759 19 90. *085004*

Meisterschwanden (Aargau)
Del Mese-Fischer, Seefeldstr 74, 5616 Meisterschwan-
den. T. (056) 6671828, Fax 6671804. - Paint - *085005*
Manazza, Mario, Kunstw 493, 5616 Meisterschwanden.
T. (057) 271039. *085006*

Mendrisio (Ticino)
L'Atelier, 3 Via Corso Bello, 6850 Mendrisio.
T. (091) 466297, 468053. *085007*
Ferrari, Gian-Mario, 2 Rue Bello, 6850 Mendrisio.
T. (091) 6468586. *085008*

Merlischachen (Schwyz)
Galerie Artes, Burgweg 11, 6402 Merlischachen.
T. (041) 8502408, Fax 8502408. - Paint /
Draw - *085009*

Meyrin (Genève)
Centre Meyrinois, 9 Ch. du Jardin-Alpin, 1217 Meyrin.
T. (022) 785 29 37. - Paint - *085010*
Galerie Bois-du-Lan, 8 Rue Bois-du-Lan, 1217 Meyrin.
T. (022) 782 60 09. *085011*
Villa du Jardin Alpin, 7 Ch. du Jardin Alpin, 1217 Meyrin.
T. (022) 782 32 87. - Paint - *085012*

Mezzovico (Ticino)
Dabbeni, Felice & Angela, 6805 Mezzovico.
T. (091) 9461757. *085013*

Minusio (Ticino)
Galleria Pegasus, 6648 Minusio. *085014*
Mediatore, Via Simen 9, 6648 Minusio.
T. (091) 7431854. - Paint - *085015*

Mollis (Glarus)
Gallarte, Seelmess 14/16, 8753 Mollis.
T. (055) 6121032. *085016*

Le Mont-Pélerin (Vaud)
Conyou Design, Chemin du Pellerin 8, 1801 Le Mont Pé-
lerin (VD). T. (021) 9212150, Fax 9212416. - Furn /
Sculp / Tex / Dec / Jew / Silv / Lights / Instr / Glass / Cu-
r - *085016a*

Le Mont-sur-Lausanne (Vaud)
Galerie L'Atelier, 45 Rte. de Lausanne, 1052 Le Mont-
sur-Lausanne. T. (021) 652 37 18. *085017*
Neuroni, Marco, 45 Rte. de Lausanne, 1052 Le Mont-
sur-Lausanne. T. (021) 652 37 18. *085018*

Montana-Vermala (Valais)
Robyr, Annie, Les Vignettes, 3962 Montana-Vermala.
T. (027) 4815118, 4811384. - Paint / Sculp / Dec /
Lights - *085019*

Montavon (Jura)
Galerie au Virage, Séprais, 2857 Montavon.
T. (032) 4267163, Fax 4267163. *085020*

Monthey (Valais)
Galerie Marmettes, 32 Av. du Crochetan, 1870 Monthey.
T. (024) 4714805. *085021*

Montreux (Vaud)
Art, 100 Grand-Rue, 1820 Montreux.
T. (021) 9635225. *085022*
ASB Galerie SA, Chemin Bottai-Chernex, 1822 Mon-
treux. T. (021) 964 37 82. *085023*
Galerie du Marché, 8 Pl. du Marché, 1820 Montreux.
T. (021) 963 05 17. *085024*
Picpus, 68 Grand-Rue, 1820 Montreux.
T. (021) 963 44 30. - Paint / Sculp - *085025*

Les Planches, 1 Ruelle Chauderon, 1820 Montreux.
T. (021) 963 78 91.   085026
Valsyra, Grand Hôtel Exelsior, 1820 Montreux.
T. (021) 3237872.   085027

Morbio Inferiore (Ticino)
Belarte, Via al Ponte, Viale Serfontana, 6834 Morbio In-
feriore. T. (091) 6831461.   085028

Morges (Vaud)
Aubry, Roger, 86 Rue Louis de Savoie, 1110 Morges.
T. (021) 801 62 27.   085029
Basilisk, 102 Grand-Rue, 1110 Morges.
T. (021) 8014764, Fax 8014764. - Paint -   085030
Galerie de Couvaloup, 1 Rue de Couvaloup, 1110 Mor-
ges. T. (021) 801 16 35.   085031
Galerie de l'Hôpital, 2 Chemin du Crêt, 1110 Morges.
T. (021) 804 22 11. - Paint -   085032
Galerie du Chêne, 1 Ch. du Chêne, 1110 Morges.
T. (021) 801 17 46. - Paint -   085033
Galerie Pro Arte Kasper, 6 Rue de la Gare, 1110 Morges.
T. (021) 8016731. - Paint / Orient / Graph -   085034

Mosnang (Sankt Gallen)
Galerie Altes Rössli, Unterdorf 60, 9607 Mosnang.
T. (071) 9833057.   085035

Môtiers (Neuchâtel)
Galerie du Château, Château, 2112 Môtiers.
T. (032) 7611754. - Paint -   085036
Galerie Golaye, Val-de-Travers, 2112 Môtiers.
T. (032) 7613610.   085037

Moudon (Vaud)
Creations d'Artisans, 7 Grand-Rue, 1510 Moudon.
T. (021) 905 34 33.   085038
Galerie d'Art Escalier 2, 2 Rue des Terreaux, 1510 Mou-
don. T. (021) 905 35 04.   085039
Grosjean, Gilbert, 12 Vieux-Bourg, 1510 Moudon.
T. (021) 905 21 68.   085040

Mühledorf (Solothurn)
Alte Seilerei, Murlistr. 97, 4583 Mühledorf.
T. (032) 6451176.   085041

Münchenstein (Basel-Land)
Oppliger, Boris, Dorfpl. 8, 4142 Münchenstein.
T. (061) 411 36 91.   085042

Münsingen (Bern)
Galerie Wagerad, Schulhausgasse 3, 3110 Münsingen.
T. (031) 721 31 24.   085043

Müselbach (Sankt Gallen)
Werkgalerie Chirchgass, Bäbikon, 9602
Müselbach.   085044

Muntelier (Fribourg)
Ruol Kunsthandel, 23 Marcoup, 3286 Muntelier.
T. (026) 6705859.   085045

Muralto (Ticino)
Galleria L, 6600 Muralto. T. (091) 7434119.   085046
Pedroni, Carlo, Postgebäude, 6600 Muralto.
T. (091) 7431247. - Paint / Graph / Furn / Orient / China /
Sculp / Arch / Eth / Jew / Fra / Silv / Rel / Glass / Mod --
085047

Muri (Aargau)
Atelier am Chelebüel, Kirchbühlstr 2a, 5630 Muri.
T. (056) 6444800. - Paint -   085048

Muri bei Bern (Bern)
Contemporary Art Gallery, Kräyigenweg 37, 3074 Muri
bei Bern. T. (031) 9514364.   085049
Mäder, Max, Walchstr 9, 3074 Muri bei Bern.
T. (031) 9516252.   085050
Mentha, Ruth, Jägerstr 21, 3074 Muri bei Bern.
T. (031) 9511121.   085051
Righetti, Thunstr 77, 3074 Muri bei Bern.
T. (031) 9516010, Fax (031) 9515412.   085052

Murten (Fribourg)
Galerie Heimatstübli, Schlossgasse 14, 3280 Murten.
T. (026) 6702809.   085053
Galerie Ringmauer, 3280 Murten.   085054

Muttenz (Basel-Land)
Erni, St. Jacobstr. 116, 4132 Muttenz.
T. (061) 461 64 52.   085055
Spreng, Katrin, Hauptstr. 65, 4132 Muttenz.
T. (061) 461 48 22. - Paint -   085056

Näfels (Glarus)
Fischli, Hans, Freulerweg 4, 8752 Näfels.
T. (055) 6122125.   085057

Naters (Valais)
Eyer-Oggier, Denise, Felsenweg 14, 3904 Naters.
T. (027) 9231341. - Paint / Graph / Mul / Draw -   085058
Kunsthaus zur Linde, Kirchstr. 21, 3904 Naters.
T. (027) 9237015.   085059

Netstal (Glarus)
Impuls-Bistro, Landstr., 8754 Netstal.
T. (055) 6408465.   085060

Neuchâtel
Ditesheim, François, 8 Rue du Château, 2000 Neuchâ-
tel. T. (032) 7245700, Fax 7212870. - Paint / Graph /
Sculp -   085061
Editions du Griffon, 17 Faubourg du Lac, 2000 Neuchâ-
tel. T. (032) 7252204. - Graph -   085062
Galerie des Amis des Arts, 1 Quai L.-Robert, 2000 Neu-
châtel. T. (032) 7241626.   085063
Galerie des Halles, 2 Rue de Flandres, 2000 Neuchâtel.
T. (032) 7247050.   085064
Galerie du Pommier, Rue du Pommier 9, 2000 Neuchâ-
tel. T. (032) 7250505, Fax 7213819. - Paint -   085065
Galerie Maison des Jeunes, 2 Rue du Tertre, 2000 Neu-
châtel. T. (032) 7254747. - Paint -   085066
Galerie Média, Moulins 29, 2000 Neuchâtel.
T. (032) 7245323.   085067
L' Orangerie Galerie d'Art, 3a Rue de l'Orangerie, 2000
Neuchâtel. T. (032) 7241010. - Paint -   085068

Neuenkirch (Luzern)
Steinemann, Tino, Rippertschwand, 6206 Neuenkirch.
T. (041) 467 12 97, Fax 4671117. - Paint / Graph / Chi-
na / Tex / Dec / Glass -   085069

Neukirch (Thurgau)
Galerie Hinterdorf, 8578 Neukirch.
T. (071) 6421028.   085070

Neukirch (Egnach) (Thurgau)
BurkARTshof, Burkartshof, 9315 Neukirch (Egnach).
T. (071) 4772831.   085071

Neunkirch (Schaffhausen)
Chelsea Gallery, Vordergasse 44, 8213 Neunkirch.
T. (052) 6813411.   085072

La Neuveville (Bern)
Galleria Noella, 14 Rue Montagu, 2520 La Neuveville.
T. (032) 7512725.   085073

Nidau (Bern)
Cooperative Kreuz Nidau, Hauptstr. 33, 2560 Nidau.
T. (032) 3319303.   085074
Patzer, Lilian, Lyssstr 21, 2560 Nidau.
T. (032) 3656748.   085075

Niedererlinsbach (Solothurn/Aargau)
Galerie Rouge, Sugenreben 16, 5015 Niedererlinsbach.
T. (064) 34 14 39. - Paint -   085076
Galerie Tresor, Hauptstr. 32, 5015 Niedererlinsbach.
T. (064) 34 24 53, 34 26 63.   085077
Roth, Oskar, Sugenreben 16, 5015 Niedererlinsbach.
T. (064) 34 14 39.   085078

Niederscherli (Bern)
Schindler, Schwarzenburgstr. 395, 3145 Niederscherli.
T. (031) 849 14 44. - Paint / Fra -   085079

Niederteufen (Aargau)
Niggli, Ida, Hauptstr. 101, 9052 Niederteufen.
T. (071) 3331244. - Paint / Graph / Sculp -   085080

Le Noirmont (Jura)
Galerie de l'Atelier, Ruelle Foltête, 2725 Le Noirmont.
T. (032) 9531331.   085081

Novaggio (Ticino)
La Galleria, Via Bertoli, 6986 Novaggio.
T. (091) 6062088.   085082

Nürensdorf (Zürich)
Galerie C, Dorfstr. 6, 8309 Nürensdorf.
T. (01) 836 63 09.   085083

Nyon (Vaud)
Atelier, 3 Rue Vieux-Marché, 1260 Nyon.
T. (022) 361 62 70.   085084
Le Coin des Artistes, r. Neuve 8, 1260 Nyon.
T. (022) 3612491. - Paint -   085085
Fischlin, Gérald & Odile, 3 Rue Vieux-Marché, 1260
Nyon. T. (022) 361 62 70. - Paint -   085086
Focale, 4 Pl. du Château, 1260 Nyon. T. (022) 3610966,
Fax 3610966. - Pho -   085087
Galerie Aurum, 1 Rue de la Gare, 1260 Nyon.
T. (022) 3617070.   085088
Galerie de la Côte, 5 Rue de la Gare, 1260 Nyon.
T. (022) 361 59 29.   085089
Galerie Rytz, 21 Rue de Rive, 1260 Nyon.
T. (022) 361 24 91.   085090
Ganslmayr, Archibald, 15 Ch. Canal, 1260 Nyon.
T. (022) 361 87 62.   085091
Morard, Claude, 58 Rue de Rive, 1260 Nyon.   085092

Oberdorf (Solothurn)
Galerie im Dokterhus, Hasenmattweg 2, 4515 Oberdorf.
T. (032) 6232421. - Paint -   085093
Künzi, Reinertstr. 6, 4515 Oberdorf.
T. (032) 6226330.   085094

Oberengstringen (Zürich)
Z Galerie, 8102 Oberengstringen.
T. (01) 750 20 28.   085095

Obererlinsbach (Solothurn/Aargau)
Galerie am Bach, Hauptstr. 11, 5016 Obererlinsbach.
T. (064) 34 15 78.   085096
Wittwer, B. & B., Hauptstr. 11, 5015 Obererlinsbach.
T. (064) 34 15 78.   085097

Oberkulm (Aargau)
Atelier Alexia, 5727 Oberkulm. T. (064) 46 11 54.   085098

Oberuzwil (Sankt Gallen)
Galerie Aukeller, Austr. 1, 9242 Oberuzwil.
T. (071) 9518038.   085099

Oberwil (Basel-Land)
Cackett, Christa, Dr., Vorderbergrain 26, 4104 Oberwil.
T. (061) 4013085. - Paint -   085100

Oensingen (Solothurn)
Schachen Galerie, Schachenstr 21, 4702 Oensingen.
T. (062) 3963355, Fax 3962410.   085101

Oetwil am See (Zürich)
Catrina, Jeannette, Schulhausstr 2, 8618 Oetwil am
See. T. (01) 9291160, Fax 9292956. - Paint -   085102

Oftringen (Aargau)
Meyer, Am Tych 14a, 4665 Oftringen. T. (062) 97 01 11.
- Paint -   085103

Ollon (Vaud)
La Magie du Verre, 1867 Ollon.
T. (024) 4992270.   085104

Olten (Solothurn)
Galerie AG, Haldenstr. 24, 4600 Olten.
T. (062) 32 46 67.   085105
Galerie im Zielemp, Zielempgasse 8, 4600 Olten.
T. (062) 32 13 82. - Graph -   085106
Galerie Martins, Ringstr. 42, 4600 Olten.
T. (062) 32 51 41.   085107
Galerie Panorama, Martin-Disteli-Str. 72, 4600 Olten.
T. (062) 26 57 92.   085108
Galerie Zeta, Hubelistr. 30, 4603 Olten.
T. (062) 2121676.   085109
Hersperger, Urs, Ringstr. 2a, 4600 Olten.
T. (062) 22 32 14. - Repr / Fra -   085110
Jacometti, Thomas, Unterführungsstr. 30, 4600 Olten.
T. (062) 26 40 88.   085111
Schneider, Hans, Konradstr. 32, 4600 Olten.   085112

Onnens (Vaud)
Galerie du Vieux Pressoir, 1425 Onnens.
T. (024) 4361376.   085113

Orbe (Vaud)
Galerie de la Tournelle, 2 Rue de la Tournelle, 1350 Orbe. T. (024) 4413966.   085114

Ostermundigen (Bern)
Bürki Galerie, Mitteldorfstr 1, 3072 Ostermundigen.
T. (031) 9342737, Fax 9342739. - Paint / Paint / Graph / Graph / Fra -   085115

Ottenbach (Zürich)
Galerie Marlène, Lanzenstr. 6, 8913 Ottenbach.
T. (01) 761 21 49.   085116

Ottoberg (Thurgau)
Steinemann, Margrith, 8561 Ottoberg.
T. (071) 6225705.   085117

Payerne (Vaud)
Grands-Magasins La Placette, 27 Grand-Rue, 1530 Payerne. T. (026) 6604444.   085118

Perrefitte (Bern)
Galerie du Tilleul, Le Clos du Tacon 18, 2742 Perrefitte.
T. (032) 4933389.   085119

Perroy (Vaud)
Galerie Zodiaque, Rue du Château, 1166 Perroy.
T. (021) 825 16 66.   085120

Pfäffikon (Zürich)
Ender, Russikerstr. 21, 8330 Pfäffikon.
T. (01) 951 05 30.   085121
Krause, Oskar, Tumbelenstr. 37, 8330 Pfäffikon.
T. (01) 950 30 66, Fax 950 30 66. - Paint -   085122

Pieterlen (Bern)
Fritz-Shaar, Robert, Hauptstr. 26, 2542 Pieterlen.
T. (032) 3771382. - Paint -   085123
Galerie zur Mühle, Bleuenweg 6, 2542 Pieterlen.
T. (032) 3772689.   085124

Pontresina (Graubünden)
Galerie Nova, Chesa Nova, 7504 Pontresina.
T. (081) 8426063, Fax 8333236. - Paint / Graph / Sculp / Draw -   085125

Porrentruy (Jura)
Atelier de Création Visuelle, Rue Pierre Préquignat 36, 2900 Porrentruy. T. (032) 4664366.   085126
Galerie Terre d'Aube, 10 Ch. de l'Ermitage, 2900 Porrentruy. T. (032) 4663638.   085127
Scalbert, Jean-François, 5 Rue de l'Ermitage, 2900 Porrentruy. T. (032) 4661795. - Paint -   085128

Poschiavo (Graubünden)
Galleria Periferia, Via di Puntanai 208, 7742 Poschiavo GR. T. (081) 8440079, Fax 4108879. - Ant / Paint / Sculp -   085130
Galerie PGI, Piazza Comunale, 7742 Poschiavo.   085129

Prato-Sornico (Ticino)
Galerie Prato Sornico, Piazza Grande, 6694 Prato-Sornico. T. (091) 7551384. - Paint -   085131

Pratteln (Basel-Land)
Galerie zem Goldrähmli, Hauptstr. 38, 4133 Pratteln.
T. (061) 821 96 28.   085132

Praz (Vully) (Fribourg)
Galerie au Poisson Rouge, 100 Rte. Principale, 1788 Praz (Vully). T. (026) 6731533, Fax 6732463. - Paint / Graph / Pho -   085133

Promontogno (Graubünden)
Galleria Curtins, Bondo, 7606 Promontogno.
T. (081) 8221734.   085134

Pully (Vaud)
Cailler, Nane, 10 Av. des Deux-Ponts, 1009 Pully.
T. (021) 7282301.   085135
Galerie Beaubourg, 8 Av. du Prieuré, 1009 Pully.
T. (021) 7297747.   085136

Galerie La Gravure, 10 Av. Deux-Ponts, 1009 Pully.
T. (021) 7282301.   085137

Ranzo (Ticino)
Galleria Castelletto al Lago, 6577 Ranzo.   085138

Rapperswil (Sankt Gallen)
Dür, Irma, Kluggasse 10, 8640 Rapperswil.
T. (052) 2109870.   085139
Galerie zum Schloss, Hauptpl. 10, 8640 Rapperswil.
T. (052) 2107453. - Ant / Paint / Graph / Jew / Mul -   085140
Spitzer, Marktgasse 6, 8640 Rapperswil.
T. (052) 2104705.   085141
Trend Art Galerie, Seestr. 7, 8640 Rapperswil.
T. (055) 2109858.   085142

Regensberg (Zürich)
Galerie rote Rose, Oberburg 16, 8158 Regensberg.
T. (01) 853 10 13.   085143
Schürer, Unterburg 141, 8158 Regensberg.
T. (01) 853 04 70.   085144

Reinach (Basel-Land)
Galerie & Möbel us dr Zyt, Hauptstr 63, 4153 Reinach.
T. (061) 7113677.   085145

Renens (Vaud)
Galerie Aurum, 9 Av. 14. Avril, 1020 Renens.
T. (021) 634 16 45.   085146

Rheinfelden (Aargau)
Galerie Salmeschüre, Kupfergasse 15, 4310 Rheinfelden.   085147

Richterswil (Zürich)
Daume, Nicole, Forbweg 10, 8805 Richterswil.
T. (01) 784 24 16.   085148
Galerie Hirt, Dorfstr 34, 8805 Richterswil.
T. (01) 7847975, 7841611. - Graph / Ant -   085149
Scheidegger Art Center, Chüngengasse 3, 8805 Richterswil. T. (01) 784 98 84.   085150
Schobinger, b., Dorfstr. 4, 8805 Richterswil.
T. (01) 784 49 79.   085151

Rickenbach (Solothurn)
A6, Belchenstr 9, 4613 Rickenbach.
T. (062) 2164771.   085152

Riedt bei Erlen (Thurgau)
Euro-Galerie KIS, Hauptstr. 16, 8586 Riedt bei Erlen.
T. (071) 6481313, Fax 6481313. - Paint / Graph / Mul / Draw -   085153

Riehen (Basel-Stadt)
Galerie der Kunst, Burgstr. 120, 4125 Riehen.
T. (061) 641 57 15.   085154
Reitz, Angela, Schmiedgasse 31, 4125 Riehen.
T. (061) 641 31 66, 67 31 67. - Paint / Graph / Sculp / Fra -   085155
Schibli, Robert, Bettingerstr.1, 4125 Riehen.
T. (061) 641 66 51.   085156
Schoeneck, Burgstr. 63, 4125 Riehen.
T. (061) 641 10 60, Fax (061) 641 10 49. - Paint / Graph / Sculp / Fra / Draw -   085157
Thommen, g., Burgstr. 120, 4125 Riehen.
T. (061) 641 57 15.   085158

Rigi Kaltbad (Luzern)
Galerie Rigi-First, Hôtel Rigi-First, 6356 Rigi Kaltbad.
T. (041) 855 14 64.   085159

Rizenbach (Bern)
Lehmann, H. & M., Gümmenen, Ferenbalm, 3206 Rizenbach.   085160

Rolle (Vaud)
Galerie Les Arcades du Port, 6 Pl. du Port, 1180 Rolle.
T. (021) 825 46 61.   085161
La Gravure d'Autrefois, 34 Grand-Rue, 1180 Rolle.
T. (021) 825 36 07.   085162

Romainmôtier (Vaud)
Galerie Le Môtier, 1323 Romainmôtier.
T. (024) 4531429.   085163

Surer, Th. D., Au Lieutenant Baillival, 1323 Romainmôtier. T. (024) 4531458, Fax 4531830. - Ant / Paint / Furn / China / Jew / Silv -   085164

Romanshorn (Thurgau)
Mathis, Rütistr. 13, 8590 Romanshorn.
T. (071) 4634938.   085165

Romont (Fribourg)
Galerie de la Ratière, 107 Rue du Château, 1680 Romont. T. (026) 6521612.   085166

Ronco sopra Ascona (Ticino)
Galleria Decorama, Via Ciseri, 6622 Ronco sopra Ascona. T. (091) 7916841.   085167
Nova, Via Nosetta, 6622 Ronco sopra Ascona.
T. (091) 7916059.   085168

Ropraz (Vaud)
Galerie d'Estre, c/o Café de la Poste, 1088 Ropraz.
T. (021) 903 18 12.   085169

Rorbas (Zürich)
Galerie Adler, Gasthof Adler, 8427 Rorbas.
T. (01) 865 01 12.   085170

Rorschach (Sankt Gallen)
Galerie im Kornhaus, Hafenpl, 9401 Rorschach.
T. (071) 8414062, Fax 8414015. - Paint / Graph / Sculp -   085171
Huber, Kunsthandlung, Trischlistr. 12, 9400 Rorschach.
T. (071) 8412993.   085172
Kunst im Kreuzgang, c/o Kant. Lehrerseminar, 9400 Rorschach.   085173
Seepark Galerie, Sankt Gallerstr. 1, 9400 Rorschach.
T. (071) 8413241, Fax 8417142.   085174

Rosé (Fribourg)
Avry-Art, Centre Commercial, Avry-sur-Matran, 1754 Rosé. T. (026) 4709111.   085175

Rothrist (Aargau)
Reist, Werner, b. Scharfen Ecken, 4852 Rothrist.
T. (062) 44 10 55, Fax 44 36 80.   085176

Rubigen (Bern)
Atelier 17, Stöcklimatte 11, 3113 Rubigen.   085177

Rue (Fribourg)
Galerie de Rue, Grand-Rue, 1671 Rue.
T. (021) 909 56 75.   085178

Rüdlingen (Schaffhausen)
Steinegger, Dorfstr. 49, 8455 Rüdlingen.
T. (01) 867 38 90.   085179

Rüti (Zürich)
Boutique-Galerie Viola, Spitalstr. 5, 8630 Rüti.
T. (01) 32 12 13.   085180

Saanen (Bern)
Saanen-Galerie, Hauptstr., 3792 Saanen.
T. (033) 7448950.   085181

Saas-Fee (Valais)
Galerie Bumann, Chalet Bergkristall, 3906 Saas-Fee.
T. (027) 9571809.   085182

Saint-Maurice (Valais)
Rohner & Berthousoz, 77 Grand-Rue, 1890 Saint-Maurice. T. (024) 4851092.   085183

Saint-Saphorin (Lavaux) (Vaud)
Galerie du Vignoble, Rte. Cantonale, 1813 Saint-Saphorin (Lavaux). T. (021) 921 41 64. - Ant / Paint / Furn -   085184

Saint-Sulpice (Vaud)
Galerie 44, 44 Rue du Centre, 1025 Saint-Sulpice.
T. (021) 691 88 17.   085185

Saint-Ursanne (Bern)
Galerie du Careau, 2882 Saint-Ursanne.   085186
Hemmi, Rolando, 95 Rte. des Malettes, 2882 Saint-Ursanne. T. (032) 4613610. - Paint -   085187

Sankt Gallen

Art Forum, Teufenerstr. 4, 9000 Sankt Gallen.
T. (071) 2229566. - Paint / Sculp / Draw - *085188*
Atelier für Bild- und Objektgestaltung, Vonwilstr. 37,
9000 Sankt Gallen. T. (071) 2778480. - Paint - *085189*
Atelier-Galerie, Greithstr. 6a, 9008 Sankt Gallen.
T. (071) 2456261. *085190*
B + W Galerie, Müller-Friedberg-Str. 34, 9000 Sankt
Gallen. T. (071) 2232364. *085191*
Boutique & Galerie a'fera, Kugelgasse 10, 9000 Sankt
Gallen. T. (071) 2233461. *085192*
Erker-Galerie, Gallusstr. 30-32, 9000 Sankt Gallen.
T. (071) 2227979, Fax 22 79 19. - Paint / Graph /
Sculp - *085193*
Galerie Adlerberg, Sankt-Jakob-Str. 60, 9000 Sankt Gal-
len. T. (071) 2448627. *085194*
Galerie am Park, Notkerstr 14, 9000 Sankt Gallen.
T. (071) 2459555. *085195*
Galerie im Erker, Gallusstr. 32, 9000 Sankt Gallen.
T. (071) 2227979. *085196*
Galerie Neubädli, Bankgasse 10, 9000 Sankt
Gallen. *085197*
Galerie Spisertor, Spisergasse 41, 9000 Sankt Gallen.
T. (071) 2225051, Fax 2225909. - Paint /
Graph - *085198*
Galerie vor der Klostermauer, Frongartenstr. 11, 9000
Sankt Gallen. T. (071) 2228608. - Paint / Graph /
Sculp - *085199*
Galerie zum Strauss, Webergasse 24a, 9000 Sankt Gal-
len. T. (071) 2235058. - Paint - *085200*
Galerie 202, Zürcher Str. 202, 9014 Sankt Gallen.
T. (071) 2775455, Fax 2775455. - Paint - *085201*
Gallery One, Sankt Leonhard-Str. 39, 9000 Sankt Gallen.
T. (071) 2224677. *085202*
Graphica Antiqua, Oberer Graben 46, 9001 Sankt Gallen.
T. (071) 2235016. *085203*
H & K Galerie, Dufourstr. 150, 9000 Sankt Gallen.
T. (071) 2770851. *085204*
Katharinen, Katharinengasse 11, 9000 Sankt Gallen.
T. (071) 2235623. - Paint - *085205*
Klopfer, Herbert, Kirchgasse 14, 9000 Sankt Gallen.
T. (071) 2225366. *085206*
Kunst und Antiquitäten, Sankt Jakob-Str. 62, 9000 Sankt
Gallen. *085207*
Lock, Wilma, Schmiedgasse 15, 9000 Sankt Gallen.
T. (071) 2226252, Fax 2226224. - Paint / Graph /
Sculp / Mul - *085208*
Raubach, Neugasse 39-41, 9000 Sankt Gallen.
T. (071) 2222766, Fax 2226842. - Paint / Fra /
Graph - *085209*
Schneeberger, Christian, Sternackerstr 3, 9000 Sankt
Gallen. T. (071) 2231350, Fax 8451355. - Paint /
Graph / Num / Pho / Draw - *085210*
Thum, Jacques, Rosenbergstr. 22, 9000 Sankt Gallen.
T. (071) 2231578. *085211*
Widmer, Neugasse 35, 9000 Sankt Gallen.
T. (071) 2221626. - Ant / Paint / Graph / Sculp /
Fra - *085212*
Zotti, Marco, Rorschacher Str. 187, 9000 Sankt Gallen.
T. (071) 2454541. - Paint - *085213*

Sankt Moritz (Graubünden)

Galerie Kunstecke, Via dal Bagn, 7500 Sankt Moritz.
T. (081) 8336775. - Paint - *085215*
Galerie Sur Punt, Via del En, 7500 Sankt Moritz.
T. (081) 8335333. *085216*
Galleria Caspar Badrutt, Via dal Bagn 52, 7500 Sankt
Moritz. T. (081) 8337769. *085217*
Galleria Curtins, Postfach 103, 7500 Sankt Moritz.
T. (081) 8332824. *085218*
Katz, David, Via Serlaz 27-29, 7500 Sankt Moritz.
T. (081) 8333090, Fax 8333090. - Paint - *085219*
Kunsthalle St. Moritz, 52 Via dal Bagn, 7500 Sankt Mo-
ritz. T. (081) 8337769. *085220*
Tscheligi, Lajos, Bahnhofstr, 7500 Sankt Moritz.
T. (081) 8332233. - Graph - *085221*
Zervudachi, Peter, Palace-Arcade, 7500 Sankt Moritz.
T. (081) 8333531. *085221a*

Savosa Paese (Ticino)

Arte Più, Via Maraini 58, 6942 Savosa Paese.
T. (091) 9664184. *085222*

Saxon (Valais)

Bovier, Danièle, Rue de Gottefrey, 1907 Saxon.
T. (027) 7443076. *085223*

Schaffhausen

Art Decor, Vordergasse 18, 8201 Schaffhausen.
T. (052) 6256142. *085224*
Einhorn, Fronwagpl 8, 8200 Schaffhausen.
T. (052) 6248172, Fax 6248163. - Paint - *085225*
Galerie an der Stadthausgasse, Stadthausgasse 2b,
8200 Schaffhausen. - Paint - *085226*
Galerie Tuskulum, Bachstr. 53, 8200 Schaffhausen.
T. (052) 6251928. *085227*
Grossmann, Ulric, Kohlfirststr 36, 8203 Schaffhausen.
T. (052) 6256055, Fax 6256055. *085228*

Schatzalp (Davos) (Graubünden)

Schatzalp Galerie, Berghotel Schatzalp, 7270 Schatzalp
(Davos). T. (081) 4138331, Fax 4131344. - Paint /
Graph / Mod - *085229*

Schenkon (Luzern)

Galerie Zum Diebeturm, Obertannberg 11, 6214
Schenkon. *085230*

Schlieren (Zürich)

Maag, Arthur, Schulstr 78, 8952 Schlieren. *085231*

Schönenwerd (Solothurn)

Galerie Zisterne, Dorf 34, 5012 Schönenwerd. *085232*

Schüpfen (Bern)

Galerie du Banneret, Bergackerweg 4, 3054 Schüpfen.
T. (031) 8792245, Fax 8792215. - Paint /
Sculp - *085233*

Schwanden (Glarus)

Galerie G, Vorderdorfstr. 31, 8762 Schwanden.
T. (058) 6442597. - Paint - *085234*

Schwarzenburg (Bern)

Bachmann, Monika, Schw'bg. Höhe, 3150 Schwarzen-
burg. T. (031) 731 14 49. *085235*
Galerie Schmiedgasse, Schmiedgasse 10, 3150
Schwarzenburg. T. (031) 7311030. *085236*

Schwyz (Schwyz)

Trütsch, Maria, Hilf Str., 6430 Schwyz.
T. (041) 811 11 67. - Graph / Fra - *085237*

Le Sentier (Vaud)

Galerie Betsaleel, 16 Grand-Rue, 1347 Le Sentier.
T. (021) 845 69 73. *085238*
Galerie de l'Essort, 2 Grand-Rue, 1347 Le Sentier.
T. (021) 845 57 22. *085239*

Servion (Vaud)

Galerie de Servion, Rte du Zoo, 1077 Servion.
T. (021) 9031914, Fax 9031914. *085240*

Sessa (Ticino)

Galleria St. Maria Sessa, 6981 Sessa.
T. (091) 6081660. *085241*

Sierre (Valais)

ASLEC, 8 Av. du Marché, 3960 Sierre.
T. (027) 4552215. *085242*
Forum d'Art Contemporain, 10 Av. du Rothorn, 3960
Sierre. T. (027) 4561514. *085243*
Galerie des Buissonnets, 31 Saint-Georges, 3960 Sierre.
T. (027) 4551504. *085244*
Galerie du Château de Villa, 4 Rue Sainte-Catherine,
3960 Sierre. T. (027) 4551896. *085245*
Galerie du Rhône, 15 Ch. des Peupliers, 3960 Sierre.
T. (027) 4553623. *085246*
Galerie Isoz, 10 Ch. des Cyprès, 3960 Sierre.
T. (027) 4557781. *085247*
Hôtel de Ville, Salle de Récréation, 3960 Sierre.
T. (027) 4567171. *085248*
Maison de Courten, 3960 Sierre.
T. (027) 4562646. *085249*

Sion (Valais)

Galerie Beaux-Arts, 30 Av. de la Gare, 1950 Sion.
T. (027) 3234969. *085250*
Galerie des Vergers, 2 Rue des Vergers, 1950 Sion.
T. (027) 3221035. *085251*

Galerie du Diable, 31 Rue des Creusets, 1950 Sion.
T. (027) 3229686. *085252*
Galerie du Midi, Ruelle du Midi 19, 1950 Sion.
T. (027) 3231751. *085253*
Galerie du Rhône, 17 Grand-Pont, 1950 Sion.
T. (027) 3220050. *085254*
Galerie du Vieux Sion, 7 Rue de Conthey, 1950 Sion.
T. (027) 3223180. *085255*
Galerie Grande Fontaine, 19 Grand-Pont, 1950 Sion.
T. (027) 3224351. - Paint / Sculp - *085256*
Galerie Theodule, 1 Pl. Cathédrale, 1950 Sion.
T. (027) 3229468. *085257*

Siselen (Bern)

Galerie 25, Juchen 25, 2577 Siselen. T. (032) 3962071,
Fax 3962071. - Paint / Graph / Sculp / Rel /
China - *085258*

Sissach (Basel-Land)

Kunsthalle Sissach, Alte Zunskerstr. 6a, 4450 Sissach.
T. (061) 382 35 52. *085259*

Sitzberg (Zürich)

Galerie Zum Tenn, Ruppen, 8495 Sitzberg.
T. (052) 3852267. *085260*

Solothurn

Chutz, Landhausquai 3, 4500 Solothurn.
T. (032) 6228929. *085261*
Gässli-Galerie, Seilergasse 6, 4500 Solothurn.
T. (032) 6226980. *085262*
Galerie Hermes, Hermesbühlstr. 23, 4500 Solothurn.
T. (032) 6235805. *085263*
Galerie Stadtbad, Klosterpl. 15, 4500 Solothurn.
T. (032) 6236817. *085264*
Goldschmiede Galerie, Hauptgasse 7, 4500 Solothurn.
T. (032) 6228979. *085265*
Imhof Galerie, Kreuzgasse 5, 4500 Solothurn.
T. (032) 6223140. *085266*
Künstlerhaus, Schmiedengasse 11, 4500 Solothurn.
T. (032) 6223140. *085267*
Medici, Römerstr. 1, 4500 Solothurn. T. (032) 6228171.
- Paint / Graph / Sculp / Draw - *085268*
Rust's Cartoonoptikum, Am Marktpl., 4500
Solothurn. *085269*
Schlüter, Bernhard, Hauptgasse 2, 4500 Solothurn.
T. (032) 6221246. *085270*
Schopfgalerie, Rötistr. 22, 4500 Solothurn.
T. (032) 6224288. *085271*

Soulce (Jura)

Huber, Camillo, 8 Rte. Principale, 2864 Soulce.
T. (032) 4265777. - Paint - *085272*

Speicher (Aargau)

Galerie Speicher, Reutenen 19, 9042 Speicher.
T. (071) 3441877. *085273*

Staad (Sankt Gallen)

Schloss Greifenstein, Steinig Tisch, 9422 Staad.
T. (071) 8551310. - Paint / Graph - *085274*

Stadel b. Niederglatt (Zürich)

Dorfgalerie, 8174 Stadel b. Niederglatt. *085275*

Stäfa (Zürich)

Atelier hrl, Rietstr. 3, 8712 Stäfa.
T. (01) 926 33 88. *085276*
Galerie Trotte im Mies, Rietstr. 3, 8712 Stäfa.
T. (01) 926 33 88. *085277*
Galerie 9, Goethestr. 9, 8712 Stäfa.
T. (01) 926 45 42. *085278*
Kehlhof-Galerie, Seestr. 185, 8712 Stäfa.
T. (01) 926 60 79. - Paint / Graph / Sculp / Pho /
Draw - *085279*
Rey, Max, Bauertacherstr. 12a, 8712 Stäfa.
T. (01) 926 61 22. *085280*

Stans (Nidwalden)

Galerie am Dorfplatz, 6370 Stans.
T. (041) 610 97 27. *085281*
Galerie Chäslager, Alter Postpl. 3, 6370 Stans.
T. (041) 610 41 60. - Paint / Graph / Sculp - *085282*

Staufen (Aargau)
Kirchhofer & Guarnieri, Wiligraben 60, 5603
Staufen. *085283*

Steckborn (Thurgau)
Galerie 73, Seestr. 73, 8266 Steckborn.
T. (052) 7612346. - Paint / Graph / Fra - *085284*

Steinach (Sankt Gallen)
Galerie Villa Weidenhof, Weidenhofstr. 14, 9323 Steinach. T. (071) 4467006. *085285*

Steinhausen (Zug)
Bell'Arte R. Orlandi, Grabenackerstr. 50, 6312 Steinhau-
sen. T. (041) 741 18 21. *085286*
Bolli, Elfi, Grabenackerstr. 46, 6312 Steinhausen.
T. (041) 741 19 55. *085287*

Sursee (Luzern)
Galerie Somehus, 6210 Sursee. *085288*

Tavannes (Bern)
Galeries Nouvelles Au Louvre, 32 Grand Rue, 2710
Tavannes. *085289*

Tenero (Ticino)
Matasci, Via alla Stazione, 6598 Tenero.
T. (091) 7356034, Fax 7356019. - Paint - *085290*

Teufen (Appenzell-Ausserrhoden)
Niggli, Ida, Hauptstr. 101, 9053 Teufen. *085291*

Thônex (Genève)
Espace Caran d'Ache, 19 Ch. du Foron, 1226 Thônex.
T. (022) 348 02 04. - Paint - *085292*
Topos Les 5 Lieux, 18 Av. Suisse, 1226 Thônex.
T. (022) 348 61 62. - Paint - *085293*

Thun (Bern)
Aarehüsli, Rathausquai 5, 3600 Thun. T. (033) 2228850.
- Paint - *085294*
Galerie Aarequai, Freienhofgasse 10, 3600 Thun.
T. (033) 2223045. *085295*
Galerie im Seewinkel 4, Im Seewinkel 4, 3645 Thun.
T. (033) 3351646. *085296*
Galerie Klubschule, Bernstr. 1a, 3600 Thun.
T. (033) 2232366. *085297*
Galerie Usco, Bälliz 67, 3601 Thun.
T. (033) 2224322. *085298*
Galerie zur alten deutschen Schule, Obere Hauptgasse
32, 3600 Thun. T. (033) 2233371. *085299*
Gunten, Wilfried von, Alte Oele, Freienhofgasse 10,
3600 Thun. T. (033) 2223045. - Paint / Graph / Sculp /
Draw - *085300*
Nielson & Wütrich, Obere Hauptgasse 32, 3600 Thun.
T. (033) 2233371. *085301*
USCO-Galerie Verlag, Obere Hauptstr. 83, 3601 Thun.
T. (033) 2224322. *085302*
Vario Deco, Rathauspl. 5, 3600 Thun. T. (033) 2224201.
- Paint - *085303*
Wermuth, P., Obere Hauptgasse 7, 3600 Thun.
T. (033) 2224740. - Paint / Fra - *085304*

Thusis (Graubünden)
Galerie zur Alten Schmiede, Feldstr. 7430 Thusis.
T. (081) 6511252. *085305*

Torricella (Ticino)
Blendinger, Paul, 6808 Torricella. T. (091) 9452568.
- Paint / Graph - *085306*

La Tour-de-Peilz (Vaud)
Chevalley, Annie, 15 Bourg-Dessous, 1814 La Tour-de-
Peilz. T. (021) 944 26 16. *085307*
De l'Artiste, 4 Av. de Traménaz, 1814 La Tour-de-Peilz.
T. (021) 944 52 80. *085308*
Galerie du Port, 15 Rue du Bourg-Dessous, 1814 La
Tour-de-Peilz. T. (021) 944 26 16. *085309*

Twann (Bern)
Galerie Salzbütti, Dorfgasse 100, 2513 Twann.
T. (032) 3151666. *085310*

Uetikon am See (Zürich)
Kronen-Galerie, Seestr. 117, 8707 Uetikon am See.
T. (01) 920 61 39. *085311*

Unterengstringen (Zürich)
Eber, Nicolas, Dr., Im Aegelsee 2, 8103 Unterengstrin-
gen. T. (01) 750 55 81. - Paint - *085312*
Galerie Bergstrasse, Bergstr. 15, 8103 Unterengstrin-
gen. T. (01) 750 38 24, Fax 750 38 24. - Paint / Graph /
Sculp - *085313*

Unterseen (Bern)
Galerie Weissenau, Weissenaustr. 6, 3800 Unterseen.
T. (033) 8221041. *085314*
Gallery Ibex, Untere Gasse 9, 3800 Unterseen.
T. (033) 8222060. *085315*

Uster (Zürich)
Atelier Armin Luginbühl, Brunnenstr. 21, 8610 Uster.
T. (01) 941 50 55. *085316*
Villa am Aabach, Brauereistr. 13, 8610 Uster.
T. (01) 940 99 91. *085317*
Villa Bianchi, Brunnenstr. 27, 8610 Uster.
T. (01) 941 51 20. - Paint / Sculp - *085318*
Zumhofen, Noëlle, Gerichtsstr. 1, 8610 Uster. *085319*

Vallorbe (Vaud)
Galerie Artcadache, 5 Rue Grandes-Forges, 1337 Vallorbe. T. (021) 8432770. *085320*

Venthône (Valais)
Gherri-Moro, Rte. de Chaloie, 3973 Venthône.
T. (027) 4555757. *085321*

Vercorin (Valais)
Galerie Fontany, 3967 Vercorin.
T. (027) 4558282. *085322*

Vésenaz (Genève)
Galerie La Collection, 151a Rte. de la Capite, 1222 Vé-
senaz. T. (022) 752 50 02. *085323*
Sedlmajer, Georges, 24 Ch. Rayes, 1222 Vésenaz.
T. (022) 752 28 31. - Paint - *085324*

Vessy (Genève)
Calimala, 25 Ch. Tour-de-Pinchat, 1234 Vessy.
T. (022) 784 01 43. *085325*

Vevey (Vaud)
Galerie du Capricorne, Rue Conseil, 1800 Vevey.
T. (021) 921 35 90. *085326*
Galerie du Théâtre de la Grenette, 1800 Vevey.
T. (021) 921 60 37. *085327*
Galerie La Lune, 5 Rue A.-Steinlen, 1800 Vevey.
T. (021) 921 85 54. *085328*
Galerie La Spirale, 26 Rue de la Madeleine, 1800 Vevey.
T. (021) 9218182. *085329*
La Lune Haralambis, 7 Quai Perdonnet, 1800
Vevey. *085330*

Veyrier (Genève)
Galerie La Mansarde, Chemin sous-Balme, 1255 Veyrier.
T. (022) 784 20 22. *085331*

Viganello (Ticino)
Galleria d'Arte, Via La Santa 17, 6962 Viganello. *085332*
Galleria La Colomba, Via al Lido 9, 6962 Viganello CP
139. T. (091) 9722181. *085333*
Monza, Emilio, Via La Santa 17, 6962 Viganello.
T. (091) 9416263. *085334*

Villars-sur-Ollon (Vaud)
Galerie Brise d'Argentine, Av Centrale, 1884 Villars-sur-
Ollon. T. (024) 4953993. *085335*
Graf, Alain, Rue Centrale, 1884 Villars-sur-Ollon.
T. (024) 4951251. *085336*

Villeneuve (Vaud)
Galerie d'Art du Vieux Villeneuve, 27 Grand-Rue, 1844
Villeneuve. T. (021) 960 23 61. *085337*

Visp (Valais)
Galerie Zur Schützenlaube, Gräfibielstr., 3930 Visp.
T. (027) 9466161. *085338*

Volketswil (Zürich)
Steinmetz, Hölzliwiesenstr. 2, 8604 Volketswil.
T. (01) 945 59 42, Fax 945 13 23. - Graph - *085339*
Vaclavik, Germaine, Rigiweg 10, 8604 Volketswil.
T. (01) 945 55 75. *085340*

Vullierens (Vaud)
Galerie Château de Vullierens, 1115 Vullierens.
T. (021) 869 94 43. *085341*
Galerie du Clocher, Rte. Grancy, 1115 Vullierens.
T. (021) 869 91 67. *085342*

Wädenswil (Zürich)
Galerie Tuchfabrik, Einsiedlerstr., 8820 Wädenswil.
T. (01) 780 63 82. *085343*

Wald (Zürich)
Zahn, Alfred & Irene, 8636 Wald.
T. (052) 2462071. *085344*

Waldstatt (Aargau)
Galerie Nördli, Dorf 171, 9104 Waldstatt.
T. (071) 3523951. *085345*

Wangen an der Aare (Bern)
Galerie W, Städtli 17, 4705 Wangen an der Aare.
T. (032) 6312323. *085346*
Städtligalerie, Vorstadt 1, 4705 Wangen an der Aare.
T. (032) 6311885. - Paint / Graph / Sculp - *085347*
Steinke, Käthy, Breitmattstr 2, 3380 Wangen an der Aa-
re. T. (032) 6311666, Fax 6311666. - Paint /
Sculp - *085348*

Wangen bei Dübendorf (Zürich)
Galerie am Dorfplatz, Dorfplatz, 8602 Wangen bei Dübendorf. T. (01) 833 34 06. *085349*

Weisslingen (Zürich)
Mülli-Galerie, Dorfstr. 65, 8484 Weisslingen.
T. (052) 3841514. *085350*

Wermatswil (Zürich)
Galerie Oswald, Vordergasse, 8615 Wermatswil.
T. (01) 940 88 47. *085351*

Wettingen (Aargau)
Atelier zum goldenen Rahmen, Bahnhofstr. 1, 5430 Wet-
tingen. T. (056) 226 20 56. *085352*
Ateliergemeinschaft Spinnerei, Klosterstr. 20, 5430 Wet-
tingen. T. (056) 226 44 19. - Paint / Sculp / Pho /
Draw - *085353*
Galerie Zum Türmli, Bahnhofstr. 1, 5430 Wettingen.
T. (056) 226 40 10. *085354*
Gluri Suter Huus Galerie, Alberich Zwyssigstr. 76, 5430
Wettingen. T. (056) 226 29 69. *085355*

Wetzikon (Zürich)
Art Cohen, Frohbergstr 32, 8620 Wetzikon.
T. (01) 9325702, Fax 9325708. *085356*
CEVO, Bahnhofstr. 289, 8623 Wetzikon. T. (01) 9304647,
9304113. *085357*

Wichtrach (Bern)
Henze & Ketterer, Kirchstr. 26, 3114 Wichtrach.
T. (031) 7810601, Fax (031) 7810722. - Paint / Graph /
Sculp / Draw - *085358*

Wil (Sankt Gallen)
Galerie am Goldenen Boden, Marktgasse 80, 9500 Wil.
T. (071) 9113966, Fax 9113966. - Paint / Graph /
Fra - *085359*
Galerie an der Marktgasse, Marktgasse 42, 9500 Wil.
T. (071) 9115558. *085360*
Galerie beim Rathaus, Marktgasse 59, 9500 Wil.
T. (071) 9111317. *085361*
Rapp, Peter, Toggenburgerstr. 139, 9500 Wil.
T. (071) 9237744, Fax 9239220. - Paint /
Graph - *085362*
Siegrist, Rudolf, Marktgasse 66, 9500 Wil.
T. (071) 9113966. - Paint - *085363*

Willisau (Luzern)
Höckli, Menznauerstr., 6130 Willisau.
T. (041) 970 27 70. *085364*

Winterthur (Zürich)
Galerie am Dorfplatz, Feldstr. 1, 8407 Winterthur.
T. (052) 213 76 67. - Ant / Paint / Furn / Sculp - *085365*
Galerie d'Art, Marktgasse 52, 8400 Winterthur.
T. (052) 2133305. *085366*
Galerie Wülfinger, Wülfingerstr. 235, 8408 Winterthur.
T. (052) 2215361. *085367*

Galerie zum Jakobskampf, Obergasse 8, 8400 Winterthur. T. (052) 212 55 34. *085368*

Wirth, Marie-Luise, Spitalgasse 3, 8400 Winterthur. T. (052) 2125520, Fax 2125520. - Paint - *085369*

Worb (Bern)

Atelier Ausstellungen, Enggisteinstr. 2, 3076 Worb. T. (031) 992 59 25. - Paint - *085370*

Galerie Farb Worb, Farbstr 23, 3076 Worb. T. (031) 8391159. - Paint / Graph / China / Sculp / Tex / Draw - *085371*

Yens (Vaud)

Cimaise, Le Carroz, 1137 Yens. T. (021) 3220544. *085372*

Yverdon-les-Bains (Vaud)

ACF Art Collector's Fund, Fabarda, 27 Ch. de Floreyres, 1400 Yverdon-les-Bains. T. (024) 4252908. *085373*

La Chaumière de Siebenthal, 21 St. Roch, 1400 Yverdon-les-Bains. T. (024) 21 27 62. *085374*

Vuille, Louis, Maison-Rouge 5, 1400 Yverdon-les-Bains. T. (024) 210626, Fax 212544. *085375*

Zell (Luzern)

Bürli, Josef, Hinterdorf, 6144 Zell. T. (041) 988 10 46. *085376*

Meier, Priska, Hauptstr., 6144 Zell. T. (041) 988 15 66. - Paint / Graph / Sculp / Draw - *085377*

Zermatt (Valais)

Schindler, Kurt, Résidence Bellevue, 3920 Zermatt. T. (027) 9671119, Fax 9675524. - Paint / Draw - *085378*

Zofingen (Aargau)

Auktionshaus Zofingen, Klösterligasse 4, 4800 Zofingen. T. (062) 7516351-53, Fax 7516354. *085379*

Galerie Media, Obere Promenade 7, 4800 Zofingen. T. (062) 516891. *085380*

Geissbühler, Pitsch, Im Talpi, Mühlethalstr. 24, 4800 Zofingen. T. (062) 51 10 80/51 78 17. *085381*

Zollikon (Zürich)

Gut, Nelly, Rietstr. 37, 8702 Zollikon. T. (01) 391 42 83. *085383*

Stummer, Jörg, Sonnenfeldstr 23, 8702 Zollikon. T. (01) 3914901. - Paint / Draw - *085383a*

Zuckenriet (Sankt Gallen)

Galerie Fueterchrippe, Unterdorf, 9526 Zuckenriet. T. (071) 9471611. - Paint / Graph / Pho / Draw - *085384*

Zürich

ACP, Viviane Ehrli, Austr 38, 8045 Zürich. T. (01) 4636353, Fax 4612552. - Paint / Sculp / Draw - *085385*

Alicana Fine Art, Sonneggstr. 84, 8006 Zürich. T. (01) 361 45 55. *085386*

Allemann, Ruth, Stampfenbachstr 38, 8006 Zürich. T. (01) 3631637. *085387*

Am Ring, Butzenstr. 40, 8038 Zürich. T. (01) 481 87 22. *085388*

Am Züriberg, Krönleinstr. 1, 8044 Zürich. T. (01) 252 70 09. *085389*

American Folk Art Gallery, Spiegelgasse 7, 8001 Zürich. T. (01) 261 58 88. *085390*

Ammann, Thomas, Restelbergstr 97, 8044 Zürich. T. (01) 2529052, Fax 2528245. - Paint - *085391*

Andersen, Annamarie M., Bodmerstr 8, 8002 Zürich. T. (01) 2811881, Fax (01) 2811882. - Paint / Graph / Sculp - *085392*

Antik-Galerie Irchel, Winterthurerstr 66, 8006 Zürich. T. (01) 3626474, Fax 3626474. - Ant / Paint / Graph / Furn / China / Silv / Glass / Mod / Draw - *085393*

Architektur Forum, Neumarkt 15, 8001 Zürich. T. (01) 2529295, Fax 2620050. *085394*

Arrigo, Alice, Hirschgraben 3, 8001 Zürich. T. (01) 262 25 44. *085395*

Art Cohen, Bahnhofstr 78, 8001 Zürich. T. (01) 2211966. *085396*

Art Poster Gallery, Stadelhoferpassage 28, 8001 Zürich. T. (01) 252 42 55. *085397*

Art-Repro, Scheideggstr. 95, 8038 Zürich. T. (01) 482 60 45. *085398*

Art Selection, Zeltweg 50, 8032 Zürich. T. (01) 261 48 11, Fax 251 09 50. *085399*

Arteba Galerie, Zeltweg 27, 8032 Zürich. T. (01) 262 32 62, Fax 262 33 63. - Paint / Pho / Draw - *085400*

Arts & Decors, Kirchgasse 33, 8001 Zürich. T. (01) 261 32 21. *085401*

Aschbacher, L., Fraumünsterstr. 9, 8001 Zürich. T. (01) 211 86 20. - Paint - *085402*

Atelier d'Art, Neumarkt 1, 8001 Zürich. T. (01) 252 66 70. *085403*

Atelier Messerli, Manessestr. 69, 8003 Zürich. T. (01) 463 55 55. *085404*

Atelier 11, Ohnstr. 16, 8050 Zürich. T. (01) 311 71 55. *085405*

Barth, Conrad-Ulrich, Schweighofstr. 206, 8045 Zürich. T. (01) 461 01 84. *085406*

Baumberger, Edward, Asylstr 58, 8032 Zürich. T. (01) 2611510. - Paint / Graph / Sculp / Tex / Draw - *085407*

Baumgartner, Werner, Schaffhauser Str. 440, 8050 Zürich. T. (01) 301 37 12. *085408*

Baviera, Peter, Segantinistr. 129, 8049 Zürich. T. (01) 341 42 51. *085409*

Baviera, Silvio R., Zwinglistr. 10, 8004 Zürich. T. (01) 241 29 96. *085410*

Bettina, Großmünsterpl. 2, 8001 Zürich. T. (01) 32 70 71. *085411*

Bilderhuus Krone, Schaffhauserstr. 6, 8006 Zürich. T. (01) 361 53 11. *085412*

Bischofberger, Bruno, Utoquai 29, 8008 Zürich. T. (01) 262 40 20, Fax 262 28 97. - Paint / Graph / Sculp / Draw - *085413*

La Bohème, Merkurstr. 31, 8032 Zürich. T. (01) 252 71 97. *085414*

Bolliger, Hans, Lenggstr 14, 8008 Zürich. T. (01) 3815888. - Graph - *085415*

Bommer, Werner, Weinbergstr 22a, 8001 Zürich. T. (01) 2518481, Fax (01) 2618770. *085416*

Brandstetter & Wyss, Limmatstr 270, 8005 Zürich. T. (01) 4404019, Fax 4404019. *085417*

Brual, Seefeldstr. 58, 8008 Zürich. T. (01) 251 44 48. *085418*

Brunner, Susi, Spitalgasse 10, 8001 Zürich. T. (01) 2512342, Fax 2612349. *085419*

Büttiker, Katharina, Wühre 9, 8001 Zürich. T. (01) 2116758, Fax 2121168. *085420*

Carrara, Austr. 22, 8045 Zürich. T. (01) 462 36 31. *085421*

Chervet, Denise, Walchestr. 17, 8006 Zürich. T. (01) 361 36 12. *085422*

City Galerie, Löwenstr. 2, 8001 Zürich. T. (01) 212 22 30. *085423*

Collection Dobe, Brunaustr 15, 8002 Zürich. T. (01) 2016767, Fax 2017158. *085424*

Cuéllar, Nathan-Arturo, Bürglistr 18, 8002 Zürich. T. (01) 2812181, Fax (01) 2812181. - Draw - *085425*

David, R., Rämistr. 33, 8024 Zürich. T. (01) 262 22 54, Fax 251 27 78. - Eth - *085426*

Derby, Sihlferdstr. 85, 8004 Zürich. T. (01) 241 83 23. *085427*

Dolejal, T., Wehntalerstr. 492, 8046 Zürich. T. (01) 371 96 11. *085428*

Dolezal, Peter, Dr., Wehntalerstr. 492, 8046 Zürich. T. (01) 371 96 11. *085429*

Dosch, Anita, Zurlindenstr. 213, 8003 Zürich. T. (01) 451 29 27. - Paint - *085430*

Dosch, Anita, Elisabethenstr. 26, 8004 Zürich. T. (01) 291 33 53. *085431*

Edition & Galerie 999, Winterthurerstr. 16, 8006 Zürich. T. (01) 362 18 76. *085432*

Ehrensperger, Franz, Rämistr. 38, 8024 Zürich. T. (01) 251 01 24. - Paint / Graph / Sculp - *085433*

Etagen-Galerie Valentin, Kirchgasse 21, 8001 Zürich. T. (01) 252 43 82. - Paint / Graph / Sculp - *085434*

Färber & Sohn, J.J., Dufourstr. 104, 8008 Zürich. T. (01) 383 66 49. *085435*

Falk + Falk, Kirchgasse 28, 8001 Zürich. T. (01) 2625657, Fax 2616202. - Graph / Draw - *085436*

Fedjuschin, Victor, Fraumünsterstr 8, 8001 Zürich. T. (01) 2213334/69, Fax 2213326. *085437*

Feilchenfeldt, Walter, Freie Str 116, 8032 Zürich. T. (01) 3837960, Fax 3839948. - Paint / Draw - *085438*

Forsblom, Kaj, Bleicherweg 7, 8002 Zürich. T. (01) 2019209. *085439*

Fortuna Galerie, Kirchgasse 31, 8001 Zürich. T. (01) 2612862. - Graph / Arch - *085440*

Forum Fine Art, Beethovenstr 3, 8002 Zürich. T. (01) 2021503, Fax (01) 2015665. - Paint / Graph / Sculp / Draw - *085441*

Fotogalerie Limmatplatz, Limmatstr 152, 8005 Zürich. T. (01) 2772744, Fax 2772897. - Pho - *085442*

Furrer, Albert, Stäbelistr. 2, 8006 Zürich. T. (01) 361 67 09. *085443*

Galerie A 16, Ausstellungsstr. 16a, 8005 Zürich. T. (01) 272 76 01. *085444*

Galerie am Hinterberg, Hinterbergstr. 15, 8044 Zürich. T. (01) 251 54 57. - Paint / Graph / Sculp / Fra - *085445*

Galerie Annapurna, Scheitergasse 10, 8001 Zürich. T. (01) 262 07 80. *085446*

Galerie Bob van Orsouw, Limmatstr 270, 8005 Zürich. T. (01) 273 11 00, Fax 2731102. *085447*

Galerie Commercio, Mühlebachstr. 2, 8008 Zürich. T. (01) 252 41 24, Fax 261 38 79. *085448*

Galerie Drei König, Beethovenstr. 20, 8002 Zürich. T. (01) 202 47 64. *085449*

Galerie Frankengasse, Frankengasse 6, 8024 Zürich. T. (01) 261 23 55. *085450*

Galerie für Glas-und Hinterglasmalerie, Sternenstr. 24, 8002 Zürich. T. (01) 202 19 51. *085451*

Galerie im Splügenschloss, Splügenstr 2, 8002 Zürich. T. (01) 2899999, Fax 2899998. *085452*

Galerie in der Kleeweid, Kleeweid 2, 8001 Zürich. T. (01) 482 43 48. *085453*

Galerie Joy, Bleicherweg 21, 8002 Zürich.
T. (01) 202 22 77. 085454
Galerie Klubschule Migros, Engelstr. 6, 8004 Zürich.
T. (01) 242 61 50. - Paint - 085455
Galerie Kranich, Selnaustr. 48-50, 8001 Zürich.
T. (01) 211 75 19. 085456
Galerie Le Clou, Birmensdorferstr. 174, 8003 Zürich.
T. (01) 463 35 36. 085457
Galerie Limmat, Rämistr. 45, 8001 Zürich.
T. (01) 252 84 33. - Paint - 085458
Galerie Margine, Stampfenbachstr. 59, 8006 Zürich.
T. (01) 362 27 66, Fax 363 34 69. - Paint / Graph / Furn /
Sculp / Draw - 085459
Galerie Médicis, Bederstr. 101, 8002 Zürich.
T. (01) 201 70 77. 085460
Galerie Palette, Zeltweg 40, 8032 Zürich.
T. (01) 252 53 43. - Paint / Sculp - 085461
Galerie Parade, Bahnhofstr. 22, 8001 Zürich.
T. (01) 221 15 25. 085462
Galerie Proarta, Bleicherweg 20, 8002 Zürich.
T. (01) 2020202, Fax (01) 2024592. - Paint / Graph /
Furn / Mul / Draw - 085463
Galerie Rämi, Rämistr. 33, 8001 Zürich.
T. (01) 251 34 06, Fax 251 91 04. - Paint - 085464
Galerie Raymond Bollag 1 und 2, Dienerstr 21, 8004 Zü-
rich. T. (01) 2428900, Fax (01) 2428942. 085465
Galerie Rindlisbacher, Zürichbergstr. 21, Postfach 331,
8028 Zürich. T. (01) 261 21 31, Fax 261 08 18. - Ant /
Paint / Sculp - 085466
Galerie Schlossgasse, Schlossgasse 28, 8003 Zürich.
T. (01) 463 99 77. 085467
Galerie sec 52, Josefstr. 52, 8005 Zürich.
T. (01) 271 18 18. 085468
Galerie Seestr. 43/BH Enge, Seestr. 43, 8002 Zürich.
T. (01) 202 85 35. 085469
Galerie Sonnhalde, Sonnhaldenstr. 6, 8032 Zürich.
T. (01) 261 67 88. - Paint / Graph / Repr /
Sculp - 085470
Galerie Trittligasse, Neustadtgasse 1, 8001 Zürich.
T. (01) 252 40 60. 085471
Galerie Vista Nova, Seefeldstr. 60, 8008 Zürich.
T. (01) 251 45 17. 085472
Galerie Walcheturm, Walchestr. 6, 8035 Zürich.
T. (01) 252 10 96. - Paint / Graph / Sculp - 085473
Galerie Walu, Rämistr. 33, 8024 Zürich.
T. (01) 262 22 54, Fax 251 27 78. - Eth - 085474
Galerie Wühre, Wühre 9, 8001 Zürich.
T. (01) 221 18 70. 085475
Galerie Ypsilon, Augustinergasse 4, 8001 Zürich.
T. 2116501. 085476
Galerie Zentrum, Gsteigstr. 2, 8049 Zürich.
T. (01) 341 65 70. 085477
Galerie zur blauen Schnecke, Oberdorfstr. 24, 8001 Zü-
rich. T. (01) 252 37 93. 085478
Galerie Zur Stockeregg, Stockerstr. 33, 8022 Zürich
Postfach. T. (01) 202 69 25, Fax 202 82 51.
- Pho - 085479
Galerie 2, Rötelsteig 4, 8037 Zürich.
T. (01) 362 33 26. 085480
Gallery Tara, Richard-Wagner-Str. 16, 8002 Zürich.
T. (01) 202 94 55. 085481
Gamberucci, Enrico, Fortunagasse 20, 8001 Zürich.
T. (01) 221 04 17. 085482
Govinda Kulturtreff, Preyergasse 16, 8025 Zürich.
T. (01) 251 88 59. 085483
Haftmann, Roswitha, Rütistr 28, 8030 Zürich.
T. (01) 2512435, Fax 2514519. 085484

Haubensack, J., Froschaugasse 11, 8001 Zürich.
T. (01) 2512618. - Graph - 085485
Heimatwerk, Rudolf-Brun-Brücke, 8001 Zürich.
T. (01) 2115780, Fax (01) 2121437. - Paint - 085486
Hipp, Wilhelm, Scheideggerstr. 120, 8038 Zürich.
T. (01) 482 65 75. 085487
Hohl, Claudine, Am Schanzengraben 15, 8002 Zürich.
T. (01) 2027243. 085488
Holckh-Falkenberg, Bahnhofstr 69, 8001 Zürich.
T. (01) 2128505, Fax 2128505. - Paint - 085489
Howeg, Waffenplatzstr 1, 8002 Zürich. T. (01) 2010650,
Fax (01) 2010650. 085490
Huber, Semiha, Talstr 16, 8001 Zürich. T. (01) 2116661,
Fax 2112674. - Paint / Sculp - 085491
Hufschmid, Esther, Predigergasse 14, 8001 Zürich.
T. (01) 252 03 66, Fax 2520366. - Paint / Graph / Sculp /
Draw - 085492
Humbel, Hans, Augustinergasse 15, 8001 Zürich.
T. (01) 2116050. 085493
Ikonen Galerie Sophia, Weggengasse 3, 8001 Zürich.
T. (01) 211 25 44, Fax 212 12 90. 085494
Im Ried, Altwiesenstr. 202, 8051 Zürich.
T. (01) 322 26 68. 085495
Ineichen, Peter, Badenerstr 75, 8004 Zürich.
T. (01) 2423944, Fax 2429141. 085496
Iseli-Moser, Marguerite, Kirchgasse 33, 8001 Zürich.
T. (01) 2613221, 2515939. 085497
Keel, Daniel, Sprecherstr 8, 8032 Zürich.
T. (01) 254 85 11, Fax 252 84 07. - Graph /
Draw - 085498
Keller, Ernst, Burstwiesenstr. 59, 8055 Zürich.
T. (01) 461 26 79. - Paint - 085499
Keller-Galerie, Gerechtigkeitsgasse 8, 8002 Zürich.
T. (01) 202 09 63. - Paint / Sculp / Tex / Jew - 085500
Kelten-Keller, Keltenstr 45, 8044 Zürich.
T. (01) 2613737, Fax 2619337. 085501
Kempf, Stephan J., Strehlgasse 19, 8001 Zürich.
T. (01) 2213830. - Paint / Graph - 085502
Klopfer, Willy, Rämistr. 33, 8001 Zürich.
T. (01) 251 34 06. 085503
Koller, Hardturmstr 102, 8031 Zürich. T. (01) 2730101,
Fax 2731966. 085504
Kornfeld & Klipstein, Titlisstr 48, 8032 Zürich.
T. (01) 2510360. - Graph - 085505
Kunst Shop Has, Weinbergstr. 15, 8001 Zürich.
T. (01) 252 69 24. 085506
Kunstfoyer Orlikon, Neumarkt Orlikon, 8050 Zürich.
T. (01) 311 50 88. - Paint / Graph / Sculp / Tex - 085507
Kunstkiosk, Im Bahnhof Enge, 8027 Zürich.
T. (01) 202 32 59. 085508
Kunstsalon Wilsberg, Bederstr. 109, 8059 Zürich.
T. (01) 2857885, Fax 2012054. - Paint / Graph / Sculp /
Tex / Draw - 085509
Latal, Merkurstr. 44, 8032 Zürich. T. (01) 261 22 91.
- Paint / Graph / Draw - 085510
Lazertis, Universitätsstr. 21, 8006 Zürich.
T. (01) 261 14 13. 085511
Leiser Wolpe, Bederstr. 28, 8002 Zürich.
T. (01) 202 91 46. 085512
Lelong, Utoquai 31, 8008 Zürich. T. (01) 2511120,
Fax 2625285. - Paint / Graph / Sculp / Draw - 085513
Leuenberger, Münsterg 10, 8001 Zürich.
T. (01) 261 68 22. 085514
Maag, Susanne, Oberdorfstr 22, 8001 Zürich.
T. (01) 2523793. - Paint / Jew - 085515
Mäusli, Susann, Klosbachstr. 144, 8032 Zürich.
T. (01) 261 05 33. 085516
Manor House Collection, Kirchgasse 25, 8001 Zürich.
T. (01) 252 05 04. 085517
von Matt, Hansjakob, Dr, Weinbergstr 20, 8001 Zürich.
T. (01) 2525277. - Paint / Graph / Repr / Sculp - 085518
Maurer, Ruth, Münstergasse 14+18, 8001 Zürich.
T. (01) 261 85 00. - Paint / Graph / Sculp - 085519
Meissner, Bruno, Bahnhofstr 14, 8001 Zürich.
T. (01) 2103355, Fax 2103357. - Paint - 085520
Meissner, Kurt, Florastr 1, 8008 Zürich. T. (01) 3835110,
Fax 3836066. - Paint / Draw - 085521

Mercator, Seefeldstr. 45, 8001 Zürich.
T. (01) 383 01 01. 085522
Modern Art Center, Werdmühlestr. 9-11, 8001 Zürich.
T. (01) 211 47 89. 085523
Mörgeli, Schipfe 3, 8001 Zürich.
T. (01) 211 91 07. 085524
Mosimann, Charles, Mühlebachstr. 126, 8008 Zürich.
T. (01) 383 36 30. 085525
Müller, Mark, Gessnerallee 36, 8001 Zürich.
T. (01) 2118155, Fax 2118220. 085526
Muhrer, Angela, Dufourstr. 134, 8008 Zürich.
T. (01) 383 76 66. - Paint / Graph / Draw - 085527
Musikgalerie Inauer, Rotbuchstr. 16, 8006 Zürich.
T. (01) 363 14 61. 085528
Nathan, Arosastr 7, 8008 Zürich. T. (01) 422 45 50,
Fax 422 45 24. 085529
Neupert AG, Genferstr. 34, 8002 Zürich.
T. (01) 201 18 48. 085530
Nievergelt, Paul, Franklinstr 23, 8050 Zürich.
T. (01) 3115866, Fax 3119055. - Graph - 085531
Nomadenschätze, Kirchgasse 36, 8001 Zürich.
T. (01) 252 55 00. 085532
Norych, Helga, Seefeldstr. 60, 8008 Zürich.
T. (01) 251 45 17. 085533
Noser, Peter, Clausiusstr. 65, 8006 Zürich.
T. (01) 262 69 56, Fax 365 77 07. - Paint / Sculp / Pho /
Draw - 085534
Payer, Fritz, Pelikanstr 6, Felsenhof, 8001 Zürich.
T. (01) 2211382, Fax 2122513. 085535
Peter, Pia, Gladbachstr. 51, 8044 Zürich.
T. (01) 361 56 42. 085536
Peter & Paul Ikonengalerie, Zähringerstr. 28, 8001 Zü-
rich. T. (01) 261 61 28. 085537
Peyer, Elisabeth, Obere Zäune 3, 8001 Zürich.
T. (01) 261 25 00. 085538
Preisig, I., Augustinergasse 52, 8001 Zürich.
T. (01) 211 34 20. 085539
Preiswerk, Irène, Cäcilienstr 3, 8032 Zürich.
T. (01) 2512639, Fax 2513419. - Paint / Graph /
Sculp - 085540
Produzentengalerie, c/o D. Leuenberger, Birchstr. 27,
8057 Zürich. T. (01) 363 64 51. 085541
Rahn, Hans Konrad, Kirchgasse 38, 8001 Zürich.
T. (01) 252 12 00. 085542
Rennweg Galerie, Rennweg 14, 8001 Zürich.
T. (01) 2115780, Fax 2121437. - Paint - 085543
Rhéa Gallery, Zürichbergstr. 26, 8032 Zürich.
T. (01) 252 06 20, Fax 252 06 26. - Ant / Paint / Furn /
China / Arch / Jew / Ico - 085544
La Rocca, Beckenhofstr. 10, 8006 Zürich.
T. (01) 361 42 20. - Paint - 085545
Römer, Rämistr 23, 8001 Zürich. T. (01) 2616087,
Fax 2610736. - Paint / Sculp - 085546

Rusterholz, Birmensdorferstr. 486, 8055 Zürich.
T. (01) 462 50 34. 085547
Saint James' Gallery, Rämistr. 5, 8001 Zürich.
T. (01) 252 24 25. - Paint - 085548
SBG-Galerie Pavillon Werd, Morgartenstr. 40, 8004 Zü-
rich. T. (01) 234 35 56, Fax 234 41 99. - Paint / Graph /
Sculp - 085549
Schade, Harald, Waaggasse 5, 8001 Zürich.
T. (01) 221 10 42. 085550
Scheidegger, Ernst, Wettingerwies 2, 8001 Zürich.
T. (01) 251 80 50, Fax 251 80 72. - Paint / Graph /
Sculp - 085551
Schenk, Dr., Paradeplatz/Bleicherweg 3, 8001 Zürich.
T. (01) 2210730/31, Fax (01) 2210761. - Paint / Furn /
Sculp / Draw - 085552

Galerie Dr. István Schlégl

Minervastrasse 119, 8032 Zürich
Telefon 01 383 49 63,
Fax 01 383 55 89

Geöffnet:
Dienstag bis Freitag 14.00–18.00 Uhr
Samstag 11.00–13.00 Uhr,
14.00–16.00 Uhr

Schlégl, István, Dr., Minervastr 119, 8032 Zürich.
T. (01) 3834963, Fax 3835589. - Paint / Graph /
Sculp - 085553
Schmuck Forum, Zollikerstr. 12, 8008 Zürich.
T. (01) 251 66 79. 085554
Schön, Roland, Granitweg 6, 8006 Zürich.
T. (01) 2619933, Fax (01) 3626905. 085555
Schweizer, Theo, Kantstr. 12, 8044 Zürich.
T. (01) 251 98 09. 085556
Seebach, Schwellistr. 34, 8052 Zürich.
T. (01) 302 24 56. 085557
Spleiss, Margrit, Freudenbergstr. 97, 8044 Zürich.
T. (01) 361 39 90. 085558
Staehelin, Theano, Freiestr 110, 8032 Zürich.
T. (01) 3836887. - Paint - 085559
Steiner, Krönleinstr. 1, 8044 Zürich. T. (01) 252 70 09.
- Paint / Graph / Sculp / Draw - 085560
Steinfels & Partner, Eric, Dr., Heinrichstr. 255, 8005 Zürich. T. (01) 272 13 31. 085561
Stibua Grischuna, Zurlindenstr. 213, 8032 Zürich.
T. (01) 35 85 91. 085562
Stiftung Binz 39, Sihlquai 133, 8005 Zürich.
T. (01) 271 18 71. 085563
Storrer Gallery, Scheuchzerstr 25, 8006 Zürich.
T. (01) 362 73 14, Fax 3627314. 085564
Strassberg, Max, Sonneggstr. 49, 8006 Zürich.
T. (01) 262 03 43. 085565
Strohschneider, Albisriederstr. 166, 8003 Zürich.
T. (01) 491 26 33. 085566
Teppich Galerie, Walchstr. 17, 8006 Zürich.
T. (01) 361 36 12. 085567
Teucher-Sánchez, Severina, Predigerpl. 14, 8001 Zürich.
T. (01) 261 95 33. - Paint - 085568
Villa Ulmberg, Thujastr. 14, 8038 Zürich.
T. (01) 481 88 33. 085569
Vita-Galerie, Austr. 46, 8003 Zürich.
T. (01) 465 65 65. 085570
Vollmoeller, Heidi, Kurhausstr 17, 8032 Zürich.
T. (01) 2513103, Fax (01) 2514249. 085571
Walu, Rämistr. 33, 8024 Zürich.
T. (01) 262 22 54. 085572
Weber, Werner Alois, Spielweg 7, 8037 Zürich.
T. (01) 362 46 90. 085573
Werkgalerie, Rämistr. 25, 8001 Zürich.
T. (01) 261 20 72. 085574
Wiedenkeller, Ursula, Neustadtgasse 2, 8001 Zürich.
T. (01) 251 69 53. - Paint / Graph / Sculp - 085575
Wimmer AG, Toblerstr. 104, 8044 Zürich.
T. (01) 251 64 71. 085576
Wirth, Marie-Louise, Lutherstr 32, 8004 Zürich.
T. (01) 2410115, Fax 2410117. - Paint - 085577
Work Gallery, Frohalpstr. 65, 8038 Zürich.
T. (01) 482 39 58. 085578
Zähringer, Gerhard, Froschaugasse 5, 8001 Zürich.
T. (01) 252 36 66, Fax 252 36 54. - Graph / Draw /
Orient - 085579
Zentrum Höngg, Gsteigstr. 2, 8049 Zürich.
T. (01) 341 65 70. 085580
Ziegler, Renée, Rämistr 34, 8001 Zürich.
T. (01) 2512322, Fax 2512546. - Paint / Graph / Sculp /
Draw - 085581
Zingg-Lamprecht, Walchestr. 9, 8006 Zürich.
T. (01) 362 36 52. 085582
Zürich Strauhof, Augustinergasse 9, 8001 Zürich.
T. (01) 216 31 39. 085583

Zug

Antik Galerie, Gotthardstr. 20, 6300 Zug.
T. (041) 711 72 17. 085584
Walter Barth Erben, Grabenstr 38, 6300 Zug.
T. (041) 7114815, Fax 7113324. 085585
Bommer, Werner, Oberaltstadt 8, 6300 Zug.
T. (041) 7103932. 085586
Galerie am Fischmarkt, Unteraltstadt 6, 6300 Zug.
T. (041) 711 02 78. 085587
Galerie am See, Seestr 17, 6300 Zug. T. (041) 7103062,
Fax 7103038. - Paint / Graph / Sculp - 085588
Galerie Proarta, Moosbachweg 12, 6300 Zug.
T. (041) 711 72 10. 085589
Galerie zur Münz, Zeughausgasse 14, 6300 Zug.
T. (041) 710 00 30. 085590
Gerber, Julia, Sankt Oswaldgasse 6, 6301 Zug.
T. (041) 710 44 41. - Jew - 085591
Horstmann, Höhenweg 3d, 6300 Zug. T. (041) 240 45 71,
Fax (041) 710 45 72. 085592
Kolin, Kirchenstr. 2, 6300 Zug.
T. (041) 711 40 47. 085593
Koller, Hermann, Baarerstr. 47, 6300 Zug.
T. (041) 711 56 18. 085594
La petite Galerie, Unter Altstadt 5, 6300 Zug.
T. (041) 7103666, Fax 7107617. - Paint / Graph /
Sculp / Jew / Fra / Rel / Glass / Draw - 085595
Pon, Nicolina, Seestr. 5, 6300 Zug. T. (041) 710 41 07,
Fax (041) 710 44 17. - Paint - 085596
Renggli, Carla, Ober-Altstadt 8, 6300 Zug.
T. (041) 7119568. - Graph / Fra / Draw - 085597
Willi, H.J. Erich, Baarerstr. 43, 6300 Zug.
T. (041) 711 53 77. 085598

Zumikon (Zürich)

Galerie Milchhütte, Dorfstr 31, 8126 Zumikon. 085599

Zurzach (Aargau)

Galerie Zum Elefanten, Hauptstr 16, 5330 Zurzach.
T. (056) 2492412. - Paint / Graph - 085600
Galerie zum oberen Schwanen, Hauptstr 28, 5330 Zurzach. T. (056) 2493838. 085601

Syria

Damas

Urnina, Shuhada Rue Abi Tammam, Damas C. P. 2886.
T. 335 392. - Paint - 085602

Thailand

Bangkok

Asia Gallery, 96-98 Rajdamr Rd., Bangkok. T. 589 63.
- Paint / Graph / Sculp - 085603
Chai Ma, 799-801 Silom Rd. Wat Dhaek, Bangkok.
T. 236-4390. - Paint / Sculp - 085604
Petchburi Gallery, 1787, 1807-17 New Petchburi Rd.,
Bangkok. T. 251 24 26, 251 30 06. - Paint / Graph /
Sculp / Fra - 085605

Turkey

Istanbul

Galeri Gezi, Taksim Gezi Dükkanlari, Istanbul. 085606

Uganda

Kampala

The Nomma Art Gallery, Plot 4 Victoria Ave., POB 6643,
Kampala. - Paint - 085607

United Kingdom

Aberchirder (Grampian)

McShane, 9 The Square, Aberchirder.
T. (01466) 780372. - Paint - 085608

Aberdeen (Grampian)

Art Attack, 32 Marischal St., Aberdeen AB1 2AJ.
T. (01224) 212708. - Paint / Graph - 085609
Heinzel, 21 Spa St., Aberdeen AB1 1PU.
T. (01224) 625629. - Paint / China - 085610
Novell-Frazer, 46a Union St., Aberdeen AB1 2BN.
T. (01224) 633752. - Paint - 085611
Peacock Print Makers, 21 Castle St., Aberdeen.
T. (01224) 639539. - Graph - 085612
Rendezvous Gallery, 100 Forest Av., Aberdeen.
T. (01224) 323247. - Paint - 085613
Rosemount Gallery, 81 Rosemount Viaduct, Aberdeen
AB1 1NS. T. (01224) 630312. - Paint - 085614
Viking Galleries, 308 George St., Aberdeen AB1 1HL.
T. (01224) 624050, Fax 624050. - Paint /
Graph - 085615
Waverley Gallery, 18 Victoria St., Aberdeen AB1 1XA.
T. (01224) 640633. - Paint / Graph - 085616

Abersoch (Gwynedd)

Artist Studio, Lou Sarn Bach Rd., Abersoch.
T. (0175881) 3622. - Paint - 085617

Aberystwyth (Dyfed)

Catherine Lewis Gallery and Print Room, Hugh Owen Library, University of Wales, Aberystwyth SY23 1HB.
T. (01970) 622460, Fax 622461. 085618
Millward, J.R., 20 Pier St., Aberystwyth.
T. (01970) 617793. - Paint - 085619

Abingdon (Oxfordshire)

Abingdon Gallery, The Precinct, Abingdon.
T. (01235) 21815. - Paint / Graph - 085620

Accrington (Lancashire)

Abbey Gallery, 65 Abbey St., Accrington.
T. (01254) 233459. - Paint - 085621
King George IV Gallery, 6 Blackburn Rd., Accrington.
T. (01254) 390898. - Paint / Graph - 085622
Stanley & Son, 4-4a Blackburn Rd., Accrington.
T. (01254) 234108. - Paint - 085623

Aislaby (Cleveland)

Jordan, T.B., Aslak, Aislaby. T. 782599. - Paint - 085624

Alcester (Warwickshire)

Coughton Galleries, Coughton Court, Alcester B49 5JA.
T. (01789) 762642. - Paint - 085625

Aldeburgh (Suffolk)

Aldeburgh Cinema Gallery, High St, Aldeburgh IP15 5AU.
T. (01728) 452996. - Paint / Graph - 085626
Thompson, 175a High St., Aldeburgh IP15 5AN.
T. (0172) 453743, Fax (0172) 453743. - Paint /
Sculp - 085627

Alderley Edge (Cheshire)

Merlin Gallery, 3 London Rd., Alderley Edge.
T. (01625) 583500. - Paint - 085628

Alderton (Suffolk)

Spring Enterprises, Spring House, Beach Lane, Alderton.
T. (0124262) 411310. - Paint - 085629

Aldworth (Berkshire)

Ker, David, Faleys Border, Aldworth. T. (01635) 578918.
- Paint - 085630

Alfreton (Derbyshire)

Horse Fair Gallery, 28 King St., Alfreton.
T. (01773) 836209. - Paint - 085631

Alfriston (East Sussex)

Alfriston Gallery, Alfriston House, High St., Alfriston.
T. (01323) 870631. - Paint - 085632

Alloway (Strathclyde)

Maclaurin, Monument Rd., Alloway. T. (01292) 43708.
- Paint / Graph - 085633

Almondsbury (Avon)

Royal Gallery, Fernhille Court, Fernhill, Almondsbury.
T. (01454) 617022. - Paint - 085634

Alnwick (Northumberland)

Gate Gallery, 12 Bondgate Within, Alnwick NE66 1TD.
T. (01665) 602165. - Paint - 085635

Hill House Gallery, 39 Bondgate Within, Alnwick NE66
1SX. T. (01665) 602352, Fax (01665) 79275.
- Paint - 085636

Alresford (Hampshire)
Alresford Gallery, 36 West St., Alresford.
T. (01962) 735286, Fax (01962) 735295. - Paint /
Sculp - 085637
Hitchcock, 11 East St, Alresford. T. (01962) 734762.
- China / Tex / Glass - 085638
ReadMolteno, 36 West St., Alresford. T. (01962) 735352.
- Tex - 085639
Stuart, 15 Broad St., Alresford SO24 9AR.
T. (01962) 735311. - Paint - 085640

Alston (Cumbria)
Gossipgate Gallery, The Butts, Alston.
T. (01434) 381806. - Paint - 085641

Alton (Hampshire)
Allen, 10-12 Church St., Alton. T. (01420) 82802.
- Paint - 085642

Altrincham (Greater Manchester)
Collectors Galleries, 28 The Downs, Altrincham WA14.
T. (0161) 9298586. - Paint - 085643
Country Galleries, 32 Railway St., Altrincham WA14.
T. (0161) 928 9942. - Paint - 085644

Alvechurch (West Midlands)
Woodland Fine Art, 16 The Square, Alvechurch B48 7LA.
T. (0121) 4455886. - Paint / Graph - 085645

Ambleside (Cumbria)
Amblocide Gallery, Zefferelis Arcade, Ambleside.
T. (015394) 34040. - Paint - 085646
Cookhouse Gallery, Church St., Ambleside.
T. (015394) 33861. - Paint - 085647
Dexterity, Kelsick Rd., Ambleside LA22 0BZ.
T. (015394) 34045. - Paint - 085648
Hobbs, 1 Church St., Ambleside. T. (015394) 32882.
- Paint - 085649
Studio House Gallery, Market Pl., Ambleside.
T. (015394) 32497. - Paint / Graph - 085650

Amersham (Buckinghamshire)
Lady Free, 11 Nightingales Corner, Amersham.
T. (01494) 764325. - Paint - 085651
Mon Galerie, Forge End, Broadway, Amersham.
T. (01494) 712468. - Paint - 085652

Amlwch (Gwynedd)
Gallery Amlwch, 8 Salem St., Amlwch.
T. (01407) 831508. - Paint - 085653

Ancrum (Borders)
Ancrum Gallery, Ancrum. T. (018353) 340. - Paint /
Sculp / Glass - 085654
Mainhill, Carnessie, Ancrum TD8 6XA. T. (018353) 518.
- Paint - 085655

Andover (Hampshire)
Andover Fine Arts, 15 London St., Andover.
T. (01264) 358424. - Paint - 085656

Andoversford (Gloucestershire)
Variete, 7 Waterside Close, Andoversford.
T. (01242) 820453. - Graph - 085657

Appledore (Devon)
Gallerie Marin, 137 Irsha St., Appledore.
T. (01237) 473679. - Paint - 085658

Armagh (Co. Armagh)
Adam, 28 Linenhall St., Armagh. T. (01861) 526908.
- Paint - 085659

Arundel (West Sussex)
Armstrong-Davis, The Square, Arundel BN18 9AB.
T. (01903) 882752. - Sculp - 085660
Arundel Gallery, 40 Tarrant St., Arundel BN18 9DN.
T. (01903) 884560. - Paint - 085661
Little Gallery, 32a High St., Arundel. T. (01903) 882642.
- Paint - 085662
River Gallery, 25 High St., Arundel BN18 9AD.
T. (01903) 882177. - Paint - 085663

Sussex Fine Art, 7 Castle Mews, Tarrant St, Arundel
BN18 9DG. T. (01903) 884055. - Paint - 085664

Ascot (Berkshire)
Austin & Desmond, 3 High St., Ascot. T. (01990) 291201.
- Paint / Graph / China - 085665

Ashbourne (Derbyshire)
Print Cellar, 35 Church St., Ashbourne. T. (01335) 42933.
- Graph - 085666
Victoria Gallery and Studio, 7a Victoria Sq., Ashbourne.
T. (01335) 46414. - Paint - 085667
Williamson, Paul, North Leys, Ashbourne.
T. (01335) 43054. - Paint - 085668

Ashby-de-la-Zouch (Leicestershire)
Hampson, South St., Ashby-de-la-Zouch.
T. (01530) 414246. - Paint - 085669

Ashford (Kent)
Ashford Gallery, Simone Weil Av, Ashford TN24 8UX.
T. (01233) 611444. - Paint / Sculp - 085670
Green, Roger, Hales Pl., Woodchurch Rd, Ashford.
T. (01233) 850219. - Paint - 085671

Ashford (Surrey)
Webster, 68 Fordbridge Rd., Ashford. T. (01784) 254877.
- Paint - 085672

Ashtead (Surrey)
Park Lane Fine Arts, 126 The Street, Ashtead.
T. (01372) 277284. - Paint - 085673

Ashton-under-Lyne (Lancashire)
Picture Shops, 7 Clarence Arcade, Stamford St., Ashton-
under-Lyne OL6. T. (0161) 339 0724. - Paint - 085674

Ashwell (Hertfordshire)
Six Bells Studio Art Gallery, 2 SwanSt., Ashwell.
T. (0146274) 2643. - Paint - 085675

Aslockton (Nottinghamshire)
Neville, Jane, Elm House, Abbey Ln., Aslockton.
T. (01949) 50220, Fax (01949) 51337. - Paint /
Graph - 085676

Astwood Bank (Hereford and Wor\-ce-ster)
Bracebridge Gallery, Robindale, 49 The Ridgeway, Ast-
wood Bank B96 6LU. T. (01527) 892819.
- Paint - 085677

Auchterarder (Tayside)
Hayes, Paul, 71 High St., Auchterarder.
T. (01764) 62320. - Paint - 085678
Shinafoot, 84 High St., Auchterarder. T. (01764) 63843.
- Paint / Graph - 085679

Aylesbury (Buckinghamshire)
Buckinghamshire County Museum, Church St, Aylesbury
HP22 5PJ, HP20 2QP. T. (01296) 331441. 085680

Aylsham (Norfolk)
Gallery at Bacon's Bookshop, 17 White Hart St., Ayls-
ham. T. (01263) 734240. - Graph - 085681
Red Lion Gallery, 56a Red Lion St., Aylsham NR11 6ER.
T. (01263) 732115. - Paint / Graph / Draw - 085682

Aylton (Hereford and Worcester)
Arcus Fine Art, Aylton Court, Aylton. T. (0153183) 785.
- Paint - 085683

Ayr (Strathclyde)
Alphabet, 68 Fort St., Ayr. T. (01292) 263653.
- Paint - 085684

Bacup (Lancashire)
Yorkshire Court Gallery, 20 Yorkshire St., Bacup.
T. (01706) 876702. - Paint - 085685

Bakewell (Derbyshire)
Bounty Gallery, Water St., Bakewell. T. (01629) 814406.
- Paint - 085686
Granby, Water Lane, Bakewell. T. (01629) 813050.
- Paint - 085687

Baldock (Hertfordshire)
Baranite, Baranite House, Whitehorse St., Baldock.
T. (01462) 895025. - Sculp - 085688

Ballater (Grampian)
McEwan, Bridge of Gairn, Ballater AB35 5UB.
T. (013397) 55429, Fax (013397) 55995. - Paint /
Graph - 085689

Ballyclare (Co. Antrim)
Lamond, 56 Main St., Ballyclare. T. (019603) 41570.
- Paint - 085690
Rafters, 77a Main St., Ballyclare. T. (019603) 41635.
- Paint - 085691

Ballymena (Co. Antrim)
Wellington Gallery, 39-41 Wellington, Ballymena.
T. (01266) 656556. - Paint - 085692

Ballymoney (Co. Antrim)
Dalriada, 1 Market St., Ballymoney. T. (012656) 62447.
- Paint - 085693

Ballynahinch (Co. Down)
Annabert, 22 Lisburn St., Ballynahinch.
T. (01238) 565186. - Paint - 085694

Bamford (Derbyshire)
Paintings & Prints, High Park Garden Centre, Mytham
Bridge, Bamford. T. (01433) 51453. - Paint /
Graph - 085695

Bampton (Oxfordshire)
West Oxfordshire Arts Association, Town Hall, Market
Sq., Bampton. T. (01993) 850137. - Paint - 085696

Banbury (Oxfordshire)
Dickens, H.C., High St, Banbury OX15 4LT.
T. (01295) 721949. - Paint / Graph - 085697

Banchory (Grampian)
Banchory Gallery, 75 High St., Banchory.
T. (013302) 4142. - Paint - 085698

Bangor (Co. Down)
Cromie, Tom, 9 Hamilton Rd., Bangor.
T. (01247) 271838. - Paint - 085699

Bangor (Gwynedd)
Windsor, David, 201 High St., Bangor LL57 1NU.
T. (01248) 364639. - Paint / Graph - 085700

Banstead (Surrey)
Mackies, 35 Nork Way, Banstead. T. (01737) 361011.
- Paint - 085701

Barking (Essex)
Amerea International, Unit 8, Portland Commercial Es-
tate, Ripple Rd., Barking IG11. T. (0181) 593 7115.
- Paint - 085702

Barnet (Greater London)
Athena Gallery, Unit 10, The Spires, High St., Barnet EN5
5XY. T. (0181) 440 5872. - Paint - 085703
Bow House Gallery, 35 Wood St., Barnet EN5 4BE.
T. (0181) 440 4672. - Paint - 085704

Barnsley (South Yorkshire)
Metro Galleries, 10 Upper Mayday Green, Barnsley.
T. (01226) 242758. - Paint - 085705
Winchester Fine Art, 339 Burton Rd., Barnsley.
T. (01226) 710816. - Paint - 085706

Barnstaple (Devon)
Blacksell, North Devon College, Barnstaple.
T. (01271) 45291. - Paint - 085707
Doidge, 19 Newport Rd., Barnstaple. T. (01271) 43194.
- Paint - 085708
Kentisbury Fine Art, Clifton Cottage, Barnstaple EX31
4LX. T. (01271) 850657. 085709

Barvas (Western Isles)
Muirneag, Brue, Barvas. T. (0185184) 240.
- Paint - 085710

Basingstoke (Hampshire)
Hoysted Watercolours, Anna, Goodchilds Farm, Basingstoke RG27 8LH. T. (01256) 882355. - Paint - 085711

Bath (Avon)
Adam, 13 John St., Bath BA1 2JL. T. (01225) 480406.
- Paint - *085712*
Artisans Gallery, 26a Belvedere, Bath.
T. (01225) 336358. - Paint - *085713*
Artsite Gallery, 1 Pierrepont Pl., Bath BA1 1JY.
T. (01225) 60394. - Paint - *085714*
Beaux Arts, 13 York St., Bath BA1 1NG.
T. (01225) 464850, Fax (01225) 422256.
- Paint - *085715*
Bridge Galleries, 2 Trim Bridge, Bath BA1 1HD.
T. (01225) 466590. *085716*
Bruton, 35 Gay St., Bath BA1 2NT. T. (01225) 466292,
Fax (01225) 461294. - Paint / Graph / Sculp /
Draw - *085717*
C.C.A. Galleries, 5 George St., Bath BA1 2EH.
T. (01225) 448121. - Paint - *085718*
Cleveland Bridge Gallery, 8 Cleveland Pl. East, Bath BA1
5DJ. T. (01225) 447885. - Paint / Sculp - *085719*
Framing Workshop & Gallery, 78 Walcot St., Bath.
T. (01225) 482748. - Graph - *085720*
Hann, 2a York St., Bath BA1 1NG. T. (01225) 466904.
- Paint - *085721*
Hayes, Peter, 2 Cleveland Bridge, Bath.
T. (01225) 466215. - Paint - *085722*
Hepworth, Anthony, 15 York St, Bath. T. (01225) 442917.
- Paint - *085723*
Hitchcock, 10 Chapel Row, Bath. T. (01225) 330646.
- Paint - *085724*
Kelston Fine Arts, Kelston House, College Rd., Bath.
T. (01225) 424224. - Paint - *085725*
Kingsley, 16 Margarets Bldgs., Brock St., Bath.
T. (01225) 448432. - Paint - *085726*
Pelly, William, Upper Langridge Farm, Bath BA1 9BW.
T. (01225) 421714, Fax (01225) 421714. - Paint /
Draw - *085727*
Porter, 19 Circus Pl., Bath BA1 2PG. T. (01225) 424910.
- Graph - *085728*
Rocksmoor Gallery, 31 Brock St., Bath.
T. (01225) 420495. - Paint - *085729*
Rooksmoor Gallery, 31 Brock St, Bath BA1 2LN.
T. (01225) 420495. - Paint / Graph - *085730*
Royal Photographic Society, The Octagon, Milson St.,
Bath. T. (01225) 462841. - Pho - *085731*
Saint James's Gallery, 96 Margarets Bldgs., Bath BA1
2LP. T. (01225) 319197. - Paint - *085732*
Saville Row Gallery, 1 Saville Row, Bath.
T. (01225) 334595. - Paint / Sculp - *085733*
Studio Prints Gallery, 2a Market Pl., Bath BA11 1AG.
T. (01225) 464528. - Graph - *085734*
University of Bath Library Gallery, Claverton Down, Bath.
T. (01225) 826420. - Paint - *085735*

Bathgate (Lothian)
Victoria Gallery, 41 King St., Bathgate.
T. (01506) 632203. - Paint - *085736*

Battle (East Sussex)
Gerrard, Alex, 2 Abbey Green, Battle. T. (014246) 4204.
- Paint - *085737*

Bawtry (South Yorkshire)
Academy Fine Arts, 1 Swan St., Bawtry.
T. (01302) 719554. - Paint - *085738*
Fine Arts of Bawtry, 4 Dower House Sq., Bawtry.
T. (01302) 710902. - Paint - *085739*

Beaconsfield (Buckinghamshire)
Cole, Christopher, 1 London End, Beaconsfield HP9 2HN.
T. (01494) 671274. - Paint - *085740*
Gallery 79, 77 Wycombe End, Beaconsfield.
T. (01494) 676811. - Paint - *085741*
Griffiths, D.L., Woodlands Farm, Burnham Rd., Beacons-
field. T. (01494) 670554. - Paint - *085742*
Messum Gallery, David, 1 Aylesbury End, Beaconsfield
HP9 1LU. T. (01494) 680880, Fax (01494) 680878.
- Paint - *085743*
Omell, 20 Aylesbury End, Beaconsfield.
T. (01494) 678097. - Paint - *085744*

Beaulieu (Hampshire)
Beaulieu Fine Arts, The Malt House, High St., Beaulieu
SO42 7YA. T. (01590) 612089. - Paint / Graph /
Draw - *085745*

Beaumaris (Gwynedd)
Oriel Fach, 46a Castle St., Beaumaris LL58 8BB.
T. (01248) 810445. - Paint - *085746*

Beccles (Suffolk)
Beccles Gallery, Saltgate House, Beccles NR34 9AN.
T. (01502) 714017. - Paint / Graph - *085747*

Beckenham (Greater London)
Art House, 100 Beckenham Rd., Beckenham BR3.
T. (0181) 663 3626. - Paint - *085748*
Camp, Richard F., 20 High St., Beckenham BR3.
T. (0181) 650 2073. - Paint - *085749*
Windmill Arts and Craft Gallery, 170 Upper Elmers End
Rd., Beckenham BR3. T. (0181) 650 0933.
- Paint - *085750*

Bedale (North Yorkshire)
Dales Gallery, 19 North End, Bedale. T. (01677) 23580.
- Paint - *085751*
Greenwood Fine Art, W., The Gallery, Oakdene, Bedale
DL8 2JE. T. (01677) 423217, 424830. - Paint - *085752*
Motif of Bedale, 17 North End, Bedale. T. (01677) 25440.
- Paint - *085753*
Thornton, Snape, Bedale DL8 2TR. T. (01677) 70318.
- Paint - *085754*

Bedford (Bedfordshire)
Art Centre, 1 Clair Court Lime St., Bedford.
T. (01234) 344784. - Paint - *085755*

Beer (Devon)
Beachcomber, Fore St., Beer. T. (01297) 20153. - Paint /
Graph - *085756*

Belfast (Co. Antrim)
Arches Art Gallery, 2 Holywood Rd., Belfast.
T. (01232) 459031. - Paint - *085757*
Athena Gallery, 6 Queen St., Belfast. T. (01232) 324764.
- Paint - *085758*
Bell Gallery, 13 Adelaide Park, Belfast BT9 6FX.
T. (01232) 662998, Fax (01232) 381524.
- Paint - *085759*
Caldwell, Tom, 40-42 Bradbury Pl., Belfast.
T. (01232) 323226, Fax (01232) 233437.
- Paint - *085760*
Cavehill Gallery, 18 Old Cavehill Rd., Belfast BT15 5GT.
T. (01232) 776784. - Paint - *085761*
Crescent Arts Centre, 2-4 University Rd., Belfast.
T. (01232) 242338. - Paint - *085762*
Crosby, 46 Belmont Rd., Belfast. T. (01232) 471626.
- Paint - *085763*
Eakin, 237 Lisburn Rd., Belfast BT9 7EN.
T. (01232) 668522. - Paint - *085764*
Emer, 110 Donegall Pass, Belfast. T. (01232) 231377.
- Paint - *085765*
Fenderesky, Upper Crescent, Belfast. T. (01232) 235245.
- Paint - *085766*
Flaxart Studios, Edenderry Industrial Estate, Crumlin
Rd., Belfast. T. (01232) 740463. - Paint - *085767*
Frame & Picture Centre, 667 Lisburn Rd., Belfast.
T. (01232) 667021. - Paint - *085768*
Kerlin, 99 Botanic Av., Belfast. T. (01232) 231222.
- Paint - *085769*
Magee, John, 455 Ormeau Rd., Belfast.
T. (01232) 693830. - Paint - *085770*
Ormonde, 195 Upper Lisburn Rd., Belfast BT10 0LL.
T. (01232) 301613. - Paint / Graph - *085771*
Orpheus Gallery, Orpheus Bldg., York St., Belfast.
T. (01232) 246259. - Paint - *085772*
Paint Box, 348 Woodstock Rd., Belfast BT6 9DP.
T. (01232) 739080. - Paint - *085773*
Priory Art Gallery, 10 Shore Rd., Holywood, Belfast.
T. (01232) 428173. - Paint - *085774*
Roma, Ryan, 73 Dublin Rd., Belfast. T. (01232) 242777.
- Paint - *085775*
Scenes, 2 North St. Arcade, Belfast. T. (01232) 247878.
- Paint - *085776*
Sheldon, 43 Great Victoria St., Belfast.
T. (01232) 330077. - Paint - *085777*
Sheldon, 29 Castle St., Belfast. T. (01232) 240762.
- Paint - *085778*
Sheldon, 1a Donegall Sq. East, Belfast.
T. (01232) 324295. - Paint - *085779*

Belford (Northumberland)
Belford Craft Gallery, 2 Market Pl., Belford NE70 7ND.
T. (016683) 213888. - Paint - *085780*
Bray, Noel, 7-9 West St., Belford. T. (016683) 213486.
- Paint - *085781*

Belper (Derbyshire)
Clusters, 114 Bridge St., Belper. T. (01773) 820833.
- Paint - *085782*

Bembridge (Isle of Wight)
Unique Crafts Gallery, 5 Foreland Rd., Bembridge.
T. (01983) 874173. - Paint - *085783*

Bentley Heath (West Midlands)
Widdas, Roger, 7 Bullivents Close, Bentley Heath.
T. (01564) 773217. - Paint / Draw - *085784*

Berkeley (Gloucestershire)
Garratt, 9 High St., Berkeley GL13 9BH.
T. (01453) 810246. - Paint - *085785*

Berkhamsted (Hertfordshire)
Gallery One Eleven, 111 High St, Berkhamsted HP4 2JF.
T. (01442) 876333, Fax (01442) 877791.
- Paint - *085786*

Berwick-upon-Tweed (Northumberland)
Quayside Gallery, 5 Chandlery, Berwick-upon-Tweed.
T. (01289) 330165. - Paint - *085787*

Betley (Staffordshire)
Betley Court Gallery, Betley Court, Main Rd., Betley.
T. (01270) 820652. - Paint - *085788*

Betws-y-coed (Gwynedd)
Gallery, Holyhead Rd., Betws-y-coed.
T. (01690) 710432. - Paint - *085789*

Beverley (Humberside)
Ladygate Gallery, 1 Ladygate, Beverley HU17 8BH.
T. (01482) 869715. - Paint / Graph / China /
Jew - *085790*
Maltings Gallery, 7 Ladygate, Beverley.
T. (01482) 862655. - Paint - *085791*
North Bar Galleries, Lairgate, Beverley.
T. (01482) 860849. - Paint - *085792*
Starkey, James, 49 Highgate, Beverley HU17 0QN.
T. (01482) 881179, Fax (01482) 861644.
- Paint - *085793*

Bewdley (Hereford & Worcester)
Bewdley Gallery, Unit 4, Lax Lane, Bewdley.
T. (01299) 400918. - Paint - *085794*
Old Bank Craft Studio, Studio 9, Severnside Sth., Be-
wdley. T. (01299) 402028. - Paint - *085795*

Bexhill-on-Sea (East Sussex)
Stewart, 48 Devonshire Rd., Bexhill-on-Sea.
T. (01424) 223410. - Paint - *085796*

Bideford (Devon)
Burton, Victoria Park, Kingsley Rd., Bideford.
T. (01237) 476713. - Paint - *085797*
Collins & Son, J., 63 High St., Bideford EX39 2AN.
T. (01237) 473103, Fax (01237) 475658.
- Paint - *085798*

Bignall End (Staffordshire)
Mirage Fine Art, 26 Megacre, Bignall End.
T. (01782) 721847. - Paint - *085799*

Billingshurst (Sussex)
Shambles, 95 High St., Billingshurst. T. (01403) 784003.
- Paint - *085800*

Binfield (Berkshire)
Traynor, V. & A., 5 Oakmede Pl., Binfield RG12 5JF.
T. (01344) 425508. - Paint / Graph / China - *085801*

Bingley (West Yorkshire)
Carrol, Edward, 5 Rishworth Hall, Bingley BD16 2EL.
T. (01274) 568800. - Paint / Graph - *085802*

Birmingham (West Midlands)
Artist's Gallery, 373 Bearwood Rd, Birmingham B66.
T. (0121) 429 2298. - Paint - *085803*

Carleton Gallery, 91 Vivian Rd., Birmingham B17.
T. (0121) 427 2487. - Paint -   085804
Craftspace Touring, 180-182 Fazeley St., Birmingham
B5 5SE. T. (0121) 766 8983. - Paint -   085805
Galaxy Galleries, 119 Alcester Rd, Birmingham B13
8DD. T. (0121) 442 4227. - Paint -   085806
Graves, 3 Augusta St, Birmingham B18 6JA.
T. (0121) 212 1635. - Paint -   085807
Halcyon Gallery, 59 The Pallasades, Birmingham.
T. (0121) 643 4474. - Paint / Graph -   085808
Ikon Gallery, 58-72 John Bright St., Birmingham B1
1BN. T. (0121) 643 0708. - Paint / Sculp / Mod / Pho /
Draw –   085809
Madden, 77 Digbeth, Birmingham B5.
T. (0121) 631 2098. - Paint -   085810
Mercia, 80 Milk St., Birmingham B5 5TL.
T. (0121) 643 5330. - Paint -   085811
Midland Pictures & Mirrors, 988 Tyburn Rd, Birmingham
B24. T. (0121) 373 9460. - Paint -   085812
Midlands Arts Centre, Cannon Hill Park, Birmingham
B12 9QH. T. (0121) 440 4221. - Paint / Sculp / Jew /
Mod / Pho -   085813
Midlands Contemporary Art, 59 George St., Birmingham
B3 1QA. T. (0121) 233 9818, Fax (0121) 2121986.
- Paint -   085814
Moseley Gallery, Woodbridge Rd., Birmingham B13.
T. (0121) 449 9456. - Paint -   085815
P & P Pictures, 3 Saint Mary's Row, Moseley, Birming-
ham B13. T. (0121) 449 5103. - Paint -   085816
Pictures, 29 Great Western Arcade, Birmingham B2 5HV.
T. (0121) 233 4255. - Paint -   085817
Public Art Commissions Agency, Studio 6, Victoria St,
Birmingham B1. T. (0121) 212 4454. - Paint -   085818
Studio Galleries, 795 WarwickRd., Tyseley, Birmingham
B11 2EL. T. (0121) 708 1809. - Paint -   085819
Warwick Fine Arts, 313 Shaftmoor Lane, Hall Green, Bir-
mingham B28 8SJ. T. (0121) 777 3178.
- Paint -   085820
Webb & Sons, A.W., 32-36 High St., Kings Heath, Bir-
mingham B14. T. (0121) 444 1553. - Paint -   085821
Windmill Gallery, 6 Ernest St., Holloway Head, Birming-
ham. T. (0121) 622 3986, Fax 666 6630. - Paint /
Draw -   085822
Woodland, 1348 Stratford Rd., Hall Green, Birmingham
B28 9EH. T. (0121) 777 2027. - Paint -   085823

Bishop's Cleeve (Gloucestershire)
Priory Gallery, Station Rd., Bishop's Cleeve.
T. (01242) 673226. - Paint -   085824

Bishop's Stortford (Hertfordshire)
Gowan, 3 Bell St, Bishops Stortford. T. (01279) 600 004.
- Paint -   085825
Visual Impressions, 94 South St., Bishops Stortford.
T. (01279) 504533. - Paint -   085826

Bishop's Waltham (Hampshire)
Bishops Waltham Gallery, Cross St., Bishops Waltham.
T. (01489) 892292. - Paint -   085827

Black Notley (Essex)
Motif Editions, 13 Bulford Ln., Black Notley.
T. (01376) 552509. - Paint -   085828

Blackburn (Lancashire)
Action Factory Cultural Community Work, Simmons St.,
Blackburn. T. (01254) 679335. - Paint -   085829
Deighton, James, 724 Whalley New Rd, Blackburn.
T. (01254) 249093. - Paint -   085830

Blackpool (Lancashire)
Chequers Gallery, 161 Church St., Blackpool.
T. (01253) 28766. - Paint -   085831
Grundy, Queen St., Blackpool. T. (01253) 751701.
- Paint -   085832
Gynn Gallery, 305 Dickson Rd., Blackpool.
T. (01253) 51233. - Paint -   085833
Halda, 318 Church St., Blackpool. T. (01253) 22918.
- Paint -   085834

Blaenau Ffestiniog (Gwynedd)
Oriel y Ddraig, 2 Diffwys Square, Blaenau Ffestiniog
LL41 3BN. T. (01766) 831777. - Paint / Graph -   085835

Blakesley (Northamptonshire)
Blakesley Gallery, 10 The Green, Blakesley.
T. (01327) 860274. - Paint -   085836

Blandford (Dorset)
Forum Gallery, 6 West St., Blandford. T. (01258) 454440.
- Paint -   085837
Hambledon Gallery, 42 Salisbury St., Blandford DT11
7PR. T. (01258) 2880. - Paint / Graph / Sculp /
Fra -   085838
Stour, 28 East St., Blandford DT11 7DR.
T. (01258) 456293. - Paint -   085839

Bletchingley (Surrey)
Cider House Galleries, 80 High St., Bletchingley RH1
4PA. T. (01883) 742198, Fax (01883) 744014.
- Paint -   085840

Bloxham (Oxfordshire)
Dickins, H.C., High St., Bloxham OX15 4LT.
T. (01295) 721949. - Paint / Graph -   085841

Bodenham (Hereford and Worcester)
Rhea Gallery, Isle of Rhea House, Bodenham.
T. (0156884) 219. - Paint -   085842

Bognor Regis (Sussex)
Felpham Galleries, 66 Felpham Rd., Bognor Regis PO22
7NZ. T. (01243) 864044. - Paint -   085843
Gough Bros., 71 High St., Bognor Regis PO21 1RZ.
T. (01243) 823773. - Paint -   085844

Bolton (Lancashire)
Barlow, Brian, Saint Georges Craft Centre, Bath St., Bol-
ton. T. (01204) 21302. - Paint -   085845
Gallery 77, 18 Princess St., Bolton BL1 1EJ.
T. (01204) 35252. - Paint -   085846
Original Art Shop, Market Pl., Bolton. T. (01204) 365556.
- Paint -   085847
Picturesque, 4 Manor St., Bolton. T. (01204) 397707.
- Paint -   085848
Stansfield, Roland, Saville Mill, Shiffnall St., Bolton.
T. (01204) 33697. - Paint -   085849

Boot (Cumbria)
Fold End Gallery, Boot CA191TG. T. (019403) 213.
- Paint -   085850

Boscastle (Cornwall)
Picture Parlour, Bridge Walk, Boscastle PL35.
T. (018405) 677. - Paint -   085851

Bosham (West Sussex)
Cumberland Gallery, High St., Bosham.
T. (01243) 573725. - Paint -   085852

Boston (Lincolnshire)
D.E.K. Supplies, 24 High St., Boston. T. (01205) 368184.
- Paint -   085853

Botley (Hampshire)
Penny Farthing Picture Framing, 31 High St., Botley.
T. (01489) 784185. - Paint -   085854

Bournemouth (Dorset)
Artists Gallery, 1125 Christchurch Rd., Bournemouth.
T. (01202) 417066. - Paint -   085855
Cutler, W., 8 Albert Rd., Bournemouth BH1 1BZ.
T. (01202) 552612. - Paint -   085856
Daler, 4 Westover Rd., Bournemouth. T. (01202) 297682.
- Paint -   085857
Galerie La France, 647 Wimborne Rd, Bournemouth.
T. (01202) 522313. - Paint / Graph -   085858
Garnet Langton, 11 Burlington Arcade, Bournemouth.
T. (01202) 552352. - Paint / Graph -   085859
Hampshire Gallery, 18 Lansdowne Rd., Bournemouth
BH1 1SD. T. (01202) 551211. - Paint -   085860
House of Pictures, 303 Charminster Rd., Bournemouth.
T. (01202) 521120. - Paint -   085861
Hunter Simmonds, 65 Seamoor Rd, Bournemouth.
T. (01202) 768525. - Paint / Graph / Sculp -   085862
Marshall, 140 Charminster Rd., Charminster, Bourne-
mouth. T. (01202) 530720. - Paint / Graph -   085863
Mayfield, 907 Wimborne Rd., Bournemouth.
T. (01202) 519044. - Paint -   085864

Pokesdown, 835 Christchurch Rd, Bournemouth.
T. (01202) 427948. - Paint -   085865
Portraits Plus, 111 Commercial Rd., Bournemouth.
T. (01202) 297321. - Paint -   085866
Wessex, 1a Rosebery Rd., Pokesdown, Bournemouth
BH5 2JH. T. (01202) 431689. - Graph -   085867
Westcliff Gallery, 7 West Cliff Rd., Bournemouth.
T. (01202) 557402. - Paint -   085868
York House Galleries, 32 Somerset Rd., Bournemouth.
T. (01202) 391035. - Paint -   085869

Bourton-on-the Water (Gloucestershire)
Chestnut Gallery, High St., Bourton-on-the Water.
T. (01451) 20017. - Paint -   085870
Connoisseur Art Gallery, 2 Victoria St., Bourton-on-the
Water. T. (01451) 20154. - Paint -   085871
James, Robert, Windrush Cottage Shop, Riverside, Bour-
ton-on-the Water. T. (01451) 22255. - Paint -   085872
Rice, R.F., 1a Victoria St., Bourton-on-the Water.
T. (01451) 22404. - Paint -   085873
Wold, Halford House, Station Rd., Bourton-on-the Water.
T. (01451) 22092. - Paint -   085874

Bovey Tracey (Devon)
Devon Guild of Craftsmen, Riverside Mill, Bovey Tracey.
T. (01626) 832223.   085875

Bowness-on-Windermere (Cumbria)
Cook House Gallery, Unit 1, Arcade Crag Brow, Bow-
ness-on-Windermere. T. 2421. - Paint -   085876
Heaton Cooper, The Studio, Bowness-on-Windermere
LA22 9SX. T. 4766. - Paint -   085877

Boxford (Suffolk)
Laurimore, 29 Swan St., Boxford. T. (01787) 210138.
- Paint -   085878

Bracknell (Berkshire)
Gallery at the Park, South Hill Park, Bracknell.
T. (01344) 427272. - Paint -   085879

Bradford (West Yorkshire)
Bull, Simon, 51 Station Rd., Clayton, Bradford.
T. (01274) 818927. - Paint -   085880
Carlton Antiques and Fine Art, 280 Keighley Rd., Brad-
ford BD9 4LH. T. (01274) 482953. - Paint -   085881
Community Arts Centre, 17-21 Chapel St., Bradford.
T. (01274) 721372. - Paint -   085882
Hindu Swayamsevak Sangh, 52 Rugby Pl., Bradford.
T. (01274) 577395. - Paint -   085883
That Picture Shop, 15-17 North Parade, Bradford.
T. (01274) 731372. - Paint -   085884
Titus Gallery, 1 Daisy Pl., Bradford. T. (01274) 581894.
- Paint -   085885
Treadwell, Upper Park Gate, Little Germany, Bradford
BD1 5DW. T. (01274) 306056, Fax (01274) 394356.
- Paint / Sculp -   085886

Bradford-on-Avon (Wiltshire)
Church Gallery, 8 MarketSt., Bradford-on-Avon.
T. (012216) 3532. - Paint -   085887

Bradstone (Devon)
Vankloof, Bradstone Coombe Mill, Bradstone.
T. (0182287) 208. - Paint -   085888

Braemar (Grampian)
Mann, Alex, Braemar Studio, Braemar AB3 5YS.
- Paint -   085889

Braintree (Essex)
Artisans Gallery, Finchingfield, Braintree CW7 4JS.
T. (01371) 810709. - Paint / Graph -   085890
Phillips, 2 George Yard, Braintree. T. (01376) 553100.
- Paint -   085891

Bramhall (Greater Manchester)
Village Gallery, 191b Moss Lane, Bramhall SK7.
T. (0161) 440 0122. - Paint -   085892

Brandon (Suffolk)
Branch, John, Officers Club, Bldg. 958, Brandon.
T. (01638) 533149. - Paint -   085893
Chinese Originals, Brandon POB 6. T. (01842) 813136.
- Paint -   085894

Brantwood (Cumbria)
Coach House Gallery, Coach House, Brantwood. T. (015394) 41426. - Paint - 085895

Braunton (Devon)
Elliott Art & Craft Exhibition Centre, Hillsview, Braunton. T. (01271) 812100. - Paint - 085896

Brecon (Powys)
Sable & Hogg, 2 Castle St., Brecon LD3 9DD. T. (01874) 625901. - Paint - 085897

Brentford (Greater London)
Syon Park Arts Centre, London Rd., Brentford TW8. T. (0181) 568 6021. - Paint - 085898
Watermans Arts Centre, 40 High St., Brentford TW8 0DS. T. (0181) 847 5651. - Paint / Sculp / Pho - 085899

Brentwood (Essex)
Brandler, 1 Coptfold Rd., Brentwood CM14 4BM. T. (01277) 222269, Fax (01277) 222786. - Paint - 085900
Brandler, 1 Coptfold Rd., Brentwood. T. (01277) 222269, Fax 222786. - Paint - 085901
Graham, Neil, 11 Ingrave Rd., Brentwood. T. (01277) 215383. - Paint - 085902

Bressingham (Norfolk)
Gallery & Things, The Street, South Lopham, Bressingham. T. (0137988) 761. - Paint - 085903

Bridge-of-Weir (Strathclyde)
Castle Art and Antiques, 4 Castle Terrace, Bridge-of-Weir. T. (01505) 690951. - Paint - 085904

Bridgend (Mid Glamorgan)
Nolton Art Gallery, 66 Nolton St., Bridgend CF313BP. T. (01656) 663278. - Paint - 085905

Bridgnorth (Shropshire)
Norton, Pauline, 1 Bank St., Bridgnorth. T. (01746) 764889. - Paint - 085906

Bridgwater (Somerset)
Amoury Gallery, 31 Saint Mary St., Bridgwater. T. (01278) 429768. - Paint - 085907
Bridgwater Arts Centre, 11 Castle St., Bridgwater. T. (01278) 422700. - Paint - 085908

Bridport (Dorset)
Allsop, Bridport Arts Centre, South St., Bridport. T. (01308) 24204. - Paint - 085909
Harbour Galleries, Clarence House, West Bay, Bridport. T. (01308) 22018. - Paint - 085910
Minstrel's Gallery, 72 West St., Bridport. T. (01308) 25734. - Paint - 085911
Old Timber Yard Gallery & Studio, Old Timber Yard, West Bay, Bridport. T. (01308) 24829. - Paint - 085912
Ommanny, O.J., 85 South St., Bridport. T. (01308) 27606. - Paint - 085913
Solid Rock Fine Art, 32 South Rd., Bridport. T. (01308) 27777. - Paint - 085914

Brighouse (West Yorkshire)
Smith, Halifax Rd., Brighouse. T. (01484) 715222. - Paint - 085915

Brightling (East Sussex)
Hunt, John, Perch Hill Farm, Willingford Ln., Brightling TN32 5HP. T. (0142482) 239. - Paint / Sculp - 085916

Brighton (East Sussex)
Barclay, Hugo, 7 East St., Brighton. T. (01273) 21694. - Paint - 085917
Clairmonte, 56 Gardner St., Brighton BN1 1UN. T. (01273) 622027. - Paint - 085918
Crinan, XV The Village Sq, Brighton. T. (01273) 620126. - Paint - 085919
Florentine Galleries, 14 Brighton Sq, Brighton BN1 1HD. T. (01273) 23730. - Paint - 085920
Gallery, Brighton Polytechnic, Grand Parade, Brighton. T. (01273) 600900. - China - 085921
Gardner Centre Gallery, Sussex University, Falmer, Brighton BN1 9RA. T. (01273) 685447. - Paint - 085922
Grange, Rottingdean, Brighton. T. (01273) 600305. - Paint - 085923
Hussey, G.F., George St., Brighton BN2. T. (01273) 681852. - Paint - 085924
Kemptown Gallery, 95 St. Georges Rd, Brighton BN2 1EE. T. (01273) 679148. - Paint - 085925
Maze, 7-8 North Rd., Brighton. T. (01273) 690089. - Paint - 085926
Nexus, 14 Broad St., Brighton BN2 1TJ. T. (01273) 684480. - Paint - 085927
Oxley, M.A., 6 Sandgate Rd., Brighton BN1 6JQ. T. (01273) 541739. - Paint - 085928
Red Herring Gallery, 10-14 Waterloo Pl., Brighton. T. (01273) 683517. - Paint - 085929
Surrounds Picture Framing, 8 Little East St., Brighton BN1 1HT. T. (01273) 27843. - Paint - 085930
Wandomir, 78 Hollingbury Rd., Brighton. T. (01273) 501629. - Paint - 085931
Window Gallery, 3 Dukes Lane, Brighton BN1 1BG. T. (01273) 726190. - Paint - 085932

Brimfield (Hereford and Worcester)
Forge House Gallery, Forge House, Brimfield. T. (0158472) 500. - Paint - 085933

Brimstage (Merseyside)
Studio Gallery, Brimstage Hall, Brimstage Rd., Brimstage L63. T. (0151) 342 7558. - Paint - 085934

Brinscall (Lancashire)
Meadow Prints, Dick Lane, Brinscall. T. (01254) 831133. - Graph - 085935

Bristol (Avon)
Alexander, 122 Whiteladies Rd., Bristol BS8 2RP. T. (0117) 9734692, 9739582, Fax (0117) 466991. - Paint - 085936
Alma Gallery, 29 Alma Vale Rd, Bristol BS8 2HL. T. (0117) 237157, Fax (0117) 732059. - Paint / Graph / Sculp - 085937
Arnolfini, 16 Narrow Quay, Bristol BS1 4QA. T. (0117) 9299191. - Paint / Graph / Sculp / Jew / Pho - 085938
Art for Business, Willow Cottage Bristol Rd., Hambrook, Bristol BS16 1SB. T. (0117) 9561031. - Paint - 085939
Art Gallery, 37c High St., Keynsham, Bristol. T. (0117) 9868230. - Paint - 085940
Art Original, 4 The New Promenade, Gloucester Rd., Bristol. T. (0117) 9420793. - Paint - 085941
Art Original, 5 Union St., Bristol. T. (0117) 9273646. - Paint - 085942
Art Plus, 70 High St., Staple Hill, Bristol. T. (0117) 9701801. - Paint - 085943
Bristol Guild of Applied Art, 68-70 Park St., Bristol BS1 5JY. T. (0117) 9265548, Fax 255659. - Paint - 085944
Business Picture Service, 22 Greenhill Gardens, Bristol BS12 2PD. T. (0117) 9414358. - Graph - 085945
Catsand Dogs Art Gallery, 167 Winchester Rd., Bristol BS4 3NJ. T. (0117) 9774334. - Paint / Graph - 085946
Cross, David, 7 Boyces Av., Bristol BS8 4AA. T. (0117) 9732614. - Paint / Fra - 085947
Designs Unlimited, 47 High St, Bristol. T. (0117) 9591497. - Graph - 085948
Dido Editions, 62 Monk Rd., Bristol. T. (0117) 9422497. - Graph - 085949
Gill, Alastair, 4 Christmas Steps, Bristol BS1 5BS. T. (0117) 9221204. - Furn / Tex / Jew - 085950
Ginger Gallery, 84 Hotwell Rd., Bristol BS8 4UB. T. (0117) 9292527. - Paint - 085951
Glevum Gallery, Merchants Quay, Bristol City Docks, Bristol BS1 4RL. T. (0117) 9227502. - Paint - 085952
Howard, Kim, 28 Gloucester Rd., Bristol BS7 8AL. T. (0117) 9424954. - Paint - 085953
K.F.C. Fine Art, 39 Fairway, Bristol BS4 5DF. T. (0117) 9723938. - Paint / Graph - 085954
Lyndon, 3 Broadweir, Bristol BS1. T. (0117) 9299823. - Paint - 085955
Mall Gallery, 16 The Mall, Bristol. T. (0117) 9736263. - Paint - 085956
Off-Centre Gallery, 13 Cotswold Rd, Bristol BS3 4NX. T. (0117) 9661782. - Graph - 085957
Pelter & Sands, 43-45 Park St., Bristol BS1 5NL. T. (0117) 9293988. - Paint / Sculp - 085958
Picture Business, 42 Downs Park East, Westbury Park, Bristol BS6 7QE. T. (0117) 9623718. - Paint - 085959
Praxis, 90 Colston St., Bristol. T. (0117) 9291538. - Paint - 085960
Royal West of England Academy, Queens Rd., Clifton, Bristol BS8. T. (0117) 9735129. - Paint - 085961
Steps Gallery, 15 Christmas Steps, Bristol BS1 5BS. T. (0117) 9298671. - Paint - 085962
Stewart Fine Art Galleries, The Georgian House, Broad St, Bristol BS18 7LA. T. (01934) 862458, Fax (01934) 863207. - Paint / Graph - 085963
Stonebridge Galleries, 233 Cheltenham Rd., Bristol BS6 5QP. T. (0117) 9241401. - Paint - 085964
Studio International, 47 High St, Bristol BS9 3ED. T. (0117) 507573, Fax (0117) 507573. - Paint - 085965
Venture Prints, Frostreed House, Orchard Rd., Saint George, Bristol. T. (0117) 9552525. - Graph - 085966
Wells Gallery, Morton House, Lower Morton, Thornbury, Bristol BS12 1RA. T. (01454) 412288. - Paint - 085967
3D Gallery, 13 Perry Rd., Bristol BS5 0SY. T. (0117) 9291363. - Paint - 085968

Broadstairs (Kent)
Bradley, 40 York St., Broadstairs. T. (01843) 68405. - Paint - 085969
Broadstairs Gallery, 10 Charlotte St., Broadstairs. T. (01843) 65849. - Paint - 085970
Tara Gallery, 16 York St., Broadstairs. T. (01843) 69041. - Paint - 085971

Broadway (Hereford and Worcester)
Bindery Galleries, 69 High St., Broadway. T. (01386) 852649. - Paint - 085972
Christie, Richard, Cotswold Court, The Green, Broadway. T. (01386) 858807. - Paint - 085973
Hagen, Richard, Yew Tree House, Broadway WR12 7DT. T. (01386) 853624, Fax (01386) 852172. - Paint / Sculp / Draw - 085973a
In the Frame, 8 Cotswold Court, The Green, Broadway. T. (01386) 858971. - Paint - 085973b
McEwen, Kennel Lane, 39b High St., Broadway. T. (01386) 858634. - Paint - 085973c
Noot Twentieth Century, John, 14 Cotswold Court, Broadway WR12 7AA. T. (01386) 858969, Fax (01386) 858348. - Paint - 085974
Noott, John, 31 High St., Broadway WR12 7NH. T. (01386) 852787. - Paint - 085975

Brobury (Hereford and Worcester)
Brobury House Gallery, Brobury House, Brobury HR3 6BS. T. (019817) 817229. - Paint / Graph - 085979

Brodick (Strathclyde)
Arran Fine Art, Douglas Centre, Brodick. T. (01770) 2578. - Paint - 085980

Bromley (Greater London)
Bromley Galleries, 37 East St., Bromley BR1. T. (0181) 466 6682. - Paint / Sculp - 085981
Lauder, Scott, 6 Bell Parade, Glebe Way, Bromley BR4. T. (0181) 777 1776. - Paint - 085982
Lombard, 6 Westmoreland Pl, Bromley BR1. T. (0181) 290 1392. - Paint - 085983

Bromsgrove (Hereford and Worcester)
Bromsgrove Fine Art Gallery, 12a Hanover St., Bromsgrove. T. (01527) 579561. - Paint - 085984

Broseley (Shropshire)
Gallery 6, 6 Church St., Broseley TF12 5DG. T. (01952) 882860. - Paint / Graph - 085985

Brougham (Cumbria)
House of Eden, Brougham Hall, Brougham. T. (01768) 899091. - Paint - 085986

Broughton (Borders)
Broughton Gallery, Broughton Pl., Broughton ML12 6HJ. T. (018994) 234. - Paint - 085987

Broughton Astley (Leicestershire)
Old Bakehouse Gallery, 10 Green Rd., Broughton Astley LE9 6RA. T. 282276. - Paint / Graph - 085988

Bruton (Somerset)
Bruton Gallery, High St., Bruton BA10 0AB. T. (01749) 812205, Fax (01749) 813303. - Paint / Sculp - 085989

Gallery 16, 16 High St., Bruton. T. (01749) 812205.
- Paint - 085990

Buchlyvie (Central)
Baxter, 29 Culbowie Crescent, Buchlyvie.
T. (0136085) 410. - Graph - 085991

Bude (Cornwall)
Trade Winds, 26 Queen St., Bude. T. (01288) 352594.
- Paint - 085992

Budleigh Salterton (Devon)
New Gallery, 9 Fore St., Budleigh Salterton EX9 6NG.
T. (013954) 443768. - Paint / Graph / Draw - 085993
New Gallery, Abele Tree House, 9 Fore St, Budleigh Sal-
terton EX9 6NG. T. (01395) 443768. - Paint /
Graph - 085994

Bulkington (Warwickshire)
Sport and Country Gallery, Northwood House, 121 West-
on Lane, Bulkington CV12 9RX. T. (01203) 314335.
- Paint - 085995

Bungay (Suffolk)
Cransford, 20 Broad St., Bungay. T. (01986) 892043.
- Paint - 085996

Burford (Oxfordshire)
Burford Gallery, Classica House, High St., Burford.
T. (01993) 822305. - Paint - 085997
Compass Art, The Forge, High St., Burford.
T. (01993) 823594. - Paint - 085998
Grafton House Gallery, 128 High St., Burford.
T. (01993) 822603. - Paint - 085999
Sinfield, Brian, 128 High St., Burford. T. (01993) 822603.
- Paint - 086000
Stone Gallery, High St., Burford. T. (01993) 3302.
- Paint - 086001
Swan Gallery, High St., Burford. T. (01993) 2244.
- Paint - 086002
Wren, 4 Bear Court, High St., Burford OX18 4RR.
T. (01993) 823495. - Paint - 086003

Burghfield Common (Berkshire)
Graham Gallery, Highwoods, Burghfield Common RG7
3BG. T. (01734) 832320, Fax (01734) 832320. - Paint /
Graph - 086004
Steeds, J. F. Graham, Highwoods, Burghfield Common.
T. (01734) 832320. - Paint - 086005

Burley (Hampshire)
Wishing Well Gallery, The Cross, Burley.
T. (014253) 2336. - Paint - 086006

Burley-in-Wharfedale (West Yorkshire)
Brook, C.A. & J., 30 Main St., Burley-in-Wharfedale.
T. (01943) 864569. - Paint - 086007

Burnham-on-Sea (Somerset)
Purcell Gallery, 10 Victoria St., Burnham-on-Sea.
T. (01278) 788587. - Paint - 086008

Burnham Overy Staithe (Norfolk)
Overy Gallery, East Harbour Way, Burnham Overy Staithe. T. (01328) 730097. - Paint - 086009

Burnley (Lancashire)
Ashenden, 161-163 Saint James St., Burnley.
T. (01282) 20563. - Paint - 086010
Coach House Craft Gallery, Gawthorpe Hall, Padiham,
Burnley. T. (01282) 78511. 086011
Portfolio Galleries, 8 Hargreaves St., Burnley.
T. (01282) 31658. - Paint - 086012

Burnsall (North Yorkshire)
Yorkshire Crafts, Old Methodist Chapel, Barden, Burnsall. T. (01756) 720659. - Paint - 086013

Burwash (East Sussex)
Martlet, High St., Burwash. T. (01435) 882995.
- Paint - 086014

Burwell (Cambridgeshire)
Abbott, Dick & Mary, 4 High St., Burwell.
T. (01638) 741787. - Paint - 086015
Infinite Art, 52a Toyse Lane, Burwell. T. (01638) 743504.
- Paint - 086016

Bury (Lancashire)
Carne Owens, 99 Crostons Rd., Bury BL8 1AL.
T. (0161) 762 9906. - Paint - 086017

Bury Saint Edmunds (Suffolk)
Guildhall Galleries, 1 Churchgate St., Bury Saint Edmunds IP32. T. (01284) 762366. - Paint - 086018
Saint John's Gallery, 26 Saint John's St., Bury Saint Edmunds. T. (01284) 769573. - Paint - 086019
Sovereign Art Studios, 107 Oakes Rd., Bury Saint Edmunds IP32 6QS. T. (01284) 761123. - Paint - 086020

Bushey (Hertfordshire)
Egerton, Haydon DellFarm, Merry Hill Rd., Bushey WD2.
T. (0181) 950 4769. - Paint - 086021

Buxton (Derbyshire)
Van Gogh Studios, 10 Cavendish Circus, Buxton.
T. (01298) 70566. - Paint - 086022

Cadeby (Leicestershire)
Stanworth, P., The Grange, Cadeby CV13 0AX.
T. (01455) 291023. - Paint - 086023

Caerleon (Gwent)
Harper, 25 High St., Caerleon. T. (01633) 42 31 32.
- Paint - 086024

Caernarvon (Gwynedd)
Williams, D.T., Dai Studios, High St., Caernarvon.
T. (01286) 77400. - Paint - 086025

Caerphilly (Mid Glamorgan)
Castle Frames, White St., Caerphilly. T. (01222) 887040.
- Paint - 086026
Coach House Gallery, Mountain Rd, Caerphilly CF8 1HH.
T. (01222) 863500. - Graph - 086027
Railway Gallery, Old Station Booking Hall, Cardiff Rd.,
Caerphilly CF8. T. (01222) 862808. - Paint /
Graph - 086028

Calne (Wiltshire)
Court Gallery, 6 London Rd., Calne. T. (01249) 812924.
- Paint - 086029

Camberley (Surrey)
Colour and Canvas, 161 London Rd., Camberley.
T. (01276) 682142. - Paint / Graph - 086030

Cambridge (Cambridgeshire)
Broughton House Gallery, 98 King St., Cambridge CB1
1LN. T. (01223) 314960, Fax (01223) 314960.
- Paint - 086031
Business Arts Conservatory Gallery, 6 Hills Av., Cambrid-
ge CB1 4XA. T. (01223) 211311. - Paint / Graph /
Sculp - 086032
Cambridge Darkroom Gallery, Unit 8, Gwydir St, Cam-
bridge. T. (01223) 350725. - Paint - 086033
Cambridge Fine Art, 33 Church St, Cambridge CB2 5HG.
T. (01223) 842866. - Paint - 086034
CCA Galleries, 6 Trinity St., Cambridge CB2 1SU.
T. (01223) 324222, Fax (01223) 315606.
- Paint - 086035
Conservatory Gallery, 6 Hills Av., Cambridge CB1 4XX.
T. (01223) 211311. - Paint / Graph / Sculp - 086036
Curwen Chilford, Chilford Hall, Cambridge CB1 6LE.
T. (01223) 893544, Fax (01223) 894054.
- Graph - 086037
Gallery on the Cam, Chesterton Rd., Cambridge CB4
3BD. T. (01223) 316901. - Paint - 086038
Ganz & Co., 2 Clare St., Cambridge CB4 3BY.
T. (01223) 316887. - Paint - 086039
Heffer, 19 Sidney St., Cambridge. T. (01223) 358241.
- Paint / Graph / Sculp - 086040
Kettle's Yard Gallery, Castle St., Cambridge CB3 0AQ.
T. (01223) 352124. - Paint - 086041
Oriel, 13 Fair St., Cambridge CB1 1HA.
T. (01223) 321027. - Paint - 086042
Pain, Jean, 7-8 Kings Parade, Cambridge CB2 1SJ.
T. (01223) 313970. - Graph - 086043
Primavera, 10 Kings Parade, Cambridge CB2 1SJ.
T. (01223) 357708. - Paint - 086044
Trumpington Gallery, 52 High St., Trumpington, Cam-
bridge CB2 2LS. T. (01223) 841656. - Paint - 086045

Warwick & Son, 102 Cherry Hinton Rd., Cambridge.
T. (01223) 246896. - Paint - 086046

Cannock (Staffordshire)
Fine Line Frames, 6-8 Wolverhampton Rd., Cannock.
T. (01543) 462570. - Paint - 086047

Canterbury (Kent)
Chaucer, 5 Iron Bar Lane, Canterbury.
T. (01227) 768222. - Paint - 086048
Drew, 16 Best Lane, Canterbury CT1 2JB.
T. (01227) 458759. - Paint - 086049
Macklin, Terence, 3 Margarets St, Canterbury.
T. (01227) 761000. - Paint - 086050
Maslen, Phillip, 60a Northgate, Canterbury.
T. (01227) 763518. - Paint - 086051
Nevill, 43 St. Peter's St, Canterbury CT1 2BG.
T. (01227) 765291. - Paint / Graph - 086052
Saint Peters Street Gallery, 42 Saint Peters St., Canter-
bury. T. (01227) 768033. - Paint - 086053
Tabor Gallery, The Barn, All Saints Lane, Canterbury CT1
2AU. T. (01227) 462570. - Paint / Sculp - 086054

Cardiff (South Glamorgan)
Albany Gallery, 74b Albany Rd., Cardiff CF2 3RS.
T. (01222) 487158. - Paint - 086055
Beere, Richard, 115-117 Woodville Rd., Cardiff.
T. (01222) 394131. - Paint - 086056
Chapter, Market Rd., Canton, Cardiff CF5 1QE.
T. (01222) 396061. - Paint - 086057
Fotogallery, 31 Charles St., Cardiff. T. (01222) 341667.
- Pho - 086058
Manor House Fine Arts, 73-75 Pontcanna St., Cardiff
CF1 9HS. T. (01222) 227787. - Paint / Furn / China /
Fra / Silv - 086059
Old Library, The Hayes, Cardiff. T. (01222) 343941.
- Paint - 086060
Oriel, The Friary, Cardiff CF1 4AA. T. (01222) 395548.
- Paint / Graph / Sculp - 086061
Saint David's Hall, The Hayes, Cardiff.
T. (01222) 342611. - Paint - 086062
Sport of Kings, 14 Balcony Castle Arcade, Cardiff.
T. (01222) 228090. - Paint / Graph 086063
Studio Gallery, 18 Llandaff Rd., Canton, Cardiff CF1 9NJ.
T. (01222) 383419. - Paint / Graph - 086064
West Wharf Gallery, Jacobs Bldg., West Canal Wharf,
Cardiff. T. (01222) T664797. - Paint / Graph / Sculp /
Draw - 086065

Cardigan (Dyfed)
Studio, 3 Cambrian Quay, Cardigan. T. (01239) 613711.
- Paint / Graph - 086066

Carleton (West Yorkshire)
Atack Fine Art, Simon, 4 Easthaugh, Carleton Rd, Carleton WF8 3RP. T. (01977) 708698. 086067

Carlisle (Cumbria)
Abbey Art Galleries, 80 Wigton Rd., Carlisle.
T. (01228) 515250. - Paint - 086068

Carnforth (Lancashire)
Haworth Gallery, Peter, Howe Hill, Cow Brow, Carnforth
LA6 1PG. T. (015395) 67656, Fax (015395) 67827.
- Paint - 086069

Carrick Fergus (Co. Antrim)
Swift, Jonathan, Kilroot Business Park, Larne Rd., Carrick Fergus. T. (012383) 67778. - Paint - 086070

Castle Ashby (Northamptonshire)
Geoffrey S. Wright Fine Paintings, Castle Ashby Gallery,
Castle Ashby NN7 1LF. T. (01604) 696787,
Fax (01604) 696787. - Paint - 086071

Castle Cary (Somerset)
Berkeley Gallery, The Old Vicarage, Castle Cary BA7
7EJ. T. (01963) 50748, Fax (01963) 50748.
- Paint - 086072

**Castle Douglas (Dumfries and Gallo\-
way)**
Framing Centre, Riverbank Industrial Unit, Gatehouse of
Fleet, Castle Douglas. T. (01556) 814737. - Paint /
Graph - 086073

McGill-Duncan, 231 King St., Castle Douglas.
T. (01556) 2468. - Paint - *086074*

Castle Hedingham (Essex)
Castle Gallery, 12 Saint James St., Castle Hedingham.
T. (01787) 60076. - Paint - *086075*

Caterham (Surrey)
Shop On The Hill, 80 High St., Caterham.
T. (01883) 349788. - Paint - *086076*

Caversham (Berkshire)
Collectors Gallery, 8 Bridge St, Caversham Bridge, Caversham RG4 8AA. T. (01734) 483663. - Paint / Graph - *086077*

Cemaes Bay (Gwynedd)
Oriel Cemaes Gallery, 5 High St., Cemaes Bay.
T. (01407) 711300. - Paint - *086078*

Cerne Abbas (Dorset)
Bairstow, 34 Long St., Cerne Abbas. T. (01300) 341336.
- Paint - *086079*

Chagford (Devon)
Chagford Galleries, 20 The Square, Chagford.
T. (01647) 433287. - Paint - *086080*

Chappel (Essex)
Chappel Galleries, 15 Colchester Rd., Chappel CO6 2DE.
T. (01206) 240326. - Paint / Sculp - *086081*

Chartham (Kent)
Master Makers, Howfield Lane, Chartham.
T. (01227) 730183. - Paint - *086082*

Chelmsford (Essex)
Gallery, 44 Moulsham St., Chelmsford.
T. (01245) 353825. - Paint / Graph - *086083*
Gallery, 43 Moulsham St, Chelmsford CM2 0HY.
T. (01245) 353825. - Paint / Graph - *086084*
Knightsbridge Fine Arts, 66 High St, Chelmsford.
T. (01245) 76305. - Paint - *086085*
Phillips, 44 Baron Rd, Chelmsford CM3 5XQ.
T. (01245) 324854. - Paint / Graph - *086086*
Phillips, 33 Springfield Rd., Chelmsford CM2 6JE.
T. (01245) 359080. - Paint / Graph - *086087*

Cheltenham (Gloucestershire)
Contemporary Art Holdings, 268 London Rd., Charlton Kings, Cheltenham GL52 6RS. T. (01242) 251657.
- Paint - *086088*
Courtgard Gallery and Studio, Bath Terrace, Leckhampton, Cheltenham GL50 2AL. T. (01242) 221711.
- Paint - *086089*
Crown Gallery, 7 Winchcombe St., Cheltenham GL52 2LZ. T. (01242) 515716. - Paint - *086090*
Howard, David, 42 Moorend Crescent, Cheltenham.
T. (01242) 243379. - Paint / Draw - *086091*
Lawrence, Clive, 12 St. James St, Cheltenham.
T. (01242) 583562. - Paint / Graph - *086092*
Manor House Gallery, Manor House, Badgeworth Rd, Cheltenham GL51 6RJ. T. (01452) 713953,
Fax (01452) 713283. - Paint - *086093*
Marler, Jane, 5 Rotunda Terrace, Cheltenham GL50 1SW. T. (01242) 221788. - Paint - *086094*
Montpellier Gallery, 27 Courtgard, Montpellier St., Cheltenham GL50 1SR. T. (01242) 515165,
Fax (01242) 515165. - Paint - *086095*
Ogle, 1 Wellington Sq., Cheltenham GL50 4JU.
T. (01242) 231011, Fax (01242) 522191.
- Paint - *086096*
Parade Gallery, 6 St. James Terrace, Suffolk Parade, Cheltenham GL50 2AB. T. (01242) 241897.
- Paint - *086097*
Picture Box, 2c Regent St., Cheltenham GL50 1HE.
T. (01242) 260682. - Paint - *086098*
Turtle, 30 Suffolk Parade, Cheltenham GL50 2AE.
T. (01242) 241646. - Paint / Graph - *086099*
Whitcombe, A. & Co, 18 Promenade, Cheltenham GL50 1LR. T. (01242) 524519. - Paint - *086100*

Chepstow (Gwent)
Old Bell Gallery, Bank Chambers, Chepstow.
T. (01291) 3400. - Paint / Graph / Sculp / Jew /
Fra - *086101*

Workshop Gallery, 13 Lower Church St., Chepstow.
T. (01291) 4836. - Paint - *086102*

Chesham (Buckinghamshire)
Monopteros Fine Art & Antiques, Trinchicunum, 1 Hunters Close, Chesham. T. (01494) 771311.
- Paint - *086103*
Waterside Gallery, Montague Mills, 32 Bois Moor Rd.,
Chesham. T. (01494) 791365. - Paint - *086104*

Chester (Cheshire)
Abbey Gallery, 7 Rufus Court Abbeygreen, Northgate St.,
Chester. T. (01244) 312770. - Paint - *086105*
Agora Contemporary Art, Canal Warehouse, Whipcord Lane, Chester. T. (01244) 382579. - Paint - *086106*
Art Shop, 38 Watergate Row, Chester.
T. (01244) 320504. - Paint - *086107*
Baron, 68 Watergate St., Chester CH1 2LA.
T. (01244) 342520. - Paint / Graph - *086108*
City Wall Galleries, 1 City Wall, Northgate St., Chester CH1 2LG. T. (01244) 349212. - Paint - *086109*
Nabis, 3 St. Werburgh St, Chester. T. (01244) 315520.
- Paint - *086110*
Nicholson of Chester, Richard, 25 Watergate St, Chester CH1 2LB. T. (01244) 326818. - Graph - *086111*
Saint Peters Fine Art Gallery, Saint Peters Churchyard,
Northgate St., Chester. T. (01244) 345500.
- Paint - *086112*

Chewton Mendip (Somerset)
Decoy, Kings Hill, Chewton Mendip. T. (01761) 241357.
- Paint - *086113*

Chichester (West Sussex)
Canon Gallery, Appledream Ln., Chichester.
T. (01243) 786063. - Paint - *086114*
Chichester Centre of Arts, Saint Andrews Court, East St.,
Chichester. T. (01243) 779103. - Paint - *086115*
Craftwork, 6 St. Peters Market, West St, Chichester PO19 1QU. T. (01243) 532588. - Paint - *086116*
Hornblower, Sadlers Walk, 44 East St, Chichester PO19 1HQ. T. (01243) 531316. - Paint - *086117*
J & G Gallery, 28 West St., Chichester PO19 1QS.
T. (01243) 788828. - Paint - *086118*

Chippenham (Wiltshire)
Celler Gallery, 58 Market Pl., Chippenham.
T. (01249) 444963. - Paint - *086119*
Framing Gallery, 149a London Rd., Chippenham.
T. (01249) 443266. - Graph - *086120*

Chipping Campden (Gloucestershire)
Camperdene Gallery, Camperdene House, High St.,
Chipping Campden. T. (01386) 841300.
- Paint - *086121*

Chorley (Lancashire)
Art Glow, 78 Bolton Rd., Chorley. T. (012572) 273892.
- Paint - *086122*
Verncraft Fine Art Gallery, 7 Saint Georges St., Chorley.
T. (012572) 274205. - Paint / Graph - *086123*
Willow House Gallery, 60 Chapel St., Chorley PR7 1BS.
T. (012572) 261618. - Paint - *086124*

Christchurch (Dorset)
Hawes, G.D., 16 Arcadia Rd., Christchurch.
T. (01202) 470733. - Paint - *086125*

Churchstoke (Powys)
Dyke, The Cwm, Mellington, Churchstoke.
T. (01588) 620453. - Paint / Graph - *086126*

Cirencester (Gloucestershire)
Cirencester Workshops, Brewery Court, Cricklade St.,
Cirencester GL7 1JH. T. (01285) 651566.
- Paint - *086127*
Colw, 19 West Market Pl., Cirencester GL7.
T. (01285) 659085. - Paint - *086128*
Delahaye, 24 Castle St., Cirencester GL7 1QH.
T. (01285) 654674. - Paint - *086129*
Marler, William, 36 Dyer St., Cirencester.
T. (01285) 641641. - Paint / Graph - *086130*
Niccol Centre, Brewery Court, Cirencester.
T. (01285) 657181. - Paint - *086131*

Clare (Suffolk)
Clare Gallery, 8 High St., Clare. T. (01787) 277825.
- Paint - *086132*

Claxby (Lincolnshire)
Terico, The Brook, Normanby Rise, Claxby.
T. (0167382) 484. - Paint - *086133*

Clevedon (Avon)
Clevedon Fine Arts, The Gallery, Cinema Bldgs., Old Church Rd., Clevedon. T. (01272) 875862.
- Paint - *086134*
Toll House Gallery, Clevedon Pier, The Beach, Clevedon BS21 7QU. T. (01275) 878846. - Paint / Graph - *086135*

Clitheroe (Lancashire)
Ethos Gallery, 4 York St., Clitheroe. T. (01200) 27878.
- Paint - *086136*

Cobham (Surrey)
Studio 54, 54 High St., Cobham. T. (01932) 865252.
- Paint - *086137*

Cockermouth (Cumbria)
Castlegate House, Castlegate, Cockermouth CA13 9HA.
T. (01900) 822149. - Paint - *086138*

Colchester (Essex)
Colchester Arts Forum, 6 Trinity St., Colchester CO1 1JN. T. (01206) 369188. - Paint - *086139*
Framing Centre, 1-2 East Bay, Colchester.
T. (01206) 868512. - Paint / Graph - *086140*
Haylett, 34 North Hill, Colchester. T. (01206) 761837.
- Paint - *086141*
Iles, Richard, 10-12 Northgate St., Colchester CO1 1HA.
T. (01206) 577877. - Paint - *086142*
Locksley, 21 Eld Lane, Colchester. T. (01206) 564011.
- Paint - *086143*
Original Art Shop, 34 Sir Isaac Walk, Colchester.
T. (01206) 571999. - Paint - *086144*
Printworks, 45 Sir Isaacs Walk, Colchester.
T. (01206) 562049. - Graph - *086145*

Collyweston (Northamptonshire)
Close, David, 27 High St., Collyweston.
T. (0178083) 245. - Pho - *086146*

Colne (Lancashire)
Wycoller Craft Centre, Wycoller, Colne.
T. (01282) 868395. - Paint - *086147*

Colyton (Devon)
Dolphin House Gallery, Dolphin St, Colyton EX13 6NA.
T. (01297) 53805. - Paint / Graph - *086148*

Comber (Co. Down)
Castle Espie Gallery, 78a Ballydrain Rd., Comber BT23 6EA. T. (01247) 872517. - Paint - *086149*
Salem Gallery, 29 Mill St., Comber. T. (01247) 874455.
- Paint - *086150*

Compton (Surrey)
Watts, Down Lane, Compton. T. (01483) 810235.
- Paint - *086151*

Congleton (Cheshire)
Carter, 54 Lawton St., Congleton. T. (01260) 298079.
- Paint - *086152*

Conwy (Gwynedd)
Conway Trading Company, High St., Conwy.
T. (01492) 593708. - Paint - *086153*
Royal Cambrian Academy of Art, Plas Mawr, High St.,
Conwy. T. (01492) 593413. - Paint - *086154*

Cookham (Berkshire)
Phillips & Sons, Dower House, Sutton Rd., Cookham.
T. (016285) 529337. - Paint - *086155*

Corpusty (Norfolk)
Old Workshop Art Gallery, The Street, Corpusty.
T. (0126387) 268. - Paint / Graph / Sculp - *086156*

Costessey (Norfolk)
Coach House, Townhouse Rd., Costessey. T. 742977.
- Paint / Graph / Draw - *086157*

Coughton (Warkwickshire)
Coughton Galleries, Coughton Court, Coughton.
T. 762542. - Paint -   *086158*

Cousley Wood (East Sussex)
Montague Ward, Lime Trees, Cousley Wood.
T. (0189288) 3673. - Paint -   *086159*

Coventry (West Midlands)
Croft Wingates, Unit 32, Cathedral Lane, Coventry.
T. (01203) 632458. - Paint -   *086160*
Friswell, 223 Albany Rd, Coventry. T. (01203) 674883.
- Paint -   *086161*
Mead, Arts Centre, University of Warwick, Coventry.
T. (01203) 523523. - Paint / Pho -   *086162*

Cowbridge (South Glamorgan)
Kingfisher, 3 Willow Walk, Cowbridge CF7 7EE.
T. (014463) 775173. - Paint -   *086163*
Owen, John, 55 Eastgate, Cowbridge CF7 7EL.
T. (014463) 774774. - Paint -   *086164*
Watercolour Gallery, Old Wool Barn, Verity's Court, Cow-
bridge CF7 7AJ. T. (014463) 773324. - Paint /
Graph -   *086165*

Cowes (Isle of Wight)
Cameron, Julia Margaret, 90b High St., Cowes.
T. (01983) 290404. - Paint -   *086166*
Marine Gallery, Bath Rd., Cowes. T. (01983) 200124.
- Paint -   *086167*

Cowling (North Yorkshire)
Brent, 60a Keighley Rd., Cowling. T. (01535) 636892.
- Paint -   *086168*

Craigavon (Co. Armagh)
Craigavon Arts, Tullygally Rd, Craigavon.
T. (01762) 341618. - Pho -   *086169*

Cranbrook (Kent)
Cranbrook Gallery, 21b Stone St., Cranbrook TN17 3HE.
T. (01580) 713021. - Paint -   *086170*

Cranham (Gloucestershire)
Heather Newmann, Milidduwa, Mill Ln., Cranham GL6
6TX. T. (01452) 812230. - Paint / Draw -   *086171*

Cranleigh (Surrey)
Cranleigh Arts Centre, High St., Cranleigh.
T. (01483) 278001. - Paint -   *086172*
Rubenstein, Barbara, Smithwood House, Smithwood
Common, Cranleigh. T. (01483) 267969, Fax 267535.
- Paint -   *086173*

Crewkerne (Somerset)
Blake, George Lane, Crewkerne. T. (01460) 76930.
- Paint -   *086174*

Criccieth (Gwynedd)
Annabelles, 15 High St., Criccieth. T. (01766) 523255.
- Paint -   *086175*

Crickhowell (Powys)
Riverside Gallery, New Road, Crickhowell NP8 1AT.
T. (01873) 810769, Fax (01873) 811531. - Paint /
Sculp -   *086176*

Crieff (Tayside)
Aiton, 63 King St., Crieff. T. (01764) 5423.
- Paint -   *086177*

Cromer (Norfolk)
Bond Street Gallery, 7 Bond St., Cromer NR27 9DA.
T. (01263) 512127. - Paint -   *086178*

Croydon (Greater London)
Apollo, 65 South End, Croydon CR0 1BF.
T. (0181) 681 3727. - Paint / Furn / Orient / China /
Sculp -   *086179*
Brown, C. W., 107 Church St., Croydon CR0.
T. (0181) 688 0919. - Paint -   *086180*
Croydon Art Gallery, 42 St. Georges Walk, Croydon CR0.
T. (0181) 680 7921. - Paint -   *086181*
Simmons, A. W. John & Son, 77 South End, Croydon
CR0. T. (0181) 688 0990. - Paint -   *086182*
Whitgift Centre Gallery, Unit 10, 49 Whitgift Centre,
Croydon CR0. T. (0181) 760 5142. - Paint -   *086183*

Whitgift Galleries, 77 South End, Croydon CR0 1BF.
T. (0181) 688 0990. - Paint -   *086184*

Cullercoats (Tyne and Wear)
Gallery 84, 52-53 Front St., Cullercoats.
T. (0191) 253 0114. - Paint -   *086185*

Cupar (Fife)
Gallery, Burnside, Cupar. T. (01334) 52353.
- Paint -   *086186*

Curry Rivel (Somerset)
Coopers Cross Gallery, High St., Curry Rivel.
T. (01458) 251116. - Paint -   *086187*

Cwmbran (Gwent)
Llantarnam Grange Art Centre, St. Davids Rd, Cwmbran.
T. (016333) 3321. - Paint -   *086188*

Darlington (Durham)
Bernhardt, 60 Coniscliffe Rd., Darlington DL3 7RN.
T. (01325) 356633. - Paint / Paint / Graph -   *086189*
Cockerton Gallery, 34 The Green, Cockerton Green, Dar-
lington. T. (01325) 469364. - Paint -   *086190*
Dodds, William, 34 Tubwell Row, Darlington.
T. (01325) 462599. - Paint / Graph -   *086191*

Dartmouth (Devon)
Drew, Simon, 13 Foss St., Dartmouth.
T. (01803) 832832. - Paint -   *086192*
Gillo, John, 3 Old Market, Dartmouth.
T. (01803) 833833. - Paint -   *086193*

Datchet (Berkshire)
Century Gallery Datchet, The Shop-on-the-Green, Dat-
chet SL3 9JH. T. (01753) 581284. - Paint -   *086194*
Marian & John Alway, Riverside Cnr, Windsor Rd, Dat-
chet SL3 9BT. T. (01753) 541163, Fax (01753) 541163.
- Paint -   *086195*

Daventry (Northamptonshire)
Evergreen Gallery, 12 Sheaf St., Daventry.
T. (01327) 78117. - Graph -   *086196*

Dawlish (Devon)
Crawshaw, 3 Priory Rd., Dawlish. T. (01626) 862032.
- Paint -   *086197*

Deal (Kent)
Joem, 14-16 Broad St., Deal. T. (01304) 368688.
- Paint -   *086198*

Debenham (Suffolk)
Debenham Gallery, 1 High St., Debenham IP14 6QL.
T. (01728) 860707. - Paint -   *086199*

Dedham (Essex)
Dedham Art and Craft Centre, High St., Dedham.
T. (0120632) 322666. - Paint -   *086200*

Derby (Derbyshire)
Classic Fine Arts, 15 Sadler Gate, Derby.
T. (01332) 294881. - Paint / Graph -   *086201*
Green Lane Art Gallery, 130 Green Lane, Derby.
T. (01332) 368652. - Paint -   *086202*
Saint Werbourghs Gallery, Saint Werbourghs Cloisters,
Friargate, Derby. T. (01332) 298207. - Paint -   *086203*
Temple Gallery, 348 Abbey St., Derby.
T. (01332) 293752. - Paint -   *086204*

Dereham (Norfolk)
Cowper Gallery, Westfield Rd, Dereham NR19 1JB.
T. (01362) 692248. - Paint -   *086205*
Portrait Artists of East Anglia, Brick Kiln Studio, Bylaugh
Park, Dereham NR20 4RL. T. (01362) 515. - Paint /
Graph -   *086206*

Dersingham (Norfolk)
Bachkauskas, R.T., 47a Chapel Rd., Dersingham.
T. (01485) 541400. - Paint -   *086207*

Devizes (Wiltshire)
Devizes Fine Art, Cornstone, Couch Lane, Devizes.
T. (01380) 729527. - Graph -   *086208*
Garton & Co., Roundway House, Devizes SN10 2EG.
T. (01380) 729624. - Graph -   *086209*

Didcot (Oxfordshire)
Rocket Contemporary Art, Millcroft Stables, Berry Lane,
Didcot OX11 9QJ. T. (01235) 851046. - Paint /
Graph -   *086210*

Dirleton (Lothian)
Dirleton Gallery, Manse Rd., Dirleton. T. (0162085) 528.
- Paint -   *086211*

Diss (Norfolk)
Falcon Gallery, Honeypot Farm, Diss IP22 1PW.
T. (01379) 783312. - Paint -   *086212*

Ditchling (East Sussex)
Chichester House Gallery, 11 High St., Ditchling BN6
8SY. T. (01273) 4167. - Paint / Repr -   *086213*
Ditchling Gallery, 30 High St., Ditchling.
T. (01273) 843342. - Graph -   *086214*

Donaghadee (Co. Down)
Dolphin Design, 15 Moat St., Donaghadee.
T. (01247) 883066. - Paint -   *086215*

Doncaster (South Yorkshire)
South Yorkshire Art, 52 Copley Rd., Doncaster DN1 2QW.
T. (01302) 329332. - Paint -   *086216*

Dorchester (Dorset)
Dorchester Gallery, 10a High East St., Dorchester DT1
1HS. T. (01305) 251144. - Paint -   *086217*
Gallery, 20 Durngate St., Dorchester. T. (01305) 297408.
- Paint -   *086218*
Manorgate Fine Art, 55 Bridport Rd., Dorchester.
T. (01305) 267779. - Paint -   *086219*

Dorchester-on-Thames (Oxfordshire)
Dorchester Galleries, Rotten Row, Dorchester-on-Thames. T. (01865) 341116. - Paint -   *086220*

Dorking (Surrey)
King's Court Galleries, 54 West St., Dorking RH4 1BS.
T. (01306) 881757, Fax (01306) 75305.
- Graph -   *086221*
Norman, 7 Old Kings Head Court, High St., Dorking.
T. (01306) 888523. - Paint -   *086222*
Spectrum Gallery, 268 High St., Dorking RH14 1QT.
T. (01306) 886088. - Paint -   *086223*

Dorridge (West Midlands)
Dorridge Gallery, 5 Arden Bldgs., Station Rd., Dorridge
B93 8HH. T. 779057. - Paint -   *086224*

Douglas (Isle of Man)
Artist, 22 Church St., Douglas. T. (01624) 29851.
- Paint / Graph -   *086225*

Dover (Kent)
Castle Fine Art Studio, 26 Castle St., Dover.
T. (01304) 206360. - Paint -   *086226*
Morrill, J.W., 437 Folkestone Rd., Dover.
T. (01304) 201989. - Paint -   *086227*

Downpatrick (Co. Down)
Down Arts Centre, 2-6 Irish St., Downpatrick.
T. (01396) 615283. - Paint -   *086228*
Scaddin, 15 Myra Rd., Downpatrick. T. (01396) 612268.
- Paint -   *086229*

Dromore (Co. Down)
Enterprise, 6 Church St., Dromore. T. (01846) 699813.
- Paint -   *086230*

Droylsden (Greater Manchester)
Wottapikture, 139 Manchester Rd., Droylsden M35.
T. (0161) 370 4913. - Paint -   *086231*

Drymen (Central)
Rowan, 36 Main St., Drymen G63 0BG.
T. (01360) 60996, Fax (01360) 70993. - Paint -   *086232*

Dudley (West Midlands)
Artist Studio M.A. Design, 6 Cotwall End Nature Centre,
Dudley. T. (01384) 880936. - Paint -   *086233*
Weetslade Fine Art, High Weetslade, Dudley.
T. (01384) 2500174. - Paint -   *086234*

Duffield (Derbyshire)
Duffield Art Gallery and Antiques, 3-5 Town St., Duffield. T. (01332) 840845. - Paint - 086235

Dulverton (Somerset)
Old Blacksmith's Gallery, Bridge St., Dulverton. T. (01398) 23699. - Paint - 086236

Dumfries (Dumfries and Galloway)
Bryden, 11 Galloway St., Dumfries. T. (01387) 67337. - Paint - 086237
Criffel, Glencaple Rd, Dumfries. T. (01387) 59379. - Paint - 086238
Gracefield, 28 Edinburgh Rd., Dumfries DG1 1JQ. T. (01387) 62084. - Paint - 086239
Maxwelltown Gallery, 12 Galloway St., Dumfries. T. (01387) 64204. - Paint / Graph - 086240
Ottersburn, 2a Nith Av., Dumfries. T. (01387) 54860. - Paint - 086241

Dunblane (Central)
Cornerstone Gallery, Cathedral Sq., Dunblane. T. (01786) 823696, Fax (0141) 3325032. - Paint - 086242

Dundee (Tayside)
Alessandro, Eduardo, 30 Gray St., Broughty Ferry, Dundee. T. (01382) 737011. - Paint - 086243
Art for All, Old Mill, 1 Guthrie St., Dundee DD1 5DY. T. (01382) 22122. - Paint / Graph - 086244
Dundee Art Society, 17 Roseangle, Dundee. T. (01382) 22429. - Paint - 086245
Dundee Arts Centre, Saint Mary Pl., Dundee. T. (01382) 201035. - Paint - 086246
Dundee Printmakers Workshop, 36-40 Seagate, Dundee. T. (01382) 26331. - Graph - 086247
Fraser & Son, 38 Commercial St., Dundee. T. (01382) 25284. - Paint - 086248
Seagate Gallery, 36-40 Seagate, Dundee. T. (01382) 26331. - Graph - 086249
West End Gallery, 85b Perth Rd., Dundee. T. (01382) 200053. - Paint / Graph - 086250
Westport Fine Art, 3 Old Hawkhill, Dundee. T. (01382) 22033. - Paint - 086251
Windsor Gallery, 61 Perth Rd., Dundee. T. (01382) 202863. - Paint - 086252

Dunfermline (Fife)
Moving Pictures, Blair Hall, Culross, Dunfermline KY12 8EP. T. (01383) 880582. - Paint - 086253

Dungannon (Co. Tyrone)
Rhoneview Art Gallery, 15 Church St., Dungannon. T. (018687) 25626. - Paint - 086254

Dunkeld (Tayside)
Atholl Gallery, 6 Atholl St., Dunkeld PH8 0AR. T. (01350) 728855. - Paint / Graph - 086255

Dunster (Somerset)
Bishop, Maurice, 6 Castle Hill, Dunster. T. (01643) 821052. - Paint / Graph - 086256

Dunvegan (Isle of Skye, Highland)
Orbost Gallery, Half Bolvean, Dunvegan IV55 8ZB. T. (0147) 022207. - Paint / Graph - 086257

Durham
Grants Galleries, 38-40 The Bank, Basrnard Castle, Co., Durham DL12 8PN. T. (01833) 37437. - Paint - 086258

Durham
Saddler Gallery, 78 Saddler St., Durham DH1 3NP. T. (0191) 384 8541. - Paint - 086259

Durley Street (Hampshire)
Stokes, Kenneth, Rodlands, Durley Street. T. (014896) 5921607 2202J. 086260

Eaglescliffe (Cleveland)
Jordan, T.B. & R., Aslak, Aislaby, Eaglescliffe. T. 782599. - Paint - 086261

East Grinstead (West Sussex)
Antique Print Shop, 11 Middle Row, High St, East Grinstead RH19 3AX. T. (01342) 410501, Fax (01342) 322149. - Paint / Graph - 086262

East Molesey (Surrey)
Court Gallery, 16 Bridge Rd, East Molesey KT8 9HA. T. (0181) 9412212. - Paint - 086263
Molesey Gallery, 46 Walton Rd., East Molesey KT8 0DQ. T. (0181) 941 2706. - Paint - 086264

Eastbourne (East Sussex)
Eastbourne Fine Art, 9 Meads St., Eastbourne BN20 7QY. T. (01323) 25634. - Paint - 086265
Penns, 3 Calverley Walk, South St., Eastbourne BN21 4UJ. T. (01323) 25204. - Paint - 086266
Picture Palace, 228 Terminus Rd., Eastbourne BN21 3DF. T. (01323) 35368. - Paint - 086267
Premier Gallery, 24-26 South St., Eastbourne BN21 4XB. T. (01323) 36023. - Paint - 086268
Stacy-Marks, E., 24 Cornfield Rd., Eastbourne BN21 4QH. T. (01323) 20429. - Paint - 086269
Stewart, 25 Grove Rd., Eastbourne BN21 4TT. T. (01323) 29588, Fax (01323) 29588. - Paint - 086270
Towner, Borough Lane, Eastbourne. T. (01323) 411688. - Paint - 086271

Eccles (Lancashire)
Art to Art, 64 Liverpool Rd., Eccles M30. T. (0161) 707 2261. - Paint - 086272

Eccleshall (Staffordshire)
Alla Prima Gallery, High St., Eccleshall. T. (01785) 850638. - Paint - 086273

Eccleston (Lancashire)
Fotheringhams, Unit 1, Carrington Centre, Eccleston. T. (01257) 453781. - Paint - 086274

Edenbridge (Kent)
Unicorn Gallery, 6 The Village, CrockhamHill, Edenbridge. T. (01732) 856226. - Paint - 086275

Edinburgh (Lothian)
Art Et Facts, 9 Roseburn Terrace, Edinburgh EH12. T. (0131) 346 7730. - Paint - 086276
Art in Partnership, 233 Cowgate, Edinburgh EH1. T. (0131) 225 4463. - Paint - 086277
Barnes & Fitzgerald, 47b George St., Edinburgh EH2 2HT. T. (0131) 220 1305. - Paint - 086278
Bourne, 4 Dundas St., Edinburgh EH3 6HZ. T. (0131) 557 4050, Fax (0131) 5578382. - Paint - 086279
Buro, 132 Queensferry Rd., Edinburgh EH4 3BG. T. (0131) 315 2288. - Paint - 086280
Calton, 10 Royal Terrace, Edinburgh EH7 5AB. T. (0131) 556 1010, Fax (0131) 5581150. - Paint - 086281
Carlyle, 19 North Bridge, Edinburgh EH1 1SD. T. (0131) 557 5068, Fax (0131) 5562691. - Paint / Graph - 086282
Carson, Clark, 173 Canongate, Edinburgh EH8 8BN. T. (0131) 556 4710. - Paint - 086283
Collective Gallery, 22-28 Cockburn St., Edinburgh EH1 1NY. T. (0131) 220 1260. - Paint - 086284
Craigmillar Festival Society, Newcraighall Rd, Edinburgh EH15. T. (0131) 669 8432. - Paint - 086285
Dalkeith Arts Centre, White Hart St, Edinburgh EH22. T. (0131) 663 6986. - Paint - 086286
Dawson, Eric D.B., 53 Corstorphine Hill Gardens, Edinburgh EH12 6LB. T. (0131) 334 7641. - Paint - 086287
Edinburgh Gallery, 18a Dundas St, Edinburgh EH3 6HZ. T. (0131) 5575227, Fax (0131) 5575227. - Paint - 086288
Edinburgh Printmakers Workshop & Gallery, 23 Union St, Edinburgh EH1 3LR. T. (0131) 5572479. - Graph - 086289
Fidelo, Tom, 49 Cumberland St., Edinburgh EH3 6RA. T. (0131) 557 2444. - Paint - 086290
Fine Art Gallery, 41 Dundas St., Edinburgh EH3 6QQ. T. (0131) 557 4569. - Paint - 086291
Fine Art Society, 137 George St., Edinburgh EH2 4JS. T. (0131) 220 6370. - Paint / Sculp - 086292
Flying Colours Gallery, 35 William St., Edinburgh EH3 7LW. T. (0131) 225 6776, Fax (0131) 2256776. - Paint / Graph - 086293
Forrest McKay, 38 Howe St., Edinburgh EH3 6TH. T. (0131) 226 2589. - Paint - 086294
Fraser & Son, Unit L2A, Waver by Market, Edinburgh EH2. T. (0131) 557 3875. - Paint - 086295
Friends of the Royal Scottish Academy, The Mound, Edinburgh EH2. T. (0131) 225 3922. - Paint - 086296
Fruitmarket Gallery, 29 Market St., Edinburgh EH1 1DF. T. (0131) 225 2385. - Paint / Sculp / Draw - 086297
Gallerie Mirages, 46a Raeburn Pl., Edinburgh EH4 1HL. T. (0131) 315 2603. - Paint - 086298
Gallery 41, 41 Dundas St, Edinburgh EH3 6QQ. T. (0131) 5574569. - Paint / Sculp - 086299
Gayfield, 77a Broughton St., Edinburgh EH1 3RJ. T. (0131) 556 2553. - Paint - 086300
Hanover Fine Arts, 22a Dundas St., Edinburgh EH3 6JN. T. (0131) 556 2181. - Paint - 086301
Hillside Gallery, 6 Hillside St., Edinburgh EH7 5HB. T. (0131) 556 6440. - Paint - 086302
Innes, 219 Bruntsfield Pl., Edinburgh EH10 4DE. T. (0131) 447 8929. - Paint - 086303
Innes, Malcolm, 67 George St., Edinburgh EH2 2JG. T. (0131) 226 4151, Fax (0131) 2264151. - Paint - 086304
Kingfisher, 5 Northumberland St., Edinburgh EH3 3JL. T. (0131) 557 5454. - Paint - 086305
La Belle Angele, 11 Hasties Close, Cowgate, Edinburgh EH1 1JD. T. (0131) 225 2774. - Paint - 086306
Mathieson, John, 48 Frederick St., Edinburgh. T. (0131) 225 6798. - Paint - 086307
Millar & Shackleton, 23 Dundas St., Edinburgh EH3 6QQ. T. (0131) 556 0234. - Paint - 086308
Nelson, John O., 22 Victoria St., Edinburgh EH1 2JN. T. (0131) 225 4413. - Graph - 086309
Open Eye Gallery, 75-79 Cumberland St., Edinburgh EH3 6RD. T. (0131) 557 1020. - Paint / Graph - 086310
Phillips, Charles, & Sons, Inveresek Industrial Estate, Edinburgh EH21. T. (0131) 665 6448. - Paint - 086311
Portfolio Gallery, 43 Candlemaker Row, Edinburgh EH1 2QB. T. (0131) 220 1911. - Pho - 086312
Printmakers Workshop, 23 Union St., Edinburgh EH1 3LR. T. (0131) 557 2479. - Graph / Fra - 086313
Quercus, 16 Howe St., Edinburgh EH3 6TD. T. (0131) 220 0147. - Paint - 086314
Royal Scottish Academy, The Mound, Edinburgh EH2. T. (0131) 225 6671. - Paint - 086315
R.S.A. Gallery Shop, The Mound, Edinburgh EH2. T. (0131) 220 2265. - Graph - 086316
Scottish Craft Centre, 140 Canongate, Edinburgh EH8 8DD. T. (0131) 5568136. - Paint - 086317
Scottish Gallery, 94 George St., Edinburgh EH2 3DF. T. (0131) 225 5955, Fax (0131) 2262312. - Paint / China / Sculp / Jew / Fra - 086318
Scottish Photographic Works, 14a Nelson St., Edinburgh EH3 6LG. T. (0131) 556 4017. - Pho - 086319
Shackleton, Daniel, 17 Dundas St, Edinburgh EH3 6QQ. T. (0131) 557 1115. - Paint - 086320
Solstice, 18a Dundas St., Edinburgh EH3 6HZ. T. (0131) 557 5227. - Paint - 086321
Step Gallery, 39 Howe St., Edinburgh EH3 6TF. T. (0131) 556 1613. - Paint - 086322
Stills, 105 High St., Edinburgh EH1 1S9. T. (0131) 557 1140. - Pho - 086323
Torrance Gallery, 29b Dundas St., Edinburgh EH3 6QQ. T. (0131) 556 6366. - Paint / Repr / Fra - 086324
Vaughan Huw, 73 Dublin St., Edinburgh EH3 6NS. T. (0131) 557 5259. - Paint - 086325
Waverley, 9 Jeffrey St., Edinburgh EH1 1DR. T. (0131) 5574757. - Paint - 086326
369 Gallery, 233 Cowgate, Edinburgh EH1 1NQ. T. (0131) 225 3013. - Paint / Graph - 086327

Egremont (Cumbria)
Lowes Court Gallery, 12 Main St., Egremont. T. (01946) 820693. - Paint - 086328

Elgin (Grampian)
Elgin Gallery, 80a South St., Elgin. T. (01343) 547153. - Paint - 086329
Moray, Birch Cottage, Findrassie, Elgin. T. (01343) 544012. - Paint - 086330

Elstree (Hertfordshire)
Hunter Fine Art Publisher, Anna, Stoneycroft House, Barnet Lane, Elstree WD6 3RQ. T. (0181) 9531307, Fax (0181) 2074989. - Graph - 086331

Ely (Cambridgeshire)
Old Fire Engine House, 25 St Mary's St, Ely CB7 4ER.
T. (01353) 662582. - Ant -   *086332*

Emsworth (Hampshire)
Screens Gallery, Malthouse, Bridgefoot Path, Emsworth
PO10 7EB. T. (01243) 377334. - Paint -   *086333*

Enfield (Greater London)
Anticacia, 57 Lancaster Rd., Enfield EN2 0BU.
T. (0181) 367 0111. - Paint -   *086334*
Hanging Around, 122 Chase Side, Enfield EN5 0QN.
T. (0181) 363 1099. - Paint -   *086335*

Enniskillen (Co. Fermanagh)
Willowisland, 25 Townhall St., Enniskillen.
T. (01365) 324733. - Paint -   *086336*

Esher (Surrey)
Kensington Sporting Paintings, Badgers Wood, West End
Lane, Esher KT10 8LB. T. (01372) 64407. - Paint /
Sculp -   *086337*
West End Galleries, 6 Winterdown Rd., Esher.
T. (01372) 464493. - Paint -   *086338*

Eton (Berkshire)
Contemporary Fine Art Gallery, 31 High St, Eton SL4
6BL. T. (01753) 854315. - Paint -   *086339*
Emgee Gallery, 60 High St, Eton SL4 6AA.
T. (01753) 856329, Fax (01753) 859889. - Paint /
Sculp -   *086340*
Eton Fine Art, 58 High St., Eton. T. (01753) 868266.
- Paint -   *086341*
Manley, J., 27 High St., Eton SL4 6AX.
T. (01753) 865647. - Paint -   *086342*
Maxwell, 3 Eton Court, Eton SL4 6BY. T. (01753) 858680.
- Paint / Graph -   *086343*

Everton (Nottinghamshire)
Tonicraft, White Lodge, Chapel Lane, Everton.
T. (0177786) 817216. - Paint -   *086344*

Evesham (Worcestershire)
Vale, 2-3 Bridge Court, Evesham WR11 9XX.
T. (01386) 45216. - Paint -   *086345*

Ewell (Surrey)
Epsom, 30 High St., Ewell KT17. T. (0181) 393 2128.
- Graph -   *086346*
Galeries des Beaux Arts, 30 High St., Ewell KT17.
T. (0181) 393 2129. - Paint -   *086347*

Exeter (Devon)
Cook, I.C., Weircliffe House, Exeter. T. (01392) 54573.
- Paint -   *086348*
Fore Street Gallery, 143b Fore St., Exeter.
T. (01392) 215789. - Paint -   *086349*
Kashan, 2 Roman Passage, High St., Exeter.
T. (01392) 213054. - Paint -   *086350*
Keetch, Fred, 21 Cathedral Yard, Exeter.
T. (01392) 74312. - Paint -   *086351*
Spacex Gallery, 45 Preston St., Exeter EX1 1DF.
T. (01392) 431786. - Paint -   *086352*
Vincent, 15 Magdalen Rd., Exeter. T. (01392) 430082.
- Paint -   *086353*

Fairburn (North Yorkshire)
Wild Goose Gallery, Silver St., Fairburn WF11 9JA.
T. (01977) 675089. - Paint -   *086354*

Falkirk (Central)
Pictorial Art, 15 Bank St., Falkirk. T. (01324) 611618.
- Paint -   *086355*
Picture Shop, 3 Kings Court High St., Falkirk.
T. (01324) 31002. - Paint -   *086356*
West End Gallery, 43 West Bridge St., Falkirk FK1 5HZ.
T. (01324) 613100. - Paint -   *086357*

Falmouth (Cornwall)
Beside the Wave, 10 Arwenack St., Falmouth TR11 3JA.
T. (01326) 211132, Fax (01326) 212212.
- Paint -   *086358*
Maggs, John, 54 Church St., Falmouth.
T. (01326) 313153. - Paint -   *086359*
Mulberry Art & Craft, 28a High St., Falmouth.
T. (01326) 312296. - Paint -   *086360*

Up and Above Gallery, 3 Market St., Falmouth.
T. (01326) 314182. - Paint -   *086361*

Fareham (Hampshire)
Coastal Galleries, Unit 91, Westbury Mall, Fareham
Shopping Centre, Fareham PO16. T. (01329) 822636.
- Paint -   *086362*
Fareham Gallery, 162b West St., Fareham PO16 0EH.
T. (01329) 281830. - Paint -   *086363*

Faringdon (Oxfordshire)
Faringdon Gallery, 21 London St., Faringdon SN7 7AG.
T. (01367) 242030. - Paint / Graph -   *086364*

Farndon (Cheshire)
Blue Dolphin Fine Art, Barn Studios, Farndon.
T. (01829) 271260. - Paint -   *086365*

Farnham (Surrey)
CCA Galleries, 13 Lion and Lamb Yard, West St., Farn-
ham GU9 7LL. T. (01252) 722231. - Graph -   *086366*
Johnson Wax Kiln Gallery, Farnham Maltings, Bridge
Sq., Farnham. T. (01252) 726234. - Paint -   *086367*
Lion & Lamb Gallery, At Biggs, West St., Farnham GU9
7HH. T. (01252) 714154. - Paint -   *086368*
Lloyd, Andrew, 17 Castle St., Farnham GU9 7JA.
T. (01252) 724333. - Paint -   *086369*
New Ashgate Gallery, Wagon Yard, Downing St., Farn-
ham GU9 7PS. T. (01252) 713208,
Fax (01252) 737398. - Paint / Graph / China / Sculp /
Jew / Fra / Silv / Glass / Draw -   *086370*

Felixstowe (Suffolk)
Norchwood, 156 Hamilton Pl., Felixstowe.
T. (01394) 671634. - Paint -   *086371*

Feock (Cornwall)
Trelissick Gallery, Trelissick Gardens, Feock.
T. (01872) 864084. - Paint -   *086372*

Fernhurst (West Sussex)
Fine Art Petworth, Upper Lodge, Henley Common, Fernhurst. T. (01428) 656177. - Paint -   *086373*

Filkins (Oxfordshire)
Cross Tree Gallery, Cross Tree Lane, Filkins.
T. (01367) 494. - Paint -   *086374*

Finedon (Northamptonshire)
F.T. Art Consultants, Cresta Service Station, Burton Rd.,
Finedon. T. 681948. - Paint -   *086375*

Fishguard (Dyfed)
Gillespie, 53 West St., Fishguard SA65 9NG.
T. (01348) 874652. - Paint -   *086376*
West Wales Arts Centre, 16 West St., Fishguard SA65
9AE. T. (01348) 873867. - Paint -   *086377*
Workshop Wales, Ty Coed Glynymel Rd., Lower Town,
Fishguard SA65 9LY. T. (01348) 872261.
- Paint -   *086378*

Fleet (Hampshire)
Fleet Fine Art & Framing Gallery, 1-2 Kings Parade,
Kings Rd., Fleet. T. (01252) 617500. - Paint /
Graph -   *086379*

Folkestone (Kent)
Metropole Arts Centre Trust, The Leas, Folkestone.
T. (01303) 55070, 44706. - Paint -   *086380*

Fordingbridge (Hampshire)
Ranita Designs, 16 Victoria Rd., Fordingbridge.
T. (01425) 653930. - Paint -   *086381*

Formby (Lancashire)
Art for Interiors, 16 Chapel Lane, Formby.
T. (017048) 31160. - Paint / Graph -   *086382*

Fort Augustus (Highland)
Meridan Fine Art, Canalside, Fort Augustus.
T. (01320) 6560. - Paint -   *086383*

Four Elms (Kent)
Elm House Gallery, Four Elms Rd., Four Elms.
T. (0173270) 201. - Paint -   *086384*

Framlingham (Suffolk)
Martin, 11 Market Hill, Framlingham. T. (01728) 723128.
- Paint -   *086385*

Frinton on Sea (Essex)
Frinton Gallery, 145 Connaught Av., Frinton on Sea.
T. (01255) 673707. - Paint / Graph -   *086386*

Frodsham (Cheshire)
Castle Park Arts Centre, Fountain Lane, Frodsham.
T. (01928) 35832. - Paint -   *086387*

Frome (Somerset)
Black Swan Guild, 2 Bridge St., Frome.
T. (01373) 473980. - Paint -   *086388*
Swale, Jill & David, 37 Butts Hill, Frome.
T. (01373) 465067. - Paint -   *086389*

Gainford (Durham)
Teesdale, 52 Balmer Hill, Gainford. T. (01325) 730404.
- Paint -   *086390*

Gainsborough (Lincolnshire)
Chameleon Gallery, 102 Trinity St., Gainsborough DN21
1HS. T. (01427) 616961. - Paint / Graph -   *086391*

Garton-on-the-Wolds (Humberside)
Copernican Connection, Church Farm, Garton-on-the-
Wolds. T. (01377) 43988. - Paint -   *086392*
Stable Gallery, Church Farm, Garton-on-the-Wolds.
T. (01377) 43988. - Paint -   *086393*

Gateshead (Tyne and Wear)
Gateshead Library Gallery, Prince Consort Rd., Gates-
head. T. (0191) 477 3478. - Graph -   *086394*
Mev, 1 Mediterranean Village, Metro Centre, Gateshead.
T. (0191) 460 9789. - Paint / Graph -   *086395*
Original Art Shop, 48 The Galleria, Metro Centre, Gates-
head NE11 9YP. T. (0191) 493 2422. - Paint -   *086396*

Gee Cross (Greater Manchester)
David, Roger, 270-272 Stockport Rd., Gee Cross SK14.
T. (0161) 368 6008. - Paint -   *086397*

Gilford (Co. Armagh)
Kristyne, Gilford Castle, Glenloughan Rd., Gilford.
T. (01762) 831108. - Paint -   *086398*

Girvan (Southclyde)
Art for Industry, 11 North Park Av., Girvan.
T. (01465) 3288. - Paint -   *086399*

Glasgow (Strathclyde)
Annan & Sons, T. & R., 16 Woodlands Rd., Glasgow G3
GLL. T. (0141) 332 0028. - Paint / Repr / Fra /
Pho -   *086400*
Art from the Billard Room, 217 Sauchiehall St., Glasgow
G2. T. (0141) 332 3711. - Paint -   *086401*
Artbank, 24 Cleveden Rd, Glasgow G12.
T. (0141) 3346180. - Paint -   *086402*
Barbizon Gallery, 40 High St., Glasgow G1 1PN.
T. (0141) 553 1990. - Paint -   *086403*
Blythswood Gallery, 161 West George St., Glasgow G2
4QN. T. (0141) 226 5529. - Paint -   *086404*
Centre Gallery, 450a SauchiehallSt., Glasgow G2 3JD.
T. (0141) 332 8880. - Paint -   *086405*
Compass Gallery, 178 West Regent St., Glasgow G2
4RL. T. (0141) 221 6370, Fax (0141) 2481322.
- Paint -   *086406*
Dick Bros., 114 Busby Rd, Glasgow G76 8BG.
T. (0141) 644 1060. - Paint -   *086407*
Fine Art Society, 134 Blythswood St., Glasgow G2 4EL.
T. (0141) 221 3095, Fax 248 1322. - Paint / Furn /
Sculp / Dec / Mod -   *086408*
Fine Portraits Paintings, Within Royal Infirmary, Castle
St., Glasgow G4. T. (0141) 552 2464. - Paint -   *086409*
Gatehouse Gallery, Rouken Glen Rd, Glasgow G46 7UG.
T. (0141) 620 0235. - Paint -   *086410*
Gerber, Cyril, 148 West Regent St., Glasgow G2 2RQ.
T. (0141) 2213095, Fax (0141) 2481322.
- Paint -   *086411*
Glasgow Print Studio, 22 King St., Glasgow G1 5QP.
T. (0141) 552 0704, Fax (0141) 5522919.
- Graph -   *086412*

Glasgow School of Art Gallery, 167 Renfrew St., Glasgow G3 6RQ. T. (0141) 332 9797. - Paint / Pho -   *086413*

Glasgow Sculpture Studios, 85 Hanson St, Glasgow G31 2HF. T. (0141) 5510562. - Sculp -   *086414*

Green, John, 203 Bath St., Glasgow G2 4HZ. T. (0141) 221 6025. - Paint -   *086415*

Hardie, William, 141 West Regent St., Glasgow G2 2SG. T. (0141) 221 6780. - Paint -   *086416*

Inprints, 253 George St., Glasgow G1. T. (0141) 552 2025. - Graph -   *086417*

J.M.K. Fine Arts, 16-18 Milnpark St., Glasgow G41. T. (0141) 429 7444. - Paint -   *086418*

Kelly, 118 Douglas St., Glasgow G2. T. (0141) 248 6386. - Paint -   *086419*

Langside, 26-28 Battlefield Rd., Glasgow G42 9QH. T. (0141) 649 8888. - Paint -   *086420*

Lennie, Barclay, 203 Bath St., Glasgow G2 4HZ. T. (0141) 226 5413, Fax (0141) 2265413. - Paint -   *086421*

Lynart, 5 Simpson Court, 11 South Av, Glasgow G71 7LH. T. (0141) 951 2065. - Paint -   *086422*

Main Fine Art, Studio Gallery, 16 Gibson St., Glasgow G12 8NX. T. (0141) 334 8858. - Paint -   *086423*

McLellan, 270 Sauchiehall St, Glasgow G2 3EH. T. (0141) 3311854, Fax (0141) 3329957. - Paint -   *086424*

Mundy, Ewan, 48 West George St., Glasgow G2 1BP. T. (0141) 331 2406, Fax (0141) 3329130. - Paint -   *086425*

Originals, 19 Mugdock Rd., Milngavie, Glasgow G62. T. (0141) 956 4850. - Paint -   *086426*

Pain, Jean, 47 Prince's Sq, Glasgow G1 3JN. T. (0141) 204 0427. - Paint -   *086427*

Pettigrew & Mail, 7 The Loaning, Whitecraigs, Glasgow. T. (0141) 639 2989. - Paint -   *086428*

Smith, Ray, 118 Haggs Rd., Glasgow G41 4AT. T. (0141) 423 1780. - Paint -   *086429*

Street Level Gallery and Workshop, 279 High St., Glasgow G4. T. (0141) 552 2151. - Paint -   *086430*

Swann, 169 Croftend Av., Glasgow G44. T. (0141) 633 3122. - Paint -   *086431*

Third Eye Centre, 346-354 Sauchiehall St., Glasgow G2 3JD. T. (0141) 332 7521. - Paint -   *086432*

Transmission, 28 King St., Glasgow G1. T. (0141) 552 4813. - Paint -   *086433*

Washington Gallery, 141 West Regent St., Glasgow G2 2SG. T. (0141) 221 6780. - Paint -   *086434*

W.A.S.P.S., 26 King St., Glasgow G1 5QZ. T. (0141) 552 0564. - Paint -   *086435*

Westmuir Art Gallery, 597 Great Western Rd., Glasgow G12 8HX. T. (0141) 339 2415. - Paint -   *086436*

World of Art, 231 Crow Rd., Glasgow G11 7PZ. T. (0141) 339 3161. - Paint -   *086437*

90s Gallery/Visual Art Scotland, 12 Otago St, Kelvinbridge, Glasgow G12 8HJ. T. (0141) 3393158, Fax (0141) 3393158. - Paint -   *086438*

Glossop (Derbyshire)
Morris, Frances, 17 Chapel St., Glossop. T. (01457) 856187. - Paint -   *086439*

Gloucester (Gloucestershire)
Art Share Gloucestershire, 23 Eastgate St., Gloucester. T. (01452) 307684. - Paint -   *086440*

Golden Vale Pictures, 4 College St., Gloucester GL1 2NE. T. (01452) 505105. - Paint -   *086441*

Medcalf, Paul, Antique Centre, Severn Rd, Gloucester GL1 2LE. T. (01452) 415186. - Paint -   *086442*

Godalming (Surrey)
Godalming Galleries, 3 Wharf St., Godalming GU7 1NN. T. (014868) 422254. - Paint / Graph / Sculp -   *086443*

Goldthorpe, P., Bicton Croft, Deanery Rd., Godalming GU7 2PG. T. (014868) 414356. - Paint -   *086444*

Gorleston-on-Sea (Norfolk)
Hardies Gallery, 205-206 High St, Gorleston-on-Sea NR31 6RR. T. (01493) 668003. - Paint -   *086445*

Gosberton (Lincolnshire)
Marlborough Fine Arts, 10 Wargate Way, Gosberton. T. (01775) 840280. - Paint -   *086446*

Gosforth (Tyne and Wear)
MacDonald, 2 Ashburton Rd., Gosforth NE3 4JB. T. (0191) 284 4214, Fax (0191) 2856188. - Paint -   *086447*

Gosport (Hampshire)
Martin, Richard, 23 Stoke Rd., Gosport PO12 1LS. T. (01705) 520642. - Paint / Graph -   *086448*

Grange-over-Sands (Cumbria)
Priory Fine Arts, Gatehouse Cavendish St, Grange-over-Sands. T. (015395) 36602. - Paint -   *086449*

Grantham (Lincolnshire)
Belvoir Gallery, 5-7 Welby St., Grantham. T. (01476) 79498. - Paint -   *086450*

Premier Framing, Unit 14, Station Rd. East, Grantham NG31 6HX. T. (01476) 590602. - Paint / Graph - *086451*

Grasmere (Cumbria)
Heaton Cooper, Grasmere. T. 280. - Paint -   *086452*

Grassington (North Yorkshire)
Logan, Pletts Barn, Garrs Lane, Grassington. T. (01756) 753043. - Paint -   *086453*

Gravesend (Kent)
Manor Gallery, 15 Manor Rd., Gravesend. T. (01474) 334392. - Paint -   *086454*

Grays (Essex)
Grays Galleries, 23 Lodge Lane, Grays. T. 374883. - Paint -   *086455*

Great Bircham (Norfolk)
Bircham Gallery, 49 Church Lane, Great Bircham PE31 6QW. T. (0148523) 604. - Paint / Graph / China -   *086456*

Great Dunmow (Essex)
Hilton Fine Art, Simon, Flemings Hill Farm, Great Dunmow CM6 2ER. T. (01279) 850107. - Paint -   *086457*

Great Eccleston (Lancashire)
Hand Made, The Square, Great Eccleston. T. (01995) 71207. - Paint -   *086458*

Great Malvern (Hereford & Worcester)
Lismore, 3 Edith Walk, Great Malvern. T. (016845) 568610. - Paint -   *086459*

Great Missenden (Buckinghamshire)
Wintgens, Elizabeth, 49 High St., Great Missenden. T. (012406) 6208. - Paint / Graph -   *086460*

Great Yarmouth (Norfolk)
Gallery 2, 27-28 Victoria Arcade, Great Yarmouth NR30. T. (01493) 330573. - Paint -   *086461*

Home Elegance, 27-28 Broad Row, Great Yarmouth NR30 1HT. T. (01493) 842793. - Paint -   *086462*

Northgate Gallery, 213 Northgate St., Great Yarmouth NR30 1DH. T. (01493) 844069. - Paint -   *086463*

Greatstone-on-Sea (Kent)
Romney Bay Galleries, 13-15 Dunes Rd., Greatstone-on-Sea. T. (01679) 66201. - Paint -   *086464*

Greenford (Greater London)
Artmaster Gallery, 378 Oldfield Lane North, Greenford UB6 8PU. T. (0181) 575 8753. - Paint -   *086465*

Greenock (Strathclyde)
First Floor Gallery, 40 West Blackhall St., Greenock. T. (01475) 27857. - Paint -   *086466*

Interior Images, 2 West Blackhall St., Greenock. T. (01475) 26618. - Paint -   *086467*

Greyabbey (County Down)
Gallery of Sporting Art, 11 Main St., Greyabbey. T. (0124774) 293. - Paint -   *086468*

Phyllis Arnold Gallery Antiques, Hoops Courtyard, Greyabbey BT22 2NE. T. (01247) 748199, 853322. - Paint / Graph -   *086469*

Greystoke (Cumbria)
Beckstones, Greystoke Gill, Greystoke. T. (018533) 83601. - Paint -   *086470*

Grimsby (Humberside)
Cassian, 27 Wellowgate, Grimsby. T. (01472) 240000. - Paint / Graph -   *086471*

Gallery, 119 Pasture St., Grimsby. T. (01472) 349197. - Paint -   *086472*

Gallery 86, 234 Freeman St, Grimsby. T. (01472) 351544. - Paint -   *086473*

Lincolnshire Fine Arts, 12 Brighowgate, Grimsby. T. (01472) 362425. - Paint -   *086474*

Yeung, 1 Freeman St., Grimsby DN32 7AB. T. (01472) 242499. - Paint -   *086475*

Guildford (Surrey)
Forest Gallery, 180 High St., Guildford. T. (01483) 506622. - Paint -   *086476*

Gallery 90, Ward St., Guildford GU1 4LH. T. (01483) 444741. - China / Tex / Jew / Silv - *086477*

Jonleigh, The Street, Wonerish, Guildford GU5 0PF. T. (01483) 893177. - Paint -   *086478*

Russell Flint, William, 61 Quarry St., Guildford. T. (01483) 504359. - Paint -   *086479*

Stewart, Michael, 61 Quarry St., Guildford. T. (01483) 504359. - Paint -   *086480*

Haddenham (Buckinghamshire)
Wellby, H.S., The Malt House, Church End, Haddenham HP17 8AH. T. (01844) 290036. - Paint -   *086481*

Haddington (Lothian)
Potter, Peter, 10 The Sands, Haddington EH41 3EY. T. (0162082) 2080. - Paint / Graph / China -   *086482*

Hale (Greater Manchester)
Hale Picture Framing, 155 Ashley Rd., Hale WA14. T. (0161) 928 7389. - Paint -   *086483*

Halesworth (Suffolk)
Halesworth Gallery, Steeple End, Halesworth 1P19 8LL. T. (019867) 3624. - Graph / Sculp -   *086484*

Halifax (West Yorkshire)
Glendale, 189 King Cross Rd., Halifax. T. (01422) 321508, 321506. - Paint -   *086485*

Howard, 18 St. James Sq, Halifax. T. (01422) 206813. - Paint -   *086486*

Riverside Gallery, 16-18 Wharf St., Sowerby Bridge, Halifax. T. (01422) 832453. - Paint -   *086487*

World Art, 16 Church St., Halifax HX1 1QY. T. (01422) 349739. - Paint / Draw -   *086488*

Hambleden (Buckinghamshire)
Luxters Fine Art, Old Luxters Gallery, Hambleden. T. (0149163) 8816, Fax 645. - Paint -   *086489*

Hampton Hill (Middlesex)
Hampton Hill Gallery, 203 & 205 High St, Hampton Hill TW12 1NP. T. (0181) 9771379. - Paint -   *086490*

Harefield (Greater London)
Amberley, 7 Summerhouse Works, Summerhouse Lane, Harefield. T. (01895) 824394. - Paint -   *086491*

Harlow (Essex)
Playhouse Gallery, The High, Harlow CM20 1LS. T. (01279) 24391. - Paint -   *086492*

Harpenden (Hertfordshire)
Knights Gallery, 38 Station Rd., Harpenden. T. (01582) 460564. - Paint -   *086493*

Select Fine Art, 24 Park Av. South, Harpenden. T. (01582) 763630. - Paint -   *086494*

Harrietsham (Kent)
Peppitt, Judith, Chegworth Manor Farm, Chegworth, Harrietsham. T. (01622) 859313. - Paint -   *086495*

Harrogate (North Yorkshire)
Amaron Arts, 6 Strawberry Dale Av., Harrogate Harrogate. T. (01423) 507949. - Paint -   *086496*

Art Connections, 4 Lancaster Rd., Harrogate. T. (01423) 563829. - Paint -   *086497*

Artful Arts, 12 High St, Harrogate. T. (01423) 712218. - Paint -   *086498*

Creskeld, 2a High St, Harrogate. T. (01423) 71 13 53. - Paint -   *086499*

Duncalfe, 34 Montpellier Parade, Harrogate.
T. (01423) 521452. - Paint -   086500
Framework Fast Framing & Gallery, 19 Station Bridge,
Harrogate HG1 1SP. T. (01423) 524851.
- Paint -   086501
Gallery Emeritus, 21-22 West Park, Harrogate.
T. (01423) 537088. - Paint -   086502
Godfrey & Twatt, 7 Westminster Arcade, Parliament St.,
Harrogate. T. (01423) 525300. - Paint -   086503
Harrogate Fine Arts, 77 Station Parade, Harrogate.
T. (01423) 530355. - Paint -   086504
Kent, Rodney, 20 West Park, Harrogate.
T. (01423) 560352. - Paint / Draw -   086505
McTague, 17 Cheltenham Mount, Harrogate.
T. (01423) 567086. - Paint -   086506
Montpellier Gallery, 12 Montpellier St., Harrogate.
T. (01423) 500460, Fax 528400. - Paint /
Sculp -   086507
Old Masters Gallery, 4 Crescent Rd., Harrogate.
T. (01423) 521142. - Paint -   086508
Sutcliffe, 5 Royal Parade, Harrogate HG1 1SZ.
T. (01423) 562976, Fax 528729. - Paint -   086509
Walker, 6 Montpellier Gardens, Harrogate HG1 2TF.
T. (01423) 567933. - Paint -   086510

Harrow (Greater London)
Charisma Picture Gallery, 57 Station Rd., HA1 Harrow.
T. (0181) 863 9560. - Paint -   086511
Ficino, 84 High St., Harrow HA1. T. (0181) 864 0865.
- Paint -   086512

Harthill (Strathclyde)
Artis, Blair House, Hirst Rd., Harthill. T. (01501) 51241.
- Paint -   086513

Hartlepool (Cleveland)
Classic Art, 21 Church Sq., Hartlepool.
T. (01429) 223949. - Paint / Graph -   086514

Hartley Wintney (Hampshire)
Century Gallery, High St, Hartley Wintney RG27 8NY.
T. (01252) 822747. - Paint -   086515
Phoenix Green Gallery, London Rd, Hartley Wintney.
T. (0125126) 2111. - Paint -   086516

Haseley Knob (Warwickshire)
Bartbright, Blackcroft Honiley Rd., Haseley Knob.
T. (01926) 484678. - Paint -   086517

Haslemere (Surrey)
Ark Gallery, 11g High St., Haslemere. T. (01428) 61808.
- Paint -   086518

Hassocks (Sussex)
Cart Lodge Gallery, Dumbrell Court Rd., Northend, Ditch-
ling, Hassocks BN6 8TG. T. (017918) 4096.
- Paint -   086519
Chichester House Gallery, Chichester House, High St.,
Ditchling, Hassocks BN6. T. (017918) 4167.
- Paint -   086520

Hatfield (Hertfordshire)
Coltsfoot, Hatfield. T. (017072) 277. - Paint -   086521

Hatfield Heath (Essex)
Barn Gallery, Parvilles Farm, Hatfield Heath.
T. (01279) 730114. - Paint / Graph -   086522

Hatherleigh (Devon)
Salar, 20 Bridge St., Hatherleigh. T. (01837) 810940.
- Paint -   086523

Havant (Hampshire)
Gardner, 35 East St., Havant PO9 1AA.
T. (01705) 475706. - Paint -   086524
Prince George Galleries, The Pallant, Havant PO9.
T. (01705) 486582. - Paint / Graph -   086525
Trentham, 40 North St., Havant PO9 1PT.
T. (01705) 484935. - Paint -   086526

Haverfordwest (Dyfed)
Old Smith Studio, Bethlehem, Cardigan Rd., Haverfordwest SA61. T. (01437) 731398. - Paint -   086527

Haverthwaite (Cumbria)
Cumbria Galleries, Clock Tower Bldg, Haverthwaite.
T. (015395) 31155. - Paint -   086528

Hawick (Borders)
Blackwood Simon Breyberry, 10-11 Bourtree Terrace,
Hawick. T. (01450) 77780. - Paint -   086529

Hawkhurst (Kent)
Moor Gallery, The Moor, Hawkhurst. T. (01580) 753277.
- Paint -   086530

Hawkshead (Cumbria)
Barn Studio, Main St., Hawkshead. T. 434.
- Paint -   086531
Cookhouse Gallery, Wordsworth St., Hawkshead. T. 502.
- Paint -   086532

Haworth (West Yorkshire)
Hutton van Mastrigt Art, 26 North View Terrace, Haworth
BD22 8HJ. T. (01535) 643882. - Paint -   086533

Hay-on-Wye (Powys)
Arvona Gallery, Arvona St, Hay-on-Wye.
T. (01497) 820415. - Paint -   086535
Bark Art, Tabbys Shed, Saint Johns Pl., Hay-on-Wye.
T. (01497) 821362. - Paint -   086536
Corner Shop, 5 Saint John's Pl., Hay-on-Wye.
T. (01497) 820045. - Paint / Graph -   086537
Forwoods, 2 Castle St., Hay-on-Wye. T. (01497) 820539.
- Paint -   086538
Hay, 9 High Town, Hay-on-Wye HR3 5AE.
T. (01497) 820172. - Graph -   086539
Kilvert, Ashbrook House, Hay-on-Wye HR3 5RZ.
T. (01497) 820831. - Paint -   086539a
Marches Gallery, 2 Lion St., Hay-on-Wye.
T. (01497) 821451. - Paint -   086540
Wye Gallery, 5 Castle St., Hay-on-Wye.
T. (01497) 821163. - Paint -   086541

Hayle (Cornwall)
Copperhouse, 14 Fore St., Hayle. T. (01736) 752787.
- Paint -   086542
Dawn's Picture Gallery, Hayle Shopping Arcade, Foundry
Sq., Hayle. T. (01736) 755433. - Paint -   086543
Dyer & Sons, W., 14 Fore St, Hayle TR27 4DX.
T. (01736) 752787. - Paint -   086544
Hayle Framecraft, Hayle. T. (01736) 756370.
- Paint -   086545

Hayling Island (Hampshire)
Morton Lee, J., Cedar House, Bacon Lane, Hayling Is-
land PO11 0DN. T. (01705) 464444,
Fax (01243) 370512. - Paint -   086546

Haywards Heath (West Sussex)
Corner House Gallery, Corner House, High St., Haywards
Heath. T. (01444) 45 22 67. - Paint -   086547
Crinan, 95 South Rd., Haywards Heath.
T. (01444) 417653. - Paint -   086548
Picturesque Gallery, 49-53 Sussex Rd., Haywards Heath
RH16 4ED. T. (01444) 412827. - Paint / Graph /
Draw -   086549

Heath and Reach (Bedfordshire)
Charterhouse, 26 Birds Hill, Heath and Reach
LU7 0AQ. T. (0152) 523379, Fax (0152) 523379.
- Paint / Fra / Draw -   086550
Trenchard, Graham, 14 Birds Hill, Heath and Reach.
T. (0152523) 379. - Paint / Graph -   086551

Hebden Bridge (West Yorkshire)
Finegold, New Oxford House, Albert St., Hebden Bridge.
T. (01422) 845659. - Paint -   086552
Sheeran Lock, West Royd Birchcliffe Rd., Hebden Brid-
ge. T. (01422) 844642. - Paint -   086553
South Bank Gallery, Stubbing Wharf, Hebden Bridge.
T. (01422) 842070. - Paint -   086554

Heckington (Lincolnshire)
Pearoom Centre for Contemporary Craft, Station Yard,
Heckington. T. (01529) 60765. - Paint -   086555

Helensburgh (Southclyde)
Helensburgh Fine Arts, 78 West Clyde St., Helensburgh
G84 8BB. T. (01436) 71821. - Paint -   086556

Helmsley (North Yorkshire)
Look Art Gallery, 20 Castlegate, Helmsley.
T. (01439) 70454. - Paint -   086557
Sissons, Williams, 23 Market Pl., Helmsley YO6 5BJ.
T. (01439) 71385. - Paint / Graph -   086558

Hemel Hempstead (Hertfordshire)
Original Art Shop, Marlowes Centre, Marlowes, Hemel
Hempstead. T. (01442) 235626. - Paint -   086559

Henbury (Cheshire)
Geldart, Chelford Rd., Henbury. T. (01625) 425392.
- Paint -   086560

Henley-in-Arden (Warwickshire)
Arden Gallery, 54 High St, Henley-in-Arden B95 5AN.
T. (01564) 792520. - Paint -   086561
Capelli, Unit 3 B, Arden Craft Centre, Little Alne, Henley-
in-Arden. T. (015642) 488437. - Paint -   086562
Chadwick, 2 Doctor's Ln., Henley-in-Arden.
T. (015642) 794820. - Paint / Graph -   086563
Colmore, 52 High St., Henley-in-Arden B95 5AN.
T. (01564) 792938. - Paint -   086564
Lacy, 56 High St., Henley-in-Arden. T. (015642) 793073.
- Paint / Graph -   086565

Henley-on-Thames (Oxfordshire)
Bohun, 15 Reading Rd., Henley-on-Thames RG9 1AB.
T. (01491) 576228. - Paint / Graph / China -   086566
Century Galleries, Thameside, Henley-on-Thames RG9
2LJ. T. (01491) 575499. - Paint -   086567
Keene, Barry, 12 Thameside, Henley-on-Thames RG9
1BH. T. (01491) 577119. - Paint / Graph /
Draw -   086568
Luxters Fine Art, Old Luxters Gallery, Henley-on-Tha-
mes. T. (01491) 638816. - Paint / Sculp -   086569
Selkirk, Christopher, 7 Friday St., Henley-on-Thames.
T. (01491) 575077. - Paint -   086570

Hereford (Hereford and Worcester)
Fine Art Studio, Unit 3, Bewell St, Hereford.
T. (01432) 354219. - Paint -   086571
Riverside Gallery, 26 Bridge st., Hereford.
T. (01432) 59428. - Paint -   086572
Tidal Wave Gallery, 3 Bridge St., Hereford HR4 9DF.
T. (01432) 352365. - Graph -   086573
Vanguard, Crossway House, Holmer Rd., Hereford.
T. (01432) 268065. - Paint -   086574

Hertford (Herfordshire)
Calvert, Coach House,, Hertford. T. (01992) 551656.
- Graph -   086575

Hessle (Humberside)
Pearson, Richard, 2a Tower Hill, Hessle.
T. (01482) 641748. - Paint -   086576

Hest Bank (Lancashire)
Hest Bank Gallery, 2a Marine Dr., Hest Bank.
T. (01524) 823883. - Paint / Graph -   086577

Heswall (Merseyside)
Dee Fine Arts, 182 Telegraph Rd., Heswall L60 0AJ.
T. (0151) 342 6657. - Paint -   086578
Landscapes, 1 Dee View Rd., Heswall L60.
T. (0151) 342 1020. - Paint -   086579

Hethersgill (Cumbria)
Sark, Hethersgill. T. (01228) 75022. - Paint -   086580

Hexham (Northumberland)
Abbey Prints, 22 Hallgate, Hexham. T. (01434) 607550.
- Graph -   086581
Beaufort, Beaumont St., Hexham NE46.
T. (01434) 605808. - Paint -   086582

High Halden (Kent)
Green, Roger, Hales Pl., High Halden.
T. (0123385) 850219. - Paint -   086583

Hillsborough (Co. Down)
Shambles, Inns Court Park Lane, Hillsborough.
T. (01846) 682946. - Paint -   086584

Hitchin (Hertfordshire)
Grosvenor Art Gallery, 11 Bridge St., Hitchin SG5 2DF.
T. (01462) 433663, Fax (01462) 420456. - Paint /
Graph - 086585
Thomas, Carole, 32a Sun St., Hitchin.
T. (01462) 436077. - Paint / Draw - 086586

Holcot (Northamptonshire)
Haig, Axel, Homestead Farm, Back Lane, Holcot.
T. (01604) 781180. - Paint - 086587

Holkham (Norfolk)
Holkham Art Gallery, Ancient House, Holkham.
T. (01328) 710783. - Paint / Graph / Sculp - 086588

Hollybush (Strathclyde)
Burns, Hollybush School, Hollybush. T. (0129256) 353.
- Paint - 086589

Holmfirth (West Yorkshire)
Jackson Ashley, 13-15 Huddersfield Rd., Holmfirth.
T. (01484) 686460. - Paint - 086590

Holt (Norfolk)
Heydon, Jolly Farmers, Langham Rd, Holt.
T. (01263) 830483. - Paint - 086591
Picturecraft of Holt, 23 Lees Yard, Bull St., Holt NR25
6HR. T. (01263) 713259. - Paint - 086592

Honiton (Devon)
Honiton Fine Art, 189 High St., Honiton EX14 8LQ.
T. (01404) 45942. - Paint / Graph - 086593
Jones, Terry, 55 Church Hill, Honiton. T. (01404) 43018.
- Paint - 086594
Newton, 116 High St., Honiton. T. (01404) 46604.
- Paint - 086595
Upper Gallery, 81 High St., Honiton. T. (01404) 41699.
- Paint - 086596

Hornchurch (Greater London)
Hornchurch Fine Art Gallery, 7 High St., Hornchurch.
T. (014024) 51080. - Paint - 086597

Horsham (West Sussex)
Gentle Gallery, 2 Shelley House, Horsham.
T. (01403) 58567. - Paint - 086598
Horsham Arts Centre, North St., Horsham.
T. (01403) 68689. - Paint - 086599

Hove (East Sussex)
Viccari, 21-23 Stirling Pl., Hove BN3 3YU.
T. (01273) 733633. - Paint - 086600

Hoylake (Merseyside)
Gerrard, John, 16 Market St., Hoylake L47.
T. (0151) 632 1799. - Paint - 086601

Huddersfield (West Yorkshire)
Byram, 5 Station St., Huddersfield HD1 1LS.
T. (01484) 425747. - Paint - 086602

Hundleby (Lincolnshire)
Lewis Fine Art, Alan, The Old Mill House, 35 Main Rd,
Hundleby PE23 5LZ. T. (01790) 52817.
- Paint - 086603

Huxham (Devon)
Austin, Desmond, Old Rectory, Huxham.
T. (01392) 841157. - Paint - 086604

Hyde (Cheshire)
Homeworks, 4 Reynold St., Hyde. T. (0161) 366 0714.
- Paint / Graph - 086605
K.T. Studios, 81 Oldham St., Hyde SK14.
T. (0161) 368 5738. - Paint - 086606

Hythe (Kent)
Windsor Gallery, 21 High St., Hythe. T. (01303) 269189.
- Paint - 086607

Ightham (Kent)
Pratt, The Street, Ightham. T. (01732) 882326.
- Paint - 086608
Retigrahic Society, The Street, Ightham.
T. (01732) 884178. - Paint - 086609

Ilford (Essex)
Picture Perfect Gallery, 171 Longwood Gardens, Ilford
IG5. T. 551 9245. - Paint - 086610

Ilfracombe (Devon)
Venucci, 9 Belgrave Promenade, Ilfracombe.
T. (01271) 862069. - Paint - 086611
Venucci, The Quay, Ilfracombe. T. (01271) 867847.
- Paint - 086612

Ilkley (West Yorkshire)
Lauron, 122 Boiling Rd, Ilkley. T. (01943) 600725.
- Paint - 086613
That Picture Shop, 22 The Grove, Ilkley.
T. (01943) 602738. - Paint - 086614

Ilminster (Somerset)
Hutchinson, Clare, 1a West St., Ilminster.
T. (01460) 53369. - Paint - 086615
Plymton, 31 West St., Ilminster. T. (01460) 54437.
- Paint - 086616

Ingatestone (Essex)
Meyers, 66 High St., Ingatestone CM4 9DW.
T. (01277) 355335. - Paint - 086617

Inkberrow (Hereford & Worcester)
New Gallery, Village Green, Inkberrow.
T. (01386) 792119. - Paint - 086618

Instow (Devon)
Waterside Gallery, 2 Marine Terrace, Instow.
T. (01271) 860786. - Paint - 086619

Inverness (Highland)
Alder, 57 Church St., Inverness. T. (01463) 243575.
- Paint - 086620
Greenfield, 3 Bow Court, Church St., Inverness.
T. (01463) 224781. - Paint - 086621
Highland Print Makers Workshop Gallery, 20 Bank St.,
Inverness. T. (01463) 712240. - Paint - 086622
Mainhill Gallery, Carnessie, Ancrum, Inverness.
T. (01463) 53518. - Paint / Graph - 086623
Renaissance Fine Art, 7 Market Hall, Inverness.
T. (01463) 713047. - Paint - 086624

Ipswich (Suffolk)
Art Shop and Haste Gallery, 3 Great Colman St., Ipswich.
T. (01473) 25 84 29. - Paint / Graph - 086625
European Visual Arts Centre, Library, Suffolk College,
Ipswich. T. (01473) 211214. - Paint - 086626
Fortescue Gallery, 27 St. Peter's St, Ipswich 1P1 1XF.
T. (01473) 51342. - Paint / Draw - 086627
M.F. Framco, 10 St Helens St, Ipswich.
T. (01473) 225544. - Paint / Graph - 086628
Russell, John, 13 Orwell Pl., Ipswich IP4 1BD.
T. (01473) 212051, Fax (01473) 212051.
- Paint - 086629

Irvine (Strathclyde)
Kuramu, 44 Forum Centre, Irvine. T. (01294) 77956.
- Paint - 086630

Jarrow (Tyne and Wear)
Bede, Springwell Park, Butchers Bridge Rd., Jarrow.
T. (0191) 489 1807. - Paint - 086631
Bede Gallery, Springwell Park, Butchersbridge Rd, Jar-
row NE32 5QA. T. (0191) 489 1807,
Fax (0191) 4891807. 086632

Jesmond (Tyne and Wear)
Brown, 15 Acorn Rd., Jesmond. T. (0191) 281 1315.
- Paint - 086633
Osborne Art & Antiques, 18c Osborne Rd., Jesmond NE2
2AD. T. (0191) 281 6380. - Paint - 086634

Keighley (West Yorkshire)
Craven, Scott St., Keighley. T. (01535) 680388.
- Paint - 086635

Kelling (Norfolk)
Picturecraft of Kelling, The Street, Kelling.
T. (0126370) 528. - Paint - 086636

Kelso (Borders)
Kelso Gallery, 5 Woodmarket, Kelso. T. (01573) 26224.
- Paint - 086637

Stichill Smithy Gallery, Stichill, Kelso. T. (01573) 346.
- Paint - 086638

Kelvedon Hatch (Essex)
Drurybond, Dodds Farm Church Rd, Kelvedon Hatch.
T. (01277) 373381. - Paint - 086639

Kempston (Bedfordshire)
Queen Adelaide Galleries, 79 High St, Kempston MK42
7BS. T. (01234) 854083. - Paint - 086640

Kendal (Cumbria)
Art Shop, 28c Finkle St., Kendal. T. (01539) 722596.
- Paint - 086641
Brewery Arts Centre, 122a Highgate, Kendal.
T. (01539) 725133. - Paint - 086642
Southgate Studios, 111 Highgate, Kendal.
T. (01539) 731552. - Paint / Graph - 086643
Talbot, 146 Highgate, Kendal. T. (01539) 724849.
- Paint / Graph - 086644
Yondell, 112 Kirkland, Kendal. T. (01539) 723728.
- Paint - 086645

Kenfig (Mid Glamorgan)
Kenfig Art Gallery, 2 Pisgah St., Kenfig.
T. (01656) 740674. - Paint - 086646

Kenilworth (Warwickshire)
Allen, 38 Castle Hill, Kenilworth. T. (01926) 851435.
- Paint / Graph - 086647
Castle Gallery, 32 Castle Hill, Kenilworth CV8 2SQ.
T. (01926) 58727. - Paint / Draw - 086648
Kenilworth Crafts, Castle Hill, Kenilworth.
T. (01926) 57666. - Paint - 086649

Kerry (Powys)
Country Works Gallery, Michaelmas Court, Sawmills,
Kerry. T. (0168668) 434. - Paint - 086650

Keswick (Cumbria)
Expressions in Art, Storms Farm, Keswick.
T. (017687) 71450. - Paint - 086651
Scott, Peter, 30 Lake Rd., Keswick. T. (017687) 71100.
- Paint - 086652
Thornthwaite Galleries, Thornthwaite Village, Keswick.
T. (0159682) 248. - Paint - 086653

Kibworth (Leicestershire)
Countrymans Gallery, 14 Harcourt Estate, Kibworth.
T. (01533) 792311. - Paint - 086654

Kidderminster (Hereford and Worcester)
Athena Galleries, Unit 5, Rowland Hill Centre, Kidderminster. T. (01562) 66072. - Paint / Graph - 086655

Kilmarnock (Southclyde)
Wellington Galleries, 23 Wellington St., Kilmarnock.
T. (01563) 23176. - Paint - 086656

King's Lynn (Norfolk)
Bachkauskas, R.T., 8 Chapel Lane, King's Lynn.
T. (01553) 760627. - Paint - 086657
Deacon & Blyth, Docking Rd, Bircham, King's Lynn PE31
6QP. T. (0148523) 779. - Paint - 086658
Galeria Reflexions, 56 Norfolk St., King's Lynn.
T. (01553) 760766. - Paint - 086659
Kings Lynn Arts Centre, King St., King's Lynn PE30 1HA.
- Paint - 086660
Lynn Prints, 15a King St., King's Lynn.
T. (01553) 774810. - Graph - 086661

Kingham (Oxfordshire)
Breyberry, Kingham House, Kingham OX7 6YA.
T. (01608) 658723, Fax (01608) 658899.
- Paint - 086662

Kingsbridge (Devon)
Mayne, 14 Fore St., Kingsbridge. T. (01548) 853848.
- Paint - 086663

Kingsclere (Hampshire)
J.B. Arts, 3 Swan St., Kingsclere. T. (01635) 297350.
- Paint - 086664

Kingston-upon-Hull (Humberside)
Dews, Steven, 66-70 Princess Av., Kingston-upon-Hull
HU5 3QJ. T. (01482) 42424, Fax (01482) 447928.
- Paint -   *086665*
Gallery, 379 Hessle Rd., Kingston-upon-Hull.
T. (01482) 29594. - Paint -   *086666*
Jolly Sixpence Gallery, 1b Packman Lane, Kingston-
upon-Hull. T. (01482) 654949. - Paint -   *086667*
Kingston Galleries, 66 George St., Kingston-upon-Hull.
T. (01482) 24910. - Paint -   *086668*
Parkin, John E., 6 Spring St., Kingston-upon-Hull.
T. (01482) 28324. - Paint -   *086669*
Posterngate Gallery, 6 Posterngate, Kingston-upon-Hull.
T. (01482) 222745. - Paint -   *086670*
Top Pictures, 7 Hepworth Arcade, Silver St., Kingston-
upon-Hull. T. (01482) 23743. - Paint -   *086671*

Kingston-upon-Thames (Surrey)
Kingston Hill Art Gallery, 9 Park Rd., Kingston-upon-Tha-
mes KT2. T. (0181) 547 2886. - Paint -   *086672*
Pictures & Frames, 6 Cambridge Rd., Kingston-upon-
Thames KT1. T. (0181) 546 3800. - Paint -   *086673*
Studio 96, 96 Richmond Rd., Kingston-upon-Thames
KT2 5EN. T. (0181) 546 3673. - Paint -   *086674*

Kingussie (Highland)
Murdoch, Colin, 56 High St., Kingussie.
T. (01540) 661552. - Paint -   *086675*

Kirkby Lonsdale (Cumbria)
Verve, 15 Main St., Kirkby Lonsdale. T. (015242) 71805.
- Paint -   *086676*

Kirkwall (Orkney Islands)
Black Pig Gallery, 60 Victoria St., Kirkwall.
T. (01856) 4328. - Paint -   *086677*
Shorelines Gallery, 25 Broad St., Kirkwall.
T. (01856) 3821. - Paint -   *086678*

Kirriemuir (Tayside)
Kirriemuir Art Gallery, 4 Reform St., Kirriemuir.
T. (01575) 74409. - Paint -   *086679*

Knaresborough (North Yorkshire)
Isis Gallery, 2a Castlegate, Knaresborough.
T. (01423) 860348. - Paint -   *086680*
Pictoriana, 88 High St., Knaresborough.
T. (01423) 866116. - Paint -   *086681*

Knowle (West Midlands)
Greswolde, 38 Knowle Shopping Precinct, Knowle.
T. (01564) 774976. - Paint -   *086682*

Knutsford (Cheshire)
Church Hill Gallery, 1a Church Hill, Knutsford.
T. (01565) 633636. - Paint / Graph -   *086683*
Cranford, 10 King St., Knutsford. T. (01565) 633646.
- Paint -   *086684*

Lamberhurst (Kent)
Montague Ward, Bartley Hill, Lamberhurst.
T. (01892) 890363. - Paint -   *086685*

Lanark (Southclyde)
Lanark Gallery, 116 North Vennel, Lanark.
T. (01555) 2565. - Paint -   *086686*

Lancaster (Lancashire)
McCormack, W.B., 6-6a Rosemary Lane, Lancaster.
T. (01524) 36405. - Graph -   *086687*
Paper Gallery, 66 Market St., Lancaster.
T. (01524) 36636. - Paint -   *086688*
Scott, Lancaster University, Bailrigg, Lancaster.
T. (01524) 65201 ext. 3182. - Paint / Graph - *086689*
Studio Arts Gallery, 6 Lower Church St., Lancaster LA1
1LT. T. (01524) 68014, Fax (01524) 844422. - Paint /
Graph -   *086690*
Talbot, 8 Cheapside, Lancaster. T. (01524) 61216.
- Paint / Graph -   *086691*
Town House Gallery, 50 Market St., Lancaster.
T. (01524) 63436. - Paint / Graph -   *086692*

Lancing (West Sussex)
Framing Studio, 2 Station Parade, Lancing BN15.
T. (01903) 766755. - Paint / Graph -   *086693*

Langholm (Dumfries and Galloway)
Tribal Art, Craigcleuch, Langholm DG13 0NY.
T. (013873) 80137. - Orient / Sculp / Arch / Eth /
Cur -   *086694*

Largs (Southclyde)
Interior Images, 33 Boyd St., Largs. T. (01475) 686666.
- Paint -   *086695*

Laugharne (Dyfed)
Powerhouse Gallery, Power House, Market Lane, Laugharne. T. (01994) 427635. - Paint -   *086696*

Launceston (Cornwall)
Tamar, 5 Church St., Launceston PL15 8AW.
T. (01566) 774233. - Paint -   *086697*

Lavenham (Suffolk)
Church Street Gallery, Church St., Lavenham.
T. (01787) 247533. - Paint -   *086698*
House Gallery, 46 Prentice St., Lavenham.
T. (01787) 248402. - Paint -   *086699*
Phoenix Art Gallery, 97 High St., Lavenham.
T. (01787) 247356. - Paint -   *086700*
Wildlife Art Gallery, 70-71 High St., Lavenham CO10
9PT. T. (01787) 248562, Fax (01787) 247057. - Paint /
Graph -   *086701*

Laxfield (Suffolk)
Mangate Gallery, Old Vicarage, Laxfield IP13 8DT.
T. (01986) 798524, Fax (01986) 798524.
- Paint -   *086702*

Leamington Spa (Warwickshire)
Craft House, 3 Satchwell Walk, Leamington Spa.
T. (01926) 451248. - Paint -   *086703*

Lechlade (Gloucestershire)
Seeba Gallery, High St., Lechlade GL7.
T. (01367) 53333. - Paint -   *086704*

Ledbury (Hereford and Worcester)
Shell House Gallery, 36 Homand, Ledbury HR8 1BT.
T. (01531) 2557. - Paint / Graph -   *086705*

Leeds (West Yorkshire)
Alcove Galleries, 332 Meanwood Rd., Leeds.
T. (0113) 2620056. - Paint / Graph -   *086706*
Craft Centre and Design Gallery, The Headrow, Leeds.
T. (0113) 2478241. - Graph -   *086707*
Headrow, 588 Harrogate Rd., Leeds LS17 8DP.
T. (0113) 2694244. - Paint / Graph -   *086708*
Jade and the Arts, Units 2-3, Arches Craft Arcade Canal
Basin, Leeds. T. (0113) 2340773. - Paint - *086709*
Oakwood Gallery, 613 Roundhay Rd, Leeds LS8 4AR.
T. (0113) 2401348. - Paint / Graph -   *086710*
Original Art Shop, 7 Theatre Walk, Schofields Centre,
Leeds. T. (0113) 2341274. - Paint / Graph - *086711*
Parker, 6 Grange Court, Alwoodly, Leeds.
T. (0113) 2662302. - Paint -   *086712*
Pavillon Company, 235 Woodhouse Lane, Leeds.
T. (0113) 2429836. - Paint -   *086713*
That Picture Shop, 59 Merrion Centre, Leeds.
T. (0113) 2455784. - Paint -   *086714*

Leek (Staffordshire)
Englands Gallery, 1 Ball Haye Terrace, Leek ST13 6AP.
T. (01538) 373451. - Paint -   *086715*
Hunt, David, The Stables, Challinor Mews, Leek.
T. (01538) 399210. - Paint -   *086716*
Wood, Pat, Stanley Bldgs., Stanley St., Leek.
T. (01538) 385696. - Paint -   *086717*
Worthy, John, 14 Saint Edward St., Leek ST13 5DS.
T. (01538) 383779. - Graph -   *086718*

Leicester (Leicestershire)
Artique Galleries, 3 Loseby Lane, Leicester.
T. (0116) 628380. - Paint -   *086719*
Caldicott, 128 Keightley Rd., Leicester.
T. (0116) 870688. - Paint -   *086720*
City Gallery, 90 Granby St., Leicester. T. (0116) 540595.
- Paint -   *086721*
Craft Gallery, 54 London Rd., Leicester.
T. (0116) 550773. - Paint -   *086722*
Feather, 3 Cherry Tree Court, Maytree Dr., Leicester.
T. (0116) 386619. - Paint -   *086723*

Frog & Mouse, 44-46 Cank St., Leicester.
T. (0116) 622151. - Paint / Graph -   *086724*
Gadsby, W.F., 22 Market Pl, Leicester LE1 5GF.
T. (0116) 517792.   *086725*
Hammond Smith, 32 West Av, Leicester LE2 1TR.
T. (0116) 709020. - Paint -   *086726*
Knighton, 360 Welford Rd., Leicester. T. (0116) 701380.
- Paint -   *086727*
West End Picture Framing Company, 2 Foxon St., Leice-
ster. T. (0116) 546546. - Paint / Graph -   *086728*
Woods, 17 King St., Leicester. T. (0116) 471067.
- Paint -   *086729*

Leigh-on-Sea (Essex)
Legra, 8 Broadway, Leigh-on-Sea. T. (01702) 713572.
- Paint -   *086730*
Selwood, 1a Leigh Park Rd., Leigh-on-Sea.
T. (01702) 74303. - Paint -   *086731*

Lenham (Kent)
Goldsmith, 3 High St., Lenham. T. (01622) 850011.
- Paint -   *086732*

Leominster (Hereford and Worcester)
Coltsfoot Gallery, Hatfield, Leominster HR6 0SF.
T. (0156) 882277. - Paint / Draw -   *086733*
Farmers Gallery, 28 Broad St, Leominster HR6 8BS.
T. (01568) 611413, Fax (01568) 611492.
- Paint -   *086734*

Letheringsett (Norfolk)
Fine Sporting Interests, Waveney House, Letheringsett.
T. (01263) 712352. - Paint -   *086735*

Leven (Fife)
Durie Street Gallery, 7 Durie St., Leven.
T. (01333) 28590. - Paint -   *086736*

Lewes (East Sussex)
Albion Gallery, 51 High St., Lewes BN7 1XE.
T. (01273) 478870. - Paint -   *086737*
Crisford, C., 175 High St., Lewes BN7 1YE.
T. (01273) 480048. - Paint -   *086738*
Felix, 2 Sun St., Lewes BN7 2QB. T. (01273) 472668.
- Paint -   *086739*
Lewes Gallery, 90 High St., Lewes BN7 1XN.
T. (01273) 473367. - Paint -   *086740*

Leyburn (North Yorkshire)
Chandler Gallery, 8 Commercial Square, Leyburn DL8
5BP. T. (01969) 23676. - Paint -   *086741*

Leyland (Lancashire)
Centurion Arts Gallery, 1 Turpin Green Lane, Leyland.
T. (01772) 424131. - Paint -   *086742*

Lichfield (Staffordshire)
Bournemouth Gallery, Lichfield POB 23.
T. (01543) 481880. - Graph -   *086743*
Exquisite Arts, 22 Bore St., Lichfield. T. (01543) 253626.
- Paint -   *086744*
Greyfriars Gallery, Old Stables Friars Alley, Lichfield.
T. (01543) 250379. - Paint -   *086745*
Guild Hall Gallery, 8 Bore St., Lichfield.
T. (01543) 414531. - Paint -   *086746*

Limpsfield (Surrey)
Limpsfield Watercolours, High St., Limpsfield.
T. 717010. - Paint -   *086747*

Lincoln (Lincolnshire)
Art Gallery, 38 Bailgate, Lincoln. T. (01522) 542717.
- Paint -   *086748*
Castle Gallery, 61 Steep Hill, Lincoln. T. (01522) 535078.
- Paint -   *086749*
Collett, Roy, 34 Steep Hill, Castle Sq., Lincoln.
T. (01522) 536250. - Paint -   *086750*
Gadsby, W. Frank, 260 High St., Lincoln.
T. (01522) 527487. - Paint -   *086751*
Lincoln Fine Art, 33 The Strait, Lincoln LN2 1JD.
T. (01522) 533029, Fax (01522) 533029.
- Paint -   *086752*
Lincolnshire County Council, Lindum Rd., Lincoln.
T. (01522) 527980. - Paint -   *086753*

Lingfield (Surrey)
Columbine Art, 4-6 Godstone Rd., Lingfield.
T. (01342) 832103. - Paint -   *086754*

Linlithgow (Lothian)
Portfolio 4, 47 High St., Linlithgow EH49 7ED.
T. (01506) 844445. - Paint -   *086755*

Lisburn (Co. Antrim)
Creevy, 33 River Rd, Lisburn BT27 6TN.
T. (01846) 638580. - Paint -   *086756*
Seymour Galleries, 20 Seymour St., Lisburn.
T. (01846) 662685. - Paint -   *086757*

Liskeard (Cornwall)
Gwaynten, 11 West St., Liskeard PL14 6BW.
T. (01579) 42314. - Paint -   *086758*
Olde Cider Press Gallery, Yolland Farm, Downgate, Lis-
keard PL14 6BW. T. (01579) 62280. - Paint -   *086759*

Liverpool (Merseyside)
Ahorn Gallery, Newington Bldgs., Newington, Liverpool
L1 4ED. T. (0151) 709 5423. - Paint -   *086760*
Bluecoat Display Centre, 50 Bluecoat Chambers, Liver-
pool L1. T. (0151) 709 4014. - Graph -   *086761*
Bluecoat Gallery, School Lane, Liverpool L1 3BX.
T. (0151) 709 5689. - Paint / Graph -   *086762*
Boydell, 15 Castle St., Liverpool L2 4SX.
T. (0151) 236 3256. - Paint / Graph -   *086763*
Davey, 44 Duke St., Liverpool L1 5AS.
T. (0151) 709 7560. - Paint -   *086764*
Green, Frank, Unit 12, Edward Pavillion, Liverpool L3
4AA. T. (0151) 709 3330. - Graph -   *086765*
Hanover Galleries, 11-13 Hanover St., Liverpool L1.
T. (0151) 709 3073. - Paint -   *086766*
Lyver & Boydell, 15 Castle St., Liverpool L2 4SX.
T. (0151) 236 3256. - Paint / Graph -   *086767*
Marita Fine Art, 502 Stanley Rd, Liverpool L20.
T. (0151) 922 0541. - Paint -   *086768*
Merkmal Gallery, 7 Falkner St, Liverpool L8 7PU.
T. (0151) 709 9633. - Paint -   *086769*
Merseyside Art, Graphic House, Duke St., Liverpool L1.
T. (0151) 709 0671. - Graph -   *086770*
Open Eye, 110 Bold St., Liverpool L1 4HY.
T. (0151) 709 2439. - Pho -   *086771*

Llanbedrog (Gwynedd)
Plas Glyn-y-Weddw Gallery, Llanbedrog LL53 7TT.
T. (01758) 740763. - Paint -   *086772*

Llanberis (Gwynedd)
Mountain Art, 64 High St, Llanberis LL55 4HA.
T. (01286) 870925. - Paint -   *086773*

Llanddeusant (Dyfed)
Country Fine Arts, Rhiwe Farm, Llanddeusant.
T. (015504) 649. - Paint -   *086774*

Llandeilo (Dyfed)
Fountain Fine Art, 115 Rhosmaen St., Llandeilo SA19
6EN. T. (01558) 823328. - Paint -   *086775*

Llandrindod Wells (Powys)
Porticus, 1 Middleton St., Llandrindod Wells.
T. (01597) 823989. - Paint -   *086776*

Llandudno (Gwynedd)
Bernards Gallery, Queen Rd., Llandudno.
T. (01492) 875852. - Paint / Graph -   *086777*
Fulmar Gallery, 44 Madoc St, Llandudno LL30 2TW.
T. (01492) 879880. - Paint -   *086778*
Mercier, 3a Oxford Rd., Llandudno. T. (01492) 870081.
- Paint -   *086779*
Oriel Mostyn, 12 Vaughan St., Llandudno LL30 1AB.
T. (01492) 879201, Fax (1492) 878869.
- Paint -   *086780*

Llandyssul (Dyfed)
Acres Beach Gallery, Derw Mill, Pentrewrt, Llandyssul.
T. (01559) 362329. - Paint -   *086781*

Llangefni (Gwynedd)
Central Gallery, Ty William Hughes Field Gallery, Llangefni.
T. (01248) 723527. - Paint -   *086782*

Llansantffraid (Powys)
Rowles Fine Art, Station House Gallery, Llansantffraid
SY22 6AD. T. (01691) 828478, Fax (01836) 348688.
- Paint -   *086783*

Llantwit Major (South Glamorgan)
Woodford, Commercial St., Llantwit Major CF6 9RB.
T. (014465) 796066. - Paint -   *086784*

London
Aaron, Didier, 21 Ryder St, London SW1Y 6PX.
T. (0171) 8394716, Fax (0171) 9306699.
- Paint -   *086785*
Abbott & Holder, 30 Museum St., London WC1A 1LH.
T. (0171) 637 3981. - Paint / Draw -   *086786*
Accademia Italiana, 24 Rutland Gate, London SW7 1BB.
T. (0171) 225 3474, Fax (0171) 589 5187.
- Paint -   *086787*
Ackermann & Johnson, 27 Lowndes St., London SW1X
9HY. T. (0171) 235 6464, Fax (0171) 8231057.
- Paint -   *086788*
A.D. Fine Art, 65 Sheen Lane, London SW14 8AD.
T. (0181) 8788800, Fax (0181) 8788744. - Paint /
Graph -   *086789*
Addison-Ross, 40 Eaton Terrace, London SW1W 8TS.
T. (0171) 730 1536. - Paint -   *086790*
Agnew's, 43 Old Bond St., London W1X 4BA.
T. (0171) 6296176, Fax 6294359. - Paint /
Graph -   *086791*

Albemarle Gallery, 18 Albemarle St., London W1X.
T. (0171) 355 1880. - Paint / Sculp -   *086792*
Alberti, 114 Albert St., London NW1 7NE.
T. (0171) 485 8976, Fax (0171) 267 7529.
- Paint -   *086793*
Alberti, 35 Dover St., London W1X 3RA.
T. (0171) 629 1052. - Paint -   *086794*
Algranti & Co, 8 Duke St, London SW1Y 6BN.
T. (0171) 9303703, Fax (0171) 3210434.
- Paint -   *086795*
Alton Gallery, 72 Church Rd, London SW13 0DQ.
T. (0181) 7480606. - Ant -   *086796*
Amadeus Gallery, 21 Saint Johns Wood High St., London
NW8. T. (0171) 722 5883. - Paint -   *086797*
Anderson O'Day, 255 Portobello Rd., London W11 1LR.
T. (0171) 221 7592, Fax (0181) 9603641. - Paint /
Graph -   *086798*
Ansdell Street Gallery, 10 Ansdell St., London W8 5BN.
T. (0171) 938 4847, Fax (0171) 937 7050.
- Paint -   *086799*
Appleby, 7 Saint James's Chambers, London SW1.
T. (0171) 839 7635. - Paint / Draw -   *086800*
Archeus, 65 New Bond St., London W1Y 9DF.
T. (0171) 499 9755, Fax (0171) 499 5964. - Paint /
Pho -   *086801*
Arena, 144 Royal College St, London NW1 0TA.
T. (0171) 2679661, Fax (0171) 2840486.
- Graph -   *086802*
Argile Gallery, 7 Blenheim Crescent, London W11 2EE.
T. (0171) 7920888. - Ant -   *086803*
Art Collection, 3-5 Elystan St., London SW3 3NT.
T. (0171) 584 4664. - Paint / Draw -   *086804*
Art of Africa, 158 Walton St., London SW3 2JZ.
T. (0171) 584 2326. - Paint / Sculp -   *086805*
Art Scene, 9/10 Grafton St, London W1X 4DA.
T. (0171) 4990314, Fax (0171) 4938635.
- Sculp -   *086806*
Art Services Grants, 8 Hoxton St, London N1.
T. (0171) 6131925, Fax (0171) 7296273.
- Paint -   *086807*

Art Space Gallery, 84 Saint Peter's St., London N1 8JS.
T. (0171) 359 7002, Fax (0171) 3597002.
- Paint -   *086808*
Artemis Fine Arts, 15 Duke St., London SW1Y 6DB.
T. (0171) 930 8733, Fax (0171) 839 5009. - Paint /
Graph / Draw -   *086809*
The Association of Illustrators Journal, 29 Bedford Squa-
re, London WC1B 3EG. T. (0171) 6364100.
- Paint -   *086810*
Austin, Desmond, & Phipps, 68-69 Great Russell St,
London WC1B 3BN. T. (0171) 242 4443,
Fax (0171) 404 4480. - Paint / Graph -   *086811*
Avivson Collection, 27 Heath St, London NW3 6TU.
T. (0171) 4351993, Fax (0171) 4351993.
- Sculp -   *086812*
Avril Noble, 2 Southampton St., London WC2.
T. (0171) 240 1970. - Graph -   *086813*
Axelson-Johnson, Charles, Flat 28, 25 Jermyn St, Lon-
don SW1Y 6HP. T. (0171) 7341834,
Fax (01932) 860331. - Paint -   *086814*
Bankside Gallery, 48 Hopton St., London SE1 9JH.
T. (0171) 928 7521. - Paint / Graph -   *086815*
Bankside Gallery, 48 Hopton St., Blackfriars, London
SE1 9JH. T. (0171) 9287521, Fax 9282820. - Paint /
Graph -   *086816*
Barbican Art Gallery, Barbican Centre, London EC2Y
8DS. T. (0171) 588 9023. - Paint -   *086817*
Barbican Concourse Gallery, Barbican Centre, London
EC2. T. (0171) 6384141. - Paint -   *086818*
Barclay-Samson, 39 Inglethorpe St, London SW6 6NS.
T. (0171) 3814341, Fax (0171) 6100434.
- Graph -   *086819*
Barkes & Barkes, 76 Parkway, London NW1.
T. (0171) 2841550. - Ant -   *086820*
Barkes & Barkes, 76 Parkway, London NW1.
T. (0171) 284 1550. - Paint -   *086821*
Battersea Arts Centre, Old Town Hall, 176 Lavender Hill,
London SW11. T. (0171) 2280741. - Paint -   *086822*
Baumkotter, 63a Kensington Church St., London W8
4BA. T. (0171) 937 5171, Fax (0171) 9382312.
- Paint -   *086823*
Bayswater Road Art Exhibition, Bayswater Rd., London
W2. - Paint -   *086824*
Beadleston, William, 13 Mason's Yard, St. James's, Lon-
don SW1Y. T. (0171) 321 0495, Fax (0171) 321 0496.
- Paint -   *086825*
Beardsmore, 22-24 Prince of Wales Rd., London NW5
3LG. T. (0171) 4850923, Fax (0171) 267 0824.
- Paint -   *086826*
Bedford Hill Gallery, 50 Bedford Hill, London SW12 9RH.
T. (0181) 6731778. - Ant -   *086827*
Belgrave Gallery, 22 Masons's Yard, Duke St, London
SW1Y 6BY. T. (0171) 9300294. - Paint -   *086828*
Berkeley Square Gallery, 23a Bruton St., London W1X
7DA. T. (0171) 493 7939, Fax (0171) 493 7798.
- Paint / Graph -   *086829*
Berning & Daw Fine Art, 8 Flitcroft St, London WC2H
8DJ. T. (0171) 4979980, Fax (0171) 3798209.
- Eth -   *086830*
Besson, 15 Royal Arcade, 28 Old Bond St, London W1X
3HB. T. (0171) 491 1706, Fax (0171) 4953203.
- Paint -   *086831*
Blackburn, Norman, 32 Ledbury Rd, London W11 2AS.
T. (0171) 2299105, Fax (0171) 2292269. - Graph /
Dec -   *086832*
Blackhealth Gallery, 34a Tranquil Vale, London SE3 0AX.
T. (0181) 8521802, 439456. - Paint / Sculp /
Graph -   *086833*
Blond Fine Art, Unit 10, Canalside Studio, 2-4 Orsman
Rd., London N1 5QJ. T. (0171) 739 4383.
- Paint -   *086834*
Bloomsbury Workshop, 12 Galen Pl., London WC1A 2JR.
T. (0171) 405 0632. - Paint / Graph / Draw -   *086835*
Bonham, Murray Feely, John, 46 Porchester Rd., London
W2 6ET. T. (0171) 221 7208. - Paint -   *086836*
Bornholt, Anna, 3-5 Weighhouse St., London W1Y 1YL.
T. (0171) 499 6114, Fax (0171) 493 8745.
- Paint -   *086837*
Boundary Gallery, 98 Boundary Rd, London NW8 0RH.
T. (0171) 6241126. - Graph -   *086838*
Bourne Fine Art, 14 Masons's Yard, Duke St, London
SW1Y 6BU. T. (0171) 930415/6, Fax (0171) 8398307.
- Paint -   *086839*

Bowmoore, 77 Peterborough Rd., London SW6. T. (0171) 736 4111. - Paint - *086840*
Boxer, Henry, 58-60 Kensington Church St, London W8 4DB. T. (0171) 3760425, 9481633, Fax (0171) 9373400. - Paint / Graph - *086841*
Boyd-Carpenter, Patrick, Grays Antique Market, 58 Davies St, London W1Y 1LB. T. (0171) 4917623. - Paint / Graph - *086842*
Brisigotti, Paolo, 44 Duke St, London SW1Y 6DD. T. (0171) 8394441, Fax (0171) 9761663. - Paint / Sculp - *086843*
Browse & Darby, 19 Cork St., London W1X 2LP. T. (0171) 734 7984, Fax (0171) 437 0750. - Paint / Graph / Sculp - *086844*
Bruton Street Gallery, 28 Bruton St., London W1X 7DB. T. (0171) 499 9747, Fax (0171) 409 7867. - Paint / Sculp - *086845*
Building Centre Gallery, 26 Store St., London WC1E 7BT. T. (0171) 637 1022. - Pho - *086846*
Burlington Gallery, 10 Burlington Gardens, London W1X 1LG. T. (0171) 734 9228, Fax (0171) 494 3770. - Graph - *086847*
Burlington Paintings, 12 Burlington Gardens, London W1X 1LG. T. (0171) 734 9984, Fax (0171) 494 3770. - Paint - *086848*
Business Art Galleries, 34 Windmill St., London W1P 1HH. T. (0171) 323 4700, Fax (0171) 436 3059. - Paint / Graph - *086849*
Buxton, Helen, 97 Mount St., London W1Y. T. (0171) 409 2685. - Paint - *086850*
C & C Master Collection, 106 Finborough Rd., London SW10 9ED. T. (0171) 373 5919. - Paint - *086851*
Cadogan, 163 Draycott Av., London SW3 3AJ. T. (0171) 581 8732, Fax (0171) 589 9120. - Paint - *086852*
Cadogan, 108 Draycott Av., London SW3. T. (0171) 581 5451, Fax (0171) 589 9120. - Paint - *086853*
Caelt, 182 Westbourne Grove, London W11 2RH. T. (0171) 229 9309, Fax (0171) 243 0215. - Paint - *086854*
Cafe By the Pool Gallery, Gomm Rd., Southwark Park, London SE16. T. (0171) 232 2170. - Paint - *086855*
California Art Galleries, 4 Royal Opera Arcade, London SW1Y. T. (0171) 930 7679. - Paint - *086856*
Camber, R.M., 28 Heath Dr., London NW3. T. (0171) 431 4553. - Paint - *086857*
Camden Art Gallery, 22 Church St., London NW8 8EP. T. (0171) 262 3613, Fax (0171) 723 2333. - Paint - *086858*
Camden Arts Centre, Arkwright Rd., London NW3. T. (0171) 4352643, Fax (0171) 794 3371. - Paint - *086859*
Camden Galleries, 70 Parkway, London NW1. T. (0171) 284 0842. - Paint - *086860*
Camerawork, 121 Roman Rd., London E2 0QN. T. (0181) 980 6256. - Paint - *086861*
Campbell, 6 Nightingale Sq., London SW12. T. (0181) 673 1136. - Paint - *086862*
Campbell, Duncan, 15 Thackeray St., London W8 5ET. T. (0171) 937 8665. - Paint / Sculp - *086863*
Campbell, John, 164 Walton St., London SW3. T. (0171) 584 9268. - Paint - *086864*
Campbell, Lucy B., 123 Kensington Church St., London W8 7LP. T. (0171) 727 2205, Fax (0171) 2294252. - Paint / Graph - *086865*
Canada House Gallery, Trafalgar Sq., London SW1Y 5BJ. T. (0171) 629 9492 ext. 2229. - Paint / Graph - *086866*
Canvas Gallery, 4 Canvas House, Queen Elizabeth St., London SE1 2LP. T. (0171) 403 4034. - Paint / Sculp / Draw - *086867*
Carina Prints, Shop 1929, Watermill Way, London SW19. T. (0181) 545 0313. - Graph - *086868*
Carlsson, Fabian, 160 New Bond St., London W1Y 0HR. T. (0171) 409 0619. - Paint / Graph / Sculp / Draw - *086869*
Carritt, David, 15 Duke St., London SW1. T. (0171) 930 8733, Fax (0171) 8395009. - Paint - *086870*
Carter, L., 313 King's Rd., London SW3 5EP. T. (0171) 351 2077. - Paint / Draw - *086871*
Carter & Brady, 119 Portobello Rd, London W11. T. (0171) 7923619. - Paint / Graph - *086872*
Cartoon Gallery, 44 Museum St., London WC1. T. (0171) 242 5335. - Paint / Graph - *086873*
Cascade Art Gallery, Pool of Little Venice, Blomfield Rd., London W9 2PA. T. (0171) 289 7050. - Paint - *086874*
Casolani, David, Alfies Antique Market, 13-25 Church St, London NW8 8DT. T. (0171) 7231370, Fax (0171) 7240999. - Paint - *086875*
Castlebar Gallery, 17 Castlebar Rd. Ealing, London W5. T. (0181) 997 6060. - Paint - *086876*
Catto, 100 Heath St., London NW3 1DP. T. (0171) 435 6660, Fax (0171) 431 5620. - Paint - *086877*
Catto Animation, 41 Heath St., London NW3 6UA. T. (0171) 431 2892, Fax (0171) 431 1831. - Graph / Draw - *086878*
Cazalet, Lumley, 24 Davies St., London W1Y 1LH. T. (0171) 491 4767, Fax (0171) 493 8644. - Graph - *086879*
CCA Galleries, 8 Dover St., London W1X 3PJ. T. (0171) 499 6701, Fax (0171) 409 3555. - Graph / Sculp - *086880*
CCA Galleries, Selfridges, Oxford St, London W1A 1AB. T. (0171) 6291234 ext 3345. - Graph - *086881*
CDR Fine Art, 97 Cambridge St., London SW1. T. (0171) 821 5861. - Paint - *086882*
Cedar, Sherena, 14 New Quebec St., London W1. T. (0171) 723 1255. - Paint - *086883*
Centaur Gallery, 82 Highgate High St., London NG 5HX. T. (0181) 340 0087. - Paint / Graph / Sculp - *086884*
Central Space Gallery, 23-29 Faroe Rd., London W14 0EL. T. (0171) 603 3039. - Paint - *086885*
Centre 181 Gallery, 181 King St., London W6 9JU. T. (0181) 748 3020 ext. 3540. - Pho - *086886*
Century Gallery, 100 Fulham Rd., London SW3 6HS. T. (0171) 581 1589, Fax (0171) 589 9468. - Paint - *086887*
Chadwick, Anna-Mei, 64 New Kings Rd, London SW6 4LT. T. (0171) 736 1928. - Paint - *086888*
Chalk Farm Gallery, 20 Chalk Farm Rd., London NW1 8AG. T. (0171) 267 3300, Fax (0171) 2673300. - Paint *086889*
Champness Canosa, 38 Saint Marys Grove, London W4 3LN. T. (0181) 747 0436, Fax (0181) 995 1099. - Paint - *086890*
Chapman, 31 Lower Richmond Rd., Putney, London SW15. T. (0181) 785 4174. - Paint - *086891*
Chat Noir, 63 Neal St., London WC2H 9PJ. T. (0171) 379 0876. - Paint - *086892*
Chaucer, 45 Pimlico Rd., London SW1W 8NE. T. (0171) 730 2972, Fax (0171) 730 5861. - Paint - *086893*
Cheatle, Zelda, 8 Cecil Court, London WC2N4HE. T. (0171) 836 0506, Fax (0171) 4978911. - Paint - *086894*
Chelsea Wharf Gallery, Chelsea Wharf, 15 Lots Rd., London SW10 0QJ. T. (0171) 351 1222. - Draw - *086895*
Chisenhale Gallery, 64-84 Chisenhale Rd., London E3 SE2. T. (0181) 981 4518. - Paint - *086896*
Churchill, 153 High Rd., London E18. T. (0181) 505 6162. - Paint - *086897*
Churzee, 17 Bellevue Rd., London SW17 7EG. T. (0181) 767 8113. - Paint - *086898*
Clarendon, 91 Jermyn St., London SW1Y. T. (0171) 839 1293. - Paint - *086899*
Clarendon, 139 Portland Rd., London W11. T. (0171) 229 5693. - Paint - *086900*
Clarges, 158 Walton Street, London SW3. T. (0171) 584 3022. - Paint / Paint - *086901*
Clark, Jonathan, 18 Park Walk, London SW10 0AQ. T. (0171) 351 3555, Fax (0171) 8233187. - Paint / Sculp - *086902*
Classic Designs, 71 Nutter Lane, London E11. T. (0181) 989 3632. - Paint - *086903*
Clouse, Wendy, 24 Church St., London TW1. T. (0181) 744 2891. - Paint - *086904*
Coakley, Tony, 183 Kings Rd., London SW3. T. (0171) 351 2914. - Paint - *086905*
Coats, Dick, 32 Grantham Rd., London W4. T. (0181) 995 9733. - Paint / Sculp - *086906*
Cobra & Bellamy, 149 Sloane St., London SW1. T. (0171) 730 2823. - Paint - *086907*
Coexistence Art, 17 Canonbury Ln., London N1 2AS. T. (0171) 226 8382, Fax (0171) 354 9610. - Paint / Graph - *086908*
Coffee Gallery, 23 Museum St., London WC1A 1JT. T. (0171) 436 0455. - Paint - *086909*
Cohen, B., & Sons, 35 Bury St., London SW1Y 6AY. T. (0171) 839 6466. - Paint - *086910*
Cohen, Edward, 40 Duke St, London SW1Y 6DF. T. (0171) 839 5180. - Paint - *086911*
Colin, Denny J., 18 Cale St., London SW3. T. (0171) 584 0240. - Paint - *086912*
Collino, Julie, 15 Glendower Pl., London SW7. T. (0171) 584 4733. - Paint / Graph - *086913*
Collyer-Bristow, 4 Bedford Row, London WC1R 4DF. T. (0171) 242 7363, Fax (0171) 405 0555. - Paint - *086914*
Colman, Cecila, 67 Saint Johns Wood High St., London NW8. T. (0171) 722 0686. - Paint - *086915*
Colnaghi, 14 Old Bond St., London W1X 1JL. T. (0171) 491 7408, Fax (0171) 491 8851. - Paint / Draw - *086916*
Commonwealth Institute, Kensington High St., London W8 6NQ. T. (0171) 603 4535. - Paint / Pho - *086917*
Connaught Brown, 2 Albemarle St., London W1X 3HF. T. (0171) 408 0362, Fax (0171) 495 3137. - Paint / Graph / Sculp / Draw - *086918*
Connaught Galleries, 44 Connaught St, London W2 2AA. T. (0171) 7231660. - Graph - *086919*
Connoisseur Gallery, 14 Halkin Arcade, Motcomb St., London SW1X 8JT. T. (0171) 245 6431, Fax (0171) 2451961. - Paint / Graph - *086920*
Contemporary Applied Arts, 43 Earlham St., London WC2H 9LD. T. (0171) 836 6993. - Graph / China - *086921*
Contemporary Art Society, 20 John Islip St., London SW1P. T. (0171) 821 5323. - Paint - *086922*
Contemporary Ceramics, William Blake House, 7 Marshall St, London W1V 1FD. T. (0171) 4377605, Fax (0171) 2879954. - China - *086923*
Contemporary Textile Gallery, 6a Vigo St., London W1X 1AH. T. (0171) 439 6971, Fax (0171) 439 2353. - Tex - *086924*
Continuum, Stall 124, Gray's Market, Davies St., London W1Y 1AR. T. (0171) 493 4909. - Paint - *086925*
Cooke, Gordon, 112 Princes House, Kensington Park Rd, London W11 3BW. T. (0171) 2212104, Fax (0171) 7929732. *086926*
Cooling, 2-4 Cork St, London W1X 1PA. T. (0171) 409 3500, Fax (0171) 6297128. - Paint - *086927*
Cooper, 768 Fulham Rd., London SW6 5SJ. T. (0171) 731 3421. - Paint - *086928*
Cooper, Jonathan, 20 Park Walk, London SW10 0AQ. T. (0171) 351 0410. - Paint - *086929*
Corbally Stourton, 2a Cork St., London W1X 1PA. T. (0171) 734 8903, Fax (0171) 7368906. - Paint - *086930*
Corporate Arts, 6 Plato Place St., Dionis Rd., London SW6. T. (0171) 384 2727. - Paint - *086931*
Corporate Office Images, 28 Nottingham Pl., London W1N. T. (0171) 224 6430. - Graph - *086932*
Cottenham, 202 Kensington Park Rd., London W11 1NR. T. (0171) 221 0394. - Paint - *086933*
Cottons Gallery Cafe, 55 Chalk Farm Rd., London NW1. T. (0171) 482 1096. - Paint - *086934*
Coventry Gallery, 7 Corsham St., London N1 6DR. T. (0171) 336 7034. - Paint - *086935*
Cox & Co., 44 Duke St., London SW1Y. T. (0171) 930 5706. - Paint / Graph - *086936*
Cox & Company, 37 Duke St, London SW1Y 6DF. T. (0171) 930 1987. - Paint - *086937*
Crafts Council Gallery, 44a Pentonville Rd., London N1 9BY. T. (0171) 278 7700. - Paint - *086938*
Crafts Council Shop, Victoria and Albert Museum, Cromwell Rd., London SW7 2RL. T. (0171) 589 5070. - China / Tex / Jew / Glass - *086939*
Craftsmen Potters Shop, William Blake House, Marshall St., London W1. T. (0171) 437 7605. - China - *086940*
Craigs Cut, 115 Shepherds Bush Rd., London W6 7LP. T. (0171) 602 7642. - Paint - *086941*
Crane, 171a Sloane St, London SW1X 9QG. T. (0171) 235 2464, Fax (0171) 5843843. *086942*

CRANE KALMAN GALLERY

178 Brompton Rd London, SW3
Tel.: 0171-584 7566
Fax: 0171-584 3843

20th CENTURY BRITISH
EUROPEAN AND
AMERICAN ART

Crane Kalman, 178 Brompton Rd., London SW3 1HQ.
T. (0171) 5847566, Fax 5843843. - Paint /
Sculp - 086943
Crawley & Asquith, 16 Savile Row, London W1X 1AE.
T. (0171) 439 2755. - Paint - 086944
Crawshaw, 180 Westbourne Grove, London W11.
T. (0171) 727 8649. - Paint - 086945
Creaser, 316 Portobello Rd., London W10.
T. (0181) 960 4928. - Graph - 086946
Crocodile Gallery, 122 Muswell Hill Broadway, London
N10 3RU. T. (0181) 444 0273, Fax (0181) 444 0223.
- Paint - 086947
Crypt Gallery, 7 Little Russell St., London WC1.
- Paint - 086948
Crystal Palace Gallery, 65 Weston St., London SE19
3RW. T. (0181) 771 1966. - Paint - 086949
Curwen, 4 Windmill St., London W1P 1HF.
T. (0171) 636 1459, Fax (0171) 436 3059. - Graph /
Graph / Draw - 086950
d'Offay, Anthony, 9 Dering St., London W1R 9AA.
T. (0171) 499 4100, Fax (0171) 493 4443. - Paint /
Sculp / Draw - 086951
d'Orsay, A., 28 Conduit St., London W1R.
T. (0171) 495 0328. - Paint - 086952
Daggett Gallery, Charles, 28 Beauchamp Pl, London
SW3 1NJ. T. (0171) 5842969, Fax (0171) 5842950.
- Paint - 086953
Danlann de Bairead, 72d Crowndale Rd., London NW1.
T. (0171) 387 6419. - Paint - 086954
Dare, George, 9 Launceston Pl, London W8 5RL.
T. (0171) 9377072. - Paint - 086955
Davenport, Sarah, 206 Walton St., London SW3 4JL.
T. (0171) 2252224, Fax (0171) 5813629.
- Paint - 086956
de Minta, 303 Munster Rd., London SW6.
T. (0171) 386 7366. - Paint - 086957
The Delfina Studios Trust, 22 Grove Crescent Rd., Lon-
don E15 1BJ. T. (0181) 5198841, Fax (0181) 5031251.
- Paint - 086958
Denham, John, 50 Mill Lane, London NW6 1NJ.
T. (0171) 7942635, Fax 7942635. - Paint - 086959
Denny, Colin, 18 Cale St., London SW3 3QU.
T. (0171) 584 0240, Fax (0171) 584 0240.
- Paint - 086960
Derek Johns, 12 Duke St., London SW1Y 6BN.
T. (0171) 8397671, Fax 9300986. - Ant - 086961

Derek Johns Ltd.

12 Duke Street
St. James's
London SW1Y 6BN
Tel: 0171-839 7671
Fax: 0171-930 0986

Old Master Paintings

Design Centre, 28 Haymarket, London SW1.
T. (0171) 839 8000. - Graph - 086962

Devereux, Vanessa, 11 Blenheim Crescent, London W11
2EE. T. (0171) 221 6836, Fax (0171) 2216481.
- Paint - 086963

Dickens, Richard, 1 Burland Rd., London SW11 6SA.
T. (0171) 223 8754. - Paint - 086964
Dickerson, Andrew, 129 Kennington Rd., London SE11
6SF. T. (0171) 587 1016. - Graph - 086965
Dodo, 286 Westbourne Grove, London W11.
T. (0171) 229 3132. - Graph - 086966
Douglas, Bryan, 16 Arcade House, Finchley Rd., London
NW11. T. (0181) 458 5911. - Paint - 086967
Douwes, 38 Duke St., London SW1 6DF.
T. (0171) 8395795, Fax 8395904. - Paint - 086968
Douwma, Robert, 173 New Bond St., London W1Y 9PB.
T. (0171) 495 4001, Fax (0171) 495 4002.
- Graph - 086969
Dover Street Gallery, 13 Dover St., London W1X 3PH.
T. (0171) 4091540, Fax 4091565. - Paint - 086970

DOVER STREET GALLERY

Old & Modern
Master Paintings

13 Dover Street
London W1X 3PH
Tel: 0171-409 1540 Fax 0171-409 1565

Drey, G., 16-17 Chenil Galleries, King's Rd., London
SW3 5EB. T. (0171) 351 2921. - Paint / China /
Sculp - 086971
Drian, 7 Porchester Pl., London W2 2BT.
T. (0171) 723 9473. - Paint / Graph / Tex - 086972
Drummond, William, 8 Saint James's Chambers, Ryder
St., London SW1Y 6QA. T. (0171) 930 9696.
- Paint - 086973
Drummond/Wrawby Moor, J.N., 6 St. John's Wood Rd,
London NW8 8RE. T. (0171) 2866452. - Paint - 086974
Dulwich Picture Gallery, College Rd., London SE21 7BG.
T. (0181) 693 5254. - Paint - 086975
Duncalfe, 5 Randolph Rd., London W9.
T. (0171) 266 2089. - Paint - 086976
Dundek Collection, 50a Kensington Church St, London
W8 4DG. T. (0171) 9383682, Fax (0171) 9378251.
- Paint - 086977
Durini, 150 Walton St., London SW3 2JJ.
T. (0171) 581 1237, Fax (0171) 584 6107.
- Paint - 086978
Duwma, Robert, 4 Henrietta St, London WC2E.
T. (0171) 836 0771. 086979
Eagle Gallery, 159 Farringdon Rd., London EC1.
T. (0171) 833 2674, Fax (0171) 8332674. - Paint /
Draw - 086980
Ealing Gallery, 78 St. Marys Rd, London W5 5EX.
T. (0181) 840 7883, Fax (0181) 8407883.
- Paint - 086981
East West, 8 Blenheim Crescent, London W11 1NN.
T. (0171) 229 7981, Fax (0171) 7274357. - Paint /
Sculp / Draw - 086982
Eaton, 34 Duke St., London SW1Y 6DF.
T. (0171) 9305950, Fax (0171) 8398076.
- Paint - 086983
Ebury Galleries, 200 Ebury St., London SW1.
T. (0171) 730 8999. - Paint / Graph - 086984
Edith Grove Gallery, 10a Edith Grove, London SW10
0NW. T. (0171) 376 3127. - Paint / Graph /
Sculp - 086985
Editions Graphiques, 3 Clifford St., London W1X.
T. (0171) 734 3944. - Graph - 086986
Edmunds, Andrew, 44 Lexington St., London W1R 3LH.
T. (0171) 437 8594, Fax (0171) 439 2551. - Paint /
Draw - 086987
Egee, 9 Chelsea Manor Studios, Flood St., London SW3
5SR. T. (0171) 351 6818. - Paint - 086988
Electrum Gallery, 21 South Molton St., London W1Y
1DD. T. (0171) 629 6325. - Jew / Fra - 086989
Eleini, Marlene, 14 New Bond St., London W1Y 9PF.
T. (0171) 408 0138. - Paint / Graph / Sculp / Pho /
Draw - 086990
Elm Lodge Gallery, 279 Fulham Rd., London SW10.
T. (0171) 351 3223. - Paint - 086991

Elms Lesters, 1-5 Flitcroft St., London WC2H 8DH.
T. (0171) 836 6747, Fax (0171) 379 0789.
- Paint - 086992
E.M. Arts, 36 Tregunter Rd., London SW10 9LQ.
T. (0171) 373 3856. - Paint - 086993
Endell Street Gallery, 27-29 Endell St., London WC2H.
T. (0171) 497 2934. - Paint - 086994
England & Co., 14 Needham Rd., London W11 2RP.
T. (0171) 221 0417. - Paint - 086995
English Heritage, Ranger's House, Chesterfield Walk,
London SE10. T. (0181) 853 0035. - Paint - 086996
Entwistle, 37 Old Bond St., London W1X 3AE.
T. (0171) 409 3484, Fax (0171) 499 5795.
- Paint - 086997
Ermitage, 14 Hay Hill, London W1X 7LJ.
T. (0171) 499 5459. - Paint - 086998
Escape Coffee House Art Gallery, 141 Greenwich South
St., London SE10. T. (0181) 692 5826. - Paint - 086999
Example Art, 903 Fulham Rd., London SW6 5HU.
T. (0171) 384 1130. - Paint - 087000
Faggionato, Anne, 20 Dering St, London W1R 9AA.
T. (0171) 493 67 32, Fax 493 96 93. - Paint - 087000a
Fairhurst, 291 New King's Rd., London SW6.
T. (0171) 736 9132. - Paint - 087001
Family Copies, 19 Brechin Pl., London SW7 4QB.
T. (0171) 373 5499. - Paint - 087002
Farren, 590 King's Rd., London SW10 2DX.
T. (0171) 371 0703. - Paint / Sculp - 087003
Faustus, 90 Jermyn St., London SW1Y.
T. (0171) 930 1864. - Graph / Draw - 087004
Federation of British Artists, 17 Carlton House Terrace,
London SW1Y 5BD. T. (0171) 930 6844,
Fax (0171) 839 7830. - Paint - 087005
Feely, Murray, 46 Porchester Rd., London W2 6ET.
T. (0171) 221 7208. - Paint / Draw - 087006
Feigen, Richard L., 6 Ryder St., London SW1Y.
T. (0171) 930 0020. - Paint - 087007
Few, Ted, 97 Drakefield Rd., London SW17.
T. (0181) 767 2314. - Paint - 087008
Fieldborne, 63 Queen's Grove, London NW8 6ER.
T. (0171) 586 3600. - Paint / Paint / Sculp - 087009
Fiell, 57a New King's Rd., London SW6 4SE.
T. (0171) 731 0546. - Furn - 087010
Finart, 4-10 Sloane Gardens, London SW1W.
T. (0171) 730 2340. - Paint - 087011
Finchley Fine Art, 48b Percy Rd., London N12.
T. (0181) 349 1211. - Paint - 087012
Finchley Fine Art Gallery, 983 High Rd, London N12
8QR. T. (0181) 446 4848. - Paint - 087013
Fine Art Associates, 229 Westbourne Grove, London
W11. T. (0171) 229 6606. - Paint - 087014
Fine Art Consultancy, 156 Tooley St., London SE1 2NR.
T. (0171) 962 0949, Fax (0171) 962 0062. - Paint /
Graph / Sculp / Draw - 087015
Fine Art Galleries, 81 Balham High Rd., London SW12.
T. (0181) 675 0884. - Paint - 087016
Fine Art Investments, 48 Kensington Church St., London
W8 4BY. T. (0171) 937 8891. - Paint - 087017
Fine Art Society, 148 New Bond St., London W1Y 0JT.
T. (0171) 629 5116, Fax (0171) 4919454. - Paint /
Sculp / Draw - 087018
Finnegan, Britannia Hotel, Grosvenor Sq., London W1A.
T. (0171) 355 3554. - Paint - 087019
Finney Antique Prints & Books, Michael, 11 Camden
Passage, London N1 8EA. T. (0171) 2269280.
- Paint - 087020
First Floor Gallery, 9 Cork St., London W1X 1PD.
T. (0171) 287 8324, Fax (0171) 287 9713.
- Paint - 087021
Flecha Gallery, Mario, 239 Liverpool Rd, London N1.
T. (0171) 6075096. - Paint - 087022
Fleur de Lys Gallery, 227a Westbourne Grove, London
W11 2SE. T. (0171) 727 8595, Fax (0171) 727 8595.
- Paint - 087023
Flower Gallery, 366 Kings Rd., London SW3.
T. (0171) 376 8766. - Paint - 087024
Flowers East, 199-205 Richmond Rd., London E8 3NJ.
T. (0181) 985 3333, Fax (0181) 985 0067. - Paint /
Graph / Sculp - 087025
Flowers Gallyer at London Fields, Angela, 282 Richmond
Rd, London E8. T. (0181) 9853333,
Fax (0181) 9850067. - Paint / Sculp / Graph - 087026

For Arts Sake, 43 The Burroughs Hendon, London NW4 4AX. T. (0181) 202 3822, Fax (0181) 202 1641. - Paint - 087027
Forest Fine Art, 20 Forest View, London E4 7AY. T. (0181) 529 8470, Fax (0171) 324 7890. - Paint - 087028
Fortune Green Gallery, 98 Fortune Green Rd., London NW6. T. (0171) 794 9381. - Paint - 087029
Fouts & Fowler, 30 Tottenham St., London W1P 9PN. T. (0171) 636 1064, Fax (0171) 388 6491. - Paint - 087030
Free Painters & Sculptors, 15 Buckingham Gate, London SW1E. T. (0171) 828 5963. - Paint - 087031
French Institute, 17 Queensberry Pl., London SW7. T. (0171) 589 6211. - Paint / Graph - 087032
Frith Street Gallery, 60 Frith St., London W1V 5TA. T. (0171) 494 1550, Fax (0171) 2873733. - Graph - 087033
Fritz-Denneville, Hildegard, 31 New Bond St., London W1Y 9HD. T. (0171) 629 2466, Fax (0171) 408 0604. - Paint / Graph - 087034
Frost & Reed, 16 Old Bond St, London W1X 3DB. T. (0171) 6292457, Fax (0171) 4990298. - Paint / Graph - 087035
Fulham Gallery, 411 Fulham Palace Rd., London SW6. T. (0171) 736 9318. - Paint - 087036
Gage, Deborah, 38 Old Bond St., London W1X 3AE. T. (0171) 493 3249. - Paint - 087037
Gage, Deborah, 38 Old Bond St, London W1X 3AE. T. (0171) 4933249, Fax (0171) 4951352. - Paint - 087038
Gagliardi, 507-509 King's Rd., London SW10 0TX. T. (0171) 352 3663. - Paint / Graph - 087039
Gale, Ira D., 42c South Audley St., London W1Y. T. (0171) 499 2030. - Paint - 087040
Galerie Dagmar, 14 Upland Rd., London SE22. T. (0181) 693 2708. - Paint - 087041
Galerie Dagmar, 14 Upland Rd, London SE22 9EE. T. (0181) 6932708. - Paint - 087042
Galerie Matisse, 17 Queensberry Pl., London SW7 2DT. T. (0171) 589 6211. - Paint - 087043
Galerie Moderne Le Style Lalique, 10 Halkin Arcade, Motcomb St., London SW1. T. (0171) 245 6907, Fax (0171) 245 6341. - Glass - 087044
Gallery, 105 Muswell Hill Broadway, London N10. T. (0181) 444 0135. - Paint - 087045
Gallery Arcticus, 176 Sloane St., London SW1X 9QG. T. (0171) 2596558, Fax (0171) 259 6080. - Paint - 087046
Gallery Downstairs, 92 Rossiter Rd., London SW12 9RX. T. (0181) 673 5150. - Paint / Graph / Draw - 087047
gallery e, 103 Greenwich South St., London SE10. T. (0181) 692 7743. - Paint - 087048
The Gallery in Cork St, 28 Cork St, London W1X 1HB. T. (0171) 2878408, Fax (0171) 2872018. 087049
Gallery K, 101-103 Heath St., London NW3 6SS. T. (0171) 794 4949, Fax (0171) 431 4833. - Paint - 087050
Gallery Kaleidoscope, 64-66 Willesden Ln., London NW6 7SX. T. (0171) 328 5833. - Paint / Graph - 087051
Gallery on Church Street, 12 Church St., London NW8. T. (0171) 723 3389, Fax (0171) 7233389. - Paint - 087052
Gallery on the Lane, 205 Acton Ln., London W4 5DA. T. (0181) 742 1754. - Paint - 087053
Gallery Shurini, 10a Charles II St, London SW1Y 4AA. T. (0171) 3210572, Fax (0171) 3210572. - Paint / Graph / Sculp - 087054
Gallery 10, 10 Grosvenor St., London W1. T. (0171) 491 8103. - Paint - 087055
Gallery 202, 202 Kensington Park Rd., London W11. T. (0171) 792 9875. - Paint - 087056
Gallery 23, 23 Copenhagen St., London N1. T. (0171) 278 2009. - Paint - 087057
Gallery 25, 4 Halkin Arcade, Motcomb St., London SW1X. T. (0171) 235 5178. - Paint - 087058
Gallery 273, Queen Mary College, Mile End Rd., London E1 4NS. T. (0171) 975 5077. - Draw - 087059
Gallery 47, 47 Great Russell St., London WC1B 3PA. T. (0171) 638 4577. - Paint - 087060
Gallery 6, 6 Kensington Pl., London W8. T. (0171) 221 6668. - Paint - 087061
Ganz, Kate, 45 South St, London W1Y 5PD. T. (0171) 4092442, Fax (0171) 4990671. - Paint / Graph - 087062
Garratt, Stephen, 60 Addison Rd., London W14. T. (0171) 603 0681. - Paint - 087063
Garton & Cooke, 39-42 New Bond St., London W1. T. (0171) 493 2820. - Paint - 087064
Gavin Graham Gallery, 47 Ledbury Rd., London W11 2AA. T. (0171) 229 4848, Fax (0171) 7929697. - Paint - 087065
Genillard, Laure, 38a Foley St., London W1P 7LB. T. (0171) 436 2300, Fax (0171) 4362300. - Paint - 087066
George, Jill, 38 Lexington St., London W1R 3HR. T. (0171) 439 7343, Fax (0171) 287 0478. - Paint / Draw - 087067
Gibson, Thomas, 44 Old Bond St., London W1 3AF. T. (0171) 4998572, Fax (0171) 4951924. - Paint / Sculp / Draw - 087068
Gill, Christopher, A14/A16 Antiquarius, 135 King's Rd., London SW3. T. (0171) 351 0150. - Paint - 087069
Gill, David, 60 Fulham Rd., London SW3 6HH. T. (0171) 589 5946. - Paint - 087070
Gillian, Jason, 42 Inverness St., London NW1. T. (0171) 267 4835. - Paint - 087071
Gimpel Fils, 30 Davies St., London W1Y 1LG. T. (0171) 493 2488, Fax (0171) 629 5732. - Paint / Sculp - 087072
Gladwell & Co., 68 Queen Victoria St., London EC4 4SJ. T. (0171) 248 3824. - Paint - 087073
Glasshouse, 65 Long Acre, London WC2. T. (0171) 836 9785. - Paint - 087074
Godfrey, 104 Mount St., London W1. T. (0171) 409 2777. - Paint / China - 087075
Goethe-Institut London, 50 Princes Gate, Exhibition Rd., London SW7 2PH. T. (0171) 581 3344, Fax (0171) 581 0974. - Paint / Graph - 087076
Goldsmith's Gallery, Lewisham Way, New Cross, London SE14 6NW. T. (0181) 6927171. - Paint - 087077
Goodwill Art Service, 4 Cowcross St., London EC1M. T. (0171) 602 6468. - Paint - 087078
Gordon, Ora, Grays Mews Antique Market, Stand J27, London W1Y. T. (0171) 499 1319. 087079
Gothick Dream, 27 Breezer's Court, 20 The Hwy, London E1 9BE. T. (0171) 2650566, Fax (0171) 2650566. - Paint - 087080
Graeme Dowling, 6 Shillingford St., London N1. T. (0171) 359 6106. - Paint - 087081
Graham-Dixon, Francis, 17-18 Great Sutton St., London EC1V 0DN. T. (0171) 250 1962, Fax (0171) 490 1069. - Paint - 087082
Graham-Stewart, 293a Westbourne Grove, London W11 2QA. T. (0171) 229 6959. - Paint - 087083
Green, Richard, 44 Dover St., London W1X 4JQ. T. (0171) 493 3939, Fax (0171) 629 2609. - Paint - 087084
Green, Richard, 33 New Bond St, London W1Y 9HD. T. (0171) 4995553, Fax (0171) 4998509. - Paint - 087085
Green, Richard, 39 Dover St, London W1X 3RB. T. (0171) 4933939, Fax (0171) 6292609. - Paint - 087086
Green, Richard, 4 New Bond St, London W1Y 9PE. T. (0171) 4933939, Fax (0171) 6292609. - Paint - 087087
Greenwich Citizens Gallery, 151 Powis St., London SE18. T. (0181) 3162752. - Paint - 087088
Greenwich Gallery, 9 Nevada St., London SE10 9JL. T. (0181) 305 1666. - Paint / Graph - 087089
Greenwich Printmakers, 1a Greenwich Market, London SE10 9HZ. T. (0181) 858 1569. - Graph - 087090
Greenwich Theatre Gallery, Crooms Hill, London SE10. T. (0181) 858 4447. - Paint - 087091
Greenwood, Nigel, 4 New Burlington St., London W1X 1FE. T. (0171) 434 3795. - Paint / Graph / Repr / Sculp / Pho - 087092
Gregory, Martyn, 34 Bury St, London SW1Y 6AU. T. (0171) 8393731, Fax (0171) 9300812. - Paint - 087093
Grenville Gibbs, 50 Sulivan Rd., London SW6 3DX. T. (0171) 731 8450. - Ant / Fra - 087094
Grodzinski, Vera, 29 Elsworthy Rd., London NW3. T. (0171) 722 6964. - Paint - 087096

GROSVENOR GALLERY

20th Century Master Paintings and Sculpture

18 Albemarle Street, London W1X 3HA
Tel: 0171-629 0891 · Fax: 0171-491 4391
Weekdays 10 - 5.00 pm

Grosvenor Gallery, 18 Albemarle St., London W1X 3HA. T. (0171) 6290891, Fax 4914391. - Paint / Graph / Sculp / Draw - 087097
Grosvenor Prints, 28-32 Shelton St., London WC2H 9HP. T. (0171) 836 1979, Fax (0171) 379 6695. - Graph - 087098
Grove Gallery, 69 The Grove, London W5. T. (0181) 567 0604. - China / Tex / Glass - 087099
Gruzelier, 16 Maclise Rd., London W14 0PR. T. (0171) 603 4540. - Paint - 087100
Guatemalan Indian Centre, 94a Wandsworth Bridge Rd., London SW6. T. (0171) 371 5291. - Paint - 087101
Guild of Aviation Artists, Bondway Business Centre, 71 Bondway, London SW8 1SQ. T. (0171) 735 0634. - Paint - 087102
Gunter, 4 Randall Av., London NW2. T. (0181) 452 3997. - Paint - 087103
Hahn Gallery, 47 Albemarle St., London W1X 3FE. T. (0171) 4939196. - Paint - 087104
Hallam, 325 Upper Richmond Rd, London SW14. T. (0181) 876 2573. - Paint - 087105
Hallam, 198 Ebury St., London SW1W. T. (0171) 730 8999. - Paint - 087106
Hamilton, 186 Willifield Way, London NW11. T. (0181) 455 7410. - Paint / Sculp - 087107
Hamilton, 61 Ledbury Rd., London W11. T. (0171) 792 8779. - Paint - 087108
Hamilton Forbes, M14 Garden Market, London SW10 0XE. T. (0171) 352 8181, Fax (0171) 351 3973. - Paint / Graph / Draw - 087109
Hamiltons Gallery, 13 Carlos Pl., London W1. T. (0171) 4999494, Fax (0171) 629 9919. - Paint - 087110
Hammond Roberts, 140 Field End Rd, London HA5. T. (0181) 868 7001. - Paint - 087111
Hancock, 184 Westbourne Grove, London W11. T. (0171) 229 7827, Fax (0171) 2293855. - Paint - 087112
Hardware, 277 Hornsey Rd., London N7 6RZ. T. (0171) 272 9651, Fax (0171) 348 0561. - Graph - 087113
Harley, 13 Overstrand Mansions, Prince of Wales Dr., London SW11 4HA. T. (0171) 622 7800, Fax (0171) 498 3978. - Paint - 087114
Harounoff, 1-7 Davies Mews, London W1Y 1AR. T. (0171) 408 0803. - Paint - 087115
Harrington, David, 27 Berkeley Sq., London W1X 5HA. T. (0171) 495 3194, Fax (0171) 409 3175. - Paint - 087116
Hartnoll, Julian, 14 Mason's Yard, London SW1Y 6BU. T. (0171) 839 3842, Fax (0171) 9308234. - Paint / Draw - 087117
Harvey-Lee, Elizabeth, 1 Belton Rd, London NW2 5PA. T. (0181) 459 7623, Fax (0171) 4598624. - Graph - 087118
Hayward, South Bank Centre, Belvedere Rd., London SE1 8XZ. T. (0171) 928 3144, Fax (0171) 928 0063. - Paint - 087119
Hazlitt, Gooden & Fox, 38 Bury St., London SW1Y 6BB. T. (0171) 930 6422, Fax (0171) 8395984. - Paint / Sculp / Draw - 087120

Heller, Kate, 5 Silver Pl., London W1R. T. (0171) 287 8328. - Paint - *087121*
Henderson, Marina, 11 Langton St., London SW10. T. (0171) 352 1667. - Paint - *087122*
Hershkowitz, Robert, 94 Queen's Gate, London SW7 5AB. T. (0171) 3738994, 044448 2240. - Pho - *087123*
Hicks, 2-4 Leopold Rd., London SW19. T. (0181) 944 7171. - Paint - *087124*
Higgins, Sandra, 31 Boundon St., London W1X. T. (0171) 629 0643. - Paint - *087125*
Higherwater, 82 Three Colts St., London E14. T. (0181) 538 3526. - Paint - *087126*
Hill Gallery, 28 Rosslyn Hill, London NW3. T. (0171) 431 5169. - Paint / Graph / Sculp - *087127*
Hill, J.K., 89 Old Brompton Rd., London SW7. T. (0171) 584 7529. - China - *087128*
Historical Portraits, 30 Old Bond St, London W1. T. (0171) 4996818, Fax (0171) 4950793. - Paint - *087129*
Holland Gallery, 129 Portland Rd., London W11 4LW. T. (0171) 727 7198, Fax (0171) 7277198. - Paint - *087130*
Hollywood Road Gallery, 12 Hollywood Rd., London SW10. T. (0171) 351 1973. - Paint - *087131*
Holtermann, Marianne, 70 South Audley St., London SW1Y. T. (0171) 491 9911. - Paint - *087132*
Honor Oak Gallery, 52 Honor Oak Park, London SE23. T. (0181) 291 6094. - Paint - *087133*
Hooper, 102 St. Johns Wood Terrace, London NW8. T. (0171) 483 0503. - Paint - *087134*
Hoppen, Stephanie, 17 Walton St., London SW3 2HX. T. (0171) 5893678. - Paint / Draw - *087135*
Hossack Gallery, Rebecca, 35 Windmill St, London W1P 1HH. T. (0171) 4093599, Fax (0171) 3233182. - Eth - *087136*
Hossack, Rebecca, 197 Piccadilly, London W1V 9LF. T. (0171) 434 4401, Fax (0171) 434 4403. - Paint / Pho - *087137*
Hossack, Rebecca, 35 Windmill St., London W1P 1HH. T. (0171) 409 3599. - Paint - *087138*
Hotz, Dennis, 9 Cork St., London W1X 1PD. T. (0171) 287 8324, Fax (0171) 287 9713. - Paint / Graph / Sculp - *087139*
Houldsworth, 46 Bassett Rd., London W10 6JL. T. (0181) 969 8197, Fax (0181) 9686829. - Paint - *087140*
Hull, Christopher, 17 Motcomb St., London SW1X 8LB. T. (0171) 235 0500. - Paint - *087141*
Humphris, Cyril, 8 Pembroke Walk, London W8 6PQ. T. (0171) 937 1719, Fax (0171) 376 1695. - Sculp - *087142*
Hunt-Jennings, 10 Bourdon St., London W1X 9HX. T. (0171) 629 3748. - Graph / Sculp - *087143*
Hunter, Sally, 11 Halkin Arcade, Motcomb St, London SW1X 8JT. T. (0171) 235 0934. - Paint - *087144*
Hurlingham & New King's Road Galleries, 297 New King's Rd., London SW6 4BR. T. (0171) 7314363. - Paint - *087145*
Hutton, Allen, Northway House, High Rd., London N20. T. (0181) 446 8450. - Paint - *087146*
Hyde Park Gallery, 16 Craven Terrace, London W2. T. (0171) 402 2904. - Paint - *087147*
I C A Galleries, Nash House, The Mall, London SW1 5AH. T. (0171) 930 3647. - Paint / Graph / Sculp / Pho - *087148*
Ice House, Holland Park, London W8. T. (0171) 603 1123. - Paint / Sculp - *087149*
Images, 19 Helenslea Av., London NW11 8NE. T. (0181) 455 3160, Fax (0181) 2090309. - Paint - *087150*
Incisioni, Alfies Antique Market, 13-25 Church St, London NW8 8DT. T. (0171) 7062970, Fax (0171) 7240999. - Graph / Dec - *087151*
Indar Posrichar, 22 Connaught St, London W2 2AF. T. (0171) 724 9541, Fax (0171) 258 0493. - Paint - *087152*
Intaglio, 15 Corsica St., London N5 1JT. T. (0171) 704 6780, Fax (0171) 7046780. - Graph - *087153*
Interim Art, 21 Beck Rd., London E8. T. (0171) 254 9607. - Paint - *087154*
Iona Antiques, POB 285, London W8 6HZ. T. (0171) 6021193, Fax (0171) 3712843. - Paint - *087155*
Islamic Arts Foundation, 144-146 Kings Cross Rd., London WC1X. T. (0171) 833 8275. - Paint - *087156*
Island Gallery, 63 Amsterdam Rd., London E14. T. (0171) 537 4398. - Paint - *087157*
Iveagh Bequest, Kenwood, Hampstead Lane, London NW3 7JR. T. (0181) 3481286. - Paint - *087158*
Jackson, William, 28 Cork St., London W1X 1HB. T. (0171) 287 2121, Fax (0171) 287 2018. - Paint - *087159*
Jacobs, Nicola, 9 Cork St., London W1. T. (0171) 437 3868. - Paint - *087160*
Jacobson, Bernard, 14a Clifford St., London W1X 1RF. T. (0171) 495 8575, Fax (0171) 495 6210. - Graph - *087161*
James, David, 3 Halkin Arcade, Motcomb St., London SW1X 8JT. T. (0171) 235 5552, Fax (0171) 235552. - Paint / Furn - *087162*
Janus Avivson, Camden Lock, Chalk Farm Rd., London NW1 8AF. T. (0171) 482 3091, Fax (0171) 284 3130. - Paint - *087163*
Japan Print Gallery, 43 Pembridge Rd., London W11. T. (0171) 221 0927. - Paint - *087164*
Japanese Gallery, 66d Kensington Church St., London W8 4BY. T. (0171) 229 2934, Fax (0171) 9383056. - Graph - *087165*
Jason, Gillian, 42 Inverness St., London NW1 7HB. T. (0171) 267 4835, Fax (0171) 284 0614. - Paint - *087166*
Jekel, Eva, 202 Kensington Park Rd., London W11. T. (0171) 792 9875. - Paint / Sculp - *087167*
Jennings, Clive, 9a Dallington St, London EC1V 0BJ. T. (0171) 6083056, Fax (0171) 2532172. - Graph - *087168*
Johnson, Oscar & Peter, 27 Lowndes St., London SW1X 9HY. T. (0171) 235 6464. - Paint - *087169*
Jonathan, Clark, 18 Park Walk, London SW10. T. (0171) 351 3555. *087170*
Jones, John, Unit 4, Finsbury Park Trading Estate, Morris Pl., London N4 3JG. T. (0171) 281 2380, Fax (0171) 281 5956. - Paint / Graph / Draw - *087171*
Jones, Robert, 6 Bury St., London SW1Y 6AB. T. (0171) 925 2079. - Paint - *087172*
Joslin, Richard, 150 Addison Gardens, London W14 0ER. T. (0171) 603 6435, Fax (0171) 603 6435. - Paint - *087173*
J.P.L. Fine Arts, 26 Davies St, London W1Y 1LH. T. (0171) 4932630, Fax (0171) 4931379. - Paint / Graph / Sculp - *087174*
J.P.L. Fine Arts, 26 Davies St, London W1Y 1LH. T. (0171) 4932630, 6299788, Fax (0171) 4931379. - Paint / Graph - *087175*
Juda, Annely, 23 Dering St, London W1R 9AA. T. (0171) 6297578, Fax (0171) 4912139. - Paint / Graph / Sculp - *087176*
Judd Street Gallery, 99 Judd St., London WC1H. T. (0171) 388 1985. - Paint - *087177*
Justin F. Skrebowski Prints, 8a Portobello Rd, London W11 2QD. T. (0171) 7929742. - Paint / Fra - *087178*
Kaleidoscope, 64-66 Willesden Lane, London NW6. T. (0171) 328 5833. - Fra / Draw - *087179*
Kaplan, Lewis M., 50 Fulham Rd., London SW3. T. (0171) 589 3108. - Paint - *087180*
Kasmin, 34 Warwick Av., London W9. T. (0171) 286 6229. - Paint - *087181*
Katz, Agi, 98 Boundary Rd., London NW8. T. (0171) 624 1126. - Paint - *087182*
Keating, Nevill, 7 Durham Pl., London SW3 4ET. T. (0171) 352 0989, Fax (0171) 376 5243. - Paint - *087183*
Kendall, Beryl, 2 Warwick Pl, London W9. T. (0171) 286 9902. - Paint - *087184*
Kennedy, Robin, 29 New Bond St., London W1Y 9HD. T. (0171) 408 1238, Fax (0171) 4911662. - Graph - *087185*
Kensington Fine Arts, 46 Kensington Church St., London W8 4BY. T. (0171) 937 5317. - Paint - *087186*
Kenwood, The Iveagh Bequest, Hampstead Lane, London NW3 7JR. T. (0181) 348 1286. - Paint - *087187*
Kepler Gallery, 36 Kepler Rd., London SW4. T. (0171) 738 6993. - Paint - *087188*
Ker, David, 85 Bourne St., London SW1W 8HF. T. (0171) 730 8365, Fax (0171) 7303352. - Paint / Graph - *087189*
Khoetsu, 22 Old Bond St., London W1X. T. (0171) 499 4469. - Paint - *087190*
King Street Galleries, 17 King St., London SW1Y 6QU. T. (0171) 930 9392, Fax (0171) 9303993. - Paint / Graph - *087191*
Kings Road Gallery, 509 Kings Rd., London SW10 0TX. T. (0171) 352 3663. - Paint - *087192*
Kings Walk Gallery, 122 Kings Rd., London SW3. T. (0171) 225 2930. - Paint - *087193*
Kleinman, Patricia, Camden Passage, 359 Upper St, London N1 0PD. T. (0171) 704 0798. - Paint / Graph - *087194*
Knapp, Regent's College, Inner Circle, London NW1 4NS. T. (0171) 487 7540. - Paint / Sculp - *087195*
Knoedler, 22 Cork St., London W1. T. (0171) 439 1096. - Paint - *087196*
Kohler, 14 Osten Mews, London SW7 4HW. T. (0171) 370 0850, Fax (0171) 370 2843. - Paint / Graph / Sculp / Pho / Draw - *087197*
Kreckovic, L., 62 Fulham High St., London SW6. T. (0171) 736 0753. - Paint - *087198*
Kufa, 26 Westbourne Grove, London W2 5RH. T. (0171) 229 1928, Fax (0171) 243 8513. - Paint - *087199*
Kyburg, 39 Duke St., London SW1Y 6DF. T. (0171) 930 9308. - Paint - *087200*
Kyle, Francis, 9 Maddox St., London W1R 9LE. T. (0171) 499 6870, Fax (0171) 495 0180. - Paint / Graph / Sculp - *087201*
La Galerie, 225 Ebury St., London SW1W 8UT. T. (0171) 730 9210, Fax (0171) 730 9206. - Paint / Draw - *087202*
Lacey, Stephen, Redcliffe Sq., London SW10. T. (0171) 370 7785. - Paint / Draw - *087203*
Lacy, 38-40 Ledbury Rd., London W11 2AB. T. (0171) 229 9105. - Paint - *087204*
Lamley & Co., 1-3 Exhibition Rd., London SW7. T. (0171) 589 9713. - Paint - *087205*
Lamont, Andrew, 65 Roman Rd., London E2 0QN. T. (0181) 981 6332, Fax (0181) 983 0144. - Paint / Graph / China - *087206*
Lampard, Charlotte, 33 Mossop St., London SW3 2NB. T. (0171) 225 2696. - Paint - *087207*
Landon, 21 Shepherd Market, London W1Y 7HR. T. (0171) 493 5616. - Paint - *087208*
Lane Fine Art, 123 New Bond St., London W1Y 9AE. T. (0171) 499 5020. - Paint - *087209*
Lanigans, 97 Prince of Wales Dr, London SW11. T. (0171) 498 6059. - Paint - *087210*
Lauderdale House & Community Arts Centre, Waterlow Park, Highgate Hill, London N6. T. (0181) 348 8716. - Paint - *087211*
Lax Fine Original Prints, Julian, Flat J, 37-39 Arkwright Rd, London NW3 6BJ. T. (0171) 7949933, Fax (0171) 4315845. - Graph - *087212*
Lefevre, 30 Bruton St., London W1X 8JD. T. (0171) 493 2107, Fax (0171) 499 9088. - Paint / Sculp / Draw - *087213*
Leger, 13 Old Bond St., London W1X 3DB. T. (0171) 629 3538, Fax (0171) 493 8681. - Paint - *087214*
Leggatt Bros., 17 Duke St., London SWIY 6DB. T. (0171) 9303772. - Paint - *087215*
Leicester Galleries, 5 Ryder St, London SW1Y 6PY. T. (0171) 9306059, Fax (0171) 9304678. - Paint / Graph - *087216*
Leigh Gallery, 17 Leigh St., London WC1H 9EW. T. (0171) 242 5177. - Paint - *087217*
Leleco Art Gallery, 5 Britannia Rd, London SW6 2HJ. T. (0171) 3715804, Fax (0171) 3715806. - Paint / Sculp - *087218*
Leopard Press, 24a Church Lane, London N2. T. (0181) 883 6140. - Paint - *087219*
Lingard, 50 Pall Mall, London SW1Y 5JQ. T. (0171) 930 1645. - Draw - *087220*
Lisson Gallery, 67 Lisson St, London NW1 5DA. - Paint - *087221*
Little Winchester Gallery, 36a Kensington Church St., London W8 4BX. T. (0171) 937 8444. - Paint - *087222*

Llewellyn, Alexander, 124-126 The Cut, London SE1 8LN. T. (0171) 620 1322, Fax (0181) 8712114.
- Paint - 087223
Lo Shan Tang, 1406 Sutherland Av., London W9.
T. (0171) 266 3158. - Paint - 087224
Locus Gallery, 116 Heath St., London NW3 1DR.
T. (0171) 7941652. - Paint / Graph - 087225
Loggia Gallery, 15 Buckingham Gate, London SW1E 6LB. T. (0171) 828 5963. - Paint / Sculp - 087226
Logos Art Gallery, 20 Barter St., London WC1A 2AH.
T. (0171) 404 7091. - Paint - 087227
London Borough of Southwark Gallery, 65 Peckham Rd., London SE5. T. (0171) 703 6120. - Paint - 087228
London Contemporary Art, 132 Lots Rd., London SW10 0RJ. T. (0171) 7318450, Fax (0171) 376 3771.
- Paint - 087229
London Ecology Centre Gallery, 45 Shelton St, London WC2H 9HJ. T. (0171) 3794324. - Ant - 087230
Long & Ryle, 4 John Islip St., London SW1P 4PX.
T. (0171) 834 1434. - Paint - 087231
Lords Gallery, 26 Wellington Rd., London NW8 9SP.
T. (0171) 722 4444. - Paint / Graph / Sculp - 087232
Lots Road Chelsea Auction Galleries, 71 Lots Rd., London SW10 0RN. T. (0171) 351 7771. - Paint - 087233
Lummis, Sandra, 17 Haslemere Rd., London N8 9QP.
T. (0181) 340 2293. - Paint / Draw - 087234
Lyons, John, 18 South Hill Park, London NW3.
T. (0171) 794 3537. - Paint / Glass - 087235
Maak, Blackburn Rd., London NW6 1RZ.
T. (0171) 372 4112, Fax (0171) 372 4205. - Paint / Sculp / Draw - 087236
Maas, 15a Clifford St., London W1X 1RF.
T. (0171) 734 2302, Fax (0171) 287 4836. - Paint / Graph / Draw - 087237
MacConnal-Mason, 15 Burlington Arcade, Piccadilly, London W1V 9AB. T. (0171) 839 7693, Fax 8396797.
- Paint - 087238
MacConnal-Mason, 14 Duke St, London SW1Y 6DB.
T. (0171) 8397693, Fax (0171) 8396797.
- Paint - 087239
Mahboubian, 65 Grosvenor St., London W1X.
T. (0171) 493 9112. - Paint - 087240
Malcolm Innes, 172 Walton St., London SW3 2JL.
T. (0171) 584 0575, Fax (0171) 589 1066.
- Paint - 087241
Malcolm Innes, 172 Walton St, London SW3.
T. (0171) 584 0575. 087242
The Mall Galleries, 17 Carlton Terrace House, London SW1Y 5BD. T. (0171) 9306844, Fax 8397830.
- Paint - 087243

Mall Gallery, 94 Leonard St., London EC2A 4RH.
T. (0171) 729 1880. - Paint - 087244
Mallett Gallery, 141 New Bond St, London W1Y 0BS.
T. (0171) 4997411, Fax 4953179. - Paint / Graph / Pho - 087245
Mangate Gallery, 3 Chiswick Lane, London W4.
T. (0181) 995 9867. - Paint - 087246
Manor House Society, 80 East End Rd., London N3 2SY.
T. (0181) 346 0307. - Paint - 087247
Mansour, 46 Davies St, London W1Y 1LD.
T. (0171) 4917444. - Arch - 087248
Manya Igel, 21-22 Peters Court, Porchester Rd., London W2 5DR. T. (0171) 229 1669, Fax (0171) 229 6770.
- Paint - 087249

Marble Arch Art Gallery, 14 Old Quebec St., London W1H. T. (0171) 629 5159. - Paint - 087250
Mark, 9 Porchester Pl., London W2 2BS.
T. (0171) 262 4906, Fax (017) 224 9416.
- Graph - 087251
Marlborough Fine Art, 6 Albemarle St., London W1X 4BY.
T. (0171) 6295161, Fax 6296338. - Paint - 087252

Marlborough Graphics, 42 Dover St., London W1X 3RB.
T. (0171) 495 2642, Fax (0171) 495 0641. - Paint / Graph - 087253
Marloes Gallery, 51 Marloes Rd., London W8.
T. (0171) 938 2150. - Paint - 087254
Marsden, 21 Dulwich Village, London SE21 7BT.
T. (0181) 693 2700. - Paint / China / Sculp - 087255
Marsham Galleries, 55 Marsham St., London SW1P.
T. (0171) 222 3882. - Paint - 087256
Martyn, Gregory, 34 Bury St., London SW1.
T. (0171) 839 3731, Fax (0171) 930 0812.
- Paint - 087257
Masks For Dreams, 80 Lupus St., London SW1V 3EL.
T. (0171) 834 3689. - Paint - 087258
Mason, Paul, 149e Sloane St., London SW1.
T. (0171) 730 3683. - Paint - 087259
Mathaf, 24 Motcomb St., London SW1X 8JU.
T. (0171) 235 0010, Fax (0171) 8231378.
- Paint - 087260
Mathon, 38 Cheyne Walk, London SW3.
T. (0171) 352 5381. - Paint / Sculp - 087261
Matt's Gallery, 10 Martello St., London E8 3PE.
T. (0171) 249 3799. - Paint / Sculp - 087262
Matthiesen, 7/8 Mason's Yard, Duke St., London SW1Y 6BU. T. (0171) 9302437, Fax 9301387.
- Paint - 087263
Mayfair Fine Art, 40-41 Conduit St., London W1R 9FB.
T. (0171) 494 0573, Fax (0171) 437 0411.
- Paint - 087264
Mayor, 22a Cork St., London W1X 1HB.
T. (0171) 734 3558, Fax (0171) 494 1377. - Paint / Sculp / Draw - 087265
Mayor Rowan, 31a Bruton Pl., London W1.
T. (0171) 499 3011, Fax (0171) 355 3486.
- Paint - 087266
McAlpine, Alistair, 33 Cork St., London W1X.
T. (0171) 437 4760. - Paint - 087267
McInnes, Ross, 16 Southerton Rd., London W6.
T. (0181) 741 5318. - Paint - 087268
McNeill, Agnès, 183-185 King's Rd., London SW3.
T. (0171) 351 5075. - Paint - 087269

Medici Gallery, 26 Thurloe St., London SW7 2LT.
T. (0171) 589 1363, Fax (0171) 581 9758. - Paint / Graph - 087270
Medici Gallery, 7 Grafton St., London W1X 3LA.
T. (0171) 629 5675, Fax (0171) 495 2997. - Paint / Graph / Repr / Fra - 087271
Mei Anna, 64 New King's Rd., London SW6.
T. (0171) 736 1928. - Paint / Sculp / Draw - 087272
Meldrum Walker, 27 Filmer Rd., London SW6.
T. (0171) 385 2305. - Paint - 087273
Mendez, Christopher, 58 Jermyn St., London SW1Y 6LP.
T. (0171) 491 0015, Fax (0171) 4954949.
- Paint - 087274
Mercury, 26 Cork St., London W1X 1HB.
T. (0171) 734 7800, Fax (0171) 287 9809. - Paint / Sculp / Draw - 087275
Merrifield Studios, 110 Heath St., London NW3 1AA.
T. (0171) 794 0343. - Paint / Sculp - 087276
Merz, 62 Kenway Rd., London SW5 0RD.
T. (0171) 244 6008. - Paint - 087277
Messum, David, 34 Saint Georges St., London W1R.
T. (0171) 408 0243. - Paint - 087278
Metro Arts, 98 Belsize Lane, London NW3.
T. (0171) 435 9766, 794 7464. - Paint - 087279
Metropolitan Fine Art, 66 St. Johns Rd, London SW11.
T. (0171) 924 5312. - Paint - 087280
Metropolitan Fine Art, 97 Lauderdale Rd, London W9 1LX. T. (0171) 266 2165. - Paint - 087281
Michael & Henrietta Spink, 91c Jermyn St, London SW1Y 6JB. T. (0171) 9308008, Fax (0171) 9302165.
- Eth - 087282
Michaelson Gallery, Maureen, 27 Daleham Gardens, London NW3 5BY. T. (0171) 4350510, Fax (0171) 4350510. - China - 087283
Michaelson & Orient, 328 Portobello Rd., London W10 5RU. T. (0181) 969 4119. - Paint - 087284
Midasland, 141 North End Rd., London W14.
T. (0171) 602 2060. - Paint - 087285
Miles, Roy, 29 Bruton St., London W1X 7DB.
T. (0171) 495 4747, Fax (0171) 495 6232.
- Paint - 087286
Miller, Duncan R., 17 Flask Walk, London NW3 1HJ.
T. (0171) 435 5462, Fax (0171) 4315352. - Paint / Sculp / Draw - 087287
Milne & Moller, 35 Colville Terrace, London W11 2BU.
T. (0171) 727 1679. - Paint / Sculp - 087288
Miro, Victoria, 21 Cork St., London W1X.
T. (0171) 734 5082. - Paint - 087289
Mistral Gallery, 10 Dover St., London W1X 3PJ.
T. (0171) 499 4701, Fax (0171) 499 0618. - Paint / Sculp / Draw - 087290
Mitchell, Paul, 99 New Bond St, London W1Y 9LF.
T. (0171) 4938732, Fax (0171) 4097136.
- Ant - 087291
Mitchell & Sons, John, 160 New Bond St., London W1Y 9PE. T. (0171) 493 7567, Fax (0171) 4935537.
- Paint - 087292
MM Arts, 248 Archway Rd, Highgate, London N6 5AX.
T. (0181) 3429301. - Paint / Sculp - 087293
Mokhtarzadeh, M., 46 Davies St., London W1Y.
T. (0171) 491 7444. - Paint - 087294
Montpelier Sandelson, 4 Montpelier St, London SW7 1EZ. T. (0171) 5840667, Fax (0171) 2252280. - Paint / Draw - 087295
Moreton Street Gallery, 40 Moreton St., London SW1V 2PB. T. (0171) 834 7773. - Paint / Graph - 087296
Morley, 61 Westminster Bridge Rd., London SE1 7HT.
T. (0171) 928 8501. - Paint - 087297
Morrison, Guy, 91 Jermyn St., London SW1 6JB.
T. (0171) 839 1454. - Paint - 087298
Moss, 2 Prebend Gardens, London W4 1TW.
T. (0181) 994 2099. - Paint - 087299
Mould, Anthony, 173 New Bond St., London W1Y 9PB.
T. (0171) 491 4627, Fax (0171) 3553865.
- Paint - 087300
Mount Gallery, 12 Heath St, London NW3 6TE.
T. (0171) 7943297, (0181) 9045184. - Paint / Graph - 087301
Moving Gallery, 17 Fairfax Rd, London W4 1EN.
T. (0181) 9942871. - Paint / Sculp - 087302
Mowbray, 6 Pilgrims Lane, London NW3.
T. (0171) 435 4741. - Paint - 087303

Mulder, Frederick, 83 Belsize Park Gardens, London NW3 4NJ. T. (0171) 722 2105. - Paint / Graph - *087304*

Mundy & Philo, 29 New Bond St., London W1. T. (0171) 499 2516. - Paint - *087305*

Music Theatre Gallery, 1 Elystan Pl., London SW3 3LA. T. (0171) 823 9880, Fax (0171) 823 9790. - Paint / Graph - *087306*

Nahum, Peter, 5 Ryder St., London SW1Y 6PY. T. (0171) 930 6059, Fax (0171) 930 4678. - Paint / Sculp / Draw - *087307*

Narwhal Inuit Art Gallery, 55 Linden Gardens, London W4 2EH. T. (0181) 747 1575, Fax (0181) 742 1268. - Graph / Sculp - *087308*

Natascha's Gallery, 39 Hyde Park Gate, London SW7 5DS. T. (0171) 235 0053. - Paint - *087309*

Nathanson, Richard, POB 575, London SW15 6LQ. T. (0181) 788 2718. *087310*

National Theatre Foyers, Upper Ground, South Bank, London SE1. T. (0171) 633 0880. - Paint - *087311*

Nevill, Guy, 251a Fulham Rd., London SW3. T. (0171) 351 4292. - Paint - *087312*

Nevill Keating, 7 Durham Pl., London SW3 4ET. T. (0171) 352 0989, Fax (0171) 3765243. - Paint - *087313*

New Academy Gallery, 34 Windmill St., London W1P 1HH. T. (0171) 323 4700, Fax (0171) 436 3059. - Paint / Graph / Sculp - *087314*

New Art Centre, 41 Sloane St., London SW1X 9LU. T. (0171) 235 5844, Fax (0171) 823 1624. - Paint / Sculp - *087315*

New City Gallery, 65 Borough High St., London SE1 1NF. T. (0171) 403 2387. - Paint - *087316*

New Grafton Gallery, 49 Church Rd, London SW13 9HH. T. (0181) 748 8850, Fax (0181) 748 9818. - Paint / Sculp - *087317*

New King's Road Gallery, 293 New King's Rd., London SW6. T. (0171) 731 4363. - Paint - *087318*

Newgate Gallery, 114 Newgate St, London EC1. T. (0171) 606 3955. *087319*

Newhart, London NW3 3LB. T. (0171) 722 2537, Fax (0171) 722 4335. - Paint - *087320*

Newman & Cooling, c/o Newhart Ltd., London W1X 4QJ. T. (0171) 722 2537. - Paint - *087321*

Noortman, 40-41 Old Bond St, London W1X 3AF. T. (0171) 4917284, Fax (0171) 4931570. - Paint - *087322*

O'Nians, Hal, 17 King St., London SW1Y 6QU. T. (0171) 930 9392/93. - Paint / Draw - *087323*

O'Shea, 89 Lower Sloane St., London SW1W 8DA. T. (0171) 730 0081, Fax (0171) 730 1386. - Graph - *087324*

Obsessions, 106 Heath St., London NW3. T. (0171) 431 4799. - Paint - *087325*

Obsidian, 13 Duke St., London SW1Y. T. (0171) 930 8606. - Paint - *087326*

October Gallery, 24 Old Gloucester St., London WC1N 3AL. T. (0171) 242 7367, Fax (0171) 405 1851. - Paint / Sculp / Draw - *087327*

Old Church Galleries, 320 Kings Rd., London SW3 5UH. T. (0171) 351 4649. - Paint / Fra - *087328*

Old London Galleries, 4 Royal Opera Arcade, Pall Mall, London SW1Y 4UY. T. (0171) 9307679. - Graph - *087329*

Omell, 43a Duke St., London SW1Y 6DD. T. (0171) 930 7744, Fax (0171) 839 1235. - Paint - *087330*

Omell, 22 Bury St., London SW1Y 6AL. T. (0171) 839 4274. - Paint - *087331*

Omell, 40 Albemarle St., London W1X. T. (0171) 499 3685. - Paint - *087332*

Omell, N.R., 6 Duke St., London SW1Y. T. (0171) 839 6223. - Paint - *087333*

One One Nine Gallery, 119 Newgate St., London EC1A 7AE. T. (0171) 600 1897. - Paint / Sculp - *087334*

Opus 1 Gallery, 25a Maddox St., London W1R. T. (0171) 495 2570. - Graph - *087335*

Orangery, Holland Park, London W8. T. (0171) 603 1123. - Paint - *087336*

Original Art Shop, Shopp. Centre, Putney High St, London SW15. T. (0181) 789 0141. - Paint - *087337*

Orms, 1 Pine St., London EC1R 0JH. T. (0171) 833 8533. - Paint - *087338*

Orssich, Paul, 117 Munster Rd, London SW6 6DH. T. (0171) 7363869, Fax (0171) 3719886. - Mod - *087339*

Osborne, 24 St. James's St, London SW1. T. (0171) 321 0448. - Paint - *087340*

Owen, Edgar, 9 West Halkin St., London SW1Y. T. (0171) 235 8989. - Paint - *087341*

Ozten Zeki, 174 Walton St., London SW3 2JL. T. (0171) 225 1624. - Paint - *087342*

Page, Desmond, 28 Eldon Rd., London W8 5PT. T. (0171) 937 0804. - Graph - *087343*

Park Galleries, 20 Hendon Ln., London N3. T. (0181) 346 2176. - Paint / Graph - *087344*

Park Walk Gallery, 20 Park Walk, London SW10. T. (0171) 351 0410. - Paint / Draw - *087345*

Parker, 28 Pimlico Rd., London SW1W 8LJ. T. (0171) 730 6768, Fax (0171) 259 9180. - Paint / Graph - *087346*

Parkin, Michael, 11 Motcomb St., London SW1X 8LB. T. (0171) 235 8144, Fax (0171) 245 9846. - Paint - *087347*

Partridge, 144-146 New Bond St., London W1Y 0LY. T. (0171) 629 0834, Fax (0171) 4956266. - Paint / Furn / Silv - *087348*

Paton, 282 Richmond Rd., London E8 3QS. T. (0181) 986 3409. - Paint - *087349*

Patterson, W.H., 19 Albemarle St., London W1X 3HA. T. (0171) 629 4119, Fax (0171) 4990119. - Paint - *087350*

Penn Road Studios, Unit 3, 59 Penn Rd., London N7. T. (0171) 607 6312. - Paint - *087351*

Pentonville, 7 Ferdinand St., London NW1. T. (0171) 482 2948. - Paint - *087352*

Perrins Art Gallery, 16 Perrins Court, London NW3. T. (0171) 794 3403. - Paint - *087353*

Petersburg Press, 59a Portobello Rd., London W11 3DB. T. (0171) 229 0105, Fax (0171) 229 4070. - Graph / Mul / Draw - *087354*

Philip, Richard, 59 Ledbury Rd., London W11. T. (0171) 727 7915. - Paint / Sculp / Draw - *087355*

Phillips, John F.C., 92 Rossiter Rd, London SW12. T. (0181) 673 5150. - Graph / Draw - *087356*

Philp, Richard, 59 Ledbury Rd, London W11 2AA. T. (0171) 7277915, Fax (0171) 7929073. - Paint / Graph - *087357*

Phipps & Co., 38 Cheyne Walk, London SW3 5HJ. T. (0171) 352 5381. - Paint / Sculp - *087358*

Phoenix Gallery, 26 Highgate High St., London N6 5JG. T. (0181) 340 7564, Fax (0181) 348 7039. - Paint - *087359*

Photographer's Gallery, 5 Great Newport St., London WC2 7HY. T. (0171) 831 1772. - Pho - *087360*

Piccadilly Gallery, 16 Cork St., London W1X 1PF. T. (0171) 629 2875, Fax (0171) 499 0431. - Paint - *087361*

Pickwick Gallery, Pickwick Walk, 286 Uxbridge Rd, London HA3. T. (0181) 421 4974. - Paint - *087362*

Picture Man, 184 Chiswick High Rd., London W4. T. (0181) 995 6359. - Paint - *087363*

Picturepoint, 122 West End Lane, London NW6. T. (0171) 435 8091. - Paint - *087364*

Piers Feetham, 475 Fulham Rd., London SW6 1HL. T. (0171) 381 5958. - Graph / Draw - *087365*

Piers Feetham Gallery, 475 Fulham Rd, London SW6 1HL. T. (0171) 3815958. - Paint - *087366*

Pigeonhole Chelsea Picture Shop, 13 Langton St, London SW10. T. (0171) 352 2677. *087367*

Pike Gallery, 145 St. John's Hill, London SW11 1TQ. T. (0171) 2236741. - Paint / Graph - *087368*

Pincus, Ben, 122 Kings Rd., London SW3. T. (0171) 584 6825. - Paint - *087369*

Pizan, 51 Mill Lane, London NW6. T. (0171) 435 8091. - Paint - *087370*

Planet Arts, 21 Kensington Park Rd., London W11. T. (0171) 229 1888. - Paint - *087371*

Plazzotta, 10 Shalcomb St., London SW10 0HY. T. (0171) 352 7493, Fax (0171) 352 7493. - Paint - *087372*

Polak, 21 King St., London SW1Y 6QY. T. (0171) 839 2871. - Paint - *087373*

Polish Cultural Institute, 34 Portland Pl., London W1. T. (0171) 636 6032. - Paint - *087374*

Polish Social & Cultural Centre, 236 King St., London W6 0RF. T. (0181) 741 1940. - Paint / Graph - *087375*

Pollard, Edward, 23 Church Rd., London SW19 5DQ. T. (0181) 946 4114. - Paint - *087376*

Porcelain & Pictures, The Studio, Gastein Rd., London W6 8LT. T. (0171) 385 7512. - Paint - *087377*

Portal Gallery, 16a Grafton St., London W1X 3LF. T. (0171) 493 0706, Fax (0171) 629 3506. - Paint - *087378*

Portfolio Gallery, 345 Portobello Rd., London W10. T. (0181) 969 0453. - Pho - *087379*

Portland Gallery, 9 Bury St., London SW1Y 6AB. T. (0171) 321 0422, Fax (0171) 321 0230. - Paint - *087380*

Portobella Group, 124-128 Barlby Rd., London W10 6BL. T. (0181) 960 9686. - Paint / Graph / Draw - *087381*

Posk, 238 King St., London W6 0RF. T. (0181) 741 1940. - Paint - *087382*

Postus-by-Post, 20 Forest View, Chingford, London E4 7AY. T. (0181) 5241032. - Graph - *087383*

Primrose Hill Gallery, 81 Regents Park Rd., London NW1 8UY. T. (0171) 586 3533. - Paint - *087384*

Print Room, 37 Museum St, London WC1A 1LP. T. (0171) 4300159, Fax (0171) 8319150. - Graph - *087385*

Profile Art, 101 Gloucester Terrace, London W2. T. (0171) 402 8841. - Paint - *087386*

Project Art, 235 Westbourne Grove, London W11. T. (0171) 299 9033. - Paint - *087387*

Pruskin, 73 Kensington Church St., London W8. T. (0171) 9371994. - Paint - *087388*

Purdy Hicks, Jacob Street Film Studios, London SE1 2BA. T. (0171) 237 6062. - Paint - *087389*

Pyms, 9 Mount Str, Mayfair, London W1Y 5AD. T. (0171) 629 2020, Fax (0171) 629 2060. - Paint - *087390*

Queen's Gallery, Buckingham Palace Rd., London SW1A 1AA. T. (0171) 799 2331. - Paint - *087391*

Raab Gallery at Millbank, 6 Vauxhall Bridge Rd., London SW1V 2SD. T. (0171) 828 2588, Fax (0171) 976 5041. - Paint - *087392*

Raab Gallery London, 9 Cork St., London W1X 1PD. T. (0171) 7346444, Fax (0171) 2871740. - Paint / Sculp / Graph - *087393*

Rabi, 94 Mount St, London W1Y 5HG. T. (0171) 499 8886/87. *087394*

Railings, 5 New Cavendish St., London W1. T. (0171) 935 1114, Fax (0171) 486 9250. - Paint - *087395*

Ranger's House, Chesterfield Walk, Blackheath, London SE10. T. (0181) 853 0035. - Ant / Lights - *087396*

Rankin, Sue, 40 Ledbury Rd., London W11 2AB. T. (0171) 229 4923. - Paint - *087397*

Ravensdale, 34-35 Dean St., London W1V 5AP. T. (0171) 734 4686. - Paint / Graph / Draw - *087398*

Red Square Gallery, 4 Whitfield St., London W1P 5RD. T. (0171) 323 3670, Fax (0171) 323 3680. - Tex - *087399*

Redfern, 20 Cork St., London W1X 2HL. T. (0171) 734 1732, Fax (0171) 494 2908. - Paint - *087400*

Reid & Lefevre, 30 Bruton St., London W1X 8JD. T. (0171) 4933 2107, Fax (0171) 499 9088. - Paint / Graph / Sculp - *087401*

Renton, Mina, 34 Moreton St., London SW1V 2PD. T. (0171) 834 7485. - Paint / Graph / China / Sculp - *087402*

Reynolds, Anthony, 5 Dering St., London W1R 9AB. T. (0171) 491 0621, Fax (0171) 495 2374. - Paint - *087403*

Rhodes, Benjamim, 4 New Burlington Pl., London W1X 1SB. T. (0171) 434 1768, Fax (017) 287 8841. - Paint / Sculp - *087404*

Riba Heinz, 21 Portman Sq., London W1H 9HF. T. (0171) 580 5593. - Paint - *087405*

Richardson, Witt & Co, 17 Leigh St., London WC1H. T. (0171) 242 5177. - Paint - *087406*

Richmond Gallery, 8 Cork St., London W1X 1PB. T. (0171) 437 9422, Fax (0171) 734 7018. - Paint - *087407*

Riverside Studios, Crisp Rd., London W6 9RL. T. (0181) 741 2251. - Paint - *087408*

Riyahi, 38 New Bond St., London W1Y.
T. (0171) 629 0143. - Paint - 087409
Romanov's, 51 Sutherland Av., London W9.
T. (0171) 286 1430. - Paint - 087410
Rona, 1-2 Weighhouse St., London W1.
T. (0171) 491 3718, Fax (0171) 491 4171.
- Paint - 087411
Ross-Hammond, 77 Saint Johns Wood High St., London
NW8. T. (0171) 722 4285. - Paint - 087412
Rossi & Rossi, 91a Jermyn St, London SW1Y 6JB.
T. (0171) 3210208, Fax (0171) 3210546. - Paint /
Eth - 087413
Rothschild, Kate de, c/o c/o National Westminster Bank
plc, 161 Old Brompton Rd, London SW3 1QU.
T. (0171) 5899440, Fax (0171) 5845253.
- Graph - 087414
Roupell Gallery, 61 Roupell St., London SE1.
T. (0171) 928 0675. - Paint - 087415
Roussos, Alexander, 22 Princes St., London W1 7RG.
T. (0171) 493 1480, Fax (0171) 493 1482.
- Paint - 087416
Route 76 Arthouse, 76 Westow St., London SE19.
T. (0181) 771 1022. - Paint - 087417
Royal Academy of Arts, Burlington House, Piccadilly,
London W1V 0DS. T. (0171) 439 7438,
Fax (0171) 434 0837. - Paint - 087418
Royal Exchange Art Gallery, 14 Royal Exchange, London
EC3V 3LL. T. (0171) 283 4400. - Paint / Graph - 087419
Royal Society of Arts Gallery, Durham House, Strand,
London. - Paint - 087420
Royston du Maurier-Lebek, Studio 323, 566 Cable St.,
London E1 9HB. T. (0171) 702 8663. - Paint - 087421
Runkel, Claus, 97 Cambridge St., London SW1V 4PY.
T. (0171) 821 5861, Fax (0171) 8215861.
- Graph - 087422
Rutherston, Max, 180 New Bond St., London W1Y 9PD.
T. (0181) 629 4189. - Paint - 087423
Rutland, 32a Saint George St., London W1R 9FA.
T. (0171) 499 5636. - Paint - 087424
Rystwood, 11 Aubrey Rd., London W8.
T. (0171) 229 9127. - Paint - 087425
Sabin, Frank T., 5 Royal Arcade, Old Bond St., London
W1X 3HB. T. (0171) 493 3288, Fax (0171) 499 3593.
- Paint / Sculp - 087426
Safari Gallery, 354 Cricklewood Lane, London NW2 2QH.
T. (0181) 455 5154. - Eth - 087427
Safari Studios, 115 Saint John St., London EC1V.
T. (0171) 250 1114. - Paint - 087428
S.A.G. Art Galleries, 589 Garratt Ln., London SW18 4DP.
T. (0181) 944 1404, Fax (0181) 947 8174. - Paint /
Graph - 087429
Saint George's Gallery, 8 Duke St., London SW1.
T. (0171) 930 0935. - Paint - 087430
Saint James's Art Group, 91 Jermyn St, London SW1Y
6JB. T. (0171) 321 0233, Fax (0171) 321 0912.
- Paint - 087431
Saint James's Gallery, 108 Hampstead Rd., London
NW1 2LS. T. (0171) 388 2588 ext. 140. - Paint / Sculp /
Mul / Draw - 087432
Saint James's Prints and Books, 15 Piccadilly Arcade off
Jermyn St, London SW1Y 6NH. T. (0171) 4956487,
Fax 4956490. - Graph - 087433

Saint Johns, Smith Sq., Westminster, London SW1.
T. (0171) 222 1061. - Paint - 087434
Salama-Caro, 5-6 Cork St., London W1.
T. (0171) 734 9179, Fax (0171) 494 2773. - Paint /
Draw - 087435
Salmon, Richard, Studio 4, 59 South Edwardes Sq., Lon-
don W8. T. (0171) 602 9494, Fax (0171) 371 6617.
- Paint / Graph / Sculp / Eth - 087436
Sammer, 101b Kensington Church St., London W8.
T. (0171) 727 2406. - Paint - 087437
Sandby, 72 Mountgrove Rd., London N5.
T. (0171) 354 3693. - Paint - 087438
Sarinda, 8 Reece Mews, London SW7.
T. (0171) 584 4307. - Paint - 087439
Savannah Gallery, 46 Derbyshire St., London E2 6HQ.
T. (0171) 613 3072, Fax (0171) 613 3072.
- Graph - 087440
Sayat Nova Gallery, 234 Archway Rd., London N6.
T. (0181) 348 0991. - Paint - 087441
Schemebest, Unit 1, 105 Blundell St., London N7.
T. (0171) 609 0096. - Paint - 087442
Scherrer, Chantal, 31 York Mansions, Prince of Wales
Dr., London SW11. T. (0171) 720 5810.
- Paint - 087443
Schubert, Karsten, 85 Charlotte St., London W1P 1LB.
T. (0171) 631 0031, Fax (0171) 436 9255.
- Paint - 087444
Schuster, 14 Maddox St., London W1R 9PL.
T. (0171) 491 2208, Fax (0171) 491 9872.
- Paint - 087445
Schwartz Sackin & Co., 17 Old Bond St., London W1X.
T. (0171) 629 4511. - Paint / Graph / Sculp - 087446
Scottish Gallery, 28 Cork St., London W1X 1HB.
T. (0171) 287 2121, Fax (0171) 287 2018.
- Paint - 087447
Senior, Mark, 240 Brompton Rd., London SW3 2BB.
T. (0171) 589 5811. - Paint / Draw - 087448
Serpentine Gallery, Kensington Gardens, London W2
3XA. T. (0171) 723 9072, Fax (0171) 402 4103.
- Paint - 087449
Seven Dials Press and Gallery, 56 Earlham St., London
WC2H. T. (0171) 836 9701. - Paint - 087450
Sharp Impressions, Unit 30, Waterside, 44-48 Wharf
Rd., London N1. T. (0171) 253 0075. - Paint - 087451
Sheen, 370 Upper Richmond Rd., London SW14.
T. (0181) 878 1100. - Paint / Graph - 087452
Shenda Amery, 25a Edith Grove, London SW10.
T. (0171) 351 1775. - Paint - 087453
Shivering Blaze, 21 Ladbroke Grove, London W11 3AY.
T. (0171) 221 1326, Fax (0171) 221 2503.
- Paint - 087454
Showroom, 44 Bonner Rd., London E2 9JS.
T. (0181) 983 4115. - Paint - 087455
Shurini, I.D.C., 10a Charles II St., London SW1Y.
T. (0171) 321 0572. - Paint - 087456
Silver Place Gallery, 6 Silver Pl., London W1.
T. (0171) 437 6332. - Paint - 087457
Simon, Julian, 70 Pimlico Rd., London SW1W 8LS.
T. (0171) 730 8673, Fax (0171) 823 6116.
- Paint - 087458
Simpson, Michael, 11 Savile Row, London W1X1 1AE.
T. (0171) 437 5414, Fax (0171) 287 5967.
- Paint - 087459
Sladmore Gallery of Animal, 32 Bruton Pl., London W1X
7AA. T. (0171) 499 0365, Fax (0171) 409 1381.
- Sculp - 087460
Slaughterhouse Gallery, 63 Charterhouse St, London
EC1M 6HJ. T. (0171) 2515888, 4900847. - Paint /
Sculp - 087461
Smith, 52-56 Earlham St., London WC2.
T. (0171) 836 6252. - Paint - 087462
Smithson & Williams, 10 Exhibition Rd., London SW7.
T. (0171) 584 1113. - Paint - 087463
Snatch Art Company, 149 Bowes Rd., London N13.
T. (0181) 881 0463. - Paint - 087464
Soar, 4 Launcester Pl., London W8 5RL.
T. (0171) 937 1602. - Paint - 087465
Society of London Art Dealers, 91a Jermyn St., London
SW1Y 6JB. T. (0171) 930 6137. - Paint - 087466
Somerville, Stephen, 32 Saint George St., London W1R
9FA. T. (0171) 493 8363, Fax (0171) 409 1814. - Paint /
Graph / Draw - 087467

Sonnet 24, 56 Westow St., London SE19.
T. (0181) 653 1669. - Paint - 087468
Sotheran, Henry, 80 Pimlico Rd, London SW1W 8PL.
T. (0171) 7308756, Fax (0171) 8236090.
- Graph - 087469
Sotheran Weinreb, 82 Pimlico Rd., London SW1W.
T. (0171) 730 8756. - Paint - 087470
South Bank Crafts Centre Gallery, 164-167 Hungerford
Arches, London SE1. T. (0171) 928 0681.
- Paint - 087471
South London Art Gallery, 65 Peckham Rd., London SE5
8UH. T. (0171) 703 6120. - Graph - 087472
Southall Arts, 1 Lancaster Rd., Southall, London UB1.
T. (0181) 843 2207. - Paint - 087473
Southey Fine Art, 74 South Audley St., London W1.
T. (0171) 409 3164. - Paint - 087474
Special Photographers Company, 21 Kensington Park
Rd., London W11. T. (0171) 221 3489. - Pho - 087475
Spectus Gallery, 298 Westbourne Grove, London W11.
T. (0171) 221 6557. - Paint - 087476
Speelman, Eduard, 175 Piccadilly, London W1V 0NP.
T. (0171) 493 0657. - Paint - 087477
Spencer, Charles, 24a Ashworth Rd, London W9 1JY.
T. (0171) 2869396. - Dec / Paint / Graph - 087478
Spink & Son, 5 King St, St. James's, London SW1Y 6QS.
T. (0171) 9307888, Fax 8394853. - Paint /
Orient - 087479
Square Gallery, 12 South Grove, London N6 6BJ.
T. (0181) 340 4983. - Paint - 087480
Stable Gallery, 15 Bellevue Rd., Wandsworth Common,
London SW17 7EB. T. (0181) 767 4688.
- Paint - 087481
Stables Gallery, Gladstone Park, Dollis Hill Ln., London
NW2 6HT. T. (0181) 452 8655. - Paint - 087482
Stern, 46 Ledbury Rd., London W11 2AB.
T. (0171) 229 6187, Fax (0171) 229 6187.
- Paint - 087483
Stern, Lynne, 43 Dover St., London W1X.
T. (0171) 491 8905. - Paint / Graph - 087484
Stevens & Capon, 28 Lower RichmondRd., London
SW15. T. (0181) 789 8374. - Paint - 087485
Stewart, Laurie, 36 Church Ln., London N2.
T. (0181) 883 7719. - Paint / Graph - 087486
Stoppenbach & Delestre, 25 Cork St., London W1X 1HB.
T. (0171) 734 3534, Fax (0171) 4943578. - Paint /
Sculp / Draw - 087487

Strange Attractions, 204 Kensington Park Rd., London
W11 1NR. T. (0171) 229 9646. - Paint - 087488
Studio, Gastein Rd., London W6. T. (0171) 385 7512.
- Graph - 087489
Studio 2000, 89 Camden High St., London NW1.
T. (0171) 387 0248. - Paint - 087490
Studio 45, 45 Dulwich Village, London SE21.
T. (0181) 693 4946. - Paint - 087491
Studio 92 Gallery, 92 Church Rd., Barnes, London
SW13. T. (0181) 741 8451. - Paint - 087492
Sunray, 46-48 Osnaburgh St., London NW1.
T. (0171) 383 3785. - Paint - 087493
Sutton, Jacob, 10 Soudan Rd., London SW11.
T. (0181) 693 7620. - Paint / Graph - 087494
Swann, Oliver, 170 Walton St., London SW3 2JL.
T. (0171) 584 8684. - Paint - 087495
Sweet Waters Gallery, 32 Crawford St., London W1H
1PL. T. (0171) 706 3166, Fax (0171) 7063166.
- Paint - 087496
Symes, Robin, 3 Ormond Yard, London SW1Y.
T. (0171) 930 9856. - Paint - 087497

Tabernacle Gallery, Powis Sq., Portobello, London W11. T. (0171) 229 1341. - Paint - *087498*
Tadema Gallery, 10 Charlton Pl., London N1 8AJ. T. (0171) 359 1055, Fax (0171) 704 9335. - Paint / Sculp - *087499*
Talent Store Gallery, 11 Eccleston St., London SW1. T. (0171) 730 8117. - Paint - *087500*
Tall House, 134 Southwark St., London SE1 0SW. - Paint - *087501*
Tallberg Taylor, 142a Greenwich High Rd., London SE10 8NN. T. (0181) 305 2113, Fax (0181) 2931268. - Sculp - *087502*
Tanous, John, 115 Harwood Road, London SW6 4QL. T. (0171) 736 7999, 1142, Fax (0171) 371 5237. - Fra - *087503*
Taylor, 4 Royal Arcade, Old Bond St., London W1X 3HD. T. (0171) 493 4111, Fax (0171) 499 3260. - Paint - *087504*
Teltscher, F., 17 Crawford St., London W1H 1PF. T. (0171) 935 0525. - Paint / Sculp - *087505*
Temple, R.C.C., 6 Clarendon Cross, London W11 4AP. T. (0171) 727 1546. - Ant / Paint - *087506*
Tesser, 106 Heath St., London NW3 1DR. T. (0171) 794 7971, Fax (0171) 794 5829. - Paint - *087507*
Thackeray Gallery, 18 Thackeray St., London W8 5ET. T. (0171) 937 5883. - Paint - *087508*
The Gallery, 74 South Adley St., London W1Y 5FF. T. (0171) 491 2948, Fax (0171) 629 0414. - Paint - *087509*
Themes & Variations, 231 Westbourne Grove, London W11. T. (0171) 727 5531. - Paint - *087510*
Thompson, 38 Albemarle St., London W1X 3FB. T. (0171) 499 1314, Fax (0171) 499 1314. - Paint / Sculp - *087511*
Thomson, Bill, 1 Bury St., London SW1. T. (0171) 839 6119. - Paint / Draw - *087512*
Thuillier, William, 10a West Halkin St., London SW1X. T. (0171) 235 3543. - Paint - *087513*
Todd, 1-5 Needham Rd., London W11 2RP. T. (0171) 792 1404, Fax (0171) 792 1505. - Paint / Ant / China - *087514*
Tooth & Sons, Arthur, 13 Dover St., London W1. T. (0171) 4996753, Fax (0171) 409 1565. - Paint / Sculp / Draw - *087515*
Totah, Edward, 13 Old Burlington St., London W1X 1LA. T. (0171) 734 0343, Fax (0171) 2872186. - Paint - *087516*
Totteridge Gallery, 61 Totteridge Lane, London N20. T. (0181) 446 7796. - Paint - *087517*
Trafalgar Galleries, 35 Bury St., London SW1Y 6AY. T. (0171) 839 6466, Fax (0171) 9761838. - Paint - *087518*
Tricycle Gallery, 269 Kilburn High Rd., London NW6 7JR. T. (0171) 372 6611, Fax (0171) 328 0795. - Paint / Pho - *087519*
Trinity Gallery, 47 Albemarle St., London W1X. T. (0171) 499 3223. - Paint - *087520*
Trowbridge Gallery, 555 King's Rd, London SW6 2EB. T. (0171) 3718733, Fax (0171) 3718138. - Graph - *087521*
Tryon, 23-24 Cork St., London W1X 1HB. T. (0171) 7346961, Fax (0171) 287 2480. - Paint / Graph / Sculp - *087522*
Underhill Leigh, 100 Islington High St., London N1. T. (0171) 226 5673. - Paint - *087523*
Uri, Ben, 21 Dean St., London W1V 6NE. T. (0171) 437 2852. - Paint / Sculp - *087524*
Usiskin, Andrew, 9-11 Flask Walk, London NW3 1HJ. T. (0171) 431 4484, Fax (0171) 4355520. - Paint - *087525*
Valcke, François, 610 King's Rd., London SW6 2DX. T. (0171) 736 6024. - Paint - *087526*
Vauxhall Gallery, 230 Vauxhall Bridge Rd., London SW1. T. (0171) 931 0481. - Paint - *087527*
Verner Amell, 4 Ryder St., London SW1Y 6QB. T. (0171) 925 2759. - Paint - *087528*
Verner Åmell, 4 Ryder St, London SW1Y 6QB. T. (0171) 9252759, Fax (0171) 3210210. - Graph - *087529*
Viart, 4 Buckingham Pl., London SW1E. T. (0171) 828 2369. - Paint - *087530*
Vortex Galleries, 139 Stoke Newington Church St., London N16. T. (0171) 254 6516. - Paint - *087531*
Waddington Galleries, 5a Cork St., London W1X 1PD. T. (0171) 4378611, Fax (0171) 734 4146. - Paint / Graph / Sculp - *087532*
Waddington, Theo, 39 Castellain Rd., London W9. T. (0171) 286 5988. - Paint - *087533*
Walker-Bagshawe, 73 Walton St., London SW3 2HT. T. (0171) 589 4582, Fax (0171) 5812573. - Paint - *087534*
Wall Game, 61 Broomwood Rd., London SW11 6HV. T. (0171) 924 1728, Fax (0171) 350 2710. - Paint / Fra - *087535*
Walpole, 38 Dover St., London 1WM 7RL. T. (0171) 499 6626, Fax (0171) 4934122. - Paint - *087536*
Warwick Arts Trust Gallery, 33 Warwick Sq., London SW1W. T. (0171) 834 7856. - Paint - *087537*
Waterhouse & Dodd, 110 New Bond St., London W1Y 9AA. T. (0171) 491 9293, Fax (0171) 491 9669. - Paint / Draw - *087538*
Waterman, 40 High St., London TW3. T. (0181) 8475651. - Paint - *087539*
Waterman, 74a Jermyn St., London SW1Y 6NP. T. (0171) 839 5203, Fax (0171) 9761628. - Paint / Draw - *087540*
Watermill Gallery, 91 The Broadway, London SW19. T. (0181) 542 2360. - Paint / Fra / Draw - *087541*
Watermill Gallery, 128 Kingston Rd., London SW19. T. (0181) 540 6479. - Paint - *087542*
Weiss, 18 Albemarle St, London W1. T. (0171) 409 0035. *087543*
Welbeck, 18 Thayer St., London W1M 5LD. T. (0171) 935 4825. - Paint - *087544*
Wengraf, Alex, The Old Knoll, Eliot Hill, London SE13 7EB. T. (0181) 8524552, Fax (0181) 8524554. - Paint / Sculp - *087545*
Westbourne Gallery, 331 Portobello Rd, London W10 5SA. T. (0181) 9601867, Fax (0181) 9609383. - Eth - *087546*
Westminster Gallery, Westminster Central Hall, Storey's Gate, London SW1H. T. (0171) 222 2723. - Paint - *087547*
Weston, William, 7 Royal Arcade, Albemarle St., London W1X 3HD. T. (0171) 493 0722, Fax (0171) 491 9240. - Graph / Draw - *087548*
Westside Gallery, 317 Upper Richmond Rd. West, East Sheen, London SW14 8QR. T. (0181) 878 6209. - Paint - *087549*
Whitechapel Art Gallery, Whitechapel High St., London E1. T. (0171) 377 0107. - Paint / Sculp - *087550*
Whitfield, 180 New Bond St., London W1X 9PD. T. (0171) 499 3592, Fax 495 6488. - Paint - *087551*
Whitford & Hughes, 6 Duke St., St. James's, London SW1. T. (0171) 930 9332. - Paint / China / Sculp - *087552*
Wiggins & Sons, Arnold, 4 Bury St, London SW1Y 6AB. T. (0171) 9250195, Fax (0171) 8396928. - Fra - *087553*
Wigmore Hall, 36 Wigmore St., London W1. T. (0171) 935 2141. - Paint / Draw - *087554*
Wild At Art, 304 Butlers Wharf Business Centre, 45 Curlew St., London SE1 2ND. T. (0171) 357 7131. - Paint - *087555*
Wildenstein & Co., 147 New Bond St, London W1Y 0NX. T. (0171) 629 0602, Fax (0171) 493 3924. - Paint / Sculp / Draw - *087556*

Wilkins & Wilkins, 1 Barrett St, London W1M 6DN. T. (0171) 9359613. - Paint - *087557*
Williams, Sue, 320 Portobello Rd., London W10 5RU. T. (0181) 960 6123. - Paint / Sculp - *087558*
Williams, Thomas, 10 Exhibition Rd., London SW7. T. (0171) 584 1113. - Draw - *087559*
Williams & Son, 2 Grafton St., London W1X 3LB. T. (0171) 493 5751, Fax (0171) 4097363. - Paint - *087560*
Wilson Hale, Unit 16, 109 Bartholomew Rd., London NW6. - Paint / Sculp - *087561*
Wilson & Gough, 106 Draycott Av., London SW3 3EA. T. (0171) 823 7082, Fax (0171) 4992558. - China / Glass - *087562*
Wimbledon Fine Art, 41 Church Rd., London SW19 5DQ. T. (0181) 944 6593. - Paint - *087563*
Wingfield, 35 Sibella Rd., London SW4. T. (0171) 622 6301. - Paint / Graph - *087564*
Winter Palace, 69 Kensington Church St., London W8. T. (0171) 937 2410. - Paint - *087565*
Wiseman, 34 West Sq, London SE11 4SP. T. (0171) 587 0747, Fax (0171) 5870747. - Paint - *087566*
Wiseman Originals, 34 West Sq, London SE11 4SP. T. (0171) 8208969, Fax (0171) 7938817. *087567*
Witch Ball, 2 Cecil Court, London WC2N 4HE. T. (0171) 836 2922, Fax (0171) 240 1630. - Graph - *087568*
Wolseley, 4 Grove Park, Camberwell, London SE5 8LT. T. (0171) 274 8788, Fax (0171) 738 4739. - Paint / Graph / Draw - *087569*
Woodlands Art Gallery, 90 Mycenae Rd., London SE3 7SE. T. (0171) 858 5847. - Paint / Sculp / Draw - *087570*
Wykeham, 51 Church Rd., London SW13 9HH. T. (0181) 741 1277. - Paint / Sculp - *087571*
Wyllie, 12 Needham Rd., London W11 2RP. T. (0171) 727 0606. - Paint / Graph - *087572*
XO Contemporary Art Gallery, 165 Draycott Av, London SW3 1AJ. T. (0171) 5842534, Fax (0171) 5810467. - Paint / Sculp - *087573*
Young Unknowns Gallery, 82 The Cut, London SE1 8LW. T. (0171) 928 3415. - Paint - *087574*
Zagon, V.E., 967 Forest Rd., London E17. T. (0181) 527 8228. - Paint - *087575*
Zangrilli & Co., 180 New Bond St., London W1Y 9PD. T. (0171) 491 1149. - Paint - *087576*
Zebra One, A/73 Hampstead High St., London NW3. T. (0171) 794 1281. - Paint - *087577*
Zella Nine, 2 Park Walk, Fulham Rd., London SW10 0AD. T. (0171) 351 0588. - Paint / Graph - *087578*
Zenith Art, 41 Balham High Rd., London SW12. T. (0181) 675 7570, Fax (0181) 673 9585. - Paint / China - *087579*
Zevi, Aroldo & Co., 3-8 Lennox Gardens, London SW1X. T. (0171) 589 5240. - Paint - *087580*
Zietz, Rainer, 1a Prairie St., London SW8 3PX. T. (0171) 4982355. - Paint - *087581*
198 Gallery, 198 Railton Rd., London SE24 0LU. T. (0171) 978 8309. - Paint - *087582*
20th Century Gallery, 821 Fulham Rd., London SW6. T. (0171) 731 5888. - Paint / Graph - *087583*
33 Mossop Street Art Gallery, 33 Mossop St., London SW3 2NB. T. (0171) 584 1954. - Paint - *087584*
9H Gallery, 26-28 Cramer St., London W1M. T. (0171) 486 3555. - Paint - *087585*

Londonderry

Foyle Art Centre, Lawrence Hill, Londonderry. T. (01504) 266657. - Paint - *087586*
Gordon Gallery, 36 Ferryquay St., Londonderry BT48 6JB. T. (01504) 266261. - Paint - *087587*

Long Compton (Warwickshire)

Yerdley House Gallery, Vicarage Lane, Long Compton. T. (0160884) 231. - Paint - *087588*

Long Crendon (Buckinghamshire)

Wintgens, Elizabeth, 20 High St., Long Crendon. T. (01844) 201617. - Paint - *087589*

Long Melford (Suffolk)

Melford Fine Arts, Little St. Mary, Long Melford. T. (0178725) 312174. - Paint - *087590*

Long Sutton (Somerset)
House of Talbot, Little Upton Bridge, Long Sutton.
T. (01458) 241445. - Paint -   087591

Longridge (Lancashire)
Charnley Fine Arts, Charnley House, Preston Rd, Longridge PR3 3BD. T. (01772) 782800,
Fax (01772) 785068. - Paint -   087592
Longridge Gallery, 78 Berry Lane, Longridge.
T. (01772) 782006. - Paint -   087593

Looe (Cornwall)
Camelot Gallery, 14 Higher Market St., Looe PL13.
T. (015036) 4581. - Paint -   087594
Clipper Art Gallery, Quay, West Looe, Looe PL13.
T. (015036) 4002. - Paint -   087595
Harbour Steps Gallery, Riverview, Quay, Looe PL13 1AQ.
T. (015036) 2999. - Paint -   087596
Waterside Gallery, 1 Seafront Court, Quayside, East
Looe, Looe PL13 1AL. T. (015036) 3375.
- Paint -   087597

Lostwithiel (Cornwall)
Ann's Gallery, 15 Fore St., Lostwithiel PL22 0BN.
T. (01208) 872828. - Paint -   087598
Treval, 7 Queen St., Lostwithiel PL22 0AB.
T. (01208) 872062. - Paint -   087599

Loughton (Essex)
Visual Impressions, 4 Lower Rd., Loughton IG10.
T. (0181) 502 2724. - Paint -   087600

Ludlow (Shropshire)
Corve Gallery, 12 Corve St, Ludlow SY8 1DA.
T. (01584) 873420. - Paint -   087601
Country Artist, 50 Bullring, Ludlow. T. (01584) 875447.
- Paint -   087602
Feathers Gallery, 20 Bullring, Ludlow SY8 1AA.
T. (01584) 875390. - Paint / Graph -   087603
Marler, Jane, Dawes Mansion, Church St., Ludlow SY8
1AP. T. (01584) 874160. - Paint / Graph -   087604
Rumens, Olivia, 30 Corve St., Ludlow SY8 1DA.
T. (01584) 873952. - Paint -   087605
Silk Top Hat Gallery, 4 Quality Sq., Ludlow SY8 1AR.
T. (01584) 875363. - Paint -   087606
York House Gallery, 69 Corve St., Ludlow.
T. (01584) 874181. - Paint -   087607

Luton (Bedfordshire)
Foye, 15 Stanley St., Luton LU1 5AL. T. (01582) 38487.
- Paint / Graph / Draw -   087608
Hayling, 27 Seaford Close, Luton. T. (01582) 481112.
- Paint -   087609
Knight, 59-61 Guildfort St., Luton. T. (01582) 36266.
- Paint -   087610

Lydford (Devon)
Skeaping, Town End House, Lydford EX20 4AR.
T. (01822) 82383. - Paint -   087611

Lyme Regis (Dorset)
Portland, 57 Broad St., Lyme Regis. T. (01297) 442061.
- Paint -   087612

Lymington (Hampshire)
Art Works, 2 High St., Lymington SO41 9AA.
T. (01590) 672764. - Paint -   087613
The Solent Gallery, 11-15 Gosport St, Lymington SO41
9BG. T. (01590) 679178, Fax (01590) 670000. - Paint /
Graph -   087614

Lyndhurst (Hampshire)
Picture Shop Lyndhurst, 48 High St., Lyndhurst SO43
7BG. T. (01703) 282483. - Paint -   087615

Lynmouth (Devon)
Lynmouth Gallery, 9 Lynmouth St., Lynmouth.
T. (01598) 53659. - Paint -   087616

Lyth (Highland)
Lyth Arts Centre, By Wick, Lyth. T. (0195584) 270.
- Paint -   087617

Lytham (Lancashire)
Number Three Gallery, Dicconson Terrace, Lytham.
T. (01253) 735290. - Paint -   087618

Macclesfield (Cheshire)
Mikulov, 38 Chestergate, Macclesfield.
T. (01625) 610321. - Paint / Graph -   087619
Paragon, Roylance Bldg., Waters Green, Macclesfield.
T. (01625) 615018. - Paint -   087620
Pictures, 14 Jordangate, Macclesfield.
T. (01625) 619203. - Paint -   087621
Pictures – Chris Crowe Fine Art, 46 Vincent St, Macclesfield SK11 6UJ. T. (01625) 427240. - Paint /
Graph -   087622
Van Gogh Studio and Showroom, 7 Bridge St., Macclesfield. T. (01625) 511189. - Paint -   087623

Machynlleth (Powys)
Spectrum Gallery, Llwyn Maengwyn St., Machynlleth.
T. (01654) 702877. - Paint -   087624

Magherafelt (Co. Londonderry)
Horner, 9 Church St., Magherafelt. T. (01648) 33466.
- Paint -   087625

Maidenhead (Berkshire)
Jaspers Fine Arts, 36 Queen St., Maidenhead SL6 1HZ.
T. (01628) 36459. - Paint / Graph -   087626
Windsor Art Studios, 25 Gloucester Rd., Maidenhead.
T. (01628) 781665. - Paint -   087627

Maidstone (Kent)
Amberfield, 6 Loose Rd., Maidstone. T. (01622) 682129.
- Paint -   087628
Clarke, Graham & Co., White Cottage, Green Lane,
Boughton Monchelsea, Maidstone ME17 4LF.
T. (01622) 743938. - Paint -   087629
Impton Studios, Penenden Heath Parade, Boxley Rd.,
Maidstone. T. (01622) 758897. - Paint -   087630

Maldon (Essex)
Mayfair Fine Art, 2 High St., Maldon. T. (01621) 859074.
- Paint -   087631
Oakwood Arts, Friars Walk, Maldon. T. (01621) 852317.
- Paint -   087632

Malmesbury (Wiltshire)
Ballantine, Belinda, Abbey Brewery, Market Cross, Malmesbury. T. (01666) 822047. - Paint -   087633

Malton (North Yorkshire)
Talents Fine Arts, 7 Market Pl., Malton YO17 0LP.
T. (01653) 600020. - Paint -   087634

Malvern (Hereford and Worcester)
Cowleigh Gallery, 14 Cowleigh Rd., Malvern.
T. (01684) 560646. - Paint -   087635
Malvern Arts, 43 Worcester Rd., Malvern.
T. (01684) 575889. - Paint -   087636
Malvern Arts Workshop, 90 Worcester Rd., Malvern.
T. (01684) 568993. - Paint -   087637
Malvern Hills Art, 32a Bellevue Terrace, Malvern.
T. (01684) 569916. - Paint -   087638

Malvern Wells (Hereford and Worcester)
Gandolfi House, 211-213 Wells Rd., Malvern Wells.
T. 569747. - Paint / Graph -   087639

Manchester (Greater Manchester)
Ad Astra Aeronautical Art, 14 Lynwood Court, Middleton
Rd., Manchester M8. T. (0161) 795 0468. - Paint /
Graph -   087640
Amber Arch, 63 Whitworth St. West, Manchester M1.
T. (0161) 236 4181. - Paint -   087641
Arts Intaglio, 69 Whitworth St. West, Manchester M1.
T. (0161) 236 9259. - Graph -   087642
Castlefield, 5 Campfield Av., Manchester M3.
T. (0161) 832 8034. - Paint -   087643
Chinese Arts Centre, 36 Charlotte St., Manchester M1.
T. (0161) 236 9251. - Paint -   087644
Concourse Enterprises, Oxford Rd., Manchester M13.
T. (0161) 273 3766. - Paint -   087645
Cornerhouse, 70 Oxford St., Manchester.
T. (0161) 228 7621. - Paint -   087646
Dixon Bate, 283 Deansgate, Manchester M3 4EW.
T. (0161) 834 0566. - Paint -   087647
Em Bee Art Galleries, 3 Broom Lane, Manchester M7.
T. (0161) 708 9408. - Paint -   087648

Exhibition Fine Art Society, 53 Cariocca Business Park,
Manchester M12. T. (0161) 273 3162. - Paint -   087649
Garson, 47 Houldsworth St., Manchester M1.
T. (0161) 236 9393, 236 5566. - Paint -   087650
Grenville, Lower Level, Royal Exchange, Manchester M2
7DB. T. (0161) 832 6002. - Paint -   087651
Jellicoe Gallery, Colin, 82 Portland St., Manchester M1
4QX. T. (0161) 236 2716. - Paint / Graph -   087652
North West Arts, 12 Harter St, Manchester M1 6HY.
T. (0161) 228 3062.   087653
Original Art Shop, R22 International Mall, Arndale Centre, Manchester M4. T. (0161) 834 3370.
- Paint -   087654
Queens Park Conservation Studios, Queens Park, Harpurhey, Manchester M9. T. (0161) 205 2645.
- Paint -   087655
T. La Art and Craft Gallery, 16 Nicholas St., Manchester
M1. T. (0161) 236 2333. - Paint -   087656
Tib Lane Gallery, 14a Tib Lane, Manchester M2 4JA.
T. (0161) 834 6928. - Paint / Sculp -   087657

Margate (Kent)
Deardens, 276 Northdown Rd, Margate.
T. (01843) 223710. - Paint -   087658
Lovely & Son, E.J., 248 Northdown Rd, Margate.
T. (01843) 202757. - Paint -   087659

Market Harborough (Leicestershire)
Coughton Galleries, The Old Manor, Arthingworth, Market Harborough LE16 8JT. T. (0185) 886436.
- Paint -   087660
Haynes Gallery, Frank, 50 Station Rd, Market Harborough LE16 7HN. T. (01858) 464862. - Paint -   087661

Markinch (Fife)
Courtyard Gallery, Balbirnie Park, Markinch.
T. (01592) 756016. - Paint -   087662

Marlborough (Wiltshire)
Lacewing Fine Art, 124 High St., Marlborough SN8 1LZ.
T. (01672) 514580. - Paint -   087663
Marlborough Studio Art Gallery, 4 Hughhenden Yard,
High St., Marlborough. T. (01672) 514848.
- Paint -   087664

Marlow (Buckinghamshire)
Messum Gallery, David, The Studio, Lordswood, Marlow.
T. (01628) 486565, Fax (01628) 890205.
- Paint -   087665

Marple Bridge (Cheshire)
Brown, Sally, 69 Lower Fold, Marple Bridge SK6.
T. (0161) 427 2654. - Paint -   087666

Martock (Somerset)
Martock Gallery, Treasurer's House, Martock TA12 6JL.
T. (01935) 823288. - Paint -   087667
Yanelle & Sons, Hurst Works, Martock.
T. (01935) 822207. - Paint -   087668

Mathon (Hereford & Worcester)
Mathon Gallery, Mathon Court, Mathon.
T. (01684) 892242. - Paint / Sculp -   087669
Phipps & Co., Mathon Court, Mathon. T. (01684) 892242.
- Paint -   087670

Matlock (Derbyshire)
Cavendish House Galleries, 24 Bank Rd., Matlock.
T. (01629) 580653. - Paint -   087671
Howard Gallery, 4 West End, Wirksworth, Matlock.
T. (01629) 823557. - Paint -   087672

Mawgan (Cornwall)
Cornwall Crafts Association, Crafts Centre, Trelowarren,
Mawgan. T. (0132622) 567. - Paint -   087673

Melbourne (Derbyshire)
Melbourne Gallery, 3 Potter St., Melbourne.
T. (01332) 864211. - Paint -   087674

Mellor (Lancashire)
Britannia Gallery, 104 Branch Rd., Melor Brook, Mellor.
T. (01254) 812579. - Paint -   087675

Melrose (Borders)
Art Aids, 12 High St., Melrose. T. 2676. - Paint - 087676

Melton Mowbray (Leicestershire)

Church Street Gallery, 18 Church St., Melton Mowbray.
T. (01664) 67001. - Paint - *087677*
Old School Gallery, Hollingshead Yard, Nottingham St.,
Melton Mowbray. T. (01664) 500729. - Paint - *087678*

Menai Bridge (Gwynedd)

Tegfryn Art Gallery, Cadnant Rd., Menai Bridge.
T. (01248) 712437. - Paint - *087679*

Metfield (Suffolk)

Fairhurst, Bramfiedl Hall, Metfield. T. (0137986) 433.
- Paint - *087680*

Mevagissey (Cornwall)

Bark House Gallery, 2 River St., Mevagissey.
T. (01726) 843933. - Paint - *087681*

Middleham (North Yorkshire)

Old School Arts Workshop, West End, Middleham.
T. 23056. - Paint - *087682*

Middlesbrough (Cleveland)

Cleveland Craft Workshops, 57 Gilkes St., Middlesbrough. T. (01642) 226351. - Paint - *087683*

Milton Keynes (Buckinghamshire)

Aim Art, 851 Silbury Blvd., Milton Keynes.
T. (01908) 696303. - Paint - *087684*
City Gallery Arts Trust, The Great Barn Great Linford,
Milton Keynes MK14 5DZ. T. (01908) 606791. - Ant /
Paint / Graph - *087685*
Hornington, 46 Aspley Hill, Woburn Sands, Milton Key-
nes. T. (01908) 585337. - Paint - *087686*
Milton Keynes Exhibition Gallery, 555 Silbury Blvd., Mil-
ton Keynes. T. (01908) 605536. - Paint - *087687*

Minehead (Somerset)

Avenue Gallery, 39 The Avenue, Minehead.
T. (01643) 707402. - Paint - *087688*
Bishop, Maurice, 39 The Avenue, Minehead.
T. (01643) 707402. - Paint / Graph - *087689*
Courtyard Gallery, 38 The Parks, Minehead.
T. (01643) 705648. - Paint - *087690*
Fallon, John, 41 The Avenue, Minehead.
T. (01643) 704486. - Paint - *087691*
Mermaid Galleries, 43 The Quay, Minehead.
T. (01643) 703538. - Paint - *087692*

Mirfield (West Yorkshire)

Kirkles Art Space Society, East Thorpe Gallery, Huddersfield Rd., Mirfield. T. (01924) 497646. - Paint - *087693*

Moffat (Dumfries and Galloway)

Bryelen, Church Gate, Moffat. T. (01683) 21298.
- Paint - *087694*

Mold (Clwyd)

Oriel, Theatr Clwyd, Clwyd, Mold. T. (01352) 756331.
- Draw - *087695*
Siop y Siswrn, 6-8 New St., Mold CH7 1NZ.
T. (01352) 753200. - Paint / Graph - *087696*

Monmouth (Gwent)

Mansard Fine Art, Mansard House, Vine Acre, Mon-
mouth. T. (01600) 6020. - Paint - *087697*
Yallup, Pat, Llandogo School, Llandogo, Monmouth.
T. (01600) 530940. - Paint - *087698*

Montrose (Tayside)

Romag, 50 High St., Montrose. T. (01674) 74227.
- Paint - *087699*
Rosemont Art Gallery, 95 Murray St., Montrose.
T. (01674) 74258. - Paint - *087700*

Moreton-in-Marsh (Gloucestershire)

Astley House Fine Art, Astley House, High St., Moreton-
in-Marsh GL56 0LL. T. (01608) 50601,
Fax (01608) 51777. - Paint - *087701*
Avon Gallery, Seaford House, High St., Moreton-in-
Marsh. T. (01608) 50614. - Paint - *087702*
Southgate Gallery, Fosse Manor Farm, Moreton-in-
Marsh GL56 9NQ. T. (01608) 50051. - Paint - *087703*
Wellington Aviation Art Gallery, British School House,
Broadway Rd., Moreton-in-Marsh. T. (01608) 50323.
- Paint - *087704*

Moretonhampstead (Devon)

Mearsdon Manor Gallery, 32 Cross St., Moretonhampstead. T. (01647) 40483. - Paint - *087705*

Morpeth (Northumberland)

Tallantyre, 43 Newgate St., Morpeth. T. (01670) 517214.
- Paint - *087706*

Much Wenlock (Shropshire)

Moel-Bryn, 3 High St., Much Wenlock.
T. (01952) 728189. - Paint - *087707*
Wenlock Fine Art, 2 The Square, Much Wenlock.
T. (01952) 728232. - Paint - *087708*

Mundesley (Norfolk)

Mundesley Gallery, 13 Station Rd., Mundesley.
T. (01263) 720907. - Paint - *087709*

Nailsworth (Gloucestershire)

Hand Prints & Watercolours Gallery, 3 Bridge St., Nailsworth. T. (0145383) 834967. - Paint / Graph - *087710*

Nannerch (Clwyd)

Wern Mill Gallery, Wern Mill, Denbigh Rd., Nannerch.
T. (01352) 741318. - Paint - *087711*

Nantlle (Gwynedd)

Wilson, Richard, Plas Baladeulyn, Nantlle.
T. (0128689) 880676. - Paint - *087712*

Nantwich (Cheshire)

Cotman, 126 Hospital St., Nantwich. T. (01270) 624567.
- Paint - *087713*
Esme, Ross, 62 Hospital St., Nantwich.
T. (01270) 628754. - Paint - *087714*
Olde Wyche Studio Gallery, 84-86 Welsh Row, Nantwich.
T. (01270) 629305. - Paint - *087715*

Narberth (Dyfed)

Hayloft, Old School, Station Rd., Narberth SA67.
T. (01834) 860797. - Paint - *087716*

Navenby (Lincolnshire)

Gallery in the Garden, 6 East Rd., Navenby.
T. (01522) 811064. - Paint - *087717*

Nelson (Lancashire)

Montage, 57 Scotland Rd., Nelson. T. (01282) 695725.
- Paint - *087718*

Neston (Cheshire)

Old Mill Gallery, Old Mill Leighton Rd., Neston L64.
T. (0151) 336 1630. - Paint - *087719*

Nether Stowey (Somerset)

Court Gallery, 18 Castle St., Nether Stowey TA5 1LN.
T. (01278) 732539, Fax (01278) 732539.
- Paint - *087720*

New Malden (Surrey)

Howard, 48 High St., New Malden KT3 4EZ.
T. (0181) 949 2125, Fax (0181) 9494277.
- Paint - *087721*

Newark (Nottinghamshire)

Mitchell, Sally, Thornlea, Eastcroft Ln., Newark NG22
0RN. T. (0177783) 234, Fax (0177783) 8198.
- Paint - *087722*
Roger Sarsby & Michael Pickering, Mill Farm, Kirkling-
ton, Newark NG22 8NF. T. (01636) 813394, 813037.
- Paint - *087723*

Newbold-on-Stour (Warwickshire)

Barrass, Sara, Define Gallery, Stratford Rd., Newbold-
on-Stour. T. 450566. - Paint - *087724*

Newbridge (Gwent)

Griffin, Tynewydd Terrace, Newbridge.
T. (01495) 247816. - Paint - *087725*

Newcastle (Co. Down)

Grant, 87c Bryansford Rd., Newcastle.
T. (013967) 22349. - Paint - *087726*
Newcastle Gallery, 18-20 Main St., Newcastle.
T. (013967) 23555. - Paint - *087727*

Newcastle-under-Lyme (Staffordshire)

Art Studio, 82 High St., Newcastle-under-Lyme.
T. (01782) 621043. - Paint - *087728*
Hobbergate Art Gallery, Hobbergate Brampton, New-
castle-under-Lyme. T. (01782) 611962.
- Paint - *087729*
Hood & Broomfield, 29 Albert St., Newcastle-under-
Lyme ST5 1JP. T. (01782) 626859,
Fax (01782) 639257. - Graph - *087730*
Lowen, 471 Hartshill Rd, Newcastle-under-Lyme.
T. (01782) 623762. - Paint - *087731*
Margaret Elizabeth Art, 14 King St., Newcastle-under-
Lyme. T. (01782) 715100. - Paint - *087732*
Wavertree, 8 Berkley Court, Borough Rd., Newcastle-un-
der-Lyme ST5 1TT. T. (01782) 712686. - Paint /
Graph - *087733*

Newcastle-upon-Tyne (Tyne and Wear)

Alder, James, 61 High Bridge, Newcastle-upon-Tyne.
T. (0191) 232 4075. - Paint - *087734*
Chameleon Gallery, Milburn House, Dean St., New-
castle-upon-Tyne NE1 3LF. T. (0191) 232 2819,
Fax (0191) 2302026. - Paint - *087735*
Corrymella, Scott, 5 Tankerville Terrace, Newcastle-
upon-Tyne. T. (0191) 281 8284. - Paint - *087736*
Cranson & Walldrige, 36-38 Grainger Park Rd., New-
castle-upon-Tyne. T. (0191) 272 1644. - Paint - *087737*
Dean Gallery, 42 Dean St., Newcastle-upon-Tyne NE1
1PG. T. (0191) 232 1208. - Paint / Graph - *087738*
Laing, Higham Pl., Newcastle-upon-Tyne NE1 8AG.
T. (0191) 2327734. - Paint - *087738a*
Newcastle Polytechnic Galleries, Library Bldg., Sand-
yford Rd., Newcastle-upon-Tyne. T. (0191) 235 8424.
- Paint - *087739*
Picture Gallery, 13 Bigg Market, Newcastle-upon-Tyne.
T. (0191) 230 1872. - Paint - *087739a*
Projects United Kingdom, 1 Black Swan Court, Westgate
Rd., Newcastle-upon-Tyne. T. (0191) 2322410.
- Paint - *087739b*
Tyne Gallery, 18 Dean St., Newcastle-upon-Tyne.
T. (0191) 230 2017. - Paint - *087740*
Tyne International, 6 Higham Pl., Newcastle-upon-Tyne.
T. (0191) 2302891. - Paint - *087741*
Tynedale Fine Art, 13 Pensford Court, Newcastle-upon-
Tyne. T. (0191) 214 0420. - Paint - *087742*
Warner, 208 Wingrove Rd., Fenham, Newcastle-upon-
Tyne NE4 9DD. T. (0191) 273 8030. - Paint /
Graph - *087743*
Weetslade, 7 Newbridge St., Newcastle-upon-Tyne.
T. (0191) 250 0174. - Paint - *087744*

Newenden (Kent)

Nilson, Ingrid, Upway Rye Rd., Newenden.
T. (01797) 252030. - Paint - *087748*

Newmarket (Suffolk)

Equus Art Gallery, Kingston Villas, Sun Ln., Newmarket
CB8 8EW. T. (01638) 560445. - Paint / Graph /
Sculp - *087749*
Sun Lane Books and Prints, Sun Lane, Newmarket CB8
8EW. T. (01638) 668587. - Graph - *087750*

Newmillerdam (West Yorkshire)

Jordan, Marie, 659 Barnsley Rd., Newmillerdam.
T. (01924) 255419. - Paint - *087751*

Newport (Dyfed)

Carningli Gallery and Craft Centre, East St., Newport
SA42 0SY. T. (01239) 820724. - Paint - *087752*

Newport (Essex)

Newport Gallery, High St., Newport CB11 3QZ.
T. (01799) 40623. - Paint - *087753*

Newport (Gwent)

Gwent Picture Framing, 18 George St., Newport.
T. (01633) 264581. - Paint - *087754*

Newport (Isle of Wight)

Gorer, 14 Holyrood St., Newport. T. (01983) 821719.
- Paint - *087755*
Holyrood Galleries, 2 Holyrood St., Newport.
T. (01983) 522467. - Paint - *087756*
New Rembrandt Gallery, 15 Scarrots Lane, Newport.
T. (01983) 529285. - Paint - *087757*

Quay Arts Centre, Little London, Newport.
T. (01983) 528825. - Paint -   *087758*

Newquay (Cornwall)
Maile, Ben, 2 Central Sq., Newquay. T. (01637) 874518.
- Paint -   *087759*
Marcelis, Georges J., 1 South Quay Hill, Newquay.
T. (01637) 850710. - Paint -   *087760*
Newquay Galleries, 6 Fore St., Newquay.
T. (01637) 874942. - Paint -   *087761*
Treasure Trove, 4 Bank St., Newquay.
T. (01637) 873678. - Paint -   *087762*

Newry (Co. Down)
Newry & Mourne Arts Centre, 1a Bank Parade, Newry.
T. (01693) 66232. - Paint -   *087763*

Newton Abbott (Devon)
Classics Devon Square Gallery, 81 Queen St., Newton
Abbott. T. (01626) 55099. - Paint -   *087764*
Newton Gallery, 2-4 East St., Newton Abbott.
T. (01626) 53208. - Paint -   *087765*

Newton St Cyres (Devon)
Hepworth Gallery, Gordon, Hayne Farm, Sandown Lane,
Newton St Cyres EX5 5DE. T. (01392) 851351.
- Paint -   *087766*

Newtown (Dyfed)
Oriel 31, Davies Memorial Gallery, The Park, Newtown.
T. (01686) 625041. - Paint -   *087767*

Newtownards (Co. Down)
Ards Art Centre, Town Hall, Conway Sq., Newtownards.
T. (01247) 810803. - Paint -   *087768*
Gillen, 38-40 High St., Newtownards BT23 3DW.
T. (01247) 812194. - Paint -   *087769*
Sheldon, 15 Mill St., Newtownards. T. (01247) 812526.
- Paint -   *087770*

North Berwick (Lothian)
Westgate Gallery, 39-41 Westgate, North Berwick.
T. (01620) 4976. - Paint -   *087771*

North Cerney (Gloucestershire)
North Cerney Gallery, North Cerney. T. (0128583) 763.
- Paint -   *087772*

North Curry (Somerset)
Ramsay, 20 Portmans, North Curry. T. (01823) 490590.
- Paint -   *087773*

North Shields (Tyne and Wear)
Collingwood, 16 Prudhoe St., North Shields.
T. (0191) 257 9541. - Paint -   *087774*
Moore, Ronald, 7 Livingstone View, North Shields NE30
2PL. T. (0191) 257 1702. - Paint -   *087775*
Thompson, 4a Albion Rd., North Shields NE30 2RJ.
T. (0191) 257 7510. - Paint -   *087776*
Vicarage Cottage Gallery, Preston Rd, North Shields
NE29 9PJ. T. (0191) 2570935. - Paint / Graph /
Sculp -   *087777*

Northampton (Northamptonshire)
Abington Galleries, 144 Abington Av., Northampton.
T. (01604) 27550. - Paint -   *087778*
Adne & Naxos, 73 Kingsthorpe Rd, Northampton.
T. (01604) 710740. - Paint -   *087779*
Art N.Z., 1 Castillian Terrace, Northampton.
T. (01604) 233885. - Paint -   *087780*
Four Seasons Gallery, 39 Saint Giles St., Northampton
NN1 1JF. T. (01604) 32287. - Paint -   *087781*
Savage, Alfred St., Northampton NN1 5EY.
T. (01604) 20327, Fax (01604) 27417. - Paint -   *087782*

Northleach (Gloucestershire)
Northleach Gallery, The Green, Northleach.
T. (01451) 60519. - Graph -   *087783*

Northwich (Cheshire)
Weaver Gallery, 12 High St., Weaverham, Northwich
CW8 3HB. T. (01606) 853585. - Paint -   *087784*

Northwood (Greater London)
Picture Scene, 64 High St., Northwood.
T. (019274) 22505. - Paint -   *087785*

Norwich (Norfolk)
A Room With A View, 20 Saint Benedicts St., Norwich
NR2 4AQ. T. (01603) 764471. - Paint -   *087786*
Bank House Gallery, 71 Newmarket Rd., Norwich NR2
2HW. T. (01603) 633380, Fax (01603) 633387.
- Paint -   *087787*
Cathedral Street Gallery, 13 Cathedral St., Norwich NR1
1LU. T. (01603) 626882. - Paint -   *087788*
Conroy-Foley, 6 Merchants Court, Saint Georges St.,
Norwich NR3. T. (01603) 630338. - Paint -   *087789*
Contact Gallery, 56 Saint Benedicts St., Norwich NR2
4AR. T. (01603) 760219. - Paint -   *087790*
Crome Gallery & Frame Shop, 34 Elm Hill, Norwich NR3
1HG. T. (01603) 622827. - Paint / Graph -   *087791*
Doyle, 155 Magdalenen St., Norwich NR3 1NF.
T. (01603) 614855. - Paint / Graph -   *087792*
Fairhurst, 13 Bedford St, Norwich NR2 1AS.
T. (01603) 614214. - Paint / Graph / Sculp -   *087793*
Gallery 45, 45 St. Benedicts St, Norwich NR2 4PG.
T. (01603) 763771. - Paint -   *087794*
Geurten, Maria, 15 Elm Hill, Norwich NR3 1HN.
T. (01603) 629442. - Paint -   *087795*
Glasshouse Gallery, 9-13 Wensum St, Elm Hill, Norwich
NR3 1LA. T. (01603) 763751. - Paint / Graph -   *087796*
King of Hearts Gallery, 13-15 Fye Bridge St., Norwich.
T. (01603) 766129. - Paint / Graph / Sculp /
Draw -   *087797*
Leveton & Sons, 31 Timberhill, Norwich NR1 3LA.
T. (01603) 625833. - Paint -   *087798*
Little Gallery, 38 Elm Hill, Norwich. T. (01603) 625809.
- Paint / Draw -   *087799*
Mandell, Elm Hill, Norwich NR3 1HN. T. (01603) 626892,
Fax (01603) 767471. - Paint / Graph -   *087800*
Norwich Gallery, Norwich School of Art and Design,
Saint George St, Norwich NR3 1BB. T. (01603) 610561,
Fax 615728. - Draw / Paint / Pho / Mod / Mul -   *087801*
Reiss, Stephen, 14 Bridewell Alley, Norwich NR2 1AQ.
T. (01603) 615357. - Paint -   *087802*
Rowans, 22 Wensum St., Norwich NR3 1HY.
T. (01603) 764135. - Paint / Graph -   *087803*
Tudor Galleries, 14 Bank St., Norwich NR2 4SE.
T. (01603) 760041, Fax (01603) 764318.
- Paint -   *087804*

Nottingham (Nottinghamshire)
Adamson, 72 Derby Rd., Nottingham NG1 5FD.
T. (0115) 9473913. - Paint / Graph -   *087805*
Angel Row Gallery, 9 Angel Row, Nottingham.
T. (0115) 9476334. - Paint / Graph / Sculp /
Pho -   *087806*
Dobbs, Southwark St, Nottingham. T. (0115) 9786654.
- Paint / Graph -   *087807*
Focus Gallery, 108 Derby Rd., Nottingham NG1 5FB.
T. (0115) 417913. - Paint / Graph / China -   *087808*
International Fine Art, 43 Milton St., Nottingham NG1
3EZ. T. (0115) 9412580. - Paint -   *087809*
Macrae, Angus, 3 Tudor Sq, Nottingham NG2 6BT.
T. (0115) 9811623, Fax 455204. - Paint /
Graph -   *087810*
Mitchell Fine Paintings, Sunnymede House, 11 Aber-
marle Rd, Nottingham NG5 4FE. T. (0115) 623865,
Fax (0115) 623865. - Paint -   *087811*
Oldknows Studio Group, Oldknows Factory, St. Anns Hill
Rd, Nottingham. T. (0115) 9413160. - Paint -   *087812*
Original Art Shop, 249 Victoria Centre, Nottingham.
T. (0115) 9419127. - Paint / Graph -   *087813*
Patchings Gallery, Patchings Farm Art Centre, Oxton Rd,
Nottingham. T. (0115) 9653479. - Paint -   *087814*
The Hart Gallery, 23 Main St., Linby, Nottingham.
T. (01602) 638707. - Paint / China -   *087815*
Zuma, 16 Stoney St., Nottingham. T. (0115) 9503667.
- Paint -   *087816*

nr Huddersfield (West Yorkshire)
Booth House Gallery & Pottery, 3 Booth House Lane, nr
Huddersfield HD7 1QA. T. (01484) 685270. - China /
Sculp -   *087817*

Oakham (Leicestershire)
Fine Art of Oakham, 4 High St., Oakham.
T. (01572) 755221. - Paint -   *087818*
Grafton Country Pictures, 153 Brooke Rd, Oakham LE15
6HQ. T. (01572) 757266. - Paint -   *087819*

Oban (Southclyde)
Art Centre, Star Brae, Oban. T. (01631) 62303.
- Paint -   *087820*
Mclan, 10 Argyll Sq., Oban. T. (01631) 66755.
- Paint -   *087821*

Ockley (Surrey)
Hannah Peschar Gallery & Sculpture Garden, Black and
White Cottage, Standon Lane, Ockley RH5 5QR.
T. (0130679) 269, Fax (0130679) 662. - Sculp /
China -   *087822*

Olney (Buckinghamshire)
Impromptu Fine Arts Gallery, 31a Market Pl., Olney.
T. (01234) 240225. - Paint -   *087823*
Olney Fine Arts, 2 Dartmouth Rd., Olney.
T. (01234) 240740. - Paint -   *087824*

Ombersley (Hereford & Worcester)
Ombersley Gallery, Worcester Rd., Ombersley WR9 0EP.
T. (01905) 620655. - Paint -   *087825*

Ormskirk (Lancashire)
National Fine Arts, 22 Beech Rd., Ormskirk L39 6SJ.
T. (01695) 424285. - Paint -   *087826*

Orpington (Greater London)
Ash, 358 Crofton Rd, Orpington. T. (01689) 860419.
- Paint -   *087827*

Oswestry (Shropshire)
Gallery, 1 Lower Brook St., Oswestry. T. (01691) 652553.
- Paint -   *087828*

Otley (West Yorkshire)
Glenrhydding, 38 Bondgate, Otley. T. (01943) 466323.
- Paint / Graph -   *087829*
Otley Originals, 6 Bay Horse Court, Otley.
T. (01943) 851112. - Paint -   *087830*

Outwood (Surrey)
Outwood Art Gallery, Shepherdshurst House, Green
Lane, Outwood. T. (01342) 842128. - Paint -   *087831*

Overton (Lancashire)
Old School House Galleries, 2 Middleton Rd., Overton.
T. (0152471) 605. - Paint -   *087832*

Oxford (Oxfordshire)
Art et Cetera, 127 Walton St., Oxford.
T. (01865) 513916. - Paint -   *087833*
Artweek Oxfordshire, 1 Saint Johns Fishers School,
Sandy Lane West, Oxford. T. (01865) 748328.
- Paint -   *087834*
C.C.A. Galleries, 276 Banbury Rd., Summertown, Oxford
OX2 7ED. T. (01865) 511556. - Paint / Graph -   *087835*
Cherwell, 16 Fairfax Centre, Kidlington, Oxford.
T. (01865) 78155. - Paint -   *087836*
Chinese Arts Centre, Gallery of Chinese Art, 50 High St.,
Oxford OX1 4AS. T. (01865) 242167. - Graph -   *087837*
City Gallery, 15 Cowley Rd., Oxford. T. (01865) 790402.
- Paint -   *087838*
East Meets West, 50 High St, Oxford OX1 4AS.
T. (01865) 242167. - Paint -   *087839*
Lawson Johnston, Philip, 307 Woodstock Rd., Oxford
OX2 7NY. T. (01865) 515417. - Paint -   *087840*
Magna Gallery, 41 High St, Oxford.
T. (01865) 245805.   *087841*
Oxford Gallery, 23 High St., Oxford OX1 4AH.
T. (01865) 242731. - Paint / Graph / China / Sculp /
Jew -   *087842*
Oxford Playhouse Gallery, Beaumont St., Oxford OX1
2LW. T. (01865) 247134. - Paint / Graph -   *087843*
Oxford Prints Shop, 46c Richmond Rd., Oxford.
T. (01865) 58695. - Paint -   *087844*
Poster Shop Retail, Shop 5, Gloucester Green, Oxford.
T. (01865) 793506. - Graph -   *087845*
Sanders, 104 High St., Oxford. T. (01865) 242590.
- Paint -   *087846*
Templecrest, 6 Boults Ln., Old Marston, Oxford.
T. (01865) 790557. - Graph -   *087847*

Oxted (Surrey)
Carter, Alan, 7 Station Rd. East, Oxted RH8 0BD.
T. (01883) 717787. - Paint / Graph -   *087848*

Padstow (Cornwall)
Artyfacts, Mill Sq., Padstow PL28 8AE.
T. (01841) 532253. - Paint - *087849*
Jason Studio, Central Sq., Padstow PL28.
T. (01841) 532099. - Paint - *087850*
Pictures of Padstow, South Quay, Padstow.
T. (01841) 532697. - Paint - *087851*
Platt, Kevin, 11 Market, Padstow PL28 8AL.
T. (01841) 532484. - Paint - *087852*
Rudge, Suzanne, 1 Market Strand, Padstow PL28 8AH.
T. (01841) 532362. - Paint - *087853*

Paignton (Devon)
Brush Strokes, 11 Hyde Rd., Paignton.
T. (01803) 550063. - Paint - *087854*
Triton Gallery, 22 Hyde Rd., Paignton.
T. (01803) 55 82 73. - Paint - *087855*

Painswick (Gloucestershire)
Yew Tree Gallery, New St., Painswick.
T. (01452) 813601. - Paint / China / Sculp /
Jew - *087856*
Zborowska, Nina, Damsels Mill, Paradise, Painswick
GL6 6UD. T. (01452) 812460, Fax (01452) 812912.
- Paint / Draw - *087857*

Par (Cornwall)
Mid-Cornwall Galleries, Biscovey, Par PL24 2EG.
T. (01726) 812131. - Paint / Sculp - *087858*

Parkgate (Cheshire)
Seel House Fine Art, Leighton Banastre, Parkgate L64.
T. (0151) 336 1710. - Paint - *087859*

Peasmarsh (Surrey)
Goldthorpe, P., Belmont Portsmouth Rd., Peasmarsh.
T. (0179721) 31718. - Paint - *087860*

Pelcomb (Dyfed)
Pembrokeshire Prints, Old School Studio, Pelcomb.
T. (01437) 710642. - Paint - *087861*

Penn (Buckinghamshire)
Penn Barn, By The Pond, Elm Rd., Penn.
T. (0149481) 485691. - Paint - *087862*

Penrith (Cumbria)
Lion Gallery, Little Dockray, Penrith. T. (01768) 67299.
- Paint - *087863*

Penryn (Cornwall)
Broad Street Gallery, 9 Broad St., Penryn TR10 8JL.
T (01326) 377216 - Paint / Graph - *087864*
Gallery Unique, 9 Higher Market St., Penryn.
T. (01326) 76124. - Paint / China / Sculp / Jew - *087865*

Penzance (Cornwall)
African Connection, 33 Fore St., Penzance.
T. (01736) 793147. - Paint - *087866*
Beaux Peep Studio, 7 Custom House Lane, Penzance.
T. (01736) 64092. - Paint - *087867*
First Legend Gallery, Unit 5, Harbour Craft Market, Pen-
zance. T. (01736) 798007. - Paint - *087868*
Newlyn Orion Gallery, Newlyn Art Gallery, Penzance.
T. (01736) 63715. - Paint - *087869*
Suddaby, Lion, 56 Chapel St., Penzance.
T. (01736) 50333. - Paint - *087870*
Wolf at the Door, Bread St., Penzance TR18 6EQ.
T. (01736) 60573. - Paint - *087871*

Perranporth (Cornwall)
Saint Pirams Art Gallery, 5 Tywarnhagle Sq., Perranporth. T. (01872) 573883. - Paint - *087872*

Pershore (Hereford and Worcester)
Classic Gallery, 48a High St., Pershore.
T. (01386) 553322. - Paint - *087873*
Hill, Jennie, 86 High St., Pershore. T. (01386) 553969.
- Paint - *087874*

Perth (Tayside)
George Street Gallery, 38 George St., Perth.
T. (01738) 38953. - Paint - *087875*
Robertson & Cox, 60 George St., Perth PH1 5JL.
T. (01738) 26300, Fax (01738) 88252. - Paint - *087876*

Ronan, 1-3 South Methven St., Perth. T. (01738) 26402.
- Paint / Graph - *087877*
Scott-Adie, John, 17 High St., Perth. T. (01738) 25550.
- Paint - *087878*

Petersborough (Cambridgeshire)
Holmes Gallery, David, 12 Eastfield Rd, Petersborough
PE1 4AN. T. (01733) 51152. - Paint / Sculp /
China - *087879*

Petworth (West Sussex)
Howes, Market Sq., Petworth. T. (01798) 43523.
- Paint - *087880*
Krüger Smith Fine Art, Tolt Coppice Farm, Hillgrove, Pet-
worth CU28 9EW. T. (01428) 78265. - Paint - *087881*
Wood, Jeremy, 19-21 East St, Petworth GU28 0AB.
T. (01798) 43408. - Paint - *087882*

Pinner (Greater London)
Blackstone, Linda, Old Slaughterhouse, R/O 13 High St.,
Pinner HA5 5QQ. T. (0181) 868 5765. - Paint /
Sculp - *087883*
Gallenti, 37 High St., Pinner HA5. T. (0181) 868 2013.
- Paint - *087884*

Plaitford (Hampshire)
Plaitford House Gallery, Gardeners Ln., Plaitford.
T. (01794) 22221. - Paint / Sculp - *087885*

Plymouth (Devon)
Athena Galleries, 3 Cornwall St., Plymouth PL1 1NL.
T. (01752) 663952. - Paint / Graph - *087886*
Barbican Gallery, 15 The Parade, Barbican, Plymouth
PL1 2JN. T. (01752) 661052. - Paint - *087887*
Mayflower Galleries, 33 Mayflower St., Plymouth PL1
1QJ. T. (01752) 662591. - Paint - *087888*
New Street Art Gallery, 38 New St., Barbican, Plymouth
PL1 2NA. T. (01752) 221450. - Paint - *087889*
Pilgrim Galleries, Island House, Barbican, Plymouth.
T. (01752) 662226. - Paint - *087890*
Plymouth Arts Centre, 38 Love St., Plymouth.
T. (01752) 660060. - Paint / Pho - *087891*
Robinson, Chris, 34 New St., Plymouth PL1 2NA.
T. (01752) 228120. - Graph - *087892*

Pocklington (North Yorkshire)
Wilton House Gallery, 95 Market St., Pocklington.
T. (01759) 304858. - Paint - *087893*

Polegate (East Sussex)
Gallery 4, 4 Grand Parade, Polegate BN26.
T. (013212) 3489. - Paint - *087894*

Pontefract (West Yorkshire)
Pomfret Gallery, Old Stables, Spring Gardens, Pontefract. T. (01977) 795009. - Paint - *087895*

Poole (Dorset)
Dolphin Gallery, Link Mall, Dolphin Centre, Poole.
T. (01202) 669299. - Paint - *087896*
Poole Arts Centre, Kingland Rd., Poole.
T. (01202) 670521. - Pho - *087897*
Quay Gallery, Coastline Bldg., The Quay, Poole.
T. (01202) 687277. - Paint - *087898*
Towngate Art Centre Gallery, 16 Wimborne Rd., Poole
BH15 2BU. T. (01202) 665495. - Paint / Graph - *087899*
Weber, Michael, 62 Danecourt Rd., Poole.
T. (01202) 731882. - Paint / Graph - *087900*

Porlock (Somerset)
Millwheel Gallery, High St., Porlock. T. (01643) 862238.
- Paint - *087901*

Port Dinorwic (Gwynedd)
Portfolio Gallery, 22 Bangor St., Port Dinorwic.
T. (01248) 671459. - Paint - *087902*

Portadown (Co. Armagh)
Edwards, Roy, Mahon Rd, Portadown BT62 4EH.
T. (01762) 339116, Fax (01762) 350179.
- Paint - *087903*

Porthcawl (Mid Glamorgan)
Well Street Gallery, 8 Well St., Porthcawl CF36 3BE.
T. 772748. - Paint - *087904*

Porthmadog (Gwynedd)
Piercy, Rob, 10 Snowdon St., Porthmadog.
T. (01766) 513833. - Paint - *087905*

Portland (Dorset)
Chesil, Chiswell, Portland. T. (01305) 822738.
- Paint - *087906*

Portree (Highland)
An Tuiremann Art Centre, Ross Memorial Bldg., Struan
Rd., Portree. T. (01478) 3306. - Paint - *087907*

Portrush (Co. Antrim)
Portrush Gallery, 93 Main St., Portrush.
T. (01265) 823739. - Paint - *087908*

Portscatho (Cornwall)
Gallery, 3 River St., Portscatho. T. (0187258) 719.
- Paint - *087909*

Portscatho (Cornwall TR2 5HQ)
Portscatho Art Society, The Gallery, Portscatho nr Truro.
T. (01872) 580719, Fax (01872) 580719.
- Paint - *087910*

Portsmouth (Hampshire)
Art Centre, 424 London Rd., Hilsea, Portsmouth.
T. (01705) 692614. - Paint - *087911*
Oldfield, 76 Elm Grove, Southsea, Portsmouth.
T. (01705) 838042. - Paint / Graph - *087912*
Scorpio, 20 Ordnance Row, Portsmouth PO1 3DN.
T. (01705) 830236. - Paint - *087913*
Screenworks Portsmouth Media Trust, 143 Kingston Rd.,
Portsmouth. T. (01705) 861851. - Paint - *087914*

Poulton-le-Fylde (Lancashire)
Strand Gallery, Village Walks, Teanlowe Centre, Poulton-
le-Fylde. T. (01253) 890810. - Paint - *087915*

Powick (Hereford & Worcester)
Ham, Martin, Sandpits Farm, Colletts Green Rd., Powick.
T. (01905) 830029. - Paint - *087916*

Poynton (Cheshire)
Harper, Overdale, Woodford Rd., Poynton SK12 1ED.
T. (01625) 879105. - Paint / Graph - *087917*
Park Lane Gallery, 222 Park Lane, Poynton. T. 878372.
- Paint - *087918*

Prestatyn (Clwyd)
Accent On Art, 156 High St., Prestatyn.
T. (017456) 886844. - Paint - *087919*

Prestbury (Cheshire)
Prestburg Gallery, Weavers House, New Rd., Prestbury.
T. (01625) 828935. - Paint - *087920*

Preston (Lancashire)
Anthony, Paul, 50a Liverpool Rd, Preston.
T. (01772) 741641. - Paint - *087921*
Barronfield, 47 Friargate, Preston PR1 2AT.
T. (01772) 563465. - Paint - *087922*
Conway Gallery, 89 Conway Dr., Futwood, Preston.
- Paint - *087923*
Dallas Inman, 36 Friargate, Preston. T. (01772) 59670.
- Paint - *087924*
Fulwood Gallery, 85 Watling Street Rd, Preston.
T. (01772) 718253. - Paint - *087925*
Hayes, 72 Friargate, Preston. T. (01772) 556412.
- Paint - *087926*
Reproduction Prints, 53a Friargate, Preston.
T. (01772) 556749. - Graph - *087927*

Prestwick (Southclyde)
Waverley, 144 Main St., Prestwick. T. (01292) 77372.
- Paint - *087928*

Princes Risborough (Buckinghamshire)
Aldus, 19 Duke St., Princes Risborough. T. 5306.
- Paint - *087929*

Purfleet (Essex)
Favorite Things, Unit 633, Lakeside Shopping Centre,
Purfleet. T. (01708) 890364. - Paint - *087930*
Gallery at Lakeside, 317 Lakeside Shopping Centre, Pur-
fleet. T. (01708) 890410. - Paint - *087931*

Purley (Greater London)
Purley Gallery, 927 Brighton Rd., Purley CR2.
T. (0181) 668 5217. - Paint -   087932

Quatford (Shropshire)
Potter, R.C., 1 Chapel Lane, Quatford.
T. (01746) 765953. - Paint -   087933

Radcliffe-on-Trent (Nottinghamshire)
Anthony, Gerald, 1 Walkers Yard, Radcliffe-on-Trent.
T. (01602) 333324. - Paint / Draw -   087934

Rainham (Kent)
Anything Goes, 164 High St., Rainham. T. 32509.
- Paint -   087935

Ramsey (Isle of Man)
Art Warehouse, 2a Water St., Ramsey.
T. (01624) 815723. - Paint -   087936

Ramsgate (Kent)
Pegram, D.G., 24 Donnahay Rd., Ramsgate.
T. (01843) 591792. - Graph -   087937
Westcliff Gallery, 1 Westcliff Arcade, Ramsgate.
T. (01843) 850921. - Paint -   087938

Raveningham (Norfolk)
Frederick, Raveningham Centre, Beccles Rd., Raveningham. T. (0150846) 688. - Graph -   087939

Rayne (Essex)
Blake End Gallery, Unit 10, Blake House Farm, Rayne.
T. (01376) 553559. - Paint -   087940

Reading (Berkshire)
Action Frame, 123 Broad St. Mall, Reading.
T. (01734) 505025. - Paint -   087941
Centaur Crafts, 137 Oxford Rd., Reading.
T. (01734) 599008. - Paint -   087942
Gryfton, 89 Mount Pleasant, Reading.
T. (01734) 751506. - Paint -   087943
Gun Street Gallery, 13-14 Gun St., Reading.
T. (01734) 571473. - Paint -   087944
Picture Framing, 14 Kings Rd., Reading.
T. (01734) 596961. - Paint   087945
Printshop Gallery, 122a Castle St., Reading.
T. (01734) 573561. - Graph -   087946

Redruth (Cornwall)
Penandrea, 12 Higher Fore St., Redruth.
T. (01209) 213134. - Paint -   087947

Reigate (Surrey)
Bourne Gallery, 31-33 Lesbourne Rd., Reigate RH2 7JS.
T. (01737) 241614. - Paint -   087948

Reymerston (Norfolk)
Reymerston Gallery, North Green Farm, Reymerston.
T. (01362) 850641. - Paint -   087949

Rhiwbina (South Glamorgan)
Millcraft Gallery, Lon Fach, Rhiwbina.
T. (01222) 613373. - Paint -   087950

Rhyl (Clwyd)
Framework, 12 Wellington Rd., Rhyl. T. (01745) 353472.
- Paint / Graph -   087951

Richmond (North Yorkshire)
Art Centre, 11 The Green, Richmond. T. (01748) 5420.
- Paint -   087952
Chiaroscuro, Greyfriars Arcade, King St., Richmond.
T. (01748) 850229. - Paint -   087953

Richmond (Surrey)
Abandon Art, 16 King St., Richmond TW9.
T. (0181) 940 9307. - Paint -   087954
Alba Gallery, 3 Station Approach, Kew Gardens, Rich-
mond TW9 3QB. T. (0181) 948 2672,
Fax (0181) 9483758. - Paint -   087955
Gallery 10, 24 Richmond Hill, Richmond TW10.
T. (0181) 948 8808. - Paint -   087956
Goslett, R.W., 139 Kew Rd., Richmond TW9.
T. (0181) 940 4009. - Paint -   087957
Kenilworth Fine Art, 53 King Rd, Richmond TW10 6EG.
T. (0181) 9402463. - Graph -   087958

Kew Gardens Gallery, Royal Botanic Gardens, Richmond
TW9 3AB. T. (0181) 3325618. - Paint / Draw - 087959
Palmer, 10 Paved Court, Richmond TW9 1LZ.
T. (0181) 948 2668. - Paint / Graph -   087960
Piano Nobile Fine Paintings, 26 Richmond Hill, Rich-
mond TW10 6QX. T. (0181) 940 2435. - Paint - 087961
Regatta, 19 King St., Richmond TW9.
T. (0181) 940 9143. - Paint -   087962
Richmond Hill Gallery, 36 Friars Stile Rd., Richmond
TW10. T. (0181) 948 9194. - Paint -   087963
Southwell Brown, 4 Friars Stile Rd., Richmond TW10.
T. (0181) 948 2776. - Paint -   087964

Rickmansworth (Hertfordshire)
McCrudden, 23 Station Rd., Rickmansworth WD3 1QP.
T. (01923) 772613. - Paint / Graph -   087965
Sheraton Galleries, 22 Church St., Rickmansworth.
T. (01923) 720261. - Paint -   087966

Ringstead (Norfolk)
Ringstead Gallery, Ringstead PE36 5JZ.
T. (0148) 525316. - Paint -   087967

Ringwood (Hampshire)
Davies, Daryl, Clayton House, Crow Hill, Ringwood.
T. (01425) 477114. - Paint -   087968

Ripley (North Yorkshire)
Chantry House Gallery, Chantry House, Main St, Ripley
HG3 3AY. T. (01423) 770141. - Paint -   087969

Ripley (Surrey)
Cedar House Gallery, High St., Ripley GU23 6AQ.
T. (01483) 211221. - Paint -   087970

Ripon (North Yorkshire)
Bromhead, 5a Kirkgate, Ripon. T. (01765) 600310.
- Paint -   087971
Ripon Galleries, 34 Kirkgate, Ripon. T. (01765) 604461.
- Paint -   087972
Rose Fine Art and Antiques, 13 Kirkgate, Ripon.
T. (01765) 690118. - Paint / Graph -   087973

Ripponden (West Yorkshire)
Glendale, 2 Spring St., Ripponden. T. (01422) 822010.
- Paint -   087974

Rochdale (Greater Manchester)
Sandiford, 78 Drake St., Rochdale. T. (01706) 46563.
- Paint -   087975

Rochester (Kent)
Copperfield, 37 High St., Rochester. T. (01634) 842910.
- Paint -   087976
Iles, Francis, 103 High St., Rochester.
T. (01634) 843081. - Paint -   087977
Just Paintings, 11 Maritime Close, Rochester ME2 4DJ.
T. (01634) 290792. - Paint -   087978
Langley, 155 High St., Rochester. T. (01634) 811802.
- Paint -   087979
Oriental Art, Maritime Close, Medway City Estate, Ro-
chester. T. (01634) 290791. - Paint -   087980
Richmond House Studio, 13 Weston Rd., Strood, Roche-
ster. T. (01634) 717236. - Paint -   087981

Romford (Essex)
Pompadour Gallery, 2 Fairview Pde. Mawney Rd., Romford. T. (01708) 723742. - Paint -   087982

Romiley (Greater Manchester)
Abacus Gallery, 28 Stockport Rd., Romiley SK6 4BN.
T. (0161) 430 7333. - Paint / Graph -   087983

Romsey (Hampshire)
First Floor Gallery, Dukes Mill, Romsey SO51 8PJ.
T. (01794) 516479. - Paint -   087984

Ross-on-Wye (Hereford and Worcester)
Bradley Hill Workshop and Gallery, 20 High St., Ross-
on-Wye. T. (01989) 65334. - Paint -   087985
Man of Ross Gallery, 1 Edde Cross St., Ross-on-Wye.
T. (01989) 768118. - Paint -   087986

Rotherham (South Yorkshire)
Harrison Proctor, 81 Wallgate, Rotherham.
T. (01709) 377788. - Paint -   087987

Rugby (Warwickshire)
Rugby Fine Art Gallery, Bilton Rd., Rugby.
T. (01788) 811500. - Paint -   087988
Windsor Gallery, 36-38 Warren Rd., Hillmorton, Rugby.
T. (01788) 56094. - Paint -   087989

Rustington (West Sussex)
Cooper, Paul, Saltings Downs View Rd., Kingston Gorse,
Rustington. T. (01903) 775550. - Paint -   087990

Ruthin (Clwyd)
Artis Gallery, 8 Market St., Ruthin LL15 1BE.
T. (018242) 4117. - Graph -   087991
Askins, J. & S., Studio 5, Ruthin Craft Centre Parc Rd.,
Ruthin. T. (018242) 5394. - Paint -   087992
Northfield, Unit 3, 55 Well St., Ruthin. T. (018242) 4841.
- Paint -   087993

Ryde (Isle of Wight)
Framers, 63 High St., Ryde. T. (01983) 66054. - Paint /
Graph -   087994
Inside Art, 24 St. Johns Rd, Ryde. T. (01983) 811942.
- Paint -   087995
Rolfe, Geoffrey, 51-52 Union St., Ryde.
T. (01983) 63646. - Paint -   087996

Rye (East Sussex)
Easton Rooms, 107 High St., Rye TN31 7JE.
T. (01797) 222433. - Paint / Graph / Sculp / Jew /
Silv -   087997
Mint Gallery, 77a High St., Rye. T. (01797) 222943.
- Paint -   087998
Rye Art Gallery, Ockmans Lane East St., Rye TN31 7JY.
T. (01797) 223218. - Paint / Graph -   087999
Stormont Studio, Ockman Lane, East St., Rye.
T. (01797) 223218. - Graph -   088000

Saffron Walden (Essex)
Twelth, August, 1 Limetree Court, Saffron Walden CB11
3LG. T. (01799) 513602. - Paint -   088001

Saint Abbs (Borders)
Kittiwake, Steading Northfield Farm, Saint Abbs.
T. (01907) 71504. - Paint -   088002

Saint Agnes (Cornwall)
Pope, John, Quay Rd., Saint Agnes. T. (0187255) 2166.
- Paint -   088003
Saffron, Peterville, Saint Agnes. T. (0187255) 3674.
- Paint -   088004

Saint Albans (Hertfordshire)
Centre of Restoration and Arts, 13 Victoria St., Saint Al-
bans. T. (01727) 51555. - Paint -   088005
Gainsborough, 46 Holywell Hill, Saint Albans.
T. (01727) 41648. - Paint / Graph -   088006
Pictures of the Past, 30 Spencer St., Saint Albans.
T. (01727) 54157. - Paint -   088007
Quartet Gallery, 21 Holywell Hill, Saint Albans.
T. (01727) 835993. - Paint -   088008

Saint Andrews (Fife)
Crawford Arts Centre, 93 North St., Saint Andrews.
T. (01334) 74610. - Paint -   088009
Forsyth, 61 South St., Saint Andrews. T. (01334) 78198.
- Paint -   088010
Saint Andrews Fine Art, 84a Market St., Saint Andrews.
T. (01334) 74080. - Paint / Draw -   088011

Saint Annes-on-Sea (Lancashire)
Halda, Saint Albans Rd., Saint Annes-on-Sea.
T. (01253) 728099. - Paint -   088012
Hazell, Mark, 9b Park Rd., Saint Annes-on-Sea.
T. (01253) 723435, Fax 728327. - Paint /
Graph -   088013

Saint Breock, Wadebridge (Cornwall)
Saint Breock Gallery, Saint Breock, Saint Breock, Wadebridge PL27 7JS. T. (01208) 812543, Fax c/o 071 -
2294918. - Paint -   088014

Saint Columb (Cornwall)
Saint Columb Gallery, 2 Bank St., Saint Columb.
T. (01637) 880887. - Paint -   088015

Saint Dogmells (Dyfed)
Corke, C. & M., 2 Ferry Terrace, Saint Dogmells.
T. 613546. - Paint -   088016

Saint Erth (Cornwall)
Clarke, Norman Stuart, 9 Fore St., Saint Erth.
T. (01736) 756577. - Ant -   088017

Saint Helier (Jersey)
Selective Eye Gallery, 50 Don St., Saint Helier.
T. (01534) 25281, Fax (01534) 58789. - Paint -   088018
Studio 18, 23a Beresford St., Saint Helier JE2 4WN.
T. (01534) 34920, Fax (01534) 34920. - Paint / Graph /
Sculp -   088019

Saint Ives (Cambridgeshire)
Burgess, 65 Fore St., Saint Ives. T. (01480) 795573.
- Paint -   088020
Crow Studios, The Warren, Saint Ives.
T. (01480) 798840. - Paint -   088021
Gallery Thirty Eight, 38 The Wharf, Saint Ives.
T. (01480) 797114. - Paint -   088022
Gower, Tom, Court Arc, Wharf Rd., Saint Ives.
T. (01480) 797939. - Paint -   088023
J.P. Fine Arts, 48 Fore St., Saint Ives. T. (01480) 795577.
- Paint -   088024
Judi, Emanuel, 30 Fore St., Saint Ives.
T. (01480) 797303. - Paint -   088025
L'Bidi, 40 Broadway, Saint Ives. T. (01480) 66886.
- Paint -   088026
Ponckle's Cat Gallery, Island Square Workshop, Saint
Ives. T. (01480) 794532. - Paint -   088027
Saint Ives Gallery, Harbour Craft Market, Wharf, Saint
Ives. T. (01480) 794665. - Paint -   088028
Suddaby, Leon, Lifeboat Hill, Saint Ives.
T. (01480) 798626. - Paint / Sculp -   088029

Saint Ives (Cornwall)
Penwith Society of Arts Gallery, Back Rd. West, Saint
Ives. T. (01736) 795579. - Paint / Graph /
Sculp -   088030
Salt House Gallery, Norway Sq., Saint Ives TR26 1NA.
T. (01736) 795003. - Paint -   088031
Wills Lane Gallery, Wills Lane, Saint Ives.
T. (01736) 795723. - Paint / Sculp -   088032

Saint Just (Cornwall)
Meridian Art Contemporary Craft, Old School House, Kel-
ynack, Saint Just. T. (01736) 788911. - Paint -   088033

Saint Lawrence (Jersey)
Exart, 3 Oaks House, Saint Lawrence. T. (01534) 62667.
- Graph / Pho -   088034
I.G.A. Old Masters, 5 Kimberley Grove, Saint Lawrence.
T. (01534) 24226. - Paint / Graph -   088035

Saint Leonards-on-Sea (East Sussex)
Galleria Fine Arts, 77 Norman Rd., Saint Leonards-on-
Sea TN38 0EG. T. (01424) 722317. - Paint -   088036
Photogallery, 2 Shepherd St., Saint Leonards-on-Sea.
T. (01424) 440140. - Pho -   088037

Saint Margaret's Bay (Kent)
Impressions Art Gallery, 1 Droveway, Saint Margaret's
Bay. T. (01304) 853102. - Paint -   088038

Saint Maughan's (Gwent)
Colourhouse, Maypole Cottage, Saint Maughan's.
T. (01600) 5788. - Paint -   088039

Saint Neots (Cambridgeshire)
Coates, Martin, 44 Market Sq., Saint Neots PE19 2AF.
T. (01480) 214832. - Paint -   088040

Saint Peter Port (Guernsey)
Channel Island Galleries, Trinity Square Centre, Saint
Peter Port. T. (01481) 723247. - Paint / Graph - 088041
Coach-house Gallery, Les Islets, Saint Peter Port.
T. (01481) 65339. - Paint / Graph / Sculp -   088042

Salcombe (Devon)
A-B Gallery, 67 Fore St., Salcombe TQ8 8BN.
T. (0154884) 2764. - Paint -   088043

Salford (Greater Manchester)
Viewpoint Photography Gallery, Old Fire Station, The
Crescent, Salford M5. T. (0161) 737 1040.
- Pho -   088044

Salisbury (Wiltshire)
Alpha Gallery, 51 Winchester St., Salisbury.
T. (01722) 414122. - Graph -   088045
Art Mart, Unit 12, Ashfield Rd, Salisbury.
T. (01722) 320310. - Paint -   088046
Art Mart, 46 Silver St., Salisbury. T. (01722) 326539.
- Paint -   088047
Carr, Ronald, 6 Saint Francis Rd., Salisbury.
T. (01722) 328892. - Graph -   088048
Courcoux & Courcoux, 90-92 Crane St., Salisbury SP1
2QD. T. (01722) 333471, Fax (01722) 333471. - Paint /
Sculp -   088049
Roche Court Sculpture Garden, East Winterslow, Salis-
bury. T. (01722) 862204. - Sculp -   088050
Saint John Street Gallery, 7 Saint John St., Salisbury.
T. (01722) 412310. - Paint -   088051
Toop, Bill, 21 New St., Salisbury SP1 1PH.
T. (01722) 320916. - Paint / Jew / Graph -   088052
Wiltshire Gallery, 22 Fisherton St., Salisbury.
T. (01722) 326346. - Paint -   088053
Winchester Street Gallery, 36 Winchester St., Salisbury.
T. (01722) 338235. - Paint -   088054

Saltney (Clwyd)
Picture This, 10 High St., Saltney. T. (01244) 675326.
- Paint -   088055

Sandown (Isle of Wight)
Casa Di Cacciato, 1 Wilkes Rd., Sandown.
T. (01963) 402788. - Paint -   088056

Sandwich (Kent)
Delf Stream Gallery, 14 New St., Sandwich.
T. (01304) 617684. - Paint / Graph -   088057

Scarborough (North Yorkshire)
Cockill, 26 Bar St., Scarborough. T. (01723) 379474.
- Graph -   088058
Crescent Arts Workshop, The Crescent, Scarborough.
T. (01723) 351461. - Paint -   088059
Hannover Arts & Book Gallery, 13a Hanover Rd., Scarbo-
rough. T. (01723) 371101. - Paint / Graph -   088060
Harbour Gallery, 40 Eastborough, Scarborough.
T. (01723) 354261. - Paint -   088061
Marine Gallery, 34 North Marine Rd., Scarborough.
T. (01723) 354080. - Paint -   088062
Saint John's Studio, 112 Victoria Rd., Scarborough.
T. (01723) 374689. - Paint -   088063

Scunthorpe (Humberside)
Art Shop, 26 Ravendale St., Scunthorpe.
T. (01724) 871158. - Paint -   088064

Seaford (East Sussex)
Alexander, Molly, Crouch House, Crouch Lane, Seaford
BN25 1PX. T. (01323) 896577. - Paint -   088065
Jane's Gallery, 18 Broad St, Seaford BN25 1 1ND.
T. (01323) 492352, Fax (01323) 29588.
- Paint -   088066

Seaton Delaval (Northumberland)
Kerr, John J., 2 Hayward Av., Seaton Delaval.
T. (0191) 237 2360. - Paint -   088067

Settle (North Yorkshire)
Gavels, 3 Commercial Courtyard, Duke St., Settle BD23
9RH. T. (017292) 824015. - Paint / Graph -   088068
Linton Court Gallery, Duke St, Settle BD24 9DS.
T. (01729) 822695. - Paint -   088069
Linton Court Gallery, Duke St, Settle BD24 9DS.
T. (01729) 822695. - Paint -   088070

Sevenoaks (Kent)
Bank Street Gallery, 3-5 Bank St., Sevenoaks TN13
1UW. T. (01732) 458063. - Paint -   088071
Gabris, 16 Weavers Lane, Sevenoaks.
T. (01732) 456527. - Paint -   088072
Pegasus Gallery, 67b London Rd., Sevenoaks TN13 1AU.
T. (01732) 450947. - Paint -   088073

Shaftesbury (Dorset)
Ashby, Mattar Arcade, High St., Shaftesbury.
T. (01747) 55125. - Paint -   088074
Grosvenor Gallery, Grosvenor Court, Parsons Rd., Shaf-
tesbury. T. (01747) 51940. - Paint -   088075
Painters Gallery, 15a High St., Shaftesbury.
T. (01747) 54564. - Paint -   088076

Sharpthorne (West Sussex)
Oakwood Fine Art, Long Meadow Station Rd., Sharpthorne. T. (01342) 810955. - Paint -   088077

Sheffield (South Yorkshire)
Book and Art Shop, 204 West St., Sheffield.
T. (0114) 757576. - Graph -   088078
Gallery Reflections, 5 Park Lane, Meadowhall, Sheffield
S9 1EL. T. (0114) 681061. - Paint / Graph -   088079
Hibbert Bros., 117 Norfolk St., Sheffield.
T. (0114) 722038. - Paint -   088080
Hinson, 290 Glossol Rd., Sheffield SI0 2HS.
T. (0114) 722082. - Paint -   088081
Simmonite, Peter, 836 Ecclesall Rd., Sheffield.
T. (0114) 663299. - Paint -   088082

Shenfield (Essex)
Shenfield Fine Art, 158 Hutton Rd., Shenfield.
T. (01742) 222333. - Paint -   088083

Shenstone (Staffordshire)
Classic Art of Shenstone, Unit 26, Birchbrook Industrial
Park, Lynn Lane, Shenstone. T. (01543) 481400.
- Paint -   088084

Shepton Mallet (Somerset)
Brunel, 19 Town St., Shepton Mallet. T. (01749) 346189.
- Paint -   088085

Sherborne (Dorset)
Alpha House Gallery, South St., Sherborne DT9 3LU.
T. (01935) 814944, Fax (01935) 816717. - Paint /
Sculp -   088086
Swan Gallery, 51 Cheap St., Sherborne DT9 3AX.
T. (01935) 814465, Fax (01308) 68195.
- Paint -   088087

Shere (Surrey)
Forge Gallery, Middle St., Shere GU5 9HF.
T. (0148641) 202388. - Sculp -   088088

Sheringham (Norfolk)
Parriss, 20 Station Rd, Sheringham.
T. (01263) 822661.   088089
Westcliffe Gallery, 2-8 Augusta St., Sheringham.
T. (01263) 824320. - Paint / Draw -   088090

Shipley (West Yorkshire)
Oak Tree Studio, 2 Wainman St., Shipley.
T. (01274) 599177. - Paint -   088091
Saltaire, 40 Westgate, Shipley. T. (01274) 531131.
- Paint -   088092
Titus Gallery, 1 Daisy Pl, Shipley BD18 4NA.
T. (01274) 581894. - Paint -   088093

Shipston-on-Stour (Warwickshire)
Fine Lines, The Old Rectory, 31 Sheep St, Shipston-on-
Stour CV36 4AE. T. (01608) 662323. - Paint /
Graph -   088094
Fine-Lines Fine Art, 31 Sheep St., Shipston-on-Stour.
T. (01608) 62323. - Paint -   088095
Gallery Four, 4 Sheep St., Shipston-on-Stour.
T. (01608) 61864. - Paint -   088096

Shipton Moyne (Gloucestershire)
Designs Unlimited, 2 The Street, Shipton Moyne.
T. (0166688) 426. - Paint -   088097

Shrewsbury (Shropshire)
Clare, 1 Butcher Row, Shrewsbury. T. (01743) 67979.
- Sculp -   088098
Severn, 67 Abbey Foregate, Shrewsbury.
T. (01743) 247514. - Paint -   088099
Severn, Perches House, Windsor Pl., Shrewsbury SY1
2BY. T. (01743) 242761. - Graph -   088100
Victorian Gallery, 16 Bugle Lane, Victorian Arcade,
Shrewsbury. T. (01743) 56351. - Paint -   088101

Wyle Cop Gallery, 13 Wyle Cop, Shrewsbury.
T. (01743) 240328. - Paint -   *088102*

Sidmouth (Devon)
Lantern Shop Gallery, 5 New St., Sidmouth.
T. (01395) 578462. - Paint -   *088103*
Ludgate, 4 Old Fore St., Sidmouth. T. (01395) 578694.
- Paint -   *088104*

Silloth (Cumbria)
Contemory, The Gale, Silloth. T. (016973) 61235.
- Paint -   *088105*

Simonsbath (Somerset)
Lethbridge, Sir Thomas, Honey mead, Simonsbath.
T. (0164383) 666. - Paint -   *088106*

Skipton (North Yorkshire)
Gallery 34, 34 Swadford St., Skipton. T. (01756) 798349.
- Paint -   *088107*
Originals Gallery, 7 Hallams Yard, Skipton.
T. (01756) 798893. - Paint -   *088108*
That Picture Shop, 16 Craven Court, High St., Skipton.
T. (01756) 700268. - Paint -   *088109*

Snaith (Humberside)
Snaith Arts and Craft, 3 High St., Snaith.
T. (01405) 860423. - Paint -   *088110*

Solihull (West Midlands)
Bucknall, Maria, Barn End Park Av., Solihull B91.
T. (0121) 705 6001. - Paint -   *088111*
Hollow, Olton Art Centre, 67 Warwick Rd., Solihull B92
7HP. T. (0121) 707 3883. - Paint -   *088112*
Solihull Art Gallery, 257 Hampton Lane, Catherine-de-
Barnes-Heath, Solihull B91. T. (0121) 705 7838.
- Paint -   *088113*

South Harting (West Sussex)
For Arts Sake, The Square, South Harting.
T. (01730) 825726. - Paint -   *088114*

South Molton (Devon)
Mole, 32 East St., South Molton. T. (017695) 573845.
- Paint -   *088115*
West Country Pictures, 10 Broad St., South Molton.
T. (017695) 572626. - Paint -   *088116*

South Petherton (Somerset)
Fantastica, The Laurels, Watergore, South Petherton.
T. (01460) 40917. - Paint / Graph -   *088117*

South Shields (Tyne & Wear)
Olley, Robert, Gambling Man Galleries, Wapping St.,
South Shields. T. (0191) 454 0360. - Paint -   *088118*

Southampton (Hampshire)
Beer, A. & E., Bridge Gallery, New Rd., Southampton.
T. (01703) 224993. - Paint -   *088119*
Hampshire Framing, 54 Bedford Pl., Southampton.
T. (01703) 631942. - Paint -   *088120*
Hamsters, Canutes Pavilion, Ocean Village, Southamp-
ton. T. (01703) 224858. - Paint -   *088121*
On Line Gallery, 76 Bedford Pl., Southampton SO1 2DF.
T. (01703) 330660. - Paint -   *088122*
Tucker, 105 Cedar Rd., Netley Viero, Hythe, Southamp-
ton SO4 6PX. T. (01703) 849015. - Paint /
Graph -   *088123*
Visage Contemporary Art, 7 Manor Farm Rd., Bitterne
Pk., Southampton. T. (01703) 582202. - Paint - *088124*

Southend-on-Sea (Essex)
Chartwell Gallery, 332 Chartwell North, Southend-on-
Sea SS2 5SR. T. (01702) 616103. - Paint -   *088125*
Poster Gallery, 8 Warrior House, Southchurch Rd., Sout-
hend-on-Sea. T. (01702) 619032. - Paint -   *088126*
Strand Gallery, 817 Southchurch Rd., Southend-on-Sea.
T. (01702) 616768. - Paint -   *088127*

Southport (Merseyside)
Gallery One, 581 Lord St., Southport. T. (01704) 534922.
- Paint -   *088128*
M & E Marketing Europe, 71 London St., Southport.
T. (01704) 532136. - Paint -   *088129*
National Fine Arts, 2a Lytham Rd., Southport.
T. (01704) 211083. - Paint -   *088130*

Studio 41, 340 Liverpool Rd., Birkdale, Southport.
T. (01704) 79132. - Paint -   *088131*

Southsea (Hampshire)
Aspex Gallery, 27 Brougham Rd., Southsea.
T. (01705) 812121. - Paint -   *088132*

Southwold (Suffolk)
Gallery Sixtyfour, 64a High St., Southwold.
T. (01502) 722911. - Paint -   *088133*
Portland Studio Art Gallery, Portland House, 43 High St.,
Southwold. T. (01502) 723689. - Paint -   *088134*

Soyland (West Yorkshire)
Harris & Holt, Dark House, Holly Royd, Soyland HX6
4NE. T. (01422) 822425. - Paint -   *088135*

Sparkford (Somerset)
Watson, P.B., Orchard Cottage, Sparkford.
T. (01963) 815067. - Paint -   *088136*

Spilsby (Lincolnshire)
Spilsby Gallery, 19 Market St., Spilsby.
T. (01790) 53864. - Paint -   *088137*

St. Helier (Jersey)
Saint Helier Galleries, 9 James St, St. Helier JE2 4TT.
T. (01534) 67048, Fax (01534) 482641.
- Paint -   *088138*

Stalybridge (Greater Manchester)
Astley Cheetham, Trinity St., Stalybridge SK15.
T. (0161) 338 3831. - Paint -   *088139*

Stansted (Essex)
Fox House Gallery, 38a Lower St., Stansted.
T. (01279) 815345. - Paint -   *088140*

Staplehurst (Kent)
Graybrook Studios, Kent Cottage, High St., Staplehurst.
T. (01580) 891961. - Paint -   *088141*

Staunton Harold (Leicestershire)
Ferrer, Melbourne Rd., Staunton Harold. T. 863337.
- Paint -   *088142*

Stenton (Lothian)
MacAulay, Stenton EH42 1TE. T. (013685) 256.
- Paint -   *088143*

Steyning (West Sussex)
Gentle Gallery, 94 High St., Steyning BN4 3RD.
T. (01903) 812933. - Paint / Graph / China / Repr /
Fra -   *088144*
Penfold, 30 High St., Steyning BN44 3GG.
T. (01903) 815595. - Paint -   *088145*

Stirling (Central)
Framed Images, 31-35 Dumbarton Rd., Stirling.
T. (01786) 51018. - Paint / Graph -   *088146*

Stockbridge (Hampshire)
Wykeham, High St., Stockbridge SO20.
T. (01264) 810364. - Paint -   *088147*

Stockport (Cheshire)
Critchley, 15 Little Underbank, Stockport SK1.
T. (0161) 480 8805. - Paint -   *088148*
Stockport Art Gallery, Willington Rd. South, Stockport.
T. (0161) 474 4453. - Paint -   *088149*
Wellington Road Gallery, 87 Wellington Rd. South,
Stockport. T. (0161) 477 6714. - Paint / Graph /
Draw -   *088150*

Stockton-on-Tees (Cleveland)
Barnard, 2 Theatre Yard, Stockton-on-Tees.
T. (01642) 616203. - Paint / Graph -   *088151*
Gemini Arts, 33 Wellington St., Stockton-on-Tees.
T. (01642) 617249. - Paint -   *088152*

Stoke-on-Trent (Staffordshire)
Bourne, 1841 Leek Rd., Milton, Stoke-on-Trent.
T. (01782) 542459. - Paint / Graph -   *088153*
Camargue Gallery, 188 Victoria Rd., Fenton, Stoke-on-
Trent. T. (01782) 744922. - Paint -   *088154*
City Framing, 9 Liverpool Rd., Stoke-on-Trent.
T. (01782) 417021. - Paint -   *088155*

Flaxman, North Staffordshire Polytechnic, College Rd.,
Stoke-on-Trent. T. (01782) 744531. - Graph - *088156*
Hydra Enterprises, Victoria House, Paxton St, Stoke-on-
Trent. T. (01782) 204016. - Paint -   *088157*
Leese, Maurice, 25 Bevan Av, Stoke-on-Trent.
T. (01782) 776665. - Paint -   *088158*
Poster Fashions, 39 Market St., Longton, Stoke-on-
Trent. T. (01782) 599185. - Graph -   *088159*
Williamson, William, 52 The Strand, Longton, Stoke-on-
Trent. T. (01782) 313505. - Paint -   *088160*

Stonehaven (Grampian)
Riverside Gallery, 28 David St., Stonehaven AB3 2AL.
T. (01569) 63931. - Paint -   *088161*

Stornoway (Western Isles)
An Lanntair, South Beach St, Stornoway.
T. (01851) 703307. - Paint / Graph -   *088162*

Storrington (West Sussex)
Milligan, 5 Eastbrook High St., Storrington.
T. (01903) 745031. - Paint -   *088163*

Stourbridge (West Midlands)
Gallery 189, 189 High St., Lye, Stourbridge.
T. (01384) 423141. - Paint -   *088164*
Oldswinford, 106 Hagley Rd., Stourbridge.
T. (01384) 395577. - Paint / Graph -   *088165*
Regent Design Gallery, 54 Hagley Rd., Stourbridge.
T. (01384) 395465. - Paint -   *088166*
Stourbridge Galleries, 58 Worchester St., Stourbridge.
T. (01384) 390170. - Paint -   *088167*

Stow-on-the-Wold (Gloucestershire)
Blockley, John, 5 Church St., Stow-on-the-Wold.
T. (01451) 31371. - Paint -   *088168*
Breock, St., Digbeth St., Stow-on-the-Wold.
T. (01451) 30424. - Paint -   *088169*
Brett, Henry, Park St., Stow-on-the-Wold.
T. (01451) 31334. - Paint -   *088170*
Church Street Gallery, Church St., Stow-on-the-Wold.
T. (01451) 31698. - Paint -   *088171*
Davies, John, Church St., Stow-on-the-Wold GL54 1BB.
T. (01451) 831698, Fax (01451) 832477.
- Paint -   *088172*
Fosse Gallery, The Square, Stow-on-the-Wold.
T. (01451) 31319. - Paint -   *088173*
Saint Breock Gallery, Digbeth St, Stow-on-the-Wold
GL54 1BN. T. (01451) 830424, Fax (0171) 2294918.
- Paint -   *088174*
Smith, G., Peppercorn House, Sheep St., Stow-on-the-
Wold. T. (01451) 31821. - Paint -   *088175*
Talbot Court Galleries, 7 Talbot Court, Stow-on-the-
Wold. T. (01451) 832169. - Ant -   *088176*

Stratford-upon-Avon (Warwickshire)
Dingley, Peter, 8 Chapel St., Stratford-upon-Avon CV37
3EP. T. (01789) 205001. - China / Sculp / Tex /
Glass -   *088177*
Montpellier Gallery, 8 Chapel St, Stratford-upon-Avon
CV37 3EP. T. (01789) 261161, Fax (01789) 261161.
- Paint / Sculp / Glass / Jew -   *088178*
Morris, Kathleen, Six Bells, Pathlow, Stratford-upon-
Avon CV37 0ES. T. (01789) 204350. - Paint -   *088179*
Studio 90, 24 Greenhill St., Stratford-upon-Avon.
T. (01789) 299669. - Paint -   *088180*
The Loquen Gallery, Minories, Stratford-upon-Avon
CV37 6NE. T. (01789) 297706. - Paint -   *088181*

Strathaven (Strathclyde)
Strathaven Arts Guild, Townmill Theatre, Stonehouse
Rd., Strathaven. T. (01357) 29411. - Paint -   *088182*

Street (Somerset)
Porcupine Gallery, 1 Bayliss Centre, High St., Street.
T. (01458) 47722. - Paint -   *088183*
Street Gallery, 86a High St., Street. T. (01458) 45301.
- Paint -   *088184*

Stretton-on-Fosse (Warwickshire)
Astley House Fine Art, Old School, CV23 Stretton-on-
Fosse. T. (01608) 50601, Fax Fax 51777.
- Paint -   *088185*

Stroud (Gloucestershire)
Sparrow, Ron & Pam, Cornermead, Gannicox Rd.,
Stroud. T. (01453) 764379. - Paint -   *088186*

Sturminster Newton (Dorset)
Market Cross Gallery, 3 Old Market Cross House, Sturminster Newton. T. (01258) 72207. - Paint -   *088187*

Sunderland (Tyne and Wear)
Davidson, R., 101 Sea Rd., Sunderland SR6 9DB.
T. (01783) 548 4060. - Paint -   *088188*
Northern Centre for Comtemporary Art, 17 Grange Terrace, Stockton Rd., Sunderland. T. (01783) 514 1214.
- Paint -   *088189*

Sundridge (Kent)
Sundridge Gallery, 9 Church St, Sundridge TN14 6DT.
T. (01959) 564104. - Paint -   *088190*

Sunninghill (Berkshire)
Austin, Desmond, 3 High St., Sunninghill.
T. (01990) 291201. - Paint -   *088191*

Sutton Coldfield (West Midlands)
de Montfort, The Keep, Weeford Rd., Sutton Coldfield
B75. T. (0121) 308 1129. - Paint -   *088192*
Driffold, 78 Birmingham Rd., Sutton Coldfield B72 1QR.
T. (0121) 355 5433. - Paint -   *088193*
Francis, C.P., Arena Studios, Marston Rd, Sutton Coldfield B73 5HH. T. (0121) 382 2415. - Paint - *088194*
Oakley Studio, 52 Bishops Way, Sutton Coldfield B74
4XS. T. (0121) 308 2072. - Paint -   *088195*
Traditional Image, 13 Queen St., Sutton Coldfield B72.
T. (0121) 355 8211. - Paint -   *088196*
Vesey, 50 Chester Rd., Sutton Coldfield B73 5DA.
T. (0121) 354 6350. - Paint -   *088197*

Sutton-upon-Derwent (Humberside)
Wild Cherries Gallery, Main St., Sutton-upon-Derwent.
T. (01904) 608466. - Paint -   *088198*

Swafield (Norfolk)
Staithe Lodge Gallery, Staithe Lodge, Mundesley Rd.,
Swafield. T. (01692) 402669. - Paint -   *088199*

Swanage (Dorset)
Alpha Gallery, 21a Commercial Rd., Swanage BH19 1DF.
T. (01929) 423692. - Paint / Sculp -   *088200*
Bourn, 57 High St., Swanage. T. (01929) 423141.
- Paint -   *088201*

Swansea (West Glamorgan)
Attic Gallery, 61 Wind St., Swansea SA1 1EG.
T. (01792) 653387. - Paint / Sculp -   *088202*
Castle Gallery, 26 Walter Rd., Swansea SA1 5NN.
T. (01792) 648377. - Paint / Graph -   *088203*
Craftsman Picture Framing and Local Artists Gallery, 58
St. Helens Rd, Swansea SA1 4BE. T. (01792) 642043.
- Paint / Graph -   *088204*
Davies, Philip, 130 Overland Rd., Swansea SA3 4EU.
T. (01792) 361766, Fax (01792) 361453.
- Paint   *088205*
Franks, S. & R., 35a Market, Swansea SA1 3HT.
T. (01792) 652852. - Graph / Pho -   *088206*
Gallery 28, 28 St. Helens Rd, Swansea SA1 4AP.
T. (01792) 465934. - Paint -   *088207*
Lawson, Edward, 110 Oxford St., Swansea SA1 3JJ.
T. (01792) 643400. - Paint -   *088208*
Mumbles Gallery, 618 Mumbles Rd., Swansea SA3 4EA.
T. (01792) 367102. - Paint -   *088209*
New Gallery, 59 Newton Rd., Mumbles, Swansea SA3
4BL. T. (01792) 367910. - Paint -   *088210*
Oasis Gallery, Piazza, Swansea SA9 1GU.
T. (01792) 474315. - Paint -   *088211*
Ocean Gallery, 1 Ocean Crescent, Maritime Quarter,
Swansea SA1 1YZ. T. (01792) 648180.
- Paint -   *088212*
Swansea Arts Workshop, Gloucester Pl., Swansea.
T. (01792) 652016. - Paint -   *088213*
Thicke Galleries, 8 Coed Mor, Derwen Fawr, Swansea
SA2 8BQ. T. (01792) 207515. - Paint -   *088214*

Swindon (Wiltshire)
Easthope & Fripp, 17 Newport St., Swindon.
T. (01793) 535069. - Paint / Graph -   *088215*

Fastframe, 456 Regent St., Swindon. T. (01793) 610471.
- Paint / Graph -   *088216*
Liden, 2-3 Lower Arcade, Brunel Pl., Swindon.
T. (01793) 693977. - Paint -   *088217*
Marlborough Sporting Gallery, 6 Milton Rd., Swindon.
T. (01793) 421458, Fax 421640. - Paint /
Graph -   *088218*

Swinton (Greater Manchester)
Le-Cira Framing Workshops, Pendleburg Rd, Swinton
M27. T. (0161) 794 7100. - Paint / Graph -   *088219*
Swinton Gallery of Fine Arts, 1 Pendlebury Rd., Swinton
M27. T. (0161) 794 5609. - Paint -   *088220*

Talbot Green (Mid Glamorgan)
Art Cetera Gallery, 85 Talbot Rd., Talbot Green.
T. (01443) 224567. - Paint -   *088221*

Tamworth (Staffordshire)
Little Pigs Art Gallery, 265 Tamworth Rd, Tamworth B77
3DG. T. (01827) 62258. - Paint -   *088222*

Tarbert (Strathclyde)
Thomas, Ann R., Ardencorrach Harbour St., Tarbert.
T. (01880) 820390. - Paint -   *088223*

Taunton (Somerset)
Anstey Place Galleries, 8a Saint James St., Taunton.
T. (01823) 254678. - Paint -   *088224*
Bishop, Maurice, Hatchers, High St., Taunton.
T. (01823) 272277. - Paint / Graph -   *088225*
Brewhouse Theatre and Arts Centre, Coal Orchard,
Taunton. T. (01823) 274608. - Paint / Sculp /
Draw -   *088226*
Frame Galleries, 9 Bath Pl., Taunton. T. (01823) 335050.
- Paint -   *088227*
Omell, 38-40 Bridge St., Taunton. T. (01823) 272234.
- Paint / Graph -   *088228*
Taunton Fine Art and Framing, 15 Paul St., Taunton.
T. (01823) 331996. - Paint / Graph -   *088229*

Tavistock (Devon)
Mayflower Galleries, 21 West St., Tavistock PL19 8AN.
T. (01822) 613665. - Paint -   *088230*
Tavistock Fine Art Gallery, 77 West St., Tavistock PL19
8AQ. T. (01822) 617952. - Paint -   *088231*

Telford (Shropshire)
Haygate Gallery, 40 Haygate Rd., Telford TF1 1QT.
T. (01952) 248553. - Paint -   *088232*

Tenby (Dyfed)
Augustus Galleries, Saint George St., Tenby SA70 7JB.
T. (01834) 5164. - Paint -   *088233*

Tenterden (Kent)
Buttonwoods, 132 High St., Tenterden.
T. (015806) 4168. - Paint -   *088234*
MacMaster, John, 5 Sayers Square, Sayers Lane, Tenterden TN30 6BW. T. (015806) 2941. - Graph / Furn /
China -   *088235*
Tenterden Gallery, Sayers Lane, Tenterden.
T. (015806) 4915. - Paint -   *088236*

Tetbury (Gloucestershire)
Gallery 123, 5 New Church St., Tetbury GL8 8DS.
T. (01666) 502413. - Paint -   *088237*
Tetbury Gallery, 18 Market Pl., Tetbury GL8 8DT.
T. (01666) 503412. - Paint -   *088238*
Upton Lodge Galleries, 6 Long St., Tetbury GL8 8AQ.
T. (01666) 503416. - Paint -   *088239*
Upton Lodge Galleries, Avening House, Avening, Tetbury
GL8 8NH. T. (01666) 3834048. - Paint -   *088240*

Thetford (Norfolk)
Thetford Art Gallery, Guildhall, Cage Lane, Thetford.
T. (01842) 766599. - Paint -   *088241*

Thirsk (North Yorkshire)
Kirkgate Picture Gallery, 18 Kirkgate, Thirsk.
T. (01845) 524085. - Paint -   *088242*
Look again, 15 Kirkgate, Thirsk. T. (01845) 522479.
- Paint -   *088243*

Thornton (Lancashire)
Artists Choice, 8-10 Marsh Mill Complex, Thornton.
T. (01253) 852700. - Paint -   *088244*

Thurso (Highland)
Toll Gallery, Bridgend, Thurso. T. (01847) 63256.
- Paint -   *088245*

Tickhill (South Yorkshire)
Davie, 8 Castlegate, Tickhill. T. (01302) 751199. - Paint /
Graph -   *088246*

Tighnabruaich (Strathclyde)
Kyleside Painting Centre, Tighnabruaich.
T. (01700) 811681. - Paint -   *088247*

Todmorden (Lancashire)
Todmorden Fine Arts, 27 Water St., Todmorden.
T. (01706) 814723. - Paint -   *088248*

Tonbridge (Kent)
Courtney, 3 Portman Park, Tonbridge.
T. (01732) 361255. - Paint / Graph / Sculp /
Draw -   *088249*

Topsham (Devon)
Ship Aground Gallery, 36 Fore St., Topsham.
T. (01392) 874505. - Paint -   *088250*

Torquay (Devon)
Bailey, 219 Union St., Torquay. T. (01803) 293318.
- Graph -   *088251*
Birbeck Gallery, 45 Abbey Rd, Torquay TQ2 2NQ.
T. (01803) 297144. - Paint -   *088252*
Devonshire Gallery, 45 Abbey Rd., Torquay.
T. (01803) 227144. - Paint / Graph / Draw -   *088253*
Farthing, Penny, 314 Teignmouth Rd., Torquay.
T. (01803) 325060. - Paint -   *088254*
Queensway Art Frames, 181 Queensway, Shiphay, Torquay. T. (01803) 614978. - Paint -   *088255*

Torrington (Devon)
Torridge, 7 South St., Torrington. T. (01805) 22100.
- Paint / Graph -   *088256*

Totland (Isle of Wight)
Afton, Broadway, Totland. T. (01983) 754664. - Paint /
Graph -   *088257*

Totnes (Devon)
Aquarelle, 3 Apple Lane, Totnes. T. (01803) 866793.
- Paint -   *088258*
Life, Mark, 29 High St., Totnes. T. (01803) 867806.
- Paint -   *088259*
Pyke, Beverley, Gothic House, Bank Ln., Totnes.
T. (01803) 864219. - Paint -   *088260*
Western Arts, 38 High St., Totnes. T. (01803) 863959.
- Paint -   *088261*

Towcester (Northamptonshire)
Clark, 215 Watling St. West, Towcester.
T. (01327) 52957. - Paint -   *088262*
Clarke, Peter, Watling St. Galleries, Towcester.
T. (01327) 51595. - Paint / Graph -   *088263*

Tring (Hertfordshire)
Spiders, 87 Akeman St., Tring. T. 8652. - Paint -   *088264*

Truro (Cornwall)
Artshop, Creation Centre, Market, Truro.
T. (01872) 78900. - Paint -   *088265*
Court Gallery, 55a Castle St., Truro. T. (01872) 41422.
- Paint -   *088266*
Gallery, 9 Calemick St., Truro. T. (01872) 77893.
- Paint -   *088267*
Gluvian, Unit 1, The Leats, Truro. T. (01872) 40567.
- Paint -   *088268*
Malpas Gallery, Malpas Village, Truro.
T. (01872) 223764. - Paint -   *088269*
New Bridge Gallery, 21 New Bridge St., Truro.
T. (01872) 75006. - Paint -   *088270*

Tunbridge Wells (Kent)
Clare Gallery, 21 High St., Tunbridge Wells TN1 1UT.
T. (01892) 538717, Fax (01323) 29588.
- Paint -   *088271*

Frankham, 4 Nevill St., Tunbridge Wells.
T. (01892) 529244. - Paint -   088272
Graham, 4 Castle St, Tunbridge Wells TN1 1XJ.
T. (01892) 526695. - Paint -   088273
Hang Ups, 19 Mount Pleasant, Tunbridge Wells.
T. (01892) 526533. - Paint -   088274
Royall Fine Art, 52 Pantiles, Tunbridge Wells TN2 5TN.
T. (01892) 536534. - Paint / Sculp -   088275

Twickenham (Greater London)
Marble Hill Gallery, 72 Richmond Rd., Twickenham TW1.
T. (0181) 8921488. - Paint -   088276

Tynemouth (Tyne & Wear)
Holly House Gallery, 14 Front St., Tynemouth NE30 4DX.
T. (0191) 259 2753. - Paint / Graph -   088277

Tywyn (Gwynedd)
Evans, G.W.D., 10 Red Lion St., Tywyn.
T. (01654) 711466. - Paint -   088278

Uckfield (East Sussex)
Ashdown Gallery, 70 Newton High St., Uckfield.
T. (01825) 767180. - Paint -   088278a
Barnes Gallery, 8 Church St., Uckfield TN22 1BJ.
T. (01825) 762066. - Paint -   088278b
Bowlby, Nicholas, Owl House, Poundgate, Uckfield TN22
4DE. T. (01892) 653722. - Paint -   088279

Upminster (Essex)
Baccarat, 179 Saint Mary's Lane, Upminster.
T. (014022) 20456. - Paint -   088282

Uppermill (Greater Manchester)
Mill Yard Gallery, Alexandra Craft Centre, High St., Uppermill. T. (01457) 870410. - Paint -   088283

Uppingham (Leicestershire)
Garner, John, 51-53 High St. East, Uppingham.
T. (01572) 823607. - Paint -   088284
Goldmark Gallery, 14 Orange St., Uppingham LE15 9SQ.
T. (01572) 821424, Fax (01572) 821503.
- Paint -   088285
Hopes Yard Gallery, 11c Hopes Yard, Uppingham.
T. (01572) 821916. - Paint -   088286
Roberts, T.J., 39-41 High St., Uppingham.
T. (01572) 821493. - Paint / Graph -   088287
Uppingham Gallery, 2 High St. West, Uppingham.
T. (01572) 822212. - Paint -   088288

**Upton-upon-Severn (Hereford and Wor-
cester)**
Arteria Galleries, 13 Old St., Upton-upon-Severn.
T. (01684) 4638. - Paint -   088289
Highway Gallery, 40 Old St., Upton-upon-Severn.
T. (01684) 592645. - Paint -   088290

Usk (Gwent)
Old Smith Gallery, Maryport St., Usk. T. 2207.
- Paint -   088291

Uttoxeter (Staffordshire)
Racecourse Gallery, 9 Queen St., Uttoxeter.
T. (01889) 566681. - Paint -   088292

Veryan (Cornwall)
Veryan Galleries, Old Thatched Cottage, Veryan Green,
Veryan. T. (01872) 501469. - Paint -   088293

Wadebridge (Cornwall)
Artyfacts, The Platts, Wadebridge PL27.
T. (01208) 812724. - Paint -   088294

Wakefield (West Yorkshire)
Art of Oak, 7 Tammyhall St., Wakefield.
T. (01924) 361933. - Paint -   088295
Dearden Gallery, Dearden House, Ventnor Way, Wake-
field. T. (01924) 265000. - Paint -   088296
Taylor Fine Arts, Robin, 36 Carter St., Wakefield WF1
1XJ. T. (01924) 381809. - Paint / Graph -   088297
Underwood, J., 7 Bread St., Wakefield.
T. (01924) 382605. - Paint -   088298

Wallasey (Merseyside)
Arte Fino Paintings, 2 Chadwick St., Moreton, Wallasey
L46. T. (0151) 606 9076. - Paint -   088299

Maritime Prints, 107 Wellington Rd., Wallasey L45 2NF.
T. (0151) 630 6563. - Graph -   088300

Wallingford (Oxfordshire)
Chilterns, 1 Saint Peters Pl., Wallingford.
T. (01491) 26440. - Paint -   088301

Wallington (Surrey)
Saint Benedicts Studio Gallery, 106 Stafford Rd., Wallington SM6. T. (0181) 647 4037. - Paint -   088302

Waltham Abbey (Essex)
Rodene, 12 Highbridge St., Waltham Abbey.
T. (01992) 712603. - Paint -   088303

Walton-on-Thames (Surrey)
Clark, Bernard E., Towpath Manor Rd., Walton-on-Thames. T. (01932) 242718. - Paint -   088304

Wantage (Oxfordshire)
Dolphin Gallery, 23-24 Market Pl., Wantage OX12 8AF.
T. 3030. - Paint -   088305

Ware (Hertfordshire)
Trading Places Gallery, 11 New Rd., Ware SG12 7BS.
T. (01920) 469620, Fax (01920) 463003. - Paint /
Sculp / Orient / Silv -   088306

Wareham (Dorset)
Hedley, Peter, 10 South St., Wareham BH20 4LT.
T. (01929) 551777. - Paint / Sculp -   088307
Trinity Art Gallery, 32a South St., Wareham.
T. (01929) 556541. - Paint -   088308

Warenford (Northumberland)
Norselands Gallery, Norselands, Warenford.
T. (01668) 213465. - Paint -   088309

Warkworth (Northumberland)
Dial Gallery, Dial Pl, Warkworth. T. (01665) 710822.
- Paint -   088310

Warminster (Wiltshire)
Touchwood, 9 Weymouth St., Warminster.
T. (01985) 846377. - Paint -   088311

Warrenpoint (Co. Down)
Brady, Denis, 7 Queen St., Warrenpoint.
T. (016937) 52915. - Paint -   088312
Narrow Water Gallery, Narrow Water Castle, Newry Rd.,
Warrenpoint. T. (016937) 53940. - Paint -   088313

Warrington (Cheshire)
Brentwood, 106-108 London Rd., Stockton Heath, War-
rington WA4 6LE. T. (01925) 601473. - Paint /
Graph -   088314

Warton (Lancashire)
Ribblefort, Bank Lane, Warton. T. (01772) 632453.
- Paint -   088315

Warwick (Warwickshire)
Eastgate Fine Arts, 6 Smith St., Warwick CV34 4HH.
T. (01926) 499777. - Paint / Graph -   088316
Mason-Watts, 60 Smith St., Warwick.
T. (01926) 403160. - Paint -   088317
Sportscene Galleries, 1 The Knibbs, Smith St., Warwick.
T. (01926) 400661. - Paint -   088318
Warwick Gallery, 12 Smith St., Warwick.
T. (01926) 495880. - Paint -   088319

Water Stratford (Buckinghamshire)
Ivers, Liam, Old Post Office, Water Stratford.
T. (01280) 848629. - Paint / Graph -   088320

Wavendon (Buckinghamshire)
Van Riemsdijk, Seven Gables, Stockwell Ln., Wavendon.
T. (01908) 582621. - Paint -   088321

Wednesbury (West Midlands)
Wednesbury Art Gallery, Holyhead Rd., Wednesbury
WS10. T. (0121) 556 0683. - Paint -   088322

Wells-next-the-Sea (Norfolk)
Stocker, 52 Staithe St., Wells-next-the-Sea NR23 1AF.
T. (01328) 710122. - Paint -   088323

Welshpool (Powys)
Oriel 31, 31 High St., Welshpool. T. (01938) 552990.
- Paint -   088324

Wembley (Greater London)
Zex Baron, 16 Stanley Av., Wembley HA0.
T. (0181) 903 7333. - Paint -   088325

Weobley (Hereford and Worcester)
Old Corner House, Broad St., Weobley.
T. (01544) 318548. - Paint -   088326

West Stow (Suffolk)
Chimney Mill Galleries, Chimney Mill, West Stow.
T. (01284) 728234. - Paint -   088327

West Wycombe (Buckinghamshire)
Black Boy Gallery, 14 High St., West Wycombe.
T. (01494) 451428. - Paint -   088328

Westcliff-on-Sea (Essex)
Beacroft, Station Rd., Westcliff-on-Sea.
T. (01702) 347418. - Paint / China / Sculp -   088329
Delta Fine Arts, 179 West Rd., Westcliff-on-Sea.
T. (01702) 333749. - Graph -   088330

Westcott (Surrey)
Westcott Gallery, 4 Guildford Rd., Westcott RH4 3NR.
T. (01306) 876261. - Paint -   088331

Westerham (Kent)
Apollo Galleries, 19-21 Market Square, Westerham
TN16 1AN. T. (01959) 562200. - Paint -   088332
Art Vaults and Exchange, The Green, Westerham TN16
1BA. T. (01959) 670 9834, Fax (01959) 6706581.
- Paint -   088333
London Art Vaults & Exchange, The Green, Westerham
TN16 1BA. T. (01959) 561806, Fax (01959) 561808.
- Paint -   088334
Wentworth, Fullers Hill, Westerham. T. (01959) 61135.
- Paint -   088335

Weston-super-Mare (Avon)
Big Splash Gallery, 8 The Centre, Weston-super-Mare.
T. (01934) 418034. - Paint -   088336
Merrick, 26 Boulevard, Weston-super-Mare BS23 1NF.
T. (01934) 620846. - Paint / Graph -   088337
Weston Galleries, The Old Bakery, Churchill Rd., West-
on-super-Mare BS23 3HD. T. (01934) 623879.
- Paint -   088338

Westwood (Nottinghamshire)
Westwood Fine Art, 59 New Westwood, Westwood.
T. (01773) 541390. - Paint -   088339

Wetherby (West Yorkshire)
Hill, Mitchell, 2 Church St., Wetherby LS22 4LD.
T. (01937) 585929. - Paint / Graph -   088340
Westgate Gallery, 10 Westgate, Wetherby.
T. (01937) 582296. - Paint -   088341

Weybridge (Surrey)
Cross Gallery, Edward, 128 Oatlands Dr., Weybridge
KT13 9HL. T. (01932) 851093. - Paint -   088342

Weymouth (Dorset)
Harbour Gallery, 6 Trinity Rd., Weymouth.
T. (01305) 772184. - Paint -   088343
Mermaid Gallery, 17 Trinity Rd., Weymouth.
T. (01305) 774679. - Paint -   088344

Whalley (Lancashire)
Frames & Pictures, 38 King St., Whalley.
T. (01254) 822620. - Paint -   088345

Whimple (Devon)
Gallery, The Square, Whimple. T. (01404) 822607.
- Paint -   088346

Whitby (North Yorkshire)
Gallery, 58 Church St., Whitby. T. (01947) 820575.
- Paint -   088347
Sutcliffe Gallery, 1 Flowergate, Whitby YO21 3BA.
T. (01947) 602239. - Pho -   088348

Whitchurch (Shropshire)
Deermoss Gallery, 2 Fletchers Court, Deermoss Lane,
Whitchurch. T. (01948) 4196. - Paint -   088349

Whitefield (Greater Manchester)
Donn, Henry, 138-142 Bury New Rd., Whitefield M25
6AD. T. (0161) 7668819. - Paint -   088350

Whitney (Hereford and Worcester)
Knight, M.R., Lower Bridge Court, Whitney.
T. (014973) 268. - Paint -   088351

Whitstable (Kent)
Pickwick, 208 Tankerton Rd., Whitstable.
T. (01227) 265801. - Paint -   088352

Whittlesey (Cambridgeshire)
Harris, W.A., 3 Queen St., Whittlesey.
T. (017314) 203356. - Paint -   088353
Letter A Gallery, 40 Whitmore St., Whittlesey.
T. (017314) 203595. - Paint -   088354

Wickham (Hampshire)
Old Exchange Art Studios & Gallery, Station Rd., Wickham. T. (01329) 833900. - Paint -   088355

Widnes (Cheshire)
Victoria Gallery, 38 Victoria Rd., Widnes WA8.
T. (0151) 495 1194. - Paint -   088356

Wigan (Lancashire)
Coach House Gallery, 1a Dicconson Terrace, Wigan.
T. (01942) 821025. - Paint -   088357
Drumc Roon Arts Centre, 2 Parsons Walk, Wigan.
T. (01942) 321840. - Paint -   088358

Wighton (Norfolk)
School House Gallery, Wighton. T. (01328) 820457.
- Graph -   088359

Wigston (Leicestershire)
Buccaneer Distributions, Whitegates Farm, Newton
Lane, Wigston. T. (01533) 571157. - Paint -   088360

Wilberfoss (Humberside)
Rentaprint, Swallow House, Middle St., Wilberfoss.
T. (017595) 8881. - Graph -   088361

Wilmslow (Cheshire)
Unicorn Gallery, 13-15 Alderley Rd., Wilmslow.
T. (01625) 525276. - Paint -   088362

Wimborne Minster (Dorset)
Bournemouth Gallery, 6 Church St., Wimborne Minster
T. (01202) 841474. - Paint -   088363
Minster, 1 Crown Court, The Square, Wimborne Minster.
T. (01202) 882775. - Paint -   088364

Winchcombe (Gloucestershire)
Kenulf, 5 North St., Winchcombe GL54 5LH.
T. (01242) 603204, Fax (01242) 604042.
- Paint -   088365
Mercia, High St., Winchcombe GL54 5LT.
T. (01242) 603877. - Graph -   088366

Winchester (Hampshire)
Bell Fine Art, 67b Parchment St, Winchester SO23 8AT.
T. (01962) 860439. - Paint -   088367
Webb, 6-8 Romsey Rd, Winchester SO23 8TP.
T. (01962) 842273.   088368
Winchester Gallery, Park Av., Winchester.
T. (01962) 852500. - Paint -   088369

Windermere (Cumbria)
Gallery 2, Beech St., Windermere. T. (019662) 88665.
- Paint -   088370
Tower Gallery of Fine Arts, 1 Saint Martin's Parade,
Lowside, Windermere. T. (019662) 3569.
- Paint -   088371

Windsor (Berkshire)
Greco, 44 Eton High St., Windsor. T. (01753) 830746.
- Paint -   088372
Omell, Shop 3, 134 Peascod St., Windsor SL4 1DR.
T. (01753) 852271. - Paint -   088373
Reynard, 14 Park St., Windsor. T. (01753) 831644.
- Paint -   088374

Wingrave (Buckinghamshire)
Arnold, Peter, 3 Knolls Close, Castle St., Wingrave.
T. (01296) 681568. - Paint -   088375

Winsford (Cheshire)
Selective Print Distributors, 122 Station Rd., Winsford.
T. (01606) 551332. - Graph -   088376

Winsford (Somerset)
Fraser, Anna, Old Village Hall, Winsford.
T. (0164385) 288. - Paint -   088377

Winslow (Buckinghamshire)
Medina, 8 High St., Winslow. T. (0129671) 712468.
- Paint -   088378
Wright, Geoffrey S., Brook Hall Gallery, 9 Sheep St.,
Winslow. T. (0129671) 4443. - Paint -   088379

Wirksworth (Derbyshire)
Gallery, 4 West End, Wirksworth. T. (01629) 823557.
- Paint -   088380
Modern Print Gallery, 25 Market Pl., Wirksworth.
T. (01629) 824525. - Graph -   088381

Wistow (Leicestershire)
Smithhurst, David, Unit 1, Wistow Gardens, Kibworth
Rd., Wistow. T. (01533) 593287. - Paint -   088382

Witney (Oxfordshire)
Bill Posters, 19 Bridge St., Witney. T. (01993) 705726.
- Graph -   088383
Cantik, Unit F3, New Yatt Business Centre, New Yatt,
Witney. T. (01993) 8167. - Sculp / Tex -   088384
Tuppence Coloured, 8 West End, Witney.
T. (01993) 772777. - Paint -   088385

Woburn (Bedfordshire)
Clifford Gallery, 11 Market Pl., Woburn MK17 9PZ.
T. (01525) 290355. - Paint -   088386
Woburn Fine Arts, 12 Market Pl., Woburn.
T. (01525) 290624. - Paint -   088387

Woking (Surrey)
Barbers Picture Framing, 18 Chertsey Rd., Woking.
T. (01483) 769926. - Paint / Graph -   088388

Wokingham (Berkshire)
T.G. Art Gallery, 7 Easthampstead Rd., Wokingham.
T. (01734) 773162. - Paint -   088389

Wolverhampton (West Midlands)
Broad Street Gallery, 16 Broad St., Wolverhampton WV1
iHP. T. (01902) 24977. - Paint / Graph / Fra -   008390
Light House Media Centre, Lichfield St., Wolverhampton.
T. (01902) 312033. - Paint -   088391

Wonersh (Surrey)
Jonleigh, The Street, Wonersh. T. (01483) 893177.
- Paint -   088392

Woodbridge (Suffolk)
Carter, Simon R., 23 Market Hill, Woodbridge.
T. (01394) 382942. - Paint / Graph -   088393
Deben Gallery, 26 Market Hill, Woodbridge IP12 4LU.
T. (01394) 383216. - Paint / Graph / Sculp /
Fra -   088394
Fraser, 62a New St., Woodbridge. T. (01394) 387535.
- Paint -   088395
Taplin, Denis, 68 Thoroughfare, Woodbridge.
T. (01394) 388603. - Paint -   088396

Woodhall Spa (Lincolnshire)
de Vere, 9 Station Rd., Woodhall Spa. T. (01526) 53404,
52892. - Paint / Graph -   088397

Woodstock (Oxfordshire)
Craftsmens Gallery, 1 Market St., Woodstock OX7 1SU.
T. (01993) 811995. - Paint -   088398
Le Print, 16 High St., Woodstock. T. (01993) 813021.
- Paint -   088399
Poole, Jonathan, 2 Market Pl., Woodstock.
T. (01993) 813381. - Paint -   088400

Woolacombe (Devon)
Chichester Gallery, 2 Westgate House, South St., Woolacombe. T. (01271) 870252. - Paint -   088401

Wooler (Northumberland)
Border Sporting Gallery, High St., Wooler NE71.
T. (01668) 81872. - Paint / Graph -   088402

Woolland (Dorset)
Old School House Gallery, Woolland. T. (01258) 817143.
- Paint -   088403

Wootton Bassett (Wiltshire)
Genie Gallery, 50 High St., Wootton Bassett.
T. (0179370) 854515. - Paint / Graph -   088404

Worcester (Hereford and Worcester)
Framed & Bee Folios Fine Art, 46 Friar St., Worcester.
T. (01905) 28836. - Paint -   088404a
Worcester Arts Workshop, 21 Sansome St., Worcester.
T. (01905) 21095. - Paint -   088405

Worsley (Lancashire)
White, G., 273 Chorley Rd., Worsley M27.
T. (0161) 794 3806. - Paint -   088407

Worthing (West Sussex)
Original Art Shop, 8 South St., Worthing BN11 3AA.
T. (01903) 820856. - Paint -   088408
Terrace Gallery, 7 Liverpool Terrace, Worthing BN11
1TA. T. (01903) 212926. - Paint / China / Sculp /
Silv -   088409
Viewpoint Gallery, 5 Stanford Sq., Worthing BN11 3EZ.
T. (01903) 205863. - Paint -   088410

Wotton-under-Edge (Gloucestershire)
Wyecliffe, 25 Long St., Wotton-under-Edge GL12 7BX.
T. (01454) 845037. - Paint -   088411

Wye (Kent)
Wye Art Gallery, 100 Bridge St., Wye TN25 5EA.
T. (01233) 812103. - Paint / Fra / Mod / Draw -   088412

Wymeswold (Leicestershire)
For Arts Sake, Wymeswold House, Far St., Wymeswold.
T. (01509) 880999. - Paint -   088413

Yarmouth (Isle of Wight)
The Gallery, High St., Yarmouth. T. (01983) 760784.
- Paint / Graph -   088414
Toms, Anne, The Quay, Yarmouth. T. (01983) 760875.
- Paint -   088415

Yateley (Hampshire)
Beaux Art, 41 Bartons Dr., Yateley. T. (01252) 871160.
- Paint -   088416

Yeovil (Somerset)
Frampton, C.J., 33 Matthews Rd., Yeovil.
T. (01935) 73522. - Paint -   088417
Yeovil Community Arts Centre, 80 South St., Yeovil.
T. (01935) 32123. - Paint -   088418

York (North Yorkshire)
Art Gallery, Exhibition Sq., York. T. (01904) 623839.
- Paint -   088419
Coulter, Robert, 19 The Horseshoe, York.
T. (01904) 702101. - Paint -   088420
French Fine Arts, Monk Bar, York YO1 2LJ.
T. (01904) 654266. - Paint -   088421
Grape Lane Gallery, 17 Grape Lane, York.
T. (01904) 643815. - Paint -   088422
Impressions Gallery of Photography, 17 Colliergate, York
YO1 2BN. T. (01904) 654724. - Pho -   088423
Kentmere House Gallery, 53 Scarcroft Hill, York YO2
1DF. T. (01904) 656507. - Paint / Graph -   088424
Miniature Gallery, 21 The Shambles, York.
T. (01904) 635187. - Paint -   088425
Pyramid Craft & Design Gallery, 10 Gillygate, York YO3
7EQ. T. (01904) 641187. - China / Tex / Jew /
Glass -   088426
Reece, Gordon, 8 Kirkgate, York. T. (01904) 868084.
- China -   088427
Rose Fine Art and Antiques, 58c Goodramgate, York.
T. (01904) 641841. - Paint / Graph -   088428
Stonegate Fine Arts, 47 Stonegate, York.
T. (01904) 643771. - Paint -   088429
Stonegate Gallery, 52a Stonegate, York YO1 2AS.
T. (01904) 635141. - Paint -   088430

Stuttle, A.T., 50 Micklegate, York. T. (01904) 624907.
 - Paint - 088431
Walmgate Gallery, 13 Walmgate, York YO1 2TX.
 T. (01904) 610345. - Paint / Sculp / Glass - 088432
York Fine Arts, 9 Grape Lane, York. T. (01904) 623182.
 - Paint - 088433

Uruguay

Montevideo

Andreoletti, 18 Julio 2108, 11.000 Montevideo. 088434
Boqui, S.A., Cerrito 623, 11.000 Montevideo. 088435
Galeria de la Ciudadela, Sarandi 688, 11000 Montevi-
deo. Fax 96 22 86. 088436
Galeria de la Ciudela, Sarandi 688, 11.000 Montevideo.
 T. (02) 91 63 01. - Paint - 088437
Galeria Rio de la Plata, Juan C. Gomez 1331, 11.000
 Montevideo. T. (02) 819 28. 088438
Meceras, Rincon 624, 11.000 Montevideo. 088439
Moretti, Ituzaingó 1431, 11.000 Montevideo.
 T. (02) 830 60. 088440
U, Gallery, Edificio Ciudadela Plaza Independencia,
 11.000 Montevideo. 088441

U.S.A.

Albany (California)

Mountain Light Photography, 1483 Solano Av, Albany,
 CA 94706. T. (510) 524-9343. 088442

Albany (New York)

McLean Gallery, 29 Dove Street, Albany, NY 12210.
 T. (518) 465-8959. - Paint - 088443

Albuquerque (New Mexico)

Adobe Gallery, 413 Romero NW, Albuquerque, NM
 87104. T. (505) 243-8485. - Graph / Eth - 088444
Mariposa Gallery, 113 Romero St. NW, Albuquerque, NM
 87104. T. (505) 842-9097. 088445
Sowers, Frank H., 3020 NW Glenwood, Albuquerque,
 NM 87104. T. (505) 344-1534. - Furn / Sculp / Silv /
 Glass / Ico - 088446
Symbolic Art Studio Gallerie, 3020 Glenwood NW, Albu-
querque, NM 87104. T. (505) 242-7662. - Paint /
 Graph / Sculp / Fra - 088447

Alexandria (Virginia)

Art League Gallery, 105 N Union St, Alexandria, VA
 22314. T. (703) 683-1780. 088448
Artworks Animation Gallery, 831 S Washington St, Ale-
xandria, VA 22314. T. (703) 836-5070. 088449
Bader, Virginia, 1305 King St, Alexandria, VA 22314.
 T. (703) 548-4440. 088450
Buffalo Gallery, 127 S Fairfax St, Alexandria, VA 22314.
 T. (703) 548-338. - Paint / China / Sculp / Tex - 088451
Discoveries, 207 Ramsey Alley, Alexandria, VA 22314.
 T. (703) 548-9448. 088452
Hensley, 1311 King St., Alexandria, VA 22314.
 T. (703) 836-1010. - Graph - 088453
Julian, 506 King St, Alexandria, VA 22314. T. (703) 548-
6203. - Graph - 088454
La Taj, 1203 King St, Alexandria, VA 22314.
 T. (703) 549-0508. - Paint / Sculp / Eth - 088455
La Taj, 1203 King St, Alexandria, VA 22314.
 T. (703) 549-0508. 088456
Marschke, Alan, 687 S Washington St, Alexandria, VA
 22314. T. (703) 548-0909. - Tex - 088457
Prince Royal Gallery, 204 S Royal St, Alexandria, VA
 22314. T. (703) 548-5151. - Paint / Graph /
 Fra - 088458
Print Room, 320 King St., Alexandria, VA 22300.
 T. (703) 549-7883. - Graph / Repr / Fra - 088459
Silverman, M.B., 110 North St. Asaph, Alexandria, VA
 22314. T. (703) 836-5363. 088460

Anchorage (Alaska)

Amniote Egg Studio, 1123 F St., Anchorage, AK 99501.
 T. (505) 272-9072. - Graph / Pho - 088461

Artique, 314 G St., Anchorage, AK 99501. T. (907) 277-
1663. - Paint / China / Repr / Sculp / Jew / Rel / Glass /
 Mod / Ico / Mul - 088462

Ann Arbor (Michigan)

Michigan Guild Gallery, 118 N Fourth Av., Ann Arbor, MI
 48104. T. (313) 662-3382. - Paint - 088463
Simsar, Alice, 301 N Main St., Ann Arbor, MI 48104.
 T. (313) 665-4883. - Paint / Graph / Sculp / Tex /
 Draw - 088464
Spitler, Clare, 2007 Pauline Court, Ann Arbor, MI 48103.
 T. (313) 662-8914. - Paint / Graph / Sculp - 088465

Annapolis (Maryland)

Dawson, 44 Maryland Av, Annapolis, MD 21401.
 T. (301) 261-2061. 088466
Dawson, 44 Maryland Av, Annapolis, MD 21401.
 T. (301) 269-1299. 088467
Middleton, 30 West St, Annapolis, MD 21401.
 T. (301) 261-2503. - Paint / Sculp - 088468

Arlington (Texas)

Rainone Galleries FNe., 1212 W. Park Row, Arlington, TX
 76013. T. (817) 261-7844. - Paint - 088469
Upstairs Gallery, 1038 W Abram St., Arlington, TX
 76013. 088470

Arlington (Virginia)

Allen, David, POB 5641, Arlington, VA 22205.
 T. (703) 536-4142. 088471

Ashland (Oregon)

Hanson, Howard, 505 Siskiyou Blvd., Ashland, OR
 97520. T. (503) 488-2562. 088472

Aspen (Colorado)

Beggs, Janie, 213 S Mill St., Aspen, CO 81611.
 T. (303) 920-2320. - Paint - 088473
Bethune & Moore, The Old Railway Station 46 Pacific
 Ave., Aspen, CO 81611. - Paint / Graph / Repr /
 Sculp - 088474
Lyon, Joanne, 525 E Cooper Av., Aspen, CO 81611.
 T. (303) 925-9044. - Paint - 088475
Mill Street Gallery, 112 S Mill St., Aspen, CO 81611.
 T. (303) 925-4988. - Paint / Sculp - 088476
Tavelli, 620 E Hyman Av., Aspen, CO 81611.
 T. (303) 920-3071. 088477

Atlanta (Georgia)

Abstein, 558 14 St NW, Atlanta, GA 30318. T. (404) 872-
8020. 088478
African Connections, 1107 Euclid Av NE, Atlanta, GA
 30307. T. (404) 589-1834. - Tex / Eth - 088479
Afrimage Arts and Promotions, 70 Fairlie St NW, Atlanta,
 GA 3030345. T. (404) 525-5758. 088480
Alford, 7513 Roswell Rd NE, Atlanta, GA 30328.
 T. (404) 393-9758. - Graph / Fra - 088481
Alias Gallery, 75 Bennett St NW, Atlanta, GA 30309.
 T. (404) 352-3532. - Paint / Graph / Draw - 088482
Aliya, 1402 N Highland Av NE, Atlanta, GA 30306.
 T. (404) 892-2835. - Paint / Graph / Sculp / Fra / Pho /
 Draw - 088483
Ancestral Arts Gallery, 780 N Highland Av NE, Atlanta,
 GA 30306. T. (404) 872-0792. - Fra - 088484
Ardavin, Anthony, 75 Bennett St NW, Atlanta, GA 30309.
 T. (404) 352-8738. 088485
Ariel Gallery at Tula, 75 Bennett St NW, Atlanta, GA
 30309. T. (404) 352-5753. 088486
Art by Design, 1054 N Highland Av NE, Atlanta, GA
 30306. T. (404) 607-0919. 088487
Art Gallery, 4575 Wieuca Rd NE, Atlanta, GA 30342.
 T. (404) 851-9808. 088488
Art Installation Services, 721 Miami Cir NE, Atlanta, GA
 30324. T. (404) 266-0990. 088489
Artist Associates, 3261 Roswell Rd NE, Atlanta, GA
 30305. T. (404) 261-4960. - Paint / Graph /
 Sculp - 088490
Artventure, 5948 Roswell Rd NE, Atlanta, GA 30328.
 T. (404) 255-3319. 088491
Atlanta Art Gallery, 262 E Paces Ferry Rd NE, Atlanta, GA
 30305. T. (404) 261-1233. 088492
Atlanta Artists Gallery, 2979 Grandview Av NE, Atlanta,
 GA 30305. T. (404) 237-2324. - Paint / Graph - 088493
Axis Twenty, 200 Peachtree Hills Av NE, Atlanta, GA
 30305. T. (404) 261-4022. 088494

Barkin-Leeds, 2280 Vinings Way NW, Atlanta, GA
 30339. T. (404) 351-2880. 088495
Berman, 1131 Euclid Av NE, Atlanta, GA 30307.
 T. (404) 525-2529. 088496
Briarcliff Frame Shop, 2187 Briarcliff Rd NE, Atlanta, GA
 30329. T. (404) 325-8454. - Fra - 088497
Brown, Sarah, 631 Miami Circle NE, Atlanta, GA 30324.
 T. (404) 262-7304. - Paint - 088498
Burnhoff, 1529 Piedmont Av NE, Atlanta, GA 30324.
 T. (404) 875-3475. - Graph / Pho - 088499
Candler Park Gallery, 1404 McLendon Av NE, Atlanta,
 GA 30307. T. (404) 522-2787. 088500
Cathreen, 2817 Peachtree Rd NE, Atlanta, GA 30305.
 T. (404) 233-2002. - Graph / Fra - 088501
Clayton Clay Worthington, 247 Buckhead Av NE, Atlanta,
 GA 30305. T. (404) 266-1934. 088502
Cone-Skelton, Annette, 1765 Peachtree St NE, Atlanta,
 GA 30309. T. (404) 874-1789. 088503
Consult Art, 3280 Farmington Dr NW, Atlanta, GA 30339.
 T. (404) 435-5180. 088504
Davis-Moye & Associates, 435 Bridges Creek Trail NE,
 Atlanta, GA 30328. T. (404) 255-5366. 088505
Dimensional Arts, 790 Huff Rd NW, Atlanta, GA 30318.
 T. (404) 355-4961. 088506
Fast Frame, 2625 Piedmont Rd NE, Atlanta, GA 30324.
 T. (404) 261-1213. - Fra - 088507
Fine Art Galleries, 650 Miami Circle NE, Atlanta, GA
 30324. T. (404) 261-1897. 088508
Folk-Art Imports, 25 Bennett St NW, Atlanta, GA 30309.
 T. (404) 352-2656. - Eth - 088509
Fox, Shirley, 1590 Piedmont Av NE., Atlanta, GA 30324.
 T. (404) 874-7294. - Paint / Graph - 088510
Frame Gallery International, 5323 Roswell Rd NE, Atlan-
ta, GA 30342. T. (404) 256-5290. - Fra - 088511
Framers on Peachtree, 2351 Peachtree Rd NE, Atlanta,
 GA 30305. T. (404) 237-2888. - Fra - 088512
Gallery 515, 515 E Paces Ferry Rd NE, Atlanta, GA
 30305. T. (404) 233-2911. 088513
Global Art Galleries, 2115 Hills Av NW, Atlanta, GA
 30318. T. (404) 351-5111. - Paint / Graph /
 Fra - 088514
Gold, Fay, 247 Buckhead Av NE, Atlanta, GA 30305.
 T. (404) 233-3843, Fax (404) 365-8633. - Paint /
 Sculp / Pho / Draw - 088515
Graphique Dujour, 2231 Faulkner Rd NE, Atlanta, GA
 30324. T. (404) 636-2782. - Graph - 088516
Greggie, 3495 Piedmont Rd NE, Atlanta, GA 30305.
 T. (404) 261-3961. - Graph / Draw - 088517
Harvey Paige, 117 Luckie St NW, Atlanta, GA 30303.
 T. (404) 577-8722. - Paint - 088518
Heath, 416 E Paces Ferry Rd NE, Atlanta, GA 30305.
 T. (404) 262-6407. - Paint / Graph / Sculp / Pho / Mul /
 Draw - 088519
Heirloom Gallery, 55 Forsyth St NW, Atlanta, GA 30303.
 T. (404) 577-0322. 088520
Hillman Holland, 2575 Peachtree Rd NE, Atlanta, GA
 30305. T. (404) 233-7494. - Paint - 088521
Image Design and Gallery, 3001 N Fulton Dr NE, Atlanta,
 GA 30305. T. (404) 365-8361. 088522
Jackson, 3115 E Shadowlawn Av, Atlanta, GA 30305.
 T. (404) 233-3739, Fax (404) 233-1205. - Pho - 088523
Japan Arts, 57 Basswood Cir NE, Atlanta, GA 30328.
 T. (404) 393-1955. - Orient - 088524
Knoke, 5325 Roswell Rd NE, Atlanta, GA 30342.
 T. (404) 252-0485. - Paint - 088525
Lambert, Marianne B., 3280 Farmington Dr NW, Atlanta,
 GA 30339. T. (404) 435-5180. 088526
Le Primitif, 631 Miami Cir NE, Atlanta, GA 30324.
 T. (404) 240-0226. - Paint - 088527
Lippitt, Linda N., 1327 Paces Forest Dr NW, Atlanta, GA
 30327. T. (404) 233-4691. 088528
Lovett, Bob, 5323 Roswell Rd NE, Atlanta, GA 30342.
 T. (404) 250-9813. 088529
Lowe, 75 Bennett St NW, Atlanta, GA 30309.
 T. (404) 352-8114. 088530
McIntosh, 587 Virginia Av NE, Atlanta, GA 30306.
 T. (404) 892-4023. - Paint / Graph / Sculp - 088531
Moore Wayland, 1687 Tully Circle NE, Atlanta, GA
 30329. T. (404) 633-0828. 088532
Myriad, 674 Miami Circle NE, Atlanta, GA 30324.
 T. (404) 364-0611. 088533
Novus, 116 Bennett St NW, Atlanta, GA 30309.
 T. (404) 355-4974. 088534

Peachtree Gallery, 2277 Peachtree Rd NE, Atlanta, GA
30309. T. (404) 355-0511. - Paint / Graph -   088535
Prestige Gallery, 6624 Dawson Blvd., Atlanta, GA 30340.
T. (404) 446-3850.   088536
Reinike, 2300 Peachtree Rd NW, Atlanta, GA 30309.
T. (404) 352-5269.   088537
Respress, 675 W Peachtree St NE, Atlanta, GA 30308.
T. (404) 874-5180.   088538
Rolling Frame Revue, 1765 Cheshire Bridge Rd NE, At-
lanta, GA 30324. T. (404) 873-5022.   088539
Rolling Stone Press, 432 Calhoun St NW, Atlanta, GA
30318. T. (404) 873-3322.   088540
Rottenberg, Fran, 602 Chestnut Oak Center NW, Atlanta,
GA 30327. T. (404) 255-6359.   088541
Signature Shop & Galleries, 3267 Roswell Rd NW, Atlan-
ta, GA 30305. T. (404) 237-4426.   088542
Solart, 240 Peachtree St NW, Atlanta, GA 30303.
T. (404) 525-7229.   088543
Steiner & Young, 2 Ravinia Dr NE, Atlanta, GA 30346.
T. (404) 390-7555.   088544
Studio L-1, 75 Bennett St NW, Atlanta, GA 30309.
T. (404) 352-5754.   088545
Swan Coach House Gallery, 3130 Slaton Dr NW, Atlanta,
GA 30305. T. (404) 266-2636. - Paint -   088546
Trinity Gallery, 249 Trinity Av SW, Atlanta, GA 30303.
T. (404) 525-7546.   088547
Vespermann, 2140 Peachtree Rd NW, Atlanta, GA
30309. T. (404) 350-9698. - Glass -   088548

Atlantic City (New Jersey)
Miller Art, 205 N. Montpelier Ave., Atlantic City, NJ
08401. T. (609) 345-5491. - Paint / Fra -   088549
Reese Palley, 1911 The Boardwalk, Atlantic City, NJ
08401. T. (609) 348-4800. - Ant / Furn -   088550

Austin (Texas)
Country Store Gallery, 1304 Lavaca St., Austin, TX
78701. T. (512) 476-1553. - Paint / Fra -   088551
Garner & Smith, 509 W 12 St., Austin, TX 78701.
T. (512) 474-1518. - Paint / Graph / Fra -   088552
Native American Images, 2104 Nueces, Austin, TX
78767. T. (512) 472-3049, 531-5008.   088553

Bakersfield (California)
Clark, C.L., 1818 V St., Bakersfield, CA 93301.
T. (805) 325-7094.   088554

Baltimore (Maryland)
Cordish, Sylvia, 519 N Charles St., Baltimore, MD
21201. T. (301) 539-6611. - Graph / Paint -   088555
Dalsheimer, G.H., 336 N Charles St., Baltimore, MD
21201. T. (301) 727-0866. - Paint / Pho -   088556
Gilden, Jerry, 303 Reisterstown Rd., Baltimore, MD
21208. T. (301) 484-1458. - Paint -   088557
Grimaldis, C., 523 N Charles St., Baltimore, MD 21201.
T. (301) 539-1080. - Paint / Sculp -   088558
McGuire, Ralph, 108 W Mulberry St, Baltimore, MD
21201. T. (301) 539-2594. - Graph / Repr /
Fra -   088559
Meredith, 805 N Charles St., Baltimore, MD 21201.
T. (301) 837-3575. - Graph -   088560
The 19th Century Shop, 1047 Hollins St, Baltimore, MD
21223. T. (301) 539-2586, Fax (301) 727-
2681.   088561
Tomlinson, 711 W 40 St., Baltimore, MD 21211.
T. (301) 338-1555. - Paint / Graph / Fra -   088562
Walters, 600 N Charles ST., Baltimore, MD 21201.
T. (301) 547-9000. - Paint / China / Sculp -   088563

Baton Rouge (Louisiana)
Clark, Taylor, 2623 Government St., Baton Rouge, LA
70806. T. (504) 342-4929. - Paint / Graph -   088564
Fetzer, Nell, 711 Jefferson Hwy., Baton Rouge, LA
70806. T. (504) 927-7420. - Paint -   088565
Lavayette Gallery, 348 Lafayette St., Baton Rouge, LA
70801. T. (504) 383-7763. - Paint / Sculp -   088566
Louisiana Art Center, 2828 Yorktown, Baton Rouge, LA
70808. T. (504) 924-1803. - Paint -   088567

Bay Harbour Islands (Florida)
Galerie Ninety-nine, 1088 Jane Concourse, Bay Harbour
Islands, FL 33154. T. (305) 865-5823. - Paint /
Sculp -   088568

Hokin, 1086 Kane Concourse, Bay Harbour Islands, FL
33154. T. (305) 861-5700.   088569
Luria, Gloria, 1033 Kane Concourse, Bay Harbour Islands, FL 33154. T. (305) 865-3060. - Paint / Graph /
Sculp -   088570
Scott, Barbara, 1055 Kane Concourse, Bay Harbour Islands, FL 33154. T. (305) 865-9393, Fax (305) 865-
9395.   088571

Bellevue (Washington)
Panaca, 376 Bellevue Sq., 98000 Bellevue, (98004).
T. (206) 454-0234. - Paint / Graph / Sculp -   088572

Belmont (Massachusetts)
East Coast Arts, 395 Belmont St., Belmont, MA 02178.
T. (617) 489-6244.   088573

Berkeley (California)
A.C.C.I. Gallery, 1652 Shattuck Av, Berkeley, CA 94709.
T. (510) 843-2527. - Paint / Graph -   088574
Ames, 2661 Cedar St, Berkeley, CA 94708. T. (510) 845-
4949. - Paint -   088575
Artworks Foundry and Gallery, 729 Heinz Av, Berkeley,
CA 94710. T. (510) 644-2735. - Sculp -   088576
Aware Designs Gallery, 2118 Vine St, Berkeley, CA
94709. T. (510) 649-1231. - Graph / Draw -   088577
Harris, 3032 Claremont Av, Berkeley, CA 94705.
T. (510) 658-6609. - Graph -   088578
White Buffalo Gallery, 900 North Point St, Berkeley, CA
94109. T. (415) 931-0665.   088579

Bethesda (Maryland)
Capricorn Galleries, 4849 Rugby Av, Bethesda, MD
20814. T. (301) 657-3477. - Paint / Sculp / Mod /
Draw -   088580
Hendricks, 5207 Crown St, Bethesda, MD 20816.
T. (301) 229-5100.   088581
Images International, 4600 East-West Hwy, Bethesda,
MD 20814. T. (301) 654-2321. - Paint / Graph -   088582
Renaissance Fine Arts, 10253 Old Georgetown Rd, Be-
thesda, MD 20814. T. (301) 564-4447. - Paint / Graph /
Fra -   088583
Snow Goose Gallery, 6831 Wisconsin Av, Bethesda, MD
20815. T. (301) 907-9241.   088584

Beverly Hills (California)
Feingarten, Beverly Hills POB 5383, CA 90209.
T. (213) 274-7042, Fax (213) 274-4255. - Paint /
Sculp -   088585
Gallery Rodeo, 421 N Rodeo Dr, Beverly Hills, CA 90210.
T. (310) 273-6615.   088586
Isenberg, Michelle, & Associates, 9233 Burton Way, Ste.
505, Beverly Hills, CA 90210. T. (213) 275-1160,
Fax (213) 388-3989.   088587
Latin American Masters, 264 N Beverly Dr, Beverly Hills,
CA 90210. T. (310) 271-4847. - Paint / Graph -   088588
Latin American Masters, 264 N Beverly Dr, Beverly Hills,
CA 90210. T. (310) 271-4847. - Paint / Graph -   088589
Latin American Masters, 264 N Beverly Drive, Beverly
Hills, CA 90210. T. (310) 271-4913, Fax (310) 278-
3932.   088590
New Renaissance Galleries, 305 N Rodeo Dr, Beverly
Hills, CA 90210. T. (310) 285-9700. - Paint /
Graph -   088591
Salander O'Reilly, 456 N Camden Dr., Beverly Hills, CA
90210. T. (213) 879-6606, Fax (213) 247-1505.
- Paint -   088592
Stern, Louis, 190 N Canon Dr, Beverly Hills, CA 90210.
T. (310) 276-0147. - Paint -   088593

Birmingham (Michigan)
Bittker, D. & J., 536 N Woodward Av., Birmingham, MI
48011. T. (313) 258-1670. - Paint / Graph / China /
Sculp -   088594
Cantor/Lemberg, 538 N Woodward Av., Birmingham, MI
48011. T. (313) 642-6623. - Paint / Graph / Sculp /
Draw -   088595
Halsted, 560 N Woodward Av., Birmingham, MI 48011.
T. (313) 644-8284. - Pho -   088596
Hilberry, Susanne, 555 S Woodward, Birmingham, MI
48011. T. (313) 642-8250.   088597
Hill, 163 Townsend, Birmingham, MI 48011.
T. (313) 540-9288. - Paint / Sculp -   088598

Jacobs, Donna, 574 N Woodward Av., Birmingham, MI
48011. T. (313) 540-1600. - Paint -   088599
Kidd, Robert, 107 Townsend St., Birmingham, MI 48011.
T. (313) 642-3909. - Paint / Graph / Sculp /
Glass -   088600
Modern Studio of Interiors, 217 Pierce St., Birmingham,
MI 48011. - Paint / Graph / Repr / Sculp / Fra -   088601
Morris, Donald, 105 Townsend, Birmingham, MI 48009.
T. (313) 642-8812. - Paint / Sculp / Eth / Draw -   088602
Pierce Street Gallery, 217 Pierce St., Birmingham, MI
48011. T. (313) 646-6950. - Pho -   088603
Ross, Sheldon, 250 Martin St., Birmingham, MI 48011.
T. (313) 258-9550. - Paint -   088604
Xochipilli, 568 N Woodward Av., Birmingham, MI 48011.
T. (313) 645-1905. - Paint / Sculp -   088605

Blacksburg (Virginia)
Miller & Main St. Galleries, 500 S Main St., Blacksburg,
VA 24060. T. (703) 552-6969. - Paint / Graph /
Sculp -   088606

Bloomington (Indiana)
Echo Press, 1805 E Tenth St., Bloomington, IN 47401.
T. (812) 335-0476. - Graph -   088607

Blytheville (Arkansas)
Deal, James R., 1145 W Hearn, Blytheville, AR 72315.
T. (501) 762-2769. - Paint / Graph / Repr / Fra -   088608

Boca Raton (Florida)
Berenson, 470 NW 20 St. Suite 105C, Boca Raton, FL
33431. T. (305) 395-0333. - Paint -   088610
Freites-Revilla, 608 Banyan Trail, Gallery Center, Boca
Ranton, FL 33431. T. (407) 241-1995, Fax (407) 241-
1998.   088610a
Martin East, 417 Town Center, Boca Raton, FL 33432.
T. (305) 395-3050. - Paint -   088611
Martin West, 169 Town Center, Boca Raton, FL 33432.
T. (305) 368-7626. - Paint -   088612
Patricia Judith Art Gallery, 720 E Palmetto Park Rd., Bo-
ca Raton, FL 33432. T. (305) 368-3316. - Paint /
Sculp -   088613

Boise (Idaho)
Art Attack Gallery, 409 S Eighth St. Suite 101, Boise, ID
83702. T. (208) 344-6422. - Paint -   088614
Ochi, 1322 Main St., Boise, ID 83702. T. (208) 342-
1314. - Paint / Graph / Sculp / Pho / Draw -   088615

Boston (Massachusetts)
A Art Collector, 382 Commonwealth Av, Boston, MA
02115. T. (617) 424-9000. - Paint / Graph -   088616
Ainsworth, 42 Bromfield St, Boston, MA 02108.
T. (617) 542-7195. - Graph -   088617
Ainswrth Gallery, The, 42 Bromfield St., Boston, MA
02108. T. (617) 542-7195. - Graph / Repr /
Fra -   088618
Akin, 164 Kneeland St, Boston, MA 02111. T. (617) 426-
2726.   088619
Alberts-Langdon, 126 Charles St, Boston, MA 02136.
T. (617) 523-5954.   088620
Aleman, 105 Charles St., Boston, MA 02114.
T. (617) 536-5978. - Paint -   088621
Alianza Contemporary Crafts, 154 Newbury St, Boston,
MA 02116. T. (617) 262-2385. - China / Jew /
Glass -   088622
Alpert, 90 Chauncy St, Boston, MY 02111. T. (617) 482-
7710.   088623
Alpha Gallery, 121 Newbury St, Boston, MA 02116.
T. (617) 536-4465. - Paint / Graph / Sculp -   088624
American Graphic Arts, 101 Merrimac St, Boston, MA
02114. T. (617) 723-7770. - Graph -   088625
Arden, 129 Newbury St, Boston, MA 02116.
T. (617) 247-0610.   088626
Ars Libri, 560 Harrison Av, Boston, MA 02118.
T. (617) 357-5212.   088627
Art Investment, 39 Newbury St, Boston, MA 02116.
T. (617) 859-3880.   088628
Arvest, 77 Newbury St, Boston, MA 02116. T. (617) 236-
1404. - Paint / Graph / Sculp -   088629
Asia Gallery, 214 Newbury St, Boston, MA 02116.
T. (617) 267-8152. - Orient -   088630
Bates, 731 Harrison Av, Boston, MA 02118. T. (617) 424-
7616.   088631

Bergh Sheldon Leigh, 502 Commercial St, Boston, MA 02109. T. (617) 367-2767. - Paint / Graph / Sculp – 088632

Bloch, 116 Newbury St, Boston, MA 02116. T. (617) 266-5575. 088633

Boston Center for the Arts, 539 Tremont St, Boston, MA 02116. T. (617) 426-7700. 088634

Caccivio & Sons, J.C., 71 Commercial St, Boston, MA 02109. T. (617) 723-4650. 088635

Canvasback Art Company, 29 Concord Sq, Boston, MA 02118. T. (617) 266-2639. 088636

Chase Gallery, 173 Newbury St, Boston, MA 02116. T. (617) 859-7222. - Paint / Graph – 088637

Childs, 169 Newbury St, Boston, MA 02116. T. (617) 266-1108, Fax (617) 266-2381. - Paint / Graph / Sculp / Draw – 088638

City Life-Boston, 45 Wareham St, Boston, MA 02118. T. (617) 350-5325. 088639

Copley, 150 Huntington Av, Boston, MA 02122. T. (617) 267-6060. - Paint / Graph / Fra – 088640

Dashow & A.D. Hilyer, R., 104 Broad St, Boston, MA 02110. T. (617) 542-2120. 088641

Different Angel Gallery, 286 Congress St, Boston, MA 02210. T. (617) 482-3343. 088642

Dyansen, 132A Newbury St, Boston, MA 02116. T. (617) 262-4800. 088643

Eugene Galleries, 76 Charles St, Boston, MA 02114. T. (617) 227-3062. - Paint / Graph / Sculp / Fra – 088644

Fenway, 50 Gloucester St, Boston, MA 02115. T. (617) 536-0127. - Paint / Repr / Fra – 088645

Fine Arts Planning Group, 71 Marlborough St, Boston, MA 02116. T. (617) 437-9807. 088646

Frame Rite Galleries, 31 Saint James Av, Boston, MA 02116. T. (617) 482-3320. - Graph / Fra – 088647

The Gallery, 99 Charles St, Boston, MA 02122. T. (617) 227-8800. 088648

Gallery at the Factory, 791 Tremont St, Boston, MA 02118. T. (617) 437-9365. 088649

Genovese, 535 Albany St, Boston, MA 02118. T. (617) 426-9738. - Graph – 088650

Ginsburg Hallowell, 125 Newbury St, Boston, MA 02116. T. (617) 266-4606. 088651

The Golden Gallery, 206 Newbury St, Boston, MA 02116. T. (617) 247-8889. 088652

Great American Picture Company, 52 Wareham St., Boston, MA 02118. T. (617) 451-1529. 088653

The Great Hang Up, 530 E Broadway S, Boston, MA 02127. T. (617) 268-1139. 088654

Grohe, Dock Sq, North St, Boston, MA 02109. T. (617) 227-4885. - Glass – 088655

Guild of Boston Artists, 162 Newbury St, Boston, MA 02116. T. (617) 536-7660. - Paint / Graph / Sculp – 088656

Haley & Steele, 91 Newbury St, Boston, MA 02116. T. (617) 536-6339. - Graph – 088657

Hamill, 2164 Washington St, Boston, MA 02119. T. (617) 442-8204. - Graph / Eth – 088658

Harcus, 6 Melrose St, Boston, MA 02116. T. (617) 262-4445, Fax (617) 451-3221. - Paint / Graph / Sculp / Arch / Pho / Mul / Draw – 088659

Harris, Liz, 711 Atlantic Av, Boston, MA 02111. T. (617) 338-1315. 088660

Heinley, 347 Marlborough St, Boston, MA 02115. T. (617) 262-0070. 088661

Iguana, 246 Newbury St, Boston, MA 02116. T. (617) 247-0211. - Paint – 088662

Kane, 115 Newbury St, Boston, MA 02116. T. (617) 536-3611. - Paint / Graph / Fra / Draw – 088663

Kanegis, 244 Newbury St, Boston, MA 02116. T. (617) 267-6735. 088664

Kennedy, 167 Newbury St, Boston, MA 02116. T. (617) 267-6589. - Paint – 088665

Kennedy, 99 High St, Boston, MA 02112. T. (617) 482-1978. - Paint – 088666

Kennedy, 200 State St, Boston, MA 02109. T. (617) 345-9533. 088667

Kingston Gallery, 129 Kingston St, Boston, MA 02111. T. (617) 423-4113. - Paint – 088668

Krakow, Barbara, 10 Newbury St, Boston, MA 02116. T. (617) 262-4490. - Paint / Graph / Sculp / Draw – 088669

Lee, 119 Charles St, Boston, MA 02114. T. (617) 227-9810. - Pho – 088670

Lopoukhine., 198 Marlborough St, Boston, MA 02116. T. (617) 262-4211. - Paint / Graph – 088671

Magnuson, 286 Commonwealth Av, Boston, MA 02115. T. (617) 262-5252. - Graph / Pho / Draw – 088672

Maritime Heritage Prints, 23 Union Wharf, Boston, MA 02109. T. (617) 227-0112. - Graph – 088673

Marlborough Galleries, 165 Newbury St, Boston, MA 02116. T. (617) 267-8350. 088674

Marquit, Andrea, 207 Newbury St, Boston, MA 02116. T. (617) 859-0190. 088675

Mirski, Boris, 166 Newbury St, Boston, MA 02116. T. (617) 267-9186. - Paint – 088676

Morgan, 222 Newbury St, Boston, MA 02116. T. (617) 536-2686. - Paint / Graph – 088677

Mourlot, 119 Newbury St, Boston, MA 02116. T. (617) 536-1177, Fax (617) 536-5466. 088678

Mourlot, 119 Newbury St, Boston, MA 02116. T. (617) 536-1177, Fax (617) 536-5466. 088679

Museum Replica Gallery, 212 Newbury St, Boston, MA 02116. T. (617) 859-7654. - Repr – 088680

Newbury Fine Arts, 133 Newbury St, Boston, MA 02116. T. (617) 536-0210. 088681

Newman, 205 Newbury St, Boston, MA 02116. T. (617) 262-9083. 088682

Nielsen, 179 Newbury St, Boston, MA 02116. T. (617) 266-4835. - Paint / Graph / Draw – 088683

Office Art, 1022 Commonwealth Av, Boston, MA 02215. T. (617) 738-7662. - Graph – 088684

One Vision, 38 Chauncy St, Boston, MA 02111. T. (617) 451-8105. 088685

Panopticon Gallery, 187 Bay State Rd, Boston, MA 02115. T. (617) 267-2961. - Pho – 088686

Pavo Real Gallery, 200 State St, Boston, MA 02109. T. (617) 951-1477. 088687

Rolly-Michaux, 290 Dartmouth St, Boston, MA 02116. T. (617) 536-9898. - Paint / Graph / Sculp – 088688

Rotenburg, J., 130 Newbury St, Boston, MA 02116. T. (617) 437-1518. 088689

Segal, Thomas, 207 South St, Boston, MA 02111. T. (617) 292-0789. 088690

Segal, Thomas, 133 Federal St, Boston, MA 02110. T. (617) 266-3500. - Paint / Graph – 088691

Signature Gallery, Dock Sq, North St, Boston, MA 02109. T. (617) 227-4885. - China / Jew / Glass – 088692

Society of Arts and Crafts, 175 Newbury St, Boston, MA 02116. T. (617) 266-1810. 088693

Stanhope, 411 Marlborough St, Boston, MA 02115. T. (617) 262-0787. - Graph / Fra – 088694

Stobart, John, 113 Lewis Wharf, Boston, MA 02110. T. (617) 227-6868. - Paint / Graph – 088695

Stylis, 45 Newbury St, Boston, MA 02116. T. (617) 859-7062. 088696

Vose, 238 Newbury St, Boston, MA 02116. T. (617) 536-6176, Fax (617) 247-8673. - Paint – 088697

Walker, Alfred J., 158 Newbury St, Boston, MA 02116. T. (617) 247-1319. - Paint – 088698

Wenniger, 174A Newbury St, Boston, MA 02116. T. (617) 536-4688. - Graph – 088699

Wolov, Judith, 1 Design Center Pl, Boston, MA 02210. T. (617) 426-5511. 088700

Yezerski, Howard, 186 South St, Boston, MA 02111. T. (617) 426-8085. 088701

Zoe Gallery, 207 Newbury St, Boston, MA 02116. T. (617) 536-6800. - Paint / Sculp / Pho – 088702

Boulder (Colorado)

MacLaren/Markowitz, 2010 Tenth St., Boulder, CO 80302. T. (303) 449-6807. 088703

Bowie (Maryland)

Baraka, 15528 Annapolis Rd, Bowie, MD 20715. T. (301) 262-6660. - Paint / Graph / Fra – 088704

Bridgehampton (New York)

Benson, Elaine, Montauk Hwy., Bridgehampton POB AJ, NY 11932. T. (516) 537-3233. - Paint / Graph / Repr / Sculp – 088705

Sterling & Hunt, Butter Lane, Bridgehampton, NY 11932. T. (516) 537-1096. - Paint / Graph / Sculp – 088706

Brisbane (California)

Trillium Graphics, 91 Park Ln, Brisbane, CA 94005. T. (415) 468-8166. - Graph – 088707

Bronxville (New York)

Art for Institutions, 46 Elm Rock Rd, Bronxville, NY 10708. T. (800) 233-2636. - Paint – 088708

Bartlett, D. & J., 50 Prescott Av., Bronxville, NY 10708. T. (914) 901-4443. - Ant / Paint / Graph / Furn / Orient / China / Repr / Sculp / Jew / Pho / Mul / Draw – 088709

Prakapas, Eugene, N Gate 6B, Alger Court, Bronxville, NY 10708. T. (914) 961-5091, Fax (914) 961-5192. 088710

Village Art Gallery, 7 Pondfield Rd., Bronxville, NY 10708. T. (914) 337-7711. - Paint – 088711

Brookline (Massachusetts)

Alon, 1665A Beacon St., Brookline, MA 02146. T. (617) 232-3388. - Paint – 088712

Beth Urdang, 77 Pond Av., Brookline, MA 02146. T. (617) 731-1915. - Paint – 088713

Brooklyn (New York)

Avery, Sharon, 175 Bergen St., Brooklyn, NY 11217. T. (718) 237-1026. - Paint – 088714

New York Experimental Glass Workshop Gallery, 647 Fulton St., Brooklyn, NY 11217. T. (718) 625-3685, Fax (718) 625-3889. - Glass – 088715

Palm Gallery, 408 Atlantic Av., Brooklyn, NY 11217. T. (718) 624-7091. - Paint / Graph / Sculp – 088716

Summa Gallery, 152 Montague St., Brooklyn, NY 11201. T. (718) 875-1647. - Graph – 088717

Wiesner, 8812 Third Av., Brooklyn, NY 11209. T. (718) 748-1324. - Paint / Graph – 088718

Buffalo (New York)

Anderson, Martha Jackson Pl., Buffalo, NY 14214. T. (716) 834-2579. - Paint / Graph / Orient / China / Repr / Sculp / Tex / Eth / Fra / Mod / Pho / Mul / Draw – – 088719

Arcangelo, d', 1740 Main St., Buffalo, NY 14208. T. (716) 885-1146. - Paint / Repr / Sculp / Fra – 088720

Art Dialogue Gallery, 403 Delaware Av., Buffalo, NY 14202. T. (716) 842-0072. 088721

Brian Art Galleries, 717 Elmwood Av., Buffalo, NY 14222. T. (716) 883-7599. 088722

Buffalo Picture Frame & Mirror Corp., 150 Allen Street, Buffalo, NY 14201. T. (716) 886-7804. - Paint / Graph / Repr / Fra – 088723

CEPA Gallery, 700 Main St., 4 Fl., Buffalo, NY 14202. T. (716) 856-2717. 088724

Dana Galleries, 417 Franklin St., Buffalo, NY 14202. T. (716) 854-5285. - Paint / Fra – 088725

Freudenheim, Nina, 560 Franklin St., Buffalo, NY 14202. T. (716) 881-1555. - Paint / Graph / Sculp / Pho – 088726

Genesee Picture Frame Co., 424 Pearl St., Buffalo, NY 14202. T. (716) 854-6295. - Paint / Fra – 088727

Hallwass, 700 Main St., 4 Fl., Buffalo, NY 14202. T. (716) 854-5828. 088728

Hyatt's Gallery 912, 914 Main St., Buffalo, NY 14202. - Graph – 088729

More-Rubin, 36 Norwood Av., Buffalo, NY 14222. T. (716) 885-1636. 088730

Tillou, Dana E., 417 Franklin St., Buffalo, NY 14202. T. (716) 854-5285. - Paint – 088731

Burbank (California)

Hillside House of Originals, 2801 W. Olive Ave., Burbank, CA 91505. T. (213) 845-3531. - Paint / Sculp – 088732

Topaz Universal, 4632 W Magnolia Blvd., Burbank, CA 91505. T. (213) 766-8660. - Paint / Graph / Sculp – 088733

Burlingame (California)

Alma, Gilbert, 1419 Burlingame Av, Burlingame, CA 94010. T. (415) 348-7266. - Paint – 088734

The Gallery, 329 Primrose Rd, Burlingame, CA 94010. T. (415) 347-9392. 088735

Gallery 30, 311 Primrose Rd, Burlingame, CA 94010. T. (415) 342-3271. - Paint / Graph – 088736

Kerwin, 1107 California Dr, Burlingame, CA 94010. T. (415) 340-8400. - Graph – 088737

Burtonsville (Maryland)

Art Resource, 2916 Cabin Creek Dr, Burtonsville, MD 20866. T. (301) 989-9589. 088738

Cambridge (Massachusetts)

Hartje, 17 Monsignor O'Brien Hwy., Cambridge, MA 02141. T. (617) 723-1414. - Paint / Sculp - *088739*

Mobilia, 348 Huron Av., Cambridge, MA 02138. T. (617) 876-2109. - Paint / Furn / China / Sculp / Tex / Jew - *088740*

Ten Arrow, 10 Arrow St., Cambridge, MA 02138. T. (617) 876-1117. - Furn / China / Jew / Glass - *088741*

Wendell Street, 17 Wendell St., Cambridge, MA 02138. T. (617) 864-9294. - Paint / Graph / Sculp / Draw - *088742*

Carmel (California)

Beeches', San Carlos St. between Ocean and 7th, P. O. Box 4092, Carmel, CA 93921. T. (408) 624-1985. - Paint / Graph / Sculp - *088743*

Carmel Gallery, 26352 Carmel Rancho Lane, Carmel, CA 93923. T. (408) 625-4226. - Paint - *088744*

Dooley, San Carlos betw. 5th & 6th, P.O.Box 5577, Carmel, CA 93921. T. (408) 624-9330. - Paint - *088745*

Galerie de France, Ocean at Monte Verde, P. O. Box 3805, Carmel, CA 93921. T. (408) 624-4808. - Paint / Graph - *088746*

Garcia Gallery, 6th Ave. and Dolores St., P. O. Box 623, Carmel, CA 93921. T. (408) 624-8338. - Paint / Graph - *088747*

Hanson, Ocean & San Carlos, Carmel, CA 93921. T. (408) 625-3111, Fax (408) 625-0123. - Paint / Graph / Sculp - *088748*

Hunter, POB 221877, Carmel, CA 93922. T. (408) 625-4130. *088749*

Jacobs, San Carlos between 7th and Ocean Ave., POB 5906, Carmel, CA 93921. T. (408) 624-5955. - Paint / Graph - *088750*

Lim, Y. S., 9 Laurel Drive and 6th, POB 331, Carmel, CA 93924. T. (408) 659-4305. *088751*

Miner's Gallery Americana, Sixth Ave & Lincoln St., POB 6146, 93921 Carmel, CA 93921. T. (408) 624-5071. - Paint / Sculp - *088752*

Norman, Emile, Carmel POB 4268, CA 93921. T. (408) 624-1434. - Sculp - *088753*

Photography West Gallery, Dolores at Ocean Av., Carmel, CA 93921. T. (408) 625-1587. - Pho - *088754*

Saint-Galy, Sixth Av. & Dolores, Carmel, CA 93921. T. (408) 624-6552. *088755*

Simic, San Carlos & Sixth St., Carmel, CA 93921. T. (408) 624-7522. - Paint / Sculp - *088756*

Skaalegaard, Dolores at Fifth, Carmel POB 6611, CA 93921. T. (408) 624-5979. - Paint / Graph - *088757*

Tudor, POB 5454, Carmel, CA 93921. T. (408) 624-6055. *088758*

Walter & White, Seventh & San Carlos, Carmel, CA 93921. T. (408) 624-4957. - Paint / Glass - *088759*

Weston, Sixth Av., Carmel, CA 93921. T. (408) 624-4453, Fax (408) 624-7190. - Pho - *088760*

Zantman, Sixth Av., Carmel, CA 93921. T. (408) 624-8314, 344-9359, Fax (408) 626-8408. - Paint - *088761*

Cedar Key (Florida)

Gallery at Cedar Key, Main St., Box 234, Cedar Key, FL 32625. T. (904) 543-5502. - Paint - *088762*

Suwannee Triangle Gallery, On the Dock, Cedar Key, FL 32625. T. (904) 543-5744. - Paint - *088763*

Cedarhurst (New York)

Daruma Custom Framing & Gallery, 554 Central Av., Cedarhurst, NY 11516. T. (212) 569-5221. *088764*

Loring, 661 Central Av., Cedarhurst, NY 11516. T. (212) 295-1919. - Paint / Graph / Sculp - *088765*

Charleston (South Carolina)

Fouche Art Gallery & Studio, Virginia Fouche Bolton, 127 Meeting St., Charleston, SC 29401. *088766*

Goin Gallery, Jan, 309 King St., Charleston, SC 29401. *088767*

Huguley, John, 269 King St., Charleston, SC 29401. *088768*

Charlottesville (Virginia)

Victorius, Paul B., 1413 University Av., Charlottesville, VA 22903. T. (804) 296-3456. - Paint / Graph / Repr / Fra - *088769*

Chautauqua (New York)

Chautauqua Art Association, Chautauqua Institution, POB 1365, Chautauqua, NY 14722. T. (716) 357-2771. *088770*

Chestnut Hill (Massachusetts)

Quadrum Gallery, The Mall, Chestnut Hill, MA 02167. T. (617) 965-5555. - Jew - *088771*

Chicago (Illinois)

AAPCO, 5137 N Saint Louis Av, Chicago, IL 60625. T. (312) 583-5066. - Graph - *088773*

Aaron, 620 N Michigan Av, Chicago, IL 60611. T. (312) 943-0660. - Ant / Paint / Graph / China / Sculp / Fra - *088774*

Adam, Alice, Chicago POB 11616, IL 60611. T. (312) 787-7295, Fax (312) 787-6083. - Paint / Graph / Draw - *088775*

Arader, W. Graham, 620 N Michigan Av, Chicago, IL 60611. T. (312) 337-6033. - Graph - *088776*

Armbruster, 1316 W Fargo Av, Chicago, IL 60626. T. (312) 743-7644. - Paint - *088777*

Armstrong, Richard R., 1446 N Dearborn Pkwy, Chicago, IL 60610. T. (312) 664-9312. - Graph / Draw - *088778*

Art Appeal, 5445 N Kenmore Av, Chicago, IL 60640. T. (312) 907-0372. - Paint - *088779*

Art Exchange, 3010 W 111 St, Chicago, IL 60655. T. (312) 779-4260. - Repr / Fra - *088780*

Art Gallery Oves, 5903 S Wentworth Av, Chicago, IL 60621. T. (312) 363-2238. - Graph / Sculp - *088781*

Baruch, Jacques, 40 E Delaware Pl, Chicago, IL 60611. T. (312) 944-3377. - Paint / Graph / Tex / Pho - *088782*

Beacon Street Gallery, 4520 N Beacon St, Chicago, IL 60640. T. (312) 784-2310. - Paint - *088783*

Brandywine Fantasy Gallery, 750 N Orleans St, Chicago, IL 60610. T. (312) 951-8466. - Paint - *088784*

Burger, W.T., Merchandise Mart Plaza, Chicago, IL 60654. T. (312) 527-1653. *088785*

Callard, 100 E Walton St, Chicago, IL 60611. T. (312) 337-4320. - Paint - *088786*

Campanile Galleries, 200 S Michigan Av, Chicago, IL 60604. T. (312) 663-3885, Fax (312) 663-3856. - Paint - *088787*

Center for Contemporary Art, 325 W Huron St, Chicago, IL 60610. T. (312) 944-0094. - Paint / Graph - *088788*

Centurion Galleries, 540 N Michigan Av, Chicago, IL 60611. T. (312) 661-0220. - Paint / Graph - *088789*

Chicago Center for the Print, 1509 W Fullerton Av, Chicago, IL 60614. T. (312) 477-1585. - Graph - *088790*

Cicero, Jan, 221 W Erie, Chicago, IL 60610. T. (312) 440-1904. - Paint / Graph / Sculp / Draw - *088791*

Circle Gallery, 540 N Michigan Av, Chicago, IL 60611. T. (312) 670-4304. - Graph / Sculp - *088792*

Contemporary Art Workshop, 542 W Grant Pl, Chicago, IL 60614. T. (312) 472-4004. - Paint / Graph / Sculp / Jew / Draw - *088793*

Cortland-Leyten, 213 N Morgan St, Chicago, IL 60607. T. (312) 733-2781. - Paint / Graph - *088794*

Creative Picture Framing, 75 E Van Buren St, Chicago, IL 60605. T. (312) 939-2071. - Graph / Fra - *088795*

Deson, Marianne, 900 N Lake Shore Dr, Chicago, IL 60611. T. (312) 266-1461. - Paint / Graph - *088796*

Diversity Fine Arts, 1010 W Diversity Pkwy, Chicago, IL 60614. T. (312) 871-3299. - Graph - *088797*

East West Contemporary Art, 311 W Superior St, Chicago, IL 60610. T. (312) 664-8003. - Paint / Graph - *088798*

Fairweather-Hardin, 101 E Ontario St, Chicago, IL 60611. T. (312) 642-0007. - Paint / Graph / Sculp / Draw - *088799*

Feigen, 325 W Huron St, Chicago, IL 60610. T. (312) 787-0500, Fax (312) 787-7261. - Ant / Paint - *088800*

Findlay, Wally, 814 N Michigan Av, Chicago, Il 60611. T. (312) 649-1500. - Paint - *088801*

Fly-by-Nite, 714 N Wells St, Chicago, IL 60610. T. (312) 664-08136. - Paint / Graph / China / Sculp / Cur / Mod - *088802*

Fraser, 209 W Goethe St, Chicago, IL 60610. T. (312) 337-0449. *088803*

From Above Gallery, 1528 W Monroe St, Chicago, IL 60607. T. (312) 733-7266. - Paint / Graph - *088804*

Gallerie Stephanie, 2123 N Clark St, Chicago, IL 60614. T. (312) 880-0995. *088805*

Gilman-Gruen, 226 W Superior St, Chicago, IL 60610. T. (312) 337-6262. - Paint / Sculp - *088806*

Goldman Kraft, 300 W Superior St, Chicago, IL 60610. T. (312) 943-9088. - Paint - *088807*

Gray, Richard, 620 N Michigan Av, Chicago, IL 60611. T. (312) 642-8877. - Paint / Graph / Sculp - *088808*

Hammer, Carl, 200 W Superior St, Chicago, IL 60610. T. (312) 266-8512. - Paint / Graph / Sculp - *088809*

Hoffman, Rhona, 215 W Superior St, Chicago, IL 60610. T. (312) 951-8828. - Paint / Sculp - *088810*

Hokin-Kaufman, 210 W Superior St, Chicago, IL 60610. T. (312) 266-1211. - Paint / Furn / Sculp / Draw - *088811*

Holland, B.C., 222 W Superior St, Chicago, IL 60610. T. (312) 664-5000. - Paint / Furn - *088812*

Horwich, Joy, 226 E Ontario St, Chicago, IL 60611. T. (312) 787-0171. - Paint / Sculp / Tex - *088813*

Houk, E., 200 W Superior St, Chicago, IL 60610. T. (312) 943-0698. - Pho - *088814*

Hyde Park Art Center, 1701 E 53 St, Chicago, IL 60615. T. (312) 324-5520. - Paint - *088815*

Jayson, 1915 N Clybourn Av, Chicago, IL 60614. T. (312) 278-9675. - Paint / Graph / Fra - *088816*

Johnson, R.S., 645 N Michigan Av, Chicago, IL 60611. T. (312) 943-1661. - Paint / Graph / Sculp / Draw - *088817*

Karkazis, R., 168 N Michigan Av, Ste 300, Chicago, IL 60601. T. (312) 346-5050. - Paint - *088818*

Kass Meridian, 215 W Superior St, Chicago, IL 60610. T. (312) 266-5999, Fax (312) 266-5931. - Paint / Graph - *088819*

Kenyon Douglas, 1357 N Wells St, Chicago, IL 60610. T. (312) 642-5300. - Repr - *088820*

Kind, Phyllis, 313 W Superior St, Chicago, IL 60611. T. (312) 642-6302. - Paint / Eth / Mod / Draw - *088821*

Klein, 400 N Morgan St, Chicago, IL 60622. T. (312) 243-0400. - Paint / Sculp - *088822*

Koehler, 175 N Franklin St, Chicago, IL 60606. T. (312) 332-7185. - Graph - *088823*

Lake Street Gallery, 660 W Lake St, Chicago, IL 60606. T. (312) 466-0664. - Paint / Graph - *088824*

Levinson, 5210 S Harper St, Chicago, IL 60615. T. (312) 288-0778. - Paint / Graph - *088825*

Lockett, R., 703 N Wells St, Chicago, IL 60610. T. (312) 649-1230. - Paint - *088826*

Love, R.H., 40 E Erie St, Chicago, IL 60611. T. (800) 437-7568. *088826a*

M K Galleries, 300 W Superior St, Chicago, IL 60610. I. (312) 944-8044. - Paint / Graph - *088827*

Mars Gallery, 1139 W Fulton St, Chicago, IL 60607. T. (312) 226-7808. - Paint - *088828*

Merrill Chase, 835 N Michigan Av, Chicago, IL 60611. T. (312) 337-6600. *088829*

Miller, Peter, 401 W Superior St, Chicago, IL 60610. T. (312) 951-0252. - Paint - *088830*

Mongerson-Wunderlich, 704 N Wells St, Chicago, IL 60610. T. (312) 943-2354. - Paint / Graph - *088831*

Name Gallery, 700 N Carpenter St, Chicago, IL 6062210. T. (312) 226-0671. - Paint - *088832*

Needlman, Phyllis, 1515 N Astor, Chicago, IL 60610. T. (312) 642-7929. - Paint / Graph / Sculp / Draw - *088833*

Neville-Sargent, 708 N Wells St, Chicago, IL 60610. T. (312) 664-2787. - Paint / Sculp - *088834*

Objects Gallery, 230 W Huron St, Chicago, IL 60610. T. (312) 664-6622. - Paint - *088835*

Okee-Chee's Wild Horse Gallery, 5337 N Clark St, Chicago, IL 60640. T. (312) 271-5882. - Eth - *088836*

Perimeter Gallery, 750 N Orleans, Chicago, IL 60610. T. (312) 266-9473. - Paint / Sculp / Draw - *088837*

Phase II Gallery, 2739 W Devon Av, Chicago, IL 60659. T. (312) 973-2544. - Paint - *088838*

Poster Plus, 2906 N Broadway, Chicago, IL 60657. T. (312) 549-2822. - Graph - *088839*

Prince Gallery, 357 W Erie St, Chicago, IL 60610. T. (312) 266-9663. - Paint - *088840*

Prints Unlimited, 28 N Wabash Av, Chicago, IL 60602. T. (312) 372-8988. - Paint / Graph / Fra - *088841*

Printworks, 311 W Superior St, Ste 105, Chicago, IL 60610. T. (312) 664-9407. - Graph / Pho / Draw - *088842*

Probst, 620 N Michigan Av, Chicago, IL 60611. T. (312) 440-1991. - Paint - 088843
Ramsay, Roger, 212 W Superior St., Ste. 503, Chicago, IL 60610. T. (312) 337-4678. - Paint / Graph / Sculp / Cur / Pho / Mul / Draw - 088844
Randolph Street Gallery, 756 N Milwaukee Av, Chicago, IL 60622. T. (312) 666-7737. - Paint - 088845
Rizzoli, 835 N Michigan Av, Chicago, IL 60611. T. (312) 642-3500. - Graph / Furn / Pho / Draw - 088846
Rosenfield, Betsy, 212 W Superior St, Chicago, IL 60610. T. (312) 787-8020. - Paint / Sculp / Pho / Draw - 088847
Rosenthal, J., 230 W Superior St, Chicago, IL 60610. T. (312) 642-2966. - Paint - 088848
Rowe, 1925 N Clybourn Av, Chicago, IL 60614. T. (312) 871-7557, Fax (312) 871-1238. - Paint / Graph / Sculp / Draw - 088849
Royal Art Gallery, 750 N Orleans St, Chicago, IL 60610. T. (312) 944-9566. - Paint - 088850
Sazama, 300 W Superior St, Chicago, IL 60610. T. (312) 951-0004. - Paint - 088851
Second Power Art Gallery, 2055 W North Av, Chicago, IL 60647. T. (312) 227-0044. - Paint - 088852
Somogyi & Co., John P., 3045 N Clark St, Chicago, IL 60657. T. (312) 248-5744. - Paint / Graph / Fra / Pho - 088853
Space 900, 900 N Franklin Sq, Chicago, IL 60610. T. (312) 944-6844. - Paint - 088854
Stein-Bartlow, 620 N Michigan Av, Chicago, IL 60611. T. (312) 337-1782. 088855
Sternberg, Maurice, 919 N Michigan Av, Chicago, IL 60611. T. (312) 642-1700. - Paint - 088856
Struve, 309 W Superior St, Chicago, IL 60610. T. (312) 787-0563. - Paint / Sculp / Draw - 088857
Ten in One Gallery, 121 E Ontario St, Chicago, IL 60611. T. (312) 850-4610. 088858
Van Straaten, 742 N Wells St, Chicago, IL 60610. T. (312) 642-2900. - Paint / Graph / Draw - 088859
Visual Graphics, 7907 S Champlain Av, Chicago, IL 60619. T. (312) 651-0072. - Graph - 088860
Volid, Ruth, 431 W Oakdale Av, Chicago, IL 60657. T. (312) 644-3180. - Paint - 088861
Walton Street Gallery, 58 E Walton St, Chicago, IL 60611. T. (312) 943-1793. 088862
Worthington, 620 N Michigan Av, Chicago, IL 60611. T. (312) 266-2424. - Paint - 088863
Zaks, 620 N Michigan Av, Chicago, IL 60611. T. (312) 943-8440. - Paint / Sculp / Draw - 088864
Zolla-Liebermann, 325 W Huron St, Chicago, IL 60610. T. (312) 944-1990. - Paint / Sculp - 088865

Cincinnati (Ohio)

Birckhead, Toni, 342 W Forth St., Cincinnati, OH 45202. T. (513) 241-0212. 088866
Blackschlaeger, Julius, 7740 Laurel Ave, Cincinnati, OH 45216. T. (513) 271-2788. - Paint / Graph / Fra - 088867
Circle Gallery, 177 Lafayette Circle, Cincinnati, OH 45220. T. (513) 221-6858. - Graph / Sculp - 088868
Closson's, 401 Race St., Cincinnati, OH 45202. T. (513) 762-5500. - Paint / Graph / Fra - 088869
Midwestern Galleries, Cincinnati POB 43088, OH 45243. T. (513) 561-2220. 088870
Miller, 2715 Erie Av., Cincinnati, OH 45208. T. (513) 871-4420. - Paint / Graph / China / Sculp / Eth / Jew / Fra / Glass / Pho / Draw - 088871
Paul, Elizabeth, 1854 Keys Crescent, Cincinnati, OH 45206. T. (513) 751-4944. 088872
Paul, Laura, 49 E Forth St., Suite 109, Cincinnati, OH 45202. T. (513) 651-5885. - Paint / Graph / Sculp / Jew / Pho - 088873
Peterson, Greta, 7696 Camargo Rd., Madeira, Cincinnati, OH 45243. T. (513) 561-6785. 088874
Solway, Carl, 314 W Fourth St., Cincinnati, OH 45202. T. (513) 621-0069, Fax (513) 621-6310. - Paint / Graph / Sculp - 088875
Suder's Art, 1309 Vine St., Cincinnati, OH 45210. T. (513) 241-0800. - Paint / Graph / Fra - 088876
Weiner, Patricia, 9352 Main St Olde Montgomery, Cincinnati, OH 45242. T. (513) 791-7717. 088877

Clayton (Missouri)

Circle Gallery, 8113 Maryland Av., Clayton, MO 63105. T. (314) 863-3373. - Paint - 088878

Cleveland (Ohio)

Bonfoey, 1710 Euclid Av., Cleveland, OH 44115. T. (216) 621-0178. 088879
Brett Mitchell Collection, 28500 Chagrin Blvd., Cleveland, OH 44122. T. (216) 831-8666. - Paint / Sculp - 088880
Fay's Art Gallery, 2869 Drummond, Cleveland, OH 44120. T. (216) 751-2706. - Paint - 088881
Feldman, Arthur, 488 The Arcade, Cleveland, OH 44114. T. (216) 861-3580. - Graph - 088882
Gabos Art Center, 2184 Warrensville Center, Cleveland, OH 44118. - Ant / Paint / Graph - 088883
Giorgi, 12720 Triskett Rd., Cleveland, OH 44111. T. (216) 251-0580. 088884
Gregorie Gallerie, 3479 Fairmouth Blvd. Cleveland Heights, Cleveland, OH 44118. T. (216) 321-4200. - Paint / Graph / Fra - 088885
Kubitz, Nelson A., 14412 Northfield Ave., Cleveland, OH 44100. 088886
Lakewood Gallery, 15500 Edgewater Dr., Cleveland, OH 44107. T. (216) 221-2222. - Paint / Graph / Fra - 088887
Linden-Kicklighter, 13010 Woodland Ave, Cleveland, OH 44120. T. (216) 791-6450. - Paint / Graph / Sculp / Fra - 088888
Pollack Studio, 14421 Cedar St., Cleveland, OH 44121. 088889
Sender, 3482 Lee St., Cleveland, OH 44120. 088890
Tregoning, Cleveland POB 20450, OH 44120. T. (216) 921-2028. 088891
Ullman, Sylvia, 13010 Woodland, Cleveland, OH 44120. 088892

Cleveland Heights (Ohio)

Vixseboxse Art Galleries, 12413 Cedar Rd., Cleveland Heights, OH 44106. T. (216) 791-2727. - Paint / Graph / Fra - 088893

Coconut Grove (Florida)

Expressions Art Gallery, 3263 Commodore Plaza, Coconut Grove, FL 33133. T. (305) 443-5719. - Paint / Sculp - 088894
Gallery One, 3109 Grand Av., Coconut Grove, FL 33133. T. (305) 442-1200. - Paint - 088895
Getz, Carol, 2843 S Bayshore Dr., Coconut Grove, FL 32133. T. (305) 446-5994. - Paint / Sculp - 088896

Coeur d'Alene (Idaho)

Drummond Gallery, The Coeur d'Alene Resort, Suite A, Coeur d'Alene, ID 83814. T. (208) 667-7732, Fax (208) 664-2091. 088897

Colorado Springs (Colorado)

Eagles Roost Gallery, 2803 N Prospect, Colorado Springs, CO 80907. T. (303) 473-8542. - Paint / Graph / Sculp - 088898
Hibbitt, 720 N Nevada Av., Colorado Springs, CO 80902. T. (303) 473-0464. - Paint / Sculp - 088899

Columbia (Missouri)

Harco Gallery, POB 1857, Columbia, MO 65205. T. (314) 443-1161. - Graph - 088900
Vincent, Arthur, 3301 Parker, Columbia, MO 65202. T. (314) 474-9908. - Paint - 088901

Columbia (South Carolina)

Hall Galleries, Charlton F.Jr., 930 Gervais St., Columbia, SC 29201. T. (803) 779-5678. 088902
House of Frames and Paintings, 2828 Devine St., Columbia, SC 29205. T. (803) 799-7405. - Paint / Fra - 088903
Pinckney Simons, 1127 Gregg St., Columbia, SC 29201. T. (803) 771-8815. 088904
Portfolio Gallery, 2007 Devine St., Columbia, SC 29205. T. (803) 256-2434. - Paint / Sculp - 088905

Columbus (Ohio)

Cultural Arts Center, 139 W Main St., Columbus, OH 43215. T. (614) 222-7047. 088906
Foley, Charles, 973 E Broad St., Columbus, OH 43205. T. (614) 253-7921. - Paint / Graph / Sculp - 088907
Gallery 200, 200 W Mound St., Columbus, OH 43215. T. (614) 224-1259. - Paint / Sculp - 088908
Kroos, Brenda, 63 Parsons Av., Columbus, OH 43215. T. (614) 221-3636. 088909
North, Paul H. Jr., 81 Bullitt Park Pl., Columbus, OH 43209. - Paint / Graph - 088910
Paul, Laura, 193 E Whittier St., Columbus, OH 43206. T. (614) 444-8808. - Paint / Graph / Sculp / Jew / Pho - 088911

Coral Gables (Florida)

Ambrosino, 3155 Ponce de Leon Boulevard, Coral Gables, FL 33134. T. (305) 4452211, Fax (305) 4440101. 088912
Elite Fine Arts, 3140 Ponce de Leon Blvd, Coral Gables, FL 33134. T. (305) 448-3800, Fax (305) 448-8147. 088913
Greene, 4200 Aurora St. Suite A, Coral Gables, FL 33146. T. (305) 448-9229. 088914
Miller, Virginia, 169 Madeira Av., Coral Gables, FL 33134. T. (305) 444-4493. - Paint / Graph / Sculp / Pho / Mul / Draw - 088915
Opus Art Studios, 1810 Ponce de Leon Blvd., Coral Gables, FL 33134. T. (305) 448-8976. - Paint / Graph / Sculp - 088916

Dallas (Texas)

Adelle, M., 3317 McKinney Av., Dallas, TX 75204. T. (214) 526-0800. - Paint / Sculp - 088917
Afterimage Photography Gallery, 250 Quadrangle, Dallas, TX 75201. - Pho - 088918
Art Center Studio and Galleries, 2408-16 McKinney Av., Dallas, TX 75201. T. (214) 747-4515. - Paint / Graph / Sculp - 088919
Bryan, Phil J., Trade Mart, Dallas, TX 75200. 088920
Conduit Gallery, 2814 Elm St., Dallas, TX 75226. T. (214) 939-0064. - Paint / Sculp - 088921
Contemporary Gallery, 4152 Shady Bend Dr., Dallas, TX 75244. T. (214) 247-5246. 088922
Florence Art Gallery, 2500 Cedar Springs, Dallas, TX 75201. T. (214) 748-6463. 088923
Fogelson, Gayle D., 300 Crescent Court, Ste. 920, Dallas, TX 75201. T. (214) 747-4588. 088924
Frame House, 2723 Routh St., Dallas, TX 75201. T. (214) 747-3189. - Fra - 088925
Gallerie International, 1170 Valley View Center, Dallas, TX 75240. T. (214) 661-8778. 088926
Hall, 2200 Cedar Springs, Ste. 212, Dallas, TX 75201. T. (214) 871-0078. 088927
Jackson, 3540 Wentwood Dr., Dallas, TX 75225. T. (214) 363-1543. - Paint / Sculp - 088928
Kahn, Ralph H., 4152 Sahdy Bend, Dallas, TX 75244. 088929
Modern Realism, 1903 McMilan Av., Rm. 1, Dallas, TX 75206. T. (214) 827-0376. 088930
Neuhoff, Donna, 2502 Cedar Springs, Dallas, TX 75201. T. (214) 871-1620. - Paint - 088931
Phillips Galleries, 2517 Fairmount St., Dallas, TX 75201. T. (214) 748-7888. - Paint - 088932
Sartor, Joseph, 4510 McKinney Av., Dallas, TX 75205. T. (214) 526-7148. - Paint - 088933
Sheraton Gallery, 400 N Olive, Dallas, TX 75201. T. (214) 922-0380. - Paint / Sculp - 088934
Southwest Gallery, 737 Preston Forest, Dallas, TX 75230. T. (214) 696-0182. - Paint / Graph / Furn / Sculp - 088935
Texas Art Gallery, 1400 Main St., Dallas, TX 75202. T. (214) 747-8158. - Paint / Repr / Fra - 088936
Valley House., 6616 Spring Valley Rd., Dallas, TX 75240. T. (214) 239-2441. - Paint / Sculp - 088937
Whistler, Barry, 2909A Canton St., Dallas, TX 75226. T. (214) 939-0242. - Paint / Graph / Sculp / Pho / Draw - 088938
Wind River Gallery, 6102 Lakehurst Av., Dallas, TX 75230. 088939
Wiseman, Ruth, 3536 Hanover Av., Dallas, TX 75225. 088940
500x Gallery, 500 Exposition Av., Dallas, TX 75226. T. (214) 828-1111. - Paint / Sculp - 088941

De Land (Florida)

Empire of America, 345 N Woodland Blvd., De Land, FL 32720. T. (904) 734-2551. 088942

Denver (Colorado)

Alpha Gallery, 959 Broadway, Denver, CO 80203.
T. (303) 623-3577. - Paint / Sculp -   *088943*

Artcraft, 383 Corona St., Denver, CO 80218.
T. (303) 722-1761. - Graph / Fra -   *088944*

Artyard, 1251 S Pearl St., Denver, CO 80210.
T. (303) 777-3219. - Sculp -   *088945*

Belding, Kyle, 1110 17 St., Denver, CO 80202.
T. (303) 825-2555.   *088946*

Bisenius, Sullivan, 3145 Larimer St., Denver, CO 80205.
T. (303) 296-9838.   *088947*

Brena, 313 Detroit St., Denver, CO 80206. T. (303) 388-0032. - Paint / Graph / Sculp -   *088948*

Camera Obscura Gallery, 1309 Bannock St., Denver, CO 80204. T. (303) 623-4059.   *088949*

Cherry Creek Gallery of Fine Art, 221 Detroit St., Denver, CO 80206. T. (303) 377-8706.   *088950*

Cohen, 108 W Byers Pl., Denver, CO 80223.
T. (303) 778-6427.   *088951*

Driscol, 555 17 St., Denver, CO 80202. T. (303) 292-5520. - Sculp -   *088952*

Gallery One Art Second Avenue, 2940 E Second Av., Denver, CO 80206. T. (303) 393-0460. - Paint / Graph / Sculp -   *088953*

Gallery 609, 609 E Speer Blvd., Denver, CO 80203.
T. (303) 733-3432. - Paint -   *088954*

Payton, Cydney, 2544 15 St., Denver, CO 80211.
T. (303) 458-6006.   *088955*

Pirate, 3659 Navajo, Denver, CO 80211. T. (303) 458-6058. - Paint / Sculp -   *088956*

Rein, C.G., 601 S Broadwy, Suite X, Denver, CO 80209.
T. (303) 744-6766. - Paint / Graph / Sculp -   *088957*

Reiss, 429 Acoma St., Denver, CO 80204. T. (303) 778-6924. - Graph / Sculp -   *088958*

Robey, Joan, 939 Broadway, Denver, CO 80203.
T. (303) 892-9600.   *088959*

Robischon, 1122 E 17 Av., Denver, CO 80218.
T. (303) 832-8899. - Paint -   *088960*

Rosenstock, Fred A., 1228 E Colfax Av., Denver, CO 80218. T. (303) 832-7190. - Paint -   *088961*

Saks, 3019 E Second Av., Denver, CO 80206.
T. (303) 333-4144. - Paint / Sculp -   *088962*

Sarkisian, H. Medill, 693 E. Speer Blvd., Denver, CO 80203. T. (303) 733-2623. - Paint / Sculp -   *088963*

Schluger, Brigitte, 929 Broadway, Denver, CO 80203.
T. (303) 320-0469. - Graph / Sculp -   *088964*

Sloane Gallery, Oxford Office Building 1612 17 St, Denver, CO 80202. T. (303) 595-4230.   *088965*

Spark, 3300 Osage, Denver, CO 80211. T. (303) 477-6782.   *088966*

Taos Connections, 162 Adams St., Denver, CO 80206.
T. (303) 393-8267. - Paint -   *088967*

Turner, 300 University Blvd., Denver, CO 80206.
T. (303) 355-1205. - Paint -   *088968*

Des Moines (Iowa)

Fernette's Gallery, Valley West Mall, Des Moines, IA 50265. T. (515) 224-9166. - Graph / Sculp -   *088969*

Olson/Larsen, 203 Fifth St., Des Moines, IA 50265.
T. (515) 277-6734. - Paint -   *088970*

Detroit (Michigan)

Arts Extended Gallery, 1553 Woodward, Suite 201, Detroit, MI 48226. T. (313) 961-5036. - Paint -   *088971*

Detroit Artists Market, 1452 Randolph St., Detroit, MI 48226. T. (313) 962-0337. - Paint / Graph / Sculp / Arch -   *088972*

Detroit Gallery of Contemp. Crafts, 301 Fisher Bldg., Detroit, MI 48202.   *088973*

Du Mouchelle, E., 409 E Jefferson Av., Detroit, MI 48226. T. (313) 963-6255. - Ant / Paint / Furn / Orient / China / Sculp / Tex / Silv / Glass / Ico -   *088974*

London Arts, 321 Fisher Bldg., Detroit, MI 48202.
T. (313) 871-2411. - Paint / Graph / Mod / Draw -   *088975*

Duncans Mills (California)

Queen, Christopher, POB 28, Duncans Mills, CA 95430.
T. (707) 865-1318.   *088976*

East Hampton (New York)

Gallery East, 257 Pantigo Rd., East Hampton, NY 11937.
T. (516) 324-9393.   *088977*

East Lansing (Michigan)

Saper, 433 Albert Av., East Lansing, MI 48823.
T. (517) 351-0815. - Paint / Graph / Sculp / Fra / Mod / Mul / Draw -   *088978*

Edina (Minnesota)

Michael, J., 3916 W 50 St., Edina, MN 55424.
T. (612) 920-6070. - Paint / Graph / Sculp / Tex -   *088979*

Rein, C.G., 3646 W 70 St., Edina, MN 55435.
T. (612) 927-4331. - Paint -   *088980*

Edmonds (Washington)

Firdale Village Gallery + Custom Framing, 9675 Firdale Ave., Edmonds, WA 98020. T. (206) 524-3007.
- Paint / Graph / Sculp / Fra -   *088981*

El Paso (Texas)

Art Center, 3019 E. Yandell Dr., El Paso, TX 79903.
T. (915) 566-2410. - Paint / Graph / Fra -   *088982*

Barrett, 2717 N Stanton, El Paso, TX 79902.
T. (915) 545-1415. - Paint / Graph / Draw -   *088983*

Margo, Adair, 415 E Yandell, Suite 10-B, El Paso, TX 79902. T. (915) 533-0048. - Paint / Graph / Sculp / Draw -   *088984*

Emeryville (California)

Osceola Vintage and Contemporary Art and Museum Quality Framing Gallery, 4053 Harian St, Emeryville, 94608. T. (510) 658-2435. - Paint / Fra -   *088985*

The Zentner Collection, 5757 Landregan St, Emeryville, CA 94608. T. (510) 653-5181, Fax (510) 653-0275.   *088986*

Encino (California)

Spring Source, 16610 Ventura Blvd, Encino, CA 91436.
T. (818) 788-5349.   *088987*

Stern, George, 17071 Ventura Blvd, Ste 106A, Encino, CA 91316. T. (818) 906-1882. - Paint / Graph -   *088988*

Englewood (New Jersey)

Print Loft, 28 N Dean St., Englewood, NJ 07631.
T. (201) 871-3661. - Paint / Repr -   *088989*

Richards, J., 64 E Palisade Av., Englewood, NJ 07631.
T. (201) 871-1050. - Paint / Graph / Sculp -   *088990*

Seraphim, 32-40 N Dean St., Englewood, NJ 07631.
T. (201) 568-4432. - Paint / Sculp -   *088991*

Spiegel, Jewel, 30 N Dean St., Englewood, NJ 07631.
T. (201) 871-3577. - Paint / Fra -   *088992*

Escondido (California)

Frazee's, 615 N. Escondido Blvd , Escondido, CA 92025.
T. (714) 745-1234. - Paint / Graph / Fra -   *088993*

Lawrence, Martin, 200 E Via Rancho Pkwy., Escondido, CA 92025. T. (714) 489-7011. - Paint / Graph -   *088994*

Evanston (Illinois)

Four Arts, 1629 Oak Av., Evanston, IL 60201.
T. (312) 328-8834. - Fra / Mod / Draw -   *088995*

Grove Street Galleries, 919 Grove St., Evanston, IL 60201. T. (312) 866-7340. - Paint -   *088996*

Mindscape Gallery, 1521 Sherman Av., Evanston, IL 60201. T. (312) 864-2660. - China / Sculp / Glass -   *088997*

Fairfax (Virginia)

Heisman, 8300 Arlington Blv, Fairfax, VA 22031.
T. (703) 641-8556.   *088998*

Us Too Studio, 10364 Main St, Fairfax, VA 22031.
T. (703) 591-5323.   *088999*

Falls Church (Virginia)

Americana Antique and Art Gallery, Patrick Henry Drive and Leesburg Pike, Falls Church, VA 22044.
T. (703) 532-8477.   *089000*

Flemington (New Jersey)

Flemington Gallery of the Arts, 150 Main St., Flemington, NJ 08822. T. (201) 782-0555. - Paint -   *089001*

Fort Lauderdale (Florida)

Carone, 600 Second Court, Fort Lauderdale, FL 33301.
T. (305) 463-8833. - Paint / Graph / Sculp / Fra -   *089002*

DeLigny, 709 E Las Olas Blvd., Fort Lauderdale, FL 33301. T. (305) 467-9303. - Paint / Sculp -   *089003*

Embrose Art, 5095 NE 12th Ave, Fort Lauderdale, FL 33300. T. (305) 772-1386. - Paint / Graph / Sculp -   *089004*

Fort Worth (Texas)

Berger, Marie, 4912 Camp Bowie, Fort Worth, TX 76107.
T. (817) 737-6062. - Graph -   *089005*

Campbell, William, 4935 Byers, Fort Worth, TX 76107.
T. (817) 737-9566. - Paint -   *089006*

Carlin, 710 Montgomery St., Fort Worth, TX 76107.
T. (817) 738-6921. - Paint / Graph / Sculp -   *089007*

Dow Frame Shop, 3330 Camp Bowie Blvd., Fort Worth, TX 76107. - Paint / Fra -   *089008*

Fenton, 1420 Shady Oaks Ln., Fort Worth, TX 76107.
T. (817) 429-0161. - Paint / Graph / Sculp / Pho / Draw -   *089009*

Fort Worth Gallery, 901 Boland St., Fort Worth, TX 76107. T. (817) 332-5603. - Paint / Sculp / Eth -   *089010*

Gallery in the Square, 1510 W. Tenth St., Fort Worth, TX 76116. T. (817) 332-5332. - Paint / Graph / Sculp -   *089011*

Jones-Blair, 4119 Camp Bowie Blvd., Fort Worth, TX 76107. T. (817) 732-3423. - Paint / Fra -   *089012*

Pierce, Jan, Fort Worth POB 331748, TX 76163.
T. (817) 292-3498. - Paint / Graph / Sculp / Draw -   *089013*

Siegel, Evelyn, 3612 W Seventh St., Fort Worth, TX 76107. T. (817) 731-6412. - Orient / Arch / Eth -   *089014*

Frankfort (Kentucky)

Capital Gallery of Contemporary Art, 314 Lewis St., Frankfort, KY 40601. T. (502) 223-2649. - Paint / Sculp / Draw -   *089015*

Fresh Meadows (New York)

Frame Art, 185-17 Union Turnpike, Fresh Meadows, NY 11366. T. (212) 454-1630. - Ant / Paint / Graph / Orient / China / Repr / Sculp / Tex / Dec / Fra / Silv / Lights / Glass / Cur / Mod / Pho / Mul / Draw -   *089016*

Fullerton (California)

Gallery 57, 204 N Harbor Blvd., Fullerton, CA 92632.
T. (714) 870-9194.   *089017*

Morico, A. M., 1072 Arroyo Dr., Fullerton, CA 92633.
T. (714) 871-5640. - Paint / Graph / Eth -   *089018*

Geneva (Illinois)

Grunwalds, A. F., 315 W State St., Geneva, IL 60134.
T. (312) 232-8040. - Paint / Tex / Jew / Silv / Glass -   *089019*

Grand Rapids (Michigan)

Bergsma, Grand Plaza Hotel, Pearl at Monroe, Grand Rapids, MI 49503. T. (616) 458-1776. - Paint / Graph / Sculp -   *089020*

Bergsma Gallery, 220 Lyon N. W., Grand Rapids, MI 49503. - Paint / Sculp -   *089021*

Hefner, 1440 SE Wealthy, Grand Rapids, MI 49506.
T. (616) 458-1715. - Paint -   *089022*

Great Neck (New York)

Artists Involvement in Art, 573 Middle Neck Rd., Great Neck, NY 11020. T. (516) 482-9005.   *089023*

Harf, Ruth, 20 Lawson Ln., Great Neck, NY 11023.
T. (516) 482-9005. - Paint / Graph / Sculp -   *089024*

Greenville (Delaware)

Gallery at Greenville, Greenville Center, Suite E129, Greenville, DE 19807. T. (302) 652-0271. - Paint / Graph / Sculp -   *089025*

Station Gallery, 3922 Kennett Pike, Greenville, DE 19807. T. (302) 654-8638. - Paint -   *089026*

Greenwich (Connecticut)

Elements, 14 Liberty Way, Greenwich, CT 06830.
T. (203) 661-0014.   *089027*

Greenwich Gallery, 6 W Putnam Av, Second Floor, Greenwich, CT 06830. T. (203) 622-1444.   *089028*

ISOA Gallery, POB 216, Greenwich, CT 06831.
T. (203) 622-6434. - Paint -   *089029*

Lublin, 95 E Putnam Av., Greenwich, CT 06830.
T. (203) 622-8777. - Graph -   *089030*

Haddam (Connecticut)
Hobart House, Route 154, POB 128, Haddam, CT 06438.
T. (203) 345-2015. *089031*

Half Moon Bay (California)
Baker, Joan, 751 Kelley Av, Half Moon Bay, CA 94019.
T. (415) 726-1519. - Paint / Graph - *089032*

Hartsdale (New York)
Artists Showcase International, 2 E Hartsdale Av., Hartsdale, NY 10530. T. (914) 948-2229, 684-8995.
- Paint / Graph - *089033*
Brown, Alan, 210 E Hartsdale Av., Hartsdale, NY 10530.
T. (914) 723-0040. - Paint / Graph / Sculp /
Pho - *089034*

Hendersonville (North Carolina)
Allen, M. Kenneth, 225 N Main St, Hendersonville, NC 28792. T. (704) 692-1350. *089035*

Holualoa (Hawaii)
Goldsmith, Hale O Kula, POB 416, Holualoa, HI 96725.
T. (808) 324-1688. - Paint / Sculp / Draw - *089036*
Studio 7 Gallery, POB 153, Holualoa, HI 96725.
T. (808) 324-1335. - Paint / Graph / China /
Sculp - *089037*

Honolulu (Hawaii)
Buntin, Robyn, 900A Maunakea St, Honolulu, HI 96817.
T. (808) 523-5913, Fax (808) 536-6305. *089038*
Gallery Eas, 1426 Makaloa St., Honolulu, HI 96814.
T. (808) 947-1426. - Graph - *089039*
Queen Emma Gallery, 1301 Punchbowl St., Honolulu, HI 96813. T. (808) 547-4397. - Paint - *089040*
Ramsay, 1128 Smith St., Honolulu, HI 96817.
T. (808) 537-2787, Fax 533-6630. - Draw - *089041*
Young, John, Kahala Hilton, 96816, Honolulu, HI 96800.
- Paint / Graph / Sculp - *089042*

Houston (Texas)
American Arts Associates, 1400 Hermann Dr., Ste. 8F, Houston, TX 77004. T. (713) 520-7157. *089043*
Archway Gallery, 2600 Montrose Blvd., Houston, TX 77006. T. (713) 522-2409. - Paint / China / Sculp /
Draw - *089044*
Barbizon, 561 Town and Country Village, Houston, TX 77024. T. (713) 467-5479. - Paint - *089045*
Benteler Morgan, 4200 Montrose, Ste. 110, Houston, TX 77006. T. (713) 522-8228. - Pho - *089046*
Burch-Wademan, 3256 Westheimer Rd., Houston, TX 77006. T. (713) JA6-1813. *089047*
Butler, Hiram, 2318-2320 Portsmouth, Houston, TX 77098. T. (713) 522-4430. *089048*
Circle Gallery, 2895 The Galleria, Houston, TX 77056.
T. (713) 961-7241. *089049*
Collins Lowell, 2903 Saint St. 0, Houston, TX 77027.
T. (713) 622-6962. - Paint - *089050*
Davis McClain, 2627 Colquitt, Houston, TX 77098.
T. (713) 520-9200. - Paint - *089051*
Diverse Works, 214 Travis, Houston, TX 77002.
T. (713) 223-8346. *089052*
Grace Collection of Popular Art in the America, 3733 Westheimer, Houston, TX 77027. T. (713) 961-5229.
- Paint / China / Sculp / Tex - *089053*
Graham, W.A, 1431 W Alabama, Houston, TX 77006.
T. (713) 528-4957. - Paint / Graph / Sculp /
Pho - *089054*
Harris, 1100 Bissonnet, Houston, TX 77005.
T. (713) 522-9116. - Paint / Graph / Pho /
Draw - *089055*
Heath & Brown, 609 Tuam Av., Houston, TX 77006.
T. (713) 529-0011. - Paint / Sculp - *089056*
Hooks Epstein, 2623 Kipling, Houston, TX 77098.
T. (713) 522-0718. - Paint / Graph / Mul /
Draw - *089057*
Kauffman, 2702 W Alabama, Houston, TX 77098.
T. (713) 528-4229. *089058*
Lee, Janie C., 1209 Berthea St., Houston, TX 77006.
T. (713) 523-7306, Fax (713) 523-0462. - Paint /
Sculp / Draw - *089059*
Meier, Jack, 2310 Bissonnet, Houston, TX 77005.
T. (713) 526-2983. *089060*
Meier, Jack, 2310 Bissonnet, Houston, TX 77005. *089061*

Meredith, Long & Co., 2323 San Felipe Rd., Houston, TX 77019. T. (713) 523-6671. - Paint / Graph /
Sculp - *089062*
Moody, 2815 Colquitt, Houston, TX 77098. T. (713) 526-9911. - Paint / Graph / Mul / Draw - *089063*
Pembroke, 1639 Bissonnet, Houston, TX 77005.
T. (713) 529-9411. *089064*
Perception Galleries, 2631 Colquitt, Houston, TX 77098.
T. (713) 527-0303. - China / Sculp - *089065*
Rice, Robert, 2627 Kipling, Ste. 201, Houston, TX 77098. T. (713) 528-0741. - Paint - *089066*
Robinson, 3514 Lake St., Houston, TX 77098.
T. (713) 526-0761, Fax (713) 526-0763.
- Paint - *089067*
Texas Gallery, 2012 Peden, Houston, TX 77019.
T. (713) 524-1593. - Paint - *089068*
Wellhausen, 2427 Rice Blvd., Houston, TX 77005.
T. (713) 524-7402. - Graph / Repr / Fra - *089069*
Wurzer, Gerhard, 5757 Memorial Dr., Ste. 200, Houston, TX 77007. T. (713) 869-9460. *089070*

Huntington Beach (California)
Bolen, John & Lynne, POB 5654, Huntington Beach, CA 92615. T. (714) 968-0806. - Paint / Graph /
Sculp - *089071*
Whitchurch, Charles, 5973 Engineer Dr., Huntington Beach, CA 92649. T. (714) 373-4459, Fax 373-4615.
- Paint / Graph / Sculp / Pho - *089072*

Indianapolis (Indiana)
Artifacts Gallery, 6327 Guilford, Indianapolis, IN 46220.
T. (317) 255-1178. - China / Jew / Glass - *089073*
Ayres & Co., L. S., 1 W. Washington St., Indianapolis, IN 46204. *089074*
Indianapolis Art League Gallery, 820 E 67 St., Indianapolis, IN 46220. T. (317) 255-2464. - Paint - *089075*
King, Patrick, 427 Massachusetts Av., Indianapolis, IN 46204. T. (317) 634-4101. - Paint / Graph / Sculp /
Tex - *089076*

Inglewood (California)
Cooper, 1043 N La Brea Av, Inglewood, CA 90302.
T. (213) 678-3116. *089077*

Ithaca (New York)
Upstairs Gallery, De Witt Office Complex, Ithaca, NY 14850. T. (607) 272-8614. *089078*

Jackson (Wyoming)
May, 172 Center St., Jackson P.O.B. 1972, WY 83001.
T. (307) 733-2625. - Paint / Sculp - *089079*
Powder River Gallery, 98 Center St., 2 Fl., Jackson, WY 83001. T. (307) 733-8258. - Paint / Sculp - *089080*

Jacksonville (Florida)
Art Sources, 1253 Southshore Dr., Jacksonville, FL 32073. T. (904) 269-2014. *089081*
Cummer, 829 Riverside Av., 32200 Jacksonville, FL 32204. T. (904) 356-6857. *089082*
Gallery Contemporanea, 526 Lancaster St., Jacksonville, FL 32204. T. (904) 359-0016. - Paint - *089083*
Reddi-Arts, 1037 Hendricks Ave., Jacksonville, FL 32207. T. (904) 398-3161. - Graph - *089084*

Jenkintown (Pennsylvania)
Langman, 218 Old York Rd., Jenkintown, PA 19046.
T. (215) 887-3500. - Paint / Sculp - *089085*
Loesch Fine Arts Ltd., 709 Washington Lane, Jenkintown, PA 19046. T. (215) 885-2414. *089086*

Kaneohe (Hawaii)
Hart & Tagami, 47-754 Lamaula Rd., Kaneohe, HI 96744. T. (808) 239-8146. - Paint / China - *089087*
International Connoisseurs, 47-421 Mahakea Rd., Kaneohe, HI 96744. T. (808) 239-9186. - Paint / Graph /
China / Sculp - *089088*

Kansas City (Missouri)
Batman, Donald, 825 Westport Rd., Kansas City, MO 64111. T. (816) 531-2588. - Paint / Sculp /
Pho - *089089*
Gates, Dorry, 5321 Belleview, Kansas City, MO 64112.
T. (816) 523-4403. - Paint / Graph / Sculp /
Draw - *089090*

Old World Art Gallery, 825 Westport Rd., 64111, Kansas City, MO 64100. T. (816) JE 1-2588. - Paint / Graph /
Fra - *089091*
Scott's, 1015 E. 75th St., 64131, Kansas City, MO 64100. T. (816) DE 3-6459. - Paint / Graph /
Fra - *089092*
Sebree, 301 E 55 St., Kansas City, MO 64113.
T. (816) 333-3387. *089093*

La Jolla (California)
Babeor, Thomas, 7470 Girard Av., La Jolla, CA 92037.
T. (619) 454-0345. - Paint / Sculp - *089094*
Casat, 5721 La Jolla Blvd., La Jolla, CA 92037.
T. (619) 454 8897. *089095*
Fraze's, 1033 Silverado Ave., La Jolla, CA 92037.
T. (619) 454-0729. - Paint / Graph / Fra - *089096*
Hanson, 1227 Prospect Pl., La Jolla, CA 92037.
T. (619) 454-9799, Fax 454-8954. - Paint / Graph /
Sculp - *089097*
Jones, 1264 Prospect St., La Jolla, CA 92037.
T. (619) 459-1370. - Paint / Graph / Sculp - *089098*
Knowles, 7422 Girard Av., La Jolla, CA 92037.
T. (619) 454-0106. - Paint / Sculp - *089099*
Mat Gallery, 1113 Wall Street, La Jolla, CA 92037.
T. (619) 459-8447. - Paint - *089100*
Prakapas, Dorothy, 800 Prospect St Apt 3C, La Jolla, CA 92037. T. (619) 454-1622, Fax (619) 454-9686. *089101*
Preisman, Fran, 1626 Buckingham Dr., La Jolla, CA 92037. T. (619) 459-2684. - Ant / Pho - *089102*
Riggs, 7463 Girard Av., La Jolla, CA 92037. T. (619) 454-3070. - Paint / Sculp / Pho - *089103*
Simic, 7925 Girard Av., La Jolla, CA 92037.
T. (619) 454-0225. - Paint / Pho - *089104*
Simic, 1205 Prospect St., La Jolla, CA 92037.
T. (619) 456-4076. - Paint / Sculp - *089105*
Tasende, 820 Prospect St., La Jolla, CA 92037.
T. (619) 454-3691, Fax 454-0589. *089106*

Lafayette (California)
Pacific Wildlife Galleries, 3420 Mount Diablo Blvd, Lafayette, CA 94549. T. (510) 283-2977. *089107*

Lafayette (Louisiana)
Heritage Art Galleries, 1009 Coolidge Blvd.,, Lafayette, LA 70503. *089108*
Live Oak Gallery, 103 Amaryllis Dr., Lafayette, LA 70503. T. (318) 233-3477. - Paint - *089109*
Rodrique, George, 1206 Jefferson St. 70501, Lafayette, LA 70501. T. (318) 232-6398. *089110*

Laguna Beach (California)
Collector's Choice, 20352 Laguna Canyon Rd., Laguna Beach, CA 92651. T. (714) 494-4515. - Paint / Sculp /
Pho - *089111*
Karavan, 1258 Brangway Way, 92651, Laguna Beach, CA 92651. - Paint - *089112*
Laguna Originals, 330 No. Coast Highway, 92651, Laguna Beach P.O.B. 984, CA 92651. *089113*
Lang Photography Gallery, 1450-A. S. Coast Highway, Laguna Beach, CA 92651. - Pho - *089114*
Yeakel Antiques, Carl, 1099 S. Coast Hwy., Laguna Beach, CA 92651. *089115*

Lahaina (Hawaii)
Lahaina Gallery, 117 Lahainaluna Rd., Lahaina, HI 96761. T. (808) 661-0839. - Paint - *089116*
Lahaina Gallery II, 728 Front St., Lahaina, HI 96761.
T. (808) 367-8047. - Paint / Graph - *089117*
Village Gallery at the Cannery, 1221 Honoapiilani Hwy., Lahaina, HI 96761. T. (808) 661-3280.
- Paint - *089118*
Village Gallery-Dickenson, 120 Dickenson, Lahaina, HI 96761. T. (808) 661-4402. - Paint - *089119*

Larchmont (New York)
Art Fair Gallery, The, 126 Larchmont Ave., Larchmont, NY 10538. T. (914) 834-9474. *089120*
Larchmont Art Gallery, 1887 Palmer Ave., Larchmont, NY 10588. T. (914) 834-0288. - Paint / Graph /
Fra - *089121*
Post Road Antiques & Gallery, 130 Boston Post Rd., Larchmont, NY 10588. T. (914) 834-7568. - Paint /
Graph - *089122*

Larkspur (California)
Lewis, R.E., POB 5325, Larkspur, CA 94939.
T. (415) 461-4161. - Paint / Draw -   *089123*

Leawood (Kansas)
Blitt, Rita, 8900 State Line Rd, Leawood, KS 66206.
T. (913) 381-3840, Fax (913) 381-5624.   *089124*

Lenox (Massachusetts)
Hand of Man, Curtis Shops, Lenox, MA 01240.
T. (413) 433-2960. - China / Glass -   *089125*
Hoadley, 17 Church St., Lenox, MA 01240. T. (413) 637-
2814. - China / Sculp / Tex / Jew -   *089126*
Lerner, Ella, 17 Franklin St., Lenox, MA 01240.
T. (413) 637-3315. - Paint -   *089127*
Towne Gallery, 28 Walker St., Lenox, MA 01240.
T. (413) 637-0053. - Graph -   *089128*
Whitney, Clark, 25 Church St., Lenox, MA 01240.
T. (413) 637-2126. - Paint / Sculp -   *089129*

Lexington (Kentucky)
Cross Gate Gallery, 219 E High St., Lexington, KY
40507. T. (606) 233-3856. - Paint / Sculp -   *089130*
Triangle Gallery, 522 W Short St., Lexington, KY 40508.
T. (606) 233-1263. - Paint -   *089131*

Locust Valley (New York)
Country Art Gallery, 198 Birch Hill Sq., Locust Valley, NY
11560. T. (516) 676-6886. - Paint / Graph /
Sculp -   *089132*

Long Island City (New York)
Oil & Steel Gallery, POB 2218, Long Island City, NY
11102. T. (212) 545-5707. - Paint / Sculp -   *089133*
Studio K, 12-15 Jackson Av., Long Island City, NY
11101. T. (212) 784-0591.   *089134*

Los Altos (California)
Sunbird Gallery, 243 Main St, Los Altos, CA 94022.
T. (415) 941-1561.   *089135*

Los Angeles (California)
A Separate Ability, 828 N Lea Brea Av, Los Angeles, CA
90038. T. (213) 464-4890. - Paint / Graph -   *089136*
AC Network, 350 S Figueroa St, Los Angeles, CA 90071.
T. (213) 680-0880. - Paint / Graph / Sculp -   *089137*
Ace Gallery, 5514 Wilshire Blvd, Los Angeles, CA 90036.
T. (213) 935-4411. - Paint / Graph -   *089138*
Adamson-Duvannes, 484 S San Vicente Blvd, Los Ange-
les, CA 90048. T. (213) 653-1015. - Paint /
Sculp -   *089139*
ADR, 605 W Olympic Blvd, Los Angeles, CA 90015.
T. (213) 629-3540.   *089140*
African Connection, 7204 Melrose Av, Los Angeles, CA
90046. T. (213) 965-8628. - Eth -   *089141*
Alitash Kebede, 964 N La Brea Av, Los Angeles, CA
90038. T. (213) 874-6269.   *089142*
Angel City Gallery, 1041 N Highland Av, Los Angeles, CA
90038. T. (213) 957-9095.   *089143*
Animation Plus Gallery, 7977 Melrose Av, Los Angeles,
CA 90046. T. (213) 852-0364. - Paint / Graph -   *089144*
Aparicio, Edgar, 1848 W Washington Blvd, Los Angeles,
CA 90007. T. (213) 733-9617.   *089145*
Arctic Circle, 464 N La Jolla Av, Los Angeles, CA 90048.
T. (213) 651-0444. - Paint -   *089146*
Art Source Los Angeles, 11901 Santa Monica Blvd, Los
Angeles, CA 90025. T. (310) 479-6649.
- Paint -   *089147*
Art Works, 1904 Bailey St, Los Angeles, CA 90033.
T. (213) 269-5437. - Paint -   *089148*
Artspace Concepts, 6623 Melrose Av, Los Angeles, CA
90038. T. (213) 939-2018.   *089149*
Asher Faure, 9519 1/2 W Olympic Blvd, Los Angeles, CA
90035. T. (310) 286-7026. - Paint / Graph /
Sculp -   *089150*
Ashkenazy, 5858 Wilshire Blvd, Los Angeles, CA 90036.
T. (213) 938-1999. - Paint / Graph -   *089151*
Bak-Tu-Jua, 4330 Degnan Blvd, Los Angeles, CA 90008.
T. (213) 295-2502.   *089152*
Baltic Crossroads Art Gallery, 4364 W Sunset Blvd, Los
Angeles, CA 90029. T. (213) 664-6216.   *089153*
Bane, Robert, 8025 Melrose Av, Los Angeles, CA 90046.
T. (213) 658-5955. - Graph -   *089154*
Bane, Tamara, 8025 Melrose Av, Los Angeles, CA
94601. T. (213) 651-1400.   *089155*

Barnes, Ernie, 8613 Sherwood Dr, Los Angeles, CA
90069. T. (310) 652-2941.   *089156*
Baum, 170 S La Brea Av, Los Angeles, CA 90036.
T. (213) 932-0170. - Paint / Graph / Eth -   *089157*
Black Gallery, 107 Santa Barbara Plaza, Los Angeles, CA
90008. T. (213) 294-9024.   *089158*
Blooming, 6623 Melrose Av, Los Angeles, CA 90038.
T. (213) 937-1171. - Paint -   *089159*
Byrnes, James B., 7820 Mulholland Dr, Los Angeles, CA
90046. T. (213) 851-0128. - Paint -   *089160*
Calif Child, 1035 N Cahuenga Blvd, Los Angeles, CA
9003838. T. (213) 462-3477.   *089161*
Champion Gallery, 8313 Beverly Blvd, Los Angeles, CA
90048. T. (213) 653-3376. - Paint -   *089162*
Chong & Thompson, 714 W Olympic Blvd, Los Angeles,
CA 90015. T. (213) 742-0707.   *089163*
Cirrus, 542 S Alameda St, Los Angeles, CA 90013.
T. (213) 680-3473, Fax (213) 680-0930. - Paint /
Graph / Sculp / Mod / Pho / Mul / Draw -   *089164*
Clark, Garth, 170 S La Brea Av, Los Angeles, CA 90036.
T. (213) 939-2189. - China -   *089165*
Cohen, Stephen, 7466 Beverly Blvd, Los Angeles, CA
90036. T. (213) 937-5525.   *089166*
Collier, 5966 Bowcroft St, Los Angeles, CA 90016.
T. (310) 204-3092. - Graph -   *089167*
Cooper, 1427 S La Brea Av, Los Angeles, CA 90019.
T. (213) 932-9150. - Repr / Fra -   *089168*
Courtright, 310 N Mansfield Av, Los Angeles, CA 90036.
T. (213) 931-7879. - Paint -   *089169*
Couturier, 166 N La Brea Av, Los Angeles, CA 90036.
T. (213) 933-5557.   *089170*
Crewe, Bob, 1155 N Las Palmas Av, Los Angeles, CA
90038. T. (213) 464-5359.   *089171*
Dassin, 8687 Melrose Av, Los Angeles, CA 90069.
T. (310) 652-0203.   *089172*
Every Picture Tells a Story, 7525 Beverly Blvd, Los Ange-
les, CA 90036. T. (213) 932-6070. - Paint -   *089173*
Fahey-Klein, 148 N La Brea Av, Los Angeles, CA 90036.
T. (213) 934-2250.   *089174*
Fluorescent Man, 6253 Hollywood Blvd, Los Angeles, CA
90028. T. (213) 962-1834.   *089175*
G & E Gift Art Gallery, 4319 Degnan Blvd, Los Angeles,
CA 90008. T. (213) 292-3567.   *089176*
Galeria Las Americas, 912 E Third St, Los Angeles, CA
90013. T. (213) 613-1347.   *089177*
Galerie Cathedrale, 1086 S Fairfax Av, Los Angeles, CA
90019. T. (213) 935-2268.   *089178*
Galerie Concrete, 201 S Santa Fe Av, Los Angeles, CA
90012. T. (213) 617-7085.   *089179*
Gallery Art, 1549 S La Cienega Blvd, Los Angeles, CA
90035. T. (310) 652-3969.   *089180*
Gallery at 777, 777 S Figueroa St, Los Angeles, CA
90017. T. (213) 955-5977.   *089181*
Gallery G, 1600 N Highland Av, Los Angeles, CA 90028.
T. (213) 469-4618.   *089182*
Gallery IV, 800 Traction Av, Los Angeles, CA 90013.
T. (213) 687-8975.   *089183*
Gallery Plus, 4333 Degnan Blvd, Los Angeles, CA
90008. T. (213) 296-2398. - Graph / Fra -   *089184*
Gallery West, 107 S Robertson Blvd, Los Angeles, CA
90048. T. (310) 271-1145. - Paint / Graph / Sculp /
Mul / Draw -   *089185*
Gemini GEL, 8365 Melrose Av, Los Angeles, CA 90069.
T. (213) 651-0513. - Graph / Mul -   *089186*
Godarm House, 3917 W Ninth St, Los Angeles, CA
90019. T. (213) 386-8833. - Paint -   *089187*
Goldfield, 8380 Melrose Av, Los Angeles, CA 90069.
T. (213) 651-1122. - Paint -   *089188*
Graphic Experience Custom Framing and Poster Studio,
8244 Santa Monica Blvd, Los Angeles, CA 90046.
T. (213) 650-3700. - Graph / Fra -   *089189*
Gray, Bruce, 688 South Av 21, Los Angeles, CA 90001.
T. (213) 223-4059.   *089190*
Hartog, 6300 Wilshire Blvd, Los Angeles, CA 90048.
T. (213) 651-2064.   *089191*
Hello Artichoke, 4655 Kingswell Av, Los Angeles, CA
90027. T. (213) 953-4835.   *089192*
Henken, 120 S Los Angeles St, Los Angeles, CA 90012.
T. (213) 626-2505.   *089193*
Heritage Gallery, 718 N La Cienega Blvd, Los Angeles,
CA 90069. T. (213) 652-7738.   *089194*
Hittleman, Michael, 8797 Beverly Blvd, Los Angeles, CA
90048. T. (213) 655-5364.   *089195*

Hollywood Cinema Arts, 6836 Lexington Av, Los Ange-
les, CA 90038. T. (213) 463-4411. - Graph -   *089196*
Hollywood Moguls, 1650 N Hudson Av, Los Angeles, CA
90028. T. (213) 465-7449.   *089197*
Holographic Visions, 115 N Normandie Av, Los Angeles,
CA 90004. T. (213) 387-0461.   *089198*
Hunsaker-Schlesinger, 812 N La Cienega Blvd, Los An-
geles, CA 90069. T. (310) 657-2557.   *089199*
Imani, 3207 W 54 St., Los Angeles, CA 90043.
T. (213) 295-0209.   *089200*
Impressions, 3630 Tyburn St, Los Angeles, CA 90065.
T. (213) 340-8251.   *089201*
Inspiration Art, 1666 1/2 N McCadden Pl, Los Angeles,
CA 90028. T. (213) 467-7390.   *089202*
International Art Connection, 420 N Poinsettia Pl, Los
Angeles, CA 90036. T. (213) 938-6581.   *089203*
Iturralde, 154 N La Brea Av, Los Angeles, CA 90036.
T. (213) 937-4267.   *089204*
Janis Aldridge, 8452 Melrose Pl, Los Angeles, CA
90069. T. (213) 658-8456.   *089205*
Jesus Jones & Justice, 7611 S San Pedro St, Los Ange-
les, CA 90003. T. (213) 971-9529.   *089206*
Kantor, Ulrike, 9143 Saint Ives Dr, Los Angeles, CA
90069. T. (310) 273-5650. - Paint -   *089207*
Kesner, Jan, 164 N La Brea Av, Los Angeles, CA 90036.
T. (213) 938-6834.   *089208*
Kizhner, Michael, 746 N La Cienega Blvd, Los Angeles,
CA 90069. T. (213) 659-5222. - Paint / Graph -   *089209*
Koan, 6109 Melrose Av, Los Angeles, CA 90038.
T. (213) 464-3735. - Eth / Jew -   *089210*
Kopelkin, Paul, 170 S La Brea Av, Los Angeles, CA
90036. T. (213) 937-0765.   *089211*
Kumon, 3921 Wilshire Blvd, Los Angeles, CA 90010.
T. (213) 389-8449.   *089212*
La Brea Art Pit Gallery, 828 N La Brea Av, Los Angeles,
CA 90038. T. (213) 464-4191.   *089213*
La Luz de Jesus Gallery, 7400 Melrose Av, Los Angeles,
CA 90046. T. (213) 651-4875. - Paint -   *089214*
Laca, 3630 Wilshire Blvd, Los Angeles, CA 90010.
T. (213) 381-1525.   *089215*
LAICAF, 333 S Spring St, Los Angeles, CA 90013.
T. (213) 626-8368.   *089216*
Lakaye, 1550 N Curson Av, Los Angeles, CA 90046.
T. (213) 850-6188.   *089217*
Leavin, Margo, 812 N Robertson Blvd, Los Angeles, CA
90069. T. (310) 273-0603, Fax (310) 273-9131.
- Paint / Graph / Sculp / Draw -   *089218*
Lee, Sabina, 3921 Wilshire Blvd, Los Angeles, CA
90010. T. (213) 380-8789.   *089219*
Light, Klm, 126 N La Brea Av, Los Angeles, CA 90036.
T. (213) 933-9816.   *089220*
Los Angeles Artcore Center, 420 E Third St, Los Angeles,
CA 90013. T. (213) 617.3274.   *089221*
Lotus House, 569 Lotus St, Los Angeles, CA 90065.
T. (213) 227-1723.   *089222*
M Oriental Art Frame, 182 S Western Av, Los Angeles,
CA 90004. T. (213) 487-9000. - Fra -   *089223*
Magic Dragon Art Gallery, 988 N Hill St, Los Angeles, CA
90012. T. (213) 626-3388.   *089224*
Maher, Daniel, 500 Molino St, Los Angeles, CA 90013.
T. (213) 617-7891.   *089225*
Mako, Gene, 430 S Burnside Av, Los Angeles, CA
90036. T. (213) 933-3151.   *089226*
Marguerite Fine Art Studio, 7507 W Sunset Blvd, Los An-
geles, CA 90046. T. (213) 876-6886.   *089227*
Marshall, 8420 Melrose Av, Los Angeles, CA 90069.
T. (213) 852-1964. - Paint -   *089228*
Menzies, Neal, 170 S La Brea Av, Los Angeles, CA
90036. T. (213) 965-1274.   *089229*
Modern Art Gallery, 607 S Oxford Av, Los Angeles, CA
90005. T. (213) 362-7038.   *089230*
Moss, Tobey C., 7321 Beverly Blvd, Los Angeles, CA
90036. T. (213) 933-5523. - Paint / Graph -   *089231*
Moving Arts, 1822 Hyperion Av, Los Angeles, CA 90027.
T. (213) 665-8961.   *089232*
Name That Toon, 8483 Melrose Av, Los Angeles, CA
90069. T. (213) 653-5633.   *089233*
Newspace, 5241 Melrose Av, Los Angeles, CA 90038.
T. (213) 469-9353. - Paint / Sculp -   *089234*
Newton, 6061 W Third St, Los Angeles, CA 90036.
T. (213) 937-2367.   *089235*

Novak, Jonathan, 10350 Wilshire Boulevard, Los Angeles, CA 90024. T. (310) 858-2918, Fax (310) 276-7381. 089236

Obatala, 758 E 14 St, Los Angeles, CA 90021. T. (213) 748-8628. 089237

Onyx Gallery, 1804 N Vermont Av, Los Angeles, CA 90027. T. (213) 660-5820. 089238

Outside-In Gallery, 6909 Melrose Av, Los Angeles, CA 90038. T. (213) 933-4096. 089239

Ovsey, Neil G., 170 S La Brea Av, Los Angeles, CA 90036. T. (213) 935-1883. - Paint / Graph / Sculp - 089240

Paideia Gallery, 765 N La Cienega Blvd, Los Angeles, CA 90069. T. (310) 652-8224. - Paint / Sculp / Jew / Draw - 089241

Pakistani American Arts Council, 689 S Sycamore Av, Los Angeles, CA 90036. T. (213) 935-1973. - Paint - 089242

Phillips, 4455 Los Feliz Blvd, Los Angeles, CA 90027. T. (213) 666-5424. 089243

Pong Nam, 3911 W Olympic Blvd, Los Angeles, CA 90019. T. (213) 933-5708. 089244

Poster Arts Distributors, 7314 Melrose Av, Los Angeles, CA 90046. T. (213) 937-0325. - Graph - 089245

Print Merchants, 8687 Melrose Av, Los Angeles, CA 90069. T. (310) 659-9260. - Graph - 089246

Ramirez, Robert, 257 Silver Lake Blvd, Los Angeles, CA 90004. T. (213) 385-8212. 089247

Random, 6040 N Figueroa St, Los Angeles, CA 90042. T. (213) 550-8000. 089248

Rock Store, 6817 Melrose Av, Los Angeles, CA 90038. T. (213) 930-2980. 089249

Rutberg, Jack, 357 N La Brea Av, Los Angeles, CA 90036-2517. T. (213) 938-5222, Fax (213) 938-0577. - Paint / Graph / Sculp / Draw - 089250

Saint Elmo's Village, 4832 1/2 Saint Elmo Dr, Los Angeles, CA 90019. T. (213) 935-6123. 089251

Sara Gallery, 2431 Colorado Blvd, Los Angeles, CA 90041. T. (213) 340-1441. - Graph / Draw - 089252

Sargent, 2750 Glendower Av, Los Angeles, CA 90027. T. (213) 660-2214. - Paint - 089253

Seven Glass, 457 N Western Av, Los Angeles, CA 90004. T. (213) 466-8973. - Glass - 089254

Solomon, Thomas, 928 N Fairfax Av, Los Angeles, CA 90046. T. (213) 654-4731. 089255

Sonrisa, 7609 Beverly Blvd, Los Angeles, CA 90036. T. (213) 935-8438. 089256

Space Art Gallery, 4277 W Third St, Los Angeles, CA 90020. T. (213) 480-6759. 089257

Space Gallery, 6015 Santa Monica Blvd, Los Angeles, CA 90038. T. (213) 461-8166. - Paint / Sculp / Draw - 089258

Spaid, Sue, 7454 Beverly Blvd, Los Angeles, CA 90036. T. (213) 935-6153. 089259

Stock, Eric, 6210 Wilshire Blvd, Ste 201, Los Angeles, CA 90048. T. (213) 217-0180. 089260

Stuart, David, 2615 La Cuesta Dr, Los Angeles, CA 90046. T. (213) 878-0330. - Paint / Sculp / Eth - 089261

Studio Sixteen-Seventeen, 1617 Silver Lake Blvd, Los Angeles, CA 90026. T. (213) 660-7991. - Paint / Graph - 089262

Sun Art Gallery, 4020 W Olympic Blvd, Los Angeles, CA 90019. T. (213) 936-9000. 089263

Swan, 6711 Forest Lawn Dr, Los Angeles, CA 90068. T. (213) 851-9326. 089264

Tanner, 5271 W Pico Blvd, Los Angeles, CA 90019. T. (213) 933-0202. - Paint / Graph / Sculp - 089265

Telles, Richard, 7380 Beverly Blvd, Los Angeles, CA 90036. T. (213) 965-5578. 089266

Third World Art Exchange, 2016 Hillhurst Av, Los Angeles, CA 90027. T. (213) 666-9357. 089267

Transmarket International Marchands, 3580 Wilshire Blvd, Los Angeles, CA 90010. T. (213) 386-7052. 089268

Turner, Steve, 7220 Beverly Blvd, Los Angeles, CA 90036. T. (213) 931-1185. 089269

Ukrainian Art Center, 4315 Melrose Av, Los Angeles, CA 90029. T. (213) 668-0172. - Paint / Graph - 089270

Up-Front Art Gallery, 7420 Santa Monica Blvd, Los Angeles, CA 90046. T. (213) 656-0913. 089271

Venger, Bob, 500 N Larchmont Blvd, Los Angeles, CA 90004. T. (213) 461-9733. 089272

Verve, 7314 Melrose Av, Los Angeles, CA 90046. T. (213) 937-0325. - Graph / Pho - 089273

Wilson & Associates, Kathleen A., 5624 Brushton St, Los Angeles, CA 90008. T. (213) 295-4278. 089274

Winn, 145 S Robertson Blvd, Los Angeles, CA 90048. T. (310) 274-0285. 089275

Z Gallery, 7555 Melrose Av, Los Angeles, CA 90046. T. (213) 655-0622. 089276

Zero One Gallery, 7025 Melrose Av, Los Angeles, CA 90038. T. (213) 965-9459. 089277

Louisville (Kentucky)

Contemporary Crafts Gallery, 2003 Frankfort Av., Louisville, KY 40206. T. (502) 896-1911. - Sculp - 089278

Hadley, 1570 Story Av., Louisville, KY 40206. T. (502) 584-2171. - Sculp - 089279

Liberty Gallery, 416 W Jefferson Av., Louisville, KY 40206. T. (502) 566-2081. - Paint / Pho - 089280

Park Gallery, 3936 Chenoweth Sq., Louisville, KY 40207. T. (502) 896-4029. - Paint / Graph / China - 089281

Rapp, Yvonne, 2007 Frankfort Av., Louisville, KY 40206. T. (502) 896-2331. 089282

Swearingen, 4806 Brownsboro Center, Louisville, KY 40207. T. (502) 893-5209. - Paint - 089283

Madison

Chosy, Grace, 218 N Henry St., Madison, WI 53703. T. (608) 255-1211. 089284

Garver, Fanny, 230 State St., Madison, WI 53703. T. (608) 256-6755. - Paint / Graph - 089285

Hastings Falk, P., 206 Boston Post Rd., Madison, CT 06443. T. (203) 245-2246. - Paint - 089286

Spaightwood Galleries, 1150 Spaight St., Madison, WI 53703. T. (608) 255-3043. - Paint / Graph - 089287

Valperine Gallery, 2608 Monroe St., Madison, WI 53711. T. (608) 233-6062. 089288

Malibu (California)

Pentimento, 6943 Grassword Av, Malibu, CA 90265. T. (213) 457-0262, Fax (213) 457-0265. 089290

Tidepool, 22762 Pacific Coast Hwy., Malibu, CA 90265. T. (213) 456-2551. - Paint / Graph / China / Sculp / Arch / Eth / Dec / Jew / Silv / Cur / Pho / Draw - 089290a

Memphis

Athens Galleries, Inc., 2116 Fox Run Cove, 38117, Memphis, TN 38100. - Paint - 089291

Garner, 1634 Union Ave, Memphis, TN 38112. T. (901) 275-8609. - Fra - 089292

Mesa

Missal Art Associates, 1357 E Enrose Circle, Mesa, AZ 85203. T. (602) 969-4969. - Paint / Graph - 089293

Miami

A & M Antiques and Gallery, 9479 S Dixie Hwy., Miami, FL 33156. T. (305) 667-4214, Fax 661-4339. - Paint / Graph - 089294

Art Place at Cauley Square, 22400 Old Dixie Hwy., Miami, FL 33170. T. (305) 258-4222. - Paint / Graph - 089295

Bacardi, 2100 Biscayne Blvd., Miami, FL 33137. T. (305) 573-8511. - Paint / Graph / Sculp / Pho / Draw - 089296

Center for the Fine Arts, 101 W Flagler St., Miami, FL 33130. T. (305) 375-1700, 375-3000. 089297

Friedman, Marvin Ross, 15451 SW 67 Court, Miami, FL 33157. T. (305) 233-4280, Fax 448-7636. - Paint / Graph / Sculp / Draw - 089298

Galerie 99, 1088 Kane Concourse, Miami, FL 33154. T. (305) 865-5823. - Paint - 089299

Gideon, 6496 Coral Way, 33155, Miami, FL 33100. T. (305) 661-9673. 089300

Gillman, Barbara, 270 NE 39 St., Miami, FL 33137. T. (305) 573-4898. - Paint / Graph / Sculp - 089301

Gillman, Barbara, 3886 Biscayne Blvd., Miami, FL 33137. T. (305) 573-4898. - Paint / Graph / Sculp - 089302

International Art Co., 1644 NE 123 St, Miami, FL 33161. T. (305) 891-4182. - Paint / Graph / Orient / Repr / Sculp / Fra - 089303

Moos, Joy, 355 NE 59 Terrace, Miami, FL 33137. T. (305) 754-9373, Fax (305) 757-2124. 089303a

Pollack's Galleries Inc., c/o Morris Pollack, 2780 N.E. 183rd St. PH14, Miami, FL 33160. T. (305) 9314476. - Ant / Paint / Furn / Orient / China / Sculp / Jew / Silv / Lights / Glass - 089304

Steiner, Berenice, Inc., 11111 Biscayne Blvd., Miami, FL 33161. T. (305) 893-3344. - Paint / Graph / Sculp - 089305

Suzanne's Gallerie, 19108 W. Dixie Hwy., Miami, FL 33160. T. (305) 931-2264. - Paint / Graph / Sculp - 089306

Windsor Arts, 6736 N. E. 4th Ave., Miami, FL 33138. - Paint / Sculp / Fra - 089307

Miami Beach (Florida)

Carel, 928 Lincoln Rd., Miami Beach, FL 33139. T. (305) 534-4384. - Paint - 089309

Rubell, Jason, 700 Lincoln Rd, Miami Beach, FL 33139. T. (305) 538-5444, Fax (305) 538-0045. 089309a

World Gallery, 945 Lincoln Rd., Miami Beach, FL 33139. T. (305) 531-3050. - Paint - 089310

Middleburg (Virginia)

Redfox, POB 385, Middleburg, VA 22117. T. (703) 687-6301, Fax (703) 687-3338. 089312

Milwaukee (Wisconsin)

Bradley, 2565 E Downer Av., Milwaukee, WI 53211. T. (414) 332-9570. - Paint / Graph / Sculp - 089313

Cudahy Gallery of Wisconsin Art, Milwaukee Art Center, 750 N. Lincoln Memorial Dr., Milwaukee, WI 53202. T. (414) 271-9508. - Paint / Graph / Sculp / Glass / Pho - 089314

Frederick, 1234 E Juneau Av., Milwaukee, WI 53202. T. (414) 271-1500. - Paint - 089315

Kondos, Peter J., 2121 East Lafayette Place, Milwaukee, WI 53202. - Ant / Paint / Graph / Furn / Num / Orient / China / Sculp / Sculp / Tex / Arch / Eth / Dec / Jew / Fra / Silv / Lights / Instr / Mil / Rel / Glass / Cur / Ico - 089316

Minneapolis

American Wildlife Art Galleries, 926 Plymouth Building, 6th St., Minneapolis, MN 55402. T. (612) 338-7247. - Paint / Graph / Sculp - 089317

Anderson & Anderson, 400 First Av. N, Minneapolis, MN 55401. T. (612) 332-4889. - Furn / China - 089318

Artbanque, 300 First Av. N, Minneapolis, MN 55401. T. (612) 342-9300. - Paint / Graph / Sculp / Pho / Draw - 089319

Barry, Thomas, 400 First Av. N, Minneapolis, MN 55401. T. (612) 338-3656. - Paint / Graph / Sculp / Pho / Draw - 089320

Bockley, 400 First Av. N, Minneapolis, MN 55401. T. (612) 339-3139. - Paint - 089321

Carver, Vern, 1018 Lasalle Av., Minneapolis, MN 55403. T. (612) 339-3449. - Graph - 089322

David, Peter M., 400 N First Av., Minneapolis, MN 55401. T. (612) 339-1825. - Paint / Graph / Sculp / Pho / Draw - 089323

Dean, 2815 S Hennepin Av., Minneapolis, MN 55408. T. (612) 822-5754. - Graph / Sculp / Fra - 089324

Fiterman, Dolly, 12 S Sixth St, Suite 238, Minneapolis, MN 55402. T. (612) 338-5358. - Paint / Graph / Sculp / Draw - 089325

Flanders, 400 First Av. N, Minneapolis, MN 55401. T. (612) 344-1700. - Paint / Sculp / Draw - 089326

Groveland Gallery, 25 Groveland Terrace, Minneapolis, MN 55403. T. (612) 377-7800. - Paint / Draw - 089327

Hui, 1225 LaSalle Av., Minneapolis, MN 55403. T. (612) 339-3399. - Paint / Graph / Sculp - 089328

Kohn, Suzanne, 100 Second Av. N, Minneapolis, MN 55401. T. (612) 341-3441. - Paint - 089329

Mamor Circle Gallery, 5300 Circle Downs, Minneapolis, MN 55416. T. (612) 544-7020. - Paint / Graph - 089330

M.C. Gallery, 400 First Av. N, Suite 332, Minneapolis, MN 55401. T. (612) 339-1480. - Paint - 089331

Nielsen's Studio, 4345 France Ave S., Minneapolis, MN 55410. 089332

Oulman, John, 400 First Av. N, Minneapolis, MN 55401. T. (612) 333-2386. - Paint / Pho - 089333

Raven, 3827 W 50 St, Minneapolis, MN 55410. T. (612) 925-4474. - Paint / Graph / Sculp / Tex - 089334

Stoller, John C., & Co., 81 S 9 St., Minneapolis, MN
55402. T. (612) 339-7060. - Paint / Furn /
Draw - 089335
Thomson, 321 Second Av. N, Minneapolis, MN 55401.
T. (612) 338-7734. - Paint / Graph / Sculp / Pho /
Draw - 089336
Vermillion, 2919 Como Av. SE, Minneapolis, MN 55414.
T. (612) 379-7281. - Graph - 089337
Wildlife of America, 2224 Grand Av., Minneapolis, MN
55405. - Paint / Graph / Repr - 089338

Montgomery (Alabama)
Haardt, Anton, 1220 S Hull St, Montgomery, AL 36104.
T. (205) 263-5494. 089339

Montgomery (New York)
Historic Importants, 198 Corbett Rd, Montgomery, NY
12549. T. (914) 457-3765. 089340

Mount Clemens
Lucier, David, 18921 Canal Rd., Mount Clemens, MJ
48044. T. (313) 263-0840. - Paint - 089341

Nantucket (Massachusetts)
Main Street Gallery, 50 Main St., Nantucket, MA 02554.
T. (617) 228-2252. - Paint / Graph / Sculp /
Pho - 089342
Sibley, 9 Union St., Nantucket, MA 02554. T. (617) 228-
4459. - Paint / Sculp / Pho / Draw - 089343
Taylor, Kenneth, POB 1104, Nantucket, MA 02554.
T. (617) 228-0722. - Paint - 089344

Napa (California)
Vianello, 2040 Oak Knoll Av W, Napa, CA 94558.
T. (415) 253-9130. 089345

Naples (Florida)
Harmon-Meek, 386 Broad Av. S, Naples, FL 33940.
T. (813) 261-2637. - Paint / Graph / Sculp /
Draw - 089346
Naples Art Gallery, 275 Broad Av. S, Naples, FL 33940.
T. (813) 262-4551. - Paint / Sculp - 089347

Nashville (Tennessee)
Cumberland Gallery, 4107 Hillsboro Circle, Nashville, TN
37215. T. (615) 297-0296. - Paint / Sculp - 089348
Lyzon Gallery, 411 Thompson Ln., Nashville, TN 37211.
T. (615) 256-7538. - Paint / Graph / Fra - 089349
Zimmerman/Saturn, 131 Second Av. N, Nashville, TN
37201. T. (615) 255-8895. - Paint / Sculp - 089350

New Haven (Connecticut)
Athena, 135 W. Elm St., New Haven, CT 06515.
T. (203) 387-8674. - Paint / Graph - 089351
Berman, Mona, 78 Lyon St., New Haven, CT 06511.
T. (203) 562-4720. - Paint / Orient / Tex / Dec / Jew /
Pho / Mul / Draw - 089352
Gallery Jazz, POB 9446, New Haven, CT 06534.
T. (203) 785-8350. - Graph - 089353
Gallery One, 1 Whitney Av., New Haven, CT 06510.
T. (203) 773-0801. - Paint - 089354
Munson, 33 Whitney Av., New Haven, CT 06511.
T. (203) 865-2121. - Paint - 089355

New Orleans (Louisiana)
A Gallery for Fine Photography, 5423 Magazine St., New
Orleans, LA 70115. T. (504) 891-1002. - Pho - 089356
Borenstein, E. Lorenz, E.L.B. Gallery, 511 Royal St., New
Orleans, LA 70130. T. (504) 525-8500. - Paint / Num /
Arch / Eth / Cur - 089357
Brenner, Ronnie R., 1213 Fourth St., New Orleans, LA
70130. T. (504) 899-6236. - Paint / Graph - 089358
Bryant, 524 Royal St., New Orleans, LA 70130. - Paint /
Graph / Sculp - 089359
Carriageway, 536 Royal St., New Orleans, LA 70100.
- Paint - 089360
Casell, 818 Royal St., New Orleans, LA 70116.
T. (504) 524-0671. - Graph - 089361
Circle Gallery, 316 Royal St., New Orleans, LA 70130.
T. (504) 523-1350. - Paint - 089362
Coghlan, 710 Toulouse St., New Orleans, LA 70100.
T. (504) 525-8550. - Paint / Sculp - 089363
Collectors Gallery of New Orleans, 537 Rue Royal, New
Orleans, LA 70130. T. (504) 524-6070.
- Paint - 089364

Davis, 3964 Magazine St., New Orleans, LA 70115.
T. (504) 897-0780. - Eth - 089365
Downtown Gallery, 532 Chartres St., New Orleans, LA
70130. T. (504) 524-1988. - Paint / Graph / Repr /
Sculp - 089366
Fine Arts Gallery of New Orleans, 614 Canal St., New Or-
leans, LA 70130. T. (504) 522-0691. - Paint / Sculp /
Draw - 089367
Gallery 539, 539 Bienville St., New Orleans, LA
70130. 089368
Hanson, 229 Royal St., New Orleans, LA 70130.
T. (504) 566-0816, Fax 525-4316. - Graph - 089369
Liberty Gallery, 628 Royal St., New Orleans, LA 70130.
T. (504) 523-4363, 283-1427. - Paint / Graph - 089370
Llewellyn, Carmen, 3901 Magazine St., New Orleans, LA
70115. T. (504) 891-5301. - Paint - 089371
Manheim Galleries, 409 Royal St., New Orleans, LA
70100. T. (504) 5681901. 089372
Monett Alexandra, 512 Saint Peter St., New Orleans, LA
70116. T. (504) 586-1011. 089373
Nahan, 540 Royal St., New Orleans, LA 70130.
T. (504) 524-8696. - Paint / Graph - 089374
Parun, Phyllis, 2109 Decatur St., New Orleans, LA
70116. T. (504) 944-2859. - Sculp / Glass - 089375
Prints International, 2034 Dublin St. N., New Orleans, LA
70118. T. (504) 861-0963. - Graph - 089376
Royal Art, 537 Rue Royal, New Orleans, LA 70130.
T. (504) 524-6070. - Paint - 089377
Schertle, 1457 1/2 Calhoun St., New Orleans, LA 70115.
- Paint / Fra - 089378
Schon, Kurt E., 510 Saint Louis St., New Orleans, LA
70130. T. (504) 525-1804. - Paint - 089379
Simms, 827 Girod, New Orleans, LA 70113.
T. (504) 528-3008. - Paint - 089380
Stern, Simonne, 518 Julia St., New Orleans, LA 70130.
T. (504) 529-1118. - Paint - 089381
Tahir, 823 Chartres St., New Orleans, LA 70116.
T. (504) 525-3095. - Graph - 089382
Tilden-Foley, 4119 Magazine St., New Orleans, LA
70115. T. (504) 897-5300. - Paint - 089383
Tilden-Foley, 4119 Magazine St., New Orleans, LA
70115. T. (504) 897-5300. 089384
Villa, Mario, 3908 Magazine St., New Orleans, LA
70115. T. (504) 895-8731. - Paint / Sculp - 089385

New York
A/C Project Program, 558 Broome St, New York, NY
10129. T. (212) 226-7271. 089389
A & B Art Gallery, 1614 Third Av, New York, NY 10013.
T. (212) 423-1861. 089390
A-1 Animation, 90 Hudson St, New York, NY 10013.
T. (212) 966-4003. - Graph - 089391
Aaron, Didier, 32 E 67 St, New York, NY 10021.
T. (212) 988-5248, Fax (212) 737-3513. 089392
Abada, Felix, 1556 Third Av, New York, NY 10128.
T. (212) 427-8731. 089393
Aber, Joshua M., 20 E 72 St, New York, NY 10023.
T. (212) 877-2071. 089394
Aberbach, 980 Fifth Av, New York, NY 10021.
T. (212) 988-1100. - Paint / Graph - 089395
Abney, 591 Broadway, New York, NY 10012.
T. (212) 941-8602. 089396
Abrons, 466 Grand St, New York, NY 10002.
T. (212) 598-0400. 089397
ACA Galleries, 41 E 57 St, New York, NY 10022.
T. (212) 644-8300. - Paint / Graph / Sculp /
Draw - 089398
Accent on Art Company, 1186A Madison Av, New York,
NY 10028. T. (212) 831-5442. - Paint / Repr /
Fra - 089399
Ace Gallery, 275 Hudson St, New York, NY 10013.
T. (212) 255-5599. 089400
Acquavella, 18 E 79 St, New York, NY 10021.
T. (212) 734-6300. - Paint / Sculp - 089401
Adams Framkin, 50 W 57 St, New York, NY 10019.
T. (212) 757-6655. 089402
Adams Fund, John, 330 W 72 St, New York, NY 10023.
T. (212) 873-2633. 089403
Addict Gallery, 542 W 27 St, New York, NY 10001.
T. (212) 629-0899. 089404
Adelson, 25 E 77 St, New York, NY 10021. T. (212) 439-
6800, Fax (212) 439-6870. - Paint - 089405

ADF International Company, 309 E 45 St, New York, NY
10017. T. (212) 557-1443. 089406
Adine, 5 E 57 St, New York, NY 10022. T. (212) 826-
9750. 089407
Adler, A.M., 150 E 74 St, New York, NY 10021.
T. (212) 249-2450. 089408
Adsit, Robert, 341 E 90 St, New York, NY 10128.
T. (212) 423-0118. 089409
Aero, 132 Spring St, New York, NY 10012. T. (212) 966-
1500. 089410
African Art Imports, 303 W 42 St, New York, NY 10036.
T. (212) 586-6322. - Eth - 089411
Afriworks Gallery, 2033 Fifth Av, New York, NY 10035.
T. (212) 876-1447. - Eth - 089412
Agora Gallery, 560 Broadway, New York, NY 10012.
T. (212) 225-4406. 089413
A.I.R. Gallery, 63 Crosby St, New York, NY 10012.
T. (212) 966-0799. - Paint - 089414
Ala, Salvatore, 560 Broadway, New York, NY 10012.
T. (212) 941-1990. 089415
Alaska Shop Gallery, 31 E 74 St, New York, NY 10021.
T. (212) 879-1782. - Eth - 089416
Alexander's, 117 E 39 St, New York, NY 10016.
T. (212) 867-8866. - Sculp - 089417
Algus Mitchell, 25 Thompson St, New York, NY 10013.
T. (212) 966-1758. 089418
Allen, Charles E., 282 W Fourth St, New York, NY 10014.
T. (212) 206-1018. 089419
Allen Wincor, 110 Greene St, New York, NY 10012.
T. (212) 334-9574. 089420
Allison, H.V., 47 E 66 St, New York, NY 10021.
T. (212) 472-1455. - Paint - 089421
Alphirst, 594 Broadway, Room 300, New York, NY
10012. T. (212) 966-7182, Fax (212) 966-
7182. 089422
Alphirst, 594 Broadway, New York, NY 10012.
T. (212) 966-7182. 089423
Alter Silver Gallery, 1050 Second Av, New York, NY
10022. T. (212) 750-1928. - Silv - 089424
Amato, Carlo, 176 E 71 St, New York, NY 10021.
T. (212) 472-0803. 089425
Ambassador Gallery, 137 Spring St, New York, NY
10012. T. (212) 431-9431. 089426
Amber Palette, 444 Madison Av, New York, NY 10022.
T. (212) 753-7338. - Graph - 089427
American European Art Associates, 22 E 72 St, New
York, NY 10021. T. (212) 517-4010. 089428
American Fine Arts Company, 22 Wooster St, New York,
NY 10013. T. (212) 941-0401. 089429
American Illustrators Gallery, 18 E 77 St, New York, NY
10021. T. (212) 744-5190. - Graph - 089430
American Indian Community House Gallery, 164 Mercer
St, New York, NY 10012. T. (212) 219-8931.
- Eth - 089431
Americas Gallery, 1015 Madison Av, New York, NY
10021. T. (212) 535-7852. 089432
An Affinity for Art, 440 E 25 St, New York, NY 10010.
T. (212) 779-2330. 089433
Ancient and Modern Art Gallery, 81 Baxter St, New York,
NY 10013. T. (212) 406-1131. 089434
Ancient Art of the New World, 42 E 76 St, New York, NY
10021. T. (212) 737-3766. 089435
Anderson, Richard, 476 Broome St, New York, NY
10013. T. (212) 431-8547. 089436
Anderson, Roy, 212 E 47 St, New York, NY 10017.
T. (212) 308-7588. 089437
Andover White, 584 Broadway, New York, NY 10012.
T. (212) 343-2316. 089438
Andre Studio and Gallery, 1567 York Av, New York, NY
10028. T. (212) 744-1627. 089439
Angel of Inventions, 81 Greene St, New York, NY 10012.
T. (212) 226-4695. 089440
Animated Classics, 399 Bleecker St, New York, NY
10014. T. (212) 255-7604. - Draw - 089441
Animation Art Guild, 330 W 45 St, New York, NY 10036.
T. (212) 765-3030. 089442
Animazing Gallery, 89 South St, New York, NY 10038.
T. (212) 964-6100. 089443
Ann's Art and Antique Gallery, 161 Ninth Av, New York,
NY 10011. T. (212) 675-9415. 089444
Anthony, Ralph, 150 E 74 St, New York, NY 10021.
T. (212) 288-5222. 089445

Arader, W. Graham, 29 E 72 St, New York, NY 10021. T. (212) 628-3668. *089446*

Aranyi, 218 E 25 St, New York, NY 10010. T. (212) 685-0655. *089447*

Archetype Gallery, 115 Mercer St, New York, NY 10012. T. (212) 334-0100. *089448*

Archi Pelago, 54 W 21 St, New York, NY 10010. T. (212) 924-1697. *089449*

Architectural Design Society of America, 106 E 60 St, New York, NY 10022. T. (212) 754-2372.
- Draw - *089450*

Ardmore Affiliates, 3 E 69 St, New York, NY 10021. T. (212) 628-0606. *089451*

Ari, Ben, Il Av A, New York, NY 10009. T. (212) 677-4730. *089452*

Arnot, Herbert, 250 W 57 St, New York, NY 10107. T. (212) 245-8287. - Paint - *089453*

Arranz, 301 Columbus Av, New York, NY 10023. T. (212) 787-9119. - Graph / Pho - *089454*

Arras, 725 Fifth Av, New York, NY 10022. T. (212) 751-0080. - Paint - *089455*

Ars Medica, 881 Seventh Av, New York, NY 10019. T. (212) 757-9247. *089456*

Art Advice, 200 E 33 St, New York, NY 10016. T. (212) 683-5611. *089457*

Art Alliance, 98 Greene St, New York, NY 10012. T. (212) 274-1704. *089458*

Art Associates, 1035 Park Av, New York, NY 10028. T. (212) 831-0402. *089459*

Art Avenues, 240 W End Av., New York, NY 10025. T. (212) 876-6305. *089460*

Art Avenues, 240 W End Av, New York, NY 10023. T. (212) 874-6305. *089461*

Art Consultants to the Trade, 60 Sutton Pl S, New York, NY 10022. T. (212) 725-4740. *089462*

Art Funding Corporation, 421 Hudson St, New York, NY 10014. T. (212) 627-4149. *089463*

Art Gallery and Framing, 765 Av of the Americas, New York, NY 10010. T. (212) 924-7380. *089464*

Art Gallery 34, 146 W 34 St, New York, NY 10001. T. (212) 967-8011. - Paint / Graph - *089465*

Art Horizons International, 1430 Broadway, New York, NY 10018. T. (212) 921-5583. *089466*

Art in General, 79 Walker St, New York, NY 10013. T. (212) 219-0473. *089467*

Art Insights, 161 W 72 St, New York, NY 10023. T. (212) 724-3715. *089468*

Art Lovers Gallery, 2418 Broadway, New York, NY 10024. T. (212) 362-2713. *089469*

Art Mine, 560 Broadway, New York, NY 10012. T. (212) 226-4151. *089470*

Art Overseas, 207 E 74 St, New York, NY 10021. T. (212) 472-9426. *089471*

Art Placement International, 178 E 73 St, New York, NY 10021. T. (212) 517-8740. *089472*

Art Projects International, 470 Broome St, New York, NY 10013. T. (212) 343-2599. *089473*

Art Renaissance, 157 Spring St, New York, NY 10012. T. (212) 925-6203. *089474*

Art Spectrum, 425 E 58 St, New York, NY 10022. T. (212) 593-1812. *089475*

Art Tours of Manhattan, 33 E 22 St, New York, NY 10010. T. (212) 254-7682. *089476*

Art Vue, 270 Lafayette St, New York, NY 10012. T. (212) 925-5671. *089477*

Art Wise, 125 W 25 St, New York, NY 10001. T. (212) 989-3348. *089478*

Art-1 Gallery, 11 E Broadway, New York, NY 10038. T. (212) 608-0068. *089479*

Arte, 21 Peck Slip, New York, NY 10038. T. (212) 608-2626. *089480*

Artifacts Collections of New York, 420 E 64 St, New York, NY 10021. T. (212) 688-2075. *089481*

Artis Group, 41 E 72 St, New York, NY 10021. T. (212) 772-2323. *089482*

Artisans Source, 920 Park Av, New York, NY 10028. T. (212) 861-6747. *089483*

Artist Space, 11 Fulton St, New York, NY 10038. T. (212) 346-9677. *089484*

Artists Rights, 250 W 57 St, New York, NY 10107. T. (212) 586-2500. *089485*

Artists Space, 38 Greene St, New York, NY 10013. T. (212) 226-3970. *089486*

Artreasury, 1185 Park Av, New York, NY 10128. T. (212) 722-1235. *089487*

Artrepreneur, 945 Fifth Av, New York, NY 10021. T. (212) 861-3156. *089488*

Arts Counsel, 116 E 27 St, New York, NY 10016. T. (212) 725-3806. *089489*

Arts du Monde, 154 Spring St, New York, NY 10012. T. (212) 226-3702. *089490*

Arts for Corporations, 57 E 11 St, New York, NY 10003. T. (212) 674-3093. - Paint / Graph / Sculp /
Pho - *089491*

Artscope, 502 Park Av, New York, NY 10022. T. (212) 838-0475. *089492*

Artweave Textile Gallery, 310 Riverside Dr, New York, NY 10025. T. (212) 864-3550. - Tex - *089493*

Asher Gallant, 62 E 55 St, New York, NY 10022. T. (212) 755-6770. *089494*

Ashione, 269 W Fourth St, New York, NY 10014. T. (212) 229-0899. *089495*

Associated American Artists, 20 W 57 St, New York, NY 10019. T. (212) 399-5510. *089496*

Associated American Artists, 20 W 57 St, New York, NY 10019. T. (212) 399-5510. *089497*

Association of Hispanic Arts, 200 E 67 St, New York, NY 10021. T. (212) 369-7054. *089498*

Astro Gallery, 185 Madison Av, New York, NY 10016. T. (212) 889-9000. - Sculp - *089499*

Atelier A/E, 323 W 22 St, New York, NY 10011. T. (212) 620-8103, Fax (212) 620-8106. *089500*

Athena Fine Arts, 38 E 57 St, New York, NY 10022. T. (212) 832-0724, Fax (212) 832-0417. *089501*

Atlantic Art Consultants, 29 Washington Sq W, New York, NY 10011. T. (212) 674-7387. *089502*

Atlantic Gallery, 475 Broome St, New York, NY 10013. I. (212) 219-3183. *089503*

Atmosphere Galleries, 81 Greene St, New York, NY 10012. T. (212) 343-9115. *089504*

Auchincloss, Pamela, 558 Broadway, New York, NY 10012. T. (212) 966-7753. *089505*

Australia Gallery, 98 Greene St, New York, NY 10012. T. (212) 274-9835. *089506*

Avanti Galleries, 22 E 72 St, New York, NY 10021. T. (212) 628-3377. *089507*

Aztec, 90 John St, New York, NY 10038. T. (212) 791-3317. *089508*

Azuma, 50 Walker St, New York, NY 10013. T. (212) 925-1381. *089509*

Babcock, 724 Fifth Av, New York, NY 10019. T. (212) 767-1852, Fax (212) 767-1857. - Paint / Sculp - *089510*

Babel, 138 W 46 St, New York, NY 10036. T. (212) 997-3580. *089511*

Bace, Bill, 39 Wooster St, New York, NY 10013. T. (212) 219-0959. *089512*

Bace, Bill, 2 Bond St, New York, NY 10012. T. (212) 388-9755. *089513*

Bag One Arts, 110 W 79 St, New York, NY 10024. T. (212) 595-5537. - Graph - *089514*

Baird, T.R., 159 W 12 St, New York, NY 10011. T. (212) 242-2498. - Paint - *089515*

Balay, Felicie, 141 E 56 St, New York, NY 10022. T. (212) 752-7567. *089516*

Bangally, 341-342 Saint Marks Pl, New York, NY 10009. T. (212) 674-1598. - Eth - *089517*

Banks, Marion, 18 E 18 St, New York, NY 10003. T. (212) 228-7354. *089518*

Banning & Associates, 138 W 18 St, New York, NY 10011. T. (212) 206-0438. - Graph / Pho - *089519*

Barclay, 985 Park Av, New York, NY 10028. T. (212) 753-7171. *089520*

Bardamu, 51 Wooster St, New York, NY 10013. T. (212) 941-7130. *089521*

Barnard-Biderman, 22 E 72 St, New York, NY 10021. T. (212) 772-2352. *089522*

Bartfield, J.N., 30 W 57 St, New York, NY 10019. T. (212) 245-8890. - Paint / Graph - *089523*

Bateau Lavoir, 182 Avenue A, New York, NY 10009. T. (212) 777-1477. *089524*

Beadleston, William, 60 E 91 St, New York, NY 10128. T. (212) 348-7234, Fax (212) 534-8623. *089525*

Beaux Arts Group, 90 Gold St, New York, NY 10038. T. (212) 962-7823. *089526*

Becker, Arlene G., 979 Third Av, New York, NY 10022. T. (212) 832-5144. *089527*

Beitzel, David, 102 Prince St, New York, NY 10012. T. (212) 219-2863. *089528*

Belgis Freidel, 77 Mercer St, New York, NY 10012. T. (212) 941-8715. *089529*

Bellardo, 100a Christopher St, New York, NY 10014. T. (212) 675-2668. *089530*

Bellette Hoffman, 480 Park Av, New York, NY 10022. T. (212) 888-1195. *089531*

Bellier, Jean Claude, 211 E 53 St, New York, NY 10022. T. (212) 752-9760. *089532*

Benedek, 3 E 75 St, New York, NY 10021. T. (212) 744-2333. *089533*

Benedetto, 52 Prince St, New York, NY 10012. T. (212) 226-2238. *089534*

Benin Gallery, 2366 Seventh Av, New York, NY 10030. T. (212) 694-9426. *089535*

Berlin-Shafir, 525 Broadway, New York, NY 10012. T. (212) 431-5503. *089536*

Berman Daferner, 568 Broadway, New York, NY 10012. T. (212) 226-8330. *089537*

Berman, E.N., 138 Greene St, New York, NY 10012. T. (212) 431-1010. *089538*

Berman & Daferner, 568 Broadway, New York, NY 10012. T. (212) 226-8330. - Paint - *089539*

Bernarducci, Frank, 560 Broadway, New York, NY 10012. T. (212) 343-1853. *089540*

Bernstein, David, 737 Park Av, New York, NY 10021. T. (212) 794-0389, Fax (212) 861-8728. - Sculp / Arch / Eth / Jew / Mil - *089541*

Berry Hill Galleries, 11 E 70 St, New York, NY 10021. T. (212) 744-2300. *089542*

Borry Hill Galleries, 983 Park Av, New York, NY 10028. T. (212) 535-4498. *089543*

Bezabel, 11 Essex St, New York, NY 10002. T. (212) 228-5982. *089544*

Bleier, Milton A., 333 Park Av S, New York, NY 10022. T. (212) 533-1730. - Paint / Fra / Mul - *089545*

Blom & Dorn, 215 E 79 St, New York, NY 10021. T. (212) 219-0761. - Paint / Sculp / Draw - *089546*

Blondies, 72 Thompson St, New York, NY 10012. T. (212) 431-8601. *089547*

Blum Helman, 80 Greene St, New York, NY 10013. T. (212) 226-8770. *089548*

Blum Helman, 20 W 57 St, New York, NY 10019. T. (212) 245-2888. - Paint / Sculp / Draw - *089549*

Blum, Peter, 99 Wooster St, New York, NY 10012. T. (212) 343-0441. *089550*

Blumka, 101 E 81 St, New York, NY 10028. T. (212) 734-3222. - Sculp - *089551*

BM Art, 375 W Broadway, New York, NY 10012. T. (212) 226-5808. *089552*

Boehm, 725 Fifth Av, New York, NY 10022. T. (212) 838-1562. *089553*

Boerner, C.G., 61 E 77 St, New York, NY 10021. T. (212) 772-7330. - Graph / Draw - *089554*

Bohen Foundation, 120 Wooster St, New York, NY 10012. T. (212) 334-2281. *089555*

Boisante, Elise, 50 W 57 St, New York, NY 10019. T. (212) 581-9191. *089556*

Bonni Benrubi, 52 E 76 St, New York, NY 110021. T. (212) 517-3766, Fax (212) 288-7815. - Pho - *089557*

Boone, Mary, 417 W Broadway, New York, NY 10012. T. (212) 431-1818. *089558*

Borden, Janet, 560 Broadway, New York, NY 10012. T. (212) 431-0166. *089559*

Borgenicht, Grace, 724 Fifth Av, New York, NY 10019. T. (212) 247-2111. - Paint / Graph / Sculp - *089560*

Borghi & Co., 26 E 80 St, New York, NY 10021. T. (212) 734-4545. - Paint - *089561*

Bowie, William, 441 Lafayette St, New York, NY 10003. T. (212) 777-1414. *089562*

Bowles Sorokko, 447 W Broadway, New York, NY 10012. T. (212) 228-4200. *089563*

Braathen, Barbara, 33 Bleecker St, New York, NY 10012. T. (212) 777-1161. *089564*

Brady, W.M., 3 E 76 St, New York, NY 10021. T. (212) 249-7212. *089565*

Bratton, 20 Cornelia St, New York, NY 10014. T. (212) 675-5203. *089566*

Brent Sikkema, 40 Wooster St, New York, NY 10013. T. (212) 941-6210. *089567*

Briet, Philippe, 558 Broadway, New York, NY 10012.
T. (212) 334-0433. *089568*

Broadway Art Expo, 2165 Broadway, New York, NY 10024. T. (212) 362-4533. *089569*

Brooke, Alexander, 476 Broome St, New York, NY 10013. T. (212) 925-2070. - Paint / Graph / Sculp - *089570*

Broome Gallery, 498 Broome St, New York, NY 10013. T. (212) 225-6085. *089571*

Brown, Diane, 620 Broadway, New York, NY 10012. T. (212) 260-8797. *089572*

Bruch, R., 66 Allen St, New York, NY 10002. T. (212) 226-4196. *089573*

Bruton, 40 E 61 St, New York, NY 10021. T. (212) 980-1640, Fax (212) 223-2593. *089574*

Bryers, Gabrielle, 111 Greene St, New York, NY 10012. T. (212) 925-8058. *089575*

Burke, Diana, 225 Liberty St, New York, NY 10281. T. (212) 233-0128. *089576*

Bustamante, Frank, 560 Broadway, New York, NY 10012. T. (212) 226-2108. *089577*

C & M, 45 E 78 St, New York, NY 10021. T. (212) 861-0020. *089578*

C & M Arts, 45 E 78 St, New York, NY 10021. T. (212) 861-0020. *089579*

C & M Fine Art, 979 Third Av, New York, NY 10022. T. (212) 421-2440. *089580*

Cadé, Denise, 1045 Madison Av, New York, NY 10021. T. (212) 734-3670. - Paint - *089581*

Cameo Art Consultants, 130 E 63 St, New York, NY 10021. T. (212) 832-7200. *089582*

Camille, Mizzi, 248 Lafayette St, New York, NY 10012. T. (212) 925-2484. *089583*

Cano, 721 Fifth Av, New York, NY 10022. T. (212) 832-8172, Fax (212) 370-9250. *089584*

Caravan Defrance Galleries, 210 E 86 St, New York, NY 10028. T. (212) 772-7160. *089585*

Carib Art Gallery, 584 Broadway, New York, NY 10012. T. (212) 343-2539. *089586*

Carpenter, Laura, 241 Lafayette St, New York, NY 10012. T. (212) 226-9292. *089587*

Carus, 872 Madison Av, New York, NY 10021. T. (212) 879-4660. *089588*

CCA Galleries, 48 Laight St, New York, NY 10013. T. (212) 274-8860. - Paint / Graph / Sculp - *089589*

CDS Gallery, 74 E 79 St, New York, NY 10021. T. (212) 772-9555. - Paint / Sculp / Draw - *089590*

Center for Book Arts, 625 Broadway, New York, NY 10012. T. (212) 460-9768. - Graph - *089591*

Central Arts, 250 W 57 St, New York, NY 10107. T. (212) 977-8675. *089592*

Century Galleries, 508 Broadway, New York, NY 10012. T. (212) 274-9189. *089593*

Ceres, 584 Broadway, New York, NY 10012. T. (212) 226-4725. *089594*

Cerutti & Miller, 40 W 17 St, New York, NY 10011. T. (212) 645-0808. *089595*

Cervera, Marta, 470 Broome St, New York, NY 10013. T. (212) 941-7135. *089596*

CFM Gallery, 112 Greene St, New York, NY 10012. T. (212) 966-3864. *089597*

Chait, Ralph M., 12 E 56 St, New York, NY 10022. T. (212) 758-0937. *089597a*

Chalette, 9 E 88 St, New York, NY 10128. T. (212) 722-8834. *089598*

Chatellier, 760 Madison Av, New York, NY 10021. T. (212) 717-5567. *089599*

Chelsea Art Galleries, 359 W 22 St, New York, NY 10011. T. (212) 691-8155. *089600*

Chelsea Ceramic Guild, 233 W 19 St, New York, NY 10011. T. (212) 243-2430. - China - *089601*

Chinoh, 69 Fifth Av, New York, NY 10003. T. (212) 255-0377. *089602*

Chinoh, 575 Fifth Av, New York, NY 10017. T. (212) 986-2420, Fax (212) 255-0377. - Paint - *089603*

Chisholm, 55 W 17 St, New York, NY 10011. T. (212) 243-8834. *089604*

Chozoco, 28 E 78 St, New York, NY 10021. T. (212) 628-2942. *089605*

Cinderella Press, 13 Laight St, New York, NY 10013. T. (212) 463-9321. - Graph - *089606*

Cinque Gallery, 560 Broadway, New York, NY 10012. T. (212) 966-3464. *089607*

Circle Gallery, 725 Fifth Av, New York, NY 10022. T. (212) 980-5455. *089608*

Circle Gallery, 468 W Broadway, New York, NY 10012. T. (212) 677-5100. - Paint - *089609*

Claude, Bernard, 900 Park Av, New York, NY 10021. T. (212) 988-2050, Fax (212) 737-2290. *089610*

Clean Well Lighted Place, 363 Bleecker St, New York, NY 10014. T. (212) 255-3656. *089611*

Club of American Collectors of Fine Arts, 20 W 64 St, New York, NY 10023. T. (212) 769-1860. *089612*

Coe Kerr, 49 E 82 St, New York, NY 10028. T. (212) 628-1340. - Paint - *089613*

Cohen, 1018 Madison Av, New York, NY 1010021. T. (212) 628-0303. *089614*

Cole, Sylvan, 101 W 57 St, New York, NY 10019. T. (212) 333-7760. *089615*

Collins, Richard J., 605 Madison Av, New York, NY 10022. T. (212) 832-1444. *089616*

Colnaghi, 21 E 67 St, New York, NY 10021. T. (212) 772-2266. - Paint - *089617*

Colorworks Studio, 114 E 32 St, New York, NY 1010016. T. (212) 481-7143. *089618*

Columbus Art Gallery, 588 Columbus Av, New York, NY 10024. T. (212) 875-1678. *089619*

Common Ground, 19 Greenwich Av, New York, NY 10011. T. (212) 366-4178. *089620*

Condeso Lawler, 524 Broadway, New York, NY 10012. T. (212) 219-1283. *089621*

Conner Rosenkranz, 16 E 73 St, New York, NY 10021. T. (212) 517-3710. *089622*

Contemporary African Art, 330 W 108 St, New York, NY 10025. T. (212) 662-8799. - Eth - *089623*

Contemporary Christian Art, 217 E 66 St, New York, NY 10021. T. (212) 288-8186. - Rel - *089624*

Conway, Catherine, 112 W 13 St, New York, NY 10011. T. (212) 627-9344. *089625*

Cooper, Paula, 155 Wooster St, New York, NY 10012. T. (212) 674-0766, Fax (212) 674-1938. - Paint / Graph / Sculp / Pho / Mul / Draw - *089626*

Cooper Seeman, 126 E 12 St, New York, NY 10003. T. (212) 475-2174. *089627*

Cordier & Ekstrom, 417 E 75 St, New York, NY 10021. T. (212) 988-8857. *089628*

Cornelius Craig, 321 W 13 St, New York, NY 10014. T. (212) 243-7171. *089629*

Corporate Art Associates, 270 Lafayette St, New York, NY 10012. T. (212) 941-9685. - Paint / Graph - *089630*

Corporate Art Directions, 41 E 57 St, New York, NY 10022. T. (212) 355-5370. *089631*

Corsini, Piero, 162 E 63 St, New York, NY 10021. T. (212) 371-6455. *089632*

Cotton, L.A., 645 Madison Av, New York, NY 10022. T. (212) 838-6390. *089633*

Cowdery, Richard, 231 E 60 St, New York, NY 10022. T. (212) 223-0726. *089634*

Cowles, Charles, 420 W Broadway, New York, NY 10012. T. (212) 925-3500. - Graph / Sculp / Instr / Pho / Draw - *089635*

Criswick, 325 F 41 St, New York, NY 10017. T. (212) 490-2337. *089636*

Crown Art Gallery, 1609 Broadway, New York, NY 10019. T. (212) 757-8255. *089637*

Cugliani, Tom, 40 Wooster St, New York, NY 10013. T. (212) 966-9006. *089638*

Culture Crossing, 40 E 94 St, New York, NY 10128. T. (212) 427-2220. *089639*

Custom Airbrush Gallery, 430 E Ninth St, New York, NY 10009. T. (212) 982-9401. *089640*

Cyn Thai Arts and Antiques, 505 Fifth Av, New York, NY 10017. T. (212) 697-0792. - Eth - *089641*

Dalva Brothers, 44 E 57 St, New York, NY 10022. T. (212) 758-2297. *089642*

Dancing Ink Art Gallery, 127 Second Av, New York, NY 10003. T. (212) 673-1607. *089643*

Danziger, James, 130 Prince St, New York, NY 10012. T. (212) 226-0056. *089644*

Daugherty, Elaine, 214 E 31 St, New York, NY 10016. T. (212) 532-3490. *089645*

David Collection, 161 W 15 St, New York, NY 10011. T. (212) 929-4602. *089646*

Davis & Langdale, 231 E 60 St, New York, NY 10022. T. (212) 838-0333. *089647*

Davlyn, 975 Madison Av, New York, NY 10021. T. (212) 879-2075. *089648*

De Mena, 179 E 93 St, New York, NY 10128. T. (212) 722-3527. *089649*

De Nagy, Tibor, 41 W 57 St, New York, NY 10019. T. (212) 421-3780. *089650*

Decor Art Gallery, 551 Third Av, New York, NY 10016. T. (212) 725-6787. *089651*

Decor Art Gallery, 1156 Second Av, New York, NY 10021. T. (212) 688-7078. *089652*

Deitch, Jeffrey, 721 Fifth Av, New York, NY 10022. T. (212) 371-2630. *089653*

Di Modica, 54 Crosby St, New York, NY 10012. T. (212) 966-6068. *089654*

Diamant Gallery, 37 W 72 St, New York, NY 10023. T. (212) 362-3434. *089655*

Dickinson, Simon, 14 E 73 St, New York, NY 10021. T. (212) 772-8083. *089656*

Dintenfass, Terry, 50 W 57 St, New York, NY 10019. T. (212) 581-2268. - Paint / Graph / Sculp - *089657*

Donahue, E.M., 560 Broadway, New York, NY 10012. T. (212) 226-1111. *089658*

Donahue, E.M., 28 E 10 St, New York, NY 10003. T. (212) 477-3442. *089659*

Donchian, Karen, 148 E 89 St, New York, NY 10128. T. (212) 369-5368. *089660*

Donson, Theodore B., 24 W 57 St, New York, NY 10019. T. (212) 245-7007. - Graph - *089661*

Dorset, 30 W 54 St, New York, NY 10019. T. (212) 956-0500. *089662*

Dorsky, 379 Broadway, New York, NY 10013. T. (212) 966-6170. *089663*

Douglas Le Roy, Joslin, 102 Christopher St, New York, NY 10014. T. (212) 242-5713. *089664*

Doyers Gallery, 14 Doyers St, New York, NY 10013. T. (212) 227-5057. *089665*

Drake, 50 W 57 St, New York, NY 10019. T. (212) 582-5930. - Paint / Graph / Sculp / Eth / Pho / Draw - *089666*

Dranoff, 588 Broadway, New York, NY 10012. T. (212) 966-0153. *089667*

Drey, Paul, 11 E 57 St, New York, NY 10022. T. (212) 753-2551, Fax (212) 838-0339. - Paint / Sculp / Draw - *089668*

Drutt, Helen, 724 Fifth Av, Ninth Floor, New York, NY 10019. T. (212) 974-7700, Fax (212) 974-9329. *089669*

Dumonde, 401 Fifth Av, New York, NY 10016. T. (212) 213-0631. *089670*

Durini Di Monza, Alessandro, 5 E 75 St, New York, NY 10021. T. (212) 744-1101. *089671*

Dyansen, Trump Tower, New York, NY 10022. T. (212) 754-3040. *089672*

Eastern Arts, 365 Bleecker St, New York, NY 10014. T. (212) 929-7460. *089673*

Eastern Arts, 68 Jane St, New York, NY 10014. T. (212) 366-5385. *089674*

Eastlake Gallery, 1078-1080 Madison Av, New York, NY 10028. T. (212) 772-8810. *089675*

Edelman, 386 W Broadway, New York, NY 10012. T. (212) 226-1198. - Paint / Fra - *089676*

Edelman, H. Heather, 386 W Broadway, New York, NY 10012. T. (212) 226-2943. *089677*

Ehrenthal, Irving, 33 E 22 St, New York, NY 10010. T. (212) 677-2527. *089678*

Einstein, G.W., 591 Broadway, New York, NY 10012. T. (212) 226-1414. *089679*

Ellis, 545 Madison Av, New York, NY 10022. T. (212) 838-8711. *089680*

Emerging Collector, 62 Second Av, New York, NY 10003. T. (212) 254-4060. *089681*

Emmerich, Andre'1, 41 E 57 St, New York, NY 10022. T. (212) 752-0124. *089682*

Empire Art Gallery, 784 Av of the Americas, New York, NY 10001. T. (212) 685-7211. *089683*

Empire Gallery, 174 Fifth Av, New York, NY 10010. T. (212) 229-0855. *089684*

Eno, Amos, 594 Broadway, New York, NY 10012. T. (212) 226-5342. *089685*

Environment Gallery, 405 E 54 St, New York, NY 10022. T. (212) 688-5880. *089686*

Equatorial America, 411 E 53 St, New York, NY 10022. T. (212) 593-3306. *089687*

Equitable Appraisal Company, 19 E 75 St, New York, NY 10021. T. (212) 535-3160. *089688*

Equity Art Brokers, 340 E 52 St, New York, NY 10022. T. (212) 593-3188. *089689*

Ergane, 469 W Broadway, New York, NY 10012. T. (212) 228-9600. *089690*

Ernst, 25 W 68 St, New York, NY 10023. T. (212) 769-1800. *089691*

Erotics Gallery, 41 Union Sq W, New York, NY 10003. T. (212) 633-2241. *089692*

Esman, Rosa, 575 Broadway, New York, NY 10012. T. (212) 219-3044, Fax (212) 941-5921. *089693*

Esskay, 51 E 42 St, New York, NY 10017. T. (212) 949-0022. *089694*

Ethnix Tribal Arts, 636 Broadway, New York, NY 10012. T. (212) 614-6610. - Eth - *089695*

Exhibition Space, 50 W 57 St, New York, NY 10019. T. (212) 315-5100. *089696*

Exotique Gallery, 90 W Houston St, New York, NY 10012. T. (212) 473-6393. *089697*

FDR Gallery, 670 Broadway, New York, NY 10012. T. (212) 777-3051. *089698*

Feature, 76 Greene St, New York, NY 10012. T. (212) 941-7077. *089699*

Fedele, Frank, 170-176 John St, New York, NY 10038. T. (212) 747-0710. *089700*

Federal Art Gallery, 102 Worth St, New York, NY 10013. T. (212) 732-7550. *089701*

Feiden, Margo, 699 Madison Av, New York, NY 10021. T. (212) 677-5330. *089702*

Feiwel, Henry, 900 Broadway, New York, NY 10003. T. (212) 777-2523. *089703*

Feldman, Ronald, 31 Mercer St, New York, NY 10013. T. (212) 226-3232. *089704*

Fendrick, Barbara, 568 Broadway, New York, NY 10012. T. (212) 966-2820. *089705*

Ferzt, Mimi, 114 Prince St, New York, NY 10012. T. (212) 343-9377. *089706*

Fielding, Natalie, 370 Lexington Av, New York, NY 10017. T. (212) 983-0850. *089707*

Fields, J., 55 W 17 St, New York, NY 10011. T. (212) 989-4520. *089708*

Fifty-Five Mercer Gallery, 55 Mercer St, New York, NY 10013. T. (212) 226-8513. *089709*

Figura, 53 E 75 St, New York, NY 10021. T. (212) 772-6627. - Repr - *089710*

Findlay, David, 219 E 81 St, New York, NY 10028. T. (212) 472-3590. *089711*

Findlay, David, 984 Madison Av, New York, NY 10021. T. (212) 249-2909. *089712*

Findlay, Peter, 1001 Madison Av, New York, NY 10021. T. (212) 772-8660. - Paint / Sculp - *089713*

Findlay, Wally, 17 E 57 St, New York, NY 10022. T. (212) 411-5390. - Paint - *089714*

Findley, Wally, 17 E 57 St., New York, NY 10022. T. (212) 421-5390. - Paint / Graph / Sculp - *089715*

Fine Art Acquisitions, 122 Spring St, New York, NY 10012. T. (212) 431-3744. *089716*

Fine Art Communications, 124 E 13 St, New York, NY 10003. T. (212) 533-2288. *089717*

Fine Art Resources, 636 Broadway, New York, NY 10012. T. (212) 533-1600. *089718*

Fine Arts of Ancient Lands, 12 E 86 St, New York, NY 10028. T. (212) 249-7442. - Paint / Pho - *089719*

First Peoples Gallery, 114 Spring St, New York, NY 10012. T. (212) 343-0166. *089720*

Fisher, M. Roy, 170 Mercer St, New York, NY 10012. T. (212) 925-9009. *089721*

Fishion, 55 Av of the Americas, New York, NY 10013. T. (212) 941-1375. *089722*

Fitch-Febvrel, 5 E 57 St, New York, NY 10022. T. (212) 688-8522. - Graph - *089723*

Flavin, Dan, 5 Worth St, New York, NY 10013. T. (212) 431-3033. *089724*

Fletcher, Michael, 382 W Broadway, New York, NY 10012. T. (212) 925-8960. *089725*

Fortuna Fine Arts, 984 Madison Av, New York, NY 10021. T. (212) 794-7272, Fax (212) 794-7275. *089726*

Forum, 745 Fifth Av at 57 St, New York, NY 10151. T. (212) 355-4545, Fax (212) 355-4547. *089727*

Four Color Images, 524 Broadway, New York, NY 10012. T. (212) 431-4234. - Graph - *089728*

Frama, 190 Tenth Av, New York, NY 10011. T. (212) 366-0700. *089729*

Framers' Workroom, 1484 Third Av, New York, NY 10028. T. (212) 570-0919. *089730*

Framers' Workroom of Chelsea, 130 W 23 St, New York, NY 10011. T. (212) 989-8900. *089731*

Frameworks New York, 51 E 19 St, New York, NY 10003. T. (212) 982-2929. - Fra - *089732*

Frankel, E. & J., 1040 Madison Av, New York, NY 10021. T. (212) 879-5733. *089733*

Franklin Parrasch, 588 Broadway, New York, NY 10012. T. (212) 925-7090. *089734*

Freire, J., 21 Mercer St, New York, NY 10013. T. (212) 941-8611. *089735*

Freund, 444 Park Av S, New York, NY 10016. T. (212) 447-6541. *089736*

Friedman, Anita, 980 Madison Av, New York, NY 10021. T. (212) 472-1527. - Fra - *089737*

Friedman, Barry, 851 Madison Av, New York, NY 10021. T. (212) 794-8950, Fax (212) 794-8889. *089738*

Friends of Bezalel Academy, 654 Madison Av, New York, NY 10021. T. (212) 935-1900. *089739*

Fulton, 799 Lexington Av, New York, NY 10021. T. (212) 832-8854. - Paint / Graph / Fra - *089740*

Fulton Street Art Gallery, 102 Fulton St, New York, NY 10038. T. (212) 587-5962. *089741*

G P L Promotions, 220 Madison Av, New York, NY 10016. T. (212) 684-1066. *089742*

Galdy, 19 E 71 St, New York, NY 10021. T. (212) 517-8576. *089743*

Galerie des Arts, 18 E 76 St, New York, NY 10021. T. (212) 861-7925. *089744*

Galerie Naive, 145 E 92 St, New York, NY 10128. T. (212) 427-9283. - Paint - *080745*

Galerie Saint Etienne, 24 W 57 St, New York, NY 10019. T. (212) 245-6734. - Paint / Graph / Sculp / Draw - *089746*

Galerie Select, 300 Mercer St, New York, NY 10003. T. (212) 529-5550. *089747*

Gallery of Contemporary Fine Art, 332 Columbus Av, New York, NY 10023. T. (212) 877-0130. *089748*

Gallery Three Zero, 30 Bond St, New York, NY 10012. T. (212) 505-9668. *089749*

Gallery 10, 7 Greenwich St, New York, NY 10004. T. (212) 206-1058. - China / Glass - *089750*

Gallery 13, 451 W Broadway, New York, NY 10012. T. (212) 387-8200. *089751*

Gallery 292, 120 Wooster St, New York, NY 10012. T. (212) 431-0292. *089752*

Gallery 84, 50 W 57 St, New York, NY 10019. T. (212) 581-6000. *089753*

Gallery 86, 208 E 86 St, New York, NY 10028. T. (212) 570-2330. *089754*

Gallery 91, 91 Grand St, New York, NY 10013. T. (212) 966-3722, Fax (212) 219-1684. *089755*

Ganz, Kate, 66 E 83 St, New York, NY 10028. T. (212) 517-4892. *089756*

Gardner & Barr, 213 E 60 St, New York, NY 10022. T. (212) 752-0555. *089757*

Garth, Clark, 24 W 57 St, New York, NY 10019. T. (212) 246-2205. *089758*

Garufi, John P., 110 Fourth Av, New York, NY 10003. T. (212) 254-0720. *089759*

Gelabert, 255 W 86 St, New York, NY 10024. T. (212) 874-7188. *089760*

Gelender, William, 457 W 57 St, New York, NY 10019. T. (212) 315-2131. *089761*

Gemini, 375 W Broadway, New York, NY 10012. T. (212) 219-1446, Fax (212) 334-3109. - Graph / Sculp - *089762*

Germans Van Eck, 420 W Broadway, New York, NY 10012. T. (212) 219-0811. *089763*

Gerst, Hilde, 685 Madison Av, New York, NY 10021. T. (212) 751-5655, Fax (212) 751-0886. - Paint - *089764*

Ghiordian Knot, 136 E 57 St, New York, NY 10022. T. (212) 371-6390. *089765*

Gibson, John, 568 Broadway, New York, NY 10012. T. (212) 925-1192. *089766*

Ginsberg, Betty, 979 Third Av, New York, NY 10022. T. (212) 980-3370. *089767*

Gladstone, Barbara, 99 Greene St, New York, NY 10012. T. (212) 431-3334. *089768*

Glass Art Gallery, 315 Central Park W, New York, NY 10025. T. (212) 787-4704. - Glass - *089769*

Godel & Co., 969 Madison Av, New York, NY 10021. T. (212) 288-7272. - Paint / Graph / Sculp - *089770*

Goffman, Judy, 18 E 77 St, New York, NY 10021. T. (212) 744-5190. *089771*

Golden, Caren, 30 W 61 St, New York, NY 10023. T. (212) 274-0080. *089772*

Goldwater, Marge, 588 Broadway, New York, NY 10012. T. (212) 966-1871. *089773*

Good, John, 532 Broadway, New York, NY 10012. T. (212) 941-8066. *089774*

Goodman, James, 41 E 57 St, New York, NY 10022. T. (212) 593-3737. - Paint / Sculp / Draw - *089775*

Gorney, Jay, 100 Greene St, New York, NY 10012. T. (212) 966-8545. *089776*

Graham & Sons, James, 1014 Madison Av, New York, NY 10021. T. (212) 535-5767. - Paint / Sculp / Pho - *089777*

Gramercy Park Art Gallery, 368 Third Av, New York, NY 10003. T. (212) 689-7680. *089778*

Grand Central Art Galleries, 24 W 57 St, New York, NY 10019. T. (212) 867-3344. *089779*

Graphic Arts Gallery, 1601 York Av, New York, NY 10028. T. (212) 988-4731. - Graph - *089780*

Grass Roots Gallery, 560 Broadway, New York, NY 10012. T. (212) 431-0144. *089781*

Great Expectations, 1310 Madison Av, New York, NY 10028. T. (212) 289-3923. *089782*

Great Modern Pictures, 48 E 82 St, New York, NY 10028. T. (212) 717-6610. - Paint / Graph / Draw - *089783*

Green Essie, 419 Convent Av, New York, NY 10031. T. (212) 368-9635. *089784*

Green, Richard, 152 Wooster St, New York, NY 10012. T. (212) 982-3993. *089785*

Greenberg, Howard, 120 Wooster St, New York, NY 10012. T. (212) 334-0010. *089786*

Greene, E., 361 Bleecker St, New York, NY 10014. T. (212) 366-0645. *089787*

Greene Space Gallery, 105 Greene St, New York, NY 10012. T. (212) 431-8720. *089788*

Greenwich House Pottery, 16 Jones St, New York, NY 10014. T. (212) 929-9091. - China - *089789*

Greenwich Village Art Gallery, 315 Bleecker St, New York, NY 10014. T. (212) 255-7711. *089790*

Greer, 81 Wooster St, New York, NY 10012. T. (212) 431-6025. - Paint / Graph / Sculp - *089791*

Greer, Jane, 611 Broadway, New York, NY 10012. T. (212) 353-0460. *089792*

Grenco, 11 E 57 St, New York, NY 10022. T. (212) 486-3434. *089793*

Grippi, 315 E 62 St, New York, NY 10021. T. (212) 759-6083. *089794*

Grossman, Shary, 128 E 72 St, New York, NY 10021. T. (212) 517-5522. *089795*

Grove Decoys, 36 W 44 St, New York, NY 10036. T. (212) 391-0688. *089796*

Gueye Ousmane, 3280 Broadway, New York, NY 10027. T. (212) 234-3345. *089797*

Guggenheim, Barbara, 63 E 82 St, New York, NY 10028. T. (212) 772-3888. *089798*

Gumilang, 1050 Second Av, New York, NY 10022. T. (212) 688-5844. *089799*

Gutierrez, Angel, 161 Chrystie St, New York, NY 10002. T. (212) 533-9380. *089800*

H. M. Art Gallery, 102 Worth St., New York, NY 10013. T. (212) 619-0959. *089801*

H & M Art Gallery, 102 Worth St, New York, NY 10013. T. (212) 619-0959. *089802*

Habart, 315 E 65 St, New York, NY 10021. T. (212) 988-5349. *089803*

Haber, Robert, 16 W 23 St, New York, NY 10010. T. (212) 243-3656. *089804*

Haenah-Kent, 568 Broadway, New York, NY 10012. T. (212) 941-6180, Fax (212) 274-8354. *089805*

Hahn, Stephem, 817 Fifth Av, New York, NY 10021. T. (212) 759-6645. *089806*

Haiti Art, 145 E 92 St, New York, NY 10128. T. (212) 427-9283. *089807*

Haitian Art World, 1595 Broadway, New York, NY 10019. T. (212) 757-0162. *089808*

Haller, Stephen, 560 Broadway, New York, NY 10012. T. (212) 219-2500. *089809*

Hamideh Bayley, 99 Greene St, New York, NY 10012.
T. (212) 334-0362. 089810
Hammer, 33 W 57 St, New York, NY 10019. T. (212) 644-
4400. - Paint - 089811
Hammerquist, 419 Third Av, New York, NY 10016.
T. (212) 889-8173. - Paint - 089812
Hanover Square Gallery, 3 Hanover Sq, New York, NY
10004. T. (212) 344-4406. - Paint - 089813
Harbor Galleries, 24 W 57 St, New York, NY 10019.
T. (212) 307-6667. - Graph - 089814
Harlan & Weaver, 83 Canal St, New York, NY 10002.
T. (212) 925-5421. 089815
Harris, Elizabeth, 524 Broadway, New York, NY 10012.
T. (212) 941-9895. 089816
Harris, Lionel H., 22 E 60 St, New York, NY 10022.
T. (212) 753-3248. 089817
Harvard Arts, 214 E 14 St, New York, NY 10003.
T. (212) 995-0653. 089818
Harvard Gallery, 315 E 86 St, New York, NY 10028.
T. (212) 722-3820. - Paint - 089819
Harvey, Emily, 537 Broadway, New York, NY 10012.
T. (212) 925-7651. 089820
Hawkins, Sally, 448 W Broadway, New York, NY 10012.
T. (212) 477-5699. 089821
Hearn, Pat, 39 Wooster St, New York, NY 10013.
T. (212) 941-7055. 089822
Heidenberg, Lillian, 50 W 57 St, New York, NY 10019.
T. (212) 586-3808. - Paint / Graph / Sculp /
Draw - 089823
Heineman, 594 Broadway, New York, NY 10012.
T. (212) 334-0821. 089824
Helander, 594 Broadway, New York, NY 10012.
T. (212) 966-9797. 089825
Heller, 71 Greene St, New York, NY 10012. T. (212) 966-
5948. 089826
Hemingway, 1050 Second Av, New York, NY 10022.
T. (212) 838-3650. - Eth - 089827
Henoch, 80 Wooster St, New York, NY 10012.
T. (212) 966-6360, Fax (212) 966-0303. 089828
Hexton, 39 E 78 St, New York, NY 10021. T. (212) 570-
9335. 089829
Hip Shop, 2228 Seventh Av, New York, NY 10027.
T. (212) 283-8527. 089830
Hirschl & Adler, 21 E 70 St, New York, NY 10021.
T. (212) 535-8810. - Paint / Graph / Sculp /
Draw - 089831
Historical Design Collection, 305 E 61 St, New York, NY
10021. T. (212) 593-4528. 089832
Hochman, Irena, 22 E 72 St, New York, NY 10021.
I. (212) 772-2227. 089833
Hoffeld & Co., Jeffrey, 360 E 88 St, New York, NY
10128. T. (212) 996-6339. 089834
Hoffman, Nancy, 429 W Broadway, New York, NY 10012.
T. (212) 966-6676. 089835
Hollis Taggart, 48 E 73 St, New York, NY 10021.
T. (212) 734-8100. 089836
Holmberg, 280 Madison Av, New York, NY 10016.
T. (212) 545-9155. 089837
Honda Fine Arts, 55 Great Jones St, New York, NY
10012. T. (212) 477-4086. 089838
Hoorn-Ashby, 766 Madison Av, New York, NY 10021.
T. (212) 628-3199. 089839
Horan, Vivian, 35 E 67 St, New York, NY 10021.
T. (212) 517-9410, Fax (212) 772-6107.
- Paint - 089840
Horodner Romley, 107 Sullivan St, New York, NY 10012.
T. (212) 274-9805. 089841
Houk Friedman, 851 Madison Av, New York, NY 10021.
T. (212) 629-5300. 089842
Howells, Henry, 137 Thompson St, New York, NY 10012.
T. (212) 533-7994. 089843
Hubert, 1046 Madison Av, New York, NY 10021.
T. (212) 628-2922. 089844
Hudson River Picture Frames, 107 W 86 St, New York,
NY 10024. T. (212) 873-2098. - Fra - 089845
Humphrey, 44 W Tenth St, New York, NY 10011.
T. (212) 226-5360. 089846
Hutton, Leonard, 41 E 57 St, New York, NY 10022.
T. (212) 751-7373. - Paint / Graph / Sculp /
Draw - 089847
I.C. Editions, 21 E 22 St, New York, NY 10010.
T. (212) 475-6990. - Graph - 089848

Igal, M., 156 Bleecker St, New York, NY 10012.
T. (212) 254-9337. 089849
Ihasa, 86 Macdougal St, New York, NY 10012.
T. (212) 228-2889. 089850
Ikeda, Akira, 130 Prince St, New York, NY 10012.
T. (212) 274-9080. - Graph - 089851
Ikkan, 77 Mercer St, New York, NY 10012. T. (212) 734-
3055. 089852
Illustration Gallery, 330 E 11 St, New York, NY 10003.
T. (212) 979-1014. - Graph - 089853
Illustration House, 96 Spring St, New York, NY 10012.
T. (212) 966-9444. - Graph - 089854
Images Art Gallery, 580 Broadway, New York, NY 10012.
T. (212) 219-8484. 089855
In te Spirit Judaica, 460 E 79 St, New York, NY 10021.
T. (212) 861-5222. 089856
Ingbar, Michael, 578 Broadway, New York, NY 10012.
T. (212) 334-1100. - Graph / Repr / Fra - 089857
Ismeco, 140 E 63 St, New York, NY 10021. T. (212) 759-
3240. 089858
Isselbacher, 41 E 78 St, New York, NY 10021.
T. (212) 472-1766. 089859
J Art Gallery, 1615 Second Av, New York, NY 10028.
T. (212) 988-5013. 089860
Jack's Art Gallery, 388 Av of the Americas, New York,
NY 10011. T. (212) 353-2220. 089861
Jack's Art Gallery, 2561 Broadway, New York, NY
10025. T. (212) 866-3500. 089862
Jack's Art Gallery, 2855 Broadway, New York, NY
10025. T. (212) 749-5554. 089863
Jacob, Yvette, 760 Madison Av, New York, NY 10021.
T. (212) 717-5162. 089864
Jadite Gallery, 415 W 50 St, 10000 New York, NY
10019. T. (212) 315-2740. 089865
Jain Marunouchi, 560 Broadway, New York, NY 10012.
T. (212) 274-8087. 089866
Jal, 655 Fifth Av, 52 St, New York, NY 10022. 089867
Japan Gallery, 1210 Lexington Av, New York, NY 10028.
T. (212) 288-2241. - Graph - 089868
Jaro, 955 Madison Av, New York, NY 10021.
T. (212) 734-5475. - Paint / Graph - 089869
Jeanmarie, 1057 Second Av, New York, NY 10022.
T. (212) 486-8150. 089870
Jensen, 48 E 73 St, New York, NY 10021. T. (212) 861-
6008. 089871
Johnpol, 127 Fulton St, New York, NY 10038.
T. (212) 267-6790. 089872
Johns, Derek, 63 E 82 St, New York, NY 10028.
T. (212) 772-3380. 089873
Johnson, Ben, 210 Central Park S, New York, NY 10019.
T. (212) 265-4389. - Paint - 089874
Johnson, Harmer F., 122 E 82 St, New York, NY 10028.
T. (212) 535-4463. - Arch / Eth - 089875
Jordan, Madelyn, 580 Broadway, New York, NY 10012.
T. (212) 343-0304. 089876
Jordan-Volpe, 958 Madison Av, New York, NY 10021.
T. (212) 570-9500. - Ant / Paint / Graph / Furn / Sculp /
Lights - 089877
Judaica Classics, 125 E 85 St, New York, NY 10028.
T. (212) 722-4271. 089878
Julie Artisans Gallery, 687 Madison Av, New York, NY
10021. T. (212) 688-2345. 089879
Jungle Studio, 200 Varick St, New York, NY 10014.
T. (212) 366-1933. 089880
Just Above Midtown, 503 Broadway, New York, NY
10012. T. (212) 966-7020. 089881
K Art Gallery, 1280 First Av, New York, NY 10021.
T. (212) 517-9620. 089882
K & M Studio, 47 W 14 St, New York, NY 10011.
T. (212) 924-2277. 089883
Kahan, 48 E 57 St, New York, NY 10022. T. (212) 355-
5110. - Eth - 089884
Kahan, Jane, 922 Madison Av, New York, NY 10021.
T. (212) 744-1490. - Paint / Graph / Sculp - 089885
Kaller-Kimche, R., 23 E 74 St, New York, NY 10021.
T. (212) 288-5698. 089886
Kalymnios, John, 9 Desbrosses St, New York, NY 10013.
T. (212) 925-0635. 089887
Kang, 24 E 81 St, New York, NY 10028. T. (212) 734-
1490. 089888
Kaplan, Leo, 965 Madison Av, New York, NY 10021.
T. (212) 535-2407. 089889

Kaplan, Leo, 967 Madison Av, New York, NY 10021.
T. (212) 249-6766, Fax (212) 249-7574. 089890
Kapoor, 40 E 78 St, New York, NY 10021. T. (212) 794-
2300. 089891
Kasmin, Paul, 74 Grand St, New York, NY 10013.
T. (212) 219-3219. 089892
K.D. Gallery, 611 Broadway, New York, NY 10012.
T. (212) 420-8011. 089893
Keats, R. Stuart, 120 E 36 St, New York, NY 10016.
T. (212) 696-5728. 089894
Keen, 423 Broome St, New York, NY 110013.
T. (212) 966-2216. - Paint / Graph - 089895
Kelly, June, 591 Broadway, New York, NY 10012.
T. (212) 226-1660. - Paint - 089896
Kempner, Jim, 1 University Pl, New York, NY 10003.
T. (212) 353-9266. 089897
Kenkeleba, 214 E Second St, New York, NY 10009.
T. (212) 674-3939. 089898
Kennedy, 40 W 57 St, New York, NY 10019.
T. (212) 514-9600. - Paint - 089899
Kensington, 157 W 57 St, New York, NY 10019.
T. (212) 489-3724. 089900
Kent, 67 Prince St, New York, NY 10012. T. (212) 966-
4500. 089901
Kery, Pat, 14 E 64 St, New York, NY 10021. T. (212) 826-
3735. 089902
Kimche, Raja, 23 E 74 St, New York, NY 10021.
T. (212) 288-5698. - Paint - 089903
Kind, Phylis, 136 Greene St, New York, NY 10012.
T. (212) 925-1200. 089904
King, 136 E 74 St, New York, NY 10021. T. (212) 249-
5010. 089905
Kjellberg, 853 Broadway, New York, NY 10003.
T. (212) 228-6200. 089906
Klagsbrun, Nicole, 51 Greene St, New York, NY 10013.
T. (212) 925-5157. 089907
Klarfeld, Perry, 472 Broome St, New York, NY 10013.
T. (212) 941-0303. 089908
Klonaridis, 50 W 57 St, New York, NY 10019.
T. (212) 541-6001. 089909
Knoedler & Co, M., 19 E 70 St, New York, NY 10021.
T. (212) 794-0550. - Paint / Sculp / Draw - 089910
Koh, 66 W Broadway, New York, NY 10007. T. (212) 619-
2180. 089911
Kostabi, 600 Broadway, New York, NY 10012.
T. (212) 925-3065. 089912
Kouros, 23 E 73 St, New York, NY 10021. T. (212) 288-
5888, Fax (212) 794-9397. 089913
Kovesdy, Paul, 30 E 81 St, New York, NY 10028.
T. (212) 737-4563. - Paint - 089914
Kramer, Ina, 104 E 40 St, New York, NY 10016.
I. (212) 599-0435. 089915
Kraushaar, 724 Fifth Av, New York, NY 10019.
T. (212) 307-5730. 089916
Kren, Alfred, 322 Eighth Av, New York, NY 10001.
T. (212) 627-7788. 089917
Krienke, Kendra, 230 Central Park W, New York, NY
10024. T. (212) 580-6516. 089918
Krugier, Jan, 41 E 57 St, New York, NY 10022.
T (212) 755-7288, Fax (212) 980-6079. 089919
Kubinski, Achim, 25 N Moore St, New York, NY 10013.
T. (212) 941-0299. 089920
Kunst Hall, 129 Greene St, New York, NY 10012.
T. (212) 598-4617, Fax (212) 598-4637. 089921
Kunstschalter, 594 Broadway, New York, NY 10012.
T. (212) 343-2153. 089922
La Belle Epoque Vintage Posters, 282 Columbus Av,
New York, NY 10023. T. (212) 362-1770. 089923
La Boetie, 9 E 82 St, New York, NY 10028. T. (212) 535-
4865, Fax (212) 650-9561. - Paint / Graph / Sculp /
Draw - 089924
La Serra, 979 Third Av, New York, NY 10022.
T. (212) 758-1335. 089925
Lafayette Parke, 58 E 79 St, New York, NY 10021.
T. (212) 517-5550, Fax (212) 734-2791. 089926
Lally & Co, J.J., 41 E 57 St, New York, NY 10022.
T. (212) 371-3380, Fax (212) 593-4699. 089927
Lamu, 161 Madison Av, New York, NY 10016.
T. (212) 889-5332. - Eth - 089928
Landau, Patrice, 568 Broadway, New York, NY 10012.
T. (212) 925-1900. 089929
Lanier, Mary, 6 Morton St, New York, NY 10014.
T. (212) 255-1674. 089930

Lawrence, 423 E 81 St, New York, NY 10028.
T. (212) 772-2325. 089931
Ledis Flam, 130 Prince St, New York, NY 10012.
T. (212) 925-2806. 089932
Lee, John, 80 Mercer St, New York, NY 10012.
T. (212) 966-2676. 089933
Lefebre, John, 47 E 77 St., New York, NY 10021.
T. (212) 744-3384. - Paint / Sculp - 089934
Lelong, 20 W 57 St, New York, NY 10019. T. (212) 315-0470. 089935
Leloup, 1080 Madison Av, New York, NY 10028.
T. (212) 772-3410. 089936
Lemonde, 40 E 76 St, New York, NY 10021.
T. (212) 744-1569. 089937
Leonard & Associates, 76 Varick St, New York, NY 10013. T. (212) 226-6709. 089938
Levine & Associates, Elizabeth, 565 West End Av, New York, NY 10024. T. (212) 874-5334. 089939
Levy, Stuart, 588 Broadway, New York, NY 10012.
T. (212) 941-0009. 089940
Lewin, Bruce R., 136 Prince St, New York, NY 10012.
T. (212) 431-4750. 089941
Lewitt, 790 Madison Av, New York, NY 10021.
T. (212) 628-0918. 089942
Lexington Art Gallery, 154 E 64 St, New York, NY 10021.
T. (212) 888-4400. - Paint / Graph / Fra - 089943
Lieberman & Saul, 560 Broadway, New York, NY 10012.
T. (212) 431-0747. 089944
Ligoa, Duncan, 22 E 72 St, New York, NY 10021.
T. (212) 988-3110. - Paint / Graph / Orient / Sculp / Pho / Draw - 089945
Limner, 598 Broadway, New York, NY 10012.
T. (212) 431-1190. 089946
Littlejohn & Daughter, 450 W 145 St, New York, NY 10031. T. (212) 368-3786. 089947
Lladro, 43 W 57 St., New York, NY 10019. T. (212) 838-9341. - Paint - 089948
LM Gallery, 8 Spring St, New York, NY 10012.
T. (212) 226-7815. 089949
Long, 24 W 57 St, New York, NY 10019. T. (212) 397-2001. 089950
Lower Manhattan Cultural Council, 1 World Trade Center, New York, NY 10048. T. (212) 432-0900. 089951
Lowinsky, 38 E 57 St, New York, NY 10022.
T. (212) 593-3320. 089952
Lowinsky, 578 Broadway, New York, NY 10012.
T. (212) 226-5440, Fax (212) 226-5442. - Pho - 089953
Lublin Collections, 131 Spring St, New York, NY 10012.
T. (203) 622-8777. - Paint / Sculp - 089954
Lucia, 150 Spring St, New York, NY 10012. T. (212) 941-9296, Fax (212) 941-9296. 089955
Luhring, Augustine, 130 Prince St, New York, NY 10012.
T. (212) 219-9600. 089956
Lumbard, Jean, 17 E 96 St, New York, NY 10128.
T. (212) 996-4484. 089957
Lumina, 251 W 19 St, New York, NY 10011.
T. (212) 807-0233. - Pho - 089958
Lumina, 137 Spring St, New York, NY 10012.
T. (212) 334-1334. 089959
Lust, Virginia, 61 Sullivan St, New York, NY 10012.
T. (212) 941-9220. 089960
Lux, Kenneth, 851 Madison Av, New York, NY 10021.
T. (212) 861-6839. 089961
M-1 Gallery, 25 E 20 St, New York, NY 10003.
T. (212) 777-1012. 089962
M-13 Gallery, 72 Greene St, New York, NY 10012.
T. (212) 925-3007. 089963
MacCallister, Cynthia, 560 Broadway, New York, NY 10012. T. (212) 925-0083. 089964
Macklowe, 667 Madison Av, New York, NY 10021.
T. (212) 644-6400. 089965
Madison Avenue Gallery, 799 Broadway, New York, NY 10003. T. (212) 535-7200. - Paint - 089966
Magidson & Associates, 1070 Madison Av, New York, NY 10021. T. (212) 744-0252. 089967
Maibaum, Walter, 50 W 57 St, New York, NY 10019.
T. (212) 541-5000. - Paint - 089968
Maison des Artistes, 492 Broome St, New York, NY 10013. T. (212) 431-9497. 089969

Malcolm, Christian, 361 W 36 St, New York, NY 10018.
T. (212) 947-3835. 089970
Manley-Riback, 201 E 79 St, New York, NY 10021.
T. (212) 861-0001. 089971
Mann, Robert, 42 E 76 St, New York, NY 10021.
T. (212) 570-1223. 089972
Mano, 164 Mercer St, New York, NY 10012.
T. (212) 219-3510. - Graph - 089973
Marbella, 28 E 72 St, New York, NY 10021. T. (212) 288-7809. 089974
March & Clothier, 210 E 68 St, New York, NY 10021.
T. (212) 794-1245. 089975
Marcus, Curt, 578 Broadway, New York, NY 10012.
T. (212) 226-3200. 089976
Maresca, Ricco, 152 Wooster St, New York, NY 10012.
T. (212) 780-0071. 089977
Maresca, Ricco, 105 Hudson St, New York, NY 10013.
T. (212) 274-0026. 089978
Marie Walsh Sharpe Art Foundation, 443 Greenwich St, New York, NY 10013. T. (212) 925-3008. 089979
Marigold, 25 E 64 St, New York, NY 10021. T. (212) 759-0777. 089980
Markel, Kathryn, 40 E 88 St, New York, NY 10128.
T. (212) 410-6931. 089981
Markel-Sears, 560 Broadway, New York, NY 110012.
T. (212) 966-7469. 089982
Markey, Lawrence, 55 Vandam St, New York, NY 10013.
T. (212) 627-4446. 089983
Markus, 145 W 57 St, New York, NY 10019.
T. (212) 956-4000. 089984
Marlborough, 40 W 57 St, New York, NY 10019.
T. (212) 541-4900. - Paint - 089985
Marqusee, Janet, 27 E 65 St, New York, NY 10021.
T. (212) 744-4070, Fax (212) 079-8514. 089986
Martin, Lawrence, 457 W Broadway, New York, NY 10012. T. (212) 995-8865. 089987
Martin, Mary-Anne, 23 E 73 St, New York, NY 10021.
T. (212) 288-2213, Fax (212) 861-7656. - Paint / Graph / Draw - 089988
Master Piece Gallery, 179 Lexington Av, New York, NY 10016. T. (212) 481-0509. 089989
Master Piece Management, 950 Third Av, New York, NY 10022. T. (212) 750-9098. 089990
Mathes, Barbara, 41 E 57 St, New York, NY 10022.
T. (212) 752-5135, Fax (212) 752-5145. 089991
Maynes, Bill, 225 Lafayette St, New York, NY 10012.
T. (212) 431-3952. 089992
McCarron, Paul, 1014 Madison Av, New York, NY 10021.
T. (212) 772-1181, Fax (212) 472-2497. - Graph / Draw - 089993

McKoy, Tim, 318 Bleecker St, New York, NY 10014.
T. (212) 242-3456. - Repr / Sculp - 089994
Mehu, 21 W 100 St, New York, NY 10025. T. (212) 222-3334. 089995
Meilman, Grete, 28 E 73 St, New York, NY 1010021.
T. (212) 570-9070. - Paint / Draw - 089996
Meisel, Louis K., 141 Prince St, New York, NY 10012.
T. (212) 677-1340. - Paint / Sculp - 089997
Meisel, Susan P., 141 Prince St, New York, NY 10012.
T. (212) 254-0137. 089998
Meisner, 96 Greene St, New York, NY 10012.
T. (212) 431-9590. 089999
Mele, 147 E 72 St, New York, NY 10021. T. (212) 517-8877. 090000
Merrin, 724 Fifth Av, New York, NY 10019. T. (212) 757-2884. - Eth - 090001
Metro Pictures, 150 Greene St, New York, NY 10012.
T. (212) 925-8335. - Paint - 090002
Metropolitan Graphic Art Gallery, 1300 Third Av, New York, NY 10021. T. (212) 737-6756. - Graph / Fra - 090003
Metropolitan Graphic Art Gallery, 2341 Broadway, New York, NY 10024. T. (212) 595-1615. - Graph / Fra - 090004
Metropolitan Graphic Art Gallery, 1457 Third Av, New York, NY 10028. T. (212) 737-9703. - Graph / Fra - 090005
Midtown Art Gallery and Framing, 231 E 34 St, New York, NY 10016. T. (212) 779-1519. - Paint / Fra - 090006
Midtown Payson Galleries, 745 Fifth Av, New York, NY 10151. T. (212) 758-1900. 090007
Millor, 560 Broadway, New York, NY 10012.
T. (212) 226-0702. 090008
Miller, Lawrence, 138 Spring St, New York, NY 10012.
T. (212) 226-1220. 090009
Miller, Robert, 41 E 57 St, New York, NY 10022.
T. (212) 980-5454. 090010
Miller & Lucy Vivante, Michael, 115 E 89 St, New York, NY 10128. T. (212) 289-7994, Fax (212) 987-0460. 090010a
Milliken, Mark, 1200 Madison Av, New York, NY 10128.
T. (212) 534-8802. 090011
Milliken, Mark, 1200 Madison Av., New York, NY 10128.
T. (212) 534-8802. 090012
M.J.M. Gallery, 1760 Broadway, New York, NY 10019.
T. (212) 247-4708. 090013
Modern Age Furniture Gallery, 795 Broadway, New York, NY 10003. T. (212) 674-5603. - Furn - 090014
Modern Art Consultants, 390 West End Av, New York, NY 10024. T. (212) 873-9576. 090015
Moeller, Achim, 52 E 76 St, New York, NY 10021.
T. (212) 988-8483, Fax (212) 439-6663. - Paint / Graph / Sculp / Draw - 090016
Mokotoff, 584 Broadway, New York, NY 10012.
T. (212) 941-1901. 090017
Montserrat, 588 Broadway, New York, NY 10012.
T. (212) 941-8899. 090018
Morante, Marta, 450 W 31 St, New York, NY 10001.
T. (212) 967-4491. 090019
Morning Star Gallery, 164 Mercer St, New York, NY 10012. T. (212) 334-9330. 090020
Morrison, Robert, 59 Thompson St, New York, NY 10012. T. (212) 274-9059. 090021
Mothers Film Stage, 210 E Fifth St, New York, NY 10003. T. (212) 260-4511. - Pho - 090022
Motion Picture Arts Gallery, 133 E 58 St, New York, NY 10022. T. (212) 223-1009. - Graph - 090023
Mulberry, 377 Broome St, New York, NY 10013.
T. (212) 941-0539. 090024
Multi Media Arts Gallery, 594 Broadway, New York, NY 10012. T. (212) 966-4080. 090025
Multiple Impressions, 128 Spring St, New York, NY 10012. T. (212) 925-1313. - Graph - 090026
Multiples, 24 W 57 St, New York, NY 10022.
T. (212) 977-7160. - Mul - 090027
Munroe, Victoria, 9 E 84 St, New York, NY 10028.
T. (212) 249-5480. 090028
Museum Gallery, 410 Columbus Av, New York, NY 10024. T. (212) 873-9446. 090029

Mythic Arts Africa, 594 Broadway, New York, NY 10012.
T. (212) 941-5968. - Eth -   *090030*

Nadler, 643 Park Av, New York, NY 10021. T. (212) 570-
4927.   *090031*

Nahan, 381 W Broadway, New York, NY 10012.
T. (212) 966-9313.   *090032*

Naiman, Lee, 300 Central Park W, New York, NY 10024.
T. (212) 362-4090.   *090033*

Naive Galerie, 145 E 92 St, New York, NY 10128.
T. (212) 427-9283. - Paint -   *090034*

Nassau Art Gallery, 75 Nassau St, New York, NY 10038.
T. (212) 962-3100.   *090035*

Nassau, Lillian, 220 E 57 St, New York, NY 10022.
T. (212) 759-6062. - Paint / Graph -   *090036*

Nation Art, 810 Second Av, New York, NY 10017.
T. (212) 687-1786.   *090037*

National Antique and Art Dealers Association of America,
15 E 57 St, New York, NY 10022. T. (212) 355-
0636.   *090037a*

National Arts Stabilization Fund, 220 E 42 St, New York,
NY 10017. T. (212) 490-1400.   *090038*

Nature Morte Gallery, 204 E Tenth St, New York, NY
10003. T. (212) 420-9544.   *090039*

Navarra, Enrico, 41 E 57 St, New York, NY 10022.
T. (212) 223-2828.   *090040*

Navin Kumar, 1001 Madison Av, New York, NY 10021.
T. (212) 734-4075.   *090041*

Neuhoff, Heidi, 1166 Second Av, New York, NY 10021.
T. (212) 838-0052.   *090042*

Neuhoff, Heidi, 999 Madison Av, New York, NY 10021.
T. (212) 879-8890.   *090043*

New Amsterdam Galleries, 140 Nassau St, New York, NY
10038. T. (212) 732-5454.   *090044*

New York Contemporary Art Observer, 101 Central Park
W, New York, NY 10023. T. (212) 724-4132.   *090045*

New York Graphic, 160 W 55 St, New York, NY 10019.
T. (212) 307-7240. - Graph -   *090046*

New York New York Gallery, 110 Greene St, New York,
NY 10012. T. (212) 941-5588.   *090047*

Newburg, Daniel, 43 Greene St, New York, NY 10013.
T. (212) 219-1885, Fax (212) 941-7980.   *090048*

Newhouse, 19 E 66 St, New York, NY 10021.
T. (212) 879-2700, Fax (212) 517-2680.
- Paint -   *090049*

Noho, 168 Mercer St, New York, NY 10012. T. (212) 219-
2210.   *090050*

Nolan & Eckman, 560 Broadway, New York, NY 10012.
T. (212) 925-6190.   *090051*

Nordenstad, Bernt, 39 Wooster St, New York, NY 10013.
T. (212) 431-1295.   *090052*

North Star Galleries, 1120 Lexington Av, New York, NY
10021. T. (212) 794-4277.   *090053*

Nosei Annina, 100 Prince St, New York, NY 10012.
T. (212) 431-9253.   *090054*

Nouveau Artist, 938 Third Av, New York, NY 10022.
T. (212) 754-1050.   *090055*

Novo Arts, 57 E 11 St, New York, NY 10003.
T. (212) 674-3093.   *090056*

O'Wyatt, Dion, 330 W 72 St, New York, NY 10023.
T. (212) 873-2633.   *090057*

Obican Lazar, 210 Fifth Av, New York, NY 10010.
T. (212) 541-4281.   *090058*

Objects and Images, 63 Wooster St, New York, NY
10012. T. (212) 431-1000.   *090059*

Objects of Bright Pride, 455a Columbus Av, New York,
NY 10024. T. (212) 721-4579.   *090060*

Odyssia, 305 E 61 St, New York, NY 10021. T. (212) 486-
7338.   *090061*

OJ Art Gallery, 1426 Av of the Americas, New York, NY
10019. T. (212) 371-4733.   *090062*

OJ Spring Street Gallery, 121 Spring St, New York, NY
10012. T. (212) 343-2706.   *090063*

OJO Art Gallery, 2341 Broadway, New York, NY 10024.
T. (212) 595-1615.   *090064*

OJS Art Gallery, 883 First Av, New York, NY 10022.
T. (212) 758-4206.   *090065*

Old World Galleries, 88 Lexington Av, New York, NY
10016. T. (212) 481-0479.   *090066*

Omaid, 244 Madison Av, New York, NY 10016.
T. (212) 983-4530.   *090067*

One Bond, 52 E 64 St, New York, NY 10021.
T. (212) 753-7040.   *090068*

One Hour Framing Shop, 131 W 45 St, New York, NY
10036. T. (212) 869-5263. - Fra -   *090069*

One Star, 325 Park Av S, New York, NY 10010.
T. (212) 254-5390.   *090070*

One Twenty Eight, 128 Rivington St, New York, NY
10002. T. (212) 674-0244.   *090071*

Optiz, Anita, 210 E 35 St., New York, NY 10016.
T. (212) 683-9680.   *090072*

Orbis International, 65 Bleecker St, New York, NY
10012. T. (212) 260-1504.   *090073*

Orion Editions, 270 Lafayette St, New York, NY 10012.
T. (212) 226-2766. - Graph -   *090074*

Owen, 762 Madison Av, New York, NY 10021.
T. (212) 879-2415.   *090075*

Pace, 32 E 57 St, New York, NY 10022. T. (212) 421-
3292, Fax (212) 421-0835. - Paint / Draw -   *090076*

Pall, William, 1175 Park Av, New York, NY 10128.
T. (212) 860-3400.   *090077*

Palmer Meredith, 30 E 85 St, New York, NY 10028.
T. (212) 472-8250. - Paint -   *090078*

Parasol Press, 289 Church St, New York, NY 10013.
T. (212) 431-9387. - Graph -   *090079*

Park South Gallery at Carnegie Hall, 885 Seventh Av,
New York, NY 10019. T. (212) 246-5900.   *090080*

Parrish, Martha, 790 Madison Av, New York, NY 10021.
T. (212) 734-7332.   *090081*

Pearl, Marilyn, 710 Park Av, New York, NY 10021.
T. (212) 734-7421.   *090082*

Peck, Ian, 163 E 61 St, New York, NY 10021.
T. (212) 980-4545. - Paint -   *090083*

Peder Bonnier, 420 W Broadway, New York, NY 10012.
T. (212) 431-1939.   *090084*

Peder Bonnier, 521 W 23 St, New York, NY 10011.
T. (212) 627-2720.   *090085*

Pelavin, 13 Jay St, New York, NY 10013. T. (212) 925-
9424. - Graph -   *090086*

Penn, S., 211 W Broadway, New York, NY 10013.
T. (212) 925-1865.   *090087*

Performer's Outlet, 222 E 85 St, New York, NY 10028.
T. (212) 249-8435.   *090088*

Perls, 1016 Madison Av, New York, NY 10021.
T. (212) 472-3200. - Paint / Graph / Sculp -   *090089*

Perry, 521 Broome St, New York, NY 10013.
T. (212) 226-8279.   *090090*

Phillips, Marguerite, 1418 Lexington Av, New York, NY
10128. T. (212) 831-1416.   *090091*

Phoenix Gallery, 568 Broadway, New York, NY 10012.
T. (212) 226-8711.   *090092*

Photocollect, 740 West End Av, New York, NY 10025.
T. (212) 932-8574. - Pho -   *090093*

Photography as Art, 141 E 33 St, New York, NY 10016.
T. (212) 686-0046. - Pho -   *090094*

Pierce, Nancy C., 48 East End Av, New York, NY 10028.
T. (212) 650-0030.   *090095*

Pietrasanta, 49 Bleecker St, New York, NY 10012.
T. (212) 477-6989.   *090096*

Place des Vosges, 42 E 12 St, New York, NY 10003.
T. (212) 995-2899.   *090097*

Plan, Lou, 20 E 63 St, New York, NY 10021.
T. (212) 752-4881.   *090098*

Pleiades Gallery, 164 Mercer St, New York, NY 10012.
T. (212) 274-8825. - Paint / Sculp / Pho -   *090099*

Pocker & Son, J., 135 E 63 St, New York, NY 10021.
T. (212) 838-5488. - Graph / Fra -   *090100*

Polansky, 20 E 69 St, New York, NY 10021. T. (212) 535-
3295.   *090101*

Pollis, John, 111 W 57 St, New York, NY 10019.
T. (212) 397-0077.   *090102*

Portraits, 985 Park Av, New York, NY 10028.
T. (212) 879-5560. - Paint / Graph -   *090103*

Poster America Gallery, 138 W 18 St, New York, NY
10011. T. (212) 206-0499. - Graph -   *090104*

Postmasters Gallery, 80 Greene St, New York, NY
10012. T. (212) 941-5711.   *090105*

PPOW, 532 Broadway, New York, NY 10012.
T. (212) 941-8642.   *090106*

Praxis International Art Gallery, 306 E 55 St, New York,
NY 10022. T. (212) 838-2748.   *090107*

Primavera, 808 Madison Av, New York, NY 10021.
T. (212) 2878-1569.   *090108*

Prince Street Gallery, 121 Wooster St, New York, NY
10012. T. (212) 226-9402. - Paint / Graph / Sculp /
Draw -   *090109*

Professional Fine Arts Services, 386 W Broadway, New
York, NY 10012. T. (212) 226-2247. - Paint / Graph /
Sculp -   *090110*

Protech, Max, 560 Broadway, New York, NY 10012.
T. (212) 966-5454.   *090111*

PS 122 Gallery, 150 First Av, New York, NY 10009.
T. (212) 228-4249.   *090112*

Q Art Trading, 1353 Second Av, New York, NY 10021.
T. (212) 734-3122.   *090113*

Quantum Gallery, 468 W Broadway, New York, NY
10012. T. (212) 260-7686.   *090114*

Quinn, Lorenzo, 55 Prince St, New York, NY 10012.
T. (212) 925-2414.   *090115*

Quintana, 9 E 84 St, New York, NY 10028. T. (212) 772-
6132.   *090116*

Raab, Rosanne, 167 E 61 St, New York, NY 10021.
T. (212) 371-6644.   *090117*

Rabenou, Yris, 249 E 61 St, New York, NY 10021.
T. (212) 486-0661.   *090118*

Raciti, Joseph, 818 Broadway, New York, NY 10003.
T. (212) 473-6460.   *090119*

Rafael, 1020 Madison Av, New York, NY 10021.
T. (212) 744-8666.   *090120*

Raku, 171 Spring St, New York, NY 10012. T. (212) 226-
6636.   *090121*

Randolph & Tate, 2095 Broadway, New York, NY 10023.
T. (212) 595-6302.   *090122*

Ravagnan, Mario, 41 E 57 St, New York, NY 10022.
T. (212) 223-1860.   *090123*

Raydon, 1091 Madison Av, New York, NY 10028.
T. (212) 288-3555. - Paint / Graph / Sculp / Mod / Ico /
Draw -   *090124*

Reece, 24 W 57 St, New York, NY 10019. T. (212) 333-
5830, Fax (212) 333-7366.   *090125*

Reed, Harold, 120 E 78 St, New York, NY 10021.
T. (212) 861-6362. - Paint / Sculp -   *090126*

Rehs, 305 E 63 St, New York, NY 10021. T. (212) 355-
5710, Fax (212) 355-5742.   *090127*

Reinhold Brown, 26 E 78 St, New York, NY 10021.
T. (212) 734-7999. - Graph -   *090128*

Resnick, Ira, 133 E 58 St, New York, NY 10022.
T. (212) 223-1009.   *090129*

Reuben, 246 E 53 St, New York, NY 10022. T. (212) 751-
6855.   *090130*

Reuben, Mark, 11 Fulton St, New York, NY 10038.
T. (212) 964-6300.   *090131*

Revel, 96 Spring St, New York, NY 10012. T. (212) 925-
0600.   *090132*

Rich Perlow, Katharina, 560 Broadway, New York, NY
10012. T. (212) 517-5858.   *090133*

Rienzo, 922 Madison Av, New York, NY 10021.
T. (212) 288-2226. - Paint -   *090134*

Rivoli Trading Corporation, 426 E 89 St, New York, NY
10128. T. (212) 876-9067.   *090135*

Ro Gallery, 300 E 74 St, New York, NY 10021.
T. (212) 732-8887. - Graph -   *090136*

Robertson, 36 W 22 St, New York, NY 10010.
T. (212) 206-0912. - Eth -   *090137*

Rolin & Co., F., 61 E 77 St, New York, NY 10021.
T. (212) 879-0077.   *090138*

Roman, Herbert, 17 E 77 St, New York, NY 10021.
T. (212) 879-4617. - Paint -   *090139*

Ronin, 605 Madison Av, New York, NY 10021.
T. (212) 688-0188. - Paint / Graph -   *090140*

Rose, Peter, 200 E 58 St, New York, NY 10022.
T. (212) 759-8173. - Paint / Sculp / Tex / Pho /
Draw -   *090141*

Rosen, Andrea, 130 Prince St, New York, NY 10012.
T. (212) 941-0203.   *090142*

Rosen, Randy, 240 E 82 St, New York, NY 10028.
T. (212) 744-7575.   *090143*

Rosenberg & Co., Paul, 20 E 79 St, New York, NY 10021.
T. (212) 472-1134. - Paint / Sculp / Draw -   *090144*

Rosenberg, Stephen, 115 Wooster St, New York, NY
10012. T. (212) 431-4838. - Paint / Graph /
Sculp -   *090145*

Rosenberg & Stiebel, 32 E 57 St, New York, NY 10022.
T. (212) 753-4368.   *090146*

Rosenberg & Stiebel, 32 E 57 St., New York, NY 10022.
T. (212) 753-4368. - Ant / Paint / Furn / China / Sculp /
Draw -   *090147*

Rosenfeld, 44 E 82 St, New York, NY 10028.
T. (212) 391-4622.   *090148*

Rosenfeld, Michael, 24 W 57 St, New York, NY 10019.
T. (212) 247-0082. *090149*

Rosenberg, Michelle, 16 E 79 St, New York, NY 10021.
T. (212) 734-0900. *090150*

Ross, Luise, 50 W 57 St, New York, NY 10019.
T. (212) 307-0400. *090151*

Rowand, J., 320 W 66 St, New York, NY 10023.
T. (212) 496-1886. *090152*

Roy, Carolyn J., 46 Greene St, New York, NY 10013.
T. (212) 941-0626. *090153*

RR Gallery, 375 W Broadway, New York, NY 10012.
T. (212) 226-6035. *090154*

Rudin, I., 20 E 74 St, New York, NY 10021. T. (212) 288-6777. *090155*

Ruesch, Jeffrey, 134 Spring St, New York, NY 10012.
T. (212) 925-1137. *090156*

Rush, 105 Hudson St, New York, NY 10013.
T. (212) 219-2420. *090157*

Sabarsky, Serge, 58 E 79 St, New York, NY 10021.
T. (212) 628-6281. *090158*

Sabbatique, 10 Waterside Plaza, New York, NY 10010.
T. (212) 213-9344. *090159*

Sacks, 50 W 57 St, New York, NY 10019. T. (212) 333-7755. *090160*

Safani Gallery, 960 Madison Av., New York, NY 10021. *090161*

Saidenberg, 1018 Madison Av, New York, NY 10021.
T. (212) 288-3387. *090162*

Saint Raphael, 207 E 30 St, New York, NY 10016.
T. (212) 886-1083. *090163*

Sander, 19 E 76 St, New York, NY 10021. T. (212) 794-4500. *090164*

Santo, Bruno, 760 Madison Av, New York, NY 10021.
T. (212) 517-8539. *090165*

Sarajo, 98 Prince St, New York, NY 10012. T. (212) 966-6156. *090166*

Sarina Tang, 3 E 76 St, New York, NY 10021.
T. (212) 517-7401. *090167*

Savacou, 240 E 13 St, New York, NY 10003.
T. (212) 473-6904. *090168*

Sayn-Wittgenstein, 155 E 72 St, New York, NY 10021.
T. (212) 288-1493. *090169*

Schaeffer, 983 Park Av, New York, NY 10028.
T. (212) 535-6410. - Paint / Graph - *090170*

Schellmann, 50 Greene St, New York, NY 10013.
T. (212) 219-1821. *090171*

Scherer, 760 Madison Av, New York, NY 10021.
T. (212) 717-6575. *090172*

Schillay, 161 E 75 St, New York, NY 10021. T. (212) 861-8353, Fax (212) 772-3758. - Paint - *090173*

Schiller & Bodo, 19 E 74 St, New York, NY 10021.
T. (212) 772-8627, Fax (212) 535-5943. *090174*

Schlesinger, 24 E 73 St, New York, NY 10021.
T. (212) 734-3600, Fax (212) 472-6519. *090175*

Schmidt Bingham, 41 W 57 St, New York, NY 10019.
T. (212) 888-1122. *090176*

Schneider, Freddie, 1272 Third Av, New York, NY 10021.
T. (212) 535-0160. *090177*

Schonfeld & Co., R.C., 349 E 49 St, New York, NY 10017. T. (212) 755-7005. *090178*

Schultz, Frederick, 41 E 57 St, New York, NY 10022.
T. (212) 758-6007, Fax (212) 832-0448. *090179*

Schwartz, Barbara E., 110 Greene St, New York, NY 10012. T. (212) 431-7452. *090180*

Schwartz, Nancy, 710 Park Av, New York, NY 10021.
T. (212) 988-6709, Fax (212) 472-4976. - Paint /
Sculp - *090180a*

Schweitzer, 18 E 84 St, New York, NY 10028.
T. (212) 535-5430. - Paint - *090181*

Scott, Alan, 524 Broadway, New York, NY 10012.
T. (212) 226-5145. *090182*

Scratch, 50 W 57 St, New York, NY 10019. T. (212) 541-9554. *090183*

Sculpture Center Gallery, 167 E 69 St, New York, NY 10021. T. (212) 879-3500. - Sculp - *090184*

Secord, William, 52 E 76 St, New York, NY 10021.
T. (212) 249-0075. *090185*

Seraphim, 780 West End Av, New York, NY 10025.
T. (212) 678-8744. *090186*

Shafrazi, Tony, 119 Wooster St, New York, NY 10012.
T. (212) 274-9300, Fax (212) 334-9499.
- Paint - *090187*

Shainman, Jack, 560 Broadway, New York, NY 10012.
T. (212) 966-3866, Fax (212) 334-8453. - Paint /
Sculp - *090188*

Shapolsky, Anita, 99 Spring St, New York, NY 10012.
T. (212) 334-9755, Fax (212) 334-6817. - Paint /
Sculp - *090189*

Shaw-Leibowitz, 212 E 47 St, New York, NY 10017.
T. (212) 759-8460. *090190*

Shepherd, 21 E 84 St, New York, NY 10028.
T. (212) 861-4050, 744-3392, Fax (212) 772-1314. *090191*

Shickman, H., 980 Madison Av, New York, NY 10021.
T. (212) 249-3800. - Paint / Graph / Sculp /
Draw - *090192*

Shorewood, 10 E 53 St, New York, NY 10022.
T. (212) 371-1500. *090193*

Shubin, Miriam, 155 E 34 St, New York, NY 10016.
T. (212) 481-8471. *090194*

Sigerson & Morrison, 611 Broadway, New York, NY 10012. T. (212) 473-2543. *090195*

Silberberg, Nathan, 16 E 79 St, New York, NY 10021.
T. (212) 861-6192. *090196*

Silencio, 40 Wooster St, New York, NY 10013.
T. (212) 219-2089. *090197*

Silver Whale Gallery, 21 Bleecker St, New York, NY 10012. T. (212) 460-8616. *090198*

Silverstein, H.E., 373 Broadway, New York, NY 10013.
T. (212) 925-1649. *090199*

Simpson Merton, D., 1063 Madison Av, New York, NY 10028. T. (212) 988-6290. - Paint / Sculp - *090200*

Simpson, Merton D., 1063 Madison Av., New York, NY 10028. T. (212) 988-6290. - Paint / Sculp /
Eth - *090201*

Sindin, 956 Madison Av, New York, NY 10021.
T. (212) 288-7902. - Paint / Graph - *090202*

Skoto, 25 Prince St, New York, NY 10012. T. (212) 226-8519. *090203*

Smith, 1045 Madison Av, New York, NY 10021.
T. (212) 941-6860. - Paint / Sculp - *090204*

Snyder, 588 Broadway, New York, NY 10012.
T. (212) 941-6860. *090205*

Soho Galleries, 147 Reade St, New York, NY 10013.
T. (212) 571-3241. *090206*

Soho Photo Gallery, 15 White St, New York, NY 10013.
T. (212) 226-8571. - Pho - *090207*

Soho 20, 469 Broome St, New York, NY 10013.
T. (212) 226-4167. *090208*

Solomon, Holly, 172 Mercer St, New York, NY 10012.
T. (212) 226-4990. *090209*

Solomon & Co., 959 Madison Av, New York, NY 10021.
T. (212) 737-8200. - Paint / Graph / Sculp - *090210*

Sonnabend, 420 W Broadway, New York, NY 10012.
T. (212) 966-6160. - Paint / Sculp / Pho / Draw - *090211*

Soroban, 205 West End Av, New York, NY 10023.
T. (212) 838-8640. *090212*

Soufer, 1015 Madison Av, New York, NY 10021.
T. (212) 628-3225. *090213*

Souyun Yi, 120 E 11 St, New York, NY 10003.
T. (212) 334-5189. *090214*

Space Time Light Gallery, 104 E Seventh St, New York, NY 10009. T. (212) 473-6366. *090215*

Spanierman, 50 E 78 St, New York, NY 10021.
T. (212) 879-7085. - Paint / Sculp - *090216*

Sportman's Edge, 136 E 74 St, New York, NY 10021.
T. (212) 249-5010. - Paint / Graph / Sculp - *090217*

Sragow, Ellen, 73 Spring St, New York, NY 10012.
T. (212) 219-1793. - Paint / Graph / Sculp / Pho / Mul /
Draw - *090218*

Staib, Philippe, 8 Greene St, New York, NY 10013.
T. (212) 941-5977. *090219*

Staley Wise, 560 Broadway, New York, NY 10012.
T. (212) 966-6223. *090220*

Starr, Herbert A., 440 E 20 St, New York, NY 10009.
T. (212) 673-7330. - Paint - *090221*

Stein, Gertrude, 998 Madison Av, New York, NY 10021.
T. (212) 535-0600. - Paint / Sculp - *090222*

Steinbaum, Bernice, 132 Greene St, New York, NY 10012. T. (212) 431-4224. *090223*

Steinhacker, Paul, 151 E 71 St, New York, NY 10021.
T. (212) 879-1245. - Eth - *090224*

Stone, Allan, 15 E 71 St, New York, NY 10021.
T. (212) 988-6870, Fax (212) 988-0936. - Paint /
Sculp - *090225*

Storefront for Art and Architecture, 97 Kenmare St, New York, NY 10012. T. (212) 431-5795. - Draw - *090226*

Stricoff, 118 Greene St, New York, NY 10012.
T. (212) 219-3977, Fax (212) 219-3240. *090227*

Stubbs, 153 E 70 St, New York, NY 10021. T. (212) 772-3120. - Graph / Draw - *090228*

Studio G, 216 E 45 St, New York, NY 10017.
T. (212) 697-6260. *090229*

Studio 827, 41 Union Sq, New York, NY 10003.
T. (212) 633-8676. *090230*

Stux, 163 Mercer St, New York, NY 10012. T. (212) 219-0010. *090231*

Sumers, Martin, 50 W 57 St, New York, NY 10019.
T. (212) 541-8334. - Graph - *090232*

Summa, 527 Amsterdam Av, New York, NY 10024.
T. (212) 787-8533. *090233*

Sutton, R.J., 455 Madison Av, New York, NY 10022.
T. (212) 223-0135. *090234*

Suzuki, 24 W 57 St, New York, NY 10019. T. (212) 582-0373. - Graph - *090235*

Sybille Gallery, 316 Bleecker St, New York, NY 10014.
T. (212) 645-0488. *090236*

Synchronicity Space, 55 Mercer St, New York, NY 10013. T. (212) 925-8645. *090237*

Szoke, John, 164 Mercer St, New York, NY 10012.
T. (212) 219-8300. - Graph - *090238*

Szoke Koo, 164 Mercer St, New York, NY 10012.
T. (212) 219-8355. *090239*

T. R. S. Gallery, 780 Seventh Av., New York, NY 10019.
T. (212) 765-6975. *090240*

Tambaran, 20 E 76 St, New York, NY 10021.
T. (212) 570-0655. *090241*

Tamenaga, 982 Madison Av, New York, NY 10021.
T. (212) 734-6789. *090242*

Tatistcheff & Co., 50 W 57 St, New York, NY 10019.
T. (212) 664-0907. *090243*

Tatyana Gallery, 145 E 27 St, New York, NY 10016.
T. (212) 683-2387. - Paint / Draw - *090244*

Tauber, 543 Eighth Av, New York, NY 10018.
T. (212) 868-0909. *090245*

Teleky, Bruce, 625 Broadway, New York, NY 10012.
T. (212) 677-2559. - Graph - *090246*

Teller, Susan, 568 Broadway, New York, NY 10012.
T. (212) 941-7335. *090247*

Terrain Gallery, 141 Greene St, New York, NY 10012.
T. (212) 777-4426. *090248*

Terry-Engell, H., 22 E 76 St, New York, NY 10021.
T. (212) 535-9800. *090249*
Thaw & Co., E.V., 726 Park Av, New York, NY 10021.
T. (212) 535-6333. *090250*
Thime is Always Now, 132 E 92 St, New York, NY
10128. T. (212) 831-1111. *090251*
Third Avenue Art Gallery, 916 Third Av, New York, NY
10022. T. (212) 371-6090. *090252*
Thomson, 19 E 75 St, New York, NY 10021.
T. (212) 249-0242. - Paint / Graph / Sculp - *090253*
Thorp, Edward, 103 Prince St, New York, NY 10012.
T. (212) 431-6880. *090254*
Three East Third Street Corporation, 3 E Third St, New
York, NY 10003. T. (212) 533-7749. *090255*
Tilton, Jack, 47 Greene St, New York, NY 10013.
T. (212) 941-1775. *090256*
Toll, Barbara, 146 Greene St, New York, NY 10012.
T. (212) 431-1788. *090257*
Tomoko Liguori, 93 Grand St, New York, NY 10013.
T. (212) 334-0190. *090258*
Ton Ying & Co., 1050 Second Av, New York, NY 10022.
T. (212) 751-0134. *090259*
Topo Look, 11 Fulton St, New York, NY 10038.
T. (212) 964-8676. *090260*
Tossan-Tossan, 305 E 50 St, New York, NY 10022.
T. (212) 6888-1574. *090261*
Town and Village Frame and Art, 217 Avenue A, New
York, NY 10009. T. (212) 677-8580. - Repr /
Fra – *090262*
Trager-Salz, Janet, 700 Park Av, New York, NY 10021.
T. (212) 744-6080. *090263*
Tregalon, 319 E 50 St, New York, NY 10022.
T. (212) 223-0337. *090264*
Trial Balloon, 484 Broadway, New York, NY 10013.
T. (212) 925-9648. *090265*
Troubetzkoy, 243 E 60 St, New York, NY 10022.
T. (212) 688-6544. - Paint - *090266*
True Fakes, 57 W 28 St, New York, NY 10001.
T. (212) 779-3215. *090267*
Tullis Garner, 10 White St, New York, NY 10013.
T. (212) 226-6665, Fax (212) 941-0678.
- Graph - *090268*
Tunick, David, 12 E 81 St, New York, NY 10028.
T. (212) 570-0090, Fax (212) 744-8931. - Graph /
Draw – *090269*
Turkana, 125 Cedar St, New York, NY 10006.
T. (212) 732-0273. *090270*
Turner, Helen, 185 E 85 St, New York, NY 10028.
T. (212) 427-5173. *090271*
Tz'art & Co., 28 Wooster St, New York, NY 10013.
T. (212) 966-9059. *090272*
Ulysses Gallery, 41 E 57 St, New York, NY 10022.
T. (212) 754-4666, Fax (212) 754-4669. *090273*
Union Square Gallery, 125 E 17 St, New York, NY 10003.
T. (212) 777-8393. *090274*
Universal Art, 443 E Ninth St, New York, NY 10009.
T. (212) 982-9793. *090275*
Uptown Gallery, 1194 Madison Av, New York, NY 10128.
T. (212) 722-3677. - Paint / Graph / Fra / Draw - *090276*
Vawter, L., 156 E 52 St, New York, NY 10022.
T. (212) 755-8577. *090277*
Venezuela Art, 335 E 46 St, New York, NY 10017.
T. (212) 983-4935. *090278*
Vercel, Felix, 17 E 64 St, New York, NY 10021.
T. (212) 744-3131. - Paint / Graph / Sculp - *090279*
V.F. Design Group, 404 E 55 St, New York, NY 10022.
T. (212) 752-0861. *090280*
Via Veneti Gallery, 382 W Broadway, New York, NY
10012. T. (212) 941-9050. *090281*
Viafora, Althea, 200 E 58 St, New York, NY 10022.
T. (212) 421-8676. *090282*
Viart, 120 E 56 St, New York, NY 10022. T. (212) 752-
3500. *090283*
Victoria, Frederick P., 154 E 55 St, New York, NY 10022.
T. (212) 755-2549. *090284*
Viewpoint Gallery, 41 Union Sq W, New York, NY 10003.
T. (212) 242-5478. *090285*
Viridian Gallery, 52 W 57 St., New York, NY 10019.
T. (212) 245-2882. *090286*
Virtual Garrison, 19 Second Av, New York, NY 10003.
T. (212) 505-6138. *090287*
Vissi, 20 W 20 St, New York, NY 10011. T. (212) 675-
7264. *090288*

Visual Arts Gallery, 137 Wooster St, New York, NY
10012. T. (212) 598-0221. - Paint / Sculp *090289*
Viva Escorts, 67 E 11 St, New York, NY 10003.
T. (212) 529-3754. *090290*
Volpe, 496 La Guardia Pl, New York, NY 10012.
T. (212) 227-7913. *090291*
Vorpal, 459 W Broadway, New York, NY 10012.
T. (212) 777-3939. - Paint / Graph / Sculp - *090292*
Wada, Steve, 48 Grand St, New York, NY 10013.
T. (212) 431-1240. *090293*
Wada, Takashi, 350 W 50 St, New York, NY 10019.
T. (212) 586-8979. *090294*
Walker Ursitti & McGuinniss, 500 Greenwich St, New
York, NY 10013. T. (212) 966-7543. *090295*
Wall Street Art Gallery, 3 Hanover Sq, New York, NY
10004. T. (212) 363-8280. *090296*
Walters, Eileen, 654 Madison Av, New York, NY 10021.
T. (212) 644-1414. *090297*
Waltzer, 262 Bowery, New York, NY 10012. T. (212) 925-
0454. *090298*
Ward, Michael, 9 E 93 St, New York, NY 10128.
T. (212) 831-4044. *090299*
Ward-Nasse, 178 Prince St, New York, NY 10012.
T. (212) 925-6951. - Paint / Graph / Sculp / Fra - *090300*
Washburn, 20 W 57 St, New York, NY 10019.
T. (212) 397-6780. *090301*
Washington Irving, 40 Union Sq W, New York, NY 10003.
T. (212) 645-9562. *090302*
Washington Square Outdoor Art Exhibit, 300 Mercer St,
New York, NY 10003. T. (212) 982-6255.
- Paint - *090303*
Watson, Simon, 44 Lispenard St, New York, NY 10013.
T. (212) 925-1955. *090304*
Wauters, A., 1014 Madison Av, New York, NY 10021.
T. (212) 988-3447. *090305*
Wazoo Dance Machine, 242 W 30 St, New York, NY
10001. T. (212) 268-3244. *090306*
Weber, John, 142 Greene St, New York, NY 10012.
T. (212) 966-6115, Fax (212) 941-8727.
- Paint - *090307*
Weintraub, 988 Madison Av, New York, NY 10021.
T. (212) 879-1195. - Paint / Graph / Sculp - *090308*
Weisbrod, Michael B., 36 E 57 St, New York, NY 10022.
T. (212) 734-6350. - Orient - *090309*
Wellesley, Ross, 77 Mercer St, New York, NY 10012.
T. (212) 941-0954. *090310*
Wender, L.J., 3 E 80 St, New York, NY 10021.
T. (212) 734-3460, Fax (212) 427-4945.
- Orient - *090311*
Werner, Michael, 21 E 67 St, New York, NY 10021.
T. (212) 988-1623, Fax (212) 988-1774. - Paint /
Sculp - *090312*
Werther, Sandra, 23 E 74 St, New York, NY 10021.
T. (212) 734-0910. *090313*
Westbeth Gallery, 55 Bethune St, New York, NY 10014.
T. (212) 989-4650. *090314*
Western Images, 125 Wooster St, New York, NY 10012.
T. (212) 966-9177. *090315*
Weybridge, 30 E 81 St, New York, NY 10028.
T. (212) 628-5445. *090316*
Weyhe, E., 101 W 57 St, New York, NY 10019.
T. (212) 333-7610. - Graph - *090317*
Wheelock & Co., Whitney, 123 E 62 St, New York, NY
10021. T. (212) 688-7780. - Paint / Draw - *090318*
White Columns, 154 Christopher St, New York, NY
10014. T. (212) 924-4212. *090319*
Wickiser, Walter, 568 Broadway, New York, NY 10012.
T. (212) 941-1817. *090320*
Wigmore, D., 22 E 76 St, New York, NY 10021.
T. (212) 794-2128. *090321*
Wildenstein & Co., 19 E 64 St, New York, NY 10021.
T. (212) 879-0500. - Paint / Sculp / Draw - *090322*
Williams, Philip, 60 Grand St, New York, NY 10013.
T. (212) 226-7830. - Repr - *090323*
Willow, 470 Broome St, New York, NY 10013.
T. (212) 941-5743. *090324*
Wimmer, Elga, 560 Broadway, New York, NY 10012.
T. (212) 274-0274. *090325*
Windwood, 1079 Third Av, New York, NY 10021.
T. (212) 355-2508. *090326*
Witkin, 415 W Broadway, New York, NY 10012.
T. (212) 925-5510, Fax (212) 925-5648. - Ant /
Pho - *090327*

Wolf, Daniel, 52 E 78 St, New York, NY 10021.
T. (212) 772-7721. *090328*
Wolff, 177 Duane St, New York, NY 10013. T. (212) 431-
7833. *090329*
Works of Heart Personal Portraits, 338 E 67 St, New
York, NY 10021. T. (212) 628-6565. - Paint - *090330*
Works on Madison Avenue, 1250 Madison Av, New York,
NY 10128. T. (212) 996-0300. *090331*
World Trade Art Gallery, 105 Greenwich St, New York,
NY 10006. T. (212) 619-5241. *090332*
World Wide Art, 24 W 57 St, New York, NY 10019.
T. (212) 581-8833. *090333*
Wrans, 1079 Av of the Americas, New York, NY 10018.
T. (212) 391-9070. *090334*
Wunderlich, 50 W 57 St, New York, NY 10019.
T. (212) 974-8444. *090335*
Yamet, 260 Fifth Av, New York, NY 10001. T. (212) 685-
3820. *090336*
Yasuda, 15 W 53 St, New York, NY 10019. T. (212) 977-
7966. *090337*
Yayoi, 30 E 85 St, New York, NY 10028. T. (212) 794-
4360. *090338*
Yong, 168 Church St, New York, NY 10007. T. (212) 964-
1209. *090339*
York, Richard, 21 E 65 St, New York, NY 10021.
T. (212) 772-9155, Fax (212) 288-0410.
- Paint - *090340*
York's, 319-321 Bleecker St, New York, NY 10014.
T. (212) 691-6944, Fax (212) 229-9541. - Sculp /
Eth - *090341*
Yoshii, 20 W 57 St, New York, NY 10019. T. (212) 265-
8876. *090342*
Young, Robert Aaron, 979 Third Av, New York, NY
10022. T. (212) 421-2440. *090343*
Yu, James, 393 West Broadway, New York, NY 10012.
T. (212) 431-7867. - Paint / Graph / Sculp - *090344*
Z Gallery, 70 Greene St, New York, NY 10012.
T. (212) 966-8836. *090345*
Zangrilli & Co., 9 E 78 St, New York, NY 10021.
T. (212) 517-2777. *090346*
Zarre, Andre, 48 Greene St, New York, NY 10013.
T. (212) 966-2222. *090347*
Zona, 97 Greene St, New York, NY 10012. T. (212) 925-
6750. *090348*
Zwirner, David, 43 Greene St, New York, NY 10013.
T. (212) 966-9074. *090349*
Zwirner, Rudolf, 99 Greene St, New York, NY 10012.
T. (212) 431-6980. *090350*
123 Co-Unit Three Corporation, 123 E 47 St, New York,
NY 10017. T. (212) 752-6246. *090351*
14 Sculptors Gallery, 164 Mercer St, New York, NY
10012. T. (212) 966-5790. - Sculp - *090352*
1405 Art Gallery, 1405 Second Av, New York, NY 10021.
T. (212) 717-4025. *090353*
18th Street Art Gallery, 112 W 17 St, New York, NY
10011. T. (212) 255-7449. *090354*
1812 Art Gallery, 1812 Second Av, New York, NY 10128.
T. (212) 410-5543. *090355*
280 Modern, 280 Lafayette St, New York, NY 10012.
T. (212) 941-5825. *090356*
303 Gallery, 89 Greene St, New York, NY 10012.
T. (212) 966-5605. *090357*
450 Broadway Gallery, 450 Broadway, New York, NY
10013. T. (212) 941-5952. *090358*

Newport (Rhode Island)
Vareika, William, 212 Bellevue Av, Newport, RI 02840.
T. (401) 849-6149. *090359*

North Bay Village ((305) 864-8064)
Vintage Animation Art, 1440 Kennedy Causeway, North
Bay Village, FL 33141. T. (800) 323-2885. *090360*

North Hollywood (California)
Corita, 5126 Vineland, North Hollywood, CA 91601.
T. (213) 985-9370. - Paint / Graph - *090361*
Flemish Artist Shop, 13059 Ventura Blvd., North Holly-
wood, CA 91604. T. (213) 788-0263. - Paint /
Graph - *090362*

Northridge (California)
Weston, Edward, 19355 Business Center Dr, Northridge,
CA 91324. T. (818) 885-1044, Fax (818) 885-1021.
- Paint / Graph / Pho - *090363*

Oakland (California)

Creative Growth Art Center, 355 24 St., Oakland, CA
94612. T. (415) 836-2340.   090364
Goldstrom, Foster, 7133 Chabrot Rd., Oakland, CA
94618. T. (415) 652-2431.   090365
Graphics International, 6353 Wood Dr, Oakland, CA
94661. T. (415) 339-9310. - Graph / Fra -   090366
Kral, 6353 Wood St, Oakland, CA 94607. T. (510) 339-
9312. - Paint -   090367

Oklahoma City (Oklahoma)

Gustafson, 9606 N May Av., Oklahoma City, OK 73120.
T. (405) 751-8466.   090368
Johns, 4325 N Western Av., Oklahoma City, OK 73118.
T. (405) 528-4275. - Paint / Graph / Fra -   090369
Shorney, 6616 N Olie, Oklahoma City, OK 73116.
T. (405) 842-6175. - Paint / China / Sculp -   090370
The Colonial Art Co., 1336 N 1st St., Oklahoma City, OK
73106. T. (405) 232-5233. - Paint / Graph /
Repr –   090371

Old Lyme (Connecticut)

Clark, J.F., POB 907, Old Lyme, CT 06371. T. (203) 434-
0790.   090372

Orinda (California)

Samimi, 105 Orinda Way, Orinda, CA 94563.
T. (510) 254-3994.   090373

Orlando (Florida)

Cashi Orlando, Ralph E. Kaschai, 1460 33rd St., POB
5672, Orlando, FL 32855. T. (305) 425-9436. - Paint /
Graph –   090374
Ivy, Texann, 120 N Orange Av., Orlando, FL 32802.
T. (305) 422-1515. - Graph / Sculp -   090375

Pacifica (California)

Periwinkle, 1305 Palmetto Av, Pacifica, CA 94044.
T. (415) 359-5230.   090376

Palm Beach (Florida)

Annex, 350 S Countay Rd, Palm Beach, FL 33480.
T. (407) 820-1490, Fax (407) 820-1488.   090377
Arij Gasiunasen, 440 S County Rd, Palm Beach, CA
33480. T. (407) 820-8920, Fax (407) 820-
8918.   090378
Findlay, Wally, 175 Worth Ave., Palm Beach, FL 33480.
T. (407) 655-2090. - Paint / Graph / Sculp -   090379
Helander, 210 Worth Av., Palm Beach, FL 33480.
T. (407) 659-1711. - Paint / Sculp / Draw -   090380
Hokin, 245 Worth Av., Palm Beach, FL 33480.
T. (407) 655-5177. - Paint / Sculp -   090381
Holsten, 206 Worth Av., Palm Beach, FL 33480.
T. (407) 833-3403.   090382
Irving, 332 Worth Av., Palm Beach, FL 33480.
T. (407) 659-6221. - Paint / Graph / Sculp / Fra - 090383
Rubell, Jason, 238 Worth Av, Palm Beach, FL 33480.
T. (407) 655-6663, Fax (407) 655-6672.   090384
Surovek, John H., 337 Worth Av., Palm Beach, FL
33480. T. (407) 832-0422. - Paint -   090385

Palm Springs

Horwitch Gallery, Elaine, 1090 North Palm Canyon Drive,
Palm Springs, CA 92262. T. (619) 3253490.   090386

Palo Alto (California)

Photographer's Gallery, 732 Emerson St, Palo Alto, CA
994301. T. (415) 328-0662. - Pho -   090387
Xanadu Gallery, 149 Stanford Shopping Center, Palo Alto, CA 94304. T. (415) 329-9999. - Eth -   090388

Pasadena (California)

Curatorial Assistance, 113 E Union St, Pasadena, CA
91103. T. (713) 681-2401.   090389
Del Mano, 33 E Colorado Blvd, Pasadena, CA 91105.
T. (818) 793-6648.   090390
Osborne, 46 N Los Robles Av, Pasadena, CA 91101.
T. (818) 795-5354.   090391

Petoskey (Michigan)

Longton Hall Galleries, 410 Rose St., Petoskey, MJ
49770. T. (616) 347-9672.   090392

Philadelphia (Pennsylvania)

Accent-Graphics, 3637 Locust Walk, Philadelphia, PA
19104. T. (215) 222-9178. - Graph / Fra -   090393

Burke, Harry, Philadelphia POB 30539, PA 19103.
T. (215) 564-1869. - Ant / Paint / Graph / Orient / China /
Sculp / Jew / Silv / Glass -   090394
Carlen, Robert, 323 S 16th St., Philadelphia, PA 19102.
T. (215) 545-1723. - Paint / Graph -   090395
Cava, 1636 Walnut St., Philadelphia, PA 19103.
T. (215) 732-5188.   090396
Custom Frame Shop and Gallery, 404 1/2 South St.,
Philadelphia, PA 19147. T. (215) 922-5708.   090397
David, David, 260 S 18 St., Philadelphia, PA 19103.
T. (215) 735-2922. - Paint / Graph / Sculp /
Draw –   090398
Dolan Maxwell, 1701 Walnut St, Philadelphia, PA 19103.
T. (215) 665-1701. - Graph / Draw -   090399
Fleisher, Janet, 211 S 17 St., Philadelphia, PA 19103.
T. (215) 545-7562. - Paint / Rel / Pho / Draw -   090400
Fuller, Jeffrey, 132 S 17 St., Philadelphia, PA 19103.
T. (215) 564-9977. - Paint / Graph / Sculp / Arch / Eth /
Pho –   090401
Gorski, 6377 Germantown Av., Philadelphia, PA 19144.
T. (215) 848-1577. - Paint / Fra -   090402
Hahn, 8439 Germantown Av., Philadelphia, PA 19118.
T. (215) 247-8439, Fax (215) 247-8849. - Paint /
Graph / Orient / Sculp / Tex / Dec / Fra / Glass / Pho / Mu-
l / Draw -   090403
LaPelle, Rodger, 122 N Third St., Philadelphia, PA
19106. T. (215) 592-0232. - Paint / Graph /
Sculp –   090404
Locks, Marian, 600 Washington Sq. S, Philadelphia, PA
19106. T. (215) 629-1000. - Paint / Graph -   090405
Makler, 225 S 18th St., Philadelphia, PA 19103.
T. (215) 735-2540. - Paint / Graph / Sculp -   090406
Newman, 1625 Walnut St., Philadelphia, PA 19103.
T. (215) 563-1779. - Paint / Graph / Fra -   090407
Revsin Art Gallery, 911 Arch St., Philadelphia, PA
19107.   090408
Rosenfeld, 113 Arch St., Philadelphia, PA 19106.
T. (215) 922-1376. - Paint / Graph / Draw -   090409
Schwarz, Frank S. & Son, 1806 Chestnut St., Philadel-
phia, PA 19103. T. (215) 563-4887. - Ant / Paint / Jew /
Silv –   090410
Sessler, Charles, 1308 Walnut St, Philadelphia, PA
19107. T. (215) 735-1086. - Paint / Repr -   090411
Snyderman, 317-319 South St., Philadelphia, PA 19147.
T. (215) 238-9576. - Sculp / Glass -   090412
Temple Gallery, 1619 Walnut St., Philadelphia, PA
19103. T. (215) 787-5041.   090413
The Print Club, 1614 Latimer St., Philadelphia, PA
19103. T. (215) 735-6090. - Graph -   090414
Webster, Sande, 2018 Locust St., Philadelphia, PA
19103. T. (215) 732-8850. - Paint / Graph /
Sculp –   090415
Works Gallery, 319 South St., Philadelphia, PA 19147.
T. (215) 922-7775.   090416

Phoenix (Arizona)

Cline, John D., 424 N Central, Phoenix, AZ 85004.
T. (602) 252-7213. - Paint / Graph / China / Sculp /
Glass –   090417
Eleven East Ashland, 11 E Ashland Av., Phoenix, AZ
85004. T. (602) 271-0831.   090418
Gallery Wall, 7122 N Seventh St., Phoenix, AZ 85020.
T. (602) 943-8183. - Paint / Graph -   090419
Gallery 3, 3819 N Third St., Phoenix, AZ 85012.
T. (602) 277-9540. - Paint / Graph / Sculp -   090420
McGoffin, 902 W Roosevelt, Phoenix, AZ 85007.
T. (602) 255-0785. - Paint / Graph / Sculp / Eth - 090421
Turner, Sally, 333 E. Beck Lane, Phoenix, AZ 85022.
T. (602) 863-3881. - Paint -   090422

Pittsburgh (Pennsylvania)

Circle Gallery, 5416 Walnut St., Pittsburgh, PA 15232.
T. (412) 687-1336.   090423
Concept Art Gallery, 1031 S Braddock Av., Pittsburgh,
PA 15218. T. (412) 242-9200.   090424
Fisher Collection, 711 Forbes Av., Pittsburgh, PA 15219.
T. (412) 562-8480.   090425
Four Winds Gallery, 5512 Walnut St., Pittsburgh, PA
15238. T. (412) 682-5092. - Paint / Graph / Sculp /
Mul –   090426
Gallery G, 211 Ninth St., Pittsburgh, PA 15222.
T. (412) 562-0912. - Paint / Sculp -   090427

Mass, Alex E., 116 Maruth Dr., Pittsburgh, PA 15237.
T. (412) 364-3458. - Paint -   090428
Mendelson, 5874 Ellsworth Av., Pittsburgh, PA 15232.
- Paint / Graph / Repr / Sculp -   090429

Pittsfield (Massachusetts)

Berkshire Artisans, 28 Renne Av., Pittsfield, 01201.
T. (413) 443-4322. - Paint -   090430

Placerville (California)

Fine Arts in Metal Art Foundry, 5271 Merchant Circle,
Placerville, CA 95667. T. (916) 626-9441.
- Sculp -   090431

Plymouth Meeting (Pennsylvania)

Plymouth Meeting Gallery, POB 756, Plymouth Meeting,
PA 19462. T. (215) 825-9068.   090432

Portland (Maine)

Elowitch, Annette & Rob, POB 9715, Portland, ME
04104. T. (207) 772-5011, Fax (207) 772-
5049.   090433
Stein, 20 Milk St., Portland, ME 04101. T. (207) 772-
9072. - Glass -   090434

Portland (Oregon)

Abanté, 124 SW Yamhill, Portland, OR 97204.
T. (503) 295-2508, Fax (503) 295-0425. - Paint / Repr /
Sculp –   090435
Attic Gallery, 206 SW First Av., Portland, OR 97204.
T. (503) 228-7830. - Paint / Graph / Sculp -   090436
Blackfish Gallery, 420 NW Ninth Av., Portland, OR
97209. T. (503) 224-2634. - Paint / Sculp -   090437
Harwin, 9101 SW 15 Av., Portland, OR 97219.
T. (503) 245-8900.   090438
Lawrence, 842 SW First Av., Portland, OR 97204.
T. (503) 224-9442. - Paint / China / Sculp -   090439
Old Masters Art Shop, 4428 SE Woodstock Blvd, Port-
land, OR 972060.   090440
The Shado' Gallery, 2910 SE Lambert St., Portland, OR
97202. - Pho -   090441
West Coast Picture Corporation, 5805 N. E. Skidmore
St., Portland, OR 97218. - Paint / Graph / Fra -   090442
Wilson W. Clark Memorial Library Gallery, 5000 N Willa-
mette Blvd., Portland, OR 97203. T. (503) 283-
7111.   090443

Raleigh (North Carolina)

Gilliam and Peden, 126 Glenwood Av., Raleigh, NC
27603. T. (919) 834-5800. - Paint / Sculp -   090444

Rancho Sante Fe (California)

Grossman, Daniel B., 6033L Paseo Delicias, Rancho
Sante Fe, CA 92067. T. (212) 861-9285.
- Paint -   090445

Ridgefield (Connecticut)

Kouros, Sculpture Center, Ridgefield, CT 06877.
T. (203) 438-7636.   090446

Rockville (Maryland)

Art Warehouse, 12015 Nebel St, Rockville, MD 20852.
T. (301) 770-5505. - Paint / Graph / Fra -   090447
Artists Circle, 11544 Springridge Rd, Rockville, MD
20854. T. (301) 921-0572.   090448
Charles, Barry, 8 Hardwicke Pl, Rockville, MD 20850.
T. (301) 340-6775. - Paint / Furn / Sculp -   090449

Saint Louis (Missouri)

Barucci, 13496 Clayton Rd., Saint Louis, MO 63131.
T. (314) 878-5090. - Paint -   090450
Barucci, 8409 OliveBlvd., Saint Louis, MO 63132.
T. (314) 993-4317. - Paint / Graph -   090451
Becker, M.J., 2010 Brentwood Blvd, Saint Louis, MO
63144. T. (314) 961-3440. - Graph / Tex -   090452
Boody, 1425 Haley Industrial Court, Saint Louis, MO
63144. T. (314) 961-5502. - Paint / Graph /
Sculp –   090453
Clayton Art Gallery, 8113 Maryland, Saint Louis, MO
63105.   090454
Delta, 1011 East Park Dr., Saint Louis, MO 63130.
T. (314) 727-2444. - Paint / Graph / Sculp /
Glass –   090455
Dietrich-Stone Ltd., 2601 S Warson, Saint Louis, MO
63124.   090456

Gallery of the Masters, 9918 Clayton Rd., Saint Louis, MO 63124. T. (314) 993-4477, Fax (314) 993-4478. - Paint / Sculp -
Greenberg, 44 Maryland Plaza, Saint Louis, MO 63108. T. (314) 361-7600, Fax (314) 361-7743. - Paint - 090458
Harmon Gallery, 8112 Maryland, Saint Louis, MO 63105. 090459
Locus, 710 N Tucker 315, Saint Louis, MO 63101. T. (314) 231-2515. - Paint / Graph / Sculp - 090460
Norton's, 325 N. Euclid Ave., Saint Louis, MO 63108. T. (314) 367-9917. - Paint / Graph / Sculp / Fra - 090461
Pepper Gallery, Edwin, 444 Brentwood Blvd., Saint Louis, MO 63105. 090462
Richelle, 6226 Forsyth Blvd., Saint Louis, MO 63105. - Paint - 090463
Samuels, Philip, 8112 Maryland Av., Saint Louis, MO 63105. T. (314) 727-2444. - Paint / Sculp / Draw - 090464
Schweig, Martin, 4658 Maryland Av., Saint Louis, MO 63108. T. (314) 361-3000. - Paint / Graph - 090465
Selkirk, 4166 Olive St., Saint Louis, MO 63108. T. (314) 533-1700. - Paint - 090466
Smith, Elliot, 360 N Skinker Blvd., Saint Louis, MO 63130. T. (314) 726-1170. - Paint - 090467

Saint Paul (Minnesota)
Billings, James E., 215 S Grotto St., Saint Paul, MN 55105. T. (612) 228-1441. - Paint / Graph / Furn / Orient / Sculp / Tex - 090468
Film in the Cities Gallery, 2388 University Av., Saint Paul, MN 55114. T. (612) 646-6104. - Pho - 090469
Kohn, Suzanne, 1690 Grand Av., Saint Paul, MN 55105. T. (612) 699-0477. - Paint / Graph / Sculp - 090470
Kramer, 229 E Sixth St., Saint Paul, MN 55101. T. (612) 228-1301. - Paint - 090471

Salt Lake City (Utah)
Appleyard Art Frame Gallery, 3096 S Highland Dr., Salt Lake City, UT 84106. T. (801) 467-3621. 090472
Gallery 56, 56 W 400 S, Salt Lake City, UT 84101. T. (801) 533-8245. - Paint / Sculp - 090473
Phillips, 444 E 200 S, Salt Lake City, UT 84111. T. (801) 364-8284. - Paint / China / Sculp / Pho / Draw - 090474

San Antonio (Texas)
Allens Flowers & Gifts, 210 McCullough, San Antonio, TX 78212. T. (512) 734-6441. - Paint / Graph / Fra - 090475
Boulephoros, POB 7120, San Antonio, TX 78207. Fax (210) 828-0231. 090476
Little Studio, 506 Villita St., San Antonio, TX 78205. - Paint / Graph / Sculp - 090477
Milagros Contemporary Art, 112 Blue Star, San Antonio, TX 78204. T. (512) 227-0001, Fax (512) 225-7015. 090478
River Art Group Gallery, 510 Paseo de la Villita, San Antonio, TX 782050. T. (512) 226-8752. - Paint / Graph / Sculp 090479
Sol del Rio, 1020 Townsend Ave, San Antonio, TX 78209. T. (512) 828-5555. - Paint / Graph - 090480
Villita Gallery, 504 Villita St., San Antonio, TX 78205. T. (512) 223-4632. - Paint / Graph / China / Repr / Sculp / Jew / Cur / Draw - 090481

San Diego (California)
Moore, Linda, 1611 W Lewis St, San Diego, CA 92103. T. (619) 260-1101, Fax (619) 260-1124. 090482

San Francisco (California)
Adams, Walter, 355 Presidio Av, San Francisco, CA 94115. T. (415) 346-2860. 090485
Addi, 400 Jefferson St, San Francisco, CA 94109. T. (415) 776-1180. - Paint / Graph / Sculp - 090486
Addi, 400 Jefferson St, San Francisco, CA 94109. T. (415) 776-1180. 090487
Albers, 251 Post St, San Francisco, CA 94108. T. (415) 391-2111. - Eth - 090488
Allrich, 251 Post St, San Francisco, CA 94108. T. (415) 398-8896, Fax (415) 398-0401. - Paint / Sculp / Tex - 090489
Alternative Design Studio, 3458 18 St, San Francisco, CA 94110. T. (415) 255-2787. 090489a

Amazing Adventures Comic Shop, 3800 Noriega St, San Francisco, CA 94122. T. (415) 661-1344. - Graph - 090490
American Indian Contemporary Arts, 685 Market St, San Francisco, CA 94105. T. (415) 495-7600. - Eth - 090491
American Masterpiece Collections, 630 Tennessee St, San Francisco, CA 94107. T. (415) 864-7790. - Paint - 090492
The Americas, 1782 Union St, San Francisco, CA 94123. T. (415) 921-4600. 090493
An American Romantic, 491 Greenwich St, San Francisco, CA 94133. T. (415) 989-1630. 090494
Anglim, Paule, 14 Geary St, San Francisco, CA 94108. T. (415) 433-2710. - Paint / Graph / Sculp - 090495
Animation USA, 222 Sutter St, San Francisco, CA 94108. T. (415) 362-3878. 090496
Ansel Adams Center for Photography, 250 Fourth St, San Francisco, CA 94107. T. (415) 495-7000. - Pho - 090497
Architects and Heroes-Annex, 580 Bush St, San Francisco, CA 94108. T. (415) 391-8833. 090498
Arkadyan, 938 Irving St, San Francisco, CA 94122. T. (415) 664-6212. - Graph - 090499
Art and Travel Gallery, 3654 Sacramento St, San Francisco, CA 94118. T. (415) 928-8095. 090500
Art-Chitecture Gallery, 211 Steiner St, San Francisco, CA 94115. T. (415) 861-6679. 090501
Art Collective, 3654 Sacramento St, San Francisco, CA 94118. T. (415) 474-9999. 090502
Art Exchange, 77 Geary St, San Francisco, CA 94108. T. (415) 956-5750. 090503
Art Group International, 251 Post St, San Francisco, CA 94108. T. (415) 981-3525. 090504
Art Options, 372 Hayes St, San Francisco, CA 94102. T. (415) 252-8334. - Paint - 090505
Arte Maya Tz'utuhil, POB 40391, San Francisco, CA 94140. T. (415) 282-7654. - Eth - 090506
Artery, 1510 Haight St, San Francisco, CA 94102. T. (415) 621-2872. 090507
Artiques, 2167 Union St, San Francisco, CA 94123. T. (415) 929-6969. 090508
Artist in Residence Gallery, 23 Grant Av, San Francisco, CA 94108. T. (415) 421-8030. 090509
Artwork, 1837 Divisadero St, San Francisco, CA 94115. T. (415) 673-3080. 090510
Asaka, 682 Post St, San Francisco, CA 94109. T. (415) 775-5343. 090511
Ashkenazie & Co, 950 Mason St, San Francisco, CA 94108. T. (415) 391-3440, Fax (415) 391-1464. 090512
Ashkenazie-Turner, Robin, 150 Post St, San Francisco, CA 94108. 090513
Aurobora, 147 Natoma St, San Francisco, CA 94105. T. (415) 546-7880. - Graph - 090514
Austerer, Eleonore, 540 Sutter St, San Francisco, CA 94102. T. (415) 986-2244. - Paint / Sculp - 090515
Avenue Art, 3060 Scott St, San Francisco, CA 94123. T. (415) 776-8108. 090516
B & W Color Images, 1286 Fillmore St, San Francisco, CA 94115. T. (415) 885-6445. - Graph / Sculp - 090517
Back to the Picture, 934 Valencia St, San Francisco, CA 94110. T. (415) 826-2321. 090518
Banaker, 251 Post St, San Francisco, CA 94108. T. (415) 397-1397. 090519
Belcher Studios Gallery, 69 Belcher St, San Francisco, CA 94114. T. (415) 863-8745. 090520
Bella Art and Frame Services, 347 Ninth Av, San Francisco, CA 94118. T. (415) 861-8389. - Paint / Graph / Fra - 090521
Bennett Hall, 41 Powell St, San Francisco, CA 94102. T. (415) 434-8745. 090522
Berggruen, John, 228 Grant Av, San Francisco, CA 94108. T. (415) 781-4629. - Paint / Graph / Sculp / Pho / Draw - 090523
Berlin, Brenda, 326 Ritch St, San Francisco, CA 94107. T. (415) 974-5961. 090524
Bernstein & Co, S., 1 Daniel Burnham Ct, San Francisco, CA 94109. T. (415) 346-9193, Fax (415) 346-9136. 090525
Blast Haus, 217 Second St, San Francisco, CA 94105. T. (415) 896-1700. 090526

Bomani, 251 Post St, San Francisco, CA 94108. T. (415) 296-8677. 090527
Bond Street Gallery, 250 Sutter St, San Francisco, CA 94108. T. (415) 362-1480. 090528
Bookstall, 570 Sutter St, San Francisco, CA 94102. T. (415) 362-6353. 090529
Bowles Sorokko, 765 Beach St, San Francisco, CA 94109. T. (415) 441-8008. 090530
Bowles Sorokko, 231 Grant Av, San Francisco, CA 94108. T. (415) 421-7770. 090531
Bowman, Leonard, 2324 Market St, San Francisco, CA 94114. T. (415) 781-2327. 090532
Boyd, David S., 101 California St, San Francisco, CA 94111. T. (415) 788-0550. 090533
Bransten, Rena, 77 Geary St, San Francisco, CA 94108. T. (415) 982-3292, Fax (415) 982-1801. - Paint / Graph / Sculp - 090534
Braunstein-Quay, 250 Sutter St, San Francisco, CA 94108. T. (415) 392-5532. - Paint / Draw - 090535
Breier, V., 3091 Sacramento St, San Francisco, CA 94115. T. (415) 929-7173. - Sculp - 090536
Breton, 2801 Leavenworth St, San Francisco, CA 94133. T. (415) 928-6334. - Paint / Graph - 090537
Bridge Gallery, 689 Bryant St, San Francisco, CA 94107. T. (415) 777-1474. 090538
Bucheon, 355 Hayes St, San Francisco, CA 94102. T. (415) 863-2891. 090539
Caldwell, Edith, 251 Post St, San Francisco, CA 94108. T. (415) 989-5414. 090540
Caldwell Snyder, 357 Geary St, San Francisco, CA 94102. T. (415) 296-7896. - Paint / Graph - 090541
Caldwell Snyder, 228 Grant Av, San Francisco, CA 94108. T. (415) 392-2299. - Paint / Graph - 090542
Camerawork Gallery, 70 12 Av, San Francisco, CA 94118. T. (415) 621-1001. - Pho - 090543
Campbell-Thiebaud, 645 Chestnut St, San Francisco, CA 94133. T. (415) 441-8680. - Paint - 090544
Canessa, 708 Montgomery St, San Francisco, CA 94111. T. (415) 296-9029. 090545
Capp Street Project, 525 Second St, San Francisco, CA 94107. T. (415) 495-7101. 090546
Castle Fine Arts, 454 Sutter St, San Francisco, CA 94108. T. (415) 956-5000. - Graph / Orient - 090547
CC & Beyond, 843 Divisadero St, San Francisco, CA 94115. T. (415) 474-0883. 090548
Cedanna, 1925 Fillmore St, San Francisco, CA 94115. T. (415) 474-7152. 090549
Chappell, Joanne, 625 Second St, San Francisco, CA 94107. T. (415) 777-5711. 090550
Chinese Culture Center, 750 Kearny St, San Francisco, CA 94108. T. (415) 986-1822. 090551
Chowning, Joseph, 1717 17 St, San Francisco, CA 94103. T. (415) 626-7496. - Paint - 090552
Chroma Art Design Company, 150 15 St, San Francisco, CA 94114. T. (415) 552-9661. - Graph - 090553
Circle Gallery, 900 North Point St, San Francisco, CA 92109. T. (415) 776-2370. 090554
Circle Gallery, 140 Maiden Ln, San Francisco, CA 94108. T. (415) 989-2100. - Sculp - 090555
Civic South International, 22 Iris Av, San Francisco, CA 94118. T. (415) 431-7271. 090556
Cobra Fine Art, 580 Sutter St, San Francisco, CA 94102. T. (415) 397-2195. 090557
Colberg, Sid, 2060 Army St, San Francisco, CA 94124. T. (415) 206-0850. 090558
Collage Gallery, 1345 18 St, San Francisco, CA 94122. T. (415) 282-4401. 090559
Color Color, 225 Gought St, San Francisco, CA 94102. T. (415) 552-0507. 090560
Compositions Gallery, 317 Sutter St, San Francisco, CA 94108. T. (415) 693-9111. - Glass - 090561
Conacher, 134 Maiden Ln, San Francisco, CA 94108. T. (415) 392-5447. - Paint / Graph / Sculp - 090562
Contemporary Realist Gallery, 23 Grant Av, San Francisco, CA 94108. T. (415) 362-7152. - Paint / Graph / Sculp - 090563
Craftsman's Guild, 300 De Haro St, San Francisco, CA 94107. T. (415) 431-5425. - Graph - 090564
Creative Spirit, 900 North Point St, San Francisco, CA 94109. T. (415) 441-1537. 090565
Crown Point Press, 20 Hawthorne St, San Francisco, CA 94105. T. (415) 974-6273, Fax (415) 495-4220. - Graph - 090566

Da Vinci, 228 Powell St, San Francisco, CA 94102.
T. (415) 397-8011. *090567*

De la Raza, 2857 24 St, San Francisco, CA 94110.
T. (415) 826-8009. *090568*

De Vera, 334 Gough St, San Francisco, CA 94102.
T. (415) 558-8865. *090569*

De Vera, 384 Hayes St, San Francisco, CA 94102.
T. (415) 861-8480. *090570*

Denenberg, 257 Grant Av, San Francisco, CA 94108.
T. (415) 788-8411. - Paint - *090571*

Deroche, 59 Grant Av, San Francisco, CA 94108.
T. (415) 989-0300. - Eth - *090572*

Discount Graphics and Framing, 34 Trinity Pl, San Francisco, CA 94104. T. (415) 788-8807. - Graph /
Fra - *090573*

Disenos Artesanales, 3072 24 St, San Francisco, CA
94110. T. (415) 641-7080. - Graph / Draw - *090574*

Dollar, Olga, 210 Post St, San Francsico, CA 94108.
T. (415) 398-2297. *090574a*

Dore, 771 Bush St, San Francisco, CA 94108.
T. (415) 391-2423. - Paint / Sculp - *090575*

Dunev, Michael, 77 Geary St, San Francisco, CA 94108.
T. (415) 398-7300, Fax (415) 398-7680. - Paint /
Graph / Sculp / Draw - *090576*

Dunk-N-Dogs, 2178 Bush St, San Francisco, CA 94115.
T. (415) 928-2159. *090577*

Dyansen, 799 Beach St, San Francisco, CA 94109.
T. (415) 928-0596. *090578*

East West Gallery, 136 Geary St, San Francisco, CA
94108. T. (415) 397-8184. *090579*

Ebert, 49 Geary St, San Francisco, CA 94108.
T. (415) 296-8405. *090580*

Editions Limited Galleries, 625 Second St, Ste 400, San
Francisco, CA 94107. T. (415) 777-5711. - Paint /
Graph *090581*

Ellese, 222 Powell St, San Francisco, CA 94102.
T. (415) 433-3060. *090582*

Erickson & Elins, 345 Sutter St, San Francisco, CA
941094108. T. (415) 981-1080. - Paint - *090583*

Ethnic Trip Cultural Art Collections, 201 Octavia St, San
Francisco, CA 94102. T. (415) 252-9493.
- Eth - *090584*

Evans, Gropper & Willis, 77 Geary St, San Francisco, CA
94108. T. (415) 398-7545. *090585*

Exhibitionism, 125 Cyril Magnin St, San Francisco, CA
94102. T. (415) 788-1825. *090586*

Eye Gallery, 1151 Mission St, San Francisco, CA 94110.
T. (415) 431-6911. *090587*

Far East Fine Arts, 518 Sutter St, San Francisco, CA
94102. T. (415) 421-0932. - Orient - *090588*

Fastframe, 1700 Market St, San Francisco, CA 94102.
T. (415) 255-1595. - Graph / Fra - *090589*

Fastframe, 1700 Lombard St, San Francisco, CA 94123.
T. (415) 563-1700. - Graph / Fra - *090590*

Fine Art Enterprises, 555 Sutter St Third Floor, San Francisco, CA 94102. T. (415) 421-5450. *090591*

First Street Gallery, 50 First St, San Francisco, CA
94105. T. (415) 512-7056. *090592*

Following Sea Gallery, 865 Market St, San Francisco, CA
94102. T. (415) 979-0933. *090593*

Fraenkel, 49 Geary St, San Francisco, CA 94108.
T. (415) 981-2661. - Paint - *090594*

Frame of Mind, 1262 Ninth Av, San Francisco, CA
94122. T. (415) 759-2000. - Fra - *090595*

Galerie Voyage, 1737 Post St, San Francisco, CA 94115.
T. (415) 567-3100. *090596*

Galleria del Sol, 381 Geary St, San Francisco, CA
94102. T. (415) 362-1820. *090597*

Gallery on the Rim, 333 Third St, San Francisco, CA
94107. T. (415) 543-7007. *090598*

Gallery 444, 444 Post St, San Francisco, CA 94102.
T. (415) 434-4477. *090599*

Gallery 524, 524 Hayes St, San Francisco, CA 94102.
T. (415) 255-9139. *090600*

Grafika, 1 Ecker Pl, San Francisco, CA 94105.
T. (415) 546-4081. - Graph - *090601*

Graystone, 250 Sutter St, San Francisco, CA 94108.
T. (415) 956-7693. - Paint / Graph - *090602*

Great Frame Up, 2358 Market St, San Francisco, CA
94114. T. (415) 863-7144. - Fra - *090603*

Greve-Hine, 357 Tehama St, San Francisco, CA 94105.
T. (415) 777-2214. *090604*

Gross, Brian, 250 Sutter St, San Francisco, CA 94108.
T. (415) 788-1050. *090605*

Gump's, 250 Post St, San Francisco, CA 94108.
T. (415) 982-1616. - Paint / Graph / Sculp - *090606*

Gump's, 250 Post St., San Francisco, CA 94108.
T. (415) 982-1616. - Paint / Graph / Sculp / Fra - *090607*

Haines, 49 Geary St, San Francisco, CA 94108.
T. (415) 397-8114. *090608*

Hanley, Jack, 41 Grant Av, San Francisco, CA 94108.
T. (415) 291-8911. *090609*

Harcourts, 460 Bush St, San Francisco, CA 94108.
T. (415) 421-3428. - Paint / Graph / Sculp /
Draw - *090610*

Harleen & Allen, 427 Bryant St, San Francisco, CA
94107. T. (415) 777-0920. - Paint - *090611*

Hermes, 2847 Clay St, San Francisco, CA 94115.
T. (415) 775-3709. - Graph - *090612*

Hertzmann, Paul M., POB 40447, San Francisco, CA
94140. T. (415) 626-2677. - Pho - *090613*

Hespe, 1764 Union St, San Francisco, CA 94123.
T. (415) 776-5918. *090614*

Holloway, Jan, 250 Sutter St, San Francisco, CA 94108.
T. (415) 398-2055. - Paint / Graph - *090615*

Hourian, 1843 Union St, San Francisco, CA 94123.
T. (415) 346-6400. *090616*

Images A Gallery, 372 Hayes St, San Francisco, CA
94102. T. (415) 626-2284. *090617*

Images of the North, 1782 Union St, San Francisco, CA
94123. T. (415) 673-1273. - Graph / Sculp /
Eth - *090618*

Immendorf, 1845 Polk St, San Francisco, CA 94109.
T. (415) 776-4178. - Graph / Fra - *090619*

International Art Gallery, 1581 Webster St, San Francisco, CA 94115. T. (415) 567-4390. - Graph /
Orient - *090620*

Intersection for the Arts, 446 Valencia St, San Francisco,
CA 94103. T. (415) 626-2787. *090621*

Jackson Square Gallery, 831 Montgomery St, San Francisco, CA 94133. T. (415) 392-0362. *090622*

Japonesque Gallery, 824 Montgomery St, San Francisco,
CA 94133. T. (415) 398-8577. - Graph - *090623*

Jewish Art Gallery, 1109 Geary Blvd, San Francisco,
94109. T. (415) 292-6500. - Paint / Graph - *090624*

Kay & Associates, Judy, 640 Davis St, San Francisco, CA
9411. T. (415) 421-3933. *090625*

Keane Eyes Gallery, 651 Market St, San Francisco, CA
94105. T. (415) 495-3263. *090626*

Keating, Michael, 442 Post St, San Francisco, CA
94102. T. (415) 391-6524. *090627*

Kertesz, 521 Sutter St, San Francisco, CA 94102.
T. (415) 626-0376. - Paint / Sculp / Draw - *090628*

Kimpton, K., 2620 Jackson St, San Francisco, CA
94115. T. (415) 563-5657. *090629*

Kimura, 1933 Ocean Av, San Francisco, CA 94127.
T. (415) 585-0052. - Graph - *090630*

Kinkade, Thomas, 876 Market St, San Francisco, CA
94102. T. (415) 788-7330. *090631*

Koch, Robert, 49 Geary St, San Francisco, CA 94108.
T. (415) 421-0122. - Pho - *090632*

Krevsky, George, 77 Geary St, San Francisco, CA 94108.
T. (415) 397-9748. *090633*

Lafayette Parke, 250 Sutter St, San Francisco, CA
94108. T. (415) 788-5050, Fax (415) 788-
5052. *090634*

Lahaina, 645 Beach St, San Francisco, CA 94133.
T. (415) 749-1000. *090635*

Lassen, 747 Beach St, San Francisco, CA 94109.
T. (415) 292-1900. *090636*

Lawson, 56 Kissling St, San Francisco, CA 94103.
T. (415) 626-1159. *090637*

Limestone Press, 357 Tehama St, San Francisco, CA
94105. T. (415) 777-2214. - Graph - *090638*

Limn, 457 Pacific Av, San Francisco, CA 94133.
T. (415) 397-7474. *090639*

Little Frankensteins, 3804 17 St, San Francisco, CA
94114. T. (415) 864-6543. *090640*

Mace Space for Art, 1319 Pine St, San Francisco, CA
94109. T. (415) 931-9670. *090641*

Mamone, 360 Jefferson St, San Francisco, CA 94133.
T. (415) 776-8001. *090642*

Mamone, 373 Geary St, San Francisco, CA 94102.
T. (415) 956-3030. *090643*

Mana, 2075 Third St, San Francisco, CA 94107.
T. (415) 621-7847. *090644*

Manuelita's Gallery, 3109 Fillmore St, San Francisco, CA
94123. T. (415) 923-0822. *090645*

Marimekko, 309 Sutter St, San Francisco, CA 94108.
T. (415) 392-1742. *090646*

Martin, Lawrence, 865 Market St, San Francisco, CA
94102. T. (415) 512-8480. *090647*

Maxwell, 551 Sutter St, San Francisco, CA 94102.
T. (415) 421-5193. - Paint / Graph / Sculp / Fra - *090648*

Meridian Gallery, 545 Sutter St, San Francisco, CA
94102. T. (415) 398-7229. *090649*

Meyerovich, 251 Post St, San Francisco, CA 94108.
T. (415) 421-7171. *090650*

Meyerovich, Erika, 231 Grant Av, San Francisco, CA
94108. T. (415) 421-9997. - Paint / Graph /
Sculp - *090651*

Minna Street Gallery, 111 Minna St, San Francisco, CA
94105. T. (415) 974-1719. *090652*

Mitre Box, 4082 24 St, San Francisco, CA 94114.
T. (415) 824-2272. *090653*

Modernism, 685 Market St, San Francisco, CA 94105.
T. (415) 541-0461, Fax (415) 541-0425.
- Paint - *090654*

Montgomery, 250 Sutter St, San Francisco, CA 94108.
T. (415) 788-8300. - Paint / Sculp / Draw - *090655*

Morphos Gallery, 544 Hayes St, San Francisco, CA
94102. T. (415) 989-4709. *090656*

Mullen, Theresa, 347 Dolores St, San Francisco, CA
94110. T. (415) 864-5283. *090657*

Mulligan-Shanoski, 747 Post St, San Francisco, CA
94109. T. (415) 771-0663. *090658*

Nevska, 353 Geary St, San Francisco, CA 94102.
T. (415) 392-4932. *090659*

Nichols, Scott, 49 Geary St, San Francisco, CA 94108.
T. (415) 788-4641. - Pho - *090659a*

North Beach Decor, 1422 Grant Av, San Francisco, CA
94133. T. (415) 989-1616. *090660*

North Beach Studio, 1817 Powell St, San Francisco, CA
94133. T. (415) 837-0505. *090661*

North Point Gallery, 872 North Point St, San Francisco,
CA 94109. T. (415) 885-0657. - Paint / Graph / Sculp /
Pho - *090662*

Opts Art, 250 Fourth St, San Francisco, 94107.
T. (415) 546-7844. *090663*

Oriental Art Gallery, 1340 Ninth Av, San Francisco, CA
94118. T. (415) 681-6448. - Orient - *090664*

Orientations, 195 De Haro St, San Francisco, CA 94107.
T. (415) 255-8277. *090665*

Owl Gallery, 465 Powell St, San Francisco, CA 94102.
T. (415) 781-5464. *090666*

Padma, 3895 18 St, San Francisco, CA 94114.
T. (415) 621-8135. *090667*

Paulson, Kristen A., 675 Carolina St, San Francisco, CA
94107. T. (415) 648-5246. *090668*

Pence, John, 750 Post St, San Francisco, CA 94109.
T. (415) 441-1138. - Paint / Sculp / Draw - *090669*

Peyton, Patricia, 1736 Stockton St, San Francisco, CA
94133. T. (415) 362-5330. *090670*

Phoenix Gallery, 301 Eighth Av, San Francisco, CA
94118. T. (415) 621-4423. *090671*

Photos Gallery, 403 Francisco St, San Francisco, CA
94133. T. (415) 986-4149. - Pho - *090672*

Pilcher, W., 372 Hayes St, San Francisco, CA 94102.
T. (415) 552-5915. *090673*

Polanco, 242 Gough St, San Francisco, CA 94102.
T. (415) 252-5753. *090674*

Polish Arts and Culture Foundation Headquarters, 1290
Sutter St, San Francisco, CA 94109. T. (415) 474-
7070. - Paint / Graph - *090675*

Print Store, 2801 Leavenworth St, San Francisco,
94133. T. (415) 771-3576. - Graph - *090676*

Prova, 2238 Fillmore St, San Francisco, CA 94115.
T. (415) 292-4010. *090677*

Refusalon, 630 Natoma St, San Francisco, CA 94105.
T. (415) 863-6157. *090678*

Regal Art Galleries, 781 Beach St, San Francisco, CA
94109. T. (415) 202-7121. - Paint - *090679*

Regal Art Galleries, 781 Beach St, San Francisco, CA
94109. T. (415) 202-7121. *090680*

Resource for Art, 200 Kansas St, San Francisco, CA
94107. T. (415) 864-2787. *090681*

Reuben, Mark, 865 Market St, San Francisco, CA 94102. T. (415) 543-5433. - Paint - *090682*

Reuben, Mark, 900 North Point St, San Francisco, CA 94109. T. (415) 346-1120. - Paint - *090683*

Reuben, Mark, 2535 Taylor St, San Francisco, CA 94133. T. (415) 563-5356. - Paint - *090684*

Reuben, Mark, 334 Grant Av, San Francisco, CA 94108. T. (415) 693-9846. - Paint - *090685*

Robert, Dana, 1849 Union St, San Francisco, CA 94123. T. (415) 749-1849. *090686*

Royal Palace, 195 Ellis St, San Francisco, CA 94102. T. (415) 362-5335. *090687*

Ruby's Clay Studio and Gallery, 552 Noe St, San Francisco, CA 94114. T. (415) 861-9779. - China - *090688*

Saint Albus, 225 Scott St, San Francisco, CA 94115. T. (415) 861-4458. *090689*

San Benigno Gallery, 601 Van Ness Av, San Francisco, CA 94102. T. (415) 928-0403. *090690*

San Francisco Art Exchange, 458 Geary St, San Francisco, CA 94102. T. (415) 441-8840. - Paint - *090691*

San Francisco Art Institute, 800 Chestnut St, San Francisco, CA 94133. T. (415) 749-4500. - Paint / Graph / Sculp / Pho / Draw - *090692*

San Francisco Women Artists' Gallery, 370 Hayes St, San Francisco, CA 94102. T. (415) 552-7392. - Paint / Graph - *090693*

Sauer, Gerald, 3271 Jackson St, San Francisco, CA 94118. T. (415) 567-6004. *090694*

Schwartz, Andrea, 333 Bryant St, San Francisco, CA 94107. T. (415) 495-2090. *090695*

Seibert, 427 Hayes St, San Francisco, CA 94102. T. (415) 431-5206. - China - *090696*

Shapiro, Michael, 250 Sutter St, San Francisco, CA 94108. T. (415) 398-6655. - Pho - *090697*

Shelter Gallery, 678 Haight St, San Francisco, CA 94102. T. (415) 487-9009. - Paint / Graph / Sculp - *090698*

Shiota, 3131 Fillmore St, San Francisco, CA 94123. T. (415) 929-7979. - Orient - *090699*

Show N Tell, 30 Rose St, San Francisco, CA 94102. T. (415) 861-6445. *090700*

Simic, 781 Beach St, San Francisco, CA 94109. T. (415) 202-1880. - Paint / Sculp - *090701*

Smile Gallery, 500 Sutter St, San Francisco, CA 94102. T. (415) 362-3436. *090702*

Snyder, Caldwell, 357 St, San Francisco, CA 94102. T. (415) 296-7896. *090703*

Snyder, Caldwell, 228 Grant Av, Fifth Floor, San Francisco, CA 94108. T. (415) 392-2299. *090704*

Soho, 548 Castro St, San Francisco, CA 94114. T. (415) 252-0294. *090705*

Soho, 2286 Market St, San Francisco, CA 94114. T. (415) 255-1525. *090706*

Soker, Don, 251 Post St, San Francisco, CA 94108. T. (415) 291-0966. *090707*

Sokoloff, 150 San Marcos Av, San Francisco, CA 94116. T. (415) 566-8177. *090708*

Southern Exposure Gallery, 401 Alabama St, San Francisco, CA 94110. T. (415) 863-2141. *090709*

Spectrum Gallery, 511 Harrison St, San Francisco, CA 94105. T. (415) 495-1113. *090710*

Squeri, Robert, 144 Funston Av, San Francisco, CA 94118. T. (415) 387-0961. *090711*

Sunrise Fine Arts Gallery, 23 Grant Av, San Francisco, CA 94108. T. (415) 398-7620. *090712*

Swanson, 3040 Larkin St, San Francisco, CA 94109. T. (415) 885-6126. *090713*

Swanson, 111 Maiden Ln, San Francisco, CA 94108. T. (415) 433-9091. *090714*

Swig, Roselyne C., 45 Belden Pl, San Francisco, CA 94104. T. (415) 956-3222. *090715*

Takata, 251 Post St, San Francisco, CA 94108. T. (415) 956-5288. *090716*

Talbot, 136 Noe St, San Francisco, CA 94114. T. (415) 552-0470. *090717*

t.c. art, 1351 Natural St, San Francisco, CA 94116. T. (415) 759-7070. - Graph - *090718*

Terehoff, Vera S., 231 12 Av, San Francisco, CA 94118. T. (415) 752-6718. *090719*

Terrain Gallery, 165 Jessie St, San Francisco, CA 94105. T. (415) 543-0636. *090720*

Thackrey & Robertson, 2266 Union St, San Francisco, CA 94123. T. (415) 567-4842. - Paint / Graph / Pho / Draw - *090721*

Thompson, 80 Maiden Ln, San Francisco, CA 94108. T. (415) 956-2114. - Paint - *090722*

Thompson, Michael, 1 Sutter St, San Francisco, CA 94104. T. (415) 391-7795. - Paint / Graph / Fra - *090723*

Thron, T., 155 S Park St, San Francisco, CA 94107. T. (415) 974-1485. *090724*

Triangle Art Gallery, 165 Post St, San Francisco, CA 941088. T. (415) 392-1686. - Paint - *090725*

Trojanowska, 2157 Union St, San Francisco, CA 94123. T. (415) 673-1971. *090726*

Turov, 337 Geary St, San Francisco, CA 94102. T. (415) 776-2298. - China - *090727*

Two of Heart Studio, 4147 19 St, San Francisco, CA 94114. T. (415) 864-5551. *090728*

Union Square Galleries, 320 Geary St, San Francisco, CA 94102. T. (415) 397-1727. - Paint / Graph - *090729*

Union Street Graphics, 1690 Union St, San Francisco, CA 94123. T. (415) 771-8180. - Graph / Fra - *090730*

Van den Berge, 855 Sansome St, San Francisco, CA 94111. T. (415) 693-9727. *090731*

Van Doren, 351 California St, San Francisco, CA 94104. T. (415) 981-5600. *090732*

Velvet, 508 Hayes St, San Francisco, CA 94102. T. (415) 626-7478. *090733*

Vission Gallery, 1155 Mission St, San Francisco, CA 94105. T. (415) 621-2107. - Pho - *090734*

Vomitus Maximus, 679 Harrison St, San Francisco, CA 94107. T. (415) 896-2956. *090735*

Vorpal, 393 Grove St, San Francisco, CA 94102. T. (415) 397-9200. - Paint / Graph / Orient / Repr / Sculp / Tex / Eth - *090736*

W & L Art Studio, 633 Fourth Av, San Francisco, CA 94118. T. (415) 221-9038. *090737*

Wah Tsui Shem, 829 Kearny St, San Francisco, CA 94108. T. (415) 421-8898. *090738*

Webber, Helen, 555 Pacific Av, San Francisco, CA 94133. T. (415) 989-5521. *090739*

Weinberg, Daniel, 49 Geary St, San Francisco, CA 94108. T. (415) 982-0180. *090740*

Weinstein, 383 Geary St, San Francisco, CA 94102. T. (415) 362-8151. *090741*

Weiss, Dorothy, 256 Sutter St, San Francisco, CA 94108. T. (415) 397-3611. - Paint - *090742*

Well Who's He, 381 Broadway St, San Francisco, CA 94133. T. (415) 362-6395. *090743*

Western Wildlife, Four Embarcadero Center-Lobby Level, San Francisco, CA 94111. T. (415) 398-4845. *090744*

Western Wildlife Gallery, 5 Embarcadero Center, San Francisco, CA 94111. T. (415) 398-4845, Fax (415) 398-5884. - Paint / Graph / Sculp - *090745*

White, 2080 Hayes St, San Francisco, CA 94102. T. (415) 752-3663. - Graph - *090746*

Winston, 780 Sutter St, San Francisco, CA 94109. T. (415) 441-3639. *090747*

Wirtz, Stephen, 49 Geary St, San Francisco, CA 94108. T. (415) 433-6879, Fax (415) 433-1608. - Paint / Graph / Sculp / Pho / Draw - *090748*

Wofsy, Alan, 1109 Geary Blvd, San Francisco, CA 91409. T. (415) 292-6500, Fax (415) 547-1623. *090749*

Womancrafts West, 1007 1/2 Valencia St, San Francisco, CA 94110. T. (415) 648-2020. - Paint / Graph / Sculp - *090750*

Yoshida, 715 Irving St, San Francisco, CA 94122. T. (415) 664-2830. - Paint / Graph / Fra - *090751*

Z Gallerie, 865 Market St, San Francisco, CA 94102. T. (415) 495-7121. *090752*

Z Gallerie, 1465 Haight St, San Francisco, CA 94102. T. (415) 863-5331. *090753*

Z Gallerie, 3251 20 Av, San Francisco, CA 95132. T. (415) 664-7891. *090754*

Zlot & Associates, Mary, 685 Market St, San Francisco. T. (415) 495-4444. *090755*

Zona Arte Gallery, 898 25 St, San Francisco, CA 94107. T. (415) 641-9208. *090756*

871 Fine Arts, 250 Sutter St, San Francisco, CA 94108. T. (415) 543-5155. *090757*

San Jose (California)
Fine Arts in Metal Art Foundry, 825 N Tenth St, San Jose, CA 95112. T. (408) 292-7628. - Sculp - *090759*

San Juan (Puerto Rico)
Botello, Cristo St. 208, San Juan, PR 00901. T. (809) 723-2879, 723-9987. - Paint / Sculp - *090760*

Galeria Colibri, 156 Calle Cristo, San Juan, PR 00903. T. (809) 725-2840. - Paint / Graph / Mul / Draw - *090761*

Galeria San Jeronimo, 999 Ashford Av., San Juan, PR 00902. T. (809) 721-1000, 722-1808. - Paint / Sculp / Draw - *090762*

Smith, Robert Lewis, 205 Cristo St., San Juan, PR 00901. T. (809) 724-0194. - Paint / Graph / Sculp - *090763*

San Rafael (California)
Garzoli, 930 B St, San Rafael, CA 94901. T. (415) 459-4321. - Paint - *090764*

Open Secret Book, Music and World Art Gallery, 923 C St, San Rafael, CA 94901. T. (415) 457-4191. *090765*

Walton-Gilbert, 50 La Crescenta Way, San Rafael, CA 94901. T. (415) 721-2466. *090766*

Santa Fe (New Mexico)
Blair, 123 W Palace Av., Santa Fe POB 2342, NM 87501. T. (505) 983-2140. - Paint / Graph / Sculp - *090767*

Butler, Marylin, 225 Galisteo, Santa Fe, NM 87501. T. (505) 988-5387. *090768*

Canfield, 414 Canyon Rd, POB 9333, Santa Fe, NM 87504. T. (505) 988-4199. *090769*

Contemporary Craftsman Gallery, 100 W San Francisco St., Santa Fe, NM 87501. T. (505) 988-1001. *090770*

Economs Work Of Art, 500 Canyon Rd, Santa Fe, NM 87501. T. (505) 982-6347, Fax (505) 982-6602. *090771*

Fenn, 1075 Paseo de Peralta, Santa Fe, NM 87501. T. (505) 982-4631. - Paint / Graph / Sculp - *090772*

Galeria Capistrano, 409 Canyon Rd., Santa Fe, NM 87501. *090773*

Gallery 10, 225 Canyon Rd., Santa Fe, NM 87501. *090774*

Gate House Gallery, 428 Camino de las Animas, Santa Fe, NM 87501. T. (505) 982-0800. - Paint / Graph / Sculp - *090775*

Graphics House Gallery, 702 Canyon Rd., Santa Fe, NM 87501. T. (505) 983-2654. - Graph - *090776*

Green, Glenn, 50 E San Francisco St., Santa Fe, NM 87501. T. (505) 988-4168. - Paint / Graph / Repr / Sculp / Pho / Mul - *090777*

Horwitch Gallery, Elaine, 129 W. Palace, Santa Fe, NM 87501. *090778*

Jamison, 111 E San Francisco St., Santa Fe, NM 87501. T. (505) 982-3666. - Paint / Graph / Sculp / Mul / Draw - *090779*

Lambert, Edith, 707 Canyon Rd, Santa Fe, NM 87501. T. (505) 984-2783. *090780*

Mayans, Ernesto, 601 Canyon Rd., Santa Fe, NM 87501. T. (505) 983-8068. *090781*

Morning Star, 513 Canyon Rd, Santa Fe, NM 87501. T. (505) 982-818/, Fax (505) 984-2388. *090782*

Peters, Gerald, 439 Camino del Monte Sol, Santa Fe, NM 87504. T. (505) 988-8961. - Paint / Sculp - *090783*

Rein, C. G., 122 W San Francisco, Santa Fe, NM 87501. T. (505) 982-6226. - Paint / Graph / Sculp - *090784*

Rettig y Martinez, 418 Montezuma St., Santa Fe, NM 87501. T. (505) 983-4640. - Paint / Graph / Sculp / Pho - *090785*

Running Ridge Gallery, 640 Canyon Rd., Santa Fe, NM 87501. T. (505) 988-2515. *090786*

Savage Galleries, 102 E Water St., Santa Fe, NM 87501. T. (505) 982-1640. - Paint / Sculp - *090787*

Scheinbaum & Russek, 328 S Guadalupe, Suite M, Santa Fe, NM 87501. T. (505) 988-5116. *090788*

Stevenson & Lipsett, 943 Canyon Rd, Santa Fe, NM 87501. T. (505) 982-8920, Fax (505) 984-2938. *090789*

Stiha, Vladan, 816 Stagecoach Dr., Santa Fe, NM 87501. T. (505) 984-1182. - Paint - *090790*

Textile Arts, 1571 Canyon Rd., Santa Fe, NM 87501. T. (505) 983-9780. - Tex - *090791*

The Munson Gallery, 225 Canyon Rd, Santa Fe, NM 87501. T. (505) 983-1657. *090792*

Throckmorton, 550 Canyon Rd, Santa Fe, NM 87501. T. (505) 988-1698, Fax (505) 982-5398. 090793
Tiqua, 812 Canyon Rd, Santa Fe, NM 87501. T. (505) 984-8704. 090794
Wilson, Woodrow, 319 Read St., Santa Fe, NM 87501. T. (505) 983-2444. - Paint / Graph / Pho - 090795
21 st Century Fox, 201 Galisteo, Santa Fe, NM 87501. T. (505) 983-2002. 090796

Santa Monica (California)

Angles Gallery, 2230 Main St., Santa Monica, CA 90405. T. (213) 396-5019. 090797
Art Source L.A., 1416 Sixth St., Santa Monica, CA 90401. T. (213) 917-6688, Fax (213) 917-6685. - Paint / Sculp / Mod / Pho / Mul / Draw - 090798
B-1 Gallery, 2730 Main St., Santa Monica, CA 90405. T. (213) 392-9625. 090799
Blum Helman, 916 Colorado Av., Santa Monica, CA 90401. T. (213) 451-0955. - Paint / Sculp - 090800
Bornstein, Karl, 1658 1/2 Tenth St., Santa Monica, CA 90404. T. (213) 452-4210. 090801
Boyd, Roy, 1547 Tenth St., Santa Monica, CA 90401. T. (213) 938-2328. - Paint / Sculp - 090802
Cherkas, Constantine, 310 15 St, Santa Monica, CA 90402. T. (213) 395-0860, 395-7036. 090803
Constantine Cherkas, 310 15th St., Santa Monica, CA 90402. - Paint - 090804
Corcoran, James, 1327 Fifth St., Santa Monica, CA 90401. T. (213) 451-4666. 090805
Cutler, Bess, 903 Colorado Av., Santa Monica, CA 90401. T. (213) 394-6673, Fax (213) 394-1419. - Paint - 090806
Hoffman, Fred, 912 Colorado Av., Santa Monica, CA 90401. T. (213) 394-4199, Fax (213) 395-8396. - Paint / Sculp - 090807
Merging One Gallery, 1547 Sixth St., Santa Monica, CA 90401. T. (213) 395-0033. - Paint / Graph / Sculp - 090808
Mirage Gallery, 1659 11 St., Santa Monica, CA 90404. 090809
Pence, 908 Colorado Av., Santa Monica, CA 90401. T. (213) 393-0069. - Paint - 090810
Santa Monica Gallery, 1109 Montana Av., Santa Monica, CA 90403. T. (213) 576-2666. - Paint - 090811
Tortue Gallery, 2917 Santa Monica Blvd., Santa Monica, CA 90404. T. (213) 828-8878. - Paint / Graph / Sculp / Draw - 090812

Sarasota (Florida)

Adley, 1620 Main St., Sarasota, FL 33577. T. (813) 366-4059. - Graph - 090813
Corbino, 69 S Palm Av., Sarasota, FL 33577. T. (813) 955-8845. - Paint - 090814
Hang-Up, 3850 S Osprey Av., Suite 100, Sarasota, FL 34239. T. (813) 953-5757. - Paint / Graph - 090815
Harmon, Forster, 1415 Main St., Sarasota, FL 33577. T. (813) 955-1002. - Paint / Sculp / China - 090816
Hodgell, Joan, 46 S Palm Av., Sarasota, FL 33577. T. (813) 366-1146. - Paint / Graph - 090817
Image Gallery, 500 N Tamiami Trail, Sarasota, FL 33577. T. (813) 366-5097. 090818
Oehlschlaeger, Frank J., 28 S Blvd. of Presidents, Sarasota, FL 33577. - Paint / Sculp - 090819

Sausalito (California)

Fine Art Collections, 686 Bridgeway, Sausalito, CA 94965. T. (415) 331-0500. 090820
Fine Woodworking Gallery, 1201c Bridgeway, Sausalito, CA 94965. T. (415) 332-5770. - Sculp - 090821
Gropper, Ursula, 10 Laurel Ln, Sausalito, CA 94965. T. (415) 331-2414. - Pho - 090822
Reuben, Mark, 34 Princess St, Sausalito, CA 94965. T. (415) 332-8815. - Paint - 090823
Studio Z, 777 Bridgeway, Sausalito, CA 94965. T. (415) 788-3461. 090824
Sumner, George, 480 Gate 5 Rd, Sausalito, CA 94965. T. (415) 332-0353. 090825

Scottsdale (Arizona)

Bentley Tomlinson, 4161 N Marshall Way, Scottsdale, AZ 85251. T. (602) 946-6060. 090826
Bishop, 7164 Main St., Scottsdale, AZ 85251. T. (602) 949-9062. - Paint / Graph / Eth - 090827
Brown, Suzanne, 7156 Main St., Scottsdale, AZ 85251. T. (602) 945-8475. - Paint / Graph / Repr - 090828
Campbell, Michael, 7824 E Lewis Av., Scottsdale, AZ 85257. T. (602) 947-5399. - Ant / Graph / Sculp / Arch / Eth / Pho / Mul / Draw - 090829
Cawley, Joan, 7137 E Main St., Scottsdale, AZ 85251. T. (602) 947-3548. - Paint / Graph / Sculp - 090830
Fagen-Peterson, 7077 Main St., Scottsdale, AZ 85251. T. (602) 941-0089. - Paint / Graph - 090831
Gallery 10 Inc., 7045 Third Avenue, Scottsdale, AZ 85251. T. (602) 994-0405. - Paint / Graph - 090832
Hand and the Spirit Gallery, 4222 N Marshall Way, Scottsdale, AZ 85251. T. (602) 949-1262. - Sculp - 090833
Horwitch, Elaine, 4211 N Marshall Way, Scottsdale, AZ 85251. T. (602) 945-0791. 090834
Ianuzzi, 7070 N 59 Pl., Scottsdale, AZ 85253. T. (602) 991-4679. - Paint / Graph - 090835
Levy, Leslie, 7141 Main St., Scottsdale, AZ 85251. T. (602) 947-0937. 090836
Mammen, 4151 N Marshall Way, Scottsdale, AZ 85251. T. (602) 949-5311. - Paint / Graph - 090837
Montgomery-Taylor, 7100 Main St., Scottsdale, AZ 85251. T. (602) 945-0111. - Paint - 090838
O'Brien, 7122 Stetson Dr., Scottsdale, AZ 85251. T. (602) 945-1082. - Paint / Sculp - 090839
Ortega von Grabill, Gilbert, 6166 N Scottsdale Rd., Ste 505, 85200 Scottsdale, AZ 85253. T. (602) 998-3836. 090840
Overland Trail Galleries, 7155 Main St., Scottsdale, AZ 85251. T. (602) 947-1934. - Paint / Graph - 090841
Phippen-O'Brien, 2926 N. Civic Center Plaza, Scottsdale, AZ 85251. T. (602) 945-1082. - Paint / Graph / Sculp - 090842
Professional Interiors and Art, 7674 E Northland Dr., Scottsdale, AZ 85251. T. (602) 946-9968. - Paint / Graph / Rel / Mod / Mul / Draw - 090843
Rein, C.G., 4235 N Marshall Way, Scottsdale, AZ 85251. T. (602) 941-0900. - Paint / Graph / Sculp - 090844
Saunders, Buck & Leo, 2724 N. Scottsdale Rd., Scottsdale, AZ 85257. T. (602) 945-9376. - Paint / Graph / Eth - 090845
Savage Galleries, 7112 Main St., Scottsdale, AZ 85251. T. (602) 945-7114. - Paint / Sculp - 090846
Sette, 4142 N Marshall Way, Scottsdale, AZ 85251. T. (602) 990-7342. - Paint / Graph - 090847
Stable Art, 7610 E. MacDonald Dr., Scottsdale, AZ 85232. T. (602) 948-5620. - Ant / Paint / Sculp - 090848
Tash, Joy, 7236 E First Av., Scottsdale, AZ 85251. T. (602) 945-0195. - Paint / Graph - 090849
Trailside Galleries, 7330 Scottsdale Mall, Scottsdale, AZ 85251. T. (602) 945-7751. 090850
Troy, 7106 Main St., Scottsdale, AZ 85251. T. (602) 946-9606. - Paint - 090851
Udinotti, 4215 N Marshall Way, Scottsdale, AZ 85251. T. (602) 946-7056. - Paint / Eth - 090852
Wagner, Odon, 4223 N Marshall Way, Scottsdale, AZ 85251. T. (602) 945-4560, Fax (602) 945-1217. 090853
Wilde-Meyer, 4151 N Marshall Way, Scottsdale, AZ 85251. T. (602) 945-6935. 090854
Wilhelm, 4142 N Marshall Way, Scottsdale, AZ 85251. T. (602) 947-4540. - Paint - 090855
Yares, 3625 Bishop Lane, Scottsdale, AZ 85251. T. (602) 947-3251. - Paint / Graph / Sculp / Mod / Draw - 090856

Seattle (Washington)

Alonso/Sullivan, 207 Harvard Av. E, Seattle, WA 98102. T. (206) 325-4186. - Paint / Sculp / Draw - 090857
Bon Marchè, 3rd Ave., Seattle, WA 98101. - Paint / Graph / Fra - 090858
Davidson, 313 Occidental Av. S, Seattle, WA 98104. T. (206) 624-7684. - Paint / Graph / Draw - 090859
Farris, Linda, 322 2nd Ave. South, Pioneer Square, Seattle, WA 98104. T. (206) 623 1110. 090860
Fifty Avenue Gallery, 1110 E Pike St., Seattle, WA 98122. T. (206) 324-7009. 090861
Foster, 311 1/2 Occidental St., Seattle, WA 98104. T. (206) 622-2833. - Paint / Graph / Sculp / Fra - 090862
Gallery Nimba, 8041 32 N. W., Seattle, WA 98107. T. (206) 783-4296. - Sculp - 090863
Haines, 8015 15th Ave. N.W., Seattle, WA 98117. T. (206) 783-7227. - Paint / Graph / Repr / Sculp / Jew - 090864
Harris, Lisa, 1922 Pike Pl., Seattle, WA 98101. T. (206) 443-3315. 090865
Haugland Art Studio, 2815 Alaskan Way, Seattle, WA 98131. - Paint - 090866
Jackson Street Gallery, 163 S Jackson St., Seattle, WA 19804. T. (206) 623-0435. 090867
Kirsten, Gallery, 5320 Roosevelt Way NE, Seattle, WA 98105. T. (206) 522-2011. 090868
McAllister, Lynn, 601 Second Av., Seattle, WA 98104. T. (206) 647-0277. 090869
Mia Gallery, 314 Occidental Av. S, Seattle, WA 98104. T. (206) 647-8283. 090870
Nimba, 8041 32 Av. NW, Seattle, WA 98107. T. (206) 783-4296. - Sculp / Eth - 090871
Seders, Francine, 6701 Greenwood Av. N, Seattle, WA 98103. T. (206) 782-0355. - Paint / Graph / Sculp - 090872
Silver Image Gallery, 318 Occidental Av. S, Seattle, WA 98104. - Pho - 090873
Snow Goose Associates, 4220 NE 125th St., Seattle, WA 98125. 090874
Stone Press Gallery, 91 Yesler Way, Seattle, WA 98104. T. (206) 624-6752. - Graph - 090875
Traver Sutton, 2219 Fourth Av., Seattle, WA 98101. T. (206) 448-4234. - Paint / Sculp / Glass - 090876
Woodside, Gordon & John Braseth, 1101 Howell St., Seattle, WA 98101. T. (206) 622-7243. - Paint / Sculp / Draw - 090877
Young, Donald, 2107 Third Av., Seattle, WA 98121. T. (206) 448-9484. - Paint - 090878

Silver Spring (Maryland)

Art Fair Galleries, 10218 New Hampshire Av, Silver Spring, MD 20903. T. (301) 439-9210. 090879
Takoma Picture Framers, 7312 Carroll Av, Silver Spring, MD 20912. T. (301) 270-4433. - Paint / Fra - 090880

Southfield (Michigan)

Habatat, 28235 Southfield Rd., Southfield, MI 48076. T. (313) 552-0515. - Glass - 090881
Park West Gallery, 29469 Northwestern Hwy., Southfield, MI 48034. T. (313) 354-2343. - Graph - 090882
Print Gallery, 29203 Northwestern Hwy., Southfield, MI 48034. T. (313) 356-5454. - Graph - 090883

Springfield (Massachusetts)

Thronja, 260 Worthington St., Springfield, MA 01103. T. (413) 732-0260. - Paint - 090884

Springfield (Missouri)

Robertson, Philip, 1055 S Glenstone Av, Springfield, MO 65804. T. (417) 869-8262. - Paint / Graph / Repr / Fra - 090885

Springfield (New Jersey)

Art Plus, 120 Morris Av, Springfield, NJ 07081. T. (212) 943-0778. 090886

Springfield (Pennsylvania)

Diana Gallery, 411 Schullar Lane, Springfield, PA 19064. - Paint / Graph / China / Repr / Sculp / Jew / Fra / Lights - 090887

Stamford (Connecticut)

Cavalier, 1 Landmark Sq., Stamford, CT 06901. T. (203) 325-8444. - Paint / Sculp - 090888
PMW Gallery, 530 Roxbury Rd., Stamford, CT 06902. T. (203) 322-5427. - Paint - 090889
Smith-Girard, 1 Strawberry Hill Av., Stamford, CT 06902. T. (203) 325-2979. - Paint / Graph - 090890
Waterfun, 323 Four Brooks Rd., Stamford, CT 06903. T. (203) 329-9826. - Paint / Graph - 090891

Syracuse (New York)

Colella Galleries, 123 E Willow St., Syracuse, NY 13202. T. (315) 474-6950. - Paint - 090892
New Acquisitions Gallery, 120 E Washington St., Suite 207, Syracuse, NY 13202. T. (315) 422-2320. 090893
Studio Gallery, 133 S Salina St., Syracuse, NY 13202. T. (315) 472-0805. - Paint / Jew / Silv / Glass / Pho - 090894

Weber, 7863 Thompson Rd., Syracuse, NY 13212.
T. (315) 458-7655. *090895*

Tampa (Florida)
Cooper, Brad, 1712 E Seventh Av., Tampa, FL 33605.
T. (813) 248-60983. - Paint / Sculp / Pho /
Draw - *090896*
Gilman-Stein, 3105 Bay to Bay Blvd., Tampa, FL 33629.
T. (813) 831-9987. *090897*
Nuance Galleries, 720 S Dale Mabry, Tampa, FL 33609.
T. (813) 875-0511. - Graph - *090898*
Realistic Artists, 705 Swann Ave, Tampa, FL 33606.
T. (813) 251-3780. - Paint / Graph - *090899*

Taos (New Mexico)
Carl's Indian Trading Post, E. Kit Carson Rd., POB 813,
Taos, NM 87571. T. (505) 758-2378. - Paint /
Graph - *090900*
Clay and Fiber Gallery, N Pueblo Rd., Taos, NM 87571.
T. (505) 758-8093. - China / Glass - *090901*
DVS Photographs, Guadelupe Pl., Taos, NM 97571.
T. (505) 758-4291. - Glass - *090902*
Gallery A., E Kit Carson Rd., Taos, NM 87571.
T. (505) 758-2343. - Paint / Graph / Sculp - *090903*
Gallery Elena, 13 Bent St., Taos, NM 87571.
T. (505) 758-9094. *090904*
Gallery of the Southwest, N Pueblo Rd., Taos, NM
87571. *090905*
Grycner, Taos POB 2107, NM 87571. T. (505) 776-1701.
- Paint / Graph / Sculp - *090906*
Holfelder, 202 Paseo del Pueblo Sur, Taos, NM
87571. *090907*
Kachina Lodge, North Pueblo Rd., Taos, NM 87571.
T. (505) 758-2275. - Paint - *090908*
Ledoux Gallery of Fine Arts, Ol Ledoux, POB 2418, Taos,
NM 87551. *090909*
Mission Gallery, E. Kit Carson Rd., Taos, NM 87571.
T. (505) 758-2861. - Paint / Graph / Sculp - *090910*
Navajo Gallery, 5 Ledoux St., POB 1756, Taos, NM
87571. T. (505) 758-3250. - Paint - *090911*
Richards, Tally, 2 Ledoux, Taos, NM 87571. T. (505) 758-
2731. *090912*
Shriver Gallery, N. Pueblo Rd., Taos, NM 87571. *090913*
Stables Gallery, North Pueblo Rd., POB 198, Taos, NM
87571. T. (505) 758-2036. - Paint / Graph / Sculp /
Pho / Draw - *090914*
Taos Art Gallery, East Kit Carson Rd, POB 1007, Taos,
NM 87571. T. (505) 758-2475. - Paint / Sculp - *090915*
The Collectores Gallery of Fine Art, North Plaza, POB
2708, Taos, NM 87571. T. (505) 758-4002. *090916*
Total Arts Gallery, E. Kit Carson Rd., POB 1744, Taos,
NM 87571. T. (505) 758-4667. - Paint / Graph / Sculp /
Pho / Draw - *090917*
Vigil, Veloy, 110 Morada Rd., Taos, NM 87571.
T. (505) 758-8384. *090918*

Tarzana (California)
Hecht, Charles, 18555 Ventura Blvd, Tarzana, CA 91356.
T. (818) 881-3218. *090919*

Tequesta (Florida)
Tomlyn, 375 Tequesta Drive, Tequesta, FL 33469.
T. (407) 747-1556. *090920*

Tucson (Arizona)
Etherton Stern, 135 S Sixth Av., Tucson, AZ 85701.
- Paint / Graph / Sculp - *090921*
Grazia, de, 3568 N Campbell Av., Tucson, AZ 85719.
- Paint / Graph / Sculp - *090922*
Hacienda Bellas Artes, 8444 Oracle Rd., Tucson, AZ
85704. T. (602) 297-0755. - Paint / Graph / China /
Sculp / Jew / Rel / Draw - *090923*
Old Town Gallery of Contemporary Art, 240 N Court Av.,
Tucson, AZ 85701. T. (602) 884-7379. *090924*
Peachin, Mary, 3955 N Speedway, Tucson, AZ 85712.
T. (602) 881-1311. *090925*
Sanders Galleries, 6420 N Campbell Av., Tucson, AZ
85718. T. (602) 299-1763. - Graph - *090926*

Tulsa (Oklahoma)
Arts Signature Gallery, 110 E Second St., Tulsa, OK
74103. T. (918) 582-7532. - Paint / Graph /
Draw - *090927*

O'Shea, Dan, 2050 Utica Sq., Tulsa, OK 74114.
T. (918) 5187. - Paint / Graph / Fra - *090928*

Tustin (California)
Buresch Fine Art, 544 El Camino Real, Tustin, CA 92680.
T. (714) 544-8873. - Paint - *090929*

Tyler (Texas)
Carmichael, F. L., Box 326, Tyler, TX 75701. *090930*

Van Nuys (California)
Lawrence, Martin, 16250 Stagg St., Van Nuys, CA
91406. T. (213) 988-0630. - Paint / China - *090931*

Venice (California)
Browne, Aldis, 1614 Crescent Pl., Venice, CA 90291.
T. (213) 301-6976, Fax 301-0698. - Paint / Graph /
Sculp / Draw - *090933*
Egenolf, Herbert, c/o Veronica Miller, POB 1439, Venice,
CA 90294. T. (310) 581-9932, Fax 581-9932. - Graph /
Orient - *090933a*
Venice Place Arts Center, 1021-1031 W Washington
Blvd., Venice, CA 90291. *090934*
Xiliary Twil Fine Arts, 202 S Main St., Suite 1, Venice,
CA 90291. T. (213) 450-1771. - Paint / Graph /
Sculp - *090935*

Vienna (Maryland)
Damon, 220 Maple Av W, Vienna, MD 21869.
T. (703) 938-7000. *090936*

Vienna (Virginia)
Andreas, 8545 Leesburg Pike, Vienna, VA 22182.
T. (703) 448-2222. - Paint - *090937*

Wailea (Hawaii)
Coast Gallery-Maui, Hotel Intercontinental, Wailea, HI
96753. *090938*

Walnut Creek (California)
Bernard, 1489 E Newell Av., Walnut Creek, CA 94596.
T. (415) 932-2738. - Paint - *090939*

Washington (District of Columbia)
A Gallerie of Fine Arts, 4620 Wisconsin Av NW, Washing-
ton, DC 20016. T. (202) 363-5062. *090942*
Aaron, 1717 Connecticut Av NW, Washington, DC
20009. T. (202) 234-3311. - Paint / Graph /
Sculp - *090943*
Accessories Unlimited, 1629 Nicholson St NW, Washing-
ton, DC 20011. T. (202) 234-3311. *090944*
Adams Davidson, 3233 P St NW, Washington, DC
20007. T. (202) 965-3800. - Paint / Fra - *090945*
Adamson, David, 406 Seventh St NW, Washington, DC
20004. T. (202) 628-0257. *090946*
Addison-Ripley, 9 Hillyer Court NW, Washington, DC
20008. T. (202) 328-2332. - Paint / Graph /
Sculp - *090947*
AFR Fine Arts, 2610 Normanstone Ln NW, Washington,
DC 20008. T. (202) 265-6191. *090948*
Africa-African Art, 2010 R St NW, Washington, DC
20009. T. (202) 745-7272. - Eth - *090949*
Africa Arts, 228 Seventh St SE, Washington, DC 20003.
T. (202) 544-8444. - Eth - *090950*
African Hands, 1851 Redwood Terrace NW, Washington,
DC 20012. T. (202) 726-2400. - Eth - *090951*
African Safari Art Gallery, 7610 Georgia Av NW, Wa-
shington, DC 20012. T. (202) 722-1619. - Eth - *090952*
Ainilian, 232 Seventh St SE, Washington, DC 20003.
T. (202) 544-5711. *090953*
ALCA, 800 K St NW, Washington, DC 20001.
T. (202) 842-0280. *090954*
Alex Gallery, 2106 R St NW, Washington, DC 20008.
T. (202) 667-2599. *090955*
Alla Rogers, 1054 31 St NW, Washington, DC 20007.
T. (202) 333-8595. *090956*
Allen, 710 Seventh St NW, Washington, DC 20001.
T. (202) 628-1389. - Paint / Fra - *090957*
American Hand, 2906 M St NW, Washington, DC 20007.
T. (202) 965-3273. *090958*
Americana West Gallery, 1630 Connectcut Av NW, Wa-
shington, DC 20009. T. (202) 265-1630. *090959*
Animation Art Sensations, 1083 Thomas Jefferson St
NW, Washington, DC 20007. T. (202) 965-
0199. *090960*

Anton, 2108 R St NW, Washington, DC 20008.
T. (202) 328-0828. - Paint / Graph / Sculp - *090961*
Ardel, 1712 21 St NW, Washington, DC 20009.
T. (202) 232-5416. *090962*
Art Alliance, 1209 East Capitol St SE, Washington, DC
20003. T. (202) 544-5505. *090963*
Art and Culture Enterprises, 504 T St NW, Washington,
DC 20001. T. (202) 332-7763. *090964*
Art in Fiber, 10218 Arizona Terrace NW, Washington, DC
20016. T. (202) 364-8404. *090965*
Art Placement International, 2811 Dumbarton Av NW,
Washington, DC 20007. T. (202) 337-5832. *090966*
Artifactory, 641 Indiana Av NW, Washington, DC 20004.
T. (202) 393-2727. *090967*
Artistic Endeavors, 1449 Roxanna Rd NW, Washington,
DC 20012. T. (212) 829-3288. *090968*
Atlantic Gallery of Georgetown, 1055 Thomas Jefferson
St NW, Washington, DC 20007. T. (202) 337-2299.
- Paint / Graph - *090969*
Attitude Exact, 739 Eighth St SE, Washington, DC
20003. T. (202) 546-7186. *090970*
Audubon Prints and Books, 499 South Capitol St SW,
Washington, DC 20032. T. (202) 484-3334.
- Graph - *090971*
Bader, Franz, 1500 K St NW, Washington, DC 20005.
T. (202) 393-6111. *090972*
Baraka, 1875 I St NW, Washington, DC 20006.
T. (202) 659-3777. - Paint / Graph / Fra - *090973*
Baumgartner, 2016 R St NW, Washington, DC 20009.
T. (202) 232-6320. - Paint - *090974*
Bird in Hand Bookstore and Gallery, 323 Seventh St SE,
Washington, DC 20003. T. (202) 543-0744. - Paint /
Graph - *090975*
Bolivar, 1918 18 St NW, Washington, DC 20009.
T. (202) 234-3088. *090976*
Brody, 1706 21 St NW, Washington, DC 20009.
T. (202) 462-4747. - Graph - *090977*
Brown, Robert, 1005 New Hampshire Av NW, Washing-
ton, DC 20037. T. (202) 822-8737. - Paint - *090978*
Browning, G.R., 3901 Cathedral Av NW, Washington, DC
20016. T. (202) 363-1963. *090979*
Buckley & Associates, 4336 Verplanck Pl NW, Washing-
ton, DC 20016. T. (202) 686-0870. *090980*
Calvert Gallery, 2500 Calvert St NW, Washington, DC
20008. T. (202) 387-8833. - Paint - *090981*
Capital Arts, 4918 Hillbrook Ln NW, Washington, DC
20016. T. (202) 966-7815. *090982*
Capitol East Graphics Gallery, 600 E St SE, Washington,
DC 20003. T. (202) 547-8246. - Graph - *090983*
Capitol Hill Art and Frane Company, 623 Pennsylvania
Av SE, Washington, DC 20003. T. (202) 546-2700.
- Graph / Fra - *090984*
Capitol Hill Arts Workshop, 545 Seventh St SE, Washing-
ton, DC 20003. T. (202) 547-6839. - Paint /
Graph - *090985*
Carega Foxley Leach, 1732 Connceticut Av NW, Wa-
shington, DC 20009. T. (202) 462-8462. *090986*
Cathedral Galleries, 3301 New Mexico Av NW, Washing-
ton, DC 20016. T. (202) 363-6936. *090987*
Chernikoff & Co., 1320 18 St NW, Washington, DC
20036. T. (202) 223-9280. *090988*
Chisholm, 4500 16 St NW, Washington, DC 20011.
T. (202) 291-5571. *090989*
Circle Fine Art Corporation, 1413 Wisconsin Av NW, Wa-
shington, DC 20007. T. (202) 338-6455. *090990*
Clay-Tor, F., 3314 14 St NW, Washington, DC 20010.
T. (202) 387-8700. *090991*
Conway Carroll, Susan, 1058 Thomas Jefferson St NW,
Washington, DC 20007. T. (202) 333-4082. *090992*
Corcoran, 1842 18 St NW, Washington, DC 20009.
T. (202) 667-0625. *090993*
Crafts Center, 1001 Connceticut Av NW, Washington, DC
20036. T. (202) 728-9603. *090994*
Creighton-Davis, 3413 Wisconsin Av NW, Washington,
DC 20016. T. (202) 966-4949. *090995*
Curl, 1801 K St NW, Washington, DC 20006.
T. (202) 833-8680. *090996*
Daley, 1230a Half St SW, Washington, DC 20024.
T. (202) 479-9483. - Paint / Graph / Fra - *090997*
Davis Wack, 3243 P St NW, Washington, DC 20007.
T. (202) 298-9225. *090998*
De Andino, 1609 Connecticut Av NW, Washington, DC
20009. T. (202) 462-4772. *090999*

De Montmollin, 1701 16 St NW, Washington, DC 20009. T. (202) 332-7556. 091000

De Pas, 5300 Wisconsin Av NW, Washington, DC 20015. T. (202) 966-7880. 091001

De Pas, 5335 Wisconsin Av NW, Washington, DC 20015. T. (202) 362-1122. 091002

Deco Gallery, 3302 M St NW, Washington, DC 20007. T. (202) 333-6060. - Graph / Sculp - 091003

Distinct Images, 210 M St SW, Washington, DC 20024. T. (202) 479-0422. 091004

Drysdale, Nancy, 2103 O St NW, Washington, DC 20037. T. (202) 466-4550. - Paint / Sculp / Pho / Draw - 091005

Dunham, 3075 Canal St NW, Washington, DC 20007. T. (202) 337-7860. - Paint - 091006

Efron, Jean, 2440 Virginia Av NW, Washington, DC 20037. T. (202) 223-1626. 091007

Evans-Tibbs, 1910 Vermont Av NW, Washington, DC 20001. T. (202) 234-8164. - Paint / Sculp - 091008

Ewing, Kathleen, 1609 Connecticut Av, Washington, DC 20009. T. (202) 328-0955. 091009

Fandra, 3112 M St NW, Washington, DC 20007. T. (202) 625-7002. 091010

Farrell, 2633 Connecticut Av NW, Washington, DC 20008. T. (202) 483-834. 091011

Fifth Column, 915 F St NW, Washington, DC 20004. T. (202) 393-3632. 091012

Fisher, 1511 Connecticut Av NW, Washington, DC 20036. T. (202) 265-6255. - Paint / Graph / Sculp - 091013

Foliograph Gallery, 1821 K St NW, Washington, DC 20006. T. (202) 296-8398. - Paint - 091014

Foundry Gallery, 9 Hillyer Court NW, Washington, DC 20008. T. (202) 387-0203. 091015

Frame Mart Gallery, 3307 Connecticut Av NW, Washington, DC 20008. T. (202) 363-5200. - Paint / Graph / Fra - 091016

Frame Shop, 1828 Wisconsin Av NW, Washington, DC 20007. T. (202) 338-6992. - Graph / Fra - 091017

Framers Workroom, 4431 Wisconsin Av NW, Washington, DC 20016. T. (202) 363-1970. - Fra - 091018

Freeman, 406 Seventh St NW, Washington, DC 20004. T. (202) 347-8934. 091019

Gallery K, 2010 R St NW, Washington, DC 20009. T. (202) 234-0339. - Paint / Graph / Sculp - 091020

Gallery 10, 1519 Connecticut Av NW, Washington, DC 20036. T. (202) 232-3326. - Paint / Graph / Sculp - 091021

Georgetown Art Center, 1046 Potomac St NW, Washington, DC 20007. T. (202) 338-0209. 091022

Georgetown Art Impressions, 4157 Chain Bridge Rd NW, Washington, DC 20016. T. (202) 342-9654. 091023

Georgetown Gallery of Art, 3235 P St NW, Washington, DC 20007. T. (202) 333-6308. 091024

Gilpin, 655 15 St NW, Washington, DC 20005. T. (202) 393-2112. - Paint / Graph - 091025

Glass Works, 1519 Connecticut Av NW, Washington, DC 20036. T. (202) 387-7125. - Glass - 091026

Govinda, 1227 34 St NW, Washington, DC 20007. T. (202) 333-1180. 091027

Graphiti Gems, 1567 Maryland Av NE, Washington, DC 20002. T. (202) 396-0888. 091028

Gregory, 3112 M St NW, Washington, DC 20007. T. (202) 625-1677. 091029

Guarisco, 2828 Pennsylvania Av NW, Washington, DC 20007. T. (202) 333-8533. - Paint - 091030

Habitat-Pelloon, 1608 U St NW, Washington, DC 20009. T. (202) 667-0789. 091031

Haslem, Jane, 2025 Hillyer Pl NW, Washington, DC 20009. T. (202) 232-4644. 091032

Hauss, 1511 H St NW, Washington, DC 20005. T. (202) 628-5938. 091033

Henri, 1500 21 St NW, Washington, DC 20036. T. (202) 659-9313. - Paint - 091034

House Wayland, 1802 11 St NW, Washington, DC 20001. T. (202) 387-8157. 091035

Hume-Christie, 1302 Rhode Island Av NW, Washington, DC 20005. T. (202) 797-0446. 091036

In Time Art Salon, 1619 Connecticut Av NW, Washington, DC 20009. T. (202) 483-2362. 091037

Indian Craft Shop, 1849 C St NW, Washington, DC 20006. T. (202) 737-4381. - Eth - 091038

Indian Craft Shop, 1050 Wisconsin Av NW, Washington, DC 20007. T. (202) 342-3918. - Eth - 091039

Induna, 2439 18 St NW, Washington, DC 20009. T. (202) 328-2133. 091040

Inner Visions, 1055 Thomas Jefferson St NW, Washington, DC 20007. T. (202) 342-6695. - Paint / Graph / Sculp / Fra - 091041

International Art Exhibition, 1326 18 St NW, Washington, DC 20036. T. (202) 785-1295. 091042

International Artifacts and Repair Shop, 2830 Georgia Av NW, Washington, DC 20001. T. (202) 387-3333. - Paint / Sculp / Tex - 091043

International Designers Corporation, 2913 P St NW, Washington, DC 20007. T. (202) 342-7111. - Graph / Draw - 091044

Jewelerswerk Gallery, 2000 Pennslyvania Av NW, Washington, DC 20006. T. (202) 293-0249. - Jew - 091045

Jones Troyer Fitzpatrick, 1614 20 St NW, Washington, DC 20009. T. (202) 328-7189. - Paint - 091046

Kimberly, 1621 21 St NW, Washington, DC 20009. T. (202) 234-1988. 091047

Kornblatt, B.R., 406 Seventh St NW, Washington, DC 20004. T. (202) 638-7657. - Paint / Graph / Sculp - 091048

L'Enfant, 2601 Connecticut Av NW, Washington, DC 20008. T. (202) 265-4096. 091048a

Lareuse, 2820 Pennsylvania Av NW, Washington, DC 20007. T. (202) 333-5704. - Paint - 091048b

Le Marie Tranier, 3304 M St NW, Washington, DC 20007. T. (202) 342-9600. - Paint / Sculp - 091049

Loophole Art Gallery, 3261 Prospect St NW, Washington, DC 20007. T. (202) 333-5187. 091050

Lyon's Den of Fine Art and Custom Framing, 3917 Georgia Av NW, Washington, DC 20011. T. (202) 726-2787. - Paint / Graph / Fra - 091051

Mahler, 406 Seventh St NW, Washington, DC 20004. T. (202) 393-5180. 091052

Mariposa, 2116 18 St NW, Washington, DC 20009. T. (202) 332-9629. 091053

Mateyka, Marsha, 2012 R St NW, Washington, DC 20009. T. (202) 328-0088. 091054

Maurine Littleton, 1667 Wisconsin Av NW, Washington, DC 20007. T. (202) 333-9307. 091055

Mehlman, Justine, 2824 Pennsylvania Av NW, Washington, DC 20007. T. (202) 337-0613. - Graph - 091056

Merrill Chase, 3300 M St NW, Washington, DC 20007. T. (202) 333-7701. 091057

Mickelson, 709 G St NW, Washington, DC 20001. T. (202) 628-1734. - Paint / Graph / Sculp - 091058

Middendorf, 2009 Columbia Rd NW, Washington, DC 20009. T. (202) 462-2009. - Paint / Graph / Repr / Sculp / Dec / Fra / Draw - 091059

Milestone Gallery, 2325 18 St NW, Washington, DC 20009. T. (202) 462-4557. 091060

Obrien, Ann, 4829 Bending Ln NW, Washington, DC 20007. T. (202) 333-4238. 091061

Oskar Gallery, 2715 M St NW, Washington, DC 20007. T. (202) 337-8299. 091062

Osuna, 1919 Q St NW, Washington, DC 20009. T. (202) 296-1963. 091063

P Street Pictures, 2621 P St NW, Washington, DC 20007. T. (202) 337-0066. - Paint - 091064

P & C Art, 2400 Wisconsin Av NW, Washington, DC 20007. T. (202) 965-2485. 091065

Parish Gallery, 1054 31 St NW, Washington, DC 20007. T. (202) 944-2310. 091066

Pavilion Gallery, 1001 Pennsylvania Av NW, Washington, DC 20004. T. (202) 393-0585. 091067

Pavo Real, 3222 M St NW, Washington, DC 20007. T. (202) 338-3128. 091068

PC Art, 3301 M St NW, Washington, DC 20007. T. (202) 963-4630. 091069

Pelloon, 1612 Seventh St NW, Washington, DC 20001. T. (202) 667-0789. - Graph / Fra - 091070

Pensler, 2029 Q St NW, Washington, DC 20009. T. (202) 328-9190. - Paint - 091071

Picture Frame Express, 2014 P St NW, Washington, DC 20036. T. (202) 775-8406. - Graph / Fra - 091072

Picture Show, 529 14 St NW, Washington, DC 20004. T. (202) 783-0371. - Paint - 091073

Picture Show, 3222 M St NW, Washington, DC 20007. T. (202) 342-2397. - Paint - 091074

Picture This Graphics, 1229 34 St NW, Washington, DC 20007. T. (202) 342-7448. - Graph - 091075

Rare Print Wagon, 1046 Potomac St NW, Washington, DC 20007. T. (202) 338-8639. - Graph - 091076

Root & Co., 445 N St SW, Washington, DC 20001. T. (202) 554-5377. 091077

Rosenberg, 3303 Porter St NW, Washington, DC 20008. T. (202) 363-3345. 091078

Ross, Holly, 516 C St NE, Washington, DC 20002. T. (202) 544-0400. 091079

S & S, 9 Hillyer Ct NW, Washington, DC 20008. T. (202) 667-1442. 091080

Saint Luke's Gallery, 1715 Q St NW, Washington, DC 20009. T. (202) 328-2424. - Paint / Graph - 091081

Sansar, 4200 Wisconsin Av NW, Washington, DC 20016. T. (202) 244-4448. - Furn / China / Jew - 091082

Sculpture Placement, 3050 K St NW, Ste 330, Washington, DC 20007. T. (202) 362-9310. - Sculp - 091083

Sherley Koteen, 2604 Tilden Pl NW, Washington, DC 20008. T. (202) 363-2233. 091084

Shogun Gallery, 1083 Wisconsin Av NW, Washington, DC 20007. T. (202) 965-5454. - Graph - 091085

Shop N Africa, 1624 Wisconsin Av NW, Washington, DC 20007. T. (202) 625-2849. - Eth - 091086

Slavin, 404 Seventh St NW, Washington, DC 20004. T. (202) 348-0473. 091087

Spectrum Gallery, 1132 29 St NW, Washington, DC 20007. T. (202) 333-0954. - Paint - 091088

Studio Gallery, 2108 R St NW, Washington, DC 20008. T. (202) 232-8734. - Paint / Graph / Sculp - 091089

Taggart & Jorgensen, 3241 P St NW, Washington, DC 20007. T. (202) 298-7676, Fax (202) 333-3087. - Paint - 091090

Tartt, 2017 Q St NW, Washington, DC 20009. T. (202) 332-5652. - Paint / Sculp - 091091

Taylor, Gary, 1843 Columbus Rd NW, Washington, DC 20009. T. (202) 483-5853. - Paint / Graph / Fra - 091092

Things, Graphics and Fine Art, 1522 14 St NW, Washington, DC 20005. T. (202) 667-4028. - Paint / Graph - 091093

Touchstone, 2009 R St NW, Washington, DC 20009. T. (202) 797-7278. - Paint / Graph / Sculp - 091094

Trocadero Far Eastern Art, 1501 Connecticut Av NW, Washington, DC 20036. T. (202) 234-5656. - Orient - 091095

Turner & Co, J.H.H., 1525 Seventh St NW, Washington, DC 20001. T. (202) 387-4441. 091095a

Uptown Arts, 3236 P St NW, Washington, DC 20007. T. (202) 337-0600. 091096

Veerhoff, 1604 17 St NW, Washington, DC 20009. T. (202) 387-2322. - Paint / Graph / Fra - 091097

Venable Neslage Galleries, 1803 Connecticut Av NW, Washington, DC 20009. T. (202) 462-1800. - Paint - 091098

Very Special Arts Gallery, 1331 F St NW, Washington, DC 20004. T. (202) 628-0800. 091099

Vidrio Vivo Contemporary Glass, 3222 M St NW, Washington, DC 20007. T. (202) 625-6062. - Glass - 091100

Wade, 1726 21 St NW, Washington, DC 20009. T. (202) 462-3576. 091101

Washington Arts Gallery, 2114 R St NW, Washington, DC 20008. T. (202) 667-3720. 091102

Washington Printmaker Gallery, 2106 R St NW, Washington, DC 20008. T. (202) 332-7757. - Graph - 091103

Washington Project for the Arts, 400 Seventh St NW, Washington, DC 20004. T. (202) 347-4813. 091104

Washington Studio School Gallery, 3232 P St NW, Washington, DC 20007. T. (202) 333-2663. - Paint / Graph - 091105

Watergate Gallery, 2552 Virginia Av NW, Washington, DC 20037. T. (202) 338-4488. - Paint / Graph / Fra - 091106

White Stewart, 52 O St NW, Washington, DC 20001. T. (202) 745-3730. 091107

Williams, Richard G., 2025 Rosemont Av NW, Washington, DC 20010. T. (202) 667-6610. 091108

Wilson-Stewart, 1423 Downing St NE, Washington, DC 20018. T. (202) 832-1902. 091109

Wohlfahrt, 3418 Ninth St NE, Washington, DC 20017. T. (202) 526-8022. 091110

Wonder Graphics and Picture Framing, 3247 Mount Pleasant St NW, Washington, DC 20010. T. (202) 328-8100. - Graph / Fra - 091111

Wonder Graphics and Picture Framing, 1000 Vermont Av NW, Washington, DC 20005. T. (202) 898-1700.
- Graph / Fra - *091112*

Worlds of Wonder, 1229 34 St NW, Washington, DC 20007. T. (202) 298-7889. *091113*

Worthy Gallery, 1020 29 St NW, Washington, DC 20007. T. (202) 342-0101. *091114*

Zenith Gallery, 413 Seventh St NW, Washington, DC 20004. T. (202) 783-2963. - Paint / Graph / Sculp / Tex / Fra - *091115*

Watchung (New Jersey)
Only Originals, 759 Somerset St., Watchung, NJ 07060. T. (201) 756-7475. - Paint / Repr - *091117*

Wellesley (Massachusetts)
Todd, J., 572 Washington St., Wellesley, MA 02181. T. (617) 237-3434. - Paint - *091118*

Wells (Maine)
Manko, Kenneth & Ida, Seabreeze Dr., Wells, ME 04090. T. (207) 646-2595. - Paint / Sculp - *091119*

West Hollywood (California)
Morseburg, 9089 Santa Monica Blvd, West Hollywood, CA 90046. T. (310) 273-5207. - Paint - *091120*

Palmer & Co., Herbert B., 9001 Melrose Av, West Hollywood, CA 90046. T. (310) 278-6407. - Paint / Graph / Sculp / Draw - *091121*

Paragone Gallery, 607 N West Knoll Dr, West Hollywood, CA 90046. T. (310) 659-0607. *091122*

Silverman, Manny, 619 N Almont Dr, West Hollywood, CA 90046. T. (310) 659-8256. *091123*

Warfield, Joanne, 508 N San Vincente Blvd., West Hollywood, CA 90048. T. (213) 855-0586. - Paint - *091124*

Yesteryear, 8816 Beverly Blvd, West Hollywood, CA 90046. T. (310) 278-2008. - Graph / Fra - *091125*

West Newton (Massachusetts)
Tepper, Martha, 120 Forest Av., West Newton, MA 02165. T. (617) 277-6612. - Paint / Graph / Sculp - *091126*

Westfield (New Jersey)
„D" Fine Arts, 133 Harrison Av., Westfield, NJ 07090. T. (201) 232-2739. - Paint / Sculp - *091127*

Westlake Village (California)
Maurice-Heyman, 813 Rim Crest Dr., Westlake Village, CA 91361. T. (805) 495-8601. - Paint / Sculp - *091128*

Westport (Connecticut)
B.E.L. Gallery, 42 Owenoke Park, Westport, CT 06880. T. (203) 226-5120. - Paint - *091129*

Connecticut Fine Arts, 2 Gorham Av., Westport, CT 06880. T. (203) 227-1302. - Paint - *091130*

Savoy Art Investment, 571 Riverside Av., Westport, CT 06880. T. (203) 222-0099. - Paint - *091131*

Van Harwegen den Breems, 2 Manitou Ct., Westport, CT 06880. T. (203) 227-8200. - Paint - *091132*

Westwood (Massachusetts)
Kiva, POB 270, Westwood, MA 02090. T. (617) 326-0177. - Pho - *091133*

White Plains (New York)
Carroll-Condit, 210 Mamaroneck Av., White Plains, NY 10601. T. (914) 946 - 1490. - Paint / Graph - *091134*

McGregor, Alexander, 90 Bryant Av., White Plains, NY 10605. T. (914) 949-5336. - Tex - *091135*

Westchester Art Workshop, Tarrytown Road County Center Building, White Plains, NY 10607. T. (914) 682-2481. - Paint / China / Sculp / Jew - *091136*

Wichita (Kansas)
Ellington, 350 N Rock Rd., Wichita, KS 67206. - Paint / Graph / Sculp - *091137*

Mid-America Fine Arts, 2601 E Central, Wichita, KS 67214. T. (316) 681-2584. - Paint - *091138*

Valhalla Gallery, 6130 E Central, Wichita, KS 67208. T. (316) 683-1131. - Paint - *091139*

Wichita Gallery of Fine Art, 100 N Broadway, Wichita, KS 67202. T. (316) 267-0243. - Paint - *091140*

Willimantic (Connecticut)
Casey-Greene, 163 Valley St., Willimantic, CT 06226. T. (203) 456-8378. - Paint - *091141*

Willow Grove (Pennsylvania)
Langman, Willow Grove Park, Willow Grove, PA 19090. T. (215) 657-8333. - Paint / Sculp - *091142*

Wilmington (Delaware)
Carspecken- Scott, 1707 N Lincoln St., Wilmington, DE 19806. T. (302) 655-7173. - Paint - *091143*

Delaware Center for the Contemporary Arts, 103 E 16 St., Wilmington, DE 19801. T. (302) 656-6466. - Paint - *091144*

Stockwell, David, 3701 Kennett Pike, Wilmington, DE 19807. T. (302) 655-4466. - Paint - *091145*

Thornapple, 1409 Silverside Rd., Wilmington, DE 19810. T. (302) 475-5096. - Paint / Graph / Sculp - *091146*

Winston-Salem (North Carolina)
Southeastern Center for the Contemporary Art, 750 Marguerite Drive, Winston-Salem, NC 27106. *091147*

Winter Park (Florida)
Albertson-Peterson, 329 Park Av. S, Winter Park, FL 32789. T. (305) 628-1258. - Paint - *091148*

Galleries International, 329 Park Av. S, Winter Park, FL 32789. T. (305) 645-0808. - Paint / Graph / Sculp - *091149*

Woodbridge (New Jersey)
Barron Arts Center, 582 Rahway Av., Woodbridge, NJ 07095. T. (201) 634-0413. - Paint - *091150*

Circle Gallery, Woodbridge Center, Woodbridge, NJ 07095. T. (201) 636-7710. - Paint - *091151*

Woodmere (New York)
Foxx Collection, 926 Mayfield Rd., Woodmere, NY 11598. T. (516) 569-1867, 687-9104. - Paint / Sculp / Pho / Draw - *091152*

Owl 57 Gallery, 1074 Broadway, Woodmere, NY 11598. T. (516) 374-5707. - Graph - *091153*

Woodstock (New York)
Night Gallery, 2 Lower Byrdcliffe Rd., Woodstock, NY 12498. T. (914) 679-7620. *091154*

Woodstock (Vermont)
Woodstock Gallery & Design Center, Route 4 E, Woodstock, VT 05091. T. (802) 457-1900. - Paint / Graph / Sculp / Pho - *091155*

Wyckoff (New Jersey)
Wyckoff Gallery, 210 Everett Av., Wyckoff, NJ 07481. T. (201) 891-7436. - Paint / Graph / Sculp - *091156*

Yountville (California)
Images Fine Art, 6540 Washington St, Yountville, CA 94599. T. (707) 944-0404. - Graph / Sculp - *091157*

Venezuela

Caracas (D.F.)
Arturo Michelena, Final Avda. Casanova, Edif. Varsovia Sabana Grande, Caracas. T. (02) 82 58 53. *091158*

Castillo, Marcos, Avda. Los Samanes 3, La Florida, Caracas. T. (02) 72 90 58. *091159*

Don Hatch, Edificio Campo Alegre, Avda. Francisco de Miranda, Caracas. T. (02) 33 48 41. *091160*

Estudio Actual, Quinta San Onofre, Tercera Av.-8/9 Transv.,Altam., Caracas. T. (02) 32 36 87, 39 15 38. *091161*

Freites, Av. Orinoco 11, 1060 Caracas. T. (02) 752 42 19, 751 93 10. - Paint - *091162*

Galeria Acquavella, Av. Principal del Bosque Edf. Torre del Bosque, PB, Caracas, 1050. T. (02) 71 36 89, 72 89 09, Fax 72 11 58. *091163*

Galeria de Arte Moderno Internacional S.R.L., Avda. Tamanaco, El Rosal, Caracas. T. (02) 71 87 78, 71 47 91. - Paint / Graph - *091164*

Galeria Siete Siete, Quinta Teca, Av. Orinoco Apart. 70574, Caracas, 107. T. (02) 91 70 75, 91 74 02. *091165*

Graphic CB2, Edf. Mohedano, Nivel Bolivar, Parque Central, Caracas. T. (02) 574 2342. *091166*

„Isla", Quinta Isla, Avda. Mèrida Urb. Las Palmas, Caracas. T. (02) 71 38 76. *091167*

Serra, Las Mercedes, Caracas. T. (02) 912 540. *091168*

Yugoslavia

Beograd (Srbija)
Galeria Cipela, Palmira Toljatija 5, 11070 Beograd. T. (011) 69 64 55. *091169*

Zimbabwe

Harare
Gallery Shona Sculpture, 56-58 Sunnyside Mansions, Samora Machel Av., Harare. T. 79 31 37. - Sculp - *091170*

Argentina

Buenos Aires

Breuer, Moreno, Libertad 1650, 1016 Buenos Aires.
T. (01) 22 85 23. *091171*

Bullrich, Adolfo, Posadas 1231, Buenos Aires, 1001.
T. (01) 22-2025. *091172*

Capdepont, A., Avda. Díaz Vélez 5250, 1405 Buenos Aires. T. (01) 982 70 71. *091173*

Comi+Pini S.R.L., Hipólito Yrigoyen 2275, Buenos Aires.
T. (01) 470 347, 474 761. *091174*

Galeria Studio, Christie's Agent, Libertad 1271, Buenos Aires. T. (01) 41 16 16, 42 20 46. *091175*

Gaona, Cesar C., Arenales 1415, Buenos Aires.
T. (01) 44 89 13. *091176*

Manzano, Maria R., Viamonte 1348, 1053 Buenos Aires.
T. (01) 45 56 48. *091177*

Naon, J. C. & Cia SRL, Guido 1785, 1016 Buenos Aires.
T. (01) 42 49 43,41 16 85, 812 6129. *091178*

Parisi, Carlos A., Austria 1998, Buenos Aires.
T. (01) 82 34 73. *091179*

Rodriguez, Pena 1673, Buenos Aires, 1021.
T. (01) 41 03 40, 42 82 10, 44 46 03, 44 54 41. *091180*

Roldán y Cia. S. R. L., Florida 141, Buenos Aires, 1005.
T. (01) 30 80 72. *091181*

Sarachaga, Juan Daniel, Juncal 1242, Buenos Aires.
T. (01) 42 87 37. *091182*

Sotheby, Libertad 846, Buenos Aires.
T. (01) PLAZA 0831. *091183*

Australia

Armadale (Victoria)

Antique Auction Galleries, 1170 High St., Armadale,
3143, Vict. T. 509 72 11. *091184*

Camperdown (New South Wales)

Hamilton & Miller, 130 Paramatta Rd., 2050 Camperdown, 2050. T. 519 63 17, 519 29 22. *091185*

Kareela (New South Wales)

Australian Art Auctions, 11 Tradewinds Pl., Kareela,
NSW 2232. T. (02) 528 4707. *091186*

Melbourne (Victoria)

Ainger, E. J., 433-435 Bridge Rd. Richmond, Melbourne,
Vic. 3000. T. (03) 4282850, 4287735. *091187*

Joel, Leonard, 174 Inkerman St., St. Kilda, Melbourne,
Vic. 3182. T. (03) 5348347. *091188*

Sotheby's, 926 High St., Armandale, Melbourne, Vic.
3143. T. (03) 5092900, Fax 5635067. *091189*

Parramatta (New South Wales)

Steers, 18-20 Hassall St., Parramatta, 2150.
T. (02) 635 59 88. *091190*

Sydney (New South Wales)

Christie, Manson & Woods, 298 New South Head Rd.,
Double Bay, Sydney, NSW 2028.
T. (02) 326 14 22. *091191*

Sotheby's, 13 Gurner St., Paddington, Sydney, NSW
2021. T. (02) 332-3500. *091192*

Austria

Kitzbühel (Tirol)

Welwert, Christine, Josef Pirchlstr. 4, 6370 Kitzbühel.
T. (05356) 24 46. *091193*

Linz (Oberösterreich)

ARTIA, Kreuzstr. 4, 4040 Linz. T. (0732) 23 92 09,
Fax 23 92 53. *091194*

Dorotheum, Fabrikstr 26, 4010 Linz. T. (0732) 773132,
Fax 77313285. *091195*

Potzneusiedl (Burgenland)

Auktionshaus im Schloß Potzneusiedl, Schloß, 2473
Potzneusiedl. T. (02145) 2249. *091196*

Salzburg

Dorotheum, Schrannengasse 7, 5027 Salzburg.
T. (0662) 871671. *091197*

Wien

Alt-Wien Kunsthandelsgesellschaft mbH, Bräunerstr. 11,
1010 Wien. T. (0222) 52 91 43. *091198*

Christie's, Kohlmarkt 4, 1010 Wien. T. (0222) 63 88 12,
Fax 63 71 66. *091199*

Dorotheum, Dorotheergasse 17, 1010 Wien.
T. (0222) 515600, 51560212,
Fax (0222) 51560474. *091200*

Hassfurther, Wolfdietrich, Hohenstaufengasse 7, 1010
Wien. T. (0222) 53509850,
Fax (0222) 535098575. *091201*

Keil, Robert, Dr., Gloriettegasse 13, 1130 Wien.
T. (0222) 8765574, Fax (0222) 8775034. *091202*

Münzenauktionsgesellschaft, Schottenring 17, 1011
Wien. T. (0222) 319 72 21. *091203*

Neumeister, Lobkowitzpl 1, 1010 Wien.
T. (0222) 5138640, Fax (0222) 5120521. *091204*

Sotheby's, Singerstr 16, 1010 Wien. T. (0222) 5124772,
5133774, Fax 513 48 67. *091205*

Wendt, Singerstr. 8, 1010 Wien. T. (0222) 53 14 62/
63. *091206*

Weywoda, Manfred, Köllnerhofg 1, 1010 Wien.
T. (0222) 5120130, Fax 5123377. *091207*

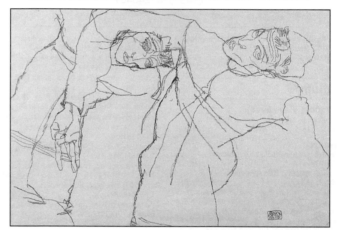

WIENER
KUNST
AUKTIONEN

Kärntnerringhof
Kärntner Ring 5–7
A - 1010 Wien

Tel. (+431) 5124540
Fax (+431) 51245409

Wiener Kunstauktionen, Kärntnerringhof, Kärntner Ring
5-7, 1010 Wien. T. (0222) 5124540,
Fax 51245409. *091208*

Belgium

Aalst (Oost-Vlaanderen)
Vandensteen, H., Leo de Bethunelaan 10, 9300 Aalst.
T. (053) 700 889. *091209*

Antwerpen
Center Galerij, Vestingstr 36, 2000 Antwerpen.
T. (03) 232 25 60. *091210*
Dixy, Handelstraat 19, 2000 Antwerpen.
T. (03) 36 38 64. *091211*
Galeries Versailles, Les, Kammenstr 36, 2000 Antwer-
pen. T. (03) 233 79 94. *091212*
Herck, Charles van, & Zoon, Leopoldstr 57, 2000 Ant-
werpen. T. (03) 233 32 75. *091213*
Keuster, de, Vrijdagmarkt 4-6, 2000 Antwerpen.
T. (03) 233 81 40. *091214*
Marnix, Terninckst 1, 2000 Antwerpen.
T. (03) 232 48 18. *091215*
Roepzaal Anselmo, Anselmostr 32-34, 2000 Antwerpen.
T. (03) 237 52 72. *091216*
Roepzaal Brabo, Melkmarkt 25a, 2000 Antwerpen.
T. (03) 32 62 33. *091217*
Sels, Kleine Markt 14, 2000 Antwerpen.
T. (03) 233 12 36. *091218*

Brugge (West-Vlaanderen)
Garnier, Korte Zilverstraat 8, 8000 Brugge.
T. (050) 33 01 95. *091219*

Bruxelles
Aberlê, 205, rue Royale, 1030 Bruxelles.
T. (02) 217 45 06. *091220*
André, 13, pl de Londres, 1050 Bruxelles.
T. (02) 511 17 18. *091221*
Auctioneer, 40 Rue A de Witte, 1050 Bruxelles.
T. (02) 640 03 09. *091222*
Chez Jean, 21, ch de Mons, 1070 Bruxelles.
T. (02) 23 14 08. *091223*
Christie's, Blvd de Waterloo 33, 1000 Bruxelles.
T. (02) 513 77 05. *091224*
Coosemans, P., 6 Rue du Grand Cerf, 1000
Bruxelles. *091225*
Du Four, Jacques, Galerie du Centre, Bureau 329, 1000
Bruxelles. *091226*

Euro Auction, 404A Av Louise, 1050 Bruxelles.
T. (02) 640 56 45, Fax 648 13 33. *091227*
Galerie Nova, 35 Rue du Pépin, 1000 Bruxelles.
T. (02) 512 24 94, 511 31 64. *091228*
Goyens de Heusch, 15 Pl du Grand Sablon, 1000
Bruxelles. *091229*
Horta, 390 Chaussée de Waterloo Post adr: 16 Av Duc-
petiaux, 1060 Bruxelles. T. (02) 539 09 89. *091230*
Hubeau, 105 Av Ch Woeste, 1050 Bruxelles. *091231*
Jourdan, 14, rue Gén-Leman, 1040 Bruxelles.
T. (02) 33 36 05. *091232*
Lempertz, 34 Rue aux Laines, 1000 Bruxelles.
T. (02) 5140586, Fax 5114824. *091233*
Moorthammers, Louis, 124, rue Lesbroussart, 1000 Bru-
xelles. T. (02) 647 85 48. *091234*
Paris, 220 Rue de Trône, 1050 Bruxelles.
T. (02) 648 02 87. *091235*
Salle de Vente du Béguinage, 10, rue du Rouleau, 1000
Bruxelles. T. (02) 218 17 42. *091236*
Salle de Vente Sainctelette, 17 Sq Sainctelette, 1000
Bruxelles. T. (02) 219 08 75. *091237*
Simonson, 38-40 Rue de l'Aqueduc, 1060 Bruxelles.
T. (02) 5383158. *091238*
Tavernier, 141 Av Victor-Rousseau, 1190 Bruxelles.
T. (02) 345 00 22. *091239*
Thémis, 13 Blvd de Waterloo, 1000 Bruxelles.
T. (02) 512 26 10. *091240*
Ventes Publiques Palais des Beaux-Arts, 10 Rue Royale,
1000 Bruxelles. T. (02) 5136080,
Fax (02) 5132165. *091241*

Ensival (Liège)
Salle de Vente Sainte-Claire, 37 Rue Maréchal, 4800
Ensival. T. (087) 33 23 00. *091242*

Gent (Oost-Vlaanderen)
Arto, Graaf v Vlaanderenpl 10-12, 9000 Gent.
T. (09) 2330240. *091243*
Dragonetti, Ajuinlei 10, 9000 Gent.
T. (09) 2251142. *091244*
Kunstcentrum Aktueel, Bij St Jacobs-St John, 9000
Gent. T. (09) 2258262. *091245*

Ladeuze
Buysscher, C. de, 32 Grande-Drève, 7950 Ladeuze.
T. (068) 65 76 78. *091246*

Lessines (Hainaut)
Galerie d'Art, 17 Rue des Combattants, 7860 Lessines.
T. (068) 33 20 85. *091247*

Leuven (Vlaams Brabant)
Hôtel des Ventes Louis-Philippe, Bondgenotenlaan 122,
3000 Leuven. T. (016) 232915. *091248*

Liège
Coronmeuse, 625 Rue Saint Léonard, 4000 Liège.
T. (04) 2270382. *091249*
Galerie du Centre, 18 rue du Pot d'Or, 4000 Liège.
T. (04) 2231714. *091250*
Hôtel des Ventes Saint-Georges, 76 Rue Hors-Château,
4000 Liège. T. (04) 2235327, 2235056. *091251*
Ista-Maréchal, 49 Rue des Champs, 4000 Liège.
T. (04) 3431765. *091252*
Salle de Vente du Paradis, 130 Rue Paradis, 4000 Liège.
T. (04) 2520407. *091253*
Salle de Vente Regina, 13, rue Soeurs-de-Hasque, 4000
Liège. T. (04) 2320077. *091254*

Limal (Liège)
Pinckaers, M., Rue Jospeh Mathieu 28, 1300
Limal. *091255*

Lokeren (Oost-Vlaanderen)
De Vuyst, Kerkstr 22-54, 9160 Lokeren.
T. (09) 3485440, Fax 09 3489218. *091256*

Marche-en-Famenne (Luxembourg)
Salle de Vente des Carmes, 11 Rue des Carmes, 6900
Marche-en-Famenne. *091257*

Marcinelle (Hainaut)
Bohen, D., 201 Av Mascaux, 6001 Marcinelle.
T. (071) 36 74 01. *091258*

Mechelen (Antwerpen)
Bernaerts, M., Overheide 34, 2800 Mechelen.
T. (015) 201532, Fax (015) 202329. *091259*

Merksem (Antwerpen)
Janssens, Patrick, Jos de Swertstr 20, 2170 Merksem.
T. (031) 6649850. *091260*

Namur (Namur)
Saint-Loup, 25-27, rue du Collège, 5000 Namur.
T. (081) 222437. *091261*
Sainte-Rita, 29 Rue de la Croix, 5000 Namur.
T. (081) 22 69 81. *091262*
Salle de Ventes Elisabeth, 15 Rue du Président, 5000
Namur. T. (081) 22 06 37. *091263*

Schoten (Antwerpen)
Schotense Roepzaal, Verbertstr 150, 2900 Schoten.
T. (031) 658 38 28. *091264*

Sint-Niklaas (Oost-Vlaanderen)
Galerij Regentie, Regentiestr 58-60, 9100 Sint-Niklaas.
T. (03) 777 63 73. *091265*

Waterloo (Brabant Wallon)
Ferme de l'ErmIte, 374 Chaussée de Bruxelles, 1410
Waterloo. T. (02) 3544114. *091266*

Wommelgem (Antwerpen)
Roepzaal Ternesse, Ternesselaan 15, 2160 Wommelgem. T. (031) 53 63 07. *091267*

Zele (Oost-Vlaanderen)
Gasthof Het Anker, Markt 10, 9240 Zele.
T. (052) 44 48 95. *091268*

Brazil

Rio de Janeiro
Bolsa de Arte, R. Texeira de Mello 53/6, 22410 Rio de
Janeiro. T. (021) 521 02 96. *091269*
Leiloeiro Alvaro Chaves, Pres. Antonio Carlos 607,
20000 Rio de Janeiro. T. (021) 224 1430. *091270*
Sotheby, Rua do Rosario 155, 20000 Rio de Janeiro,
20041. T. (021) 222-7771. *091271*

Canada

Dartmouth (Nova Scotia)
Dartmouth Auction Centre, 389 Windmill Rd., Dartmouth. T. (902) 463 2599.   *091272*

Montreal (Québec)
Fraser-Pinneys, 8290 Devonshire, Montreal, P.Q. H4P 2P7. T. (514) 731-4312, 345-0571, Fax 731-4081.   *091273*
Fraser-Pinneys, 5627 Ferrier, Montreal, P.Q. H4P 1N1. T. (514) 731-4312, 345-0571, Fax 731-4081.   *091274*
Saint Hippolyte, Iégor de, 2825 Bates, Montreal, P.Q. H3S 1B3. T. (514) 344-4081, Fax 344-4125.   *091275*

Ottawa (Ontario)
Walker, W. S., 125 Mountbatten Ave., Ottawa.   *091276*

Toronto (Ontario)
Christie's, 170 Bloor W, Toronto. T. (416) 960-2063.   *091277*
Deveau, Robert, 297-299 E Queen St., Toronto, M5A 1S7. T. (416) 364-6271.   *091278*
Dupuis, 104 Lowther, Toronto. T. (416) 926-8091.   *091279*
Gallery Sixtyeight, 3 Southvale Dr., Toronto, M4G 1G1. T. (416) 421-7614.   *091280*
Phillips Ward-Price, 5a Thorncliffe Av., Toronto, M4K 1V4. T. (416) 462-9044.   *091281*
Ritchie, D. & J., 288 King E, Toronto, M5A 1K4. T. (416) 364-1864, Fax (416) 364-0704.   *091282*
Sotheby, 9 Hazelton Av., Toronto, M5R 2E1. T. (416) 926-1774.   *091283*
Waddington, McLean & Co., 189 E Queen St., Toronto, M5A 1S2. T. (416) 362-1678.   *091284*

Vancouver (British Columbia)
Maynard, 445 W Second, Vancouver. T. (604) 876-8787.   *091285*
Semiahmoo, 826 Parker St. W, Vancouver. T. (604) 536-9231.   *091286*

Victoria (British Columbia)
Lund's Auctioneers, 926 Fort St., Victoria. T. (604) 386 3308.   *091287*

China, People's Republic

Beijing
China International Auction, 21st Century Hotel, 40 Liang Ma Qiao, 100016 Beijing. T. (10) 4663311, Fax (10) 4664812.   *091288*

Denmark

Hørsholm
Auktionshuset, Christianshusv. 185, 2970 Hørsholm. T. 45 76 70 80.   *091289*

København
Bukowski Danmark, Kongens Nytorv. 22, 1050 København.   *091290*
Christie's, Dronningens Tvaerg. 10, 1302 København. T. 33 32 70 75.   *091291*
Due, Ole, Östbanegade 169, 2100 København Ø. T. 42 61 11.   *091292*
Københavns Auktioner Chr. Hee's Eftf., Aebeløgade 4, 2100 København. T. 31 29 90 00.   *091293*
Kunsthallen Kunstauktioner, Købmagergade 11, 1150 København K. T. 33 13 85 69.   *091294*
Rasmussen, Bruun, Bredgade 33, 1260 København K. T. 33136911, Fax 33324920.   *091295*
Sagførernes Auktioner, N. Farimagsg. 43-45, 1364 København K. T. 33 11 45 30.   *091296*

Lyngby
Boye, Jernbanepl, 2800 Lyngby. T. 42 87 45 55.   *091297*

Nærum
Herholdt Jensen's, Rundforbivej 188, 2850 Nærum. T. 45505288.   *091298*

Bruun Rasmussen
Auctioneers of Fine Art
Bredgade 33, 1260 Copenhagen K
Tel. +45 33136911, Fax +45 33324920
Pedersholms Allé 42, 7100 Vejle
Tel. +45 75827722, Fax +45 75724722

Valby
Lauridsens, Stuer, Skolegade 12c, 2500 Valby. T. 17 07 00.   *091299*

Vejle (Jütland)
Rasmussen, Bruun, Pedersholms Allé 42, 7100 Vejle. T. 75827722, Fax 75724722.   *091300*

Viby
Nellemann & Thomsen, Skanderborgvej 104-106, 8260 Viby J. T. 86 11 47 11, Fax 86 11 46 66.   *091301*

Finland

Helsinki
Bukowskis, Aleksanterinkatu 19 A, 00100 Helsinki. T. (09) 631 061, Fax 633 994.   *091302*

France

Agen (Lot-et-Garonne)
Hôtel des Ventes, 462 Av Docteur-Jean-Bru, 47000 Agen. T. 0553661092, Fax 0553964061.   *091303*

Aix-en-Provence (Bouches-du-Rhône)
Christie's, 28 Rue Lieutaud, 13100 Aix-en-Provence. T. 0492724331, Fax 0492725365.   *091304*
Hours & De Valaurie, 7 Chemin de la Vierge Noire, 13090 Aix-en-Provence. T. 0442640237, Fax 0442592912.   *091305*

Albi (Tarn)
Joanny, Jacques, 14 Rue Bernard-de-Castanet, 81000 Albi. T. 0563380305, Fax 0563471838.   *091306*

Amiens (Somme)
Salle des Ventes, 237 Rue Jean-Moulin, 80000 Amiens. T. 0322952015, Fax 0322951506.   *091307*

Angers (Maine-et-Loire)
Courtois & Chauviré, 52 Rue Maine, 49100 Angers. T. 41605519.   *091308*
Hôtel des Ventes des Arènes, 12 Rue Arènes, 49000 Angers. T. 41886389, Fax 41810307.   *091309*

Angoulême (Charente)
Hôtel des Ventes, 14 Rue Remparts-de-l'Est, 16000 Angoulême. T. 0545921463, Fax 0545384171.   *091310*

Annecy (Haute-Savoie)
Teulère, Michel, 93 Blvd Fier, 74000 Annecy. T. 0450572505, Fax 0450574261.   *091311*

Antibes (Alpes-Maritimes)
Conseil, Philippe, 8 Av Pasteur, 06600 Antibes. T. 0493340852.   *091312*
Philippe, 8 Av Pasteur, 06600 Antibes. T. 0493340852.   *091313*

Arcachon (Gironde)
Toledano, Jean-Daniel, 135 Cours Lamarque-de-Plaisance, 33120 Arcachon. T. 0556836567, Fax 0556012265.   *091314*

Argentan (Orne)
Audhoui, Antony, 11 Rue Georges-Méheudin, 61200 Argentan. T. 0233670996, Fax 0233362717.   *091315*

Argenteuil (Val-d'Oise)
Régis, Valérie & Marie-Laure Thiollet, 19 Rue Denis-Roy, 95100 Argenteuil. T. 0139610150, Fax 0139613477.   *091316*

Arles (Bouches-du-Rhône)
Holz, Françoise, 28 Rue Jean Lebas, 13200 Arles. T. 0490498470, Fax 0490938941.   *091317*

Armentières (Nord)
Dessaut, Benoît, 154 Rue Nationale, 59280 Armentières. T. 0320772191, Fax 0320777024.   *091318*

Arras (Pas-de-Calais)
Bertrand & Catteau, 7 Rue Emile-Legrelle, 62000 Arras. T. 0321715716, Fax 0321715538.   *091319*

Ascain (Pyrénés-Atlantiques)
Mouël-Chouffot, Lucienne, Beherko Errota, 64310 Ascain. T. 0559540630.   *091320*

Aubagne (Bouches-du-Rhône)
Germain, Elisabeth, 22 Av Jeanne-d'Arc, 13400 Aubagne. T. 0442038036, Fax 0442038460.   *091321*

Aubervilliers (Seine-Saint-Denis)
Compagnie des Commissaires-Priseurs, 30 Rue Fillettes, 93300 Aubervilliers. T. 0148333506, Fax 0148330801.   *091322*
Salle des Ventes, 10 Rue Léopold-Réchossière, 93300 Aubervilliers. T. 0148346262.   *091323*

Aubignan (Vaucluse)
Hôtel des Ventes, Quart Bouteille Rte Carpentras, 84810 Aubignan. T. 0490626230, Fax 0490626237.   *091324*

Auch (Gers)
Hôtel des Ventes, 129-131 Rue Victor-Hugo, 32000 Auch. T. 0562054120, Fax 0562059158.   *091325*

Aurillac (Cantal)
Jalenques, Philippe, 37 Av Aristide-Briand, 15000 Aurillac. T. 0471480823, Fax 0471648672.   *091326*

Auxerre (Yonne)
Sineau, Alain, 21 Av Pierre Larousse, 89000 Auxerre. T. 0386521798, Fax 0386516674.   *091327*

Auxonne (Côte-d'Or)
Droin, Gérard, 60 Rue Antoine-Masson, 21130 Auxonne. T. 0380311445, Fax 0380311834.   *091328*

Avignon (Vaucluse)
Salle des Ventes Armengau, 21 Av Sources, 84000 Avignon. T. 0490863535, Fax 0490866761.   *091329*

Avize (Marne)
Salle des Ventes, 6 Pl Charles-de-Gaulle, 51190 Avize. T. 0326579099.   *091330*

Avranches (Manche)
Poulain, Pierre, Rue Nationale, 50300 Avranches. T. 0233580834, Fax 0233584248.   *091331*

Bar-le-Duc (Meuse)
Salle des Ventes, 40 Quai Victor-Hugo, 55000 Bar-le-Duc. T. 0329792064, Fax 0329796571.   *091332*

Bayeux (Calvados)
Bailleul, Régis, 7 Rue Bouchers, 14400 Bayeux. T. 0231920447, Fax 0231922127.   *091333*

Bayonne (Pyrénés-Atlantiques)
Carayol, Jean, 24 Av Card-Lavigerie, 64100 Bayonne. T. 0559592944.   *091334*
Hôtel des Ventes Mobilières, 22 Av Dubrocq, 64100 Bayonne. T. 0559598873, Fax 0559243582.   *091335*

Beaune (Côte-d'Or)
Herry, Daniel, 23 Rue Richard, 21200 Beaune. T. 0380222887, Fax 0380247058.   *091336*

Beauvais (Oise)
Salles des Ventes, 103 Rue Madeleine, 60000 Beauvais.
T. 0344450471. *091337*

Beauzelle (Haute-Garonne)
Centre de Vente aux Enchères, ZI Garossos, 31700
Beauzelle. T. 0561594040, Fax 0561592359. *091338*

Bédarieux (Hérault)
Salle des Ventos, 4 Rue Chapelle, 34600 Bédarieux.
T. 0467950893. *091339*

Belfort (Territoire-de-Belfort)
Gauthier, Patrick, 29 Av Wilson, 90000 Belfort.
T. 0384280071, Fax 0384550585. *091340*

Bergerac (Dordogne)
Biraben, Aurèle, 84 Rue Professeur-Pozzi, 24100 Berge-
rac. T. 0553585751, Fax 0553571667 *091341*
Biraben, Aurèle, 31 Rue José-Maria-de-Hérédia, 24100
Bergerac. T. 0553279933, Fax 0553613747. *091342*

Bernay (Eure)
Hôtel des Ventes, 1 Rue Guy-Pépin, 27300 Bernay.
T. 0232434741, Fax 0232440003. *091343*

Besançon (Doubs)
Peretz, Eric, 11 Rue Eglise, 25000 Besançon.
T. 0381803737, Fax 0381534190. *091344*
Renoud-Grappin, Jean-Paul, 13 Rue Pasteur, 25000 Be-
sançon. T. 0381821414, Fax 0381821415. *091345*

Béthune (Pas-de-Calais)
Duhamel, Alexis, Av Ferme-du-Roi, 62400 Béthune.
T. 0321576318. *091346*

Béziers (Hérault)
Abraham, Isabelle, 1 Zac Montimaran, 34500 Béziers.
T. 0467622014, Fax 0467760447. *091347*

Blois (Loir-et-Cher)
Pousse-Cornet, Marie-Edith, 32 Av Maunoury, 41000
Blois. T. 0254784558, Fax 0254786801. *091348*

Bolbec (Seine-Maritime)
Hermonville, Anne, 36 Rue Léon-Gambetta, 76210 Bolbec. T. 0235310653. *091349*

Bordeaux (Gironde)
Bailly-Pommery & Mathias, 63 Cours Xavier-Arnozan,
33000 Bordeaux. T. 0556527889,
Fax 0556526388. *091350*
Christie's, 49 Cours Xavier-Arnozan, 33000 Bordeaux.
T. 0556816547. *091351*
Commissaires-Priseurs des Chartrons, 136 Quai des
Chartrons, 33000 Bordeaux. T. 0556111191,
Fax 0556111192. *091352*
Hôtel de Ventes des Chartrons, 136 Quai Chartrons,
33300 Bordeaux. T. 0556111191,
Fax 0556111192. *091353*
Hôtel des Ventes Bordeaux Rive Droite, 276 et 280 Av
Thiers, 33300 Bordeaux. T. 0556323232,
Fax 0556409283. *091354*
Toledano, Jean-Daniel, 26 Cours Martinique, 33000 Bor-
deaux. T. 0556792405, Fax 0556012265. *091355*

Boulogne-Billancourt (Hauts-de-Seine)
Jonquet, Etienne, 23bis Rue Longs-Prés, 92100 Boulo-
gne-Billancourt. T. 0141410739,
Fax 0141419041. *091356*

Boulogne-sur-Mer (Pas-de-Calais)
Salle des Ventes, 12 Rue Pot-d'Etain, 62200 Boulogne-
sur-Mer. T. 0321313951. *091357*

Bourg-en-Bresse (Ain)
Hôte des Ventes, 1bis Rue Général-Debeney, 01000
Bourg-en-Bresse. T. 0474233018,
Fax 0474221025. *091358*

Bourges (Cher)
Hôtel des Ventes, 11 Rue Fulton, 18000 Bourges.
T. 0248240290, Fax 0248653751. *091359*

Bourgoin-Jallieu (Isère)
Champion, Gondrand, 8 Rue Joseph-Seigner, 38300
Bourgoin-Jallieu. T. 0474438010. *091360*

Brest (Finistère)
Hôtel des Vente de Brest, 26 Rue Château, 29200 Brest.
T. 0298462150, Fax 0298462155. *091361*

Brive-la-Gaillarde (Corrèze)
Gillardeau, Charles, 143 Av 8-Mai-1945, 19100 Brive-
la-Gaillarde. T. 0555241112,
Fax 0555740507. *091362*

Bucéels (Calvados)
Havard, André, La Croix, 14250 Bucéels.
T. 0231808007, Fax 0231081369. *091363*

Caen (Calvados)
Dumont, Tancrède & Lô Dumont, 7 Rue Mélingue,
14000 Caen. T. 0231860813,
Fax 0231866787. *091364*
Hôtel des Ventes, 16 Rue Marais, 14000 Caen.
T. 0231830101, Fax 0231839657. *091365*

Cagnes-sur-Mer (Alpes-Maritimes)
Courchet, Thierry, 23 Av Fauvettes, 06800 Cagnes-sur-
Mer. T. 0493070597. *091366*

Cahors (Lot)
Hôtel des Ventes, 44 Av Jean-Jaurès, 46000 Cahors.
T. 0565301380, Fax 0565239481. *091367*

Calais (Pas-de-Calais)
Salle des Ventes, 24 Rue Delaroche, 62100 Calais.
T. 0321973376, Fax 0321960231. *091368*

Cambrai (Nord)
Bertrand, Dominique, 26 Rue Cordiers, 59400 Cambrai.
T. 0327812047. *091369*

Cannes (Alpes-Maritimes)
Hôtel des Ventes, 20 Rue Jean-Jaurès, 06400 Cannes.
T. 0493384147, Fax 0493393393. *091370*
Issaly, François, 31 Blvd Alsace, 06400 Cannes.
T. 0493390135, Fax 0493682832. *091371*

Carcassonne (Aude)
Deleau, Jacques, 7bis Rue Jean-Jacques-Rousseau, 11000 Carcassonne. T. 0468726931, Fax 0468476288. *091372*

Carpentras (Vaucluse)
Hôtel des Ventes du Ventoux, Quart Rossan Rte Bédoin, 84200 Carpentras. T. 0490606788. *091373*

Castres (Tarn)
Hôtel des Ventes, 21 Rue Trésor, 81100 Castres. T. 0563597543, Fax 0563721729. *091374*

Caudan (Morbihan)
Guignard, Rue Kerpont, 56850 Caudan. T. 0297768282, Fax 0297813760. *091375*

Chalon-sur-Sâone (Saône-et-Loire)
Hôtel des Ventes, 9 Rue Félix-Renaud, 71100 Chalon-sur-Sâone. T. 0385463998, Fax 0385432225. *091376*

Châlons-sur-Marne (Marne)
Casini-Vitalis, Patricia, 42 Rue Martyrs-de-la-Résistance, 51000 Châlons-sur-Marne. T. 0326658394. *091377*

Champigny-sur-Marne (Val-de-Marne)
Morlot, Jean-Louis, 26 Rue Verdun, 94500 Champigny-sur-Marne. T. 0147068070. *091378*

Chantilly
Muizon, Vincent de, 12bis rue Connétable, 60500 Chantilly. T. 0344574052, Fax 0344587800. *091379*

Charleville-Mézières (Ardennes)
Hôtel des Ventes, 20 Rue Alsace, 08000 Charleville-Mézières. T. 0324574266, Fax 0324571544. *091380*

Chartres (Eure-et-Loir)
Galerie de Chartres, 1bis Pl Gén de Gaulle, 28000 Chartres. T. 0237360433, Fax 0237363471. *091381*

Châteaudun (Eure-et-Loir)
Trapenat, Jean-Pascal, 19 Rue Madeleine, 28200 Châteaudun. T. 0237451574. *091382*

Châteauroux (Indre)
Lane, André, 8 Rue Palais-de-Justice, 36000 Châteauroux. T. 0254341106, Fax 0254342891. *091383*

Châtellerault (Vienne)
Hôtel des Ventes, 6 Rue Cognet, 86100 Châtellerault. T. 0549212887, Fax 0549232454. *091384*

Chatou (Yvelines)
Hôtel des Ventes, 33 Rue Général-Colin, 78400 Chatou. T. 0139521040. *091385*

Chaumont (Haute-Marne)
Duvillier, Arnaud, 3bis Blvd Thiers, 52000 Chaumont. T. 0325031291, Fax 0325324152. *091386*

Cherbourg (Manche)
Boscher, Samuel, 4 Rue Noyon, 50100 Cherbourg. T. 0233205968, Fax 0233200331. *091387*

Chinon (Indre-et-Loire)
Alix, Pierre, Rte Tours, Les Plaines-des Vaux, 37500 Chinon. T. 0547931264, Fax 0547983320. *091388*

Clamecy (Nièvre)
Bourgartchev, Veni, 8 Rue Pressures, 58500 Clamecy. T. 0386271900. *091389*

Clermont-Ferrand (Puy-de-Dôme)
Aguttes & Vassy, 19 Rue des Salles, 63000 Clermont-Ferrand. T. 0473934486. *091390*
Hôtel des Ventes, 19 Rue Salins, 63000 Clermont-Ferrand. T. 0473934486, Fax 0473355434. *091391*

Cognac (Charente)
Champion, René-Paul, 19 Rue François-Porché, 16100 Cognac. T. 0545821378, Fax 0545820798. *091392*

Compiègne (Oise)
Loizillon, Dominique, 18 Rue Cordeliers, 60200 Compiègne. T. 0344400616, Fax 0344400173. *091393*

Corbeil-Essonnes (Essonne)
Bonduelle, Jean-Pierre & Jean-Marc Lancry, 10 Quai Essonne, 91100 Corbeil-Essonnes. T. 0164960308. *091394*

Cosne-Cours-sur-Loire (Nièvre)
Hautin, Jean-Louis, 33 Av 14-Juillet, 58200 Cosne-Cours-sur-Loire. T. 0386280197. *091395*

Coulommiers (Seine-et-Marne)
Dapsens-Bauve, Françoise, 1 Pl 27-Août, 77120 Coulommiers. T. 64031090. *091396*

Coutances (Manche)
Boureau, Eric, 14 Rue Ecluse-Chette, 50200 Coutances. T. 0233070733, Fax 0233077640. *091397*

Davézieux (Ardèche)
Blanc, Bernard, Espace Jean-Monnet, 07100 Davézieux. T. 0475675993, Fax 0475676477. *091398*

Dax (Landes)
Donzeau, Marie-Claire, 171bis Av Saint-Vincent-de-Paul, 40100 Dax. T. 0558749005, Fax 0558561594. *091399*

Deauville (Calvados)
Deauville Auction, 31 Av Florian-de-Kergorlay, 14800 Deauville. T. 0231818100. *091400*
Le Houelleur, Guy, 16 Rue Général-Leclerc, 14800 Deauville. T. 0231882192, Fax 0231888206. *091401*

Dieppe (Seine-Maritime)
Giffard, Patrick, 10 Rue Houard, 76200 Dieppe. T. 0235841033, Fax 0235060248. *091402*

Dijon (Côte-d'Or)
Hôtel des Ventes, 44 Rue Gray, 21000 Dijon. T. 0380731764. *091403*
Levitte, Christian, 46 Rue des Godrans, 21000 Dijon. T. 0380305941, Fax 0380301150. *091404*
Sadde, Philippe, 13 Rue Paul-Cabet, 21000 Dijon. T. 0380661917, Fax 0380678199. *091405*

Dole (Jura)
Macaigne, Claude, Cité Barberousse, 39100 Dole. T. 0384722527. *091406*

Doullens (Somme)
Herbette, Denis, 19 Rue André-Temez, 80600 Doullens. T. 0322324381. *091407*

Draguignan (Var)
Charbit, Adolphe, Pass Industrie, 83300 Draguignan. T. 0494681917. *091408*

Dreux (Eure-et-Loir)
Granger, Jean-Claude, 4 Rue Tanneurs, 28100 Dreux. T. 0237460422. *091409*

Duclair (Seine-Maritime)
Seguinet, Arnaud, 129 Rue Jules-Ferry, 76480 Duclair. T. 0235375061, Fax 0235377188. *091410*

Dunkerque (Nord)
Girard, Jean-Jacques, Rue Gustave-Degans, 59140 Dunkerque. T. 0328634269. *091411*

Elbeuf (Seine-Maritime)
Dupeyroux, Jean, 85 Rue Martyrs, 76500 Elbeuf. T. 0235770381. *091412*

Enghien-les-Bains (Val-d'Oise)
Hôtel des Ventes, 2 Rue Docteur-Leray, 95880 Enghien-les-Bains. T. 0134126816, Fax 0134128964. *091413*

Entzheim (Bas-Rhin)
Hôtel des Ventes, All Europe, 67960 Entzheim. T. 0388686363, Fax 0388686048. *091414*

Epernay (Marne)
Petit, Antoine, 25 Blvd Motte, 51200 Epernay. T. 0326552344, Fax 0326544408. *091415*

Epinal (Vosges)
Hôtel des Ventes, 10 Av Général-de-Gaulle, 88000 Epinal. T. 0329825408, Fax 0329350275. *091416*

Etampes (Essonne)
Colobert, Michel, 6 Av Paris, 91150 Etampes. T. 0164940233. *091417*
Salle Ventes Enchères Publiques, Pl Jeu-de-Paume, 91150 Etampes. T. 0160800001. *091418*

Evreux (Eure)
Hôtel des Ventes, 63 Rue Isambard, 27000 Evreux. T. 0232331359. *091419*

Fécamp (Seine-Maritime)
Madec, Eliane, 51 Rue Jules-Ferry, 76400 Fécamp. T. 0235281084, Fax 0235283799. *091420*

Fleury-les-Aubrais (Loiret)
C.V.P., 17 Rue Montaran, 45400 Fleury-les-Aubrais. T. 0238841352, Fax 0238841310. *091421*

Fontainebleau (Seine-et-Marne)
Osenat, Jean Pierre, Jean-Pierre, 5 Rue Royale, 77300 Fontainebleau. T. 0164222762. *091422*

Fontenay-le-Comte (Vendée)
Thélot, Frank, 16 Pl Saint-Jean, 85200 Fontenay-le-Comte. T. 0251690410, Fax 0251510679. *091423*

Fougères (Ille-et-Vilaine)
Hôtel des Ventes Mobilières, 7 Rue Pipon, 35300 Fougères. T. 0299944411. *091424*

Génicourt (Val-d'Oise)
Hôtel des Ventes, Rue Fossettes, 95650 Génicourt. T. 0134421450, Fax 0134421421. *091425*

Gien (Loiret)
Renard, Jean-Claude, 35 Quai Nice, 45500 Gien. T. 0238670183, Fax 0238676650. *091426*

Granville (Manche)
Robin, Didier, 175 Rue Jeanne-Jugan, 50400 Granville. T. 0233500391, Fax 0233904992. *091427*

Grasse (Alpes-Maritimes)
Vilatte Fabre, Agnès, 14 Blvd Maréchal-Leclerc, 06130 Grasse. T. 0493706853. *091428*

Grenoble (Isère)
Blache, Pierre, 15 Rue de Bonne, 38000 Grenoble. T. 0476467366, Fax 0476873010. *091429*
Gaucher, Francis & Torossian, Armand, 6 Rue Thiers, 38100 Grenoble. T. 0476466661, Fax 0476472167. *091430*

Guéret (Creuse)
Turpin, Alain, 15 Bd de la Gare, 23000 Guéret. T. 0555528362. *091431*

Honfleur (Calvados)
Hôtel des Ventes, 7 Rue Saint-Nicol, 14600 Honfleur. T. 0231890106. *091432*

Houdon (Yvelines)
Faure & Rey, 57 Rue Paris, 78550 Houdon. T. 0130461212. *091433*
Hôtel des Ventes, Rte Prévauté, 78550 Houdon. T. 0130597778. *091434*

Issoudun (Indre)
Sarget, Denis, 22 Rue Puits-à-Cognet, 36100 Issoudun. T. 0254031228, Fax 0254031789. *091435*

Joigny (Yonne)
Sausverd, Patrick, 34 Rue Aristide Briand, 89300 Joigny. T. 0386620075 k703 86624900. *091436*

L'Aigle (Orne)
Blanchetière, Yves, 18 Av du Mont-Saint-Michel, 61300 L'Aigle. T. 0233240511, Fax 0233242732. *091437*

L'Isle-Adam (Val-d'Oise)
Elkaim, Jean-Marc, 1 Rue Mellet, 95290 L'Isle-Adam. T. 0134690083, Fax 0134693930. *091438*

La Baule (Loire-Atlantique)
Hôtel des Ventes, Pl A.-Perrière, 44500 La Baule. T. 40113710, Fax 40113712. *091439*

La Châtre (Indre)
Sarget, Denis, Rue Jean-Pacton, 36400 La Châtre. T. 0254481965. *091440*

La Flèche (Sarthe)
Manson, Yves, 5 Rue pape-Carpantier, 72200 La Flèche. T. 0243940381, Fax 0243944363. *091441*

La Madeleine-de-Nonancourt (Eure)
Hôtel des Ventes de Nonancourt, Rte Evreux, 27320 La Madeleine-de-Nonancourt. T. 0232583612, Fax 0232600319. *091442*

La Roche-sur-Yon (Vendée)
Raynaud, Jean, 31 Rue Lorraine, 85000 La Roche-sur-Yon. T. 0251052984, Fax 0251460821. *091443*

La Rochelle (Charente-Maritime)
Hôtel des Ventes, 18 Rue Saint-Louis, 17000 La Rochelle. T. 0546411362, Fax 0546416491. *091444*

La Turbie (Alpes-Maritimes)
Salle des Ventes, 1521 Rte Beausoleil, 06320 La Turbie. T. 0492108888, Fax 0492108889. *091445*

La Varenne-Saint-Hilaire (Val-de-Marne)
Lombrail, Franck & Jean-Pierre Teucquam, 21 Av Balzac, 94210 La Varenne-Saint-Hilaire. T. 0143972993, Fax 0142836848. *091446*

Lombrail, Franck & Jean-Pierre Teucquam, 3 Av Marie-Louise, 94210 La Varenne-Saint-Hilaire. T. 0143979129, Fax 0142836848. *091447*

Langres (Haute-Marne)
Bertrand-Vannier, Pl Saint-Ferjeux, 52200 Langres. T. 0325876404. *091448*

Duvillier, Arnaud, Rte Poterne, 52200 Langres. T. 0325873593. *091449*

Lannion (Côtes-d'Armor)
Hôtel des Ventes, 5 Rue 73ème-Territorial, 22300 Lannion. T. 0296464875. *091450*

Laval (Mayenne)
Daveau, Jean-Michel, 5 Allée Saint-Vincent-de-Paul, 53000 Laval. T. 0243660238. *091451*

Hiret & Nugues, 17 Rue nantes, 53000 Laval. T. 0243682903, Fax 0243029630. *091452*

Salle des Ventes du Britais, 4 Rue Britais, 53000 Laval. T. 0243661778. *091453*

Le Bourget (Seine-Saint-Denis)
Centre de Ventes aux Enchères, Aéroport du Bourget, 93350 Le Bourget. T. 0148359119. *091454*

Le Havre (Seine-Maritime)
Lesieur, Robert & Maryvonne Le Bars, 77 Rue Louis-Brindeau, 76600 Le Havre. T. 0235225452, Fax 0235210623. *091455*

Mabille-Vankemmel, Nelly & Philippe-Jean Revol, 203 Blvd Strasbourg, 76600 Le Havre. T. 0235212127, Fax 0234432428. *091456*

Le Mans (Sarthe)
Butant, Jean, Rue Ursulines, 72000 Le Mans. T. 0243244707. *091457*

Hervouin, Serge, 20 Rue de Wagram, 72000 Le Mans. T. 0243233611, Fax 0243236731. *091458*

Longin, M., 165 Rue Maillets, 72000 Le Mans. T. 0243813450. *091459*

Sanson, Xavier, 16 Rue Bon-Pasteur, 72000 Le Mans. T. 0243770791, Fax 0243771962. *091460*

Le Puy-en-Velay (Haute-Loire)
Lafon, François, 10 Blvd République, 43000 Le Puy-en-Velay. T. 0471090385, Fax 0471022601. *091461*

Le Raincy (Seine-Saint-Denis)
Touati, François-Léopold, 7 All Fontaine, 93340 Le Raincy. T. 0143018471. *091462*

Les Andelys (Eure)
Cousin, Jacqueline, 1 Rue Sadi-Carnot, 27700 Les Andelys. T. 0232543004, Fax 0232544695. *091463*

Libourne (Gironde)
Devilder-Durand, Nadia, 2 Quai de l'Isle, 33500 Libourne. T. 0557512980. *091464*

Lille (Nord)
Desbuisson, Philippe, 2 Rue Sainte-Anne, 59800 Lille. T. 0320062581, Fax 0320744956. *091465*

Issaly, François, 14 Rue Jardins, 59800 Lille. T. 0320061014. *091466*

Mercier & Cie, 14 Rue Jardins, 59800 Lille. T. 0320061014, Fax 0320510662. *091467*

Limoges (Haute-Vienne)
Rollin, Philippe, 12 Rue Réforme, 87000 Limoges. T. 0555776000, Fax 0555777678. *091468*

Lisieux (Calvados)
Lebrun, Jean, 114 Blvd Herbét-Fournet, 14100 Lisieux. T. 0231621748. *091469*

Salle des Ventes, Pl Hennuyer, 14100 Lisieux. T. 0231621203. *091470*

Lons-le-Saunier (Jura)
Fernaux, Brigitte, 145 Chemin Ferté, 39000 Lons-le-Saunier. T. 0384244178, Fax 0384248152. *091471*

Louviers (Eure)
Salle des Ventes de Louviers, 28 Rue Pierre-Mendès-France, 27400 Louviers. T. 0232402230, Fax 0232251505. *091472*

Lunéville (Meurthe-et-Moselle)
Hôtel des Ventes, 42 Rue Sainte-Anne, 54300 Lunéville. T. 0383744251. *091473*

Lyon (Rhône)
Anaf, Jean-Claude, 13bis Pl Jules-Ferry, 69456 Lyon Cedex 6. T. 0478650505, Fax 0478650909. *091474*

Chenu, Jean & Benoît Scrive, 19 Rue Prof Louis Paufique, 69002 Lyon. T. 0478420134, Fax 0478376817. *091475*

Christie's France, 36 Pl Bellecour, 69002 Lyon. T. 0478428382, Fax 0478428384. *091476*

Conan, Loïc & Marie-France Auclair, 1 Rue de Cronstadt, 69007 Lyon. T. 0472734567, Fax 0478610795. *091477*

Dumas, André, 19 Rue Prof Louis Paufique, 69002 Lyon. T. 0478420134. *091478*

Guillaumot, Georges, Georges, 19 Rue Prof Louis Paufique, 69002 Lyon. T. 0478378808, Fax 0478376817. *091479*

Hôtel des Ventes de Lyon, 3 Av Sidoine-Apollinaire, 69009 Lyon. T. 0478477818, Fax 0478838034. *091480*

Hôtel des Ventes des Tuiliers, 31 Rue des Tuiliers, 68008 Lyon. T. 0478008665, Fax 0478003217. *091481*

Mâcon (Saône-et-Loire)
Lopard-Dessolin, Mme, 1054 Quai de Lattre-de-Tassigny, 71000 Mâcon. T. 0385387507, Fax 0385386554. *091482*

Manosque (Alpes-de-Haute-Provence)
Leclerc, marie-Sylvie, Av 1er Mai, 04100 Manosque. T. 0492876269, Fax 0492728048. *091483*

Mantes-la-Jolie (Yvelines)
Fillaire, Marie-Christine, 12bis Rue Léon-Marie-Cesné, 78200 Mantes-la-Jolie. T. 0130335050, Fax 0130333799. *091484*

Marseille (Bouches-du-Rhône)
Authier de Sisgaw & Christian Ribière, 19 Rue Borde, 13008 Marseille. T. 0491794630, Fax 0491798014. *091485*

Berquat, Pascal, 47 Rue Falque, 13006 Marseille. T. 0491811081, Fax 0491539898. *091486*

Clavel, Pierre-Yves, 102 Av Jules-Cantini, 13008 Marseille. T. 0491783357. *091487*

Clavel & Bonnaz, 74 Av Alfred Curtel, 13010 Marseille. T. 0491259140. *091488*

Fleck, François, 10 Rue Jean-Martin, 13005 Marseille. T. 0491850897, Fax 0491494208. *091489*

Tabutin, Hervé & Gérard de Dianous, 102 Av Jules Cantini, 13008 Marseille. T. 0491791993, Fax 0491259741. *091490*

Marssac-sur-Tarn (Tarn)
Salle des Ventes, ZAC Vialette, 81150 Marssac-sur-Tarn. T. 0563532718. *091491*

Maubeuge (Nord)
Entrepot, 79 Rte Elesmes, 59600 Maubeuge. T. 0327640903. *091492*

Mayenne (Mayenne)
Blouet, Pascal, 12 Rue Réaumur, 53100 Mayenne. T. 0243041374, Fax 0243002502. *091493*

Meaux (Seine-et-Marne)
Corneillan, Arnaud de, 21 Rue Isaac-Newton, 77100 Meaux. T. 64365930. *091494*

Melun (Seine-et-Marne)
Peron & Champin, 19 Rue de Dammarie, 77000 Melun. T. 0164370212 k703 (1) 64376199. *091495*

Mende (Lozère)
Meissonnier, Henri, 13 Rue Basse, 48000 Mende. T. 0466493099. *091496*

Menton (Alpes-Maritimes)
Biaggi, Anne-Marie, 4 Av Edouard-VII, 06500 Menton. T. 0493575857, Fax 0493576630. *091497*

Salle des Ventes, 12 Rue Albert-1er, 06500 Menton. T. 0493416444, Fax 0493284418. *091498*

Metz (Moselle)
Salle des Ventes Actipole, 5 Rue Nonnetiers, 57070 Metz. T. 0387372057. *091499*

Mirande (Gers)
Beaudran, Pierre, Rte Tarbes, ZI, 32300 Mirande. T. 0562667675. *091500*

Mont-de-Marsan (Landes)
Hôtel des Ventes, 4 B Rue Saint-François, 40000 Mont-de-Marsan. T. 0558759273. *091501*

Montargis (Loiret)
Baron, Jean, Ecluse Reinette, 45200 Montargis. T. 0238850799, Fax 0238987896. *091502*

Montauban (Tarn-et-Garonne)
Cohet, Chantal & Robert Feraud, 24 Rue Fort, 82000 Montauban. T. 0563200600. *091503*

Montluçon (Allier)
Dagot, Sylvie, 2 Pl Poterie, 03100 Montluçon. T. 0470051134. *091504*

Pierre-Petit, 9 Rue Pierre-Petit, 03100 Montluçon. T. 0470050507. *091505*

Montpellier (Hérault)
Commissaires-Priseurs de Montpellier, Chemin Poutingon, 34000 Montpellier. T. 0467472800, Fax 0467474774. *091506*

Marques, Louis, 121 Av de Lodève, 34000 Montpellier. T. 0467756555. *091507*

Montreuil-sur-Mer (Pas-de-Calais)
Anton, Henri, 20 Rue Pierre-Ledent, 62170 Montreuil-sur-Mer. T. 0321060570, Fax 0321815345.   *091508*

Morlaix (Finistère)
Boscher & Oriot, 37 Rue de Paris, 29210 Morlaix.
T. 0298880839, Fax 0298881582.   *091509*

Moulins (Allier)
Pellegrino, Jean-Claude, 5 Rue Pasteur, 03000 Moulins.
T. 0470443322.   *091510*

Nancy (Meurthe-et-Moselle)
Hertz, Eric, 107 Rue Sergent Blandan, 54000 Nancy.
T. 0383901920, Fax 0383412435.   *091511*
Hôtel des Ventes Blandan-Thermal, 12 Rue Placieux,
54000 Nancy. T. 0383281331,
Fax 0383903014.   *091512*
Hôtel des Ventes Nabécor, 52 Rue Nabécor, 54000 Nancy. T. 0383579957, Fax 0383545267.   *091513*

Nanterre (Hauts-de-Seine)
Gillet-Seurat, Anne, 15 Rue Raymond-Poincaré, 92000
Nanterre. T. 0147250087.   *091514*

Nantes (Loire-Atlantique)
Antonietti & Kaczorowski, 7 Rue Nicolas-Appert, 44100
Nantes. T. 40693900, Fax 40691860.   *091515*
Hôtel des Ventes Talma, 3 Rue François-Joseph-Talma,
44000 Nantes. T. 40744128, Fax 40140771.   *091516*
Talandier & Couton & Veyrac, 10-14 Rue Miséricorde,
44000 Nantes. T. 40892444, Fax 40470999.   *091517*

Narbonne (Aude)
Laudet, Jacques, 1 Quai Alsace, 11100 Narbonne.
T. 0468321033.   *091518*

Neuilly-sur-Seine (Hauts-de-Seine)
Hôtel des Ventes de Neuilly, 185 Av Charles-de-Gaulle,
92200 Neuilly-sur-Seine. T. 0147455555,
Fax 0147455431.   *091519*

Nevers (Nièvre)
Michaud & Michaud & Michaud, 7 Rue Saint-Didier,
58000 Nevers. T. 0386612828,
Fax 0386215404.   *091520*

Nice (Alpes-Maritimes)
Fusade, Bernard & Yves Wetterwald, 11bis Rue Pertinax,
06000 Nice. T. 0493621471,
Fax 0493669997.   *091521*
Hôtel des Ventes Gioffredo, 50 Rue Gioffredo, 06000 Nice. T. 0493858650, Fax 0493624511.   *091522*
Licorne, 14 Rue Alexandre-Mari, 06300 Nice.
T. 0493134749, Fax 0493925792.   *091523*
Moulierac, Jean-Marie, Av Saint-Antoine, 06000 Nice.
T. 0493018035.   *091524*
Nice Hôtel des Ventes, 15 Rue Dante, 06000 Nice.
T. 0493972929, Fax 0493864676.   *091525*
Palloc, Philippe, 5 Rue Rossini, 06000 Nice.
T. 0493889591.   *091526*

Niort (Deux-Sèvres)
Dezamy, Jacques-Marie, 52 Rue Gare, 79000 Niort.
T. 0549240303.   *091527*

Nîmes (Gard)
Champion, Pierre & Françoise Kusel, 69 Rue Nationale,
30000 Nîmes. T. 0466675274,
Fax 0466762096.   *091528*

Nogent-le-Rotrou (Eure-et-Loir)
Ecklé, Bruno, 4 Rue Tochon, 28400 Nogent-le-Rotrou.
T. 0237520185, Fax 0237523964.   *091529*

Nogent-sur-Marne (Val-de-Marne)
Berlinghi, Muriel & Christophe Lucien, 17 Rue Port,
94130 Nogent-sur-Marne. T. 0148720733,
Fax 0148726471.   *091530*
CM, 6 Av Joinville, 94130 Nogent-sur-Marne.
T. 0149749240, Fax 0149749241.   *091531*

Orléans (Loiret)
Binoche, Xavier & Ghislain de Maredsous, 39 Rue du
Pot-de-Fer, 45000 Orléans. T. 0238530025,
Fax 0238812576.   *091532*

Dard, Jean, 13 Rue Parisie, 45000 Orléans.
T. 0238531105.   *091533*
Galerie des Ventes, 2 Imp Notre-Dame-du-Chemin,
45000 Orléans. T. 0238538093,
Fax 0238537380.   *091534*

Ourville-en-Caux (Seine-Maritime)
Roquigny, Bruno, Rue Dames, 76450 Ourville-en-Caux.
T. 0235284497, Fax 0235283657.   *091535*

Palaiseau (Essonne)
Bouvet, Olivier de, 66 Rue Sablière, 91120 Palaiseau.
T. 0160148938.   *091536*
Martin du Nord, Denis, 66 Rue Sablière, 91120 Palaiseau. T. 0160148938.   *091537*

Pamiers (Ariège)
Ribaute, Roger, 23 Pl Marché-au-Bois, 09100 Pamiers.
T. 0561671186.   *091538*

Paris
Ader-Rémi, 14 Rue Favart, 75002 Paris. T. 0142606256,
Fax 0142606255.   *091539*
Allardi, Jean-Philippe, 15 Rue Grange-Batelière, 75009
Paris. T. 0147703070.   *091541*
Artus & Associés, 15 Rue de la Grange-Batelière, 75009
Paris. T. 0147708729, Fax 0142467144.   *091542*
Audap-Solanet, Godeau-Velliet, 32 Rue Drouot, 75009
Paris. T. 0147706768, Fax 0142470576.   *091543*
Binoche & Godeau, 5 Rue La-Boétie, 75008 Paris.
T. 0142657950.   *091544*
Boisgirard, Claude, 2 Rue de Provence, 75009 Paris.
T. 0147708136, Fax 0142470584.   *091545*
Bondu, 17 Rue Drouot, 75009 Paris.
T. 0147703616.   *091546*
Boscher, Studer, Fromentin, 3 Rue d'Amboise, 75002
Paris. T. 0142608787, Fax 0142603644.   *091547*
Briest, Francis, 24 Av Matignon, 75008 Paris.
T. 0142681130, Fax 0142681267.   *091548*
Cagny, Yves de, 4 Rue Drouot, 75009 Paris.
T. 0142460007, Fax 0145233321.   *091549*
Chambellan, Giaferri, Veyrac, 117 Rue Saint-Lazare,
75008 Paris. T. 0142941024.   *091550*
Charbonneaux, Catherine, 134 Rue Fbg Saint-Honoré,
75008 Paris. T. 0143596656,
Fax 0142565257.   *091551*
Cheval, H.P. & M.F. Robert, 33 Rue Fbg Montmartre,
75009 Paris. T. 0147705626,
Fax 0142467956.   *091552*
Chochon-Chochon, Barré-Allardi, 15 Rue de la Grange-Batelière, 75009 Paris. T. 0147703837,
Fax 0148009654.   *091553*
Christie's France, 6 Rue Paul-Baudry, 75008 Paris.
T. 0140768585, Fax 0142562601.   *091554*
Compagnie des Commissaires-Priseurs de la Région Parisienne, 10 Rue Docteur-Lancereaux, 75008 Paris.
T. 0140750485, Fax 0140750482.   *091555*
Cornette de Saint-Cyr, Pierre, 44 Av Kléber, 75016 Paris.
T. 0147271124, Fax 0145534524.   *091556*
Coutau-Bégarie, Olivier, 60 Av La-Bourdonnais, 75007
Paris. T. 0145561220, Fax 0145557045.   *091557*
Couturier, Eric & Jean Hoebanx, 23 Rue Le Peletier,
75009 Paris. T. 0147708266,
Fax 0142463582.   *091558*
Dayen, Patrick & Jacques Lenormand, 12 Rue Hippolyte
Lebas, 75009 Paris. T. 0142815091.   *091559*
Delorme & Fraysse, 14 Av de Messine, 75008 Paris.
T. 0145623119, Fax 0145622920.   *091560*
Depretz, Bernard, 5 Rue Artois, 75008 Paris.
T. 0142563775.   *091561*
Deurberge & Delvaux, 29 Rue Drouot, 75009 Paris.
T. 0140220040, Fax 0140220083.   *091562*
Drouot Montaigne, 15 Av Montaigne, 75008 Paris.
T. 0148000080, Fax 0148002086.   *091563*
Drouot Richelieu, 9 Rue Drouot, 75009 Paris.
T. 0148002020.   *091564*
Dumousset & Deburaux, 105 Rue Pompe, 75116 Paris.
T. 0147048403.   *091565*
Ferri, Marc, 53 Rue Vivienne, 75002 Paris.
T. 0142331124, Fax 0142334000.   *091566*
Galateau, Bernard, 52 Av Breteuil, 75007 Paris.
T. 0147832997, Fax 0145660445.   *091567*
Godeau, Antoine, 14 Rue Favart, 75002 Paris.
T. 0142616426.   *091568*

Grandin, Christian, 18 Rue Mazarine, 75006 Paris.
T. 0146340150, Fax 0143545234.   *091569*
Gros, Henri & Georges Delettrez, 22 Rue Drouot, 75009
Paris. T. 0147708304, Fax 0145230164.   *091570*
Habsburg, 2 Villa Violet, 75015 Paris.
T. 0145759683.   *091571*
Jutheau, Viviane, 13 Rue Grange-Batelière, 75009 Paris.
T. 0148009522.   *091572*
Kohn, Marc-Arthur, 16 Rue Drouot, 75009 Paris.
T. 0142464608, Fax 0142464615.   *091573*
Langlade, Emmanuel, 12 Rue Vivienne, 75002 Paris.
T. 0140159955.   *091574*
Laurin & Guilloux & Buffetaud & Tailleur, 12 Rue Drouot,
75009 Paris. T. 0142466116,
Fax 0147701251.   *091575*
LC Promotion, 38 Rue Varenne, 75007 Paris.
T. 0145493839, Fax 0145484560.   *091576*
Le Blanc, Hubert, 32 Av de l'Opéra, 75002 Paris.
T. 0142662448.   *091577*
Le Mouël, Jean-Marie, 22 Rue Chauchat, 75009 Paris.
T. 0147708636, Fax 0147704326.   *091578*
Le Roux, Yves-Marie, 18 Rue de la Grange-Batelière,
75009 Paris. T. 0147708300,
Fax 0142466063.   *091579*
Lefèvre, Pierre-Yves, 46 Rue Victoire, 75009 Paris.
T. 0140239212.   *091580*
Libert, Etienne & Alain Castor, 3 Rue Rossini, 75009 Paris. T. 0148245120, Fax 0148009107.   *091581*
Loudmer, 7 Rue Rossini, 75009 Paris. T. 0144795050,
Fax 0143438933.   *091582*
Mathias, Jean-Jacques, 18 Rue de la Grange-Batelière,
75009 Paris. T. 0147700036,
Fax 0142466063.   *091583*
Mercier, Etienne, 132 Blvd Raspail, 75006 Paris.
T. 0143261715.   *091584*
Mercier & Cie, 26 Rue Washington, 75008 Paris.
T. 0145619659, Fax 0145619670.   *091585*
Millon & Robert, 19 Rue de la Grange-Batelière, 75009
Paris. T. 0148009944.   *091586*
Morand, Richard, 7 Rue Ernest-Renan, 75015 Paris.
T. 0147348113.   *091587*
Morelle & Marchandet, 8 Rue Rossini, 75009 Paris.
T. 0144830003, Fax 0144839388.   *091588*
Neret-Minet, 8 Rue Saint-Marc, 75002 Paris.
T. 0140130779, Fax 0142336194.   *091589*
Oger & Dumont, 22 Rue Drouot, 75009 Paris.
T. 0142469695, Fax 0145231632.   *091590*
Pescheteau-Badin & Godeau & Leroy, 16 Rue de la
Grange-Batelière, 75009 Paris. T. 0147708838,
Fax 0148010445.   *091591*
Picard, Jean-Louis, 5 Rue Drouot, 75009 Paris.
T. 0147707722, Fax 0147707749.   *091592*
Poulain, Hervé & Rémy Le Fur, 20 Rue de Provence,
75009 Paris. T. 0142468181,
Fax 0142460009.   *091593*
De Quai Lombrail, 22 Rue Courcelles, 75008 Paris.
T. 0145615454.   *091594*
Rabourdin, Yves & Olivier Choppin de Janvry, 4 Rue Rossini, 75009 Paris. T. 0147703491,
Fax 0147703886.   *091595*
Renaud, Paul, 6 Rue de la Grange-Batelière, 75009 Paris. T. 0142467425, Fax 0148009575.   *091596*
Ribeyre, Dominique, 5 Rue de Provence, 75009 Paris.
T. 0142460077, Fax 0145232292.   *091597*
Rieunier Bailly Pommery, 25 Rue Le-Peletier, 75009 Paris. T. 0145234440, Fax 0148242595.   *091598*
Robert, Claude, 5 Av d'Eylau, 75016 Paris.
T. 0147279534, Fax 0147277089.   *091599*
Robert, Marie-Françoise, 18 Rue Cadet, 75009 Paris.
T. 0142465451, Fax 0142465446.   *091600*
Rogeon, Pierre-Marie, 16 Rue Milton, 75009 Paris.
T. 0142803455, Fax 0142851412.   *091601*
Rostand, Michel, 30bis Rue Bergère, 75009 Paris.
T. 0147705011, Fax 0147701932.   *091602*
Roux Troostwijk, 13 Rue Eugène-Flachat, 75017 Paris.
T. 0147632727, Fax 0147632728.   *091603*
Salle de Vente Saint Honoré, 214 Rue Fbg Saint-Honoré,
75008 Paris. T. 0143596863,
Fax 0142568507.   *091604*
Sotheby's, 3 Rue de Miromesnil, 75008 Paris.
T. 0142664060, Fax 0147422232.   *091605*

Tajan, 37 Rue Mathurins, 75008 Paris. T. 0153303030, Fax 0153303031. *091605a*

Tripier, Antoinette, 26 Rue Malar, 75007 Paris. T. 0140629717, Fax 0140629678. *091606*

Wapler, Vincent, 16 Pl des Vosges, 75004 Paris. T. 0142785710, Fax 0142788980. *091607*

Watine-Arnault, Dominique, 41 Av Montaigne, 75008 Paris. T. 0147239387, Fax 0147239389. *091608*

Parthenay (Deux-Sèvres)
Tesson, Serge, 78 Rue Bourg-Belais, 79200 Parthenay. T. 0549952421, Fax 0549643446. *091609*

Pau (Pyrénées-Atlantiques)
Hôtel des Ventes, 33 Rue Emile-Guichenné, 64000 Pau. T. 0559271081, Fax 0559828361. *091610*

Périgueux (Dordogne)
Suze, Jean-Michel, 9 Rue Bodin, 24000 Périgueux. T. 0553086084, Fax 0553074532. *091611*

Péronne (Somme)
Salle des Ventes, 23 Rue Georges-Clémenceau, 80200 Péronne. T. 0322844012. *091612*

Perpignan (Pyrénées-Orientales)
Pujol & Revoul, Etienne & Isabelle, 4 Av Ribière, 66000 Perpignan. T. 0468540910, Fax 0468554345. *091613*

Pithiviers (Loiret)
Ducellier, Hugues, 2 Blvd Beauvallet, 45300 Pithiviers. T. 0238300379. *091614*

Plérin (Côtes-d'Armor)
Gay-Lussac, 16 Rue Montesquieu, 22190 Plérin. T. 0296744835, Fax 0296747921. *091615*

Podensac (Gironde)
Hôtel des Ventes des Graves, 29 Rue François-Mauriac, 33720 Podensac. T. 0556272186, Fax 0556272801. *091616*

Poitiers (Vienne)
Chevalier, Isabelle, 22 Blvd Grand-Cerf, 86000 Poitiers. T. 0549378082, Fax 0549371380. *091617*

Plassart, Ch., 4 Rue Gaillards, 86000 Poitiers. T. 0549017124, Fax 0549416500. *091618*

Pont-Audemer (Eure)
Desbenoît, Olivier, 13 Rue Doult-Vitran, 27500 Pont-Audemer. T. 0232411408. *091619*

Pont-l'Evêque (Calvados)
Le Houelleur, Guy, 16 Rue Thouret, 14130 Pont-l'Evêque. T. 0231640026. *091620*

Pontoise (Val-d'Oise)
Hôtel des Ventes de Pontoise, 3bis Rue Saint-Martin, 95300 Pontoise. T. 0130310183. *091621*

Provins (Seine-et-Marne)
Feletin, Thierry, 1 Av Gén de Gaulle, 77160 Provins. T. 0164001714. *091622*

Quetigny (Côte-d'Or)
Sadde, Philippe, Rue La-Gouge, 21800 Quetigny. T. 0380469109. *091623*

Quimper (Finistère)
Salle des Ventes, 1bis Rue Pont-l'Abbé, 29000 Quimper. T. 0298529797, Fax 0298557644. *091624*

Rambouillet (Yvelines)
Faure, Francis & Bernard Rey, 14 Rue d'Angiviller, 78120 Rambouillet. T. 0134830132, Fax 0134830045. *091625*

Hôtel des Ventes, 14 Rue Angiviller, 78120 Rambouillet. T. 0134830132. *091626*

Réalville (Tarn-et-Garonne)
Cohet, Chantal & Robert Feraud, Moulin de Sadoul, 82440 Réalville. T. 0563671079. *091627*

Reims (Marne)
Damoisy, Christian & Pierre-Pascal Guizzetti, 25 Rue Temple, 51100 Reims. T. 0326473259, Fax 0326404487. *091628*

Dapsens, Ludovic, 31 Rue Chativesle, 51100 Reims. T. 0326472637, Fax 0326977426. *091629*

Rennes (Ille-et-Vilaine)
Livinec & Pincemin & Gauducheau, 30-32 Pl des Lices, 35000 Rennes. T. 0299315800, Fax 0299655264. *091630*

Riom (Puy-de-Dôme)
Jalenques, Philippe, 23bis Rue Dellile, 63200 Riom. T. 0473382431. *091631*

Roanne (Loire)
Engles-Lanfrey, Martine, 23 Rue Benoît-Malon, 42300 Roanne. T. 0477725222, Fax 0477701523. *091632*

Rochefort (Charente-Maritime)
Dijeau, René, 32 Av Camille-Pelletan, 17300 Rochefort. T. 0546990046. *091633*

Rodez (Aveyron)
Falabrègues, Pascal, Bel Air, Rue Artisans, 12000 Rodez. T. 0565782178, Fax 0565782179. *091634*

Romans-sur-Isère (Drôme)
Cassagne, Corinne, 26 Rue République, 26100 Romans-sur-Isère. T. 0475020926, Fax 0475059328. *091635*

Roubaix (Nord)
Issaly, François, 22 Rue Curé, 59100 Roubaix. T. 0320730030. *091636*

Mercier, Jacques, 22 Rue Curé, 59100 Roubaix. T. 0320730030. *091637*

Rouen (Seine-Maritime)
Anjou, Bernard d', 20 Rue Croix-de-Fer, 76000 Rouen. T. 0235987349, Fax 0235898765. *091638*

Bisman, Jean-Jacques, 25 Rue Général-Giraud, 76000 Rouen. T. 0235711350. *091639*

Denesle, Christian, 20 Rue Croix-de-Fer, 76000 Rouen. T. 0235715448. *091640*

Wemaere, Max & Arnaud de Beaupuis, 20 Rue Croix-de-Fer, 76000 Rouen. T. 0235703289, Fax 0235880129. *091641*

Royan (Charente-Maritime)
Geoffroy, Jean-Pierre & Jean-Renaud, 6 Rue Président-Raymond-Poincaré, 17200 Royan. T. 0546386935, Fax 0546392805. *091642*

Saint-Amand-Montrond (Cher)
Hôtel des Ventes du Boischaut, 57 Av Général-de-Gaulle, 18200 Saint-Amand-Montrond. T. 0248964173. *091643*

Saint-Brieuc (Côtes-d'Armor)
Hôtel des Ventes, 12 Rue Gouët, 22000 Saint-Brieuc. T. 0296331591, Fax 0296338057. *091644*

Saint-Dié (Vosges)
Guérin, Michel, 65 Rue Prairie, 88100 Saint-Dié. T. 0329561334. *091645*

Saint-Dizier (Haute-Marne)
Armengau, Gilbert, 19 Rue Vergy, 52100 Saint-Dizier. T. 0325566707, Fax 0325050996. *091646*

Saint-Etienne (Loire)
Hôtel des Ventes de la Terrasse, 7 Rue Léon-Lamaizière, 42000 Saint-Etienne. T. 0477934276, Fax 0477937700. *091647*

Hôtel des Ventes Parc Giron, Rue Richelandière, All Drouot, 42100 Saint-Etienne. T. 0477325312, Fax 0477375493. *091648*

Saint-Germain-en-Laye (Yvelines)
Loiseau, Jean & Alain Schmitz & Marielle Digard, 13 Rue Thiers, 78100 Saint-Germain-en-Laye. T. 0139739564, Fax 0139730314. *091649*

Saint-Lô (Manche)
Morin, Victor, 18 Rue Carnot, 50000 Saint-Lô. T. 0233570135. *091650*

Saint-Malo (Ille-et-Vilaine)
Salle des Ventes Mobilières, 14 Rue Alphonse-Thébault, 35400 Saint-Malo. T. 0299564618. *091651*

Saint-Nazaire (Loire-Atlantique)
Hôtel des Ventes, 78 Rue Aristide-Briand, 44600 Saint-Nazaire. T. 40223951. *091652*

Saint-Omer (Pas-de-Calais)
Fourquet, Patrick, 165 Rue Dunkerque, 62500 Saint-Omer. T. 0321932311, Fax 0321937575. *091653*

Saint-Pierre-d'Oleron (Charente-Maritime)
Dijeau, René, 17 Rue Docteur-Delteil, 17310 Saint-Pierre-d'Oleron. T. 0546473299. *091654*

Saint-Priest (Rhône)
Lyonnaise des Ventes Publiques, 6 Rue Pierre-et-Marie-Curie, 69800 Saint-Priest. T. 0478906464, Fax 0478908330. *091655*

Saint-Quentin (Aisne)
Muné Mercédès, 14 Rue Mulhouse, 02100 Saint-Quentin. T. 0323622830, Fax 0323676936. *091656*

Saint-Raphaël (Var)
Salle Ventes, Imp Bellay, 83700 Saint-Raphaël. T. 0494958581. *091657*

Saint-Valery-en-Caux (Seine-Maritime)
Roquigny, Bruno, 8 Rue Ravine, 76460 Saint-Valery-en-Caux. T. 0235978552. *091658*

Saint-Vincent-de-Tyrosse (Landes)
Donzeau, Marie-Claire & Rue Métiers, 40230 Saint-Vincent-de-Tyrosse. T. 0558773694. *091659*

Saintes (Charente-Maritime)
Geoffroy, Jean-Pierre & Jean-Renaud, 38 Blvd Guillet-Maillet, 17100 Saintes. T. 0546933914. *091660*

Sarlat-la-Canéda (Dordogne)
Biraben, Aurèle, Rue Jean-Bernard-Delpeyrat, 24200 Sarlat-la-Canéda. T. 0553285990, Fax 0553294785. *091661*

Saumur (Maine-et-Loire)
Nouvel Hôtel des Ventes de Saumur, 2 Rue Dupetit-Thouars, 49400 Saumur. T. 41510317, Fax 41672816. *091662*

Sceaux (Hauts-de-Seine)
Hôtel des Ventes de Sceaux, 27 Av Georges-Clemenceau, 92330 Sceaux. T. 0146608425. *091663*

Sedan (Ardennes)
Hôtel des Ventes, 4bis Rue Mirbritz, 08200 Sedan. T. 0324270874, Fax 0324295298. *091664*

Semur-en-Auxois (Côte-d'Or)
Colliette, Marie-Agnès, 10 Rue Vaux, 21140 Semur-en-Auxois. T. 0380972160. *091665*

Senlis (Oise)
May, Thierry & Vincent Muizen, 63 Rue Fbg-Saint-Martin, 60300 Senlis. T. 0344530342, Fax 0344530194. *091666*

Sens (Yonne)
Vivier, Gilles, 61 Rue République, 89100 Sens. T. 0386651537, Fax 0386954490. *091667*

Soissons (Aisne)
Collignon & Laurent, Hervé, 2bis Rue Charliers, 02200 Soissons. T. 0323537901, Fax 0323594310. *091668*

Soyaux (Charente)
Salle des Ventes, Av Général-de-Gaulle, 16800 Soyaux. T. 0545956292. *091669*

Tarbes (Hautes-Pyrénées)
Adam, Henry, 22 Rue Docteur-Roux, 65000 Tarbes. T. 0562361985, Fax 0562361827. *091670*

Thonon-les-Bains (Haute-Savoie)
Holtz, Albert, 4 Av Clos-Rouge, 74200 Thonon-les-Bains. T. 0450262736, Fax 0450262767. *091671*

Tonnerre (Yonne)
Devilleneuve, Philippe, 47 Rue La-Bonneterie, 89700 Tonnerre. T. 0386551249, Fax 0386544745. *091672*

Toulon (Var)
Couret, Pierre & Jacques Bourcier & Richard Maunier, 54 Blvd Georges-Clemenceau, 83000 Toulon. T. 0494926286, Fax 0494916101. *091673*

Toulouse (Haute-Garonne)
Arnaune, Paul & Eric Prim, 4 Rue Trois-Journées, 31000 Toulouse. T. 0561234000, Fax 0561218601. *091674*

Fouré-Labrot, Gérard & Nicolas Bignon, 4 Rue Trois-Journées, 31000 Toulouse. T. 0561224192, Fax 0561213600. *091675*

Hôtel des Ventes Saint-Georges, 7 Rue Astorg, 31000 Toulouse. T. 0561233055. *091676*

Lavail & Tajan-Blondeau, 8 Rue Labéda, 31000 Toulouse. T. 0561235878, Fax 0562272928. *091677*

Tours (Indre-et-Loire)
Hôtel des Ventes, 20 Rue Michel-Colombe, 37000 Tours. T. 0547666364, Fax 0547664500. *091678*

Hôtel des Ventes Giraudeau, 248 Rue Giraudeau, 37000 Tours, BP 2027, 37020 Tours Cédex. T. 0547377171, Fax 0547392555. *091679*

Trouville-sur-Mer (Calvados)
Jouet, Jacques, 10 Rue Am-de-Maigret, 14360 Trouville-sur-Mer. T. 0231881354. *091680*

Valence (Drôme)
Hôtel des Ventes, 11 Rue Alpes, 26000 Valence. T. 0475565827, Fax 0475552661. *091681*

Valenciennes (Nord)
Enault, Bernard, 27 Blvd Carpeaux, 59300 Valenciennes. T. 0327469892. *091682*

Valognes (Manche)
Salle des Ventes de Valognes, 16 Rue 20-Juin-1944, 50700 Valognes. T. 0233401035. *091683*

Vannes (Morbihan)
Maître Ruellan, 17 Rue Joseph-le-Brix, 56000 Vannes. T. 0297472632, Fax 0297479182. *091684*

Vendôme (Loir-et-Cher)
Rouillac, Philippe, Rue Albert-Einstein, 41100 Vendôme. T. 0254802424, Fax 0254776110. *091685*

Vernon (Eure)
Châtain, Lydie, 12 Av Pierre-Mendès-France, 27200 Vernon. T. 0232216723, Fax 0232213666. *091686*

Verrières-le-Buisson (Essonne)
Martin du Nord & Bouvet, 2 Rue D'Estienne d'Orves, 91370 Verrières-le-Buisson. T. 0169201891. *091687*

Versailles (Yvelines)
Bailly, François & Stanislas Machoir, 4 Rue Abbé-de-l'Epée, 78000 Versailles. T. 0139505506. *091688*

Martin, J. & G. Chausselat, 11 Rue Ploix, 78000 Versailles. T. 0130210339, Fax 0130216249. *091689*

Martin, J. & G. Chausselat, 6bis Av Sceaux, 78000 Versailles. T. 0130217005. *091690*

Martin, Jacques & Gilles Chausselat, 3 Imp des Chevau-Légers, 78000 Versailles. T. 0239505808, Fax 0230213248. *091691*

Perrin, Paul & Olivier Perrin & Philippe Royère & Antoine Lajeunesse, 3 Imp des Chevau-Légers, 78000 Versailles. T. 0139506982, Fax 0139507504. *091692*

Vervins (Aisne)
Valentin, Antoine, 8 Rue République, 02140 Vervins. T. 0323983434. *091693*

Vesoul (Haute-Saône)
Jivoult, Boris, 10 Rue Banque, 70000 Vesoul. T. 0384754646, Fax 0384752323. *091694*

Vichy (Allier)
Laurent, 16 Av de Lyon, 03200 Vichy. T. 0470983848. *091695*

Laurent, Guy, 16 Av de Lyon, 03200 Vichy. T. 0470590940. *091696*

Salle des Ventes, 16 Av Lyon, 03200 Vichy. T. 0470590940. *091697*

Villefranche-sur-Saône (Rhône)
Salle des Ventes, 1725 Rte Riottier, 69400 Villefranche-sur-Saône. T. 0474656039, Fax 0474681695. *091698*

Villeneuve-sur-Lot (Lot-et-Garonne)
Salle des Ventes, 7 Rue Navrelle, 47300 Villeneuve-sur-Lot. T. 0553015756. *091699*

Salle des Ventes, 34 Rue Grelot, 47300 Villeneuve-sur-Lot. T. 0553400528. *091700*

Villers-Semeuse (Ardennes)
Salles des Ventes des Ayvelles, zi Rte Les-Ayvelles, 08000 Villers-Semeuse. T. 0324377588, Fax 0324339584. *091701*

Vire (Calvados)
Toutain, Gilles, 2 Rue Varende, 14500 Vire. T. 0231681719, Fax 0231675477. *091702*

Viry-Châtillon (Essonne)
Bouvet, Olivier de, 32 Rue Victor-Basch, 91170 Viry-Châtillon. T. 0169244442. *091703*

Martin du Nord, Denis, 32 Rue Victor-Basch, 91170 Viry-Châtillon. T. 0169244442. *091704*

Vitry-le-François (Marne)
Archambault, Guy, 9 Fbg-Léon-Bourgeois, 51300 Vitry-le-François. T. 0326747502, Fax 0326741779. *091705*

Yvetot (Seine-Maritime)
Anjou, Elisabeth d', 6 Rue Félix-Faure, 76190 Yvetot. T. 0235950796. *091706*

Germany

Ahlden (Niedersachsen)
Kunstauktionshaus Schloß Ahlden, Schloß, 29693 Ahlden. T. (05164) 575, Fax 522. *091707*

Ahlerstedt (Niedersachsen)
Hinck, C., Neues Feld 1, 21702 Ahlerstedt. T. (04166) 246. *091708*

Albersdorf (Schleswig-Holstein)
Kunstauktionshaus Albersdorf, Kapellenpl. 2, 25767 Albersdorf. T. (04835) 231. *091709*

Anröchte (Nordrhein-Westfalen)
Gerwin, H., Beleckerstr. 55, 59609 Anröchte. T. (02947) 32 47. *091710*

Augsburg (Bayern)
Augsburger Kunstauktionshaus Petzold, Maximilianstr 53, 86150 Augsburg. T. (0821) 33715. *091711*

Boegler, Peter, Mennwarthstr 12, 86154 Augsburg. *091712*

Kunsthaus im Welserhof, Jakoberstr 49a, 86152 Augsburg. T. (0821) 30100. *091713*

VILLA GRISEBACH
AUKTIONEN

Kunst des 19. und 20. Jahrhunderts

Erich Heckel. „Rote Dächer
(Häusergruppe Dangast)"
1909. Öl auf Leinwand
67,5 x 75,5 cm

Verkauft auf der
50. Auktion am 7. Juni 1996
zum neuen Weltrekordpreis von
DM 1.782.500,- (incl. Aufgeld)

München
Peter Graf zu Eltz
Villa Grisebach Auktionen
Prannerstraße 13
D - 80333 München
Tel.: 089 - 22 76 32 / 33
Fax: 089 - 22 37 61

Stephanie Gräfin Wolff
Metternich
Seestr. 7
D - 80802 München
Tel.: 089 - 34 02 99 50
Fax: 089 - 34 02 99 51

Baden-Württemberg
Dr. Suse Pfäffle
Immergrünweg 1
D - 70771 Leinfelden-
Echterdingen
Tel.: 0711 - 754 32 29
Fax: 0711 - 754 37 43

Köln
Gabriele Bierbaum
Bonner Landstraße 43
D - 50996 Köln
Tel.: 02236 - 3 12 38
Fax: 02236 - 3 12 38

Dortmund
Wilfried Utermann
Galerie Utermann
Betenstraße 12
D - 44137 Dortmund
Tel.: 0231 - 57 89 41
Fax: 0231 - 52 50 26

Norddeutschland
Dr. Rainer Horstmann
Hofweg 69
D - 22085 Hamburg
Tel.: 040 - 270 04 28
Fax: 040 - 22 18 42

Großbritannien
Vivien Reuter
5, The Keir
Westside Common
GB - London SW19 4UG
Tel.: 0044 - 181 - 944 18 58
Fax: 0044 - 181 - 879 08 62

Österreich
Andrea Temt
Landstraßer Hauptstraße 1/4
A - 1030 Wien
Tel.: 0043 - 1 - 715 23 32
Fax: 0043 - 1 - 714 14 54

Schweiz / Italien
Claudia Baronin von Schilling
Casa Serena
CH - 6922 Morcote-
Arbostora/Tessin
Tel.: 0041 - 91 - 996 31 04
Fax: 0041 - 91 - 996 31 05

Israel
Schmuel Kaufmann
P.O.B. 1514
IL - 47114 Ramat Hasharon
Tel.: 00972 - 3 - 549 28 87
Fax: 00972 - 3 - 549 74 62

Südamerika
Ursula Maiweg
Apartado 80072
YV - Caracas 1080 A
Venezuela
Tel.: 0058 - 2 - 962 11 59
Fax: 0058 - 2 - 962 11 59

USA / Kanada
Andrea Crane
120 East 56th Street, # 635
USA - New York, NY 10022
Tel.: 001 - 212 - 308 07 62
Fax: 001 - 212 - 308 06 55

Villa Grisebach Auktionen · Fasanenstraße 25 · D - 10719 Berlin · Tel 030 - 885 915-0 · Fax 030 - 885 41 45

Rehm, Georg, Provinostr 47, 86153 Augsburg.
T. (0821) 551001/02.   *091714*

Bad Bevensen (Niedersachsen)
Hille, Henning, Medinger Str 18, 29549 Bad Bevensen.
T. (05821) 2474, Fax 42474.   *091715*

Bad Breisig (Rheinland-Pfalz)
Pauken, E., Rheinalstr. 10, 53498 Bad Breisig. *091716*

Bad Mergentheim (Baden-Württemberg)
Partin & Co., Bahnhofpl 1, 97980 Bad Mergentheim.
T. (07931) 5920, Fax 592445.   *091717*

Bad Oeynhausen (Nordrhein-Westfalen)
Wolf, Cäcilia, Am Kurpark 5, 32545 Bad Oeynhausen.
T. (05731) 2460, Fax (05731) 246105.   *091718*

Bad Oldesloe (Schleswig-Holstein)
Hanseatisches Auktionshaus für Historica, Ratzeburger
Str 54, 23843 Bad Oldesloe. T. (04531) 81092,
Fax 82563.   *091719*

Bad Vilbel (Hessen)
Blank, Friedrich-Ebert-Str 2, 61118 Bad Vilbel.
T. (06101) 8211, Fax 12313.   *091720*

Baden-Baden (Baden-Württemberg)
Albrecht, Friedrich, & E. Koehler, Kreuzstr. 7, 76530 Ba-
den-Baden. T. (07221) 22110.   *091721*
Hanisch, Peter, Weinbergstr. 10, 76530 Baden-Baden.
T. (07221) 32655, 32666.   *091722*
Kolb, Erich, Lichtentaler Str. 56, 76530 Baden-Baden.
T. (07221) 38972, 25575, Fax (07221) 38982. *091723*

Bamberg (Bayern)
Lüffe, Friedrich-Wilhelm, Karolinenstr 24, 96049 Bam-
berg. T. (0951) 54489, (09544) 7796,
Fax 59439.   *091724*
Rammel, Gerhard, Geyerswörthpl. 2, 96047 Bamberg.
T. (0951) 55529, Fax (0951) 57539.   *091725*
Sebök, Untere Königstr. 21, 96052 Bamberg.
T. (0951) 202593, Fax (09519 200491.   *091726*

Bayreuth (Bayern)
Boltz, Waltraud, Brandenburger Str. 36, 95448 Bayreuth.
T. (0921) 20616.   *091727*
Hemmungen, Friedrichstr. 27, 95444 Bayreuth.
T. (0921) 65933.   *091728*
Rothenbücher, Peter, Schloßhof Birken, 95447 Bayreuth.
T. (0921) 61878, Fax (0921) 58911.   *091729*

Berlin
Altus, Kalckreuthstr 4-5, 10777 Berlin.
T. (030) 2181818, Fax 2187430.   *091730*
Bassenge, Gerda, Erdener Str 5a, 14193 Berlin.
T. (030) 8912909, Fax 8918025.   *091731*

Beier, Ulrich, Eldenaer Str. 36, 10247 Berlin. *091732*
Berliner Auktionshaus, Ringbahnstr. 36, 10711 Berlin.
T. (030) 752 60 12.   *091733*
Berliner Auktionshaus für Geschichte, Motzstr 22,
10777 Berlin. T. (030) 2119538, Fax 2110480. *091734*
Berliner Münzauktion, Chausseestr. 16, 10115 Berlin.
T. (030) 2829920, Fax 8030) 2829920.   *091735*
Bertram, Karin, Bundesallee 193, 10717 Berlin.
T. (030) 2135334, Fax (030) 2118572.   *091736*
Blome, Ulrike, Paderborner Str. 7f, 10709 Berlin.
T. (030) 891 52 02.   *091737*
Christie's, Fasanenstr 72, 10719 Berlin.
T. (030) 8856950, Fax 88569595.   *091738*
Dannenberg, Reiner, Wiesbadener Str. 82, 12161 Berlin.
T. (030) 821 69 79, Fax (030) 822 00 28. *091739*

Dietzel, Goethestr. 6, 10623 Berlin.
T. (030) 31 06 10.   *091740*
Dorau, Gernot, Beusselstr 65, 10553 Berlin.
T. (030) 3911488, Fax (030) 3922984.   *091741*
Hadersbeck, Wolfgang, Koppenstr. 47, 10243 Berlin.
T. (030) 436 15 07.   *091742*
Henzel, Gerd, Rinkartstr. 20, 12437 Berlin.
T. (030) 632 05 39.   *091743*
Hirts, Henry E., Sybelstr. 67, 10629 Berlin.
T. (030) 883 53 24.   *091744*
Jeschke, Meinke & Hauff, Habsburgerstr 14, 10781 Ber-
lin. T. (030) 2161584, Fax 2169594, 2170874. *091745*
Kraus + Silbernagel, Fritschestr. 77, 10585 Berlin.
T. (030) 341 12 32.   *091746*
Kunstkabinett, Kaiserdamm 32, 14057 Berlin.
T. (030) 301 66 13.   *091747*
Lach, Schönwalder Str. 35, 13347 Berlin.
T. (030) 336 40 07.   *091748*
Laurisch, Horst D., Wildenbruchpl. 7, 10115
Berlin.   *091749*
Lempertz, Am Kupfergraben 6, 10117 Berlin.
T. (030) 2084244.   *091750*
Neumeister, Meinekestr. 7, 10719 Berlin.
T. (030) 883 42 33, Fax (030) 883 57 82. *091751*
Plohmann, Horst, Wintersteinstr. 22, 10587 Berlin.
T. (030) 341 87 92.   *091752*
Prinz-Dunst, Karin, Schlüterstr. 16, 10625 Berlin.
T. (030) 3135965, Fax (030) 3137310.   *091753*
Prucha, Theodor, Rankestr 3, 10789 Berlin.
T. (030) 881 47 21, Fax 8814721.   *091754*
Schmidt, Wolfgang, Mehringdamm 117, 10965 Berlin.
T. (030) 6912357, Fax (030) 6941327.   *091755*
Schönberger & Co., Fuggerstr. 23, 10777 Berlin.
T. (030) 213 90 11.   *091756*
Schreyer, Chr., Manfred-von-Richthofen-Str. 19, 12101
Berlin. T. (030) 785 88 84.   *091757*
Schulze, Keithstr. 21, 10787 Berlin.
T. (030) 213 26 32.   *091758*
Schweppenhäuser, Johannes G.B., Düsseldorfer Str. 10,
10719 Berlin. T. (030) 883 47 43.   *091759*
Senger, Heinz, Bacharacher Str. 39, 12099 Berlin.
T. (030) 626 33 59, Fax (030) 625 77 30. *091760*
Sotheby's, Am Festungsgraben, Unter den Linden, Neue
Wache, 10117 Berlin.   *091761*
Spik, Leo, Kurfürstendamm 66, 10707 Berlin.
T. (030) 8836170, 8836179,
Fax (030) 8839734.   *091762*
Villa Grisebach Auktionen, Fasanenstr 25, 10719 Berlin.
T. (030) 8859150, Fax 8854145.   *091763*

Bernkastel-Kues (Rheinland-Pfalz)
Masuhr, Erhard, Römerstr. 39, 54470 Bernkastel-
Kues.   *091764*

Bielefeld (Nordrhein-Westfalen)
Granier, Jochen, Otto-Brenner-Str 186, 33604 Bielefeld.
T. (0521) 285005, Fax (0521) 285015.   *091765*
Schielmann, K., Beckhausstr. 105, 33611 Bielefeld.
T. (0521) 857 15.   *091766*
Winkel, Wolfgang, Hagenkamp 157, 33609 Bielefeld.
T. (0521) 332758, Fax 3369984.   *091767*

Billerbeck (Nordrhein-Westfalen)
Antik- und Auktionshaus, Holthauser Str 29, 48727 Billerbeck. T. (02543) 4086, Fax (02543) 4075. *091768*

Bobenheim (Rheinland-Pfalz)
Heissler, Willi F. G., Haardtweg 7, 67273 Bobenheim.
T. (06353) 65 18, 16 66.   *091769*

Bochum (Nordrhein-Westfalen)
Bochumer Auktionshaus, Nehringskamp 1, 44879 Bo-
chum. T. (0234) 494444, Fax (0234) 494426. *091770*
Descho, Brückstr. 55, 44787 Bochum.
T. (0234) 64774.   *091771*

Bönningstedt (Schleswig-Holstein)
Kuhlmann & Struck, Hasloher Weg 1a, 25474 Bönningstedt. T. (0411) 5566633.   *091772*

Bonn (Nordrhein-Westfalen)
Bödiger, August, Franziskanerstr 17-19, 53113 Bonn.
T. (0228) 604200, Fax 6042099.   *091773*

Christoph, Holger A., Goethestr. 15, 53113 Bonn.
T. (0228) 21 09 73.   *091774*
Zengen, Dietrich B. von, Friedrich-Breuer-Str. 105,
53225 Bonn. T. (0228) 46 19 55.   *091775*

Boppard (Rheinland-Pfalz)
Breitbach, Norbert, Rheinallee 62, 56154 Boppard.
T. (06742) 50 22, Fax 5022.   *091776*

Braunschweig (Niedersachsen)
Behrens, Rolf Friedrich, An der Trift 22a, 38124 Braun-
schweig. T. (0531) 61 21 42.   *091777*
Brandes, W., Wolfenbütteler Str 12, 38102 Braun-
schweig. T. (0531) 75003, Fax (0531) 75015. *091778*
Kranz, Kristina & Sohn, Rankestr. 5, 38102 Braun-
schweig. T. (0531) 33 57 30.   *091779*
Mühlenberg, Petritorwall 9, 38118 Braunschweig.
T. (0531) 400733, Fax 126303.   *091780*

Bremen
Auktionshaus Hansa, Friesenstr. 4-5, 28203 Bremen.
T. (0421) 73462.   *091781*
Auschwitz, W., Parkallee 105, 28209 Bremen.
T. (0421) 346 94 72.   *091782*
Biebl, Jürgen, Hermann-Böse-Str. 11a, 28209 Bremen.
T. (0421) 34 58 66.   *091783*
Bolland & Marotz, Fedelhören 19, 28203 Bremen.
T. (0421) 328282, Fax 328543.   *091784*
Ghodoussi, Ebrahim, Am Wall 190, 28195 Bremen.
T. (0421) 32 84 02.   *091785*
Roland, Admiralstr. 19, 28215 Bremen.
T. (0421) 32 82 86.   *091786*
Tröndle, R., Violenstr. 19, 28195 Bremen.
T. (0421) 32 70 34.   *091787*

Ziemann, Außer der Schleifmühle 40, 28203 Bremen.
T. (0421) 324432, Fax 323828. *091788*

Buchholz in der Nordheide (Niedersachsen)
Ziemer, L., Dibbeser Mühlenweg 85a, 21244 Buchholz in der Nordheide. T. (04181) 34166. *091789*

Büsingen (Baden-Württemberg)
Hochleitner, Josef F., Höhenstr 36, 78266 Büsingen.
T. (07734) 6778. *091790*

Cloppenburg (Niedersachsen)
Lorenz & Meyer, Dr, Löninger Str 15, 49661 Cloppenburg. T. (04471) 7800, 84411, Fax 6112. *091791*

Coburg (Bayern)
Happernagl, M., Am Rödlein 13, 96450 Coburg.
T. (09561) 604 72. *091792*

Darmstadt (Hessen)
Wendt, Heinz-D., Elisabethenstr. 46, 64283 Darmstadt.
T. (06151) 29 35 15. *091793*

Detmold (Nordrhein-Westfalen)
Pilling, Paulinenstr 7, 32756 Detmold. T. (05231) 21141, Fax 29827. *091794*

Dormagen (Nordrhein-Westfalen)
Weinel, Christel, Turmstr. 20, 41541 Dormagen.
T. (02133) 466 91, 47 07 86. *091795*

Dortmund (Nordrhein-Westfalen)
Auktionshaus am Krückenweg, Krückenweg 93, 44225 Dortmund. T. (0231) 71 64 06. *091796*
Bange, W., Karl-Funke-Str. 128, 44149 Dortmund.
T. (0231) 17 28 74. *091797*
Huste, Liebigstr. 46-48, 44139 Dortmund.
T. (0231) 12 26 38, Fax 12 94 95. *091798*

Dresden (Sachsen)
Dresdner Münzhandlung, Dr.-Külz-Ring 11, 01067 Dresden. T. (0351) 4952217. *091799*
Neumeister, Bautzner Landstr 7, 01324 Dresden.
T. (0351) 2640995, Fax 2640995. *091800*

Düren (Nordrhein-Westfalen)
Auktion & Galerie, Alte Jülicher Str. 232/234, 52353 Düren. T. (02421) 82116, 88 04 73. *091801*
Fornara, P.A., Kölnstr. 74, 52351 Düren.
T. (02421) 159 07. *091802*

Düsseldorf (Nordrhein-Westfalen)
Bach, Hans Jürgen, Königsallee 30, 40212 Düsseldorf.
T. (0211) 325832, Fax (0211) 6798736. *091803*
Christie's, Inselstr 15, 40479 Düsseldorf.
T. (0211) 4982986, Fax 4920339. *091804*
Düsseldorfer Auktionshaus, Sternstr. 14, 40479 Düsseldorf. T. (0211) 443422. *091805*
Felzmann, U., Bismarckstr. 96, 40210 Düsseldorf.
T. (0211) 353258. *091806*
Karbstein, Peter, Hohenzollernstr. 36, 40211 Düsseldorf.
T. (0211) 9061610, Fax (0211) 3613232. *091807*

Krauth, Th., Duisburger Str. 19, 40477 Düsseldorf.
T. (0211) 4982961/2, Fax (0211) 4981438. *091808*
Niedheidt, Klaus, Niederdonker Str. 34, 40547 Düsseldorf. T. (0211) 59 44 01. *091809*
Phillips, Duisburger Str. 19, 40477 Düsseldorf.
T. (0211) 4982961, Fax (0211) 4981438. *091810*
Valenta, Sigrid, Kaiser-Wilhelm-Ring 34, 40545 Düsseldorf. T. (0211) 57 04 32. *091811*

Duisburg (Nordrhein-Westfalen)
Pöersch, W., Ziegelhorststr. 113, 47169 Duisburg.
T. (0203) 59 06 33. *091812*
Ruhrorter Kunstauktionshaus, Hafenstr. 35, 47119 Duisburg. T. (0203) 855 55. *091813*

Durmersheim (Baden-Württemberg)
Kowalewski, V., Werderstr. 48a, 76448 Durmersheim.
T. (07245) 824 04. *091814*

Edingen-Neckarhausen (Baden-Württemberg)
Walter, W., Hundert Morgen 3, 68535 Edingen-Neckarhausen. T. (0621) 833 61. *091815*

Eislingen (Baden-Württemberg)
Belger, K.-R., Salacher Str 85, 73054 Eislingen.
T. (07161) 83339. *091816*

Ellwangen (Baden-Württemberg)
Eckart, Karl-Heinz, Höhenweg 2, 73479 Ellwangen.
T. (07961) 90450, Fax 904545. *091817*

Erlangen (Bayern)
Bergmann, Möhrendorfer Str 4, 91056 Erlangen.
T. (09131) 450666, Fax 450204. *091818*

Essen (Nordrhein-Westfalen)
Bertermann, W., Ulmenstr. 12, 45133 Essen.
T. (0201) 77 54 53. *091819*
Göhlmann, Heinrich, Kölner Str. 14, 45145 Essen.
T. (0201) 77 08 53. *091820*
Hänisch, Malmedystr. 36a, 45259 Essen.
T. (0201) 46 61 16. *091821*
Peinelt, Kennedyplatz 5, 45127 Essen.
T. (0201) 22 72 78. *091822*
Schenk-Behrens, Karla W., Moltkepl. 9, 45127 Essen.
T. (0201) 26 23 90. *091823*

Frankfurt am Main (Hessen)
Arnold, Bleichstr 42, 60313 Frankfurt am Main.
T. (069) 282779, Fax 2977929. *091825*
Auktionshaus Höchst, Hostatostr 3, 65929 Frankfurt am Main. T. (069) 303030, Fax (069) 319013. *091826*
Bel'Arte, Kaiserstr. 42, 60329 Frankfurt am Main.
T. (069) 23 77 29, Fax (069) 23 95 40. *091827*
Christie's, Arndtstr. 18, 60325 Frankfurt.
T. (069) 74 50 21, Fax 75 20 79. *091827a*
Döbritz, Wilhelm M., Braubachstr 10-12, 60311 Frankfurt am Main. T. (069) 721118, 287733. *091828*
Kegelmann, P. Michael, Saalgasse 3, 60311 Frankfurt am Main. T. (069) 288461, Fax 288462. *091829*
Peus, Busso, Dr., Bornwiesenweg 34, 60322 Frankfurt am Main. T. (069) 9596620, Fax 555995. *091830*
Sotheby's, Beethovenstr. 71, 60325 Frankfurt am Main.
T. (069) 74 07 87, Fax (069) 74 69 01. *091831*

Freiburg (Baden-Württemberg)
Peege, F., Dreikönigstr. 43, 79102 Freiburg.
T. (0761) 755 56. *091832*

Garbsen (Niedersachsen)
Auktionshaus Schloß Ricklingen, Schloß-Ricklinger-Str., 30826 Garbsen. T. (05131) 710 66. *091833*

Gescher (Nordrhein-Westfalen)
Glockenmuseum, Lindenstr 4, 48712 Gescher.
T. (02542) 1848, 7144, Fax (02542) 60123. *091834*

Glashütten (Hessen)
Auvermann & Reiss, Zum Talblick 2, 61479 Glashütten.
T. (06174) 6947, Fax (06174) 63612. *091835*

Grafenau (Baden-Württemberg)
Klöter, Peter, Schloß Dätzingen, 71117 Grafenau.
T. (07033) 43484, Fax 44619. *091836*

Grünwald (Bayern)
Phillips, Robert-Koch-Str 5, 82031 Grünwald.
T. (089) 6410338, Fax (089) 6410339. *091837*

Gütersloh (Nordrhein-Westfalen)
Jentsch, Detlef, Kahlertstr 2, 33330 Gütersloh.
T. (05241) 13168, Fax 13168. *091838*

Strothotte, B., Andreasweg 8, 33335 Gütersloh.
T. (05241) 784 83. *091839*

Hamburg
Bergstädt, Jens B., Lippeltstr. 1, 20097 Hamburg.
T. (040) 32 73 28. *091840*
Bernhard, M., Saselheider Str 68, 22159 Hamburg.
T. (040) 6444566, Fax 6444568. *091841*
Buchholz, K.-D., Brandstwiete 4, 20457 Hamburg.
T. (040) 33 50 91. *091842*
Christie's, Wentzelstr 21, 22301 Hamburg.
T. (040) 2794073, Fax 2704497. *091843*
Dechow, Wilhelm, Neuer Pferdemarkt 23, 20359 Hamburg. T. (040) 433016, Fax (040) 431430. *091844*
Dörling, F., Neuer Wall 40, 20354 Hamburg.
T. (040) 37496160, Fax 37496166. *091845*
Galerie Condor, Volksdorfer Damm 33, 22359 Hamburg.
T. (040) 6039816, Fax (040) 6036158. *091846*
Günnemann, Peter, Ehrenbergstr. 57, 22767 Hamburg.
T. (040) 3893995, Fax (040) 384089. *091847*
Haus Wandsbek, Wandsbeker Allee 15-19, 22041 Hamburg. T. (040) 6587780. *091848*

AUKTIONSHAUS ARNOLD

Inh. K. H. Arnold

KUNSTAUKTIONEN
SCHMUCKAUKTIONEN
Frankfurt am Main

Vereidigte und öffentlich bestellte
Auktionatoren

Bleichstraße 42, 60313 Frankfurt am Main
Telefon (0 69) 28 27 79 und 28 31 39
Fax (0 69) 2 97 79 29

50 Jahre

Hauswedell & Nolte, Pöseldorfer Weg 1, 20148 Hamburg. T. (040) 4132100, Fax 41321010. *091849*

Heuser & Grethe, Dr., Hohe Bleichen 14-16, 20354 Hamburg. T. (040) 354649, Fax 352668. *091850*

Kendzia, Klaus D., Hofweg 52, 22085 Hamburg. T. (040) 229 97 67. *091851*

Landjunk, Arthur, Bogenstr. 45, 20144 Hamburg. T. (040) 44 70 07. *091852*

F. DÖRLING

Auctioneers in Hamburg

RARE BOOKS

OLD MASTERS
MODERN ART

Auctions in
May and November
– catalogues on request –

We always accept consignments for
our specialized auctions.

NEUER WALL 40 · 20354 HAMBURG
TEL(+49-40) 374961-0 · FAX -66

Hauswedell & Nolte

Buch- und Kunstantiquariat
Buch- und Kunstauktionen

20148 Hamburg, Pöseldorfer Weg 1
Tel. (0 40) 41 32 10-0
Telefax (0 40) 41 32 10-10

New York branch office:
225 Central Park West
New York, N.Y. 10024, USA
Tel. (2 12) 5 95-08 06
Fax (2 12) 5 95-08 32

Lempertz, Mathias, Parkberg 24, 22397 Hamburg. T. (040) 607 27 72. *091853*

Meyer, Walter H. F., Woltmanstr. 27-29, 20097 Hamburg. T. (040) 23 17 91/92. *091854*

Nattenheimer, Herbert, Bei St. Johannis 10, 20148 Hamburg. T. (040) 45 05 12. *091855*

Neumeister, Monetastr 6, 20144 Hamburg. T. (040) 446584, Fax 446598. *091856*

Scheil, P., Gertigstr. 4a, 22303 Hamburg. T. (040) 272126. *091857*

Schlüter, Carl F., Alsterufer 12, 20354 Hamburg. T. (040) 410 10 49/40. *091858*

Schopmann, Wandsbeker Allee 15-19, 22041 Hamburg. T. (040) 65877821, Fax 65877828. *091859*

Schopmann & Sohn, Speersort 1, 20095 Hamburg. T. (040) 3232390, Fax 3232398. *091860*

Stahl, Hans, Hohe Bleichen 28, 20354 Hamburg. T. (040) 342325, Fax 3480432. *091861*

Tietjen & Co., Spitalerstr 30, 20095 Hamburg. T. (040) 330368, Fax 323035. *091862*

Wacker, Karl, Volksdorfer Damm 33, 22359 Hamburg. T. (040) 603 03 23, Fax (040) 603 61 58. *091863*

Hannover (Niedersachsen)

Brenske, Helmut, Machandelweg 11, 30419 Hannover. T. (0511) 633667, Fax 633667. *091864*

Erdmann, Am Kröpcke, 30159 Hannover. T. (0511) 32 03 03. *091865*

Fellechner, T. H., Gifhorner Str. 14, 30625 Hannover. T. (0511) 57 58 14. *091866*

Rödiger, Ernst-August, Schellingstr. 1, 30625 Hannover. T. (0511) 556870, Fax (0511) 556877. *091867*

Weigelt, Jörg, Oskar-Winter-Str. 3, 30161 Hannover. T. (0511) 628375, 628376, Fax (0511) 628377. *091868*

Haßloch (Rheinland-Pfalz)

Stahler, Arno, Langgasse 61, 67454 Haßloch. T. (06324) 1531. *091869*

Heidelberg (Baden-Württemberg)

AH Auktionen in Heidelberg, Rischerstr. 3, 69123 Heidelberg. T. (06221) 84 08 40,
Fax (06221) 83 13 35. *091870*

---

since 1823

SCHOPMANN

The most traditional and oldest auctioning company in Germany

Art • Furniture • Jewellery
Silver • Porcelain • Paintings
Oriental • Carpets
Properties and Estimates
Auctions and
continual sales

NEW ADDRESS

Speersort 1, Pressehaus
D-20095 Hamburg
Tel.: +49.40.3232 39-0 (Fax:-8)

W.C.H. Schopmann & Sohn, Prop.: Ralf-Matthias Kuball

Bücherwurm, Heiliggeiststr. 5, 69117 Heidelberg.
T. (06221) 122 02. 091871

Eid, Sengle & Kraus, Bergheimer Str. 101a, 69115 Heidelberg. T. (06221) 227 84. 091872

Hörrle, Oskar, Kaiserstr. 70, 69115 Heidelberg.
T. (06221) 209 14. 091873

Lux, Michael, Akademiestr 1, 69117 Heidelberg.
T. (06221) 23851. 091874

Metz, Friedrich-Ebert-Anlage 5, 69117 Heidelberg.
T. (06221) 23571, Fax 183231. 091875

Winterberg, Arno, Hildastr 12, 69115 Heidelberg.
T. (06221) 22631, Fax 164631. 091876

Heidenheim an der Brenz (Baden-Württemberg)

Neils, Elfriede/Tatjana, Leonhardstr 39, 89518 Heidenheim an der Brenz. T. (07321) 44614. 091877

Heilbronn (Baden-Württemberg)

Heilbronner Kunst- und Auktionshaus, Trappensee, 74074 Heilbronn. T. (07131) 173064,
Fax (07131) 177428. 091878

Krieg, Alfred, Brahmsstr 14, 74078 Heilbronn.
T. (07131) 7021. 091879

Hiddenhausen (Nordrhein-Westfalen)

Onken, Peter, Ziegelstr. 177, 32120 Hiddenhausen.
T. (05221) 32069. 091880

Hilden (Nordrhein-Westfalen)

Hildener Auktionshaus und Galerie, Klusenhof 12, 40723 Hilden. T. (02103) 602 00. 091881

Hof (Bayern)

Lankes, Heinz-Dieter, Klosterstr 22, 95028 Hof.
T. (09281) 18200. 091882

Ingelheim (Rheinland-Pfalz)

Leimer, Hochstr 44, 55218 Ingelheim. T. (06132) 8094, Fax (06132) 86563. 091883

Itzehoe (Schleswig-Holstein)

Reimers, H., Nordschleswiger Str. 15, 25524
Itzehoe. 091884

Kaarst (Nordrhein-Westfalen)

Tschöpe, Reinhild, Bruchweg 8, 41564 Kaarst.
T. (021 01) 60 27 56. 091885

Karlsruhe (Baden-Württemberg)

Auctions Contor, Hirschstr. 164, 76137 Karlsruhe.
T. (0721) 81 39 93. 091886

Früh, A., Scheffelstr. 66, 76135 Karlsruhe.
T. (0721) 84 36 39. 091887

Saheli, A., Winterstr. 24a, 76137 Karlsruhe.
T. (0721) 38 75 72. 091888

Terminus, Zähringer Str. 47, 76133 Karlsruhe.
T. (0721) 37 58 36. 091889

Kiel (Schleswig-Holstein)

Auktionshaus Alte Lübecker, Alte Lübecker Chaussee 26, 24113 Kiel. T. (0431) 687574,
Fax (0431) 687596. 091890

Köln (Nordrhein-Westfalen)

Auction Team Köln, Bonner Str 528-530, 50968 Köln.
T. (0221) 387049, Fax 374878. 091891

Auktionshaus Süd, Gladbacher Str. 32, 50672 Köln.
T. (0221) 51 40 40. 091892

Cornwall, Heckhofweg 146, 50739 Köln.
T. (0221) 176011, Fax (0221) 173253. 091893

Devroede-Missinne, Zeughausstr 14-22, 50667 Köln.
T. (0221) 131417, 134702. 091894

Franke, A., Blaubach 30a, 50676 Köln. 091895

Gordon, J., Zeughausstr. 10, 50667 Köln.
T. (0221) 12 46 06, Fax (0221) 13 84 65. 091896

Gutkäss, J., Christinastr. 31, 50733 Köln.
T. 73 64 74 (739 26 64). 091897

Herr, W.G., Friesenwall 35, 50672 Köln.
T. (0221) 254548, Fax 254548. 091898

Hilgers, H., Niehler Kirchweg 155, 50735 Köln.
T. (0221) 74 43 21. 091899

Hüll, Dr., Berrenrather Str 138, 50937 Köln.
T. (0221) 444026. 091900

Klefisch, Ubierring 35, 50678 Köln. T. (0221) 32 17 40,
Fax (0221) 32 52 17. 091901

Knopek, Hans Jürgen, Alter Markt 55, 50667 Köln.
T. (0221) 253600. 091902

Kölner Münzkabinett, Neven-du-Mont-Str. 15, 50667
Köln. T. (0221) 2574238, 211438,
Fax (0221) 254175. 091903

Kunsthaus am Museum, Drususgasse 1-5, 50667 Köln.
T. (0221) 9258620, Fax (0221) 92586230. 091904

Lempertz, Neumarkt 3, 50667 Köln. T. (0221) 9257290,
Fax 9257296. 091905

Ling, D., Bachemer Str. 143, 50931 Köln.
T. (0221) 40 39 77. 091906

Schenkel, W., Karl-Marx-Allee 15, 50769 Köln.
T. (0221) 70 51 63. 091907

Schmitz, K., Wendelinusstr. 46, 50933 Köln.
T. (0221) 49 17 21. 091908

Schmitz, K.H., Auf dem Hügel 19, 50933 Köln.
T. (0221) 49 39 13. 091909

Sotheby's, St.-Apern-Str. 21, 50667 Köln.
T. (0221) 257 49 56, Fax (0221) 21 77 59. 091910

Venator & Hanstein, Cäcilienstr 48, 50667 Köln.
T. (0221) 2575419, Fax 2575526. 091911

Konstanz (Baden-Württemberg)

Karrenbauer, Obere Laube 46, 78462 Konstanz.
T. (07531) 27202, Fax 16596. 091912

Krefeld (Nordrhein-Westfalen)

Warth, Willy von der, Burgstr. 21a, 47829 Krefeld.
T. (02151) 44 19 0. 091913

Kürnbach (Baden-Württemberg)

Frank, T.H., Deutschherrenhaus, 75057 Kürnbach.
T. (07258) 12 30. 091914

REPRÄSENTANZEN

BRÜSSEL
34, rue aux Laines
B-1000 Bruxelles
Tel. 02/514 05 86 · Fax 511 48 24

HAMBURG
Heimhuder Straße 81
D-20148 Hamburg
Tel. 040/45 03 61 52 · Fax 45 03 61 53

BERLIN
Am Kupfergraben 6
D-10117 Berlin
Tel. u. Fax 030/208 42 44
(Mi 14.30-17.30)

DRESDEN
Hubertusstr. 46b
D-01129 Dresden
Tel. 0351/858 08 05

MÜNCHEN
Rümelinstr. 12
D-81925 München
Tel. 089/98 52 01 · Fax 982 71 66

NEW YORK
181 East 73rd Street,
NewYork, N.Y. 10021
Tel. u. Fax 001/212/861 44 13

TOKYO
Toshi-international
Nichieiakebonobashi Bldg. 3F
1-18 Sumiyoshi-cho, Shinjuku-ku
J-162 Tokyo · Tel. 0081/3/33 52 37 97
Fax 0081/3/33 52 38 29

BUENOS AIRES
San Martin 793 · Piso 20
1004 Buenos Aires
Tel. 541/313/66 18 95 06
Fax 541/312/52 53

LEMPERTZ
gegründet 1845

KUNSTHAUS LEMPERTZ
NEUMARKT 3 · 50667 KÖLN
TEL. 0049/221 / 92 57 29-0
FAX 92 57 29 6

Landau (Rheinland-Pfalz)
Hammel, H., Ostring 1a, 76829 Landau.
T. (06341) 89756. 091915

Leinfelden-Echterdingen (Baden-Württemberg)
Uebersalz, H., Bussardweg 9, 70771 Leinfelden-Echterdingen. T. (0711) 75 66 92. 091916

Leipzig (Sachsen)
Galerie am Sachsenplatz, Katharinenstr. 11/I, 04109 Leipzig. T. (0341) 29 22 31. 091917
Höhn, Heidrun, Brühl 52, 04109 Leipzig.
T. (0341) 9602386, 9613464, Fax 2117245. 091918
Numismatik & Auktionen, Nikolaistr. 47, 04109 Leipzig.
T. (0341) 20 08 31. 091919
Sächsisches Auktionshaus und Antiquariat, Sebastian-Bach-Str 28, 04109 Leipzig. T. (0341) 9832015,
Fax 470680. 091920

Stuttgarter Kunstauktionshaus Dr. Fritz Nagel, Eilenburger Str 39-39a, 04317 Leipzig. T. (0341) 2615161,
Fax 2615162. 091921

Lindau, Bodensee (Bayern)
Zeller, Michael, Bindergasse 7, 88131 Lindau, Bodensee. T. (08382) 93020, Fax 26535. 091922

Lindenthal (Sachsen)
Lindenthal, Bahnhofstr 47, 04466 Lindenthal.
T. (0341) 4614666, Fax (0341) 4612660. 091923

Lippstadt (Nordrhein-Westfalen)
Menke, K., Traberweg 7, 59557 Lippstadt.
T. (02941) 121 34. 091924

Ludwigsburg (Baden-Württemberg)
Reimann & Monatsberger, Palais Graevenitz, Marstallstr. 5, 71634 Ludwigsburg. T. (07141) 90955,
Fax (07141) 901071. 091925
Reimann & Monatsberger, Marstallstr. 5, 71634 Ludwigsburg. T. (07141) 90955, Fax 901071. 091926
Waldner, Erich R., Robert-Mayer-Str. 9, 71636 Ludwigsburg. T. (07141) 87 03 98. 091927

Lüneburg (Niedersachsen)
Brüns, A., Soltauer Str. 71, 21335 Lüneburg.
T. (04131) 442 00. 091928
Lindberg, H.-H., Reiherstieg 21, 21337 Lüneburg.
T. (04131) 438 53. 091929

Mainz (Rheinland-Pfalz)
Nürnberger, J. A., Am Sportfeld 42, 55124 Mainz.
T. (06131) 427 62. 091930
Wenz, R., Am Rathaus 8, 55116 Mainz.
T. (06131) 22 77 94, Fax (06131) 22 89 08. 091931

Malsch (Baden-Württemberg)
Maier, H., Birkenweg 20, 69254 Malsch.
T. (07253) 21 69. 091932

Meerbusch (Nordrhein-Westfalen)
Meerbuscher Kunstauktionshaus, Kanzlei 3, 40667
Meerbusch. T. (02132) 5711, Fax 5337. 091933

MEERBUSCHER KUNST AUKTIONSHAUS
ROSTHAL

Kanzlei 3 · 40667 Meerbusch
Ruf (021 32) 5711 · Fax (021 32) 5337

ALTE und NEUERE KUNST
MODERNE und ZEITGENÖSSISCHE KUNST
MOBILIAR, TEPPICHE, VARIA

Mettmann (Nordrhein-Westfalen)
Rasel, Walter, Ekkehardstr. 16, 40822 Mettmann.
T. (02104) 746 93. 091934

Monsheim (Rheinland-Pfalz)
Lösch, Erich, Postfach 44, 67590 Monsheim.
T. (06243) 8144, Fax (06243) 5934. 091935

Mülheim an der Ruhr (Nordrhein-Westfalen)
Löhr, G., Buggenbeck 32, 45470 Mülheim an der Ruhr.
T. (0208) 32772. 091936

München (Bayern)
Arco & Flotow, Briennerstr 10/V, 80333 München.
T. (089) 284089, Fax (089) 285696. 091937
Athena Galerie, Ottostr 5, 80333 München.
T. (089) 591147, Fax 598220. 091938
Auktionshaus Maximilians, Viktualienmarkt 6, 80331
München. T. (089) 260 54 40, 260 58 88,
Fax (089) 26 78 79. 091939

Brockmann, G., Guntherstr. 15, 80639 München.
T. (089) 17 70 80. 091940
Christie's, Residenzstr 27, Preysing Palais, 80333 München. T. (089) 229539, Fax 296302. 091941
Ehrlich & Langwieser, Landwehrstr. 39a, 80336 München. T. (089) 59 25 30. 091942
Giessener Münzhandlung, Maximilianspl 20, 80333
München. T. (089) 226876, Fax 2285513. 091943

GIESSENER
MÜNZHANDLUNG
Dieter Gorny GmbH
80333 München
Maximiliansplatz 20

Münzen
Medaillen
mehrere
Auktionen
jährlich

Tel.: 0 89 – 22 68 76
Fax: 0 89 – 22 85 55 13

Hampel, Holger J., Prinzregentenstr 68, 81675 München. T. (089) 473067, Fax 479899. 091944
Hartung & Hartung, Karolinenpl 5a, 80333 München.
T. (089) 284034, Fax (089) 285569. 091945
Hermann, Sandstr 33, 80335 München.
T. (089) 5237296, Fax (089) 5237103. 091946
Hoyer, H., Hohenaschauer Str. 10, 81669 München.
T. (089) 68 44 68. 091947
Kaiser, Kurt, Nymphenburger Str. 115, 80636 München.
T. (089) 129 29 66, 129 74 75. 091948
Karl & Faber, Amirapl 3, 80333 München.
T. (089) 221865/66, Fax 2283350. 091949
Ketterer, Wolfgang, Brienner Str 25, 80333 München.
T. (089) 552440, Fax (089) 55244166. 091950
Kube, Jan K., Thomas-Wimmer-Ring 17, 80539 München. T. (089) 296659. 091951
Lanz, Hubert, Dr., Maximiliansplatz 10, 80331 München.
T. (089) 299070, Fax (089) 220762. 091952
Müller, Josef, Daiserstr. 24, 81371 München.
T. (089) 721 16 11. 091953
Münchner Spielzeugauktion, Guntherstr. 15, 80639
München. T. (089) 17 70 80, Fax 178 38 13. 091954
Neumeister, Barer Str 37, 80799 München.
T. (089) 2317100, Fax 23171055. 091955
Nusser, Ursula, Nordendstr. 46-48, 80801 München.
T. (089) 272 21 50, Fax 271 88 29. 091956

NEUMEISTER
Alte und Neue Kunst

Annahme und Schätzung
für unsere Auktionen
in München
jederzeit

Repräsentanzen
Berlin
Dresden
Hamburg
Wien
Zürich

Barer Str. 37 · 80799 München
Tel. (0 89) 23 17 10-0 · Fax 23 17 10-55

HARTUNG & HARTUNG

Antiquariat · Auktionen

D-80333 MÜNCHEN · KAROLINENPLATZ 5 A
Telefon (0 89) 28 40 34 · Telegramme: »Buchauktion München«

Wertvolle alte Bücher

Illuminierte Handschriften
Inkunabeln – Holzschnittbücher
Kupferstichwerke – Schöne Einbände
Alte kolorierte Atlanten und Tafelwerke
Alte Medizin und Naturwissenschaften
Deutsche Literatur in Erstausgaben – Autographen
Illustrierte Bücher des 18.–20. Jahrhunderts

Graphik · Städteansichten · Landkarten

AUKTIONEN
jeweils im Mai und November
Anmeldung von Beiträgen, möglichst unter vorheriger Einsendung von
Listen, jederzeit erbeten. Besichtigung größerer Objekte an Ort und Stelle.
Reich illustrierte Kataloge auf Anforderung gegen Unkostenbeitrag erhältlich.
Unverbindliche Beratung.

Prandtl, Michael, Neusser Str 21, 80807 München.
   T. (089) 36101462, Fax 364710.　　　*091957*
Queens Auktionshaus, Landsberger Str 146, 80339
   München. T. (089) 5021313, Fax 501916.　*091958*
Reibnitz, S. Baron von, Dachauer Str 7a, 80335 Mün-
   chen. T. (089) 598783, Fax 553988.　　*091959*

Ruef, Hugo, Gabelsbergerstr 28, 80333 München.
   T. (089) 524084, Fax 5236936.　　　*091960*
Schöninger & Co., Ottostr 10, 80333 München.
   T. (089) 596872, Fax 5503616.　　　*091961*
Sotheby's, Odeonspl. 16, 80539 München.
   T. (089) 2913151, Fax 299271.　　　*091962*

AUKTIONSHAUS MICHAEL PRANDTL

Für unsere regelmäßig stattfindenden
Versteigerungen nehmen wir Ihre
Einlieferungen immer gerne entgegen.

Neusser Straße 21, 80807 München
Tel. (089) 36 10 14 62, Fax 36 47 10

Sprink, Hans U., Dachauer Str 14, 80335 München.
   T. (089) 598908.　　　　　　　*091963*
Villa Grisebach Auktionen, Prannerstr 13, 80333 Mün-
   chen. T. (089) 227632, Fax 223761.　　*091964*
Zaun, Willy, Geiselgasteigstr. 30, 81545 München.
   T. (089) 64 77 84.　　　　　　*091965*
Zisska & R. Kistner, F., Unterer Anger 15, 80331 Mün-
   chen. T. (089) 263855, Fax 269088.　　*091966*

Münster (Nordrhein-Westfalen)
Münstersches Kunst- und Auktionshaus, Buddenstr. 27,
   48143 Münster. T. (0251) 51356, Fax 294478. *091967*

Mutterstadt (Rheinland-Pfalz)
Henry's Auktionshaus, An der Fohlenweide 12-14,
   67112 Mutterstadt. T. (06234) 80110,
   Fax 801150.　　　　　　　　*091968*

Nahrendorf (Niedersachsen)
Schmidt, O., Oldendorf, 21369 Nahrendorf.
   T. (05855) 219.　　　　　　　*091969*

Natendorf (Niedersachsen)
Kleingärtner, Lothar, Golster Str 10, 29587 Natendorf.
   T. (0581) 15996, Fax 78583.　　　*091970*

Kunstauktionen

HUGO RUEF

seit 1844

Alte und Moderne Kunst

**Gemälde · Skulpturen · Möbel
Kunstgewerbe · Volkskunst
Teppiche · Ostasiatica
Schmuck**

Gabelsbergerstr. 28
80333 München
Telefon (0 89) 52 40 84
Telefax (0 89) 523 6936

Karl & Faber

AUKTIONEN in MÜNCHEN

ALTE MEISTER MODERNE KUNST GEMÄLDE HANDZEICHNUNGEN GRAPHIK

Karl & Faber · Amiraplatz 3 · 80333 München · Telefon 0 89-22 18 65/66 · Fax 0 89-2 28 33 50

Neuburg (Bayern)
Schorer, Walter, Gustav-Philipp-Str. 26, 86633 Neuburg.
T. (08431) 72 86. *091971*

Neuenstein, Hessen
Antikhof Neuenstein, Domäne, 36286 Neuenstein, Hessen. T. (06677) 1212, 472, Fax 633. *091972*

Neuss (Nordrhein-Westfalen)
Neusser Auktionshaus, Weingartstr. 37, 41464 Neuss.
T. (02131) 453 29. *091973*

Neustadt an der Weinstraße (Rheinland-Pfalz)
Denzinger, Herbert, Hauptstr 63, 67433 Neustadt an der Weinstraße. *091974*

Nürnberg (Bayern)
Bamberger, Peter, Karolinenstr. 6, 90402 Nürnberg.
T. (0911) 22 21 20, Fax 20 85 74. *091975*
Germanisches Nationalmuseum, Kartäusergasse 1, 90402 Nürnberg. T. (0911) 13310,
Fax (0911) 1331200. *091976*
König, Bucher Str 17, 90419 Nürnberg.
T. (0911) 338182, Fax (0911) 337960. *091977*
Kracheel, Klaus, Obere Wörthstr. 7, 90403 Nürnberg.
T. (0911) 22 38 08, 20 87 31, Fax 22 38 08. *091978*
Nowak, Bruno, Karolinenstr. 14, 90402 Nürnberg.
T. (0911) 20 81 49. *091979*
Schulz, G., Jauerstr. 21, 90473 Nürnberg.
T. (0911) 80 54 40. *091980*
Weidler, Albrecht-Dürer-Platz 8, 90403 Nürnberg.
T. (0911) 22 25 25/45, Fax 24 38 51. *091981*

Nürtingen (Baden-Württemberg)
Kersten, Hellmut, Forststr. 13, 72622 Nürtingen.
T. (07022) 82 95. *091982*
Stark, A., Grünewaldstr. 26, 72622 Nürtingen.
T. (07022) 46092. *091983*
Thies, Andreas, Kirchstr. 28, 72622 Nürtingen.
T. (07022) 359 59. *091984*

Offenbach (Hessen)
Mars + Merkur, Parkstr. 37, 63067 Offenbach. *091985*

Oldenburg, Oldenburg (Schleswig-Holstein)
Kaluza, Peter, Alexanderstr 13, 26121 Oldenburg, Oldenburg. T. (0441) 82870, Fax 86500. *091986*

Osnabrück (Niedersachsen)
Wenner, H.Th., Heger Str 2-3, 49074 Osnabrück.
T. (0541) 3310366, Fax (0541) 201113. *091987*

Pforzheim (Baden-Württemberg)
Bode, Michael, Wilhelmshöhe 2, 75173 Pforzheim.
T. (07231) 24347. *091988*
Kiefer, Peter, Kaiser-Friedrich-Str. 10, 75172 Pforzheim.
T. (07231) 92320, Fax 923216. *091989*
Müller, Klaus Emanuel, Würmtalstr 11b, 75181 Pforzheim. T. (07231) 69343, 680485, Fax 67166. *091990*

Pinneberg (Schleswig-Holstein)
Heidorn, C., Haidloh 24, 25421 Pinneberg.
T. (04101) 729 63. *091991*

Radolfzell (Baden-Württemberg)
Geble, Schützenstr. 15, 78315 Radolfzell.
T. (07732) 3175, Fax 6833. *091992*

Recklinghausen (Nordrhein-Westfalen)
Pfeil, W.P. Graf von, Beisinger Weg 2a, 45657 Recklinghausen. T. (02361) 234 74. *091993*

Regensburg (Bayern)
Schmidt, Stefan, Schwandorfer Str. 30, 93059 Regensburg. T. (0941) 89 77 78. *091994*

Rendsburg (Schleswig-Holstein)
Schaar, G., Nobiskrüger Allee 27, 24768 Rendsburg.
T. (04331) 277 41. *091995*

Reutlingen (Baden-Württemberg)
Galerie unter den Linden, Bahnhofstr. 30, 72764 Reutlingen. T. (07121) 408 76. *091996*
Heck, Thomas, Kaiserstr 64, 72764 Reutlingen.
T. (07121) 370911, Fax 87408. *091997*

Rosenheim (Bayern)
Hetzel & Klinger, Schießstattstr. 1a, 83024 Rosenheim.
T. (08031) 338 88, Fax 32988. *091998*

Rudolstadt (Thüringen)
Wendl, Martin, August-Bebel-Str 4, 07407 Rudolstadt.
T. (03672) 424350, Fax 412296. *091999*

KUNST-AUKTIONSHAUS – Antiquitäten-Stube

Martin Wendl
August-Bebel-Str. 4,
07407 Rudolstadt (Thüringen):
Tel.-Vorwahl 0 36 72
Tel.: 42 43 50, Fax: 41 22 96

Rüsselsheim (Hessen)
Friedrichs, Heinz A., Danziger Str. 24, 65428 Rüsselsheim. T. (06142) 422 85. *092000*

Saarbrücken (Saarland)
Perc-Peretz, M., Dudweilerstr. 9, 66111 Saarbrücken.
T. (0681) 356 97. *092001*

Saarburg (Saarland)
Beissel, W., Hubertusstr 79, 54439 Saarburg.
T. (06581) 99258, Fax 95110. *092002*

Saarlouis (Saarland)
Schirra, Provinzialstr 244, 66740 Saarlouis.
T. (06831) 49449, Fax 41524. *092003*

Sande (Niedersachsen)
Wolff, Wilfried, Sanderahmer Str. 33a, 26452 Sande.
T. (04422) 40 00, Fax 40 00. *092004*

Schwetzingen (Baden-Württemberg)
Bölts, S., Scheffelstr. 79, 68723 Schwetzingen.
T. (06202) 241 59. *092005*

Seeheim-Jugenheim (Hessen)
Poorhosaini, Hauptstr 48, 64342 Seeheim-Jugenheim.
T. (06257) 7809. *092006*

Singen (Baden-Württemberg)
Lenz, Heinrich, Thurgauer Str 1, 78224 Singen. *092007*

Solingen (Nordrhein-Westfalen)
Solinger Auktionshaus, Merscheider Str 316, 42699 Solingen. T. (0212) 331124, Fax (0212) 333131. *092008*

Stuttgart (Baden-Württemberg)
Dietrich, Walter, Alte Weinsteige 113, 70597 Stuttgart.
T. (0711) 76 28 45. *092009*
Feil, I., Auf dem Haigst 11, 70597 Stuttgart.
T. (0711) 64 37 18. *092010*
Kötter, Johannes, & Sohn, Erbsenbrunnengasse 9-11, 70372 Stuttgart. T. (0711) 56 32 62. *092011*
Rieber, Bernd, Rotebühlstr 108-110, 70197 Stuttgart.
T. (0711) 618633, Fax 610353. *092012*
Stuttgarter Kunstauktionshaus Dr. Fritz Nagel, Adlerstr 31-33, 70199 Stuttgart. T. (0711) 649690,
Fax 6496969. *092013*

Sugenheim (Bayern)
Kube, Jan K., Altes Schloss, 91484 Sugenheim.
T. (09165) 650, Fax 1292. *092014*

Tübingen (Baden-Württemberg)
Heck, Thomas, Hafengasse 10, 72070 Tübingen.
T. (07071) 26306, Fax 87408. *092015*

Überlingen (Baden-Württemberg)
Zadick, Lion B., Nußdorfer Str 39, 88662 Überlingen.
T. (07551) 7447, Fax (07551) 7447. *092016*

Viersen (Nordrhein-Westfalen)
Viersener Auktionshaus, Oberstr. 2, 41749 Viersen.
T. (02162) 80864, 77059, Fax 81385. *092017*

Villmar (Hessen)
Müller, Karlheinz, Lahnstr. 14, 65606 Villmar.
T. (06474) 8038, Fax 1337. *092018*

Walldorf (Baden-Württemberg)
Berlinghof, Heinrich-Hertz-Str. 7, 69190 Walldorf.
T. (06227) 4043, Fax 63642. *092019*

Weinheim (Baden-Württemberg)
Richter, Rolf, Karlsruher Str 2-8, 69469 Weinheim.
T. (06201) 15997. *092020*
Weinheimer Auktionshaus, Karlsruher Str 2-8, 69469 Weinheim. T. (06201) 15997. *092021*

Wiesbaden (Hessen)
Jäger, Julius, Luisenstr. 6, 65185 Wiesbaden.
T. (0611) 30 41 02, Fax 308 11 52. *092022*
Kunz, Taunusstr. 24, 65183 Wiesbaden.
T. (0611) 518 09. *092023*
Rippon Boswell & Co., Friedrichstr 45, 65185 Wiesbaden. T. (0611) 372062, Fax 307369. *092024*

Wietze (Niedersachsen)
Auktionshaus Villa Steinförde, Steinförderstr. 126, 29323 Wietze. T. (05146) 14 44. *092025*

Wilnsdorf (Nordrhein-Westfalen)
Faak, Claus-Dieter, Postfach 1219, 57226 Wilnsdorf. *092026*

Wolfenbüttel
Freunde Historischer Wertpapiere, Am Hogrevenkamp 4, 38302 Wolfenbüttel. T. (05331) 72890,
Fax 31575. *092027*

Würzburg (Bayern)
Kunst- und Auktionshaus, Hörleingasse 3-5, 97070 Würzburg. T. (0931) 17736. *092028*
Mars, Roland, Ludwigstr. 4, 97070 Würzburg.
T. (0931) 55688, Fax 57554. *092029*

Zwingenberg (Hessen)
Marmulla, Brunhilde, Annastr. 60, 64673 Zwingenberg.
T. (06251) 775 41. *092030*

Hong Kong

Hong Kong
Hong Kong Auctioneers, Arts Department, 36 Queen's Rd., Room 205, Central, Hong Kong. T. 5-229446, 5-229430. *092031*
Sotheby, 901-5 Queen's Rd. Central, Hong Kong. T. 524-8121. *092032*

Iceland

Reykjavik
H. S. B. Art Auctions, Ltd., Hafnarstraeti 11, P. O. Box 154, Reykjavik. T. (91) 1 48 24. *092033*

Ireland

Blackrock (Co. Dublin)
Hazley Godsil, 4 Main St, Blackrock.
T. (01) 88 50 22. *092034*

Dublin
Adam, James, 26 Saint Stephen's Green North, Dublin 2. T. (01) 76 02 61, 76 48 91, Fax 68 01 01. *092035*
Allen & Townsend, 10 Saint Stephen's Green, Dublin 2.
T. (01) 71 00 33, Fax 71 08 25. *092036*
Balfe, 4 Lower Ormond Quay, Dublin 1.
T. (01) 72 74 01. *092037*
Christie's, 52 Waterloo Rd, Dublin 4.
T. (01) 68 05 85. *092038*
Duffy, John, & Sons, 10 Parnell St, Dublin 1.
T. (01) 72 89 28. *092039*
Herman & Wilkinson, 161 Lower Rathmines Rd, Dublin 6. T. (01) 97 22 45, 97 23 41. *092040*

O'Reilly, 1-2 Upper Exchange St, Dublin 8.
T. (01) 77 20 27. *092041*
Sotheby's, 51 Dawson St, Dublin 2.
T. (01) 71 17 86. *092042*
Taylor DeVere, 15 Molesworth St, Dublin 2.
T. (01) 679 7433. *092043*
Tormey Bros., 27 Lower Ormond Quay, Dublin 1.
T. (01) 72 67 81. *092044*

Dun Laoghaire (Co. Dublin)
Buckley, 27-28 Sandycove Rd, Dun Laoghaire.
T. (01) 80 54 08. *092045*

Israel

Tel Aviv
First International Antiques House, 52 Ben Yehuda St,
Tel Aviv. T. (03) 288454. *092046*
Sotheby's, 19 Dov Hoz St, 63416 Tel Aviv.
T. (03) 5226616. *092047*

Italy

Brescia
Capitolium, Via Cattaneo 55, 25121 Brescia.
T. (030) 48400, 53090, Fax 53090. *092048*
Michelangelo, Viale Venezia 90, 25100 Brescia.
T. (030) 521 56. *092049*
Michelangelo Casa d'Aste, Via Cavour 4, 25100 Brescia.
T. (030) 28 90 57. *092050*

Brugine (Padova)
Ifarte, Via Roma 122, 35020 Brugine.
T. (049) 580 60 70. *092051*

Chiavari (Genova)
Casa delle Aste, Corso Valparaiso 28, 16043 Chiavari.
T. (0185) 30 30 44. *092052*

Firenze
Galleria Giorgi, Via della Vigna Nuova 51, 50123 Firenze.
T. (055) 21 16 31. *092053*
Gazzi, Alberto, Borgo Santi Apostoli 18, 50123 Firenze.
T. (055) 28 23 45. *092054*
Instituto Vendite Giudiziarie, Pandolfini Cav. Luigi, 26
Borgo Albizi, 50122 Firenze. T. (055) 2340830. *092055*
Istituto Vendite Giudiziarie, Pandolfini Cav. Luigi, 26 Via
Poggio Bracciolini, 50126 Firenze.
T. (055) 6580242. *092056*
Istituto Vendite Giudiziarie Pandolfini Cav. Luigi, 26 Via
Poggio Bracciolini, 50126 Firenze.
T. (055) 685698. *092057*
Palazzo Internazionale delle Aste ed Esposizioni, Via
Maggio 11, 50125 Firenze. T. (055) 29 30 00,
28 29 05. *092058*
Pandolfini, Borgo degli Albizi 26, 50127 Firenze.
T. (055) 26 32 98. *092059*
Pitti, Via Maggio 15, 50125 Firenze.
T. (055) 29 63 82. *092060*
Semenzato, Franco, Palazzo Michelozzi, Via Maggio 11,
50125 Firenze. T. (055) 28 29 05,
Fax 29 30 00. *092061*
Sotheby, Via Gino Capponi 26, 50121 Firenze.
T. (055) 57 14 10. *092062*
Sotheby's Italia, 16 Borgo Albizi, 50122 Firenze.
T. (06) 2340504. *092063*

Genova
Boetto Aste di Antiquariato, Via Garibaldi, 16124 Geno-
va. T. (010) 292584. *092064*
Ghiglione, Piero, Palazzo Doria, Pzza San Matteo 6/b/r,
16123 Genova. T. (010) 20 55 30, 20 87 07. *092065*
SO.VE.MO, 2c/r Via Romani, 16122 Genova.
T. (010) 814594, 88206, 88642. *092066*

Lucca
Vangelisti, Bruno, Piazza dei Servi 11, 55100 Lucca.
T. (0583) 413 40. *092067*

Lurago d'Erba (Como)
Il Mercatino, Via Roma 4, 22040 Lurago d'Erba.
T. (031) 60 97 26. *092068*

Milano
Arphil, Via Salvini 3, 20122 Milano. T. (02) 70 62 24,
70 64 76. *092069*
Asta Ambrosiana, 64 Corso B. Aires, 20124 Milano.
T. (02) 2049071. *092070*
Asta Ambrosiana, 4 Viale Valtellina, 20159 Milano.
T. (02) 66013127. *092071*
Aste Mecenate, 30/2 Via Mecenate, 20138 Milano.
T. (02) 58012061. *092072*
Auction Phila, Corso di Porta Romana 132, 20122 Mila-
no. T. (02) 546 65 06, Fax 545 79 12. *092073*
Brera Arte, Piazza San Marco 1, 20121 Milano.
T. (02) 655 50 40/1957, Fax 29 00 01 85. *092074*
Casa delle Aste Nuova Ifir, Alz. Nav. Grande 98, 20144
Milano. T. (02) 89405858, 89405862. *092075*
Copello & Rizzo, Via G de Castillia 21, 20124 Milano.
T. (02) 688 20 61. *092076*
De Rosa, R., 8/6 Via Pellegrini, 20122 Milano.
T. (02) 58318051. *092077*
Farsettiarte di Franco Farsetti, 52 Via Spiga, 20121 Mi-
lano. T. (02) 76013228. *092078*
Finarte, Piazzetta Maurilio Bossi 4, 20121 Milano.
T. (02) 87 70 41, Fax 86 73 18. *092079*

Finarte Casa d'Aste S.p.A.
Milano
Piazzetta Bossi 4, (20121)
tel. 2/877041 - telefax 2/867779
Internet: http://www.vol.it/finarte/

Finarte S.A.
Londra
7/8 Mason's Yard, Duke Street,
St. James's, (SW1Y 6BU)
tel. 171/8397233
telefax 171/8395433

Finarte España S.A.
Madrid
Velazquez 7, (28001)
tel. 1/5754300
telefax 1/5753847

Finarte
CASA D'ASTE

Frearte, Viale Sabotino 22, 20135 Milano.
T. (02) 58 30 49 55, Fax 58 30 53 83. *092080*
Geri, Via Bagutta 13, 20121 Milano.
T. (02) 70 07 85. *092081*
Il Ponte, Via Pontaccio 12, 20121 Milano.
T. (02) 72 00 37 49, Fax 72 02 20 83. *092082*
I.R.VE.G. Instituti Riuniti Vendite Giudiziarie, 87/2 Via
Mecenate, 20138 Milano. T. (02) 58010627,
58010636. *092083*
Irveg Istituti Riuniti Vendite Giudiziarie, 18 Via Andegari,
20121 Milano. T. (02) 72022642. *092084*
Manzoni Finarte, Via Manzoni 38, 20121 Milano.
T. (02) 70 11 17. *092085*

Milano 02 Antiquarum Italia, Piazza Duomo 21, 20121
Milano. T. (02) 876625, Fax (02) 877915. *092086*
Motta, Luigi, Via San Giovanni sul Muro 3, 20121 Mila-
no. T. (02) 87 86 51. *092087*
Pizzigoni, Marco, Gall Buenos Aires 13, 20124 Milano.
T. (02) 271 60 98. *092088*
Il Ponte – Casa D'Aste, 3 Via Tazzoli, 20154 Milano.
T. (02) 6597465. *092089*
Rerum, 61 Via Torino, 20123 Milano. T. (02) 72000074,
72021079, 72021085. *092090*
Semenzato, Franco, Palazzo Fontana Silvestri, Corso Ve-
nezia 10, 20121 Milano. T. (02) 7600 2939, 79 44 79,
Fax 79 65 81. *092091*
Semenzato SpA Casa D'Aste, Franco, S. Paolo Conveso,
Via Sant'Eufemia 25, 20122 Milano. T. (02) 809191,
809192, Fax (02) 8055837. *092092*
Sicit, 17 Via Conservatorio, 20122 Milano.
T. (02) 76021416, 76021662, 76022874. *092093*
Sotheby's Italia, 19 Via Broggi, 20129 Milano.
T. (06) 29518371, 29518372. *092094*
Taylor's Europa, 18 Corso di Porta Vittoria, 20122 Mila-
no. T. (02) 55193797, 55193896, 55194017. *092095*
Trading Art Invest, 5 Via Tazzoli, 20154 Milano.
T. (02) 6551262, 6551295. *092096*
Zara Aste di Danielli Massimo, 50 Viale Brianza, 20127
Milano. T. (02) 66015757. *092097*

Napoli
Nuova Bianchi d'Espinosa, Via Vito Fornari 9, 80121 Napoli. T. (081) 41 45 01. *092098*

Palermo (Sicilia)
Sarno, Via Amari 148, 90139 Palermo. T. (091) 58 18 48,
58 54 42. *092099*

Piacenza
Cò Attilio, Via Leopardi 29, 29100 Piacenza.
T. (0523) 68156. *092100*
Oppizzi, Via Cittadella 39, 29100 Piacenza.
T. (0523) 349 71. *092101*

Pisa
Casa delle Aste, Via Catalani 19, 56100 Pisa.
T. (050) 240 04. *092102*

Roma
A. De Crescenzio, 61 Via Margutta, 00187 Roma.
T. (06) 3214365. *092103*
A. de Crescenzo, 3 Piazza Cavour, 00193 Roma.
T. (06) 68802946. *092104*
A. De Crescenzo, 61 Via Margutta, 00187 Roma.
T. (06) 3212657, 3213465, 3215051. *092105*
Antonina, La, Piazza di Spagna 93, 00187 Roma.
T. (06) 679 40 09, 679 20 64. *092106*
Arcadia, L', Via del Babuino 70, 00187 Roma.
T. (06) 679 10 23. *092107*
Aste Guidiziaria, via della Cava Aurelia, 98, 00165 Ro-
ma. T. (06) 637 42 69, 637 56 47. *092108*
Barbuino, Via dei Greci 2, 00187 Roma.
T. (06) 678 59 75. *092109*
Christie's, Piazza Navona 114, 00186 Roma.
T. (06) 654 27 85, 656 40 32. *092110*
Cimino, L. ed A. Fratelli, via Basento 52d, 00198 Roma.
T. (06) 85 67 71. *092111*
di Castro, Adolfo, via Babuino 81/62, 00100 Roma.
T. (06) 67 57 92. *092112*
Finarte, Via Margutta 54, 00187 Roma.
T. (06) 678 65 57, Fax 678 84 03. *092113*
Galleria dei Cosmati, Via Vittoria Colonna 11, 00193 Ro-
ma. T. (06) 361 11 41. *092114*
Galleria del Corso, c Vittorio Emanuele 4-6, 00186
Roma. T. (06) 65 21 94. *092115*
Martinoja, Socrate, v della Stelletta 13, 00186 Roma.
T. (06) 65 21 94. *092116*
Righetti, Tullio, v Babuino 96, 00187 Roma.
T. (06) 679 01 92. *092117*
Romana Aste, Via del Babuino 96, 00187 Roma.
T. (06) 679 01 92. *092118*
Semenzato, Franco, Piazza di Spagna 93, 00187 Roma.
T. (06) 679 64 79, 678 38 12, Fax 679 64 79. *092119*
Sotheby's, Piazza di Spagna, 00187 Roma.
T. (06) 678 17 98, 678 27 34. *092120*
Studio G.S., Viale Parioli 168, 00197 Roma.
T. (06) 804697. *092121*

Saint-Pierre (Aosta)
Museo di Storia Naturale, Castello di Saint-Pierre,
11010 Saint-Pierre. T. (0165) 90 34 85.   *092122*

Torino
Aste – Ifir Piemonte, Via Bonzanigo 16, 10144 Torino.
T. (011) 485338, 482822, Fax (011) 488913.   *092123*
Della Rocca, Via della Rocca 33, 10128 Torino.
T. (011) 839 80 62, Fax 83 62 44.   *092124*
Fiver Fiduciaria Vendite e Realizzi, 117 Via S. Paolo,
10141 Torino. T. (011) 334086.   *092125*
Ifir Piemonte Istituto Vendite Giudiziarie, 16 Via Bonzani-
go, 10144 Torino. T. (011) 485338, 482822.   *092126*
Ifir Piemonte Istituto Vendite Giudizirie, 10 Via Corte
d'Appello, 10122 Torino. T. (011) 4367070.   *092127*
Robert Louis, Corso Vittorio Emanuele 109, 10128 Tori-
no. T. (011) 54 11 50.   *092128*
S. Mauro Torinese to 011 Panebianco G., 61 Corso Ca-
sale, 10131 Torino. T. (011) 10131.   *092129*
Sant'Agostino Arte, Corso Tassoni 56, 10144 Torino.
T. (011) 4377770, Fax (011) 4377577.   *092130*
Sotheby's Italia, 18b Corso Ferraris, 10121 Torino.
T. (011) 542869.   *092131*

Trieste
Zucco, de, Riva Nazario Sauro 6/A e B, 34121 Trieste.
T. (040) 30 82 99, Fax 30 83 99.   *092132*

Udine
Marchetti & C., Via Bonaldo Stringher 25/3, 33100
Udine. T. (0432) 29 91 29.   *092133*

Venezia
Galleria d'Arte Cesana, Ponte Consorzi Calle Larga S
Marco, 30124 Venezia. T. (041) 239 05.   *092134*
Istituto Vendite Giudiziarie, 2292 Cannaregio, 10 Via
Rossetto – Mestr, 30121 Venezia. T. 721811,
5312266.   *092135*
Nummus et Ars, 106 Via S. Dona' Mestre, 30030 Vene-
zia. T. 611844.   *092136*
Semenzato, Franco, Cannaregio 2292, 30121 Venezia.
T. (041) 722 18 11, Fax 72 18 11.   *092137*
Vidali G., 1022g S. Polo, 30125 Venezia.
T. 5239981.   *092138*

Vercelli
Meeting Art, Corso Libertà 89, 13100 Vercelli.
T. (0161) 20 66.   *092139*

Zola Predosa (Bologna)
Villa Albergati, Via Masini 46, 40069 Zola Predosa.
T. (051) 75 02 47.   *092140*

Japan

Nagoya (Aichi-ken)
Japanese Art Gallery, 401 Takara Dai-ichi Bldg., 2-5-1
Sakae, Naka-ku, Nagoya 460. T. (052) 231-
0855.   *092141*

Tokyo
Sotheby, Seibu Pisa Tokyo Prince Hotel, Shiba-koen 3-
3-1, Minato-ku, Tokyo 105. T. (03) 3434 5511,
3437 1916.   *092142*

Lebanon

Beirut
Atallah, Mounis, P. O. Box 7095, Beirut.
T. (961) 25 71 50, 25 79 70.   *092143*

Malaysia

Ipoh (Malaya)
Hup Hin, Co., 22 Lbh Hale, Ipoh.   *092144*
Simon, James, 4 Po Gdns, Ipoh.   *092145*

Kuala Lumpur (Selangor)
DAS K.R., 46 Jalan T. Abdul Rahman, Kuala
Lumpur.   *092146*

Lew Chin Chuan & Co., 108 Jalan Bandar, Kuala
Lumpur.   *092147*

Malacca (Malaya)
Town Auctioneer, 30 Jalan Laksamana,
Malacca.   *092148*

Mexico

México (D.F.)
Christie's, Schiller 325, México. T. 531 16 86. *092149*

Monaco

Monte Carlo
Monte Carlo Art Gallery, 42 Blvd d'Italie, 98000 Monte
Carlo. T. 93 50 10 32.   *092150*
Sotheby, Sporting d'Hiver, Pl du Casino, 98000 Monte
Carlo. T. 93 30 88 80.   *092151*
Sotheby's, 5bis Av Saint Michel, 98000 Monte Carlo.
T. 93 25 19 33.   *092152*

Netherlands

Amsterdam
Brandt, Paul, Reguliersdwarsstr 50, 1017 BM Amster-
dam. T. (020) 624 86 62.   *092153*
Christie's, Cornelis Schuytstr 57, 1071 JG Amsterdam.
T. (020) 664 20 11.   *092154*
Dullaert Taxaties, Keizersgracht 570, 1017 EM Amster-
dam. T. (020) 620 30 47, 673 41 87.   *092155*
Gijselman, Loth, Overtoom 197, 1267 HT Amsterdam.
T. (020) 618 32 47.   *092156*
Mensing & Zn., W., Pijperstraat 3, 1077 XK Amsterdam.
T. (020) 671 79 41.   *092157*
Philips, Nwe Spiegelstr 38, 1017 DG Amsterdam.
T. (020) 622 94 10.   *092158*
Rommelmarkt Looiersgracht, Looiersgracht 38, 1016 VS
Amsterdam. T. (020) 627 47 62.   *092159*
Sotheby, Rokin 102, 1012 KZ Amsterdam.
T. (020) 624 62 15/16, 624 31 88, 622 54 91.   *092160*
Veilinggebouw De Zwaan, Keizersgracht 474, 1017 EG
Amsterdam. T. (020) 622 04 47.   *092161*
Zwaan, De, Keizersgracht 474, 1017 EG Amsterdam.
T. (020) 622 04 47.   *092162*

Arnhem (Gelderland)
Notarishuis, Het, Bakkerstr 19, 6811 EH Arnhem.
T. (026) 4425900.   *092163*

Dordrecht (Zuid-Holland)
Mak, A., Visstr 25, 3311 KX Dordrecht.
T. (078) 6133344, 6133412.   *092164*

Den Haag (Zuid-Holland)
Centrum 't Veilinghuis, Nassau Dillenburgstr 3, 2596 AB
Den Haag. T. (070) 324 42 71.   *092165*
Diederiks, Marcel, Noordeinde 128, 2514 GN Den Haag.
T. (070) 365 56 33.   *092166*
Glerum CS Kunst en Antiekveilingen, Westeinde 12,
2512 DH Den Haag. T. (070) 356 01 65.   *092167*
Phillips, L Vijverberg 4-5, 2513AC Den Haag.
T. (070) 363 99 00.   *092168*
Stockum, van, Prinsegracht 15, 2512 EW Den Haag.
T. (070) 364 98 40/41.   *092169*
Venduhuis der Notarissen, Nobelstr 5, 2513 BC Den
Haag. T. (070) 365 88 57.   *092170*

Haarlem (Noord-Holland)
Kuijper, Bubb, Jansweg 39, 2011 KM Haarlem.
T. (023) 5323986.   *092171*
Notarishuis Haarlem, Bilderdijkstraat 1a, 2013 EG Haar-
lem. T. (023) 5316486.   *092172*

Hoorn (Noord-Holland)
Veilinghuis De Eenhoorn, Appelhaven 5, 1621 BB Hoorn.
T. (0229) 219933, 216023.   *092173*

Ijlst (Friesland)
Baerveldt, Roodhemsterweg 8, 8650 AA Ijlst.   *092174*

Laren (Noord-Holland)
Gijselman, Loth, Drift 6, 1251 CC Laren.
T. (035) 5315677.   *092175*

Rotterdam (Zuid-Holland)
Veiling, Mira, Stationsplein 45, 3001 GA Rotterdam.
T. (010) 433 02 38.   *092176*
Vendue Notarishuis, Kipstr 54, 3011 RT Rotterdam.
T. (010) 411 85 44.   *092177*

Utrecht
Beijers, J.L., Achter Sint Pieter 140, 3512 HT Utrecht.
T. (030) 2310958.   *092178*

Voorburg (Zuid-Holland)
Vanderstelt, v. Deventerlaan 51, 2271 TW Voorburg.
T. (070) 386 90 45.   *092179*

Zutphen (Gelderland)
Jurrissen, M., Halterstraat 22, 7201 MX
Zutphen.   *092180*

New Zealand

Wellington
General Auctioneers Association of New Zealand, Wellington POB 11-253.   *092181*

Norway

Gjøvik
Hoels, Ö Torvgt. 17, 2800 Gjøvik.   *092182*

Haugesund (Rogaland)
Røvaer, Karl Fr., Strandgt. 115, 5500
Haugesund.   *092183*

Kristiansand S. (Vest-Agder)
Kristiansands Auksjons-Forretning, Festningsgt. 52,
4600 Kristiansand S.   *092184*

Mandal (Vest-Agder)
Mandal Auksjonsforretning, Slettev. 6, 4500
Mandal.   *092185*

Mysen
Borger, Bjørn, 1850 Mysen.   *092186*

Oslo
Aktiv Auksjon, Trondheimsv. 13, 0560 Oslo.
T. 22 68 43 03.   *092187*
Børsum, Oscarsgt. 59, 0258 Oslo.
T. 22 56 34 50.   *092188*
City Auksjon, Madserudallé 23, 0268 Oslo.
T. 22 44 99 91.   *092189*
Oslo Auksjonsforretning Blomqvist, Tordenskioldsgt. 5,
0160 Oslo. T. 22 41 26 31.   *092190*

Sandefjord (Vestfold)
Liverød, A., & Co., Kongensgt. 4, 3200 Sandefjord.
T. 33462117.   *092191*

Skien (Telemark)
Eek, Marth., Lundegt. 2, 3700 Skien.
T. 35523831.   *092192*

Steinkjer
Steinkjer Auktionsforr., Kongensgt. 15, 7700
Steinkjer.   *092193*

Stord (Hordaland)
Stord Auksjonsforretning, 5400 Stord.
T. 53411726.   *092194*

Tønsberg
Berg, Sigmund, Ö. Langgt. 15, 3100 Tønsberg.   *092195*

Philippines

Manila
The Auction House, Manila Garden Hotel, Makati, Manila. T. 817 12 36, 85 79 11.   *092196*

Portugal

Lisboa
Dinastia-Antiquarios, Rua da Escola Politecnica 183,
1200 Lisboa. T. (01) 66 89 73, 66 83 44. *092197*
Leiria & Nascimento, Rua da Emenda 30, 1200 Lisboa.
T. (01) 36 94 98. *092198*
Soares e Mendonça, Lda., Rua Luz Soriano 53, 1200
Lisboa. T. (01) 32 13 12. *092199*

Porto
Casa Tem Tudo, Av. da Boavista 881, 4100 Porto.
T. (02) 622 17. *092200*

Réunion

Saint-Pierre
Jaubert, Didier, Rte ZI 2, 97410 Saint-Pierre.
T. (262) 356909, Fax (262) 356908. *092201*

Russia

Moskva
Aktsiya, Bryusov per 6, 103009 Moskva.
T. (095) 2291975. *092202*
Alfa-Art, Krymski val 10, 117049 Moskva.
T. (095) 2384029. *092203*
Antikvar, Kozikhinski per 15, 103001 Moskva.
T. (095) 2991865. *092204*
Baskom, ul Pokrovka 9, 101000 Moskva.
T. (095) 9230242. *092205*
Chetyre Iskusstva, ul Krasnokazarmennaya 17a, Mos-
kva. T. (095) 2911124, 3611678, 2006747,
Fax 3611678, 2006747. *092206*
Knizhny Auktsion v Tsentralnom dome literatorov, ul
Bolshaya Nikitskaya 53, Moskva.
T. (095) 2916600. *092207*
Magnum-Ars, 1-y Spasonalivkovski per 4, Moskva.
T. (095) 2292370. *092208*

Sankt-Peterburg
Alfa Art, ul Saltykova-Shchedrina 43a, 193015 Sankt-
Peterburg. T. (812) 2793913. *092209*
Antikvarny auktsion, ul Nalichnaya 21, Sankt-Peterburg.
T. (812) 2171010. *092210*

South Africa

Cape Town (Cape Province)
Ashbey, 43 Church St., Cape Town, 8001.
T. (021) 22 75 27. *092211*
Ashbey's Galleries, 43 Church St., Cape Town, 8001.
T. (021) 23 80 60. *092212*
Sotheby, 37 Burg St., Cape Town, 8001.
T. (021) 23 47 28. *092213*

Spain

Barcelona
Balcli's, Rosellón 227, 08008 Barcelona. *092214*
Barna, San Eusebio 57, 08006 Barcelona.
T. (93) 200 57 99. *092215*
Brok, Pau Claris 167, 08037 Barcelona.
Calicó, X. & F., Pl. del Angel 2, 08002 Barcelona. *092216*
T. (93) 310 55 12/16, Fax 310 27 56. *092217*
Canuda, Sala d' Arte, Canuda, 4, 08002 Barcelona.
T. (93) 302 38 31. *092218*
Miro, Ramon, Floridablanca 110-112, 08015 Barcelona.
T. (93) 223 41 40. *092219*
Prestige, Valencia 277, 08009 Barcelona. *092220*
Sala Vayreda, Rambla de Cataluña 116, 08008 Barcelo-
na. T. (93) 218 2960. *092221*
Subastas de Barcelona, Provenza 257, 08008
Barcelona. *092222*
Valenti Valro, Provenza 308-310, 08037 Barcelona.
T. (93) 216 07 50/54. *092223*

Madrid
Alonso Jimnéz, Ezequiel, Jorge Juan 56, 28001 Madrid.
T. (91) 22 62 219. *092224*
Ansorena, Alcalá 52, 28014 Madrid. T. (91) 222 0158,
231 6353. *092225*
Christie's, Casado del Alisal 5, 28014 Madrid.
T. (91) 228 39 00. *092226*
Duran, Fernando, Conde de Aranda 23, 28001
Madrid. *092227*
Duran Subastas de Arte, Serrano, 12, 28001 Madrid.
T. (91) 401 3400. *092228*
Galeria, La, Colmenares 7, 28004 Madrid. *092229*
Julie, Ribera de Curtidores 29 Nuevas Galerias, 28005
Madrid. T. (91) 239 00 11. *092230*
Muebles Castellanos, Ribera de Curtidores 29, and Gale-
rias Piquer, Naves 17, 28005 Madrid.
T. (91) 2 28 65 34. *092231*
Peel, Edmund, Pza. de la Indipendencia 8, 28001
Madrid. *092232*
Sala Faberge, Gran Vía 1, 28013 Madrid.
T. (91) 521 10 82. *092233*
Siena, Jeramagos 23, 28029 Madrid. *092234*
Sotheby, Plaza de la Independencia 8, 28001 Madrid.
T. (91) 232 65 72, 522 29 02. *092235*

Sevilla
Sodartys, Vírgen de Luján 39, 41011 Sevilla. *092236*

Torrejon de Ardoz (Madrid)
La Casa Grande, Calle Madrid, 2, 28850 Torrejon de Ar-
doz. T. (91) 675 3900. *092237*

Sweden

Borås
Auktionskammaren, Bryggareg. 22, 502 30
Borås. *092238*

Djursholm (Stockholm)
Christie's, Hildingavagen 19, 18262 Djursholm.
T. 755 57 33. *092239*

Gävle
Auktionsverket i Gävle, S. Skeppsbron 6, 802 33
Gävle. *092240*

Göteborg
Antik-City AB, V. Hamngatan 6, 41117 Göteborg.
T. (031) 13 55 13. *092241*
Göteborgs Auktionsverk, Geijersg 14, 411 34 Göteborg.
T. (031) 206110, Fax (031) 209160. *092242*
Mölndals Auktionsbyra AB, Fridkullagatan 15, 41262
Göteborg. T. (031) 18 46 64. *092243*

Helsingborg
Hälsingborg Stads Auktionskammare, Kungsg. 16, 251
01 Helsingborg. *092244*

Löddeköping
Albumet, Malmövägen 8, 240 21 Löddeköping.
T. 70 50 01. *092245*

Malmö
Falkkloos, Hamngatan 2, 211 22 Malmö.
T. (040) 23 52 70, Fax 30 37 62. *092246*
Malmö Auktionsverk, Engelbrektsg 7, 211 33 Malmö.
T. (040) 112026, Fax (040) 115313. *092247*

Norrköping
Norrköpings Kommunala Auktionskammare, Tunnbindar-
eg. 37, 602 21 Norrköping. T. (011) 15 19 42. *092248*

Sala
Eriksson & Enagrius, Ringg. 25, 733 00 Sala. *092249*

Stockholm
Bukowski, Arsenalsgt. 4, 111 47 Stockholm.
T. (08) 810 25 95, Fax 11 46 74. *092250*
Jakobssons, E. A., S:t Eriksgatan 70, 10090
Stockholm. *092251*
Nordén Auctioner, Arsenalsgt 1, 111 47 Stockholm.
T. (08) 6788800, Fax (08) 6788820. *092252*

Sotheby, Arsenalsgatan 4, 11147 Stockholm.
T. (08) 10 14 78. *092253*
Stockholms Auktionsverk, Jakobsg. 10, 103 25 Stock-
holm. T. (08) 4536700, Fax (08) 102845. *092254*
Strandvägen Auktioner, Strandvägen 7a, 114 56 Stock-
holm. T. (08) 661 62 62. *092255*

Switzerland

Allaman (Vaud)
Artal, Château d'Allaman, 1165 Allaman.
T. (021) 807 38 05. *092256*
Grand Argentier, Château, 1165 Allaman.
T. (021) 807 37 09, 36 54 62. *092257*

Bad Ragaz
Numis-Post, Postfach, 7310 Bad Ragaz.
T. (081) 3022429, Fax 3025984. *092258*

Basel
Auktionshaus zum Dorenbach, Holeestr 6, 4054 Basel.
T. (061) 4218718, Fax (061) 4218720. *092259*
Graf & Raaflaub, Rheingasse 31, 4051 Basel.
T. (061) 6818020, Fax 2721383. *092260*
Kronenberg AG, Hirschgässlein 44/4, Postfach 320,
4010 Basel. T. (061) 271 26 26, Fax 271 26 25. *092261*
Kübli, Josua, Kornhausgasse 8, 4051 Basel.
T. (061) 261 51 67. *092262*
Rusterholz Kunstauktionen, Hammerstr. 108, 4057 Ba-
sel. T. (061) 691 14 14, Fax (061) 691 14 61. *092263*
Ségal, M. & G., Aeschengraben 14-16, 4051 Basel.
T. (061) 272 39 08, Fax (061) 272 29 84. *092264*
Sotheby's, Schifflände 2, 4051 Basel. T. (061) 2611020,
Fax 2611077. *092265*

Bern
City Auktion, Kramgasse 29, 3011 Bern.
T. (031) 312 28 38. *092266*
Dobiaschofsky, Monbijoustr 30, 3001 Bern.
T. (031) 3812372, Fax 3812374. *092267*
Kornfeld, Laupenstr 41, 3008 Bern. T. (031) 3814673,
Fax 3821891. *092268*
Stuker, Jürg, Alter Aargauerstalden 30, 3006 Bern.
T. (031) 352 00 44, Fax (031) 352 78 13. *092269*

Bevaix (Neuchâtel)
Arts Anciens, 2022 Bevaix. T. (032) 8461353. *092270*

Chêne-Bourg (Genève)
Lopez, Jacques, Rue Péillonnex 39, 1225 Chêne-Bourg.
T. (022) 3490326. *092271*

Collonge-Bellerive (Genève)
Patrizzi, Osvaldo, 5 Ch. Marly, 1254 Collonge-Bellerive.
T. (022) 752 13 01. *092272*

Ebmatingen (Zürich)
Baehler, Steinmueri 24a, 8123 Ebmatingen.
T. (01) 980 19 53, Fax 980 38 49. *092273*

Genève
Antiquorum, 2 Rue du Mont-Blanc, 1201 Genève.
T. (022) 9092850, Fax 9092860. *092274*
Christie's, 8 Pl de la Taconnerie, 1204 Genève.
T. (022) 3111766, Fax (022) 3115559. *092275*
Christin, Jean, 8 Pl. Eaux Vives, 1207 Genève.
T. (022) 736 22 55. *092276*
Cigarini, Romano, 1 Rue Rôtisserie, 1204 Genève.
T. (022) 329 29 33. *092277*
Habsburg, Quai du Mont-Blanc 1, 1201 Genève.
T. (022) 7572530, Fax (022) 7572530. *092278*
Hôtel de Ventes, 51 Rue Prévost-Martin, 1205 Genève.
T. (022) 320 11 77. *092279*
Koller, 2 Rue de l'Athénée, 1205 Genève.
T. (022) 3210385, Fax (022) 3287872. *092280*
Naville, Claude, 2 Rue Fontaine, 1204 Genève.
T. (022) 321 33 12. *092281*
Nessim, Gabriel & Isabelle, 8 Rue Goetz-Monin, 1205
Genève. T. (022) 320 62 43. *092282*
Pantet, René, 6 Rue Rôtisserie, 1204 Genève.
T. (022) 328 60 78. *092283*

Rosset, Christian, 29 Rue du Rhône, 1204 Genève.
T. (022) 3109633, Fax 3102854. 092284
Scagliola, Henri, 6 Rue Rôtisserie, 1204 Genève.
T. (022) 328 60 77. 092285
Sotheby's, Quai du Mont Blanc 13, 1201 Genève.
T. (022) 7328585, Fax (022) 7316594. 092286
Tradart Genève, 29 Quai des Bergues, 1201 Genève.
T. (022) 7313831, Fax (022) 7314590. 092287

Gossau (Sankt Gallen)
Chiani-Auktionen, Hochschorenstr 31, 9201 Gossau.
T. (071) 3858566, Fax 3858566. 092288

Lausanne (Vaud)
Beney, Daniel, 7 Avant-Poste, 1005 Lausanne.
T. (021) 3222864. 092289

Lucens (Vaud)
Koller, Château de Lucens, 1522 Lucens. 092290

Lugano (Ticino)
Galleria d'Arte, Via Ginevra 4, 6900 Lugano.
T. (091) 9227589. 092291
Sotheby's, Via Peri 21, 6900 Lugano. T. (091) 9238562,
Fax (091) 9238563. 092292

Luzern
Burkard Galerie + Auktion, Schützenstr. 6, 6003 Luzern.
T. (041) 2405022, 2403188,
Fax (041) 240 82 52. 092293
Meyer, Marken, Klosterstr. 15, 6003 Luzern.
T. (041) 240 87 10. 092234

Lyss (Bern)
Gnägi, Bendicht, Herrengasse 38, 3250 Lyss.
T. (032) 3848270, Fax 3841157. 092295

Morges (Vaud)
Meigniez, A., 5 Ch. du Moulin, 1110 Morges.
T. (021) 801 00 33. 092296

Onex (Genève)
Feldmann, David, 175 Rte. Chancy, 1213 Onex.
T. (022) 757 39 01. 092297

Rapperswil (Sankt Gallen)
Spitzer, Marktgasse 6, 8640 Rapperswil.
T. (052) 2104705. 092298

Sankt Gallen
Widmer, Hans, Löwengasse 3, 9004 Sankt Gallen.
T. (071) 2233581, Fax 2234280. 092299
Widmer, Hans, Löwengasse 3, 9004 Sankt Gallen.
T. (071) 2233581, Fax 2234280. 092300

Vevey (Vaud)
Stirt, James, 4 Rue Léman, 1800 Vevey.
T. (021) 921 60 61. 092301

Wil (Sankt Gallen)
Rapp, Peter, Toggenburgerstr. 139, 9500 Wil.
T. (071) 9237744, Fax 9239220. 092002

Wolfhausen (Zürich)
Bühler, Edy, Hauptstr. 1, 8633 Wolfhausen.
Fax 552431455. 092303

Zofingen (Aargau)
Auktionshaus Zofingen, Klösterligasse 4, 4800 Zofingen.
T. (062) 7516351-53, Fax 7516354. 092304

Zürich
Bollag, Max G., Werdmühlestr 11, 8001 Zürich.
T. (01) 2114789. 092305

CHRISTIE'S
(International) AG

Steinwiesplatz
8032 Zürich

Tel. 01/2681010
Fax 01/2681011

CHRISTIAN ROSSET

Huissier judiciaire, 29, rue du Rhône – 1204 Genève
Tél.: 022/310 96 33 – Fax: 022/310 28 54

SALLE DES VENTES AUX ENCHERES

tableaux anciens et modernes
meubles anciens, porcelaines, argenterie,
livres et gravures
bibelots, extrême-orient, archéologie

*Si vous désirez être tenu au courant des ventes de l'Etude, une simple carte
postale vous permettra de recevoir gratuitement les catalogues.*

Bommer, Werner, Weinbergstr 22a, 8001 Zürich.
T. (01) 2518481, Fax (01) 2618770. 092306
Christie's, Steinwiesplatz, 8032 Zürich. T. (01) 2681010,
Fax 2681011. 092307
Dolezal, Peter, Dr., Wehntalerstr. 492, 8046 Zürich.
T. (01) 371 96 11. 092308
Germann, Zeltweg 67, 8032 Zürich. T. (01) 251 83 58,
Fax 2518358. 092309
Ineichen, Peter, Badenerstr 75, 8004 Zürich.
T. (01) 2423944, Fax 2429141. 092310
Koller, Hardturmstr 102, 8031 Zürich. T. (01) 2730101,
Fax 2731966. 092311

GALERIE KOLLER
AUKTIONEN

Hardturmstrasse 102
CH-8031 Zürich
Tel. 01/273 01 01
Fax. 01/273 19 66

Neumeister, Hinterbergstr. 68, 8044 Zürich.
T. (01) 262 51 50, Fax 262 51 56. 092312
Phillips, Rämistr. 27, 8001 Zürich.
T. (01) 252 69 62. 092313
Schuler, Philippe, Seestr. 341, 8038 Zürich.
T. (01) 482 47 48, Fax 482 48 07. 092314
Schweizerische Gesellschaft der Freunde von Kunstauktionen, Werdmühlestr. 11, 8001 Zürich.
T. (01) 2114789. 092315
Sotheby's, Bleicherweg 20, 8022 Zürich.
T. (01) 2020011, Fax (1) 2012042. 092316
Steinfels, Eric, Dr., Limmatstr 264, 8005 Zürich.
T. (01) 2732236, Fax 2733235. 092317
Sternberg, Frank, Schanzengasse 10, 8001 Zürich.
T. (01) 2523088, Fax 2524067. 092318
Villa Ulmberg, Thujastr. 14, 8038 Zürich.
T. (01) 481 88 33. 092319

Zug
BKB Gant, Baarerstr. 79, 6300 Zug.
T. (041) 711 10 24. 092320
Willi, H.J. Erich, Baarerstr. 43, 6300 Zug.
T. (041) 711 53 77. 092321

Thailand

Bangkok
River City, 23 Trok Rongnamkaeng, Yota Rd. Sampanta-
wong, Bangkok, 10100. T. 237 00 77-8. 092322

United Kingdom

Abergavenny (Gwent)
Rennies, Lion Street, Abergavenny NP7 5NT.
T. (01873) 859331, Fax (01873) 859958. 092323

Aberystwyth (Dyfed)
Watkins & Co., John, 22 Terrace Rd, Aberystwyth SY23
1NP. T. (01970) 612464. 092324

Amersham (Buckinghamshire)
Amersham, Station Rd, Amersham HP7 0AH.
T. (01494) 729292, Fax (01494) 722337. 092325

Ascot (Berkshire)
Elliott, Robin, 32 High St, Ascot SL5 7HG.
T. (01990) 872588, Fax (01990) 24700. 092326

Ashby-de-la-Zouch (Leicestershire)
Taylor Scott, 1a Upper Church St, Ashby-de-la-Zouch
LE65 1BX. T. (01530) 416665,
Fax (01530) 560417. 092327

Ashford (Kent)
Hobbs Parker, Rommey House, Ashford Market, Ashford
TN23 1PG. T. (01233) 622222,
Fax (01233) 646642. 092328

Axbridge (Somerset)
Richards, Town Hall, Axbridge BS26 2AR.
T. (01934) 732969, Fax (01934) 490434. 092329

Ayr (Strathclyde)
Callan, Thomas R., 22 Smith St, Ayr KA7 4HW.
T. (01292) 267681. 092330
Sandgate, 42 Fort St, Ayr KA7 1DE.
T. (01292) 263263. 092331

Banbury (Oxfordshire)
Holloway, 49 Parsons St, Banbury OX16 8PF.
T. (01295) 253197, Fax (01295) 22642. 092332

Barnsley (South Yorkshire)
BBR Auctions, c/o c/o Elsecar Project, Wath Rd, Barnsley S74 8HJ. T. (01226) 745156,
Fax (01226) 745156. *092333*

Barnstaple (Devon)
South Street Auctions, South St, Barnstaple EX32 9DT.
T. (01271) 850337. *092334*

Barton-upon-Humber (Humberside)
A.E. Dowse & Son, Foresters' Galleries, Falkland Way, Barton-upon-Humber DN18 5RL. T. (01652) 32335,
Fax (01652) 32335. *092335*

Bath (Avon)
Aldridges of Bath, 130-132 Walcot St, Bath BA1 5BG.
T. (01225) 462830. *092336*
Gardiner Houlgate, Upper Bristol Rd, Bath BA1 3AJ.
T. (01225) 447933, Fax (01225) 448365. *092337*
Philips Bath, 1 Old King St, Bath BA1 2JT.
T. (01225) 310609, Fax (1225) 446675. *092338*

Battle (Sussex)
Burstow & Hewett, Abbey Galleries, Battle TN38 0AT.
T. (014246) 2302. *092339*

Beaumont St Peter (Channel Islands)
Jones, Michael, Plaisance, Beaumont St Peter.
T. (01534) 73958, Fax (01534) 73958. *092340*

Beccles (Suffolk)
Durrant, 10 New Market, Beccles NR34 9HA.
T. (01502) 712122. *092341*

Belfast (Co. Antrim)
Andersons, 28 Linenhall St, Belfast BT2 8BG.
T. (01232) 321401. *092342*
Ross's, 37 Montgomery St, Belfast BT1 4NX.
T. (01232) 325448, Fax (01232) 333642. *092343*

Berkhamsted (Hertfordshire)
Berkhamsted Auctions Rooms, Middle Rd, Berkhamsted HP4 3EQ. T. (01442) 865169. *092344*

Bicester (Oxfordshire)
Messenger, 27 Sheep St, Bicester OX6 7JF.
T. (01869) 252901, Fax (01869) 320283. *092345*

Billinghurst (West Sussex)
Bellman's, Wisborough Green, Billinghurst RH14 0AY.
T. (01403) 700858, Fax (01403) 700814. *092346*

Billingshurst (Sussex)
Sotheby's, Summers Pl, Billingshurst RH14 9AD.
T. (01403) 783933, Fax (01403) 785153. *092347*

Birmingham (West Midlands)
Biddle & Webb, Ladywood Middleway, Birmingham B16 0PP. T. (0121) 455 8042, Fax (0121) 4549615. *092348*
Fellows & Sons, 19 Augusta St, Hockley, Birmingham B18 6JA. T. (0121) 212 2131,
Fax (0121) 2121249. *092349*

Bishops Stortford (Hertfordshire)
G.E. Sworder & Sons, 15 Northgate End, Bishops Stortford CM23 2ET. T. (01279) 651388,
Fax (01279) 467467. *092350*

Blackpool (Lancashire)
Smythe, Son & Walker, 174 Victoria Rd West, Blackpool FY5 3NE. T. (01253) 852184,
Fax (01253) 854084. *092351*

Bletchingley (Surrey)
Lawrence, 80 High St, Bletchingley RH1 4PA.
T. (01883) 743323, Fax (01883) 744578. *092352*

Bognor Regis (West Sussex)
Summerley Auction Rooms, 96 Limmer Lane, Bognor Regis PO22 7LF. T. (01243) 821212. *092353*

Bourne (Lincolnshire)
Richardsons, Spalding Rd, Bourne PE10 9LE.
T. (01778) 422686, Fax (01778) 425726. *092354*

Bourne End (Buckinghamshire)
Bourne End Auction Rooms, Station Approach, Bourne End SL8 5QH. T. (01628) 531500,
Fax (01494) 433031. *092355*

Bournemouth (Dorset)
Dalkeith Auctions, POB 4, Bournemouth BH1 1YL.
T. (01202) 292905, Fax (01202) 292905. *092356*
House & Son, Lansdowne House, Christchurch Rd, Bournemouth BH1 3JW. T. (01202) 556232,
Fax (01202) 292668. *092357*
Riddett, 20 Richmond Hill, Bournemouth BH2 6EJ.
T. (01202) 555686, Fax (01202) 311004. *092358*

Bradford (West Yorkshire)
Raby & Son, John H., 21 St Mary's Rd, Bradford BD8 7QL. T. (01274) 491121, Fax (01274) 544203. *092359*

Brentwood (Essex)
Brentwood Auctions, 45 North Rd, Brentwood CM14 4YZ. T. (01277) 224599, Fax (01277) 261502. *092360*

Bridgwater (Somerset)
Tamlyn & Son, 56 High St, Bridgwater TA6 3BN.
T. (01278) 458241, Fax (01278) 458242. *092361*

Bridport (Dorset)
Morey & Sons, William, Saint Michaels Ln, Bridport DT6 3RB. T. (01308) 22078. *092362*

Brigg (Humberside)
Dickinson, Davy & Markham, Old Courts Rd, Brigg.
T. (01652) 653666, Fax 801652) 650085. *092363*

Brighton (East Sussex)
Messrs Raymond P. Inman, 35 & 40 Temple St, Brighton BN1 3BH. T. (01273) 774777. *092364*

Bristol (Avon)
Allen & Harris, Apsley Rd, Bristol BS8 2ST.
T. (0117) 737201, Fax (0117) 735671. *092365*
Taviners, Prewett St, Redcliffe, Bristol BS1 6PB.
T. (01272) 265996, Fax (01272) 272290. *092366*

Buntingford (Hertfordshire)
Bayles, Childs Farm, Buntingford SG9 9PU.
T. (0176) 381256. *092367*

Burnley (Lancashire)
Walton & Walton, 23 St James Row, Burnley BB11 1EY.
T. (01282) 23247, Fax (01282) 832814. *092368*

Bury Saint Edmunds (Suffolk)
Lacy Scott, 10 Risbygate St, Bury Saint Edmunds IP33 3AA. T. (01284) 763531, Fax (01284) 704713. *092369*

Cambridge (Cambridgeshire)
Cheffins, Grain & Comins, 2 Clifton Rd, Cambridge CB1 4BW. T. (01223) 213343. *092370*

Canterbury (Kent)
Canterbury Auction Galleries, 40 Station Rd, Canterbury CT2 8AN. T. (01227) 763337,
Fax (01227) 456770. *092371*

Cardiff (South Glamorgan)
Phillips Cardiff, 9-10 Westgate St, Cardiff CF1 1DA.
T. (01222) 396453, Fax (01222) 222625. *092372*

Carlisle (Cumbria)
Thomson, Roddick & Laurie, 24 Lowther St, Carlisle CA3 8DA. T. (01228) 28939, Fax (01228) 592128. *092373*

Carmarthen (Dyfed)
Francis, Peter, 19 King St, Carmarthen SA31 1BH.
T. (01267) 233456. *092374*

Chelmsford (Essex)
Cooper Hirst, Granary Salerooms, Victoria Rd,, Chelmsford CM2 6LH. T. (01245) 260535,
Fax (01245) 345185. *092375*
Rowland, Simon H., 42 Mildmay Rd, Chelmsford CM2 0DZ. T. (01245) 354251, Fax (01245) 344466. *092376*

Cheltenham (Gloucestershire)
Hobbs & Chambers, 15 Royal Crescent, Cheltenham GL50 3DA. T. (01242) 513722,
Fax (01242) 227175. *092377*
Mallam, 26 Grosvenor St, Cheltenham GL52 2SG.
T. (01242) 235712, Fax (01242) 241943. *092378*

Chester (Cheshire)
Heyes, Robert I., Hatton Bldgs, Lightfoot St, Hoole, Chester CH2 3AL. T. (01244) 328941,
Fax (01244) 310898. *092379*

Chichester (West Sussex)
Phillips, Baffins Hall, Baffins Ln, Chichester PO19 1UA.
T. (01243) 787548. *092380*
Stride & Son, Southdown House, St John's St, Chichester PO19 1XQ. T. (01243) 780207,
Fax (01243) 786713. *092381*

Chippenham (Wiltshire)
Dreweatt Neate, St Mary St, Chippenham SN15 3JM.
T. (01249) 447886, Fax (01249) 654848. *092382*

Cirencester (Gloucestershire)
Fraser Glennie & Partners, Old Rectory, Siddington, Cirencester GL7 6HL. T. (01285) 659677,
Fax (01285) 642256. *092383*
Hobbs & Chambers, Market Pl, Cirencester GL7 1QQ.
T. (01285) 654736, Fax (01285) 885818. *092384*
Moore Allen & Innocent, 33 Castle St, Cirencester GL7 1QD. T. (01285) 651831, Fax (1285) 640494. *092385*

Clare (Suffolk)
Suffolk Sales, Half Moon House, Clare CO10 8NY.
T. (01787) 277993. *092386*

Cockermouth (Cumbria)
Mitchells, 47 Station Rd, Cockermouth CA13 9PZ.
T. (01900) 827800, Fax (01900) 826780. *092387*

Colchester (Essex)
Brown, William H., 11-14 East Hill, Colchester CO1 2QX.
T. (01206) 868070, Fax (01206) 869590. *092388*

Congleton (Cheshire)
Whittaker & Biggs Auction Room, Macclesfield Rd, Congleton CW12 4AP. T. (01260) 279858,
Fax (01260) 271629. *092389*

Cranbrook (Kent)
Mervyn Carey, Twysden Cottage, Cranbrook TN7 4LD.
T. (01580) 240283. *092390*
Wealden Auction Galleries, Marden Rd, Cranbrook TN17 2LP. T. (01580) 714522, Fax (01580) 715266. *092391*

Crewkerne (Somerset)
Lawrence, South St, Crewkerne TA18 8AB.
T. (01460) 73041, Fax (01460) 74627. *092392*

Crieff (Tayside)
Neils of Crieff, 22 Galvelmore St, Crieff PH7 4DN.
T. (01764) 3276, Fax (01764) 3276. *092393*

Diss (Norfolk)
Gaze & Son, Thomas William, Roydon Rd, Diss IP22 3LN. T. (01379) 650306, Fax (01379) 651936. *092394*

Doncaster (South Yorkshire)
Doncaster Auction Rooms, Unit 2a, Queens Rd, Doncaster. T. (01302) 328664. *092395*

Dorchester (Dorset)
Hy Duke & Son, Weymouth Av, Dorchester DT1 1DG.
T. (01305) 265080, Fax (01305) 260313. *092396*

Dorking (Surrey)
Crow's, Reigate Rd, Dorking RH4 1SG.
T. (01306) 740382. *092397*
Windibank, P.F., 18-20 Reigate Rd, Dorking RH4 1SG.
T. (01306) 884556, Fax (01306) 876280. *092398*

Driffield (Humberside)
Dee & Atkinson, Exchange St, Driffield YO25 7JL.
T. (01377) 43151, Fax (01377) 241041. *092399*

Dumfries (Dumfries and Galloway)
Thomson, Roddick & Laurie, 60 Whitesands, Dumfries DG1 2RS. T. (01387) 55366,
Fax (01387) 66236. *092400*

Easingwold (North Yorkshire)
Summersgill, Geoffrey, Market Pl, Easingwold.
T. (01347) 21366. *092401*

East Boldon (Tyne and Wear)
Boldon Auction Galleries, 24a Front St, East Boldon
NE36 0SJ. T. (0191) 5372630,
Fax (0191) 5363875. *092402*

Eastbourne (East Sussex)
Horn, Edgar, 46-50 South St, Eastbourne BN21 4XB.
T. (01323) 419410, Fax (01323) 416540. *092403*

Edinburgh (Lothian)
Phillips, 65 George St, Edinburgh EH2 2JL.
T. (0131) 225 2266, Fax (0131) 2202547. *092404*

Exeter (Devon)
Phillips, Alphin Brook Rd, Alphington, Exeter EX2 8TH.
T. (01392) 439025, Fax (01392) 410361. *092405*

Fareham (Hampshire)
West Hoe Auctions, 1a Queens Crescent, Fareham PO14
2QA. T. (01329) 664806. *092406*

Folkestone (Kent)
H. & H. Auctioneers, Saint Johns St, Folkestone CT21
3JU. T. (01303) 269323. *092407*
Phillips, 11 Bayle Parade, Folkestone CT20 ISQ.
T. (01303) 245555. *092408*
Valley Auctions, Brady Rd, Folkestone CT18 8EU.
T. (01303) 862134. *092409*

Forres (Grampian)
Forres Saleroom, Tytler St, Forres IV36 0EL.
T. (01309) 672422. *092410*

Frome (Somerset)
Nationwide Fine Art and Furniture, Frome Market, Stan-
derwick, Frome BA11 2PY. T. (01373) 831010,
Fax (01373) 831103. *092411*

Gateshead (Tyne & Wear)
Phillips North East, St Mary's, Oakwellgate, Gateshead
NE8 2AX. T. (0191) 4776688,
Fax (0191) 4787754. *092412*

Glasgow (Strathclyde)
Christie's Scotland, 164-166 Bath St, Glasgow G2 4TG.
T. (0141) 3328134, Fax (0141) 3325759. *092413*
Great Western Auctions, 29-37 Otago St, Glasgow.
T. (0141) 3393290, Fax (0141) 3348615. *092413a*
McTear, 6 North Court, St Vincent Pl, Glasgow G1 2DS.
T. (0141) 221 4456. *092414*
Phillips, 207 Bath St, Glasgow G2 4HD.
T. (0141) 2218377, Fax (0141) 2264441. *092415*

Gloucester (Gloucestershire)
Bruton Knowles, 111 Eastgate St, Gloucester GL1 1PZ.
T. (01452) 521267, Fax (01452) 300184. *092417*
Short, Graham & Co., 4-6 Clarence St, Gloucester GL1
1DX. T. (01452) 521177. *092418*

Godalming (Surrey)
Hampton, 93 High St, Godalming GU7 1AL.
T. (01483) 423567, Fax (01483) 426392. *092419*

Gosport (Hampshire)
Coates Auctions of Gosport, 15 South Loading R, Gos-
port PO12 1BL. T. (01705) 589418,
Fax (01705) 521358. *092420*

Grantham (Lincolnshire)
Goldings, Old Wharf Rd, Grantham. T. (01476) 65118,
Fax (01476) 590998. *092420a*
Marilyn Swain Auctions, Westgate Hall, Westgate, Gran-
tham NG31 GLT. T. (01476) 68861. *092421*

Great Dunmow (Essex)
Hampton, Old Town Hall, Great Dunmow CM6 1AU.
T. (01371) 872117, Fax (01371) 873014. *092423*

Great Malvern (Hereford & Worcester)
Hamptons, 69 Church St, Great Malvern WR14 2AE.
T. (01684) 892314, Fax (01684) 569832. *092424*

Guildford (Surrey)
Clarke Gammon, Bedford Rd, Guildford GU1 4SJ.
T. (01483) 66458, Fax (01483) 34835. *092425*
Ewbank Auctioneers, Welbeck House, High St, Guildford
GU1 3JF. T. (01483) 232134,
Fax (01483) 236671. *092426*
Phillips Guildford, Millmead, Guildford GU2 5BE.
T. (01483) 504030. *092427*
South East Marts, Cattle Market, Guildford GU1 1SG.
T. (01483) 573386, Fax (01483) 301994. *092428*

Haddington (Lothian)
Leslie & Leslie, 77 Market St, Haddington EH41 3JJ.
T. (0162) 0822241, Fax (0162) 0822241. *092429*

Hamilton (Strathclyde)
Smellie's, Hamilton, Lower Auchingromont Rd, Hamilton
ML3 6HW. T. (01698) 282007,
Fax (01357) 29797. *092430*

Harrogate (North Yorkshire)
Morphets/William H. Brown, 4-6 Albert St, Harrogate
HG1 1JL. T. (01423) 530030,
Fax (01423) 531685. *092431*

Hartley Wintney (Hampshire)
Odiham Auctions Sales, High St, Hartley Wintney RG27
8PU. T. (01252) 844410, Fax (01252) 843195. *092432*

Henley-on-Thames (Oxfordshire)
Simmons & Sons, 32 Bell St, Henley-on-Thames RG9
2BH. T. (01491) 571111, Fax (01491) 579833. *092433*

Honiton (Devon)
Bonhams West Country, Dowell St, Honiton EX14 0LX.
T. (01404) 41872, Fax (01404) 43137. *092434*
Taylor, 205 High St, Honiton EX14 8LF. T. (01404) 42404,
Fax (01404) 46510. *092435*

Horncastle (Lincolnshire)
Bell & Co., Robert, Old Bank Chambers, Horncastle LN9
5HY. T. (01507) 522222. *092436*

Horsham (West Sussex)
Denham's, Horsham Auction Galleries, Durfold Hill,
Horsham RH12 3RZ. T. (01403) 55699,
Fax (01403) 53837. *092437*

Hove (East Sussex)
Graves Son & Pilcher, 71 Church Rd, Hove BN3 2GL.
T. (01273) 735266, Fax (801273) 723813. *092438*

Hull (Humberside)
Baitson, Gilbert, Wiltshire Rd, Hull HU4 6PG.
T. (01482) 500500, Fax (01482) 500501. *092439*

Hythe (Kent)
Butler & Co., Lawrence, 86 High St, Hythe CT21 5AJ.
T. (01303) 266022/3, Fax (01303) 260063. *092440*

Ilkley (West Yorkshire)
Hartley, Andrew, Victoria Hall Salerooms, Little Ln, Ilkley
LS29 8EA. T. (01943) 816363,
Fax (01943) 816086. *092441*

Inverness (Highland)
Fraser, 28-30 Church St, Inverness IV1 1EH.
T. (01463) 232395. *092442*

Ipswich (Suffolk)
Phillips, Dover House, Wolsey St, Ipswich IP1 1UD.
T. (01473) 255137, Fax (01473) 251924. *092443*

Kettering (Northamptonshire)
Southams, The Corn Exchange, Kettering NN14 4JJ.
T. (01832) 734486, Fax (01832) 732409. *092444*

Kilgetty (Dyfed)
Evans & Co., Graham H., The Market Pl, Kilgetty SA69
0UG. T. (01834) 811151, Fax (01834) 813649. *092445*

Kingston-upon-Thames (Surrey)
Chancellors Auctions, 74 London Rd., Kingston-upon-
Thames KT2 6PX. T. (0181) 5414139,
Fax (0181) 5470210. *092446*

Knowle (West Midlands)
Phillips Knowle, Station Rd, Knowle B93 0HT.
T. (01564) 776151, Fax (01564) 778069. *092447*

Lampeter (Dyfed)
King, Thomas, 36 High St, Lampeter SA48 7BB.
T. (01570) 422550, Fax (01570) 422071. *092448*

Leamington Spa (Warwickshire)
Black Horse Agencies – Locke & England, 18 Guy St,
Leamington Spa CV32 4RT. T. (01926) 889100,
Fax (01926) 470608. *092449*

Leeds (West Yorkshire)
Phillips, 17a East Parade, Leeds LS1 2BU.
T. (0113) 448011, Fax (0113) 429875. *092450*

Leicester (Leicestershire)
Brown, William H., 16-18 Halford St, Leicester LE1 1JB.
T. (0116) 519777, Fax (0116) 510078. *092451*

Leigh-on-Sea (Essex)
Leigh Auction Rooms, 86-90 Pall Mall, Leigh-on-Sea
SS9 1RG. T. (01702) 77051,
Fax (01702) 470141. *092452*

Leominster (Hereford and Worcester)
Russell, Baldwin & Bright, Fine Art Saleroom, Ryelands
Rd, Leominster HR6 8NZ. T. (01568) 611166,
Fax (01568) 611802. *092453*

Leven (Fife)
Dowie, Robert, Station Rd, Leven.
T. (01333) 423438. *092454*

Lewes (East Sussex)
Dann, Clifford, 20-21 High St, Lewes BN7 2LN.
T. (01273) 480111, Fax (01273) 480345. *092455*
Gorringe, 15 North St, Lewes BN7 2PD.
T. (01273) 472503, Fax (1273) 479559. *092456*
Lewes Auction Rooms, 56 High St, Lewes BN7 1XE.
T. (01273) 478221. *092457*
Wallis & Wallis, West St, Lewes BN7 2NJ.
T. (01273) 480208, Fax (01273) 476562. *092458*

Leyland (Lancashire)
Warren & Wignall, The Mill, Earnshaw Bridge, Leyland
PR5 3PH. T. (01772) 451430/453252,
Fax (01772) 454516. *092459*

Lichfield (Staffordshire)
Wintertons, Lichfield Auction Centre, Woodend Ln, Lich-
field WS13 8NF. T. (01543) 263256,
Fax (01543) 415348. *092460*

Lincoln (Lincolnshire)
Walter's, 1 Mint Lane, Lincoln LN1 1UD.
T. (01522) 525454, Fax (01522) 512720. *092461*

Lisburn (Northern Ireland)
Temple Auctions, 133 Carryduff Rd, Lisburn BT27 6YL.
T. (01846) 638777, Fax (01846) 638777. *092462*

Liverpool (Merseyside)
Cato Crane & Co., 6 Stanhope St, Liverpool L8 5RF.
T. (0151) 7095509, Fax (0151) 7072454. *092463*
Outhwaite & Litherland, Kingsway Galleries, Fontenoy
St, Liverpool L3 2BE. T. (0151) 2366561,
Fax (0151) 2361070. *092464*

London
Academy Auctioneers & Valuers, Northcote House,
Northcote Av, London W5 3UR. T. (0181) 579 7466,
Fax (0181) 5790511. *092465*
Bainbridge's, St John's Parade, Mattock Lane, London
W13. T. (0181) 5792966. *092466*
Bonhams, Montpellier St., London SW7 1HH.
T. (0171) 3933900, Fax (0171) 3933905. *092467*
Bonhams Chelser, 65-69 Lots Rd, London SW10 0RN.
T. (0171) 351 7111, Fax (0171) 351 7754. *092468*
Christie's, 8 King St, London SW1Y 6QT.
T. (0171) 839 9060, Fax (0171) 8391611. *092469*
Christie's South Kensington, 85 Old Brompton Rd, Lon-
don SW7 3LD. T. (0171) 581 7611,
Fax (0171) 3213321. *092470*
Criterion Auction Rooms, 53 Essex Rd, London N1 2BN.
T. (0171) 3595707, Fax (0171) 3549843. *092471*

Dowell Lloyd & Co., 118 Putney Bridge Rd, London SW15 2NQ. T. (0181) 788 7777, Fax (0181) 8745390. *092472*

Glendining & Co., 101 New Bond St, London W1Y 9LG. T. (0171) 493 2445, Fax (0171) 4919181. *092473*

Gray's, 34-36 Jamestown Rd, London NW1 7BY. T. (0171) 2842026, Fax (0171) 2842015. *092474*

Lewisham Auction Rooms, 165 Lee High Rd, Lewisham, London SE13 5PF. T. (0181) 8523145. *092475*

Lloyd Park Auction Rooms, 89 Grange Rd, London E17. T. (0181) 5209878. *092476*

Lots Road Galleries, 71 Lots Rd, London SW10 0RN. T. (0171) 351 7771, Fax (0171) 3768349. *092477*

MacGregor Nash & Co., 9-17 Lodge Lane, London N12 8JH. T. (0181) 4459000/5153, Fax (0181) 4466068. *092478*

Merton Abbey Mills, Watermill Way, London SW19 2RD. T. (0181) 5437266. *092479*

Phillips, 101 New Bond St, London W1Y 0AS. T. (0171) 629 6602, Fax (0171) 629 8876. *092480*

Phillips West Two, 10 Salem Rd, London W2 4DL. T. (0171) 229 9090, Fax (0171) 7929201. *092481*

Rosebery, Old Railway Station, Crystal Palace, Station Rd, London SE19 2AZ. T. (0181) 778 4024, Fax (0181) 6596023. *092482*

Sotheby's, 34-35 New Bond St, London W1A 2AA. T. (0171) 493 8080, Fax (0171) 409 3100. *092483*

LOCAL SERVICE,
INTERNATIONAL
PRICES

SOTHEBY'S

34-35 New Bond Street,
London W1A 2AA
Tel: 0171 493 8080

Southgate Auction Rooms, 55 High St, London N14 6LD. T. (0181) 886 7888, Fax (0181) 8867287. *092484*

Lostwithiel (Cornwall)
Jefferys, 5 Fore St, Lostwithiel PL22 0BP. T. (01208) 872245, Fax (801208) 873260. *092485*

Loughton (Essex)
Black Horse Agencies, 149 High Rd, Loughton IG10 4LZ. T. (0181) 508 2121, Fax (0181) 5089516. *092486*

Ludlow (Shropshire)
Ludlow Antique Auctions, 29 Corve St, Ludlow SY8 1DA. T. (01584) 875157, Fax (01584) 876491. *092487*

McCartneys, 25 Corve St, Ludlow SY8 1DA. T. (01584) 872636, Fax (01584) 875727. *092488*

Mear & Co., Timothy, Temeside Salerooms, Ludford Bridge, Ludlow SY8 1PE. T. (01584) 876081. *092489*

Luton (Bedfordshire)
Frank & Shirley's Auctions, 37 John St, Luton LU1 2JE. T. (01582) 405281/38624. *092490*

Luton Multi-Auctions, 37 John St, Luton LU1 2JE. T. (01583) 405281. *092491*

Lymington (Hampshire)
Kidner, George, The Old School, The Square, Lymington SO41 8GN. T. (01590) 670070, Fax (01590) 675167. *092492*

Manchester (Greater Manchester)
Capes, Dunn & Co., 38 Charles St, Manchester M1 7DB. T. (0161) 273 1911, Fax (0161) 2733474. *092493*

Marlborough (Wiltshire)
Hamptons Pocock & Lear, 20 High St, Marlborough SN8 1AA. T. (01672) 516161, Fax (01672) 515882. *092494*

Midhurst (West Sussex)
Nationwide Midhurst Auction Rooms, West St, Midhurst GU29 9NG. T. (01730) 812456, Fax (01730) 814514. *092495*

Milton Keynes (Buckinghamshire)
Downer Ross, 426 Avebury Blvd, Milton Keynes MK9 2HS. T. (01908) 679900, Fax (01908) 678242. *092496*

Minehead (Somerset)
Mart Road Salerooms, Mart Rd, Minehead TA24 5SR. T. (01643) 703646, Fax (01643) 707523. *092497*

Mold (Clwyd)
Dodd, Chester St, Mold CH7 1EB. T. (01352) 752552. *092498*

Nantwich (Cheshire)
Wilson, Peter, Market St, Nantwich CW5 5DG. T. (01270) 623878. *092499*

Newbury (Berkshire)
Dreweatt Neate, Donnington Priory, Newbury RG13 2JE. T. (01635) 31234, Fax (01635) 528195. *092500*

Newcastle-upon-Tyne (Tyne and Wear)
Anderson & Garland, Marlborough House, Marlborough Crescent, Newcastle-upon-Tyne NE1 4EE. T. (0191) 2326278, Fax (0191) 2618665. *092501*

Newton Abbot (Devon)
Rendells, 13 Market St, Newton Abbot TQ12 2RL. T. (01626) 53881, Fax (01626) 65030. *092502*

Newtown (Powys)
Morris Marshall & Poole, The Smithfield Saleroom, Newtown SY16 2LZ. T. (01686) 625900, Fax (01686) 623783. *092503*

Northampton (Northamptonshire)
Merry's, 14 Bridge St, Northampton NN1 1NJ. T. (01604) 32266, Fax (01604) 231566. *092504*

Norwich (Norfolk)
Key's, 8 Market Pl, Norwich NR11 6EH. T. (01263) 733195, Fax (01263) 732140. *092505*

Oakham (Leicestershire)
Oakham Auction Centre, 78 South St, Oakham LE15 6BQ. T. (01572) 723569. *092506*

Oxford (Oxfordshire)
Mallams, 24 Saint Michael's St, Oxford OX1 2EB. T. (01865) 241358, Fax (01865) 725483. *092507*

Phillips, 39 Park End St, Oxford OX1 1JD. T. (01865) 723524, Fax (01865) 791064. *092508*

Par (Cornwall)
Phillips, Cornubia Hall, Par PL24 2AQ. T. (0172681) 814047, Fax (0172681) 817979. *092509*

Penrith (Cumbria)
Penrith Farmers & Kidds, Devonshire St, Penrith CA11 2SS. T. (01768) 62135, Fax (01768) 62135. *092510*

Penzance (Cornwall)
Lane & Son, W.H., 64 Morrab Rd, Penzance TR18 2QT. T. (01736) 61447, Fax (01736) 50097. *092511*

Lay, David, Penzance Auction House, Alverton, Penzance TR18 4RE. T. (01736) 61414, Fax (01736) 60035. *092512*

Perth (Tayside)
Lindsay Burns & Co., 6 King St, Perth PH2 8JA. T. (01738) 33888, Fax (01738) 441322. *092513*

Love, 52-54 Canal St, Perth PH2 8LF. T. (01738) 33337, Fax (01738) 29830. *092514*

Petersfield (Hampshire)
Jacobs & Hunt, 26 Lavant St, Petersfield GU32 3EF. T. (01730) 262744, Fax (01730) 231393. *092515*

Plymouth (Devon)
Eldred, Anthony, The Drill Hall, 13-15 Ridge Park Rd, Plymouth PL7 3BS. T. (01752) 340066. *092516*

Poole (Dorset)
Alder King, 13 St Peters Rd, Poole BH14 0PH. T. (01202) 748567, Fax (01202) 716258. *092517*

Pulborough (West Sussex)
South Coast Auctions, Red Lion, Lower Rd, Pulborough. T. (01273) 509214. *092518*

Ramsey (Isle of Man)
Chrystals Auctions, The Mart, Bowring Rd, Ramsey. T. (01624) 673986. *092519*

Ringwood (Hampshire)
Phillips, 54 Southampton Rd, Ringwood BH24 1JD. T. (01425) 473333, Fax (01425) 470989. *092520*

Romsey (Hampshire)
Romsey Auction Rooms, 86 The Hundred, Romsey SO51 8BX. T. (01794) 513331, Fax (01794) 511770. *092521*

Rotherham (South Yorkshire)
Wilkinson & Beighton Auctioneers, Woodhouse Green, Thurcroft, Rotherham S66 9AQ. T. (01709) 700005, Fax (01709) 700244. *092522*

Ryde (Isle of Wight)
Way, Garfield Rd, Ryde PO33 2PT. T. (01983) 562255. *092523*

Saffron Walden (Essex)
Saffron Walden Auctions, 1 Market St, Saffron Walden CB10 1JB. T. (01799) 513281, Fax (01799) 513334. *092524*

St Andrews (Fife)
MacGregor Auctions, 56a Largo Rd, St Andrews KY16 8RP. T. (01334) 72431. *092525*

Saint Helier (Jersey)
Langlois, Westaway Chambers, 39 Don St, Saint Helier JE2 4TR. T. (01534) 22441, Fax (1534) 59354. *092526*

St Leonards-on-Sea (East Sussex)
Ascent Auction Galleries, 11-12 East Ascent & 1 Mews Rd, St Leonards-on-Sea TN38 0DS. T. (01424) 420275. *092527*

Salisbury (Wiltshire)
Woolley & Wallis, 51-61 Castle St, Salisbury SP1 3SU. T. (01722) 411422, Fax (01722) 411426. *092528*

Saltburn-by-the-Sea (Cleveland)
Simmons & Son, J.C., Saltburn Salerooms, Diamond St, Saltburn-by-the-Sea TS12 1EB. T. (01287) 622366. *092529*

Sandbach (Cheshire)
Andrew, Hilditch & Son, 1a The Square, Sandbach CW11 0AP. T. (01270) 762048, 767246, Fax (01270) 762048. *092530*

Sandwich (Kent)
Halifax Property Services, 15 Cattle Market, Sandwich. T. (01304) 611044/614369. *092531*

Scarborough (North Yorkshire)
Chapman & Son, H.C., Auction Mart, North St, Scarborough YO11 1DL. T. (01723) 372424, Fax (01723) 500697. *092532*

Seaton (Devon)
Lyme-Bay Auction Galleries, 28 Harbour Rd, Seaton EX12 2JA. T. (01297) 22453. *092533*

Sevenoaks (Kent)
Ibbett Mosely, 125 High St, Sevenoaks TN13 1UT. T. (01732) 456731, Fax (01732) 740910. *092534*

Phillips, Son & Neale, 49 London Rd, Sevenoaks TN13 1AR. T. (01732) 740310, Fax (01732) 741842. *092535*

Shaftesbury (Dorset)
Semley Auctioneers, Station Rd, Semley, Shaftesbury SP7 9AN. T. (01747) 55122/55222. *092536*

Shanklin (Isle of Wight)
Watson Bull & Porter, 79 Regent St, Shanklin PO37 7AP. T. (01983) 863441, Fax (01983) 863890. *092537*

Sheffield (South Yorkshire)
Dowse & Son, A.E., Cornwall Galleries, Scotland St, Sheffield S3 7DE. T. (0114) 725858. *092538*
Ellis, Willis & Beckett, 54 Campo Lane, Sheffield S1 1FU. T. (0114) 729667, Fax (0114) 767160. *092539*

Sherborne (Dorset)
Phillips Sherborne, Long Street Salerooms, Sherborne DT9 3BS. T. (01935) 815271,
Fax (01935) 816416. *092540*

Shrewsbury (Shropshire)
Halls, Welsh Bridge Salerooms, Shrewsbury SY3 8LA. T. (01743) 231212, Fax (01743) 271014. *092541*

Southport (Merseyside)
Cobern, A.J., 93b Eastbank St, Southport PR8 1DG. T. (01704) 500515, Fax (01704) 500254. *092542*

Southsea (Hampshire)
Nesbit's, 7 Clarendon Rd, Southsea PO5 2ED. T. (01705) 864321, Fax (01705) 295522. *092543*

Stoke-on-Trent (Staffordshire)
Taylor, Louis, Louis, 10 Town Rd, Stoke-on-Trent ST1 2QG. T. (01782) 260222, Fax (01782) 287874. *092544*

Stratford-upon-Avon (Warwickshire)
Bigwood, Old School, Tiddington, Stratford-upon-Avon CV37 7AW. T. (01789) 269415. *092545*
Phillips Bros Auctioneers, Bearley Rd, Stratford-upon-Avon CV37 0EZ. T. (01789) 731114. *092546*

Stroud (Gloucestershire)
Trinity Auction Rooms, Field Rd, Stroud.
T. (01452) 812487. *092547*

Sudbury (Suffolk)
Brown, William H., Olivers Rooms, Burkitts Ln, Sudbury CO10 6HB. T. (01787) 880305,
Fax (01787) 880052. *092548*

Sutton-in-Ashfield (Nottinghamshire)
Sheppard & Son, C.B., Chatsworth St, Sutton-in-Ashfield NG17 4GG. T. (01773) 872419. *092549*

Swaffham (Norfolk)
Heritage Auctions, 5 Latimer Way, Swaffham PE37 8JY. T. (01760) 440384. *092550*

Swindon (Wiltshire)
Allen & Harris, Planks Salerooms, Old Town, Swindon SN3 1QP. T. (01793) 615915. *092551*

Tarporley (Cheshire)
Wright Manley, 63 High St, Tarporley CW6 0DR. T. (01829) 260318, Fax (01829) 261208. *092552*

Taunton (Somerset)
Greenslade Hunt Fine Art, Magdalene House, Church Square, Taunton TA1 1SB. T. (01823) 332525,
Fax (01823) 323923. *092553*

Tavistock (Devon)
Fenner & Company, The Stannary Gallery, Drake Rd, Tavistock PL19 0AX. T. (01822) 617799/617800,
Fax (01822) 617595. *092554*
Ward & Chowen, Tavistock Auction Rooms, Market Rd, Tavistock PL19 0BW. T. (01822) 612603,
Fax (01822) 615635. *092555*

Tenterden (Kent)
Halifax Property Services, 53 High St, Tenterden TN30 6BG. T. (015806) 3200. *092556*

Tetbury (Gloucestershire)
Tetbury Auctions, 2 Baytree Court, Tetbury GL8 8EU. T. (01666) 505695. *092557*

Torquay (Devon)
Bearne's, Rainbow, Avenue Rd, Torquay TQ2 5TG. T. (01803) 296277, Fax (01803) 291565. *092558*

Tring (Hertfordshire)
Tring Auctions, Brook St, Tring HP23 5EF. T. (0144) 2826446, Fax (0144) 2827743. *092559*

Truro (Cornwall)
Truro Auction Centre, Calenick St, Truro TR1 2SG. T. (01872) 260020, Fax (01872) 261794. *092560*

Tunbridge Wells (Kent)
Bracketts, 27-29 High St, Tunbridge Wells TM1 1UU. T. (01892) 533733, Fax (01892) 512201. *092561*

Uttoxeter (Staffordshire)
Bagshaw, 17 High St, Uttoxeter ST14 7HP. T. (01889) 562811, Fax (01889) 563795. *092562*

Wadebridge (Cornwall)
Lambrays, Polmorla Walk, Wadebridge PL27 7AE. T. (01208) 8813593. *092563*

Wakefield (West Yorkshire)
Walsh & Co., John, 48 Woodlands, Wakefield WF4 5HH. T. (01924) 271710/264030,
Fax (01924) 279710. *092564*

Wallasey (Merseyside)
Kent, J., 2-6 Valkyrie Rd, Wallasey L45 4RQ. T. (0151) 6383107, Fax (0151) 6383107. *092565*

Warnham (West Sussex)
Denham, Garth, Horsham Auction Galleries, Warnham RH12 3RZ. T. (01403) 55699, Fax 53837. *092566*

Wellingborough (Northamptonshire)
Wilford, H., 76 Midland Rd, Wellingborough NN8 1NB. T. (01933) 222760. *092567*

Wells (Somerset)
Allen & Harris Wells Auction Rooms, 66-68 Southover, Wells BA5 1UH. T. (01749) 678094/678884. *092568*

Westcliff-on-Sea (Essex)
Chalkwell Auctions, 66 The Ridgeway, Westcliff-on-Sea SS0 8NU. T. (01702) 710383. *092569*

Weymouth (Dorset)
Hy, Duke, & Son, Saint Nicholas St, Weymouth. T. (01305) 761499. *092570*

Whitby (North Yorkshire)
Nationwide Fine Art and Furniture, 27 Flowergate, Whitby YO21 3AX. T. (01947) 603433,
Fax (01947) 601868. *092571*
Richardson & Smith incorporating Robert Gray & Sons, West Cliff Saleroom, 19 Silver St, Whitby YO21 1EA. T. (01947) 602298, Fax (01947) 820594. *092572*

Wigton (Cumbria)
Thomson Roddick & Laurie, 25 King St, Wigton CA7 9DT. T. (016973) 43348. *092573*

Winchester (Hampshire)
Phillips, Red House, Hyde St, Winchester SO23 7DX. T. (01962) 862515, Fax (01962) 865166. *092574*

Winslow (Buckinghamshire)
Winslow Saleroom – Geo. Wigley & Sons, 12 Market Square, Winslow MK18 3AG. T. (01296) 712717,
Fax (01296) 713561. *092575*

Woking (Surrey)
Barbers, The Mayford Centre, Smarts Heath Rd, Woking GU22 0PP. T. (01483) 728939. *092576*

Woodbridge (Suffolk)
Abbotts, Campsea Ashe, Woodbridge IP13 0PS. T. (01728) 746323, Fax (01728) 746880. *092577*
Neal Sons & Fletcher, 26 Church St, Woodbridge IP12 1DP. T. (01394) 382263, Fax (01394) 383030. *092578*

Woodford (Cheshire)
Maxwell of Wilmslow, John, 133a Woodford Rd, Woodford SK7 1QD. T. (0161) 4395182,
Fax (0161) 4395182. *092579*

Worcester (Hereford & Worcester)
Andrew Grant Fine Art Auctions, St Marks House, St Marks Close, Worcester WR5 3DJ. T. (01905) 357547,
Fax (01905) 726213. *092580*

Worthing (West Sussex)
Worthing Auction Galleries, 31 Chatsworth Rd, Worthing BN11 1LY. T. (01903) 205565. *092581*

Wotton-under-Edge (Gloucestershire)
Wotton Auction Rooms, Tabernacle Rd, Wotton-under-Edge GL12 7EB. T. (01454) 844733,
Fax (01454) 845448. *092582*

Uruguay

Montevideo
Adami Casaravilla, H., Calle 25 de Mayo No. 582-64, 11.000 Montevideo. T. (02) 95 79 29. *092583*
Barrios, J.G. Gómez 1282, 11000 Montevideo.
T. (02) 95 81 66. *092584*
Bavastro, Eugenio, Misiones 1376, 11000 Montevideo.
T. (02) 95 58 01. *092585*
Belveder, San Quintin 4326, 11900 Montevideo.
T. (02) 39 82 42. *092586*
Benech Gardiol, Ruben, Bartolomé Mitre 1475, 11000 Montevideo. T. (02) 95 82 79/80. *092587*
Bentancour, César, Bartolomé Mitre 1437, 11000 Montevideo. T. (02) 95 91 97. *092588*
Cabrera Delfa, Pres. Gral. Gestido 2851, 11300 Montevideo. T. (02) 77 15 80. *092589*
Carballo y Carballo, Cno. Maldonaldo 6269, 12200 Montevideo. T. (02) 54 71 60. *092590*
Castells & Castells, Galicia 1069, 11100 Montevideo.
T. (02) 90 73 00, 98 02 51, Fax 90 54 30. *092591*
Corbo, José Enrique Rodo 1671, 11200 Montevideo.
T. (02) 41 35 15, 41 93 64. *092592*
Fernández, Jacinto, J.P. Lamolle 1903, 12500 Montevideo. T. (02) 32 84 42. *092593*
Ferrari Sarzábal, Aldo, Avda. Millán 2371, 11800 Montevideo. T. (02) 20 13 20. *092594*
Ferretjans, Gral. Flores 2673, 11800 Montevideo.
T. (02) 20 26 10. *092595*
Gomensoro, Paraguay 1924, 11800 Montevideo.
T. (02) 944000, Fax 949050. *092596*
Gómez, Blanca Martinez de, Avda. Gral. Flores 4105, 12300 Montevideo. T. (02) 25 30 79. *092597*
Infante Panaro Mónica R., Avda. Gral. Flores 3839, 12300 Montevideo. T. (02) 25 38 54. *092598*
Izquierdo, Alberto, J. Roldós YP 4253, 12000 Montevideo. T. (02) 25 67 11. *092599*
La Catedral, Sarandi 536, 11000 Montevideo.
T. (02) 95 87 65, 95 90 72. *092600*
Mauad Juan, Omar & Michel, Bartolomé Mitre 1567, 11000 Montevideo. T. (02) 96 39 97. *092601*
Milán, San Quintin 4293, 11900 Montevideo.
T. (02) 39 80 37. *092602*
Nuñez, Elena, Avda. Italia 4364, 11400 Montevideo.
T. (02) 69 72 10. *092603*
Piñeyro, Horacio, Piedras 274, 11000 Montevideo.
T. (02) 95 53 22. *092604*
Remates 488, Sarandi 488, 11000 Montevideo.
T. (02) 95 26 12. *092605*
Sabas, Gaboto 1543, 11200 Montevideo.
T. (02) 41 88 14. *092606*
Straumann, Werther, Tristán Narvaja 1729, 11200 Montevideo. T. (02) 49 09 94, 49 05 35,
Fax 48 70 07. *092607*
Szenker, Max Anrique, Misiones 1348, 11000 Montevideo. T. (02) 95 26 64. *092608*
Tambasco, Yaro 1121, 11200 Montevideo.
T. (02) 48 30 02, 40 19 35. *092609*
Vargha & Bettega, Dr. J. de Salterain 1019, 11200 Montevideo. T. (02) 49 93 38. *092610*
Viviano, Gomez, Gral. Flores 4105, 12000 Montevideo.
T. (02) 25 30 79. *092611*

Wolf, Rodriguez, Solis 1463, 11000 Montevideo.
T. (02) 95 85 46.   *092612*

U.S.A.

Alexandria (Virginia)
Yudkin, Samuel, & Associates, 2109 Popkins Lane, Alexandria, VA 22307. T. (703) 768-1858.   *092613*

Annapolis (Maryland)
Theriault, POB 151, Annapolis, MD 21404. T. (301) 269-
0680.   *092614*

Antioch (Illinois)
Larson, Jo Anna, 60002 Antioch, IL 60002. T. (312) 395-
0963.   *092615*

Atlanta (Georgia)
Depew, Jim, 1860 Piedmont Rd., Atlanta, GA 30324.
T. (404) 874-2286.   *092616*
Gold, 1149 Lee St. SW, Atlanta, GA 30310. T. (404) 752-
5660.   *092617*
Howe, Clive, 778 Adair Av. NE, Atlanta, GA 30306.
T. (404) 872-8600.   *092618*

Auburn (Indiana)
Kruse, POB 190, Auburn, IN 46706. T. (219) 925-
5600.   *092619*

Baltimore (Maryland)
Harris, 975 N Howard St., Baltimore, MD 21201.
T. (301) 847-2045.   *092620*

Baton Rouge (Louisiana)
Louisiana Auction Exchange, 2031 Government St., Baton Rouge, LA 70806. T. (504) 924-1803.   *092621*

Bay City (Michigan)
Butterfield, L., 605 W Midland, Bay City, MI 48706.
T. (517) 684-3229.   *092622*

Belvidere (New Hampshire)
Hampton Auction Gallery, 201 Hardwick St, Belvidere,
NH 07823. T. (201) 4752928.   *092623*

Bethesda (Maryland)
Old World Mail Auction, 5614 Northfield Rd., Bethesda,
MD 20817. T. (301) 657-9074.   *092624*
Waverly, 4931 Cordell Av, Bethesda, MD 20814.
T. (301) 951-8883.   *092625*

Beverly Hills (California)
Superior Stamp and Coin Company, 9478 W Olympic
Blvd., Beverly Hills, CA 90212-4299.   *092626*

Birmingham (Alabama)
Alabama Auction Room, Inc., 2112 Fifth Ave. North, Birmingham, AL 35203. T. (205) 2524073.   *092627*

Bloomfield Hills (Michigan)
Boos, Frank H., 420 Enterprise Court, Bloomfield Hills,
MI 48302. T. (313) 332-1500, Fax (313) 332-
6370.   *092628*

Bolton (Massachusetts)
Skinner, 357 Main St., Bolton, MA 01740. T. (508) 779-
6241, Fax (508) 779-5144.   *092629*

Boston (Massachusetts)
Grogan & Co, 890 Commonwealth Av, Boston, MA
02215. T. (617) 566-4100, Fax (617) 566-
7715.   *092630*
Skinner, 2 Newbury St., Boston, MA 02116.
T. (617) 236-1700, Fax 247-2903.   *092631*
Sotheby, 101 Newbury St., Boston, MA 02116.
T. (617) 247-2851.   *092632*

Brooklyn (New York)
Rasmussen, Birgit, 50 Sterling Pl., Apt 3, Brooklyn, NY
11217. T. (718) 857-0151.   *092633*

Buskirk (New York)
Siefert, Ronald, RFD Buskirk, Buskirk, NY 12028.
T. (518) 686-9375.   *092634*

Cambridge (Massachusetts)
Bakker, James R., 370 Broadway, Cambridge, MA
02139. T. (617) 864-7067, Fax (617) 864-
6626.   *092635*
Hubley Et Co, F.B., 364 Broadway, Cambridge, MA
02100. T. (617) 876-2030.   *092636*

Carmel (Indiana)
Acorn Fam Antiques, 15466 Oak Rd., Carmel, IN 46032.
T. (317) 846-2383.   *092637*

Century City (California)
Goodman, J.M., 1888 E Century Park, Suite 10, Century
City, CA 90067. T. (213) 556-3033.   *092638*

Chattanooga (Tennessee)
Northgate, 5520 Hwy. 153, Chattanooga, TN 37343.
T. (615) 877-6114.   *092639*

Chicago (Illinois)
Gilmore, Chase, 724 W Washington Blvd., Chicago, IL
60606. T. (312) 648-1690.   *092640*
Hanzel, 1120 South Michigan Ave, Chicago, IL 60605.
T. (312) 922-6234, Fax (312) 922-6972.   *092641*
Hindman, Leslie, 215 W Ohio St., Chicago, IL 60610.
T. (312) 670-0010, Fax (312) 670-4248.   *092642*
Shore Galleries, Inc., 3318 W. Devon Ave., Chicago, IL
60645. T. (312) 676 2900.   *092643*

Cincinnati (Ohio)
Main Auction Galleries, 137 W. 4th St., Cincinnati, OH
45202. T. (513) 621-1280.   *092644*
Treadway, Don, 2128 Madison Rd, Cincinnati, OH
45208. T. (513) 321-6742, Fax (513) 871-
7722.   *092645*

Cleveland (Ohio)
Wolf's, 1239 W 6th St, Cleveland, OH 44113.   *092646*

Cogan Station (Pennsylvania)
Roan, Bob, Chuck & Rich, RD3, Box 118, Cogan Station,
PA 17728. T. (717) 494-0170.   *092647*

Columbia (South Carolina)
Charlton, 929 Gervais St., Columbia, SC 29201.
T. (803) 779-5678.   *092648*

Dallas (Texas)
Garrett, 1800 Irving Blvd., Dallas, TX 75207.
T. (214) 742-4343.   *092649*
Heritage Numismatic Auctions, 311 Market St., Dallas,
TX 75202. T. (214) 742-2200.   *092650*

Delaware (Ohio)
Garth's Auction Barn, 1570 Stratford Rd., Delaware, OH
43015. T. (614) 362 4771.   *092651*

Denmark (Maine)
Guarino, C.E., POB 49, Denmark, ME 04022.
T. (207) 452-2123.   *092652*

Denver (Colorado)
Rosvall Auction, 1238 S. Broadway, Denver, CO
80210.   *092653*

Detroit (Michigan)
DuMouchelle, 409 E Jefferson Av., Detroit, MI 48226.
T. (313) 963-6255.   *092654*

Dover (New Jersey)
Bermans, 33 W Blackwell St., Dover, NJ 07801.
T. (201) 361-3110.   *092655*

East Dennis (Massachusetts)
Eldred, Robert C., Rte. 6A, Box 796, East Dennis, MA
02641. T. (617) 385-3116.   *092656*

Elgin (Illinois)
Dunning, 755 Church Rd., Elgin, IL 60120. T. (312) 741-
3483.   *092657*

Encino (California)
Malter, Joel L., & Co., 16661 Ventura Blvd., Encino, CA
91316. T. (818) 784-7772.   *092658*

Essex (Massachusetts)
Landry, L.A., 94 Main St., Essex, MA 01929.
T. (617) 744-5811.   *092659*

Fairfield (Maine)
Julia, James D., Rte. 201, Fairfield, ME 04937.
T. (207) 453-9725.   *092660*

Forney (Texas)
Clements, POB 727, Forney, TX 75126. T. (214) 226-
1520.   *092661*

Glen Falls (New York)
Tyrer, H.R., 707 Upper Glen St., Glen Falls, NY 12801.
T. (518) 793-2244.   *092662*

Glencoe (Illinois)
It's about time, 375 Park Ave., Glencoe, IL 60022.
T. (312) 8352012.   *092663*

Hillsboro (New Hampshire)
Withington, Richard W., Hillsboro, NH 03244.
T. (603) 464-3232.   *092664*

Honolulu (Hawaii)
ALA Moanastampt Coin, 1236 Ala Moana Blvd., Honolulu, HI 96814.   *092665*
Lipton, 1108 Fort St., Honolulu, HI 96813. T. (808) 533-
4320.   *092666*

Houston (Texas)
Hart, 2311 Westheimer, Houston, TX 77098.
T. (713) 524-2979.   *092667*
Hart, 2301 S Voss Rd, Houston, TX 77057. T. (713) 266-
3500, Fax (713) 266-1013.   *092668*
Peyton Place Antiques, 819 Lovett Blvd., Houston, TX
77006. T. (713) 523-4841.   *092669*

Hyannis Port (Massachusetts)
Bourne, Richard A., Co., Inc, Corporation St., P. O. Box
141/A, Hyannis Port, MA 02647.
T. (617) 775 0797.   *092670*

Kennebunk (Maine)
Oliver, Richard W., Plaza 1, Rte. 1, Kennebunk, ME
04043. T. (207) 985-3600.   *092671*

Lebanon (New Jersey)
Heller, Elwood + Son Auctioneer, 151 Main St., Lebanon,
NJ 08833. T. (201) 23 62 195.   *092672*

Lee (Massachusetts)
Caropreso, 136 High St., Lee, MA 01238. T. (413) 243-
3424.   *092673*

Litchfield (Connecticut)
Litchfield Auction Gallery, Rte. 202, Litchfield, CT
06759. T. (203) 567-3126.   *092674*

Los Angeles (California)
Butterfield & Butterfield, Sunset Boulevard, Los Angeles,
CA 90046.   *092675*
Numismatic Fine Arts, 10100 Santa Monica Blvd., Los
Angeles, CA 90067. T. (213) 278-7535.   *092676*

Lucas (Kansas)
Palmer Auction Service, Lucas, KS 67648.   *092677*

Mamaroneck (New York)
Chatsworth Auction Rooms, 151 Mamaroneck Ave., Mamaroneck, NY 10543.   *092678*

Marshalltown (Iowa)
Harris, Gene, 203 S 18 Av, Marshalltown, IA 50158.
T. (515) 752-0600, Fax (515) 753-0226.   *092679*

Marshfield (Massachusetts)
Willis, Henry, 22 Main St, Marshfield, MA 02050.
T. (617) 834-7774.   *092680*

Milford (Ohio)
Early Auctions Company, 123 Main St, Milford, OH
45150. T. (513) 831-4833.   *092681*

Montpelier (Ohio)
Huber, Col. Raymond W., 211 N Monroe, Montpelier, OH
43543.   *092682*

Montville (New Jersey)
Manning, Greg, 115 Main Rd, Montville, NJ 07045.
T. (201) 299-1800.   *092683*

New Orleans (Louisiana)
Alford, Neal, 4139 Magazine St., New Orleans, LA 70115. T. (504) 899-5329.   092684
Levin's Auction Exchange, 414 Camp St., New Orleans, LA 70130.   092685
Neal Auction Company, 4038 Magazine St, New Orleans, LA 70115. T. (504) 899-5329, Fax (504) 897-3808.   092686

New York
Altman, B., & Co., 34th and Fifth Ave, New York, NY 10016. T. (212) OR 9 7800 Ext. 550 + 322.   092687
Ariadne Galleries, 970 Madison Av, New York, NY 10021. T. (212) 772-3388.   092688
Birkenstaff & Knowles, 1290 Avenue of the Americas, 10000 New York, NY 10104. T. (212) 757-7998.   092689
Christie's, 502 Park Av, New York, NY 10022. T. (212) 546-1000.   092690
Christie's East, 219 E 67 St, New York, NY 10021. T. (212) 606-0400.   092691
Doyle, William, 175 E 87 St, New York, NY 10028. T. (212) 427-2730, Fax (212) 369-0892.   092692
Edelmann, 523 E 73 St., New York, NY 10021. T. (212) 628-1700.   092693
Ettinger, Arian, 253 E 77 St., New York, NY 10021. T. (212) 628-1702.   092694
Gotham, 80 Fourth Av., New York, NY 10003. T. (212) 677-3303.   092695
Grand Auction Art, 54 Suffolk St., New York, NY 10002. T. (212) 533-4640.   092696
Greenwich Auction Room, 110 E 13 St., New York, NY 10003. T. (212) 533-5550.   092697
Guernsey, 136 E 73 St., New York, NY 10021. T. (212) 794-2280.   092698
Haboldt & Co, Bob P., 42 E 76 St, New York, NY 10021. T. (212) 249-1183, Fax (212) 472-2413.   092699
Habsburg, Feldman, 36 E 75 St., New York, NY 10021. T. (212) 570-4040.   092700
Harmer, 14 E 33 St., New York, NY 10036. T. (212) 532-3700.   092701
Harmer Rooke, 32 E 57 St., New York, NY 10022. T. (212) 751-1900.   092702
Hausewedell & Nolte, 225 W Central Park, New York, NY 10024. T. (212) 787-7245.   092703
Kaldewey, Sibylle, 225 W Central Park, New York, NY 10024. T. (212) 787-7245.   092704
Ketterer, 790 Madison Av., New York, NY 10021. T. (212) 570-1221.   092705
Ketty Maisonrouge, 16 E 65 St., New York, NY 10021. t. (212) 737-3597, Fax (212) 861-1434.   092705a
Landau, William & Co., 1365 York Av., New York, NY 10021. T. (212) 570-6784.   092706
Leontis, George & Co., 152 Madison Av., New York, NY 10016. T. (212) 683-9200.   092707
Lubin, 30 W 26 St., New York, NY 10001. T. (212) 254-1080.   092708
Muller, Adrian H. & Son, 363 Seventh Av., New York, NY 10001. T. (212) 947-9100.   092709
Phillips, 406 E 79 St, New York, NY 10021. T. (212) 570-4830.   092710
Rothschild, Sigmund, 27 W 67 St., New York, NY 10023. T. (212) 873-5522.   092711
Saint Hippolyte, légor de, 129 E 61 St., New York, NY 10021. T. (212) 980-2003, Fax 980-2004.   092712
Siegel, Robert A., 160 E 56 St., New York, NY 10022. T. (212) 753-6421.   092713
Smythe, R.M., & Co., 24 Broadway, New York, NY 10004. T. (212) 943-1880.   092714
Sotheby, 1334 York Av., New York, NY 10021. T. (212) 606-7000.   092715
Sotheby's, 411 E 76 St., New York, NY 10021. T. (212) 606-7800.   092716

Stack, 123 W 57 St., New York, NY 10019. T. (212) 582-2580.   092717
Swann, 104 E 25 St, New York, NY 10010. T. (212) 254-4710.   092718
Tepper, 110 E 25 St., New York, NY 10010. T. (212) 677-5300.   092719

Newcastle (Maine)
Foster, Robert, POB 203, Newcastle, ME 04553. T. (207) 563-8150.   092720

Newport (Rhode Island)
Sotheby, 228 Spring St., Newport POB 1499, RI 02840. T. (401) 846-8668.   092721

Otego (New York)
Hesse, 53 Main St., Otego, NY 13825. T. (607) 988-6322.   092722

Paramount (California)
Bakers Auction, 14100 Paramount Blvd., Paramount, CA 90723. T. (213) 531-1524.   092723

Pasadena (California)
Sotheby, 507 Bellefontaine, Pasadena, CA 91105. T. (818) 799-8715.   092724

Philadelphia (Pennsylvania)
Freeman, S. T. & Co, 1808-10 Chestnut Street, Philadelphia, PA 19103. T. (215) 563-9275, Fax (215) 563-8236.   092725
Sotheby, 1811 Chestnut St., Philadelphia, PA 19103. T. (215) 751-9540.   092726
Traiman, Louis, Auction Co, 1519 Spruce St, Philadelphia, PA 19102. T. (215) 545-4500.   092727

Plainville (Connecticut)
Winter, 21 Cook St, Plainville, CT 06062. T. (203) 793-0288.   092728

Pompano Beach (Florida)
Charles, C.B., 750 E Sample Rd, Ste. 6, Pompano Beach, FL 33064. T. (305) 946-1800.   092729

Portland (Maine)
Bailey, F.O. & Co, 137-141 Middle St, Portland, ME 04104. T. (207) 774-1479.   092730

Portland (Oregon)
O'Gallerie, 228 NE Seventh St., Portland, OR 97232. T. (503) 238-0202.   092731

Richmond (Virginia)
Shield, 1515 W Broad St, Richmond, VA 23220. T. (804) 359-2493.   092732

Rome (Georgia)
Rome Auction Gallery, Rt.2, Highway 53, Rome, GA 30161.   092733

Saint Ignatius (Montana)
Allard, POB 460A, Saint Ignatius, MT 59865. T. (406) 745-2951.   092734

Saint Louis (Missouri)
Selkirk, B.J., & Sons, 4166 Olive St., Saint Louis, MO 63108. T. (314) 533-1700.   092735

San Francisco (California)
Butterfield & Butterfield, 220 San Bruno Av, San Francisco, CA 94103. T. (415) 861-7500, Fax (415) 861-8951.   092736
California Book Auction Galleries, 965 Mission St, Suite 730, San Francisco, CA 94103. T. (415) 243-0650.   092737
Pacific Book Auction Galleries, 139 Townsend St, San Francisco, CA 94107. T. (415) 896-2665.   092738

Sotheby, 3667 Sacramento St, San Francisco, CA 94118. T. (415) 561-8400.   092739
Wolffers, Richard, 133 Kearny St, San Francisco, CA 94108. T. (415) 781-5127.   092740

Sandwich (Massachusetts)
Sandwich Auction House, 15 Tupper Rd, Sandwich, MA 02563. T. (617) 888-1926.   092741

Saratoga (California)
Neale & Sons, 14320 S Saratoga-Sunnyvale Rd, Saratoga, CA 95071. T. (408) 867-3751.   092742

Seattle (Washington)
Satori, 2305 Fifth Av, Seattle, WA 98121. T. (206) 233-9505.   092743

Sheffield (Massachusetts)
Bradford, Rte. 7, Sheffield, MA 01257. T. (413) 229-6667.   092744

Solvang (California)
Gade, POB 555, Solvang, CA 93463. T. (308) 688-5675.   092745

South Burlington (Vermont)
Merrill, Duane E., 32 Beacon St, South Burlington, VT 05401. T. (802) 878-2625.   092746

South Cairo (New York)
Savoia & Fromm, Rte. 23, South Cairo, NY 12482. T. (518) 622-8000.   092747

South Deerfield (Massachusetts)
Douglas, Rtes. 5 & 10, South Deerfield, MA 01373. T. (413) 665-2877.   092748

South Essex (Massachusetts)
Landry, L. A., 164 Main St., South Essex, MA 01929. T. (617) 768-6233, 744-5811.   092749

South Glastonbury (Connecticut)
Riba-Mobley, POB53, South Glastonbury, CT 06073. T. (203) 633-3076.   092750

Summit (New Jersey)
Summit Auction Rooms, 47-49 Summit Av, Summit, NJ 07901.   092751

Vestal (New York)
Mapes, 1600 W Vestal Pkwy, Vestal, NY 13850. T. (607) 754-9193.   092752

Washington (District of Columbia)
Weschler's, 905 E St NW, Washington, DC 20004. T. (202) 628-1281.   092753
Yudkin, 3636 16 St NW, Washington, DC 20010. T. (202) 232-6249.   092754

Wolfeboro (New Hampshire)
Bowers & Merena, POB 1224, Wolfeboro, NH 03894. T. (603) 569-5095.   092755

Woodstock (Connecticut)
Arman, David & Linda, RD1, Box 174, Woodstock, CT 06281. T. (203) 928-5838.   092756

York (Maine)
Maritime Antique Auctions, RR 2, Box 45A, York, ME 03909. T. (207) 363-4247.   092757

Ypsilanti (Michigan)
Schmidt's Inc., 5138 W Michigan Av, Ypsilanti, MI 48197.   092758

Das Register zum *Thieme-Becker, Vollmer* und zum *Allgemeinen Künstlerlexikon* – jetzt inklusive der vollständigen Lexikonartikel aus dem *Allgemeinen Künstlerlexikon!*

Allgemeines Künstlerlexikon – Internationale Künstlerdatenbank

AKL – World Biographical Dictionary of Artists

3. CD-ROM-Ausgabe 1996
DM 2.400,–*
(DM 498,–* für Bezieher der Buchausgabe *Allgemeines Künstlerlexikon*)
(DM 796,–* für Bezieher der *IKD II*)

Die dritte erheblich erweiterte Ausgabe enthält nun neben den Strukturdaten aus den 37 Bänden des *Thieme-Becker* und den 6 Bänden des *Vollmer* die Strukturdaten und die **vollständigen Texteinträge** aus den ersten 12 Bänden des *Allgemeinen Künstlerlexikons*.
Maler, Graphiker, Bildhauer, Architekten – die Vertreter der bildenden Künste aller Kulturräume der Erde von der Antike bis zur Gegenwart können hier nach den verschiedensten Kriterien gesucht und ihre biographischen Daten abgerufen werden.

* unverbindliche Preisempfehlung

Bitte fordern Sie einen ausführlichen Prospekt bei uns an!

 K•G•Saur Verlag
Postfach 701620 · D-81316 München · Tel. (089) 7 69 02-0
Fax (089) 7 69 02-150 · E-mail: 100730.1341@compuserve.com

Selhamin-LACKE
Selhamin-POLIMENT

in verschiedenen
Farben
für die Leisten-,
Rahmen- und
Vergolderindustrie

Ernst Sonderhoff
GmbH & Co. KG

Richard-Byrd-Straße 26
D-50829 Köln

Telefon 02 21 / 95 68 5-0
Telefax 02 21 / 95 68 5-1 99
Telex 8 883 528 seso d

Vangerow

weltweiter Partner für

RESTAURATOREN

- über 100 Japan/Chinapapiere
- REMAY, in schwarz und weiß und in verschiedenen Qualitäten
- Löschkarton in verschiedenen Abmessungen und Stärken
- Säurefreier Museumskarton
- Passepartoutkarton, Künstler-Pinsel, Malspachteln, Schnitzwerkzeuge u. v. m.

Fordern Sie unsere speziellen Unterlagen für Restauratoren an.

Oskar Vangerow – München
Postf. 14 51, 85506 Ottobrunn,
Fax 0 89/60 81 22 22

NORIS
BLATTGOLD

seit 1876

blatt gold
spezialfabrik

Wir produzieren für Ihren besonderen Bedarf in gleichbleibend bester Qualität

Blattgold in 25 verschiedenen Farben

Blattsilber – Blattmetalle

und alle Vergolder-Artikel

Noris Blattgold GmbH
Rennmühle 3
D-91126 Schwabach
Tel. 0 91 22/9 89 30
Fax 0 91 22/7 32 45

Argentina

Buenos Aires
Arte Antica, Defensa 1133, 1065 Buenos Aires.
T. (01) 362 08 61. (Antigüedades, Muebles)   092759
Casa Veltri, Juncal 1642, Buenos Aires. T. (01) 44 41 74.
(Cadres, Tableaux, Gravures)   092760
Corradini, Juan, Avda. Santa Fé 3527 A., Buenos Aires.
T. (01) 83 31 87. (Examen Técnico, Restauracion Pintu-
ras, Dibujos, Grabados)   092761
Giovannini, Mi gucl, Avda. Libertador 15365 Acassuso,
Buenos Aires. T. (01) 743 03 62. (Antigüedades, mueb-
les, porcelana)   092762
Manzanel da Torrellardona, Prof. Orfelia, c/o Museo Poli-
cia Federal, San Martin 353, Buenos Aires.
(Pintura)   092763
Segal, Luis, 11 de Septiembre 920, 1426 Buenos Aires.
T. (01) 772 83 77. (Antigüedades)   092764

Australia

Goulburn (New South Wales)
Shaw, G., 261 Auburn St., Goulburn, 2580.
T. (048) 21 16 90. (Furniture)   092765

Melbourne (Victoria)
Wiesel, Michael, 256 Toorak Rd., South Yarra, Mel-
bourne, Vic. 3141. T. (03) 2415143. (Clocks, Watches
Gold & Silver.)   092766

North Sydney (New South Wales)
Painting Conservation Company, 28 Pacific St., Bronte,
2060 North Sydney, 2024. T. 387 2669.
(Paintings)   092767

Sydney (New South Wales)
Feuerring, Maximilian, Prof., 6 Russell St. woollahra,
Sydney, NSW 2000. T. (02) 389 70 38.
(Paintings)   092768
Grant & Lindner, Sydney POB 69, Woolahra, NSW 2025.
(Furniture, Gilts)   092769
Macedo, G.L., 2 Sydenham Rd., Brookvale, Sydney,
NSW 2100. T. (02) 93 37 62. (Antiques)   092770
williams, I.B. & P.A., 95 Moorefields Rd., Kingsgrove,
Sydney, NSW 2208. T. (02) 759 50 81.
(Metalwork)   092771

Austria

Bad Vöslau (Niederösterreich)
Wächter, Andrea, Penzigstraße 4, 2540 Bad Vöslau.
T. (02252) 764 51.   092772

Feistritz an der Drau (Kärnten)
Campidell, Walter, Feistritz/Drau 11, 9710 Feistritz an
der Drau. T. (04245) 22 48.   092773

Feldkirchen bei Graz (Steiermark)
Meder-Weitzl, M. & B., Sandgrubenweg 7, 8073 Feldkirchen bei Graz. T. 29 61 10.   092774

Graz (Steiermark)
Herzberg, Riesstr. 181, 8047 Graz.
T. (0316) 30 17 05.   092775
Pichler, Günther, Sporgasse 29b, 8010 Graz.
T. (0316) 76 90 32.   092776
Rohrer, Erich, Pachernweg 5, 8010 Graz.
T. (0316) 44 572.   092777
Schäffer, Thomas, Kollonitschstr. 9a, 8010 Graz.
T. (0316) 35 97 52.   092778
Stampfer, Georg, Josefigasse 45, 8020 Graz.
T. (0316) 91 38 59.   092779

Hörsching (Oberösterreich)
Zdeb, Haidstr. 3, 4063 Hörsching.
T. (07221) 722 57.   092780

Innsbruck
Wall-Beyerfels, Frambert, Allerheiligenhöfe, Sankt Geor-
gsweg 22, 6020 Innsbruck. T. (0512) 584609.   092781

Innsbruck (Tirol)
Margreiter, Kurt, Höhenstr. 42a, 6020 Innsbruck.
T. (0512) 84 20 83.   092782

Linz (Oberösterreich)
Hahmann, Clara, Prof., Bürgerstr. 5/3, 4020 Linz.
T. (0732) 28 38 07.   092783
Meindl, H. Georg, Steingasse 1, 4020 Linz.
T. (0732) 783754, Fax 783754.   092784

Mödling (Niederösterreich)
Hanzl, Stefan, Elsa Brandström-Gasse 4, 2340 Mödling.
T. (02236) 45569, Fax 45569.   092785

Neu-Purkersdorf (Niederösterreich)
Kosensky, Hugo, Prof, Steinerg 5, 3011 Neu-Purkers-
dorf. T. (02231) 66508.   092786

Pörtschach (Kärnten)
Leder, Wilhelm A., Rumpeleweg 25, 9210 Pörtschach.
T. (04272) 3850.   092787

Salzburg
Costal, Robert, Esch 115, 5023 Salzburg.
T. (0662) 66 13 52.   092788
Fiebich-Ripke, Annemarie, Wolfsgartenweg 16, 5020
Salzburg. T. (0662) 20 78 09.   092789
Fortmann, Evamarie, Augustinergasse 11a, 5020 Salz-
burg. T. (0662) 84 44 77.   092790
Gürtlerwerkstatt, vorm. G. Simon, Zallweingasse 4,
5020 Salzburg. T. (0662) 829133,
Fax (0662) 8291334.   092791
Mair, Ursula, Kirchengasse 37 A, 5020 Salzburg.
T. (0662) 53150.   092792
Prinz, Josef, Almgasse 3, 5020 Salzburg.
T. (0662) 841452.   092793
Wilfing, Josef, Moosstr. 47, 5020 Salzburg.
T. (0662) 842 82 83.   092794

Strobl (Salzburg)
Holzmann-Keller, Ruth, 5350 Strobl.
T. (06137) 208.   092795

Wels (Oberösterreich)
Födisch, Helga, Alois-Auerstr. 7, 4600 Wels.
T. (07242) 46780.   092796
Saminger, Erich, Flugplatzstr. 3, 4601 Wels.
T. (07242) 5458.   092797

Wien
Böck, Anton, Währinger Str. 27, 1090 Wien.
T. (0222) 405 02 46, Fax (0222) 405 02 46.   092798
Brandner, Wilhelm, Einsiedlerpl. 4, 1050 Wien.
T. (0222) 55 51 71.   092799
Braunshör, Peter, Bennogasse 6, 1080 Wien.
T. (0222) 4050242.   092800
Csutak, Magdolna, Fuhrmannsg. 2/15, 1080 Wien.
T. (0222) 402 84 923.   092801
Dockal, Reinhard, Gamandergasse 9, 1140 Wien.
T. (0222) 9146178-0.   092802
Dokulil, Wolfgang, Schumanngasse 81, 1170 Wien.
T. (0222) 46 23 41.   092803
Donau, Erich Josef, Liechtensteinstr. 117/18, 1090
Wien. T. (0222) 34 43 91.   092804
Dunkel, Walter, Bäckerstr. 7, 1010 Wien.
T. (0222) 527 02 95.   092805
Franek, Walter, Ullmannstr. 6, 1150 Wien.
T. (0222) 83 89 305.   092806
Hanisch, J., Gatterburggasse 6, 1190 Wien.
T. (0222) 36 44 82.   092807
v. Harten, Beate, Burggasse 24/12, 1070 Wien.
T. (0222) 5229683, Fax 5238768.   092808
Havlik, R., Chromygasse 38, 1230 Wien.
T. (0222) 804 04 15.   092809
Hegenbarth, Werner, Weihburgg. 20, 1010 Wien.
T. (0222) 520 88 13.   092810
Heher, Heinz, Reindorfgasse 15/3, 1150 Wien.
T. (0222) 83 97 624.   092811
Heiner, Gernot M., Vinzenzgasse 28, 1180 Wien.
T. (0222) 43 67 14.   092812
Hengl, Klaus, Taubstummengasse 8, 1040 Wien.
T. (0222) 5057516, 5055696, Fax 5055696.   092813
Hillinger, Gustav, Ausstellungsstr. 63, 1020 Wien.
T. (0222) 240 43 53.   092814

Hübner, Rudolf, Am Graben 28, 1010 Wien.
T. (0222) 5338065, Fax 533806522.   092815

Ständige Ausstellung antiker
Meisterwerke der Uhrmacherkunst

Rudolf Hübner
Spezialwerkstätte
zur Restaurierung antiker Uhren

A-1010 Wien,   Tel. 533 80 65
Am Graben 28   Fax 533 80 65 22

Iges, Stumpergasse 14, 1060 Wien.
T. (0222) 5978660.   092816
Jahoda, Karin, Wehlistr. 180, 1020 Wien.
T. (0222) 26 66 25.   092817
Kabele, Vinzenz, Penzingerstr. 23, 1140 Wien.
T. (0222) 894 31 89.   092818
Der Kachelofen, Sechsschimmelgasse 3, 1090 Wien.
T. (0222) 34 72 94.   092819
Kalousek, Franz, Ratschkygasse 42, 1120 Wien.
T. (0222) 8131373.   092820
Kaufmann, Karl, Mayerhofgasse 12, 1040 Wien.
T. (0222) 505 19 11.   092821
Krehon, Verena, Bernardgasse 4/2, 1070 Wien.
T. (0222) 5264424, Fax 5264424.   092822
Laslin, Andrej N., Ungargasse 27, 1030 Wien.
T. (0222) 715 31 05, 713 24 76.   092823
Limberger-Dachauer, Wilfriede, Himmelstr. 30, 1190
Wien. T. (0222) 322 81 72.   092824
Machowetz, Senta, Johannesg. 3, 1010 Wien.
T. (0222) 523 03 33.   092825
Maegle, Rudolf, Freyung 1, 1010 Wien.
T. (0222) 5354361, Fax (0222) 5354361.   092826
Makovec, J., Hauptstr. 90, 1030 Wien.
T. (0222) 712 32 32.   092827
Miel, Ingo, Riemergasse 2, 1010 Wien.
T. (0222) 512 48 69.   092828
Mönnig, F.A., Schönbrunner Str. 74, 1050 Wien.   092829
Montibeller, C., Favoritenstr. 2, 1040 Wien.
T. (0222) 505 88 03.   092830
Mucnjak-Hochland, Riemergasse 1, 1010 Wien.
T. (0222) 525 09 94.   092831
Novak, Erika, Wurlitzergasse 13, 1160 Wien.
T. (0222) 46 86 21.   092832
Oberauer, Herbert, Blindengasse 42/5, 1080 Wien.
T. (0222) 428 87 95.   092833
Parisini, Währinger Str. 67, 1090 Wien.
T. (0222) 408 79 87.   092834
Perko, Friedrich E., Goldschlagstr. 97, 1150 Wien.
T. (0222) 952 31 94.   092835
Pillisz, Johann, Margaretenstr. 119, 1050 Wien.
T. (0222) 55 89 322.   092836
Pitz, Richard, Erlgasse 44, 1120 Wien.
T. (0222) 85 52 79.   092837
Röder, Kurt, Trautmannsdorffgasse 11, 1130 Wien.
T. (0222) 8775301.   092838
Schmidt, Friedrich Otto, Währinger Str. 28, 1091 Wien.
T. (0222) 34 93 48/49, Fax 310 76 12.   092839
Schmidt, Johann, Kochstr. 3, 1236 Wien.
T. (0222) 889 25 35.   092840
Schmiedmaier, Schulgasse 53, 1180 Wien.
T. (0222) 4064171, 4026088.   092841
Schügerl, F. u. A., Gerlgasse 9-13, 1030 Wien.
T. (0222) 78 44 065.   092842
Siems-Afuhs, Waaggasse 14/19, 1040 Wien.
T. (0222) 57 48 925.   092843
Smolka, Wilhelm, Möllwaldpl 1, 1040 Wien.
T. (0222) 5054851. (Gilding)   092844
Smolka, Wilhelm, Spiegelgasse 25, 1010 Wien.
T. (0222) 5120283, 5046414, Fax 5120283. (framing,
gilding)   092845
Stranski, Edith, Singerstr 26A, 1010 Wien.
T. (0222) 5126850.   092846
Stransky, Ferdinand, Prof., Favoritenstr. 38/19, 1040
Wien. T. (0222) 656 08 22.   092847
Tartler, I., Mariahilfer Str. 64, 1070 Wien.
T. (0222) 93 48 964.   092848

TecnoArt, Testarellogasse 24/16, 1130 Wien.
T. (0222) 8773801, Fax (0222) 8773802. *092849*
Theuermann, Valentin & Georg, Zitterhofg. 4, 1070
Wien. T. (0222) 93 73 44. *092850*
Valta, H. & J., Rotenlöwengasse 7, 1090 Wien.
T. (0222) 31 64 29. *092851*
Vytiska, Ruckergasse 24, 1120 Wien.
T. (0222) 83 91 76. *092852*
Wagner, Johann, Lienfeldergasse 74, 1160 Wien.
T. (0222) 4858141. *092853*

Belgium

Aalst (Oost-Vlaanderen)
Van Lierde, J., Pontstr 65-71, 9300 Aalst.
T. (053) 70 02 31. (Meubelen) *092854*

Antwerpen
Avonds, H. & Zn., Mechelsesteenweg 78, 2018 Antwer-
pen. T. (03) 238 51 86. (Meubles et Métal) *092855*
C&R Eykelberg-Van Herck, Bolwerkstr 8, 2018 Antwer-
pen. T. (03) 238 62 60, Fax 237 36 33. (Conservation
and restoration of paintings and sculptures) *092856*
Meier, Bernard, Grote Pieter Potstr 13, 2000 Antwerpen.
T. (03) 232 65 70, 091/21 41 20. (Antike
Klokken) *092857*
Putcuyns, Constant, St Thomasstr 31, 2000 Antwerpen.
T. (03) 230 82 56. (Meubles) *092858*
De Ridder, Terliststr 26, 2018 Antwerpen.
T. (03) 2264578, 2301581. (conservation and restorati-
on of paintings) *092859*

Bertem (Vlaams Brabant)
Indekeu, J Ginisstr 25, 3060 Bertem. T. (016) 480000.
(Meubelen) *092860*

Bierbeek (Vlaams Brabant)
Lucas, Zwartehoekstr 24, 3360 Bierbeek.
T. (016) 463864. (Meubelen) *092861*

Borgerhout (Antwerpen)
Cuyvers, Georges, Plantin en Moretuslei 135, 2140 Bor-
gerhout. T. (031) 234 12 74. (Jewellery, Silver,
Sculpture) *092862*

Braine-l'Alleud (Brabant Wallon)
Art-Clinique, 14 Rue de la Gare, 1420 Braine-l'Alleud.
T. (02) 3846307. (Tableaux, Porcelaines) *092863*

Braine-le-Comte ('s-Gravenbrakel) (Hai-naut)
Lechêne, C., 43 Rue E Etienne, 7090 Braine-le-Comte
('s-Gravenbrakel). T. (067) 555191. (Polissage,
Marqueterie) *092864*

Brugge (West-Vlaanderen)
Lisabeth, Ph., Ezelstr 78, 8000 Brugge.
T. (050) 33 71 08. (Eik, Mahonie) *092865*
Mullem, van, Kraanplats 1, 8000 Brugge.
T. (050) 305 94. (Meubles) *092866*
Poly, P., Vestingstr 28, 8000 Brugge. T. (050) 36 36 81.
(Meubelen, Marqueterie) *092867*
Van Lerberghe, K., Garenmarkt 26, 8000 Brugge.
T. (050) 33 19 58. (Keramiek, Porselein) *092868*

Bruxelles
Art-Artisanat, 73 Blvd S Dupuis, 1070 Bruxelles.
T. (02) 523 93 04. (Meubles, tableaux, cardres-
Marquetterie) *092869*
Artibois, 67 Rue du Page, 1050 Bruxelles.
T. (02) 537 23 63. (Meubles) *092870*
Atelier Adam, 83 Rue van Aa, 1050 Bruxelles.
T. (02) 649 60 77. (Bijoux, Pieces precieuses) *092871*
Atelier de Conservations & Restauration, 19 Rue des
Chartreux, 1000 Bruxelles. T. (02) 513 50 24.
(Sculptur) *092872*
Atelier de l'Horlogerie Ancienne, 71 Rue du Sceptre,
1050 Bruxelles. T. (02) 648 89 14. (Clocks) *092873*
Bedane, 40 Rue de la Vallée, 1050 Bruxelles.
T. (02) 640 10 30. (Restauration & polishing of
Furniture) *092874*
Bekaert, 47 Av G Demey, 1160 Bruxelles.
T. (02) 672 06 66. (Ebenisterie) *092875*

Bousson, Frederic, 8a Rue de Suède, 1060 Bruxelles.
T. (02) 735 88 01. (Tableaux) *092876*
Brabant, van, 393 Chaussée de Gand, 1080 Bruxelles.
T. (02) 427 01 77, Fax 465 91 06. (Meubles) *092877*
Brackmann, C., 31 Rue Vandernoot, 1080 Bruxelles.
T. (02) 425 06 09. (Polissage, Marqueterie) *092878*
Carton & Taquin, 27 Rue Ducale, 1000 Bruxelles.
T. (02) 513 58 31. (Furniture) *092879*
Codt, de, 99 Rue Charles-Quint, 1000 Bruxelles.
T. (02) 734 93 78. (Meubles, Marqueterie) *092880*
Copet, Christian, 155 Rue Ph Baucq, 1040 Bruxelles.
T. (02) 640 53 75. (Meubles, Sculptures) *092881*
Dekens, L., 155 Rue de Linthout, 1200 Bruxelles.
T. (02) 734 59 69. (Meubles) *092882*
Delvaulx, L., 54 Rue Th Vander Elst, 1170 Bruxelles.
T. (02) 672 16 63. (Tableaux) *092883*
Depuydt, L., 60 Av V Rousseau, 1190 Bruxelles.
T. (02) 346 23 56. (Tableaux) *092884*
Devaux, F.J., 4 Sq Larousse, 1190 Bruxelles.
T. (02) 347 47 48. (Tableaux) *092885*
Favresse, Mathieu, 1348 Ch de Waterloo, 1180 Bruxel-
les. T. (02) 375 43 65. (Porcelaine & Faïences) *092886*
Galerie Carrette, 257 Ch de Charleroi, 1060 Bruxelles.
T. (02) 534 03 25. (Tableaux) *092887*
Gerin, F., 38 Rue Paul Lauters, 1050 Bruxelles.
T. (02) 374 08 29. (Tableaux) *092888*
Gigot, R., 39 Av A Buyl, 1050 Bruxelles.
T. (02) 640 40 05. (horlogerie) *092889*
Goossens, D.&H., 11 Quai au Foin, 1000 Bruxelles.
T. (02) 218 13 82. (Tableaux) *092890*
Imberechts, E., Belforststr 12, 1000 Bruxelles.
T. (02) 736 33 60. (Tableaux) *092891*
Jonckheere, de, 55 Blvd de Waterloo, 1000 Bruxelles.
T. (02) 512 99 48. (Tableaux) *092892*
Lebeau, 27 Rue Gachard, 1050 Bruxelles.
T. (02) 647 76 79. (Tableaux) *092893*
Mets, de, 86 Rue de Haerne, 1040 Bruxelles.
T. (02) 647 56 79. (Tableaux) *092894*
Moulart, Thierry, 27 Rue de Parme, 1060 Bruxelles.
T. (02) 539 20 46. (Marqueterie, Ebenisterie, Meubles,
Sculptures) *092895*
Nelis, J., 124 Av Couronne, 1050 Bruxelles.
T. (02) 649 00 21. (Tableaux) *092896*
Oppitz, Philippe, 30 Av J de Bologne, 1020 Bruxelles.
T. (02) 268 42 30. (Meubles) *092897*
Paalman, F., 45 Rue H Wafelaerts, 1060 Bruxelles.
T. (02) 537 85 22. (Tableaux) *092898*
Pierot, D., 21 Rue P-EJanson, 1050 Bruxelles.
T. (02) 539 21 06. (Tableaux) *092899*
Poncelet, T., 24 Rue Bosquet, 1060 Bruxelles.
T. (02) 537 12 31. (Tableaux) *092900*
Renaissance du Meubles, 36 Rue Belle Vue, 1000 Bru-
xelles. T. (02) 647 56 96. (Furniture) *092901*
Saffa-Janssen, 34 Rue de Broyer, 1180 Bruxelles.
T. (02) 376 74 21. (Meubles) *092902*
Schleiper, 149 Ch de Charleroi, 1060 Bruxelles.
T. (02) 538 60 50. (Tableaux) *092903*
Thienen, C. van, 28 Rue de l'Enclume, 1210 Bruxelles.
T. (02) 230 27 16. (Rest.of gilding) *092904*
Trouveres, Les, 85-87 Av R Vanderbruggen, 1070 Bru-
xelles. T. (02) 520 42 34. (Meubles) *092905*
Vanderkerkhove, M., Coppensstr 3, 1000 Bruxelles.
T. (02) 511 02 41. (Tableaux) *092906*
Vercruysse, 1214 Ch de Gand, 1082 Bruxelles.
T. (02) 465 31 57. (Tableaux) *092907*
Villers, T. de, 67 Rue Véronèse, 1000 Bruxelles.
T. (02) 735 76 00. (Tableaux) *092908*
Vyve, van, 25 Rue C Franck, 1050 Bruxelles.
T. (02) 640 76 87. (Tableaux) *092909*
Willems, M., 9 Rue Crocq, 1200 Bruxelles.
T. (02) 771 93 81. (Tableaux) *092910*

De Haan
Vanhalst, R., Batterijstr 55, 8420 De Haan. T. 23 41 90.
(Meubelen) *092911*

Deurne (Antwerpen)
Engels, J., Boterlaarbaan 171, 2100 Deurne.
T. (03) 322 41 86. (Porcelain, Faience, Enamel, recon-
struction of Tiles, also Marble and Ivory) *092912*

Dottignies
Union des Ebénistes, Barrière Leclerq, 7711 Dottignies.
(Meubles) *092913*

Drongen (Oost-Vlaanderen)
Moens, A., Oude Abdijstr 24, 9031 Drongen.
T. (091) 26 16 15. (Klokken) *092914*

Ekeren (Antwerpen)
Lemmens, Didier, Kapelsestr 215, 2180 Ekeren.
T. (031) 647 32 17. (Meubelen) *092915*
Van Laer, F., Prinshoeveweg 42, 2180 Ekeren.
T. (031) 647 18 61. (Meubelen) *092916*

Emblem
Kammen, de, Oostmallestw 118, 2520 Emblem.
T. (031) 4857035. (Meubelen) *092917*

Erpent
Pompier, E., 578 Chaussée de Marche, 5101 Erpent.
T. (081) 30 15 37. (Meubles) *092918*

Essene (Vlaams Brabant)
Sompel, J. van, 1 Karlemeersbaan, 1790 Essene.
T. (02) 5822641. (Meubelen) *092919*

Evergem (Oost-Vlaanderen)
Verougstraete, Thierry, Spoorwegstr 2, 9940 Evergem.
T. (091) 53 74 06. (Meubelen) *092920*

Geel (Antwerpen)
Geels Restauratieatelier, Antwerpsedries 9, 2440 Geel.
T. (014) 58 42 35. (Meubelen) *092921*

Gent (Oost-Vlaanderen)
Fielding, Blekerijstr 33, 9000 Gent. T. (09) 3845829.
(Meubelen, Kaders, Schilderijen) *092922*
Lagrain, P., Oude Vest 10, 9000 Gent. T. (09) 2242717.
(Tableaux) *092923*
Meignen, Christian, Oolevaarstr 64, 9000 Gent.
T. (09) 2275442. (Marqueterie) *092924*
Nieuwenhuyse, H. van, Prinsenhof 55, 9000 Gent.
T. (09) 2232522. (Meubelen) *092925*
Vandenputte, G., Zwijnaardsestw 525, 9000 Gent.
T. (09) 2220115. (Boeken) *092926*
Verdonck & Zn., Ganzendries 31, 9000 Gent.
T. (09) 2223340. (Koper, Tin, Zilver) *092927*
Vietti, Zwarte Zusterstraat 24, 9000 Gent.
(Faiences) *092928*
Witte, Georges de, Walpoortstr 30, 9000 Gent.
T. (09) 2230287. (Meubelen) *092929*

Geraardsbergen (Oost-Vlaanderen)
Van Quickelberghe, Lessensestr 30, 9500 Geraardsber-
gen. T. (054) 41 27 33. (Schilderijen,
Kunstvoorwerpen) *092930*

Gistel (West-Vlaanderen)
Sculptura – Meub, Schoolstr 17, 8470 Gistel.
T. (059) 27 79 70. (Meubelen) *092931*

Harelbeke (West-Vlaanderen)
Dilux, Kortrijksestw 162, 8530 Harelbeke.
T. (056) 71 09 36. (Schilderijen) *092932*
Ostyn, A., Tramstraat 33, 8530 Harelbeke.
T. (056) 71 40 61. (Sculptures) *092933*

Hasselt (Limburg)
Minnaert, Alain, Boostr 79, 3500 Hasselt.
T. (011) 22 72 65. (Meubelen) *092934*

Herstal (Liège)
Decap Bois, 153 Rue Hurbise, 4040 Herstal.
T. (041) 64 51 37. (Meubelen) *092935*

Ieper (West-Vlaanderen)
Degraeve-Gillebert, Hoornwerk 14, 8900 Ieper.
T. (057) 20 84 45. (Meubelen) *092936*

Kortrijk (West-Vlaanderen)
Beche's Wood – Strip Shop, Vlaanderenkaai 7, 8500
Kortrijk. T. (056) 22 94 56. (Meubles) *092937*
Epoque Fine Old Jewels, Voorstr 12, 8500 Kortrijk.
T. (056) 21 01 02. (Medieval Sculptures Fourniture, Old
Master Paintings, Jewels, Tapestries) *092938*

Liège
Bailly, rue Daussoigne Mehul, 4000 Liège. (Monuments
historiques)   *092939*
Eymael, F., 85 rue Henri Maus, 4000 Liège.
T. (04) 2523916. (Furniture rest.)   *092940*
Foulon, 50 Rue du Calvaire, 4000 Liège. (Monuments
historiques)   *092941*
Jongen, Henri, 51, rue Chartreuse Grivegnée, 4000 Liè-
ge. T. (04) 3422623. (Tableaux)   *092942*
Tercaefs, G., 2, rue St Thomas, 4000 Liège.
T. (04) 2230209. (Sculptures)   *092943*

Londerzeel (Vlaams Brabant)
Tierens, Hugo, Schoolstr 12-14, 1840 Londerzeel.
T. (052) 303284. (Antiquiteiten, Meubelen)   *092944*

Lovendegem
Moens, Romain, Binnenslag 48, 9920 Lovendegem.
T. (091) 72 84 27. (Meubelen)   *092945*

Maldegem (Oost-Vlaanderen)
Rodts, M., Edestr 35, 9990 Maldegem. T. (050) 71 46 52.
(Meubelen)   *092946*

Mechelen (Antwerpen)
Op de Beek, J., Lange Schipstr 13, 2800 Mechelen.
T. (015) 211894. (Horlogerie)   *092947*

Namur (Namur)
Gourdin, 13, rue Haute-Marcelle, 5000 Namur.
(Antiquités)   *092948*

Oostende (West-Vlaanderen)
Seghers, P. & L., Kerkstr 29, 8400 Oostende.
T. (059) 507564, Fax (059) 267107.   *092948a*
Seynaeve, J., Nieuwe Dokstr 44, 8400 Oostende.
T. (059) 504847.   *092948b*
Stantschev, Matey, Leopold van Tyghemlaan 6, 8400
Oostende. T. (059) 806507, Fax 806856. (paintings,
icons)   *092951*

Roeselare (West-Vlaanderen)
Dewulf, Schoolstr 105, 8800 Roeselare.
T. (051) 20 61 74. (Meubelen)   *092952*

Rossignol
Baille, Viviane, 166 Rue de la Chauss Romaine, 6730
Rossignol. T. (063) 41 13 85, 41 19 15. (Porcelaines et
Faïences)   *092953*

Sclayn
Jambe, Willy, 128 Rue Gouverneur Glose, 5300 Sclayn.
T. (081) 58 91 64. (Tapis d'Orient, Tapisserie)   *092954*

Sint-Martens-Latem (Oost-Vlaanderen)
Buysse, George, Nemeleersstraat 53, 9830 Sint-Martens-Latem. T. (091) 82 47 04. (Tableaux et
meubles)   *092955*

Sint-Niklaas (Oost-Vlaanderen)
Buytaert, Jan-F. E., Plezantstr 57, 9100 Sint-Niklaas.
T. (03) 76 09 90. (Gravures)   *092956*

Soignies (Hainaut)
Podevyn, 125, ch de Mons, 7060 Soignies. (Monuments
historiques, sculptures)   *092957*

Tintigny (Luxembourg)
Jacqemin, Georges, 25 b 46 et 84, Grand-Route, 6730
Tintigny. T. (063) 441 62. (Meubles)   *092958*

Turnhout (Antwerpen)
Avonds, Pierre, de Merodelei 172, 2300 Turnhout.
T. (014) 41 18 65. (Meubles)   *092959*

Veurne (West-Vlaanderen)
Godderis, E., Ooststr 9, 8630 Veurne. T. (058) 31 19 29.
(Klokken)   *092960*

Vilvoorde (Vlaams Brabant)
Idee International, Harensestw 522, 1800 Vilvoorde.
T. (02) 2521405. (Meubles)   *092961*

Waterloo (Brabant Wallon)
Atelier Richard, 327 Ch de Bruxelles, 1410 Waterloo.
T. (02) 3545172. (Meubles, ebenisterie)   *092962*

Wijnegem
Janssens, J., Schijnbeemdenlaan 36, 2110 Wijnegem.
T. (031) 353 91 04. (Meubelen)   *092963*

Canada

Calgary (Alberta)
Bashford, 736 17th Ave. S.W., Calgary. T. (403) 269-
3560. (Furniture)   *092964*

Montreal (Québec)
Galerie Rolland, 2350 Guy St., Montreal. T. (514) 932-
9739. (Paintings)   *092965*
Gemst, 5380 Sherbrooke St.W., Montreal. T. (514) 488-
5104. (Paintings)   *092966*
Klinkhoff, Walter, 1200 Ouest Rue Sherbrooke, Montreal,
P.Q. H3A 1H6. T. (514) 288-7306. (Paintings) *092967*
Plomer, Hubert, 1226 Bishop St., Montreal. T. (514) 866-
0837. (Furniture)   *092968*

Ottawa (Ontario)
Austrian Furniture and Cabinet Making, 3740 Revelstoke
Dr., Ottawa. T. (613) 733-6474. (Antiques, Books,
Furniture)   *092969*
Gora, J., 484 King Edward Ave, Ottawa. T. (613) 235-
4572. (Furniture, China)   *092970*
Jarman, Frank, 1622 Carling St., Ottawa. T. (613) 728-
6546. (Paintings)   *092971*
Nicholas Art Gallery, 5 Nicholas (Ontario), Ottawa.
T. (613) 232-6515. (Paintings)   *092972*
Robertson, 162 Laurier Ave. W., Ottawa. T. (613) 235-
6426. (Paintings)   *092973*
Saint Laurent Art Centre, Saint Laurent Shopping Centre,
Ottawa, Ont. T. (613) 745-0613. (Paintings)   *092974*
Wallack, 203 Bank Street, Ottawa, Ont. K2P 1W7.
T. (613) 235-4339. (Paintings)   *092975*

Philipsburg (Québec)
Lemquerme, Frederic, Rte. 133, Philipsburg, JOJ 1NO.
(Furniture)   *092976*

Toronto (Ontario)
Abulnar, Franc, 40 Croham, Toronto. T. (416) 783-2401.
(Antiques)   *092977*
Braemar, 2585 Yonge St., Toronto. T. (416) 483-2415.
(Furniture)   *092978*
Mazelow, 3463 Yonge St., Toronto. T. (416) 481-7711,
481-3876. (Paintings)   *092979*
Pilarski, 19 Macauley, Toronto. T. (416) 534-2488.
(Furniture)   *092980*
Roberts, 641 Yonge St., Toronto, M4Y 1Z9. T. (416) 924-
8731. (Paintings)   *092981*
Thom, Frederick, 194 W Bloor St., Toronto, M5S 1T8.
T. (416) 921-3522. (Paintings)   *092982*

Vancouver (British Columbia)
Boulevard Furniture Finishers, 5439 W Boulevard, Van-
couver. T. (604) 261-7920. (Furniture)   *092983*
Collectors Custom Furniture, 8920 Shaughnessy, Van-
couver. T. (604) 321-51712. (Furniture)   *092984*
Dai, 8606 Fraser, Vancouver. T. (604) 327-3002.
(Furniture)   *092985*
Fabian, 7507 Victoria Dr., Vancouver. T. (604) 327-9601.
(China, glass)   *092986*
Fraser, Alex, 2027 W. 41st St., Vancouver.
(Paintings)   *092987*
Inter-Continental Art Agency Ltd., P.H.2, Park Royal
Towers, 935 Marine Drive, Vancouver, B.C., V7T 1A7.
T. (604) 922 3409. (Paintings & sculptures)   *092988*
Leif's Custom Upholstery, 1558 W Sixth, Vancouver.
T. (604) 738-1716. (Furniture)   *092989*
Modern Done Upholstery, 3666 W Fourth, Vancouver.
T. (604) 733-9422. (Furniture)   *092990*
Northland, 502 20 St. NW, Vancouver. T. (604) 521-3333.
(Furniture)   *092991*
Olympic Upholsterers, 3315 Victoria Dr., Vancouver.
T. (604) 324-4050. (Furniture)   *092992*
Swift, 8211 Granville St., Vancouver. T. (604) 261-1616.
(Furniture)   *092993*
Tapping, 821 W First, Vancouver. T. (604) 988-1730.
(Furniture)   *092994*

Victoria (British Columbia)
Craven, Wolf A., 1037 Fort St., Victoria. (Clocks) *092995*
Leaf Hill Galleries, 47 Bastion Sq., Victoria. T. (604) 384-
1311. (Paintings, Frames)   *092996*

Winnipeg (Manitoba)
Petrov, Ferdinand, 83 Kingsway, Winnipeg. T. (204) 475-
1785. (Paintings)   *092997*

Chile

Santiago
Campos Larenas del Rio, Ramon, Victorino Lastarria 307
E., Santiago. T. 33 19 46. (Pinturas)   *092998*
Razeto, Adriano, Pocuro 2826, Santiago. (Antigüedades,
Cuadros)   *092999*

Czech Republic

Břeclav
Art & Antik, c/o Fosfa, Poštorná, 69141 Břeclav.
T. (0627) 415-159.   *093000*

Denmark

København
Fritzsche, C.E., Kompagnistraede 12, 1208 København.
T. 15 17 88. (Chandeliers)   *093001*
Hjorth, Emil, & Sønner, Ny Verstergade 1, 1471 Køben-
havn. T. 33 12 39 89, Fax 33 13 90 30. (Violinmaker-
restorer)   *093002*
Hougaard, Sv., Ved Vigen 4, 2400 København.
T. 67 87 53. (Möbel)   *093003*
Jall, Erik Heide, Nansensgade 43, 1366 København K.
T. 33 13 18 67. (Europäische Porzellane und
Fayencen)   *093004*
Reitzel, C.A., Norregade 20, 1165 København K.
T. 12 24 00. (Bücher)   *093005*

France

Abbeville (Somme)
Bois Détail Marchandin, 139 Chemin Rouvroy, 80100
Abbeville. T. 0322242186. (Encadrements)   *093006*
Cajon, Lucien, 4 Rue Général-Leclerc, 80100 Abbeville.
T. 0322235431. (Meubles)   *093007*
Décapage de la Maye, Rue Bois-Fontaine-sur-Maine,
80100 Abbeville. T. 0322236345.   *093008*
Garbe, Francis, 12 Rte Crécy, 80100 Abbeville.
T. 0322298979. (Meubles)   *093009*
Oger & Fils, 80100 Abbeville. T. 0322251142.
(Meubles)   *093010*
Petit, Jacky, 3 Pl Clemenceau, 80100 Abbeville.
T. 0322240028. (Encadrements)   *093011*

Acquigny (Eure)
Jaillette, François, 45 B Rue Aristide-Briand, 27400 Acquigny. T. 0232407744.   *093012*

Agde (Hérault)
Canton, Dalio, 25 Rue Rabelais, 34300 Agde.
T. 0467947051.   *093013*

Agen (Lot-et-Garonne)
Bareyre, Martine & Gérard, 12 Rue Garonne, 47000
Agen. T. 0553669645, Fax 0553967394.   *093014*
Caillon, 4 Rue Généraux-Arlabosse, 47000 Agen.
T. 0553665733.   *093015*
Galerie Anton, 87 Rue Montesquieu, 47000 Agen.
T. 0553474070.   *093016*

Aigues-Mortes (Gard)
Babinot, Francine, 30 Rue Emile-Jamais, 30220 Aigues-
Mortes. T. 0466536936.   *093017*

Aix-en-Provence (Bouches-du-Rhône)
Dubruel, Dorothée, Chemin Croix-Verte, 13100 Aix-en-
Provence. T. 0442201655.   *093018*

Mivière, Valérie, 7 Rue Griffon, 13100 Aix-en-Provence.
T. 0442235401.   *093019*

Ajaccio (Corse)
Peretti, Sylvie, 1 Rue Forcioli-Conti, 20000 Ajaccio.
T. 0495215102.   *093020*
Sicurani, 12 et 14 Cours Grandval, 20000 Ajaccio.
T. 0495213274.   *093021*

Albi (Tarn)
Alibert, Daniel, 4 Chemin Bellevue, 81000 Albi.
T. 0563544729.   *093022*
Bordes, Michèle, 118 Rue Commandant-Blanché, 81000
Albi. T. 0563470915.   *093023*

Alès (Gard)
Belle Epoque, 33 Av Carnot, 30100 Alès.
T. 0466867389.   *093024*
Domergue, Jean-Pierre, 6 Rue Napoléon, 30100 Alès.
T. 0466528226.   *093025*

Alfortville (Val-de-Marne)
Fancelli & Cie, 31 Rue Marcel-Bourdarias, 94140 Alfortville. T. 0143754787, Fax 0143752472. (Sculptures
sur Bois)   *093026*

Alzen (Ariège)
Noblens, Cécile de, Peydanes, 09240 Alzen.
T. 0561645805.   *093027*

Ambert (Puy-de-Dôme)
Bois, Jacques, 21 Rue Lafayette, 63600 Ambert.
T. 0473821066. (encadrements)   *093028*

Amboise (Indre-et-Loire)
Dibon-Béacco, 22 Rue Jules-Ferry, 37400 Amboise.
T. 0547231147.   *093029*

Amiens (Somme)
Atelier G, 15 Rue Chaudronniers, 80000 Amiens.
T. 0322918575. (Encadrements)   *093030*
Boiself, 154 Rue Rouen, 80000 Amiens. T. 0322950913.
(Meubles)   *093031*

Bouthors, René, 15 Rue Macquet-Vion, 80000 Amiens.
T. 0322451322. (Meubles)   *093032*
Dersigny, Patrice, 11bis Rue Cozette, 80000 Amiens.
T. 0322452077, Fax 0322893190. (Meubles)   *093033*
Emielot, François, 28 Rue Berryer, 80080 Amiens.
T. 0322453164. (Faience, Porcelaine, Objet
d'art)   *093034*
Galerie des Beaux Arts, 106 Rue Maréchal-de-Lattre-
de-Tassigny, 80000 Amiens. T. 0322916599.
(Encadrements)   *093035*
Onichimiuk, Halina, 12 Rue Santons, 80000 Amiens.
T. 0322472324. (Tableaux)   *093036*
Payen, Michel, 89 Rue Dreuil, 80000 Amiens.
T. 0322444056.   *093037*

Andainville (Somme)
Scellier, Michel, Rue Villers, 80140 Andainville.
T. 0322258256. (Meubles)   *093038*

Andéchy (Somme)
Alluard, Regis, 5 Rue Eglise, 80700 Andéchy.
T. 0322374857. (Maître ébéniste, sculpteur, tourneur,
restauration, copie d'ancien)   *093039*

Andrésy (Yvelines)
Aux Mains de Bronze, 13 Rue Ormeteaux, 78570 Andrésy. T. 0139749664.   *093040*

Angers (Maine-et-Loire)
Bouloux, Sylvie, 7 Rue Lionnaise, 49100 Angers.
T. 41877220.   *093041*
Erbs-Mailleux, E., 65 Chemin Vieilles-Carrières, 49000
Angers. T. 41666190.   *093042*
Ilias, Antonis, 1 Rue Aristide-Justeau, 49100 Angers.
T. 41432562.   *093043*
Machefer, Pierre, 100 Rue Bressigny, 49100 Angers.
T. 41874576.   *093044*

Anglet (Pyrénées-Atlantiques)
Peyrecave, Lachiste, Rte Cambo, 64600 Anglet.
T. 0559424175.   *093045*

Annecy (Haute-Savoie)
Allard, Isabelle, 23 Rue Fraternité, 74000 Annecy.
T. 0450577703.   *093046*

Anneyron (Drôme)
Thomas, Bernard, Béraudière, 26140 Anneyron.
T. 0475315408.   *093047*

Appoigny (Yonne)
Cordier, Maurice, 39 Rte Branches, 89380 Appoigny.
T. 0386530384.   *093048*

Arcey (Doubs)
Daguet, Christophe, 35 Rue 5ème DB, 25750 Arcey.
T. 0381934144.   *093049*

Argelès-sur-Mer (Pyrénées-Orientales)
Lopinski, Michel, 1 Rue Victor-Hugo, 66700 Argelès-
sur-Mer. T. 0468815476. (encadrements)   *093050*

Argent-sur-Sauldre (Cher)
Antiquité La Croix Verte, Av Paris, 18410 Argent-sur-
Sauldre. T. 0248733264.   *093051*

Armentières (Nord)
Sainte-Anne, 2 Quai Beauvais, 59280 Armentières.
T. 0320441733.   *093052*

Arnas (Rhône)
Fleurieu, Patrick de, Les Rues, 69400 Arnas.
T. 0474650376.   *093053*

Arques (Pas-de-Calais)
Dufay, René, 8 Av Pierre-Mendès-France, 62510 Arques. T. 0321988570.   *093054*

Artix (Pyrénées-Atlantiques)
Abadie, Alain, Av République, 64170 Artix.
T. 0559603734.   *093055*

Asques (Gironde)
Malmezat, Thierry, 79 Le Bourg, 33240 Asques.
T. 0557581257.   *093056*

Athies (Somme)
Verbrugghe, Claude, 21 Rue Ham, 80200 Athies.
T. 0322856254, Fax 0322856221. *093057*

Athies-sous-Laon (Aisne)
Levent, Alain, 2 Rue des Ecoles, 02840 Athies-sous-Laon. T. 0323245545. *093058*

Aubais (Gard)
Felix Restauration, Quartier Oreille, Rte Gallargues,
30250 Aubais. T. 0466807572. *093059*

Aubervilliers (Seine-Saint-Denis)
Starosciak, Christian, 50 Rue Colbert, 93300 Aubervilliers. T. 0143524069. *093060*

Aubusson (Creuse)
Dessemond, J. – P., 30 Av Jean-Jaurès, 23200 Aubusson. T. 0555838745. *093061*

Auch (Gers)
Bérenguer, Joseph, 7bis Rue Blazy, 32000 Auch.
T. 0562630622. *093062*

Auray (Morbihan)
Hier-Aujourd'hui, 7 Pl République, 56640 Auray.
T. 0297507600. *093063*
Le Serrec, Yvonnick, 7 Pl République, 56640 Auray.
T. 0297563090. *093064*

Autun (Saône-et-Loire)
Gras, Bernard, 2 Rue Changarnier, 71400 Autun.
T. 0385520966. *093065*
Marbres, 15 Rue Marbres, 71400 Autun.
T. 0385862834. *093066*

Auxerre (Yonne)
Dagron, Benoît, 5 Rue Valmy, 89000 Auxerre.
T. 0386522816, Fax 0386511892. *093067*
Martinet, Dominique, 5 Rue Valmy, 89000 Auxerre.
T. 0386526636, Fax 0386511892. *093068*

Avignon (Vaucluse)
Centre Régional d'Etude et de Traitement des Œuvres
d'Art, 47 Rue Teinturiers, 84000 Avignon.
T. 0490851806, Fax 0490868942. *093069*
Guerre, Gérard, 1 Plan-Lunel, 84000 Avignon.
T. 0490864267, Fax 0490856462. *093070*
Hazaël-Massieux, Philippe, 47 Rue Teinturiers, 84000
Avignon. T. 0490868827. *093071*
Hubert, Patrick-Charles, 12 Rue Louis-Pasteur, 84000
Avignon. T. 0490866559. *093072*

Baden (Morbihan)
Kerhervé Antiquités, 56870 Baden.
T. 0297571237. *093073*

Balma (Haute-Garonne)
Catala d'Oc, 44 Chemin Arènes, 31130 Balma.
T. 0561365139. *093074*
Palmada, J., 44 Chemin Arènes, 31130 Balma.
T. 0561243727. *093075*
Rico, Gérard, Quint-Fonsegrives, 31130 Balma.
T. 0561241844. *093076*

Bar-le-Duc (Meuse)
Ricard, Claude, 6 Rue Horloge, 55000 Bar-le-Duc.
T. 0329790898. (lustres, bronze, cristaux) *093077*

Bardouville (Seine-Maritime)
Delaunay, Virginie, Beaulieu, 76480 Bardouville.
T. 0235370869. *093078*

Barr (Bas-Rhin)
Grewey, Marcel, 4 Rue Gare, 67140 Barr.
T. 0388089664. *093079*
Mangold, Alfred, 15 Grand'Rue, 67140 Barr.
T. 0388080004. *093080*

Bastelicaccia (Corse)
Arrighi, Mascarone, 20129 Bastelicaccia.
T. 0495200856, Fax 0495238105. *093081*

Bastia (Corse)
Buckland, Richard, Rte Inférieure-Cardo, Villa Gradic-
chia, 20200 Bastia. T. 0495327849. *093082*

Beaumettes (Vaucluse)
Hervé-Thibault, 100 Rte Nationale, 84220 Beaumettes.
T. 0490722878. *093083*

Beaune (Côte-d'Or)
Girard, Jean-Luc, 6 Rempart Madeleine, 21200 Beaune.
T. 0380241754. *093084*

Beautiran (Gironde)
Atelier du Rostu, Le Couloumey, 14 Rte Landes, 33640
Beautiran. T. 0556675351. *093085*

Beauvais (Oise)
Debruyn, Isabelle, 194 Rue de-Notre-Dame-du-Thil,
60000 Beauvais. T. 0344458999. *093086*
Gorostarzu, Marie-Odile de, 40 Rue de la Madeleine,
60000 Beauvais. T. 0344455383. *093087*
Institut de Restauration et de Recherches Archéologi-
ques et Paléométallurgiques (I.R.R.A.P), 21 Rue Corde-
liers, 60000 Beauvais. T. 0344202024,
Fax 0344200896. *093088*
Jolibois-Chevalier, 24 Rue Jean-Baptiste-Ballière,
60000 Beauvais. T. 0344484310. *093089*
Pradel, Claude, 5 Rue Chenevières, 60000 Beauvais.
T. 0344889108. *093090*

Béhen (Somme)
Hétroy, Hugues, 1 Rte Nationale, Les Croisettes, 80870
Béhen. T. 0322317314. (Ebénisterie, placage, marque-
terie, sculpture) *093091*

Belabre (Indre)
Chatenet, Jacky, Les Chirons, 36370 Belabre.
T. 0254376034. *093092*

Belfort (Territoire-de-Belfort)
Cerf, 51 Fbg Montbéliard, 90000 Belfort.
T. 0384280591. *093093*

Bergerac (Dordogne)
Pimouguet, Elisabeth, 8 Rue Saint-Martin, 24100 Bergerac. T. 0553270390. *093094*

Bernin (Isère)
France Antique, 19 Chemin Bas-Bernin, 38190 Bernin.
T. 0476088648. *093095*

Besançon (Doubs)
Laurent, Jean-Paul, 23 Av Chardonnet, 25000 Besan-
çon. T. 0381501655. *093096*
Morel, Olivier, 9 Rue Mégevand, 25000 Besançon.
T. 0381813279, Fax 0381816924. *093097*

Bessoncourt (Territoire-de-Belfort)
Bourquin, René, 11 Rue Eglantines, 90160 Bessoncourt.
T. 0384299395, Fax 0384299123. *093098*

Bétaille (Lot)
Renov Meubles, Ménoire, 46110 Bétaille.
T. 0565324757. *093099*

Beton-Bazoches (Seine-et-Marne)
Marteau, William, 6 Pl Eglise-Saint-Denis, 77320 Beton-
Bazoches. T. 64010196. *093100*

Béziers (Hérault)
Au Petit Noyer, 56 Rue Casimir-Péret, 34500 Béziers.
T. 0467490151. *093101*
Berte, Henri, 28 Rue Debès, 34500 Béziers.
T. 0467306796. *093102*
Ferreiro-Cros, Martine, 8 Rue Jules-Ferry, 34500 Bé-
ziers. T. 0467286554. *093103*

Biarritz (Pyrénées-Atlantiques)
Atelier de la Porcelaine, 41a Rue Courasson, 64200
Biarritz. T. 0559222214. *093104*
Chapelet, Albert, 18 Rue Borde-Saraspe, 64200 Biarritz.
T. 0559230336. *093105*
Jobbe-Duval, Xavier, 11 Rue Courasson, 64200 Biarritz.
T. 0559221139, Fax 0559221429. *093106*
Macé, Christophe, 77 Blvd Marcel-Dassault, 64200 Biar-
ritz. T. 0559439370. *093107*
Poydenot, Geneviève, 31 Rue Marie-Hope-Vère, 64200
Biarritz. T. 0559240713. *093108*

Bignan (Morbihan)
Atelier Régional de Restauration, Kerguehennec, 56500
Bignan. T. 0297604646. *093109*

Billac (Corrèze)
Gonnet, Jean-Louis, Bourg, 19120 Billac.
T. 0555912195, Fax 0555912640. *093110*

Bitche (Moselle)
Au Chardon Lorrain, 17 Rue Saint-Augustin, 57230 Bit-
che. T. 0387962465. *093111*
Peiffer, Yves, 14 Rue Sarreguemines, 57230 Bitche.
T. 0387961891. *093112*

Blaslay (Vienne)
Groux, 65 Av Saumur-Etables, 86170 Blaslay.
T. 0549511111, Fax 0549600713. *093113*

Bletterans (Jura)
Monloubou, Dominique, 2bis Rue Amont, 39140 Bletterans. T. 0384850240. *093114*

Blois (Loir-et-Cher)
Antiquité Blésoise, 30 Quai Aristide-Briand, 41000 Blois.
T. 0254743862. *093115*

Bois-Colombes (Hauts-de-Seine)
Au Fil des Ans, 5 Rue Victor-Hugo, 92270 Bois-Colombes. T. 0147843537. *093116*

Bois-Guillaume (Seine-Maritime)
Pottier, Marie-Hélène, 1060 Chemin Clères, 76230 Bois-
Guillaume. T. 0235981046. *093117*

Bonne (Haute-Savoie)
Meubles Style Restauration, Chemin Prés-Potex, 74380
Bonne. T. 0450362320, Fax 0450392267. *093118*

Bonnefontaine (Jura)
Pagnier, Jean, Rte Mirebel, 39800 Bonnefontaine.
T. 0384853006, Fax 0384853224. *093119*

Bordeaux (Gironde)
Atelier d'Ornano, 126bis Rue Ornano, 33000 Bordeaux.
T. 0556991614. *093120*
Atelier de la Licorne, 22 Rue Barreyre, 33300 Bordeaux.
T. 0556792187. *093121*
Atelier de Lerme, 19 Rue Lacroix, 33000 Bordeaux.
T. 0556819181. *093122*
Atelier du Rostu, 7 Rue Cerf-Volant, 33000 Bordeaux.
T. 0556519694. *093123*
Atelier du Village, 61 Rue Notre-Dame, 33000 Bordeaux.
T. 0556790942. *093124*
Bronze et Cuivre, 262 Rue Pasteur, 33000 Bordeaux.
T. 0556423856. *093125*
Centre International des Artisans d'Art, 13bis Rue Notre-
Dame, 33000 Bordeaux. T. 0556592222. *093126*
Fau, Marie-Noëlle, 37 Rue Condorcet, 33000 Bordeaux.
T. 0556873231. *093127*
Grimard, 138 Rue Notre-Dame, 33000 Bordeaux.
T. 0556444599. *093128*
Hérati, 14 Rue Sicard, 33000 Bordeaux.
T. 0556512417. *093129*
Hilber, 9 Pl Parlement, 33000 Bordeaux.
T. 0556524813. *093130*
Louwerse, Brigitte, 8 Rue La Boétie, 33000 Bordeaux.
T. 0556445308. *093131*
Montaut, 87 Rue Course, 33000 Bordeaux.
T. 0556819638. *093132*
Rougier, 29 Rue Bouffard, 33000 Bordeaux.
T. 0556525752. *093133*
Vuillier, Cécile, 77 Rue Saint-Joseph, 33000 Bordeaux.
T. 0556482971. *093134*
Wustner, Patrick, 41 Rue Notre-Dame, 33000 Bordeaux.
T. 0556446817. *093135*

Borgo (Corse)
Tudisco, Pascal, Les Chênes-Valrose, 20290 Borgo.
T. 0495307243. *093136*

Bouafle (Yvelines)
Atelier de la Renaissance, 27 Rue Maurice-Berteaux,
78410 Bouafle. T. 0130958499. *093137*

Boudreville (Côte-d'Or)
Echoppe, 21520 Boudreville. T. 0380935216. *093138*

Bougival (Yvelines)
Pelzer, Alice Hélène, Gérard, 4 Rue du Gén Leclerc,
78380 Bougival. T. 0139690857. (Meubles) *093139*

Bougnon (Haute-Saône)
Bernard, Michel, Grande Rue, 70170 Bougnon.
T. 0384916526. *093140*

Boulogne-Billancourt (Hauts-de-Seine)
Coquetterie du Logis, 61bis Rte Reine, 92100 Boulogne-
Billancourt. T. 0146041573. *093141*
Villeneuve, Arnaud de, 3 Sq Frères-Farman, 92100 Bou-
logne-Billancourt. T. 0146037832. *093142*

Boulogne-sur-Mer (Pas-de-Calais)
Bridenne, Franck, 13 All Alma, 62200 Boulogne-sur-
Mer. T. 0321306258. *093143*
Leleu, Gérald, 18 Rue du Doyen (Pl Dalton), 62200 Bou-
logne-sur-Mer. T. 0321872448. *093144*

**Bourcefranc-le-Chapus (Charente-Mari-
time)**
Antiquités L'Astelle, 13 Rue Léon-Oriou, 17560 Bourcefranc-le-Chapus. T. 0546853828. *093145*

Bourges (Cher)
Devulder, Jean-Marc, 33 Rue Bourbonnoux, 18000
Bourges. T. 0248651763. *093146*
Frères Nordin, 10 Rue Emile-Zola, 18000 Bourges.
T. 0248690416. *093147*
Le Taxin, Delphine, 28 Rue Auron, 18000 Bourges.
T. 0248709103. *093148*
Souvenance, 93 Rue Auron, 18000 Bourges.
T. 0248704847. *093149*

Bourron-Marlotte (Seine-et-Marne)
Poinsard, Eric, 14 Rue Bois, 77780 Bourron-Marlotte.
T. 64458525. *093150*

Bousbecque (Nord)
Six, Luc, 126 Rue de Linselles, 59166 Bousbecque.
T. 0320030405. (Vitraux) *093151*

Boutigny-Prouais (Eure-et-Loir)
Ronssin, Bertrand, 2 Rue Vignes-Rosay, 28410 Boutigny-Prouais. T. 0237431714. *093152*

Brantôme (Dordogne)
Auchère-Merle, Marie-Hélène, 19 Rue Victor-Hugo,
24310 Brantôme. T. 0553058613. *093153*

Brenthonne (Haute-Savoie)
Fauvergue, Arnaud, Puard, 74890 Brenthonne.
T. 0450363460. *093154*

Brest (Finistère)
Arats, 2bis Rue Jean-le-Gail, 29200 Brest.
T. 0298436000. *093155*
Buit, Hervé du, 40 Rue Vauban, 29200 Brest.
T. 0298450120. *093156*
Grenier de Recouvrance, 32 Rue Saint-Exupéry, 29200
Brest. T. 0298457666. *093157*
Talec, Pierre, 15 Rue Galliéni, 29200 Brest.
T. 0298053344. *093158*

Brioude (Haute-Loire)
Mollon, Av Velay, 43100 Brioude.
T. 0471749944. *093159*

Brive-la-Gaillarde (Corrèze)
Atelier Doménat, 6 Rue République, 19100 Brive-la-
Gaillarde. T. 0555242149. *093160*
Teillard, Roland, 84 Rue Martial-Brigouleix, 19100 Bri-
ve-la-Gaillarde. T. 0555872563. *093161*

Brux (Vienne)
Hapel, François, Bourg, 86510 Brux.
T. 0549590343. *093162*

Buc (Yvelines)
Perrault, Gilles, 27 Rue Alsace-Lorraine, 78530 Buc.
T. 0139561163. *093163*

Caen (Calvados)
Ali Adel, 50 Rue Ecuyère, 14300 Caen. T. 0231853746,
Fax 0231864813. *093164*

Au Cherche Hier, 19 Rue Teinturiers, 14021 Caen Cédex.
T. 0231856076. *093165*
Hubert, Marie, 9 Rue Québec, 14000 Caen.
T. 0231744454. *093166*
Mesnil, Bruno, 46 Passage Grand-Turc, 14000 Caen.
T. 0231772592. *093167*
Reine Mathilde, 47 Rue Saint-Jean, 14000 Caen.
T. 0231854552, Fax 0231866493. *093168*

Cahors (Lot)
Descroix, Alain, 76 Rue Soubirous, 46000 Cahors.
T. 0565350277. *093169*

Cambrai (Nord)
Relais d'Art, 13 Rue Tavelle, 59400 Cambrai.
T. 0327812330. (antiquités) *093170*

Cannes (Alpes-Maritimes)
Antiquaires Associés, 101 Blvd République, 06400 Can-
nes. T. 0493992230. *093171*
Castellano, Nicolas, 5 Rue Docteur-Calmette, 06400
Cannes. T. 0493395769. *093172*
Cluzel, Patrick, 50 Rue Léon-Noël, 06400 Cannes.
T. 0493991213. *093173*
Desaunay, 103 Blvd Paul-Doumer, 06400 Cannes.
T. 0493465610. *093174*
Gallard, François, 17 Blvd Strasbourg, 06400 Cannes.
T. 0493391228. *093175*
Lauretta, 105 Blvd République, 06400 Cannes.
T. 0493680535. *093176*
Lebraly, Guy, 113 Blvd République, 06400 Cannes.
T. 0493380430. *093177*

Carcassonne (Aude)
Rouch, Yves, 19 Rue Myrtilles, 11000 Carcassonne.
T. 0468711155. *093178*

Carnac (Morbihan)
Le Poher, 1 Av Druides, 56340 Carnac.
T. 0297521181. *093179*

Carpentras (Vaucluse)
Augier, Albert, 261 Blvd Alfred-Naquet, 84200 Carpentras. T. 0490632309. *093180*
Marty, Robert, 124 Blvd Waldeck-Rousseau, 84200 Carpentras. T. 0490600684. *093181*

Castelnau-le-Lez (Hérault)
Atelier de la Porte, 355 Rte Nîmes, 34170 Castelnau-le-
Lez. T. 0467722513, Fax 0467721667. *093182*
Curabet, Philippe, 17 Av Jean-Jaurès, 34170 Castelnau-
le-Lez. T. 0467724496. *093183*
Nicolet, Chantal, 3 Rue Grenouillère, 34170 Castelnau-
le-Lez. T. 0467729701. *093184*

Castres (Tarn)
Belle Epoque, 72 Av Albi, 81100 Castres.
T. 0563597656. *093185*
Lauret, Gérard, 34 All Corbière, 81100 Castres.
T. 0563720622. *093186*
Sales, Patrick, 11 Rue Cambos, 81100 Castres.
T. 0563478324. *093187*

Cauneille (Landes)
Carrau, Gilbert, Villa Thiena, RN 117, 40300 Cauneille.
T. 0558730710, Fax 0558731534. *093188*

Cavaillon (Vaucluse)
Atelier Allégro, Lot Les Peupliers, 96 Imp Arbousiers,
84300 Cavaillon. T. 0490780081. *093189*

Céret (Pyrénées-Orientales)
Catalane, 30 Blvd Maréchal-Joffre, 66400 Céret.
T. 0468872173. (encadrements) *093190*
Degeorge, Charles, 72 Saint-Férréol, 66400 Céret.
T. 0468870793. (encadrements) *093191*
Rossignol & Fils, 24 Pl Liberté, 66400 Céret.
T. 0468870572, Fax 0468873057.
(encadrements) *093192*

Challans (Vendée)
Brunet, Guy, 3 Rue Pasteur, 85300 Challans.
T. 0251353204. *093193*

Chalon-sur-Saône (Saône-et-Loire)
Jusselin, Dominique, 6 Rue Edgar-Quinet, 71100 Chalon-sur-Saône. T. 0385935182. *093194*

Chamalières (Puy-de-Dôme)
Artiste, 5 Rue Arsenal, 63400 Chamalières.
T. 0473313159. (encadrements; beaux arts;
affiches) *093195*
Atelier Dorures, 66 Av Joseph-Claussat, 63400 Chama-
lières. T. 0473369023. *093196*
Georges, Annick, 16bis Av Thermes, 63400 Chamaliè-
res. T. 0473371828. (encadrements) *093197*

Chambéria (Jura)
Chauvin, Didier, Chemin Chambéria-Messia, 39270
Chambéria. T. 0384357175. *093198*

Chambéry (Savoie)
Bard, Philippe, 2 Pass Henri-Murger, 73000 Chambéry.
T. 0479337483. *093199*
Bonheur du Jour, 68 Rue Dacquin, 73000 Chambéry.
T. 0479852131. *093200*
Chiodero, Serge, 71 Chemin Grive-Sac, 73000 Cham-
béry. T. 0479722677. *093201*
Moleins, Daniel, 189 Rue Dacquin, 73000 Chambéry.
T. 0479705536. *093202*
Moreaux-Jouannet, Isabelle, 131 All Grand-Parc, 73000
Chambéry. T. 0479626627. (tableaux) *093203*

Chambray-lès-Tours (Indre-et-Loire)
Carré, Jean, 25 Av République, 37170 Chambray-lès-
Tours. T. 0547283134. *093204*

Champagnole (Jura)
Deniset, René, 5 Rue Lavoisier, 39300 Champagnole.
T. 0384520707. *093205*

Chantilly
Chantebois Restauration, 4 Rue Otages, 60500 Chantilly.
T. 0344581725. *093206*

Chard (Creuse)
Aphecca Aubail, Bourg, 23700 Chard. T. 0555672671,
Fax 0555672675. *093207*

Charlieu (Loire)
Ducher, Charles, 29 Rue Chanteloup, 42190 Charlieu.
T. 0477600116. *093208*

Charmoille (Haute-Saône)
Jaccachoury, Jean-Paul, 6 Rue Puits-Salé, 70000 Charmoille. T. 0384752148. *093209*

Chartres (Eure-et-Loir)
Brunet, Jany, 19 Rue Epervier, 28000 Chartres.
T. 0237214158. *093210*
Devillers, Bernard, 13 Rue Grenets, 28000 Chartres.
T. 0237212285. *093211*

Châteaudun (Eure-et-Loir)
Au Sourire du Passé, 8 Rue Moulin, 28200 Châteaudun.
T. 0237458900. *093212*

Châteauroux (Indre)
Delloye Thoumyre, Anne-Marie, 34 Rue Pavillons,
36000 Châteauroux. T. 0254342483,
Fax 0254342483. *093213*
Jaeger, Gertrude, 104 Av Marins, 36000 Châteauroux.
T. 0254076508. *093214*
Perreau, Patrick, 58 Av John-Kennedy, 36000 Château-
roux. T. 0254270945. *093215*
Soria, 28 Rue Grande, 36000 Châteauroux.
T. 0254340860. *093216*

Châtelus-le-Marcheix (Creuse)
L'Atelier, 29bis Rue Deux-Ponts, 23430 Châtelus-le-
Marcheix. T. 0555643239. *093217*

Châtenois (Bas-Rhin)
Herrbach, Pl de la Mairie, 67730 Châtenois.
T. 0388820369. *093218*

Châtillon (Hauts-de-Seine)
Virmaux, Christine, 70 Blvd Vanves, 92320 Châtillon.
T. 0140848567. *093219*

Chauray (Deux-Sèvres)
Beaufort, Robert, 39 Rue Château, 79180 Chauray.
T. 0549080307. *093220*

Chavéria (Jura)
Gand, Philippe, Grand Chavéria, 39270 Chavéria.
T. 0384355421. *093221*

Chaville (Hauts-de-Seine)
Keramos, 22 Rue Lamennais, 92370 Chaville.
T. 0147508870. *093222*

Chazey-sur-Ain (Ain)
Auffray-Vuichard, Guy, 01150 Chazey-sur-Ain.
T. 0474619323. *093223*

Chevry-Cossigny (Seine-et-Marne)
Matthey, Alain, 19 Rue Chemin-Vert, 77173 Chevry-Cossigny. T. 0360284854. *093224*

Chomérac (Ardèche)
Ferrière de Lassus, André de, Château de Mauras,
07210 Chomérac. T. 0475651180. (Antiquité,
Archéologie) *093225*

Choux (Jura)
Orfila, Antoine, 20 Rte Perrine, 39370 Choux.
T. 0384411493. *093226*

Clamart (Hauts-de-Seine)
Atelier, 106 Av Marguerite-Renaudin, 92140 Clamart.
T. 0146489641. *093227*
Gallot, Germain, 7 Rue Montoir, 92140 Clamart.
T. 0140958708. *093228*
Lepainteur, Patrick, 15 Rue Chef-de-Ville, 92140 Clam-
art. T. 0146459507. *093229*

Clermont-Ferrand (Puy-de-Dôme)
Alban Ebéniste, 59 Rue Henri-Barbusse, 63000 Cler-
mont-Ferrand. T. 0473922993. *093230*
Barrière, Luc, Villerose, 63000 Clermont-Ferrand.
T. 0473385352. (meubles) *093231*
Boulet, Nicole, 87bis Av Libération, 63000 Clermont-
Ferrand. T. 0473355745. (encadrements) *093232*
Cadre a l'Orange, 3 Rue Boucherie, 63000 Clermont-
Ferrand. T. 0473925569. (encadrements) *093233*
Col, Bernard, 8 Rue Francisque-Bathol, 63000 Cler-
mont-Ferrand. T. 0473934130. (Ebénisterie d'art;
meubles) *093234*
CO.R.O.ART, 10 Pl Thomas, 6300 Clermont-Ferrand.
T. 0473914224. (Glaces; Statuaires; Bois doré; Ta-
bleaux; Affiches; Gravures) *093235*
Création Gérard, 15 Rue Savaron, 63000 Clermont-Fer-
rand. T. 0473906294. *093236*
Damit, Jean-Michel, 11 Rue Savaron, 63000 Clermont-
Ferrand. T. 0473907262. (Ebénisterie d'art;
meubles) *093237*
Dautrait, Daniel, 12 Rue Savaron, 63000 Clermont-Fer-
rand. T. 0473915589. (Ebénisterie d'art;
meubles) *093238*
Ebénisterie Plasse, Le Clos, 63000 Clermont-Ferrand.
T. 0473629331. (copie d'ancien-restauration) *093239*
Lamare, Patrick, 39 Rue Dominique, 63000 Clermont-
Ferrand. T. 0473373190. (Ebénisterie d'art;
meubles) *093240*
Lavigne, Jean-Michel, 38 Rue Port, 63000 Clermont-
Ferrand. T. 0473916363. (encadrements) *093241*
Leblay, Bernard, 5 Rue Abbé-Girard, 63000 Clermont-
Ferrand. T. 0473902942. (Ebénisterie d'art;
meubles) *093242*
Lopez, Pierre, 20 Rue Eugène-Gilbert, 63000 Clermont-
Ferrand. T. 0473352265. (Doreur sur bois) *093243*
Monnet, François, 10 Rue Savaron, 63000 Clermont-
Ferrand. T. 0473924995. (Ebénisterie d'art;
meubles) *093244*
Perrin, Patrick, 29 Rue Pascal, 63000 Clermont-Ferrand.
T. 0473917052. (dorure; argenture) *093245*
Porte, Henri, 1 Rue Ancien-Poids-de-Ville, 63000 Cler-
mont-Ferrand. T. 0473374751. *093246*
Rigaud, Pascal, 21 Rue Vieillards, 63000 Clermont-Fer-
rand. T. 0473309514. (Ebénisterie d'art;
meubles) *093247*
Rousset, Didier, 10 Pl Thomas, 63000 Clermont-Ferrand.
T. 0473914224. (Doreur sur bois) *093248*

Clichy (Hauts-de-Seine)
Hogommat, Yves-Laurent, 15 Rue Victor-Méric, 92110
Clichy. T. 0142709502. *093249*

Cluses (Haute-Savoie)
Verbièse, P., 614 Av Noiret, 74300 Cluses.
T. 0450981835. *093250*

Cogna (Jura)
Richard, Claude, 3 Rue Montrichard, 39130 Cogna.
T. 0384258334. *093251*

Colayrac-Saint-Cirq (Lot-et-Garonne)
Paoli, Bruno de, Cours Libération, 47450 Colayrac-
Saint-Cirq. T. 0553875054. *093252*

Combs-la-Ville (Seine-et-Marne)
Bernhardt, Claude, 17 Rue Pierre-et-Marie-Curie, 77380
Combs-la-Ville. T. 64888013. *093253*

Compiègne
Duchenne, Daniel, 360 Rue République, 60200 Compiègne. T. 0344830489. *093254*
Hyart & Fils, 7 Rue-du-Four-Saint-Jacques, 60200 Compiègne. T. 0344202305. *093255*
Metais, Claude, 44 Rue Saint-Germain, 60200 Compiègne. T. 0344230034. *093256*

Condamine (Jura)
Behem, Norbert, Rue Ecole, 39570 Condamine.
T. 0384353030. *093257*

Corbeil-Essonnes (Essonne)
Didier, 9 Rue Tisseurs, 91100 Corbeil-Essonnes.
T. 0160884605, Fax 0160884605. *093258*

Cosges (Jura)
Vergon, Vincent, Chemin Garenne, 39140 Cosges.
T. 0384851033, Fax 0384850413. *093259*

Cosne-Cours-sur-Loire (Nièvre)
Borde, Thierry, RN 7, Bois Maillard, 58200 Cosne-
Cours-sur-Loire. T. 0386261221. *093260*

Couhé (Vienne)
Liévens, Av de Paris, 86700 Couhé. T. 0549432156.
(meubles) *093261*

Coupvray (Seine-et-Marne)
Mondon, François, 3 Imp Pierres, 77450 Coupvray.
T. 0360044307. *093262*

Courbevoie (Hauts-de-Seine)
Chevalier, Georges, 64 Blvd de la Mission-Marchand,
92400 Courbevoie. T. 0147884141, Fax 0143340899.
(tapis) *093263*
Lumont, 12 Rue Cacheux, 92400 Courbevoie.
T. 0147895690. *093264*

Coutevroult (Seine-et-Marne)
Gingras, Colette, 20 Rue Tillaye, 77580 Coutevroult.
Fax 64635621. *093265*

Craponne (Rhône)
Passé Composé, 120 Av Dumont, 69290 Craponne.
T. 0478448956. *093266*

Crastatt (Bas-Rhin)
Richert, Gilbert, 3 Rue Principale, 67310 Crastatt.
T. 0388872815. *093267*

Crécy-la-Chapelle (Seine-et-Marne)
Chapelle Antique, 31 Rue Abbesse, 77580 Crécy-la-
Chapelle. T. 64636134. *093268*

Crest (Drôme)
Gilles, Gilbert, 17 Rue Sadi-Carnot, 26400 Crest.
T. 0475253053. *093269*

Creuzier-le-Vieux (Allier)
Valentin, Jean-Claude, 38 Rue de l'Industrie, 03000
Creuzier-le-Vieux. T. 0470315513. *093270*

Crolles (Isère)
Warren, Renaud de, Château de Crolles, 38190 Crolles.
T. 0476088741. *093271*

Cuguen (Ille-et-Vilaine)
Antiquités de la Villate, La Villate, 35270 Cuguen.
T. 0299733334, Fax 0299732979. *093272*

Darnétal (Seine-Maritime)
Legrand, B., 27 Rue Lucien-Fromage, 76160 Darnétal.
T. 0232830070. *093273*

Darvault (Seine-et-Marne)
Servas, François, 18 All Château, 77140 Darvault.
T. 64282664. *093274*

Dax (Landes)
Bordenave, Pierre, 8 Blvd Forceries, 40100 Dax.
T. 0558745824. *093275*
Gensous, Jean, 21 Centre Artisanal, 40100 Dax.
T. 0558744818. *093276*

Dijon (Côte-d'Or)
Chancenotte, Jacques, 37 Blvd Thiers, 21000 Dijon.
T. 0380316900. *093277*
Deiller-Ducatel, 17 Rue Blériot, 21000 Dijon.
T. 0380744846. *093278*
Fouchet, 11 Rue Bons-Enfants, 21000 Dijon.
T. 0380637004. *093279*
Galerie 6, 6 Rue Auguste-Comte, 21000 Dijon.
T. 0380716846. *093280*
Laserblast, 23 Rue René-Coty, 21000 Dijon.
T. 0380662600, Fax 0380673250. *093281*
Nouvelle Héloïse, 95 Rue Jean-Jacques-Rousseau,
21000 Dijon. T. 0380316090. *093282*
Renard, René, 5 Pl 30-Octobre, 21000 Dijon.
T. 0380653043. *093283*

Dinan (Côtes-d'Armor)
Morin, François, 6 Rue Guichet, 22100 Dinan.
T. 0296392520. *093284*

Dole (Jura)
Dorée, Jacques, 45 Rue Fourches, 39100 Dole.
T. 0384824504. *093285*
Mercier, Denis, 51 Rue Mont-Roland, 39100 Dole.
T. 0384723752. *093286*

Domblans (Jura)
Tignolet, André, Rue Ligne, 39210 Domblans.
T. 0384852133. *093287*

Doué-la-Fontaine (Maine-et-Loire)
Moisson, Dominique, 35bis Rue Soulanger, 49700
Doué-la-Fontaine. T. 41590200. *093288*

Doullens (Somme)
Vasseur, Frédéric, 1 Av Général-de-Gaulle, 80600 Doullens. T. 0322772331. (Meubles) *093289*

Dourges (Pas-de-Calais)
Labaère Lustrerie, Rte Hénin-Beaumont, 62119 Dourges. T. 0321495178. *093290*

Draguignan (Var)
Tilbury, Av Général-de-Gaulle, 83300 Draguignan.
T. 0494681385. *093291*

Eaubonne (Val-d'Oise)
Passé Simple, 1 Rue Jeanne-Robillon, 95600 Eaubonne.
T. 0139592958, Fax 0139598854. *093292*

Ennordres (Cher)
Laurent, Jean-Claude, Le Grand-Lieu, 18380 Ennordres.
T. 0248583202, Fax 0248583242. *093293*

Epinal (Vosges)
Atelier, 52 Quai Bons-Enfants, 88000 Epinal.
T. 0329820406. *093294*
Passé Simple, 77 Rue Neuve-Grange-Saint-Laurent,
88000 Epinal. T. 0329641017. *093295*
Tisserant, Jean-Marie, 16 Rue Louis-Blériot, 88000 Epi-
nal. T. 0329343144. *093296*
Viant, André, 47 Rue Remiremont, 88000 Epinal.
T. 0329353485. *093297*

Ermont (Val-d'Oise)
Combey, Claude, 37 Rue Gros-Noyer, 95120 Ermont.
T. 0134144833. *093298*

Esbly (Seine-et-Marne)
Fessenmeyer, Christian, 28 Av Foch, 77450 Esbly.
T. 0360041270. *093299*

Esparron-de-Verdon (Alpes-de-Haute-Provence)
Seehof, Sascha, Rue Mairie, 04550 Esparron-de-Verdon. T. 0492771366. *093300*

Espinasse-Vozelle (Allier)
Germain-Vizade, Le Bourg, 03110 Espinasse-Vozelle.
T. 0470565755. (Gravures, Encadrements, Meubles, Tableaux, Dessins) *093301*
Goliard, Paul, Rte Nationale 209, 03110 Espinasse-Vozelle. T. 0470565032. *093302*

Espondeilhan (Hérault)
Charme d'Antan, Rue Notre-Dame-des-Pins, 34290 Espondeilhan. T. 0467391190. *093303*

Essey-lès-Nancy (Meurthe-et-Moselle)
Restauration de vos Meubles, 101 Av 69ème-RI, 54270 Essey-lès-Nancy. T. 0383212109. *093304*

Evette-Salbert (Territoire-de-Belfort)
Allemann, Pierre, 17 Rue Clarines, 90350 Evette-Salbert. T. 0384260931. *093305*

Evreux (Eure)
Ménard, Christophe, 13 Rue Verdun, 27000 Evreux.
T. 0232386780. *093306*

Fabrègues (Hérault)
Damiean, Pierre-Jean, 2 Imp Presbytère, 34690 Fabrègues. T. 0467851211. *093307*

Fegersheim (Bas-Rhin)
Grimm, Henri, 116 Rue Général-de-Gaulle, 67640 Fegersheim. T. 0388685730. *093308*

Ferrette (Haut-Rhin)
Galerie Mazarin, 3 Carrefour Rte Lucelle, 68480 Ferrette. T. 0389403277. *093309*

Flayosc (Var)
D'Aubreby, Vincent, Chemin Martelle, 83780 Flayosc.
T. 0494703591. *093310*

Fontaine-lès-Dijon (Côte-d'Or)
Antiquités Le Bail, 2 Rue Chambertin-Hauteville, 21121 Fontaine-lès-Dijon. T. 0380564100. *093311*

Fontenay-le-Comte (Vendée)
Au Temps Jadis, La Garde, Rte Nantes, 85200 Fontenay-le-Comte. T. 0251692530. *093312*
Legroux, Pascale, 6 Rue Arsène-Charrier, 85200 Fontenay-le-Comte. T. 0251698264. *093313*
Luminaires de Prestige, 67 Rue Tiraqueau, 85200 Fontenay-le-Comte. T. 0251690322. *093314*

Fougerolles (Haute-Saône)
Oudot & Fils, 10 Rue Parc, 70220 Fougerolles.
T. 0384491316. *093315*

Fronsac (Gironde)
Montion, Jean-Pierre, 10 Av Général-de-Gaulle, 33126 Fronsac. T. 0557514249. *093316*

Gap (Hautes-Alpes)
Gap Antiquités, Zone Artisanale Eyssagnières, 05000 Gap. T. 0492534014. *093317*
Parruzot, W., 43 Av d'Embrun, 05000 Gap.
T. 0492537619. *093318*

Gaujacq (Pyrénées-Atlantiques)
Thomas, Frédérique, Château Gaujacq, 40330 Gaujacq.
T. 0558892112. *093319*

Gémenos (Bouches-du-Rhône)
Amathieux, Suzanne, 103 Chemin Saint-Jean Garguier-à-Gémen, 13420 Gémenos. T. 0442322543. *093320*
Gibelli, Richard, 112 Chemin Départemental 2, 13420 Gémenos. T. 0442322096. *093321*
Rouvière, Michel, 1476 Chemin République, 13420 Gémenos. T. 0442320569. *093322*

Genay (Rhône)
Carret, Jean, 273 Rue Proulieu, 69730 Genay.
T. 0478915562. *093323*

Gençay (Vienne)
Valade, François, Rue Usson, 86160 Gençay.
T. 0549594549. *093324*

Genillé (Indre-et-Loire)
Estève, Brigitte, 24 Rue Jeanne-d'Arc, 37460 Genillé.
T. 0547595555. *093325*

Gentilly (Val-de-Marne)
Burgues, Catherine, 155 Av Paul-Vaillant-Couturier, 94250 Gentilly. T. 0149850819. *093326*

Gétigné (Loire-Atlantique)
Papis, Louis, 5 Pl Foumil, 44190 Gétigné.
T. 40544960. *093327*

Giromagny (Territoire-de-Belfort)
Menuiserie Claude, 11 Av Gare, 90200 Giromagny.
T. 0384271588. *093328*

Givet (Ardennes)
Migeon, Benoît, 65 Rte Bon-Secours, 08600 Givet.
T. 0324418140, Fax 0324418236. *093329*

Gouesnou (Finistère)
Roudaut, Robert, Ker-Loïs Rte Brest, 29850 Gouesnou.
T. 0298077645. *093330*

Grasse (Alpes-Maritimes)
Antiquités Douce France, 12bis Av Chiris, 06130 Grasse.
T. 0493401418. *093331*
Legrain, Alain, Rue Tunnel, 06130 Grasse.
T. 0493401172. *093332*

Grenade-sur-l'Adour (Landes)
Dauriac, Annie, 1 Rue Monseigneur-Cassaigne, 40270 Grenade-sur-l'Adour. T. 0558459045. *093333*

Grenoble (Isère)
Armentero, Albert, 5 Rue Camille-Desmoulins, 38000 Grenoble. T. 0476871458. *093334*
Atelier de l'Arno, 7 Rue Lieutenant-Chanaron, 38000 Grenoble. T. 0476562993. (tableaux) *093335*
Chimène, 3 Rue des Bergers, 38000 Grenoble.
T. 0476431221. *093336*
Eleouet, Catherine, 4bis Rue Nicolas-Chorier, 38000 Grenoble. T. 0476474446. *093337*
Prince, Michèle, 2 Rue Saint-Laurent, 38000 Grenoble.
T. 0476426076. (cuirs décorés pour meubles) *093338*
Rapin, Jean-François, 7 Rue Voltaire, 38000 Grenoble.
T. 0476638234. *093339*
Thomasson, Gérard, 8 Rue du Vieux-Temple, 38000 Grenoble. T. 0476420755. (meubles anciens) *093340*
Torelli & Pétrella, 13 Rue Roger-Ronserail, 38100 Grenoble. T. 0476210090. *093341*
Viguier, Henry, 6 Rue Dominique-Villars, 38000 Grenoble. T. 0476426916. *093342*

Grésy-sur-Aix (Savoie)
Sarret, Yvan, La Chevret, Rte Annecy, 73100 Grésy-sur-Aix. T. 0479880402. *093343*

Grignan (Drôme)
Styl'Créations, Quart Tuilière, 26230 Grignan.
T. 0475469082. *093344*

Grosbliederstroff (Moselle)
Schmid, Ralf, 15 Rue Liberté, 57520 Grosbliederstroff.
T. 0387092951. *093345*

Guémené-Penfao (Loire-Atlantique)
Hermon, Philippe, Rue Chateaubriant, 44290 Guémené-Penfao. T. 40792658. *093346*

Guérande (Loire-Atlantique)
Lechat, Bernard, 1bis Fbg-Saint-Armel, 44350 Guérande. T. 40248408. *093347*
Mamy Ateliers, La Noette, Rte Clis, 44350 Guérande.
T. 40248930. *093348*

Guiseniers (Eure)
Pouvreau, Paul, 47 Rue Pierre-Simon, 27700 Guiseniers.
T. 0232543688. *093349*

Gujan-Mestras (Gironde)
Antunes, Pedro, 55 Cours Verdun, 33470 Gujan-Mestras. T. 0556660713. *093350*

Haguenau (Bas-Rhin)
Au Fil du Temps, 113 Rte Strasbourg, 67500 Haguenau.
T. 0388932722, Fax 0388061159. *093351*
Entre-Temps, 14 Rue de la Redoute, 67500 Haguenau.
T. 0388733566. *093352*
Riff, 22 Rte Soufflenheim, 67500 Haguenau.
T. 0388909413. *093353*

Hallivillers (Somme)
Joubert, Anne, 21 Rue Eglise, 80250 Hallivillers.
T. 0322094589. (Tableaux) *093354*

Hautefort (Dordogne)
Férignac, Jean, Gare, 24390 Hautefort. T. 0553504475, Fax 0553502626. *093355*

Hédé (Ille-et-Vilaine)
Annic, Patrice, 18 Pl Mairie, 35630 Hédé.
T. 0299454126. *093356*

Hégenheim (Haut-Rhin)
Riedlin, Marcel, 29 Rue Hagenthal, 68220 Hégenheim.
T. 0389697650. *093357*

Hérouville (Val-d'Oise)
Royer, Rémy, 18 Rue Georges-Duhamel, 95300 Hérouville. T. 0134662265. *093358*

Héry (Yonne)
Artop, 2 Rue Seignelay, 89550 Héry. T. 0386479551, Fax 0386479125. *093359*
Yeremiyew, Luc, 10 Rue du Moutier, 89550 Héry.
T. 0386477298. *093360*

Huismes (Indre-et-Loire)
Bondy, Eliane de, Le Bourg, 37420 Huismes.
T. 0547954054. *093361*

Hyères (Var)
D'Hyères et d'Aujourd'hui, Rue Séré-de-Rivière, 83400 Hyères. T. 0494655670. *093362*
Galerie des Iles d'Or, 16 Av des Iles-d'Or, 83400 Hyères.
T. 0494651955. *093363*

Issoire (Puy-de-Dôme)
Allemand, Philippe, Zi la Maze, 63500 Issoire.
T. 0473550206. (Ebénisterie d'art; meubles) *093364*
Erard, Patrick, 4 Chemin Croisettes, 63500 Issoire.
T. 0473551376. (Ebénisterie d'art; meubles) *093365*
Fontanon, Jean-Michel, 2 Rue Pierre-Antoine-Rouvet, 63500 Issoire. T. 0473896127. (Ebénisterie d'art; meubles) *093366*
Karoutzos, Ch., 10 Imp Emile-Zola, 63500 Issoire.
T. 0473895931, Fax 0473892874. (Arts; Bâtiments) *093367*
Lagière, Jacques, 5 Rue Auguste-Bravard, 63500 Issoire. T. 0473891018. (Ebénisterie d'art; meubles) *093368*

Jaujac (Ardèche)
Musso, Joseph, Quart Roudils, 07380 Jaujac.
T. 0475932087. *093369*

Joigny (Yonne)
Friess, Jean-Pierre, 13 Av Forêt-d'Othe, 89300 Joigny.
T. 0386622245. *093370*
Friess, Jean-Pierre, Rte Dixmont, 89300 Joigny.
T. 0386623724. *093371*

Jonzac (Charente-Maritime)
Antiquités du Cloître, 29 Rue Carmes, 17500 Jonzac.
T. 0546482683. *093372*

Jouars-Pontchartrain (Yvelines)
Tardif, François, 6 Rte Paris, 78760 Jouars-Pontchartrain. T. 0134890259. *093373*

Joué-lès-Tours (Indre-et-Loire)
Khallouf, Faddoui, 6 All Alphonse-Riverain, 37300 Joué-lès-Tours. T. 0547520661, Fax 0547272828. *093374*

Jouy (Eure-et-Loir)
GLB Création, 5 Rue Berchères, 28300 Jouy.
T. 0237222972. *093375*

L'Escarène (Alpes-Maritimes)
Peluet-Altobianchi, César de, Col de Nice, 06440 L'Escarène. T. 0493795048. *093376*

L'Isle-Adam (Val-d'Oise)
Chevrier, Françoise, 3 Rue Nogent, 95290 L'Isle-Adam.
T. 0134690271. *093377*

L'Isle-Jourdain (Gers)
Maimponte, Marcel, Av Toulouse, 32600 L'Isle-Jourdain.
T. 0562071593, Fax 0562072485. *093378*

La Baule (Loire-Atlantique)
Atelier de l'Ebéniste, 37 Av Georges-Clemenceau,
44500 La Baule. T. 40110417. *093379*
Célette, René, Esplanade François-André, 44500 La
Baule. T. 40242091. *093380*

La Calmette (Gard)
Atelier de la Regordane, Plan Croix, 30190 La Calmette.
T. 0466810203, Fax 0466810167. *093381*

La Charité-sur-Loire (Nièvre)
Bétabois, 19 Cour Château, 58400 La Charité-sur-Loire.
T. 0386696238. *093382*
Timoléonthos, François, 64 Rue Hôtelleries, 58400 La
Charité-sur-Loire. T. 0386701190. *093383*

La Crau (Var)
Village Saint-Pierre, 22 Av Gare, 83260 La Crau.
T. 0494661194. *093384*

La Garenne Colombes (Hauts-de-Seine)
Nucci, 27 Av Joseph-Froment, 92250 La Garenne-Colombes. T. 0142421975. *093385*

La Londe-les-Maures (Var)
Varlope, Rte Cabasson, Quartier Moulières, 83250 La
Londe-les-Maures. T. 0494666307. *093386*

La Monnerie (Puy-de-Dôme)
Dumas, Jean & Fils, Rue de la Roulière, 63650 La Monnerie. T. 0473514030, Fax 0473514505. (Argenture;
reargenture; dorure) *093387*

La Montagne (Loire-Atlantique)
Revalor, 9 Rue de la Roserai, 44620 La Montagne.
T. 40329492. *093388*

La Riche (Indre-et-Loire)
Boutillier, Frédéric, 46 Rue Mairie, 37520 La Riche.
T. 0547371156. *093389*

La Rochelle (Charente-Maritime)
Reix, Chantal, 125 Blvd André-Sautel, 17000 La Rochelle. T. 0546341670, Fax 0546003568. *093390*

La Seyne-sur-Mer (Var)
Art Utile, 51 Blvd 4-Septembre, 83500 La Seyne-sur-Mer. T. 0494879659, Fax 0494879954. *093391*

La Teste-de-Buch (Gironde)
Mauron, 651 Av Denis-Papin, 33260 La Teste-de-Buch.
T. 0556547038. *093392*
Mauron, Pierre, 221 Av Gustave-Eiffel, 33260 La Teste-de-Buch. T. 0556547260. *093393*

La Turballe (Loire-Atlantique)
Martin, Jean-Noël, Rue Roëllo, 44420 La Turballe.
T. 40118034, Fax 40118536. *093394*

La Verpillière (Isère)
Brocantine, 44 Rue du Batou, 38290 La Verpillière.
T. 0474944771. *093395*

Labarde (Gironde)
Proniewski, Serge, 32 B Rte Château, 33460 Labarde.
T. 0557889046, Fax 0557883629. *093396*

Labastide-d'Armagnac (Landes)
Grange Notre Dame, Rue Notre-Dame, 40240 Labastide-d'Armagnac. T. 0558446666. *093397*

Lachapelle (Lot-et-Garonne)
Keuten, Viviane, Bourg, 47350 Lachapelle.
T. 0553836567. *093398*

Lagny-sur-Marne (Seine-et-Marne)
Desroches, Françoise, 10 Rue Jacques-Le-Paire, 77400
Lagny-sur-Marne. T. 64305498. *093399*

Laissey (Doubs)
Entre-Deux, Prés Docks, 25820 Laissey.
T. 0381632084. *093400*

Lambesc (Bouches-du-Rhône)
Imbert, J.K., 28 Av Verdun, 13410 Lambesc.
T. 0442928830. *093401*

Lancon-Provence (Bouches-du-Rhône)
Art du Bois, Chemin Ratonneaux, Quartier du Riou,
13680 Lancon-Provence. T. 0490427567. *093402*

Langres (Haute-Marne)
Macheret, Philippe, 16 Rue Terreaux, 52200 Langres.
T. 0325874016. *093403*

Lapalme (Aude)
Delacour, Jean-Claude, RN 9, Carrefour Port-La-Nouvelle, 11480 Lapalme. T. 0468481555. *093404*

Laragne-Montéglin (Hautes-Alpes)
Crédence, 9 Av Provence, 05300 Laragne-Montéglin.
T. 0492651290. *093405*

Lardy (Essonne)
Crison-Brière, ZA, Vieux-Fourneaux, 91510 Lardy.
T. 0160826437. *093406*

Lattes (Hérault)
Genin, 98 Rue Vieux-Chêne, 34970 Lattes.
T. 0467201874. *093407*

Launaguet (Haute-Garonne)
Raymond, André, 209 Chemin Boudou, 31140 Launaguet. T. 0561705964. *093408*

Lautrec (Tarn)
Aufranc, Michèle, Rue Cordeliers, 81440 Lautrec.
T. 0563753160. *093409*

Lavaveix-les-Mines (Creuse)
Bour, Michel, Rte Aubusson, 23150 Lavaveix-les-Mines.
T. 0555624365. *093410*

Lavergne (Lot)
Fraux, Patrice, Mirabel, 46500 Lavergne.
T. 0565387604. *093411*

Lavérune (Hérault)
Lagarde, Yannick, 3 Av Mosson, 34880 Lavérune.
T. 0467690346. *093412*

Le Bignon (Loire-Atlantique)
Bastard, Paul, 10 Rue Cormier, 44140 Le Bignon.
T. 40781283. *093413*

Le Boulou (Pyrénées-Orientales)
Marchais, Guy, 20 Imp Albères-Catalanes, 66160 Le
Boulou. T. 0468877524. (doreur sur bois) *093414*

Le Foeil (Côtes-d'Armor)
Bullier, Daniel, Ville Orhan, 22800 Le Foeil.
T. 0296748369. *093415*

Le Fugeret (Alpes-de-Haute-Provence)
Ricard, Claude, Grande-Rue, 04240 Le Fugeret.
T. 0492833283. *093416*

Le Garric (Tarn)
Farenc, Michel, 84 RN 88, 81450 Le Garric.
T. 0563367437. *093417*

Le Havre (Seine-Maritime)
Antiquités de l'Isle, 40 Quai Michel-Féré, 76600 Le Havre. T. 0235424285. *093418*
Atelier du Patrimoine, 11 Rue Bastion, 76600 Le Havre.
T. 0235432328. *093419*
Galerie Saint-Philibert, 15 Pl Halles-Centrales, 76600 Le
Havre. T. 0235213945. *093420*

Le Luc (Var)
Kockler, Paul, Quartier Grimaudet, 83340 Le Luc.
T. 0494608550. *093421*

Le Mans (Sarthe)
Richard-Ricordeau, Caroline, 87 Grande Rue, 72000 Le
Mans. T. 0243287734. *093422*

Le Merlerault (Orne)
Saint-Christophe Antiquités, 3 Rue Granville, 61240 Le
Merlerault. T. 0233354375. *093423*

Le Pailly (Haute-Marne)
Chez Desserey, Rue Breuil-Saint-Germain, 52600 Le
Pailly. T. 0325874268. *093424*

Le Pecq (Yvelines)
Kerlan, Gwenaëlle de, 34 Rue Président-Wilson, 78230
Le Pecq. T. 0139763630. *093425*

Le Perray-en-Yvelines (Yvelines)
Matagne, Dominique, 28bis Petite-Rue-Verte, 78610 Le
Perray-en-Yvelines. T. 0134841876. *093426*

Le Poinçonnet (Indre)
Dallier, C.Y., 3 Imp Ormes, La Brauderie, 36330 Le Poinçonnet. T. 0254223132. *093427*

Le Pré-Saint-Gervais (Seine-Saint-Denis)
Alm Déco, 10 Rue André-Joineau, 93310 Le Pré-Saint-Gervais. T. 0148919864, Fax 0148910271. *093428*

Le Puy-en-Velay (Haute-Loire)
Benoît, Xavier, 29 Rue Farges, 43000 Le Puy-en-Velay.
T. 0471022868. *093429*
Centrale de l'Occasion, Rue Latour-Maubourg, 43000 Le
Puy-en-Velay. T. 0471096189. *093430*
Habauzit, Robert, 46 Chemin Sainte-Catherine, 43000
Le Puy-en-Velay. T. 0471091010. *093431*
Servoir, 40 Blvd Saint-Louis, 43000 Le Puy-en-Velay.
T. 0471093694. *093432*

Le Quesnoy (Nord)
Galland, Jacques, 3 Rue Chevray, 59530 Le Quesnoy.
T. 0327276139. *093433*

Le Taillan-Médoc (Gironde)
Sydor, Michel, 23 Rue Docteur-Romefort, 33320 Le Taillan-Médoc. T. 0556570103. *093434*

Lempaut (Tarn)
Franceschin, Philippe, Peyrelade, 81700 Lempaut.
T. 0563754235. *093435*

Léon (Landes)
Roulhac, 6 Rue Ecoles, 40550 Léon.
T. 0558492219. *093436*

Les Andelys (Eure)
Tuffier, Thierry, 22 Rue Marcel-Lefèvre, 27700 Les Andelys. T. 0232540957, Fax 0232545044. *093437*

Les Damps (Eure)
Duchemin, Claire, 10 Rue Ecoles, 27340 Les Damps.
T. 0232232224. *093438*

Les Essards (Charente-Maritime)
Orgé, Claude, 9 Rue Chez-Belat, 17250 Les Essards.
T. 0546939384, Fax 0546955858. *093439*

Les Essards (Vendée)
Au Mobilier Vendéen, 1 Rue Sables, 85140 Les Essards.
T. 0251629264. *093440*

Lesneven (Finistère)
Calves Yvon, 27 Pl Château, 29260 Lesneven.
T. 0298211552. *093441*

Lézat-sur-Lèze (Ariège)
Gaubert, 28 Av Pyrénées, 09210 Lézat-sur-Lèze.
T. 0561691435. *093442*

Lezoux (Puy-de-Dôme)
Raynaud, Agnès, 57 Av Verdun, 63190 Lezoux.
T. 0473731134. (estampe; peinture; dessin; pastel;
gravure) *093443*

Libourne (Gironde)
Largeteau, Michel, 8 Rue Orbe, 33500 Libourne.
T. 0557510268. *093444*

Liesse-Notre-Dame (Aisne)
Collignon, David, Rte Regain, 02350 Liesse-Notre-
Dame. T. 0323221348. *093445*

Lille (Nord)
Incartade, 17 Rue Halle, 59800 Lille. T. 0320558294.
(cinéma-restauration d'affiches) *093446*

Limoges (Haute-Vienne)
Cilyan's Europ Collections, 86 Av Garibaldi, 87000 Limo-
ges. T. 0555776929. *093447*
Clinique de la Poupée, 9 Rue Allois, 87000 Limoges.
T. 0555325400. *093448*
Debort, Jean-Claude, 13 Rue Jules-Claretie, 87000 Li-
moges. T. 0555013732. *093449*
Reliure d'Art du Centre, 39 Rue Henri-Giffard, BP 1016,
87050 Limoges Cedex. T. 0555372690,
Fax 0555383887. *093450*
Vieille Epoque, 285 Rue François-Perrin, 87000 Limo-
ges. T. 0555508684. *093451*

Liverdun (Meurthe-et-Moselle)
Claude, Alain, 6 Rue Gare, 54460 Liverdun.
T. 0383245216. *093452*

Logrian-Florian (Gard)
Chavan, Christian, Le Mas des Elfes, 30610 Logrian-Florian. T. 0466774516. *093453*

Loix (Charente-Maritime)
Quillet, 27 Rue Perthuis, 17111 Loix. T. 0546290425,
Fax 0546290425. *093454*

Lommoye (Yvelines)
Saule, Armand, 1 Chemin Melotterie-Mesnil-Guyon,
78270 Lommoye. T. 0134761186. *093455*

Longueil (Seine-Maritime)
Poupée Passion, 76860 Longueil.
T. 0235830072. *093456*

Lons-le-Saunier (Jura)
Aux Meubles Thibert, 72 Rue Salines, 39000 Lons-le-
Saunier. T. 0384471058. *093457*

Loulay (Charente-Maritime)
Logis de Loulay, 6 Rue 8-Mai-1945, 17330 Loulay.
T. 0546339065. *093458*

Louvigné-du-Désert (Ille-et-Vilaine)
Logeais, Georges, 16 Rue Monseigneur-Gry, 35420 Louvigné-du-Désert. T. 0299980134. *093459*

Luçon (Vendée)
Thimoléon, Jean-Luc, 3 Chemin Saint-James, 85400
Luçon. T. 0251568157. *093460*

Lumbin (Isère)
Atelier R.O.C.S., 8 Rue Ancienne-Boucherie, 38660
Lumbin. T. 0476924104. *093461*

Luppy (Moselle)
Nowicki, Jean, 10 Petite Rue, 57580 Luppy.
T. 0387577352, Fax 0387577876. *093462*

Lutterbach (Haut-Rhin)
Goffinet, Bernard, 23 Rue Aristide-Briand, 68460 Lutterbach. T. 0389524782. *093463*

Luzillé (Indre-et-Loire)
Bellon, 8 Rue Temple, 37150 Luzillé.
T. 0547578810. *093464*

Lyon (Rhône)
Adhoc Broc, 26 Rue Camille-Roy, 69007 Lyon.
T. 0478725991. *093465*
Adhoc Broc, 98 Rue Chevreul, 69007 Lyon.
T. 0478690032. *093466*
Amiens Yves Asta Richard Patrick Restauration, 25 Rue
Vaubecour, 69002 Lyon. T. 0478929571. *093467*
Atelier du Temps, 6 Av Berthelot, 69007 Lyon.
T. 0478721442. *093468*

Bidaud, Toussaint, 1 Rue Antonins, 69005 Lyon.
T. 0478375898. *093469*
Boccard, Sybille de, 16 Rue Capucins, 69001 Lyon.
T. 0478272054. *093470*
Bottaz, Bousson, 6 Pl Raspail, 69007 Lyon.
T. 0478721896. *093471*
Brunet, Patrick, 73 Rue Tronchet, 69006 Lyon.
T. 0472430232. *093472*
Clinique des Poupées, 2 Rue Chavanne, 69001 Lyon.
T. 0478281093. *093473*
Cuyl, Chantal, 7 Rue Tramassac, 69005 Lyon.
T. 0472417513. *093474*
Damidot, Daniel, 38 Rue Auguste Comte, 69002 Lyon.
T. 0478378929. (meubles, sculptures) *093475*
Dhikéos, Georges & Michel, 24 Rue Auguste-Comte,
69002 Lyon. T. 0478377556. *093476*
Dolls-Toys, 38 Rue Auguste-Comte, 69002 Lyon.
T. 0478429151. *093477*
Dumas, Jean-Paul, 8 Rue Auguste Comte, 69002 Lyon.
T. 0478371118. (bois doré) *093478*
Fontaine, Gérard, 43 Av Frères-Lumière, 69008 Lyon.
T. 0478003901. *093479*
Kostia, Jacques, 68bis Rue Pierre-Delore, 69008 Lyon.
T. 0472800660. *093480*
Lafay, Benoît, 15 Rue Charlot-d'Or, 69004 Lyon.
T. 0478283743. *093481*
Mathon, Helga, 56 Rue Auguste-Comte, 69002 Lyon.
T. 0478424773. *093482*
Miaz, Pierre, 94 Av Frères-Lumière, 69008 Lyon.
T. 0478007738. *093483*
Moreteau, Paule, 3 Rue Remparts-d'Ainay, 69002 Lyon.
T. 0478374867. *093484*
Nicod, Nicole, 4 Rue Dumont-d'Urville, 69004 Lyon.
T. 0478270538. *093485*
Pivard, Xavier, 60 Rue Auguste-Comte, 69002 Lyon.
T. 0478376483. *093486*
Rougier, 17 Cours Liberté, 69003 Lyon.
T. 0478606431. *093487*
Victoire, 36 Rue Auguste-Comte, 69002 Lyon.
T. 0478421988. *093488*

Maisons-Laffitte (Yvelines)
Girandole, 18 Rue Plantes, 78600 Maisons-Laffitte.
T. 0139620457, Fax 0139628850. *093489*

Malemort-sur-Corrèze (Corrèze)
Astéggiano, 45 Rue Industrie, 19360 Malemort-sur-Corrèze. T. 0555920390. *093490*
Barreau, Michel, 29 Rue Charles-Dickens, 19360 Malemort-sur-Corrèze. T. 0555232187. *093491*

Malicorne (Sarthe)
Arts et Techniques, Gare de Malicorne, 72270 Malicorne. T. 0243947192. *093492*

Manigod (Haute-Savoie)
Catrice, Nicolas, Villard Dessus, 74230 Manigod.
T. 0450449559. *093493*
Ferry, François, Villard Dessus, 74230 Manigod.
T. 0450449557, Fax 0450449558. *093494*

Marcy-l'Etoile (Rhône)
Ponvianne, André, 1 Chemin Grange-Neuve, 69280 Marcy-l'Etoile. T. 0478442489. *093495*

Mareuil (Dordogne)
Servolle, Pierre, Le Clos-du-Roy, 24340 Mareuil.
T. 0553609913. *093496*

Mareuil-sur-Lay-Dissais (Vendée)
Faucher, Henry, Rue Barres, 85320 Mareuil-sur-Lay-Dissais. T. 0251972197. *093497*

Marly (Nord)
Beaupuy, Patrice, 5 Rue Gare-Dérivation, 59770 Marly.
T. 0327360652. *093498*

Marly-le-Roi (Yvelines)
Chauplanaz, Jean, 18 Rue Montagne, 78160 Marly-le-
Roi. T. 0139586520. *093499*

Marmande (Lot-et-Garonne)
Act'Art, 14 Rue Hirondelle, 47200 Marmande.
T. 0553202904. *093500*

Marnes-la-Coquette (Hauts-de-Seine)
Riesen, Didier, 9 Rue Gabriel-Sommer, 92430 Marnes-
la-Coquette. T. 0147012461. *093501*

Marquise (Pas-de-Calais)
Leleu, Gérald, Grande-Place, 62250 Marquise.
T. 0321337076. *093502*

Marseille (Bouches-du-Rhône)
Galerie d'Art La Poutre, 206 Rue Paradis, 13006 Mar-
seille. T. 0491371093. (tableaux) *093503*
Glotin, Frédéric, 26 Blvd Verd, 13013 Marseille.
T. 0491669166. *093504*
Mouret, Gilbert, 4 Rue Guy-Fabre, 13001 Marseille.
T. 0491507219. *093505*
Nadjarian, 137 Rue Paradis, 13006 Marseille.
T. 0491370449. *093506*
Ozenda, Gérard, 105 Rue Liandier, 13008 Marseille.
T. 0491801344. *093507*
Parent, Xavier, 29 Rue Neuve-Sainte-Catherine, 13007
Marseille. T. 0491332177. *093508*
Spindler, Thomas, 1 Rue Bergers, 13006 Marseille.
T. 0491485393. *093509*

Martigues (Bouches-du-Rhône)
Arche de Noë, Chemin Saint-Lazare, 13500 Martigues.
T. 0442070565. *093510*

Massy (Essonne)
Armand, 25 Av Carnot, 91300 Massy. T. 0169321484,
Fax 0169321483. *093511*

Maubeuge (Nord)
Duval, Luc, 2 Rue Gippus, 59600 Maubeuge.
T. 0327643431. *093512*

Melun (Seine-et-Marne)
Mobilier Service 77, 24 Rue Dammarie, 77000 Melun.
T. 64395293. *093513*

Menthonnex-en-Bornes (Haute-Savoie)
Bro, Jean-Pierre, Chef Lieu, 74350 Menthonnex-en-Bornes. T. 0450680281. *093514*

Menton (Alpes-Maritimes)
Bonnery, Jacques, 4 Traverse Bastion, 06500 Menton.
T. 0493579736. *093515*

Mercin-et-Vaux (Aisne)
Reflex, 44 Rue de Vaux, 02200 Mercin-et-Vaux.
T. 0323734379. (vehicules de collection) *093516*

Mésanger (Loire-Atlantique)
Lépinay, Cécile, La Coindière, 44522 Mésanger.
T. 40967545. *093517*
Ménoret, Hervé, La Coindière, 44522 Mésanger.
T. 40967545. *093518*

Metz (Moselle)
A La Vieille France, 31 Rue des Jardins, 57000 Metz.
T. 0387366338. *093519*
Au Chlabout, 74 Rue des Allemands, 57000 Metz.
T. 0387360934. *093520*
Cartophila, 49 Rue Allemands, 57000 Metz.
T. 0387366644. *093521*

Meudon (Hauts-de-Seine)
Atelier de Conservation et de Restauration d'Ile de Fran-
ce, 50bis Rue Paris, 92190 Meudon. T. 0145079191,
Fax 0146231770. *093522*
Etude et Conservation des Anciens Textiles, 50bis Rue
Paris, 92190 Meudon. T. 0146263638. *093523*

Meylan (Isère)
Michel Antiquités, 23 Chemin Chaumetière, 38240 Meylan. T. 0476410343. *093524*

Miramont-de-Guyenne (Lot-et-Garonne)
Keuten, Viviane, 24 Rue Viguerie, 47800 Miramont-de-
Guyenne. T. 0553834937. *093525*

Mollégès (Bouches-du-Rhône)
Lestoquoit, Denise, 14 Av Lauron, 13940 Mollégès.
T. 0490954870, Fax 0490954164. *093526*

Mollkirch (Bas-Rhin)
Lickel, Patrick, 8 Rue Source-Laubenheim, 67190 Moll-kirch. T. 0388500707, Fax 0388490109.　093527

Moncayolle-Larrory-Mendibi (Pyrénées-Atlantiques)
Caudin, Alain, Maison Pastou, 64130 Moncayolle-Larro-ry-Mendibi. T. 0559283281. (horloge comtoise)　093528

Mons (Haute-Garonne)
Guy, Jean, 20 Av Lauragais, 31280 Mons.
T. 0561833420.　093529

Mont-de-Marsan (Landes)
Poydenot, Jean, 7 Pl Nonères, 40000 Mont-de-Marsan.
T. 0558060619.　093530

Mont-sous-Vaudrey (Jura)
Revy, Jacques, Rue Léon-Guignard, 39380 Mont-sous-Vaudrey. T. 0384815212.　093531

Montbéliard (Doubs)
Daguet, Christophe, 29 Rue Château, 25200 Montbé-liard. T. 0381953209.　093532

Montereau-Fault-Yonne (Seine-et-Mar-ne)
Jessa, Denise, 15 Rue Docteur-Arthur-Petit, 77130 Montereau-Fault-Yonne. T. 64329132.　093533

Montfort-sur-Argens (Var)
Gérard, Emond, 10 Rue Logis, 83570 Montfort-sur-Ar-gens. T. 0494595142, Fax 0494595529.　093534

Montguyon (Charente-Maritime)
Poirrier, Christian, Montguyon, 17270 Montguyon.
T. 0546044329.　093535

Montignac (Dordogne)
Requier, Jean-Pierre, Pl Carnot, 24290 Montignac.
T. 0553518210.　093536

Montlieu-la-Garde (Charente-Maritime)
Maillet, Jean-Pierre, 11 Av Général-Leclerc, 17210 Montlieu-la-Garde. T. 0546044696, Fax 0546040384.　093537

Montlouis-sur-Loire (Indre-et-Loire)
Lévêque, André, 29 Quai Albert-Baillet, 37270 Mont-louis-sur-Loire. T. 0547451188.　093538

Montmarault (Allier)
Billon, 1 Rte de Montluçon, 03390 Montmarault.
T. 0470076669.　093539

Montmorot (Jura)
Renard, Joël, ZA Les Toupes, 39570 Montmorot.
T. 0384245488.　093540

Montpellier (Hérault)
Atelier, 16 Rue Alexis-Alquié, 34000 Montpellier.
T. 0467646779.　093541
Genin, 8 Pl Alexandre-Laissac, 34000 Montpellier.
T. 0467922792.　093542
Géraud, Guy, 5 Rue Alger, 34000 Montpellier.
T. 0467587666.　093543
Hélian, Martin, 8 Rue Etienne-Antoine, 34000 Montpel-lier. T. 0467581891.　093544
Levy, Luc, 25ter Rue Haguenot, 34000 Montpellier.
T. 0467584547.　093545
Roche, Patrick, 8 Blvd Pasteur, 34000 Montpellier.
T. 0467603089.　093546
Susini, Pierre, 20 Rue Valfère, 34000 Montpellier.
T. 0467603848.　093547

Montreuil (Seine-Saint-Denis)
Clément, Thierry, 33 Rue Fernand-Combette, Bât B, 93100 Montreuil. T. 0148708797.　093548
Gracieuse Orient, 14 Rue Kléber, 93100 Montreuil.
T. 0148583929, Fax 0148583955.　093549
Ottin, Michel, 20 Rue Meuniers, 93100 Montreuil.
T. 0149880022.　093550
Tarabiscot, 32 Rue Raspail, 93100 Montreuil.
T. 0149887305.　093551

Montrouge (Hauts-de-Seine)
Caudine, Alain, 45 Rue Carvès, 92120 Montrouge.
T. 0142534443.　093552

Montry (Seine-et-Marne)
Vermandé, Patrick, 7 Rue Paul-Doumer, 77450 Montry.
T. 0360041719.　093553

Morangis (Essonne)
Copeau d'Ebène, 4 Rue Général-Leclerc, 91420 Moran-gis. T. 0164485835.　093554

Mornant (Rhône)
Broallier, Jean, Les Platières, 69440 Mornant.
T. 0478487450.　093555

Mornas (Vaucluse)
Amis de Mornas, Rue Herni-Thynel, 84550 Mornas.
T. 0490370126, Fax 0490370988.　093556

Mougins (Alpes-Maritimes)
Ranc, 19 Rue Orfèvres, 06250 Mougins.
T. 0493901388.　093557

Mougon (Deux-Sèvres)
Prest, Nathalie, 1 Rte Trois-Bois-Montaillon, 79370 Mougon. T. 0549058787.　093558

Moulins (Allier)
Wagram, 1 Rue Wagram, 03000 Moulins.
T. 0470201773.　093559

Mouzay (Meuse)
Didiot, William, Rte Charmois, 55700 Mouzay.
T. 0329806525.　093560

Mulhouse (Haut-Rhin)
Arbalete Antiquites, 10 Rue Loi, 68100 Mulhouse.
T. 0389454979.　093561
Chaiseland, 2 Rue Vergers, 68100 Mulhouse.
T. 0389600232.　093562
Jess, André, 10 Rue Jacquard, 68200 Mulhouse.
T. 0389423852.　093563
Karm, Pierre, 1 Rue Port, 68100 Mulhouse.
T. 0389456997.　093564

Mussy-sur-Seine (Aube)
Pin, Maurice, Chemin Mezes, 10250 Mussy-sur-Seine.
T. 0325384150.　093565

Muzillac (Morbihan)
Arbre aux Quarante Ecus, Le Pont-Chaland, 56190 Mu-zillac. T. 0297414343.　093566
Guillouzouic, Pascal, 10 Rue Général-de-Gaulle, 56190 Muzillac. T. 0297415621.　093567

Nancy (Meurthe-et-Moselle)
Clinique des Poupées, 5 Rue Saint-Nicolas, 54000 Nan-cy. T. 0383352774.　093568
Huel, Didier, 18 Rue La Salle, 54000 Nancy.
T. 0383374933.　093569

Nanterre (Hauts-de-Seine)
Légende des Siècles, 12 Av Maréchal-Joffre, 92000 Nanterre. T. 0141370223.　093570

Nantes (Loire-Atlantique)
ARC Antique Laboratoire de Restauration, 26 Rue Haute-Forêt, 44000 Nantes. T. 0251810940, Fax 0251810936.　093571
Charron, Michèle, 1 Rue Jean-Baptiste-Corot, 44100 Nantes. T. 40469752.　093572
Soulard Varanne, Marie-Hélène, 144 Blvd Fraternité, 44100 Nantes. T. 40430236.　093573
Vent d'Ouest, 10 Rue Rubens, 44000 Nantes.
T. 40893707.　093574

Nérac (Lot-et-Garonne)
Verdier, Jacques, Rte Condom, 47600 Nérac.
T. 0553654811.　093575

Nevers (Nièvre)
Atelier du 18ème, 23 Rue Jean-Desveaux, 58000 Ne-vers. T. 0386570949.　093576
Philippe, Alain, 8 Pl Mossé, 58000 Nevers.
T. 0386360075.　093577

Timoléonthos, François, 23 Rue Jean-Desveaux, 58000 Nevers. T. 0386570836.　093578

Nice (Alpes-Maritimes)
Arnoul, Daniel, 5 Rue Joseph-Bres, 06000 Nice.
T. 0493877281.　093579
Atelier Carina, 3 Rue de France, 06000 Nice.
T. 0493889339.　093580
Bellino, Rodolphe, 1 Rue Molière, 06100 Nice.
T. 0493846256.　093581
Clinique de Poupées, 22 Rue Lépante, 06000 Nice.
T. 0493854384.　093582
Daverio, Chrisgeni, 16 Rue Hôtel-des-Postes, 06000 Ni-ce. T. 0493921253.　093583
Dupuis, Bernard, 10 Blvd Dubouchage, 06000 Nice.
T. 0493852877.　093584
Estela, Lucien, 4 Rue Antoine-Gautier, 06300 Nice.
T. 0493557567.　093585
Kiseljakovic, Kemal, 6bis Rue Lascaris, 06300 Nice.
T. 0493624576.　093586
Monier, Patrice, 7 Rue Docteur-Albert-Balestre, 06000 Nice. T. 0493622910.　093587
Paties, Claire, 2 Rue Droite, 06300 Nice.
T. 0493858822.　093588
Véronèse, 3 Rue André-Poullan, 06000 Nice.
T. 0493963684.　093589

Niederhausbergen (Bas-Rhin)
Haug, Tania, 18 Rue Mercière, 67200 Niederhausber-gen. T. 0388563833.　093590

Niort (Deux-Sèvres)
Marquois, Jacky, 172 Av Limoges, 79000 Niort.
T. 0549284478.　093591
Sigogneau, Claude, 39 Rue Bas-Sablonnier, 79000 Niort.
T. 0549734804, Fax 0549091813.　093592
Sigogneau, Claude, 28 Rue Brisson, 79000 Niort.
T. 0549249579, Fax 0549091813.　093593

Nîmes (Gard)
Atelier Peinture Décorative, 17 Rue Porte-d'Alés, 30000 Nîmes. T. 0466360500.　093594
Charmoy, Xavier, 9 Rue Guizot, 30000 Nîmes.
T. 0466360747.　093595
Charrasse, Edith, 81 Rue République, 30900 Nîmes.
T. 0466298013, Fax 0466292971.　093596
Rainer-Small, 6 Rue Servie, 30000 Nîmes.
T. 0466845111, Fax 0466842385.　093597

Nohant-Vic (Indre)
Bouquin, Patrick, La Petite Maison, 36400 Nohant-Vic.
T. 0254311044.　093598

Nonancourt (Eure)
Fréminet, Alain, 8 Pl Aristide-Briand, 27320 Nonancourt.
T. 0232580492.　093599

Nostang (Morbihan)
Ordécor Bouesnard, Legevin, 56690 Nostang.
T. 0297657059.　093600

Notre-Dame-de-Bondeville (Seine-Mari-time)
Renault, Daniel, 415 Rue Longs-Vallons, 76960 Notre-Dame-de-Bondeville. T. 0235757440.　093601

Noyal-Pontivy (Morbihan)
Jubin, Jean, Sainte-Noyale, 56920 Noyal-Pontivy.
T. 0297383977, Fax 0297382130.　093602

Nuits-Saint-Georges (Côte-d'Or)
Carrières de Nuits, Rte Beaune, 21700 Nuits-Saint-Ge-orges. T. 0380611076.　093603

Nyons (Drôme)
Vande Pitte, Philippe, 22 Rue Bas-Bourgs, 26110 Nyons.
T. 0475264217.　093604
Vande Pitte, Philippe, 1 Rue Camille-Bréchet, 26110 Nyons. T. 0475264474.　093605

Oberhoffen-sur-Moder (Bas-Rhin)
Riff, Etienne, 78 Rue Principale, 67240 Oberhoffen-sur-Moder. T. 0388538652.　093606

Odos (Hautes-Pyrénées)
Moreno & Fils, Av Pène, 65310 Odos.
T. 0562347222. *093607*

Offendorf (Bas-Rhin)
Offendorf, 23 Rte Gambsheim, 67850 Offendorf.
T. 0388964607. *093608*

Olivet (Loiret)
Huillery, Eric, 71 Rue Ecoles, 45160 Olivet.
T. 0238638621. *093609*

Omerville (Val-d'Oise)
Rouland, Bertrand, 7 Ruelle Eglise, 95420 Omerville.
T. 0134677930. *093610*

Onet-le-Château (Aveyron)
Atelier, Rte de Vabre, 12850 Onet-le-Château.
T. 0565780845. *093611*

Oppède (Vaucluse)
Thoumyre, Perrine, Quartier Malpertuis, Rte Carrières,
84580 Oppède. T. 0490769506. *093612*

Orléans (Loiret)
Anchier, Danielle, 82 Rue Bretonnerie, 45000 Orléans.
T. 0238621618. *093613*
Maupin, Olivier, 14 Rue Saint-Marceau, 45100 Orléans.
T. 0238566173. *093614*

Ossès (Pyrénées-Atlantiques)
Chow-Chuen, Alain, Maison Tano Eyherra, 64780 Ossès.
T. 0559377301. (tableuax retables feuille d'or) *093615*

Ougney (Jura)
Chauvey, Claude, Rue Barboux, 39350 Ougney.
T. 0384810205. *093616*

Ougney-Douvot (Doubs)
Gagnon, Jean-Paul, Douvot, 25640 Ougney-Douvot.
T. 0381555587. *093617*

Oullins (Rhône)
Jaboulet, Jean-Paul, 86 Rue Francisque-Jomard, 69600
Oullins. T. 0478517233, Fax 0478517233. *093618*

Pacy-sur-Eure (Eure)
Leveillé, Eric, 103 Rue Isambard, 27120 Pacy-sur-Eure.
T. 0232360853. *093619*

Pagney (Jura)
Chauvey, Claude, Grande Rue, 39350 Pagney.
T. 0384810105, Fax 0384810805. *093620*

Paray-le-Monial (Saône-et-Loire)
Dufayet, Patrick, 136 Rte Saint-Germain, 71600 Paray-
le-Monial. T. 0385815601. *093621*

Paris
A.C.R., 86 Rue Charonne, 75011 Paris.
T. 0143710033. *093622*
Afi, 16 Rue Rocroy, 75010 Paris.
T. 0142855443. *093623*
Agneray, Josette, 90 Rue Charonne, 75011 Paris.
T. 0140098647. *093624*
Agostinho, Orlanda, 18 Rue Henri-Chevreau, 75020 Pa-
ris. T. 0146362826. *093625*
Alabastri, Anne, 4 Rue Hermann-Lachapelle, 75018 Pa-
ris. T. 0142555560. *093626*
Alal, 83 Rue Bagnolet, 75020 Paris.
T. 0143735441. *093627*
Alencar, 28 Rue Sedaine, 75011 Paris.
T. 0143559733. *093628*
Alix, Jean-Bernard, 52 Rue Saint-André-des-Arts,
75006 Paris. T. 0143542817. *093629*
Alot, Jean, 101 Rue Patay, 75013 Paris. T. 0145828032,
Fax 0144245190. *093630*
Ameline, Paule, 320 Rue Saint-Honoré, 75001 Paris.
T. 0142605065. *093631*
André, 107 Blvd Charonne, 750011 Paris.
T. 0143704020, Fax 0143703205. *093632*
Antic-Tac, Louvre des Antiquaires, 2 Pl Palais-Royal,
75001 Paris. T. 0142615716,
Fax 0142617586. *093633*
Apelle, 55 Rue Pergolèse, 75016 Paris.
T. 0140679836. *093634*

Ardouin, J. & Cie, 40 Rue Folie-Regnault, 75011 Paris.
T. 0143795251. *093635*
Ars longa, 5 Rue Gît-le-Coeur, 75006 Paris.
T. 0146331975. *093636*
Art 3, 92 Rue Archives, 75003 Paris.
T. 0148873019. *093637*
Artcurial, 9 Av Matignon, 75008 Paris.
T. 0142991616. *093638*
Artel, 25 Rue Bonaparte, 75006 Paris.
T. 0143549377. *093639*
Arts et Antiques, 16 Rue Sédillot, 75007 Paris.
T. 0147054588. *093640*
Arts et Marines, 8 Rue Miromesnil, 75008 Paris.
T. 0142652785, Fax 0142653059. *093641*
Arts et Techniques, 9 Rue Deux-Ponts, 75004 Paris.
T. 0143256715. *093642*
Assay, Caroline d', 53bis Rue Roquette, 75011 Paris.
T. 0147002640, Fax 0147001831. *093643*
Atelier d'Art des Compagnons de la Tradition, 33 Blvd
Beaumarchais, 75003 Paris. T. 0142772222. *093644*
Atelier Damrémont, 28 Rue Damrémont, 75018 Paris.
T. 0142556838. *093645*
Atelier de la Feuille d'Or, 3 Rue Titon, 75011 Paris.
T. 0143561632. *093646*
Atelier de Maître Paolo, 151 Rue Fbg-Saint-Antoine,
75012 Paris. T. 0143431498. *093647*
Atelier de Restauration des Oeuvres d'Art, 125 Rue Tu-
renne, 75003 Paris. T. 0142723000,
Fax 0142725864. *093648*
Atelier de Restauration et Conservation d'Objets d'Art, 3
Rue Buisson-Saint-Louis, 75010 Paris.
T. 0142024982, Fax 0142021100. *093649*
Atelier des Arts et Techniques, 13 Rue Docteur-Potain,
75019 Paris. T. 0142491418. *093650*
Atelier des Marches, 4 Rue Malebranche, 75005 Paris.
T. 0146331683. *093651*
Atelier du Bois Doré, 80 Av Ternes, 75017 Paris.
T. 0145746758. *093652*
Atelier du Fou, 10 Rue Gustave-Doré, 75017 Paris.
T. 0142274012. *093653*
Atelier du Peintre, 2 Rue Bastien-Lepage, 75016 Paris.
T. 0142887259. *093654*
Atelier du Temps Passé, 173 Rue Fbg-Saint-Antoine,
75011 Paris. T. 0143468627. *093655*
Atelier du Val de Grace, 22 Rue Henri-Barbusse, 75005
Paris. T. 0146332201. *093656*
Atelier Genovesio, 2 Rue Valois, 75001 Paris.
T. 0142613585, Fax 0142961233. *093657*
Atelier RTCD, 123 Rue Lamarck, 75018 Paris.
T. 0142294184. *093658*
Atelier 91, 72 Rue Jouffroy-d'Abbans, 75017 Paris.
T. 0142671477. *093659*
Ateliers A.C., 28 Rue Sedaine, 75011 Paris.
T. 0148062973, Fax 0148070717. *093660*
Ateliers Brocard, 1 Rue Jacques-Coeur, 75004 Paris.
T. 0142721638, Fax 0142720477. *093661*
Ateliers de Restauration de Tableaux, 35 Av Théophile-
Gautier, 75016 Paris. T. 0145209639. *093662*
Au Chirurgien Assassiné, 9 Blvd Pereire, 75017 Paris.
T. 0142270270. *093663*
Bailly, Jean-Jacques, 12 Rue Perdonnet, 75010 Paris.
T. 0142400098. *093664*
Balcaen, 5 Rue Charonne, 75011 Paris. T. 0148065944,
Fax 0148062061. *093665*
Bardez, Jean-François, 23 Rue Tocqueville, 75017 Paris.
T. 0142275332. *093666*
Bastien & Associés, 13 Rue Lille, 75007 Paris.
T. 0142602422. *093667*
Baudouin, Robert, 6 Rue Ballu, 75009 Paris.
T. 0148746821. *093668*
Baudrillart, Jean-E., 59 Rue Saint-André-des-Arts,
75006 Paris. T. 0146331988. *093669*
Bauer, Christophe, 50 Rue Bidassoa, 75020 Paris.
T. 0143580958. *093670*
Baxter, 15 Rue Dragon, 75006 Paris.
T. 0145490134. *093671*
Belcour, 28 Rue Sedaine, 75011 Paris.
T. 0149299413. *093672*
Belle Epoque, 99 Rue Bobillot, 75013 Paris.
T. 0145653737. *093673*
Bellou, Didier, 1 Passage Rauch, 75011 Paris.
T. 0143482062. *093674*

Bellucci, S., 61 Av République, 75011 Paris.
T. 0140210447. *093675*
Bembnista, Henri, 10 Rue Flatters, 75005 Paris.
T. 0147078783. *093676*
Benadava, V., 28 Rue La-Boétie, 75008 Paris.
T. 0143591221. *093677*
Béné, 10ter Rue Bisson, 75020 Paris.
T. 0147970536. *093678*
Benedetti & Estève, 80 Rue Charonne, 75011 Paris.
T. 0143674244, Fax 0143676334. *093679*
Besenval, Jean-Pierre, 32 Rue Pastourelle, 75003 Paris.
T. 0142726981. *093680*
Bettencourt Frères, 12 Rue Saint-Gilles, 75003 Paris.
T. 0142723404, Fax 0142728302. *093681*
Bianco & Péry, 89 Rue Fbg-Saint-Antoine, 75011 Paris.
T. 0146286055. *093682*
Bissonnet, André, 6 Rue Pas-de-la-Mule, 75003 Paris.
T. 0148872015. *093683*
Blaise, Benoit, 173 Rue Fbg-Saint-Antoine, 75011 Paris.
T. 0143416086. *093684*
Blaise, Laurent, 157 Rue Temple, 75003 Paris.
T. 0142717526. *093685*
Blassiaux, Richard, 23 Rue Seine, 75006 Paris.
T. 0143265353. *093686*
Bodin-Landrein, Isabelle, 52 Rue Fontaine, 75009 Paris.
T. 0148741994. *093687*
Bon Marché, 22 Rue Sèvres, 75007 Paris.
T. 0144398090. *093688*
Bonanni, Emmanuel, 4 Rue Arquebusiers, 75003 Paris.
T. 0148872882. *093689*
Bonfini, Gabriel, 18 Rue Jules-Vallès, 75011 Paris.
T. 0140091790. *093690*
Bonnimond, F., 16 Rue Saint-Charles, 75015 Paris.
T. 0145792993. *093691*
Bouillon, Dominique, 100 Rue Théâtre, 75015 Paris.
T. 0145779393. *093692*
Bouin & Gardon, 4 Passage Josset, 75011 Paris.
T. 0147005652, Fax 0160805934. *093693*
Boulanger & Fils, 22 Rue Folie-Méricourt, 75011 Paris.
T. 0143555296. *093694*
Bourdariat, Albert, 75 Rue Chardon-Lagache, 75016 Pa-
ris. T. 0145240262. *093695*
Boutin, 1 Rue Pondichéry, 75015 Paris.
T. 0140569333. *093696*
Brans, Sylvaine, 15 Rue Grange-Batelière, 75009 Paris.
T. 0148000476. *093697*
Brenot, André & Michèle, 12 Rue Christiani, 75018 Pa-
ris. T. 0142541364, Fax 0142555122. *093698*
Brillet, Muriel, 1 Rue Châteaudun, 75009 Paris.
T. 0149950151. *093699*
Brodard, Pierre, 7bis Rue Alexandre-Parodi, 75010 Pa-
ris. T. 0142096712. *093700*
Broves, Anne de, 11 Rue Géricault, 75016 Paris.
T. 0142248458. *093701*
Brugier, A., 74 Rue Sèvres, 75007 Paris. T. 0147348327,
Fax 0140569140. *093702*
Brunetti, S., 11 Rue Cassette, 75006 Paris.
T. 0145440355. *093703*
Bruno, André & Fils, 29 Cours Vincennes, 75020 Paris.
T. 0143481103. *093704*
Buisson, Roger, 4 Rue Aligre, 75012 Paris.
T. 0143071925. *093705*
Caisse, Jean-François, 10 Rue Pierre-Larousse, 75014
Paris. T. 0145429653. *093706*
Capia, Robert, 26 Gal Véro-Dodat, 75001 Paris.
T. 0142362594. *093707*
Chalard, Denis, 10 Rue Bourg-Tibourg, 75004 Paris.
T. 0142721271. *093708*
Charbonnier, Noël, 187 Rue Fbg-Saint-Honoré, 75008
Paris. T. 0143597355. *093709*
Chauvel, Catherine, 30 Rue Ernest-Renan, 75015 Paris.
T. 0145672196. *093710*
Chef, Jean-Louis, 55 Rue Popincourt, 75011 Paris.
T. 0147005153. *093711*
Chevalier, Jean-Pierre, 27 Rue Dauphine, 75006 Paris.
T. 0146330739. *093712*
Chollet, Stéphane, 28bis Rue Montreuil, 75011 Paris.
T. 0143482084. *093713*
Cletienne, Olivia, 23 Rue Saint-Paul, 75004 Paris.
T. 0142711908. *093714*
Cocault, Frédéric, 5 Rue Ernest-Lefèvre, 75020 Paris.
T. 0140315423. *093715*

Coiffard, Jean-Marc, 114bis Rue Moines, 75017 Paris.
T. 0142280463. *093716*
Coin de Montcalm, 28 Rue Montcalm, 75018 Paris.
T. 0142586327. *093717*
Compagnie Française de Bijouterie, 139 Rue Temple,
75003 Paris. T. 0144788810. *093718*
Compagnons Ebénistes Associés, 145 Rue Saussure,
75017 Paris. T. 0147630182. *093719*
Compagnons Ebénistes Associés, 62 Rue Legendre,
75017 Paris. T. 0143804633. *093720*
Congé, Michèle, 9 Rue Grenelle, 75007 Paris.
T. 0142228874. *093721*
Conservation Restauration de Tableaux, 42 Rue Fon-
taine, 75009 Paris. T. 0148780304. *093722*
Coquery, Jean-Jacques, 45 Rue Amelot, 75011 Paris.
T. 0143575272. *093723*
Cordié, Jérome, 76 Rue Dutot, 75015 Paris.
T. 0144198310. *093724*
Corlouer, Gilbert, 140 Av Victor-Hugo, 75016 Paris.
T. 0147045265. *093725*
Coroller & Gilbon, 4 Rue De-Cotte, 75012 Paris.
T. 0143439455, Fax 0143439687. *093726*
Cottage de Deborah, 29bis Rue Pierre-Demours, 75017
Paris. T. 0142275550. *093727*
Cotte, Sabine, 157 Rue Temple, 75003 Paris.
T. 0142717526. *093728*
Couleur des Choses, 7 Rue Plantes, 75014 Paris.
T. 0145453505. *093729*
C.T.S. France, 26 Passage Thiéré, 75011 Paris.
T. 0143556044, Fax 0143556687. *093730*
Dagoneau, Gérard, 138 Rue Fbg-Saint-Antoine, 75012
Paris. T. 0143445131. *093731*
Daubrée, Valérie, 17 Rue Larrey, 75005 Paris.
T. 0145352912. *093732*
Debladis, 50 Rue Sévigné, 75003 Parls. T. 0148870824,
Fax 0148874143. *093733*
Deglise, Nicolas, 13 Pl Commerce, 75015 Paris.
T. 0145312028. *093734*
Delalande, 87 Rue Dessous-des-Berges, 75013 Paris.
T. 0145708008. *093735*
Delarue, 4 Rue Bac, 75007 Paris. T. 0145485674,
Fax 0145480242. *093736*
Denova-Tésar, Olga, 189 Rue Ordener, 75018 Paris.
T. 0142621567. *093737*
Depretz, Bernard, 30 Rue Jacob, 75006 Paris.
T. 0143266014. *093738*
Deroyan, Armand, 13 Rue Drouot, 75009 Paris.
T. 0148000785, Fax 0148000634. *093739*
Desserme, 17 Rue Pont-aux-Choux, 75003 Paris.
T. 0142720266, Fax 0142725091. *093740*
Devauchelle, Alain, 98 Rue Fbg-Poissonnière, 75010 Pa-
ris. T. 0148786712. *093741*
Dieutegard (Fille du Pirate), Village Suisse N 38, 78 Av
Suffren, 75015 Paris. T. 0147340676. *093742*
Dieutegard (Fille du Pirate), Louvre des Antiquaires, 2 Pl
Palais-Royal, 75001 Paris. T. 0142602031. *093743*
Dieutegard (Fille du Pirate), Aux Armes de Furstenberg,
1 Rue Furstenberg, 75006 Paris.
T. 0143297951. *093744*
Diolosa, Gesualdo, 59 Rue Fbg-Saint-Antoine, 75011
Paris. T. 0143472406. *093745*
Dmitrenko, Youri, 26 Rue Montiboeufs, 75020 Paris.
T. 0140304083. *093746*
Doison, Christine, 121 Rue Raymond-Losserand, 75014
Paris. T. 0145398513. *093747*
Dreux, Liliane, 231 Rue Marcadet, 75018 Paris.
T. 0142639574. *093748*
Dromard, Jean, 6 Rue Louis-Thuillier, 75005 Paris.
T. 0143545468. *093749*
Dubuy, Lucie, 160 Rue Saint-Denis, 75002 Paris.
T. 0145089205. *093750*
Duchâteau, Monique, 4 Rue Casimir-Périer, 75007 Paris.
T. 0145550840, Fax 0145515699. *093751*
Dupard, Henri, 105 Rue Fbg-Saint-Honoré, 75008 Paris.
T. 0142256815. *093752*
Dupin, Juliette, 18 Rue Chappe, 75018 Paris.
T. 0142595301. *093753*
Dupont, Marlène Edith, 8 Passage Bonne-Graine, 75011
Paris. T. 0147006052, Fax 0148053770. *093754*
Ebéniste, 157 Rue Marcadet, 75018 Paris.
T. 0142511926. *093755*
Endemann, J., 92 Rue Miromesnil, 75008 Paris.
T. 0145637702. *093756*

Espace Temps, 27 Rue Saint-Dominique, 75007 Paris.
T. 0145511839. *093757*
Estève, Jacqueline, 24 Rue Juge, 75015 Paris.
T. 0145791544. *093758*
Fabry, 4 Rue Gramme, 75015 Paris.
T. 0142509464. *093759*
Feret, Marc, 158 Rue Damrémont, 75018 Paris.
T. 0142574105. *093760*
Ferreira da Silva, Rodolfo, 5 Rue Saint-Bernard, 75011
Paris. T. 0143707278. *093761*
Fey, A., 11 Passage Chantier, 75012 Paris.
T. 0143438039, Fax 0143410405. *093762*
Fey, Michel, 1 Rue Charonne, 75011 Paris.
T. 0143556846, Fax 0143558381. *093763*
Flahaut, Michel, 3 Passage Vierge, 75007 Paris.
T. 0145511552. *093764*
Flé, Martine, 26 Rue Charonne, 75011 Paris.
T. 0147008122, Fax 0147008485. *093765*
Fortin, Evelyne, 12 Rue Froidevaux, 75014 Paris.
T. 0143351673. *093766*
François, Michel, 36 Rue Chardon-Lagache, 75016 Pa-
ris. T. 0145204424. *093767*
Fromaget, Régis, 145 Rue Belleville, 75019 Paris.
T. 0140189973. *093768*
Futur Antérieur, 9 Rue Buffault, 75009 Paris.
T. 0142810523. *093769*
Futur Antérieur, 77 Rue Broca, 75013 Paris.
T. 0143311212. *093770*
Gaillard, Christian, 37 Rue Montreuil, 75011 Paris.
T. 0143562185. *093771*
Galbert, Sophie de, 13 Rue Lille, 75007 Paris.
T. 0142975230. *093772*
Galerie de Beaune, 10 Rue Beaune, 75007 Paris.
T. 0142860572, Fax 0140159681. *093773*
Galerie de l'Orcine, 77 Rue Broca, 75013 Paris.
T. 0143311212. *093774*
Galerie du Cherche-Midi, 17 Rue Dupin, 75006 Paris.
T. 0142227479. *093775*
Galerie H.M., 185 Blvd Saint-Germain, 75007 Paris.
T. 0142220114. *093776*
Galerie 91, 91 Rue Saint-Honoré, 75001 Paris.
T. 0145081339. *093777*
Garcia, Maud, Village Suisse, 78 Av Suffren, 75015 Pa-
ris. T. 0147839303, Fax 0147832610. *093778*
Gavallet, Nicole, 128 Rue Théâtre, 75015 Paris.
T. 0145751430. *093779*
Ged, Arielle, 42 Rue Cardinet, 75017 Paris.
T. 0142276062. *093780*
Gérard, Nicole, 28 Rue Jacob, 75006 Paris.
T. 0143262643. *093781*
Germond, Michel, 78 Quai Hôtel-de-Ville, 75004 Paris.
T. 0142780478, Fax 0142782274. *093782*
Gohard, Robert, 90-92 Rue Entrepreneurs, 75015 Paris.
T. 0145788968, Fax 0145797809. *093783*
Goubault, Francis, 2 Passage Saint-Sébastien, 75011
Paris. T. 0143382364. *093784*
Goujon, Jacques, 5 Villa Guelma, 75018 Paris.
T. 0142527515, Fax 0142239550. *093785*
Grandière Frères, 12 Rue Martel, 75010 Paris.
T. 0147706598. *093786*
Grenier de Grand-Mère, Village Suisse, 78 Av Suffren,
75015 Paris. T. 0147833284. *093787*
Grimaud, Marie-Noëlle, 8 Rue Grands-Augustins, 75006
Paris. T. 0143268796. *093788*
Grivois, Paul, 81 Rue Archives, 75003 Paris.
T. 0142721417, Fax 0142726559. *093789*
Groubetitch, Marie-Pierre, 3 Rue Roule, 75001 Paris.
T. 0142338649. *093790*
Guichard, Henriette, 8 Rue Pyramides, 75001 Paris.
T. 0142604040. *093791*
Guigne, Constance de, 11 Rue Saint-Simon, 75007 Pa-
ris. T. 0145486786. *093792*
Guigue, 11 Rue Saint-Gilles, 75003 Paris.
T. 0148040495. *093793*
Guigue, Jean-François & Muriel, 4 Pl Edmond-Michelet,
75004 Paris. T. 0142728874. *093794*
Guigue, Locca, 81 Av Daumesnil, 75012 Paris.
T. 0143449955. *093795*
Guyomard, Gérard, 1 Rue Petits-Carreaux, 75002 Paris.
T. 0145088915. *093796*
Hadjer, Reynold & Fils, 102 Rue Fbg-Saint-Honoré,
75008 Paris. T. 0142666113,
Fax 0142666603. *093797*

Hanaire, Madeleine, 18 Rue Rochebrune, 75011 Paris.
T. 0148065724. *093798*
Heckmann, Pierre, 57 Rue Bonaparte, 75006 Paris.
T. 0143547109. *093799*
Hémery, Paul, 186 Rue Rivoli, 75001 Paris.
T. 0142604013. *093800*
Hervé, Geneviève, 73 Rue Cherche-Midi, 75006 Paris.
T. 0145489658. *093801*
Hervé, Jeannine, 15 Rue Molière, 75001 Paris.
T. 0142960874. *093802*
Honnelaitre, Claude, 14 Rue Cardinal-Lemoine, 75005
Paris. T. 0143548988. *093803*
Hourrière, Jacques-Denis, 18 Rue Biot, 75017 Paris.
T. 0143870393. *093804*
Huber, Laurent, 17 Rue Charonne, 75011 Paris.
T. 0148068823, Fax 0147000703. *093805*
Huot, Claude & Didier Bellou, 1 Pass Rauch, 75011 Pa-
ris. T. 0143482062. *093806*
Institut d'Art Conservation et Couleur, 15 Rue Grange-
Batelière, 75009 Paris. T. 0148009354. *093807*
Jakubowski, B. & Grégor de Weydenthal, 176 Av Italie,
75013 Paris. T. 0145889263. *093808*
Josnin, 8 Rue Immeubles-Industriels, 75011 Paris.
T. 0143737830, Fax 0143734242. *093809*
Jouan, Jean-Paul, 10 Rue Perronet, 75007 Paris.
T. 0145486420. *093810*
Jung-Pignatta, 61 Rue Petits-Champs, 75001 Paris.
T. 0142968529. *093811*
Kachtanoff, Nadia, 218 Rue Pyrénées, 75020 Paris.
T. 0146367938. *093812*
Keller & Ass, 15 Av Friedland, 75008 Paris.
T. 0145631569, Fax 0145612058. *093813*
Kéramos, 24 Rue Violet, 75015 Paris.
T. 0145796847. *093814*
Kesteven, Evelyne, 41 Rue Joseph-de-Maistre, 75018
Paris. T. 0142630311. *093815*
Klein, François, 55 Rue Orsel, 75018 Paris.
T. 0142595200. *093816*
Kleinert-Nicolas, Isabelle, 63 Rue Daguerre, 75014 Pa-
ris. T. 0143207880. *093817*
Klotz, 9 Rue Belloy, 75016 Paris.
T. 0147279264. *093818*
Kraftchik, Jean-Claude, 6 Rue Bonaparte, 75006 Paris.
T. 0140518007, Fax 0144071345. *093819*
Krzysko, Miroslava, 179 Av Maine, 75014 Paris.
T. 0145396133. *093820*
Laederich, Jehanne, 22 Blvd Edgar-Quinet, 75014 Paris.
T. 0143209232. *093821*
Lambert-Barnett, G., 4 Rue Monsieur-le-Prince, 75006
Paris. T. 0146330884. *093822*
Lanzani, Gaëtan, 19 Rue Basfroi, 75011 Paris.
T. 0143790074, Fax 0143792608. *093823*
Laurenchet, 4 Rue Elisa-Lemonnier, 75012 Paris.
T. 0143072539. *093824*
Laurent-Lasson, Eric, 159 Rue Saint-Charles, 75015 Pa-
ris. T. 0145546522, Fax 0144261865. *093825*
Laurent, Philippe, 2 Rue Regard, 75006 Paris.
T. 0142229872. *093826*
De Lazuli, 9 Blvd Pereire, 75017 Paris.
T. 0142270270. *093827*
De Lazuli, 39 Rue Saint-Georges, 75009 Paris.
T. 0142852446. *093828*
Le Dantec, Bertrand, 71 Rue Mare, 75020 Paris.
T. 0144627263, Fax 0144627345. *093829*
Lebrun, 155 Rue Fbg-Saint-Honoré, 75008 Paris.
T. 0145610065, Fax 0145619749. *093830*
Ledeur, Jean-Paul, 61 Rue Raymond-Losserand, 75014
Paris. T. 0143200022, Fax 0143204115. *093831*
Leegenhoek, Joseph, 23 Quai Voltaire, 75007 Paris.
T. 0142963608. *093832*
Lefeuvre, Solange, 21 Rue Brézin, 75014 Paris.
T. 0145433551. *093833*
Lefortier, 54 Rue Fbg-Saint-Honoré, 75008 Paris.
T. 0142654374. *093834*
Leger, Marianine, 17 Blvd Bourdon, 75004 Paris.
T. 0142784987. *093835*
Legrand, Catherine, 35 Rue Grange-aux-Belles, 75010
Paris. T. 0142450098. *093836*
Legrand-Tardif, 29 Rue Bayen, 75017 Paris.
T. 0145720077. *093837*
Lemaire, Gérard, 18 Rue Lappe, 75011 Paris.
T. 0148072494. *093838*

Lepage, Raymond, 5 Rue Christine, 75006 Paris.
T. 0143269093. *093839*

Lepavec, Yves, 28 Rue Sedaine, 75011 Paris.
T. 0143389547. *093840*

Letailleur, Maurice, 36 Rue Hamelin, 75016 Paris.
T. 0147204832. *093841*

Levoir, Rose, 22 Rue Théophraste-Renaudot, 75015 Paris. T. 0145321178. *093842*

Lévy, Nathalie, 185bis Rue Ordener, 75018 Paris.
T. 0142577101. *093843*

Lewis & Fils, 18 Rue Moulin-Joly, 75011 Paris.
T. 0143574528, Fax 0147004233. *093844*

Lobstein, Alain, 5 Rue Félix-Faure, 75015 Paris.
T. 0145583125. *093845*

Lubrano, Michel, 5 Rue Lions, 75004 Paris.
T. 0148874188. *093846*

Luchini, Sophie, 24 Rue Lebrun, 75013 Paris.
T. 0143367459. *093847*

Lumière de l'Oeil, 4 Rue Flatters, 75005 Paris.
T. 0147076347. *093848*

Mahieu, 15 Imp Primevères, 75011 Paris.
T. 0143558825, Fax 0148069299. *093849*

Malavoy, Brigitte, 19 Rue Bréa, 75006 Paris.
T. 0146330133. *093850*

Malavoy, Brigitte, 21 Rue Drouot, 75009 Paris.
T. 0142461525. *093851*

Malmanche, Catherine, 12 Rue Bernardins, 75005 Paris. T. 0143549958. *093852*

Malouvier, Celia, 18 Rue Saintonge, 75003 Paris.
T. 0142783869. *093853*

Manic, Louvre des Antiquaires, 2 Pl Palais-Royal, 75001 Paris. T. 0142615812, Fax 0142970014. *093854*

Marchais, Jean-Paul, 61 Rue Guy-Moquet, 75017 Paris. T. 0146275302. *093855*

Marine d'Autrefois, 80 Av Ternes, 75017 Paris.
T. 0145742397, Fax 0145746170. *093856*

Marquisat, 96 Av Mozart, 75016 Paris.
T. 0142246729. *093857*

Marsaleix, Pierre, 113 Rue Cherche-Midi, 75006 Paris. T. 0142221213. *093858*

Martel, Thierry, 346 Rue Saint-Honoré, 75001 Paris.
T. 0142960809. *093859*

Martial, Philippe, 8 Rue Général-Guilhem, 75011 Paris. T. 0147007172, Fax 0143554156. *093860*

Martin, Jean, 9 Imp Lamier, 75011 Paris.
T. 0143798419. *093861*

Mativet, Georges, 46 Rue Lamartine, 75009 Paris.
T. 0145267076. *093862*

Maître, Anne-Marie, 127 Rue Château, 75014 Paris.
T. 0143219347. *093863*

Maulet, Didier, 74 Rue Charenton, 75012 Paris.
T. 0143444408. *093864*

Maury, P.C., 47 Rue Saint-Sabin, 75011 Paris.
T. 0143382212, Fax 0140213584. *093865*

Maury, Pierre, 4 Rue Pas-de-la-Mule, 75003 Paris.
T. 0148879589. *093866*

Mellier, Guilhem, 19 Rue Exposition, 75007 Paris.
T. 0145552904. *093867*

Miallier, Laurent, 13 Rue Cavallotti, 75018 Paris.
T. 0142936541, Fax 0142936549. *093868*

Michel, Colette, 5 Rue Campagne-Première, 75014 Paris. T. 0143202467. *093869*

Mikaeloff, Robert, 23 Rue La-Boétie, 75008 Paris.
T. 0142652455, Fax 0149240516. *093870*

Montier, Nicole, 7 Rue Moulinet, 75013 Paris.
T. 0145804444. *093871*

Moran, Miguel, 22 Rue Mayet, 75006 Paris.
T. 0143064790. *093872*

Moreira, Fernando, 8 Blvd Ménilmontant, 75020 Paris. T. 0143729172, Fax 0143791148. *093873*

Moretti, Raymonde, 50 Rue Doudeauville, 75018 Paris. T. 0142640104. *093874*

Mors Doré, 16 Pl Dauphine, 75001 Paris.
T. 0146340632. *093875*

Moustier, Pierre de, 4 Rue Dupin, 75006 Paris.
T. 0145488292. *093876*

Muguet-Lhermine, Daniele, 173 Rue Fbg-Saint-Antoine, 75011 Paris. T. 0143423946. *093877*

Nguyen, Serge, 2 Rue Réunion, 75020 Paris.
T. 0143677153. *093878*

Nordin Frères, 215 Rue Fbg-Saint-Antoine, 75011 Paris. T. 0143723835, Fax 0143568950. *093879*

Nouaille, 11 Rue Edouard-Jacques, 75014 Paris.
T. 0143203935. *093880*

Nouvelle Tendance, 9 Rue Tour, 75016 Paris.
T. 0145206498. *093881*

Octernaud, Pierre, 71 Rue Rennes, 75006 Paris.
T. 0142224778. *093882*

Oliver, Lucile, 45 Rue Madame, 75006 Paris.
T. 0145483806. *093883*

Orlaque, 42 Rue Saint-Bernard, 75011 Paris.
T. 0143714014. *093884*

Ortmann, Jan, 8 Cité Joly, 75011 Paris.
T. 0147009207. *093885*

Ottocento, Village Saint-Paul, 4 Rue Ave-Maria, 75004 Paris. T. 0142718190. *093886*

Ouvrez les Guillemets, 10 Rue Jean-Jacques-Rousseau, 75001 Paris. T. 0140266959. *093887*

Padilla, Clotilde, 33 Rue Berthe, 75018 Paris.
T. 0142624562. *093888*

Palissandres, 15 Rue Damrémont, 75018 Paris.
T. 0142237353. *093889*

Palma-Vata, Marianne, 66 Rue Regnault, 75013 Paris. T. 0145849600. *093890*

Panhard, Gilles, 59bis Rue Bonaparte, 75006 Paris.
T. 0143257031, Fax 0146333898. *093891*

Parant, Marie, 37 Rue Charonne, Bâtiment E, 75011 Paris. T. 0148065651. *093892*

Parin, Marie-Madeleine, 44 Rue Notre-Dames-des-Champs, 75006 Paris. T. 0145481744. *093893*

Paris American Art, 2 Rue Bonaparte, 75006 Paris.
T. 0143260993. *093894*

Peintre Déco, 12 Rue Saint-Bernard, 75011 Paris.
T. 0143719126. *093895*

Pellas, Frédéric, 157 Rue Temple, 75003 Paris.
T. 0142717526. *093896*

Pellet, Patrice, 17 Rue Saint-Paul, 75004 Paris.
T. 0142715145. *093897*

Perolari, Sergio, 339 Rue Pyrénées, 75020 Paris.
T. 0143662612. *093898*

Peyruseigt, Jean, 35 Rue Rousselet, 75007 Paris.
T. 0142730902. *093899*

Pianos Hista, 1 Rue Louis-Ganne, 75020 Paris.
T. 0143640027. *093900*

Pierre, Alain, 107 Rue Blomet, 75015 Paris.
T. 0148287521, Fax 0148289694. *093901*

Pierre, Alain, 132 Rue Lecourbe, 75015 Paris.
T. 0148287131. *093902*

Pierre, Daniel, 22 Rue Boulangers, 75005 Paris.
T. 0143541415. *093903*

Pinault, 27 Rue Bonaparte, 75006 Paris. T. 0143548999, Fax 0143298169. *093904*

Pinault, Jacques-Henri, 30 Rue Jacob, 75006 Paris.
T. 0143269056. *093905*

Pincas, Nathalie, 11 Rue Schoelcher, 75014 Paris.
T. 0143275227, Fax 0143217090. *093906*

Poisat, Daniel, 24 Rue Gravilliers, 75003 Paris.
T. 0148874973, Fax 0148877460. *093907*

Poissant, Pierre, 59 Rue Charonne, 75011 Paris.
T. 0148057554. *093908*

Poisson de Souzy, François, 54 Av La-Motte-Picquet, 75015 Paris. T. 0145672939. *093909*

Poisson, Jacques, 17 Cité-Aubry, 75020 Paris.
T. 0143717309, Fax 0140242620. *093910*

Polack, Michèle, 27 Rue Chazelles, 75017 Paris.
T. 0146227093, Fax 0146227093. *093911*

Portier-Boucard, Michelle, 75 Rue Avron, 75020 Paris. T. 0143560466. *093912*

Priscilla, 178 Quai Jemmapes, 75010 Paris.
T. 0142490446. *093913*

Provost, Michel, 83 Rue Vieille-du-Temple, 75003 Paris. T. 0142774392. *093914*

Rabu, Rémi, 28 Rue Sedaine, 75011 Paris.
T. 0140217970, Fax 0143289547. *093915*

Ratz, Peter, 66 Rue Condorcet, 75009 Paris.
T. 0142804677. *093916*

Raymond Corte Real Pinto, Claire, 37 Rue Blancs-Manteaux, 75004 Paris. T. 0148048012. *093917*

Reinold, 233 Rue Fbg-Saint-Honoré, 75008 Paris.
T. 0142273940. *093918*

Rennotte, 161 Rue Fbg-Saint-Antoine, 75011 Paris.
T. 0143433958, Fax 0143415027. *093919*

Renouvel, Alain, 3 Rue Elzevir, 75003 Paris.
T. 0142721528. *093920*

Réquiston, Mireille, 28 Rue Sedaine, 75011 Paris.
T. 0143389547. *093921*

Riot, 24 Rue Folie-Méricourt, 75011 Paris.
T. 0147003447. *093922*

Rocher, Alain, 23 Rue Faidherbe, 75011 Paris.
T. 0143568240. *093923*

Roig & Léger, 15 Rue Henri-Monnier, 75009 Paris.
T. 0142801204. *093924*

Ronsard, 70 Rue Lecourbe, 75015 Paris.
T. 0145666004. *093925*

Rose des Vents, 25 Rue Beaune, 75007 Paris.
T. 0142601117. *093926*

Rostain, 17 Quai Grands-Augustins, 75006 Paris.
T. 0143267610. *093927*

Rouge Pullon, 189 Rue Temple, 75003 Paris.
T. 0142727541, Fax 0144780383. *093928*

Rousseau, Florent, 34 Rue Ballu, 75009 Paris.
T. 0145267058. *093929*

Roy, Martine, 80 Rue Joseph-de-Maistre, 75018 Paris. T. 0146272374. *093930*

Royer, Jean Pierre, 20 Rue Chabrol, 75010 Paris.
T. 0147704674. *093931*

Ruch, René, 3bis Rue Capri, 75012 Paris.
T. 0143445505. *093932*

Sarre, Léonce, 3 Rue Péclet, 75015 Paris.
T. 0145323846. *093933*

Sassénus, 49 Av Parmentier, 75011 Paris.
T. 0148058915. *093934*

Saunier, Maryvonne, 11 Passage Kracher, 75018 Paris. T. 0142594051. *093935*

Schlissinger, Michèle, 111 Av Victor-Hugo, 75116 Paris. T. 0153708848. *093936*

Schneider, Annick, 42 Rue Mazarine, 75006 Paris.
T. 0143251852. *093937*

Séguier, Claudie de, 20 Rue Berthe, 75018 Paris.
T. 0142557279. *093938*

Senac, Anna, 32 Rue Orteaux, 75020 Paris.
T. 0143484048. *093939*

Serod, 42 Rue Varenne, 75007 Paris.
T. 0145445478. *093940*

Sindaco Domas, Claudia, 157 Rue Temple, 75003 Paris. T. 0142717526. *093941*

Société Européenne de Restauration et de Services, 5 Rue Hanovre, 75002 Paris. T. 0142662728. *093942*

Sophie du Bac, 109 Rue Bac, 75007 Paris.
T. 0145484901. *093943*

Souchet, Fabien, 18 Rue Biot, 75017 Paris.
T. 0145225347. *093944*

Soufflard, Catherine, 21 Rue Lepic, 75018 Paris.
T. 0142579121. *093945*

Soutumier, Suzanne, 28 Rue Réaumur, 75003 Paris.
T. 0148877114. *093946*

Taillefert, Geneviève, 18 Rue Moulin-de-la-Vierge, 75014 Paris. T. 0145411765. *093947*

Tayrac, Régine de, 31 Av Félix-Faure, 75015 Paris.
T. 0140600230. *093948*

Terre de Sienne, 74 Rue Cherche-Midi, 75006 Paris.
T. 0145491815. *093949*

Thellier, 13 Rue Titon, 75011 Paris.
T. 0143713125. *093950*

Thellier, 64 Rue Longchamp, 75116 Paris.
T. 0147043283. *093951*

Tilmant d'Auxy, Bruno, 8 Cité Joly, 75011 Paris.
T. 0143553315. *093952*

Torlet, 27 Rue Mayet, 75006 Paris.
T. 0147345101. *093953*

Torrens, Jean, 8 Rue Lakanal, 75015 Paris.
T. 0148284708. *093954*

Toulouse, 10 Rue Beautreillis, 75004 Paris.
T. 0148878285. *093955*

Tourenne, Robin, 71 Av Daumesnil, 75012 Paris.
T. 0143075925. *093956*

Tournay, Nicole, 42 Rue Meslay, 75003 Paris.
T. 0142778030. *093957*

Triptyque, 91 Rue Saint-Honoré, 75001 Paris.
T. 0142332374. *093958*

Trouillard, Didier, 1 Rue Faidherbe, 75011 Paris.
T. 0143710358. *093959*

Univers du Livre, 5 Rue Bièvre, 75005 Paris.
T. 0143268241. *093960*

Vassallo Paléologo, Renato, 125 Blvd Montparnasse, 75006 Paris. T. 0143208677. *093961*

Vatelot, Etienne, 11bis Rue Portalis, 75008 Paris.
T. 0145221725, Fax 0145220972.   *093962*
Verbizier, Eugène de, 75 Rue Buffon, 75005 Paris.
T. 0143312526.   *093963*
Verbizier, Solange de, 75 Rue Buffon, 75005 Paris.
T. 0143375368.   *093964*
Vergain, Philippe, 10 Rue Maître-Albert, 75005 Paris.
T. 0146334792.   *093965*
Vernier, Roger, 43 Rue Crozatier, 75012 Paris.
T. 0143443343.   *093966*
Veron, Yvon, 28 Rue Petits-Champs, 75002 Paris.
T. 0142968564.   *093967*
Vieil Orfèvre, 22 Rue Vieux-Colombier, 75006 Paris.
T. 0145491140.   *093968*
Villermet, Rolande, 18 Rue Plâtrières, 75020 Paris.
T. 0143667549.   *093969*
Viret, Jacques, 26 Rue Gravilliers, 75003 Paris.
T. 0148872777, Fax 0148047598.   *093970*
Voeltzel, Thierry, 171 Rue Fbg Saint-Antoine, 75011 Paris. T. 0143431128.   *093971*
Voldère, Isabelle de, 238 Rue Fbg-Saint-Antoine, 75012 Paris. T. 0143489339.   *093972*
Volmers, Philippe, 99 Rue Vaugirard, 75006 Paris.
T. 0145490414.   *093973*
Votat, Pierre, 133 Rue Michel-Ange, 75016 Paris.
T. 0147430064.   *093974*
Walle, Gisèle, 157 Rue Fbg-Saint-Honoré, 75008 Paris.
T. 0145634757.   *093975*
Watrelos, Paule, 12 Rue Bernardins, 75005 Paris.
T. 0143549958.   *093976*
Wrobel, Claude, 63 Rue Daguerre, 75014 Paris.
T. 0143222393, Fax 0143203245.   *093977*

Passenans (Jura)
Marotte, Pascal, Rte Frontenay, 39230 Passenans.
Fax 84446664.   *093978*

Pau (Pyrénées-Atlantiques)
Ateliers Maysounabe, 15 Rue Orléans, 64000 Pau.
T. 0559837951.   *093979*
Pendulerie, 30 Rue Monpezat, 64000 Pau.
T. 0559273077.   *093980*

Peillac (Morbihan)
Atelier le Bot et Chesnais, 8 Rue Jeanne-d'Arc, 56220 Peillac. T. 0299913763.   *093981*

Pellegrue (Gironde)
Chassé, Gérard, 1 Raymond-Bérard, 33790 Pellegrue.
T. 0556616114.   *093982*

Périgueux (Dordogne)
Atelier de la Cité, 19 Rue Cité, 24000 Périgueux.
T. 0553353711, Fax 0553353712.   *093983*
Navarro, Pierre, 8 Rue Farges, 24000 Périgueux.
T. 0553532343.   *093984*

Péronne (Somme)
Atelier, 12 Pl André-Audinot, 80200 Péronne.
T. 0322842684. (Encadrements)   *093985*

Pérouges (Ain)
Vénard „La Barbacane", La Porte-d'en-Haut, 01800 Pérouges. T. 0474618427.   *093986*

Perpignan (Pyrénées-Orientales)
Asparre, 7 Rue Emile-Zola, 66000 Perpignan.
T. 0468347380. (encadrements, fourniture, sous-verre)   *093987*
Buforn, Francis, 6 Rue Tour-du-Mir, 66000 Perpignan.
T. 0468612103. (encadrements)   *093988*
Costal, Jacques, 32 Rue Claude-Bernard, 66000 Perpignan. T. 0468352146. (encadrements)   *093989*
Delonca, 65 Av Victor-Dalbiez, 66000 Perpignan.
T. 0468546578. (bois, quincaillerie, decoration)   *093990*
Feuille d'Or, Av Grande-Bretagne, 66000 Perpignan.
T. 0468352886. (doreur sur bois)   *093991*
Gomez, Manuel, La Vigneronne Av Doct-Torreilles, 66000 Perpignan. T. 0468353543. (meubles anciennes et objets d'art)   *093992*
Larrey-Bernat, Paule, 13 Pl Poilus, 66000 Perpignan.
T. 0468355515. (reliure, dorure artisanale)   *093993*
Martin, Henri, 5 Rue Lanterne, 66000 Perpignan.
T. 0468353960. (dorure, argenture)   *093994*

Parot, 11 Rue Pierre-Cartelet, 66000 Perpignan.
T. 0468342425.   *093995*
Serra, 22 Rue Fusterie, 66000 Perpignan.
T. 0468347215. (encadrements)   *093996*
Seus, Serge, 5 Av Emile-Roudayre, 66000 Perpignan.
T. 0468611690.   *093997*
Soulé-Roig, Béatrice, 40 Rue Courteline, 66000 Perpignan. T. 0468356835. (tableaux)   *093998*
Structure 17, 17 Rue Ange, 66000 Perpignan.
T. 0468511407. (affiches, gravures)   *093999*
Temps qui Passe, 3 Rue Fontaine-Napincarda, 66000 Perpignan. T. 0468354331. (tableaux, cadres) *094000*
Torrella, Carl, 5 Rue Révolution-Française, 66000 Perpignan. T. 0468510060. (encadrements d'art) *094001*

Pesmes (Haute-Saône)
Girardot, Jacques, Rue Tanneurs, 70140 Pesmes.
T. 0384312023.   *094002*

Pessac (Gironde)
Boivin, Jean, 64 Rue Bougnard, 33600 Pessac.
T. 0556451716.   *094003*

Petite-Chaux (Doubs)
Todeschini, Claude, 25240 Petite-Chaux.
T. 0381692132.   *094004*

Peypin (Bouches-du-Rhône)
Fabre, Etienne, Chemin Départemental 8, Verclos, 13124 Peypin. T. 0442629711.   *094005*

Peyrat-la-Nonière (Creuse)
Calard, Jacques, Bourg, 23130 Peyrat-la-Nonière.
T. 0555623730.   *094006*

Pierrefontaine-les-Varans (Doubs)
Barret, Jean-Marie, 7 Rue Pavre, 25510 Pierrefontaine-les-Varans. T. 0381560642.   *094007*

Pinsac (Lot)
Société d'Investissement et de Restauration (S.I.R.), Terregaye, 46200 Pinsac. T. 0565326534.   *094008*

Pithiviers (Loiret)
Touzeau, André, 6 Rue Croissant, 45300 Pithiviers.
T. 0238304967.   *094009*

Plaisance-du-Touch (Haute-Garonne)
Lis, Vincent, 44bis Chemin Guis, 31830 Plaisance-du-Touch. T. 0561864540.   *094010*

Pleslin-Trigavou (Côtes-d'Armor)
Hogué, Robert, Gervily Trigavou, 22490 Pleslin-Trigavou. T. 0296271341, Fax 0296271668.   *094011*

Ploudalmézeau (Finistère)
Arielle, 5 Rue Yves-Talarmain, 29262 Ploudalmézeau.
T. 0298480127.   *094012*

Plougastel-Daoulas (Finistère)
Miossec, André, 22bis Passage, 29213 Plougastel-Daoulas. T. 0298042636.   *094013*

Plouider (Finistère)
Deniaux, Françoise, 3 Allée Lilas, 29260 Plouider.
T. 0298254217.   *094014*

Pointis-Inard (Haute-Garonne)
Samuel, André, Rue En-Bas, 31800 Pointis-Inard.
T. 0561955167.   *094015*

Poisy (Haute-Savoie)
Buttet, Pierre de, 75 Ancienne Rte Monod, 74330 Poisy.
T. 0450462628.   *094016*

Poitiers (Vienne)
Baillet, Françoise, 154 Grand-Rue, 86000 Poitiers.
T. 0549602343.   *094017*
Burgues, Yves, 17 Rue René-Descartes, 86000 Poitiers.
T. 0549880730.   *094018*

Poligny (Jura)
Sejac, Rue Le Corbusier, 39800 Poligny. T. 0384371178, Fax 0384370543.   *094019*

Pompey (Meurthe-et-Moselle)
Antic Services Conseil, 1 Rue Alsace, 54340 Pompey.
T. 0383247287.   *094020*

Pont-de-Beauvoisin (Isère)
Bertholier, 12 Rue Porte-de-la-Ville, 73330 Pont-de-Beauvoisin. T. 0476372607.   *094021*

Pont-de-Vaux (Ain)
Colin, Jean-Pierre, Rte de Saint-Trivier-de-Courtes, 01190 Pont-de-Vaux. T. 0385309306.   *094022*

Pont-l'Abbé (Finistère)
Biger, Yves-Marie, 16 Rue Kérentré, 29120 Pont-l'Abbé.
T. 0298872658.   *094023*
Bittner, Imogen, Kernel-Vian, 29120 Pont-l'Abbé.
T. 0298870702.   *094024*

Pontorson (Manche)
Nougues, Henri, 17 Rue Saint-Michel, 50170 Pontorson.
T. 0233601253.   *094025*

Ponts (Manche)
Angélique, Jean-Claude, Maréchalerie, 50300 Ponts.
T. 0233582624.   *094026*

Pouilly-sur-Loire (Nièvre)
Garnier, Lucien, 89 Rue Waldeck-Rousseau, 58150 Pouilly-sur-Loire. T. 0386390131.   *094027*

Pouzac (Hautes-Pyrénées)
Abadie, Clément, 65 Av La-Mongie, 65200 Pouzac.
T. 0562951243.   *094028*

Prades (Pyrénées-Orientales)
Mandragore, 25 Rue Palais-de-Justice, 66500 Prades.
T. 0468963813. (encadrements)   *094029*
Mesalles, Rosendo, Imp Gibraltar, 66500 Prades.
T. 0468962025.   *094030*

Prey (Vosges)
Cendre, Jean-Luc, 3 Rte Fiménil, 88600 Prey.
T. 0329368537.   *094031*

Quesnoy-sur-Deûle (Nord)
Feuille d'acanthe, 30 Rue Verlinghem, 59890 Quesnoy-sur-Deûle. T. 0320398042.   *094032*

Quiers-sur-Bézonde (Loiret)
Pelletier, Claude, 984 Rte Auvilliers, 45270 Quiers-sur-Bézonde. T. 0238901850.   *094033*

Quimper (Finistère)
Bars, Yvon le, 13 Chemin Kervouyec-Nevez, 29000 Quimper. T. 0298953232.   *094034*
Corre, Françoise le, 6 Rue Auguste-Dupouy, 29000 Quimper. T. 0298557433.   *094035*
Jardin des Arts, 35 Rue Aristide-Briand, 29000 Quimper.
T. 0298904771.   *094036*
Nodé, Christian, 19 Rue Douves, 29000 Quimper.
T. 0298951279.   *094037*

Ravilloles (Jura)
Colin, René, 1 Imp Sous-la-Chapelle, 39170 Ravilloles.
T. 0384428676.   *094038*

Redon (Ille-et-Vilaine)
Le Bot, Jean-Yves, 17 Rue Général de La-Ferrière, 35600 Redon. T. 0299727986.   *094039*

Reims (Marne)
A l'Iris de Florence, 8 Rue Talleyrand, 51100 Reims.
T. 0326473085, Fax 0326473332.   *094040*
Atelier de la Renaissance, 96 Rue Gambetta, 51100 Reims. T. 0326501655.   *094041*
Berteaux, 28 Rue Maucroix, 51100 Reims.
T. 0326476766.   *094042*
Blanckaert, Alain, 51 Rue Neuvillette, 51100 Reims.
T. 0326885252.   *094043*
Cocusse, Claudine, 7 Rue Marlot, 51100 Reims.
T. 0326403149.   *094044*

Remiremont (Vosges)
Lanterne, 22 Rue La Xavée, 88200 Remiremont.
T. 0329622436.   *094045*

Rennes (Ille-et-Vilaine)
Arcades, 23 Rue Hypolite-Vatar, 35000 Rennes.
T. 0299389779.   *094046*
Atelier Cabane, 16 Rue Pré-Botte, 35000 Rennes.
T. 0299796950.   *094047*

Réflexions, 9 Pl Lices, 35000 Rennes.
T. 0299781466. *094048*

Rezé (Loire-Atlantique)
Atelier des Arts, 20 Rue Alsace-Lorraine, 44400 Rezé.
T. 40041120. *094049*

Ribérac (Dordogne)
Atelier du Moulin, Rte d'Angoulême-Villetoureix, 24600
Ribérac. T. 0553902516. *094050*

Ris-Orangis (Essonne)
Collard, Françoise, 5 Av Parmentier, 91130 Ris-Orangis.
T. 0169065736. *094051*

Rivesaltes (Pyrénées-Orientales)
Galerie, 5 Rue Armand-Barbès, 66600 Rivesaltes.
T. 0468385736. *094052*

Rochecorbon (Indre-et-Loire)
Art Partners International, 37210 Rochecorbon.
T. 0547525965, Fax 0547525097. *094053*

Rochefort (Charente-Maritime)
Duffour, Pierre, 15 Rue Grimaux, 17300 Rochefort.
T. 0546874377. *094054*

Rochemaure (Ardèche)
Fabre, Régis, Mte Château, 07400 Rochemaure.
T. 0475490610. *094055*

Rodez (Aveyron)
Lacombe, Ulysse, 4 Av Durand-de-Gros, 12000 Rodez.
T. 0565671708, Fax 0565671869. *094056*

Rognac (Bouches-du-Rhône)
Récréation, 517 Av Général-Leclerc, 13340 Rognac.
T. 0442786361. *094057*

Romilly-sur-Seine (Aube)
Guillemin, Alain, 37 Rue Milford-Haven, 10100 Romilly-
sur-Seine. T. 0325248217. *094058*

Romorantin-Lanthenay (Loir-et-Cher)
Au Reflet de Sologne, 5 Rue Notre-Dame, 41200 Romorantin-Lanthenay. T. 0254769570. *094059*

Roquevaire (Bouches-du-Rhône)
Amodéo, Salvatore, RN 96, Quartier Saint-Vincent,
13360 Roquevaire. T. 0442042222. *094060*

Rosay-sur-Lieure (Eure)
Depierre, Rodolphe, 25 Côte Eglise, 27790 Rosay-sur-
Lieure. Fax 32499663. *094061*

Rouen (Seine-Maritime)
Bais, Patrick, 69 Rue Saint-Maur, 76000 Rouen.
T. 0235713655. *094062*
Charles, Françoise, 249 Rue Eau-de-Robec, 76000
Rouen. T. 0235715052. *094063*
Galerie Géricault, 111 Blvd Yser, 76000 Rouen.
T. 0235715159. *094064*
Hesse, Claire, 194 Rue Eau-de-Robec, 76000 Rouen.
T. 0235980030. *094065*
Or et Bleu, 249 Rue Eau-de-Robec, 76000 Rouen.
T. 0235715052. *094066*
Renault, Daniel, 1 Pl Lieutenant-Aubert, 76000 Rouen.
T. 0235896171. *094067*
Rollin, 31 Rue Ecuyère, 76000 Rouen.
T. 0235701072. *094068*
Vigreux, Jean-Jacques, 5 Rue Boucheries-Saint-Ouen,
76000 Rouen. T. 0235715110. *094069*

Royan (Charente-Maritime)
Favre, Christian, 8 Rue Edouard-Branly, 17200 Royan.
T. 0546054377. *094070*

Roye (Somme)
Pécriaux, Henri, 20 Rue Noyon, 80700 Roye.
T. 0322873067. *094071*

Saint-Alban-Leysse (Savoie)
Goy, Patrick, 258 Rte Verel, 73230 Saint-Alban-Leysse.
T. 0479700823, Fax 0479704818. *094072*

Saint-André-de-l'Eure (Eure)
Lancelin, Pascal, Rue Damville, 27220 Saint-André-de-
l'Eure. T. 0232371968. *094073*

Saint-André-lez-Lille (Nord)
Acanthe Antiquités Service, 30 Rue Brune, 59350 Saint-
André-lez-Lille. T. 0320517979. *094074*

Saint-Aubin-d'Ecrosville (Eure)
Jaillette, Pierre, 22 Rue Château, 27110 Saint-Aubin-
d'Ecrosville. T. 0232350025. *094075*

Saint-Ay (Loiret)
1900, 98 Rte Nationale, 45130 Saint-Ay.
T. 0238806517. *094076*

Saint-Bris-le-Vineux (Yonne)
Durot, Gilles, 33 Rue Gouaix, 89530 Saint-Bris-le-Vineux. T. 0386533977. *094077*

**Saint-Christophe-sur-Roc (Deux-Sè-
vres)**
Antiquités Saint-Christophe, La Truite, 79220 Saint-
Christophe-sur-Roc. T. 0549052054. *094078*

Saint-Claude (Jura)
Meyer, Christian, Prés-Valfin, 39200 Saint-Claude.
T. 0384456328. *094079*

Saint-Cristol-lès-Alès (Gard)
Galerie Coup d'Oeil, 544 Av Général-de-Gaulle, 30380
Saint-Cristol-lès-Alès. T. 0466608045. *094080*
Genolhac, Olivier, Château de Montmoirac, 30380 Saint-
Cristol-lès-Alès. T. 0466608238. *094081*

Saint-Denis (Seine-Saint-Denis)
Unité de Traitement d'Information en Conservation Ar-
chéologique (U.T.I.C.A.), 8 Rue Franciade, 93200
Saint-Denis. T. 0148208316. *094082*

Saint-Denis-de-l'Hôtel (Loiret)
Renaud, Catherine, 36 Av Orléans, 45550 Saint-Denis-
de-l'Hôtel. T. 0238591158. *094083*

**Saint-Denis-lès-Rebais (Seine-et-Mar-
ne)**
De Abreu, La Brosse, 77510 Saint-Denis-lès-Rebais.
T. 64209302. *094084*

Saint-Doulchard (Cher)
Bobin, Guy, 8 Rue Pierre-Desbois, 18230 Saint-Doulchard. T. 0248246712. *094085*

Saint-Estève (Pyrénées-Orientales)
Colomb, Olivier, 21 Av Gilbert-Brutus, 66240 Saint-Estève. T. 0468920419. (Meubles) *094086*

Saint-Etienne (Loire)
Gousset, 30 Rue Paul-Bert, 42000 Saint-Etienne.
T. 0477325192. *094087*
Nicosia, Carmélo, 55 Rue République, 42000 Saint-
Etienne. T. 0477388030. *094088*
Passé Recomposé, 12 Rue Grand-Gonnet, 42000 Saint-
Etienne. T. 0477419072. *094089*
Raveyre, Antoine, 34 Rue Mulatière, 42100 Saint-
Etienne. T. 0477251861. *094090*
Thiollière, Philippe, 3 Rue Marcellin-Champagnat,
42100 Saint-Etienne. T. 0477255898. *094091*

Saint-Flour (Cantal)
Bonnet, Christian, 40 Av Verdun, 15100 Saint-Flour.
T. 0471602087. *094092*

Saint-Fons (Rhône)
Krass, Olivier, 23 Rue Carnot, 69190 Saint-Fons.
T. 0478701875. *094093*

Saint-Gaudens (Haute-Garonne)
Berdou, Yves, Blvd Sommer, 31800 Saint-Gaudens.
T. 0561950559. *094094*

**Saint-Genis-de-Saintonge (Charente-
Maritime)**
Renoux, Yves, RN 137, 17240 Saint-Genis-de-Sainton-
ge. T. 0546498891. *094095*

Saint-Genis-Laval (Rhône)
Antiquités Beau-Versant, Chemin Beauversant, 69230
Saint-Genis-Laval. T. 0472399700. *094096*

**Saint-Germain-de-Longue-Chaume
(Deux-Sèvres)**
Merceron, Le Patis, 79200 Saint-Germain-de-Longue-
Chaume. T. 0549700114. *094097*

Saint-Germain-du-Puy (Cher)
Dauchel, Eric, Nérigny, 18390 Saint-Germain-du-Puy.
T. 0248307061. *094098*

Saint-Germain-en-Laye (Yvelines)
Atelier de Restauration de Tableaux, 21 Rue Danès-de-
Montardat, 78100 Saint-Germain-en-Laye.
T. 0139211939. *094099*
Galerie des Coches, 12 Rue Coches, 78100 Saint-Ger-
main-en-Laye. T. 0130615528. *094100*
Marotte, 20 Rue Danès-de-Montardat, 78100 Saint-Ger-
main-en-Laye. T. 0130611610. *094101*
Mertens, Juliette, 14bis Rue Pontel, 78100 Saint-Ger-
main-en-Laye. T. 0139585170. *094102*

Saint-Germain-Laprade (Haute-Loire)
Masson, Olivier, La Chaux-Marnhac, 43700 Saint-Germain-Laprade. T. 0471030644. *094103*

Saint-Hilaire-de-Riez (Vendée)
Lucas, Joël, 68bis Rue Georges-Clemenceau, 85270
Saint-Hilaire-de-Riez. T. 0251556728. *094104*
Migné, Théophile, 283 Rte Perrier-La-Fradinière, 85270
Saint-Hilaire-de-Riez. T. 0251683344. *094105*

Saint-Hilaire-du-Harcouët (Manche)
Antiquités Saint-Hilaire, Goberie, 50600 Saint-Hilaire-
du-Harcouët. T. 0233495061. *094106*

Saint-Jean (Haute-Garonne)
Clinique des Objets Anciens, 2 Rue Coteaux, 31240
Saint-Jean. T. 0561354788. *094107*

Saint-Jean-de-Braye (Loiret)
Chauveau, Yves, 65 Chemin Halage, 45800 Saint-Jean-
de-Braye. T. 0238842482. *094108*

Saint-Jean-de-Moirans (Isère)
Berthelet, Anne, Rue Billoud, 38430 Saint-Jean-de-Moirans. T. 0476534999. (céramique) *094109*

Saint-Jean-de-Monts (Vendée)
Galeyrand, Philippe, 200 Rue Sables-Beaulieu, 85160
Saint-Jean-de-Monts. T. 0251586726. *094110*

**Saint-Jeoire-en-Faucigny (Haute-Sa-
voie)**
Perron, Ralph, 1 Rue Melchior, 74490 Saint-Jeoire-en-
Faucigny. T. 0450358139. *094111*

Saint-Juery (Tarn)
Farenc, Michel, Rte Ambialet, Les Avalats, 81160 Saint-
Juery. T. 0563551209. *094112*

Saint-Laurent-d'Agny (Rhône)
Broallier, Jean, Pl By, 69440 Saint-Laurent-d'Agny.
T. 0478482617. *094113*

Saint-Laurent-du-Var (Alpes-Maritimes)
Brelaz, Armand, Chalet Printemps, Rte Nationale, 06700
Saint-Laurent-du-Var. T. 0493311226. *094114*
Ceppa, Guy, Collet Rouge, Chalet Plateaux-Fleurie,
06700 Saint-Laurent-du-Var. T. 0493073592. *094115*

Saint-Léon-sur-l'Isle (Dordogne)
Aviles, Pascal, 7 Rue Pierre-Sémard, 24110 Saint-Léon-
sur-l'Isle. T. 0553806017. *094116*

Saint-Léonard-en-Beauce (Loir-et-Cher)
Taillefert, Geneviève, 39 Grande Rue, 41370 Saint-Léonard-en-Beauce. T. 0254723864. *094117*

Saint-Leu-la-Forêt (Val-d'Oise)
Jouvert, Pascale, 6 Rue Hoche, 95320 Saint-Leu-la-Fo-
rêt. T. 0139608597. *094118*
Martin, Bruno, 150 Rue Général-Leclerc, 95320 Saint-
Leu-la-Forêt. T. 0130401093. *094119*

Saint-Lô (Manche)
Bergmann, Christian, 35 Rue Havin, 50000 Saint-Lô.
T. 0233050668. *094120*

Saint-Loup (Nièvre)
Brouard, Frantz, Grands Maraux, 58200 Saint-Loup.
T. 0386399088. 094121

Saint-Martin-de-Crau (Bouches-du-Rhône)
Tacher, Aimé, Rte Craponne, 13310 Saint-Martin-de-Crau. T. 0490473480. 094122

Saint-Martin-le-Beau (Indre-et-Loire)
Capredon, Bruno, 2 Rue Caves, 37270 Saint-Martin-le-Beau. T. 0547506460. 094123

Saint-Maur-des-Fossés (Val-de-Marne)
Diamin, Jean-Claude, 5 Pl Tilleuls, 94100 Saint-Maur-des-Fossés. T. 0142834043. 094124
Lutet Toti, 31 Av Port-au-Fouarre, 94100 Saint-Maur-des-Fossés. T. 0143971854. 094125

Saint-Max (Meurthe-et-Moselle)
Pardo, Grégoire, 5 Ruelle Saint-Médard, 54130 Saint-Max. T. 0383214663. 094126

Saint-Michel-l'Observatoire (Alpes-de-Haute-Provence)
Collines de Provence, RN 100, 04870 Saint-Michel-l'Ob-servatoire. T. 0492766902. (Dorures, Meubles) 094127

Saint-Nabord (Vosges)
Au Réveil du Temps, 24 Rue Centre, 88200 Saint-Na-bord. T. 0329233201. 094128

Saint-Ouen (Seine-Saint-Denis)
Claude & Martine, 7 Rue Edgar-Quinet, 93400 Saint-Ouen. T. 0140117046. 094129
Daveau, Pierre, 3 Rue Louis-Dain, 93400 Saint-Ouen. T. 0140117713. 094130
Delpierre, Philippe, 113 Rue Docteur-Bauer, Lot 33, 93400 Saint-Ouen. T. 0140118502. 094131
Digiart, 15 Rue Maréchal-Leclerc, 93400 Saint-Ouen. T. 0140116134. 094132
Doinet, Thierry, 11 Rue Voltaire, 93400 Saint-Ouen. T. 0140100322. 094133
Krougly, 41 Rue Rosiers, 93400 Saint-Ouen. Fax (1) 40115501. 094134
Lepage, Raymond, 22 Imp Aubert, 93400 Saint-Ouen. T. 0140117583. 094135
Steger, André, 76 Av Michelet, 93400 Saint-Ouen. T. 0140125378. 094136
Steger, Marie-Claude, 76 Av Michelet, 93400 Saint-Ouen. T. 0140125378. 094137

Saint-Ouen (Somme)
Jacmaire & Buteux, 22 Rue Vignacourt, 80610 Saint-Ouen. T. 0322529130. (Meubles) 094138

Saint-Paul-Trois-Châteaux (Drôme)
Antiquités des Remparts, 6 Rte Garde-Adhémar, 26130 Saint-Paul-Trois-Châteaux. T. 0475967151. 094139

Saint-Pierre-de-Jards (Indre)
Rabaté, Pierre, Le Bourg, 36260 Saint-Pierre-de-Jards. T. 0254492321. 094140

Saint-Pourçain-sur-Sioule (Allier)
Bruchet, Jean-Pierre, 44 Fbg National, 03500 Saint-Pourçain-sur-Sioule. T. 0470454398. 094141

Saint-Pryvé-Saint-Mesmin (Loiret)
Casciello, Domenico, 223 Rte Saint-Mesmin, 45750 Saint-Pryvé-Saint-Mesmin. T. 0238519801. 094142

Saint-Quentin (Aisne)
Dupuis, Dominique, 3bis Rue Georges-Pompidou, 02100 Saint-Quentin. T. 0323082904. (ebenisterie d'art; re-stauration meubles anciens) 094143
Gressier, Sylvie, 2 Av Aristide-Briand, 02100 Saint-Quentin. T. 0323626222. 094144

Saint-Règle (Indre-et-Loire)
Joubert, Robert, 10 Rue Petit-Pont, 37530 Saint-Règle. T. 0547574672. 094145

Saint-Rémy (Côte-d'Or)
L.P.3 Conservation, Château, 21500 Saint-Rémy. T. 0380924503. 094146

Saint-Rémy-lès-Chevreuse (Yvelines)
Riesen, Didier, 7 Rue Victor-Hugo, 78470 Saint-Rémy-lès-Chevreuse. T. 0130529329. 094147

Saint-Sever (Landes)
Loupret, Patrick, Rue du Bellocq, 40500 Saint-Sever. T. 0558762449. 094148

Saint-Tropez (Var)
Roehrig, Jean-François, Chemin Ay-Parcs-Saint-Tropez, 83000 Saint-Tropez. T. 0494977638. 094149

Saint-Uze (Drôme)
Tracol, Roger, Quart Combe-Tourmente, 26240 Saint-Uze. T. 0475032582. 094150

Saint-Vincent-de-Mercuze (Isère)
Fayolle, Véronique, Rue du Bourg, 38660 Saint-Vincent-de-Mercuze. T. 0476085687. (céramique) 094151

Saint-Vincent-Sterlanges (Vendée)
Aux Vieux Meubles, Rue Malvoisine, 85110 Saint-Vin-cent-Sterlanges. T. 0251402319. 094152
Fallourd, Claude, 30 Rue Nationale, 85110 Saint-Vin-cent-Sterlanges. T. 0251402696, Fax 0251402001. 094153

Sainte-Feyre (Creuse)
Catinat, Maurice, Rte Saint-Laurent, 23000 Sainte-Fey-re. T. 0555522391. 094154

Saintes (Charente-Maritime)
Toujouse, Jean-Yves, 25 Rue Saint-Michel, 17100 Sain-tes. T. 0546933641. 094155

Salins-les-Bains (Jura)
Chatelain, Marcel, 6 Rue Préval, 39110 Salins-les-Bains. T. 0384731202. 094156

Sallanches (Haute-Savoie)
A la Belle Epoque, 24 Rte Fayet, 74700 Sallanches. T. 0450585461. 094157

Salon-de-Provence (Bouches-du-Rhône)
Antiquités du Château, 42 Rue Moulin-d'Isnard, 13300 Salon-de-Provence. T. 0490567422. 094158

Salouel (Somme)
Thierry, Bruno, 9 Rue Denis-Sevin, 80480 Salouel. T. 0322954872. (Meubles) 094159

Sanary-sur-Mer (Var)
Bisogno, Denis, 194 Ancien Chemin de Toulon, 83110 Sanary-sur-Mer. T. 0494881037. 094160
Grand Bazar, 194 Ancien Chemin de Toulon, 83110 Sa-nary-sur-Mer. T. 0494347884, Fax 0494881034. 094161

Sannerville (Calvados)
Chereau, Jacques, 3 Rue Maréchal-Leclerc, 14940 San-nerville. T. 0231237730. 094162

Saou (Drôme)
Luce, Jean-Marc, Chantebise, 26400 Saou. T. 0475760388. 094163

Sarreguemines (Moselle)
A la Belle Epoque, 8 Rue Bac, 57200 Sarreguemines. T. 0387957065. 094164

Sarzeau (Morbihan)
Le Boulicaut, Henri, Bourg Saint-Colombier, 56370 Sar-zeau. T. 0297264456. 094165

Sathonay-Camp (Rhône)
Agnès Frères, 38 Av Boutarey, 69580 Sathonay-Camp. T. 0478237433. 094166

Saules (Doubs)
Vignal, Hélène, Village, 25580 Saules. T. 0381622878. 094167

Saumur (Maine-et-Loire)
Atelier Opus, 35 Rue Saint-Nicolas, 49400 Saumur. T. 41513663. 094168
Greffier, Marie-Sophie, 5 Quai Comte-Lair, 49400 Sau-mur. T. 41504003. 094169

Scey-sur-Saône-et-Saint-Albin (Haute-Saône)
Gavoille, Alain, Rue Mécorne, Rte Ferrières-lès-Scey, 70360 Scey-sur-Saône-et-Saint-Albin. T. 0384688893. 094170

Schiltigheim (Bas-Rhin)
Feldmann, 3 A Rue Faisans, 67300 Schiltigheim. T. 0388833580. 094171

Sciez (Haute-Savoie)
Fauvergue, Arnaud, RN 5, Bonnatrait, 74140 Sciez. T. 0450725808. 094172

Semoussac (Charente-Maritime)
Isodéco l'Enclouse, L'Enclouse, 17150 Semoussac. T. 0546860696, Fax 0546861274. 094173

Semur-en-Auxois (Côte-d'Or)
Diebold, Pascal, 4 Rue Liberté, 21140 Semur-en-Auxois. T. 0380970862. 094174
Père, 13 Rue Paris, 21140 Semur-en-Auxois. T. 0380970251. 094175

Senlis (Oise)
Bouchardon, Alain, 2 Rue Lavarde, 60300 Senlis. T. 0344531015. 094176
Parot, Marguerite, 13 Rue Corne-de-Cerf, 60300 Senlis. T. 0344600694. 094177
Restauration Meubles Anciens (S.R.M.A), 7 Rue Châtel, 60300 Senlis. T. 0344600603. 094178

Sens (Yonne)
Roques, Fabienne, 7bis Rue Puits-de-la-Chaîne, 89100 Sens. T. 0386952204. 094179

Sériers (Cantal)
Bonnet, Christian, Peireladès, 15100 Sériers. T. 0471730044. 094180

Serres-sur-Arget (Ariège)
Morère, Jacques, Cambié, 09000 Serres-sur-Arget. T. 0561028911. 094181

Solesmes (Sarthe)
Beaugey, Pierre, Clos-Messu, 72300 Solesmes. T. 0243920507. 094182

Sorel-Moussel (Eure-et-Loir)
Chatelain, Bertrand, 2 Rte Anet, 28520 Sorel-Moussel. T. 0237418292. 094183

Souvigné (Indre-et-Loire)
Quesson, La Joinière, 37330 Souvigné. T. 0547247335. 094184

Stains (Seine-Saint-Denis)
Thomas, Daniel, 120 Rue Jean-Durand, 93240 Stains. T. 0148211731. 094185

Strasbourg (Bas-Rhin)
Aktuaryus, 23 Rue Nuée-Bleue, 67000 Strasbourg. T. 0388323938. 094186
Atelier du Bibliophile, 26 Quai Bateliers, 67000 Stras-bourg. T. 0388242300, Fax 0388240009. 094187
Balboni, 9 Rue Klein, 67000 Strasbourg. T. 0388361903. 094188
Berauer, 7 A Rue des Frères, 67000 Strasbourg. T. 0388250646. 094189
Blum, 17 Rue Rosheim, 67000 Strasbourg. T. 0388223840. 094190
Eichwald, Huguette, 47 Rue Finkwiller, 67000 Stras-bourg. T. 0388250189. 094191
Galerie Sum Qui Sum, 20 Pl Cathédrale, 67000 Stras-bourg. T. 0388221117. 094192
Husser, 8 Rue Hallebardes, 67000 Strasbourg. T. 0388322968. 094193
Macquet, Cécile, 39 Rue Petites-Fermes, 67200 Stras-bourg. T. 0388297287, Fax 0388297281. 094194

Talasani (Corse)
Oliver, Jacques, Fiume Olmo, Sud Folelli, RN 198, 20230 Talasani. T. 0495368795. 094195

Talence (Gironde)
Campo, André, Résidence Michel-Montaigne, 33400 Ta-lence. T. 0556370737. 094196

Tarascon (Bouches-du-Rhône)
Art Plus, 14 Rue Château, 13150 Tarascon.
T. 0490911414. *094197*

Tarbes (Hautes-Pyrénées)
Garay, 12 Rue Massey, 65000 Tarbes.
T. 0562930696. *094198*

Taulignan (Drôme)
Atelier D.L., Rte Valréas, 26770 Taulignan.
T. 0475535063. *094199*

Thairé (Charente-Maritime)
Chaussat, Dominique, 9 Rue Dirac, 17290 Thairé.
T. 0546563645. *094200*

Thann (Haut-Rhin)
Briswalter, Jacques, 14 Rue Cigognes, 68800 Thann.
T. 0389370882. *094201*

Thiais (Val-de-Marne)
Stossel, Willy, 28 Av République, 94320 Thiais.
T. 0146818140. *094202*

Thiers (Puy-de-Dôme)
Art cadrerie, 9 Rue Grenette, 63300 Thiers.
T. 0473800879. (encadrements) *094203*

Thivars (Eure-et-Loir)
Madelin, Christophe, 37 Rue Chanoine-Vergez, 28630 Thivars. T. 0237264174. *094204*

Thonon-les-Bains (Haute-Savoie)
Grapin, Joël, 24 Chemin Froid-Lieu, 74200 Thonon-les-Bains. T. 0450710544. *094205*

Thorigné-Fouillard (Ille-et-Vilaine)
Helleux, Thierry, Zone Activité Bellevue, 35235 Thorigné-Fouillard. T. 0299624659. *094206*

Thuir (Pyrénées-Orientales)
Atelier du Tapis, 4 Pl René-Crabos, 66300 Thuir.
T. 0468533602. *094207*

Tilques (Pas-de-Calais)
Dubois, Dominique, 77 RN 43, 62500 Tilques.
T. 0321959526. *094208*

Tinqueux (Marne)
Lambiet Audurenq, Cécile, 1 Rue Haute-Borne, 51430 Tinqueux. T. 0326087504. *094209*

Torigni-sur-Vire (Manche)
Bergmann, Christian, 23 Rue Notre-Dame, 50160 Torigni-sur-Vire. T. 0233567523. *094210*

Toulon (Var)
Atelier d'Art, 3 Rue Réhel, 83000 Toulon.
T. 0494037221. *094211*
Boeuf, Robert, 49 Rue Jean-Jaurès, 83000 Toulon.
T. 0494931105, Fax 0494930093. *094212*
Fouasse, Dominique, 268 Rue Docteur-Barrois, 83000 Toulon. T. 0494466240. *094213*
Mevel, Jean-Pierre, 113 Rue Edouard-Perrichi, 83000 Toulon. T. 0494911202. *094214*
Nannini, Nathalie, 25 Av Lazare-Carnot, 83000 Toulon.
T. 0494245943. *094215*
Ruiz, Ramon, 8 Rue Alexandre-Borrely, 83100 Toulon.
T. 0494928511, Fax 0494915207. *094216*

Toulouse (Haute-Garonne)
Akademia, 20 Rue Couteliers, 31000 Toulouse.
T. 0561551512. *094217*
Baudouy, 171 Chemin Lanusse, 31200 Toulouse.
T. 0561575906. *094218*
Canillo, Philippe, 234 Av Castres, 31500 Toulouse.
T. 0561348574. *094219*
Châteauvieux, 14 Rue Poids-de-l'Huile, 31000 Toulouse.
T. 0561219948. *094220*
Corbarieu, Didier, 100bis Rue Fontaines, 31300 Toulouse. T. 0561427660. *094221*
Courtiade, Bernard, 40 Rue Couteliers, 31000 Toulouse. T. 0561251425. *094222*
Etabli, 13 Rue Industrie, 31000 Toulouse.
T. 0561996005. *094223*
Furgadou, 231 Av Saint-Exupéry, 31400 Toulouse.
T. 0561203059, Fax 0562720006. *094224*

Grenier de la Ramée, 362 Chemin Tucaut, 31000 Toulouse. T. 0561075414. *094225*
Laid Vaurien, 8 Rue Boyer-Fonfrede, 31000 Toulouse.
T. 0561139413. *094226*
Martin, Chantal, 31 Port Saint-Sauveur, 31000 Toulouse. T. 0561996414. *094227*
Milhes, Bruno, 3 Rue Trois-Banquets, 31000 Toulouse.
T. 0561258983. *094228*
Naa, M., 13 Rue Rempart-Saint-Etienne, 31000 Toulouse. T. 0561218407. *094229*
Restauratore, 9 Rue Trois-Banquets, 31000 Toulouse.
T. 0561522100. *094230*
Savard, Jean-Christophe, 38 Chemin Moulis, 31200 Toulouse. T. 0561704561. *094231*
Savard, Jean-Christophe, 15 Av Minimes, 31200 Toulouse. T. 0561470047. *094232*
Stambak, Jean-Marc, 14bis Rue Chant-du-Merle, 31000 Toulouse. T. 0561348434. *094233*
Sverko, Mario, 96 Chemin Lanusse, 31200 Toulouse.
T. 0561582383. *094234*

Tourcoing (Nord)
Tradition, 40 Blvd Gambetta, 59200 Tourcoing.
T. 0327748729. (meubles) *094235*

Tournon-sur-Rhône (Ardèche)
Millers, Max, 47 Av Maréchal-Foch, 07300 Tournon-sur-Rhône. T. 0475083429. *094236*

Tournus (Saône-et-Loire)
Vidgrain, Paul, 3 Imp Amandiers, 71700 Tournus.
T. 0385510682. *094237*

Tourrettes (Var)
Bihan, Anne-Marie, Quartier Turquières, 83440 Tourrettes. T. 0494762870. *094238*

Tours (Indre-et-Loire)
Art Rénovation, 92 Rue James-Cane, 37000 Tours.
T. 0547391773. *094239*
Asfeld-Bidal, Arnaud de, 17 Pl Foire-Le-Roi, 37000 Tours. T. 0547649088. *094240*
Lemaire, Bernard, 6 Rue Lamartine, 37000 Tours.
T. 0547380366. *094241*
Maudet, Bruno, 9 Rue Monnaie, 37000 Tours.
T. 0547662272. *094242*

Tréguier (Côtes-d'Armor)
Atelier du Cuir, 22 Rue Saint-André, 22220 Tréguier.
T. 0296929333. *094243*

Treillières (Loire-Atlantique)
Piolot, François, 17 Rue Etienne-Sebert, 44119 Treillières. T. 40946276. *094244*

Trets (Bouches-du-Rhône)
Pichot, Patrice, RN 7, Quartier Verlaque, 13530 Trets.
T. 0442293037. *094245*

Troyes (Aube)
Au Point du Jour, 7 Rue Urbain IV, 10000 Troyes.
T. 0325730902. (Tableaux, gravures, cadres) *094246*
Sandri, Eric, 6 Rue Demi-Lune, 10000 Troyes.
T. 0325813685. *094247*

Turenne (Corrèze)
Baillot, Bernard, Borie Basse, 19500 Turenne.
T. 0555859732. *094248*

Urçay (Allier)
Auvity, Jean-Claude, Le Bourg, 03360 Urçay.
T. 0470069787. *094249*

Val-d'Epy (Jura)
Atelier des Petites Vallées, Rue Bordeaux, 39160 Val-d'Epy. T. 0384854450. *094250*

Valdoie (Territoire-de-Belfort)
Allemann, Jean-Pierre, 14 Rue Gare, 90300 Valdoie.
T. 0384265251. *094251*

Valence (Drôme)
Capron, Philippe, 88bis Rue Pont-du-Gât, 26000 Valence. T. 0475552226. *094252*
Gormand, Odile, 5 Pl Clercs, 26000 Valence.
T. 0475568401. *094253*

Jouve, Dominique, 88bis Rue Pont-du-Gât, 26000 Valence. T. 0475552226. *094254*
Jouve, Dominique, 2 Av Pierre-Semard, 26000 Valence.
T. 0475812185. *094255*
Rollet, Isabelle, 39 Grande Rue, 26000 Valence.
T. 0475565686. *094256*
Sauret, Noël, 2 Rue Hôpital, 26000 Valence.
T. 0146449852. *094257*

Valognes (Manche)
Duteurtre, Philippe, 40bis Rue Poterie, 50700 Valognes.
T. 0233403416. *094258*

Vannes (Morbihan)
Clinique Poupées Anciennes, 28 Rue Boucherie, 56000 Vannes. T. 0297471555. *094259*

Vanves (Hauts-de-Seine)
Domergue, Margaret, 52 Rue Mary-Besseyre, 92170 Vanves. T. 0146449852. *094260*

Varces-Allières-Risset (Isère)
Ricciardi, Lucienne, 40 Gal Saint-Ange, 38760 Varces-Allières-Risset. T. 0476729089. *094261*

Vaux-sur-Mer (Charente-Maritime)
Toujouse, Jean-Yves, Rocade Palmyre, ZA, Rte La Tremblade, 17640 Vaux-sur-Mer. T. 0546390869, Fax 0546381862. *094262*

Veigné (Indre-et-Loire)
Asquier, Marie-Pierre, La Chataigneraie, 37250 Veigné.
T. 0547. *094263*

Velogny (Côte-d'Or)
Sennelier, Pierre, RD 119, 21350 Velogny.
T. 0380646467. *094264*

Vence (Alpes-Maritimes)
Gastaud, Jean-Marie, 19 Pl Antony-Mars, 06140 Vence.
T. 0493580595. *094265*
Valette, Jean, 885 Chemin Siné, 06140 Vence.
T. 0493246990. *094266*
Wulleman, Pierre, 95 Av Général-Leclerc, 06140 Vence.
T. 0493580853. *094267*

Vendenheim (Bas-Rhin)
Maser, Francis, 3 Rue Lignée, 67550 Vendenheim.
T. 0388594840. *094268*

Venelles (Bouches-du-Rhône)
Dunoyer de Segonzac, Sylvie, Les Gailles, 13770 Venelles. T. 0442540622. *094269*

Venette
Martins, Henri, 526 Rue République, 60200 Venette.
T. 0344900361. *094270*

Vercia (Jura)
Maschio, Fernand, Chemin Fontaine-Paisia, 39190 Vercia. T. 0384250560. *094271*

Véretz (Indre-et-Loire)
Maintenant, Hubert de, Le Château de Véretz, 37270 Véretz. T. 0547505160. *094272*

Vernon (Eure)
Guérin, Joël, 12 Rue Docteur-Burnet, 27200 Vernon.
T. 0232519630. *094273*

Vernouillet (Yvelines)
Magagnini, Vittorio, 5 Av Auguste-Hottot, 78540 Vernouillet. T. 0139710017. *094274*

Versailles (Yvelines)
Athis, Claude d', Passage Geôle, 78000 Versailles.
T. 0139490088. *094275*
Beugnot, Claire & Xavier, 33 Rue Albert-Joly, 78000 Versailles. T. 0139250185. *094276*
Galerie Saint-Louis, 11 Rue Orient, 78000 Versailles.
T. 0130215494. *094277*
Katana-ya, 14 Rue Baillet-Reviron, 78000 Versailles.
T. 0139027979. *094278*
Nollinger, Marie-Christine, 33 Av Normandie, 78000 Versailles. T. 0139558675. *094279*
Pendule, 5 Rue Baillage, 78000 Versailles.
T. 0139506431. *094280*

Perrault, Gilles, 12 Rue Montbauron, 78000 Versailles. T. 0139022429, Fax 0130212447. (furniture, sculptures) *094281*

Verteillac (Dordogne)
Loubiat, Alain, Fons-de-la-Brousse, 24320 Verteillac. T. 0553915204. *094282*

Vesoul (Haute-Saône)
Centre Régional de Restauration d'Oeuvres d'Art, Rte Saint-Loup, 70000 Vesoul. T. 0384766330, Fax 0384768752. *094283*

Vic-Fezensac (Gers)
Fauroux, Philippe, Rte Auch, 32190 Vic-Fezensac. T. 0562064676. *094284*

Vichy (Allier)
Mar, Manuel, Bât B Cité Ailes, 03200 Vichy. T. 0470598267. *094285*
Rodenas, Philippe, 14 Rue Lavoisier, 03200 Vichy. T. 0470316009. *094286*

Vieux-Thann (Haut-Rhin)
Mobiliocase, 35 Rue Charles-de-Gaulle, 68800 Vieux-Thann. T. 0389375314. *094287*

Vigneux-sur-Seine (Essonne)
Anson, Marceline, 22 Rue Prés-Lakota, 91270 Vigneux-sur-Seine. T. 0169034492. *094288*
Pellet, Patrice, 105bis Av Paul-Vaillant-Couturier, 91270 Vigneux-sur-Seine. T. 0169405409. *094289*

Vignoles (Côte-d'Or)
Atelier Régional de Restauration des Eléments du Patrimoine (A.R.R.E.P.), 5 Rue Châteaux, Château de Vignoles, 21200 Vignoles. T. 0380246816. *094290*

Ville-d'Avray (Hauts-de-Seine)
Antonoff, Oleg, 64 Rue Saint-Cloud, 92410 Ville-d'Avray. T. 0147503084. *094291*
Cuvillier, Christine, 41 Rue Corot, 92410 Ville-d'Avray. T. 0147093687. *094292*

Villeblevin (Yonne)
Clastres, Jacques, 80 Grande Rue, 89720 Villeblevin. T. 0386961022. *094293*

Villeneuve-d'Ascq (Nord)
Chris'Ary, 114 Rue Jean-Jaurès, 59650 Villeneuve-d'Ascq. T. 0320984365. *094294*

Villeneuve-le-Roi (Val-de-Marne)
Etat d'Art, Pass Paul-Barrou, 94290 Villeneuve-le-Roi. T. 0145970464. *094295*

Villeneuve-sur-Lot (Lot-et-Garonne)
Américi, Francis, 42 Rue Agen, 47300 Villeneuve-sur-Lot. T. 0553701425. *094296*
Atelier Aquitain de Restauration, Etude Patrimoine Archéologique (A.A.R.E.P.A.), 1 Pl Saint-Sernin, 47300 Villeneuve-sur-Lot. T. 0553706519. *094297*
Deloubes, Marie Noëlle, 5 Pl Egalité, 47300 Villeneuve-sur-Lot. T. 0553491527. *094298*
Leclerc, Alain, 194 Av Eysses, 47300 Villeneuve-sur-Lot. T. 0553704053. *094299*

Villersexel (Haute-Saône)
Garcia, José, 553 Rue 13-Septembre-1944, 70110 Villersexel. T. 0384634513. *094300*

Villetoureix (Dordogne)
Carvalho, Francisco de, Le Moulin-du-Pont-La-Borie, 24600 Villetoureix. T. 0553902516, Fax 0553905627. *094301*

Villeurbanne (Rhône)
Atelier Dedieu, 20 Rue Dedieu, 69100 Villeurbanne. T. 0472744928. *094302*
Seguin, 43 Rue Hippolyte-Kahn, 69100 Villeurbanne. T. 0478848884, Fax 0478685170. *094303*

Vincennes (Val-de-Marne)
ABP, 8 Rue Giraudineau, 94300 Vincennes. T. 0143982377. *094304*
ABP, 177 Rue Diderot, 94300 Vincennes. T. 0148081447. *094305*

Buche, Pierre, 63 Rue Jarry, 94300 Vincennes. T. 0148085041. *094306*
Grise, 19 Av Franklin-Roosevelt, 94300 Vincennes. T. 0143983036. *094307*
Poinsard, Roland, 5 Rue Fraternité, 94300 Vincennes. T. 0143288761. *094308*

Viroflay (Yvelines)
Collot, Henri, 5 All Belvédère, 78220 Viroflay. T. 0130245161. *094309*

Vitry-sur-Seine (Val-de-Marne)
Dominguez-Lesage, Maryse, 22bis Rue Malassis, 94400 Vitry-sur-Seine. T. 0149606960. *094310*
Hejtmanek, Regina, 104 Av Colonel-Fabien, 94400 Vitry-sur-Seine. T. 0146777239. *094311*

Voiron (Isère)
Foralosso, Michel, 53 Av Paviot, 38500 Voiron. T. 0476056705. *094312*

Voulx (Seine-et-Marne)
Ribot, Christian, 4 Rue Merdereau, 77940 Voulx. T. 64319452. *094313*

Vouvray (Indre-et-Loire)
Gicquel, Pierre, 4 Rue Commerce, 37210 Vouvray. T. 0547527786, Fax 0547526827. *094314*

Yerres (Essonne)
Corvaisier, Pierre, 52 Rue Charles-de-Gaulle, 91330 Yerres. T. 0169480297. *094315*

Ymeray (Eure-et-Loir)
Domenech, Jean-Paul, 5 Rue Chapitre, 28320 Ymeray. T. 0237316166. *094316*

Yvetot-Bocage (Manche)
Nouvelle Bodin, 7 Tapotin, 50700 Yvetot-Bocage. T. 0233402033. *094317*

Germany

Aachen (Nordrhein-Westfalen)
Schoenen, Wilhelmstr 103, 52070 Aachen. T. (0241) 504561, Fax 902061. (Gemälde, Skulpturen, Rahmen) *094318*

Aichhalden (Baden-Württemberg)
Vaia, E., Uhlandstr. 3, 78733 Aichhalden. T. (07422) 8932. *094319*

Aichtal (Baden-Württemberg)
Weihs, Fritz, Gemeindeberg, 72631 Aichtal. T. (07127) 7400. *094320*

Altenburg (Thüringen)
Kohlbach, Thomas, Kreuzstr. 3, 04600 Altenburg. T. (03447) 314044, Fax (03447) 314044. *094321*

Altendorf (Bayern)
Frenzel, Rainer, Birkenstr. 1, 96146 Altendorf. T. (09545) 5586. *094322*

Alzey (Rheinland-Pfalz)
Müller, Rudolf, Hermann-Ehler-Str. 4, 55232 Alzey. T. (06731) 435 76. *094323*

Ampfing (Bayern)
Holzner, K., Am Vorland 10, 84539 Ampfing. T. (08636) 5586, Fax 698996. *094324*

Arnsdorf (Sachsen)
Schwarzmeier, Hauptstr 10, 01475 Arnsdorf. T. (035200) 24279, Fax 23235. (Furniture) *094325*

Auerbach, Kr. Deggendorf (Bayern)
Beer, Franz X., Zolling 3, 94530 Auerbach, Kr. Deggendorf. T. 74 16. *094326*

Baar-Ebenhausen (Bayern)
Wiedemann, Konrad, Werkstr 33, 85107 Baar-Ebenhausen. T. (08453) 330008, Fax (08137) 2543. *094327*

Bad Bevensen (Niedersachsen)
Hille, Henning, Medinger Str 18, 29549 Bad Bevensen. T. (05821) 2474, Fax 42474. (Carpets, furniture) *094328*

Bad Ems (Rheinland-Pfalz)
Wegmann, Hans, Otto-Balzer-Str 16, 56130 Bad Ems. T. (02603) 2725. *094329*

Bad Homburg vor der Höhe (Hessen)
Antik-Möbel-Restaurierung, Dorotheenstr 21, 61348 Bad Homburg vor der Höhe. T. (06172) 690150, Fax (06172) 690150. *094330*

Bad Oeynhausen (Nordrhein-Westfalen)
Schmidt, Karin, Auf der Brake 16, 32549 Bad Oeynhausen. T. (05731) 529 55. *094331*
Sturhan, Alter Rehmer Weg 163,, 32547 Bad Oeynhausen. T. (05731) 22972. *094332*

Bad Oldesloe (Schleswig-Holstein)
Mannewitz, Botho, Robert-Koch-Str. 29, 23843 Bad Oldesloe, T. (04531) 35 62. *094333*

Bad Schönborn (Baden-Württemberg)
Arnold, Gotthard, 76669 Bad Schönborn. *094334*

Bad Soden (Hessen)
Sommer, Harald, Königsteiner Str 20A, 65812 Bad Soden. T. (06196) 21719. *094335*

Bad Tölz (Bayern)
Eichmann, Gerd-Michael, Königsdorferstr. 4, 83646 Bad Tölz. T. (08041) 410 27. *094336*

Bad Vilbel (Hessen)
Umlauf, Osswald, Nidderstr. 19, 61118 Bad Vilbel. T. (06101) 326 55. *094337*

Baden-Baden (Baden-Württemberg)
Benner, Gloria, Maria-Viktoria-Str. 12, 76530 Baden-Baden. T. (07221) 26999. *094338*
Kolb, Erich, Lichtentaler Str 56, 76530 Baden-Baden. T. (07221) 25575. *094339*
Kolb, Erich, Lichtentaler Str. 56, 76530 Baden-Baden. T. (07221) 38972, 25575, Fax (07221) 38982. *094340*
Runge, K., Stolzenbergstr. 13, 76532 Baden-Baden. T. (07221) 53704. *094341*

Batzdorf (Sachsen)
Schmidt, Joseph-Dieter, Schloß, 01665 Batzdorf. T. (03521) 453210. *094342*

Bayreuth (Bayern)
Lehr, Erwin, Quellhöfe 5, 95447 Bayreuth. T. (0921) 65825. *094343*

Bergheim (Nordrhein-Westfalen)
Hirsch & Söhne, H., Oswaldstr 5, 50126 Bergheim. T. (02271) 64844. *094344*

Berlin
Andro, Willi, Lützowstr. 22, 10785 Berlin. T. (030) 2614194, Fax (030) 2628602. *094345*
Antikwerkstatt, Waldemarstr. 24, 10999 Berlin. T. (030) 651146. *094346*
Apel, Hans, Thorwaldsenstr. 4, 12157 Berlin. T. (030) 7964124. *094347*
Bär, Manfred, Gäblerstr. 16, 13086 Berlin. T. (030) 3662449. *094348*
Bild & Rahmen, Ludwigkirchstr. 9, 10719 Berlin. T. (030) 891 64 92. *094349*

Böhm, Hans, Borstellstr. 55, 12167 Berlin.
T. (030) 796 47 96. *094350*
Bondzio, Ulrich, Oranienburger Str. 53, 10115 Berlin.
T. (030) 282 86 95. *094351*
Budig, Robert, Schlüterstr. 65, 10625 Berlin.
T. (030) 313 47 58. *094352*
Demmin, Erich, Otto-Suhr-Allee 25, 10585 Berlin.
T. (030) 341 41 36. *094353*
Derz, Ralf, Massolleweg 11b, 14089 Berlin.
T. (030) 365 88 73. *094354*
Dillmann, H., Schlüterstr. 48, 10629 Berlin.
T. (030) 881 93 02. *094355*
Döbler, R.H., Keithstr. 8, 10787 Berlin.
T. (030) 211 93 44. *094356*
Fesseler, K., Stromstr. 35, 10551 Berlin.
T. (030) 395 11 98. *094357*
Feyerabend, Karl, Naumannstr. 33, Haus 3, 10829
Berlin. *094358*
Franke, Hans-Joachim, Winterfeldtstr 46, 10781 Berlin.
T. (030) 2162625, Fax 2169249. (Bücher) *094359*
Fuhrmann, Jacob, Mommsenstr. 43, 10629 Berlin.
T. (030) 323 57 24. *094360*
Giegold, Edgar, Neue Schönholzer Str. 13, 13187 Berlin.
T. (030) 482 65 30. *094361*
Grafe, Gottfried, Schönhauser Allee 65, 10437 Berlin.
T. (030) 4297106, Fax (030) 4297106. *094362*
Grundemann, Rudolf, Markelstr. 1, 12163 Berlin.
T. (030) 792 19 19. *094363*
Haack, Lars, Bergmannstr. 2, 10961 Berlin.
T. (030) 693 07 58. *094364*
Heider, Jörn, Schliemannstr. 5, 10437 Berlin.
T. (030) 449 66 39. *094365*
Hein, Jörg, Schreinerstr. 11, 10247 Berlin.
T. (030) 588 85 39. *094366*
Herrmann, Gunter, Lienhardweg 11, 12557 Berlin.
T. (030) 656 92 98. *094367*
Herwig, Anna, Bogotastr. 4, 14163 Berlin.
T. (030) 801 32 40. *094368*
Hirschfeld, A. & W., Hauptstr. 72, 10827 Berlin.
T. (030) 8523014. *094369*
Hohlfeld, Johannes, Nordufer 40, 13351 Berlin.
T. (030) 451 66 89. *094370*
Homburger, Hildegard, Krefelder Str 17, 10555 Berlin.
T. (030) 3912503. (Papier) *094371*
Keller-Kempas, Ruth, Prof., Bergengruenstr 27, 14129
Berlin. T. (030) 8014322, Fax 8028362.
(Papier) *094372*
Klein, Corinna von, Brandenburgische Str. 38, 10707
Berlin. T. (030) 891 90 90. *094373*
Klix, U., Steglitzer Damm 25, 12169 Berlin.
T. (030) 795 43 40. *094374*
König, Katrin, Metzer Str 24, 10405 Berlin.
T. (030) 4422011. (Gemälde) *094375*
Kohnert, Jacob, KG, Wilmersdorfer Str. 60/61, 10627
Berlin. T. (030) 323 40 64. *094376*
Korbel, Barbara, Großgörschenstr. 5, 10827 Berlin.
T. (030) 782 05 49. *094377*
Krassnig & Sturm-Larondelle, Oppelner Str. 33, 10997
Berlin. T. (030) 611 53 06. *094378*
Krüger, Meinhard, Wendenschloßstr. 95, 12559 Berlin.
T. (030) 6543349, Fax (030) 6540154. *094379*
Kunze, Gerhard, Frankfurter Allee 59, 10247 Berlin.
T. (030) 5890936, Fax (030) 6097588. *094380*
Lärisch, Alfred, Keithstr. 8, 10787 Berlin.
T. (030) 24 65 54. *094381*
Lampertius, Jörg, Fichtestr. 3, 10967 Berlin.
T. (030) 3138070, 6923385, 6933530. *094382*
Langfeld, Heinz, Lichtenrader Damm 41-43, 12305
Berlin. *094383*
Lapadula, Francesco, Beckerstr. 2, 12157 Berlin.
T. (030) 855 38 08. *094384*
Lehmann, Rosemarie, Saarower Weg 2, 12589 Berlin.
T. (030) 648 01 96, Fax 6480196. *094385*
Leonhardt, Rainer W., Gierkeplatz 11, 10585 Berlin.
T. (030) 342 10 48. *094386*
Malfatti, Nino, Schillerstr. 94, 10625 Berlin.
T. (030) 31 72 20. *094387*
Mangold, Heinz, Gustav-Müller-Platz 2, 10829 Berlin.
T. (030) 782 94 61. *094388*
Möller, Rudolf, Einsteinufer 63-65, 10587 Berlin.
T. (030) 341 62 50. *094389*
Müller, Marie, Fischerinsel 2, 10179 Berlin.
T. (030) 2011353. *094390*

Niederhäusern, Rudolf von, Krumme Str. 52, 10585 Berlin. T. (030) 312 98 99. *094391*
Nitsch, Brigitte, Ansbacher Str. 65, 10777 Berlin.
T. (030) 213 84 72. *094392*
Noack, Hermann, Fehlerstr 8, 12161 Berlin.
T. (030) 8216387, Fax 8214922. (Brass sculptures and
monuments) *094393*
Olczak, D. Ewa, Bleibtreustr 42, 10623 Berlin.
T. (030) 8834960, Fax 8834828. (Gemälde, Ikonen,
Holzskulpturen mit Fassung) *094394*
Palitza, Ulf, Detmolder Str. 64b, 10715 Berlin.
T. (030) 854 25 08. *094395*
Prückner, Gerhard, Nollendorfstr 20, 10777
Berlin. *094396*
Ritscher-Sandkuhl, Helga, Prinz-Friedrich-Leopold-Str.
5, 14129 Berlin. T. (030) 8034598,
Fax (030) 8035152. *094397*
Rockel, Roland, Parforceheide 102, 14163 Berlin.
T. (030) 796 55 56. *094398*
Ruthenberg von Klein, Ruth, Brandenburgische Str. 38,
10707 Berlin. T. (030) 891 90 90. *094399*
Scheuer, Cynthia, Fritschestr. 60a, 10627 Berlin.
T. (030) 317100. *094400*
Schleede, Jens, Pestalozzistr 88b, 10625 Berlin.
T. (030) 3128435, Fax 3139270. *094401*
Schütze, Alwin, Landauer Str. 9, 14197 Berlin.
T. (030) 8214927. (Clocks, brass, metall
objects) *094402*
Schulz, Michael, Breite Str. 18, 12167 Berlin.
T. (030) 822 85 51. *094403*
Specht, P.-M., Freiheit 28, 12057 Berlin.
T. (030) 332 83 57. *094404*
Stantschew, Matey, Rigaerstr 39, 10247 Berlin. (paintings, icons) *094405*
Stenzel, Willi, Donaustr. 24, 12043 Berlin.
T. (030) 624 24 42. *094406*
Stolle, Wolf-Rüdiger, Bayreuther Str. 9a, 10789 Berlin.
T. (030) 2181666. *094407*
Suckau, Irmgard, Torstr 231, 10115 Berlin.
T. (030) 2822822, Fax 2822822. (Gemälde) *094408*
Thurow, Gerhard, Marienburger Str 27, 10405 Berlin.
T. (030) 4413018, Fax 4413118. (Möbel,
Holzobjekte) *094409*
Tiemeyer, Ria, Damaschkestr. 22, 10711 Berlin.
T. (030) 324 62 91, Fax (030) 324 39 12. *094410*
Titzke, Bernard, Boxhagener Str. 117, 10245 Berlin.
T. (030) 589 58 59. *094411*
Wessling, Robert, Gerichtstr. 45, 13347 Berlin.
T. (030) 4622481, Fax (030) 4627844. *094412*
Winkler, Klaus, Burgwallstr. 57, 13129 Berlin.
T. (030) 481 79 88. *094413*
Wittkowoki, Evolyn, Am Ficchtal 28, 14169 Berlin.
T. (030) 8132316. *094414*
Wolff, R., Geisbergstr. 29, 10777 Berlin.
T. (030) 2111861, Fax (030) 2111861. *094415*

Berne (Niedersachsen)
Lohrengel, Manfred, Bettingbühren 25, 27804 Berne.
T. (04406) 1828. *094416*
Skrypzak, Georg, Schlüterdeich 7, 27804 Berne.
T. (04406) 1588. *094417*

Bernkastel-Kues (Rheinland-Pfalz)
Becker, Otmar, Cusanusstr. 6, 54470 Bernkastel-Kues.
T. (06531) 8327, 3926. *094418*
Kullmann, Wuppertalstr. 14, 54470 Bernkastel-Kues.
T. (06531) 8399. *094419*

Besigheim (Baden-Württemberg)
Wengerter, Horst, & Annette Rothmayr, Heckenweg 1,
74354 Besigheim. T. (07143) 349 34,
Fax 349 34. *094420*

Bexbach (Saarland)
Geldermans, Eleonore, Banatstr 9, 66450 Bexbach.
T. (06826) 800308. (Paintings) *094421*

Biebesheim (Hessen)
Becker, Bernd, Breslauerstr. 10, 64584 Biebesheim.
T. (06258) 7114. *094422*

Bielefeld (Nordrhein-Westfalen)
Nonnenbruch, Splittenbrede 11, 33613 Bielefeld.
T. (0521) 88 79 70. *094423*

Nonnenbruch, Splittenbrede 11, 33613 Bielefeld.
T. (0521) 88 79 70, Fax 887970. *094424*
Spiegel, A. von, Senne 1, 33602 Bielefeld.
T. (0521) 49 11 01. *094425*
Stehr, Volker J., Gehrenberg 15, 33602 Bielefeld.
T. (0521) 619 62, 838 70. *094426*

Bietigheim-Bissingen (Baden-Württemberg)
Heiland, Stefan, Hauptstr. 17, 74321 Bietigheim-Bissingen. T. (07142) 413 09. *094427*

Billerbeck (Nordrhein-Westfalen)
Müthing, Gerleve 15, 48727 Billerbeck.
T. (02541) 85237. (Furniture) *094428*

Binzen (Baden-Württemberg)
Messerschmidt, Cornelius, Basel Str. 7, 79589 Binzen.
T. (07621) 6 23 11. *094429*

Bippen (Niedersachsen)
Markau, Heinz, Am Feldkamp 18, 49626 Bippen.
T. (05909) 285. *094430*

Bochum (Nordrhein-Westfalen)
Heinsch, Jakobstr. 15, 44789 Bochum.
T. (0234) 30 82 15. *094431*

Bonn (Nordrhein-Westfalen)
Andersen-Bergdoll, Greta, Arndtstr 29, 53113 Bonn.
T. (0228) 217809. *094432*
Eiblmaier, Josef, Gudenauer Weg 34, 53127 Bonn.
T. (0228) 28 14 48. *094433*
Kieszkowska, J., Prinz-Albert-Str. 47, 53113 Bonn.
T. (0228) 21 09 94. *094434*
Kurek, Stanislaw, Bonner Str 23, 53173 Bonn.
T. (0228) 314260, Fax 314260. (Gemälde) *094435*
Leogrande, Vitantonio, Elsässer Str. 33-39, 53175 Bonn.
T. (0228) 35 24 05. *094436*
Mertes-Schön, Eva, Wiedemannstr. 28, 53173 Bonn.
T. (0228) 36 16 46. *094437*
Müller, Ernst Ludwig, Niebuhrstr. 12, 53113 Bonn.
T. (0228) 21 57 19. *094438*
Müller, Siegfried, Gotenstr. 136, 53175 Bonn.
T. (0228) 37 57 62. *094439*
Nobis & Lancier, Wallfahrtsweg 10-12, 53115 Bonn.
T. (0228) 22 31 46. *094440*
Procner-Matusiak, Halina, Postfach 200942, 53139
Bonn. T. (0228) 325151, Fax 354810.
(Textilien) *094441*
Sobeck, R., Sternenburgstr 62, 53115 Bonn.
T. (0228) 9140092, Fax 9140093. (Antiquitäten,
Uhren) *094442*

Bramsche (Niedersachsen)
Icks, Horst, An der Schule 23, 49565 Bramsche.
T. (05468) 468. *094443*

Braunfels (Hessen)
Schlafke, 35619 Braunfels. T. (06442) 4457.
(Furniture) *094444*

Braunschweig (Niedersachsen)
Jaeschke, Olaf, Schuhstr. 42, 38100 Braunschweig.
T. (0531) 243120, Fax 2431222. *094445*

Lauschke, Erna, Ritterbrunnen 1, 38100 Braunschweig.
T. (0531) 497 49. *094446*

Bremen
Beihl, Werner, Vor dem Steintor 34, 28203 Bremen.
T. (0421) 76971, Fax 70 54 80. *094447*

Boekholt, Lockwood, Platz, Am Hilgeskamp 42, 28325
Bremen. T. (0421) 40 40 34. *094448*
Boldizsar, Zoltan, Borgfelder Deich 21, 28357 Bremen.
T. (0421) 27 22 20. *094449*
von der Brüggen, Falk, Marschstr 35, 28309 Bremen.
T. (0421) 453040, Fax 453040. *094450*
D'Agostino, N./ L. Miessner, Gastfeldstr. 91/Hof, 28201
Bremen. T. (0421) 53 04 84. *094451*
Gérard, Parkstr 73, 28209 Bremen.
T. (0421) 342260, Fax 342260. (Uhren, Antike
Mechanik) *094452*
Grüttert, Sögestr. 70, 28195 Bremen.
T. (0421) 13056. *094453*
Heuer, Peter, Zur Munte 6, 28213 Bremen.
T. (0421) 211126, Fax 2239599. *094454*
Hoffmann, Anne, Franz-Grashof-Str. 11-15, 28201 Bre-
men. T. (0421) 87 47 31. *094455*
Kossann, Roger, Stader Str 35, 28205 Bremen.
T. (0421) 4988809, Fax 434746. (Möbel,
Holzobjekte) *094456*
Mertens, Andreas, Rockwinkeler Heerstr. 42, 28355
Bremen. T. (0421) 25 91 02, Fax 25 05 73. *094457*
Roche, Thomas, Fedelhören 30, 28203 Bremen.
T. (0421) 32 37 47. *094458*
Thiessen, H.-G., Franz-Grashof-Str. 11-15, 28201 Bre-
men. T. (0421) 87 07 61. *094459*

Briedel (Rheinland-Pfalz)
Lawen, Ferdinand, Eltzerhofstr 3, 56867 Briedel.
T. (06542) 4827, Fax 5835. *094460*

Bruchhausen (Rheinland-Pfalz)
Hartmann, Johannes, Orsberger Str. 1, 53572 Bruchhausen. T. (02224) 29 95. *094461*

Bruchhausen-Vilsen (Niedersachsen)
Reinhardt, Wilhelm, Syker Str 22-24, 27305 Bruchhausen-Vilsen. T. (04252) 1666, Fax 1666. *094462*

Brühl (Nordrhein-Westfalen)
Müller, Karl-Heinz, Pingsdorferstr 143, 50321 Brühl.
T. (02232) 44143. *094463*

**Buchholz in der Nordheide (Niedersach-
sen)**
Ohl, Leo, Roßdorfstr 6, 21244 Buchholz in der Nordheide. T. (04181) 7179. *094464*

Burgen (Rheinland-Pfalz)
Theuer-Grings, Claudia, Frankenweg 7, 56332 Burgen.
T. (02605) 43 72. *094465*

Burgwedel (Niedersachsen)
Schmalstieg, Schulze-Delitzsch-Str. 19, 30938 Burgwedel. T. (05139) 7027, 7028, Fax 2454. *094466*

Buxtehude (Niedersachsen)
Senger, Karl Heinrich, Kellerkuhle 8, 21614 Buxtehude.
T. (04161) 8 23 23. *094467*

Calw (Baden-Württemberg)
Maschke, Walter, Schafackerweg 20, 75365 Calw.
T. (07051) 510 45. *094468*

Clausthal-Zellerfeld (Niedersachsen)
Gisevius, Bernhard, Klepperberg 4, 38678 Clausthal-
Zellerfeld. T. (05323) 35 53. *094469*

Cloppenburg (Niedersachsen)
Frederichs, Josef, Molberger Str. 13, 49661 Cloppenburg. T. (04471) 37 30. *094470*

Coburg (Bayern)
Lüdeke, Mohrenstr. 10, 96450 Coburg.
T. (09561) 39605, Fax 18464. *094471*

Cramberg (Rheinland-Pfalz)
Meffert, Erwin, Hauptstr. 6, 65558 Cramberg.
T. (06439) 269. *094472*

Dänischenhagen (Schleswig-Holstein)
Poley, Doris, Zum Wasserwerk 57, 02301 Dänischenhagen. T. (04349) 12 22. *094473*

Darmstadt (Hessen)
Eisenhauer, Wolfgang, Glockengartenweg 12, 64291
Darmstadt. T. (06151) 378 09. *094474*

Grobbauer, Adelungstr. 15, 64283 Darmstadt.
T. (06151) 29 19 70. *094475*
Höfler, Heinz, Haardtring 154, 64295 Darmstadt.
T. (06151) 31 53 16. *094476*
Schulz, Barbara, Wilhelminenstr 16, 64283 Darmstadt.
T. (06151) 291911. *094477*

Dasing (Bayern)
Schmied, Horst, Alpenstr,. 47, 86453 Dasing.
T. (08205) 15 61. *094478*

Deggendorf (Bayern)
Motz, Anton, Bergerstr. 14, 94469 Deggendorf.
T. (0991) 262 59, Fax 22250. *094479*

Delmenhorst (Niedersachsen)
Usenko, H., Jägerstr. 9, 27755 Delmenhorst.
T. (04221) 622 09. *094480*

Dessau (Sachsen-Anhalt)
Ardelt, Frank, Werderstr 29, 06844 Dessau.
T. (0340) 2201162. *094481*

Dielheim (Baden-Württemberg)
Fuchs, Eugen, Kolpingstr. 6, 69234 Dielheim.
T. (06222) 73833. *094482*

Dießen am Ammersee (Bayern)
Fehler, Frank, Currypark 15, 86911 Dießen am Ammersee. T. (08807) 77 80. *094483*
Fischer, Arno, Stagurastr 13, 86911 Dießen am Ammersee. T. (08807) 1640. (Gemälde) *094484*

Dinkelsbühl (Bayern)
Ramms, Manfred, Neustädtlein 20, 91550
Dinkelsbühl. *094485*

Dissen (Niedersachsen)
Fark & A. Osterheider, F., Große Str 14, 49201 Dissen.
T. (05421) 2146, Fax (05421) 4196. *094486*

Dorfen (Bayern)
Münzenloher, Franz, Furth 1, 84405 Dorfen.
T. (08081) 571, Fax (08081) 1840. *094487*

Drensteinfurt (Nordrhein-Westfalen)
Schöttelndreyer, Eickendorf 21, 48317 Drensteinfurt.
T. (02508) 509, Fax (02508) 1049. *094488*

Dresden (Sachsen)
Flade, Jochen, Eichbuschweg 3, 01326 Dresden.
T. (0351) 2610804, Fax 2610804. (Holz,
Möbel) *094489*
Friedrich, Barbara & Susanne, Liliensteinstr. 16a, 01277
Dresden. T. (0351) 2361525,
Fax (0351) 495 23 40. *094490*
Gabriel, Peter, Dölzschener Str. 49, 01159 Dresden.
T. (0351) 4116234. *094491*
Gommlich, Torstr. 36, 01127 Dresden.
T. (0351) 57 77 38. *094492*
Hempel, Christian, Sierksstr 25, 01279 Dresden.
T. (0351) 376939. *094493*
Kless, Elvira, Neubertstr 21, 01307 Dresden.
T. (0351) 4408687, Fax 4408687. *094494*
Lang, Münchner Str 26, 01187 Dresden.
T. (0351) 4715096, Fax 4715096. *094495*
Liebner, Günther, Pillnitzer Landstr. 29, 01326
Dresden. *094496*
Mohrmann, Robert-Matzke-Str. 34, 01127
Dresden. *094497*
Sandner, Ingo, Prof. Dr., Ingo, Prof.Dr., Schwenkstr. 5,
01326 Dresden. T. (0351) 370 16. *094498*
Sperling, Reinhard, Hosterwitzer Str. 22, 01259 Dres-
den. T. (0351) 2013559, Fax (0351) 2013559. *094499*
Wolf & Eckert, Quohrener Str. 31, 01324 Dresden.
T. (0351) 4605687, Fax (0351) 4695687. *094500*

Düsseldorf (Nordrhein-Westfalen)
Ackens, Gregor, Herzogstr 47, 40215 Düsseldorf.
T. (0211) 3850506, Fax 3850507. *094501*
Barro, Maria M., Dr., Cecilienallee 62, 40474 Düsseldorf.
T. (0211) 4708128, Fax 4708328. (Gemälde) *094502*
Breitenstein, Anne, Poststr. 13, 40213 Düsseldorf.
T. (0211) 326934. *094503*
Eckhardt, Alfred, Metzkauser Str. 44, 40625 Düsseldorf.
T. (0211) 29 32 33. *094504*

Euler & Roswitha Friedelt, Sabine, Dr, Jülicher Str 14,
40477 Düsseldorf. T. (0211) 461832,
Fax 461832. *094505*
Falkenberg, P., Langerstr. 38, 40233 Düsseldorf.
T. (0211) 7331939. *094506*
Heller, Hans-Jürgen, Schwelmer Str. 2, 40235 Düssel-
dorf. T. (0211) 675741, Fax (0211) 604464. *094507*
Hennigs, Claudia Michaela von, Arnheimer Str 74,
40489 Düsseldorf. T. (0211) 4080103. *094508*
Hentschel, G., Volmerswerther Str. 32, 40221 Düssel-
dorf. T. (0211) 39 37 41. *094509*
Lappe, K., Auf'm Hennekamp 23, 40225 Düsseldorf.
T. (0211) 33 10 11. *094510*
Löffelsend, Rolf, Lanker Str. 8, 40545 Düsseldorf.
T. (0211) 57 86 79. *094511*
Luckow, Kai H., Karl-Anton-Str. 6, 40211 Düsseldorf.
T. (0211) 16 12 34. *094512*
Nowack, J. & G. Cattafesta, Spichernstr. 35, 40476 Düs-
seldorf. T. (0211) 48 88 03. *094513*
Parl-Guntermann, Käthe, Lambertusstr. 6, 40213 Düs-
seldorf. T. (0211) 19847. *094514*
Reuter, Walter, Leuchtenberger Kirchweg 14, 40489
Düsseldorf. T. (0211) 40 22 17. *094515*
Söhn-Veigl, Barbara, Jülicher Str 14, 40476 Düsseldorf.
T. (0211) 446132. *094516*
Uhlig, Bernd, Kronprinzenstr. 116, 40217 Düsseldorf.
T. (0211) 34 17 18. *094517*
Van Eick, Manfred, Germaniastr. 35, 40223 Düsseldorf.
T. (0211) 39 11 88. *094518*
Vierth, Hans-Heinrich, Kaiserstr 28, 40479 Düsseldorf.
T. (0211) 4912414. *094519*

Ebern (Bayern)
Zeidler, Ulrike, Karlsbader Str. 2, 96106 Ebern.
T. (09531) 6531. *094520*

Eglfing (Bayern)
Mack, Toni, Hauptstr. 12, 82436 Eglfing. T. (08847) 315,
Fax (08847) 254. *094521*

Egling (Bayern)
Bleymaier, E. A., Schallkofen, 82544 Egling.
T. (08176) 7403. *094522*

Eichenau (Bayern)
Stemp, Alfred, Schillerstr 39, 82223 Eichenau.
T. (08141) 80293, Fax 70400. *094523*

Eicklingen (Niedersachsen)
Eipper, Paul-Bernhard, Höfnerwinkel 11b, 29358 Eicklingen. T. (05149) 1648, Fax 1648. (Paintings,
sculptures) *094524*

Eilsleben (Sachsen-Anhalt)
Wagener, Günter, R.-Breitscheid-Str 4, 39365 Eilsleben.
T. (039409) 6634, Fax 6634. (Polstermöbel) *094525*

Elze (Niedersachsen)
Bohland, Joseph, Dr., Am Knick 1, 31008 Elze.
T. (05124) 2154. *094526*

Emkendorf (Schleswig-Holstein)
Seebach, Jochen, Schloß, 24802 Emkendorf.
T. (04330) 240, Fax (04330) 725. *094527*

Engelskirchen (Nordrhein-Westfalen)
Odendahl & Kretschmer, Im Auel 38, 51766 Engelskirchen. T. (02263) 21 62, Fax 801024. *094528*

Eppstein (Hessen)
Castle, Ian, Schäfergasse 3, 65817 Eppstein.
T. (06198) 33525. *094529*

Erbes-Büdesheim (Rheinland-Pfalz)
Heinz, Damaris, Schloss, 55234 Erbes-Büdesheim.
T. (06731) 417 29. *094530*

Erfurt (Thüringen)
Buse, Adelheid, Johann-Sebastian-Bach-Str 11, 99096
Erfurt. T. (0361) 3731992. *094531*

Erlangen (Bayern)
Barthelmeß, Eugen, Heuwaagstr. 12, 91054 Erlangen.
T. (09131) 2 14 50. *094532*
Hoffmann, Claudia, Luitpoldstr 6, 91054 Erlangen.
T. (09131) 24762. (Gemälde) *094533*

Esens (Niedersachsen)
Lehmann, Detlef, Westerstr. 13, 26427 Esens. *094534*

Essen (Nordrhein-Westfalen)
Herz, W., Veronikastr 69, 45131 Essen.
T. (0201) 79 26 85, Fax 792685. *094535*
Kaufhold, Heinz-Josef, Keplerstr. 104/06, 45147 Essen.
T. (0201) 70 62 02. *094536*
Tröstrum, Eva, Isenbergstr. 39, 45130 Essen.
T. (0201) 78 22 34. *094537*

Esslingen (Baden-Württemberg)
Cabanis & Troschke, Weilerweg 22-1, 73732 Esslingen.
T. (0711) 375381, Fax (0711) 378817. *094538*
Riehle, B., Kupfergasse 6, 73728 Esslingen.
T. (0711) 350131. *094539*

Euerdorf (Bayern)
Halbig, Georg & Sohn, Kissinger Str. 38, 97717 Euerdorf.
T. (09704) 219. *094540*

Feldafing (Bayern)
Froidl, Christian, Aumillerstr. 1, 82340 Feldafing.
T. (08157) 35 46. *094541*

Flonheim (Rheinland-Pfalz)
Höhn, Ulrich, Alzeyer Str. 13, 55237 Flonheim.
T. (06734) 431, Fax (06734) 8996. *094542*

Frankfurt am Main (Hessen)
Adrian, Johannes M., Am Waldgraben 12, 60529 Frankfurt am Main. T. (069) 666 78 69. *094543*
Antik, Gutzkowstr. 1, 60594 Frankfurt am Main.
T. (069) 61 83 28. *094544*
Berner, Reinhard, Eckenheimer Schulstr 22, 60435 Frankfurt am Main. T. (069) 5485922,
Fax 675622. *094545*
Dettmering, Christoph, Rotlintstr 14, 60316 Frankfurt am Main. T. (069) 447757, Fax 4304649. (Holzobjekte, Möbel) *094546*
Falkenau, Alte Gasse 6, 60313 Frankfurt am Main.
T. (069) 282750. (Glass) *094547*
Gamp, Corinna, Scheusenstr 11, 60327 Frankfurt am Main. T. (069) 233906. (Ceramics, China, Glass) *094548*
Herrlein, Klaus, Schulstr 1a, 60594 Frankfurt am Main.
T. (069) 613933, 624928. *094549*
Himmighoffen, Schillerstr 28, Steinkleestr 15, 60313 Frankfurt am Main. T. (069) 284066, 542054, Fax (069) 541523. *094550*
Kähler, Cordula, c/o Städt. Galerie Liebighaus, Schaumainkai 71, 60311 Frankfurt am Main.
T. (069) 62 13 89. *094551*
Krause, Helmut, Postfach 160454, 60067 Frankfurt am Main. T. (06105) 74306, Fax 74190. (Paintings) *094552*
Kress, Matthias, Eschersheimer Landstr 554b, 60433 Frankfurt am Main. T. (069) 526434. *094553*
Leonhardi, Friedrich, Altkönigstr. 11, 60323 Frankfurt am Main. T. (069) 72 70 60. *094554*
Muhle, Benedikt, Eckenheimer Schulstr. 22, 60435 Frankfurt am Main. T. (069) 548 59 22. *094555*
Nouri, N., Bornheimer Landstr. 18, 60316 Frankfurt am Main. T. (069) 59 85 57. *094556*
Osten, Detlef von der, Georg-Speyer-Str. 7, 60487 Frankfurt am Main. T. (069) 70 15 45. *094557*
Saalig, Heinrich, Lassallestr 1, 60386 Frankfurt am Main. T. (069) 413472. (Gemälde, Fresken) *094558*
Schramm, Otto, Niddastr. 64, 60329 Frankfurt am Main.
T. (069) 23 49 34. *094559*
Siebert, Fritz, Berliner Str 68, 60311 Frankfurt am Main.
T. (069) 284685, Fax (069) 541523. *094560*
Stapp, Rudolf hr, Berger Str. 21, 60316 Frankfurt am Main. T. (069) 49 41 65. *094561*
Tello, Helene, Eckenheimer Landstr. 318, 60435 Frankfurt am Main. T. (069) 54 11 30. *094562*
Vadala, Christina, Heidestr. 12, 60312 Frankfurt am Main. T. (069) 446549. *094563*
Wagner, Mörfelder Landstr. 116, 60598 Frankfurt am Main. T. (069) 62 58 80. *094564*
Wagner, Stephanie, Gartenstr. 70, 60596 Frankfurt am Main. T. (069) 61 87 21. *094565*

Freiburg (Baden-Württemberg)
Bauernfeind, Michael, Hofackerstr. 1, 79110 Freiburg.
T. (0761) 827 42. *094566*

Dold, Tony, Gerberau 2, 79098 Freiburg.
T. (0761) 241 17. *094567*
Ehret, Lucia, Dr., Dischlerstr. 21, 79117 Freiburg.
T. (0761) 690 15. *094568*
Gschöll, Emil Josef, Wippertstr. 3, 79100 Freiburg.
T. (0761) 40 23 43. *094569*

Friedberg (Bayern)
Binapfl, Alfred, Arthur Pichlerstr. 29/8, 86316 Friedberg.
T. (0821) 612 86. *094570*
Külmer, Renate von, Thomas-Mann-Str. 23, 86316 Friedberg. T. (0821) 635 40. *094571*

Friedrichsdorf, Taunus (Hessen)
Foucar, Ingeborg, Wilhelmstr 12, 61381 Friedrichsdorf, Taunus. *094572*
Schmid, Klaus-Peter, Nelkenweg 17, 61381 Friedrichsdorf, Taunus. T. (06175) 78493. *094573*

Füssen (Bayern)
Gingele, Gerhard, Tirolerstr. 11, 87629 Füssen.
T. (08362) 59 39. *094574*

Fulda (Hessen)
Kramer, Jean, Neuenberger Str 28, 36041 Fulda.
T. (0661) 97200, Fax 75670. (Paintings, stone, wood, metal) *094575*

Garbsen (Niedersachsen)
Dettmer, Berthold, Langestr. 5, 30827 Garbsen.
T. (05131) 62 93. *094576*

Geislingen an der Steige (Baden-Württemberg)
Hauke-Sommer, Renate, Südmährenstr 53, 73312 Geislingen. T. (07331) 60717. *094576a*
Steck, Wolfgang, Stuttgarter Str 50, 73312 Geislingen an der Steige. T. (07331) 63538. *094578*

Gelnhausen (Hessen)
Helmdach, G., Tolnauer Str. 15, 63571 Gelnhausen.
T. (06051) 611 99. (Paper) *094579*

Geltendorf (Bayern)
Höricht, Nikolai, Schloß Kaltenberg, 82269 Geltendorf.
T. (08193) 7977, Fax 5687. *094580*

Gernlinden (Bayern)
Herbich, Karl, R.-Diesel-Str 25, 82216 Gernlinden.
T. (08142) 14418, Fax 12704. (Metal art works) *094581*

Karl Herbich
Herstellung und
Restaurierung
von Metallkunstwerken

82216 Gernlinden, R.-Diesel-Str. 25
Fax 12704 ☎ (08142) 1 44 18

Gernsbach (Baden-Württemberg)
Panowsky, Alfred, Scheuernerstr. 34, 76593 Gernsbach.
T. (07224) 78 82. *094582*

Gescher (Nordrhein-Westfalen)
Lehmkuhl, Porsche Str. 5, 48712 Gescher. *094583*

Glauburg (Hessen)
Spruck, Gisela, Hof Leustadt, 63695 Glauburg.
T. (06041) 206. *094584*

Göttingen (Niedersachsen)
Mannig, Kurt, Calsowstr. 37, 37085 Göttingen.
T. (0551) 433 39. *094585*

Goslar (Niedersachsen)
Bacmeister, Ursula, Beuthener Weg 10, 38642 Goslar.
T. (05321) 831 50. *094586*
Flügge, Hans R., Wittenstr. 7, 38640 Goslar.
T. (05321) 220 17. *094587*

Grasberg (Niedersachsen)
Dietzsch, Paul-Uwe, Deepen, Wisch 11, 28879 Grasberg. T. (0408) 1813. *094588*

Grassau (Bayern)
Blüml, J. & A., Achentalstr. 11, 83224 Grassau.
T. (08641) 14 57. *094589*

Hagen (Nordrhein-Westfalen)
Cercle d'Art Orthodoxe du Sud-Est, Bolohstr. 39, 58093 Hagen. T. (02331) 520 60. *094590*

Haigerloch (Baden-Württemberg)
Kotalla, Ralf, Kätzling 2, 72401 Haigerloch.
T. (07474) 95360, Fax 953610. *094591*
Naeschke, Matthias, Fliederstr 7, 72401 Haigerloch.
T. (07474) 2613, Fax 2613. (Clocks) *094592*

Halblech (Bayern)
Fischer, Werner, Kulturenweg 4, 87642 Halblech.
T. (08368) 517. *094593*
Mahler, Xaver, Sonnenstr. 10, 87642 Halblech.
T. (08368) 446. *094594*

Hallbergmoos (Baden-Württemberg)
Schmidt, Horst, Forsthaus, Grüneckstr. 60, 85399 Hallbergmoos. T. (08169) 217. *094595*

Halle (Sachsen-Anhalt)
Schöne, Peter, Ulestr 2-3, 06114 Halle.
T. (0345) 3880450, Fax 3881851. *094596*

Hamburg
Bachem, Borselstr. 16, 22765 Hamburg.
T. (040) 390 69 12. *094597*
Böhler, Petra, Papenhuder Str 22, 22087 Hamburg.
T. (040) 2277787, Fax 2277787. *094598*
Brune, Matthias, Borselstr. 16, 22765 Hamburg.
T. (040) 390 03 09. *094599*
Dickel, Martin, Sillemstr 60, 20257 Hamburg.
T. (040) 495885, Fax 4916531. *094600*
Eith, Nicole, Usdorfer Landstr. 245, 22549 Hamburg.
T. (040) 800 22 95. *094601*
Frahm-Hessler, Franz, Radenwisch 45, 22457 Hamburg. *094602*
Guckel, Anna M., Stresemannstr 109, 22769 Hamburg.
T. (040) 435453, Fax 4304445. *094603*
Helwig, Monika, Müllenhoffweg 60, 22607 Hamburg.
T. (040) 828551, Fax (040) 8226118. *094604*
Hinkel, Ada, & Wihke Röh, Koppel 66, 20099 Hamburg.
T. (040) 24 69 13. *094605*
Hoppe, Thomas, Friedensallee 26, 22765 Hamburg.
T. (040) 3902112, Fax (040) 397192. *094606*
Jacobs, Erika, Johnsweg 2, 21077 Hamburg.
T. (040) 760 20 38. *094607*
Klack-Eitzen, Charlotte, Dr., Glindersweg 64, 21029 Hamburg. T. (040) 7211754, Fax 7211754. (Gemälde, Skulpturen) *094608*
Klement, Ina, Eppendorfer Weg 2, 20259 Hamburg.
T. (040) 439 89 57. *094609*
Metz, Anke & Günther, Kirchenredder 20, 22339 Hamburg. T. (040) 538 32 53. *094610*
Meyer, Harry, Haydnstr. 21, 22761 Hamburg.
T. (040) 899 13 31. *094611*
Motzek, Robert, Windmühlenweg 31, 22607 Hamburg.
T. (040) 82 52 23. *094612*
Offern, Franziska van, Prof., Eppendorfer Baum 4, 20249 Hamburg. T. (040) 48 42 10. *094613*
Reinecke, Kurt, Hopfensack 22, 20457 Hamburg.
T. (040) 32 40 83. *094614*
Rogalsky, Wandsbeker Allee 62, 22041 Hamburg.
T. (040) 68 20 16. *094615*

Roß, Betina, Borselstr. 16, 22765 Hamburg.
T. (040) 390 68 68. 094616
Rüsch, Andreas, Fabriciusstr. 121, 22177 Hamburg.
T. (040) 642 72 64. 094617
Scheidemann, Christian, Michaelisbrücke 1, 20459
Hamburg. T. (040) 363572, Fax 363573. 094618
Schleede, Thomas, Billw. Billdeich 330, 21033 Hamburg. T. (040) 7398366, Fax (040) 7340752. 094619
Schreiber, H., Brödermannsweg 55a, 22453 Hamburg.
T. (040) 553 24 83. 094620
Spies, V., Borselstr. 16, 22765 Hamburg.
T. (040) 390 68 78. 094621
Stritzky, Matthias von, Inselstr. 37, 22297 Hamburg.
T. (040) 511 02 80. 094622
Sudbrak, Uwe, Wandsbeker Königstr. 3, 22041 Hamburg. T. (040) 652 89 43. 094623
Weber, Helga Maria, Eppendorfer Baum 23, 20249 Hamburg. T. (040) 478593. 094624
Zwang, Christian, Paulinenallee 28, 20259 Hamburg.
T. (040) 43 76 43, Fax 4304207. 094625

Hannover (Niedersachsen)
Ansorge, Werner, Podbielskistr. 199, 30177 Hannover.
T. (0511) 69 17 27. 094626
Blome, Manfred Th., Hallerstr. 4, 30161 Hannover.
T. (0511) 77 61 06, 31 43 74. 094627
Brenske, Helmut, Machandelweg 11, 30419 Hannover.
T. (0511) 633667, Fax 633667. 094628
Canbaz, Lange-Feld-Str. 60, 30559 Hannover.
T. (0511) 51 71 43. 094629
Furmanek, P., Seelhorststr. 6, 30175 Hannover.
T. (0511) 81 84 76, Fax (0511) 28 11 10. 094630
Heller, Reinhold, Robertstr. 4, 30161 Hannover.
T. (0511) 66 46 98. 094631
Herbart, Wolfgang, Rotermundstr. 13d, 30165 Hannover. T. (0511) 350 23 70. 094632
Lamazza, Francesco, Podbielskistr. 3a, 30163 Hannover. T. (0511) 66 92 50. 094633
Mogge, Martina, Podbielskistr 48, 30177 Hannover.
T. (0511) 66 32 45. 094634
Schreiber, Irmgard, Zeppelinstr. 5, 30175 Hannover.
T. (0511) 28 15 28. 094635
Seemeyer, Adolf, Podbielskistr. 5, 30163 Hannover.
T. (0511) 66 14 57. 094636
Seidemann, Max, Friesenstr 22, 30161 Hannover.
T. (0511) 345171. 094637
Vogt, Bettina, Auf dem Lärchenberge 6, 30161 Hannover. T. (0511) 31 15 12. 094638
Voigt, Gerhard, Limmerstr. 44, 30451 Hannover.
T. (0511) 45 66 40. 094639
Weinhöppel, Joachim, Gretchenstr. 31,, 30161 Hannover. T. (0511) 348 12 34. 094640
Zurmöhle, Brabeckstr. 9, 30559 Hannover.
T. (0511) 51 25 46. 094641

Heidelberg (Baden-Württemberg)
Mabarez, Esmat, Friedrich-Ebert-Anlage 53b, 69117
Heidelberg. T. (06221) 28424, Fax 28424. (Orientteppiche, Kelims) 094642
Merkler, Josef, Gutenbergstr. 10, 69120 Heidelberg.
T. (06221) 76 80 45. 094643
Rotberg, H. W. Frhr. v., Landhausstr. 17, 69115 Heidelberg. T. (06221) 205 29. 094644
Stadler, Jonny, Lindengasse 1, 69121 Heidelberg.
T. (06221) 411191, Fax 411191. (Möbel, Holzobjekte, Rahmen) 094645

Heilbronn (Baden-Württemberg)
Blech, Wolfgang, Allee 12, 74072 Heilbronn.
T. (07131) 84151. 094646

Heiligenberg (Baden-Württemberg)
Hummel, Adi, Betenbrunnerstr. 8, 88633 Heiligenberg.
T. (07554) 85 77. 094647

Heiligenhaus (Nordrhein-Westfalen)
Fuchs, Hans, Langenbügeler Str. 101, 42579 Heiligenhaus. T. (02126) 697 33. 094648

Hemmingen (Baden-Württemberg)
Dietrich, Horst, Frh. v. Vambüler Str 6, 71282 Hemmingen. T. (07150) 959800. 094649

Hemmingen (Niedersachsen)
Kitzig, Erdmann, Alte Dorfstr 12, 30966 Hemmingen.
T. (0511) 424400. 094650

Hochheim (Hessen)
Textor, Wilma, Laternengasse 1, 65239 Hochheim.
T. (06146) 6692. 094651

Hofheim (Bayern)
Meindl, P., Eichelsdorf 28, 97461 Hofheim.
T. (09523) 432. 094652

Holzminden (Niedersachsen)
Nauwald, Heinz, Schlesierstr. 12, 37603 Holzminden.
T. (05531) 62 19. 094653

Hüfingen (Baden-Württemberg)
Sigwart, Klaus, Pfarrhausstr. 6, 78183 Hüfingen.
T. (0771) 75 56. 094654

Inzigkofen (Baden-Württemberg)
Heinzler, Franz, Kreuzäcker 4, 72514 Inzigkofen.
T. (07571) 51258, Fax 51258. (Gemälde) 094655

Jena (Thüringen)
Bruhm, Wolfgang, Ziegenhainer Str. 9, 07749
Jena. 094656

Kandern (Baden-Württemberg)
Volz, Stephanie, H.-Burte-Str 9, 79400 Kandern.
T. (07626) 6887. 094657

Karben (Hessen)
Kern, Wolfgang, Solmserweg 10, 61184 Karben.
T. (06039) 73 13. 094658

Karlsruhe (Baden-Württemberg)
Ferstl, Robert, Enzstr. 2, 76199 Karlsruhe.
T. (0721) 887368, Fax (0721) 885000. 094659
Leyendecker, Horst, Kirchstr. 20, 76229 Karlsruhe.
T. (0721) 48 24 81. 094660

Kassel (Hessen)
Bunge, Kurt, Prof., Kuhbergstr. 21, 34131 Kassel.
T. (0561) 3 25 13. 094661
Landgrebe, Georg, Harleshäuser Str. 11, 34130 Kassel.
T. (0561) 3 27 73. 094662
Wiegel, Heinz, Wolfhager Str. 357, 34128 Kassel.
T. (0561) 653 07. 094663

Kelkheim (Hessen)
Antikes & Kreatives im Holunderhof, Frankfurter Str 21, 65779 Kelkheim. T. (06195) 2000. 094664

Kempten (Bayern)
Opitz, Willi, Ankergässele 3, 87435 Kempten.
T. (0831) 28388. 094665

Kerpen (Nordrhein-Westfalen)
Kurth, Franz, Kolpingstr 21, 50171 Kerpen. 094666

Kevelaer (Nordrhein-Westfalen)
Janssen, H., Hoogeweg 16, 47623 Kevelaer.
T. (02832) 2281, Fax (02832) 3902. 094667

Kiel (Schleswig-Holstein)
Rendtorff, Barbara, Muhliusstr. 49, 24103 Kiel.
T. (0431) 55 23 22. 094668

Köln (Nordrhein-Westfalen)
Dautzenberg, Bruno, St.-Apern-Str. 56, 50667 Köln.
T. (0221) 257 70 60. 094669
Gerber, Am Römerturm 7, 50667 Köln.
T. (0221) 257 50 87. 094670
Großer Bachem, Großer Griechenmarkt 39, 50676 Köln.
T. (0221) 21 59 56, Fax (0221) 215668. 094671
Kelemen, Gabor, Hochstadenstr. 29, 50674 Köln.
T. (0221) 24 66 01. 094672
Keulen, R. & D., Am Rinkenpfuhl 49, 50676 Köln.
T. (0221) 21 94 08. 094673
Koepsell & Schulz, Kartäuserhof 11, 50678 Köln.
T. (0221) 318668, Fax 319289. 094674
Laufenberg, Christian, Breite Str. 159, 50667 Köln.
T. (0221) 24 44 54. 094675
Maul, Georg, Kartäuserhof 7, 50678 Köln.
T. (0221) 32 81 51. 094676

Meul, Theodor, Paulstr. 10, 50676 Köln.
T. (0221) 31 72 41. 094677
Müller, Alfred Otto, Sternengasse 1, 50676 Köln.
T. (0221) 231513. 094678
Müller-Herrmann, Irma, Faßbenderkaul 1, 50968 Köln.
T. (0221) 38 59 79. 094679
Musto, M., Ferdinand-Porsche-Str. 7, 51149 Köln.
T. (0221) 381 69. 094680
Nowaczynski, Adam, Höninger Weg 145, 50969 Köln.
T. (0221) 360 39 11. 094681
Oelerich & Troltsch, Moltkestr 149, 50674 Köln.
T. (0221) 511732, Fax 511761. (Gemälde, Skulpturen) 094682
Rotmann, E., St.-Apern-Str. 11, 50667 Köln.
T. (0221) 2574827, 2574874,
Fax (0221) 2574874. 094683
Schwarz, Ewald, Jessestr. 19, 50823 Köln.
T. (0221) 55 74 36. 094684
Sievers, Johannes, Diözesanbibliothek, Kard.-Frings-Str. 1-3, 50667 Köln. T. (0221) 164 27 89,
Fax (0221) 1642783. 094685
Steinnus, Johann, Vitalisstr. 227, 50827 Köln.
T. (0221) 580 21 83, Fax (0221) 580 23 98. 094686
Topcu, Breite Str. 159, 50667 Köln. T. (0221) 24 85 46,
257 61 45. 094687
Trier, Michael, Maria-Hilf-Str. 17, 50677 Köln.
T. (0221) 32 75 41, Fax (0221) 32 64 40. 094688
Werner, Fleischmengergasse 33, 50676 Köln.
T. (0221) 232617, 393315, Fax 249035. 094689

Königstein (Hessen)
Halbach, Helmuth, Ölmühlweg 2a, 61462 Königstein.
T. (06174) 1665, Fax 1234. 094690
Knüttel, Kurt & Maria, Im Eck 5, 61462 Königstein.
T. (06174) 6320, 21633. 094691

Konstanz (Baden-Württemberg)
Leber, Peter, Schwaketenstr. 9, 78467 Konstanz.
T. (07531) 786 62. 094692
Repphun, Kreuzlinger Str 37-39, 78462 Konstanz.
T. (07531) 24665, Fax 27355. (Paintings, graphics, furniture) 094693
Scheideck, Andreas, Kindlebildstr 5, 78467 Konstanz.
T. (07531) 927272, Fax 927274. 094694

Korntal-Münchingen (Baden-Württemberg)
Mai, Zuffenhauser Str 54, 70825 Korntal-Münchingen.
T. (0711) 834615. 094695
Schempp, N., Kallenbergstr 43, 70825 Korntal-Münchingen. T. (0711) 802949. 094696

Krefeld (Nordrhein-Westfalen)
Oelgart, D., Moerser Str. 502, 47802 Krefeld.
T. (02151) 56 22 59. 094697
Gebr. Schleiffenbaum, Vinzenzstr 16, 47799 Krefeld.
T. (02151) 22569, Fax 22569. 094698
Steinbach, Hans & Sohn, Rheinstr. 38 u. 39, 47799 Krefeld. T. (02151) 265 34. 094699

Kreuth (Bayern)
Mayr, Hans, Tegernseerstr 46, 83708 Kreuth.
T. (08022) 2806, Fax 2806. (Bemalte und gefaßte Möbel, Skulpturen) 094700

Kronberg (Hessen)
Cropp, W., An der Stadtmauer 15, 61476 Kronberg.
T. (06173) 5531. (Möbel) 094701

Krummhörn (Niedersachsen)
Buhr, Jan de, Harringa Haus, 26736 Krummhörn.
T. (04926) 04923/16 43. 094702

Kupferzell (BaWü)
Müller, Walter K.F., Seestr 11, 74635 Kupferzell.
T. (07944) 1290, Fax 8232. 094703

Lahnstein (Rheinland-Pfalz)
Hardy, Franz Josef, Blücherstr. 15, 56112 Lahnstein.
T. (02621) 7315. 094704

Landau (Rheinland-Pfalz)
Müller, Kirchstr 49, 76829 Landau. T. (06341) 63658,
Fax 62740. (Bücher, Buch-Beschläge) 094705

Langenhagen (Niedersachsen)
Gerlich, G.-Ch., Wachtelsteig 4, 30455 Langenhagen.
T. (0511) 784922. *094706*

Lankau (Schleswig-Holstein)
Bock von Wülfingen, Regina, Tannenweg 9, 23881 Lankau. T. (04543) 665. *094707*

Leer (Niedersachsen)
Pache, Johannes, Neuestr 42, 26789 Leer.
T. (0491) 3291. *094708*

Leinfelden-Echterdingen (Baden-Württemberg)
Schlachtberger, U., Filderstr. 42, 70771 Leinfelden-Echterdingen. T. (0711) 754 21 18. *094709*
Tomanek, Sigrid, Wiesentalstr 22, 70771 Leinfelden-Echterdingen. T. (0711) 795148. (Textiles) *094710*

Leipzig (Sachsen)
Bielitz, Volker, Eilenburger Str 19, 04317 Leipzig.
T. (0341) 2619668, Fax 9804048. (Holzobjekte, Möbel) *094711*
Mahn, Rainer, Feuerbachstr 28, 04105 Leipzig.
T. (0341) 9803479, Fax 9803479. (Gemälde) *094712*

Lemwerder (Niedersachsen)
Reiners-Kimmich, Helmut, Kirchstr. 4, 27809 Lemwerder. T. (0421) 67 90 90. *094713*

Lenggries (Bayern)
Gerg, Michael, Kapellengasse 21, 83661 Lenggries.
T. (08042) 34 28. *094714*

Leutkirch im Allgäu (Baden-Württemberg)
Lutz, Joseph, Kemptener Str 29, 88299 Leutkirch im Allgäu. T. (07561) 2615. *094715*

Linnich (Nordrhein-Westfalen)
Oidtmann, Friedrich, Rurdorferstr 9-11, 52441 Linnich.
T. (02462) 6350, Fax 5503. *094716*

Lohfelden (Hessen)
Wolfram, Michelskopfweg 1, 34253 Lohfelden.
T. (0561) 514717, Fax (0561) 5101683. *094717*

Ludwigshafen am Rhein (Rheinland-Pfalz)
Siller, Klaus, Altriper Str 56, 67065 Ludwigshafen am Rhein. T. (0621) 573896, Fax 573896. (Wandmalerei, Skulpturen, Vergoldungen) *094718*

Lübeck (Schleswig-Holstein)
Gusewski, Siegfried, An der Hülshorst 8, 23568 Lübeck.
T. (0451) 825 36. *094719*
Saß, Linde & Karl Heinz, Medenbreite 47, 23556 Lübeck. T. (0451) 49 21 29. *094720*
Ziegler, Eva M., Hohelandstr. 58, 23564 Lübeck.
T. (0451) 79 33 59. *094721*

Magdeburg (Sachsen-Anhalt)
Kaminski, Dieter, Dr.-Eisenbart-Ring 36, 39120 Magdeburg. T. (0171) 3617903. *094722*
Schneider, Michael J., Hecklinger Str. 15, 39112 Magdeburg. T. (0391) 44657. *094723*

Maintal (Hessen)
Topitsch, Edwin, Goethestr. 55, 63477 Maintal.
T. (06181) 63626. *094724*

Mainz (Rheinland-Pfalz)
Buse, Heidelbergerfaßgasse 8, 55005 Mainz.
T. (06131) 234015, Fax 236594. *094725*
Metzner, Wolfgang Jakob, Liebfrauenstr. 1, 55116 Mainz. T. (06131) 22 82 54. *094726*
Recker, M., Zeystr 8, 55120 Mainz. T. (06131) 688000. (Furniture) *094727*
Schramm, Elisabeth, Leibnizstr. 43, 55118 Mainz.
T. (06131) 67 49 88. *094728*

Mainz-Kastel (Hessen)
Münch, In der Witz 38, 55252 Mainz-Kastel.
T. (06134) 652 91. *094729*

Malsch (Baden-Württemberg)
Göckel, Hauptstr. 30, 69254 Malsch.
T. (07253) 221 40. *094730*

Mannheim (Baden-Württemberg)
Hauck, Dietrich, Am Bogen 6, 68259 Mannheim.
T. (0621) 79 69 56, 49 45 47. *094731*
Hua, Hai-Yen, Karl-Kuntz-Weg 9, 68163 Mannheim.
T. (0621) 413631, Fax 413632. (Paper, silk works) *094732*

Restaurierung
Kunst auf Papier und Seide

Zeichnungen, Aquarelle,
Druckgrafiken, Plakate,
Pastelle, Gouache, Miniaturen,
Globen, Landkarten, Tapeten,
Moderne Kunst,
Ostasiatische Rollbilder,
Paravans, Bücher

Betreuung von Ausstellungen
und Schadensfällen
Beratung zur Konservierung
und Aufbewahrung

Hai-Yen Hua
Karl Kuntz Weg 9
D-68163 Mannheim
Tel.: 49 - (0)621 - 41 36 31
Fax: 49 - (0)621 - 41 36 32

Kauffelt, Matthias, Zähringer Str. 101, 68239 Mannheim.
T. (0621) 48 11 57, 47 73 41. *094733*
Kurpfälzische Münzhandlung, Augusta-Anlage 52, 68159 Mannheim. T. (0621) 44 95 66, 44 88 99, Fax (0621) 40 37 52. *094734*
Pfleger, Lothar, Robert-Blum-Str. 22, 68199 Mannheim.
T. (0621) 40 61 33. *094735*

Mauer (Baden-Württemberg)
Thoma-Flade, Schubertstr. 6, 69256 Mauer.
T. (06226) 64 88. *094736*

Meckesheim (Baden-Württemberg)
Haaf, Franz-Josef, Hauptstr 50, 74909 Meckesheim.
T. (06226) 8174. *094737*

Memmelsdorf (Bayern)
Török, Johann, Hauptstr. 46, 96117 Memmelsdorf.
T. (0951) 43524. *094738*

Miesbach (Bayern)
Schwab, Eckhard, Waldecker Höhe 6, 83714 Miesbach.
T. (08025) 3967, Fax 5468. (Gemälde, Möbel) *094739*

Möhrendorf (Bayern)
Hahm, H.-H., Waldstr. 1, 91096 Möhrendorf.
T. (09131) 48870. *094740*

Mönchengladbach (Nordrhein-Westfalen)
Meinz, Friedrich-K., Mühlenstr. 174, 41236 Mönchengladbach. *094741*

Moers (Nordrhein-Westfalen)
Perret, Richard, Rheinberger Str. 56-58, 47441 Moers.
T. (02841) 232 36. *094742*

Möser (Sachsen-Anhalt)
Korbmacher, Christa, Thälmannstr. 58, 39291 Möser.
T. (039222) 411. *094743*

Mössingen (Baden-Württemberg)
Atelier und Werkstätte für Restaurierungen, Mittelgasse 3, 72116 Mössingen. T. (07473) 8938. (Paintings, sculptures, furniture) *094744*

Mühlheim (Hessen)
Atelier Carta, Zimmerstr 44a, 63165 Mühlheim.
T. (06108) 77337. *094745*

Mülheim an der Ruhr (Nordrhein-Westfalen)
Buchmüller, J., Dümptener Str 64, 45476 Mülheim an der Ruhr. T. (0208) 407101. *094746*
Peichert, Uwe, Ruhrorter Str 6, 45478 Mülheim an der Ruhr. T. (0208) 55212. *094747*

München (Bayern)
Adams, Schellingstr. 24, 80799 München.
T. (089) 28 21 07. *094748*
Atelier Neugebauer, Albrechtstr. 37, 80636 München.
T. (089) 129 91 78. *094749*
Ballack, F.H.H., Bismarckstr 6, 80803 München.
T. (089) 335138, Fax 342095. *094750*
Bear Gallery, The, Gabelsbergerstr. 7, 80333 München.
T. (089) 280 03 33, Fax (089) 641 31 18. *094751*
Becker, Michael, Hohenwarter Str. 4, 80686 München.
T. (089) 58 68 71. *094752*
Beer, Franz X., Schraudolphstr. 26, 80799 München.
T. (089) 278 00 89. *094753*
Berendes, Lüder, Innere Wiener Str 24, 81667 München.
T. (089) 482512. *094754*
Bissinger, George C., Klenzestr. 12, 80469 München.
T. (089) 22 35 67. *094755*
Bogner, Willi, Thierschstr. 31, 80538 München.
T. (089) 29 32 35. *094756*
Braunmüller, Atelier, Ismaninger Str. 102, 81675 München. T. (089) 98 59 77. *094757*
Brigl, G., Warngauer Str. 45, 81539 München.
T. (089) 691 16 98. *094758*
Fischer, Wolfgang, Holzhofstr. 4, 81667 München.
T. (089) 48 97 79, 48 11 12. *094759*
Frewel, B., Bauerstr. 2, 80796 München.
T. (089) 272 22 93. *094760*
Galland, Heinrich, Blütenstr. 10, 80799 München.
T. (089) 272 34 67. *094761*
Gerstenberger, Manfred, Otkerstr. 27, 81547 München.
T. (089) 692 12 84. *094762*
Goering Institut e.V., Giselastr 7, 80802 München.
T. (089) 3839500, Fax 396781. *094763*
Götz, Fritz, Clemensstr. 24, 80803 München.
T. (089) 34 74 92. *094764*
Götz, Heinrich, Weltistr. 61, 81477 München.
T. (089) 79 86 52. *094765*
Gottwald, Hans, Robert-Koch-Str. 13, 80538 München.
T. (089) 29 68 54. *094766*
Grams, Brita, Aberlestr 18, 81371 München.
T. (089) 765361, Fax 765320. (Furniture) *094767*

20 Jahre   Brita Grams
Mitglied BVFR

Möbel - Holzobjekte - Gutachten
81371 Mü., Aberlestr. 18 (Rgb.)
Tel. 76 53 61 + Fax 76 53 20

Grams, Ulrich, Marsstr 13, 80335 München.
T. (089) 594452, Fax 5504310. *094768*
Gruber, Hans, Am Hackelanger 16, 81241 München.
T. (089) 88 64 74. *094769*
Hager, Christine, Fürstenrieder Str. 145, 80686 München. T. (089) 56 38 09. *094770*
Hauser, Josef, Gottschalkstr. 2a, 81825 München.
T. (089) 42 35 11. *094771*
Hermann, Walter, Reichenbachstr. 22, Rgb., 80469 München. T. (089) 692 29 17. *094772*
Hiebl, Hans, Am Glockenbach 11, 80469 München.
T. (089) 26 59 82. *094773*

Kellner, Hans, Augustenstr 15, 80333 München.
T. (089) 595094, Fax 595094.								094774
Kirsch, H., Talstr. 59, 80331 München.
T. (089) 292907.									094775
Kirschner, Ludwig, Leopoldstr. 76, 80802 München.
T. (089) 34 86 55.									094776
Klein, G., Triebstr. 4, 80993 München.
T. (089) 1495879.									094777
Knörle-Jahn, Cornelia, Walpurgisstr. 4, 81677 München.
T. (089) 470 49 11.									094778
Knörle, Lieselotte, Dr., Unertlstr. 40, 80803 München.
T. (089) 30 98 69, 470 49 11.							094779
Köck, Beichstr 5, 80802 München. T. (089) 337538,
Fax 337538.										094780

Günter Frank Köck

GEMÄLDE-STUDIO-KÖCK

**ATELIER FÜR RESTAURIERUNGEN
VON GEMÄLDEN UND PLASTIKEN
BERATUNG · EXPERTISEN**

80802 München, Beichstr. 5, Tel+Fax 33 75 38

Köppel, Max, Amalienstr. 15, 80333 München.
T. (089) 28 13 68.									094781
Komarek, L., Maxburgstr. 4, 80333 München.
T. (089) 293270.									094782
Kottulinsky, Louisette, Lohengrinstr. 36, 81925 Mün-
chen. T. (089) 95 38 19.								094783
Lerch, Ottostr. 1, 80333 München.
T. (089) 59 37 67.									094784
Lermer, Michael J., Nymphenburger Str. 106, 80636
München. T. (089) 123 11 26.							094785
Lilienthal-Plate, Margarete von, Winthirstr. 31, 80639
München. T. (089) 16 77 62.							094786
Luhn, Albert, Münchner Freiheit 4, 80802 München.
T. (089) 34 44 20.									094787
Majer-Trendel, Helga, Gustav-Freytag-Str. 6, 81925
München. T. (089) 98 32 17.							094788
Mandl, Helmut, Amalienstr. 14, 80333 München.
T. (089) 28 53 86.									094789
Mastellari, Divina-Beatrice, Friedrich-Herschel-Str. 5,
81679 München. T. (089) 98 57 93.						094790
Mayer, Franz, Seidlstr. 25, 80335 München.
T. (089) 59 54 84.									094791
Mittl, L., Knöblestr. 18, 80538 München.
T. (089) 22 51 70.									094792
Mory, Ludwig, Kunsthandwerkl. Zinngießerei, Rathaus-
gasse 8, 81241 München. T. (089) 22 45 42.			094793
Müller, Karl, Risserkogelstr 3, 81673 München.
T. (089) 4311468, Fax 4312300.						094794
Münchener Gobelin-Manufaktur, Notburgastr. 5, 80639
München. T. (089) 17 03 61.							094795
Neudhart, Ingrid, Münchner Freiheit 6, 80802 München.
T. (089) 39 39 27 35.									094796
Oexmann, Knuth H., Franz-Josef-Strauß-Ring 4, 80539
München. T. (089) 22 19 67.							094797
Ostler, Thomas-Wimmer-Ring 3, 80539 München.
T. (089) 2289264, Fax 220377.							094798
Poel, Karl te, St.-Pauls-Platz 6, 80336 München.
T. (089) 53 11 90.									094799
Privatinstitut zur Untersuchung von Gemälden und
Kunstwerken, Dachauer Str 111, 80636 München.
T. (089) 2907570, Fax 29075729.						094800
Rahmen-Siegert, Amalienstr. 43, 80799 München.
T. (089) 28 11 67.									094801
Rau, Regina, Am Harras 12, 81373 München.
T. (089) 77 83 00, 18 47 49.							094802
Reichert, Barbara, Thierschstr. 20, 80538
München.											094803
Restauro, Dachauer Str 111, 80335 München.
T. (089) 5236411, Fax 29075729.						094804
Riggauer, Konrad, Lilienstr. 11-13, 81669 München.
T. (089) 48 15 85, Fax 481587. (Antiques, sculptures,
frames)											094805
Romann, Henri, Blumenstr. 25, 80331 München.
T. (089) 26 40 29.									094806

Sason, Ch., Schleißheimer Str. 124, 80797 München.
T. (089) 18 97 90.									094807
Scheel von Rodenberg, Jan, Auenstr 2, 80469 München.
T. (089) 2022617.									094808
Schindelhauer, Manfred, Schleißheimer Str. 501, 80933
München. T. (089) 313 89 67.							094809
Schoeller, Thomas, Corneliusstr 23, 80469 München.
T. (089) 2016578, 2603116, Fax 2608267.			094810
Scholl, Sonnfriede, Josef-Vötter-Str 18, 81545 Mün-
chen. T. (089) 644144.								094811
Sindel, Heinz, Fürstenstr. 8, 80333 München.
T. (089) 28 06 55.									094812
Sohlern, Luise von, Lindwurmstr. 195, 80337 München.
T. (089) 76 67 34.									094813
Stage, Ulrike, Hiltenspergerstr. 53, 80796 München.
T. (089) 300 12 57.									094814
Streck, Ernst, Kaulbachstr. 77, 80802 München.
T. (089) 33 21 71.									094815
Strobl, Ingrid, Ebenböckstr. 16, 81241 München.
T. (089) 88 08 14, 834 45 03.							094816
Strübe, Henning, Turnerstr. 1a, 81827 München.
T. (089) 430 99 35.									094817
Vinzenz, Rolf, Morassistr 22, 80469 München.
T. (089) 296603.									094818
Vring, Cornelia von der, Hohenschwangaustr. 8, 81549
München. T. (089) 690 52 55.							094819
VV-Möbelrestaurierung, Schellingstr. 24, 80799 Mün-
chen. T. (089) 28 21 07.								094820
Waber, G., Parkstr. 2, 80339 München.
T. (089) 50 59 20.									094821
Wilm, Joh. Mich., Mauerkircherstr. 26, 81679 München.
T. (089) 98 68 96.									094822
Winzinger-Schnack, Katharina, Nebelhornstr. 22, 80686
München. T. (089) 57 77 53.							094823
Zauner, Albert, Ysenburgstr. 7, 80634 München.
T. (089) 470 36 87.									094824
Zilken, Uta, Brunnerstr. 5, 80804 München.
T. (089) 308 48 76, Fax 308 48 76.					094825

Münster (Nordrhein-Westfalen)
Bröker, Georgskommende 9, 48143 Münster.
T. (0251) 4 53 82.									094826
Clasing, Prinzipalmarkt 37, 48143 Münster.
T. (0251) 441 65, Fax 518911.							094827
Der Restaurator, Schadowstr. 8, 48163 Münster.
T. (0251) 02501/58683.								094828
Etage, Prinzipalmarkt 37, 48143 Münster.
T. (0251) 454 42, Fax 518911.							094829
Teufel, Alter Fischmarkt 7, 48143 Münster.
T. (0251) 546 18.									094830
Topp & Bußkamp, Neustr. 24, 48167 Münster.
T. (0251) 02506/7803.								094831
Wohl, Dietmar, Rothenburg 45, 48143 Münster.
T. (0251) 58762, Fax 58762. (Gemälde,
Skulpturen)										094832

Munderkingen (Baden-Württemberg)
Kneer, Hans-Peter, Breslauer Str. 11-13, 89597 Munder-
kingen. T. (07393) 309.								094833

Naila (Bayern)
Höhne, B., Berliner Str. 8, 95119 Naila.
T. (09282) 3135.									094834

Neckarsteinach (Hessen)
Feuerstein, Peter Valentin, Kirchenstr. 20, 69239 Nek-
karsteinach. T. (06229) 580.							094835

Neu-Anspach (Hessen)
Herles, Michael, Feldbergstr. 2, 61267 Neu-Anspach.
T. (06081) 41020.									094836
Heuner, Jürgen, Am Dorfbrunnen 1, 61267 Neu-An-
spach. T. (06081) 7053, Fax 42644.					094837

Neu-Isenburg (Hessen)
Fetschele, Helmut, Hirtengasse 15, 63263 Neu-Isen-
burg. T. (06102) 33853, Fax 31744.					094838

Neuenstein, Hessen (Hessen)
Hess, H., Domäne 2, 36286 Neuenstein, Hessen.
T. (06677) 1212, Fax 633.							094839

Neufahrn (Bayern)
Zauner, Albert, Ahornweg 46, 85375 Neufahrn.	094840

Neuhausen (Baden-Württemberg)
Schaller, Alfons, Wilhelmstr. 22, 73765 Neuhausen.
T. (07158) 536.										094841

Neuss (Nordrhein-Westfalen)
Stader, Johann Joseph, Virchowstr 13, 41464 Neuss.
T. (02131) 82697. (Bücher, Graphik)				094842

Neustadt an der Weinstraße (Rheinland-Pfalz)
Scheike, Siegfried G., Weinstr 514, 67434 Neustadt an
der Weinstraße. T. (06321) 31404.					094843

Neuwied (Rheinland-Pfalz)
Failer, Marktstr. 52, 56564 Neuwied.
T. (02631) 25750.									094844

Niederjahna (Sachsen)
Winkelgrund, Stefan H., Querstr 1, 01665 Niederjahna.
T. (03521) 451354. (China, glass, ceramics)		094845

Winkelgrund

PORZELLAN
GLAS / KERAMIK

Konservierung / Restaurierung

Stefan H. Winkelgrund

Dipl.-Ing. (FH) Restaurator
Querstraße 1
01665 Niederjahna / Meißen
Tel.: (03521) 45 13 54

Niederzier (Nordrhein-Westfalen)
Hertel, Niederfeld 2, 52382 Niederzier.
T. (02428) 3454.									094846

Nierstein (Rheinland-Pfalz)
Schiffel, B., Langgasse 4, 55283 Nierstein.
T. (06133) 591 10.									094847

Nordhackstedt (Schleswig-Holstein)
Werner, F. W., & Sohn, Rugenbarg 66c, 22848 Nord-
hackstedt. T. (04639) 523 39 44, 44 04 92.			094848

Nottuln (Nordrhein-Westfalen)
Gausepohl, Bernhard, Liebigstr. 20, 48301
Nottuln.											094849
Tischlerei im Stevertal, Stockum 7, 48301 Nottuln.
T. (02502) 8574.									094850

Nürnberg (Bayern)
Augustiner-Galerie, Augustinerstr. 11, 90403 Nürnberg.
T. (0911) 22 61 26, Fax 241 90 83.					094851
Bach, Guido & Peter, Peter-Henlein-Str. 71, 90459 Nürn-
berg. T. (0911) 45 89 09.								094852
Barthelmeß, Eugen, Vordere Ledergasse 4-6, Kaiserstra-
ße 32, 90403 Nürnberg. T. (0911) 22 72 42 /
22 45 58.											094853
Ehmann, Rudolf, Kraftshofer Hauptstr. 162a, 90427
Nürnberg. T. (0911) 30 61 63, Fax 30 21 79.			094854
Frenzel, Gottfried, Dr., Holzstatt 4, 90475 Nürnberg.
T. (0911) 83 17 02.									094855
Haisch, Karl-Anton, Bergstr. 10, 90403 Nürnberg.
T. (0911) 23 28 59.									094856
Krauss, Gebersdorfer Str. 71, 90449 Nürnberg.
T. (0911) 68 78 71.									094857
Nürnberger Gobelin-Manufaktur, Bingstr. 40, 90480
Nürnberg. T. (0911) 40 75 66.							094858
Reichel, Robert, Bessemerstr 52, 90411 Nürnberg.
T. (0911) 512556, Fax 512556.						094859
Russo, Anton, Albrecht-Dürer-Str. 4, 90403 Nürnberg.
T. (0911) 20 84 43.									094860
Verenkotte-Engelhardt, Magdalena, Unterreichenbacher
Str. 7-9, 90455 Nürnberg.							094861
Wiedl, Hermann, Adamstr. 14, 90489 Nürnberg.
T. (0911) 55 86 85, Fax 581181.						094862
Wilcke, Holger, Kraftshofer Hauptstr. 214, 90427 Nürn-
berg. T. (0911) 30 58 86.								094863

Oberhausen, Rheinland (Rheinland-Pfalz)
Nagel, Debra, Sofienstr 45, 46049 Oberhausen,
Rheinland.										094864

Obermichelbach (Bayern)
Breil, E., Weichselleite 10, 90587 Obermichelbach.
T. (0911) 76 29 79. *094865*

Oettingen (Bayern)
Götz, Kornelius, Schloßstr 41, 86732 Oettingen.
T. (09082) 4763, Fax 4763. *094866*

RESTAURIERUNGS-
B E R A T U N G

Kornelius Götz
Schloßstr. 41
D-86732 Oettingen
Tel.: 09082/ 4763
Fax.: 09082/ 4763

Offenbach (Hessen)
Gantzert-Castrillo, Erich, Ludwigstr. 64, 63067 Offen-
bach. T. (069) 80 11 67. *094867*
Günther, J., Weinbergstr. 1, 63073 Offenbach.
T. (069) 89 14 89. *094868*
Herold, Manfred & Christa, Ludwigstr 151, 63067 Offen-
bach. T. (069) 821556, Fax 821556. *094869*
Sommer, R., Weinbergstr. 10, 63073 Offenbach.
T. (069) 89 82 77. *094870*

Ohmden (Baden-Württemberg)
Bohring, Lothar, Stahlackerweg 91, 73275 Ohmden.
T. (07023) 2715. *094871*

Opfenbach (Bayern)
Steinbauer, Franz, Allgäustr 2-4, 88145 Opfenbach.
T. (08385) 544, Fax 544. *094872*

Osnabrück (Niedersachsen)
Böggemeyer, Walter, Lönsweg 20, 49076 Osnabrück.
T. (0541) 43 33 78. *094873*
Clasing, Heger Str. 21, 49074 Osnabrück.
T. (0541) 252 57. *094874*
Deppen, Hannoversche Str 43, 49084 Osnabrück.
I. (0541) 5848/0, Fax 5848/33. (Glasmalerei) *094875*

Osterholz-Scharmbeck (Niedersachsen)
Meyer-Graft, Reinhardt, Teufelsmoor 47, 27711 Osterholz-Scharmbeck. T. (04791) 287. *094876*

Ostrach (Baden-Württemberg)
Heine, Arthur, Postfach 2, 88354 Ostrach.
T. (07585) 21 73, Fax 1030. *094877*

Ottersberg (Niedersachsen)
Reuter, Jochen, Benkel 11, 28870 Ottersberg.
T. (04205) 425. *094878*

Ottweiler (Saarland)
Schöndorf, Manfred, Schäfereistr 37, 66564 Ottweiler.
T. (06824) 3170. *094879*

Paderborn (Nordrhein-Westfalen)
Janssen, Grube 9, 33098 Paderborn. T. (05251) 25444.
(Paintings, graphics, frames) *094880*

Parsberg (Bayern)
Fromm, Albert, Jurastr 4, 92331 Parsberg.
T. (09492) 220, Fax 7426. *094881*

Pattensen (Niedersachsen)
Kummer, Wolfram, Amtsrichterweg 1, 30982 Pattensen.
T. (05101) 05069/28 88. *094882*

Pforzheim (Baden-Württemberg)
Atzig, Peter, Pforzheimer Str 45, 75180 Pforzheim.
T. (07231) 767985, Fax 765118. (Furniture) *094883*

Leiter, Alfred, Gesellstr. 67a, 75175 Pforzheim.
T. (07231) 62845. *094884*
Schäfer, Otto Herbert, Schellingstr. 8, 75175 Pforzheim.
T. (07231) 637 35. *094885*
Wolf, Joachim, Allensteiner Str 28, 75181 Pforzheim.
T. (07231) 96290, Fax 962920. *094886*

Pfungstadt (Hessen)
Schilke, Richard, Am Hintergraben 6, 64319 Pfungstadt.
T. (06157) 37 72, 846 96. *094887*

Planegg (Bayern)
Oheimb, Rüdiger von, Hörwarthstr. 11, 82152 Planegg.
T. (089) 859 93 88, 859 61 36. *094888*

Pöcking (Bayern)
Manninger, Karl, 82343 Pöcking. T. (08157) 462. *094889*

**Preußisch Oldendorf (Nordrhein-Westfa-
len)**
Rohlfing, K.-H., Kleiner Maschweg 1, 32361 Preußisch
Oldendorf. T. (05742) 31 07. *094890*

Pullach (Bayern)
Cichon, Manfred, Tannenstr 16, 82049 Pullach.
T. (089) 7932368. *094891*

Rastatt (Baden-Württemberg)
Semsei, C., Hauptstr. 51, 76437 Rastatt.
T. (07222) 825 06. *094892*

Rastede (Niedersachsen)
Kieler, Dieter, Am Nordkreuz 6, 26180 Rastede.
T. (04402) 814 43. *094893*

Rattenkirchen (Bayern)
Kallenbach, Gabriele, Feldbergstr 10, 84431 Rattenkirchen. T. (08082) 5525, Fax (08638) 81517. *094894*

Ravensburg (Baden-Württemberg)
Leinmüller, Reinhold, Henri-Dunant-Str. 35, 88213 Ravensburg. T. (0751) 918 64. *094895*

Regensburg (Bayern)
Insam, Tändlergasse 11, 93047 Regensburg.
T. (0941) 510 74. *094896*
Kallinger, Johannes, Sigenhofferstr. 2, 93055 Regens-
burg. T. (0941) 406 51. *094897*
Otto, R., Pürkelgutweg 12, 93055 Regensburg.
T. (0941) 79 36 63, Fax 53649. *094898*
Preis, Hugo, Kapellengasse 2, 93047 Regensburg.
T. (0941) 5 26 69. *094899*

Remchingen (Baden-Württemberg)
Zurell, Markt-Str 8, 75196 Remchingen.
T. (07232) 71751, Fax 70420. *094900*

Remscheid (Nordrhein-Westfalen)
Fuentes, Antonio, Dorfstr. 16, 42897 Remscheid.
T. (02191) 633 19. *094901*

Remshalden (Baden-Württemberg)
Porzellanklinik, Kanalstr. 10, 73630 Remshalden.
T. (07181) 73505, Fax 74933. *094902*
Winter, Ernst, Königsteinstr. 20, 73630 Remshalden.
T. (07181) 736 02. *094903*

Ritterhude (Niedersachsen)
Börnsen, Ulrike, Seefahrerstr. 4, 27721 Ritterhude.
T. (04292) 63 75 13. *094904*

Ronnenberg (Niedersachsen)
Piepo, Wolfgang, Vörier Str. 5, 30952 Ronnenberg.
T. (05109) 34 36. *094905*

Rosenheim (Bayern)
Reheis, Erich, Färberstr. 35, 83022 Rosenheim.
T. (08031) 412 11. *094906*

Rostock (Mecklenburg-Vorpommern)
Schmidt, Martin-Christian, Tannenweg 19B, 18059
Rostock. *094907*

Rotthalmünster (Bayern)
Fessler, Paul, Am Markt, 94094 Rotthalmünster.
T. (08533) 315. *094908*

Saarbrücken (Saarland)
Kampschulte, I., Bruchwiesenanlage 1, 66125 Saar-
brücken. T. (06897) 767005. *094909*
Seekatz, Konrad, Bahnhofstr. 34, 66111
Saarbrücken. *094910*

Schleching (Bayern)
Klampfer, Felix, Mühlbachweg 10, 83259
Schleching. *094911*

Schönebeck (Brandenburg)
Jahn, Peter, Akazienstr. 2, 39218 Schönebeck.
T. (03928) 5329. *094912*
Jahn, Peter, Akazienstr. 2, 39218 Schönebeck.
T. (03928) 5329. *094913*

**Schwäbisch Gmünd (Baden-Württem-
berg)**
Lipp, C., Robert-Schumann-Str. 8, 73525 Schwäbisch
Gmünd. T. (07171) 20 08. *094914*

Seefeld (Bayern)
Niemann Atelier, Stampfgasse 3, 82229 Seefeld.
T. (08152) 7 84 46. *094915*

Siegburg (Nordrhein-Westfalen)
Müllerke, Horst, Siegdamm 30, 53721
Siegburg. *094916*

Siegen (Nordrhein-Westfalen)
Bossmann, Am Lohgraben 8, 57074 Siegen.
T. (0271) 57597. *094917*

Sigmaringen (Baden-Württemberg)
Lorch, Ernst, Gorheimer Str. 2, 72488 Sigmaringen.
T. (07571) 520 70. *094918*

Sinzheim (Baden-Württemberg)
Hillert, G., Weinbergstr. 24, 76547 Sinzheim.
T. (07221) 851 28. *094919*
Krause, Bernd, Im Niederfeld 2, 76547 Sinzheim.
T. (07221) 852 45. *094920*

Solingen (Nordrhein-Westfalen)
Hoch, Alois, Dr., Wilhelmstr 33, 42697 Solingen.
T. (0212) 71129. *094921*

Sontheim (Bayern)
Harzenetter, Richard, Bergstr. 9, 87776 Sontheim.
T. (08336) 345. *094922*

Spahnharrenstätte (Niedersachsen)
Bley, Bernhard, Hauptstr. 81, 49751 Spahnharrenstätte.
T. (05951) 662, Fax 1202. *094923*

Speicher (Rheinland-Pfalz)
Kleinschmidt, Gisbert, Kapellenstr. 39, 54662 Speicher.
T. (06562) 85 13. *094924*

Staig (Baden-Württemberg)
Rau, Peter, Kirchstr 18, 89195 Staig. T. (07346) 5501,
Fax 2142. *094925*

Starnberg (Bayern)
Gantner, Benno Michael, Würmstr. 7a, 82319 Starnberg.
T. (08151) 1 24 74. *094926*
Lippe, Chlodwig Prinz zur, Riedener Weg 34, 82319
Starnberg. T. (08151) 85 66. *094927*

Staufen (Baden-Württemberg)
Kästner, Anita, Jägerhäusleweg 1, 79219 Staufen.
T. (07633) 6141. *094928*

**Steinbach, Kreis Heiligenstadt (Thürin-
gen)**
Gritsch, E., Dorfstr. 78, 37308 Steinbach, Kreis Heiligenstadt. T. 0551/48 67 72. *094929*

Steinfurt (Nordrhein-Westfalen)
Brücker, Ursula, Kroosgang 33, 48565 Steinfurt.
T. (02551) 616 80. *094930*

Steinheim (Baden-Württemberg)
Schmautz, Dieter, Kleinbottwarer Str 31, 71711 Steinheim. T. (07144) 24373, Fax 208154. (Möbel, Innen-
räume, Holzobjekte) *094931*

Stetten am kalten Markt (Baden-Württemberg)
Oswald, Albin, Westerstetterstr 8, 72510 Stetten am kalten Markt. T. (07573) 2448. *094932*

Stuttgart (Baden-Württemberg)
Bischoff, Barbara, Industriestr. 24, 70565 Stuttgart. T. (0711) 73 24 78. *094933*
Breunig, Eugen, Hauptstätter Str. 37, 70173 Stuttgart. T. (0711) 24 56 04. *094934*
Fabian, H., Wagnerstr. 38, 70182 Stuttgart. T. (0711) 24 20 46. *094935*
Heiland, Hans, Zazenhäuser Str. 16, 70437 Stuttgart. T. (0711) 87 32 59. *094936*
Keller, Berthold, Leibnizstr. 51, 70193 Stuttgart. T. (0711) 65 01 06. *094937*
Siller, Manfred, Neue Weinsteige 23/1, 70180 Stuttgart. T. (0711) 60 98 16, Fax 6490148. *094938*
Weinbrenner, Ulrike, Tuttlinger Str. 90, 70619 Stuttgart. T. (0711) 47 44 66. *094939*

Sulzbach (Baden-Württemberg)
Erkert, Hermann, Hauffweg 7, 71560 Sulzbach. T. (07193) 6106. *094940*

Sylt-Ost (Schleswig-Holstein)
Nordfriesische Kunstwerkstätten, Kampende 17, 25980 Sylt-Ost. T. (04651) 60 88. *094941*

Telgte (Nordrhein-Westfalen)
Dondrup, Eduard, Dorf 32a, 48291 Telgte. T. (02504) 74 73. *094942*
Willach, Gabriele, Grevener Str. 10, 48291 Telgte. T. (02504) 881 84. *094943*

Teningen (Baden-Württemberg)
Haas, Peter, Dr., Blochmatten 7, 79331 Teningen. T. (07641) 55956, 55532, Fax (07641) 55950. *094944*

Tholey (Saarland)
Mrziglod, Günter, Grimostr 9, 66636 Tholey. T. (06853) 5210. *094945*
Mrziglod, Martin, Varuswaldstr 21, 66636 Tholey. I. (06853) 5210. *094946*

Thyrnau (Bayern)
Kellhammer, Bernhard, Unteres Bergfeld 10, 94136 Thyrnau. T. (08501) 1586. *094947*

Überlingen (Baden-Württemberg)
Sebastiani, Martin, Owinger Str 1, 88662 Überlingen. T. (07551) 61925. *094948*

Ulm (Baden-Württemberg)
Kneer, Kurt, Karlstr 28/2, 89073 Ulm. T. (0731) 63553. *094949*

Utting (Bayern)
Lehner, Dieter, Dießener Str. 19, 86919 Utting. T. (08806) 75 37. *094950*

Villingen-Schwenningen (Baden-Württemberg)
Thomas, Georg, Vöhrenbacher Str. 18, 78050 Villingen-Schwenningen. T. (07721) 5 31 20. *094951*

Villmar (Hessen)
Müller, Karlheinz, Lahnstr. 14, 65606 Villmar. T. (06474) 238, Fax 1337. *094952*

Vreden (Nordrhein-Westfalen)
Jetter, Edgar, Ölbachstr. 72, 48691 Vreden. T. (02564) 40 82. *094953*

Waldbronn (Baden-Württemberg)
Petersohn, Jürgen, Birkelweg 4, 76337 Waldbronn. T. (07243) 67250. (Wandmalereien) *094954*

Waldshut-Tiengen (Baden-Württemberg)
Atelier Aureus, Wallstr. 18, 79761 Waldshut-Tiengen. T. (07741) 61 13. *094955*

Walsdorf (Bayern)
Reiß, Ludwig, Kolmsdorfer Hauptstr. 13, 96194 Walsdorf. T. (09549) 7107. *094956*

Warendorf (Nordrhein-Westfalen)
Röttger, F., Beckumer Str. 21, 48231 Warendorf. T. (02581) 60238. *094957*

Wasenbach (Rheinland-Pfalz)
Dick, Walter, Mühlweg 2, 56370 Wasenbach. T. (06432) 811 23. *094958*

Weilersbach (Bayern)
Stegmeyer, Jürgen, Schloßpl. 8, 91365 Weilersbach. T. (09194) 657 94. *094959*

Weiterstadt (Hessen)
Felderhoff, Günter, Frankensteiner Str 5, 64331 Weiterstadt. T. (06150) 4844. *094960*

Wendelstein (Bayern)
Meissel, Oskar, Georg-Löhlein-Str. 15, 90530 Wendelstein. T. (09129) 77 69. *094961*

Wennigsen (Niedersachsen)
Hattendorf, Willy, Hülsebrinkstr 21, 30974 Wennigsen. *094962*

Westoverledingen (Niedersachsen)
Wall, Heinz de, Reinkeburg, 26810 Westoverledingen. T. (04955) 13 04. *094963*

Wiesbaden (Hessen)
Herrchen, Andreas, Kettenbornstr. 4, 65201 Wiesbaden. T. (0611) 20702. *094964*
Tremus, Karl, Nerostr. 22, 65183 Wiesbaden. T. (0611) 517 69. *094965*
Weller-Plate, P., Steingasse 1, 65183 Wiesbaden. T. (0611) 52 77 62. *094966*

Wilhelmsdorf (Baden-Württemberg)
Usenbenz/Urbanski, Pfrungener Str. 5, 88271 Wilhelmsdorf. T. (07503) 1552. *094967*

Willich (Nordrhein-Westfalen)
Kamphof, Günter, Martin-Rieffert-Str. 11, 47877 Willich. T. (02154) 21 64. *094968*

Witten (Nordrhein-Westfalen)
Frigge, Gleiwitzer Str. 6, 58454 Witten. T. (02302) 14871. *094969*

Wolfenbüttel (Niedersachsen)
Petersen, Dag-Ernst, Lessingpl 1, 38304 Wolfenbüttel. T. (05331) 808217, Fax 808173. *094970*

Worpswede (Niedersachsen)
Nitze, Isabella, Bergedorfer Str 38, 27726 Worpswede. T. (04792) 3273, 2797. *094971*

Würzburg (Bayern)
Pracher, Peter R., Weingartenstr. 39 a, 97072 Würzburg. T. (0931) 721 97. *094972*
Sämann-Schellenberger, Hans, Bibrastr. 3, 97070 Würzburg. T. (0931) 532 63. *094973*
Schnellenberger & Sämann, Bibrastr. 3, 97070 Würzburg. T. (0931) 532 63. *094974*

Wuppertal (Nordrhein-Westfalen)
Abeler, Heinrich, Poststr. 11, 42103 Wuppertal. T. (0202) 493990, Fax 45 67 10. *094975*
Schmidt & Green, Herbringhausen 10, 42399 Wuppertal. T. (0202) 612061, Fax 613740. *094976*

Zell (Rheinland-Pfalz)
Niespor, Franz, Marienthaler Au 20, 56856 Zell. T. (0654) 43 23. *094977*

Zellingen (Bayern)
Felgenhauer, Joachim, Mähderweg 32, 97225 Zellingen. T. (09364) 98 76. *094978*

Zierenberg (Hessen)
Tippl, Gerd, Berliner Str. 27, 34289 Zierenberg. T. (05606) 8641. *094979*

Zwingenberg, Bergstr. (Hessen)
Sperling, Bodo D., Postfach 1147, 64669 Zwingenberg, Bergstr. T. (06251) 788582, Fax 788583. *094980*

Ireland

Dublin
Antiquarian Bookcrafts, Craft Centre, Marlay Park, Dublin 16. T. (01) 97 28 34. (Books) *094981*
Atha Cliath, Belvedere Av off NCR, Dublin, 1. T. (01) 36 42 39, 30 53 93. (Furniture) *094982*
Castle Upholstery, 80 Drimenagh Rd, Dublin 12. T. (01) 55 73 26. (Furniture) *094983*
Dalymount, 337 North Circular Rd, Dublin 7. T. (01) 30 37 26. (Furniture) *094984*
Fagan, J. & J., 121-122 The Coombe, Dublin 8. T. (01) 54 09 00. (Furniture) *094985*
Mitchell, T.J., 4 Lower Pembroke St, Dublin 2. T. (01) 76 68 81. (Furniture) *094986*
O'Reilly & Son, 24 Clarence Mangan Rd, Dublin 8. T. (01) 53 69 30. (Furniture) *094987*
Ross, 73 Grange Park Rd, Dublin 5. T. (01) 47 16 71. (Furniture) *094988*

Dun Laoghaire (Co. Dublin)
A Restoration Centre, 7 Cumberland St, Dun Laoghaire. T. (01) 80 16 35. (Furniture) *094989*
Clock Centre, 71 York Rd, Dun Laoghaire. T. (01) 80 36 67. (Clocks) *094990*

Enniskerry (Co. Wicklow)
Bushy Park Engineering, The Forge, Enniskerry. T. (01) 86 90 77. (Gates, railings, garden furniture) *094991*

Sandycove (Co. Dublin)
Old Irish Pine, Islington Av, Sandycove. T. (01) 80 49 60. (Furniture, doors, fireplaces) *094992*

Italy

Bari
Coluccia, Piero, Via Dante Alighieri 330, 70122 Bari. I. (080) 521 28 02. (Dispinti, Mobili) *094993*
Il Federico, Via Putignani 122, 70121 Bari. T. (080) 521 60 35. (Mobili, Cornici) *094994*

Bergamo
Staffanoni, Franco, via Matris Domini 21, 24100 Bergamo. T. (035) 23 27 27. (Antichità) *094995*

Bologna
Sibani, Ferruccio, via Belle Arti 52, 40126 Bologna. (Antichità) *094996*

Bolzano
Kronau, Rudolf, Dominikanerpl 17, 39100 Bolzano. (Gemälde) *094997*

Brescia
Navoni, Via Milano 20c, 25126 Brescia. T. (030) 54023. (Mobili, Oggetti d'Arte) *094998*

Busto Arsizio (Varese)
Montalto, Franco, Via Palestro 14, 21052 Busto Arsizio. T. (0331) 63 23 42. (Mobili, Tappeti) *094999*

Cagliari
Cao Marino, Via Bonaria 58, 09100 Cagliari. T. (070) 65 78 27. (Antichità, Dorature, Mobili, Tappeti) *095000*

Cuneo
Fulcheri, Giuseppe, corso Francia 48, 12100 Cuneo. T. (0171) 31 71. (Mobili) *095001*
Garello, Pietro, Corso JF Kennedy 5, 12100 Cuneo. T. (0171) 42 96, 624 70. (Antichità, Dorature, Mobili, Quadri, Sculture) *095002*

Domodossola (Novara)
Paggi, Remy, Via Gramsci 38, 28037 Domodossola. T. (0324) 28 35. (Antichità, Quadri, Sculture) *095003*

Firenze
Boschini & Galeotti, Borgo Allegri 27/r, 50122 Firenze. T. (055) 234 11 73. (Mobili) *095004*

Chiarantini, Giacomo, piazza Pitti 8r, 50125 Firenze.
T. (055) 28 44 40. (Mobili) *095005*
Crudeli, dott. arch. Guido, via Piana 18, 50124 Firenze.
T. (055) 22 22 84. (Antichità, Chiese) *095006*
Cuniberti, Beatrice, Via Maggio 7, 50125 Firenze.
T. (055) 28 59 32. (Carta) *095007*
Galleria Giorgi, Via della Vigna Nuova 51, 50123 Firenze.
T. (055) 21 16 31. (Quadri) *095008*
Gennarini, Giuseppe, via G Zanella 21, 50124 Firenze.
(Ceramiche e pulitura bronzi) *095009*
Migliorini, Lorenzo, Via F Zanetti 10, 50123 Firenze.
T. (055) 21 20 44. (Dipinti, Miniature) *095010*
Nocentini, Paolo, Piazza Ghiberti 14/r, 50122 Firenze.
(Mobili) *095011*
Piccini, Dante, via G Ancillotto 18, 50127 Firenze. (Dipinti, Sculture e Calchi) *095012*
Poggiali & Grossi, Via Sprone 19-21r, 50125 Firenze.
T. (055) 21 48 73. (Maioliche, Porcellane, Ceramiche, Terracotte) *095013*
Rossi, Dr. Arch. Ferdinando, Via degli Alfani 76-78, 50121 Firenze. ((Pietre Dure)) *095014*
Schiavoncini, Via Faetina 244b, 50133 Firenze.
T. (055) 57 18 08. (Libri, Documenti, Stampe) *095015*
Ticci & Falteri, F., Via delle Belle Donne 14, 50123 Firenze. T. (055) 28 70 20. (Dipinti) *095016*
Vannacci, Piero, Via Giuliani 66r, 50141 Firenze.
T. (055) 41 29 96, 70 22 25. (Mobili) *095017*

Fonte (Treviso)
Gazzola, Francesco Ampelio, via Crespano 2 b37 b39, 31010 Fonte. T. (0423) 58 079. (Mobili) *095018*

Genova
Cassan, Maria Luisa, Via A. Carrara 226-227, 16147 Genova. T. (010) 38 82 47. (Ceramiche) *095019*
Cortile, Il, Vico Falamonica 6/r, 16123 Genova.
T. (010) 29 85 22. (Mobili) *095020*

Milano
Arte Persiana, Corso Venezia 25, 20121 Milano.
T. (02) 79 33 97. (Tappeti) *095021*
Cesari, Orfelio, Ripa Ticinese 97, 20143 Milano.
T. (02) 848 56 40. (Quadri) *095022*
Colombo, Carlo, Via Gesù 1, 20121 Milano.
T. (02) 70 20 69. (Tappeti, Antichi, Arazzi, Tessuti) *095023*
Il Capitello, Via Montegani 1, 20141 Milano.
T. (02) 89 50 05 63. (Mobili) *095024*
Maltinti, Bruno, Via Fratelli Bronzetti 26, 20129 Milano.
T. (02) 749 25 80. (Mobili) *095025*
Pippa, Luigi, Via Durini 26, 20122 Milano.
T. (02) 79 42 97. (Orologi antichi e istrumenti scientifici) *095026*
Zardin, via Majno 16, 20129 Milano. T. (02) 70 69 51.
(Mobili, Quadri, Tappeti) *095027*

Montevarchi (Arezzo)
Donati, Antonio & Figli, via Ammiraglio Burz 40, 52025 Montevarchi. T. (055) 98 02 44, 98 02 33, 98 21 35.
(Mobili) *095028*

Napoli
Bowinkel, U., Via S Lucia, 80132 Napoli.
T. (081) 41 77 39. (Incisioni, Sculture, Stampe, Aquarelli, Gouache, Litografie) *095029*
Sebastiano 36, Via Sant Anna dei Lombardi 58-59, 80134 Napoli. T. (081) 32 72 81. (Mobili) *095030*

Niardo (Brescia)
Fedele, Bucci, Via Nazionale 48, 25050 Niardo.
T. (0364) 47 90 72, 33 90 72. (Mobili) *095031*

Padova (Belluno)
Galleria d'Arte Antica, via Altinate 45, 35100 Padova.
T. (049) 394 74. (Vetro, Porcellana) *095032*

Palermo (Sicilia)
Dima, Via Gaetano Daita 12-12/a, 90139 Palermo.
T. (091) 33 49 63. (Antichità) *095033*
L'Oro dei Farlocchi, Via Florestano Pepe 12, 90139 Palermo. T. (091) 32 54 57. (Mobili) *095034*
Villarà, Giuseppe, via Simone da Bologna 3, 90134 Palermo. (Libri) *095035*

Perugia
Legart, Borgo XX Giugno 74, 06124 Perugia.
T. (075) 30991. (Libri) *095036*

Roma
Amadio, Manlio, via Margutta 50, 00187 Roma.
(Quadri) *095037*
Bizarri, Francesco, piazza Giuditta Tavani Arquati 104, 00153 Roma. (Mobili antichi) *095038*
Conti, Fernando, via della Gensola 3, 00153 Roma.
(Mobili) *095039*
Crisostomi, Paolo, Via del Boschetto 60, 00100 Roma.
(Prints and Drawings) *095040*
Fontana, Pierino, via Nomentana 233, 00161 Roma.
(Mobili) *095041*
Leali, Bernardiono, via del Babuino 16, 00187 Roma.
(Ceramiche) *095042*
Mata, A. de, via Babuino 55, 00187 Roma.
T. (06) 68 08 39. (Quadri) *095043*
Nichilò G., via dei Coronari 209, 00186 Roma.
T. (06) 56 40 85. (Dipinti) *095044*
Petrosemolo, Arnoldo, Via del Lupo 11, 00186 Roma.
(Mobili) *095045*

Siena
CMC Antichità, Piazza Indipendenza 3-4, 53100 Siena.
T. (0577) 28 44 80. (Mobili) *095046*
Taddeucci, D., Via di Città 136, 53100 Siena.
T. (0577) 28 91 60. (Dipiuti, Mobili) *095047*

Spoleto (Perugia)
Coo. Be. C., Largo Possenti 4, 06049 Spoleto.
T. (0743) 49850, Fax 49850. (Dipinti, Sculture) *095048*

Suzzara (Mantova)
Negri, Roberto, Via Pasine 73, 46029 Suzzara.
T. (0376) 53 46 12. (Dipinti, Scultura) *095049*

Torino
Asero, Angelo, via Acc Albertina 28, 10123 Torino.
T. (011) 83 23 96. (Scultore, restauratore Oggetti d'Arte) *095050*
Breuza & Larizza, Via Monginevro 8, 10138 Torino.
T. (011) 44 12 43. (Mobili) *095051*
Cohen, Maria, Galleria S Federico 41, 10121 Torino.
T. (011) 51 87 69. (Tappeti) *095052*
Emprin-Gilardini & Bersano, Via della Rocca 41, 10123 Torino. T. (011) 87 46 18. (Dipinti) *095053*
Frisano, F., Via Perosa 12, 10139 Torino.
T. (011) 44 67 76. (Mobili) *095054*
Gamarra, Elvio, Via dei Faggi 7, 10156 Torino.
T. (011) 26 07 38. (Antichità, Quadri, Chiese) *095055*
Minerva, Michele Lacidogna, Corso Giulio Cesare 20A, 10125 Torino. (Antichi, Mobili, Dipinti, Cornici) *095056*
Neirotti, Via Gradisca 52, 10136 Torino.
T. (011) 36 55 89. (Mobili d'epoca) *095057*
Vecchie Idee, Via Americo Vespucci 36, 10129 Torino.
T. (011) 58 40 22. (Mobili, Oggetti d'Arte) *095058*

Treviso
Fabris, Paolo, Via Gobetti 6, 31100 Ireviso.
T. (0422) 26 21 10, 517 43. (Dipinti) *095059*

Trezzano (Milano)
Gregorio, Guiseppe, Via Pirandello 8, Cascina Mezzetta, 20090 Trezzano. T. (02) 48 40 07 96, 488 31 97. (Mobili, Lucidatura) *095060*

Trieste
D'Ercole, Renato, Via Patrizio 6/1, 34137 Trieste.
T. (040) 94 22 89. (Legni) *095061*

Udine
Boschi Brollo, Giuliana, via Cavour 7, 33100 Udine.
T. (0432) 577 37. (Antichità, Quadri) *095062*

Venezia
Guarinoni, Giancarlo, San Tomà 2862, 30125 Venezia.
T. (041) 522 42 86. (Mobili) *095063*
Longo, Giancarlo, Via Giudecca San Giacomo 885, 30100 Venezia. T. (041) 378 27. (Antichità, Vetro/Porcellane) *095064*
Parenti, Prof. Nino, Santa Croce 314, 30125 Venezia.
(Quadri) *095065*

Verona
Rossignoli, Marino & C., Corso Sant' Anastasia 25, 37121 Verona. T. (045) 30701. (Orologi, Gioielli) *095066*

Japan

Mitaka
Yoshimura, Emile, 5-24-15 Inokashira, Mitaka.
T. (0422) 483180, Fax (0555) 621883. *095067*

Tokyo
Heisando Co. Ltd., 13, 5-gochi Shiba Park, Minato-ku, Tokyo. T. (03) 3434-0588. (Paintings) *095068*
Mori, Kyoko, 3-15-27-102, Syoan Suginami-ku, Tokyo 167. T. (03) 53704083. *095069*

Liechtenstein

Schaan
Heeb, Iris, Im Bretscha 1, 9494 Schaan.
T. (075) 285 95. *095070*

Martinique

Fort-de-France
Renaissance, Rue Professeur-Raymond-Garcin, 97200 Fort-de-France. T. (596) 630850. *095071*

Le Lamentin
Aire, Basse Gondeau, 97232 Le Lamentin.
T. (596) 500511. *095072*

Mexico

México (D.F.)
Lopez, Carlos, Gemelos 33 Col. Prado-Churubusco, México. (Arqueologia) *095073*

Monaco

Monte Carlo
Lanteri et Fils, 26, rue des Remparts, 98000 Monte Carlo. T. 93 30 31 01. (Fresques) *095074*
Van Deudekom, J.J., La Victoria, bd Princesse-Charlotte, 98000 Monte Carlo. T. 93 30 76 68. (Porcelaines, tableaux anciens) *095075*

Netherlands

Amstelveen (Noord-Holland)
Bos, Amsterdamseweg 376, 1182 HS Amstelveen.
T. (020) 643 17 52. (Meubelstoffeerderij) *095076*
Kruymel, Gebr., Ouderkerkerlaan 23, 1185 HC Amstelveen. T. (020) 641 20 80. (Meubelstoffeerderij) *095077*

Amsterdam
Antiquariaat Sint Joris, Reestr 3, 1016 DM Amsterdam.
T. (020) 623 54 66. (Graphic doll's houses) *095078*
A.R.R., Zakslootje 12, 1011 NE Amsterdam.
T. (020) 6274415, Fax 6274415. (paintings, research) *095079*
Bosschaert, Louise C.E., 2e Anjeliersdwarsstr 20, 1015 NT Amsterdam. T. (020) 627 60 46. (Antique Textiles) *095080*
Dood, P. de, Rokin 74-76, 1012 KW Amsterdam.
T. (020) 623 47 26. (Schilderijen, tekeningen en prenten) *095081*
Fetter & Zn., Gasthuismolensteeg 5, 1016 AM Amsterdam. T. (020) 623 09 92. (Schilderijen) *095082*
Gude & Meijer, Overtoom 152, 1054 HP Amsterdam.
T. (020) 6129742, Fax (020) 6850112. (Antieke Klokken) *095083*

Lingbeek, Nico, Amaliastr 5, 1052 GM Amsterdam.
T. (020) 684 10 74. (Papieren, Boeken)   *095084*
Marcus, Johannes, N.Z. Voorburgwal 284, 1012 RT Amsterdam. T. (020) 6236920. (Papierrestaurator) *095085*
Mel, G., 2e Kostverlorenkade 120, 1053 SC Amsterdam.
T. (020) 612 06 41. (Meubelen)   *095086*
Stambolov, Todor, Scheldestr 96, 1078 GP Amsterdam.
T. (020) 671 32 81. (Porselein, Bronzen,
Sculptur)   *095087*

Breda (Noord-Brabant)
Schreurs, M. H., Catharinastr 40-42, 4811 XJ Breda.
T. (076) 5219024. (Antieke klokken)   *095088*

Delft (Zuid-Holland)
Ruyter, Pieter de, Donkerstr 3, 2611 TE Delft.
T. (015) 2122017. (Schilderijen)   *095089*
Sittekist, De, Hovenierstr 1, 2613 RM Delft.
T. (015) 2140605. (Meubelen)   *095090*

Ede (Gelderland)
Simonis & Bunk, Notaris Fischerstr 30-32, 6711 BD Ede.
T. (0318) 614511. (Paintings)   *095091*

Eijsden (Limburg)
Driessen, P.A.Ph., Spriemenstr 2, 6245 BX Eijsden.
T. (043) 4092047. (Schilderijendeskundige taxatie en
expertise)   *095092*

Eindhoven (Noord-Brabant)
Bies, J. H. P., Boschdijk 221a, 5612 HC Eindhoven.
T. (040) 2431377. (Gemälde)   *095093*
Teunis, F., Thomas A Kempislaan 68, 5643 NV Eindhoven. T. (040) 2115379. (Porselein)   *095094*
Verspaget, Jean-Pierre, Heezerweg 278d, 5643 KL Eindhoven. T. (040) 212001. (Schilderijen)   *095095*

Gasteren (Drenthe)
Jobing & Zonen, Brink 6, 9466 PE Gasteren.
T. (0592) 231363. (Meubelen)   *095096*

Gendringen (Gelderland)
Brunsveld, hoek Ulftsestr- Grotestr Oldheid, 7081 CE
Gendringen. T. (0315) 681423. (Meubel)   *095097*

Den Haag (Zuid-Holland)
Andelos, Dr. Lelykade 54, 2583 CM Den Haag.
T. (070) 358 56 08. (Antiek Textiel)   *095098*
Au Domicile Ancien, Spekstr 7, 2514 BL Den Haag.
T. (070) 346 09 72, 387 11 01. (antike Möbel)   *095099*
Baranyi, Loosduinsekade 51, 2571 AA Den Haag.
T. (070) 389 93 60. (Meubelstoffering)   *095100*
Bosch, W.S. ten, Meppelweg 868, 2544 BW Den Haag.
(Schilderijen)   *095101*
Dam & Stücken, Assendelftstr 13, 2512 VS Den Haag.
T. (070) 389 44 64. (Möbel)   *095102*
Dereumaux, Noordeinde 168-180, 2514 GR Den Haag.
T. (070) 341 65 64. (Meubel, Schilderijen)   *095103*
Gaemers, A., Noordeinde 155, 2514 GG Den Haag.
T. (070) 346 38 68. (Antike Uhren)   *095104*
Heymans, Slijkeinde 11a, 2513 VC Den Haag. (Porselein,
metaal, ivoor, sieraden)   *095105*
Kettenis, Sandor, Javastr 116, 2858 Den Haag.
T. (070) 365 47 98. (Porzellan)   *095106*
Klijn, Johan, Noordeinde 172-178, 2514 GR Den Haag.
T. (070) 364 91 81. (Möbel, Polster)   *095107*
Koch, Gebr., Hoogstraat 7, 2513 AN Den Haag.
T. (070) 313 56 37. (Schilderijen)   *095108*
Krans, Altingstr 8, 2593 SX Den Haag.
T. (070) 347 96 89. (Holz, Schnitzereien)   *095109*
Moesman, Assendelftstr 28-28A, 2512 VW Den Haag.
T. (070) 364 80 55. (Antike Möbel)   *095110*
Schoonens, Zuidwal 101a, 2512 XV Den Haag.
T. (070) 360 08 33. (algemeen)   *095111*
Tigges, Renee, W-de-Withstr 131-133, 2518 CS Den
Haag. T. (070) 345 62 32. (Alte Rahmen)   *095112*
Treffers, J.H., Molenstraat 9a-11, 2513 BH Den Haag.
(Schilderijen)   *095113*
Vermolen, J. A., Molenstr 23, 2513 BH Den Haag.
(Schilderijen)   *095114*
Vlam, Michiel de, Sumatrastr 200, 2585 CV Den Haag.
T. (070) 358 56 33. (Meubelen)   *095115*
Vrolijk en Zn., Koppelstokstr 120, 2583 CG Den Haag.
(Meubel, sculptuur)   *095116*

Haarlem (Noord-Holland)
Heerkens Thijssen, Wagenweg 6, 2012 ND Haarlem.
T. (023) 5312725. (Meubel, Antiquiteiten en
Schilderijen)   *095117*
Stichting Werkplaatstextiel, Leidseplein 36, 2013 PZ
Haarlem. T. (023) 5325949. (Tapestries, Flags) *095118*

Maartensdijk (Utrecht)
Barometermuseum, Dorpsweg 187, 3738 CD Maartensdijk. T. (0346) 212400, Fax 211280.   *095119*

Maastricht (Limburg)
Mares, W. J., Vossenvoetpad 13, 6213 GE Maastricht.
T. (043) 331807. (Oude Sculpturen)   *095120*

Meerssen (Limburg)
Hermesdorf, P. F. J. M., Bokstr 2, 6235 NM Meerssen.
T. (043) 3642398. (Schilderijen)   *095121*

Mierlo (Noord-Brabant)
Huybregts, J.H., Pastoor de Winterstraat 16, 5731 EJ
Mierlo. (Möbel)   *095122*

Oosterbeek (Gelderland)
Holtrop, Jan, Stationsweg 17, 6861 EA Oosterbeek.
T. (026) 3333241. (Schilderijen)   *095123*

Oss (Noord-Brabant)
Poezenest, 't, Kortfoortstr 85, 5342 AC Oss.
T. (0412) 625108. (Möbel)   *095124*

Prinsenbeek (Noord-Brabant)
Well, van, Klaverveld 53, 4841 RK Prinsenbeek.
(Furniture)   *095125*

Rotterdam (Zuid-Holland)
Au Caveau, Nieuwe Binnenweg 158c, 3015 BG Rotterdam. T. (010) 436 31 41. (Gemälde, Graphiken) *095126*
Banis, H.F.G., Zwaanshals 81c + 99, 3036 KD Rotterdam. T. (010) 465 77 66. (Meubel)   *095127*
Koch, Gebr., Lijnbaan 78, 3012 ER Rotterdam.
T. (010) 413 59 92. (Schilderijen)   *095128*
Refinishing Touch, W van Hillegaersbergstr 135a, 3051
RG Rotterdam. T. (010) 422 03 51, 456 20 18.
(Meubel)   *095129*
Vis, D.C. van der, Oudedijkse Schiekade 98, 3043 LC
Rotterdam. T. (010) 466 57 07. (Meubel)   *095130*

Schiedam (Zuid-Holland)
Bijl, Simon A., Boterstr 2, 3111 NC Schiedam.
T. (010) 426 22 42. (Barometers, Clocks,
Antiques)   *095131*

Sint Michielsgestel (Noord-Brabant)
Van Dijk, Jaap, Schijndelseweg 40, 5271 SB Sint Michielsgestel. T. (073) 5515093. (Antike Bouwmaterialien, Betimmeringen, Meubelen, Taxaties,
Expertises)   *095132*

Sint Nicolaasga
Douwes Atelier, Kade 11, 8251 JR Sint Nicolaasga.
T. (05134) 31821.   *095133*

Utrecht
Aandacht, Oudegracht 239 adWerf, 3511 NK Utrecht.
T. (030) 2322796. (Meubelen)   *095134*
Bergsma, W., Bemuurde Weerd oostzijde 1bis, 3514 AN
Utrecht. T. (030) 2319643. (Meubelen)   *095135*
Jansen, Nieuwegracht 77, 3512 LH Utrecht.
T. (030) 2317158. (Meubelen)   *095136*
Kleef, R. van, Biltstr. 73, 3572 AJ Utrecht.
T. (030) 2318509. (Koperwerk)   *095137*

Venlo (Limburg)
Knippenberg, L. van, Straelseweg 566-568, 5916 AD
Venlo. T. (077) 315936. (meubles)   *095138*

Zeist (Utrecht)
Becker, J.H. Hendr., Zn., Tweede Hogeweg 119, 3701
AX Zeist. T. (030) 6912767. (Meubel, antieke klokken,
sieraden)   *095139*

New Zealand

Christchurch
Fisher, H., & Son, 691 Colombo St., Christchurch.
T. (03) 401 61. (Paintings)   *095140*

Dunedin (Otago)
Lloyd, L. Charles, Dunedin POB 1392. (Paintings, Works
on Paper)   *095141*

Wellington
McGregor Wright's Ltd., 115 Lambton Quay, Wellington.
T. (04) 409 24. (Paintings)   *095142*

Norway

Bergen
Kaland, Björn, Brattlien 26, 5000 Bergen. (Paintings and
polychrome wooden Sculpture)   *095143*

Peru

Lima
Univeros, Fidel, Venezuela 135, Chosica, Lima.
T. 23 4732, 23 6332. (Madera y Tejidos
antiguos)   *095144*

Poland

Kraków
Błyskosz, Jan, Wawel 9, 30-960 Kraków. T. 22 92 66.
(easel and mural paintings, polychrome
sculpture)   *095145*
Kostecka, Anna, ul. Senatorska 25 m. 67, 30-106 Kraków. T. 21 53 04 party-line. (easel and mural paintings,
polychrome sculpture)   *095146*
Otlowska, Maria, Al. Pokoju 24 m. 5, 31-548 Kraków.
(easel and mural paintings, polychrome
sculpture)   *095147*
Wagner, Wacław, ul Kasztelańska 32 m. 1, 30-116 Kraków. (easel paintings, old and modern
cordovans)   *095148*

Legnica
Renopol Przedsiębiorstwo Zagraniczne, ul. Chojnowska
2, 59-200 Legnica. T. 28576. (Steinskulptur, architektonische Details, Metallobjekte)   *095149*

Łódź
Kamwiszer, Andrzej, ul Piotrkowska 204/210 m. 131,
90-369 Łódź. T. 362437. (archaeological objects, metal, textiles, analysis C-14)   *095150*
Olawa-Oławiński, Bogumił, ul. Zamenhofa 1/3 m. 32,
90-431 Łódź. T. 32 78 21. (easel and mural paintings,
polychrome sculpture)   *095151*
Potemska, Maria, ul. Narutowicza 127 m. 18, 90-146
Łódź. (easel and mural paintings, graphics, polychrome sculpture)   *095152*

Toruń
Renbud Przedsiębiorstwo Badań i Konserwacji Zabytków, ul Kościuszki 17, 87-100 Toruń. T. 33886. (conservation and restoration of old architecture and monuments of art)   *095153*

Warszawa
Buraczewska, Grażyna, ul Częstochowska 16/18 m. 3,
02-344 Warszawa. T. (022) 22 79 63. (graphics, watercolour drawings, cordovans)   *095154*
Jaworski, Jacek, ul Płocka 39 m. 57, 01-231 Warszawa.
T. (022) 32 30 01. (ceramics, glass, gilding, wood
sculpture)   *095155*
Jaworski, Piotr, ul Widawska 7/11, 01-494 Warszawa.
(Furniture)   *095156*
Pełczyński, Maciej, ul. Górczewska 90 a m. 29, 01-117
Warszawa. T. (022) 37 68 64. (clocks)   *095157*

Portugal

Lisboa

Alves Gama, Jose, Rua da Rosa 235/237, 1200 Lisboa.
T. (01) 36 81 13. (Moveis) *095158*

Bourgard, Pedro, Cidade Luanda 482 r/c-A., 1800 Lisboa. T. (01) 31 61 57. (Pintura) *095159*

Corvélho, A., Rua Angelina Vidal 84, 1.0, 1100 Lisboa.
T. (01) 84 30 75. (Porcelana, faiança) *095160*

Fundação Ricardo do Espirito Santo Silva, Museu – Escola de Artes Decorativas Portuguesas, Largo das Portas do Sol 2, 1100 Lisboa. T. (01) 8862183/4/5,
Fax 8874930. *095161*

Mural da História, Rua Serpa Pinto 5,1#Et E-T, 1200 Lisboa. T. (01) 3470032, Fax 3470032. (mural painting) *095162*

MURAL DA HISTÓRIA-RESTAURO DE PINTURA
MURAL LDA

PINTURA DECORATIVA
FRESCOS
REVESTIMENTOS MURAIS
TRABALHOS EM TODO O PAIS
FAX: (01)3470032

5,1°-E-T Serpa Pinto(1200 LISBOA).....................347 00 32

Ramalho, Cabo 49 B, 1200 Lisboa. T. (01) 67 92 02.
(Antiguidades) *095163*

Russia

Moskva

Gosudarstvenny nauchno-issledovatelski institut restovratsii, ul Gastello 44, Moskva.
T. (095) 2615814. *095164*

Mosoblrestavratsiya, ul Mantulinskaya 10, 123100 Moskva. T. (095) 2565050. *095165*

Resma, ul Shkolnaya 48, 109544 Moskva.
T. (095) 2788178. *095166*

Rosrestavratsiya, Kadashevskaya naberezhnaya 24, Moskva. T. (095) 2311358. *095167*

Starina, ul Petrovka 24, 103051 Moskva.
T. (095) 2093215. *095168*

Target, Barykovski per 4, 119034 Moskva.
T. (095) 2030903. *095169*

Vserossiski khudozhestvenny nauchno-restavratsionny tsentr im akademika Igorya Grabarya, ul Bolshaya Ordynka, Moskva. T. (095) 2310284. *095170*

Sankt-Peterburg

Antik, Chernyshevskogo pr 3, Sankt-Peterburg.
T. (812) 2750800. *095171*

Ermitazh, Dvortsovaya nab 34, 190000 Sankt-Peterburg.
T. (812) 2198693. *095172*

Remont antikvarnykh izdeli, Svechnoi per 7, Sankt-Peterburg. T. (812) 1132627. *095173*

Restamp, ul Dnepropetrovskaya 12B, Sankt-Peterburg.
T. (812) 1663597. *095174*

Restavrator, ul Marshala Govorova 43, Sankt-Peterburg.
T. (812) 2525425. *095175*

South Africa

Cape Town (Cape Province)

Rebok, T.H., 14 Scott Rd, Cape Town 7925.
T. (021) 4483842. *095176*

Johannesburg (Tvl.)

Lesser, Stanley, 19 Third Ave. Parktown North, Johannesburg. (Antiques) *095177*

Spain

Bañolas (Gerona)

Constants, Juan Mayor, Bañolas. (Varios) *095178*

Barcelona

Aragonés Corominas, Veguer, 12, 08002 Barcelona.
T. (93) 221 42 04. (Varios) *095179*

Camarasa, Hércules, 1, 08002 Barcelona.
(Varios) *095180*

Casa Alia, San Severo, 2, 08002 Barcelona.
(Varios) *095181*

Cuyas, Juan, Casanova, 31, 08011 Barcelona.
(Varios) *095182*

Gotico, Avda. Catedral, 3, 08002 Barcelona.
T. (93) 222 70 67. (Cuadros) *095183*

Grau Mas, Manuel, Aragon, 216, 08007 Barcelona.
(Varios) *095184*

Grifé y Escoda, Passaje del Credito, 8, 08002 Barcelona.
(Varios) *095185*

Guart, Ramon, Dagueria, 14, 08002 Barcelona.
T. (93) 231 51 20. (Muebles) *095186*

Gudiol, Ricart, Ramon, Anselmo, Clavé, 4, pral., 08002 Barcelona. T. (93) 222 39 15. (Quadros, tablas, pinturas, esculturas) *095187*

Ibars, J., Alfonso 12, 26, 08006 Barcelona.
(Varios) *095188*

LLuis Monllao, Ramón, Plaza San Justo 3, 08002 Barcelona. T. (93) 318 12 31. (Cuadros, retablos, esculturas, muebles policromados) *095189*

Miranda Valdes, Carlos, San Paciano, 19, pral., 08001 Barcelona. (Ceramica, escultura) *095190*

Moix Bajad, Bajada Santa Eulalia, 2, 08002 Barcelona.
(Pintura, varios) *095191*

Morato Ojer, Modesto, Leon 13, 08022 Barcelona.
T. (93) 247 15 05. (Esmaltes, Sobre) *095192*

Navarro, Margarit, 10, 08004 Barcelona.
(Varios) *095193*

Portobello, Tuset, 38, 08006 Barcelona.
T. (93) 228 95 58. (Varios) *095194*

Priu Marine, T., Arco de San Marco del Call, 11, 08002 Barcelona. (Varios) *095195*

Sala Parés, Petritxol 5, 08002 Barcelona.
T. (93) 318 70 24. (Pintura, Marcos) *095196*

Santi Vallve, Valencia, 391, 08013 Barcelona.
(Barometros) *095197*

Urgell Llorens, Lorenzo, Piedad, 9, 08002 Barcelona.
T. (93) 221 75 95. (Varios) *095198*

Villaro, Fernando, Canuda, 35, 2.0 1.à, 08002 Barcelona. (Pintura) *095199*

Burgos

Lomillo Andrés, Florentino, Plaza Santa Maria, 6, 09003 Burgos. (Policromios) *095200*

Serna Revilla, José, Lain Calvo, 31, 09003 Burgos.
T. (947) 49 65. (Varios) *095201*

Cádiz

Antigua Casa Roquero, Rosario, 25, 11004 Cádiz.
(Varios) *095202*

Córdoba

Casa Adarve Gonzalez, Magistral Gonzalez Francés 11, 14003 Córdoba. T. (957) 22 64 91. (Varios) *095203*

Corella (Navarra)

Siete Villas, Pérez Onate, 37 y Ramon y Cajal, 8, Corella.
T. (948) 194. (Varios) *095204*

La Coruña

Galerias Casimiro, Marcial del Adalid, 19, 15005 La Coruña. T. (981) 23 20 90. (Varios) *095205*

Logroño (La Rioja)

Santos, José, Mayor, 181, Logroño. (Varios) *095206*

Madrid

Abascal, Carlos, Olmo 12, 28012 Madrid.
(Pinturas) *095207*

Alcaraz Gonzalez, Francisco, Prim 17, 5.0, 28004 Madrid. T. (91) 222 16 97. (Dorados, Policromias, Tallas) *095208*

Arte y Restauracion Escriba, Hortaleza, 102, 28004 Madrid. (Varios) *095209*

Berriobena, J., Zorilla, 23, 28014 Madrid.
T. (91) 222 26 86. (Pinturas) *095210*

Biquert Pérez, Antonio, Goya, 27, 28001 Madrid.
T. (91) 226 61 18, 415 25 64. (Varios) *095211*

Bonal, Ana Maria, Gral. Oráa, 82, 28006 Madrid.
(Pinturas) *095212*

Casas, M.à del Carmen, Vallehermoso, 108, 3.0, 28003 Madrid. T. (91) 233 02 34. (Pinturas) *095213*

Diaz Rull, Emilia, Entrevias, 213, n.0 12, 28018 Madrid.
(Pinturas) *095214*

Fabriciano, Fomento, 12, 28013 Madrid. (Ceramica, Porcelana) *095215*

García, Yudez, Juan, Gustavo Fernandez Vallbuena, 34, 28002 Madrid. (Escultura) *095216*

Gonzalez, Alfredo, Meson de Paredes, 35, 28012 Madrid. (Varios) *095217*

Gonzalez Queseda, Christobal, Ardemans, 83, 28028 Madrid. (Pinturas) *095218*

Gracia, Irene, Princesa, 81, 28008 Madrid.
(Pinturas) *095219*

Herranz Garcia, Eugenio, Casado del Alisal 6, 28014 Madrid. T. (91) 227 15 07. (Antiguas, Tallas) *095220*

Instituto de Conservación y Restauración de Bienes Culturales, Calle Greco 4 Edificio Circular, 28040 Madrid.
(Varios) *095221*

Juaréz, Cecilia, Juan de Austria, 3, 28010 Madrid.
(Pinturas) *095222*

Lapausa Miralles, Andrés, Huerta del Bayo, 8, 28005 Madrid. (Varios) *095223*

Lapayesa, José, Alameda, 3, 28014 Madrid.
(Varios) *095224*

Lopez Pingarron, J., Almansa, 48, 28039 Madrid.
T. (91) 254 20 36. (Tallas) *095225*

Lopez Reiz, Enrique, Gal. Piquer, tda. 59 Ribera de Curtidores, 29, 28005 Madrid. T. (91) 239 50 80.
(Varios) *095226*

Martinez Chumila, Antonia, Larra, 12, 28004 Madrid.
(Pinturas) *095227*

Melchor Rodriguez, Leocadio, Camino de los Vinateros, 108, 28030 Madrid. T. (91) 439-30-85. (Lienzos, tablas) *095228*

Menéndez Moran, José Antonio, Lilas, 9, 28036 Madrid.
(Pinturas) *095229*

Moret, Aurelio, Clara del Rey, 79, 28036 Madrid.
(Pinturas) *095230*

Nunez de Celis, Francisco, Lopez de Hoyos, 394, 28043 Madrid. (Pinturas) *095231*

Pardo de Cela, César F., Avda. del Manzanares, 4, 28011 Madrid. T. (91) 266 69 39, 221 04 19.
(Pinturas) *095232*

Perales Soriano, Gonzalo, Rufina Blanco, 6, 28028 Madrid. (Pinturas) *095233*

Pérez Tormo, Manuel, Hermosilla, 55, 28001 Madrid.
(Pinturas) *095234*

Permas, Isabel, Ferraz, 94, 28008 Madrid.
(Pinturas) *095235*

Quemada, Angel, Campomanes, 3, 28013 Madrid.
(Varios) *095236*

Rodriguez Mostacero, Pablo, San Mateo, 30, 28004 Madrid. (Pinturas) *095237*

Selgas, Cervantes, 44, 28014 Madrid. (Varios) *095238*

Talleres de Arte Granda, S.A., Serrano, 56, 28001 Madrid. T. (91) 275 90 15. (Varios) *095239*

Torron Duran, Francisco, Felipe Moratilla, 8, 28008 Madrid. (Escultura, Pinturas) *095240*

Vinals Coma, José, Ferraz, 65, 5.0, 28008 Madrid.
(Varios) *095241*

Wortham, Harold, Serrano, 63, 28006 Madrid.
T. (91) 226 68. (Pinturas) *095242*

Sagunto (Valencia)

Roca Ribelles, Facundo, Josefa Daroqui 10, Sagunto.
T. (96) 358. (Arqueologia) *095243*

Salamanca

Albarran Chacon, Alfonso, Sanchez Llevot, 1, 6.0, 37005 Salamanca. (Varios) *095244*

San Sebastián (Guipuzcoa)

Gallego Rodriguez, Isabel II, 6, 20011 San Sebastián.
(Varios) *095245*

Sevilla
San Isidro, Luchana, 14, 41004 Sevilla.
T. (954) 22 42 61, 21 22 21, 21 30 69. (Varios) *095246*

Tarragona
Castellarnau, Fernando de, Caballeros, 11, 43003 Tarragona. T. (977) 20 30 61. (Varios) *095247*

Teruel
Punter Loscos, Domingo, Mayor, 6, Teruel. (Arqueologia, ceramica, varios) *095248*

Valencia
Artesania Puerto, Tejedores, 5, 46001 Valencia.
(Varios) *095249*
Valencia, Manuel de, Nave, 1, 46003 Valencia.
T. (96) 33 61 32, Fax 2419224. (Pintura) *095250*

Valladolid
Castilla, Portugalete, 1, 47002 Valladolid.
T. (983) 22 30 04. (Varios) *095251*

Vic (Barcelona)
Punti Costa, Pedro, Plaza San Felipe 10, Vic.
(Varios) *095252*

Zaragoza
Alvareda Hnos., Allué Salvador, 9, 50001 Zaragoza.
T. (976) 22 57 02. (Varios) *095253*
Vargas, Carlos B. & Grasa Jordan, Eloisa, Costa 3, 50000 Zaragoza. T. (976) 23 85 67. (Pintura, Obra Grafica) *095254*

Sweden

Stockholm
Falk, Ake, Nybrogatan 5, 11440 Stockholm.
T. (08) 11 37 65, 11 37 66. (Clocks) *095255*
Gamla Ting, Hästholmsv. 16, 116 44 Stockholm.
T. (08) 714 8899. (Möbel) *095256*
Salvén, Bernh., & Söhner, Tulegatan 19, 113 53 Stockholm. T. (08) 31 11 18. (Möbel) *095257*

Sundsvall
Dahlin, Bengt, Mosjön, 85590 Sundsvall.
(Paintings) *095258*

Switzerland

Allschwil (Basel-Land)
Hofstetter, Emil, Binningerstr. 112, 4123 Allschwil.
T. (061) 481 00 15. *095259*

Andeer (Graubünden)
Rampa, Ivano, Rotes Haus, 7440 Andeer.
T. (081) 6611909, Fax 6611909. (mural painting, canvas, sculptures) *095260*

Appenzell (Appenzell Innerrhoden)
Faessler, Adalbert, Hauptgasse 44, 9050 Appenzell.
T. (071) 7871113. *095261*

Arcegno (Ticino)
Fornera, Eros, Via Cantonale 2, 6618 Arcegno.
T. (091) 7914589. *095262*

Arzo (Ticino)
Baretta, Anna-Martina, Bonaga, 6864 Arzo.
T. (091) 6461131. *095263*

Ascona (Ticino)
Centro Del Bel Libro, Via Collegio, 6612 Ascona.
T. (091) 7917234, Fax 7917254. *095264*
Consonni, Carlo, Via Muraccio 7, 6612 Ascona.
T. (091) 7917226. *095265*
Meschini-Broggini, Linda, Villa Baraggie 38, 6612 Ascona. T. (091) 7912259. *095266*
Mordasini, Alfredo, Via Muraccio 66, 6612 Ascona.
T. (091) 7912386. *095267*

L'Auberson (Vaud)
Baud Frères, 1454 L'Auberson.
095268

Auvernier (Neuchâtel)
Uhler-Stähli, Les Lerins 1, 2012 Auvernier.
T. (032) 7319585. *095269*

Avenches (Vaud)
Chevalley, Christian, 83 Rue Centrale, 1580 Avenches.
T. (026) 6751730. *095270*
Fischbacher, Verena, Musée Romain, 1580 Avenches.
T. (026) 6751730. *095271*

Balerna (Ticino)
Castane, Maria-J., Via Ciarello 19, 6828 Balerna.
T. (091) 6835054. *095272*

Barbengo (Ticino)
Salzmann, Jürg, Casa Balmelli, 6917 Barbengo.
T. (091) 9951580. *095273*

Basel
Berkes, Peter, Sankt Albangraben 16, 4010 Basel.
T. (061) 2710828, Fax 2710845. (202) *095274*
Brunner, Walter, Burgfeldstr. 1, 4055 Basel.
T. (061) 381 49 04. *095275*
Cadorin, Paolo, Dr., Picassopl. 8, 4052 Basel.
T. (061) 272 68 90, Fax (061) 272 68 90. *095276*
Cimicchi, Sandro, Angensteinerstr. 15, 4052 Basel.
T. (061) 312 85 46. *095277*
Faller, Dieter, Grellingerstr. 48, 4052 Basel.
T. (061) 312 41 86. *095278*
Faltermeier, Karl, Sankt Alban-Graben 5, 4051 Basel.
T. (061) 7212202, Fax 2721861. *095279*
Graf & Raaflaub, Rheingasse 31, 4051 Basel.
T. (061) 6818020, Fax 2721383. *095280*
Heydrich, Christian, Dr., Marschalkenstr. 56, 4054 Basel.
T. (061) 281 42 35. *095281*
Holenweg, Hans, Augustinergasse 2, 4051 Basel.
T. (061) 261 83 83. *095282*
Meier, Egon H., Allschwilerstr. 30, 4055 Basel.
T. (061) 302 53 50. *095283*
Mettler, Johann, Steinbühlallee 51, 4054 Basel.
T. (061) 302 68 10. *095284*
Pawelzik, Martin, Isteiner Str 86, 4058 Basel.
T. (061) 6929613. *095285*
Perret, Ernst, Seinenberg 4, 4051 Basel.
T. (061) 22 05 05. *095286*
Rahmenatelier G., Heuberg 24, 4051 Basel.
T. (061) 261 50 24. *095287*
Schroth, Ernst, Eisengasse 5, 4051 Basel.
T. (061) 261 96 62. *095288*
Senn, Rudolf, Klosterberg 7, 4051 Basel.
T. (061) 2726262. *095289*
Snétivy, J.K., Falknerstr. 36, 4001 Basel.
T. (061) 261 32 46. *095290*
Stieger, Hans, Unterer Rheinweg 118, 4057 Basel.
T. (061) 692 95 23. *095291*
Tschanz, Peter, Schauenburgerstr. 20, 4052 Basel.
T. (061) 311 33 00. *095292*
Veillon, Monique, Picassopl. 8, 4052 Basel.
T. (061) 272 68 90, Fax (061) 272 68 90. *095293*
Wagner, Carl, Güterstr. 201, 4053 Basel.
T. (061) 361 74 30. *095294*
Wissel-Eggimann, S., Kapellenstr. 18, 4052 Basel.
T. (061) 313 15 78. *095295*

Bellinzona (Ticino)
Giovannini, Andrea Mr., Via Mesolcina 1, 6500 Bellinzona. T. (091) 8262680, Fax 8262680. *095296*

Berg (Sankt Gallen)
Kurer, Bernadette, Brühl, 9305 Berg.
T. (071) 4551255. *095297*

Bern
Berthold, Romy, Rosenweg 20, 3007 Bern.
T. (031) 371 38 82. *095298*
Bürki, Annagret, Murifeldweg 66, 3006 Bern.
T. (031) 351 59 72. *095299*
Dällenbach, Walter, c/o Kunstmuseum Bern, Hodlerstr. 8-12, 3011 Bern. T. (031) 311 09 44,
Fax (031) 311 72 63. *095300*
Dobi, Daniel, Nydeggstalden 10, 3011 Bern.
T. (031) 311 38 01. *095301*
Drembley, Anne, Hodlerstr. 12, 3011 Bern.
T. (031) 311 09 46. *095302*

Fischer-Scherler, Michael, Mattenenge 5, 3011 Bern.
T. (031) 3116820, Fax 3116847. *095303*
Freyer, Ulli, Altenbergstr. 60B, 3013 Bern.
T. (031) 331 13 14. *095304*
Irmak, Abdulkadir, Kramgasse 47, 3011 Bern.
T. (031) 3120604. (carpets) *095305*
Maurer, Bernhard, Forsthausweg 4, 3008 Bern.
T. (031) 372 01 29. *095306*
Alfred Müllers Söhne, Aebistr. 10, 3012 Bern.
T. (031) 301 12 72. *095307*
Piller, Ferdinand, Bernastr. 5, 3005 Bern.
T. (031) 351 01 27. *095308*
Robert, Henri, Tscharnerstr. 12a, 3007 Bern.
T. (031) 372 05 10. *095309*
Rolli, Bernard, Breiteweg 28, 3006 Bern.
T. (031) 9315488. *095310*
Schiessl, Ulrich, Dr., Studerstr. 56, 3004 Bern.
T. (031) 331 05 75. *095311*
Stettler, Amthausgasse 1, 3000 Bern. T. (031) 312 03 33,
Fax 3112329. *095312*
Streit, Ursula, Brunngasse 25, 3011 Bern.
T. (031) 3116906. *095313*

Bernex (Genève)
Tanner, Claude, 96 Chemin de Saule, 1233 Bernex.
T. (022) 757 16 67. *095314*

Bettlach (Solothurn)
Bischof, Cesar, Bischmattstr 7, 2544 Bettlach.
T. (032) 6452574. *095315*

Bettwil (Aargau)
Wohlgemuth, Urs, Hinterdorf 42, 5618 Bettwil.
T. (056) 6272423. *095316*

Bevaix (Neuchâtel)
Artho, Edwin, Miremont, 2022 Bevaix.
T. (038) 461917. *095317*

Biasca (Ticino)
Pierini, Giorgio, Via Stazione, 6710 Biasca.
T. (091) 8621118. *095318*

Biel (Bern)
Rettenmund, Peter, Montozweg 17, 2504 Biel.
T. (032) 3418860. *095319*

Binningen (Basel-Land)
Kämpfer, Horst, Hauptstr. 57, 4102 Binningen.
T. (061) 421 85 86. *095320*

Birrwil (Aargau)
Zum blauen Pfauen, In den Ländern 79, 5708 Birrwil.
T. (064) 74 12 67. *095321*

Birsfelden
Steiner, Martin P., Am Stausee 27/10, 4127 Birsfelden.
T. (061) 3132000, Fax 3132000. (paintings; gildings; drawings; etchings; watercolours) *095322*

Bremgarten (Aargau)
Bürger, Ulrike, Seftaustr. 40, 3047 Bremgarten.
T. (031) 3010357, Fax 3203299. *095323*

Brig (Valais)
Fischer-Burgener, D., Sennereigasse 3, 3900 Brig.
T. (027) 9230269. *095324*
Furrer, Walter J., Saflischstr 2, 3900 Brig.
T. (027) 9235276. *095325*

Brunnen (Schwyz)
Gisler, Hubert, Wylenstr 6, 6440 Brunnen.
T. (041) 8205110. *095326*

Canobbio (Ticino)
Cantoni, Marco, Via Chiosso 17, 6952 Canobbio.
T. (091) 9411776. *095327*
Ferrari, Franco, Via Viganelli 2, Al Maglio, 6952 Canobbio. T. (091) 9410520. *095328*

Carouge (Genève)
Casagrande, Pierre-A., 5 Clos-Fonderie, 1227 Carouge.
T. (022) 343 19 65. *095329*
Conte, Salvatore, 9 Clos-Fonderie, 1227 Carouge.
T. (022) 343 85 77, Fax 43 79 97. *095330*
Dick, Caroline, 2 Pl de l'Octroi, 1227 Carouge.
T. (022) 3435923. *095331*

Dunand & Reymond, 8 Rue Ancienne, 1227 Carouge.
T. (022) 342 08 21.   *095332*
Henry, Arthur, 32 Rue des Noirettes, 1227 Carouge.
T. (022) 342 02 01.   *095333*
Magnin, Michel, 5 Rue Ancienne, 1227 Carouge.
T. (022) 342 53 67.   *095334*
Perino, Marcel, 20 Rue St. Victor, 1227 Carouge.
T. (022) 342 11 98.   *095335*
Travagli, Jacques, 4 Rue St. Joseph, 1227 Carouge.
T. (022) 343 52 91.   *095336*
Travagli, Pietro, Rue Saint-Joseph 13, 1227 Carouge.
T. (022) 3473320, 3433118.   *095337*

Caslano (Ticino)
Alberti, Pierluigi, P. Lago, 6987 Caslano.
T. (091) 6063719.   *095338*

Chardonne (Vaud)
Pelot, Anne-Françoise, 10 Rte de Bellevue, 1803 Char-
donne. T. (021) 9235349.   *095339*

Château-d'Oex (Vaud)
Mottier, Philippe, Atelier la Place, 1837 Château-d'Oex.
T. (026) 9246482.   *095340*

La Chaux-de-Fonds (Neuchâtel)
Eisenegger, Erwin, Rue des Musées 26, 2300 La Chaux-
de-Fonds. T. (032) 9138526.   *095341*
Institut l'homme et le temps, Centre de Restauration, 29
Rue des Musées, 2301 La Chaux-de-Fonds.
T. (032) 9676861, Fax 9676889.   *095342*

Chêne-Bougeries (Genève)
Bionda, François, Rue de Chêne-Bougeries 14, 1224
Chêne-Bougeries. T. (022) 3481349.   *095343*
Etienne, Danielle, Chemin de Grange-Bonnet 10, 1224
Chêne-Bougeries. T. (022) 3490044.   *095344*

Chêne-Bourg (Genève)
Cerutti-Anchisi, Dante, Av Bel-Air 72, 1225 Chêne-
Bourg. T. (022) 3480055.   *095345*

Cheseaux-sur-Lausanne (Vaud)
Mietta, Pierre, 6 Ch. des Chalets, 1033 Cheseaux-sur-
Lausanne. T. (021) 731 18 78.   *095346*

Chur (Graubünden)
Lengler, Josef Maria, Luzistr. 6, 7000 Chur.
T. (081) 2520506.   *095347*

Clugin (Graubünden)
Demarmels, Fritz, 7442 Clugin.
T. (081) 6611733.   *095348*

Cologny (Genève)
Denis, Christiane, Ch. Nant d'Argent, 1223 Cologny.
T. (022) 752 42 31.   *095349*

Coppet (Vaud)
Boissonnas, Alain G., 16 Chemin des Grands Huttins,
1296 Coppet. T. (022) 776 21 28.   *095350*

Crans-sur-Sierre (Valais)
Barras, Martine, Chalet Bruno, 3963 Crans-sur-Sierre.
T. (027) 4812036.   *095351*

Crémines (Bern)
Spart, Michel, Zatte 4, 2746 Crémines.
T. (032) 4999548.   *095352*

La Croix-de-Rozon (Genève)
Micheli, Béatrice, 50 Rte. du Prieur, 1257 La Croix-de-
Rozon. T. (022) 771 14 58.   *095352a*

Deitingen (Solothurn)
Kofmel, Walter, Baschistr 231, 4707 Deitingen.
T. (032) 6141686.   *095353*

Les Diablerets (Vaud)
Rouiller, Willy, 1865 Les Diablerets.
T. (024) 4923980.   *095353a*

Dübendorf (Zürich)
Wyss, Jaime, Zürichstr 98, 8600 Dübendorf.
T. (01) 8213366, Fax 8213354.   *095354*

Echallens (Vaud)
Galaud, Michel, Pl. de la Gare, 1040 Echallens.
T. (021) 731 18 78.   *095355*

Ennetbaden (Aargau)
Runte, Hélène, Trottestr. 2, 5400 Ennetbaden.
T. (056) 2221931.   *095356*

Faido (Ticino)
Bertini, Patrizio, 6760 Faido. T. (091) 8661893.   *095357*

Fischingen (Thurgau)
Ressel, Erhard, Rudlenstr. 5, 8376 Fischingen.
T. (071) 9771609.   *095358*

Flaach (Zürich)
Zimmermann-Kretz, Kurt & Silvia, Oberdorfstr 9, 8416
Flaach. T. (052) 3181147, Fax 3181969.
(furniture)   *095359*

Forch (Zürich)
Brodbeck, Sabina, Alte Forchstr. 55, 8127 Forch.
T. (01) 918 09 10.   *095360*

Frauenfeld (Thurgau)
Hauser, Janina, Zürcherstr. 218, 8500 Frauenfeld.
T. (052) 7216052.   *095361*
Warger, Doris, Industriestr. 21, 8500 Frauenfeld.
T. (052) 7218055.   *095362*

Fribourg
Atelier Conservation / Restauration du Livre, 14 Stalden,
1700 Fribourg. T. (026) 3221124.   *095363*
Egger, André, 8 Rue de l'Industrie, 1700 Fribourg.
T. (026) 3249874.   *095364*
Horky, Jan, 61 Grand-Rue, 1700 Fribourg.
T. (026) 3228469, Fax 3228469.   *095365*
Neuhaus, Beat, 7 Imp. Forêt, 1700 Fribourg.
T. (026) 4812142.   *095366*
Page, André E., 1 Rte. Nicolas-Chenaux, 1700 Fribourg.
T. (026) 3247563.   *095367*
Rossier, Claude, c/o Musée d'Art et d'Histoire, 12 Rue
de Morat, 1700 Fribourg. T. (037) 228571, 228140,
Fax 231672.   *095368*

Frick (Aargau)
Wahl-Lang, Esther, Geissgasse 5, 5070 Frick.
T. (062) 8710337.   *095369*

Gais (Aargau)
Knechtle, Rudolf, Langasse 74, 9056 Gais.
T. (071) 7932448.   *095370*

Genève
Anex, Isabelle, 5 Rue Simplon, 1207 Genève.
T. (022) 735 16 25.   *095371*
Atelier Arte, Rte des Jeunes 4ter, 1211 Genève 26.
T. (022) 301 30 00, Fax 3013000. (Paintings)   *095372*
Beguin, René, Rue Etienne Dumont 1, 1204 Genève.
T. (022) 3291308.   *095373*
Cottier, Fiorella, 62 Rte. de Frontenex, 1207 Genève.
T. (022) 736 74 20.   *095374*
Diotalleri, Italo, 11 Rue Royaume, 1201 Genève.
T. (022) 732 82 27.   *095375*
Dufour, Claude, 9 Rlle. du Couchant, 1207 Genève.
T. (022) 736 98 79.   *095376*
Gagnebin-Bang, Cécilie, 28 Av. Crets de Champel, 1206
Genève. T. (022) 346 30 31.   *095377*
Hakkak, Betty, Musée Ariana – 10, Av de la Paix, 1202
Genève. T. (022) 4185450, Fax 4185451. (Ceramiques
verre)   *095378*
Houriet, Claude, 9-11 Rue du Clos, 1207 Genève.
T. (022) 735 96 13.   *095379*
Huber, Christian, 31 Rue Lausanne, 1201 Genève.
T. (022) 732 56 48.   *095380*
Laboratoire du Musée d'Art et d'Histoire, 9-11 Rue du
Clos, 1207 Genève. T. (022) 7359613,
Fax 7365416.   *095381*
Lahusen, Aliska, 47 Quai du Rhône, 1205 Genève.
T. (022) 349 61 26.   *095382*
Lerik, Rozalia, 1 Av. Mail, 1205 Genève.
T. (022) 328 11 80.   *095383*
Micara-Granelli, Lisa, 14 Rue Jean-Sénébier, 1205 Ge-
nève. T. (4122) 3208943, Fax 3208943.   *095384*

Obermann, Pierre, 12 Rue du Perron, 1204 Genève.
T. (022) 3213654, 3113654.   *095385*
Overney, Arlette J., 39 Grand-Rue, 1204 Genève.
T. (022) 320 42 59.   *095386*
Pologruto, Marziale, 48 Rue Maunoir, 1207 Genève.
T. (022) 735 59 90.   *095387*
Strasser, Véronique, 5 Rue le Corbusier, 1208 Genève.
T. (022) 3470560.   *095388*

Genthod (Genève)
Orange-Fischer, C., 11 Ch. de la Dime, 1294 Genthod.
T. (022) 774 29 17.   *095389*

Geuensee (Luzern)
Albisser, Egon, Oberdorf, 6232 Geuensee.
T. (041) 921 25 24.   *095390*

Giubiasco (Ticino)
Fasciani, Leonardo, 2 Strada delle Gaggiole, 6512 Giu-
biasco. T. (091) 8576480, Fax 8577850.   *095391*
Melchioretto, Corrado, Via Ferriere 5, 6512 Giubiasco.
T. (01) 27 31 15.   *095392*

Gland (Vaud)
Bondi, Delmo, Ch. Vermy, 1196 Gland.
T. (022) 364 23 71.   *095393*

Grand-Lancy (Genève)
Giorgi, Fres de, 6 Ch. Ramboussons, 1212 Grand-Lancy.
T. (022) 794 73 20.   *095394*

Grens (Vaud)
Glardon, Marcel, Le Pâ, 1261 Grens.
T. (022) 361 25 69.   *095395*

Grüningen (Zürich)
Oberli, Fritz, Bühl, 8627 Grüningen.
T. (01) 935 11 81.   *095396*

Herrenschwanden (Bern)
Schaible, Volker, Mettlenwaldweg 30, 3037 Herren-
schwanden. T. (031) 302 46 74.   *095397*

Herrliberg (Zürich)
Steinlin, Robert, Felsenaustr. 2, 8704 Herrliberg.
T. (01) 915 02 42.   *095398*

Hunzenschwil (Aargau)
Strebel, Martin, Bahnhofstr 15, 5502 Hunzenschwil.
T. (062) 8973970, Fax 8970046.   *095399*

Ittigen (Bern)
Cuany, Françoise, Vord. Schermen 6, 3063 Ittigen.
T. (031) 921 20 89.   *095400*
Nussli, Stefan, Worblentalstr. 8, 3063 Ittigen.
T. (031) 921 85 84, Fax (031) 921 87 55.   *095401*

Jona (Sankt Gallen)
Baldiger, Hugo, Rütistr. 60, 8645 Jona.
T. (052) 2103162.   *095402*

Kloten (Zürich)
Stohler, Alice, Dietlikerstr. 43, 8302 Kloten.
T. (01) 813 26 50.   *095403*

Köniz (Bern)
Berthold, Romy, Schloßstr. 18, 3098 Köniz.
T. (031) 971 75 25.   *095404*

Kriens (Luzern)
Kammermann, Werner, Luzernerstr. 71, 6010 Kriens.
T. (041) 311 17 28.   *095405*

Küsnacht (Zürich)
Carol, Reto, Rainweg 17, 8700 Küsnacht.
T. (01) 910 09 39.   *095406*
Tuchschmid, Anne, Rietstr. 20, 8700 Küsnacht.
T. (01) 910 86 20.   *095407*

Lamone (Ticino)
Bocchi, Adriano, 6814 Lamone.
T. (091) 9432035.   *095409*

Le Landeron (Neuchâtel)
Holweger, Günther, Nugerol 6, 2525 Le Landeron.
T. (032) 7514724.   *095410*

Lausanne (Vaud)
A l'Antiquaille, 17 Blvd. de Grancy, 1006 Lausanne.
T. (021) 616 22 01. *095411*
Baechtold, Brigitte, 19 Av. Villamont, 1005 Lausanne.
T. (021) 312 62 17. *095412*
Benois, Patrick, 17 Bd. de Grancy, 1006 Lausanne.
T. (021) 616 22 01. *095413*
Fuchs, Michel, 1bis Av du Rond-Point, 1006 Lausanne.
T. (021) 6164242, Fax (021) 6164242. (roman mural
painting) *095414*
Lena, Mario, Rue César-Roux 7, 1005 Lausanne.
T. (021) 320 07 41. *095415*
Michel, Claude, Musée Cantonal, 1014 Lausanne.
T. (021) 312 83 34. *095416*

Lausen (Basel-Land)
Möbel- und Teppich-Markt, Rolleweg 5, 4415 Lausen.
T. (061) 921 20 10. *095417*

Liestal (Basel-Land)
Ohlhorst, Dieter, Kesselweg 43a, 4410 Liestal.
T. (061) 901 79 58. *095420*

Le Lignon (Genève)
Hermanès, Théo-Ant., Atelier Crephart 19 Ch. Château-
Bloc, 1219 Le Lignon. T. (022) 7969380,
Fax 7973130. *095421*

Locarno (Ticino)
Bellerio, Timothy & Atsuko, Via Sant'Antonio 11, 6600
Locarno. T. (091) 7515794, Fax 7515774. (Furniture,
silver, jewels) *095422*
Grimbühler, Gabriele, Via ai Monti Trinita 33, 6600 Lo-
carno. T. (091) 7516187. *095423*
Ledermann, Leo, Castelrotto, 6600 Locarno.
T. (091) 7511716. (paintings, graphics) *095424*

Le Locle (Neuchâtel)
Huguenin-Zryd, A., 30 Mi-Côte, 2400 Le Locle.
T. (032) 9312420. *095425*

Losone (Ticino)
Gallina, Silvia, Via Barchée 16, 6616 Losone.
T. (091) 7913564. *095426*

Lüchingen (Sankt Gallen)
Grabherr-Häfliger, W., Rorschacher Str. 114, 9438 Lüchingen. T. (071) 7552036. *095427*

Lugano (Ticino)
Passardi, Gabriele, C. Pestalozzi 25, 6900 Lugano.
T. (091) 9451288. *095428*
Pierini & Rossini, Via Lavizzari 10, 6900 Lugano.
T. (091) 9237569. *095429*

Luzern
Achermann-von Segesser, Jeanette, Pfistergasse 15,
6003 Luzern. T. (041) 240 63 35. *095430*
Eckert, Georges, St. Karli-Str 13c, 6004 Luzern.
T. (041) 2409080. *095431*
Galerie Meile, Rosenberghöhe 4a, 6004 Luzern.
T. (041) 4203318, Fax 4202169. *095432*
Tiffany, Schwanenpl. 7, 6004 Luzern.
T. (041) 410 43 00. *095433*

Männedorf (Zürich)
Englisch, Gabriele, Bergstr. 79, 8708 Männedorf.
T. (01) 920 17 50. *095434*

Martigny (Valais)
Favre-Bulle, Gisèle, Les Rappes, 1920 Martigny. *095435*

Meinier (Genève)
Rod, Richard, 11 Ch. Stade, 1252 Meinier.
T. (022) 752 45 10. *095436*

Mendrisio (Ticino)
Gilardi, Silvano, Via Franchini 19, 6850 Mendrisio.
T. (091) 6467731. *095437*

Minusio (Ticino)
Pedroia, Piero, Via Pozzaracchia 5, 6648 Minusio.
T. (091) 7433927. *095438*

Mönchaltorf (Zürich)
Frehner, Ernst, Bruggächerstr. 10, 8617 Mönchaltorf.
T. (01) 948 03 43. *095439*

Mörel (Valais)
Mutter, Otto, Furkastr., 3983 Mörel.
T. (027) 9271236. *095440*

Mollis (Glarus)
Kamm, Hans-Rudolf, Hinterdorfstr. 14, 8753 Mollis.
T. (055) 6124063. *095441*

Montalchez (Neuchâtel)
Gabus-Thevenaz, 2027 Montalchez.
T. (032) 8551776. *095442*

Morges (Vaud)
Perugini, Giuseppe, 39 Rue Fossés, 1110 Morges.
T. (021) 802 12 31. *095443*

Muri bei Bern
Burkhard, Susi, Villettengässli 31, 3074 Muri bei Bern.
T. (031) 3515972. (watercolours, pastels) *095444*
Kolb, Anne-J., Reutigenweg 7, 3074 Muri bei Bern.
T. (031) 9515622. *095445*

Muttenz (Basel-Land)
Bernard, Peter, Hauptstr. 2, 4132 Muttenz.
T. (061) 461 02 33. *095446*

Naters (Valais)
Rossi, Mario, Furkastr. 50, 3904 Naters.
T. (027) 9231124. *095447*

Neuchâtel
Hug, Beat, 22 Ruelle Vaucher, 2000 Neuchâtel.
T. (032) 7247212, 7242816. *095448*
De Montmollin, 3 Rue Louis Favre, 2000 Neuchâtel.
T. (032) 8451152. *095449*
Piller, Yves, Rue des Saavs 18, 2000 Neuchâtel.
T. (032) 7252019. *095450*
Salis, Isabelle de, 29 Trois-Portes, 2000 Neuchâtel.
T. (032) 7252591. *095451*

Neuhausen am Rheinfall (Schaffhausen)
Bührer, Barbara, Zentralstr 25, 8212 Neuhausen am
Rheinfall. T. (052) 6721508, Fax 6724583. *095452*
Hug, Aldo, Zentralstr 25, 8212 Neuhausen am Rheinfall.
T. (052) 6724583, Fax 6724583. *095453*

Nyon (Vaud)
Dabre, Florence, 8b Ch. de la Dôle, 1260 Nyon.
T. (022) 362 25 49. *095454*

Obbürgen (Obwalden)
Ettlin, Werner, Diethelmstr. 16, 6363 Obbürgen.
T. (041) 610 64 94. *095455*

Oberwangen bei Bern
Bellwald & Partner, Alte Mühle, 3173 Oberwangen bei
Bern. T. (031) 981 27 24. *095456*

Onex (Genève)
Meister, Richard, 15 Rue du Vieux-Moulin, 1213 Onex.
T. (022) 792 89 80. *095457*

Onnens (Vaud)
Ashdown, Ian, Centre de restauration et conservation,
1425 Onnens. T. (024) 4361712, Fax 4361945. *095458*

Orbe (Vaud)
Pittet, Christian, 40 Rue Terreaux, 1350 Orbe.
T. (024) 4414040. *095459*

Orient (Vaud)
LM Laser, 1341 Orient. T. (021) 845 46 20. *095460*

Orselina (Ticino)
Pedrocchi, Sabrina, Via al Parco 20, 6644 Orselina.
T. (091) 7437905. *095461*

Les Ponts-de-Martel (Neuchâtel)
Benoit & Gentil, 5 Rue de la Prairie, 2316 Les Ponts-de-
Martel. T. (032) 9371458. *095461a*

Porrentruy (Jura)
Villoz, Jean-Philippe, Quai de l'Allaine 4, 2900 Porrentruy. T. (032) 4665866. *095462*

Présinge (Genève)
Carbonnel, Katrina de, 200 Rte. de Jussy, 1243 Présin-
ge. T. (022) 759 14 16, Fax 759. *095463*

Pully (Vaud)
Tafelmacher, Georges, 22 Rte. du Port, 1009 Pully.
T. (021) 7286571. *095464*
Tissières, Floriane, 4 Av. de Lavaux, 1009 Pully.
T. (021) 7298276. *095465*

Raron (Valais)
Lochmatter, Roland, Bietschgärten, 3942 Raron.
T. (027) 9341939. *095466*

Reinach (Basel-Land)
Bernard, Robert, Baselstr 108, 4153 Reinach.
T. (061) 711 01 76, Fax 7110565. *095467*

Riehen (Basel-Stadt)
Buder, Susanne, Rössligasse 9, 4125 Riehen.
T. (061) 641 50 49. (202; 209) *095468*
Waldner, Sigrid, Rheinsprung 7, 4126 Riehen.
T. (061) 261 58 95. *095469*

Riggisberg (Bern)
Schorta, Regula, Dr., c/o Abegg-Stiftung, 3132 Riggis-
berg. T. (031) 8081201, Fax 8081200. *095470*

Rotkreuz (Zug)
Meierhans, Jakob, Waldetenstr. 7, 6343 Rotkreuz.
T. (041) 790 21 12. *095471*

Rudolfstetten (Aargau)
Remigius Sep & Elisabeth Graf, Mühlegasse 10, 8964
Rudolfstetten. T. (056) 6330360. *095472*

Rüdlingen (Schaffhausen)
Rüfenacht, Fritz, Im Chapf, 8455 Rüdlingen.
T. (01) 867 05 52. *095473*

Rünenberg (Baselland)
Bieri, Doris, Hundsbrunn 91c, 4497 Rünenberg.
T. (061) 991 49 82. *095474*

Rüschlikon (Zürich)
Höhn, Ernst, Alte Landstr 73, 8803 Rüschlikon.
T. (01) 724 03 05. *095475*

Rupperswil (Aargau)
Brücker, Daniela, Auweg 6, 5102 Rupperswil.
T. (064) 47 24 54. *095476*
Ineichen, Josef, Bruggerstr 26, 5102 Rupperswil.
T. (064) 473480. *095477*

Russin (Genève)
Mühlethaler, Marie-J., 313 Rte. du Mandement, 1281
Russin. T. (022) 754 15 68. *095478*

Saint-Saphorin (Lavaux) (Vaud)
Genton, Annette, 1813 Saint-Saphorin (Lavaux).
T. (021) 921 18 15. *095479*

Sainte-Croix (Vaud)
Mannella, Antoine, 2 Rue Industrie, 1450 Sainte-Croix.
T. (024) 4541956. *095480*

Sankt Gallen
Eichholzer, Werner, Goliathgasse 33, 9006 Sankt Gallen.
T. (071) 2440641, Fax 2440641. *095481*
Niedermann, Urs, Zürcherstr 178, 9014 Sankt Gallen.
T. (071) 2778591. *095482*
Sennhauser & Partner, Altenwegenstr. 71, 9015 Sankt
Gallen. T. (071) 3113579. *095483*

La Sarraz (Vaud)
Bonard, Pierre, 19 Grand-Rue, 1315 La Sarraz.
T. (021) 866 63 20. *095484*

Schlatt bei Winterthur (Zürich)
Vogel, Fritz, In der Säge, 8418 Schlatt bei Winterthur.
T. (052) 3631060. *095485*

Schwarzenegg (Bern)
Salzmann, Hans, Allmend 41, 3616 Schwarzenegg.
T. (033) 4532608. *095486*

Servion (Vaud)
Delanoê, Michel, Le Praz-du-Perey, 1077 Servion.
T. (021) 903 19 34. *095487*

Siebnen (Schwyz)
Salvaggio, Aldo, Zürcherstr 26, 8854 Siebnen.
T. (052) 4401594. *095488*

Sion (Valais)
Meyer-de Weck, Madeleine, La Muraz, 1950 Sion.
T. (027) 3953060, Fax 3953060. (202) *095489*

Solothurn
Kocher, Kathrin, Werkhofstr. 52, 4500 Solothurn.
T. (032) 6233474. *095490*

Staad (Sankt Gallen)
Sigi's Antiquitäten, Schlössliweg 6, 9422 Staad.
T. (071) 8551888. *095491*

Stäfa (Zürich)
Hediger, Max, Glärnischstr 48b, 8712 Stäfa.
T. (01) 9263696. *095492*

Stans (Nidwalden)
Stöckli, Tottikonstr 5, 6370 Stans. T. (041) 6101635,
Fax 6100036. *095493*

Steffisburg (Bern)
Brechbühl, Christof, Hombergstr. 56, 3612 Steffisburg.
T. (033) 4378000. *095494*

Steinen (Schwyz)
Schibig, Josef, Bitzistr. 11, 6422 Steinen.
T. (041) 832 14 39, Fax (041) 832 14 57. *095495*

Tafers (Fribourg)
Kappeler, Urs, Wolgiswil, 1712 Tafers.
T. (026) 4942874. *095496*
Meucelin, Myriam, Thunstr. 2, 1712 Tafers.
T. (026) 4941647. *095497*

Thalwil (Zürich)
Höhn, Ernst, Alte Landstr. 191a, 8800 Thalwil.
T. (01) 721 00 06. *095498*
Pegurri, Giacomo, Gotthardstr. 34, 8800 Thalwil.
T. (01) 721 04 32. *095499*

Thônex (Genève)
Wyss-Chodat, Yvonne, 16b Rte. de Jussy, 1226 Thônex.
T. (022) 348 71 45. *095500*

La Tour-de-Peilz (Vaud)
Domingo, Louis, 20 Rue du Château, 1814 La Tour-de-
Peilz. T. (021) 944 60 31. *095501*

Tremona (Ticino)
Gianola, Luigi, 6865 Tremona. T. (091) 6466601. *095502*

Uetikon am See (Zürich)
Blum, Michael, Auf der Rüti, 8707 Uetikon am See.
T. (01) 9204979. *095503*

Untereggen (St. Gallen)
Engler, Bonifaz, Vorderhof, 9033 Untereggen.
T. (071) 8661455. *095504*

Vaglio (Ticino)
Graf, Mario, Lab. di restauro, 6947 Vaglio.
T. (091) 9434488. *095505*

Vandoeuvres (Genève)
Cotton, Yvonne, 183 Rte. Mon-Idée, 1253 Vandoeuvres.
T. (022) 750 24 32, Fax 750 24 48. *095506*

Vernier (Genève)
Stocker, Suzanne, 22 Chemin de la Greube, 1214 Vernier. T. (022) 341 22 35, Fax 341 23 73. *095507*

Vevey (Vaud)
Dik, Jan, 31 Rue de la Madeleine, 1800 Vevey.
T. (021) 922 92 11. *095508*
Héritier, Pierre-Ant., 45 Av. Général Guisan, 1800 Vevey.
T. (021) 921 35 94, Fax 921 03 97. *095509*

Veyrier (Genève)
Gottret, Maurice, 16 Ch. Jules-Ed-Gottret, 1255 Veyrier.
T. (022) 784 20 48. *095510*
White, Loren, 12 Ch. Fléchère, 1255 Veyrier.
T. (022) 784 17 18. *095511*

Vezia (Ticino)
Righini, Nicola, Via Morbio 13, 6943 Vezia.
T. (091) 9663942. *095512*

Villars-sur-Glâne (Fribourg)
von Imhoff, Hans-Christoph, Chemin des Rochettes 6,
1752 Villars-sur-Glâne. T. (026) 4010777, Fax 410888.
(Paintings, wood sculpture) *095513*

Villmergen (Aargau)
Gall, Ernst, In den Reben 16, 5612 Villmergen.
T. (056) 6228332, Fax 6228332. (Books) *095514*

Volketswil (Zürich)
Elmer, Jörg-Thomas, Bachstr. 13, 8604 Volketswil.
T. (01) 945 41 38. *095515*

Vordemwald (Aargau)
Roudnicky, Zdenek, Rüti 297, 4803 Vordemwald.
T. (062) 52 15 72. *095516*

Wabern (Bern)
Jordi, Peter, Seftigenstr. 309, 3084 Wabern.
T. (031) 961 42 53. *095517*

Worben (Bern)
Arn, Willy, Alkernweg 2, 3252 Worben.
T. (032) 3845850, Fax 3851809. *095518*

Zizers (Graubünden)
Emmenegger, Oskar, Stöcklistr, 7205 Zizers.
T. (081) 3223081, Fax 3072250. *095519*

Zollikerberg (Zürich)
Scheidegger, René Ferdinand, Postfach 223, 8125 Zoll-
ikerberg. T. (01) 391 67 45. *095520*
Téoh, Geneviève, Am Brunnbächli 12, 8125 Zollikerberg.
T. (01) 391 99 43. *095521*

Zollikofen (Bern)
Restaur' Art, Eichenweg 2, 3052 Zollikofen.
T. (031) 9116116, Fax 9116117. (Paintings, stones,
gilding) *095522*

Zollikon (Zürich)
Rietmann, René, Buchholzstr. 3, 8702 Zollikon.
T. (01) 391 89 54. *095523*
Wohlgemuth, Luise, Witellikerstr. 9, 8702 Zollikon.
T. (01) 391 44 22. *095524*

Zürich
Aladin Antik, Seefeldstr 226, 8008 Zürich.
T. (01) 3815380, Fax 3822913. (lights) *095525*
Atelier d'Art, Neumarkt 1, 8001 Zürich.
T. (01) 252 66 70. *095526*
Beyer, Bahnhofstr. 31, 8001 Zürich.
T. (01) 221 10 80. *095527*
Biondi, Massimo, Trittligasse 36, 8001 Zürich.
T. (01) 221 02 03. *095528*
Boissonnas, Baschligpl 1, 8032 Zürich. T. (01) 2514739,
Fax 2612787. (202) *095529*
Büren, Fritz von, Museumstr. 2, 8023 Zürich.
T. (01) 221 10 10. *095530*
Bürki, Fritz, Thurgauerstr. 76, 8050 Zürich.
T. (01) 302 00 11. *095531*
Canetti, Hera, Klosbachstr. 88, 8032 Zürich.
T. (01) 261 09 36. *095532*
Davite, Giulio, Riedtlistr. 30/34, 8006 Zürich.
T. (01) 363 52 40, 361 53 19. *095533*
Dorigo, Richard, Tobelhofstr. 320, 8044 Zürich.
T. (01) 251 98 34. *095534*
Frey, Charles, Kreuzpl 9, 8032 Zürich.
T. (01) 2516868. *095535*
Graf, Max, Froschaugasse 9, 8001 Zürich.
T. (01) 252 14 75. *095536*
Grimbühler, Bruno, Fabrikstr. 12, 8005 Zürich.
T. (01) 272 22 03, Fax 272 22 03. *095537*
Häusler, Albert, Zedernstr. 4, 8032 Zürich.
T. (01) 261 41 57. *095538*
Hediger, Max, Limmatquai 100, 8025 Zürich.
T. (01) 251 64 78. *095539*
Heuberger, Jakob, Rindermarkt 17, 8001 Zürich.
T. (01) 251 67 91. *095540*
Hug, Aldo, Wildbachstr 80, 8008 Zürich.
T. (01) 3839313, Fax 3839033. *095541*

Hug, Max, Neumarkt 25, 8001 Zürich.
T. (01) 251 61 36. *095542*
Invernizzi, Osvaldo, Rotbuchstr. 54, 8037 Zürich.
T. (01) 363 23 53. *095543*
Kiener, Martin, Neumarkt 23, 8001 Zürich.
T. (01) 2624221 (Antiquitäten), 2624235 (Antiquariat),
Fax 2624275. (silver) *095544*
Koenig, Peter, Kreuzpl 5, 8032 Zürich.
T. (01) 2513261. *095545*
Lorenzi, Franz, Letzigraben 22, 8003 Zürich.
T. (01) 492 91 97. *095546*
Lunin, Serge, Zeltweg 9, 8032 Zürich.
T. (01) 261 94 33. *095547*
Mäder, Peter M., c/o Schweizerisches Landesmuseum,
Museumstr. 2, 8001 Zürich. T. (01) 221 10 10. *095548*
Marty, Hanspeter, Kunsthaus, Heimpl. 1, 8024 Zürich.
T. (01) 251 67 65, Fax 251 24 64. *095549*
Masson, Olivier, Baschligpl. 1, 8032 Zürich.
T. (01) 251 47 39. *095550*
Meier, Erich und Irma, Haldenbachstr. 34, 8006 Zürich.
T. (01) 261 92 30. *095551*
Minder, Daniel, Zeltweg 42, 8032 Zürich.
T. (01) 2517533. *095552*
Münger, Heinrich, Rindermarkt 11, 8001 Zürich.
T. (01) 252 20 52. *095553*
Nefer, Glockengasse 18/II, 8001 Zürich. T. (01) 2114805,
Fax (01) 2115947. *095554*
Pictet, Françoise, Baschligplatz 1, 8032 Zürich.
T. (01) 251 47 39. *095555*
Ries, Judith, Hüslibachstr 11, 8041 Zürich.
T. (01) 4824710. *095556*
Saint James' Workshop, Hardpl 21, 8004 Zürich.
T. (01) 4015365, Fax 4015365. *095557*
Schweidler, Gerd, Tobelhofstr. 335, 8044 Zürich.
T. (01) 821 06 24. *095558*
Sturzenegger, Markus, Weggengasse 3, 8001 Zürich.
T. (01) 2115925. (Möbel) *095559*
Tanner, Robert, Forchstr 19, 8032 Zürich.
T. (01) 3837072. *095560*
Wild, Wolfgang, Wuhrstr. 27, 8003 Zürich.
T. (01) 463 12 42. *095561*
Wohlgemuth, Urs, Pelikanstr. 40, 8001 Zürich.
T. (01) 221 31 91. *095562*

Zug
Aschwanden, Rolf, St Johannstr 26, 6300 Zug.
T. (041) 7416694. *095563*
Bohren, Beatrice, Aegeristr. 76, 6300 Zug.
T. (041) 711 37 12, Fax (041) 711 37 14. *095564*
Gerber, Julia, Sankt Oswaldgasse 6, 6301 Zug.
T. (041) 710 44 41. *095565*
Trojanowski, Albisstr 7, 6300 Zug. T. (041) 7114818,
Fax 7116392. *095566*

United Kingdom

Aberdare (Mid Glamorgan)
Pinewood Studios, 26b Weatherall St, Aberdare.
T. (01685) 872158. (Furniture) *095567*

Aberdeen (Grampian)
Aberdeen Antiques, 75 Skene St, Aberdeen AB1 1QD.
T. (01224) 639093. (Furniture, silver,
porcelain) *095568*
Art Attack, 32 Marischal St, Aberdeen.
T. (01224) 212708. (Paintings) *095569*
Belgrave French Polishing, 1 Belgrave Terrace, Aber-
deen. T. (01224) 624384. (Furniture) *095570*
Clock Repair Service, 197 King St, Aberdeen.
T. (01224) 637495. (Clocks) *095571*
Gallery, 41 Justice St, Aberdeen. T. (01224) 625909.
(Jewellery) *095572*
George, Arthur F., Granitehill Enterprise Centre, Granite-
hill, Northfield, Aberdeen. T. (01224) 698545.
(Furniture) *095573*
Interior Stripping and Decorating Services, 610 King St,
Aberdeen AB2 1SN. T. (01224) 488509.
(Furniture) *095574*
Watt, Elizabeth, 69 Thistle St, Aberdeen.
T. (01224) 647232. (China, glass) *095575*
Waverley, 18 Victoria St, Aberdeen. T. (01224) 640633.
(Oil paintings, watercolours, prints) *095576*

Aberfeldy (Tayside)
Barclay, Jane, Blackhill House, Aberfeldy.
T. (01887) 840276. (Paintings)   095577

Abertillery (Gwent)
David's Antiques, 64-66 Somerset St, Abertillery.
T. (01495) 215888. (Furniture)   095578

Aberystwyth (Dyfed)
Furniture Cave, 33 Cambrian St, Aberystwyth.
T. (01970) 611234. (Furniture)   095579

Abingdon (Oxfordshire)
Faulkner, Ian, 2 Hedgemead Av, Abingdon.
T. (01235) 529453. (Furniture)   095580

Ablington Bibury (Gloucestershire)
Robertson, Godfrey, Fourwinds, Ablington Bibury GL7
5NX. T. (0128574) 740355, Fax 740355. (Antiques, furniture, clocks, instruments)   095581

Acle (Norfolk)
Lion Antiques, Old Sale Ring, Cattle Market, Acle.
T. 751836. (Furniture)   095582

Addingham (West Yorkshire)
Addingham Antiques, 70-72 Main St, Addingham.
T. (01943) 830788. (Clocks, musical boxes, furniture,
paintings)   095583
Manor Barn Pine, Burnside Mill, Main St, Addingham.
T. (01943) 830176. (Furniture)   095584

Albrighton (Shropshire)
Doveridge House of Neachley, Long Lane, Albrighton
TF11 8PJ. T. (01902) 3131. (Furniture, oils)   095585

Alcester (Warwickshire)
Malthouse Antiques Centre, Market Pl, Alcester.
T. (01789) 764032. (Furniture)   095586

Aldeburgh (Suffolk)
Thompson, 175 High St, Aldeburgh. T. (0172) 453743.
(Oils, watercolours)   095587

Alderley Edge (Cheshire)
Broomhead, Sara, West St, Alderley Edge.
T. (01625) 829625. (Furniture, silver)   095588

Alnwick (Northumberland)
Country Pine Antiques, 22 Bailiffgate, Alnwick.
T. (01665) 603616. (Furniture)   095589

Alresford (Hampshire)
Studio Bookshop and Gallery, 17 Broad St, Alresford.
T. (01962) 732188. (Oil paintings, prints)   095590

Althorne (Essex)
Bailey, John, 5 Austral Way, Althorne.
T. (01621) 740279. (Clocks)   095591

Altrincham (Greater Manchester)
New Street Antiques, 48 New St, Altrincham.
T. (0161) 929 8171. (Furniture, textiles,
porcelain)   095592
Woodcare Restoration, 12 Arnolds Yard, Altrincham
WA15. T. (0161) 928 5579. (Furniture)   095593

Amersham (Buckinghamshire)
Collectors Treasures Ltd., 91 High St, Amersham HP7
0DU. T. (01494) 7213. (Prints and Antique maps o
prints, Antique wall paper print roller lamps)   095594
Mon Galerie, The Old Forge, The Broadway, Old Amersham, Amersham. T. (01494) 721705. (Watercolours,
engravings)   095595

Ampthill (Bedfordshire)
Ampthill Antiques, Market Sq, Ampthill.
T. (01525) 403344. (Clocks)   095596
Ampthill Emporium, 6 Bedford St, Ampthill.
T. (01525) 402131. (Furniture)   095597
D.M.E. Restorations, 11 Church St, Ampthill.
T. (01525) 405819. (Furniture)   095598
Harman, Robert, 11 Church St, Ampthill.
T. (01525) 402322. (Furniture)   095599

Annahilt (Co. Down)
Period Architectural Features and Antiques, 263 Ballynahich Rd, Annahilt. T. (01846) 638091. (Marble) 095600

Ardersier (Highland)
Ardersier Antiques, Ardersier Cottage, Ardersier.
T. (01667) 62237. (Paintings, furniture)   095601

Arnesby (Leicestershire)
Leycester Map Galleries, Well House, Arnesby.
T. (01533) 478462. (Maps)   095602

Arthog (Gwynedd)
Gothick Dream Fine Art, Arthog Hall, Arthog.
T. (0175881) 250168. (Paintings, frames)   095603

Arundel (West Sussex)
Pepperall, Noel & Eva-Louise, Dairy Lane Cottage, Wal-
berton, Arundel BN18 0PT. T. (01903) Yapton 551282.
(Furniture, Paintings)   095604
Roseland Restoration, The Studio, Arundel Station Cau-
seway, Arundel. T. (01903) 883672. (Furniture) 095605
Serendipity Antiques, 27 Tarrant St, Arundel.
T. (01903) 882047. (Oil paintings)   095606

Ascot (Berkshire)
Woodley, A. R., 140 Locks Ride, Ascot SL5 8QX.
T. (01990) Winkfield Row 2458. (Antique
Furniture)   095607

Ash Vale (Surrey)
House of Christian Antiques, 5-7 Vale Rd, Ash Vale.
T. (01252) 314478. (Furniture)   095608

Ashfield (Suffolk)
Ponsonby, A.M., Upham House, Ashfield.
T. (0172882) 200. (Furniture)   095609

Askham (Nottinghamshire)
Mitchell, Salley, Thornlea, Askham. T. (0177783) 234.
(Paintings, prints)   095610

Aslockton (Nottinghamshire)
Neville, Jane, Elm House, Abbey Lane, Aslockton.
T. (01949) 50220. (Paintings, prints)   095611

Attleborough (Norfolk)
Bush, A.E., & Partners, Vineyards, Leys Lane, Attleborough. T. (01953) 454239, 452175. (Furniture) 095612

Auchterarder (Tayside)
Times Past Antiques, Broadfold Farm, Auchterarder.
T. (01764) 63166. (Furniture)   095613

Auchtertool (Fife)
Castle Restoration, Auchtertool House, Auchtertool KY2
5XW. T. 780371. (Furniture)   095614

Axbridge (Somerset)
Number One, 1 High St, Axbridge. T. (01934) 732130.
(Ceramics, Textiles)   095615
Omri, Kirklea Farm, Badgworth, Axbridge BS26 2QH.
T. (01934) 732323. (Mirrors)   095616

Axminster (Devon)
Potter, W.G., & Son, West St, Axminster.
T. (01297) 32063. (Furniture)   095617

Ayr (Strathclyde)
Old Curiosity Shop, 27 Crown St, Ayr. T. (01292) 280222.
(Furniture)   095618

Bacup (Lancashire)
English Squirrel Woodcraft, Unit 2, Pioneer Buildings, Alma St, Bacup. T. (01706) 874191. (Furniture) 095619

Bakewell (Derbyshire)
Harper, Martin & Dorothy, King St, Bakewell.
T. (01629) 814757. (Furniture)   095620
Water Lane Antiques, Water Ln, Bakewell.
T. (01629) 814161. (Furniture, metalware)   095621

Balcombe (West Sussex)
Pine and Design, Haywards Heath Rd, Balcombe.
T. (01444) 811700. (Furniture)   095622

Baldock (Hertfordshire)
Howards, 33 Whitehorse St, Baldock. T. (01462) 892385.
(Clocks)   095623
Porter, Arthur, 31 Whitehorse St, Baldock.
T. (01462) 895351. (Furniture)   095624

Ballyclare (Co. Antrim)
Antique Shop, 64a Main St, Ballyclare.
T. (019603) 52550. (Clocks, furniture)   095625

Banbury (Oxfordshire)
Hume, P., 78b Almoral Av, Banbury. T. (01295) 257810.
(Clock cases)   095626

Bangor (Co. Down)
Arnold, Phyllis, 24 Dufferin Av, Bangor.
T. (01247) 469899. (Maps, prints,
watercolours)   095627

Bangor (Gwynedd)
Windsor, David, 201 High St, Bangor. T. (01248) 364639.
(Oil paintings, watercolours, engravings)   095628

Bankfoot (Tayside)
Antiques and Bygones, Tighvallich, Dunkeld Rd, Bank-
foot. T. (0173) 87452. (Oil lamps, small
furniture)   095629
Athollbank, Main St, Bankfoot. T. (0173) 87253.
(Furniture)   095630

Banwell (Avon)
Textile Conservation, Ivy Studios, Ivy House Farm, Banwell. T. (01934) 822449. (Textiles)   095631

Barford (Warwickshire)
Goodson, Ingsley Bank, Wellesbourne Rd, Barford.
T. (01926) 624044. (Furniture)   095632

Barkham (Berkshire)
Barkham Antiques and Craft Centre, Barkham St, Bark-
ham. T. (01734) 761355. (Furniture)   095633
Davis, John E., Edneys Hill Farm, Edneys Hill, Barkham.
T. (01734) 783181. (Furniture, clocks,
metalwork)   095634

Barnard Castle (Durham)
Collector, Douglas House, The Bank, Barnard Castle.
T. (01833) 37783. (Furniture, watercolours, oil pain-
tings, silver, rugs)   095635
Grant, Stephanie, 38-40 The Bank, Barnard Castle.
T. (01833) 37437. (Furniture, paintings, prints) 095636

Barnoldswick (Lancashire)
Bunn, Roy W., 34-36 Church St, Barnoldswick BB8 5UT.
T. (01282) 813703. (Ceramics)   095637

Barnsley (South Yorkshire)
Northern Arts, 36 Doncaster Rd, Barnsley.
T. (01226) 282182. (Paintings)   095638
Summer Lane Antiques, 87a Summer Ln, Barnsley.
T. (01226) 293013. (Furniture)   095639

Barnstaple (Devon)
Blue Gallery, Joy St, Barnstaple. T. (01271) 3536.
(Paintings)   095640
Webb, H., Little Barn, Eastcombe, Barnstaple.
T. (01271) 73413. (Furniture)   095641

Barnt Green (Hereford and Worcester)
Barnt Green Antiques, 93 Hewell Rd, Barnt Green B45
8NE. T. (0121) 445 4942. (Furniture, clocks, oil
paintings)   095642

Barrhead (Strathclyde)
C.P.R. Antiques and Services, 96 Main St, Barrhead.
T. (0141) 881 5379. (Brass, copper, pewter)   095643

Barry (Tayside)
Irena Arts and Crafts, 111 Broad St, Barry. T. 747626.
(Furniture)   095644

Barton (Cheshire)
Rayment, Derek, Orchard House, Barton Rd, Barton.
T. (01829) 270429. (Barometers)   095645

Barton-upon-Humber (Humberside)
Elegance Antiques, Brigg Rd, Barton-upon-Humber.
T. (01652) 635012. (Furniture)   095646

Bath (Avon)
Abbey Galleries, 9 Abbey Churchyard, Bath.
T. (01225) 460565. (Jewellery, clocks)   095647
Adam, 13 John St, Bath. T. (01225) 480406.
(Paintings)   095648
Arts of Living Decor Lighting and Oriental Rugs, 57 Walcot St, Bath. T. (01225) 462441. (Old columns,
vases)   095649
Bayntun, George, Manvers St, Bath BA1 1JW.
T. (01225) 466000, Fax Fax 482122. (Books)   095650
Bean Nash House Antiques, Bean Nash House, Union
Passage, Bath. T. (01225) 447806. (Furniture,
pictures)   095651
Brass, Lawrence, & Son, 93-95 Walcot St, Bath BA1
5BW. T. (01225) 464057. (Traditional upholstery, gilding, lacquer & decorative furniture, statuary, metal,
ivories, clocks, barometers)   095652
Dollin & Daines, 2 Church St, Bath. T. (01225) 462752.
(Violins, violas, cellos, bows)   095653
Dux, Frank, 33 Belvedere, Lansdown Rd, Bath.
T. (01225) 312367. (Furniture)   095654
Gregory, George, 98 Walcot St, Bath. T. (01225) 466055.
(Books)   095655
Haliden Oriental Rug Shop, 98 Walcot St, Bath.
T. (01225) 469240. (Carpets, rugs, textiles,
porcelain)   095656
Hood, Helena, & Co., 3 Margarets Buildings, Brock St,
Bath. T. (01225) 424438. (Furniture, prints, paintings,
porcelain)   095657
Kwik Strip, Unit 3, Lymore Gardens, Oldfield Park, Bath.
T. (01225) 315541. (Furniture)   095658
Pennard House Antiques, 3-4 Piccadilly, London Rd,
Bath. T. (01225) 313791, Fax 448196.
(Furniture)   095659
Saville Row Gallery, 1 Saville Row, Bath.
T. (01225) 334595. (Oil paintings, frames)   095660
Walcot Reclamation, 108 Walcot St, Bath.
T. (01225) 444404, 335532. (Architectural items,
chimney pieces, ironwork)   095661

Battle (East Sussex)
Campbell, Duncan, Prior's Lodge, Upper Lake (Sussex),
Battle. T. (014246) 2888. (Armour, Arms,
Weapons)   095662

Beachport (Southern Australia)
Cleve, Church Rd, Beachport. T. (0187) 3226. (Oils, watercolours, prints)   095663

Beaconsfield (Buckinghamshire)
Messum, David, 1 Aylesbury End, Beaconsfield.
T. (01494) 680878. (English pictures)   095664
Period Furniture Showrooms, 49 London End, Beaconsfield. T. (01494) 674112. (Furniture)   095665

Beaminster (Dorset)
Good Hope Antiques, 2 Hogshill St, Beaminster.
T. (01308) 862119. (Clocks)   095666

Beccles (Suffolk)
Andrew's Gallery, 6 Ingate, Beccles. T. (01502) 713263.
(Furniture)   095667
Beccles Gallery, Saltgate House, Beccles.
T. (01502) 714017. (Oils, watercolours)   095668
Besley, 4 Blyburgate, Beccles. T. (01502) 715762.
(Books)   095669

Beckenham (Greater London)
Horton, 428 Croydon Rd., Beckenham.
T. (0181) 658 8418. (Jewellery)   095670

Bedale (North Yorkshire)
Thornton, Snape, Bedale. T. (01677) 70318. (Oil
paintings)   095671

Bedford (Bedfordshire)
A.B. Upholstery, Unit 7, Cauldwell Walk, Cauldwell County, Bedford. T. (01234) 344234. (Furniture)   095672
Antique Furniture Restoration, 45 Saint Michaels Rd, Bedford. T. (01234) 359976. (Furniture)   095673

George, J., & Son, 23 Fountains Rd, Bedford MK41 8NU.
T. (01234) 353080, 216811. (Furniture)   095674

Bedingfield (Suffolk)
Old Red Lion, The Street, Bedingfield. T. (0172876) 491.
(Furniture, oil paintings, ceramics)   095675

Beeston (Nottinghamshire)
Bailey, Elizabeth, 33 Chilwell Rd, Beeston. T. 259259.
(Furniture)   095676

Belfast (Co. Antrim)
Bell, 13 Adelaide Park, Belfast. T. (01232) 662998.
(Paintings)   095677
Treasure House, 123 University St, Belfast.
T. (01232) 231055. (Furniture)   095678

Belper (Derbyshire)
Sweetings, 1-1a The Butts, Belper. T. (01773) 825930,
822780. (Furniture)   095679

Bembridge (Isle of Wight)
Solent, 1 Dennett Rd, Bembridge. T. (01983) 872107.
(Clocks, furniture)   095680
Vectis, 71 High St, Bembridge. T. (01983) 872316. (Paintings, watercolours, engravings)   095681

Berkhamsted (Hertfordshire)
Yesterday's Pine, 61 High St, Berkhamsted.
T. (01442) 862042. (Furniture)   095682

Berry Hill (Gloucestershire)
Forest, Dean, Corner House, Berry Hill.
T. (01594) 833211. (Furniture)   095683

Berwick-upon-Tweed (Northumberland)
Treasure Chest, 44 Castlegate St, Berwick-upon-Tweed.
T. (01289) 307736. (China)   095684

Bethersden (Kent)
Luckhurst, Bruce, Little Surrenden Workshops, Ashford
Rd, Bethersden TN26 3BG. T. (01233) 820589.
(Furniture)   095685

Bethesda (Gwynedd)
Ogwen, 10 High St, Bethesda. T. (01248) 600460,
600549. (Oil paintings, watercolours)   095686

Beverley (Humberside)
Starkey, James H., 49 Highgate, Beverley HU17 0QN.
T. (01482) 881179. (Paintings)   095687

Bewdley (Hereford and Worcester)
Bewdley Antiques, 28 Load St, Bewdley.
T. (01299) 403731. (Furniture)   095688

Bexhill-on-Sea (East Sussex)
Stewart, 48 Devonshire Rd, Bexhill-on-Sea.
T. (01424) 223410. (Paintings, frames)   095689
Village Antiques, 2-4 Cooden Sea Rd, Bexhill-on-Sea.
T. (01424) 5214. (Furniture)   095690

Bicester (Oxfordshire)
Barn, Crumps Butts, Bell Ln, Bicester.
T. (01869) 252958. (Furniture)   095691

Bideford (Devon)
Acorn Antiques, 11 Rope Walk, Bideford.
T. (01237) 470177. (Furniture)   095692
Collins, J., & Son, The Studio, 63 High St, Bideford.
T. (01237) 473103, Fax 475658. (Furniture, paintings,
watercolours)   095693
Petticombe Manor Antiques, Petticombe Manor, Monkleigh, Bideford. T. (01237) 475605.
(Furniture)   095694

Bildeston (Suffolk)
Carapace, 100 High St, Bildeston. T. (01449) 740125.
(Furniture)   095695

Birchington (Kent)
Chawner, John, 36 Station Approach, Birchington.
T. (01843) 43309. (Clocks)   095696

Birmingham (West Midlands)
Albert House Interiors, 23-25 Albert Rd, Harborne, Birmingham B17 0AP. T. (0121) 426 5616.
(Furniture)   095697

Ashleigh House Antiques, 5 Westbourne Rd, Birmingham. T. (0121) 454 6283. (Furniture, paintings) 095698
Barnt Green Antiques, 93 Hewell Rd, Barnt Green, Birmingham B45 8NE. T. (0121) 445 4942.
(Furniture)   095699
Beasley, B.S., 542 Aldridge Rd, Great Barr, Birmingham
B44 8ND. T. (0121) 360 9518. (Furniture)   095700
Clark, Peter, 36 Saint Mary's Row, Moseley, Birmingham
B13 8JG. T. (0121) 449 8245. (Furniture)   095701
Classic French Polishing, 5 Warstone Ln, Birmingham
B18. T. (0121) 233 4005. (Furniture)   095702
Cole, S.J., 20 Sark Dr, Birmingham B36 0NU.
T. (0121) 770 8929. (Furniture)   095703
Collyer, R., 185 New Rd, Rubery, Birmingham.
T. (0121) 453 2332. (Clocks, watches,
barometers)   095704
Edgbaston Gallery, 42 Islington Row, Five Ways, Edgbaston, Birmingham. T. (0121) 454 4244.
(Paintings)   095705
Fellows, Maurice, 21 Vyse St, Hockley, Birmingham.
T. (0121) 554 0211, Fax Fax 507 0807.
(Jewellery)   095706
Gale & Co., 12 Lee Bank House, Holloway Head, Birmingham B1. T. (0121) 643 6639. (Furniture)   095707
Good Wood Furniture Restoration, Unit 7, Middleway Industrial Estate, Moseley Rd, Birmingham B12 0EA.
T. (0121) 440 5688. (Furniture)   095708
Harborne Place Antiques, 22-24 Northfield Rd, Harborne, Birmingham. T. (0121) 427 5788.
(Furniture)   095709
Hill, E., 11a Caroline St, Birmingham.
T. (0121) 236 28 29. (Silver)   095710
Hubbard, John, 224-226 Court Oak Rd, Harborne, Birmingham. T. (0121) 426 1694. (Furniture)   095711
Kestrel House Antiques, 72 Gravelly Hill North, Erdington, Birmingham. T. (0121) 373 2375. (Oil paintings,
frames)   095712
Martin & Co., 97 Camden St, Birmingham B1 3DG.
T. (0121) 2332111. (Reproduction Brass Cabinet
Hardware)   095713
Midland Antiques Furniture Restorations, The Prior Industrial Estate, Electric Av, Birmingham B6.
T. (0121) 327 1213. (Furniture)   095714
Moseley Gallery, 6 Ernest St, Holloway Head, Birmingham. T. (0121) 622 3986. (Watercolours,
drawings)   095715
Neilson, Ivor, 48 School Rd, Moseley, Birmingham.
T. (0121) 449 3633. (Furniture)   095716
Old Clock Shop, 32 Stephenson St, Birmingham.
T. (0121) 632 4864. (Clocks)   095717
Parr, Alan, 73 Electric Av, Witton, Birmingham B6 7ED.
T. (0121) 326 6253. (Furniture)   095718
Popular Choice Antiques, 15 Shaw's Passage, Digbeth,
Birmingham B5 5JG. T. (0121) 633 4529.
(Furniture)   095719
Russell, Simon, 112-116 Park Hill Rd, Birmingham B17
9HD. T. (0121) 427 4363. (Furniture)   095720
Stuart House Fine Art, 123 Queens Park Rd, Harborne,
Birmingham. T. (0121) 426 3300. (Furniture,
paintings)   095721
Woodland, 1348 Stratford Rd, Hall Green, Birmingham.
T. (0121) 777 2027. (Oil paintings, watercolours,
prints)   095722

Birstwith (North Yorkshire)
Pearson, John, Church Cottage, Birstwith.
T. (01423) 770828. (Clocks)   095723

Bishop Monkton (North Yorkshire)
Pine Finds, Old Cornmill, Bishop Monkton.
T. (01765) 87159. (Furniture)   095724

Bishop's Cleeve (Gloucestershire)
Cleeve Picture Framing, Church Rd, Bishop's Cleeve.
T. (01242) 672785. (Oil paintings, watercolours,
prints)   095725
Priory Gallery, Priory, Station Rd, Bishop's Cleeve.
T. (01242) 673226. (Watercolours, prints, oils) 095726

Bishops Stortford (Hertfordshire)
Dragon's Antiques, 1 Church St, Bishops Stortford.
(Porcelain)   095727
Restoration, 46-48 Hockerill St, Bishops Stortford.
T. (01279) 813098. (Furniture)   095728

Bishops Waltham (Hampshire)
Pinecrafts, 4 Brook St, Bishops Waltham.
T. (01489) 892878. (Furniture)   095729

Blackburn (Lancashire)
Ancient and Modern, 56 Bank Top, Blackburn.
T. (01254) 263256. (Jewellery, watches, longcase
clocks)   095730
Connor, L., 36 Mowbray Av, Blackburn BB2 3ET.
T. (01254) 670174. (Furniture)   095731
Eccles, D.R., 256 Whalley New Rd, Blackburn.
T. (01254) 662951. (Furniture)   095732
Furniture Care, 186 Redlam, Blackburn BB2 1XQ.
T. (01254) 261467. (Furniture)   095733
Walmsley, Anthony, 93 Montague St, Blackburn.
T. (01254) 698755. (Furniture, clocks)   095734

Blackpool (Lancashire)
Handsworth Restorers, Unit 9, Caunce Street, Saw Mills,
Blackpool. T. (01253) 24994. (Furniture)   095735
Pine Dresser, 1 Ball St, South Shore, Blackpool.
T. (01253) 403862. (Furniture)   095736

Blairmore (Strathclyde)
Fyne, 2 Pierhead, Blairmore. T. (0136984) 563.
(Furniture)   095737

Blakedown (Worcestershire)
Hay, 20 Birmingham Rd, Blakedown. T. (01562) 700791.
(Furniture)   095738

Blandford (Dorset)
Stone, Ramon, Thyme Cottage, 8 Alfred St, Blandford.
T. (01258) 455469. (Clocks)   095739
Stour, 28 East St, Blandford. T. (01258) 456293. (Oils,
watercolours, wash line Mounts)   095740

Bletchingley (Surrey)
Marsh, Simon, Old Butchers Shop, High St, Bletchingley
RH1 4PA. T. (0188384) 843350. (Furniture,
Clocks)   095741

Bognor Regis (Sussex)
Gough Bros., 71 High St, Bognor Regis.
T. (01243) 823773. (Oils, watercolours,
frames)   095742

Bolton (Lancashire)
Bolton Furniture Restorers, 160 Tonge Moor Rd, Bolton
BL2 2HN. T. (01204) 24909. (Furniture)   095743
Doffcocker Antiques, 813 Chorley Old Rd, Bolton BL1
1AA. T. (01204) 4 3666. (Barometers)   095744
Drop Dial Antiques, Last Drop Village, Hospital Rd,
Bromley Cross, Bolton. T. (01204) 57186. (Clocks,
barometers)   095745
Gallery 77, 18 Princess St, Bradshawgate, Bolton.
T. (01204) 35252. (Oil Paintings, watercolours) 095746
Park Galleries Antiques, 167 Mayor St, Bolton.
T. (01204) 29827. (Brass, porcelain, furniture, metal-
work, pottery, paintings, frames, clock
mouvements)   095747

Borough Green (Kent)
Tillman, William, Crouch Lane, Borough Green.
T. (01732) 88 3278. (Furniture)   095749

Boroughbridge (North Yorkshire)
Galloway, High St, Boroughbridge. T. (01423) 324602.
(Furniture)   095750
Saint James House Antiques, Saint James Sq, Borough-
bridge. T. (01423) 322508. (Furniture)   095751

Boston (Lincolnshire)
Boston Antiques Centre, 12 West St, Boston.
T. (01205) 361510. (Jewellery, Silver)   095752

Boston Spa (West Yorkshire)
London House Oriental Rugs and Carpets, London House, High St, Boston Spa. T. (01937) 845123. (Rugs,
carpets)   095753

Bottesford (Leicestershire)
Keen, Thomas, 51 High St, Bottesford. T. (01949) 42177.
(Furniture)   095754

Boughton (Kent)
Clock Shop Antiques, 187 The Street, Boughton.
T. (0122775) 751258. (Clocks)   095755

Bournemouth (Dorset)
Antique Centre, 837-839 Christchurch Rd, East Boscom-
be, Bournemouth. T. (01202) 421052. (Silver, jewellery,
replating)   095756
Blackwoods, 21 Bethia Rd, Bournemouth.
T. (01202) 395467. (Furniture)   095757
Blackwoods, 805 Christchurch Rd, Boscombe, Bourne-
mouth. T. (01202) 434800. (Furniture)   095758
Blade & Bayonet, 884 Christchurch Rd, Boscombe,
Bournemouth. T. (01202) 429891. (Weapons)   095759
Bournemouth Framing and Fine Art, 821 Wimborne Rd,
Bournemouth. T. (01202) 535951. (Paintings)   095760
Crosscut, The Old Coach House, Robert Louis Stevenson
Av, Bournemouth. T. (01202) 760731.
(Furniture)   095761
Cutler, 8 Albert Rd, Bournemouth. T. (01202) 552612.
(Paintings)   095762
Galerie Lafrance, 647 Wimborne Rd, Bournemouth.
T. (01202) 522313. (Paintings)   095763
Green Room, 796 Christchurch Rd, Boscombe, Bourne-
mouth. T. (01202) 392634. (Silver, metalware)   095764
Hampshire Gallery, 18 Lansdowne Rd, Bournemouth.
T. (01202) 551211. (Paintings, watercolours)   095765
Mitchell, G.H., & Co., 266 Holdenhurst Rd, Bournemouth.
T. (01202) 396527. (Furniture)   095766
Payne, G.A., & Son, 742 Christchurch Rd, Boscombe,
Bournemouth. T. (01202) 394954. (Silver, jewellery,
clocks, watches)   095767
Sainsbury, Jonathan L.F., 21-22 The Arcade, Bourne-
mouth. T. (01202) 557633. (Furniture)   095768
Shippey, 15-16 Royal Arcade, Boscombe, Bournemouth.
T. (01202) 396548. (Jewellery)   095769
Victorian Chairman, 883 Christchurch Rd, Bournemouth.
T. (01202) 420996. (Furniture)   095770
Victorian Parlour, 874 Christchurch Rd, Boscombe, Bour-
nemouth. T. (01202) 433928. (Cane, rush
seating)   095771

Bourton-on-the Water (Gloucestershire)
Angus, Stewart, Sycamore Barn, Industrial Park, Bour-
ton-on-the Water GL54 2HQ. T. (01451) 21611.
(Furniture)   095772

Bovey Tracey (Devon)
Thomas & James, 6a Station Rd, Bovey Tracey.
T. (01626) 835350. (Furniture, ceramics)   095773

Bowness-on-Windermere (Cumbria)
White Elephant, 66 Quarry Rigg, Lake Rd, Bowness-on-
Windermere. T. 46962. (Rugs)   095774

Brackley (Northamptonshire)
Brackley Antiques, 69 High St, Brackley.
T. (01280) 703362. (Furniture)   095775
Jackson, Peter, 3 Market Pl, Brackley.
T. (01280) 703259. (Porcelain, pottery)   095776

Bradfield Saint George (Suffolk)
Grant, Denzil, Hubbards Corner, Bradfield Saint George.
T. (014493) 576. (Furniture, tapestry)   095777

Bradford (West Yorkshire)
Carlton Antiques and Fine Art, 1 Hammond Sq, Emm
Lane, Heaton, Bradford. T. (01274) 496853.
(Porcelain)   095778
Easy-Strip, 2 Vivien Rd, Bradford. T. (01274) 544021.
(Furniture)   095779
Hazelmount, 160 Allerton Rd, Bradford.
T. (01274) 547172. (Furniture)   095780

Bradford-on-Avon (Wiltshire)
Rooths, 18 Market St, Bradford-on-Avon BA15 1LL.
T. (012216) 4191. (Paintings)   095781

Braintree (Essex)
Frame It, Unit 24, Warner Dr, Springwood Industrial Es-
tate, Braintree. T. (01376) 553590. (Paintings) 095782
Kwik Strip, Unit 27, Springwood Industrial Estate, Finch
Dr, Braintree. T. (01376) 550535. (Furniture)   095783

Bramley (Surrey)
Drummond, Birtley Farm, Horsham Rd, Bramley.
T. (01256) 898766. (Blacksmithing, stone
work)   095784

Brampton (Cumbria)
Fell, Mary, 32-34 Main St, Brampton. T. (016977) 22224.
(Furniture)   095785

Branksome (Dorset)
Mack, David, 434-437 Poole Rd, Branksome.
T. (01202) 760005. (Furniture)   095786
Mack, David, 43a Langley Rd, Branksome.
T. (01202) 760005. (Furniture)   095787

Brasted (Kent)
Courtyard Antiques, High St, Brasted. T. (01959) 564483.
(Furniture, metalware)   095788
Weald, High St, Brasted. T. (01959) 562627. (Oil pain-
tings, watercolours, prints)   095789

Brentwood (Essex)
Brandler, 1 Coptfold Rd, Brentwood. T. (01277) 222269,
Fax Fax 222786. (Pictures)   095790

Bridge-of-Allan (Central)
Athole House Antiques, 64 Henderson St, Bridge-of-Allan. T. (01786) 833959. (Furniture)   095791

Bridge-of-Weir (Strathclyde)
Castle Fine Art, 4-5 Castle Terrace, Bridge-of-Weir.
T. (01505) 690951. (Paintings, watercolours)   095792

Bridgnorth (Shropshire)
Norton, Pauline, Bank St, Bridgnorth. T. (01746) 4889.
(Paintings)   095793

Bridport (Dorset)
Batten, 26 South St, Bridport. T. (01308) 56910. (Jewel-
lery, silver)   095794
Westdale Antiques, 4a Saint Michael's Trading Estate,
Bridport. T. (01308) 27271. (Ceramics)   095795

Brierfield (Lancashire)
Blakey, J.H., & Sons, Church St, Brierfield BB9 5AD.
T. (01282) 691655, 602493. (Furniture, brass, copper,
pewter, clocks)   095796

Brighton (East Sussex)
Artists and Restorers Studios, 30 Sillwood St, Brighton.
T. (01273) 720165. (Paintings)   095797
Cowen, Christopher G., 60 Middle St, Brighton.
T. (01273) 205757. (Furniture)   095798
Douglas, Terry, 71a Hollingbury Rd, Brighton.
T. (01273) 558905, 604014. (Furniture)   095799
Fine Restorations, 43-45 Bonchurch Rd, Brighton.
T. (01273) 623937. (Furniture)   095800
Fitchett, Alan, 5-5a Upper Gardner St, Brighton.
T. (01273) 600894. (Furniture)   095801
G.T. French Polishing, Unit E4, Meridian Ind Est, Hoyle
Rd, Peacehaven, Brighton. T. (01273) 586038.
(Furniture)   095802
Hale, Robert, 38 Robertson Rd, Brighton.
T. (01273) 566479. (Furniture)   095803
Hartnett, A. & J., & Son, 2 Victoria St, Brighton BW1 3FP.
T. (01273) 328793. (Furniture)   095804
Hatchwell, Simon, 94 Gloucester Rd, Brighton.
T. (01273) 691164. (Barometers, furniture)   095805
Hook, Albert G., & Son, 37b Duke St, Brighton.
T. (01273) 323836. (Furniture)   095806
Leoframes, 70 North Rd, Brighton. T. (01273) 695862.
(Frames)   095807
Oasis Antiques, 39 Kensington Gardens, Brighton.
T. (01273) 683885. (Furniture, metals,
ceramics)   095808
Pearson, Sue, 13 1/2 Prince Albert St, Brighton.
T. (01273) 29247. (Dolls, bears)   095809
Prinny, 3 Meeting House Lane, The Lanes, Brighton.
T. (01273) 204554. (Watches, clocks)   095810
Recollections, 1a Sydney St, Brighton.
T. (01273) 681517. (Metal, china, oil lamps)   095811
Resner, 1 Meeting House Lane, Brighton.
T. (01273) 29127. (Jewellery)   095812

Rogers, Clive, 22 Brunswick Rd, Hove, Brighton. T. (01273) 738257, Fax Fax 738687. (Rugs, carpets, textiles) *095813*

Sentry Box, 3 Meeting House Lane, The Lanes, Brighton. T. (01273) 204554. (Weapons) *095814*

Shelton Arts, 4 Islingwood Rd, Brighton BN2 2SE. T. (01273) 698345. (Pictures, prints, framing, wash and line work) *095815*

Shop of the Yellow Frog, 10-11 The Lanes, Brighton. T. (01273) 25497. (Watches, jewellery, furniture) *095816*

Sussex Fine Art, 29 Gloucester Rd Brighton BN1 1HF. T. (01273) 26135. (Paintings) *095817*

Tyldesley, Margot, 1 Adelaide Crescent, Hove, Brighton. T. (01273) 21307. (Clocks, paintings, porcelain) *095818*

Yellow Lantern Antiques, 34 Holland Rd, Brighton. T. (01273) 771572. (Furniture) *095819*

Brinscall (Lancashire)
Cardy, Brian, 2 Churchill Rd, Brinscall. T. (01254) 831949. (Paintings) *095820*

Bristol (Avon)
Alexander, 122 Whiteladies Rd, Bristol BS8 2RP. T. (0117) 9734692, 9739582. (Paintings, watercolours) *095821*

Brass, Lawrence, & Son, 96 Redland Rd, Bristol. T. (0117) 9241987. (Traditional upholstery, gilding, lacquer & decorative furniture, statuary, metal, ivories) *095822*

Bristol Restoration, 8 Devon Rd, Whitehall, Bristol BS5 9AE. T. (0117) 9542114. (Furniture) *095823*

Coggins, Anthony, 26 Roseville Av, Bristol. T. (0117) 9324032. (Furniture) *095824*

Cross, David, 7a Boyces Av, Clifton, Bristol. T. (0117) 9732614. (Paintings, prints) *095825*

Down, Charles, 1 Wilson St, Bristol BS2 9HH. T. (0117) 9428764. (Furniture) *095826*

Gill, Jennifer, 56 Colston St, Bristol. T. (0117) 9276285. (Textiles) *095827*

Haskins, Simon, & S. Poyntz, Kennel Lodge Rd, Bristol. T. (0117) 9632563. (Furniture) *095828*

Historic Interiors, 43-45 Park St, Bristol. T. (0117) 9272953. (Furniture) *095829*

Holcombe, Colin, 54 Alcove Rd, Fishponds, Bristol BS16 3DT. T. (0117) 9651299. (Furniture) *095830*

Hosegood, Alan, 4 Colston Yard, Bristol. T. (0117) 9268719. (Furniture) *095831*

Kohn, Simon, No 3 Riverside Business Park, Saint Annes Rd, Bristol BS4 4ED. T. (0117) 9721366. (Furniture) *095832*

Kwik Strip, Units 1-2, 242 Broomhill Rd, Bristol. T. (0117) 9772470, 9716537. (Furniture) *095833*

Metal Restoration Workshop, 8 Devon Rd, Bristol. T. (0117) 9542114. (Metalware) *095834*

Pelter & Sands, 43-45 Park St, Bristol. T. (0117) 9293988. (Oil paintings, watercolours, sculptures) *095835*

Saunders, R.A., 162 Raleigh Rd, Bedminster, Bristol. T. (0117) 9631268. (Silver, gold plating) *095836*

Wells, Patricia, Morton House, Lower Morton, Thornbury, Bristol BS12 1RA. T. (0117) 9412288. (Paintings) *095837*

Brixworth (Northamptonshire)
Brixworth Upholstery, 27 Grass Slade, Brixworth. T. (01604) 881488. (Furniture) *095838*

Broad Oak (East Sussex)
Reid, A.G.D., The Firs, Chitcombe, Broad Oak. T. (01424) 882097. (General restorer) *095839*

Broadstone (Dorset)
Galerie Antiques, 4-4a Station Approach, Broadstone. T. (01202) 695428. (Clocks, watches, jewellery) *095840*

Broadway (Hereford and Worcester)
Branch, Olive, 80 High St, Broadway. T. (01386) 853831. (Furniture) *095841*

Broadway Old Books, 45 High St, Broadway. T. (01386) 853668. (Books, maps, prints) *095842*

Ewart, Gavina, 60 High St, Broadway. T. (01386) 853371, Fax Fax 858948. (Clocks, furniture, barometers) *095843*

Hagen, Richard, Yew Tree House, Broadway. T. (01386) 853624, 858561, Fax Fax 852172. (Oil paintings, watercolours) *095844*

Hay Loft Gallery, Berry Wormington, Broadway. T. (01242) 621202. (Paintings, watercolours) *095845*

Haynes, 69 High St, Broadway. T. (01386) 852649. (Paintings) *095846*

Howards of Broadway, 27a High St, Broadway. T. (01386) 858924. (Jewellery, silver) *095847*

Noott, John, 14 Cotswold Court, The Green, Broadway. T. (01386) 852787, 858969, Fax Fax 858348. (Paintings, watercolours) *095848*

Noott, John, 31 High St, Broadway. T. (01386) 852787, 858969, Fax 858348. (Paintings, watercolours) *095849*

Picton House Antiques, High St, Broadway. T. (01386) 853807. (Furniture) *095850*

Stratford Trevers, 45 High St, Broadway. T. (01386) 853668. (Books) *095851*

Brobury (Hereford and Worcester)
Brobury House Gallery, Brobury HR3 6BS. T. (019817) 229. (Old Prints, watercolours) *095852*

Brockdish (Norfolk)
Brockdish Antiques, Commerce House, Brockdish 1P21 45L. T. (01379) 498. (Furniture) *095853*

Eekhout, Rosebrook, Grove Rd, Brockdish. T. (01379) 575. (Paintings, prints) *095854*

Bromley (Greater London)
China Restoration, 1c Avondale Rd., Bromley BR1. T. (0181) 460 1776. (Ceramics) *095855*

Taurus Antiques, 145 Masons Hill, Bromley. T. (0181) 464 8746. (Furniture) *095856*

Bromyard (Hereford and Worcester)
Lennox, 3 Broad St, Bromyard. T. (01885) 483432. (Pottery, porcelain, cloisonné) *095857*

Buckie (Grampian)
Duncan, Alan S., The Smiddy, Drybridge, Buckie. T. (01542) 32271. (Furniture) *095858*

Sherman, 31 Commercial Rd, Buckie. T. (01542) 34680. (Furniture) *095859*

Buckingham (Buckinghamshire)
Picture Conservation and Restoration Studios, 9 Bridge St, Buckingham MK18 1EW. T. (01280) 815478. (Paintings, watercolours, prints, frames) *095860*

Webster, Stuart, 2 Greenway Walk, Buckingham. T. (01280) 816555. (Furniture) *095861*

Bucks Green (West Sussex)
Kings Antiques, Guildford Rd, Bucks Green. T. (0140372) 2084. (Furniture) *095862*

Budleigh Salterton (Devon)
Quinney's, High St, Budleigh Salterton. T. (013954) 442793. (Furniture, porcelain, glass) *095863*

Talisman, Salterton Workshops, Station Rd, Budleigh Salterton. T. (013954) 442251. (Paintings) *095864*

Bures (Suffolk)
Bures Antiques, 1 Bridge St, Bures. T. (01787) 227858. (Furniture, metalwork) *095865*

Burford (Oxfordshire)
Burford Antiques, 134 High St, Burford. T. (01993) 822552, 822135. (Metalwork, ceramics) *095866*

Crypt Antiques, 109 High St, Burford. T. (01993) 2302. (Furniture) *095867*

Denver House Antiques and Collectables, Denver House, Witney St, Burford. T. (01993) 822040, Fax - Fax 822769. (Maps, bank notes) *095868*

Schotten, Manfred, 109 High St, Burford. T. (01993) 822302, Fax 822055. (Furniture, sporting collectables) *095869*

Swan Gallery, High St, Burford. T. (01993) 822244. (Furniture) *095870*

Wren, 4 Bear Court, High St, Burford. T. (01993) 823495. (Watercolours) *095871*

Burgess Hill (West Sussex)
British Antiques Interiors, School Close, Queen Elizabeth Av, Burgess Hill. T. (01444) 245577. (Furniture) *095872*

Cruttenden, 95 Church Rd, Burgess Hill. T. (01444) 232329. (Clocks) *095873*

Burghfield Common (Berkshire)
Graham, Highwoods, Burghfield Common. T. (01734) 832320. (Paintings, frames) *095874*

Burley (Leicestershire)
Burley Workshops, Home Farm, Burley on the Hill, Burley. T. (01572) 757333. (Furniture) *095875*

Burneston (North Yorkshire)
Greenwood, W., Oak Dene, Church Wynd, Burneston. T. (01677) 24830. (Paintings) *095876*

Burnley (Lancashire)
Dewar, Arthur, & Co., 149 Nairne St, Burnley. T. (01282) 421866, Fax 424149. (Furniture) *095877*

Dewar, Arthur, & Co., 38 Prairie Crescent, Burnley. T. (01282) 24149. (Furniture) *095878*

Burton-upon-Trent (Staffordshire)
Richards, H.J. & Son, Abbey Arcade, High St, Burton-upon-Trent. T. (01283) 65921. (Silver, jewellery, clocks) *095879*

Burwash (East Sussex)
Chaunt House, High St, Burwash. T. (01435) 882221. (Clocks, watches, barometers) *095880*

Lime Tree Antiques, High St, Burwash. T. (01435) 882385. (Paintings, prints, furniture) *095881*

Burwell (Cambridgeshire)
Hayward, Maurice, Orchard Cotage, 100 Silver St, Burwell CB5 0EF. T. (01638) 741657. (Furniture) *095882*

Norman, Peter, 57 North St, Burwell. T. (01638) 742197. (Furniture, oil paintings, clocks, arms) *095883*

Bury (Lancashire)
Newton, 151 The Rock, Bury. T. (0161) 764 1863. (Furniture) *095884*

Bury Saint Edmunds (Suffolk)
Guildhall Gallery, 1-1a Churchgate St, Bury Saint Edmunds. T. (01284) 762366. (Oil paintings, watercolours, prints) *095885*

Mac, Winston, 65 Saint John's St, Bury Saint Edmunds. T. (01284) 767910. (Silver, plating) *095886*

Murfet, Graham, Saint Andrews St, Bury Saint Edmunds. T. (01284) 700244. (Furniture) *095887*

Pepper, 23 Churchgate St, Bury Saint Edmunds. T. (01284) 762366. (Furniture) *095888*

Saint Edmunds Antique Centre, 30 Saint John's St, Bury Saint Edmunds. T. (01284) 764469. (Furniture, oil paintings, ceramics) *095889*

Usher, R.N., 42 Southgate St, Bury Saint Edmunds. T. (01284) 762366. (Furniture) *095890*

Bushey (Hertfordshire)
Thwaites & Co., 33 Chalk Hill, Oxhey, Bushey. T. (01923) 32412. (Stringed instruments) *095891*

Bushmills (Co. Antrim)
Dunlace, 33 Ballytober Rd, Bushmills. T. (012657) 31140. (Porcelain) *095892*

Buxton (Derbyshire)
Antiques Warehouse, 25 Lightwood Rd, Buxton. T. (01298) 72967. (Furniture, paintings, brass, beds) *095893*

Buxton (Norfolk)
Buxton Mill Galleries, Buxton Mill, Buxton NOR 62Y. T. (0160546) 337. (Paintings) *095894*

Caernarvon (Gwynedd)
Revival, 60 Pool St, Caernarvon. T. (01286) 397. (Furniture) *095895*

Camberley (Surrey)
235 Antiques, 235 London Rd, Camberley.
T. (01276) 32123. (Furniture, clocks) *095896*

Cambridge (Cambridgeshire)
Antiques, 18 King St, Cambridge. T. (01223) 62825.
(Wood, metalware, silver, china) *095897*
Belgrave Plate Company, Dove House, New Park St,
Cambridge CB5 8AT. T. (01223) 62771. (Pewter, metal,
brass, copper, silver, gold, old plate) *095898*
Buckies, 31 Trinity St, Cambridge. T. (01223) 357910.
(Jewellery, silver, objets d'art) *095899*
Cambridge Fine Art, Priesthouse, 33 Church St, Little
Shelford, Cambridge. T. (01223) 842866, 843537.
(Paintings) *095900*
Collectors Centre, The Old Stables, Hope Saint Yard,
Cambridge. T. (01223) 211632. (Furniture, general
antiques) *095901*
Cut Throat & Co., 551 Newmarket Rd, Cambridge.
T. (01223) 410222. (Wood) *095902*
Hyde Park Corner Antiques, 12 Lensfield Rd, Cambridge.
T. (01223) 353654. (Pottery, porcelain,
furniture) *095903*
Oriel Gallery, 13 Fair St, Cambridge. T. (01223) 321027.
(Oil paintings) *095904*
Rose Cottage Antiques, Rose Cottage, Brewery Rd, Pam-
pisford, Cambridge. T. (01223) 834631.
(Furniture) *095905*

Canterbury (Kent)
Antique and Design, Unit 14, Graham Bell House, Roper
Close, Canterbury. T. (01227) 762871.
(Furniture) *095906*
Burgate Antiques, 10 Burgate, Canterbury.
T. (01227) 456500. (Furniture) *095907*
Chaucer, 6 Beer Cart Lane, Canterbury.
T. (01227) 453912. (Books) *095908*
Cloisters, 26 Palace St, Canterbury. T. (01227) 462729.
(Oil paintings, watercolours, prints) *095909*
Greenfield, H.S., & Son, 4-5 Upper Bridge St, Canterbu-
ry. T. (01227) 45659. (Firearms) *095910*
Mynheer, J.W., 14 Kirbys Ln, Canterbury.
T. (01227) 762133. (Furniture) *095911*
Mynheer, J.W., 7-8 Roper Close, Canterbury.
T. (01227) 764933. (Furniture) *095912*
Nevill, John, 43 Saint Peter's St, Canterbury CT1 2BG.
T. (01227) 65291. (Paintings, Drawings, Sculptures,
Textiles) *095913*
Pearson, Michael, 2 The Borough, Northgate, Canterbu-
ry. T. (01227) 459939. (Clocks) *095914*
Victorian Fireplace, 92 Broad St, Canterbury.
T. (01227) 767723. (Fireplaces, shipping
furniture) *095915*

Cardiff (South Glamorgan)
Back to the Wood, rear of 3 Talygarn St, Heath, Cardiff.
T. (01222) 342247. (Fireplaces, doors) *095916*
Fiddes & Son, Brindley Rd, Cardiff. T. (01222) 340323,
Fax 343235. (Wood) *095917*
Heritage Antiques and Stripped Pine, 83 Pontcanna St,
Cardiff. T. (01222) 390097. (Furniture) *095918*
King, 163 Cowbridge Rd East, Canton, Cardiff.
T. (01222) 225014. (Furniture, fireplaces) *095919*
Manor House Fine Arts, 73-75 Pontcanna St, Cardiff CF1
9HS. T. (01222) 227787. (Paintings, watercolours,
prints) *095920*
Past and Present, 242 Whitchurch Rd, Heath, Cardiff.
T. (01222) 621443. (Furniture, clocks) *095921*
Salisbury Square Antiques, 5 Miskin St, Cathays, Cardiff.
T. (01222) 226889. (Furniture) *095922*
San Domenico Stringed Instruments, 175 Kings Rd, Can-
ton, Cardiff. T. (01222) 235881. (Stringed
instruments) *095923*
S.M. Upholstery, 212a Whitchurch Rd, Cardiff.
T. (01222) 617579. (Furniture) *095924*
Studio Galleries, 18 Llandaff Rd, Cardiff.
T. (01222) 383419. (Paintings) *095925*
Timberstrip, Unit 4a, Victoria Wharf, Ferry Rd, Cardiff.
T. (01222) 664650. (Furniture) *095926*

Carlisle (Cumbria)
Carlisle Furniture Restoration Centre, 2b Orfeur St, Carlisle. T. (01228) 512440. (Furniture) *095927*

Castle Antiques, 16 Fisher St, Carlisle. T. (01228) 49001.
(Furniture, paintings, pottery, linen) *095928*
Layne, A.C., 48 Cecil St, Carlisle. T. (01228) 45019.
(Clocks, watches) *095929*
Second Sight, 4a Mary St, Carlisle. T. (01228) 591525.
(Furniture, porcelain, paintings) *095930*
Strip Clean, Holme Works, Norfolk St, Carlisle.
T. (01228) 23743. (Furniture, doors) *095931*

Cassington (Oxfordshire)
old School House Antiques, The Green, Cassington.
T. Oxford 880 943. (Furniture, Glass, Paintings,
Textiles) *095932*

Castle Ashby (Northamptonshire)
Ashby Antique Restoration, Unit 2, The Woodyard, Castle
Ashby. T. 304. (Furniture) *095933*

Castle Cary (Somerset)
Boyd, John, Higher Flax Mills, Castle Cary BA7 7DY.
T. (01963) 50451. (Furniture) *095934*
Cary Antiques, 2 High St, Castle Cary. T. (01963) 50437.
(China) *095935*

Castle Hedingham (Essex)
Orbell House Gallery, Orbell House, Castle Hedingham.
T. (01787) 60298. (Oriental rugs) *095936*

Cerne Abbas (Dorset)
Bungay, M.J., The Buthery, Wills Ln, Cerne Abbas.
T. (01300) 341222. (Furniture) *095937*

Chagford (Devon)
Meredith, John, 41 New St, Chagford TQ13 8AB.
T. (01647) 3405. (Oak refectory tables, court cup-
boards, coffers and chests in oak only) *006038*

Chapel-en-le-Frith (Derbyshire)
Clock House, 48 Manchester Rd, Chapel-en-le-Frith.
T. (01298) 815174, Fax 816192. (Clocks) *095939*

Cheadle (Greater Manchester)
Foott, Andrew, 4 Claremont Rd, Cheadle Hulme, Cheadle
SK8 6EG. T. (0161) 485 3559. (Furniture) *095940*

Chelmsford (Essex)
Baddow Antique and Craft Centre, The Bringy, Church
St, Great Baddow, Chelmsford. T. (01245) 76159. (Fur-
niture, general antiques) *095941*
Baddow Antique and Craft Centre, The Bringy, Church
St, Great Baddow, Chelmsford. T. (01245) 76159.
(Furniture) *095942*

Cheltenham (Gloucestershire)
Cocoa, 7 Queens Circus, Cheltenham.
T. (01242) 233588. (Period textiles) *095943*
Homer Oriental Rugs, Parabola Rd, Stoneleigh, Chelten-
ham. T. (01242) 234243. (Rugs) *095944*
Keil, H.W., 129-131 Promenade, Cheltenham GL50 1NW.
T. (01242) 522509. (Furniture, glass, rugs) *095945*
Kyoto House Antiques, 14 Suffolk Rd, Cheltenham.
T. (01242) 262549. (Furniture) *095946*
Pride, Eric, 44 Suffolk Rd, Cheltenham.
T. (01242) 580822. (Rugs) *095947*
Scott-Cooper, 52 The Promenade, Cheltenham.
T. (01242) 522580. (Silver, jewellery) *095948*
Tapestry, 33 Suffolk Parade, Cheltenham.
T. (01242) 512191. (Furniture) *095949*

Chepstow (Gwent)
Glance, 16a Saint Mary St, Chepstow. (Prints,
maps) *095950*
Plough House Interiors, 11 Upper Church St, Chepstow.
T. (01291) 625200. (Furniture) *095951*

Chesham (Buckinghamshire)
Bartram, Albert, 177 Hivings Hill, Chesham HP5 2PN.
T. (01494) 783271. (Antique pewter and early
brass) *095952*
Chess Antiques, 85 Broad St, Chesham.
T. (01494) 783043. (Furniture, clocks) *095953*
Rewcastle, Geraldinge, 1 Mineral Lane, Chesham.
T. (01494) 56 48. (Porcelain, Pottery) *095954*
Tooley, M.V., 85 Broad St, Chesham. T. (01494) 783043.
(Clocks, barometers) *095955*

Chester (Cheshire)
A.C. Upholstery, Dale House, Dale St, Boughton, Chester.
T. (01244) 313263. (Furniture) *095956*
Adams, 65 Watergate Row, Chester. T. (01244) 319421.
(Furniture, clocks, oil paintings) *095957*
Baron, 68 Watergate St, Chester. T. (01244) 342520,
349212. (Watercolours, oil paintings,
etchings) *095958*
Green, Mike, Dale House, Dale St, Boughton, Chester
CH3 5EQ. T. (01244) 313263. (Furniture) *095959*
Grosvenor Antiques of Chester, 22 Watergate St, Che-
ster. T. (01244) 315201. (Jewellery) *095960*
Kayes, 9 Saint Michaels Row, Chester.
T. (01244) 327149. (Silver, jewellery, plate) *095961*

Chesterfield (Derbyshire)
Coleman, Polly, 424 Chatsworth Rd, Brampton, Chester-
field. T. (01246) 278146. (Furniture) *095962*
Times-Past, 13 Chatsworth Rd, Chesterfield.
T. (01246) 557077. (Furniture, paintings) *095963*
Yates, Brian, 420 Chatsworth Rd, Chesterfield.
T. (01246) 220395. (Furniture) *095964*

Chichester (West Sussex)
Canon Gallery, 4 Newtown, Chichester.
T. (01243) 786063. (Watercolours, oils) *095965*
Fowler, A., & Sons, 18 Greenfield Rd, Chichester.
T. (01243) 528903, Fax 783294. (Furniture) *095966*
Saint Pancras Antiques, 150 Saint Pancras, Chichester.
T. (01243) 787645. (Arms, armour) *095967*

Chilham (Kent)
Chilham Antiques, The Square, Chilham.
T. (01227) 730250. (Pictures) *095968*

Chipping Campden (Gloucestershire)
School House Antiques, School House, High St, Chipping
Campden. T. (01386) 841474, Fax 841367.
(Furniture) *095969*
Stuart House Antiques, High St, Chipping Campden.
T. (01386) 840995. (Ceramics) *095970*

Chipping Norton (Oxfordshire)
Howard, Jonathan, 21 Market Pl, Chipping Norton.
T. (01608) 643065. (Clocks) *095971*
West Street Antiques, 30 West St, Chipping Norton.
T. (01608) 644205. (Furniture) *095972*
Wiggins, Peter, Raffles, Southcombe, Chipping Norton.
T. (01608) 642652. (Barometers, clocks,
automata) *095973*

Chipping Sodbury (Avon)
Southall, Edward, Serridge House, Chipping Sodbury.
T. (01454) 322887. (Furniture) *095974*

Chislehurst (Greater London)
Sim, Michael, 1 Royal Parade, Chislehurst.
T. (0181) 467 7040. (Furniture) *095975*

Chobham (Surrey)
Hedgecoe, Michael, Burrow Hill Green, Chobham.
T. (01276) 838206. (Furniture) *095976*

Chorley (Lancashire)
Charisma Curios and Antiques, 91 Wigan Rd, Euxton,
Chorley. T. (012572) 76845. (Furniture) *095977*

Christchurch (Dorset)
Arditti, J.L., 88 Bargates, Christchurch.
T. (01202) 485414. (Carpets, rugs) *095978*

Chulmleigh (Devon)
Bagnall, W., Lingfiled, Chulmleigh. T. (01769) 80576.
(Furniture) *095979*

Church Stretton (Shropshire)
Antiques on the Square, 2 Sandford Court, Sandford Av,
Church Stretton. T. (01694) 724111. (Furniture,
ceramics) *095980*

Cirencester (Gloucestershire)
Beech, Jonathan, Nurses Cottage, Ampney Crucis, Ci-
rencester. T. (01285) 851495. (Clocks) *095981*
Bull, Walter, & Son, 10 Dyer St, Cirencester.
T. (01285) 653875. (Jewellery, silver) *095982*

Cirencester Antiques Centre, The Waterloo, Cirencester.
T. (01285) 644040. (Furniture, silver, jewellery) *095983*
Colborne, 15 Gosditch St, Cirencester.
T. (01285) 657557. (Furniture) *095984*
Forum Antiques, 20 West Way, Cirencester.
T. (01285) 658406. (Furniture) *095985*
Hares, 17-19 Gosditch St, Cirencester.
T. (01285) 640077. (Furniture) *095986*
Holzgräwe, W.W., Unit 3, Beeches Workshops, Beeches
Rd, Cirencester. T. (01285) 659351, 658625. (Furniture, metalwork) *095987*
Lammers, R., Broadbridge Cottage, Cirencester.
T. (01285) 326. (Clockmaker) *095988*
Legg, E.C., & Son, Unit 3, College Farm Workshops, Tetbury Rd, Cirencester. T. (01285) 650695. (Furniture, gilt frames) *095989*
Ponsford, A. J., 51-53 Dollar St, Cirencester GL7 2AS.
T. (01285) 652355. (Furniture, oil paintings) *095990*
Rivers, John D., 1 Ashcroft Rd, Cirencester.
T. (01285) 657616. (Jewellery) *095991*
Thornborough Galleries, 28 Gloucester St, Cirencester
GL7 2DH. T. (01285) 2055. (Old Oriental
carpets) *095992*
Traditional Woodskills, 4 Carpenters Buildings, 25 The
Avenue, Cirencester. T. (01285) 640840.
(Wood) *095993*
Ward, P.J., 11 Gosditch St, Cirencester.
T. (01285) 658499. (Paintings) *095994*

Clacton-on-Sea (Essex)
Sharman, L.R., 80b Rosemary Rd, Clacton-on-Sea.
T. (01255) 424620. (Furniture, jewellery) *095995*

Clare (Suffolk)
Salter, F.D., 1-2 Church St, Clare. T. (01787) 277693.
(Furniture) *095996*

Clayton-le-Moors (Lancashire)
Kwik Strip, Unit 10, Petre Rd, Clayton-le-Moors.
T. (01254) 235253. (Furniture) *095997*

Cle Elum (Washington)
Cobweb, The Old Tannery, Exeter Rd, Cle Elum.
T. (509) 38207. (Furniture) *095998*

Clitheroe (Lancashire)
Ethos Gallery, 4 York St, Clitheroe. T. (01200) 27878.
(Oils, watercolours) *095999*

Clutton (Avon)
McCarthy, Ian & Dianne, 112 Station Rd, Clutton.
T. (01761) 53188. (Metalware) *096000*

Coalville (Leicestershire)
Galleon Antiques, 195 Belvoir Rd, Coalville.
T. (01530) 37431. (Furniture) *096001*

Cobham (Surrey)
Speed, J. & J., Fox House, Pains Hill, Cobham.
T. (01932) 63333. (Watercolours, oils) *096002*
Taylor & Parry, Norwood Farm, Portsmouth Rd, Cobham.
T. (01932) 868308. (Furniture) *096003*

Coggeshall (Essex)
Lindsell, 11 Market Hill, Coggeshall. T. (01376) 562766.
(Seatings) *096004*
Marchant, Mark, 3 Market Sq, Coggeshall.
T. (01376) 561188. (Clocks, decorative works) *096005*
Smith, John, 1 Church St, Coggeshall.
T. (01376) 561365. (Pictures) *096006*

Colchester (Essex)
Badger, The Old House, The Street, Elmstead Market,
Colchester. T. (01206) 822044. (Furniture,
clocks) *096007*
Bond, S., & Son, 14 North Hill, Colchester.
T. (01206) 572925. (Furniture, oil paintings,
watercolours) *096008*
Coggeshall, Upp Hall Farm, Salmons Ln, Colchester CO6
1RY. T. (01206) 210020. (Furniture) *096009*
Davana, 88 Hythe Hill, Colchester. T. (01206) 577853.
(Metalware) *096010*
Graham, 19 Short Wyre St, Colchester.
T. (01206) 576808. (Jewellery, silver) *096011*

Iles, Richard, 10,10a,12 Northgate St, Colchester.
T. (01206) 577877. (Oils, engravings,
watercolours) *096012*
Rowell, Mary, 33 Cowdray Av, Colchester.
T. (01206) 769664. (Paintings) *096013*
Taber, Jacqueline, Jaggers Fingringhoe, Colchester.
T. (01206) 729334. (Paintings) *096014*
Trinity Clocks, 29 East Hill, Colchester.
T. (01206) 868623. (Clocks, watches) *096015*

Colne (Lancashire)
Enloc, Birchenlee Mill, Lenches Rd, Colne.
T. (01282) 861417, 867101. (Furniture) *096016*

Colsterworth (Lincolnshire)
Underwood, Clive, 46 High St, Colsterworth.
T. (0147687) 860689. (Furniture) *096017*

Coltishall (Norfolk)
Allpot, Elizabeth, Church St, Coltishall.
T. (01603) 737597. (Pottery, porcelain,
furniture) *096018*
Bates, Eric, & Sons, High St, Coltishall.
T. (01603) 738716. (Furniture) *096019*

Combe Martin (Devon)
Britannia Restorations, Old Britannia House, Castle St,
Combe Martin. T. (01271) 882887. (Furniture) *096020*

Congleton (Cheshire)
Syson, L., Church House Eaton, Congleton.
T. (01260) 274 331. (Furniture) *096021*

Coniston (Cumbria)
Old Man Antiques, Yewdale Rd, Coniston.
T. (015394) 41389. (Barometers, barographs,
thermographs) *096022*

Cookham (Berkshire)
Phillips & Sons, The Dower House, Cookham.
T. (016285) 529337. (Pictures) *096023*

Corringham (Essex)
Bush House, Church Rd., Corringham.
T. (01375) 673463. (Pottery, porcelain) *096024*

Cottingham (Humberside)
Sirrs, J., 100 Golf Links Rd, Cottingham.
T. (01482) 841940. (Furniture) *096025*

Coulsdon (Greater London)
Knightsbridge Pine, 39 Chipstead Valley, Coulsdon.
T. (0181) 660 0148. (Furniture) *096026*
Potashnik, David, 7 The Parade, Stoats Nest Rd, Coulsdon. T. (0181) 660 8403. (Furniture) *096027*

Coventry (West Midlands)
Parke, Regency Works, Shakleton Rd, Coventry.
T. (01203) 691199. (Furniture) *096028*

Cowes (Isle of Wight)
Marine Gallery, 1 Bath Rd, Cowes. T. (01983) 200124.
(Oils, watercolours, prints) *096029*

Cowfold (West Sussex)
Cowfold Clocks, Old House, The Street, Cowfold.
T. (0140386) 864505. (Clocks) *096030*

Cranbrook (Kent)
Wooden Choir Antiques, Waterloo Rd, Cranbrook.
T. (01580) 713671. (Furniture) *096031*

Cranleigh (Surrey)
Mann, David, & Sons, High St, Cranleigh.
T. (01483) 3777. (Furniture, Tapestries) *096032*

Cremyll (Cornwall)
Cremyll Antiques, The Cottage, Cremyll Beach, Cremyll.
T. (01752) 822934. (Barometers, barographs, watches,
clocks, jewellery) *096033*

Criccieth (Gwynedd)
Burridge, L., Portmadoc Rd, Criccieth.
T. (01766) 522955. (Paintings) *096034*

Crieff (Tayside)
Aiton, 63 King St, Crieff. T. (01764) 5423. (Paintings,
frames) *096035*

Cromer (Norfolk)
Bond Street Antiques, 6 Bond St, Cromer.
T. (01263) 513134. (Watches, jewellery) *096036*
Rust, Benjamin, 3 Saint Margaret's Rd, Cromer.
T. (01263) 511452. (Glass, clocks) *096037*

Crosby Ravensworth (Cumbria)
Grayling, David A.H., Lyvennet, Crosby Ravensworth.
T. (019315) 282, Fax 282. (Books) *096038*

Croydon (Greater London)
Apollo Galleries, 65-67 South End, Croydon.
T. (0181) 681 3727. (Pictures) *096039*
Dumont-Smith, Robert, 119 Cherry Orchard Rd East
Croydon, Croydon CR0 6BE. T. (0181) 688 0672. (Oil
Paintings) *096040*
Griffin, G.E., 43a Brighton Rd., Croydon.
T. (0181) 688 3130. (Furniture) *096041*
Venetian French Polishers, 11 Inglewood, Pixton Way,
Croydon CR0 9LN. T. (0181) 651 5223.
(Furniture) *096042*
Whitgift, 77 South End, Croydon. T. (0181) 688 0990.
(Paintings) *096043*

Cuckfield (West Sussex)
Sussex Conservation Studio, Hill Bank, Broad St, Cuckfield RH17 5DX. T. (01444) 451964. (Prints, watercolours, drawings) *096044*
Usher, Richard, 23 South St, Cuckfield.
T. (01444) 451699. (Furniture) *096045*

Cullompton (Devon)
Clock Shop, The Old Tannery Exeter Rd, Cullompton.
T. (01884) 34585. (Clocks) *096046*
Sunset Country Antiques, Old Tannery, Exeter Rd, Cullompton. T. (01884) 32890. (Furniture) *096047*

Culross (Fife)
Gunn, Alastair, Dunimarle Castle, Culross KY12 8JN.
T. (01383) 881515. (Furniture) *096048*

Darlington (Durham)
Nichol & Hill, 20 Grange Rd, Darlington.
T. (01325) 357431. (Furniture) *096049*

Deal (Kent)
Serendipity, 168-170 High St, Deal. T. (01304) 369165.
(Paintings, watercolours) *096050*

Debenham (Suffolk)
Debenham Gallery, 1 High St, Debenham.
T. (01728) 860827. (Oil paintings) *096051*

Deddington (Oxfordshire)
Tucker, Market Pl, Deddington. T. (01869) 38215. (Oil
paintings) *096052*

Denby Dale (West Yorkshire)
The Restoration Workshop, 11 Dearneside Rd, Denby
Dale HD8 8TP. T. (01484) Hudd. 86 4400. (Antique furniture, french polishing, wood turning) *096053*

Denham Village (Buckinghamshire)
Elmes, Margaret, Denham Gallery, Denham Village.
T. (0189583) 832244. (Furniture) *096054*

Derby (Derbyshire)
Abbey House, 115 Woods Ln, Derby. T. (01332) 31426.
(Dolls, teddies) *096055*
Derby Antique Centre, 11 Friargate, Derby.
T. (01332) 385002. (Furniture, clocks) *096056*
Ward, Charles H., 12 Friargate, Derby. T. (01332) 42893.
(Oil paintings, watercolours) *096057*

Disley (Cheshire)
Mill Farm Antiques, 50 Market St, Disley.
T. (01663) 764045. (Clocks, watches, barometers,
musicboxes) *096058*

Diss (Norfolk)
Diss Antiques, 2-3 Market Pl, Diss IP22 3YT.
T. (01379) 642213. (Furniture, barometers,
clocks) *096059*

Doddington (Cambridgeshire)
Doddington House, 2 Benwick Rd, Doddington.
T. (01354) 740755. (Chairs, barometers) *096060*

Dorchester (Dorset)
Colliton Antique and Craft Centre, Colliton St, North Square, Dorchester. T. (01305) 269398. (Cabinet work, upholstery, metalware) *096061*
Legg, Michael, 15 High East St, Dorchester.
T. (01305) 4596. (Furniture) *096062*

Dorchester-on-Thames (Oxfordshire)
Dorchester Galleries, Rotten Row, Dorchester-on-Thames. T. (01865) 341116. (Paintings, prints) *096063*
Giffengate Antiques, 16 High St, Dorchester-on-Thames.
T. (01865) 340028. (Porcelain) *096064*

Dorking (Surrey)
Collins, T.M., 70 High St, Dorking. T. (01306) 880790.
(Jewellery) *096065*
Hollander, E., Dutch House, Horsham Rd, Dorking RH5 4NF. T. (01306) 888921. (Clocks, barometers) *096066*
Hutton, Eleanor, 59 West St, Dorking. T. (01306) 886466.
(Jewellery, silver) *096067*
Oriental Carpets and Decorative Arts, 37 West St, Dorking. T. (01306) 76370. (Rugs, carpets) *096068*
Saunderson, Elaine, 18-18a Church St, Dorking.
T. (01306) 881231, 886082. (Furniture) *096069*
Upstairs, Downstairs Antiques, Old King's Head Court, High St, Dorking. T. (01306) 888849. (Furniture, porcelain) *096070*
Watson, Pauline, Old King's Head Court, High St, Dorking. T. (01306) 885452. (Jewellery, silver) *096071*

Douglas (Isle of Man)
Corrin, John, 73 Circular Rd, Douglas. T. (01624) 29655.
(Furniture, clocks, barometers) *096072*
Hamilton, 68 Derby Rd, Douglas. T. (01624) 662483.
(Furniture) *096073*

Dover (Kent)
Bonnies, 18 Bartholomew St, Dover. T. (01304) 204206, 830116. (Furniture) *096074*
Dover Furniture Restorers, 4 Branch St, Dover.
T. (01304) 205666. (Furniture) *096075*
Morrill, W.J., 437 Folkstone Rd, Dover.
T. (01304) 201989. (Paintings) *096076*

Droitwich (Hereford and Worcester)
Ainsworth, 14 Ombersley St West, Droitwich WR9 8HZ.
T. (01905) 778216. (Furniture) *096077*

Dudley (West Midlands)
Weetslade Fine Art, High Weetslade, Dudley.
T. (0191) 250 0174. (Oils, watercolours) *096078*

Dulverton (Somerset)
Dulverton Antique Centre, Lower Town Hall, Dulverton.
T. (01398) 23522. (Furniture) *096079*

Dundee (Tayside)
McIntyre, 8 Prospect Pl, Dundee. T. (01382) 26751. (Oil paintings) *096080*
Westport, 3 Old Hawkhill, Dundee. T. (01382) 22033.
(Furniture, ceramics, paintings) *096081*

Dunmow (Essex)
Hilton, Simon, Flemings Hill Farm, Great Easton, Dunmow. T. (01279) 850107, 850279. (Oil paintings, watercolour, drawings) *096082*

Duns (Borders)
Wedderburn Castle Antiques, Wedderburn Castle, Duns.
T. (01361) 82981. (Furniture, clocks, musical boxes) *096083*

Dunstable (Bedfordshire)
McLeay, Andrew, 98 Lowther Rd, Dunstable.
T. (01582) 661701. (Furniture) *096084*

Easingwold (North Yorkshire)
Davies, Pamela, 56-58 Long St, Easingwold.
T. (01347) 21251. (Oil paintings) *096085*

East Grinstead (West Sussex)
Antique Print Shop, 11 Middle Row, East Grinstead.
T. (01342) 410501. (Prints, watercolours, drawings) *096086*
Atkinson, Keith, Moorhawes Farm, East Grinstead.
T. (0134287) 765. (Furniture) *096087*

Spectrum, Oasted House, Lewes Rd, East Grinstead.
T. (01342) 325622. (Paintings) *096088*

East Molesey (Surrey)
B.S. Antiques, 39 Bridge St., East Molesey.
T. (0181) 941 1812. (Clocks, barometers) *096089*
Court Gallery, 16 Bridge Rd., East Molesey.
T. (0181) 941 2212. (Oils, watercolours) *096090*
May, R.J., 248 Fleetside, East Molesey.
T. (0181) 979 3826. (Furniture) *096091*

East Peckham (Kent)
North, Desmond & Amanda, The Orchard, Hale St, East Peckham. T. (01622) 871353. (Rugs, carpets) *096092*

Eastbourne (East Sussex)
Anglo Am Warehouse, 2a Beach Rd, Eastbourne.
T. (01323) 648661, Fax 648658. (Furniture) *096093*
Brufords of Eastbourne, 11-13 Cornfield Rd, Eastbourne.
T. (01323) 25452. (Clocks, silver) *096094*
Cowderoy, John, 42 South St, Eastbourne BN21 4XB.
T. (01323) 20058. (Clocks, musical boxes, furniture) *096095*
Eastbourne Clocks Restoration, 9 Victoria Dr, Eastbourne. T. (01323) 642650. (Clocks) *096096*
Eastbourne Fine Art, 9 Meads St, Eastbourne.
T. (01323) 25634. (Oils, watercolours) *096097*
Holder Gallery, 66 Grove Rd, Eastbourne.
T. (01323) 26565. (Paintings) *096098*
Premier Gallery, 24-26 South St, Eastbourne.
T. (01323) 36023. (Oil paintings, watercolours) *096099*
Romans, Colin, 154 Longland Rd, Eastbourne.
T. (01323) 645390. (Furniture) *096100*
Stacy-Marks, E., 24 Cornfield Rd, Eastbourne BN21 4QH. T. (01323) 20429, 32653. (Paintings, Prints) *096101*
Stewart, 25 Grove Rd, Eastbourne. T. (01323) 29588.
(Paintings, frames) *096102*
Time for Everyone, 44 Ocklynge Rd, Eastbourne.
T. (01323) 35714. (Clocks) *096103*
Weller, W.H., 12 North St, Eastbourne BN21 1AA.
T. (01323) 23592. (Polishing, silver plating, engraving) *096104*
Williams, Robert, 27 South St, Eastbourne.
T. (01323) 25337. (Paintings) *096105*

Edenbridge (Kent)
Unicorn Gallery, 6 Main Rd, Edenbridge.
T. (01732) 866226. (Paintings) *096106*

Edinburgh (Lothian)
Beaver, 23 Hatton Pl, Edinburgh EH9.
T. (0131) 667 8996. (Glass) *096107*
Behar, 12a Howe St, Edinburgh. T. (0131) 225 1069.
(Carpets, rugs) *096108*
Blair, Celia, Cramond Brig Farm, Edinburgh EH4.
T. (0131) 339 6502. (Paintings) *096109*
Bourne, 4 Dundas St, Edinburgh. T. (0131) 557 4050, 557 4874. (Paintings) *096110*
Brien, Kenneth & Stewart, Units 2-3, Saint Mary's Workshop, Henderson St, Edinburgh. T. (0131) 553 6811.
(Paintings) *096111*
Calton, 10 Royal Terrace, Edinburgh. T. (0131) 556 1010.
(Oils, watercolours) *096112*
Dovesi, Luciano, 3 Buckstane Park, Edinburgh EH10.
T. (0131) 445 1087. (Paintings) *096113*
Essex, A. & Co., 1 Hope Park Terrace, Edinburgh EH8 9LZ. T. (0131) 667 5387. (Paintings) *096114*
Fine Art Gallery, 41 Dundas St, Edinburgh.
T. (0131) 557 4569. (Pictures) *096115*
Georgian Antiques, Poplar Lane, Pattison St, Leith, Edinburgh. T. (0131) 553 6299. (Furniture) *096116*
Hardie, J.J., 222 Newhaven Rd, Edinburgh EH6.
T. (0131) 552 7080. (Furniture) *096117*
Herrald, 38 Queen St, Edinburgh EH2.
T. (0131) 225 5939. (Furniture) *096118*
Innes, Malcolm, 67 George St, Edinburgh.
T. (0131) 226 4151. (Pictures) *096119*
Jones, Simon, 65 Ratcliffe Terrace, Edinburgh EH9 1SU.
T. (0131) 662 0705. (Furniture) *096120*
McLuskie, Frank, The Studio, 5-7 Kings Stables Ln, Edinburgh EH1 2LQ. T. (0131) 226 6949.
(Paintings) *096121*

Mulherron, 83 Grassmarket, Edinburgh.
T. (0131) 226 5907. (Furniture, rugs) *096122*
Neilson, T. & J.W., 192-194 Morrison St, Edinburgh EH1 1AA. T. (0131) 229 5591. (Fenders, dog grates, hobs, interiors in steel, cast iron and brass) *096123*
Open Eye Gallery, 75-79 Cumberland St, Edinburgh.
T. (0131) 557 1020. (Paintings, ceramics) *096124*
Parkes & Bordone, Unit 01, St Mary's Workshop, Henderson St, Edinburgh EH6. T. (0131) 553 5111.
(Paintings) *096125*
Siller & Donaldson, 58 Grove St, Edinburgh EH3.
T. (0131) 229 5870. (Furniture) *096126*
Trist & McBain, 9 Canongate Venture, New St, Edinburgh EH8 8BH. T. (0131) 557 3828. (Furniture) *096127*
Whytock & Reid, Sunbury House, Belford Mews, Edinburgh EH4. T. (0131) 226 4911. (Furniture, rugs) *096128*
Whytock & Reid, Sunbury House, Belford Mews, Edinburgh EH4 3DN. T. (0131) 226 4911. (Furniture, persian, carpets, textiles) *096129*

Egham (Surrey)
Pastimes, 86 High St, Egham. T. (01784) 436290. (Pictures, furniture) *096130*

Ellesmere (Shropshire)
Wharf Road Antiques, Wharf Rd, Ellesmere.
T. (01691) 623227. (Furniture) *096131*

Empingham (Leicestershire)
Old Bakery Antiques, Church St, Empingham.
T. (0178086) 243. (Furniture) *096132*

Emsworth (Hampshire)
Tiffins, 12 Queen St, Emsworth. T. (01243) 372497.
(Clocks) *096133*

Errol (Tayside)
Errol Antiques, The Cross, High St, Errol. T. 642391.
(Furniture) *096134*

Esher (Surrey)
Kensington Galleries, Badgers Wood, West End Lane, Esher. T. (01372) 64407. (Oil paintings) *096135*

Eton (Berkshire)
Manley, J., 27 High St, Eton. T. (01753) 865647. (Watercolours, old prints) *096136*
Martin, Peter J., 40 High St, Eton. T. (01753) 864901.
(Furniture) *096137*
Mostly Boxes, 92 High St, Eton. T. (01753) 858470.
(Boxes) *096138*
Times Past Antiques, 59 High St, Eton.
T. (01753) 857018. (Clocks, watches) *096139*

Evenlode (Gloucestershire)
Jerram, E. J., The Studio, Poplars Farmhouse, Evenlode GL56 0NR. T. Moreton-in-Marsh 5 1009. (Oil paintings) *096140*

Eversley (Hampshire)
Kingsley Barn, Church Ln, Eversley. T. (01734) 328518.
(Furniture) *096141*

Evesham (Worcestershire)
Port Street Antiques, 18 Port St, Evesham.
T. (01386) 442023. (Furniture) *096142*

Exeter (Devon)
Bruford, William, & Son, 1 Bedford St, Exeter.
T. (01392) 54901. (Clocks, silver, jewellery) *096143*
Holmdale, 4 New Bridge St, Exeter. T. (01392) 77270.
(Paintings) *096144*
Keetch, Fred, 21 Cathedral Yard, Exeter EX1 1HB.
T. (01392) 74312. (Paintings) *096145*
Nathan, John, 153-154 Cowick St, Saint Thomas, Exeter. T. (01392) 78216. (Silver, jewellery) *096146*
Samuels, C., & Sons, 17-19 Waterbeer St, Guildhall Shopping Centre, Exeter. T. (01392) 73219. (Watercolours, prints, maps) *096147*
Southards, 119 Fore St, Exeter. T. (01392) 213680.
(Wood) *096148*
Trinity Pine, 31 Okehampton Rd, Saint Thomas, Exeter.
T. (01392) 221649. (Furniture) *096149*

Eynsham (Oxfordshire)
Juno Furniture Restorers, Eynsham Malthouse, Newland St, Eynsham OX8 1LA. T. (01865) 880008. (Furniture) *096150*

Falmouth (Cornwall)
Maggs, John, 54 Church St, Falmouth.
T. (01326) 313153. (Prints, bindings) *096151*
Rosina's, 4 High St, Falmouth. T. (01326) 311406. (Dolls, toys, clothes) *096152*

Faringdon (Oxfordshire)
Faringdon Gallery, 21 London St, Faringdon.
T. (01367) 22030. (Paintings, prints) *096153*
La Chaise Antique, 30 London St, Faringdon SN7 7AA.
T. (01367) 240427, Fax 241001. (Furniture) *096154*

Farnham (Surrey)
Casque and Gauntlet Antiques, 55-59 Badshot Lea Rd, Farnham. T. (01252) 20745. (Metals) *096155*
Christopher's Antiques, 39a West St, Farnham.
T. (01252) 713794. (Furniture) *096156*
Lion and Lamb Gallery, West St, Farnham.
T. (01252) 714154. (Oils, watercolours) *096157*
New Ashgate Gallery, Wagon Yard Car Park, Downing St, Farnham GU9 7PS. T. (01252) 0252/713208. (Painting, Prints, Drawings, Ceramics, Jewellery, Textiles) *096158*
Putnam, R. & M., 60 Downing St, Farnham.
T. (01252) 715769. (Furniture) *096159*
Weijand, Karel, Lion and Lamb Courtyard, Farnham.
T. (01252) 726215. (Rugs, carpets) *096160*

Farningham (Kent)
Finch, Matthew, 7 High St, Farningham. T. (01322) 2029. (Furniture) *096161*

Felpham (West Sussex)
Botting, Susan & Robert, 38 Firs Av, Felpham.
T. (012433) 584515. (Watercolours, oil paintings) *096162*

Finedon (Northamptonshire)
Thorpe, 12-20 Regent St, Finedon. T. 681688. (Furniture) *096163*

Fishguard (Dyfed)
Hermitage Antiques, 10 West St, Fishguard.
T. (01348) 873037. (Arms, woodwork) *096164*

Folkestone (Kent)
Keller & Partridge, 3 Sandgate High St, Folkestone. (Antiques, Porcelain, Paintings) *096165*
Marrin, G. & D.I., & Sons, 149 Sandgate Rd, Folkestone.
T. (01303) 53016. (Paintings, engravings, prints) *096166*
Tontine Antiques, 77-81 Tontine St, Folkestone.
T. (01303) 53077. (Antiques, Paintings) *096167*

Fordingbridge (Hampshire)
Fox, J.G., 2 Roman Quay, High St, Fordingbridge.
T. (01425) 653033. (Furniture) *096168*

Forres (Grampian)
Traditional Antique Restoration, The Stable, Altyre Estate, Forres IV36 0SH. T. (01309) 72572. (Furniture, Frames, Marble, Staircases, General Fittings, Painted Ceilings and Walls) *096169*

Framlingham (Suffolk)
Bed Bazaar, 29 Double St, Framlingham.
T. (01728) 723756. (Beds) *096170*
Fleming, T., Church St, Framlingham. T. (01728) 553. (Antiques, furniture) *096171*

Freshwater (Isle of Wight)
Aladdin's Cave, 1-2 School Green Rd, Freshwater.
T. (01983) 752934. (China) *096172*

Frome (Somerset)
Sutton & Sons, 15 Vicarage St, Frome. T. (01373) 62062. (Furniture) *096173*

Galston (Southclyde)
Fresner, Cessnock Castle, Galston. T. (01563) 820314. (Paintings) *096174*

Gants Hill (Greater London)
Antique Clock Repair Shoppe, 26 Woodford Av., Gants Hill. T. (0181) 550 9540. (Clocks) *096175*

Gargrave (North Yorkshire)
Dickinson, Bernard, 88 High St, Gargrave.
T. (0175678) 749285. (Furniture) *096176*

Garlinge (Kent)
Watson, R.W., 33 Crow Hill Rd, Garlinge CT9 5PF. T. Thanet 3 3833. (Marquetry work of all periods, motive work) *096177*

Gateshead (Tyne and Wear)
Windmill, 223 Coatsworth Rd, Gateshead.
T. (0191) 477 2300. (Oil paintings, watercolours) *096178*

Gillingham (Kent)
Lake, Daniel, 2 Star Ln, Hempstead, Gillingham.
T. (01634) 375832. (Furniture) *096179*

Glasgow (Strathclyde)
Behar, 15 Bath St, Glasgow. T. (0141) 332 2858. (Carpets, rugs) *096180*
Brown, 63 Admiral St, Glasgow G41. T. (0141) 429 6007. (Furniture) *096181*
Brown, 1060 Argyle St, Glasgow. T. (0141) 248 6760. (Specialists in fine Clocks for ower forty Years – complete) *096182*
Heritage House, 59/73 James St, Glasgow G40 1BZ.
T. (0141) 550 2221. (Furniture) *096183*
Keep Sakes, 27 Gibson St, Glasgow. T. (0141) 334 2264. (Jewellery) *096184*
Kettlewell, Piers, 10 Robertson St, Barrhead, Glasgow G78. T. (0141) 881 8166. (Furniture) *096185*
Langside, 26-28 Battlefield Rd, Glasgow.
T. (0141) 649 8888, Fax 632 5590. (Paintings) *096186*
Malloy, Fran, Suite 1, 66 Dora St, Glasgow G40.
T. (0141) 551 0616. (Furniture) *096187*
Morton, Sherron, Unit 24, 42 Dalsetter Av, Glasgow G15.
T. (0141) 334 9685. (Furniture) *096188*
Muirhead Moffat & Co., 182 West Regent St, Glasgow.
T. (0141) 226 4683. (Furniture, clocks, barometers, jewellery) *096189*
Pettigrew & Mail, 7 The Loaning, Whitecraigs, Giffnock, Glasgow. T. (0141) 639 2989. (Paintings) *096190*
Rose, R.L., & Co., 19 Waterloo St, Glasgow.
T. (0141) 248 3313. (Carpets, rugs) *096191*

Glastonbury (Somerset)
Glastonbury Framing, 65 High St, Glastonbury.
T. (01458) 33161. (Paintings) *096192*

Glossop (Derbyshire)
Derbyshire Clocks, 104 High St West, Glossop.
T. (01457) 862677. (Clocks) *096193*
Old Cross Gallery, Church St South, Old Glossop, Glossop. T. (01457) 862555. (Furniture, pictures, mirrors) *096194*

Gloucester (Gloucestershire)
Bartrick, Douglas J., Antique Centre, Severn Rd, Gloucester. T. (01452) 29716. (Clocks) *096195*
Cook, E.J., & Son, Antique Centre, Severn Rd, Gloucester. T. (01452) 529716. (Furniture, clocks) *096196*

Godalming (Surrey)
Cry for the Moon, 31 High St, Godalming.
T. (014868) 426201. (Jewellery) *096197*
Heath-Bullock, 8 Meadrow, Godalming GU7 3HN.
T. (014868) 22562, Fax 426077. (Furniture) *096198*

Gosforth (Tyne and Wear)
Harrison, Anna, Grange Park, Great North Rd, Gosforth.
T. (0191) 284 3202. (Furniture) *096199*
MacDonald, 2 Ashburton Rd, Gosforth.
T. (0191) 284 4214. (Watercolours, oils) *096200*

Gosport (Hampshire)
Alverstoke Antiques, 47 Village Rd, Alverstoke, Gosport.
T. (01705) 582204. (Furniture) *096201*

Goudhurst (Kent)
Burnett, Richard, Finchcocks, Goudhurst TN17 1HH.
T. (01580) 211702. (Antique Keyboard and Musical Instruments) *096202*

Grantham (Lincolnshire)
Grantham Clocks, 30 Lodge Way, Grantham.
T. (01476) 61784. (Clocks) *096203*

Great Bardfield (Essex)
Markswood, Great Bardfield. T. (0137181) 810106. (Oil paintings, watercolours) *096204*

Great Bookham (Surrey)
Davis, Roger A., 19 Dorking Rd, Great Bookham.
T. 57655. (Clocks) *096205*

Great Malvern (Hereford and Worcester)
Malvern Antiques, Lyttleton House, Abbey Arch Abbey Rd, Great Malvern. T. (016845) 575889. (Paintings) *096206*
Malvern Studios, 56 Cowleigh Rd, Great Malvern.
T. (016845) 574913. (Furniture) *096207*

Great Missenden (Buckinghamshire)
Farrow, Peter, The Ashlands, Ballinger Common, Great Missenden. T. (012406) 403. (Furniture) *096208*
Heritage Restorations, 36b High St, Great Missenden.
T. (012406) 5710. (Clocks, furniture) *096209*

Great Yarmouth (Norfolk)
Ferrow, David, 77 Howard St South, Great Yarmouth.
T. (01493) 843800. (Books, prints) *096210*
Haven, 6-7 Hall Quay, Great Yarmouth.
T. (01493) 855391. (Oils, watercolours, prints) *096211*
Howkins, John, 137-138 King St, Great Yarmouth.
T. (01493) 855330. (Furniture, clocks) *096212*
Howkins, Peter, 39-41 King St, Great Yarmouth.
T. (01493) 844639. (Jewellery, furniture, silver, gold) *096213*
Lawson, Keith, 7 White Horse Plain, Northgate St, Great Yarmouth. T. (01493) 843679. (Clocks) *096214*

Greyabbey (Co. Down)
Greyabbey Timecraft, 18 Main St, Greyabbey.
T. (0124774) 416. (Clocks, watches) *096215*

Guildford (Surrey)
Traylen, Charles W., 49-50 Quarry St, Guildford.
T. (01483) 572424. (Books) *096216*

Guilsborough (Northamptonshire)
Goodwin, Nick, The Firs, Nortoft Rd, Guilsborough.
T. 813115. (Furniture) *096217*

Haddenham (Cambridgeshire)
Potts, Ludovic, Unit 1, Haddenham Bus Park, Station Rd, Haddenham CB6 3XD. T. (01353) 741537. (Furniture) *096218*
Wellby, H.S., Malt House, Church End, Haddenham.
T. (01353) 290036. (Paintings) *096219*

Hadleigh (Suffolk)
Randolph, 97-99 High St, Hadleigh. T. (01473) 823789. (Furniture) *096220*

Hadlow (Kent)
Langold, Oxon Heath, Hadlow TN11 9SS.
T. (01732) Plaxtol 810577. (Antique Furniture) *096221*

Halesowen (West Midlands)
Country Chaircraft, 12 Waxland Rd, Halesowen.
T. 550 9519. (Furniture) *096222*

Halstead (Essex)
Heather Cottage Cabinet Makers, School Rd, Halstead.
T. (01787) 269528. (Furniture) *096223*

Harbertonford (Devon)
Fine Pine Antiques, Woodland Rd, Harbertonford.
T. (01803) 732465. (Furniture) *096224*

Harlow (Essex)
Millside Antique Restoration, Studio 3, Parndon Mill, Parndon Mill Ln, Harlow. T. (01279) 428148. (Porcelain) *096225*

Harpenden (Hertfordshire)
Knights, 38 Station Rd, Harpenden. T. (01582) 460564.
(Watercolours, oils, prints) 096226

Harrogate (North Yorkshire)
Antique Pine, Library House, Regent Parade, Harrogate.
T. (01423) 560452. (Furniture) 096227
Bentley, Bill, 41 Cheltenham Crescent, Harrogate HG1
2TG. T. (01423) 546084. (Furniture) 096228
Haworth, 26 Cold Bath Rd, Harrogate.
T. (01423) 521401. (Clocks) 096229
London House Oriental Rugs and Carpets, 9 Montpellier
Parade, Harrogate. T. (01423) 567167. (Rugs) 096230
Mason, D., & Son, 7-8 Westmoreland St, Harrogate.
T. (01423) 567305. (Clocks, jewellery) 096231
Omar, 8 Crescent Rd, Harrogate. T. (01423) 567968.
(Carpets) 096232
Pearson, John, Church Cottage, Birstwith, Harrogate
HG3 2NG. T. (01423) 770828. (Longcase and Wall-
Clocks) 096233
Regency Fine Art, 123 Wetherby Rd, Harrogate.
T. (01423) 883178. (Oil paintings) 096234
Rippon, 6 Station Bridge, Harrogate. T. (01423) 501835.
(Books) 096235
Sutcliffe, 8 Albert St, Harrogate. T. (01423) 62976.
(Paintings) 096236
Walker, 6 Montpellier Gardens, Harrogate.
T. (01423) 567933. (Oil paintings,
watercolours) 096237
Warner, Christopher, 15 Princes St, Harrogate.
T. (01423) 503617. (Silver, jewellery) 096238

Harrow (Greater London)
Browne, Maurice & Anna, 46 High St, Harrow.
T. (0181) 422 4820. (Furniture) 096239

Hartley Wintney (Hampshire)
Atelier Fine Art Castings, Hulfords Lane, Hartley Wintney
RG27 8AG. T. (0125126) 844388, Fax 842709.
(Metalwork) 096240
Cedar Antiques, High St, Hartley Wintney.
T. (0125126) 843252. (Clocks, furniture) 096241
Clisby, Bryan, High St, Hartley Wintney.
T. (0125126) 842305. (Clocks, barometers) 096242
Porter, A.W., & Son, High St, Hartley Wintney.
T. (0125126) 842676, Fax 842064. (Clocks) 096243
Willson, Anthony, 22 High St, Hartley Wintney.
T. (0125126) 4499. (Oil paintings,
watercolours) 096244

Haslemere (Surrey)
Saint Barbe Spurr, Ursula, The Fourth House, Petworth
Rd, Haslemere GU27 3AF. T. (01428) 5 2428. (Gilding,
Lacquerwork, hand-painted finishing) 096245
Surrey Clock Centre, 3 Lower St, Haslemere.
T. (01428) 4547. (Clocks) 096246

Haslingden (Lancashire)
Doran, Paul, 196 Blackburn Rd, Haslingden. T. 827423.
(Furniture) 096247

Hastings (Sussex)
Wren, R.W., 3 The Ridge, Hastings. T. (01424) 445248.
(Clocks) 096248

Hatfield Heath (Essex)
Barn Gallery, Parvilles Farm, Hatfield Heath.
T. (01279) 730114. (Oil paintings, watercolours,
prints) 096249

Hawick (Borders)
Blackwood, Simon, 10-11 Bourtree Terrace, Hawick.
T. (01450) 378547. (Paintings) 096250

Hawkhurst (Kent)
Hawkhurst Antiques, Cranbrook Rd, Hawkhurst.
T. (01580) 752277. (Furniture) 096251

Haworth (West Yorkshire)
Haworth Antiques, Lees Mill, Lees Lane, Haworth.
T. (01535) 43535. (Furniture) 096252

Hay-on-Wye (Powys)
Wigington, 15 Broad St, Hay-on-Wye.
T. (01497) 820545. (Furniture) 096253

Haydon Bridge (Northumberland)
Haydon Gallery, 3 Shaftoe St, Haydon Bridge.
T. (014984) 648200. (Oil paintings) 096254

Haynes (Bedfordshire)
Hagen, Ann & Richard, Bakehouse Cottage Northwood
End Rd, Haynes MK45 3PS. T. (0123066) 424. (Period
furniture, primitive items, treen, tools, painted woodwork, antique maps and prints) 096255

Haywards Heath (West Sussex)
Cruttenden's, 14 South Rd, Haywards Heath.
T. (01444) 441447. (Clocks) 096256

Headcorn (Kent)
Brown, Ken, Unit 7, Tong Farm, Headcorn.
T. (01622) 890926. (Furniture) 096257

Heath and Reach (Bedfordshire)
Antique Metal Polishing Company, 14 Birds Hill, Heath
and Reach LU7 0AQ. T. (0152523) 379. (Copper and
brass) 096258
Trenchard, Graham, 14 Birds Hill, Heath and Reach.
T. (0152523) 379. (Oil Paintings, watercolours, prints,
pastels) 096259

Helmsley (North Yorkshire)
Westway Cottage Restored Pine, Ashdale Rd, Helmsley.
T. (01439) 70172. (Furniture) 096260

Hemel Hempstead (Hertfordshire)
Abbey Antiques and Fine Art, 97 High St, Hemel Hemp-
stead. T. (01442) 64667. (Watercolours,
furniture) 096261
Carousel, 59 High St, Hemel Hempstead.
T. (01442) 219772. (Dolls) 096262

Hempstead (Essex)
Beaumont, Michael, Hempstead Hall, Hempstead.
T. (01440) 730239. (Furniture) 096263

Henfield (West Sussex)
Clockwise, 6 London Rd, Henfield. T. (01273) 492568.
(Clocks) 096264

Henley-in-Arden (Warwickshire)
Colmore Galleries, 52 High St, Henley-in-Arden.
T. (015642) 792938. (Paintings) 096265

Henley-on-Thames (Oxfordshire)
Keene, Barry M., 12 Thameside, Henley-on-Thames.
T. (01491) 577119. (Paintings, watercolours,
prints) 096266
Kingston, Richard J., 95 Bell St, Henley-on-Thames.
T. (01491) 574535. (Furniture) 096267
Selkirk, 7 Friday St, Henley-on-Thames.
T. (01491) 574077. (Paintings) 096268
Thames Oriental Rug Company, 48-56 Reading Rd, Hen-
ley-on-Thames. T. (01491) 574676. (Carpets) 096269

Hereford (Hereford and Worcester)
Brown, L. & J.L., 58-59 Commercial Rd, Hereford.
T. (01432) 358895, Fax 275338. (Furniture) 096270

Hertford (Herfordshire)
Beckwith & Son, Saint Nicholas Hall, Saint Andrew St,
Hertford. T. (01992) 582079. (Porcelain, furniture, sil-
ver, clocks) 096271
Georgian House Antiques, 42 Saint Andrew St, Hertford.
T. (01992) 583508. (Furniture) 096272
Partridge, L., 25 Saint Andrew St, Hertford.
T. (01992) 584385. (Oil paintings, prints, silver,
jewellery) 096273

Hest Bank (Lancashire)
Kelsall, T.H., 82 Main Rd, Hest Bank. T. (01524) 822347.
(Furniture) 096274

Hexham (Northumberland)
Caris, Gordon, 16 Market Pl, Hexham.
T. (01434) 602106. (Clocks, watches) 096275
Hedley, J.A. & T., 3 Saint Mary's Chare, Hexham.
T. (01434) 602317. (Furniture) 096276

High Wycombe (Buckinghamshire)
Brown, Church Lane, West Wycombe, High Wycombe.
T. (01494) 24537. (Furniture) 096277

Burrell, Kitchener Works, Kitchener Rd, High Wycombe.
T. (01494) 23619. (Furniture) 096278
Kwik Strip, Kitchener Works, Kitchener Rd, High Wycom-
be HP11 2SJ. T. (01494) 520230. (Furniture) 096279

Highbridge (Somerset)
Treasure Chest, 19 Alstone Lane, Highbridge. T. 787267.
(Pictures) 096280

Hillsborough (Co. Down)
Period Architectural Features and Antiques, 5 The Square, Hillsborough. T. (01846) 683703. (Marble) 096281

Hinckley (Leicestershire)
Lycett, 1 Bradgate Rd, Hinckley. T. (01455) 637629.
(Porcelain) 096282

Hindhead (Surrey)
Borton, Peter, Moorlands, Linkside West, Hindhead.
T. (0142873) 5033. (Paintings, watercolours) 096283

Hinton Waldrist (Oxfordshire)
Davenport, Antony, The Grange, Hinton Waldrist.
T. 820227. (Furniture, pictures) 096284

Hitchin (Hertfordshire)
Countrylife Gallery, 41-43 Portmill Ln, Hitchin.
T. (01462) 433267. (Watercolours, paintings) 096285
Green & Cockburn, Fore St., Weston, Hitchin.
T. (0146279) 646. (Clocks, furniture, churches and pe-
riod premises) 096286
Hitchin Antiques Gallery, 37 Bridge St, Hitchin.
T. (01462) 434525. (Furniture, clocks, glass) 096287
Perry, R.J., 38 Bridge St, Hitchin. T. (01462) 434525.
(Furniture, metalware) 096288
Phillips, The Manor House, Hitchin. T. (01462) 432067.
(Furniture) 096289
Thomas, Carole, 32a Sun St, Hitchin. T. (01462) 436077.
(Watercolours, oils) 096290

Hollinwood (Lancashire)
Abbey Antiques, 299-301 Manchester Rd, Hollinwood.
T. 681 6538. (Clocks) 096291

Holme (Cumbria)
JBW Antiques, Green Farm, Duke St, Holme.
T. (01524) 781377. (Pottery, porcelain, glass, silver,
plate, furniture) 096292
Utopia Antiques, Holme Mills, Holme. T. (01524) 781739.
(Pine) 096293

Holmfirth (West Yorkshire)
Easy Strip, 77 Dunford Rd, Holmfirth. T. (01484) 682129.
(Furniture) 096294

Holsworthy (Devon)
Victoria Antiques, Victoria Hill, Holsworthy.
T. (01409) 253815. (Furniture) 096295

Holt (Norfolk)
Antiques, 12 Chapel Yard, Albert St, Holt.
T. (01263) 712975. (Furniture, jewellery) 096296
Humbleyard Fine Art, 3 Fish Hill, Holt.
T. (01263) 713362. (Watercolours, prints) 096297

Honiton (Devon)
Honiton Fine Art, 189 High St, Honiton.
T. (01404) 45942. (Oil paintings) 096298
Oakfields, 46 High St, Honiton. T. (01404) 46858.
(Furniture) 096299
Vine Furniture Services, Vine Yard, Vine Passage, High
St, Honiton. T. (01404) 44876. (Furniture) 096300

Horley (Surrey)
Horley Gallery, 39 Victoria Rd, Horley RH6 7NL.
T. (01293) 772879. (Paintings) 096301

Horsham (West Sussex)
Crown Woodcraft, 29 Hill Mead, Horsham.
T. (01403) 265959. (Furniture) 096302

Hove (East Sussex)
ABC & Viccari Restoration, 21-23 Stirling Pl, Hove.
T. (01273) 720165. (Paintings) 096303
Hove Antique Clocks, 68 Western Rd, Hove.
T. (01273) 722123. (Clocks) 096304

Hoylake (Merseyside)
Clock Shop, 7 The Quadrant, Hoylake.
T. (0151) 632 1888. (Clocks, jewellery)   096305
Crewel Frederick, 75 Market St, Hoylake.
T. (0151) 632 1647. (Needlework)   096306

Huddersfield (West Yorkshire)
Fillans, 2 Market Walk, Huddersfield. T. (01484) 531609.
(Silver, jewellery)   096307
Hemingway, 221 Meltham Rd, Huddersfield.
T. (01484) 662806. (Furniture)   096308
Paragon Antiques, 90 Acre St, Lindley, Huddersfield.
T. (01484) 542789. (Furniture)   096309
Picture Framing, Cloth Hall St, Huddersfield.
T. (01484) 546075. (Paintings, frames)   096310

Hungerford (Berkshire)
Ashley, 129 High St, Hungerford. T. (01488) 682771.
(Furniture)   096311
Harris, Bibi, 1 Church St, Hungerford. T. (01488) 685189.
(Textiles)   096312
Styles, 12 Bridge St, Hungerford. T. (01488) 683922.
(Silver)   096313

Hunstanton (Norfolk)
Woodhouse, R.C., 10 Westgate, Hunstanton.
T. (01485) 2903. (Clocks)   096314

Huntingdon (Cambridgeshire)
Kendal, 2 Clifton Rd, Huntingdon. T. (01480) 411811.
(Furniture)   096315

Hursley (Hampshire)
Hursley Antiques, Hursley. T. (01962) 75488.
(Metalware)   096316

Hurstpierpoint (West Sussex)
Clock Shop, 36 High St, Hurstpierpoint.
T. (01273) 832081. (Clocks, furniture)   096317

Hyde (Cheshire)
Bunting, Peter, 238 Higham Ln, Werneth Low, Hyde.
T. (0161) 368 5544. (Furniture)   096318
Bunting, Peter, 274 Stockport Rd, Hyde.
T. (0161) 368 5544. (Furniture)   096319

Hythe (Kent)
Barclay, J., Unit 9, Kengate Ind Est, 142 Dymchurch Rd,
Hythe. T. (01303) 264800. (Furniture)   096320

Ickleton (Cambridgeshire)
Abbey Antiques, 18 Abbey St, Ickleton.
T. (01799) 30637. (Furniture)   096321

Ilkley (West Yorkshire)
Cooper, J.H., & Sons, 33 Church St, Ilkley.
T. (01943) 608020. (Furniture)   096322
Coopers of Ilkley, 46-50 Leeds Rd, Ilkley.
T. (01943) 608020. (Furniture)   096323
Russell, M.J., Booth's Yard, Nile Rd, Ilkley.
T. (01943) 607165. (Furniture)   096324

Ilminster (Somerset)
Hutchinson, Clare, 1a West St, Ilminster.
T. (01460) 53369. (Pictures, frames)   096325
Plympton, 31 West St, Ilminster. T. (01460) 54437. (Watercolours, prints, china)   096326

Ingatestone (Essex)
Meyers, 66 High St, Ingatestone. T. (01277) 355335. (Oil paintings, watercolours)   096327

Inverness (Highland)
Fraser, 28-30 Church St, Inverness. T. (01463) 32395,
32625. (Antiques, Furniture)   096328

Ipswich (Suffolk)
Art Shop, 3 Great Colman St, Ipswich.
T. (01473) 258429. (Paintings)   096329
Atfield & Daughter, 17 Saint Stephen's Lane, Ipswich.
T. (01473) 251158. (Furniture)   096330
Cottage Collections, 46a Bolton Ln, Ipswich IP4 2BT.
T. (01473) 211032. (Furniture)   096331
Cox, Claude, 3 Silent St, Ipswich. T. (01473) 254776.
(Books)   096332

Croydon & Sons, 50-56 Tavern St, Ipswich.
T. (01473) 256514. (Silver, plate, clocks, watches,
jewellery)   096333
Gazeley, John W., 17 Fonnereau Rd, Ipswich.
T. (01473) 252420. (Paintings)   096334
Hubbard, 16 Saint Margarets Green, Ipswich.
T. (01473) 226033. (Furniture)   096335
Kwik Strip, Unit 5, Penny Corner, Farthing Rd, Ipswich.
T. (01473) 743734. (Furniture)   096336
Orwell, 427 Wherstead Rd, Ipswich. T. (01473) 680091.
(Furniture)   096337
Weir, Gerald, Bond Str, Ipswich. T. (01473) 214621.
(Wood)   096338

Iron Bridge (Shropshire)
Ironbridge Antique Centre, Dale End, Iron Bridge.
T. (01952) 3784. (Furniture)   096339

Irvine (Strathclyde)
Kelley, 100 Bank St, Irvine. T. (01294) 79128.
(Furniture)   096340

Iver (Buckinghamshire)
Yester-Year, 12 High St, Iver. T. (01753) 652072. (Furniture, pictures)   096341

Jedburgh (Borders)
Turner, R. & M., 34-36 High St, Jedburgh.
T. (01835) 518. (Furniture, pottery, porcelain)   096342

Jesmond (Tyne and Wear)
Humble, Owen, 11-12 Clayton Rd, Jesmond.
T. (0191) 281 4602. (Furniture)   096343
Osborne Art and Antiques, 18c Osborne Rd, Jesmond.
T. (0191) 281 6380. (Oil paintings, watercolours,
drawings)   096344

Kedington (Suffolk)
Suffolk House, Kedington. T. (01440) 703 803.
(Furniture)   096345

Keighley (West Yorkshire)
Pine Stripping, Unit 6, Eastburn Mills Main Rd, Keighley.
T. (01535) 656297. (Furniture)   096346

Kempston (Bedfordshire)
Queen Adelaide, 79 High St, Kempston. T. 854083.
(Paintings, frames)   096347

Kendal (Cumbria)
Georgian House, 99 Highgate, Kendal.
T. (01539) 724527. (Furniture)   096348
Kendal Studios Antiques, Wildman St, Kendal.
T. (01539) 723291. (Ceramics, maps, prints, paintings,
furniture)   096349

Kenilworth (Warwickshire)
Paull, Janice, 125 Warwick Rd, Kenilworth.
T. (01926) 497194. (Pottery, porcelain)   096350

Kettering (Northamptonshire)
Albion Antiques, 36 Duke St, Kettering.
T. (01536) 516220. (Furniture)   096351
Dinsdale, F.L., 3 Horsemarket, Kettering.
T. (01536) 513046. (Paintings)   096352
Rockingham Road Antiques, 103 Rockingham Rd, Kettering. T. (01536) 511842. (Marble, stone)   096353
Ward, C.W., 40 Lower St, Kettering. T. (01536) 513537.
(Furniture, silver, porcelain)   096354

Kidderminster (Hereford and Worcester)
B.B.M. Jewellery and Antiques, 8-9 Lion St, Kidderminster. T. (01562) 744118. (Jewellery, porcelain,
silver)   096355
Gorst Hall Restoration, Gorst Hall, Barnetts Ln, Kidderminster. T. (01562) 515880. (Furniture)   096356
Rea, Lower St., Cleobury Mortimer, Kidderminster.
T. (01299) 271099. (Furniture)   096357

Kilmacolm (Southclyde)
Kilmacolm Antiques, 29 Stewart Pl, Kilmacolm.
T. (0150587) 3149. (Furniture, silver, jewellery,
porcelain)   096358

King's Lynn (Norfolk)
Clayton, Tim, 23 Chapel St, King's Lynn.
T. (01553) 772329. (Silver)   096359

Silverton, 23 Chapel St, King's Lynn. T. (01553) 772329.
(Clocks)   096360

Kingston-upon-Hull (Humberside)
Academy Upholstery, 54 Holderness Rd, Kingston-upon-
Hull. T. (01482) 210628. (Furniture)   096361
Burdett & Rawling, 83-85 Reynoldson St, Kingston-
upon-Hull. T. (01482) 493246. (Furniture)   096362
Classique Upholstery, Unit 7, English St, Kingston-upon-
Hull HU3 2BE. T. (01482) 218666. (Furniture)   096363
Hawthorne, 277-279 North Rd, Kingston-upon-Hull.
T. (01482) 568355. (Furniture)   096364
New English Art Galleries, 66-70 Princes Av, Kingston-
upon-Hull. T. (01482) 42424. (Paintings,
furniture)   096365
55 Antiques, 55 Spring-Bank, Kingston-upon-Hull HU3
1AG. T. (01482) 224510. (Furniture, paintings, clocks,
china)   096366

Kingston-upon-Thames (Surrey)
Glydon & Guess, 14 Apple Market, Kingston-upon-Thames. T. (0181) 546 3758. (Jewellery, silver)   096367
Kingston Antiques, 170 London Rd., Kingston-upon-Thames. T. (0181) 549 5876. (Furniture)   096368
Rich, John & William, 17 Wolverton Ave, Kingston-upon-
Thames. T. (0181) 5464651. (Paintings)   096369

Kingussie (Highland)
Mostly Pine, Gynack Cottage, High St, Kingussie.
T. (01540) 661838. (Furniture)   096370

Kinross (Tayside)
Miles, 16 Mill St, Kinross. T. (01577) 64858.
(Furniture)   096371

Kirkby Lonsdale (Cumbria)
Adamson, Alexander, Tearnside Hall, Kirkby Lonsdale.
T. (015242) 71989. (Furniture)   096372

Kirkby-on-Bain (Lincolnshire)
Kirkby Antiques, Highfield, Roughton Rd, Kirkby-on-
Bain. T. (01526) 52119, 53461. (Furniture)   096373

Kirton Lindsey (Humberside)
Sargent, J., Market Pl, Kirton Lindsey.
(Furniture)   096374

Knaresborough (North Yorkshire)
Bowkett, 9 Abbey Rd, Knaresborough.
T. (01423) 866112. (Furniture)   096375
Northern Kilim Centre, 24 Finkle St, Knaresborough.
T. (01423) 866219. (Rugs, carpets)   096376
Pictoriana, 88 High St, Knaresborough.
T. (01423) 866116. (Furniture)   096377

Knebworth (Hertfordshire)
Hamilton & Tucker, Park Ln, Knebworth.
T. (01438) 811995. (Billiard tables)   096378

Knowle (West Midlands)
Lukeman, Richard, 1673-1675 High St, Knowle.
T. (01564) 774302. (Paintings)   096379

Knutsford (Cheshire)
Cranford Clocks, 12 Princess St, Knutsford.
T. (01565) 633331. (Clocks)   096380
Glynn Interiors, 92 King St, Knutsford WA16 6EW.
T. (01565) 634418. (Furniture incl. upholstery)   096381
Lion Gallery and Bookshop, 15a Minshull St, Knutsford.
T. (01565) 650575, Fax 750142. (Maps, prints, books,
watercolours, oil paintings)   096382

Lamberhurst (Kent)
Lamberhurst Antiques, Upwey House, School Hill, Lamberhurst TN3 8DF. T. (01892) 890993.
(Furniture)   096383

Lampeter (Dyfed)
Barn Antiques, 2 Market St, Lampeter.
T. (01570) 423526. (Furniture)   096384

Lancaster (Lancashire)
Christie, White Cross Mill, Lancaster. T. (01524) 32607.
(Furniture)   096385
G.W. Antiques, 4 Saint Georges Quay Works, Saint Georges Quay, Lancaster. T. (01524) 841148.
(Furniture)   096386

Studio Arts Gallery, 6 Lower Church St, Lancaster.
T. (01524) 68014. (Paintings, frames) 096387

Largs (Southclyde)
Winestone, S., & Son, 2 May St, Largs. T. (01475) 2517.
(Furniture restored and polished) 096388

Launceston (Cornwall)
Tamar, 5 Church St, Launceston. T. (01566) 774233.
(Watercolours) 096389

Lavenham (Suffolk)
Antique Renovations, Unit 1, Lavenham Craft Units,
Brent Eleigh Rd, Lavenham. T. (01787) 248511.
(Furniture) 096390
Smith, Tom, 36 Market Pl, Lavenham.
T. (01787) 247463. (Furniture) 096391

Leamington Spa (Warwickshire)
Charles Antiques, Blackdown Mill, Leamington Spa.
T. (01926) 22614. (Furniture, Paintings) 096392
Wale, Percy F., 32-34 Regent St, Leamington Spa CV32
5EG. T. (01926) 421288. (Furniture) 096393

Lechlade (Gloucestershire)
Serle, Mark A., 6 Burford St, Lechlade.
T. (01367) 53145. (Furniture) 096394

Ledbury (Hereford and Worcester)
Forge Antiques, 21 High St, Ledbury. T. (01531) 650520,
652976. (Furniture) 096395
Nash, John, 17c High St, Ledbury. T. (01531) 5714.
(Furniture) 096396
Old George Antiques, 17c High St, Ledbury HR8 1DS.
T. (01531) 5299. (Furniture) 096397
Serendipity, The Tythings, Preston Court, Ledbury HR8
2LL. T. (0153184) 380, 245. (Furniture) 096398

Leeds (West Yorkshire)
Boston Pine Company, Unit 9, Globe Mills, Back Row,
Leeds. T. (0113) 2441650. (Furniture) 096401
Calverley Antiques, 34 Salisbury St, Calverley, Leeds.
T. (0113) 2562779. (Furniture) 096402
Goldsmith, William, 23 County Arcade, Leeds.
T (0113) 2451345. (Jewellery, clocks) 096403
Henson, H.J.S., 7a Chapel Pl, Leeds LS6 3HY.
T. (0113) 275 1914. (Furniture) 096404
Herail, B., 30 Davies Ave, Leeds LS8 1JY. (Oil
paintings) 096405
Oakwood Gallery, 613 Roundhay Rd, Oakwood, Leeds.
T. (0113) 2401348. (Paintings, prints) 096406
Piano Shop, 39 Holbeck Lane, Leeds.
T. (0113) 2443685. (Pianos) 096407
Solden, P.D. & S., 65 Mabgate, Leeds LS9 7DR.
T. (0113) 2452229. (Silver, Jewellery) 096408

Leek (Staffordshire)
Aspley, Compton Mill, Compton, Leek.
T. (01538) 373396. (Furniture) 096409
England's Gallery, 4-6 Brook St, Leek.
T. (01538) 373451. (Paintings) 096410
Johnson, Park Works, Park Rd, Leek. T. (01538) 386745.
(Furniture) 096411
Wood, Pat, Stanley St, Leek. T. (01538) 385696.
(Pictures) 096412

Leicester (Leicestershire)
Smith, Hammond, 32 West Av, Claredon Park, Leicester.
T. (0116) 709020. (Watercolours, prints) 096413
Withers, 142a London Rd, Leicester LE2 1EB.
T. (0116) 544836. (Furniture) 096414

Leigh-on-Sea (Essex)
Downes, Bill, 36 Marine Parade, Leigh-on-Sea SS9 2HG.
T. (01702) Southend-on-Sea 7 8412.
(Ceramics) 096415
Tilly's Antiques, 1801 London Rd, Leigh-on-Sea.
T. (01702) 557170. (Furniture, dolls) 096416

Leighton Buzzard (Bedfordshire)
Charterhouse Gallery, 14 Birds Hill, Leighton Buzzard.
T. (01525) 379. (Paintings) 096417

Leiston (Suffolk)
Leiston Furniture Warehouses, High St, Leiston.
T. (01728) 831414. (Furniture) 096418

Lenzie (Southclyde)
Fraser, Daphne, 58 Victoria Rd, Lenzie G66 5AP.
T. 7761281. (Dolls, Rocking Horses) 096419

Leominster (Hereford and Worcester)
Barometer Shop, New St, Leominster.
T. (01568) 613652. (Clocks, barometers) 096420
Chapman, 2 Bridge St, Leominster. T. (01568) 5803.
(Furniture) 096421
Coltsfoot, Hatfield, Leominster HR6 0SF.
T. (0156882) 277. (Works of art on paper) 096422
Courtyard Antiques, 28 Broad St, Leominster.
T. (01568) 611413. (China) 096423
Crofts, Geoffrey, 10 South St, Leominster.
T. (01568) 611580. (Furniture) 096424
Highbury House Antiques, 25 Broad St, Leominster.
T. (01568) 611725. (Furniture, oil paintings) 096425
Jennings, 30 Bridge St, Leominster. T. (01568) 612946.
(Furniture, clocks) 096426
Kimberley, Andrew, Lion Yard, Broad St, Leominster.
T. (01568) 611688. (Furniture, porcelain) 096427
Mayfield, 13 South St, Leominster. T. (01568) 2127.
(Furniture) 096428

Leuchars (Fife)
Earlshall Castle, Leuchars. T. (01334) 205. (Wood,
metal) 096429

Lewes (East Sussex)
Coombe House Antiques, 121 Malling St, Lewes.
T. (01273) 472319. (Furniture) 096430
Dennison, H.P., & Son, 22 High St, Lewes.
T. (01273) 480655. (Furniture) 096431
Justice, George, 12a Market St, Lewes BN7 1AA.
T. (01273) 4174. (Split cane, rush seating, antique
furniture) 096432

Lichfield (Staffordshire)
Jones, K.R., & Co., 7 Jackson Rd, Lichfield.
T. (01543) 252837. (Furniture) 096433

Limpsfield (Surrey)
Limpsfield Watercolours, High St, Limpsfield. T. 717010.
(Prints, watercolours, oils) 096434

Lincoln (Lincolnshire)
Castle Gallery, 61 Steep Hill, Lincoln. T. (01522) 535078.
(Oils, watercolours) 096435
Dorrian Lambert, 64-65 Steep Hill, Lincoln.
T. (01522) 545916. (Clocks) 096436
Pine Cone, 25 Steep Hill, Lincoln. T. (01522) 200 79.
(Furniture) 096437
Pullen, Richard, 28 The Strait, Lincoln.
T. (01522) 537170. (Jewellery) 096438

Liss (Hampshire)
Liss Bookshop and Gallery, 71-73 Station Rd, Liss.
T. (01730) 892406. (Books) 096439
Pine Collection, 71 Station Rd, Liss. T. (01730) 893743.
(Furniture) 096440

Little Haywood (Staffordshire)
Jalna, Coley Lane, Little Haywood. T. (01889) 881381.
(Furniture) 096441

Littlebourne (Kent)
Warren, Jimmy, 28 The Hill, Littlebourne.
T. (0122778) 721510. (Furniture) 096442

Liverpool (Merseyside)
Delta Antiques, 175-177 Smithdown Rd, Liverpool.
T. (0151) 734 4277. (Furniture) 096443
Hughes, Harriet, 41 Bluecoat Chambers, School Lane,
Liverpool LI 3BX. T. (0151) 7086808. (Paintings in
Oil) 096444
Lyver & Boydell, 15 Castle St, Liverpool.
T. (0151) 236 3256. (Paintings, watercolours) 096445
Maggs, 26-28 Fleet St, Liverpool. T. (0151) 708 0221.
(Furniture) 096446
Ryan-Wood, 102 Seel St, Liverpool. T. (0151) 709 7776.
(Furniture) 096447
Stefani, 497 Smithdown Rd, Liverpool.
T. (0151) 734 1933. (Furniture, jewellery) 096448

Llandeilo (Dyfed)
Jones, Glyn, Caebach Villa, Penybanc, Llandeilo.
T. (01558) 822043. (Furniture) 096449

Llandudno (Gwynedd)
Madoc Antiques and Art Gallery, 48 Madoc St, Llandud-
no. T. (01492) 79754. (Clocks) 096450
North Wales Paint Stripping, Masonic St, Llandudno.
T. (01492) 878207. (Furniture) 096451

Llanrwst (Gwynedd)
Snowdonia Antiques, Bank Buildings, Station Rd,
Llanrwst. T. (01492) 640789. (Clocks) 096452
Williams, K. and M., Ty Uchaf, Melin-y-Coed, Llanrwst
LL26 09W. (Furniture, f. ex. stools, dining chairs,
tables) 096453

London
A. & R. French Polishers, 407 Long St, London E2.
T. (0171) 739-1478. (Furniture) 096454
Ablett, Anne, 15 Kings St, London SW1Y.
T. (0171) 359 8046. (Picture Frames) 096455
Acanthus, 171 Arthur Rd, Wimbledon Park, London
SW19. T. (0181) 944 8404. (Pianos) 096456
Ackerman & Johnson, 27 Lowndes St, London SW1.
T. (0171) 235 6464. (Paintings) 096457
Adam & Sheridan, 7 Ashbourn Parade, Finchley Rd, Lon-
don NW1 0AD. T. (0181) 455-69760.
(Furniture) 096458
Adams, G.H., & Co., Coach House, Askham Rd, London
W12 0NW. T. (0181) 743 2261. (Furniture) 096459
A.D.C. Heritage, 2 Old Bond St, London W1X 3TD.
T. (0171) 493 5088, Fax (0171) 495 0062.
(Silver) 096460
Addison, 57 Addison Av, London W11.
I. (0171) 603 2374. (Paintings) 096461
Albemarle Gallery, 18 Albemarle St, London W1X.
T. (0171) 355 1880. (Paintings) 096462
Albion Clocks, 4 Grove End, Grove Hill, London E18 2LE.
T. (0181) 530-5570. (Clocks) 096463
Aldridge, F.W., 199-201 Wood St, London E17.
T. (0171) 621 5045. (Blue Glass Liners, Glass
Repairs) 096464
Alexander, Norman, 304 Old Brompton Rd, London SW5.
T. (0171) 373 5113. (Furniture) 096465
Allpine, 129a Broadway, London W13. T. (0181) 567-
2231. (Furniture) 096466
Amadeus Gallery, 21 Saint John's Wood, High St, Lon-
don NW8. T. (0171) 722 5883. (Paintings, works of
art) 096467
Amazing Grates, 61-63 High Rd, London N2.
T. (0181) 883 9590, 883 6017. (Ironwork) 096468
And So To Bed, 638-640 King's Rd, London SW6.
T. (0171) 731 3593. (Beds) 096469
Andipa, Maria, 162 Walton St, London SW1.
T. (0171) 589 2371. (Icons) 096470
Andy's Largest Drive In Stripper, 70 Russell Rd, Olympia
Bridge Quay, London W14. T. (0171) 602-0856,
Fax (0171) 602-8655, 602-2105. (Furniture) 096471
Anglo – Persian Carpet Co., 6 South Kensington Station
Arcade, London SW7 2NA. T. (0171) 589 5457. (Fine
Oriental Carpets) 096472
Antique Carpets Gallery, 150 Wandworth Bridge Rd, Ful-
ham, London SW6. T. (0171) 371 9619, 371 9620.
(Carpets, rugs, textiles, tapestries) 096473
Antique Furniture Restoration, 87 Maple Rd., Penge,
London SE20 8LN. T. (0181) 659 2702.
(Furniture) 096474
Antique Leathers, 4 Park End, South Hill Park, London
NW3 2SE. T. (0171) 435 7799, 435 8582,
Fax (0171) 435 7799. (Leather goods, backgammon
and chessboards, table liners and
upholsterers) 096475
Antique Porcelain Company, 149 New Bond St, London
W1Y 0HY. T. (0171) 629 1254. (Porcelain) 096476
Antiques, 18 Parson St, Hendon, London NW4.
T. (0181) 203 1194. (Furniture, furniture) 096477
Antiques and Piano, 90 Lots Rd, Chelsea, London SW10.
T. (0171) 352-9876. (Furniture, pianos) 096478
Archaize, 17c Oval Rd, London NW1. T. (0171) 261 8692.
(Ceramics) 096479
Archer Gallery, 303 Westbourne Grove, London W11.
T. (0171) 727 8761. (Paintings) 096480

Architectural Antiques, 351 King St, London W5.
T. (0181) 741 7883, Fax 741 1109. (Furniture)   *096481*
Art Furniture, 158 Camden St, London NW1.
T. (0171) 267 4324. (Furniture, fixtures,
fittings)   *096482*
Art Restoration Services, 16a Church Rd, London NW10.
T. (0181) 961-0043. (Paintings)   *096483*
Asprey, 153 Fenchurch St, London EC3.
T. (0171) 626 2160. (Silver, clocks, jewellery)   *096484*
B. & H., Unit H6, Hastingwood, Trading Est, Harbert Rd,
Edmonton, London N18. T. (0181) 803-6292.
(Furniture)   *096485*
Badger, 12 Saint Mary's Rd, London W5.
T. (0181) 567 5601. (Furniture, clocks,
ceramics)   *096486*
Badger, 320-322 Creek Rd, London SE10.
T. (0181) 853 1394. (Furniture)   *096487*
Bardawil, Eddy, 106 Kensington Church St, London W8.
T. (0171) 221 3967, Fax 221 5124. (Furniture,
brassware)   *096488*
Barewood, 58 Mill Lane, London NW6. T. (0171) 435-
7244. (Furniture)   *096489*
Barnett, Olaf Blayney, 89 Portobello Rd, London SW19.
T. (0171) 727 1403. (Paintings, Drawings)   *096490*
B.C. Metalcrafts, 69 Tewkesbury Gardens, London NW9.
T. (0181) 204 2446, Fax 206 2871. (Lighting, vases,
clocks)   *096491*
Beare, John & Arthur, 7 Broadwick St, London W1V 1FJ.
T. (0171) 437 1449. (Rare Violins)   *096492*
Beech, Nicholas, 787,789 Wandsworth Rd, London
SW8. T. (0171) 720-8552. (Pine)   *096493*
Belton, Anthony, 14 Holland St, London W8.
T. (0171) 937 1012. (Pottery, furniture,
paintings)   *096494*
Benardout, 31a Buckingham Palace Rd, London SW1.
T. (0171) 834 8241. (Carpets)   *096495*
Benardout, Raymond, 4-5 William St, London SW1X
9HL. T. (0171) 235 3360, 235 9588,
Fax (0171) 823 1345. (Rugs, Carpets, Tapestries,
Furniture)   *096496*
Benardout & Benardout, 18 Grosvenor St, Mayfair, Lon-
don W1. T. (0171) 355 4531, Fax Fax 491 9710.
(Carpets)   *096497*
Big Ben, 5 Broxholme House, New King's Rd, London
SW6. T. (0171) 736 1770, Fax 384 1957.
(Clocks)   *096498*
Black, David, 96 Portland Rd, London W11 4LN.
T. (0171) 727 2566. (Carpets)   *096499*
Blackett, P., Unit 16, Imperial Stu, Imperial Rd, London
SW6. T. (0171) 736-0173. (Paintings)   *096500*
Bloomfield, 58 Davies St, London W1Y. T. (0171) 493-
4456. (Ceramics)   *096501*
Bookham, 164 Wandsworth Bridge Rd, London SW6.
T. (0171) 736-5125. (Paintings)   *096502*
Boswell, Peter, 67 b69 Beak St, London W1.
(Furniture)   *096503*
Boswell & Davis, 1 Phipp St, London EC2A 4PS.
T. (0171) 739-5738. (Furniture)   *096504*
Bourdon-Smith, J.H., 24 Mason's Yard, Duke St, Saint
James's, London SW1. T. (0171) 839 4714/5.
(Silver)   *096505*
Bourne, 14 Mason's Yard, Duke St, Saint James's, Lon-
don SW1. T. (0171) 930 4215. (Paintings)   *096506*
Bowmoore, 77 Peterborough Rd, Fulham, London SW6.
T. (0171) 736 4111. (Paintings, watercolours)   *096507*
Brady & Turner, 34 Ellanby Crescent, London N18.
T. (0181) 884 4394. (Furniture)   *096508*
Brocklehurst, Aubrey, 124 Cromwell Rd, London SW7
4ET. T. (0171) 373 0319. (Clocks)   *096509*
Brown, Alasdair, 560 King's Rd, London SW6.
T. (0171) 736 8077. (Furniture)   *096510*
Brown, I. & J.L., 632-636 King's Rd, London SW6.
T. (0171) 736 4141. (Furniture)   *096511*
Burne, W.G.T., 11 Elystan St, London SW3.
T. (0171) 589 6074, Fax (0181) 944 1977. (Glass,
chandeliers)   *096512*
Burnett, Richard, 3 Macaulay Rd, London SW4 0QP.
T. (0171) 622 9393. (Antique keybords and musical
instruments)   *096513*
C. & A., 199 Southfield Rd, London W4. T. (0181) 994-
9067. (Furniture)   *096514*
Cameron, Michael, 115 Pancra Rd, London NW1 1UN.
T. (0181) 388-6446. (Musical Instruments)   *096515*

Campbell, John, 164 Walton St, London SW3.
T. (0171) 584 9268. (Paintings)   *096516*
Cane & Rush, 6c Sylvan Rd, London E11. T. (0181) 530-
7052. (Furniture)   *096517*
Canonbury Antiques, 13 Canonbury Pl, London N1.
T. (0171) 359 2246. (Upholstery)   *096518*
Capital Clocks, 190 Wandsworth Rd, London SW8.
T. (0171) 720 6372. (Clocks)   *096519*
Capon, Patric, 350 Upper St, Islington, London N1.
T. (0171) 354 0487. (Clocks, barometers)   *096520*
Carleton, Michael, 77, 79, 81 Haverstock Hill, London
NW3 4SL. T. (0171) 722 2277, 586 4458.
(Antiques)   *096521*
Chanticleer, 105 Portobello Rd, London W11.
T. (0171) 385 0919. (Oriental works)   *096522*
Chapman, Peter, 10 Theberton St, Islington, London N1.
T. (0171) 226 5565, Fax (0181) 348 4846.
(Furniture)   *096523*
Chelsea Bric-a-Brac Shop, 16 Hartfield Rd, London
SW19. T. (0181) 946 6894. (Furniture)   *096524*
China Repairers, 64 Charles Lane, London NW8 7SB.
T. (0171) 722 8407. (Porcelain, Pottery, Glass and
Enamels)   *096525*
Chinamend, 54 Walton St, London SW3.
T. (0171) 589 1182. (Porcelain and Pottery)   *096526*
City Clocks, 31 Amwell St, London EC1.
T. (0171) 278 1154. (Clocks, watches)   *096527*
Clarke-Hall, J., 7 Bride Court, London EC4.
T. (0171) 353 4116. (Books)   *096528*
Clock Clinic, 85 Lower Richmond Rd, London SW15.
T. (0181) 788 1407, Fax Fax 780 2838. (Antique
clocks)   *096529*
Clock Gallery, 58 Saint Marys Rd, London W5.
T. (0181) 579-3367. (Clocks)   *096530*
Coats Oriental Carpets, 4 Kensington Church Walk, Lon-
don W8. T. (0171) 937 0983. (Carpets,
embroideries)   *096531*
Cocks, Alan, 279 Liverpool, London N1. T. (0171) 607-
6594. (Furniture)   *096532*
Cohn, George & Peter, Unit 21, Wren St, London WC1X
OHF. T. (0171) 278 3749. (Chandeliers,
walllights)   *096533*
Cole, A.E., 27 Russell Gardens Mews Kensington, Lon-
don W14. T. (0171) 602 2283. (Furniture)   *096534*
Conservation Studio, 17 Pennybank Chambers, 33-35
Saint John's Sq, London EC1. T. (0171) 251 6853.
(Glass, ceramics)   *096535*
Cooke, Mary, 121a Kensington Church St, London W8.
T. (0171) 792 8077. (Silver)   *096536*
Cooper, 768 Fulham Rd, London SW6.
T. (0171) 731 3421. (Paintings, watercolours)   *096537*
Corner Portobello, 282-284 Westbourne Grove, London
W11. T. (0171) 727 2027. (Silver, jewellery)   *096538*
Countrystyle, Arch 153, Deptford Market, Deptford High
St, London SE8. T. (0181) 469-3110.
(Furniture)   *096539*
Coutts, 75 Blythe Rd, London W14. T. (0171) 602-3980.
(Paintings)   *096540*
Cox, Robert, 2 Border Rd, London SE26 6HB.
T. (0181) 778 0712. (Furniture)   *096541*
Cox & Co., 37 Duke St, Saint James's, London SW1.
T. (0171) 930 1987. (Paintings)   *096542*
Crawford, Matthew, 74-77 White Lion St, London N1
9PF. T. (0171) 278-7146. (Furniture)   *096543*
Crawley, 39 Wood Vale, London SE23 30S.
T. (0181) 299 4121, Fax (0181) 299 0754.
(Furniture)   *096544*
Crispin J., & Sons, 92-96 Curtain Rd Shoreditch, London
EC2A 3AA. T. (0171) 739 4857. (Veneer)   *096545*
Crotty, J., & Son, 74 New King's Rd, Parsons Green,
London SW6. T. (0171) 731 4209. (Antique metal fire-
place equipment)   *096546*
Crouch End Antiques, 47 Park Rd, Crouch End, London
N8. T. (0181) 348 7652. (Furniture)   *096547*
Curious Grannies, 2 Middleton Rd, Hackney, London E8.
T. (0171) 254 7074. (Musical Instruments)   *096548*
Cuss, Camerer, & Co., 17 Ryder St, Saint James's, Lon-
don SW1. T. (0171) 930 1941. (Clocks,
watches)   *096549*
D'Orsai, Sebastian, 39 Theobalds Rd, London WC1.
T. (0171) 405 6663. (Paintings, prints)   *096550*
D & Y Furniture, 137 Tredegar Rd, London E3.
T. (0181) 980-2755. (Furniture)   *096551*

Daborn, J.A.P. Ltd., 9 Broadway, London NW7.
(Paintings)   *096552*
Daggett, 153 Portobello Rd, London W11.
T. (0171) 229 2248. (Paintings, frames, furniture,
carpets)   *096553*
Daggett, Charles, 28 Beauchamp Pl, Knightsbridge, Lon-
don SW3. T. (0171) 584 2969, Fax 584 2950. (Pictures,
frames)   *096554*
Dare, George, 9 Launceston Pl, Kensington, London W8.
T. (0171) 937 7072. (Watercolours, paintings)   *096555*
David, Alexander, 102 Waterford Rd, London SW6.
T. (0171) 731 4644. (Furniture)   *096556*
Davighi, N., 117 Shepherd's Bush Rd, London W6.
T. (0171) 603 5357. (Chandeliers)   *096557*
Davis & Davis, Arch 266, Urlwin St, Camberwell, London
SE5. T. (0171) 703 6525. (Fireplaces)   *096558*
Dehn, Hannerle, Studio 7, Studio Centre, Ranelagh Gar-
dens, London SW6. T. (0171) 746-5171.
(Furniture)   *096559*
Denham, John, 50 Mill Ln, West Hampstead, London
NW6. T. (0171) 794 2635. (Paintings, drawings,
prints)   *096560*
Denny, Colin, 18 Cale St, Chelsea Green, London SW3
3QU. T. (0171) 584 0240. (Pictures, particularly
marines)   *096561*
Dining Room Shop, 62-64 White Hart Ln, Barnes, Lon-
don SW13. T. (0181) 878 1020. (Furniture,
glass)   *096562*
Drescher, Arthur B. Ltd., 17 Alverstone Rd, London NW2.
T. (0181) 459 5543. (Old & Modern Master Drawings,
Watercolours, Prints and Pastels)   *096563*
Drown, William R., 41 Saint James's Pl, London SW1.
T. (0171) 493 9820. (Paintings)   *096564*
Drummond, Nicholas, 6 Saint John's Wood Rd, London
NW8. T. (0171) 286 6452. (Paintings)   *096565*
Ealing Gallery, 78 Saint Marys Rd, Ealing, London W5.
T. (0181) 840 7883. (Paintings)   *096566*
Fagiani, A., 30 Wagner St, London SE15.
T. (0171) 732 7188. (Furniture)   *096567*
Fairfax, 568 King's Rd, London SW6. T. (0171) 736 5023,
Fax 736 5023. (Fireplaces)   *096568*
Fairman, Jack, 218 Westbourne Grove, London W11.
T. (0171) 229 2262, Fax 229 2263. (Carpets)   *096569*
Feekery, Liam & Associates, 41 Silvester Rd, London
SE22 9PB. T. (0181) 299 3129. (Furniture)   *096570*
Femandes & Marche, 80 Islington High St, London N1.
T. (0171) 837 8768. (Furniture)   *096571*
Fiddes-Watt, 66 Ledbury Rd, London W11.
T. (0171) 727 2511. (Paintings and Prints)   *096572*
Finchley Fine Art Galleries, 983 High Rd, North Finchley,
London N12. T. (0181) 446 4848. (Watercolours, pain-
tings, prints, porcelain, musical and scientific
instruments)   *098573*
Fine China Restoration, 21 Alkerden Rd, London W4
2HP. T. (0181) 994 8990. (Ceramics)   *096574*
Fisher & Sperr, 46 Highgate High St, London N6.
T. (0181) 340 7244. (Books)   *096575*
Fleamarket, 7 Pierrepont Row, Camden Passage, Isling-
ton, London N1. T. (0171) 226 8211.
(Weapons)   *096576*
Foster, Michael, 118 Fulham Rd, Chelsea, London SW3
6HU. T. (0171) 373-3636, 373-3040.
(Furniture)   *096577*
FPS, Unit 21, Sulivan Centre, Sulivan Rd, London SW6.
T. (0171) 371-9246. (Furniture)   *096578*
Frans, 73 Fulham Park Gardens, London SW6 8LQ.
T. (0171) 731 5770. (Furniture)   *096579*
Frans, Murtex House, Bollo Ln, London W3 8QU.
T. (0181) 992 5347. (Furniture)   *096580*
Franses, Victor, 57 Jermyn St, Saint James's, London
SW1. T. (0171) 493 6284, 629 1144, Fax 629 1144.
(Bronzes, carpets)   *096581*
Fuller, Clifford, 7 Kingsmere Park, Kingsbury, London
NW9. T. (0181) 205-0329. (Furniture)   *096582*
Furniture Renovations Company, 76 Arnos Grove, Lon-
don. T. (0181) 886 3596. (Furniture)   *096583*
Game Advice, 23 Holmes Rd, London NW5.
T. (0171) 485 4226. (Games, toys, children
books)   *096584*
Garbe, G., 23 Charlotte St, London W1P 1HB.
T. (0171) 636 1268. (Porcelain, Ivories, Furniture, Pic-
tures, Bronze, Boulle, Jewellery and Objects of
Art)   *096585*

Get Stuffed, 105 Essex Rd, Islington, London N1.
T. (0171) 226 1364. (Stuffed objects) 096586
Giaccherini, Riccardo, 39 Newman St, London W1P.
T. (0171) 580-1783. (Frames) 096587
Goodall & Co. Ltd., 24 & 26 Chiswick High Rd, London
W4. T. (0181) 994 1729. (Furniture) 096588
Gould, Betty, & Julian Gonnermann, 408-410 Archway
Rd, Highgate, London N6. T. (0181) 340 4987.
(Furniture) 096589
Gould, Francis, 29 Old Fold Ln, London.
T. (0181) 449 3623. (Furniture) 096590
Gray, Marion, 33 Crouch Hill, London N4.
T. (0171) 935 6161. (Furniture) 096591
Green & Stone, 259 Kings Rd, London SW3.
T. (0171) 352 0837, 352 6521. (Watercolours,
paintings) 096592
Greenwich Antiques and Ironware, 14-15 King William
Walk, Greenwich, London SE10. T. (0181) 858 7557,
Fax 293 4135. (Furniture, pictures) 096593
Greenwich Gallery, 9 Nevada St, London SE10 9JL.
T. (0171) 305 1666. (Paintings) 096594
Gridley, Gordon, 41 Camden Passage, Islington, London
N1. T. (0171) 226 0643. (Furniture, paintings, metal-
work, instruments) 096595
Grosvenor Prints, 28-32 Shelton St, London WC2H 9HP.
T. (0171) 836 1979, Fax 379 6695. (Prints) 096596
Hahn, 47 Albemarle St, London W1X 3FE.
T. (0171) 493 9196. (Paintings) 096597
Hale, Patricia H., 64 Chester Row, London SW1.
T. (0171) 730 4605. (China) 096598
Hall, Robert, 140 Sutherland Av, London W9.
T. (0171) 286 0809, Fax 289 3287. (Chinese snuff bott-
les, oriental works) 096599
Halliday's, 28 Beauchamp Pl, London SW3.
T. (0171) 589 5534, Fax 589 2477. (Fireplace
equipment) 096600
Hamilton, 186 Willifield Way, London NW11.
T. (0181) 455 7410. (Paintings, watercolours,
bronzes) 096601
Hamilton, Rosemary, 44 Moreton St, London SW1.
T. (0171) 828 5018. (Furniture, porcelain) 096602
Harbottle, Patricia, Stand 16, Geoffrey Van Arcade, 107
Portobello Rd, London W11. T. (0171) 731 1972.
(Glass) 096603
Harbud, E.J., & Partners, 7 Warwick Pl, London W9 2PX.
T. (0171) 289-0876. (Furniture) 096604
Hares, 498 King's Rd, London SW10.
T. (0171) 351 1442. (Furniture) 096605
Harris, Nicholas, 564 King's Rd, London SW6.
T. (0171) 371 9711, Fax 371 9537. (Silver) 096606
Harvey, W.R., 70 Chalk Farm Rd, London NW1 8AN.
T. (01712) 485-1504. (Furniture) 096607
Hatfield, H.J. & Sons Ltd., 42 St Michael St Norfolk Pl,
London W2. T. (0171) 723 8265/66. (Antiques and
Furniture) 096608
Hazlitt, Gooden, & Fox, 38 Bury St, Saint James's, Lon-
don SW1. T. (0171) 930 6422. (Paintings, drawings,
sculpture) 096609
Henham, Martin, 218 High Rd, East Finchley, London
N2. T. (0181) 444 5274. (Furniture, paintings) 096610
Hennell, 12 New Bond St, London W1.
T. (0171) 629 6888. (Silver, jewellery) 096611
Heskia, 19 Mount St, London W1. T. (0171) 629 1483.
(Carpets) 096612
Hicks, 2-4 Leopold Rd, London SW19.
T. (0181) 944 7171. (Paintings, watercolours) 096613
Hollingshead & Co., 783 Fulham Rd, London SW6.
T. (0171) 385 8519. (Marblework, wood
mantelpieces) 096614
Holmes, 29 Old Bond St, London W1.
T. (0171) 493 1396. (Jewellery, silver) 096615
Holmes, 24 Burlington Arcade, London W1.
T. (0171) 629 8380. (Jewellery, silver) 096616
Holmes, D., 47c Earls Court Rd, Kensington, London W8.
T. (0171) 937 3415. (Furniture) 096617
Holmes, Richard, 1 Baronsmead Rd, London SW13.
T. (0181) 748-6816. (Furniture) 096618
Home to Home, 355c Archway Rd, London N6.
T. (0181) 340 8354. (Furniture, books) 096619

Hordern, David, 1a Codrington Mews, Blenheim, London
W11 2EH. T. (0171) 7278855, Fax (0171) 7929164.
(Boulle, Cabinetwork, Carving, Gilding, Ivory, Lacquer,
Leather, Marble, Marquetry, Metalwork, Ormolu, Polis-
hing, Upholstery) 096620
Howard, Valerie, 131e Kensington Church St, London
W8. T. (0171) 792 9702. (China, French faience,
mirrors) 096621
Jefferson, Patrick, 572 King's Rd, London SW6.
T. (0171) 371 9088. (Furniture) 096622
Jeffs, Peter, c/o N Harris, 564 King's Rd, London SW6.
T. (0171) 371 9711. (Silver) 096623
Jewell, S. & H., 26 Parker St, London WC2B 5PH.
T. (0171) 405 8520. (Antique Furniture) 096624
Jones, 194 Westbourne Grove, London W11.
T. (0171) 229 6866, Fax 229 6866. (Lamps) 096625
Jones, John, Unit 4, Finsbury Park Trading Estate, Morris
Pl, London N4 3JG. T. (0171) 281 5439,
Fax (0171) 281 5956. (Frames) 096626
Joslin, Richard, 150 Addison Gardens, London.
T. (0171) 603 6435, Fax 603 6435. (Paintings) 096627
Juran, Alexander, & Co., 74 New Bond St, London W1Y
9DD. T. (0171) 629 2550, 493 4484. (Old and Decorati-
ve Carpets) 096628
Kaleidoscope, 66 Willesden Ln, London NW6.
T. (0171) 328 5833. (Oilpaintings, watercolours,
prints) 096629
Kasia & Ela, Studio 11, 63 Jeddo Rd, London W12 9EE.
T. (0181) 740 4977. (Tapestries, aubussons, needle-
works, kilims) 096630
Keil, John, 154 Brompton Rd, London SW3.
T. (0171) 589 6454. (Furniture) 096631
Kemp, Peter, 170 Kensington Church St, London W8.
T. (0171) 229 2988. (Porcelain) 096632
Kendal, 91a Heath St, Hampstead, London NW3 033.
T. (0171) 435 4351. (Furniture, porcelain,
watercolours) 096633
Kendal, 91a Heath St, Hampstead, London NW3 6SS.
T. (0171) 435 4351. (Furniture) 096634
Kennedy, 9a Vigo St, London W1. T. (0171) 439 8873,
Fax 437 1201. (Carpets, kelims) 096635
Kensington Fine Arts, 46 Kensington Church St, London
W8. T. (0171) 937 5317. (Paintings) 096636
Ker, David, 85 Bourne St, London SW1.
T. (0171) 730 8365, Fax 730 3352. (Watercolours,
prints, paintings) 096637
Kettle, Thomas, 53a Neal St, London WC2.
T. (0171) 379 3579. (Watches) 096638
Kihl, Richard, 164 Regents Park Rd, London NW1.
T. (0171) 586 5911, Fax 586 2960. (Glass) 096639
Kilim Warehouse, 28a Pickets St, London SW12.
T. (0181) 675 3122, Fax 675 8494. (Kilims) 096640
Klaber & Klaber, 2a Bedford Gardens, Kensington Church
St, London W8. T. (0171) 727 4573. (Porcelain) 096641
Kwik Strip, Unit 9, Whiteheater Industrial Estate, Brent-
field Rd, London NW10. T. (0181) 451 7949.
(Furniture) 096642
Lamp Gallery, 355 New King's Rd, London SW6.
T. (0171) 736 6188. (Lamps) 096643
Lampard, S., & Son, 32 Notting Hill Gate, London W11.
T. (0171) 229 5457. (Jewellery, silver, clocks) 096644
Langford, 535 King's Rd, London SW10.
T. (0171) 352 4881, Fax (0171) 352 0763. (Shipmodels,
marine objects) 096645
Lassalle, Judith, 7 Pierrepont Arcade, Camden Passage,
London N1. T. (0171) 607 7121. (Maps, prints, children
games) 096646
Laurie, John, 352 Upper St, Islington, London N1.
T. (0171) 226 0913, 226 6969. (Silver) 096647
Lavian, Joseph, Block F, 53-79 Highgate Rd, London
NW5. T. (0171) 485 7955, 482 1234, Fax 267 9222.
(Carpets, needlework, textiles) 096648
Lee, A., 122 St John St, London EC1.
T. (0171) 253 6901. (Antique Clocks, watches and
Automata) 096649
Leger, 13 Old Bond St, London W1. T. (0171) 629 3538.
(Paintings) 096650
Lev, 97 Kensington Church St, London W8.
T. (0171) 727 9248. (Paintings) 096651
Lion Witch and Lampshade, 89 Ebury St, London SW1W
9QU. T. (0171) 730 1774. (Ceramics) 096652
Llewellyn, Alexander, 124-126 The Cut, London SE1.
T. (0171) 620-1322. (Paintings) 096653

Lloyd, John, 101 Hydethorpe Rd, London SW12.
T. (0181) 673-7483. (Furniture) 096654
Locus Gallery, 116 Heath St, London NW3 1DR.
T. (0171) 435 4005. (Sculptures, Paintings) 096655
Loveless, Clive, 29 Kelfield Gardens, North Kensington,
London W10. T. (0181) 969 5831. (Rugs,
textiles) 096656
Lowe & Butcher, Unit 23, Abbey Business Centre, Ingate
Pl, London SW8 3NS. T. (0171) 498-6981.
(Paintings) 096657
Lowe, William Fraser, 75 Randolph Ave, Maida Vale,
London W9. T. (0171) 286 5018. (Paintings, Relining,
credling of panels, Drawings, Watercolours,
Engravings) 096658
Lucas, J.E. & Sons, 3 Swanscombe Rd Holland Park,
London W11. T. (0171) 603 7543. (Furniture,
Pinework) 096659
M & D Furniture, 269 Putney Bridge Rd, London SW15
2PT. T. (0181) 789-3022. (Furniture) 096660
MacConnal-Mason, 15 Burlington Arcade, London W1Y
9AB. T. (0171) 499 6991. (Paintings) 096661
MacConnal-Mason, 14 Duke St, London SW1.
T. (0171) 839 7693, 499 6991. (Paintings) 096662
Maecenas, 13 Crescent Pl, London SW3. T. (0171) 581-
1083. (Furniture) 096663
Major, C.H., 154 Kensington Church St, London W8 4BN.
T. (0171) 229 1162. (Furniture) 096664
Manners, E. & H., 66a Kensington Church St, London
W8. T. (0171) 229 5516. (Ceramics) 096665
Mansell, William C., 24 Connaught St, London W2.
T. (0171) 723 4154. (Silver, clocks, jewellery) 096666
Marc, 9 Porchester Pl, London W2. T. (0171) 262 4906,
Fax (0171) 224 9416. (Icons, graphics) 096667
Marchant & Son, 120 Kensington Church St, London
W8. T. (0171) 229 5319, 229 3770. (Chinese and japa-
nese pottery, porcelain, furniture, paintings) 096668
Marriott, Michael, 588 Fulham Rd, London SW6.
T. (0171) 736 3110, 736 0568. (Furniture) 096669
Mason, Paul, 149 Sloane St, London SW1.
T. (0171) 730 3683, 730 7359. (Paintings, prints, ship
models) 096670
Massada Antiques, 45 New Bond St, London W1.
T. (0171) 493 4792, 493 5610. (Jewellery) 096671
Maurice Antiques, 202 Brecknock Rd, London N19.
T. (0171) 607 2371. (Furniture) 096672
Mayorcas Ltd., 38 Jermyn St, London SW1Y 6DN.
T. (0171) 629 4195. (Tapestries, textiles, European Car-
pets & Rugs) 096673
McDonald, Joy, 50 Station Rd, Barnes, London SW13.
T. (0181) 876 6184. (Furniture) 096674
McKenna & Co, 28 Beauchamp Pl, London SW3.
T. (0171) 584 1966, Fax 225 2893. (Jewellery) 096675
Messum, David, 34 Saint George St, London W1.
T. (0171) 408 0243. (Paintings) 096676
Milne & Moller, 35 Colville Terrace, London W11.
T. (0171) 727 1679. (Watercolours, paintings,
sculpture) 096677
Mitchell, John, & Son, 160 New Bond St, London W1.
T. (0171) 493 7567. (Paintings, drawings) 096678
Mitchell, Paul, 99 New Bond St, London W1Y 9LF.
T. (0171) 493 8732, 493 0860. (Paintings, Antique Pic-
ture Frames) 096679
Monro, 16 Motcomb St, London SW1.
T. (0171) 235 0326. (Furniture, china, rugs,
prints) 096680
Moreton Street Gallery, 40 Moreton St, London SW1.
T. (0171) 834 7773/5, 834 7834. (Paintings, waterco-
lours, engravings) 096681
Morley, Robert, & Co., 34 Engate St, Lewisham, London
SE13. T. (0181) 318 5838, Fax 297 0720. (Musical
instruments) 096682
Moss, 2 Prebend Gardens, London W4 1TW.
T. (0181) 994 2099. (Watercolours) 096683
Moy, J., 9 Greenwich South St, London SE10.
T. (0181) 858-0072. (Paper) 096684
Mueller, Ceridwen, 22 Sulivan Enterprise Centre, Sulivan
Rd, London SW6. T. (0181) 371-5191.
(Paintings) 096685
Napier, Sylvia, 554 King's Rd, London SW6.
T. (0171) 371 5881. (Furniture, objets d'art) 096686
New Century, 69 Kensington Church St, London W8.
T. (0171) 937 2410. (Furniture) 096687

Newhart, PO Box 1608, London NW3.
T. (0171) 722 2537, Fax 722 4335. (Oil paintings, watercolours) *096688*

Newland, L., & Son, 17 Picton Pl, London W1.
T. (0171) 935 2864. (Clocks, jewellery) *096689*

Noller, Bertram Ltd., 25 Walton St, London SW3.
T. (0171) 589 3795. (Furniture, Porcelain) *096690*

North London Clock Shop, 72 Highbury Park, London N5. T. (0171) 226 1609. (Clocks, barometers) *096691*

Nunheadgreen Clocks, 30 Nunhead Green, London SE15. T. (0171) 639-2506. (Clocks) *096692*

O'Donnell, Brian, 1 Waterfall Rd, Colliers Wood, London SW19. T. (0181) 543 1369, 648 2684. (Turnery, gilding, carving, framing) *096693*

Oakstar, Clarendon Rd, London W11. T. (0171) 630 1822. (Furniture, mirrors, prints) *096694*

Omell, 22 Bury St, London SW1Y 6AL.
T. (0171) 839 4274. (Paintings) *096695*

Orsai, Sebastian d', 8 Kensington Mall, London W8 4EA.
T. (0171) 229 3888. (Picture Frames, Pictures, Mirror Glass) *096696*

Ossowski, A. & M., 83 Pimlico Rd, London SW1.
T. (0171) 730 3256. (Mirrors, wood carvings) *096697*

Osterley, 595 King's Rd, London SW6.
T. (0171) 731 0334. (Furniture) *096698*

Out of the Ark, 50 Royal Parade Mews, London SE3 0TN. T. (0181) 852-6222. (Furniture) *096699*

Palmer, B., 77 Jeddo Rd, London W12 9ED.
T. (0181) 749-2013. (Metal) *096700*

Paragon Furniture, Unit 2c, Asleigh Commercial Estate, Westmoor St, London SE7 8NB. T. (0181) 305-2332. (Furniture) *096701*

Parish Leathers, Unit K, Canada House, Blackburn Rd, London NW6. T. (0171) 328-4261. (Leather) *096702*

Parker, 28 Pimlico Rd, London SW1. T. (0171) 730 6768, Fax (0171) 259 9180. (Prints, paintings, chip models) *096703*

Patchworks, 62 South Parade, London W4 5LG.
T. (0181) 747 8910. (Furniture) *096704*

Period Brass Lights, 9A Thurloe Place, Brompton Rd, London SW7. T. (0171) 589 8305. (Metalware) *096705*

Persian Market, 48 Upper St, Islington, London N1.
T. (0171) 226 7927. (Porcelain, bronze) *096706*

Petherton Antiques, 124 Petherton Rd, London N5.
T. (0171) 226 6597. (Furniture) *096707*

Philip, Trevor, & Sons, 75a Jermyn St, Saint James's, London SW1. T. (0171) 930 2954, Fax 321 0212. (Scientific instruments, clocks, globes) *096708*

Phillips, S.J., 139 New Bond St, London W1A 3DL.
T. (0171) 6296261, Fax (0171) 4956180. (Silver, jewellery) *096709*

Phoenix Antique Furniture Restoration, 96 Webber St, Southwark, London SE1. T. (0171) 928-3624. (Furniture) *096710*

pH7, Business Village, Broomhill Rd, London SW18.
T. (0181) 871-5075. (Paper) *096711*

Pine Designs, 325 Katherine Rd, London E7 8PJ.
T. (0181) 471-5495. (Furniture) *096712*

Pine Stripping, Arch 212, Trussly Rd, London W6.
T. (0181) 741 4440. (Furniture) *096713*

Pine Stripping Specialists, 46 The Drive, South Woodford, London E18 2BL. T. (0181) 530-7758.
(Furniture) *096714*

Plowden & Smith, 190 Saint Ann's Hill, London SW18 2RT. T. (0181) 874 4005, Fax 874 7248. (Antiques, bronzes, sculptures, glass, churches) *096715*

Pollak, F. A., 20 Blue Ball Yard, London SW1.
T. (0171) 493 1434. (Picture Frames) *096716*

Potter, Jonathan, 21 Grosvenor St, Mayfair, London W1.
T. (0171) 491 3520, Fax 491 9754. (Maps, prints, atlases) *096717*

Poulter, H.W., & Son, 279 Fulham Rd, London SW10 9PZ. T. (0171) 352 7268. (Antique Marbles and Sculpture) *096718*

Priest, Michael, 27a Motcomb St, Belgrave Sq, London SW1. T. (0171) 235 7241. (Furniture, paintings) *096719*

Priory Antiques, 45 Cloth Fair, West Smithfield, London EC1. T. (0171) 606 9060. (Jewellery, silver) *096720*

Pryce & Brise, 79 Moore Park Rd, Fulham, London SW6.
T. (0171) 736 1864. (Glass) *096721*

Pyms, 9 Mount Str, Mayfair, London W1Y 5AD.
T. (0171) 629 2020, Fax (0171) 629 2060.
(Paintings) *096722*

Rare Carpets Gallery, 496 King's Rd, Chelsea, London SW10. T. (0171) 351 3296, Fax 376 4876.
(Carpets) *096723*

Real, A.M., Unit 4, 3 Glebe Rd, London E8 4BD.
T. (0171) 254 8683, Fax Fax 923 2489.
096724

Real French Polishers, Unit 153, 99-103 Lomond Grove, London SE5 7HN. T. (0171) 252 5505.
(Furniture) *096725*

Real French Polishers, 288 Richmond Rd, London E8.
T. (0171) 249 4374. (Furniture) *096726*

Regent Antiques, 9-10 Chester Court, Albany St, London NW1 4BU. T. (0171) 935 6944, Fax 935 7814.
(Furniture) *096727*

Relcy, 9 Nelson Rd, Greenwich, London SE10.
T. (0181) 858 2812. (Furniture, pictures) *096728*

Restoration Studio, 15 Chatsworth Rd, London W4.
T. (0181) 994 3582. (Ceramics) *096729*

Richards, David, & Sons, 12 New Cavendish St, London W1. T. (0171) 935 3206, 935 0322, Fax 224 4423.
(Silver) *096730*

Robin Hood's Workshop, 18 Bourne St, London SW1W 8JR. T. (0171) 730 0425. (Porcelain, pottery, objets d'art) *096731*

Rochefort, 32-34 The Green, Winchmore Hill, London N21. T. (0181) 886 4779. (Clocks, metalware) *096732*

Roderick, 23 Vicarage Gate, London W8.
T. (0171) 937 8517. (Clocks) *096733*

Ronald Bock Restorations, 3 Gresham Gardens, London WC2. T. (0181) 455 7395. (Ethnographica, Far East, Porcelain ceramics, sculptures, fossils) *096734*

Rose, R.E., 731 Sidcup Rd, London SE9 3SA.
T. (0181) 859 4754. (Clocks, barometers) *096735*

Rowley, 115 Kensington Church St, London SW8.
T. (0171) 727 6495. (Paintings and Frames) *096736*

Saint Peters Organ Works, Saint Peters Close, Warner Pl, London E2. T. (0171) 739 4747. (Pipe organs) *096737*

Scallywag, 224 Clapham Rd, London SW8.
T. (0171) 735 2444, Fax (0171) 735 0787.
(Furniture) *096738*

Scarisbrick & Bate, 111 Mount St, London W1.
T. (0171) 499 2043/4/5, Fax 499 2897.
(Furniture) *096739*

Schell, Christine, 15 Cale St, London SW3.
T. (0171) 352 5563. (Tortoiseshell, ivory, shagreen, crocodile, leather, enamel, silver) *096740*

Scope Antiques, 64-66 Willesden Ln, London NW6.
T. (0171) 328 5833. (Silver) *096741*

Seagar, R.C., 275 Lillie Rd, London SW6.
T. (0171) 385 7941. (Antique Furniture and polisher) *096742*

Seager, Arthur, 25a Holland St, London W8.
T. (0171) 937 3262. (Furniture, carvings, pottery) *096743*

Searle & Co., 1 Royal Exchange, Cornhill, London EC3.
T. (0171) 626 2456. (Silver, jewellery) *096744*

Senior, Mark, 240 Brompton Rd, London SW3.
T. (0171) 589 5811. (Watercolours) *096745*

Sensation, 66 Fulham Rd, London SW6.
T. (0171) 736 0586, Fax 385 4218. (Furniture, porcelain, silver, objets d'art) *096746*

Servisco, Unit 11, 58 Sandgate St, London SE15.
T. (0171) 732-1378. (Furniture) *096747*

Shaikh & Son, 16 Brook St, London W1.
T. (0171) 629 3430. (Carpets) *096748*

Shrubsole, S.J., 43 Museum St, London WC1 A1LY.
T. (0171) 405 2712. (Silver, Sheffield plate) *096749*

Silver, 3-5 Burlington Gardens, London W1.
T. (0171) 437 7034. (Jewellery) *096750*

Silver Belle, 48 Church St, London NW8.
T. (0171) 723 2908. (Silver, china) *096751*

Silver Mouse Trap, 56 Carey St, London WC2.
T. (0171) 405 2578. (Jewellery, silver) *096752*

Sitch, W., & Co., 48 Berwick St, London W1.
T. (0171) 437 3776. (Lamps) *096753*

Sladmore, 32 Bruton Pl, London W1. T. (0171) 499 0365.
(Sculptures) *096754*

Smyth, Peter, 42 Moreton St, Pimlico, London SW1.
T. (0171) 630 9898. (Textiles) *096755*

Somlo, 7 Piccadilly Arcade, London SW1.
T. (0171) 499 6526. (Watches) *096756*

Sotheran, Henry, 2-5 Sackville St, Piccadilly, London W1. T. (0171) 439 6151. (Books, prints) *096757*

Speelman, Edward, 175 Piccadilly, London W1.
T. (0171) 493 0657. (Paintings) *096758*

Spink, Michael & Henrietta, 91c Jermyn St, Saint James's, London SW1. T. (0171) 930 8008. (Islamic and Indian jewellery, paintings) *096759*

Spread Eagle Antiques, 1 Stockwell St, London SE10.
T. (0181) 692 1618. (Pictures, furniture) *096760*

Spread Eagle Antiques, 8 Nevada St, London SE10.
T. (0181) 305 1666. (Furniture, china, pictures) *096761*

Squibbs, 32 Danbury St, London N1. T. (0171) 359-8025. (Ceramics) *096762*

Stair & Co., 120 Mount St, London W1.
T. (0171) 499 1784, Fax (0171) 629 1050. (Furniture, barometers, lamps, clocks) *096763*

Stapleton, Serena, 75 Lower Richmond Rd, Putney, London SW15. T. (0181) 789 4245. (Furniture, pictures, objects) *096764*

Stern, 46 Ledbury Rd, London W11 2AB.
T. (0171) 229 6187. (Paintings) *096765*

Strike One, 33 Balcombe St, London NW1.
T. (0171) 224 9719. (Clocks, barometers) *096766*

Strip Joint, 128 Askew Rd, London W12. T. (0181) 749-1813. (Furniture) *096767*

Strip Shop, Unit 9, Rosebank Works, Rosebank Way, London W3. T. (0181) 992-0093. (Furniture) *096768*

Stuart, 12-14 Greenwich Church St, London SE10.
T. (0181) 858 1975. (Furniture, pictures) *096769*

Sugar Antiques, 8-9 Pierrepont Arcade, Islington, London N1. T. (0171) 354 9896. (Watches, pens, lighters, jewellery) *096770*

Surridge, 443 High St North, London E12 6TJ.
T. (0181) 472 5638. (Furniture) *096771*

Swann, Oliver, 170 Walton St, London SW3.
T. (0171) 581 4229, 584 8684. (Paintings, ship models) *096772*

Taleghani, Vahid S., 6 Vicars Rd, London NW5 4NL.
T. (0171) 284 3030. (Carpets, textiles) *096773*

Tanous, John, 115 Harwood Rd, London SW6.
T. (0171) 736-7999, 736-1142. (Paintings) *096774*

Taylor, 4 Royal Arcade, Old Bond St, London W1.
T. (0171) 734 3534. (Paintings) *096775*

Teltscher, F., 17 Crawford St, London W1.
T. (0171) 935 0525. (Paintings, wood carvings) *096776*

Temple Gallery, 6 Clarendon Cross, London W11.
T. (0171) 727 3809, Fax 727 1546. (Icons) *096777*

Tessiers, 26 New Bond St, London W1Y 0JY.
T. (0171) 629 0458, Fax Fax 629 5110. (Silver, jewellery) *096778*

Theobald, A.J., 120 Wandsworth Rd, London SW8 3lT.
T. (0171) 720 6509. (Furniture) *096779*

Thomas, Frank, Unit 13, Enterprise Way, Osier Industrial Estate, Wandsworth, London SW18.
T. (0181) 871 1196, 870 7998. (Fine Art Objects) *096780*

Thornhill, 76 New King's Rd, London SW6.
T. (0171) 736 5830. (Architectural items) *096781*

Thornhill, 78 Deodar Rd, London SW15.
T. (0181) 874 2101, 874 5669. (Architectural items) *096782*

Through the Looking Glass, 563a King's Rd, London SW6. T. (0171) 736 7799. (Mirrors) *096783*

Titian, Salvatore, 89 Lansdowne Rd Holland Park, London W11. T. (0171) 727 5742. (Antiques, Paintings, Gilding, Jvory) *096784*

Titian Studio, Unit 4, 326 Kensal Rd, London W10 5BN.
T. (0181) 960-6247, 969-6126. (Furniture) *096785*

Tociapski, Igor, 39 Ledbury Rd, London W11.
T. (0171) 229 8317. (Clocks, scientific instruments) *096786*

Tomkinson, 87 Portobello Rd, London W11.
T. (0171) 727 1304. (Stained glass windows) *096787*

Totteridge Gallery, 61 Totteridge Ln, London N20.
T. (0181) 446 7896. (Watercolours, paintings, prints) *096788*

Toucan, Gardeners Cottage, Spencer Rd, Chiswick, London W4. T. (0181) 994-5515. (Frames) *096789*

Tower Antiques, 463 Harrow Rd, London W10.
T. (0181) 969 0535. (Furniture, pine, paintings, prints) *096790*

Tracy, Simon, 18 Church St, London NW8.
T. (0171) 724 5890, Fax 262 0275. (Furniture) *096791*

Trade Picture Services, Neckinger Mills, Abbey St, London SE1. T. (0171) 237-4388. (Paintings) 096792

Trender, Robert, 33d Holland St, London W8 4LX.
T. (0171) 937-3247. (Antique Musical Boxes) 096793

Trove, 71 Pimlico Rd, London SW1. T. (0171) 730 6514.
(Paintings, furniture) 096794

Trowbridge, 17 Turret Grove, London SW4.
T. (0171) 738 8354. (Paper) 096795

Tsar Architectural, 487 Liverpool Rd, London N7.
T. (0171) 609 4238. (Fireplaces) 096796

Tulissio de Beaumont, 277 Lillie Rd, London SW6.
T. (0171) 385 0156. (Chandeliers) 096797

Ullmann, A.R., 10 Hatton Garden, London EC1.
T. (0171) 405 1877. (Jewellery, Silver) 096798

Valcke, François, 610 King's Rd, London SW6.
T. (0171) 736 6024, Fax 731 8302. (Oil paintings, drawings, prints) 096799

Van Haeften, Johnny, 13 Duke St, Saint James's, London SW1. T. (0171) 930 3062/3, Fax 839 6303.
(Paintings) 096800

Victorian Pine Paint Stripping Specialisty, 298 Brockley Rd, London SE4. T. (0181) 691-7162.
(Furniture) 096801

Village Time, 43 The Village Charlton, London SE7.
T. (0181) 858 2514. (Clocks, jewellery) 096802

Walker-Bagshawe, 73 Walton St, London SW3.
T. (0171) 589 4582. (Paintings, watercolours, prints) 096803

Walker, Johnson, & Tolhurst, 64 Burlington Arcade, London W1. T. (0171) 629 2615. (Jewellery) 096804

Walker, W.E., 277-279 Camden High St, London NW 1.
T. (0171) 485 6210, 485 4433. (China) 096805

Warder, G.D., & Son, 14 Hanway Pl, London W1P 9DG.
T. (0171) 636 1867. (Gilding of Mirrors, Furniture etc.) 096806

Waroujian, M.L., 110-112 Hammersmith Rd, London W6. T. (0181) 748 7509. (Carpets) 096807

Wartski, 14 Grafton St, London W1. T. (0171) 493 1141.
(Jewellery, silver) 096808

Waterhouse & Dodd, 110 New Bond St, London W1.
T. (0171) 491 9293. (Paintings, Drawings, Watercolours) 096809

Wates, E. & A., 82-84 Mitcham Ln, Streatham, London SW16 6NR. T. (0181) 769 2205. (Furniture) 096810

Wates, E. & A., 82-84 Mitcham Ln, London SW16 6NR.
T. (0181) 769 2205. (Furniture) 096811

Weiss, 16 Albemarb St, London W1X 3HF. T. (0171) 409-0035, Fax (0171) 491-9604. (Paintings) 096812

Whatling, R., Unit U 05, Acton Workshop, School Rd, London NW10. T. (0181) 961-2642. (Paintings) 096813

Whitworth & O'Donnell, 282 Lewisham High St, London SE13. T. (0181) 690 1282. (Jewellery) 096814

Wibroe, Neil, 185 Westbourne Grove, London W11.
T. (0171) 229 6334. (Furniture) 096815

Wilkins & Wilkins, 1 Barrett St, London W1.
T. (0171) 935 9613. (Furniture) 096816

Wilkinson, 5 Catford Hill, London SE6.
T. (0181) 314 1080. (Glass, metalwork) 096817

Wilson & Buttle, 310 Worple Rd, London SW20 8QU.
T. (0181) 947-4568. (Furniture) 096818

Winchmore Antiques, 14 The Green, Winchmore Hill, London N21. T. (0181) 882 4800. (Metal polishing, silver plating, oil lamps) 096819

Witch Ball, 51a Blackbird Hill, Kingsbury, London NW9.
T. (0181) 200 4937. (Furniture) 096820

Wolff, J., & Son., 82 Troutbeck Albany St, London NW1 4EJ. T. (0171) 388 3588. (Antiques) 096821

Wood Works, 72 Fulham Palace Rd, London W6.
T. (0181) 741-5626. (Furniture) 096822

Wren, 49b Church Rd, Barnes, London SW13.
T. (0181) 741 7841. (Furniture) 096823

Wynter, Harriet, 50 Redcliffe Rd, London SW10.
T. (0171) 352 6494, Fax 352 9312. (Globes, instruments) 096824

Wynyards, 5 Ladbroke Rd, London W11.
T. (0171) 221 7936. (Furniture) 096825

Yesterday Child, Angel Arcade, 118 Islington High St, London N1. T. (0171) 354 1601. (Dolls) 096826

Zanelli, 71 Chalk Farm Rd, London NW1 8AN.
T. (0171) 267-2456, Fax (0171) 267-9337.
(Furniture) 096827

Zebrak, Stand 41, 284 Westbourne Grove, London W11.
T. (01273) 202929, Fax 21021. (Jewellery, silver, watches) 096828

Zoulfaghari, Unit D, 53-79 Highgate Rd, London NW5.
T. (0171) 267 5973. (Persien carpets, rugs) 096829

20th Century Gallery, 821 Fulham Rd, London SW6.
T. (0171) 731 5888. (Paintings) 096830

Long Crendon (Buckinghamshire)
Wintgens, Michael & Elizabeth, 20 High St, Long Crendon. T. (01844) 201617. (Paintings) 096831

Long Eaton (Derbyshire)
Goodacre, Thrumpton Av, Long Eaton.
T. (01602) 734387. (Clock movements, silvering, engraving, dial repainting) 096832

Long Melford (Suffolk)
Antique Clocks, Little Saint Mary's Court, Hall St, Long Melford. T. (0178725) 880040. (Clocks) 096833

Chater-House, Foundry House, Hall St, Long Melford.
T. (0178725) 79831. (Furniture) 096834

Lyall, Alexander, Belmont House, Hall St, Long Melford.
T. (0178725) 75434. (Furniture) 096835

Marney, Patrick, Gate House, Melford Hall, Long Melford. T. (0178725) 880533. (Barometers) 096836

Simpson, Oswald, Hall St, Long Melford.
T. (0178725) 77523. (Furniture) 096837

Suthburgh, Red House, Hall St, Long Melford.
T. (0178725) 310140. (Furniture, barometers) 096838

Tudor Antiques, Little Saint Mary's, Long Melford.
T. (0178725) 75896. (Metal, clocks, barometers) 096839

Village Clocks, Little Saint Mary's, Long Melford.
T. (0178725) 75896. (Clocks) 096840

Ward, Hall St, Long Melford. T. (0178725) 78265.
(Furniture) 096841

Long Sutton (Lincolnshire)
Gardiner, John, 1 The Green, Long Sutton.
T. (01406) 72238. (Furniture) 096842

Longridge (Lancashire)
Charnley Fine Arts, Charnley House, Preston Rd, Longridge. (Paintings) 096843

Loughborough (Leicestershire)
Abbey Cane and Rush Seaters, Moat House, Bramcote Rd, Loughborough. T. (01509) 214154.
(Furniture) 096844

Lowe, 37-40 Church Gate, Loughborough LE11 1UE.
T. (01509) 212554. (Furniture) 096845

Lubenham (Leicestershire)
Stevens & Son, 61 Main St, Lubenham.
T. (01858) 63521. (Furniture) 096846

Ludlow (Shropshire)
Corve Galleries, 12 Corve St, Ludlow.
T. (01584) 873420. (Furniture) 096847

Marler, Jane, Dawes Mansion, Church St, Ludlow.
T. (01584) 874160. (Oil paintings, watercolours, prints) 096848

Pepper Lane Antiques Centre, Pepper Lane, Ludlow.
T. (01584) 876494. (Furniture, clocks) 096849

Rumens, Olivia, 30 Corve St, Ludlow. T. (01584) 873952.
(Paintings) 096850

Saint Leonards Antiques, Corve St, Ludlow.
T. (01584) 875573. (Clocks, furniture) 096851

Lustleigh (Devon)
Connell, S., Lower Wreyland, Lustleigh. T. (016477) 262.
(Paintings) 096852

Luton (Bedfordshire)
Foye, 15 Stanley St, Luton. T. (01582) 38487.
(Paintings) 096853

Knight, 59-61 Guildford St, Luton. T. (01582) 36266.
(Watercolours) 096854

Lymington (Hampshire)
Captain's Cabin Antiques, 1 Quay St, Lymington.
T. (01590) 672912. (Furniture, pictures, ceramics, silver) 096855

Corfield, 120 High St, Lymington. T. (01590) 673532, 675359. (Furniture, paintings) 096856

Hughes & Smeeth, 1 Gosport St, Lymington.
T. (01590) 676324. (Oil paintings) 096857

Lyndhurst (Hampshire)
Antiques Gallery, 76 High St, Lyndhurst. T. (01703) 2693.
(Furniture) 096858

Macclesfield (Cheshire)
Bagshaw, G., 74 Mill Ln, Macclesfield.
T. (01625) 421642. (Clocks, pottery, porcelain) 096859

Brooks, Philip, 6 West Bank Rd, Macclesfield.
T. (01625) 426275. (Watercolours, oil paintings, prints) 096860

Cheshire Antiques, 88-90 Chestergate, Macclesfield.
T. (01625) 423268. (Porcelain, clocks) 096861

Maidenhead (Berkshire)
Jaspers, 36 Queen St, Maidenhead. T. (01628) 36459.
(Victorian watercolours, paintings, maps, prints) 096862

Strippers, 85 Pinkneys Rd, Maidenhead.
T. (01628) 21341. (Furniture) 096863

Maldon (Essex)
Antique Workshop, Mill Works, Hazleigh, Maldon.
T. (01621) 828686. (Furniture) 096864

Beardall, Clive, 104b High St, Maldon.
T. (01621) 857890. (Furniture) 096865

Malmesbury (Wiltshire)
Kadwell, J.P., Silver St, Malmesbury. T. (01666) 823589.
(Wood) 096866

Malvern (Hereford and Worcester)
Malvern Bookshop, 5-7 Abbey Rd, Malvern WR14 3ES.
T. (01684) 5915. (Books) 090007

Malvern Link (Hereford and Worcester)
Kimber & Son, 6 Lower Howsell Rd, Malvern Link.
T. 574339. (Furniture) 096868

Manchester
Albion Antiques, 643 Stockport Rd, Longsight, Manchester M12. T. (0161) 225 4957. (Furniture, wooden items) 096869

Authentiques, 403 Bury New Rd, Prestwich, Manchester.
T. (0161) 773 9601. (Silver) 096870

Baron, 373 Bury New Rd, Prestwich, Manchester M25.
T. (0161) 773 9929. (Furniture) 096871

Blackley, 1139 Rochdale Rd, Manchester.
T. (0161) 721 4546. (Furniture) 096872

Bulldog Antiques, 393 Bury New Rd, Prestwich, Manchester M25 5AW. T. (0161) 798 9277.
(Furniture) 096873

Fulda, 19 Vine St, Salford, Manchester.
T. (0161) 792 1962. (Oil paintings, watercolours) 096874

Mansfield (Nottinghamshire)
Antiques Warehouse, 375 Chesterfield Rd North, Pleasley, Mansfield. T. (01623) 810480. (Furniture) 096875

Margate (Kent)
Furniture Mart, Grotto Hill, Margate. T. (01843) 220653.
(Furniture) 096876

Market Harborough (Leicestershire)
Stamp, J., & Son, 15 Kettering Rd, Market Harborough.
T. (01858) 62524. (Furniture) 096877

Market Weighton (Humberside)
Dyson, C.G., & Sons, 51 Market Pl, Market Weighton.
T. (01430) 810284. (Paintings) 096878

Houghton Hall Antiques, Houghton Hall, Cliffe Rd, Market Weighton. T. (01430) 873234. (Furniture) 096879

Marlborough (Wiltshire)
Cook, High Trees House, Savernake Forest, Marlborough. T. (01672) 513017. (Furniture) 096880

Marlow (Buckinghamshire)
Hogarth, 11 New Court Stables, High St, Marlow.
T. (016284) 73 424. (Picture framing, colouring of maps and prints) 096881

Messum, David, The Studio, Lords Wood, Marlow.
T. (016284) 44 6284, 44 6565. (Paintings) 096882

Marnhull (Dorset)
Brazier, Peter, Nash Court Farmhouse, Marnhull DT10 1JZ. T. (01258) 820255. (Furniture)   096883

Melbourn (Cambridgeshire)
Hardiman, P.N., 62 High St, Melbourn. T. 260093. (Furniture, general antiques)   096884

Merton (Devon)
Merton Antiques, Quicksilver Barn, Merton. T. (018053) 443. (Barometers)   096885

Midhurst (West Sussex)
Church Hill Clocks, Church Hill, Midhurst. T. (01730) 813891. (Clocks, watches, barometers)   096886

Milton Keynes (Buckinghamshire)
Campbell, Common Farm, West Hill, Milton Keynes. T. (01908) 583665. (Furniture)   096887

Minchinghampton (Gloucestershire)
Mason, Kenneth, 13 Windmill Rd, Minchinghampton GL6 9DX. T. 883 099. (Oak, mahagony, walnut, leather, leather cloth fitted)   096888

Minster (Kent)
Lamb, Michael, 2 Church St, Minster. T. (01843) 821666. (Furniture)   096889

Modbury (Devon)
Fourteen A, 14a Broad St, Modbury. T. (01548) 830732. (Boxes, furniture)   096890
Ye Little Shoppe, 1b Broad St, Modbury. T. (01548) 830732. (Furniture)   096891

Monmouth (Gwent)
Monmouth Antiques, 1 Agincourt Sq, Monmouth. T. (01600) 6568. (Furniture, clocks)   096892

Montrose (Tayside)
Heritage Centre, Balmain House, Lower Balmain St, Montrose DD10 8AZ. T. (01674) 77173. (Doors, furniture)   096893

Moreton-in-Marsh (Gloucestershire)
Astley House Fine Art, Astley House, High St, Moreton-in-Marsh. T. (01608) 50601, Fax Fax 51777. (Paintings)   096894
Astley House Fine Art, Astley House, High St, Moreton-in-Marsh. T. (01608) 50601. (Paintings)   096895

Much Wenlock (Shropshire)
Wenlock, 2 The Square, Much Wenlock. T. (01952) 728232. (Paintings)   096896

Nailsworth (Gloucestershire)
Hand Prints and Watercolours Gallery, 3 Bridge St, Nailsworth. T. (0145383) 4967. (Watercolours, prints)   096897

Nantwich (Cheshire)
Adams, 57 Welsh Row, Nantwich. T. (01270) 625643. (Furniture)   096898
Chapel Antiques, 47 Hospital St, Nantwich. T. (01270) 629508. (Furniture, clocks)   096899
Richardson, 89 Hospital St, Nantwich. T. (01270) 625963. (Oil paintings, furniture, clocks)   096900

Narberth (Dyfed)
Cheriton, 32 High St, Narberth. T. (01834) 860660. (Furniture, pictures)   096901

Nelson (Lancashire)
Blakey, Colin, 115 Manchester Rd, Nelson. T. (01282) 64941. (Furniture)   096902
Classic Restorations, 141 Napier St, Nelson. T. (01282) 611949. (Furniture)   096903
Wildman, Barbara, 9 Woodside Terrace, Nelson. T. (01282) 699679. (Paintings)   096904

Nettlebed (Oxfordshire)
Ferry, Harvey, & William Clegg, 1 High St, Nettlebed. T. (01491) 641780. (Furniture)   096905

Newark-on-Trent (Nottinghamshire)
D. and G. Antiques, 11 Kings Rd, Newark-on-Trent. T. (01636) 702782. (Furniture)   096906
TGM Antiques Warehouse, 5 Victoria St, Newark-on-Trent NG24 4UU. T. (01636) 701686. (Furniture)   096907

Newbury (Berkshire)
Baker, John, 20 George St, Kingsclere, Newbury RG14 5BS. T. (01635) 298 744. (Furniture)   096908

Newby Bridge (Cumbria)
Shire Antiques, Post House, High Newton, Newby Bridge. T. (015395) 31431. (Furniture)   096909

Newcastle-under-Lyme (Staffordshire)
Hood & Broomfield, 29 Albert St, Newcastle-under-Lyme. T. (01782) 626859. (Oils, watercolours)   096910
Midwinter, Richard, 13 Brunswick St, Newcastle-under-Lyme. T. (01782) 712483. (Clocks)   096911

Newcastle-upon-Tyne (Tyne and Wear)
Dean Gallery, 42 Dean St, Newcastle-upon-Tyne. T. (0191) 232 1208. (Oils, watercolours)   096912

Newhaven (Sussex)
Russell, Leonard, 21 Kings Av, Mount Pleasant, Newhaven. T. (01273) 515153. (Pottery)   096913

Newmarket (Suffolk)
Newmarket Gallery, 156 High St, Newmarket. T. (01638) 661183. (Prints, drawings, pictures)   096914
Northwold Gallery, 30 High St, Newmarket. T. (01638) 668758. (Oils, watercolours, prints)   096915

Newnham-on-Severn (Gloucestershire)
Cottonwood, High St, Newnham-on-Severn. T. (01594) 516633. (Furniture)   096916

Newport (Essex)
Brown House Antiques, High St, Newport. T. (01799) 40238. (Furniture)   096917

Newport (Gwent)
Country Pine, 210 Chepstow Rd, Newport. T. (01633) 272091. (Furniture)   096918
Moreton, Rex, Mountjoy Rd, Newport. T. (01633) 255078. (Furniture)   096919
Newport Restoration, 86 Operation Rd, Newport. T. (01633) 267960. (Furniture)   096920
Pinewood Stripping and Restoration, Dudley St, Newport. T. (01633) 274535. (Furniture)   096921
Stuart, Herbert, Unit 1a, Enterprise Way, Bolt St, Newport. T. (01633) 841829. (Furniture)   096922

Newport (Isle of Wight)
Heath, Mike, 3-4 Holywood St, Newport. T. (01983) 525748. (Copper, brass)   096923

Newton Abbott (Devon)
De Paul, 132 Queen St, Newton Abbott. T. (01626) 65678. (Paintings)   096924

Newton Stewart (Dumfries and Galloway)
Brown, 44 Queen St, Newton Stewart. T. (01671) 3968. (Furniture)   096925
Galloway, 110 Queen St, Newton Stewart. T. (01671) 3968. (Paintings)   096926

North Berwick (Lothian)
Fraser, 129 High St, North Berwick. T. (01620) 2722. (Paintings, clocks, furniture)   096927

North Shields (Tyne and Wear)
May, Maggie, 3-4 Kirton Park Terrace, North Shields. T. (0191) 257 0076. (Furniture)   096928

North Walsham (Norfolk)
Bates, Eric, & Sons, Melbourne House, Bacton Rd, North Walsham. T. (01692) 403221. (Furniture)   096929

Northallerton (North Yorkshire)
Alverton, 7 South Parade, Northallerton. T. (01609) 780402. (Clocks)   096930

Northampton (Northamptonshire)
Savage, R.S.J., & Son, Alfred St, Northampton. T. (01604) 20327. (Paintings)   096931

Northchapel (West Sussex)
Callingham, N. & S., London Rd 5 Miles, North of Petworth, Northchapel. T. (0142878) 379. (Furniture)   096932

Northfleet (Kent)
McClelland, 2 Dover Rd, Northfleet. T. (01474) 568234. (Paintings)   096933

Northleach (Gloucestershire)
Harding, Keith, Oak House, High St, Northleach. T. (01451) 60181. (Musical boxes, clocks)   096934

Norwich (Norfolk)
As Time Goes By Antique Clocks, 5 Wrights Court, Elm Hill, Norwich. T. (01603) 666508. (Clocks)   096935
Bank House Gallery, 71 Newmarket Rd, Norwich. T. (01603) 633380. (Paintings)   096936
Carrow Hill Antique and Bygone Centre, Carrow Hill, Norwich. T. (01603) 628628, 615943. (Furniture)   096937
Crome, 34 Elm Hill, Norwich. T. (01603) 622827, 614781. (Oils, watercolours, prints)   096938
D'Amico, 20 Highland Rd, Norwich. T. (01603) 624315, 622049. (Clocks)   096939
Design House, 29 Saint Georges St, Norwich. T. (01603) 623181. (Furniture)   096940
Fairhurst, 13 Bedford St, Norwich. T. (01603) 614214. (Paintings)   096941
Hallam, Michael, 17 Magdalen St, Norwich. T. (01603) 621163. (Porcelain, pottery)   096942
Leveton & Sons, 31 Timberhill, Norwich NR1 3LA. T. (01603) 625833. (Paintings)   096943
Mandell, Elm Hill, Norwich NR3 1HN. T. (01603) 626892, 629810. (Paintings, watercolours)   096944
Mann, Anthony, 22-24 Saint Benedicts St, Norwich. T. (01603) 660046. (Metal work)   096945
Reiss, Stephen, 14 Bridewell Alley, Norwich. T. (01603) 615357. (Oils, watercolours)   096946
Sebley, Oswald, 20 Lower Goat Lane, Norwich. T. (01603) 632201. (Silver, jewellery)   096947
Tillett, James & Ann, 12-13 Tombland, Norwich. T. (01603) 624914. (Silver)   096948
Tillett, Thomas, & Co., 17 Saint Giles St, Norwich. T. (01603) 625922. (Jewellery, silver)   096949

Nottingham (Nottinghamshire)
Antiques and General Trading Company, 145 Lower Parliament St, Nottingham. T. (0115) 9585971. (Furniture)   096950
Cowley, Heather, 237 Mansfield Rd, Nottingham. T. (0115) 9473836. (Books, oil paintings)   096951
Kemp, Melville, 79-81 Derby Rd, Nottingham. T. (0115) 9417055. (Silver, china, jewellery)   096952
Lustre Metal Antiques, Canning Circus, Derby Rd, Nottingham. T. (0115) 9704385. (Copper, brass, silver)   096953
Mitchell, Anthony, 11 Albemarle Rd, Nottingham. T. (0115) 9628865. (Oil paintings, watercolours)   096954

Nuneaton (Warwickshire)
Vivian Antiques, 32 Coton Rd, Nuneaton. T. (01203) 381945. (Furniture)   096955

Oakham (Leicestershire)
Flore's House Antiques, 34 High St, Oakham. T. (01572) 757207. (Furniture)   096956
Merchant, S. A., 28 Cricket Lawns, Oakham LE15 6MT. T. (01572) 2768. (Antique specimens, natural history specimens and sporting trophies)   096957
Old House Gallery, 13 Market Pl, Oakham. T. (01572) 755538. (Oils, watercolours, prints)   096958
Rutland, 38a Melton Rd, Oakham. T. (01572) 757661. (Paintings, prints, maps)   096959
Swans Antique Centre, 27 Mill St, Oakham. T. (01572) 724364. (Furniture)   096960

Oban (Southclyde)
Mclan, 10 Argyll Sq, Oban. T. (01631) 66755, 62303. (Watercolours, oil paintings)   096961

Oldham (Lancashire)
Howell, Charles, 2 Lord St, Oldham. T. (0161) 624 2479.
(Jewellery, watches)   096962
Valley Antiques, Soho St, Oldham. T. (0161) 624 5030.
(Furniture, clocks)   096963

Ollerton (Nottinghamshire)
Hamlyn Lodge, Station Rd, Ollerton. T. (01623) 323600.
(Furniture)   096964

Olney (Buckinghamshire)
Market Square Antiques, Olney. T. (01234) 712172. (Fur-
niture, clocks, china, silver, glass, copper,
brass)   096965
Martin, Alan, Farthing Cottage, Clickers Yard, Olney.
T. (01234) 712446. (Clocks)   096966
Overland, John, Rose Court, Market Pl, Olney.
T. (01234) 269790. (Furniture, clocks)   096967

Ombersley (Hereford and Worcester)
Stables Antiques, Blacksmiths Cottage, Chatley, Ombersley. T. (01905) 620353. (China, paintings)   096968

Ormskirk (Lancashire)
Grice, Alan, 106 Aughton St, Ormskirk L39 3BS.
T. (01695) 572007. (Antique Furniture)   096969

Otley (West Yorkshire)
Butterchurn, 32-36 Bondgate, Otley. T. (01943) 462579.
(Furniture)   096970

Overton (Hampshire)
Anton Galleries, 21 a High St, Overton. T. 406.
(Furniture)   096971

Oxford (Oxfordshire)
Bibb, Barbara, 149 Kineton Rd, Oxford.
T. (01865) 512128. (Paintings)   096972
Davis, Reginald, 34 High St, Oxford OX1 4AN.
T. (01865) 248347. (Silver, jewellery)   096973
Desk Shop, 41 Saint Clements, Oxford.
T. (01865) 245524. (Furniture)   096974
Keyboard Instruments, 27 Northmoor Rd, Oxford.
T. (01865) 55651. (Organs, harpsichords,
harps)   096975
Legge, Christopher, 25 Oakthorpe Rd, Summertown, Ox-
ford. T. (01865) 57572. (Carpets)   096976
Oxford Architectural Antiques, Old Depot, Nelson St, Je-
richo, Oxford. T. (01865) 53310. (Architectural
items)   096977
Park, Kathryn, 5 North Parade, Oxford. T. (01865) 56026.
(Oil paintings, parchments)   096978
Payne & Son, 131 High St, Oxford. T. (01865) 243787.
(Silver)   096979
Rowell & Son, 12 Turl St, Oxford. T. (01865) 242187.
(Silver, jewellery, clocks, watches)   096980

Oxted (Surrey)
Antiques and Interiors, 34 Station Rd, Oxted.
T. (01883) 712806. (Furniture)   096981

Paisley (Strathclyde)
Heritage Antiques, Walker St, Paisley.
T. (0141) 889 3661. (Furniture)   096982

Pamber Heath (Hampshire)
Smith, D.J., 34 Silchester Rd, Pamber Heath RG26 6EF.
T. Silchester 700595. (Woodcarving repairs,
mirrors)   096983

Pateley Bridge (North Yorkshire)
Squirrels and Early Days, 4 King's Court, Pateley Bridge.
T. 711661. (Furniture)   096984

Peasenhall (Suffolk)
Peasenhall Art and Antiques Gallery, The Street, Peasenhall. T. (0172879) 224. (Oils, watercolours,
furniture)   096985

Peel (Isle of Man)
Mannin, 5 Castle St, Peel. T. (01624) 843897.
(Paintings)   096986

Penmaenmawr (Gwynedd)
Gay, Ynys-Las, Conway Rd, Penmaenmawr.
T. (01492) 622850. (Clocks, oil paintings)   096987

Penn (Buckinghamshire)
Penn Barn, By the Pond, Elm Rd, Penn.
T. (0149481) 5691. (Books, maps, prints)   096988

Penrith (Cumbria)
James, Joseph, Corney Sq, Penrith. T. (01768) 62065.
(Furniture, porcelain, pottery, silver, pictures)   096989
Penrith Coin and Stamp Centre, 37 King St, Penrith.
T. (01768) 64185. (Coins, jewellery, stamps)   096990
Pollock, Jane, 4 Castlegate, Penrith. T. (01768) 67211.
(Silver, blue glass, liners)   096991

Penzance (Cornwall)
Ashbrook, Ken, Leskinnick Pl, Penzance.
T. (01736) 65477. (Cabinet work)   096992
New Street Antiques, 26 New St, Penzance.
T. (01736) 60173. (Furniture)   096993

Pershore (Hereford and Worcester)
Hansen Chard Antiques, 126 High St, Pershore.
T. (01386) 553423. (Clocks, barometers)   096994

Perth (Tayside)
Love, Thomas, & Sons, 51-53 South St, Perth.
T. (01738) 24111. (Furniture, Antiques)   096995

Peterborough (Cambridgeshire)
Smith, G., & Sons, 1379 Lincoln Rd, Werrington, Peterborough. T. (01733) 71630. (General antiques, furniture, clocks)   096996

Peterhead (Grampian)
Crofters, 28 Kirktown, Peterhead. T. (01779) 838702.
(Clocks, paintings, porcelain, furniture,
weapons)   096997

Petersfield (Hampshire)
Petersfield Bookshop, 16a Chapel St, Petersfield.
T. (01730) 63438. (Books)   096998

Petworth (West Sussex)
Amini, Majid, Church St, Petworth. T. (01798) 43344.
(Rugs)   096999
Baskerville, Saddlers House, Saddlers Row, Petworth.
T. (01798) 42067. (Clocks, furniture)   097000
Bragge, Lesley, Fairfield House, High St, Petworth.
T. (01798) 42324. (Furniture)   097001
Chapman, Mark, New St, Petworth. T. (01798) 42283.
(Furniture, metal, paintings)   097002
Davidson, Richard, Pettifers, Lombard St, Petworth.
T. (01798) 42508. (Furniture)   097003
Granville, High St, Petworth. T. (01798) 43250.
(Furniture)   097004
Grove House Antiques, Middle St, Petworth.
T. (01798) 43151. (Furniture, paintings)   097005
Madison Gallery, Swan House, Market Sq, Petworth.
T. (01798) 43638. (Furniture)   097006

Pinner (Greater London)
Artbry, 44 High St, Pinner. T. (0181) 868 0834.
(Clocks)   097007

Plaitford (Hampshire)
Plaitford House Gallery, Plaitford. T. (01794) 22221.
(Paintings, watercolours)   097008

Polegate (East Sussex)
Corbell, A.B., Unit 2, Windsor Way, Polegate.
T. (013212) 485277. (Furniture)   097009

Poole (Dorset)
Burgess, D.J., 116-116a Ashley Rd, Parkstone, Poole.
T. (01202) 730542. (Clocks, watches)   097010
Canners & Upholders, 42 Farnham Rd, Parkstone, Poole.
T. (01202) 733407. (Furniture)   097011
Clegg, G.D., & Sons, 29a Gladstone Rd, Poole.
T. (01202) 744003. (Furniture)   097012
Corbin, D.A., 32 Morrison Av, Poole. T. (01202) 744419.
(Furniture)   097013
D'Ardenne, 7 North Lodge Rd, Poole. T. (01202) 743505.
(Furniture)   097014
D.J. Jewellery, 166-168 Ashley Rd, Parkstone, Poole.
T. (01202) 745148. (Clocks, watches,
jewellery)   097015
Mailins, John, 16 Orchard Av, Parkstone, Poole.
T. (01202) 737510. (Clocks)   097016

Marples, D.A., 9 Inverclyde Rd, Poole BH14 8PB.
T. (01202) 744914. (Furniture)   097017
Weber, Michael, 62 Danecourt Rd, Parkstone, Poole.
T. (01202) 731882, 721183. (Paintings)   097018
Wiffen, 99-101 Bournemouth Rd, Poole.
T. (01202) 736567. (Furniture, porcelain, pictures, sil-
ver, clocks)   097019

Port Erin (Isle of Man)
Spinning Wheel, Church Rd, Port Erin.
T. (01624) 833137, 835020. (Furniture)   097020

Portslade (West Sussex)
Powell, J., 20 Wellington Rd, Portslade. T. 411599.
(Furniture)   097021

Portsmouth (Hampshire)
Fleming, A., Clock Tower, Castle Rd, Portsmouth.
T. (01705) 822934. (Furniture, silver, china, porcelain,
jewellery)   097022
Leslie's, 107 Fratton Rd, Portsmouth. T. (01705) 825952.
(Jewellery)   097023
Oldfield, 76 Elm Grove, Portsmouth. T. (01705) 838042.
(Maps, prints)   097024

Potters Bar (Hertshire)
Rodwell, 94 High St, Potters Bar. T. (01707) 55402.
(Furniture)   097025

Powick (Hereford and Worcester)
Barn Gallery, Sandpits Farm, Colletts Green Rd, Powick.
T. (01905) 830029. (Paintings, watercolours)   097026

Poynton (Cheshire)
Harper, Overdale, Woodford Rd, Poynton. T. 879105.
(Watercolours, oil paintings, prints)   097027

Preston (Lancashire)
Allison, C.W., & Sons, 107 New Hall Lane, Preston.
T. (01772) 701805. (Furniture, porcelain,
pictures)   097028
Swag, 24 Leyland Rd, Penwortham, Preston.
T. (01772) 744970. (Dolls)   097029
Treasure, Frederick, 274-278 New Hall Lane, Preston
PR1 4SU. T. (01772) 70 0216. (Furniture)   097030
Wade, Ray, 111 New Hall Lane, Preston.
T. (01772) 792950. (Furniture, paintings,
porcelain)   097031

Prestwich (Greater Manchester)
Heritage, 373 Bury New Rd, Prestwich.
T. (0161) 773 0500. (Furniture)   097032

Prestwick (Southclyde)
Pine Village, 399-413 Spey Rd, Prestwick Airport, Prest-
wick. T. (01292) 74377. (Furniture)   097033
Yer Granny's Attic, 176 Main St, Prestwick.
T. (01292) 76312. (Stained glass)   097034

Princes Risborough (Buckinghamshire)
Farelly, The Barns, Old Cross Keys, New Rd, Princes Risborough. T. 7044. (Furniture)   097035

Puckeridge (Hertfordshire)
Saint Ouen, Vintage Corner, Old Cambridge Rd, Puckeridge. T. (01920) 821336. (Furniture)   097036

Pudsey (West Yorkshire)
Geary, 114 Richardshaw Lane, Stanningley, Pudsey.
T. (01532) 564122. (Furniture)   097037

Purley (Greater London)
Addison, House, 28-30 Godstone Rd., Purley.
T. (0181) 668 6714. (Furniture)   097038

Ramsbury (Wiltshire)
Inglenock, 59 High St, Ramsbury. T. (01672) 20 261.
(Clocks)   097039

Ramsey (Cambridgeshire)
Yesteryear Antiques, 79-81 High St, Ramsey.
T. (01487) 815006. (Watercolours, oil paintings, prints,
furniture)   097040

Reach (Cambridgeshire)
Furniture and Classic Car Clinic, Vine House, Fair Green,
Reach. T. (01638) 741989. (Furniture, cars)   097041

Furniture Clinic, Vine House, Fair Green, Reach.
T. (01638) 741989, Fax Fax 743239.
(Furniture)   *097042*

Reading (Berkshire)
Clock Workshop, 17 Prospect St, Caversham, Reading.
T. (01734) 470741. (Clocks, barometers)   *097043*
Collectors Gallery, 8 Bridge St, Caversham, Reading.
T. (01734) 483663. (Paintings)   *097044*
French Blake, R. L. V., Loddon Lower Farm, Spencer's
Wood, Reading RG7 1JE. T. (01734) 883 212. (Oil pain-
tings, gilt frames)   *097045*
Havers, Hamilton, 58 Conisboro Av, Caversham, Reading
RG4 7JE. T. (01734) 47 3379. (Boulle, Marquetry,
French Polishing, Brass Inlay etc.)   *097046*

Redditch (Hereford and Worcester)
Lower House, Far Moor Ln, Winyates Green, Redditch.
T. (01527) 25117. (Furniture, paintings, silver,
pewter)   *097047*

Redruth (Cornwall)
Penandrea, 12 Higher Fore St, Redruth.
T. (01209) 213134. (Oil paintings,
watercolours)   *097048*

Reigate (Surrey)
Bourne Gallery, 31-33 Lesbourne Rd, Reigate.
T. (01737) 241614. (Oil paintings)   *097049*
Noller, Bertram, 14a London Rd, Reigate.
T. (01737) 242548. (Furniture, clocks, marble) *097050*
Trevers, P. Stratford, 45 Bell St, Reigate.
T. (01737) 46055. (Books, Prints, Documents) *097051*

Retford (Nottinghamshire)
Franco, Riverside Lodge, London Rd, Retford.
T. (01777) 705688. (Porcelain)   *097052*

Richmond (North Yorkshire)
Brown, 2 New Rd, Richmond. T. (01748) 4095.
(Furniture)   *097053*

Richmond (Surrey)
Goslett, Roland, 139 Kew Rd, Richmond.
T. (0181) 940 4009. (Watercolours, oil
paintings)   *097054*
Hugh, Evelyn, 36a Friar Stile Rd, Richmond.
T. (0181) 948 4031. (Prints, watercolours,
pastels)   *097055*

Rickmansworth (Hertfordshire)
McCrudden, 23 Station Rd, Rickmansworth.
T. (01923) 772613. (Pictures, frames)   *097056*

Ringwood (Hampshire)
Pine Company, 104 Christchurch Rd, Ringwood.
T. (01425) 476705, Fax Fax 480467. (Furniture, model
railways, silver, china)   *097057*
Robinson, Glen, 82 Christchurch Rd, Ringwood.
T. (01425) 480450. (Furniture, porcelain) *097058*

Ripley (Surrey)
Ripley Antiques, 67 High St, Ripley.
T. (0148643) 224981. (Furniture)   *097059*
Sage, Green Cottage, High St, Ripley.
T. (0148643) 224981. (Furniture, pictures) *097060*

Ripon (North Yorkshire)
Rose, 13 Kirkgate, Ripon. T. (01765) 690118.
(Pictures)   *097061*

Riverhead (Kent)
Mandarin Gallery, 32 London Rd, Riverhead. T. 457399.
(Chinese, furniture)   *097062*

Rochdale (Greater Manchester)
Owen, 189-193 Oldham Rd, Rochdale.
T. (01706) 48138. (Clocks, furniture)   *097063*

Rochester (Kent)
Iles, Francis, Rutland House, La Providence, High St, Ro-
chester. T. (01634) 843081. (Watercolours, oil
paintings)   *097064*
Kwik Strip, Unit 3, Bardell Terrace, Rochester.
T. (01634) 841212. (Furniture)   *097065*
Langley, 153 High St, Rochester. T. (01634) 811802.
(Watercolours, oil paintings)   *097066*

Northgate Antiques, 48 High St, Rochester.
T. (01634) 65428. (Porcelain, furniture)   *097067*

Rolvenden (Kent)
Walters, J.D. & R.M., 10 Regent St, Rolvenden.
T. (01580) 241563. (Furniture)   *097068*

Romsey (Hampshire)
Robinson, Tim, 25 Bell St, Romsey. T. (01794) 523985.
(Paintings)   *097069*

Ross-on-Wye (Hereford and Worcester)
Fryer, Fritz, 12 Brookend St, Ross-on-Wye.
T. (01989) 67416. (Metalware, glass
chandeliers)   *097070*
Old Chop Shop, Gloucester Rd, Ross-on-Wye.
T. (01989) 64738. (Furniture)   *097071*
Relics, 19 High St, Ross-on-Wye. T. (01989) 64539.
(Clocks, jewellery)   *097072*
Trecilla, 36 High St, Ross-on-Wye. T. (01989) 63010.
(Furniture, clocks)   *097073*

Rotherham (South Yorkshire)
South Yorkshire Antiques, 88-94 Broad St, Rotherham.
T. (01709) 585854, 526514. (Furniture)   *097074*

Ruddington (Nottinghamshire)
Rodgers, Arthur & Ann, 7 Church St, Ruddington.
T. (01602) 216214. (Pottery, china)   *097075*

Rugby (Warwickshire)
Wood, P. N., 3a King St, Rugby CV21 2LT.
T. (01788) 6 1644. (General furniture, regency brass
grills, leather table linings)   *097076*

Ruthin (Clwyd)
Porter, Liz, Unit 1, Ruthin Craft Centre, Park Rd, Ruthin.
T. (018242) 3575. (Paintings)   *097077*

Ryde (Isle of Wight)
Vanner Mews Workshop, 3 Newport St, Ryde.
T. (01983) 562140. (Furniture)   *097078*

Rye (East Sussex)
Bragge & Sons, Landgate House, Rye.
T. (01797) 223358. (Furniture)   *097079*
Gasson, Herbert Gordon, Lion Galleries, Lion St, Rye.
T. (01797) 222208. (Furniture)   *097080*

Saffron Walden (Essex)
Sleven, Robert, Unit 3, Hall Farm, Little Walden, Saffron
Walden CB10 1XA. T. (01799) 513206, 584654.
(Furniture)   *097081*

Saint Albans (Hertfordshire)
Clock Shop, 161 Victoria St, Saint Albans AL1 3TA.
T. (01727) 56633. (Clocks, watches,
barometers)   *097082*
Leaside Antiques, Shop 5, George St, Saint Albans.
T. (01727) 40653. (Jewellery)   *097083*

Saint Andrews (Fife)
Old Saint Andrews Gallery, 9 Albany Pl, Saint Andrews.
T. (01334) 77840. (Jewellery, silver)   *097084*

Saint Austell (Cornwall)
Furniture Store, 37-39 Truro Rd, Saint Austell.
T. (01726) 63178. (Furniture)   *097085*

Saint Helier (Jersey)
Grange, 30 New St, Saint Helier. T. (01534) 20077.
(Pictures)   *097086*
Saint Helier Galleries, 9 James St, Saint Helier.
T. (01534) 67048. (Paintings, watercolours,
drawings)   *097087*
Selective Eye Gallery, 50 Don St, Saint Helier.
T. (01534) 25281. (Pictures)   *097088*

Saint Ives (Cornwall)
Read, Mike, Ayia Napa, Wheal Whidden, Carbis Bay,
Saint Ives. T. (01736) 798219. (Scientific
instruments)   *097089*

Saint Leonards-on-Sea (East Sussex)
Aarquebus Antiques, 46 Norman Rd, Saint Leonards-on-
Sea. T. (01424) 433267. (Furniture)   *097090*

Chapel Antiques, 1 London Rd, Saint Leonards-on-Sea.
T. (01424) 440025. (Furniture)   *097091*
Galleon Antiques, 19 Marina, Saint Leonards-on-Sea.
T. (01424) 424145. (Furniture)   *097092*
South East Conservation Centre, 5 North St, Saint Leo-
nards-on-Sea. T. (01424) 431157. (Paintings) *097093*

Saint Peter Port (Guernsey)
Blower, Mark, 3 Tower Hill, Saint Peter Port.
T. (01481) 25638. (Furniture)   *097094*
Saint James's Gallery, 18-20 The Bordage, Saint Peter
Port. T. (01481) 720070. (Furniture, pictures) *097095*

Salisbury (Wiltshire)
Micawber, 73 Fisherton St, Salisbury. T. (01722) 337822.
(Furniture, watches, jewellery)   *097096*
Salisbury Clock Shop, 107 Exeter St, Salisbury.
T. (01722) 337076. (Clocks)   *097097*

Saltney (Clwyd)
Chester Furniture and Door Stripping, Unit 1, Bryman, 3
River Ln, Saltney. T. (01244) 674737. (Furniture,
doors)   *097098*

Sandhurst (Berkshire)
Berkshire Metal Finishers, Swan Lane Trading Estate,
Sandhurst. T. (01252) 873475, Fax 875434.
(Metalware)   *097099*

Sandhurst (Kent)
Forge Antiques and Restorations, Rye Rd, Sandhurst.
T. (01580) 850308, 850665. (Furniture)   *097100*

Sandwich (Kent)
Atkinson, James, 38 King St, Sandwich.
T. (01304) 617216. (Oils, watercolours)   *097101*

Sawbridgeworth (Hertfordshire)
G. & J. Restoration, Allens Green, Sawbridgeworth.
T. (01279) 726217. (Furniture)   *097102*

Scunthorpe (Humberside)
Guns and Tackle, 251a Ashby High St, Scunthorpe.
T. (01724) 865445. (Guns)   *097103*

Seaford (East Sussex)
Old House, 15-17 High St, Seaford BN25 1PD.
T. (01323) 892091, 893795. (Furniture)   *097104*
Steyne House Antiques, 35 Steyne Rd, Seaford.
T. (01323) 895088. (China)   *097105*

Sevenoaks (Kent)
Field, G.E., 27 London Rd, Sevenoaks. T. (01732) 52167.
(Furniture)   *097106*
Ward, Sheldon, 57 Saint John's Hill, Sevenoaks.
T. (01732) 455311. (Inlay, marquetry)   *097107*

Sharpthorne (West Sussex)
Thayre, Roger, 23 Hamsey Rd, Sharpthorne.
T. (01342) 810641. (Furniture)   *097108*

Sheffield (South Yorkshire)
Anita's Holme Antiques, 144 Holme Lane, Hillsborough,
Sheffield. T. (0114) 336698. (Pottery)   *097109*
Arcade Antiques, Unit 14, Sheaf Market, Sheffield.
T. (0114) 737651. (Jewellery)   *097110*
Door Stripping, 314-318 Langsett Rd, Sheffield.
T. (0114) 346088. (Doors)   *097111*
Dovetail, 112-114 London Rd, Sheffield S2 4LR.
T. (0114) 700273, 561013. (Furniture)   *097112*
Fulwood, 7 Brooklands Av, Sheffield. T. (0114) 307387.
(Ceramics, metal, pictures)   *097113*
Hibberts Bros., 117 Norfolk St, Sheffield.
T. (0114) 722038. (Paintings)   *097114*
Hinson, 290 Glossop Rd, Sheffield. T. (0114) 722082.
(Paintings)   *097115*
Jameson & Co., A.E., 257 Glossop Rd, Sheffield.
T. (0114) 723846. (Furniture)   *097116*
Peter James Antiques, 112-114 London Rd, Sheffield.
T. (0114) 700273. (Furniture)   *097117*
Richards, 94 Abbeydale Rd, Sheffield. T. (0114) 550720.
(Furniture)   *097118*

Shepperton (Surrey)
Rickett & Co., Church Sq, Shepperton. T. 222508.
(Metalware)   *097119*

Shepshed (Leicestershire)
Hadfield, G.K., Blackbrook Hill House, Tickow Lane, Shepshed LE12 9GY. T. (01509) 503014, Fax 600136. (Clocks)   *097120*

Sherborne (Dorset)
Antiques of Sherborne, 1 The Green, Sherborne.
T. (01935) 816549. (Furniture, paintings)   *097121*
Heygate Browne, South St, Sherborne.
T. (01935) 815487. (Furniture, pottery, porcelain)   *097122*
Johnson, South St, Sherborne. T. (01935) 812585. (Furniture)   *097123*
Swan Gallery, 51 Cheap St, Sherborne.
T. (01935) 814465. (Paintings, watercolours, prints)   *097124*

Sheringham (Norfolk)
Westcliffe Gallery, 2-8 Augusta St, Sheringham.
T. (01263) 824320. (Oils, watercolours, prints) *097125*

Shipston-on-Stour (Warwickshire)
Fine-Lines, 31 Sheep St, Shipston-on-Stour.
T. (01608) 62323. (Paintings, watercolours, drawings)   *097126*
Time in Hand, 11 Church St, Shipston-on-Stour.
T. (01608) 62578. (Clocks, watches, barometers, mechanical instruments)   *097127*

Shoreham (Kent)
Porcelain Collector, 29 High St, Shoreham TN14 7TD.
T. 3416. (Porcelain)   *097128*

Shrewsbury (Shropshire)
Jones, J.A., 38 Wyle Cop, Shrewsbury SY1 1AA.
T. (01743) 53 234. (Furniture, walnut a speciality)   *097129*
Manser, F.C., & Son, 53-54 Wyle Cop, Shrewsbury.
T. (01743) 51120. (Furniture)   *097130*
Nevill, 9-10 Milk St, Shrewsbury. T. (01743) 51013. (Furniture)   *097131*
Pritchard, C.J., 11 Fish St, Shrewsbury SY1 1UH.
T. (01743) 2854. (Furniture)   *097132*
Raleigh House, 23 Belle Vue Rd, Shrewsbury.
T. (01743) 59552. (Furniture, clocks)   *097133*
Severn Fine Art, 67 Abbey Foregate, Shrewsbury.
T. (01743) 247514. (Paintings, watercolours) *097134*

Sible Hedingham (Essex)
Churchgate Antiques, 150 Swan St, Sible Hedingham.
T. (01787) 62269. (Furniture)   *097135*
Hedingham Antiques, 100 Swan St, Sible Hedingham.
T. (01787) 60360. (Furniture, china, glass, silver)   *097136*

Sidmouth (Devon)
Lantern Shop, 4 New St, Sidmouth. T. (01395) 516320. (Lamps, oil paintings)   *097137*

Silchester (Hampshire)
Smith, D.J., 34 Silchester Rd Pamber Heath, Silchester.
T. 70 0595. (Antiques)   *097138*

Sittingbourne (Kent)
Periwinkle Press, 23 East St, Sittingbourne.
T. (01795) 426242. (Prints, oils)   *097139*

Skegness (Lincolnshire)
Romantiques, 87 Roman Bank, Skegness.
T. (01754) 67879. (Clocks, furniture)   *097140*

Skipton (North Yorkshire)
Dales, Unit 47, Craven Yard, Craven St, Skipton.
T. (01756) 701570. (Furniture)   *097141*

Soham (Cambridgeshire)
Galloway, Ursula, 9 Great Fen Rd, Soham.
T. (01353) 722435. (Furniture, paintings)   *097142*

Solihull (West Midlands)
Hassall, Geoffrey, 20 New Rd, Solihull.
T. (0121) 705 0068. (Furniture)   *097143*
Renaissance, 18 Marshall Lake Rd, Shirley, Solihull.
T. (0121) 745 5140. (Furniture)   *097144*

Somerton (Somerset)
Ribbons, James, Unit 7, Bancombe Rd Trading Estate, Somerton. T. (01458) 74257, 73964. (Furniture)   *097145*

South Brent (Devon)
Wootton, L.G., 2 Church St, South Brent.
T. (01364) 72553. (Clocks)   *097146*

South Molton (Devon)
Great Western Pine, 99 East St, South Molton.
T. (017695) 572689. (Furniture)   *097147*
Lace Shop, 33 East St, South Molton.
T. (017695) 573184. (Lace, embroidery)   *097148*
Mole, 32 East St, South Molton. T. (017695) 573845. (Prints, frames)   *097149*
Tredantiques, 50-50a South St, South Molton.
T. (017695) 3006. (Furniture)   *097150*

South Walsham (Norfolk)
Pratt, Leo, & Son, South Walsham. T. (0160549) 204. (Furniture)   *097151*

Southampton (Hampshire)
Parkhouse & Wyatt, 96 Above Bar, Southampton.
T. (01703) 226653. (Silver, jewellery)   *097152*
Parkhouse & Wyatt, 96 Above Bar, Southampton.
T. (01703) 226653. (Silver, jewellery)   *097153*
Swaythling Woodcrafts, 340 Burgess Rd, Swaythling, Southampton. T. (01703) 551515. (Furniture) *097154*

Southport (Merseyside)
Anderson, 14 Wesley St, Southport. T. (01704) 40024. (Watches, clocks)   *097155*
Weldon, 567 Lord St, Southport. T. (01704) 32469. (Watches, jewellery)   *097156*

Southsea (Hampshire)
Fleming, A., Clock Tower, Castle Rd, Southsea PO5 3DE.
T. (01705) 822934. (Furniture)   *097157*

Stafford (Staffordshire)
Browse, 127 Lichfield Rd, Stafford. T. (01785) 41097. (Furniture)   *097158*

Staines (Surrey)
Ivydale Joinery, Unit 18, Staines Central Trading Estate, Staines TW18 4UX. T. (01784) 463166. (Furniture)   *097159*

Stalham (Norfolk)
Stalham Antique Gallery, High St, Stalham.
T. (01692) 80636. (Furniture)   *097160*

Stamford (Lincolnshire)
George Clocks, 9 George Mews, Stamford.
T. (01780) 66068. (Clocks, barometers)   *097161*

Stansted (Essex)
Wiskin, 18 Silver St, Stansted. T. (01279) 812376. (Furniture)   *097162*

Staveley (Cumbria)
Hall, Peter, & Son, Danes Rd, Staveley LA8 9PL.
T. (01539) 821633. (Furniture)   *097163*

Steyning (West Sussex)
Fileman, David R., Squirrels, Bayards, Steyning.
T. (01903) 813229. (Chandeliers, candelabra) *097164*

Stirling (Central)
Campbell, 35 Friars St, Stirling. T. (01786) 71832. (China, furniture, jewellery)   *097165*

Stock (Essex)
Sabine Antiques, 38 High St, Stock. T. (01277) 840553. (Furniture)   *097166*

Stockbridge (Hampshire)
Mahy, Victor, Mulberry House, Stockbridge.
T. (01264) 466. (Oil Paintings)   *097167*
Mulberry House Antiques, High St, Stockbridge.
T. (01264) 810357. (Furniture)   *097168*
Strawberry Fayre, High St, Stockbridge. T. (01264) 629. (Furniture, Antiques,Churches)   *097169*

Stockport (Cheshire)
Booth, L., 137 Wellington Rd North, Stockport.
T. (0161) 431 7494. (Furniture)   *097170*
Bright Antiques, 6 Portland Grove, Stockport.
T. (0161) 442 9334. (Furniture, pottery, glass) *097171*
Highland Antiques, 65a Wellington Rd North, Stockport.
T. (0161) 476 6669, Fax 476 6669. (China, pottery, porcelain, furniture)   *097172*
Hole in the Wall Antiques, 370 Buxton Rd, Great Moor, Stockport. T. (0161) 483 6603. (Furniture)   *097173*
Strippadoor, Victoria House, Higher Bury St, Stockport SK4 1BJ. T. (0161) 477 8980, 477 6612. (Doors)   *097174*
Swift Fit, Warburtons Yard, Higher Bury St, Stockport SK4 1BJ. T. (0161) 477 0405. (Furniture)   *097175*

Stoke-on-Trent (Staffordshire)
Antiques Workshop, 43-45 Hope St, Hanley, Stoke-on-Trent. T. (01782) 273645. (Furniture)   *097176*
Old Flames Architectural Antiques, 133-139 Church St, Stoke-on-Trent. T. (01782) 744985. (Marble decoration, graining and rag work)   *097177*

Stone (Staffordshire)
Bridle, Bro-Dawel House, Kettlebrook Rd, Stone.
T. (01785) 5303. (Furniture, paintings)   *097178*

Storrington (West Sussex)
Thakeham, Orchardway Stables, Rock Rd, Storrington.
T. (01903) 745464. (Furniture)   *097179*

Stourbridge (West Midlands)
Oldswinford Gallery, 106 Hagley Rd, Oldswinford, Stourbridge. T. (01384) 395577. (Oil paintings, watercolours, prints)   *097180*

Stow-on-the-Wold (Gloucestershire)
Acorn Antiques, Sheep St, Stow-on-the-Wold.
T. (01451) 831519. (Ceramics)   *097181*
Cotswold Galleries, The Square, Stow-on-the-Wold.
T. (01451) 30586. (Paintings)   *097182*
Davies, John, Church St, Stow-on-the-Wold.
I. (01451) 31698, Fax 32477. (Oil paintings, watercolours, prints, drawings)   *097183*
Otto, Rudolph, The Little House, Sheep St, Stow-on-the-Wold. T. (01451) 30455. (Furniture)   *097184*
Otto, Rudolph, The Little House, Sheep St, Stow-on-the-Wold. T. (01451) 30455. (Furniture)   *097185*
Saint Breock Gallery, Digbeth St, Stow-on-the-Wold.
T. (01451) 30424. (Watercolours, furniture)   *097186*
Saint Breock Gallery, Digbeth St., Stow-on-the-Wold.
T. (0171) 229 4918. (Furniture)   *097187*
Samarkand Galleries, 2 Brewery Yard, Sheep St, Stow-on-the-Wold. T. (01451) 32322. (Carpets, rugs, kelims)   *097188*
Talbot Court Galleries, Talbot Court, Stow-on-the-Wold.
T. (01451) 32169. (Prints, maps, engravings) *097189*
Touchwood International, 9 Park St, Stow-on-the-Wold.
T. (01451) 30221. (Furniture)   *097190*

Stradbroke (Suffolk)
Palmer, Mary, Cottage Farm, Stradbroke.
T. (0137984) 8100. (Furniture)   *097191*

Stratford-upon-Avon (Warwickshire)
Burman, 5a Chapel St, Stratford-upon-Avon.
T. (01789) 293917, 295164. (Furniture, porcelain, silver)   *097192*
Howard, 44a Wood St, Stratford-upon-Avon.
T. (01789) 205404. (Jewellery, silver)   *097193*
La-di-da, 6c Union St, Stratford-upon-Avon.
T. (01789) 67521. (Furniture)   *097194*
Loquens, The Minories, Rother St, Stratford-upon-Avon.
T. (01789) 297706. (Oils, watercolours)   *097195*

Streatley (Berkshire)
Vine Cottage Antiques, High St, Streatley.
T. (01491) 872425. (Furniture)   *097196*

Stretton-on-Fosse (Warwickshire)
Astley House Fine Art, Old School, CV23 Stretton-on-Fosse. T. (01608) 50601, Fax Fax 51777. (Oil paintings)   *097197*

Sturminster Newton (Dorset)
Quarter Jack Antiques, Bridge St, Sturminster Newton.
T. (01258) 72558. (Glass, furniture, pictures)   *097198*
Tribe, Tom, & Son, Bridge St, Sturminster Newton.
T. (01258) 72311. (Clocks)   *097199*

Sudbury (Suffolk)
Charles, Simon, 72 Melford Rd, Sudbury.
T. (01787) 75931. (Clocks)   *097200*
Clare Hall Company, The Barns, Clare Hall, Sudbury
CO10 8PJ. T. (01787) 277510. (Furniture,
paintings)   *097201*
Clock and Barometer Studio, 100 Ballington St, Sudbury.
T. (01787) 77467. (Clocks, barometers)   *097202*
Dales, Colin, 115 Melford Rd, Sudbury.
T. (01787) 78434. (Paintings)   *097203*
Hillside Upholstery, 28 Hillside Rd, Sudbury.
T. (01787) 880489. (Furniture)   *097204*
Marney, Patrick, The Gate House, Melford Hall, Long
Melford, Sudbury. T. (01787) 880533.
(Barometers)   *097205*

Sunderland (Tyne and Wear)
Smith, Peter, 12-14 Borough Rd, Sunderland.
T. (01783) 567 3537, 567 7842. (Clocks)   *097206*

Sutton (Surrey)
Flynn, Norman, 37 Lind Rd, Sutton SM1 4PP.
T. (0181) 6619505. (Ceramics)   *097207*
Warrender S., & Co., 4-6 Cheam Rd., Sutton.
T. (0181) 643 4381. (Jewellery, silver, clocks)   *097208*

Sutton Bridge (Lincolnshire)
Old Barn Antiques Warehaoue, New Rd, Sutton Bridge.
T. (01406) 350435. (Furniture)   *097209*

Sutton Coldfield (West Midlands)
Coulborn, Thomas, & Sons, 64 Birmingham Rd, Sutton
Coldfield. T. (0121) 354 3974. (Furniture,
paintings)   *097210*
D.J. & Co., 10a-b Marston Rd, Sutton Coldfield B73.
T. (0121) 350 2861, 354 5937. (Furniture)   *097211*
Osborne, 91 Chester Rd, New Oscott, Sutton Coldfield.
T. (0121) 355 6667. (Clocks, barometers)   *097212*

Swafield (Norfolk)
Straithe Lodge Gallery, Straithe lodge, Swafield.
T. (01692) 402669. (Paintings, watercolours,
prints)   *097213*

Swanage (Dorset)
Georgian Gems, 28 High St, Swanage.
T. (01929) 424697. (Jewellery, silver)   *097214*

Swansea (West Glamorgan)
Davies, Philip, 29 Saint Helens Rd, Swansea.
T. (01792) 651446. (Paintings, frames)   *097215*
Scurlock, Kim, 25 Russell St, Swansea.
T. (01792) 643085. (Furniture)   *097216*
Timberstrip, 87-88 Saint Helens Av, Swansea.
T. (01792) 465240. (Furniture)   *097217*

Swindon (Wiltshire)
Smith, Allan, 162 Beechcroft Rd, Upper Stratton, Swindon. T. (01793) 822977. (Clocks)   *097218*

Swinton (Greater Manchester)
Casements, Slack Ln Workshops, Swinton M27 2QT.
T. (0161) 794 1610. (Furniture)   *097219*

Tain (Highland)
Logie, 11 Stafford St, Tain. T. (01862) 4148. (Paintings,
watercolours, prints)   *097220*

Teddington (Greater London)
Crisp, J.W., 166 High St, Teddington. T. (0181) 977 4309.
(Furniture)   *097221*

Teignmouth (Devon)
Old Passage, 13a Bank St, Teignmouth.
T. (01626) 772634. (Furniture)   *097222*

Tetbury (Gloucestershire)
Balmuir House Antiques, 14 Long St, Tetbury.
T. (01666) 503822. (Furniture, paintings)   *097223*
Bristow, Daniel, 54 Long St, Tetbury GL8 8AQ.
T. (01666) 503946. (violins, violas, cellos)   *097224*

Colleton House Gallery, 16 Long St, Tetbury.
T. (01666) 502048. (Watercolours)   *097225*
Gastrell House, 33 Long St, Tetbury. T. (01666) 502228.
(furniture, clocks, paintings)   *097226*
Old George Antiques and Interiors, 3 The Chipping, Tet-
bury GL8 8EU. T. (01666) 503405. (Furniture)   *097227*
Williamson & Crocker, 1 The Chiping, Tetbury.
T. (01666) 504533. (Furniture)   *097228*
Yeo Antiques, 6 Westonbirt, Tetbury GL8 5QG.
T. (01666) 88388. (Furniture, metalware, clocks, por-
celain, pottery)   *097229*

Tewkesbury (Gloucestershire)
Berkeley Antiques and Replay, 132 High St, Tewkesbury.
T. (01684) 292034. (Furniture)   *097230*
Gainsborough House Antiques, 81 Church St, Tewkesbu-
ry. T. (01684) 293072. (Furniture)   *097231*

Teynham (Kent)
Jackson-Grant, 133 London Rd, Teynham.
T. (01795) 522027. (Furniture)   *097232*

Thame (Oxfordshire)
Rosemary and Time, 42 Park St, Thame.
T. (01844) 6923. (Clocks, watches,
barometers)   *097233*

Thames Ditton (Surrey)
Gant, Elizabeth, 52 High St, Thames Ditton.
T. (0181) 398 5107. (Books)   *097234*

Thaxted (Essex)
Turpin, 4 Stoney Lane, Thaxted. T. (01371) 830495.
(Furniture)   *097235*

The Lee (Buckinghamshire)
Tooley, M.V., The Guildroom, The Lee HP16 9LZ.
T. (0124020) 463. (Clocks)   *097236*

Theale (Berkshire)
Theale Fireplaces, Mile House Farm, Bath Rd, Theale
RG7 5AH. T. Reading 302232, Fax 323344. (Antique
Fireplaces)   *097237*

Thirsk (North Yorkshire)
Kirkgate Picture Gallery, 18 Kirkgate, Thirsk.
T. (01845) 24085. (Oil paintings)   *097238*

Thorpe-le-Soken (Essex)
Beale, G.S., Rose Cottage, Argyle Rd, Thorpe-le-Soken.
T. (01255) 861483. (Furniture)   *097239*

Thurso (Highland)
Thurso Antiques, Drill Hall, Sinclair St, Thurso.
T. (01847) 63291. (Paintings, silver, jewellery)   *097240*

Tingewick (Buckinghamshire)
Tingewick Antiques Centre, Main St, Tingewick.
T. (01280) 847922. (Cooper, brass, spelter)   *097241*

Tisbury (Wiltshire)
Pearson, Carol, 4 High St, Tisbury. T. (01747) 870710.
(Ceramics, furniture)   *097242*

Titchfield (Hampshire)
Titchfield Antiques, 15 South St, Titchfield.
T. (01329) 43402. (Art nouveau, art deco, silver,
glass)   *097243*

Tiverton (Devon)
Chandler, R.A., 17 Angel Hill, Tiverton.
T. (01884) 257784. (Paintings)   *097244*

Todmorden (Lancashire)
Todmorden Fine Art, 27 Water St, Todmorden.
T. (01706) 814723. (Oil paintings,
watercolours)   *097245*

Topsham (Devon)
Vernon, Tony, 15 Follett Rd, Topsham.
T. (01392) 874635. (Furniture)   *097246*

Torquay (Devon)
Birbeck, 45 Abbey Rd, Torquay. T. (01803) 297144,
214836. (Paintings, drawings, prints)   *097247*
Cane Corner, Cockington Court, Cockington Village, Torquay. T. (01803) 605377. (Chairs)   *097248*

Pine Connection, Unit 6, Coventry Farm Estate, Newton
Rd, Torquay. T. (01803) 874184. (Furniture)   *097249*

Towcester (Northamptonshire)
Acorn Country Furniture, Old Mill, Moat Ln, Towcester
NN12 7AD. T. (01327) 52788. (Furniture)   *097250*
Clark, 215 Watling St, Towcester. T. (01327) 52957. (Oil
paintings)   *097251*
Watling Street Galleries, 116 Watling St East, Towcester.
T. (01327) 51595. (Paintings)   *097252*

Tring (Hertfordshire)
Country clocks, 3 Pendley Bridge Cottages, Tring Sta-
tion, Tring HP23 5QU. T. 5090. (Clocks)   *097253*
Farrelly, 50 High St, Tring. T. 891905. (Furniture) *097254*

Truro (Cornwall)
Pine Parlour, 1 Coronation Terrace, Truro.
T. (01872) 560919. (Furniture)   *097255*
Stanton, Peter, Old Pottery, Chapel Hill, Truro TR1 3BN.
T. (01872) 70262. (Furniture)   *097256*

Tunbridge Wells (Kent)
Clare Gallery, 21 High St, Tunbridge Wells TN1 1UT.
T. (01892) 38717, Fax 29588. (Oil Paintings, waterco-
lours, prints, frames)   *097257*
Hadlow, 1 The Pantiles, Tunbridge Wells.
T. (01892) 29858. (Clocks, watches)   *097258*
Thompson, John, 27 The Pantiles, Tunbridge Wells.
T. (01892) 547215. (Furniture)   *097259*

Twickenham (Greater London)
Phelps, 133-135 Saint Margaret's Rd, Twickenham TW1
1RG. T. (0181) 892 1778. (Furniture)   *097260*
Zafer, 36 Church St, Twickenham. T. (0181) 891 3183.
(Furniture)   *097261*

Twyford (Hampshire)
Twyford Antiques, High St, Twyford SO21 1NH.
T. (01962) 713484. (clocks, furniture)   *097262*

Uckfield (Sussex)
Barnes, 8 Church St, Uckfield. T. (01825) 762066. (Wa-
tercolours, oils)   *097263*
Bowlby, Nicholas, Owl House, Poundgate, Uckfield.
T. (01892) 653722. (Watercolours, drawings)   *097264*
Ringless Cross Antiques, Ringles Cross, Uckfield.
T. (01825) 762909. (Furniture)   *097265*

Uley (Gloucestershire)
Old Chapel Antiques, Uley GL11 5SP. T. (01453) Durs-
ley 860 656. (Antique furniture)   *097266*

Ulverston (Cumbria)
A1A Antiques, 59b Market St, Ulverston.
T. (01229) 869745. (Furniture, clocks,
pictures)   *097267*

Uppingham (Leicestershire)
Clutter, 14 Orange St, Uppingham. T. (01572) 823745.
(Furniture, brass, copper, silver)   *097268*
Garner, John, 51-53 High St, Uppingham.
T. (01572) 823607. (Pictures, furniture)   *097269*
Lapwing Antiques, 10 Orange St, Uppingham.
T. (01572) 821260. (Pottery, porcelain)   *097270*
Tattersall, 14b Orange St, Uppingham.
T. (01572) 821171. (Rush and cane work,
rugs)   *097271*

Upton-upon-Severn (Hereford and Wor-
cester)
Highway Gallery, 40 Old St, Upton-upon-Severn.
T. (01684) 592645. (Paintings)   *097272*

Uxbridge (Greater London)
Manton, F.T., 12 Windsor St, Uxbridge. T. (01895) 32812.
(Silver)   *097273*

Ventnor (Isle of Wight)
Lord, Derek R., 81 Leeson Rd, Ventnor.
T. (01983) 854749. (Weapons)   *097274*

Waddington (Lincolnshire)
Baldam, Pam, Hillyfield, Somerton Gate Lane, Waddington LN5 9RN. T. Lincoln 6 5895. (reseats chairs in rush
or cane)   *097275*

Wadebridge (Cornwall)
Victoria Antiques, 21 Molesworth St, Wadebridge.
T. (01208) 814160. (Furniture)   *097276*

Wallingford (Oxfordshire)
Lester, Anthony J., The Dower House, Hithercroft, Wallingford OX10 9ES. T. (01491) 37552, 36683. (oil
paintings)   *097277*

Wallington (Surrey)
Sainsbury, R.P., 57 Woodcote Av, Wallington SM6.
T. (0181) 773 0771. (Furniture)   *097278*

Walmer (Kent)
Deal, 116 Downs Rd, Walmer. T. (01304) 372297.
(Furniture)   *097279*

Walsall (West Midlands)
Furniture Restoration Services, 99a Bentley Ln, Walsall
WS2 8SS. T. (01922) 614523. (Furniture)   *097280*
Furniture Workshop, 47-49 Bath St, Walsall.
T. (01922) 615579. (Furniture)   *097281*

Walton-on-Thames (Surrey)
Boathouse Gallery, The Towpath, Manor Rd, Walton-on-
Thames. T. (01932) 242718. (Oil paintings, watercolours, engravings)   *097282*

Walton-on-the-Hill (Surrey)
Caldwell, Ian, 9a Tadworth Green, Dorking Rd, Walton-
on-the-Hill. T. (01823) 813968. (Furniture)   *097283*

Wantage (Oxfordshire)
Arts and Antiques, 33 Wallingford St, Wantage. T. 2676.
(Oil paintings)   *097284*

Wareham (Dorset)
Hedley, Peter, 10 South St, Wareham.
T. (01929) 551777. (Paintings)   *097285*
Heirlooms, 21 South St, Wareham. T. (01929) 554207.
(Jewellery, silver)   *097286*

Wargrave (Berkshire)
Millgreen Antiques, 86 High St, Wargrave.
T. (01734) 402955. (Furniture)   *097287*

Warley (West Midlands)
Gullheath, Heath St, Rowley Regis, Warley B65 0AT.
T. (0121) 559 2555. (Furniture)   *097288*

Warminster (Wiltshire)
Wood, Trevor, 6 Silver St, Warminster.
T. (01985) 213961. (Furniture)   *097289*

Warwick (Warwickshire)
Payne, Martin, 30 Brook St, Warwick.
T. (01926) 494948. (Silver)   *097290*
Warwick Antiques, 16-18 High St, Warwick.
T. (01926) 492482, Fax 493867. (Furniture)   *097291*
Westgate Antiques, 28 West St, Warwick.
T. (01926) 494106. (Silver, furniture)   *097292*

Watlington (Oxfordshire)
Cross Antiques, 37 High St, Watlington.
T. (0149161) 2324. (Furniture, procelain)   *097293*

Welbeck (Nottinghamshire)
Roberts, Mark, Unit 1, West Workshops, Tan Gallop,
Welbeck. T. (01909) 484270. (Paintings)   *097294*
Textile Conservation Services, 3-4 West Workshop Tan
Gallop, Welbeck. T. (01909) 481655. (Textiles)   *097295*

Wellingborough (Northamptonshire)
Perkins, Bryan, 52 Cannon St, Wellingborough.
T. (01933) 228812. (Furniture)   *097296*

Wellington (Somerset)
Lewis, Michael & Amanda, 8 North St, Wellington.
T. (01823) 667430. (Carpets, rugs)   *097297*

Wells (Somerset)
House, Bernard G., Market Pl, Wells. (Barometers,
clocks)   *097298*
Nowell, Edward A., Tor St, Wells. T. (01749) 675586.
(Furniture, silver, clocks, jewellery)   *097299*

Nowell, Marcus, 21 Market Pl, Wells. T. (01749) 78051.
(Furniture)   *097300*

Welshpool (Powys)
School House Antiques, 21 High St, Welshpool.
T. (01938) 554858. (Furniture)   *097301*

Welwyn (Hertfordshire)
Bowden, Burnham Green, Welwyn. T. 716, 265.
(Furniture)   *097302*

West Bridgford (Nottinghamshire)
Fraser, Alastair, 2a Rushworth Av, West Bridgford.
T. 821835. (Furniture)   *097303*
Moulton, 5 Portland Rd, West Bridgford. T. 814354.
(Furniture)   *097304*

West Kirby (Merseyside)
Bennett, Michael, 2a Alexandra Rd, West Kirby L48 0RT.
T. (0151) Liverpool 6257888. (Engl. furniture of the
16th-18th cent., marquetry, inlay, boulle
furniture)   *097305*

West Peckham (Kent)
Persian, Rugs, Vines Farm, Matthews Lane, West Peckham. T. 850228. (Oriental carpets)   *097306*

West Wycombe (Buckinghamshire)
Brown, Church Lane, West Wycombe HP14 3AG.
T. (01494) High 24537. (Antique Sets)   *097307*

Westbury (Wiltshire)
Booth Gallery, 30 Edenvale Rd, Westbury.
T. (01373) 826574. (Maps, prints)   *097308*

Westcliff-on-Sea (Essex)
David, Jean & John, 587 London Rd, Westcliff-on-Sea.
T. (01702) 339106, Fax 560536. (Clocks, barometers,
small furniture)   *097309*

Westcott (Surrey)
Westcott Antiques, The Studio, Parsonage Lane, West-
cott. T. (01306) 881900. (Furniture)   *097310*
Westcott Gallery, 4 Guildford Rd, Westcott.
T. (01306) 76261. (Oils, watercolours, frames)   *097311*

Westerham (Kent)
London House Antiques, 4 Market St, Westerham.
T. (01959) 64479. (Furniture)   *097312*
Sargeant, Denys, 21 The Green, Westerham.
T. (01959) 62130. (Chandeliers)   *097313*

Weston-super-Mare (Avon)
D.M. Restorations, 3 Laburnum Rd, Weston-super-Mare.
T. (01934) 631681. (Furniture)   *097314*
Merrick, 26 Boulevard, Weston-super-Mare BS23 1NF.
T. (01934) 620846. (Paintings)   *097315*

Wetherby (West Yorkshire)
Tomlinson, Raymond, Northfield Bldgs, Northfield Pl,
Wetherby. T. (01937) 64866. (Furniture)   *097316*

Weybridge (Surrey)
Caenshill, 271 Brooklands Rd, Weybridge KT13 0RB.
T. (01932) 849432. (Furniture)   *097317*
Clock Shop Weybridge, 64 Church St, Weybridge.
T. (01932) 840407, 855503. (Clocks)   *097318*
Cross, Edward, 128 Oatlands Dr, Weybridge.
T. (01932) 851093. (Watercolours, oil
paintings)   *097319*
Hatch, 49 Church St, Weybridge. T. (01932) 846782.
(Furniture, clocks)   *097320*
Not Just Silver, 16 York Rd, Weybridge.
T. (01932) 842468. (Replating, metalwork, glass,
procelain)   *097321*
Saunders, R., 71 Queen's Rd, Weybridge.
T. (01932) 842503. (Furniture)   *097322*
Weybridge Antiques, 244 Brooklands Rd, Weybridge.
T. (01932) 852503. (Furniture)   *097323*

Weymouth (Dorset)
Strippers, 17 Chickerell Rd, Weymouth.
T. (01305) 783732. (Furniture)   *097324*

Whaley Bridge (Derbyshire)
Nimbus, 5 Lower Macclesfield Rd, Whaley Bridge.
T. (01663) 734248. (Furniture)   *097325*

Wheathampstead (Hertfordshire)
Collins, F.G., & C., Corner House, Wheathampstead.
T. 3111. (Furniture)   *097326*

Whitby (North Yorkshire)
Bobbins, Wesley Hall, Church St, Whitby.
T. (01947) 600585. (Oil lamps)   *097327*
Caedmon House, 14 Station Sq, Whitby.
T. (01947) 602120. (Furniture, porcelain)   *097328*

White Colne (Essex)
Fox and Pheasant Antique Pine, White Colne.
T. (01787) 223297. (Furniture)   *097329*

Whitefield (Lancashire)
Donn, Henry, 138-142 Bury New Rd, Whitefield.
T. 766 8819. (Pictures)   *097330*

Whitstable (Kent)
Laurens, 17 Harbour St, Whitstable. T. (01227) 261940.
(Cabinet work)   *097331*

Whitwell (Hertfordshire)
Boosey, Simon, Tun House, Whitwell. T. (01438) 871563.
(Carpets)   *097332*

Wigan (Lancashire)
Polished with Pride, Unit 3, Peppermill, Darlington Rd,
Wigan. T. (01942) 820795. (Furniture)   *097333*

Willerby (North Yorkshire)
Glenway, 20 Palmer Av, Willerby. T. (01482) 654195.
(Furniture)   *097334*

Williton (Somerset)
Venn, Edward, 52 Long St, Williton. T. (01984) 32631.
(Furniture, barometers, clocks)   *097335*

Wilmslow (Cheshire)
Bosson, Peter, 10b Swan St, Wilmslow.
T. (01625) 525250. (Clocks)   *097336*
Stott, F.V., 12c Kennerleys Ln, Wilmslow SK9 5EQ.
T. (01625) 527437. (Furniture)   *097337*

Wilton (Wiltshire)
Pearson, Carol, 14 West St, Wilton. T. (01722) 742451.
(Ceramics, furniture)   *097338*

Wimborne Minster (Dorset)
Brights, 61-63 Leigh Rd, Wimborne Minster.
T. (01202) 884613. (Furniture, clocks,
paintings)   *097339*
Hicklenton & Phillips, 19 Colborne Av, Wimborne Minster
BH21 2PZ. T. (01202) 88 2040. (Jewellery and
Silver)   *097340*
J.B. Antiques, 10a West Row, Wimborne Minster.
T. (01202) 882522. (Metalware)   *097341*

Wincanton (Somerset)
Sainsbury, Barry M., 17 High St, Wincanton.
T. (01963) 32289. (Furniture)   *097342*

Winchcombe (Gloucestershire)
Kenulf Fine Arts, 5 North St, Winchcombe.
T. (01242) 602776, 603204. (Oil paintings, watercolours, period framing)   *097343*
Spinks, 16 Stancombe View, Winchcombe GL54 5PS.
T. (01242) 60 3391. (Period chimney pieces, overman-
tels, carved wood work, plaster mouldings, cornice,
architrave)   *097344*

Winchester (Hampshire)
Bell, 67b Parchment St, Winchester. T. (01962) 860439.
(Oil paintings, watercolours)   *097345*
Gallery Antiques, Saint Thomas St, Winchester.
T. (01962) 865039, Fax 867019. (Furniture)   *097346*
Gilbert, H.M., 19 The Square, Winchester.
T. (01962) 852832. (Books)   *097347*
Marsh, Gerald E., 32a The Square, Winchester SO23
9EX. T. (01962) 844443. (Clocks)   *097348*

Printed Page, 2-3 Bridge St, Winchester.
T. (01962) 854072, Fax 862995. (Prints, oil paintings, watercolours) *097349*

Skipwith, W.G., 5 Parchment St, Winchester.
T. (01962) 852911. (Oil paintings, watercolours, prints) *097350*

Todd & Austin, 2 Andover Rd, Winchester.
T. (01962) 869824. (Clocks) *097351*

Webb, 6-8 Romsey Rd, Winchester. T. (01962) 842273.
(Oil paintings) *097352*

Windsor (Berkshire)

Collectors Treasures, 8-9 Church St, Windsor.
T. (01753) 60157. (Furniture) *097353*

Parterre, 28 Beaumont Rd, Windsor. T. (01753) 851548.
(Mansonry, lead, wrought iron) *097354*

Wisbech (Cambridgeshire)

Wilding, R., Lanes End, Gadds Ln, Wisbech.
T. (01945) 588204. (Furniture) *097355*

Witney (Oxfordshire)

Country Pine Antiques, 14a West End, Witney.
T. (01993) 778584. (Furniture) *097356*

Witney Antiques, 96-98 Corn St, Witney OX8 7BU.
T. (01993) 703902, 703887, Fax Fax 779852.
(Furniture) *097357*

Wiveliscombe (Somerset)

Carousel Pig, 19 High St, Wiveliscombe.
T. (01984) 23097. (China) *097358*

Heads n' Trails, 41 Church St, Wiveliscombe.
T. (01984) 23097. (Taxidermy) *097359*

Woburn (Bedfordshire)

Butterworths, 14 Bedford St, Woburn.
T. (01525) 290545. (Furniture) *097360*

Ford, G.W., & Son, Shop 25, Woburn Abbey Antiques Centre, Woburn Abbey, Woburn MK43 0TP.
(Furniture) *097361*

Woburn Fine Arts, 12 Market Pl, Woburn.
T. (01525) 290624. (Oil paintings, watercolours) *097362*

Woking (Surrey)

Chattel, 156 High St, Woking. T. (01483) 771310.
(Clocks, furniture) *097363*

Manor Antiques, 2 The New Shops, Woking.
T. (01483) 724666. (Furniture) *097364*

Wokingham (Berkshire)

Thomas, Paul, 27 Glebelands Rd, Wokingham.
T. (01734) 794671. (Pictures) *097365*

Wolverhampton (West Midlands)

Broad Street Gallery, 16 Broad St, Wolverhampton.
T. (01902) 24977. (Prints, watercolours, oils) *097366*

Newbridge Antiques, 281a Tettenhall Rd, Wolverhampton. T. (01902) 746242. (Furniture) *097367*

Wonersh (Surrey)

Odell, Millmead, Wonersh GU5 0QL. T. (01483) Guildford 89 2375. (Roman, Greek, Egyptian and other antiquities, icons) *097368*

Woodbridge (Suffolk)

Carter, Simon, 23 Market Hill, Woodbridge IP12 4LX.
T. (01394) 382242. (Paintings, watercolours, furniture) *097369*

Hurst, Anthony, 13 Church St, Woodbridge.
T. (01394) 2500. (Furniture) *097370*

Manson, Edward, 8 Market Hill, Woodbridge.
T. (01394) 380235. (Clocks) *097371*

Voss, Anthony Gordon, 24 Market Hill, Woodbridge.
T. (01394) 385830. (Furniture) *097372*

Woodstock (Oxfordshire)

Fox House, 30-32 Oxford St, Woodstock.
T. (01993) 811377. (Silver, furniture) *097373*

Wooler (Northumberland)

Border Sporting Gallery, 25 High St, Wooler.
T. (01668) 81872. (Oils, prints) *097374*

Wootton Bassett (Wiltshire)

Manley, Neil, 1 Clarendon Dr, Wootton Bassett SN4 8BT.
T. (0179370) 848074. (Copper and brass) *097375*

Worcester (Hereford and Worcester)

Antiques and Interiors, 41 Upper Tything, Worcester.
T. (01905) 29014. (Furniture) *097376*

Barn Antiques, Paynes Heath Farm, Martley Rd, Lower Broadheath, Worcester. T. (01905) 355997. (Clocks, furniture) *097377*

Meriden House Antiques, 41 Upper Tything, Worcester.
T. (01905) 29014. (Furniture) *097378*

Robinson, Keith, 49 Upper Tything, Worcester.
T. (01905) 25357. (Furniture) *097379*

Tolley, T.M., 26 College St, Worcester WR1 2LS.
T. (01905) 26632. (Oriental Art) *097380*

W.H.E.A.P. Antiques, 17 Bromyard Rd, Worcester.
T. (01905) 427796. (Furniture) *097381*

Worcester Antiques Centre, Reindeer Court, Mealcheapen St, Worcester. T. (01905) 610680, 610681, Fax 610681. (Furniture, porcelain) *097382*

Wortham (Suffolk)

Falcon Gallery, Honeypot Farm, Wortham.
T. (01379) 312. (Oils, watercolours) *097383*

Worthing (West Sussex)

Q.D. Metalcraft, 98 Dominion Rd, Worthing.
T. (01903) 207715. (Metalware) *097384*

Willard, Paul, 29 Goring Rd, Worthing.
T. (01903) 244053. (Furniture) *097385*

Wilson, 57-59 Broadwater Rd, Worthing.
T. (01903) 202059. (Furniture) *097386*

Wotton-under-Edge (Gloucestershire)

Bell Passage Antiques, 36-38 High St, Wickwar, Wotton-under-Edge. T. (01454) 294251. (Furniture, glass, watercolours, prints, oil paintings) *097387*

Wraysbury (Berkshire)

Wyrardisbury, 23 High St, Wraysbury. T. (01784) 3225.
(Clocks) *097388*

Wrexham (Clwyd)

Smith, 2 New Rd, Rhosddu, Wrexham.
(Furniture) *097389*

Wymeswold (Leicestershire)

Bryan-Peach, N., 28 Far St, Wymeswold.
T. (01509) 880425. (Clocks, furniture) *097390*

Yarmouth (Isle of Wight)

Gallery, High St, Yarmouth. T. (01983) 760784. (Oil, watercolours, prints) *097391*

Yeovil (Somerset)

Hamblin, John, Unit 3, 15 Oxford Rd, Yeovil.
T. (01935) 71154. (Furniture) *097392*

York (North Yorkshire)

Aitken, 120 The Mount, York. T. (01904) 656211.
(Furniture) *097393*

Clocks and Gramophones, 11 Walmgate, York.
T. (01904) 611924. (Clocks, gramophones) *097394*

Minster Gate Bookshop, 8 Minster Gate, York.
T. (01904) 621812. (Books) *097395*

Stonegate Fine Arts, 47 Stonegate, York.
T. (01904) 643771. (Pictures) *097396*

U.S.A.

Aldie (Virginia)

MacDowell, Robert & Karin, Oakwood, Aldie, VA 22001.
T. (703) 777-6644. (Fine Arts Conservators, Ceramics, Dolls) *097397*

Altamont (New York)

Frinta, Mojmir S., 150 Maple Ave., Altamont, NY 12009.
T. (518) 861-6942. (Paintings & Sculpture) *097398*

Atlas (Michigan)

Reid, Maurice E., 8470 Perry Rd., Atlas, MI 48411.
T. (313) 636-2240. (Furniture) *097399*

Atwater (Ohio)

The Antique Nook, 6226 Waterloo St., Atwater POB 338, OH 44201. (Scientific Instruments, Clocks) *097400*

Audubon (Pennsylvania)

The Conservation Studio, POB 7128, Audubon, PA 19407. T. (215) 489-7140. *097401*

Austin (Texas)

Country Store Gallery, Inc., 1304 Lavaca St., Austin, TX 78701. T. (512) GR 6-1663, GR 6-2019.
(Paintings) *097402*

Baltimore (Maryland)

London Shop, 1500-1502 Bolton St., Baltimore, MD 21217. T. (301) 523-3330. (Paintings, Glass, China) *097403*

Packard, Elisabeth C.G., c/o Walters Art Gallery, 600 N Charles St., Baltimore, MD 21201. (Antiques, Paintings) *097404*

Bayside (New York)

Workman, Ron, 209-33 26th Ave, Bayside, NY 11360.
T. (718) 279-1551. *097405*

Beverly Hills (California)

Szymanski, 9510 Wilshire Blvd., Beverly Hills, CA 90212. T. (213) 276-0507. (Paintings) *097406*

Birmingham (Michigan)

Little Gallery, 915 E Maple St., Birmingham, MI 48011.
T. (313) 644-5566. (Paintings) *097407*

Boonville (New York)

Fynmore Studios, 101 Post St., Boonville, NY 13309.
T. (315) 942-2825. (Paintings, Antiques) *097408*

Boston (Massachusetts)

Ainsworth, 42 Bromfield St, Boston, MA 02108.
T. (617) 542-7195. (Graphics) *097409*

Childs, 169 Newbury St, Boston, MA 02116.
T. (617) 266-1108, Fax (617) 266-2381. (Paintings, Graphics, Sculptures, Drawings) *097410*

Fenway, 50 Gloucester St, Boston, MA 02115.
T. (617) 536-0127. (Paintings) *097411*

Haley & Steele, 91 Newbury St., Boston, MA 02116.
(Paintings) *097412*

Vose, Robert C., 238 Newbury St., Boston, MA 02116.
T. (617) 536-6176. (Paintings) *097413*

Brooklyn (New York)

Rosenstiel, Helene von, 382 11 St., Brooklyn, NY 11215.
T. (718) 788-7909. (Garments, textiles) *097414*

Buffalo (New York)

Comfort, 1310 Broadway, Buffalo, NY 14212.
T. (716) 892-0600. (Furniture) *097415*

D'Arcangelo, L., 1740 Main St., Buffalo, NY 14208.
T. (716) 885-1146. (Paintings) *097416*

Tillou, Dana E., 417 Franklin St., Buffalo, NY 14202.
T. (716) 854-5285. (Paintings) *097417*

Carolina (Rhode Island)

Scudder, James E., Rte. 112, Carolina, RI 02812.
T. (401) 364-7228. (Furniture) *097418*

Chicago (Illinois)

Creative Arts Gallery, 6107 W. Addison St., Chicago, IL 60634. T. (312) 685-0203. (Paintings) *097419*

Lee, Armand & Co., 350 W. Erie St., Chicago, IL 60610.
T. (312) 787-3830. (Paintings) *097420*

Waller Art Shop, 5300 S. Blackstone Ave. Hyde Park, Chicago, IL 60615. T. (312) 363-7446.
(Paintings) *097421*

Cleveland (Ohio)

Fay's Art Galleries, 2869 Drummond Rd., Cleveland, OH 44120. T. (216) 751-2706. (Paintings) *097422*

Colorado Springs (Colorado)
Hibbitt, 720 N Nevada Av., Colorado Springs, CO 80902.
T. (303) 473-0464. (Paintings)   097423

Columbia (South Carolina)
McCarthy, Robert C., 2008 Shadowood Ct., Columbia,
SC 29210. T. (803) 781-5674. (Furniture)   097424

Dallas (Texas)
Shuttles, 9431 Paramount St., Dallas, TX 75217. (Paintings, Frames)   097425

Dania (Florida)
Arthur's Antiques, 51 N. Federal Hwy, Dania, FL 33004.
(Antiques)   097426

Dayton (Ohio)
King, John M., 215 Kenwood Ave., Dayton, OH 45405.
(Paintings)   097427
Raffel, Alvin, 6720 Mad River Rd., Dayton, OH 45459.
T. (513) 433-3071. (Paintings)   097428

Deansboro (New York)
Sanders, Arthur H., South Main St., Deansboro, NY
13328. T. (315) 841-8774. (Music boxes)   097429

Fayetteville (New York)
Drake Gallery, 304 E. Genesee St., Fayetteville, NY
13066. T. (315) NE 7-6442. (Paintings)   097430

Fort Worth (Texas)
Dow Frame Shop, 3330 Camp Bowle Blvd., Fort Worth,
TX 76107. (Paintings)   097431

Framingham (Massachusetts)
Schiff, Lonny, Framingham POB 2156, MA 01701.
(paintings)   097432

Glencoe (Illinois)
It's about Time, 375 Park Ave., Glencoe, IL 60022.
T. (312) 8352012. (Clocks)   097433

Jacksonville (Florida)
Lamp Post Antiques, 3955 Riverside Ave, Jacksonville,
FL 32205. (Lamps)   097434

Kansas City (Missouri)
Allen's Antique Shop, 8102 Evanston Av., Kansas City,
MO 64138. (Antiques)   097435
Scott's Custom Picture Framing, 1015 E. 75th St., Kansas City, MO 64131. T. (816) 333-6459.
(Paintings)   097436

Long Island City (New York)
Oxford Antique Restorers, Ltd., 37 b. 20 48th Ave., Long
Island City, NY 11100. T. (212) 355-7620.
(Antiques)   097437

Los Angeles (California)
Goldfield, 8380 Melrose Av, Los Angeles, CA 90069.
T. (213) 651-1122. (Paintings)   097438
Marks Studio, 12209 Wilshire Blvd., Los Angeles, CA
90025. (Paintings)   097439

Los Gatos (California)
Montgomery Antiques, 140 W. Main St. and 262 E. Main
St., Los Gatos, CA 95030. (Antiques)   097440

Lowell (Massachusetts)
Kostoulakos, Peter, 15 Sayles St., Lowell, MA 01851.
T. (617) 453-8888. (Paintings)   097441

Mercerville (New Jersey)
Johnson Atelier, 60 Ward Av Extension, Mercerville, NJ
08619. T. (609) 890-7777, Fax (609) 890-
1816.   097442

Miami (Florida)
Windsor Arts, 6736 NE 4th Av, Miami, FL 33138.
(Paintings)   097443

Middletown (Connecticut)
Wasicki Art Center, 681 Saybrook Rd, Middletown, CT
06457. T. (203) 347-0140. (Paintings, Sculpture,
Frames)   097444

Milwaukee (Wisconsin)
Kondos, Peter J., E Wisconsin Av at N Water First Saving
Bldg. 2nd Fl., Milwaukee, WI 53202. T. (414) 271-
8000. (Paintings)   097445

Minneapolis (Minnesota)
Erickson's Interiors, 2735 Nicollet Av, Minneapolis, MN
55408. T. (612) 827-2911. (Furniture)   097446

New Boston (Michigan)
Escher, 19224 Craig, New Boston, MI 48164.
T. (313) 753-4112. (Clocks)   097447

New Orleans (Louisiana)
Downtown Gallery, 420 Julia St., New Orleans, LA
70130. T. (504) 522-5308. (Paintings)   097448

New York
Alexander's Sculptural Service, 117 E. 39th St., New
York, NY 10016. T. (212) 867-8866. (Ceramics,
Metals)   097449
American-Swiss Watch Hospital, 42 University Pl., New
York, NY 10003. (Clocks)   097450
Antique Furniture Workroom, 225 E 24 St., New York, NY
10010. T. (212) 683-0551. (Furniture)   097451
Bartfield, J.N., 30 W 57 St, New York, NY 10019.
T. (212) 245-8890. (Paintings)   097452
Bulfair, John, 252 E. 77th St., New York, NY 10021.
T. (212) 288-9540. (Paintings)   097453
Findlay, Wally, 17 E 57 St, New York, NY 10022.
T. (212) 411-5390. (Paintings)   097454
Fulton, 799 Lexington Av, New York, NY 10021.
T. (212) 832-8854. (Paintings)   097455
Gracie, Charles R., & Sons, 979 3rd Ave., New York, NY
10022. T. (212) 213-5350. (Screens, Wallpaper, Furniture, Paintings, Porcelain, All Oriental)   097456
Heydenryk, 417 E 76 St., New York, NY 10021.
T. (212) 249-4903. (Frames)   097457
Korany, Edward O., 227 E. 57th St., New York, NY
10022. (Paintings)   097458
Lexington Art Gallery, 154 E 64 St, New York, NY 10021.
T. (212) 888-4400. (Paintings)   097459
Lindemann, Grete, 333 E 83 St., New York, NY 10028.
T. (212) 737-5626. (Paintings, Sculpture)   097460
Lowengard, Sarah, 1080 Park Av. 5W, New York, NY
10128. T. (212) 860-2386. (Textile
Conservation)   097461
Lowy, 28 West End Av., New York, NY 10023.
(Frames)   097462
Montaperto, Angelo L., 131 Varick St, New York, NY
10013. T. (212) 255-8626. (Furniture)   097463
Morse, Michael, 334 E 59 St., New York, NY 10022.
T. (212) 593-1812. (Paintings)   097464
Oestreicher„s, 43 W. 46th, New York, NY 10036.
T. (212) 757-1190. (Paintings)   097465
Papp, Florian, 962 Madison Av., New York, NY 10021.
T. (212) 288-6770. (Antiques, furniture, china,
lamps)   097466
Rios, Eli C., 515 W 29 St, New York, NY 10001.
T. (212) 643-0388.   097467
Rosselli, John, 255 E 72 St., New York, NY 10021. (Furniture, Paintings, Prints, Sculpture)   097468
Rothschild, Sigmund, 27 W 67 St., New York, NY 10023.
T. (212) 873-5522. (Furniture, Paintings, Prints,
Sculptures)   097469
Sack, Israel, 15 E 57 St., New York, NY 10022.
T. (212) 753-6562. (Furniture)   097470
Scott, John C., 519 W 26 St., New York, NY 10001.
T. (212) 714-0620, Fax 714-0149. (Sculptures)   097471
Signorelli, Gloria, 1100 Madison Av., Apt. 8-K, New York,
NY 10028. T. (212) 288-4683. (Paintings)   097472
Thompson, 20 Cornelia St., New York, NY 10014.
T. (212) 243-5610. (Paintings)   097473

Norfolk (Virginia)
Monticello, 227 W. York St., Norfolk, VA 23510.
(Antiques)   097474

Oceanside (New York)
Crescent Plating Co, Inc., 101 Bayfield Blvd, Oceanside,
NY 11572. (Antiques, Silver)   097475

Palm Beach (Florida)
Findlay, Wally, Galleries, 175 Worth Av, Palm Beach, FL
33480. T. (407) 655-2090. (Paintings)   097476

Philadelphia (Pennsylvania)
Capuzzi, 1820 Ludlow St, Philadelphia, PA 19100.
T. (215) 564-4994. (Paintings)   097477
Eberhardt, Harry A. & Son, 2010 Walnut St, Philadelphia,
PA 19103. T. (215) 568-4144. (Porcelain)   097478
Fiorillo, Michael, 1120 Pine St (19107), Philadelphia, PA
19100. (Paintings)   097479
Gorski, 6377 Germantown Av, Philadelphia, PA 19144.
T. (215) 848-1577. (Paintings)   097480
Newman, 1625 Walnut St, Philadelphia, PA 19103.
T. (215) 563-1779. (Paintings)   097481
Shatalow, Vladimir, 2104 Poplar St, Philadelphia, PA
19130. (Paintings)   097482

Pittsburgh (Pennsylvania)
Mass, Alex E., 116 Maruth Dr, Pittsburgh, PA 15237.
T. (412) 364-3458. (Paintings)   097483
McNeish, Ronald F., 5424 Walnut St, Pittsburgh, PA
15232. T. (412) 361-6666. (Goldsmith,
Silversmith)   097484

Portland (Maine)
Bailey, F.O. Co, 141 Middle St, Portland, ME 04111.
T. (207) 774-1479. (Antiques)   097485

Rochester (New York)
Nova Finishing, 1922 South Av., Rochester, NY 14620.
(Furniture)   097486

Saint Louis (Missouri)
Master Slide, 118 E Lockwood Av, Saint Louis, MO
63119. T. (314) 961-4463. (Photo)   097487

San Diego (California)
Orr, 2222 Fourth Av, San Diego, CA 92101. T. (619) 234-
4765. (Paintings)   097488

San Francisco (California)
Campero's, 350 Florida St, San Francisco, CA 94110.
I. (415) 863-7793.   097489
Cow Hollow Woodworks, 3100 Steiner St, San Francisco, CA 94123. T. (415) 929-0218.   097490
Lengfeld, K.H. Inc., 1409 Sutter St, San Francisco, CA
94109. T. (415) 775-3040. (Antiques,
Furniture)   097491
Lesser, E., 2158 41st Av, San Francisco, CA 94116.
T. (415) 885-5903. (Paintings)   097492

Santa Monica (California)
Cherkas, Constantine, 310 15th St., Santa Monica, CA
90402. T. (213) 395-7036. (Paintings)   097493

Santa Rosa (California)
Venerable Classics, 645 Fourth St, Santa Rosa, CA
95404. T. (707) 531-2891. (Porcelain, crystal, jade,
ivory, marble)   097494

Schenectady (New York)
Skype's Gallery, 140 N Broadwy, Schenectady, NY
12305. T. (518) 372-1870. (Antiques,
Furniture)   097495

Southold (New York)
The Jellett Studio, Glenn Rd, Southold, NY 11971.
T. (516) 765-5481. (Antiques, Glass, Porcelain)   097496

Springfield (Missouri)
Robertson, Philip, 1055 South Glenstone Av., Springfield,
MO 65804. T. (417) 8698262. (Paintings,
Frames)   097497

Syracuse (New York)
Paglia Furniture Refinishing, 826 N Townsend St, Syracuse, NY 13208. T. (315) 471-1469.
(Furniture)   097498
Worfel, J. Sons, 934 Oak St., Syracuse, NY 13208.
T. (315) 479-6431. (Furniture)   097499

Uniondale (New York)
Roman Arts, Inc., 904 Nassau Rd, Uniondale, NY 11553.
(Antiques)   097500

Washington (District of Columbia)

Allen, 710 Seventh St NW, Washington, DC 20001.
T. (202) 628-1389. (Paintings)   *097501*

Corcoran Gallery of Art, Dept. of Restoration, 17 St, Washington, DC 20006. T. (202) 638-3211.
(Paintings)   *097502*

International Artifacts and Repair Shop, 2830 Georgia Av NW, Washington, DC 20001. T. (202) 387-3333. ((Paintings, Sculptures, Textiles))   *097503*

Keshishian, Mark, & Sons, 6930 Wisconsin Av. NW, Washington, DC 20015. (Carpets, Rugs)   *097504*

Mickelson, 707 NW G St, Washington, DC 20001.
T. (202) 628-1735. (Paintings)   *097505*

Saint Luke's Gallery, 1715 Q St NW, Washington, DC 20009. T. (202) 328-2424. (Paintings, Works on Paper))   *097506*

Williamstown (Massachusetts)

Williamstown Regional Art Conservation Laboratory, 225 South St, Williamstown, MA 01267. T. (413) 458-5741. (Parchment, bio-degraded art works on paper and parchment)   *097507*

ALLGEMEINES KÜNSTLERLEXIKON
Die Bildenden Künstler aller Zeiten und Völker

(General dictionary of artists. Artists of the world throughout all ages)

Edited by K.G. Saur Publishers. Founded and co-edited by Günter Meißner
1991ff. c. 78 volumes. c. 700 pages per volume. Half leather-bound with dust cover.
DM 398.00 per volume
ISBN 3-598-22740-X

◆ A total of nearly 500,000 artist entries with c. 7,000 articles per volume

◆ Precise biographical and bibliographical information on representatives of the fine arts

◆ No comparable work exists whose information on artists throughout the world and
from every age is as extensive, up-to-date, and authoritative as that in the **Allgemeines Künstlerlexikon**

◆ For further information, please send for our brochure, our 32-page sample booklet
or a volume on approval.

K•G•Saur Verlag
Postfach 701620 · D-81316 München · Tel. (089) 7 69 02-232 · Fax (089) 7 69 02-150/250
E-mail: 100730.1341@compuserve.com

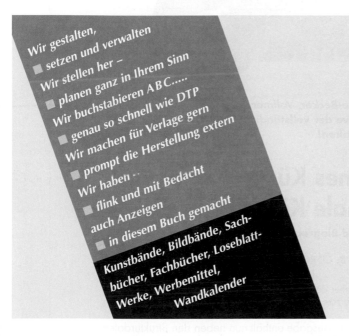

Das Register zum *Thieme-Becker, Vollmer* und zum *Allgemeinen Künstlerlexikon* – jetzt inklusive der vollständigen Lexikonartikel aus dem *Allgemeinen Künstlerlexikon!*

Allgemeines Künstlerlexikon – Internationale Künstlerdatenbank

AKL – World Biographical Dictionary of Artists

3. CD-ROM-Ausgabe 1996
DM 2.400,–*
(DM 498,–* für Bezieher der Buchausgabe *Allgemeines Künstlerlexikon*)
(DM 796,–* für Bezieher der *IKD II*)

Die dritte erheblich erweiterte Ausgabe enthält nun neben den Strukturdaten aus den 37 Bänden des *Thieme-Becker* und den 6 Bänden des *Vollmer* die Strukturdaten und die **vollständigen Texteinträge** aus den ersten 12 Bänden des *Allgemeinen Künstlerlexikons.*
Maler, Graphiker, Bildhauer, Architekten – die Vertreter der bildenden Künste aller Kulturräume der Erde von der Antike bis zur Gegenwart können hier nach den verschiedensten Kriterien gesucht und ihre biographischen Daten abgerufen werden.

* unverbindliche Preisempfehlung

Bitte fordern Sie einen ausführlichen Prospekt bei uns an!

K • G • Saur Verlag
Postfach 701620 · D-81316 München · Tel. (089) 7 69 02-0
Fax (089) 7 69 02-150 · E-mail: 100730.1341@compuserve.com

Argentina

Buenos Aires
Editorial Contempora S.R.L., Sarmiento 643, Buenos Aires, 1382. *097508*
Hachatte S. A., Rivadavia 739/43, Buenos Aires.
T. (01) 34 84 81/5. *097509*

Australia

Kareela (New South Wales)
Australian Art Sales, 11 Tradewinds Pl., Kareela, 2232.
T. (02) 528 47 07. *097510*

Melbourne (Victoria)
Australian Video Magazine, 257 Coventry St., Melbourne, Vic. 3205. T. (03) 69994247. - Mul - *097511*
Oxford University Press, 7 Bowen Crescent, Melbourne, Vic. 3004. - ArtBk - *097512*
Thames & Hudson, 86 Stanley St., Melbourne, WA 3003.
T. (03) 3298454. *097513*

Mulgrave (Victoria)
Images Publishing Group, 6 Barstow Pl., 3170 Mulgrave, 3170. T. (03) 561 55 44, Fax 561 48 60. *097514*

Netley
Griffin Press Pty. Ltd., 262 Marion Rd., 5152 Netley.
T. 53 22 71. - ArtBk / Graph / Repr / Card / Card / Sli / Cal - *097515*

Sydney (New South Wales)
Boronia, 768 Military Rd., Mosman, Sydney, NSW 2088.
T. (02) 969 2100. *097516*
Edwards & Shaw, Pty. Ltd., 171 Sussex St., Sydney, NSW 2000. *097517*
Gallery A., 21 Gipps St., Paddington, Sydney, NSW 2021.
- Graph - *097518*
Legend Press, 479 Pacific Hwy., Artarmon, Sydney, NSW 2064. - ArtBk / Repr - *097519*
Oswald-Sealy, 251 Clarence St., Sydney, NSW 2000.
T. (02) 29 65 61. - Graph / Repr / Card / Sli / Cal / Mul - *097520*

Austria

Baden bei Wien
Grasl, Gottfried, Wassergasse 1, 2500 Baden bei Wien.
T. (02252) 70 20 10. - ArtBk / Graph - *097521*

Dornbirn (Vorarlberg)
Sedlmayr, Hugo, Schulgasse 20, 6850 Dornbirn. *097522*

Graz (Steiermark)
Akademische Druck- und Verlagsanstalt, ADEVA, Auersperggasse 12, 8010 Graz. T. (0316) 364433, Fax 364424. - ArtBk - *097523*
Drosch, Maximilian, Bischofpl 1, 8010 Graz.
T. (0316) 831857, Fax 34071. - ArtBk - *097524*
Galerie & Edition Artelier, Eisengasse 3, 8020 Graz.
T. (0316) 585036, Fax 58503650. *097525*
Stocker, Leopold, Hofgasse 5, 8011 Graz.
T. (0316) 821636, Fax 835612. - ArtBk / Cal - *097526*
Verlag für Sammler, St. Peter Hauptstr 35e, Postfach 54, 8042 Graz. T. (0316) 472230, Fax 673987.
- ArtBk - *097527*

Hall (Tirol)
Stockhammer, Stadtgraben 16, 6060 Hall.
T. (05223) 57378, Fax 57378. - Card / Sli - *097528*

Höchst (Vorarlberg)
Seeverlag, H. Schneider, Dr.-Schneider-Str 94, Postfach 72, 6973 Höchst. T. (05578) 75217, Fax (05578) 75217. - Card - *097529*

Horn (Niederösterreich)
Thurnhof, Wiener Str. 2, 3580 Horn.
T. (02982) 3333. *097530*

ADEVA Der weltgrößte Faksimile-Verlag

und Hersteller originalgetreu reproduzierter bibliophiler Editionen. – Bildbände zur Kunst Europas, Asiens und Amerikas.

AKADEMISCHE DRUCK- u. VERLAGSANSTALT
A 8011 Graz / Austria POB 598

Innsbruck (Tirol)
Forum für Aktuelle Kunst, Adolf-Pichler-Pl. 8, 6020 Innsbruck. T. (0512) 22 21 55. *097531*
Tyrolia Verlagsanstalt GmbH, M.-Theresienstr. 15, 6020 Innsbruck. T. (0512) 59611/630, Fax 58 20 50. *097532*

Klagenfurt (Kärnten)
Carinthia Verlag, Völkermarkter Ring 25, 9020 Klagenfurt. T. (0463) 5880210, Fax 5880214.
- ArtBk - *097533*
Ritter Klagenfurt, Hermann-Gmeiner-Str, 9020 Klagenfurt. T. (0463) 36800, Fax 3680017. - ArtBk / Graph / Repr / Mul - *097534*

Krems an der Donau (Niederösterreich)
Galerie Rabe, Wachtbergstr. 42, 3500 Krems an der Donau. T. (02732) 82980. - ArtBk / Graph / Repr - *097535*

Lustenau (Vorarlberg)
Neufeld Verlag & Galerie, Schillerstr. 7, 6890 Lustenau.
T. (05577) 84657, Fax 84657-20. - ArtBk / Graph / Repr / Card / Sli / Cal / Mul - *097536*

Maria Enzersdorf (Niederösterreich)
Edition art actuell, Wienerbrückstr. 104, 2344 Maria Enzersdorf. *097537*
Severin Presse, Urlaubskreuzstr 34/3, 2346 Maria Enzersdorf. T. (02236) 811744. - Graph - *097538*

Mödling (Niederösterreich)
Weiss, H., Dr-Rieger-Str 10, 2340 Mödling.
T. (02236) 44672, Fax 23086. - Graph - *097539*

Reutte (Tirol)
Milz, Franz, Lindenstr 14, 6600 Reutte. T. (05672) 2831, Fax 5174. *097540*

Salzburg
Cosy Kunstverlag, Münchner Bundesstr. 152/156, 5020 Salzburg. *097541*
Edition Noema, Lessingstr. 2, 5021 Salzburg.
T. (0662) 87 97 84, Fax 87 97 89. *097542*
Galerie Weihergut, Linzerg 25, 5020 Salzburg.
T. (0662) 879119, Fax 879119. - Graph - *097543*
Graphische Werkstatt im Traklhaus, Waagplatz 1a, 5020 Salzburg. T. (0662) 84 65 19. - Graph - *097544*
Jordis & Sohn, Salzburger Handdrucke, Pausingerstr. 6, 5020 Salzburg. *097545*
Müller, Otto, Ernest-Thun-Str 11, 5021 Salzburg.
T. (0662) 8819740, Fax 872387. - ArtBk / Card - *097546*
Residenz Verlag, Gaisbergstr 6, 5020 Salzburg.
T. (0662) 641986, Fax 643548. - ArtBk / Cal - *097547*
Sankt Peter, Postfach 113, 5010 Salzburg. *097548*
Welz, Sigmund-Haffner-Gasse 16, Postfach 123, 5010 Salzburg. T. (0662) 841771-0, Fax 84177120. - ArtBk / Repr / Card / Cal - *097549*

Schärding (Oberösterreich)
Heindl, Josef, Linzertor 2-3, 4780 Schärding.
T. (07712) 3035, Fax 4708. - ArtBk / Graph - *097550*

Siegendorf
NN-fabrik, GZO Fabriksgelände 17, 7011 Siegendorf. *097551*

Telfs (Tirol)
Hörtenbergverlag, Postfach 25, 6410 Telfs.
T. (05262) 27 12. *097552*

Wels (Oberösterreich)
Nöttling & Fasser, Anzengruberstr. 6-10, 4600 Wels.
T. (07242) 69 67. - Graph / Repr - *097553*

Wien
Amalthea-Verlag, Am Heumarkt 19, 1030 Wien.
T. (0222) 712 35 60, Fax 7138995. - ArtBk - *097554*
Ars Hungarica, Heumühlgasse 12, 1040 Wien.
T. (0222) 56 14 58. *097555*
Ars Nova, Panikengasse 41/11-15, 1160 Wien.
T. (0222) 4923726, Fax 4923726. - Sli - *097556*
Artaria, Kohlmarkt 9, 1010 Wien. T. (0222) 533 09 36.
- Graph - *097557*
Basic, Luka, Gaullachergasse 15, 1160 Wien.
T. (0222) 408 39 74, Fax 4088127. - Graph / Repr / Card - *097558*
Böhlau, Sachsenpl 4-6, 1201 Wien. T. (0222) 3302427-0, Fax (0222) 3302432. - ArtBk - *097559*
Brandstätter, Christian, Wickenburggasse 26, 1080 Wien. T. (0222) 4083814/15, Fax 408 72 00. - ArtBk / Card - *097560*
Bukum Verlag, Pulverturmgasse 7, 1090 Wien.
T. (0222) 34 16 58. - ArtBk - *097561*
Chobot, Manfred & Dagmar, Domgasse 6, 1010 Wien.
T. (0222) 5125332, Fax 512 20 38. - Graph - *097562*
Eberle, Seilergasse 12, 1010 Wien. *097563*
Editio Totius Mundi, Gussenbauergasse 5-9, 1090 Wien.
T. (0222) 34 73 46. - Graph - *097564*
Edition Das fröhliche Wohnzimmer, Fuhrmannsgasse 1a, 1080 Wien. T. (0222) 408 01 40. - Graph / ArtP - *097565*
Edition Freibord, Postfach 281, 1181 Wien.
T. (0222) 4083178. *097566*
Edition Graphischer Zirkel, Lange Gasse 14/44, 1080 Wien. T. (02773) 46615. - ArtBk / Graph / Card - *097567*
Edition Tusch, Wilhelminenstr 80, 1160 Wien.
T. (0222) 4855334, Fax (0222) 4860287. - ArtBk / Graph - *097568*
Falter-Verlag, Marc-Aurel-Str. 9, 1010 Wien.
T. (0222) 533 46 37, Fax 533 46 37 12.
- ArtBk - *097569*
Fesch Buchdienst, Dannebergplatz 11, 1030 Wien. *097570*
Flutlicht, Harmonieg 2, 1090 Wien. T. (0222) 3197375, Fax 3197374. *097571*
Fuchs, Heinrich, Dr., Thimiggasse 82, 1180 Wien.
- ArtBk - *097572*
Herbstpresse, Arndtstr. 87, 1120 Wien. *097573*
Hilger Verlag, Dorotheergasse 5, 1010 Wien.
T. (0222) 512 53 15, Fax 513 91 26. - ArtBk - *097574*
Irsa Verlag, Rüdengasse 6, 1030 Wien.
T. (0222) 713 01 36, Fax 713 01 30. - ArtBk / ArtP - *097575*
Knoll, Hans, Esterházygasse 29, 1060 Wien.
T. (0222) 587 50 52, Fax 587 59 66. - ArtBk / Graph / Card / Mul - *097576*
Krieg, Walter, Kärntner Str 4, 3. Stock, 1010 Wien.
T. (0222) 5121093, Fax 5123266. *097577*
Krinzinger, Seilerstätte 16, 1010 Wien.
T. (0222) 5133006, Fax 513300633. *097578*
Löcker Verlag, Annagasse 3a, 1010 Wien.
T. (0222) 512 02 82, Fax 512 02 82 22.
- ArtBk - *097579*
Luka Basic Edition, Gaullachergasse 15, 1160 Wien.
T. (0222) 408 39 74. - Graph / Card / Cal - *097580*
Medusa Verlag, Leberstr. 122, 1110 Wien.
T. (0222) 74 15 95-0, Fax 74 15 95-183.
- ArtBk - *097581*

Minimal Edition, Kohlgasse 11, 1050 Wien.
T. (0222) 545 28 31, Fax 55 06 25. - ArtBk / Graph /
Repr / Card / Sli / Mul - *097582*
Modulverlag, Mahlerstr 3, 1010 Wien.
T. (0222) 512 98 92, Fax 512 98 93. - ArtBk - *097583*
Mündel, Ferry, Blumauergasse 9, 1020 Wien.
T. (0222) 214 74 34. - Graph - *097584*
Neuwirth, Waltraud, Dr., Weinzingergasse 10/18, 1190
Wien. T. (0222) 32 73 23. - ArtBk - *097585*
Österreichischer Bundesverlag, Schwarzenbergstr. 5,
1015 Wien. T. (0222) 51405, Fax 51405-210.
- ArtBk - *097586*
Österreichischer Kunst- und Kulturverlag, Freundg 11,
1040 Wien, POB 17, 1016 Wien. T. (0222) 5878551,
Fax 5878552. - ArtBk / Card / Cal - *097587*
Parnass Verlag, Porzellangasse 43/19, 1090 Wien.
T. (0222) 3195375, Fax 3108272. - ArtBk - *097588*
Reisser, M. & D., Braunschweigg 12, 1130 Wien.
T. (0222) 87754870, Fax 87754875. - Repr /
Card - *097589*
Schaufler, Karin, Löwengasse 51, 1030 Wien.
T. (0222) 947 29 52. - ArtBk - *097590*
Schroll, Anton, Spengergasse 39, 1051 Wien.
T. (0222) 555641, Fax (0222) 55564166. - ArtBk /
Graph - *097591*
Sonderzahl Verlag, Grosse Neugasse 35, 1040 Wien.
T. (0222) 5868070, Fax 58680704. - ArtBk - *097592*
Tromayer, Erich, Dorotheerg 7, 1010 Wien.
T. (0222) 5131075, Fax 5138107. - Graph /
Repr - *097593*
Verlag Der Apfel, Schottenfeldgasse 51, 1070
Wien. *097594*
Werkstattpresse, Maria-Treu-Gasse 6, 1080 Wien.
T. (0222) 408 29 60. - ArtBk / Graph - *097595*
Wolfrum, Augustinerstr 10, 1010 Wien.
T. (0222) 51253980, Fax 5121557. - ArtBk / Graph /
Repr / Card / Cal - *097596*

Belgium

Antwerpen
Mercatorfonds, Meir 85, 2000 Antwerpen.
T. (03) 231 38 40. - ArtBk - *097597*
Morguen V.Z.W., Waalse Kaai 22, 2000 Antwerpen.
T. (03) 248 08 45, 226 52 77. - ArtBk - *097598*
Velde van de, Ronny, Ijzerenpoortkaai 3, 2000 Antwer-
pen. T. (03) 2163047, Fax (03) 2372516.
- ArtBk - *097599*

Berchem (Antwerpen)
Schraenen, G., Uitbreidingsstr. 552, 2600 Berchem.
T. (03) 235 85 96. - ArtBk - *097600*

Bruxelles
Artis-Historia, 1 Rue Carli, 1140 Bruxelles.
T. (02) 242 23 20, Fax 242 18 18. *097601*
Atelier 340, 340 Drève de Rivieren, 1090 Bruxelles.
T. (02) 424 24 12. *097602*
Centre International de Recherches Primitifs Flamands,
1 Parc du Cinquantenaire, 1000 Bruxelles.
T. (02) 739 68 66. *097603*
Collections Livres, 26 Rue du Collège, 1050 Bruxelles.
T. (02) 512 85 29, Fax 512 85 29. *097604*
Cosmos, 23 rue de la Vallée, 1050 Bruxelles.
T. (02) 648 80 23. *097605*
Daled, 200 Av de Messidor, 1180 Bruxelles.
T. (02) 344 02 20. *097606*
Editions Arto, 85 Av Winston Churchill, 1180 Bruxelles.
T. (02) 3459583. - ArtBk - *097607*
Editions Camomille, 30 Rue Vilain XIV, 1050 Bruxelles.
T. (02) 649 23 68, Fax 731 90 09. *097608*
Editions de Lassa, 26 Rue Vilain XIV, 1050 Bruxelles.
T. (02) 648 38 07, Fax 648 39 33. *097609*
Editions G. Blanchart, 15 Av Ernest Masoin, 1090 Bru-
xelles. T. (02) 478 37 06, Fax 478 64 29. *097610*
Eiffel Editions, 7 Rue Charles Hanssens, 1000 Bruxelles.
T. (02) 513 55 10, Fax 512 13 65. *097611*
Europalia International, Biennial of Culture and the Arts,
Palais des Beaux-Arts, 10 Rue Royale, 1000 Bruxelles.
T. (02) 5078550, Fax (02) 5135488. *097612*
Fondation André Hallet, 1 Rue Pierre Theunis, Boite 80,
1030 Bruxelles. T. (02) 242 56 33. - ArtBk - *097613*

Fondation Egyptologique Reine Elisabeth, 10 Parc du
Cinquantenaire, 1000 Bruxelles. T. (02) 733 96 10.
- ArtBk - *097614*
Fondations Hergé, 162 Av. Louise, Bte. 7, 1050 Bruxel-
les. T. (02) 647 51 90, Fax 640 41 20. - Graph - *097615*
Galerie 2016, 5 Av. G. Macau, 1050 Bruxelles.
T. (02) 647 11 36. - ArtBk / Graph - *097616*
Institut Royal du Patrimoine Artistique/Koninklijk Insti-
tuut voor het Kunstpatrimonium, 1, Parc du Cinquante-
naire, 1000 Bruxelles. T. (02) 7354160.
- Card - *097617*
Institut Supérieur pour l'Etude du Langage Plastique –
I.S.E.L.P., 31 Blvd de Waterloo, 1000 Bruxelles.
T. (02) 5135662, Fax (02) 5024526. - ArtBk - *097618*
La Renaissance du Livre, 203 Av. Louise, Bte 9, 1050
Bruxelles. T. (02) 627 35 11, Fax 627 36 50.
- ArtBk - *097619*
Larousse Belgique, 25-27 Rue Godefroid Kurth, 1140
Bruxelles. T. (02) 242 77 00, Fax 242 78 69. *097620*
Lebeer Hossmann, 124 Av. de Boetendael, 1180 Bruxel-
les. T. (02) 345 95 66. - ArtBk / Graph / Mul - *097621*
Loock, A. van, 51 Rue Saint-Jean, 1000 Bruxelles.
T. (02) 512 74 65. *097622*
Meddens, 141-145 Av. de Scheut, 1070 Bruxelles.
- Graph - *097623*
Mont des Arts, 72 Coudenberg, 1000 Bruxelles.
T. (02) 25 13 57 44. - ArtBk - *097624*
Post-Scriptum, 37 Rue des Eperonniers, 1000 Bruxelles.
T. (02) 511 96 43. - ArtBk - *097625*
Sisley, 27-29 Rue St.-Jean, 1000 Bruxelles.
T. (02) 511 40 36, 511 46 69. - ArtBk / Repr - *097626*
Synthèse, 24 Rue E Allard, 1000 Bruxelles.
T. (02) 514 40 55. *097627*
Vander-Chine Editions, 321 Av des Volontaires, Bte 28,
1150 Bruxelles. T. (02) 762 98 04,
Fax 762 06 62. *097628*

Deurne (Antwerpen)
Bakelants, Ivo, Manebruggestr. 247, 2100 Deurne.
T. (03) 321 09 81. - ArtBk - *097629*

Gent (Oost-Vlaanderen)
Imschoot, Burggravenlaan 20, 9000 Gent.
T. (09) 2225508, 2225518, Fax 2225507. - ArtBk /
Repr - *097630*

Knokke (West-Vlaanderen)
Berko, Kustlaan 163, 8300 Knokke.
T. (050) 60 57 90. *097631*

La Louvière (Hainaut)
Daily-Bul, 29 Eue Daily-Bul, 7100 La Louvière.
T. (064) 22 29 73. *097632*

Leuven (Vlaams Brabant)
Peeters, Bondgenotenlaan 153, 3000 Leuven.
T. (016) 235170, Fax 481486. *097633*

Liège
Lizène, Jacques, 349 Rue Basse-Wez, 4020 Liège.
T. (04) 3433101. - ArtBk / Graph / Repr / Card - *097634*

Louvain-La-Neuve (Brabant)
Duculot, 65 Av de Lauzelle, 1348 Louvain-La-Neuve.
T. (010) 47 19 11, Fax 47 19 25. *097635*
Editions d'Archéologie et d'Histoire de l'Art de L'UCL, 1
Pl. Blaise Pascal, 1348 Louvain-la-Neuve.
T. (010) 47 48 80. - Graph - *097636*

Malle
Sikkel, de, Nijverheidsstr 8, 2390 Malle.
T. (03) 312 47 61. *097637*

Mouscron (Hainaut)
Vanbraekel, A., 230 Coquinie, 7700 Mouscron.
T. (056) 33 64 85. - Card / Cal - *097638*

Ougrée
Varlez, Robert, 36 Rue des Ramons, 4102 Ougrée.
T. (041) 36 37 22. - ArtBk - *097639*

Overijse (Vlaams Brabant)
Editions König, Justus Lipsiusplein 11, 3090 Overijse.
T. (02) 6877700. *097640*

Schelderode
Kunstforum, Meersstr1, 9820 Schelderode.
T. (091) 62 59 58. *097641*

Tielt (West-Vlaanderen)
Lannoo, Kasteelstr. 97, 8700 Tielt. T. (051) 424211,
Fax 401152. - ArtBk - *097642*

Tournai (Hainaut)
Casterman, 28 Rue des Soeurs Noirs, 7500 Tournai.
T. (069) 25 42 11, Fax 25 42 29. *097643*

Turnhout (Antwerpen)
Brepols, 8 Rue Baron Frans du Four, 2300 Turnhout.
T. (014) 41 54 63, Fax 42 89 19. *097644*

Zandhoven
Groep Interecho, Hof van Lyere, Hofeinde 2, 2240 Zandhoven. T. (03) 484 55 11. *097645*

Bolivia

Cochabamba
Amigos del Libro, Av. las Heroinas 3712, 450 Cocha-
bamba. T. (042) 229 20. - ArtBk / ArtBk - *097646*

Brazil

Rio de Janeiro
Artes Graficas Industrias Reunidas S. A., Rua dos Inváli-
dos 198, 20000 Rio de Janeiro, CEP 20231.
T. (021) 252 04 10, 221 64 24. - ArtBk - *097647*
Bloch, Praia do Russel, 814, 20000 Rio de Janeiro.
- ArtBk / Graph / Repr / Card / Sli / Cal / Mul - *097648*
Livraria Agir Editora, Rua México 98 B, 20000 Rio de Ja-
neiro. T. (021) 240-1978. - ArtBk - *097649*

São Paulo
Editora Abril, Avda. O. A. Lima, 800, São Paulo, 01390.
- ArtBk / Repr - *097650*
Editora Cultrix Ltda., Rua Dr. Mario Vicente 374 Ipiranga,
São Paulo. T. (011) 63 31 41. - ArtBk - *097651*

Bulgaria

Sofia
Bulgarski Houdozhnik, 1 Rue Assene Zlatarov, 1504 So-
fia. T. 89 31 97, 87 66 57, Fax 46 72 85. - ArtBk /
Graph / Repr - *097652*
Darjavno izdatelstvo Nauka i izkustvo, bul. Ruski 6,
1000 Sofia. T. 87 57 01. - ArtBk / ArtBk - *097653*
Editions Bulgarski Houdojnik, 6 place Slaveikov, 1000
Sofia. T. 89 77 46, Fax 88 47 49. *097654*
Izdatelstvo na Balgarskata akademija na naukite, ul.
Akademik Georgi Bontchev blok 6, 1113 Sofia.
T. 72 09 22. - ArtBk - *097655*

Canada

Halifax (Nova Scotia)
Nova Scotia College of Art and Design Press, 5163 Duke
St, Halifax, N.S. B3J 3J6. T. (902) 422-7381.
- ArtBk - *097656*

Markham (Ontario)
Fairmount, 120 Duffield Dr, Markham, Ont. L6G 1B5.
T. (905) 475-0988, Fax (905) 475-1072.
- ArtBk - *097657*

Montréal (Québec)
Beauchemin, 281 Av Av Jean Bévaud, Montréal, Que'1.
H7T 2L2. T. (514) 334-5912, Fax (514) 688-6269.
- ArtBk / Sli - *097658*
Graff, 963 Rue Rachel Est, Montreal.
T. (514) 526 26 16. *097659*
Gravure, 489 Rue Saint-Joseph Est, Montréal, Qué. H2J
2J4. T. (514) 526-2616. *097660*

Toronto (Ontario)
Art Metropole, 788 King St W, Toronto, Ont. M5V 1N6.
T. (416) 367-2304, Fax (416) 365-9205.
- ArtBk -   097661
Coach House Press, 401 Hurton St, Toronto.
T. (416) 979-7374.   097662
Little, Brown & Co., 146 Davenport Rd, Toronto, Ont.
M5R 1J1. T. (416) 967-3888, Fax (416) 967-4591.
- ArtBk -   097663
Madison Press Books, 40 Madison Av, Toronto, Ont.
M5R 2S1. T. (416) 923-5027, Fax (416) 923-9708.
- ArtBk -   097664
McClelland & Stewart, 481 University Av, Toronto, Ont.
M4G 2E9. T. (416) 598-1114, Fax (416) 598-7764.
- ArtBk -   097665
Open Studio, 520 King St West, Toronto, Ont. M5V 1L7.
T. (416) 368-8238.   097666
University of Toronto Press, 700-10 Saint Mary St, To-
ronto, Ont. M4Y 2W8. T. (416) 978-6817,
Fax (416) 978-4738. - ArtBk -   097667

Vancouver (British Columbia)
Talon, 201-1019 E Cordova, Vancouver. T. (604) 253-
5261, Fax (604) 255-5755.   097668

Chile

Santiago
Ediciones Gráficas Escuela de Arte, El Comendador
1926, Santiago. T. 232 58 13.   097669
Editorial Andres Bello, Ricardo Lyon 946, Santiago.
T. 223 45 65.   097670
Editorial Universitaria S. A., San Francisco 454, Santia-
go. T. 39 34 61.   097671

China, People's Republic

Beijing
The People's Fine Arts, 32 Baizhongbu Hutong, Beijing.
T. (10) 5722367.   097672

China, Republic

Taipei
Art Book Co., 18 Lane, 283 Roosevelt Rd., Sec. 3, Tai-
pei. T. (02) 362 05 78, 362 97 69,
Fax 362 35 94.   097673
Artist Publishing, Chung Ching S. Rd., 6Fl. N. 147, Sec.
1, Taipei. T. (02) 371 96 92, Fax 331 70 96.   097674
Wen-kai, 493 Fu-hsing N Rd., Taipei, 112.   097675

Colombia

Bogotá
Arte dos Grafico, Cra. 14, 75-35, Bogotá. T. 212 87 81,
Fax 211 93 58. - ArtBk / Graph / Repr -   097676
Herder Editorial y Liberia Ltda., Apdo. Aereo 6855, Bo-
gotá. T. 42 27 06. - ArtBk -   097677
Liberia Buchholz, Avda. Jiménez de Quesada 8-40,
Bogotá.   097678

Croatia

Rijeka
Otokar, Keršovani, Korzo narodne revolucije 24, 51000
Rijeka. - ArtBk -   097679

Zagreb
Grafički zavod Hrvatske, Frankopanska 26, 10000 Za-
greb. T. (01) 41 86 00. - ArtBk -   097680
Mladost, Ilica 28-30 P.O.B. 1028, 10000 Zagreb.
T. (01) 43 32 22, Fax 43 48 78. - ArtBk -   097681
Skolska knjiga, Masarykova 28, 10000 Zagreb.
T. (01) 42 91 11. - ArtBk -   097682

Svevčilišna Naklada Liber, Savska Cesta 16, 10000 Zagreb. T. (01) 44 78 16. - ArtBk -   097683

Czech Republic

Praha
ARTIA, Ve Smečkách 30, Praha. T. (02) 24 60 41.
- ArtBk -   097684
Nakladatelstvi Československých výtvarných umělců,
Mikulandska 10, Praha.   097685
Odeon, Národní tř 36, 115 87 Praha. T. (02) 26 01 68,
236 68 85. - ArtBk / Repr -   097686
Orbis, Vinohradská tr. 46, Praha.   097687
Panton, Říční 12, 118 39 Praha. T. (02) 53 81 51-5.
- ArtBk -   097688
Supraphon, Palackého 1, Praha. T. (02) 26 81 41-
9.   097689

Denmark

Allerød
Grønlund, Svanevang 4, 3450 Allerød. T. 42 27 60 99,
Fax 42 27 54 21. - ArtBk / Card / Sli -   097690

Brøndby
Storm Pedersen, Henn., Vibeholmsallée 8, 2605 Brønd-
by. T. 45 88 73.   097691

Farum
a2-grafik, Paltholmterr. 46f, 3520 Farum. T. 42 95 50 16.
- Repr -   097692
Original Graphic Studio, Paltholmterrasserne 46f, 3520
Farum. T. 42 95 50 16. - Graph -   097693
Rimfaxe Esben, Paltholmterrasserne 46F, 3520 Farum.
T. 42 95 50 16. - Graph -   097694

Glostrup
Storm, Vibeholms Allé 8, 2600 Glostrup. T. 45 88 73.
- Repr / Card -   097695

Hellerup
Olsen, I. Chr., AN Hansensallé 38, 2900 Hellerup.
T. 62 66 33.   097696

København
Amager Kunst Forlag, Svinget 17, 1000 København.
T. 54 61 82.   097697
Augustinus Forlag, Amaliegade 47, 1256 København.
T. 125 221.   097698
Billeder, G. & C., P. Bangsv. 47, 1000 København.
T. 34 47 99.   097699
Dansk Grafisk Kunstforlaget, Gammel Strand 44, 1202
København K. T. 15 83 01. - Graph -   097700
Edition Siljan, Siljangade 1-3, 2300 København S.
T. 57 40 40.   097701
Hexagon, Mikkel Bryggers Gade 10, 1003 København K.
T. 13 53 11. - ArtBk / Graph / Repr / Cal -   097702
Kunstkredsen for Grafik og Skulptur, Gammel Strand 44,
1202 København K. T. 15 83 01. - Graph / Repr /
Sli -   097703
Nyt Nordisk Forlag, Kobmagergade 49, 1150 København
K. T. 33 11 11 03, Fax 33 93 44 90. - ArtBk -   097704
Olsen, Rudolf, Sturlasgade 14, 1000 København.
T. 57 64 73.   097705
Rapp, M.C., Hesseløg. 3, 1000 København.
T. 20 05 11.   097706
Reitzel, C. A., Nørregade 20, 1165 København.
T. 12 24 00.   097707
Scannex Art, Købmagerg. 50, 1004 København K.
T. 33 14 76 80. - Graph / Repr / Card -   097708
Skandinavisk Kunstforlag, Hesseløg. 3, 1000 København.
havn. T. 20 05 11.   097709
Sommersko, Kronprinsensgade 6, 1114 København
K.   097710
U. M. Grafik Editions, Nørrebrog. 20, 2200 København N.
T. 31 37 05 61. - Graph -   097711
Wilking & Landsbo, Njalsg. 17, 2300 København S.
T. 54 67 33.   097712

Lyngby
Stok-Art, Kaerparken 6, 2800 Lyngby. T. 87 60 07.
- ArtBk / Graph / Cal -   097713

Odense
Galleri & Edition Torso, Vintapperstr. 57, 5000 Odense C.
T. 6613 4466, 6594 2495. - ArtBk / Graph -   097714
Odense Universitetsforlag, 55, Campusvej, 5230
Odense. T. 66157999, Fax 66158126.   097715

Ringkjøbing
Editon After Hand, Oster No, 6950 Ringkjøbing. - ArtBk /
Graph / Mul / ArtP -   097716

Skørping
Forlaget Cordelia, Hellum Byvej 9, 9520 Skørping.
T. 98 39 81 39, Fax 98 39 80 19. - ArtBk /
Graph -   097717
Heede & Moestrup, Hellum Byvej 9, 9520 Skørping.
T. 98398139, Fax 98398019. - ArtBk / Graph -   097718

Tølløse
Stok-Art Danmark, Stengårdsvej 25, 4340 Tølløse.
T. 48 69 69.   097719

Valby
Borgens Forlag, Valbygaardsvej 33, 2500 Valby.
T. 31 46 21 00, Fax 36 44 14 88.   097720

Egypt

Cairo
Dar al Maaref, Corniche el Nil 1119, Cairo.   097721
Institut Français d'Archéulugle Orientale, 37 Rue El-
Cheik Aly Youssef, Cairo. T. (2) 55 71 42.   097722

Finland

Espoo (Uudenmaan lääni)
Amer, Ahertajantie 5, 02100 Espoo. - ArtBk / Repr /
Cal -   097723

Helsinki (Uudenmaan lääni)
Kirjapaja, Pohjoiskaari 15, 00200 Helsinki.
T. (09) 692 25 91, Fax 67 44 17. - ArtBk -   097724
Kustannus Oy Taide Art Publishers, Kasarmikatu 23 A,
00130 Helsinki. T. (09) 62 64 59. - ArtBk -   097725
Schildts, Holger, Nylandsgatan 17B, 00120 Helsinki.
T. (09) 60 48 92.   097726
Söderström, Werner, Bulevardi 12, 00 121 Helsinki.
T. (09) 61 681. - ArtBk / Repr -   097727

France

Aix-en-Provence (Bouches-du-Rhône)
Art de Voir, 39 Rue Garnet, 13100 Aix-en-
Provence.   097728
Editions Edisud, RN 7, La Calade, 13090 Aix-en-Proven-
ce. T. 0442216144, Fax 0442215620. - ArtBk - 097729

Antibes (Alpes-Maritimes)
Editions Henry, 884 Chemin-de-Rabiac-Estagnol, 06600
Antibes. T. 0493742286. - Repr -   097730

Arcueil (Val-de-Marne)
Anthèse, 30 Av Jean-Jaurès, 94117 Arcueil Cedex.
T. 0146560667, Fax 0149850992. - ArtBk -   097731

Arles (Bouches-du-Rhône)
Actes Sud, Le Méjan, 43-47 Rue Docteur-Fanton, 13200
Arles. T. 0490498691, Fax 0490964974.
- ArtBk -   097732

Bagnolet (Seine-Saint-Denis)
Critiques Livres Distribution, 56 Rue Malmaison, 93172
Bagnolet Cedex. T. 0143603910, Fax 0148973706.
- ArtBk -   097733

Beaumes-de-Venise (Vaucluse)
Atelier des Grames, Gigondas, 84190 Beaumes-de-Ve-
nise. T. 0490658205. - ArtBk / Graph -   097734

Bièvres (Essonne)
Moulin de Vauboyen, Porte de Châtillon, 91570 Bièvres.
T. 0169410121.   *097735*

Bordeaux (Gironde)
Féret & Fils, 9 Rue Grassi, 33000 Bordeaux.
T. 0556481781, Fax 0556481863.   *097736*

Briare (Loiret)
Chimères, Château de Beau-Chêne, 45250 Briare.
T. 0238296121, Fax 0238296291. - ArtBk -   *097737*

Carnac (Morbihan)
Grassin, Jean, Pl Port-en-Dro, 56342 Carnac.
T. 0297529363, Fax 0297528390. - ArtBk /
Graph -   *097738*

Champigny-sur-Marne (Val-de-Marne)
Editions Lito-Jesco, 41 Rue Verdun, BP 363, 94503
Champigny-sur-Marne Cedex. T. 0145161700,
Fax 0148820085.   *097739*

Clermont-Ferrand (Puy-de-Dôme)
Instant Durable, 5 Rue Treille, 63007 Clermont-Ferrand
Cedex. T. 0473920789, Fax 0473911387. - ArtBk /
Graph -   *097740*

Combeaufontaine (Haute-Saône)
Porro, René, Fedry, 70120 Combeaufontaine.
T. 0384920018, Fax 0384920930. - ArtBk - *097741*

Coupvray (Seine-et-Marne)
Colibri Edition Service, 8 Rue Eglise, 77700 Coupvray.
T. 0160040059, Fax 0160040059.   *097742*

Courbevoie (Hauts-de-Seine)
Art Création et Réalisation (ACR), 20ter Rue Bezons,
1192 Tour-les-Poissons, 92400 Courbevoie.
T. 0147881492, Fax 0143333881. - ArtBk /
Repr -   *097743*

Dijon (Côte-d'Or)
Editions Faton, 25 Rue Berbisey, BP 669, 21017 Dijon
Cedex. T. 0380404100, Fax 0380301537.
- ArtBk -   *097744*

Dourdan (Essonne)
Vial, Henri, 8 Rue Moines, 91410 Dourdan.
T. 0164597048, Fax 0164595296. - ArtBk - *097745*

Drémil-Lafage (Haute-Garonne)
Briand, Daniel, Panayrac, 31280 Drémil-Lafage.
T. 0561839578, Fax 0561839790. - ArtBk - *097746*

Echiré (Deux-Sèvres)
Aubisse, Gérard, Logis de Beaulieu, 79410 Echiré.
T. 0549257199. - ArtBk -   *097747*

Epinal (Vosges)
Imagerie Pellerin, 42bis Quai Dognoville, 88000 Epinal.
T. 0329822189. - ArtBk / Graph / Card -   *097748*

Fontenay-le-Comte (Vendée)
Société Historique de Radio, 1 Pl Puits-Lavaud, 85200
Fontenay-le-Comte. T. 0450695085. - ArtBk - *097749*

Grenoble (Isère)
Glénat, 6 Rue Lieutenant-Chanaron, BP 177, 38008 Gre-
noble Cedex. T. 0476887575, Fax 0476887570.
- Graph -   *097750*

Issy-les-Moulineaux (Hauts-de-Seine)
Vents d'Ouest, 31-33 Rue Ernest-Renan, 92130 Issy-
les-Moulineaux. T. 0141461146, Fax 0140930558.
- ArtBk -   *097751*

La Bouilladisse (Bouches-du-Rhône)
Garçon, Jean-Michel, Plan de la Bourine, 13720 La
Bouilladisse. T. 0491333465, Fax 0491852793.
- ArtBk -   *097752*

Laval (Moselle)
Siloé, 22 Rue Jeu-de-Paume, 53000 Laval Cedex.
T. 0243671717, Fax 0243535601. - ArtBk - *097753*

Le Mans (Sarthe)
Arbre aux Papiers, BP 121, 72003 Le Mans Cedex.
T. 0243853120, Fax 0243852741. - Repr /
Mul -   *097754*

Le Mesnil-Esnard (Seine-Maritime)
Dabek, Yolande, 17-19 Rue Perrets, 76240 Le Mesnil-
Esnard. T. 0235798308. - ArtBk -   *097755*

Lentillères (Ardèche)
Galerie La Serre, La Serre, 07200 Lentillères.
T. 0475355114, Fax 0475350153. - ArtBk - *097756*

Levallois-Perret (Hauts-de-Seine)
Editions EFFA, 75bis Rue Rivay, 92300 Levallois-Perret.
T. 0142709602. - Graph -   *097757*

Libourne (Gironde)
Arts Graphiques d'Aquitaine, 94 Rue Président-Carnot,
BP 169, 33501 Libourne Cedex.
T. 0557514346.   *097758*

Lichtenberg (Bas-Rhin)
Lettrimages, 24 Vieux Chemin, 67340 Lichtenberg.
T. 0388899177, Fax 0388899178. - ArtBk - *097759*

Limoges (Haute-Vienne)
Reliure d'Art du Centre, 39 Rue Henri-Giffard, 87050 Li-
moges. T. 0555372690, Fax 0555383887.
- ArtBk -   *097760*

Limours (Essonne)
Studio X, La Benerie, 91470 Limours. T. 0164911090,
Fax 0164912327. - ArtBk -   *097761*

Lorient (Morbihan)
Art Média, 1 Rue Corenton-Le-Floch, 56100 Lorient.
T. 0297374666, Fax 0297833013. - ArtBk - *097762*

Luzarches (Val-d'Oise)
Morcrette, Daniel, 4 Av Joffre, 95270 Luzarches.
T. 0134710158. - ArtBk -   *097763*

Lyon (Rhône)

Chomarat, Michel, 160 Rue Vendôme, 69003 Lyon.
T. 0478628859. - ArtBk - *097764*
Ulysse Diffusion, 101 Quai Pierre-Scice, 69005 Lyon.
T. 0478306660, Fax 0478278071. - ArtBk - *097765*

Maisons-Alfort (Val-de-Marne)

Arts Graphiques, c/o Martine Bouveret, 15 Rue Masséna, 94700 Maisons-Alfort. T. 0148994471. *097766*

Malakoff (Hauts-de-Seine)

Lanore, J. & H. Laurens, 131 Rue Paul-Vaillant-Couturier, 92240 Malakoff. T. 0146542707,
Fax 0146542193. - ArtBk - *097767*

Marseille (Bouches-du-Rhône)

Art-Transit, 11-19 Blvd Boisson, 13004 Marseille.
T. 0491854278, Fax 0491851347. *097768*
Editions Méditerranéennes du Prado, Le Magellan, 352
Av Prado, 13008 Marseille. T. 0491774730,
Fax 0491711430. - ArtBk - *097769*
Galerie d'Art La Poutre, 206 Rue Paradis, 13006 Mar-
seille. T. 0491371093. - ArtBk / Graph / Repr /
Mul - *097770*
Tacussel, Paul, 191 Blvd Baille, 13005 Marseille.
T. 0491477206, Fax 0491420344. - ArtBk /
Graph - *097771*

Maubec (Vaucluse)

Eme, André, Le Devens, 84660 Maubec.
T. 0239683455. - ArtBk - *097772*

Meudon (Hauts-de-Seine)

Editions du CNRS, 1 Pl Aristide-Briand, 92195 Meudon
Cedex. T. 0145075050, Fax 0145075900. *097773*

Millemont (Yvelines)

Editions Moundarren, 3 Chemin Bois, 78940 Millemont.
T. 0134864950. - ArtBk - *097774*

Montreuil (Seine-Saint-Denis)

Argraphie, 56 Rue Paris, 93100 Montreuil.
T. 0148577849, Fax 0148574645. - ArtBk /
Graph - *097775*

Montrouge (Hauts-de-Seine)

Maeght Editeur, 12 Rue Carvès, 92120 Montrouge.
T. 0145484515, Fax 0142222283. *097776*

Mulhouse (Haut-Rhin)

A.M.C., 7 Rue Alfred Engel, 68100 Mulhouse.
T. 0389456395. - ArtBk - *097777*

Nancy (Meurthe-et-Moselle)

Berger-Levrault, 10 Rue Glacis, 54000 Nancy.
T. 0383356144. - ArtBk - *097778*

Nérac (Lot-et-Garonne)

Vers les Arts, 79 Av Georges-Clemenceau, 47600 Nérac.
T. 0553653613, Fax 0553659164. - ArtBk - *097779*

Neuilly-sur-Seine (Hauts-de-Seine)

Compagnie Française des Arts Graphiques, 129-131 Av
Achille-Peretti, 92200 Neuilly-sur-Seine.
- ArtBk - *097780*

Nice (Alpes-Maritimes)

Culture Sud, c/o Myriam Orbau, 44 Av Marne, Résidence
Cimiez-le-Haut, 06100 Nice. T. 0493530982.
- ArtBk - *097781*
Editions Bélisane, 11 Rue Gutenberg, 06100 Nice.
T. 0493849830. - ArtBk - *097782*
Villa Arson, 20 Av Stephen-Liégard, 06105 Nice Cedex
2. T. 0493844004, Fax 0493844155. - ArtBk /
Graph - *097783*

Ozoir-la-Ferrière (Seine-et-Marne)

In Fine, 22 Av Hoche, 77330 Ozoir-la-Ferrière.
T. 0164404172, Fax 0164404211. - ArtBk - *097784*

Paris

Abbéville, 6 Rue Casimir-Delavigne, 75006 Paris.
T. 0144070085, Fax 0143298002. - ArtBk - *097785*
Académie des Inscriptions et des Belles-Lettres, 23 Quai
Conti, 75270 Paris Cedex 06. T. 0143269282.
- ArtBk - *097786*

Agence Culturelle de Paris, 6 Rue François-Miron,
75004 Paris. T. 0144788050, Fax 0144788055.
- ArtBk - *097787*
A.L.T. Production, 63 et 68 Blvd Voltaire, 75011 Paris.
T. 0143557755, Fax 0143381624. - Graph /
Repr - *097788*
Altinéa, 169 Rue Rennes, 75006 Paris. T. 0145490100,
Fax 0145492867. - ArtBk - *097789*
Anon, c/o David Nosek, 44 Rue Quincampoix, 75004 Pa-
ris. T. 0148043098. - ArtBk - *097790*
Arche, 86 Rue Bonaparte, 75006 Paris. T. 0143266072,
Fax 0146335640. *097791*
Armand, Colin, 103 Blvd Saint-Michel, 75240 Paris Ce-
dex 05. T. 0146341219, Fax 0143269638. - ArtBk /
Sli - *097792*
Art Concorde, 36 Rue Penthièvre, 75008 Paris.
T. 0145620044, Fax 0142257938. - ArtBk / Graph /
Mul - *097793*
Art Conseil, 69 Rue Université, 75007 Paris.
T. 0147059764. *097794*
Art Estampe, 67 Blvd Général-Martial-Valin, 75015 Pa-
ris. T. 0140607797, Fax 0140607339.
- Graph - *097795*
Art International Publishers, 49 Rue Héricart, 75015 Pa-
ris. T. 0145781292, Fax 0145750567. *097796*
Art Moderne, 17 Rue Voltaire, 75011 Paris.
T. 0143483545, Fax 0143481840. *097797*
Art Public Contemporain, 108 Rue Vieille-du-Temple,
75003 Paris. T. 0144598800,
Fax 0144598801. *097798*
Art Publications, 2 Rue Saint-Simon, 75007 Paris.
T. 0145441200, Fax 0142221236. *097799*
Art Vivant, c/o Aimé Maeght, 26 Rue Treilhard, 75008
Paris. *097800*
Art 204, 204 Blvd Saint-Germain, 75007 Paris.
T. 0142222629, Fax 0145484848. *097801*
Artabras, 6 Rue Casimir-Delavigne, 75006 Paris.
T. 0144070085, Fax 0143298002. - ArtBk - *097802*
Artcurial, 9 Av Matignon, 75008 Paris. T. 0142991616.
- ArtBk - *097803*
Arte Mundi France, 134 Blvd Haussmann, 75008 Paris.
T. 0145631278, Fax 0145633431. *097804*
Arted, 6 Av Coq, 75009 Paris. T. 0148747184,
Fax 0142811534. *097805*
Artes France, c/o Galerie Claudine Lustman, 11 Rue
Quincampoix, 75003 Paris. T. 0142777800. *097806*
Arthaud, 20 Rue Monsieur-le-Prince, 75006 Paris.
T. 0140513100, Fax 0143292148. - ArtBk - *097807*
Arts et Métiers Graphiques, 26 Rue Racine, 75278 Paris
Cedex 06. T. 0140513100, Fax 0143292148.
- ArtBk - *097808*
Arts Publishing Company, 54 Rue Seine, 75006 Paris.
T. 0140460216. *097809*
Assouline, 26 Rue Daniel-Casanova, 75001 Paris.
T. 0142603384, Fax 0142603385. - ArtBk - *097810*
Atelier Alpha Bleue, 5 Rue Sainte-Anastase, 75003 Pa-
ris. T. 0142727462, Fax 0142727982.
- ArtBk - *097811*
Atelier Bordas, 2 Rue Roquette, 75011 Paris.
T. 0147003161, Fax 0143381831. - Graph - *097812*
Atelier de Recherche et de Création, des Arts et Métiers
(ARCAM), 40 Rue Bretagne, 75003 Paris.
T. 0142729312. - ArtBk - *097813*
Autrement, 4 Rue Enghien, 75010 Paris. T. 0147701250,
Fax 0147709752. - ArtBk - *097814*
Aveline, Michel, 5 Rue Charonne, 75011 Paris.
T. 0147003558, Fax 0147003522. - ArtBk - *097815*
Bailly, Jacques, 36 Av Matignon, 75008 Paris.
T. 0143590918, Fax 0145635671. - ArtBk - *097816*
Baranès, Martine, 6 Rue Maître-Albert, 75005 Paris.
T. 0143269618. - ArtBk - *097817*
Baschet & Cie, 13 Rue Saint-Georges, 75009 Paris.
T. 0142806118. - ArtBk - *097818*
Bateau Lavoir, 18 Rue Seine, 75006 Paris.
T. 0143251387. - Graph / Repr - *097819*
Berès, Pierre, 14 Av Friedland, 75008 Paris.
T. 0145638553. - ArtBk - *097820*
Berg International, 129 Blvd Saint-Michel, 75005 Paris.
T. 0143267273, Fax 0146339499. - ArtBk - *097821*
Berger-Levrault, 5 Rue Auguste-Comte, 75007 Paris.
T. 0146341235. - ArtBk - *097822*
Berggruen & Cie, 70 Rue Université, 75007 Paris.
T. 0142220212, Fax 0142225743. - Graph - *097823*

Bernheim-Jeune, 83 Rue Fbg-Saint-Honoré, 75008 Pa-
ris. T. 0142666031. - Graph - *097824*
Bibliothèque des Arts, 3 Pl Odéon, 75006 Paris.
T. 0146331818, Fax 0140469556. - ArtBk - *097825*
Biro, Adam, 28 Rue Sévigné, 75004 Paris.
T. 0144598459, Fax 0144598414. - ArtBk - *097826*
Blaizot, Claude, 164 Rue Fbg-Saint-Honoré, 75008 Pa-
ris. T. 0143593658, Fax 0142259027. - ArtBk /
Graph - *097827*
de Boccard, 11 Rue Médicis, 75006 Paris.
T. 0143260037, Fax 0143548583. - ArtBk - *097828*
Bookking International, 60 Rue Saint-André-des-Arts,
75006 Paris. T. 0144416531, Fax 0143256492.
- ArtBk - *097829*
Bordas, 17 Rue Rémy-Dumoncel, BP 50, 75661 Paris
Cedex 14. T. 0142796200, Fax 0143228518.
- ArtBk - *097830*
Bosquet, 44 Av Bosquet, 75007 Paris. T. 0145515586.
- ArtBk / Graph - *097831*
Bréhéret, René, 9 Quai Malaquais, 75006 Paris.
T. 0142607474. - ArtBk / Graph / Repr - *097832*
Broutta, Michèle, 31 Rue Bergers, 75015 Paris.
T. 0145779371, Fax 0140590432. - Graph /
Repr - *097833*
Bucher, Jeanne, 53 Rue Seine, 75006 Paris.
T. 0143262232, Fax 0143294704. - ArtBk - *097834*
Butman, Alexander, 4 Pl Vendôme, 75001 Paris.
T. 0140159283, Fax 0140150548. *097835*
Caisse Nationale des Monuments Historique et des Si-
tes, Hôtel de Sully, 62 Rue Saint-Antoine, 75004 Paris.
T. 0144612000. - ArtBk - *097836*
Carlimpex Reproduction, 33 Rue Ponthieu, 75008 Paris.
T. 0142255251. - Repr - *097837*
Carpentier-Bachelet, 4 Rue Laferrière, 75009 Paris.
T. 0148787936, Fax 0142829199. - ArtBk - *097838*
Centre National de la Photographie, 42 Av Gobelins,
75013 Paris. T. 0145354303, Fax 0143360534.
- ArtBk - *097839*
Centre National de la Photographie, 11 Rue Berryer,
75008 Paris. T. 0153761232, Fax 0153761233.
- ArtBk - *097840*
Centre National des Arts Plastiques (CNAP), 27 Av Opé-
ra, 75001 Paris. T. 0140157473, Fax 0140157376.
- ArtBk - *097841*
Champvallins, Jacqueline de, 83 Rue Javel, 75015 Pa-
ris. T. 0145778833, Fax 0145775867.
- Graph - *097842*
Cheneau, Christian, 30 Rue Lisbonne, 75008 Paris.
T. 0145633606. - Graph - *097843*
Circonflexe, 26 Rue Ecoles, 75005 Paris.
T. 0146347777, Fax 0143253467. - ArtBk - *097844*
Citadelles & Mazenod, 33 Rue Naples, 75008 Paris.
T. 0145222366, Fax 0145220427. - ArtBk - *097845*
Claude, Bernard, 5-9 Rue Beaux-Arts, 75006 Paris.
T. 0143269707. - Graph - *097846*
Club du Livre, 28 Rue Fortuny, 75017 Paris.
T. 0147638055, Fax 0144404865. - ArtBk - *097847*
Cohen-Aloro, Claude, 11 Rue Tronchet, 75008 Paris.
T. 0144402525, Fax 0149240780. - ArtBk - *097848*
Connaissance des Arts, 25 Rue Ponthieu, 75008 Paris.
T. 0143596200, Fax 0142564335. - ArtBk /
Graph - *097849*
Copyright, 55 et 57 Rue Brillat-Savarin, 75013 Paris.
T. 0144169200, Fax 0144169214. - ArtBk - *097850*
Damase, Jacques, 61 Rue Varenne, 75007 Paris.
T. 0147055504, Fax 0145513371. - ArtBk / Graph /
Card / Mul - *097851*
Delille, Francis, 15 Rue Mézières, 75006 Paris.
T. 0145493751. - ArtBk - *097852*
Delpha, 71bis Rue Cardinal-Lemoine, 75005 Paris.
T. 0144411616, Fax 0144411600. - ArtBk - *097853*
Delpire, 13 Rue Abbaye, 75006 Paris. T. 0146342727,
Fax 0143266534. - ArtBk - *097854*
Delvaux, Véronique, 76 Rue Seine, 75006 Paris.
T. 0143299004, Fax 0143268968. - ArtBk - *097855*
Despalles, F., 21 Rue Saint-Jacques, 75005 Paris.
T. 0146330937. - ArtBk / Graph - *097856*
Dessain & Tolra, 17 Rue Rémy-Dumoncel, 75661 Paris
Cedex 14. T. 0142796200, Fax 0143228518.
- ArtBk - *097857*
Didier Erudition, 6 Rue Sarbonne, 75005 Paris.
T. 0143544757, Fax 0140517385. *097858*

Documentation Française, 29-31 Quai Voltaire, 75340 Paris Cedex 07. T. 0140157000, Fax 0140157230.
- Repr - *097859*
Dorotheum, 42 Rue Lauriston, 75116 Paris.
T. 0147556700. *097860*
Edimedia, 58 Rue Beaubourg, 75003 Paris.
T. 0148877373, Fax 0148877975. *097861*
Edipresse France, 16 Rue Guillaume-Tell, 75017 Paris.
T. 0147660005, Fax 0147664694. - ArtBk / Graph - *097862*
Edition et Diffusion M.P., 6 Rue Clodion, 75015 Paris.
T. 0145792549. *097863*
Editions Albin Michel, 22 Rue Huyghens, 75014 Paris.
T. 0142791000, Fax 0143272158. - ArtBk - *097864*
Editions Alternatives, 9bis Rue Abel-Hovelacque, 75013 Paris. T. 0144088380, Fax 0144088428.
- ArtBk - *097865*
Editions Atlas, 89 Rue Boétie, 75008 Paris.
T. 0140743838, Fax 0145611985. - ArtBk - *097866*
Editions Cahiers d'Art, 14 Rue du Dragon, 75006 Paris.
T. 0145487673, Fax 0145449850. *097866a*

> **Editions «Cahiers d'Art»**
> **14 Rue du Dragon**
> **75006 - Paris**
> **Tel: 01.45.48.76.73**
> **Fax: 01.45.44.98.50**

Editions Carré, 33 Rue Fbg-Saint-Antoine, 75011 Paris.
T. 0143466924, Fax 0143468565. - ArtBk - *097867*
Editions Citadelles & Mazenod Edition, 33 Rue Naples, 75008 Paris. T. 0145222366, Fax 0145220427.
- ArtBk - *097868*
Editions Clivages, 5 Rue Sainte-Anastase, 75003 Paris.
T. 0142724002. - ArtBk - *097869*
Editions de Grenelle, 14 Rue Grenelle, 75007 Paris.
T. 0145444190, Fax 0145491898. - ArtBk / Graph - *097870*
Editions de l'Amateur, 25 Rue Ginoux, 75737 Paris Cedex 15. T. 0145770805, Fax 0145799715.
- ArtBk - *097871*
Editions de l'Ermitage, 33 Rue Henri-Barbusse, 75005 Paris. T. 0143547144, Fax 0146338903.
- Graph - *097872*
Editions de la Fenêtre, 67 Rue Gergovie, 75014 Paris.
T. 0145412162. *097873*
Editions de la Martinière, 27 Rue Saint-André-des-Arts, 75006 Paris. T. 0146330423,
Fax 0143370816. *097874*
Editions de la Réunion des Musées Nationaux, 49 Rue Etienne-Marcel, 75039 Paris Cedex 01.
T. 0140134800, Fax 0140134814. - ArtBk / Repr / Card / Sli / Cal - *097875*
Editions du Beau Livre de France, 22 Rue Colonnes-du-Trône, 75012 Paris. T. 0143078874,
Fax 0143075337. *097876*
Editions du Centre Pompidou, Service Commercial, 75191 Paris Cedex 04. T. 0144781233,
Fax 0144781205. - ArtBk - *097877*
Editions du Cercle d'Art, 10 Rue Sainte-Anastase, 75003 Paris. T. 0148879212, Fax 0148874779.
- ArtBk / Graph / Repr - *097878*
Editions du Chêne, 43 Quai Grenelle, 75905 Paris Cedex 15. T. 0143923000, Fax 0143923381.
- ArtBk - *097879*
Editions du Félin, Philippe Lebaud Editeur, 10 Rue La-Vacquerie, 75011 Paris. T. 0144641180,
Fax 0143735510. - ArtBk - *097880*
Editions du Jeu de Paume, 20 Rue Royale, 75008 Paris.
T. 0147031325, Fax 0147031251. - ArtBk / Repr / Card - *097881*
Editions du Moniteur, 17 Rue Uzès, 75002 Paris.
T. 0140133376, Fax 0140410887. - ArtBk / Graph - *097882*
Editions du Regard, 14 Rue Mail, 75002 Paris.
T. 0142336157, Fax 0142337286. - ArtBk - *097883*

Editions du Seuil, 27 Rue Jacob, BP 80, 75261 Paris Cedex 06. T. 0140465050, Fax 0143290829.
- ArtBk - *097884*
Editions E.C.A. France, 21 Rue Saint-Roch, 75001 Paris.
T. 0149270173, Fax 0149270174. - Graph - *097885*
Editions EFFA, 12 Av Franklin-Roosevelt, 75008 Paris.
T. 0142894985. *097886*
Editions Emer, 47 Rue Tournelles, 75003 Paris.
T. 0142742715, Fax 0142740799. *097887*
Editions F.B., 85 Blvd Pasteur, 75015 Paris.
T. 0143354495. *097888*
Editions Flammarion, 26 Rue Racine, 75278 Paris Cedex 06. T. 0140513100, Fax 0143292148.
- ArtBk - *097889*
Editions Fleurus, 11 Rue Dugnay-Trouin, 75006 Paris.
T. 0145443834, Fax 0145499392. - ArtBk - *097890*
Editions Galilée, 9 Rue Linné, 75005 Paris.
T. 0143312384, Fax 0145355368. *097891*
Editions Hermé, 3 Rue Regard, 75006 Paris.
T. 0145491250, Fax 0145499536. - ArtBk - *097892*
Editions Hoëbecke, 12 Rue Dragon, 75006 Paris.
T. 0142228381, Fax 0145440496. - ArtBk / Graph - *097893*
Editions Memoire Vivante, 3 Rue Ormesson, 75004 Paris. T. 0148589000. *097894*
Editions Pygmalion, 70 Av Breteuil, 75007 Paris.
T. 0145674077, Fax 0147345152. - ArtBk - *097895*
Editions Revue Noire, 8 Rue Cels, 75014 Paris.
T. 0143202814, Fax 0143229260. - ArtBk - *097896*
Editions Saint Germain des Près, 17 Rue Grands-Augustins, 75006 Paris. T. 0143268272. - ArtBk - *097897*
Editions Tallandier, 25 Blvd Malesherbes, 75008 Paris.
T. 0144510101, Fax 0144510100. - ArtBk - *097898*
Editions Terre des Arts, 34 Rue Peringnon, 75015 Paris.
T. 0142731122. - Graph - *097899*
Editions Traversière, 167 Blvd Vincent-Auriol, 75013 Paris. T. 0145849455. - ArtBk - *097900*
Editions Vision Nouvelle, 62 Rue Pierre-Charron, 75008 Paris. T. 0142257025, Fax 0142254085. - ArtBk / Graph - *097901*
Editions 3A, 3 Rue Chauveau-Lagarde, 75008 Paris.
T. 0142652000. *097902*
Editions 666, c/o Studio 666, 6 Rue Maître-Albert, 75005 Paris. T. 0143545929. - ArtBk - *097903*
ERFI, 68 Rue Vaugirard, 75006 Paris. T. 0145442777, Fax 0145487611. - ArtBk - *097904*
Errance, 7 Rue Arsenal, 75004 Paris. T. 0142786212, Fax 0142745702. - Graph / Repr - *097905*
Exhibition International, c/o Géraldine Martin, 57 Rue Claude-Decaen, 75012 Paris. T. 0143075592, Fax 0143075881. - ArtBk - *097906*
Fall, Georges, 37 Quai Grands-Augustins, 75006 Paris.
T. 0142096640, Fax 43298063. - ArtBk / Graph - *097907*
Fayard, 75 Rue Saints-Pères, 75006 Paris.
T. 0145443845, Fax 0142224017. - ArtBk - *097908*
Fildier-Cartophilié, 4 Blvd Morland, 75004 Paris.
T. 0142720964. - Card - *097909*
Fischbacher, 33 Rue Seine, 75006 Paris.
T. 0143268487, Fax 0143264887. - ArtBk / Cal - *097910*
Forum des Arts, Forum des Halles, 11 Grande Galerie, 75001 Paris. T. 0140265390. - Graph / Mul - *097911*
Fragments, 5 Rue Charonne, 75011 Paris.
T. 0147007648, Fax 0147002204. - ArtBk - *097912*
Gadgets Arts Collections, 96 Rue Legendre, 75017 Paris. T. 0146279830. *097913*
Galanis, 8 Rue Duras, 75008 Paris. T. 0142654096.
- ArtBk / Mul - *097914*
Galerie de France, 52 Rue Verrerie, 75004 Paris.
T. 0142743800, Fax 0142743467. - ArtBk / Graph - *097915*
Galerie de Varenne, 61 Rue Varenne, 75007 Paris.
T. 0147055504. - ArtBk / Graph - *097916*
Galerie Lelong, 13-14 Rue Téhéran, 75008 Paris.
T. 0145631319, Fax 0142633643. - ArtBk - *097917*
Galfard, Eric, 2 Rue Messine, 75008 Paris.
T. 0145624560. - ArtBk / Graph - *097918*
Gallimard/ Electa, 5 Rue Sébastien-Bottin, 75328 Paris Cedex 07. T. 0149544200, Fax 0145449403.
- ArtBk - *097919*
Geuthner, Paul, 12 Rue Vavin, 75006 Paris.
T. 0146347130, Fax 0143297564. - Sli - *097920*

Girandon, 92 Rue Richelieu, 75002 Paris.
T. 0142961044. - ArtBk - *097921*
Grancher, Jacques, 98 Rue Vaugirard, 75006 Paris.
T. 0142226480, Fax 0145482503. - ArtBk - *097922*
Graphique de France, 6 Rue Braque, 75003 Paris.
T. 0144543232, Fax 0144543220. - Cal - *097923*
Gravure, 41 Rue Seine, 75006 Paris. T. 0143260544.
- ArtBk / Graph - *097924*
Gründ, 60 Rue Mazarine, 75006 Paris. T. 0143298740.
- ArtBk - *097925*
Gutenberg Reprints Bailly, 20 Rue Savoie, 75006 Paris.
T. 0143548927. - ArtBk - *097926*
Hachette, 43 Quai Grenelle, 75905 Paris Cedex 15.
T. 0143923000, Fax 0143923030. - ArtBk - *097927*
Hautôt, Pierre, 36 Rue Bac, 75007 Paris.
T. 0142611015. - Graph / Repr - *097928*
Hazan, 35 et 37 Rue Seine, 75006 Paris.
T. 0144411700, Fax 0144411909. - ArtBk / Repr - *097929*
Hermann, 293 Rue Lecourbe, 75015 Paris.
T. 0145574540, Fax 0140601293. - ArtBk / Graph - *097930*
Herscher, 8 Rue Férou, 75278 Paris Cedex 04.
T. 0146342142, Fax 0143251829. - ArtBk - *097931*
Hervas, 123 Av Philippe-Auguste, 75011 Paris.
T. 0143791095, Fax 0143797710. - ArtBk - *097932*
Herzog, Lucette, 157 Rue Saint-Martin, 75003 Paris.
T. 0148873994. - ArtBk / Graph - *097933*
Horay, Pierre, 22bis Passage Dauphine, 75006 Paris.
T. 0143545390, Fax 0140510637. - ArtBk - *097934*
Hubschmid & Bouret, 11 Rue Sèvres, 75006 Paris.
T. 0145482495. *097935*
Hugues, Jean, 1 Rue Furstenberg, 75006 Paris.
T. 0143267476. *097936*
Imprimerie Nationale, 27 Rue Convention, 75732 Paris Cedex 15. T. 0140583000, Fax 0140583064.
- ArtBk - *097937*
Inter-Livres, 55 Passage Jouffroy, 75009 Paris.
T. 0148245414, Fax 0145230823. *097938*
J.B.F., 12 Rue de Miromesnil, 75008 Paris.
T. 0147427000, Fax 0147420925. - Graph - *097939*
Joubert, Jean-Pierre, 18 Av Matignon, 75008 Paris.
T. 0142650079, Fax 0147426381. - ArtBk / Graph - *097940*
Klincksieck, 8 Rue Sorbonne, 75005 Paris.
T. 0143545953, Fax 0143252553. - ArtBk - *097941*
Lacourière & Frelaut, 11 Rue Foyatier, 75018 Paris.
T. 0146061770. - ArtBk - *097942*
Lahumière, 88 Blvd Courcelles, 75017 Paris.
T. 0147630395, Fax 0140530078. - Graph / Repr - *097943*
Lalique, 11 Rue Royale, 75008 Paris. - ArtBk - *097944*
Langloys, Regis, 169 Rue Saint Honoré, 75001 Paris.
T. 0142605694. - Graph - *097945*
Le Prat, Guy, 5 Rue Grands-Augustins, 75006 Paris.
T. 0143265782. - ArtBk - *097946*
Lecuire, Pierre, 14bis Rue Pierre-Nicole, 75005 Paris.
T. 0146337608. - ArtBk / Graph - *097947*
Leiris, Louise, 47 Rue Monceau, 75008 Paris.
T. 0145632056, Fax 0145637613. - ArtBk / Repr - *097948*
Leroy, Dominique, 61 Rue Monsieur-le-Prince, 75006 Paris. T. 0143297233, Fax 0143548913.
- ArtBk - *097949*
Levasseur & Fils, 232 Rue Rivoli, 75001 Paris.
T. 0142607759. - Graph - *097950*
Lit du Vent, 11 Rue Beaux-Arts, 75006 Paris.
T. 0143293460, Fax 0143293460. - ArtBk - *097951*
Loeb, Frédéric, 15 Rue Grands-Augustins, 75006 Paris.
T. 0143299539. - ArtBk - *097952*
Macula, 9 Rue Coëtlogon, 75006 Paris. T. 0145485870, Fax 0145485870. - ArtBk - *097953*
Maeght, 42 Rue Bac, 75007 Paris. T. 0145484515, Fax 0142222283. - ArtBk - *097954*
Magna Carta Productions, 3 Imp Royer-Collard, 75005 Paris. T. 0143542411, Fax 0143547643.
- ArtBk - *097955*
Maisonneuve, Jean, 11 Rue Saint-Sulpice, 75006 Paris.
T. 0143268635, Fax 0143545954. - ArtBk - *097956*
Manière, Diane, 11 Rue Pastourelle, 75003 Paris.
T. 0142770426. - ArtBk - *097957*
Marval, 7 Pl Saint-Placide, 75006 Paris. T. 0143253333, Fax 0143258888. - ArtBk - *097958*

Massin, 16-18 Rue Amiral-Mouchez, 75686 Paris Cedex 14. T. 0145654848, Fax 0145654700.
- ArtBk -   *097959*
Matignon, 32 Av Matignon, 75008 Paris.
T. 0142662012. - Graph -   *097960*
Mazo, Alain, 15 Rue Guénégaud, 75006 Paris.
T. 0143263984. - Graph / Repr -   *097961*
Millet, Didier, 77 Rue Cherche-Midi, 75006 Paris.
T. 0145492550, Fax 0145492546. - ArtBk -   *097962*
Minkoff France, c/o Librairie à la Règle d'Or, 23 Rue Fleurus, 75006 Paris. T. 0145449433,
Fax 0145449430. - ArtBk -   *097963*
Musée-Galerie de la Seita, 12 Rue Surcouf, 75007 Paris.
T. 0145566017, Fax 0145566569. - ArtBk /
Graph -   *097964*
Nagel, 48 Rue Galande, 76005 Paris. T. 0143269091,
Fax 0140510099. - ArtBk -   *097965*
Navarra, Enrico, 34 Rue Bac, 75007 Paris.
T. 0142617320, Fax 0142869653. - ArtBk -   *097966*
Neudin, Gérard & Noëlle, 35 Rue Geoffroy-Saint-Hilaire, 75005 Paris. - Card -   *097967*
Nobele, F. de, 35 Rue Bonaparte, 75006 Paris.
T. 0143260862, Fax 0140468596. - ArtBk -   *097968*
Nouvelles Editions Françaises, 152 Rue Picpus, 75583 Paris Cedex 12. T. 0144741600, Fax 0140049803.
- ArtBk / Repr -   *097969*
Nouvelles Editions Séguier, 3 Rue Séguier, 75006 Paris.
T. 0146331950, Fax 0140460775. - ArtBk /
Graph -   *097970*
Nouvelles Images, 6 Rue Dante, 75005 Paris.
T. 0143256243. - Repr -   *097971*
Nvision Grafix France, 16 Av Friedland, 75008 Paris.
T. 0145614308, Fax 0145612627.   *097972*
Oeuvres Graphiques Contemporaines, 31 Rue Bergers, 75015 Paris. T. 0145779379. - ArtBk / Graph /
Mul -   *097973*
Opus International, 1 Rue Dauphine, 75006 Paris.
T. 0143290950, Fax 0146342683. - ArtBk / Graph /
Mul -   *097974*
Papierski, Daniel, 5 Rue Labrouste, 75015 Paris.
T. 0145406392, Fax 0145391948. - Graph -   *097975*
Paris-Musées, 31 Rue Francs-Bourgeois, 75004 Paris.
T. 0142766796 / 95, Fax 0142766622.
- ArtBk -   *097976*
Peuples du Monde, 8 Rue François-Villon, 75015 Paris.
T. 0145311300. - ArtBk -   *097977*
Picard, 82 Rue Bonaparte, 75006 Paris. T. 0143264871,
Fax 0143264264. - ArtBk -   *097978*
Plume, 51 Rue Turenne, 75003 Paris. T. 0140299609,
Fax 0140299611. - ArtBk -   *097979*
Point Cardinal, 3 Rue Jacob, 75006 Paris.
T. 0140333208. - ArtBk / Graph -   *097980*
Postcard Selection, 75 Rue Amsterdam, 75008 Paris.
T. 0145261357. - Card -   *097981*
Presses Universitaires de France, 17 Rue Souflot, 75005 Paris. T. 0143267741. - ArtBk -   *097982*
Prints etc., 57 Quai Grands-Augustins, 75006 Paris.
T. 0143254458. - ArtBk -   *097983*
Quintette, 6 Rue Uzès, 75002 Paris. T. 0142362662,
Fax 0142211884. - ArtBk / Graph -   *097984*
Rec, 7 Rue Charlemagne, 75004 Paris.
T. 0142773363.   *097985*
René, Denise, 196 Blvd Saint-Germain, 75007 Paris.
T. 0142227757, Fax 0145448918. - ArtBk /
Repr -   *097986*
Ricci, Franco Maria, 12 Rue Beaux-Arts, 75006 Paris.
T. 0146339631, Fax 0147469680. - ArtBk -   *097987*
Rivière, Yves, 117 Rue Vieille-du-Temple, 75003 Paris.
T. 0142747784, Fax 0142781265. - ArtBk / Graph /
Repr / Mul -   *097988*
Salachas, Gilbert, 22 Av Porte-Brunet, 75019 Paris.
T. 0142031896, Fax 0142030301. - ArtBk /
Graph -   *097989*
Scala, 14bis Rue Berbier-du-Mets, 75013 Paris.
T. 0143311451, Fax 0143311705. - ArtBk -   *097990*
Sermadiras, 11 Rue Arsène-Houssaye, 75008 Paris.
T. 0147665121, Fax 0147641056. - ArtBk -   *097991*
Service Photographique des Musées Nationaux, 89 Av Victor-Hugo, 75116 Paris. T. 0145007557,
Fax 0145009239. - Sli -   *097992*
Seydoux, Arnaud, 137 Rue Fbg-Saint-Antoine, 75011 Paris. T. 0143458228. - ArtBk -   *097993*

Skira, 34 Rue Serpente, 75006 Paris. T. 0146345689,
Fax 0144071088. - ArtBk -   *097994*
Somogy, 20 Av Rapp, 75007 Paris. T. 0145555874,
Fax 0147537657. - ArtBk / Graph / Repr /
Card -   *097995*
Sous le Vent, 10 Rue Lisbonne, 75008 Paris.
T. 0142931318. - ArtBk -   *097996*
Taschen France, 17 Rue Buci, 75006 Paris.
T. 0140517093, Fax 0143267380. - ArtBk -   *097997*
Teisseire, A., 13 Av Mozart, 75016 Paris.
T. 0145270868. - Graph -   *097998*
Terrail, Pierre, 1 Rue Bayard, 75008 Paris.
T. 0144356245, Fax 0144356026. - ArtBk -   *097999*
Textuel, 29 Blvd Bourdon, 75004 Paris. T. 0148049819,
Fax 0148049740. - ArtBk -   *098000*
Thames & Hudson, 4 Imp Peintres, 75002 Paris.
T. 0142219515, Fax 0142213336. - ArtBk -   *098001*
Thibaud, Dany, 52 Rue Labrouste, 75015 Paris.
T. 0142507211. - ArtBk -   *098002*
UNESCO Publishing, 7 Pl Fontenoy, 75352 Paris.
T. 0145681000, Fax 0142733007. - ArtBk -   *098003*
Van Wilder, 8 Rue Prague, 75012 Paris. T. 0140190679,
Fax 0140190474. - ArtBk -   *098004*
Vilo Diffusion, 25 Rue Ginoux, 75737 Paris Cedex 15.
T. 0145770805, Fax 0145799715. - ArtBk /
Card -   *098005*
Weill, Lucie, 6 Rue Bonaparte, 75006 Paris.
T. 0143547195. - ArtBk -   *098006*
Wildenstein, 57 Rue Boétie, 75008 Paris.
T. 0145630100, Fax 0145614653.   *098007*

Périgueux (Dordogne)

Faulac, Pierre, 12 Rue Professeur-Peyrot, BP 2043, 24000 Périgueux. T. 0553534190, Fax 0553080585.
- ArtBk / Graph -   *098008*

Poitiers (Vienne)

Brissaud, 162 Grand-Rue, 86000 Poitiers.
T. 0549880181, Fax 0549525329. - ArtBk -   *098009*

Portet-sur-Garonne (Haute-Garonne)

Loubatières, Francis, 10bis Blvd Europe, BP 27, 31122 Portet-sur-Garonne Cedex. T. 0561725390,
Fax 0561722370. - ArtBk -   *098010*

Ramatuelle (Var)

Edition Lithelle, Juliane Schack, Les Romarins, 83350 Ramatuelle. T. 0494792031. - Graph -   *098011*

Romorantin-Lanthenay (Loir-et-Cher)

Martinsart, 58 Rue Capucins, BP 7, 41200 Romorantin-Lanthenay. T. 0254760808, Fax 0254965172.   *098012*

Roudouallec (Morbihan)

Atelier d'Endoume, Le Queidel, 56110 Roudouallec.
T. 0297345299, Fax 0297345299. - Graph -   *098013*

Rouen (Seine-Maritime)

Imprimerie Lecerf, 22-26 Rue Bons-Enfants, 76000 Rouen. T. 0235714451. - ArtBk -   *098014*

Saint-Amand-en-Puisaye (Nièvre)

Cercle International de la Pensée et des Arts Français (CIPAF), Arquian, 58310 Saint-Amand-en-Puisaye.
T. 0386396332. - ArtBk / Graph -   *098015*

Saint-Clément-la-Rivière (Hérault)

Fata Morgana, Fontfroide-le-Haut, 34980 Saint-Clément-la-Rivière. T. 0467544040. - ArtBk /
Graph -   *098016*

Saint-Didier-des-Bois (Eure)

Fine Arts Books, 1 Pl Eglise, 27370 Saint-Didier-des-Bois. T. 0232505949, Fax 0232505947.
- ArtBk -   *098017*

Saint-Julien-aux-Bois (Corrèze)

Sers, Philippe, Lecouf, 19220 Saint-Julien-aux-Bois.
T. 0555282022, Fax 0555284877. - ArtBk -   *098018*

Saint-Malo (Ille-et-Vilaine)

Derveaux, Daniel, 5 Rue Charles-Cunat, 35400 Saint-Malo. T. 0299400357. - ArtBk / Repr -   *098019*

Saint-Nazaire (Loire-Atlantique)

Arcane 17, 1 Blvd René-Loty, 44600 Saint-Nazaire.
T. 40666320, Fax 40224175. - ArtBk -   *098020*

Saint-Rémy-en-l'Eau (Oise)

Hayot, Monelle, Château-de-Saint-Rémy-en-l'Eau, 60130 Saint-Rémy-en-l'Eau. T. 0344787961,
Fax 0344787859. - ArtBk -   *098021*

Sens (Yonne)

Bianchini, Paul, 5 Rue Jules Verne, 89100 Sens.
T. 0386552720, Fax 0386642709. - ArtBk /
Mul -   *098021a*

Strasbourg (Bas-Rhin)

Oberlin, 19 Rue Francs-Bourgeois, 67000 Strasbourg Cedex. T. 0388324583. - ArtBk / Repr -   *098022*

Toucy (Yonne)

Theimer, François, 4 Rue Cavaliers, 89130 Toucy.
T. 0386743176, Fax 0386743213. - ArtBk -   *098023*

Toulouse (Haute-Garonne)

Privat, 14 Rue Arts, 31068 Toulouse Cedex.
T. 0561230926, Fax 0561215603. - ArtBk -   *098024*

Valenciennes (Nord)

Editions Aquarium Agnostique, 8 Rue Ferrand, 59300 Valenciennes. T. 0327332202,
Fax 0327452425.   *098025*

Vannes (Hauts-de-Seine)

Giraudon, 70 Rue Jean-Bleuzen, 92170 Vannes.
T. 0141237840, Fax 0141237841. - Repr / Sli -   *098026*

Vidauban (Var)

Sèbe, Alain, 128 Av Président-Wilson, BP 37, 83550 Vidauban Cedex. T. 0494731280, Fax 0494735887.
- ArtBk / Repr -   *098027*

Villemandeur (Loiret)

Nouvelles Images, Lombreuil, 45700 Villemandeur.
T. 0238962662, Fax 0238963200. - Graph / Repr /
Mul -   *098028*

Villeurbanne (Rhône)

Art-Edition, 11 Rue Docteur-Dolar, BP 30-77, 69605 Villeurbanne Cedex. T. 0478034700,
Fax 0478034709.   *098029*

Germany

Aachen (Nordrhein-Westfalen)

Edition Galerie 33, I. Rote-Haag-Weg 17, 52076 Aachen.
T. (0241) 60 77 38, Fax 275 30. - Graph / Repr /
Mul -   *098030*
Edition R. de Bernardi, Ludwigsallee 99, 52062 Aachen.
T. (0241) 153238, Fax 151977. - Graph -   *098031*
Georgi, Theaterstr. 77, 52062 Aachen.
T. (0241) 47 79 10, Fax (0241) 477 91 60. - ArtBk /
Graph / Repr / Card / Cal / Mul -   *098032*
Rimbaud, Postfach 86, 52001 Aachen. T. (0241) 542532,
Fax (0241) 514117.   *098033*

Abtsgmünd (Baden-Württemberg)

Sowa & Reiser, Hinterbüchelberg 10, 73453 Abtsgmünd.
T. (07975) 799. - Graph -   *098034*

Achim (Niedersachsen)

Berlin Design, Theodor-Barth-Str. 30, 28832 Achim.
T. (04202) 48 31 24. - Mul -   *098035*

Ahnatal (Hessen)

Vereinigung Malerstübchen Willingshausen e.V., Bergstr 13, 34292 Ahnatal.   *098036*

Aichwald (Baden-Württemberg)

Imago-Verlag, Schurwaldstr 70, 73773 Aichwald.
T. (0711) 361044, Fax 364117. - Repr / Card / Sli /
Mul -   *098037*

Alfeld (Niedersachsen)

Schaper, M. & H., Kalandstr 4, 31061 Alfeld.
T. (05181) 80090.   *098038*

Alfter (Nordrhein-Westfalen)
Conrad, Hans, Oberdorf 18, 53347 Alfter.
T. (0228) 642291, Fax 642295. - Graph -   *098039*

Alsfeld (Hessen)
Arbeitskreis Stadtzeichner, Postfach 527, 36295 Alsfeld.
T. (06631) 3294. - ArtBk / Card -   *098040*

Altenmünster (Bayern)
Edition Sprachlos, Johann-Wisrich-Str. 52, 86450 Alten-
münster. T. (08295) 399, Fax (08295) 399. - Graph /
Cal / Mul / ArtP -   *098041*

Amöneburg (Hessen)
Galerie Verlag, Kappeweg 5, 35287 Amöneburg.
T. (06422) 45 45. - Graph / Card / Cal -   *098042*

Aschaffenburg (Bayern)
Atelier SpessArt, Friedhofstr. 28, 63741 Aschaffenburg.
T. (06021) 415 56. - Graph -   *098043*
May, Goldbacher Str. 25-27, 63739 Aschaffenburg.
- Graph / Repr / Card / Mul -   *098044*

Augsburg (Bayern)
art lab, Jan Prein, An der Blauen Kappe 16, 86152
Augsburg. T. (0821) 33797. - Graph -   *098045*
Augustus Verlag, Aindlinger Str 16, 86167 Augsburg.
T. (0821) 7004538, Fax 7004540. - ArtBk -   *098046*
Battenberg, Aindlinger Str 16, 86167 Augsburg.
T. (0821) 7004341, Fax 7004279. - Graph -   *098047*
Brigg Verlag, Zusamstr 9, 86165 Augsburg.
T. (0821) 711347. - ArtBk -   *098048*
Weltbild Verlag, Aindlinger Str 16, 86167 Augsburg.
T. (0821) 70040, Fax 7004279. - ArtBk -   *098049*

Babenhausen (Bayern)
Reiner, Hermann, Silcherweg 3, 87727 Babenhausen.
T. (08333) 1255.   *098050*

Bad Homburg vor der Höhe (Hessen)
New Art Consulting & Edition, Kisseleffstr 11a, 61348
Bad Homburg vor der Höhe. T. (06172) 46056,
Fax (06172) 25832. - ArtBk / Graph / Repr / Cal /
Mul -   *098051*

Bad Honnef (Nordrhein-Westfalen)
Bock & Herchen, Reichenberger Str. 11e, 53604 Bad
Honnef. T. (02224) 54 43, 57 75, Fax (02224) 78310.
- ArtBk -   *098052*
Maas & Burbach, Rhöndorfer Str. 29 A, 53604 Bad Hon-
nef. T. (02224) 78352, Fax (02224) 78490.
- ArtBk -   *098053*
Overmans, Angelika, Luisenstr. 23, 53604 Bad Honnef.
T. (02224) 744 90.   *098054*

Bad Kreuznach (Rheinland-Pfalz)
Burkart, Rolf A., Neunmorgen 12, 55545 Bad Kreuznach.
T. (0671) 36715. - ArtBk / Graph -   *098055*

Bad Münster (Rheinland-Pfalz)
Neue Plakat Kunst, Berliner Str 60, 55583 Bad Münster.
T. (06708) 3808, Fax 4200. - Repr -   *098056*

Bad Neustadt an der Saale (Bayern)
Pfaehler, Dietrich, Berliner Str 37, 97616 Bad Neustadt
an der Saale. T. (09771) 8142. - ArtBk / Card / Mul /
ArtP -   *098057*

Bad Rappenau (Baden-Württemberg)
Steiner, Schloss Babstadt, 74906 Bad Rappenau.
T. (07264) 597. - ArtBk -   *098058*

Bad Schussenried (Baden-Württemberg)
Kasper, Alfons, Dr., Rohrerstr. 12, 88427 Bad Schussen-
ried. T. (07583) 24 15. - ArtBk -   *098059*

Bad Vilbel (Hessen)
Groth, Memelweg 11, 61118 Bad Vilbel.
T. (06101) 8121, Fax 83200. - Graph / Repr /
Card -   *098060*

Bad Zwischenahn (Niedersachsen)
Edition Galerie Moderne, Am Delf 37, 26160 Bad Zwi-
schenahn. T. (04403) 5429, Fax 63450.
- Repr -   *098061*

Baden-Baden (Baden-Württemberg)
Agis-Verlag, Ooser Luisenstr. 23, 76532 Baden-Baden.
T. (07221) 640 24/25. - ArtBk -   *098062*
Colorprint Seidendruck, Rheinstr. 219-221, 76532 Ba-
den-Baden. T. (07221) 500 40. - Repr / Mul -   *098063*
Klimas-Panten, Rheinstr. 13, 76532 Baden-Baden.
T. (07221) 53065, Fax (07221) 53062, 17965. - ArtBk /
Repr / Card -   *098064*
Koerner, Valentin, Hermann-Sielcken-Str 36, 76530 Ba-
den-Baden. T. (07221) 22423, Fax (07221) 38697.
- ArtBk -   *098065*

Bayreuth (Bayern)
Bear Press, Schlegelstr. 10, 95447 Bayreuth.
T. (0921) 81418. - Graph -   *098066*

Bensheim (Hessen)
Böhler, Wolfgang, Marktpl. 6, 64625 Bensheim.
T. (06251) 39600. - Graph / Card -   *098067*
Edition Galerie Mobil, Bauer + Bauer, Hauptstr. 21,
64625 Bensheim. T. (06251) 64992, Fax (06251) 2765.
- Graph -   *098068*

Berg (Bayern)
Keller, Josef, Seebreite 9, 82335 Berg. T. (08151) 7710,
Fax (08151) 771-190. - ArtBk / Graph -   *098069*

Bergheim (Nordrhein-Westfalen)
Edition Gabriele Krombholz, Im Brauweiler Feld 29,
50129 Bergheim. T. (02271) 42104,
Fax (0221) 4009687. - Graph -   *098070*
Schmiedel, Karlheinz, Mandelweg 7, 50127 Bergheim.
T. (02271) 94538. - Graph -   *098071*

Bergisch Gladbach (Nordrhein-Westfa-
len)
Edition Schlinkhoff, Alter Traßweg 10, 51427 Bergisch
Gladbach. T. (02202) 623 38. - Graph -   *098072*
Gruppen-Grafik, Edition für künstlerisches Teamwork,
Gemarkenweg 1, 51467 Bergisch Gladbach.
T. (02202) 815 66. - Graph / Mul -   *098073*

Berlin
Ahnert, Knut, Sybelstr 58, 10629 Berlin.
T. (030) 3240907, Fax (030) 3239754. - ArtBk /
Repr -   *098074*
Akademie Verlag, Mühlenstr 33-34, 13187 Berlin.
T. (030) 47889300, Fax 47889357. - ArtBk -   *098075*
Album Verlag, Prinz-Friedrich-Leopold-Str 34, 14129
Berlin. T. (030) 8037092, Fax 81699435. - Repr / Sli /
Cal -   *098076*
Alexander Verlag, Fredericiastr 12, 14050 Berlin.
T. (030) 3021826, Fax 3029408.   *098077*
Aphaia Verlag, Riemeisterstr. 113, 14169 Berlin.
T. (030) 8133998, Fax 8133998. - Graph /
ArtBk -   *098078*
Ararat Curiosity Shop, Bergmannstr 99a, 10961 Berlin.
T. (030) 6935080, Fax (030) 6930229. - Card -   *098079*
Archibook Verlag, Westendallee 97e, 14052 Berlin.
T. (030) 3046578, Fax (030) 3049902. - ArtBk -   *098080*
Arenhövel, Willmuth, Dr., Treuchtlinger Str 4, 10779 Ber-
lin. T. (030) 2132803, Fax 2181995. - ArtBk /
ArtP -   *098081*
Argon Verlag, Potsdamer Str. 77-87, 10785 Berlin.
T. (030) 26009393, Fax (030) 2617620.
- ArtBk -   *098082*
Ars Nicolai, Neuenburger Str 17, 10969 Berlin.   *098083*
artery berlin, Nestorstr 14, 10709 Berlin.
T. (030) 8911888, Fax (030) 8911750.   *098084*
Atelier-Handpresse, Neuenburger Str. 17, 10969 Berlin.
T. (030) 251 15 84. - ArtBk / Graph / Repr -   *098085*
Aufbau-Verlag, Französische Str. 32, 10117 Berlin.
T. (030) 22350, Fax 8030) 2298637. - ArtBk /
Cal -   *098086*
Berliner Handpresse, Naunynstr 69, 10997 Berlin.
T. (030) 6142605, 6148728. - Graph / Repr -   *098087*
Block, René, Schaperstr 11, 10719 Berlin.
T. (030) 2113145, Fax 2176432. - ArtBk / Graph /
Mul -   *098088*
Boettcher, H., Meinekestr 4, 10719 Berlin.
T. (030) 8813815. - ArtBk -   *098089*
Burgert Handpresse, Lassenstr 22, 14193 Berlin.
T. (030) 8264348. - ArtBk / Graph -   *098090*

Casablanca Verlag, Postfach 310344, 10633 Berlin.
T. (030) 8919569, Fax (030) 8919569. - ArtBk / Graph /
Mul -   *098091*
Columbus Communication, Oranienstr 25, 10999 Berlin.
T. (030) 630050, Fax (030) 63005298.   *098092*
D & D Verlags- und Ausstellungs GmbH, Bülowstr 66,
10783 Berlin. T. (030) 2173830,
Fax (030) 21738393.   *098093*
Dahmann, Kurt, Fuggerstr. 38, 10777 Berlin.
T. (030) 24 42 18. - Graph -   *098094*
Deutscher Verlag der Wissenschaft, Taubenstr. 10,
10117 Berlin. T. (030) 229 00.   *098095*
Deutscher Verlag für Kunstwissenschaft, Charlottenstr
13, 10969 Berlin. T. (030) 25913864/65,
Fax 25913537. - ArtBk -   *098096*
Dietrich, Horst, Giesebrechtstr 19, 10629 Berlin.
T. (030) 3245345, Fax (030) 3243151. - ArtBk / Graph /
Repr / Card -   *098097*
Druckwerkstatt Bethanien, Mariannenpl 2, 10997 Berlin.
T. (030) 6148003, Fax 6157315. - Graph -   *098098*
Edition Divan, Reichsstr. 104, 14052 Berlin.
T. (030) 302 20 57, 301 52 48. - ArtBk -   *098099*
Edition Graph Druckula, Gneisenaustr. 2A, 10961 Berlin.
T. (030) 693 44 14/74, Fax (030) 694 12 18.
- Graph -   *098100*
Edition Hentrich, Albrechtstr. 111-112, 12167 Berlin.
T. (030) 792 70 11, Fax (030) 792 94 28. - ArtBk /
Cal -   *098101*
Edition Lidiarte, Knesebeckstr 13-14, 10623 Berlin.
T. (030) 3137420, Fax 3127117. - ArtBk / Repr /
Card -   *098102*
Edition Messer-Ladwig, Nollendorfstr. 15, 10777 Berlin.
T. (030) 215 58 70. - Graph / Card / Mul -   *098103*
edition q, Ifenpfad 2-14, 12107 Berlin. T. (030) 76180635,
Fax 76180692. - ArtBk -   *098104*
Edition Schoen, Wilmersdorfer Str. 94, 10629 Berlin.
- Graph -   *098105*
Edition Sirene, Köpenicker Str. 145, 10997
Berlin.   *098106*
Elefanten Press Verlag, Oranienstr 25, 10999 Berlin.
T. (030) 650050, Fax (030) 65005298. - ArtBk /
Card -   *098107*
Ergo-Verlag, Wielandstr. 16, 10625 Berlin.
T. (030) 324 47 89. - Graph / Repr -   *098108*
Ernst & Sohn, Mühlenstr 33-34, 13187 Berlin.
T. (030) 47889284, Fax 47889240. - ArtBk -   *098109*
Eulenspiegel, Das Neue Berlin, Kronenstr. 73-74, 10117
Berlin. T. (030) 2202126, Fax (030) 6093187.
- ArtBk -   *098110*
FAB-Verlag, Kantstr. 152, 10623 Berlin.
T. (030) 3135064, Fax (030) 310781. - ArtBk -   *098111*
Fahnemann, Fasanenstr 61, 10719 Berlin.
T. (030) 8839897, Fax 8824572. - Graph -   *098112*
Falk, Christoph, Kastanienallee 22, 14052 Berlin.
T. (030) 3023234, Fax 8137621. - Graph -   *098113*
Fannei & Walz, Kantstr. 152, 10623 Berlin.
T. (030) 313 86 30, Fax (030) 31 07 81.
- Graph -   *098114*
Fischer, Carmerstr 14, 10623 Berlin. T. (030) 3131371,
Fax 3131860.   *098115*
Frieling & Partner, Hünefeldzeile 18, 12247 Berlin.
T. (030) 7742911, Fax (030) 7744103. - ArtBk / Graph /
Repr -   *098116*
Frölich & Kaufmann, Willdenowstr. 5, 12203 Berlin.
T. (030) 465 10 01/02.   *098117*
Gerhardt, Greifenhagener Str 7, 10437 Berlin.
T. (030) 4445506. - ArtBk -   *098118*
Göpfert Handpresse, Skalitzer Str. 101, 10997 Berlin.
T. (030) 618 22 98, 211 66 11. - Graph -   *098119*
Grauert & Zink, Lindenthaler Allee 4, 14163 Berlin.
T. (030) 802 50 88.   *098120*
Henschel, Weydingerstr. 14-16, 10178 Berlin.
T. (030) 28409421, Fax (030) 28409433.
- ArtBk -   *098121*
Hulsch, Gebr., Emser Str 43, 10719 Berlin.
T. (030) 8822842, Fax 8822844. - Graph / Repr / Card /
Mul -   *098122*
Imprimatur, Meinekestr. 6, 10719 Berlin.
T. (030) 8836415. - Graph / Mul -   *098123*
Janssen, Volker, Pfalzburger Str 76, 10719 Berlin.
T. (030) 8811590, Fax (030) 8854344. - ArtBk / Repr /
Card -   *098124*

Paul Pfisterer (Editor)

Monogrammlexikon 2 / Dictionary of Monograms 2

Internationales Verzeichnis der Monogramme bildender Künstler des 19. und 20. Jahrhunderts

International List of Monograms in the Visual Arts of the 19th and 20th Centuries

1995. 24 x 17 cm. XX, 1067 pages. Cloth.
DM 638,– / öS 4.657,– / sFr 568,–
• ISBN 3-11-014300-3

The "Dictionary of Monograms 2" is a cultural-historically valuable list of monograms in the visual arts of the 19th and 20th centuries. It is a continuation of Franz Goldstein's "Monogramm Lexikon -

Internationales Verzeichnis der Monogramme bildender Künstler seit 1850" published by Walter de Gruyter in 1964, and contains about 25,000 monograms. These were collected from books, second-hand bookshops, museums, directly from the artists themselves, etc. The monograms are easily to reference and are comprehensive, making them invaluable to those producing or collecting work in the visual arts.
Paul Pfisterer, Graphic Artist, Painter and Etcher, Writer on Art, Gießen, Germany

WALTER DE GRUYTER & CO
Genthiner Straße 13 · D–10785 Berlin
Tel. +49 (0)30 2 60 05–130
Fax +49 (0)30 2 60 05–352
Internet: http://www.deGruyter.de

W DE G de Gruyter
Berlin · New York

Junghans, Karl, Heesestr. 10, 12169 Berlin.
T. (030) 791 31 64. - Graph / Repr –   098125
Kluge & Morgenstern, Trabener Str 39, 14193 Berlin.
T. (030) 8913001, Fax 8918315. - Repr –   098126
Koehler & Amelang, Zimmerstr. 79-80, 10117 Berlin.
T. (030) 20369233, Fax (030) 20369232.
- ArtBk –   098127
KONTEXTverlag, Husemannstr 7, Berlin.
T. (030) 4429082, Fax (030) 4429083.   098128
Kropp, Rolf, Bozener Str. 13-14, 10825 Berlin.
T. (030) 854 47 96. - Graph –   098129
Kunst und Bild, Großbeerenstr 31, 10963 Berlin.
T. (0311) 320203.   098130
Kunsthaus am Moritzplatz, Oranienstr 46, 10969 Berlin.
T. (030) 6145577, Fax (030) 6141791. - Card /
Mul –   098131
Kupfergraben Verlagsgesellschaft, Lützowstr 105,
10785 Berlin. T. (030) 2621990, Fax 2621990.
- ArtBk –   098132
Langner & Bose, Hauptstr 136, 10115 Berlin.
T. (030) 7828925, 6154892. - ArtBk / Repr –   098133
Lindner, M.+ W., Klosterstr. 12, 13581 Berlin.
T. (030) 332 15 03. - Graph –   098134
Mainz, Zossener Str 40, 10961 Berlin.
T. (030) 69409277/78, Fax 69409279.
- Graph –   098135
Gebr. Mann, Charlottenstr 13, 10969 Berlin.
T. (030) 25913865, Fax 25913537. - ArtBk –   098136
Merve, Crellestr 22, 10827 Berlin. T. (030) 7848433,
Fax (030) 7881074.   098137
Mikro, Carmerstr. 1, 10623 Berlin. T. (030) 312 58 65.
- ArtBk / Graph / Mul –   098138
Nicolaische Verlagsbuchhandlung, Neuenburger Str 17,
10969 Berlin. T. (030) 2537380, Fax 25373839.
- ArtBk –   098139
Nierendorf, Hardenbergstr 19, 10623 Berlin.
T. (030) 8325013, Fax 3129327. - ArtBk / Graph /
Repr –   098140
Nishen, Dirk, Bülowstr. 66, 10783 Berlin.
T. (030) 21738345, Fax (030) 21738393.
- ArtBk –   098141

Parkett-Verlag, Motzstr. 30, 10783 Berlin.
T. (030) 211 07 59, Fax (030) 211 07 46.
- ArtBk –   098142
Pescars, Cranachstr. 17, 12157 Berlin.
T. (030) 855 29 75.   098143
Pfeiffer, Claus Jürgen, Bleibtreustr. 53, 10623 Berlin.
T. (030) 312 38 04.   098144
Phoenix Press, Fasanenstr. 61, 10719 Berlin.
T. (030) 883 89 34, Fax (030) 882 45 72.
- Graph –   098145
Propyläen-Verlag, Lindenstr. 76, 10969 Berlin.
T. (030) 25 91 35 91, Fax (030) 25 91 35 33. - ArtBk /
Graph / Mul –   098146
Rainer Verlag, Körtestr. 10, 10967 Berlin.
T. (030) 691 65 36. - ArtBk / Graph –   098147
Reimer, Dietrich, Unter den Eichen 57, 12203 Berlin.
T. (030) 8314081, Fax 8316323. - ArtBk –   098148
Ruksaldruck, Hagelberger Str. 53-54, 10965 Berlin.
T. (030) 786 50 50, Fax 786 19 82. - Cal –   098149
Schultz, Michael, Mommsenstr 32, 10629 Berlin.
T. (030) 3241591, Fax 3231575.   098150
Stapp, Lützowstr 105, 10785 Berlin. T. (030) 2622097,
Fax 2621990. - ArtBk –   098151
Verlag der Beeken, Jürgen Eckhardt, Tempelhofer Ufer
36, 10963 Berlin. T. (030) 262 52 54.   098152
Verlag für zeitgenössische Kunst, Landergerstr. 5,
14195 Berlin. T. (030) 832 58 48. - ArtBk –   098153
Verlag Haus am Checkpoint Charlie, Friedrichstr 43-44,
10969 Berlin. T. (030) 2511031, Fax 2512075.
- ArtBk –   098154
Warnke, Uwe, Wühlischstr 30, 10245 Berlin.
T. (030) 2928570. - Graph / Mul –   098155
Wehner, F., Oranienstr 183, 10999 Berlin.
T. (030) 6169510, Fax 61695125. - Repr –   098156
Wever, Peter, Gustav-Freytag-Str. 5A, 10827 Berlin.
T. (030) 784 72 76. - Graph –   098157
Wewerka, Homeyerstr 32, 13156 Berlin.
T. (030) 4826662, Fax 4829261. - ArtBk –   098158
Wiens, Gleditschstr 37, 10781 Berlin. T. (030) 2170837,
Fax 2172923. - ArtBk / Graph / Mul / ArtP –   098159

Zunker, P., Werner-Voß-Damm 54b, 12101 Berlin.
T. (030) 785 20 18. - Graph –   098160
7. Produzentengalerie, Schaperstr. 19, 10719 Berlin.
T. (030) 881 74 31. - ArtBk –   098161

Beuron (Baden-Württemberg)

Beuroner Kunstverlag, Erzabtei St. Martin, 88631 Beuron. T. (07466) 17228, Fax (07466) 17209. - ArtBk /
Repr / Card / Cal –   098162

Bielefeld (Nordrhein-Westfalen)

Jesse, Jürgen, Dr., Neustädter Str 16, 33602 Bielefeld.
T. (0521) 177924, Fax 24051. - ArtBk / Graph / Sli /
Mul –   098163
Keilich & Biasci, Werthestr. 167, 33615 Bielefeld.
T. (0521) 17 94 67. - Graph –   098164
Kerber, Windelsbleicher Str 166-170, 33659 Bielefeld.
T. (0521) 9500810, Fax 9500888. - ArtBk –   098165
Luther-Verlag, Cansteinstr. 1, 33647 Bielefeld.
T. (0521) 448 60. - ArtP –   098166

Bietigheim-Bissingen (Baden-Württemberg)

Verlag im Unteren Tor, Platanenweg 16, 74321 Bietigheim-Bissingen. T. (07142) 920011, Fax 31594.
- ArtBk / Graph / Cal –   098167

Bocholt (Nordrhein-Westfalen)

Art House, Raiffeisenring 21, 46395 Bocholt.
T. (02871) 8822, Fax 18 34 22. - Repr / Card –   098168
Neue Tendenzen Verlagsgesellschaft, Osterstr. 53,
46397 Bocholt. - Graph / Repr / Card –   098169

Bochum (Nordrhein-Westfalen)

Edition Bochumer Glashausatelier, Josephinenstr. 44,
44807 Bochum. T. (0234) 59 45 37. - Graph –   098170
Schwarz Edition, Unterm Kolm 4a, 44797 Bochum.
T. (0234) 79 15 83. - Graph / Mul –   098171

Bonn (Nordrhein-Westfalen)
Deutsche UNESCO-Kommission e.V., Colmantstr 15,
53115 Bonn. T. (0228) 69 20 91, Fax 636912.
- Sli - 098172
Dümmler, Ferdinand, Kaiserstr 31-37, 53113 Bonn.
T. (0228) 91340, Fax 213040. - Repr - 098173
Habelt, Rudolf, Dr., Am Buchenhang 1, 53115 Bonn.
T. (0228) 232015/16, Fax 232017. - ArtBk - 098174
Hennes, Karin, Malteserstr. 24, 53115 Bonn.
T. (0228) 63 62 04. 098175
Marco Edition, Händelstr 12, 53115 Bonn.
T. (0228) 651208. - ArtBk / Graph / Card / Sli /
Mul - 098176
Steinmetz, Bernhard-Michael, Ermekeilstr. 25, 53113
Bonn. T. (0228) 21 51 01, Fax 26 11 14. - ArtBk /
Graph / Card / Mul - 098177
Zytglogge Verlag, Cäsariusstr. 18, 53173 Bonn.
T. (0228) 52 20 30/40, Fax 52 25 24. - ArtBk - 098178

Borken (Nordrhein-Westfalen)
Heimath, H. M., Graf Landsbergstr. 4, 46325 Borken.
T. (02861) 2173, Fax 666 60. - ArtBk / Graph - 098179

Bottrop (Nordrhein-Westfalen)
Pomp, Peter, Gabelsberger Str 4, 46238 Bottrop.
T. (02041) 747110, Fax 747150. - ArtBk / Mul - 098180

Brackenheim (Baden-Württemberg)
Taurus-Kunstkarten, Wurmbachstr 6, 74336 Bracken-
heim. T. (07135) 4055, Fax (07135) 12773.
- Card - 098181

Braunschweig (Niedersachsen)
Archiv Verlag, Kocherstr 2, 38120 Braunschweig.
T. (0531) 12220, Fax 1222199. - Mul - 098182
Fischer, Manfred, Auerstr. 5, 38112 Braunschweig.
T. (0531) 31 15 37. - Graph / Repr - 098183
Kuhle, Michael, Ottmerstr. 7, 38102 Braunschweig.
T. (0531) 787 48. 098184
Masuch & Schnell, Ägidienmarkt 14, 38100 Braun-
schweig. T. (0531) 4 96 04. 098185
Schmücking, Lessingpl 12, 38100 Braunschweig.
T. (0531) 449 60, Fax 44960. - Graph - 098186

Bremen
Art' n Card, Am Dobben 69, 28203 Bremen.
T. (0421) 76713. - Repr / Card - 098187
Banane Design, Außer der Schleifmühle 51, 28203 Bre-
men. T. (0421) 3398490, Fax 3398492. - ArtP - 098188
Brauer, Gustav Art Printing, Wüstestätte 2, 28195 Bre-
men. T. (0421) 32 42 19, Fax 32 08 50. 098189
Der Rote Faden, Werner-von-Siemens-Str. 37, 28357
Bremen. T. (0421) 2574737, Fax 2574738.
- Repr - 098190
edition CON, Benquestr. 29, 28209 Bremen.
T. (0421) 34 11 73. - ArtBk - 098191
Hertz, Michael, Richard-Wagner-Str. 22, 28209 Bremen.
T. (0421) 34 16 70. - Graph - 098192
Krebs & Co., Am Markt 11, 28195 Bremen.
T. (0421) 32 10 13, Fax 32 49 42. 098193
Kunstbuch im Neuen Museum Weserburg, Teerhof 20d,
28199 Bremen. T. (0421) 598 39 14. 098194
Schünemann, Carl Ed., Zweite Schlachtpforte 7, 28195
Bremen. T. (0421) 3690371, Fax 3690339. - ArtBk /
Repr / Cal - 098195
Wassmann, Bettina, Am Wall 164, 28195 Bremen.
T. (0421) 32 76 27. - ArtBk / Graph / Repr - 098196
Wüstenbecker, Karl, Hansestr. 20, 28217
Bremen. 098197

Buchenbach (Baden-Württemberg)
Edition im Höllental, Höllentalstr. 16, 79256 Buchenbach. T. (07661) 07661/4866. 098198

Bühl (Baden-Württemberg)
Konkordia Verlag, Eisenbahnstr 31, 77815 Bühl.
T. (07223) 98890, Fax 988945. 098199

Coburg (Bayern)
Verlag des Kunstvereins Coburg, Hans-Holbein-Weg 10,
96450 Coburg. T. (09561) 28285. - Repr - 098200

Cochem (Rheinland-Pfalz)
Steib, Brunhilde, Moselpromenade 22, 56812 Cochem.
T. (02671) 86 27. 098201

Darmstadt (Hessen)
Bischoff, Annette, Viktoriastr 58, 64293 Darmstadt.
T. (06151) 294139. 098202
Edition Beckers, Rheinstr 99, 64295 Darmstadt.
T. (06151) 899704, Fax 899706. - Graph - 098203
Häußer, Jürgen, Frankfurter Str. 64, 64293 Darmstadt.
T. (06151) 22824, Fax 26854. - ArtBk / Mul - 098204
Roether, Eduard, Berliner Allee 56, 64295 Darmstadt.
T. (06151) 332 55. - ArtBk - 098205
Steindruck-Presse, Müllerstr. 41, 64289 Darmstadt.
T. (06151) 77475. - Graph / Repr - 098206
Verlag der Saalbau-Galerie, Adelungstr. 16, 64283
Darmstadt. T. (06151) 249 39, Fax 29 52 80. - ArtBk /
Graph - 098207
Verlag Kunst und Literatur, Postfach 230 161, 64245
Darmstadt. - ArtBk - 098208
Wissenschaftliche Buchgesellschaft, Hindenburgstr 40,
64295 Darmstadt. T. (06151) 33 08-0, Fax 314128.
- ArtBk / Graph - 098209

Datteln (Nordrhein-Westfalen)
Mertins, Jürgen, Provinzialstr 51, 45711 Datteln.
T. (02363) 66867, Fax 771926. - Repr / Card / Sli /
Mul - 098210

Deisenhofen (Bayern)
Dennoch-Verlag, Gleisental 18, 82041 Deisenhofen.
T. (089) 6131724. - Graph / Card / Cal - 098211

Dessau (Sachsen-Anhalt)
Anhaltische Verlagsgesellschaft, Oechelhaeuserstr 19,
06846 Dessau. T. (0340) 6504323, Fax 6504345.
- Graph / Repr / Cal / ArtBk - 098212

Dielheim (Baden-Württemberg)
König, Edmund von, Schillerstr. 48, 69234 Dielheim.
T. (06222) 720 18, Fax 748 46. - ArtBk / Card /
Sli - 098213

Dießen am Ammersee (Bayern)
D.A. Keramik Kabinett, Postfach 87, 86908 Dießen am
Ammersee. T. (08807) 08807/363. - ArtBk - 098214
Lama-Verlag, Probst-Herkulan-Karg-Str. 22, 86911 Die-
ßen am Ammersee. T. (08807) 18 73. 098215

Dietzenbach (Hessen)
Technical Art, Dreieichstr 50, 63128 Dietzenbach.
T. (06074) 25033, Fax 25066. 098216

Ditzingen (Baden-Württemberg)
Reclam jun., Philipp, Siemensstr 32, 71254 Ditzingen.
T. (07156) 1630, Fax 163197. - ArtBk - 098217

Dortmund (Nordrhein-Westfalen)
Harenberg, Die bibliophilen Taschenbücher, Westfalen-
damm 67, 44141 Dortmund. T. (0231) 4344-0,
Fax 434 42 14. - ArtBk - 098218
Internationale Kunstedition Jürgen Mertins, Blickstr 251,
44227 Dortmund. T. (0231) 770234, Fax 771926.
- ArtBk / Graph - 098219
Lamers, Leni-Rommel-Str. 145, 44309 Dortmund.
T. (0231) 25 10 71/72. - Graph - 098220
Wortkötter, Paul, Gnadenort 3-5, 44135 Dortmund.
T. (0231) 811749. - Graph / Repr - 098221
Zorzycki, Regina, Körner Hellweg 11, 44143 Dortmund.
T. (0231) 59 73 98. - ArtBk / Graph / Repr - 098222

Dreieich (Hessen)
Melzer, Abi, Wildscheuerweg 1, 63303 Dreieich.
T. (06103) 630 61/62. 098223
Schierlingspresse, Postfach 102171, 63267 Dreieich.
T. (06103) 62375. - Graph - 098224

Dresden (Sachsen)
Obergrabenpresse, Ritzenbergstr 5, 01067 Dresden.
T. (0351) 8010865, Fax 8010865. - Graph - 098225
Verlag der Kunst, Glashütter Str 55, 01309 Dresden.
T. (0351) 30052, Fax 35245. - ArtBk / Cal /
Mul - 098226

Düsseldorf (Nordrhein-Westfalen)
Achenbach, Cuxhavener Str 6a, 40221 Düsseldorf.
T. (0211) 9302113, Fax 9302114. - ArtBk / Graph /
Repr / Card / Mul - 098227
Blaeser, Norbert, Bilker Str 5, 40213 Düsseldorf.
T. (0211) 323180, Fax 328887. 098228

Chaos Editions, Kölner Str. 26, 40211 Düsseldorf.
T. (0211) 369041, Fax (0211) 357824. 098229
Cosat Verlag, Paul-Thomas-Str. 1, 40589 Düsseldorf.
T. (0211) 7185159, Fax (0211) 7185273.
- ArtBk - 098230
Droste Verlag, Pressehaus, 40210 Düsseldorf.
T. (0211) 505 26 06. - ArtBk - 098231
Edition Fils, Postfach 230147, 40087 Düsseldorf.
T. (0211) 672063, Fax 672065. - Graph / Repr /
Mul - 098232

Edition GS, Robert-Reinick-Str 2, 40474 Düsseldorf.
T. (0211) 4380092, Fax 4350889. - ArtBk - 098233
Eremiten-Presse, Fortunastr. 11, 40235 Düsseldorf.
T. (0211) 66 05 90. - ArtBk / Graph / Mul - 098234
Grupello Verlag, Schwerinstr 55, 40476 Düsseldorf.
T. (0211) 4912558, Fax 4912558. - ArtBk - 098235
Neumann, Michael, Orangeriestr 6, 40213 Düsseldorf.
T. (0211) 325550, Fax (0211) 324625. 098236
Phil Artes Kunst Editionen, Rethelstr. 20, 40237 Düssel-
dorf. T. (0211) 622509, Fax (0211) 671112.
- Repr - 098237
Rau, Walter, Benderstr. 168a, 40625 Düsseldorf.
T. (0211) 28 30 95. - ArtBk / Graph / Repr /
Card - 098238
Scheelen, Heinz, Akazienstr. 37, 40627 Düsseldorf.
T. (0211) 20 19 29. 098239
Schulgen, A.W., Alte Landstr. 77, 40489 Düsseldorf.
T. (0211) 40 12 06. - Repr - 098240
Thiemig, Karl, Hans-Endt-Str. 69, 40210 Düsseldorf.
T. (0211) 71 57 55. 098241
Verlag des Kunstvereins für die Rheinlande und Westfa-
len, Grabbepl 4, 40213 Düsseldorf. T. (0211) 327023,
Fax 329070. - ArtBk / Graph / Mul - 098242

Duisburg (Nordrhein-Westfalen)
Edition Phönix Shanti, Postfach 101 210, 47012 Duis-
burg. T. (0203) 23785. - ArtBk / Graph / Repr /
Card - 098243
Orober, Bismarckpl. 3, 47051 Duisburg. T. (0203) 7165/
67. 098244
Tushita, Schifferstr. 170a, 47059 Duisburg.
T. (0203) 33 10 66, Fax (0203) 34 35 71. - Graph /
Card - 098245

Ebenhausen (Bayern)
Langewiesche-Brandt, Lechnerstr 27, 82067 Ebenhau-
sen. T. (08453) 4857, Fax 7388. - Repr - 098246

Eckernförde (Schleswig-Holstein)
NEMO – Kunst in Nordeuropa, Bootshaus am Südstrand,
24340 Eckernförde. T. (04351) 712500, Fax 712501.
- ArtBk / Graph - 098247

Eggenstein-Leopoldshafen (Baden-Württemberg)
International Graphics, Dieselstr 7, 76344 Eggenstein-
Leopoldshafen. T. (0721) 978060, Fax 786064.
- Graph / Repr - 098248

Eltville (Hessen)
Bechtermünz Verlag, Rheingauer Str 54, 65343 Eltville.
T. (06123) 2312, 1031. - ArtBk - 098249

Emmerich (Nordrhein-Westfalen)
Graphik Edition Dornick, Dornicker Str. 52, 46446 Emmerich. T. (02822) 8767. - ArtBk / Repr - 098250

Eschborn (Hessen)
Edition Haag, Hinter der Heck 7, 65760 Eschborn.
T. (06196) 41760. - Card - 098251

Essen (Nordrhein-Westfalen)

Bacht, Richard, Heererstr. 26, 45145 Essen.
T. (0201) 74 98 80. *098252*
Burkhard-Verlag, Moltkepl. 63, 45127 Essen.
T. (0201) 25 25 87, Fax (0201) 25 25 31.
- ArtBk - *098253*
Galerie KK, Rüttenscheider Str. 73, 45130 Essen.
T. (0201) 78 82 66. *098254*
Margreff, H.G., Heidhauser Str. 135, 45239 Essen.
T. (0201) 400 52/53. - ArtBk - *098255*
Triptychon Verlag, In der Borbeck 50, 45239 Essen.
T. (0201) 49 47 01, Fax (0201) 49 45 58. - ArtBk / Repr /
Card / Sli - *098256*
Westrich, Josh, Berliner Str. 204, 45144 Essen.
T. (0201) 74 83 40. - Repr / Card - *098257*
Woensampresse, Werkgemeinschaft Deutscher Graphi-
ker, Rosastr 46, 45130 Essen. T. (0201) 776554/55.
- Graph / Card / Cal - *098258*

Esslingen (Baden-Württemberg)

Bechtle, Richard, Zeppelinstr 116, 73730 Esslingen.
T. (0711) 93100, Fax (0711) 3180510. - ArtBk /
Card - *098259*
Berner, Gebr., Obertürkheimer Str 62, 73733
Esslingen. *098260*
Huggele, Küferstr 52, 73728 Esslingen.
T. (0711) 359036. - Graph / Repr / Card - *098261*
Langer, Bruno, Ludwig-Jahn-Str 37, 73732 Esslingen.
T. (0711) 372151, Fax 3701330. - ArtBk - *098262*
Schönemann, Michael, Obertorstr 32a, 73728 Esslingen.
T. (0711) 357293, Fax 355962. - ArtBk /
Graph - *098263*

Ettal (Bayern)

Buch-Kunstverlag Ettal, Benedictinor Abtei Ettal, 82488
Ettal. T. (08822) 67 35, Fax (08822) 74215. - ArtBk /
Repr / Card - *098264*

Feldafing (Bayern)

Buchheim, Biersackstr. 23, 82340 Feldafing.
T. (08157) 12 21. - ArtBk / Graph / Repr / Card /
Cal - *098265*

Feldkirchen (Bayern)

Aries Verlag, Postfach 226, 85619 Feldkirchen, Kr Mün-
chen. T. (089) 9032382, Fax 9030713. - Repr / Card /
Cal - *098266*
Oktogon Verlag, Feldkirchner Str. 2, 85622 Feldkirchen,
Kr. München. T. (089) 904 38 30, Fax (089) 903 07 13.
- ArtBk - *098267*

Fellbach (Baden-Württemberg)

Edition P, Cannstatter Str 84, 70734 Fellbach.
T. (0711) 583799. - ArtBk - *098268*

Filderstadt (Baden-Württemberg)

Domberger, Uhlbergstr. 36-40, 70794 Filderstadt.
T. (0711) 77 10 77, Fax (0711) 777 58 70. - ArtBk /
Graph / Card / Cal / Mul - *098269*

Flensburg (Schleswig-Holstein)

MM-Kunstverlag, Hirschbogen 16, 24941
Flensburg. *098270*

Forchheim, Oberfranken (Bayern)

Schiffmann, Reinhard, Hauptstr 54, 91301 Forchheim,
Oberfranken. - ArtBk - *098271*

Frankenthal, Pfalz (Rheinland-Pfalz)

Edition Dr. O.H. Schindler, Postfach 2133, 67211 Fran-
kenthal, Pfalz. T. (06233) 41317. - ArtBk / Repr /
Card - *098272*
Stocké, Rainer, Eisenbahnstr 30, 67227 Frankenthal,
Pfalz. T. (06233) 20760, Fax (06233) 22262.
- Graph - *098273*

Frankfurt am Main (Hessen)

Alpha-Presse, August-Siebert-Str. 9, 60323 Frankfurt
am Main. T. (069) 55 53 25, Fax (069) 72 07 74.
- ArtBk / Repr - *098274*
Anabas-Verlag, Friesstr 20-24, 60388 Frankfurt am
Main. T. (069) 94219871, Fax 94219872.
- ArtBk - *098275*

Antonow, Alexander, Friedrichstr. 30, 60323 Frankfurt
am Main. T. (069) 17 24 22, Fax (069) 17 22 49.
- ArtBk - *098276*
Art Alt Praunheim, Alt Praunheim 28, 60488 Frankfurt
am Main. T. (069) 76 58 03. - Graph - *098277*
Art System, Stegstr. 53, 60594 Frankfurt am Main.
T. (069) 62 38 14. *098278*
Bockenheimer Presse, c/o T. Jensch, Kiesstr. 15, 60311
Frankfurt am Main. T. (069) 70 28 97. - Graph - *098279*
Büchergilde Gutenberg, Untermainkai 66, 60311 Frank-
furt am Main. T. (069) 27 39 08 40,
Fax (069) 27 39 08 24. - ArtBk - *098280*
Deutsches Architektur Museum, Schaumainkai 43,
60596 Frankfurt am Main. T. (069) 2123 8471,
Fax (069) 2123 7721. *098281*
Edition Atelier Stephan, Corneliusstr. 19, 60325 Frank-
furt am Main. T. (069) 74 53 24. - ArtBk /
Graph - *098282*
Edition Farangis Yegane, Bundenweg 7, 60320 Frankfurt
am Main. T. (069) 56 22 41. - Graph / Repr /
Repr - *098283*
Edition Irmgard Flemming, Blanchardstr. 17, 60487
Frankfurt am Main. T. (069) 70 14 33. - Graph - *098284*
Edition Kimmel, Schifferstr. 42, 60594 Frankfurt am
Main. T. (069) 61 48 88. - Graph / Repr / Card - *098285*
Edition Peter Lugert, Siesmayerstr. 9, 60323 Frankfurt
am Main. T. (069) 75 23 37. *098286*
Edition Zwo, Stegstr. 53, 60594 Frankfurt am Main.
T. (069) 62 38 14. - Graph / Repr / Mul - *098287*
Fahrner & Fahrner, Gerhart-Hauptmann-Ring 228,
60439 Frankfurt am Main. T. (069) 584777,
Fax 584777. - Graph / ArtBk - *098288*
Frankfurter Kunstverein, Markt 44, 60311 Frankfurt am
Main. T. (069) 285330, 285339,
Fax (069) 28 12 53. *098289*
Gierig, Timm, Weckmarkt 17, 60311 Frankfurt am Main.
T. (069) 287111, Fax (069) 283687. - ArtBk /
Graph - *098290*
Grafik Verlag, Friedrichstr 8, 60323 Frankfurt am Main.
T. (069) 723949, Fax 172799. - Graph / Mul - *098291*
Hoeppner, Hans, Bockenheimer Landstr 2-4, 60323
Frankfurt am Main. T. (069) 724420. *098292*
Hunt, Leslie G., Schwanthaler Str. 10, 60594 Frankfurt
am Main. T. (069) 61 59 80, Fax (069) 62 02 85.
- Graph - *098293*
Insel Verlag, Lindenstr. 29-35, 60325 Frankfurt am
Main. T. (069) 756010, Fax (069) 75601522.
- ArtBk - *098294*
Klosterpresse, Seckbächer Gasse 4, 60311 Frankfurt
am Main. - ArtBk / Graph - *098295*
Kramer, Waldemar, Bornheimer Landwehr 57a, 60385
Frankfurt am Main. T. (069) 44 90 45,
Fax (069) 44 90 64. - ArtBk - *098296*
Lang, Peter, Eschborner Landstr 42-50, 60489 Frankfurt
am Main. T. (069) 7807050, Fax 785893.
- ArtBk - *098297*
Materialis Verlag, Rendeler Str. 9-11, 60385 Frankfurt
am Main. T. (069) 65 52 65, 45 08 82. - ArtBk / Graph /
Repr / Cal - *098298*
McBride, Will, Leipziger Str 36, 60487 Frankfurt am
Main. T. (069) 708974, Fax (069) 708974.
- ArtBk - *098299*
Michel & Co., Bertramstr. 73, 60320 Frankfurt am Main.
T. (069) 56 16 46. *098300*
Nesselbusch Presse, Nesselbuschstr. 1, 60439 Frankfurt
am Main. T. (069) 57 49 57. - ArtBk / Card - *098301*
Portikus, Schöne Aussicht 2, 60311 Frankfurt am Main.
T. (069) 60500830, Fax 60500831. - ArtBk / Graph /
Repr - *098302*
Raphael, Domstr 6, 60311 Frankfurt am Main.
T. (069) 291338, Fax 2977532. - Graph - *098303*
Societäts-Verlag, Frankenallee 71-81, 60327 Frankfurt
am Main. T. (069) 75011, Fax 7306965. - ArtBk /
Cal - *098304*
Umschau Buchverlag, Stuttgarter Str. 18-24, 60329
Frankfurt am Main. T. (069) 26000, Fax (069) 2600559.
- ArtBk / Cal - *098305*
Verlag des Kunstgeschichtlichen Instituts der J.-W.-Goe-
the-Universität, Hausener Weg 120/II, 60489 Frankfurt
am Main. T. (069) 79828336, Fax 79828428.
- ArtBk - *098306*
Weidlich, Wolfgang, Savignystr. 59, 60325 Frankfurt am
Main. T. (069) 74 62 15. *098307*

Frauenchiemsee (Bayern)

Kunstverlag Frauenwörth, 83256 Frauenchiemsee.
T. (08054) 653. *098308*

Frechen (Nordrhein-Westfalen)

Ritterbach, Rudolf-Diesel-Str. 10-12, 50226 Frechen.
T. (02234) 18660, Fax (02234) 186690. *098309*

Freiburg (Baden-Württemberg)

Bild-Verlag, Hermann-Herder-Str. 4, 79104 Freiburg.
T. (0761) 271 71. - Card / Sli - *098310*
Edition Abstracta, Sebastian-Kneipp-Str. 28, 79104 Frei-
burg. T. (0761) 248 41. - ArtBk / Graph - *098311*
Herder, Hermann-Herder-Str. 4, 79104 Freiburg.
T. (0761) 27170, Fax 2717520. - ArtBk - *098312*
Historia Verlag, In den Weihermatten 13, 79108 Frei-
burg. T. (0761) 54821, Fax 57994. - Mul - *098313*

Freudenstadt (Baden-Württemberg)

Altendorf, Irmeli & Wolfgang, Wittlensweiler, 72250
Freudenstadt. T. (07441) 7864, Fax 951031. - Repr /
Card - *098314*

Friedberg (Hessen)

Draier, Görbelheimer Mühle 1, 61169 Friedberg.
T. (06031) 24 29. - ArtBk / Graph - *098315*
Edition Hoffmann, Görbelheimer Mühle, 61169 Fried-
berg. T. (06031) 2443, Fax (06031) 62965. - Graph /
Mul - *098316*
Edition Potratz, Römerstr. 47, 61169 Friedberg.
T. (06031) 74 61. - Graph / Repr - *098317*

Friedland (Niedersachsen)

Bartels, Fahrt 4, 37133 Friedland. T. (05509) 1821.
- Repr - *090318*

Friedrichsdorf, Taunus (Hessen)

Edition Marguerite, Adalbert-Stifter-Str 16, 61381 Fried-
richsdorf, Taunus. *098319*
Edition Paul Robert Wilk, Industriestr 18c, 61381 Fried-
richsdorf, Taunus. T. (06175) 5160, Fax (06175) 5398.
- ArtBk / Graph - *098320*
Eschwege & Wölbing, Im Dammwald 16, 61381 Fried-
richsdorf, Taunus. T. (06175) 5763. - Graph /
Card - *098321*

Friedrichshafen (Baden-Württemberg)

Gessler, Robert, Friedrichstr 53, 88045 Friedrichshafen.
T. (07541) 700614, Fax (07541) 700610. *098322*

Füssen (Bayern)

Milz, Franz, Schrundenweg 1 1/2, 87623 Füssen.
T. (08362) 6008/09, Fax (08362) 38754.
- Card - *098323*

Fulda (Hessen)

Sippel, Heuss-Str. 23, 36043 Fulda. T. (0661) 414 78,
Fax (0661) 457 63. - Graph - *098324*

Garching bei München (Bayern)

Poster-Galerie-München, Carl-von-Linde-Str 33, 85748
Garching bei München. T. (089) 3205026,
Fax (089) 3203567. *098325*

Garmisch-Partenkirchen (Bayern)

Lübbert, Ulrich, Dr., Klarweinstr. 39, 82467 Garmisch-
Partenkirchen. T. (08821) 563 01. - Sli - *098326*

Gießen (Hessen)

Mittelhessische Druck- und Verlagsgesellschaft mbH,
Marburger Str. 18-20, 35390 Gießen. T. (0641) 300 30.
- ArtBk - *098327*
Schäfer, K.G., Gartenstr 13, 35390 Gießen.
T. (0641) 33999, Fax 390439. - ArtBk / Graph /
Mul - *098328*

Gilching (Bayern)

Korsch, A., Landsberger Str 77, 82205 Gilching.
T. (08105) 720, Fax 7245. - Repr / Card / Cal - *098329*

Glashütten, Taunus (Hessen)

Gleissner, Ginsterweg 12, 61479 Glashütten, Taunus.
T. (06174) 63652, Fax (06174) 63502. - Repr - *098330*

Göttingen (Niedersachsen)

European Photography, Postfach 3043, 37020 Göttingen. T. (0551) 24820, Fax 25224. - ArtBk - *098331*

Graphikum-Verlag, Wilhelm-Baum-Weg 31, 37077 Göttingen. T. (0551) 37 30 74. - ArtBk / Graph / Repr / Card - 098332

Goslar (Niedersachsen)
Edition Kemenate, Hokenstr. 6, 38640 Goslar.
T. (05321) 2 36 97. - ArtBk / Graph / Cal / Mul - 098333

Gotha (Thüringen)
Edition Balance, Brunnenstr 12, 99867 Gotha.
T. (03621) 750061, Fax 750061. - ArtBk / Graph / Mul - 098334

Gräfelfing (Bayern)
Urbes Verlag, Maria-Eich-Str 78, 82166 Gräfelfing.
T. (089) 85210, Fax 8542291. - ArtBk - 098335

Grafenau (Baden-Württemberg)
Edition Schlichtenmaier, Schloß Dätzingen, 71117 Grafenau. T. (07033) 41394, Fax (07033) 44923.
- ArtBk - 098336

Grafenau (Bayern)
Morsak, Wittelsbacher Str. 2-8, 94481 Grafenau.
T. (08552) 4200, Fax (08552) 42050. - Graph / Card / Cal / Mul - 098337

Grafing (Bayern)
Aquamarin Verlag, Voglherd 1, 85567 Grafing.
T. (08092) 9444, Fax 1614. - ArtBk / Repr / Card - 098338

Grevenbroich (Nordrhein-Westfalen)
Krapohl, Jakob, Schloß Hülchrath, 41516 Grevenbroich.
T. (02181) 7104, Fax 69149. - Repr / Card / Sli / Cal - 098339

Grönenbach (Bayern)
AC-Kunstverlag, Bahnhofsstr. 16, 87730 Grönenbach.
T. (08334) 69 37, Fax (08334) 66 88. - Repr / Card - 098340

Großpösna (Sachsen)
Müller, Christian, Damaschkestr. 47, 04463 Großpösna.
T. (04297) 27 77. 098341

Gütersloh (Nordrhein-Westfalen)
Artico Kunstgrafik, Auf der Horst 17, 33335 Gütersloh.
T. (05241) 73403, Fax (05241) 77268.
- Graph - 098342
Edition Kurze, Spiekergasse 12, 33330 Gütersloh.
T. (05241) 279 71. - ArtBk / Graph / Repr / Card / Cal / Mul - 098343

Haiger (Hessen)
Weber, Rolf, Bahnhofstr 33, 35708 Haiger.
T. (02773) 4548. - Graph / Repr - 098344

Hamburg
Art Service, Heidacker 7e, 22523 Hamburg.
T. (040) 574577, Fax (040) 574577. 098345
art & book edition, Grindelallee 132, 20146 Hamburg.
T. (040) 447936, Fax (040) 4102906. - ArtBk / Graph / Repr / Card / Mul - 098346
Bartkowiak, Heinz Stefan, Körnerstr 24, 22301 Hamburg. T. (040) 2793674, Fax 2704397. - Mul - 098347
Breuel, Ernst, Breite Str 159, 22767 Hamburg.
T. (040) 3898698, Fax 387305. - Mul - 098348
Broschek, Bargkoppelweg 61, 22145 Hamburg.
T. (040) 679 61. 098349
Christians, Hans, Kleine Theaterstr. 10, 20354 Hamburg. T. (040) 35 60 06 35. - ArtBk / Graph / Repr / Card - 098350
Dörrie/Priess, Admiralitätstr 71, 20459 Hamburg.
T. (040) 364131, Fax 362877. - ArtBk / Graph / Mul - 098351
Gingko Press, Hamburger Str 180, 22083 Hamburg.
T. (040) 291425, Fax (040) 291055. - ArtBk - 098352
Glass Expressions, Robert Butt, Mundsburger Damm 54, 22087 Hamburg. T. (040) 220 33 65. 098353
Hanseatischer Verlag, Schallnsteed 6, 21129 Hamburg.
T. (040) 742 78 74. 098354
HB Verlags- und Vertriebsgesellschaft, Alsterufer 4, 20354 Hamburg. T. (040) 4151890. 098355

Hochhuth, Walter D., Poststr 11, 20354 Hamburg.
T. (040) 342211, Fax 352020. - Graph / Repr / Card - 098356
Hoeppner, Hans, Rothenbaumchaussee 103, 20148 Hamburg. T. (040) 453362. - Graph / Repr - 098357
Kellner, Admiralitätstr 71, 20459 Hamburg.
T. (040) 37519825, Fax 37519626. - ArtBk - 098359
Klosterfelde, Helga Maria, Admiralitätsstr 71, 20459 Hamburg. T. (040) 37500754, Fax 37500753. 098360
Kronen-Verlag, Donnerstr. 5-7, 22763 Hamburg.
T. (040) 39 12 07. 098361
Krüger, Arthur F., Erdkampsweg 134, 22335 Hamburg.
T. (040) 59 78 13 / 14. - Repr - 098362
Laurence Art Products, Hofweg 22, 22085 Hamburg.
T. (040) 220 28 59. - Repr - 098363
Lebeer & Hossmann, Rutschbahn 37, 20146 Hamburg.
T. (040) 4104937. - ArtBk / Graph / Mul - 098364
Lochte, Mittelweg 164, 20148 Hamburg.
T. (040) 457851. - Graph - 098365
Museum für Kunst und Gewerbe, Verlagsabteilung, Steintorpl, 20099 Hamburg. T. (040) 24862732, Fax 24862834. - ArtBk - 098366
Rogner & Bernhard, Fettstr 6, 20357 Hamburg.
T. (040) 4302110, Fax 4302716. - ArtBk - 098367
Rohse, Otto, Klotzenmoor 54, 22453 Hamburg.
T. (040) 511 65 06. - Graph - 098368
Schultz, Lohseplatz 2, 20457 Hamburg.
T. (040) 83 40 54. - Graph - 098369
Schwarze Kunst, Stresemannstr 384a, 22761 Hamburg.
T. (040) 8901732, Fax 894084. - Graph - 098370
Svato, Missundestr 18, 22769 Hamburg.
T. (040) 4390004. - ArtBk / Graph - 098371
Verlag Sammlerfreund, Poststr 3, 20354 Hamburg.
T. 01725105216. - ArtBk - 098372
Verlag St. Gertrude, Goldbachstr. 9, 22765 Hamburg.
T. (040) 378 28 47, Fax (040) 38 88 27. - ArtBk / Graph / Repr / Card - 098373
Xenos, Am Hehsel 40, 22339 Hamburg.
T. (040) 538 19 09, 538 23 66, Fax (040) 538 60 00.
- ArtBk - 098374

Hamm (Nordrhein-Westfalen)
Artcolor, Ostenallee 78, 59071 Hamm.
T. (02381) 980190, Fax 9801999. - ArtBk / Repr / Card - 098375
Kley, Werner, Werler Str 304, 59008 Hamm.
T. (02381) 9504040, Fax 9504019. - ArtBk / Graph - 098376

Hamminkeln (Nordrhein-Westfalen)
Stöver, L., Waldstr. 16, 46499 Hamminkeln.
- Graph - 098377

Hanau (Hessen)
Dausien, Werner, Burgallee 67, 63454 Hanau.
T. (06181) 25 90 52. - ArtBk - 098378
Forum Bildkunstverlag, Postfach 700210, 63427 Hanau.
T. (06181) 6760, Fax 676264. - Cal - 098379
Galerie 88, Gustav-Adolf-Str. 9, 63452 Hanau.
T. (06181) 857 88, Fax (06181) 83027. - ArtBk / Graph / Mul - 098380
Peters, Hans, Dr., Saliisweg 56, 63452 Hanau.
T. (06181) 21632, Fax 257064. - ArtBk / Card / Cal - 098381

Hannover (Niedersachsen)
Ars Mundi Collection, Bödekerstr. 13, 30161 Hannover.
T. (0511) 348 43 43. 098382
Bauer, J.H., Holzmarkt 4, 30159 Hannover.
T. (0511) 324485, Fax 324452. - ArtBk / Graph - 098383
Brenske, Helmut, Machandelweg 11, 30419 Hannover.
T. (0511) 633667, Fax 633667. - ArtBk / Repr / Cal - 098384
Cartoonage Galerie und Versand, Wedekindstr 32, 30161 Hannover. T. (0511) 990560, Fax 9905620.
- Repr / Card - 098385
Edition Ars Antiqua, Bödekerstr. 3, 30161 Hannover.
T. (0511) 34 57 01. 098386
Jaeger, Ch., & Co., Hurlebuschweg 7, 30453 Hannover.
T. (0511) 210 09 70. - Sli / Cal / Mul - 098387
Just, Gerald, Postfach 890109, 30514 Hannover.
T. (0511) 9849615, Fax 9849640. - ArtBk - 098388

Lüpfert, Turnierweg 11, 30916 Hannover.
T. (0511) 73 61 78. 098389
Schäfer, Th., Tivolistr 3, 30161 Hannover.
T. (0511) 9909977, Fax (0511) 9909999.
- ArtBk - 098390
Schlüter, Georgswall 4, 30159 Hannover.
T. (0511) 123 60. - ArtBk - 098391
Stübler, Langensalzastr. 1a, 30169 Hannover.
T. (0511) 880066, Fax (0511) 9805177.
- ArtBk - 098392
Taubitz & Sohn, Benno, Tiestestr 14, 30171 Hannover.
T. (0511) 882904, Fax 2834433. - Card / Cal - 098393
Textilwerkstatt-Verlag, Friedenstr 5, 30175 Hannover.
T. (0511) 81 70 06, Fax 813108. - ArtP - 098394
Touristbuch Reise- und Kunstbuchverlagsgesellschaft, Helmstedter Str. 40, 30519 Hannover.
T. (0511) 83 25 40. - ArtBk - 098395
Ulrichs, Timm, Sodenstr. 6, 30161 Hannover.
T. (0511) 31 28 23. - ArtBk / Graph / Mul - 098396
Verlag Plakat-Konzepte, Oskar-Winter-Str 3, 30161 Hannover. T. (0511) 628376, Fax (0511) 628377.
- ArtBk - 098397

Hardheim (Baden-Württemberg)
Kalligraphie Edition, Bretzinger Str 7, 74736 Hardheim.
T. (06283) 6777, Fax 6777. - Repr - 098398

Harsefeld (Niedersachsen)
Albert, Fritz, Horneburger Str. 26, 21698 Harsefeld.
T. (04164) 6221. 098399

Heidelberg (Baden-Württemberg)
Edition Braus, Hebelstr 10, 69115 Heidelberg.
T. (06221) 14080, Fax 14086. - ArtBk - 098400
Edition Günter Gastrock, Hauptstr. 79, 69117 Heidelberg. T. (06221) 24849, Fax (06221) 20519.
- Mul - 098401
Galeria Palatina, Hildastr 12, 69115 Heidelberg.
T. (06221) 168588, Fax 164631. 098402
Galerie Edition Signum, Brückenstr 35, 69120 Heidelberg. T. (06221) 451490, Fax 451491. 098403
Hüthig, Alfred, Dr., Im Weiher 10, 69121 Heidelberg.
T. (06221) 48 92 80, Fax (06221) 48 92 79. - Mul / ArtP - 098404
Jedermann-Verlag, Kaiserstr 6, 69115 Heidelberg.
T. (06221) 14510, Fax 27870. - ArtP - 098405
Museo, Plöck 54, 69117 Heidelberg. T. (06221) 28801, Fax (06221) 28701. 098406
Popp-Verlag, Oberer Gaisbergweg 2, 69115 Heidelberg.
T. (06221) 2 24 57. - Card / Cal - 098407
Vogel, Hauptstr 25, 69117 Heidelberg. T. (06221) 22821, Fax 162142. 098408
Winter, Carl, Lutherstr. 59, 69120 Heidelberg.
T. (06221) 491 11. - ArtBk - 098409

Heidenheim an der Brenz (Baden-Württemberg)
Heidenheimer Verlagsanstalt, In den Seewiesen 16-18, 89520 Heidenheim an der Brenz. T. (07321) 350015, Fax (07321) 350015. - ArtBk - 098410

Heiligenhaus (Nordrhein-Westfalen)
Müller, H.-J., Gohrstr 10, 42579 Heiligenhaus.
T. (02126) 23466/67. - Repr / Cal - 098411

Heitersheim (Baden-Württemberg)
X für U – Schuwald und Pröfrock, Kirchgasse 10, 79423 Heitersheim. T. (07634) 4893, Fax (07634) 4883. 098412

Herten (Nordrhein-Westfalen)
Typos-Verlag, Eschenweg 2, 45699 Herten.
T. (02366) 81805, Fax (02366) 36774. 098413

Hildesheim (Niedersachsen)
Gebr. Gerstenberg, Rathausstr 18-20, 31134 Hildesheim. T. (05121) 1060, Fax 106498. - ArtBk - 098414
Olms, Georg, Hagentorwall 7, 31134 Hildesheim.
T. (05121) 15010, Fax 150150. - ArtBk - 098415
Verlag El Puente, Bischofskamp 42a, 31137 Hildesheim.
T. (05121) 51 41 21. - ArtBk - 098416

Höhr-Grenzhausen (Rheinland-Pfalz)
Starczewski, Hans Joachim, Im Silbertal 4a, 56195
Höhr-Grenzhausen. T. (02624) 2052, Fax 6762.
- ArtBk / Graph / Card / Cal / Mul -   098417

Hohenfelde (Schleswig-Holstein)
Degkwitz, Hermann, Prof., Oberreihe 2, 25358 Hohenfelde. T. (04121) 504. - Graph -   098418

Holzkirchen, Oberbayern (Bayern)
Magdalenen-Verlag, Tölzer Str 13, 83601 Holzkirchen,
Oberbayern. T. (08024) 5051, Fax (08024) 7064.
- Card -   098419

Homburg (Saarland)
Beck, Monika, Am Römermuseum, 66424 Homburg.
T. (06848) 6527. - Graph / Repr -   098420

Hünfelden (Hessen)
Präsenz Galerie Edition, Gnadenthal, 65597 Hünfelden.
T. (06438) 81266, Fax (06438) 81270.
- Graph -   098421

Hürtgenwald (Nordrhein-Westfalen)
Pressler, Guido, Auf dem Strifft, 52393 Hürtgenwald.
T. (02429) 1385. - ArtBk -   098422

Ingelheim (Rheinland-Pfalz)
Kyma, Binger Str 22, 55218 Ingelheim. T. (06132) 3266,
Fax (06132) 3266. - Graph -   098423

Ingolstadt (Bayern)
Rewa Verlag, Neubaustr 2, 85049 Ingolstadt.
T. (0841) 32079. - Card -   098424

Jüchen (Nordrhein-Westfalen)
Condor-Prell, Kölner Str. 28, 41363 Jüchen.
T. (02165) 70 81. - Graph / Repr / Cal -   098425
Eder, K.B., Niersstr. 24, 41363 Jüchen. T. (02165) 2030,
Fax (02165) 7632. - Graph -   098426

Jülich (Nordrhein-Westfalen)
Cieslik, Marianne, Theodor-Heuss-Str. 3, 52428 Jülich.
- ArtBk -   098427

Karlsruhe (Baden-Württemberg)
Braun, G., Karl-Friedrich-Str 14-18, 76133 Karlsruhe.
T. (0721) 1651, Fax 1657308. - ArtBk -   098428
Herr, Harald, Kübelkopfstr. 21, 76189 Karlsruhe.
T. (0721) 57 27 94. - Graph -   098429
Karlsruher Radierpresse, Luisenstr. 14, 76137 Karlsru-
he. T. (0721) 30010.   098430
Rottloff, Sophienstr. 105, 76135 Karlsruhe.
T. (0721) 84 32 25.   098431
Thoma, Hans, Blumenstr. 7, 76133 Karlsruhe.
T. (0721) 147408, Fax (0721) 147406. - Repr - 098432

Kassel (Hessen)
Edition Reichenberger, Pfannkuchstr. 4, 34121
Kassel.   098433
Evangelischer Presseverband Kurhessen-Waldeck e. V.,
Heinrich-Wimmer-Str. 4, 34131 Kassel.
- ArtBk -   098434
Güler, Mehmet, Johann-Hermann-Schein-Str. 8, 34131
Kassel. T. (0561) 345 19. - Graph / Repr -   098435
Sander, Siegfried, Schönfelder Str 3, 34121 Kassel.
T. (0561) 24494, Fax 26049. - ArtBk / Graph / Repr /
Card / Cal / Mul -   098436
Schmitz, Martin, Goethestr 44, 34119 Kassel.
T. (0561) 104734, Fax 713041. - ArtBk -   098437
Thiele & Schwarz, Werner-Heisenberg-Str. 7, 34123
Kassel. T. (0561) 589090, Fax (0561) 5890968.
- ArtBk -   098438
Weber & Weidemeyer, Friedrich-Ebert-Str. 161, 34119
Kassel. T. (0561) 20 32 77-79. - ArtBk -   098439
Wenderoth, Georg, Schillerstr. 36, 34117 Kassel.
T. (0561) 15209. - ArtBk -   098440

Kehl (Baden-Württemberg)
MA-Buch-Marketing, Postfach 1480, 77674 Kehl.
T. (07851) 71034, Fax (07851) 75955.   098441
Wagner, Hildegard, Jahnstr 16, 77694 Kehl.
T. (07851) 482902, Fax (07851) 482902.   098442

Kempen (Nordrhein-Westfalen)
Regrafo, Kerkener Str 23, 47906 Kempen.
T. (02152) 1529. - Cal -   098443
te Neues, Am Selder 37, 47906 Kempen.
T. (02152) 9160, Fax 916111. - Repr / Card / Mul /
Cal -   098444

Kempten (Bayern)
Verlag für Heimatpflege, Westendstr 21, 87439 Kempten. T. (0831) 26775, Fax 15108. - ArtBk -   098445

Kevelaer (Nordrhein-Westfalen)
Anrich, Egmontstr. 28, 47623 Kevelaer.
T. (02832) 70014, Fax (02832) 50094. - Repr - 098446
Butzon & Bercker, Hoogeweg 71, 47623 Kevelaer.
T. (02832) 2906, Fax (02832) 40321. - ArtBk /
Card -   098447

Kiel (Schleswig-Holstein)
Edition Carsten Koch, Seeblick 11, 24106 Kiel.
T. (0431) 333080, Fax 333025. - Graph / Mul - 098448
Künstlerhaus Kiel, Schönkirchener Str. 48, 24149 Kiel.
T. (0431) 287 73, 20 28 68. - ArtBk -   098449
Verlag der Kunsthalle zu Kiel, Düsternbrooker Weg 1,
24105 Kiel. T. (0431) 5973751, Fax 5973754.
- ArtBk -   098450
Wittig, Friedrich, Fleethörn 32, 24103 Kiel.
T. (0431) 51970, Fax 5197292. - ArtBk -   098451
          098451a

Kindsbach (Rheinland-Pfalz)
Wagner, T.E., Kaiserstr. 35, 66862 Kindsbach.
T. (06371) 151 44.   098452

Kippenheim (Baden-Württemberg)
Treichel, Gerhard, Bachgasse 14, 77971 Kippenheim.
T. (07826) 75 47, Fax 5348. - Repr -   098453

Kirchdorf am Inn (Bayern)
Berghaus Oberauer, Hauptstr 19, 84375 Kirchdorf am
Inn. T. (08571) 2868, Fax 6550. - ArtBk -   098454

Koblenz (Rheinland-Pfalz)
Edition Görg, Rathauspassage 6, 56068 Koblenz.
T. (0261) 15487. - Graph -   098455

Köln (Nordrhein-Westfalen)
artQuisit-Edition, Mittelstr 52-54, 50672 Köln.
T. (0221) 257 60 30, 257 36 36, Fax 257 34 97.
- Graph / Mul -   098455a
Baukunst-Galerie, Theodor-Heuss-Ring 7, 50668 Köln.
T. (0221) 7713335, Fax 7713380. - Graph -   098456
Böhlau, Theodor-Heuss-Str 76, 51149 Köln.
T. (0221) 307021, Fax 307349. - ArtBk -   098457
CCA Galleries, Braugasse 14h, 50859 Köln.
T. (02234) 71836, Fax (02234) 4156.   098458
Delphin Verlag, Emil-Hoffmann-Str 1, 50996 Köln.
T. (02236) 39990, Fax (02236) 399997.   098459
Dreiseitel, Aachener Str 1013, 50858 Köln.
T. (0221) 483888, Fax 4844452. - Graph / Mul - 098460
DuMont, Mittelstr. 12-14, 50672 Köln. T. (0221) 2053-1,
Fax (0221) 2053-281. - ArtBk / Graph / Cal -   098461
Edition Alectri, Postfach 45 03 63, 50878 Köln.
T. (0221) 493047, Fax (0221) 493047. - ArtBk / Graph /
Repr / Card / Cal -   098462
Edition Berend von Nottbeck, Salierring 14-16, 50677
Köln. T. (0221) 312878, Fax (0221) 315787.
- ArtBk -   098463
Edition d'Art Cologne, Bobstr. 9, 50676 Köln.
T. (0221) 234946, Fax (0221) 213022.
- Graph -   098464
edition fundamental, Gellertstr. 31, 50733 Köln.
T. (0221) 72 45 93. - ArtBk / Mul -   098465
Edition Kölnischer Kunstverein, Cäcilienstr 33, 50667
Köln. T. (0221) 217021, Fax 210651. - ArtBk - 098466
Edition People Art Animals, Renate Spekowius, Wormser
Str. 25, 50677 Köln. T. (0221) 376 19 47. - Repr /
Card -   098467
Edition Zufall, Mauenheimer Str 32, 50733 Köln.
T. (0221) 7604944. - ArtBk / Graph / Mul -   098468
Editionen der Museen der Stadt Köln, St.-Apern-Str. 17-
21, 50667 Köln. T. (0221) 2214919,
Fax (0221) 2214005. - Repr -   098469
Fritzsche, B., Zülpicher Str 272, 50937 Köln.
T. (0221) 410177, Fax 410177.   098470

Galerie und Edition Hundertmark, Brüsseler Str 29,
50674 Köln. T. (0221) 237944, Fax 249146.
- Graph -   098471
Gesellschaft für Literatur und Bildung, Zollstockgürtel 5,
50969 Köln. T. (0221) 342092, Fax 384040.   098472
Gestlo, de, Aachener Str. 21, 50674 Köln.
T. (0221) 21 91 27. - Graph / Sli / Mul -   098473
Greven, Neue Weyerstr. 1-3, 50676 Köln.
T. (0221) 203 30, Fax (0221) 2033162.
- ArtBk -   098474
Hake, Wolfgang, Pantaleonswall 36, 50676 Köln.
T. (0221) 212726, Fax 239764. - ArtBk / Graph /
Mul -   098475
Haschemi Edition Cologne, Mechternstr. 44, 50823 Köln.
T. (0221) 56 10 07, Fax (0221) 52 92 82. - Card /
Cal -   098476
Holtmann, Heinz, Richartzstr 10, 50667 Köln.
T. (0221) 2578607, 2578716, Fax 2578724.
- Graph -   098477
Kai Yeh Verlag und Offsetdruckerei, Ohmstr 30, 50677
Köln. T. (0221) 385964, Fax (0221) 385561.   098478
Naturalis Verlags- und Vertriebsgesellschaft, Emil-Hoff-
mann-Str 1, 50996 Köln. T. (02236) 39990,
Fax (02236) 399999.   098479
Nauck, Albert, Luxemburger Str 449, 50939 Köln.
T. (0221) 460100, Fax (0221) 4601069.   098480
Post, Constantin, Sachsenring 73, 50677 Köln.
T. (0221) 319529, Fax 328924. - ArtBk / Mul - 098481
Selbstverlag Kunsthaus am Museum, Drususgasse 1-5,
50667 Köln. T. (0221) 9258620, Fax 92586230.
- ArtBk -   098482
Stenvert-Mittrowsky, Antonia, Johanniterstr 2a, 50859
Köln. T. (02234) 70304, Fax 700305. - Graph - 098483
Taschen, Benedikt, Hohenzollernring 53, 50672 Köln.
T. (0221) 201800, Fax (0221) 254919. - ArtBk / Card /
Cal -   098484
Tinaia 9-Verlag, Neusser Str 27-29, 50670 Köln.
T. (0221) 720173. - ArtBk -   098485
Vista Point, Engelhardtstr 38a, 50674 Köln.
T. (0221) 210587/88, Fax 234191. - ArtBk / Card /
Sli -   098486
Vitt, Walter, Maternusstr 29, 50678 Köln.
T. (0221) 314641, Fax 315337. - ArtBk -   098487
Wasserturm Edition, Birkenstr. 9, 50996 Köln.
T. (0221) 35 37 58.   098488
Wienand, Weyertal 59, 50937 Köln. T. (0221) 9440900,
Fax 448911. - ArtBk / Graph -   098489
Wilbrand, Dieter, Lindenstr 20, 50674 Köln.
T. (0221) 244904, Fax (0221) 237592. - Graph /
Repr -   098490
ZYpresse, Mathias Pohlmann, Zülpicher Str. 253, 50937
Köln. T. (0221) 41 70 18. - ArtBk / Repr -   098491

Königstein (Hessen)
Langewiesche, Karl Robert, Grüner Weg 6, 61462 Kö-
nigstein. T. (06174) 7333, Fax 933039. - ArtBk /
Cal -   098492

Königswinter (Nordrhein-Westfalen)
Heel, F.Ch., Hauptstr. 354, 53639 Königswinter.
T. (02223) 266 67. - ArtBk / Cal -   098493

Konstanz (Baden-Württemberg)
Deike, Horst, Robert-Bosch-Str 18, 78467 Konstanz.
T. (07531) 81550, Fax 815581. - ArtBk /
Graph -   098494

Kornwestheim (Baden-Württemberg)
Siebdruck-Atelier Roland Geiger, Verlag für Druckgrafik,
Enzstr. 9, 70806 Kornwestheim. T. (07154) 72 23.
- Graph -   098495

Krefeld (Nordrhein-Westfalen)
Peerlings, Friedrichstr 49, 47798 Krefeld.
T. (02151) 29743, Fax 28524. - ArtBk / Graph - 098496

Kronberg (Hessen)
Opper, Uwe, Tanzhausstr 1, 61476 Kronberg.
T. (06173) 640518, Fax 940194. - ArtBk -   098497

Krummwisch (Schleswig-Holstein)
Blödorn & Ewert, Königstr 15, 24796 Krummwisch.
T. (04334) 623, Fax 704. - Graph / Cal / Card - 098498

HANDBUCH DER EDITIONEN

HANDBOOK OF EDITIONS

MANUEL DES EDITIONS

MANUALE DELLE EDIZIONI

MANUAL DE EDICIONES

DRUCKGRAPHIK · SKULPTUR · PHOTOGRAPHIE · MULTIPLES

GRAPHIC PRINT · SCULPTURE · PHOTOGRAPHY · MULTIPLES

GRAVURE · SCULPTURE · PHOTOGRAPHIE · MULTIPLES

STAMPA D'ARTE · SCULTURA · FOTOGRAFIA · MULTIPLI

GRAFICO IMPRESO · ESCULTURA · FOTOGRAFIA · MULTIPLE

1995-1996

Verlag Depelmann

in Zusammenarbeit mit dem
Bundesverband Deutscher Kunstverleger e.V.

FORUM KULTUR

Kreissparkasse Hannover

Band I 1989-1994, Band II 1994-1995, Band III 1995-1996 (ab Sept. 1996) je Band DM 44,-CD Rom Band I bis III DM 88,- zuzüglich Porto. Zu bestellen über den Buchhandel oder direkt beim Verlag: Galerie Depelmann · Edition · Verlag GmbH, Walsroder Str. 305, 30855 Langenhagen. Tel. 05 11/73 36 93, Fax 05 11/72 36 29

Lamspringe (Niedersachsen)
Quensen, Bismarckstr 8, 31195 Lamspringe.
T. (05183) 94040, Fax 940444. - ArtBk / Repr /
Mul -   *098499*

Landau (Rheinland-Pfalz)
Verlag Pfälzer Kunst, Liebigstr 11, 76829 Landau.
T. (06341) 32609.   *098500*

Langenhagen (Niedersachsen)
Depelmann, Walsroder Str 305, 30855 Langenhagen.
T. (0511) 733693, Fax 723629. - ArtBk /
Graph -   *098501*

Lauda-Königshofen (Baden-Württemberg)
Aquarell Verlag, Deubacher Str. 7, 97922 Lauda-Königshofen. T. (09343) 7665, Fax 4846. - ArtBk / Graph /
Repr / Cal / Mul -   *098502*

Leinfelden-Echterdingen (Baden-Württemberg)
Lucas, Kolumbusstr 25, 70771 Leinfelden-Echterdingen.
T. (0711) 792121, Fax (0711) 7978844. - ArtBk /
Graph / Repr / Card -   *098503*

Leipzig (Sachsen)
Beck, Michael, Naunhofer Str 24, 04299 Leipzig.
T. (0341) 8622550, Fax 8622803.   *098504*
Edition Leipzig, Karlstr. 20, 04103 Leipzig.
T. (0341) 7631, Fax 29 24 35. - ArtBk / Cal /
Mul -   *098505*
edtion m, Matthias Kleindienst, Coppistr. 91, 04157
Leipzig. - Graph -   *098506*
Evangelische Verlagsanstalt, Burgstr 1-5, 04109 Leipzig. T. (0341) 711410. - ArtBk -   *098507*
Kretschmar, Hubert, Prager Str 163, 04299 Leipzig.
T. (0341) 89644, Fax (0341) 89644. - ArtBk -   *098508*
Miniaturbuchverlag Leipzig, Perthesstr. 3, 04317 Leipzig. T. (0341) 686 72 01, 60904, Fax 60290.
- ArtBk -   *098509*
Reclam-Verlag Leipzig, Nonnenstr. 38, 04229 Leipzig.
T. (0341) 47 45 01, Fax 401 25 08. - ArtBk /
Graph -   *098510*
Sammlung Dieterich, Mottelerstr. 8, 04155 Leipzig.
T. (0341) 58726, Fax 5640835. - ArtBk -   *098511*
Sankt Benno-Verlag, Thüringer Str. 1-3, 04179 Leipzig.
T. (0341) 47 41 61, Fax 470802. - ArtBk / Card /
Cal -   *098512*
Schmiedicke, H. C., Kreuzstr. 20, 04103 Leipzig.
T. (0341) 28 24 85. - Repr / Card / Cal / Mul -   *098513*
Seemann, E.A., Jacobstr 6, 04105 Leipzig.
T. (0341) 7736, Fax (0341) 295820. - ArtBk / Repr /
Card / Cal -   *098514*

Leonberg (Baden-Württemberg)
Walter, Hans-Willi, Postfach 1804, 71208 Leonberg.
T. (07152) 24800, Fax (07152) 24698. - ArtBk -   *098515*
Wulff, Dieter, Untere Burghalde 48, 71229 Leonberg.
T. (07152) 6947, Fax 6947. - ArtBk / Graph / Repr /
Card -   *098516*
Zwingmann, Robert, Hertichstr 37, 71229
Leonberg.   *098517*

Lich (Hessen)
Zartbitter, Ettingshäuser Str. 8, 35423 Lich.
- Graph -   *098518*

Lilienthal (Niedersachsen)
Worpsweder Verlag, Alten Eichen 2, 28865 Lilienthal.
T. (04298) 7937, Fax 2862. - ArtBk -   *098519*

Limburg an der Lahn (Hessen)
Edition Phoenix, Hospitalstr 1, 65549 Limburg an der
Lahn. T. (06431) 3168. - Graph -   *098520*

Lingen (Niedersachsen)
Luca Verlag, Wesel 3a, 49811 Lingen. T. (05906) 667,
Fax 2414. - ArtBk -   *098521*

Ludwigsburg (Baden-Württemberg)
Edition Libri Illustri, Neißestr 31, 71638 Ludwigsburg.
T. (07141) 84720, Fax 875117. - ArtBk -   *098522*
Frank, Günther, Mühlstr. 4, 71640 Ludwigsburg.
T. (07141) 23473.   *098523*

Waldner, Erich R., Robert-Mayer-Str. 9, 71636 Ludwigsburg. T. (07141) 87 03 98.   *098524*
Waldner, Erich R., Robert-Mayer-Str. 9, 71636 Ludwigsburg. T. (07141) 87 03 98.   *098525*

Ludwigshafen am Rhein (Rheinland-Pfalz)
Saal, Marsstr 14-16, 67065 Ludwigshafen am Rhein.
T. (0621) 578670.   *098526*

Lübbecke (Nordrhein-Westfalen)
Tantius, Hans-Gerd, Andreasstr 6, 32312 Lübbecke.
T. (05741) 31877, Fax 318799.   *098527*

Lübeck (Schleswig-Holstein)
Kunsthaus Lübeck, Königstr 20, 23552 Lübeck.
T. (0451) 75700, Fax 73755.   *098528*
Luciferlag im Kunsthaus Lübeck, Königstr 20, 23552 Lübeck. T. (0451) 75700, Fax 73755. - ArtBk / Graph /
Repr / Card / Cal / Mul -   *098529*
Möller, Ludwig, Herderstr. 2, 23564 Lübeck.
T. (0451) 79 73 62, Fax (0451) 79 15 77. - Graph /
Repr -   *098530*
Steintor-Verlag, Grapengießerstr 30, 23566 Lübeck.
T. (0451) 8798849, Fax 8798834. - ArtBk / Graph /
Repr / Card / Mul -   *098531*
Verlag Jugend in der Kunst, Moislinger Allee 191, 23558
Lübeck. T. (0451) 89 32 70,
Fax (0451) 89 25 90.   *098532*

Lüdinghausen (Nordrhein-Westfalen)
Barbara Kunsthandels- und Verlagsgesellschaft, Hans-Böckler-Str., Ind.gebiet, 59348 Lüdinghausen.   *098533*

Magdeburg (Sachsen-Anhalt)
Bleimond, c/o Anette Groschopp, Alt Benneckenbeck
28, 39116 Magdeburg. T. (0391) 6312177,
Fax 6312177. - ArtBk / Graph / Mul -   *098534*
Grimm, Jean-Burger-Str. 2, 39112 Magdeburg.
T. (0391) 482 24.   *098535*
Verlag Blaue Äpfel, c/o Michael Groschopp, Benneckenbeck 28, 39116 Magdeburg. T. (0391) 6312177,
Fax 6312177. - ArtBk / Graph / Mul -   *098536*

Mainhardt (Baden-Württemberg)
Verlag im Atelierhaus, Keltenring 60, 74535 Mainhardt.
T. (07903) 688. - ArtBk / Repr / Card / Cal -   *098537*

Mainz (Rheinland-Pfalz)
Edition Brönner, Augustinerstr. 43, 55116 Mainz.
T. (06131) 22 46 93. - Graph -   *098538*
Edition Euro Art, Große Langgasse, 55116 Mainz.
T. (06131) 1522, Fax (06131) 8231. - Graph -   *098539*
Edition F. Despalles, Kirchstr. 44, 55124 Mainz.
T. (06131) 42683, Fax (06131) 42170. - Graph /
Mul -   *098540*
van der Koelen, Dorothea, Dr., Hinter der Kapelle 54,
55128 Mainz. T. (06131) 34664, 834380, Fax 369076.
- ArtBk / Graph / Card / Mul -   *098541*
Schmidt, Hermann, Robert-Koch-Str 8, 55129 Mainz.
T. (06131) 50600, Fax 506070. - ArtBk / Graph /
Cal -   *098542*
Weber, Augustinerstr. 43, 55116 Mainz.
T. (06131) 2246 93. - Graph -   *098543*
Zabern, Philipp von, Welschnonnengasse 13A, 55116
Mainz. T. (06131) 28 74 70, Fax (06131) 22 37 10.
- ArtBk / Repr / Cal -   *098544*

Mannheim (Baden-Württemberg)
Amiralai, Wilhelm-Busch-Str 23, 68259 Mannheim.
T. (0621) 795203, Fax (0621) 797279.   *098545*
Art-U6, Antonitsch, Augusta-Anlage 3, 68159 Mannheim. T. (0621) 41 49 96. - Graph -   *098546*
Edition Galeria Panetta, Augusta-Anlage 54-56, 68159
Mannheim. T. (0621) 44 84 41, 89 19 35.   *098547*
Holme, Peter, Waldfrieden 58, 68305 Mannheim.
T. (0621) 75 61 58. - ArtBk / Repr -   *098548*
Multimedia Publikations- und Verlagsgesellschaft, Augartenstr 86, 68165 Mannheim. T. (0621) 4400999,
Fax 4400915.   *098549*

Marburg (Hessen)
Basilisken-Presse, Hirschberg 5, 35037 Marburg.
T. (06421) 15188. - ArtBk / Graph -   *098550*

Hitzeroth, Wolfram, Dr., Franz-Tuczek-Weg 1, 35039
Marburg. T. (06421) 409261, Fax (06421) 409262.
- ArtBk -   *098551*
Jonas Verlag, Weidenhäuser Str 88, 35037 Marburg.
T. (06421) 25132. - ArtBk -   *098552*

Marktheidenfeld (Bayern)
Bröstler, Horst, Petzoltstr. 14, 97828 Marktheidenfeld.
T. (09391) 4055, Fax (09391) 5959. - ArtBk -   *098553*

Mechernich
Kagyü-Dharma Verlag, Schloß Wachendorf, 53894 Mechernich. T. (02256) 850, Fax (02256) 1757.   *098554*

Meerbusch (Nordrhein-Westfalen)
B9 Gemälde, Moerser Str 74, 40667 Meerbusch.
T. (02132) 5449, Fax 5449. - Graph -   *098555*
Staedtner,F.,Dr., Wienenweg 3a, 40670 Meerbusch.
T. (02159) 528288, Fax (02159) 528391.   *098556*
Stoedtner, F., Dr., Wienenweg 3a, 40670 Meerbusch.
T. (02159) 528288, Fax 528391. - Sli -   *098557*

Melle (Niedersachsen)
Mergus Verlag, Im Wiele 27, 49328 Melle.
T. (05422) 3636, Fax 1404. - Repr -   *098558*

Memmingen (Bayern)
Dietrich, Maximilian, Weberstr 36, 87700 Memmingen.
T. (08331) 2853, Fax 490364. - ArtBk -   *098559*
Edition Curt Visel, Weberstr 36, 87700 Memmingen.
T. (08331) 2853, Fax 490364. - ArtBk / Graph / Cal /
ArtP -   *098560*

Meudt (Rheinland-Pfalz)
Edition Tietze, Nachtigallenweg 10, 56414 Meudt.
T. (06435) 88 22. - Graph -   *098561*

Minden (Nordrhein-Westfalen)
Bruns, J. C. C., Obermarktstr 26-30, 32423 Minden.
T. (0571) 8820. - ArtBk -   *098562*
Edition Lübking, Alemannstr 2, 32423 Minden.
T. (0571) 23536, 28826. - ArtBk -   *098563*

Möckmühl (Baden-Württemberg)
Aue Verlag, Korberstr 20, 74219 Möckmühl.
T. (06298) 1328, Fax 4298. - Graph / Cal -   *098564*

Mönchengladbach (Nordrhein-Westfalen)
Blaumond, Windthorststr 2, 41061 Mönchengladbach.
T. (02161) 4162. - Graph / Card -   *098565*
Zimmermann & Franken, Lürriper Str. 228, 41065 Mönchengladbach. T. (02161) 66 44 27, 44960, Fax 48412.
- ArtBk / Graph / Mul -   *098566*

Moers (Nordrhein-Westfalen)
edition aragon, Neumarkt 7-9, 47441 Moers.
T. (02841) 16561, Fax (02841) 24336. - ArtBk -   *098567*

Mossautal (Hessen)
White Light Verlag, Neudorf 3, 64756 Mossautal.
- Repr -   *098568*

Mülheim an der Ruhr (Nordrhein-Westfalen)
Dohrenbusch, Josef, Kuhlendahl 98, 45470 Mülheim an
der Ruhr.   *098569*

München (Bayern)
Ackermanns, F.A., Wiener Pl 7-8, 81667 München.
T. (089) 4890880, Fax 48908848. - Cal -   *098570*
Antiquitäten-Zeitung Verlag, Nymphenburger Str 84,
80636 München. T. (089) 1269900,
Fax 12699048.   *098571*
arsEdition, Friedrichstr 9, 80801 München.
T. (089) 38100677, Fax (089) 38100655.
- ArtBk -   *098572*
Art Hilscher, Keuslinstr 1, 80798 München.
T. (089) 2719446, Fax 2780017. - Repr / Card -   *098573*
Artemis & Winkler Verlag, Hackenstr. 5, 80331 München. T. (089) 2311980, Fax (089) 264499.
- ArtBk -   *098574*
Arts & Antiques Edition, Postfach 400128, 80701 München. T. (089) 349830, Fax (089) 349834.
- ArtBk -   *098575*

Bangert, Albrecht, Dr., Peter-Paul-Althaus-Str 9f, 80805 München. T. (089) 365372. - ArtBk - *098576*

Beck, C.H., Wilhelmstr. 9, 80801 München. T. (089) 381890, Fax (089) 38189398. - ArtBk - *098577*

Bizarr-Verlagsgesellschaft, Kreuzstr. 23, 80331 München. T. (089) 26 39 29. *098578*

Blanc & Haenle, Ismaninger Str. 58-60, 81675 München. T. (089) 470 80 84, Fax (089) 47 12 77. - Graph / Repr - *098579*

Bühn, Josef, Jollystr. 5, 81545 München. T. (089) 64 86 12, Fax (089) 642 19 35. - ArtBk - *098580*

Calig, Landsberger Str. 77, 80339 München. T. (089) 502 60 25. - Sli - *098581*

Callwey, Georg D.W., Streitfeldstr. 35, 81673 München. T. (089) 4360050, Fax (089) 43600513. - ArtBk - *098582*

CCC-Cartoon-Caricature-Contor, Rosmarinstr 4, 80939 München. T. (089) 3233669, Fax 3226859. - ArtBk - *098583*

Collection Rolf Heyne, Türkenstr. 5-7, 80323 München. T. (089) 23 17 170, Fax (089) 280 09 43. - ArtBk - *098584*

Deutscher Kunstverlag, Nymphenburger Str 84, 80636 München. T. (089) 1215160, Fax 12151610. - ArtBk / Card - *098585*

Dry, Amalienstr 71, 80799 München. T. (089) 280623, 3397472, Fax 2805332. - ArtBk - *098586*

Duncker, Alexander, Hollerstr. 4, 80995 München. T. (089) 1502185. - ArtBk - *098587*

Edition de Beauclair, Gabelsbergerstr. 17, 80333 München. T. (089) 281500, Fax (089) 286063. - ArtBk / Graph / Mul - *098588*

Edition Galerie Hermeyer, Wilhelmstr. 3, 80801 München. T. (089) 39 61 96. - Repr - *098589*

Edition Gross, Thierschstr. 51, 80538 München. T. (089) 29 62 72, Fax (089) 29 55 10. - Graph / Repr - *098590*

Edition Helga Lengenfelder, Schönstr. 51, 81543 München. T. (089) 66 38 45. - ArtBk - *098591*

Edition Kunstpodium, Postfach 430101, 80731 München. T. (089) 344520. - ArtBk / Card - *098592*

Edition Michael Fischer, Postfach 140266, 80452 München. T. (089) 2913386, Fax 2913642. - ArtBk - *098593*

Edition Pfefferle, Maximilianstr 16, 80539 München. T. (089) 297969, Fax (089) 2913571. - ArtBk / Graph - *098594*

Edition Siegfried Hafner, Münchner Freiheit 7, 80802 München. T. (089) 34 56 72. *098595*

Frühmorgen, Schwindstr 5, 80798 München. T. (089) 5427220, Fax 54272244. *098596*

Gruber, Werkstattpresse, Hermann, Bereiteranger 15, 81541 München. T. (089) 65 67 00. - ArtBk - *098597*

Hahn, Mauerkircherstr 102, 81925 München. T. (089) 985524, Fax (089) 4704860. *098598*

Hartmann, Richard P., Franz-Joseph-Str. 20, 80801 München. T. (089) 347967, Fax (089) 349694. - ArtBk / Graph - *098599*

Hatzfeld, Georg von, Elisabethstr. 42, 80796 München. T. (089) 271 42 49, Fax 33 11 09. - ArtBk - *098600*

Herbig, F. A., Thomas-Wimmer-Ring 11, 80539 München. T. (089) 2350080, Fax 23500844. - ArtBk / Repr - *098601*

Hirmer, Nymphenburger Str 84, 80636 München. T. (089) 1215160, Fax 12151610. - ArtBk / Card - *098602*

Jahn, Fred, Maximilianstr 10, 80539 München. T. (089) 220714, 220117, Fax 221541. - ArtBk - *098603*

Keller, Dany, Buttermelcherstr 11, 80469 München. T. (089) 226132, Fax 295508. - ArtBk / Card - *098604*

Keysersche Verlagsbuchhandlung, Landshuter Allee 38, 80637 München. T. (089) 12 69 04-0, Fax 12 69 04 25. - ArtBk - *098605*

Klinkhardt & Biermann, Landshuter Allee 38, 80637 München. T. (089) 1269040, Fax 12690425. - ArtBk - *098606*

Knaus, Albrecht, Neumarkter Str 18, 81673 München. T. (089) 431890. *098607*

Kotziok, Roman, Theresienhöhe 3, 80339 München. T. (089) 502 30 73. - ArtBk / Graph - *098608*

kunst publik, Konradstr. 10a, 80801 München. T. (089) 34 53 50, 33 82 22. - Graph - *098609*

Langen-Müller, Thomas-Wimmer-Ring 11, 80539 München. T. (089) 235 00 80. - ArtBk - *098610*

Leger, Helmut, Herzogstr 41, 80803 München. T. (089) 393930, Fax (089) 334033. - ArtBk / Graph - *098611*

Lipp, Karl M., Postfach 710624, 81456 München. T. (089) 7858080. - ArtBk / Repr / Card / Cal / Mul - *098612*

List Verlag, Goethestr 43, 80336 München. T. (089) 51480. - ArtBk - *098613*

Loo, Otto van de, Maximilianstr 27, 80539 München. T. (089) 226270, Fax (089) 2285599. - ArtBk / Graph - *098614*

Magazinpresse Verlag, Elisenstr. 3, 80335 München. T. (089) 55 13 50. *098615*

Maximilian Verlag, Possartstr 12, 81679 München. T. (089) 4708051, Fax 471260. - Graph - *098616*

Mosel und Tschechow, Winterstr 7, 81543 München. T. (089) 6515621, Fax (089) 669350. *098617*

Münchener Bildkunst Verlag, Scherrstr. 6, 80639 München. T. (089) 17 15 50. - Card - *098618*

Nazraeli, Siegfriedstr 17, 80803 München. T. (089) 395099. - ArtBk - *098619*

Neuland-Bund und Verlag, Feichthofstr. 165, 81247 München. T. (089) 88 07 61. - Repr - *098620*

Nöttling & Fasser, Marbachstr. 2, 81369 München. T. (089) 760 23 85. - Repr - *098621*

Nymphenburger Verlagshandlung, Thomas-Wimmer-Ring 11, 80539 München. T. (089) 290880, Fax 29088144. - ArtBk - *098622*

Oldenbourg, R., Rosenheimer Str. 145, 81671 München. T. (089) 411 21. *098623*

Omnibus Press, Hohenstaufenstr 7, 80801 München. *098624*

Orbis Verlag, Neumarkter Str 18, 81673 München. T. (089) 43189577. - ArtBk - *098625*

Pantheon Verlag, Nymphenburger Str 86, 80636 München. T. (089) 1257302, Fax 1257269. - ArtBk / ArtP - *098626*

Porta-Verlag, Tangastr. 22, 81827 München. T. (089) 430 22 01. - Repr - *098627*

Praun, Nebelhornstr 22a, 80686 München. T. (089) 54729570. - Repr / Card / Sli - *098628*

Prestel, Mandlstr. 26, 80802 München. T. (089) 38 17 090, Fax 38 17 09 35. - ArtBk - *098629*

Puluj, Georg, Widenmayerstr. 49, 80538 München. T. (089) 29015692, Fax 220629. - ArtP - *098630*

Rose Verlag, Oettingenstr 62, 80538 München. T. (089) 359 73 77. - Graph - *098631*

Sandor, L., Ingolstädter Str. 40, 80807 München. T. (089) 8641189, Fax 8632310. - Repr / Card - *098632*

Schild-Verlag, Henschelstr 7, 81249 München. T. (089) 39 30 37/38, Fax 338695. - ArtBk / Graph / Mul - *098633*

Schirmer/Mosel, Franz-Joseph-Str. 12, 80801 München. T. (089) 297299, Fax 2904515. *098634*

Schneider-Henn, Galeriestr 2b, 80539 München. T. (089) 2710180, Fax 2716957. - ArtBk - *098635*

Schreiber, Silke, Agnesstr 12, 80798 München. T. (089) 65 35 90. - ArtBk / Graph - *098636*

Schroll, Anton & Co., Boosstr. 15, 81541 München. T. (089) 291738, Fax (089) 291507. *098637*

Spielvogel, Gudrun, Oettingenstr 22, 80538 München. T. (089) 8115289. - ArtBk / Graph / Card / Mul - *098638*

Stöberlein, Günter, Niethammerstr 15, 80997 München. T. (089) 41902828, Fax 41902829. - ArtBk / Graph - *098639*

Storms, Walter, Ismaninger Str 51, 81675 München. T. (089) 185871. *098640*

Studio Bruckmann, Nymphenburger Str 84, 80636 München. T. (089) 51480. - ArtBk - *098641*

Südwest-Verlag, Goethestr. 43, 80336 München. T. (089) 280 90 95, Fax 280 95 28. *098642*

tuduv Verlagsgesellschaft, Gabelsbergerstr. 15, 80333 München. T. (089) 39 43 66. *098643*

Verlag Galerie B.O.A., Siegfriedstr. 19, 80803 München. T. (089) 799011, Fax 7918988. - ArtBk - *098644*

Verlag Laterna Magica, c/o Callwey, Wolfratshauser Str 278, 81479 München. *098645*

Waldrich, Joachim, Belgradstr 9, 80796 München. T. (089) 30778440, Fax 30778148. - ArtBk - *098646*

WB Verlag, Nymphenburger Str 84, 80636 München. T. (089) 12699031, Fax 12699011. - ArtBk - *098647*

Weber, Annerose, Metzstr 5, 81667 München. T. (089) 4801801. *098648*

Weltkunst Verlag, Nymphenburger Str 84, 80636 München. T. (089) 1269900, Fax 12699011. - ArtBk / ArtP - *098649*

Wittenbrink, Bernhard, Jahnstr 18, 80469 München. T. (089) 2605580, Fax (089) 2605868. - ArtBk / Graph / Mul - *098650*

Wolfrum, Boosstr 15, 81541 München. T. (089) 653590. *098651*

Münster (Nordrhein-Westfalen)

Artdata Verlag, Ottmarsbocholter Str 6, 48163 Münster. T. (02501) 58036, Fax 58636. - ArtBk - *098652*

Edition Schnake, Windthorststr 37, 48143 Münster. T. (0251) 518363, Fax 518364. - Graph / Repr / ArtBk / Mul - *098653*

Hüning, Bernhard, Grevener Str. 343, 48159 Münster. T. (0251) 21 56 40, 21 16 68, Fax 215640. - ArtBk / Graph / Mul - *098654*

Inventa, Grevener Str. 353, 48159 Münster. T. (0251) 21 80 18/19, Fax 26 11 58. - Card - *098655*

Kleinheinrich, Königsstr 42, 48143 Münster. T. (0251) 55572, Fax 55572. - ArtBk - *098656*

Mandragora Verlag, Höltenweg 65, 48155 Münster. T. (0251) 61 49 19, Fax 61 78 12. - ArtBk - *098657*

Wienhausen, Rosenplatz 10, 48143 Münster. T. (0251) 42433, Fax 58584. - Graph - *098658*

Neu-Isenburg (Hessen)

Edition Tiessen, Postfach 2179, 63243 Neu-Isenburg. T. (06102) 53335. - ArtBk / Graph - *098659*

Patio, Waldstr 115, 63263 Neu-Isenburg. T. (06103) 373949. - ArtBk / Graph / Mul - *098660*

Neubrandenburg (Mecklenburg-Vorpommern)

federchen Verlag, Dahlener Weg, 17034 Neubrandenburg. T. (0395) 4224287, Fax (0395) 4224287. *098661*

Neumünster (Schleswig-Holstein)

Wachholtz, Karl, Rungestr. 4, 24537 Neumünster. T. (04321) 56720, Fax 56778. - ArtBk - *098662*

Neusäß (Bayern)

Hannesschläger, Josef, Siemensstr 2, 86356 Neusäß. T. (0821) 465015, Fax (0821) 469153. - ArtBk / Cal - *098663*

Neuss (Nordrhein-Westfalen)

Hanke, Gerhard, Postfach 210554, 41431 Neuss. T. (02137) 7840, Fax 784150. - ArtBk - *098664*

Niederdorfelden (Hessen)

art design, Erika Steidten, Altkönigstraße, 61138 Niederdorfelden. *098665*

Nördlingen (Bayern)

Uhl, Alfons, Dr., Mittlere Gerbergasse 1, 86720 Nördlingen. T. (09081) 872 48, Fax 23710. - ArtBk - *098666*

Norderstedt (Schleswig-Holstein)

Patzwall, Klaus D., Tangstedter Weg 52, 22851 Norderstedt. *098667*

Nürnberg (Bayern)

afv-Verlag, Postfach 820119, 90252 Nürnberg. T. (0911) 612219, Fax 652046. - ArtBk / ArtP - *098668*

arte factum Verlagsgesellschaft, Winterstr 1, 90431 Nürnberg. T. (0911) 612219, Fax 652046. - ArtBk / Repr / Card / Cal / Mul / ArtP - *098669*

Bode, Klaus D., Elbinger Str 11, 90491 Nürnberg. T. (0911) 5109200, Fax (0911) 5109108. - Graph - *098670*

Carl, Hans, Andernacher Str 33a, 90411 Nürnberg. T. (0911) 952850, Fax 9528547. - ArtBk / ArtP - *098671*

DA Verlag, Röthensteig 15, 90408 Nürnberg. T. (0911) 993540, Fax 352958. - ArtBk - *098672*

DMK Verlag, Hutergasse 4, 90403 Nürnberg. T. (0911) 22 76 98, Fax 20 88 97. - ArtBk / Graph / Repr / Card / Sli / Mul - *098673*

Glock und Lutz, Bayreuther Str. 25, 90409 Nürnberg. T. (0911) 55 62 38. - ArtBk - *098674*

Liebermann & Co., Merianstr. 36, 90409 Nürnberg. *098675*

Miba, Schanzäckerstr. 24-26, 90443 Nürnberg. - ArtBk - *098676*

Puhlfürst, Curt, Wodanstr 75, 90461 Nürnberg. T. (0911) 465131, Fax 465131. - Card / Sli - *098677*

RE-AL Kunstverlag, Burgstr 21, 90403 Nürnberg. T. (0911) 222999, Fax 222455. - Repr / Card / Sli / Cal - *098678*

Ringer, Angela, Obere Wörthstr. 13, 90403 Nürnberg. T. (0911) 22 42 17. - Graph - *098679*

Ulrich, Karl, Wodanstr. 34, 90461 Nürnberg. T. (0911) 496 55. - Repr - *098680*

Verlag für Moderne Kunst, Königstr 51, 90402 Nürnberg. T. (0911) 227623, Fax 2419224. - ArtBk - *098681*

Wolff, Jürgen, Keplerstr 17, 90478 Nürnberg. T. (0911) 463927. - Graph / Repr / Mul - *098682*

Ober-Mörlen (Hessen)
Scheibel, Dieter, Nauheimer Str 26, 61239 Ober-Mörlen. T. (06002) 7396, (06032) 3650. - Graph - *098683*

Obertshausen (Hessen)
Avanlache NCG, Seligenstädter Str 85, 63179 Obertshausen. T. (06104) 72357. - Repr / Card - *098684*

Oberursel (Hessen)
Edition Articon, Köhlerweg 16, 61440 Oberursel. T. (06171) 52508, Fax 56812. *098685*

Offenbach (Hessen)
Bintz, Große Marktstr. 36-44, 63065 Offenbach. T. (069) 806 31. - ArtBk - *098686*

Die Galerie, Berliner Str 218, 63067 Offenbach. T. (069) 816466. *098687*

Holz-Vonderbeck, Dielmannstr. 45, 63069 Offenbach. - Graph - *098688*

Huber, Volker, Berliner Str 218, 63067 Offenbach. T. (069) 814523, Fax 880155. - ArtBk / Graph - *098689*

Hügelow, Manfred, Kaiserstr. 94, 63065 Offenbach. T. (069) 62 62 73. *098690*

Lineart-Gesellschaft für Sammlereditionen, Berliner Str. 218, 63067 Offenbach. T. (069) 82 44 02, Fax 88 01 55. - ArtBk / Graph / Repr - *098691*

Unica T, Domstr 57, 63067 Offenbach. T. (069) 825782, Fax 824762. - Mul / Graph - *098692*

Offenburg (Baden-Württemberg)
Huber, Franz, Hauptstr 128, 77652 Offenburg. T. (0781) 72038, Fax 72039. *098693*

Oldenburg, Oldenburg (Schleswig-Holstein)
Isensee, Haarenstr. 20, 26122 Oldenburg, Oldenburg. T. (0441) 25388, Fax 17872. - ArtBk - *098694*

Vondrlik, J., Wiesenstr. 34, 26135 Oldenburg, Oldenburg. T. (0441) 129 20, 16431. - Repr - *098695*

Osnabrück (Niedersachsen)
Zeller, Otto, Jahnstr. 15, 49080 Osnabrück. T. (0541) 412 17. - ArtBk - *098696*

Ostfildern (Baden-Württemberg)
Cantz, Senefelderstr 9, 73760 Ostfildern. T. (0711) 449930, Fax 4414579. - ArtBk - *098697*

Hatje, Gerd, Senefelderstr 9, 73760 Ostfildern. T. (0711) 449930, Fax 4414579. - ArtBk / Graph - *098698*

Kühnle, Carl, Maybachstr. 11, 73760 Ostfildern. *098699*

Ottersberg (Niedersachsen)
Verlag Atelier im Bauernhaus, In der Bredenau 6, 28870 Ottersberg. T. (04293) 491, Fax 1238. - ArtBk / Repr / Card / Cal - *098700*

Passau (Bayern)
Verlag Passavia, Vornholzstr 40, 94036 Passau. T. (0851) 700215, Fax 700257. - ArtBk - *098701*

Peißenberg (Bayern)
Artothek, Fendt 4a, 82380 Peißenberg. T. (08803) 9214, Fax 9213. - Sli - *098702*

Pfaffenweiler (Baden-Württemberg)
Pfaffenweiler Presse, Mittlere Straße 23, 79292 Pfaffenweiler. T. (07664) 8999. - Graph - *098703*

Pforzheim (Baden-Württemberg)
Hertenstein-Presse, Mathystr 36, 75173 Pforzheim. T. (07231) 27084. - ArtBk / Graph - *098704*

Piesport (Rheinland-Pfalz)
Ottenhausen Verlag, 54498 Piesport. T. (06507) 935615, Fax 935688. - ArtBk / Mul - *098705*

Pinneberg (Schleswig-Holstein)
Raecke, Renate, Amselstieg 31, 25421 Pinneberg. T. (04101) 654 72. - ArtBk - *098706*

Pöcking (Bayern)
Kirchner, Bernd H.D., Lindenberg 5, 82343 Pöcking. T. (08157) 1498, Fax 1616. - Mul - *098707*

Pulheim (Nordrhein-Westfalen)
Rheinland-Verlag, Abtei Brauweiler, 50250 Pulheim. T. (02238) T02234/8051. - ArtBk / Graph / Card / Sli / Mul - *098708*

Rangendingen-Höfendorf (Baden-Württemberg)
Edition Automobile, Kesslerstr 21, 72414 Rangendingen-Höfendorf. T. (07471) 1597, Fax 8197. - ArtBk / Repr / Card - *098709*

Rastatt (Baden-Württemberg)
Moewig, Arthur, Karlsruher Str. 31, 76437 Rastatt. T. (07222) 13-1, Fax 13218. - ArtBk - *098710*

Neff, Paul, Karlsruher Str. 31, 76437 Rastatt. T. (07222) 131, Fax 13218. - ArtBk - *098711*

Recklinghausen (Nordrhein-Westfalen)
Bongers, Aurel, Dortmunder Str. 67, 45665 Recklinghausen. T. (02361) 410 01, Fax 41004. - ArtBk / Repr / Card / Cal - *098712*

Musarion Verlag, Speckhorner Str 262, 45659 Recklinghausen. - ArtBk / Graph - *098713*

Paulus-Verlag K. Bitter KG, Löhrhofstr. 10, 45657 Recklinghausen. T. (02361) 230 94. - ArtBk - *098714*

Regensburg (Bayern)
Bäumler, Peter, Obere Bachgasse 9, 93047 Regensburg. T. (0941) 560263, Fax (0941) 566097. *098715*

Lankes & Spaan, Sedanstr 21, 93055 Regensburg. T. (0941) 7957397, Fax 7957592. *098716*

Pustet, Friedrich, Gutenbergstr 8, 93051 Regensburg. T. (0941) 920220, Fax 948652. - ArtBk - *098717*

Schnell & Steiner, Leibnizstr 13, 93055 Regensburg. T. (0941) 7878516, Fax 7878516. - ArtBk - *098718*

Reinbek (Schleswig-Holstein)
Dialog-Verlag, Haidkoppelweg 24, 21465 Reinbek. T. (040) 711 14 24. - ArtBk - *098719*

Remagen (Rheinland-Pfalz)
Marschner, Günter, Kölner Str. 3, 53424 Remagen. T. (02642) 3527, Fax 23463. *098720*

Remscheid (Nordrhein-Westfalen)
Vice-Versand, Postfach 100343, 42803 Remscheid. T. (02191) 330 49. *098721*

Remseck (Baden-Württemberg)
RVG Rheingauer Verlagsgesellschaft, Hofener Weg 33a, 71686 Remseck. T. (07146) 998-0, Fax 91617. - ArtBk - *098722*

Rendsburg (Schleswig-Holstein)
Jerenstedt, Kuhler Weg 16, 24768 Rendsburg. T. (04331) 813. *098723*

Schleswiger Druck- und Verlagshaus, Bahnhofstr. 12-16, 24768 Rendsburg. T. (04331) 59102, Fax 59 13 45. - ArtBk - *098724*

Rheda-Wiedenbrück (Nordrhein-Westfalen)
Artes, Berliner Str 52, 33378 Rheda-Wiedenbrück. T. (05242) 410720. *098725*

Rhede (Nordrhein-Westfalen)
Edition S. Siedlaczek, Krommert 9a, 46414 Rhede. T. (02872) 32 68. *098726*

Rheinbach (Nordrhein-Westfalen)
CMZ-Verlag, Kallenturm 2, 53359 Rheinbach. T. (02226) 912626, Fax 912627. - ArtBk - *098727*

Rimpar (Bayern)
Krackenberger, Helmut, Riemenschneiderstr. 18, 97222 Rimpar. T. (09365) 18 81, Fax 3581. - ArtBk / Card / Cal - *098728*

Rinteln (Niedersachsen)
Bösendahl, C., Klosterstr. 32-33, 31737 Rinteln. T. (05751) 400 00, Fax 40 00 77. - ArtBk - *098729*

Rodewald (Niedersachsen)
Hauck, Norma C. & Bernd, Dorfstr. 45, 31637 Rodewald. T. (05074) 13 42. - Graph / Card - *098730*

Rodgau (Hessen)
Gaumer, Elbestr 6, 63110 Rodgau. T. (06106) 72337. - Card - *098731*

Röthenbach an der Pegnitz (Bayern)
Wollinger, H., Tannenstr. 6, 90552 Röthenbach an der Pegnitz. T. (09120) 57 70 10. - Graph / Repr - *098732*

Rosbach (Hessen)
Hirsch-Post, Dagmar, Taunusblick 6, 61191 Rosbach. T. (06003) 930333, Fax 930332. - Graph - *098733*

Rosenheim (Bayern)
Edition Scheuer, Hohenzollernstr. 8, 83022 Rosenheim. T. (08031) 150 15, 881 22. *098734*

Gartner, Alois, Ludwigsplatz 17, 83022 Rosenheim. *098735*

Rosenheimer Verlagshaus, Am Stocket 12, 83022 Rosenheim. T. (08031) 28380, Fax 283844. - ArtBk - *098736*

Rostock (Mecklenburg-Vorpommern)
Hinstorff Verlag, Lagerstr. 7, 18055 Rostock. T. (0381) 34441, Fax 34601. - ArtBk - *098737*

Rothenburg ob der Tauber (Bayern)
Geissendörfer, Ernst, Obere Schmiedgasse 1, 91541 Rothenburg ob der Tauber. T. (09861) 2005, Fax 2009. - Graph - *098738*

Rottach-Egern (Bayern)
Edition G.A. Richter, Pitscherweg 2, 83700 Rottach-Egern. T. (08022) 52 22, Fax 26591. - ArtBk - *098739*

Rottendorf (Bayern)
Verlag für Originalgraphik, Am Grasholz 6h, 97228 Rottendorf. T. (09302) 437. - Graph - *098740*

Rudolstadt (Thüringen)
Burgart-Presse, Ortsstr 45a, 07407 Rudolstadt. T. (03672) 412214, Fax 412214. - ArtBk / Graph - *098741*

Rüsselsheim (Hessen)
Brün, Weserstr 22, 65428 Rüsselsheim. T. (06142) 61434, Fax 61259. - ArtBk - *098742*

Saarbrücken (Saarland)
AQ-Verlag, Weinbergweg 16, 66119 Saarbrücken. T. (0681) 55118, Fax 581772. - ArtBk - *098744*

SDV Saarbrücker Druckerei und Verlag, Halbergstr 3, 66121 Saarbrücken. T. (0681) 6650135, Fax (0681) 6650110. *098744a*

Sankt Augustin-Niederberg (Nordrhein-Westfalen)
Edition Meyring, Siebengebirgsstr. 34, 53757 Sankt Augustin-Niederberg. T. (02241) 34 31 48, Fax 34 32 45. - Repr / Card / Cal - *098745*

Sankt Ottilien (Bayern)
Eos Verlag, Erzabtei, 86941 Sankt Ottilien. T. (08193) 71261, Fax (08192) 6844. - Cal - *098746*

Schöneck (Hessen)
Atelier Edition Wölbing, Hinter den Zäunen 1b, 61137 Schöneck. T. (06187) 8133. - ArtBk / Graph - *098747*

Kunsthaus Hinter den Zäunen, Hinter den Zäunen 1b, 61137 Schöneck. T. (06187) 8133. - Graph / ArtBk - *098748*

Ich bestelle _____ Expl.

Gerhard Hoehme:
8. Druck der Belser Presse

Die letzten numerierten und signierten Exemplare

Olaf Römer/Gerhard Hoehme/Wernher von Braun
Die Entdeckung und Berechnung der Lichtgeschwindigkeit (1676)
Mit fünf Farbradierungen von Gerhard Hoehme, und einem Faksimiledruck
der schriftlichen Aufzeichnungen Olaf Römers.
Buchformat 43 x 31,5 cm, von Hand auf sichtbare flache Bünde geheftet,
Einband aus fünffach geleimtem Pergaminpapier. In einer Acrylglas-Kassette im
Format 44,5 x 33 cm, Deckel mit einer Hoehme-Schnur befestigt.

Einmalige Auflage von 65 (50 +15) arabisch numerierten Exemplaren.

DM 4.900,–

_____ Expl. **Roman Norbert Ketterer:**
Dialoge
Zwei Bände ca. 880 Seiten, Leinen.
Format 20,5 x 27,3 cm
Preis 198,– DM / Fr.175,– / öS 1545,–
ISBN 3-7630-1724-0

Ich bestelle zur sofortigen Lieferung an die angegebene Adresse:

Absender:

Name   Vorname

Straße

PLZ Ort

Datum   Unterschrift

Belser Verlag

**Pfizerstraße 5–7
70184 Stuttgart
Tel.: 07 11 / 2 19 14 01
Fax: 07 11 / 2 19 13 55**

Mayer, Wahrmut, Brunnengasse 6, 61137 Schöneck.
T. (06187) 6367. *098749*

Schöneiche (Brandenburg)
K + D, K., Mozartstr 23, 15566 Schöneiche.
T. (030) 6498341, Fax 6498341. - Cal - *098750*

Schopfheim (Baden-Württemberg)
Edition Bruna Haas, Inselstr. 3a, 79650 Schopfheim.
T. (07622) 61600. - Graph / Repr / Card / Cal - *098751*

Schwäbisch Hall (Baden-Württemberg)
Eppinger, Brenzstr. 16, 74523 Schwäbisch Hall.
T. (0791) 530 61. - ArtP - *098752*
Journal-Verlag Schwend, Schmollerstr 31, 74523
Schwäbisch Hall. T. (0791) 404500, Fax 404111.
- ArtBk / ArtP - *098753*

Schwalbach (Saarland)
Deutsch, Rudolf-Diesel-Str. 6, 66773 Schwalbach.
T. (06834) 554 54/57. - Card - *098754*

Schwanau ((Baden-Württemberg))
Nouvelles Images, Unterdorfstr 6a, 77963 Schwanau.
T. (07824) 4954, Fax 4959. - Graph / Card /
Cal - *098755*

NOUVELLES IMAGES
Kunstverlag

Seit 1957
der Name
für Stil und Qualität

Siebdrucke
Plakate
Karten
Kunstkalender

NOUVELLES IMAGES
GmbH
77963 Schwanau
Tel. 0 78 24 / 49 54
Fax 0 78 24 / 49 59

Schweinfurt (Bayern)
Verlag Palette, Metzgergasse 14, 97421 Schweinfurt.
T. (09721) 21973, Fax 18 54 32. - ArtBk - *098756*

Schwetzingen (Baden-Württemberg)
Schimper, K.F., Scheffelstr. 55, 68723 Schwetzingen.
T. (06202) 205600, Fax 205206. *098757*

Seelze (Niedersachsen)
Kall'meyersche Verlagsbuchhandlung, Im Brande 19,
30926 Seelze. T. (0511) 4000475,
Fax (0511) 4000476. *098758*

Siegen (Nordrhein-Westfalen)
Galerie Hansahaus, Leokadia Wolfers, Hindenburgstr 1,
57072 Siegen. T. (0271) 57795. - Repr - *098759*

Sigmaringen (Baden-Württemberg)
Thorbecke, Jan, Karlstr 10, 72488 Sigmaringen.
T. (07571) 728100, Fax 728280. - ArtBk - *098760*

Sindelfingen (Baden-Württemberg)
Galerie Tendenz, Rathauspl 4, 71063 Sindelfingen.
T. (07031) 878170, Fax 873580. *098761*

Solingen (Nordrhein-Westfalen)
Mertens, Sabine, Gasstr 66, 42657 Solingen.
T. (0212) 814150, Fax 870455. - ArtBk /
Graph - *098762*

Sonneberg (Sachsen)
Edition Kunst der Comics, Köppelsdorfer Str 197a,
96515 Sonneberg. T. (03675) 40900, Fax 409020.
- Graph / ArtBk / Cal - *098763*

Soyen (Bayern)
Dietz Offizin, Lengmoos, 83564 Soyen. T. (08072) 10 62.
- Graph / Repr - *098764*

Speyer (Rheinland-Pfalz)
Jaeger Druck Selbin, Daimlerstr. 7, 67346 Speyer.
T. (06232) 32041. - ArtBk - *098765*

Stadtoldendorf (Niedersachsen)
Hinrichsen, Ursula, Ziegeleistr, 37627 Stadtoldendorf.
T. (05532) 2021, Fax (05532) 1290. *098766*

Starnberg (Bayern)
Wiechmann, Josef-Fischhaber-Str 31, 82319 Starnberg.
T. (08151) 12511, Fax 2395. - Card / Cal - *098767*

Staufenberg (Hessen)
Minerva International, Gartenstr 1, 35460 Staufenberg.
T. (06406) 5898, Fax 71999. - Repr - *098768*
Objects and Posters, Mainzlerstr 6, 35460 Staufen-
berg. T. (06406) 4971, Fax 71999. - Repr - *098769*

Stuttgart (Baden-Württemberg)
AL Galerie, Mittlere Str 8, 70597 Stuttgart.
T. (0711) 767183, Fax 7671814. *098770*
Apostroph Verlag, Arminstr. 13, 70178 Stuttgart.
T. (0711) 640 63 87. - ArtBk - *098771*
Arnold'sche Verlagsanstalt, Senefelderstr 8, 70178
Stuttgart. T. (0711) 612460, Fax 6159843.
- ArtBk - *098772*
AT-Fachverlag, Postfach 50 01 80, 70331 Stuttgart.
T. (0711) 9529510, Fax 95295199. *098773*
Behrndt, Malte, Hasenbergstr. 95, 70176
Stuttgart. *098774*
Belser, Pfizerstr 5-7, 70184 Stuttgart. T. (0711) 21910,
Fax 2191355. - ArtBk / Cal - *098775*
Cotta'sche Buchhandlung, J.G., Adolf-Kröner-Str 24,
70184 Stuttgart. T. (0711) 240159. - Mul - *098776*
Daco Verlag, Richard-Wagner-Str 10, 70184 Stuttgart.
T. (0711) 2105752, Fax 2360938. - ArtBk / Graph /
Repr / Card / Mul - *098777*
Der Neue Schulmann, Pfizerstr. 5-7, 70184 Stuttgart.
- Repr - *098778*
Deutscher Bücherbund, Wolframstr. 36, 70191 Stuttgart.
T. (0711) 258 00. *098779*
Edition Camu, Im Schellenkönig 56, 70184
Stuttgart. *098780*
Edition Hans-Jörg Mayer, Postfach 131113, 70069
Stuttgart. T. (0711) 166560, Fax 1665610.
- ArtBk - *098781*
Edition Patricia Schwarz, Schwabstr. 2, 70197 Stuttgart.
T. (0711) 62 53 13. *098782*
Fink, Emil, Heidehofstr. 15, 70184 Stuttgart.
T. (0711) 46 53 30, Fax 48 76 36. - ArtBk / Repr / Card /
Cal - *098783*
Graphik International, Lieschingstr. 6, 70567 Stuttgart.
T. (0711) 71 30 36. - Graph - *098784*
Hauswedell & Co., Henrstr. 29, Rosenbergstr 113, 70193
Stuttgart. T. (0711) 638264/65, Fax 6369010.
- ArtBk - *098785*
Hiersemann, Anton, Rosenbergstr 113, 70193 Stuttgart.
T. (0711) 638264/65, Fax 6369010. - ArtBk - *098786*
Hoffmann, Julius, Neckarstr. 121, 70190 Stuttgart.
T. (0711) 26310, Fax 263 12 92. - ArtBk - *098787*
Kaufmann GmbH, Franz, Breitwiesenstr. 9, 70565 Stutt-
gart. - ArtBk / Graph / Repr / Card / Cal / Mul - *098788*
Kohlhammer, W., Heßbrühlstr 69, 70565 Stuttgart.
T. (0711) 78630, Fax 7863263. - ArtBk / Mul - *098789*
Korn, Felix, Ebinger Weg 21, 70567 Stuttgart.
T. (0711) 71 12 20. - Repr / Card / Mul - *098790*
Krämer, Hugo-Poster Scan, Aixheimer Str. 12, 70619
Stuttgart. T. (0711) 47 51 48/49, Fax 47 45 60. *098791*
Krämer, Karl, Schulze-Delitzsch-Str 15, 70565 Stuttgart.
T. (0711) 784960, Fax 7849620. - ArtBk - *098792*

Kreuz-Verlag, Breitwiesenstr 30, 70565 Stuttgart.
T. (0711) 788030, Fax 7880310. - ArtBk / Cal - *098793*
Kunst und Wissen, Wilhelmstr. 4, 70182 Stuttgart.
T. (0711) 24 11 52/54. *098794*
Lithopresse, Reinsburgstr. 102, 70197 Stuttgart.
T. (0711) 62 63 92, Fax 628849. - Repr - *098795*
Manus Presse GmbH, Lieschingstr. 6, 70567 Stuttgart.
T. (0711) 713036, Fax (0711) 717618. - ArtBk /
Graph - *098796*
Müller & Schindler, Sonnenbergstr 55, 70184 Stuttgart.
T. (0711) 233204, Fax 2369977. *098797*
Neff, Paul, Relenbergstr. 72, 70174 Stuttgart.
T. (0711) 29 71 34. - ArtBk - *098798*
Neske, Günther, Rotebühlstr. 72, 70178 Stuttgart.
T. (0711) 667 20, Fax 615 97 02. - ArtBk /
Graph - *098799*
Oktagon, Ehrenstr 4, 70193 Stuttgart.
T. (0221) 2059630, Fax 2059643. *098800*
Parkland Verlag, Lindenspürstr. 22, 70176 Stuttgart.
T. (0711) 638248, Fax 636 81 76. - ArtBk - *098801*
Porupsky, Karl, Ohmstr. 10, 70435 Stuttgart. *098802*
Reisacher Repro, Gustav, Breitscheidstr. 86/1, 70176
Stuttgart. *098803*
Schmid, Gerold, Wiener Str. 93A, 70469
Stuttgart. *098804*
Schuler, Lenzhalde 28, 70192 Stuttgart.
T. (0711) 2573058/59, Fax 2566360. - Graph /
Repr - *098805*
Stähle & Friedel, Neue Weinsteige 36, 70180 Stuttgart.
T. (0711) 60 44 64/65. - Cal - *098806*
Stähle, Walter, Prof., Landauer Str. 59b, 70499 Stuttgart.
T. (0711) 889 19 09. - ArtBk / Mul - *098807*
Steiner, Franz, Birkenwaldstr 44, 70191 Stuttgart.
T. (0711) 25820, Fax 2582290. - ArtBk - *098808*
Strache, Wolf, Dr., Friedhofstr. 11, 70191 Stuttgart.
T. (0711) 25 60 10, 25 62 17. - ArtBk - *098809*
Theiss, Konrad, Villastr 11, 70190 Stuttgart.
T. (0711) 2686101, Fax 2686127. - ArtBk - *098810*
Verlag Urachhaus, Urachstr. 41, 70190 Stuttgart.
T. (0711) 26 05 89, 26 59 39. - ArtBk - *098811*
Witthoeft, Traubenstr. 51, 70176 Stuttgart. - Graph /
Repr - *098812*
Wortwerkstatt Poesie und Politik, Schwarenbergstr 83,
70188 Stuttgart. T. (0711) 281809. *098813*

Süßen (Baden-Württemberg)
Edition Dietmar Gürtler, Bachstr. 45, 73079 Süßen.
T. (07162) 76 17. *098814*

Sylt-Ost (Schleswig-Holstein)
Cicero Presse, Morsum, 25980 Sylt-Ost.
T. (04651) 890305, Fax 890885. - ArtBk - *098815*

Traben-Trarbach (Rheinland-Pfalz)
Gasters und Marien, Wolferweg 3, Villa Sonora, 56841
Traben-Trarbach. - ArtBk / Graph / Repr / Cal - *098816*

Trendelburg (Hessen)
Hofeditz, Oberer Weg 23,, 34388 Trendelburg.
T. (05675) 1514. - Repr - *098817*

Trier (Rheinland-Pfalz)
Sauerwein, Hans, Eurener Str. 193a, 54294 Trier.
- Graph - *098818*

Tübingen (Baden-Württemberg)
konkursbuch, Garmerstr 29, 72070 Tübingen.
T. (07071) 66551, Fax (07071) 63539. *098819*
Wasmuth, Ernst, Fürststr 133, 72072 Tübingen.
T. (07071) 35071, 33658, Fax 35776. - ArtBk /
Graph - *098820*

Ulm (Baden-Württemberg)
Gröner, Karl, Riedweg 37, 89081 Ulm.
T. (0731) 331057. *098821*
Süddeutsche Verlagsgesellschaft, Sedelhofgasse 19-21,
89073 Ulm. T. (0731) 1430-0, Fax (0731) 1430-49.
- ArtBk - *098822*

Unterwössen (Bayern)
Plischke, Raitner Str 32, 83246 Unterwössen.
T. (08641) 8250, Fax 61484. - Cal - *098823*

Vastorf (Niedersachsen)
Merlin Verlag, Gifkendorf 38, 21397 Vastorf.
T. (04137) 7207, Fax (04137) 7948. - ArtBk / Graph /
Cal / Mul -   *098824*

Veitshöchheim (Bayern)
Zettner, Andreas, Hofweg 12, 97209 Veitshöchheim.
T. (0931) 91970, Fax 960097. - ArtBk / Card -   *098825*

Versmold (Nordrhein-Westfalen)
Werkstatt-Galerie, Ravensberger Str. 10, 33775 Versmold. T. (05423) 418 22. - Graph -   *098826*

Waghäusel (Baden-Württemberg)
Graphik-Verlag, Wagbachstr. 20, 68753 Waghäusel.
T. (07254) 66 36. - Graph -   *098827*

Walldürn (Baden-Württemberg)
Edition Peter Lugert, Geisberg 29, 74731
Walldürn.   *098828*

Wedel (Schleswig-Holstein)
Jacob, Martin, Bündtwiete 1, 22880 Wedel.
T. (04103) 34 30.   *098829*
Kröger, Kronskamp 138, 22880 Wedel.
T. (04103) 80 80.   *098830*

Weil am Rhein (Baden-Württemberg)
Edition Vitra Design Museum, Charles-Eames-Str 1,
79576 Weil am Rhein. T. (07621) 702514, Fax 702146.
- ArtBk -   *098831*

Weimar (Thüringen)
Böhlaus, Hermann, Nachf., Meyerstr. 50 a, 99423 Weimar. T. (03643) 20 71. - ArtBk / Card -   *098832*

**Weingarten, Württemberg (Baden-Würt-
temberg)**
Kunstverlag Weingarten, Lägelerstr 31, 88250 Weingarten, Württemberg. T. (0751) 41039, Fax 48735.
- ArtBk / Cal / Card -   *098833*

Weinheim (Baden-Württemberg)
VCH Verlagsgesellschaft, Pappelallee 3, 69469 Weinheim. T. (06201) 6020. - ArtBk -   *098834*

Weißenhorn (Bayern)
Konrad, Anton H., Schulstr. 5, 89264 Weißenhorn.
T. (07309) 26 57, Fax 6069. - ArtBk -   *098835*

Wernau (Baden-Württemberg)
QNST-Verlag, Martinstr 3, 73249 Wernau.
T. (07153) 31660, Fax 38169. - ArtBk -   *098836*

Werther (Nordrhein-Westfalen)
Graue, Postfach 1195, 33824 Werther. T. (05203) 66 66,
Fax 66 64. - Repr -   *098837*

Wesel (Nordrhein-Westfalen)
Hülsey, Karnannga 52, 46483 Wesel.
T. (0281) 27227, Fax 24682. - ArtBk -   *098838*
Verkerke, Schepersweg 35, 46485 Wesel.
T. (0281) 8060, Fax 89121. - ArtBk / Repr / Card /
Cal -   *098839*

Weßling (Bayern)
Krause, Grämer & Co., Kunst- und Verlagsanstalt, 82234
Weßling. - Repr -   *098840*

Westerkappeln (Nordrhein-Westfalen)
Johann-to-Settel, Fillkampstr. 56, 49492 Westerkappeln. T. (05404) 2979. - Graph / Repr -   *098841*

Wetzlar (Hessen)
Pegasus Verlag, Krämerstr. 19, 35578 Wetzlar.
- ArtBk -   *098842*

Wiesbaden (Hessen)
Atelier Phönix, Tannhäuserstr. 6, 65203 Wiesbaden.
T. (0611) 667 55.   *098843*
Cumic, Ingeborg, Oestricher Str. 22, 65197 Wiesbaden.
T. (0611) 44 24 46. - Graph / Card -   *098844*
Drews, Alfons, Veilchenweg 36B, 65201 Wiesbaden.
T. (0611) 25774. - ArtBk -   *098845*
Gantzert, Carmen, Danziger Str. 96, 65191 Wiesbaden.
T. (0611) 54 24 53.   *098846*

Harlekin Art, Wandersmannstr 39, 65205 Wiesbaden.
T. (0611) 740 01, Fax 711406.   *098847*
Heymer, Jürgen, Werner-Hilpert-Str. 171, 65197 Wies-
baden. T. (0611) 46 62 12, Fax 46 44 53.
- Graph -   *098848*
Neue Edition Hans-Joachim Finke, Schillerstr. 36, 65207
Wiesbaden. T. (0611) 613 76. - Graph -   *098849*
Orell Füssli & Parabel, Gaabstr. 6, 65195 Wiesbaden.
T. (0611) 40 10 62. - ArtBk -   *098850*
Reichert, Ludwig, Dr., Tauernstr. 11, 65199 Wiesbaden.
T. (0611) 46 18 51, Fax 46 86 13. - ArtBk -   *098851*
Vieweg & Sohn, Friedrich, Abraham-Lincoln-Str 46,
65189 Wiesbaden. T. (0611) 78780, Fax 7878470.
- ArtBk -   *098852*

Wilhelmshaven (Niedersachsen)
Noetzel, Florian, Valoisstr. 11, 26382 Wilhelmshaven.
T. (04421) 43003, Fax 42985. - ArtBk -   *098853*

Willebadessen (Nordrhein-Westfalen)
Zwiebelzwerg Verlag, Klosterstr 23, 34439 Willebadessen. T. (05646) 1261, Fax 1261. - ArtBk -   *098854*

Winnenden (Baden-Württemberg)
Scriptorum R, R. Mildner-Müller, Storm 2, 71364 Winnenden. T. (07195) 64355. - ArtBk / Graph -   *098855*

Witzwort (Berlin)
Quetsche, Verlag für Buchkunst, Riesbülldeich 2, 25889
Witzwort. T. (04864) 660. - ArtBk / Graph -   *098856*

Wörthsee (Bayern)
Groh, Hauptstr 15, 82237 Wörthsee. T. (08153) 8830,
Fax 88348. - ArtBk / Card / Cal -   *098857*

Worms (Rheinland-Pfalz)
Werner'sche Verlagsgesellschaft, Liebfrauenring 17-19,
67547 Worms. T. (06241) 435 74. - ArtBk /
Mul -   *098858*

Worpswede (Niedersachsen)
Art Expo Catalogs, Schlussdorfer Str 46, 27726 Wor-
pswede. T. (04792) 3972, Fax 3972. - ArtBk -   *098859*
Blome, Dietmar, Auf der Dohnhorst 3d, 27726 Worpswe-
de. T. (04792) 662. - Graph / Repr / Card -   *098860*
Girschner, Alfred, Findorffstr. 1, 27726 Worpswede.
T. (04792) 77 38.   *098861*

Würzburg (Bayern)
Biblia Rara, Kopenhagener Str. 66, 97084 Würzburg.
T. (0931) 695 55. - ArtBk -   *098862*
Kunstverlag Würzburg, Postfach 5823, 97008 Würzburg.
T. (0931) 12011/12, Fax 17806.   *098863*
Stürtz, H., Beethovenstr. 5, 97080 Würzburg.
T. (0931) 3850, Fax 38 53 05. - ArtBk -   *098864*
Weidlich/Flechsig, Beethovenstr. 5, 97080 Würzburg.
T. (0931) 38 53 73, Fax 38 53 05. - ArtBk -   *098865*

Wuppertal (Nordrhein-Westfalen)
Artcards Kunst- und Verlagsgesellschaft, Varresbecker
Str. 27-31, 42115 Wuppertal. T. (0202) 71 17 56.
- ArtBk / Cal -   *098866*
Edition des Kunst- und Museumsvereins Wuppertal,
Turmhof 8, 42103 Wuppertal.
T. (0202) 563 2191.   *098867*
Kiefel, Linderhauser Str. 62, 42279 Wuppertal.
T. (0202) 64 20 84/85. - Card -   *098868*
Schmidt & Green, Herbringhausen 10, 42399 Wuppertal.
T. (0202) 612061, Fax 613740.   *098869*
Schwarze, Wolfgang, Dr, Richard-Strauß-Allee 35,
42289 Wuppertal. T. (0202) 622005/06, Fax 63631.
- ArtBk / Repr / Cal / Mul -   *098870*
Wicher, Helga, Gräfrather Str 43a, 42327 Wuppertal.
T. (0202) 738217, Fax 738440. - Graph / ArtBk / Repr /
Card / Mul -   *098871*

Zierenberg (Hessen)
Brede, Horst, Schlagweg 5, 34289 Zierenberg.
T. (05606) 1869. - ArtBk -   *098872*

Zweibrücken (Rheinland-Pfalz)
Nickel, Heinz, Oselbachstr 72, 66482 Zweibrücken.
T. (06332) 16384.   *098873*

Greece

Athinai
Adam, Costas, Mesogeion 275, 15231 Athinai.
T. (01) 672 1801, Fax 672 5015.   *098874*
Alta Grafica, V. Voulgaroktonou 19, 11472 Athinai.
T. (01) 363 70 98. - ArtBk -   *098875*
Atlantis, M. Pechlivanidis, 8 Korai, 105 64 Athinai.
T. (01) 32 22 846, 32 31 624.   *098876*
Bernier, Jean, Marasli 51, 10676 Athinai.
T. (01) 723 56 57, Fax 722 61 89. - ArtBk /
Graph -   *098877*
IOLAS-Galerie Zoumboulakis, 20, Kolonaki Square, 106
73 Athinai. T. (01) 608 278, 324 8039. - ArtBk - *098878*
Melissa Publishing House, Navarinou 10, 10680 Athinai.
T. (01) 360 08 65. - ArtBk -   *098879*
Phorkys Publishing House, 51 Od. Methymnis, 11252
Athinai. T. (01) 864 10 62. - ArtBk -   *098880*
Pleias Editions, Sergios Raftanis, Od. Skoufa 35, 10673
Athinai. T. (01) 361 34 98. - ArtBk / Graph -   *098881*
Poliplano, 16 Lykavittou, 106 73 Athinai.
T. (01) 36 37 859. - ArtBk / Graph / Card / Mul - *098882*
Tria Phylla, Agras 25, 116 35 Athinai. T. (01) 722 47 63.
- ArtBk -   *098883*

Guatemala

Guatemala City
Libreria Guatemala-Tuncho Granados, 10 Calle 6-56,
Zona 1, Guatemala City. T. 2-47 36, 2-72 69, 2-
11 81.   *098884*

Hong Kong

Hong Kong
Chung Hwa Book Co., 7/F Kati It Bldg., 58 Pak Tai St.,
Tokwawan, Hong Kong. T. 71 50 176, Fax 765 84 68.
- ArtBk -   *098885*
Commercial Press, 2D Finnie St., Quarry Bay, Hong
Kong. T. 565 1371, Fax 565 1113. - ArtBk -   *098886*
Joint Publishing Co., 9 Queen Victoria St. 4/F, Hong
Kong. T. 23 01 05, 21 05 61, Fax 581 04 201.
- ArtBk -   *098887*

Hungary

Budapest
Akademiai Kiado, Prielle K. u. 19-35, 1117 Budapest.
T. (01) 181 21 34. - ArtBk -   *098888*
Corvina Books, Vörösmarty tér 1, 1051 Budapest.
T. (01) 1184-148.   *098889*
Helikon Publishing House, Eötvös L. u. 8, 1053 Buda-
pest. T. (01) 1147-987. - ArtBk / Repr -   *098890*
Hungarian Publicity Co., Felszabadulás tér 1,
Budapest.   *098891*
Képzömüveszeti Kiadó, Vörösmarty tér 1, 1051 Buda-
pest. T. (01) 184-981. - ArtBk / Repr / Card /
Cal -   *098892*
Kultúra, Budapest, 1051. T. (01) 359370. - ArtBk /
Graph -   *098893*
Studio Vizio, Patko utca 13, 1125 Budapest.
T. (01) 75 83 75. - Graph / Card -   *098894*

India

Bombay (Maharashtra)
Jaisingh & Mehta, 18/20 K. Dubash Marg, Bombay,
400023. T. (022) 262831. - ArtBk -   *098895*
Taraporevala, D.B., 210 Dr. Dababhai Naroji Rd, 40001
Bombay.   *098896*
Vakil & Sons, 18 Ballard Estate, Bombay, 400038.
T. (022) 269121. - ArtBk / Graph / Repr / Card /
Cal -   *098897*

Calcutta (West Bengal)

Indian Publications, 3 British Indian St. Abdul Hamid Street, Calcutta, 700069. T. 236 334, 344 733.
- ArtBk -   *098898*
KLM Private Ltd., 257B, B. B. Ganguly St., Calcutta, 700012. T. 27 43 91, 27 41 60.   *098899*
Mukhopadhyay, K. L., 6/1-A Dhiren Dhar Sarani, Calcutta. T. 24 18 24. - ArtBk / Graph / Repr / Card -   *098900*
Newman & Co. Ltd., W., 3 Old Court House Street, 700001 Calcutta. T. 23-9436/8. - ArtBk -   *098901*
Saraswaty, 32 Acharya Prafulla Chandra Rd, Calcutta.
T. 35 41 71. - ArtBk -   *098902*

Delhi (Delhi)

Kumar, Ashok Hotel, Delhi, 110021. T. 60 27 14.
- ArtBk -   *098903*
Kumar, Virendra, 11 Sundar Nagar Market, Delhi, 110003. T. 61 88 75, 61 11 13. - ArtBk -   *098904*

Hyderabad (Andhra Pradesh)

Orient Longman, 5-9-41/1 Bashir Bagh, Hyderabad, 500 029. T. 23 03 43, 23 79 36.   *098905*

New Delhi

Dhoomi Mal Gallery, 8A Connaught Pl, New Delhi.
T. (011) 3320839. - ArtBk -   *098906*

Iran

Teheran

Iran Caligraphers Cociety, No. 9-4th Av. Bissotoon, Teheran. T. (021) 65 66 91, 65 18 18. - ArtBk -   *098907*
Soroush Press, 228 Motahari Av., Teheran.
T. (021) 83 07 71, Fax 29 40 24.   *098908*
Sulivan Gallery, 136 Fakhrerazy Ave. Shahreza Ave, Teheran. T. (021) 649751. - Repr -   *098909*

Ireland

Blackrock (Co. Dublin)

Irish Academic Press, Kill Ln., Blackrock.
T. (01) 2892922, Fax 2893072. - ArtBk -   *098910*

Cork (Co. Cork)

Cork University Press, University College, Cork.
T. (021) 276871 ext. 2163. - ArtBk -   *098911*
Mercier Press, 4 Bridge St., Cork. T. (021) 504022.
- ArtBk -   *098912*

Dublin

ERA-Maptec International, 5 South Leinster St., Dublin 2. T. (01) 766266, Fax 619785. - Graph -   *098913*
National Gallery of Ireland Publications, Merrion Sq., Dublin 2. T. (01) 615133, Fax (01) 615372.
- ArtBk -   *098914*
O'Brien, 20 Victoria Rd., Dublin 6. T. (01) 979598, Fax (01) 97924. ArtBk -   *098915*
Project Arts Center, 39 East Essex St., Dublin 2.
T. (01) 712321. - ArtBk -   *098916*
Wolfhound, 68 Mountjoy Sq., Dublin 1. T. (01) 740354, Fax (01) 720207. - ArtBk -   *098917*

Israel

Jerusalem

Israel Museum Product, POB 71117, 91710 Jerusalem.
T. (02) 708883, Fax (02) 630764.   *098918*
Soussana, Jacques, 37 P. Koenig St. Talpioth, 91041 Jerusalem. T. (02) 78 26 78, Fax 78 24 26.   *098919*

Ramat Gan

I.G.A., 11 Nahum St., Ramat Gan POB 926, 52233.
T. 74 70 95. - Repr -   *098920*
Rolnik, 10 Dov Fridman St., Ramat Gan. T. 751 08 48, Fax 751 08 58. - Graph / Card / Cal -   *098921*

Tel Aviv

B. L. D., 17 Weisel St, Tel Aviv. T. (03) 5246483.
- Graph -   *098922*

Har-El, 11 Soncino St, Tel Aviv, 67216. T. (03) 984152.
- ArtBk -   *098923*
Turnowsky, W., 17a Nahmani St, Tel Aviv.
T. (03) 297462/64, Fax (03) 283218. - Graph / Card / Cal -   *098924*

Italy

Aglientu (Sassari)

Edition J. Gabriel, Corri Bassu 406, 07020 Aglientu.
- ArtBk / Graph -   *098925*

Ancona

Biblo Manifesti, Via Matteotti 105, 60121 Ancona.
T. (071) 87 10 87, Fax 89 74 58. - Repr -   *098926*

Antella (Firenze)

Scala Istituto Fotografico Editoriale, Via Chiantigiana Ponte a Niccheri, 50011 Antella. T. 64 15 41.
- Sli -   *098927*

Appiano Gentile (Como)

Baldini, Via Lecco 23, 22070 Appiano Gentile.
T. (031) 93 10 63. - ArtBk -   *098928*

Assisi (Perugia)

Casa Editrice Francescana, Convento di S Francesco, 06082 Assisi. T. (075) 81 30 98.   *098929*
Minerva Editrice, Vicolo degli Archi 1, 06081 Assisi.
T. (075) 81 23 81. - ArtBk -   *098930*

Bari

Laterza, Giuseppe, & Figli, Via Dante Alighieri 51, 70121 Bari. T. (080) 521 34 13. - ArtBk -   *098931*

Bergamo

Bolis, Via Zanica 58, 24100 Bergamo. T. (035) 31 73 33, Fax 31 69 38.   *098932*
El Bagatt, Via S Martino della Pigrizia 22/A, 24100 Bergamo. T. (035) 25 33 66, 25 37 35.   *098933*
Grafica e Arte Bergamo, Via Coghetti 108, 24100 Bergamo. T. (035) 25 50 14, Fax 25 01 64. - ArtBk -   *098934*
Lucchetti, Via Ghezzi 22, 24100 Bergamo.
T. (035) 22 61 18, Fax 23 43 14, 22 67 83.
- ArtBk -   *098935*
Nuovo Istituto Italiano d'Arti Grafiche, Via Zanica 92, 24100 Bergamo. T. (035) 32 91 11, Fax 31 13 49.
- ArtBk -   *098936*
Walk over Italiana, Via May 24, 24100 Bergamo.
T. (035) 22 00 91.   *098937*

Biella (Vercelli)

Dialoghi, Via C. Colombo 4, 13051 Biella.
T. (015) 34017, 34186. - Graph -   *098938*

Bologna

Alfa, Via S. Stefano 13, 40125 Bologna.
T. (051) 26 28 05. - ArtBk -   *098939*
Atesa, Via della Beverara 96, 40131 Bologna.
T. (051) 37 21 82.   *098940*
Bora, Via Jacopo di Paolo 42, 40128 Bologna.
T. (051) 35 61 33.   *098941*
Cappelli, Licinio, Via Marsili 2, 40124 Bologna.   *098942*
Istituto Beni Artistici, Via Farini 28, 40124 Bologna.   *098943*
Nuova Editrice di Luigi Benassi, via S Mamolo 2, 40136 Bologna. T. (051) 58 03 85.   *098944*
Nuova Alfa Editoriale, Via Marsili 15, 40100 Bologna.
T. (051) 23 88 70. - ArtBk -   *098945*
Parma, Luigi, via Collamarini 23, 40138 Bologna.
T. (051) 53 12 14. - Graph -   *098946*
Patron, Prof. Riccardo, via Badini 12 bis 14, 40127 Bologna. T. (051) 76 70 03. - ArtBk -   *098947*
Stamparte, Via Morandi 4, 40124 Bologna.
T. (051) 22 19 13, Fax 26 94 12. - ArtBk / Graph -   *098948*
Tamari Editori, via Carracci 7, 40129 Bologna.
T. (051) 35 64 59.   *098949*

Bolzano

Athesia, Via Portici 41, 39100 Bolzano.
T. (0471) 92 51 11. - ArtBk / Card / Cal -   *098950*

Ferrari-Auer, Waltherpl 12, 39100 Bolzano.
T. (0471) 232 66.   *098951*

Borgo di Trevi (Perugia)

Politi, Giancarlo, POB 36, 06032 Borgo di Trevi.
Fax 6680 1290. - ArtBk -   *098952*

Brescia

Grafo, Via Bassi 20, 25124 Brescia.
T. (030) 39 32 21.   *098953*

Bressanone (Bolzano)

Egger, O. von Wolkenstein-Str. 161, 39042 Bressanone.
T. (0472) 307 90. - Card -   *098954*

Busto Arsizio (Varese)

Bramante, Via Generale Biancardi 1, 21052 Busto Arsizio. T. (0331) 62 03 24. - ArtBk -   *098955*

Caltanissetta

Sciascia, Salvatore, corso Umberto 111, 93100 Caltanissetta. T. (0934) 219 46. - ArtBk / Graph -   *098956*

Campobasso

Enne, Viale U Petrella 22, 86100 Campobasso.
T. (0874) 937 40.   *098957*

Casalecchio di Reno (Bologna)

Grafis, Via 2 Giugno, 40033 Casalecchio di Reno.
T. (051) 58 24 29.   *098958*

Casellina-Scandicci (Firenze)

Nuova Italia, Via E. Codignola, 50018 Casellina-Scandicci. T. 279 81. - ArtBk -   *098959*

Castellarano (Reggio Emilia)

Mascal, Via Radici Sud 114, 42014 Castellarano.
T. (0536) 85 93 82, Fax 85 06 99.   *098960*

Catania (Sicilia)

Giannotta, Nicolò, Via R Margherita 2, 95125 Catania.
T. (095) 44 76 29.   *098961*

Cava dei Tirreni (Salerno)

Di Mauro, Via XXV Luglio, 34/D, 84013 Cava dei Tirreni.
T. (089) 46 25 70. - ArtBk / Cal / Mul -   *098962*
Pubblicazioni della Badia, Badia di Cava 7 bis 11, 84013 Cava dei Tirreni.   *098963*

Cavriago (Reggio Emilia)

Pari Editori & Dispari, via Tornara 3, 42025 Cavriago.
T. (0522) 575780. - ArtBk / Graph / Repr / Mul -   *098964*

Cinisello Balsamo (Milano)

Edizioni Paoline, Piazza Soncino 5, 20092 Cinisello Balsamo. T. (02) 660 06 21. - ArtBk -   *098965*

Cittadella (Padova)

Artegrafica Sociale, Via Alfieri 5, 35013 Cittadella.
T. (049) 940 10 20, Fax 597 13 97. - ArtBk / Graph / Repr -   *098966*

Collecchio (Parma)

Silva Arte Grafica, Localita-Cavalli, 43044 Collecchio.
T. (0521) 80 41 06, Fax 80 44 06.   *098967*

Como

Casa Editrice Pietro Cairoli, via Giuseppe Rovelli 32, 22100 Como. T. (031) 27 50 60.   *098968*

Fagagna (Udine)

Magnus Edizioni, Via Spilimbergo 180, 33034 Fagagna.
T. (0432) 80 00 81, Fax 73 15 79. - ArtBk -   *098969*

Ferrara

Belriguardo, Via Mascheraio 29, 44100 Ferrara.
T. (0532) 20 21 70, Fax 20 53 32.   *098970*

Fiesole (Firenze)

Opus Libri, Via Benedetto da Maiano 3, 50014 Fiesole.
T. (055) 59 87 57.   *098971*

Firenze

Alinari Fratelli, via Nazionale 6, 50123 Firenze.
T. (055) 21 78 42. - ArtBk / Sli / Mul -   *098972*
Arnaud, Casa Editrice, Via XXVII Aprile 13, 50129 Firenze. T. (055) 49 63 33. - ArtBk -   *098973*

Artificio, Borgo Santissimi Apostoli 40R, 50123 Firenze.
T. (055) 21 02 70, Fax 29 54 14. *098974*
Bonechi, Via dei Rustici 5, 50122 Firenze. *098975*
Cantini, Borgo Santa Croce 8, 50122 Firenze.
T. (055) 24 47 26. *098976*
Centro Di, Piazza di Mozzi 1, 50125 Firenze.
T. (055) 232 12. *098977*
Edizioni Ponte Vecchio, Via Colleram. 9-10, 50125 Firenze. T. (055) 203 46 55. - Repr - *098978*
Giunti Publishing Group, Via V Gioberti, 34, 50121 Firenze. T. (055) 67 04 51. *098979*
Hopeful Monster editore, 19 Via Ginori, 50123 Firenze.
T. (055) 21 05 76, Fax 51 92 46. - ArtBk - *098980*
„Il Bargello", via le Petrarca 88, 50124 Firenze. *098981*
Il Bisonte, via S. Niccoló 24, 50125 Firenze.
T. (055) 234 25 85. - Graph - *098982*
Le Lettre, Viale Gramsci 18, 50132 Firenze.
T. (055) 234 27 10, Fax 234 60 10. - ArtBk - *098983*
Le Nuove Edizioni, viale Milton 7, 50129
Firenze. *098984*
Nardini, Via Scipione Ammirato 37, 50136 Firenze.
T. (055) 67 03 30, 67 99 97, Fax 67 04 60.
- ArtBk - *098985*
Nova Lux di s. Becocci, Via Canto dei Nelli, 10r, 50123
Firenze. T. (055) 212478. *098986*
Olschki, Leo S., Viuzzo del Pozzetto, Viale Europa,
50100 Firenze CP 66. T. (055) 653 06 84,
Fax 653 02 14. - ArtBk - *098987*
Salani Editore, Cittadella 7, 50144 Firenze. *098988*
Sansoni, Via Varchi 47, 50132 Firenze.
T. (055) 24 33 34. *098989*
Sansoni, G. C., Viale Mazzini 46, 50132 Firenze.
T. (055) 67 74 51. - ArtBk / Graph - *098990*
Schema, Via Vigna Nuova 17, 50123 Firenze.
T. (055) 284090. - ArtBk / Graph / Card / Mul - *098991*
Torchio, Via Francavilla 10a-10b, 50142 Firenze.
- Repr / Mul - *098992*

Foligno (Perugia)
Editoriale Umbra, Via Pignattara 38, 06034 Foligno.
T. (0742) 35 73 74, Fax 35 31 74. *098993*
Edizioni dell'Arquata, Via Nazario Sauro 21, 06034
Foligno. *098994*

Galatina (Lecce)
Congedo, Via Marche 24, 73013 Galatina.
T. (0836) 635 43. *098995*

Genova
Sagep, Piazza Merani 1, 16145 Genova.
T. (010) 31 34 53. *098996*

La Spezia
Taschen, Benedikt, Corso Cavour 108, 19100 La Spezia.
T. (0187) 63 12 11-8, Fax 63 01 24. *098997*

Lallio – Grumello del Piano (Bergamo)
Grafica Gutenberg, Via Provinciale 8, 24040 Lallio –
Grumello del Piano. T. (035) 69 20 45. *098998*

Lecce
Centro di Studi Salentini, Palazzo Adorni via Umberto I,
32, 73100 Lecce. T. (0832) 41 938. - ArtBk - *098999*
Salentini, Via Umberto I 32, 73100 Lecce.
T. (0832) 419 38. *099000*
Studio Gi, Via T. Tasso 12, 73100 Lecce.
T. (0832) 404 50. - Graph / Mul - *099001*

Lerici (La Spezia)
Il Campanile Arte, Via tra il Campanile 1, 19032
Lerici. *099002*

Livorno
Graphis Arte, Via Roma 84, 57126 Livorno.
T. (0586) 80 85 18, Fax 81 32 19. - ArtBk - *099003*
Toninelli Arte Moderna, Via Roma 45, 57100 Livorno.
- ArtBk / Graph / Repr - *099004*

Lucca
Fazzi, P., via P Guidi 10, 55100 Lucca.
T. (0583) 457 36. *099005*

Macerata
L'Arco, Studio Internazionale d'Arte Grafica, via Crispi
36, 62100 Macerata. T. (0733) 21 14. - Graph /
Mul – *099006*

Mantova
Galleria l'Inferriata, Consol., Nedo Sottoportico Lattonai
4, 46100 Mantova. T. (0376) 36 63 67. - Graph / Repr /
Sli / Cal – *099007*

Milano
Adelphi, Via S. Giovanni sul Muro 14, 20121 Milano.
T. (02) 720 00 975, Fax 890 10 337. - ArtBk - *099008*
Alfieri, Via Trentacoste 7, 20134 Milano. T. (02) 21 56 31,
Fax 215 49 40. - ArtBk - *099009*
Alfieri & Lacroix, via Fermi 12, 20019 Milano.
T. (02) 328 49 80. - ArtBk / Graph / Cal / Mul – *099010*
Alma Grafiche, Via F. Brioschi 65, 20141 Milano.
T. (02) 843 55 41. - ArtBk / Repr / Cal - *099011*
Arcadia Edizioni, Via Torino 44, 20123 Milano.
T. (02) 877623, 804353, Fax (02) 72021006. *099012*
Aristea S. E. C. I., via Saldini 25, 20100 Milano.
T. (02) 73 01 03. *099013*
Arte Lombarda, Via Lovanio 4, 20121 Milano.
T. (02) 659 99 60. *099014*
Arte Struktura, Via Mercato 1, 20121 Milano.
T. (02) 805 44 69, Fax 87 58 84. *099015*
BCM, Corso Vercelli 2, 20145 Milano.
T. (02) 43 45 20. *099016*
Centro Internazionale di Brera, Via Formentini 10, 20121
Milano. T. (02) 80 84 78. *099017*
Clup, Piazza Leonardo da Vinci 7, 20133 Milano.
T. (02) 23 53 20. - ArtBk - *099018*
Cortina-Cavour, Piazza Cavour 1, 20121 Milano.
T. (02) 66 77 05, 659 56 44. - Graph – *099019*
Dalla Costa, Via G. Leopardi 21, 20123 Milano.
T. (02) 86 42 75. - Graph / Repr / Card - *099020*
Daverio, Philippe, Via Montenapoloene 6A, 20121 Milano. T. (02) 79 86 95, 76 00 17 48,
Fax 76 02 15 07. *099021*
Del Duca, Cino, via Borgogna 5, 20122 Milano. *099022*
Electa, Via Trentacoste 7, 20134 Milano.
- ArtBk – *099023*
Ermes, Via Timavo 12, 20124 Milano.
T. (02) 607 3892. *099024*
Fabbri, Fratelli, via Mecenate 91, 20138 Milano.
T. (02) 509 51. - ArtBk – *099025*
Feltrinelli, Giangiacomo, via Andegari 6, 20121 Milano.
T. (02) 86 61 96. - ArtBk - *099026*
Fenice 200, Via Resi 32, 20125 Milano.
T. (02) 688 98 73, Fax 688 24 94. *099027*
Garzanti, Via Senato 25, 20121 Milano. T. (02) 778 71.
- ArtBk – *099028*
Gruppo Editoriale Electa, Trentacoste 7, 20134 Milano.
T. (02) 236 93. - ArtBk – *099029*
Hoepli, Ulrico, Via Hoepli 5, 20121 Milano.
T. (02) 86 54 46. - ArtBk – *099030*
Humor Graphic, via Arzaga 28, 20146 Milano.
T. (02) 415 29 50. - ArtBk / Graph – *099031*
Idea Books, Via Vigevano 41, 20144 Milano.
T. (02) 8373949, 8360395, 8390284,
Fax (02) 8357776. - ArtBk / Cal – *099032*
Idea Libri, Via S.Tommaso 10, 20129 Milano.
T. (02) 871915, Fax (02) 72022752. *099033*
Il Quadrato, Via Cimarosa13, 20144 Milano.
T. (02) 498 44 13. - ArtBk / Graph / Mul – *099034*
Inedita, Corso Venezia 46, 20121 Milano.
T. (02) 79 68 08, Fax 7600 0823. - ArtBk – *099035*
Jaca Book, Via Aurelio Saffi 19, 20123 Milano.
T. (02) 498 23 41, Fax 4819 3361. - ArtBk - *099036*
Johnson, Stefano, Via Terraggio 15, 20123 Milano.
T. (02) 805 96 23. - ArtBk – *099037*
Krachmalmicoff, via G Carcano 32, 20141 Milano.
T. (02) 843 95 95. *099038*
L'Affiche Uno, Via Nirone 11, 20123 Milano.
T. (02) 80 73 80. *099039*
La Grafica, Piazza Cavour 1, 20121 Milano.
T. (02) 654 002. *099040*
Leonardo- De Luca, Via Borgonuovo 3, 20121 Milano.
T. (02) 72 00 37 00, Fax 72 00 37 00. - ArtBk - *099041*
Longanesi, Via T Salvini 3, 20122 Milano.
T. (02) 78 25 51. *099042*

m'arte, Via Carlo Poerio 3, 20129 Milano.
T. (02) 79 40 34. - ArtBk / Graph - *099043*
Maeght Edizioni, Piazza del Carmine 6, 20121 Milano.
T. (02) 87 98 66. *099044*
Marconi, Via Tadino 15, 20129 Milano.
T. (02) 22 55 43. *099045*
Mazzotta, Gabriele, Foro Bonaparte 52, 20121 Milano.
T. (02) 869 00 50, 805 58 03, Fax 869 30 46. - ArtBk /
Repr / Mul - *099046*
Miano, Guido, viale Caldara 13, 20122 Milano.
T. (02) 58 42 23. *099047*
Mondadori, Arnoldo, Via Cadore 19, 20135 Milano.
T. (02) 545 64 21. - ArtBk – *099048*
Mursia, Ugo e Co. Edizioni A. R. E., Corticelli, via Tadino
29, 20124 Milano. T. (02) 20 93 41. *099049*
Nuova Prearo, Via Filippo Juvara 9, 20129 Milano.
T. (02) 29 86 25. *099050*
Offset Giemme, Via Guerzoni 42, 20158 Milano.
T. (02) 607 3202. *099051*
Perotto, Via Gesù 17, 20121 Milano. T. (02) 76 00 83 38,
Fax 76 02 05 27. *099052*
Pizzi, Amilcare, Arti Grafiche, Cinisello Balsamo Via de
Vizzi 86, 20092 Milano. T. (02) 61 88 821.
- ArtBk – *099053*
Plura Edizioni, Via Salvini 1, 20122 Milano.
T. (02) 70 12 87. *099054*
Polifilo, Via Borgonuovo 2, 20121 Milano.
T. (02) 655 15 49. - ArtBk – *099055*
Politi, Giancarlo, Via Farini 68, 20159 Milano.
T. (02) 688 73 41. - ArtBk / Graph / Repr - *099056*
Ricci, Franco Maria, via Durini 19, 20122 Milano.
T. (02) 7702. - ArtBk – *099057*
Ricordi, Vla Quaranta 44, 20139 Milano. T. (02) 53 63 55,
Fax 525 9249. - Repr / Cal / Card - *099058*
Rizzardi, Via Solferino 56, 20121 Milano.
T. (02) 657 05 63, Fax 657 05 63. *099059*
Rizzoli, Via A. Rizzoli 2, 20132 Milano. T. (02) 25 88.
- ArtBk / Graph - *099060*
Rusconi, Via Livraghi 1/b, 20126 Milano.
T. (02) 257 41 41-44, Fax 255 20 98. - ArtBk – *099061*
Scheiwiller, Vanni, Via Sacchi 3, 20121 Milano.
T. (02) 86 55 90. - ArtBk / Graph / Repr / Card - *099062*
Sisar, via M. Agrate 35, 20139 Milano. T. (02) 539 38 46/
718. - ArtBk – *099063*
Top Graphic, Via G Modena 15, 20129 Milano.
T. (02) 204 62 36. *099064*
Torcular Spa, Via Bixio 37, 20159 Milano.
T. (02) 29 40 57 41, Fax 204 73 33. *099065*

Modena
Panini, Franco Cosimo, Viale Corassori 24, 41100 Modena. T. (059) 34 35 72, Fax 34 42 74. - ArtBk - *099066*

Moncalieri (Torino)
ILTE- Industria Libraria Tipografica Editrice S.p.A., Via F
Postiglione 14, 10024 Moncalieri.
T. (011) 639 51. *099067*

Montale Rangone (Modena)
Ferrari, Giorgio, Via Sicilia 7, 41050 Montale Rangone.
T. (059) 53 01 56. - Repr – *099068*

Napoli
Gallina, Via S Anna dei Lombardi 10, 80134 Napoli.
T. (081) 32 09 95. *099069*
Guida Editori, Via Domenico Morelli, 80121 Napoli.
T. (081) 764 42 88, Fax 764 44 14. - ArtBk - *099070*
Macchiaroli, Gaetano, Via Michetti 11, 80127 Napoli.
T. (081) 24 05 68. *099071*
Società Editrice Napoletana, Corso Umberto I 84, 80138
Napoli. T. (081) 40 68 66. *099072*

Novara
Istituto Geografico, Via Giovanni da Verrazano 15, 28100
Novara. T. (0321) 47 12 01. - ArtBk / Graph /
Repr– *099073*

Padova (Belluno)
Mastrogiacomo Editore, Galleria Images 70, Via delle
Piazze 13, 35100 Padova. T. (049) 22707. *099074*

Palermo (Sicilia)
Flaccovio, Salvatore Fausto, Via Ruggiero Settimo 37,
90139 Palermo. T. (091) 58 94 42. - ArtBk – *099075*

IPSA Editore, Via Remo Sandron 61, 90143 Palermo.
T. (091) 34 74 78/43. - ArtBk - *099076*
Novecento Editrice, VIa Siracusa 16, 90141 Palermo.
T. (091) 58 74 17, 32 35 13, Fax 58 57 02.
- ArtBk - *099077*
Sellerio, Via Siracusa 50, 90141 Palermo.
T. (091) 625 41 10, 625 94 75, Fax 625 88 02.
- ArtBk - *099078*

Parma
Battei, Luigi, Strada Cavour 5/c, 43100 Parma.
T. (0521) 33733-28 30 77. - ArtBk - *099079*
Studium Parmense, piazzale Serventi 5, 43100 Parma.
T. (0521) 272 59. *099080*

Pavone (Torino)
Pheljna, Stradale Torino 11, 10018 Pavone.
T. (0125) 23 41 14, Fax 23 00 85. - Graph - *099081*
Priuli & Verlucca, Stradale Torino 11, 10018 Pavone.
T. (0125) 23 99 29. *099082*

Perugia
Volumnia, Via Baldeschi 2, 06100 Perugia.
T. (075) 249 50. *099083*

Pesaro
La Pergola, Via Diaz 14, 61100 Pesaro.
T. (0721) 68604. *099084*

Pisa
Giardini Editori e Stampatori in Pisa S. P. A., via Santa
Bibbiana 28, 56100 Pisa. T. (050) 2 45 27. - ArtBk /
Graph / Repr - *099085*
Nistri-Lischi, piazza Castelletto 7, 56100 Pisa.
T. (050) 280 31. - ArtBk - *099086*

Ponzano (Treviso)
Vianello Libri, Via Postioma 85, 31050 Ponzano.
T. (0422) 96 96 77, Fax 96 94 10. - ArtBk /
Graph - *099087*

Ravenna
Longo, Angelo, Via Paolo Costa 33, 48100 Ravenna.
T. (0544) 270 26. - ArtBk / Repr / Card / Sli - *099088*

Reggio Emilia
Age, Via Casorati 29, 40200 Reggio Emilia.
T. (0522) 422 27. *099089*
Edizioni Civici Musei, Via Spallanzani 1, 42100 Reggio
Emilia. T. (0522) 43 77 75. - ArtBk / Graph /
Mul - *099090*
Liberia Antiquaria Prandi, viale Timavo 75, 42100 Reg-
gio EmIlla. T. (0522) 3 49 73. - ArtBk / Graph /
Repr - *099091*

Rimini (Forli)
Luisé Editore, Viale Tiberio, 25, 47037 Rimini.
T. (0541) 287 55. - ArtBk - *099092*

Roma
Accademia Nazionale dei Lincei, Via della Lungara 10,
00165 Roma. T. (06) 65 08 31. *099093*
Ages, Via Reggio Emilia 16, 00198 Roma.
T. (06) 845 38 64. *099094*
Bardi, Salita Crescenzi 16, 00186 Roma.
T. (06) 654 14 90. *099095*
Belvedere, Piazzale Flaminio 19, 00196 Roma.
T. (06) 360 44 88, 360 29 60. *099096*
Bestetti + C. sas, Carlo E., Via di S. Giacomo, 18, 00187
Roma. - ArtBk - *099097*
Bianconero Spa, Via Bertolini 19, 00197 Roma.
T. (06) 87 75 05. *099098*
Bozzi, Ugo, Edizioni per la Storia dell'Arte, Via Paisiello
41, 00198 Roma. T. (06) 844 05 64. - ArtBk - *099099*
Bretschneider, Giorgio, Dr., Via Cassiodoro 19, 00193
Roma. T. (06) 687 41 27, 38 85 00, Fax 687 41 29.
- ArtBk - *099100*
Bulzoni, Editore S. R. L., via dei Liburni 14, 00185 Ro-
ma. T. (06) 495 52 07. *099101*
Carte Segrete, Via Garibaldi 153, 00153 Roma.
T. (06) 589 97 07, Fax 589 62 29. *099102*
Curcio, Armando, via Arno 64, 00198 Roma.
T. (06) 848 71. - ArtBk - *099103*
Editalia-Edizioni d'Italia, Via di Pallacorda 7, 00186 Ro-
ma. T. (06) 654 15 92, 656 95 37. - ArtBk - *099104*

Edition Belvedere, Piazzale Flaminio 19, 00196 Roma.
T. (06) 360 44 88, 360 29 60. - ArtBk - *099105*
Editori Riuniti, Via Serchio 9-11, 00198 Roma.
T. (06) 854 63 83. - ArtBk - *099106*
Edizioni Arte Molica, Via Crescenzio 46A, 00193 Roma.
T. (06) 68 30 84 23, Fax 68 30 84 23. *099107*
Europa Edizioni, via G B Martini 6, 00198 Roma.
T. (06) 844 91 24. *099108*
Giorgi Rossi, Gianfranco, Via G Arrivabene 57, 00191
Roma. T. (06) 239 49 37. *099109*
Grafica d'Arte Lombardi, Via Salaria 222, 00198 Roma.
T. (06) 841 63 92, 808 29 52. *099110*
Grafica dei Greci, Via dei Greci 33, 00187 Roma.
T. (06) 679 60 97, Fax 678 94 13. - Graph - *099111*
Herder, Piazza Montecitorio 117-120, 00186 Roma.
T. (06) 679 46 28. - ArtBk - *099112*
Il Nuovo Torcoliere, Via del Babuino 89, 00187 Roma.
T. (06) 679 47 94. - Graph - *099113*
Il Ponte, Via Sant'Ignazio 6, 00186 Roma.
T. (06) 679 61 14, Fax 679 61 14. *099114*
Il Rinoceronte d'Oro, Via dei Coronari 26, 00186 Roma.
T. (06) 656 90 41. *099115*
Istituto della Enciclopedia Italiana, fondata da Giovanni
Treccani, piazza Paganica 4, 00186 Roma. *099116*
Istituto Nazionale di Archeologiae Storia dell'Arte, Piazza
S Marco 49, 00186 Roma. T. (06) 679 88 04,
678 08 17. *099117*
Joyce & Co., Via San Francesco a Ripa 18, 00153 Roma.
T. (06) 589 92 85, Fax 588 06 07. *099118*
Kappa, Piazza Borghese 6, 00186 Roma.
T. (06) 679 03 56. *099119*
Luca, De, Via S. Anna 16, 00186 Roma.
T. (06) 687 79 09, Fax 656 44 30. - ArtBk / Graph /
Repr / Mul - *099120*
Marteau, Pierre, Via Metastasio 19, 00186 Roma.
T. (06) 653 08 11. - ArtBk - *099121*
Multigrafica, Viale dei 4 Venti 52a, 00152 Roma.
T. (06) 589 28 39, 589 14 96. *099122*
Newton Compton, Via Germanico 197, 00192 Roma.
T. (06) 370 02 05, Fax 31 69 00. *099123*
Palombi, via dei Gracchi 181 bis 185, 00192 Roma.
T. (06) 321 41 50. - ArtBk - *099124*
Pozzilli, Fabrizio, Via della Lungara 3, 00165 Roma.
T. (06) 589 58 95. *099125*
Santamaria, Pio & Pietro, Piazza di Spagna 35, 00187
Roma. T. (06) 679 04 16. *099126*
Semar, Via Reginella 29A, 00186 Roma.
T. (06) 687 93 33, 686 91 51, Fax 654 86 01. *099127*
Tomo Edizioni, Vila dei Piceni 5, 00185 Roma.
T. (06) 494 10 88. *099128*
Trec, Via Cassia Antica 132, 00191 Roma.
T. (06) 328 83 61. - Repr - *099129*

Rozzano (Milano)
Editoriale Domus, Via Achille Grandi 5-7, 20089 Rozza-
no. T. (02) 82 47 21. *099130*

Santa Cristina Gela (Palermo)
Edizioni Labrarie Siciliane, C. da Portella, 90030 Santa
Cristina Gela. T. (091) 34 26 70, 857 02 21.
- ArtBk - *099131*

Torino
Allemandi, Umberto, Via Mancini 8, 10131 Torino.
T. (011) 88 25 56-58. - ArtBk / Mul - *099132*
Edizioni Seat, Via A Saffi 18, 10138 Torino.
T. (011) 33301. *099133*
Einaudi, Giulio, Via Umberto Biancamano 1, 10121 Tori-
no. - ArtBk - *099134*
Eri, Via Arsenale 41, 10121 Torino.
T. (011) 571 01. *099135*
Fogola, Piazza Carlo Felice 19, 10123 Torino.
T. (011) 53 58 97. *099136*
Grafica Internazionale, Corso Re Umberto 23, 10128 To-
rino. T. (011) 54 38 91. - ArtBk - *099137*
Gribaudi, Piero, Via Galileo Ferraris 67, 10128 Torino.
T. (011) 50 03 60. *099138*
Guernica, Via Gioberti 40, 10128 Torino.
T. (011) 53 34 18. *099139*
Lo Scarabeo, Via Miglietti 5, 10144 Torino.
T. (011) 473 00 70, Fax 48 88 22. - Graph - *099140*
Musolini, Tommaso, Via Rubiana 47, 10149 Torino.
T. (011) 33 77 82. *099141*

S.A.I.E. Editrice, corso Regina Margherita 2, 10153
Torino. *099142*
Salamon, Via Cosseria 6, 10131 Torino.
T. (011) 669 22 26, Fax 312 17 61. - ArtBk / Graph /
Mul - *099143*
Società Editrice Internazionale, Corso Regina Margherita
176, 10152 Torino. T. (011) 521 14 41.
- ArtBk - *099144*
Stamperia Artistica Nazionale, Corso Siracusa 37,
10136 Torino. T. (011) 329 00 31. - Graph /
Repr - *099145*
Studio Piergiorgio Firinu, Via M. Vittria 46d, 10123 Tori-
no. T. (011) 885968. - ArtBk / Graph / Card / Sli /
Mul - *099146*
U. T. E. T., corso Raffello 28, 10125 Torino.
T. (011) 65291, Fax 652 92 40. - ArtBk - *099147*

Treviso
Canova, Via Calmaggiore 31, 31100 Treviso.
T. (0422) 38 23 83. - ArtBk - *099148*

Trieste
Edizioni Lint, Via di Romagna 30, 34134 Trieste.
T. (040) 360396, 360421. - ArtBk - *099149*

Udine
Art & s.r.l., Via del Sale 2a, 33100 Udine.
T. (0432) 29 29 66, 50 67 58. - ArtBk - *099150*
Arti Grafiche Friulane, Via Treppo 1, 33100 Udine.
T. (0432) 29 18 28. *099151*
Del Bianco, Via S. Daniele 11, 33100 Udine CP 40.
T. (0432) 50 11 34. - ArtBk / Graph - *099152*

Urbino (Pesaro e Urbino)
Istituto Statale d'Arte, piazza Duca Federico, 61029
Urbino. *099153*

Venezia
Alfieri Edizioni d'Arte, San Marco 1991, 30124 Venezia.
T. (041) 233 23. *099154*
Arsenale Editrice, S Marco 4708, POB 720, 30124 Vene-
zia. T. (041) 520 59 03, Fax 522 15 79. *099155*
Cluva, Sta Croce 197, 30125 Venezia.
T. (041) 269 10. *099156*
Edizioni del Cavallino, S. Marco 1725, 30124 Venezia.
T. (041) 521 0488, Fax 521 06 42. - ArtBk / Graph /
Mul - *099157*
Edizioni L'Altra Riva, Dorsoduro 1470, 30123 Venezia.
T. (041) 521 05 95, Fax 538 10 75. *099158*
Marsilio, Via Sta Chiara 518, 30125 Venezia.
T. (041) 70 71 88. *099159*
Stamperia di Venezia, S Croce 649A, 30100 Venezia.
T. (041) 251 84. *099160*
Torchio, San Marco 1389/B, 30124 Venezia.
T. (041) 28 742. *099161*

Vercelli
White Fotolibri, Via C. Sassone 22, 13100 Vercelli.
T. (0161) 29 42 03. - ArtBk - *099163*

Verona
Edizioni Futuro, Viale G. D'Annuzio 3, 37126 Verona.
T. (045) 45955, 91 56 22, Fax 830 02 61.
- ArtBk - *099164*
Mondadori, Arnoldo, Via G. V. Zeviani 2, 37131 Verona.
T. (045) 93 41 11. - Graph - *099165*
Valdonega, Via Marsala 71, 37128 Verona.
T. (045) 48501. - ArtBk - *099166*

Vicenza
Pozza, Neri, Contra'Oratorio dei Servi 19, 36100 Vicenza. T. (0444) 32 07 87. - ArtBk - *099167*

Japan

Kyoto
Kyoto Shoin Co., Ltd. Shijo Agaru, Kawaramachi, Naka-
gyo-ku, Kyoto 604. T. (075) 221-1062. *099168*
Tankosha Publishing Co., Horikawa, Kuramaguchi-agaru
Kita-ku, Kyoto 603. *099169*
Unsodo Co. Ltd., Nijo Tera-machi, Kyoto 604.
T. (075) 231 36 13. - ArtBk / Repr - *099170*

Miki

Yuyudo Art Gallery, 1-51 Otsuka 2-chome Hyogo, 673
Miki 673-04. T. (081) 273 73. - Repr -   *099171*

Niigata (Niigata-ken)

Nishimura Co., 1-754-39 Asahimachi-dori, Niigata 951.
T. (0252) 223 2388, Fax 224 7165. - ArtBk -   *099172*

Osaka

Hoikusha, 4-8-6 Tsurumi, Tsurumi-ku, Osaka 538.
T. (06) 932 66 01, Fax 933 85 77. - ArtBk -   *099173*

Tokyo

Art Life, 1-5 Motoakasaka, 1-chome, Minato-ku, Tokyo
107. T. (03) 3497-5671. - ArtBk / Graph -   *099174*
Bijutsu Shuppan-sha, 2-36 Kanda Jinbo-cho Chiyoda-ku
101, Tokyo. T. (03) 3234 2151. - ArtBk / Graph / Repr /
Sli -   *099175*
Christie's, 1414 Akasaka, 1-chome, Minato-ku, Tokyo.
- Graph -   *099176*
Gakken Co., 4-28-5, Nishi Gotanda, Shinagawa-ku, To-
kyo 141. T. (03) 3493 3352. - ArtBk -   *099177*
Geijutsu Shinbun Sha, 3-17-28, Kanda Jinbocho Chiyo-
da-ku, Tokyo 101. T. (03) 3263-1637. - ArtBk - *099178*
Graphic Arts Japan, 16-8, 1-chome, Shintomi Chuo-ku,
Tokyo 104. - Graph / Repr -   *099179*
Interface, 7-5-56 Akaska, Minato-ku, Tokyo 107.
T. (03) 3587-1307. - ArtBk / Graph -   *099180*
Kodansha International Ltd., 2-12-21, Otowa. Bunkyo-
ku, Tokyo 112. T. (03) 3944-6491-3. - ArtBk - *099181*
Kohan Densitograph, 19-11 Kasuga, 2-chome Bunkyo-
ku, Tokyo 112. T. (03) 3813 4488. - Repr -   *099182*
Mitsumura Graphique, 1-4-1, Higashi-Azabu, Minato-ku,
Tokyo 106.   *099183*
Nigensha Publishing Co., Ltd., 4-6, Misaki-cho 2-cho-
me, Chiyoda-ku, Tokyo 101. T. (03) 3239-0141.
- ArtBk -   *099184*
Nippon Shuppan Hanbai, 3, 4-chome, Kandasurugadai,
Chiyoda-ku, Tokyo. T. (03) 3233 1111.
- ArtBk -   *099185*
Robundo Publishing, 2-4-9 Shinguku, Tokyo 160.
T. (03) 3352 5070, Fax 3352 5859. - ArtBk -   *099186*
Tokuma Shoten, 4-10-1, Shinbashi, Minato-ku, Tokyo
105. T. (03) 3433 6231, Fax 3433 0608.
- ArtBk -   *099187*
Tuttle, Charles E., Suido 1-chome 2-6 Bunkyo-ku, Tokyo
112. T. (03) 38 11 71 06, Fax 03 3811 6953.
- ArtBk -   *099188*
Weatherhill, John, Nibancho Onuma Bldg. 2F, 8-3 Niban-
cho, Chiyoda-ku, Tokyo (106). T. (03) 3263 4391,
Fax 03 3263 4392. - ArtBk / Graph -   *099189*
Yoseido, 5-5-9 Ginza, Chuo-ku, Tokyo 104. T. (03) 3571-
4493. - ArtBk -   *099190*
Zokeisha Publications, 1-10-3 Minami-Aoyama Minato-
ku, Tokyo 107. T. (03) 3404 44 45, Fax 03 3475 58 74.
- ArtBk -   *099191*

Yamanashi

Edition Nikoh International, 1297 Ichikawadaimon-cho,
409 Yamanashi 409-36. T. (0522) 72 13 71,
Fax 72 13 73. - ArtBk / Graph -   *099192*

Lebanon

Beirut

Dar-Al-Maaref Liban S. A. L., P. O. Box 2320,
Beirut.   *099193*
Khayats Publishers, 90 à 94, rue Bliss, Beirut. *099194*

Liechtenstein

Triesen

Eck, Frank P. van, Haldenweg 8, 9495 Triesen.
T. (075) 3922277, Fax (075) 3922277. - ArtBk - *099195*

Vaduz

Grafos Verlag, Pflugstr. 20, 9490 Vaduz.
T. (075) 232 24 11, Fax 233 25 10. - Graph -   *099196*
Perspective, Kirchstr. 1, 9490 Vaduz. - ArtBk / Graph /
Mul -   *099197*

Sändig, Am Schrägen Weg 12, 9490 Vaduz.
T. (075) 2323627. - ArtBk -   *099198*
Saendig Reprint (Hans R. Wohlwend), Hans Rainer, Am
schrägen Weg 12, 9490 Vaduz. T. (075) 2323627,
Fax (075) 2323627. - ArtBk -   *099199*

Luxembourg

Luxembourg

Biver, Fons, 11 Rue Sigismond, 2537 Luxembourg.
- ArtBk / Graph / Repr / Card -   *099200*
Editeurs Réunis, 23 Allée Scheffer, 2520 Luxembourg.
- ArtBk -   *099201*
Edition Articon, 6 Av du X Septembre, 2550 Luxem-
bourg. T. (0352) 45 24 60, Fax 45 83 46.   *099202*
Editions Saint-Paul, 2 Rue Christophe Plantin, 2339 Lu-
xembourg. T. (0352) 49931, Fax 499 32 62.
- ArtBk -   *099203*
NUMA-Revue internationale de numismatique, 12, Rue
Duchscher, Luxembourg. T. (0352) 48 17 65.   *099204*
RTL Edition, 26 Blvd. Grande-Duchesse Charlotte, 1330
Luxembourg. T. (0352) 45 28 88. - ArtBk -   *099205*

Macedonia

Skopje

Misla, Maksim Gorki 18, 91000 Skopje.
- ArtBk -   *099206*

Mexico

México (D.F.)

Artes de Mexico y del Mundo, Amores 262, México.
T. 536 20 31, 543 83 91. - ArtBk -   *099207*
Artes Graficas y Venereo S. de R. L., Lago Norgis 32,
Col. Veronica Anzures 5, México.   *099208*
Diaz, Juan Luis, Rio Balsas 106, México, D.F. 06500.
T. 514 1434. - ArtBk -   *099209*
Editorial Hermes, Castilla 229, México. T. 696 35 22.
- ArtBk -   *099210*
Grupo Azabache, Dallas 85-40 Piso, Col. Napoles,
03810 México. T. 543 26 34, Fax 543 29 49.
- ArtBk -   *099211*
Herrero, Amazonas 44, México. T. 566 49 00.
- ArtBk -   *099212*
Instituto Nacional de Bellas Artes, México.
T. 518 01 80.   *099213*
Libreria Anticuaria Echaniz, Mar Arafura 8, México.
T. 527 29 51.   *099214*
Lito Offset Nacional, Avda. Sur 16, México.
- Repr -   *099215*
Misrachi, Enrique Beraha, Genova 20, México.
T. 511 90 88.   *099216*

Monaco

Monte Carlo

Hals, Christian, Palais de la Scala, 98000 Monte Carlo.
T. 93 50 66 14.   *099217*
Sauret, André, Les Editions du Livre, 17, bd de Suisse,
BP 164, 98000 Monte Carlo.   *099218*

Netherlands

Aerdenhout (Noord-Holland)

Abrams, Harry N., POB 34, 2110 AA
Aerdenhout.   *099219*

Alkmaar (Noord-Holland)

Arti, Emmastr. 11, 1814 DL Alkmaar. T. (072) 5117506.
- ArtBk -   *099220*

Alphen a/d Rijn (Zuid-Holland)

Dobbenburgh, van, Saffierstr. 129, 2403 XP Alphen a/d
Rijn. T. (0172) 430413. - ArtBk -   *099221*

Amersfoort (Utrecht)

Museum Cards, Pr. Frederiklaan 10a, 3818 KC Amersfoort. T. (033) 4613718. - Card -   *099222*

Amsterdam

Architectura & Natura, Leliegracht 44, 1015 DH Amster-
dam. T. (020) 623 61 86, Fax 638 23 03.   *099223*
Art Book, Prinsengracht 645, 1016 HV Amsterdam.
T. (020) 625 93 37. - ArtBk -   *099224*
Art Unlimited, Overtoom 31, 1054 HB Amsterdam.
T. (020) 685 10 11. - ArtBk / Repr / Card / Cal - *099225*
Becht, H. J. W., Keizergracht 810, 1000 AD Amsterdam.
T. (020) 624 24 49. - ArtBk -   *099226*
Benjamin's, John, Amsteldijk 44, POBox 75577, 1074
HV Amsterdam. T. (020) 676 23 25, 673 81 56,
Fax 673 97 73.   *099227*
Boekie Woekie, Gasthuismolensteg 16, 1016 AN Am-
sterdam. T. (020) 625 93 60.   *099228*
Bussy, J.H. de, Keizergracht 810, 1017 ED Amsterdam.
T. (020) 624 24 49. - ArtBk -   *099229*
Castrum Peregrini Presse, Herengracht 401, 1017 BP
Amsterdam. T. (020) 623 52 87. - ArtBk -   *099230*
Drukwerk in de Marge, 1001 RN Amsterdam.
T. (020) 671 90 86. - Graph -   *099231*
Fragment Uitgeverij Publishers, Conraadstr. 23, 1018 NE
Amsterdam. T. (020) 626 71 33. - ArtBk -   *099232*
Gennep, van, 283 Spuistraat, 1012 VR Amsterdam.
T. (020) 624 70 33, Fax 24 70 35. - ArtBk -   *099233*
Gieben, J.C., Nieuwe Herengracht 35, 1011 RM Amster-
dam. T. (020) 627 51 70. - ArtBk -   *099234*
Huisman, Hetty, Anjelierstr. 153, 1015 NG Amsterdam.
T. (020) 626 79 68. - ArtBk -   *099235*
Idea Books, Nieuwe Herengracht 11, 1011 RK Amster-
dam. T. (020) 622 61 54, 624 73 76,
Fax 20 92 99.   *099236*
Israel, B. M., N.Z. Voorburgwal 264, 1012 RS Amster-
dam. T. (020) 624 70 40. - ArtBk -   *099237*
Kehwa Art, Jan van der Neuthof 37, 1106 WL Amster-
dam. T. (020) 697 83 13. - Graph -   *099238*
Kuurstra, J. J., Amsteldam 113, 1078 AR Amsterdam.
T. (020) 679 00 61. - Card / Cal -   *099239*
Lange, Allert de, Damrak 62, 1012 LM Amsterdam.
T. (020) 624 67 44. - ArtBk -   *099240*
Lieve Hemel, Vijzelgracht 6-8, 1017 HR Amsterdam.
T. (020) 623 00 60, Fax 27 26 63.   *099241*
Meulenhoft/Landshoft, Herengracht 507, 1000 AC Am-
sterdam. T. (020) 626 75 55, Fax 20 55 16.
- ArtBk -   *099242*
Picaron Editions, Binnenkant 29, 1011 BJ Amsterdam.
T. (020) 620 14 84, Fax 625 12 58.   *099243*
Ploughman Art Productions, Geldersekade 89, 1011 EL
Amsterdam. T. (020) 638 15 13, Fax 620 84 72.
- ArtBk -   *099244*
Positionem, Keizersgracht 82, 1015 CT Amsterdam.
T. (020) 622 47 27.   *099245*
Printshop, Prinsengracht 845, 1017 KB Amsterdam.
T. (020) 625 16 56. - Graph -   *099246*
Saundarya Lahari, Reestr. 19, 1016 DM Amsterdam.
T. (020) 626 97 75. - ArtBk -   *099247*
Sparts, Utrechtsestr. 139, 1017 VM Amsterdam.
T. (020) 627 44 82, Fax 638 00 37. - Graph / Card / Cal /
Mul -   *099248*
Steltman Editions, Spuistr. 330, 1012 VX Amsterdam.
T. (020) 622 86 83. - ArtBk / Graph / Card -   *099249*
Veen/Reflex Publishers, Herengracht 481, 1017 BT Am-
sterdam. T. (020) 626 17 71, Fax 627 68 51.
- ArtBk -   *099250*

Assen (Drenthe)

Gorcum, van & Comp., Industrieweg 38, 9403 AB Assen.
T. (0592) 346846, Fax 372064. - ArtBk -   *099251*

Assendelft (Noord-Holland)

International Art Products, Dorpsstr. 684, 1566 EN As-
sendelft. T. (075) 6874508. - Graph -   *099252*

Benteld (Noord-Holland)

Abrams, Harry N., Bentveldweg 19, 2116 EG Benteld.
T. (023) 5249031. - ArtBk -   *099253*

Bergeijk

Society for Japanese Arts, Mr. Pankenstr. 12, 5571 CP
Bergeijk. - ArtBk / ArtP -   *099254*

Blaricum (Noord-Holland)

Hamer Graphics, Langeweg 1, 1261 EL Blaricum.
T. (035) 5312678. *099255*

Bodegraven (Zuid-Holland)

Hart, Gerard 't, Zuidzijde 72, 2411 RT Bodegraven.
- ArtBk - *099256*

De Bilt (Utrecht)

Cantecleer, Dorpsstr. 74, 3730 AA De Bilt.
T. (030) 2204014, Fax 2210106. - ArtBk - *099257*

Doornspijk (Gelderland)

Davaco, Beukenlaan 3, 8085 RK Doornspijk.
T. (0525) 661823, Fax 2153. - ArtBk - *099258*

Ede (Gelderland)

Verkerke, Morsestr. 9-11, 6716 AH Ede.
T. (0318) 677911. - Repr / Card / Sli - *099259*

Eindhoven (Noord-Brabant)

Lande, Hadewych van der, Vesaliuslaan 50, 5644 HL
Eindhoven. T. (040) 2117108. - ArtBk - *099260*

Groningen

Verkerke, Zwanestraat 13, 9712 CJ Groningen.
T. (050) 3126875. *099261*

Den Haag (Zuid-Holland)

Schwartz, Gary, Christ. Plantijnstr. 2, 2005 EA Den Haag.
T. (070) 370 99 11. - ArtBk - *099262*
Sdu Verlag, Postbus 30446, 2500 GK Den Haag.
T. (070) 342 97 33, Fax 363 49 03. *099263*
Verboon, Leo, Paviljoensgracht 68-70, 2512 BR Den
Haag. T. (070) 346 54 16. - ArtBk / Graph /
Mul - *099264*
Verkerke, Papestraat 5, 2513 AV Den Haag.
T. (070) 346 70 11. *099265*

Haarlem (Noord-Holland)

Toorts, Nijverheidsweg 1, 2031 CN Haarlem. *099266*

Hilversum (Noord-Holland)

EG-atelier, 1200 BH Hilversum Postbus 1311.
T. (035) 6233180. - Graph - *099267*

Hoorn (Noord-Holland)

Edecea, Italiaanse Zeedijk 16a, 1621 AH Hoorn. *099268*

Huizen (Noord-Holland)

EG-Atelier, Wedekuil 7, 1273 SB Huizen.
- Graph - *099269*

Kampen (Overijssel)

La Rivière & Voorhoeve, Gildestr. 5, 8263 AH Kampen.
T. (038) 3313545. - Cal - *099270*

Leiden (Zuid-Holland)

Brill, E. J., Plantijnstr 2, 2321 JC Leiden.
T. (071) 5312624, Fax 5317532. *099271*

Leidschendam (Zuid-Holland)

Aalbers, Ben, Westvlietweg 33, 2267 AB Leidschendam.
T. (070) 386 42 29. - Graph - *099272*

Maarssen (Utrecht)

Apa-Academic Publ. Assoc., Postbus 122, 3600 AC
Maarssen. *099273*

Maastricht (Limburg)

Adelt, Wilhelminasingel 80, 6202 NA Maastricht.
T. (043) 316707. - Graph / Repr / Card / Cal - *099274*

Middelburg (Zeeland)

Art Information Centre, Breestraat 79, 4331 TT Middelburg. T. (0118) 611210. - ArtBk / Graph / Card - *099275*

Naarden (Noord-Holland)

Bekhoven, Anton W. van, Nieuwe Haven 27a, 1411 SG
Naarden. T. (035) 6947638. *099276*

Nijmegen (Gelderland)

Holland-Imparch Art Publishing, Prins Bernhardstr. 8,
6576 BB-001J bij Nijmegen. Fax 22550. - Graph /
Repr - *099277*
Uitgeverij Sun, Bijleveldsingel 9, 6521 AM Nijmegen.
T. (024) 3221700, Fax 3235742. - ArtBk - *099278*

Ochten (Gelderland)

Brunott Fitting Image, Mercuriusweg 42, 4050 EA Ochten. T. (0344) 643333, Fax 642700. - Graph / Repr /
Card - *099279*

Oss (Noord-Brabant)

Lennart Publicity, Kruisstr. 62, 5340 AC Oss.
T. (0412) 622135. - Cal - *099280*

Rotterdam (Zuid-Holland)

Balkema, A. A., Vijverweg 8, 3000 BR Rotterdam.
T. (010) 414 58 22. - ArtBk / Repr - *099281*
Bébert, Westersingel 22, 3014 GP Rotterdam.
T. (010) 436 15 55, Fax 436 40 92. *099282*
Donker, Ad., Koningin Emmapl 1, 3016 AA Rotterdam.
T. (010) 436 30 09. *099283*
Heer, Joh. de, & Zn., Rozenlaan 113, 3051 LP Rotter-
dam. T. (010) 422 09 88. *099284*
Museum Boymans-van Beuningen, Editionen, Mathe-
nesserlaan 18-20, 3015 CK Rotterdam.
T. (010) 4419400, Fax (010) 4360500. - Repr / Card /
Cal - *099285*

Utrecht

Catch Publishing, Mississippidreef 50, 3565 CG Utrecht.
T. (030) 2621654. - Graph / Repr / Card - *099286*
Haentjens Dekker & Gumbert, Achter Sint Pieter 140,
3512 HT Utrecht. T. (030) 2310958. - ArtBk - *099287*
Reflex, Maliebaan 45, 3581 CD Utrecht. - ArtBk /
Graph - *099288*
Spectrum, P. O. Box 2073, 3500 GB Utrecht. *099289*

Voorburg (Zuid-Holland)

Lande, Hadewych van der, Postbus 263, 2270 AG Voorburg. - ArtBk - *099290*

Weert (Limburg)

Smeets Illustrated Projects, Molenveldstr. 90, 6001 HL
Weert. T. (0495) 570911, Fax 542905. - ArtBk - *099291*

Zaltbommel (Gelderland)

Europese Bibliotheek, Waalkade 34, 5300 AA Zaltbom-
mel. - ArtBk - *099292*

Norway

Oslo

Abel, Kristian IV's g. 15, 0164 Oslo.
T. 22 20 25 02. *099293*
Acanthus, Nobels G. 37, Oslo. T. 22 55 28 79. *099294*
Aqva Art, Tårnv. 1e, Oslo. T. 22 69 20 38. - Repr - *099295*
Aschehoug, H., & Co., Sehestedsgate 3, 0102 Oslo.
T. 22 42 94 90. - ArtBk / Repr - *099296*
Borsum, Fridtjof Nansens plass 2, Oslo. T. 22 41 04 33.
- Graph - *099297*
Cappelen, J.W., Kirkegaten 15, 0101 Oslo.
T. 22 42 94 40. *099298*
Grøhndahl & Dreyers Forlag, Fred. Olsensgate 5, 0152
Oslo. T. 22 33 58 50, Fax 22 42 12 58. - ArtBk / Graph /
Repr / Card - *099299*
Halvorsen, Brödr., Stansevn. 4, 0975 Oslo.
T. 22 16 38 10, Fax 22 16 50 58. - Repr - *099300*
Munchforlaget, Behrens gt. 8, 0257 Oslo. T. 22 55 77 30,
Fax 22 55 77 32. - Repr / Card - *099301*
Universitetsforlaget, Scandinavian University Press, POB
2959 Tøyen, 0608 Oslo. T. 22575400,
Fax 22575353. *099302*

Pakistan

Lahore

Ferozsons, 60, Shahrah-e-Quaid-e-Azam, Lahore.
T. 30 11 96/98. - Graph - *099303*

Poland

Kraków

Wydawnictwo Literackie, ul Długa 1, 31-147 Kraków.
T. 22 46 44. - ArtBk - *099304*

Łódź

CDA, ul Ks. Brzoski 34a/62, 91-315 Łódź.
T. 55 16 18. *099305*

Warszawa

Państwowe Wydawnictwo Naukowe, ul Miodowa 10,
00-251 Warszawa. T. (022) 26 71 63. - ArtBk - *099306*
Wydawnictwa Artystyczne i Filmowe, ul Puławska 61,
02-595 Warszawa. T. (022) 45 53 01. - ArtBk - *099307*
Wydawnictwo Arkady, ul Sienkiewicza 14, 00-950 War-
szawa. T. (022) 26 93 16. - ArtBk / Graph /
Card - *099308*
Wydawnictwo Interpress, ul Bagatela 12, 00-585 War-
szawa. T. (022) 28 22 21. - ArtBk / Graph / Repr / Card /
Cal - *099309*

Wrocław

Ossolineum – Wydawnictwo Polskiej Akademii Nauk,
Rynek 9, 50 106 Wrocław. T. 3 86 25. *099310*

Portugal

Braga (Minho)

Livraria Cruz, Cruz & Cia. Lda., Rua de D. Diogo de Sousa 127-133, 4700 Braga. T. 220 11, 223 98.
- Graph - *099311*

Lisboa

Biblarte, Rua São Pedro Alcântara 71, 1200 Lisboa.
T. (01) 36 37 02. - ArtBk - *099312*
Centro de Arte, Sociedade Tipográfica, Rua de D. Estefâ-
nia 195 D, 1000 Lisboa. T. (01) 54 32 80,
Fax 57 79 26. *099313*
Editora Cosmos, Rua da Emenda 111, 1200 Lisboa.
T. (01) 32 20 50. - ArtBk - *099314*
Gravura, Tv. do Sequeiro 4r/c, Lisboa.
T. (01) 363 437. *099315*
Imprensa Nacional Casa da Moeda, Rua D. Fr. Manuel
de Melo 5, 1092 Lisboa, Codex. - ArtBk - *099316*
Parceria A. M. Pereira, Lda., Rua Augusta 44 bis 54,
1200 Lisboa. T. (01) 36 17 10, 36 17 30. *099317*
Sousa, Ernesto de, Tv. Fala – So 15, 1. E/C, 1200 Lis-
boa. T. (01) 361 994. *099318*

Portimao

Galeria Portimao, Rua Santa Isabel 5, 8500 Portimao.
T. (082) 229 65. - ArtBk - *099319*

Romania

Bucuresti

Editura Academiei Române, Calea Victoriei 125, 79717
Bucuresti. T. (01) 6507 680. - ArtBk - *099320*
Editura Meridiane, Piata Scînteii 1, 71341 Bucuresti.
T. (01) 6181 087. - ArtBk - *099321*

Russia

Moskva

Planeta, 8/11 Petrovka St., Moskva, 103031.
T. (095) 924 64 04. - ArtBk - *099322*

Sankt-Peterburg

Aurora-Kunstverlag, Newsky Prospekt 7-9, 191065
Sankt Peterburg. T. 312 37 53. - ArtBk / Repr / Card /
Cal / Mul - *099323*

Singapore

Singapore

Alpha Gallery, 7 Alexandra Av., Singapore, 0315.
T. 63 53 11. - Card - *099324*
Sun Tree Publisher, Block 6 No. 152, Singapore, 2678.
T. 452 26 77, Fax 455 37 58. - ArtBk - *099325*

Slovenia

Ljubljana
Cankarjeva založba, Kopitarjeva 2, 1000 Ljubljana.
T. (061) 323841. - ArtBk -   *099326*
Državna Založba, Mestni trg 28, 1000 Ljubljana POB
501. T. (061) 310736. - ArtBk -   *099327*
Mladinska Knjiga, Prešernova 5, 1000 Ljubljana.
T. (061) 212211, Fax 224454. - ArtBk -   *099328*

South Africa

Craighall
Gallery 21, 88 Fox Street, Craighall, 2001. T. 838-66 30.
- Graph / Card -   *099329*

Maitland
Struik Book Distributors, Upper Camp Rd., 7405 Mai-
tland. T. 511 0935, Fax 511 0972.   *099330*

Pretoria (Tvl.)
Schweickerdt, E., 89 Queen St., Pretoria, 0002.
T. (012) 21 65 57. - Repr -   *099331*

Spain

Barcelona
ADOGI, POB 9319, 08080 Barcelona. T. (93) 211 26 24.
- Graph / Repr / Mul -   *099332*
Afha Internacional S. A., 08006 Barcelona B. P.
75.   *099333*
Argos Vergara, Aragón 390, 08013 Barcelona.   *099334*
Binomi, Sant Lluís 63, 08024 Barcelona.
T. (93) 210 81 01. - Graph -   *099335*
Blume, Milanesado 21-23, 08017 Barcelona.
T. (93) 204 23 00. - ArtBk / Graph -   *099336*
Bosch, Comte d'Urgell 51 bis, 08011 Barcelona.
T. (93) 254 84 37, 254 46 29. - ArtBk -   *099337*
Castro Graphic, Noguera Pallaresa 44, ático 2, 08014
Barcelona. T. (93) 432 17 94. - ArtBk -   *099338*
Cayfosa Industria Grafica, Ctra. de Caldes Km 3 Sta.
Perpetua de Mogoda, Barcelona. T. (93) 56 00 851,
Fax 56 03 724. - ArtBk -   *099339*
Destino, Consejo de Ciento, 425, 08009 Barcelona.
T. (93) 246 23 05. - ArtBk -   *099340*
Edart, Ediciones de Arte, Muntaner, 177, 08036 Barcelo-
na. - ArtBk -   *099341*
Ediciones Atrium, Muntaner 483, ático 4a, 08021 Barce-
lona. T. (93) 212 71 54, Fax 418 52 87.
- ArtBk -   *099342*
Ediciones Poligrafa, Balmes, 54, 08007 Barcelona.
T. (93) 301 91 00. - ArtBk / Graph / Card / Cal -   *099343*
Ediciones 62, Provenza, 278, 08008 Barcelona.
T. (93) 216 00 62, Fax 215 54 68. - ArtBk -   *099344*
Editions de l'Eixample, Mallorca 297, Pral., 08037 Bar-
celona. T. (93) 258 94 05, Fax 207 62 48.
- ArtBk -   *099345*
Editora Nacional, Muntaner, 221, 08036 Barcelona.
T. (93) 250 64 53.   *099346*
Editorial Labor, Calabria 235-239, 08029 Barcelona.
T. (93) 322 05 51. - ArtBk -   *099347*
Editorial Lumen, Ramón Miquel y Planas 10, 08034 Bar-
celona. T. (93) 204 34 96, 204 21 39,
Fax 205 56 19.   *099348*
Editorial Planeta, Córcega 273-277, 08008 Barcelona.
T. (93) 217 90 50. - ArtBk -   *099349*
Editorial Teide, Viladomat 291, 08029 Barcelona.
T. (93) 410 45 07. - ArtBk -   *099350*
Fundacio Caixa de Pensions, Via Laietana 56, 08003
Barcelona. T. (93) 404 60 07. - Graph -   *099351*
Gaspar, Consejo de Ciento 323, 08007 Barcelona.
T. (93) 318 87 01. - Graph -   *099352*
Gili, Gustavo, S. A., Calle Rosellon, 87 y 89, 08029 Bar-
celona. T. (93) 322 81 61, Fax 322 92 05. - ArtBk /
Graph -   *099353*
Juventud, Provenza 101, 08029 Barcelona.
T. (93) 439 20 00. - ArtBk -   *099354*
La Poligrafa, Balmes 54, 08007 Barcelona.
T. (93) 301 91 00. - ArtBk -   *099355*

Marcombo, Ediciones Tecnicas, S. A. de Boixareu Edito-
res, Gran Via de les Corts Catalanes, 594, 08007 Bar-
celona. T. (93) 318 00 79. - Graph -   *099356*
Morón, Andres, Gerona 122, 08009 Barcelona.
T. (93) 207 74 42, Fax 257 60 29.   *099357*
Omega, S. A., Platón, 08006 Barcelona.
T. (93) 201 38 07. - ArtBk -   *099358*
Pigmalion, Av. Diagonal 442-3o-2a, 08037 Barcelona.
T. (93) 238 05 34. - ArtBk -   *099359*
Pintó, Ramon, Passeig Sant Joan 176, 08037 Barcelona.
T. (93) 258 38 16. - Graph -   *099360*
Porter Libros, Avda. Puerta del Angel, 9, 08002 Barcelo-
na. T. (93) 301 2700.   *099361*
Promotora Editorial Europea, Calle D, Sector C Parcela
28, 08040 Barcelona. T. (93) 263 03 04,
Fax 263 16 20.   *099362*
Rauter, Rda. Gral. Mitre 206, 08006 Barcelona.
T. (93) 217 65 26. - ArtBk / Repr -   *099363*
Salvat, Mallorca 45-49, 08029 Barcelona.
T. (93) 230 36 07. - ArtBk -   *099364*
Seix Barral, S. A., Provenza, 219, 08008 Barcelona.
- ArtBk / Graph / Repr -   *099365*
Sopéna, Ramon, S. A., Provenza, 95, 08029 Barcelona.
- ArtBk -   *099366*
Taché Editor, J. Sebastian Bach 22, 08021 Barcelona.
T. (93) 202 29 16.   *099367*
Taller, C. Cadiz 9, 08023 Barcelona. T. (93) 211 26 24.
- Graph -   *099368*

Burgos
„Hijos de Santiago Rodriguez", Aptdo. 55, Burgos.
- Graph -   *099369*

Cadaques (Gerona)
Galeria Cadaques, Hort d'en Sanos 9, 17400 Cadaques.
T. (972) 25 82 44. - Graph / Mul -   *099370*

Esplugas de Llobregat (Barcelona)
Plaza & Janes, Virgen de Guadaloupe 21-23, 08950 Es-
plugas de Llobregat. T. (93) 371 02 00.   *099371*

Figueres (Girona)
Art-3, Pujada del Castell 41, 17600 Figueres.
T. (972) 50 35 16.   *099372*
Ediciones Tristan, Pere III 36, 17600 Figueres.
T. (972) 51 02 94, Fax 67 24 68.   *099373*

Girona
Dalmau Carles Pla, S. A., Juan Maragall 34 x 36 Aptdo.
3, 17002 Girona. - ArtBk -   *099374*

Madrid
Aguilar Ediciones, Juan Bravo, 38, Aptdo. 14241, 28006
Madrid. T. (91) 578 31 59, Fax 578 32 20.
- ArtBk -   *099375*
Alianza Editorial, Milán 38, 28043 Madrid.
T. (91) 200 00 45. - ArtBk -   *099376*
Catolica, S. A., Mateo Inurrio, 15, Aptdo. 466, 28036
Madrid. - ArtBk -   *099377*
Dossat, S. A., Plaza de Santa Ana, 9 Aptdo. 12040,
28012 Madrid. - ArtBk / Graph -   *099378*
Ediciones Catedra, Josef Valcárcel 27, 28027 Madrid.
T. (91) 32 00 119, Fax 742 66 31. - ArtBk -   *099379*
Ediciones L, Gravina 10, 28004 Madrid.
T. (91) 222 29 71/72. - ArtBk / Graph / ArtP -   *099380*
Edition Emilio Alvarez, Arturo Soria 187, 28043 Madrid.
T. (91) 0413 6178.   *099381*
Espasa-Calpe, Gran Via 29, 28013 Madrid. - ArtBk /
Graph / Repr / Card -   *099382*
Esti-Arte, Almagro 44, 28010 Madrid.
T. (91) 419 76 69.   *099383*
Gredos, Sanchez Pacheco 81, 28002 Madrid.
T. (91) 415 74 12, 415 74 08. - ArtBk -   *099384*
Kreisler, Jorge, C/ Prim 13, 28004 Madrid.
T. (91) 522 05 34, Fax 522 06 85. - ArtBk / Graph /
Repr / Card / Sli / Mul -   *099385*
Lunwerg Editores, Manuel Silvela 12, 28010 Madrid.
T. (91) 593 00 58. - ArtBk -   *099386*
Magisterio Espanol, Quevedo 1-3, 28014
Madrid.   *099387*
Mundiarte, Julián Romea, 7, 28003 Madrid.
T. (91) 254 17 10, 254 76 65. - Graph / Mul -   *099388*
Publicaciones Europaes de Arte, Cid 3, 28001 Madrid.
T. (91) 276 93 45. - Graph -   *099389*

Pueyo, S. L., Arenal, 6, 28013 Madrid. - ArtBk -   *099390*
Reproart, Av. Menendez Pelayo 2, 28009 Madrid.
T. (91) 431 72 24.   *099391*
Santo Grial, El, Santiago Bernabeu 4, 28036 Madrid.
T. (91) 411 60 53.   *099392*
Silex Ediciones, Alcalá 202, 28028 Madrid.
T. (91) 356 69 09, 356 69 09, Fax 361 00 75.
- ArtBk -   *099393*
Tecnos, Josefa Valcárcel 27, 28027 Madrid.
T. (91) 742 22 15, 742 91 11. - ArtBk -   *099394*
Turner, Génova 3, 28004 Madrid. T. (91) 419 20 37,
531 77 22, Fax 419 39 30. - ArtBk / Graph /
Repr -   *099395*

Málaga (Malaga)
Editiones El Pesebre, Monte de Miramar, Camino de Sta.
Paula 1, 29018 Málaga. T. (952) 221 99 76.
- Mul -   *099396*

Oviedo (Asturias)
Ediciones Naranco, S. A., B.P. 542, 33000
Oviedo.   *099397*

Pamplona (Navarra)
Salvat S. A. de Ediciones, Arrieta 25, Pamplona.   *099398*

Sant Andreu de Llavaneres (Barcelona)
Parthenon, Camí del Plà de Sanç 24, 08392 Sant Andreu
de Llavaneres. T. (93) 795 20 08, Fax 795 20 08.
- ArtBk / Graph -   *099399*

Valencia
Vicent, Fuente del Jarro, Poligono Industr., Ciudad de
Sevilla 10, 46006 Valencia. T. (96) 138 83 11,
Fax 138 89 00. - ArtBk / Graph / Repr -   *099400*

Vitoria (Alava)
Heraclio Fournier SA, Heraclio Fournier 17, 01006 Vitoria. T. (945) 25 11 00, Fax 26 49 47. - ArtBk -   *099401*

Sweden

Akersberga
Semmann, Lerviksvägen 19, 184 00 Akersberga.
T. (0764) 242 64. - Repr / Card -   *099402*

Lidingö
Sonet Editions, Atlasvägen 1, 181 23 Lidingö.
T. (08) 767 01 50. - ArtBk / Graph -   *099403*

Lund
Lund Art Press, Box 1517, 221 00 Lund.
T. (046) 14 17 29, Fax (046) 4646-104545.   *099404*
Sellem Edition, POB 1507, 22101 Lund.
T. (046) 147676.   *099405*

Malmö
Adlers Editions, Henrik Smithsgatan 3, 21156 Malmö.
T. (040) 111 592.   *099406*
Börjeson, Hamngatan4, 211 22 Malmö. T. (040) 711 00.
- ArtBk -   *099407*
Hommage aux Prix Nobel, Hamngatan 4, 211 22 Malmö.
T. (040) 711 00. - ArtBk -   *099408*
Refek, Roslinväg 4, 217 55 Malmö. T. (040) 643 52.
- ArtBk / Graph -   *099409*

Norrköping
Guteförlaget, Hospitalsgatan 16, 602 27 Norrköping.
T. (011) 18 19 19, 13 12 12. - Graph / Repr -   *099410*

Stockholm
Ahlén & Akerlunds, Torsgatan 21, 113 21 Stockholm.
- ArtBk -   *099411*
Alfabeta, P.O.Box 4284, 10266 Stockholm.
T. (08) 714 93 53/36, Fax 643 24 31.   *099412*
Arkitektur Förlag, P.O.Box 1742, 11187 Stockholm.
T. (08) 679 61 05, Fax 611 52 70.   *099413*
Fischer & Rye, Adolf Fredriks Kyrkogata 13, 111 37
Stockholm. T. (08) 24 21 60, Fax 24 78 25.
- ArtBk -   *099414*
Futura, Grafikhuset, Karlaplan 14, 10055 Stockholm.
T. (08) 24 46 55. - Graph / Mul -   *099415*
Galerie Aix, Karlpl. 7, 114 60 Stockholm.
T. (08) 667 23 05. - Graph -   *099416*

Galleri Klara, Beridarebanan 1, 111 51 Stockholm.
T. (08) 11 08 03. - Graph -   *099417*
Guterstam, Turingevägen 33, 125 42 Stockholm.
T. (08) 86 17 44. - Graph / Repr -   *099418*
Raster Förlag, Götgatan 34, 116 21 Stockholm.
T. (08) 42 20 16, Fax 42 41 23. - ArtBk -   *099419*
Scandinavian University Press, POB 3255, 103 65
Stockholm. T. (08) 4408040, Fax 4408050.   *099420*

Uppsala

Scandecor International, Seminariegatan 33, 751 27
Uppsala. T. (018) 17 11 00, Fax 12 57 70. - Graph /
Card -   *099421*

Switzerland

Aarau (Aargau)

Huber & Amacker AG, Graphische Kunstanstalt, Schö-
nenwerderstr. 40, 5000 Aarau. T. (064) 24 15 51.
- Repr / Card -   *099422*

Adliswil (Zürich)

Schenker, U. & U., Rütistr. 4c, 8134 Adliswil.
T. (01) 710 99 22.   *099423*

Allschwil (Basel-Land)

Hinz, Hans, Herrenweg 119, 4123 Allschwil.
T. (061) 301 61 81, Fax (061) 301 66 90. - Sli -   *099424*
Schwitter, Lilienstr. 114, 4123 Allschwil.
T. (061) 481 06 00.   *099425*

Alpnach Dorf (Obwalden)

Wallimann, Martin, 6055 Alpnach Dorf.
T. (041) 670 26 36.   *099426*

Arbon (Thurgau)

Arben-Press, Alemannenstr. 13, 9320 Arbon.
T. (071) 4461460.   *099427*

Ascona (Ticino)

Arte e Scienza, Passagio San Pietro 8, 6612 Ascona.
T. (091) 7914666, Fax 7922187.   *099428*
Noack, Via Moscia 61, 6612 Ascona.
T. (091) 7916335.   *099429*
Ambrogio Pellegrini, S. Progetti Culturali, Via San Pietro,
6612 Ascona. T. (091) 7921528.   *099430*

Au (Sankt Gallen)

Neufeld, Hauptstr 2, 9434 Au. T. (071) 7442303,
Fax 7443412. - Card / Cal -   *099431*

Auvernier (Neuchâtel)

Numaga 2, 24 Grand-Rue, 2012 Auvernier.
T. (032) 7314490. - ArtBk / Cal -   *099432*
Rosselet, André, 76 Rte. des Clos, 2012
Auvernier.   *099433*

Baden (Aargau)

Müller, Lars, POB 912, 5401 Baden. T. (056) 822700,
Fax 822701.   *099434*

Basel

Beyeler, Ernst, Bäumleing 9, 4001 Basel.
T. (061) 2725412, Fax 2719691. - ArtBk /
Graph -   *099435*
Brunnen-Verlag, Wallstr 6, 4002 Basel.
T. (061) 2956000, Fax 2956068. - ArtBk -   *099436*
Galerie d'Analytica Art, Hermann-Albrecht-Str. 17, 4002
Basel. T. (061) 681 76 66, 681 76 55. - ArtBk / Repr /
Card -   *099437*
Lilian, Andrée, Socinstr. 60, 4051 Basel.
T. (061) 2722600, 232600.   *099438*
Littmann, Klaus, Elisabethenstr. 44, 4051 Basel.
T. (061) 272 87 67.   *099439*
Mäder, Franz, Claragraben 45, 4005 Basel.
T. (061) 691 89 47. - ArtBk / Graph / Mul -   *099440*
Pep & No Name Gallery, Güterstr. 153, 4053 Basel.
T. (061) 361 20 65, Fax 3612065. - ArtBk /
Card -   *099441*
Schmücking, Sattelg 2, 4051 Basel. T. (061) 2613705,
Fax 2613705. - ArtBk / Graph -   *099442*
Schwabe & Co., Steinentorstr 13, 4010 Basel.
T. (061) 2725523, Fax 2725573. - ArtBk / ArtP - *099443*

Sphinx Verlag, Freie Str. 84, 4051 Basel.
T. (061) 272 82 66, Fax (061) 272 11 50. - ArtBk /
Sli -   *099444*
Vogelsperger, Grenzacherstr 481, 4058 Basel.
T. (061) 6016650. - Graph -   *099445*
Wiese Verlag AG, Hochbergerstr. 15, 4002 Basel.
T. (061) 661350, Fax (061) 661343. - ArtBk -   *099446*

Bern

Art + Vision, Junkerngasse 34, 3011 Bern.
T. (031) 3113191. - ArtBk / Card / Cal -   *099448*
Edition Tanner, Postfach 8455, 3001 Bern.
T. (031) 381 44 46. - ArtBk / Graph / Card / Cal - *099449*
Gerber, Toni, Gerechtigkeitsgasse 62, 3011 Bern.
T. (031) 311 36 50.   *099450*
Haupt, Paul, Falkenpl 11, 3000 Bern. T. (031) 3012345,
Fax 3014669. - ArtBk / Card -   *099451*
Kornfeld, Laupenstr 41, 3008 Bern. T. (031) 3814673,
Fax 3821891. - Graph / Repr -   *099452*
Lang, Peter, Jupiterstr 15, 3000 Bern. T. (031) 9402121,
Fax 9402131. - ArtBk -   *099452a*
Oeuvre Gravée, Rathausgasse 30, 3011 Bern.
T. (031) 311 44 80, Fax (031) 311 44 70.
- Graph -   *099453*
Scherz, Alfred, Marktgasse 25, 3011 Bern.
T. (031) 311 68 34. - ArtBk -   *099454*
Suti Galerie und Edition, Gerberngasse 15, 3011 Bern.
T. (031) 3110966, 3312007.   *099455*

Boudry (Neuchâtel)

Editions de la Baconnière, La Baconnière, 2017 Boudry.
T. (032) 8421004. - ArtBk -   *099457*

Brig (Valais)

Rotten Verlag, Sonnenstr. 7, 3900 Brig.
T. (027) 9234122.   *099458*

La Chaux-de-Fonds (Neuchâtel)

Editions d'en haut, Postfach 825, 2301 La Chaux-de-
Fonds. T. (032) 9267638, Fax 9265412. - ArtBk /
Graph / Cal / Mul -   *099459*

Chiasso (Ticino)

Fotografia Oltre, Via Bossi 13, 6830 Chiasso.
T. (091) 6828655.   *099460*

Dietikon (Zürich)

Stocker, Josef, Hasenbergstr. 7, 8953 Dietikon.
T. (01) 740 44 44. - ArtBk -   *099461*
Verlag Bibliophile Drucke von Josef Stocker AG, Hasen-
bergstr. 7, 8953 Dietikon. T. (01) 740 44 44.
- ArtBk -   *099462*

Disentis/Mustér (Graubünden)

Desertina Verlag, Carcarola, 7180 Disentis/Mustér.
T. (081) 9475441, Fax 947 49 42. - ArtBk -   *099463*

Döttingen (Aargau)

Object Art, Berg 848, 5312 Döttingen.
T. (056) 245 26 87. - Graph / Mul -   *099464*

Dornach (Solothurn)

Rudolf Steiner Verlag, Haus Duldeck, Postfach 135,
4143 Dornach. T. (061) 701 22 40, Fax 7012534.
- ArtBk / Repr -   *099465*

Dübendorf (Zürich)

Gysin, Bob, Oberdorfstr. 113, 8600 Dübendorf.
T. (01) 821 52 66, Fax 8215272. - Graph /
Cal -   *099466*

Ebmatingen (Zürich)

Baehler, Steinmueri 24a, 8123 Ebmatingen.
T. (01) 980 19 53, Fax 980 38 49. - Graph /
Repr -   *099467*

Egg bei Zürich

Manus Verlag, Zelgmatt 14, 8132 Egg bei Zürich.
T. (01) 9841242, Fax 9840764. - Graph / Card /
Cal -   *099468*

Emmenbrücke (Luzern)

beag Kunstverlag, 6021 Emmenbrücke.
T. (041) 2686868, Fax 2686800. - ArtBk -   *099469*

Erlach (Bern)

Steiner, René, Mayhaus, 3235 Erlach. T. (032) 3382088,
Fax 3382033. - ArtBk / Graph -   *099470*

Feldmeilen (Zürich)

Vontobel, General-Wille-Str 144, 8706 Feldmeilen.
T. (01) 9255333, Fax 9255570. - Repr / Card - *099471*

Forch (Zürich)

Abderhalden, Emil, Hans-Roelli-Str. 16, 8127 Forch.
T. (01) 980 00 81.   *099472*

Frauenfeld (Thurgau)

Huber, Promenadenstr 16, 8500 Frauenfeld.
T. (052) 7235511, Fax 7213573. - ArtBk -   *099473*

Fribourg

Artcurial Suisse, Villars-les-Joncs, 1700 Fribourg.
T. (026) 4814877.   *099474*
Fragnière, Henri, 31 Rte. de la Glâne, 1700 Fribourg.
T. (026) 4222525.   *099475*

Genève

Asia-Africa Museum, 30 Grand-Rue Vieille Ville, 1204
Genève. T. (022) 311 71 90.   *099476*
Bronze Gallery, 12 Rue Kléberg, 1201 Genève.
T. (022) 732 63 33.   *099477*
Cramer, Patrick, 13, Chantepoulet, 1201 Genève.
T. (022) 7325432, Fax 7314731.   *099478*
Droz, 11 Rue Massot, 1211 Genève. T. (022) 3466666,
Fax 3472391. - ArtBk -   *099479*
Ecart, 6 Rue Plantamour, 1211 Genève BP 1438.
T. (022) 7311400, Fax (022) 7316709. - ArtBk /
Mul -   *099480*
Editart, 17 Av. Pictet-de-Rochemont, 1207 Genève.
T. (022) 7369603, Fax (022) 7369703. - ArtBk /
Graph -   *099481*
Etablissement Alice Editions, 1, Place du Port, 1204 Ge-
nève. - ArtBk / Graph / Repr / Card -   *099482*
GVA SA Editions, 16 Rue des Granges, 1211 Genève.
T. (022) 3470847, Fax (022) 3112556. - ArtBk - *099483*
Koller, 2 Rue de l'Athénée, 1205 Genève.
T. (022) 3210385, Fax (022) 3287872.   *099484*
Letu, Bernard, Rue Calvin 2, 1204 Genève.
T. (022) 3104757, Fax 3108492. - ArtBk /
Graph -   *099485*
Minkoff, 8 Rue Eynard, 1211 Genève. T. (022) 3104660,
Fax (022) 3102857. - ArtBk -   *099486*
Albert Skira, Editions d'Art, 89 Rte. de Chêne, 1208 Ge-
nève. T. (022) 3495533, Fax (022) 3495535.
- ArtBk -   *099487*
Weber, 13 Rue de Monthoux, 1201 Genève.
T. (022) 7326450, Fax 7384305.   *099488*

Glarus (Glarus)

Tschudi, Lill, Eichenstr. 26, 8750 Glarus.
T. (055) 6406360. - ArtBk -   *099489*

Gossau (Zürich)

Bukal Verlag, Industriestr., 8625 Gossau.
T. (01) 935 26 77, Fax 935 32 47. - Cal -   *099490*
Neugebauer, Michael, 8625 Gossau. - ArtBk / Graph /
Repr / Card / Cal -   *099491*

Grand-Lancy (Genève)

Richert, Albert, 22 Av. Curé-Baud, 1212 Grand-Lancy.
T. (022) 794 06 26.   *099492*

Hindelbank (Bern)

Edition Grafic d'Or, Moosweg 66, 3324 Hindelbank.
T. (034) 51 15 47, Fax 4110610. - Graph -   *099493*

Hochdorf (Luzern)

Impuls, An der Ron, 6280 Hochdorf.
T. (041) 910 33 55.   *099494*

Ittigen (Bern)

Raffael-Verlag, Stockhornstr 5, 3063 Ittigen.
T. (031) 9217700, Fax 9220192. - Repr / Card /
Cal -   *099495*

Kreuzlingen (Thurgau)

Ariston, Hauptstr 14, 8280 Kreuzlingen.
T. (071) 6727218, Fax 6727219. - ArtBk -   *099496*
Edition du Carrois, Postfach 710, 8280
Kreuzlingen.   *099497*

Signer, Werner, Haus Avantgarde, 8280 Kreuzlingen.
T. (071) 6724383. - Graph / ArtBk / Mul / ArtP -   *099498*

Küsnacht (Zürich)
Weber, Heidi, Seestr. 13a, 8700 Küsnacht.
T. (01) 383 64 70.   *099499*

Küssnacht am Rigi (Schwyz)
Verkerke, Im Fänn, 6403 Küssnacht am Rigi.
T. (041) 850 52 52. - Graph -   *099500*

Lachen (Schwyz)
Fretz & Wasmuth, Marktstr. 2, 8853 Lachen.
T. (052) 4425394, Fax 4425435. - ArtBk -   *099501*

Le Landeron (Neuchâtel)
Schneider & Steiner, Vieille Ville 32, 2525 Le Landeron.
T. (032) 7513820. - ArtBk -   *099502*

Lausanne (Vaud)
Acatos, Av Villamont 17, 1005 Lausanne.
T. (021) 3205901, Fax (021) 3129108.   *099503*
Collection de l'art brut, 11 Av. des Bergières, 1004 Lausanne. T. (021) 6475435, Fax (021) 6485521.   *099504*
Daulte & Cie, 50 Av. Rumine, 1005 Lausanne.
T. (021) 323 93 34, Fax 3123750.   *099505*
Edition Rosset, 16 Ch du Parc Rouvraie, 1018 Lausanne.
T. (021) 647 15 72.   *099506*
Editions Favre, 29 Rue de Bourg, 1002 Lausanne.
T. (021) 221717, Fax 3205059. - Graph -   *099507*
Editions Rencontre, 31 Ch. d'Entre-Bois, 8 Bellevaux, 1000 Lausanne. T. (021) 647 38 41,
Fax (021) 647 38 40. - ArtBk -   *099508*
Gonin, Pierre, 41 Rue du Valentin, 1004 Lausanne.
T. (021) 3129996.   *099509*
Payot, Rue de Bourg 1, 1003 Lausanne.
T. (021) 320 33 31. - ArtBk -   *099510*
Who's Who International Art, 20 Av. de la Gare, 1001 Lausanne. T. (021) 733 11 19.   *099511*

Lugano (Ticino)
Centro della Stampa Azed, Via Magatti 2, 6900 Lugano.
T. (091) 9231618.   *099512*
Dabbeni, Felice & Angela, Corso Pestalozzi 1, 6900 Lugano. T. (091) 9232980, Fax 9231211.   *099513*
Fidia Edizioni d'arte, Via Frasca 3, 6900 Lugano.
T. (091) 9235677, Fax 9220171.   *099514*
Giampiero Casagrande, Via Frasca 3, 6900 Lugano.
T. (091) 9235677, Fax 9220171.   *099515*

Lutry (Vaud)
White Gallery, Grand-Rue, 1095 Lutry. T. (021) 7297099.
- Graph / Mul -   *099516*

Luzern
Bessa Verlagsgesellschaft, Grendelstr. 15, 6004 Luzern.
T. (041) 4109515, Fax 4109516. - ArtBk -   *099517*
Editions Aujourd'hui, Abendweg 9, 6006 Luzern.
T. (041) 347 87 38.   *099518*
Faksimile Verlag, Maihofstr 25, 6006 Luzern.
T. (041) 4200380, Fax 4200606. - ArtBk /
Repr -   *099519*
Kunstbilderverlag, Kreuzbuchstr. 27, 6006 Luzern.
T. (041) 370 41 22.   *099520*
Lion's Art, Werchlaubengässli 8, 6004 Luzern.
T. (041) 4102331.   *099521*
Raeber AG, Frankenstr. 7-9, 6002 Luzern.
T. (041) 210 53 63.   *099522*

Mönchaltorf (Zürich)
Nord-Süd Verlag, Industriestr. 837, 8625 Mönchaltorf.
T. (01) 935 13 35, Fax 935 17 00. - Repr / Cal - *099523*

Le Mont-sur-Lausanne (Vaud)
Guide Emer – Ed. R. Chevalley, 35 Ch. de Pernessy, 1052 Le Mont-sur-Lausanne.
T. (021) 652 62 15.   *099524*

Montreux (Vaud)
Editions Udrisard, 1 Eglise-Catholique, 1820 Montreux.
T. (021) 963 45 11.   *099525*

Neuchâtel
Attinger, Victor, 149 Av des Portes-Rouges, 2009 Neuchâtel. T. (032) 7530101, Fax 7530103.
- ArtBk -   *099526*

Editions du Griffon, 17 Faubourg du Lac, 2000 Neuchâtel. T. (032) 7252204. - ArtBk / Card -   *099527*
Editions Ides et Calendes, 19 Evole, BP 752, 2001 Neuchâtel. T. (032) 7253861, Fax 7255880.
- ArtBk -   *099528*
Média, 29 Rue des Moulins, 2000 Neuchâtel.
T. (032) 7245323.   *099529*

Niederteufen (Aargau)
Niggli, Arthur, Hauptstr. 101, 9052 Niederteufen.
T. (071) 3331772. - ArtBk / Graph / Card -   *099530*

Nyon (Vaud)
Armenia Editions, CP 2621, 1260 Nyon 2.
T. (022) 3615833, Fax 3648632. - ArtBk -   *099531*
Publication G.V. Service, 5 Rue César-Soulié, 1260 Nyon. T. (022) 361 26 76.   *099532*

Pfäffikon (Zürich)
Krause, Oskar, Tumbelenstr. 37, 8330 Pfäffikon.
T. (01) 950 30 66, Fax 950 30 66.   *099533*

Pully (Vaud)
Krafft, Anthony, Av du Tirage 13, 1009 Pully.
T. (021) 7280462, Fax 7280136. - ArtBk -   *099534*

Regensberg (Zürich)
Knebel, Sven, Im Höfli, 8158 Regensberg.
T. (01) 853 14 74.   *099535*

Riehen (Basel-Stadt)
Edition Schöneck, Burgstr. 63, 4125 Riehen.
T. (061) 641 10 60.   *099536*

Romanshorn (Thurgau)
Fatzer Verlag, Amriswilerstr, 128, 8590 Romanshorn.
l. (071) 4631043, Fax 4631936. - Repr / Card /
Cal -   *099537*

Sankt Gallen
Schneeberger, Christian, Sternackerstr 3, 9000 Sankt Gallen. T. (071) 2231350, Fax 8451355.
- ArtBk -   *099538*
Vexer Verlag, Brauer Str. 27b, 9000 Sankt Gallen.
T. (071) 2457966, Fax 2447987. - ArtBk / Mul - *099539*

Schaffhausen
Meili, Peter, Am Fronwagplatz 13, 8200 Schaffhausen.
T. (052) 6254144. - ArtBk / Graph / Repr / Cal - *099540*

Schönbühl-Urtenen (Bern)
A Boss & Co AG, Kunst- und Glückwunschkartenverlag, Grubenstr 22, 3322 Schönbühl-Urtenen.
T. (033) 8596111, Fax 8592985. - Card -   *099541*

Seuzach (Zürich)
Seedorn Verlag, Postfach 174, 8472 Seuzach. - ArtBk /
Graph -   *099542*

Stäfa (Zürich)
Zürichsee Zeitschriftenverlag, Seestr 86, 8712 Stäfa.
T. (01) 9285611, Fax 9285600. - ArtP -   *099543*

Unterägeri (Zug)
Groth, Gewerbestr. 19, 6314 Unterägeri.
T. (041) 750 45 72.   *099544*

Unterengstringen (Zürich)
Eber, Nicolas, Dr., Im Aegelsee 2, 8103 Unterengstringen. T. (01) 750 55 81.   *099545*

Visp (Valais)
Rotten Verlag, Terbinerstr 2, 3930 Visp.
T. (027) 9483030, Fax 9462128. - ArtBk / Repr /
Card -   *099546*

Wabern (Bern)
Benteli Verlags AG, Grünaustr. 5, 3084 Wabern.
T. (031) 961 84 84, Fax (031) 961 74 14.
- ArtBk -   *099547*

Zürich
Amman, Thomas, Restelbergstr 97, 8044 Zürich.
T. (01) 2529052, Fax 2528254.   *099548*
Ammann, Neptunstr 20, Postfach 163, 8032 Zürich.
T. (01) 2681040, Fax 2681050. - ArtBk -   *099549*

Artibus Asiae, c/o Museum Rietberg, Gablerstr 15, 8002 Zürich. T. (01) 2024528, Fax 2025201. - Sli / Cal /
Mul -   *099550*
Belser, Chr., Tödistr 18, 8002 Zürich. T. (01) 2014323.
- ArtBk -   *099551*
Bischofberger, Bruno, Utoquai 29, 8008 Zürich.
T. (01) 262 40 20, Fax 262 28 97. - ArtBk /
Repr -   *099552*
Brunnenturm Presse, Napfgasse 4, 8001 Zürich.
T. (01) 853 14 74. - ArtBk / Graph / Repr -   *099553*
Caspari Gallery, Bederstr 109, 8002 Zürich.
T. (01) 2017055.   *099554*
Diogenes Verlag, Sprecherstr. 8, 8032 Zürich.
T. (01) 254 85 11, Fax 252 84 07. - ArtBk / Graph /
Repr / Card / Mul -   *099555*
Edition C, Postfach 822, 8024 Zürich. T. (01) 4627366,
Fax 4620112. - ArtBk -   *099556*
Edition Marlene Frei, Dienerstr. 21, 8004 Zürich.
T. (01) 242 89 00, Fax 241 82 79.   *099557*
Edition & Galerie 999, Winterthurerstr. 16, 8006 Zürich.
T. (01) 362 18 76. - ArtBk / Repr / Mul -   *099558*
Graphis-Verlag, Dufourstr. 107, 8008 Zürich.
T. (01) 251 92 11.   *099559*
Howeg, Waffenplatzstr 1, 8002 Zürich. T. (01) 2010650,
Fax (01) 2010650.   *099560*
Künstlertreff, Kleeweidstr. 61, 8041 Zürich.
T. (01) 481 90 41.   *099561*
Leu, Postfach 1704, 8048 Zürich. T. (01) 4330313,
(077) 392215, Fax 8103201. - ArtBk -   *099562*
Lutz, Hans-Rudolf, Lessingstr. 11, 8002 Zürich.
T. (01) 201 76 72, Fax 201 76 72. - Repr -   *099563*
Münsterhof Verlag, Neptunstr. 82, 8032 Zürich.
T. (01) 261 14 93.   *099564*
Orell Füssli, Dietzingerstr. 3, 8036 Zürich.
T. (01) 466 77 11, Fax 466 74 12. - ArtBk -   *099565*
Papageien-Verlag, Salvatorstr. 28, 8050 Zürich.
T. (01) 311 43 50.   *099566*
Parkett-Verlag, Quellenstr. 27, 8005 Zürich.
T. (01) 271 81 40/41, Fax 272 43 01. - ArtBk / Graph /
Mul -   *099567*
Photoglob, Grubenstr. 37, 8045 Zürich.
T. (01) 463 76 76.   *099568*
Rabe Verlag Zürich, Frankengasse 6, 8001 Zürich.
T. (01) 261 85 40, Fax 261 85 41. - ArtBk / Graph /
Repr / Card -   *099569*
Rentsch, Eugen, Nüschelerstr. 22, 8022 Zürich.
T. (01) 211 36 30.   *099570*
Ruff Edition, Theo, Rosengartenstr 66, 8037 Zürich.
T. (01) 2730353, Fax 2730410. - ArtBk / Card - *099571*
Scalo Verlag, Weinbergstr 22a, 8001 Zürich.
T. (01) 2610910, Fax 2619262. - ArtBk -   *099572*
Scheidegger, Ernst, Wettingerwies 2, 8001 Zürich.
T. (01) 251 80 50, Fax 251 80 72. - ArtBk -   *099573*
Schlégl, István, Dr., Minervastr 119, 8032 Zürich.
T. (01) 3834963, Fax 3835589. - Graph -   *099574*
W. Schmitt Verlag, Affolternstr. 96, 8050 Zürich.
T. (01) 311 27 56.   *099575*
Verein für Originalgraphik, Verena Conzett Str 7, 8004 Zürich. T. (01) 2415300, Fax 2415300.
- Graph -   *099576*
Verlag Freie Kunstschule Zürich, Mutschellenstr. 27, 8002 Zürich. T. (01) 2014691. - ArtBk -   *099577*
Verlag Um die Ecke, Dienerstr. 21, 8000 Zürich.
T. (01) 241 29 96.   *099578*
Viernheim S. A. W. Schmitt-Verlag, Affolternstr. 96, 8050 Zürich. T. (01) 311 27 56. - ArtBk / Graph /
Repr -   *099579*
Weltwoche-ABC-Verlag, Edenstr. 20, 8021 Zürich.
T. (01) 207 86 43.   *099580*
Wolfsbergverlag, Bederstr 109, 8059 Zürich.
T. (01) 2857878, Fax 2012054. - Graph / Repr - *099581*
Ziegler, Renée, Rämistr 34, 8001 Zürich.
T. (01) 2512322, Fax 2512546.   *099582*

Zug
Ars Edition & Ars Sacra Verlag, Baarerstr 59, 6301 Zug.
T. (041) 7118355, Fax 7118310.   *099583*
Edition Crocodile, Postfach 4031, 6304 Zug.
T. (01) 4627366, Fax 4620112. - ArtBk -   *099584*
Kalt-Zehnder-Druck, Grienbachstr 11, 6301 Zug.
T. (041) 761 66 66, Fax 7616665. - ArtBk / Repr /
Card -   *099585*

Musarion Verlag, Bahnhofstr 11, 6300 Zug.
T. (041) 7115070, Fax 7116505. - ArtBk / Graph /
Repr - *099586*
Sunart, Unter Altstadt 5, 6300 Zug. T. (041) 7103666,
Fax 7107617. - ArtBk / Card / Cal - *099587*

Turkey

Istanbul
Archeology & Art Publications, Hayriye Cad. Apt. 3/5,
80060 Istanbul. T. 245 68 38, Fax 245 68 77. *099588*

United Kingdom

Aberdeen (Grampian)
Peacock, 21 Castle St., Aberdeen AB1 1AJ.
T. (01224) 639539. - Graph - *099589*

Aldershot (Hampshire)
Ashgate Publishing Company, Gower House, Croft Rd.,
Aldershot GU11 3HR. T. (01252) 331551,
Fax (01252) 344405. - ArtBk - *099590*
Gower, Gower House, Croft Rd., Aldershot GU11 3HR.
T. (01252) 331551, Fax (1252) 344405.
- ArtBk - *099591*
Scholar Press, Gower House, Croft Rd., Aldershot GU11
3HR. T. (01252) 331551, Fax (01252) 344405.
- ArtBk - *099592*
Scolar Press, Gower House, Croft Rd, Aldershot GU11
3HR. T. (01252) 331511, Fax (01252) 317446. *099593*
Variorum, Gower House, Croft Rd., Aldershot GU11 3HR.
T. (01252) 331551, Fax (01252) 344405.
- ArtBk - *099594*
Wildwood House, Gower House, Croft Rd., Aldershot
GU11 3HR. T. (01252) 331551, Fax (01252) 344405.
- ArtBk - *099595*

Aylesbury (Buckinghamshire)
Shire Publications, Cromwell House, Church St., Ayles-
bury HP17 9AJ. T. (01296) 4301, Fax (01296) 7030.
- ArtBk - *099596*

Basildon (Essex)
Kingfisher, 1 Christy Court, Southfields Business Park,
Basildon. T. (01268) 411191. - ArtBk - *099597*

Bath (Avon)
Mindata, Bathwick Hill, Bath BA2 6LA.
I. (01225) 468447, Гах (01225) 482841. *099598*

Bedford (Bedfordshire)
Fraser, Gordon, Eastcotts Rd., Bedford MK42 0JX.
T. (01234) 272800, Fax (01234) 55981.
- ArtBk - *099599*

Belfast (Co. Antrim)
Appletree Press, 7 James St., Belfast BT2 8DL.
T. (01232) 243074, Fax 246756. - ArtBk - *099600*
Belfast Print Workshop, 181a Stranmillis Rd., Belfast
BT9 5DU. T. (01232) 381591. - Graph - *099601*
Blackstaff Press, 3 Galway Park, Dundonald, Belfast
BT16 0AN. T. (01232) 487161, Fax (01232) 489552.
- ArtBk - *099602*
Circa Publications, 67 Donegall Passage, Belfast.
T. (01232) 230375. - ArtBk - *099603*

Birmingham (West Midlands)
Birmingham Museums and Art Gallery Shops, Chamber-
lain Sq., Birmingham B3 3DH. T. (0121) 235 2843.
- ArtBk - *099604*
Washington Green Fine Art Publishing Company, 30 Mar-
shall St., Birmingham B1. T. (0121) 616 1313.
- ArtBk - *099605*

Bradford (West Yorkshire)
Treadwell's Art Mill, Upper Park Gate, Bradford BD1
5DW. T. (01274) 306065, Fax (01274) 394356.
- ArtBk - *099606*

Brighton (East Sussex)
Hendon Press, 36 Hendon St., Brighton BN2 2EG.
T. (01273) 690271. - ArtBk - *099607*

North Star Studios, 65 Ditchling Rd., Brighton.
T. (01273) 601041. - Graph - *099608*

Buckhurst Hill (Essex)
Scorpion Publishing, Victoria House, Victoria Rd., Buck-
hurst Hill IG9 5ES. T. (0181) 506 0606,
Fax (0181) 506 0553. - ArtBk - *099609*

Calne (Wiltshire)
Hilmarton Manor Press, Calne SN11 8SB.
T. (01249) 76208, Fax (01249) 76379. *099610*

Cambridge (Cambridgeshire)
Cambridge University Press, Edinburgh Bldg., Shaftes-
bury Rd., Cambridge CB2 2RU. T. (01223) 312393,
Fax (01223) 315052. - ArtBk - *099611*
Chadwyck-Healey, Cambridge Pl., Cambridge CB2 1NR.
T. (01223) 311479, Fax (01223) 66440.
- ArtBk - *099612*
Curwen Chilford, Chilford Hall, Linton, Cambridge CB1
6LE. T. (01223) 893544, Fax (01223) 894056.
- Graph - *099613*
Lutterworth, 50-52 Kingston St., POB 60, Cambridge
CB1 2NT. T. (01223) 350865, Fax (01223) 66951.
- ArtBk - *099614*
Silent Books, Boxworth End, Swavesey, Cambridge CB4
5RA. T. (01223) 31000, Fax (01223) 32199.
- ArtBk - *099615*

Canterbury (Kent)
Oaten Hill Press, 254 Broad Oak Rd., Canterbury.
T. (01227) 767856. - Graph - *099616*

Cardiff (South Glamorgan)
University of Wales Press, 6 Gwennyth St., Cardiff CF2
4YD. T. (01222) 231919, Fax (01222) 230908.
- ArtBk - *099617*

Colchester (Essex)
Austin, John, 48 Scarletts Rd., Colchester CO1 2HA.
T. (01206) 540225. - Graph / Repr / Card - *099618*

Drewsteignton (Devon)
Cambrooke, Woodbrooke Cottage, Drewsteignton.
T. (01647) 24474. - ArtBk - *099619*

Dundee (Tayside)
Dundee Printmakers Workshop, 36-40 Seagate, Dundee
DD1 2EG. T. (01382) 26331. - Graph - *099620*

East Grinstead (Sussex)
British Leisure Publications, Windsor Court, East Grin-
stead House, East Grinstead RH19 1XA.
T. (01342) 26972. - ArtBk - *099621*

Eastbourne (East Sussex)
Monarch Publications, 1 Saint Anne's Rd., Eastbourne
BN21 3UN. T. (01323) 410930, Fax (01323) 411970.
- ArtBk - *099622*

Edinburgh (Lothian)
Edinburgh Printmakers, 23 Union St., Edinburgh EH1
3l R. T. (0131) 557 2479. - Graph - *099623*
Edinburgh University Press, 22 George Sq., Edinburgh
EH8 9LF. T. (0131) 662 0553, Fax (0131) 6620053.
- ArtBk - *099624*
Fruitmarket Gallery Publications, 29 Market St., Edin-
burgh EH1 1DF. T. (0131) 225 2383,
Fax (0131) 2203130. - ArtBk - *099625*
Graeme Murray, 15 Scotland St., Edinburgh EH3 6PU.
T. (0131) 556 6020. - ArtBk - *099626*
Mainstream Publishing Company, 7 Albany St., Edin-
burgh EH1 3UG. T. (0131) 557 2959,
Fax (0131) 5568720. - ArtBk - *099627*
National Galleries of Scotland, Publications Department,
The Mound, Edinburgh EH2 2EL. T. (0131) 5568921.
- ArtBk - *099628*
Ramsay Head, 15 Gloucester Pl., Edinburgh EH3 6EE.
T. (0131) 225 5646. - ArtBk - *099629*
Saltire Society, 22 High St., Edinburgh EH1 1TF.
T. (0131) 556 1836. - ArtBk - *099630*

Exeter (Devon)
University of Exeter Press, Reed Hall, Streatham Dr.,
Exeter EX4 4QR. T. (01392) 263066,
Fax (01392) 263108. - ArtBk - *099631*

Folkestone (Kent)
Dawson & Sons, William, Cannon House, Park Farm Rd.,
Folkestone CT19 5EE. T. (01303) 850101,
Fax (801303) 850440. - ArtBk - *099632*

Forest Row (Sussex)
Artists Bookworks, 28 Freshfield Bank, Forest Row
RH18 5HG. T. (01342) 823568. *099633*

Galashiels (Borders)
Lyle, Glennmayne, Galashiels TD1 3NR. T. (01896) 2005,
Fax (01896) 4696. - ArtBk - *099634*

Gerrards Cross (Buckinghamshire)
Smythe, Colin, POB 6, Gerrards Cross SL9 8XA.
T. (01753) 886000, Fax (01753) 886469.
- ArtBk - *099635*

Girton (Cambridgeshire)
Cambrooke, Trinity Farm, Huntingdon Rd., Girton.
T. (01223) 276441. - ArtBk - *099636*

Glasgow (Strathclyde)
Eastwood, 450a Sauchiehall St., Glasgow G2.
T. (0141) 332 9901. - ArtBk - *099637*
Glasgow Print Studio, 22 King St., Glasgow G1 5QP.
T. (0141) 552 0704, Fax (0141) 5522919.
- Graph - *099638*
Third Eye Centre, 346-354 Sauchiehall St., Glasgow G2
3JD. T. (0141) 332 7521, Fax (0141) 3323226.
- ArtBk - *099639*

Godalming (Surrey)
Colour Library Books, Business Center, Woodsack Way,
Godalming GU7 1XW. T. (014868) 426277,
Fax (014868) 426947. - ArtBk - *099640*

Guildford (Surrey)
Circle Press, 22 Sydney Rd., Guildford GU1 3LL.
T. (01483) 50 48 43. - Graph - *099641*
Genesis Publications, 51 Lynwood, Guildford GU2 5NY.
T. (01483) 37431, Fax (01483) 304709.
- ArtBk - *099642*

Harlow (Essex)
Longman, Longman House, Burnt Mill, Harlow CM20
2JE. T. (01279) 28721. - ArtBk - *099643*
Motif Editions, Shenval House, South St., Harlow.
T. (01279) 444214. - ArtBk - *099644*

Haslemere (Surrey)
Emmett Publishing, Westhouse, 21 West St, Haslemere
GU27 2AB. T. (01428) 654443,
Fax (01428) 665082. *099645*

Havant (Hampshire)
Art Trade Press, 9 Brockhampton Rd., Havant PO9 1NU.
T. (01705) 484943. - ArtBk - *099646*

Hemel Hempstead (Hertfordshire)
Prentice-Hall, Wolsey House, Wolsey Rd., Hemel Hemp-
stead HP2 4SS. T. (01442) 231900,
Fax (01442) 221485. - ArtBk - *099647*

Henley-on-Thames (Oxfordshire)
Ellis, Aidan, Cobb House, Nutfield, Henley-on-Thames
RG9 5RT. T. (01491) 641496, Fax (01491) 573649.
- ArtBk - *099648*
Gresham, POB 61, Henley-on-Thames RG9 3LQ.
T. (01491) 403789, Fax (01491) 403789.
- ArtBk - *099649*

Hove (Sussex)
Wayland, 61 Western Rd., Hove BN3 1JD.
T. (01273) 722561, Fax (01273) 29314.
- ArtBk - *099650*

Hurstpierpoint (West Sussex)
Lyon, Richard, 17 Old High St., Hurstpierpoint BN6 9WH.
T. (01273) 832255, Fax (01273) 833250.
- ArtBk - *099651*

Ightham (Kent)
Pratt, The Gallery, Ightham TN15 9HH.
T. (01732) 882326, Fax (01732) 885502.
- Graph - *099652*

Inverness (Highland)

Highland Printmakers, 20 Bank St., Inverness IV1 1QE. T. (01463) 712240. - Graph - 099653

Lanark (Southclyde)

Geddes & Grosset, David Dale House, New Lanark, Lanark ML11 9DJ. T. (01555) 65008, Fax (01555) 65694. - ArtBk - 099654

Leicester (Leicestershire)

Leicester University Press, Johnson Bldg., University Rd., Leicester LE1 7RH. T. (0116) 523334, Fax (0116) 522200. - ArtBk - 099655

Lewes (East Sussex)

Guild of Master Craftsman Publications, 166 High St., Lewes BN7 1XU. T. (01273) 477374. - ArtBk - 099656

Limpsfield (Surrey)

Dragon's World, High St., Limpsfield RH8 0DY. T. (0171) 976 5477. - ArtBk - 099657

Liverpool (Merseyside)

Liverpool University Press, POB 147, Liverpool L69 3BX. T. (0151) 794 2232, Fax (0151) 7086502. - ArtBk - 099658

London

Academic and University Publishers Group, 1 Gower St., London WC1E 6HA. T. (0171) 580 3994, Fax (0171) 580 3995. - ArtBk - 099659
Academy Editions, 42 Leinster Gardens, London W2 3AN. T. (0171) 402 2141, Fax (0171) 7239540. - ArtBk - 099660
Academy Group, 42 Leinster Gardens, London W2 3AN. T. (0171) 4022141, Fax 7239540. - ArtBk - 099661
Advanced Graphics, 812 Creekside, London SE8 3DX. T. (0181) 691 1330. - Graph - 099662
Alexandria Press, 43 Pembridge Villas, London W11 3EP. T. (0171) 727 9724. - ArtBk - 099663
Alpine Fine Arts Collection, 43 Manchester St., London W1M 5PE. T. (0171) 935 0797, Fax (0171) 935 0636. - ArtBk - 099664
Anaya, 44-50 Osnaburgh St., London NW1 3ND. T. (0171) 383 2997, Fax (0171) 383 3076. - ArtBk - 099665
Anderson O'Day, 5 Saint Quintin Av., London W10 6NX. T. (0181) 969 8085, Fax (0181) 960 3641. - Graph - 099666
Angus & Robertson, 77-85 Fulham Palace Rd., London W6 8JB. T. (0181) 741 7070, Fax (0181) 307 4440. - ArtBk - 099667
Antiques Trade Gazette, 17 Whitcomb St, London WC2H 7PL. T. (0171) 9304957, Fax (0171) 9306391. - ArtP - 099668
Apple Press, 6 Blundell St., London N7 9BH. T. (0171) 700 6700, Fax (0171) 700 4191. - ArtBk - 099669
Architectural Association Publications, 34-36 Bedford Sq., London WC1B 3ES. T. (0171) 636 0974. - ArtBk - 099670
Art Group, 146 Royal College St, London NW1 0TA. T. (0171) 4823206, Fax (0171) 2840435. - Repr - 099671
The Art Newspaper, 27-29 Vauxhall Grove, London SW8 1SY. T. (0171) 7353331, Fax (0171) 7353332. 099672
Arts Council of Great Britain, 14 Great Peter St, London SW1P 3NQ. T. (0171) 3330100, Fax (0171) 9736590. - ArtBk - 099673
Arts Review, 20 Prescott Pl, London SW4 6BT. T. (0171) 9781000, Fax (0171) 9781102. - ArtP - 099674
Associated University Presses, 25 Sicilian Av., London WC1A 2QH. T. (0171) 405 7979. - ArtBk - 099675
Athena Reproductions, 82 Gower St., London WC1E. T. (0171) 631 1188. - Graph - 099676
Athlone Press, 1 Park Dr., London NW11 7SG. T. (0181) 458 0888. - ArtBk - 099677
Bamboo Publishing, 719 Fulham Rd., London SW6 5UL. T. (0171) 731 2447, Fax (0171) 731 8009. - ArtBk - 099678
Barrie & Jenkins, 289 Westbourne Grove, London. T. (0171) 727 9636, Fax (0171) 229 4571. - ArtBk - 099679
Barrington, 54 Uxbridge Rd., London W12 8LP. T. (0181) 740 7020, Fax (0181) 740 7020. - ArtP - 099680
Batsford, B.T., 4 Fitzhardinge St., London W1H 0AH. T. (0171) 486 8484, Fax (0171) 487 4296. - ArtBk / Graph - 099681
BBC Books, 80 Wood Ln., London W12 0TT. T. (0181) 576 2536, Fax (0181) 749 8766. - ArtBk - 099682
Bellew, 8 Balham Hall, London SW12 9EA. T. (0181) 673 5611, Fax (0181) 675 3542. - ArtBk - 099683
Bestseller Publications, 50 Eastcastle St, London W1N 7AP. T. (0171) 636 5070, Fax (0171) 580 3001. - ArtBk - 099684
Black, A. & C., 35 Bedford Row, London WC1R 4JH. T. (0171) 242 0946, Fax (0171) 831 8478. - ArtBk - 099685
Blandford Publishing, 41-47 The Strand, London WC2N 5JE. T. (0171) 839 4900, Fax (0171) 839 1804. - ArtBk - 099686
Book Works, 1 Arch, Bedale St, London SE1 9AH. T. (0171) 407 1692, Fax (0171) 378 6799. - ArtBk - 099687
BPL Remainders, 50 Eastcastle St., London W1N 7AP. T. (0171) 636 5070, Fax (0171) 580 3001. - ArtBk - 099688
British Academy Publications, 20-21 Cornwall Terrace, London NW1 4QP. T. (0171) 487 5966, Fax (0171) 224 3807. - ArtBk - 099689
British Council, Visual Arts Department, 11 Portland Pl., London W1N 4EJ. T. (0171) 930 8466. - ArtBk - 099690
British Library, 41 Russell Square, London WC1B 3DG. T. (0171) 3237704, Fax (0171) 3237736. - ArtBk - 099691
British Museum Press, 46 Bloomsbury St., London WC1B 3QQ. T. (0171) 323 1234, Fax (0171) 4367313. - ArtBk / Card / Sli / Cal - 099692
Burlington Magazine Publications, 14-16 Duke's Rd, London WC1H 9AD. T. (0171) 3888157, 3881228, Fax 3881230, 3881229. - ArtP - 099693
Business Art Galleries, 34 Windmill St., London W1P 1HH. T. (0171) 323 4700, Fax (0171) 436 3059. - Graph - 099694
Camden Press, 46 Colebrook Row, London N1 8AS. T. (0171) 226 2061, Fax (0171) 226 2418. - ArtBk - 099695
Cape, Jonathan, 20 Vauxhall Bridge Rd., London SW1V 2SA. T. (0171) 973 9730, Fax (0171) 233 6117. - ArtBk - 099696
Cassell, 41-47 The Strand, London WC2N 5JE. T. (0171) 839 4900, Fax (0171) 839 1804. - ArtBk - 099697
CCA Galleries, 8 Dover St., London W1X 3PJ. T. (0171) 499 6701, Fax (0171) 409 3555. - Graph - 099698
Chatto & Windus, 20 Vauxhall Bridge Rd., London SW1W 2SA. T. (0171) 973 9740. - ArtBk - 099699
Christies Publications, 8 King St., London SW1. T. (0171) 839 9060. - ArtBk - 099700
Circle Press Publications, 26 Saint Lukes Mews, London W11. T. (0171) 792 9298. - ArtBk - 099701
Clematis Press, 18 Old Church St., London SW3 5DQ. T. (0171) 352 8755. - ArtBk - 099702
Cleverdon, Douglas, 27 Barnsbury Sq., London N1 1JP. T. (0171) 607 7392. - ArtBk / Graph - 099703
Conran Octopus, 37 Shelton St., London WC2H 9HN. T. (0171) 240 6961, Fax (0171) 836 9951. - ArtBk - 099704
Constable & Co., 162 Fulham Palace Rd., London W6 9ER. T. (0181) 741 3663, Fax (0181) 748 7562. - ArtBk - 099705
Crompton, Paul H., 102 Felsham Rd., London SW15 1DQ. T. (0181) 780 1063, Fax (0181) 318 1439. - ArtBk - 099706
Dauphin Publishing, 118a Holland Park Av., London W11 4PA. T. (0171) 727 0715, Fax (0171) 221 8371. - ArtBk - 099707
Dent & Sons, J.M., 91 Clapham High St., London SW4. T. (0171) 622 9933. - ArtBk - 099708
Deutsch, André, 105-106 Great Russell St., London WC1B 3LJ. T. (0171) 580 2746, Fax (0171) 6313253. - ArtBk - 099709
Devon Publishing Group, 47 Barnsbury St., London N1. T. (0171) 700 4085. - ArtBk - 099710
Directory of Social Change, Arts Units, 69 Queen's Crescent, London NW5 4DS. T. (0171) 2842229, Fax (0171) 2843445. 099711
Editions Alecto, 46 Kelso Pl., London W8 5QG. T. (0171) 937 6611. - ArtBk / Graph / Card - 099712
Essendine Lithographic Workshop and Art Studios, Essendine Rd, London W9. T. (0171) 286 4475. - Graph - 099713
Faber & Faber, 3 Queen Sq., London WC1N 3AU. T. (0171) 465 0045, Fax (0171) 4650034. - ArtBk / Graph - 099714
Facsimile Editions, 40 Hamilton Terrace, London NW8 9UJ. T. (0171) 286 0071, Fax (0171) 266 3927. - ArtBk - 099715
Fine Art Journals, 10 Barley Mow Passage, London W4. T. (0181) 995 1909. - ArtP - 099716
Flowers Graphics, 199-205 Richmond Rd., London E8 3NJ. T. (0181) 985 3333. - Graph - 099717
Folio Society, 202 Great Suffolk St., London SE1 1PR. T. (0171) 407 7411. - ArtBk - 099718
Fourth Estate, 289 Westbourne Grove, London S11 2QA. T. (0171) 727 8993, Fax (0171) 792 3176. - ArtBk - 099719
Frost & Reed, 12 Old Bond St., London W1X 3DB. T. (0171) 629 2457, Fax (0171) 499 0299. - Graph / Repr - 099720
Fudge & Co., 2 Caversham St., London SW3. T. (0171) 351 4995. - ArtBk - 099721
Garton & Co., 39-42 New Bond St., London W1Y 9HB. T. (0171) 493 2820. - Graph - 099722
GMP Publishers, POB 247, London N17 9QR. T. (0181) 365 1545, Fax (0181) 365 1252. - ArtBk - 099723
Golden Cockerel Press, 25 Sicilian Av., London WC1A 2QH. T. (0171) 405 7979, Fax (0171) 405 7979. - ArtBk - 099724
Gollancz, Victor, 14 Henrietta St., London WC2E 8QL. T. (0171) 836 2006, Fax (0171) 3790934. - ArtBk - 099725
Green, 2a Queensdale Rd., London W11. T. (0171) 792 2272. - ArtBk - 099726
Greenwich Printmakers, 1a The Market, Greenwich, London SE10. T. (0181) 858 1569. - Graph - 099727
Greenwood, Nigel, 4 New Burlington St., London W1X 1FE. T. (0171) 434 3795. - ArtBk / Graph - 099728
Grosvenor Gallery, 48 South Molton St., London W1Y 2JU. T. (0171) 629 0891, Fax (0171) 491 4391. - Graph - 099729
Halban, Peter, 42 South Molton St., London W1Y 1HB. T. (0171) 491 1582, Fax (0171) 629 5381. - ArtBk - 099730
Hale, Robert, 45-47 Clerkenwell Green, London EC1R 0HT. T. (0171) 251 2661, Fax (0171) 4904958. - ArtBk - 099731
Hali Publications, Kingsgate House, Kingsgate Pl, London NW6 4TA. T. (0171) 3289341, Fax (0171) 3725924. - ArtBk / Repr / Card / Sli - 099732
Hamilton, Hamish, 27 Wright's Ln., London W8 5TZ. T. (0171) 4163000, Fax (0171) 4163298. - ArtBk - 099733
Hamlyn Publishing, 81 Fulham Rd., London SW3 6RB. T. (0171) 581 9393, Fax (0171) 5898419. - ArtBk - 099734
Harper Collins Publishers, 77-85 Fulham Palace Rd, London W6 8JB. T. (0181) 7417070, Fax (0181) 3074440. 099735
Harvard University Press, 14 Bloomsbury Sq, London WC1A 2LP. T. (0171) 404 0712, Fax (0171) 4040601. - ArtBk - 099736
Hawk, 222 Kensal Rd, London W10 5BN. T. (0181) 969 8091, Fax (0181) 968 9012. - ArtBk - 099737
Heinemann, William, 81 Fulham Rd., London SW3 6RB. T. (0171) 581 9393. - ArtBk - 099738
Her Majesty's Stationery Office, 51 Nine Elms Ln., London SW8 5DR. T. (0171) 211 5148, Fax (0171) 372 5924. - ArtBk - 099739
Herbert Press, 46 Northchurch Rd., London N1 4EJ. T. (0171) 254 4379, Fax (0171) 2544332. - ArtBk - 099740

Holland Park Studio, 50 Queensdale Rd., London W11
4SA. T. (0171) 602 1563. - Graph -   099741
Imperial Publishing, 40 Dunton Rd., London E10.
T. (0181) 518 7722. - ArtBk -   099742
Johnson, 24-28 Oval Rd., London NW1 7DX.
T. (0171) 267 4466. - ArtBk -   099743
Joseph, Michael, 27 Wright's Ln., London W8 5TZ.
T. (0171) 937 7255, Fax (0171) 937 8704. - ArtBk /
Repr / Card -   099744
Journeyman Press, 97 Ferme Park Rd., London N8 9SA.
T. (0181) 348 9261. - ArtBk -   099745
Laurence King Publishing, 71 Great Russell St, London
W1B 3BN. T. (0171) 8316351,
Fax (0171) 8318356.   099746
Little, Brown & Co, 165 Great Dover Rd, London SE1
4YA. T. (0171) 3344800, Fax (0171) 3344905.   099747
London Contemporary Art, 132 Lots Rd., London SW10
0RJ. T. (0171) 352 7694. - Graph -   099748
Lund Humphries Publishers, Park House, 1 Russell Gar-
dens, London NW11 9NN. T. (0181) 4586314,
Fax (0181) 9055245.   099749
Macmillan, 4 Little Essex St., London WC2R 3LF.
T. (0171) 836 6633, Fax (0171) 3794204.
- ArtBk -   099750
Marlborough Graphics, 42 Dover St., London W1X 3RB.
T. (0171) 495 2642, Fax (0171) 495 0641.
- Graph -   099751
Matt's Gallery, 10 Martello St., London E8 3PE.
T. (0171) 249 3799. - ArtBk -   099752
Medici Society, 34-42 Pentonville Rd., London N1 9HG.
T. (0171) 837 7099, Fax (0171) 837 9152. - ArtBk /
Repr / Card / Cal -   099753
Merrion, 16 Groveway, London SW9 0AR.
T. (0171) 735 7791, Fax (0171) 735 4842.
- ArtBk -   099754
Miller, Harvey, 20 Marryat Rd., London SW19 5BD.
T. (0181) 946 4426, Fax (0181) 9446082.
- ArtBk -   099755
Miller, Harvey, 20 Marryat Rd., London SW19 5BD.
T. (0181) 946 4426, Fax (0181) 944 6082.
- ArtBk -   099756
MIT Press, 14 Bloomsbury Sq, London WC1A 2LP.
T. (0171) 404 0712, Fax (0171) 4040601.
- ArtBk -   099757
Mitchell Beazley, 81 Fulham Rd., London SW3 6RB.
T. (0171) 581 9393, Fax (0171) 5848268.
- ArtBk -   099758
Mitchell Street Print Studio, 39 Mitchell St., London EC1.
T. (0171) 253 8930. - Graph -   099759
Murray, John, 50 Albemarle St., London W1X 4BD.
T. (0171) 493 4361, Fax (0171) 4991792.
- ArtBk -   099760
National Gallery Publications, 5-6 Pall Mall East, London
SW1Y 5BA. T. (0171) 839 8544, Fax (0171) 9300108.
- ArtBk -   099761
National Magazine Company, 72 Broadwick St., London
W1V 2BP. T. (0171) 439 7144, Fax (0171) 437 6886.
- ArtP -   099762
New Leaf Books, BCM-New Leaf, London WC1N 3XX.
T. (0171) 435 3056. - ArtBk -   099763
Norton & Co., W.W., 10 Coptic St., London WC1A 1PU.
T. (0171) 323 1579, Fax (0171) 436 4553.
- ArtBk -   099764
Octopus Illustrated Publishing, 81 Fulham Rd., London
SW3 6RB. T. (0171) 581 9393, Fax (0171) 589 8419.
- ArtBk -   099765
Owen, Peter, 73 Kenway Rd., London SW5 0RE.
T. (0171) 373 5628, Fax (0171) 373 6760.
- ArtBk -   099766
Pallas Gallery, 3 Rufus St., London N1 6PE.
T. (0171) 729 4343. - Graph -   099767
Penguin Books, 27 Wright's Ln., London W8 5TZ.
T. (0171) 4163000, Fax (0171) 4163099.
- ArtBk -   099768
Petersburg Press, 59a Portobello Rd., London W11 3DB.
T. (0171) 229 0105, Fax (0171) 229 4070. - ArtBk /
Graph -   099769
Phaidon Press, 140 Kensington Church St., London W8
4BN. T. (0171) 221 5656, Fax (0171) 2218474.
- ArtBk -   099770
Picture Man, 184 Chiswick High Rd., London W4 1PP.
T. (0181) 995 6359. - Graph -   099771

Pindar Press, 66 Lyncroft Gardens, London NW6 1JY.
- ArtBk -   099772
Principia Press, Unit 100, 99 Lomond Grove, London
SE5. T. (0171) 708 1050. - ArtBk -   099773
Printers Inc. and Associates, 27 Clerkenwell Close, Lon-
don EC1. T. (0171) 251 1923. - Graph -   099774
Quartet Books, 27-29 Goodge St., London W1P 1FD.
T. (0171) 636 3992, Fax (0171) 637 1866.
- ArtBk -   099775
Quintet Publishing, 6 Blundell St., London N7 9BH.
T. (0171) 700 6700, Fax (0171) 700 4191.
- ArtBk -   099776
Ramboro, Unit 5A, 202-208 New North Rd., London N1
7BJ. T. (0171) 226 7777, Fax (0171) 704 6442.
- ArtBk -   099777
Random Century, 20 Vauxhall Bridge Rd., London SW1V
2SA. T. (0171) 973 9000, Fax (0171) 233 6058.
- ArtBk -   099778
Reaktion Books, 11 Rathbone Place, London W1P 1DE.
T. (0171) 5809928, Fax (0171) 5809935.   099779
Redfern, 20 Cork St., London W1. T. (0171) 734 1732,
Fax (0171) 494 2908. - Graph -   099780
RIBA Publications, Finsbury Mission, Moreland St., Lon-
don EC1V 8BB. T. (0171) 251 0791,
Fax (0171) 6082375. - ArtBk -   099781
Rizzoli International Publications, London Office, 40 Vol-
taire Rd, London SW4 6DH. T. (0171) 4980115,
Fax (0171) 4982245.   099782
Routledge, 11 New Fetter Ln., London EC4P 4EE.
T. (0171) 583 9855, Fax (0171) 583 0701.
- ArtBk -   099783
Royal Academy Graphics, Burlington House, Picadilly,
London W1. T. (0171) 734 7764. - Graph -   099784
Royle, W.R., Royle House, Wenlock Rd., London N1 7ST.
T. (0171) 253 7654. - Graph / Repr / Card / Cal - 099785
Saint George's Gallery Books, 8 Duke St., London SW1.
T. (0171) 930 0935. - ArtBk -   099786
Sarema Press, 15 Beeches Ln., London.
T. (0181) 770 1953. - ArtBk -   099787
School of Oriental and African Studies Publications,
Thornhaught St., London WC1H 0XG.
T. (0171) 637 2388, Fax (0171) 436 3844.
- ArtBk -   099788
Seaby, B.A., 7 Davies St., London W14 1LL.
T. (0171) 495 2590, Fax (0171) 491 1595. - ArtBk /
Graph -   099789
Secker & Warburg, Martin, 81 Fulham Rd., London SW3
6RB. T. (0171) 581 9393, Fax (0171) 589 8411.
- ArtBk -   099790
Serindia Publications, 10 Parkfields, London SW15 6NH.
T. (0181) 788 1966, Fax (0181) 785 4789.
- ArtBk -   099791
Skilton, Charles, 2 Caversham St., London SW3.
T. (0171) 351 4995. - ArtBk -   099792
Souvenir Press, 43 Great Russell St., London WC1B 3PA.
T. (0171) 580 9307, Fax (0171) 589 5064.
- ArtBk -   099793
Studio Editions, 50 Eastcastle St., London W1N 7AP.
T. (0171) 636 5070, Fax (0171) 580 3001.
- ArtBk -   099794
Studio Prints, 159 Queen's Crescent, London NW5 4EA.
T. (0171) 485 4527. - Graph -   099795
Tate Gallery Publications, Millbank, London SW1P 4RG.
T. (0171) 834 5651, Fax (0171) 8287357.
- ArtBk -   099796
Tesser, 106 Heath St., London NW3 1DR.
T. (0171) 794 7971, Fax (0171) 794 5829.
- Graph -   099797
Tetrad Press, 3 Hega House, Ullin St., London E14 6PN.
T. (0171) 515 7783. - Graph -   099798
Thames & Hudson, 30-34 Bloomsbury St., London
WC1B 3QP. T. (0171) 636 5488, Fax (0171) 6364799.
- ArtBk / Graph -   099799
Thumb, 38 Lexington St., London W1R 3HR.
T. (0171) 439 7343, Fax (0171) 287 0478.
- Graph -   099800
Times Books, 77-85 Fulham Palace Rd., London W6
6JB. T. (0181) 741 7070, Fax (0181) 307 4440.
- ArtBk -   099801
Trefoil Publications, 108 Blackhorse Ln., London E17
6AB. T. (0181) 527 5823, Fax (0181) 527 6631.
- ArtBk -   099802

Trodd, Brian, 27 Swinton St., London WC1X 9NW.
T. (0171) 837 8820, Fax (0171) 837 1331.
- ArtBk -   099803
Victoria and Albert Museum Publications, Cromwell Rd.,
London SW7 2RL. T. (0171) 589 6371.
- ArtBk -   099804
Viking, 27 Wright's Ln., London W8 5TZ.
T. (0171) 4163000, Fax (0171) 4163193.
- ArtBk -   099805
Visual Arts Publishing, 82 Sinclair Rd, London W14 0NJ.
T. (0171) 6037945, Fax (0171) 6037945.   099806
Waddington Graphics, 16 Clifford St., London W1X 1RG.
T. (0171) 439 1866. - Graph -   099807
Warburg Institute Publications, University of London,
Woburn Sq., London WC1H 0AB. T. (0171) 580 9663,
Fax (0171) 436 2852. - ArtBk -   099808
Ward Lock, 41-47 Strand, London WC2N 5JE.
T. (0171) 839 4900, Fax (0171) 839 1804.
- ArtBk -   099809
Weidenfeld & Nicolson, Orion House, 5 Upper St Martin's
Lane, London WC2A 5EA. T. (0171) 2403444,
Fax (0171) 2404822/3.   099810
White, John, 9 Manville Rd., London SW17 8JW.
T. (0181) 672 3461. - Graph -   099811
Wilson, Philip, 26 Litchfield St., London WC2H 9NJ.
T. (0171) 379 7886, Fax (0171) 8367049.
- ArtBk -   099812
Wingfield, 35 Sibella Rd., London SW4 6JA.
T. (0171) 622 6301. - Graph -   099813
Woodlands Prints and Publications, 13 Firs Av., London
N10. T. (0181) 365 2379. - ArtBk / Graph -   099814
World of Islam Festival Trust, 33 Thurloe Pl., London
SW7 2HQ. T. (0171) 581 3522, Fax (0171) 584 1977.
- ArtBk -   099815
Yale University Press, 23 Pond St., London NW3 2PN.
T. (0171) 431 4422, Fax (0171) 431 3755.
- ArtBk -   099816
Zella Nine, 2 Park Walk, London SW10 0AD.
T. (0171) 351 0588. - Graph -   099817

Maidenhead (Berkshire)
McGraw-Hill, Shoppenhangers Rd., Maidenhead SL6
2QL. T. (01628) 23432, Fax (01628) 35895. - ArtBk /
Sli -   099818

Maldon (Essex)
Artwork Publishing, 8 Galliford Rd., Maldon CM9 7XD.
T. (01621) 851646, Fax (01621) 850862.
- ArtBk -   099819

Manchester
Manchester Etching Workshop, 3-5 Union St., Manche-
ster. T. (0161) 832 5439. - Graph -   099820
Manchester University Press, Oxford Rd, Manchester
M13 9PL. T. (0161) 2735539,
Fax (0161) 2743346.   099821

Margate (Kent)
Matthew, Alexander, 30a Thanet Rd., Margate.
T. (01843) 297207. - ArtBk -   099822

Milton Keynes (Buckinghamshire)
Open University Educational Enterprises, 12 Cofferidge
Close, Milton Keynes MK11 1BY. T. (01908) 261662,
Fax (01908) 261001. - ArtBk -   099823

Moffat (Dumfries and Galloway)
Cameron, POB 1, Moffat DG10 9SU. T. (01683) 20808,
Fax (01683) 20012. - ArtBk -   099824

Newcastle-upon-Tyne (Tyne and Wear)
Projects U.K., 1 Black Swan Court, Westgate Rd., New-
castle-upon-Tyne NE1 1SG. T. (0191) 232 2410,
Fax (0191) 2210492. - Graph -   099825

Newton Abbott (Devon)
David & Charles, Brunel House, Forde Close, Newton Ab-
bott TQ12 4PU. T. (01626) 61121, Fax (01626) 64463.
- ArtBk -   099826

Norwich (Norfolk)
Collectair Limited Editions, 26 Cambridge St., Norwich.
T. (01603) 610759. - Graph -   099827
HMSO Books, St Crispins, Duke St, Norwich NR3 1PD.
T. (01603) 694497, Fax (01603) 695317.   099828

Mainstone Publications, Old Rectory, Sparham, Norwich.
T. (0136288) 395. - ArtBk -   *099829*
Norwich Gallery, Norwich School of Art and Design,
Saint George St, Norwich NR3 1BB. T. (01603) 610561,
Fax 615728. - ArtBk -   *099830*
Sainsbury Centre for Visual Arts, Norwich NR4 7TJ.
T. (01603) 592470, 456060,
Fax (01603) 259401.   *099831*

Oxford (Oxfordshire)
ARTbibliographies, 55 Saint Thomas' St., Oxford OX1
1JG. T. (01865) 250333. - ArtBk -   *099832*
Ashmolean Museum Publications, Ashmolean Museum,
Beaumont St., Oxford OX1 2PH. T. (01865) 278010,
Fax (01865) 270018. - ArtBk -   *099833*
Blackwell Publishers, 108 Cowley Rd, Oxford OX4 1JF.
T. (01865) 791100, Fax (01865) 791347.   *099834*
Clio Press, 55 Saint Thomas' St., Oxford OX1 1JG.
T. (01865) 250333, Fax (01865) 790358.
- ArtBk -   *099835*
Oxford Printmakers, Christadelphian Hall, Tyndale Rd.,
Oxford OX4 1JL. T. (01865) 728472. - Graph - *099836*
Oxford University, Walton St, Oxford OX2 6DP.
T. (01865) 56767.   *099837*
Phaidon Press, Musterlin House, Jordan Hill Rd., Oxford
OX2 8DP. T. (01865) 310664, Fax (01865) 310662.
- ArtBk / Sli -   *099838*
Previous Parrot Press, The Foundry, Church Hanborough,
Oxford OX7 2AB. T. (01865) 881260. - Graph - *099839*
Templecrest, 6 Boults Ln, Oxford. T. (01865) 790557.
- Repr -   *099840*

Portsmouth (Hampshire)
Milestone Publications, 62 Murray Rd., Portsmouth PO8
9JL. T. (01705) 592255, Fax (01705) 591975.
- ArtBk -   *099841*

Reading (Berkshire)
Gordon & Breach, POB 90, Reading RG1 8JL.
T. (01734) 560080, Fax (01734) 568211.
- ArtBk -   *099842*

Richmond (Surrey)
Regatta, 48 Hill Rise, Richmond. T. (0181) 940 9143.
- Graph -   *099843*

Saint Austell (Cornwall)
Gluvian, Saint Columb Rd, Saint Austell.
T. (01726) 861151. - ArtBk -   *099844*

Saint Ives (Cornwall)
Penwith Print Workshop, Back Rd. West, Saint Ives.
T. (01736) 795579. - Graph -   *099845*

Scarborough (North Yorkshire)
Crescent Arts Workshop, The Crescent, Scarborough.
T. (01723) 351461. - Graph -   *099846*

Sessay (North Yorkshire)
Potterton, Old Rectory, Sessay YO7 3LZ.
T. (01845) 401218, Fax (01845) 401439.
- ArtBk -   *099847*

Sevenoaks (Kent)
Hodder & Stoughton, Mill Rd., Dunton Green, Sevenoaks
TN13 2YA. T. (01732) 450111, Fax (01732) 460134.
- ArtBk -   *099848*

Shaftesbury (Dorset)
Element Books, Longmead, Shaftesbury SP7 8PL.
T. (01747) 51339, Fax (01747) 51394. - ArtBk - *099849*

Sheffield (South Yorkshire)
Northend, J.W., Clyde Rd. off Broadfield Rd., Sheffield.
T. (0114) 500331, Fax (0114) 500676. - ArtBk - *099850*

Shenstone (Staffordshire)
Solomon & Whitehead, Lynn Ln., Shenstone.
T. (01543) 480696. - Graph -   *099851*

Shepton Beauchamp (Somerset)
Dennis, Richard, Old Chapel, Middle St., Shepton Beauchamp TA19 0LE. T. (01460) 42009. - ArtBk - *099852*

Sherborne (Dorset)
Alphabet and Image, Alpha House, South St., Sherborne
DT9 3LU. T. (01935) 814944, Fax (01935) 816717.
- ArtBk -   *099853*

Stevenage (Hertfordshire)
Croft, 28 Whitney Dr., Stevenage. T. (01438) 367032.
- ArtBk -   *099854*
SPA Books, POB 47, Stevenage SG2 8UH.
T. (01438) 310009, Fax (01438) 310104.
- ArtBk -   *099855*

Sunderland (Tyne and Wear)
AN Publications, POB 23, Sunderland SR4 6DG.
T. (01783) 5673589, Fax (01783) 5641600.
- ArtBk -   *099856*

Surbiton (Surrey)
Fountain Press, 2 Claremont Rd., Surbiton KT6 4QU.
T. (0181) 390 7768, Fax (0181) 390 8062.
- ArtBk -   *099857*

Tonbridge (Kent)
The Art Newspaper, PO Box 1, Tonbridge TN9
1HW.   *099858*

Torquay (Devon)
Triton Publications, 1 Manor Rd., Torquay.
T. (01803) 311098. - ArtBk -   *099859*

Tunbridge Wells (Kent)
Costello, 43 High St., Tunbridge Wells TN1 1XL.
T. (01892) 45355. - ArtBk -   *099860*
Search Press, Wellwood, North Farm Rd., Tunbridge
Wells TN2 3DR. T. (01892) 510850,
Fax (01892) 515903. - ArtBk -   *099861*

Wellingborough (Northamptonshire)
Collett, Denington Estate, Wellingborough NN8 2QT.
T. (01933) 224351, Fax (01933) 27602.
- ArtBk -   *099862*

Weston-super-Mare (Avon)
Avon-Anglia Publications, 4 Woodspring Av., Weston-su-
per-Mare BS22 9RG. T. (01934) 631616.
- ArtBk -   *099863*

Weybridge (Surrey)
Art Sales Index, 1 Thames St., Weybridge KT13 8JG.
T. (01932) 856426, Fax (01932) 842482.
- ArtBk -   *099864*

Whitby (North Yorkshire)
Sutcliffe Gallery, 1 Flowergate, Whitby YO21 3BA.
T. (01947) 602239. - ArtBk / Card -   *099865*

Woodbridge (Suffolk)
Antique Collectors' Club, 5 Church St., Woodbridge IP12
1DS. T. (01394) 385501, Fax (01394) 384434. - ArtBk /
Graph -   *099866*
Boydell & Brewer, POB 9, Woodbridge IP12 3DF.
T. (01394) 411320, Fax (01394) 411477.
- ArtBk -   *099867*

Uruguay

Montevideo
Barreiro y Ramos, 25 de Mayo Esq. J.C. Gómez, 11 000
Montevideo. T. (02) 95 01 50, 95 82 83.   *099868*

U.S.A.

Albuquerque (New Mexico)
Tamarind Institute, 108 SE Cornell Av, Albuquerque, NM
87106. T. (505) 277-3901. - Graph -   *099869*

Ann Arbor (Michigan)
University of Michigan Press, POB 1104, Ann Arbor, MI
48106. T. (313) 764-4388, Fax (313) 936-0456.
- ArtBk -   *099870*

Asheville (North Carolina)
Lark, 50 College St, Asheville, NC 28801. T. (704) 253-
0476, Fax (704) 253-7952. - ArtBk -   *099871*

Atglen (Pennsylvania)
Schiffer, 77 Lower Valley Rd, Atglen, PA 19310.
T. (215) 593-1777, Fax (215) 593-2002.
- ArtBk -   *099872*

Avenel (New Jersey)
Outlet Book Company, 34 Englehard Av, Avenel, NJ
07001. T. (212) 572-2600, Fax (212) 572-8700.
- ArtBk -   *099873*

Berkeley (California)
Dharma, 2910 San Pablo Av, Berkeley, CA 94702.
T. (510) 548-5407, Fax (510) 548-2230.
- ArtBk -   *099874*
McCutchan, 2940 San Pablo Av, Berkeley, CA 94702.
T. (510) 841-8616, Fax (510) 841-7787.
- ArtBk -   *099875*
University of California Press, 2223 Fulton St, Berkeley,
CA 94720. T. (415) 642-4247, Fax (415) 642-7127.
- ArtBk -   *099876*

Blauvelt (New York)
Garber Communications, 5 Garber Hill Rd, Blauvelt, NY
10913. T. (914) 359-9292, Fax (914) 353-2880.
- ArtBk -   *099877*

Bloomington (Indiana)
Indiana University Press, 601 N Morton St, Bloomington,
IN 47404. T. (812) 855-4203. - ArtBk -   *099878*

Boston (Massachusetts)
Houghton, Mifflin, 222 Berkeley St, Boston, MA 02116.
T. (617) 351-5000, Fax (617) 331-1100.
- ArtBk -   *099879*
Little, Brown, 34 Beacon St, Boston, MA 02108.
T. (617) 227-0730, Fax (617) 227-3519.
- ArtBk -   *099880*
Pucker, 171 Newbury St, Boston, MA 02116.
T. (617) 267-9473, Fax (617) 424-9759. - Graph /
Card -   *099881*
Shambhala, 300 Massachusetts Av, Boston, MA 02115.
T. (617) 424-0030, Fax (617) 236-1563.
- ArtBk -   *099882*

Cambridge (Massachusetts)
M.I.T. Press, 55 Hayward St, Cambridge, MA 02142.
T. (617) 625-8569, Fax (617) 258-6779.
- ArtBk -   *099883*

Captiva Island (Florida)
Untitled Press, Inc., POB 54, Captiva Island, FL 33924.
T. (813) 427-1265. - Graph -   *099884*

Carmel (California)
Merrill-West, POB 1227, Carmel, CA 93921.
T. (408) 625-5792, Fax (408) 625-3502.
- ArtBk -   *099885*

Chicago (Illinois)
Art Institute of Chicago, Publications Department, 111 S
Michigan Av, Chicago, IL 60603. T. (312) 443-3600,
Fax (312) 443-0849. - ArtBk -   *099886*
Fawcett, 1100 W Cermak Rd, Chicago, IL 60608.
T. (312) 243-5660, Fax (312) 243-4847.
- ArtBk -   *099887*

Cincinnati (Ohio)
Cincinnati Art Museum, Publications Department, Eden
Park, Cincinnati, OH 45202. T. (513) 721-5204.
- ArtBk -   *099888*
Seven Hills Books, 49 Central Av, Cincinnati, OH 45202.
T. (513) 381-3881, Fax (513) 381-0753.
- ArtBk -   *099889*

Clarence (New York)
West-Art, POB 279, Clarence, NY 14031. T. (716) 634-
8805.   *099890*

Corte Madera (California)
Gingko Press, 5768 Paradise Dr, Ste J, Corte Madera,
CA 94925. T. (415) 924-9615, Fax (415) 924-9608.
- ArtBk -   *099891*

Portal Publications, 21 Tamal Vista, POB 659, Corte Madera, CA 94925. T. (415) 924-5652. - Repr - *099892*

Denver (Colorado)
Old West Publishing Company, 1228 E Colfax Av, Denver, CO 80218. T. (303) 832-7190. - ArtBk - *099893*

Detroit (Michigan)
Saint James Press, 835 Penobscot Bldg, Detroit, MI 48226. T. (313) 961-2242, Fax (313) 961-6637. - ArtBk - *099894*

Dubuque (Iowa)
Brown, William C., 2460 Kerper Blvd, Dubuque, IA 52001. T. (319) 588-1451, Fax (319) 589-4657. - ArtBk - *099895*

East Hampton (New York)
Sequoia, 10 Underwood Dr, East Hampton, NY 11937. T. (516) 324-6063. - ArtBk - *099896*

Fort Worth (Texas)
Kimbell Art Museum, Publications Department, 3333 Camp Bowie Blvd, Fort Worth, TX 76107. T. (817) 332-8451, Fax (817) 877-1264. - ArtBk - *099897*

Greenwich (Connecticut)
Bison Group-Brompton Books, 15 Sherwood Pl, Greenwich, CT 06830. T. (203) 661-9551, Fax (203) 629-1436. - ArtBk - *099898*

Hanover (New Hampshire)
University Press of New England, 23 S Main St, Hanover, NH 03755. T. (603) 643-7100, Fax (603) 643-1540. - ArtBk - *099899*

Hollywood (California)
Hawley, 8200 Gould Av, Hollywood, CA 90046-1573. T. (213) 654-1573, Fax (213) 650-7629. - ArtBk - *099900*

Honolulu (Hawaii)
University of Hawaii Press, 2840 Kolowalu St, Honolulu, HI 96822. T. (808) 956-8697, Fax (808) 988-6052. - ArtBk - *099901*

Houston (Texas)
Arte Publico Press, University of Houston, Houston, TX 77204-2090. T. (713) 743-2841, Fax (713) 743-2847. - ArtBk - *099902*
Houston Fine Art Press, 7331 Rampart St, Houston, TX 77081. T. (713) 981-1009. - ArtBk - *099903*

Iola (Wisconsin)
Krause, 700 E State St, Iola, WI 54990. T. (715) 445-2214, Fax (715) 445-4087. *099904*

Ithaca (New York)
Cornell University Press, 512 E State St, Ithaca, NY 14850. T. (607) 277-2338, Fax (607) 277-2374. - ArtBk - *099905*

Jersey City (New Jersey)
Booksmith, 100 Paterson Plank Rd, Jersey City, NJ 07307. T. (718) 782-0405, Fax (201) 659-3631. - ArtBk - *099906*

Kingston (New York)
McPherson & Co., POB 1126, Kingston, NY 12401. T. (914) 331-5807, Fax (914) 331-5807. - ArtBk - *099907*

La Jolla (California)
McGilvery, Laurence, POB 852, La Jolla, CA 92038. T. (619) 454-4443. - ArtBk - *099908*

Lincoln (Nebraska)
University of Nebraska Press, 901 N 17 St, Lincoln, NE 68588. T. (402) 472-3581, Fax (402) 472-6214. - ArtBk - *099909*

Los Angeles (California)
Arundel Press, 8300 Beverly Blvd, Los Angeles, CA 90048. T. (213) 852-9852, Fax (213) 852-9853. - ArtBk - *099910*

Leavin, Margo, 812 N Robertson Blvd, Los Angeles, CA 90069. T. (310) 273-0603, Fax (310) 273-9131. - Graph - *099911*
Questron, 11150 Olympic Blvd, Ste 650, Los Angeles, CA 90064. T. (310) 477-6100, Fax (310) 445-3933. - ArtBk - *099912*

Madison (Connecticut)
Sound View Press, 170 Boston Post Rd, Ste 150, Madison, CT 06443. T. (203) 245-2246, Fax (203) 245-3589. - ArtBk - *099913*

Malibu (California)
J. Paul Getty Trust Publications, 401 Wilshire Blvd, Malibu, CA 90401. T. (310) 451-6536, Fax (310) 395-0461. - ArtBk - *099914*

Metuchen (New Jersey)
Scarecrow, 52 Liberty St, POB 4167, Metuchen, NJ 08840. T. (908) 548-8600, Fax (908) 548-5767. - ArtBk - *099915*

Miami Beach (Florida)
Gordon, Conni, 427 22 St, Miami Beach, FL 33139. T. (305) 532-1001. - ArtBk / Repr - *099916*

Minneapolis (Minnesota)
Walker Art Center, Vineland Pl, Minneapolis, MN 55403. T. (612) 377-7500. - ArtBk / Repr / Card - *099917*

New Haven (Connecticut)
Yale University Press, 92a Yale Station, New Haven, CT 06520. T. (203) 432-0940. - ArtBk - *099918*

New York
Abaris Books, 42 Memorial Plaza, New York, NY 10570. T. (914) 747-9298, Fax (914) 747-4166. - ArtBk - *099920*
Abbeville, 488 Madison Av, New York, NY 10022. T. (212) 888-1969, Fax (212) 644-5085. - ArtBk - *099921*
Abrams, Harry N., 100 Fifth Av, New York, NY 10011. T. (212) 206-7715, Fax (212) 645-8437. - ArtBk / Repr / Cal - *099922*
American Showcase, 915 Broadway, New York, NY 10010. T. (212) 673-6600, Fax (212) 673-9795. - ArtBk - *099923*
Arcadia Press, 37 W Washington Sq, New York, NY 10011. T. (212) 477-5331. - ArtBk - *099924*
Art Directions Book Company, 10 E 39 St, New York, NY 10016. T. (212) 889-6500, Fax (212) 889-6504. - ArtBk - *099925*
Artisan, c/o Workman Publishing Company, 708 Broadway, New York, NY 10003. T. (212) 254-5900, Fax (212) 677-6692. - ArtBk / Cal - *099926*
Ballantine, 201 E 50 St, New York, NY 10022. T. (212) 572-2600, Fax (212) 572-8700. - ArtBk - *099927*
Bleier, Milton A., 333 Park Av S, New York, NY 10022. T. (212) 533-1730. - Graph / Repr / Mul - *099928*
Brant, 575 Broadway, New York, NY 10012. T. (212) 941-2800, Fax (212) 941-2897. - ArtBk - *099929*
Braziller, George, 60 Madison Av, New York, NY 10010. T. (212) 889-0909, Fax (212) 689-5405. - ArtBk - *099930*
Cambridge University Press, 40 W 20 St, New York, NY 10011. T. (212) 924-3900, Fax (212) 691-3239. - ArtBk / Repr - *099931*
Carr, James F., 227 E 81 St, New York, NY 10028. T. (212) 535-8110. - ArtBk - *099932*
Columbia University Press, 562 W 113 St, New York, NY 10025. T. (212) 316-7129, Fax (212) 316-7169. - ArtBk - *099933*
Consultant Press, 163 Amsterdam Av, New York, NY 10023. T. (212) 838-8640, Fax (212) 873-7065. - ArtBk - *099934*
Continuum Publishing Group, 370 Lexington Av, New York, NY 10017-6503. T. (212) 953-5858, Fax (212) 953-5944. - ArtBk - *099934a*
Crown Publishing Group, 201 E 50 St, New York, NY 10022. T. (212) 572-2600, Fax (212) 572-8700. - ArtBk - *099935*

Daheshist, POB 875, Grand Central Station, New York, NY 10163-0875. T. (212) 371-7436, Fax (212) 832-7413. - ArtBk - *099936*
D.A.P., 636 Broadway, New York, NY 10012. T. (212) 473-5119, Fax (212) 673-2887. - ArtBk - *099937*
Definition Press, 141 Greene St, New York, NY 10012. T. (212) 777-4490, Fax (212) 777-4426. - ArtBk - *099938*
Dell, 1540 Broadway, New York, NY 10036. T. (212) 354-6500, Fax (212) 782-9597. - ArtBk - *099939*
Facts on File Publications, 460 Park Av S, New York, NY 10016. T. (212) 683-2244, Fax (212) 213-4578. - ArtBk - *099940*
Farrar, Straus & Giroux, 19 Union Sq W, New York, NY 10003. T. (212) 741-6900, Fax (212) 633-9385. - ArtBk / Graph - *099941*
Felicie Press, 141 E 56 St, New York, NY 10022. T. (212) 752-6567. - ArtBk / Graph - *099942*
Gordon, Martin, 1000 Park Av, New York, NY 10028. T. (212) 249-7350. *099943*
Harmony Books, 201 E 50 St, New York, NY 10022. T. (212) 572-2600, Fax (212) 572-8700. - ArtBk - *099944*
Harper Collins, 10 E 53 St, New York, NY 10022. T. (212) 207-7000, Fax (212) 207-7433. *099945*
Hearst, 1350 Av of the Americas, New York, NY 10019. T. (212) 261-6770, Fax (212) 261-6795. - ArtBk - *099946*
Hill & Wang, 19 Union Sq, New York, NY 10003. - ArtBk - *099947*
Hudson Hills Press, 230 Fifth Av, Ste 1308, New York, NY 10001-7704. T. (212) 889-3090, Fax (212) 889-3091. - ArtBk - *099948*
Kaldewey, Poestenkill, New York, NY 12140. T. (518) 283-5152. - ArtBk - *099949*
Klayman, Leon, POB 281, Prince Station, New York, NY 10012. T. (212) 645-4037, Fax (212) 924-7365. *099950*
Knoedler & Co, M., 19 E 70 St, New York, NY 10021. T. (212) 794-0550. - Graph - *099951*
Knopf, Alfred A., 201 E 50 St, New York, NY 10022. T. (212) 572-2600, Fax (212) 572-8700. - ArtBk - *099952*
Konecky, William S., 156 Fifth Av, New York, NY 10010. T. (212) 807-8230, Fax (212) 807-8239. - ArtBk - *099953*
Logo Art Corporation, 472 Broome St, New York, NY 10013. T. (212) 925-6796, Fax (212) 925-0849. - ArtBk / Graph - *099954*
Lucas, Phyllis, 981 Second Av, New York, NY 10022. T. (212) 753-1441. - Graph - *099955*
Mano, 164 Mercer St, New York, NY 10012. T. (212) 219-3510. *099956*
M.A.S de Reinis, POB 1500, Grand Central Station, New York, NY 10163. T. (718) 625-4336. *099957*
Master Drawings Association, 29 E 36 St, New York, NY 10016. T. (212) 685-0008. - Graph - *099958*
McGaw, Bruce, 230 Fifth Av, New York, NY 10001. T. (212) 679-7823. - Graph - *099959*
McGraw-Hill, 1221 Av of the Americas, New York, NY 10020. T. (212) 512-4471, Fax (212) 512-2186. - ArtBk - *099960*
Midmarch Arts Press, 300 Riverside Dr, New York, NY 10025. T. (212) 666-6990. *099961*
Multiples, 24 W 57 St, New York, NY 10022. T. (212) 977-7160. - Mul - *099962*
Museum of Modern Art, Publications Department, 11 W 53 St, New York, NY 10019. T. (212) 708-9733, Fax (212) 708-9779. - ArtBk / Repr / Card / Sli / Cal - *099963*
New Press, 450 W 41 St, New York, NY 10036. T. (212) 629-8802, Fax (212) 629-8617. - ArtBk - *099964*
Orion Editions, 270 Lafayette St, New York, NY 10012. T. (212) 226-2766. - Graph - *099965*
Oxford University Press, 200 Madison Av, New York, NY 10016. T. (212) 679-7300, Fax (212) 725-2972. - ArtBk / Graph - *099966*
Pantheon Books, 201 E 50 St, New York, NY 10022. T. (212) 572-2600, Fax (212) 572-8700. - ArtBk - *099967*

Parasol Press, 289 Church St, New York, NY 10013.
T. (212) 431-9387. - Graph -   *099968*

Pelavin, 13 Jay St, New York, NY 10013. T. (212) 925-
9424. - Repr -   *099969*

Petersburg Press, 380 Lafayette St, New York, NY
10003. T. (212) 420-0890, Fax (212) 420-1617.
- ArtBk / Graph / Cal -   *099970*

Rizzoli, 300 Park Av S, New York, NY 10010.
T. (212) 387-3400, Fax (212) 387-3535.
- ArtBk -   *099971*

Rose, Peter, 200 E 58 St, New York, NY 10022.
T. (212) 759-8173.   *099972*

Saint Martin's Press, 175 Fifth Av, New York, NY 10010.
T. (212) 674-5151, Fax (212) 677-7456.
- ArtBk -   *099973*

Sterling Publishing Company, 387 Park Av S, New York,
NY 10017. T. (212) 532-7160, Fax (212) 213-2495.
- ArtBk / Graph -   *099974*

Stewart, Tabori & Chang, 575 Broadway, New York, NY
10012. T. (212) 941-2929, Fax (212) 941-2982.
- ArtBk -   *099975*

Thames and Hudson, 500 Fifth Av, New York, NY 10110.
T. (212) 354-3763, Fax (212) 398-1252.   *099976*

Tullis Garner, 10 White St, New York, NY 10013.
T. (212) 226-6665, Fax (212) 941-0678. - Graph /
Mul -   *099977*

Universe Publishing, 300 Park Av S, New York, NY
10010. T. (212) 387-3400, Fax (212) 387-3644.
- ArtBk / Cal -   *099978*

Viking Penguin, 375 Hudson St, New York, NY 10014.
T. (212) 366-2000, Fax (212) 366-2933.
- ArtBk -   *099979*

Watson-Guptill, 1515 Broadway, New York, NY 10036.
T. (212) 764-7300, Fax (212) 536-5359. - ArtBk /
Graph -   *099980*

Wilson, H.W., 950 University Av, New York, NY 10452.
T. (212) 590-8400, Fax (212) 590-1617.   *099981*

World Arts Registry, Dept. ADM 2, Times Square Station,
POB 334, New York, NY 10108. T. (914) 624-2222,
Fax (914) 624-1212.   *099982*

Northridge (California)
Weston, Edward, 19355 Business Center Dr, Northridge,
CA 91324. T. (818) 885-1044, Fax (818) 885-1021.
- ArtBk / Graph / Repr / Card / Cal / Mul -   *099983*

Norwalk (Connecticut)
Abaris Books, 70 New Canaan Av, Norwalk, CT 06850.
T. (203) 849-1655, Fax (203) 849-9181.
- ArtBk -   *099984*

Gibson, C.R., 32 Knight St, Norwalk, CT 06856.
T. (203) 847-4543, Fax (203) 847-1165.
- Graph -   *099985*

Orleans (Massachusetts)
Parnassus Imprints, 210 Main St, POB 1036, Orleans,
MA 02643. - ArtBk -   *099986*

Pleasantville (New York)
Abaris Books, 42 Memorial Plaza, Pleasantville, NY
10570. T. (914) 747-9298, Fax (914) 747-
4166.   *099987*

Princeton (New Jersey)
American School of Classical Studies, Institute for Ad-
vanced Study, Princeton, NJ 08540. T. (609) 734-8387,
Fax (609) 924-0578.   *099988*

Princeton University Press, 41 William St, Princeton, NJ
08540. T. (609) 258-4900, Fax (609) 258-6305.
- ArtBk -   *099989*

Rockport (Massachusetts)
Rockport Publishers, 146 Granite St, Rockport, MA
01966. T. (508) 546-9590, Fax (508) 546-7141.
- ArtBk / Graph -   *099990*

Rutland (Vermont)
Tuttle, 26 S Main St, Rutland, VT 05701. T. (802) 773-
8229. - ArtBk -   *099991*

Salisbury (Connecticut)
Lime Rock Press, Mount Riga Rd, POB 363, Salisbury,
CT 06068. T. (203) 435-9458.   *099992*

San Francisco (California)
Arti Grafiche, 2140 Bush St, San Francisco, CA 94115-
3166. T. (415) 928-8732, Fax (415) 928-8539.
- ArtBk / Graph / Card -   *099993*

San Francisco Art Exchange, 458 Geary St, San Francis-
co, CA 94102. T. (415) 441-8840. - Graph -   *099994*

Wofsy, Alan, 1109 Geary Blvd, San Francisco, CA
91409. T. (415) 292-6500, Fax (415) 547-1623.
- ArtBk -   *099995*

San Marino (California)
Huntington Library Press, 1151 Oxford Rd, San Marino,
CA 91108. T. (818) 405-2172, Fax (818) 405-0225.
- ArtBk -   *099996*

San Rafael (California)
Gilden, 4172 Redwood Hwy, San Rafael, CA 94903.
T. (972) 350-57833. - Graph -   *099997*

Santa Monica (California)
Hennessy & Ingalls, 1254 Santa Monica Mall, Santa Monica, CA 90401. T. (213) 458-9074, Fax (213) 394-
2928.   *099998*

Seattle (Washington)
University of Washington Press, POB 50096, Seattle, WA
98145. T. (206) 543-4050, Fax (206) 543-3932.
- ArtBk -   *099999*

Stamford (Connecticut)
Reinhold, 600 Summer St, Stamford, CT 06904.
- ArtBk -   *100000*

Storrs (Connecticut)
William Benton Museum of Art, Publications Depart-
ment, University of Connecticut, Storrs, CT 06268.
T. (203) 486-4520. - ArtBk -   *100001*

Sun Valley (California)
Caler, John W., 7506 Clybourn, Sun Valley, CA 91352.
T. (213) 765-1210. - ArtBk / ArtP -   *100002*

Syracuse (New York)
Syracuse University Press, 1600 Jamesville Av, Syracuse, NY 13244. T. (315) 443-2597, Fax (315) 443-
5545. - ArtBk -   *100003*

Taos (New Mexico)
Taos/Western Fine Arts Publishing Company, Sagebrush
Inn, Taos POB 1566, NM 87571. T. (505) 758-
0680.   *100004*

Tucson (Arizona)
Nazraeli, 1955 W Grant Rd, Ste 230, Tucson, AZ 85745.
T. (520) 798-1513, Fax (520) 798-1514.
- ArtBk -   *100005*

University Park (Pennsylvania)
Pennsylvania State University Press, 820 N University
Dr, Ste C, University Park, PA 16802. T. (814) 865-
1327, Fax (814) 863-1408. - ArtBk -   *100006*

Venice (California)
Martin, Susan, 28 A 25 Av, Venice, CA 90291.
T. (310) 577-7680, Fax (310) 577-7682.   *100007*

Washington (District of Columbia)
National Gallery of Art Publications, Fourth and Constitu-
tion Av NW, Washington, DC 20565. T. (202) 842-6466,
Fax (202) 408-8530. - ArtBk -   *100008*

Preservation Press, 1785 Massachusetts Av NW, Washington, DC 20036. T. (202) 673-4058, Fax (202) 673-
4172. - ArtBk -   *100009*

Smithsonian Institution Press, 470 L'Enfant Plaza, Ste
7100, Washington, DC 20560. T. (202) 287-3738,
Fax (202) 287-3184. - ArtBk -   *100010*

Watkins Glen (New York)
Century House Publishing, POB 349, Watkins Glen, NY
14891. T. (607) 535-4737. - ArtBk -   *100011*

Worcester (Massachusetts)
Davis, 50 Portland St, Worcester, MA 01608.
T. (508) 754-7201, Fax (508) 753-3834.
- ArtBk -   *100012*

York (Pennsylvania)
Shumway, George, 3900 Deep Run Lan, York, PA 17402.
T. (717) 755-1196. - ArtBk -   *100013*

Vatican City

Città del Vaticano
Vaticana, Via della Tipografia, 00120 Città del Vaticano.
T. (06) 69 83 345. - ArtBk -   *100014*

Venezuela

Caracas (D.F.)
Armitano, Ernesto, 4a Transversal de Boleita, Centro Industrial de Boleita, Caracas. T. (02) 34 25 65, 34 08 65,
34 08 70, Fax 241 50 91. - ArtBk / ArtP -   *100015*

Yugoslavia

Beograd (Srbija)
Prosveta, Cika Ljubina 1, 11000 Beograd.
- ArtBk -   *100016*

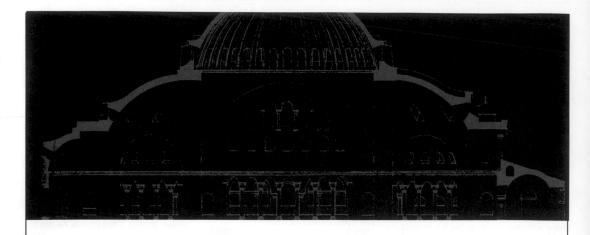

Hans F. Schweers

GEMÄLDE IN DEUTSCHEN MUSEEN

Paintings in German Museums

Katalog der ausgestellten und depotgelagerten Werke

2. völlig aktualisierte, erheblich erweiterte und verbesserte Ausgabe 1994
Teil I: Bde. 1-4 (Künstler und ihre Werke)
Teil II: Bde. 5-7 (Ikonographisches Verzeichnis)
Teil III: Bde. 8-10 (Verzeichnis der Museen mit ihren Bildern)
10 Bände CCCXXIV, 4.871 Seiten. Gebunden. DM 3.900,– (Unverb. Preisempf.)
ISBN 3-598-10927-X

Teil I des bewährten Standardwerks beschränkt sich nicht nur auf die ausgestellten Werke, sondern verzeichnet zum ersten Mal auch Depotbestände. Damit und mit den über **10.000 Gemälden** aus den wichtigsten Museen der neuen Bundesländer vergrößert sich der Umfang des Katalogs auf jetzt nahezu **110.000 Gemälde** von annähernd **18.000 Malern aus über 420 Museen und Galerien**. Die Einträge enthalten den Titel des Gemäldes, Entstehungsjahr, Material, Format und besondere Hinweise wie Kopie, Werkstattarbeit, Zuschreibung usw.

Über **250 Motivgruppen** stellen im Teil II, dem ikonographischen Verzeichnis, eine sinnvolle Aufschlüsselung der Bildthemen sicher.

In Teil III, einem umfangreichen Register der Museen, finden sich alle im Hauptteil aufgeführten Gemälde (zum Teil mit Inventarnummer ihres Museums) nach Museen und Galerien geordnet.

K·G·Saur Verlag
Postfach 701620 · D-81316 München
Tel. (089) 7 69 02-232 · Fax (089) 7 69 02-150/250 · E-mail: 100730.1341@compuserve.com

Art Periodicals
Kunstzeitschriften
Journaux d'Arte
Periodice d'Arte
Revistas de Arte

Das Register zum *Thieme-Becker, Vollmer* und zum *Allgemeinen Künst-lerlexikon* – jetzt inklusive der vollständigen Lexikonartikel aus dem *Allgemeinen Künstlerlexikon!*

Allgemeines Künstlerlexikon – Internationale Künstlerdatenbank

AKL – World Biographical Dictionary of Artists

3. CD-ROM-Ausgabe 1996
DM 2.400,–*
(DM 498,–* für Bezieher der Buchausgabe *Allgemeines Künstlerlexikon*)
(DM 796,–* für Bezieher der *IKD II*)

Die dritte erheblich erweiterte Ausgabe enthält nun neben den Strukturdaten aus den 37 Bänden des *Thieme-Becker* und den 6 Bänden des *Vollmer* die Struktur-daten und die **vollständigen Texteinträge** aus den ersten 12 Bänden des *Allgemeinen Künstlerlexikons*.
Maler, Graphiker, Bildhauer, Architekten – die Vertreter der bildenden Künste aller Kulturräume der Erde von der Antike bis zur Gegenwart können hier nach den verschiedensten Kriterien gesucht und ihre biographischen Daten abgerufen werden.

* unverbindliche Preisempfehlung

Bitte fordern Sie einen ausführlichen Prospekt bei uns an!

K•G•Saur Verlag
Postfach 701620 · D-81316 München · Tel. (089) 7 69 02-0
Fax (089) 7 69 02-150 · E-mail: 100730.1341@compuserve.com

Argentina

Arte al Dia, Bolívar 1542, 1141 Buenos Aires. *100017*
Horizontes, Bartolomé Mitre 2061, Buenos Aires.
T. (01) 492713. *100018*
Sudamerica, Casilla de Correo 426, Buenos
Aires. *100019*

Australia

Art Almanac, 96 Canterbury Rd., Middle Park, Vic. 3206.
T. 6907036. *100020*
Art and Australia, 653 Pacific Hwy., Killara, NSW 2071.
T. 4984933, 4984656. *100021*
Australian Antique Collector, 3-13 Queen St., Chippen-
dale, NSW 2008. *100022*
Australian Numismatic Journal, GPO Box 80, Adelaide,
SA 5001. *100023*
Ceramics Art and Perception, 35 Williams St., Sydney,
NSW 2021. T. (02) 361-5286, Fax (02) 361-
5402. *100024*
Mankind, Depturture of Anthropology University of Syd-
ney, Sydney, NSW 2006. T. (02) 6922360. *100025*
Pottery in Australia, 2/68 Alexander St., Crows Nest,
Sydney, NSW 2065. T. (02) 4361681,
4361184. *100026*
University Union, Parkville, Vict. 3052. *100027*

Austria

Adler, Haarhof 4a, 1014 Wien. *100028*
Anzeiger des Verbandes der Antiquare Österreichs, Die
Fachzeitschriften des österreichischen Buchhandels,
Grünangergasse 4, 1010 Wien. T. (0222) 5121535,
Fax 5128482. *100029*
ARAM Kunstmagazin, Neustiftgasse 5, 1070 Wien.
T. (0222) 5234242-0, Fax (0222) 5234242-42. *100030*
Artibus et Historiae, Rüdengasse 6, 1030 Wien.
T. (0222) 7130136, Fax (0222) 7130130. *100031*
Camera Austria, Sparkassenpl 2, 8010 Graz.
T. (0316) 8155500, Fax 8155509. *100032*
Corpus der Mittelalterlichen Glasmalerei Österreichs, c/
o Hofburg, Schweizerhof, 1010 Wien. T. (0222) 53415-
116/124, Fax (0222) 53415-252. *100033*
Eikon, Internationale Zeitschrift für Photographie & Me-
dienkunst, Gumpendorfer Str 118 A/12, 1060 Wien.
T. (0222) 5977088, Fax 5977087. *100034*
Imagination, Zeitschrift für Freunde des Alten Buches, c/
o Akademische Druck- und Verlagsanstalt, Schönau-
gasse 6, 8010 Graz. T. (0316) 813460,
Fax (0316) 813460-24. *100035*
Kunst und Kirche, c/o Landesverlag, Hafenstr. 1-3, 4020
Linz. T. (070) 278121-223. *100036*
Linzer Archäologische Forschungen, c/o Stadtmuseum,
Bethlehemstr 7, 4020 Linz. T. (0732) 70701918,
Fax 793518. *100037*
Mitteilungen der Gesellschaft für Vergleichende Kunst-
forschung in Wien, c/o Hofburg, Säulenstiege, 1010
Wien. T. (0222) 53415-120. *100038*
Mitteilungen der Österreichischen Numismatischen Ge-
sellschaft, c/o Österreichische Numismatische Gesell-
schaft, Burgring 5, 1010 Wien. T. (0222) 52524383,
Fax 52524501. *100039*
Mühlviertler Heimatblätter, c/o Mühlviertler Künstlergil-
de, Rudolfstr. 70, 4020 Linz. T. (070) 347855. *100040*
Museum, Hyrtlgasse 28/13, 1160 Wien.
T. (0222) 4924546. *100041*
Neues Museum, Burgring 5, 1010 Wien.
T. (0222) 52177, Fax 5232770. *100042*
Nomea Art Journal, Lessingstr. 2, 5021 Salzburg.
T. (0662) 879784, Fax (0662) 879789. *100043*
Numismatische Zeitschrift, c/o Österreichische Numis-
matische Gesellschaft, Burgring 5, 1010 Wien.
T. (0222) 52524383, Fax 52524501. *100044*
Österreichische Kunsttopographie, c/o Hofburg, Schwei-
zerhof, 1010 Wien. T. (0222) 534150. *100045*
Österreichische Zeitschrift für Kunst und Denkmalpflege,
c/o Verlag Anton Schroll & Co., Sprengersgasse 39,
1051 Wien. T. (0222) 555641,
Fax (0222) 55564166. *100046*

EIKON
Internationale Zeitschrift für Photographie & Medienkunst

EIKON

INTERNATIONALE ZEITSCHRIFT FÜR PHOTOGRAPHIE & MEDIENKUNST

Das Periodikum **EIKON** widmet sich der Präsentation von und der
Auseinandersetzung mit österreichischer und internationaler Photographie,
ihrer Bedeutung im Kontext der Bildenden Kunst, neuen Medien
und Medienkunst generell. Regelmäßig erscheinen auch Themenhefte.

Seit 1996 bietet das *Österreichische Institut für Photographie (ÖIP)* in den
Räumlichkeiten von **EIKON** den *Info-Service-Center Photographie (ISCP)* an,
der eine Mediathek (Video, CD-Rom, Photo-CD, Internet), Infothek und
Bibliothek (ca. 7.000 Publikationen) zur Information über und Vermittlung
von v.a. künstlerischer Photographie beinhaltet.

Mediadaten/Informationen
Herausgeber: ÖIP/Carl Aigner
Erscheinungsweise: vierteljährlich; Umfang ca. 100 Seiten, ca. 80 Abbildungen (SW,Farbe).
1 Heft ATS 210,–/ DM 30,– plus Porto/Verpackung; Jahresabonnement (4 Hefte)
ATS 490,–/ DM 70,– plus Porto/Verpackung
Verlag Turia & Kahn, Wien
Gumpendorfer Straße 118A/19, A-1060 Wien, Tel +43-1/597 7088, Fax 597 7087
e-mail: eikon@thing.at, http://www.eikon.or.at/eikon/

Parnass, Porzellangasse 43/19, 1090 Wien.
T. (0222) 3195375, Fax 3108272. *100047*
Public Art Gallery – Gebhard Schatz, Pfarrgasse 8, 6460
Imst. T. (05412) 64317, Fax 64317. *100048*
Studien zu Denkmalschutz und Denkmalpflege, c/o Hof-
burg, Schweizerhof, 1010 Wien.
T. (0222) 534150. *100049*
Studien zur Österreichischen Kunstgeschichte, Hofburg,
1010 Wien. T. (0222) 534150. *100050*
Vernissage, Miesbachgasse 15, 1020 Wien.
T. (0222) 331186. *100051*
Wiener Kunsthefte, c/o Kleine Galerie, Neudeggerg. 8,
1080 Wien. *100052*

Belgium

Annuaire General des Beaux-Arts, 85, av. Winston-Chur-
chill, 1180 Bruxelles. *100053*
Antique Classique, 28a Av Léopold, 1330 Rixensart.
T. (02) 6539691. *100054*
Archives et Bibliotheques de Belgique, 4 Blvd de l'Em-
pereur, 1000 Bruxelles. T. (02) 5195351. *100055*
Art d'Eglise, Monastère Saint-André, 1340 Ottignies.
T. 417464. *100056*
Artefactum, Amerikalei 125, 2000 Antwerpen.
T. (03) 2382089. *100057*
Arts, Antiques & Auctions, 79 Blvd E Machtens, Boite
22, 1080 Bruxelles. T. (02) 4108686,
Fax (02) 4108289. *100058*
Bulletin de l'Institut Royal du Patrimoine Artistique, 1
Parc du Cinquantenaire, 1000 Bruxelles.
T. (02) 7396711. *100059*
Chronique d'Egypte, 10 Parc du Cinquantenaire, 1000
Bruxelles. T. (02) 7339610. *100060*
Graphia, Lange Rekstr 13, 9100 Sint Niklaas.
T. (03) 7764515. *100061*
Hoog, Ketsstr 25, 2018 Antwerpen.
T. (03) 2360016. *100062*
Institut Supérieur pour l'Etude du Langage Plastique –
I.S.E.L.P., 31 Blvd de Waterloo, 1000 Bruxelles.
T. (02) 5135662, Fax (02) 5024526. *100063*
Kunstecho's, Keizer Karelstr 199, 9000 Gent.
T. (09) 2233889, 3625958. *100064*
PACT, 28a Av Léopold, 1330 Rixensart.
T. (02) 6539691. *100065*
Patrimonium, Westerlosteenweg 32, 2220 Heist o.d.
Berg. T. (015) 246797. *100066*

Publications d'Historie de l'Art et d'Archeologie de l'Uni-
versite Catholique de Louvain, 31 Pl Blaise Pascal Col-
lege Erasme, 1348 Louvain-La-Neuve.
T. (016) 474880, Fax (016) 472999. *100067*
Revue Belge d'Archeologie et d'Histoire de l'Art, c/o Mu-
sée Bellevue, 7 Pl des Palais, 1000 Bruxelles. *100068*
Revue Belge de Numismatique et de Sigillographie, c/o
Musée de la Banque Nationale, 28a Av Léopold, 1330
Rixensart. *100069*
Revue Des Archeologues et Historiens d'Art de Louvain,
c/o Collège Erasme, Place Blaise Pascal 1, 1348 Lou-
vain-la-Neuve. T. (016) 6539691. *100070*
Revue l'Apart de l'Oeil, 144 Rue du Midi, 1000 Bruxel-
les. T. (02) 5141841, 7332437. *100071*
Vlaanderen, Hondstraat 6, 8700 Tielt.
T. (051) 401108. *100072*
Wavriensia, 23 Rue de l'Ermitage, 1300 Wavre (Waver).
T. (010) 223846. *100073*

Brazil

Arte Vogue, Av. Brasil 1456, Sao Paulo. *100074*
Dedalo, Cidade Universitária, São Paulo Caixa Postal
8105. T. (011) 211-0011 r. 335. *100075*
GAM, Av. G.Freire 663, Sala 1001, Rio de Janeiro, 20
000. T. (021) 2424217. *100076*
Revista de Historia, Rua do Lago, 717, 05508 São Paulo
Caixa Postal 8105. T. (011) 813-3222. *100077*

Bulgaria

Izkustvo, Ul Shipka 18, 1404 Sofia.
T. (02) 430192. *100078*
Spisanie Karikatura, ul Nikolai Pavlovitsh 6, 1000 Sofia.
T. (02) 661826. *100079*
Spisanie Kartinna Galeriia, pl Slaveikov 2-a, 1000 Sofia.
T. (02) 870701. *100080*
Spisanie Obzor, Bul Dondukov 39, 1080 Sofia.
T. (02) 873390. *100081*
Spisanie Panorama, ul Tsanko Tserkovski 16, 1421 So-
fia. T. (02) 655940. *100082*
Spisanie Plamak, ul Angel Kantshev 5, 1000 Sofia.
T. (02) 880031. *100083*
Vestnik Ab, pl Slaveikov 11, 1000 Sofia.
T. (02) 879111. *100084*
Vestnik Narodna Kultura, ul Sofiiska Komuna 4, 1040
Sofia. T. (02) 883322. *100085*
Vestnik Zname na Mira, ul Oborishte 17, 1504 Sofia.
T. (02) 441994, 4300-01/03. *100086*

Canada

Applied Arts, 885 Don Mills Rd, Ste 324, Don Mills, Ont. M3C 1V9. T. (416) 510-0913, Fax (416) 510-0913. *100087*

Art Impressions, 22 Keele St S, King City, Ont. L0G 1K0. T. (416) 833-2737, Fax (416) 833-3763. *100088*

Inuit Art Quarterly, c/o Inuit Art Foundation, 2081 Merivale Rd, Nepean, Ont. K2G 1G9. T. (613) 224-8189, Fax (613) 224-2907. *100089*

Journal of Canadian Art History, c/o Concordia University, 1455 Blvd de Maisonneuve Ouest, Montre'1al, Qué. H3G 1M8. T. (514) 848-4699, Fax (514) 848-3494. *100090*

Journal of Canadian Studies/Revue d'Etudes Canadiennes, Trent University, Peterborough, K9J 7B8. *100091*

Parachute, 4060 Blvd Saint-Laurent, Montréal, P.Q. H2W 1Y9. T. (514) 842-9805, Fax (514) 287-7146. *100092*

The Structurist, University of Saskatchewan, Saskatoon, Sask. S7N 0W0. T. (306) 966-4198, Fax (306) 966-8670. *100093*

China, Republic

National Palace Museum Monthly of Chinese Art, Wai-shuang-hsi, Shih-lin, 11102 Taipei. T. (02) 88212-30/33. *100094*

The National Palace Museum Bulletin, Wai-shuang-hsi, Shih-lin, 111 02 Taipei. T. (02) 88212-30/33. *100095*

The National Palace Museum Newsletter & Gallery Guide, Wai-shuang-hsi, Shih-lin, Taipei. T. (02) 88212-30/33. *100096*

The National Palace Museum Research Quarterly, Wai-shuang-hsi, Shih-lin, 111 02 Taipei. T. (02) 88212-30/33. *100097*

Colombia

Boletin de Historia y Antiguedades, c/o Academia Colombiana de Historia, Calle 10, No. 8 – 95, Bogota. *100098*

Czech Republic

Slezsky Numismatik, Tyrsova 33, Opava. T. 2184. *100099*

STUDIA COMENIANA ET HISTORICA, Museum J. A. Komenskeho, Přemysla Otakara II. 36, 688 12 Uherský. T. 2288, 2289. *100100*

TVAR, Gottwaldovo nabř 250, Praha. *100101*

UMĚNÍ, Haštalská 6, 116 92 Praha. T. (02) 231 29 51, 231 29 09, 231 28 40. *100102*

UMĚNÍ A ŘEMESLA, Sněmovní 9, 118 00 Praha. T. (02) 53 68 02. *100103*

Výtvarná Práce, Gottwaldovo nabř 250, Praha. *100104*

Výtvarné Umění, Gottwaldovo nábř 250, Praha. *100105*

Denmark

Arkitektur-DK, Nyhavn 43, 1051 København K. *100106*

Hvedekorn, Valbygaardsvej 33, 2500 Valby. T. 31462100, Fax 36441488. *100107*

International Grafik, POB 109, 9900 Frederikshavn. *100108*

Louisiana Revue, c/o Louisiana Museum, Gl Strandvej 13, 3050 Humlebaek. *100109*

Estonia

E & F Der Estnische Sammler, Pärnu maantee 102, 0013 Tallinn. T. (02) 556504, Fax (02) 556828. *100110*

Ethiopia

Annales d'Ethiopie, POB 1907, Addis Abeba. *100111*

Finland

Siksi-Nordic Arts Review, c/o Nordic Arts Centre, Suomenlinna, 00190 Helsinki. T. (09) 668143. *100112*

Taide, Kasarmikatu 23 A, 00130 Helsinki. T. (09) 626459. *100113*

France

A-Ya, Editions A-Ya, Chapelle de la Villedieu, 78310 Elancourt. *100114*

Actualité des Arts Plastiques, Centre National de Documentation Pédagogique, 29 Rue d'Ulm, 75230 Paris Cedex 05. *100115*

Actuels, Editions Comp'Act, 9 Pl de la République, 01420 Seyssel. T. 0450561312, Fax 0450590290. *100116*

Amis du Château de Pau: Bulletin, Château, 64000 Pau. T. 0559823810, Fax 0559823818. *100117*

Art de Basse Normandie, 49 Rue Canchy, 14000 Caen. *100118*

Art et Poésie, 11 Rue de la Fontaine-Saint-Laurent, 58200 Cosne-sur-Loire. *100119*

Art International, Archive Press, 77 Rue des Archives, 75003 Paris. T. 0148048454, Fax 0148048200. *100120*

Art Plein Cadre, 67 Rue de Provence, 75009 Paris. T. 0142802777, Fax 0140230875. *100121*

Arts Asiatiques, Editions d'Amérique et d'Orient, 11 Rue Saint-Sulpice, 75006 Paris. T. 0143268635, Fax 0143545954. *100122*

Beaux Arts Magazine, 9 Rue Christiani, 75880 Paris Cedex 18. T. 0149251717, Fax 0149251721. *100123*

Get a closer look at things with DAIDALOS

Gehen Sie den Dingen auf den Grund mit DAIDALOS

Lieferbare Hefte / Available Issues

Im Jahresabonnement (4 Ausgaben) 184 DM. Für Studenten 140 DM. Einzelheft 50 DM.
Leseproben erhältlich. Bestellungen bitte an:
Bertelsmann-Verlag, Carl-Bertelsmann-Straße 270, Postfach 120, 33311 Gütersloh, Telefon: (05241) 80-2165, Fax: 73055
Redaktion: Schlüterstraße 42, 10707 Berlin, Telefon: (030) 88 67 18 – 80-83 Fax: 88 67 19 66

B.H.A., Bibliography of the History of Art, Institut de l'Information Scientifique et Technique, 2 Allée du Parc du Brabois, 54514 Vandœuvre-Les-Nancy.
T. 0383504600, Fax 0383504615.   *100124*
Bulletin de l'Antiquaire et du Brocanteur, 18 Rue de Provence, 75009 Paris. T. 0147708878.   *100125*
Céramique Moderne, Editions Techniques et Artistiques, 22 Rue Le Brun, 75013 Paris. T. 0145871748.   *100126*
Cimaise, 3 Rue Maurice-Loewy, 75014 Paris.
T. 0143277540, Fax 0143228663.   *100127*
Le Collectionneur Français, 10 Rue du Pont-Louis-Philippe, 75004 Paris. T. 0142780417.   *100128*
Connaissance des Arts, 25 Rue de Ponthieu, 75008 Paris. T. 0143596200, Fax 0142564335.   *100129*
La Côte des Arts, 31 Rue Dieude'1, 13006 Marseille.
T. 0491339162, Fax 0491333664.   *100130*
Le Courrier des Galeries, 14 Rue de Thionville, 75019 Paris.   *100131*
Créations, BP 109, 06322 Cannes.   *100132*
Dossier de l'Art, BP 90, 21803 Quetigny Cedex.
T. 0380709346.   *100133*
Les Dossiers de l'Art Public, 71 Rue d'Hautpoul, 75019 Paris. T. 0142411361, Fax 0142417718.   *100134*
Editions Cahiers d'Art, 14 Rue du Dragon, 75006 Paris.
T. 0145487673, Fax 0145449850.   *100135*
Eléments, 41 Rue Barrault, 75013 Paris.
T. 0169260521.   *100136*
Faïences Patriotiques, 3 Rue de l'Abbé-Gregoire, 75006 Paris. T. 0142229387.   *100137*
FMR, 5 Rue Félicité, 75015 Paris.
T. 0142506920.   *100138*
Gazette de l'Hôtel Drouot, 10 Rue du Faubourg-Montmartre, 75009 Paris. T. 0147709300.   *100139*
Gazette des Beaux-Arts, BP 87, 05003 Gap Cedex.
T. 0442890804, Fax 0445614653.   *100140*
Histoire de l'Art, Centre d'Histoire, 3 Rue Michelet, 75006 Paris. T. 0143252323.   *100141*
ICOM News, 1 Rue Miollis, 75732 Paris. T. 0147340500, Fax 0143067862.   *100142*
Impressions, 49 Rue Etienne-Marcel, 75001 Paris.
T. 0140134800, Fax 0140134814.   *100143*
L'Art et la Mer, Musée de la Marine, 2 Rue Royale, 75200 Paris. T. 0142603330.   *100144*
L'Objet d'Art, 25 Rue Berbisey, 21000 Dijon.
T. 0380404113, Fax 0380301537.   *100145*
L'Oeil, 10 Rue Guichard, 75116 Paris. T. 0145258560, Fax 0142886587.   *100146*
Langouste, Model-Peltex Association, 3 Rue des Couples, 67000 Strasbourg.   *100147*
Macula, 6 Rue Coëtlogon, 75006 Paris. T. 0145485870, Fax 0145485870.   *100148*
Mausolée, BP 8, 69702 Givors Cedex.
T. 0472248933.   *100149*
Métiers d'Art, 20 Rue La Boëtie, 75008 Paris.
T. 0149240103, Fax 0149249854.   *100150*
Le Monde de l'Art Tribal, 29 Rue Saint-Amand, 75015 Paris. T. 0148425776.   *100151*
Musée Ingres: Bulletin, Société des Amis du Musée d'Ingres, 7 Rue Emile-Pouvillon, 82000 Montauban.   *100152*
Musée National d'Art Moderne: Cahiers, Editions du Centre Georges-Pompidou, 75191 Paris Cedex 04.
Fax 0142772949.   *100153*
Musées et Collections Publiques de France, Editions Person, Palais du Louvre, Pavillon Mollien, 75001 Paris. T. 0142603926.   *100154*
Musées et Monuments Lyonnais: Bulletin, 20 Pl des Terreaux, 69001 Lyon. T. 0478280766, Fax 0478281245.   *100155*
Ninety, 33 Rue de la Brèche-aux-Loups, 75012 Paris.
T. 0143408082.   *100156*
Nouvelles de l'Estampe, 58 Rue de Richelieu, 75084 Paris Cedex 02. T. 0147038388.   *100157*
Officiel des Galeries, 15 Rue du Temple, 75014 Paris.   *100158*
Peinture – Cahiers Théoriques, Edition Louis Cane, 37 Rue d'Enghien, 75010 Paris.   *100159*
La Recherche Photographique, 35 Rue La Boëtie, 75008 Paris. T. 0144359336.   *100160*
Revue de l'Art, C.N.R.S. Editions, 20-22 Rue Saint-Armamd, 75015 Paris. T. 0145331010, Fax 0145339213.   *100161*

Revue de la Céramique et du Verre, 61 Rue Marconi, 62880 Vendin-le-Vieil. T. 0321794444, Fax 0321794445.   *100162*
Revue du Louvre, 60ter Rue de Lille, 75007 Paris.
T. 0142223936.   *100163*
Revue Noire, 8 Rue Cels, 75014 Paris. T. 0143202814, Fax 0143229260.   *100164*
Science et Technologie de la Conservation et de la Restoration des Œuvres d'Art et du Patrimoine, E.R.E.C., 68 Rue Jean-Jaurès, 92800 Puteaux. T. 0547730123, Fax 0549000591.   *100165*
Son!, 63 Av des Champs-Elysées, 75008 Paris. *100166*
Techne, 6 Rue des Pyramides, 75041 Paris.
T. 0140205654, Fax 0147033246.   *100167*
Trouvailles, 1-3 Rue du Départ, 75014 Paris.   *100168*
Zodiaque, Abbaye de la Pierre Qui Vire, 89630 Saint-Leger-Vauban. T. 0386322123, Fax 0386322233.   *100169*

Germany

Aachener Kunstblätter, c/o Verlag DuMont, Mittelstr. 12-14, 50672 Köln. T. (0221) 20530.   *100170*
Acta Praehistorica et Archaeologica, c/o Museum für Vor- und Frühgeschichte, Spandauer Damm 19, 14059 Berlin. T. (030) 32091233, Fax 3226422.   *100171*
AK-Express, Postfach 11606, 45001 Essen.   *100172*
AKK – Architektur-, Kunst- und Kulturgeschichte in Nord- und Westdeutschland, c/o Tosch Verlag, Hindenburgpl. 26, 48143 Münster. T. (0251) 54163, Fax (0251) 55428.   *100173*
Alte und Neue Kunst, c/o Verein für christl. Kunst, Dompl. 3, 33098 Paderborn. T. (05251) 125216, Fax (05251) 207470.   *100174*
Antike Welt, c/o Verlag Philipp von Zabern, Phlipp von Zabern-Pl 1-3, 55116 Mainz. T. (06131) 2874719, Fax 223710.   *100175*
Antiquitäten Zeitung, c/o Antiquitäten-Zeitung Verlag, Nymphenburger Str 84, 80636 München.
T. (089) 1269900, Fax 12699048.   *100176*
Architectura, Nymphenburger Str 84, 80636 München.
T. (089) 12151650, Fax 12151610.   *100177*
Der Architekt, Ippendorfer Allee 14b, 53127 Bonn.
T. (0228) 285011, Fax 285465.   *100178*
Archiv Frankfurter Künstler, c/o Dr. Reinhold Schmitt-Thomas, Gottfried-Keller-Str 23, 60431 Frankfurt am Main.   *100179*
Der Archivar, Schloss Kalkum, Oberdorfstr 10, 40489 Düsseldorf. T. (0211) 940750, Fax 9407599.   *100180*
Art, Am Baumwall 11, 20459 Hamburg.
T. (040) 37032562, Fax 37035618.   *100181*
Artei-Kunstbrief, Postfach 450116, 80901 München.
T. (089) 3138192, Fax 3149674.   *100182*
artist Kunstmagazin, Außer der Schleifmühle 51, 28203 Bremen. T. (0421) 3398491, Fax 3398492.   *100183*
artist window, Außer der Schleifmühle 51, 28203 Bremen. T. (0421) 3398472, Fax 3398492.   *100184*
Artium Art Collection, Köhlerweg 16, 41440 Oberursel.
T. (06171) 52508, Fax (06171) 56812.   *100185*
Atelier, c/o Atelier Verlag, Industriestr 170, 50999 Köln.
T. (0221) 410177, Fax 410177.   *100186*
Aus dem Antiquariat, Großer Hirschgraben 17-21, 60311 Frankfurt am Main. T. (069) 13060/353, Fax 13060/394.   *100187*
Ausgrabungen in Berlin, c/o Archäolog. Landesamt Berlin, Schloß Charlottenburg, 14059 Berlin.
T. (030) 32091231, Fax (030) 3221504.   *100188*
Bateria – Zeitschrift für Kunst und Literatur, Hardenbergstr 31, 90768 Fürth. T. (0911) 7234752.   *100189*
Belser Kunst Katalog, c/o Verlag Chr. Belser, Pfizerstr 5-7, 70184 Stuttgart. T. (0711) 2191410, Fax 2191413.   *100190*
Belser Kunst Quartal, c/o Verlag Chr. Belser, Pfizerstr 5-7, 70184 Stuttgart. T. (0711) 2191410, Fax 2191413.   *100191*
Blätter für Grafik und Literatur, Weberbach, 54290 Trier.
T. (0651) 42505, Fax (0651) 300699.   *100192*
Burgen und Schlösser, c/o Deutsche Burgenvereinigung, Marksburg, 56338 Braubach. T. (02627) 536, Fax (02627) 8866.   *100193*

Byzantinische Zeitschrift, c/o B.G. Teubner Verlag, Industriestr 15, 70565 Stuttgart. T. (0711) 789010, Fax 7890110.   *100194*
Daidalos, Schlüterstr 42, 10707 Berlin.
T. (030) 88410634/35, Fax 8832538.   *100195*
Design Report, Mitteilungen über den Stand der Dinge, Ludwig-Erhard-Anlage 1, 60327 Frankfurt am Main.
T. (069) 747919, Fax (069) 7410911.   *100198*
Deutsche Kunst und Denkmalpflege, Nymphenburger Str 84, 80636 München. Fax (089) 12151610.   *100199*
Eins und ... Zeitschrift für Kunst und Gestaltung, Bebelstr 121, 70193 Stuttgart. T. (0711) 654844, Fax 812710.   *100200*
Ethnographisch-Archäologische Zeitschrift, Friedenstr 3, 10249 Berlin. T. (030) 4265162, Fax (030) 4261153.   *100201*
Ethnologica, c/o Gesellschaft zur Förderung des Rautenstrauch-Joest-Museums, Ubierring 45, 50678 Köln.
T. (0221) 33694018, Fax 3369410.   *100202*
European Photography, Postfach 3043, 37020 Göttingen. T. (0551) 24820, Fax 25224.   *100203*
Form, Ernsthöfer Str 12, 64342 Seeheim-Jugenheim.
T. (06257) 81395.   *100204*
Graphische Kunst, c/o Edition Curt Visel, Weberstr 36, 87700 Memmingen. T. (08331) 2853, Fax 490364.   *100205*
Hamburger Beiträge zur Numismatik, Holstenwall 24, 20355 Hamburg. T. (040) 35042360, Fax (040) 34973103.   *100206*
Haus der Geschichte – Magazin, c/o Medienhaus Bonn, Europäische Medienagentur, Oststr 6, 53173 Bonn.
T. (0228) 9561140, Fax 9561141.   *100207*
Hermeneia – Zeitschrift für Ostkirchliche Kunst, Grüner Weg 40 a, 44791 Bochum. T. (0234) 501932, Fax 503576.   *100208*
Die Horen, Bgm.-Smidt-Str 74-76, 27568 Bremerhaven.
T. (0471) 945440, Fax 9454477.   *100209*
Illustration 63, c/o Edition Curt Visel, Weberstr 36, 87700 Memmingen. T. (08331) 2853, Fax 490364.   *100210*
Informationsdienst Kunst, Margaretenstr 8, 93047 Regensburg. T. (0941) 22177, Fax 270377.   *100211*
Insider's Guide, Sigmaringer Str 242, 70597 Stuttgart.   *100212*
International Journal of Cultural Property, c/o Verlag Walter de Gruyter & Co., Postfach 303421, 10728 Berlin. T. (030) 260050, Fax 26005222.   *100213*
Junge Kunst, c/o vgr Verlagsgesellschaft Ritterbach, Rudolf-Diesel-Str 5-7, 50226 Frechen. T. (02234) 18660, Fax 186690.   *100214*
Keramik-Magazin, c/o vgr Verlagsgesellschaft Ritterbach, Rudolf-Diesel-Str 5-7, 50226 Frechen.
T. (02234) 18660, Fax 186690.   *100216*
Keramos, Körnerstr 21, 63067 Offenbach.
T. (069) 880869, Fax 824667.   *100217*
Kinky Beaux Arts, Eisenbahnstr 58, 70372 Stuttgart.   *100218*
Kölner Museums-Bulletin, Schaevenstr 1b, 50676 Köln.
T. (0221) 2214076, 2213467, Fax 2214544.   *100219*
Kölner Museumszeitung, c/o Heinen Verlag, Richartzstr 2-4, 50667 Köln. Fax (0221) 2214544.   *100220*
Kritische Berichte, c/o Jonas Verlag, Weidenhäuser Str 88, 35037 Marburg. T. (06421) 25132.   *100221*
Der Künstler, Postfach 429, 76483 Baden-Baden.
T. (07221) 53065, 61985, Fax (07221) 53062, 17965.   *100221a*
KULIMU, Zeitschrift für Kunst & Literatur & Musik, Pielmühler Str 6, 93138 Lappersdorf. T. (0941) 897381, Fax 894918.   *100222*
kultur politik, Weberstr 61, 53113 Bonn.
T. (0228) 216107, Fax 216105.   *100223*
Kunst + Unterricht, c/o Friedrich Verlag, Im Brande 17, 30926 Seelze. T. (0511) 40004-0, Fax (0511) 40004-19.   *100225*
KUNST-aktuell, c/o afv-Verlag, Postfach 820119, 90252 Nürnberg. T. (0911) 612219, Fax 652046.   *100226*
Kunst Bulletin, Schöne Aussicht 7, 65193 Wiesbaden.
T. (0611) 525391, Fax (0611) 524870.   *100227*
Kunst Kurier, Kapellstr 24, 40479 Düsseldorf.
T. (0211) 4921324.   *100228*
Kunst und Kirche, Spreestr 9, 64295 Darmstadt.
T. (06151) 33557, Fax (06151) 313089.   *100229*

Walter de Gruyter
Berlin • New York

International Journal of Cultural Property

Published for the International Cultural Property Society

Editor-in-Chief: Professor Patty Gerstenblith (USA).

Editorial Board: Professor John Henry Merryman (USA), Chairman of the International Cultural Property Society; Dr. Claude Daniel Ardouin (Senegal); Professor Sabino Cassese (Italy); Professor Clemency Coggins (USA); Richard Crewdson (England); Professor Patty Gerstenblith (USA); Professor Vassos Karageorghis (Cyprus); Dr. Patrick O'Keefe (Australia); Professor Pierre Lalive (Switzerland); Professor David Lowenthal (England); Professor Lyndel Prott (Australia); Professor Dr. Kurt Siehr (Germany/Switzerland); Daniel Shapiro (USA); Stephan Urice (USA); Thomas Weyland (Netherlands).

Two issues per volume. 24 x 17 cm. Approx. 400 pages per volume. ISSN 0940-7391.
Volume 6 (2 issues). 1997. (Approx. 400 pages.)
Subscription rate: DM 250.00/US $ 170.00 per volume, single issue price: DM 150.00/ US $ 93.00 plus postage.
Volumes 1 (1992) to 5 (1996) are also available.

The *International Journal of Cultural Property* is a unique multidisciplinary periodical which addresses the concerns of people in all fields of learning and professional activity that touch on cultural property: anthropologists, archaeologists, art historians, auctioneers, collectors, conservators, cultural historians, curators, dealers, economists, gov-ernment officials, international organizations, lawyers and judges, museum directors, museum trustees, foundation staff and trustees.

The Journal was founded in the belief that questions of cultural property policy, ethics, economics, and law are in urgent need of continuing scholarly attention. The editors intend that the Journal will be the leading international forum for discussion among all who are interested in cultural property matters. All are welcome within its pages and will profit from subscribing.

Cultural property can generate disputes in many forms: problems of contested attribution and of the ethics of the art historian; the legitimacy of treating human remains as a species of cultural property or archaeological material; the perennial clashes between conservation and development, or between professional and commercial archaeology; even the meaning of truth in art.

The members of the Editorial Board represent a diversity of interests within the fields of art and antiquity such as history, anthropology, archaeology, museum administration, and law. The Board is drawn from a wide variety of nations, reflecting the international aims and character of the Journal.

The Editor-in-Chief is backed by a team of expert assistant editors, national and international correspondents who are responsible for covering such subjects as legislation, case law, treaties and EC matters, official documents, book reviews and bibliography. The Journal is further supported by a network of international correspondents based in most of the major jurisdictions, whose task is to inform about events of interest and provide periodic surveys of developments within their region.

Prices are subject to change

Please visit us in the World Wide Web at http://www.deGruyter.de
Walter de Gruyter & Co., P.O. Box 30 34 21, D - 10728 Berlin

Kunst zur Zeit, Dianastr 13, 40223 Düsseldorf.
T. (0211) 309710, Fax (0211) 309710.   *100230*
Der Kunstblitz, c/o Edition Helga Wicher, Krutscheider
Weg 82, 42327 Wuppertal. T. (0202) 736554, 738217,
Fax 738440.   *100231*
Kunstchronik, c/o Verlag Hans Carl, Andernacher Str
33a, 90411 Nürnberg. T. (0911) 95285-0,
Fax 9528547.   *100232*
Kunstforum, Nidegger Str 21, 50937 Köln.   *100233*
Kunsthandel, Im Weiher 10, 69121 Heidelberg.
T. (06221) 489293, Fax 489481.   *100234*
Kunsthandwerk & Design, c/o vgr Verlagsgesellschaft
Ritterbach, Rudolf-Diesel-Str 5-7, 50226 Frechen.
T. (02234) 18660, Fax 186690.   *100235*
Kunstmagazin, 38226 Salzgitter.
T. (05341) 394233.   *100236*
Kunstmarkt, Winterstr 1, 90431 Nürnberg.
T. (0911) 612219, Fax (0911) 652046.   *100237*
Kunstzeitung, c/o Lindinger & Schmid, Margaretenstr 8,
93047 Regensburg. T. (0941) 22177,
Fax 270377.   *100238*
Münchner Jahrbuch der Bildenden Kunst, Mandlstr 26,
80802 München.   *100239*
Das Münster, c/o Verlag Schnell & Steiner, Leibnizstr 13,
93055 Regensburg. T. (0941) 7878516,
Fax 7878516.   *100240*
Der Münzen- und Medaillensammler, Günterstalstr 16,
79100 Freiburg. T. (0761) 73913.   *100240a*
Museums-Journal, c/o Museumspädagogischer Dienst
Berlin, Chausseestr 123, 10115 Berlin.
T. (030) 283973, Fax 2826183.   *100241*
Museumskunde, c/o Rheinland-Verlag, Postfach 2140,
50250 Pulheim.   *100242*
neue bildende kunst, Christburger Str 11, 10405 Berlin.
T. (030) 4413177, Fax 4413176.   *100243*
Neues Glas / New Glass, c/o vgr Verlagsgesellschaft Rit-
terbach, Rudolf-Diesel-Str 5-7, 50226 Frechen.
T. (02234) 18660, Fax 186690.   *100244*
Neues Rheinland, c/o Rhein-Eifel-Mosel-Verlag, Abtei
Brauweiler, 50250 Pulheim. T. (02234) 8051,
Fax (02234) 82503.   *100245*
The New Blind Man, c/o Hans-Werner Kalkmann,
Kirchstr 25, 31162 Bad Salzdetfurth. T. (05060) 2649,
Fax 2575.   *100246*
Niederdeutsche Beiträge zur Kunstgeschichte, Nym-
phenburger Str 84, 80636 München. T. (089) 121516-
0, Fax (089) 121516-10.   *100247*
Nike, Leopoldstr 62, 80802 München. T. (089) 339381,
397708, 340013, 340072.   *100248*
Nostalgie-Revue, Goebenstr 22a, 32052 Herford.
T. (05221) 58669.   *100249*
Numismatisches Nachrichtenblatt, Hans-Purrmann-Allee
26, 67346 Speyer. T. (06232) 92458,
Fax 98989.   *100250*
Passage, Greifenhagenerstr 49, 10437 Berlin.
T. (030) 4459709.   *100251*
Philobiblon, c/o Dr. Ernst Hauswedell & Co., Postfach
140155, 70071 Stuttgart. T. (0711) 638264/65,
Fax 6369010.   *100252*
Plakatjournal, c/o Verlag Plakat-Konzepte, Oskar-Win-
ter-Str 3, 30161 Hannover. T. (0511) 628376,
Fax (0511) 628377.   *100253*
Portraits, Im Silbertal 4a, 56203 Höhr-
Grenzhausen.   *100254*
Projekt, 38685 Langelsheim.   *100255*
Puppen & Spielzeug, c/o Verlag Gert Wohlfarth, Strese-
mannstr 20-22, 47051 Duisburg. T. (0203) 305270,
Fax 337765.   *100256*
Restauro, c/o Verlag G.D.W. Callwey, Streitfeldstr 35,
81673 München. T. (089) 4360050,
Fax 43600513.   *100257*
Rogue, Burgstr 5, 60316 Frankfurt am Main.
T. (069) 445550, Fax (069) 4909427.   *100258*
Sammler Journal, Schmollerstr 31, 74523 Schwäbisch
Hall. T. (0791) 404500, Fax 404111.   *100259*
Signatur, c/o Verlag Rommerkirchen, Rolandshof, 53424
Rolandseck. T. (02228) 931144,
Fax (02228) 931149.   *100260*
Speculum Orbis, c/o Verlag Dietrich Pfaehler, Berliner
Str 37, 97616 Bad Neustadt an der Saale.   *100262*
Stein, Postfach 1170, 82411 Murnau.
T. (08841) 612020, Fax 612030.   *100263*

Textilforum, Friedenstr 5, 30175 Hannover.
T. (0511) 817006, Fax 813108.   *100264*
Textilkunst, Kalandstr 4, 31061 Alfeld.
T. (05181) 800914, Fax 800933.   *100265*
Trödler & Sammeln, Postfach, 85291 Reichertshausen.
T. (08441) 40220, Fax 71846.   *100266*
Volksfoto, Schaperstr 19, 10719 Berlin.   *100267*
Weltkunst, c/o Weltkunst Verlag GmbH, Nymphenburger
Str 84, 80636 München. T. (089) 1269900,
Fax 12699011.   *100268*
Wolfenbütteler Barock-Nachrichten, c/o Herzog August
Bibliothek, Postfach 1364, 38299 Wolfenbüttel.
T. (05331) 8080, Fax 808266.   *100269*
Wolfenbütteler Renaissance Mitteilungen, c/o Herzog
August Bibliothek, Postfach 1364, 38299 Wolfenbüttel.
T. (05331) 8080, 808210, Fax 808266.   *100270*
Zeitschrift für Kunstgeschichte, Dompl 23, 48143 Mün-
ster. T. (0251) 834171, Fax 834538.   *100271*
Zeitschrift für Kunsttechnologie und Konservierung,
Liebfrauenring 17-19, 67547 Worms.
T. (06241) 43574.   *100272*
2029 Magazin, Poolstr 7, 20355 Hamburg.   *100273*

Greece

Architecture in Greece, 5 Kleomenous St, 106 75 Athi-
nai. T. (01) 7213916, 7225930.   *100274*
Bibliofilia, 23 Hippocrates St, 106 79 Athina.   *100275*
Design + Art in Greece, 5 Kleomenous St, 106 75 Athi-
nai. T. (01) 7213916, 7225930.   *100276*
SIMA, 16 Od Lykavittou, 106 73 Athina.
T. (01) 3629822.   *100277*

Hong Kong

Arts of Asia, Suite 1309 Kowloon Centre 29-39 Ashley
Road, Kowloon, Hong Kong. T. 3-692228.   *100278*
HAN MO, A Magazine of Chinese Brush Art, 2-4 Hysan
St., Rm.208-210, Causeway Bay, Hong Kong.   *100279*
Orientations, 200 Lockhart Rd., Hong Kong. T. 5-
8921368.   *100280*

Hungary

Acta Historiae Artium/Academiae Scientiarium Hungari-
cae, Alkotmany utca 21, 1363 Budapest.
T. (01) 111063, 176149.   *100281*
Antik Tanulmanyok, Alkotmany utca 21, 1363 Budapest.
T. (01) 111010, 176149.   *100282*
AZ Erem, Nepköztarsasag u. 77, 1062 Budapest.
T. (01) 411007.   *100283*
Fotomüveszet, Lenin körut 9-11, 1073
Budapest.   *100284*
Müveszet, Agancs u. 26-28, 1126 Budapest.
T. (01) 75 77 64.   *100285*
Müveszettörteneti Ertesitö, Alkotmany utca 21, 1363
Budapest V. T. (01) 111010, 176149.   *100286*

India

Folklore, 3 British Indian St., Calcutta 700069.   *100287*
Human Events, 3 British Indian St., Calcutta.   *100288*
Indian Ceramics, 7 Sourin Roy Rd., Calcutta.   *100289*
Roopa-Lekha, Rafi Marg 1, New Delhi.   *100290*
Sangeet Natak, Rabindra Bhawan, New Delhi,
110001.   *100291*

Iran

Banstan-Chenassi va Honare-Iran, Av. du Professeur Ro-
lin, Teheran. T. (021) 303708.   *100292*
Hafte Honar, no 2 du Ministère de la Culture et des Arts,
Téhéran.   *100293*
Honar va Memari, 256 Chah Reza Ave., Teheran B.P.
1418. T. (021) 41417.   *100294*

Iraq

Sumer, Mathaf Sq., Baghdad. T. (01) 36121.   *100295*

Ireland

Crane Bag, Trinity College, Dublin.   *100296*
Introspect, 23 Annesley Park, Dublin 6.   *100297*

Israel

Painting and Sculpture, 9 Alharizi St, Tel Aviv.   *100298*

Italy

Aegyptus – Rivista Italiana di Egittologia e Papirologia,
Largo A Gemelli 1, 20123 Milano. T. (02) 8856323,
88561.   *100299*
A.E.I.U.O., Piazza del Grillo 10, 00184 Roma.
T. (06) 6798006.   *100300*
Anima, via Port'Alba 30, 80134 Napoli.   *100301*
Annali, Palazzo Barberini, via Fontane 13, 00186 Roma.
T. (06) 4743603.   *100302*
Annuario della Pittura Italiana, piazzale Giulio Cesare
12, 20145 Milano.   *100303*
Annuario della Scultura Italiana, 1965, piazzale Giulio
Cesare 12, 20145 Milano.   *100304*
Anoir, Eblanc, Irouge, Uvert, Obleu, Piazza del Grillo 10,
00184 Roma. T. (01) 6798006.   *100305*
Antiqua, Arco de' Banchi 8, 00186 Roma.   *100306*
Archeo Club, Arco de' Banchi 8, 00186 Roma.
T. (06) 655838.   *100307*
Archeologia Classica, Via Cassiodoro 19, 00193
Roma.   *100308*
Armi Antiche, Via Pietro Micca 17, 10121 Torino.
T. (011) 543590.   *100309*
Arte, Via Cadore 19, 20135 Milano. T. (02) 5456421,
Fax (02) 5469150.   *100310*
Arte Argomenti, Piazza G Tavani Arquati 103, 00153 Ro-
ma. T. (06) 6884004.   *100311*
Arte Contemporanea, Via di Pallacorda 7, 00186
Roma.   *100312*
Arte Cristiana, via S. Gimignano 19, 20146
Milano.   *100313*
Arte Illustrata, Via Cosseria 6, 10131 Torino.
T. (011) 6692226, Fax (011) 3121761.   *100314*
Arte in Friuli-Arte a Trieste, Via Treppo 1, 33100
Udine.   *100315*
Arte Italia Illustrata, Via Gigliarelli 6, 06100
Perugia.   *100316*
Arte Lombarda, Via Vitruvio 39, 20124 Milano.
T. (02) 2846903.   *100317*
Arte Nuova Oggi, corso G. Matteotti 11, 60035
Iesi.   *100318*
Arte Roma, Piazza S Francesca Romana 1, 20129
Milano.   *100319*
Arte Veneta, San Marco 1991, 30124 Venezia.   *100320*
Artforum, Villa Paran Cadessino 11, 28050 Oggebbio.
T. 48468.   *100321*
Athenaeum, Università, 27100 Pavia.   *100322*
Bollettino d'Arte, Via di S Michele 22, 00153 Roma.
T. (06) 5819353.   *100323*
Capitolium, via Scala dell'Arce Capitolina 7, 00186
Roma.   *100324*
Cenacolo, via Madama Cristina 90, 10126
Torino.   *100325*
Città Eterna, Via Brunacci 15, 00146 Roma.
T. (06) 5576604.   *100326*
Comanducci, Via Chiossetto 18, 20122 Milano.
T. (02) 780630, 781141.   *100327*
Comed, Via Visconti di Modrone 8/6, 20122 Milano.
T. (02) 791402.   *100328*
Contemporanea, San Marco 4255, 30124
Venezia.   *100329*
Corpus Nummorum Romanorum, Piazza Stazione,
50123 Firenze. T. (055) 215831.   *100330*
Cutla Bononia, Via Badini 12 Quarto Interiore, 40127 Bo-
logna. T. (051) 767003.   *100331*
D'Ars, Via S Agnese 3, 20123 Milano.
T. (02) 860290.   *100332*

ART DIARY INTERNET: http://www.art-diary.com

WOULDN'T YOU LIKE TO BE IN ART DIARY INTERNET ?

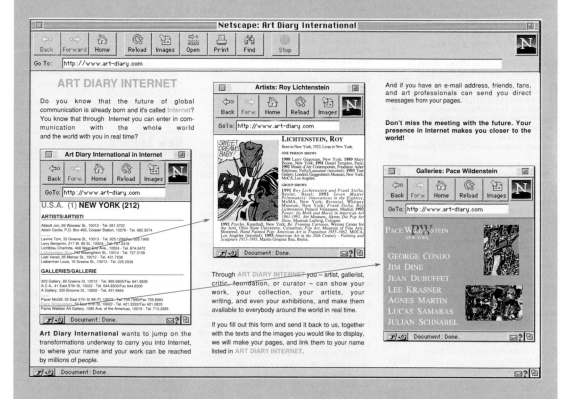

For more information:

E-mail: artdiary@internetforce.com
Phone: +39 (2) 688 7341
Fax: +39 (2) 6680 1290
Address: Giancarlo Politi Editore
68, Via Carlo Farini
20159 Milan ITALY

Domus, Via Manzoni 37, 20121 Milano.
T. (02) 638227. *100333*

East and West, Via Merulana 248, 00185 Roma.
T. (06) 732741. *100334*

En Plein Air, via Milano, 23032 Bormio.
T. (0342) 91666. *100335*

Etra Arte, Via Tito Angelini, 80129 Napoli.
T. (081) 368175. *100336*

Faenza, via Campidori 2, 48018 Faenza.
T. (0546) 21240. *100337*

Flash Art, Via Carlo Farini 68, 20159 Milano.
T. (02) 6686150, 6687341, Fax 66801290. *100337a*

FMR, Via Montecuccoli 30-32, 20122 Milano.
T. (02) 4151846, Fax (02) 656372. *100338*

G 7, Via Val d'Aposa 7 /c, 40123 Bologna.
T. (051) 266497. *100339*

Gala International, Via Turati 3, 20121 Milano.
T. (02) 639768. *100340*

Gazzetta Antiquaria, Lung Soderini 5, 50124 Firenze.
T. (055) 282635. *100341*

Gazzetta del Bibliofilo, Via Cino del Duca 8, 20122
Milano. *100342*

Histonium, via Catanzaro 9, 00161 Roma. *100343*

Humor Graphic, via Arzaga 28, 20146 Milano. *100344*

il Bolaffio, 22016 Lenno. T. 55146. *100345*

Il Cigno, via Stefano Jacini 4, 20121 Milano.
T. (02) 871622. *100346*

Il Diaframma-Kodak Cultura, Via degli Imbriani 15,
20158 Milano. T. (02) 3760535,
Fax (02) 375626. *100347*

Il Giornale dell'Arte, Via Mancini 8, 10131 Torino. *100348*

Il Giornale delle Aste, Via Felice Romani 8, 10131 Torino.
T. (011) 81244-73/6, Fax (011) 81244-79. *100349*

Il Mercato dell' Arte e News, Via Roma 102, 35020 Brugine. T. 580 60 48. *100350*

Il Noncello, Via della Ferriera 12, 33170 Pordenone.
T. 220 30. *100351*

Il Notiziario, Palazzo del Teatro Comunale piazza del Giglio, 55100 Lucca. *100352*

L'Erma, via Cassiodoro 19, 00193 Roma.
T. (06) 6874127, 388500, Fax (06) 6874129. *100353*

L'Organo, Via Badini 12, 40127 Bologna.
T. (051) 767003. *100354*

La Filanda, c/o Centro Culturale la Filanda, via N. Sauro,
19, 20050 Verano Brianza, Mil. T. (02) 37326. *100355*

La Numismatica, Via Ferramola 1a, 25121 Brescia.
T. (030) 56211. *100356*

La Permanente, via Filippo Turati 34, 20121
Milano. *100357*

La Voce Degli Idit, via delle Vigne Nuove 250, 00139 Roma. T. (06) 8871341. *100358*

Lo Spazio, Via Roma 82, 04022 Fondi.
T. 501053. *100359*

Medaglia, Via Terraggio 15, 20123 Milano.
T. (02) 8059623. *100360*

Mela, Via Marsala 4, 50137 Firenze.
T. (055) 679378. *100361*

Museo Teo, Viale Padova 133, 20127 Milano.
T. (02) 2824652. *100362*

NEXT, Via San Francesco a Ripa 18, 00153 Roma.
T. (06) 5899285, Fax (06) 5880607. *100363*

Novità Bibliografiche, Via Crescenzio 43, 00193 Roma.
T. (06) 659361. *100364*

Nuova Rassegna, Periodico Pellegrini via Parisio 4,
87100 Cosenza Cas. Post. 158. T. (0984) 25245,
25066. *100365*

Nuovi Orrizonti, Via Verdi 34, 80055 Portici. *100366*

Old Gallery, Via Castel Maraldo 19, 41100 Modena.
T. (059) 214161. *100367*

OP. CIT, Via V Padula 2, 80123 Napoli.
T. (081) 7690783. *100368*

Opening, Piazzale di Ponte Milvio 14, 00191 Roma.
T. (06) 3331776. *100369*

Orientalia, via della Pilotta 25, 00187 Roma.
T. (06) 6796453. *100370*

Pact Education, Centro Universitario, 84010 Ravello.
T. 857669, Fax 857711. *100371*

Pact News, Centro Universitario, 84010 Ravello.
T. 857669, Fax 857711. *100372*

Parametro, Via P De Crescenzi 44, 48018 Faenza.
T. (0546) 663488. *100373*

Prospettive d'Arte, Via Carlo Torre 29, 20143 Milano.
T. (02) 89408327, Fax (02) 89408329. *100374*

Prova d'Autore, Via Caposile 2, 00195 Roma.
T. (06) 3605302. *100375*

Qui Arte Contemporanea, Via di Pallacorda 7, 00186 Roma. T. (06) 6541592, 6569537. *100376*

Rivista di Psicologia dell'Arte, Via dei Pianellari 20,
00186 Roma. *100377*

Rivista Italiana di Numismatica, via Orti 3, 20122
Milano. *100378*

Rivista Pensiero ed Arte, via Calefati 379, 70123 Bari.
T. 21 02 59. *100379*

Saggi e Memorie di Storia dell'Arte, Isola di San Giorgio
Maggiore, 30124 Venezia. T. (041) 5289900. *100380*

Scultura, Via S Spirito, 10, 20121 Milano. *100381*

Segno, Via Modesto della Porta 35, 65100 Pescara.
T. (085) 61712. *100382*

Storia dell'Arte, Via E Codignola, 50018 Scandicci (Fi).
T. (055) 75901. *100383*

T, Via Carlo Farini 68, 20159 Milano. T. (02) 6887341,
Fax (02) 68801290. *100384*

Tema Celeste, Via Augusta 17, 96100 Siracusa.
T. 757219. *100385*

Terzo Occhio, Via Jacopo di Paolo, 40128 Bologna.
T. (051) 356133. *100386*

Verso il Duemila, via L Guercino 136, 84100
Salerno. *100387*

VIP Gran Premio, Via Brunacci 15, 00146 Roma.
T. (06) 5577188. *100388*

Japan

Asahi Graph Bessatsu, 5-3-2 Tsukiji, Chuo-ku, Tokyo
104-11. T. (03) 3545-0131, Fax (03) 3545-
0311. *100389*

Bijutsu, 1-3-9 Ginza, Chuo-ku, Tokyo 104. T. (03) 3562-
1021, Fax (03) 3562-4312. *100390*

Bijutsu Techo, Inaoka Bldg., 2-36, Kanda, Jinbo-cho,
Chiyoda-ku, Tokyo. T. (03) 3234 2151. *100391*

Geijutsu Shincho, 71 Yarai-cho, Shinjuku-ku, Tokyo 162.
T. (03) 3266-5101, Fax (03) 3266-5234. *100392*

IDEA, 1-5 Kanda Nishiki-cho, Chiyoda-ku, Tokyo 101.
T. (03) 3292-1211, Fax (03) 3291-3170. *100393*

KOKKA, 5-3-2 Tsukiji, Chuo-ku, Tokyo 104-11. *100394*

MIZUE, c/o Bijutsu Shuppan-sha Co. Ltd., 2-36, Kanda,
Jinbo-cho, Chiyoda-ku, Tokyo. T. 03 3234-
2151. *100395*

Museum, Suido I-chome, 2 6 Bunkyo-ku, Tokyo
112. *100396*

Portfolio, 1-5 Kanda Nishiki-cho, Chiyoda-ku, Tokyo
101. T. (03) 3292-1211, Fax (03) 3291-3170. *100397*

Science of Performing Arts, 13-27 Ueno Parku, Taito-ku,
Tokyo. *100398*

Soshoku Design, 4-40-5 Kamiikedai, Ota-ku, Tokyo 145.
T. (03) 3726-8111, Fax (03) 3726-8862. *100399*

Taiyo, 5 Sanban-cho, Chiyoda-ku, Tokyo 102.
T. (03) 3265 0451, Fax (03) 3265 0477. *100400*

Year-Book of Japanese Art, 13-27, Ueno Park, Taito-ku,
Tokyo 110. T. (03) 3823 2241. *100401*

Luxembourg

Artium Art Center, B.P. 1183, 1011 Luxembourg.
T. (00352)452460, Fax (00352)458346. *100402*

NUMA, 12, Rue Duchscher, Luxembourg.
T. 481765. *100403*

Mexico

Arquitectura Mexico, Calle de Rio Volga 77, México City,
D.F. 5. T. (05) 115428. *100404*

Artes Plasticas, Paseo de la Reforma y Gandhi, Chapultepec, México City, D.F.5. T. (05) 553 8118. *100405*

Cuadernos de Bellas Artes, Instituto Nacional de Bellas
Artes, México City. *100406*

Monaco

International Art Bulletin, Palais de la Scala, 98000
Monte Carlo. T. 93256614. *100407*

Netherlands

Het Blad, B.P. 307, 6800 AH Arnham.
T. (026) 3511300. *100407a*

Bulletin van het Rijksmuseum, B.P. 50673, 1077 DD
Amsterdam. *100408*

CASTRUM PEREGRINI, Herengracht 401, B.P. 645, 1017
BP Amsterdam. *100409*

Home Art, Laanakkerweg 14-16, 4124 PB Vianen.
T. 79210. *100412*

Kunst & Antiekrevue, B.P. 85994, 2508 CR Den Haag.
T. (070) 3648800. *100413*

Kunst- & Museumjournaal, Keizersgracht 609, 1017 DS
Amsterdam. *100414*

Kunstbeeld, Pr Margrietlaan 3, 2400 MA Alphen a/d Rijn.
T. (0172) 466508. *100415*

Mnemosyne, Lindenlaan 8, 3707 ER Zeist. *100416*

De Muntkoerier, Canadalaan 8A, 7316 BX Apeldoorn.
T. (055) 5216629, Fax 5223963. *100416a*

Oud-Holland, Prins Willem-Alexanderhof 5, 2509 LK Den
Haag. *100417*

Palet en Tekenstift, Emmastr 11, 1814 DL
Alkmaar. *100418*

Perspektief, Sint Jobseg 30, 3024 EJ Rotterdam.
T. (010) 4780655, Fax (010) 4772072. *100419*

Simiolus, Kromme Nieuwegracht 29, 3512 HD Utrecht.
T. (030) 2392326, 2717377. *100420*

New Zealand

New Zealand Numismatic Journal, 2 Sylvan Ave., Milford, Auckland. *100421*

Norway

F 15 Kontakt, Jeloy, 1501 Moss. T. (09) 71033. *100422*

Kunst, St. Olavsgt. 13, Oslo. *100423*

Kunst og Kultur, Kolstadgt. 1, 0608 Oslo.
T. (02) 677600. *100424*

Nye Bonytt., Bygdö Allé 9, Oslo. *100425*

Poland

Archeologia Polski, al K. Świerczewskiego 105, 00-140
Warszawa. T. (022) 202881. *100426*

Archiwa Biblioteki i Muzea Kościelne, ul Faraona 6, 20-
635 Lublin. *100427*

Biblioteka Muzealnictwa i Ochrony Zabytków, ul Brzozowa 35, 00-258 Warszawa. T. (022) 311491. *100428*

Biuletyn Historii Sztuki, ul Długa 26/28, 00-950 Warszawa. T. (022) 202881. *100429*

Biuletyn Informacyjny, ul Krakowskie Przedmieście 15/
17, 00-950 Warszawa. I. (022) 260637. *100430*

Bulletin du Musee National de Varsovie, Al. Jerozolims-
kie 3, 00-495 Warszawa. T. (022) 211031. *100431*

Fontes Archaeologici Posnanienses, ul Wodna 27, 61-
781 Poznań. T. (061) 526430. *100432*

Informator Muzeum w Grudziądzu, ul Wodna 3/5, 86-
300 Grudziądz. T. 3139. *100433*

Katalog Zabytkow Sztuki w Polsce, c/o Instytut Sztuki
PAN, ul Długa 26/28, 00-950 Warszawa.
T. (022) 313149, 313271. *100434*

Kwartalnik Architektury i Urbanistyki, ul. Koszykowa 55,
00-659 Warszawa. T. (022) 21007 int. 1547. *100435*

Kwartalnik Historii Kultury Materialnej, ul Świerczewskiego 105, 00-140 Warszawa. T. (022) 202881. *100436*

Materiały Archeologiczne, ul Senacka 3, 31-002 Kraków. T. (012) 315031. *100437*

Materiały Starożytne, ul Długa 52, 00-950 Warszawa.
T. (022) 313221. *100438*

Monografie Muzeum Narodowego w Poznaniu, Al Marcinkowskiego 9, 61-745 Poznań.
T. (061) 528011. *100439*

Konsthistorisk tidskrift

This journal is intended for an audience interested in art historical research, i.e. scholars, university institutions, libraries etc. However, it also has the ambition to reach readers with general cultural interests.

Readers generally expect to find articles on European art in Konsthistorisk Tidskrift, but the journal is also open for studies in non-European art. Since the journal is internationally oriented, it welcomes contributions by foreign scholars.

Most of the articles are in English or Swedish, occasionally also in German and French. With its wide range of topics it can be said to reflect the breadth of art historical research today.

Representative articles in recent issues of Konsthistorisk Tidskrift

Vad berättar Midvinterblot? No. 1, 1995
Per Bjurström, Stockholm, Sweden

Hieronymus Bosch's Venetian St. Jerome. No. 2, 1995
Martha Moffitt Peacock, Provo, USA

Ein wiederentdeckter Hainhoferschrank. No, 3, 1995
Hans-Olof Boström, Hammarö, Sweden

The Idea of "Gesamtkunstwerk" - Lenbachhaus and Stuckvilla in Munich. No. 3, 1995
Udo Kultermann, New York, USA

A "Mithraic Formula" in Renaissance Images of the Christ Child. No. 4, 1995
Avigdor W.G. Posèq, Jerusalem, Israel

About an Unsolved Jacob Jordaens Problem. No. 4, 1995
Minna Heimbürger, Rome, Italy

"Drottning Margaretas gyllene kjortel" - än en gång. No 1, 1996
Arne Danielsson, Vikbolandet, Sweden

❑ **Please enter my subscription to Konsthistorisk Tidskrift, starting with No 1, 1997, ISSN 0023-3609**
Postage included. Air speed delivery worldwide.

❑ Please send me a **free sample copy** of Konsthistorisk Tidskrift.

Subscription rates Vol. 66, 1997:

❑ Institutions: USD 99 (in Scandinavia NOK 545,-)   ❑ Individual: USD 58 (in Scandinavia NOK 315,-)

Please tick one box:
❑ Send invoice ❑ Cheque enclosed   ❑ AmEx   ❑ Diners   ❑ Euro/Mastercard ❑ VISA

Card No.: | | | | | | | | | | | | | | | | | | | Exp.date:_____/_____
Please make the cheque payable to Scandinavian Univeristy Press and staple it to your order form.

Name:_____

Address:_____

_____

Signature:_____

Send to: Scandinavian University Press, Journals Customer Services, P.O.Box 2959 Tøyen, N-0608 Oslo, Norway
Fax: +47 22 57 53 53

SCANDINAVIAN
UNIVERSITY PRESS

Oslo, Stockholm,
Copenhagen, Oxford, Boston

6435 S

Muzealnictwo, ul Brzozowa 35, 00-258 Warszawa.
T. (022) 311491, 313377. *100440*
Ochrona Zabytków, Brzozowa 35, 00-258 Warszawa.
T. (022) 311491, 313377. *100441*
Opolski Rocznik Muzealny, ul Mały Rynek 7, 45-020
Opole. T. (077) 36677. *100442*
Polska Sztuka Ludowa, ul Długa 26/28, 00-950 Warsza-
wa. T. (022) 313271. *100443*
Prace i Materiały Muzeum Archeologicznego i Etnogra-
ficznego w Łodzi, Pl Wolności 14, 91-415 Łódź.
T. (042) 328440. *100444*
Rocznik Białostocki, Rynek Kościuszki, 19-091 Biały-
stok. T. 21440. *100445*
Rocznik Muzeum Narodowego w Kielcach, Pl Partyzan-
tów 3-5, 25-303 Kielce. T. 46764. *100446*
Rocznik Muzeum Narodowego w Warszawie, Al. Jerozo-
limskie 3, 00-495 Warszawa. T. (022) 211031. *100447*
Rocznik Muzeum w Toruniu, Ratusz, 87-100 Toruń.
T. (056) 27038. *100448*
Rocznik Etnografii Śląskiej, Pl. Powstańców Warszawy
5, 50-153 Wrocław. T. (071) 38830. *100449*
Roczniki Sztuki Śląskiej Muzeum Narodowe, Pl Pow-
stańców Warszawy 5, 50-153 Wrocław.
T. (071) 38830. *100450*
Rozprawy i Sprawozdania, ul. Manifestu Lipcowego 12,
30-960 Kraków. T. (012) 228140. *100451*
Silesia Antiqua, ul Kazimierza Wielkiego 34, 50-077
Wrocław. T. (071) 34924. *100452*
Studia i Materiały do Dziejów Dawnego Uzbrojenia, ul
Manifestu Lipcowego 12, 30-960 Kraków.
T. (012) 225434. *100453*
Studia i Materiały do Dziejów Wielkopolski i Pomorza,
Stary Rynek 78/79, 61-772 Poznań.
T. (061) 316341. *100454*
Studia i Materiały Lubelskie, ul Zamkowa 9, 20-117
Lublin. T. (081) 25001. *100455*
Studia Muzealne, Al Marcinkowskiego 9, 61-745 Poz-
nań. T. (061) 522035. *100456*
Sztuka, ul Puławska 61, 02-595 Warszawa.
T. (022) 444031. *100457*
Wiadomości Archeologiczne, ul Długa 52, 00-950 War-
szawa. T. (022) 313221. *100458*
Z Otchłani Wieków, ul. Jezuicka 6, 00-281 Warszawa.
T. (022) 313928. *100459*
Zeszyty Państwowego Muzeum Etnograficznego w War-
szawie, ul Kredytowa 1, 00-056 Warszawa.
T. (022) 277641. *100460*

Portugal

Belas Artes, R. Alegria 117, 4000 Porto.
T. (02) 23696. *100461*

Romania

Arhitectura, Str. Academiei 18-20, 70109 Bucuresti.
T. (01) 139880. *100462*
Arta, Str. C. A. Rosetti 39, 70205 Bucuresti.
T. (01) 6131380. *100463*
Revista Muzeelor, Calea Victoriei 174, 71014 Bucuresti.
T. (01) 650 48 68. *100464*
Revue Roumaine d'Histoire de l'Art-Série Beaux-Arts,
Série Théatre, Musique, Cinéma, Calea Victoriei 196,
71104 Bucuresti. T. (01) 6505 680. *100465*

Slovakia

ARS, Fajnorovo nábrežie 1, 81364 Bratislava.
T. (07) 332302. *100466*
Výtvarný Život, 811 04, Bratislava.
T. (07) 48193. *100467*

South Africa

Samab, c/o South African Museum, Queen Victoria St.,
8000 Cape Town POB 61. T. (021) 243330. *100468*

Spain

Ampurias, Parque de Montjuich, 08004 Barcelona.
T. (03) 2232149, 2235601. *100469*
Archivo Espanol de Arte, Duque de Medinaceli 6, 28014
Madrid. T. (01) 4292017. *100470*
Ceramica, Paseo de las Acacias 9, 28005 Madrid.
T. (91) 5173239. *100471*
Cimal, Av. Republica Argentina 42, 46700 Gandia.
T. (01) 2862589. *100472*
DANES – Directorio de Anticuarios Españoles, Rafael
San Narciso 9, 20018 Madrid. T. (01) 7777015,
Fax (01) 7783312. *100473*
Estudios pro Arte, Lauria 112, 1., 08037 Barcelona 37.
T. (03) 2577805. *100475*
GOYA, Serrano, 122, 28006 Madrid.
T. (01) 5635535. *100476*
De Museus, Portaferrissa 1, 08002 Barcelona.
T. (03) 3021522. *100476a*
ORGON, Coslada 26, 28028 Madrid.
T. (01) 2556792. *100477*

Sweden

ARIS, Kyrkogatan 19, 222 22 Lund.
T. (046) 108396. *100478*
Fornvannen, Box 200, 221 01 Lund. *100479*
Konsthistorisk tidskrift, c/o Scandinavian University
Press, Stockholms Universitet, POB 3255, 103 65
Stockholm. T. (08) 4408047, Fax 4408050. *100480*
Paletten, Karl Gustavsgatan 10c, 411 25 Göteborg.
T. (031) 117873. *100481*
Svenska Museer, Alsnögatan 7, Box 4715, 116 92
Stockholm. T. (08) 435041. *100482*

Switzerland

Anthropos, c/o Editions Saint Paul, 42 Pérolles, 1705
Fribourg. T. (037) 864331, Fax 864330. *100483*
Antike Kunst, c/o Archäologisches Seminar der Universi-
tät, Schönbeinstr 20, 4056 Basel.
T. (061) 2673063. *100484*
Archaeologie der Schweiz, c/o Schweiz. Ges. f. Ur- und
Frühgesch., Petersgraben 9-11, 4001 Basel.
T. (061) 2613078, Fax (061) 2672341. *100485*
Art & Presse Diffusion, L'Adeu 1, 2416 Les Brenets.
T. (032) 9321177, Fax 9321177. *100486*
Artibus Asiae, c/o Museum Rietberg, Gablerstr 15, 8002
Zurich. T. (01) 2024528, Fax 2025201. *100487*
Artis, c/o Hallwag Verlag, Nordring 4, 3001 Bern.
T. (031) 3323131, Fax 3314133. *100488*
Berner Kunstmitteilungen, c/o Kunstmuseum Bern, Hod-
lerstr 8-12, Postfach 3000, 3011 Bern.
T. (031) 3110944, Fax 3117263. *100489*
Bulletin du Centre Genevois d'Anthropologie, c/o Dép.
d'Anthro. et d'Ecologie, 12 Rue Gustave-Revilliod,
1227 Carouge. T. (021) 7026967,
Fax 3000351. *100490*
Collections-Passions, CP 322, 2072 Saint-Blaise.
T. (032) 7531212. *100491*
Du, Baslerstr 30, Postfach, 8048 Zürich.
T. (01) 4046030, Fax (01) 4046040. *100492*
Fotoheft, Schlagbaumstr 6, 8201 Schaffhausen.
T. (052) 6250003. *100493*
Graphis – Graphis Press Corp., c/o B. Martin Pedersen,
Dufourstr 107, 8008 Zürich. T. (01) 3838211,
Fax (01) 3831643. *100494*
Kunst-Bulletin, Zeughausstr 55, Postfach, 8004 Zürich.
T. (01) 2416300, Fax 2416373. *100495*
Kunst und Stein, Effingerstr 3, Postfach 6922, 3001
Bern. T. (031) 3822322, Fax (031) 3822670. *100496*
Librarium, c/o Prof Dr Martin Bircher, Köllikerstr 25,
8044 Zürich. T. (01) 2515995. *100497*
Money Trend, Postfach 146, 9401 Rorschach.
T. (071) 8440402, Fax 8440414. *100498*
Münzen Revue, Blotzheimerstr 40, 4055 Basel.
T. (061) 3825504, Fax 3825542. *100499*
Musées de Genève, Chemin Voil-Creusel 16, 1202 Ge-
nève. T. (022) 7332600. *100500*

Numis-Post, Postfach, 7310 Bad Ragaz.
T. (081) 3022429, Fax 3025984. *100501*
L'Oeil, 5 Ch. du Closel, 1020 Renens. T. (021) 6350427,
Fax (021) 6359646. *100502*
Parkett, c/o Parkett-Verlag, Quellenstr 27, 8005 Zürich.
T. (01) 2718140, Fax (01) 2724301. *100503*
Photoamateur, Promoguide, 3 Rue de la Vigle, 1003
Lausanne. T. (021) 3121552. *100504*
Photographie, Schlagbaumstr 6, 8201 Schaffhausen.
T. (052) 6248891. *100505*
Spektrum, Internationale Vierteljahresschrift für Dich-
tung und Originalgrafik, c/o Sven Knebel, Napfgasse 4,
8001 Zürich. T. (01) 8531474. *100506*
Stehplatz, Postfach 478, 3000 Bern 14.
T. (031) 3820003, Fax 3820465. *100507*
Tribune des Arts, 42 Rue du Stand, 1211 Genève.
T. (022) 3212121. *100508*
Werk, c/o Verlegergemein. Werk, Bauen + Wohnen, Vo-
gelsangstr 48, 8006 Zürich. T. (01) 3629566. *100509*
Zürcher Chronik, Ernst Jäggli, 8405 Winterthur (Zürich).
T. (052) 2322121, Fax 2322126. *100510*

Turkey

Archaeology and Art Magasin, Hayriye Cad. Corlu Apt. 3/
5, 80060 Istanbul. T. (01) 2456838,
Fax (01) 2456877. *100511*

United Kingdom

Ambit, 17 Priory Gardens, London N6 5QY.
T. (0181) 3403566. *100512*
Annual Review, c/o National Art Collections Fund, 20
John Islip St, London SW1P 4JX. T. (0171) 8210404,
Fax (0171) 6387715. *100513*
Antiquaries Journal, c/o Oxford University Press, Pinkill
House, Southfield Rd., Oxford OX8 1JJ.
T. (01865) 882283, Fax (01865) 882890. *100514*
Antique Collecting, 5 Church St, Woodbridge 1P12 1OS.
T. (01394) 385501, Fax (01394) 384434. *100515*
Antique Dealer and Collectors' Guide, P.O.Box 805, Lon-
don SE10 8TD. T. (0181) 3185868,
Fax (0181) 6912489. *100516*
Antique & New Art, 10-11 Lower John St, London W1R
3PE. T. (0171) 4349180, Fax (0171) 2875488. *100517*
Antiques Bulletin, c/o H.P. Publishing, 2 Hampton Court,
Harborne, Birmingham B17 2AE. T. (0121) 4263300,
Fax (0121) 4281214. *100518*
Antiques Trade Gazette, 17 Whitcomb St, London WC2H
7PL. T. (0171) 9304957, Fax (0171) 9306391. *100519*
Antiquity, c/o Oxford University Press, Pinkhill House,
Southfield Rd., Oxford OX8 1JJ. T. (01865) 882283,
Fax (01865) 882890. *100520*
Apollo. The International Magazine of the Arts, 29 Ches-
ham Pl, London SW1X 8HB. T. (0171) 2351998,
Fax (0171) 2351689. *100521*
Architects' Journal, 9 Queen Anne's Gate, London SW1H
9BY. T. (0171) 2224333. *100522*
Architectural Design, 42 Leinster Gardens, London W2
3AN. T. (0171) 4022141, Fax (0171) 7239540. *100523*
Architectural Monographs, 42 Leinster Gardens, London
W2. T. (0171) 4022141. *100524*
Architectural Review, 9 Queen Anne's Gate, London
SW1H 9BY. T. (0171) 2224333. *100525*
ARLIS News-sheet, 18 College Road, Bromsgrove B60
2NE. T. (01527) 579298. *100526*
Arms and Armour Society Journal, c/o Victoria and Al-
bert Museum, Cromwell Rd., London SW7 2RL.
T. (0171) 938850. *100527*
Art and Design, 42 Leinster Gardens, London W2 3AN.
T. (0171) 4022141, Fax (0171) 7239540. *100528*
The Art Book, 133 North End Rd, London NW11 7HT.
T. (0181) 9055900, Fax 9055999. *100529*
Art Business Today, c/o Fine Art Trade Guild, 16-18 Em-
press Pl., London SW6 1TT. T. (0171) 3816616,
Fax (0171) 3812596. *100530*
Art History, 108 Cowley Rd, Oxford OX4 1JF.
T. (01865) 791100. *100531*
Art Libraries Journal, c/o Lancashire Polytechnic Library,
Saint Peter's Sq., Preston PR1 7BB.
T. (01772) 201201 ext. 2323. *100532*

Art Line, Phoenix House, Phoenix St, London WC2.
T. (0171) 4973545, Fax (0171) 3794846. *100534*

Art Monthly, c/o Britannia Art Publications, Charing Cross Rd, London WC2H 0DG. T. (0171) 2400389, Fax (0171) 2405958. *100535*

The Art Quarterly, c/o National Art Collections Fund, 20 John Islip St, London SW1P 4JX. T. (0171) 8210404, Fax (0171) 6307715. *100536*

Art & Architecture, 43 Courtfield Gdns, London SW5OLZ. *100537*

Art & Craft, c/o Scholastic Publications, Villiers House, Clarendon Av., Leamington Spa CV32 5PR. T. 887799, Fax 883331. *100538*

Art Workers Guild Annual Report, 6 Queen Sq, London WC1N 3AR. *100539*

Artery, 19 Lyme St, London NW1 0EH.
T. (0171) 2675803. *100540*

Artist, 63-65 High St, Tenterden TN30 6BD.
T. (015806) 3673, Fax (015806) 5411. *100541*

The Artist's & Illustrator's Magazine, 4 Brandon Road, London N7 9TP. T. (0171) 6092177, Fax (0171) 7004985. *100542*

Artists Newsletter, Sunderland SR4 6DG.
T. (0191) 5673589, Fax (0191) 5641600. *100543*

Artrage, 26 Shacklewell Lane, London E8 2EZ.
T. (0171) 2547295, Fax (0171) 9234465. *100544*

Arts Council of Great Britain Annual Report and Accounts, 14 Great Peter St, London SW1P 3NQ.
T. (0171) 3330100, Fax (0171) 9736590. *100545*

Arts Express, 43 Camden Lock, London NW1 8AF.
T. (0171) 2870972. *100546*

Arts Management Weekly, c/o Rhinegold Publishing, 241 Shaftesbury Avenue, London WC2H 8EH.
T. (0171) 8362384, Fax (0171) 5287991. *100547*

Arts Review, 20 Prescott Pl, London SW4 6BT.
T. (0171) 9781000, Fax (0171) 9781102. *100548*

Arts & The Islamic World, c/o Islamic Arts Foundation, 144-146 King's Cross Road, London WC1X 9DH.
T. (0171) 8338275, Fax (0171) 2784797. *100549*

Artyfacts, c/o Brighton University, Grand Parade, Brighton BN2 2JY. T. (01273) 643187. *100550*

Asian Art, c/o Oxford University Press, Walton St., Oxford OX2 6DP. T. (01865) 56767, Fax (01865) 56646. *100551*

Aspects, 3 Roseworth Terrace, Gosforth, Newcastle-upon-Tyne NE3 1LU. T. (0191) 854914. *100552*

Association of Art Historians Bulletin, c/o Dept. of History of Art and Design, College Rd., Stoke-on-Trent ST4 2DE. *100553*

Association of Independent Museums Bulletin, Park Cottage, West Dean, Chichester PO18 0RX.
T. 63364. *100554*

Audio Arts, 6 Briarwood Rd, London SW4.
T. (0171) 7209129. *100555*

Block, c/o Middlesex Polytechnic, Cat Hill, Cockfoster, East Barnet EN4 8HT. T. (0181) 4405181. *100556*

Blueprint, 26 Cramer St, London W1M 3HE.
T. (0171) 4867419, Fax (0171) 4861451. *100557*

BM Magazine, c/o British Museum Society, Great Russell St., London WC1B 3DG. T. (0171) 6379983. *100558*

The British Journal of Aesthetics, c/o Oxford University Press, Walton St., Oxford OX2 6DP. T. (01865) 56767, Fax (01865) 56646. *100559*

Burlington Magazine, 14-16 Duke's Rd, London WC1H 9AD. T. (0171) 3888157, 3881228, Fax 3881230, 3881229. *100560*

Ceramic Review, 21 Carnaby St, London W1V 1PH.
T. (0171) 4393377, Fax (0171) 2879954. *100561*

Circa Art Magazine, 67 Donegall Pass, Belfast BT7 1DR.
T. (01232) 230375, Fax (01232) 230375. *100562*

City Limits, 115 Shaftesbury Av, London WC2H 8AD.
T. (0171) 3791010, Fax (0171) 3791653. *100563*

Classical Quarterly, c/o Oxford University Press, Pinkhill House, Southfield Rd., Oxford OX8 1JJ.
T. (01865) 882283, Fax (01865) 882890. *100564*

Classical Review, c/o Oxford University Press, Pinkhill House, Southfield Rd., Oxford OX8 1JJ.
T. (01865) 882283, Fax (01865) 882890. *100565*

Connoisseur, 50 Marshall St, London W1V 1LR.
T. (0171) 4395000. *100566*

Contemporary Art, 2 Sydney Pl, Bath BA2 6NF.
T. (01225) 332527, Fax (01225) 332527. *100567*

Control Magazine, 5 London Mews, London W2. *100568*

Counter Culture, POB 1234, London SW7 3PB.
T. (0171) 3733432, Fax (0171) 3733432. *100569*

Country Life, Stamford St, London SE1 9LS.
T. (0171) 2617058, Fax (0171) 2615139. *100570*

The Craftsman Magazine, Lowthorpe, POB 5, Driffield YO25 8JD. T. (01377) 45213, Fax (01377) 45730. *100571*

Creative Camera Magazine, c/o CC Publishing, Business Arts Centre, Lavender Hill, London SW1 1SF.
T. (0171) 9243017. *100572*

Crested Circle, c/o F.Owen, 26 Urswick Rd., Dagenham RM9 6EA. *100573*

CTO, 149 Kathleen Rd, Sholing, Southampton SO2 8LP. *100574*

Cultural Trends, c/o Policy Studies Institute, 100 Park Village East, London NW1 3SR. T. (0171) 3872171, Fax (0171) 3880914. *100575*

Design, 28 Haymarket, London SW1.
T. (0171) 8398000. *100576*

Design Week, 50 Poland St, London W1V 4AX.
T. (0171) 4394222, Fax (0171) 7341770. *100577*

Designers' Journal, 9 Queen Anne's Gate, London SW1H 9BY. T. (0171) 2224333. *100578*

Drawing Paper, 172-174 Brent Crescent, North Circular Rd, London NW10 7XA. *100579*

Eastern Art Report, c/o Centre for Near East, Asia & Africa Research, 172 Castelnau, London SW13 9DH.
T. (0181) 7415878, Fax (0181) 7415671. *100580*

Estetika/Aesthetics, c/o Academic Press, 24-28 Oval Rd., London NW1 7DX. T. (0171) 2674466, Fax (0171) 4822293. *100581*

European Illustration, c/o Polygon Editions, 80 Charlotte St, London W1A 1AQ. *100582*

Exeter Museums News, c/o Royal Albert Memorial Museum, Queen St., Exeter EX4 3RX. T. (01392) 265858, Fax (01392) 421252. *100583*

Feminist Art News, 30-38 Dock St, Leeds LS7 3NE.
T. (0113) 429964. *100584*

Fine Art Trade Guild Journal, 16-18 Empress Pl, London SW6 1TT. T. (0171) 3816616, Fax (0171) 3812596. *100585*

FMR, 16 Royal Arcade, Old Bond St, London W1X 3HB.
T. (0171) 4998363, Fax (0171) 4910662. *100586*

Framework, 40a Topsfield Parade, London N8 8QA.
T. (0181) 348 1977. *100587*

Framing and Art, c/o Framing Publications, 48 Longfield Dr., Amersham HP6 5HE. T. 722696, Fax 432411. *100588*

Framing & Art Buyers World, 3 Colleton Crescent, Exeter EX2 4DG. T. (01392) 79589. *100589*

frieze, c/o Durian Publications, 6 Denmark St, London WC2H 8NE. T. (0171) 3791533, Fax (0171) 3791521. *100590*

Galleries, c/o Barrington Publications, 54 Uxbridge Rd, London W12 8LP. T. (0181) 7407020, Fax (0181) 7407020. *100591*

Graphics World, c/o Datateam Publishing, 21-25 Tovil Hill, Maidstone ME15 6QS. T. (01622) 50882, Fax (01622) 57646. *100592*

Green Book, 49 Park St, Bristol BS1 5NT.
T. (0117) 9290158, Fax (0117) 215431. *100593*

HALI, The International Magazine of Fine Carpets and Textiles, Kingsgate House, Kingsgate Pl, London NW6 4TA. T. (0171) 3289341, Fax (0171) 3725924. *100594*

HBSA Newsletter, Imperial War Museum, Lambeth Rd, London SE1 6HZ. T. (0171) 416 5000. *100595*

Historic Houses, Castles and Gardens, c/o British Leisure Publications, East Grinstead House, East Grinstead RH19 1XA. T. (01342) 26972. *100596*

Historical Commercial News, c/o Iden Grange, Cranbrook Rd, Staplehurst, Tonbridge TN12 0ET.
Fax (01732) 893227. *100597*

History of Photography, c/o Tayolr & Francis, 4 Saint John St., London WC1N 2ET.
T. (0171) 4052237. *100598*

ICA Monthly Bulletin, c/o Institute of Contemporary Arts, The Mall, London SW1. Fax (0171) 8730051. *100599*

Imperial War Museum Review, Lambeth Rd, London SE1 6HZ. T. (0171) 4165000. *100600*

International Arts Manager, c/o Martin Huber, 4 Assam St., London E1 7QS. T. (0171) 2470066. *100601*

International Journal of Museum Management and Curatorship, Thrupp House, Abingdon OX14 3NE.
T. (0181) 20595. *100602*

International Who's Who in Art and Antiques, c/o Melrose Press, 3 Regal Ln., Soham, Ely CB7 5BA.
T. 721091, Fax 721839. *100603*

Irish Arts Review, c/o Eton Enterprises, Stokes House, College Sq., Belfast. T. (01232) 2808415, Fax (01232) 2808309. *100604*

Journal of Art and Design Education, c/o Carfax Publishing Company, POB 25, Abingdon OX14 3UE.
T. (0181) 555335, Fax (0181) 553559. *100605*

Journal of Design History, c/o Oxford University Press, Walton St., Oxford OX2 6DP. T. (01865) 56767, Fax (01865) 56646. *100606*

Journal of Education in Museums, c/o Susan Morris, 63 Navarino Rd., London E8 1AG. *100607*

Journal of Egyptian Archaeology, 3 Doughty Mews, London WC1N 2PG. T. (0171) 2421880. *100608*

Journal of Garden History, c/o Taylor & Francis, 4 John St., London WC1N 2ET. T. (0171) 4052237. *100609*

Journal of Philosophy and the Visual Arts, c/o Academy Group, 42 Leinster Gardens, London W12 3AN.
T. (0171) 4022141, Fax (0171) 7239540. *100610*

Journal of Stained Glass, 23 Balmoral Rd, Hitchin SG5 1XG. *100611*

Journal of the Decorative Arts Society, POB 844, Lewes BN7 3NG. T. (01273) 474245. *100612*

Journal of the History of Collections, c/o Oxford University Press, Walton St, Oxford OX2 6DP.
T. (01865) 56767, Fax (01865) 56646. *100613*

Journal of the Warburg and Courtauld Institutes, c/o Warburg Institute, Woburn Sq, London WC1H 0AB.
T. (0171) 5809663, Fax (0171) 4362852. *100614*

The Journal ot the William Morris Society, 26 Upper Mall, Hammersmith, London W6 9TA.
T. (0181) 7413735. *100615*

Landscape Research, c/o Exeter College of Art and Design, Earl Richards Rd., Exeter EX2.
T. (01392) 273519. *100616*

Leeds Arts Calendar, c/o Leeds Arts Collection Fund, Temple Newsam House, Leeds.
Fax (0113) 602285. *100617*

Leisure Painter, 63-65 High St, Tenterden TN30 6BD.
T. (015806) 3673, Fax (015806) 5411. *100618*

The List, 14 High St, Edinburgh EH1 1TE.
T. (0131) 5581191, Fax (0131) 5578500. *100619*

London Federation of Museum and Art Galleries Newsletter, Saint John's Gate, London WC1M 4DA. *100620*

Medieval World, POB 1871, London N3 2NY.
T. (0181) 3466348, Fax (0181) 3466348. *100621*

Minerva. The International Review of Ancient Art and Archaeology, 7 Davies St, London W1Y 1LL.
T. (0171) 4952590, Fax (0171) 4911595. *100622*

Modern Painters, c/o Fine Art Journal, 10 Barley Mow Passage, Chiswick, London W4 4PH. T. (0181) 0909, Fax (0181) 7421462. *100623*

Museum, 108 Cowley Rd, Oxford OX4 1JF.
T. (01865) 791100, Fax (01865) 791347. *100624*

Museum Abstracts, Routledge, 11 New Fetter Ln, London EC4P 4EE. T. (0171) 5839855, Fax (0171) 5830701. *100625*

Museum Management and Curatorship, c/o Butterworth-Heinemann, Linacre House, Jordan Hill, Oxford OX2 8DP. T. (01865) 310366, Fax (01865) 310898. *100626*

Museum Reporter, c/o National Museums of Scotland, Chambers St., Edinburgh EH1 1JF. T. (0131) 2257534, Fax (0131) 2257534. *100627*

Museums & Galleries, c/o British Leisure Publications, East Grinstead House, East Grinstead RH19 1XA.
T. (01342) 26972. *100628*

National Galleries of Scotland Bulletin, c/o Information Departure, Belford Rd., Edinburgh EH4 3DR.
Fax (0131) 3432802. *100629*

National Gallery, London, Technical Bulletin, Trafalgar Sq, London WC2N 5DN. T. (0171) 8393321. *100630*

NEMS Annual Report, c/o North of England Museum Service, Bath Ln., Newcastle-upon-Tyne NE4 5SQ.
T. (0191) 2221661, Fax (0191) 2614725. *100631*

NEMS News, c/o North of England Museum Service, Bath Ln., Newcastle-upon-Tyne NE4 5SQ.
T. (0191) 2221661, Fax (0191) 2614725. *100632*

New English Art Club, c/o Federation of British Artists, 17 Carlton House Terrace, London SW1Y 5BD. T. (0171) 9306844, Fax (0171) 8397830. *100633*

New Exhibitions of Contemporary Art, 152 Narrow St, London E14 8BP. *100634*

New Research in Museum Studies, c/o Athlone Press, 1 Park Dr., London NW11 7SG. T. (0181) 4580888. *100635*

Oxford Art Journal, c/o Oxford University Press, Walton St., Oxford OX2 6DP. T. (01865) 56767, Fax (01865) 56646. *100636*

Phillips Preview, 101 New Bond St, London W1Y 0AS. T. (0171) 6296602. *100637*

Print Quarterly, 80 Charlton Hill, London NW8 0ER. T. (0171) 6256332, Fax (0171) 6240960. *100638*

RA magazine, c/o Royal Academy of Arts, Piccadilly, London W1V 0DS. T. (0171) 4397438 ext. 256, Fax (0171) 2879023. *100640*

RAC Historic Britain, c/o British Leisure Publications, East Grinstead House, East Grinstead RH19 1XA. T. (01342) 26972. *100641*

Real Pottery, c/o Northfields Studio, Northfields, Tring Herts. *100642*

RSA Journal, c/o Royal Society of Arts, 8 John Adam St, London WC2N 6EZ. T. (0171) 9305715, Fax (0171) 8395805. *100643*

Saleroom & Auction Monthly, POB 107, Guildford GU1 1EB. T. (0181) 3360393, Fax (0181) 3360365. *100644*

Scottish Art Review, c/o Glasgow Art Gallery and Museums Assoc., Kelvingrove, Glasgow G3 8AG. T. (0141) 3573929, Fax (0141) 3574537. *100645*

Scottish Museum News, c/o Scottish Museums Council, 20-22 Tophichen St., Edinburgh EH3 8JB. T. (0131) 2297465. *100646*

Scottish Pottery Historical Review, 21 Warrender Park Terrace, Edinburgh. *100647*

Screen, 29 Old Compton St, London W1V 5PL. T. (0171) 7345455. *100648*

Sponsorship News, c/o Charterhouse Business Publications, POB 66, Wockingham RG11 4RQ. T. (01734) 772770, Fax (01734) 774522. *100649*

SSCR Journal, 33 Barony St, Edinburgh EH3 6NX. T. (0131) 5568417, Fax (0131) 3313019. *100650*

Studies in Conservation, c/o International Institute for Conservation of Historic and Artistic Works, 6 Buckingham St, London WC2N 6BA. T. (0171) 8395975, Fax (0171) 9761564. *100652*

Survey of London, c/o Athlone Press, 1 Park Dr., London NW11 7SG. T. (0181) 4580888. *100653*

TFN 8, 9 Key Hill Dr, Hockley, Birmingham B18 5NY. T. (0121) 5542237. *100654*

Third Text. Third World Perspectives on Contemporary Art and Culture, 120 Greencroft Gardens, London NW6 3PJ. T. (0171) 4353748, Fax (0171) 4353748. *100655*

Time Out, c/o Time Out Publications, Southampton St, London WC2E 7HD. T. (0171) 8364411, Fax (0171) 8367118. *100656*

Torquay Pottery Collectors Society Magazine, c/o Virginia Brisco, 218 Sandridge Rd., Saint Albans Herts. *100657*

Trace, 38 New St, Plymouth PL1 2NA. T. (01752) 228727, Fax (01752) 226911. *100658*

Tuition, Entertainment, News, Views, Oxford Area Arts Council, Old Fire Station Arts Centre, Oxford. *100659*

Turner, R.A., J.M.W., 153 Cromwell Rd, London SW5 0TQ. T. (0171) 3735560. *100660*

Turner Studies, c/o Carfax Publishing Company, POB 25, Abingdon OX14 3UE. T. (0181) 9927985. *100661*

Variant, 73 Robertson St, Glasgow G2 8QD. T. (0141) 2216380, Fax (0141) 2217775. *100662*

Watercolours, Drawings and Prints, 2 Barb Mews, Brook Green, London W6 7PA. T. (0171) 6029117, Fax (0171) 6020298. *100663*

The Watteau Society Bulletin, 153 Cromwell Rd, London SW5 0TQ. T. (0171) 3735560. *100664*

What's On in London, 182 Pentonville Rd, London N1 9LB. T. (0171) 2784393, Fax (0171) 8375838. *100665*

Who's Who in Art, 9 Brockhampton Rd, Havant PO9 1NU. T. (01705) 484943. *100666*

Women's Art Magazine, c/o Women Artists Slide Library, Fulham Palace, Bishop's Avenue, London SW6 6EA. T. (0171) 7317618, Fax (0171) 3841110. *100667*

Word & Image, c/o Taylor & Francis, 4 John St., London WC1N 2ET. T. (0171) 4052237. *100668*

U.S.A.

ACA Update, c/o American Council for the Arts, 1 E 53 St, New York, NY 10022-4201. T. (800) 321-4510, Fax (212) 245-4415. *100669*

Access (Seattle), c/o Allied Arts of Seattle, 107 S Main St, Ste 201, Seattle, WA 98104. T. (206) 624-0432. *100670*

AFAS Quarterly, c/o Bort Productions, POB 325, Lake Orion, MI 48361-0325. T. (313) 391-1378. *100671*

African Arts, c/o African Studies Center, University of California-Los Angeles, 405 Hilgard Av, Los Angeles, CA 310) 825-1218. *100672*

AHA! Hispanic Art News, c/o Association of Hispanic Arts, 173 E 116 St, New York, NY 10029. T. (212) 860-5445, Fax (212) 427-2787. *100673*

AIC News, c/o American Institute for Conservation of Historic and Artistic Works, 1400 16 St NW, Ste 340, Washington, DC 20036. T. (202) 232-6636, Fax (202) 232-6630. *100674*

Airbrush Action, POB 2052, Lakewood, NJ 08701. T. (908) 364-2111, Fax (908) 367-5908. *100675*

Alabama Arts, c/o State Council on the Arts, 1 Dexter Av, Montgomery, AL 36130. T. (205) 242-4076, Fax (205) 240-3269. *100676*

Alaska State Council on the Arts Bulletin, 411 W Fourth Av, Ste 1E, Anchorage, AK 99501-2343. T. (907) 279-1558, Fax (907) 279-4330. *100677*

All Area, POB 1042, Canal Street Station, New York, NY 10013. *100678*

AMACADMY, 41 E 65 St, New York, NY 10021. T. (212) 517-4200, Fax (212) 517-4893. *100679*

American Academy in Rome Memoirs, c/o Pennsylvania State University Press, Barbara Bldg, Ste C, 820 N University Dr, University Park, PA 16802-1003. T. (814) 865-1327, Fax (814) 863-1408. *100680*

American Art, c/o Rizzoli International Publications, 300 Park Av S, New York, 10010. T. (212) 387-3400, Fax (212) 387-3535. *100681*

American Art Journal, c/o Kennedy Galleries, 40 W 57 St, New York, NY 10019. T. (212) 541-9600, Fax (212) 333-7451. *100682*

American Artist, c/o BPI Communications, 1515 Broadway, New York, NY 10036. T. (212) 764-7300, Fax (212) 536-5351. *100683*

American Indian Art Magazine, 7314 E Osborn Dr, Scottsdale, AZ 85251. T. (602) 994-5445. *100684*

American Institute for Conservation of Historic and Artistic Works Journal, 1400 16 St NW, Washington, DC 20036. T. (202) 232-6636, Fax (202) 232-6630. *100685*

American Living Press, POB 901, Allston, MA 02134. T. (617) 522-7782. *100686*

American Review, 15 Burchfield Av, Cranford, NJ 07016. T. (201) 276-6222. *100687*

Antique Review, 12 E Stafford Av, POB 538, Worthington, OH 43085. T. (614) 885-9758. *100688*

Antique Trader Weekly, 100 Bryant St, POB 1050, Dubuque, IA 52004-1050. T. (319) 588-2073, Fax (319) 588-2073. *100689*

Antiques and Auction News, c/o Engle Publishing Company, Rte 230 W, POB 500, Mount Joy, PA 17552. T. (800) 482-2886, Fax (717) 653-6165. *100690*

Antiques and Fine Arts, c/o Fine Arts Publishing, 25200 La Paz Rd, Ste 210, Laguna Hills, CA 92653-5135. Fax (408) 298-3057. *100691*

Antiques & Collectibles Magazine, c/o Branciforte Communications, POB 33, Westbury, NY 11590. T. (516) 334-9650, Fax (516) 334-5740. *100692*

Antiquing America, c/o Web Publications, 650 Westdale Dr, Wichita, KS 67209. T. (316) 946-0600, Fax (316) 946-0675. *100693*

Antropology Newsletter, 1703 New Hampshire Ave. N. W., Washington, DC 20009. *100694*

Anyone, c/o Rizzoli International Publications, 300 Park Av, New York, NY 10010. T. (212) 387-3400, Fax (212) 387-3535. *100695*

APAA Newsletter, c/o American Physicians Art Association, 1130 N Cabrillo, San Pedro, CA 90731. T. (310) 436-9645, Fax (310) 436-7119. *100696*

Archives of American Art Journal, 1285 Av of the Americas, New York, NY 10019. T. (202) 357-2781. *100697*

Aristos, POB 1105, Radio City Station, New York, NY 10101. T. (212) 678-8550. *100698*

Arsenal, c/o Black Swan Press-Surrealist Editions, 1726 W Jarvis Av, Chicago, IL 60626. *100699*

Art Alliance Bulletin, 251 S 18 St, Philadelphia, PA 19103. Fax (215) 545-0767. *100700*

Art Alternatives, c/o Outlaw Biker Enterprises, 450 Seventh Av, Ste 2305, New York, NY 10001. T. (212) 564-0112, Fax (212) 465-8350. *100701*

Art Bulletin, c/o College Art Association, 275 Seventh Av, New York, NY 10001. T. (212) 691-1051, Fax (212) 627-2381. *100702*

Art Business News, c/o Advanstar Communications, 7500 Old Oak Blvd, Cleveland, OH 44130. T. (216) 826-2839, Fax (216) 891-2726. *100703*

Art Calendar, POB 199, Upper Fairmount, MD 21856. T. (410) 651-9150, Fax (410) 657-5313. *100704*

Art Cellar Exchange, c/o Token Art Corporation, 2171 India St, Ste H, San Diego, CA 92101. T. (619) 338-0797, Fax (619) 338-0826. *100705*

Art COM: Contemporary Art Communications, c/o Contemporary Arts Press, POB 3123, San Francisco, CA 94119. T. (415) 431-7524, Fax (415) 431-7841. *100706*

Art Directors Annual, c/o A.D.C. Publications, 250 Park Av S, New York, NY 10003. T. (212) 674-0500, Fax (212) 228-0649. *100707*

Art Gallery Magazine, Main St, Ivoryton, CT 06442. *100707a*

Art in America, c/o Brant Publications, 575 Broadway, New York, NY 10021. T. (212) 941-2800, Fax (212) 941-2819. *100708*

Art Issues, c/o Foundation for Advanced Critical Studies, 8721 Santa Monica Blvd, Ste 6, West Hollywood, CA 90069. T. (213) 876-4508, Fax (213) 876-5061. *100709*

Art Journal, c/o College Art Association, 275 Seventh Av, New York, NY 10001. T. (212) 691-1051, Fax (212) 627-2381. *100710*

Art Lover's Art and Craft Fair Bulletin, c/o American Society of Artists, POB 1326, Palatine, IL 60078. T. (312) 751-2500. *100711*

Art New England, 425 Washington St, Brighton, MA 02135. T. (617) 782-3008. *100712*

Art of the West, c/o Duerr & Tierney, 15612 Hwy 7, Ste 235, Minnetonka, 55345. T. (612) 935-5850, Fax (612) 935-6546. *100713*

Art Papers, c/o Atlanta Art Papers, POB 77348, Atlanta, GA 30357. T. (404) 588-1837, Fax (404) 588-1836. *100714*

Art Students League News, 215 W 57 St, New York, NY 10019. T. (212) 247-4510. *100715*

Art-Talk, POB 8508, Scottsdale, AZ 85252-8508. T. (602) 948-1799. *100716*

Art & Artists, c/o Foundation for the Community od Artists, 280 Broadway, Ste 412, New York, NY 10007. T. (212) 227-3770. *100717*

Art & Auction, 250 W 57 St, New York, NY 10107. T. (212) 447-9555, Fax 447-5221. *100718*

Art & Design News, c/o Boyd Publishing Co., 5783 Park Plaza Ct, Indianapolis, IN 46220. T. (317) 849-6110, Fax (317) 576-5859. *100719*

Art-World, c/o Arts Review Inc, 55 Wheatley Rd, Glen Head, NY 15545. T. (516) 626-0914. *100720*

Artist's Magazine, c/o F & W Publications, 1507 Dana Av, Cincinnati, OH 45207. T. (513) 531-2222. *100721*

ARTnews, 48 W 38 St, New York, NY 10018. T. (212) 398-1690. *100722*

Arts Education Policy Review, c/o Heldref Publications, 1319 18 St NW, Washington, DC 20036-1802. T. (202) 296-6267, Fax (202) 296-5149. *100723*

Arts in Virginia, c/o Virginia Museum of Fine Arts, 2800 Grove Av, Richmond, VA 23221. T. (804) 367-0534. *100724*

Arts Quarterly, c/o New Orleans Museum of Art, POB 19123, New Orleans, LA 70179. T. (504) 488-2631, Fax (504) 484-6662. *100725*

Arts & Cultural Times, 75 Fountain St, Providence, RI 02902. T. (401) 277-3880, Fax (401) 277-7804. *100726*

Artspeak, c/o Art Liaison, 245 Eighth Av, Ste 285, New York, NY 10011. T. (212) 924-6531. *100727*

Artweek, c/o Spaulding-Devlin Inc, 12 S First St, Ste 520, San Jose, CA 95113-2404. T. (408) 279-2293, Fax (408) 279-2432. *100728*

ASA Artisan, c/o American Society of Artists, POB 1326, Palatine, IL 60078. T. (312) 751-2500. *100729*

ASMA News, c/o American Society of Marine Artists, POB 90, Ambler, PA 17002-0090. T. (215) 646-1440, Fax (215) 646-1581. *100730*

A.W. Mellon Lectures in the Fine Arts, c/o Princeton University Press, 3175 Princeton Pike, Lawrenceville, NJ 08648. T. (609) 896-1344, Fax (609) 895-1081. *100731*

Carnegie Magazine, 4400 Forbes Av, Pittsburgh, PA 15213. T. (412) 622-3315, Fax (412) 622-1970. *100732*

Chicago Art Review, c/o American References Publishing Corporation, 2210 N Burling St, Chicago, IL 60614-3712. *100733*

Chicago Artists' News, c/o Chicago Artists' Coalition, 5 W Grand, Chicago, IL 60610. T. (312) 670-2060. *100734*

China Painter, c/o World Organization of China Painters, 2641 NW Tenth, Oklahoma Coty, OK 73107. T. (405) 521-1234, Fax (405) 521-1265. *100735*

Corporate Artnews, 48 W 38 St, New York, NY 10018. T. (212) 398-1690. *100736*

Getty Conservation Institute Newsletter, 4503 Glencoe Av, Marina del Rey, CA 90292-6537. T. (213) 822-2299, Fax (213) 821-9409. *100737*

Glass Art Society Journal, 1305 Fourth Av, Ste 711, Seattle, WA 98101-2401. T. (206) 382-1305. *100738*

IFAR Reports, c/o International Foundation for Art Research, 46 E 70 St, New York, NY 10021. T. (212) 879-1780, Fax (212) 734-4174. *100739*

Illustrator, c/o Art Instruction Schools, 500 S Fourth St, Minneapolis, MN 55415. T. (612) 339-8721, Fax (612) 339-3455. *100740*

International Auction Records, c/o Editions Publisol, POB 339, Gracie Station, New York, NY 10028. T. (212) 289-3981. *100741*

International Review of African American Art, POB 1, Hollywood, FL 33022-9967. T. (800) 828-2536, Fax (305) 983-8441. *100742*

Journal of Aesthetics and Art Criticism, 114N Murray St, Madison, WI 53715. T. (608) 262-4952. *100743*

Journal of Contemporary Art, POB 1472, New York, NY 10023-1472. T. (212) 799-1435, Fax (212) 873-0401. *100744*

Journal of Decorative and Propaganda Arts, c/o Wolfson Foundation of Decorative and Propaganda Arts, 2399 NE Second Av, Miami, FL 33137. T. (305) 573-9170, Fax (305) 573-0409. *100745*

Journal of Regional Criticism, c/o Arjuna Library Press, 1025 Garner St, Space 18, Colorado Springs, CO 80905-1774. T. (719) 475-2787. *100746*

Journal of Southern Decorative Arts, POB 10310, Winston-Salem, NC 27108-0310. T. (919) 721-7360. *100747*

Journal of the Walters Art Gallery, 600 N Charles St, Baltimore, MD 21201. T. (410) 547-9000, Fax (410) 783-7969. *100748*

Lightworks Magazine, POB 1202, Birmingham, MI 48012-1202. T. (313) 626-8026. *100749*

Master Drawings, c/o Master Drawings Association, 29 E 36 St, New York, NY 10016. T. (212) 685-0008, Fax (212) 685-4740. *100750*

Mundus Artium, c/o The University of Texas at Dallas, Richardson, POB 830688, Richardson, TX 75083. *100750a*

Numismatic Literature, Broadway at 155th St, New York, NY 10032. *100750b*

Numismatic News, 700 E State St, Iola, WI 54990. T. (713) 445-2214, Fax (713) 445-4087. *100751*

Numismatic Review, 123 W 57th St, New York, NY 10019. T. 582-2580. *100751a*

Numismatic Scrapbook Magazine, 7320 Milwaukee Av, Chicago, IL 60648. *100751b*

Photograph Collector, c/o Consultant Press, 163 Amsterdam Av, New York, NY10023. T. (212) 838-8640, Fax (212) 873-7065. *100751c*

Plateau, Fort Valley Rd, Flagstaff, Route 4, Box 720, Flagstaff, AZ 86001. *100751d*

School Arts, 50 Portland St, Worcester, MA 01608. *100751e*

Southwest Art, c/o C.B.H. Publishing, POB 460535, Houston, TX 77256-0535. T. (713) 850-0990, Fax (713) 850-1314. *100752*

Southwestern Art Magazine, 1304 Lavaca St, Austin, TX 78701. T. (512) 476-1810. *100752a*

Southwestern Historical Quarterly, 2-306 Sid Richardson Hall University Station, Austin, TX 78712. T. (512) 471-1525. *100752b*

Speculum, 1430 Massachusetts Av, Cambridge, MA 02138. *100752c*

Washington Artists Equity Ass., 3106 P St N W, Washington, DC 20007. T. (202) 333-5156. *100752d*

Winterthur Portfolio, Winterthur Museum, Winterthur, DE 19735. T. 888-4803. *100752e*

World Coin News, Iola, WI 54990. *100753*

Antiquarian and Art Booksellers
Antiquariate und Kunstbuchhandlungen
Librairies Anciennes et d'Art
LibrerieAntiquarie e Librerie d'Arte
Librerías Anticuarias y Librerías de Arte

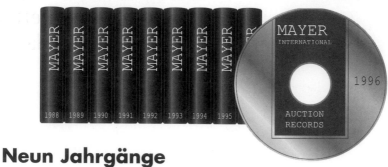

Argentina

Buenos Aires
Atlantida, Florida 643, Buenos Aires.
T. (01) 314 284. *100754*
Bullrich, Adolfo, Posadas 1231, Buenos Aires, 1001.
T. (01) 22-2025. *100755*
Casa Pardo S.R.L., Defensa 1170, Buenos Aires.
T. (01) 30 05 83. - Print - *100756*
Henschel, Juan, Reconquista 533 10P, 1003 Buenos Aires. - Engr - *100757*
Hirsch, Carlos, Florida 165, 4, Of. 453/465, Buenos Aires. T. (01) 30-7122, 331-1787, 331-2391.
- ArtBk - *100758*
Keins, Dr. J. Pablo, Tucuman 653 Galeria Ergon, Buenos Aires. T. (01) 392-94 70. *100759*
Kramer, Lil Garcia Beniter de, M.T. de Alvear 624, 6. Suite 48, 4058 Buenos Aires. T. (01) 312-8363,
Fax 312 5891. - Engr - *100760*
L'Amateur, Esmeralda 882, 1007 Buenos Aires.
T. (01) 312 76 35. *100761*
Librart S.R.L., Corrientes 127, Buenos Aires. *100762*
Librería Colonial, Paraná 1233, 1018 Buenos Aires.
T. (01) 812 03 26. *100763*
Librería El Ateneo, Florida 340, 1005 Buenos Aires.
T. (01) 46 68 01. - ArtBk / Engr / Autogr - *100764*
Libreria de Antaño, A. Breitfeld, S. de Bustamante 1876, 1425 Buenos Aires. T. (01) 83 71 78, Fax 824 90 67.
- Print / ArtBk / Engr / Autogr - *100765*
Libreria L'Amateur, Esmeralda 882, 1007 Buenos Aires.
T. (01) 312 76 35. *100766*
Petti Américo, Belgrano 2934, 1209 Buenos Aires.
T. (01) 748 44 40. *100767*
Talner, Beatriz & Mauricio, 1000 Buenos Aires Casilla 4146. T. (01) 394 07 00. - Print / ArtBk / Engr / Autogr / Map - *100768*
Viau, S.R. de, Florida 971, Buenos Aires.
T. (01) 31 42 97. - ArtBk - *100769*

Australia

Adelaide (South Australia)
Treloar, Michael, 10 Pitt St., 5000 Adelaide, 5000.
T. (08) 410 08 66. *100770*

Balgowlah (New South Wales)
Rocks Bookshop, P.O.Box 25, 2093 Balgowlah, 2093.
T. 94 18 05. *100771*

Berrima (New South Wales)
Berkelouw, Bendooley, Hume Hwy., 2577 Berrima, 1370. T. (048) 77 13 70, Fax 77 10 02. *100772*

Brisbane (Queensland)
Read's Rare Bookshop, 40 George St., 4000 Brisbane, 4000. T. (07) 229 32 78, Fax 221 92 31. *100773*

Broadway (New South Wales)
Vickery, Herbert, P.O.Box 102, Broadway, 2007.
T. 560 03 50. *100774*

Canberra (Australian Capital Territory)
Weekend Gallery, 5 Birdwood St, Hughes, Canberra, ACT 2605. T. (06) 2812745, Fax (06) 2851074. *100775*

Collingwood (Victoria)
Renard, Gaston, 51 Sackville St., 3066 Collingwood, 3066. T. 417 10 44, Fax 417 30 25. *100776*

Hobart (Tasmania)
Astrolabe, 81 Salamanca Pl., 7000 Hobart, 7000.
T. (002) 23 86 44. *100777*

Melbourne (Victoria)
Arnold, Peter, 463 High St., Prahran, Melbourne, Vic. 3181. T. (03)5292933, Fax (03)5211079. *100778*
Batman Book Club, 303 Elizabeth St., Melbourne, Vic. 3000. T. (03) 671622. *100779*
Bradstreet's Books, 9 Railway Arcade South, Glenferrie Rd. Hawthorn, Melbourne, Vic. 3122.
T. (03) 8193600. *100780*

17. INTERNATIONALE ANTIQUARIATSMESSE WIEN 1998

October 9 – 11

Campbell, Elizabeth, 146 Greville St., Prahran, Melbourne, Vic. 3181. *100781*
Craddock, Kay, Assembley Hall, 156 Collins St., Melbourne, Vic. 3000. T. (03) 6548506, 6547530,
Fax (03)6547351. *100782*
Gallery Shop, 180 St. Kilda Rd., Melbourne, Vic. 3004.
T. (03) 6180205. *100783*
Grant's Bookshop, 161 Commercial Rd., South Yarra, Melbourne, Vic. 3141. T. (03) 2401779. *100784*
Isles, Andrew, 113-115 Greville St., Prahran, 3000 Melbourne, 3181. T. (03) 51 57 50, 529 68 50,
Fax 529 12 56. *100785*
Old, Kenneth Hince, 485 High St., Prahran, Melbourne, Vic. 3181. T. (03) 5251649,
Fax (03) 35291298. *100786*
Printed Image Bookshop, 232 Chapel St., Prahran, Melbourne, Vic. 3181. T. (03) 5211244. - ArtBk - *100787*
Spencer Scott Sandilands, 546 High St., Prahran, Melbourne, Vic. 3181. T. (03) 5298011,
Fax (03) 5211754. *100788*

North Sydney (New South Wales)
Hawk, 370 Pacific Hwy., Crows Nest, 2060 North Sydney, 2065. T. 436 2350. *100789*

Perth (Western Australia)
Muir, Robert, 15/145 Stirling Hwy., Nedlands, 6000 Perth, 6009. T. (09) 386 58 42, 386 61 03,
Fax 386 37 87. *100790*
Serendipity Books, 256 Railway Parade, 6000 Perth, 6007. T. (09) 382 22 46, Fax 388 27 28. *100791*

Sydney (New South Wales)
Bibliophile, 24 Glenmore Rd., Paddington, Sydney, NSW 2021. T. (02) 331 14 11, Fax 361 33 71. *100792*
Cornstalk, 112 Glebe Point Rd., Glebe, Sydney, NSW 2037. T. (02) 660 48 89, Fax 552 26 70. *100793*
Hordern House, 77 Victoria St, Potts Point, Sydney, NSW 2011. T. (02) 3564411, Fax (02) 3573635. *100794*
Kerr, Louella, 26 Glenmore Rd., Paddington, Sydney, NSW 2021. T. (02) 361 46 64, Fax 564 17 60. *100795*
McCormick, Tim, 53 Queen St., Woollahra, Sydney, NSW 2025. T. (02) 363 53 83, Fax 326 27 52. *100796*
McCormick, Tim, 53 Queen St., Woollahra, Sydney, NSW 2025. T. (02) 32 5383. - Print / Engr - *100797*
McCormicks, 2 Regent St., Paddington, Sydney, NSW 2021. T. (02) 357 6541. *100798*
Pounder, Nicholas, 298 Victoria St., Kings Cross, Sydney, NSW 2011. T. (02) 331 54 80, Fax 360 54 56. *100799*
Stewart, K.R., 284 Pitt St., Sydney, (N.South Wales) 2000. T. (02) 26 56 80. - Print - *100800*

34·ILAB·KONGRESS WIEN 1998

October 4 – 7

The Antique Bookshop, 66 Victoria St., McMahons Point, Sydney, NSW 2060. T. (02) 959 56 65,
Fax (02) 959 33 52. *100801*
The Old Church Bookshop, 346 A Marsden Rd., Carlingford, Sydney, NSW 2118. T. (02) 872 38 02. *100802*
Tyrrell, 328 Pacific Hwy., Crows Nest, 2000 Sydney, 2065. T. (02) 438 59 20, 439 36 58. *100803*
University Bookshop, Univ. of Sydney, Sydney, N.S.W. 2006. *100804*

Toowoomba (Queensland)
Pollard, 2 St. Louis St., 4350 Toowoomba, 4350.
T. (076) 32 28 62. *100805*

Austria

Amstetten (Niederösterreich)
Sankt Georgs Antiquariat, Brandströmstr 20, 3300 Amstetten. T. (07472) 3565. - Print / Engr / Map - *100806*

Bad Goisern (Oberösterreich)
Zopf, Alois, Hauptstr. 327, 4822 Bad Goisern.
T. (06135) 8254, Fax 7409. - Map - *100807*

Baden bei Wien (Niederösterreich)
Bibliographicum, Rathausgasse 3, 2500 Baden bei Wien. T. (02252) 41587. - Engr / Map - *100808*

Feldkirch (Vorarlberg)
Montfort, Neustadt 36, 6800 Feldkirch Postfach 570.
T. (05522) 21783. - Print / Engr / Map - *100809*

Graz (Steiermark)
Alpenland Buchhandlung, Joanneumring 11, 8010 Graz.
T. (0316) 82 60 89, Fax 83 17 43. - ArtBk - *100810*
Alpenland Buchhandlung, Kaiserfeldgasse 13, 8010 Graz. T. (0316) 794 64. *100811*
Möhler, Brandhofgasse 12, 8020 Graz.
T. (0316) 38 10 41. - Print - *100812*
Moser, Hans-Sachs-Gasse 14, Passage, I.Stock, 8010 Graz. T. (0316) 82982123, 830110 (Antiquariat), 825696 (Galerie u. Antiquitäten), Fax 83011020.
- Print - *100813*
Pock, Max, Hauptpl. 1, 8010 Graz.
T. (0316) 790 42. *100814*
Regner, Johann, Bischofpl. 5, 8010 Graz.
T. (0316) 82 60 17, Fax 82 60 17. - ArtBk - *100815*
Truppe, Matthäus, Stubenberggasse 7, 8010 Graz.
T. (0316) 82 95 52. - Print / ArtBk / Engr / Autogr / Map - *100816*

Wildner, L., Stempfergasse 8, 8010 Graz.
T. (0316) 824216. - Print / Engr / Autogr / Map - *100817*

Großgmain (Salzburg)
Wessiak, Ferdinand, 5084 Großgmain. T. (06247) 217.
- Print / Autogr / Map - *100818*

Innsbruck (Tirol)
Antiquariat Gallus, Anichstr 25, 6020 Innsbruck.
T. (0512) 584343, Fax 588143. - Print / Engr /
ArtBk - *100819*
Boschi, Rudolf, Kiebachgasse 8 u. 14, 6020 Innsbruck.
T. (0512) 29224, 21386. *100820*
Hasenöhrl, Maria, Museumstr.4, 6020 Innsbruck.
T. (0512) 59505-0. - ArtBk - *100821*
Hofinger, Tempelstr. 5, 6010 Innsbruck.
T. (0512) 57 71 82, Fax 57 22 06. - Engr / Map - *100822*
Tausch, Dieter, Adolf Pichler Pl 12, 6020 Innsbruck.
T. (0512) 562769, Fax 582132. - Print / Engr /
Autogr - *100823*
Unterberger, Fr., Burggraben 10, 6020 Innsbruck.
T. (0512) 320 88. - Print / Engr / Map - *100824*
Widmoser, Herwig, Maria-Theresien-Str. 8, 6020 Innsbruck. T. (0512) 58 48 48, Fax 58 48 48. - Print / ArtBk /
Engr / Map - *100825*

Klagenfurt (Kärnten)
Haid, Josef, Villacher Str. 4, 9020 Klagenfurt.
T. (0463) 51 21 92. *100826*
Kärntner Antiquariat, A.-Lemisch Pl. 2, 9020 Klagenfurt.
T. (0463) 51 67 85. - Print / ArtBk / Map - *100827*

Leoben (Steiermark)
Nüssler, Hauptstr. 16, 8700 Leoben. T. (03842) 2347.
- Print / Engr - *100828*

Linz (Oberösterreich)
Eigl, Alois, Dametzstr. 25, 4020 Linz. T. (0732) 77 02 70,
Fax 78 56 12. - Engr / Map - *100829*
Kolarik, Walter, Tummelpl. 4, 4040 Linz.
T. (0732) 27 16 42. *100830*
Neugebauer, W., Landstr. 1, Postfach 380, 4010 Linz.
T. (0732) 77 17 66-0, Fax 77 17 66-19. - Print /
Map - *100831*
Scheuringer & Weinek, Bischofstr. 9, 4020 Linz.
T. (0732) 276 98 73. - Print / Map - *100832*

Rattenberg (Tirol)
Armütter, Robert, Bienerstr. 11, 6240 Rattenberg.
T. (05337) 2417. - ArtBk / Engr / Map - *100833*

Salzburg
Aschenbrenner, Franz, Wolf-Dietrich-Str. 25, 5020
Salzburg. *100834*
Franklin Mint, Zillnerstr 18, 5020 Salzburg.
T. (0662) 39661. *100835*
Höllrigl, Eduard, Sigmund-Haffner-Gasse 10, 5020 Salzburg. T. (0662) 84 26 51, 84 11 46. - Engr - *100836*
Matern, Peter, Linzer Gasse 5, 5024 Salzburg.
T. (0662) 873795, Fax (0662) 873795. - Print / Engr /
Autogr / Map - *100837*
Mayrische Buchhandlung, Theatergasse, 5024 Salzburg.
T. (0662) 873596. - Print - *100838*
Menzel, Michael, Getreidegasse 13, 5020 Salzburg.
T. (0662) 84 33 93. - Engr / Autogr - *100839*
Müller, Johannes, Hildmannpl 1A, 5020 Salzburg.
T. (0662) 846338, Fax 846338. - Print / Engr /
Map - *100840*
Schwaighofer, G., Giselakai 15, 5020 Salzburg.
T. (0662) 871127, Fax (0662) 871127. - Print - *100841*
Weinek, Steingasse 21 + 27, 5020 Salzburg.
T. (0662) 88 29 49. - Print / Engr / Autogr /
Map - *100842*
Welz, Sigmund-Haffner-Gasse 16, Postfach 123, 5010
Salzburg. T. (0662) 841771-0, Fax 84177120. - Print /
ArtBk / Engr / Map - *100843*

Sankt Pölten (Niederösterreich)
Sydy's Buchhandlung, J.G., Wiener Str. 19, 3100 Sankt
Pölten. T. (02742) 53189. - Print / Engr - *100844*

Seekirchen (Salzburg)
Klügel, Walter, Wimm 15, 5201 Seekirchen.
T. (06212) 7133. - Print / ArtBk - *100845*

Steyr (Oberösterreich)
Ennsthaler, Wilhelm, Stadtpl. 26, 4402 Steyr.
T. (07252) 220 53. *100846*

Villach (Kärnten)
Baier, Adalbert-Stifter-Str. 1, 9500 Villach.
T. (04242) 24268. - ArtBk - *100847*

Völkermarkt (Kärnten)
Kärntner Antiquariat, Hauptpl. 29, 9100 Völkermarkt.
T. (04232) 2444, Fax 2444-13. - Engr / Autogr - *100848*

Wien
Aichinger & Co, Bernhard, Weihburggasse 16, 1010
Wien. T. (0222) 512 88 53, Fax 512 88 53-13. - Print /
Engr - *100849*
Altbuchdienst Luegerplatz, Dr. Karl Lueger Platz 3, 1010
Wien. T. (0221) 52 64 00. - Print / Map - *100850*
Bartsch, Georg, Lerchenfelder Str. 138, 1081 Wien.
T. (0222) 43 12 75, Fax 43 12 84. - Print - *100851*
Berger, J., Kohlmarkt 3, 1010 Wien. T. (0222) 533 60 01,
Fax 533 60 01/15. - ArtBk - *100852*
Bourcy & Paulusch, Wipplingerstr 5, 1010 Wien.
T. (0222) 5337149. - Print / Engr / Map - *100853*
Buchfreund, Sonnenfelsgasse 4, 1010 Wien.
T. (0222) 5124856. - Print / ArtBk - *100854*
Buchfreund, Lugeck 7/17, 1010 Wien.
T. (0222) 5138289. - Print / ArtBk - *100855*
Buchhandlung Opernpassage, Opernpassage 18, 1010
Wien. T. (0222) 587 31 03. *100856*
Bücher-Ernst Handeslges. m.b.H., Gumpendorfer Str. 84,
1060 Wien. T. (0222) 597 42 57, 56 85 00. - Print /
Map - *100857*
Cottage, Gymnasiumstr 17, 1180 Wien.
T. (0222) 4707022, Fax 4707023. - Print - *100858*
Cudek, Erwin A., Garnisongasse 3, 1090 Wien.
T. (0222) 402 38 632. *100859*
Der Buchfreund, Sonnenfelsgasse 4, 1010 Wien.
T. (0222) 512 48 56, Fax 513 82 89. - Print /
ArtBk - *100860*
Derflinger & Fischer, Neulerchenfelder Str. 8, 1100 Wien.
T. (0222) 43 21 26. *100861*
Deuticke, Franz, Helferstorferstr 4, Postfach 761, 1011
Wien. T. (0222) 5336429, 5331535, Fax 5332347.
- Print - *100862*

Diehl, Ingeborg, Märzstr. 15, 1150 Wien.
T. (0222) 95 81 13. *100863*
Doblinger, Ludwig, Dorotheergasse 10, 1010 Wien.
T. (0222) 515030, Fax 5150351. - Print - *100864*
Dom-Buchhandlung, Stephanspl. 5, 1010 Wien.
T. (0222) 52 37 09. *100865*
Editio Totius Mundi, Gussenbauergasse 5-9, 1090 Wien.
T. (0222) 34 73 46. - Print / Engr / Map - *100866*
Entzmann & Sohn, Reinhold, Seilerstätte 21, 1010 Wien.
T. (0222) 512 18 90. - Engr / Map - *100867*
Fritsch, Georg, Schönlaterngasse 7, 1011 Wien.
T. (0222) 5126294, Fax 5138814. - Print /
Autogr - *100868*
Fritsch, Georg, Schönlaterngasse 7, 1010 Wien.
T. (0222) 5126294, Fax 5138814. - ArtBk /
Autogr - *100869*
Fritsch, Georg, Döblinger Hauptstr 61, 1190 Wien.
T. (0222) 365683. - Print - *100870*
Fröhlich, Helmut, Floriangasse 36, 1080 Wien.
T. (0222) 4023906, Fax 4023906. - Print / ArtBk /
Autogr - *100871*

Gerold & Co., Graben 31, 1011 Wien.
T. (0222) 533 50 14, Fax 533 50 14 12. - Print - *100872*
Gilhofer, Bognergasse 2, 1010 Wien. T. (0222) 5334285,
Fax 5350902. - Print / Engr - *100873*
Godai, Helmut, Mariahilfer Str. 169, 1150 Wien.
T. (0222) 83 82 95. - Print - *100874*
Gottschalk, Friedrich, Krugerstr. 10, 1010 Wien.
T. (0222) 512 73 32. - Print / ArtBk - *100875*
Grass, Roman, Freyung 1, 1014 Wien.
T. (0222) 535 42 76. - Print / ArtBk / Engr /
Map - *100876*
Halosar, Karl M., Margaretenstr. 35, 1040 Wien.
T. (0222) 56 13 53. - Print - *100877*
Handelsgesellschaft für historische Wertpapiere, Kärntner Str. 21, 1010 Wien. T. (0222) 512 88 22. *100878*
Hartleben, A., Walfischgasse 14, 1015 Wien.
T. (0222) 512 62 41, Fax 513 94 98. - Print - *100879*
Hasbach, A.L., Wollzeile 9 u. 29, 1010 Wien.
T. (0222) 5128876, 5128932, Fax 512887683.
- Print - *100880*
Hassfurther, Wolfdietrich, Hohenstaufengasse 7, 1010
Wien. T. (0222) 53509850, Fax (0222) 535098575.
- Print / Engr / Autogr / Map - *100881*
Heck, V.A., Kärntnerring 14, 1010 Wien.
T. (0222) 5055152. - Print / Engr / Autogr - *100882*
Heger, Rudolf, Wollzeile 2, 1010 Wien.
T. (0222) 52 63 98. - ArtBk - *100883*
Heidrich, Leopold, Plankengasse 7, 1010 Wien.
T. (0222) 5123701. - Print / ArtBk - *100884*
Hintermayer, Karl, Neubaugasse 29 u. 36, 1070 Wien.
T. (0222) 52302250, 5231057. - ArtBk - *100885*
Hölzl, Carl, Seilergasse 3, 1010 Wien.
T. (0222) 5122896. - Engr - *100886*
Huhold, Joachim, Schönbrunner Graben 104, 1180
Wien. T. (0222) 4700566. - Print - *100887*
Informatio Antiquariat-Buchhandlung, Seilergasse 19,
1010 Wien. T. (0222) 512 82 68. - Print - *100888*
Internumis, Grabnergasse 15/2, 1061 Wien.
T. (0222) 56 46 372. *100889*
Kantner, Hermann, Windmühlgasse 10, 1060 Wien.
T. (0222) 587 09 49. *100890*
Kleemann, Robert, Hietz. Hauptstr. 6, 1130 Wien.
T. (0222) 829 56 12, 877 56 12. *100891*
Klügel, Walter, Gumpendorfer Str 33, 1060 Wien.
T. (0222) 5730342. - Print - *100892*
Krey, Rudolf, Graben 13, 1010 Wien.
T. (0222) 512 59 02. - ArtBk - *100893*
Krieg, Walter, Kärntner Str 4, 3. Stock, 1010 Wien.
T. (0222) 5121093, Fax 5123266. - Print / Engr / Autogr / Map - *100894*
Kuppitsch, Schottengasse 4, 1010 Wien.
T. (0222) 63 02 44, 63 94 30. - Print - *100895*
Lücker, Annagasse 5, Postfach 101, 1015 Wien.
T. (0222) 5127344, 5129888, Fax 5128742. - Print /
Autogr - *100896*
Lugmair, Hans, Seilergasse 19, 1010 Wien.
T. (0222) 512 82 68. - Print - *100897*
Lugmair, Hans, Linke Wienzeile 40, 1060 Wien.
T. (0222) 56 71 68. - Print - *100898*
Maenner, Emil K., Gussenbauergasse 5, 1090 Wien.
T. (0222) 34 73 46. *100899*
Malota, Wiedner Haupstr 22, 1040 Wien.
T. (0222) 5879275, Fax 5879275. - Print - *100900*
Maudrich, Wilhelm, Spitalgasse 21a, 1097 Wien.
T. (0222) 4024712/13, Fax 4085080. - Print - *100901*
Minerva im MAK, Stubenring 5, 1200 Wien, Postfach 88,
1201 Wien. T. (0222) 3302433-155,
Fax (0222) 3302439-159. - ArtBk - *100902*
Minichbauer, Rudolf, Walfischgasse 12, 1010 Wien.
T. (0222) 52 37 16. *100903*
Müller, Gerhard, Dr., Im Burgdurchgang 6, 1010 Wien.
T. (0222) 587 61 04. *100904*
Ferdinand Rudolf Müller's Nachf., Ungargasse 50, 1030
Wien. T. (0222) 713 63 13. *100905*
Nebehay, Christian M., Annagasse 18, Postfach 303,
1015 Wien. T. (0222) 5121801, Fax 5135038. - Print /
Engr / Autogr - *100906*
Poxleitner-Blasl, Alois, Strozzigasse 32, 1080 Wien.
T. (0222) 402 82 17. *100907*
Prachner, Georg, Kärntnerstr. 30, 1015 Wien.
T. (0222) 512 85 49. - ArtBk - *100908*
Reichmann, Alois, Wiedner Hauptstr 18-20, 1040 Wien.
T. (0222) 5878118. - Print - *100909*

Sallmayer, Marco d'Aviano-Gasse 2, 1010 Wien.
T. (0222) 52 21 81. *100910*
Schiebl, Franz, Laxenburger Str. 48, 1100 Wien.
T. (0222) 64 12 30. - Print - *100911*
Schöfegger, Rupert, Schaumburgerg. 5, 1040 Wien.
T. (0222) 504 26 60. *100912*
Schottenfeld & Partner, Kaiserstr. 32/1/2, 1070 Wien.
T. (0222) 526 15 09, Fax 526 39 39. - Print / ArtBk /
Autogr - *100913*
Seemann, H., Seilergasse 19, 1010 Wien.
T. (0222) 513 64 91. *100914*
Smolders, Wilhelm, Weyprechtg. 6, 1160 Wien.
T. (0222) 43 44 65. *100915*
Steinbach, Michael, Salmannsdorfer Str. 64, 1190 Wien.
T. (0222) 44 11 39. *100916*
Steiner, Helmut, Sampogasse 4, 1142 Wien.
T. (0222) 95 97 77. - Print / ArtBk - *100917*
Stöhr, Heide, Lerchenfelder Str. 78-80, 1080 Wien.
T. (0222) 0222/43 13 49, Fax 403 04 10.
- Print - *100918*
Stropek, Karl, Dr., Währinger Str. 122, 1180 Wien.
T. (0222) 479 54 95, Fax 479 62 30. - Print - *100919*
Theuermann, Monika, Sellergasse 16, 1010 Wien.
T. (0222) 52 20 864. - Engr / Map - *100920*
Wiener Antiquariat, Seilergasse 16, 1014 Wien.
T. (0222) 5125466. - Print / Engr / Autogr - *100921*
Wögenstein, Walter, Singerstr 13, 1010 Wien.
T. (0222) 5131472, Fax 5122620. - Print /
ArtBk - *100922*
Wolfrum, Augustinerstr 10, 1010 Wien.
T. (0222) 51253980, Fax 5121557. - Engr /
Map - *100923*
Würthle & Sohn Nfg, Kaasgraben 108, 1190 Wien.
T. (0222) 3181685, Fax 3181685. - ArtBk - *100924*

Belgium

Aarschot (Vlaams Brabant)
Buvens, Testeltsestw 34, 3200 Aarschot.
T. (016) 562246. *100925*

Antwerpen
Antorff, St-Jorispoort 35, 2000 Antwerpen.
T. (03) 233 18 44. *100926*
Beo, Hopland 15, 2000 Antwerpen.
T. (03) 232 62 74. *100927*
Bladel, R. van, St Kathelijnevest 57, 2000 Antwerpen.
T. (03) 233 00 39. *100928*
Ceuleers, Schildersstr. 2, 2000 Antwerpen.
T. (03) 216 41 90, Fax 238 94 08. - Print /
ArtBk - *100929*
Cosy Corner, Leeuw van Vlanderenstr. 4, 2000 Antwer-
pen. T. (03) 232 05 00. - Print / ArtBk - *100930*
Goeij, W. de, Tolstr. 11, 2000 Antwerpen.
T. (03) 238 21 15. - Print - *100931*
Jennes, Lge. Nieuwstr. 91, 2000 Antwerpen.
T. (03) 231 90 23. - ArtBk - *100932*
Joyce-Royce, Lge. Leemstr. 144 b, 2018 Antwerpen.
T. (03) 218 75 73. - Print / ArtBk - *100933*
Laurijssens, Hoogstr 34, 2000 Antwerpen.
T. (03) 232 33 56. *100934*
Librije, de, Gierstr 11, 2000 Antwerpen.
T. (03) 233 78 64. *100935*
Mammoet, de, Van Kerckhovenstr 53, 2008 Antwerpen.
T. (03) 225 11 99. *100936*
Mekanik-Strip, St-Jacobsmarkt 73, 2000 Antwerpen.
T. (03) 233 23 47. *100937*
Oude Borze, de, Oude Beurs 62, 2000 Antwerpen.
T. (03) 231 94 74. *100938*
Slegte, de, Meir 40, 2000 Antwerpen.
T. (03) 233 29 14. *100939*
Sternberg, Leon, Hertoginstr 11, 2018 Antwerpen.
T. (03) 233 56 81, Fax 231 77 63. *100940*
Tendeloo, L. van, De Pretstr. 6, 2008 Antwerpen.
T. (03) 232 76 26. - Print / Engr - *100941*
Ulysses, St. Katelijnevest 14, 2000 Antwerpen.
T. (03) 232 42 91. - Print / Engr / Map - *100942*

Berchem (Antwerpen)
't Flodderke, Statiestr 111, 2600 Berchem.
T. (03) 239 49 55. *100943*

Beverlo (Limburg)
Mangelschots, F., Beverpad 41, 3581 Beverlo.
T. (011) 346373. *100944*

Borgerhout (Antwerpen)
Daneels, D., Herentalsebaan 18, 2140 Borgerhout.
T. (031) 22 49 28. *100945*

Borsbeek (Antwerpen)
Hertogh, de, Corluylei 47, 2150 Borsbeek.
T. (03) 3218132. *100946*

Brasschaat (Antwerpen)
Tweede Lezer, Bredabn 501, 2930 Brasschaat.
T. (031) 652 13 62. *100947*

Brugge (West-Vlaanderen)
In den Eenhoorn, Ezelstr. 84, 8000 Brugge.
T. (050) 33 42 46. - Print - *100948*
Marechal, Frans, Mariastr 10, 8000 Brugge.
T. (050) 33 13 05, 33 00 23, Fax 33 55 79. *100949*
Pollentier-Marechal, G. & M., St Salvatorskerkhof 8,
8000 Brugge. T. (050) 33 18 04. *100950*
Reyghere, Markt 12, 8000 Brugge. T. (050) 33 34 03.
- Print - *100951*
Wiele, M. van de, St. Salvatorkoorstr. 3, 8000 Brugge.
T. (050) 33 63 17. - Print / ArtBk / Engr / Map - *100952*

Bruxelles
Abelard, 7 Rue F Dons, 1050 Bruxelles.
T. (02) 649 75 84, 640 48 42. *100953*
ABMC, 14 Rue Saint-Jean, 1000 Bruxelles.
T. (02) 640 22 53, 511 63 88. *100954*
Aladin, 8 Rue de la Tulipe, 1050 Bruxelles.
T. (02) 514 02 49. *100955*
Archives, 76 Rue de la Montange, 1000 Bruxelles.
T. (02) 511 52 67. *100956*
Arnoldi, 46 Blvd de l'Empereur, 1000 Bruxelles.
T. (02) 502 07 70. *100957*
Art Shop de la Société des Expositions du Palais des
Beaux-Arts, 10 Rue Royale, 1000 Bruxelles.
T. (02) 5120403. *100958*
Arts & Livres, 6 Rue de l'Enseignement, 1000 Bruxelles.
T. (02) 217 77 18. *100959*
Bande des Six Nez, La, 179 Chaussée de Wavre, 1050
Bruxelles. T. (02) 513 72 58. *100960*
Boite à Bouquins, 8 Blvd Anspach, 1000 Bruxelles.
T. (02) 217 45 17. *100961*
Book Market, 47 Rue de la Madeleine, 1000 Bruxelles.
T. (02) 512 92 53. *100962*
Bouquinerie Le Meridien, 15 Rue de la Vierge Noire,
1000 Bruxelles. T. (02) 511 70 64. *100963*
Buchet, 166 Av de la Reine, 1000 Bruxelles.
T. (02) 242 63 05. *100964*
Cabinet de Curiosité, Le, 25 Rue de la Madeleine, 1000
Bruxelles. T. (02) 512 89 64. *100965*
Chabanne, 41, 26b Rue du Fort, 1060 Bruxelles.
T. (02) 537 73 32. *100966*
Chasseur d'Images, 148 Rue du Midi, 1000 Bruxelles.
T. (02) 511 54 05. *100967*
Chevreuille, D., 71-73 Rue des Eperonniers, 1000 Bru-
xelles. T. (02) 512 97 44. *100968*
Codire, 109 Av Louis Lepoutre, 1050 Bruxelles.
T. (02) 347 28 00, 347 42 43. *100969*
Collet, G., 15 Rue de la Vièrge Noire, 1000 Bruxelles.
T. (02) 511 70 64. *100970*
Cox, 47 Chaussée de Charleroi, 1060 Bruxelles.
T. (02) 538 18 25. - ArtBk - *100971*
Crucis, Gérard, 41 Rue Saint Jean, 1000 Bruxelles.
T. (02) 512 12 00. *100972*
Deprins, Y., 36 Rue St-Lambert, 1200 Bruxelles.
T. (02) 771 33 04. *100973*
Dichotoma, 294 Blvd Lambermont, 1030 Bruxelles.
T. (02) 215 69 35. *100974*
Discosold, 105 Blvd A Max, 1000 Bruxelles.
T. (02) 217 16 13. *100975*
Dupontcheel, Adam, 42 Rue Mellery, 1020 Bruxelles.
T. (02) 4787902. *100976*
Ex-Libris, 109 Av Louis Lepoutre, 1050 Bruxelles.
T. (02) 347 28 00. *100977*
Ferraton, A., 162 Ch de Charleroi, 1060 Bruxelles.
T. (02) 538 69 17. *100978*
Galerie Bortier, 55 Rue de la Madeleine, 1000 Bruxelles.
T. (02) 511 82 54. *100979*

Gehain, M., 122 Rue Blaes, 1000 Bruxelles.
T. (02) 514 11 20. *100980*
Gevaert, Yves, 160 Rue du Pinson, 1170 Bruxelles.
T. (02) 660 23 72, Fax 660 23 72. *100981*
Hankard, Jean-Jacques, 25 Rue de la Paix, 1050 Bru-
xelles. T. (02) 512 36 42. *100982*
Heyde, Jacques van der, 21 Rue du Chêne, 1000 Bruxel-
les. T. (02) 513 05 25. *100983*
Jonas-Ansaldi, 4 Pl F Cocq, 1050 Bruxelles.
T. (02) 513 46 22. *100984*
La Mine de Papier, 246 Ch de Waterloo, 1060 Bruxelles.
T. (02) 5341908. *100985*
Le Bâteau-Livre, 14 Rue des Eperonniers, 1000 Bruxel-
les. T. (02) 511 98 08. *100986*
Le Charabia, 15 Rue du Page, 1050 Bruxelles.
T. (02) 539 20 28. *100987*
Le Grenier du Collectionneur, 88A Av du Polo, 1150
Bruxelles. *100988*
Librairie Arte, 36 Pl. du Grand Sablon, 1000 Bruxelles.
T. (02) 512 87 36. - ArtBk - *100989*
Librairie de Rome, 50 Ave Louise, 1050 Bruxelles.
T. (02) 511 79 37. *100990*
Librairie des Eléphants, 19 Pl Van Meenen, 1060 Bruxel-
les. T. (02) 539 06 01. *100991*
Librairie des Galeries, 2 Galerie du Roi, 1000 Bruxelles.
T. (02) 511 24 12. *100992*
Little Memo, 132 Rue du Trône, 1000 Bruxelles.
T. (02) 646 53 45. *100993*
Ma Maison de Papier, 6 Gal Rue de Ruysbroeck, 1000
Bruxelles. T. (02) 5122249. *100994*
Maréchal, Yvon, 41 Rue des Deux Gares, 1070 Bruxel-
les. T. (02) 522 25 67. *100995*
Michotte, J.L., 32 Rue des Gravelines, 1000 Bruxelles.
T. (02) 230 23 55. *100996*
Minet Frères, 60-62 Rue des Eperonniers, 1000 Bruxel-
les. T. (02) 513 45 42, Fax 513 86 75. *100997*
Mont des Arts, 72 Coudenberg, 1000 Bruxelles.
T. (02) 25 13 57 44. - ArtBk - *100998*
Moorthamers, Louis, 124 Rue Lesbroussart, 1000 Bru-
xelles. T. (02) 647 85 48. - Print / Map - *100999*
Morel de Westgaver, Evelyn & Alain, 14 Rue Saint Jean,
1000 Bruxelles. T. (02) 511 63 88. *101000*
Myriades, Les, 197 Av Goerges Henri, 1200 Bruxelles.
T. (02) 770 55 79. *101001*
Noir sur Blanc, 38 Rue des Chapeliers, 1000 Bruxelles.
T. (02) 511 00 08. *101002*
Office International de Librairie, 30, av. Marnix, 1000
Bruxelles. T. (02) 513 66 75. - Print - *101003*
Onckelinx, H., 9 Pl Sablon, 1000 Bruxelles.
T. (02) 3753070. - Print / Engr - *101004*
Outre Mer Bouquins, 25 Av A Bertrand, 1190 Bruxelles.
T. (02) 347 45 01. *101005*
Papivore, Le, 67 Pl du Jeu de Balle, 1000 Bruxelles.
T. (02) 514 46 93. *101006*
Papyrus, Le, 16 Gal Bortier, 1000 Bruxelles.
T. (02) 512 38 91. *101007*
Paradis des Chercheurs, 245 Chaussée de Charleroi,
1060 Bruxelles. T. (02) 538 52 35. - Print - *101008*
Pêle-Mêle, 55 Blvd M Lemonnier, 1000 Bruxelles.
T. (02) 512 29 91. *101009*
Pique-Puces, 204 Ch de Wavre, 1050 Bruxelles.
T. (02) 673 57 16. *101010*
Posada, 29 Rue de la Madeleine, 1000 Bruxelles.
T. (02) 511 08 34, Fax 512 78 52. - Engr - *101011*
Rouge et Le Noir, Le, 53 Rue Saint-Jean, 1000 Bruxel-
les. T. (02) 511 66 97. *101012*
Schwilden, 5 Galerie Bortier, 1000 Bruxelles.
T. (02) 512 21 81. - Print - *101013*
Simonson, 227 Ch de Charleroi, 1060 Bruxelles.
T. (02) 538 31 58, Fax 538 24 13. *101014*
Sisley, 27-29 Rue St.-Jean, 1000 Bruxelles.
T. (02) 511 40 36, 513 46 69. - ArtBk - *101015*
Smith, W.H. & Son, Bd. Adolphe Max 71 b.75, 1000 Bru-
xelles. T. (02) 17 67 22, 19 27 07. - Print - *101016*
Speeckaert, E., 53 Blvd. Saint-Michel, 1040 Bruxelles.
T. (02) 736 43 29. - Print - *101017*
Stiernet, M., 8 Rue Moissonneurs, 1040 Bruxelles.
T. (02) 735 61 91. *101018*
Thanh-Long, 34 Rue Dekens, 1040 Bruxelles.
T. (02) 733 16 18. - Print - *101019*
Transatlantique, 126 Ch de Wavre, 1050 Bruxelles.
T. (02) 512 49 30. *101020*

Trouvaille, La, 289 Chaussee d'Ixelles, 1050 Bruxelles.
T. (02) 648 28 62. - Print / Autogr / Map -   *101021*
Tulkens, Florimond, 21, rue du Chène, 1000 Bruxelles.
T. (02) 513 05 25. - Engr -   *101022*
Van Balberghe, Emile, 4 Rue Vautier, 1050 Bruxelles.
T. (02) 649 46 08.   *101023*
Van Berchem, J., 68 Rue de la Fauvette, 1180 Bruxelles.
T. (02) 374 47 81.   *101024*
Van der Elst, 55 Rue de la Madeleine, 1000 Bruxelles.
T. (02) 511 82 54.   *101025*
Van der Perre, Francine, 23 Rue de la Madeleine, 1000
Bruxelles. T. (02) 511 75 59. - Print -   *101026*
Van der Perre, Micheline, 6 Rue van Moer, 1000 Bruxel-
les. T. (02) 512 14 33. - Print / Engr / Autogr /
Map -   *101027*
Van Hoeter, F., 61 Rue St.-Quentin, 1000 Bruxelles.
T. (02) 647 30 49. - Print / Engr / Map -   *101028*
Van Loock, A., 51, rue St.-Jean, 1000 Bruxelles.
T. (02) 512 7465. - Print / Engr -   *101029*
Vandeplas, 10 Rue des Eperonniers, 1000 Bruxelles.
T. (02) 512 22 96.   *101030*
Vokaer, Michel, Chausse'1e de Charleroi 169, 1060 Bru-
xelles. T. (02) 512 13 53.   *101031*
Wilbert, 35 Rue du Prévot, 1050 Bruxelles.
T. (02) 537 65 64.   *101032*
Wyngaert, De, 127a Rue R Vandevelde, 1030 Bruxelles.
T. (02) 242 80 76.   *101033*

Deinze (Oost-Vlaanderen)
Centre de Scriptophilie, Kouter 126, 9800 Deinze.
T. (091) 86 90 91.   *101034*

Deurne (Antwerpen)
Trefpunt, Boterlaarbaan 98, 2100 Deurne.
T. (03) 22 46 35.   *101035*
Vilain, M., Ten Eekhovelei 287, 2100 Deurne.
T. (03) 24 21 28. - Print / ArtBk / Engr -   *101036*

Gent (Oost-Vlaanderen)
Copyright Artbookshop, Jakobijnenstr 8, 9000 Gent.
T. (09) 2235794, Fax 33 31 73.   *101037*
Deene, R., Hoogpoort 83, 9000 Gent.
T. (09) 2250248.   *101038*
Intellect, Kalandenstr. 1, 9000 Gent. T. (09) 2257351.
- ArtBk -   *101039*
Kunstmarkt, Bij Sint Jacobs 17, 9000 Gent.
T. (09) 2401260, 2237696.   *101040*
Renaissance van het Boek, Walpoortstr. 7, 9000 Gent.
T. (09) 2254808. - Print / Map -   *101041*
Rombaut, Alexander, Lievestr. 14, 9000 Gent
T. (09) 2235646. - ArtBk / Map -   *101042*
Sion, M., Steendam 13, 9000 Gent.
T. (09) 2254399.   *101043*

Haasrode (Brabant)
Devroe, J., Dalemstr 27, 3053 Haasrode.
T. (016) 46 36 61.   *101044*

Hasselt (Limburg)
Griffel, de, Minderbroederstr 42, 3500 Hasselt.
T. (011) 22 24 49.   *101045*
Hermans, E., Guffensln 50, 3500 Hasselt.
T. (011) 22 74 45.   *101046*

Knokke (West-Vlaanderen)
Mappamundi, Ebbestr 2, 8300 Knokke.
T. (050) 60 85 44, Fax 61 55 58.   *101047*

Kortrijk
Antiquariaat Sanderus, Brugsestraat 88, 8500 Kortrijk.
T. (056) 352541.   *101048*

Kortrijk (West-Vlaanderen)
Speybrouck, B. & A., Onze-Lieve-Vrouwestr 37, 8500
Kortrijk. T. (056) 20 20 60.   *101049*

Lanaken
Hester, Maastrichterstw 189, 3620 Lanaken.
T. (011) 71 47 37.   *101050*

Leuven (Vlaams Brabant)
Tweedehandels Boekhuis, Muntstr 16, 3000 Leuven.
T. (016) 237614.   *101051*

Liège
Bouquinerie des Carmes, 35b Rue St-Paul, 4000
Liège.   *101052*
Grommen, Michel, 159 A Rue Saint Gilles, 4000 Liège.
T. (04) 2222448.   *101053*
La Sirène, 17bis Quai sur Meuse, Henri Thyssens, 4000
Liège. T. (04) 2229047.   *101054*
Lhomme, 9 Rue des Carmes, 4000 Liège.
T. (04) 2232463.   *101055*

Lier (Antwerpen)
d'Oude Postkaart, Antwerpsestw 20, 2500 Lier.
T. (03) 489 06 25.   *101056*
Schoon, F Van Cauwenberghstr 32, 2500 Lier.
T. (03) 480 76 36.   *101057*

Mechelen (Antwerpen)
Boektiekske, Hoogstr 51, 2800 Mechelen.
T. (015) 41 47 96.   *101058*
Garcia, St. Katelijnestr. 1 & 10, 2800 Mechelen.
T. (015) 29 09 85. - Print / Engr / Map -   *101059*

Mons (Hainaut)
Librairie du Miroir, 9-11 Rue du Miroir, 7000 Mons.
T. (065) 34 69 02.   *101060*

Mortsel (Antwerpen)
Woefke, Antwerpsestr 185, 2640 Mortsel.
T. (031) 449 15 60.   *101061*

Namur (Namur)
Au Vieux Quartier, Adrienne Goffin, 30, rue de la Croix,
5000 Namur. T. (081) 22 19 94. - Print -   *101062*
Contrepoint, Pl Marché aux Légumes, 5000 Namur.
T. (081) 22 50 55.   *101063*

Peer (Limburg)
Pen, de, Bomerstr 55, 3990 Peer.
T. (011) 631913.   *101064*

Redu
Anselot, Noël, 18 Rue de Transinne, 6890 Redu.
T. (061) 65 54 02, 65 60 91.   *101065*
Boite aux Lettres, 14 Rue St-Hubert, 6890 Redu.
T. (061) 65 62 28.   *101066*
Dailly, P., 14 Rue de St-Hubert, 6890 Redu.
T. (061) 65 61 84.   *101067*
Feuillet Jauni, Au, 38 Rue de la Prairie, 6890 Redu.
T. (061) 65 64 42.   *101068*
Griffel, de, 34 Rue de Transinne, 6890 Redu.
T. (061) 65 52 51.   *101069*
La Forge, 72 Rue Neuve, 6890 Redu.
T. (061) 65 61 4b.   *101070*
Le Rat des Champs, 53B Rue Hamaïde, 6890 Redu.
T. (061) 65 60 34.   *101071*

Sint-Truiden (Limburg)
Gallier's Stripwinkel, Beekstr 46, 3800 Sint-Truiden.
T. (011) 67 17 39.   *101072*

Tervuren (Vlaams Brabant)
Exhibitions International Foundation, Leuvensesteenweg
18, 3080 Tervuren. T. (02) 7679414,
Fax 7675115.   *101073*

Tongeren (Limburg)
Boekenwurm, Stationsln 30, 3700 Tongeren.
T. (012) 23 42 27.   *101074*

Waterloo (Brabant Wallon)
Feuillet Jauni, Au, 396 Chaussée de Bruxelles, 1410
Waterloo. T. (02) 3547160.   *101075*

Brazil

Petrópolis (Rio de Janeiro)
Sebo Fino, Rua Santos Dumont 677, 25625 Petrópolis.
T. (0242) 43 66 54, Fax 43 66 54.   *101076*

Porto Alegre (Rio Grande do Sul)
Livraria Kosmos Editora, Rua dos Andradas 1644,
90000 Porto Alegre, 90000. T. (0512) 21 24 14,
25 91 12. - Print -   *101077*

Rio de Janeiro
Bach, Susanne, Rua Martins Ferreira 32, 22271 Rio de
Janeiro. T. (021) 226 35 90.   *101078*
Kosmos, R. do Rosario 155, 20041 Rio de Janeiro,
20041. T. (021) 222-7771. - Print / ArtBk / Engr /
Map -   *101079*
Leonardo da Vinci, Av. Rio Branco 185/2, 20000 Rio de
Janeiro, 20000. T. (021) 2527172.   *101080*

São Paulo
Bach, Susan, Alameda Campinas 1127, 01404 São Pau-
lo. T. (011) 887 85 49, Fax 814 31 01.   *101081*
Gaudi, Rua Augusta 2872, São Paulo. T. (011) 881-1010,
881-1877.   *101082*
Kosmos Editora, Pracã Dom José Gaspar 134, São Pau-
lo. T. (011) 34 35 48. - Print -   *101083*
Livraria Parthenon Ltda., Av. Paulista, 820, 01310 São
Paulo. T. (011) 289 2113.   *101084*
Livraria São Paulo, Rua São Bento 370 9.0 Andar, Sala
1, São Paulo. T. (011) 32 38 05.   *101085*

Bulgaria

Sofia
Antikvarni Knigi, ul. Graf Ignatiev 18, 1000 Sofia.
T. 87 62 73. - Print -   *101086*
Hemus, 6 Bd Rouskv, 1000 Sofia. T. 66 57 50.   *101087*
Knijarnitsa Balgarski hudojnik, ul. Levski 21, 1000 Sofia.
T. 88 29 26. - Engr -   *101088*

Canada

Montreal (Québec)
Hachette Librairie Ltd., 554 Ste. Catherine St.E., Mont-
real. T. (514) 842-3857.   *101089*
Nova, 2100 Rue Crescent, Montreal, H3G 2B8.
T. (514) 845-1221. - ArtBk -   *101090*
Renaud-Bray, 5219 Côte des Neiges, Montreal.
T. (514) 342 1515.   *101091*

Ottawa (Ontario)
The Bookstore, National Gallery of Canada, Albert & Elgin St., Ottawa, K1A OM8. T. (613) 992-7189.   *101092*

Québec (Québec)
Librairie du Nouveau Monde, 103 Rue Saint-Pierre, Québec, Qué. G1K 7A1 T. (418) 694-9475, Fax 694-
9486.   *101093*

Saskatoon (Saskatchewan)
Buller, E., 204 A 2nd Ave. N., Saskatoon, S7K 2B5.
T. (306) 242-0294. - Print -   *101094*

Toronto (Ontario)
Alexandre, 1543 Bayview Av., Toronto. T. (416) 489-
6701. - Print / Engr -   *101095*
Book Shop, Art Gallery of Ontario, 317 Dundas St. W, To-
ronto, Ont. M5T 1G4. T. (416) 979-6609.
- ArtBk -   *101096*
Britnell, Albert, Book Shop, 765 Yonge St., Toronto,
M4W 2G6. T. (416) 924-3321.   *101097*
Mirvish, David, 596 Markham St., Toronto, M6G 2L8.
T. (416) 531-9975. - Print / ArtBk -   *101098*
Movements in Time, POB 6629, Station A, Toronto, M5W
1X4. T. (905) 883-1924.   *101099*
Patrick, Joseph, POB 100 Stn. V, Toronto. T. (416) 766-
3357. - Print -   *101100*
Wallrich, 280 Queen St. West, Toronto.   *101101*

Victoria (British Columbia)
Vanhall Antiques Ltd., 1023 Fort St., Victoria.
T. (604) 382-7643. - Print -   *101102*

Winnipeg (Manitoba)
Curiosity Shop, 266 Edmonton St., Winnipeg, Manitoba
R3C 1R9. T. (204) 943-2734. - Print -   *101103*

Chile

Santiago
Editorial Universitaria, S.A., San Francisco 454, Santiago. T. 39 34 61. - Print / Map - 101104
Libreria Andres Bellos, Huéfanos 1156, Santiago.
T. 72 21 16. 101105
Razeto, Adriano, Pocuro 2826, Santiago. - Print / Engr / Map - 101106

China, Republic

Taipei
Chang, W.C., East and West Book Co. Ltd., Taipei P.O.B. 1655. T. (02) 381-8589;Telex 22192 NEWORLD.
- ArtBk - 101107
New City International Book Company, 2F, No. 34, Lane 25, Tai-Shung St., Taipei. T. (02) 396-7588. 101108

Colombia

Bogotá
Herder Editorial y Libreria Ltda., Apdo. Aereo 6855, Bogotá. T. 42 27 06. 101109
Libreria Central, Avenida 82, No. 11-18, Bogotá.
T. 256 21 20, 236 84 31. 101110

Croatia

Rijeka
Knjižara nakladnog zavoda Matice Hrvatske, Djure Djakovića 20, 51000 Rijeka. T. (051) 252 70.
- ArtBk - 101111

Zagreb
Antikvarijat Tin Ujević, Nakladni zavod Znanje, Trg Nik. Subića Zrinjskog 16, 10000 Zagreb. T. (01) 44 22 86.
- Print / ArtBk / Engr / Map - 101112
Knjižara i antikvarijat nakladnog zavoda Matice Hrvatske, Ilica 62, 10000 Zagreb. T. (01) 44 20 64. 101113
Mladost-Znanstvena knjizara, Preradoviceva 2, 10000 Zagreb. T. (01) 41 82 87. - ArtBk - 101114
Tehnička knjiga i antikvarijat, Gundulićeva 19, 10000 Zagreb. T. (01) 44 85 26. - Print / ArtBk - 101115

Czech Republic

Brno
Kniha n. p., ul. 9 Května 1, Brno. T. (05) 248 63. 101116
Kniha n. p., Česká ul. 28, Brno. T. (05) 225 01. 101117

České Budějovice
Kniha n. p., Žižkovo nám 31, České Budějovice.
T. (038) 27 91. 101118

Dvůr Králové n./L.
Kniha n. p., Gottwaldovo nam. 37, Dvůr Králové n./L.
T. 25 13. 101119

Hodonín
Kniha n. p., Stalingradska 4, Hodonín. T. 21 95. 101120

Hradec Králové
Kniha n. p., 169 V. Kopecky, Hradec Králové.
T. (049) 53 25. 101121

Jablonec nad Nisou
Kniha n. p., Komenského 2, Jablonec nad Nisou.
T. 43 70. 101122

Jihlava
Kniha n. p., Palackého 29, Jihlava. T. 220 03. 101123

Karlovy Vary
Kniha n. p., Čs. Armády 12, Karlovy Vary.
T. (17) 34 13. 101124

Kroměříž
Kniha n. p., Riegrovo nam. 10, Kroměříž.
T. 30 00. 101125

Liberec
Kniha n. p., 4 Pražská, Liberec. T. (048) 42 04. 101126

Louny
Kniha, Beneše z Loun 137, 440 01 Louny. T. 2063.
- Print / ArtBk - 101127

Most
Kniha n. p., Bezručova 1, Most. T. (035) 21 26. 101128

Náchod
Antikvariát, nám TGM 58, 547 01 Náchod. T. 23443.
- Print / ArtBk / Engr - 101129

Olomouc
Kniha n. p., 9 Ostružnická, Olomouc. T. 55 79. 101130

Opava
Kniha n. p., Ostrožná, Opava. T. (0653) 26 35. 101131

Ostrava
Kniha n. p., Zámecká ul. 4, Ostrava.
T. (069) 218 71. 101132

Pardubice
Antikvariát, Zelenbranská 2, 530 98 Pardubice.
T. 202 70. - Print / ArtBk - 101133

Plzeň
Kniha n. p., nám. Republiky 42, Plzeň.
T. (019) 35493. 101134

Praha
ARTIA, Ve Smečkách 30, Praha. T. (02) 24 60 41.
- Print - 101135
Kniha, Vinohradska 20, Praha. T. (02) 24 42 26. 101136
Kniha, ul. 28 Října 13, Praha. T. (02) 23 72 57/8. 101137
Kniha, Kírovova 32, Praha. T. (02) 53 35 60. 101138
Kniha, Dlážděná 5, 110 00 Praha.
T. (02) 221861. 101139
Kniha, Myslikova 10, Praha. T. (02) 23 44 02. 101140
Kniha, Ječná 36, Praha. T. (02) 22 22 26. 101141
Kniha, Skořepka 2, Praha. T. (02) 24 77 08. 101142
Kniha, Malé nám. 11, Praha. T. (02) 23 39 18.
- Map - 101143
Kniha, Karlova ul. 2, Praha. T. (02) 23 42 82. - Print / Engr - 101144
Kniha, Karlova ul. 16, Praha. T. (02) 24 02 75. - Print / Engr / Autogr - 101145
Knižní velkoobchod, Spálená 55, Praha.
T. (02) 23 23 23. 101146
Knižní velkoobchod, Stěpánská 65, Praha.
T. (02) 246561. 101147

Prostějov
Kniha n. p., nam. 9 Května 30, Prostějov.
T. 38 12. 101148

Tábor
Kniha n. p., Palackého 6, Tábor. T. 42 19. 101149

Teplice
Kniha, Masarykova tř. 15, 415 01 Teplice. T. 23966.
- ArtBk - 101150

Ústí nad Labem
Kniha n. p., 12 Pařížská, 400 01 Ústí nad Labem.
T. 228 70. - Print - 101151

Zlín
Kniha n. p., 15 Leninova 212, Zlín. T. 27 12. 101152

Znojmo
Kniha n. p., Kollárová 13, Znojmo. T. 32 07. 101153

Denmark

Ålborg
Pilegaard, G., Algade 65, 9000 Ålborg. T. 98 13 90 00.
- Print - 101154

Århus (Jütland)
Aabenhus Aarhus Antikvariat, Aaboulevarden 39, 8000 Århus C. T. 86 12 02 78. - Print / Engr - 101155
Christensen, J.E., L. Hammerichsvej 5, 8200 Århus N.
T. 648 94. - Print - 101156
Jydsk Antikvariat, PP Orumsgade 18, 8000 Århus C.
T. 11 07 89. 101157

Hillerød
Frederiksborg, Aeblehaven 10, 3400 Hillerød.
T. 26 07 58. - Print - 101158
Hillerød Antikvariat, Slotsg. 57, 3400 Hillerød.
T. 42 26 14 98. 101159

København
ABC-Antikvariatet, Skt. Hans Torv 3, 2200 København.
T. 31 35 00 17. 101160
Aeseløret, Nordre Fihavnsg. 18, 1000 København.
T. 38 45 98. - Print - 101161
Andersens Antikvariat, Alhambravej 22, 1826 København. T. 31 24 88 33. - Print - 101162
Antikvar-Nyt, Studiestr. 41, 1455 København K.
T. 33 13 66 24. - Print - 101163
Antikvarboden, Gl. Jernbanev. 4, 1000 København.
T. 31 17 48 32. - Print - 101164
Antikvariatet Hyltebro 3, Hyltebro 3, 1000 København.
T. 31 81 40 62. - Print - 101165
Antikvariatet Jagtvej 94, Jagtv. 94, 1000 København.
T. 31 35 94 02. 101166
Blågårdsplads Antikvariat, Blågårdspl., 1000 København. T. 31 39 69 24. 101167
Blume, Vaernedamsvej 9, 1619 København V.
T. 31 31 04 53. - Print - 101168
Bog-Børsen, Studiestr. 10, 1455 København.
T. 33 13 25 80. 101169
Boghallens Antikvariat, Radhuspladsen 37, 1585 København. T. 33 11 85 11. - Print / Engr / Autogr / Map - 101170
Bogormen, Vennemindevej 65, 1000 København.
T. 31 18 30 03. - Print - 101171
Booktrader, Skinderg. 23, 1159 København.
T. 33 12 06 69. - Print / ArtBk / Engr - 101172
Branner, Bredgade 10, 1260 København K.
T. 33 15 91 87. - Print / Engr / Map - 101173
Brøndum, Askildrupv. 23, 1000 København.
T. 98 33 95 59. 101174
Busck, Arnold, Købmagerg. 49, 1150 København K.
T. 12 24 53. - Print - 101175
Busck, Arnold, Fiolstraede 24, 1171 København K.
T. 33 13 49 90. - Print - 101176
Dansk Bogservice, Amg.faelledv. 9, 1000 København.
T. 31 57 10 56. 101177
Dansk Bogservice, Amg. faelledv. 9, 1000 København.
T. 57 10 56. - Print - 101178
Dr. Octopus, Århusg. 2, 1000 København. T. 26 28 48.
- Print - 101179
Enghave Plads Antikvariat, Enghavepl. 3, 1670 København V. T. 31 24 92 84. - Print - 101180
Fantask, Sankt Pederstr. 18, 1453 København.
T. 33 11 85 38. - Print - 101181
Fog Dan Musikantikvariat, Gråbrødretorv 7, 1154 København K. T. 33 11 40 60. - Print - 101182
Frederiksberg Antikvariat, Gl. Kongevej 120, 1850 København. T. 31 24 97 08. 101183
Girsel, Max & Käthe, Silkeg. 11 (K), 1113 København K.
T. 13 53 35. - Print - 101184
Gladsaxe, Søb. Hovedg. 195, 1000 København.
T. 67 16 46. - Print - 101185
Grosell, Peter, Laederstr. 15, 1201 København K.
T. 33 93 45 05. - Print - 101186
Harck, Einar, Fiolstr. 34, 1171 København K.
T. 33 12 13 44. - Print - 101187
Hartmund, Nils, Gl. Kongev. 163, 1000 København.
T. 31 31 63 56. - Print - 101188
Hieroglyffen, Howitzvej 27, 1000 København.
T. 31 87 12 60. - Print - 101189
Jensen, Helge S., Fasanv. 95, 1000 København.
T. 31 16 04 01. - Print - 101190
Jensen, Solveig, Borgbjerv. 11, 1000 København.
T. 31 21 01 77. - Print - 101191
Kaaber, Skindergade 34, 1159 København K.
T. 33 15 41 77. - Print / Engr / Autogr / Map - 101192

Suomen Antikvariaattiyhdistys ry.
Finska Antikvariatföreningen rf.

The Antiquarian Booksellers Association of Finland

Founded 1941

Fredrikinkatu 63 , FIN-00100, Helsinki, Finland
Tel: +358 9 694 33 06
Member of ILAB. International League of Antiquarian Booksellers

---

Kjaer, Blågradsg. 25, 1000 København. T. 31 39 69 24.
- Print - *101193*

Knagsted, Kompagnistr. 8, 1208 København K.
T. 33 13 37 70. - Print - *101194*

Knagsted, Gert, Dr.-Priemev. 11, 1854 København.
T. 31 22 62 64. - Print - *101195*

Kobberstikhuset, Kronprinsensg. 4, 1114 København K.
T. 33 14 91 72. - Print - *101196*

Købes, Strandboulevarden 166, 2100 København Ø.
T. 29 40 77. - Print - *101197*

Larsen, Kjeld, Enghavev. 5, 1674 København V.
T. 31 24 06 00. - Print - *101198*

Lynge & Søn, Silkegade 11, 1113 København K.
T. 33 15 53 35. *101199*

Muleposen, Godthåbsv. 126, 1000 København.
T. 31 86 54 71. - Print - *101200*

Nansensgade Antikvariat, Nansensgade 70, 1366 København K. T. 33 14 24 26. - Print - *101201*

Nørballe, Leif, Gl. Kongev. 120, 1850 København V.
T. 31 24 97 08. - Print - *101202*

Notabene, Österbrogade 96, 2100 København Ø.
T. 31 26 12 03. - Print - *101203*

Oasen, Vigerslevv. 39, 1000 København.
T. 31 30 41 42. *101204*

Österbro, Strandboul. 166, 2100 København Ø.
T. 31 29 40 77. - Print - *101205*

Olsen Marinus, Studiestraede 41, 1455 København K.
l. 33 13 66 24. - Print - *101206*

Ordrup Antikvariat, Ordrupv. 70A, 1000 København.
T. 63 03 61. *101207*

Paludan, Erik, Fiolstraede 10, 1171 København.
T. 33 15 06 75. *101208*

Penny Lane, P. Bangsv. 2, 1000 København K.
T. 31 86 65 42. - Print - *101209*

Pinkerton, Nansensgade 66, 1366 København K.
T. 33 13 95 40. - Print - *101210*

Pixi, Enghavevej 28B, 1674 København V.
T. 31 23 36 40. *101211*

Puk, Hans-Egedesg. 13, 1000 København.
T. 31 37 37 54. *101212*

Rosenkilde & Bagger, Kron-Prinsens-Gade 3, 1017 København K. T. 33 15 70 44. - Engr / Autogr /
Map - *101213*

Samson, Torben, Ole Suhrs G. 4, 1354 København.
T. 33 32 05 05. *101214*

Seismograaf, Larsbjørnsstr. 17, 1454 København K.
T. 33 14 41 90. *101215*

Skovle & Skovle, Dag Hammarskjöldsallé 42 + 40, 1000 København. T. 26 00 03. - Print - *101216*

Thuesen, Fiolstr. 23, 1171 København K. T. 33 11 99 62.
- ArtBk - *101217*

Nykøbing

Skafte, K. E., Falster, 4800 Nykøbing.
T. 54 85 15 06. *101218*

Randers

Randers Antikvariat, J. Nielsen Schirmer, Hospitalsgade 3, 8900 Randers. T. 86 41 00 29. *101219*

Roskilde

Hedenborgs Antikvariat, Dr. Margrethesvej 4, 4000 Roskilde. T. 35 89 13. - Print - *101220*

Skørping

Brøndum Antikvariat, Askildrupvej 23 St. Brøndum, 9520 Skørping. T. 98 33 95 59. - Print - *101221*

Sorø

Soro Antikvariat, Frederiksbergvej 8, 4180 Sorø.
T. 63 35 85. - Print - *101222*

Viborg

Kjaer, Sankt Mathiasg. 29, 8800 Viborg. T. 86 61 39 00.
- Print - *101223*

Egypt

Cairo

Lehnert & Landrock, 44 Sherif Pasha St., Cairo.
T. (2) 392 7606. - ArtBk - *101224*

Finland

Espoo (Uudenmaan lääni)

Tapiola-antikvariaatti, Suvikuja 4a, 02120 Espoo.
T. (09) 42 58 47. *101225*

Hanko

Marian Antikvariaatti, Marias Antikvariat, Bulevardi 3, 10900 Hanko. T. (019) 2487225. *101226*

Helsinki

Antiikki-Kartta Jan Strang, Jatasalmentie 1, 00830 Helsinki. T. (09) 7554929, Fax 7554929. *101227*

Antikvaarinen Kirjakauppa, Klaarantie 4 A 1, 00200 Helsinki. Fax (09) 499930. *101228*

Antikvaarinen Kirjakauppa Johannes oy, Yrjönkatu 1, 00120 Helsinki. T. (09) 605675. - Print - *101229*

Antikvaarinen Kirjakauppa Kimmo Välkesalmi, Pursimiehenkatu 11, 00150 Helsinki. T. (09) 627657. *101230*

Antikvariaatti Lukeva Toukka, Fleminginkatu 9, 00530 Helsinki. T. (09) 730284. *101231*

C. Hagelstamin Antikvaarinen Kirjakauppa, Antikvariska Bokhandel, Fredrikinkatu 35, 00120 Helsinki.
T. (09) 649291, Fax 602785. - Print / Map - *101232*

Itä-Helsingin Antikvariaatti, Hansasilta 4, 00930 Helsinki. T. (09) 336668. *101233*

Yrjönkadun Antikvariaatti, Yrjönkatu 21, 00100 Helsinki. T. (09) 611499. *101234*

Helsinki (Uudenmaan lääni)

Aarnio, Liiketie 21, 00730 Helsinki.
T. (09) 36 46 88. *101235*

Akateeminen Kirjakauppa, Keskuskatu 1, 00100 Helsinki. T. (09) 65 11 22. - ArtBk - *101236*

Antikvaari, Kasarmikatu 26, 00130 Helsinki.
T. (09) 65 40 41. *101237*

Antikvaarinen Kirjakauppa, Albertinkatu 18, 00120 Helsinki. T. (09) 66 63 49. *101238*

Antikvaria Bökkeri, Vironkatu 11, 00170 Helsinki.
T. (09) 135 68 00. *101239*

Antikvariaatti, Hämeentie 77, 00550 Helsinki.
T. (09) 76 00 98. *101240*

Antikvariaatti Kauppamakasiini, Vuorimiehenkatu 10, 00140 Helsinki. T. (09) 62 80 04. *101241*

Antikvariaatti Kirjakamari, Uudenmaankatu 15, 00120 Helsinki. T. (09) 693 26 71. *101242*

Antikvariaatti Putiikki, Viipurinkatu 16, 00510 Helsinki.
T. (09) 146 32 31. *101243*

Antikvariaatti Syvä uni oy, Fredrikinkatu 55, 00100 Helsinki. T. (09) 60 11 24. - Print - *101244*

Arohonka, Cygnaeuksenkatu 12, 00100 Helsinki.
T. (09) 49 34 83. *101245*

Diivari, Viiskulma Laivurinrinne 2, 00120 Helsinki.
T. (09) 63 88 16. *101246*

Divary, Kirstinkatu 13, 00510 Helsinki.
T. (09) 71 29 25. *101247*

Ervasti, K., Torkkelinkatu 4, 00500 Helsinki.
T. (09) 753 05 09. *101248*

Haapanen, Takaniityntie 5k, 00700 Helsinki.
T. (09) 35 67 11. *101249*

Hagelstam, C., Fredrikinkatu 35, 00120 Helsinki.
T. (09) 64 92 91, Fax 60 27 85. *101250*

Helsingin Antikvariaatti Ky, Mechelininkatu 17, 00100 Helsinki. T. (09) 40 76 56, Fax 407206. - Print / Map - *101251*

Helsingin Levy- ja Kirjapörssi, Helsinginkatu 7, 00500 Helsinki. T. (09) 76 85 28. *101252*

Hiltunen, Viherniemenkatu 3, 00530 Helsinki.
T. (09) 753 64 35. *101253*

Kampintorin Antikvaarinen Kirjakauppa Oy, Fredrikinkatu 63, 00100 Helsinki. T. (09) 694 33 06, Fax 6943650.
- Print - *101254*

Karhupuiston Antikvaarinen Kirjakauppa, Fleminginkatu 5, 00530 Helsinki. T. (09) 753 18 48. *101255*

Keskustan Antikvaarinen Kirjakauppa, Yrjönkatu 1, 00120 Helsinki. T. (09) 60 56 75. *101256*

Laterna Magica, Rauhankatu 7, 00170 Helsinki.
T. (09) 66 95 59, Fax 8043949. - Print - *101257*

Lehti-Fennica, Kalevankatu 40, 00180 Helsinki.
T. (09) 64 51 61. *101258*

Lukutoukka, Fleminginkatu 8, 00530 Helsinki.
T. (09) 73 02 84. *101259*

Malmin Lehti- ja Kirja, Markkinatie 2, 00700 Helsinki.
T. (09) 35 34 72. *101260*

Malminrinteen Vanhakirja, Malminrinne 4, 00100 Helsinki. T. (09) 694 90 68. *101261*

Pohjoismainen Antikvaarinen Kirjakauppa, Nordiska Antikvariska Bokhandeln, Pohjoinen Makasiinikatu 6, 00130 Helsinki. T. (09) 62 63 52. - Print / Engr /
Map - *101262*

Presentti, Pikku Roba 2, 00100 Helsinki.
T. (09) 63 88 77. *101263*

Punavuori, Iso Roobertinkatu 42, 00120 Helsinki.
T. (09) 62 60 89. *101264*

Runebergin Antikvariaatti, Runebergs Antikvariat, Runeberginkatu 37, 00100 Helsinki. T. (09) 49 90 30, Fax 499930. - Print - *101265*

Samaletdin, B., Iso Roobertinkatu 9, 00120 Helsinki.
T. (09) 64 58 86. *101266*

Savolainen, Sakari, Mannerheimintie 33, 00250 Helsin-
ki. T. (09) 41 47 88.   *101267*

Seppo Hiltunen Ky, Sofiankatu 6, 00170 Helsinki.
T. (09) 62 71 61.   *101268*

Strindberg, Pohjoisesplanadi 33, 00100 Helsinki.
T. (09) 61 84 04.   *101269*

Suomalainen Kirjakauppa, Vanha Ylioppilastalo, 00100
Helsinki. T. (09) 60 28 55. - ArtBk / Engr -   *101270*

Tapiiri, Eerikinkatu 10, 00100 Helsinki.
T. (09) 60 23 68.   *101271*

Tapiola-antikvariaatti, Malminrinne 3, 00100 Helsinki.
T. (09) 694 47 79.   *101272*

Tavela, Tiina, Albertinkatu 18, 00120 Helsinki.
T. (09) 66 63 49.   *101273*

Ilomantsi (Pohjois-Karjalan lääni)
Antikvaarinen Osto- ja myyntiliike, 82900 Ilomantsi.
T. (013) 21129.   *101274*

Jämsä (Keski-Suomen lääni)
Kalevala, Koskentie 6, 42100 Jämsä.
T. (014) 12490.   *101275*

Joensuu (Pohjois-Karjalan lääni)
Suvantodivari, Suvantokatu 12, 80100 Joensuu.
T. (013) 12 73 95.   *101276*

Jyväskylä (Keski-Suomen lääni)
Jyväskylän Vanha Antikvariaatti, Kauppakatu 2, 40100
Jyväskylä. T. (014) 21 68 75.   *101277*
Keski-Suomen Antikvaarinen Kirjakauppa, Yliopistonkatu
30, 40100 Jyväskylä. T. (014) 61 60 86.   *101278*

Kemi (Lapin lääni)
Kemin kirjadivari, Valtakatu 30, 94100 Kemi.
T. (016) 16798.   *101279*

Kerava (Uudenmaan lääni)
Kersa, Aleksanterintori, 04200 Kerava.
T. (09) 294 42 10.   *101280*

Kouvola (Kymen lääni)
Kouvolan Lukusoppi, Torikatu 2, 45100 Kouvola.
T. (05) 17604.   *101281*
Novgorod, Kauppalankatu 8, 45100 Kouvola.
T. (05) 16161.   *101282*

Kuopio (Kuopion lääni)
Kirja- ja Lehtilinna, Kuninkaankatu 23, 70100 Kuopio.
T. (017) 11 97 95.   *101283*

Lahti (Hämeen lääni)
Antikvariaatti Lehtitori, Rautatienkatu 14, 15110 Lahti.
T. (03) 48901.   *101284*
Ex Libris, Hämeenkatu 24, 15110 Lahti.
T. (03) 51 51 95.   *101285*
Ex Libris, Linja-Autoasema, 15110 Lahti.
T. (03) 83 41 14.   *101286*
Lahden Antikvaarinen Kirjakauppa, Vesijärvenkatu 12,
15110 Lahti. T. (03) 40295.   *101287*
Suuronen, Vesijärvenkatu 12, 15110 Lahti.
T. (03) 40295.   *101288*
Vaihtolehdet, Rautatienkatu 10, 15110 Lahti.
T. (03) 82 75 50.   *101289*

Lappeenranta (Kymen lääni)
Suma, Kirkkokatu 9b, 53100 Lappeenranta.
T. (05) 17761.   *101290*

Leppävaara (Uudenmaan lääni)
Merja, Vartia, Timpurinkuja 2, 97100 Leppävaara.
T. (09) 51 39 60.   *101291*

Lohja (Uudenmaan lääni)
Lohjan Antikvaarinen Kirjakauppa, Nahkurinkatu 10,
08100 Lohja. T. (019) 21084.   *101292*

Mikkeli (Mikkelin lääni)
Heinikainen, A., Maaherrankatu 30, 50100 Mikkeli.
T. (015) 21 37 71.   *101293*
Kulma-Antikvari, Hallituskatu 2, 50100 Mikkeli.
T. (015) 16 21 11.   *101294*

Myyrmäki
Marleenan Aitta, Vuollemutka 9, Myyrmäki.
T. 566 12 72.   *101295*

Oulu (Oulun lääni)
Ale-Kirja, Rautatienkatu 16, 90100 Oulu.
T. (08) 22 06 85.   *101296*
Kirja-Antikvariaatti, Pakkahuoneenkatu 21, 90100 Oulu.
T. (08) 311 23 44.   *101297*

Paimio (Turun ja Porin lääni)
Marjo, K., Meijeritie, 21530 Paimio.
T. (02) 73 20 11.   *101298*

Pietarsaari /Jakobstad (Vaasan lääni)
City Divary, Isokatu 17, 68600 Pietarsaari /Jakobstad.
T. (06) 18300.   *101299*

Raisio (Turun ja Porin lääni)
Raision Antikvariaatti, Kauppakatu 3, 21200 Raisio.
T. (02) 78 36 64.   *101300*

Riihimäki (Hämeen lääni)
Riihimäen Antikva, Hämeenkatu 24-26, 11100 Riihimä-
ki. T. (019) 72 11 40.   *101301*
Väisänen, P. M., Torikatu 3, 11100 Riihimäki.
T. (019) 72 10 11.   *101302*

Rovaniemi (Lapin lääni)
Kriivari, Korkalonkatu 34, 96200 Rovaniemi.
T. (016) 23220.   *101303*

Seinäjoki (Vaasan lääni)
Seinäjoen Lehti- ja Kirjapörssi, Koulukatu 7, 60100 Seinäjoki. T. (06) 14 77 30.   *101304*

Siilinjärvi (Kuopion lääni)
Siilin Divari, Kasurilantie 6, 71800 Siilinjärvi.
T. (017) 42 44 62.   *101305*
Siivari, Asematie 11, 71800 Siilinjärvi.
T. (017) 42 30 10.   *101306*

Sysmä (Mikkelin lääni)
Vanha Kerttu, Sysmäntie 29, 19700 Sysmä.
T. (014) 171717. *101307*

Tampere (Hämeen lääni)
A & O Antikva, Verkatehtaankatu 13, 33100 Tampere.
T. (03) 13 00 78. *101308*
Alarannan Antikvariaatti, Laukontori 6, 33200 Tampere.
T. (03) 14 78 23. *101309*
Antikvaarinen Kirjahuone Libris, Hämeenkatu 19, 2nd
floor, 33200 Tampere. T. (03) 14 92 95. *101310*
Divari Tammer-Kanava, Ratinankuja 4, 33100 Tampere.
T. (03) 22 51 27. *101311*
Komisario Palmu, Itsenäisyydenkatu 18, 33500 Tampe-
re. T. (03) 61 35 44. *101312*
Kukunor, Rautatienkatu 22, 33100 Tampere.
T. (03) 13 12 87. *101313*
Kulkukirja, Pirkankatu 10, 33230 Tampere.
T. (03) 12 18 04. *101314*
Lukulaari, Kauppakatu 15, 33200 Tampere.
T. (03) 14 25 60. *101315*
Tammer-Divari, Tammelanpuistokatu 34, 33500 Tampe-
re. T. (03) 14 20 67. *101316*
Tampereen Kirja- ja Lehtiantikva, Hämeenpuisto 17-19,
33210 Tampere. T. (03) 14 79 95. *101317*
Timisto, Ojakatu 2, 33100 Tampere.
T. (03) 14 14 32. *101318*

Tapiola
Mäntyviidan Kirjakauppa, Mäntyviita 4, Tapiola.
T. 455 24 62. *101319*

Turku (Turun ja Porin lääni)
AAA Antikka, Verkatehtaankatu 8, 20300 Turku.
T. (02) 51 04 20. *101322*
ABC-Kirja, Linnankatu 33, 20100 Turku. T. (02) 51 72 52.
- Print / Engr - *101323*
Abiskukko ja Levylautanen, Humalistonkatu 12, 20100
Turku. T. (02) 2511224, Fax 2511430. *101323a*
Alfa Antikva, Puistokatu 8, 20140 Turku.
T. (02) 32 59 89. *101324*
Antikka 32, Puutarhakatu 32, 20140 Turku.
T. (02) 30 31 06. *101325*
Antikvaari-Aitta, Rauhankatu 12a, 20100 Turku.
T. (02) 33 63 57. *101326*
Antikvaarinen Kirjakauppa, Brahenkatu 9, 20110 Turku.
T. (02) 32 58 90. *101327*
Brahen Antikvariaatti, Brahenkatu 2, 20110 Turku.
T. (02) 32 22 44. *101328*
Kaarinan Antikka, Kaarinan tori, 20000 Turku.
I. (02) 43 31 51. *101329*
Kaskenkulma Antikvariaatti, Kaskenkatu 15b, 20700
Turku. T. (02) 33 00 16. *101330*
Kvariaatti, Hämeenkatu 16, 20500 Turku.
T. (02) 33 16 68. *101331*
Läntisenkadun Antikvariaatti, Läntinen Pitkäkatu 26,
20100 Turku. T. (02) 32 37 84. *101332*
Myllynpuoti, Martinkatu 7, 20810 Turku.
T. (02) 35 72 23. *101333*
Narikka, Maariankatu 1, 20100 Turku.
T. (02) 51 08 35. *101334*
Omituisten Opusten Kauppa, Sibeliuksenkatu 2, 20110
Turku. T. (02) 2516794. *101334a*
Pansion Taide-Antika, Hyrköisentie 26-28, 20240 Turku.
T. (02) 40 43 49. *101335*
Parkin Antikvaari, Verkatehtaankatu 6, 20110 Turku.
T. (02) 51 04 20. *101336*
Turun Antiikki ja Raha, Läntinen Pitkäkatu 14, 20100
Turku. T. (02) 50 02 35. *101337*
Turun Vaihtotalo, Läntinen Pitkäkatu 15, 20100 Turku.
T. (02) 32 95 97. *101338*
Varissuon Antikvariaatti, Itäkeskus, 20000 Turku.
T. (02) 44 11 98. *101339*
Vetus et Nova, Uudenmaankatu 12b, 20500 Turku.
T. (02) 51 01 41. *101340*

Vaasa (Vaasan lääni)
Antikvariaatti Lafkan, Antikvariat Lafkan, Hovioikeudenpuistikko 5, 65100 Vaasa. T. (06) 12 16 76. *101341*

Vaasa/Vasa (Vaasan lääni)
Pohjanmaan Antikvariaatti, Pitkäkatu 43, 65100 Vaasa/
Vasa. T. (06) 17 79 88. *101342*

Vantaa (Uudenmaan lääni)
Malin, A., Kytötie 17, 01640 Vantaa.
T. (09) 874 73 63. *101343*

France

Agen (Lot-et-Garonne)
Gauzy, J.L., 1 Rue Courteline, 47000 Agen.
T. 0553663889, Fax 0553660328. - Print /
Engr - *101344*
Jooris, Patrice, 71 Rue La-Fayette, 47000 Agen.
T. 0553470699. *101345*

Aix-en-Provence (Bouches-du-Rhône)
Borréani, Laurent, 11 Cours Saint-Louis, 13100 Aix-en-
Provence. T. 0442214028. *101346*
K Livres, 8 Rue Cardinale, 13100 Aix-en-Provence.
T. 0442263511. *101347*

Ajaccio (Corse)
Arte et Opara, 16 Rue Bonaparte, 20000 Ajaccio.
T. 0495212254. - Print - *101348*
Bouquinerie du Palais, 1 Rue Comte-Bacciochi, 20000
Ajaccio. T. 0495222119. *101349*
Temps Retrouvé, 1 Rue Sainte-Lucie, 20000 Ajaccio.
T. 0495201730, Fax 0495209168. *101350*

Alençon (Orne)
Art et Collection, 4 Pl du 103 RI, 61000 Alençon.
T. 0233321725. - Autogr / Print - *101351*

Allerey-sur-Saône (Saône-et-Loire)
Guillemin, Hervé, Le Lary, Rte de Verdun, 71350 Aller-
ey-sur-Saône. T. 0385918558. - Print / Engr - *101352*

Amiens (Somme)
Langlois, Danièle, 11 Rue Hotoie, 80000 Amiens.
T. 0322912090. - Print - *101353*
Or du Temps, 7 Pl Don, 80000 Amiens. T. 0322923949.
- Print - *101354*
Temps Livre, 41 Rue 3-Cailloux, 80000 Amiens.
T. 0322922643. - Print - *101355*

Angers (Maine-et-Loire)
Alphabet, 8 Rue 2-Haies, 49100 Angers.
T. 41880613. *101356*
Candide, 7 Rue Montault, 49100 Angers.
T. 41861500. *101357*

Angoulême (Charente)
Calliope, 38 Rue Beaulieu, 16000 Angoulême.
T. 0545958636. *101358*
Livres d'Autrefois, 23 Rue Beaulieu, 16000 Angoulême.
T. 0545957775. *101359*

Annecy (Haute-Savoie)
Chaminade, Jacques, 2 Rue Jean-Jacques-Rousseau,
74000 Annecy. T. 0450515731, Fax 0450456153.
- Print - *101360*
Librairie des Arts, 12 Rue Sommeiller, 74000 Annecy.
T. 0450512335. - ArtBk - *101361*
Reflets d'Epoques, 4 Rue Jean-Jacques-Rousseau,
74000 Annecy. T. 0450527096. *101362*

Annemasse (Haute-Savoie)
Hermès, 17 Av Pasteur, 74100 Annemasse.
T. 0450920443, Fax 0450958069. - Print /
Engr - *101363*

Antibes (Alpes-Maritimes)
Librairie de l'Olympe, 1 Rue Tourraque, 06600 Antibes.
T. 0493341411. *101364*
Maurel, Brigitte, 594 Chemin Combes, Bleuets, Pav. 31,
06600 Antibes. T. 0493749688. - Print - *101365*

Aubagne (Bouches-du-Rhône)
Marques, Maxime, 14bis Rue Laget, 13400 Aubagne.
T. 0442030465. - Print - *101366*

Auch (Gers)
Dupuy-Cyrille, Claude, 10 Rue Gambetta, 32000 Auch.
T. 0562054381. *101367*
Mauvin, Pascal, 3 Rue Espagne, 32000 Auch.
T. 0562618157. *101368*

Auray (Morbihan)
Le Guennec, Jean-Louis, 36 Rue Georges-Clemenceau,
56400 Auray. T. 0297507314. - Print - *101369*

Autun (Saône-et-Loire)
Metra, Guy, 11 Pl du Terreau, 71400 Autun.
T. 0385861951. - Print - *101370*

Auxerre (Yonne)
Cheminant, Sylvie, 77 Rue Paris, 89000 Auxerre.
T. 0386511406. *101371*

Avignon (Vaucluse)
Ami Voyage, 5 Rue Prévot, 84000 Avignon.
T. 0490824151. *101372*
Bouguen, Bernard, 43 Rue Teinturiers, 84000 Avignon.
T. 0490829330. *101373*
Galerie des Augustins, 1 Rue Louis-Pasteur, 84000 Avi-
gnon. T. 0490859178. - Engr - *101374*
Paroles, 6 Petite-Saunerie, 84000 Avignon.
T. 0490852357. *101375*

Avillers-Sainte-Croix (Meuse)
Boux, Jean, 33 Grande Rue, 55210 Avillers-Sainte-
Croix. T. 0329875625. - Print - *101376*

Bagneux (Hauts-de-Seine)
Dimp, 34 Rue Alphonse-Pluchet, 92220 Bagneux.
Fax (1) 46543403. *101377*

Baume-les-Messieurs (Jura)
Noir, André, Abbaye, 39570 Baume-les-Messieurs.
T. 0384446187. *101378*

Bavay (Nord)
Duriez, François, 5 Rue Soupirs, 59570 Bavay.
T. 0327631789, Fax 0327668375. - Print - *101379*

Bayonne (Pyrénées-Atlantiques)
Bouquiniste, 36 Rue Bourgneuf, 64100 Bayonne.
T. 0559254372. - Print - *101380*
Librairie Cadier, 11 Rue Vieille-Boucherie, 64100
Bayonne. T. 0559597749. - Print - *101381*
Librairie des Pyrénées, 21 Rue Vieille-Boucherie, 64100
Bayonne. T. 0559597874. - Print - *101382*

Bazincourt-sur-Epte (Eure)
Jakubowicz, Le Plateau, 27140 Bazincourt-sur-Epte.
T. 0232555476, Fax 0232271012. - Print /
Engr - *101383*

Beaulieu-sur-Mer (Alpes-Maritimes)
Rocchietti, 50 Blvd Général-Leclerc, 06310 Beaulieu-
sur-Mer. T. 0493012558. - ArtBk - *101384*

Beaune (Côte-d'Or)
Ancienne Guillemin, 24 Pl Carnot, Passage Sainte-Hé-
lène, 21200 Beaune. T. 0380227553. - Print /
Engr - *101385*
Mille et Une Feuilles, 20 Rue Maufoux, 21200 Beaune.
T. 0380246771. - Print / Engr - *101386*
Musée du Livre, 7 Av République, 21200 Beaune.
T. 0380221395. - Print - *101387*

Beauvais (Oise)
Géody, 84 Rue Amiens, 60000 Beauvais.
T. 0344056502. - Print - *101388*

Bécherel (Ille-et-Vilaine)
Ambassade de Hay on Wye, 20 Rue Libération, 35190
Bécherel. T. 0299667196. *101389*
Guimard, Edith, 1 Rue Porte-Saint-Michel, 35190 Bé-
cherel. T. 0299667448. *101390*
Gwrizienn, 3 Rue Chanvrerie, 35190 Bécherel.
T. 0299668709. - Print - *101391*
Librairie de la Porte Bertault, 5 Rue Fbg-Bertault, 35190
Bécherel. T. 0299667330. *101392*
Librairie du Pied de l'Eglise, 3 Porte Saint-Michel,
35190 Bécherel. T. 0299667333. - Print - *101393*
Séanachi, 7 Rue Fbg-Bertault, 35190 Bécherel.
T. 0299667442. *101394*

Belfort (Territoire-de-Belfort)
Caricatures, 5 Av Wilson, 90000 Belfort. T. 0384213623.
- Print - *101395*

Bergerac (Dordogne)
Arcane, 33 Rue Fontaines, 24100 Bergerac.
T. 0553575838. *101396*

Bernay (Eure)
Charrette, 18 Rue Bernard-Gombert, 27300 Bernay.
T. 0232430548. - Print - *101397*
Herbert, Michel, 5 Rue Alexandre, 27300 Bernay.
T. 0232436578. *101398*

Besançon (Doubs)
Barthélémy, J., 8 Rue Liberté, 25000 Besançon, BP 125,
25014 Besançon Cédex. T. 0381808031. - Print /
ArtBk - *101399*
Bouquinerie Comtoise, 9 Rue Morand, 25000 Besançon.
T. 0381810293. - Print - *101400*
Cité des Vieux Livres, 139 Grande Rue, 25000 Besan-
çon. T. 0381813807. - Print / Engr - *101401*

Besse-sur-Issole (Var)
Editions du Forum, Quartier Ferraille-Rousse, Av Gare,
83890 Besse-sur-Issole. T. 0494698232. *101402*

Béthune (Pas-de-Calais)
Bel Régis, 78 Rue Arras, 62400 Béthune.
T. 0321571450, Fax 0321653637. - ArtBk - *101403*

Biarritz (Pyrénées-Atlantiques)
Jeu de l'Oie, 10 Av Louis-Barthou, 64200 Biarritz.
T. 0559245865. *101404*

Biesles (Haute-Marne)
Delbos, Frédéric, 15bis Rue Verdun, 52340 Biesles.
T. 0325037198. *101405*

Biot (Alpes-Maritimes)
Librairie du Musée Fernand Léger, 255 Chemin Val-de-
Pôme, 06410 Biot. T. 0493655070. - ArtBk - *101406*

Blagnac (Haute-Garonne)
Servettaz, Christian, 7 Chemin Barrieu, 31700 Blagnac.
T. 0561716441. - Print - *101407*

Blaye (Gironde)
Bouquinerie, 2 Rue Neuve, 33390 Blaye.
T. 0557428085. - Print - *101408*

Bléré (Indre-et-Loire)
Mathis, Jean-Louis, 12 Rue Madame, 37150 Bléré.
T. 0547303182. *101409*

Blois (Loir-et-Cher)
Charmoy, Xavier, 11 Rue Cobaudière, 41000 Blois.
T. 0254744529. *101410*
Librairie du Palais, 14 Rue Palais, 41000 Blois.
T. 0254560082, Fax 0254561702. - Print - *101411*

Bois-Colombes (Hauts-de-Seine)
Marges, 27 Rue Mertens, 92270 Bois-Colombes.
T. 0142427830. *101412*
Passages, 19 Rue Mertens, 92270 Bois-Colombes.
T. 0147609519. *101413*

Bordeaux (Gironde)
Aner, Michel, 20 Cours Somme, 33800 Bordeaux.
T. 0556313522. *101414*
Art and Arts Editeur, 15 Rue Maubec, 33000 Bordeaux.
T. 0556314547. - Print - *101415*
Au Vieux Grimoire, 13 Rue Parlement-Saint-Pierre,
33000 Bordeaux. T. 0556813750. - Print - *101416*
Au Vieux Grimoire, 46 Rue Bahutiers, 33000 Bordeaux.
T. 0556448940. - Print - *101417*
Bédélire, 249 Rue Sainte-Catherine, 33000 Bordeaux.
T. 0556314639, Fax 0557959050. - ArtBk - *101418*
Besançon, Jacques, 2ter Rue Mably, 33000 Bordeaux.
T. 0556816320. *101419*
Chat Noir, 45 Rue Remparts, 33000 Bordeaux.
T. 0556446763. *101420*
Espace BD, 33 Pass Galerie Bordelaise, 33000 Bor-
deaux. T. 0556481109, Fax 0556446905.
- ArtBk - *101421*
Fety, Margaret, 71 Rue Lafaurie-de-Monbadon, 33000
Bordeaux. T. 0556444380. *101422*
Foot, Johnny B., 20 Rue Menuts, 33000 Bordeaux.
T. 0556945126. *101423*

Librairie à Micita, 7 Pl Ferme-de-Richemont, 33000 Bor-
deaux. T. 0556480989. *101424*
Librairie Ancienne Laurencier, 7 Rue Chai-des-Farines,
33000 Bordeaux. T. 0556816879, Fax 0556818341.
- Print - *101425*
Librairie du Glorit, 20 Cours Pasteur, 33000 Bordeaux.
T. 0556793536, Fax 0556516860. *101426*
Librairie Populaire Castera, 4 Rue Saint-Nicolas, 33800
Bordeaux. T. 0556916290. *101427*
Maronne, Elisabeth, 37 Rue Bouffard, 33000 Bordeaux.
T. 0556443360. *101428*
Menelik, 66 et 70 Cours Argonne, 33000 Bordeaux.
T. 0556918760. *101429*
Montaut, Denis, 87 Rue de la Course, 33000 Bordeaux.
T. 0556819638. - Print / Engr - *101430*
Pagès, Jean, 11 Rue Maucoudinat, 33000 Bordeaux.
T. 0556790662. - Print / Engr - *101431*
Petit Saint-James, 2 Rue Saint-Nicolas, 33800 Bor-
deaux. T. 0556312266, Fax 0556312300. *101432*
Pictures, 25 Cours Pasteur, 33000 Bordeaux.
T. 0556445088. *101433*
Roche, Stéphane, 2bis Rue Tourat, 33000 Bordeaux.
T. 0556811720. - Print - *101434*
Salle des Ventes Libres, 29 Rue de Cheverus, 33000
Bordeaux. T. 0556442046. - Print - *101435*

Boulogne-Billancourt (Hauts-de-Seine)
Sapajou, 93 Rte Reine, 92100 Boulogne-Billancourt.
T. 0146031804. *101436*

Bourges (Cher)
Cartier, Philippe, 13 Rue Geoffroy-Tory, 18000 Bourges.
T. 0248653790. *101437*
Futur Archaïque, 15 Rue Littré, 18000 Bourges.
T. 0248706636. - Print - *101438*
Jardin des Lettres, 5 Rue Bourbonnoux, 18000 Bourges.
T. 0248246855, Fax 0248698663. *101439*

Brest (Finistère)
Bouquinerie in l'Occasion d'un Livre, 2 Rue Ducouëdic,
29200 Brest. T. 0298805490. - Print - *101440*
Ty Korn, 25 Rue Danton, 29200 Brest. T. 0298432631.
- Print - *101441*

Brignoles (Var)
Brignolaise de Presse, 10 Pl Caramy, 83170 Brignoles.
T. 0494694425. *101442*

Brive-la-Gaillarde (Corrèze)
Lemarie, Sylvie, 14bis Rue Elie-Breuil, 19100 Brive-la-
Gaillarde. T. 0555245649, Fax 0555170495.
- Print - *101443*
Nuits Blanches, 14 Rue Jaubertie, 19100 Brive-la-Gail-
larde. T. 0555171508. *101444*

Caen (Calvados)
Aux Collectionneurs, 30 Rue Froide, 14000 Caen.
T. 0231860229. - Print - *101445*
Frérot, 32 Pl Saint-Sauveur, 14000 Caen.
T. 0231863638. - Print - *101446*
Hamminoff, Chris, 50 Rue Ecuyère, 14000 Caen.
T. 0231866273. - Print - *101447*
Lang, François, 15 Rue Ecuyère, 14000 Caen.
T. 0231865218. - Print - *101448*
Siméon, Daniel, 59 Rue Jacobins, 14000 Caen.
T. 0231866688. *101449*

Cahors (Lot)
Charbonneau, Loys, 3 et 17 Rue Clément-Marot, 46000
Cahors. T. 0565355194, Fax 0565355194. - Print /
Autogr - *101450*
Rapaud, Valérie, 1 Pl Libération, 46000 Cahors.
T. 0565357130. - Print - *101451*

Calvi (Corse)
Broc'Art de Livres, Rue Alsace-Lorraine, Les Remparts, 20260 Calvi. T. 0495653587. - Map - *101452*

Calvisson (Gard)
Gandini, Jacques, 11 Grand'Rue, 30420 Calvisson.
T. 0466014042, Fax 0466014339. *101453*

Cannes (Alpes-Maritimes)
Beres, Pierre, 24 Rue Antibes, 06400 Cannes.
T. 0492983470. *101454*

Gagé, Pierre, 89 Blvd République, 06400 Cannes.
T. 0493383671. - Print - *101455*
Librairie Ancienne Carterie, 5 Rue Allieis, 06400 Can-
nes. T. 0493381777. *101456*
Rossignol, Henri, 1 Rue Jean-Daumas, 06400 Cannes.
T. 0493397055. - Print - *101457*

Carcassonne (Aude)
Amateur de Livres, 43 Rue Docteur-Albert-Tomey,
11000 Carcassonne. T. 0468718734. - Print - *101458*

Cardet (Gard)
Gauville, Thierry, Grand'Rue, 30350 Cardet.
T. 0466838561. *101459*

Carnac (Morbihan)
Grassin, Jean, Pl Port-en-Dro, 56342 Carnac.
T. 0297529363, Fax 0297528390. - ArtBk - *101460*

Castelnau-le-Lez (Hérault)
Lefèvre, Michel, Chemin Amandiers, Villa Virginia,
34170 Castelnau-le-Lez. T. 0467790248. *101461*

Cély-en-Bière (Seine-et-Marne)
Schoenmaeker, Bernard, 2 Rue Eglise, 77930 Cély-en-
Bière. T. 64380214. *101462*

Chalaines (Meuse)
Bibliomax-Office, 14 Rue Enfer, 55140 Chalaines.
T. 0329895013. - Print - *101463*

Challans (Vendée)
Antiquités Les 3 Moulins, 149 Rte Saint-Jean-de-Monts,
85300 Challans. T. 0251931377. - Print - *101464*

Châlons-sur-Marne (Marne)
Orfeuil Antiquités, 12 Rue Orfeuil, 51000 Châlons-sur-
Marne. T. 0326210404. - Print - *101465*

Chambéry (Savoie)
Cérino, 13 Rue De-Boigne, 73000 Chambéry.
T. 0479332760. *101466*

Chamonix-Mont-Blanc (Haute-Savoie)
Galerie Mont Blanc, 65 Av Michel-Croz, 74400 Chamo-
nix-Mont-Blanc. T. 0450531650,
Fax 0450532501. *101467*

Charleville-Mézières (Ardennes)
Page 17, Pass Ducale 10 Rue Irénée-Carré, 08000 Charleville-Mézières. T. 0324592116. *101468*
Temps de Cérises, 3 Rue Aubilly, 08000 Charleville-Mézières. T. 0324335622, Fax 0324599567. *101469*

Chartres (Eure-et-Loir)
Garnier, Jean-Michel, 3 C Cloître Notre-Dame, 28000
Chartres. T. 0237219089. *101470*

Château-Guibert (Vendée)
Boucquier, Gérard, La Reynière, 85320 Château-Guibert.
T. 0251972212. *101471*

Châteauroux (Indre)
Plantureux, Serge, 43 Rue Lamartine, 36000 Châteauroux. T. 0254074679. *101472*

Chef-Boutonne (Deux-Sèvres)
Librairie Griffes, 15 Rue Fontaine, 79110 Chef-Boutonne. T. 0549298743. *101473*

Cheillé (Indre-et-Loire)
Lesecq, Bernard, 46 Rue Chinon, 37190 Cheillé.
T. 0547452217. *101474*

Chinon (Indre-et-Loire)
Barreau, Jean-Louis, 28 Rue Commerce, 37500 Chinon.
T. 0547931289. *101475*

Cholet (Maine-et-Loire)
Librairie Mielle, 50 Rue Scellerie, 49300 Cholet.
T. 41622706. - ArtBk - *101476*

Clermont-Ferrand (Puy-de-Dôme)
Argus des Monnaies-Curiosités, 30bis Rue Pascal,
63000 Clermont-Ferrand. T. 0473925891.
- Print - *101477*

Duclos la Chine, 4 Pl Gras, 63000 Clermont-Ferrand.
T. 0473918140, Fax 0473913439. - Print /
Engr - 101478
Fil du Temps, 19 Rue Pascal, 63000 Clermont-Ferrand.
T. 0473900555. - Print - 101479
Librairie Averne, 11bis Rue Pascal, 63000 Clermont-Ferrand. T. 0473921018. - Print - 101480
Musée du Livre, 3 Pl Terrail, 63000 Clermont-Ferrand.
T. 0473917322. - Print / Engr / Map - 101481
Papyvore, 3 Rue Ente, 63000 Clermont-Ferrand.
T. 0473913924. - Print - 101482
Pochothèque, 29 Rue Treille, 63000 Clermont-Ferrand.
T. 0473913501. - Print - 101483

Colmar (Haut-Rhin)
Bouquiniste, 10 Rue Porte-Neuve, 68000 Colmar.
T. 0389245575. - Print - 101484
Caminade, 10 Rue Porte-Neuve, 68000 Colmar.
T. 0389245575. - Print / Engr - 101485
Lire et Chiner, 36 Rue Marchands, 68000 Colmar.
T. 0389241678. - Print - 101486

Combreux (Loiret)
Fleur de Lys, 32 Chemin Moulins, 45530 Combreux.
T. 0238593290. - Print - 101487

Compiègne
Hallmark Cards, Rue Gustave-Eiffel, 60200 Compiègne.
T. 0344303535, Fax 0344860433. - Autogr - 101488

Corbeil-Essonnes (Essonne)
Bouquinerie, 7 Rue Laminoir, 91100 Corbeil-Essonnes.
T. 0164962559. 101489
Tailliez, Michèle, 37 Rue Feray, 91100 Corbeil-Essonnes. T. 0164962602. - Print - 101490

Coulon (Deux-Sèvres)
Galerie du Marais, 7 Pl Coutume, 79510 Coulon.
T. 0549358550. 101491

Courbevoie (Hauts-de-Seine)
Encre et la Plume, 6 Av Séverine, 92400 Courbevoie.
T. 0147688577. 101492

Créteil (Val-de-Marne)
Joyen, Claude, 74bis Rue Général-Leclerc, 94000 Créteil. T. 0142074816. 101493

Dieupentale (Tarn-et-Garonne)
Dauriac, Jean-Louis, RN 113, 82170 Dieupentale.
T. 0563025094. - Print - 101494

Dijon (Côte-d'Or)
Le Meur, 12 Pl Théâtre, 21000 Dijon. I. 0380671303,
Fax 0380637513. - Print / Engr - 101495
Librairie Heurtebise, 23 Rue Gambetta, 21000 Dijon.
T. 0380676560. 101496

Dinan (Côtes-d'Armor)
Davy, Serge, 4 Pl Saint-Sauveur, 22100 Dinan.
T. 0296396300. 101497

Donzy (Nièvre)
Crépin, Serge, 21 Rue Etape, 58220 Donzy.
T. 0386394387. - Print - 101498

Draguignan (Var)
Raizman, Adolphe, 10 Av Carnot, 83300 Draguignan.
T. 0494680566. - Print - 101499

Dreux (Eure-et-Loir)
Au Grenier Durocasse, 50 Rue Orfeuil, 28100 Dreux.
T. 0237467318. 101500

Epernay (Marne)
Cosmographe, 37 Rue Thiercelin-Parrichault, 51200
Epernay. T. 0326554073. 101501

Evreux (Eure)
Floréal, 41 Rue Harpe, 27000 Evreux. T. 0232332233.
- Print / Engr - 101502

Figeac (Lot)
Magne, 1 Rue Gambetta, 46100 Figeac. T. 0565346666,
Fax 0565344015. - Print - 101503
Serra, Christian, 8bis Rue Clermont, 46100 Figeac.
T. 0565347772. - Print - 101504

Flayosc (Var)
Soulard, Jacqueline & Christian, Château du Deffends,
83780 Flayosc. T. 0494704037, Fax 0494703893.
- Print / ArtBk / Engr - 101505

Foix (Ariège)
Ivre Livre, 3 Rue Pénitents, 09000 Foix. T. 0561653654.
- Print - 101506

Fontainebleau (Seine-et-Marne)
Bouquins, 2 Rue Guérin, 77300 Fontainebleau.
T. 0360725856. - Print - 101507

Fontenay-sous-Bois (Val-de-Marne)
Alain, Bernard, 2 Rue Réunion, 94120 Fontenay-sous-
Bois. T. 0148737340. - Print - 101508

Fressenneville (Somme)
Pruvot, Jean, 60 Rue Jean-Jaurès, 80390 Fressenneville. T. 0322303664. - Print - 101509

Gap (Hautes-Alpes)
Librairie des Hautes-Alpes, 16 Rue Jean-Eymar, 05000
Gap. T. 0492524300. - Print - 101510

Gardouch (Haute-Garonne)
Latude, Hugues de, Castillon, 31290 Gardouch.
T. 0561815121, Fax 0561815144. 101511

Granville (Manche)
Grizzli, 22 Rue Paul-Poirier, 50400 Granville.
T. 0233614801. - Print - 101512
Lemberger, Anne, 4 Rue Général-Patton, 50400 Granville. T. 0233506803. 101513

Grenoble (Isère)
Librairie des Alpes, 1 Rue Casimir-Périer, 38000 Grenoble. T. 0476515798. - Print - 101514
Munari Librairie, 9 Rue Bayard, 38000 Grenoble.
T. 0476445784. - Print - 101515
Nouvelle Sainson, 2 Rue Voltaire, 38000 Grenoble.
T. 0476512373. - Print - 101516
Stendhal, 4 Rue Sault, 38000 Grenoble. T. 0476464169,
Fax 0476474142. - Print - 101517

Grimaud (Var)
Porte du Soleil, 11 Rte Nationale 558, 83310 Grimaud.
T. 0494568011. - Print - 101518

Ham (Somme)
Maquet, Jean, 23 Rue Notre-Dame, 80400 Ham.
T. 0323363233. - Print - 101519

Herm (Landes)
Troc 40, Cluquelardit, Rte Dax-Castets, 40990 Herm.
T. 0558915360. - Print - 101520

Issoire (Puy-de-Dôme)
Grenier aux Livres, 61 Rue Berbiziale, 635000 Issoire.
T. 0473551446. - Print - 101521

Janville-sur-Juine (Essonne)
Monod, Luc, 127 Grande Rue, 91510 Janville-sur-Juine.
T. 0160822971. 101522

Joigny (Yonne)
Arbre de Jessé, 12 Rue Montant-au-Palais, 89300 Joigny. T. 0386917202, Fax 0386917215. 101523

Jouarre (Seine-et-Marne)
Mahieu, 27 Rue Pierre, 77640 Jouarre. T. 0360222484.
- Print - 101524

L'Isle-d'Espagnac (Charente)
Dupeux, 148 Av République, 16340 L'Isle-d'Espagnac.
T. 0545681728. 101525

La Bastide-de-Besplas (Ariège)
Vamos, Marie-Claire, Village, 09350 La Bastide-de-Besplas. T. 0561698870. - Print - 101526

La Baule (Loire-Atlantique)
Séguineau, Eric, 2 Av Pierre-Percé, 44500 La Baule.
T. 40240462. 101527
Séguineau, Eric, 24 Blvd Hennecart, 44500 La Baule.
T. 07065384. 101528

La Cadière-d'Azur (Var)
Graffan, Roger, Le Vieux Presbytère, Rue République,
83740 La Cadière-d'Azur. T. 0494900731.
- Print - 101529

La Colle-sur-Loup (Alpes-Maritimes)
Maurel, 30 Rue Maréchal-Foch, 06480 La Colle-sur-
Loup. T. 0493320694. - Print / ArtBk - 101530

La Ferté-sous-Jouarre (Seine-et-Marne)
Leglaive, Jacques, 31 Av Franklin Roosevelt, 77260 La
Ferté-sous-Jouarre. T. 0160220242. - Print - 101531

La Flocellière (Vendée)
Bouquineux, La Sicotière, 85700 La Flocellière.
T. 0251577247. 101532

La Gacilly (Morbihan)
Pressensé, Jean-Louis, 9 Rue Relais-Postal, 56200 La
Gacilly. T. 0299081991. - Print - 101533

La Garenne-Colombes (Hauts-de-Seine)
Cambon, Alain, 88 Rue Sartoris, 92250 La Garenne-Colombes. T. 0142428428. 101534

La Mothe-Achard (Vendée)
Antiqvaria, 24 Rue Victor-Hugo, 85150 La Mothe-
Achard. T. 0251059309. 101535

La Rochelle (Charente-Maritime)
Bouquiniste, 4 Rue Saint-Nicolas, 17000 La Rochelle.
T. 0546417775. - Print - 101536

Landerneau (Finistère)
Rohan, 9 Rue Saint-Thomas, 29220 Landerneau.
T. 0298213888. - Print - 101537

Lansargues (Hérault)
Minotaure, 2 Lot Plants, 34130 Lansargues.
T. 0467867981. 101538

Le Creusot (Saône-et-Loire)
Bouquiniste, 14 Rue Maréchal-Leclerc, 71200 Le Creusot. T. 0385804460. - Print - 101539

Le Havre (Seine-Maritime)
Au Bouquiniste, 139 Cours de la République, 76600 Le
Havre. T. 0235531777. 101540
Coquenet, Gérald, 23 Rue Paris, 76600 Le Havre.
T. 0235424453, Fax 0235432234. 101541
Echo du Passé, 62 Rue Maréchal-Gallieni, 76600 Le
Havre. T. 0235214271. - Print - 101542
Le Marignier, Jean-Pierre, 99 Cours de la République,
76600 Le Havre. T. 0235250645. 101543
Normandie, 153 Rue Victor-Hugo, 76600 Le Havre.
T. 0235430511. 101544

Le Mans (Sarthe)
Broceliande, 21 Rue Reine-Bérangère, 72000 Le Mans.
T. 0243241827. 101545
Denis, 50 Rue Scellerie, 72000 Le Mans.
T. 0547641277. - Print - 101546

Le Poët-Laval (Drôme)
Dit-Elle, Maison Vieux Village, 26160 Le Poët-Laval.
T. 0475462305. 101547

Le Puy-en-Velay (Haute-Loire)
Arkham, 42 Rue Raphaël, 43000 Le Puy-en-Velay.
T. 0471026398. 101548
Bertrandy, Philippe, 27 Rue Raphaël, 43000 Le Puy-en-
Velay. T. 0471028523. - Print / Engr - 101549
Bouquineur, 58 Rue Grangevieille, 43000 Le Puy-en-Velay. T. 0471026668. - Print - 101550

Les Arcs (Var)
Rossignol, Daniel, Quartier Saint-Pierre, 83460 Les
Arcs. T. 0494733017, Fax 0494474379. 101551

Les Eyzies-Tayac-Sireuil (Dordogne)
Archéos, Rte Sarlat, 24620 Les Eyzies-Tayac-Sireuil.
T. 0553069365. 101552

Les Herbiers (Vendée)
Herbadilla, 29 La Gare, 85500 Les Herbiers.
T. 0251671019, Fax 0251668400. 101553

Lille (Nord)
ABC Livres, 33 Rue Clef, 59800 Lille. T. 0320632308,
Fax 0320319263. - Map -   101554
Eclipse Librairie Godon, 10 Rue de-la-Barre, 59000 Lille.
T. 0320315619. - Print -   101555
Montupet, Béatrice, 8 Rue Monnaie, 59800 Lille.
T. 0320553439.   101556

Limoges (Haute-Vienne)
Livresse, 12 Rue de la Boucherie, 87000 Limoges.
T. 0555342332. - Print -   101557

Lorient (Morbihan)
Musilivres, 61 Rue Port, 56100 Lorient. T. 0297211186.
- Print -   101558

Lormaye (Eure-et-Loir)
Librairie des Arts et Métiers, 20 Rue Verdun, 28210 Lormaye. T. 0237514429.   101559

Lormont (Gironde)
Proust, Jean-Luc, 32 Rue Michel-Montaigne, 33310 Lor-
mont. T. 0556068728.   101560

Lumio (Corse)
Boutet, Lionel, Rte Calvi, Clos des Fleurs, 20260 Lumio.
T. 0495607708. - Print -   101561

Luzarches (Val-d'Oise)
Morcrette, Daniel, 4 Av Joffre, 95270 Luzarches.
T. 0134710158. - Print / Autogr -   101562

Lyon (Rhône)
Abatemps, 6 Pl Saint-Jean, 69005 Lyon.
T. 0478426677. - Map -   101563
Abecedaire, 34 Rue Saint-Jean, 69005 Lyon.
T. 0478929063.   101564
Agora, 24 Rue Remparts d'Ainay, 69002 Lyon.
T. 0478382149. - Print -   101565
Ajasse, 62 Rue Tramassac, 69005 Lyon. T. 0478379967,
Fax 0472409873.   101566
Alcade, 1 Quai Fulchiron, 69005 Lyon.
T. 0478428817.   101567
Ancre Aldine, 62 Rue Auguste-Comte, 69002 Lyon.
T. 0478420760. Print / Engr -   101568
Chaminade, Jacques, 54 Rue Auguste Comte, 69002
Lyon. T. 0478928740. - Print -   101569
Clagahé, 27 Quai Gailleton, 69002 Lyon.
T. 0478372135. - Print -   101570
Defournel, Philippe, 43 Rue Auguste-Comte, 69002
Lyon. T. 0478380564.   101571
Descours, Michel, 31 Rue Auguste-Comte, 69002 Lyon.
T. 0478426567. - ArtBk -   101572
Fournier, 6 Quai Jules-Courmont, 69002 Lyon.
T. 0478374495, Fax 0478928325.   101573
Grande Fenêtre, 3 Quai Pêcherie, 69001 Lyon.
T. 0478274371.   101574
Histoire Ancienne, 13 Montée Carmélites, 69001 Lyon.
T. 0478285156.   101575
J.P.C., 38 Rue Saint-Jean, 69005 Lyon.
T. 0478378304.   101576
Laurencin, 1 Pl du Change, 69005 Lyon. T. 0478378619,
Fax 0478429185.   101577
Librairie Ancienne Chambefort, 26 Pl Bellecour, 69002
Lyon. T. 0478373215. - Print / Engr / Autogr /
Map -   101578
Librairie des Terreaux, 20 Rue Algérie, 69001 Lyon.
T. 0478281069. - Print -   101579
Librairie Diogène, 29 Rue Saint-Jean, 69005 Lyon.
T. 0478422941.   101580
Librairie du Bâtiment d'Argent, 38 Rue des Remparts-
d'Ainay, 69002 Lyon. T. 0478374153,
Fax 0478424947. - Print / Map -   101581
Librairie La Bourse, 8 Rue Lanterne, 69001 Lyon.
T. 0478394976.   101582
Librairie Méridiés, 36 Rue Sainte-Hélène, 69002 Lyon.
T. 0478375846, Fax 0478380865.   101583
Lips Arts Graphiques, 88 Av Saxe, 69003 Lyon.
T. 0478603070. - ArtBk -   101584
Livre à Lili, 5 Rue de Belfort, 69004 Lyon.
T. 0478278321. - Print -   101585
Loulou Cinéma, 58 Rue Saint-Jean, 69005 Lyon.
T. 0478428628.   101586
Lucas & Vermorel, 9 Quai Pêcherie, 69001 Lyon.
T. 0478309484.   101587

Miraglia, Salvador, 24 Rue Remparts d'Ainay, 69002
Lyon. T. 0478421462, Fax 0472402590.   101588
Parchemine, 8 Rue Palais-de-Justice, 69005 Lyon.
T. 0478422314. - Print -   101589
Perras, Bernard, 56 Rue Molière, 69006 Lyon.
T. 0478247179. - Print -   101590
Revel, Sylvain, 8 Rue Juiverie, 69005 Lyon.
T. 0472070157.   101591

Machecoul (Loire-Atlantique)
Coutumier, La Boisvélerie, 44270 Machecoul.
T. 40785449.   101592

Mâcon (Saône-et-Loire)
Librairie Ancienne Darreau, 9 Pl Saint-Pierre, 71000
Mâcon. T. 0385392800. - Print -   101593

Maisons-Alfort (Val-de-Marne)
Thiot, Agnès, 8 Rue Eugène-Renault, 94700 Maisons-Alfort. T. 0143683101, Fax 0148935485.   101594

Maisons-Laffitte (Yvelines)
Hunold, Gyan, 8 Av Sully, 78600 Maisons-Laffitte.
T. 0142454767. - Print -   101595

Marcq-en-Barœul (Nord)
Maître Mot, 188 Rue Jules-Delcenserie, 59700 Marcq-
en-Barœul. T. 0320458371, Fax 0320897911.
- Print -   101596

Marly-le-Roi (Yvelines)
Quadrature, 3 Sq Montferrands, 78160 Marly-le-Roi.
T. 0139589295, Fax 0139583349.   101597

Marmande (Lot-et-Garonne)
Vitrat, Francis, RN 113, 47200 Marmande.
T. 0553642193. - Print -   101598

Marseille (Bouches-du-Rhône)
Accents Toniques, 52 Rue Grignan, 13001 Marseille.
T. 0491335618, Fax 0491549275. - Print -   101599
Aquitaine Provence Collection, 2 Blvd Théodore-Thurner,
13006 Marseille. T. 0491484550,
Fax 0491427633.   101600
Battini, François, 13 Rue Jean-Roque, 13001 Marseille.
T. 0491330133.   101601
Bouquineur, 78 Rue Breteuil, 13006 Marseille.
T. 0491816339.   101602
Brés, Martin, 60 Rue Grignan, 13001 Marseille.
T. 0491330292. - Print / ArtBk / Engr -   101603
Eupalinos, 72 Cours Julien, 13006 Marseille.
T. 0491487444, Fax 0491426806. - ArtBk -   101604
Gégé le Chinois, 26 Rue Trois-Mages, 13006 Marseille.
T. 0491422607. - ArtBk -   101605
Laffitte, Jeanne, 25 Cours Honoré d'Estienne d'Orves,
13001 Marseille. T. 0491543937, Fax 0491547633.
- Print -   101606
Lettre et l'Image, 31 Rue des Trois Rois, 13006 Marseil-
le. T. 0491483517.   101607
Librairie La Légende, 58 Rue Aubagne, 13001 Marseille.
T. 0491543634.   101608
Tour d'Oriol, 248 Chemin Vallon-de-l'Oriol, 13007 Mar-
seille. T. 0491522800. - Print -   101609

Martigues (Bouches-du-Rhône)
Ecritoire, 30 Blvd Camille-Pelletan, 13500 Martigues.
T. 0442810531, Fax 0442810043.   101610

Mauzens-et-Miremont (Dordogne)
Archéos, Margnol, 24260 Mauzens-et-Miremont.
T. 0553032674, Fax 0553035669.   101611

Melun (Seine-et-Marne)
Temps Retrouvé, 10 Rue Boissettes, 77000 Melun.
T. 64520229.   101612

Ménerval (Seine-Maritime)
Pério-Jade, Village, 76220 Ménerval.
T. 0235906336.   101613

Menton (Alpes-Maritimes)
Falconnet, Pierre, 7 Av Edouard-VII, 06500 Menton.
T. 0493359240. - Print -   101614
Scrudato, Robert, 3 Av Thiers, 06500 Menton.
T. 0493577567. - Print -   101615

Mer (Loir-et-Cher)
Portheault, Bernard, 8 Rue Pichots, 41500 Mer.
T. 0254812433, Fax 0254813983. - Print -   101616

Merfy (Marne)
Lecrocq, Jean-Jacques, Chemin Entredeux, 51220 Mer-
fy. T. 0326030071.   101617

Metz (Moselle)
Bédébulles, 20 Rue Sainte-Marie, 57000 Metz.
T. 0387369055.   101618
Best Seller, 27 Rue Jardins, 57000 Metz.
T. 0387365724.   101619
Galerie du Bibliophile, 3bis Rue Wad-Billy, 57000 Metz.
T. 0387746610.   101620
Librairie Ancienne, 37 Rue Mazelle, 57000 Metz.
T. 0387740014.   101621
Librairie Mnemosyne, 18 Rue Sainte-Marie, 57000
Metz. T. 0387364979.   101622
Moresi, J.L., 11 Rue des Clercs, 57000 Metz.
T. 0387751217.   101623
Viola, André, 79 Rte de Plappeville, 57050 Metz.
T. 0387304949. - Print -   101624

Millau (Aveyron)
Alauzet, Yvon, 25 Blvd Ayrolle, 12100 Millau.
T. 0565601039. - Print -   101625

Montauban (Tarn-et-Garonne)
Layan, Roseline, 28 Fbg-Lacapelle, 82000 Montauban.
T. 0563637268.   101626

Montcuq (Lot)
Chimera, Fbg Saint-Privat, 46800 Montcuq.
T. 0565229701   101027

Montgeron (Essonne)
Kronis, Stéphane, 6 Av Sénart, 91230 Montgeron.
T. 0169831777.   101628

Montigny-sur-Canne (Nièvre)
Oberlé, Gérard, Manoir Pron, 58340 Montigny-sur-
Canne. T. 0386500522.   101629

Montmorot (Jura)
Rousseau, Nadine, 43 Rue Aristide-Briand, 39570 Montmorot. T. 0384245782. - Print -   101630

Montolieu (Aude)
Bibliotaphe Converti, Rue Tour, 11170 Montolieu.
T. 0468248110. - Print -   101631
Chouette, Rue Nationale, 11170 Montolieu.
T. 0468248063.   101632
Dilettante, Imp Ferradou, 11170 Montolieu.
T. 0468248060.   101633
Ile Lettrée, Rue Saint-André, 11170 Montolieu.
T. 0468248411.   101634
Ornière Bleue, Rue Paix, 11170 Montolieu.
T. 0468248525, Fax 0468248625.   101635

Montpellier (Hérault)
Anagramme, 5 Rue Gagne-Petit, 34000 Montpellier.
T. 0467527384. - Print -   101636
Clerc, Pierre, 13 Rue Alexandre Cabanel, 34000 Mont-
pellier. T. 0467660597, Fax 0467606878. - Print /
Autogr -   101637
Collin, Gérard, 12 Rue Université, 34000 Montpellier.
T. 0467606757. - Print -   101638
Glénat, 5 Rue Aiguillerie, 34000 Montpellier.
T. 0467663440. - ArtBk -   101639
Haffner, Hervé, 27 Rue Maguelone, 34000 Montpellier.
T. 0467925632.   101640
Librairie Bouquinerie du Languedoc, 12 Rue de l'Univer-
sité, 34000 Montpellier. T. 0467606757.
- Print -   101641
Librairie Jean-Jacques Rousseau, 11 Rue Jean-Jac-
ques-Rousseau, 34000 Montpellier.
T. 0467662595.   101642
Livres Anciens et Modernes, 16 Rue Claret, 34000
Montpellier. T. 0467920305.   101643
Moustache et Trottinette, 5 Rue Jules-Latreilhe, 34000
Montpellier. T. 0467607977.   101644
Rouchaléou, 4 Blvd Jeu-de-Paume, 34000 Montpellier.
T. 0467583860, Fax 0467924727. - Print -   101645

Séranne 2, 13 Rue Jules-Latreilhe, 34000 Montpellier.
T. 0467607080, Fax 0467609142. *101646*

Montreuil (Seine-Saint-Denis)
Elzevir, 1 Rue François-Debergue, 93100 Montreuil.
T. 0148588583. *101647*

Morlaix (Finistère)
Bouquiniste, 22 Pl AAende, 29210 Morlaix.
T. 0298881382. - Print - *101648*

Mouans-Sartoux (Alpes-Maritimes)
Librairie Acloque, 2 Av Marcel-Journet, 06370 Mouans-Sartoux. T. 0493753157. *101649*

Moulins (Allier)
Devaux, Jean-Luc, 26 Rue François Péron, 03000 Moulins. T. 0470440265, Fax 0470209675. - Print /
ArtBk - *101650*
Foucher, Jacques, 47 Rue Allier, 03000 Moulins.
T. 0470444970. *101651*

Moulis (Ariège)
Wallez, Edgard, 09200 Moulis. T. 0561667180.
- Print - *101652*

Mulhouse (Haut-Rhin)
Alsaticarta, 31 Av Clemenceau, 68100 Mulhouse.
T. 0389461357. - Print - *101653*
Coral, 18 Av Clemenceau, 68100 Mulhouse.
T. 0389563777. - Print / Engr - *101654*
Gangloff, 13 Av Auguste-Wicky, 68100 Mulhouse.
T. 0389465225. - Print - *101655*
Neff, Charles, 21 Rue Synagogue, 68100 Mulhouse.
T. 0389466138. - Print - *101656*

Nancy (Meurthe-et-Moselle)
Au Cartophile, 105 Grande Rue, 54000 Nancy.
T. 0383350919. - Print / Map - *101657*
Dornier, Vincent, 74 Grande Rue, 54000 Nancy.
T. 0383365062. - Print - *101658*
Librairie L'Abri du Temps, 21 Grande Rue, 54000 Nancy.
T. 0383370633. - Print / ArtBk - *101659*
Nancéide, 19 Grande Rue, 54000 Nancy.
T. 0383372552. *101660*
Rémy, Albert, 25 Rue Stanislas, 54000 Nancy.
T. 0383356423. - Print - *101661*
Thinus, Emmanuel, 93 Grande Rue, 54000 Nancy.
T. 0383351348. - Print - *101662*

Nantes (Loire-Atlantique)
Bachelier Foucauld, 28 Rue Jean-Jaurès, 44000 Nantes.
T. 40484364. - Print / Engr - *101663*
Bachelier, Pierre, 6 Rue Neuve-des-Capucins, 44000
Nantes. T. 40697919. *101664*
Bellanger, 4 et 6 Pass Pommeraye, 44000 Nantes.
T. 40695170, Fax 40719274. - Print / Engr - *101665*
Bocquier, G., 18 Rue Franklin, 44000 Nantes.
T. 0251889708. *101666*
Brocante, 2 Rue Château, 44000 Nantes. T. 40203160.
- Print / Engr - *101667*
Durance, G., 5 All Orléans, 44000 Nantes. T. 40487245,
Fax 40486896. - Print - *101668*
Guimard, 23bis Rue Jean-Jaurès, 44000 Nantes.
T. 40082120. - Print / Engr - *101669*
Librairie Ancienne du Casoar, 7 Rue Chateaubriand,
44000 Nantes. T. 40895043. *101670*
Librairie du Musée des Beaux-Arts, 10 Rue Georges-Clemenceau, 44000 Nantes. T. 0251819741.
- ArtBk - *101671*
Librairie Mercoeur, 18 Rue Mercoeur, 44000 Nantes.
T. 40893612. *101672*
Vachon, Yves, 14 Rue Racine, 44000 Nantes.
T. 40731013. - Print - *101673*

Neuilly-sur-Seine (Hauts-de-Seine)
Blackburn, Charles, 27 Rue Pierret, 92200 Neuilly-sur-Seine. T. 0147228230, Fax 0140883513. *101674*
Gorvitz, Guy, 203 Av Charles-de-Gaulle, 92200 Neuilly-sur-Seine. T. 0146372673. *101675*

Kaufmann, Jean, 108 Av Charles-de-Gaulle, 92200 Neuilly-sur-Seine. T. 0147450121. *101676*

Neuville-lès-Decize (Nièvre)
Lorient, Emmanuel, Domaine Tallet, 58300 Neuville-lès-Decize. T. 0386506402, Fax 0386506422. *101677*

Nevers (Nièvre)
Belles Lettres, 11 Rue Ardilliers, 58000 Nevers.
T. 0386610848, Fax 0386610848. - ArtBk - *101678*
Galerie Saint-Cyr, 18 Rue Cathédrale, 58000 Nevers.
T. 0386574565. - ArtBk - *101679*
Ver Vert, 32 Rue Saint-Etienne, 58000 Nevers.
T. 0386369541, Fax 0386215807. - Print - *101680*

Nice (Alpes-Maritimes)
Art et l'Affiche, 17 Rue Alfred-Mortier, 06000 Nice.
T. 0493623655. - Print - *101681*
Art et Lettres, 3 Rue Alberti, 06000 Nice.
T. 0493622058, Fax 0493850663. *101682*
Bouquinerie, 18 Rue Delille, 06000 Nice.
T. 0493809176. - Print - *101683*
Bouquinerie Bonaparte, 10 Rue Gioffredo, 06000 Nice.
T. 0493138070. - Print - *101684*
Bouquiniste, 24 Rue Cassini, 06300 Nice.
T. 0493552589. - Print - *101685*
Chapuis, 62 Blvd Risso, 06300 Nice. T. 0493555313.
- Print / Engr / Autogr - *101686*
D'Un Livre l'Autre, 11 Rue Biscara, 06000 Nice.
T. 0493130306. *101687*
Edition du Ricochet, 1 Rue Spitaliéri, 06000 Nice.
Fax 93134302. *101688*
Hirlam, Gérard, 8 Av Auber, 06000 Nice. T. 0493889351,
Fax 0493889701. - Print - *101689*
Librairie de l'Escurial, 29 Rue Alphonse-Karr, 06000 Nice. T. 0493884244, Fax 0493874337. *101690*
Librairie du Musée Matisse, 164 Av des Arènes, 06000
Nice. T. 0493535096, Fax 0493532147.
- ArtBk - *101691*
Librairie Niçoise, 2 Rue Defly, 06000 Nice.
T. 0493853669. - Print / Autogr - *101692*
Meyer, Michel, 3 Rue Défly, 06000 Nice.
T. 0493858044. *101693*
Ségur, Anne, 9 Rue Défly, 06000 Nice.
T. 0493854832. *101694*
Tiberti, Marguerite, 1 Rue Spitaliéri, 06000 Nice.
T. 0493130400. *101695*

Niort (Deux-Sèvres)
Au Cri de la Chouette, 13 Rue Basse, 79000 Niort.
T. 0549770925, Fax 0549770925. *101696*
Tribout, 2 Rue Basse, 79000 Niort.
T. 0549285333. *101697*

Nîmes (Gard)
Autour du Monde, 11 Rue Tédenat, 30000 Nîmes.
T. 0466214811. *101698*
Fleurs du Mal, 30 Rue Grand-Couvent, 30000 Nîmes.
T. 0466360628. *101699*
Librairie de Carré d'Art, Pl Maison-Carrée, Carré d'Art,
30000 Nîmes. T. 0466677814. - ArtBk - *101700*

Nogent-le-Rotrou (Eure-et-Loir)
Livres et Collections, 25 Rue Giroust, 28400 Nogent-le-Rotrou. T. 0237529459, Fax 0237529481. *101701*

Nogent-sur-Marne (Val-de-Marne)
Maitre-Allain, Micheline, 162 Grande Rue Charles-de-Gaulle, 94130 Nogent-sur-Marne.
T. 0148710610. *101702*

Nointel (Val-d'Oise)
Trovero, Pascal, 25 Rue Bohémies, 95590 Nointel.
T. 0130345354. - Print - *101703*

Noyers (Yonne)
Chanut, François, Pl de la Madeleine, 89310 Noyers.
T. 0386828232. - Print - *101704*
Chanut, François, Pl Madeleine, 89310 Noyers.
T. 0386828232. *101705*

Nyons (Drôme)
Fert, Nathalie, 30 Pl Docteur-Bourdongle, 26110 Nyons.
T. 0475261380. - Print - *101706*
Ramette, Dominique, 11 Rue Colonel-Barillon, 26110
Nyons. T. 0475260126. *101707*

Orléans (Loiret)
A l'Enseigne du Forgeron Bonheur, 53 Rue Saint-Marceau, 45100 Orléans. T. 0238560610. *101708*
Au Coeur du Monde, 261 Rue Bourgogne, 45000 Orléans. T. 0238543759. *101709*
Bouquinistes, 217 Rue Bourgogne, 45000 Orléans.
T. 0238543488. *101710*
Foire aux Images, 200 Rue Bourgogne, 45000 Orléans.
T. 0238622640. *101711*
Malle du Martroi, 14 Rue Adolphe-Crespin, 45000 Orléans. T. 0238535036, Fax 0238540398. *101712*
Maxi Livres, 33 Rue Jeanne-d'Arc, 45000 Orléans.
T. 0238538018, Fax 0238536851. *101713*

Paimpol (Côtes-d'Armor)
Bateau-Livre, 9 Rue Vieille-Poissonnerie, 22500 Paimpol. T. 0296204613. - Print - *101714*

Pantin (Seine-Saint-Denis)
Thomas, Simone, 60 Rue Marcelle, 93500 Pantin.
T. 0148442758. *101715*

Paris
A l'Image du Grenier sur l'Eau de Maria, 45 Rue Francs-Bourgeois, 75004 Paris. T. 0142710231.
- Print - *101716*
A la Librairie, 6bis Imp Guémenée, 75004 Paris.
T. 0144610490, Fax 0144610492. *101717*
A la Libre Errance, 5 Rue Echaudé, 75006 Paris.
T. 0146331984. *101718*
A la Nef des Fous, 53 Rue Manin, 75019 Paris.
T. 0142455251, Fax 0142455058. - Print - *101719*
Abbey Bookshop, 29 Rue Parcheminerie, 75005 Paris.
T. 0146331624, Fax 0146330333. *101720*
Age d'Or, 59 Rue Raymond-Losserand, 75014 Paris.
T. 0142798989. - Print / Engr - *101721*
Agnes B., 7 Rue Saint-Sulpice, 75006 Paris.
Fax (1) 46335124. *101722*
Albertine, 9 Rue Maître-Albert, 75005 Paris.
T. 0143293920. - Engr - *101723*
Album, 6 Rue Dante, 75005 Paris. T. 0143546709.
- Print - *101724*
Alcandre, 46 Rue Léon-Frot, 75011 Paris.
T. 0140091373. - Print - *101725*
Alias, 21 Rue Boulard, 75014 Paris. T. 0143212982,
Fax 0143213240. - Print - *101726*
Alphée, 25 Rue Grands-Augustins, 75006 Paris.
T. 0143269470. - Print - *101727*
Arcades, 8 Rue Castiglione, 75001 Paris.
T. 0142606296, Fax 0142974356. - Print /
ArtBk - *101728*
Archives, 52 Rue Mazarine, 75006 Paris.
T. 0143541264, Fax 0140468422. *101729*
Arenthon, 3 Quai Malaquais, 75006 Paris.
T. 0143268606, Fax 0143266208. - Print / ArtBk /
Engr - *101730*
Argences, 38 Rue Saint-Sulpice, 75006 Paris.
T. 0143540560, Fax 0146347498. *101731*
Argonautes, 74 Rue Seine, 75006 Paris. T. 0143267069,
Fax 0143269988. - Print / Engr / Autogr - *101732*
Armes de la Nuit, 41 Rue Jean-Pierre-Timbaud, 75011
Paris. T. 0147006434. *101733*
Arnaqueur, 3 Rue Papillon, 75009 Paris.
T. 0142465313. *101734*
Arnaud, Florence, 10 Rue Saintonge, 75003 Paris.
T. 0142770179. - Engr / Autogr - *101735*
Art Estampe, 67 Blvd Général-Martial-Valin, 75015 Paris. T. 0140607797, Fax 0140607339. - ArtBk /
Engr - *101736*
Art et Scène, 161 Rue Saint-Martin, 75003 Paris.
T. 0148871899. - Print / ArtBk - *101737*
Artcurial, 9 Av Matignon, 75008 Paris. T. 0142991616.
- ArtBk - *101738*
Artem, 9 Blvd Sébastopol, 75001 Paris. T. 0142362420.
- Print - *101739*

Association Liko, 161 Rue Rennes, 75005 Paris.
T. 0145486949. - ArtBk - *101740*
Atmosphère, 7 Rue Francis-de-Pressensé, 75014 Paris.
T. 0145422926. - ArtBk - *101741*
Au Vieux Document, 6bis Rue Châteaudun, 75009 Paris.
T. 0148787784. *101742*
Autrefois, 6bis Rue Baigneur, 75018 Paris.
T. 0142620898. *101743*
Balabanian, Emile, 3 Rue Cluny, 75005 Paris.
T. 0143262754. - Print - *101744*
Barbéry, Jean-Louis, 2 Rue Grands-Degrés, 75005 Pa-
ris. T. 0143253376. - Print / Engr - *101745*
Bayarré, Fabrice, 21 Rue Tournon, 75006 Paris.
T. 0143549199, Fax 0143545878. *101746*
Benedetti & Estève, 80 Rue Charonne, 75011 Paris.
T. 0143674244, Fax 0143676334. *101747*
Benelli, Jacques, 244 Rue Saint-Jacques, 75005 Paris.
T. 0146337351, Fax 0140510139. - Print /
Autogr - *101748*
Berche & Pagis, 60 Rue Mazarine, 75006 Paris.
T. 0143542767. - Print - *101749*
Berès, Pierre, 14 Av Friedland, 75008 Paris.
T. 0145638553. - Print / Engr / Autogr - *101750*
Berggruen & Cie, 70 Rue Université, 75007 Paris.
T. 0142220212, Fax 0142225743. - ArtBk - *101751*
Berton, Gérard, 97 Rue Bagnolet, 75020 Paris.
T. 0143674289. *101752*
Bibliophile Russe, 12 Rue Lamartine, 75009 Paris.
T. 0148789102, Fax 0149950805. - Print - *101753*
Bibliothèque des Arts, 3 Rue Corneille, 75005 Paris.
T. 0146340862. - ArtBk - *101754*
Bibliothèque des Arts, 3 Pl Odéon, 75006 Paris.
T. 0146331818, Fax 0140469556. - Print - *101755*
Blaizot, Claude, 164 Rue Fbg-Saint-Honoré, 75008 Pa-
ris. T. 0143593658, Fax 0142259027. - Print / ArtBk /
Autogr - *101756*
Bloody Mary, 18 Rue Linné, 75005 Paris.
T. 0143360426. - Print - *101757*
Bonnefoi, Henri, 1 Rue Médicis, 75006 Paris.
T. 0146335722, Fax 0143540543. *101758*
Bouquinerie de l'Institut, 12 Rue Seine, 75006 Paris.
T. 0143266349. - ArtBk / Engr - *101759*

LIBRAIRIE FISCHBACHER

33, rue de Seine, 75006 PARIS
BEAUX-ARTS
ARTS PRIMITIFS
Distribution tous livres d'art français
et étrangers

Annuaire international des Ventes
International Directory of Arts 1997/1998

Catalogue de Livres d'Art Primitif N° 9
Tél. 0143 26 84 87 – Fax 0143 26 48 87

Bourguignat, Pierre, 10bis Rue Châteaudun, 75009 Pa-
ris. T. 0148747680, Fax 0148784150. - Print - *101760*
Boutique de l'Histoire, 24 Rue Ecoles, 75005 Paris.
T. 0146340336, Fax 0143268396. *101761*
Boutique Paris-Musées, c/o Musée Carnavalet, 23 Rue
Sévigné, 75003 Paris. T. 0142740800,
Fax 0142740408. - ArtBk - *101762*
Boutique Paris-Musées, c/o Forum des Halles, 1 Rue
Pierre-Lescot, 75001 Paris. T. 0140265665.
- ArtBk - *101763*
Boutique Paris-Musées, 29bis Rue Francs-Bourgeois,
75004 Paris. T. 0142741302. - ArtBk - *101764*
Bouvier, Michel, 11 Rue Daguerre, 75014 Paris.
T. 0142790938. - Print - *101765*
Bouvier, Michel, 14 Rue Visconti, 75006 Paris.
T. 0146346453, Fax 0140469140. - Print - *101766*
Brieux, Alain, 48 Rue Jacob, 75006 Paris.
T. 0142602198, Fax 0142605524. - Print /
Autogr - *101767*
Brimo de Laroussilhe, 11 Rue Lille, 75007 Paris.
T. 0142607476. *101768*
Buffet, Claude, 7 Rue Saint-Sulpice, 75006 Paris.
T. 0143266179. - Print - *101769*
Buret, Roland, 6 Passage Verdeau, 75009 Paris.
T. 0147706299, Fax 0142460075. *101770*

Cahiers d'Art

14 Rue du Dragon

75006 – Paris

Tel: 01.45.48.76.73

Cahiers d'Art, 14 Rue du Dragon, 75006 Paris.
T. 0145487673. *101770a*
Cambon, Alain, 30 Rue Monsieur-le-Prince, 75006 Paris.
T. 0143257625, Fax 0144071535. - Print - *101771*
Carlier, Philippe, 11 Rue Lille, 75007 Paris.
T. 0142605392, Fax 0142605392. - Print /
ArtBk - *101772*
Carnavalette, 2 Rue Francs-Bourgeois, 75003 Paris.
T. 0142729192. - Print / Engr - *101773*
Cart-Tanneur, Didier, 11bis Rue Vauquelin, 75005 Paris.
T. 0143360285, Fax 0143318602. - Print - *101774*
Castaing, Frédéric, 13 Rue Chapon, 75003 Paris.
T. 0142746909, Fax 0142740089. - Autogr - *101775*
Causse, Javelle, 24 Passage Verdeau, 75009 Paris.
T. 0148241871. - Print - *101776*
Chamonal, François & Rodolphe, 5 Rue Drouot, 75009
Paris. T. 0147708487, Fax 0142463547.
- Print - *101777*
Chanut, François, 41 Rue Mazarine, 75006 Paris.
T. 0143540470, Fax 0143547984. *101778*
Charavay, 3 Rue Furstenberg, 75006 Paris.
T. 0143545989. - Autogr - *101779*
Chastenay, Florence de, 76 Rue Gay-Lussac, 75005 Pa-
ris. T. 0143540578, Fax 0143257695. - Print - *101780*
Chrétien, Jean, 178 Rue Fbg-Saint-Honoré, 75008 Paris.
T. 0145635266, Fax 0145636587. - Print /
Autogr - *101781*
Cinédoc, 45 Passage Jouffroy, 75009 Paris.
T. 0148247136. - ArtBk - *101782*
Citadelles & Mazenod, 33 Rue Naples, 75008 Paris.
T. 0145222366, Fax 0145220427. - ArtBk - *101783*
Clavreuil, Jean, 37 Rue Saint-André-des-Arts, 75006
Paris. T. 0143267117, Fax 0143549537.
- Print - *101784*
Clio, 38 Av Villemain, 75014 Paris. T. 0145415920.
- Print - *101785*
Cluzel, René, 61 Rue Vaugirard, 75006 Paris.
T. 0142223871, Fax 0145447966. - Print - *101786*
Collectionneur Impuni, 11 Rue Berzélius, 75017 Paris.
T. 0142261530. - Print - *101787*
Compagnie des Libraires Experts de France, 164 Rue
Fbg-Saint-Honoré, 75008 Paris.
T. 0143593658. *101788*
Conservatoire, 98bis Blvd Latour-Maubourg, 75007 Pa-
ris. T. 0144180865. - Print - *101789*
Couailhac, Paul-Louis, Louvre des Antiquaires, 2 Pl Pa-
lais-Royal, 75001 Paris. T. 0142615691,
Fax 0142611070. *101790*
Coulet, Laurent, 166 Blvd Haussmann, 75008 Paris.
T. 0142895159, Fax 0142891481. - Print - *101791*
Coulet & Faure, 1 Rue Dauphine, 75006 Paris.
T. 0143264240. *101792*
Courant d'Art, 79 Rue Vaugirard, 75006 Paris.
T. 0145493008. *101793*
Creuzevault, Colette, 58 Rue Mazarine, 75006 Paris.
T. 0143266785, Fax 0143252570. - Print / ArtBk /
Engr - *101794*
Delamain, 155 Rue Saint-Honoré, 75001 Paris.
T. 0142614878. - Print - *101795*
Delmas, Solange, 62 Rue Vaneau, 75007 Paris.
T. 0145483781. *101796*
Delon, Jean-Paul, 10 Rue Buffault, 75009 Paris.
T. 0145230442, Fax 0145231909. *101797*
Delvaux, Véronique, 76 Rue Seine, 75006 Paris.
T. 0143299004, Fax 0143268968. - Print /
ArtBk - *101798*
Dhennequin, Michèle, 76 Rue Cherche-Midi, 75006 Pa-
ris. T. 0142221853, Fax 0145440879. - Autogr /
Map - *101799*

Documentec, 58 Blvd Batignolles, 75017 Paris.
Fax (1) 42939262. *101800*
Drouet, Juliette, 111 Av Victor-Hugo, 75016 Paris.
T. 0147277720. *101801*
Dudragne, 86 Rue Maubeuge, 75010 Paris.
T. 0148785095. *101802*
Dutel, Jean-Pierre, 16 Rue Jacques-Callot, 75006 Paris.
T. 0143541777, Fax 0143258301. *101803*
Edition et Diffusion M.P., 6 Rue Clodion, 75015 Paris.
T. 0145792549. - Print - *101804*
Editions Flammarion, 26 Rue Racine, 75278 Paris Cedex
06. T. 0140513100, Fax 0143292148.
- ArtBk - *101805*
Elbé, 213bis Blvd Saint-Germain, 75007 Paris.
T. 0145487797. - Print - *101806*
Epigrammes, 85 Rue Dunkerque, 75009 Paris.
T. 0142820845. *101807*
Eppe, Christian, 3 Rue Maubeuge, 75009 Paris.
T. 0148746668. *101808*
Europ'Espace Communication, 150 Rue Rivoli, 75001
Paris. T. 0142860521. *101809*
Ex Libris, 60 Rue Moines, 75017 Paris. T. 0142283241.
- Print - *101810*
Expressions, 54 Blvd Reuilly, 75012 Paris.
T. 0143074563. - Print - *101811*
Fabius Frères, 152 Blvd Haussmann, 75008 Paris.
T. 0145623918, Fax 0145625307. - Engr /
Autogr - *101812*
Fager, 5 Rue Mansart, 75009 Paris.
T. 0142802022. *101813*
Fantasmak, 17 Rue Belzunce, 75010 Paris.
T. 0148787244. *101814*
Fata Libelli, 9 Rue Médicis, 75006 Paris.
T. 0144071644, Fax 0144071645. *101815*
Filloux, Georges, 4 Rue Université, 75007 Paris.
T. 0142602650. *101816*
Fischbacher, 33 Rue Seine, 75006 Paris.
T. 0143268487, Fax 0143264887. - Print / ArtBk /
Engr / Autogr - *101817*

BOUQUINERIE DE L'INSTITUT
MAZO, LEBOUC S.A.

12, rue de Seine
Paris-6ᵉ
Tél.: 01.43.26.63.49

Flachard, Rémi, 9 Rue Bac, 75007 Paris.
T. 0142868687. *101818*
Flak, 8 Rue Beaux-Arts, 75006 Paris. T. 0146337777,
Fax 0146332757. - Print - *101819*
Fleurs du Mal, 24 Rue Chaligny, 75012 Paris.
T. 0143406334. *101820*
Foma France, 31 Rue Fleurus, 75006 Paris.
T. 0145440637. *101821*
Fourcade, Jean-François, 27 Rue Saint-Paul, 75004 Pa-
ris. T. 0148048215. *101822*
Fourquier, Stanislas, 40 Rue Gay-Lussac, 75005 Paris.
T. 0143542470. *101823*
Galcante, 43 Rue Arbre-Sec, 75001 Paris.
T. 0144778740. *101824*
Gallimard, 15 Blvd Raspail, 75007 Paris.
T. 0145482484, Fax 0142841697. - Print / ArtBk /
Autogr - *101825*
Ganet, Gérard, 10 Pass Verdeau, 75009 Paris.
T. 0142463115. - Print / Engr - *101826*
Garnier Arnoul, 5 Rue Montfaucon, 75006 Paris.
T. 0143548005, Fax 0143548292. *101827*
Geuthner, Paul, 12 Rue Vavin, 75006 Paris.
T. 0146347130, Fax 0143297564. *101828*
Gilot, Jean-Pierre, 4 Rue de Provence, 75009 Paris.
T. 0142248027, Fax 0148248027. *101829*
Giraud & Badin, 1 Rue Fleurus, 75006 Paris.
T. 0145490924, Fax 0145491925. *101830*
Goudemare, S., 9 Rue Cardinal-Lemoine, 75005 Paris.
T. 0146340476. *101831*

Graphes, 13 Rue Buci, 75006 Paris. T. 0146335757.
- ArtBk - *101832*
Grenier à Livres, 50 Passage Jouffroy, 75009 Paris.
T. 0148249889. - Print - *101833*
Grolée-Virville, Alain de, 19 Rue Valois, 75001 Paris.
T. 0142960159. *101834*
Guilbert, Benoît, 137 Blvd Montparnasse, 75006 Paris.
T. 0143268602, Fax 0140460743. *101835*
Guillou, 9 Rue Eperon, 75006 Paris. T. 0140510555,
Fax 0146333968. *101836*
H Livres, 13 Rue Cardinal-Lemoine, 75005 Paris.
T. 0146347434. *101837*
Hebraica Judaica, 12 Rue Hospitalières-Saint-Gervais,
75004 Paris. T. 0148873220. *101838*
Herbinet, Jacques, 39 Rue Constantinople, 75008 Paris.
T. 0145226115. *101839*
Hugues, Jean, 1 Rue Furstenberg, 75006 Paris.
T. 0143267476. - Print / Autogr - *101840*
I.A.C., 6bis Rue Forez, 75003 Paris.
T. 0140279013. *101841*
Impact Livres, 24 Rue Nevers, 75006 Paris.
T. 0142345454, Fax 0142345459. *101842*
Inde Editions, 22 Rue Descartes, 75005 Paris.
T. 0143546729. *101843*
Intemporel, 22 Rue Saint-Martin, 75004 Paris.
T. 0142725541. - Engr - *101844*
Intemporel, Louvre des Antiquaires, 2 Pl Palais-Royal,
75001 Paris. T. 0142602265. - Engr - *101845*
Intermédiaire du Livre, 88 Rue Bonaparte, 75006 Paris.
T. 0146330050. - Print - *101846*
Intersigne Livres Anciens, 66 Rue Cherche-Midi, 75006
Paris. T. 0145442454, Fax 0145445055.
- Print - *101847*
Introuvable, 23 Rue Juliette-Dodu, 75010 Paris.
T. 0142006143. *101848*
Jadis et Naguère, 166 Rue Fbg-Saint-Honoré, 75008
Paris. T. 0143594052, Fax 0145629354.
- Print - *101849*
Jammes, P., 3 Rue Gozlin, 75006 Paris. T. 0143264771.
- Print - *101850*
Jardin de Flore, 24 Pl Vosges, 75004 Paris.
T. 0142776190. *101851*
Jardin des Philosophes, 62 Rue Pierre-Larousse, 75014
Paris. T. 0145433137. *101852*
Jonard, Robert, 80 Rue Joseph-de-Maistre, 75018 Pa-
ris. T. 0142293797. *101853*
Jours Anciens, 57 Rue Rome, 75008 Paris.
T. 0145226886. - Engr - *101854*
Jousseaume, Dominique & François, 45 Gal Vivienne,
75002 Paris. T. 0142960624. - Print / ArtBk - *101855*
Katz, Raphaël, 40 Rue Saints-Pères, 75007 Paris.
T. 0145443363. *101856*
Kérangue & De Pollès, 34 Rue Vivienne, 75002 Paris.
T. 0142362311. - Print - *101857*
Kieffer, 46 Rue Saint-André-des-Arts, 75006 Paris.
T. 0143264711. - Print - *101858*
Klincksieck, 8 Rue Sorbonne, 75005 Paris.
T. 0143545953, Fax 0143252553. - ArtBk - *101859*
Laget, Léonce, 76 Rue Seine, 75006 Paris.
T. 0143299004, Fax 0143268968. - Print /
ArtBk - *101860*
Laib, Maherzia, 95 Rue Clignancourt, 75018 Paris.
T. 0142542328. *101861*
Lardanchet, 100 Rue Fbg-Saint-Honoré, 75008 Paris.
T. 0142666832, Fax 0149240787. *101862*
De Lattre, 56 Rue Université, 75007 Paris.
T. 0145448353. - Engr - *101863*
Laucournet, Dominique, 2 Rue Rossini, 75009 Paris.
T. 0145233928. *101864*
Le Fell, Jean-Marie, 16 Rue Tournon, 75006 Paris.
T. 0143265289. *101865*
Le Prat, Guy, 5 Rue Grands-Augustins, 75006 Paris.
T. 0143265782. - Print - *101866*
Lecomte, Marcel, 17 Rue Seine, 75006 Paris.
T. 0143268547. - Engr - *101867*
Lefèbvre, Marc, 69 Blvd Beaumarchais, 75003 Paris.
T. 0142713669, Fax 0142715494. *101868*
Lelong, 12 et 13 Rue Téhéran, 75008 Paris.
T. 0145631319, Fax 0142893433. - ArtBk - *101869*
Lepert & Scheler, 42 Rue Jacob, 75006 Paris.
T. 0142614270. *101870*
Lettre Ecarlate, 114 Rue Blomet, 75015 Paris.
T. 0145332111. *101871*

Lévy, Jacques, 46 Rue Alésia, 75014 Paris.
T. 0143270879. - Print - *101872*
Liber, 52 Rue Montparnasse, 75014 Paris.
T. 0143203207. *101873*
Librairie Abencerage, 177 Rue Jeanne-d'Arc, 75013 Pa-
ris. T. 0147073032, Fax 0147073067. *101874*
Librairie Ancienne, 68 Rue Arras, 75006 Paris.
T. 0145486412. *101875*
Librairie Andante, 6 Rue Dante, 75005 Paris.
T. 0143262488. *101876*
Librairie de Châteaudun, 17 Rue Châteaudun, 75009 Pa-
ris. T. 0148787469, Fax 0148784245. - Print - *101877*
Librairie de l'Ameublement et de la Décoration, 23 Rue
Joubert, 75009 Paris. T. 0142820921.
- ArtBk - *101878*
Librairie de l'Imprimerie Nationale, 2 Rue Paul-Hervieu,
75015 Paris. T. 0140583275. - ArtBk - *101879*
Librairie de l'Inde, 20 Rue Descartes, 75005 Paris.
T. 0143258338, Fax 0143257952. *101880*
Librairie de la Seine, 5 Rue Lagrange, 75005 Paris.
T. 0143543222, Fax 0144073369. - Print - *101881*
Librairie des Alpes, 6 Rue Seine, 75006 Paris.
T. 0143269011, Fax 0144070366. - Print /
Map - *101882*
Librairie des Antiquaires, Louvre des Antiquaires, 2 Pl
Palais-Royal, 75001 Paris. T. 0142615679.
- ArtBk - *101883*
Librairie des Arts et Métiers, 33 Rue Réaumur, 75003
Paris. T. 0142721243. *101884*
Librairie des Galeries Nationales du Grand Palais, Av Gé-
néral-Eisenhower, 75008 Paris. T. 0144131717.
- ArtBk - *101885*
Librairie des Musées, 10 Rue Abbaye, 75006 Paris.
T. 0143292145. - ArtBk - *101886*
Librairie du Camée, 76 Rue Saint-André-des-Arts,
75006 Paris. T. 0143262170,
Fax 0143293888. *101887*
Librairie du Cygne, 17 Rue Bonaparte, 75006 Paris.
T. 0143263245, Fax 0143269268. *101888*
Librairie du Musée d'Art Moderne de la Ville de Paris, 11
Av Président-Wilson, 75116 Paris. - ArtBk - *101889*
Librairie du Musée d'Orsay, Parvis de Bellechasse,
75007 Paris. T. 0140494999. - ArtBk - *101890*
Librairie du Musée des Monuments Français, Pl du Tro-
cadéro, Palais de Chaillot, 75116 Paris.
T. 0144053910. - ArtBk - *101891*
Librairie du Musée du Louvre, Pyramide du Louvre,
75001 Paris. T. 0140205353. - ArtBk - *101892*
Librairie du Musée du Moyen-Age, Thermes de Cluny, 6
Pl Paul-Painlevé, 75005 Paris. T. 0143257561.
- ArtBk - *101893*
Librairie du Musée du Petit Palais, Av Winston-Churchill,
75008 Paris. - ArtBk - *101894*
Librairie du Passage, 111 Av Victor-Hugo, 75116 Paris.
T. 0147558933, Fax 0144059272. - Print - *101895*
Librairie du Spectacle, 5 Rue Montfaucon, 75006 Paris.
T. 0143548005, Fax 0143548292. - Print / ArtBk /
Engr / Autogr - *101896*
Librairie Epsilon, 33 Rue Vaugirard, 75006 Paris.
T. 0145445300. *101897*
Librairie Farfouille, 27 Pass Verdeau, 75009 Paris.
T. 0147702115. *101898*
Librairie Flammarion du Centre National d'Art, et de Cul-
ture Georges Pompidou, 19 Rue Beaubourg, 75004
Paris. T. 0142786740, Fax 0142785059.
- ArtBk - *101899*
Librairie François 1er, 46 Rue Pierre Charron, 75008 Pa-
ris. T. 0147204267, Fax 0147206773. *101900*
Librairie Godot de Mauroy, 34 Rue Godot-de-Mauroy,
75009 Paris. T. 0147421741. *101901*
Librairie Gourmande, 4 Rue Dante, 75005 Paris.
T. 0143543727, Fax 0143543116. - Print /
ArtBk - *101902*
Librairie Graphigro, 120 Rue Damrémont, 75018 Paris.
T. 0146067773. - ArtBk - *101903*
Librairie Guénégaud, 10 Rue de l'Odéon, 75006 Paris.
T. 0143260791. *101904*
Librairie Henner, 9 Rue Henner, 75009 Paris.
T. 0148746038. - Print / Autogr - *101905*
Librairie Jules Verne, 7 Rue Lagrange, 75005 Paris.
T. 0143255970. *101906*
Librairie L'Harmattan, 48 Rue Bernardins, 75005 Paris.
T. 0146341371. *101907*

Librairie Les Deux Mondes, 84 Rue Vaugirard, 75006
Paris. T. 0145440433. *101908*
Librairie Marco Polo, 25 Rue Saint-Marc, 75002 Paris.
T. 0142968283. *101909*
Librairie Mazarine, 78 Rue Mazarine, 75006 Paris.
T. 0143299107. - Print - *101910*
Librairie Métamorphoses, 76 Av Ledru-Rollin, 75012 Pa-
ris. T. 0143436830. *101911*
Librairie Monte Cristo, 5 Rue Odéon, 75006 Paris.
T. 0143264903. *101912*
Librairie Orientale Samuelian, 51 Rue Monsieur-Le-Prin-
ce, 75006 Paris. T. 0143268865. *101913*
Librairie Palladio, 83 Blvd Richard-Lenoir, 75011 Paris.
T. 0148059972. *101914*
Librairie Paris-Musées, c/o Musée Carnavalet, 23 Rue
Sévigné, 75003 Paris. T. 0142740800,
Fax 0142740408. - ArtBk - *101915*
Librairie Paris-Musées, c/o Bibliothèque Historique de la
Ville de Paris, 22 Rue Malher, 75003 Paris.
- ArtBk - *101916*
Librairie Picasso, 5 Rue Thorigny, 75003 Paris.
T. 0142719715. - ArtBk - *101917*
Librairie Pont-Neuf, 1 Rue Dauphine, 75006 Paris.
T. 0146335782, Fax 0143253460. - Print - *101918*
Librairie Puce, 30 Rue Bouret, 750019 Paris.
T. 0142407021. *101919*
Librairie Recherche, 238 Rue Croix-Nivert, 75015 Paris.
T. 0145324272. *101920*
Librairie Romain, 62 Av Italie, 75013 Paris.
T. 0145808069. - Print - *101921*
Librairie Rostain, 3 Rue Ave-Maria, 75004 Paris.
T. 0142745018. *101922*
Librairie Sainte-Marie, 25 Blvd Port-Royal, 75013 Paris.
T. 0143369050, Fax 0143369300. *101923*
Librairie Sevilla, 29 Rue Fontarabie, 75020 Paris.
T. 0143723842. *101924*
Librairie Uniformologique International, 111 Av Victor-
Hugo, 75016 Paris. T. 0147555574. *101925*
Librairie Valette, 11 Rue Vaugirard, 75006 Paris.
T. 0143264564. *101926*
Librairie Vers et Prose, 23 Rue Boulangers, 75005 Paris.
T. 0143260042, Fax 0146337341. *101927*
Librairie Violet, 41 Rue Violet, 75015 Paris.
T. 0145777879. *101928*
Livre Mon Ami, 24 Passage Verdeau, 75009 Paris.
T. 0148241871. *101929*
Livres de A à Z, 3 Rue Moines, 75017 Paris.
T. 0142294919. *101930*
Loliée, Bernard, 72 Rue de Seine, 75006 Paris.
T. 0143265382. - Print / Autogr - *101931*
Lühl, Jan & Hélène, 19 Quai Malaquais, 75006 Paris.
T. 0142607697. - Print - *101932*
Lutèce-BD, 29 Rue Monge, 75005 Paris.
T. 0143263216. *101933*
Lutèce-BD, 5 Rue Arras, 75005 Paris.
T. 0146333356. *101934*
Maeght, Adrien, 42 Rue Bac, 75007 Paris.
T. 0145481955, Fax 0145484515. - Print /
ArtBk - *101935*
Magis, Jean-Jaques, 47 Rue Saint-André-des-Arts,
75006 Paris. T. 0143265057, Fax 0143261138.
- Print - *101936*
Magnin, François, 25 Rue Charles-V, 75004 Paris.
T. 0142726700. *101937*
Maille, Bernard, 3 Rue Dante, 75005 Paris.
T. 0143255173. *101938*
Maison de l'Autographe, 328 Rue Saint-Jacques, 75005
Paris. T. 0140518259, Fax 0143257814.
- Autogr - *101939*
Maisonneuve, Jean, 11 Rue Saint-Sulpice, 75006 Paris.
T. 0143268635, Fax 0143545954. *101940*
Manière Noire, 46 Rue Caulaincourt, 75018 Paris.
T. 0146061848. *101941*
Margo, Thierry, 13 Rue Médicis, 75006 Paris.
T. 0143297991. *101942*
Marine et Voyages, 8 Rue Echaudé, 75006 Paris.
T. 0143260591, Fax 0146346140. - Print - *101943*
Marraine du Sel, 24 Rue Taillandiers, 75011 Paris.
T. 0148067511. *101944*
Martin, Guy, 56 Rue Saint-Georges, 75009 Paris.
T. 0148787842, Fax 0145262347. - Autogr - *101945*
Martinez, Fernand, 97 Rue Seine, 75006 Paris.
T. 0146330812. - Engr - *101946*

Mazo Lebouc, 15 Rue Guénégaud, 75006 Paris.
T. 0143263984. - Engr -   *101947*
Mécène, 109 Rue Lemercier, 75017 Paris.
T. 0142263777.   *101948*
Médicis 26, 26 Pl Vosges, 75003 Paris.
T. 0148871188.   *101949*
Minotaure, 2 Rue Beaux-Arts, 75006 Paris.
T. 0143253537, Fax 0143546293.   *101950*
Mode Information, 67 Blvd Sébastopol, 75002 Paris.
T. 0140138150, Fax 0145084577. - ArtBk -   *101951*
Montbel, E. de, 1 Rue Paul-Cézanne, 75008 Paris.
T. 0145639564, Fax 0145639564. - Print -   *101952*
Morel, Jean, 19 Rue Vieux-Colombier, 75006 Paris.
T. 0145444326.   *101953*
Muses Galantes, 111 Rue Legendre, 75017 Paris.
T. 0142289287, Fax 0142285959.   *101954*
Myers, Myrna, 11 Rue de Beaune, 75007 Paris.
T. 0142611108.   *101955*
Neuf Muses, 41 Quai Grands Augustins, 75006 Paris.
T. 0143263871. - Print / Autogr -   *101956*
Nobele, F. de, 35 Rue Bonaparte, 75006 Paris.
T. 0143260862, Fax 0140468596. - Print / ArtBk /
Engr -   *101957*
Odyssée, 160 Av Parmentier, 750010 Paris.
T. 0142401068. - Print -   *101958*
Or du Temps, 53 Rue Cardinal-Lemoine, 75005 Paris.
T. 0143269518.   *101959*
Oriens, 10 Blvd Arago, 75013 Paris. T. 0145358028,
Fax 0143360150. - Print -   *101960*
Oterelo, Claude, 159bis Blvd Montparnasse, 75006 Pa-
ris. T. 0143266229.   *101961*
Pabian, Stéphane, 4 Rue de Clichy, 75009 Paris.
T. 0145266130. - Print -   *101962*
Pages d'Histoire, 8 Rue Bréa, 75006 Paris.
T. 0143544361, Fax 0143549640.   *101963*
Pages Volantes, 7 Rue Auguste-Bartholdi, 75015 Paris.
T. 0140598846.   *101964*
Passagère, 25 Rue Echaudé, 75006 Paris.
T. 0143256666, Fax 0144070870.   *101965*
Petit Prince, 121 Blvd Saint-Michel, 75005 Paris.
T. 0143544560, Fax 0140510751. - Print /
ArtBk -   *101966*
Petitot, Pierre, 234 Bdvd Saint-Germain, 75007 Paris.
T. 0145480527.   *101967*
Picard, 82 Rue Bonaparte, 75006 Paris. T. 0143264871,
Fax 0143264264. - Print / ArtBk -   *101968*
Picard, Henri & Fils, 126 Rue Fbg Saint-Honoré, 75008
Paris. T. 0143592811, Fax 0143590402.   *101969*
Pinault, 27 Rue Bonaparte, 75006 Paris. T. 0143548999,
Fax 0143298169. - Print / Autogr -   *101970*
Pinault, 36 Rue Bonaparte, 75006 Paris. T. 0146330424,
Fax 0143298169. - Print / Autogr -   *101971*
Plantureux, Serge, 61 Rue Fbg-Poissonnière, 75009 Pa-
ris. T. 0144790713, Fax 0144790819.   *101972*
Pont Traversé, 62 Rue Vaugirard, 75006 Paris.
T. 0145480648.   *101973*
Porte Etroite, 10 Rue Bonaparte, 75006 Paris.
T. 0143542603, Fax 0140460655. - Print /
ArtBk -   *101974*

---

*Livres anciens et modernes sur
les Beaux-Arts*

LA PORTE
ETROITE

10, rue Bonaparte - 75006 Paris
Tél.: 01 43 54 26 03
Fax: 01 40 46 06 55

Poussière du Temps, 9 Rue Odéon, 75006 Paris.
T. 0143264954.   *101975*
Privat, B. & D., 162 Blvd Haussmann, 75008 Paris.
T. 0145622564, Fax 0149530525. - Print -   *101976*
Prouté, Paul, 74 Rue Seine, 75006 Paris.
T. 0143268980, Fax 0143258341. - Engr /
Map -   *101977*
Regard Moderne, 10 Rue Gît-le-Coeur, 75006 Paris.
T. 0143291393, Fax 0143291394.   *101978*

Rieffel, Alain Delbes, 15 Rue Odéon, 75006 Paris.
T. 0143549223.   *101979*
Rossignol, Emile, 8 Rue Bonaparte, 75006 Paris.
T. 0143267431. - Print -   *101980*
Rouillon, Jean-Paul, 27 Rue Seine, 75006 Paris.
T. 0143267300. - Print / Engr / Map -   *101981*
Roux Devillas, Olivier, 12 Rue Bonaparte, 75006 Paris.
T. 0143546932, Fax 0140469150. - Print -   *101982*
Saffroy, Gaston, 4 Rue Clément, 75006 Paris.
T. 0143262592. - Print / Autogr -   *101983*
Saffroy, Gaston, 3 Quai Malaquais, 75006 Paris.
T. 0143260919. - Print / Autogr -   *101984*
Sartoni-Cerveau, 15 Quai Saint-Michel, 75005 Paris.
T. 0143547573, Fax 0146341288. - Print /
Engr -   *101985*
Sepulchre, Bruno, 7 Rue Cassette, 75006 Paris.
T. 0145441514, Fax 0145490823.   *101986*
Sieur, Pierre, 3 Rue de l'Université, 75007 Paris.
T. 0142607594. - Print / Engr -   *101987*
Sportsman, 7bis Rue Henri-Duchêne, 75015 Paris.
T. 0145793893.   *101988*
Sudestasie, 17 Rue Cardinal-Lemoine, 75005 Paris.
T. 0143251804, Fax 0146347275. - Print -   *101989*
Sylva Sylvarum, 64 Rue Vieille-du-Temple, 75003 Paris.
Fax (1) 42718841.   *101990*
Table d'Emeraude, 21 Rue Huchette, 75005 Paris.
T. 0143549096, Fax 0140510267. - Print -   *101991*
Table d'Emeraude, 8 Rue Trois-Portes, 75005 Paris.
T. 0143254032.   *101992*
Tea and Tatterd Pages, 24 Rue Mayet, 75006 Paris.
T. 0140659435.   *101993*
Téboul, Francis, 9 Rue Odéon, 75006 Paris.
T. 0146339323.   *101994*
Teissèdre, F., 102 Rue Cherche-Midi, 75006 Paris.
T. 0145480391, Fax 0145443552.   *101995*
Thomas-Scheler, 19 Rue Tournon, 75006 Paris.
T. 0143269769, Fax 0140469146. - Print /
Autogr -   *101996*
Thomas, Simone, 46 Rue Saint-André-des-Arts, 75006
Paris. T. 0143263032.   *101997*
Tour du Monde, 9 Rue Pompe, 75016 Paris.
T. 0142885806, Fax 0142884057.   *101998*
Troisième Veille, 40 Rue Milton, 75009 Paris.
T. 0140161387. - Print -   *101999*
Urubamba, 4 Rue Bûcherie, 75005 Paris.
T. 0143540824, Fax 0143299180. - Print /
ArtBk -   *102000*
Valleriaux, Christian, 98 Blvd Voltaire, 75011 Paris.
T. 0147005043.   *102001*
Vertige, 45 Rue Pouchet, 75017 Paris.
T. 0142263187.   *102002*
Vieux Persan, 10 Rue Victor Massé, 75009 Paris.
T. 0145268493. - Print -   *102003*
Vignes, Henri, 1 Quai Austerlitz, 75013 Paris.
T. 0145846730. - Print -   *102004*
Volume, 110 Rue Olivier-de-Serres, 75015 Paris.
T. 0145324229, Fax 0145320531.   *102005*
Vouivre, 11 Rue Saint-Martin, 75004 Paris.
T. 0142713239, Fax 0142720283.   *102006*
Vrain, Jean Claude, 12 Rue Saint-Sulpice, 75006 Paris.
T. 0143293688, Fax 0144072271. - Print -   *102007*
Weill, Lucie, 6 Rue Bonaparte, 75006 Paris.
T. 0143547195. - Engr -   *102008*
Weissert, Friedrich, 22 Rue Savoie, 75006 Paris.
T. 0143297259, Fax 0146346063.   *102009*

Pau (Pyrénées-Atlantiques)
Librairie Clemenceau, 4 Rue Bordenave-d'Abère, 64000
Pau. T. 0559274662. - Print -   *102010*

Périgueux (Dordogne)
Ami de Passage, 1 Rue Clarté, 24000 Périgueux.
T. 0553352461.   *102011*
Hélénie de Pommier, 7 Rue Metz, 24000 Périgueux.
T. 0553532597. - Print -   *102012*
Lamongie, 2 Rue Nation, 24000 Périgueux.
T. 0553532245.   *102013*
Millescamps, Henri-Pierre, 7 Rue Saint-Front, 24000
Périgueux. T. 0553095325, Fax 0553098538.   *102014*
Sèze, Christian de, 52 Rue Michel-Roulland, 24000 Péri-
gueux. T. 0553534073.   *102015*

Perpignan (Pyrénées-Orientales)
Editions Dino, 14 Av Ampère-Cabestany, 66000 Perpig-
nan. T. 0468670607. - Print -   *102016*
Histoire de Lire, 5 Pl Grétry, 66000 Perpignan.
T. 0468342992. - Print -   *102017*
Mariany, Robert, 8 Rue Théâtre, 66000 Perpignan.
T. 0468346598. - Print -   *102018*
Point Virgule, 17 Rue Mar-Foch, 66000 Perpignan.
T. 0468343223. - Print -   *102019*
Tardy, Raymond, 19 Rue Castillet, 66000 Perpignan.
T. 0468345471. - Print -   *102020*

Pézenas (Hérault)
Aparté, 13 Rue Foire, 34120 Pézenas.
T. 0467980304.   *102021*
Haut Quartier, 44 Rue Conti, 34120 Pézenas.
T. 0467982741.   *102022*

Pia (Pyrénées-Orientales)
Arboux Diffusion, 1 Rue Perpignan, 66380 Pia.
T. 0468633625. - Print -   *102023*

Plateau-d'Assy (Haute-Savoie)
Jiguet, Philippe, 719 Chemin Cran, 74480 Plateau-d'Assy. T. 0450938723. - Print -   *102024*

Pléneuf-Val-André (Côtes-d'Armor)
Turcas, Flore, 132 Rue Georges-Clemenceau, 22370
Pléneuf-Val-André. T. 0296722146.   *102025*

Poitiers (Vienne)
Brissaud Librairie Ancienne, 162 Grand'Rue, 86000 Poi-
tiers. T. 0549880181, Fax 0549525329. - Print /
Engr -   *102026*

Poligny (Jura)
Saint-Priest, Mireille, 6 Rue Victor-Hugo, 39800 Poligny.
T. 0384373246. - Print -   *102027*

Port-de-Bouc (Bouches-du-Rhône)
Port des Bouquins, Rue Charles-Nédélec, 13110 Port-
de-Bouc. T. 0442060120.   *102028*

Pouilly-sur-Loire (Nièvre)
Orcet, Anne, 21ter Quai Docteur-Jules-Sebillotte, 58150
Pouilly-sur-Loire. T. 0386391314.   *102029*

Provins (Seine-et-Marne)
Lecoq, Francis, 2 Rue Loups, 77160 Provins.
T. 0360677850.   *102030*

Quimper (Finistère)
Aularge-Danigo, 16 Rue Marc-Sangnier, 29000 Quimper.
T. 0298642242. - Print -   *102031*
Glanerie, 49 Blvd Am-de-Kerguelen, 29000 Quimper.
T. 0298643250.   *102032*

Reims (Marne)
Bibliothème, 4 Rue Colbert, 51100 Reims.
T. 0326884342.   *102033*
Librairie Courcelles, 58 Rue Courcelles, 51100 Reims.
T. 0326477300.   *102034*

Rennes (Ille-et-Vilaine)
Au Vieux Saint-Melaine, 29 Rue Saint-Melaine, 35000
Rennes. T. 0299387332. - Print -   *102035*
Bouquinerie des Quais, 6 Quai Emile-Zola, 35000 Ren-
nes. T. 0299793664. - Print -   *102036*
Bréhélin, Jean, 22 Pl Sainte-Anne, 35000 Rennes.
T. 0299387095.   *102037*
Corre, François, 18 Rue Hoche, 35000 Rennes.
T. 0299387887. - Print -   *102038*
Moisan, Philippe, 9 Rue Victor-Hugo, 35000 Rennes.
T. 0299781116.   *102039*
Poste du Village, 6 Rue Edith-Cavell, 35000 Rennes.
T. 0299792702, Fax 0299794516.   *102040*

Riom (Puy-de-Dôme)
Légende Dorée, 22 Blvd Clémentel, 63200 Riom.
T. 0473387309. - Print -   *102041*

Roanne (Loire)
Mot Passant, 14 Rue Cadore, 42300 Roanne.
T. 0477672700.   *102042*

Rodez (Aveyron)
Librairie Ancienne et Cabinet Généalogique, 1 Rue Barrière, Pl du Bourg, 12000 Rodez. T. 0565429521.
- Print - *102043*

Roinville-sur-Auneau (Eure-et-Loir)
Abbaye, 9 Rue Eglise, 28700 Roinville-sur-Auneau.
T. 0237318844. - Print - *102044*

Rouen (Seine-Maritime)
Belle Page, 19 Rue Alsace-Lorraine, 76000 Rouen.
T. 0235704701. *102045*
Bertran, Etienne, 110 Rue Molière, 76000 Rouen.
T. 0235707996. - Print - *102046*
Brunet, Elisabeth, 70 Rue Ganterie, 76000 Rouen.
T. 0235986306. - Print - *102047*
Colportages, 2 Pl 39ème-Régiment-d'Infanterie, 76000 Rouen. T. 0235983075. - Print - *102048*
Librairie du Musée des Beaux-Arts, 26bis Rue Jean-Lecanuet, 76000 Rouen. T. 0235711317.
- ArtBk - *102049*
Magne, Michel, 20 Rue Hôpital, 76000 Rouen.
T. 0235887631. *102050*
Mémoires, 210 Rue Martainville, 76000 Rouen.
T. 0235075305, Fax 0235895147. *102051*
Métais, Henri, 2 Pl Barthélemy, 76000 Rouen.
T. 0235709433, Fax 0235711148. - Print - *102052*
Palier, Denise, 180 Rue Martainville, 76000 Rouen.
T. 0235070933. - Print - *102053*
Sciardet, Daniel, 138 Rue Eau-de-Robec, 76000 Rouen.
T. 0235892378. *102054*
Vigreux, Jean-Jacques, 5 Rue Boucheries-Saint-Ouen, 76000 Rouen. T. 0235715110. - Print - *102055*

Rueil-Malmaison (Hauts-de-Seine)
Bug-Auto-Moto, 15 Rue Yser, 92500 Rueil-Malmaison.
T. 0147495629. *102056*

Rully (Saône-et-Loire)
Gros, André-Charles, Pl Eglise, 71150 Rully.
T. 0385871951. - Print - *102057*

Saint-Brieuc (Côtes-d'Armor)
Grenier Robien, 21 Blvd Carnot, 22000 Saint-Brieuc.
T. 0296782367. - Print - *102058*
Sofec, 13 Rue Saint-François, 22000 Saint-Brieuc.
T. 0296613205. - Print - *102059*

Saint-Cernin-de-Larche (Corrèze)
Mauranges, Hélène, Château Pommier, 19600 Saint-Cernin-de-Larche. T. 0555853139. *102060*

Saint-Cyr-sur-Loire (Indre-et-Loire)
Veyssière, Jean-Paul, 19 Rue Victor-Hugo, La Moisanderie, 37540 Saint-Cyr-sur-Loire. T. 0547548454.
- Print / Engr - *102061*

Saint-Didier-des-Bois (Eure)
Fine Arts Books, 1 Pl Eglise, 27370 Saint-Didier-des-Bois. T. 0232505949, Fax 0232505947.
- Print - *102062*

Saint-Etienne (Loire)
Bouquiniste, 34 Rue Michelet, 42000 Saint-Etienne.
T. 0477326369, Fax 0477320830. - Print - *102063*
Imagine, 11 Rue Pierre-Bérard, 42000 Saint-Etienne.
T. 0477418070. *102064*
Odyssée, 15 Rue Mi-Carême, 42000 Saint-Etienne.
T. 0477332150. *102065*
Tropique Bouquinerie, 18 Rue Elise-Gervais, 42000 Saint-Etienne. T. 0477411190. *102066*

Saint-Flour (Cantal)
Ajalbert, René, 13 et 18 Rue Rollandie, 15100 Saint-Flour. T. 0471604438. - Print - *102067*

Saint-Germain-en-Laye (Yvelines)
Collections du Passé, 5 Rue Vieil-Abreuvoir, 78100 Saint-Germain-en-Laye. T. 0134519612.
- Print - *102068*
Marque Jaune, 10 Rue Salle, 78100 Saint-Germain-en-Laye. T. 0139211938, Fax 0139219218. *102069*
Raux, Jean-Emmanuel, 5 Rue Vieil-Abreuvoir, 78000 Saint-Germain-en-Laye. T. 0134519612,
Fax 0134514229. - Autogr - *102070*

Saint-Jean-de-Védas (Hérault)
Bateau Livre, La Lauze, 11 Rue Jean-Mermoz, 34430 Saint-Jean-de-Védas. T. 0467276722. *102071*

Saint-Julien-en-Genevois (Haute-Savoie)
Sphinx d'Or, 4 Le Mail, 74160 Saint-Julien-en-Genevois.
T. 0450350507. - ArtBk - *102072*

Saint-Maixent (Sarthe)
Montescot, Bruyère, 72320 Saint-Maixent.
T. 0243710070. *102073*

Saint-Martin-de-la-Lieue (Calvados)
Legeleux, Nadine, Eglise, 14100 Saint-Martin-de-la-Lieue. T. 0231624407. *102074*

Saint-Martin-de Ré (Charente-Maritime)
Quillet, Cour Cinéma, 17410 Saint-Martin-de-Ré.
T. 0546091055. - Print / Engr - *102075*

Saint-Ouen (Seine-Saint-Denis)
Haulle, Jean-Claude, 136 Av Michelet, 93400 Saint-Ouen. T. 0140108116. - Print - *102076*
Lattre, Dominique de, 99 Rue Rosiers, 93400 Saint-Ouen. T. 0140126889. *102077*
Librairie de l'Avenue, 31 Rue Lecuyer, 93400 Saint-Ouen. T. 0140100765, Fax 0140100789. - Print /
ArtBk - *102078*
Maurel, Isabelle, Marché Vernaison, 93400 Saint-Ouen.
T. 0140111159. *102079*
Rémon, Nicolas, 95 Rue Rosiers, 93400 Saint-Ouen.
T. 0140102932. *102080*

Saint-Pryvé-Saint-Mesmin (Loiret)
Lefèbvre, 1 Rue Lucien-Péan, 45750 Saint-Pryvé-Saint-Mesmin. T. 0238666324, Fax 0238582831. *102081*

Saint-Quentin (Aisne)
Crespin, Jean-Claude, 23 Rue Bouchers, 02100 Saint-Quentin. T. 0323642320. - Print - *102082*

Saint-Raphaël (Var)
Cassandre, 115 Av Victor-Hugo, 83700 Saint-Raphaël.
T. 0494831171. *102083*

Saint-Rémy-de-Provence (Bouches-du-Rhône)
Tetragramme, 12 Blvd Gambetta, 13210 Saint-Rémy-de-Provence. T. 0490926091. *102084*

Saint-Yrieix-sous-Aixe (Haute-Vienne)
Jouhate, Annette, Le Gué-de-la-Roche, 87420 Saint-Yrieix-sous-Aixe. T. 0555038306. *102085*

Saintes (Charente-Maritime)
Saliba, Gérard, 28 Av Gambetta, 17100 Saintes.
Fax 46740443. *102086*

Sallanches (Haute-Savoie)
Aux 3 Siècles, 68 Av Genève, 74700 Sallanches.
T. 0450937548, Fax 0450939716. - Print /
Engr - *102087*

Sannerville (Calvados)
Chereau, Jacques, 3 Rue Maréchal-Leclerc, 14940 Sannerville. T. 0231237730. - Print - *102088*

Sarzeau (Morbihan)
Chassaniol, Robert, Bourg-Saint-Colombier, 56370 Sarzeau. T. 0297264809. - Print - *102089*
Recherche du Passé, Bourg-Saint-Colombier, 56370 Sarzeau. T. 0297264150, Fax 0297264529. *102090*

Sauliac-sur-Célé (Lot)
Ménard, Jean-Yves, Montagnac, 46330 Sauliac-sur-Célé. T. 0565312870, Fax 0565302269. *102091*

Scy-Chazelles (Moselle)
Boux, Jean, 9 Rue Saint-Nicolas, 57160 Scy-Chazelles.
T. 0387601294, Fax 0387600525. *102092*

Seix (Ariège)
Gourgues, Nelly, Rue Clemenceau, 09140 Seix.
T. 0561669333. - Print - *102093*

Seraincourt (Val-d'Oise)
Tourret, 1 Imp Saint-Jean-Rueil, 95450 Seraincourt.
T. 0134754502. *102094*

Sévrier (Haute-Savoie)
Juillet, L., Létraz, 74320 Sévrier. T. 0450526040.
- Print - *102095*

Soissons (Aisne)
Rayon Vert, 14 Rue Pot-d'Etain, 02200 Soissons.
T. 0323534860. - Print - *102096*

Strasbourg (Bas-Rhin)
Atelier du Bibliophile, 26 Quai Bateliers, 67000 Strasbourg. T. 0388242300, Fax 0388240009.
- Print - *102097*
Brocantique, 125 Rte Schirmeck, 67200 Strasbourg.
T. 0388285878. - Print - *102098*
Elegia, 28 Rue des Tonneliers, 67000 Strasbourg.
T. 0388223865. - Engr - *102099*
Galerie du Quai, 14 Quai Saint-Nicolas, 67000 Strasbourg. T. 0388361329. - Print / Engr / Autogr - *102100*
Galerie Oberlin, 19 Rue Francs-Bourgeois, 67000 Strasbourg. T. 0388324583, Fax 0388210587.
- ArtBk - *102101*
Gangloff, 20 Pl de la Cathédrale, 67000 Strasbourg.
T. 0388324052, Fax 0388225756. - Print /
Engr - *102102*
Image et le Livre, 12 Rue Jacques-Peirotes, 67000 Strasbourg. T. 0388360160, Fax 0388379526. *102103*
Librairie de l'Amateur, 24bis Rue Orfèvres, 67000 Strasbourg. T. 0388321172, Fax 0388321922. *102104*
Librairie L'Autodidacte, 14 Rue Roses, 67000 Strasbourg. T. 0388446670, Fax 0388440903. *102105*
Librairie Le Temps Retrouvé, 5 Rue Veaux, 67000 Strasbourg. T. 0388353757. *102106*
Tiresias, 12 Rue Vieil-Hôpital, 67000 Strasbourg.
T. 0388226959. *102107*

Tarbes (Hautes-Pyrénées)
Au Bouquiniste, 75 Av Bertrand-Barère, 65000 Tarbes.
T. 0562933822. - Print - *102108*
Chilperic, 28 Av Régiment-de-Bigorre, 65000 Tarbes.
T. 0562936097. - Print - *102109*

Tassin-la-Demi-Lune (Rhône)
Bertrand, 2 All Ecureuils, 69160 Tassin-la-Demi-Lune.
T. 0478344111. *102110*

Thann (Haut-Rhin)
Dannenberger, Michel, 20 Rue 1ère-Armée-Française, 68800 Thann. T. 0389372466. - Print - *102111*

Toulon (Var)
Kiosques, Rue Prosper-Ferréro, 83000 Toulon.
T. 0494913130, Fax 0494091032. - Print - *102112*
Montbarbon, 1 Rue Richard-Andrieu, 83000 Toulon.
T. 0494934939. *102113*
Passé Retrouvé, 5 Rue Corneille, 83000 Toulon.
T. 0494242079. - Print / Engr - *102114*
Vieux Ordinaires, 8 Rue Jean-Baptiste-Baudin, 83000 Toulon. T. 0494895924. - Print / Engr - *102115*

Toulouse (Haute-Garonne)
Aminotaur, 36 Rue Taur, 31000 Toulouse.
T. 0561231272. - Print - *102116*
Cau, Jean, 52 Rue Taur, 31000 Toulouse.
T. 0561233494. *102117*
Cau, Jean, 52 Rue Peyras, 31000 Toulouse.
T. 0561219350. *102118*
Champavert, 2 Rue Périgord, 31000 Toulouse.
T. 0561219596, Fax 0561121178. *102119*
Hartmann, Frédéric, 6 Rue Gestes, 31000 Toulouse.
T. 0561231912. *102120*
Jamois, Jean-Luc, 63 Rue Pargaminières, 31000 Toulouse. T. 0561230978. *102121*
Juaniquet, Jean, 22 Rue Rempart-Saint-Etienne, 31000 Toulouse. T. 0561218079. - Print / Engr /
Autogr - *102122*
Lestrade, Michel, 2 Rue Philippe-Feral, 31000 Toulouse.
T. 0561250880. *102123*
Maison de l'Etameur, 12 Rue Jean-Rancy, 31000 Toulouse. T. 0561226614. - Print - *102124*
Maldoror, 1 Rue Jean-Suau, 31000 Toulouse.
T. 0561234982. *102125*

Marnières, Pierre, 5 Rue Poids-de-l'Huile, 31000 Tou-
louse. T. 0561233433. - ArtBk -　　　　　　*102126*
Marnières, Pierre, 13 Rue Metz, 31000 Toulouse.
T. 0561219298. - ArtBk -　　　　　　　　　*102127*
Occitania, 46 Rue Taur, 31000 Toulouse.
T. 0561214900. - Print / Engr -　　　　　　　*102128*

Tours (Indre-et-Loire)
Amours, 72 Rue Nationale, 37000 Tours.
T. 0547660685. - Print -　　　　　　　　　*102129*
Antiquaria, 56 Rue Scellerie, 37000 Tours.
T. 0547050931. - Print -　　　　　　　　　*102130*
Bienvault, Odile, 3 Rue Corneille, 37000 Tours.
T. 0547610071, Fax 0547618902.　　　　　　*102131*
Boireau, Benoît, 83 Rue Scellerie, 37000 Tours.
T. 0547052681.　　　　　　　　　　　　*102132*
Denis, Marie-Thérèse, 14bis Blvd Heurteloup, 37000
Tours. T. 0547050279.　　　　　　　　　　*102133*
Librairie Denis, 50 Rue Scellerie, 37000 Tours.
T. 0547641277. - Print -　　　　　　　　　*102134*
Librairie du Théâtre, 2 Rue Corneille, 37000 Tours.
T. 0547612185.　　　　　　　　　　　　*102135*

Trédarzec (Côtes-d'Armor)
Debeir, France-Lise, Traou Meur, 22220 Trédarzec.
T. 0296293028. - Print -　　　　　　　　　*102136*

Trédias (Côtes-d'Armor)
Davy, Serge, Le Bourg, 22250 Trédias.
T. 0296848233.　　　　　　　　　　　　*102137*

Trévou-Tréguignec (Côtes-d'Armor)
Paternotte, Gérard, 2 Rue Moulin, 22660 Trévou-Tré-
guignec. T. 0296237854.　　　　　　　　　*102138*

Triel-sur-Seine (Yvelines)
Encausticup, 177 Rue Paul-Doumer, 78510 Triel-sur-
Seine. T. 0139707767. - Print -　　　　　　　*102139*

Troyes (Aube)
Au Bouquiniste, 51 Rue Simart, 10000 Troyes.
T. 0325805490. - Print -　　　　　　　　　*102140*
Prod'Homme, Jean-René, 1 Rue Urbain, 10000 Troyes.
T. 0325432682. - Print / Engr / Autogr / Map -　*102141*

Tulle (Corrèze)
Boulet, Olivier, 33 Quai Aristide-Briand, 19000 Tulle.
T. 0555203537. - Print -　　　　　　　　　*102142*
O.K.B.D., 4 Rue Solane, 19000 Tulle.
T. 0555265200.　　　　　　　　　　　　*102143*

Valbonne (Alpes-Maritimes)
Livres d'Or, 6 Pl Carrée, 06560 Valbonne.
T. 0492960538.　　　　　　　　　　　　*102144*

Valence (Ardèche)
Bouquinerie, Pl Pierre, 26000 Valence.
T. 0475437571.　　　　　　　　　　　　*102145*

Valence (Drôme)
Bouquinerie, 9 Pl Pierre, 26000 Valence.
T. 0475437571. - Print -　　　　　　　　　*102146*

Vallauris (Alpes-Maritimes)
Librairie du Musée Picasso, Pl Libération, 06220 Vallauris. T. 0493649742. - ArtBk -　　　　　　　*102147*

Vannes (Hauts-de-Seine)
Giraudon, 70 Rue Jean-Bleuzen, 92170 Vannes.
T. 0141237840, Fax 0141237841.　　　　　　*102148*

Vanves (Hauts-de-Seine)
Dimp, 58 Rue Jean-Bleuzen, 92170 Vanves.
T. 0146452046.　　　　　　　　　　　　*102149*

Varages (Var)
Charrot, Jean-Louis, 4 Pl République, 83670 Varages.
T. 0494776337, Fax 0494776338.　　　　　　*102150*

Vence (Alpes-Maritimes)
Galerie Librairie de la Basse Fontaine, 2 Pl Antony-Mars,
06140 Vence. T. 0493580480. - Print -　　　　*102151*
Librairie du Château de Villeneuve, 3 Pl du Frêne, 06140
Vence. T. 0493585212. - ArtBk -　　　　　　*102152*

Verdun (Meuse)
Bouquinerie, 3 Rue Gros-Degrès, 55100 Verdun.
T. 0329847169. - Print -　　　　　　　　　*102153*

Vernon (Eure)
Librairie Atelier du Chapitre, 14 Rue Saint-Sauveur,
27200 Vernon. T. 0232514588. - Print -　　　　*102154*

Vernou-sur-Brenne (Indre-et-Loire)
Portal, Sylviane, 4 La Rauderie, 37210 Vernou-sur-
Brenne. T. 0547521510, Fax 0547521520.　　　*102155*

Versailles (Yvelines)
Analecta, 108 Blvd Reine, 78000 Versailles.
T. 0130218413. - Print -　　　　　　　　　*102156*
Betis, Jean-François, 2 Rue Magenta, 78000 Versailles.
T. 0139027619. - Print -　　　　　　　　　*102157*
Interphase, 2bis Rue Limoges, 78000 Versailles.
T. 0139531469.　　　　　　　　　　　　*102158*
Lefebvre, Michel, 38 Rue Paroisse, 78000 Versailles.
T. 0139504484. - Print / ArtBk -　　　　　　　*102159*
Librairie des Carrés, 42 Rue Royale, 78000 Versailles.
T. 0139200632. - Print -　　　　　　　　　*102160*
Planète, 33 Av Saint-Cloud, 78000 Versailles.
T. 0139533227.　　　　　　　　　　　　*102161*
Puzin, Georges, 30 Rue Paroisse, 78000 Versailles.
T. 0139504375. - Print / Engr -　　　　　　　*102162*
Traineau, 33 Rue Royal, 78000 Versailles.
T. 0139507413.　　　　　　　　　　　　*102163*
Witte, Loïc-Marie de, 7 Rue Deux-Portes, 78000 Versail-
les. T. 0139021754.　　　　　　　　　　　*102164*

Vézelay (Yonne)
Bleu du Ciel, Rue Saint-Etienne, 89450 Vézelay.
T. 0386333030, Fax 0386333570.　　　　　　*102165*

Viabon (Eure-et-Loir)
Leseur, Daniel, 8 Rue Conie, 28150 Viabon.
T. 0237990812.　　　　　　　　　　　　*102166*

Vichy (Allier)
Condé, Monica de, 16 Rue Source-Hôpital, 03200 Vichy.
T. 0470325783.　　　　　　　　　　　　*102167*
Faye, Jean, 30 Rue Montaret, 03200 Vichy.
T. 0470974016.　　　　　　　　　　　　*102168*
Librairie de la Tour, Louis de Condé, 16 Rue Source de
l'Hôpital, 03200 Vichy. T. 0470325783,
Fax 0470325783.　　　　　　　　　　　　*102169*

Vignory (Haute-Marne)
Duplessis, J.V., Rue Général-Leclerc, Le Prieuré, 52320
Vignory. T. 0325318185, Fax 0325312735.
- Print -　　　　　　　　　　　　　　　*102170*

Villars (Vaucluse)
La Marge, Pl Fontaine, 84400 Villars.
T. 0490755511.　　　　　　　　　　　　*102171*

Villebon-sur-Yvette (Essonne)
Ryckelynck, Alain, 1 Rue Basse-Roche, 91140 Villebon-
sur-Yvette. T. 0160103501.　　　　　　　　*102172*

Villefranche-de-Rouergue (Aveyron)
Lesueur, Patrice, 12 Rue Sénéchal, 12200 Villefranche-
de-Rouergue. T. 0565453246.　　　　　　　*102173*

Villemolaque (Pyrénées-Orientales)
A.B.L. Editions, 2 Pl de la Marqueta, 66300 Villemola-
que. T. 0468217005. - Print -　　　　　　　*102174*

Villeneuve-de-Berg (Ardèche)
Carle, Patrick, Pl Obélisque, 07170 Villeneuve-de-Berg.
T. 0475948045.　　　　　　　　　　　　*102175*

Villeneuve-lès-Avignon (Gard)
Michel, Robert, 57 Rue Récollets, 30400 Villeneuve-lès-
Avignon. T. 0490254411.　　　　　　　　　*102176*

Villeneuve-sur-Lot (Lot-et-Garonne)
Galerie Edera, 21 Blvd Palissy, 47300 Villeneuve-sur-
Lot. T. 0553704399. - Print -　　　　　　　*102177*

Villenouvelle (Haute-Garonne)
Duchêne, 4 Rue Nationale, 31290 Villenouvelle.
T. 0561270903, Fax 0561271044.　　　　　　*102178*

Villeurbanne (Rhône)
Loison, Jean, Cité des Antiquaires, 117 Blvd Stalingrad,
2.14, 69100 Villeurbanne. - ArtBk -　　　　　*102179*
Mazoyer, Georges, 35 Rue Fontanières, 69100 Villeurbanne. T. 0478841947. - Print -　　　　　　*102180*

Vincennes (Val-de-Marne)
Milles et un Livres, 114 Rue Diderot, 94300 Vincennes.
T. 0143280109.　　　　　　　　　　　　*102181*

Vire (Calvados)
A la Recherche du Passé, 13 Rue Armand-Gasté, 14500
Vire. T. 0231680585. - Print / Engr -　　　　　*102182*
Chassaniol Bénard, Elisabeth, 13 Rue Armand-Gasté,
14500 Vire. T. 0231680585.　　　　　　　　*102183*

Vitry-sur-Seine (Val-de-Marne)
Reisz, Gilles, 41 Av Paul-Vaillant-Couturier, 94400 Vitry-
sur-Seine. T. 0146805545.　　　　　　　　*102184*

Vivières (Aisne)
Editions du Bien Aller, Ferme Epine, 02600 Vivières.
T. 0323964080. - Print -　　　　　　　　　*102185*

Yvoire (Haute-Savoie)
Boutique de l'Enluminure, Rue Principale, 74140 Yvoire.
T. 0450729423, Fax 0450729423.　　　　　　*102186*

Germany

Aachen (Nordrhein-Westfalen)
Antiquariat Aix-la-Chapelle, Markt 36, 52062 Aachen.
T. (0241) 30872, Fax 20786. - Print / Engr -　*102187*
Augustinus-Buchhandlung, Pontstr. 66, 52062 Aachen.
T. (0241) 310 51. - ArtBk -　　　　　　　　*102188*
Collectors Cabinet, Pontstr. 38, 52062 Aachen.
T. (0241) 37930.　　　　　　　　　　　*102189*
Henninghaus, L., Dr., Pontdriesch 19, 52062 Aachen.
T. (0241) 25340.　　　　　　　　　　　*102190*
Schmetz am Dom, Rennbahn 13, 52062 Aachen.
T. (0241) 32528, Fax (0241) 403877. - Print -　*102191*

Aalen (Baden-Württemberg)
Scientia, Adlerstr 65, 73434 Aalen. T. (07361) 41700,
Fax (07361) 45620.　　　　　　　　　　　*102192*

Ahrenshoop (Mecklenburg-Vorpommern)
Bunte Stube Andreas Wegscheider, Dorfstr. 24, 18347
Ahrenshoop. T. (038220) 238,
Fax (038220) 80472.　　　　　　　　　　*102193*

Ainring (Bayern)
Schindegger, Paul, Haller Str 11, 83404 Ainring.
T. (08654) 64185, Fax (08654) 66185. - Print -　*102194*

Albstadt (Baden-Württemberg)
Renner, Gerhard, Auf dem Unteren Berg, 72461 Albstadt.
T. (07431) 51 14, Fax 5567. - Print -　　　　　*102195*

Allensbach (Baden-Württemberg)
Graphica, Kirchgasse 1, 78476 Allensbach.
T. (07533) 07531/261 36.　　　　　　　　　*102196*
Herzog von Hinterskirch, Brigitte, Zur Halde 26, 78476
Allensbach. T. (07533) 58 10. - Print / Engr /
Map -　　　　　　　　　　　　　　　　*102197*

Allershausen (Bayern)
Scharnagi, G. Graphisches Antiquariat, von-Behring-Str.
4, 85391 Allershausen. T. (08166) 71 32.
- Engr -　　　　　　　　　　　　　　　*102198*

Allmendingen (Baden-Württemberg)
Feucht, R.G., Hauptstr. 18, 89604 Allmendingen.
T. (07391) 12 76, Fax 83 24.　　　　　　　　*102199*

Altenbeken (Nordrhein-Westfalen)
Wichert-Pollmann, Dr., Hammer 16, Haus Durbeke,
33184 Altenbeken. T. (05255) 69 55.　　　　　*102200*

Altenberg (Sachsen)
Schnuphase'sche Buchhandlung, Moskauer Str. 49,
04600 Altenberg.　　　　　　　　　　　*102201*

Ammerbuch (Baden-Württemberg)
Appelkamp, Dieter, Obere Str. 51, 72119 Ammerbuch.
T. (07073) 61 26. *102202*

Amorbach (Bayern)
Emig, Hermann, 63916 Amorbach. - Print /
Engr - *102203*

Ansbach (Bayern)
Heubeck, Sonja, Kronenstr 16, 91522 Ansbach.
T. (0981) 17360, (09872) 2600. *102204*

Arnstein (Bayern)
Mergenthaler, W., Eulenbergstr 3, 97450 Arnstein.
T. (09363) 5406. *102205*

Arolsen (Hessen)
Kirstein, Waldemar, 34454 Arolsen. - Print - *102206*

Aschaffenburg (Bayern)
Gerster, Karl-Heinz, Ligusterweg 5, 63741 Aschaffenburg. T. (06021) 89360. - Print - *102207*

Aschersleben (Sachsen-Anhalt)
Ascherslebener Bücherstube, Tie 11, 06433 Aschersle-
ben. T. (03473) 3557. - Print / ArtBk - *102208*

Augsburg (Bayern)
Antiquariat Büchertürmle, Bäckergasse 7, 86150 Augs-
burg. T. (0821) 519898. - Print - *102209*
Beier, K., Bäckergasse 7, 86150 Augsburg. *102210*
Hassold, Peter Wilhelm, Grottenau 6, 86150 Augsburg.
T. (0821) 514941, Fax (0821) 36150. - Map / Engr /
Print - *102211*
Scharnhorst, Dominikanergasse 12, 86150 Augsburg.
T. (0821) 511931. *102212*
Schreyer, Hartmut R., Ulrichspl 12, 86150 Augsburg.
T. (0821) 36468. - Print / ArtBk / Engr / Map - *102213*

Augustusburg (Sachsen)
Klis'sche Buchhandlung, Chemnitzer Str. 2, 09573 Au-
gustusburg. T. (037291) 348. *102214*

Aystetten (Bayern)
Lörcher, Margot, Gartenstr 13, 86482 Aystetten.
T. (0821) 489028, Fax (0821) 485741. - Engr - *102215*

Bad Honnef (Nordrhein-Westfalen)
Meuschel, Konrad, Hauptstr 19a, 53604 Bad Honnef.
T. (02224) 78485, Fax (02224) 5642. - Print /
Autogr - *102216*

Bad Karlshafen (Hessen)
Schäfer, Bernhard, Conradistr 2, 34385 Bad Karlshafen.
T. (05672) 503. - Print / ArtBk / Map - *102217*

Bad Kissingen (Bayern)
Badorrek, Manfred, Kurhausstr. 22, 97688 Bad Kissingen. T. (0971) 632 92. - Print - *102218*

Bad Marienberg (Rheinland-Pfalz)
Goeltzer, Konrad, Schillerstr 3, 56470 Bad Marienberg.
T. (02661) 3814. *102219*

Bad Münder (Niedersachsen)
Filmwelt Berlin, Im Bracken 2, 31848 Bad Münder.
T. (05042) 7202, Fax 7205. *102220*

Bad Nauheim (Hessen)
Deutsches Buch-Kontor, Stresemannstr. 5, 61231 Bad
Nauheim. T. (06032) 26 66. - ArtBk - *102221*
Schwab, G., Sudetenring 9, 61231 Bad Nauheim.
T. (06032) 847 82. *102222*

Bad Neuenahr-Ahrweiler (Rheinland-Pfalz)
Müller-Feldmann, Annemarie, Telegrafenstr. 21, 53474
Bad Neuenahr-Ahrweiler. T. (02641) 263 39,
Fax 287 95. *102223*

Bad Neustadt an der Saale (Bayern)
Pfaehler, Dietrich, Berliner Str 37, 97616 Bad Neustadt
an der Saale. T. (09771) 8142. - Print / Engr /
Map - *102224*

Bad Segeberg (Schleswig-Holstein)
Schatulle, Lübecker Str. 10a, 23795 Bad Segeberg.
T. (04551) 926 22. *102225*

Bad Soden (Hessen)
Nolting, Hans Joachim von, Oranienstr 16, 65812 Bad
Soden. T. (06196) 23832, 24892, Fax (06196) 28769.
- Print / ArtBk - *102226*

Baden-Baden (Baden-Württemberg)
Koerner, Valentin, Hermann-Sielcken-Str 36, 76530 Ba-
den-Baden. T. (07221) 22423, Fax (07221) 38697.
- Print - *102227*
Thelen, Gertrud, Büttenstr 11, Kurgarten 6, 76530 Ba-
den-Baden. T. (07221) 33398, Fax (07221) 38518.
- Print / ArtBk - *102228*
Weber, Peter, Eichstr 12, 76530 Baden-Baden.
T. (07221) 25571. *102229*

Badenweiler (Baden-Württemberg)
Sasse, Kaiserstr. 1, 79403 Badenweiler.
T. (07632) 1355. - Print - *102230*
Terl, Margarete, Luisenstr. 2, 79410 Badenweiler.
T. (07632) 327. - Print - *102231*

Bamberg (Bayern)
Antiquariat am Maxplatz, Fleischstr. 19, 96047 Bam-
berg. T. (0951) 230 52. *102232*
Görres Buch- und Kunsthandlung, Lange Str. 22, 96047
Bamberg. T. (0951) 2 52 52. - Print - *102233*
Kohr, A., Zinkenwörth 9, 96047 Bamberg.
T. (0951) 286 29. - Print / Engr - *102234*
Kunstkontor, Obere Brücke 5, 96047 Bamberg.
T. (0951) 230 27, 557 27, Fax 20 28 13. - Print / ArtBk /
Autogr / Map - *102235*
Messidor, Lugbank 6, 96049 Bamberg.
T. (0951) 58236. *102236*
Murr, Karlheinz, Karolinenstr 4, Untere Brücke 3-5,
96049 Bamberg. T. (0951) 57728, Fax (0951) 56221.
- ArtBk / Engr / Autogr / Map - *102237*

Bayreuth (Bayern)
Bösch, W., Carl-Schüller-Str. 9, 95444 Bayreuth.
T. (0921) 82196. *102238*
Boltz, Hartwig, Brandenburger Str. 36, 95448 Bayreuth.
T. (0921) 206 16. *102239*
Hagen, H.J., Ludwigstr 6, 95444 Bayreuth.
T. (0921) 56488, Fax (0921) 8365. - Print - *102240*
Kohler, P. & I., Am Sachsenberg 7, 95448 Bayreuth.
T. (0921) 99265. *102241*

Bedburg (Nordrhein-Westfalen)
Haas, Gebr, Sonnenblick 8a, 47551 Bedburg.
T. (02821) 6336, Fax (02821) 6739. - Print / Engr /
Map - *102242*
Schmidt, Marianne, Bahnstr 10, 50181 Bedburg.
T. (02272) 81390. *102243*

Bensheim (Hessen)
Böhler, Wolfgang, Marktpl. 6, 64625 Bensheim.
T. (06251) 396 00. - ArtBk - *102244*

Bergisch Gladbach (Nordrhein-Westfalen)
Bergische Bücherstube, Hauptstr. 247, 51465 Bergisch
Gladbach. T. (02202) 39834, Fax 42846. *102245*

Berlin
Ahnert, Knut, Sybelstr 58, 10629 Berlin.
T. (030) 3240907, Fax (030) 3239754. *102246*
Albrecht-Antiquariat, Albrechtstr. 111, 12167 Berlin.
T. (030) 7929119. - Print - *102247*
Antiquariat, Schönhauser Allee 126, 10437
Berlin. *102248*
Antiquariat Pankow, Schönholzer Str. 1, 13187 Berlin.
T. (030) 482 80 03. - Print / ArtBk / Engr / Autogr /
Map - *102249*
Barasch, Rüdiger, Stierstr. 6, 12159 Berlin.
T. (030) 852 03 09. - Print / ArtBk - *102250*
Bassenge, Gerda, Erdener Str 5a, 14193 Berlin.
T. (030) 8912909, Fax 8918025. - Print - *102251*
Bauer, Arthur, Nestorstr. 1, 10711 Berlin.
T. (030) 323 47 58. - Print - *102252*
Berlin-Antiquariat, Zimmermannstr. 17, 12163 Berlin.
T. (030) 792 05 20. *102253*
Bibliographikon, Das, Carmerstr. 19, 10623 Berlin.
T. (030) 313 82 72. - Engr - *102254*

Bickhardt, Karl-Marx-Str. 168, 12043 Berlin.
T. (030) 687 4078/79, Fax 681 55 44. - Print / Engr / Au-
togr / Map - *102255*
Blöcker, Thomas, Nürnberger Str. 50-56, 10777 Berlin.
T. (030) 24 31 45. *102256*
Böhme, Sybille, Bülowstr 55, 10783 Berlin.
T. (030) 2163378, Fax (030) 2167418. - Print / ArtBk /
Engr - *102257*
Braecklein, Wolfgang, Dickhardtstr 48, 12159 Berlin.
T. (030) 8516613, Fax (030) 8592369. - Print /
Autogr - *102258*
Buch und Kunst an der Kaiserdammbrücke, Kaiserdamm
19, 14057 Berlin. T. (030) 321 63 75. - ArtBk - *102259*
Bücherbogen am Savignyplatz, Stadtbahnbogen 593,
10623 Berlin. T. (030) 312 19 32, Fax 313 72 37.
- ArtBk - *102260*
Bücherbogen in der Nationalgalerie, Potsdamer Str. 50,
10783 Berlin. T. (030) 261 10 90. - ArtBk - *102261*
Bürck, Winterfeldtstr. 44, 10781 Berlin.
T. (030) 216 45 28. - Print - *102262*
Düwal, Schlüterstr 17, 10625 Berlin. T. (030) 3133030.
- Print / Engr / Autogr - *102263*
Eckardt, Hans-Georg, Dr., Dimitroffstr. 52, 10435 Berlin.
T. (030) 609 75 98. - Print / ArtBk / Engr / Autogr /
Map - *102264*
Einhorn, Günther, Richardstr. 6, 12043 Berlin.
- Print - *102265*
Fontane-Antiquariat, Eberstr. 59, 10827 Berlin.
T. (030) 782 33 31. - Print / ArtBk - *102266*
Friedländer, R., & Sohn, Schlesische Str. 26, 10997 Ber-
lin. T. (030) 6124034. - Print - *102267*
Frieling & Partner, Liliencronstr. 8, 12167 Berlin.
T. (030) 795 50 75. - Engr / Autogr - *102268*
Frölich & Kaufmann, Willdenowstr. 5, 12203 Berlin.
T. (030) 465 10 01/02. *102269*
Gadegust, Gerald, Fasanenstr. 11, 10623 Berlin.
T. (030) 312 22 06. *102270*
Galerie der Berliner Graphikpresse und bibliophiles Anti-
quariat, Brunnenstr 165, 10119 Berlin.
T. (030) 2818106, Fax (030) 2818106. *102271*
Goethe & Co., S. Geißler/C. Sauter, Wilhelm-Pieck-Str.
147 und Große Hamburger Str. 29, 10119 Berlin.
T. (030) 281 70 84. - Print / ArtBk / Engr / Map - *102272*
Grandé, Manfred, Blankenburger Str. 8, 10115 Berlin.
T. (030) 483 14 85. *102273*
Hartwig, Robert, Pestalozzistr. 23, 10625 Berlin.
T. (030) 312 91 24. *102274*
Hartwig, Robert, Pestalozzistr. 23, 10625 Berlin.
T. (030) 312 91 24. *102275*
Henke, Motzstr. 59, 10777 Berlin. *102276*
Hennig, Renate, Motzstr. 25, 10777 Berlin.
T. (030) 211 54 56, Fax 211 57 37. - Print /
Engr - *102277*
Hentrich, Plantagenstr. 21, 12169 Berlin.
T. (030) 792 91 19, Fax 792 46 57. - Print / ArtBk /
Autogr - *102278*
Hermes, Martin-Luther-Str. 125, 10825 Berlin.
T. (030) 782 28 49, Fax 782 28 97. *102279*
Hinterhof Antiquariat, Czarnikauer Str. 19, 10439 Berlin.
T. (030) 448 99 17. - Print / ArtBk - *102280*
Holstein, Jürgen, Wildpfad 8, 14193 Berlin.
T. (030) 8259933, Fax (030) 8266009. - ArtBk /
Autogr - *102281*
Junghans, Karl, KG, Heesestr. 10, 12169 Berlin.
T. (030) 791 31 64. - Engr / Map - *102282*
Karl-Marx-Buchhandlung, Karl-Marx-Allee 78-84/I,
10243 Berlin. T. (030) 591 91 455. *102283*
Koch, Hans Horst, Kurfürstendamm 216, 10719 Berlin.
T. (030) 8826360, Fax (030) 8824066. *102284*
Kunstbuchhandlung Galerie 2000, Knesebeckstr. 56-58,
10623 Berlin. T. (030) 883 84 67, Fax 822 44 32.
- ArtBk - *102285*
Kunze, Kathrin, Weinmeisterstr. 9b, 10178 Berlin.
T. (030) 281 73 31. - Print / ArtBk - *102286*
Lange & Springer, Otto-Suhr-Allee 26/28, 10585 Berlin.
T. (030) 3422011, Fax (030) 3410440. - Print - *102287*
Linden-Antiquariat, Friedrichstr. 165, 10117 Berlin.
T. (030) 229 19 39. - Engr / Autogr / Map - *102288*
Meyer, Rainer, Schillerstr. 22, 10625 Berlin.
T. (030) 31 67 14, Fax 31 60 09. - Print - *102289*
Mikro, Carmerstr. 1, 10623 Berlin. T. (030) 312 58 65.
- ArtBk - *102290*

Nierendorf, Hardenbergstr. 19, 10623 Berlin.
T. (030) 785 60 60, Fax 312 93 27. - ArtBk - *102291*
Richter, Bernard, Marie-Elisabeth-Lüders-Str. 3, 10625
Berlin. T. (030) 342 74 52. *102292*
Rosenfeld, Drakestr. 35a, 12205 Berlin.
T. (030) 831 50 01. - ArtBk - *102293*
Ruff, Rheinstr. 45, 12161 Berlin.
T. (030) 859 10 50. *102294*
Schaaf, Geraldine, Berliner Str. 140, 10713 Berlin.
T. (030) 87 88 71. - ArtBk - *102295*
Schmidt, Wolfgang, Mehringdamm 117, 10965 Berlin.
T. (030) 691 23 57, Fax 694 13 27. *102296*
Schomaker & Niederstrasser, Niedstr. 24, 12159 Berlin.
T. (030) 851 62 22, Fax 859 44 78. - Print /
Engr - *102297*
Senzel, Knesebeckstr. 13/14, 10623 Berlin.
T. (030) 312 58 87. *102298*
Skowronska, Schustehrusstr. 28, 10585 Berlin.
T. (030) 341 58 33, Fax 348 25 83. *102299*
Sonnenthal, Cauerstr. 20, 10587 Berlin.
T. (030) 342 56 38. *102300*
Speth, Camilla, Kurfürstendamm 38-39, 10719 Berlin.
T. (030) 881 15 45. - Engr / Map - *102301*
Springer, Fasanenstr 13, 10623 Berlin.
T. (030) 3127063, Fax (030) 3131308. - Print /
Engr - *102302*
Stadnik & Stadnik, Kantstr. 39, 10623 Berlin.
T. (030) 31 04 30. - Print / Engr / Map - *102303*
Stargardt, J.A., Clausewitzstr. 4, 10629 Berlin.
T. (030) 8822542, Fax (030) 8822466.
- Autogr - *102304*
Staschen, Wolfgang, Potsdamer Str. 138, 10783 Berlin.
T. (030) 262 20 75. - Print / ArtBk / Engr / Autogr /
Map - *102305*
Stodieck, Richard-Wagner-Str. 39, 10585 Berlin.
T. (030) 341 10 40. *102306*
Sundberg, Alan Frederick, Niebuhrstr. 3, 10629 Berlin.
- Print - *102307*
Tepper, Gustav A., Droysenstr. 19, 10629 Berlin.
T. (030) 323 15 65. - ArtBk - *102308*
Wasmuth, Hardenbergstr. 9a, 10623 Berlin.
T. (030) 3131920, Fax (030) 3126370. - ArtBk - *102309*
Wegner, Carl, Martin-Luther-Str. 113, 10825 Berlin.
T. (030) 782 24 91. - ArtBk - *102310*
Zeisig, Kurt-Georg, Ebertystr. 51, 10249 Berlin.
T. (030) 437 37 54. - Print / ArtBk - *102311*
Zentrales Antiquariat Berlin, Rungestr. 20, 10179 Berlin.
T. (030) 279 21 95. - Engr / Map - *102312*

Bernburg (Sachsen-Anhalt)
Kunst und Musik, Lindenstr. 14, 06406
Bernburg. *102313*

Bielefeld (Nordrhein-Westfalen)
Altenhein, Manfred, Am Tiefen Weg 9, 33604 Bielefeld.
- Engr - *102315*
Granier, Welle 9, 33602 Bielefeld. T. (0521) 67148,
Fax (0521) 67146. - Print / Engr / Map - *102315a*
Oetzmann, K., Mühlenstr. 19, 33607 Bielefeld.
T. (0521) 616 06. *102316*
Valentien, Heinrich, Niederwall 14, 33602 Bielefeld.
T. (0521) 644 20. - Print / Engr / Map - *102317*
Wäger, Hans, In der Arcade, 33602 Bielefeld.
T. (0521) 17 79 94. *102318*
Wäger, Hans, In der Arcade, 33602 Bielefeld.
T. (0521) 17 79 94. *102319*

Bienenbüttel (Niedersachsen)
Grewe, Hans, Zum Lietzberg 22, 29553
Bienenbüttel. *102320*

Bischberg (Bayern)
Keller, Jean, 96120 Bischberg. T. (0951) 669 65. *102321*

Bisingen (Baden-Württemberg)
Schmidt, H. & E., Untere Klingen 2, 72406 Bisingen.
T. (07476) 1609. *102322*

Bitburg (Rheinland-Pfalz)
Zimmer, Heinrich, Trierer Str. 40, 54634 Bitburg.
T. (06561) 31 92. *102323*

Bochum (Nordrhein-Westfalen)
Bochumer Antiquariat, Universitätsstr. 150, 44801 Bochum. T. (0234) 70 60 40. *102324*

Bochumer Antiquariat, Brüderstr. 7, 44787 Bochum.
T. (0234) 68 24 88. *102325*
Hellwig, Haferweg 13d, 44797 Bochum.
T. (0234) 79 78 39. *102326*
Jöst, W., Universitätsstr. 16, 44789 Bochum.
T. (0234) 33 16 24. *102327*
Lorych, S., Rathauspl. 8, 44787 Bochum.
T. (0234) 68 24 21. *102328*
Orientalia Christiana, Grüner Weg 40a, 44791 Bochum.
T. (0234) 59 65 45, Fax 50 35 76. - Print /
ArtBk - *102329*
Stobbe, Westenfelder Str. 89, 44867 Bochum.
T. (0234) 023 27/32 01 32. *102330*
Ubu, Universitätsstr. 16, 44789 Bochum.
T. (0234) 33 16 24. - Print - *102331*

Bodelshausen (Baden-Württemberg)
Wachter, Manfred, Bahnhofstr. 73, 72411 Bodelshausen.
T. (07471) 715 85. *102332*

Bötzingen (Baden-Württemberg)
Bernecker, Johann, Schwimmbadstr. 14, 79268
Bötzingen. *102333*

Bonn (Nordrhein-Westfalen)
Behrendt, Hermann, Am Hof 5a, 53113 Bonn.
T. (0228) 65 80 21. - Print - *102334*
Bonner Kunsthaus, Bonner Talweg 70, 53113 Bonn.
T. (0228) 21 17 70. - ArtBk - *102335*
Bouvier, Am Hof 32, 53113 Bonn. T. (0228) 72 90 10.
- ArtBk - *102336*
Bücher Etage, Martinsplatz 2, 53113 Bonn.
T. (0228) 63 87 61. - Print / ArtBk - *102337*
Christoph, Holger A., Goethestr. 15, 53113 Bonn.
T. (0228) 21 09 73. *102338*
Habelt, Gero, Gartenweg 15, 53229 Bonn.
T. (0228) 43 19 20, Fax 43 28 17. - Print /
ArtBk - *102339*
Habelt, Rudolf, Dr., Am Buchenhang 1, 53115 Bonn.
T. (0228) 23 20 15, Fax 23 20 17. - Print - *102340*
Lempertz, Mathias, Fürstenstr. 1, 53111 Bonn.
T. (0228) 63 29 73, 69 44 86, Fax 65 10 97.
- ArtBk - *102341*
Niemeyer, Lüder H., Simrockallee 34, 53173 Bonn.
T. (0228) 35 12 77. - Print / Engr / Autogr /
Map - *102342*
Nosbüsch, Mandfred, Bonner Talweg 14, 53113 Bonn.
T. (0228) 229251, Fax (0228) 217591. - Print /
ArtBk - *102343*
Sawhney, Christiane, Reuterstr. 4a, 53113 Bonn.
T. (0228) 21 66 22. - Print / ArtBk - *102344*
Schreyer, Hanno, Euskirchener Str 57-59, 53121 Bonn.
T. (0228) 621059, Fax (0228) 613029. - Print / Engr /
Map - *102345*
Siebengebirg-Buchhandlung Bosch, 53111
Bonn. *102346*
Skali, N., Maxstr. 68, 53117 Bonn.
T. (0228) 63 57 80. *102347*
Wollner, Wilhelm, Königstr. 40, 53115 Bonn.
T. (0228) 22 91 90. *102348*

Brandenburg (Brandenburg)
Kunstkabinett, Hauptstr. 17, 14776
Brandenburg. *102349*

Braunschweig (Niedersachsen)
Anglewitz, B., Bernerstr. 2, 38106 Braunschweig.
T. (0531) 34 35 08. *102350*
Antiquariat im Hopfengarten, Hopfengarten 3, 38102
Braunschweig. T. (0531) 79 56 85. *102351*
Bilder-Etage, Schuhstr. 42, 38100
Braunschweig. *102352*
Brandes, W., Wolfenbütteler Str 12, 38102 Braun-
schweig. T. (0531) 75003, Fax (0531) 75015. - Print /
Engr - *102353*
Buch & Kunst, Kasernenstr. 12, 38102 Braunschweig.
T. (0531) 34 73 32. - Print / ArtBk - *102354*
Graff, A., Neue Str. 23, 38100 Braunschweig.
T. (0531) 49271. *102355*
Jaeschke, Am Ringerbrunnen, 38100 Braunschweig.
T. (0531) 443 87. *102356*
Klittich-Pfankuch, Adelheid, Kleine Burg 12, 38100
Braunschweig. T. (0531) 242880, Fax (0531) 13505.
- Print / Engr - *102357*

Kuhle, Michael, Ottmerstr. 7, 38102 Braunschweig.
T. (0531) 787 48. *102358*
Trivial Book Shop, Bohlweg 46, 38100 Braunschweig.
T. (0531) 40 02 88. *102359*

Bremen
Albatros Buchhandlung, Fedelhören 91, 28203 Bremen.
T. (0421) 32 72 48. - ArtBk - *102360*
Antiquariat Beim Steinernen Kreuz, Beim Steinernen
Kreuz 1, 28203 Bremen. T. (0421) 701515,
Fax (0421) 72171. - Print / ArtBk - *102361*
Antiquariat im Schnoor, Hinter der Balge 1, 28195 Bre-
men. T. (0421) 32 34 16. - Print / ArtBk - *102362*
Bolland & Marotz, Fedelhören 19, 28203 Bremen.
T. (0421) 32 82 82, Fax 32 85 43. *102363*
Brinkhus, Heike, Fedelhören 92, 28203 Bremen.
T. (0421) 32 36 02. - Print - *102364*
Dürerhaus Bremen, Faulenstr. 108, 28195 Bremen.
T. (0421) 17 16 18. - ArtBk - *102365*
Eckert, D., Am Dobben 36, 28203 Bremen.
T. (0421) 72204. *102366*
Gerling, Rolf-Peter, Fedelhören 89, 28203 Bremen.
T. (0421) 32 58 62. *102367*
Graphik & Buch, St.-Pauli-Str 44, 28203 Bremen.
T. (0421) 74793. *102368*
Kunstbuch, Vor dem Steintor 136, 28203 Bremen.
T. (0421) 70 45 31, Fax 70 45 32. - ArtBk - *102369*
Libretto, Lehmstr., 28199 Bremen. T. (0421) 505477.
- Print / ArtBk - *102370*
Libretto, Am Dobben 58, 28203 Bremen.
T. (0421) 71717. - Print / ArtBk - *102371*
Oertel, Peter, St.-Pauli-Str. 44, 28203 Bremen.
T. (0421) 74793. - Print - *102372*
Plöger, T., Leher Heerstr. 44, 28359 Bremen.
T. (0421) 23 30 76. *102373*
Puck & Hornberg, Buntentorsteinweg 323, 28201 Bre-
men. T. (0421) 55 81 30. *102374*
Schmidt, Götz-R., Nernststr 16, 28357 Bremen.
T. (0421) 256242, Fax (0421) 254138. - Print /
Engr - *102375*
Theimann, S. Dr., Violenstr. 33-35, 28195 Bremen.
T. (0421) 32 59 03. *102376*

Bückeburg (Niedersachsen)
Scheck, M., Lange Str. 67, 31675 Bückeburg.
T. (05722) 34 93. *102377*

Bühl (Baden-Württemberg)
Unitas GmbH, Hauptstr 44, 77815 Bühl. *102378*

Bürstadt (Hessen)
Schubert, Erhard, Klarastr. 21, 68642 Bürstadt.
T. (06206) 8935. - Print - *102379*

Calw (Baden-Württemberg)
Großmann, Brudersteige 7, 75365 Calw.
T. (07051) 67 76. *102380*

Celle (Niedersachsen)
Das Bücherhaus, Im Beckfeld 48, 29351 Celle.
T. (05148) 1248, Fax (05148) 4232. - Print / ArtBk /
Autogr - *102381*
Lützau, R. von, Brauhausstr. 2, 29221 Celle.
T. (05141) 6644. *102382*

Chemnitz (Sachsen)
Klis'sche Buchhandlung, Zwickauer Str. 409, 09117
Chemnitz. T. (0371) 85 27 75. *102383*
Müller, Max, Reitbahnstr. 23, 09002 Chemnitz.
T. (0371) 624 16, Fax 304 95. - Print / ArtBk - *102384*

Coswig (Sachsen)
Tharandt, Ernst, Bahnhofstr. 3, 01640 Coswig.
T. (03523) 74577. *102385*

Cottbus (Brandenburg)
Heron, Karl-Liebknecht-Str. 127, 03046 Cottbus.
T. (0355) 249 76, Fax 224 79. - Print / Engr /
Map - *102386*

Cuxhaven (Niedersachsen)
Rauschenplat, Deichstr. 21, 27472 Cuxhaven.
T. (04721) 371 37. - Print - *102387*

Dachau (Bayern)

Bavaria Antiquariat, Konrad-Adenauer-Str. 23, 85221
Dachau. T. (08131) 829 29.　　　　　102388

Darmstadt (Hessen)

Lehr, K., Sandstr. 38, 64283 Darmstadt.
T. (06151) 209 48. - Print / Engr / Map -　　102389
Wellnitz, Rudolf, Lauteschlägerstr. 4, 64289 Darmstadt.
T. (06151) 765 48.　　　　　102390

Dedelstorf (Niedersachsen)

Pohl, Gabriele, 29386 Dedelstorf.　　　102391

Detmold (Nordrhein-Westfalen)

Antiqua, Lemgoer Str. 62, 32756 Detmold.
T. (05231) 297 93.　　　　　102392
Gebrauchtbuchhandlung, Lange Str. 81a, 32756 Det-
mold. T. (05231) 29652.　　　　　102393
Meyersche Hofbuchhandlung, Krumme Str. 26, 32756
Detmold. T. (05231) 221 31. - Print / Engr /
Autogr -　　　　　102394
Schmitt, Curt L., 32756 Detmold. - Print -　102395
Winands, Ralph, Schülerstr. 28, 32756 Detmold.
T. (05231) 342 33, Fax 34233.　　　　102396

Diez (Rheinland-Pfalz)

Meckel, Wilhelmstr. 2, 65582 Diez.　　　102397

Dinslaken (Nordrhein-Westfalen)

Falkenstein, Klaus, Dr., Friedrich-Ebert-Str. 96, 46535
Dinslaken. T. (02064) 56440, Fax 70229.
- ArtBk -　　　　　102398

Dippoldiswalde (Sachsen)

Buchhandlung Erich Kästner, Platz des Friedens 14,
01744 Dippoldiswalde.　　　　　102399

Donaueschingen (Baden-Württemberg)

Ruby, J., Karlstr. 16, 78166 Donaueschingen.
T. (0771) 13999. - Print -　　　　102400

Dortmund (Nordrhein-Westfalen)

Huste, Liebigstr. 46-48, 44139 Dortmund.
T. (0231) 12 26 38, Fax 12 94 95. - Print / ArtBk / Engr /
Autogr / Map -　　　　　102401
Kirchner, R., Hoher Wall 30, 44137 Dortmund.
T. (0231) 14 99 57, Fax 14 99 57. - Print / Engr /
Map -　　　　　102402
Wortkötter, Paul, Gnadenort 3-5, 44135 Dortmund.
T. (0231) 811749. - Print / Engr -　　102403

Drelsdorf (Schleswig-Holstein)

Der Büchergarten, Dorfstr. 29, 25853 Drelsdorf.
T. (04671) 721.　　　　　102404

Dresden (Sachsen)

Adler, Carl, Leisniger Str 25, 01127 Dresden.
T. (0351) 5023363. - Print -　　　　102405
Buchhandlung Heinrich Mann, Prager Str. 7, 01069
Dresden. T. (0351) 495 51 08, 495 40 30.
- ArtBk　　　　　102406
Das Internationale Buch, Kreuzstr. 4, 01067 Dresden.
T. (0351) 495 41 90, Fax 51147. - ArtBk -　102407
Dresdener Antiquariat, Bautzener Str 11, 01099 Dres-
den. T. (0351) 8043970. - Print / Engr / Autogr /
Map -　　　　　102408
Fundus, Augsburger Str 79-81, 01277 Dresden.
T. (0351) 35759. - Print -　　　　102409
Historica, Helgolandstr. 17, 01097 Dresden.
T. (0351) 4114757. - Print / Engr -　　102410
Richter, Gemäldegalerie, Theaterplatz, 01067 Dresden.
- ArtBk -　　　　　102411
Richter, Schloß Pillnitz, 01326 Dresden.
- ArtBk -　　　　　102412
Richter, Albertinum, Brühlsche Terrasse, 01067 Dres-
den. - ArtBk -　　　　　102413

Düsseldorf (Nordrhein-Westfalen)

Ahrens & Hamacher, Bilker Allee 168, 40217 Düsseldorf.
T. (0211) 31 89 60. - ArtBk -　　　102414
Bender, Königsallee 21-23, 40212 Düsseldorf.
T. (0211) 325112, Fax (0211) 325112. - Print -　102415
Boerner, C.G., Kasernenstr 13, 40213 Düsseldorf.
(0211) 131805, Fax (0211) 132177. - Engr -　102416

Daehne, Wilfried, Hermannstr. 22a, 40233 Düsseldorf.
T. (0211) 66 57 91. - Print / ArtBk / Engr / Autogr /
Map -　　　　　102417
Daras & Gilbert, Bismarckstr. 67, 40210 Düsseldorf.
T. (0211) 16 16 19. - Print / Engr / Map -　102418
Egenolf, Herbert, Citadellstr 14, 40213 Düsseldorf.
T. (0211) 320550, Fax 131291. - Print / Engr -　102419
Eickhoff, Peter, Germaniastr. 28, 40223 Düsseldorf.
T. (0211) 37 58 09.　　　　　102420
Förster, Sabrina, Poststr 3, 40213 Düsseldorf.
T. (0211) 323413, Fax (0211) 328218.　　102421
Graphik Kabinett, Humboldtstr. 80, 40237 Düsseldorf.
T. (0211) 67 31 36. - Print / Engr / Map -　102422
Guderian, L., An St. Swidbert 67, 40489 Düsseldorf.
T. (0211) 40 73 95.　　　　　102423
Heinrich Heine Antiquariat, Citadellstr. 9, 40213 Düssel-
dorf. T. (0211) 13 26 12, Fax 32 22 57. - Print -　102424
Hofladen-Antiquariat Ganseforth, Hohe Str. 47, 40213
Düsseldorf. T. (0211) 13 16 76. - Print / Engr -　102425
Hoppe & Haeffele, Bruchhausenstr. 37, 40591 Düssel-
dorf. T. (0211) 229 38 50.　　　　102426
König, Walther, Heinrich-Heine-Allee 15, 40213 Düssel-
dorf. T. (0211) 13 62 10, Fax 13 47 46. - ArtBk -　102427
Koop, W., Florastr. 9, 40217 Düsseldorf.
T. (0211) 37 64 38.　　　　　102428
Loy, Roswitha, Poststr. 8, 40213 Düsseldorf.
T. (0211) 32 31 50. - Print / ArtBk / Engr /
Autogr -　　　　　102429
Marcus, Ange, Ritterstr 10, 40213 Düsseldorf.
T. (0211) 325940, Fax (0211) 327633. - Print /
Engr -　　　　　102430
Mehs, P., Frankenstr. 7, 40476 Düsseldorf.
T. (0211) 454 32 96.　　　　　102431
Mollenhauer, J.W., Unterrather Str. 92, 40468 Düssel-
dorf. T. 42 36 41 (432 06 41).　　　　102432
Pascher, Arnold, Oststr. 36, 40211 Düsseldorf.
T. (0211) 36 35 94. - Engr / Map -　　102433
Schoppmann, Wolfgang, Düsseldorfer Str 105, 40545
Düsseldorf. T. (0211) 555281.　　　　102434
Schrobsdorff, Königsallee 22, 40212 Düsseldorf.
T. (0211) 25820. - Print / Engr / Autogr -　102435
Stern-Verlag Janssen & Co., Friedrichstr. 24-26, 40217
Düsseldorf. T. (0211) 388 10, Fax 3881-200. - Print /
ArtBk / Engr / Map -　　　　　102436
Vester, Helmut, Dr., Friedrichstr 7, 40217 Düsseldorf.
T. (0211) 382843. - Print -　　　　102437
Vömel, Alex, Königsallee 30, 40212 Düsseldorf.
T. (0211) 327422, Fax (0211) 135267.　　102438
Weber, Hans-Joachim, Hohenzollernstr. 23-25, 40211
Düsseldorf. T. (0211) 35 75 81, Fax 164 98 57.
- Engr -　　　　　102439
Wehrens, Horst, Oststr. 13, 40211 Düsseldorf.
T. (0211) 36 34 38.　　　　　102440

Duisburg (Nordrhein-Westfalen)

Collet, H., Tilsiter Ufer 4, 47279 Duisburg.
- Print -　　　　　102441
Keune, Sabine, Friedrich-Alfred-Str 79, 47226 Duisburg.
T. (02065) 59619, Fax (02065) 56827. - Print /
Autogr -　　　　　102442

Eberbach (Baden-Württemberg)

Polygraphicum, Backgasse 1, 69412 Eberbach.
T. (06271) 1387. - Print / ArtBk / Engr / Map -　102443

Ebersbach an der Fils (Baden-Württem-berg)

Bretz, P.F., Ziegelstr 30, 73061 Ebersbach an der Fils.
T. (07163) 2247.　　　　　102444

Eckernförde (Schleswig-Holstein)

Kunsthaus Eckernförde, Amselweg 3, 24340
Eckernförde.　　　　　102445

Eichstätt (Bayern)

Boegl, Bruno, Weissenburger Str 16, 85072 Eichstätt.
T. (08421) 4987. - Engr / Map -　　　102446

Elsdorf (Nordrhein-Westfalen)

Fußwinkel, Karlheinz, Rotdornweg 26, 50189 Elsdorf.
T. (02274) 635 58. - Engr -　　　　102447

Erfurt (Thüringen)

Antiquariat Buch Kunst Graphik, Paulstr. 29/30, 99084
Erfurt. T. (0361) 60 23 94. - Print / Engr / Map -　102448
Antiquariat Erfurt, Eveline Müller, Schlösserstr. 34,
99084 Erfurt. T. (0361) 60 23 94. - Print -　102449

Erkrath (Nordrhein-Westfalen)

Heitmann, Heinfried, Gruitener Str. 32, 40699 Erkrath.
T. (0211) 45103.　　　　　102450

Erlangen (Bayern)

Buch- und Kunstantiquariat, Wasserturmstr. 14, 91054
Erlangen.　　　　　102451
Krische, Theodor, Krankenhausstr. 6, 91054 Erlangen.
T. (09131) 229 40. - ArtBk -　　　102452
Kurta, A., Friedrichstr. 38, 91054 Erlangen.
T. (09131) 20 74 70.　　　　　102453
Rudolph, E., Dompfaffstr. 42, 91056 Erlangen.
T. (09131) 437 35. - Print / Engr / Map -　102454
Schmidt, F., Martin-Luther-Platz 5, 91054 Erlangen.
T. (09131) 28811.　　　　　102455
Wünschmann, Wasserturmstr 14, 91054 Erlangen.
T. (09131) 26827.　　　　　102456

Erlenbach (Bayern)

Keip, Ulrich, Am Sportplatz 2, 63906 Erlenbach.
T. (09372) 5063, Fax (09372) 73258.　　102457
Pfeffer, Am Brückensteg 5, 63906 Erlenbach.
T. (093 72) 727 86.　　　　　102458

Eschborn (Hessen)

Debus, Karl F., Hamburger Str 1-3, 65760 Eschborn.
T. (06196) 46937. - Print -　　　　102459

Essen (Nordrhein-Westfalen)

Götzhaber, L., Dr., Hufelandstr. 32, 45147 Essen.
T. (0201) 70 13 44, Fax 70 73 51.　　　102460
Die Gravüre, Rüttenscheider Str 56, 45130 Essen.
T. (0201) 793182, Fax (0201) 794949.　　102461
Grimmeisen, Ralf, Kurfürstenstr. 23, 45138 Essen.
T. (0201) 27 21 87. - Print -　　　　102462
Krüger, Limbecker Str. 8, 45127 Essen.
T. (0201) 23 26 15.　　　　　102463
Scharioth'sche Buchhandlung, Huyssenallee 58, 45128
Essen. T. (0201) 22 49 06.　　　　102464
Wirmsberger oHG, Hufelandstr. 15 u. 32, 45147 Essen.
T. (0201) 77 90 61, 77 61 83.　　　　102465
Wünnenberg, Eckhard, Hollestr 1, 45127 Essen.
T. (0201) 239700. - Print -　　　　102466

Esslingen (Baden-Württemberg)

Stahl, Adolf, Bahnhofstr 19, 73728 Esslingen.
T. (0711) 357590　　　　　102467
Suevia, Franziskanergasse 6, 73728 Esslingen.
T. (0711) 359288. - Print -　　　　102468

Ettlingen (Baden-Württemberg)

Bartsch, Erika, Gottfried-Keller-Str. 10, 76275 Ettlingen.
T. (07243) 34 26. - Print -　　　　102469

Eurasburg (Bayern)

Bierl, Peter, Hauptstr. 29, 82547 Eurasburg.
T. (08179) 82 82, Fax 8009. - Print -　　102470
Schwabinger Bilderbogen, Hauptstr. 29, 82547 Euras-
burg. T. (08179) 8282, Fax 8009. - Print -　102471

Feldafing (Bayern)

Walz, Ed.a., Maffeistr. 9, 82340 Feldafing.
T. (08157) 83 40. - Engr / Map -　　　102472

Feuchtwangen (Bayern)

Kohlhauer, Carl-Ernst, Graserweg 2, 91555 Feuchtwan-
gen. T. (09852) 9292, Fax (09852) 4037.　102473
Tenner, Margit, Graserweg 2, 91555 Feuchtwangen.
T. (09852) 1539, Fax (09852) 4037.　　102474

Flammersfeld (Rheinland-Pfalz)

Buschulte, H., Alter Bahnhof, 57632 Flammersfeld.
T. (02685) 12 86.　　　　　102475

Flensburg (Schleswig-Holstein)

Hattesen, Peter, Holm 76, 24937 Flensburg.
T. (0461) 250 77.　　　　　102476
Rojahn, Rote Str. 14, 24937 Flensburg. T. (0461) 25643.
- Print / Engr / Map -　　　　　102477

Flörsheim am Main (Hessen)
China Antiquaria, Weilbacher Str. 38, 65439 Flörsheim
am Main. T. (06145) 53536, Fax 53536.
- Print - *102478*

Frankenberg (Sachsen)
Klis'sche Buchhandlung, Markt 11a, 09669 Frankenberg. T. (037206) 2313. *102479*

Frankfurt am Main (Hessen)
Alicke, Paul, Elisabethenstr 2, 60594 Frankfurt am Main.
T. (069) 6031825. *102480*
Antiquariat Alpha, Homburger Str 34, 60486 Frankfurt
am Main. T. (069) 773323. *102481*
Antiquariat Walkmühle, Am Hollerbusch 7, 60437 Frank-
furt am Main. T. (069) 5077197. *102482*
Brumme, Siegfried, Braubachstr 34, 60311 Frankfurt
am Main. T. (069) 287263, Fax (069) 296682. - Print /
Engr / Map - *102483*
Buch-Café im Jüdischen Museum, Untermainkai 14/15,
60311 Frankfurt am Main. T. (069) 23 49 21.
- ArtBk - *102484*
Buchhandlung am Goethe-Haus, Am Salzhaus 1-3,
60311 Frankfurt am Main. T. (069) 28 11 43. - Engr /
Map - *102485*
Epicerie, Wiesenstr. 11, 60385 Frankfurt am Main.
T. (069) 45 62 80. *102486*
Ewald, Georg, Große Bockenheimer Str 29, 60313
Frankfurt am Main. T. (069) 287413. *102487*
Fach, Joseph, Fahrgasse 8, 60311 Frankfurt am Main.
T. (069) 287761, Fax 285844. - Print / Engr /
Map - *102488*
Flach, Werner, Heddernheimer Landstr. 78 a, 60439
Frankfurt am Main. T. (069) 581018,
Fax (069) 573002. *102489*
Francofurtensien, Bethmannstr 11, 60311 Frankfurt am
Main. T. (069) 292324. - Print - *102490*
Frankfurter Bücherstube, Schuhmann und Cobet, Lin-
denstr 30, 60325 Frankfurt am Main. T. (069) 727940,
Fax (069) 727947. *102491*
Frankfurter Kunstkabinett Hanna Bekker vom Rath,
Braubachstr 14-16, 60311 Frankfurt am Main.
T. (069) 281085, Fax 280687. *102492*
Galerie 410, Eschersheimer Landstr 410, 60433 Frank-
furt am Main. T. (069) 511180. - ArtBk - *102493*
Greul, A., Am Goldsteinpark 28, 60529 Frankfurt am
Main. T. (069) 6661817. *102494*
Guttzeit, H.E., Homburger Str 34, 60486 Frankfurt am
Main. T. (069) 773323. *102495*
Haschtmann, W., Bornwiesenweg 53, 60322 Frankfurt
am Main. T. (069) 613298. *102496*
Heidekorn, K.-U., Schenckstr 26, 60489 Frankfurt am
Main. T. (069) 784925. *102497*
Henle, Ruth, Zeil 24, 60313 Frankfurt am Main. *102498*
Historisches Portfolio, Kaiserstr 24, 60311 Frankfurt am
Main. T. (069) 231010. *102499*
Hoffmann, Ernst, Weißadlergasse 3, 60311 Frankfurt am
Main. T. (069) 283781. - Print / Engr / Map - *102500*
Kerst, Rudolf, Klingerstr 23, 60313 Frankfurt am Main.
T. (069) 287870. - Print - *102501*
Koch, Jürgen, Eckenheimer Landstr 42, 60318 Frankfurt
am Main. T. (069) 592009. *102502*
König, Walther, Hasengasse 5-7, 60311 Frankfurt am
Main. T. (069) 2979905, Fax (069) 296587. *102503*
König, Walther, Domstr 6, 60311 Frankfurt am Main.
T. (069) 296588, Fax (069) 296587. - ArtBk - *102504*
Korenke-Bücher, Höhenblick 33, 60311 Frankfurt am
Main. *102505*
Kunst-Buch, Römerberg 7, 60311 Frankfurt am Main.
T. (069) 29988244, Fax (069) 75089. - Print /
ArtBk - *102506*
Makol, Schweizer Str. 19, Hinterh., 60594 Frankfurt am
Main. T. (069) 613298. *102507*
Marx, Jordanstr 11, 60486 Frankfurt am Main.
T. (069) 778803. - Print / ArtBk - *102508*
Meichsner & Dennerlein, Dreieichstr 52, 60594 Frank-
furt am Main. T. (069) 616965. *102509*
Missirloglou, Christos, Alte Gasse 67, 60313 Frankfurt
am Main. T. (069) 283579. - Print / ArtBk /
Engr - *102510*
Otto, Manfred, Schwanthaler Str 53, 60596 Frankfurt
am Main. T. (069) 617350. *102511*

Pölck, Rainer, Alt Rödelheim 15, 60489 Frankfurt am
Main. T. (069) 7893945, Fax (069) 7893945. - Print /
ArtBk / Engr / Autogr / Map - *102512*
Rabeneck, L., Homburger Str 12, 60486 Frankfurt am
Main. T. (069) 700850. *102513*
Rausch, Uwe, Westenberger Str 17, 60489 Frankfurt am
Main. T. (069) 64378812. *102514*
Rumbler, Helmut H., Börsenstr 7-11, 60313 Frankfurt
am Main. T. (069) 291142, Fax (069) 289975.
- Engr - *102515*
Sämann, W., Bolongarostr 136, 65929 Frankfurt am
Main. T. (069) 312144. *102516*
Samland, D., Storchgasse 5, 65929 Frankfurt am Main.
T. (069) 332663. *102517*
Schuhmann, Richard, Windmühlstr 7, 60329 Frankfurt
am Main. *102518*
Schutt, H., Arnsburger Str 76, 60385 Frankfurt am Main.
T. (069) 439543. *102519*
Seiffert & Medeke, Berger Str 31, 60316 Frankfurt am
Main. T. (069) 449998. *102520*
Stelzner, Horst, Braubacher Str 48, 60389 Frankfurt am
Main. T. (069) 455599. *102521*
Stolzenberg, Kurt G., Große Seestr 63, 60486 Frankfurt
am Main. T. (069) 701379. *102522*
Thinius, A., Wingert 13, 60316 Frankfurt am Main.
T. (069) 498290, 444115. *102523*
Tresor am Römer, Braubachstr 15, 60311 Frankfurt am
Main. T. (069) 281248, Fax (069) 282160. - Print /
Engr / Map - *102524*
Vonderbank, Goethestr 11, 60313 Frankfurt am Main.
T. (069) 282490, Fax (069) 296148. - ArtBk / Engr /
Map - *102525*
Weger, Schlosserstr 4, 60322 Frankfurt am Main.
T. (069) 15680990, Fax (069) 15680928.
- ArtBk - *102526*
Weidlich, Weidlich, Savignystr 59, 60325 Frankfurt am
Main. T. (069) 746215. *102527*
Wötzel, Paul-Ehrlich-Str 24, 60596 Frankfurt am Main.
T. (069) 637014, Fax (069) 638080. *102528*

Frankfurt/Oder (Brandenburg)
Antiquariat, Große Scharrnstr. 17a, 15230 Frankfurt/
Oder. T. (0335) 23452. *102529*
Buchhandlung Ulrich von Hutten, Am Platz der Republik,
15230 Frankfurt/Oder. *102530*

Frasdorf (Bayern)
Katzbichler, Emil, Dr., Wilhelming 7, 83112 Frasdorf.
T. (08051) 2595, Fax (08051) 64113. - Print /
ArtBk - *102531*

Frechen (Nordrhein-Westfalen)
Brauns, Thomas & Curt, Keimesstr. 22, 50226 Frechen.
T. (02234) 57691. *102532*

Freiberg (Sachsen)
Büchereck, Aug.-Bebel-Str. 20a, 09599
Freiberg. *102533*

Freiburg (Baden-Württemberg)
Badenia-Antiquariat, Lerchenstr. 21, 79104 Freiburg.
T. (0761) 55 34 36, Fax 55 42 24. - Print / Engr /
Map - *102534*
Bauch, H., Basler Str. 20, 79100 Freiburg.
T. (0761) 70 28 15. *102535*
Bernecker, J., Gerberau 7 b, 79098 Freiburg.
T. (0761) 26137, Fax 34268. - Engr / Map - *102536*
Forster, Heinrich, Grünwälderstr. 6, 79098
Freiburg. *102537*
Fritz, Jos, Moltkestr. 31, 79098 Freiburg.
T. (0761) 34008, Fax 38 14 14. - Print / ArtBk - *102538*
Kolb, Lina, Gabelsbergerstr 18, 79112 Freiburg.
T. (07665) 51953, Fax (07665) 51996. - Print - *102539*
Rombach, Bertoldstr. 10, 79098 Freiburg.
T. (0761) 4909 434, Fax 4909 413. - ArtBk - *102540*
Sasse & Lubahn, Quäkerstr. 11, 79102 Freiburg.
T. (0761) 73295. - Print / Autogr - *102541*
Simmermacher, René, Talstr 5, 79102 Freiburg.
T. (0761) 73676. - ArtBk / Engr - *102542*
Spittka, M., Günterstalstr. 27, 79102 Freiburg.
T. (0761) 71989, 70 24 56. - Print / ArtBk / Engr /
Map - *102543*
Uhl, Peter, Werthmannpl. 2, 79098 Freiburg.
T. (0761) 38 27 75, Fax 415 42. - Print - *102544*

Freising (Bayern)
Antik-Palette, Ziegelgasse 17, 85354 Freising.
T. (08161) 13410, Fax 50000. - Print / Engr /
Map - *102545*

Freital (Sachsen)
Antiquitätenmarkt, Dresdner Str. 55, 01705 Freital.
T. 641865. *102546*

Friedberg (Hessen)
Heckner, E., Leonhardstr. 30, 61169 Friedberg.
T. (06031) 5501. *102547*
Marel, Karel, Benrathweg 36a, 61169 Friedberg.
T. (06031) 61560. - Print - *102548*

Fronhausen (Hessen)
Schenk zu Schweinsberg, Ekkehard, Giessener Str. 4,
35112 Fronhausen. T. (06426) 63 43. - Print / ArtBk /
Engr - *102549*

Fürth (Bayern)
Schrepf, R., Nürnberger Str. 31, 90762 Fürth.
T. (0911) 77 31 88. - Print / Engr - *102550*

Füssen (Bayern)
Bruhns, E., Reichenstr. 10, 87629 Füssen. *102551*
Raffin, A., Schwangauerstr. 3 1/2, 87629 Füssen.
T. (08362) 79 31. *102552*

Fulda (Hessen)
Schmidt, J. & E., Abtstor 41, 36037 Fulda.
T. (0661) 723 43. - Print / Engr - *102553*
Ulenspiegel, Löherstr. 13, 36037 Fulda.
T. (0661) 216 86, Fax 24 25 56. - Print / ArtBk - *102554*

Garmisch-Partenkirchen (Bayern)
Benkert, R., Ludwigstr. 25, 82467 Garmisch-Partenkir-
chen. T. (08821) 71949. - Print / Engr / Map - *102555*
Gräfe und Unzer, Ludwigstr. 39, 82467 Garmisch-
Partenkirchen. *102556*

Gehrden, Hannover (Niedersachsen)
Preidel, Herbert, Bismarckstr 20, 30989 Gehrden, Han-
nover. T. (05108) 4766, Fax (05108) 8501.
- Print - *102557*

Gelnhausen (Hessen)
Schoemer, N., Waldstr. 12, 63571 Gelnhausen.
T. (06051) 132 36. *102558*

Gelsenkirchen (Nordrhein-Westfalen)
Döme, B., Am Fettingkotten 1, 45891 Gelsenkirchen.
T. (0209) 78 68 92. *102559*

Gerlingen (Baden-Württemberg)
Veit, Günther, Burgklinge 33, 70839 Gerlingen.
T. (07156) 23209, Fax 23209. - Print / Autogr - *102560*

Gießen (Hessen)
Die Buche, Ludwigstr. 40, 35390 Gießen.
T. (0641) 73830. - Print / ArtBk - *102561*
Gießener Kunstantiquariat, Seltersweg 55, 35390 Gie-
ßen. T. (0641) 742 22. *102562*
Sammlerzentrale, Frankfurter Str. 11, 35390 Gießen.
T. (0641) 745 45. *102563*
Schneider, Karl Friedrich, Seltersweg 38, 35390 Gießen.
T. (0641) 743 52. - Print / Engr - *102564*

Gilching (Bayern)
MNA, Postfach 1408, 82199 Gilching. *102565*

Glashütten (Hessen)
Auvermann & Reiss, Zum Talblick 2, 61479 Glashütten.
T. (06174) 6947, Fax (06174) 63612. - Print - *102566*

Glauchau (Sachsen)
Evangel. Buch- und Kunsthandlung, Theaterstr. 43,
08371 Glauchau. *102567*

Gmund (Bayern)
Inter Art, Mühlthalstr. 16, 83703 Gmund.
T. (08022) 74350, Fax 74340. - Print / ArtBk /
Map - *102568*

Göppingen (Baden-Württemberg)
Kümmerle, H., Schillerstr. 8, 73033 Göppingen.
T. (07161) 750 20. - Engr / Map - *102569*

Reichsdorfstuben, Reichsdorfstr. 25, 73037
Göppingen. *102570*

Göttingen (Niedersachsen)

Dörrie, Hans H., Düstere Str. 8, 37073 Göttingen.
T. (0551) 47597. *102571*

Geibel, E., Burgstr. 11, 37073 Göttingen.
T. (0551) 58705. - Print - *102572*

Groß, Erich, Mauerstr. 16-17, 37073 Göttingen.
T. (0551) 57503, Fax (0551) 57500. - ArtBk / Engr /
Map - *102573*

Hölty-Stube, Johannisstr. 28, 37073 Göttingen.
T. (0551) 56368. *102574*

Kunstbuchhandlung Eulenspiegel, Gotmarstr. 1, 37073
Göttingen. T. (0551) 47387,
Fax (0551) 485524. *102575*

Goldbach (Bayern)

Keip, Ulrich, Bayernstr 9, 63773 Goldbach.
T. (06021) 59050, Fax (06021) 590542.
- Print - *102576*

Goslar (Niedersachsen)

Antiquariat Bäringerstrasse, Bäringerstr. 4, 38640 Goslar. T. (05321) 25825. - Print - *102577*

Gotha (Thüringen)

Höck, Hannah, Marktstr. 15, 99867 Gotha.
T. (03621) 29674, Fax 29674. - Print / ArtBk - *102578*

Gräfelfing (Bayern)

Bornheims Kupferstich-Kabinett, Grosostr. 18, 82166
Gräfelfing. T. (089) 85 51 79. *102579*

Greifswald (Mecklenburg-Vorpommern)

Norddeutsches Antiquariat, Friedrich-Loeffler-Str. 13a,
17489 Greifswald. T. (03834) 4039. *102580*

Großhansdorf (Schleswig-Holstein)

Antiquariat-Union, Sieker Landstr. 90, 22927 Großhansdorf. T. (04102) 61131, Fax 64932. *102581*

Gütersloh (Nordrhein-Westfalen)

Dempwolf, Ursula, Elbrachtsweg 46, 33332 Gütersloh.
T. (05241) 48114. - Print / Engr / Map - *102582*

Haiger (Hessen)

Nowakiewitsch, Ernst, Birkenweg 1, 35708 Haiger.
T. (02773) 3941. - Print / Engr / Map - *102583*

Hallbergmoos (Baden-Württemberg)

Schnittger, Ute, Weidenweg 5, 85399 Hallbergmoos.
T. (08169) 0011/8632. - Print / Engr / Map - *102584*

Halle (Nordrhein-Westfalen)

Lohmann, Günther, Talstr 10, 33790 Halle.
T. (05201) 7483. - Print - *102585*

Reinhardt, J., Bredenstr 15, 33790 Halle.
T. (05201) 2261, Fax (05201) 2238. - Print / ArtBk /
Engr / Autogr - *102586*

Hamburg

ABC Antiquariat, Hohe Bleichen 20, 20354 Hamburg.
T. (040) 35 23 34. *102587*

ABS-Altonaer-Gebraucht-Bücher und Schallplatten-
markt, Neue Große Bergstr. 11, 22767 Hamburg.
T. (040) 38 80 98. *102588*

Altonaer Antiquariat, Am Felde 91, 22765 Hamburg.
T. (040) 39 69 70. *102589*

Andere Welten, Rappstr. 15, 20146 Hamburg.
T. (040) 44 31 18. *102590*

Antiquariat am Grindelhof, Grindelhof 62, 20146 Hamburg. T. (040) 410 72 81. *102591*

Antiquariat am Hofweg, Hofweg 57, 22085 Hamburg.
T. (040) 22 28 67. *102592*

Antiquariat Hoheluft, Hoheluftchaussee 29, 20253 Hamburg. T. (040) 420 02 53. *102593*

Antiquariat im Alstertal, Wellingsbüttler Weg 134, 22391
Hamburg. T. (040) 536 10 98. - Print / ArtBk / Engr /
Map - *102594*

Antiquariat Sankt Gertrude, Gertrudenkirchhof 4, 20095
Hamburg. T. (040) 33 60 50. - Print / Engr /
Map - *102595*

art & book, Grindelallee 132, 20146 Hamburg.
T. (040) 44 79 36. - ArtBk / Engr - *102596*

Barme, Walter, Krumdal 24, 22587 Hamburg.
T. (040) 86 29 41. *102597*

Bartkowiak, Heinz Stefan, Körnerstr 24, 22301 Hamburg. T. (040) 2793674, Fax 2704397. - ArtBk - *102598*

Behncke-Brahmer, D., Hoheluftchaussee 29, 20253
Hamburg. T. (040) 420 02 53. *102599*

Bock von Wülfingen, Ernst, Dehnhaide 1, 22081 Hamburg. T. (040) 299 58 07. *102600*

Bücherkabinett, Emkendorfstr 1, 22605 Hamburg.
T. (040) 882055, Fax (040) 8801342. - Print - *102601*

Cabinett der Geschichte, Esplanade 17, 20354 Hamburg. T. (040) 34 56 21. *102602*

Der Bücherwurm, Ottenser Hauptstr. 60, 22765 Hamburg. T. (040) 390 02 50. *102603*

Dörling, F., Neuer Wall 40, 20354 Hamburg.
T. (040) 3749610, Fax 37496166. - Print /
Engr - *102604*

Engel Sammlerhaus, Methfesselhaus, 20257 Hamburg.
T. (040) 491 10 71. *102605*

Freitag, Am Felde 91, 22765 Hamburg.
T. (040) 39 69 70. *102606*

Frensche, Martin H., Hermannstr. 46, 20095
Hamburg. *102607*

Frisch, Dieter, Im Tale 17, 20251 Hamburg.
T. (040) 48 15 20. *102608*

Fundgrube für Bücherfreunde, Dammtordamm 4, 20354
Hamburg. T. (040) 34 50 16. *102609*

Gätjens, Dieter, Brahmsallee 28, 20144 Hamburg.
T. (040) 418009, Fax (040) 456165. *102610*

Günnemann, Peter, Ehrenbergstr. 57, 22767 Hamburg.
T. (040) 38 59 67. - Print / ArtBk / Engr - *102611*

Günther, Jörn, Dr., Reichskanzlerstr 6, 22609 Hamburg.
T. (040) 8005656, Fax (040) 8005625. *102612*

Hamburger Antiquariat Keip, Grindelhof 48, 20146 Hamburg. T. (040) 443234, Fax (040) 445972. - Print /
Engr / Map - *102613*

Hamburger Bücherstube Felix Jud & Wilfried Weber,
Neuer Wall 13, 20354 Hamburg. T. (040) 34 34 09.
- ArtBk / Engr - *102614*

Hauswedell & Nolte, Pöseldorfer Weg 1, 20148 Hamburg. T. (040) 4132100, Fax 41321010. - Print / ArtBk /
Engr / Autogr / Map - *102615*

Hauswedell & Nolte

Buch- und Kunstantiquariat
Buch- und Kunstauktionen

20148 Hamburg, Pöseldorfer Weg 1
Tel. (0 40) 41 32 10-0
Telefax (0 40) 41 32 10-10

New York branch office:
225 Central Park West
New York, N.Y. 10024, USA
Tel. (2 12) 5 95-08 06
Fax (2 12) 5 95-08 32

Heinen, Paul, Huusbarg 14, 22359 Hamburg. *102616*

Heinrich-Heine-Buchhandlung, Grindelallee 26-28,
20146 Hamburg. T. (040) 44 97 78. *102617*

Hennings, Paul, Altstädter Str. 15, 20095 Hamburg.
T. (040) 32 60 74. - Print / ArtBk - *102618*

Heymann, Kurt, Eppendorfer Baum 27-28, 20249 Hamburg. T. (040) 47 00 25. *102619*

Hochhuth, Walter D., Poststr 11, 20354 Hamburg.
T. (040) 342211, Fax 352020. - ArtBk / Engr /
Map - *102620*

Höh, Helmut von der, Große Bleichen 21, 20354 Hamburg. T. (040) 34 63 88, Fax 34 62 72. - ArtBk - *102621*

Huelsmann, F.K.A., Hohe Bleichen 15, 20354 Hamburg.
T. (040) 342017, Fax 354534. - Print / Engr / Autogr /
Map - *102622*

Jaeger, Roland, Michaelisbrücke 3, 20459 Hamburg.
T. (040) 37 11 94, Fax 37 11 03. - Print / ArtBk - *102623*

Kaak, Elbchaussee 583, 22587 Hamburg.
T. (040) 86 77 26. *102624*

Kemmer, Eberhard, Eppendorfer Weg 248, 20251 Hamburg. T. (040) 420 39 61. *102625*

Kirk, J., Schwarzenbergstr. 16, 21073 Hamburg.
T. (040) 766 57 15. *102626*

Koppel, Susanne, Parkallee 4, 20144 Hamburg.
T. (040) 454407, Fax (040) 453013. - Print /
Autogr / *102627*

Laatzen, Hermann, Warburgstr. 18, 20354 Hamburg.
T. (040) 44 41 60. *102628*

Le Bouquiniste, Postfach 670502, 22345 Hamburg.
T. (040) 603 41 13. - Print - *102629*

Le Claire, Thomas, Elbchaussee 156, 22605 Hamburg.
T. (040) 8810646, Fax (040) 8804612. - Engr - *102630*

Libresso – Antiquariat an der Universität, Binderstr. 24,
20146 Hamburg. T. (040) 45 16 63. - Print / ArtBk /
Engr - *102631*

Lüders, Axel, Heußweg 33, 20255 Hamburg.
T. (040) 40 57 27. *102632*

Lührs, Joachim, Michaelisbrücke 3, 20459 Hamburg.
T. (040) 371194, Fax 371103. - Print / ArtBk / Engr /
Autogr - *102633*

Malinowski, G., Bahrenfelder Str. 11, 22765 Hamburg.
T. (040) 39 23 59. *102634*

Marissal Bücher, Gerhart-Hauptmann-Platz 48k, 20095
Hamburg. *102635*

Mauke, W., Söhne, Karl-Muck-Platz 12, 20355 Hamburg. T. (040) 34 52 41. *102636*

Moeller, Martin, Klosterallee 78, 20144 Hamburg.
T. (040) 420 63 88. *102637*

Noritz, N., Weidenstieg 14, 20259 Hamburg.
T. (040) 40 02 72, Fax 453 24. *102638*

Pabel, Reinhold, Krayenkamp 10b, 20459 Hamburg.
T. (040) 36 48 89, Fax 374 33 91. - Print /
ArtBk - *102639*

Paulusbuchhandlung, Alsterarkaden 21, 20354 Hamburg. T. (040) 36 78 01, Fax 374 32 59. *102640*

Pfeiffer, E., Wilhelm-Strauß-Weg 12, 21109 Hamburg.
T. (040) 754 33 75. *102641*

Prager & Prinz, Neue ABC-Str. 8, 20354 Hamburg.
T. (040) 34 48 82. - Print / Engr / Map - *102642*

Rabe, Bellealliancestr. 32, 20259 Hamburg.
T. (040) 430 29 35. *102643*

Recht-Ullrich, Wilhelm, Fuhlsbüttler Str. 386, 22309
Hamburg. T. (040) 630 98 18. *102644*

Riepen, R., Raamstieg 8, 22397 Hamburg.
T. (040) 608 02 16. *102645*

Ritter-Volkmann, Vera, Gravensteiner Str. 7, 20259
Hamburg. T. (040) 4396701. *102646*

Salchow, R., Hohenzollernring 27, 22763 Hamburg.
T. (040) 881 14 88. *102647*

Sammlerhaus Engel, Methfesselstr. 60, 20257 Hamburg.
T. (040) 491 10 71. *102648*

Sautter & Lackmann, Admiralitätstr. 71/72, 20459 Hamburg. T. (040) 37 31 96, Fax 36 54 79. - ArtBk - *102649*

Schöningh, B., Ottenser Marktplatz 15, 22765 Hamburg.
T. (040) 3906949, Fax (040) 397160. *102650*

Schütte, P., Ottenser Hauptstr. 62, 22765 Hamburg.
T. (040) 390 02 50. *102651*

Stammerjohann, Jürgen, Hohenzollernring 27, 22763
Hamburg. T. (040) 8805425, Fax (040) 8811533.
- Print / ArtBk - *102652*

Straube, Martha, Weidestr. 24, 22083 Hamburg.
T. (040) 29 50 93. *102653*

Tepper, Burkhardt, Isestr. 56, 20149 Hamburg.
T. (040) 48 41 08, Fax 48 41 68. *102654*

Tiedemann, H.-H., Am Felde 91, 22765 Hamburg.
T. (040) 39 69 70. *102655*

Tiedtke, Wolfgang, Soltaustr. 27, 21029 Hamburg.
T. (040) 724 38 79. *102656*

Tietjen & Co., Spitalerstr 30, 20095 Hamburg.
T. (040) 330368, Fax 323035. *102657*

Uhlenhorster Antiquariat, Mozartstr. 11, 22083 Hamburg. T. (040) 220 66 53. *102658*

Wiedebusch, Max, Dammtorstr. 20, 20354 Hamburg.
T. (040) 34 50 01/02. *102659*

Wohlers, Dr., & Co., Lange Reihe 68-70, 20099 Hamburg. T. (040) 24 77 15. - Print - *102660*

Zimmerling, Günter, Johanniswall 3, 20095 Hamburg.
T. (040) 33 63 03. *102661*

Hamm (Nordrhein-Westfalen)

Classics Mine, Erlenkamp 2, 59071 Hamm.
T. (02381) 81016. *102662*

Hanau (Hessen)
Dausien, Werner, Burgallee 67, 63454 Hanau.
T. (06181) 25 90 52, Fax 25 73 87. - Print / Engr /
Map - *102663*
Hanauer Kunstkabinett, Burgallee 65, 63454 Hanau.
T. (06181) 21632, Fax 25 70 64. - ArtBk - *102664*

Hann. Münden (Niedersachsen)
Beume, Karen, Rosenstr. 5, 34346 Hann. Münden.
T. (05541) 8686. - Print / Engr / Map - *102665*

Hannover (Niedersachsen)
Antiquariat am Weißekreuzplatz, Lister Meile 17, 30161
Hannover. T. (0511) 33 15 15. *102666*
Antiquariat Buchfink, Charlottenstr 81, 30449 Hannover.
T. (0511) 483506. *102667*

Antiquariat Die Silbergäule, Marienstr. 6, 30171 Hanno-
ver. T. (0511) 85 18 81. *102668*
Antiquariat im Internationalismus Buchladen, Engelbo-
steler Damm 10, 30167 Hannover.
T. (0511) 70 98 99. *102669*
Aschenbrenner, Peter, Ferdinand-Wallbrecht-Str. 23,
30163 Hannover. T. (0511) 62 07 52. *102670*
Bauer, J.H., Holzmarkt 4, 30159 Hannover.
T. (0511) 324485, Fax 324452. - Print / ArtBk / Engr /
Autogr / Map - *102671*
Becker, Ingeborg, Lister Meile 49, 30161 Hannover.
T. (0511) 31 28 34. *102672*
Buchhandlung im Sprengel Museum, Kurt-Schwitters-
Platz 1, 30169 Hannover. T. (0511) 809 37 37.
- ArtBk - *102673*
Gärtner, Heinz, Marienstr. 105-107, 30171 Hannover.
T. (0511) 85 12 10. *102674*
Hartmann, Gebr., Schwarzer Bär 7, 30449 Hannover.
T. (0511) 44 18 93. *102675*
Hennies & Zinkeisen, Marienstr. 14-18, 30171 Hanno-
ver. T. (0511) 85 10 98. *102676*
Internationalismus, Engelbosteler Damm 10, 30167
Hannover. T. (0511) 70 98 99. *102677*
Karicartoon, Fössestr. 12, 30451 Hannover.
T. (0511) 44 26 25. *102678*
Koechert, C., Böckerstr. 11, 30659 Hannover.
T. (0511) 649 83 21. *102679*
Küster, K., Gustav-Adolf-Str. 12, 30167 Hannover.
T. (0511) 32 35 11. *102680*
Mielke, M., Schlägerstr. 33, 30171 Hannover.
T. (0511) 88 49 60. *102681*
Müller-Kilian, Klaus, Asternstr. 33, 30167 Hannover.
T. (0511) 70 37 67. - Print / Map - *102682*
Mueller, Robert A., Ricklinger Stadtweg 24, 30459 Han-
nover. T. (0511) 42 56 76. - Print - *102683*
Müller's Antiquariat, Marienstr. 81, 30171 Hannover.
T. (0511) 81 44 25, Fax 23 27 29. - Print / Engr /
Autogr - *102684*
Rosenbach, Detlev, Walderseestr 24, 30177 Hannover.
T. (0511) 669348, Fax (0511) 621285. - Engr /
Autogr - *102685*

Sachse & Heinzelmann, Georgstr. 34, 30159 Hannover.
T. (0511) 32 64 74. - ArtBk - *102686*
Schröder & Weise, Lehrter Str., 30559 Hannover.
T. (0511) 51 70 37. *102687*
Seemeyer, Podbielskistr. 5, 30163 Hannover.
T. (0511) 66 14 57. *102688*
Timme, H.F., Lange Laube 29, 30159 Hannover.
T. (0511) 32 95 57. *102689*
Trivial Book Shop, Marienstr. 3, 30171 Hannover.
T. (0511) 32 90 97. *102690*
Wäger, Hans, Lavesstr. 6, 30159 Hannover.
T. (0511) 32 17 25. *102691*
Wiehe, Irene, Hildesheimer Str. 46, 30169 Hannover.
T. (0511) 88 84 34. *102692*

Hattingen (Nordrhein-Westfalen)
Die Gravüre, Nierenhofer Str 109, 45529 Hattingen.
T. (02324) 27821. *102693*

Heidelberg (Baden-Württemberg)
Bibliographicum, Hauptstr 194, 69117 Heidelberg.
T. (06221) 26252. - Print / Engr - *102695*
Biehn, Ingeborg, Steingasse 3, 69117 Heidelberg.
T. (06221) 129 08. - Print / Map - *102696*
Braun, Gustav, Sofienstr. 3, 69115 Heidelberg.
T. (06221) 200 74. *102697*
Bücherwurm, Heiliggeiststr. 5, 69117 Heidelberg.
T. (06221) 122 02. - Print / Engr - *102698*
Goethe und Compagny, Ingrimstr. 20a, 69117 Heidel-
berg. T. (06221) 16 61 14. *102699*
Greiser, Olaf, Schröderstr 14, 69120 Heidelberg.
T. (06221) 401587. - Engr / Map - *102700*
Hassbecker, Haspelgasse 12, 69117 Heidelberg.
T. (06221) 24466. - ArtBk - *102701*
Hatry, T., Plöck 93/Friedrichstr., 69117 Heidelberg.
T. (06221) 26202. - Print - *102702*
Ingrim-Antiquariat, Ingrimstr. 26, 69117 Heidelberg.
T. (06221) 26299. - ArtBk - *102703*
Kerle, F. H., Plöck 101, 69117 Heidelberg.
T. (06221) 226 11, Fax 16 42 10. - Print - *102704*
Kulbach, Neugasse 19, 69117 Heidelberg.
T. (06221) 236 14, Fax 121 13. - Print / ArtBk - *102705*
Kulbach, Richart, Neugasse 19, 69117 Heidelberg.
T. (06221) 236 14. *102706*
Lang, P. & B., Heiliggeiststr. 5, 69117 Heidelberg.
T. (06221) 122 02. *102707*
Rehberger, R., Heiliggeistkirche, 69117 Heidelberg.
T. (06221) 128 42. *102708*
Schwing, Rolf, Gaisbergstr 29, 69115 Heidelberg.
T. (06221) 28314, Fax (06221) 167829. - Print /
Engr - *102709*
Weiss'sche Universitätsbuchhandlung, Universitätsplatz
8, 69117 Heidelberg. T. (06221) 221 60.
- Print - *102710*
Welz, F., Oberbadgasse 8, 69117 Heidelberg.
T. (06221) 152 08. - Print / ArtBk - *102711*
Wiemann, Wolfgang, Dr., Bergstr 49, 69120 Heidelberg.
T. (06221) 413030, Fax (06221) 474442. *102711a*
Winterberg, Arno, Hildastr 12, 69115 Heidelberg.
T. (06221) 22631, Fax 164631. *102712*

ARNO WINTERBERG
KUNSTANTIQUARIAT
VERSTEIGERUNGEN
☎ (0 62 21) **2 26 31**
Fax (0 62 21) 16 46 31
69115 Heidelberg · Hildastraße 12

Heilbronn (Baden-Württemberg)
Gruber, Gerhard, Neuwiesenstr 16, 74078 Heilbronn.
T. (07131) 45245, Fax (07131) 910474. *102713*
Mehrdorf, R., Reutlinger Str 7, 74074 Heilbronn.
T. (07131) 75775. *102714*
Wahl, M., Cäcilienstr 58, 74072 Heilbronn.
T. (07131) 84617. - Print - *102715*

Helgoland (Schleswig-Holstein)
Knauß, Maren, Siemensterrasse 140, 27498 Helgoland.
T. (04725) 78 66. - Print / Engr - *102716*

Herford (Nordrhein-Westfalen)
Antiquariat in der Radewig, Löhrstr. 3, 32052 Herford.
T. (05221) 534 55. - Print - *102717*

Herne (Nordrhein-Westfalen)
Lorych, S., Gartenstr. 69, 44625 Herne.
T. (02323) 448 94. *102718*

Hildesheim (Niedersachsen)
Vree, H.G., Orleanstr. 26, 31135 Hildesheim.
T. (05121) 554 29. - Print - *102719*
Vree, H.G., Hoher Weg 32-33, 31134 Hildesheim.
T. (05121) 32423. - Print - *102720*

Hohenschäftlarn (Bayern)
Renner, Klaus, Am Sonenhang 8, 82069
Hohenschäftlarn. *102721*

Hohenstein-Ernstthal (Sachsen)
Klis'sche Buchhandlung, Weinkellerstr. 20, 09337 Ho-
henstein-Ernstthal. T. (03723) 3307. *102722*

Homburg (Saarland)
Keweloh, N., Dr., Hopfenweg 9, 66424 Homburg.
T. (06841) 68086. *102723*
Kopatz-Baumann, S., Marktstr. 5, 66424 Homburg.
T. (06841) 68409. *102724*
Raueiser, H., Untergasse 4, 66424 Homburg.
T. (06841) 64805. *102725*

Horb (Baden-Württemberg)
Vogel, I., Mühlgäßle 19, 72160 Horb.
T. (07451) 8533. *102726*

Husum (Schleswig-Holstein)
Husumer Antiquariat, Wasserreihe 48, 25813 Husum.
T. (04841) 81199. *102727*

Ingolstadt (Bayern)
Steinbeißer, K.-H. & W., Fraunhoferstr 6, 85053 Ingolstadt. T. (0841) 69259. *102728*

Iserlohn (Nordrhein-Westfalen)
Broich, Josef, Hans-Böckler-Str. 52, 58638 Iserlohn.
T. (02371) 27154. - Print / ArtBk / Engr / Map - *102729*

Ismaning (Bayern)
Milo Antiquariat, Böhmerwaldstr. 59, 85737 Ismaning.
T. (089) 96 54 49. *102730*

Jameln (Niedersachsen)
Historia Medicinae Antiquariat, Dobro 14, 29479 Ja-
meln. T. (058 64) 230. *102731*

Kaiserslautern (Rheinland-Pfalz)
Gondrom KG, Fruchthallstr. 22, 67655 Kaiserslautern.
T. (0631) 65077, Fax 65076. - Print / Engr - *102732*
Schmidt, Geschw., Karl-Marx-Str. 15, 67655 Kaiserslau-
tern. T. (0631) 920 25. *102733*
Winkelmann, P., Rudolf-Breitscheid-Str. 45, 67655 Kai-
serslautern. T. (0631) 18605. *102734*

Karlsfeld (Bayern)
Handwerker, Helmut, Peter-Rosegger-Str. 4, 85757
Karlsfeld. T. (08131) 950 95. - ArtBk - *102735*

Karlsruhe (Baden-Württemberg)
Art Service, Ochsentorstr. 13, 76227 Karlsruhe.
T. (0721) 434 52, 49 46 06. - ArtBk - *102736*
Braun, Kaiserstr. 120, 76133 Karlsruhe.
T. (0721) 232 96, 260 27, Fax 291 16. - Print / Engr /
Map - *102737*
Damsons, Sophienstr. 116, 76135 Karlsruhe.
T. (0721) 85 53 57. *102738*
Gromer, Herta, Tulpenstr. 39, 76199 Karlsruhe.
T. (0721) 302 42. - Engr / Map - *102739*
Krieg, G., Ludwig-Wilhelm-Str. 3, 76131 Karlsruhe.
T. (0721) 69 67 54. *102740*

Kundt, Ernst, Kaiserstr. 124b, 76133 Karlsruhe.
T. (0721) 242 08. *102741*

Menzel, U., Bonhoefferstr. 5, 76189 Karlsruhe.
T. (0721) 86 14 76. - ArtBk / Autogr - *102742*

Stuckhardt, W., Gartenstr. 1, 76133 Karlsruhe.
T. (0721) 37 44 00. *102743*

Kassel (Hessen)
Freyschmidt, A., Königstr. 23, 34117 Kassel. *102744*

Hamecher, Horst, Goethestr. 74, 34119 Kassel.
T. (0561) 131 79. - Print / ArtBk - *102745*

Hühn, Ernst, Friedrich-Ebert-Str. 137, 34119 Kassel.
T. (0561) 126 47. *102746*

Jenior & Pressler, Lassallestr. 15, 34119 Kassel.
T. (0561) 176 55. - Print / ArtBk - *102747*

Loida, E., Friedrich-Ebert-Str. 95, 34119 Kassel.
T. (0561) 77 77 77. *102748*

Lometsch, Kölnische Str. 5, 34117 Kassel.
T. (0561) 143 58. - ArtBk - *102749*

Makrocki, A., Quellenstr. 14, 34134 Kassel.
T. (0561) 456 09. *102750*

Vietor, Carl, Ständepl. 17, 34117 Kassel.
T. (0561) 130 85, Fax 71 04 42. - ArtBk - *102751*

Kaufbeuren (Bayern)
Montazer, Kaiser-Max-Str. 16, 87600 Kaufbeuren.
T. (08341) 139 16. *102752*

Kehl (Baden-Württemberg)
Art Stock Vertrieb Internationaler Kunstbücher, Gold-
scheuerstr 16, 77694 Kehl. T. (07851) 71034,
Fax (07851) 75955. - Print - *102753*

Kelkheim (Hessen)
Schmidt & Günther, Bahnstr 25, 65779 Kelkheim.
T. (06192) 74124, Fax (06192) 74291. - Print /
ArtBk - *102754*

Schmidt & Günther, Bahnstr 25, 65779 Kelkheim.
T. (06195) 74124, Fax (06195) 74291. - Print /
ArtBk - *102755*

Kelsterbach (Hessen)
Nold, Rainer, Feldstr. 29, 65451 Kelsterbach. *102756*

Kempen (Nordrhein-Westfalen)
Rössler, S., Peterstr 30, 47906 Kempen.
T. (02152) 53328. *102757*

Kevelaer (Nordrhein-Westfalen)
Janssen, H., Busmannstr. 2, 47623 Kevelaer.
T. (02832) 6966, Fax 3902. - Engr / Map - *102758*

Kiel (Schleswig-Holstein)
Antiquariat Bücherwurm, Knooper Weg 28, 24103 Kiel.
T. (0431) 96925. *102759*

Eschenburg, Holtenauer Str. 109, 24105 Kiel.
T. (0431) 81772. *102760*

Schramm, Bernd, Dänische Str 26, 24103 Kiel.
T. (0431) 94367, Fax (0431) 801066. - Print / Engr /
Map - *102761*

Kirchbrak (Niedersachsen)
Brunnarius, Karl, Westerbraker Str. 4, 37619 Kirchbrak.
T. (05533) 4220. - Engr / Map - *102762*

Kirchheim (Baden-Württemberg)
Hauff, Fritz oHG, Marktstr. 1 b.3, 73230 Kirchheim.
T. (07021) 26 24. - Print - *102763*

Kirchheim am Neckar (Baden-Württemberg)
Randebrock, E., Finkenweg 5, 74366 Kirchheim am
Neckar. T. (07143) 339 54. - Print / Engr / Map - *102764*

Kleve (Nordrhein-Westfalen)
Antiquariat am Schloßtor, Schloßstr 19, 47533 Kleve.
T. (02821) 21903. - Engr / Map - *102765*

Koblenz (Rheinland-Pfalz)
Struck, Nikolaus, An der Liebfrauenkirche 6, 56068 Koblenz. T. (0261) 32898, Fax (06746) 1568. *102766*

Köln (Nordrhein-Westfalen)
Boisserée, Drususgasse 7-11, 50667 Köln.
T. (0221) 2578519, Fax 2578550. - Engr - *102767*

Buchholz, Neven-DuMont-Str 17, 50667 Köln.
T. (0221) 2576251, Fax (0221) 253351. *102768*

Capitain, Gisela, Apostelnstr. 19, 50667 Köln.
T. (0221) 256676, Fax (0221) 256593. - ArtBk - *102769*

Das Bücherparadies, Eigelstein 50, 50668 Köln.
T. (0221) 12 15 93. - Print - *102770*

Dinter, Jürgen, Buchholzstr 8, 51061 Köln.
T. (0221) 646001, Fax (0221) 646018. - Print - *102771*

Franke, H., Hirschgäßchen 2a, 50678 Köln.
T. (0221) 31 99 31. - Print / ArtBk - *102772*

Galerie Orangerie-Reinz, Helenenstr 2, 50667 Köln.
T. (0221) 2575038, Fax (0221) 2575132. *102773*

Gelbert, Gundel, St.-Apern-Str. 4, 50667 Köln.
T. (0221) 2576131, Fax (0221) 254885.
- Print - *102774*

Herder, Komödienstr. 11, 50667 Köln.
T. (0221) 257 75 44, Fax 257 75 56. - ArtBk /
Engr - *102775*

Heuberger, Roman, Düppelstr 20, 50679 Köln.
T. (0221) 884914/810439, Fax (0221) 885483. *102776*

Heybutzki, Gerd, Pfeilstr 8, 50672 Köln.
T. (0221) 256531. - ArtBk - *102777*

König, Walther, Ehrenstr. 4, 50672 Köln.
T. (0221) 20 59 60, Fax 205 96 40. - ArtBk - *102778*

König, Walther, Breite Str. 79, 50667 Köln.
T. (0221) 205 96 32. *102779*

Krause, Hermann, Thürmchenswall 6, 50668 Köln.
T. (0221) 12 43 15, Fax 13 17 15. - Print /
ArtBk - *102780*

Kuhn, H. & R., Lützowstr. 13, 50674 Köln.
T. (0221) 24 67 26. - Engr - *102781*

Kunsthandlung Goyert, Hahnenstr 18, 50667 Köln.
T. (0221) 2570330, Fax (0221) 2570339. - Print / Engr /
Autogr / Map - *102782*

Kutsch, Wilhelm, Komödienstr. 19, 50667 Köln.
T. (0221) 2576711. - Print / Engr / Autogr /
Map - *102783*

Lehmann, Dorothea, Weyertal 30, 50937 Köln.
T. (0221) 41 96 74. *102784*

Lésabendio, Gereonswall 5c, 50668 Köln.
T. (0221) 13 63 03. - Print / ArtBk / Engr - *102785*

Pflips, Rolf, Limburger Str. 25, 50672 Köln.
T. (0221) 25 15 25. - Print - *102786*

Post, Constantin, Auf dem Berlich 26, 50667 Köln.
Fax (0221) 257 62 26. - Print / Engr - *102787*

Roemke, C., & Cie., Apostelnstr. 7, 50667 Köln.
T. (0221) 257 37 17, Fax 25 51 08. - ArtBk / Engr /
Map - *102788*

Sasserath & Winges, Hahnenstr. 2, 50667 Köln.
T. (0221) 255979. *102789*

Schulz, Apostelnstr. 12, 50667 Köln.
T. (0221) 2578009. *102790*

Unverzagt, Siegfried, Limburger Str. 10, 50672 Köln.
T. (0221) 25 15 15, Fax (0221) 25 13 44. - Print /
ArtBk - *102791*

Unverzagt, Siegfried, Zülpicher Str. 68, 50937 Köln.
T. (0221) 512437. *102792*

Venator & Hanstein, Cäcilienstr 48, 50667 Köln.
T. (0221) 2575419, Fax 2575526. - Print / ArtBk / Engr /
Autogr / Map - *102793*

Weber, Peter, Mauritiussteinweg 108, 50676 Köln.
T. (0221) 24 13 84. - Print - *102794*

Weyers, A., Steinweg 3, 50667 Köln.
T. (0221) 2582359. *102795*

Königstein (Hessen)
Koeltz, Sven, Herrnwaldstr 6, 61462 Königstein.
T. (06174) 4492, 3189, Fax 1634. - Print - *102796*

Küchler, Walther, Dr., Klosterstr 3, 61462 Königstein.
T. (06174) 7079, Fax 21189. - ArtBk - *102797*

Reiss & Auvermann, Adelheidstr 2, 61462 Königstein.
T. (06174) 1017, Fax (06174) 1602. - Print - *102798*

Konstanz (Baden-Württemberg)
Buch und Kunst, Münzgasse 16, 78462 Konstanz.
T. (07531) 241 71. - Print / ArtBk - *102799*

Bücherstube am See, Kreuzlinger Str 11, 78462 Konstanz. T. (07531) 22176, Fax (07531) 21190.
- Print - *102800*

Gsellius, Münzgasse 16, 78462 Konstanz.
T. (07531) 23138. *102801*

Kunst-Antiquariat, Emmishofer Str. 3, 78462 Konstanz.
T. (07531) 261 36. - Print / Engr - *102802*

Müsken, H., Zollernstr. 3, 78462 Konstanz.
T. (07531) 246 31. *102803*

Patzer & Trenkle, Hussenstr 45, 78462 Konstanz.
T. (07531) 21337, Fax (07531) 16256. - Print /
ArtBk - *102804*

Scheringer, Georg, Münzgasse 16, 78462 Konstanz.
T. (07531) 24171. *102805*

Kornwestheim (Baden-Württemberg)
Brockhaus Antiquarium, Kreidlerstr 9, 70806 Kornwest-
heim. T. (07154) 132751, Fax (07154) 132713.
- Print - *102806*

Kottgeisering (Bayern)
Ricke, Walter, Villenstr. Süd 30, 82288 Kottgeisering.
T. (08144) 553, Fax 1309. - Print - *102807*

Krefeld (Nordrhein-Westfalen)
Biermann, J., Ostwall 64, 47798 Krefeld.
T. (02151) 23927. *102808*

Greven, J., Hochstr. 52, 47798 Krefeld.
T. (02151) 232 85, 298 92. - ArtBk - *102809*

Storch, E., & H. Radojcic, Ostwall 50, 47798 Krefeld.
T. (02151) 203 11. *102810*

Kronberg (Hessen)
Bauer, Michael, Dr., Pferdstr 3, 61476 Kronberg.
T. (06173) 4914. *102811*

Lage, Lippe (Nordrhein-Westfalen)
Boer, Jan Berndt de, 32791 Lage, Lippe.
T. (05232) 4219. *102812*

Langenbach (Bayern)
Bärwinkel, Elfriede & Eike, Angerstr. 24, 85416
Langenbach. *102813*

Langenfeld (Nordrhein-Westfalen)
Holtum, Manfred von, Ursulaweg 53, 40764 Langenfeld.
- Print / Engr / Map - *102814*

Holtum, Roswitha von, Ursulaweg 53, 40764 Langenfeld. T. (02173) 70708. - Map - *102815*

Laupheim (Baden-Württemberg)
Genth, Frischweid 12, 88471 Laupheim.
T. (07392) 80991. - Print / Engr / Map - *102816*

Lebrade (Schleswig-Holstein)
Rohlmann, Heinz, Dörpstraat 12, 24306 Lebrade.
T. (04383) 893, Fax 1350. *102817*

Leinfelden-Echterdingen (Baden-Würt-temberg)
Knirck, Andreas, Raichbergweg 2, 70771 Leinfelden-
Echterdingen. T. (0711) 7542928,
Fax (0711) 7545931. *102818*

Leipzig (Sachsen)
Franz-Mehring-Haus, Goethestr. 3/5, 04109 Leipzig.
T. (0341) 29 26 45, Fax 20 01 54. *102819*

Leipziger Antiquariat, Ritterstr 16, 04109 Leipzig.
T. (0341) 9602229. - Print - *102820*

Musik-Antiquariat, Thomaskirchhof 15, 04109 Leipzig.
T. (0341) 9604843. - Print - *102821*

Musikalien Antiquariat, Thomaskirchhof 15, 04109 Leipzig. T. (0341) 28 94 06. *102822*

Sächsisches Auktionshaus und Antiquariat, Sebastian-
Bach-Str 28, 04109 Leipzig. T. (0341) 9832015,
Fax 470680. *102823*

Syndikat, Grassistr. 10, 04107 Leipzig.
T. (0341) 27 18 07. - ArtBk - *102824*

Trier, Dieter, Tschaikowskistr 9, 04105 Leipzig.
T. (0341) 273277, Fax (0341) 273277. *102825*

Universum, Karl-Liebknecht-Str. 105, 04275 Leipzig.
T. (0341) 32 33 10. - Print - *102826*

Zentralantiquariat Leipzig GmbH
An- und Verkauf

- Antiquariat
  Talstr. 29   ☎ (03 41) **2 16 17 28**

- „Leipziger Antiquariat"
  Ritterstr. 16 ☎ (03 41) **9 60 22 29**

- Musik-Antiquariat
  Thomaskirchhof 15, Leipzig
       ☎ (03 41) **9 60 48 43**

- „Dresdener Antiquariat"
  Bautzener Str. 11, Dresden
       ☎ (03 51) **8 04 39 70**

- „Dresdener Bücher-Fundus"
  Augsburger Str. 79 - 81
  01277 Dresden
       ☎ (03 51) **3 57 59**

Zentrale: Talstraße 29
☎ **(03 41) 21 61 70**
Fax (03 41) 9 60 28 19

Zentralantiquariat Leipzig, Talstr 29, 04103 Leipzig.
T. (0341) 2161728, Fax 9602819. - Print -   *102827*

Lenningen (Baden-Württemberg)
Löffler, Julius-von-Jan-Pl. 8, 73252 Lenningen.
T. (07026) 4116.   *102828*

Limburg an der Lahn (Hessen)
Topp, Hans-Jürgen, Grabenstr 31, 65549 Limburg an
der Lahn. T. (06431) 6490, Fax 24172. - Engr / Autogr /
Map -   *102829*

Lindau, Bodensee (Bayern)
Zeller, Klaus Robert, Dr., Fischergasse 13, 88131 Lind-
au, Bodensee. T. (08382) 27113,
Fax (08382) 5589.   *102830*

Lörzweiler (Rheinland-Pfalz)
Kandel, J., Ruländerweg 2, 55296 Lörzweiler.
T. (06138) 64 36. - Print -   *102831*

Ludwigsburg (Baden-Württemberg)
Aigner, J., Am Arsenalplatz, 71638 Ludwigsburg.
T. (07141) 23 323, Fax 90 27 93. - Print / ArtBk /
Engr -   *102832*

Beuttler, H. & P. Bewer, Untere Gasse 29, 71642 Ludwigsburg. T. (07141) 56144.   *102833*

Fetzer, J., Bogenstr. 1, 71634 Ludwigsburg.
T. (07141) 92 99 86. - Print / ArtBk -   *102834*

Hieronymus, Seestr. 5, 71638 Ludwigsburg.
T. (07141) 92 96 04. - Print / ArtBk -   *102835*

Ludwigshafen am Rhein (Rheinland-
Pfalz)
Hofmann, Wilhelm, Bismarckstr 98, 67059 Ludwigsha-
fen am Rhein. T. (0621) 516001.   *102836*

Jaeger, Bismarckstr 112, 67059 Ludwigshafen am
Rhein. T. (0621) 512234. - ArtBk / Engr -   *102837*

Pfister, A., Bismarckstr 34, 67059 Ludwigshafen am
Rhein. T. (0621) 512792. - ArtBk -   *102838*

Lübeck (Schleswig-Holstein)
Adler, Arno, Hüxstr 55, 23552 Lübeck. T. (0451) 74466,
Fax (0451) 7063762. - Print -   *102839*

Babendererde, Peter, Große Burgstr 35, 23552 Lübeck.
T. (0451) 7060666, Fax (0451) 706755. - Print / Engr /
Map -   *102840*

Bücherwurm, Engelsgrube 85, 23552 Lübeck.
T. (0451) 78913.   *102841*

Gaulin & Oestmmann, Königstr. 20, 23552 Lübeck.
T. (0451) 702 95, Fax 73755. - Print / Engr / Autogr /
Map -   *102842*

Oestmann, Königstr. 20, 23552 Lübeck. - Print / ArtBk /
Engr / Autogr / Map -   *102843*

Weiland, Gustav, Nachf., Königstr. 67a, 23552 Lübeck.
T. (0451) 16 00 60, Fax 160 06 77. - ArtBk -   *102844*

Lüdenscheid (Nordrhein-Westfalen)
Melzer, Sauerfelder Str. 8, 58511 Lüdenscheid.
T. (02351) 22464. - Print / ArtBk -   *102845*

Lüneburg (Niedersachsen)
Diemke, Siegmar, Uelzener Str. 28, 21335 Lüneburg.
T. (04131) 41890.   *102846*

Jäger, Ruthild, Steinweg 17, 21335 Lüneburg.
T. (04131) 42797, Fax (04131) 42798. - Print / Engr /
Map -   *102847*

Magdeburg (Sachsen-Anhalt)
Glaser, Schönebecker Str. 104, 39104
Magdeburg.   *102848*

Magdeburger Antiquariat, Leibnizstr. 21, 39104 Magdeburg. T. (0391) 32902. - Print / Engr -   *102849*

Mauritius Buch- und Kunsthandlung, Max-Josef-Metzger-Str. 2, 39104 Magdeburg.
T. (0391) 34 43 39.   *102850*

Trigon, Feuerbachstr. 1, 39104 Magdeburg.
T. (0391) 561 30 23. - Print / Engr -   *102851*

Mainburg (Bayern)
Lindner, Hans, Sandolfstr 32c, 84048 Mainburg.
T. (08751) 5617, Fax (08751) 5418. - Print -   *102852*

Mainz (Rheinland-Pfalz)
Brumme, Siegfried, Kirschgarten 11, 55116 Mainz.
T. (06131) 228074, Fax (06131) 230717.   *102853*

Czernik-Schild, G., Gaustr. 24, 55116 Mainz.
T. (06131) 22 08 28. - Print -   *102854*

Dumjahn, Immenhof 12, 55128 Mainz.
T. (06131) 356 00, Fax 35659. - Print -   *102855*

Johannes-Gutenberg-Buchhandlung, Große Bleiche 29,
55116 Mainz. T. (06131) 38 70 12, 22 63 01. - ArtBk /
Engr / Map -   *102856*

Sellin, Wilfried, Fischtorstr. 4-8, 55116 Mainz.
T. (06131) 22 19 62.   *102857*

Windfelder, Norbert, Hintere Bleiche 3, 55116 Mainz.
T. (06131) 22 93 98. - Print -   *102858*

Mannheim (Baden-Württemberg)
Bender, A., O 4,2, 68161 Mannheim. T. (0621) 108 24,
Fax 10 61 65.   *102859*

Kaeflein, Walter, M 2, 10, 68161 Mannheim.
T. (0621) 15 14 54.   *102860*

Schubert, K., Friedrichsring 40, 68161 Mannheim.
T. (0621) 147 56.   *102861*

Marburg (Hessen)
Antiquariat Roter Stern, Am Grün 30, 35037 Marburg.
T. (06421) 24786. - ArtBk -   *102862*

Elwert, N.G., Reitgasse 7-9, 35037 Marburg.
T. (06421) 17090. - Print / Engr / Map -   *102863*

Söhn, Fritz-Dieter, Renthof 8, 35037 Marburg.
T. (06421) 66002, Fax (06421) 62977. - Print -   *102864*

Wolpert, Fritz, 35037 Marburg 2353. T. (06421) 32395,
Fax 32395. - Engr / Map -   *102865*

Marquartstein (Bayern)
Mengedoht, Werner, Bahnhofstr. 1a, 83250 Marquartstein. T. (08641) 83 61. - ArtBk -   *102866*

Marxzell (Baden-Württemberg)
Lange, Horst-Joachim, Hirschweg 15, 76359 Marxzell.
T. (07248) 5417.   *102867*

Mechernich (Nordrhein-Westfalen)
Claassen, Aribert D., Rochusstr. 11, 53894 Mechernich.
T. (02256) 637. - Print / Engr / Map -   *102868*

Meckenheim, Rheinland (Nordrhein-
Westfalen)
Urbs et Orbis, Klaus Semmel, Göddertzgarten 42, 53340
Meckenheim, Rheinland. T. (02225) 3588.   *102869*

Meerbusch (Nordrhein-Westfalen)
Mönter, Konrad, Kirchplatz 1-5, 40670 Meerbusch.
T. (02132) 35 30. - Print / ArtBk / Engr / Map -   *102870*

Meersburg (Baden-Württemberg)
List & Francke, Stettener Str 33, 88709 Meersburg.
T. (07532) 5534, Fax (07532) 1381. - Print -   *102871*

Meiningen (Thüringen)
Dietzel, Ludwig-Chronegk-Str. 14, 98617 Meiningen.
T. (03693) 2615, Fax 2615. - Print / ArtBk / Engr /
Map -   *102872*

Mindelheim (Bayern)
Rittinghaus, Rudolf Carl, Maximilianstr. 42, 87719 Mindelheim. - ArtBk -   *102873*

Minden, Westfalen (Nordrhein-Westfa-
len)
Bücherinsel, Ritterstr. 40, 32423 Minden, Westfalen.
T. (0571) 21126. - Print / Engr / Map -   *102874*

SBS Minden, Paulinenstr 3, 32427 Minden, Westfalen.
T. (0571) 27702.   *102875*

Mönchengladbach (Nordrhein-
Westfalen)
Gerlach, B., & M. Lebbing, Rathausstr. 10, 41061 Mön-
chengladbach. T. (02161) 39 39 57. - Print /
ArtBk -   *102876*

Stodieck, Marcel, Bismarckstr. 38, 41061 Mönchengladbach. T. (02161) 234 43, Fax 20 56 43.
- ArtBk -   *102877*

Mörfelden-Walldorf (Hessen)
Alicke, P., Frankfurterstr. 107a, 64546 Mörfelden-Walldorf. T. (06105) 339 44. - Print -   *102878*

Moers (Nordrhein-Westfalen)
Altstadt-Antiquariat, Friedrichstr. 28, 47441 Moers.
T. (02841) 212 60, 638 63. - Print / Engr / Map -   *102879*

Moosinning (Bayern)
Billesberger, Siegfried, Billesberger Hof, 85452 Moosin-
ning. T. (08123) 1477, Fax (08123) 8399.
- Engr -   *102880*

Mudershausen (Rheinland-Pfalz)
Hertling, Edmund, Taunusblick 4, 65623 Mudershausen.
T. (06430) 6242. - Print -   *102881*

Mülheim an der Ruhr (Nordrhein-West-
falen)
Wünschmann & Co., Edith, Leineweberstr 68-70, 45468
Mülheim an der Ruhr. T. (0208) 37836.
- ArtBk -   *102882*

München (Bayern)
Ackermann, Theodor, Ludwigstr 7, 80539 München.
T. (089) 284787, Fax (089) 280172. - Print -   *102883*

ad artem, Pütrichstr. 4, 81667 München.
T. (089) 48 59 97.   *102884*

Akademische Buchhandlung, Veterinärstr. 1, 80539
München. T. (089) 3816160.   *102885*

Andersch, N., Volkartstr 46, 80636 München.
T. (089) 1233091.   *102886*

Antiquariat am Viktualienmarkt, Rosental 3-4, 80331
München. T. (089) 2604813.   *102887*

Antiquariat an der Universität, Veterinärstr. 1, 80539
München. T. (089) 33 66 51. - Print / ArtBk -   *102888*

Antiquitäten-Schatzkammer, Herzogstr. 77, 80796 München. T. (089) 58 22 21.   *102889*

Arco & Flotow, Briennerstr 10/V, 80333 München.
T. (089) 284089, Fax (089) 285696.   *102890*

Avalun, Friedenspromenade 25, 81827 München.
T. (089) 4307654. - Print / ArtBk -   *102891*

Bach, Susanne, Jakob-Klar-Str. 10, 80796 München.
T. (089) 271 86 48.   *102892*

Basis

Antiquariat

Wissenschaft · Kunst
Architektur · Literatur

Adalbertstraße 43
80799 München
Telefon 089/272 00 33
Fax 089/271 34 63

Basis Antiquariat, Adalbertstr. 43, 80799 München.
T. (089) 2720033, Fax 2713463. - Print /
ArtBk - *102893*
Bauer, A., Augsburgerstr. 1, 80337 München.
T. (089) 26 54 76. *102894*
Bauer, Gretel, Hohenzollernstr. 122, 80796 München.
T. (089) 308 90 48. *102895*
Beisler, Hermann, Oskar-von-Miller-Ring 33, 80333
München. T. (089) 283452. - Print / Engr /
Map - *102896*
Brehmer, R., Gebsattelstr. 15, 81541 München.
T. (089) 448 91 54. - Print / ArtBk / Engr - *102897*
Brincken, Klaus von, Salvatorstr 2, 80333 München.
T. (089) 298815, Fax (089) 222983. *102898*
BS-Buchservice, Postfach 701943, 81319 München.
T. (089) 717058, Fax (089) 712751. *102899*
Büchergalerie Westend, Ligsalzstr. 25, 80339 München.
T. (089) 502 73 73. *102900*
Bücherkabinett am Prinzregentenplatz, Lucille-Grahn-
Str 43, 81675 München. T. (089) 477036.
- Print - *102901*
Buk-Antiquariat, Gebsattelstr. 15, 81541 München.
T. (089) 448 91 54. - Print - *102902*
Dietz, Klaus, Oettingenstr. 62, 80538 München.
T. (089) 22 65 05, Fax 22 65 05. - Engr - *102903*
Dössinger, Franz, Hohenzollernstr. 156, 80797 München.
T. (089) 3081602. - ArtBk / Autogr - *102904*
Euro-Art, Josephsburgstr. 85, 81673 München.
T. (089) 43 48 24. *102905*
Gabelsberger Antiquariat, Gabelsbergerstr. 72, 80333
München. T. (089) 52 67 57. *102906*
Garwood & Voigt, Langerstr. 2, 81675 München.
T. (089) 4703066. - Print / Engr / Map - *102907*
Götz, Max, Frauenplatz 14, 80331 München.
T. (089) 22 00 65. *102908*
Goltz, Türkenstr. 54, 80799 München. T. (089) 284906,
Fax (089) 2802244. - Print - *102909*
Haeusgen, Ursula, Maximilianstr 38, 80539 München.
T. (089) 346299, Fax (089) 345395. *102910*
Hammerstein, Hans, Türkenstr. 37, 80799 München.
T. (089) 285183. - ArtBk - *102911*
Hartung & Hartung, Karolinenpl 5a, 80333 München
T. (089) 284034, Fax (089) 285569. *102912*

HARTUNG
&
HARTUNG

Wertvolle Bücher · Manuskripte
Autographen · Graphik
Auktionen (siehe dort)
D-80333 München · Karolinenplatz 5 a
Tel. (0 89) 28 40 34

Hauser, Schellingstr. 17, 80799 München.
T. (089) 281159. - Engr / Map - *102913*
Hellwig, R., Rosental 3, 80331 München.
T. (089) 2604813. *102914*

Hillenbrand, Rosental 3-4, 80331 München.
T. (089) 260 48 13. *102915*
Hoch, A., Schwanthalerstr 86, 80336 München.
T. (089) 532533. *102916*
Höchtberger, Hans, Mauerkircherstr. 28, 81679 Mün-
chen. T. (089) 983686. - Engr / Autogr - *102917*
Hollerbach-Schliebener, Görresstr. 33, 80798 München.
T. (089) 52 68 92. - ArtBk - *102918*
Hugendubel, Heinrich, Salvatorplatz 2, 80333 München.
T. (089) 2389330, Fax (089) 2389319. - Print /
Engr - *102919*
Husslein, Richard, Schellingstr. 129, 80798 München.
T. (089) 5234732. - Print / ArtBk / Autogr - *102920*
Iliu, Julia F., Barerstr 46, 80799 München.
T. (089) 2800688. - Engr / Map - *102921*
Johannes-Buchhandlung, Kreuzstr. 6, 80331 München.
T. (089) 26 61 86, 26 88 20. - ArtBk - *102922*
Karl & Faber, Amirapl 3, 80333 München.
T. (089) 221865/66, Fax 2283350. - Print / Engr /
Autogr - *102923*
Ketterer, Wolfgang, Brienner Str 25, 80333 München.
T. (089) 552440, Fax (089) 55244166. *102924*
Kitzinger, J., Schellingstr 25, 80799 München.
T. (089) 283537, 283561, Fax (089) 281394.
- ArtBk - *102925*
Köbelin, Rainer, Schellingstr 99, 80799 München.
T. (089) 285640, Fax (089) 5237404. *102926*
Koenig, Ilka, Feilitzschstr. 26, 80802 München.
T. (089) 34 55 75, Fax 39 21 49. - Print - *102927*
Koropp, E. M., Theatinerstr. 40-42, 80333 München.
T. (089) 229542. - Engr / Map - *102928*
Krauss, T., Maillingerstr. 3, 80636 München.
T. (089) 123 13 43. *102929*
Kreussel, Lutz-Peter, Occamstr. 10, 80802 München.
T. (089) 39 51 21, Fax 39 09 07. - Print - *102930*
Kuhn, H., Augsburgerstr. 2, 80337 München. *102931*
Kunstantiquariat Am Gasteig, Rosenheimer Str. 8, 81669
München. T. (089) 8112250, 4486260,
Fax 8111336. *102932*
Lachner, Universitätsbuchhandlung, Theresienstr. 43,
80333 München. T. (089) 52 13 40, 52 22 33. *102933*
Leissle, Peter, Daiserstr. 40, 81371 München.
T. (089) 77 55 78, 780 99 36. *102934*
Lentner, Marienpl. 8, 80331 München. T. (089) 22 79 67,
Fax 22 41 96. - Print / Engr - *102935*
List, Stephan, Barerstr 39/Rgb, 80799 München.
T. (089) 281960. - Engr - *102936*
Madison, Alexander, Lindwurmstr. 69, 80337 München.
T. (089) 533049. - ArtBk - *102937*
Mathes, Rudolf, Amalienstr. 63, 80799 München.
T. (089) 282547. - ArtBk - *102938*
Michalek, Eva, Lucille-Grahn-Str. 43, 81675 München.
T. (089) 47 70 36. *102939*
Mikorey, H., Theresienstr. 51, 80333 München.
T. (089) 52 53 22. *102940*
Müller, Eva, Metzstr. 2, 81667 München.
T. (089) 485696. - Print / ArtBk - *102941*
Müller, Josef, Daiserstr. 24, 81371 München.
T. (089) 721 16 11. *102942*
Müller, S. & D., Liesl-Karlstadt-Str. 19, 81476 München.
T. (089) 75 13 30. *102943*
Neithardt, Heinrich, Ainmillerstr. 35/3, 80801 München.
T. (089) 36 89 36. *102944*
Ohme, Peter, Oberföhringer Str 177, 81925 München.
T. (089) 92962473. *102945*
Paepcke, H. von, Görresstr. 17, 80798 München.
T. (089) 52 93 37. *102946*
Pfadenhauer, Karl, Hackenstr. 4, 80331 München.
T. (089) 263619. - Engr / Map - *102947*
Philographikon, Pfisterstr. 11, 80331 München.
T. (089) 225082, Fax 225791. - Engr / Map - *102948*
Pressler, Karl H., Dr., Römerstr 7, 80801 München.
T. (089) 341331/398430. - Print - *102949*
Rauscher, Franz, Maximilianspl 20, 80331
München. *102950*
Rietzschel & Ruß, Daiserstr. 24, 81371 München.
T. (089) 721 16 11. *102951*
Robertson, Michael, Wolfratshauser Str. 278, 81479
München. T. (089) 791 79 91. - ArtBk - *102952*
Rosenthal-Dürr, Dr. Arthur, Sachsenkamstr. 26, 81369
München. T. (089) 760 67 87. - Map - *102953*
Sapunaru, A., Heerstr. 12, 81247 München.
T. (089) 811 22 50. - Engr / Map - *102954*

Scheppler, G., & M. Müller, Giselastr 25, 80802 Mün-
chen. T. (089) 348174, Fax (089) 398214.
- Print - *102955*
Schild-Buch-Dienst, Federseestr. 1, 81249 München.
T. (089) 8641189, Fax 8632310. - Print / Engr - *102956*
Schmidt, Monika, Türkenstr 48, 80799 München.
T. (089) 284223, Fax (089) 2800044. - Print / Engr /
Map - *102957*
Schmitt, Schellingstr 15, 80798 München.
T. (089) 28 12 38. *102958*
Schneider-Henn, Galeriestr 2b, 80539 München.
T. (089) 297299, Fax 2904515. *102959*
Schott, Alexander, St.-Anna-Str 29, 80538 München.
T. (089) 297436. - Engr / Map - *102960*
Schwarz, G. W., Orleansstr. 63, 81667 München.
T. (089) 448 14 76. *102961*
Shakespeare & Co., Rindermarkt 10, 80331 München.
T. (089) 260 50 34. *102962*
Spatz, Otto, Schillerstr 51, 80336 München.
T. (089) 557696. *102963*
Steinbach, Michael, Demollstr 1, 80638 München.
T. (089) 1571691, Fax (089) 1577096. - Print /
ArtBk - *102964*
Taiping, Gabelsbergerstr. 17, 80333 München.
T. (089) 28 23 23. *102965*
Weishäupl, K.-H., Mitteisstr. 19, 80935 München.
T. (089) 313 24 01. *102966*
Werner, L., Residenzstr. 18, 80333 München.
T. (089) 22 57 70, 22 69 79, Fax 228 91 67.
- ArtBk - *102967*
Werner, L., Türkenstr. 80, 80333 München.
T. (089) 2805448. - ArtBk - *102968*
Wöhler, Thomas, Isabellastr 27, 80798 München.
T. (089) 2718285. - Print - *102969*
Wölfle, Robert, Amalienstr 65, 80799 München.
T. (089) 283626, Fax (089) 284308. - Print / Engr / Au-
togr / Map - *102970*
Zisska & R. Kistner, F., Unterer Anger 15, 80331 Mün-
chen. T. (089) 263855, Fax 269088. - Print /
Autogr - *102971*

Münster (Nordrhein-Westfalen)
Döme, Frauenstr. 49, 48143 Münster.
T. (0251) 45339. *102972*
Extrabuch, Spiekerhof, 48143 Münster. *102973*
Geisenheyner, Winfried, Roseneck 6, 48165 Münster.
T. (02501) 7884, Fax (02501) 13657. - Print / Autogr /
Map - *102974*
Hüning, Bernhard, Grevener Str. 343, 48159 Münster.
T. (0251) 21 56 40, 21 16 68. - Print - *102975*
Ketz, Hans-Jürgen, Scharnhorststr 92, 48151 Münster.
T. (0251) 521082, Fax (0251) 525851. - Print /
Engr - *102976*
Knirim, Ingrid, Kanalstr. 113, 48147 Münster.
T. (0251) 22682. *102977*
Medium Buchmarkt, Rosenstr. 5 – 6, 48143 Münster.
T. (0251) 46000, Fax 46745. *102978*
Modernes Antiquariat Comedia, Frauenstr. 9, 48143
Münster. T. (0251) 460 00, Fax 46745. *102979*
Modernes Antiquariat Medium, Rosenstr. 5-6, 48143
Münster. T. (0251) 460 00, Fax 46745. - Print /
ArtBk - *102980*
Poertgen-Herder, Salzstr. 56, 48143 Münster.
T. (0251) 49 01 40, Fax 490 14 63. - ArtBk - *102981*
Rosta, Aegidiistr. 12, 48143 Münster. T. (0251) 44926,
Fax 544 97. - ArtBk - *102982*
Ruck, Helmut, Staufenstr. 45, 48145 Münster.
T. (0251) 39 31 02. *102983*
Rüttger, Ortwin, Alter Fischmarkt 8, 48143 Münster.
T. (0251) 45307, Fax 45392. - Print / ArtBk /
Engr - *102984*
Stenderhoff, Theresia, Alter Fischmarkt 21, 48143 Mün-
ster. T. (0251) 44749, Fax (0251) 51526. - Print / Engr /
Map - *102985*

Murnau (Bayern)
Erdlen, Georg J., Obermarkt 5, 82418 Murnau.
T. (08841) 5109, Fax (08841) 90257. - Print - *102986*
Hannak, G., Schloßbergstr 4, 82418 Murnau.
T. (08841) 8224, Fax 8224. - ArtBk - *102987*

Naumburg (Sachsen-Anhalt)
Kockler, A., Steinweg 32, 06618 Naumburg.
T. (03445) 31 25. - Print - *102988*
Metzner's Buchhandlung, Wilhelm-Pieck-Pl. 14, 06618
Naumburg. *102989*

Nettetal (Nordrhein-Westfalen)
Matussek, Hans K., Marktstr 13, 41334 Nettetal.
T. (02153) 4525, Fax (02153) 13363. - Print - *102990*

Neuss (Nordrhein-Westfalen)
Hildebrandt, H., Tiberiusstr. 12, 41468 Neuss.
T. (02131) 12 01 49. *102991*
Kowallik, Brigitta, Klarissenstr 10, 41460 Neuss.
T. (02131) 24832, Fax (02131) 278114. *102992*
Symanczyk, Wolfgang, Hubertusweg 32, 41466 Neuss.
T. (02131) 46 43 23. - Print - *102993*

Neuwied (Rheinland-Pfalz)
Kehrein, Peter, Engerser Str. 39-40, 56564 Neuwied.
T. (02631) 9883-0, Fax 9883-69. - Print / ArtBk / Engr /
Map - *102994*

Nürnberg (Bayern)
Barth, Fürther Str. 89, 90429 Nürnberg.
T. (0911) 28 99 66. *102995*
Behringer, E. & W., Krelingstr. 47, 90408 Nürnberg.
T. (0911) 35 49 79. *102996*
Campe, Karolinenstr. 13, 90402 Nürnberg.
T. (0911) 99 20 80. - Print / ArtBk - *102997*
Edelmann, M., Kommarkt 8, im Maximum, 90402 Nürn-
berg. T. (0911) 99 20 60, Fax 992 06 60.
- ArtBk - *102998*
Eule, Mostgasse 4, 90402 Nürnberg.
T. (0911) 22 10 51. *102999*
Hartor, Heinz, Austl. 42, 90429 Nürnberg.
T. (0911) 26 21 56. *103000*
Hofner, Gerhard, Emmericher Str 21, 90411 Nürnberg.
T. (0911) 523234, Fax (0911) 525675. - Print /
ArtBk - *103001*
Jakob, Emil, Hefnersplatz 8, 90402 Nürnberg.
T. (0911) 22 47 18. *103002*
Kistner, E. & R., Weinmarkt 6, 90403 Nürnberg.
T. (0911) 203482, Fax (0911) 203484. - Print / Engr /
Map - *103003*
König, Bucher Str 17, 90419 Nürnberg.
T. (0911) 338182, Fax (0911) 337960. - Print /
Engr - *103004*
Korn & Berg, Hauptmarkt 9, 90403 Nürnberg.
T. (0911) 229 80, Fax 20 31 76. - ArtBk - *103005*
Kuhn, Breitscheidstr. 49, 90459 Nürnberg.
T. (0911) 44 71 60. *103006*
Paul, G., Allersberger Str. 6, 90461 Nürnberg.
T. (0911) 45 75 53. *103007*
Stein, J.A., Hauptmarkt 25, 90403 Nürnberg.
T. (0911) 22 63 85. - ArtBk / Engr / Map - *103008*
Wild, H., Obere Wörthstr. 22, 90403 Nürnberg.
T. (0911) 22 41 36. *103009*

Oberhausen, Rheinland (Rheinland-Pfalz)
Wiebus, Arndt, Steinbrinkstr 249, 46145 Oberhausen,
Rheinland. T. (0208) 668255. *103010*

Oberlahr (Rheinland-Pfalz)
Buschulte, H., Brucherstr. 7, 57641 Oberlahr.
T. (02685) 1286. *103011*

Oberried (Baden-Württemberg)
Bauch, H., Seppelhof, 79254 Oberried.
T. (07602) 514. *103012*

Obertshausen (Hessen)
Antiquariat Glas + Keramik, Laakirchener Str 60, 63179
Obertshausen. T. (06104) 490422. - Print - *103013*

Obing (Bayern)
Feurer, Reto, Dr., Wanningerstr. 7, 83119 Obing.
T. (08624) 16 04. - Print / ArtBk / Autogr - *103014*

Ockenheim (Rheinland-Pfalz)
Geib, Renate, Am St. Jakobsberg 33, 55437 Ockenheim.
T. (06725) 1704, Fax 3749. *103015*

Odenthal (Nordrhein-Westfalen)
Leisten, Günther, St. Engelbert-Str 24, 51519 Odenthal.
T. (02202) 78540. - Print / Engr / Autogr / Map - *103016*

Oelde (Nordrhein-Westfalen)
Wilsmann, Manfred, Zur Dicken Linde 70, 59302 Oelde.
T. (02522) 1386. - Print / ArtBk / Engr / Autogr /
Map - *103017*

Offenbach (Hessen)
Ott, W., Frankfurter Str. 56, 63067 Offenbach.
T. (069) 81 63 79. *103018*

Olching (Bayern)
Benner, L., Prof.-Schmid-Str. 25, 82140 Olching.
T. (08142) 3251. *103019*

Oldenburg, Oldenburg (Schleswig-Holstein)
Ebel, Rudolf, 26121 Oldenburg, Oldenburg.
T. (0441) 147 92. *103020*
Heinze, Walter, Lindenallee 14, 26122 Oldenburg, Ol-
denburg. T. (0441) 77521. - Print - *103021*
Schroeder's Sammler Bücher, 26121 Oldenburg, Olden-
burg. T. (0441) 850 56, Fax 83606. - ArtBk - *103022*
Völker, Ernst, Lange Str. 45, 26122 Oldenburg, Olden-
burg. T. (0441) 264 06. - Engr / Map - *103023*

Olpe (Nordrhein-Westfalen)
Schneider, Gerhard, Dr., Rhode-Goldsiepen 12, 57462
Olpe. T. (02761) 61215, Fax (02761) 61215. *103024*

Osnabrück (Niedersachsen)
Bojara & Kellinghaus, Katharinenstr. 26, 49078 Osna-
brück. T. (0541) 462 40. *103025*
Harlinghausen, Klaus, Arndtstr 5, 49078 Osnabrück.
I. (0541) 433929. - Engr - *103026*
Kraemer & Hansen, Laischaftsstr 17, 49080 Osnabrück.
T. (0541) 88372, Fax (0541) 801622. - Print - *103027*
Kuballe, Reinhard, Sutthauser Str 19, 49074 Osnabrück.
T. (0541) 804387. - Print / Engr / Map - *103028*
Liebmann, Konrad, Dr., Lortzingstr. 1, 49074 Osnabrück.
T. (0541) 261 76. *103029*
Wenner, H.Th., Heger Str 2-3, 49074 Osnabrück.
T. (0541) 3310366, Fax (0541) 201113. - Print / Engr /
Map - *103030*
Zeller, Otto, Jahnstr. 15, 49080 Osnabrück.
T. (0541) 412 17. *103031*

Osterode am Harz (Sachsen-Anhalt)
Elchlepp, Alice, Schillerstr 14a, 37520 Osterode am
Harz. T. (05522) 4660. - Engr / Map - *103033*

Paderborn (Nordrhein-Westfalen)
Buchhandlung am Dom, Markt 10, 33098
Paderborn. *103034*
Harlingshausen, Fritz, Giersstr. 29, 33098 Paderborn.
T. (05251) 2 34 37. - Print / Engr - *103035*
Janssen, Grube 9, 33098 Paderborn. T. (05251) 25444.
- Engr / Map - *103036*

Passau (Bayern)
Buch- und Kunstantiquariat am Domplatz, Dompl.,
94032 Passau. T. (0851) 21 41. - Print / Engr /
Map - *103037*

Pattensen (Niedersachsen)
Wellm, Horst, Bennigser Weg 1, 30982 Pattensen.
T. (05101) 13361. - Print - *103038*

Peine (Niedersachsen)
Gillmeister, Ferdinand, Breite Str. 8, 31224 Peine.
T. (05171) 170 26-27. - ArtBk / Engr - *103039*

Pfaffenhofen an der Ilm (Bayern)
Pennarz, Rainer, Gundamsried, Alte Schule, 85276 Pfaf-
fenhofen an der Ilm. T. (08441) 72952,
Fax (08441) 83875. - Engr / Map - *103040*

Pforzheim (Baden-Württemberg)
Brechsprecher, Bodo, Östl Karl-Friedr-Str. 11, 75175
Pforzheim. *103041*
Fischer, Rudolf, Blumenheckstr. 25, 75177 Pforzheim.
T. (07231) 515 47. *103042*
Kiefer, Peter, Kaiser-Friedrich-Str. 10, 75172 Pforzheim.
T. (07231) 92320, Fax 923216. *103043*

Plauen (Sachsen)
Trommer, Jeannette, Dr., Marktstr. 15, 08523
Plauen. *103044*
Vogtlandverlag, Nobelstr. 18, 08523 Plauen. *103045*

Potsdam (Brandenburg)
Potsdamer Antiquariat, Friedrich-Ebert-Str. 27-28,
14467 Potsdam. T. (0331) 218 75, Fax 218 75.
- ArtBk - *103046*

Quedlinburg (Sachsen-Anhalt)
Gebede's Buchhandlung, Pölkenstr. 3, 06484
Quedlinburg. *103047*

Quickborn, Kreis Pinneberg (Schleswig-Holstein)
Tessin, Heinz, Harksheider Weg 138, 25451 Quickborn,
Kreis Pinneberg. T. (04106) 2453, Fax 2453. - Print /
Engr / Autogr - *103048*

Rauenberg (Baden-Württemberg)
Siegle, Franz, Erlenweg 6, 69231 Rauenberg.
T. (06222) 63082, Fax (06222) 60364. - Print - *103049*

Ravensburg (Baden-Württemberg)
Blank, Rüdiger, Gespinstmarkt 17, 88212 Ravensburg.
T. (0751) 266 76. - Print - *103050*
Genth, H., Gespinstmarkt 17, 88212 Ravensburg.
T. (0751) 266 76. - Print / Engr - *103051*
Rieser, Rudolf, Eichelstr. 8, 88212 Ravensburg.
T. (0751) 2 27 61. - Print / Engr - *103052*
Schmitt, A.F., Schulgasse 6, 88214 Ravensburg.
T. (0751) 329 83. *103053*

Recklinghausen (Nordrhein-Westfalen)
Streubel, Paul, Kunibertistr. 30, 45657 Recklinghausen.
T. (02361) 24 361. - Engr / Map - *103054*

Rednitzhembach (Bayern)
König, M., Am Rothbuck 6a, 91126 Rednitzhembach.
T. (09122) 78440. *103055*

Regensburg (Bayern)
Berg, R., Wahlenstr. 6, 93047 Regensburg.
T. (0941) 52229. *103056*
Hackel-Bleibtreu, Christine, Wöhrdstr 7, 93059 Regens-
burg. T. (0941) 560674, Fax (0941) 57199. - Print /
ArtBk / Engr - *103057*
Wagner, H.-J., Hackengäßchen 6, 93047 Regensburg.
T. (0941) 536 69. - Print - *103058*

Reichenbach (Vogtland) (Sachsen)
Vogtländische Buchhandlung, Zenkergasse 2, 08468
Reichenbach (Vogtland). *103059*

Reinbek (Schleswig-Holstein)
Fotobuch-Versandantiquariat punctum, Klosterbergenstr.
34, 21465 Reinbek. T. (040) 722 26 26.
- Print - *103060*

Remshalden (Baden-Württemberg)
A und B, Antiquitäten und Bücher, Haus der Kunst, Ka-
nalstr. 10, 73630 Remshalden. T. (07181) 749 71.
- Print - *103061*

Rennerod (Rheinland-Pfalz)
Westerwald-Antiquariat, Hauptstr. 71, 56477 Rennerod.
T. (02664) 227, Fax 300850. - Print / ArtBk / Engr / Au-
togr / Map - *103062*

Reutlingen (Baden-Württemberg)
Heck, Thomas, Kaiserstr 64, 72764 Reutlingen.
T. (07121) 370911, Fax 87408. *103063*
Knödler, Karl, Katharinenstr 8-10, 72764 Reutlingen.
T. (07121) 38770, Fax 387777. - ArtBk - *103064*

Rielasingen-Worblingen (Baden-Württemberg)
Klock, E., Leutenweg 23, 78239 Rielasingen-
Worblingen. *103065*

Rochlitz (Sachsen)
Klis'sche Buchhandlung, Burgstr. 1, 09306 Rochlitz.
T. (03737) 2877. *103066*

Rodgau (Hessen)
Niesen, Hubert, Postfach 300447, 63091 Rodgau.
T. (06106) 73164, Fax (06106) 79667. - Print / ArtBk /
Autogr -   *103067*

Rödermark (Hessen)
Grass, A., Im Taubhaus 11, 63322 Rödermark.   *103068*

Rosenheim (Bayern)
Antiquariat im Mail Keller, Schmettererstr. 20, 83022
Rosenheim. T. (08031) 12817, Fax 38 02 56.
- Print -   *103069*

Rostock (Mecklenburg-Vorpommern)
Norddeutsches Antiquariat, Kröpeliner Str. 73, 18055
Rostock. T. (0381) 34052.   *103070*

Rothenburg ob der Tauber (Bayern)
Geissendörfer, Ernst, Obere Schmiedgasse 1, 91541 Ro-
thenburg ob der Tauber. T. (09861) 2005, Fax 2009.
- Engr / Map -   *103071*

Rotthalmünster (Bayern)
Tenschert, Heribert, Kirchpl 14-15, 94094 Rotthalmün-
ster. T. (08533) 1881/83, Fax 2129. - Print /
Autogr -   *103072*

Rottweil (Baden-Württemberg)
Traxler, H., Tuttlinger Str. 17-19, 78628 Rottweil.
T. (0741) 235 28.   *103073*

Saarbrücken (Saarland)
Akademische Buchandlung, Kaiserstr. 2a, 66111 Saar-
brücken. - Autogr -   *103074*
Barbian, M., Türkenstr. 7a, 66111 Saarbrücken.
T. (0681) 31877, Fax 31877. - Print -   *103075*
Buchladen, Försterstr. 14, 66111 Saarbrücken.
T. (0681) 31171, Fax 33814. - ArtBk -   *103076*
Comic Antiquariat, Breite Str. 9, 66115 Saarbrücken.
T. (0681) 49 83 81.   *103077*
Görres-Buchhandlung GmbH, Kaiserstr. 16 b.18, 66111
Saarbrücken. T. (0681) 3 20 37. - Engr -   *103078*
Jura, Talstr. 58, 66119 Saarbrücken.
T. (0681) 584 61 16, 584 61 94.   *103079*
Kiefer, H. & D., Berliner Promenade 12, 66111 Saarbrük-
ken. T. (0681) 390 43 33.   *103080*
Köhl, Peter H., St. Johanner Markt 20, 66111 Saarbrük-
ken. T. (0681) 33242, Fax (0681) 33242. - Print / Engr /
Map -   *103081*
Krämer, Peter, Beethovenstr., 66111
Saarbrücken.   *103082*
Raueiser, H., Viktoriastr. 3, 66111 Saarbrücken.
T. (0681) 31955, Fax 31895. - Print -   *103083*

Saarlouis (Saarland)
Schwarwarth, H., Dr., Silberherz-Str. 17, 66740 Saarlouis. T. (06831) 21 14.   *103084*

Sande (Niedersachsen)
Wolff, Wilfried, Sanderrahmer Str. 33a, 26452 Sande.
T. (04422) 4000, Fax 4000. - Print / Engr /
Map -   *103085*

Sangerhausen (Sachsen-Anhalt)
Sankt-Michael-Buchhandlung, Kylische Str. 52, 06526
Sangerhausen.   *103086*

Sankt Ingbert (Saarland)
St. Ingberter Antiquariat, Ensheimer Str 34, 66386 Sankt
Ingbert.   *103087*

Sankt Peter (Baden-Württemberg)
Schiller, Ludwig, Am Birkenrain 28, 79271 Sankt Peter.
T. (07660) 308, Fax (07660) 1762. - Print -   *103114*

Sankt Wendel (Saarland)
Hackhofer, Barbara & Peter, Am Schlaufenglan 75,
66606 Sankt Wendel. T. (06851) 706 90. - Print /
Engr -   *103115*

**Sasbach, Kaiserstuhl (Baden-Württem-
berg)**
Sonntag, A., Dorfstr. 16, 79361 Sasbach, Kaiserstuhl.
T. (07662) 14 53. - Engr / Map -   *103088*

Antiquariat Heribert Tenschert

Kirchplatz 14–15
D-94094 Rotthalmünster
Telefon: (0 85 33) 18 81-18 83 · Telefax: (0 85 33) 21 29

Mittelalterliche Manuskripte
Schöne und seltene Bücher

Schleswig (Schleswig-Holstein)
Liesegang, Karl, Stadtweg 8, 24837 Schleswig.
T. (04621) 2 31 18. - Print / Engr / Map -   *103089*

Schmitten (Hessen)
Auvermann, Dominik, Hauptstr 86, 61389 Schmitten.
T. (06082) 930044, Fax (06082) 930045.   *103090*

Schneverdingen (Niedersachsen)
Hartung, L., Junkershof, 29640 Schneverdingen.
T. (05193) 6043.   *103091*
Uranus Buchhandlung, Lärchenhof, 29640 Schneverdin-
gen. T. (05193) 1829, Fax 50754. - ArtBk -   *103092*

Schönberg (Schleswig-Holstein)
Haschtmann, Werner, Alte Apotheke, 24217
Schönberg.   *103093*

Schopfheim (Baden-Württemberg)
Donald Cuntz, Im Grund 12, 79650 Schopfheim.   *103094*

Schriesheim (Baden-Württemberg)
Albrecht, Frank, Panoramastr 4, 69198 Schriesheim.
T. (06203) 65713. - Print / Autogr -   *103095*

**Schwäbisch Gmünd (Baden-Württem-
berg)**
Lang, Fritz, Karl-Lüllig-Str 56, 73527 Schwäbisch
Gmünd. T. (07117) 71584. - Print -   *103096*
Schmidt, Wolfgang, Wilhelmstr. 38, 73525 Schwäbisch
Gmünd. T. (07171) 64528.   *103097*

Schwäbisch Hall (Baden-Württemberg)
Zeughaus Buchshop, Gelbinger Gasse 87, 74523
Schwäbisch Hall. T. (0791) 83 84. - ArtBk -   *103098*

Schwalmstadt (Hessen)
Antiquariat der Schwalm, Industriestr. 1a, 34613
Schwalmstadt. T. (06691) 2988, Fax 24224. - Engr /
Autogr -   *103099*

Schweinfurt (Bayern)
Hansen, Julius, Zehntstr. 2, 97421 Schweinfurt.
T. (09721) 180 47.   *103100*
Rückert-Buchhandlung, Keßlergasse 9, 97421 Schwein-
furt. T. (09721) 18063, Fax 28313. - Map -   *103101*
Seitz, Ingo, Merckstr. 15, 97421 Schweinfurt.
T. (09721) 282 46.   *103102*

Schwerin (Mecklenburg-Vorpommern)
Svensdotter, H., Buschstr. 14, 19053 Schwerin.
T. (0385) 86 47 61.   *103103*

Selters (Hessen)
Beckers, Hinterstr. 11, 65618 Selters.
T. (06483) 76 26.   *103104*

Siegburg (Nordrhein-Westfalen)
Buch- und Kunsthandlung der Benediktinerabtei St. Mi-
chael, Bergstr. 26, 53721 Siegburg.
T. (02241) 12 91 80, Fax 12 91 32. - ArtBk -   *103105*

Siegen (Nordrhein-Westfalen)
Reibetanz, H., Sandstr 129, 57072 Siegen.
T. (0271) 42805.   *103106*

Sindelfingen (Baden-Württemberg)
Bissinger, H., Weberstr. 18, 71063 Sindelfingen.
T. (07031) 80 49 81.   *103107*
Strehler, Brigitte, Hermelinweg 7, 71063 Sindelfingen.
T. (07031) 801043, Fax (07031) 806906.   *103108*

Sinsheim (Baden-Württemberg)
Doll, Julius, Bahnhofstr 17, 74889 Sinsheim.
T. (07261) 2322. - ArtBk -   *103109*

Sinzig (Rheinland-Pfalz)
Haselhoff, B., Hunsrückstr 15, 53489 Sinzig.
T. (02642) 41712. - ArtBk / Autogr -   *103110*

Solingen (Nordrhein-Westfalen)
Kiene, H., Katharinenstr. 19, 42653 Solingen.
T. (0212) 59 19 46, Fax 59 41 99. - Print /
ArtBk -   *103111*

Speyer (Rheinland-Pfalz)
Dusch, Peter, Gutenbergstr. 19, 67346 Speyer.
T. (06232) 745 72. - Print / ArtBk -   *103112*
Versandbuchhandlung für handsignierte Bücher, Am
Renngraben 2, 67346 Speyer.
T. (06232) 67 68.   *103113*

Stadtoldendorf (Niedersachsen)
Hinrichsen, Ursula, Ziegeleistr, 37627 Stadtoldendorf.
T. (05532) 2021, Fax (05532) 1290.   *103116*

Staffelstein (Bayern)
Möhrstedt, U. & G., Angerstr. 50, 96231 Staffelstein.
T. (09573) 65 04.   *103117*

Straubing (Bayern)
Stöcker, E., Ludwigspl., 94315 Straubing.
T. (09421) 101 20.   *103118*
Völkl, I., Mühlweg 34, 94315 Straubing.
T. (09421) 812 30. - Print -   *103119*

Stuttgart (Baden-Württemberg)
Alte Stiche, Eberhardstr. 3, 70173 Stuttgart.
T. (0711) 24 00 39.   *103120*
AS-Alte Stiche, Eberhardstr. 3, 70173 Stuttgart.
T. (0711) 24 00 39. - Print -   *103121*
Barth, Elisabeth, Konradstr. 10, 70327 Stuttgart. *103122*
Bermoser, L., Kyffhäuserstr. 81, 70469 Stuttgart.
T. (0711) 889 19 77.   *103123*
Bermoser, L., Kyffhäuserstr. 81, 70469 Stuttgart.
T. (0711) 889 19 77.   *103124*
Blank, Herbert, Melonenstr 54, 70619 Stuttgart.
T. (0711) 472130, Fax (0711) 478408. - Print /
Autogr -   *103125*
Braun, Bernd, Wagnerstr. 47, 70182 Stuttgart.
T. (0711) 236 97 53. - Print -   *103126*
Breitsprecher, Manfred, Paulinenstr. 44, 70178 Stutt-
gart. T. (0711) 61 73 63.   *103127*
Drüner, Ulrich, Dr., Ameisenbergstr 65, 70188 Stuttgart.
T. (0711) 486165, Fax (0711) 4800408. - Print / Engr /
Autogr -   *103128*
Engel & Co., Alexanderstr 11, 70184 Stuttgart.
T. (0711) 240413, Fax (0711) 2360021.
- Print -   *103129*
Fischer, Torstr. 23, 70173 Stuttgart. T. (0711) 24 41 63,
Fax 26 45 62. - Engr / Map -   *103130*
Franz, H., Jakobstr. 8, 70182 Stuttgart.
T. (0711) 24 52 08.   *103131*
Heinzelmann & Hermann, Alexanderstr. 157, 70180
Stuttgart. T. (0711) 640 65 31.   *103132*
Held, Reuchlinstr. 10, 70178 Stuttgart.
T. (0711) 62 60 32.   *103133*
Hohmann, Wilhelm, Rotenwaldstr. 41, 70197 Stuttgart.
T. (0711) 657 23 28, Fax 657 29 14. - Print -   *103134*
Julius, Charlottenstr. 12, 70182 Stuttgart.
T. (0711) 24 07 09.   *103135*

Lindemanns, H., Nadlerstr. 10, 70173 Stuttgart.
T. (0711) 23 34 99, Fax 236 96 72. *103136*
Lörcher, Dorrit, Heubergstr 42, 70188 Stuttgart. *103137*
Müller & Gräff, Calwer Str 54, 70173 Stuttgart.
T. (0711) 294174, Fax (0711) 2268280. - Print / Engr /
Map - *103138*
Neidhardt, Fritz, Fleckenweinberg 12, 70192 Stuttgart.
T. (0711) 8567173, Fax (0711) 8178870. - Print /
Engr - *103139*
Röth, L.G., Pfarrstr 21, 70182 Stuttgart.
T. (0711) 241852/241873,
Fax (0711) 2360310. *103140*
Steinkopf, J.F., Marienstr 3, 70178 Stuttgart.
T. (0711) 2264021, Fax (0711) 2264023. *103141*
Stuttgarter Antiquariat, Rathenaustr 21, 70191 Stuttgart.
T. (0711) 2568402, Fax (0711) 2576174.
- Print - *103142*
Utzt, Inge, Rippoldsauer Str 9, 70372 Stuttgart.
T. (0711) 562949. - Print - *103143*
Valentien, Freerk C., Dr., Königstr 28, 70173 Stuttgart.
T. (0711) 221625, Fax (0711) 297918. - ArtBk - *103144*
Voerster, J., Relenbergstr 20, 70174 Stuttgart.
T. (0711) 297186. - Print / Autogr - *103145*
Weissert, Nikolaus, Ahornstr 31, 70597 Stuttgart.
T. (0711) 766282, Fax (0711) 7657454. - Print /
ArtBk - *103146*
Wertpapier-Antiquariat, Olgastr. 125, 70180 Stuttgart.
T. (0711) 60 60 69. *103147*
Witthoeft, Traubenstr. 51, 70176 Stuttgart. - ArtBk /
Engr - *103148*

Sylt-Ost (Schleswig-Holstein)
Cicero Presse, Morsum, 25980 Sylt-Ost.
T. (04651) 890305, Fax 890885. - Print - *103149*

Traunstein (Bayern)
Stifel, G.H., 83278 Traunstein. *103150*

Trier (Rheinland-Pfalz)
Antiquariat am Dom, Sternstr. 4, 54290 Trier.
T. (0651) 48425, Fax 45974. - Print / ArtBk / Engr /
Map - *103151*
Berens, Palaststr. 3, 54290 Trier.
I. (0651) 767 44. *103152*
Kottmeier, H.J., Bitburger Str. 2, 54294 Trier.
T. (0651) 83300, Fax 84622. - Print / Engr / Autogr /
Map - *103153*

Tübingen (Baden-Württemberg)
Gastl, Neue Str. 1, 72070 Tübingen. T. (07071) 51641,
Fax 27613. - ArtBk - *103154*
Heck, Hafengasse 10, 72070 Tübingen.
T. (07071) 26306, Fax 87408. *103155*
Heckenhauer, J.J., Holzmarkt 5, 72070 Tübingen.
T. (07071) 23018, (07572) 5807, Fax (07572) 5807.
- Print / Engr / Map - *103156*
Noûs-Verlag, Eichhalde 19, 72074 Tübingen.
T. (07071) 87408, Fax 87408. - Print / ArtBk - *103157*
Osiandersche Buchhandlung, Wilhelmstr. 12, 72074 Tü-
bingen. T. (07071) 92010, Fax (07071) 920192.
- ArtBk - *103158*
Schwarz, K.- H., Münzgasse 5, 72070 Tübingen.
T. (07071) 23100. - Engr - *103159*
Seuffer, Fritz, Neue Str. 4, 72070 Tübingen.
T. (07071) 225 50. - Engr / Map - *103160*
Szakacs, A. & A. Brenner, Bachgasse 13, 72070 Tübin-
gen. T. (07071) 237 35. *103161*
Tübinger Antiquariat, Wilhelmstr. 3, 72074 Tübingen.
T. (07071) 514 27. - Print - *103162*

Tutzing (Bayern)
Held, Gebhard, Hauptstr 54, 82327 Tutzing.
- Print - *103163*
Schneider, Hans, Dr., Mozartstr 6, 82327 Tutzing.
T. (08158) 3050, Fax (08158) 7636. - Print / Engr /
Autogr - *103164*

Überlingen (Baden-Württemberg)
Mathias, Gotthold B., Münsterstr 10, 88662 Überlingen.
T. (07551) 63413. - Print / Engr / Map - *103165*

Ulm (Baden-Württemberg)
Braun, Georg, Sterngasse 15, 89073 Ulm.
T. (0731) 67139. *103166*

Eichhorn, Manfred, Herrenkellergasse 10, 89073 Ulm.
T. (0731) 64610. - ArtBk - *103167*
Kerler, Heinrich, Platzgasse 26, 89073 Ulm.
T. (0731) 63978. - Print - *103168*

Varel (Niedersachsen)
Lehmann & Co, Osterstr 8, 26316 Varel.
T. (04451) 83151, Fax (04451) 82961. - Print /
ArtBk - *103169*

Vechta (Niedersachsen)
Korth, Werner, Grosse Str. 95, 49377 Vechta.
T. (04441) 29 28. *103170*

Velbert (Nordrhein-Westfalen)
Fuchs, Günter, Zum Hardenberger Schloß 1-3, 42553
Velbert. T. (02124) 406 12. - ArtBk / Autogr - *103171*

Verl (Nordrhein-Westfalen)
Dingwerth, Eichendorffstr 77, 33415 Verl.
T. (05246) 4102, Fax 8483. *103172*

Vettweiß (Nordrhein-Westfalen)
Reimersdahl, Dieter van, Amselweg 16, 52391 Vettweiß.
T. (02424) 2685, Fax (02424) 7590. *103173*

Viersen (Nordrhein-Westfalen)
Jansen, H., Ummerstr. 4, 41748 Viersen.
T. (02162) 206 05. *103174*

Villingen-Schwenningen (Baden-Würt-
temberg)
Flaig, W., Rosengasse 20, 78050 Villingen-Schwenningen. - Print / ArtBk - *103175*

Villmar (Hessen)
Müller, Karlheinz, Lahnstr. 14, 65606 Villmar.
T. (06474) 80 38/39, Fax 1337. - Print - *103176*

Walluf (Hessen)
Sändig, Elmar, Postfach 007, 65392 Walluf.
T. (06123) 71527. - Print / Engr / Autogr / Map - *103177*

Waltrop (Nordrhein-Westfalen)
Spenner, H., Stratmannsweg 10, 45731 Waltrop.
T. (02309) 755 72. *103178*

Weidenthal (Rheinland-Pfalz)
Patzer, Rudolf, Mainzer Berg 23, 67475 Weidenthal.
T. (06329) 362, Fax (06329) 362. - Print - *103179*

Weilburg (Hessen)
Hild, Bernd Uwe, Kirschweg 4, 35781 Weilburg. *103180*

Weimar (Thüringen)
Bernau, Kirsten, Schillerstr. 10, 99423 Weimar. *103181*
Hoffmann's Buch & Kunsthandlung, Chr. Gräf, gegenüber
dem Schillerhaus, 99423 Weimar.
T. (03643) 3921. *103182*
Thelemanns Buch- und Kunsthandlg., Rittergasse 21,
99423 Weimar. *103183*

Weinheim (Baden-Württemberg)
Weise, H.-D., Sommergasse 137, 69469 Weinheim.
T. (06201) 58773. - Print - *103184*

Wernigerode (Sachsen-Anhalt)
Jüttner, Westernstr. 10, 38855 Wernigerode.
T. (03943) 33050, Fax 32469. - Print / ArtBk / Engr /
Map - *103185*

Wiesbaden (Hessen)
Czenkusch, Eva, Museumsreplikate, Beethovenstr. 14,
65189 Wiesbaden. T. (0611) 30 09 94,
30 69 33. *103186*
Goetz, Hans J. von, Rheinstr. 101, 65185 Wiesbaden.
T. (0611) 37 23 58. - Print - *103187*
Harrassowitz, Otto, Taunusstr 5, 65183 Wiesbaden.
T. (0611) 5300, Fax (0611) 530560. - Print - *103188*
Köhler, Pamela, Nerostr. 10, 65183 Wiesbaden.
T. (0611) 52 85 24. - Print / Engr - *103189*
Lang, Heinrich. 104, 60311 Wiesbaden.
T. (0611) 37 69 31, Fax 300850. - Print / ArtBk / Engr /
Autogr / Map - *103190*
Mohr, Heinz, Kleine Weinbergstr. 1, 65193 Wiesbaden.
T. (0611) 52 12 12. *103191*

Panorama, Möhringstr. 6a, 65187 Wiesbaden.
T. (0611) 84 40 21, Fax 80 79 84. - Print - *103192*
Rinnelt, C., Taunusstr 36, 65183 Wiesbaden.
T. (0611) 523307, Fax (0611) 9590951. - Print / ArtBk /
Engr / Autogr / Map - *103193*
Sändig, Martin, Dr., Sonnenberger Str 64a, 65193 Wies-
baden. T. (0611) 521029, Fax (0611) 527913.
- Print - *103194*
Schwaedt, Arthur, Rheinstr. 43, 65185 Wiesbaden.
T. (0611) 30 14 89. - Map - *103195*
Simon, Taunusstr. 34, 65183 Wiesbaden.
T. (0611) 59 92 10, Fax 52 89 01. - Print / ArtBk / Engr /
Autogr - *103196*
Suppes WWA, Am Schloßpark 121, 65203 Wiesbaden.
T. (0611) 960 08 30, Fax 69 23 09. - Print - *103197*
VMA, Langgasse 35, 65183 Wiesbaden.
T. (0611) 390 81. *103198*

Wilhelmsfeld (Baden-Württemberg)
Stephan, W., Richard-Wagner-Str. 16c, 69259 Wilhelms-
feld. T. (06220) 89 16. *103199*

Witten (Nordrhein-Westfalen)
Ullrich, W. & R., Ruhrstr. 81, 58452 Witten.
T. (02302) 880 56. *103200*

Würzburg (Bayern)
Arena-Buchhandlung, Domstr. 26, 97070 Würzburg.
T. (0931) 503 66. - ArtBk - *103201*
Becker, Ulrich, Am Rubenland 13, 97084 Würzburg.
T. (0931) 62251. - Print / Engr / Map - *103202*
Bub, Oberthürstr 9, 97070 Würzburg. T. (0931) 12867,
Fax (0931) 571417. - Engr - *103203*
Meixner, A., Spessartstr. 27a, 97082 Würzburg.
T. (0931) 422 49. - Autogr - *103204*
Müller, Franz X., Kardinal-Faulhaber-Platz 2, 97070
Würzburg. T. (0931) 526 24. *103205*
Schland, Josef, Eichhornstr. 23, 97070 Würzburg.
T. (0931) 525 23. - ArtBk - *103206*
Schöneborn, Klaus, Arndtstr. 22, 97072 Würzburg.
T. (0931) 87355. - Print / ArtBk - *103207*

Wunsiedel (Bayern)
Böhringer, Heinrich, Marktpl. 2, 95632 Wunsiedel.
T. (09232) 21 17, Fax 1774. - Print / ArtBk / Engr / Au-
togr / Map - *103208*

Wunstorf (Niedersachsen)
Anspach, Angelika, Neustädter Str. 21, 31515
Wunstorf. *103209*
Scholl, Winfried, Heinrichstr 2, 31515 Wunstorf.
T. (05031) 74757, Fax (05031) 909013.
- Print - *103210*

Wuppertal (Nordrhein-Westfalen)
Burchard, Friedrich, Sonnborner Str 144, 42327 Wup-
pertal. T. (0202) 740337, 742696, Fax (0202) 742185.
- Print / Engr - *103211*
Elberfelder Bücherkiste, Kleine Klotzbahn 2, 42105
Wuppertal. T. (0202) 44 94 91. *103212*
Ex Libris, Sonnborner Str. 93, 42327 Wuppertal.
T. (0202) 74 53 76. *103213*
Köndgen, Heinrich, Werth 75, 42275 Wuppertal.
T. (0202) 59 10 46. - Print - *103214*
Mackensen, Klaus von, Friedrich-Ebert-Str. 10, 42103
Wuppertal. T. (0202) 30 40 01. - ArtBk - *103215*
Müller, Clemens, Kapellenweg 59, 42285 Wuppertal.
T. (0202) 598911. - Print - *103216*
Offermann & Schmitz, Wittelsbacherstr 31, 42287 Wup-
pertal. T. (0202) 555873, Fax (0202) 572267. *103217*
Schmidt & Green, Herbringhausen 10, 42399 Wuppertal.
T. (0202) 612061, Fax 613740. - Print /
Autogr - *103218*

Xanten (Nordrhein-Westfalen)
Antiquariat am Mitteltor, Klever Str.6, 46509 Xanten.
T. (02801) 17 04. - Engr - *103219*

Zapfendorf (Bayern)
Gunzelmann, Gartenstr. 16, 96199 Zapfendorf. *103220*

Zweibrücken (Rheinland-Pfalz)
Nickel, Heinz, Oselbachstr 72, 66482 Zweibrücken.
T. (06332) 16384. *103221*

Zwickau (Sachsen)

Gutenberg Buchhandlung OHG Kozok & Unger, Galerie &
Buch „Peter Breuer", Hauptstr. 22, 08056 Zwickau.
T. (0375) 25992, Fax (0375) 25429. - ArtBk -   *103222*

Marx Nachf. E. Walter, Dr.-Friedrichs-Ring 23, 08056
Zwickau. T. (0375) 22131. - Print / ArtBk -   *103223*

Greece

Athinai

Dimakarakos, Evagelos, Od. Normanou 6, 105 55 Athinai. T. (01) 324 52 41. - Print / Engr / Map -   *103224*

Kallitsas, P.N., University Books, 25, Solonos St., 106 71
Athinai. T. (01) 629-556. - ArtBk -   *103225*

Kauffmann, 28 Rue du Stade, 105 59 Athinai.
T. (01) 62 42 52. - Engr / Map -   *103226*

Koutsikos, Georgios, Salongou 9, 106 78 Athinai.
T. (01) 36 10 379.   *103227*

Le Bibliophile, 14 Massalias St., 106 80 Athinai.
T. (01) 361 4531. - Map -   *103228*

Les Amis du Livre, 9 Od. Valaoritou, 10671 Athinai.
T. (01) 615 562. - Print / Map -   *103229*

Retsas, Dimitris, Astingos 6A, 105 55 Athinai.
T. (01) 32 51 405. - Print / Map -   *103230*

Stravridis, Stravros, Panaghitsas 18, 145 62 Athinai.
T. (01) 801 70 79. - Print / Engr -   *103231*

Tsanetis, Charl., Astingos 16, 105 55 Athinai.
T. (01) 32 42 053.   *103232*

Guadeloupe

Pointe-à-Pitre

A la Recherche du Passé, Centre Commercial La Marina,
97110 Pointe-à-Pitre. T. (590) 908415,
Fax (590) 909739. - Print -   *103233*

Guatemala

Guatemala City

Tuncho Granados Libreria Gustemala, 10 Calle 6 b.56
Zona 1, Guatemala City Apartado Postal 13. T. 2 11 81,
2 47 36, 2 72 69.   *103234*

Hong Kong

Hong Kong

Coleman, Teresa, 37 Wyndham St., Ground Fl., Hong
Kong. T. 526 2450, Fax 845 0793. - Engr /
Map -   *103235*

Keng Seng, Loon San Bldg. Rm. 103, 140-142 Connaught Rd., Hong Kong. T. 45 50 08.   *103236*

Swindon Book Co., 13 b.15 Lock Rd., Hong Kong.
- Print -   *103237*

Tai Yip, 30A Stanley St., Hong Kong. T. 5-
250496.   *103238*

Hungary

Budapest

Kultura, Fö u. 11, Budapest. T. (01) 15 94 50.   *103239*

Iceland

Reykjavik

Benediktsson, Sigurdur, Hafnarstraeti 11, P.O.Box 154,
Reykjavik. - Print -   *103240*

Kristjonsson, Bragi, Vatnsstigur 4, Box 775, 121 Reykjavik. T. (91) 12 97 20.   *103241*

India

Ahmedabad (Gujarat)

New Order Book Company, Ellisbridge, Ahmedabad,
380006. T. 79 065, 44 54 09. - Print -   *103242*

Bombay (Maharashtra)

Lalvani, 210 Dr Dadabhoy Naoroji Rd, Bombay, 400001.
T. (022) 2046811/12.   *103243*

Calcutta (West Bengal)

Newman & Co., 3 Old Court House St., Calcutta, 70001.
T. 23-9436. - Print -   *103244*

Oxford Book and Stationery Company, 17 Park St, Calcutta. T. 23 60 87.   *103245*

New Delhi

Oxford Book & Stationery, Scindia House, New Delhi.
T. (011) 47388.   *103246*

Indonesia

Jakarta

Java Books, 15 Cempaka Putih Barat 17, P.O. Box 55
JKCP, Jakarta. T. 420 92 79. - Print -   *103247*

Iraq

Baghdad

Hasso, N.A. & Co., Hasso Building, Baghdad.
- Print -   *103248*

Ireland

Blackrock (Co. Dublin)

Carraig, 73 Main St., Blackrock. T. (01) 88 25 76.
- Print -   *103249*

de Burca, 27 Priory Dr., Blackrock. T. (01) 288 2159,
Fax 283 4080. - Print -   *103250*

Cork (Co. Cork)

Feehan & Co., 2 Bridge St., Cork. T. (021) 260 79.
- Print -   *103251*

Lee, 10 Lavitt's Quay, Cork. T. (021) 223 07.
- Print -   *103252*

Dalkey (Co. Dublin)

Exchange Bookshop, 34 Castle St., Dalkey.
T. (01) 85 38 06. - Print -   *103253*

Dublin

Banba, 45 Chapel St., Dublin 1. T. (01) 72 55 84.
- Print -   *103254*

Banba, 210 Lower Rathmines Rd., Dublin 6.
T. (01) 97 41 52. - Print -   *103255*

Banba, 9 Tara St., Dublin 2. T. (01) 77 24 15.
- Print -   *103256*

Banba, 17 Talbot St., Dublin 1. T. (01) 78 87 14.
- Print -   *103257*

Bookworm, 53 Patrick St., Dublin 8. T. (01) 53 36 82.
- Print -   *103258*

Cathach, 10 Duke St., Dublin 2. T. (01) 71 86 76.
- Print -   *103259*

Cathair, 1 Essex Gate, Dublin 2. T. (01) 679 2406.
- Print -   *103260*

Chapters Bookshop, 70 Middle Abbey St., Dublin 2.
T. (01) 72 32 97. - Print -   *103261*

Chapters Bookshop, 21 Wicklow St., Dublin 2.
T. (01) 68 83 28. - Print -   *103262*

Corr, Kevin, 61 Lower Mespil Rd., Dublin 4.
T. (01) 60 93 21. - Print -   *103263*

Figgis, 53 Pembroke Rd., Dublin 4. T. (01) 60 94 91.
- Print -   *103264*

Halfpenny Bridge Books, 1 Merchants Arch, Dublin 2.
T. (01) 77 52 06. - Print -   *103265*

Hanna, Fred, 29 Nassau St., Dublin 2. T. (01) 77 12 55.
- Print / Map -   *103266*

Ranelagh Bookshop, 26 Ranelagh Village, Dublin 6.
T. (01) 96 20 64. - Print -   *103267*

Webb, George, 5 Crampton Quay, Dublin 1.
T. (01) 77 74 89. - Print -   *103268*

Winding Stair Bookshop, 40 Lower Ormond Quay, Dublin
1. T. (01) 73 32 92. - Print -   *103269*

Dun Laoghaire (Co. Dublin)

Fenning, James, 12 Glenview Rochestown Av., Dun
Laoghaire. T. (01) 85 78 55. - Print -   *103270*

Naughton, 8 Marine Terrace, Dun Laoghaire.
T. (01) 80 43 92. - Print -   *103271*

Galway (Co. Galway)

Kenny's Antiquarian Bookshop and Art Galleries, High
St., Galway. T. (091) 62793. - Engr / Autogr /
Map -   *103272*

Kilkenny (Co. Kilkenny)

Ossory, 67 High St., Kilkenny. T. (056) 218 93.
- Print -   *103273*

Limerick (Co. Limerick)

Stacpoole, George, 35 Cecil St., Limerick.
T. (061) 45 433. - Print / ArtBk / Engr / Autogr /
Map -   *103274*

Israel

Jerusalem

Collector, Jerusalem Hilton Hotel, PO Box 4075, 91000
Jerusalem, 91040. T. (02) 53 38 90. - ArtBk / Engr /
Map -   *103275*

Mayer, Ludwig, 4 Shlomzion Hamalka, 91000 Jerusalem, 91010. T. (02) 22 26 28.   *103276*

Tel Aviv

Pollak, 36 and 42 King George St, 63298 Tel Aviv.
T. (03) 288613.   *103277*

Richter, Horace, 24 Simtat-Mazal-Arieh, Tel Aviv.
T. (03) 5229045. - ArtBk -   *103278*

Wiluzanski, W., 58 Ben Yehuda St, 61031 Tel Aviv.
T. (03) 297073. - Print / Map -   *103279*

Italy

Arezzo

Perlini, Via Cavour 33, 52100 Arezzo. T. (0575) 206 13,
335 55.   *103280*

Stradivarius, Via Madonna del Prato 28, 52100 Arezzo.
T. (0575) 22010.   *103281*

Bari

Adriatica, Via Andrea da Bari 119, 70121 Bari.
T. (080) 521 13 41.   *103282*

Cavalieri, Via Putignani 50, 70121 Bari.
T. (080) 521 41 45.   *103283*

Fortunato, Francesco, Via De Rossi 175, 70122 Bari.
T. (080) 521 11 08. - Print -   *103284*

Laterza, Via Sparano 134, 70121 Bari.
T. (080) 521 17 80.   *103285*

Milella, Salvatore, Corso Cavour 64, 70121 Bari.
T. (080) 33 92 33.   *103286*

Bassano del Grappa (Vicenza)

Ottocento, Via Parolini 1, 36061 Bassano del Grappa.
T. (0424) 22452. - ArtBk / Engr / Map -   *103287*

Bergamo

Bolis, Via Tasso 68, 24100 Bergamo.
T. (035) 24 44 26.   *103288*

Lorenzelli, Enrico, Via Giovanni XXIII, 74, 24100 Bergamo. T. (035) 24 34 26. - Print -   *103289*

Tarantola, Luigi, Via Petrarca 8, 24100 Bergamo.
T. (035) 24 99 26.   *103290*

Bologna

Aesse, Via Castiglione 30, 40124 Bologna.
T. (051) 27 77 79.   *103291*

Antiquariato d'Epoca, Via de'Toschi 2, 40124 Bologna.
T. (051) 27 52 74.   *103292*

Antiquariato San Stefano, Via Santo Stefano 15, 40125
Bologna. T. (051) 27 12 57. *103293*
Bagnolati, Giancarlo, Via Castiglione 50, 40124 Bologna.
T. (051) 27 09 62. *103294*
Banco, Via Marsala 6, 40126 Bologna.
T. (051) 27 64 15. *103295*
Bertocchi, Strada Maggiore 70, 40125 Bologna.
T. (051) 23 37 57. *103296*
Bottega del Libro, Via San Vitale 24, 40125 Bologna.
T. (051) 27 09 74. *103297*
Brighenti, Gino, Via Malpertuso 1, 40123 Bologna.
T. (051) 58 40 70. - Autogr / Map - *103298*
D.E.A., Via Belle Arti 48, 40126 Bologna.
T. (051) 23 61 00. *103299*
Docet, Francesco Rabiti, Via A. Righi 9, 40126 Bologna.
T. (051) 23 07 57. - Print - *103300*
Feltrinelli, Pzzadi Porta Ravegnana 1, 40126 Bologna.
T. (051) 266 891. *103301*
Garisenda, Strada Maggiore 14, 40125 Bologna.
T. (051) 23 18 93. - Print / Map - *103302*
Grifoni, Giancarlo, Via Emilia Levante 13, 40139 Bolo-
gna. T. (051) 54 93 78. - Print / Map - *103303*
Matteuzzi, Piazza Aldrovandi 5, 40125 Bologna.
T. (051) 22 16 87. *103304*
Novissima, Via Castiglione 1, 40124 Bologna.
T. (051) 232 329. *103305*
Palmaverde, Via Castiglione 35, 40124 Bologna.
T. (051) 23 20 85. - Print - *103306*
Parolini, Antonia, Via Ugo Bassi 14, 40121 Bologna.
T. (051) 23 41 40. *103307*
Sermoneta, Emma, Via C Battisti 2, 40123 Bologna.
T. (051) 27 84 74. *103308*
Stamparte, Via Morandi 4, 40124 Bologna.
T. (051) 22 19 13, Fax 26 94 12. - Print / ArtBk - *103309*
Veronese, Via de'Foscherari 19, 40124 Bologna.
T. (051) 23 64 92. *103310*
Zanichelli, Piazza Galvani 1, 40124 Bologna.
T. (051) 23 73 89. - Print - *103311*

Bolzano
Athesia, Via Portici 41, 39100 Bolzano.
T. (0471) 92 51 11. - Print / Map - *103312*
Cappelli, Piazza Vittoria 41, 39100 Bolzano.
T. (04/1) 420 41. *103313*
Emeri, Galleria Europa 13, 39100 Bolzano.
T. (0471) 40272. *103314*
Ferrari Auer, Piazza Walther 12, 39100 Bolzano.
T. (0471) 97 32 66. *103315*

Borgo di Trevi (Perugia)
Politi, Giancarlo, POB 36, 06032 Borgo di Trevi.
- ArtBk - *103316*

Brescia
Argentario, L', Paolo Tonini, Via Franzinetti 7, 25100
Brescia. T. (030) 31 59 64. *103317*
Cantoni, Andrea, Via San Zeno 201/b, 25100 Brescia.
T. (030) 34 77 61, 34 77 20. *103318*
Cavriolo, Via Elia Capriolo 16/D, 25122 Brescia.
T. (030) 29 57 32. *103319*
Ersego, C., Via Capriolo 16d, 25122 Brescia.
T. (030) 29 57 32. *103320*
Malatesta, Via dei Musei 50, 25100 Brescia. *103321*

Caltanissetta
Cavallotto, Corso Vitt Emanuele 133, 93100 Caltanissetta. T. (0934) 20081. *103322*
Sciascia, Salvatore, Corso Umberto 117, 93100 Caltanissetta. T. (0934) 219 46. *103323*

Catania (Sicilia)
Cavallotto, Corso Sicilia 89, 95131 Catania.
T. (095) 31 06 00. *103324*
Crisafulli, G. Dott., Via Etnea 280, 95131 Catania.
T. (095) 31 70 25. *103325*
Musumeci, Via Caronda 16, 95129 Catania.
T. (095) 22 06 81. *103326*

Cerea (Verona)
Elite Antiquariato, Via F Filzi 4, 37053 Cerea.
T. (0442) 821 04. *103327*

Chiavari (Genova)
Flumen Dantis, Piazza Mazzini 12, 16043 Chiavari.
T. (0185) 30 66 30. *103328*

Chiesina Uzzanese (Pistoia)
Falco, Giovanni, Via Vitt Veneto 27, 51013 Chiesina Uzzanese. Fax 63 64 53. *103329*

Fano (Pesaro e Urbino)
Soncino, Piazza Costanzi 20, 61032 Fano.
T. (0721) 87 79 19. *103330*

Firenze
Arnaud, Edizione, via 27 Aprile 13, 50129 Firenze.
T. (055) 49 63 33. - ArtBk - *103331*
Arrigucci, Daniela, Via Oriuolo 315, 50122 Firenze.
T. (055) 234 02 75. *103332*
Baccani, Bruno, via Porta Rossa 99r, 50123
Firenze. *103333*
Cappellini, Corso Tintori 31, 50122 Firenze.
T. (055) 24 09 89. *103334*
Casalini, Libreria, Via Benedetto da Maiano 3, 50137 Fi-
renze. T. (055) 599941. *103335*
Centro Di, Piazza dei Mozzi 1, 50125 Firenze.
T. (055) 21 32 12. - ArtBk / Engr - *103336*
Conforti, Via Ginori 53r, 50123 Firenze.
T. (055) 230 26 35. *103337*
Del Re, Via dei Pucci 45, 50122 Firenze. *103338*
Dilaghi, N., via 27 Aprile 4r, 50129 Firenze. *103339*
Fallani, Alessandro, Via Pergola 21a, 50121 Firenze.
T. (055) 247 88 86. *103340*
Feltrinelli Libreria Internazionale, via Cavour 12, 50129
Firenze. T. (055) 29 21 96. - Engr - *103341*
Ferrini, Rossella, Via Ghibellina 91r, 50122 Firenze.
T. (055) 234 47 33. *103342*
Fortuna, Via de Pucci 4, 50122 Firenze.
T. (055) 28 49 07. *103343*
Giorni, Maria, Via Martelli 35, 50129 Firenze.
T. (055) 28 49 67. - Engr - *103344*
Gonnelli, via Ricasoli 14, 50122 Firenze.
T. (055) 21 68 35. - Print / ArtBk / Engr - *103345*
Grifo 32, Via Ghibellina 135, 50122 Firenze.
T. (055) 21 64 70. *103346*
Le Monnier, via S. Gallo 49r., 50129 Firenze.
- ArtBk - *103347*
Libreria del Porcellino, Piazza Mercato Nuovo 6-8,
50123 Firenze. T. (055) 21 25 35. - ArtBk - *103348*
Libreria dello Stato, via Cavour 46r., 50129 Firenze.
- Print - *103349*
Libreria dello Studente, Via Laura 68/A, 50121 Firenze.
T. (055) 247 87 55. *103350*
Libreria Fiorentina, Via Ricasoli 107, 50122 Firenze.
T. (055) 21 65 33. *103351*
Marzocco, Via Martelli 22, 50129 Firenze.
T. (055) 21 45 68. - ArtBk - *103352*
Opus Libri, Via della Torretta 16, 50137 Firenze.
T. (055) 66 08 33, Fax 67 06 04. - Print - *103353*
Palatina, Francesco Masini, Via Stracciatella 13/r,
50125 Firenze. T. (055) 21 81 35. *103354*
Salimbeni, Via Palmieri 14-16 R, 50122 Firenze.
T. (055) 234 09 04/05. - Print / ArtBk - *103355*
Seeber, Via Tornabuoni 70, 50123 Firenze.
T. (055) 21 56 27. - ArtBk - *103356*
Studio Bibliografico Fortuna, Via de' Pucci 4, 50122 Fi-
renze. T. (055) 28 49 07. - Print / ArtBk / Autogr /
Map - *103357*
Valleri, Via Ricasoli 168, Via degli Alfani 135, 50121 Fi-
renze. T. (055) 29 61 92. - Print / Engr - *103358*
Vittorio, Via Verdi 33r, 50122 Firenze. T. (055) 234 48 36.
- Print - *103359*

Genova
Ardy, Claudio e Bernardino, Piazza Sauli 4, 16123 Geno-
va. T. (010) 29 55 08. *103360*
Bardini, Salita del Fondaco 32/r, Via XII Octobre, 16121
Genova. T. (010) 29 89 56. *103361*
Dallai, Piazza De Marini 11, 16123 Genova.
T. (010) 29 83 38. - Print / Engr - *103362*
di Stefano, Via Roccatagliata 40, 16138 Genova.
T. (010) 59 38 21. - ArtBk - *103363*
Libreria Antica, Vico Falamonica 15, 16123 Genova.
T. (010) 20 38 21. *103364*
Lunigiana, Vico Fiascaie 7, 16123 Genova.
T. (010) 29 89 56. *103365*
Micheloni, W., Via Falamonica 15, 16123 Genova.
T. (010) 20 38 21. - Print - *103366*
Pasta, Edmondo, Via Stefanina Moro 21, 16144 Genova.
- ArtBk / Engr - *103367*

Salotto del Bibliofilo, Via Luccoli 21, 16123 Genova.
T. (010) 29 44 80. *103368*
Sileno, Il, Galleria Mazzini 13, 16121 Genova.
T. (010) 59 05 20. - Print - *103369*

Giovinazzo (Bari)
Peucetia, Vicento Luisi, Via Giovanni XXIII 19, 74054
Giovinazzo. T. (080) 894 38 82. *103370*

Livorno
Belforte, Via Grande 91, 57123 Livorno.
T. (0586) 88 73 79, Fax 88 96 68. - ArtBk - *103371*

Lodi (Milano)
Zazzera, Giampiero, Via Milite Ignoto 9, 20075 Lodi.
T. (0371) 43 11 03, Fax 43 11 02. *103372*

Lucca
Baroni, Via Fillungo 51, 55100 Lucca. T. (0583) 465 79.
- ArtBk - *103373*

Magliano Alpi (Cuneo)
Bosio Giovanni, Via Langhe 400, 12060 Magliano Alpi.
T. (0174) 66502. - Print - *103374*

Mantova
Arcari, Gianluigi, Via Cappello 10, 46100 Mantova.
T. (0376) 36 84 58. *103375*

Messina
Libreria C.I.O.F.A.L.O., Piazza Municipio 37, 98100 Messina. T. (090) 77 53 11. *103376*

Milano
Antichità della Moscova, Via Moscova 47A, 20121 Mila-
no. T. (02) 29 00 07 63. *103377*
Antiqua Libri, Via Borgogna 2, 20122 Milano.
T. (02) 70 44 57. - Print / ArtBk / Engr / Autogr - *103378*
Bocca, Galleria Vitt. Emanuele 12, 20121 Milano.
T. (02) 87 15 36. - Print / ArtBk - *103379*
Boldi, Lea, Foro Bonaparte 12, 20121 Milano.
T. (02) 80 27 03. - ArtBk - *103380*
Bonfanti, Via M. Melloni 19, 20129 Milano.
T. (02) 749 61 81. - Print - *103381*
Chiesa, Carlo Alberto, Via Bigli 11, 20121 Milano.
T. (02) 79 86 78. - Print / Engr / Autogr / Map - *103382*
Daverio, Philippe, Via Monte Napoleone 6A, 20121 Mi-
lano. T. (02) 79 86 95, 76 00 17 48, Fax 76 02 15 07.
- ArtBk - *103383*
Feltrinelli, Libreria, Via Manzoni 12, 20121 Milano.
T. (02) 76 00 03 86. *103384*
Finzi, Foro Bonaparte 12, 20121 Milano.
T. (02) 86 25 79. - Print - *103385*
Gallini, Via Gorani 8, 20123 Milano. T. (02) 72 000 398.
- Print - *103386*
Garzanti, Via Senato 25, 20121 Milano. T. (02) 778 71.
- Print - *103387*
Hoepli, Ulrico, Via Hoepli 5, 20121 Milano.
T. (02) 86 54 46. - ArtBk - *103388*
Idea Books, Via Vigevano 41, 20144 Milano.
T. (02) 8373949, 8360395, 8390284,
Fax (02) 8357776. - ArtBk - *103389*
Il Collezionista, Via Madonnina 9, 20121 Milano.
T. (02) 86 66 65. *103390*
Il Labirinto, Via Spartaco 33, 20135 Milano.
T. (02) 548 45 55. *103391*
Il Milione, Via Bigli 19, 20121 Milano. T. (02) 78 15 90,
Fax 78 15 90. - ArtBk / Engr - *103392*
Incisione Muhely Art, Via Spiga 33, 20100 Milano.
T. (02) 70 59 93. - Engr - *103393*
Libraria L'Archivolto, Silvio San Pietro, Via Marsala 2,
20121 Milano. T. (02) 659 08 42, 659 55 52,
Fax 659 55 52. *103394*
Libreria Al Castello, Via San Giovanni sul Muro 9, 20121
Milano. T. (02) 80 00 52. - ArtBk - *103395*
Libreria Antiquaria Mediolanum, Via Montebello 24,
20121 Milano. T. (02) 65 36 37, 659 23 20. *103396*
Libreria dello Stato, Galleria Vittorio Emanuele 3, 20121
Milano. *103397*
Libreria di Piazza San Babila, Corso Monforte 2, 20122
Milano. T. (02) 79 92 19. - Print / ArtBk - *103398*
Libreria Internazionale Cavour, Piazza Cavour 1, 20121
Milano. T. (02) 66 77 05. - ArtBk - *103399*

Libreria Internazionale di Piazza San Babila, corso Monforte 2, 20122 Milano. T. (02) 79 92 19.
- Engr - *103400*
Libreria Mediolanum, L. Pozzi, Via Montebello 24, 20121 Milano. T. (02) 65 36 37, 659 23 20, Fax 659 23 20. *103401*
Malavasi, Via S. Tecla 2, 20122 Milano. T. (02) 80 46 07.
- Print - *103402*
Manusé, Gaetano, Galleria Hoepli 3, 20121 Milano.
T. (02) 80 72 46, 539 31 52. - Print / ArtBk - *103403*
Mercante di Stampe, Il, Corso Venezia 29, 20121 Milano. T. (02) 70 44 02. - Autogr / Map - *103404*
Milano Libri, Via Verdi 2, 20121 Milano.
T. (02) 875 871. *103405*
Moretti, Via Lusardi 8, 20122 Milano. T. (02) 839 12 75.
- Engr - *103406*
Mottola, Via S Marta 21, 20123 Milano.
T. (02) 869 10 53. *103407*
Nicholls, Paul, Via Manzoni 41, 20121 Milano.
T. (02) 657 58 74. *103408*
Nuova Milano Libri, Via Verdi 2, 20121 Milano.
T. (02) 87 58 71. - ArtBk - *103409*
Polifilo, Via Borgonuovo 3, 20121 Milano.
T. (02) 87 11 89. - Engr - *103410*
Radaeli, Via Manzoni 39, 20121 Milano.
T. (02) 659 00 55. - Print / ArtBk / Engr / Autogr / Map - *103411*
Rizzi, Renzo, Via Cernaia 4, 20121 Milano.
T. (02) 29 00 27 05. - Print / Autogr - *103412*
Rovello, Via Rovello 1, 20121 Milano.
T. (02) 87 39 78. *103413*
Sibrium, Via Bigli 21, 20121 Milano. T. (02) 76 00 56 69.
- Print / Engr / Autogr - *103414*
Studio Al Borgonuovo, Via Borgonuovo 27, 20121 Milano. T. (02) 86 26 62. *103415*
Studio Bibliografico Lidis, Foro Bonaparte 12, 20121 Milano. T. (02) 80 27 03. - Print / Engr - *103416*
Tomasetig, Andrea, Via Caccialepori 3, 20148 Milano.
T. (02) 403 24 33. *103417*
Valeria Bella Stampe, Via S. Cecilia 2, 20122 Milano.
T. (02) 76 00 44 13, Fax 76 00 65 05. - Autogr - *103418*

VALERIA BELLA STAMPE

Via S. Cecilia 2
Grafica antica e moderna
20122 MILANO
Tel. (02) 76 00 44 13
Fax (02) 76 00 65 05

Modena

Broseghini, Marcello, Viale Storchi 26, 41100 Modena.
T. (059) 21 94 52. *103419*
Govi, Alberto, Via S Pietro 18, 41100 Modena.
T. (059) 23 64 20, 21 81 70. *103420*
Mezzacqui, Tino, Via dei Servi 45, 41100 Modena.
T. (059) 21 10 55. *103421*

Montecatini Terme e Tettuccio (Pistoia)

Michelotti, Giuliano, Corso Roma 18, 51016 Montecatini Terme e Tettuccio. T. (0572) 793 29. *103422*

Napoli

Arti Visive, Via dei Mille 40, 80121 Napoli.
T. (081) 42 12 07. - ArtBk - *103423*
Berisio Arturo, Via Port'Alba, 80134 Napoli.
T. (081) 34 44 01. *103424*
Biblio Sud, Via Morghen 72, 80134 Napoli.
T. (081) 32 47 85. *103425*
Cassela, Gaspare, Via Carlo Poerio 92 E-F, 80121 Napoli. T. (081) 764 2627. - Print / Autogr - *103426*
Cassitto, Ermanno, Via Port'Alba 10, 80134 Napoli.
T. (081) 45 90 68. *103427*
Cicerano e Grimaldi, Via Bausan 61, 80121 Napoli.
T. (081) 40 60 21. *103428*
Colonnese, Via S. Pietro a Majella 33, 80138 Napoli.
T. (081) 45 98 58. - Print / Engr - *103429*

Deperro, Libreria, via dei Mille 17 b19, 80121 Napoli.
T. (081) 41 86 87. *103430*
Fiorentino, Fausto, Calata Trinità Maggiore 36, 80134 Napoli. T. (081) 552 20 05. *103431*
Grimaldi, Alfonso, Via Bausan 61, 80121 Napoli.
T. (081) 40 60 21. *103432*
Guida, Port' Alba 20-24, 80134 Napoli.
T. (081) 44 63 77. *103433*
L'Incontro, Libreria, via Kerbaker 19/21, 80129 Napoli.
T. (081) 24 35 34. - Print / Engr - *103434*
Libreria dello Stato, via Chiaia 5, 80121 Napoli. *103435*
Miliano, Mario, Via Benedetto Croce 60, 80134 Napoli.
T. (081) 551 65 55. *103436*
Pucci, Bruno, Via Fern Russo 31, 80123 Napoli.
T. (081) 769 58 78. *103437*
Regina, Luigi, Via Constantinopoli 51, 80138 Napoli.
T. (081) 45 99 83. *103438*

Padova (Belluno)

Bado & Mart, Via Dietro Duomo 14/1, 35100 Padova.
T. (049) 875 09 63, Fax 875 53 17. *103439*
Buzzanca, Giampaolo, Via San Andrea 5, 35100 Padova.
T. (049) 65 18 31. - Print / Engr - *103440*
Draghi-Randi, Via Cavour 17-19, 35122 Padova.
T. (049) 875 13 53, 39447, Fax 875 18 25. - ArtBk / Map - *103441*
Libreria ai due Santi, M.&G. Negriolli, Via del Santo 43, 35100 Padova. T. (049) 65 66 81. *103442*
Libreria Universitaria, Via VIII Febbraio 10, 35100 Padova. *103443*
Mussato, A., Corso Vittorio Emanuele II 20, 35100 Padova. T. (049) 459 32. - Print / Autogr - *103444*

Palermo (Sicilia)

Flaccovio, S.F., via Ruggiero Settimo 37, 90139 Palermo. T. (091) 58 94 42. - ArtBk - *103445*
Libreria L'Aleph, L. Giordano, Via Vinc Di Marco 24, 90143 Palermo. T. (091) 625 79 35, 34 44 93. *103446*
Novecento, via Siracusa 7, 90141 Palermo.
T. (091) 26 83 58. *103447*

Parma

Aurea Parma, Via al Duomo 5, 43100 Parma.
T. (0521) 389 08. *103448*
Battei, Luigi, Via Brigida 1, 43100 Parma.
T. (0521) 230 77. *103449*
Battei, Luigi, Via Cavour 5, 43100 Parma.
T. (0521) 337 33. *103450*
Montanini, Gian Paolo, Strada Nino Bixio 58, 43100 Parma. T. (0521) 68662. - Print - *103451*
Oliva, Via al Duomo 1, 43100 Parma.
T. (0521) 33920. *103452*
Palatina Editrice, Borgo G Tommasini 9, 43100 Parma. *103453*

Perugia

Le Muse Libreria, Corso Vannucci 51, 06100 Perugia.
T. (075) 209 60. - ArtBk - *103454*
Monticelli, Giancarlo, Via Baldeschi 16, 06100 Perugia.
T. (075) 26894. *103455*

Pisa

Goliardica Libreria, via Oberdan 2 b.4, 56100 Pisa.
- Print - *103456*
Vallerini, Andrea, Via dei Mille 7a-13, 56126 Pisa.
T. (050) 403 93, Fax 56 27 52. - Print / ArtBk / Autogr - *103457*

Pompei (Napoli)

Studio Bibliografico Pompeiana, Via Lepanto 54, 80045 Pompei. T. (081) 863 71 74, Fax 863 71 72. *103458*

Ravenna

Tonini, Matteo, Via Mazzini 18, 48100 Ravenna.
T. (0544) 303 97. - Print - *103459*

Reggio Emilia

Prandi, Viale Timavo 75, 42100 Reggio Emilia.
T. (0522) 349 73. - Engr - *103460*

Rimini (Forli)

Luisè Editore, Viale Tiberio 25, 47037 Rimini.
T. (0541) 28755. - ArtBk - *103461*

Roma

Antiquariato Babuino, Via del Babuino 73, 00187 Roma.
T. (06) 678 97 06. *103462*
Antiquariato 2 P, Piazzale Roberto Ardigò 36-37, 00142 Roma. T. (06) 540 97 16. *103463*
Bocca, Libreria Internazionale, piazza di Spagna 84, 00187 Roma. T. (06) 679 09 88. *103464*
Bretschneider, Giorgio, Dr., Via Cassiodoro 19, 00193 Roma. T. (06) 687 41 27, 38 85 00, Fax 687 41 29.
- Print - *103465*
Cascianelli, Eugenio, largo Febo 15, 00186 Roma.
T. (06) 55 28 06. - Map - *103466*
Centro Di, Via San Giacomo 18, 00187 Roma.
T. (06) 678 6963. *103467*
Cesaretti, Via Piè di Marmo 27, 00186 Roma. *103468*
Club dell'Antiquariato Internazionale, Via Ramazzini 91, 00151 Roma. T. (06) 534 69 30, 537 30 87. *103469*
Di Cave, Giuliana, Via dei Pastini 23, 00186 Roma.
T. (06) 678 02 97. - Print - *103470*
Dotti, Via della Scrofa 58, 00186 Roma.
T. (06) 686 47 55. - Print - *103471*
Feltrinelli, Via del Babuino 41, 00187 Roma.
T. (06) 687 058. *103472*
Ferro di Cavallo, Via Ripetta 67, 00186 Roma.
T. (06) 687 269. *103473*
Galleria del Libro, via Nazionale 246, 00184 Roma.
T. (06) 46 48 53, 48 64 80. - Print - *103474*
Librars & Antiquaria, Via Zanardelli 3-4, 00186 Roma.
T. (06) 65 59 31. *103475*
Libreria Al Vascello, Via Giuseppe Dezza 15, 00152 Roma. T. (06) 589 86 68. *103476*
Libreria Antiquaria Ex Libris, Via dell'Umiltà 77, 00187 Roma. T. (06) 679 15 40. *103477*
Libreria dell'Impero, Corso Rinascimento 63, 00186 Roma. T. (06) 654 29 41. *103478*
Libreria dello Stato, via Tritone 61, 00187 Roma.
- Print - *103479*
Libreria Sant'Agostino, Via Sant'Agostino 17, 00186 Roma. T. (06) 65 54 70. *103480*
Lombardi, Pasquale Libreria, via S Eufemia 11, 00187 Roma. T. (06) 756 76 49. *103481*
Montenegro, Via dei Gracchi 291a, 00192 Roma.
T. (06) 38 63 42. - ArtBk - *103482*
Nardecchia, Plinio, piazza Navona 25, 00186 Roma.
T. (06) 55 63 18. - Print / Engr - *103483*
Pacitti, N. A., Via dei Banchi Vechi 59, 00186 Roma.
T. (06) 654 03 91. - Print / Map - *103484*
Primo Piano, Via Panisperna 203, 00184 Roma.
T. (06) 488 03 09, Fax 488 18 94. *103485*
Rappaport, C. E., Via Sistina 23, 00187 Roma.
T. (06) 48 38 26. - Print / Engr - *103486*
Riccardi, Maresca, Via del Banco di S Spirito 61, 00186 Roma. T. (06) 656 59 44. *103487*
Rizzoli, Largo Chigi 15, 00187 Roma. T. (06) 679 66 41.
- ArtBk - *103488*
Scarpignato, Giuseppe, Via di Ripetta 156, 00186 Roma.
T. (06) 65 59 23. *103489*
Sforzini, Via della Vite 43, 00187 Roma.
T. (06) 678 91 70. *103490*
Shakespeare & Co., Via Tor Millina 10-11, 00186 Roma.
T. (06) 659 94 07. *103491*
Soave, Fiammetta, Via Leccosa 4-6, 00186 Roma.
T. (06) 686 42 85, Fax 686 42 85. *103492*
Venza, Salvatore, Via Busiri Vici 34, 00152 Roma.
T. (06) 581 63 50. *103493*

Sala Bolognese (Bologna)

Forni, Arnaldo, Via Gramsci 164, 40010 Sala Bolognese.
T. (051) 95 41 45. *103494*

Savona

Dedalo, Piazza del Vescovato, 17100 Savona.
T. (019) 343 27. *103495*

Tavarnuzze (Firenze)

Pampaloni, Paolo, Prof., Vicolo delle Rose 6, 50029 Tavarnuzze. T. (055) 203 40 71, Fax 203 42 90. *103496*

Torino

Aretusa, Via Po 2, 10123 Torino.
T. (011) 518 264. *103497*
Avignone, Rossa, Piazza Carlo Felice 67, 10123 Torino.
T. (011) 557 53 61. *103498*

Bergoglio, Via Moncalvo 53bis, 10131 Torino.
T. (011) 839 72 95. *103499*
Bertola, Carlo, Via Silvio Pellico 29, 10125 Torino.
T. (011) 68 97 12. *103500*
Biggio, G., Via San Franc da Paolo 14, 10123 Torino.
T. (011) 83 03 06. *103501*
Bourlot, Caesare Birocco, piazza S. Carlo 183, 10123
Torino. T. (011) 53 74 05. - Print / Engr / Map - *103502*
Brambilla, A., Via Carlo Alberto 7, 10123 Torino.
T. (011) 839 77 20. *103503*
Casanova, F., & C., Via Po 39, 10124 Torino.
T. (011) 88 23 68. *103504*
„Dante Alighieri". Libreria, piazza Carlo Felice 19,
10123 Torino. - Print / ArtBk - *103505*
Gatto, G., Via S. Francesco da Paola 10bis, 10123 Tori-
no. T. (011) 839 66 36. - Print - *103506*
Grosso Libreria, Via San Dalmazzo 14, 10122 Torino.
T. (011) 54 49 18. *103507*
Hellas, Via Bertola 6, 10121 Torino.
T. (011) 546 941. *103508*
Il Cartiglio, Roberto Cena, Via Po 32D, 10123 Torino.
T. (011) 83 91 11. *103509*
Il Delfino, via Cesare Battisti 19A, 10123 Torino.
T. (011) 54 04 11. *103510*
Il Putto, Magno Facheris, Via Battisti 7, 10123 Torino.
T. (011) 51 83 77. *103511*
Il Vecchio Melo, Via San Dalmazzo 6, 10122 Torino.
T. (011) 54 36 41. *103512*
Libreria Antiquaria Soave, Via Po 48, 10123 Torino.
T. (011) 87 89 57, Fax 812 30 77. - Print / Engr - *103513*
Libreria dello Stato, via Roma 80, 10100 Torino.
- Print - *103514*
Libreria Piemontese, Via Monte di Pietà 13 H, 10122 To-
rino. T. (011) 53 54 72. *103515*
Mantua, Isidoro, Via Andrea Doria 6, 10123 Torino.
T. (011) 53 87 44. *103516*
Masi, D. de, Piazza Carlo Felice 48, 10121 Torino.
T. (011) 54 03 34. *103517*
Peyrot, Piazza Savoia 8, 10122 Torino.
T. (011) 436 96 54. - Print - *103518*
Pregliasco, Via Accademia Albertina 3bis, 10123 Torino.
T. (011) 87 71 14, Fax 87 92 14. - Print / Engr / Autogr /
Map - *103519*
Salamon, Via Cosseria 6, 10131 Torino.
T. (011) 669 22 26, Fax 312 17 61. *103520*
Salamon, Silverio, Via A Volta 9, 10121 Torino.
T. (011) 562 58 34, 54 90 41, Fax 53 41 54. *103521*
Soave, Via Po 48, 10123 Torino.
T. (011) 87 89 57. *103522*
Viglongo, Andrea e C., Via Genova 266, 10127 Torino.
T. (011) 60 60 421. *103523*
Visani, M., Via Battisti 19, 10123 Torino.
T. (011) 839 67 75. *103524*

Travagliato (Brescia)
Cadeo, S. & A., Via Santa Caterina 13, 25039 Travaglia-
to. T. (030) 66 01 47. *103525*

Trieste
Libreria Achille, Piazza Vecchia 4, 34121 Trieste.
T. (040) 685 25, 76 81 68. *103526*
Misan, Tullio, Via dei Rettori 1, 34121 Trieste.
T. (040) 607 58. *103527*
Rigatteria, Via Malcanton 12, 34121 Trieste.
T. (040) 65491. *103528*
Saba, Umberto, Via San Nicolò 30, 34121 Trieste.
T. (040) 63 17 41. *103529*

Udine
Arti Antiche, Via Giusto Muratti 35, 33100 Udine.
T. (0432) 29 78 00. *103530*
Serenissima, Via Aquileia 113, 33100 Udine.
T. (0432) 233 88. *103531*
Tarantola, R., Via Vittorio Veneto 20, 33100 Udine.
T. (0432) 50 24 59. - Print - *103532*

Venezia
Cassini, Giocondo, Via San Marco 2424, 30124 Venezia.
T. (041) 318 15. - Print / Engr / Map - *103533*
Kleine Galerie, Prof. Cl. Gorini, C delle Botteghe 2972,
30124 Venezia. T. (041) 522 21 77. *103534*
La Fenice, San Marco 1850, 30124 Venezia.
T. (041) 523 80 06. - Print - *103535*

Libreria del Cavallino, S. Marco 1725, 30124 Venezia.
T. (041) 521 04 88, Fax 521 06 42. - ArtBk - *103536*
Penso, Manlio, S Tomà 2916/a, 30121 Venezia.
T. (041) 523 82 15. *103537*
Rigattieri, Calle della Mandola 3713, 30124 Venezia.
T. (041) 313 21. *103538*
San Giorgio, Via XXII Marzo 2087, S Marco, 30124 Vene-
zia. T. (041) 38 451. *103539*
Sansovino, S Marco 84, 30124 Venezia.
T. (041) 522 26 23. *103540*
Serenissima, Libreria, San Marco 739, 30124 Venezia.
T. (041) 230 50. *103541*

Verona
Perini, Via A Sciesa 11, 37122 Verona.
T. (045) 300 73. *103542*
Porta Borsari, Corso Porta Borsari 15 c, 37121 Verona.
T. (045) 31679. *103543*

Vicenza
Libraio, Il, Corso Fogazzaro 159, 36100 Vicenza.
T. (0444) 5452 47. - Print - *103544*

Japan

Kyoto
Kyoto Shoin, Sanjo Agaru, Horikawa, Nakagyo-ku, Kyoto
604. T. (075) 841-9123, Fax 841-9127. *103545*
Kyoto Shoten, Shijo Agaru, Kawaracho Dori, Nakakyo-ku
Kyoto-shi, Kyoto. T. (075) 221-1062. *103546*
Rinsen Book, Imadegawa-Dori, Kawabat- Higashi-Iru,
Sakyo-ku, Kyoto 606. T. (075) 721-7111, Fax 781-
6168. *103547*
Shinbunkatu, 2-7 Tanaka-Sekiden-cho, Sakyo-ku, Kyoto
606. T. (075) 751-1781, Fax 752-0723. *103548*
Shobo, Sylvan, Higashi-iru, Higashinotoin, Bukkoji Shi-
mogyo-ku, Kyoto 600. T. (075) 341-8793, Fax 361-
0480. *103549*

Mie
Art Index, 1-5-1 Horiki, Yokkaichi, 510 Mie 510. T. 53-
6178. - Print / ArtBk - *103550*

Nagoya (Aichi-ken)
Maruzen Company, 2-Ban 7-Go, 2-Ban 7-Go 3-chome,
Sakae Naka-ku, Nagoya 460.
T. (052) 261 22 51. *103551*

Osaka
Librairie Arcade, Hankyu Koshono-machi 6, 1-6-2 Shi-
bata, Kita-ku, Osaka 530. T. (06) 374-2524, Fax 374-
2524. *103552*
Manjiya, 3 Umeda, Kita-ku, Osaka 530.
T. (06) 34130 93. *103553*
Nakao Shosen-do, 3-4-4 Awaji-machi, Higashi-ku, Osa-
ka 541. T. (06) 231-8797, Fax 231-4105. *103554*
Nakao Shoten, 1-2-14 Shinsaibashisuji, Chuo-ku, Osaka
542. T. (06) 271-0843. *103555*

Tokyo
Academia Music Ltd., 16-5, Hongo 3-chome Bunkyo-ku,
Tokyo 113, Tokyo 113. T. (03) 3813-6751. *103556*
Art Information, Sanko Bldg. 1F, Meguro-ku, 2-13-29
Meguro, Tokyo 153. T. (03) 3716 3960,
Fax 3716 3960. *103557*
Azuchi-do, 6-8-21-102 Honkomagome, Bunkyo-ku, To-
kyo 113. T. (03) 3943-8925, Fax 03 3943-
8925. *103558*
Bunryu, 704 Heiwa Sogo Bldg., 1-33-6 Takatanobaba,
Tokyo 160. T. (03) 3208-5445, Fax 3208-
5863. *103559*
Europe Art, Kamiogi 4-16-4 Suginami-Ku, Tokyo 167.
T. (03) 3397 9796, Fax 3397 5109. - ArtBk - *103560*
Fuji-Yosho, Daiichi Yamamoto Bldg., 1 b.11 Akihabara
Taito-ku, Tokyo. T. (03) 3253-8481. *103561*
Gyokuei-do Shoten, 1-1 Jimbocho, Kanda Chiyoda-ku,
Tokyo 101. T. (03) 3294-8045, Fax 3219-
5313. *103562*
Hakwo, Kojinachi Shine Bldg. 8F, 4, Kojimachi 4-chome,
Chiyoda-ku, Tokyo 102. T. (03) 3329-0666. *103563*
Heisando Co., Ltd., 13, 5-gochi, Shiba Park Minato-ku,
Tokyo. T. (03) 3434 0588. *103564*

Inoue Book Co., 6-2-8 Hongo Bunkyo-ku, Tokyo 113.
T. (03) 3811-4354, Fax 03 3811-8148. *103565*
Isseido, 1-7 Kanda-Jimbocho, Chiyoda-ku, Tokyo 101.
T. (03) 3292-0071, Fax 3292-0095. *103566*
Jena Co., Ltd., No. 6-1, Ginza 5-Chome Chuo-ku, Tokyo
104. T. (03) 3571-2980. *103567*
Kinokuniya, 38-1 Sakuragoaka 5, Setagaya-ku, Tokyo
156. T. (03) 3439-0161, Fax 3439-0839. *103568*
Kitazawa, 2-5 Jimbocho, Kanda chiyoda-ku, Tokyo 101.
T. (03) 3263-0017, 3263-0018, Fax 3263-
0015. *103569*
Komiyama, 1-7 Kanda-Jimbocho, Chiyoda-ku, Tokyo
101. T. (03) 3291-0495, Fax 3291-0498. *103570*
Maruzen Co. Ltd., 3-10, Nihonbashi 2-chome Chuo-ku,
Tokyo 103. T. (03) 3272-7211. - Print - *103571*
Matsumura, 1-7 Kanda-Jimbocho, Chiyoda-ku, Tokyo
101. T. (03) 3291-2410. *103572*
Meiji Shobo, 2-4, Surugadai Kanda, Chiyoda-ku, Tokyo
101. T. (03) 3291-0726. *103573*
Naigai, 7-3-107 Hiroo, 1-chome, Shibuya-ku, Tokyo.
T. (03) 3400-2326, Fax 3400-2036. *103574*
Ohya-Shobo, 1, 1-chome, Jimbocho Kanda, Chiyoda-ku,
Tokyo 101. T. (03) 3291-0062. - Map - *103575*
Orion Press, 1-58 Kanda-Jimbocho Chiyoda-ku, Tokyo
101. T. (03) 3295-4008. *103576*
Sanseido, 1-19 Kanda-Jimbocho, Chiyoda-ku, Tokyo
101. T. (03) 3233-0395. *103577*
Subun-so, 3-3 Ogawa machi Kanda, Tokyo 101.
T. (03) 3292-7877, Fax 3292-7878. *103578*
Sugihara, 1-2-5 Nishikata, Bunkyo-ku, Tokyo 113.
T. (03) 3816-0283, Fax 3811-4209. *103579*
Tamura-Shoten, 1-7 Kanda-Jimbocho, Chiyoda-ku, To-
kyo 101. T. (03) 3291-0563, Fax 3295-0039. *103580*
Tokodo Shoten, Nakauchi Bldg., 7 b.6 Nihonbashi 1-
chome Chuoku, Tokyo. T. (03) 3272-1966. *103581*
Tomaru, 3-1-16 Koenji-kita, Suginami-ku, Tokyo 166.
T. (03) 3337-3690, Fax 03 3337-6610. *103582*
Tuttle, Charles E., 2-6, Suido 1-chome Bunkyo-ku, To-
kyo 112. T. (03) 811 7106. - Engr - *103583*
Yagi Book Store, 3-8 Kanda Ogawamachi, Chiyoda-ku,
Tokyo 101. T. (03) 3291-2965, Fax 03 3291-
2963. *103584*
Yamada Shoten, 1-8 Kanda-Jimbocho, Chiyoda-ku, To-
kyo 101. T. (03) 3295-0552, Fax 03 3295-
0061. *103585*
Yamamoto Shoten, 2-7 Kanda-Jimbocho, Chiyoda-ku,
Tokyo 101. T. (03) 3261-0847, Fax 03 3261-
6276. *103586*

Latvia

Riga
Antikvariat S, Peteris Stuckas Ilea 5, Riga. *103587*
Centralis Antikvariats, Lenina Ilea 46, Riga. *103588*

Lebanon

Beirut
Abousleiman, Farid, rue de Damas, Beirut B.P. 3939.
T. (961) 22 52 85, 23 57 15. - Print - *103589*

Liechtenstein

Balzers
Wolfinger, Willy, Pädergross 20, 9496 Balzers.
T. (075) 3841392, Fax 3841889. *103590*

Schaan
Blackford, John, Im Bretscha, 9494 Schaan.
T. (075) 21326, Fax 24305. - Print / Engr /
Map - *103591*

Vaduz
Interlibrum, Schloßstr. 6, 9490 Vaduz. T. (075) 23261,
Fax 82102. - Engr - *103592*
Saendig Reprint (Hans R. Wohlwend), Hans Rainer, Am
schrägen Weg 12, 9490 Vaduz. T. (075) 2323627,
Fax (075) 2323627. *103593*

Lithuania

Vilnius
Senamiesčio Antikvariatas, Universiteto 10, 2001 Vilnius. T. (02) 629146, Fax 628138. *103594*

Luxembourg

Luxembourg
Librairie du Centre, bd. Royal 49, Luxembourg.
T. (0352) 279 99/289 66. - Engr / Autogr - *103595*

Mexico

México (D.F.)
Dalis, Amberes 12c, 06600 México.
T. 511 52 54. *103596*
Francesca, Paseo de la Reforma 250-A, México, D.F. 6.
T. 533 5490. *103597*
Libreria Alemana de Ultramar S. de R.L., Benjamin Hill 19b, México, 06170. - Print - *103598*
Libreria Anticuaria Echaniz, Mar Arafura 8 Popotla, México. T. 527 29 51. - Engr - *103599*
Libreria de Bellas Artes S.A., Avda. Juarez 18D, México.
- Print - *103600*
Libreria de Cristal, Avda. Ejército Nacional 826B, México. - Print - *103601*
Libreria del Prado, Avda. Juarez 70H, México.
- Print - *103602*
Porrua Hnos. y Cia. S.A., Argentina y Justo Sierra, México. - Print - *103603*
Porrua, Manuel, 5 de Mayo 49, México. T. 10-26 34, 18-46 43. - ArtBk - *103604*

Monaco

Monte Carlo
Librairie Les Beaux Livres Aymé Oberthur, 4, rue des Iris, 98000 Monte Carlo. T. 93 30 73 90. *103605*

Nepal

Kathmandu
Bhakta Bahadur Sreshtha, 20/239 Sano Gaucharan, Gyaneswor, Naksal, P.O. Box 699, Kathmandu. T. 4-14665. - Print - *103606*
Handicrafts Impex Enterprises, G.P.O.Box 1069, Kathmandu. *103607*

Netherlands

Aalsmeer
Maas, Zijdstraat 8, 1431 EC Aalsmeer. *103608*

Amersfoort (Utrecht)
Koppelpoort, Krommestr 68-77, 3811 CD Amersfoort.
T. (033) 415687. *103609*

Amsterdam
Agora, Corn. Schuytstr. 9, 1071 JC Amsterdam.
T. (020) 679 92 34. - Print - *103610*
Antiquariaat Antiqua, Herengracht 159, 1015 BH Amsterdam. T. (020) 624 59 98. - Print - *103611*
Ariëns Kappers, E.H., Nieuwe Spiegelstr. 32, 1017 DG Amsterdam. T. (020) 623 53 56, Fax 638 43 71. - Engr / Map - *103612*
Art Book, Prinsengracht 645, 1016 HV Amsterdam.
T. (020) 625 93 37. *103613*
Art Medical Livres Anciens, Hasebroekstr. 9, 1053 CL Amsterdam. T. (020) 685 28 47. - Print - *103614*
Asher, A., & Co., Keizersgracht 489-91, 1017 DM Amsterdam. T. (020) 622 22 55. - Print - *103615*

Athenaeum Antiquarian Booksellers, Reguliersgracht 50, 1017 LT Amsterdam. T. (020) 622 62 88.
- Print - *103616*
Bakker, Gebr., Gasthuismolensteeg 7, 1016 AM Amsterdam. T. (020) 623 97 03. - Print - *103617*
Benjamins, John, Amsteldijk 44, PO Box 75577, 1070 AN Amsterdam. T. (020) 676 23 25, 673 81 56, Fax 673 97 73. - Print / Engr - *103618*
Beokentoko, Oude Hoogstr. 14-18, 1012 CE Amsterdam.
T. (020) 623 11 91. - Print - *103619*
Berensluis, De, Prinsengracht 288, 1016 HJ Amsterdam.
T. (020) 624 67 69. *103620*
Berg, van, Oude Schans 8-10, 1011 KX Amsterdam.
T. (020) 624 08 48. - ArtBk - *103621*
Bergmans & Brouwer, Rustenburgerstr. 291, 1073 GE Amsterdam. T. (020) 679 55 00. - Print - *103622*
Boekencasa, Haarlemmerdijk 133, 1013 KG Amsterdam.
T. (020) 622 58 92. - Print - *103623*
Boekwinkel & Antiquariaat Vrouwen in Druk, Westermarkt 5, 1016 DH Amsterdam.
T. (020) 624 50 03. *103624*
Bolland, Prinsengracht 493, 1016 HR Amsterdam.
T. (020) 622 19 21. - Print - *103625*
Buijs, J., Kloveniersburgwal 44, 1012 CW Amsterdam.
T. (020) 622 38 28. - Print - *103626*
Burnet, R. Claeszenstr. 96, 1056 WS Amsterdam.
T. (020) 685 36 89. - Print - *103627*
Charbo's Antiquariaat, Koninginneweg 79, 1075 CJ Amsterdam. T. (020) 676 12 29. *103628*
Cine-Qua-Non Film Boekwinkel, Staalstr. 14, 1011 JL Amsterdam. T. (020) 625 55 88. - Print - *103629*
Clingeborg, Gravenstr 26, 1012 NM Amsterdam.
T. (020) 623 64 72. *103630*
Colombine, Ceintuurbaan 37, 1072 ET Amsterdam.
T. (020) 662 13 94. *103631*
Die Schmiede, Brouwersgracht 4, 1013 GW Amsterdam.
T. (020) 625 05 01. - Print - *103632*
Dishoeck, E.A.E. van, Oudemanhuispoort 8, 1012 CN Amsterdam. T. (020) 626 14 38. - Print - *103633*
Dishoeck, E.A.E. van, Raamsteeg 1, 1012 VZ Amsterdam. T. (020) 624 71 90. - Print - *103634*
Dorsman, T., Kloveniersburgwal 35, 1011 JV Amsterdam. T. (020) 622 40 40. - Print - *103635*
Egidius, Nieuwez Voorburgwal 334, 1012 RW Amsterdam. T. (020) 624 39 29. - Print - *103636*
Emmering, S., N.Z. Voorburgwal 304, 1012 RV Amsterdam. T. (020) 6231476, Fax (020) 6245487. - Print / Engr / Map - *103637*
Erasmus, Postbus 19140, 1000 GC Amsterdam.
T. (020) 627 69 52. - ArtBk - *103638*
Erlemann, Hartmut, Keizersgracht 258, 1016 EV Amsterdam. T. (020) 625 97 68, Fax 638 61 40. *103639*
Flint, J.H., Dikninge 119, 1083 VA Amsterdam.
T. (020) 642 36 46. *103640*
Fragmenta Selecta, Postbus 6489, 1005 EL Amsterdam.
T. (020) 612 25 98. - Print - *103641*
Friedesche Molen, De, Rosmarijnsteeg 6, 1012 RP Amsterdam. T. (020) 625 59 47. - Print - *103642*
Gennep, Van, Nieuwez Voorburgwal 330, 1012 RW Amsterdam. T. (020) 626 44 48. - Print - *103643*
Gerits, A., & Sons, Prinsengracht 445, 1000 AR Amsterdam. T. (020) 627 22 85, Fax 25 89 70. - Print / ArtBk - *103644*
Gerits, A., & Sons, Prinsengracht 445, 1016 HN Amsterdam. T. (020) 627 22 85. - Print - *103645*
Gerritsma, B., Herengracht 350, 1016 CG Amsterdam.
T. (020) 626 14 35. - Print - *103646*
Goltzius, Nieuwe Spiegelstr. 37-I, 1017 DC Amsterdam.
T. (020) 6380094. *103647*
Gouw, J. ter, Overtoom 480, 1054 JZ Amsterdam.
T. (020) 616 64 26. *103648*
Hagen, Bert, Herengracht 38, 1015 CB Amsterdam.
T. (020) 626 39 82. - Print - *103649*
Hieronymus Bosch, Leliegracht 36, 1015 DH Amsterdam. T. (020) 623 71 78. - Print - *103650*
Hondius, Nieuwe Spiegelstr 59, 1017 DD Amsterdam.
T. (020) 625 86 39. *103651*
Hoogkamp, Spiegelgracht 27, 1017 JP Amsterdam.
T. (020) 625 88 52. - Print - *103652*
Houthakker, Bernard, Rokin 98, 1012 KZ Amsterdam.
T. (020) 623 39 39. - Print / Engr - *103653*
Huijr, W., Grubbehoeve 307, 1000 Amsterdam.
T. (020) 699 71 35. - Print - *103654*

Huizenga, M. L., OZ Achterburgwal 156, 1012 DW Amsterdam. T. (020) 623 75 66. *103655*
Humaniora Antiqua, Herengracht 242, 1016 BT Amsterdam. T. (020) 626 15 85. - Print - *103656*
Israel, B. M., Singel 379, 1012 WL Amsterdam.
T. (020) 622 55 00. - Engr / Map - *103657*
Israel, Nico, Keizersgracht 489-491, 1017 DM Amsterdam. T. (020) 622 22 55. - Print / Map - *103658*
Jimmink, Rooseveltin 62, 1078 NL Amsterdam.
T. (020) 679 12 44. - Print - *103659*
Jonge, P. de, Zweerskade 18b, 1077 TZ Amsterdam.
T. (020) 664 08 41. - Print - *103660*
Junk, Van Eeghenstr. 129, 1017 GA Amsterdam.
T. (020) 676 31 85. *103661*
Kenter, Willemsparkw. 37, 1071 GP Amsterdam.
T. (020) 672 99 50. - Print - *103662*
Kok, A. & Zn., Oude Hoogstr 14-18, 1012 CE Amsterdam. T. (020) 623 11 91. *103663*
Kool & Hoedeman, Singel 348, 1016 AG Amsterdam.
T. (020) 624 62 89, 618 91 90. - Print - *103664*
Koolemans, C., Willemsparkweg 164, 1071 HT Amsterdam. T. (020) 673 28 42. - Print - *103665*
Kuik, Paul von, Lastmankade, p. 178, 1075 KT Amsterdam. T. (020) 662 96 17. - Print - *103666*
Landré, G.N., 1e Anjeliersdwarsstr. 36, 1015 NR Amsterdam. T. (020) 624 70 56. - Print - *103667*
Lankamp & Brinkman, Spiegelgracht 19, 1017 JP Amsterdam. T. (020) 623 45 12. *103668*
Le Canard Blue, Sarphatiepark 107, 1073 CW Amsterdam. T. (020) 679 60 76. - Print - *103669*
Leeuwen, W.J. van, Binnenkant 17, 1011 BG Amsterdam. T. (020) 622 66 12. - Print - *103670*
Linz, P.H.B., Amsteldijk 108, 1078 RP Amsterdam.
T. (020) 671 77 05. - Print - *103671*
Lorelei, Prinsengracht 495, 1016 HR Amsterdam.
T. (020) 623 43 08. - Print - *103672*
Loutron, van, Baerlestr. 166, 1071 BH Amsterdam.
T. (020) 664 88 57. - Print - *103673*
Marcus, Johannes, N.Z. Voorburgwal 284, 1012 RT Amsterdam. T. (020) 6236920. - Print / Engr / Map - *103674*
Meer, A. van der, P.C. Hooftstr. 112, 1071 CD Amsterdam. T. (020) 662 19 36. - Engr / Map - *103675*
Meyer, S.S., J. van Eyckstr. 22a, 1077 LL Amsterdam.
T. (020) 671 57 82. - Print - *103676*
Nabrink, Gé., Korte Korsjespoortsteeg 8, 1012 TC Amsterdam. T. (020) 622 30 58. - Print - *103677*
Nijhof & Lee, Staalstr 13a, 1011 JK Amsterdam.
T. (020) 620 39 80, Fax 639 32 94. *103678*
Opus, Rustenburgerstr. 391, 1072 GW Amsterdam.
T. (020) 676 66 73. - Print - *103679*
Peel, C.P.J. van der, Nieuwe Spiegelstr 33-35, 1017 DC Amsterdam. *103680*
Poelgeest, W. van, Overtoom 85, 1054 HC Amsterdam.
T. (020) 616 31 03. - Print - *103681*
Postma, G., O.Z. Voorburgwal 249, 1012 EZ Amsterdam. T. (020) 624 57 81. - Print - *103682*
Premsela, Robert, Van Baerlestr 78, 1071 BB Amsterdam. T. (020) 662 42 66. *103683*
Printroom-Prentenkabinet, Singel 379, 1012 WL Amsterdam. T. (020) 622 55 00. - Print - *103684*
Quest, Oude Hoogstr. 12, 1012 CE Amsterdam.
T. (020) 625 00 66. - Print - *103685*
Schierenberg, Dieter, Prinsengracht 485-487, 1016 HP Amsterdam. T. (020) 6225730, Fax (020) 6265650. *103686*
Schierenberg, Ineke, Leidsegracht 42, 1016 CM Amsterdam. T. (020) 623 61 78. - Print - *103687*
Schippers, P., Keizersgracht 302-304, 1016 EX Amsterdam. T. (020) 622 75 07. *103688*
Schors, W.N., Reguliersgracht 52-54, 1017 LT Amsterdam. T. (020) 626 41 21. - Print - *103689*
Schuhmacher, Gelderschekade 107, 1011 EM Amsterdam. T. (020) 622 16 04, Fax 620 66 20. - Print / ArtBk - *103690*
Silbernberg, M. Dr., 1e vd. Helststr. 74, 1072 NZ Amsterdam. T. (020) 673 29 15. - Print - *103691*
Slegte, J. de, Kalverstr. 48-52, 1012 PE Amsterdam.
T. (020) 622 59 33. - Print / Engr / Map - *103692*
Speculum Orbis Terrrarum, Nieuwe Herengracht 235, 1011 SP Amsterdam. T. (020) 626 78 74.
- Map - *103693*

Spinoza, Den Textstr. 26, 1017 ZB Amsterdam.
T. (020) 624 23 73. - Print -   *103694*
Steiner-Asher, Keizersgracht 489, 1017 EH
Amsterdam.   *103695*
Straat Antiquaren, Rosmarijnsteeg 8, 1012 RP Amster-
dam. T. (020) 822 79 04. - Print -   *103696*
Valerius Muziekhandel en Antiquariaat, Koninginneweg
145, 1075 CM Amsterdam. T. (020) 662 36 29.
- Print -   *103697*
Verbeelding, Utrechtsestr. 40, 1017 VP Amsterdam.
T. (020) 626 53 85. - Print -   *103698*
Vermeulen, Arno S., Herengracht 453, 1001 NC
Amsterdam.   *103699*
Vrouwen in Druck, Westermarkt 5, 1016 DH Amsterdam.
T. (020) 624 50 03.   *103700*
Witcard, St. Antoniesbreestr. 9, 1011 HB Amsterdam.
T. (020) 620 98 90. - Print -   *103701*
Wout Vuyk Boeken, Spuistr. 316, 1012 VX Amsterdam.
T. (020) 622 04 61. - Print -   *103702*
Wout Vuyk Boeken, Singel 367-383, 1012 WL Amster-
dam. T. (020) 622 04 61. - Print -   *103703*
Zuiderwijk, W., Linnaeusparksweg 95 hs, 1098 CT Am-
sterdam. T. (020) 665 11 41. - Print -   *103704*

Arnhem (Gelderland)
Gysbers & van Loon, Bakkerstr 7-7a, 6800 AJ Arnhem.
T. (026) 4424421.   *103705*
Slegte, J. de, Janstr. 28, 6811 GJ Arnhem.
T. (026) 4420597. - Print / Map -   *103706*

Baarn (Utrecht)
Argus, Prof. Drionlaan 6, 3741 XE Baarn.
- Print -   *103707*
Hertzberger, Menno, Eemnesserweg 81, 3743 AG Baarn.
T. (035) 5414938. - Print / ArtBk / Autogr /
Map -   *103708*

Barneveld (Gelderland)
Beek, Johan, Graaf van Lyndenlaan 55, 3771 JB Barne-
veld. T. (0342) 415118. - Print -   *103709*

Bilthoven (Utrecht)
IKAVO, 1. Brandenburgerweg 24, 3721 MJ Bilthoven.
T. (030) 2211754. - Print / ArtBk / Engr / Map -   *103710*

Blaricum (Noord-Holland)
Gendt, A.L. van, Oud Huizerweg 4, 1261 BD Blaricum.
T. (035) 5314683. - Print -   *103711*

Breda (Noord-Brabant)
Couvreur, Smaragdstr 33, 4817 JL Breda.   *103712*
Turnhout, van, Grote Markt 18, 4811 XR Breda.
T. (076) 5134772. - ArtBk -   *103713*

Buren (Gelderland)
Knuf, Frits, Postbus 720, 4116 ZJ Buren.
T. (0344) 571255. - Print -   *103714*

Bussum (Noord-Holland)
Book Exchange, Kapelstr 15a, 1404 HT Bussum.
T. (035) 6930828.   *103715*
Carpinus, Kerkstr. 26, 1404 HJ Bussum.
T. (035) 6914996. - ArtBk -   *103716*
Notebaart, P.C., Postbus 280, 1400 AG Bussum.
T. (035) 6945801. - Print / ArtBk -   *103717*
Peet, Jan, Koningslaan 16, 1405 GL Bussum.
T. (035) 6919350.   *103718*
Verhoeven, Thierensstr 3, 1404 CZ Bussum.
T. (035) 6918352.   *103719*

Castricum (Noord-Holland)
Hagen, Bert, Molenweide 24, 1902 CH Castricum.
T. (0251) 656734. - Print -   *103720*

Delft (Zuid-Holland)
Boekenbeurs Haagse, Hippolytusbuurt 26, 2611 HN
Delft.   *103721*
Geur Van Vergetelheid, De, Rietveld 2a, 2611 LL Delft.
T. (015) 2131788.   *103722*

Den Burg (Noord-Holland)
Klift, Hans van der, Weverstr. 28, 1791 AD Den Burg.
- Print / Engr / Map -   *103723*

Doornspijk (Gelderland)
Coevorden, van, Beukenlaan 3, 8085 RK Doornspijk.
T. (0525) 661823.   *103724*

Eindhoven (Noord-Brabant)
Slegte, J. de, Rechtestr 36a, 5611 GP Eindhoven.
T. (040) 2447419.   *103725*

Enschede (Overijssel)
Slegte, J. de, Marktstr. 13, 7511 GC Enschede.
T. (053) 4319200. - Print -   *103726*

Franeker (Friesland)
Wever, Zilverstraat 16, 8801 KC Franeker.   *103727*

Geldrop (Noord-Brabant)
Swaen, Paulus, Hofstr 19, 5664 HS Geldrop.
T. (040) 2853571, Fax 2854075.   *103728*

Gorinchem (Zuid-Holland)
Bergmans & Brouwer, W de Vries Robbeweg 40, 4206
AM Gorinchem. T. (0183) 621471.   *103729*

Grave (Noord-Brabant)
Alfa, Brugstr. 5, 5361 GT Grave. T. (0486) 473966.
- Print -   *103730*

Groningen
Bouma, Turfsingel 3, 9712 KG Groningen.
T. (050) 3123037. - Print -   *103731*
Onder de Galerij, Brugstraat 23, 9712 AB Groningen.
T. (050) 528656.   *103732*
Slegte, J. de, Herestr. 30, 9711 LJ Groningen.
T. (050) 521422. - Print / Engr / Map -   *103733*

Grouw (Friesland)
Frisco, Hoofdstraat 5, 9001 AM Grouw.
T. (0566) 621316.   *103734*

Den Haag (Zuid-Holland)
Aagje Deken, Celebesstr. 13, 2585 TB Den Haag.
T. (070) 350 39 68. - Print -   *103735*
Alfa Haganum, Ln. v. Meerdervoort 245, 2563 AC Den
Haag. T. (070) 360 12 85. - Print -   *103736*
Cycnus, Ln de Colignystr. 122a, 2595 ST Den Haag.
T. (070) 383 81 72. - Print -   *103737*
De Prins Hendrik, Prins Hendrikstr. 111, 2518 HM Den
Haag. T. (070) 345 40 94. - Print -   *103738*
Haags Antiquariaat, Bentinckstr. 107, 2582 SZ Den
Haag. T. (070) 358 54 80. - Print -   *103739*
Heeneman, M., Prinsestr 47, 2513 CA Den Haag.
T. (070) 364 47 48.   *103740*
Heenemann, Jan, Bezuidenhoutseweg 86A, 2594 AX
Den Haag. T. (070) 385 87 18, 385 41 88.
- Map -   *103741*
Imagerie, Spekstr. 2, 2514 BL Den Haag.
T. (070) 365 11 37. - Engr -   *103742*
Janbroers, J.W., Sweelinckplein 2, 2517 GK Den Haag.
T. (070) 345 61 44. - Print -   *103743*
Juridisch Antiquariaat, Noordeinde 39, 2514 GC Den
Haag. T. (070) 346 89 08. - Print -   *103744*
Leest, K. Poten 7b, 2511 EB Den Haag.
T. (070) 345 38 38. - Print -   *103745*
Leest, Fred Hendriklaan 81a, 2582 BV Den Haag.
T. (070) 354 03 45. - Print -   *103746*
Lelieveld Muziekantiquaariat, Stationsweg 70, 2515 BP
Den Haag. T. (070) 388 81 31.   *103747*
Loose, R., Papestr. 3, 2513 AV Den Haag.
T. (070) 346 04 04. - Print / Engr / Map -   *103748*
Minverva Antiquariaat, Pyrmontkd 884b, 2518 JT Den
Haag. T. (070) 346 18 11.   *103749*
Nijhoff, Martinus, Lange Voorhout 9-11, 2501 CN Den
Haag. T. (070) 346 94 60. - Print -   *103750*
Porto Bello, Atjehstr. 46, 2585 VL Den Haag.
T. (070) 350 54 28. - Print -   *103751*
Schoonbeek, Pynboomstr. 34, 2565 ZS Den Haag.
T. (070) 360 05 05. - Print -   *103752*
Slegte, J. de, Spuistr. 21, 2511 BC Den Haag.
T. (070) 363 97 12. - Print / Engr / Map -   *103753*
Vere, Eline, P. Heinstr. 47, 2518 CB Den Haag.
T. (070) 346 62 70. - Print -   *103754*
Vloemans, H. A., Anna Paulownastr 10, 2518 BE Den
Haag. T. (070) 360 78 86.   *103755*
Vorkink-Heeneman, Beeklaan 327-329, 2562 AJ Den
Haag. T. (070) 363 44 28. - Print / Engr / Map -   *103756*

Vos, W.R., Laan van Meerdervoort 394, 2563 BC Den
Haag. T. (070) 345 11 98. - Engr -   *103757*

Haarlem (Noord-Holland)
Becker, H., Gierstr 50, 2011 GE Haarlem.
T. (023) 5312839.   *103758*
Coebergh, H., Gedempte Oude Gracht 74, 2011 GT
Haarlem. T. (023) 5319198.   *103759*
Hovingh, C., & Zoon, Kleine Houtstr 50, 2011 DP Haar-
lem. T. (023) 5310714.   *103760*
Kuijper, Bubb, Jansweg 39, 2011 KM Haarlem.
T. (023) 5323986. - Print -   *103761*
Slegte, J. de, Grote Houtstr. 100, 2011 SR Haarlem.
T. (023) 5315250. - Print -   *103762*
Vries, H. de, Ged. Oude Gracht 27, 2000 AG Haarlem.
T. (023) 5319458. - ArtBk -   *103763*

Heemstede (Noord-Holland)
Marel, A. A. W. J. Jac van der, van Ruisdaellaan 30,
2102 AP Heemstede. T. (023) 5285800. - Engr / Au-
togr / Map -   *103764*

's-Hertogenbosch (Noord-Brabant)
Brabant Antiquariaat, Lange Putstraat 14, 5211 KN 's-
Hertogenbosch. T. (073) 6141915. - Print / ArtBk /
Engr / Map -   *103765*

Hilversum (Noord-Holland)
Vuyk, Wout, Leeuwenstr. 13, 1211 ES Hilversum.
T. (035) 647236. - ArtBk -   *103766*

Hoorn (Noord-Holland)
Hoorn's Antiquariaat, Gedempte Turfhaven 50, 1621 HG
Hoorn. T. (0229) 216529.   *103767*

Kampen (Overijssel)
Dijk, van, Dieselstraat 1, 8263 AE Kampen.
T. (038) 3315757.   *103768*

Leeuwarden (Friesland)
Tille, de, Weerd 11, 8911 HL Leeuwarden.
T. (058) 2135500. - Print -   *103769*

Leiden (Zuid-Holland)
Brill, E.J., Nieuwe Rijn 2, 2300 PA Leiden.
T. (071) 5312624. - Print -   *103770*
Burgerdijk & Niermans, Nieuwsteeg 1, 2311 RW Leiden.
T. (071) 5121067. - Print -   *103771*
Hotei Japanese Prints, Breestraat 113a, 2311 CL Lei-
den. T. (071) 5124459, Fax 5141488.   *103772*
Jongbloed, A., & Zoon, Kloksteeg 4, 2311 SL Leiden.
T. (071) 5122570. - Print -   *103773*
Sint Lucas Society, Rapenburg 83, 2311 GK Leiden.
T. (071) 5125540. - Print / Engr -   *103774*
Slegte, J. de, Breestr 73, 2311 CJ Leiden.
T. (071) 5122007.   *103775*

Lisse (Zuid-Holland)
Lemmers, S.C., van Bönninghausenlaan 16, 2161 ET
Lisse. T. (0252) 415332. - Print -   *103776*
Swets & Zeitlinger, Heereweg 347b, 2161 CA Lisse.
T. (0252) 419113. - Print -   *103777*

Maastricht (Limburg)
Slegte, J. de, Grote Str. 53, 6211 CV Maastricht.
T. (043) 3217296. - Print -   *103778*

Middelburg (Zeeland)
Benthem, van, & Jutting, Lange Delft 64, 4331 AR Mid-
delburg. T. (0118) 612630. - ArtBk / Engr /
Map -   *103779*
Icon, Wagenaarstr. 16, 4331 CZ Middelburg.
T. (0118) 624216. - Engr / Map -   *103780*

Mijnsherenland (Zuid-Holland)
Troost, Eendrachtslaan 59, 3271 AB Mijnsherenland.
T. (0186) 601397. - Print -   *103781*

Naarden (Noord-Holland)
Bekhoven, Anton W. van, Nieuwe Haven 27a, 1411 SG
Naarden. T. (035) 6947638. - Print / ArtBk -   *103782*

Nieuwkoop (Zuid-Holland)
Graaf, de, Zuideinde 40, 2421 AK Nieuwkoop. - Print /
Engr -   *103783*

Rotterdam (Zuid-Holland)

Blokken, Zaagmolenstr. 165, 3036 HK Rotterdam.
T. (010) 467 75 19. - Print -   *103784*
Boer, H., Dr Zamenhofstr 56, 3061 SK Rotterdam.
T. (010) 412 85 27.   *103785*
Lindenberg, Slaak 4-14, 3061 CS Rotterdam.
T. (010) 411 16 07. - Print -   *103786*
Louters, Postbus 2790, 3000 CT Rotterdam.
T. (010) 411 54 00. - Print -   *103787*
Manutius, Postbus 4041, 3006 AA Rotterdam.
T. (010) 465 38 37. - Print -   *103788*
Nierop, C.J. van, Rodenrijselaan 47C, 3037 XD Rotter-
dam. T. (010) 466 51 67.   *103789*
Opbouw, Bergweg 60A, 3036 BC Rotterdam.
T. (010) 467 14 64. - Print -   *103790*
Quist, Nieuwe Binnenweg 110, 3015 BE Rotterdam.
T. (010) 436 43 98. - Print / Engr -   *103791*
Republik der Letteren, Boorn 92, 3068 LA Rotterdam.
T. (010) 420 88 18. - Print -   *103792*
Seij, Peter, Strevelsweg 35A, 3073 DS Rotterdam.
T. (010) 484 12 25. - Print -   *103793*
Slegte, J. de, Coolsingel 83, 3012 AE Rotterdam.
T. (010) 413 83 05. - Print / Engr / Map -   *103794*
Thisbe, v. Oldenbarnev. Str. 126-128, 3012 GW Rotter-
dam. T. (010) 433 09 45. - Print -   *103795*
Willemsen, Guus, Postbus 21791, 3001 AT Rotterdam.
T. (010) 412 97 62. - ArtBk -   *103796*

Schiedam (Zuid-Holland)

Interbook International, Langehaven 97, 3111 CC Schiedam. - Print -   *103797*

Stadskanaal (Groningen)

Ossel, Max, Handelsstraat 42, 9501 EV Stadskanaal.
- ArtBk -   *103798*

Tilburg (Noord-Brabant)

Antiquaariat De Rijzende Zon, Poststr. 8, 5038 DH Tilburg. T. (013) 5360337. - Print -   *103799*

Utrecht

Acanthus, Oudegracht 232, 3511 NT Utrecht.
T. (030) 2314949. - Print -   *103800*
Aleph, Vismarkt 9, 3511 KR Utrecht. T. (030) 2322069.
- Print / ArtBk -   *103801*
Beijers, J. L., Achter Sint Pieter 140, 3512 HT Utrecht.
T. (030) 2310958. - Print -   *103802*
Boer, Springweg 7a, 3511 VH Utrecht. T. (030) 2328888.
- Print -   *103803*
Curio, Voorstraat 55, 3512 AK Utrecht.
T. (030) 223895.   *103804*
De Lichte Gaard, Lichte Gaard 5, 3511 KT Utrecht.
T. (030) 213626.   *103805*
Eureka, Nachtegaalstr. 28, 3581 AJ Utrecht.
T. (030) 2340169. - Print -   *103806*
Het Bisschopshof, Buurkerhof 6, 3511 KC Utrecht.
T. (030) 2318618. - Print / Engr / Map -   *103807*
Het Bisschopshof, J.W. Kervezee, Lichte Gaard 1, 3511
KT Utrecht. I. (030) 2314093.   *103808*
Hinderickx en Winderichx, Oudegracht 324, 3511 NT Ut-
recht. T. (030) 2322771. - Print -   *103809*
Interscientia, W.-v.-Noortplein 3, 3514 GK Utrecht.
T. (030) 2733804. - Print -   *103810*
Israel, B., Drs., K. Smeestr. 10, 3512 NX Utrecht.
T. (030) 2369194. - Print -   *103811*
Lapoutre, Schoutenstr 5, 3512 GA Utrecht.
T. (030) 2317480.   *103812*
Mercator, Achter Clarenburg 2, 3511 JJ Utrecht.
T. (030) 2321342. - Map -   *103813*
Reflex, Achter Sint Pieter 4, 3512 HS Utrecht.
T. (030) 2315291. - Print / ArtBk -   *103814*
Slavenburg, M.M.E., Donkere Gaard 9, 3511 KV Utrecht.
T. (030) 2314820. - Print -   *103815*
Slegte, J. de, Oude Gracht 121, 3511 AH Utrecht.
T. (030) 2313001.   *103816*
Swertz, André, Achter St Pieter 4,, 3500 AL Utrecht.
T. (030) 2315291, Fax 2369015.   *103817*
Waterbolk, Niek, Schoutenstr. 7, 3512 GA Utrecht.
T. (030) 2314861. - Print -   *103818*
Wolvekamp, J., Servetstr. 3-5, 3512 JG Utrecht.
T. (030) 227138. - Print / Engr / Map -   *103819*

Warmenhuizen

Soest, Arthur van, De Baan 1, 1749 VR Warmenhuizen.
T. (0226) 393900.   *103820*

Wassenaar (Zuid-Holland)

Picker, Otto, Groot Hoefijzerlaan 3, 2244 GD Wassenaar.
- Print -   *103821*

Zandvoort (Noord-Holland)

Bonset, E.J., Patrijzenstraat 8, 2042 CM Zandvoort.
T. (023) 5713906. - Print -   *103822*

Zeist (Utrecht)

Heeneman, Marloes, Steynlaan 64, 3701 EH Zeist.
T. (030) 6920126. - Engr / Map -   *103823*

Zutphen (Gelderland)

Jongh, Matthijs de, Coehoornsingel 28/A, 7201 AC Zutphen. T. (0575) 543136, Fax 543182. - Print -   *103824*

Zwijndrecht (Zuid-Holland)

Antiekkooi, Ringdijk 386, 3331 LK Zwijndrecht.
T. (078) 6126815. - Engr / Map -   *103825*

Zwolle (Overijssel)

Boer, Theo de, Nagellstr. 28, 8011 EB Zwolle.
T. (038) 4217524, Fax 4221867.   *103826*
Slegte, J. de, Melkmarkt 10, 8011 MC Zwolle.
T. (038) 4214408, 4212789. - Print -   *103827*

New Zealand

Auckland (Auckland)

Dunsheath, Anah, 6 High St., Auckland, 1.
T. (09) 79 03 79, 54 37 88.   *103828*

Wellington

Quilter, John, Plimmer Steps P.O.Box 958, Wellington.
T. (04) 72 27 67.   *103829*
Smith's Bookshop, P.O.Box 10-265, Wellington.
T. (04) 84 32 22.   *103830*

Norway

Bergen

Eiken, Lille Ovregt. 19, 5000 Bergen. - Print -   *103831*
Holberg, Lille Ovregt. 15, 5000 Bergen. - Print -   *103832*

Fredrikstad

Fredrikstad Antikvariat, Torvgaten 64, 1601
Fredrikstad.   *103833*

Grimstad (Aust-Agder)

Thorsen, Skaregrøm, 4890 Grimstad. - Print -   *103834*

Oslo

Adamstuen, Thereses G. 14, 0452 Oslo. T. 22 46 30 79.
- Print -   *103835*
Alva, Skipperg. 19, Oslo. T. 22 41 84 15. - Print - *103836*
Atlantis Antikvariat, Frognerv. 30a, Oslo. T. 22 44 63 55.
- Print -   *103837*
Børsum, Baltzer M., Oscarsgt. 59, 0258 Oslo.
T. 22 56 34 50. - Engr / Autogr -   *103838*
Cappelen, J.W., Kirkegaten 15, 0101 Oslo, (1).
T. 22 42 94 40. - Map -   *103839*
Damm, Tollbodgaten 25, 0157 Oslo. T. 22 41 04 02.
- Print / Engr / Autogr / Map -   *103840*
Lies, Rolv, Nedre Prinsdalsv. 61, 1263 Oslo.
- Print -   *103841*
Lucky Eddie, Trondheimsv. 10, Oslo. T. 22 38 12 90.
- Print -   *103842*
Majorstuen, Vibesg. 15, 0356 Oslo. T. 22 60 06 48.
- Print -   *103843*
Majorstuen, Trudvang. 41, 0363 Oslo.
T. 22 60 80 28.   *103844*
Messel & Wildhagens, Briskebyv. 30, 1182 Oslo.
T. 22 44 25 55.   *103845*
Møller, Juul, Nedre Slottsgt. 11, Oslo. T. 22 41 19 00.
- ArtBk -   *103846*
Norlis, Universitetsgt. 18, 0162 Oslo. T. 22 33 43 47.
- Print -   *103847*

Oslo Nye Antikvariat, Majorstuvn. 15, 0367 Oslo.
T. 22 46 67 38. - Print -   *103848*
Ringstrøm, Bjørn, Ullevålsveien 1, 0165 Oslo.
T. 22 20 78 05.   *103849*
Ruuds Antikvariat, Ullevålsv. 35, 0131 Oslo.
T. 22 46 34 75. - Print -   *103850*
Ruuds Antikvariat, Sigurds G. 20, Oslo. T. 22 67 59 21.
- Print -   *103851*
Vinderen, Slemdalsv. 63, 0373 Oslo. T. 22 14 80 75.
- Print -   *103852*

Trondheim

Adamstuen, Dag Rolfsen, Kongensgt. 68, 7012
Trondheim.   *103853*
Wangsmo, Vår Frue Str. 1, 7000 Trondheim.
- Print -   *103854*

Pakistan

Lahore

Ferozsons, 60 Shara-e-Quaid-i-Azim, Lahore.
T. 30 11 96/98.   *103855*

Paraguay

Asuncíon

Libreria Universal, Mcal Estigarribia 430, Asuncíon.
T. (021) 90633. - Print -   *103856*

Philippines

Manila

Casalinda, G/F, Philbanking Bldg. Ayala Av., Makati, Manila. T. 816-2524, 815-4440/41.   *103857*

Poland

Bydgoszcz

Antykwariat Naukowy „Dom Książki", ul. Armii Czerwonej 2, 85-070 Bydgoszcz.   *103858*

Częstochowa

„Dom Książki", antykwariat, ul. N. Marii Panny 27, 42-
200 Częstochowa.   *103859*

Gdańsk

Księgarski Antykwariat, ul. Grunwaldzka 76, 80-244
Gdańsk.   *103860*

Kraków

Antykwariat Naukowy, ul Sławkowska 10, 31-014
Kraków.   *103861*
Antykwariat Naukowy, ul. Podwale 4, 31-118
Kraków.   *103862*
„Dom Książki", księgarnia-antykwariat współczesny, ul
Szpitalna 19, 31-024 Kraków. T. 2 18 61.   *103863*
Kamiński, Stefan, ul Św. Jana 3, 31-136
Kraków.   *103864*
Pelc, K., ul. Karmelicka 21a, 31-131 Kraków.   *103865*

Nowy Sącz

Kubrycht, ul Dunajewskiego 6, 33-300 Nowy
Sącz.   *103866*

Poznań

Antykwariat Naukowy, ul Stary Rynek 53/54, 61-772
Poznań.   *103867*

Radom

Antykwariat Naukowy, Żeromskiego 89, 26-601
Radom.   *103868*

Warszawa

Księgarnia Antykwaryczna, Nowy Świat 61, 60-583
Warszawa.   *103869*
Warszawski Antykwariat Naukowy, ul Świętokrzyska 14,
00-050 Warszawa. T. (022) 26 89 23.   *103870*

Wrocław

Antykwariat, 8 Pl. Universytecki, 50-137
Wrocław. 103871
Dom Książki Antykwariat, Rynek 6, 50-106
Wrocław. 103872

Portugal

Carcavelos

Estúdio Antiquário Conde da Folgosa, Av. Maria da Conceiçao 8, 2775 Carcavelos. T. (01) 247 02 39. 103873

Coimbra

Vicente, Maria Luisa D.A., Trav. de Ladeira de eminario 32, 3000 Coimbra. - ArtBk - 103874

Lisboa

Antiquário do Chiado, Rua Anchieta 7, 1200 Lisboa.
- Print - 103875
Barateira Ltda., Rua Nova da Trindade 16A, 1200 Lisboa. - Print - 103876
Bertrand, R. Garrett 73, 1200 Lisboa.
T. (01) 320 081. 103877
Biblarte Ltda., Rua de Sao Pedro de Alcântara 71, 1200 Lisboa. T. (01) 337 02. - Engr / Autogr / Map - 103878
Buchholz, Rua Duque de Palmela 4, 1296 Lisboa.
T. (01) 54 73 58, 52 48 59. - ArtBk - 103879
Centro de Arte, Sociedade Tipográfica, Rua de D. Estefânia 195 D, 1000 Lisboa. T. (01) 54 32 80,
Fax 57 79 26. 103880
Duff, George Robert, Rua Artilharia 34 R/C, 1200 Lisboa.
T. (01) 68 43 40. - Engr - 103881
Ediçoes Universo a Bibliofila, Lda., Rua da Misericordia 102, 1200 Lisboa. T. (01) 334 76. - Engr /
Map - 103882
Holtreman, Joao Lopes, Rua da Misericordia 145 b.147, 1200 Lisboa. T. (01) 36 15 64, 32 72 72.
- Print - 103883
Livraria Castro e Silva, Rua da Rosa 31, 1200 Lisboa.
T. (01) 346 73 80. - Print - 103884
Livraria Historica e Ultramarina, Travessa da Queimada 26-28, 1200 Lisboa. T. (01) 346 85 89. - Engr / Autogr /
Map - 103885
Livraria Petrony, Rua da Assunçao 90, 1100 Lisboa. 103886
Livraria Portugal, Rua do Carmo 70, 1200 Lisboa.
T. (01) 36 05 82, 36 05 83, 32 82 20. - Print /
ArtBk - 103887
Livraria Sa da Costa, Rua Garrett 100-102, 1200 Lisboa. 103888
Marques, Americo Francisco, Rua da Misericordia 92, 10, 1200 Lisboa. T. (01) 349 77. - Print / Engr /
Map - 103889
O Mundo do Livro, Largo da Trindade 11 b. 13, 1200 Lisboa. T. (01) 36 99 51. - Print / Autogr - 103890
Pereira,A.M., Rua Augusta 44-54, Lisboa.
T. (01) 36 17 10, 36 17 30. 103891
Tavares de Carvalho, A., Av. da República 46, 1000 Lisboa. T. (01) 77 03 77. - Print / Engr / Map - 103892
Telles da Sylva, Jose Antonio, Travessa Marquês sá da Bandeira 19-3, 1000 Lisboa. T. (01) 77 87 54. 103893

Porto

Candelabro, Rua da Conceiçao 3, 4000 Porto.
T. (02) 224 49. - Print / Engr - 103894
Costa, Eduardo Honorio,Dr., Rua Cedofeita 403, 4000 Porto. T. (02) 216 67. - ArtBk - 103895
Ferreira, Manuel, Rua Formosa 19, 4000 Porto.
T. (02) 56 32 37. - Print / ArtBk / Engr / Autogr - 103896
Livraria Academica, Rua Mártires da Liberdade 10, 4000 Porto. 103897

Romania

Arad (judetul Arad)

Anticariat, Str. Miron Constantinescu 2-4, 2900 Arad.
T. (0966) 14196. - Print / ArtBk - 103898

Bacau (judetul Bacau)

Anticariat, Str. N. Bălcescu nr. 5, 5500 Bacau.
T. (0931) 22161. - Print / ArtBk - 103899

Baia Mare (judetul Maramures)

Anticariat, Pta. Libertatii nr. 5, 4800 Baia Mare. - Print /
ArtBk - 103900

Bistrita (judetul Bistrita-Nasaud)

Anticariatul, Calea Armatei Rosii 2, 4400 Bistrita.
- Print - 103901

Botosani (judetul Botosani)

Anticariatul, Str. N. Balcescu Bloc 7, 6800 Botosani.
T. (0985) 17260. - Print / ArtBk - 103902

Braila (judetul Braila)

Anticariat, Str. Republicii nr. 2, 6100 Braila. - Print /
ArtBk - 103903

Brasov (judetul Brasov)

Anticariat, Str. Ciucas nr. 4, 2200 Brasov. - Print /
ArtBk - 103904

Bucuresti

Anticariat nr. 1, Calea Victoriei nr. 45, sector 1, 70101 Bucuresti. T. (01) 615 46 00. - Print / ArtBk - 103905
Anticariat nr. 10, Calea Victoriei nr. 46, sector 1, 70101 Bucuresti. - Print / ArtBk - 103906
Anticariat nr. 11, Calea Mosilor nr.330, sector 1, 73252 Bucuresti. - Print / ArtBk - 103907
Anticariat nr. 13, Calea Rahovei nr. 302, sector 5, 76402 Bucuresti. - Print / ArtBk - 103908
Anticariat nr. 15, Bd. 1 Mai, nr. 42-45, Bl. 2/35, sector 1, 78209 Bucuresti. - Print / ArtBk - 103909
Anticariat nr. 17, Bdul. Republicii nr. 72, sector 2, 70334 Bucuresti. - Print / ArtBk - 103910
Anticariat nr. 2, Str. Academiei nr. 7, sector 1, 70108 Bucuresti. - Print / ArtBk - 103911
Anticariat nr. 3, Bd. Magheru nr. 2, 70156 Bucuresti.
- Print / ArtBk - 103912
Anticariat nr. 5, Calea Victoriei nr. 12, sector 1, 70412 Bucuresti. - Print / ArtBk - 103913
Anticariat nr. 7, Sos. Stefan cel Mare nr.10, sector 2, 71133 Bucuresti. - Print / ArtBk - 103914
Anticariat nr. 8, B-dul. 1848 nr. 14, sector 3, 70427 Bucuresti. - Print / ArtBk - 103915
Anticariat nr. 9, Str. 30 Decembrie nr. 9, sector 3, 70002 Bucuresti. T. (01) 616 32 31. - Print / ArtBk - 103916
U.C.E. Artexim, 1, Piata Scinteii, 70 055 Bucuresti.
T. (01) 617 13 13. - Print - 103917

Buzau (judetul Buzau)

Anticariatul, Piata Daciei Bloc 3 B, 5100 Buzau.
- Print - 103918

Cluj-Napoca

Anticariat, Pta. Libertatii nr. 16, 3400 Cluj-Napoca.
- Print / ArtBk - 103919

Constanta (judetul Constanta)

Anticariat, Bd. Republicii nr. 7a, 8700 Constanta.
- Print - 103920

Craiova (judetul Dolj)

Anticariatul, Str. Ion Maiorescu Bloc 7-14, 1100 Craiova.
T. (0941) 12588. - Print - 103921

Deva (judetul Hunedoara)

Anticariat, Pta. Unirii nr. 4, 2700 Deva. - Print - 103922

Focsani (judetul Vrancea)

Anticariat, Str. Alexandru Vlahuta nr. 30, 5300 Focsani.
- Print / ArtBk - 103923

Galati (judetul Galati)

Anticariat, Str. Republicii nr. 59, 6200 Galati. - Print /
ArtBk - 103924

Iasi

Anticariat, Str. Stefan cel Mare nr. 67, 6600 Iasi.
T. (0981) 42471. - Print / ArtBk - 103925

Miercurea Ciuc (judetul Harghita)

Anticariatul, Str. Petöfi Sandor 6, 4100 Miercurea Ciuc.
T. (0958) 11452. - Print / ArtBk - 103926

Oradea (judetul Bihor)

Anticariat, Calea Republicii nr. 14, 3700 Oradea.
T. (0991) 18920. - Print - 103927

Piatra Neamt (judetul Neamt)

Anticariatul, Bd. Chimiei Bloc C 6, 5600 Piatra Neamt.
T. (0936) 15182. - Print - 103928

Pitesti (judetul Arges)

Anticariat, Str. 1 Mai Bl. B 3-4, 0300 Pitesti. - Print /
ArtBk - 103929

Ploiesti (judetul Prahova)

Anticariat, Str. Republicii nr. 104, Bl. 12c, 2000 Ploiesti.
- Print - 103930

Satu Mare (judetul Satu Mare)

Anticariatul, Bd. Eliberarii 12, 3900 Satu Mare.
- Print - 103931

Sfintu Gheorghe (judetul Covasna)

Anticariatul, Piata Gabor Aron 2, 4000 Sfintu Gheorghe.
T. (0923) 14142. - Print / ArtBk - 103932

Sibiu (judetul Sibiu)

Anticariat, Str. N. Bălcescu nr. 43, 2400 Sibiu.
T. (0924) 11657. - Print - 103933

Suceava (judetul Suceava)

Anticariat, Piata 23 August, 5800 Suceava.
T. (0987) 12726. - Print - 103934

Timisoara (judetul Timis)

Anticariat, Str. Bastion ul Cetatii, 1900 Timisoara.
T. (0961) 30355. - Print / ArtBk - 103935

Tirgu Mures (judetul Mures)

Anticariat, Str. Cálárasilor nr. 14, 4300 Tirgu Mures.
T. (0954) 17192. - Print / ArtBk - 103936

Russia

Moskva

Akademkniga, ul Tverskaya 19a, Moskva.
T. (095) 2996242. - ArtBk - 103937
Akademkniga, Michurinski prosp 12, Moskva.
T. (095) 9327479. - Print - 103938
Akademkniga, ul Vavilova 55-7, Moskva.
T. (095) 124 5500. - ArtBk - 103939
Arbatskaya nakhodka, ul Arbat 11, 121019 Moskva.
T. (095) 2917038. 103940
Biblio-Globus Torgovy Dom, ul Myasnitskaya 6, Moskva.
T. (095) 9283567. - ArtBk - 103941
Bukinist, ul Arbat 36, 121002 Moskva.
T. (095) 2413387. 103942
Bukinist 28 600-Stoleshnikov per 14, 103031 Moskva.
T. (095) 9233771. 103943
Bukinist 37, Kotelnicheskaya naberezhnaya 1-15, 109240 Moskva. T. (095) 9154320. 103944
Bukinist 7, ul Sretenka 9, 103045 Moskva.
T. (095) 9289636. 103945
Buks, ul Tverskaya 18b, Moskva. T. (095) 2090105.
- ArtBk - 103946
Dom Knigi v Sokolnikakh, ul Rusakovskaya 27, Moskva.
T. (095) 2648121. 103947
Elina, ul Novaya Basmannaya 10, Moskva.
T. (095) 2659128. - ArtBk - 103948
Fakel, ul Pervomaiskaya 52, Moskva. T. (095) 4653647.
- ArtBk - 103949
Knizhnaya Lavka, ul Pogodinskaya 18, Moskva.
T. (095) 2468970. - ArtBk - 103950
Knizhnaya Lavka Arkhitektora, ul Rozhdestvenka 11, Moskva. T. (095) 9289374. - ArtBk - 103951
Knizhnaya lavka pisatelei, ul Kuznetski Most 18, Moskva. T. (095) 9212298. - ArtBk - 103952
Knizhnaya lavka vostokoveda, Tsvetnoi bulvar 21 stroenie2, Moskva. T. (095) 9254725. - ArtBk - 103953
Knizhnaya Nakhodka, ul Nikolskya 23, 103012 Moskva.
T. (095) 9256690. - ArtBk - 103954
Krymski brod, ul Ostozhenka 53, 119021 Moskva.
T. (095) 2468431. - ArtBk - 103955
Kutuzovski Torgovy Dom, Kutuzovski prosp 4-2, Moskva.
T. (095) 2433256. 103956

Lavka knigolyuba, ul 1-ya Tverskaya-Yamskaya 22, 125147 Moskva. T. (095) 2510904. - ArtBk - *103957*
Lubyanski dvorik, ul Bolshaya Lubyanka 17, Moskva. T. (095) 9210801. - ArtBk - *103958*
Moskovski dom knigi, ul Novy Arbat 8, Moskva. T. (095) 2903580. - ArtBk - *103959*
Moskva Torgovy Dom, ul Tverskaya 8, Moskva. T. (095) 2296483. - ArtBk - *103960*
Nadezhda Torgovy Dom, ul Sretenka 9, Moskva. T. (095) 9232867. - ArtBk - *103961*
Nadezhda Torgovy Dom, ul Sretenka 9, Moskva. T. (095) 9232867. *103962*
Nika, Leninski prosp 85, Moskva. T. (095) 1346038. - ArtBk - *103963*
Progres Torgovy Dom, Zubovski bulvar 17, Moskva. T. (095) 2467741. *103964*
Pushkinskaya lavka, ul Bolshaya Dmitrovka 7-5stroenie 1, 103009 Moskva. T. (095) 2293842. - ArtBk - *103965*
Raduga, ul Profsoyuznaya 7-12, Moskva. T. (095) 1250361. - ArtBk - *103966*
Ukrainskaya kniga, ul Gilyarovskogo 1, Moskva. T. (095) 2075362. - ArtBk - *103967*
Vedy, ul Kuznezki most 18, Moskva. T. (095) 9231705. - ArtBk - *103968*

Sankt-Peterburg

Akademkniga magazin N1, Liteiny prosp 57, Sankt-Pe- terburg. T. (812) 2723665. - ArtBk - *103969*
Alkonost, Grazhdanski proezd 33, Sankt-Peterburg. T. (812) 5350504. - ArtBk - *103970*
Bibliopolis, Moskovski prosp 41, Sankt-Peterburg. T. (812) 3167101. - ArtBk - *103971*
Bukinist na Liteinom, Liteiny prosp 59, Sankt-Peterburg. T. (812) 2732504. - ArtBk - *103972*
Dom knigi, Nevski prosp 28, Sankt-Peterburg. T. (812) 2199440. - ArtBk - *103973*
Iskusstvo, Nevski prosp 16, Sankt-Peterburg. T. (812) 3128535. - ArtBk - *103974*
Iskusstvo, Nevski prosp 52, Sankt-Peterburg. T. (812) 3111651. - ArtBk - *103975*
Knizhnaya lavka, Bankovski per 3, Sankt-Peterburg. T. (812) 3105161. - ArtBk - *103976*
Knizhny magazin N60, Nevski prosp 94, Sankt-Peter- burg. T. (812) 2737734. - ArtBk - *103977*
Mir, Nevski prosp 16, Sankt-Peterburg. T. (812) 3126773. - ArtBk - *103978*
Na Liteinom, Liteiny prosp 61, Sankt-Peterburg. T. (812) 2753873. - ArtBk - *103979*
Na Staronevskom, Nevski prosp 122, Sankt-Peterburg. T. (812) 2772686. - ArtBk - *103980*
Natasha, Rizhski proezd 19, Sankt-Peterburg. T. (812) 2514863. - ArtBk - *103981*
Palech, Ligovski prosp 120, Sankt-Peterburg. T. (812) 1645787. - ArtBk - *103982*
Petrodvorets, ul Avrova 10, Sankt-Peterburg. T. (812) 4279956. - ArtBk - *103983*
Staraya kniga, Nevski pr 18, Sankt-Peterburg. T. (812) 3122081. - ArtBk - *103984*
Staraya kniga, Bolshoi pr B.O. 29, Sankt-Peterburg. T. (812) 2184286. - ArtBk - *103985*
Staraya kniga, ul Marata 43, Sankt-Peterburg. T. (812) 1649415. - ArtBk - *103986*
Staraya kniga, Bolshoi pr P.S.19, Sankt-Peterburg. T. (812) 2321765. - ArtBk - *103987*
Staraya kniga, Moskovski pr 153, Sankt-Peterburg. T. (812) 2981845. - ArtBk - *103988*
U Parnasa, Kultury pr 21 korp 1, Sankt-Peterburg. T. (812) 5576784. - ArtBk - *103989*

Singapore

Singapore

Antiques of the Orient, 21 Cuscaden Rd. 01-02, Ming Ar- cade, Singapore, 1024. *103990*

Slovakia

Bratislava

Slovenská kniha n. p., Mickiewiczova 10, 811 07 Brat- islava. T. (07) 501 64. - Print / ArtBk - *103991*

Slovenska Kniha n. p., Sedliarski 9, Bratislava. T. (07) 301 17. *103992*
Slovensky knizny velkoobehod n. p., Dunajska 21, Brat- islava. T. (07) 512 64. *103993*

Košice

Slovenská kniha n. p., Leninova 29, Košice. T. 24 27. *103994*

Nitra

Slovenská kniha n. p., Leninova 45, Nitra. T. 22 04. *103995*

Trnava

Slovenská Kniha n. p., Hviezdoslavova 2, Trnava. T. 24 23. *103996*

Žilina

Slovenska Kniha n. p., Marx Engelsova 4, Žilina. T. (089) 200 67. *103997*

Slovenia

Ljubljana

Cankarjeva založba, Kopitarjeva 2, 1000 Ljubljana. T. (061) 323841. - ArtBk - *103998*
Cankarjeva založba, Antikvarijat, Mestni trg 25, 1000 Ljubljana. T. (061) 20352. - Print / ArtBk / Engr / Map - *103999*
Državna založba Slovenije, Mestni trg 28, 1000 Ljublja- na POB 50 I. T. (061) 310736. - ArtBk - *104000*
Mladinska knjiga, Prešernova 5, 1000 Ljubljana. T. (061) 212211, Fax 224454. - ArtBk - *104001*

South Africa

Cape Town (Cape Province)

Clarke's Bookshop, 211 Long St., 8001 Cape Town. T. (021) 23 57 39. *104002*
Naumann, Ulrich, 17 Burgstr., 8001 Cape Town. T. (021) 41 12 79. - Engr / Map - *104003*

Johannesburg (Transvaal)

Vanguard, 123 Commissioner Str., Johannesburg. T. (011) 23 35 11. - Print - *104004*

Johannesburg (Tvl.)

Thorold, Frank R., Meischke Bldg. 42, 3.Fl., 2001 Jo- hannesburg. T. (011) 838 59 03. *104005*

Pretoria (Tvl.)

Schaik, van, 270 Church. St., Pretoria P.O.B. 724, 0001. T. (012) 212 441. - ArtBk - *104006*

Randburg (Transvaal)

Real Books, 44 Randarcade, Randburg, 2125. T. 787 8018. *104007*

Spain

Almeria (Almeria)

Libreria Sol, Obispo Orbera, 33, 04001 Almeria. T. (951) 21 56 96. *104008*

Barcelona

Antigua Libreria Sala, Boters, 8, 08002 Barcelona. T. (93) 231 95 49. - Print - *104009*
Aristeucos, Paseo de la Bonanova 14, 08022 Barcelona. T. (93) 247 82 55. - Print - *104010*
Batlle, Angel, Paja 23, 08002 Barcelona. T. (93) 301 58 84. - Print / ArtBk / Engr / Autogr / Map - *104011*
Bosch, Ronda Universidad 11, 08007 Barcelona. T. (93) 317 53 08. - ArtBk - *104012*
Cinc d'Oros, Diagonal 462, 08006 Barcelona. T. (93) 217 00 59. *104013*
Herder, Balmes 26, 08007 Barcelona. T. (93) 317 05 78. - ArtBk - *104014*
Italiana, Rambla Ciatalunya 33, 08007 Barcelona. T. (93) 301 7579. *104015*

Libreria Castells, S.A., Ronda de la Universidad 13 b. 15, 08007 Barcelona. T. (93) 317 06 46. *104016*
Libreria de Tomas Trallero Bardaji, Paja, 33, 08002 Barcelona. *104017*
Libreria Fabre, Rambla de Cataluña 52, 08007 Barcelo- na. T. (93) 216 02 25. *104018*
Martinez Pérez, Valencia 246, 08007 Barcelona. T. (93) 215 19 33. *104019*
Novecientos, Libreria, Libreteria 10 + 12, 08002 Barce- lona. T. (93) 315 39 04. *104020*
Puvill, Boters 10, 08002 Barcelona. T. (93) 318 29 86, 318 18 48. *104021*
Sala Gaspar, Consejo de Ciento 323, 08007 Barcelona. T. (93) 487 71 57, Fax 487 41 21. - Print / Engr / Autogr - *104022*

Lérida

Oliva, Sala, Luciano, San Antonio, 42, 25002 Lérida. T. (973) 1 18 16. *104023*

Madrid

Libreria Callejon, Callejon de Preciados, 2, 28013 Madrid. *104024*
Libreria la Casa de la Troya, Libreros, 6, 28004 Madrid. T. (91) 221 94 10 y 221 94 78. *104025*
Libreria Mirto, Ruiz de Alarcon, 27, 28014 Madrid. T. (91) 239 83 31. *104026*
Libreria para Bibliofilos Luis Bardon Lopez, Plaza de San Martin, 3, 28013 Madrid. T. (91) 221 55 14. - Print / Autogr - *104027*
Libreria Universal de Garcia Rico, Desengano, 13, 28013 Madrid. *104028*
Libreria Vda. de Estanislau Rodriguez, San Bernardo, 27, 28015 Madrid. *104029*
Libros Argensola, Argensola 20, 28004 Madrid. T. (91) 410 48 68. *104030*
Molina, Gabriel, Suc., Travesia del Arenal, 1, 28013 Ma- drid. T. (91) 266 44 43. *104031*
Naos, Quintana 12, 28008 Madrid. T. (91) 247 39 16. *104032*

Palamós (Gerona)

Ripoll, San Miguel 12, 07002 Palamós. T. (972) 22 13 55. - Print / Autogr / Map - *104033*

Palma de Mallorca (Baleares)

Fiol, Oms 45a, 07003 Palma de Mallorca. T. (971) 72 14 28. - Print - *104034*

Sevilla

Munoz, Sebastian Rodriguez, Amparo, 20, 41003 Sevil- la. T. (954) 22 38 75. - Print - *104035*

Tarragona

Javier, Portella, 2, 43003 Tarragona. T. (977) 20 54 75. *104036*

Valencia

Libreria Bonaire, Nave, 21, 46003 Valencia. *104037*
Marti Belda, Lope de Vega, 9, 46001 Valencia. T. (96) 22 22 46. - Print - *104038*

Zaragoza

Hesperia, Pl. de los Sitios 10, 50001 Zaragoza. T. (976) 23 53 67, 22 82 39. - Print - *104039*
Ruiz Lasala, Inocencio, Cuatro de Agosto, 7 + 9, 50003 Zaragoza. T. (976) 22 89 08. - Print - *104040*

Sri Lanka

Colombo

Lake House Bookshop, P.O.Box 244, Colombo. *104041*

Sweden

Årsta

Olof Edlund, POB 723, 120 02 Årsta. T. (08) 811718, Fax 811678. - Print / ArtBk - *104042*

Eslöv

Crafoord, Kastberga Slott, POB 40, 241 21 Eslöv. T. (0413) 13040, Fax 60960. *104043*

Gunnar Johanson-Thor, Nämndemansvägen 5, 241 37
Eslöv. T. (0413) 60100, 60101. - Print / Engr /
Map - *104044*

Färila
Hälsinglands, Härjedalsvägen 12, 820 41 Färila.
T. (0651) 20179, Fax 14237. *104045*

Falköping
Carl Hellmor, Hasselgatan 10 (S. Bestorp), POB 644, 521
21 Falköping. T. (0515) 19899, 19707, Fax 8105686.
- Print / ArtBk - *104046*

Göteborg
Antiquaria Bok- & Bildantikvariat AB, Kristinelundsgatan
7, 411 37 Göteborg. T. (031) 161415, Fax 161415.
- Print / Map - *104047*
Lundquists, Geijersgatan 5, 411 34 Göteborg.
T. (031) 189719. *104048*
Styrbjörn Öhman AB, Västra Hamngatan 24, 411 17 Gö-
teborg. T. (031) 110066, Fax 171804. - Print - *104049*
Wettergrans Bokhandel, Västra Hamngatan 22, 411 17
Göteborg. T. (031) 10 10 60. - ArtBk - *104050*

Helsingborg
AB Killsberg Bokhandel, Stortorget 4, 25223 Helsingborg. T. (042) 12 00 85. *104051*
Lundgrens Antikvariat, Romares Stifelse, Romares Väg,
250 03 Helsingborg. T. (042) 11 73 86. *104052*

Järpås
Andreassons, Höra Stommen, 531 94 Järpås.
T. (0510) 91783. - Print - *104053*

Karlstad
Karlstads Antikvariat, Per Bredberg, Kungsgatan 2, POB
509, 651 11 Karlstad. T. (054) 154313/42. *104054*

Lidingö
Enhörningen Antikvariat, Bo Löwenström, Stockhol-
msvägen 60, 181 42 Lidingö. T. (08) 7676411. *104055*

Linköping
Antikvariska Bokhandeln, Nygatan 33, 582 24 Linköping. T. (013) 121408. *104056*

Ljusdal
Hälsinglands Antik, Slottegatan 15, 827 00 Ljusdal.
T. (0651) 10559, Fax 14237. *104057*

Lund
Åkarps Antikvariat, P. Dethorey, Klostergatan 11, POB
1129, 221 04 Lund. T. (046) 112499,
Fax 142786. *104058*
Barnboksantikvariatet Piraten, St. Gråbrödersgatan 17,
222 22 Lund. T. (046) 140606, Fax 142786. *104059*
Bokkultur, Charlotte du Rietz, Pålsjövägen 7, 223 62
Lund. T. (046) 130420, 158298. *104060*
Roger Jacobsson, Klostergatan 11, 2 tr, 222 22 Lund.
T. (046) 149133, Fax 142533. - Print - *104061*
Lengertz' Antikvariat i Lund, Kjell Askagården, St. Grå-
brödersgatan 13, 222 22 Lund. T. (046) 110345.
- Print / Engr / Map - *104062*
Olins Antikvariat, Klostergatan 11, 222 22 Lund.
T. (046) 112499. - Print - *104063*

Malmö
Jonny Ambrius, Davidshallsgt. 28, 211 45 Malmö.
T. (040) 232713. *104064*
Lengertz', Gösta Janson, Regementsgatan 56A, 217 48
Malmö. T. (040) 915620. *104065*
Lilla, Djäknegatan 4, 211 35 Malmö. T. (040) 128778,
Fax 142786. *104066*

Mörbylånga
Ölands Antikvariat, Storgatan 22, Mörbylånga.
T. (0485) 40705. *104067*

Örebro
Bergslagens, Kungsgatan 3, POB 208, 701 44 Örebro.
T. (019) 148990. *104068*

Österbymo
Antikvariatet Bokkultur AB, Charlotte Du Rietz, 57060
Österbymo. T. (0140) 83021, Fax 83027.
- Print - *104069*

Thulins, Tångarp, 570 60 Österbymo. T. (0140) 83021,
Fax 83027. - Engr / Autogr - *104070*

Stockholm
Alla Tiders Böcker, Kungsg. 90, 100 90 Stockholm.
T. (08) 54 53 25. *104071*
Andra, Rörstrandsgatan 25, 113 40 Stockholm.
T. (08) 310707. *104072*
Antikvariat Antiqua, Karlavägen 12, 114 31 Stockholm.
T. (08) 100996. - Print / ArtBk - *104073*
Antikvariat Erato, Norrtullsgatan 12, POB 6329, 102 35
Stockholm. T. (08) 311960. *104074*
Antikvariat Gallerian, Hamng. Gallerian, 100 90 Stock-
holm. T. (08) 21 34 20. *104075*
Antikvariska Bokcentralen A/B, Kornhamnstorg 47,
11127 Stockholm. T. (08) 20 27 69. *104076*
Antiquariat Athenæum, Strandvägen 11, 114 59 Stock-
holm. T. (08) 6677840, Fax 6677840. - Engr /
Map - *104077*
Appelholt, J., Regeringsg. 71, 100 90 Stockholm.
T. (08) 21 49 94. *104078*
Aspingtons, Västerlånggatan 54, 111 29 Stockholm.
T. (08) 201100, Fax 205200. - Print / ArtBk / Engr /
Map - *104079*
Axen, Gunnar, Alströmerg. 6, 100 90 Stockholm.
T. (08) 54 81 56. *104080*
Björck & Börjesson, Odengatan 23, 114 24 Stockholm.
T. (08) 4119042, Fax 149702. - Print - *104081*
Blå Tornet, Drottningatan 85, 111 60 Stockholm.
T. (08) 20 21 43 , 775 31 11. *104082*
Böhme, Stella, Hantverkarg. 30, 100 90 Stockholm.
T. (08) 50 47 04. *104083*
Bok & Antik, Tegnerg. 14, 100 90 Stockholm.
T. (08) 30 39 61. *104084*
Boksarmabete, Antikvariatet Sten Thunvik, Tegnergatan
17, 10090 Stockholm. *104085*
Bokslussen, Götgatan 17 (T-banan Slussen), POB
15102, 104 65 Stockholm. T. (08) 6409615. *104086*
Boulard, Frejg. 32, 100 90 Stockholm.
T. (08) 33 65 92. *104087*
Bouquiniste, S:t Paulsg. 13, 100 90 Stockholm.
T. (08) 714 09 80. *104088*
Celi, Götg. 24, 100 90 Stockholm.
T. (08) 41 14 50. *104089*
Central Antikvariatet, Drottninggatan 73 B, 111 36
Stockholm. T. (08) 4119136, Fax 209308. *104090*
Codex, Grevg. 32, 100 90 Stockholm.
T. (08) 660 98 01. *104091*
Diefenbronner, Eric, Sibyllegatan 13, 10243 Stockholm.
T. (08) 60 76 79. - Print - *104092*
Ellehöjs Antikvariat, John O. E. Ellehöj, S:t Eriksgatan
92, 10090 Stockholm. *104093*
Engberg, Bergsg. 49, 100 90 Stockholm.
T. (08) 52 41 15. *104094*
ERA Bok- & Bildantikvariat, Drottninggatan 83 ö.g., POB
45197, 104 30 Stockholm. T. (08) 4110891, 7581412,
Fax 7925440. - Print / Engr / Map - *104095*
Europa Antikvariat, Sibylleg. 51, 100 90 Stockholm.
T. (08) 661 94 58. *104096*
Evas Antikvariat, Ringv. 143, 100 90 Stockholm.
T. (08) 43 30 50. *104097*
Flodin, Västerlångg. 37, 111 29 Stockholm.
T. (08) 20 48 81, 20 61 95. - Engr / Map - *104098*
Fynd, Karla, Karlav. 73, 100 90 Stockholm.
T. (08) 661 52 70. *104099*
Grafik-Antikvariatet, Ove G. Renqvist, POB 2271, 103 16
Stockholm. T. (08) 6694430, Fax 7206460. - Print /
Map - *104100*
Gunnars Antikvariat, Gunnar Ohlsson, Bergsgatan 49,
10090 Stockholm. *104101*
Hagelin, POB 3321, 103 66 Stockholm. T. (08) 6737505,
Fax 6737505. - Print - *104102*
Halléns, Tegnérgatan 17, 111 40 Stockholm.
T. (08) 200270, 207819, 7179331. *104103*
Hyllan, Årstav. 57, Johanneshov, 100 90 Stockholm.
T. (08) 81 53 73. *104104*
Inger Johanson-Thor, Riddargatan 28, 114 57 Stock-
holm. T. (08) 6617024. - Print / ArtBk / Map - *104105*
Jones, Norrtullsgatan 3, 113 29 Stockholm.
T. (08) 307697. *104106*
Kåbe, Högbergsg. 64, 100 90 Stockholm.
T. (08) 42 53 65. *104107*

Karlsson, Bo Rainer, Braheg. 5, 100 90 Stockholm.
T. (08) 661 66 91. *104108*
Katarina-Antikvariatet, Katarina bang. 17, 100 90 Stock-
holm. T. (08) 40 78 68. *104109*
Kokora Asian Art, Österlangg. 12, 111 31 Stockholm.
T. (08) 11 68 87, Fax 758 46 49. - ArtBk - *104110*
Konst-Bibliofilen, Västerlanggatan 6, 111 29 Stockholm.
T. (08) 21 27 68. *104111*
Kornhamnstorgs Antikvariat, L. Nygatan 11, 100 90
Stockholm. T. (08) 20 24 72. *104112*
Läseleket Barnboksantikvariat, Hornsgatan 80, 118 21
Stockholm. T. (08) 6680580. *104113*
Libris Antikvariatet, Nybrogatan 64, POB 5123, 102 43
Stockholm. T. (08) 6622131, 6609262. - Print / Engr /
Map - *104114*
Lindbergh, Nils, Tegnérgatan 10, 113 58 Stockholm.
T. (08) 31 20 20. - Print - *104115*
Lyktan, Bergsg. 20, 100 90 Stockholm.
T. (08) 51 43 91. *104116*
Moderna Museet Bookshop, Skeppsholmen, Box 16382,
103 27 Stockholm. T. (08) 666 43 76. *104117*
Nya Antikvariatet, Renstiernasg. 28, 100 90 Stockholm.
T. (08) 44 31 43. *104118*
Parnassen, Regeringsg. 54, 100 90 Stockholm.
T. (08) 21 10 66. *104119*
PRA Antikvariat, Birger Jarlsgatan 44, 114 29 Stock-
holm. T. (08) 6110372, Fax 6110372. - Print /
Map - *104120*
Mats Rehnström, Torbjörn Klockares Gata 11, 113 30
Stockholm. T. (08) 326985. - Print - *104121*
Rönnells, Birger Jarlsgatan 32, 114 29 Stockholm.
T. (08) 6797550, Fax 6114162. - Map - *104122*
Ryös, Hantverkargatan 21, 112 21 Stockholm.
T. (08) 6548086, Fax 6548006. - ArtBk - *104123*
Sörhuus, Riddargatan 3 A, 114 35 Stockholm.
T. (08) 6115595, Fax 6114875. *104124*
Solna-Sundyberg, Förrådsg. 3, 100 90 Stockholm.
T. (08) 82 07 11. *104125*
Tidevarvet, Hornsgatan 80, 118 21 Stockholm.
T. (08) 6682450. *104126*
Karna Wachtmeister, Storgatan 1/IV, 114 44 Stockholm.
T. (08) 6619197. - Engr / Map - *104127*

Sundsvall
Sundsvalls Antikvariat AB, Kyrkogatan 5, 852 31 Sundsvall. T. (060) 124202, Fax 557037. *104128*

Umeå
Antikvariat Bocum, Björn Olofsson, Esplanaden 6, POB
4102, 904 04 Umeå. T. (090) 121577,
Fax 125577. *104129*

Umeå (Västerbotten)
Bothnia, Jan Berglund, Kullavägen 73, 903 62 Umeå.
T. (090) 148990, Fax 148990. *104130*
Umeå Antikvariat, POB 415, 901 08 Umeå.
T. (090) 135850, 32054, Fax 135855. *104131*

Uppsala
Ola Eng, Kyrkogatan 23, 753 12 Uppsala.
T. (018) 108763, Fax 108763. - Print - *104132*
Olofsson, Dragarbrunnsgatan 53, 753 20 Uppsala.
T. (018) 127504. *104133*
Redins, Drottninggatan 11, 753 10 Uppsala.
T. (018) 117000, Fax 117014. *104134*
Roda Rummet, Dragarbrunnsgatan 56, POB 1207, 751
42 Uppsala. T. (018) 133295. *104135*

Västerås
Leanders, Stora Gatan 44 B, POB 333, 721 07 Västerås.
T. (021) 119900. *104136*

Västra Frölunda
H. Mellgrens, Dingegatan 10, 421 76 Västra Frölunda.
T. (031) 298636. *104137*

Vallentuna
Bokantikvaria, Miguel Dethorey, Åbyholmsvägen PL 219,
186 36 Vallentuna. T. (08) 51171037. *104138*

Varberg
Waldrapp, Kungsgatan 9, 432 41 Varberg.
T. (0340) 84568, Fax 84568. *104139*

Visby (Gotland)

Gotlands Antikvariat, Stora Torget 10, 621 56 Visby.
T. (0498) 18802. *104140*

Switzerland

Aathal-Seegräben (Zürich)

EOS-Buchantiquariat Benz, Aathalstr., 8607 Aathal-Seegräben. T. (01) 932 30 22. - Print / Map - *104141*

Ascona (Ticino)

Centro del Bel Libro Ascona, Via Collegio Centro Culturale, Postfach 2600, 6612 Ascona. T. (091) 7917234,
Fax 7917254. *104142*

Baden (Aargau)

Antiquariat mittlere Mühle, Kronengasse 35, 5400 Ba-
den. T. (056) 222 97 80. - Print - *104143*
Doppler zum Pflug, Weite Gasse 31, 5401 Baden.
T. (056) 2227464. - Print - *104144*
Mittlere Mühle, Kronengasse 35, 5400 Baden.
T. (056) 2229780. *104145*

Basel

Antiquariat am Klosterberg, Klosterberg 21, 4051 Basel.
T. (061) 271 33 67. *104146*
Antiquariat Austrasse 66, Austr. 66, 4003 Basel.
T. (061) 271 47 72. - Print / Autogr - *104147*
Antiquariat Oriflamme, Postfach 4065, 4002 Basel.
T. (061) 401 01 00. - Print / ArtBk / Engr / Map - *104148*
Beran, Georg, Kartausgasse 1, 4005 Basel.
T. (061) 692 62 84, Fax (061) 692 62 63. *104149*
Beyeler, Ernst, Bäumleing 9, 4001 Basel.
T. (061) 2725412, Fax 2719691. - Print / Engr - *104150*
Buchantiquariat am Rhein, Kartausgasse 1, 4058 Basel.
T. (061) 6926284, Fax (061) 6926263. - Print - *104151*
Cachet, Münsterberg 13, 4051 Basel.
T. (061) 2723594. *104152*
Erasmushaus, Haus der Bücher, Bäumleingasse 18,
4001 Basel. T. (061) 2723088, Fax (061) 2723041.
- Print / ArtBk / Engr / Autogr - *104153*
Erlanger, Marc, Klybeckstr. 29, 4057 Basel.
T. (061) 692 32 18. - Print / ArtBk / Map - *104154*
Gerber, Waldemar, Schneidergasse 18, 4001 Basel.
T. (061) 2611773, Fax 2614150. - Print / Engr - *104155*
Jäggi, W., Freie Str 32, 4001 Basel. T. (061) 2615200,
Fax 2615205. *104156*
Koechlin, Heinrich, Dr., Spalenberg 34, 4051 Basel.
T. (061) 261 55 94. *104157*
Kronenberg AG, Hirschgässlein 44/4, Postfach 320,
4010 Basel. T. (061) 271 26 26, Fax 271 26 25. - Print /
Engr / Autogr / Map - *104158*
Mohler, Karl, Rheinsprung 7, 4051 Basel.
T. (061) 2619882, Fax (061) 2619881. - Print / Engr /
Map - *104159*
Mohler, Karl, Rheinsprung 7, 4051 Basel.
T. (061) 2619882, Fax 2619881. *104160*
Pegasus Buch- und Kunsthandlung, Leonhardsgraben
52, 4051 Basel. T. (061) 261 59 55. *104161*
Pep & No Name Gallery, Güterstr. 153, 4053 Basel.
T. (061) 361 20 65, Fax 3612065. - ArtBk - *104162*
Riggenbach, H., Dr., Morgartenring 144, 4054 Basel.
T. (061) 301 82 42. *104163*
Ruetz, Karl, Dr., Postfach 103, 4009 Basel.
T. (061) 302 53 28, Fax (061) 302 53 52.
- Print - *104164*
Schenk & Stehlin, Freie Str. 20, 4001 Basel.
T. (061) 261 23 21. *104165*
Schiess, Patricia, Güterstr. 122, 4053 Basel.
T. (061) 361 14 19. *104166*
Schlöhlein, Schützenmattstr. 15, 4003 Basel.
T. (061) 261 43 17, Fax (061) 261 45 95.
- Print - *104167*
Simmermacher, René, Augustinergasse 7, 4001 Basel.
T. (061) 2611848. - Print / ArtBk / Engr - *104168*
Stampa, Spalenberg 2, 4051 Basel. T. (061) 2617910,
Fax 2617919. *104169*
Tschirren, René, Spalenberg 29, 4051 Basel.
T. (061) 261 58 31. - Engr - *104170*
Wepf & Co., Eisengasse 5, 4001 Basel.
T. (061) 261 63 77, Fax (061) 261 35 97.
- ArtBk - *104171*

Zum Basilisk, Kohlenberg 4, 4051 Basel.
T. (061) 281 71 55. - Print - *104172*

Beinwil am See (Aargau)

Eichenberger, Walter, Dr., Aarauerstr 12, 5712 Beinwil
am See. T. (062) 7714421, Fax 7714421. - Print /
Engr - *104173*

Bern

Berger, Rudolf, Gerechtigkeitsgasse 47, 3011 Bern.
T. (031) 311 41 76. *104174*
Bolsoni Antik AG, Postfach 5575, 3001 Bern.
T. (031) 3027778, Fax 3027774. *104175*
Hegnauer & Schwarzenbach, Kramgasse 16, 3011 Bern.
T. (031) 311 64 15/22 74 00, Fax (031) 311 96 53.
- Print / Engr / Map - *104176*
Hofer, Münstergasse 56, 3011 Bern. T. (031) 3117897.
- Print / Engr / Map - *104177*
Huber, Hans, Marktgasse 59, 3011 Bern.
T. (031) 312 14 14, Fax (031) 312 25 71.
- ArtBk - *104178*
Iberia Centro del Libro Espanol, Hirschengraben 6, 3001
Bern. T. (031) 381 59 43. - Print - *104179*
Kampf, Heinz Hubertus, Wasserwerkgasse 31, 3011
Bern. T. (031) 311 33 73. *104180*
Kiener, Martin, Postfach 6912, 3001 Bern.
T. (031) 332 66 44, Fax (031) 332 11 60. *104181*
Kornfeld, Laupenstr 41, 3008 Bern. T. (031) 3814673,
Fax 3821891. - Engr - *104182*
Laeri, Gerechtigkeitsgasse 13, 3011 Bern.
T. (031) 312 08 30. *104183*
Lang & Cie., Herbert, Münzgraben 2, 3011 Bern.
T. (031) 311 88 71, Fax (031) 3123183. - Print - *104184*
Pulitzer & Knöll, Kramgasse 62, 3011 Bern.
T. (031) 311 56 91, 22 93 33. *104185*
Stauffacher, Hodlerstr. 12, 3011 Bern.
T. (031) 311 14 23. - ArtBk - *104186*
Thierstein, Daniel, Gerechtigkeitsgasse 60, 3011 Bern.
T. (031) 312 37 11. - Print / ArtBk / Autogr - *104187*
Wild, Alexander, Rathausgasse 30, 3011 Bern.
T. (031) 311 44 80, Fax (031) 311 44 70.
- Print - *104188*

Biberist (Solothurn)

Kurmann, Schachenstr. 23, 4562 Biberist.
T. (032) 6724250. - Print / Engr / Map - *104189*

Biel (Bern)

Patzer, Lilian, BP 408, 2501 Biel.
T. (032) 3656748. *104190*
Thierstein, Daniel, Obergasse 27, 2502 Biel.
T. (032) 3232937, Fax 3232937. - Print / ArtBk /
Autogr - *104191*

Birsfelden (Basel-Land)

Schibli-Doppler, Eichenstr. 14, 4127 Birsfelden.
T. (061) 313 15 04, Fax (061) 313 15 33. *104192*

Blonay (Vaud)

Kellenberger, Eric, 22 Ch. Planaz, 1807 Blonay.
T. (021) 943 44 44, Fax 9437777. - Print /
ArtBk - *104193*

Les Brenets (Neuchâtel)

Art & Presse Diffusion, L'Adeu 1, 2416 Les Brenets.
T. (032) 9321177, Fax 9321177. - ArtBk - *104194*

Burgdorf (Bern)

Fink, Eduard, Metzgergasse 18, 3400 Burgdorf.
T. (034) 4226044, 4224711. - Engr - *104195*

Carouge (Genève)

Leuba, Sonja, 20 Pl. du Marché, 1227 Carouge.
T. (022) 343 67 85. *104196*

Chernex (Vaud)

Paratte, Serge, Le Couvent, 1822 Chernex.
T. (021) 964 60 10. *104197*

Chur (Graubünden)

Narrenschiff, Reichsgasse, 7000 Chur.
T. (081) 2523029. *104198*
Schmid, Mia & Hans, Obere Gasse 38, 7000 Chur.
T. (081) 2521058. *104199*
Schuler, F., Postpl., 7002 Chur. T. (081) 2521160,
Fax 2528473. - ArtBk / Engr / Map - *104200*

Cornol (Jura)

Schnoebelen, Gérard, Rte. St. Gilles, 2952 Cornol.
T. (032) 4622774. *104201*

Emmetten (Nidwalden)

Müller, Kurt, Gumprechtstr. 39, 6376 Emmetten.
T. (041) 620 10 62. - Engr - *104202*

Les Evouettes (Valais)

Ostertag, R., Bouveret, Villa Domino, 1891 Les
Evouettes. *104203*

Fribourg

Altstadt Antiquariat, 47 Rue des Alpes, 1700 Fribourg.
T. (026) 3223808, Fax 3228893. - Print / ArtBk / Engr /
Map - *104204*
Bouquin Librairie, 62 Rue des Alpes, 1700 Fribourg.
T. (026) 3223808. *104205*
Cabinet d'Estampes, Grand-Rue 56, 1700 Fribourg.
T. (026) 3227156. *104206*
Intermède Belleroche, 6 Pl. Notre Dame, 1700 Fribourg.
T. (026) 3232552. *104207*

Genève

Au Temps Perdu, Rue Georges-Leschot 6, 1205 Genève.
T. (022) 329 29 50. *104208*
Autographe, 5 Ch. de la Chevillarde, 1208 Genève.
T. (022) 348 77 55. - Autogr - *104209*
Cramer, Patrick, 13, Chantepoulet, 1201 Genève.
T. (022) 7325432, Fax 7314731. *104210*
Descombes S.A., Rue du Vieux-Collège 6, 1204 Genève.
T. (022) 3215656. - Map - *104211*
Dike, Catherine, 4 Rue de Hesse, 1204 Genève.
T. (022) 7218888. - ArtBk - *104212*
Droz, 11 Rue Massot, 1211 Genève. T. (022) 3466666,
Fax 3472391. - ArtBk - *104213*
Engelberts, Edwin, 3 Grand-Rue, 1204 Genève.
T. (022) 3116192, Fax 3116192. - Print /
ArtBk - *104214*
Exemplaire, 12 Rue du Perron, 1204 Genève.
T. (022) 328 84 65. *104215*
Faure, Jean-Jacques, 4 Rue Georges Leschot, 1205 Ge-
nève. T. (022) 320 87 59. *104216*
Forum, 35 Rue Terrassière, 1207 Genève.
T. (022) 736 86 86. *104217*
Galerie de Loës, 9 Rue Beauregard, 1204 Genève.
T. (022) 3116001, 3206001, Fax (022) 3124704.
- Engr / Map - *104218*
Galerie Grand-Rue, 25 Grand-Rue, 1204 Genève.
T. (022) 3117685. - Print / Engr / Map - *104219*
Grand-Rue, 25 Grand-Rue, 1204 Genève.
T. (022) 3117685. - Engr / Map - *104220*
Gras, 1 Pl. Ile, 1204 Genève. T. (022) 3208777. *104221*
Illi, Raymond, 20 Rue de l'Arquebuse, 1204 Genève.
T. (022) 321 43 47. - Print / Autogr - *104222*
Jullien, 32 Pl. Bourg-de-Four, 1211 Genève.
T. (022) 320 36 70. *104223*
Letu, Bernard, Rue Calvin 2, 1204 Genève.
T. (022) 3104757, Fax 3108492. - ArtBk - *104224*
Literart, 15 Blvd. Georges-Favon, 1204 Genève.
T. (022) 321 40 80. *104225*
Molènes, Pl. de la Fusterie 9-11, 1204 Genève.
T. (022) 3211433, Fax (022) 7814659. - Print - *104226*
Montparnasse, 39 Grand-Rue, 1204 Genève.
T. (022) 321 67 19. - Print / Map - *104227*
Novel, Jean, 1 Rue de la Muse, 1205 Genève.
T. (022) 328 15 57. *104228*
Payot & Naville, 7 Rue Ami-Lévrier, 1211 Genève CP
887. T. (022) 732 24 00. *104229*
Payot & Naville, 6 Rue Grenus, 1201 Genève CP 381.
T. (022) 731 89 50. - ArtBk - *104230*
Payot & Naville, 5 Rue de la Conféderation, 1204 Genè-
ve. T. (022) 328 92 66. *104231*
Quentin, Molènes, 7 Pl. Fusterie, 1204 Genève.
T. (022) 321 14 33. *104232*
Slatkine Reprints, 5 Rue des Chaudronniers, 1211 Genè-
ve. T. (022) 7762551, Fax (022) 7763527.
- Print - *104233*
Suisse Librairie, 3 Rue Saint Lèger, 1205 Genève.
T. (022) 320 04 76. *104234*
Talisman, 2 Pl. Grand-Mezel, 1204 Genève.
T. (022) 321 97 77. *104235*
Weber, 13 Rue de Monthoux, 1201 Genève.
T. (022) 7326450, Fax 7384305. - ArtBk - *104236*

Genève (11)
Skorianetz, Werner, 4 Pl. Neuve, 1211 Genève.
T. (022) 3280667, Fax 8001703.   *104237*

Interlaken (Bern)
Tantra-Buchhandlung, Jungfraustr. 29, 3800 Interlaken.
T. (033) 8227414.   *104238*

Ittigen (Bern)
Spalinger, Th., Stockhornstr. 5, 3063 Ittigen.
T. (031) 921 77 00, Fax (031) 922 01 92.
- Print -   *104239*

Lausanne (Vaud)
Aubaine, Rue du Tunnel 11, 1005 Lausanne.
T. (021) 3223033.   *104240*
Bridel, Maurice, Cité Derrière 10, 1002 Lausanne.
T. (021) 323 77 35. - Print -   *104241*
Gismondi, 1 Ch. Beau-Rivage, 1006 Lausanne.
T. (021) 616 24 14. - ArtBk -   *104242*
Guillod, Frédéric, 10 Blvd. de Grancy, 1004 Lausanne.
T. (021) 616 95 93.   *104243*
Lehmann, 10 Rue de la Cité-Derrière, 1005 Lausanne.
T. (021) 311 80 21.   *104244*
Payot & Naville, 1 Rue de Bourg, 1002 Lausanne.
T. (021) 341 33 31.   *104245*
Ségalat, Roger J., 4 Rue Pontaise, 1018 Lausanne.
T. (021) 6483601, Fax 6482585. - Print -   *104246*

Liebefeld (Bern)
Stähli, Simon, Hangweg 46, 3097 Liebefeld.
T. (031) 971 86 31. - Print / ArtBk / Engr /
Autogr -   *104247*

Lugano (Ticino)
Bredford Libri Rari, Via Molinazzo 2, 6900 Lugano.
T. (091) 9702081/2, Fax 9702624. - Print -   *104248*
Fiera del Libro, Via Marconi 2, 6900 Lugano.
T. (091) 9227649. - Print / Engr -   *104249*
Fuchs & Reposo, via Nassa 21, 6900 Lugano.
T. (091) 9231606. - Print / Engr / Map -   *104250*

Luzern
Gilhofer & Ranschburg, Trüllhofstr 20a, 6004 Luzern.
T. (041) 2401015, Fax 2405001. - Print -   *104251*
Stocker, Josef, Weinmarkt 8, Postfach 5166, 6005 Luzern. T. (041) 240 49 48. - ArtBk -   *104252*
Die Wolkenpumpe, Steinenstr. 2, 6004 Luzern.
T. (041) 410 18 84. - Print / ArtBk -   *104253*

Meilen (Zürich)
Komatzki, Dorfstr. 140, 8706 Meilen. T. (01) 9234512,
Fax (01) 9236158.   *104254*

Morges (Vaud)
Galerie de Couvaloup, 1 Rue de Couvaloup, 1110 Morges. T. (021) 801 16 35.   *104255*

Muralto (Ticino)
Antiquario alla stazione, Palazzo della Posta, 6600 Muralto. T. (091) 7431247. - Print / Engr / Map -   *104256*

Muri bei Bern (Bern)
Kampf, Heinz Hubertus, Ob. Wehrliweg 2, 3074 Muri bei Bern. T. (031) 9515580. - Print / Engr / Autogr /
Map -   *104257*

Neuchâtel
Du Banneret, 2 Rue du Château, 2000 Neuchâtel.
T. (032) 7246724.   *104258*
Meylan, Jacques-E., Pl. des Halles 2, 2000 Neuchâtel.
T. (032) 7252806.   *104259*

Neuhausen am Rheinfall (Schaffhausen)
Bücherwurm, Bahnhofstr. 8, 8212 Neuhausen am Rheinfall. T. (052) 6725527. - Print / ArtBk / Engr / Autogr /
Map -   *104260*

Nidau (Bern)
Patzer, Paul & Lilian, Lyssstr. 21, 2560 Nidau.
T. (032) 3656748.   *104261*

Nyon (Vaud)
Galerie de la Côte, 5 Rue de la Gare, 1260 Nyon.
T. (022) 361 59 29. - ArtBk -   *104262*

Richterswil (Zürich)
Galerie Hirt, Dorfstr 34, 8805 Richterswil.
T. (01) 7847975, 7841611. - Print / Map -   *104263*

Riehen (Basel-Stadt)
Schibli, Robert, Bettingerstr.1, 4125 Riehen.
T. (061) 641 66 51.   *104264*

Saanen (Bern)
Au Foyer, Hauptstr., 3792 Saanen.
T. (033) 7442607.   *104265*

Saint-Gingolph (Valais)
Werlen, René, 1898 Saint-Gingolph.
T. (024) 4812382.   *104266*

Saint-Prex (Vaud)
Bloch, F., 10 Rte. de Rolle, 1162 Saint-Prex.
T. (021) 806 16 62, Fax 806 30 59. - Print -   *104267*

Sankt Gallen
Galerie an der Löwengasse, Löwengasse 3, 9004 Sankt Gallen. T. (071) 2233581, 2231958, Fax 2234280.
- Print / Print / Engr / Map -   *104268*
Graphica Antiqua, Oberer Graben 46, 9001 Sankt Gallen.
T. (071) 2235016. - Engr / Autogr -   *104269*
Hartmann, Roland, Dr., Zwinglistr. 3, Postfach 213, 9004 Sankt Gallen. T. (071) 2221870. - Print / Map -   *104270*
Lüchinger, Magnihalde 3, 9000 Sankt Gallen.
T. (071) 2226074.   *104271*
Osvald, Niklaus von, Dr., Sankt Jakobstr. 61, 9000 Sankt Gallen. T. (071) 2455011.   *104272*
Osvald, Olivier, Obere Graben 46, 9001 Sankt Gallen.
T. (071) 2235016, Fax 2235094. - Engr -   *104273*
Ribaux, Vadianstr. 8, 9001 Sankt Gallen.
T. (071) 2221660, Fax 2221688. - ArtBk -   *104274*
Widmer, Neugasse 35, 9000 Sankt Gallen.
T. (071) 2221626. - Engr / Map -   *104275*

Schaffhausen
Buch-Antiquariat T. Müller, Korallenstr. 17, 8200 Schaffhausen. T. (052) 6246170. - Print -   *104276*
Meili, Peter, Am Fronwagplatz 13, 8200 Schaffhausen.
T. (052) 6254144.   *104277*

Solothurn
Lüthy, Gurzelngasse 17, 4500 Solothurn.
T. (032) 6223522. - ArtBk / Engr -   *104278*

Stans (Nidwalden)
Matt, Josef von, Poststr. 1, 6370 Stans.
T. (041) 610 11 15/16, Fax (041) 610 80 28. - Print /
Engr -   *104279*

Steffisburg (Bern)
Krebser, Bernerstr. 85, 3612 Steffisburg.
T. (033) 2221922.   *104280*

Tagelswangen (Zürich)
Struchen, Rietstr 3, 8317 Tagelswangen.
T. (052) 3435331, Fax 3434930.   *104281*

Thalwil (Zürich)
Ideereal, Dorfstr. 17, 8800 Thalwil.
T. (01) 720 10 16.   *104282*

Thun (Bern)
Krebser, Bälliz 64, 3601 Thun. T. (033) 2221922.
- Engr -   *104283*
Lüthi, Heinz, Bälliz 35, Postfach 1249, 3600 Thun.
T. (033) 2223938. - Print -   *104284*

La Tour-de-Peilz (Vaud)
Bircher, Frédéric, 7 Rue de la Gare, 1814 La Tour-de-Peilz. T. (021) 944 98 52.   *104285*
Graf, Frédéric, 12 Rue Anciens-Fosses, 1814 La Tour-de-Peilz. T. (021) 944 48 09.   *104286*
Wieland, Nicolas, 80 Av. Bel-Air, 1814 La Tour-de-Peilz.
T. (021) 944 28 31.   *104287*

Vernier (Genève)
Renova-Libris, 5 Chemin des Coquelicots, 1214 Vernier.
T. (022) 3411015.   *104288*

Vouvry (Valais)
Gillioz, Maurice, La Praise, 1896 Vouvry.
T. (024) 4812203.   *104289*

Winterthur (Zürich)
Hoster, Alexandre-Michel, Marktgasse 57, 8400 Winterthur. T. (052) 212 57 22, Fax 213 24 75. - Print /
Map -   *104290*
Müller, Henry, Arbergstr 17, 8405 Winterthur.
T. (052) 2329903, Fax 2336780. - Print -   *104291*

Yverdon-les-Bains (Vaud)
Vuille, Louis, Maison-Rouge 5, 1400 Yverdon-les-Bains.
T. (024) 210626, Fax 212544.   *104292*

Yvonand (Vaud)
Altmann, René, Maison du Pont, 1462 Yvonand.
T. (024) 4301475.   *104293*

Zermatt (Valais)
Taugwalder, German, Haus Don Bosco, 3920 Zermatt.
T. (027) 9672793. - ArtBk -   *104294*

Zürich
ABC Antiquariat, Zähringerstr 31, 8001 Zürich.
T. (01) 2527145, Fax 2526132. - ArtBk -   *104295*
Ammann, Daniel C., Postfach 163, 8026 Zürich.
T. (01) 2418561, Fax (01) 2412774. - Print / Engr / Autogr / Map -   *104296*
Benz, Willy, Universitätsstr 29, 8006 Zürich.
T. (01) 2617954, Fax (055) 2464349.   *104297*
Bibliotheca Gastronomica, Winzerstr. 5, 8049 Zürich.
T. (01) 341 97 84, Fax 341 97 84. - Print / Engr - *104298*
Bodmer, Stadelhoferstr 34, 8001 Zürich.
T. (01) 251 93 54, Fax 2512905.   *104299*
Bolliger, Hans, Lenggstr 14, 8008 Zürich.
T. (01) 3815888. - Print / Engr -   *104300*
Buchantiquariat am Stauffacher, Badenerstr. 41, 8004 Zürich.   *104301*
Buchhandlung am Waffenplatz, Waffenplatzstr. 1, 8002 Zürich. T. (01) 201 06 50, Fax 201 06 50. *104302*
Buchhandlung zum Elsässer, Limmatquai 18, 8022 Zürich. T. (01) 261 08 47. - ArtBk -   *104303*
Buchhandlung zum Rennwegtor, Oetenbachgasse 11, 8001 Zürich. T. (01) 221 39 19, Fax 212 14 40.
- ArtBk -   *104304*
Falk + Falk, Kirchgasse 28, 8001 Zürich.
T. (01) 2625657, Fax 2616202. - Print / ArtBk / Engr /
Map -   *104305*

Fortuna Galerie, Kirchgasse 31, 8001 Zürich.
T. (01) 2612862. - Engr -   *104306*
Freistadt, Lydia, Alderstr. 38, 8008 Zürich.
T. (01) 208 07 08.   *104307*
Galerie Fortuna, Kirchgasse 31, 8001 Zürich.
T. (01) 261 28 62. - Print -   *104308*
Das gute Buch, Rosengasse 10, 8001 Zürich.
T. (01) 251 70 72. - Print / Engr / Map -   *104309*
Guyer, Annemarie, Auf der Mauer 1, 8001 Zürich.
T. (01) 261 33 43.   *104310*
Haubensack, J., Froschaugasse 11, 8001 Zürich.
T. (01) 2512618. - ArtBk -   *104311*
Kaudel, Otto, Rislingstr. 3, 8044 Zürich.
T. (01) 201 25 70.   *104312*
Kempf, Stephan J., Strehlgasse 19, 8001 Zürich.
T. (01) 2213830. - Print / Engr / Map -   *104313*

Kiener, Martin, Neumarkt 23, 8001 Zürich.
T. (01) 2624221 (Antiquitäten), 2624235 (Antiquariat),
Fax 2624275. - ArtBk -
Krauthammer, Robert, Obere Zäune 24, 8001 Zürich.
T. (01) 251 20 10. - ArtBk -							104315
KunstKiosk, c/o Helmhaus, Limmatquai 31, 8001 Zürich.
T. (01) 261 56 52, Fax 2615652. - ArtBk -					104316
Langer, Wolfgang, Predigerpl 26, 8001 Zürich.
T. (01) 2526950.								104317
Laube, Dr, Trittligasse 19, 8001 Zürich. T. (01) 2518550,
Fax 2527527. - Print / Engr -						104318
Libresso, Rindermarkt 8, 8001 Zürich.
T. (01) 252 73 58.								104319
Madliger-Schwab, Wohllebgasse 8, 8001 Zürich.
T. (01) 221 06 86. - Print / ArtBk / Engr -					104320
Muhrer, Angela, Dufourstr. 134, 8008 Zürich.
T. (01) 383 76 66.								104321
Orell Füssli, Füsslistr. 4, 8022 Zürich. T. (01) 211 80 11,
Fax 211 34 11. - ArtBk -							104322
Payot & Naville, Bahnhofstr. 9, 8001 Zürich.
T. (01) 211 54 52. - Print / Engr -						104323
Petrej, Peter, Sonneggstr 29, 8006 Zürich.
T. (01) 2513608, Fax 2513608. - Print / ArtBk -				104324
Pinkus-Genoss. Antiquariat, Froschaugasse 7, 8001 Zü-
rich. T. (01) 251 26 47.							104325
Rohr, Hans, Oberdorfstr. 5, 8024 Zürich.
T. (01) 251 36 36, Fax 251 33 44.						104326
Scalo Books & Looks, Weinbergstr 22a, 8001 Zürich.
T. (01) 2610910, Fax (01) 2619262. - ArtBk -				104327
Schäfer, Jörg, Alfred-Escher-Str. 76, 8002 Zürich.
T. (01) 202 69 75, Fax 201 05 38. - Print / Engr -				104328
Schlégl, István, Dr., Minervastr 119, 8032 Zürich.
T. (01) 3834963, Fax 3835589. - ArtBk -					104329
Schöni, Sankt-Petersstr. 16, 8001 Zürich.
T. (01) 211 10 19.								104330
Schumann, Hellmut, Rämistr 25, Postfach, 8024 Zürich.
T. (01) 2510272, Fax (01) 2527961. - Print / ArtBk /
Engr / Autogr / Map -							104331
Scialom, Jean-Pierre, Höschgasse 80, 8024 Zürich.
T. (01) 383 42 13, Fax 383 50 46. - Print / ArtBk /
Engr -									104332
Simmermacher, René, Kirchgasse 25, 8024 Zürich.
T. (01) 2525512. - Print / ArtBk / Engr -					104333
Trösch, Armin, Rämistr. 33, 8001 Zürich.
T. (01) 261 56 32. - ArtBk -							104334
Zähringer, Gerhard, Froschaugasse 5, 8001 Zürich.
T. (01) 252 36 66, Fax 252 36 54. - Print / ArtBk / Engr /
Autogr / Map -								104335
Zell, Werner, Zeltweg 12, 8032 Zürich.
T. (01) 261 13 30.								104336

Zug

Balmer, Neugasse 12, 6301 Zug. T. (041) 711 41 41,
Fax (041) 711 09 17. - ArtBk -						104337
Walter Barth Erben, Grabenstr 1a, 6300 Zug.
T. (041) 7114815, Fax 7113324.						104338

Thailand

Bangkok
Chalermnit, 1 b.2 Erawan Arcade, Bangkok.		104339

United Kingdom

Aberdeen (Grampian)
Aberdeen Art Gallery Shop, City Arts Department,
Schoolhill, Aberdeen AB9 1FQ. T. (01224) 646333,
Fax (01224) 632133. - ArtBk -						104340

Abergavenny (Gwent)
Lockyer, H.K., Monk St, Abergavenny.
T. (01873) 855825. - Print -							104341

Aberystwyth (Dyfed)
Ystwyth Bookshop, 7 Princess St., Aberystwyth.
T. (01970) 617511. - Print -							104342

Accrington (Lancashire)
Bookstall, D. & J., Stall 2g, Market Hall, Accrington.
T. (01254) 385935. - Print -							104343

Alresford (Hampshire)
Oxley The Studio Bookshop, Laurence, 17 Broad St, Al-
resford. T. (01962) 2188.							104344
Studio Bookshop and Gallery, 17 Broad St., Alresford.
T. (01962) 732188. - Print -							104345

Altrincham (Greater Manchester)
Abacus Bookshop, 24 Regent Rd, Altrincham WA14.
T. (0161) 928 5108.								104346

Ambergate (Derbyshire)
Hatcher, J. & V., 31 Derby Rd., Ambergate.
T. (01773) 856653. - Print -							104347

Ambleside (Cumbria)
Hebden, M., 1 Cheapside, Ambleside.
T. (015394) 32094. - Print -							104348

Arundel (West Sussex)
Arundel Bookshop, 10 High St., Arundel.
T. (01903) 882680. - Print -							104349
Baynton-Williams, 37a High St., Arundel BN18 9AG.
T. (01903) 883588. - Print -							104350

Ashburton (Devon)
Ashburton Rare Books, 20 West St., Ashburton.
T. (01364) 53341. - Print -							104351
Dartmoor Bookshop, 2 Kingsbridge Ln., Ashburton.
T. (01364) 313464. - Print -							104352

Ashby-de-la-Zouch (Leicestershire)
Croft Books, 55 Market St, Ashby-de-la-Zouch.
T. (01530) 417034. - Print -							104353

Aylesbury (Buckinghamshire)
Square Edge, 38 Kingsbury, Aylesbury. T. (01296) 89480.
- Print -									104354

Bakewell (Derbyshire)
Hill, Alan, 3 Buxton Rd., Bakewell. T. (01629) 814841.
- Print -									104355

Ballynahinch (Co. Down)
Davidson, 34 Broomhill Rd., Ballynahinch.
T. (01238) 562502. - Print -							104356

Bangor (Gwynedd)
Bangor Books, 122 High St., Bangor. T. (01248) 352695.
- Print -									104357

Barnstaple (Devon)
Roberts & Young, Unit H, Gammon Walk, Barnstaple.
T. (01271) 23591. - Print -							104358
Tarka, 5 Bear St., Barnstaple. T. (01271) 74997.
- Print -									104359

Barrow-in-Furness (Cumbria)
Mostly Books, 247 Rawlinson St., Barrow-in-Furness.
T. (01229) 836808. - Print -							104360

Bassingbourn (Cambridgeshire)
Bickersteth, David, 4 South End, Bassingbourn.
T. (01763) 245619. - Print -							104361

Bath (Avon)
Bath Old Books, 9c Margarets Bldgs., Bath.
T. (01225) 422244. - Print -							104362
Bayntun, George, Manvers St., Bath BA1 1JW.
T. (01225) 466000. - Print -							104363
Garwood & Voigt, 15 Devonshire Bldgs., Bath BA2 4SP.
T. (01225) 424074. - Print / ArtBk / Engr -					104364
Gregory, George, Manvers St., Bath. T. (01225) 466055.
- Print -									104365
Pathway Books, 1 Grove St., Bath. T. (01225) 463917.
- Print -									104366
Patterson & Little, 10 Margaret's Bldg., Brock St., Bath.
T. (01225) 426722. - Print -							104367
Rainsford, P.R., 23a Manvers St., Bath BA1 1JW.
T. (01225) 445107. - Print -							104368
Wallis, Derek & Glenda, 6 Chapel Row, Queen Sq., Bath.
T. (01225) 424677. - Print -							104369

Beccles (Suffolk)
Besley, 4 Blyburgate, Beccles. T. (01502) 715762.
- Print -									104370

Bedford (Bedfordshire)
Eagle Bookshop, 103 Castle Rd., Bedford.
T. (01234) 269295. - Print -							104371

Belfast (Co. Antrim)
Antiquarian Booksellers, 93 Dublin Rd., Belfast BT2 7HF.
T. (01232) 245787. - Print -							104372
Arts Council Gallery Bolkshop, 56-60 Dublin Rd, Belfast
BT2 7HP. T. (01232) 381591, Fax (01232) 661715.
- ArtBk -									104373
Bookfinders, 47 University Rd., Belfast.
T. (01232) 328269. - Print -							104374
Emerald Isle Books, 539 Antrim Rd., Belfast.
T. (01232) 370798. - Print -							104375
Evangelical Bookshop, 15 College Sq. East, Belfast.
T. (01232) 320529. - Print -							104376
Gamble, J.A., 539 Antrim Rd., Belfast BT15 3BU.
T. (01232) 370798. - Print -							104377
Mews Books, 260 Antrim Rd, Belfast.
T. (01232) 751319. - Print -							104378
Prospect House Books, 93 Dublin Rd., Belfast.
T. (01232) 245787. - Print -							104379
Rowan, P. & B., 92 Malone Rd., Belfast.
T. (01232) 666448. - Print -							104380
World of Books, 329 Woodstock Rd., Belfast.
T. (01232) 454272. - Print -							104381

Belper (Derbyshire)
Bodkin, 101 Bridge St., Belper. T. (01773) 820181.
- Print -									104382

Berkhamsted (Hertfordshire)
Wilson, J., 22 Castle St., Berkhamsted.
T. (01442) 873396. - Print -							104383

Berwick-upon-Tweed (Northumberland)
Jones, F.J., Bridge St., Berwick-upon-Tweed.
T. (01289) 307749. - Print -							104384

Bethesda (Gwynedd)
Bethesda Books and Antiques, 44 High St., Bethesda.
T. (01248) 602384. - Print -							104385
Morris, A.E., 40 High St., Bethesda. T. (01248) 602533.
- Print -									104386

Bewdley (Hereford and Worcester)
Clent, Habberley Rd, Bewdley. T. (01299) 401090.
- Print -									104387

Bideford (Devon)
Hames, P., 8 Eastbourne Terrace, Bideford.
T. (01237) 421065. - Print -							104388

Birmingham (West Midlands)
Beech, 28b Oldbury Rd, Birmingham B65.
T. (0121) 559 9822. - Print -							104389
Birmingham Bookshops, 565-567 Bristol Rd., Birming-
ham B29. T. (0121) 472 8556. - Print -					104390
Midlands Arts Centre Bookshop, Midlands Arts Centre,
Cannon Hill Park, Birmingham B12 9QH.
T. (0121) 4406722. - ArtBk -						104391
Readers World, 11 Saint Martins Parade, Birmingham
B5 5LD. T. (0121) 643 8664. - Print -					104392
Readers World, 4 Hurst St., Birmingham B5 4HJ.
T. (0121) 643 7464. - Print -							104393
Taplin, 62 Station Rd., Birmingham B37.
T. (0121) 779 6505. - Print -							104394
Temperley, David, 19 Rotten Park Rd, Birmingham.
T. (0121) 454 0135, Fax (0121) 4541124.
- Print -									104395
Wycherley, Stephen, 508 Bristol Rd, Birmingham B29.
T. (0121) 471 1006. - Print -							104396

Bournemouth (Dorset)
Ashley Bookshop, 30b Ashley Rd, Bournemouth.
T. (01202) 302499. - Print -							104397
Bizzy Lizzy, 708 Christchurch Rd, Bournemouth.
T. (01202) 303942. - Print -							104398
Booksbought, 1 Jewelbox Bldg., Cardigan Rd., Bourne-
mouth. T. (01202) 521373. - Print -					104399
Holdenhurst Books, 275 Holdenhurst Rd., Bournemouth
BH8 8BZ. T. (01202) 397718. - Print -					104400
Markland, 136 Charminster Rd., Bournemouth.
T. (01202) 531414. - Print -							104401

Movieland, 19 Queens Rd., Bournemouth.
T. (01202) 768706. - Print -   *104402*
Rowan, H., 459 Christchurch Rd., Bournemouth.
T. (01202) 398820. - Print -   *104403*
Shickell, 869 Christchurch Rd, Bournemouth.
T. (01202) 418497. - Print -   *104404*
Wright, Sidney, 12-13 Royal Arcade, Bournemouth.
T. (01202) 37153.   *104405*
Yesterdays Books, 65-67 Bennet Rd., Bournemouth BH8
8RH. T. (01202) 302023. - Print -   *104406*

Boxford (Suffolk)
Abbey Book Buyers, 3 Firs Farm, Boxford.
T. (01787) 210810. - Print -   *104407*

Brackley (Northamptonshire)
Old Hall Bookshop, 32 Market Pl., Brackley.
T. (01280) 704146. - Print / ArtBk -   *104408*

Bradford-on-Avon (Wiltshire)
Books and Prints, 15 Church St., Bradford-on-Avon.
T. (012216) 868300. - Print -   *104409*

Brasted (Kent)
Attic, Village House, Brasted TN16 1HU.
T. (01959) 563507. - Print -   *104410*

Braunton (Devon)
Book Cellar, 5a The Square, East St., Braunton EX33
2EA. T. (01271) 815655. - Print -   *104411*

Brecon (Powys)
Maps, Prints and Books, 7 The Struet, Brecon.
T. (01874) 622714. - Print / Engr -   *104412*

Bridgnorth (Shropshire)
Bookstack Bridgnorth, 2a Castle Terrace, Bridgnorth.
T. (01746) 767089. - Print -   *104413*

Bridgwater (Somerset)
Brook House, 13 Friarn St., Bridgwater.
T. (01278) 422282. - Print -   *104414*

Bridport (Dorset)
PIC's Bookshop, 11 South St., Bridport.
T. (01308) 25689. - Print -   *104415*

Brighton (East Sussex)
Brighton Bargain Books, 33 Saint James St., Brighton.
T. (01273) 679249. - Print -   *104416*
Brookes, N.F., 12a Queens Rd., Brighton.
T. (01273) 23105. - Print -   *104417*
Davids Book Exchange, 3-5 Sydney St., Brighton.
T. (01273) 690223. - Print -   *104418*
Hunter, Simon, 3 Meeting House Ln., Brighton.
T. (01273) 736983. - Print -   *104419*
Page, Colin, 36 Duke St., Brighton BN1 1AG.
T. (01273) 25954, Fax 746246. - Print -   *104420*
Robinson, 11 Bond St., Brighton. T. (01273) 29012.
- Print -   *104421*
Tenpenny Book Exchange, 95 North d., Brighton.
T. (01273) 691012. - Print -   *104422*
Trafalgar Bookshop, 44 Trafalgar St., Brighton.
T. (01273) 684300. - Print -   *104423*
Walton, C., 31 Trafalgar St., Brighton.
T. (01273) 600400. - Print -   *104424*
Witchball, 48 Meeting House Lane, Brighton BN1 1HB.
T. (01273) 26618. - Engr / Map -   *104425*

Bristol (Avon)
Arnolfini, Arnolfini Gallery, 16 Narrow Quay, Bristol BS1
4QA. T. (0117) 299191. - ArtBk -   *104426*
Beware of the Leopard Books, Saint Nicholas St, Bristol.
T. (0117) 9257277. - Print -   *104427*
Bristol, 1806 Cheltenham Rd., Bristol.
T. (0117) 9245458. - Print -   *104428*
Cotham Hill Bookshop, 39a Cotham Hill, Bristol.
T. (0117) 9732344. - Print -   *104429*
George's Antiquarian & Secondhand Bookshop, 52 Park
St., Bristol BS1 5PW. T. (0117) 9276602, Fax 251854.
- Print -   *104430*
Heath, A.R., 3/62 Pembroke Rd, Bristol.
T. (0117) 9741183. - Print -   *104431*
Roberts, John, 43 Triangle West, Clifton, Bristol BS8
1ES. T. (0117) 9268568. - Print -   *104432*

Symes, John & Sheila, 93 Charleton Mead Dr., Bristol.
T. (0117) 9501074. - Print -   *104433*
Twiggers, 108 Reedley Rd., Bristol. T. (0117) 9682155.
- Print -   *104434*
Uta's Bookshop, 68 Park Row, Bristol.
T. (0117) 9272996. - Print -   *104435*
Wise Owl Bookshop, 26 Upper Maudlin St., Bristol BS2
8DJ. T. (0117) 9262738. - Print / ArtBk -   *104436*

Brixham (Devon)
Book Warren, 9a Bolton St., Brixham.
T. (01803) 858531. - Print -   *104437*

Broadway (Hereford and Worcester)
Stratford Trevers, 45 High St, Broadway.
T. (01386) 853668. - Print / Engr -   *104438*

Bungay (Suffolk)
Greyfriars Books, 4 Upper Olland St., Bungay.
T. (01986) 895600. - Print -   *104439*
Scorpio Books, 1 Nethergate St., Bungay.
T. (01986) 895743. - Print -   *104440*

Burntwood (Staffordshire)
About Books, Saint Matthews Rd., Burntwood.
T. (01543) 682217. - Print -   *104441*
Smith Royden, Farewell Ln., Burntwood.
T. (01543) 682217. - Print -   *104442*

Burton-upon-Trent (Staffordshire)
Needwood, 55 New St., Burton-upon-Trent.
T. (01283) 41641. - Print -   *104443*

Burwash (East Sussex)
Whittaker, Anthony, High St., Burwash.
T (01435) 882636. Print -   *104444*

Bury Saint Edmunds (Suffolk)
Crawford, John, 55 Av. Approach, Bury Saint Edmunds.
T. (01284) 704453. - Print -   *104445*
Wakerley, J.A., 28a Hatter St., Bury Saint Edmunds.
T. (01284) 755936. - Print -   *104446*

Buscot (Oxfordshire)
Jobson, N.J., 8 Weston Cottages, Buscot.
T. (01367) 252240. - Print -   *104447*

Buxton (Derbyshire)
Hall Bank Books, 9 Hall Bank, Buxton.
T. (01298) 570889. - Print -   *104448*
Pavillon, 60 West Rd., Buxton. T. (01298) 577465.
- Print -   *104449*

Calne (Wiltshire)
Farahar, Clive & Sophie Dupré, 14 The Green, Calne.
T. (01249) 821121.   *104450*
Hilmarton Manor Press, Calne SN11 8SB.
T. (01249) 024976/208. - ArtBk -   *104451*

Cambridge (Cambridgeshire)
Alister & Garon, 70 King St., Cambridge.
T. (01223) 62086. - Print -   *104452*
Bookroom, 13 Saint Eligius St., Cambridge.
T. (01223) 69694. - Print -   *104453*
Bookshop, 24 Magdalene St., Cambridge.
T. (01223) 62457. - Print -   *104454*
David, G., 16 Saint Edwards Passage, Cambridge CB2
3PJ. T. (01223) 354619. - Print -   *104455*
Deighton, Bell & Co., 13 Trinity St., Cambridge CB2 1TD.
T. (01223) 353939, Fax (01223) 410464.
- Print -   *104456*
Fitzwilliam Museum Shop, Strumpington St, Cambridge
CB2 1RB. T. (01223) 332914, Fax (01223) 332923.
- ArtBk -   *104457*
Galloway & Porter, 3 Green St., Cambridge.
T. (01223) 67876, Fax (01223) 60705. - Print - *104458*
Galloway & Porter, 30 Sidney St., Cambridge CB2 3HS.
T. (01223) 67876. - Print -   *104459*
Gibbons, Derek, 9 Saint Edwards Passage, Cambridge.
T. (01223) 312913. - Print -   *104460*
Haunted Bookshop, 9 Saint Edwards Passage, Cambrid-
ge. T. (01223) 312913.   *104461*
Kettles's Yard Bookshop, Kettle's Yard, Castle St, Cam-
bridge CB3 0AQ. T. (01223) 352124,
Fax (01223) 324377. - ArtBk -   *104462*

Quinto, 34 Trinity St., Cambridge. T. (01223) 358279.
- Print / Engr -   *104463*
Trotman, Ken, Unit 11, 135 Ditton Walk, Cambridge.
T. (01223) 211030. - Print -   *104464*

Canterbury (Kent)
Chaucer, 6 Beer Cart Lane, Canterbury.
T. (01227) 453912. - Print / Engr / Map -   *104465*
Holcombe, Paul, 5 North Ln., Canterbury CT2 7EB.
T. (01227) 457913. - Print -   *104466*
Miles, David, 37 Northgate, Canterbury CT1 1BL.
T. (01227) 464773. - Print -   *104467*

Cardiff (South Glamorgan)
Capital Bookshop, 27 Morgan Arcade, Cardiff.
T. (01222) 388423. - Print -   *104468*
Oriel, The Friary, Cardiff CF1 4AA. T. (01222) 395548,
Fax (01222) 221447. - ArtBk -   *104469*
Out of Print Book Service, 13 Pantbach Rd., Cardiff.
T. (01222) 627703. - Print -   *104470*
Roath, 188 City Rd., Cardiff. T. (01222) 490523.
- Print -   *104471*
Zwemmer at the Fotogallery, 30 Charles St, Cardiff CF1
4EA. T. (01222) 665377, Fax (01222) 341672.
- ArtBk -   *104472*

Carlisle (Cumbria)
Bookcase, 17 Castle St., Carlisle. T. (01228) 44560.
- Print -   *104473*
Dodd, Maurice, 112 Warwick Rd, Carlisle.
T. (01228) 22087.   *104474*
Kinnaird, Jane and John, 18 Houghton Rd., Carlisle CA3
0LA. T. (01228) 28567. - Print -   *104475*
Thomson, Roddick & Laurie, 24 Lowther St., Carlisle.
T. (01228) 28939. - Print -   *104476*

Carmarthen (Dyfed)
Carmarthen Bookshop, 1 Saint Marys St., Carmarthen.
T. (01267) 235676. - Print -   *104477*
Corran, King St., Carmarthen SA33 4RY.
T. (01267) 427444, Fax (01267) 427709.
- Print -   *104478*

Cartmel (Cumbria)
Bain Smith, Peter, Bank Court, Market Sq., Cartmel.
T. (015395) 36369. - Print -   *104479*
Kerr, Norman, The Square, Cartmel. T. (015395) 36247.
- Print -   *104480*

Castle Cary (Somerset)
Bailey Hill, Fore St., Castle Cary. T. (01963) 50917.
- Print -   *104481*

Chard (Somerset)
Chard Bookshop, 2 Pig Ln., Chard. T. (01460) 67046.
- Print -   *104482*

Cheddleton (Staffordshire)
Wragg, R.G., 319 Cheadle Rd., Cheddleton.
T. (01782) 360044. - Print -   *104483*

Cheltenham (Gloucestershire)
Banister, David, 26 Kings Rd., Cheltenham.
T. (01242) 514287, Fax 513890. - Print / Engr - *104484*
Bennett, Graham, 17 Montpellier Villas, Cheltenham
GL50 2XE. T. (01242) 232429. - Print -   *104485*
Bradbury & Son, Edward, 32 High St., Cheltenham.
T. (01242) 221486. - Print -   *104486*
Hancox, Alan, Montpellier St, Cheltenham.
T. (01242) 513204. - Print -   *104487*
Rayner, Michael, 11 Saint Lukes Rd., Cheltenham GL53
7JQ. T. (01242) 512806. - Print -   *104488*
Second Storey Book, 7 Shelkirk St., Cheltenham.
T. (01242) 570754. - Print -   *104489*

Chepstow (Gwent)
Glance Back, 17-17a Upper Church St., Chepstow.
- Print -   *104490*
Hyland, C.P., 6 Saint Mary St., Chepstow.
T. (01291) 622817. - Print -   *104491*

Chesham (Buckinghamshire)
Omniphil Prints, Germains Lodge, Fullers Hill, Chesham.
T. (01494) 771851. - Print -   *104492*

Chester (Cheshire)
Earls Eye Books, Princess St, Chester.
T. (01244) 319688. - Print -   *104493*
S.P.C.K. Bookshop, 7 Saint Werburgh St., Chester.
T. (01244) 323753. - Print -   *104494*
Stothert, 4 Nicholas St., Chester. T. (01244) 340756.
- Print -   *104495*

Chesterfield (Derbyshire)
Hill, Alan, 8 Falcon Yard, Chesterfield.
T. (01246) 231158. - Print -   *104496*
Tilley, 29-31 South St, Chesterfield. T. (01246) 454270.
- Print -   *104497*

Chichester (West Sussex)
Chichester Bookshop, 39 Southgate, Chichester PO19
1DP. T. (01243) 785473. - Print / ArtBk -   *104498*
Hancock, Peter, 40 West St., Chichester.
T. (01243) 786173. - Print -   *104499*
Saint Peter's Bookshop, Saint Peter's Arcade, Chichester. T. (01243) 778477. - Print -   *104500*

Chipping Norton (Oxfordshire)
Trada, 21 High St., Chipping Norton. T. (01608) 644325.
- Print -   *104501*

Cirencester (Gloucestershire)
Period Book Simulations, 51-53 Dollar St., Cirencester.
T. (01285) 641919. - Print -   *104502*
Thompson, Park St, Cirencester. T. (01285) 655239.
- Print -   *104503*

Clare (Suffolk)
Trinder, Malting Ln., Clare. T. (01787) 277130.
- Print -   *104504*

Cleethorpes (Humberside)
Lafayette, 6 High St., Cleethorpes. T. (01472) 699244.
- Print -   *104505*

Cleobury Mortimer (Shropshire)
Baldwin, M. & M., 24 High St., Cleobury Mortimer.
T. (01299) 270110. - Print -   *104506*

Clevedon (Avon)
Clevedon Books, 14 Woodside Rd., Clevedon.
T. (01272) 872304. - Print / Engr -   *104507*

Clitheroe (Lancashire)
Bowland, 64 Highfield Rd., Clitheroe BB7 1NE.
T. (01200) 26492. - Print -   *104508*

Cobham (Surrey)
Joppa, 29 Milner Dr., Cobham. T. (01932) 868269.
- Print -   *104509*

Cockermouth (Cumbria)
Winkworth, D.R. & A.P., 102 Main St., Cockermouth.
T. (01900) 824984. - Print -   *104510*

Coggeshall (Essex)
Mathews, Elkin, 16 Stoneham St., Coggeshall.
T. (01376) 561730. - Print -   *104511*

Colchester (Essex)
Abacus Book Buyers, 37 North Hill, Colchester.
T. (01206) 577520. - Print -   *104512*
Alphabets Books, 13 Trinity St., Colchester.
T. (01206) 572751. - Print -   *104513*
Book Exchange, 48 East Hill, Colchester.
T. (01206) 867242. - Print -   *104514*
Castle Bookshop, 37 North Hill, Colchester C01 1QR.
T. (01206) 577520. - Print / Engr -   *104515*
Taylor, 92b East Hill, Colchester C01 2QN.
T. (01206) 563138. - Print -   *104516*

Coleraine (Co. Londonderry)
Coleraine Bookshop, 5 Stow Row, Coleraine BT52 1EP.
T. (01265) 52557. - Print -   *104517*

Colne (Lancashire)
Colne Books, Colne. T. (01282) 870952. - Print -   *104518*

Colwyn Bay (Clwyd)
Bay Bookshop, 14 Seaview Rd., Colwyn Bay.
T. (01492) 531642. - Print -   *104519*

Colwyn Books, 66 Abergele Rd., Colwyn Bay.
T. (01492) 530683. - Print -   *104520*
Jones, Elfed, 43 Dundonald Rd., Colwyn Bay.
T. (01492) 531303. - Print -   *104521*

Congleton (Cheshire)
Morten, E.J., Brookland House, Congleton.
T. (01260) 277959. - Print -   *104522*

Conwy (Gwynedd)
Bookshop, 21 High St., Conwy. T. (01492) 592137.
- Print -   *104523*

Coventry (West Midlands)
Armstrong, 163a Sovereign Rd., Coventry.
T. (01203) 714344. - Print -   *104524*
Gosford Books, 116 Gosford St., Coventry.
T. (01203) 220813. - Print -   *104525*
Sports Programmes, 3 Chapel St, Coventry POB 74.
T. (01203) 228672.   *104526*

Cowes (Isle of Wight)
Cameron, Julia Margaret, 90b High St., Cowes.
T. (01983) 290404. - Engr -   *104527*
Charles Dickens Bookshop, 65 High St., Cowes.
T. (01983) 293598. - Print -   *104528*

Cranleigh (Surrey)
Books and Bits, The Common, Cranleigh.
T. (01483) 275895. - Print -   *104529*

Crieff (Tayside)
Crieff Cinema Bookshop, High St., Crieff.
T. (01764) 3673. - Print -   *104530*

Crosby Ravensworth (Cumbria)
Grayling, David A.H., Lyvennet, Crosby Ravensworth.
T. (019315) 282. - Print -   *104531*

Croydon (Greater London)
Howard, Peter, 15 Beech House Rd., Croydon CR0 1JQ.
T. (0181) 681 1627. - Print -   *104532*
Plus Books, 341 London Rd., Croydon CR0.
T. (0181) 684 4651. - Print -   *104533*

Darlington (Durham)
Bentley-Swift, 6 Tower Rd., Darlington.
T. (01325) 480561. - Print -   *104534*
Vokes & Sons, 44 Bondgate, Darlington DL3 7JJ.
T. (01325) 359790. - Print -   *104535*

Davenham (Cheshire)
Forest Books, 4 Church St., Davenham.
T. (01606) 260360. - Print -   *104536*

Deal (Kent)
Golden Hind Bookshop, 85 Beach St., Deal.
T. (01304) 37086. - Print -   *104537*
The Print Room, 95a Beach St, Deal.
T. (01304) 368904.   *104538*

Derby (Derbyshire)
Neales, Becket St., Derby DE1 1HT. T. (01332) 43286.
- Print -   *104539*

Dersingham (Norfolk)
Torc, 9 Hall Rd., Dersingham. T. (01485) 541188.
- Print -   *104540*

Devizes (Wiltshire)
D'Arcy, 16 High St, Devizes. T. (01380) 726922.
- Print -   *104541*

Didcot (Oxfordshire)
Lawson, E.M., Kingsholme, East Hagbourne, Didcot.
T. (01235) 812033. - Print -   *104542*

Disley (Cheshire)
Davis, John, 45 Buxton Rd., Disley. T. (01663) 428 0012.
- Print -   *104543*

Dorchester (Dorset)
Johnston, D.G.L., 8 Church St., Dorchester.
T. (01305) 262517. - Print -   *104544*

Dorking (Surrey)
Hill, T.S., 122 South St., Dorking RH4 2EU.
T. (01306) 886468. - Print -   *104545*

Douglas (Isle of Man)
Garrett, Peter, 9 Duke St., Douglas. T. (01624) 629660.
- Print -   *104546*

Downpatrick (Co. Down)
Bookline, 35 Farranfad Rd., Downpatrick.
T. (01396) 712. - Print -   *104547*

Droitwich (Hereford and Worcester)
Grant, Victoria Sq., Droitwich. T. (01905) 778155.
- Print -   *104548*

Dulverton (Somerset)
Rothwell & Dunworth, 2 Bridge St., Dulverton.
T. (01398) 23169. - Print -   *104549*

Dumfries (Dumfries and Galloway)
Anderson, I.G., Gribton, Dumfries DG2 0AJ.
T. (01387) 721071. - Print -   *104550*

Durham (Durham)
Bookstall, New Markets, Durham. T. (0191) 386 1491.
- Print -   *104551*
Cosmic Fantasy, Dunelm House, New Elvet, Durham.
T. (0191) 384 5222. - Print -   *104552*
Shotton, J., 89 Elvet Bridge, Durham.
T. (0191) 386 4597.   *104553*

East Hagbourne (Oxfordshire)
Lawson & Co, E.M., Kingsholm, East Hagbourne OX11
8LN. T. (01235) 812033. - Print -   *104554*

Eastbourne (East Sussex)
Camilla's Bookshop, 57 Grove Rd., Eastbourne BN21
4TX. T. (01323) 36001. - Print -   *104555*
Roderick, Dew, 10 Furness Rd., Eastbourne.
T. (01323) 20239. - Print -   *104556*
Smith, Raymond, 30 South St., Eastbourne BN21 4XB.
T. (01323) 34128. - Print / Engr -   *104557*

Edinburgh (Lothian)
Armchair Books, 72 West Port, Edinburgh EH1.
T. (0131) 229 5927. - Print -   *104558*
Bell, Peter, 68 West Port, Edinburgh EH1 2LD.
T. (0131) 2290562. - Print -   *104559*
Bon Accord Enterprises, 14 Pentland Av, Edinburgh
EH13. T. (0131) 441 5655. - Print -   *104560*
Bookfare, 8 Victoria St., Edinburgh EH1.
T. (0131) 225 9237. - Print -   *104561*
Broughton Books, 2a Broughton Pl., Edinburgh EH1.
T. (0131) 557 8010. - Print -   *104562*
Campbell & Stillwell, 19 Queen Charlotte St., Edinburgh
EH6. T. (0131) 553 5317. - Print -   *104563*
Castle Books, 204 Canongate, Edinburgh EH8 8D0.
T. (0131) 556 0624. - Print -   *104564*
Cluny, 4 Cluny Terrace, Edinburgh EH10 4SW.
T. (0131) 4478618. - ArtBk -   *104565*
Grant & Shaw, 62 West Port, Edinburgh EH1 2LD.
T. (0131) 229 8399. - Print -   *104566*
Jay, 1 Roull Grove, Edinburgh EH12. T. (0131) 316 4034.
- Print -   *104567*
MacCormick, Donald, 19 Braid Cr, Edinburgh.
T. (0131) 447 2889.   *104568*
MacNaughtan, 3a-4a Haddington Pl, Edinburgh EH7
4AE. T. (0131) 556 5897.   *104569*
McNaughtan, 3a-4a Haddington Pl., Edinburgh.
T. (0131) 556 5897. - Print -   *104570*
Nelson, John O., 84 West Bow, Edinburgh EH1 2JW.
T. (0131) 225 4413. - Engr -   *104571*
Old Grindles Bookshop, 3 Spittal St., Edinburgh EH3.
T. (0131) 229 7252. - Print -   *104572*
Pringle, Andrew, 7 Dundas St., Edinburgh EH3 6AG.
T. (0131) 556 9698. - Print -   *104573*
Ramsay, Jain G.M., 29a Dundas St., Edinburgh EH3.
T. (0131) 557 4485. - Print -   *104574*
Rankin, Alan, 72 Dundas St., Edinburgh EH3 6QZ.
T. (0131) 556 3705. - Print -   *104575*
Thin, James, 53-59 South Bridge, Edinburgh.
T. (0131) 556 6743. - Print -   *104576*
Thrift Book Centre, 26 Lochrin Bldgs., Edinburgh EH3.
T. (0131) 229 6939. - Print -   *104577*
Till's Bookshop, Buccleuch St, Edinburgh EH8 9NA.
T. (0131) 667 0895. - Print -   *104578*
Updike, John, 7 Saint Bernard's Row, Edinburgh EH4
1HW. T. (0131) 332 1650. - Print -   *104579*

West Port Books, 151 West Port, Edinburgh EH3.
T. (0131) 229 4431. - Print -   104580

Egham (Surrey)
Blacklock, 8 Victoria St., Egham. T. (01784) 438025.
- Print -   104581

Elgin (Grampian)
Nik Nak Stores, 41c South St., Elgin. T. (01343) 548897.
- Print -   104582

Ely (Cambridgeshire)
Ely Bookshop, 11a Saint Marys St., Ely.
T. (01353) 661824. - Print -   104583
Hereward, 32 High St., Ely. T. (01353) 740821.
- Print -   104584
Lewcock, John, 6 Chewells Ln., Ely. T. (01353) 741152.
- Print -   104585

Emsworth (Hampshire)
Hubbard, Mary, 10 South St., Emsworth.
T. (01243) 377394. - Print -   104586

Epping (Essex)
Browser, 9 Station Rd, Epping. T. (01378) 572260.
- Print -   104587

Epsom (Surrey)
Vandeleur, 6 Seaforth Gardens, Epsom KT19 0NR.
T. (01372) 393 7752. - Print / ArtBk / Engr /
Map -   104588

Eton (Berkshire)
Eton Antique Bookshop, 88 High St., Eton.
T. (01753) 855534. - Print -   104589

Evesham (Worcestershire)
Bookworm, 81 Port St., Evesham. T. (01386) 45509.
- Print -   104590

Exeter (Devon)
Dickens, Fore St, Exeter. T. (01392) 431587.
- Print -   104591
Exeter Rare Books, Guildhall Shopping Centre, Exeter
EX4 3HG. T. (01392) 436021. - Print -   104592

Eye (Suffolk)
Gippeswic, Church St, Eye. T. (01379) 871439.
- Print -   104593

Falmouth (Cornwall)
Browser, 13-15 Saint Georges Arcade, Church St, Fal-
mouth. T. (01326) 313464. - Print -   104594
Maggs, John, 54 Church St., Falmouth.
T. (01326) 313153. - Engr / Map -   104595
Price, R.W., 13 Budock Terrace, Falmouth.
T. (01326) 314080. - Print -   104596

Farnborough (Hampshire)
Farnborough Gallery and Bookshop, 26 Guildford Rd.
West, Farnborough. T. (01252) 518033.
- Print -   104597
Wicks, E.S., 48 Peabody Rd, Farnborough.
T. (01252) 544876. - Print -   104598

Farnham (Surrey)
Cobweb, 29 The Woolmead, East St., Farnham.
T. (01252) 734531. - Print -   104599

Faversham (Kent)
Bookshop, 1a Gatefield Ln., Faversham.
T. (01795) 532873. - Print -   104600
Periwinkle, 119 West St., Faversham.
T. (01795) 533086. - Print -   104601
Phoenix Books, 8 Preston St., Faversham.
T. (01795) 536064. - Print -   104602

Felixstowe (Suffolk)
Abacus Book Buyers, 78 Hamilton Rd., Felixstowe.
T. (01394) 270717. - Print -   104603
Treasure Chest, 78 Hamilton Rd., Felixstowe.
T. (01394) 270717. - Print -   104604

Fochabers (Grampian)
Simpson, Marianne, 61-63 High St., Fochabers.
T. (01343) 821192. - Print -   104605

Folkestone (Kent)
Marrin, G. & D.I., 149 Sandgate Rd., Folkestone CT20
2DA. T. (01303) 53016, Fax (01303) 57403. - Print /
ArtBk / Engr / Map -   104606

Fowey (Cornwall)
Bookends, 4 South St., Fowey. T. (01726) 833361.
- Print -   104607

Framlingham (Suffolk)
Bell, V., 19 Market Hill, Framlingham.
T. (01728) 723046. - Print -   104608

Freshford (Avon)
Clarke, Janet, 3 Woodside Cottages, Freshford.
T. (01225) 723186. - Print -   104609

Frome (Somerset)
Old Curiosity Shop, 15 Catherine Hill, Frome.
T. (01373) 464482. - Print -   104610

Glasgow (Strathclyde)
Caledonia Books, 483 Great Western Rd, Glasgow.
T. (0141) 334 9663. - Print -   104611
Cooper Hay, 203 Bath St., Glasgow G2.
T. (0141) 226 3074. - Print -   104612

Glastonbury (Somerset)
Haddans, 30 Benedict St., Glastonbury.
T. (01458) 31753. - Print -   104613

Gloucester (Gloucestershire)
Quayside Bookshop, 2 Severn Rd., Gloucester.
T. (01452) 300422. - Print -   104614

Godalming (Surrey)
Eureka Bookroom, 19a Church St., Godalming.
T. (014868) 426968. - Print -   104615

Godmanchester (Cambridgeshire)
Bookshop, 11 Post St., Godmanchester. - Print -   104616

Goole (Humberside)
Howden, 5b Vicar Ln., Goole. T. (01405) 432071.
- Print -   104617

Gosport (Hampshire)
Richard, Martin, 23 Stoke Rd., Gosport PO12 1LS.
T. (01705) 520642. - Print -   104618

Grays (Essex)
Dunsford Emporium, College Av., Grays. - Engr /
Map -   104619

Great Ayton (North Yorkshire)
Great Ayton Bookshop, 47 High St., Great Ayton.
T. (01642) 723358. - Print / Engr -   104620

Great Yarmouth (Norfolk)
Ferrow, David, 77 Howard St. South, Great Yarmouth.
T. (01493) 843800. - Print / Engr -   104621

Greenock (Strathclyde)
Westwords, 14 Newton St., Greenock.
T. (01475) 892467. - Print -   104622

Guildford (Surrey)
Stewart, Michael, 61 Quarry St., Guildford.
T. (01483) 504359. - Print -   104623
Thorp, Thomas, 170 High St., Guildford GU1 3HP.
T. (01483) 62770. - Print -   104624
Traylen, Charles W., 49A-50 Quarry St., Guildford GU1
3UA. T. (01483) 572424. - Print -   104625

Hale (Greater Manchester)
Book Shop, 64a Park Rd., Hale WA15.
T. (0161) 980 8064. - Print -   104626
Davis, John, 64a Park Rd., Hale. T. (0161) 980 8064.
- Print -   104627

Halesowen (West Midlands)
Clent, 52a Summerhill, Halesowen B63. - Print -   104628

Halifax (West Yorkshire)
Collector Books, 39 The Colonade, Piece Hall, Halifax.
T. (01422) 363895. - Print -   104629

Harleston (Norfolk)
Hermitage Bookshop, 4c Church St., Harleston.
T. (01379) 853376. - Print -   104630

Harpenden (Hertfordshire)
Book Cabin, 379 Luton Rd., Harpenden.
T. (01582) 768581. - Print -   104631

Harrogate (North Yorkshire)
Bookstop, 11 Mayfield Grove, Harrogate.
T. (01423) 505817. - Print -   104632
Harrogate Bookshop, 29 Cheltenham Crescent, Harro-
gate. T. (01423) 500479. - Print -   104633
Merchant, Nicholas, 3 Promenade Court, Promenade
Square, Harrogate HG1 2PJ. T. (01423) 505370,
Fax (01423) 506183. - Print / ArtBk -   104634
Rippon, 6 Station Bridge, Harrogate. T. (01423) 501835.
- Print -   104635

Haslemere (Surrey)
Holmes, Julia, Muirfield Pl, Haslemere. T. (01428) 2153.
- Engr -   104636

Hastings (Sussex)
Howes, Trinity Hall, Hastings TN34 1HQ.
T. (01424) 423437. - Print -   104637
Old Hastings Bookshop, 15 George St., Hastings.
T. (01424) 425989. - Print -   104638
Riches, Brian, 15 George St., Hastings.
T. (01424) 425989. - Print -   104639
Tamarisk Bookshop, 80 High St, Hastings TN34 3EL.
T. (01424) 420591. - Print -   104640
Wilbraham, J. & S., 16 George St, Hastings.
T. (01424) 446413. - Print -   104641

Hatfield (Hertfordshire)
Old Cathay Fine Books, 43 Park St, Hatfield.
T. (017072) 274200. - Print -   104642

Havant (Hampshire)
Bookends, 2 North St., Havant. T. (01705) 470094.
- Print -   104643

Haverfordwest (Dyfed)
Seafarer Books, 18 Riverside Market, Haverfordwest.
T. (01437) 768359. - Print -   104644

Hay-on-Wye (Powys)
Addyman, 39 Lion St., Hay-on-Wye. T. (01497) 821136.
- Print -   104645
Aspin, J. Geoffrey, 27 Castle St., Hay-on-Wye.
T. (01497) 820437. - Print -   104646
Book Shop, Pavement House, Hay-on-Wye.
T. (01497) 821341. - Print -   104647
Booksearch, 1 Saint Marys Rd., Hay-on-Wye.
T. (01497) 820828. - Print -   104648
Boz, 13 Castle St., Hay-on-Wye. T. (01497) 821277.
- Print -   104649
Hay Cinema Bookshop, Castle St., Hay-on-Wye.
T. (01497) 820071. - Print -   104650
Rose's Bookshop, 14 Broad St., Hay-on-Wye.
T. (01497) 820013. - Print -   104651
Westwood, Mark, High Town, Hay-on-Wye.
T. (01497) 820068. - Print -   104652

Hebden Bridge (West Yorkshire)
Books and Collectors Centre, 16 Market St., Hebden
Bridge. T. (01422) 844600. - Print -   104653
Hatchard & Daughters, 56 Market St., Hebden Bridge.
T. (01422) 845717. - Print -   104654

Helensburgh (Southclyde)
McLaren, 91 Clyde St West, Helensburgh.
T. (01436) 76453.   104655

Helmsley (North Yorkshire)
Helmsley Bookshop, The Old Fire Station, Helmsley YO6
5BN. T. (01439) 70014. - Print -   104656
Rievaulx, 18 High St., Helmsley. T. (01439) 70912.
- Print -   104657

Henley-on-Thames (Oxfordshire)
Attic Bookshop, 4 Station Rd., Henley-on-Thames.
T. (01491) 579107. - Print -   104658
Way, Richard, 54 Friday St., Henley-on-Thames RG9
1AH. T. (01491) 576663. - Print -   104659

Hereford (Hereford and Worcester)
Chapters Bookshop, 17 Union St., Hereford.
T. (01432) 341302. - Print -   *104660*
Latcham, Paul, 25 Church St., Hereford.
T. (01432) 353586. - Print -   *104661*
Pierpont, 10 Church St., Hereford. T. (01432) 267002.
- Print -   *104662*

Hertford (Herfordshire)
Castle Bookshop, 25 Castle St., Hertford SG14 1HH.
T. (01992) 586537. - Print -   *104663*
Oxfam, 8 Railway St., Hertford. T. (01992) 583221.
- Print -   *104664*

Hindhead (Surrey)
Beacon Hill Bookshop, Brackendene, Beacon Hill Rd.,
Hindhead. T. (0142873) 606783. - Print -   *104665*

Hindley (Greater Manchester)
Arcadia Bookshop, 34 Cranstall Dr., Hindley.
T. (01942) 523627. - Print -   *104666*

Hitchin (Hertfordshire)
Book Bug, 1 The Arcade, Hitchin. T. (01462) 431309.
- Print -   *104667*
Moore, Eric T., 24 Bridge St., Hitchin. T. (01462) 450497.
- Print / Engr -   *104668*
Wheldon & Wesley, Lytton Lodge, Codicote, Hitchin SG4
8TE. T. (01462) 820370, Fax (01462) 821478.
- Print -   *104669*

Holmfirth (West Yorkshire)
Toll House Bookshop, 32-34 Huddersfield Rd., Holmfirth.
T. (01484) 686541. - Print -   *104670*

Holt (Norfolk)
Cook, Robert, 10 Heathfield Rd, Holt. T. (01263) 711163.
- Print -   *104671*
Gough, Simon, 5 Fish Hill, Holt. T. (01263) 712650.
- Print -   *104672*

Holyhead (Gwynedd)
Anglesey Books, 1 Thomas St., Holyhead.
T. (01407) 760988. - Print -   *104673*

Holywood (Co. Down)
World of Books, 13 Downshire Rd., Holywood.
- Print -   *104674*

Honiton (Devon)
Brockwell, 174 High St., Honiton. T. (01404) 43460.
- Print -   *104675*
Honiton Old Bookshop, 51 High St., Honiton.
T. (01404) 47180. - Print -   *104676*
Woodhead, Geoffrey M., 53 High St., Honiton.
T. (01404) 42969. - Print -   *104677*

Horncastle (Lincolnshire)
Jabberwock, 14 Saint Lawrence St., Horncastle.
T. (016582) 522112. - Print -   *104678*

Horsham (West Sussex)
Horsham Bookshop, 4 Park St., Horsham.
T. (01403) 52187. - Print -   *104679*
Murray & Kennett, 102 Bishopric, Horsham.
T. (01403) 54847. - Print -   *104680*

Huddersfield (West Yorkshire)
Roblyn, 18 Westgate, Huddersfield. T. (01484) 516793.
- Print -   *104681*

Hurstpierpoint (West Sussex)
Chimera Books, 17 High St., Hurstpierpoint.
T. (01273) 832255. - Print -   *104682*
Lyon, Richard, 17 High St, Hurstpierpoint BN6 9TT.
T. (01273) 832255.   *104683*

Hythe (Kent)
Old Gallery Bookshop, 125 High St., Hythe.
T. (01303) 269339. - Print -   *104684*

Ilfracombe (Devon)
Fitzjohn, 44 Fore St., Ilfracombe. T. (01271) 866888.
- Print -   *104685*
Lowe, Susan, Myrtle Cottage, Kiln Close Ln., Ilfracombe.
T. (01271) 861158. - Print -   *104686*

Instow (Devon)
Porcupine, Instow. T. (01271) 861158. - Print -   *104687*

Inverness (Highland)
Leakey, Charles, 10 Bank St, Inverness.
T. (01463) 23 99 47.   *104688*

Ipswich (Suffolk)
College Gateway Bookshop, 3 Silent St., Ipswich.
T. (01473) 254776. - Engr / Map -   *104689*

Irún (San Sebastian)
Spike Hughes, Leithen Rd, Irún EH44 6HY.
T. (943) 830019. - Print -   *104690*

Kelso (Borders)
Border Books, 21 The Tofts, Kelso. T. (01573) 25861.
- Print -   *104691*

Kendal (Cumbria)
Kerr, Ewen, No. 1, Yard 51, Stramongate, Kendal LA9
4BH. T. (01539) 720659, Fax (01539) 730739. - Engr /
Autogr / Map -   *104692*
Kirkland Books, 68 Kirkland, Kendal. T. (01539) 740841.
- Print -   *104693*

Kettering (Northamptonshire)
Kettering Bookshop, 14 Horsemarket, Kettering.
T. (01536) 84987. - Print -   *104694*

Kew (Greater London)
Lloyd, 9 Mortlake Terrace, Kew. T. (0181) 940 2512.
- Print -   *104695*

Kingsbridge (Devon)
Room at the Top, Fore St, Kingsbridge.
T. (01548) 856364. - Print -   *104696*

Kingston-upon-Hull (Humberside)
Cottingham, Unit 4, 169-171 Hallham, Kingston-upon-
Hull. T. (01482) 845567. - Print -   *104697*
F.J. Bookshop, Unit 24, Hull Microfirms Centre, Kings-
ton-upon-Hull. T. (01482) 585290. - Print -   *104698*
Sheridan, 19 Anlaby Rd., Kingston-upon-Hull.
T. (01482) 28759. - Print -   *104699*

Kirkby-in-Ashfield (Nottinghamshire)
Kyrios Books, 32b Kingsway, Kirkby-in-Ashfield.
T. 750966. - Print -   *104700*

Kirkby Lonsdale (Cumbria)
Beck Head Books and Gallery, 10 Beck Head, Kirkby
Lonsdale. T. (015242) 71314. - Print -   *104701*

Kirkby Stephen (Cumbria)
Wright, Vivian, Market St, Kirkby Stephen.
T. (017683) 71735. - Print -   *104702*

Kirkcaldy (Fife)
Book-Ends, 449-High St., Kirkcaldy. T. (01592) 205294.
- Print -   *104703*

Knaresborough (North Yorkshire)
Pennymead Bookshop, Scotton, Knaresborough.
T. (01423) 865962. - Print -   *104704*

Knutsford (Cheshire)
Lion Gallery and Bookshop, 15a Minshull St., Knutsford.
T. (01565) 652915, Fax (01565) 750142. - Print /
Engr -   *104705*

Lancaster (Lancashire)
Atticus Bookshop, 26 King St., Lancaster.
T. (01524) 381413. - Print -   *104706*
McCormack, W.B., 6-6a Rosemary Ln., Lancaster.
T. (01524) 36405. - Print -   *104707*

Langport (Somerset)
Old Bookshop, Bow St, Langport. T. (01458) 252644.
- Print -   *104708*

Lanreath (Cornwall)
A & R Booksearch, Highclose, Winnick Cross, Lanreath.
T. (01503) 220246, Fax 220965. - Print -   *104709*

Launceston (Cornwall)
Hutton, 8 Race Hill, Launceston. T. (01566) 776503.
- Print -   *104710*

Lavenham (Suffolk)
Archer, R.G., 7 Water St., Lavenham CO10 9RW.
T. (01787) 247229. - Print -   *104711*

Leamington Spa (Warwickshire)
Devitt, Nial, 217 Leam Terrace, Leamington Spa.
T. (01926) 315533. - Print -   *104712*
Portland, 5 Spencer St., Leamington Spa.
T. (01926) 338793. - Print -   *104713*

Ledbury (Hereford and Worcester)
Smith, Keith, 78b The Hammend, Ledbury.
T. (01531) 5336. - Print -   *104714*

Leeds (West Yorkshire)
Alerton, 11a Headingley Ln., Leeds LS6 1BL.
T. (0113) 2695012. - Print -   *104715*
Almar, 10 Commercial Rd, Leeds. T. (0113) 2780937.
- Print -   *104716*
Bookside, Midland Rd., Leeds LS6 1BQ.
T. (0113) 2744021. - Print -   *104717*
Miles, 12 Great George St., Leeds LS1 3DW.
T. (0113) 2455327. - Print -   *104718*

Leek (Staffordshire)
Abbey Bookshop, 17 Russel St., Leek.
T. (01538) 372092. - Print -   *104719*
Stockwell, 43 Bath St., Leek. T. (01538) 399033.
- Print -   *104720*

Leicester (Leicestershire)
Albion Books, 9 Thurlow Rd, Leicester.
T. (0116) 701914. - Print -   *104721*
Black Cat Bookshop, 37-38 Silver Arcade, Leicester.
T. (0116) 512756. - Print -   *104722*
Clarendon Books, 144 Clarendon Park Rd., Leicester
LE2 3AE. T. (0116) 701856. - Print -   *104723*
Forest Books, 41-42 Silver Arcade, Leicester.
T. (0116) 627171. - Print -   *104724*
Lenton, A., 27 Saint Nicholas Pl., Leicester.
T. (0116) 627827. - Print -   *104725*
Tin Drum Books, 68 Narborough Rd., Leicester.
T. (0116) 548236. - Print -   *104726*

Leighton Buzzard (Bedfordshire)
Books-a-Daisy, 23 Bell Alley, Leighton Buzzard.
T. (01525) 851380. - Print -   *104727*

Leominster (Hereford and Worcester)
Mainly Books, 7 School Ln., Leominster.
T. (01568) 615722. - Print -   *104728*

Letchworth (Hertfordshire)
Davids Bookshop, 7 Eastcheap Letchworth, Letchworth.
T. (01462) 686764. - Print -   *104729*

Lewes (East Sussex)
Bow Windows Book Shop, 128 High St., Lewes BN7
1XL. T. (01273) 480780. - Print -   *104730*
Chapter Two Bookshop, 18 Landsdown Pl., Lewes.
T. (01273) 477488. - Print -   *104731*
Cumming, A.J., 84 High St., Lewes BN7 1XN.
T. (01273) 472319. - Print -   *104732*
Fifteenth Century Bookshop, 99 High St., Lewes BN7
1XH. T. (01273) 474160. - Print -   *104733*

Leyland (Lancashire)
Great Grandfathers Bookshop, 82 Towngate, Leyland.
T. (01772) 422268. - Print -   *104734*

Lichfield (Staffordshire)
Abrahams, Mike, Cranmere Court, Walsall Rd., Lichfield.
T. (01543) 256200. - Print -   *104735*
Images, 4-6 Dam St., Lichfield. T. (01543) 264093.
- Print -   *104736*
Ridware, 8 Saint Margerets Rd., Lichfield.
T. (01543) 414112. - Print -   *104737*
Staffs Bookshop, 4-6 Dann St., Lichfield WS13 6AA.
T. (01543) 264093. - Print -   *104738*

Lincoln (Lincolnshire)
Golden Goose Books, 20-21 Steep Hill, Lincoln.
T. (01522) 522589. - Print -   *104739*
Readers Rest, 13 Steep Hill, Lincoln. T. (01522) 543217.
- Print -   *104740*

Lisburn (Co. Antrim)

Book Nook, 15 Antrim St., Lisburn. T. (01846) 607394.
- Print - *104741*

Little Walsingham (Norfolk)

Walsingham Books, Saint Peter's Rd, Little Walsingham.
T. (01328) 820892. - Print - *104742*

Liverpool (Merseyside)

Bohn, Henry, 32 Berry St., Liverpool L1.
T. (0151) 709 4501. - Print - *104743*
Bookcase, 45 Seaview Rd, Liverpool L4S.
T. (0151) 630 6334. - Print - *104744*
Crosby David E., 39 Crosby Rd. North, Liverpool L22.
T. (0151) 920 7738. - Print - *104745*
Hulse, D., Leighton Lodge, The Runnel, Liverpool.
T. (0151) 336 2023. - Print - *104746*
Leon, 111 Banks Rd, Liverpool L48. T. (0151) 625 2039.
- Print - *104747*
Out of Print Bookshop, 97 Renshaw St., Liverpool L1.
T. (0151) 708 9700. - Print - *104748*
Roles, John D., 55 Mount Pleasant, Liverpool L22.
T. (0151) 920 6801. - Print - *104749*
Walker Art Gallery Shop, Walker Art Gallery, William
Brown St, Liverpool L3 8EL. T. (0151) 2070001,
Fax (0151) 2981816. - ArtBk - *104750*

Llandudno (Gwynedd)

Hughes, David E., 21 Madoc St., Llandudno LL30 2TL.
T. (01492) 877700. - Print - *104751*

Llanidloes (Powys)

Great Oak Bookshop, 35 Great Oak St., Llanidloes.
T. (015512) 2959. - Print - *104752*

Llanrwst (Gwynedd)

Prospect Books and Prints, 18 Denbigh St., Llanrwst.
T. (01492) 640111. - Print - *104753*

London

Alexandra Books, 3 Chimes Av, London N13 5HT.
T. (0181) 447 9105. - Print - *104754*
Allen, J.A., 1 Lower Grosvenor Pl., London SW1W 0EL.
T. (0171) 834 5606, Fax (71) 834 5836. - Print - *104755*
Angelini, Marco, 7 Ulundi Rd., London SE3 70Q.
T. (0181) 858 3491. - ArtBk - *104756*
Antiquarius, 135 King's Rd., London SW3.
T. (0171) 351 0963. - Print - *104757*
Antique Books, 101 Whipps Cross Rd., London E11.
T. (0181) 530 7472. - Print - *104758*
Any Amount of Books, 62-56 Charing Cross Rd., London
WC2H 0BB. T. (0171) 2408140. - Print - *104759*
Archive Books and Music, 83 Bell St, London NW1 6TB.
T. (71) 402 8212. - Print - *104760*
Arts Bibliographic, 37 Cumberland Business Park, Cum-
berland Av, London NW10 7SL. T. (0181) 9614277,
Fax (0181) 9618246. - ArtBk - *104761*
Ash, J., 25 Royal Exchange, London EC3V 3LP.
T. (0171) 626 2665, Fax (0171) 623 9052.
- Print - *104762*
Atlantis Bookshop, 49a Museum St., London WC1.
T. (0171) 405 2120. - ArtBk - *104763*
Baddiel, Sarah, B12 Grays Antique Market, London W1Y.
T. (0171) 408 1239. - Print - *104764*
Baldwin & Sons, A.H., 11 Adelphi Terrace, London WC2N
6BJ. T. (0171) 930 6879. - Print - *104765*
Ballantyne & Date, 38 Museums St, London WC1A 1LP.
T. (0171) 242 4249, Fax (0171) 4300684.
- Print - *104766*
Bankside Gallery Bookshop, 48 Hopton St, London SE1
9JH. T. (0171) 9287521, Fax (0171) 9282820.
- ArtBk - *104767*
Baron, H., 76 Fortune Green Rd., London NW6 1DS.
T. (0171) 794 4041, Fax (0181) 459 2035. - Print /
Autogr - *104768*
Batbooks, 29 Museum St., London WC1A.
T. (0171) 436 5501. - Print - *104769*
Bayswater Books, 27a Craven Terrace, London W2 3EL.
T. (0171) 402 7398. - Print / ArtBk / Engr - *104770*
Beacon Hill Books, 11a Aberdeen Rd., London N7.
T. (0171) 609 4378. - Print - *104771*
Bell, Book & Radmell, 4 Cecil Court, London WC2N.
T. (0171) 2402161. - Print - *104772*

Biltcliffe, 2a Eynham Rd., London W12 0HA.
T. (0181) 740 5326. - Print - *104773*
Blackheath, 74 Tranquil Vale, London SE3.
T. (0181) 852 4786. - Print - *104774*
Books and Lyrics, Merton Abbey Mill, London SW19
2RD. T. (0181) 543 0625. - Print - *104775*
Books and Things, 292 Westbourne Grove, London W11.
T. (0171) 370 5593. - Print - *104776*
Books of Asia, 717 Fulham Rd., London SW6 5UL.
T. (0171) 731 2447, Fax (0171) 731 8009.
- ArtBk - *104777*
Boutle & King, 23 Arlington Way, London EC1R.
T. (0171) 278 4497. - Print - *104778*
Boyle & Co, John, 40 Drayton Gardens, London SW8.
T. (0171) 373 8247. - Print - *104779*
Brett, Alan, 24 Cecil Court, London WC2N.
T. (0171) 836 8222. - Print - *104780*
British Museum Bookshop, Great Russel St, London
WC1B 3DG. T. (0171) 3238587, Fax (0171) 4367315.
- ArtBk - *104781*
Bromley Bookshop, 39-41 High St., London.
T. (0181) 313 0242. - Print - *104782*
Brotherton, 77 Walton St., London SW3 LJ2.
T. (0171) 589 6848. - Print - *104783*
Burgess Browning, 25 Blue Ball Yard, Saint Jame's St.,
London SW1A. T. (0171) 491 1811. - Print - *104784*
Cambell, Marcus, 46 Maddox St, London W1R 9PB.
T. (0171) 4954412, Fax (0171) 4954425. - ArtBk /
Print - *104785*
Camberwell Bookshop, 28 Camberwell Grove, London
SE5 8RE. T. (0171) 7013450. - Print - *104786*
Camden Arts Centre Bookshop, Arkwright Rd, London
NW3 6DG. T. (0171) 4352643, Fax (0171) 7943371.
- ArtBk - *104787*
Cassidy, 20 College Approach, London SE10.
T. (0181) 858 7197. - Print - *104788*
Cavendish, 2 Sackville St, London W1X.
T. (0171) 439 6151. - Print - *104789*
Chapter One, 2 Pierrepont Row, Camden Passage, Lon-
don N1. T. (0171) 359 1185. - Print - *104790*
Chelsea Rare Books, 313 Kings Rd., London SW3 5EP.
T. (0171) 351 0950. - ArtBk - *104791*
Cherrington, 58 Davies St, London W1.
T. (0171) 495 1630. - Print - *104792*
Chichester Gallery, 20a Oakley St, London SW3 5NT.
T. (0171) 3525981, Fax (0171) 3520732. - Print /
ArtBk - *104793*
Cinema Bookshop, 13-14 Great Russell St., London
WC1B 3NH. T. (0171) 637 0206. - ArtBk - *104794*
Clarke-Hall, J., 7 Bride Court, London EC4Y.
T. (0171) 353 4116. - Print - *104795*
Classic Bindings, 23 Montford Pl., London SE11.
T. (0171) 735 1872. - Print - *104796*
Collinge & Clark, 13 Leigh St., London WC1H 9EW.
T. (0171) 387 7105. - Print - *104797*
Connelly, Robert, 31-35 Great Ormond St., London
WC1N. T. (0171) 430 1394. - Print - *104798*
Constant Reader Bookshop, 627 Fulham Rd., London
SW6 5UQ. T. (0171) 731 0218. - Print - *104799*
Contemporary Ceramics, 7 Marshall St, London W1V
1FD. T. (0171) 4377605, Fax (0171) 2879954.
- ArtBk - *104800*
Design Council Bookshop, 28 Haymarket, London SW1Y
4SU. T. (0171) 839 8000, Fax (0171) 9252130.
- ArtBk - *104801*
Dicken's Old Curiosity Shop, 13-14 Portsmouth St.
Kingsway, London WC2A 2ES. T. (0171) 405 9891.
- Print / Engr - *104802*
Dillon, 82 Gower St., London WC1E 6EQ.
T. (0171) 636 1577. - Print - *104803*
Dillons Arts Bookshop, 8 Long Acre, London WC2E 9LG.
T. (0171) 8361359. - Print - *104804*
Dixon, Charles, 132 Tranmere Rd, London SW18 3QU.
T. (0181) 946 9677. - Print - *104805*
Donovan Military Books, 52 Willow Rd, London NW3.
T. (0171) 431 2474. - Print - *104806*
Drummond, David, 11 Cecil Court, London WC2N 4EZ.
T. (0171) 836 1142. - Print - *104807*
Eastern Books, 125a Astonville St., London SW18.
T. (0181) 871 0880. - Print - *104808*
Edrich, I.D., 17 Selsdon Rd., London E11.
T. (0181) 989 9541. - Print - *104809*

Edwards, Christopher, 63 Jermyn St., London SW1Y.
T. (0171) 495 4263. - Print - *104810*
Europa Books, 15 Luttrell Av, London SW15 6PD.
T. (0181) 788 0312. - Print - *104811*
Fantasy Centre, 157 Holloway Rd., London N7 8LX.
T. (0171) 607 9433. - Print - *104812*
Fawkes, Keith, 1-3 Flash Walk, London NW3.
T. (0171) 435 0614. - Print - *104813*
Finch, Simon, 10 New Bond St., London W1Y.
T. (0171) 499 0974. - Print - *104814*
Fine Books Oriental, 46 Great Russell St., London
WC1B. T. (0171) 636 6068. - Print - *104815*
Finney, Michael, 11 Camden Passage, London N1.
T. (0171) 226 9280. - Print - *104816*
First Issues, 17 Alfoxton Av., London N15.
T. (0181) 881 6931. - Print - *104817*
Fisher & Sperr, 46 Highgate High St., London N6 5JB.
T. (0181) 340 7244. - Print / ArtBk - *104818*
Fitzjohn, 27a Northways Parade, London NW3.
T. (0171) 722 9864. - Print - *104819*
Fletcher, H.M., 201 Cardamon Bldg., 31 Shad Thames,
London SE1 2YR. T. (0171) 378 1350,
Fax (0171) 403 2044. - Print / Engr - *104820*
Fogg, Sam, 14 Old Bond St., London W1X.
T. (0171) 495 2333. - Print - *104821*
Forster, W., 83a Stamford Hill, London N16 5TP.
T. (0181) 800 3919. - Engr / Autogr / Map - *104822*
Foster, Stephen, 95 Bell St., London NW1.
T. (0171) 724 0876. - Print - *104823*
Foster, W.A., 183 Chiswick High Rd., London W4.
T. (0181) 995 2768. - Print - *104824*
Foyle, W. & G., 113-119 Charing Cross Rd, London WC2.
T. (0171) 437 5660. *104825*
Franks, J.A.L., 7 Allington St., London SW1.
T. (0171) 834 8697. - Map - *104826*
Frew Mackenzie, 106 Great Russell St., London WC1B.
T. (0171) 580 2311. - Print - *104827*
Fuller d'Arch Smith, 37b New Cavendish St., London
W1. T. (0171) 722 0063. - Print - *104828*
Gardner, Walter H., 16 Chalton Dr., London N2.
T. (0181) 458 3202. - Print - *104829*
Gekoski, R.A., 33b Chalcot Sq., London NW1 8YA.
T. (0171) 722 9037. - Print - *104830*
Gibbons, Starley, 399 Strand, London WC2.
T. (0171) 836 8444, Fax (0171) 836 7342.
- Print - *104831*
Gloucester Road Bookshop, 123 Gloucester Rd., London
SW7 4TE. T. (0171) 370 3503. - Print - *104832*
Graves-Johnston, Michael, 54 Stockwell Park Rd., Lon-
don SW9 0DR. T. (0171) 274 2069,
Fax (0171) 738 3747. - ArtBk - *104833*
Great Russell Street Books, 44 Great Russell St., London
WC1B. T. (0171) 637 7635. - Print - *104834*
Green, G.L., 104 Pitshanger Ln., London W5.
T. (0181) 997 6454. - Print - *104835*
Greer, Robin, 30 Sloane Court West, London SW3 4T3.
T. (0171) 730 7392. - Print - *104836*
Grigor-Taylor, Barbara, 15 Frith St., London W1V.
T. (0171) 287 3721. - Print - *104837*
Haas, Otto, 49 Belsize Park Gardens, London NW3 4JL.
T. (0171) 722 1488, Fax (0171) 722 2364. - Print /
Autogr - *104838*
Hammersmith Bookshop, Barnes High St., London
SW13. T. (0181) 876 7254. - Print - *104839*
Han-Shan Tang, 42 Westleigh Av., London SW15 6RL.
T. (0181) 788 4464, Fax (0181) 780 1565.
- Print - *104840*
Harlequin Books, 68 Greenwich High Rd., London SE10.
T. (0181) 692 7170. - Print - *104841*
Harrington Brothers, 253 Kings Rd, London SW3 5EL.
T. (0171) 3525689. - Print - *104842*
Harrington Brothers, 253 Kings Rd, London SW3 5EL.
T. (0171) 352 5689, Fax (0171) 823 3449. *104843*
Hatchards, 187 Piccadilly, London W1V 9DA.
T. (0171) 439 9921, Fax (0171) 287 2638.
- ArtBk - *104844*
Hayward Gallery Bookshop, Belvedere Rd, London SE1
8XZ. T. (0171) 9283144. - ArtBk - *104845*
Heneage Art Books, Thomas, 42, Duke Street, St. Ja-
mes's, London SW1Y 6DJ. T. (0171) 9309223,
Fax (0171) 8399223. - ArtBk - *104846*
Heywood Hill, 10 Curzon St, London W1Y 7FJ.
T. (0171) 629 0647, Fax (0171) 408 0286. *104847*

Hilton, P.J., Charing Cross Rd, London WC2N.
T. (0171) 379 9825. - Print - *104848*

History Bookshop, 2 The Broadway, London N11.
T. (0181) 368 8568. - Print - *104849*

Holstein, Florian, 15 Piccadilly Arcade, London SW1Y
6NH. - ArtBk - *104850*

Home to Home, 355c Archway Rd., London N6.
T. (0181) 340 8354. - Print - *104851*

Hosains Rare Books, 25 Connaught St., London W2 2AY.
T. (0171) 262 7900. - Print / ArtBk / Engr - *104852*

Hünersdorff, Richard von, 57 Drayton Gardens, London
SW10 9RU. T. (0171) 373 3899, Fax (0171) 370 1244.
- Print - *104853*

ICA Bookshop, 12 Carlton House Terrace, London SW1Y
5AH. T. (0171) 930 0493, Fax (0171) 8730051.
- ArtBk - *104854*

Imprints London, 42 Bonner Rd., London E2 9JS.
T. (0181) 980 9427. - Print - *104855*

International Book Exchange, 213 Garratt Ln., London
SW18. T. (0181) 877 3043. - Print - *104856*

Jarndyce, 46 Great Russell St., London WC1B.
T. (0171) 631 4220. - Print - *104857*

Joseph, E., 1 Vere St., London W1M 9HQ.
T. (0171) 493 8353, Fax (0171) 629 2759.
- Print - *104858*

Kennedy, Peter, 305 Westbourne Grove, London W11
2QA. T. (0171) 243 1416, Fax (0171) 243 2271. - Print /
Engr / Map - *104859*

Kirkdale Bookshop, 272 Kirkdale, London SE26.
T. (0181) 778 4701, Fax (0181) 460 4548.
- Print - *104860*

Korn, M.E., 47 Tetherdown Muswell Hill, London N10
1NH. T. (0181) 883 5251. - Print - *104861*

Landry, Harold, 19 Tanza Rd., London NW3 2UA.
T. (0171) 435 6167. - Print - *104862*

Leicester Art Books, POB 4YT, London W1A 4YT.
T. (0171) 485 7073, Fax (0171) 485 7075.
- Print - *104863*

MacDonnell, Finbar, 17 Camden Passage, London N1.
T. (0171) 226 0537. *104864*

Maggs Brothers, 50 Berkeley Sq., London W1X 6EL.
T. (0171) 493 7160, Fax (0171) 499 2007. - Print /
Engr / Autogr - *104865*

Manheim Bookseller, Carol, 31 Ennismore Av, London
W4 1SE. T. (0181) 9949740, Fax (0181) 9955396.
- Print / ArtBk - *104866*

Map House, 54 Beauchamp Pl, London SW3.
T. (0171) 5894325, Fax (0171) 589 1041. *104867*

Marcet, 4a Nelson Rd, London SE10 9JB.
T. (0181) 8535408. - Print - *104868*

Marchmont, 39 Burton St., London WC1H 9AL.
T. (0171) 387 7989. - Print / ArtBk - *104869*

Marchpane, E.W., 16 Cecil Court, London WC2N.
T. (0171) 836 8661. - Print - *104870*

Marks, Barrie, 11 Laurier Rd, London NW5 1SD.
T. (0171) 482 5684, Fax (0171) 284 3149. *104871*

Marlborough Rare Books, 144-146 New Bond St., London W1Y 9FD. T. (0171) 493 6993. - Print - *104872*

Marsden, Francis, 59a King's Rd., London SW3 4ND.
T. (0171) 730 2836. - Engr - *104873*

Matthews, Lisa, 213 Garratt Ln., London SW18 4DS.
T. (0181) 877 3043. - Print - *104874*

Maude, Richard, 22 Parkfields, London SW13.
T. (0181) 788 2991. - Print - *104875*

Mulder, Frederick, 83 Belsize Park Gardens, London
NW3. T. (0171) 435 4228. - Print - *104876*

Museum Bookshop, 36 Great Russell St., London WC1B.
T. (0171) 580 4086. - Print - *104877*

My Back Pages, Unit 318, Elephant & Castle, London
SE1. T. (0171) 252 6889. - Print - *104878*

My Back Pages, 8-10a Balham Station Rd., London
SW12. T. (0181) 675 9346. - Print - *104879*

National Gallery Shop, The National Gallery, Trafalgar
Square, London WC2N 5DN. T. (0171) 3891770,
Fax (0171) 9300108. - ArtBk - *104880*

Old Ephemera and Newspaper Shop, 37 Kinnerton St.,
London SW1X 8ED. T. (0171) 235 7788.
- ArtBk - *104881*

Old Town Books, 30 Old Town, London SW4.
T. (0171) 498 0998. - Print - *104882*

Olimpia Theodoli, 55 Cambridge St, London SW1V4PS.
T. (0171) 8397805. - ArtBk / Engr / Print / Map - *104883*

Orrsich, Paul, 117 Munster Rd., London SW6.
T. (0171) 736 3869. - Print - *104884*

Oxus, 121 Astonville St., London SW18.
T. (0171) 870 3854. - Print - *104885*

Parikian, D., 3 Caithness Rd, London W14.
T. (0171) 603 8375, Fax (0171) 602 1178. *104886*

Pendlebury, Portland Av, London N16.
T. (0181) 809 4922. - Print - *104887*

Phelps, Michael, 19 Chelverton Rd., London SW15.
T. (0181) 785 6766. - Print - *104888*

Pickering & Chatto, 17 Pall Mall, London SW1.
T. (0171) 930 2515, Fax (0171) 930 8627.
- Print - *104889*

Pleasures of Past Times, 11 Cecil Court, London WC2N
4EZ. T. (0171) 836 1142. - ArtBk - *104890*

Plus Books, 19 Abbey Parade High St, London SW19.
T. (0181) 542 1665. - Print - *104891*

Pordes, Henry, 58-60 Charing Cross Rd, London WC2.
T. (0171) 836 9031. *104892*

Primrose Hill Books, 134 Regent Park Rd., London NW1.
T. (0171) 586 2022. - Print - *104893*

Print Room, 37 Museum St., London WC1A.
T. (0171) 430 0159. - Print - *104894*

Probsthain, Arthur, 41 Great Russell St, London WC1B
3PH. T. (0171) 636 1096. *104895*

Quaritch, Bernard, 5-8 Lower John St., London W1R
4AU. T. (0171) 734 2983, Fax (0171) 437 0967. - Print /
Autogr - *104896*

Randall, John, 47 Moreton St., London SW1V 2NY.
T. (0171) 630 5331. - Print - *104897*

Reeves, William, 1a Norbury Crescent, London SW16
4JR. T. (0181) 764 2108. - ArtBk - *104898*

Remington, Reg & Philip, 18 Cecil Court, London WC2.
T. (0171) 836 9771. - Print - *104899*

Ripping Yarns, 355 Archway Rd., London N6.
T. (0181) 341 6111. - Print - *104900*

Robbie's Bookshop, 118a Alexandra Park Rd., London
N10. T. (0181) 444 6957. - Print - *104901*

Rogers Turner, 22 Nelson Rd., London SE10 9JB.
T. (0181) 853 5271. - Print - *104902*

Rota, Bertram, 9-11 Langley Court, London WC2E 9RX.
T. (0171) 836 0723. - Print / Autogr / Map - *104903*

Royal Academy Shop, Royal Academy of Arts, Burlington
House, Piccadilly, London W1V 0DS.
T. (0171) 4945757, Fax (0171) 4390837.
- ArtBk - *104904*

Russell, 18 Queen St., London W1X. T. (0171) 629 0532.
- Print - *104905*

Saint George's Gallery Books, 8 Duke St., London SW1Y
6BN. T. (0171) 930 0935, Fax (0171) 9761832.
- ArtBk - *104906*

Saint James's Prints and Books, 15 Piccadilly Arcade off
Jermyn St, London SW1Y 6NH. T. (0171) 4956487,
Fax 4956490. - ArtBk - *104907*

Saint Martins Prints, 5 Cecil Court, London WC2N.
T. (0171) 240 1844. - Print - *104908*

Sawyer, Charles J., 30 Dover St., London W1X 4BX.
T. (0171) 493 3810, Fax (0171) 491 3098.
- Print - *104909*

Schmidt-Gotz, C., 57 Drayton Gardens, London SW10.
T. (0171) 373 3979. - Print - *104910*

Schuster, Thomas E., 14 Maddox, London SW1V 1HN.
T. (0171) 491 2208. - Print / Engr / Map - *104911*

Scott, K., 27 Romford Rd., London E15.
T. (0181) 519 1593. - Print - *104912*

Serpentine Gallery Trust, Kensington Gardens, London
W2 3XA. T. (0171) 4026075/0343,
Fax (0171) 4024103. - ArtBk - *104913*

Shapero, Bernard T., 80 Holland Park Av., London W11
3RE. T. (0171) 493 0876. - Print - *104914*

Shipley, Specialist Art Booksellers, 70 Charing Cross Rd,
London WC2H 0BB. T. (0171) 8364872,
Fax (0171) 4972486. - Print / ArtBk - *104915*

Silverman, Michael, POB 350, London SE3.
T. (0181) 319 4452, Fax (0181) 856 6006.
- Print - *104916*

Sims Reed, 58 Jermyn St., London SW1Y 6LX.
T. (0171) 493 5660, Fax (0171) 493 8468. - Print /
ArtBk - *104917*

Skoob, 11a-15 Sicilian Av., London WC1A 2QH.
T. (0171) 404 3063, Fax (0171) 404 4398.
- Print - *104918*

South London Antique and Bookcentre, 18-19 Stockwell
St., London SE10 9JN. T. (0181) 853 2151.
- Print - *104919*

Speed, John, 97 Vanbrough Court, London SE11.
T. (0171) 820 1639. *104920*

Spread Eagle Bookshop, 8 Nevada St., London SE10
9JL. T. (0181) 6921618. - Print / ArtBk - *104921*

Stage Door Prints, 1 Cecil Court, London WC2N.
T. (0171) 240 1683. *104922*

Stevens, Eric & Joan, 74 Fortune Green Rd, London
NW6 1DS. T. (0171) 435 7545. *104923*

Stone Trough Books, 59 Camberwell Grove, London
SE5. T. (0171) 708 0612. - Print - *104924*

Storey, Harold T., 3 Cecil Court Charing Cross Rd., London WC2N 4EZ. T. (0171) 836 3777. - Print / Engr /
Map - *104925*

Stroh, M.A., 98a Blackstock Rd., London N4 2DR.
T. (0171) 359 7666. - Print - *104926*

Tate Gallery Shop, Tate Gallery, Millbank, London SW1P
4RG. T. (0171) 8345651, Fax (0171) 8287357.
- ArtBk - *104927*

Thomas, Alan G., c/o National Westminster Bank, 300
King's Rd., London SW3 0HT.
T. (0171) 352 5130. *104928*

Tooley, Adams & Co., 13 Cecil Court, London WC2.
T. (0171) 240 4406, Fax (0171) 240 8058.
- Print - *104929*

Travis & Emery, 17 Cecil Court, London WC2N 4EZ.
T. (0171) 240 2129. - Print - *104930*

Ulysses Bookshop, 31/40 Museum St., London WC1A.
T. (0171) 6368206. - Print - *104931*

Unsworth, Rice & Coe, 12 Bloomsbury St., London
WC1B. T. (0171) 637 7334. - Print - *104932*

Upper Street Bookshop, 182 Upper St., London N1.
T. (0171) 359 3785. - Print - *104933*

Vanbrugh, 40a Museum St., London WC1A.
T. (0171) 404 0733. - Print - *104934*

Vandeleur, 69 Sheen Ln., London SW14.
T. (0181) 878 6837. - Print - *104935*

Victoria and Albert Museum Bookshop, Victoria and Al-
bert Museum, Cromwell Rd, London SW7 2RL.
T. (0171) 9388500, Fax (0171) 9388623.
- ArtBk - *104936*

Village Bookshop, 46 Belsize Ln., London NW3.
T. (0171) 794 3180. - Print - *104937*

Vortex, 139-141 Church St., London N1 0UH.
T. (0171) 254 6516. - Print - *104938*

Walden, 38 Harmood St., London NW1.
T. (0171) 267 8146. - Print - *104939*

Walford, G.W., 15 Calabria Rd., London N5.
T. (0171) 226 5682. - Print - *104940*

Warwick Leadlay, 5 Nelson Rd., London SE10 9JB.
T. (0181) 858 0317. - Engr / Autogr - *104941*

Waterstone, 193 Kensington High St., London W8.
T. (0171) 937 8432. - Print - *104942*

Waterways, 59 Tottenham Ln., London N8.
T. (0181) 348 3459. - Print - *104943*

Watkins, 19-21 Cecil Court, London WC2.
T. (0171) 836 2182. - Print - *104944*

Whetstone, 368 Oakleigh Rd. North, London N20.
T. (0181) 368 8338. - Print - *104945*

Whitehart, F.E., 40 Priestfield Rd., London SE23 2RS.
T. (0181) 699 3225, Fax (0181) 291 1605.
- Print - *104946*

World of Books, 39 Woborn Pl., London WC1H.
T. (0171) 436 0027. - Print - *104947*

Zeno Booksellers, 6 Denmark St., London WC2H 8LP.
T. (0171) 836 2522. - Engr / Map - *104948*

Zwemmer, A., 24 Litchfield St., London WC2H 9NJ.
T. (0171) 3797886, Fax (0171) 4973290.
- ArtBk - *104949*

Zwemmer at the Courtauld Institute Galleries, Sommer-
set House, Strand, London WC2R 0RN.
T. (0171) 872 0217, Fax (0171) 8732579.
- ArtBk - *104950*

Zwemmer at the Whitechapel Art Gallery, 80 Whitechapel High St, London E1 7QX. T. (0171) 247 6924.
- ArtBk - *104951*

Zwemmer Media Bookshop, 80 Charing Cross Rd., London WC2H 0BE. T. (0171) 379 7886,
Fax (0171) 8367049. - ArtBk - *104952*

Looe (Cornwall)
Booksearch, A. & R., Highclose, Looe PL13 2PF.
T. (015036) 220246, Fax (015036) 220965.
- Print -   *104953*
Old Hall Bookshop, Shutta Rd, Looe.
T. (015036) 263700. - Print -   *104954*

Loughborough (Leicestershire)
Sparrow Hill Books, 3 Sparrow Hill, Loughborough.
T. (01509) 263080. - Print -   *104955*

Lowestoft (Suffolk)
Curfew, 44 High St., Lowestoft. T. (01502) 589496.
- Print -   *104956*
Rolph, John, Pakefield St, Lowestoft. T. (01502) 572039.
- Print -   *104957*

Lubenham (Leicestershire)
Brown, Jack, 62 Main St., Lubenham.
T. (01858) 465787. - Print -   *104958*

Ludlow (Shropshire)
Books and Chattles, 107 Corve St., Ludlow.
T. (01584) 876191. - Print -   *104959*
Offa's Dyke, 5 Bull Ring, Ludlow. T. (01584) 873854.
- Print -   *104960*
20th Century Books, 132 Corve St., Ludlow.
T. (01584) 874441. - Print -   *104961*

Luton (Bedfordshire)
Foye, 15 Stanley St., Luton. T. (01582) 38487.
- Print -   *104962*

Lyme Regis (Dorset)
Long, 40 Silver St., Lyme Regis. T. (01297) 443111.
- Print -   *104963*

Lymington (Hampshire)
Hughes & Smeeth, 1 Gosport St., Lymington.
T. (01590) 676324. - Print / Engr -   *104964*

Macclesfield (Cheshire)
Bridgewater, 28 Sunderland St., Macclesfield.
T. (01625) 424763. - Print -   *104965*
Macclesfield Bookshop, 124 Chestergate, Macclesfield.
T. (01625) 425352. - Print -   *104966*
Treglown, Roger J., 28 Landsdowne St., Macclesfield
SK10 SQZ. T. (01625) 618978. - Print -   *104967*

Maidstone (Kent)
Antiquarian Book Company, 258 Upper Fant Rd., Maidstone. T. (01622) 728525. - Print -   *104968*
Maidstone Bookshop, 38 Union St., Maidstone ME14
1ED. T. (01622) 662878. - Print -   *104969*

Maldon (Essex)
All Books, 2 Mill Rd., Maldon. T. (01621) 856214.
- Print -   *104970*
Beeleigh Abbey Books, Beeleigh Abbey, Maldon CM3
4AD. T. (01621) 856308, Fax (01621) 850064.
- Print -   *104971*

Malmesbury (Wiltshire)
Batstone, 12 Gloucester St., Malmesbury SN16 0AA.
T. (01666) 823072. - ArtBk -   *104972*

Malvern (Hereford and Worcester)
Malvern Bookshop, 5-7 Abbey Rd., Malvern WR14 3ES.
T. (01684) 575915. - Engr / Map / Print -   *104973*
Priory Bookshop, Church Walk, Malvern.
T. (01684) 560258. - Print -   *104974*

Manchester (Greater Manchester)
Browzers, 14 Warwick St, Manchester M25 7HN.
T. (0161) 7980626. - Print / Engr -   *104975*
Fennel Bookshop, 23 Fennel St., Manchester M4.
T. (0161) 835 3759. - Print -   *104976*
Forest Books, 16 Lloyd St., Manchester.
T. (0161) 833 9037. - Print -   *104977*
Gibb, 10 Charlotte St., Manchester. T. (0161) 236 7179.
- Print -   *104978*
McGill, 115 Princess Rd., Manchester M14 4RB.
T. (0161) 232 9620. - Print -   *104979*
Morton, Eric J., 4-6 Warburton St., Manchester M20
ORA. T. (0161) 445 7629. - Print -   *104980*

Paramount Book Exchange, 25 Shudehill, Manchester
M4. T. (0161) 834 9509. - Print -   *104981*
Secondhand & Rare Books, Corner of Church St./High
St., Manchester. T. (0161) 834 5964. - Print -   *104982*
Talisman Books, 42 Town St., Manchester SK6.
T. (0161) 449 9271. - Print -   *104983*

Mansfield (Nottinghamshire)
Book Shelf, 16 Albert St., Mansfield. T. (01623) 648231.
- Print -   *104984*

Market Deeping (Lincolnshire)
Bridge Bookshop, 106 Church St., Market Deeping PE6
8HB. T. (01778) 343175. - Print -   *104985*

Market Drayton (Shropshire)
Second Chapter, 5 Queen St., Market Drayton.
T. (01630) 657410. - Print -   *104986*

Marlborough (Wiltshire)
Antique and Book Collector, Katherine House, Marlborough. T. (01672) 514040. - Print -   *104987*
Military Parade Bookshop, The Parade, Marlborough.
T. (01672) 515470. - Print -   *104988*

Matlock (Derbyshire)
Jarvis, 57-59 Smedley St. East, Matlock DE4 3FQ.
T. (01629) 55322. - Print -   *104989*

Midhurst (West Sussex)
Browse Awhile, Mint Market, Grange Rd., Midhurst.
T. (01730) 815425. - Print -   *104990*
Cameo Bookshop, 3 Knockhundred Market, Midhurst.
T. (01730) 815221. - Print -   *104991*

Minehead (Somerset)
Alcombe Bookshop, 26 Alcombe Rd., Minehead.
T. (01643) 703425. - Print -   *104992*

Montrose (Tayside)
Jordan, S., 91 Murray St., Montrose. T. (01674) 72252.
- Print -   *104993*

Moreton-in-Marsh (Gloucestershire)
Four Shire Books, 17 High St., Moreton-in-Marsh.
T. (01608) 51451. - Print -   *104994*

Nailsworth (Gloucestershire)
Valentine, Day's Mill, Old Market, Nailsworth.
T. (0145383) 832483. - Print -   *104995*

Nether Stowey (Somerset)
House of Antiquity, Saint Mary St., Nether Stowey.
T. (01278) 732426. - Print -   *104996*

New Milton (Hampshire)
Books and Things, 99 Milton Rd., New Milton.
T. (01425) 617521. - Print -   *104997*

Newark-on-Trent (Nottinghamshire)
Lawrence, Lombard St, Newark-on-Trent.
T. (01636) 605865. - Print -   *104998*

Newbury (Berkshire)
Invicta Bookshop, 8 Cromwell Pl., Newbury.
T. (01635) 31176. - Print -   *104999*

Newcastle-upon-Tyne (Tyne and Wear)
Bookworms Paradise, 33 Green Market, Newcastle-
upon-Tyne. T. (0191) 232 3196. - Print -   *105000*
Steedman, Robert D., 9 Grey St., Newcastle-upon-Tyne
NE1 6EE. T. (0191) 232 6561. - Print -   *105001*
Thorne, Grand Hotel Bldg., Haymarket, Newcastle-upon-
Tyne. T. (0191) 2326421. - Print -   *105002*

Newmarket (Suffolk)
Way, R.E. & G.B., Brettons, Burrough Green, Newmarket.
T. (01638) 507217. - Print -   *105003*

Newton Abbott (Devon)
Lindy's Books, 58a Queen St., Newton Abbott.
T. (01626) 63221. - Print -   *105004*

North Harrow (Middlesex)
Zip, 39 Sta Rd, North Harrow HA2 7SU.
T. (0181) 8630155, Fax (0181) 8631227.
- ArtBk -   *105005*

North Shields (Tyne and Wear)
Keel Row, 57 Kirton Park Terrace, North Shields.
T. (0191) 296 1952. - Print -   *105006*
Keel Row, 11 Fenwick Terrace, Preston Rd., North
Shields. T. (0191) 296 0664. - Print -   *105007*

Northampton (Northamptonshire)
Abington, 327 Bellingborough Rd., Northampton.
T. (01604) 32932. - Print -   *105008*
Occultique, 73 Kettering Rd., Northampton.
T. (01604) 27727. - Print -   *105009*
Talent Pastimes Bookshop, 85 Kettering Rd., Northampton. T. (01604) 36396. - Print -   *105010*

Northleach (Gloucestershire)
Loveday, Peter & Sarah, The Green, Northleach GL54
3EX. T. (01451) 60519. - Print / ArtBk / Engr -   *105011*

Norwich (Norfolk)
Crowe, 75-77 Upper Saint Giles St., Norwich NR2 1BA.
T. (01603) 624800. - Print / Engr -   *105012*
Crowe, Denise, 64-65 Provision Market, Norwich.
T. (01603) 764265. - Print -   *105013*
Ellis, J.R. & R.K., 53 Saint Giles St., Norwich NR2 1JR.
T. (01603) 623679. - Print -   *105014*
Hull, T. & J., 72 Saint Benedicts St., Norwich.
T. (01603) 624890. - Print -   *105015*
Movie Shop, 11 Saint Gregorys Alley, Norwich.
T. (01603) 615239. - Print -   *105016*
Scientific Anglian, 30-30a Saint Benedict St., Norwich.
T. (01603) 624079. - Print -   *105017*
Tombland Bookshop, 8 Tombland, Norwich.
T. (01603) 760610. - Print / Engr -   *105018*

Nottingham (Nottinghamshire)
Blore, 484 Mansfield Rd., Nottingham.
T. (0115) 9691441. - Print -   *105019*
Jermy & Westerman, 203 Mansfield Rd., Nottingham.
T. (0115) 9474522. - Print -   *105020*
Maynard & Bradley, 30 Friar Ln., Nottingham NG1 6DZ.
T. (0115) 9484824. - Print -   *105021*
Neales, 192-194 Mansfield Rd., Nottingham NG1 3HU.
T. (0115) 9624141. - Print -   *105022*

Oakham (Leicestershire)
Old House Gallery, 13 Market Pl, Oakham.
T. (01572) 755538.   *105023*

Ombersley (Hereford and Worcester)
Slim, R.T., Boreley Cottage, Ombersley.
T. (01905) 620697. - Print -   *105024*

Ormskirk (Lancashire)
Mere, 48 Southport Rd., Ormskirk L39 1QR.
T. (01695) 577570. - Print -   *105025*

Orpington (Greater London)
J.C. Antiquarian Books, 115 Crofton Ln., Orpington BR5
1HB. T. (01689) 830938. - Print -   *105026*

Oswestry (Shropshire)
Newgate Bookshop, 59 Church St., Oswestry.
T. (01691) 650178. - Print -   *105027*

Otford (Kent)
Darenth, 8 High St., Otford. T. (019592) 922430. - Print /
Engr -   *105028*

Oxford (Oxfordshire)
Arcadia Booksellers, 4 Saint Michaels St., Oxford.
T. (01865) 241757. - Print -   *105029*
Ars Artis, 31 Abberbury Rd., Oxford OX4 4ET.
T. (01865) 770714. - ArtBk -   *105030*
Artemis Books, 76 Cowley Rd., Oxford.
T. (01865) 726909. - Print -   *105031*
Blackwell's Art and Poster Shop, 27 Broad St, Oxford
OX1 2AS. T. (01865) 794143, Fax (01865) 248833.
- ArtBk / Print -   *105032*
Bookshop at the Plain, 11 Cowley Rd., Oxford.
T. (01865) 790285. - Print -   *105033*
Clark, Robert, 6a King St, Oxford. T. (01865) 52154.
- Print -   *105034*
Classics Bookshop, 3 Turl St., Oxford.
T. (01865) 726466. - Print -   *105035*
Ferrini, Bruce, 88 Old High St., Oxford.
T. (01865) 741924. - Print -   *105036*

Little Bookshop, Lane 2, Covered Market, Oxford.
T. (01865) 59176. - Print - 105037
Magna Gallery, 41 High St., Oxford. T. (01865) 245805.
- Engr - 105038
Museum of Modern Art Bookshop, Museum of Modern
Art, 30 Pembroke Street, Oxford OX1 1BP.
T. (01865) 722733, Fax (01865) 722573.
- ArtBk - 105039
Niner & Hill, 43 High St., Oxford OX1 4AP.
T. (01865) 726105. - Print - 105040
Rosenthal, A., 9-10 Broad St., Oxford OX1 3AP.
T. (01865) 243093, Fax 794197. - Print - 105041
Sanders of Oxford, 104 High St., Oxford OX1 4BW.
T. (01865) 242590. - Print / Engr - 105042
Thornton, 11 Broad St., Oxford OX1 3AR.
T. (01865) 242939. - Print - 105043
Titles Old and Rare Books, 15/1 Turl St., Oxford.
T. (01865) 727928. - Print - 105044
Waterfield's Bookshop, 36 Park End St., Oxford.
T. (01865) 721809. - Print - 105045

Padstow (Cornwall)
Strand Bookshop, 4 The Strand, Padstow.
T. (01841) 532236. - Print - 105046

Paignton (Devon)
Biddy, 99c Dartmouth Rd., Paignton. T. (01803) 556151.
- Print - 105047
Pocket Bookshop, 159 Winner St., Paignton.
T. (01803) 529804. - Print - 105048

Paisley (Strathclyde)
Paisley Fine Books, 17 Corsebar Crescent, Paisley.
T. (0141) 884 2661. - Print / ArtBk - 105049
Wordsworth, 4 Johnston St., Paisley PA1.
T. (0141) 887 7303. - Print - 105050

Parkstone, nr. Poole (Dorset)
Haskell, R.H. & P., 64 Winston Av., Parkstone, nr. Poole.
T. (01202) 744310. - Print - 105051

Peel (Isle of Man)
Golden Past, 18a Michael St., Peel. T. (01624) 842170.
- Print - 105052

Penn (Buckinghamshire)
Cottage Bookshop, Elm Rd., Penn HP10 8LB.
T. (0149481) 812632. - Print - 105053
Penn Barn, Elm Rd, Penn. T. (0149481) 5691. - Print /
Engr - 105054

Penrith (Cumbria)
Phenotype Books, 39 Arthur St., Penrith.
T. (01768) 63049. - Print - 105055

Penzance (Cornwall)
New Street Books, 4 New St., Penzance.
T. (01736) 62758. - Print - 105056
Penzance Bookshop, 43 Causewayhead, Penzance.
T. (01736) 62140. - Print - 105057

Pershore (Hereford and Worcester)
Pugh, Jan K., 40 Bridge St., Pershore.
T. (01386) 552681. - Print - 105058

Perth (Tayside)
Perth Bookshop, 3a Abbot St., Perth. T. (01738) 33970.
- Print - 105059

Peterborough (Cambridgeshire)
Colest, T.V., 981 Lincoln Rd., Peterborough.
T. (01733) 577268. - Print - 105060
Old Soke Books, 68 Burghley Rd., Peterborough PE1
2QE. T. (01733) 64147. - Print - 105061

Petersfield (Hampshire)
Petersfield Bookshop, 16a Chapel St., Petersfield GU32
3DS. T. (01730) 63438. - Print / Engr - 105062

Plymouth (Devon)
Clement, A., 46 Southside St., Plymouth.
T. (01752) 664957. - Print - 105063
Harrison, F., 43 Bridwell Rd., Plymouth.
T. (01752) 365595. - Print - 105064
Universal Book Store, 24 Frankfort Gate, Plymouth.
T. (01752) 223841. - Print - 105065

Poole (Dorset)
Castle Books, 2 North St., Poole. T. (01202) 660295.
- Print - 105066

Portsmouth (Hampshire)
Gibbs, E., 166 New Rd., Portsmouth. T. (01705) 812265.
- Print - 105067

Prestatyn (Clwyd)
Wilde Rice, D., Southwind, Meliden, Prestatyn.
T. (017456) 854777. - Print - 105068

Presteigne (Powys)
Monckton & Fraser, 47 High St., Presteigne.
T. (01544) 260102. - Print - 105069

Preston (Lancashire)
Book House, 63-67 Fylde Rd., Preston PR1 2XQ.
T. (01772) 201576. - Print - 105070
Halewood & Sons, 37 Friargate, Preston PR1 2AT.
T. (01772) 52603. - Print - 105071
Preston Book Company, 68 Friargate, Preston PR1 2ED.
T. (01772) 52603. - Print / Engr / Map - 105072

Radnor
Keegan, Friar St, Radnor RG1 1DT. T. (215) 587253.
- Print - 105073

Ramsbury (Wiltshire)
Heraldry Today, Parliament Piece, Back Ln., Ramsbury
SN8 2QH. T. (01672) 20617, Fax (01672) 20163.
- Print / Engr - 105074

Ramsgate (Kent)
Michaels Bookshop, 72 King St., Ramsgate.
T. (01843) 589500. - Print - 105075
Mullen, P. & M., Goodwin Rd, Ramsgate.
T. (01843) 587283. - Print - 105076

Reading (Berkshire)
Victoria Books, 14-16 Eldon Terrace, Reading.
T. (01734) 500303. - Print - 105077

Redhill (Surrey)
Ivelet, 18 Fairlawn Dr., Redhill RH1 6JP.
T. (01737) 768282. - Print - 105078

Reigate (Surrey)
Reigate Galleries, 45a Bell St., Reigate RH2 7AQ.
T. (01737) 246055. - Print - 105079
Southdown Bookshop, 26 Doversgreen Rd., Reigate.
T. (01737) 552907. - Print - 105080

Richmond (North Yorkshire)
Five Owls Bookshop, 28 Victoria Rd., Richmond.
T. (01748) 823648. - Print - 105081

Rickmansworth (Hertfordshire)
Burden, Clive A., 46 Talbot Rd, Rickmansworth WD3
1HE. T. (01923) 772387, Fax (01923) 896520. - Print /
Engr / Map - 105082

Ripponden (West Yorkshire)
Old Apothecary Bookshop, 121 Halifax Rd., Ripponden.
T. (01422) 822214. - Print - 105083

Rochdale (Greater Manchester)
North West Book Buyers, 399 Oldham Rd., Rochdale
OL16 5LN. T. (01706) 31136. - Print - 105084

Rochester (Kent)
Baggin, 19 High St., Rochester. T. (01634) 811651.
- Print - 105085
Hearts of Oak Bookshop, 63 High St., Rochester.
T. (01634) 841851. - Print - 105086

Romsey (Hampshire)
Ruskin, 27 Bell St., Romsey. T. (01794) 523881.
- Print - 105087

Ross-on-Wye (Hereford and Worcester)
Ross Old Book and Print Shop, 51-52 High St., Ross-on-
Wye. T. (01989) 67458. - Print - 105088

Ryde (Isle of Wight)
Heritage Books, 7 Cross St., Ryde. T. (01983) 562933.
- Print - 105089

Ryde Bookshop, 135 High St., Ryde. T. (01983) 565227.
- Print - 105090

Rye (East Sussex)
Books and Prints, Tower Forge, Hilders Clif, Rye.
T. (01797) 222280. - Print - 105091
Neville, Anthony, Arling House, Rye Hill, Rye TN31 3NH.
T. (01797) 222123. - Print - 105092

Saint Albans (Hertfordshire)
Abbey Bookshop, 36 Sopwell Rd., Saint Albans.
T. (01727) 867904, 832514. - Print - 105093
Paton, 34 Holywell Hill, Saint Albans. T. (01727) 53984.
- Print - 105094
Thorp, Thomas, 9 George St., Saint Albans AL3 4ER.
T. (01727) 865576. - Print - 105095

Saint Andrews (Fife)
Bilson, 15 Greyfriars Gardens, Saint Andrews.
T. (01334) 75063. - Print - 105096
Bouquiniste, 31 Market St., Saint Andrews.
T. (01334) 76724. - Print - 105097
McIlreavy, A. & F., 57 South St., Saint Andrews.
T. (01334) 72487. - Print - 105098
Quarto Bookshop, 8 Golf Pl., Saint Andrews KY16 9JA.
T. (01334) 74616. - Print - 105099

Saint Helier (Jersey)
Selective Eye Gallery, 50 Don St., Saint Helier.
T. (01534) 25281. - Print - 105100
Thesaurus, 3 Burrad St., Saint Helier. T. (01534) 37045.
- Print - 105101

Saint Leonards-on-Sea (East Sussex)
Book Jungle, 24 North St., Saint Leonards-on-Sea.
T. (01424) 421187. - Print - 105102
Bookmans Halt, 127 Bohemia Rd., Saint Leonards-on-
Sea. T. (01424) 421413. - Print - 105103
Hoovey, 9 Kings Rd., Saint Leonards-on-Sea.
T. (01424) 430398. - Print - 105104
Springfield, 269 London Rd., Saint Leonards-on-Sea.
T. (01424) 718848. - Print - 105105

Salisbury (Wiltshire)
Barn Book Supply, 88 Crane St., Salisbury.
T. (01722) 327767. - Print - 105106
Beach, D.M., 52 High St., Salisbury SP1 2PG.
T. (01722) 333801. - Print / Engr / Map - 105107
Head, John & Judith, 88 Crane St., Salisbury SP1 2QD.
T. (01722) 327767, Fax 339888. - Print - 105108

Sandwich (Kent)
Judd, Simon, Shuttlecote, Ramsgate Rd., Sandwich.
T. (01304) 617170. - Print - 105109
Strand Books, 21 Strand St., Sandwich.
T. (01304) 611948. - Print - 105110

Scarborough (North Yorkshire)
Bar Bookstore, 4 Swanhill Rd., Scarborough.
T. (01723) 500141. - Print - 105111
Hanover Bookshop, 13a Hanover Rd., Scarborough.
T. (01723) 371101. - Print - 105112
Mellor, L. & M., Cromwell Parade, Scarborough.
T. (01723) 371045. - Print - 105113
Past and Presents, 11a Ramshill Rd, Scarborough.
T. (01723) 364215. - Print - 105114
Scarborough Bookshop, 55 Castle Rd., Scarborough.
T. (01723) 368813. - Print - 105115

Scunthorpe (Humberside)
Atlas Book Exchange, 1b Oswald Rd., Scunthorpe.
T. (01724) 282196. - Print - 105116

Seaford (East Sussex)
Harpen, J.M. & B.H., 11 Lullington Close, Seaford.
T. (01323) 898316. - Print - 105117

Sedbergh (Cumbria)
Hollet & Son, R.F.G., 6 Finkle St., Sedbergh LA10 5BZ.
T. (015396) 20298, Fax 21396. - Print - 105118

Settle (North Yorkshire)
Bookend, The Shambles, Market Sq., Settle.
T. (017292) 823879. - Print - 105119

Shaftesbury (Dorset)
Book in Hand, 17 Bell St., Shaftesbury. - Print -   *105120*

Sharnbrook (Bedfordshire)
Ouse Valley Books, 16 Home Close, Sharnbrook.
T. (01234) 782411. - Print -   *105121*

Sheffield (South Yorkshire)
Book and Art Shop, 204 West St., Sheffield.
T. (0114) 757576. - Print -   *105122*
Hill, Alan, 261 Glossop Rd, Sheffield. T. (0114) 780594.
- Print / Engr -   *105123*
Porter, 227 Sharrow Vale Rd., Sheffield.
T. (0114) 667762. - Print -   *105124*
Rare and Racy Bookshop, 164-166 Devonshire St.,
Sheffield. T. (0114) 701916. - Print -   *105125*
Tilley, 281 Shoreham St., Sheffield. T. (0114) 752442.
- Print -   *105126*
Y.S.F. Bookshop, 365 Sharrowvale Rd., Sheffield.
T. (0114) 680687. - Print -   *105127*

Sherborne (Dorset)
Booklore, 2 Hound St., Sherborne. T. (01935) 814191.
- Print -   *105128*
Chapter House, Trendle St., Sherborne.
T. (01935) 816262. - Print -   *105129*

Sheringham (Norfolk)
Cox, P.D., 19 Saint Peters Rd., Sheringham.
T. (01263) 823008. - Print -   *105130*
Peters Bookshop, 19 Saint Peters Rd., Sheringham.
T. (01263) 823008. - Print -   *105131*

Shipley (West Yorkshire)
Bodhran, 9 Victoria Rd., Shipley. T. (01274) 530102.
- Print -   *105132*

Shrewsbury (Shropshire)
Candle Lane Books, 28-31 Princess St., Shrewsbury
SY1 1LW. T. (01743) 365301. - Print -   *105133*
Quarry Bookshop, 24 Claremont Hill, Shrewsbury.
T. (01743) 361404. - Print -   *105134*

Sidmouth (Devon)
Antique Book Shop, All Saints Rd., Sidmouth.
T. (01395) 516028. - Print -   *105135*
Sidmouth Old Books, 14 Temple St., Sidmouth.
T. (01395) 514461. - Print -   *105136*

Sittingbourne (Kent)
Periwinkle, 23 East St., Sittingbourne.
T. (01795) 426242. - Print -   *105137*

Skipton (North Yorkshire)
Box of Delights, 25 Otley St., Skipton.
T. (01756) 790111. - Print -   *105138*
Craven, 23 Newmarket St., Skipton. T. (01756) 792677.
- Print / Engr -   *105139*

Somerton (Somerset)
Simon, Broad St., Somerton. T. (01458) 72313.
- Print -   *105140*

South Brent (Devon)
Mitchell, James A., 1 The Manor, North Huish, South
Brent TQ10 9NQ. T. (01364) 72288. - Print -   *105141*
Pollak, P.M., Plymouth Rd., South Brent.
T. (01364) 73457. - Print -   *105142*

Southampton (Hampshire)
Gilbert & Son, H.M., 2 1/2 Portland St., Southampton
SO1 0EB. T. (01703) 226428. - Print -   *105143*
Wonderworld Bookshop, Unit 2, Bevois St., Southampton. T. (01703) 234815. - Print -   *105144*

Southend-on-Sea (Essex)
Barrie, E. Ellen, 262 London Rd., Southend-on-Sea.
T. (01702) 338763. - Print -   *105145*
Leigh Bookshop, 137 Leigh Rd., Southend-on-Sea SS9
1JQ. T. (01702) 715477. - Print -   *105146*

Southport (Merseyside)
Kernaghan, Bryan, Lord St, Southport.
T. (01704) 546329. - Print -   *105147*
Parkinson, Anthony, 359-363 Lord St, Southport PR8
1NH. T. (01704) 547016. - Print -   *105148*

Southsea (Hampshire)
Book Academy, 13 Marmion Rd., Southsea.
T. (01705) 816632. - Print -   *105149*
Minotaure, 26 Collingwood Rd, Southsea PO5 2QY.
T. (01705) 753325. - ArtBk -   *105150*
Mirrow, 55 Fawcett Rd., Southsea. T. (01705) 755796.
- Print -   *105151*
New To You, Albert Rd, Southsea. T. (01705) 871942.
- Print -   *105152*
Star Bookshop, 69 Fawcett Rd., Southsea.
T. (01705) 737077. - Print -   *105153*

Stafford (Staffordshire)
Picken, Robert A., 11 Goal Rd., Stafford.
T. (01785) 53425. - Print -   *105154*

Stamford (Lincolnshire)
Humm, Robert, Station House, Station Yard, Stamford.
T. (01780) 66266. - Print -   *105155*
Staniland, 4-5 Saint George St., Stamford PE9 2BJ.
T. (01780) 55800. - Print -   *105156*

Stirling (Central)
Book Shop, 30 Spittal St., Stirling. T. (01786) 461771.
- Print -   *105157*
Corn Exchange Bookshop, 53 King St., Stirling.
T. (01786) 473112. - Print -   *105158*

Stockport (Cheshire)
Grenville Street Bookshop, 105 Grenville St, Stockport.
T. (0161) 477 1909. - Print -   *105159*

Stokesley (North Yorkshire)
Stokesley Bookshop, 63 High St., Stokesley.
T. (01642) 712514. - Print -   *105160*

Stourbridge (West Midlands)
Painter, J., 8 Church St., Stourbridge. T. (01384) 377824.
- Print -   *105161*

Stow-on-the-Wold (Gloucestershire)
Bookbox, Chantry House, Sheep St., Stow-on-the-Wold.
T. (01451) 31214. - Print -   *105162*
Four Shire Books, 4 Talbot Court, Stow-on-the-Wold.
T. (01451) 30755. - Print   *105163*
Wychwood, Sheep St., Stow-on-the-Wold.
T. (01451) 31880. - Print -   *105164*

Stowmarket (Suffolk)
Webster, E.T., Millbarn Church Ln., Stowmarket.
T. (01449) 711397. - Print -   *105165*

Stratford-upon-Avon (Warwickshire)
Anticus-BDC, 59 Ely St., Stratford-upon-Avon.
T. (01789) 266950. - Print -   *105166*
Chaucer-Head Bookshop and Art Gallery, 21 Chapel St.,
Stratford-upon-Avon CV37 6EP. T. (01789) 415691.
- Print / Map -   *105167*
Vaughan, Robert, 20 Chapel St., Stratford-upon-Avon
CV37 6EP. T. (01789) 205312. - Print / Engr -   *105168*

Stroud (Gloucestershire)
Hodkins, Ian, Upper Vatch Mill, Stroud.
T. (01453) 764270. - Print -   *105169*
Imprint Books, 31 High St., Stroud. T. (01453) 759731.
- Print -   *105170*

Sudbury (Suffolk)
Entente Books, 18 Gainsborough St., Sudbury.
T. (01787) 72102. - Print -   *105171*
Suffolk Rare Books, 7 New St., Sudbury.
T. (01787) 72075. - Print -   *105172*

Sunderland (Tyne and Wear)
Bookshop, 5 Crowtree Rd., Sunderland.
T. (01783) 565 7343. - Print -   *105173*
Durham Book Centre, Vine Pl., Sunderland.
T. (01783) 567 4389. - Print -   *105174*

Swanage (Dorset)
Blanchard, M., 55 High St., Swanage.
T. (01929) 424088. - Print -   *105175*
Reference Works, 12 Commercial Rd., Swanage.
T. (01929) 424423, Fax 422597. - Print -   *105176*

Swansea (West Glamorgan)
Dylan, Salubrious Passage, Swansea SA1 3RT.
T. (01792) 655255. - Print -   *105177*
Old Book Mart, 37 Saint Helens Rd., Swansea.
T. (01792) 474919. - Print -   *105178*
Robert, 12 Dillwyn St., Swansea. T. (01792) 655525.
- Print -   *105179*
Rowland, 16 Saint Helens Rd., Swansea.
T. (01792) 654427. - Print -   *105180*

Sway (Hampshire)
Beagle, 1 Middle Rd., Sway. T. (0159068) 683421.
- Print -   *105181*

Swindon (Wiltshire)
Arts Guild, POB 199, Swindon SN3 4BR.   *105182*
Victoria Bookshop, 30 Wood St., Swindon.
T. (01793) 527364. - Print -   *105183*

Taunton (Somerset)
Rothwell & Dunworth, 14 Paul St., Taunton.
T. (01823) 282476. - Print -   *105184*

Tavistock (Devon)
Harden, J.L., 41 Courtsland Rd., Tavistock PL19 0EF.
T. (01822) 616094. - Print -   *105185*

Teignmouth (Devon)
Bookworm, 26 Regent St., Teignmouth.
T. (01626) 775177. - Print -   *105186*

Tenby (Dyfed)
Albatross Bookshop, 1 Bridge St., Tenby.
T. (01834) 842113. - Print -   *105187*

Tenterden (Kent)
Bookshelves, 33 High St., Tenterden.
T. (015806) 763325. - Print -   *105188*

Tewkesbury (Gloucestershire)
Wayfarer, 19 Church St., Tewkesbury.
T. (01684) 293337. - Print -   *105189*

Thames Ditton (Surrey)
Gant k5060 Elizabeth, 52 High St., Thames Ditton KT7.
T. (0181) 398 5107. - Print -   *105190*

Thirsk (North Yorkshire)
Potterton, The Old Rectory, Sessay, Thirsk YO7 3LZ.
T. (01845) 401218, Fax (01845) 401439.
- ArtBk -   *105191*
Potterton Books, Old Rectory, Sessay, Thirsk YO7 3LZ.
T. (01845) 401218, Fax 401439. - Print -   *105192*

Todmorden (Lancashire)
Pangolin, 17 Water St., Todmorden OL14 5AB.
T. (01706) 817945. - Print -   *105193*

Tonbridge (Kent)
Barmby, C. & A.J., 140 Lavender Hill, Tonbridge.
T. (01732) 771590. - Print -   *105194*

Torquay (Devon)
Book Barn, 53 Market St., Torquay. T. (01803) 298160.
- Print -   *105195*
Fitzjohn, 286 Union St., Torquay. T. (01803) 212565.
- Print -   *105196*
Magpie, 22 Perinville Rd., Torquay. T. (01803) 325944.
- Print -   *105197*

Totland (Isle of Wight)
Bookshop, The Broadway, Totland. T. (01983) 754960.
- Print -   *105198*

Totnes (Devon)
Collard, 4 Castle St., Totnes. T. (01803) 550246.
- Print -   *105199*
Pedlar's Pack Books, 4 The Plains, Totnes TQ9 5DR.
T. (01803) 866423. - Print -   *105200*

Towcester (Northamptonshire)
Shelron, 9 1/2 Brackley Rd., Towcester.
T. (01327) 50242. - Print -   *105201*

Tring (Hertfordshire)
Gresham, 15a Albert St., Tring. T. 828519.
- Print -   *105202*

Truro (Cornwall)
Just Books, Pydar Mews, Truro. T. (01872) 42532.
- Print -   *105203*

Tunbridge Wells (Kent)
Baskerville, 13 Neville St., Tunbridge Wells.
T. (01892) 526776. - Print -   *105204*
Hall, 20 Chapel Pl., Tunbridge Wells. T. (01892) 27842.
- Print -   *105205*
Mount Ephraim Books, 25-27 Mount Ephraim, Tunbridge
Wells. T. (01892) 521888. - Print -   *105206*
Stead, Graham, The Pantiles, Union Sq., Tunbridge
Wells. T. (01892) 533708. - Print -   *105207*
Whittaker, Anthony, 64 Pantiles, Tunbridge Wells.
T. (01892) 539652. - Print -   *105208*

Twickenham (Greater London)
Hall, Anthony C., 30 Staines Rd., Twickenham TW2 5AH.
T. (0181) 898 2638. - Print -   *105209*
Ives, John, 5 Normanhurst Dr., Twickenham TW1 1NA.
T. (0181) 892 6265. - Print -   *105210*
Shenton, Rita, 148 Percy Rd., Twickenham TW26 3B.
T. (0181) 894 6888, Fax (0181) 893 8766.
- Print -   *105211*

Uppermill (Greater Manchester)
Moorland, Mill St, Uppermill. T. (01457) 871306.
- Print -   *105212*

Uppingham (Leicestershire)
Goldmark Bookshop, 14 Orange St., Uppingham.
T. (01572) 822694. - Print -   *105213*

Uxbridge (Greater London)
Barnard, Thomas, 11 Windsor St., Uxbridge.
T. (01895) 258054. - Print / Engr -   *105214*

Ventnor (Isle of Wight)
Ventnor Rare Books, 19 Pier St., Ventnor.
T. (01983) 853706. - Print -   *105215*

Wallingford (Oxfordshire)
Toby English, Lamp Arcade, Wallingford OX10 0BS.
T. (01491) 36389. - Print -   *105216*

Warwick (Warwickshire)
Allsop, Duncan M., 26 Smith St., Warwick.
T. (01926) 493266. - Print / Engr -   *105217*

Watford (Hertfordshire)
Taylor, Peter, 4a Ye Corner, Aldenham Rd., Watford.
T. (01923) 250342. - Print -   *105218*
Weston, 44 Stratford Rd., Watford. T. (01923) 229081.
- Print -   *105219*

Wednesbury (West Midlands)
Simmons, 37 Lower High St., Wednesbury WS10.
T. (0121) 502 4622. - Print -   *105220*

Weedon (Buckinghamshire)
Eaton, Peter, Lilies, Weedon HP22 4NS.
T. (01296) 641393. - Print -   *105221*

Wellingborough (Northamptonshire)
Collet, Denington Estate, Wellingborough NN8 2QT.
T. (01933) 224351. - ArtBk -   *105222*
Park Book Shop, 12 Park Rd., Wellingborough.
T. (01933) 222592. - Print / Engr -   *105223*

Wells-next-the-Sea (Norfolk)
Cook, 65 Staithe St., Wells-next-the-Sea.
T. (01328) 710419. - Print -   *105224*

Wendover (Buckinghamshire)
Wendover Bookshop, 35 High St., Wendover HP22 6DU.
T. (01296) 696204. - Print -   *105225*

West Malling (Kent)
Foxed and Bound Bookshop, 8 West St., West Malling
ME19 6QZ. T. (01732) 847 886. - Print -   *105226*

Westerham (Kent)
Taylor-Smith, 2 High-St., Westerham TN16 1RF.
T. (01959) 561561. - Print -   *105227*
Taylor-Smith, 1 High St, Westerham TN16 1AH.
T. (01959) 563100.   *105228*

Weston-super-Mare (Avon)
Manna, 30 Orchard St., Weston-super-Mare.
T. (01934) 636228. - Print -   *105229*
Severn Books, 48 Severn Rd., Weston-super-Mare.
T. (01934) 635389. - Print -   *105230*
Sterling Books, 43a Locking Rd., Weston-super-Mare
BS23 3DG. T. (01934) 625056. - Print / ArtBk -   *105231*

Wetherby (West Yorkshire)
Words and Music, 3a Church St., Wetherby LS22 4LP.
T. (01937) 586009. - Print -   *105232*

Weymouth (Dorset)
Books Afloat, 66 Park St., Weymouth.
T. (01305) 779774. - Print -   *105233*

Whitchurch (Shropshire)
Barn Bookshop, Pear Tree, Farm Norbury, Whitchurch.
T. (01948) 3742. - Print -   *105234*
Parish Bookshop, 47 High St., Whitchurch.
T. (01948) 4115. - Print -   *105235*

Whitehaven (Cumbria)
Moon, Michael, 41-43 Roper St., Whitehaven.
T. (01946) 62936. - Print -   *105236*

Whitley Bay (Tyne and Wear)
Olivers Bookshop, 48a Whitley Rd., Whitley Bay.
T. (0191) 251 3552. - Print -   *105237*

Whitstable (Kent)
Books and Pieces, 48 Oxford St., Whitstable.
T. (01227) 771333. - Print -   *105238*

Wigan (Lancashire)
Book House, 8 The Wiend, Wigan. T. (01942) 44648.
- Print -   *105239*
Bookstall, Wallgate Railway Station, Wigan.
T. (01942) 322935. - Print -   *105240*

Wigtown (Dumfries and Galloway)
Baker, A.P. & R., Laigh House, Church Ln., Wigtown.
T. (0169) 403348. - Print -   *105241*

Wimborne Minster (Dorset)
Minster, 12 Corn Market, Wimborne Minster.
T. (01202) 883355. - Print -   *105242*

Winchester (Hampshire)
Daly, Peter, 20a Jewry St., Winchester.
T. (01962) 867732. - Print -   *105243*
Gilbert, H.M., 19 The Square, Winchester.
T. (01962) 852832. - Print -   *105244*
Printed Page, 2-3 Bridge St., Winchester SO23 9BH.
T. (01962) 854072, Fax 862995. - Engr -   *105245*
SPCK Bookshop, 24 The Square, Winchester.
T. (01962) 866617. - Print -   *105246*
Upcroft, 66 Saint Cross Rd., Winchester SQ23 9PS.
T. (01962) 852679. - Print -   *105247*
Winchester Bookshop, 10a Saint Georges St., Winche-
ster. T. (01962) 855630. - Print -   *105248*

Wingham (Kent)
Lloyd, 27 High St., Wingham. T. (01227) 720774.
- Print / Engr -   *105249*

Winslow (Buckinghamshire)
Medina Antiquarian Maps and Prints, 8 High St., Winslow. T. (0129671) 2468. - Engr -   *105250*

Wirksworth (Derbyshire)
Scarthin, The Promenade, Wirksworth DE4 3QF.
T. (01629) 823272. - Print -   *105251*

Wisbech (Cambridgeshire)
Golding, Eric, 12 North Brink, Wisbech.
T. (01945) 582927. - Print -   *105252*

Wolstanton (Staffordshire)
Pomes Penyeach, 63 High St., Wolstanton.
T. (0193363) 630729. - Print -   *105253*

Wolverhampton (West Midlands)
Berry Street Bookshop, 35 Berry St., Wolverhampton.
T. (01902) 28939. - Print -   *105254*
Bookstack Wolverhampton, 53 Bath Rd., Wolverhamp-
ton. T. (01902) 21055. - Print -   *105255*

Woodbridge (Suffolk)
Abacus Book Buyers, 88 Thoroughfare, Woodbridge.
T. (01394) 380302. - Print -   *105256*
Blake, 88 Thoroughfare, Woodbridge.
T. (01394) 380302. - Print -   *105257*

Woodstock (Oxfordshire)
Afternoon Bookshop, 21 Oxford St., Woodstock.
T. (01993) 813445. - Print -   *105258*
Museum Bookshop, County Museum, Fletcher's House,
Woodstock. T. (01993) 811456. - ArtBk -   *105259*
Woodstock Bookshop, 3 Marchet Pl., Woodstock.
T. (01993) 811005. - Print -   *105260*

Worcester (Hereford and Worcester)
Abookortwo, 6 The Tything, Worcester.
T. (01905) 20816. - Print -   *105261*
Boyle, Andrew, 21 Friar St., Worcester.
T. (01905) 611700. - Print -   *105262*
Holbourne, 47a Upper Tything, Worcester.
T. (01905) 27824. - Print -   *105263*

Worthing (West Sussex)
Badger, 8 Gratwicke Rd., Worthing. T. (01903) 211816.
- Print -   *105264*
Frances, 54a Homefield Rd., Worthing.
T. (01903) 236437. - Print -   *105265*
Kim's Bookshop, 33 West Bldg., Worthing BN11 3BS.
T. (01903) 206282. - Print -   *105266*
Steyne, 5 High St., Worthing. T. (01903) 206216.
- Print -   *105267*

Wrexham (Clwyd)
Glyn, 4 Bryn Draw Terrace, Wrexham LL13 7DF.
T. (01978) 364473. - Print -   *105268*
Tegs, 3 King St., Wrexham. T. (01978) 354224.
- Print -   *105269*

Wymondham (Norfolk)
Crowe, 4 Estelle Way, Wymondham. T. (01953) 607338.
- Print -   *105270*
Turret House Bookshop, 27 Middleton St., Wymondham
NR18 0AB. T. (01953) 603462. - Print -   *105271*

Yatton (Avon)
Bevon, John, Saint Francis St., Yatton.
T. (01934) 890878. - Print -   *105272*

York (North Yorkshire)
Barbican Bookshop, 24 Fossgate, York Y01 2TA.
T. (01904) 653643. - Print -   *105273*
Caduceus, 14 Holgate Rd., York. T. (01904) 628021.
- Print -   *105274*
Duncan, Jack, 36 Fossgate, York. T. (01904) 641389.
- Print -   *105275*
Goodramgate Bookshop, 58c Goodramgate, York.
T. (01904) 641841. - Print -   *105276*
Inch's Books, 82 The Mount, York Y02 2AR.
T. (01904) 627082, Fax (01904) 639424 - Print /
ArtBk -   *105277*
Minster Gate Bookshop, 8 Minster Gates, York.
T. (01904) 621812. - Print -   *105278*
O'Flynn, 35 Micklegate, York. T. (01904) 641404.
- Print / Engr -   *105279*
Spelman, Ken, 70 Micklegate, York Y01 1LF.
T. (01904) 624414, Fax (01904) 626276.
- Print -   *105280*
Stone Trough Bookshop, 38 Fossgate, York.
T. (01904) 670323. - Print -   *105281*
Taikoo, 29 High Petergate, York. T. (01904) 641213.
- Print -   *105282*
York City Art Gallery Shop, York City Art Gallery, Exhibi-
tion Square, York Y01 2EW. T. (01904) 623839,
Fax (01904) 654981. - ArtBk -   *105283*

Yoxford (Suffolk)
Riderless Horse Books, The Old Wool Shop, High St.,
Yoxford. T. (0172877) 439. - Print -   *105284*
Stevens, Joan, Rosslyn House, High St., Yoxford.
T. (0172877) 77368. - Print -   *105285*

Uruguay

Montevideo
Cabral, Jorge, Bartolomé Mitre 1385, 11000 Montevideo. T. (02) 95 96 70. *105286*
Libreria Mosca Hns, Juan M. Blanes 1170, 11.000 Montevideo. T. (02) 40 99 54, 49 96 86,
Fax 48 89 50. *105287*
Linardi & Risso, Juan Carlos Gomez 1435, 11.000 Montevideo. T. (02) 95 71 29, Fax 95 74 31. - Print - *105288*
Marotti, Silvio, Bacacay 1326, 11000 Montevideo.
T. (02) 95 96 75. *105289*
Monteverde, A., Libr. – 25 de Mayo 577 Palacio del Libro, 11.000 Montevideo Casilla de Correo 371.
T. (02) 902 473, 902 228. *105290*
Valiño, Alicia & Jorge, Bartolomé Mitre 1324, 11000 Montevideo. T. (02) 96 27 11. *105291*

Punta del Este
Marotti, Silvio, Galeria Concorde, Loc. 9, 20.100 Punta del Este. T. (042) 43613. *105292*
Marotti, Silvio, Galerie del Torreon, Loc. 13, 20100 Punta del Este. T. (042) 43613. *105293*

U.S.A.

Alexandria (Virginia)
Air, Land and Sea, 1215 King St, Alexandria, VA 22314.
T. (703) 684-5118. - Print / Engr - *105294*
Book Stop, 3640a King St, Alexandria, VA 22302.
T. (703) 578-3292. - Print - *105295*
Comics Center and Book Niche, 2008 Mount Vernon Av, Alexandria, VA 22301. T. (703) 548-3466.
- Print - *105296*
From Out of the Past, 6440 Richmond Hwy, Alexandria, VA 22306. T. (703) 768-7827. - Print - *105297*

Aptos (California)
Rare Oriental Book Company, POB 1599, Aptos, CA 95001. T. (408) 724-4911, Fax (408) 761-1350.
- Print - *105298*

Arlington (Virginia)
Book Ends, 2710 Washington Blvd, Arlington, VA 22201.
T. (703) 524-4976. - Print - *105299*
Bookhouse, 805 N Emerson St, Arlington, VA 22205.
T. (703) 527-7797. - Print - *105300*

Atlanta (Georgia)
Books and Cases, 715 Miami Circle NE, Atlanta, GA 30324. T. (404) 231-9107. - Print - *105301*
Buckhead, 47 W Paces Ferry Rd NW, Atlanta, GA 30305.
T. (404) 814-1025. - Print - *105302*
Dickens, C., 3393 Peachtree Rd NE, Atlanta, GA 30326.
T. (404) 231-3825, Fax (404) 364-0713.
- Print - *105303*
Old New York Book Shop, 1069 Juniper St NE, Atlanta, GA 30309. T. (404) 881-1285. - Print - *105304*
Yesteryear Book Shop, 3201 Maple Dr NE, Atlanta, GA 30305. T. (404) 237-0163. - Print - *105305*

Baltimore (Maryland)
Second Story Books, 3302 Greenmount Av, Baltimore, MD 21218. T. (410) 467-4344. - Print - *105306*
19th Century Shop, 1047 Hollins St, Baltimore, MD 21223. T. (410) 727-2665. - Print - *105307*

Bellmore (New York)
Booklovers Paradise, 2956 Merrick Rd, Bellmore, NY 11710. T. (516) 221-0994. - Print - *105308*

Berkeley (California)
Adams, 1170 Keeler Av, Berkeley, CA 94708.
T. (510) 849-1324. - Print - *105309*
Anacapa, 3090 Claremont Av, Berkeley, CA 94705.
T. (510) 654-3517. - Print - *105310*
Black Oak Books, 1491 Shattuck Av, Berkeley, CA 94709. T. (510) 486-0698. - Print - *105311*
Moe, 2476 Telegraph Av, Berkeley, CA 94704.
T. (510) 849-2087. - Print - *105312*
Serendipity Books, 1201 University Av, Berkeley, CA 94702. T. (510) 841-7455. - Print - *105313*

Turtle Island Booksellers, 2067 Center St, Berkeley, CA 94704. T. (510) 541-5422. - Print - *105314*

Bethesda (Maryland)
Bartley, 4823 Fairmont Av, Bethesda, MD 20814.
T. (301) 654-4373. - Print - *105315*
Big Planet Comics, 4908 Fairmont Av, Bethesda, MD 20814. T. (301) 654-6856. *105316*
Book Cellar, 8227 Woodmont Av, Bethesda, MD 20814.
T. (301) 654-1898. - Print - *105317*
Curious Books, 7921 Norfolk Av, Bethesda, MD 20814.
T. (301) 656-2668. - Print - *105318*
Georgetown Book Shop, 7770 Woodmont Av, Bethesda, MD 20814. T. (301) 907-6923. - Print - *105319*
Lamson, 4823 Fairmont Av, Bethesda, MD 20814.
T. (301) 654-4373. - Print - *105320*
Second Story Books, 4836 Bethesda Av, Bethesda, MD 20814. T. (301) 656-0170. - Print - *105321*
Stone Ridge Used Book Sale, 9101 Rockville Pike, Bethesda, MD 20814. T. (301) 657-4322. - Print - *105322*
Waverly, 4931 Cordell Av, Bethesda, MD 20814.
T. (301) 951-8883. - Print / Engr / Autogr - *105323*

Boston (Massachusetts)
Ars Libri, 560 Harrison Av, Boston, MA 02118.
T. (617) 357-5212, Fax (617) 338-5763. - Print / ArtBk - *105324*
Avenue Victor Hugo Bookshop, 339 Newbury St, Boston, MA 02115. T. (617) 266-7746. - Print - *105325*
Boston Book Annex, 906 Beacon St, Boston, MA 02215.
T. (617) 266-1090. - Print - *105326*
Boston Book Company, 705 Centre St, Boston, MA 02130. T. (617) 522-2100, Fax (617) 522-9359. *105327*
Brattle, 9 West St, Boston, MA 02111. T. (617) 542-0210. - Print - *105328*
Bromer, 607 Boylston St., Boston, MA 02161.
T. (617) 247-2818. *105329*
Buddenbrooks, 753 Boylston St, Boston, MA 02116.
T. (617) 536-4433. - Print - *105330*
Goodspeed, 7 Beacon St, Boston, MA 02108.
T. (617) 523-5970. - Engr / Autogr / Map - *105331*
Nostalgia Factory, 324 Newbury St, Boston, MA 02115.
T. (617) 236-8754. - Print - *105332*
O'Neal, David L., 234 Clarendon St, Boston, MA 02116.
T. (617) 266-5790. - Print - *105333*
Pepper & Stern, 355 Boylston St, Boston, MA 02159.
T. (617) 421-1880. - Print - *105334*

Brinklow (Maryland)
Old Hickory Bookshop, 20225 New Hampshire Av, Brinklow, MD 20862. T. (301) 924-2225. - Print - *105335*

Brooklyn (New York)
Biegeleisen, J., 4409 16 Av, Brooklyn, NY 11204.
T. (718) 436-1165. - Print - *105336*

Burlingame (California)
Historicana, 1200 Edgehill Dr, Burlingame, CA 94010.
T. (415) 343-9578. - Print - *105337*

Cambridge (Massachusetts)
Harvard Book Stores, 1256 Massachusetts Av, Cambridge, MA 02138. T. (617) 661-1616. - Print / ArtBk - *105338*
Starr, 29 Plympton St, Cambridge, MA 02138.
T. (617) 547-6864. - Print - *105339*
Worldwide Antiquarian, 357 Cambridge St, Cambridge, MA 02141. T. (617) 876-6220. - Print - *105340*

Chicago (Illinois)
Abraham Lincoln Book Shop, 357 W Chicago Av, Chicago, IL 60610. T. (312) 944-3085. - Print / Engr / Autogr - *105341*
Behnke, Dan, 2463 N Lincoln Av, Chicago, IL 60614.
T. (312) 404-0403. - Print - *105342*
Booksellers Row, 408 S Michigan Av, Chicago, IL 60605. T. (312) 427-4242. - Print - *105343*
Booksellers Row, 2445 N Lincoln Av, Chicago, IL 60614.
T. (312) 348-1170. - Print - *105344*
O'Gara & Wilson, 1311 E 57 St, Chicago, IL 60637.
T. (312) 363-0993. - Print - *105345*
Paragon, 21 W Illinois St, Chicago, IL 60610.
T. (312) 527-5355, Fax (312) 527-5007. *105346*

Paragon Book Gallery, 21 W Illinois St, Chicago, IL 60610. T. (312) 527-5155, Fax (312) 527-5007. *105347*
Powell, 1501 E 57 St, Chicago, IL 60637. T. (312) 955-77800. - Print - *105348*
Powell, 2850 N Lincoln Av, Chicago, IL 60657.
T. (312) 248-1444. - Print - *105349*
Powell, 828 S Wabash Av, Chicago, IL 60605.
T. (312) 341-0748. - Print - *105350*
Rizzoli, 835 N Michigan Av, Chicago, IL 60611.
T. (312) 642-3500. - ArtBk / Engr - *105351*

College Park (Maryland)
Book Nook, 9933 Rhode Island Av, College Park, MD 20740. T. (301) 474-4060. - Print - *105352*

Cooperstown (New York)
Classical Forms Bookstore, 90 Main St, Cooperstown, NY 13326. T. (800) 781-2665. - Print - *105353*

Dania (Florida)
Art World International, 69 N Federal Hwy., 33004 Dania, 33004. T. (305) 923-3001. - ArtBk - *105354*

Denver (Colorado)
Abracadabra Booksearch International, 3827 W 32 Av, Denver, CO 80211. T. (800) 545-2665. - Print - *105355*

Falls Church (Virginia)
Laubert, Alexander, 1073 Broad St W, Falls Church, VA 22046. T. (703) 533-1699. - Print - *105356*

Frederick (Maryland)
Wonder Books and Video, 1306 Patrick St W, Frederick, MD 21702. T. (301) 694-5955. - Print - *105357*

Gaithersburg (Maryland)
Olde Soldier Books, 18779b N Frederick Av, Gaithersburg, MD 20879. T. (301) 963-2929. - Print - *105358*
Van Sickle, Ron, 9605 Duffer Way, Gaithersburg, MD 20879. T. (301) 330-2400. - Print - *105359*

Glen Ellen (California)
Jack London Bookstore, 14300 Arnold Dr, Glen Ellen, CA 95442. T. (707) 996-2888. - Print - *105360*

Haddonfield (New Jersey)
BTC Between the Covers, 132 Kings Hwy E, Haddonfield, NJ 08033. T. (609) 354-7665. - Print / Autogr - *105361*

Hastings-on-Hudson (New York)
Riverrun Books, 7 Washington Av, Hastings-on-Hudson, NY 10706. T. (914) 478-4307. - Print - *105362*

Houston (Texas)
Booked-Up, 711 Studewood St, Houston, TX 77007.
T. (713) 868-3910. - Print - *105363*
Books Bought and Sold, 1305 S Shepherd Dr, Houston, TX 77019. T. (713) 529-1059. - Print - *105364*
Colleen, 6880 Telephone Rd, Houston, TX 77061.
T. (713) 641-1753. - Print - *105365*
Detering, 2311 Bissonnet St, Houston, TX 77005.
T. (713) 526-6974. - Print / ArtBk - *105366*

Hughsonville (New York)
Art Book Services, POB 360, Hughsonville, NY 12537.
T. (800) 247-9955. *105367*

Lafayette (California)
Docheff, Carol, 1390 Reliez Valley Rd, Lafayette, CA 94549. T. (510) 935-9595. - Print - *105368*

Lambertville (New Jersey)
Phoenix Books, 49 N Union St, Lambertville, NJ 08530.
T. (609) 397-4960. - Print - *105369*

Land O'Lakes (Florida)
Dealer's Choice Books, Land O'Lakes POB 710, FL 34639. T. (813) 996-6599. - ArtBk - *105370*

Larchmont (New York)
Bernett, F.A., 2001 Palmer Av, Larchmont, NY 10538.
T. (914) 834-3026, Fax (914) 834-0084. - Print / ArtBk - *105371*

Laurel (Maryland)
Attic Books, 100 Washington Blvd, Laurel, MD 20723.
T. (301) 725-3725. - Print -   *105372*

Los Angeles (California)
Caravan Book Store, 550 S Grand Av., Los Angeles, CA
90071. T. (213) 626-9944. - Engr / Autogr /
Map -   *105373*
Dailey, William & Victoria, 8216 Melrose Av., Los Ange-
les, CA 90046. T. (213) 658-8515. - Print / ArtBk /
Engr -   *105374*
Dawson's Book Shop, 535 N. Larchmont Blvd., Los An-
geles, CA 90004. T. (213) 469-2186. - Print -   *105375*
Edmunds, Larry, Bookshop, 6658 Hollywood Blvd., Los
Angeles, CA 90028. T. (213) 463-3273. - Print /
Autogr -   *105376*
Heritage Bookshop. Inc., 847 North La Cienega Blvd.,
Los Angeles, CA 90069. T. (213) 6593674.
- Print -   *105377*
Houle, 7260 Beverly Blvd, Los Angeles, CA 90036.
T. (213) 937-5858. - Print / ArtBk / Autogr -   *105378*
Pickwick, 6743 Hollywood Blvd., Los Angeles, CA
90028. T. (213) 469-8191. - Print -   *105379*
Zeitlin & Ver Brugge, 815 N La Cienega Blvd., Los Ange-
les, CA 90069. T. (213) 652-0784. - Print / ArtBk /
Engr / Autogr / Map -   *105380*

Malibu
J. Paul Getty Museum Bookstore, 17985 Pacific Coast
Hwy., Malibu, CA 90406. T. (213) 459-7611.
- ArtBk -   *105381*

Martinez (California)
California Collectible Books, 3503 Alhambra Av, Martinez, CA 94553. T. (510) 229-4878. - Print -   *105382*

Menlo Park (California)
Wessex, 558 Santa Cruz Av, Menlo Park, CA 94025.
T. (415) 321-1333. - Print -   *105383*

Montclair (New Jersey)
Montclair Book Center, 221 Glenridge Av, Montclair, NJ
07042. T. (201) 703-3630. - Print -   *105384*

Montgomery (New York)
Historic Importants, 198 Corbett Rd, Montgomery, NY
12549. T. (914) 457-3765.   *105385*

Mountain View (California)
Shasky, Florian J., 970 Terra Bella Av, Mountain View,
CA 94043. T. (415) 967-5330. - Print -   *105386*

New York
Academy Book Store, 10 W 18 St, New York, NY 10011.
T. (212) 242-4848. - Print / ArtBk / Autogr -   *105387*
Acanthus Books, 54 W 21 St, New York, NY 10010.
T. (212) 463-0750. - Print / ArtBk -   *105388*
Appelfeld, 1372 York Av, New York, NY 10021.
T. (212) 988-7835. - Print / Autogr -   *105389*
Archivia, 944 Madison Av, New York, NY 10021.
T. (212) 439-9194, Fax (212) 744-1626.
- Print -   *105390*
Argosy, 116 E 59 St, New York, NY 10022. T. (212) 753-
4455. - Print / Engr / Map -   *105391*
Art Books, 45 W 57 St, New York, NY 10019.
T. (212) 688-7600. - Print / ArtBk -   *105392*
Arte Primitivo, 3 E 65 St, New York, NY 10021.
T. (212) 570-0393. - Print -   *105393*
Aurora Fine Books, 548 W 28 St, New York, NY 10001.
T. (212) 947-0422. - Print -   *105394*
Bartfield, J.N., 30 W 57 St, New York, NY 10019.
T. (212) 245-8890. - Print -   *105395*
Bauman, c/o Waldorf-Astoria Hotel, Lobby Level, 301
Park Av, New York, NY 10022. T. (212) 759-8300.
- Print / Autogr -   *105396*
Biography House, 547 W 27 St, New York, NY 10001.
T. (212) 714-2004. - Print / Autogr -   *105397*
Black Sun Books, 157 E 57 St, New York, NY 10022.
T. (212) 688-6622. - Print -   *105398*
Bohemian Bookworm, 110 W 25 St, New York, NY
10001. T. (212) 620-5627. - Print -   *105399*
Book-Friends Cafe, 16 W 18 St, New York, NY 10011.
T. (212) 255-7407. - Print -   *105400*
Book Ranger, 105 Charles St, New York, NY 10014.
T. (212) 924-4957. - Print -   *105401*

Bookleaves, 304 W Fourth St, New York, NY 10014.
T. (212) 924-5638. - Print -   *105402*
Books of Wonder, 132 Seventh Av, New York, NY 10011.
T. (212) 989-3270. - Print -   *105403*
Books & Binding, 33 W 17 St, New York, NY 10011.
T. (212) 229-0004. - Print -   *105404*
Bryn Mawr Book Shop, 502 E 79 St, New York, NY
10021. T. (212) 744-7682. - Print -   *105405*
Carr, James F., 227 E 81 St, New York, NY 10028.
T. (212) 535-8110. - Print / Engr -   *105406*
El Cascajero, 506 La Guardia Pl, New York, NY 10012.
T. (212) 473-1576. - Print -   *105407*
Chancellor, John, 667 Madison Av, New York, NY 10021.
T. (212) 308-4014. - Print -   *105408*
Chelsea Books and Records, 111 W 17 St, New York, NY
10011. T. (212) 645-4340. - Print -   *105409*
Comic Art Gallery, 940 Third Av, New York, NY 10022.
T. (212) 759-6255. - ArtBk -   *105410*
Complete Traveller Bookshop, 199 Madison Av, New
York, NY 10016. T. (212) 685-9007. - Print /
Map -   *105411*
Compulsive Collector, 1082 Madison Av, New York, NY
10021. T. (212) 473-1576. - Print -   *105412*
Cummins, James, 699 Madison Av, New York, NY
10021. T. (212) 688-6441. - Print -   *105413*
Demes, 109 W 105 St, New York, NY 10025.
T. (212) 865-1273. - Print -   *105414*
Forbidden Planet Store, 821 Broadway, New York, NY
10003. T. (212) 473-1576. - Print -   *105415*
Fox, Leonard, 790 Madison Av, New York, NY 10021.
T. (212) 879-7077. - Print -   *105416*
Fred's Used Books, 249 E Tenth St, New York, NY
10009. T. (212) 228-4998. - Print -   *105417*
Gotham, 41 W 47 St, New York, NY 10036. T. (212) 719-
4448. - Print -   *105418*
Gryphon Bookshop, 2246 Broadway, New York, NY
10024. T. (212) 362-0706. - Print -   *105419*
Hacker, 45 W 57 St, New York, NY 10019. T. (212) 688-
7600. - Print / ArtBk -   *105420*
Hayden & Fandetta, POB 1549, Radio City Station, New
York, NY 10101-1549. T. (212) 582-2505.   *105421*
Imperial Fine Books, 690 Madison Av, New York, NY
10021. T. (212) 861-6620. - Print -   *105422*
Inner Circle Books, 6 W 18 St, New York, NY 10011.
T. (212) 691-2596. - Print -   *105423*
Johnson Harmer, 21 E 65 St, New York, NY 10021.
T. (212) 535-9118. - Print -   *105424*
Jonah's Whale, 935 Eighth Av, New York, NY 10019.
T. (212) 581-8181. - Print -   *105425*
Kisluk, Eugene J., 315 W 74 St, New York, NY 10023.
T. (212) 875-0252. - Print -   *105426*
Kolwyck-Jones, 588 Broadway, New York, NY 10012.
T. (212) 966-8698. - Print / ArtBk -   *105427*
Kraus, H.P., 16 E 46 St, New York, NY 10017.
T. (212) 687-4808, Fax (212) 983-4790. - Print / Au-
togr / Map -   *105428*
Landy, 80 Fifth Av, New York, NY 10011. T. (212) 647-
0743. - Print -   *105429*
Last Word, 1181 Amsterdam Av, New York, NY 10027.
T. (212) 864-0013. - Print -   *105430*
Lawbook Exchange, 135 W 29 St, New York, NY 10001.
T. (212) 594-4241. - Print -   *105431*
Lion Heart Autographs, 470 Park Av S, New York, NY
10016. T. (212) 779-7050. - Autogr -   *105432*
Magazine Center, 1133 Broadway, New York, NY 10010.
T. (212) 929-5255. - Print -   *105433*
Manhattan Comics and Cards, 228 W 23 St, New York,
NY 10011. T. (212) 243-9349. - Print -   *105434*
Martayan Lan, 48 E 57 St, New York, NY 10022.
T. (212) 308-0018. - Print / Map -   *105435*
Mercer Street Books and Records, 206 Mercer St, New
York, NY 10012. T. (212) 505-8625. - Print -   *105436*
Metropolis Comics and Collectibles, 7 W 18 St, New
York, NY 10011. T. (212) 627-9691. - Print -   *105437*
Metropolitan Antiques Pavilion, 110 W 19 St, New York,
NY 10011. T. (212) 463-0200, Fax (212) 463-7099.
- Print / Autogr / Map -   *105438*
Military Bookman, 29 E 93 St, New York, NY 10128.
T. (212) 348-1280. - Print -   *105439*
Minters, Arthur H., 96 Fulton St, New York, NY 10038.
T. (212) 587-4014. - Print / ArtBk / Engr -   *105440*
Murder Ink, 2486 Broadway, New York, NY 10025.
T. (212) 362-8905. - Print -   *105441*

Mysterious Book Shop, 129 W 56 St, New York, NY
10019. T. (212) 765-0900. - Print -   *105442*
Nathanson, Louis, 219 E 85 St, New York, NY 10028.
T. (212) 249-3235. - Print -   *105443*
New York Bound Bookshop, 50 Rockefeller Plaza, New
York, NY 10020. T. (212) 245-8503. - Print -   *105444*
Oaklander, Irving, 547 W 27 St, New York, NY 10001.
T. (212) 594-4210. - Print / ArtBk / Engr -   *105445*
OAN/Oceanie Afrique Noire, 15 W 39 St., New York, NY
10018-3806. T. (212) 840-8844, Fax 840-3304.
- Print / ArtBk -   *105446*
Old Print Shop, 150 Lexington Av, New York, NY 10016.
T. (212) 686-2111. - Print / Map -   *105447*
Pageant, 109 E Ninth St, New York, NY 10003.
T. (212) 674-5296. - Engr / Autogr / Map -   *105448*
Pak, 137 E 27 St, New York, NY 10016. T. (212) 213-
2177. - Print -   *105449*
Reference Book Center, 175 Fifth Av, New York, NY
10010. T. (212) 677-2160. - Print -   *105450*
Riverside Book Co, 250 W 57 St, New York, NY
10107.   *105451*
Rizzoli, 300 Park Av S, New York, NY 10010.
T. (212) 387-3400, Fax (212) 387-3535. - ArtBk / Engr /
Autogr -   *105452*
Ruby's Book Sale, 119 Chambers St, New York, NY
10007. T. (212) 732-8672. - Print -   *105453*
Saint Marks Comics, 11 Saint Marks Pl, New York, NY
10003. T. (212) 598-9439. - Print -   *105454*
Schiller, Justin G., 135 E 57 St, New York, NY 10022.
T. (212) 832-8231. - Print -   *105455*
Schulson, David, 11 E 68 St, New York, NY 10021.
T. (212) 517-8300. - Autogr -   *105456*
Science Fiction Mysteries and More, 140 Chambers St,
New York, NY 10007. T. (212) 385-8798.
- Print -   *105457*
Shakespeare & Co., 2259 Broadway, New York, NY
10024. T. (212) 580-7800. - Print -   *105458*
Skyline Books, 13 W 18 St, New York, NY 10011.
T. (212) 759-5463. - Print -   *105459*
Sports Series, 145 Hester St, New York, NY 10002.
T. (212) 226-8831. - Print -   *105460*
Stoddard, Richard, 18 E 16 St, New York, NY 10003.
T. (212) 645-9576. - Print -   *105461*
Strand Book Store, 828 Broadway, New York, NY 10003.
T. (212) 473-1452. - Print / ArtBk -   *105462*
Stubbs, 153 E 70 St, New York, NY 10021. T. (212) 772-
3120. - Print -   *105463*
Swann, 104 E 25 St, New York, NY 10010. T. (212) 254-
4710. - Print / Engr / Autogr -   *105464*
Third Avenue Book Store, 127 Third Av, New York, NY
10003. T. (212) 533-6550. - Print -   *105465*
Tumarkin, Peter, 310 E 70 St, New York, NY 10021.
T. (212) 737-8783. - Print -   *105466*
Union Square Art Books, 33 Union Sq W, New York, NY
10003. T. (212) 989-3083. - Print / ArtBk -   *105467*
University Place Book Shop, 821 Broadway, New York,
NY 10003. T. (212) 254-5998. - Print -   *105468*
Ursus Books, 981 Madison Av, New York, NY 10021.
T. (212) 772-8787, Fax (212) 737-9306.
- ArtBk -   *105469*
Weintraub, Michael, 263 W 90 St, New York, NY 10024.
T. (212) 769-1178. - Print -   *105470*
Weiser, Samuel, 132 E 24 St, New York, NY 10010.
T. (212) 777-6363. - Print -   *105471*
Weitz & Coleman, 1377 Lexington Av, New York, NY
10128. T. (212) 831-2213. - Print -   *105472*
Wendell, 302 W 12 St, New York, NY 10001.
T. (212) 675-0877. - Print -   *105473*
Wendell, 23 Eighth Av, New York, NY 10014.
T. (212) 675-6718. - Print -   *105474*
Wilson, Fred, 80 E 11 St, New York, NY 10003.
T. (212) 533-6381. - Print -   *105475*
Witkin, 415 W Broadway, New York, NY 10012.
T. (212) 925-5510, Fax (212) 925-5648.   *105476*
Ximenes, 19 E 69 St, New York, NY 10021.
T. (212) 19 E 69 St. - Print -   *105477*
Zucker, 303 Fifth Av, New York, NY 10016. T. (212) 679-
6332. - Print / ArtBk -   *105478*

Oakland (California)
Bibliomania, 1539 San Pablo Av, Oakland, CA 94612.
T. (510) 835-5733. - Print -   *105479*

Nightmares and Notions, 5904 Foothill Blvd, Oakland, CA 94605. T. (510) 562-0956. - Print -   105480

Palo Alto (California)
Connie's Cookbooks, 4121 Old Trace Rd, Palo Alto, CA 94306. T. (415) 948-2524. - Print -   105481
Wreden, POB 56, Palo Alto, CA 94302. T. (415) 233-0508. - Print / Autogr -   105482

Passaic (New Jersey)
Book Center of Passaic, 594 Main Av, Passaic, NJ 07055. T. (201) 778-6646. - Print -   105483

Philadelphia (Pennsylvania)
Allen, William H., 2031 Walnut St, Philadelphia, PA 19103. T. (215) 563-3398. - Print -   105484
Bauman, 1215 Locust St, Philadelphia, PA 19107. T. (215) 546-6466. - Print / Engr / Autogr / Map -   105485
Book Mark, 2049 W Rittenhouse Sq, Philadelphia, PA 19103. T. (215) 735-5546. - Print -   105486
Book Trader, 501 South St, Philadelphia, PA 19147. T. (215) 925-0219. - Print -   105487
Bookfinders, 1018 Pine St, Philadelphia, PA 19106. T. (215) 238-1262. - Print -   105488
Fran's Bookhouse, 6601 Greene St, Philadelphia, PA 19119. T. (215) 438-2729. - Print -   105489
Hibberd, 1310 Walnut St, Philadelphia, PA 19107. T. (215) 546-8811. - Print -   105490
MacManus, George S., 1317 Irving St, Philadelphia, PA 19107. T. (215) 735-4456. - Print / Autogr -   105491

Portland (Oregon)
Abanté, 124 SW Yamhill, Portland, OR 97204. T. (503) 295-2508, Fax (503) 295-0425.   105492

Poughkeepsie (New York)
Apollo Book, POB 3839, Poughkeepsie, NY 12603. T. (800) 942-8222.   105493

Reston (Virginia)
Book Alcove, 2337 Hunters Woods Plaza, Reston, VA 22090. T. (703) 620-6611. - Print -   105494

Rockville (Maryland)
Book Alcove, 5210 Randolph Rd, Rockville, MD 20852. T. (301) 770-5590. - Print -   105495
Dabney & Co., Q.M., 11910 Parklawn Dr, Rockville, MD 20852. T. (301) 881-1470. - Print -   105496
Quill & Brush, 14717 Janice Dr, Rockville, MD 20853. T. (301) 460-3700. - Print -   105497
Second Story Books, 12160 Parklawn Av, Rockville, MD 20852. T. (301) 770-0477. - Print -   105498

Rutland (Vermont)
Tuttle, 26 S Main St, Rutland, VT 05701. T. (802) 773-8229. - Print -   105499

Sacramento (California)
Crocker Art Museum Shop, 216 O St, Sacramento, CA 95814. T. (916) 446-0943. - ArtBk -   105500

San Anselmo (California)
Good, Michael, 35 San Anselmo Av, San Anselmo, CA 94960. T. (415) 459-6092. - Print -   105501

San Carlos (California)
Antique Trove, 1119 Industrial Way, San Carlos, CA 94070. T. (415) 593-1300. - Print -   105502

San Diego (California)
The Prince and the Pauper, 3201 Adams Av, San Diego, CA 92116. T. (800) 454-3726. - Print -   105503

San Francisco (California)
Aaben, 1546 California St, San Francisco, CA 94109. T. (415) 563-3525. - Print -   105504
About Music, POB 31415, San Francisco, CA 94131. T. (415) 647-3343. - Print -   105505
Acorn Books, 740 Polk St, San Francisco, CA 94109. T. (415) 563-1736. - Print -   105506
Adobe, 3166 16 St, San Francisco, CA 94114. T. (415) 864-3936. - Print -   105507
Albatross Book Store, 166 Eddy St, San Francisco, CA 94102. T. (415) 885-6501. - Print -   105508

Albatross Book Store, 143 Clement St, San Francisco, CA 94118. T. (415) 752-8611. - Print -   105509
Anthill, 237 Church St, San Francisco, CA 94114. T. (415) 626-2665. - Print -   105510
Arader, W. Graham, 435 Jackson St, San Francisco, CA 94111. T. (415) 788-5115. - Print -   105511
Argonaut Book Shop, 786 Sutter St, San Francisco, CA 94109. T. (415) 474-9067. - Engr / Autogr / Map -   105512
Arkadyan, 938 Irving St, San Francisco, CA 94122. T. (415) 664-6212. - Print / Engr -   105513
Arkadyan, 938 Irving St, San Francisco, CA 94122. T. (415) 664-6212. - Print / ArtBk / Engr -   105514
Around the World Books, 1346 Polk St, San Francisco, CA 94109. T. (415) 474-5568. - Print -   105515
Austen, 1687 Haight St, San Francisco, CA 94102. T. (415) 552-4122. - Print -   105516
Beard, 637 Irving St, San Francisco, CA 94122. T. (415) 566-0507. - Print -   105517
Bolerium, 2141 Mission St, San Francisco, CA 94110. T. (415) 863-6353. - Print -   105518
Book Bay, Fort Mason, San Francisco, CA 94123. T. (415) 771-1076. - Print -   105519
Bookmonger, 2411 Clement St, San Francisco, CA 94118. T. (415) 387-2332. - Print -   105520
Books & Company, 1323 Polk St, San Francisco, CA 94109. T. (415) 441-2929. - Print -   105521
Bookstall, 570 Sutter St, San Francisco, CA 94102. T. (415) 362-6353. - Print -   105522
Brick Row Book Shop, 278 Post St, San Francisco, CA 94108. T. (415) 398-0424. - Print -   105523
Califia, 657 Howard St, San Francisco, CA 94105. T. (415) 346-9740. - Print -   105524
Carroll's Bookshop, 1193 Church St, San Francisco, CA 94114. T. (415) 647-3020. - Print -   105525
Dog Eared Books, 1173 Valencia St, San Francisco, CA 94110. T. (415) 282-1901. - Print -   105526
Elsewhere Books, 260 Judah St, San Francisco, CA 94122. T. (415) 661-2535. - Print -   105527
Fantasy etc, 808 Larkin St, San Francisco, CA 94109. T. (415) 441-7617. - Print -   105528
Field, 1419 Polk St, San Francisco, CA 94109. T. (415) 673-2027. - Print -   105529
Forest Books, 3080 16 St, San Francisco, CA 94114. T. (415) 863-2755. - Print -   105530
Forever After Books, 1475 Haight St, San Francisco, CA 94102. T. (415) 431-8299. - Print -   105531
Goldwasser, Thomas A., 126 Post St, San Francisco, CA 94108. T. (415) 981-4100. - Print -   105532
Goldwasser & Wilkinson, 486 Geary St, San Francisco, CA 94102. T. (415) 292-4698. - Print -   105533
Green Apple Books, 506 Clement St, San Francisco, CA 94118. T. (415) 387-2272. - Print -   105534
Hilkert, Richard, 333 Hayes St, San Francisco, CA 94102. T. (415) 863-3339. - Print -   105535
Kuhn, 695 Sutter St, San Francisco, CA 94102. T. (415) 474-6981. - Autogr -   105536
Limelight Film and Theatre Bookstore, 1803 Market St, San Francisco, CA 94102. T. (415) 864-2265. - Print -   105537
Lodestar, 313 Noe St, San Francisco, CA 94114. T. (415) 864-3746. - Print -   105538
Lubbe, 807 347294, San Francisco, CA 94134. T. (415) 467-0811. - Print -   105539
Maelstrom, 572 Valencia St, San Francisco, CA 94110. T. (415) 863-9933. - Print -   105540
Magazine, 920 Larkin St, San Francisco, CA 94109. T. (415) 441-7737. - Print -   105541
Manning, 209 Corbett Av, San Francisco, CA 94114. T. (415) 621-3565. - Print -   105542
Manzanita, 3686 20 St, San Francisco, CA 94110. T. (415) 648-0957. - Print -   105543
McDonald, 48 Turk St, San Francisco, CA 94102. T. (415) 673-2235. - Print -   105544
Meyer Boswell, 2141 Mission St, San Francisco, CA 94110. T. (415) 255-6400. - Print -   105545
Ninth Avenue Book Store, 1348 Ninth Av, San Francisco, CA 94122. T. (415) 665-2938. - Print -   105546
Norman & Co., Jeremy, 720 Market St, San Francisco, CA 94102. T. (415) 781-6402. - Print / Autogr -   105547
Old and Rare Prints, 209 Corbett Av, San Francisco, CA 94114. T. (415) 621-3565. - Print -   105548

Pacific Book Auction Galleries, 139 Townsend St, San Francisco, CA 94107. T. (415) 896-2665. - Print -   105549
Phoenix Books and Records, 3850 24 St, San Francisco, CA 94110. T. (415) 821-3477. - Print -   105550
Red House Books, POB 460267, San Francisco, CA 94146. T. (415) 282-8933. - Print -   105551
Russian Hill Bookstore, 2234 Polk St, San Francisco, CA 94109. T. (415) 929-0997. - Print -   105552
Stephen, 837 Jones St, San Francisco, CA 94109. T. (415) 928-5287. - Print -   105553
Stout, William K., 804 Montgomery St, San Francisco, CA 94133. T. (415) 391-6757. - Print -   105554
Sunset Bookstore, 2161 Irving St, San Francisco, CA 94122. T. (415) 664-3644. - Print -   105555
Tall Stories, 2141 Mission St, San Francisco, CA 94110. T. (415) 255-1915. - Print -   105556
Thomas, Jeffrey, 49 Geary St, San Francisco, CA 94108. T. (415) 956-3272. - Map -   105557
Transition Books, 2626 Filbert St, San Francisco, CA 94123. T. (415) 346-2629. - Print -   105558
West Portal Books, 111 West Portal Av, San Francisco, CA 94127. T. (415) 731-5291. - Print -   105559
Wofsy, Alan, 1109 Geary Blvd, San Francisco, CA 91409. T. (415) 292-6500, Fax (415) 547-1623. - Print / ArtBk / Engr / Autogr -   105560
Writer's Bookstore, 2848 Webster St, San Francisco, CA 94123. T. (415) 921-2620. - Print -   105561
871 Fine Arts Book Store, 250 Sutter St, San Francisco, CA 94108. T. (415) 543-5812. - Print / ArtBk -   105562

San Rafael (California)
Books Revisted, 921 C St, San Rafael, CA 94901. T. (415) 459-5788. - Print -   105563
West Wind Books, 1006 Tamalpais Av, San Rafael, CA 94901. T. (415) 456-6322. - Print -   105564

Santa Monica (California)
Levin, Barry R., 726 Santa Monica Blvd, Santa Monica, CA 90401. T. (310) 458-6111. - Print / Autogr -   105565

Silver Spring (Maryland)
Barbarian, 11254 Triangle Ln, Silver Spring, MD 20902. T. (301) 946-4184. - Print -   105566
Bonifant Books, 11240 Georgia Av, Silver Spring, MD 20902. T. (301) 946-1526. - Print -   105567
Ground Zero Books, 946 Sligo Av, Silver Spring, MD 20910. T. (301) 589-2223. - Print -   105568
Imagination Books, 946 Sligo Av, Silver Spring, MD 20910. T. (301) 589-2223. - Print -   105569

Vienna (Maryland)
Reisler, Jo Ann, 360 Glyndon St NE, Vienna, MD 21869. T. (703) 938-2237. - Print / Engr -   105570

Waldorf (Maryland)
Ellie's Paperback Shack, Acton Sq, Waldorf, MD 20601. T. (301) 843-3676. - Print -   105571

Washington (District of Columbia)
Adams, 2912 M St NW, Washington, DC 20007. T. (202) 337-2665. - Print -   105572
Another World, 1504 Wisconsin Av NW, Washington, DC 20007. T. (202) 333-8650. - Print -   105573
Audubon Prints and Books, 499 South Capitol St SW, Washington, DC 20032. T. (202) 484-3334. - ArtBk -   105574
Bird in Hand Bookstore and Gallery, 323 Seventh St SE, Washington, DC 20003. T. (202) 543-0744. - ArtBk -   105575
Book Market, 2602 Connecticut Av NW, Washington, DC 20008. T. (202) 332-2310. - Print -   105576
Booked Up, 1209 31 St NW, Washington, DC 20007. T. (202) 965-3244. - Print -   105577
Capitol Hill Books, 657 C St SE, Washington, DC 20003. T. (202) 544-1621. - Print -   105578
Fuller & Saunders, 3238 P St NW, Washington, DC 20007. T. (202) 337-3235. - Print -   105579
Hale, William F., 1222 31 St NW, Washington, DC 20007. T. (202) 338-8272. - Print -   105580
Heller, Joshua, 3720 Albemarle St NW, Washington, DC 20016. T. (202) 966-9411. - Print -   105581
Idle Time Books, 2410 18 St NW, Washington, DC 20009. T. (202) 232-4774. - Print -   105582

Key Bridge News Stand, 3326 M St NW, Washington, DC 20007. T. (202) 338-2626. - Print - *105583*

Kulturas Books and LP's, 1621 Connecticut Av NW, Washington, DC 20009. T. (202) 462-2541. - Print - *105584*

Lambda Rising Book Store, 1625 Connecticut Av NW, Washington, DC 20009. T. (202) 462-6969. - Print - *105585*

Lantern Bryn Mawr Bookshop, 3222 O St NW, Washington, DC 20007. T. (202) 333-3222. - Print - *105586*

Logic and Literature Bookstore, 3034 M St NW, Washington, DC 20007. T. (202) 625-1668. - Print - *105587*

Old Forest Book Shop, 3145 Dumbarton St NW, Washington, DC 20007. T. (202) 965-3842. - Print - *105588*

Old Print Gallery, 1220 31 St NW, Washington, DC 20007. T. (202) 965-1818. - Engr / Map - *105589*

Rock Creek Bookshop, 1214 Wisconsin Av NW, Washington, DC 20007. T. (202) 342-8046. - Print - *105590*

Science, 1531 33 St NW, Washington, DC 20007. T. (202) 337-2878. - Print - *105591*

Second Story Books, 2000 P St NW, Washington, DC 20036. T. (202) 659-8884. - Print - *105592*

Secondhand Prose, 5010 Connecticut Av NW, Washington, DC 20008. T. (202) 364-8280. - Print - *105593*

Vassar, 2737 Devonshire Pl NW, Washington, DC 20008. T. (202) 667-1592. - Print - *105594*

Wayward, 325 Seventh St SE, Washington, DC 20003. T. (202) 546-2719. - Print - *105595*

Yawa, 2206 18 St NW, Washington, DC 20009. T. (202) 483-6805. - Print - *105596*

Yesterday's Books, 4702 Wisconsin Av NW, Washington, DC 20016. T. (202) 363-0581. - Print - *105597*

Yudkin, 3636 16 St NW, Washington, DC 20010. T. (202) 232-6249. - Print - *105598*

Winterthur (Delaware)

Winterthur Museum Book Store, Winterthur, DE 19735. - ArtBk - *105599*

Venezuela

Caracas (D.F.)
Libreria Unica, Edif. Capriles local 13, Pl. Venez, Ap. 3956, Caracas, 1010. T. (02) 72 78 51. *105600*

Yugoslavia

Beograd (Srbija)
Antikvarijat i knjižara Matice srpske, Knez Mihajlova 35, 11000 Beograd. - Print / ArtBk / Engr - *105601*

Knjižara i antikvarijat Srpske književne zadruge, Maršala Tita 19, 11000 Beograd. T. (011) 33 15 93. *105602*

Knjizara i antikvarnica Matice srpske, Knez Mihajlova 40, 11000 Beograd. T. (011) 62 33 68. - Print / ArtBk / Engr - *105603*

Novi Sad (Srbija)
Antikvarijat Matice srpske, Matičina 1, 21000 Novi Sad. - Print / ArtBk / Engr - *105604*

FACHADRESSEN
für gezielte
Werbemaßnahmen vom

K·G·Saur Verlag

Optimieren Sie Ihren Werbeerfolg mit den Fachadressen des K.G. Saur Verlags!

Wir bieten Ihnen:

- **rund 120.000 Kunstadressen aus 175 Ländern, darunter**
  - **ca.   26.500 Museen**
  - **ca.   19.000 Galerien**
  - **ca.   1.500 Auktionatoren**
  - **ca.   2.000 Kunstvereinigungen**
  - **ca.   2.500 Kunstverlage**
  - **ca.   4.500 Antiquariate und Kunstbuchhandlungen**
  - **ca.   35.000 Kunst- und Antiquitätenhandlungen**

- **rund 55.000 Bibliotheksadressen weltweit**

- **mehr als 10.000 Adressen von Hochschulinstituten und ihren Leitern im deutschsprachigen Raum**

- **Adressen von über 17.000 wissenschaftlichen Gesellschaften und Vereinigungen sowie rund 22.000 Wirtschaftsverbänden in aller Welt**

Die Fachadressen basieren auf den Datenbanken des K. G. Saur Verlags für so renommierte Nachschlagewerke wie *International Directory of Arts, Museums of the World, World Guide to Libraries, Handbuch der Universitäten und Fachhochschulen, World Guide to Scientific Associations and Learned Societies* und *World Guide to Trade Associations.*

Nähere Informationen über unser Angebot an Fachadressen sowie einen Spezialprospekt erhalten Sie bei Herrn Hans-Peter Golla: Telefon 089/76902-239, Telefax 089/76902-250

 K • G • Saur Verlag
Postfach 701620 · D-81316 München · Tel. (089) 7 69 02-232 · Fax (089) 7 69 02-150/250
E-mail: 100730.1341@compuserve.com